Tolley's Orange Tax Handbook 2015–16

42nd Edition

Part 1: Value Added Tax

CONSULTANT EDITOR

Roderick Cordara QC SC(NSW) MA(Cantab) FIIT

Barrister
Essex Court Chambers

LexisNexis®

Members of the LexisNexis Group worldwide

United Kingdom	Reed Elsevier (UK) Limited trading as LexisNexis, 1-3 Strand, London WC2N 5JR
Australia	LexisNexis Butterworths, Chatswood, New South Wales
Austria	LexisNexis Verlag ARD Orac GmbH & Co KG, Vienna
Canada	LexisNexis Butterworths, Markham, Ontario
Czech Republic	Nakladatelství Orac sro, Prague
France	LexisNexis SA, Paris
Germany	LexisNexis Deutschland GmbH, Frankfurt and Munster
Hong Kong	LexisNexis Butterworths, Hong Kong
Hungary	HVG-Orac, Budapest
India	LexisNexis Butterworths, New Delhi
Italy	Giuffrè Editore, Milan
Malaysia	Malayan Law Journal Sdn Bhd, Kuala Lumpur
New Zealand	LexisNexis Butterworths, Wellington
Poland	Wydawnictwo Prawnicze LexisNexis, Warsaw
Singapore	LexisNexis Butterworths, Singapore
South Africa	LexisNexis Butterworths, Durban
Switzerland	Stämpfli Verlag AG, Berne
USA	LexisNexis, Dayton, Ohio

First published in 1976

Published by LexisNexis Butterworths

ISBN: 9781405788007 (for set); 9781405795074 (for Part 1)
A CIP Catalogue record for this book is available from the British Library.

Visit Tolley at www.tolley.co.uk or email the editorial department on: yellowandorange@lexisnexis.co.uk

Contents

CLIMATE CHANGE LEVY

Detailed contents lists are provided at the beginning of each subject group.

Contents

Contents

Value Added Tax Statutes

Value Added Tax

TAX CREDITS

Annual amounts	*2015–16*	*2014–15*
	£	£
Child tax credit		
Family element	545	545
Child element (for each child)	2,780	2,750
Addition for disabled child	3,140	3,100
Severely disabled child enhancement	1,275	1,255
Working tax credit		
Basic element	1,960	1,940
Lone parent and couple element	2,010	1,990
30-hour element	810	800
Disability element	2,970	2,935
Severe disability element	1,275	1,255
Childcare element (up to 70% of costs)	Weekly	Weekly
maximum eligible cost (1 child)	175	175
maximum eligible cost (2 or more children)	300	300
Income thresholds		
First income threshold	6,420	6,420
eligible for child tax credit only	16,105	16,010
Withdrawal rate	41%	41%
Income rise disregard	5,000	5,000
Income fall disregard	2,500	2,500

Summer Budget 2015 announced various changes from 6 April 2016, including—

- first income threshold to be reduced to £3,850;
- withdrawal rate to be increased to 48%;
- income rise disregard to be reduced to £2,500;

and the following changes from 6 April 2017—

- child element of child tax credit to be limited to two children, in relation to children born after 6 April 2017;
- family element of child tax credit to be withdrawn.

Child tax credit and working tax credit will be subject to the benefits uprating freeze, for four years from April 2016 (except for disability elements which will increase by CPI).

CAPITAL ALLOWANCES

	Rate %
Dredging (straight-line basis)	
Writing-down allowance	4
Business premises renovation	
Initial allowance	100
Writing-down allowance for unrelieved expenditure (straight-line basis)	25
Know-how (reducing balance basis)	
Writing-down allowance	25
Mineral extraction (reducing balance basis)	
Writing-down allowances	
General	25
Acquisition of mineral asset	10
Patent rights (reducing balance basis)	
Writing-down allowance	25
Plant and machinery (reducing balance basis)	
Annual investment allowance (max £500,000 for qualifying expenditure incurred between April 2014 and December 2015; max £200,000 from 1 January 2016)	100
First-year allowances	
Energy-saving or environmentally-beneficial assets	100
New low-emission cars	100
New zero-emission goods vehicles	100
New assets for use in designated areas of enterprise zones	100
Writing-down allowances	
General	18
Cars (other than low-emission cars)	8
Special rate expenditure (including integral features and thermal insulation)	8
Long-life assets	8
Research and development	
Allowance	100

REGISTERED PENSION SCHEMES

2015–16	£
Annual allowance	£40,000
Lifetime allowance	£1,250,000
2014–15	£
Annual allowance	£40,000
Lifetime allowance	£1,250,000

Budget 2015 announced the intention to reduce the lifetime allowance to £1 million from 6 April 2016.

Summer Budget 2015 announced the intention to taper the annual allowance by £1 for every £2 that an individual's income exceeds £150,000 (income including pension contributions), subject to a maximum reduction of £30,000, from 6 April 2016.

VAT

Standard rate	20%
Lower rate	5%
Registration level from 1 April 2015	£82,000 pa
Deregistration limit from 1 April 2015	£80,000 pa

Summer Budget 2015 announced that the standard and reduced rates of VAT would be capped at current levels for the duration of the current Parliament.

VAT CAR FUEL SCALE CHARGES FROM 1 MAY 2015

Description of vehicle: vehicle's CO_2 emissions figure	VAT inclusive consideration for a 12 month prescribed accounting period £	VAT inclusive consideration for a 3 month prescribed accounting period £	VAT inclusive consideration for a 1 month prescribed accounting period £
120 or less	536.00	133.00	44.00
125	802.00	200.00	66.00
130	857.00	213.00	70.00
135	909.00	227.00	75.00
140	965.00	240.00	80.00
145	1,016.00	254.00	84.00
150	1,072.00	267.00	88.00
155	1,123.00	281.00	93.00
160	1,179.00	294.00	97.00
165	1,231.00	308.00	102.00
170	1,286.00	320.00	106.00
175	1,338.00	334.00	111.00
180	1,393.00	347.00	115.00
185	1,445.00	361.00	119.00
190	1,501.00	374.00	124.00
195	1,552.00	388.00	129.00
200	1,608.00	401.00	133.00
205	1,660.00	415.00	138.00
210	1,715.00	428.00	142.00
215	1,767.00	441.00	146.00
220	1,822.00	455.00	151.00
225 or more	1,874.00	468.00	155.00

STAMP TAXES

Shares and marketable securities	.5%*

* Rounded up to the nearest multiple of £5 and subject to exemption where consideration is less than £1,000 or nil.

STAMP DUTY LAND TAX

Residential	*Rate*
£125,000 or less	Nil
£125,001–£250,000	2%
£250,001–£925,000	5%
£925,001–£1,500,000	10%
Over £1,500,000	12%

For residential property, rates are charged on the portion of the consideration that falls within each rate band.

For residential property, a 15% rate applies if purchase by, or by a partnership including, a company or collective investment scheme enveloping the property.

Non-residential	*Rate*
£150,000 or less	Nil
£150,001–£250,000	1%
£250,001–£500,000	3%
Over £500,000	4%

Leases

Residential	*Non-residential*	*Rate*
Up to £125,000	Up to £150,000	Nil
Over £125,000	Over £150,000	1%

ANNUAL TAX ON ENVELOPED DWELLINGS

Property value	*Charge for tax year 2015–16*	*Charge for tax year 2014–15*
Less than £1m	0	0
£1m – £2m	£7,000	0
£2m – £5m	£23,350	£15,400
£5m – £10m	£54,450	£35,900
£10m – £20m	£109,050	£71,850
£20m +	£218,200	£143,750

TAX-FREE MILEAGE ALLOWANCES

Employee's own vehicle

Motorcars and vans	*2015–16*
Up to 10,000 business miles	45p
Over 10,000 business miles	25p
Passenger making same trip	5p
Motorcycles	24p
Cycles	20p

Advisory fuel rates for company car (from 1 June 2015)

Cylinder capacity	*Petrol*	*LPG*
Up to 1,400 cc	12p	8p
1,401 cc to 2,000 cc	14p	9p
Over 2,000 cc	21p	14p

	Diesel
Up to 1,600 cc	10p
1,601 cc to 2,000 cc	12p
Over 2,000 cc	14p

Hybrid cars are treated as petrol or diesel cars accordingly.

INHERITANCE TAX

Transfers made after 5 April 2015 and before 6 April 2016.

Death rates

Gross transfer	*Rate %*
Up to £325,000	Nil
Over £325,000	40

Unused nil rate band is transferable to spouse or civil partner.

Chargeable lifetime transfers are initially charged at 20%.

Annual gifts of up to £3,000 per donor are exempt.

A reduced rate of 36% applies where 10% or more of the net estate is left to charity.

Summer Budget 2015 announced an additional nil rate band for the main residence, transferable to a surviving spouse/civil partner, to be phased in from 6 April 2017. This will be set at £100,000 for 2017–18, £125,000 for 2018–19, £150,000 for 2019–20 and £175,000 for 2020–21. The basic nil rate band will remain at £325,000 until 5 April 2021. After that, both nil rate bands will increase in line with CPI.

BANK LEVY

	1.1.2011–28.2.2011	1.3.2011–30.4.2011	1.5.2011–31.12.2011	1.1.2012–31.12.2012	1.1.2013–31.12.2013	1.1.2014–31.3.2015	1.4.2015–31.12.2015	1.1.2016–31.12.2016
short-term chargeable liabilities	.05%	.1%	.075%	.088%	.130%	.156%	.21%	.18%
long-term chargeable equity and liabilities	.025%	.05%	.0375%	.044%	.065%	.078%	.105%	.09%

CAR BENEFIT

CO_2 emissions (2015–16) grams per kilometre	*% of list price*	
	Petrol	*Diesel*
50	5	8
75	9	12
94	13	16
95	14	17
100	15	18
105	16	19
110	17	20
115	18	21
120	19	22
125	20	23
130	21	24
135	22	25
140	23	26
145	24	27
150	25	28
155	26	29
160	27	30
165	28	31
170	29	32
175	30	33
180	31	34
185	32	35
190	33	36
195	34	37
200	35	37
205	36	37
210 and above	37	37

A 5% charge applies for cars incapable of producing CO_2 emissions.

CAR FUEL BENEFIT

For 2015–16, car fuel benefit is calculated by applying the above car benefit percentage to a figure of £22,100.

INDIVIDUAL SAVINGS ACCOUNTS

	Overall limit	*Cash limit*	*Junior ISA limit*
	£	£	£
2015–16	15,240	15,240	4,080
2014–15			
From 1 July 2014	15,000	15,000	4,000
Before 1 July 2014	11,880	5,940	3,840

Savings are exempt from income tax and capital gains tax.

CAPITAL GAINS TAX

	2015–16	*2014–15*
Annual exempt amount	£	£
Individuals, disabled trusts, personal representatives for year of death and two years thereafter	11,100	11,000
Trusts generally	5,550	5,500
Rates		
Individuals		
Standard rate	18%	18%
Higher rate	28%	28%
Trustees and personal representatives	28%	28%

Entrepreneurs' relief Qualifying gains charged at 10% (subject to £10 million lifetime limit).

CORPORATION TAX

Financial year to—	*31 March 2016*	*31 March 2015*
Full rate	20%	21%
Small profits rate	N/A	20%
Small profits rate limit	N/A	£300,000
Marginal relief limit	N/A	£1,500,000
Marginal relief fraction	N/A	1/400
Effective marginal rate	N/A	21.25%

The main rate for ring-fence profits is 30% and the small profits rate for ring-fence profits is 19%. Ring fence profits above £300,000 but not exceeding £1.5m attract marginal relief. The marginal relief ring-fence fraction is 11/400.

The patent box will provide a 10% rate of corporation tax on profits from patents from April 2017, and is being phased in from April 2013. Companies are able to claim 60% of the benefit in 2013–14, 70% in 2014–15, 80% in 2015–16, 90% in 2016–17 and 100% in 2017–18.

Starting rate for savings income

Taxable income £	*Band £*	*Rate %*	*Tax on band £*	*Total tax £*
2015–16				
0–5,000	5,000	0	0	0
2014–15				
0–2,880	2,880	10	288	288

Savings income is generally treated as the highest part of total income.

Where taxable non-savings income exceeds £5,000 the special 0% starting rate for savings income does not apply.

Budget 2015 announced the intention to introduce a new Personal Savings Allowance from 6 April 2016. This would exempt from income tax the first £1,000 of savings income (£500 for higher rate taxpayers). The allowance would not be available to additional rate taxpayers.

NATIONAL INSURANCE CONTRIBUTIONS 2015–16

Class 1 (Earnings related)

	Not contracted out (NCO)	*Contracted out (salary-related schemes only) (SRS)*
Employees		
Weekly earnings		
First £155	Nil	Nil
£155.01–£770	12%	10.6%
£770.01–£815	12%	12%
Over £815	2%	2%

Employers	*NCO*	*SRS*
Weekly earnings		
First £156	Nil	Nil
£156.01 to £770	13.8%	10.4%
On balance over £770	13.8%	13.8%

Class 1A and 1B: 13.8%.

Class 2 (self-employed): flat rate £2.80 a week (small earnings exemption £5,965 a year).

Class 3 (voluntary contributions): £14.10 a week.

Class 4 (self-employed): 9% of profits between £8,060 and £42,385 a year (2% of profits above £42,385 a year).

Summer Budget 2015 announced that Class 1 NICs rates (employers and employees) would not be increased for the duration of the current Parliament.

TAX TABLES

INCOME TAX ALLOWANCES

	2015–16	2014–15
Personal allowance	£	£
general (born after 5 April 1948)	10,600	10,000
born after 5 April 1938 but before 6 April 1948**	10,600	10,500
born before 6 April 1938**	10,660	10,660
general income limit*	100,000	100,000
age allowance income limit	27,700	27,000
minimum where income exceeds limit (subject to general income limit)	10,600	10,000

* Where income is above £100,000, personal allowances are reduced by £1 for every £2 of income above the £100,000 limit. This reduction applies irrespective of age.

** Age-related personal allowances are restricted from the 2013–14 tax year onwards.

MARRIED COUPLE'S ALLOWANCE* (RELIEF AT 10%)

either partner born before 6 April 1935*	8,355	8,165
age allowance income limit	27,700	27,000
minimum where income exceeds limit	3,220	3,140

* Available for civil partners.

BLIND PERSON'S ALLOWANCE

Blind person's allowance	2,290	2,230

INCOME TAX RATES

Non-savings income

Taxable income £	*Band £*	*Rate %*	*Tax on band £*	*Total tax £*
2015–16				
0–31,785	31,785	20%	6,357	6,357
31,786–150,000	118,215	40%	47,286	53,643
Over 150,000	—	45%	—	—
2014–15				
0–31,865	31,865	20	6,373	6,373
31,866–150,000	118,135	40	47,254	53,627
Over 150,000	—	45%	—	—

Summer Budget 2015 announced that the basic, higher and additional rates of income tax would not increase above current levels for the duration of the current Parliament. Different provision may apply in Scotland.

Retrospective legislation

Subscribers are advised to retain Handbooks for earlier years to use when dealing with tax for those years. Each Handbook shows the legislation operative for the corresponding year so far as it was known at the time of the passing of the Finance Act of that year. In view of the increasing practice of passing tax legislation with retrospective effect, it is necessary when dealing with past years to consider whether the provisions have been affected or amended by subsequent legislation.

NHA 1980	National Heritage Act 1980
OJ	Official Journal of the European Communities
para	paragraph(s)
PAYE	Pay as you earn
PCTA 1968	Provisional Collection of Taxes Act 1968
PEP	Personal equity plan
PET	Potentially exempt transfer
PR	Press releases
Pt	Part(s)
r	rule(s)
RA 1898	Revenue Act 1898
reg	regulations
RD	Revenue decisions
Regulations	EC Regulations
RI	Revenue interpretation
s	section(s)
SA 1891	Stamp Act 1891
Sch	Schedule
SDMA 1891	Stamp Duties Management Act 1891
SDLT	Stamp duty land tax
SDRT	Stamp duty reserve tax
SD(TP)A 1992	Stamp Duty (Temporary Provisions) Act 1992
SI	Statutory Instrument
SP	Statement of Practice
STC	Simon's Tax Cases
STI	Simon's Tax Intelligence
sub-para	sub-paragraph(s)
sub-s	sub-section(s)
TA	Income and Corporation Taxes Act
Taxes Act 1970	Income and Corporation Taxes Act 1970
Taxes Act 1988	Income and Corporation Taxes Act 1988
TMA 1970	Taxes Management Act 1970
VAT	Value added tax
VATA 1994	Value Added Tax Act 1994
vol	volume(s)

List of abbreviations

art	article
ATED	annual tax on enveloped dwellings
CA 1985	Companies Act 1985
CAA 2001	Capital Allowances Act 2001
CCL	Climate change levy
CED(GR)A 1979	Customs & Excise Duties (General Relief) Act 1979
CEMA 1979	Customs & Excise Management Act 1979
CGTA 1979	Capital Gains Tax Act 1979
Ch	Chapter(s) of statute
col	column(s)
Comrs	Commissioners
CPA 1947	Crown Proceedings Act 1947
CTA 2009/2010	Corporation Tax Act 2009/2010
DLT	Development land tax
edn	edition
EEC	European Economic Community
ESC	Extra-statutory concession
FA	Finance Act
F(No 2)A	Finance (No 2) Act
Gp	Group (VAT legislation)
HA 1980	Highways Act 1980
HM	Her Majesty
HMRC	Her Majesty's Revenue & Customs
HMSO	Her Majesty's Stationery Office
IA	Interpretation Act
ICAEW	Institute of Chartered Accountants in England & Wales
IOM	Isle of Man
IoT	Institute of Taxation
IPT	Insurance Premium Tax
IR	Inland Revenue
LIFFE	London International Financial Futures and Options Exchange
LPA 1925	Law of Property Act 1925
NB	(nota bene) note well

remains generally unaffected. In this case, the original provision is printed without modification but a **Cross reference** to the later Act or statutory instrument is provided, see below.

Prospective amendments

The Handbook sets out the text of the legislation as it applies for the current tax year. Amendments which are stated to come into effect on a specified future date, or with effect from a date to be appointed, are therefore strictly outside the scope of the current edition and are not made in the text of the Act affected. However, a **Prospective amendment** note is provided to indicate the existence of the amendment and the provision making the prospective amendment is retained in full in successive editions of the Handbook until the amendment becomes effective.

Retrospective amendments

For the tax legislation as it applied in an earlier year, reference should be made to the appropriate earlier edition of the Orange Tax Handbook. Care must be taken, however, to ensure that amendments made retrospectively are not overlooked.

Repealed legislation

Generally, repealed legislation is omitted. However, where it may be necessary to refer to the repealed text in dealing with tax liabilities for the current year, the text is retained and is printed in italics.

Defined terms

Where a word or phrase used in the main Acts has been defined elsewhere, a cross-reference to the definition is provided in a **Definitions** note below the text.

Cross references

The notes under each section or Schedule paragraph include references to commentary and to relevant statutory provisions, statutory instruments, published HMRC practice and other published or unpublished official and professional bodies' views. These are presented under the following headings—

Commentary—refers to paragraph numbers for commentary relating to the provision in *De Voil Indirect Tax Service* or *Simon's Taxes*.

Concession; Statement of Practice; HMRC Interpretations—refer to published official practice separately reproduced in the same section of this Handbook.

Press releases etc—refer to published or unpublished official and professional bodies' views reproduced in this Handbook or *MHA MacIntyre Hudson's Orange Tax Guide*.

Cross reference—refers to provisions in the same or another Act or statutory instrument.

Simon's Tax Cases—provides references to the most significant cases reported in *Simon's Tax Cases* and *Simon's First-tier Tax Decisions*. Cases decided on the previous corresponding statutory provision are marked by an asterisk.

Note—introduces other references not within any of the above categories.

July 2015

Publishers' Note

Finance Act 2015—key dates

Budget Day	18 March 2015
Finance Act 2015 passed	26 March 2015
Summer Budget Day	8 July 2015

Tax legislation

Tolley's Yellow and Orange Tax Handbooks are indispensable to the practitioner who needs to refer to the tax legislation as currently in force. Each year the legislation is augmented and amended by one or more Finance Acts and lesser amendments are made from time to time by a variety of other statutes. An increasing amount of the detailed regulation of taxes is contained in statutory instruments—orders or regulations—which are also amended frequently. The Handbooks are normally published annually. They contain the text of the relevant statutes and statutory instruments as amended together with current texts of extra-statutory concessions, statements of practice, published official interpretations and decisions, selected press releases and internal guidance where available.

Tolley's Orange Tax Handbook covers value added tax (Part 1), and stamp taxes (including land and buildings transaction tax in Scotland), insurance premium tax, landfill tax (including Scottish landfill tax), aggregates levy and climate change levy (Part 2). Its companion volume, Tolley's Yellow Tax Handbook, covers income tax, corporation tax, capital gains tax, inheritance tax, National Insurance contributions, tax credits and petroleum revenue tax and other direct taxes.

This edition of the Orange Tax Handbook contains texts as they applied at July 2015, although later amendments have been taken into account where possible.

Organisation

The contents of this Handbook are arranged in separate sections for each of the taxes covered. The start of each section is marked with a grey tab on the front edge of the book. The texts in each section are arranged in the following order — UK statutes, statutory instruments, European legislation for VAT, extra-statutory concessions, statements of practice, VAT Notices with the force of law, press releases. Within each of those categories, items are printed in chronological order. To enable individual items to be located quickly, an item reference is printed in bold type in the outside top corner of each page.

Amendments and modifications

Amendments to existing legislation which take effect for the current year are made in the text of the amended legislation. An **Amendment** note under the amended text indicates the authority for the amendment and, where appropriate, the timing of its commencement. All relevant provisions of the current Finance Act are reproduced in full but otherwise the text of provisions which merely amend other Acts is generally omitted and replaced by a note indicating the legislation amended.

Sometimes the effect of a provision is modified by a later Act or statutory instrument but the scope of the modification is limited in some way so that the original provision

PROVISIONAL COLLECTION OF TAXES ACT 1968

(1968 Chapter 2)

An Act to consolidate the Provisional Collection of Taxes Act 1913 and certain other enactments relating to the provisional collection of taxes or matters connected therewith.

[1st February 1968]

1 Temporary statutory effect of House of Commons resolutions affecting . . . , [value added tax][1], . . .

(1) This section applies only to . . . , [value added tax][1], . . .

[(1A) . . .][2]

(2) Subject to that, and to the provisions of subsections (4) to [(9)][6] below, where the House of Commons passes a resolution which—

(*a*) provides for the renewal for a further period of any tax in force or imposed during the previous financial year (whether at the same or a different rate, and whether with or without modifications) or for the variation or abolition of any existing tax, and

(*b*) contains a declaration that it is expedient in the public interest that the resolution should have statutory effect under the provisions of this Act,

the resolution shall, for the period specified in the next following subsection, have statutory effect as if contained in an Act of Parliament and, where the resolution provides for the renewal of a tax, all enactments which were in force with reference to that tax as last imposed by Act of Parliament shall during that period have full force and effect with respect to the tax as renewed by the resolution. In this section references to the renewal of a tax include references to its reimposition, and references to the abolition of a tax include references to its repeal.

[(3) The period is one expiring at the end of seven months after the date on which the resolution is expressed to take effect or, if no such date is expressed, after the date on which the resolution is passed.][6]

(4) A resolution shall cease to have statutory effect under this section unless within the next [thirty][3] days on which the House of Commons sits after the day on which the resolution is passed—

(*a*) a Bill renewing, varying or, as the case may be, abolishing the tax is read a second time by the House, or

(*b*) a Bill is amended by the House [in Committee or on Report, or by any [Public Bill Committee][5] of the House][4] so as to include provision for the renewal, variation or, as the case may be, abolition of the tax.

(5) A resolution shall also cease to have statutory effect under this section if—

(*a*) the provisions giving effect to it are rejected during the passage of the Bill containing them through the House, or

(*b*) an Act comes into operation renewing, varying or, as the case may be, abolishing the tax, or

(*c*) Parliament is dissolved...[6][, or

(*d*) Parliament is prorogued.][6]

[(5A) Subsection (5B) applies in relation to a resolution instead of subsection (5) (*d*) where Parliament is prorogued at the end of a session if—

(*a*) one of the following happens during the session—

(i) a Bill renewing, varying or, as the case may be, abolishing the tax is read a first time by the House, or

(ii) a Bill is amended by the House in Committee or on Report or by any Public Bill Committee of the House so as to include provision for the renewal, variation or, as the case may be, abolition of the tax,

(*b*) the Standing Orders or Sessional Orders of the House provide, or during the session the House orders, that proceedings on the Bill not completed before the end of the session shall be resumed in the next session, and

(*c*) proceedings on the Bill are not completed during the session.

(5B) The resolution shall cease to have statutory effect under this section if, during the period of thirty sitting days beginning with the first sitting day of the next session, no Bill renewing, varying or, as the case may be, abolishing the tax is presented to the House.

(5C) In subsection (5B) "sitting day" means a day on which the House sits.

(5D) Where a Bill is amended as mentioned in subsection (5A)(*a*)(ii), it does not matter for the purposes of subsection (5A)(*b*) if the House orders as mentioned in subsection (5A)(*b*) before the amendment to the Bill is made.][6]

(6) Where, in the case of a resolution providing for the renewal or variation of a tax, the resolution ceases to have statutory effect by virtue of subsection [(4), (5) or (5B)][6] above, or the period specified in subsection (3) above terminates, before an Act comes into operation renewing or varying the tax, any money paid in pursuance of the resolution shall be repaid or made good, and any deduction made in pursuance of the resolution shall be deemed to be an unauthorised deduction.

(7) Where any tax as renewed or varied by a resolution is modified by the Act renewing or varying the tax, any money paid in pursuance of the resolution which would not have been payable under the new conditions affecting the tax shall be repaid or made good, and any deduction made in pursuance of the resolution shall, so far as it would not have been authorised under the new conditions affecting the tax, be deemed to be an unauthorised deduction.

(8) When during any session a resolution has had statutory effect under this section, statutory effect shall not be again given under this section in the same session to the same resolution or to a resolution having the same effect.

[(9) Subsection (8) does not apply where the later resolution is passed in a different calendar year from that in which the earlier resolution is passed.][6]

Commentary—*De Voil Indirect Tax Service* **V1.131**.

Note—Words and any subsection not relevant for the purposes of VAT have been omitted.

Sub-s (3A), which was to have been inserted by the Scotland Act 2012 s 26(7) with effect in relation to the tax year appointed by the Treasury under Scotland Act 2012 s 25(5) and subsequent tax years, repealed by FA 2014 s 296, Sch 38 para 13 with effect from 17 July 2014. Sub-s (3A) was to have read as follows—

"(3A) If a resolution specifies the basic rate, higher rate or additional rate of income tax, the resolution has effect in relation to Scottish taxpayers (within the meaning of Chapter 2 of Part 4A of the Scotland Act 1998) as if it specified the rate calculated in accordance with section 6(2A) to (2C) of the Income Tax Act 2007.".

Cross references—See VATA 1994 s 90(1) (VAT paid by virtue of a resolution under this Act becoming repayable under sub-ss (6) or (7) above).

Amendments—[1] Words in the heading and in sub-s (1) added by virtue of VATA 1983 Sch 9 para 1.

[2] Sub-s (1A) repealed by FA 1993 ss 205(1), (3), 213, Sch 23 Pt VI, in relation to resolutions passed after 27 July 1993. Further repealed by the Statute Law (Repeals) Act 2013 s 1, Sch 1 Pt 10.

[3] Word in sub-s (4) substituted by FA 1993 s 205 in relation to resolutions passed after 27 July 1993.

[4] Words in sub-s (4)(*b*) inserted by FA 1968 s 60.

[5] Words in sub-s (4)(*b*) substituted by FA 2007 s 112(1) with effect from 19 July 2007.

[6] In sub-s (2) reference substituted for "(8)"; sub-s (3) substituted; in sub-s (5), words "or prorogued" in para (*c*) repealed, and words at end of that para and para (*d*) inserted; sub-ss (5A)–(5D) inserted; in sub-s (6), references substituted for "(4) or (5)"; and sub-s (9) inserted; by FA 2011 s 88 (1)–(8) with effect from 30 December 2011 (by virtue of SI 2011/2934). These amendments do not apply to any resolution passed before 30 December 2011. Subsection (3) previously read as follows—

"(3) The said period is—

(*a*) in the case of a resolution passed in November or December in any year, one expiring with 5th May in the next calendar year;

(*aa*) in the case of a resolution passed in February or March in any year, one expiring with 5th August in the same calendar year; and

(*b*) in the case of any other resolution, one expiring at the end of four months after the date on which it is expressed to take effect or, if no such date is expressed, after the date on which it is passed.".

5 House of Commons resolution giving provisional effect to motions affecting taxation

(1) This section shall apply if the House of Commons resolves that provisional statutory effect shall be given to one or more motions to be moved by the Chancellor of the Exchequer, or some other Minister, and which, if agreed to by the House, would be resolutions—

(*a*) to which statutory effect could be given under section 1 of this Act, or

(*b*), (*c*) . . .[1]

(2) Subject to subsection (3) below, on the passing of the resolution under subsection (1) above, sections 1 . . . of this Act, . . . shall apply as if each motion to which the resolution applies had then been agreed to by a resolution of the House.

(3) Subsection (2) above shall cease to apply to a motion if that motion, or a motion containing the same proposals with modifications, is not agreed to by a resolution of the House (in this section referred to as "a confirmatory resolution") within the next ten days on which the House sits after the resolution under subsection (1) above is passed, and, if it ceases to apply, all such adjustments, whether by way of discharge or repayment of tax, or discharge of security, or otherwise, shall be made as may be necessary to restore the position to what it would have been if subsection (2) above had never applied to that motion, and to make good any deductions which have become unauthorised deductions.

(4) . . .

Commentary—*De Voil Indirect Tax Service* **V1.131**.

Note—Sub-ss (1)(*b*), (4) and words omitted from sub-s (2) are not relevant to VAT.

Cross references—See VATA 1994 s 90(1) (VAT paid by virtue of a resolution under this Act becoming repayable under sub-s (3) above).

Amendments—[1] Sub-s (1)(*c*) and the word "or" immediately preceding it repealed by FA 1993 ss 205(6), (7), 213, Sch 23 Pt VI, in relation to resolutions passed after 27 July 1993.

6 Short title, repeals and saving as respects Northern Ireland

(1) This Act may be cited as the Provisional Collection of Taxes Act 1968.

(2) . . .

(3) . . .[1]

Note—Sub-s (2) repeals enactments specified in Schedule.

Amendments—[1] Sub-s (3) repealed by Northern Ireland Constitution Act 1973 s 41(1)(*a*), Sch 6 Pt 1, with effect from 18 July 1973.

INTERPRETATION ACT 1978

(1978 Chapter 30)

ARRANGEMENT OF SECTIONS

An Act to consolidate the Interpretation Act 1889 and certain other enactments relating to the construction and operation of Acts of Parliament and other instruments, with amendments to give effect to recommendations of the Law Commission and the Scottish Law Commission.

[20th July 1978]

General provisions as to enactment and operation

1 Words of enactment

Every section of an Act takes effect as a substantive enactment without introductory words.

3 Judicial notice

Every Act is a public Act to be judicially noticed as such, unless the contrary is expressly provided by the Act.

4 Time of commencement

An Act or provision of an Act comes into force—

(*a*) where provision is made for it to come into force on a particular day, at the beginning of that day;

(*b*) where no provision is made for its coming into force, at the beginning of the day on which the Act receives the Royal Assent.

Interpretation and construction

5 Definitions

In any Act, unless the contrary intention appears, words and expressions listed in Schedule 1 to this Act are to be construed according to that Schedule.

Note—Omitted provisions are outside the scope of this publication.

Simon's Tax Cases—*IRC v Clydebridge Properties Ltd* [1980] STC 68*; *IRC v Frampton (Trustees of the Worthing Rugby Football Club)* [1985] STC 186*; *Starke (executors of Brown decd) v IRC* [1995] STC 689.

6 Gender and number

In any Act, unless the contrary intention appears,—

(*a*) words importing the masculine gender include the feminine;

(*b*) words importing the feminine gender include the masculine;

(*c*) words in the singular include the plural and words in the plural include the singular.

Note—Omitted provisions are outside the scope of this publication.

Simon's Tax Cases—*Floor v Davis* [1976] STC 475*.

7 References to service by post

Where an Act authorises or requires any document to be served by post (whether the expression "serve" or the expression "give" or "send" or any other expression is used) then, unless the contrary intention appears, the service is deemed to be effected by properly addressing, pre-paying and posting a letter containing the document and, unless the contrary is proved, to have been effected at the time at which the letter would be delivered in the ordinary course of post.

Note—Omitted provisions are outside the scope of this publication.

Simon's Tax Cases—*Wing Hung Lai v Bale* [1999] STC (SCD) 238; *Holly v Inspector of Taxes* [2000] STC (SCD) 50.

10 References to the Sovereign

In any Act a reference to the Sovereign reigning at the time of the passing of the Act is to be construed, unless the contrary intention appears, as a reference to the Sovereign for the time being.

11 Construction of subordinate legislation

Where an Act confers power to make subordinate legislation, expressions used in that legislation have, unless the contrary intention appears, the meaning which they bear in the Act.

Statutory powers and duties

12 Continuity of powers and duties

(1) Where an Act confers a power or imposes a duty it is implied, unless the contrary intention appears, that the power may be exercised, or the duty is to be performed, from time to time as occasion requires.

(2) Where an Act confers a power or imposes a duty on the holder of an office as such, it is implied, unless the contrary intention appears, that the power may be exercised, or the duty is to be performed, by the holder for the time being of the office.

13 Anticipatory exercise of powers

Where an Act which (or any provision of which) does not come into force immediately on its passing confers power to make subordinate legislation, or to make appointments, give notices, prescribe forms or do any other thing for the purposes of the Act, then, unless the contrary intention appears, the power may be exercised, and any instrument made thereunder may be made so as to come into force, at any time after the passing of the Act so far as may be necessary or expedient for the purpose—

(*a*) of bringing the Act or any provision of the Act into force; or

(*b*) of giving full effect to the Act or any such provision at or after the time when it comes into force.

14 Implied power to amend

Where an Act confers power to make—

(*a*) rules, regulations or byelaws; or

(*b*) Orders in Council, orders or other subordinate legislation to be made by statutory instrument,

it implies, unless the contrary intention appears, a power, exercisable in the same manner and subject to the same conditions or limitations, to revoke, amend or re-enact any instrument made under the power.

[14A Power to include sunset and review provisions in subordinate legislation

(1) This section applies where an Act confers a power or a duty on a person to make subordinate legislation except to the extent that—

(*a*) the power or duty is exercisable by the Scottish Ministers, or

(*b*) the power or duty is exercisable by any other person within devolved competence (within the meaning of the Scotland Act 1998).

(2) The subordinate legislation may include—

(*a*) provision requiring the person to review the effectiveness of the legislation within a specified period or at the end of a specified period;
(*b*) provision for the legislation to cease to have effect at the end of a specified day or a specified period;
(*c*) if the power or duty is being exercised to amend other subordinate legislation, provision of the kind mentioned in paragraph (*a*) or (*b*) in relation to that other legislation.

(3) The provision that may be made by virtue of subsection (2)(*a*) includes provision requiring the person to consider whether the objectives which it was the purpose of the legislation to achieve remain appropriate and, if so, whether they could be achieved in another way.

(4) Subordinate legislation including provision of a kind mentioned in subsection (2) may make such provision generally or only in relation to specified provisions of the legislation or specified cases or circumstances.

(5) Subordinate legislation including provision of a kind mentioned in subsection (2) may make transitional, consequential, incidental or supplementary provision or savings in connection with such provision.

(6) In this section, "specified" means specified in the subordinate legislation.][1]

Amendments—[1] Section 14A inserted by the Enterprise and Regulatory Reform Act 2013 s 59(1), (2) with effect from 25 April 2013.

Repealing enactments

15 Repeal of repeal

Where an Act repeals a repealing enactment, the repeal does not revive any enactment previously repealed unless words are added reviving it.

16 General savings

(1) Without prejudice to section 15, where an Act repeals an enactment, the repeal does not, unless the contrary intention appears,—
(*a*) revive anything not in force or existing at the time at which the repeal takes effect;
(*b*) affect the previous operation of the enactment repealed or anything duly done or suffered under that enactment;
(*c*) affect any right, privilege, obligation or liability acquired, accrued or incurred under that enactment;
(*d*) affect any penalty, forfeiture or punishment incurred in respect of any offence committed against that enactment;
(*e*) affect any investigation, legal proceeding or remedy in respect of any such right, privilege, obligation, liability, penalty, forfeiture or punishment;

and any such investigation, legal proceeding or remedy may be instituted, continued or enforced, and any such penalty, forfeiture or punishment may be imposed, as if the repealing Act had not been passed.

(2) This section applies to the expiry of a temporary enactment as if it were repealed by an Act.

17 Repeal and re-enactment

(1) Where an Act repeals a previous enactment and substitutes provisions for the enactment repealed, the repealed enactment remains in force until the substituted provisions come into force.

(2) Where an Act repeals and re-enacts, with or without modification, a previous enactment then, unless the contrary intention appears,—
(*a*) any reference in any other enactment to the enactment so repealed shall be construed as a reference to the provision re-enacted;
(*b*) in so far as any subordinate legislation made or other thing done under the enactment so repealed, or having effect as if so made or done, could have been made or done under the provision re-enacted, it shall have effect as if made or done under that provision.

Cross references—ITA 2007 Sch 2 para 6 (ITA 2007 Sch 2 paras 1–5 have effect instead of sub-s (2) above (but are without prejudice to any other provision of this Act). ITA 2007 Sch 3 paras 4 and 5 apply only so far as the context permits).
FA 2012 s 147, Sch 17 para 36(8) (insurance companies carrying out long-term business: transitional provisions (disapplication of sub-s (2))).

Miscellaneous

18 Duplicated offences

Where an act or omission constitutes an offence under two or more Acts, or both under an Act and at common law, the offender shall, unless the contrary intention appears, be liable to be prosecuted and punished under either or any of those Acts or at common law, but shall not be liable to be punished more than once for the same offence.

19 Citation of other Acts

(1) Where an Act cites another Act by year, statute, session or chapter, or a section or other portion of another Act by number or letter, the reference shall, unless the contrary intention appears, be read as referring—

(*a*) in the case of Acts included in any revised edition of the statutes printed by authority, to that edition;

(*b*) in the case of Acts not so included but included in the edition prepared under the direction of the Record Commission, to that edition;

(*c*) in any other case, to the Acts printed by the Queen's Printer, or under the superintendence or authority of Her Majesty's Stationery Office.

(2) An Act may continue to be cited by the short title authorised by any enactment notwithstanding the repeal of that enactment.

20 References to other enactments

(1) Where an Act describes or cites a portion of an enactment by referring to words, sections or other parts from or to which (or from and to which) the portion extends, the portion described or cited includes the words, sections or other parts referred to unless the contrary intention appears.

(2) Where an Act refers to an enactment, the reference, unless the contrary intention appears, is a reference to that enactment as amended, and includes a reference thereto as extended or applied, by or under any other enactment, including any other provision of that Act.

[20A References to [EU instruments][2]

Where an Act passed after the commencement of this section refers to an [EU instrument][2] that has been amended, extended or applied by another such instrument, the reference, unless the contrary intention appears, is a reference to that instrument as so amended, extended or applied.][1]

Amendments—[1] This section inserted by the Legislative and Regulatory Reform Act 2006, s 25(1) with effect from 8 January 2007.

[2] In section heading and in main text, words substituted by the European Union (Amendment) Act 2008, s 3(3), Schedule, Pt 2 with effect from 1 December 2009 (by virtue of SI 2009/3143 art 2).

Supplementary

21 Interpretation etc

(1) In this Act "Act" includes a local and personal or private Act; and "subordinate legislation" means Orders in Council, orders, rules, regulations, schemes, warrants, byelaws and other instruments made or to be made under any Act.

(2) This Act binds the Crown.

26 Commencement

This Act shall come into force on 1st January 1979.

27 Short title

This Act may be cited as the Interpretation Act 1978.

SCHEDULES

SCHEDULE 1

WORDS AND EXPRESSIONS DEFINED

Section 5

Note—Omitted provisions are outside the scope of this publication.

Simon's Tax Cases—*IRC v Clydebridge Properties Ltd* [1980] STC 68*; *IRC v Frampton (Trustees of the Worthing Rugby Football Club)* [1985] STC 186*; *Starke (executors of Brown decd) v IRC* [1995] STC 689.

Note: The years or dates which follow certain entries in the Schedule are relevant for the purposes of paragraph 4 of Schedule 2 (application to existing enactments).

Definitions

"Associated state" means a territory maintaining a status of association with the United Kingdom in accordance with the West Indies Act 1967. [16th February 1967]

"Bank of England" means, as the context requires, the Governor and Company of the Bank of England or the bank of the Governor and Company of the Bank of England.

"Bank of Ireland" means, as the context requires, the Governor and Company of the Bank of Ireland or the bank of the Governor and Company of the Bank of Ireland.

"British Islands" means the United Kingdom, the Channel Islands and the Isle of Man. [1889]

["British overseas territory" has the same meaning as in the British Nationality Act 1981.]

"British possession" means any part of Her Majesty's dominions outside the United Kingdom; and where parts of such dominions are under both a central and a local legislature, all parts under the central legislature are deemed, for the purposes of this definition, to be one British possession. [1889]

. . .

"Building regulations", in relation to England and Wales, [has the meaning given by section 122 of the Building Act 1984].

"Central funds", in an enactment providing in relation to England and Wales for the payment of costs out of central funds, means money provided by Parliament.

["Charity Commission" means the Charity Commission for England and Wales (see section 13 of the Charities Act 2011).]

"Church Commissioners" means the Commissioners constituted by the Church Commissioners Measure 1947.

["Civil partnership" means a civil partnership which exists under or by virtue of the Civil Partnership Act 2004 (and any reference to a civil partner is to be read accordingly).]

"Colonial legislature", and "legislature" in relation to a British possession, mean the authority, other than the Parliament of the United Kingdom or Her Majesty in Council, competent to make laws for the possession. [1889]

"Colony" means any part of Her Majesty's dominions outside the British Islands except—

(*a*) countries having fully responsible status within the Commonwealth;

(*b*) territories for whose external relations a country other than the United Kingdom is responsible;

(*c*) associated states;

and where parts of such dominions are under both a central and a local legislature, all parts under the central legislature are deemed for the purposes of this definition to be one colony. [1889]

"Commencement", in relation to an Act or enactment, means the time when the Act or enactment comes into force.

"Committed for trial" means—

(*a*) *in relation to England and Wales, committed in custody or on bail by a magistrates' court pursuant to [section 6 of the Magistrates' Courts Act 1980], or by any judge or other authority having power to do so, with a view to trial before a judge and jury; [1889]*

(*b*) in relation to Northern Ireland, committed in custody or on bail by a magistrates' court pursuant to [Article 37 of the Magistrates' Courts (Northern Ireland) Order 1981], or by a court, judge, resident magistrate, . . . or other authority having power to do so, with a view to trial on indictment. [1st January 1979]

["The EU" or "the EU Treaties"] and other expressions defined by section 1 of and Schedule 1 to the European Communities Act 1972 have the meanings prescribed by that Act.

"Comptroller and Auditor General" means the Comptroller-General of the receipt and issue of Her Majesty's Exchequer and Auditor-General of Public Accounts . . . .

"Consular officer" has the meaning assigned by Article 1 of the Vienna Convention set out in Schedule 1 to the Consular Relations Act 1968.

["The Corporation Tax Acts" means the enactments relating to the taxation of the income and chargeable gains of companies and of company distributions (including provisions relating to income tax).]

"County court" means—

(*a*) in relation to England and Wales, [the county court established under section A1 of] [the County Courts Act 1984]; [1846]

(*b*) in relation to Northern Ireland, a court held for a division under the County Courts [(Northern Ireland) Order 1980]. [1889]

"Court of Appeal" means—

(*a*) in relation to England and Wales, Her Majesty's Court of Appeal in England;

(*b*) in relation to Northern Ireland, Her Majesty's Court of Appeal in Northern Ireland.

["Court of Judicature" means the Court of Judicature of Northern Ireland.]

"Court of summary jurisdiction", "summary conviction" and "Summary Jurisdiction Acts", in relation to Northern Ireland, have the same meanings as in Measures of the Northern Ireland Assembly and Acts of the Parliament of Northern Ireland.

"Crown Court" means—

(*a*) in relation to England and Wales, the Crown Court constituted by section 4 of the Courts Act 1971;

(*b*) in relation to Northern Ireland, the Crown Court constituted by section 4 of the Judicature (Northern Ireland) Act 1978.

"Crown Estate Commissioners" means the Commissioners referred to in section 1 of the Crown Estate Act 1961.

["EEA agreement" means the agreement on the European Economic Area signed at Oporto on 2nd May 1992, together with the Protocol adjusting that Agreement signed at Brussels on 17th March 1993, as modified or supplemented from time to time. [The date of the coming into force of this paragraph.]

"EEA state", in relation to any time, means—

(*a*) a state which at that time is a member State; or

(*b*) any other state which at that time is a party to the EEA agreement. [The date of the coming into force of this paragraph.]]

["Enactment" does not include an enactment comprised in, or in an instrument made under, an Act of the Scottish Parliament.]

"England" means, subject to any alteration of boundaries under Part IV of the Local Government Act 1972 the area consisting of the countries established by section 1 of that Act, Greater London and the Isles of Scilly. [1st April 1974]

"Financial year" means, in relation to matters relating to the Consolidated Fund, the National Loans Fund, or moneys provided by Parliament, or to the Exchequer or to central taxes or finance, the twelve months ending with 31st March. [1889]

"Governor-General" includes any person who for the time being has the powers of the Governor-General, and "Governor", in relation to any British possession, includes the officer for the time being administering the government of that possession. [1889]

["Her Majesty's Revenue and Customs" has the meaning given by section 4 of the Commissioners for Revenue and Customs Act 2005.]

"High Court" means—

(*a*) in relation to England and Wales, Her Majesty's High Court of Justice in England;

(*b*) in relation to Northern Ireland, Her Majesty's High Court of Justice in Northern Ireland.

"The Income Tax Acts" means all enactments relating to income tax, including any provisions of the Corporation Tax Acts which relate to income tax.

"Land" includes buildings and other structures, land covered with water, and any estate, interest, easement, servitude or right in or over land. [1st January 1979]

"Land Clauses Acts" means—

(*a*) in relation to England and Wales, the Land Clauses Consolidation Act 1845 and the Lands Clauses Consolidation Acts Amendment Act 1860, and any Acts for the time being in force amending those Acts; [1889]

(*b*) in relation to Scotland, the Lands Clauses Consolidation (Scotland) Act 1845 and the Lands Clauses Consolidation Acts Amendment Act 1860, and any Acts for the time being in force amending those Acts; [1889]

(*c*) in relation to Northern Ireland, the enactments defined as such by section 46(1) of the Interpretation Act (Northern Ireland) 1954. [1889]

"Local land charges register", in relation to England and Wales, means [the register] kept pursuant to section 3 of the Local Land Charges Act 1975 . . . .

["Local policing body" has the meaning given by section 101(1) of the Police Act 1996.]

"London borough" means a borough described in Schedule 1 to the London Government Act 1963 "inner London borough" means one of the boroughs so described and numbered from 1 to 12 and "outer London borough" means one of the boroughs so described and numbered from 13 to 32, subject (in each case) to any alterations made under Part IV of the Local Government Act 1972[, Part 2 of the Local Government Act 1992 or Part 1 of the Local Government and Public Involvement in Health Act 2007].

"Lord Chancellor" means the Lord High Chancellor of Great Britain.

"Magistrates' court" has the meaning assigned to it—

(*a*) in relation to England and Wales, by [section 148 of the Magistrates' Courts Act 1980];

(*b*) in relation to Northern Ireland, by [Article 2(2) of the Magistrates' Courts (Northern Ireland) Order 1981].

"Month" means calendar month. [1850]

"National Debt Commissioners" means the Commissioners for the Reduction of the National Debt.

"Northern Ireland legislation" has the meaning assigned by section 24(5) of this Act. [1st January 1979]

"Oath" and "affidavit" include affirmation and declaration, and "swear" includes affirm and declare.

["Officer of a provider of probation services" in relation to England and Wales, has the meaning given by section 9(1) of the Offender Management Act 2007;]

["Officer of Revenue and Customs" has the meaning given by section 2(1) of the Commissioners for Revenue and Customs Act 2005.]

"Ordnance Map" means a map made under powers conferred by the Ordnance Survey Act 1841 or the Boundary Survey (Ireland) Act 1854.

"Parliamentary Election" means the election of a Member to serve in Parliament for a constituency. [1889]

["PAYE income" has the meaning given by section 683 of the Income Tax (Earnings and Pensions) Act 2003.]

["PAYE regulations" means regulations under section 684 of that Act.]

"Person" includes a body of persons corporate or unincorporate. [1889]

["Police and crime commissioner" means a police and crime commissioner established under section 1 of the Police Reform and Social Responsibility Act 2011]

"Police area" . . . and other expressions relating to the police have the meaning or effect described—

(*a*) in relation to England and Wales, by [section 101(1) of the Police Act 1996];

(*b*) in relation to Scotland, by sections 50 and 51(4) of the Police (Scotland) Act 1967.

["Police authority", in relation to Scotland, has the meaning or effect described by sections 50 and 51(4) of the Police (Scotland) Act 1967.]

["Police Service of Northern Ireland" and "Police Service of Northern Ireland Reserve" have the same meaning as in the Police (Northern Ireland) Act 2000.]

"The Privy Council" means the Lords and others of Her Majesty's Most Honourable Privy Council.

["Provider of probation services", in relation to England and Wales, has the meaning given by section 3(6) of the Offender Management Act 2007;]

[Registered" in relation to nurses and midwives, means registered in the register maintained under article 5 of the [Nursing and Midwifery Order 2001] by virtue of qualifications in nursing or midwifery, as the case may be.]

"Registered medical practitioner" means a fully registered person within the meaning of the Medical Act 1983 who holds a licence to practise under that Act.".

["Registered provider of social housing"'has the meaning given by section 80(2) of the Housing and Regeneration Act 2008 (and "non-profit" and "profit-making" in connection with a provider have the meanings given by section 115 of that Act).]

"Rules of Court" in relation to any court means rules made by the authority having power to make rules or orders regulating the practice and procedure of that court, and in Scotland includes Acts of Adjournal and Acts of Sederunt; and the power of the authority to make rules of court (as above defined) includes power to make such rules for the purpose of any Act which directs or authorises anything to be done by rules of court. [1889]

"Secretary of State" means one of Her Majesty's Principal Secretaries of State.

["Senior Courts"'means the Senior Courts of England and Wales.]

["Sent for trial" means, in relation to England and Wales, sent by a magistrates' court to the Crown Court for trial pursuant to section 51 or 51A of the Crime and Disorder Act 1998.]

["Sewerage undertaker, in relation to England and Wales, shall be construed in accordance with [section 6 of the Water Industry Act 1991].]

["Sheriff' is to be construed in accordance with section 134(2) and (3) of the Courts Reform (Scotland) Act 2014.]

["The standard scale", with reference to a fine or penalty for an offence triable only summarily,—

(*a*) in relation to England and Wales, has the meaning given by section 37 of the Criminal Justice Act 1982;

(*b*) in relation to Scotland, has the meaning given by section 289G of the Criminal Procedure (Scotland) Act 1975;

(*c*) in relation to Northern Ireland, has the meaning given by Article 5 of the Fines and Penalties (Northern Ireland) Order 1984.]

"Statutory declaration" means a declaration made by virtue of the Statutory Declarations Act 1835.

["Statutory maximum", with reference to a fine or penalty on summary conviction for an offence,—

(*a*) in relation to England and Wales, means the prescribed sum within the meaning of section 32 of the Magistrates' Courts Act 1980;

(*b*) in relation to Scotland, means the prescribed sum within the meaning of section 289B(6) of the Criminal Procedure (Scotland) Act 1975; and

(*c*) in relation to Northern Ireland, means the prescribed sum within the meaning of Article 4 of the Fines and Penalties (Northern Ireland) Order 1984.]

["Supreme Court" means the Supreme Court of the United Kingdom.]

["The Tax Acts" means the Income Tax Acts and the Corporation Tax Acts.]

["Transfer for trial" means the transfer of proceedings against an accused to the Crown Court for trial under section 7 of the Magistrates' Courts Act 1980.]

"The Treasury" means the Commissioners of Her Majesty's Treasury.

["Trust of land" and "trustees of land", in relation to England and Wales, have the same meanings as in the Trusts of Land and Appointment of Trustees Act 1996.]

"United Kingdom" means Great Britain and Northern Ireland. [12th April 1927]

["Wales" means the combined area of counties which were created by section 20 of the Local Government Act 1972, as originally enacted, but subject to any alteration made under section 73 of that Act (consequential alteration of boundary following alteration of watercourse).]

["Water undertaker", in relation to England and Wales, shall be construed in accordance with [section 6 of the Water Industry Act 1991].]

"Writing" includes typing, printing, lithography, photography and other modes of representing or reproducing words in a visible form, and expressions referring to writing are construed accordingly.

. . .

Construction of certain expressions relating to offences

In relation to England and Wales—

(*a*) "indictable offence" means an offence which, if committed by an adult, is triable on indictment, whether it is exclusively so triable or triable either way;

(*b*) "summary offence" means an offence which, if committed by an adult, is triable only summarily;

(*c*) "offence triable either way" means an offence [, other than an offence triable on indictment only by virtue of Part V of the Criminal Justice Act 1988] which, if committed by an adult, is triable either on indictment or summarily;

and the terms "indictable", "summary" and "triable either way", in their application to offences, are to be construed accordingly.

In the above definitions references to the way or ways in which an offence is triable are to be construed without regard to the effect, if any, of [section 22 of the Magistrates' Courts Act 1980] on the mode of trial in a particular case.

[Construction of certain references to relationships

In relation to England and Wales—

(*a*) references (however expressed) to any relationship between two persons;

(*b*) references to a person whose father and mother were or were not married to each other at the time of his birth; and

(*c*) references cognate with references falling within paragraph (b) above,

shall be construed in accordance with section 1 of the Family Law Reform Act 1987. [4th April 1988]]

Note—Omitted provisions are outside the scope of this publication.

Cross references—See TA 1988 s 834(1) (meaning of "financial year" for the purposes of Corporation Tax Acts).

Modifications—See the Police and Fire Reform (Scotland) Act 2012 (Consequential Provisions and Modifications) Order, SI 2013/602 art 26, Sch 2 para 15 (modification of this Schedule in its application to Scotland).

Amendments—The definition of "British overseas territory" inserted by the British Overseas Territories Act 2002 s 1(3) with effect from 26 February 2002.

The definitions of "British subject" and "Commonwealth citizen" repealed by the British Nationality Act 1981 Sch 9.

Words in the definition of "Building regulations" substituted by the Building Act 1984 Sch 6 para 19.

Definition "Charity Commission" substituted by the Charities Act 2011 s 354, Sch 7, para 34 with effect from 16 January 2012.

Definition "Civil partnership" inserted by the Civil Partnership Act 2004 s 261(1), Sch 27 para 59 with effect from 5 December 2005 (by virtue of SI 2005/3175).

Words in the definition of "Committed for trial" substituted by the Magistrates' Courts Act 1980 Sch 7 para 169 and the Magistrates' Courts (Northern Ireland) Order, SI 1981/1675 Sch 6 para 56. The whole of para (*a*) of this definition is repealed by the Criminal Justice and Public Order Act 1994 Sch 4 para 28(*a*), Sch 11 with effect for certain purposes from 8 June 2012 (see SI 2012/1320 art 4(1)(*a*), (*b*), (*c*)(iii)–(v), (*d*), for certain other purposes from 5 November 2012 (see SI 2012/2574 art 2(1)(*a*)–(*d*), (2), (3), Schedule, and for remaining purposes from a date to be appointed.

Words in the definition of "Committed for trial" repealed by the Justice (Northern Ireland) Act 2002 s 86, Sch 13 with effect from 1 April 2005 (by virtue of SR 2005/109).

In definition of "Committed for trial", para *(a)* repealed by the Criminal Justice Act 2003 ss 41, 332, Sch 3 para 49*(a)*, Sch 37 Pt 4. This amendment has effect from 28 May 2013 in relation to certain local justice areas (see SI 2013/1103).
Words in definition of "Comptroller and Auditor General" repealed by the Budget Responsibility and National Audit Act 2011 s 26, Sch 5 para 12 with effect from 1 April 2012 (SI 2011/2576 art 5).
The definition of "The Corporation Tax Acts" substituted by FA 1987 s 71 Sch 15 para 12.
Words in the definition of "County court" substituted by the County Courts Act 1984 Sch 2 para 68 and the County Courts (Northern Ireland) Order, SI 1980/397 Sch 1 Pt II.
In definition of "County court", in para *(a)*, words substituted by the Crime and Courts Act 2013 s 17, Sch 9 para 94 with effect from 22 April 2014 (by virtue of SI 2014/954 art 2*(c)*).
The definition of "Court of Judicature" inserted by the Constitutional Reform Act 2005 s 59, Sch 11 para 24*(b)* with effect from 1 October 2009 (by virtue of SI 2009/1604 art 2(d)).
Definitions "EEA agreement" and "EEA state" inserted by the Legislative and Regulatory Reform Act 2006, s 26(1) with effect from 8 January 2007.
Definition "Enactment" inserted by the Scotland Act 1998 s 125, Sch 8 para 16(3) with effect from 1 July 1999 (SI 1998/3178, art 2(1)).
In definition "The EU" or "the EU Treaties", those words substituted for words ""The Communities", "the Treaties" or "the Community Treaties"', by the European Union (Amendment) Act 2008, s 3(3), Schedule, Pt 2 with effect from 1 December (by virtue of SI 2009/3143 art 2).
Definition of "Her Majesty's Revenue and Customs" inserted by CRCA 2005 s 4(3) with effect from 7 April 2005 (by virtue of SI 2005/1126).
Words in the definition "local land charges register" substituted for words "a register", and words "and "the appropriate local land charges register" has the meaning assigned by section 4 of that Act" repealed by the Infrastructure Act 2015 s 34(1), (2)*(c)*, Sch 5 para 34 with effect from 12 April 2015.
Definitions "Local Policing Body and "Police Authority" inserted by Police Reform and Social Responsibility Act 2011 s 97(1), (2), (5) with effect from 16 January 2012 (by virtue of SI 2011/3019 art 2, Sch 1*(aaa)*).
Words in the definition of "London borough" substituted by the Local Government and Public Involvement in Health Act 2007 s 22, Sch 1 para 14 with effect from 1 November 2007 (by virtue of SI 2007/3136, art 2*(b)*).
Words in para *(a)* of the definition of "Magistrates' court" substituted by the Magistrates' Courts Act 1980 s 154 Sch 7 para 169 and, in para *(b)*, by the Magistrates' Court (Northern Ireland) Order, SI 1981/1675 art 170(2) Sch 6 Pt I para 56.
Definition of "Officer of a provider of probation services" inserted by the Offender Management Act 2007 s 39, Sch 3 para 2 with effect from 1 April 2008 (by virtue of SI 2008/504 art 3(l)).
Definition of "Officer of Revenue and Customs" inserted by CRCA 2005 s 2(7) with effect from 7 April 2005 (by virtue of SI 2005/1126).
Definitions of "PAYE income" and "PAYE regulations" inserted by ITEPA 2003 s 722, Sch 6 para 148 with effect, for income tax purposes, from 2003–04; and for corporation tax purposes, for accounting periods ending after 5 April 2003. For transitional provisions and savings see ITEPA 2003 s 723, Sch 7.
Definition of "police and crime commissioner" inserted by Police Reform and Social Responsibility Act 2001, s 97(3) with effect from 22 November 2012 (by virtue of SI 2012/2892 art 2*(a)*).
Words in the definition of "police area" substituted by the Police Act 1996 Sch 7 para 32.
Words in the definition of "Police area" repealed by Police Reform and Social Responsibility Act 2011 s 97(1), (4), with effect from 16 January 2012 (by virtue of SI 2011/3019 art 2, Sch 1*(aaa)*).
Definition of "Police authority" inserted by the Police Reform and Social Responsibility Act 2011 s 97(1), (5) with effect from 16 January 2012 (by virtue of SI 2011/3019 art 3, Sch 1 para *(aaa)*).
Definition of "Police Service of Northern Ireland" and "Police Service of Northern Ireland Reserve" inserted by the Police (Northern Ireland) Act 2000 s 78(1), Sch 6 para 5 with effect from 4 December 2001 (by virtue of SR 2001/396).
Definition of "Provider of probation services" inserted by the Offender Management Act 2007 s 39, Sch 3 para 2 with effect from 1 April 2008 (by virtue of SI 2008/504 art 3(l)).
Definition of "Registered" substituted by the Nursing and Midwifery Order 2001, SI 2002/253, art 54, Sch 5 para 7 with effect from 1 August 2004 (London Gazette, 21 July 2004). Words in this definition substituted by the Health Act 1999 (Consequential Amendments) (Nursing and Midwifery) Order, SI 2004/1771 art 3, Schedule para 7 with effect from 1 August 2004.
"Registered" in relation to nurses and midwives, means registered in the register maintained under article 5 of the Nurses and Midwives Order 2001 by virtue of qualifications in nursing or midwifery, as the case may be.".
Definition of "Registered medical practitioner" substituted by the Medical Act 1983 (Amendment) Order, SI 2002/3135 art 16(1), Sch 1 para 10 with effect from 16 November 2009.
The definition of "Registered provider of social housing" inserted by the Housing and Regeneration Act 2008 s 277, Sch 9 para 5 with effect from 1 April 2010 (by virtue of SI 2010/844, art 1(2)
The definition of "Senior Courts" inserted by the Constitutional Reform Act 2005 s 59, Sch 11 para 24*(b)* with effect from 1 October 2009 (by virtue of SI 2009/1604 art 2(d)).
The definition of "Sent for trial" inserted by the Criminal Justice Act 2003 s 41, Sch 3, Pt 2, para 49*(b)* with effect from 9 May 2005 (by virtue of SI 2005/1267).
The definition of "Sewerage undertaker" inserted by the Water Act 1989 s 190(1), Sch 25 para 55(1), (2), as amended by the Water Consolidation (Consequential Provisions) Act 1991 s 2(1) Sch 1 para 32.
Definition of "Sheriff" substituted by the Courts Reform (Scotland) Act 2014 (Consequential Provisions and Modifications) Order, SI 2015/700 art 10, Schedule para 10, with effect for certain purposes from 11 November 2014 and for remaining purposes from a date to be appointed (see SI 2015/700 art 1(11)*(h)* and the Court Reform Act ss 134, 138). Definition previously read as follows—

""Sheriff", in relation to Scotland, includes sheriff principal."

The definition of "The standard scale" inserted by the Criminal Justice Act 1988 s 170(1) Sch 15 para 58*(a)*.
The definition of "Statutory maximum" inserted by the Criminal Justice Act 1988 s 170(1) Sch 15 para 58*(b)*.
The definition of "Supreme Court" substituted by the Constitutional Reform Act 2005 s 59, Sch 11 para 24*(a)* with effect from 1 October 2009 (by virtue of SI 2009/1604 art 2(d)).
The definition of "The Tax Acts" substituted by FA 1987 s 71 Sch 15 para 12.

The definition "Transfer for trial" inserted by the Criminal Justice and Public Order Act 1994 Sch 4 para 28(*b*), as from a day to be appointed.

The definitions of "Trust of land" and trustees of land" inserted by the Trusts of Land and Appointment of Trustees Act 1996 s 25(1), Sch 3 para 16, as from a day to be appointed.

The definition of "Wales" substituted by the Local Government (Wales) Act 1994 Sch 2 para 9.

The definition of "Water undertaker" substituted for the definitions "Water authority" and "Water authority area" by the Water Act 1989 s 190(1) Sch 25 para 55(1), (3), as amended by the Water Consolidation (Consequential Provisions) Act 1991 s 2(1) Sch 1 para 32.

The entry relating to the construction of certain expressions relating to children is repealed by the Children Act 1989 s 108(7) Sch 15.

In the entry relating to the construction of certain expressions relating to offences (i) the words in the definition "offence triable either way" inserted by the Criminal Justice Act 1988 s 170(1) Sch 15 para 59; (ii) the words "section 22 of the Magistrates' Courts Act 1980" substituted by the Magistrates' Courts Act 1980 s 154 Sch 7 para 169.

The entry relating to the construction of references to relationships added at the end by the Family Law Reform Act 1987 s 33(1), Sch 2 para 73.

SCHEDULE 2

APPLICATION OF ACT TO EXISTING ENACTMENTS

PART I

ACTS

1 The following provisions of this Act apply to Acts whenever passed—

Section 6(*a*) and (*c*) so far as applicable to enactments relating to offences punishable on indictment or on summary conviction

Section 9

Section 10

Section 11 so far as it relates to subordinate legislation made after the year 1889

[Section 14A][1]

Section 18

Section 19(2).

Amendments—[1] Entry for "Section 14A" inserted by the Enterprise and Regulatory Reform Act 2013 s 59(1), (3) with effect from 25 April 2013.

2 The following apply to Acts passed after the year 1850—

Section 1

Section 3

Section 6(*a*) and (*c*) so far as not applicable to such Acts by virtue of paragraph 1

Section 15

Section 17(1)

3 The following apply to Acts passed after the year 1889—

Section 4

Section 7

Section 12

Section 13

Section 14 so far as it relates to rules, regulations or byelaws

Section 16(1)

Section 17(2)(*a*)

Section 19(1)

Section 20(1)

4—(1) Subject to the following provisions of this paragraph—

(*a*) paragraphs of Schedule 1 at the end of which a year or date . . .[1] is specified [or described][2] apply, so far as applicable, to Acts passed on or after the date, or after the year, so specified [or described][2]; and

(*b*) paragraphs of the Schedule at the end of which no year or date is specified [or described][2] apply, so far as applicable, to Acts passed at any time.

(4) The definition of "Lord Chancellor" does not apply to Acts passed before 1st October 1921 in which that expression was used in relation to Ireland only.

(5) The definition of "person", so far as it includes bodies corporate, applies to any provision of an Act whenever passed relating to an offence punishable on indictment or on summary conviction.

Note—Omitted provisions are outside the scope of this publication.

Amendments—[1] Words in sub-para (1)(*a*) repealed by the Family Law Reform Act 1987 s 33(1) Sch 2 para 74, Sch 4, with effect from 4 April 1988, by virtue of the Family Law Reform Act 1987 (Commencement No 1) Order, SI 1988/425.

2 Words in sub-para (1)(*a*), (*b*) inserted by the Family Law Reform Act 1987 s 33(1) Sch 2 para 74, Sch 4, with effect from 4 April 1988, by virtue of the Family Law Reform Act 1987 (Commencement No 1) Order, SI 1988/425.

5 The following definitions shall be treated as included in Schedule 1 for the purposes specified in this paragraph—

(*a*) in any Act passed before 1st April 1974, a reference to England includes Berwick upon Tweed and Monmouthshire and, in the case of an Act passed before the Welsh Language Act 1967 Wales;

(*b*) in any Act passed before the commencement of this Act and after the year 1850, "land", includes messuages, tenements and hereditaments, houses and buildings of any tenure;

(*c*) in any Act passed before the commencement of the Criminal Procedure (Scotland) Act 1975 "the Summary Jurisdiction (Scotland) Acts" means Part II of that Act.

PART II

SUBORDINATE LEGISLATION

7 The definition in Schedule 1 of "county court", in relation to England and Wales, applies to Orders in Council made after the year 1846.

CUSTOMS AND EXCISE MANAGEMENT ACT 1979

(1979 Chapter 2)

ARRANGEMENT OF SECTIONS

PART XII

GENERAL AND MISCELLANEOUS

General powers, etc

An Act to consolidate the enactments relating to the collection and management of the revenues of customs and excise and in some cases to other matters in relation to which the Commissioners of Customs and Excise for the time being perform functions, with amendments to give effect to recommendations of the Law Commission and the Scottish Law Commission.

[22nd February 1979]

Construction—FA 1988 s 8 to be construed as one with this Act; see FA 1988 s 8(4).

Cross references—See VATA 1994 s 16(1) (application of this Act with certain exceptions for the purposes of value added tax).

PART I

PRELIMINARY

1 Interpretation

(1) In this Act, unless the context otherwise requires—

"aerodrome" means any area of land or water designed, equipped, set apart or commonly used for affording facilities for the landing and departure of aircraft;

. . .[15]

"approved wharf" has the meaning given by [section 20A][8] below;

"armed forces" means the Royal Navy, the Royal Marines, the regular army and the regular air force, and any reserve or auxiliary force of any of those services which has been called out on permanent service, [. . .][24] or embodied;

["assigned matter" means any matter in relation to which the Commissioners, or officers of Revenue and Customs, have a power or duty[, except that it does not include any matter relating to a devolved tax within the meaning of the Scotland Act 1998][32] [or the Government of Wales Act 2006][37];][27]

"boarding station" means a boarding station for the time being appointed under section 19 below;

"boundary" means the land boundary of Northern Ireland;

"British ship" means a British ship within the meaning of the [Merchant Shipping Act 1995][21];

"claimant", in relation to proceedings for the condemnation of any thing as being forfeited, means a person claiming that the thing is not liable to forfeiture;

"coasting ship" has the meaning given by section 69 below;

"commander", in relation to an aircraft, includes any person having or taking the charge or command of the aircraft;

["the Commissioners" means the Commissioners for Her Majesty's Revenue and Customs;][27]

"Community transit goods"—

(*a*) in relation to imported goods, means—

(i) goods which have been imported under the internal or external Community transit procedure for transit through the United Kingdom with a view to exportation where the importation was and the transit and exportation are to be part of one Community transit operation; or

(ii) goods which have, at the port or airport at which they were imported, been placed under the internal or external Community transit procedure for transit through the United Kingdom with a view to exportation where the transit and exportation are to be part of one Community transit operation;

(*b*) in relation to goods for exportation, means—

(i) goods which have been imported as mentioned in paragraph (*a*)(i) of this definition and are to be exported as part of the Community transit operation in the course of which they were imported; or

(ii) goods which have, under the internal or external Community transit procedure, transited the United Kingdom from the port or airport at which they were imported and are to be exported as part of the Community transit operation which commenced at that port or airport;

[and for the purposes of para (*a*)(i) above the Isle of Man shall be treated as if it were part of the United Kingdom;][1]

"container" includes any bundle or package and any [baggage,][29] box, cask or other receptacle whatsoever;

"the customs and excise Acts" means the Customs and Excise Acts 1979 and any other enactment for the time being in force relating to customs or excise;

"the Customs and Excise Acts 1979" means—

this Act,

the Customs and Excise Duties (General Reliefs) Act 1979

the Alcoholic Liquor Duties Act 1979

the Hydrocarbon Oil Duties Act 1979

. . . [13] and

the Tobacco Products Duty Act 1979;

"customs warehouse" means a place of security approved by the Commissioners under subsection (2) (whether or not it is also approved under subsection (1)) of section 92 below;[9]

"customs and excise airport" has the meaning given by section 21(7) below;

"customs and excise station" has the meaning given by section 26 below;

["designation order" has the meaning given by section 100A(5);][4]

"drawback goods" means goods in the case of which a claim for drawback has been or is to be made;

"dutiable goods", except in the expression "dutiable or restricted goods", means goods of a class or description subject to any duty of customs or excise, whether or not those goods are in fact chargeable with that duty, and whether or not that duty has been paid thereon;

"dutiable or restricted goods" has the meaning given by section 52 below;

"examination station" has the meaning given by [section 22A][8] below;

["excise duty point" has the meaning given by section 1 of the Finance (No 2) Act 1992;][11]

"excise licence trade" means, subject to subsection (5) below, a trade or business for the carrying on of which an excise licence is required;

"excise warehouse" means a place of security approved by the Commissioners under subsection (1) (whether or not it is also approved under subsection (2)) of section 92 below, and, except in that section, also includes a distiller's warehouse;

"exporter", in relation to goods for exportation or for use as stores, includes the shipper of the goods and any person performing in relation to an aircraft functions corresponding with those of a shipper;

["free zone" has the meaning given by section 100A(2);][4]

["free zone goods" are goods which are within a free zone][18]

. . . [10]

"goods" includes stores and [containers][34];

"holiday", in relation to any part of the United Kingdom, means any day that is a bank holiday in that part of the United Kingdom under the Banking and Financial Dealings Act 1971 Christmas Day, Good Friday and the day appointed for the purposes of customs and excise for the celebration of Her Majesty's birthday;

"hovercraft" means a hovercraft within the meaning of the Hovercraft Act 1968;

"importer", in relation to any goods at any time between their importation and the time when they are delivered out of charge, includes any owner or other person for the time being possessed of or beneficially interested in the goods and, in relation to goods imported by means of a pipe-line, includes the owner of the pipe-line;

"justice" and "justice of the peace" in Scotland includes a sheriff and in Northern Ireland, in relation to any powers and duties which can under any enactment for the time being in force be exercised and performed only by a resident magistrate, means a resident magistrate;

"land" and "landing", in relation to aircraft, include alighting on water;

"law officer of the Crown" means the Attorney General or [for the purpose of criminal proceedings in Scotland, the Lord Advocate or, for the purpose of civil proceedings in Scotland, the appropriate Law Officer within the meaning of section 4A of the Crown Suits (Scotland) Act 1857][25] or in Northern Ireland the Attorney General for Northern Ireland;

"licence year", in relation to an excise licence issuable annually, means the period of 12 months ending on the date on which that licence expires in any year;
"master", in relation to a ship, includes any person having or taking the charge or command of the ship;
. . . [6]
"night" means the period between 11 pm and 5 am;
["nuclear material" has the same meaning as in the Nuclear Material (Offences) Act 1983 (see section 6 of that Act);][31]
"occupier", in relation to any bonded premises, [includes any][12] person who has given security to the Crown in respect of those premises;
"officer" means, subject to section 8(2) below, a person commissioned by the Commissioners;
"owner", in relation to an aircraft, includes the operator of the aircraft;
"owner", in relation to a pipe-line, means (except in the case of a pipe-line vested in the Crown which in pursuance of arrangements in that behalf is operated by another) the person in whom the line is vested and, in the said excepted case, means the person operating the line;
"perfect entry" means an entry made in accordance with [regulation 5 of the Customs Controls on Importation of Goods Regulations 1991][14] or warehousing regulations, as the case may require;[20]
"pipe-line" has the meaning given by section 65 of the Pipe-lines Act 1962 (that Act being taken, for the purposes of this definition, to extend to Northern Ireland);
"port" means a port appointed by the Commissioners under section 19 below;
"prescribed area" means such an area in Northern Ireland adjoining the boundary as the Commissioners may by regulations prescribe;
"prescribed sum", in relation to the penalty provided for an offence, has the meaning given by section 171(2) below;
"prohibited or restricted goods" means goods of a class or description of which the importation, exportation or carriage coastwise is for the time being prohibited or restricted under or by virtue of any enactment;
"proper", in relation to the person by, with or to whom, the place at which, anything is to be done, means the person or place appointed or authorised in that behalf by the Commissioners;
"proprietor", in relation to any goods, includes any owner, importer, exporter, shipping or other person for the time being possessed of or beneficially interested in those goods;
"Queen's warehouse" means any place provided by the Crown or appointed by the Commissioners for the deposit of goods for security thereof and of the duties chargeable thereon;
["registered excise dealer and shipper" means a revenue trader approved and registered by the Commissioners under section 100G below;
"registered excise dealers and shippers regulations" means regulations under section 100G below;][19]
"the revenue trade provisions of the customs and excise Acts" means—

(*a*) the provisions of the customs and excise Acts relating to the protection, security, collection or management of the revenues derived from the duties of excise on goods produced or manufactured in the United Kingdom;

(*b*) the provisions of the customs and excise Acts relating to any activity or facility for the carrying on or provision of which an excise licence is required; . . . [16]

(*c*) the provisions of [the Betting and Gaming Duties Act 1981][3] (so far as not included in paragraph (*b*) above); . . . [22]

[(*d*) the provisions of Chapter II of Part I of the Finance Act 1993;][16]

[(*e*) the provisions of section 10 to 15 of, and Schedule 1 to, the Finance Act 1997;][22]

[(*f*) the provisions of Part 1 of Schedule 24 to the Finance Act 2012;][33]

[(*g*) the provisions of Part 3 of the Finance Act 2014;][35]

"revenue trader" means—

[(*a*)] [2]any person carrying on a trade or business subject to any of the revenue trade provisions of the customs and excise Acts, [or which consists of or includes—

(i) the buying, selling, importation, exportation, dealing in or handling of any goods of a class or description which is subject to a duty of excise (whether or not duty is chargeable on the goods);][7] . . . [17]

[(ia) the buying, selling, importation, exportation, dealing in or handling of tickets or chances on the taking of which lottery duty is or will be chargeable;][17] . . . [23]

[(ib) being (within the meaning of sections 10 to 15 of the Finance Act 1997) the provider of any premises for gaming;][23]

[(ic) the organisation, management or promotion of [any activity that constitutes betting or gaming for the purposes of Part 3 of the Finance Act 2014 (see sections 150, 183 and 188)][35]; . . . [3]][23]

[(id)being responsible for premises where relevant machines are located (within the meaning of Part 1 of Schedule 24 to the Finance Act 2012); or][3]

[(*ie*)the management or administration of any Chapter 1 stake fund, Chapter 2 stake fund or gaming prize fund within the meaning of Part 3 of the Finance Act 2014 (see sections 134, 143 and 154);][35]

[(ii) the financing or facilitation of any such transactions or activities][7] [as are mentioned in sub-paragraph (i)[, (ia), (ib) [(ic)[, (*id*) or (*ie*)][35]][33]][23] above][17]

whether or not that trade or business is an excise licence trade[; and[2]

[(*b*) any person who is a wholesaler or an occupier of an excise warehouse (so far as not included in paragraph (*a*) above),

and includes a registered club;][2]

"ship", and "vessel" include any boat or other vessel whatsoever (and, to the extent provided in section 2 below, any hovercraft);

"shipment" includes loading into an aircraft, and "shipped" and cognate expressions shall be construed accordingly;

"stores" means, subject to subsection (4) below, goods for use in a ship or aircraft and includes fuel and spare parts and other articles of equipment, whether or not for immediate fitting;

"tons register" means the tons of a ship's net tonnage as ascertained and registered according to the tonnage regulations of the [Merchant Shipping Act 1995][21] or, in the case of a ship which is not registered under that Act, ascertained in like manner as if it were to be so registered;

"transit goods", except in the expression "Community transit goods", means imported goods entered on importation for transit or transhipment;

"transit or transhipment", in relation to the entry of goods, means transit through the United Kingdom or transhipment with a view to the re-exportation of the goods in question [or transhipment of those goods for use as stores][5];

"transit shed" has the meaning given by [section 25A][8] below;

["tribunal" means the First-tier Tribunal or, where determined by or under Tribunal Procedure Rules, the Upper Tribunal;][30]

["United Kingdom waters" means any waters (including inland waters) within the seaward limits of the Territorial sea of the United Kingdom.][6]

"vehicle" includes a railway vehicle;

["victualling warehouse" means a place of security approved by the Commissioners under subsection (2) (whether or not it is also a place approved under subsection (1) of section 92 below).][9]

"warehouse", except in the expressions "Queen's warehouse" and "distiller's warehouse", means a place of security approved by the Commissioners under subsection (1) or (2) or subsections (1) and (2) of section 92 below and, except in that section, also includes a distiller's warehouse; and "warehoused" and cognate expressions shall, subject to subsection (4) of that section [and any regulations made by virtue of section 93(2)(*da*)(i) or (*ee*) or (4) below][11], be construed accordingly;

"warehousing regulations" means regulations under section 93 below.

(2) This Act and the other Acts included in the Customs and Excise Acts 1979 shall be construed as one Act but where a provision of this Act refers to this Act that reference is not to be construed as including a reference to any of the others.

(3) Any expression used in this Act or in any instrument made under this Act to which a meaning is given by any other Act included in the Customs and Excise Acts 1979 has, except where the context otherwise requires, the same meaning in this Act or any such instrument as in that Act; . . .

[(4) Goods for use in a ship or aircraft as merchandise for sale to persons carried in the ship or aircraft shall be treated for the purposes of the customs and excise Acts as stores if, and only if—

(*a*) the goods are to be sold by retail either—

(i) in the course of a [journey made by the ship or aircraft][36], or

(ii) for consumption on board;

and

(*b*) the goods are not treated as exported by virtue of regulations under section 12 of the Customs and Excise Duties (General Reliefs) Act 1979 (goods for use in naval ships or establishments).

(4A) . . . [36]

(4B) In relation to goods treated as stores by virtue of subsection (4) above, any reference in the customs and excise Acts to the consumption of stores shall be construed as referring to the sale of the goods as mentioned in paragraph (*a*) of that subsection.][26]

(5) A person who deals in or sells tobacco products in the course of a trade or business carried on by him shall be deemed for the purposes of this Act to be carrying on an excise licence trade (and to be a revenue trader) notwithstanding that no excise licence is required for carrying on that trade or business.

(6) In computing for the purposes of this Act any period expressed therein as a period of clear days no account shall be taken of the day of the event from which the period is computed or of any Sunday or holiday.

(7) The provisions of this Act in so far as they relate to customs duties apply, notwithstanding that any duties are imposed for the benefit of the Communities, as if the revenue from duties so imposed remained part of the revenues of the Crown.

Notes—Words omitted from sub-s (3) are not relevant to VAT.

Cross references—See Police and Criminal Evidence Act 1984 s 114 (application of that Act to Customs and Excise).

Amendments—[1] Words in the definition of "Community transit goods" in sub-s (1) inserted by Isle of Man Act 1979 s 13, Sch 1.

[2] "(a)", para (b) and the word "and" preceding it in the definition of "revenue trader" in sub-s (1) inserted by FA 1981 Sch 8 para 1(1).

[3] Words in para (c) of the definition of "the revenue trade provisions of the customs and excise Acts" in sub-s (1) substituted by Betting and Gaming Duties Act 1981 Sch 5 para 5(a).

[4] Definitions inserted by FA 1984 Sch 4 Pt II, para 1.

[5] Words in the definition of "transit or transhipment" added by F(No 2)A 1987 s 103(3).

[6] Definition of "United Kingdom waters" inserted, and definition of "nautical mile" repealed, by Territorial Sea Act 1987 s 3(1), (4), Sch 1 para 4(1), Sch 2 with effect from 1 October 1987; see SI 1987/1270.

[7] Words in the definition of "revenue trader" inserted by FA 1991 s 11(2).

[8] Words in the definitions of "approved wharf", "examination station", "transit shed" in sub-s (1) substituted by Customs Controls on Importation of Goods Regulations, SI 1991/2724 reg 6(1), (2).

[9] Definition of "customs warehouse" repealed and definition of "victualling warehouse" inserted by Customs Warehousing Regulations, SI 1991/2725 regs 3(1), (2), 4, except in relation to its application to VAT by virtue of VATA 1994 s 16.

[10] Definition of "free zone regulations" repealed by Free Zone Regulations, SI 1991/2727 reg 4, with effect from 1 January 1992.

[11] Definition of "excise duty point" and words in the definition of "warehouse" in sub-s (1) inserted by F(No 2)A 1992 ss 1(8), 3 and Sch 1 para 1 and Sch 2 para 1 with effect from 9 December 1992 by virtue of F(No 2)A 1992 (Commencement No 3) Order, SI 1992/3104.

[12] Words in the definition of "occupier" in sub-s (1) substituted for the words "means the" by F(No 2)A 1992 s 3 and Sch 2 para 1 with effect from 9 December 1992 by virtue of F(No 2)A 1992 (Commencement No 3) Order, SI 1992/3104.

[13] Words omitted from the definition of "the Customs and Excise Acts 1979" in sub-s (1) repealed by F(No 2)A 1992 Sch 18 Pt II with effect from 1 January 1993.

[14] Words in the definition of "perfect entry" in sub-s (1) substituted by the Customs and Excise (Single Market etc) Regulations, SI 1992/3095 Sch 1 para 2 with effect from 1 January 1993.

[15] Definition of "approved route" in sub-s (1) repealed by the Customs and Excise (Single Market etc) Regulations, SI 1992/3095 regs 2, 3(1) and Sch 2 with effect from 1 January 1993.

[16] Word "and" in the definition of "revenue trade provisions of the customs and excise Acts" repealed and para (d) added to that definition by FA 1993 ss 30(1), (2), 41, 213, Sch 23 Pt I.

[17] Word "or" in the definition of "revenue trader" repealed and sub-para (ia) and the words in sub-para (ii) inserted in that definition by FA 1993 ss 30(1), (2)(a), (b), 41, 213, Sch 23 Pt I.

[18] Definition "free zone goods" substituted by VATA 1994 s 100, Sch 14 para 6.

[19] Definitions "registered excise dealer and shipper" and "registered excise dealers and shippers regulations" inserted by FA 1991 s 11(1).

[20] Definition "perfect entry" in sub-s (1) is repealed with effect from a day to be appointed by C & E Commissioners by FA 1981 Sch 19 Pt I.

[21] Words in the definitions of "British ship" and "tons register" substituted by Merchant Shipping Act 1995 Sch 13 para 53(1), (2) with effect from 1 January 1996.

[22] Word "and" in the definition of "revenue trade provisions of the customs and excise Acts" repealed and para (e) added to that definition by FA 1997 s 13, Sch 2 para 2, Sch 18 Pt II with effect from 19 March 1997.

[23] Word "or" in the definition of "revenue trader" repealed, sub-paras (a)(ib)and (a)(ic) inserted and words in sub-para (a)(ii) substituted by FA 1997 s 13, Sch 2 para 2, Sch 18 Part II with effect from 19 March 1997.

[24] Words "or called into actual service" in the definition of "armed forces" repealed by The Reserved Forces Act 1996 (Consequential Provisions etc.) Regulations 1998 reg 10(3), with effect from 1 January 1999.

[25] Words in the definition "law officer of the Crown" substituted by Scotland Act 1998 (Consequential Modifications) (No 1) Order, SI 1999/1042 Article 4 Sch 2 Part 1 para 6 with effect from 20 May 1999.

[26] Sub-ss (4), (4A), (4B) substituted by FA 1999 s 10 with effect from 1 July 1999.

[27] Definitions of "assigned matter" and "the Commissioners" substituted by Commissioners for Revenue and Customs Act 2005 s 50, Sch 4 para 22 with effect from 18 April 2005 by virtue of the Commissioners for Revenue and Customs Act 2005 (Commencement) Order, SI 2005/1126, art 2(2).

[29] Word in definition of "container" inserted by FA 2008 s 117(1), (2) with effect from 21 July 2008.

[30] Definition of "tribunal" inserted by the Transfer of Tribunal Functions and Revenue and Customs Appeals Order, SI 2009/56 art 3, Sch 1 paras 88, 89 with effect from 1 April 2009.

[31] In sub-s (1), definition of "nuclear material" inserted by the Criminal Justice and Immigration Act 2008 s 75, Sch 17 para 8(1), (2) with effect from 30 November 2009 (by virtue of SI 2009/3074 art 2(*i*), (*q*)).

[32] In sub-s (1), in definition of "assigned matter", words inserted by the Scotland Act 2012 s 24(7) with effect from 1 July 2012.

[33] In sub-s (1), in definition of "the revenue trade provisions of the customs and excise Acts", para (f) inserted; in definition of "revenue trader", word at end of para (a)(ic) repealed, para (a)(id) inserted, and in sub-para (ii), words substituted by FA 2012 s 191, Sch 24 para 41 with effect in relation to the playing of machine games on or after 1 February 2013.

[34] In sub-s (1) in definition of "goods", word substituted for word "baggage" by FA 2013 s 225 with effect from 17 July 2013.

[35] In sub-s (1) in definition of "the revenue trade provisions of the customs and excise Acts", para (*g*) inserted, in definition of "revenue trader", in para (*a*)(ic) words substituted for words "gaming within the meaning of the Betting and Gaming Duties

Act 1981 (see section 33(1))", para (*a*)(ie) inserted, and in para (ii) words substituted for words "or (id)", by FA 2014 s 196, Sch 28 paras 10, 11 with effect from 1 December 2014 (FA 2014 s 198(2)), subject to transitional provisions and savings in FA 2014 Sch 29.

36 In sub-s (4)(*a*)(i), words substituted, and subs (4A) repealed, by FA 2014 s 101, Sch 21 para 1 with effect from 1 April 2015 (by virtue of SI 2015/812 art 2).

37 In definition of "assigned matter", words inserted by the Wales Act 2014 s 7(1) with effect from 17 February 2015 (Wales Act 2014 s 29(2)(*b*)).

5 Time of importation, exportation, etc

(1) The provisions of this section shall have effect for the purposes of the customs and excise Acts.

(2) Subject to subsections (3) and (6) below, the time of importation of any goods shall be deemed to be—

(*a*) where the goods are brought by sea, the time when the ship carrying them comes within the limits of a port;

(*b*) where the goods are brought by air, the time when the aircraft carrying them lands in the United Kingdom or the time when the goods are unloaded in the United Kingdom, whichever is the earlier;

(*c*) where the goods are brought by land, the time when the goods are brought across the boundary into Northern Ireland.

(3) In the case of goods brought by sea of which entry is not required under [regulation 5 of the Customs Controls on Importation of Goods Regulations 1991][1], the time of importation shall be deemed to be the time when the ship carrying them came within the limits of the port at which the goods are discharged.

(4) Subject to subsections (5) and (7) below, the time of exportation of any goods from the United Kingdom shall be deemed to be—

(*a*) where the goods are exported by sea or air, the time when the goods are shipped for exportation;

(*b*) where the goods are exported by land, the time when they are cleared by the proper officer at the last customs and excise station on their way to the boundary.

(5) In the case of goods of a class or description with respect to the exportation of which any prohibition or restriction is for the time being in force under or by virtue of any enactment which are exported by sea or air, the time of exportation shall be deemed to be the time when the exporting ship or aircraft departs from the last port or customs and excise airport at which it is cleared before departing for a destination outside the United Kingdom.

(6) Goods imported by means of a pipe-line shall be treated as imported at the time when they are brought within the limits of a port or brought across the boundary into Northern Ireland.

(7) Goods exported by means of a pipe-line shall be treated as exported at the time when they are charged into that pipe-line for exportation.

(8) A ship shall be deemed to have arrived at or departed from a port at the time when the ship comes within or, as the case may be, leaves the limits of that port.

Commentary—*De Voil Indirect Tax Service* **V3.307, V4.307**.

Cross references—See VATA 1994 Sch 13 para 19 (importation of goods around that date; determination of time of importation);
Postal Packets (Customs and Excise) Regulations, SI 1986/260 reg 5(*a*) (modification of this section in its application to goods contained in postal packets).
Postal Packets (Customs and Excise) Regulations, SI 2011/3036 regs 9, 10 (modification of this section in its application to foreign postal packets carried by a universal service provider acting in that capacity).

Amendments—[1] Words in sub-s (3) substituted by Customs and Excise (Single Market etc) Regulations, SI 1992/3095 Sch 1 para 3 with effect from 1 January 1993.

PART II
ADMINISTRATION

Appointment and duties of Commissioners, officers, etc

6 . . . [1]

Commentary—*De Voil Indirect Tax Service* **V1.264, V1.265**.

Amendments—[1] Section repealed by Commissioners for Revenue and Customs Act 2005 ss 50, 52, Sch 4 para 21 and Sch 5 with effect from 18 April 2005 by virtue of the Commissioners for Revenue and Customs Act 2005 (Commencement) Order, SI 2005/1126, art 2(2).

Offences in connection with Commissioners, officers, etc

15 . . . [1]

Commentary—*De Voil Indirect Tax Service* **V5.303**.

Amendments—[1] Section repealed by the Commissioners for Revenue and Customs Act 2005 s 52, Sch 5 with effect from 18 April 2005 (by virtue of SI 2005/1126, art 2(2)(i)).

16 . . . [1]

Commentary—*De Voil Indirect Tax Service* **V5.303**.

Amendments—[1] Section repealed by Commissioners for Revenue and Customs Act 2005 ss 50, 52, Sch 4 para 21 and Sch 5 with effect from 18 April 2005 by virtue of the Commissioners for Revenue and Customs Act 2005 (Commencement) Order, SI 2005/1126, art 2(2).

Commissioners' receipts and expenses

17 . . .[1]

Commentary—*De Voil Indirect Tax Service* **V1.264**.
Amendments—[1] Section repealed by Commissioners for Revenue and Customs Act 2005 ss 50, 52, Sch 4 para 21 and Sch 5 with effect from 18 April 2005 by virtue of the Commissioners for Revenue and Customs Act 2005 (Commencement) Order, SI 2005/1126, art 2(2).

PART III
CUSTOMS AND EXCISE CONTROL AREAS

19 Appointment of ports, etc

(1) The Commissioners may by order made by statutory instrument appoint and name as a port for the purposes of customs and excise any area in the United Kingdom specified in the order.
(2) The appointment of any port for those purposes made before 1st August 1952 may be revoked, and the name or limits of any such port may be altered, by an order under subsection (1) above as if the appointment had been made by an order under that subsection.
(3) The Commissioners may in any port from time to time appoint boarding stations for the purpose of the boarding of or disembarkation from ships by officers.

Commentary—*De Voil Indirect Tax Service* **V3.307, V4.251**

21 Control of movement of aircraft, etc into and out of the United Kingdom

(1)–(6) . . .
(7) In this Act "customs and excise airport" means an aerodrome for the time being designated as a place for the landing or departure of aircraft for the purposes of the customs and excise Acts by an order made by the Secretary of State with the concurrence of the Commissioners which is in force under an Order in Council made in pursuance of [section 60 of the Civil Aviation Act 1982][1].
(8) . . .

Commentary—*De Voil Indirect Tax Service* **V3.307**.
Note—Sub-ss (1)–(6), (8) are not relevant to VAT.
Amendments—[1] Words substituted by Civil Aviation Act 1982 Sch 15 para 23.

PART IV
CONTROL OF IMPORTATION

Inward entry and clearance

37 . . .

Amendments—This section repealed by Customs and Excise (Single Market etc) Regulations, SI 1992/3095 regs 2, 3(5) and Sch 2 with effect from 1 January 1993.

[37A Initial and supplementary entries

[(1) The Commissioners may—
- (*a*) give such directions as they think fit for enabling an entry under regulation 5 of the Customs Controls on Importation of Goods Regulations 1991 to consist of an initial entry and a supplementary entry where the importer is authorised for the purposes of this section in accordance with the directions; and
- (*b*) include in the directions such supplementary provision in connection with entries consisting of initial and supplementary entries as they think fit.][5]

[(1A) Without prejudice to section 37 above, a direction under that section may—
- (*a*) provide that where the importer is not authorised for the purposes of this section but a person who is so authorised is appointed as his agent for the purpose of entering the goods, the entry may consist of an initial entry made by the person so appointed and a supplementary entry so made; and
- (*b*) make such supplementary provision in connection with entries consisting of initial and supplementary entries made as mentioned in paragraph (*a*) above as the Commissioners think fit.][2]

[(2) Where—
- (*a*) an initial entry made under subsection (1) above has been accepted and the importer has given security by deposit of money or otherwise to the satisfaction of the Commissioners for payment of the unpaid duty, or
- (*b*) an initial entry made under subsection (1A) above has been accepted and the person making the entry on the importer's behalf has given such security as is mentioned in paragraph (*a*) above,

the goods may][3] be delivered without payment of any duty chargeable in respect of the goods, but any such duty shall be paid within such time as the Commissioners may direct.
(3) An importer who makes an initial entry [under subsection (1) above][2] shall complete the entry by delivering the supplementary entry within such time as the Commissioners may direct.

[(3A) A person who makes an initial entry under subsection (1A) above on behalf of an importer shall complete the entry by delivering the supplementary entry within such time as the Commissioners may direct.][2]

(4) For the purposes of the customs and excise Acts an entry of goods shall be taken to have been delivered when an initial entry of the goods has been delivered, and accepted when an initial entry has been accepted.][1]

Commentary—*De Voil Indirect Tax Service* **V3.308**

Amendments—[1] This section inserted by FA 1984 Sch 5 para 2.

[2] Sub-ss (1A), (3A) and words in sub-s (3) inserted by FA 1990 s 7 and Sch 3 paras 1, 2(1), (3), (6), in relation to goods imported after 25 July 1990.

[3] Words in sub-s (2) substituted by FA 1990 s 7 and Sch 3 paras 1, 2(1), (4) in relation to goods imported after 25 July 1990.

[37B Postponed entry

(1) The Commissioners may, if they think fit, direct that where—

(*a*) such goods as may be specified in the direction are imported by an importer authorised for the purposes of this subsection;

(*b*) the importer has delivered a document relating to the goods to the proper officer, in such form and manner, containing such particulars and accompanied by such documents as the Commissioners may direct; and

(*c*) the document has been accepted by the proper officer,

the goods may be delivered before an entry of them has been delivered or any duty chargeable in respect of them has been paid.

[(1A) The Commissioners may, if they think fit, direct that where—

(*a*) such goods as may be specified in the direction are imported by an importer who is not authorised for the purposes of this subsection;

(*b*) a person who is authorised for the purposes of this subsection is appointed as his agent for the purpose of entering the goods;

(*c*) the person so appointed has delivered a document relating to the goods to the proper officer, in such form and manner, containing such particulars and accompanied by such documents as the Commissioners may direct; and

(*d*) the document has been accepted by the proper officer,

the goods may be delivered before an entry of them has been delivered or any duty chargeable in respect of them has been paid.][2]

(2) The Commissioners may, if they think fit, direct that where—

(*a*) such goods as may be specified in the direction are imported by an importer authorised for the purposes of this subsection;

(*b*) the goods have been removed from the place of importation to a place approved by the Commissioners for the clearance out of charge of such goods; and

(*c*) the conditions mentioned in subsection (3) below have been satisfied,

the goods may be delivered before an entry of them has been delivered or any duty chargeable in respect of them has been paid.

(3) The conditions are that—

(*a*) on the arrival of the goods at the approved place the importer delivers to the proper officer a notice of the arrival of the goods in such form and containing such particulars as may be required by the directions;

(*b*) within such time as may be so required the importer enters such particulars of the goods and such other information as may be so required in a record maintained by him at such place as the proper officer may require; and

(*c*) the goods are kept secure in the approved place for such period as may be required by the directions.

[(3A) The Commissioners may, if they think fit, direct that where—

(*a*) such goods as may be specified in the direction are imported by an importer who is not authorised for the purposes of this subsection;

(*b*) a person who is authorised for the purposes of this subsection is appointed as his agent for the purpose of entering the goods;

(*c*) the goods have been removed from the place of importation to a place approved by the Commissioners for the clearance out of charge of such goods; and

(*d*) the conditions mentioned in subsection (3B) below have been satisfied,

the goods may be delivered before an entry of them has been delivered or any duty chargeable in respect of them has been paid.][2]

[(3B) the conditions are that—

(*a*) on the arrival of the goods at the approved place the person appointed as the agent of the importer for the purpose of entering the goods delivers to the proper officer a notice of the arrival of the goods in such form and containing such particulars as may be required by the directions;

(b) within such time as may be so required the person appointed as the agent of the importer for the purpose of entering the goods enters such particulars of the goods and such other information as may be so required in a record maintained by him at such place as the proper officer may require; and

(c) the goods are kept secure in the approved place for such period as may be required by the directions.][3]

(4) The Commissioners may direct that the condition mentioned in subsection (3)(*a*) [or (3B) (*a*)][3] above shall not apply in relation to any goods specified in the direction and such a direction may substitute another condition.

(5) No goods shall be delivered under [subsection (1) or (2) above][4] unless the importer gives security by deposit of money or otherwise to the satisfaction of the Commissioners for the payment of any duty chargeable in respect of the goods which is unpaid.

[(5A) No goods shall be delivered under subsection (1A) or (3A) above unless the person appointed as the agent of the importer for the purpose of entering the goods gives security by deposit of money or otherwise to the satisfaction of the Commissioners for the payment of any duty chargeable in respect of the goods which is unpaid.][2]

(6) Where goods of which no entry has been made have been delivered under [sub-section (1) or (2) above][4], the importer shall deliver an entry of the goods under [regulation 5 of the Customs Controls on Importation of Goods Regulations 1991][5] within such time as the Commissioners may direct.

[(6A) Where goods of which no entry has been made have been delivered under sub-section (1A) or (3A) above, the person appointed as the agent of the importer for the purpose of entering the goods shall deliver an entry of the goods under section 37(1) above within such time as the Commissioners may direct.][2]

(7) For the purposes of section 43(2)(*a*) below such an entry shall be taken to have been accepted—

(*a*) in the case of goods delivered by virtue of a direction under subsection (1) [or (1A)][3] above, on the date on which the document mentioned in that subsection was accepted; and

(*b*) in the case of goods delivered by virtue of a direction under subsection (2) above, on the date on which particulars of the goods were entered as mentioned in subsection (3)(*b*) above;][1] [and][2]

[(*c*) in the case of goods delivered by virtue of a direction under subsection (3A) above, on the date on which particulars of the goods were entered as mentioned in subsection (3B)(*b*) above.][2]

Commentary—*De Voil Indirect Tax Service* **V3.308, V3.313.**

Amendments—[1] This section inserted by FA 1984 Sch 5 para 2.

[2] Sub-ss (1A), (3A), (3B), (5A), (6A), (7)(c) inserted by FA 1990 s 7 and Sch 3 paras 1, 3(1), (2), (3), (6), (8), (9)(b) in relation to goods imported after 25 July 1990.

[3] Words in sub-ss (4), (7)(a) inserted by FA 1990 s 7 and Sch 3 paras 1, 3(1), (4), (9)(a).

[4] Words in sub-ss (5), (6) substituted by FA 1990 s 7 and Sch 3 paras 1, 3(1), (5), (7).

[5] Words in sub-s (6) substituted by Customs and Excise (Single Market etc) Regulations, SI 1992/3095 Sch 1 para 6 with effect from 1 January 1993.

[37C Provisions supplementary to ss 37A and 37B

(1) The Commissioners may, if they think fit—

(*a*) authorise any [person][2] for the purposes of section 37A, or 37B(1) [, (1A), (2) or (3A)][3] above; and

(*b*) suspend or cancel the authorisation of any [person][2] where it appears to them that he has failed to comply with any requirement imposed on him by or under this Part of this Act or that there is other reasonable cause for suspension or cancellation.

(2) The Commissioners may give directions—

(*a*) imposing such requirements as they think fit on any [person][2] authorised under this section; or

(*b*) varying any such requirements previously imposed.

(3) If any person without reasonable excuse contravenes any requirement imposed by or under section 37A, 37B or this section he shall be liable on summary conviction to a penalty of level 4 on the standard scale.][1]

Commentary—*De Voil Indirect Tax Service* **V3.308.**

Amendments—[1] This section inserted by FA 1984 Sch 5 para 2.

[2] Word in sub-ss (1)(a), (b), (2)(a) substituted by FA 1990 s 7 and Sch 3 paras 1, 4 in relation to goods imported after 25 July 1990.

[3] Words in sub-s (1)(a) substituted by FA 1990 s 7 and Sch 3 paras 1, 4 in relation to goods imported after 25 July 1990.

[38B Correction and cancellation of entry

(1) Where goods have been entered for home use or for free circulation the importer may correct any of the particulars contained in an entry of the goods after it has been accepted if—

(*a*) the goods have not been cleared from customs and excise charge;

(*b*) he has not been notified by an officer that the goods are to be examined; and

(*c*) the entry has not been found by an officer to be incorrect.

(2) The proper officer may permit or require any correction allowed by subsection (1) above to be made by the delivery of a substituted entry.
(3) An entry of goods may at the request of the importer be cancelled at any time before the goods are cleared from customs and excise charge if the importer proves to the satisfaction of the Commissioners that the entry was delivered by mistake or that the goods cannot be cleared for free circulation.][1]

Commentary—*De Voil Indirect Tax Service* **V3.308**.
Amendments—[1] This section inserted by FA 1981 s 10(1), Sch 6 para 4 with effect from 1 April 1982; see FA 1981 (Import Procedures) (Commencement) Order, SI 1982/205.

41 Failure to comply with provisions as to entry

Without prejudice to any liability under any other provision of the Customs and Excise Acts 1979, any person making entry of goods on their importation who fails to comply with any of the requirements of this Part of this Act in connection with that entry shall be liable on summary conviction to a penalty of [level 2 on the standard scale][2] and the goods in question shall be liable to forfeiture [but this section shall not apply to—][1]

[(*a*) any failure which has been or may be remedied by virtue of section 38B(1); or][1]
[(*b*) any failure in respect of an entry which by virtue of section 38B(3) has been or may be cancelled at his request.][1]

Amendments—[1] Paras (a), (b) and the preceding words added by FA 1981 s 10(1), Sch 6 para 6 with effect from 1 April 1982; see FA 1981 (Import Procedures) (Commencement) Order, SI 1982/205.
[2] Words substituted by virtue of Criminal Justice Act 1982 ss 37, 46.

42 Power to regulate unloading, removal, etc of imported goods

(1) The Commissioners may make regulations—
(*a*) prescribing the procedure to be followed by a ship arriving at a port, an aircraft arriving at a customs and excise airport, or a person conveying goods into Northern Ireland by land;
(*b*) regulating the unloading, landing, movement and removal of goods on their importation;
and different regulations may be made with respect to importation by sea, air or land respectively.
(2) If any person contravenes or fails to comply with any regulation made under this section or with any direction given by the Commissioners or the proper officer in pursuance of any such regulation, he shall be liable on summary conviction to a penalty of [level 3 on the standard scale][1] and any goods in respect of which the offence was committed shall be liable to forfeiture.
[(3) Subsection (1)(*b*) above shall not apply in relation to goods imported on or after 1st January 1992 from a place outside the customs territory of the Community][2] [or to any goods which are moving under the procedure specified in [Article 165 of Council Regulation (EEC) No 2913/92 and Article 311 of Commission Regulation (EEC) No 2454/93][4] (transit procedures).][3]

Cross references—See Channel Tunnel (Customs and Excise) Order, SI 1990/2167 Schedule, para 6 (modification of sub-s (1)(*a*) above to extend its application to a vehicle arriving at a Customs approved area in France or through the tunnel from France).
FA 1994 s 14(1)(*d*) and Sch 5 para 2(3) (decisions by Commissioners for the purposes of regulations under this section; Commissioners' obligation to review certain decisions if required by any person affected by them).
Amendments—[1] Words in sub-s (2) substituted by virtue of Criminal Justice Act 1982 ss 37, 38, 46.
[2] Sub-s (3) added by Customs Controls on Importation of Goods Regulations, SI 1991/2724 reg 6(1), (9).
[3] Words in sub-s (3) added by Customs and Excise (Single Market etc) Regulations, SI 1992/3095 reg 3(2) with effect from 1 January 1993.
[4] Words in sub-s (3) substituted by Community Customs Code (Consequential Amendment of References) Regulations, SI 1993/3014 reg 2(1), (2).

Provisions as to duty on imported goods

43 Duty on imported goods

(1) Save as permitted by or under the customs and excise Acts or section 2(2) of the European Communities Act 1972 or any Community regulation or other instrument having the force of law, no imported goods shall be delivered or removed on importation until the importer has paid to the proper officer any duty chargeable thereon, and that duty shall, in the case of goods of which entry is made, be paid on making the entry.
(2) [Subject to subsections (2A), (2B) [(2C) and (2D)][7] below,][3] the duties of customs or excise and the rates thereof chargeable on imported goods—
[(*a*) if entry is made thereof, except where the entry is for warehousing, or if they are declared under section 78 below, shall be those in force with respect to such goods at the time when the entry is accepted or the declaration is made;][1]
(*b*) if entry *or, in the case of goods entered by bill of sight, perfect entry* is made thereof for warehousing, shall be ascertained in accordance with warehousing regulations;
[(*c*) if no entry is made thereof and the goods are not declared under section 78 below shall be—
(i) as respects Community customs duties, those in force with respect to such goods at the time of their entry into the customs territory of the Community; and
(ii) as respects other duties, those in force with respect to such goods at the time of their importation.][4]

44 Exclusion of section 43(1) for importers etc keeping standing deposits

Where the Commissioners so direct, section 43(1) above shall not apply if and so long as the importer or his agent pays to, and keeps deposited with, the Commissioners a sum by way of standing deposit sufficient in their opinion to cover any duty which may become payable in respect of goods entered by that importer or agent, and if the importer or agent complies with such other conditions as the Commissioners may impose.

Commentary—*De Voil Indirect Tax Service* **V5.117, V5.118**.

45 Deferred payment of customs duty

(1) The Commissioners may by regulations provide for the payment of customs duty to be deferred in such cases as may be specified by the regulations and subject to such conditions as may be imposed by or under the regulations; and duty of which payment is deferred under the regulations shall be treated, for such purposes as may be specified thereby, as if it had been paid.

(2) Regulations under this section may make different provision for goods of different descriptions or for goods of the same description in different circumstances.

Commentary—*De Voil Indirect Tax Service* **V5.117**.

Regulations—See Customs Duties (Deferred Payment) Regulations, SI 1976/1223.

Customs and Excise (Deferred Payment) (RAF Airfields and Offshore Installations) (No 2) Regulations, SI 1988/1898.

Excise Duties (Deferred Payment) Regulations, SI 1992/3152.

46 Goods to be warehoused without payment of duty

Any goods which are on their importation permitted to be entered for warehousing shall be allowed, subject to such conditions or restrictions as may be imposed by or under warehousing regulations, to be warehoused without payment of duty.

Commentary—*De Voil Indirect Tax Service* **V3.332**.

47 Relief from payment of duty of goods entered for transit or transhipment

Where any goods are entered for transit or transhipment, the Commissioners may allow the goods to be removed for that purpose, subject to such conditions and restrictions as they see fit, without payment of duty.

Commentary—*De Voil Indirect Tax Service* **V3.333**.

Cross references—See FA 1994 s 14(1)(*d*) and Sch 5 para 2(1)(*j*) (decisions by Commissioners for the purposes of this section; Commissioners' obligation to review any decision if required by any person affected by it).

48 Relief from payment of duty of goods temporarily imported

In such cases as the Commissioners may by regulations prescribe, where the Commissioners are satisfied that goods are imported only temporarily with a view to subsequent re-exportation, they may permit the goods to be delivered on importation, subject to such conditions as they see fit to impose, without payment of duty.

Commentary—*De Voil Indirect Tax Service* **V3.338**.

Cross references—See FA 1994 s 14(1)(*d*) and Sch 5 para 2(1)(*k*) (decisions by Commissioners for the purposes of this section; Commissioners' obligation to review any decision if required by any person affected by it).

Forfeiture, offences, etc in connection with importation

49 Forfeiture of goods improperly imported

(1) Where—

(*a*) except as provided by or under the Customs and Excise Acts 1979, any imported goods, being goods chargeable on their importation with customs or excise duty, are, without payment of that duty—

(i) unshipped in any port,

(ii) unloaded from any aircraft in the United Kingdom,

(iii) unloaded from any vehicle in, or otherwise brought across the boundary into, Northern Ireland, or

(iv) removed from their place of importation or from any approved wharf, examination station or transit shed; or

(*b*) any goods are imported, landed or unloaded contrary to any prohibition or restriction for the time being in force with respect thereto under or by virtue of any enactment; or

(*c*) any goods, being goods chargeable with any duty or goods the importation of which is for the time being prohibited or restricted by or under any enactment, are found, whether before or after the unloading thereof, to have been concealed in any manner on board any ship or aircraft or, while in Northern Ireland, in any vehicle; or

(*d*) any goods are imported concealed in a container holding goods of a different description; or

(*e*) any imported goods are found, whether before or after delivery, not to correspond with the entry made thereof; or

(*f*) any imported goods concealed or packed in any manner appearing to be intended to deceive an officer,

those goods shall, subject to subsection (2) below, be liable to forfeiture.

[(2A) Where the Commissioners require a duty of customs to be paid because of a failure to comply with a condition or other obligation imposed under section 47 or 48 below (not being a condition or obligation required to be complied with before the goods were allowed to be removed or delivered) the duty shall be charged as if entry of the goods had been accepted at the time when the non-compliance occurred.][5]
[(2B) Where any duties of customs are chargeable in respect of waste or debris resulting from the destruction of imported goods in free circulation, those duties and their rates shall be those in force at the time when the goods were destroyed.][5]
[(2C) As respects goods which have been unlawfully removed from customs charge, subsection (2)(*c*) above shall have effect with respect to any duties of customs as if they had entered the customs territory of the Community, or, as the case may be, had been imported at the time of their removal.][5]
[(2D) Nothing in the provisions of subsections (1) and (2) above or of subsection (6) below or in any exception to any of those provisions made by or under any of sections 44 to 48 below shall have effect for the purposes of any duty of excise chargeable on any goods for which—

(*a*) the excise duty point is fixed by regulations under section 1 of the Finance (No 2) Act 1992; and

(*b*) the applicable rate of duty is determined in accordance with subsection (2) of that section.][6]

(3) Any goods brought or coming into the United Kingdom by sea otherwise than as cargo, stores or baggage carried in a ship shall be chargeable with the like duty, if any, as would be applicable to those goods if they had been imported as merchandise; and if any question arises as to the origin of the goods they shall, unless that question is determined under section 120 below, section 14 of the Customs and Excise Duties (General Reliefs) Act 1979 (produce of the sea or continental shelf) or under a Community regulation or other instrument having the force of law, be deemed to be the produce of such country as the Commissioners may on investigation determine.

(4) Where, in accordance with approval given by the Commissioners, entry of goods is made by any method involving the use of a computer, subsection (2) above shall have effect as if the reference in paragraph (a) to the time of the delivery of the entry were a reference to the time when particulars contained in the entry are accepted by the computer.

(5) . . .

[(6) Where entry of goods is made otherwise than for warehousing and there is a reduction in the rate of duty of customs or excise chargeable on the goods between—

(*a*) the time mentioned in subsection (2)(*a*) above; and

(*b*) the time when the goods are cleared from customs and excise charge,

the rate of the duty chargeable on the goods shall, if the importer so requests, be that in force at the time mentioned in paragraph (b) above unless clearance of the goods has been delayed by reason of any act or omission for which the importer is responsible.][2]

[(7) Notwithstanding section 6(5) of the European Communities Act 1972 "duty of customs" in subsection (6) above does not include any agricultural levy.][2]

[(8) Where samples are taken of goods under section 38A above and the quantity of the goods covered by the entry which is subsequently delivered does not include the samples the duties of customs and the rates of those duties chargeable on the samples shall be those in force at the time when the application under subsection (1) of that section was made and shall be determined by reference to the particulars contained in the application.][2]

[(9) Where a substituted entry is delivered under section 38(2) or 38B(2) above the entry referred to in subsection (2)(*a*) above is the original entry.][2]

Commentary—*De Voil Indirect Tax Service* **V3.312.**

Notes—Sub-s (5) does not apply to VAT; see VAT Regulations, SI 1995/2518 reg 118(*c*)(i).

Cross references—See VATA 1994 s 16(1) and VAT Regulations, SI 1995/2518 reg 118(*c*)(i) (this section not to apply in relation to any tax chargeable on importation of goods from non-EEC countries with effect from 1 December 1992);

Postal Packets (Customs and Excise) Regulations, SI 1986/260 reg 5(*d*) (modification of this section in its application to goods contained in postal packets).

Postal Packets (Customs and Excise) Regulations, SI 2011/3036 regs 9, 12 (modification of this section in its application to foreign postal packets carried by a universal service provider acting in that capacity).

Amendments—[1] Sub-s (2)(a) substituted by FA 1981 s 10(3) and Sch 6 para 7(2) with effect from 1 April 1982; see FA 1981 (Import Procedures) (Commencement) Order, SI 1982/205.

[2] Sub-ss (6)–(9) added by FA 1981 s 10(3) and Sch 6 para 7(2) with effect from 1 April 1982; see FA 1981 (Import Procedures) (Commencement) Order, SI 1982/205.

[3] Words at the beginning of sub-s (2) substituted by Customs Duty Regulations, SI 1982/1324 reg 2(2).

[4] Sub-s (2)(c) substituted by Customs Duty Regulations, SI 1982/1324 reg 2(3) with effect from 15 October 1982.

[5] Sub-ss (2A)–(2C) inserted by Customs Duty Regulations, SI 1982/1324 reg 2(4) with effect from 15 October 1982.

[6] Sub-s (2D) inserted by F(No 2)A 1992 s 1(8) and Sch 1 para 2 with effect from 1 December 1992 by virtue of F(No 2)A 1992 (Commencement No 2 and Transitional Provisions) Order, SI 1992/2979 art 4 and Schedule, Pt II.

[7] Words in sub-s (2) substituted by F(No 2)A 1992 s 1(8) and Sch 1 para 2 with effect from 1 December 1992 by virtue of F(No 2)A 1992 (Commencement No 2 and Transitional Provisions) Order, SI 1992/2979 art 4 and Schedule, Pt II.

Prospective amendment—Words in italics in sub-s (2)(*b*) and whole of sub-s (4) repealed by FA 1981 Sch 19 Pt I, with effect from a date to be appointed.

(*b*) within such time as may be so required the person appointed as the agent of the importer for the purpose of entering the goods enters such particulars of the goods and such other information as may be so required in a record maintained by him at such place as the proper officer may require; and

(*c*) the goods are kept secure in the approved place for such period as may be required by the directions.][3]

(4) The Commissioners may direct that the condition mentioned in subsection (3)(*a*) [or (3B) (*a*)][3] above shall not apply in relation to any goods specified in the direction and such a direction may substitute another condition.

(5) No goods shall be delivered under [subsection (1) or (2) above][4] unless the importer gives security by deposit of money or otherwise to the satisfaction of the Commissioners for the payment of any duty chargeable in respect of the goods which is unpaid.

[(5A) No goods shall be delivered under subsection (1A) or (3A) above unless the person appointed as the agent of the importer for the purpose of entering the goods gives security by deposit of money or otherwise to the satisfaction of the Commissioners for the payment of any duty chargeable in respect of the goods which is unpaid.][2]

(6) Where goods of which no entry has been made have been delivered under [sub-section (1) or (2) above][4], the importer shall deliver an entry of the goods under [regulation 5 of the Customs Controls on Importation of Goods Regulations 1991][5] within such time as the Commissioners may direct.

[(6A) Where goods of which no entry has been made have been delivered under sub-section (1A) or (3A) above, the person appointed as the agent of the importer for the purpose of entering the goods shall deliver an entry of the goods under section 37(1) above within such time as the Commissioners may direct.][2]

(7) For the purposes of section 43(2)(*a*) below such an entry shall be taken to have been accepted—

(*a*) in the case of goods delivered by virtue of a direction under subsection (1) [or (1A)][3] above, on the date on which the document mentioned in that subsection was accepted; and

(*b*) in the case of goods delivered by virtue of a direction under subsection (2) above, on the date on which particulars of the goods were entered as mentioned in subsection (3)(*b*) above;][1] [and][2]

[(*c*) in the case of goods delivered by virtue of a direction under subsection (3A) above, on the date on which particulars of the goods were entered as mentioned in subsection (3B)(*b*) above.][2]

Commentary—*De Voil Indirect Tax Service* **V3.308, V3.313.**

Amendments—[1] This section inserted by FA 1984 Sch 5 para 2.

[2] Sub-ss (1A), (3A), (3B), (5A), (6A), (7)(c) inserted by FA 1990 s 7 and Sch 3 paras 1, 3(1), (2), (3), (6), (8), (9)(b) in relation to goods imported after 25 July 1990.

[3] Words in sub-ss (4), (7)(a) inserted by FA 1990 s 7 and Sch 3 paras 1, 3(1), (4), (9)(a).

[4] Words in sub-ss (5), (6) substituted by FA 1990 s 7 and Sch 3 paras 1, 3(1), (5), (7).

[5] Words in sub-s (6) substituted by Customs and Excise (Single Market etc) Regulations, SI 1992/3095 Sch 1 para 6 with effect from 1 January 1993.

[37C Provisions supplementary to ss 37A and 37B

(1) The Commissioners may, if they think fit—

(*a*) authorise any [person][2] for the purposes of section 37A, or 37B(1) [, (1A), (2) or (3A)][3] above; and

(*b*) suspend or cancel the authorisation of any [person][2] where it appears to them that he has failed to comply with any requirement imposed on him by or under this Part of this Act or that there is other reasonable cause for suspension or cancellation.

(2) The Commissioners may give directions—

(*a*) imposing such requirements as they think fit on any [person][2] authorised under this section; or

(*b*) varying any such requirements previously imposed.

(3) If any person without reasonable excuse contravenes any requirement imposed by or under section 37A, 37B or this section he shall be liable on summary conviction to a penalty of level 4 on the standard scale.][1]

Commentary—*De Voil Indirect Tax Service* **V3.308.**

Amendments—[1] This section inserted by FA 1984 Sch 5 para 2.

[2] Word in sub-ss (1)(a), (b), (2)(a) substituted by FA 1990 s 7 and Sch 3 paras 1, 4 in relation to goods imported after 25 July 1990.

[3] Words in sub-s (1)(a) substituted by FA 1990 s 7 and Sch 3 paras 1, 4 in relation to goods imported after 25 July 1990.

[38B Correction and cancellation of entry

(1) Where goods have been entered for home use or for free circulation the importer may correct any of the particulars contained in an entry of the goods after it has been accepted if—

(*a*) the goods have not been cleared from customs and excise charge;

(*b*) he has not been notified by an officer that the goods are to be examined; and

(*c*) the entry has not been found by an officer to be incorrect.

(2) The proper officer may permit or require any correction allowed by subsection (1) above to be made by the delivery of a substituted entry.
(3) An entry of goods may at the request of the importer be cancelled at any time before the goods are cleared from customs and excise charge if the importer proves to the satisfaction of the Commissioners that the entry was delivered by mistake or that the goods cannot be cleared for free circulation.][1]

Commentary—*De Voil Indirect Tax Service* **V3.308**.
Amendments—[1] This section inserted by FA 1981 s 10(1), Sch 6 para 4 with effect from 1 April 1982; see FA 1981 (Import Procedures) (Commencement) Order, SI 1982/205.

41 Failure to comply with provisions as to entry

Without prejudice to any liability under any other provision of the Customs and Excise Acts 1979, any person making entry of goods on their importation who fails to comply with any of the requirements of this Part of this Act in connection with that entry shall be liable on summary conviction to a penalty of [level 2 on the standard scale][2] and the goods in question shall be liable to forfeiture [but this section shall not apply to—][1]

[(*a*) any failure which has been or may be remedied by virtue of section 38B(1); or][1]

[(*b*) any failure in respect of an entry which by virtue of section 38B(3) has been or may be cancelled at his request.][1]

Amendments—[1] Paras (a), (b) and the preceding words added by FA 1981 s 10(1), Sch 6 para 6 with effect from 1 April 1982; see FA 1981 (Import Procedures) (Commencement) Order, SI 1982/205.
[2] Words substituted by virtue of Criminal Justice Act 1982 ss 37, 46.

42 Power to regulate unloading, removal, etc of imported goods

(1) The Commissioners may make regulations—

(*a*) prescribing the procedure to be followed by a ship arriving at a port, an aircraft arriving at a customs and excise airport, or a person conveying goods into Northern Ireland by land;

(*b*) regulating the unloading, landing, movement and removal of goods on their importation;

and different regulations may be made with respect to importation by sea, air or land respectively.
(2) If any person contravenes or fails to comply with any regulation made under this section or with any direction given by the Commissioners or the proper officer in pursuance of any such regulation, he shall be liable on summary conviction to a penalty of [level 3 on the standard scale][1] and any goods in respect of which the offence was committed shall be liable to forfeiture.
[(3) Subsection (1)(*b*) above shall not apply in relation to goods imported on or after 1st January 1992 from a place outside the customs territory of the Community][2] [or to any goods which are moving under the procedure specified in [Article 165 of Council Regulation (EEC) No 2913/92 and Article 311 of Commission Regulation (EEC) No 2454/93][4] (transit procedures).][3]

Cross references—See Channel Tunnel (Customs and Excise) Order, SI 1990/2167 Schedule, para 6 (modification of sub-s (1)(*a*) above to extend its application to a vehicle arriving at a Customs approved area in France or through the tunnel from France).
FA 1994 s 14(1)(*d*) and Sch 5 para 2(3) (decisions by Commissioners for the purposes of regulations under this section; Commissioners' obligation to review certain decisions if required by any person affected by them).
Amendments—[1] Words in sub-s (2) substituted by virtue of Criminal Justice Act 1982 ss 37, 38, 46.
[2] Sub-s (3) added by Customs Controls on Importation of Goods Regulations, SI 1991/2724 reg 6(1), (9).
[3] Words in sub-s (3) added by Customs and Excise (Single Market etc) Regulations, SI 1992/3095 reg 3(2) with effect from 1 January 1993.
[4] Words in sub-s (3) substituted by Community Customs Code (Consequential Amendment of References) Regulations, SI 1993/3014 reg 2(1), (2).

Provisions as to duty on imported goods

43 Duty on imported goods

(1) Save as permitted by or under the customs and excise Acts or section 2(2) of the European Communities Act 1972 or any Community regulation or other instrument having the force of law, no imported goods shall be delivered or removed on importation until the importer has paid to the proper officer any duty chargeable thereon, and that duty shall, in the case of goods of which entry is made, be paid on making the entry.
(2) [Subject to subsections (2A), (2B) [(2C) and (2D)][7] below,][3] the duties of customs or excise and the rates thereof chargeable on imported goods—

[(*a*) if entry is made thereof, except where the entry is for warehousing, or if they are declared under section 78 below, shall be those in force with respect to such goods at the time when the entry is accepted or the declaration is made;][1]

(*b*) if entry *or, in the case of goods entered by bill of sight, perfect entry* is made thereof for warehousing, shall be ascertained in accordance with warehousing regulations;

[(*c*) if no entry is made thereof and the goods are not declared under section 78 below shall be—

(i) as respects Community customs duties, those in force with respect to such goods at the time of their entry into the customs territory of the Community; and

(ii) as respects other duties, those in force with respect to such goods at the time of their importation.][4]

(2) Where any goods, the importation of which is for the time being prohibited or restricted by or under any enactment, are on their importation either—

(*a*) reported as intended for exportation in the same ship, aircraft or vehicle; or

(*b*) entered for transit or transhipment; or

(*c*) entered to be warehoused for exportation or for use as stores,

the Commissioners may, if they see fit, permit the goods to be dealt with accordingly.

Cross references—See Postal Packets (Customs and Excise) Regulations, SI 1986/260 (modification of this section in its application to postal packets).

Channel Tunnel (Customs and Excise) Order, SI 1990/2167 Schedule, para 7 (modification of sub-s (1) above to extend its application to goods unloaded from or concealed on a train or vehicle arriving through the tunnel from France or Belgium).

Postal Packets (Customs and Excise) Regulations, SI 2011/3036 regs 9, 13 (modification of this section in its application to foreign postal packets carried by a universal service provider acting in that capacity).

Simon's Tax Cases—*R (on the application of Eastenders Cash and Carry plc and anor) v R&C Comrs* [2010] EWHC 2797 (Admin), [2011] STC 64.

50 Penalty for improper importation of goods

(1) Subsection (2) below applies to goods of the following descriptions, that is to say—

(*a*) goods chargeable with a duty which has not been paid; and

(*b*) goods the importation, landing or unloading of which is for the time being prohibited or restricted by or under any enactment.

(2) If any person with intent to defraud Her Majesty of any such duty or to evade any such prohibition or restriction as is mentioned in subsection (1) above—

(*a*) unships or lands in any port or unloads from any aircraft in the United Kingdom or from any vehicle in Northern Ireland any goods to which this subsection applies, or assists or is otherwise concerned in such unshipping, landing or unloading; or

(*b*) removes from their place of importation or from any approved wharf, examination station, transit shed or customs and excise station any goods to which this subsection applies or assists or is otherwise concerned in such removal,

he shall be guilty of an offence under this subsection and may be [arrested.][3]

(3) If any person imports or is concerned in importing any goods contrary to any prohibition or restriction for the time being in force under or by virtue of any enactment with respect to those goods, whether or not the goods are unloaded, and does so with intent to evade the prohibition or restriction, he shall be guilty of an offence under this subsection and may be [arrested.][3]

(4) Subject to subsection [(5), (5A)[, (5B) or (5C)][7]][1] below, a person guilty of an offence under subsection (2) or (3) above shall be liable—

(*a*) on summary conviction, to a penalty of [£20,000][8] or of three times the value of the goods, whichever is the greater, or to imprisonment for a term not exceeding 6 months, or to both; or

(*b*) on conviction on indictment, to a penalty of any amount, or to imprisonment for a term not exceeding [7 years][4], or to both.

(5) In the case of an offence under subsection (2) or (3) above in connection with a prohibition or restriction on importation having effect by virtue of section 3 of the Misuse of Drugs Act 1971 subsection (4) above shall have effect subject to the modifications specified in Schedule 1 to this Act.

[(5A) In the case of—

(*a*) an offence under subsection (2) or (3) above committed in Great Britain in connection with a prohibition or restriction on the importation of any weapon or ammunition that is of a kind mentioned in section 5(1)(*a*), (*ab*), (*aba*), (*ac*), (*ad*), (*ae*), (*af*) or (*c*) or (1A)(*a*) of the Firearms Act 1968,

(*b*) any such offence committed in Northern Ireland in connection with a prohibition or restriction on the importation of any weapon or ammunition that is of a kind mentioned in [Article 45(1)(*a*), (*b*), (*c*), (*d*), (*e*) or (*g*) or (2)(*a*)][6] of the Firearms (Northern Ireland) Order [2004][6], or

(c) any such offence committed in connection with the prohibition contained in section 20 of the Forgery and Counterfeiting Act 1981,

subsection (4)(b) above shall have effect as if for the words "7 years" there were substituted the words "10 years".][5]

[(5B) In the case of an offence under subsection (2) or (3) above in connection with the prohibition contained in regulation 2 of the Import of Seal Skins Regulations 1996, subsection (4) above shall have effect as if—

(*a*) for paragraph (*a*) there were substituted the following—

"(*a*) on summary conviction, to a fine not exceeding [£20,000][8] or to imprisonment for a term not exceeding three months, or both"; and

(*b*) in paragraph (*b*) for the words "7 years" there were substituted the words "2 years".".][1]

[(5C) In the case of an offence under subsection (2) or (3) above in connection with a prohibition or restriction relating to the importation of nuclear material, subsection (4)(*b*) above shall have effect as if for the words "7 years" there were substituted the words "14 years".][7]

(6) If any person—

(*a*) imports or causes to be imported any goods concealed in a container holding goods of a different description; or

(*b*) directly or indirectly imports or causes to be imported or entered any goods found, whether before or after delivery, not to correspond with the entry made thereof,

he shall be liable on summary conviction to a penalty of three times the value of the goods or [level 3 on the standard scale][2], whichever is the greater.

(7) In any case where a person would, apart from this subsection, be guilty of—

(*a*) an offence under this section in connection with the importation of goods contrary to a prohibition or restriction; and

(*b*) a corresponding offence under the enactment or other instrument imposing the prohibition or restriction, being an offence for which a fine or other penalty is expressly provided by that enactment or other instrument,

he shall not be guilty of the offence mentioned in paragraph (a) of this subsection.

Cross references—See Channel Tunnel (Customs and Excise) Order, SI 1990/2167 Schedule, para 8 (extension of the application of sub-ss (1), (2) above to a person who unloads etc goods brought on a vehicle arriving through the tunnel from France or is concerned with bringing goods into a control zone in France or Belgium).

FA 2014 Sch 34 para 6(4)(*f*) (application of sub-section (2) above in relation to the issue of conduct notices to promoters of tax avoidance schemes).

Legal Aid, Sentencing and Punishment of Offenders Act 2012 (Fines on Summary Conviction) Regulations, SI 2015/664 reg 2(1), Sch 1 (offences under sub-ss (2), (3) do not apply for the purposes of the Legal Aid, Sentencing and Punishment of Offenders Act 2012 s 85(1))

Modification—Controlled Drugs (Drug Precursors) (Community External Trade) Regulations, SI 2008/296 reg 7 (modification of sub-s (4)(*a*), (*b*) in relation to breaches of Articles 20 and 12 of Council Regulation (EC) No 111/2005).

Forest Law Enforcement, Governance and Trade Regulations, SI 2012/178 reg 12 (modification of sub-s (4)(*b*) in relation to breaches of Article 4(1) of the FLEGT Regulation (EC) No 2173/2005).

Export Control (North Korea and Ivory Coast Sanctions and Syria Amendment) Order, SI 2013/3182 reg 12 (modification of sub-s (4)(*b*) in relation to the prohibitions of importation in Articles 2(3) or 4a(1)(*b*) of the North Korea Regulation (Council Regulation (EC) No 329/2007)).

Export Control (Syria Sanctions) Order, SI 2013/2012 reg 17 (modification of sub-s (4)(*b*) in relation to the prohibitions of importation in Articles 6(*a*) or 11(*a*)(1)(*b*) of the Syria Regulation (Council Regulation (EU) No 36/2012)).

Amendments—[1] Words in sub-s (4) substituted, and sub-s (5B) inserted, by the Import of Seal Skins Regulations, SI 1996/2686 reg 4(1), with effect from 15 November 1996.

[2] Words in sub-s (6) substituted by virtue of Criminal Justice Act 1982 ss 37, 38, 46.

[3] Words in sub-ss (2), (3) substituted by Police and Criminal Evidence Act 1984 s 114(1) with effect from 1 January 1986; see Police and Criminal Evidence Act 1984 (Commencement No 3) Order, SI 1985/1934.

[4] Words in sub-s (4)(b) substituted by FA 1988 s 12(1)(a).

[5] Sub-s (5A) substituted by the Criminal Justice Act 2003 s 293(1), (2) with effect from 22 January 2004 (by virtue of SI 2004/81), except in relation to any offences committed before that date.

[6] Words and figure in sub-s (5A) substituted by the Firearms (Northern Ireland) Order, SI 2004/702 art 82(1), Sch 7 para 3 with effect from 1 February 2005 (by virtue of SR 2005/4).

[7] In sub-s (4) words substituted for words "or (5B)", and sub-s (5C) inserted, by the Criminal Justice and Immigration Act 2008 s 75, Sch 17 para 8(1), (3) with effect from 30 November 2009 (by virtue of SI 2009/3074 art 2(*i*), (*q*)).

[8] In sub-ss (4)(*a*) and para (*a*) of inserted text in (5B)(*a*), figure substituted by the Legal Aid, Sentencing and Punishment of Offenders Act 2012 (Fines on Summary Conviction) Regulations, SI 2015/664 reg 2(2), Sch 2 paras 1, 3 with effect from 12 March 2015 in relation to England and Wales only.

PART VII

CUSTOMS AND EXCISE CONTROL: SUPPLEMENTARY PROVISIONS

Additional provisions as to information

77 Information in relation to goods imported or exported

(1) An officer may require any person—

(*a*) concerned with the . . . [2] shipment for carriage coastwise of goods of which [for that purpose an entry is required by regulation 5 of the Customs Controls on Importation of Goods Regulations 1991 or an entry or specification is required by or under this Act][3]; or

(*b*) concerned in the carriage, unloading, landing or loading of goods which are being or have been imported or exported,

to furnish in such form as the officer may require any information relating to the goods and to produce and allow the officer to inspect and take extracts from or make copies of any invoice, bill of lading or other book or document whatsoever relating to the goods.

(2) If any person without reasonable cause fails to comply with a requirement imposed on him under subsection (1) above he shall be liable on summary conviction to a penalty of [level 3 on the standard scale.][1]

(3) Where any prohibition or restriction to which this subsection applies, that is to say, any prohibition or restriction under or by virtue of any enactment with respect to—

(*a*) the exportation of goods to any particular destination; or

(*b*) the exportation of goods of any particular class or description to any particular destination,

is for the time being in force, then, if any person about to ship for exportation or to export any goods or, as the case may be, any goods of that class or description, in the course of making entry thereof before shipment or exportation makes a declaration as to the ultimate destination thereof, and the Commissioners have reason to suspect that the declaration is untrue in any material particular, the goods may be detained until the Commissioners are satisfied as to the truth of the declaration, and if they are not so satisfied the goods shall be liable to forfeiture.

(4) Any person concerned in the exportation of any goods which are subject to any prohibition or restriction to which subsection (3) above applies shall, if so required by the Commissioners, satisfy the Commissioners that those goods have not reached any destination other than that mentioned in the entry delivered in respect of the goods.

(5) If any person required under subsection (4) above to satisfy the Commissioners as mentioned in that subsection fails to do so, then, unless he proves—

(*a*) that he did not consent to or connive at the goods reaching any destination other than that mentioned in the entry delivered in respect of the goods; and

(*b*) that he took all reasonable steps to secure that the ultimate destination of the goods was not other than that so mentioned,

he shall be liable on summary conviction to a penalty of three times the value of the goods or [level 3 on the standard scale][2], whichever is the greater.

Cross references—See Postal Packets (Customs and Excise) Regulations, SI 1986/260 (modification of this section in its application to postal packets).

FA 1994 s 14(1)(*d*) and Sch 5 para 2(1)(*m*) (decisions by Commissioners for the purposes of this section; Commissioners' obligation to review any decision if required by any person affected by it).

Postal Packets (Customs and Excise) Regulations, SI 2011/3036 regs 9, 15 (application of this section to any foreign postal packet and its contents).

Amendments—[1] Words in sub-ss (2) and (5) substituted by virtue of Criminal Justice Act 1982 ss 37, 38, 46.

[2] Words in sub-s (1)(a) repealed by FA 1987 ss 10, 72(7) and Sch 16 Pt III.

[3] Words in sub-s (1) substituted by Customs and Excise (Single Market etc) Regulations, SI 1992/3095 reg 10(1), Sch 1 para 7.

[77A Information powers

(1) Every person who is concerned (in whatever capacity) in the importation or exportation of goods for which [for that purpose an entry is required by regulation 5 of the Customs Controls on Importation of Goods Regulations 1991 or an entry or specification is required by or under this Act][2] shall—

(*a*) furnish to the Commissioners, within such time and in such form as they may reasonably require, such information relating to the goods or to the importation or exportation as the Commissioners may reasonably specify; and

(*b*) if so required by an officer, produce or cause to be produced for inspection by the officer—

(i) at the principal place of business of the person upon whom the demand is made or at such other place as the officer may reasonably require, and

(ii) at such time as the officer may reasonably require,

any documents relating to the goods or to the importation or exportation.

(2) Where, by virtue of subsection (1) above, an officer has power to require the production of any documents from any such person as is referred to in that subsection, he shall have the like power to require production of the documents concerned from any other person who appears to the officer to be in possession of them; but where any such other person claims a lien on any document produced by him, the production shall be without prejudice to the lien.

(3) An officer may take copies of, or make extracts from, any document produced under subsection (1) or subsection (2) above.

(4) If it appears to him to be necessary to do so, an officer may, at a reasonable time and for a reasonable period, remove any document produced under subsection (1) or subsection (2) above and shall, on request, provide a receipt for any document so removed; and where a lien is claimed on a document produced under subsection (2) above, the removal of the document under this subsection shall not be regarded as breaking the lien.

(5) Where a document removed by an officer under subsection (4) above is reasonably required for the proper conduct of a business, the officer shall, as soon as practicable, provide a copy of the document, free of charge, to the person by whom it was produced or caused to be produced.

(6) Where any documents removed under the powers conferred by this section are lost or damaged, the Commissioners shall be liable to compensate their owner for any expenses reasonably incurred by him in replacing or repairing the documents.

(7) If any person fails to comply with a requirement under this section, he shall be liable on summary conviction to a penalty of level 3 on the standard scale.][1]

Amendments—[1] This section inserted by FA 1987 s 10.

[2] Words in sub-s (1) substituted by virtue of Customs and Excise (Single Market etc) Regulations, SI 1992/3095 reg 10(1) and Sch 1 para 7.

78 Customs and Excise control of persons entering or leaving the United Kingdom

(1) Any person entering the United Kingdom shall, at such place and in such manner as the Commissioners may direct, declare any thing contained in his baggage or carried with him which—

(*a*) he has obtained outside the United Kingdom; or

(*b*) being dutiable goods or chargeable goods, he has obtained in the United Kingdom without payment of duty or tax,

and in respect of which he is not entitled to exemption from duty and tax by virtue of any order under section 13 of the Customs and Excise Duties (General Reliefs) Act 1979 (personal reliefs).

In this subsection "chargeable goods" means goods on the importation of which value added tax is chargeable or goods obtained in the United Kingdom before 1st April 1973 which are chargeable goods within the meaning of the Purchase Tax Act 1963; and "tax" means value added tax or purchase tax.

[(1A) Subsection (1) above does not apply to a person entering the United Kingdom from the Isle of Man as respects anything obtained by him in the Island unless it is chargeable there with duty or value added tax and he has obtained it without payment of the duty or tax.][1]

[(1B) Subsection (1) above does not apply to a person entering the United Kingdom from another member State, except—

(*a*) where he arrives at a customs and excise airport in an aircraft in which he began his journey in a place outside the member States; or

(*b*) as respects such of his baggage as—

(i) is carried in the hold of the aircraft in which he arrives at a customs and excise airport, and

(ii) notwithstanding that it was transferred on one or more occasions from aircraft to aircraft at an airport in a member State, began its journey by air from a place outside the member States.][4]

(2) Any person entering or leaving the United Kingdom shall answer such questions as the proper officer may put to him with respect to his baggage and any thing contained therein or carried with him, and shall, if required by the proper officer, produce that baggage and any such thing for examination at such place as the Commissioners may direct.

[(2A) Subject to subsection (1A) above, where the journey of a person arriving by air in the United Kingdom is continued or resumed by air to a destination in the United Kingdom which is not the place where he is regarded for the purposes of this section as entering the United Kingdom, subsections (1) and (2) above shall apply in relation to that person on his arrival at that destination as they apply in relation to a person entering the United Kingdom.][3]

(3) Any person failing to declare any thing or to produce any baggage or thing as required by this section shall be liable on summary conviction to a penalty of three times the value of the thing not declared or of the baggage or thing not produced, as the case may be, or [level 3 on the standard scale][2], whichever is the greater.

(4) Any thing chargeable with any duty or tax which is found concealed, or is not declared, and any thing which is being taken into or out of the United Kingdom contrary to any prohibition or restriction for the time being in force with respect thereto under or by virtue of any enactment, shall be liable to forfeiture.

Commentary—*De Voil Indirect Tax Service* **V3.345, V3.346.**

Cross references—See F(No 2)A 1992 s 4(3)(*g*) (restriction of enforcement powers under this section with effect from 1 January 1993 in relation to movements of persons or things between member States).

Amendments—[1] Sub-s (1A) inserted by Isle of Man Act 1979 s 13, Sch 1.

[2] Words in sub-s (3) substituted by virtue of Criminal Justice Act 1982 ss 37, 38, 46.

[3] Sub-s (2A) inserted by F(No 2)A 1992 s 5 with effect from 1 January 1993.

[4] Sub-s (1B) inserted by Customs and Excise (Single Market etc) Regulations, SI 1992/3095 reg 3(10) with effect from 1 January 1993.

79 Power to require evidence in support of information

(1) The Commissioners may, if they consider it necessary, require evidence to be produced to their satisfaction in support of any information required by or under Parts III to VII of this Act to be provided in respect of goods imported or exported.

(2) Without prejudice to subsection (1) above, where any question as to the duties chargeable on any imported goods, or the operation of any prohibition or restriction on importation depends on any question as to the place from which the goods were consigned, or any question where they or other goods are to be treated as grown, manufactured or produced, or any question as to payments made or relief from duty allowed in any country or territory, then—

(*a*) the Commissioners may require the importer of the goods to furnish to them, in such form as they may prescribe, proof of—

(i) any statement made to them as to any fact necessary to determine that question, or

(ii) the accuracy of any certificate or other document furnished in connection with the importation of the goods and relating to the matter in issue, and if such proof is not furnished to their satisfaction, the question may be determined without regard to that statement or to that certificate or document; and

(*b*) if in any proceedings relating to the goods or to the duty chargeable thereon the accuracy of any such certificate or document comes in question, it shall be for the person relying on it to furnish proof of its accuracy.

Cross references—See FA 1994 s 14(1)(*d*) and Sch 5 para 2(1)(*m*) (decisions by Commissioners for the purposes of this section; Commissioners' obligation to review any decision if required by any person affected by it).

PART VIII
WAREHOUSES AND QUEEN'S WAREHOUSES AND RELATED PROVISIONS ABOUT PIPE-LINES

92 Approval of warehouses

(1) The Commissioners may approve, for such periods and subject to such conditions as they think fit, places of security for the deposit, keeping and securing—

(*a*) of imported goods chargeable as such with excise duty (whether or not also chargeable with customs duty) without payment of the excise duty;

(*b*) of goods for exportation or for use as stores, being goods not eligible for home use;

(*c*) of goods manufactured or produced in the United Kingdom [or the Isle of Man][1] and permitted by or under the customs and excise Acts to be warehoused without payment of any duty of excise chargeable thereon;

(*d*) of goods imported into or manufactured or produced in the United Kingdom [or the Isle of Man][1] and permitted by or under the customs and excise Acts to be warehoused on drawback,

subject to and in accordance with warehousing regulations; and any place of security so approved is referred to in this Act as an "excise warehouse".

(2) The Commissioners may approve, for such periods and subject to such conditions as they think fit, places of security for the deposit, keeping and securing—

(*a*) of imported goods chargeable with customs duty or otherwise not for the time being in free circulation in member States (whether or not also chargeable with excise duty) without payment of the customs duty;

[(*b*) of such other goods as the Commissioners may allow to be warehoused—

(i) for exportation or for use as stores in cases where relief from or repayment of any customs duty or other payment is conditional on their exportation or use as stores; or

(ii) for exportation or for use for a purpose referred to in a Community regulation in cases where payment of an export refund under such a regulation is conditional on their exportation or use for such a purpose,][2]

subject to and in accordance with warehousing regulations; and any place of security so approved is referred to in this Act as a "customs warehouse".

(3) The same place may be approved under this section both as a customs and as an excise warehouse.

(4) Notwithstanding subsection (2) above and the terms of the approval of the warehouse but subject to directions under subsection (5) below, goods of the following descriptions, not being goods chargeable with excise duty which has not been paid, that is to say—

(*a*) goods originating in member States;

(*b*) goods which are in free circulation in member States; and

(*c*) goods placed on importation under a customs procedure (other than warehousing) involving the suspension of, or the giving of relief from, customs duties,

may be kept, without being warehoused, in a customs warehouse.

(5) The Commissioners may from time to time give directions—

(*a*) as to the goods which may or may not be deposited in any particular warehouse or class of warehouse;

(*b*) as to the part of any warehouse in which any class or description of goods may be kept or secured.

(6) If, after the approval of a warehouse as an excise warehouse, the occupier thereof makes without the previous consent of the Commissioners any alteration therein or addition thereto, [the making of the alteration or addition shall attract a penalty under section 9 of the Finance Act 1994 (civil penalties).][3]

(7) The Commissioners may at any time for reasonable cause revoke or vary the terms of their approval of any warehouse under this section.

[(8) Where any person contravenes or fails to comply with any condition imposed or direction given by the Commissioners under this section, his contravention or failure to comply shall attract a penalty under section 9 of the Finance Act 1994 (civil penalties).][3]

Commentary—*De Voil Indirect Tax Service* **V3.138, V3.332, V5.141**.

Notes—By virtue of Customs Warehousing Regulations, SI 1991/2725 regs 3(1), (4), 4 the following provisions of this section apply for VAT purposes only—

(i) sub-s (2)

(ii) the word "customs" in sub-s (3)
(iii) the words "customs warehouse" in sub-s (4).

Cross references—See FA 1994 s 14(1)(*d*) and Sch 5 para 2(1)(*n*) (decisions by Commissioners for the purposes of this section; Commissioners' obligation to review certain decisions if required by any person affected by them).

Amendments—[1] Words in sub-s (1)(c), (d) inserted by Isle of Man Act 1979 s 13, Sch 1 para 21.
[2] Sub-s (2)(b) substituted by FA 1988 s 9(1).
[3] Sub-s (8) and words in sub-s (6) substituted by FA 1994 Sch 4 paras 1, 2.

PART VIIIA
FREE ZONES

Amendments—This Part (ie ss 100A–100F) inserted by FA 1984 Sch 4 Pt I.

[100A Designation of free zones

(1) The Treasury may by order designate any area in the United Kingdom as a special area for customs purposes.
(2) An area so designated shall be known as a "free zone".
(3) An order under subsection (1) above—
(*a*) shall have effect for such period as shall be specified in the order;
(*b*) may be made so as to take effect, in relation to the area or any part of the area designated by a previous order under this section, on the expiry of the period specified in the previous order;
(*c*) shall appoint one or more persons as the responsible authority or authorities for the free zone;
(*d*) may impose on any responsible authority such conditions or restrictions as may be specified; and
(*e*) may be revoked if the Commissioners are satisfied that there has been a failure to comply with any condition or restriction.
(4) The Treasury may by order—
(*a*) from time to time vary—
(i) the conditions or restrictions imposed by a designation order; or
(ii) with the agreement of the responsible authority, the area designated; or
(*b*) appoint one or more persons as the responsible authority or authorities for a free zone either in addition to or in substitution for any person appointed as such by a designation order.
(5) In this Act "designation order" means an order made under subsection (1) above.
(6) Any order under this section shall be made by statutory instrument.][1]

Commentary—*De Voil Indirect Tax Service* **V3.331**.

Orders—See Free Zone (Birmingham Airport) Designation Order, SI 1991/1737; Free Zone (Humberside) Designation Order, SI 1994/144; Free Zone (Port of Sheerness) Designation Order, SI 1994/2898; Free Zone (Southampton) Designation Order, SI 2001/2880; Free Zone (Liverpool) Designation Order, SI 2001/2881; Free Zone (Prestwick Airport) Designation Order, SI 2001/2882; Free Zone (Port of Tilbury) Order, SI 2002/1418.

Amendments—[1] This section inserted by FA 1984 Sch 4 Pt I.

[100B Free zone regulations][1]

Commentary—*De Voil Indirect Tax Service* **V3.331**.

Amendments—[1] This section inserted by FA 1984 Sch 4 Pt I.
This section repealed by Free Zone Regulations, SI 1991/2727 reg 3(1) with effect from 1 January 1992, but subject to reg 3(2); and repealed fully by VATA 1994 s 100(2) and Sch 15, with effect from 1 September 1994.

[100C Free zone goods: customs duties, etc][1]

Commentary—*De Voil Indirect Tax Service* **V3.331**

Amendments—[1] This section inserted by FA 1984 Sch 4 Pt I.
This section repealed by VATA 1994 s 100(2), Sch 15, with effect from 1 September 1994.

[100D Free zone regulations: supplemental][1]

Commentary—*De Voil Indirect Tax Service* **V3.331**.

Amendments—[1] This section inserted by FA 1984 Sch 4 Pt I.
This section repealed by Free Zone Regulations, SI 1991/2727 reg 3(1) with effect from 1 January 1992.

[100E Control of trading in free zones]

Commentary—*De Voil Indirect Tax Service* **V3.331**.

Amendments—This section inserted by FA 1984 Sch 4 Pt I.
This section repealed by the Free Zone Regulations, SI 1991/2727 reg 3(1) with effect from 1 January 1992.

[100F Powers of search

(1) Any person entering or leaving a free zone shall answer such questions as any officer may put to him with respect to any goods and shall, if required by the officer, produce those goods for examination at such place as the Commissioners may direct.
(2) At a time while a vehicle is entering or leaving a free zone, any officer may board the vehicle and search any part of it.
(3) Any officer may at any time enter upon and inspect a free zone and all buildings and goods within the zone.][1]

Commentary—*De Voil Indirect Tax Service* **V3.331**.

Amendments—[1] This section inserted by FA 1984 Sch 4 Pt I.

PART X
DUTIES AND DRAWBACKS—GENERAL PROVISIONS
General provisions relating to imported goods

125 Valuation of goods for purposes of ad valorem duties

(1), (2) . . .

(3) The Commissioners may make regulations for the purpose of giving effect to the *foregoing provisions of this section*, and in particular for requiring any importer or other person concerned with the importation of goods—

(*a*) to furnish to the Commissioners in such form as they may require, such information as is in their opinion necessary for a proper valuation of the goods; and

(*b*) to produce any books of account or other documents of whatever nature relating to the purchase, importation or sale of the goods by that person.

(4) If any person contravenes or fails to comply with any regulation made under sub-section (3) above he shall be liable on summary conviction to a penalty of [level 3 on the standard scale].[1]

Commentary—*De Voil Indirect Tax Service* **V3.314**.

Notes—Sub-ss (1) and (2) are excepted from the enactments which apply to value added tax by virtue of VATA 1994 s 16(1): VAT Regulations, SI 1995/2518 reg 118(*c*)(ii).

Sub-s (3) has effect in its application to value added tax by virtue of VATA 1994 s 16(1) as if the reference to the preceding subsections of s 125 (ie the italicised words) included a reference to VATA 1983 s 11: VAT Regulations, SI 1995/2518 reg 121.

Amendments—[1] Words in sub-s (4) substituted by virtue of Criminal Justice Act 1982 ss 37, 38, 46.

PART XI
[ARREST] OF PERSONS, FORFEITURE AND LEGAL PROCEEDINGS
[Arrest] of persons

Amendments—Words in square brackets substituted by Police and Criminal Evidence Act 1984 s 114(1) with effect from 1 January 1986; see Police and Criminal Evidence Act 1984 (Commencement No 3) Order, SI 1985/1934.

138 Provisions as to [arrest][1] of persons

(1) Any person who has committed, or whom there are reasonable grounds to suspect of having committed, any offence for which he is liable to be [arrested][1] under the customs and excise Acts may be [arrested][1] by any officer . . . [2]or any member of Her Majesty's armed forces or coastguard at any time within [20 years][4] from the date of the commission of the offence.

(2) Where it was not practicable to [arrest][1] any person so liable at the time of the commission of the offence, or where any such person having been then or subsequently [arrested][1] for that offence has escaped, he may be [arrested][1] by any officer . . . [2] or any member of Her Majesty's armed forces or coastguard at any time and may be proceeded against in like manner as if the offence had been committed at the date when he was finally [arrested][1].

(3) Where any person who is a member of the crew of any ship in Her Majesty's employment or service is [arrested][1]by an officer for an offence under the customs and excise Acts, the commanding officer of the ship shall, if so required by the [arresting][1]officer, keep that person secured on board that ship until he can be brought before a court and shall then deliver him up to the proper officer.

[(4) Where any person has been arrested by a person who is not an officer—

(*a*) by virtue of this section; or

(*b*) by virtue of section 24 [or 24A][6] of the Police and Criminal Evidence Act 1984 in its application to offences under the customs and excise Acts, [or][5]

[(*c*) by virtue of Article 26 of the Police and Criminal Evidence (Northern Ireland) Order 1989 in its application to such offences][5]

the person arresting him shall give notice of the arrest to an officer at the nearest convenient office of customs and excise.][3]

Cross reference—Nuclear Material (Offences) Act 1983 s 1D(2) (as inserted by Criminal Justice and Immigration Act 2008 s 75, Sch 17 para 3) (Offences of importing or exporting etc nuclear material: extended jurisdiction).

Amendments—[1] Words in sub-ss (1)–(3) substituted by Police and Criminal Evidence Act 1984 s 114(1) with effect from 1 January 1986; see Police and Criminal Evidence Act 1984 (Commencement No 3) Order, SI 1985/1934.

[2] Words in sub-ss (1), (2) repealed by Police and Criminal Evidence Act 1984 ss 26(1), 119(2), 120, Sch 7 with effect from 1 January 1986; see Police and Criminal Evidence Act 1984 (Commencement No 3) Order, SI 1985/1934.

[3] Sub-s (4) substituted by Police and Criminal Evidence Act 1984 s 119(1), Sch 6 Pt II, para 37 with effect from 1 January 1986; see Police and Criminal Evidence Act 1984 (Commencement No 3) Order, SI 1985/1934.

[4] Words in sub-s (1) substituted by FA 1988 s 11(1), (2).

[5] Words in sub-s (4) inserted by Police and Criminal Evidence (Northern Ireland) Order, SI 1989/1341 art 90(1), Sch 6 para 9.

[6] In sub-s (4)(b), words inserted by the Serious Organised Crime and Police Act 2005 s 111, Sch 7 para 54 with effect from 1 January 2006, see Serious Organised Crime and Police Act 2005 (Commencement No 4 and Transitory Provision), SI 2005/3495, art 2(1)(m).

Forfeiture

139 Provisions as to detention, seizure and condemnation of goods, etc

(1) Any thing liable to forfeiture under the customs and excise Acts may be seized or detained by any officer or constable or any member of Her Majesty's armed forces or coastguard.

[(1A) A person mentioned in subsection (1) who reasonably suspects that any thing may be liable to forfeiture under the customs and excise Acts may detain that thing.

(1B) References in this section and Schedule 2A to a thing detained as liable to forfeiture under the customs and excise Acts include a thing detained under subsection (1A).][2]

(2) Where any thing is seized or detained as liable to forfeiture under the customs and excise Acts by a person other than an officer, that person shall, subject to subsection (3) below, [deliver that thing to an officer][2]

(3) Where the person seizing or detaining any thing as liable to forfeiture under the customs and excise Acts is a constable and that thing is or may be required for use in connection with any proceedings to be brought otherwise than under those Acts it may, subject to subsection (4) below, be retained in the custody of the police until either those proceedings are completed or it is decided that no such proceedings shall be brought.

(4) The following provisions apply in relation to things retained in the custody of the police by virtue of subsection (3) above, that is to say—

(*a*) notice in writing of the seizure or detention and of the intention to retain the thing in question in the custody of the police, together with full particulars as to that thing, shall be given to [an officer][2];

(*b*) any officer shall be permitted to examine that thing and take account thereof at any time while it remains in the custody of the police;

(*c*) nothing in the Police (Property) Act 1897 shall apply in relation to that thing.

(5) Subject to subsections (3) and (4) above and to [Schedules 2A and 3][2] to this Act, any thing seized or detained under the customs and excise Acts shall, pending the determination as to its forfeiture or disposal, be dealt with, and, if condemned or deemed to have been condemned or forfeited, shall be disposed of in such manner as the Commissioners may direct.

[(5A) Schedule 2A contains supplementary provisions relating to the detention of things as liable to forfeiture under the customs and excise Acts.][2]

(6) Schedule 3 to this Act shall have effect for the purpose of forfeitures, and of proceedings for the condemnation of any thing as being forfeited, under the customs and excise Acts.

(7) If any person, not being an officer, by whom any thing is seized or detained or who has custody thereof after its seizure or detention, fails to comply with any requirement of this section or with any direction of the Commissioners given thereunder, he shall be liable on summary conviction to a penalty of [level 2 on the standard scale][1].

(8) Subsections (2) to (7) above shall apply in relation to any dutiable goods seized or detained by any person other than an officer notwithstanding that they were not so seized as liable to forfeiture under the customs and excise Acts.

Commentary—*De Voil Indirect Tax Service* **V4.309, V4.346**.

Simon's Tax Cases—*Demand & Supply Cash & Carry Ltd v R&C Comrs* [2010] STC 832, *R (on the application of Eastenders Cash and Carry plc and anor) v R&C Comrs* [2010] EWHC 2797 (Admin), [2011] STC 64.

Amendments—[1] Reference to level 2 on the standard scale substituted by virtue of Criminal Justice Act 1982 ss 37, 46.
[2] Sub-ss (1A), (1B), (5A) inserted, and words in sub-ss (2), (4), (5) substituted, by FA 2013 s 226(1)–(6) with effect in relation to things detained on or after 17 July 2013.

General provisions as to legal proceedings

Cross references—See VATA 1994 s 72(12) (ss 145–155 of this Act to apply in relation to offences under the value added tax legislation);

Free Zone Regulations, SI 1991/2727 reg 7 (ss 145–155 of this Act to apply in relation to offences and penalties under reg 6 of the Regulations).

Statistics of Trade (Customs and Excise) Regulations, SI 1992/2790 (ss 145–148, 150–154 of this Act apply to these regulations).

145 Institution of proceedings

(1) Subject to the following provisions of this section, no proceedings for an offence under the customs and excise Acts or for condemnation under Schedule 3 to this Act shall be instituted [except—

(*a*) by or with the consent of the Director of Revenue and Customs Prosecutions, or

(*b*) by order of, or with the consent of, the Commissioners for Her Majesty's Revenue and Customs.][2]

(2) Subject to the following provisions of this section, any proceedings under the customs and excise Acts instituted [by order of the Commissioners][2]in a magistrates' court, and any such proceedings instituted [by order of the Commissioners][2] in a court of summary jurisdiction in Northern Ireland, shall be commenced in the name of an officer [of Revenue and Customs][2].

(3) Subsections (1) and (2) above shall not apply to proceedings on indictment in Scotland.

[(4) In the case of the death, removal, discharge or absence of the officer in whose name any proceedings were commenced under subsection (2) above, those proceedings may be continued by any officer authorised in that behalf by the Commissioners.] [2]

(5) Nothing in the foregoing provisions of this section shall prevent the institution of proceedings for an offence under the customs and excise Acts by order and in the name of a law officer of the Crown in any case in which he thinks it proper that proceedings should be so instituted.

(6) Notwithstanding anything in the foregoing provisions of this section, where any person has been [arrested][1] for any offence for which he is liable to be [arrested][1] under the customs and excise Acts, any court before which he is brought may proceed to deal with the case although the proceedings have not been instituted [in accordance with this section][2]or have not been commenced in the name of an officer.

Commentary—*De Voil Indirect Tax Service* **V5.304**.

Cross reference—Nuclear Material (Offences) Act 1983 s 1D(3) (as inserted by Criminal Justice and Immigration Act 2008 s 75, Sch 17 para 3) (Offences of importing or exporting etc nuclear material: extended jurisdiction).

Amendments—[1] Words in sub-s (6) substituted by Police and Criminal Evidence Act 1984 s 114(1) with effect from 1 January 1986; see Police and Criminal Evidence Act 1984 (Commencement No 3) Order, SI 1985/1934.

[2] Words in sub-ss (1), (6) substituted, words in sub-s (2) inserted, and words in sub-s (4) repealed, by Commissioners for Revenue and Customs Act 2005 ss 50, 52, Sch 4 para 23 and Sch 5 with effect from 18 April 2005 by virtue of the Commissioners for Revenue and Customs Act 2005 (Commencement) Order, SI 2005/1126, art 2(2).

146 Service of process

(1) Any summons or other process issued anywhere in the United Kingdom for the purpose of any proceedings under the customs and excise Acts may be served on the person to whom it is addressed in any part of the United Kingdom without any further endorsement, and shall be deemed to have been duly served—

(*a*) if delivered to him personally; or

(*b*) if left at his last known place of abode or business or, in the case of a body corporate, at their registered or principal office; or

(*c*) if left on board any vessel or aircraft to which he may belong or have lately belonged.

(2) Any summons, notice, order or other document issued for the purposes of any proceedings under the customs and excise Acts, or of any appeal from the decision of the court in any such proceedings, may be served by an officer.

In this subsection "appeal" includes an appeal by way of case stated.

(3) This section shall not apply in relation to proceedings instituted in the High Court or Court of Session.

Commentary—*De Voil Indirect Tax Service* **V5.304**.

Cross references—See Channel Tunnel (Customs and Excise) Order, SI 1990/2167 Schedule, para 22 (process deemed to have been duly served if left on the vehicle of a person using the tunnel; service in the United Kingdom includes a control zone in France within the tunnel system).

Nuclear Material (Offences) Act 1983 s 1D(3) (as inserted by Criminal Justice and Immigration Act 2008 s 75, Sch 17 para 3) (Offences of importing or exporting etc nuclear material: extended jurisdiction).

[146A Time limits for proceedings

(1) Except as otherwise provided in the customs and excise Acts, and notwithstanding anything in any other enactment, the following provisions shall apply in relation to proceedings for an offence under those Acts.

(2) Proceedings for an indictable offence shall not be commenced after the end of the period of 20 years beginning with the day on which the offence was committed.

(3) Proceedings for a summary offence shall not be commenced after the end of the period of 3 years beginning with that day but, subject to that, may be commenced at any time within 6 months from the date on which sufficient evidence to warrant the proceedings came to the knowledge of the prosecuting authority.

(4) For the purposes of subsection (3) above, a certificate of the prosecuting authority as to the date on which such evidence as is there mentioned came to that authority's knowledge shall be conclusive evidence of that fact.

(5) In the application of this section to Scotland—

(*a*) in subsection (2), "proceedings for an indictable offence" means proceedings on indictment;

(*b*) in subsection (3), "proceedings for a summary offence" means summary proceedings.

(6) In the application of this section to Northern Ireland—

(*a*) "indictable offence" means an offence which, if committed by an adult, is punishable on conviction on indictment (whether only on conviction on indictment, or either on conviction on indictment or on summary conviction);

(*b*) "summary offence" means an offence which, if committed by an adult, is punishable only on summary conviction.

(7) In this section, "prosecuting authority" means—

[(*a*) in England and Wales, means the Director of Revenue and Customs Prosecutions,

(*b*) in Scotland, means the Commissioners or the procurator fiscal, and

(*c*) in Northern Ireland, means the Commissioners.][2]][1]

Commentary—*De Voil Indirect Tax Service* **V5.304**.

Cross reference—Nuclear Material (Offences) Act 1983 s 1D(3) (as inserted by Criminal Justice and Immigration Act 2008 s 75, Sch 17 para 3) (Offences of importing or exporting etc nuclear material: extended jurisdiction).

Amendments—[1] This section inserted by FA 1989 s 16(1), (4) in relation to offences committed after 26 July 1989.

[2] Words in sub-s (7) inserted by the Commissioners for Revenue and Customs Act 2005 s 50, Sch 4 para 24 with effect from 18 April 2005 (by virtue of SI 2005/1126).

147 Proceedings for offences

(1) . . . [2]

(2) . . . [3]

(3) In the case of proceedings in England or Wales, without prejudice to any right to require the statement of a case for the opinion of the High Court, the prosecutor may appeal to the Crown Court against any decision of a magistrates' court in proceedings for an offence under the customs and excise Acts.

(4) In the case of proceedings in Northern Ireland, without prejudice to any right to require the statement of a case for the opinion of the High Court, the prosecutor may appeal to the county court against any decision of a court of summary jurisdiction in proceedings for an offence under the customs and excise Acts.

(5) . . . [1]

Commentary—*De Voil Indirect Tax Service* **V5.304, V5.308**.

Cross reference—Nuclear Material (Offences) Act 1983 s 1D(3) (as inserted by Criminal Justice and Immigration Act 2008 s 75, Sch 17 para 3) (Offences of importing or exporting etc nuclear material: extended jurisdiction).

Amendments—[1] Sub-s (5) repealed by Criminal Justice Act 1982 Sch 16.

[2] Sub-s (1) repealed by FA 1989 s 16(2), (4) and Sch 17 Pt I in relation to offences committed after 26 July 1989.

[3] Sub-s (2) repealed (except in relation to Northern Ireland) by the Criminal Justice Act 2003 ss 41, 332, Sch 3 para 50, Sch 37 Pt 4 with effect from 18 June 2012 (the date appointed by SI 2013/1320 art 2).

148 Place of trial for offences

(1) Proceedings for an offence under the customs and excise Acts may be commenced—

(*a*) in any court having jurisdiction in the place where the person charged with the offence resides or is found; or

(*b*) if any thing was detained or seized in connection with the offence, in any court having jurisdiction in the place where that thing was so detained or seized or was found or condemned as forfeited; or

(*c*) in any court having jurisdiction anywhere in that part of the United Kingdom, namely—

(i) England and Wales,

(ii) Scotland, or

(iii) Northern Ireland,

in which the place where the offence was committed is situated.

(2) Where any such offence was committed at some place outside the area of any commission of the peace, the place of the commission of the offence shall, for the purposes of the jurisdiction of any court, be deemed to be any place in the United Kingdom where the offender is found or to which he is first brought after the commission of the offence.

(3) The jurisdiction under subsection (2) above shall be in addition to and not in derogation of any jurisdiction or power of any court under any other enactment.

Commentary—*De Voil Indirect Tax Service* **V5.304**.

Cross reference—Nuclear Material (Offences) Act 1983 s 1D(3) (as inserted by Criminal Justice and Immigration Act 2008 s 75, Sch 17 para 3) (Offences of importing or exporting etc nuclear material: extended jurisdiction).

149 Non-payment of penalties, etc: maximum terms of imprisonment

(1) Where, in any proceedings for an offence under the customs and excise Acts, a magistrates' court in England or Wales or a court of summary jurisdiction in Scotland, in addition to ordering the person convicted to pay a penalty for the offence—

(*a*) orders him to be imprisoned for a term in respect of the same offence; and

(*b*) further (whether at the same time or subsequently) orders him to be imprisoned for a term in respect of non-payment of that penalty or default of a sufficient distress to satisfy the amount of that penalty,

the aggregate of the terms for which he is so ordered to be imprisoned shall not exceed 15 months.

[(1A) [2]

(2) . . . [1]

(3) Where, under any enactment for the time being in force in Northern Ireland, a court of summary jurisdiction has power to order a person to be imprisoned in respect of the non-payment of a penalty, or of the default of a sufficient distress to satisfy the amount of that penalty, for a term in addition and succession to a term of imprisonment imposed for the same offence as the penalty, then in relation to a sentence for an offence under the customs and excise Acts the aggregate of those terms of imprisonment may, notwithstanding anything in any such enactment, by any period not exceeding 15 months.

Commentary—*De Voil Indirect Tax Service* **V5.308**.

Amendments—[1] Sub-s (2) repealed by Criminal Justice (Scotland) Act 1980 Sch 8.

[2] Sub-s (1A) inserted by the Tribunals, Courts and Enforcement Act 2007 s 50, Sch 10 paras 44 with effect from 6 April 2014 (by virtue of SI 2014/768).

150 Incidental provisions as to legal proceedings

(1) Where liability for any offence under the customs and excise Acts is incurred by two or more persons jointly, those persons shall each be liable for the full amount of any pecuniary penalty and may be proceeded against jointly or severally as [the Director of Revenue and Customs Prosecutions (in relation to proceedings instituted in England and Wales) or the Commissioners (in relation to proceedings instituted in Scotland or Northern Ireland)][1] may see fit.

(2) In any proceedings for an offence under the customs and excise Acts instituted in England, Wales or Northern Ireland, any court by whom the matter is considered may mitigate any pecuniary penalty as they see fit.

(3) In any proceedings for an offence or for the condemnation of any thing as being forfeited under the customs and excise Acts, the fact that security has been given by bond or otherwise for the payment of any duty or for compliance with any condition in respect of the non-payment of which or non-compliance with which the proceedings are instituted shall not be a defence.

Commentary—*De Voil Indirect Tax Service* **V5.304, V5.307**.

Cross reference—Nuclear Material (Offences) Act 1983 s 1D(3) (as inserted by Criminal Justice and Immigration Act 2008 s 75, Sch 17 para 3) (Offences of importing or exporting etc nuclear material: extended jurisdiction).

Amendment—[1] Words in sub-s (1) substituted by Commissioners for Revenue and Customs Act 2005 s 50, Sch 4 para 25 with effect from 18 April 2005 by virtue of the Commissioners for Revenue and Customs Act 2005 (Commencement) Order, SI 2005/1126, art 2(2).

151 Application of penalties

The balance of any sum paid or recovered on account of any penalty imposed under the customs and excise Acts, after paying any such compensation or costs as are mentioned in [section 139 of the Magistrates' Courts Act 1980][1] to persons other than the Commissioners shall, notwithstanding any local or other special right or privilege of whatever origin, be accounted for and paid to the Commissioners or as they direct.

Cross reference—Nuclear Material (Offences) Act 1983 s 1D(3) (as inserted by Criminal Justice and Immigration Act 2008 s 75, Sch 17 para 3) (Offences of importing or exporting etc nuclear material: extended jurisdiction).

Amendments—[1] Words substituted by Magistrates' Courts Act 1980 Sch 7 para 177.

152 Power of Commissioners to mitigate penalties, etc

The Commissioners may, as they see fit—

(*a*) stay, sist or [compound an offence (whether or not proceedings have been instituted in respect of it) and compound proceedings][1] or for the condemnation of any thing as being forfeited under the customs and excise Acts; or

(*b*) restore, subject to such conditions (if any) as they think proper, any thing forfeited or seized under those Acts; or

(*c*), (*d*) . . . [2]

but paragraph (*a*) above shall not apply to proceedings on indictment in Scotland.

Commentary—*De Voil Indirect Tax Service* **V5.308**.

Cross references—See FA 1994 s 14(1)(*d*) and Sch 5 para 2(1)(*r*) (decisions by Commissioners under para (*b*) above; Commissioners' obligation to review any decision if required by any person affected by it).

Nuclear Material (Offences) Act 1983 s 1D(3) (as inserted by Criminal Justice and Immigration Act 2008 s 75, Sch 17 para 3) (Offences of importing or exporting etc nuclear material: extended jurisdiction).

Amendments—[1] Words substituted by Commissioners for Revenue and Customs Act 2005 s 50, Sch 4 para 26 with effect from 18 April 2005 by virtue of the Commissioners for Revenue and Customs Act 2005 (Commencement) Order, SI 2005/1126, art 2(2).

[2] Paras (*c*), (*d*) repealed by the Commissioners for Revenue and Customs Act 2005 s 52, Sch 5 with effect from 18 April 2005 by virtue of SI 2005/1126, art 2(2)(i).

153 . . . [1]

Amendments—[1] Section repealed by Commissioners for Revenue and Customs Act 2005 ss 50, 52, Sch 4 para 21 and Sch 5 with effect from 18 April 2005 by virtue of the Commissioners for Revenue and Customs Act 2005 (Commencement) Order, SI 2005/1126, art 2(2).

154 Proof of certain other matters

(1) An averment in any process in proceedings under the customs and excise Acts—

(*a*) that those proceedings were instituted by the order of the Commissioners; or

(*b*) that any person is or was a Commissioner, officer or constable, or a member of Her Majesty's armed forces or coastguard; or

(*c*) that any person is or was appointed or authorised by the Commissioners to discharge, or was engaged by the orders or with the concurrence of the Commissioners in the discharge of, any duty; or

(*d*) that the Commissioners have or have not been satisfied as to any matter as to which they are required by any provision of those Acts to be satisfied; or

(*e*) that any ship is a British ship; or

(*f*) that any goods thrown overboard, staved or destroyed were so dealt with in order to prevent or avoid the seizure of those goods,

shall, until the contrary is proved, be sufficient evidence of the matter in question.

(2) Where in any proceedings relating to customs or excise any question arises as to the place from which any goods have been brought or as to whether or not—

(*a*) any duty has been paid or secured in respect of any goods; or

(*b*) any goods or other things whatsoever are of the description or nature alleged in the information, writ or other process; or

(*c*) any goods have been lawfully imported or lawfully unloaded from any ship or aircraft; or

(*d*) any goods have been lawfully loaded into any ship or aircraft or lawfully exported or were lawfully waterborne; or

(*e*) any goods were lawfully brought to any place for the purpose of being loaded into any ship or aircraft or exported; or

(*f*) any goods are or were subject to any prohibition of or restriction on their importation or exportation,

then, where those proceedings are brought by or against the Commissioners, a law officer of the Crown or an officer, or against any other person in respect of anything purporting to have been done in pursuance of any power or duty conferred or imposed on him by or under the customs and excise Acts, the burden of proof shall lie upon the other party to the proceedings.

Commentary—*De Voil Indirect Tax Service* **V5.305**.

Cross references—See VATA 1994 s 72(12) (application of ss 145–155 of this Act to offences in relation to value added tax and accordingly "duty" in sub-s (2) above to include a reference to value added tax);

Channel Tunnel (Customs and Excise) Order, SI 1990/2167 Schedule, para 23 (extension of the application of sub-s (2) above to goods on a vehicle using the tunnel).

Nuclear Material (Offences) Act 1983 s 1D(3) (as inserted by Criminal Justice and Immigration Act 2008 s 75, Sch 17 para 3) (Offences of importing or exporting etc nuclear material: extended jurisdiction).

155 Persons who may conduct proceedings

[(1) An officer of Revenue and Customs or other person authorised by the Commissioners may conduct criminal proceedings relating to an assigned matter before a court of summary jurisdiction in Scotland or Northern Ireland.][1]

[(2) Any person who has been admitted as a solicitor and is employed by the Commissioners may act as a solicitor in any proceedings in England, Wales or Northern Ireland relating to any assigned matter notwithstanding that he does not hold a current practising certificate.][2]

Commentary—*De Voil Indirect Tax Service* **V5.305**.

Nuclear Material (Offences) Act 1983 s 1D(3) (as inserted by Criminal Justice and Immigration Act 2008 s 75, Sch 17 para 3) (Offences of importing or exporting etc nuclear material: extended jurisdiction).

Amendments—[1] Sub-s (1) substituted by Commissioners for Revenue and Customs Act 2005 s 50, Sch 4 para 27 with effect from 18 April 2005 by virtue of the Commissioners for Revenue and Customs Act 2005 (Commencement) Order, SI 2005/1126, art 2(2).

[2] Sub-s (2) repealed by Commissioners for Revenue and Customs Act 2005 ss 50, 52, Sch 4 para 21 and Sch 5 with effect from 18 April 2005 by virtue of the Commissioners for Revenue and Customs Act 2005 (Commencement) Order, SI 2005/1126, art 2(2).

Saving for outlying enactments of certain general provisions as to offences

156 Saving for outlying enactments of certain general provisions as to offences

(1) In subsections (2), (3) and (4) below (which reproduce certain enactments not required as general provisions for the purposes of the enactments re-enacted in the Customs and Excise Acts 1979) "the outlying provisions of the customs and excise Acts" [means the provisions][1] of the customs and excise Acts, as for the time being amended, which were passed before the commencement of this Act and are not re-enacted in the Customs and Excise Acts 1979 [or the Betting and Gaming Duties Act 1981][1].

(2) It is hereby declared that any act or omission in respect of which a pecuniary penalty (however described) is imposed by any of the outlying provisions of the customs and excise Acts is an offence under that provision; and accordingly in this Part of this Act any reference to an offence under the customs and excise Acts includes a reference to such an act or omission.

(3) Subject to any express provision made by the enactment in question, an offence under any of the outlying provisions of the customs and excise Acts—

(*a*) where it is punishable with imprisonment for a term of 2 years, with or without a pecuniary penalty, shall be punishable either on summary conviction or on conviction on indictment;

(*b*) in any other case, shall be punishable on summary conviction.

. . . [2]

[(4) The maximum term of imprisonment which may be imposed on summary conviction in the sheriff court of an offence under any of the outlying provisions of the customs and excise Acts shall be 6 months.

(5) Where, in Scotland, an offence under any of the outlying provisions of the customs and excise Acts is triable only summarily by virtue of subsection (3)(b) above, the penalty for the offence shall be that to which a person was liable on summary conviction of the offence immediately before 29th

July 1977 (the date of the passing of the Criminal Law Act 1977) subject to any increase by virtue of section 289C(5) of the Criminal Procedure (Scotland) Act 1975 or Part IV of the Criminal Justice Act 1982.][3]

Amendments—[1] Words sub-s (1) substituted by the Betting and Gaming Duties Act 1981, s 34(1), Sch 5, para 5.
[2] Words omitted repealed by the Criminal Justice Act 1982, ss 77, 78, Sch 14, para 43, Sch 16.
[3] Sub-ss (4), (5) substituted for original sub-s (4) by the Criminal Justice Act 1982, s 77, Sch 14, para 43.

PART XII
GENERAL AND MISCELLANEOUS

General powers, etc

157 Bonds and security

(1) Without prejudice to any express requirement as to security contained in the customs and excise Acts, the Commissioners may, if they see fit, require any person to give security [(or further security) by bond, guarantee][1] or otherwise for the observance of any condition in connection with customs or excise.

[(1A) For the purposes of this section "condition in connection with excise" includes a condition in connection with excise duty charged, under the law of a member State other than the United Kingdom, on—

(*a*) manufactured tobacco,
(*b*) alcohol or alcoholic beverages, or
(*c*) [energy products][6].

The expressions used in paragraphs (a) to (c) above have the same meaning as in Council Directive [2008/118/EC][6].][2]

(2) Any bond[, guarantee or other security][3] taken for the purposes of any assigned matter—

(*a*) shall be taken [either on behalf of Her Majesty or on behalf of Her Majesty and the tax authorities of each member State other than the United Kingdom][4]; and
(*b*) shall be valid notwithstanding that it is entered into by a person under full age; and
(*c*) may be cancelled at any time by or by order of the Commissioners.

[In this subsection "assigned matter" includes any excise duty charged as mentioned in subsection (1A) above.][5]

Amendments—[1] Words in sub-s (1) substituted by the Finance Act 2000, s 27(1), (2) with effect from 28 July 2000.
[2] Sub-s (1A) inserted by the Finance Act 2000, s 27(1), (3) with effect from 28 July 2000.
[3] Words in sub-s (2) inserted by the Finance Act 2000, s 27(1), (4) with effect from 28 July 2000.
[4] Words in sub-s (2) inserted by the Finance Act 2000, s 27(1), (5) with effect from 28 July 2000.
[5] Words substituted by the Finance Act 2000, s 27(1), (6) with effect from 28 July 2000.
[6] In sub-s (1A), words substituted for words "mineral oils", and reference substituted for reference "92/12/EEC", by the Excise Goods (Holding, Movement and Duty Point) Regulations, SI 2010/593 reg 90, Sch 2 para 3 with effect from 1 April 2010 (by virtue of SI 2010/593 reg 2).

[157A General information powers in relation to persons entering or leaving the United Kingdom

(1) The proper officer of Revenue and Customs may require any person entering or leaving the United Kingdom—

(*a*) to produce the person's passport or travel documents for examination, or
(*b*) to answer any questions put by the proper officer of Revenue and Customs about the person's journey.

(2) In subsection (1) "passport" means—

(*a*) a United Kingdom passport (within the meaning of the Immigration Act 1971),
(*b*) a passport issued by or on behalf of the authorities of a country or territory outside the United Kingdom, or by or on behalf of an international organisation, or (c) a document that can be used (in some or all circumstances) instead of a passport.

(3) Subsections (1) and (2) apply in relation to a transit air passenger arriving at the passenger's final destination in the United Kingdom as they apply in relation to a person entering the United Kingdom.

(4) For the purposes of subsection (3) a transit air passenger is a person—

(*a*) who has arrived by air in the United Kingdom; and
(*b*) whose journey is continued or resumed by air to a destination in the United Kingdom which is not the place where the person is regarded for the purposes of this section as entering the United Kingdom; and the passenger's final destination is the destination of the continued or resumed journey.][1]

Amendments—[1] This section inserted by the Policing and Crime Act 2009 s 98(1) with effect from 25 January 2010 (by virtue of SI 2010/52 art 2).

158 Power to require provision of facilities

(1) A person to whom this section applies, that is to say, a revenue trader and any person required by the Commissioners under the Customs and Excise Acts 1979 to give security in respect of any premises or place to be used for the examination of goods by an officer, shall—

(*a*) provide and maintain such appliances and afford such other facilities reasonably necessary to enable an officer to take any account or make any examination or search or to perform any other of his duties on the premises of that trader or at the bonded premises or place as the Commissioners may direct;

(*b*) keep any appliances so provided in a convenient place approved by the proper officer for that purpose; and

(*c*) allow the proper officer at any time to use anything so provided and give him any assistance necessary for the performance of his duties.

(2) Any person who contravenes or fails to comply with any provision of subsection (1) above shall be liable on summary conviction to a penalty of [level 3 on the standard scale][1].

(3) A person to whom this section applies shall provide and maintain any fitting required for the purpose of affixing any lock which the proper officer may require to affix to the premises of that person or any part thereof or to any vessel, utensil or other apparatus whatsoever kept thereon, and in default—

(*a*) the fitting may be provided or any work necessary for its maintenance may be carried out by the proper officer, and any expenses so incurred shall be paid on demand by that person; and

(*b*) if that person fails to pay those expenses on demand, he shall in addition be liable on summary conviction to a penalty of [level 3 on the standard scale][1].

(4) If any person to whom this section applies or any servant of his—

(*a*) wilfully destroys or damages any such fitting as is mentioned in subsection (3) above or any lock or key provided for use therewith, or any label or seal placed on any such lock; or

(*b*) improperly obtains access to any place or article secured by any such lock; or

(*c*) has any such fitting or any article intended to be secured by means thereof so constructed that that intention is defeated,

he shall be liable on summary conviction to a penalty of [£20,000][3] and may be [arrested][2].

Cross references—See the Legal Aid, Sentencing and Punishment of Offenders Act 2012 (Fines on Summary Conviction) Regulations, SI 2015/664 reg 2(1), Sch 1 (offences under sub-s (4) do not apply for the purposes of the Legal Aid, Sentencing and Punishment of Offenders Act 2012 s 85(1))

Amendments—[1] References in sub-ss (2), (3) to level 3 on the standard scale substituted by virtue of the Criminal Justice Act 1982, ss 37, 38, 46.

[2] In sub-s (4), word substituted by the Police and Criminal Evidence Act 1984, s 114(1).

[3] In sub-s (4), figure substituted by the Legal Aid, Sentencing and Punishment of Offenders Act 2012 (Fines on Summary Conviction) Regulations, SI 2015/664 reg 2(2), Sch 2 paras 1, 17 with effect from 12 March 2015 in relation to England and Wales only.

159 Power to examine and take account of goods

(1) Without prejudice to any other power conferred by the Customs and Excise Acts 1979, an officer may examine and take account of any goods—

(*a*) which are imported; or

(*b*) which are in a warehouse or Queen's warehouse; or

[(*bb*) which are in a free zone; or][2]

(*c*) which have been loaded into any ship or aircraft at any place in the United Kingdom [or the Isle of Man][1]; or

(*d*) which are entered for exportation or for use as stores; or

(*e*) which are brought to any place in the United Kingdom for exportation or for shipment for exportation or as stores; or

(*f*) in the case of which any claim for drawback, allowance, rebate, remission or repayment of duty is made;

and may for that purpose [open or unpack any container or][5] require any container to be opened or unpacked [and search it or anything in it.][5]

(2) Any examination of goods by an officer under the Customs and Excise Acts 1979 shall be made at such place as the Commissioners appoint for the purpose.

(3) In the case of such goods as the Commissioners may direct, and subject to such conditions as they see fit to impose, an officer may permit goods to be skipped on the quay or bulked, sorted, lotted, packed or repacked before account is taken thereof.

(4) Any opening, unpacking, weighing, measuring, repacking, bulking, sorting, lotting, marking, numbering, loading, unloading, carrying or landing of goods or their containers for the purposes of, or incidental to, the examination by an officer, removal or warehousing thereof shall be done, and any facilities or assistance required for any such examination shall be provided, by or at the expense of the proprietor of the goods[; but if an officer opens or unpacks any container, or searches it or anything in it, the Commissioners are to bear the expense of doing so.][5]

(5) If any imported goods which an officer has power under the Customs and Excise Acts 1979 to examine are without the authority of the proper officer removed from customs and excise charge before they have been examined, those goods shall be liable to forfeiture.

(6) If any goods falling within subsection (5) above are removed by a person with intent to defraud Her Majesty of any duty chargeable thereon or to evade any prohibition or restriction for the time being in force with respect thereto under or by virtue of any enactment, that person shall be guilty of an offence under this subsection and may be [arrested][3].

(7) A person guilty of an offence under subsection (6) above shall be liable—

(*a*) on summary conviction, to a penalty of [£20,000][6] or of three times the value of the goods, whichever is the greater, or to imprisonment for a term not exceeding 6 months, or to both; or

(*b*) on conviction on indictment, to a penalty of any amount, or to imprisonment for a term not exceeding [7 years][4], or to both.

(8) Without prejudice to the foregoing provisions of this section, where by this section or by or under any other provision of the Customs and Excise Acts 1979 an account is authorised or required to be taken of any goods for any purpose by an officer, the Commissioners may, with the consent of the proprietor of the goods, accept as the account of those goods for that purpose an account taken by such other person as may be approved in that behalf by both the Commissioners and the proprietor of the goods.

Cross references—See Channel Tunnel (Customs and Excise) Order, SI 1990/2167 Schedule, para 24 (extension of the application of sub-s (1) above to goods loaded on a vehicle for exportation through the tunnel).

Legal Aid, Sentencing and Punishment of Offenders Act 2012 (Fines on Summary Conviction) Regulations, SI 2015/664 reg 2(1), Sch 1 (offences under sub-s (6) do not apply for the purposes of the Legal Aid, Sentencing and Punishment of Offenders Act 2012 s 85(1))

Amendments—[1] Words in sub-s (1)(*c*) inserted by Isle of Man Act 1979 s 13, Sch 1, para 22.

[2] Sub-s (1)(*bb*) inserted by FA 1984 Sch 4 Pt II, para 5.

[3] Word in sub-s (6) substituted by Police and Criminal Evidence Act 1984 s 114(1) with effect from 1 January 1986; see Police and Criminal Evidence Act 1984 (Commencement No 3) Order, SI 1985/1934.

[4] Words in sub-s (7)(*b*) substituted by FA 1988 s 12(1)(a).

[5] Words in sub-ss (1), (4) inserted by FA 2008 s 117(3)–(5) with effect from 21 July 2008.

[6] In sub-s (7)(*a*), figure substituted by the Legal Aid, Sentencing and Punishment of Offenders Act 2012 (Fines on Summary Conviction) Regulations, SI 2015/664 reg 2(2), Sch 2 paras 1, 18 with effect from 12 March 2015 in relation to England and Wales only.

164 Power to search persons

(1) Where there are reasonable grounds to suspect that any person to whom this section applies [(referred to in this section as "the suspect")][2]is carrying any article—

(*a*) which is chargeable with any duty which has not been paid or secured or

(*b*) with respect to the importation or exportation of which any prohibition or restriction is for the time being in force under or by virtue of any enactment,

[an officer may exercise the powers conferred by subsection (2) below and, if the suspect is not under arrest, may detain him for so long as may be necessary for the exercise of those powers and (where applicable) the exercise of the rights conferred by subsection (3) below.][3]

[(2) The officer may require the suspect—

(*a*) to permit such a search of any article which he has with him; and

(*b*) subject to subsection (3) below, to submit to such searches of his person, whether rub-down, strip or intimate,

as the officer may consider necessary or expedient; but no such requirement may be imposed under paragraph (b) above without the officer informing the suspect of the effect of subsection (3) below.][4]

[(3) If the suspect is required to submit to a search of his person, he may require to be taken—

(*a*) except in the case of a rub-down search, before a justice of the peace or a superior of the officer concerned; and

(*b*) in the excepted case, before such a superior;

and the justice or superior shall consider the grounds for suspicion and direct accordingly whether the suspect is to submit to the search.][4]

[(3A) A rub-down or strip search shall not be carried out except by a person of the same sex as the suspect; and an intimate search shall not be carried out except by a suitably qualified person.][4]

(4) This section applies to the following persons, namely—

(*a*) any person who is on board or has landed from any ship or aircraft;

(*b*) any person entering or about to leave the United Kingdom;

(*c*) any person within the dock area of a port;

(*d*) any person at a customs and excise airport;

(*e*) any person in, entering or leaving any approved wharf or transit shed which is not in a port;

[(*ee*) any person in, entering or leaving a free zone;][1]

(*f*) in Northern Ireland, any person travelling from or to any place which is on or beyond the boundary.

[(5) In this section—

"intimate search" means any search which involves a physical examination (that is, an examination which is more than simply a visual examination) of a person's body orifices;

"rub-down search" means any search which is neither an intimate search nor a strip search;

"strip search" means any search which is not an intimate search but which involves the removal of an article of clothing which—

(*a*) is being worn (wholly or partly) on the trunk; and

(*b*) is being so worn either next to the skin or next to an article of underwear;

"suitably qualified person" means a registered medical practitioner or a registered nurse.][5]

[(6) Notwithstanding anything in subsection (4) of section 48 of the Criminal Justice (Scotland) Act 1987 (detention and questioning by customs officers), detention of the suspect under subsection (1) above shall not prevent his subsequent detention under subsection (1) of that section.][5]

Cross references—See Channel Tunnel (Customs and Excise) Order, SI 1990/2167 Schedule, para 25 (this section to apply to any person in the tunnel system in the United Kingdom, in a through train in the United Kingdom, in, entering or leaving a customs approved area in the United Kingdom or in a control zone in France or Belgium).

F(No 2)A 1992 s 4(3)(*h*) (restriction on powers under this section with effect from 1 January 1993 in relation to movements of persons and things between member States).

Amendments—[1] Sub-s (4)(*ee*) inserted by FA 1984 Sch 4 Pt II, para 6.

[2] Words in sub-s (1) inserted by FA 1988 s 10(1)(*a*).

[3] Words in sub-s (1) substituted by FA 1988 s 10(1)(*b*).

[4] Sub-ss (2), (3), (3A) substituted for sub-ss (2), (3) by FA 1988 s 10(2).

[5] Sub-ss (5), (6) inserted by FA 1988 s 10(3).

[164A Powers to search for cash

(1) The provisions of this Act which fall within subsection (2) (search powers for officers of Revenue and Customs etc) apply in accordance with subsection (3)—

(*a*) for the purposes of searching for cash—

(i) which is recoverable property or is intended by any person for use in unlawful conduct; and

(ii) the amount of which is not less than the minimum amount;

(*b*) for the purposes of searching for cash to ensure compliance with the Cash Control Regulation; or

(*c*) for purposes connected to any such purposes.

(2) The provisions of this Act which fall within this subsection are—

(*a*) section 28(1) (powers of access etc);

(*b*) section 77(1) and (2) (information powers);

(*c*) section 159(1) to (4) (powers to examine and take account of goods); and

(*d*) section 164 (power to search persons including intimate searches).

(3) Those provisions apply for the purposes mentioned in subsection (1) as if—

(*a*) any reference in them to goods included a reference to cash; and

(*b*) in section 164(1)—

(i) the reference to an article were a reference to cash; and

(ii) paragraphs (*a*) and (*b*) were omitted.

(4) The Treasury may by regulations provide for—

(*a*) any provision of this Act to apply with modifications for the purposes of the provisions applied by subsections (1) to (3), or

(*b*) any other enactment to apply, with or without modifications, for the purposes of the provisions so applied.

(5) This section does not limit the scope of any powers that exist apart from this section (whether under this Act or otherwise).

(6) In this section—

"the 2002 Act" means the Proceeds of Crime Act 2002;

"cash"—

(*a*) so far as relating to purposes falling within subsection (1)(*a*) above, has the meaning given by section 289(6) and (7) of the 2002 Act; and

(*b*) so far as relating to purposes falling within subsection (1)(*b*) above, has the same meaning as in the Cash Control Regulation;

"the Cash Control Regulation" means Regulation (EC) No 1889/2005 of the European Parliament and of the Council of 26 October 2005 on controls of cash entering or leaving the Community;

"minimum amount" has the meaning given by section 303 of the 2002 Act;

"modifications" includes omissions;

"recoverable property" has the meaning given by section 316(1) of the 2002 Act;

"unlawful conduct" has the meaning given by section 241 of the 2002 Act.][1]

Amendments—[1] This section inserted by the Policing and Crime Act 2009 s 99(1) with effect from 25 January 2010 (by virtue of SI 2010/52 art 2).

General offences

167 Untrue declarations, etc

(1) If any person either knowingly or recklessly—

(*a*) makes or signs, or causes to be made or signed, or delivers or causes to be delivered to the Commissioners or any officer, any declaration, notice, certificate or other document whatsoever; or

(*b*) makes any statement in answer to any question put to him by an officer which he is required by or under any enactment to answer,

being a document or statement produced or made for any purpose of any assigned matter, which is untrue in any material particular, he shall be guilty of an offence under this subsection and may be [arrested][2]; and any goods in relation to which the document or statement was made shall be liable to forfeiture.

(2) Without prejudice to subsection (4) below, a person who commits an offence under subsection (1) above shall be liable—

(*a*) on summary conviction, to a penalty of [£20,000][2], or to imprisonment for a term not exceeding 6 months, or to both; or

(*b*) on conviction on indictment, to a penalty of any amount, or to imprisonment for a term not exceeding 2 years, or to both.

(3) If any person—

(*a*) makes or signs, or causes to be made or signed, or delivers or causes to be delivered to the Commissioners or an officer, any declaration, notice, certificate or other document whatsoever; or

(*b*) makes any statement in answer to any question put to him by an officer which he is required by or under any enactment to answer,

being a document or statement produced or made for any purpose of any assigned matter, which is untrue in any material particular, then, without prejudice to subsection (4) below, he shall be liable on summary conviction to a penalty of [level 4 on the standard scale.][1]

(4) Where by reason of any such document or statement as is mentioned in subsection (1) or (3) above the full amount of any duty payable is not paid or any overpayment is made in respect of any drawback, allowance, rebate of repayment of duty, the amount of the duty unpaid or of the overpayment shall be recoverable as a debt to the Crown or may be summarily recovered as a civil debt.

[(5) An amount of excise duty, or the amount of an overpayment in respect of any drawback, allowance, rebate or repayment of any excise duty, shall not be recoverable as mentioned in subsection (4) above unless the Commissioners have assessed the amount of the duty or of the overpayment as being excise duty due from the person mentioned in subsection (1) or (3) above and notified him or his representative accordingly.][3]

Commentary—*De Voil Indirect Tax Service* **V5.304**.

Note—Statistics of Trade (Customs and Excise) Regulations, SI 1992/2790 reg 12 modifies sub-s (2)(*a*) above by substituting "3 months" for "6 months" when a person is convicted under sub-s (1) above under the Intrastat System.

Cross references—See FA 1985 s 10(5), (6)(*c*) (meaning of document).

CRCA 2005 Sch 2 para 6 (this section does not apply in relation to a declaration, document or statement for a function relating to a matter to which CRCA 2005 s 7 applies).

FA 2014 Sch 34 para 6(4)(*f*) (application of this section in relation to the issue of conduct notices to promoters of tax avoidance schemes).

Legal Aid, Sentencing and Punishment of Offenders Act 2012 (Fines on Summary Conviction) Regulations, SI 2015/664 reg 2(1), Sch 1 (offences under sub-s (1) do not apply for the purposes of the Legal Aid, Sentencing and Punishment of Offenders Act 2012 s 85(1))

Amendments—[1] Words in sub-s (3) substituted by virtue of Criminal Justice Act 1982 ss 37, 38, 46.

[2] Word in sub-s (1) substituted by Police and Criminal Evidence Act 1984 s 114(1) with effect from 1 January 1986; see Police and Criminal Evidence Act 1984 (Commencement No 3) Order, SI 1985/1934.

[3] Sub-s (5) inserted by FA 1997 s 50(2), Sch 6 para 5 with effect from a date to be appointed by the Commissioners.

[4] In sub-s (2)(*a*), figure substituted by the Legal Aid, Sentencing and Punishment of Offenders Act 2012 (Fines on Summary Conviction) Regulations, SI 2015/664 reg 2(2), Sch 2 paras 1, 19 with effect from 12 March 2015 in relation to England and Wales only.

168 Counterfeiting documents, etc

(1) If any person—

(*a*) counterfeits or falsifies any document which is required by or under any enactment relating to an assigned matter or which is used in the transaction of any business relating to an assigned matter; or

(*b*) knowingly accepts, receives or uses any such document so counterfeited or falsified; or

(*c*) alters any such document after it is officially issued; or

(*d*) counterfeits any seal, signature, initials or other mark of, or used by, any officer for the verification of such a document or for the security of goods or for any other purpose relating to an assigned matter,

he shall be guilty of an offence under this section and may be [arrested.][1]

(2) A person guilty of an offence under this section shall be liable—

(*a*) on summary conviction, to a penalty of [£20,000][2], or to imprisonment for a term not exceeding 6 months, or to both; or (*b*) on conviction on indictment, to a penalty of any amount, or to imprisonment for a term not exceeding 2 years, or to both.

Commentary—*De Voil Indirect Tax Service* **V5.304**.

Note—Statistics of Trade (Customs and Excise) Regulations, SI 1992/2790 reg 12 modifies sub-s (2)(*a*) above by substituting "3 months" for "6 months" when a person is convicted under sub-s (1) above under the Intrastat System.

Cross references—See FA 1985 s 10(5), (6)(*d*) (meaning of document).

FA 2014 Sch 34 para 6(4)(*f*) (application of this section in relation to the issue of conduct notices to promoters of tax avoidance schemes).

Legal Aid, Sentencing and Punishment of Offenders Act 2012 (Fines on Summary Conviction) Regulations, SI 2015/664 reg 2(1), Sch 1 (offences under sub-s (1) do not apply for the purposes of the Legal Aid, Sentencing and Punishment of Offenders Act 2012 s 85(1))

Amendments—[1] Word in sub-s (1) substituted by Police and Criminal Evidence Act 1984 s 114(1) with effect from 1 January 1986; see Police and Criminal Evidence Act 1984 (Commencement No 3) Order, SI 1985/1934.

[2] In sub-s (2)(*a*), figure substituted by the Legal Aid, Sentencing and Punishment of Offenders Act 2012 (Fines on Summary Conviction) Regulations, SI 2015/664 reg 2(2), Sch 2 paras 1, 20 with effect from 12 March 2015 in relation to England and Wales only.

171 General provisions as to offences and penalties

(1) Where—

(*a*) by any provision of any enactment relating to an assigned matter a punishment is prescribed for any offence thereunder or for any contravention of or failure to comply with any regulation, direction, condition or requirement made, given or imposed thereunder; and

(*b*) any person is convicted in the same proceedings of more than one such offence, contravention or failure,

that person shall be liable to that punishment for each such offence, contravention or failure of which he is so convicted.

(2) In this Act the "prescribed sum", in relation to the penalty provided for an offence, means—

(*a*) if the offence was committed in England [or Wales][2], the prescribed sum within the meaning of [section 32 of the Magistrates' Courts Act 1980 (£1,000 or other sum substituted by order under section 143(1) of that Act)][1];

(*b*) if the offence was committed in Scotland, the prescribed sum within the meaning of section 289B of the Criminal Procedure (Scotland) Act 1975 (£1,000 or other sum substituted by order under section 289D(1) of that Act);

[(*c*) if the offence was committed in Northern Ireland, the prescribed sum within the meaning of Article 4 of the Fines and Penalties (Northern Ireland) Order 1984 ([£5,000][3] or other sum substituted by order under Article 17 of that Order);][2]

and in subsection (1)(a) above, the reference to a provision by which a punishment is prescribed includes a reference to a provision which makes a person liable to a penalty of the prescribed sum within the meaning of this subsection.

[(2A) . . .][5]

(3) Where a penalty for an offence under any enactment relating to an assigned matter is required to be fixed by reference to the value of any goods, that value shall be taken as the price which those goods might reasonably be expected to have fetched, after payment of any duty or tax chargeable thereon, if they had been sold in the open market at or about the date of the commission of the offence for which the penalty is imposed.

(4) Where an offence under any enactment relating to an assigned matter which has been committed by a body corporate is proved to have been committed with the consent or connivance of, or to be attributable to any neglect on the part of, any director, manager, secretary or other similar officer of the body corporate or any person purporting to act in any such capacity, he as well as the body corporate shall be guilty of that offence and shall be liable to be proceeded against and punished accordingly.

In this subsection "director", in relation to any body corporate established by or under any enactment for the purpose of carrying on under national ownership any industry or part of an industry or undertaking, being a body corporate whose affairs are managed by the members thereof, means a member of that body corporate.

[(4A) Subsection (4) shall not apply to an offence which relates to a matter listed in Schedule 1 to the Commissioners for Revenue and Customs Act 2005 (former Inland Revenue matters).][6]

(5) Where in any proceedings for an offence under the customs and excise Acts any question arises as to the duty or the rate thereof chargeable on any imported goods, and it is not possible to ascertain the relevant time specified in section 43 above [or the relevant excise duty point][4], that duty or rate shall be determined as if the goods had been imported without entry at the time when the proceedings were commenced [or, as the case may be, as if the time when the proceedings were commenced was the relevant excise duty point][4].

Commentary—*De Voil Indirect Tax Service* **V5.306, V5.307**.

Simon's Tax Cases—*Chaudhry v R&C Prosecution Office* [2008] STC 2357.

Amendments—[1] Words in sub-s (2)(*a*) substituted by Magistrates' Courts Act 1980 Sch 7 para 178.

2 Words in sub-s (2)(*a*) substituted and sub-s (2)(*c*) inserted by Fines and Penalties (Northern Ireland) Order, SI 1984/703 art 19(1), Sch 6 para 7 with effect from 19 July 1984.
3 Figure in square brackets in sub-s (2)(*c*) substituted for the figure "£2,000" by virtue of Criminal Justice (Northern Ireland) Order, SI 1994/2795 art 3(1) with effect from a day to be appointed.
4 Words in sub-s (5) inserted by F(No 2)A 1992 s 3 and Sch 2 para 9 with effect from 9 December 1992 by virtue of F(No 2)A 1992 (Commencement No 3) Order, SI 1992/3104.
5 Sub-s (2A) repealed by Statute Law (Repeals) Act 1993 s 1(1), Sch 1 Pt XIV.
6 Sub-s (4A) inserted by Commissioners for Revenue and Customs Act 2005 s 50, Sch 4 para 28 with effect from 18 April 2005 by virtue of the Commissioners for Revenue and Customs Act 2005 (Commencement) Order, SI 2005/1126, art 2(2).

SCHEDULES

[SCHEDULE 2A

SUPPLEMENTARY PROVISIONS RELATING TO THE DETENTION OF THINGS AS LIABLE TO FORFEITURE]

Section 139(5A)

Amendments—Schedule 2A inserted by FA 2013 s 226(7) with effect in relation to things detained on or after 17 July 2013.

[Interpretation

1 In this Schedule, references (however expressed) to a thing being detained are references to a thing being detained as liable to forfeiture under the customs and excise Acts.][1]

Amendments—[1] Schedule 2A inserted by FA 2013 s 226(7) with effect in relation to things detained on or after 17 July 2013.

[Period of detention

2—(1) This paragraph applies where a thing is detained.

(2) The thing may be detained for 30 days beginning with the day on which the thing is first detained.

(3) The thing is deemed to be seized as liable to forfeiture under the customs and excise Acts if its detention ceases to be authorised under this paragraph.][1]

Amendments—[1] Schedule 2A inserted by FA 2013 s 226(7) with effect in relation to things detained on or after 17 July 2013.

[Notice of detention

3—(1) The Commissioners must take reasonable steps to give written notice of the detention of any thing, and of the grounds for the detention, to any person who to their knowledge was, at the time of the detention, the owner or one of the owners of the thing.

(2) But notice need not be given under sub-paragraph (1) if the detention occurred in the presence of—

(*a*) the person whose offence or suspected offence occasioned the detention,

(*b*) the owner or any of the owners of the thing detained or any servant or agent of such an owner, or

(*c*) in the case of any thing detained on a ship or aircraft, the master or commander.][1]

Amendments—[1] Schedule 2A inserted by FA 2013 s 226(7) with effect in relation to things detained on or after 17 July 2013.

[Unauthorised removal or disposal: penalties etc

4—(1) This paragraph applies where a thing is detained and, with the agreement of a person within sub-paragraph (2) ("the responsible person"), the thing remains at the place where it is first detained (rather than being removed and detained elsewhere).

(2) A person is within this sub-paragraph if the person is—

(*a*) the owner or any of the owners of the thing at the time it was detained or any servant or agent of such an owner, or

(*b*) a person whom the person who detains the thing reasonably believes to be a person within paragraph (*a*).

(3) If the responsible person fails to prevent the unauthorised removal or disposal of the thing from the place where it is detained, that failure attracts a penalty under section 9 of the Finance Act 1994 (civil penalties).

(4) The removal or disposal of the thing is unauthorised unless it is done with the permission of a proper officer of Revenue and Customs.

(5) Where any duty of excise is payable in respect of the thing—

(*a*) the penalty is to be calculated by reference to the amount of that duty (whether it has been paid or not), and

(*b*) section 9 of the Finance Act 1994 has effect as if in subsection (2)(*a*) the words "5 per cent of" were omitted.

(6) If no duty of excise is payable in respect of the thing, that section has effect as if the penalty provided for by subsection (2)(*b*) of that section were whichever is the greater of—

(*a*) the value of the thing at the time it was first detained, or

(*b*) £250.][1]

Amendments—[1] Schedule 2A inserted by FA 2013 s 226(7) with effect in relation to things detained on or after 17 July 2013.

[5—(1) This paragraph applies where—

(*a*) a thing is detained at a revenue trader's premises,

(*b*) the thing is liable to forfeiture under the customs and excise Acts, and

(*c*) without the permission of a proper officer of Revenue and Customs, the thing is removed from the trader's premises, or otherwise disposed of, by any person.

(2) The Commissioners may seize, as liable to forfeiture under the customs and excise Acts, goods of equivalent value to the thing, from the revenue trader's stock.

(3) For the purposes of this paragraph, a revenue trader's premises include any premises used to hold or store anything for the purposes of the revenue trader's trade, regardless of who owns or occupies the premises.][1]

Amendments—[1] Schedule 2A inserted by FA 2013 s 226(7) with effect in relation to things detained on or after 17 July 2013.

SCHEDULE 3

PROVISIONS RELATING TO FORFEITURE

Sections 139, 143, 145

Notice of seizure

1—(1) The Commissioners shall, except as provided in sub-paragraph (2) below, give notice of the seizure of any thing as liable to forfeiture and of the grounds therefor to any person who to their knowledge was at the time of the seizure the owner or one of the owners thereof.

(2) Notice need not be given under this paragraph if the seizure was made in the presence of—

(*a*) the person whose offence or suspected offence occasioned the seizure; or

(*b*) the owner or any of the owners of the thing seized or any servant or agent of his; or

(*c*) in the case of any thing seized in any ship or aircraft, the master or commander.

2 Notice under paragraph 1 above shall be given in writing and shall be deemed to have been duly served on the person concerned—

(*a*) if delivered to him personally; or

(*b*) if addressed to him and left or forwarded by post to him at his usual or last known place of abode or business or, in the case of a body corporate, at their registered or principal office; or

(*c*) where he has no address within the United Kingdom [or the Isle of Man][1], or his address is unknown, by publication of notice of the seizure in the London, Edinburgh or Belfast Gazette.

Amendments—[1] Words in para 2(*c*) inserted by Isle of Man Act 1979 s 13 and Sch 1, para 23.

Notice of claim

3 Any person claiming that any thing seized as liable to forfeiture is not so liable shall, within one month of the date of the notice of seizure or, where no such notice has been served on him, within one month of the date of the seizure, give notice of his claim in writing to the Commissioners at any office of customs and excise.

Simon's Tax Cases—*R&C Comrs v Jones & anor* [2011] EWCA Civ 824, [2011] STC 2206.

4—(1) Any notice under paragraph 3 above shall specify the name and address of the claimant and, in the case of a claimant who is outside the United Kingdom [and the Isle of Man][1], shall specify the name and address of a solicitor in the United Kingdom who is authorised to accept service of process and to act on behalf of the claimant.

(2) Service of process upon a solicitor so specified shall be deemed to be proper service upon the claimant.

Amendments—[1] Words in para 4(1) inserted by Isle of Man Act 1979 s 13 and Sch 1. para 24.

Condemnation

5 If on the expiration of the relevant period under paragraph 3 above for the giving of notice of claim in respect of any thing no such notice has been given to the Commissioners, or if, in the case of any such notice given, any requirement of paragraph 4 above is not complied with, the thing in question shall be deemed to have been duly condemned as forfeited.

Simon's Tax Cases—*R&C Comrs v Jones & anor* [2011] EWCA Civ 824, [2011] STC 2206.

6 Where notice of claim in respect of any thing is duly given in accordance with paragraphs 3 and 4 above, the Commissioners shall take proceedings for the condemnation of that thing by the court, and if the court finds that the thing was at the time of seizure liable to forfeiture the court shall condemn it as forfeited.

7 Where any thing is in accordance with either of paragraphs 5 or 6 above condemned or deemed to have been condemned as forfeited, then, without prejudice to any delivery up or sale of the thing by the Commissioners under paragraph 16 below, the forfeiture shall have effect as from the date when the liability to forfeiture arose.

Proceedings for condemnation by court

8 Proceedings for condemnation shall be civil proceedings and may be instituted—

(*a*) in England or Wales either in the High Court or in a magistrates' court;

(*b*) in Scotland either in the Court of Session or in the sheriff court;

(*c*) in Northern Ireland either in the High Court or in a court of summary jurisdiction.

9 Proceedings for the condemnation of any thing instituted in a magistrates' court in England or Wales, in the sheriff court in Scotland or in a court of summary jurisdiction in Northern Ireland may be so instituted—

(*a*) in any such court having jurisdiction in the place where any offence in connection with that thing was committed or where any proceedings for such an offence are instituted; or

(*b*) in any such court having jurisdiction in the place where the claimant resides or, if the claimant has specified a solicitor under paragraph 4 above, in the place where that solicitor has his office; or

(*c*) in any such court having jurisdiction in the place where that thing was found, detained or seized or to which it is first brought after being found, detained or seized.

10—(1) In any proceedings for condemnation instituted in England, Wales or Northern Ireland, the claimant or his solicitor shall make oath that the thing seized was, or was to the best of his knowledge and belief, the property of the claimant at the time of the seizure.

(2) In any such proceedings instituted in the High Court, the claimant shall give such security for the costs of the proceedings as may be determined by the Court.

(3) If any requirement of this paragraph is not complied with, the court shall give judgment for the Commissioners.

11—(1) In the case of any proceedings for condemnation instituted in a magistrates' court in England or Wales, without prejudice to any right to require the statement of a case for the opinion of the High Court, either party may appeal against the decision of that court to the Crown Court.

(2) In the case of any proceedings for condemnation instituted in a court of summary jurisdiction in Northern Ireland, without prejudice to any right to require the statement of a case for the opinion of the High Court, either party may appeal against the decision of that court to the county court.

12 Where an appeal, including an appeal by way of case stated, has been made against the decision of the court in any proceedings for the condemnation of any thing, that thing shall, pending the final determination of the matter, be left with the Commissioners or at any convenient office of customs and excise.

Provisions as to proof

13 In any proceedings arising out of the seizure of any thing, the fact, form and manner of the seizure shall be taken to have been as set forth in the process without any further evidence thereof, unless the contrary is proved.

14 In any proceedings, the condemnation by a court of any thing as forfeited may be proved by the production either of the order or certificate of condemnation or of a certified copy thereof purporting to be signed by an officer of the court by which the order or certificate was made or granted.

Special provisions as to certain claimants

15 For the purposes of any claim to, or proceedings for the condemnation of, any thing, where that thing is at the time of seizure the property of a body corporate, of two or more partners or of any number of persons exceeding five, the oath required by paragraph 10 above to be taken and any other thing required by this Schedule or by any rules of the court to be done by, or by any person authorised by, the claimant or owner may be taken or done by, or by any other person authorised by, the following persons respectively, that is to say—

(*a*) where the owner is a body corporate, the secretary or some duly authorised officer of that body;

(*b*) where the owners are in partnership, any one of those owners;

(*c*) where the owners are any number of persons exceeding five not being in partnership, any two of those persons on behalf of themselves and their co-owners.

Power to deal with seizures before condemnation, etc

16 Where any thing has been seized as liable to forfeiture the Commissioners may at any time if they see fit and notwithstanding that the thing has not yet been condemned, or is not yet deemed to have been condemned, as forfeited—

(*a*) deliver it up to any claimant upon his paying to the Commissioners such sum as they think proper, being a sum not exceeding that which in their opinion represents the value of the thing, including any duty or tax chargeable thereon which has not been paid;

(*b*) if the thing seized is a living creature or is in the opinion of the Commissioners of a perishable nature, sell or destroy it.

17—(1) If, where any thing is delivered up, sold or destroyed under paragraph 16 above, it is held in proceedings taken under this Schedule that the thing was not liable to forfeiture at the time of its seizure, the Commissioners shall, subject to any deduction allowed under sub-paragraph (2) below, on demand by the claimant tender to him—

(*a*) an amount equal to any sum paid by him under sub-paragraph (*a*) of that paragraph; or

(*b*) where they have sold the thing, an amount equal to the proceeds of sale; or

(*c*) where they have destroyed the thing, an amount equal to the market value of the thing at the time of its seizure.

(2) Where the amount to be tendered under sub-paragraph (1)(*a*), (*b*) or (*c*) above includes any sum on account of any duty or tax chargeable on the thing which had not been paid before its seizure the Commissioners may deduct so much of that amount as represents that duty or tax.

(3) If the claimant accepts any amount tendered to him under sub-paragraph (1) above, he shall not be entitled to maintain any action on account of the seizure, detention, sale or destruction of the thing.

(4) For the purposes of sub-paragraph (1)(*c*) above, the market value of any thing at the time of its seizure shall be taken to be such amount as the Commissioners and the claimant may agree or, in default of agreement, as may be determined by a referee appointed by the Lord Chancellor (not being an official of any government department [or an office-holder in, or a member of the staff of, the Scottish Administration][1]), whose decision shall be final and conclusive; and the procedure on any reference to a referee shall be such as may be determined by the referee.

[(5) The Lord Chancellor may make an appointment under sub-paragraph (4) only with the concurrence—

(*a*) where the proceedings referred to in sub-paragraph (1) were taken in England and Wales, of the Lord Chief Justice of England and Wales;

(*b*) where those proceedings were taken in Scotland, of the Lord President of the Court of Session;

(*c*) where those proceedings were taken in Northern Ireland, of the Lord Chief Justice of Northern Ireland.

(6) The Lord Chief Justice of England and Wales may nominate a judicial office holder (as defined in section 109(4) of the Constitutional Reform Act 2005) to exercise his functions under this paragraph.

(7) The Lord President of the Court of Session may nominate a judge of the Court of Session who is a member of the First or Second Division of the Inner House of that Court to exercise his functions under this paragraph.

(8) The Lord Chief Justice of Northern Ireland may nominate any of the following to exercise his functions under this paragraph—

(*a*) the holder of one of the offices listed in Schedule 1 to the Justice (Northern Ireland) Act 2002;

(*b*) a Lord Justice of Appeal (as defined in section 88 of that Act).][2]

Amendments—[1] Words in para (4) inserted by The Scotland Act 1998 (Consequential Modifications) (No 2) Order, SI 1999/1820 s 59, which comes into force on the "principle appointed day", currently 1 July 1999, by virtue of the Scotland Act 1998 (Commencement) Order 1998/3178.

[2] Sub-paras (5)–(8) inserted by the Constitutional Reform Act 2005 s 15, Sch 4 para 97 with effect from 3 April 2006 (by virtue of SI 2006/1014, art 2(a), Sch 1, para 11).

CUSTOMS AND EXCISE DUTIES (GENERAL RELIEFS) ACT 1979

(1979 Chapter 3)

Cross references—See VATA 1994 s 16(1), (application of the following provisions of this Act for the purposes of

value added tax),
VAT Regulations, SI 1995/2518 reg 118(*d*) (this Act, except ss 8, 9(*b*), not to apply in relation to any tax chargeable on importation of goods from non-EEC countries with effect from 1 December 1992).

Miscellaneous reliefs from customs and excise duties

[7 Power to provide for reliefs from duty and value added tax in respect of imported legacies

(1) The Commissioners may by order make provision for conferring reliefs from duty and value added tax in respect of goods imported into the United Kingdom by or for any person who has become entitled to them as legatee.
(2) Any such relief may take the form either of an exemption from payment of duty and tax or of a provision whereby the sum payable by way of duty or tax is less than it would otherwise be.
(3) The Commissioners may by order make provision supplementing any Community relief, in such manner as they think necessary or expedient.
(4) An order under this section—
(*a*) may make any relief for which it provides or any Community relief subject to conditions, including conditions which are to be complied with after the importation of the goods to which the relief applies;
(*b*) may, in relation to any relief conferred by order made under this section, contain such incidental and supplementary provisions as the Commissioners think necessary or expedient; and
(*c*) may make different provision for different cases.
(5) In this section—
"Community relief " means any relief which is conferred by a Community instrument and is of a kind, or of a kind similar to that, which could otherwise be conferred by order made under this section;
"duty" means customs or excise duty chargeable on goods imported into the United Kingdom and, in the case of excise duty, includes any addition to the duty by virtue of section 1 of the Excise Duties (Surcharges or Rebates) Act 1979;
"legatee" means any person taking under a testamentary disposition or donatio mortis causa or on an intestacy; and
"value added tax" means value added tax chargeable on the importation of goods.][1]

Commentary—*De Voil Indirect Tax Service* **V3.341**.
Orders—See Customs and Excise Duties (Personal Reliefs for Goods Permanently Imported) Order, SI 1992/3193.
Amendments—[1] This section substituted by FA 1984 s 14(1), (3) with effect from 1 July 1984.

8 Relief from customs or excise duty on trade samples, labels, etc

The Commissioners may allow the delivery without payment of customs or excise duty on importation, subject to such conditions and restrictions as they see fit—
(*a*) of trade samples of such goods as they see fit, whether imported as samples or drawn from the goods on their importation;
(*b*) of labels or other articles supplied without charge for the purpose of being re-exported with goods manufactured or produced in, and to be exported from, the United Kingdom [or the Isle of Man.][1]

Commentary—*De Voil Indirect Tax Service* **V3.342, 3.343**.
Amendments—[1] Words in para (*b*) inserted by Isle of Man Act 1979 s 13, Sch 1 para 26.

9 Relief from customs or excise duty on antiques, prizes, etc

The Commissioners may allow the delivery without payment of customs or excise duty on importation—
(*a*) of any goods (other than spirits or wine) which are proved to the satisfaction of the Commissioners to have been manufactured or produced more than 100 years before the date of importation;
(*b*) of articles which are shown to the satisfaction of the Commissioners to have been awarded abroad to any person for distinction in art, literature, science or sport, or for public service, or otherwise as a record of meritorious achievement or conduct, and to be imported by or on behalf of that person.

Commentary—*De Voil Indirect Tax Service* **V3.344**.

Personal reliefs

13 Power to provide, in relation to persons entering the United Kingdom, for reliefs from duty and value added tax and for simplified computation of duty and tax

(1) The Commissioners may by order make provision for conferring on persons entering the United Kingdom reliefs from duty and value added tax; and any such relief may take the form either of an exemption from payment of duty and tax or of a provision whereby the sum payable by way of duty or tax is less than it would otherwise be.
[(1A) The Commissioners may by order make provision supplementing any Community relief, in such manner as they think necessary or expedient.][1]

(2) Without prejudice to subsection (1) above, the Commissioners may by order make provision whereby, in such cases and to such extent as may be specified in the order, a sum calculated at a rate specified in the order is treated as the aggregate amount payable by way of duty and tax in respect of goods imported by a person entering the United Kingdom; but any order making such provision shall enable the person concerned to elect that duty and tax shall be charged on the goods in question at the rate which would be applicable apart from that provision.

(3) An order under this section—

(*a*) may make any relief for which it provides [, or any Community relief,][1] subject to conditions, including conditions which are to be complied with after the importation of the goods to which the relief applies [and conditions with respect to the conduct in relation to the goods of persons other than the person on whom the relief is conferred and of persons whose identity cannot be ascertained at the time of importation][2];

(*b*) may [, in relation to any relief conferred by order made under this section,][1] contain such incidental and supplementary provisions as the Commissioners think necessary or expedient, including [provisions requiring any person to whom a condition of the relief at any time relates to notify the Commissioners of any non-compliance with the condition and][2]provisions for the forfeiture of goods in the event of non-compliance with any condition subject to which they have been relieved from duty or tax; and

(*c*) may make a different provision for different cases,

[(3A) An order under this section may provide, in relation to any relief which under such an order is made subject to a condition, for there to be a presumption that, in such cases as may be described in the order by reference—

(*a*) to the quantity of goods in question; or

(*b*) to any other factor which the Commissioners consider appropriate,

the condition is to be treated, unless the Commissioners are satisfied to the contrary, as not being complied with.][3]

[(3B) An order under this section may provide, in relation to any requirement of such an order for the Commissioners to be notified of non-compliance with a condition to which any relief from payment of any duty of excise is made subject, for goods to be exempt from forfeiture under section 124 of the Customs and Excise Management Act 1979 (forfeiture for breach of certain conditions) in respect of non-compliance with that condition if—

(*a*) the non-compliance is notified to the Commissioners in accordance with that requirement;

(*b*) any duty which becomes payable on those goods by virtue of the non-compliance is paid; and

(*c*) the circumstances are otherwise such as may be described in the order.][3]

[(3C) If any person fails to comply with any requirement of an order under this section to notify the Commissioners of any non-compliance with a condition to which any relief is made subject—

(*a*) he shall be liable, on summary conviction, to a penalty of an amount not exceeding [£20,000][6]; and

(*b*) the goods in respect of which the offence was committed shall be liable to forfeiture.][3]

(4) In this section—

["Community relief" means any relief which is conferred by a Community instrument and is of a kind, or of a kind similar to that, which could otherwise be conferred by order made under this section;][1]

["conduct", in relation to any person who has or may acquire possession or control of any goods, includes that person's intentions at any time in relation to those goods;][4]

"duty" means customs or excise duty chargeable on goods imported into the United Kingdom and, in the case of excise duty, includes any addition thereto by virtue of section 1 of the Excise Duties (Surcharges or Rebates) Act 1979; and

"value added tax" or "tax" means value added tax chargeable on the importation of goods [from places outside the member States or on the acquisition of goods from member States other than the United Kingdom][5].

(5) Nothing in any order under this section shall be construed as authorising any person to import any thing in contravention of any prohibition or restriction for the time being in force with respect thereto under or by virtue of any enactment.

Commentary—*De Voil Indirect Tax Service* **V3.345, 3.346**.

Orders—See Customs and Excise Duties (Personal Reliefs for Goods Permanently Imported) Order, SI 1992/3193; Travellers' Allowances Order, SI 1994/955; Travellers' Reliefs (Fuel and Lubricants) Order, SI 1995/1777.

Cross reference—See VATA 1994 Sch 8, Group 14 (tax-free shops).

Amendments—[1] Sub-s (1A) and words in sub-ss (3)(*a*), (*b*), (4) inserted by FA 1984 s 15(1)–(5), (8) with effect from 31 March 1984.

[2] Words in sub-s (3)(*a*), (*b*) inserted by F(No 2)A 1992 s 1(8), Sch 1 para 8 with effect from 1 December 1992 by virtue of F(No 2)A 1992 (Commencement No 2 and Transitional Provisions) Order, SI 1992/2979 art 4 and Schedule, Pt II.

[3] Sub-ss (3A)–(3C) inserted by F(No 2)A 1992 s 1(8), Sch 1 para 8 with effect from 1 December 1992 by virtue of F(No 2)A 1992 (Commencement No 2 and Transitional Provisions) Order, SI 1992/2979 art 4 and Schedule, Pt II.

[4] Definition of "conduct" in sub-s (4) inserted by F(No 2)A 1992 s 1(8), Sch 1 para 8 with effect from 1 December 1992 by virtue of F(No 2)A 1992 (Commencement No 2 and Transitional Provisions) Order, SI 1992/2979 art 4 and Schedule, Pt II.

5 Words in the definition of "value added tax" in sub-s (4) added by F(No 2)A 1992 s 14(3), Sch 3 para 93 with effect from 1 January 1993 by virtue of F(No 2)A 1992 (Commencement No 4 and Transitional Provisions) Order, SI 1992/3261.

6 In sub-s (3C)(*a*), figure substituted by the Legal Aid, Sentencing and Punishment of Offenders Act 2012 (Fines on Summary Conviction) Regulations, SI 2015/664 reg 2(2), Sch 2 para 2(1), (2) with effect from 12 March 2015 in relation to England and Wales only.

[13A Reliefs from duties and taxes for persons enjoying certain immunities and privileges

(1) The Commissioners may by order make provision for conferring in respect of any persons to whom this section applies reliefs, by way of remission or repayment, from payment by them or others of duties of customs or excise, value added tax or car tax.

(2) An order under this section may make any relief for which it provides subject to such conditions binding the person in respect of whom the relief is conferred and, if different, the person liable apart from the relief for payment of the tax or duty (including conditions which are to be complied with after the time when, apart from the relief, the duty or tax would become payable) as may be imposed by or under the order.

(3) An order under this section may include any of the provisions mentioned in subsection (4) below for cases where—

(*a*) relief from payment of any duty of customs or excise, value added tax or car tax chargeable on any goods, or on the supply of any goods or services or the importation of any goods has been conferred (whether by virtue of an order under this section or otherwise) in respect of any person to whom this section applies, and

(*b*) any condition required to be complied with in connection with the relief is not complied with.

(4) The provisions referred to in subsection (3) above are—

(*a*) provision for payment to the Commissioners of the tax or duty by—

(i) the person liable, apart from the relief, for its payment, or

(ii) any person bound by the condition, or

(iii) any person who is or has been in possession of the goods or has received the benefit of the services,

or for two or more of those persons to be jointly and severally liable for such payment, and

(*b*) in the case of goods, provision for forfeiture of the goods.

(5) An order under this section—

(*a*) may contain such incidental and supplementary provisions as the Commissioners think necessary or expedient, and

(*b*) may make different provision for different cases.

(6) In this section and section 13C of this Act—

"duty of customs" includes any agricultural levy within the meaning of section 6 of the European Communities Act 1972 chargeable on goods imported into the United Kingdom, and "duty of excise" means any duty of excise chargeable on goods and includes any addition to excise duty by virtue of section 1 of the Excise Duties (Surcharges or Rebates) Act 1979.

(7) For the purposes of this section and section 13C of this Act, where in respect of any person to whom this section applies relief is conferred (whether by virtue of an order under this section or otherwise) in relation to the use of goods by any persons or for any purposes, the relief is to be treated as conferred subject to a condition binding on him that the goods will be used only by those persons or for those purposes.

(8) Nothing in any order under this section shall be construed as authorising a person to import any thing in contravention of any prohibition or restriction for the time being in force with respect to it under or by virtue of any enactment.][1]

Commentary—*De Voil Indirect Tax Service* **V3.347**.

Orders—See Customs and Excise (Personal Reliefs for Special Visitors) Order, SI 1992/3156.

Amendments—[1] This section inserted by FA 1989 s 28(1).

[13B Persons to whom section 13A applies

(1) The persons to whom section 13A of this Act applies are—

(*a*) any person who, for the purposes of any provision of the Visiting Forces Act 1952 or the International Headquarters and Defence Organisations Act 1964 is—

(i) a member of a visiting force or of a civilian component of such a force or a dependant of such a member, or

(ii) a headquarters, a member of a headquarters or a dependant of such a member,

(*b*) any person enjoying any privileges or immunities under or by virtue of—

(i) the Diplomatic Privileges Act 1964

(ii) the Commonwealth Secretariat Act 1966

(iii) the Consular Relations Act 1968

(iv) the International Organisations Act 1968 or

[(v) the International Development Act 2002.][2]

(*c*) any person enjoying, under or by virtue of section 2 of the European Communities Act 1972 any privileges or immunities similar to those enjoyed under or by virtue of the enactments referred to in paragraph (*b*) above.

(2) The Secretary of State may by order amend subsection (1) above to include any persons enjoying any privileges or immunities similar to those enjoyed under or by virtue of the enactments referred to in paragraph (*b*) of that subsection.

(3) No order shall be made under this section unless a draft of the order has been laid before and approved by resolution of each House of Parliament.][1]

Commentary—*De Voil Indirect Tax Service* **V3.347**.

Amendments—[1] This section inserted by FA 1989 s 28(1).

[2] In sub-s (1), para (*b*)(v) substituted by the International Development Act 2002 s 19, Sch 3 para 7 with effect from 17 June 2002 (by virtue of SI 2002/1408).

[13C Offence where relieved goods used, etc, in breach of condition

(1) Subsection (2) below applies where—

(*a*) any relief from payment of any duty of customs or excise, value added tax or car tax chargeable on, or on the supply or importation of, any goods has been conferred (whether by virtue of an order under section 13A of this Act or otherwise) in respect of any person to whom that section applies subject to any condition as to the persons by whom or the purposes for which the goods may be used, and

(*b*) if the tax or duty has subsequently become payable, it has not been paid.

(2) If any person—

(*a*) acquires the goods for his own use, where he is not permitted by the condition to use them, or for use for a purpose that is not permitted by the condition or uses them for such a purpose, or

(*b*) acquires the goods for use, or causes or permits them to be used, by a person not permitted by the condition to use them or by a person for a purpose that is not permitted by the condition or disposes of them to a person not permitted by the condition to use them,

with intent to evade payment or any tax or duty that has become payable or that, by reason of the disposal, acquisition or use, becomes or will become payable, he is guilty of an offence.

(3) For the purposes of this section—

(*a*) in the case of a condition as to the persons by whom goods may be used, a person is not permitted by the condition to use them unless he is a person referred to in the condition as permitted to use them, and

(*b*) in relation to a condition as to the purposes for which goods may be used, a purpose is not permitted by the condition unless it is a purpose referred to in the condition as a permitted purpose,

and in this section "dispose" includes "lend" and "let on hire", and "acquire" shall be interpreted accordingly.

(4) A person guilty of an offence under this section may be detained and shall be liable—

(*a*) on summary conviction, to a penalty of [£20,000][3] or of three times the value of the goods (whichever is the greater), or to imprisonment for a term not exceeding six months, or to both, or

(*b*) on conviction on indictment, to a penalty of any amount, or to imprisonment for a term not exceeding seven years, or to both.][1]

[(5) Where any person is guilty of an offence under this section, the goods in respect of which the offence was committed shall be liable to forfeiture.][2]

Commentary—*De Voil Indirect Tax Service* **V5.303**.

Amendments—[1] This section inserted by FA 1989 s 28(1), (2) and has effect where relief is conferred after 26 July 1989.

[2] Sub-s (5) added by F(No 2)A 1992 s 3, Sch 2 para 10 with effect from 9 December 1992 by virtue of F(No 2)A 1992 (Commencement No 3) Order, SI 1992/3104.

[3] In sub-s (4)(*a*), figure substituted by the Legal Aid, Sentencing and Punishment of Offenders Act 2012 (Fines on Summary Conviction) Regulations, SI 2015/664 reg 2(2), Sch 2 para 2(1), (3) with effect from 12 March 2015 in relation to England and Wales only.

ISLE OF MAN ACT 1979

(1979 Chapter 58)

ARRANGEMENT OF SECTIONS

An Act to make such amendments of the law relating to customs and excise, value added tax, car tax and the importation and exportation of goods as are required for giving effect to an Agreement between the government of the United Kingdom and the government of the Isle of Man signed on 15th October 1979; to make other amendments as respects the Isle of Man in the law relating to those matters; to provide for the transfer of functions vested in the Lieutenant Governor of the Isle of Man or, as respects that Island, in the Commissioners of Customs and Excise; and for purposes connected with those matters.

[20th December 1979]

1 Common duties

(1) Subject to subsection (2) below, in this Act "common duties" means—

(*a*)–[(*ca*)] . . .

(*d*) value added tax chargeable under the law of the United Kingdom or the Isle of Man except tax chargeable in accordance with [section][1] [23 of the Value Added Tax Act 1994][2] (gaming machines);

(*e*) . . .

(2) The Treasury may by order amend subsection (1) above by adding or deleting any duty or tax which is under the care and management of the Commissioners of Customs and Excise (in this Act referred to as "the Commissioners") or any corresponding duty or tax chargeable under the law of the Isle of Man; and any such order may apply to a duty or tax generally or in such cases or subject to such restrictions as may be specified in the order.

(3) The power to make orders under subsection (2) above shall be exercisable by statutory instrument subject to annulment in pursuance of a resolution of the House of Commons.

Commentary—*De Voil Indirect Tax Service* **V1.217**.

Note—Sub-s (1)(*a*)–(*ca*), (*e*) are not relevant to this work.

Amendments—[1] Word in sub-s (1)(*d*) substituted by VATA 1983 Sch 9 para 3(a).

[2] Words in sub-s (1)(*d*) substituted by VATA 1994 s 100, Sch 14 para 7(1).

2 Isle of Man share of common duties

(1) Of the moneys standing to the credit of the General Account of the Commissioners an amount ascertained for each financial year in accordance with subsection (2) below shall be paid by the Commissioners, at such times and in such manner as they may determine, to the Treasurer of the Isle of Man.

(2) There shall be calculated in such manner as the Treasury may direct—

(*a*) the amount of common duties, whether collected in the United Kingdom or the Isle of Man, which is attributable to goods consumed or used in the Island, to services supplied in the Island or (as respects pool betting duty) to bets placed by persons in the Island;

(*b*) the cost incurred by the Commissioners in collecting the amount so attributable together with the amount of any drawback or repayment referable to that amount;

and the amount arrived at by deducting from the amount calculated under paragraph (a) above the amount calculated under paragraph (b) above shall be known as the net Isle of Man share of common duties; and the amount mentioned in subsection (1) above shall be the excess of the net Isle of Man share of common duties over the common duties collected in the Island.

(3) For the purposes of this section the amount of common duties collected in the Isle of Man and the United Kingdom, or in the Isle of Man, shall be calculated by reference to the amount so collected in respect of such duties after giving effect to any addition or deduction provided for under section 1 of the Excise Duties (Surcharges or Rebates) Act 1979 or any Isle of Man equivalent.

(4) The Commissioners shall for each financial year prepare, in such form and manner as the Treasury may direct, an account showing the payments made by them under this section and shall send it, not later than the end of November in the following financial year, to the Comptroller and Auditor General, who shall examine and certify the account.

(5) The Comptroller and Auditor General shall send every account examined and certified by him under this section and his report thereon to the Treasury and a copy of every such account and report to the Treasurer of the Isle of Man; and the Treasury shall lay copies of the account and report before Parliament.

Commentary—*De Voil Indirect Tax Service* **V1.262**.

3 Recovery of common duties chargeable in Isle of Man

(1) Any liability to pay an amount on account of a common duty chargeable under the law of the Isle of Man shall, to the extent to which it has not been discharged or enforced there, be enforceable in the United Kingdom as if it were a liability to pay an amount on account of the corresponding common duty chargeable under the law of the United Kingdom.

(2) Any amount recoverable by the Commissioners from any person under subsection (1) above may be set off against any amount recoverable by him from the Commissioners on account of a common duty chargeable under the law of the United Kingdom.

Commentary—*De Voil Indirect Tax Service* **V1.271**.

4 Enforcement of Isle of Man judgments for common duties

(1) Subject to subsection (2) below, the provisions of sections 2 to 5 of the Foreign Judgments (Reciprocal Enforcement) Act 1933 shall have effect in relation to any judgment or order given or made by the High Court of Justice of the Isle of Man under which an amount is payable on account of—

(*a*) a common duty chargeable under the law of the Island; or

(*b*) a fine or penalty imposed in connection with such a duty,

as if the judgment or order were a judgment to which Part I of that Act applied.

(2) Subsection (1) above does not apply to a judgment or order given or made on appeal from a lower court but, except when given or made in criminal proceedings, applies notwithstanding that it is subject to appeal or that an appeal against it is pending.

(3) In their application by virtue of subsection (1) above the provisions there mentioned shall have effect—

(*a*) with the omission of so much of section 2(1) as imposes a time-limit for applications for registration;

(*b*) with the omission of section 4(1)(*a*)(v) and (vi); and

(*c*) as if the Commissioners were the judgment creditor and any criminal proceedings in which the judgment or order was given or made were an action.

(4) The reference in subsection (1) above to sections 2 to 5 of the said Act of 1933 includes a reference to so much of sections 11 to 13 of that Act as is relevant to those sections and the definition of "appeal" in section 11 shall apply for the purposes of subsection (2) above.

(5) The reference in subsection (1) above to the High Court of Justice of the Isle of Man includes a reference to the Court of General Gaol Delivery.

Commentary—*De Voil Indirect Tax Service* **V1.271**.

5 Offences relating to common duties etc

(1) Any summons or other process requiring a person in the Isle of Man to appear before a court in the United Kingdom—

(*a*) to answer a charge that he has committed an offence relating to a common duty chargeable under the law of the United Kingdom or to the importation or exportation of anything into or from the United Kingdom; or

(*b*) to give evidence or to produce any document or thing in proceedings for any such offence,

may be served by being sent to him by registered post or the recorded delivery service.

(2) In relation to proceedings for any such offence as is mentioned in subsection (1) above—

(*a*) [section 97 of the Magistrates' Courts Act 1980][1] (summons to witness and warrant for his arrest) shall have effect as if the reference in subsection (1) of that section to a person in England and Wales included a reference to a person in the Isle of Man;

(*b*) in Scotland a warrant for the citation of accused persons and witnesses shall include a warrant to cite accused persons and witnesses in the Isle of Man.

(3) In relation to proceedings for any such offence as is mentioned in subsection (1) above—

(*a*) [section 9 of the Criminal Justice Act 1967 and section 102 of the Magistrates' Courts Act 1980][1] (admission of written statements) shall apply also to written statements made in the Isle of Man but with the omission of subsections (2)(*b*) and (3A) of [section 102][1] and subsections (2)(*b*) and (3A) of section 9;

(*b*) section 1 of the Criminal Justice (Miscellaneous Provisions) Act (Northern Ireland) 1968 and section 3 of the Criminal Procedure (Committal for Trial) Act (Northern Ireland) 1968 (which contain corresponding provisions) shall apply also to written statements made in the Isle of Man but with the omission of subsection (2)(*b*) of section 1 and subsection (2)(*c*) of section 3.

(4) Subject to subsection (5) below, a warrant issued in the Isle of Man for the arrest of—

(*a*) a person charged with an offence relating to a common duty chargeable under the law of the Isle of Man or to the importation or exportation of anything into or from the Island; or

(*b*) a person required to give evidence or to produce any document or thing in proceedings for any such offence,

may be executed in England and Wales by any constable acting within his police area, in Scotland by any officer of law as defined in [section 307(1) of the Criminal Procedure (Scotland) Act 1995][2] and in Northern Ireland by any member of the Royal Ulster Constabulary or the Royal Ulster Constabulary Reserve.

(5) A warrant, other than one for the arrest of a person charged with an offence punishable with at least two years' imprisonment, shall not be executed under subsection (4) above unless it has been endorsed for execution under that subsection by a justice of the peace in England, Wales, Scotland or Northern Ireland, as the case may be; and any warrant which purports to have been issued as mentioned in that subsection may be so endorsed without further proof.

(6) A warrant for the arrest of a person charged with an offence may be executed by a constable under subsection (4) above notwithstanding that it is not in his possession at the time but the warrant shall, on demand of that person, be shown to him as soon as practicable.

(7) Subsections (1) and (4) above are without prejudice to any other enactment enabling any process to be served or executed otherwise than as provided in those subsections.

(8) References in this section to a warrant for the arrest of any person include references to any process for that purpose available under the law of the Isle of Man; and references to an offence relating to a common duty or to importation or exportation include references to any offence which relates to any of those matters whether or not it is an offence under a provision dealing specifically with that matter.

Commentary—*De Voil Indirect Tax Service* **V1.217, 1.263**.

Amendments—[1] Words in sub-ss (2)(*a*) and (3)(*a*) substituted by Magistrates' Courts Act 1980 s 154, Sch 7 para 198.

[2] Words in sub-s (4) substituted by Criminal Procedure (Consequential Provisions) (Scotland) Act 1995 Sch 4 para 25.

6 Value added tax

(1) For the purpose of giving effect to any Agreement between the government of the United Kingdom and the government of the Isle of Man whereby both countries are to be treated as a single area for the purposes of value added tax charged under [the Value Added Tax Act [1994][2]][1] and value added tax charged under the corresponding Act of Tynwald, Her Majesty may by Order in Council make provision for securing that tax is charged under [the Act of [1994][2]][1] as if all or any of the references in it to the United Kingdom included both the United Kingdom and the Isle of Man but so that tax is not charged under both Acts in respect of the same transaction.

(2) An Order in Council under this section may make provision—

(*a*) for determining, or enabling the Commissioners to determine, under which Act a person is to be registered and for transferring a person registered under one Act to the register kept under the other;

(*b*) for treating a person who is a taxable person for the purposes of the Act of Tynwald as a taxable person for all or any of the purposes of [the Act of [1994][2]][1];

(*c*) for extending any reference in [the Act of [1994][2]][1] to tax under that Act so as to include tax under the Act of Tynwald;

(*d*) for treating any requirement imposed by or under either Act as a requirement imposed by or under the other;

(*e*) for treating any permission, direction, notice, determination or other thing given, made or done under the Act of Tynwald by the Isle of Man authority corresponding to the Commissioners as given, made or done by the Commissioners under [the Act of [1994][2]][1];

(*f*) for enabling the Commissioners to determine for the purposes of [section [43][2]][1] of [the Act of [1994][2]][1] (groups of companies) which member of a group is to be the representative member in cases where supplies are made both in the United Kingdom and the Isle of Man;

(*g*) for modifying or excluding, as respects goods removed from the Isle of Man to the United Kingdom or from the United Kingdom to the Isle of Man, any provision relating to importation or exportation contained in [the Act of [1994][2]][1] or in the customs and excise Acts as applied by that Act;

(*h*) for any supplementary, incidental or transitional matter.

(3) An Order in Council under this section may make such modifications of any provision contained in or having effect under any Act of Parliament relating to value added tax as appears to Her Majesty to be necessary or expedient for the purposes of the Order.

(4) While an Order in Council under this section is in force and without prejudice to the powers conferred by the foregoing provisions—

(*a*) [section [30(10)][2]][1] of [the Act of [1994][2]][1] (forfeiture of zero-rated goods) shall have effect as if the reference to goods zero-rated under the regulations there mentioned included a reference to goods zero-rated under any corresponding regulations made under the Act of Tynwald;

(*b*) [paragraph 10(3) of [Schedule 11][2]][1] to] [the Act of [1994][2]][1] (search of premises where offence is suspected) shall have effect as if the references to an offence in connection with the tax included references to an offence in connection with the tax charged under the Act of Tynwald;

(*c*) [section [72(8)][2]][1] of [the Act of [1994][2]][1] (course of conduct involving offences) shall have effect as if the reference to offences under the provisions there mentioned included a reference to offences under the corresponding provisions of the Act of Tynwald.

(5) Provision may be made by or under an Act of Tynwald for purposes corresponding to those of this section and of any Order in Council made under it.

Commentary—*De Voil Indirect Tax Service* **V1.236**.
Orders—See VAT (Isle of Man) Orders: SI 1982/1067; (No 2) Order, SI 1982/1068.
Cross references—See VATA 1994 Sch 13 para 23 (validity of orders made under this section prior to coming into force of VATA 1994 not affected).
Amendments—[1] Words in sub-ss (1), (2), (4) substituted by VATA 1983 Sch 9 para 3.
[2] Word and figures in sub-ss (1), (2), (4) substituted by VATA 1994 s 100, Sch 14 para 7(2).

10 Exchange of information

No obligation as to secrecy or other restriction on the disclosure of information imposed by statute or otherwise shall prevent the Commissioners or any officer of the Commissioners from disclosing information to the Isle of Man customs and excise service for the purpose of facilitating the proper administration of common duties and the enforcement of prohibitions or restrictions on importation or exportation into or from the Isle of Man or the United Kingdom.

11 Transfer of functions to Isle of Man authorities

(1) Her Majesty may by Order in Council make such modifications in any provision contained in or having effect under any Act of Parliament extending to the Isle of Man as appear to Her Majesty to be appropriate for the purpose of transferring to any authority or person constituted by or having functions under the law of the Island—

(*a*) any functions under that provision of the Lieutenant Governor of the Isle of Man (whether referred to by that title or otherwise) or of a deputy governor of the Island;

(*b*) any functions under that provision, so far as exercisable in relation to the Island, of the Commissioners or an officer of the Commissioners.

(2) Any statutory instrument made by virtue of this section shall be subject to annulment in pursuance of a resolution of either House of Parliament.

12 Proof of Acts of Tynwald etc

(1) Without prejudice to the Evidence (Colonial Statutes) Act 1907 any Act of Tynwald or other instrument forming part of the law of the Isle of Man may, in any proceedings in the United Kingdom relating to a common duty or to importation or exportation into or from the United Kingdom or the Isle of Man, be proved by producing a copy of the Act or instrument authenticated by a certificate purporting to be signed by or on behalf of the Attorney General for the Island.

(2) Any provision contained in or having effect under an Act of Tynwald which—

(*a*) prescribes the mode or burden of proof with respect to any matter in proceedings relating to a common duty chargeable under the law of the Isle of Man; and

(*b*) corresponds to a provision of United Kingdom law for similar purposes,

shall apply to any proceedings in the United Kingdom relating to that duty.

(3) For the purposes of any proceedings in the United Kingdom relating to a common duty an order may be made under the Bankers' Books Evidence Act 1879 in respect of books and persons in the Isle of Man.

13 Amendments of customs and excise Acts etc

The enactments mentioned in Schedule 1 to this Act shall have effect with the amendments there specified, being amendments which—

(*a*) extend certain references to the United Kingdom in the customs and excise Acts so as to include the Isle of Man; or

(*b*) are otherwise consequential on the provisions of this Act.

14 Short title, interpretation, repeals, commencement and extent

(1) This Act may be cited as the Isle of Man Act 1979.

(2) In this Act—

"the Commissioners" means the Commissioners of Customs and Excise;

"common duties" has the meaning given in section 1 above and "common duty" shall be construed accordingly;

"customs duty" includes any levy or other charge which is treated as a customs duty by section 6 of the European Communities Act 1972.

(3) . . .

(4) Without prejudice to section 2(3) above,—

(*a*) . . .

(*b*) any sum recoverable as a debt due to the Crown under [paragraph 5(3) of Schedule 11 to the Value Added Tax Act 1994][1] (sums shown in invoices as value added tax) or any Isle of Man equivalent, shall be treated for the purposes of this Act as an amount of excise duty or value added tax chargeable under the law of the United Kingdom or, as the case may be, the Isle of Man.

(5) The enactments mentioned in Schedule 2 to this Act (which include spent provisions) are hereby repealed to the extent specified in the third column of that Schedule.

(6) Subject to subsection (7) below, this Act shall come into force on 1st April 1980.

(7) Sections 6, 7, 10 and 11 above shall come into force on the passing of this Act but no Order in Council shall be made under section 6, 7 or 11, and no provision shall by virtue of section 6(5) or 7(5) be made by or under an Act of Tynwald, so as to come into force before 1st April 1980.

(8) Except for sections 6, 7, 11 and this section, this Act does not extend to the Isle of Man as part of the law of the Island.

Note—Sub-ss (3) and (4)(*a*) are not relevant to VAT.
Amendments—[1] Words in sub-s (4)(*b*) substituted by VATA 1994 s 100, Sch 14 para 7(3).

COMPANIES ACT 1985

(1985 Chapter 6)

PART XXVI

INTERPRETATION

736 "Subsidiary", "holding company" and "wholly owned subsidiary"

Note—This section was rewritten to Companies Act 2006 s 1159(1), (2), (4).
Cross references—See VATA 1994 s 43A (Groups: eligibility).

736A Provisions supplementing s 736

Note—This section was rewritten to Companies Act 2006 s 1159(3) and Sch 6.
Cross references—See VATA 1994 s 43A (Groups: eligibility).

INCOME AND CORPORATION TAXES ACT 1988

(1988 Chapter 1)

PART XIX

SUPPLEMENTAL

Interpretation

839 Connected persons

Commentary—*Simon's Taxes* **A1.156**.
Rewrite destinations—Sub-s (1) rewritten to ITA 2007 ss 993(1), 994(4), Sch 1 para 411 and CTA 2010 ss 1122(1), 1123(4).
Sub-s (2) rewritten to ITA 2007 s 993(2), Sch 1 para 411 and CTA 2010 s 1122(5).
Sub-ss (3), (3A) rewritten to ITA 2007 ss 993(3), 994(1), Sch 1 para 411 and CTA 2010 s 1122(6), 1123(1).
Sub-s (3B) rewritten to ITA 2007 s 994(1), (3) and CTA 2010 s 1123(1), (3).
Sub-ss (4)–(7) rewritten to ITA 2007 s 993(4)–(7), Sch 1 para 411 and CTA 2010 s 1122(2)–(4), (7), (8).
Sub-s (8) rewritten to ITA 2007 s 994(1), (2), Sch 1 para 411 and CTA 2010 s 34(7), 1123(1), (2).

FINANCE ACT 1988

(1988 Chapter 39)

An Act to grant certain duties, to alter other duties, and to amend the law relating to the National Debt and the Public Revenue, and to make further provision in connection with Finance.

[29th July 1988]

PART I

CUSTOMS AND EXCISE

Management

8 Disclosure of information as to imports

(1) The Commissioners may, for the purpose of supplementing the information as to imported goods which may be made available to persons other than the Commissioners, disclose information to which this section applies to such persons as they think fit.

(2) Such information may be so disclosed on such terms and conditions (including terms and conditions as to the payment of fees or charges to the Commissioners and the making of the information available to other persons) as the Commissioners think fit.

(3) This section applies to information consisting of the names and addresses of persons declared as consignees in entries of imported goods, arranged by reference to such classifications of imported goods as the Commissioners think fit.

(4) This section shall be construed as if it were contained in the Customs and Excise Management Act 1979.

PART IV

MISCELLANEOUS AND GENERAL

Miscellaneous

149 Short title

This Act may be cited as the Finance Act 1988.

FINANCE ACT 1989

(1989 Chapter 26)

An Act to grant certain duties, to alter other duties, and to amend the law relating to the National Debt and the Public Revenue, and to make further provision in connection with Finance.

[27th July 1989]

PART III

MISCELLANEOUS AND GENERAL

Miscellaneous

182 Disclosure of information

(1) A person who discloses any information which he holds or has held in the exercise of tax functions . . . is guilty of an offence if it is information about any matter relevant, for the purposes . . . of those functions—

[(*a*) to tax . . . in the case of any identifiable person, ...

[(*ab*),] [4] (*b*), (*c*) . . .][3]

(2) In this section "tax functions" means functions relating to tax . . . —

(*a*) of the Commissioners, . . . and their officers,

(*aa*) . . .

(*b*) of any person carrying out the administrative work of any tribunal mentioned in subsection (3) below, and

(*c*) of any other person providing, or employed in the provision of, services to any person mentioned in paragraph (*a*) or (*b*) above.

. . .

(3) The tribunals referred to in subsection (2)(b) above are—

(*a*) . . .

(*b*) any value added tax tribunal,

(*c*), (*d*) . . . [6]

(4) A person who discloses any information which—

(*a*) he holds or has held in the exercise of functions—

(ia) [of the Comptroller and Auditor General for Northern Ireland and any member of the staff of the Northern Ireland Audit Office,][7],

(i) of the Comptroller and Auditor General[, of the National Audit Office and any member or employee of that Office or of any member of the staff of the National Audit Office that was established by section 3 of the National Audit Act 1983][7],

(ii) of the Parliamentary Commissioner for Administration and his officers,

[(iii) of the Auditor General for Wales and any member of his staff, . . . [3]

[(iv) of the Public Services Ombudsman for Wales and any member of his staff, or][5]

(v) of the Scottish Public Services Ombudsman and any member of his staff,][3]

(*b*) is, or is derived from, information which was held by any person in the exercise of tax functions . . . , and

(*c*) is information about any matter relevant, for the purposes of tax functions . . . —

[(i) to tax . . . in the case of any identifiable person . . . ,

. . .

is guilty of an offence.

(5) Subsections (1) and (4) above do not apply to any disclosure of information—

(*a*) with lawful authority,

(*b*) with the consent of any person in whose case the information is about a matter relevant to tax . . . , or

(*c*) which has been lawfully made available to the public before the disclosure is made.

(6) For the purposes of this section a disclosure of any information is made with lawful authority if, and only if, it is made—

(*a*) by a Crown servant in accordance with his official duty,

(*b*) by any other person for the purposes of the function in the exercise of which he holds the information and without contravening any restriction duly imposed by the person responsible,
(*c*) to, or in accordance with an authorisation duly given by, the person responsible,
(*d*) in pursuance of any enactment or of any order of a court, or
(*e*) in connection with the institution of or otherwise for the purposes of any proceedings relating to any matter within the general responsibility of the Commissioners . . . ,

and in this subsection "the person responsible" means the Commissioners, . . . the Comptroller[and Auditor General, the Comptroller and Auditor General for Northern Ireland][7] [, the Parliamentary Commissioner, the Auditor General for Wales[, [the Public Services Ombudsman for Wales][5] or the Scottish Public Services Ombudsman][3],][2] as the case requires.

(7) It is a defence for a person charged with an offence under this section to prove that at the time of the alleged offence—
(*a*) he believed that he had lawful authority to make the disclosure in question and had no reasonable cause to believe otherwise, or
(*b*) he believed that the information in question had been lawfully made available to the public before the disclosure was made and had no reasonable cause to believe otherwise.

(8) A person guilty of an offence under this section is liable—
(*a*) on conviction on indictment, to imprisonment for a term not exceeding two years or a fine or both, and
(*b*) on summary conviction, to imprisonment for a term not exceeding six months or a fine not exceeding the statutory maximum or both.

(9) No prosecution for an offence under this section shall be instituted in England and Wales or in Northern Ireland except—
(*a*) by the Commissioners . . . , or
(*b*) by or with the consent of the Director of Public Prosecutions or, in Northern Ireland, the Director of Public Prosecutions for Northern Ireland.

(10) In this section—

. . .

"the Commissioners" means the Commissioners of Customs and Excise,

. . . [3]

"Crown servant" has the same meaning as in the Official Secrets Act 1989 and

"tax . . . " means any tax . . . within the general responsibility of the Commissioners

. . .

[(10A) In this section, in relation to the disclosure of information "identifiable person" means a person whose identity is specified in the disclosure or can be deduced from it.][4]

(11) In this section—
(*a*) . . . [7]
(*b*) . . . [7]
(*c*) references to the Parliamentary Commissioner for Administration include the Health Service Commissioner for England . . . [5], . . . [3] the [Assembly Ombudsman for Northern Ireland][1] and the Northern Ireland Commissioner for Complaints.

. . .

(12) This section shall come into force on the repeal of section 2 of the Official Secrets Act 1911.

Note—This section came into force on 1 March 1990 when the repeal of Official Secrets Act 1911 came into force by virtue of the Official Secrets Act 1989 (Commencement) Order, SI 1990/199.

Words omitted in various places are not relevant to VAT.

Amendments—[1] Words substituted by Ombudsman (Northern Ireland) Order, SI 1996/1298 (NI 8) art 21(1), Sch 5.

[2] Sub-ss (4)(*a*)(iii) and (iv) inserted and words in sub-s (6) substituted by the Government of Wales Act 1998, Sch 12 para 31 with effect from 1 February 1999 by virtue of The Government of Wales Act 1998 (Commencement No 3) Order, SI 1999/118.

[3] Word "or" in sub-s (4)(a)(iii) repealed, sub-s (4)(*a*)(v) and words in sub-s (6) inserted, words in sub-s (11)(c) repealed by Scottish Public Services Ombudsman Act 2002 (Consequential Provisions and Modifications) Order, SI 2004/1823 with effect from 14 July 2004.

[4] Sub-s (10A) inserted by CRCA 2005 s 50, Sch 4 para 39 with effect from 18 April 2005 (by virtue of SI 2005/1126).

[5] Sub-s (4)(*a*)(iv) substituted, words in sub-s (6) substituted, and words omitted from sub-s (11)(*c*) repealed, by Public Services Ombudsman (Wales) Act 2005 s 39, Sch 6 para 22, Sch 7 with effect from 1 April 2006 (by virtue of SI 2005/2800, art 5(1)).

[6] Sub-s (3) repealed by the by the Transfer of Tribunal Functions and Revenue and Customs Appeals Order, SI 2009/56 art 3, Sch 1 paras 166, 167 with effect from 1 April 2009.

[7] In sub-s (4), in para (*a*)(i), words substituted and sub-para (i *a*) inserted, in sub-s (6), words inserted, and sub-s (11)(*a*), (*b*) repealed by the Budget Responsibility and National Audit Act 2011 s 26, Sch 5 para 14 with effect from 1 April 2012 by virtue of SI 2011/2576 art 5, subject to savings in SI 2011/2576 art 6.

General

186 Interpretation etc

(1) In this Act "the Taxes Act 1970" means the Income and Corporation Taxes Act 1970 and "the Taxes Act 1988" means the Income and Corporation Taxes Act 1988.

(2), (3) . . .

Note—Sub-ss (2), (3) are not relevant to VAT.

188 Short title
This Act may be cited as the Finance Act 1989.

CHARITIES ACT 1993

(1993 Chapter 10)

Amendments—This Act repealed by the Charities Act 2011 s 354, Sch 10 with effect from 14 March 2012.

FINANCE ACT 1994

(1994 Chapter 9)

CHAPTER II

APPEALS AND PENALTIES

[The meaning of tribunal

7 Meaning of tribunal
In the following provisions of this Chapter references to an appeal tribunal are references to the First-tier Tribunal or, where determined by or under Tribunal Procedure Rules, the Upper Tribunal.][1]

Amendments—[1] Section 7 substituted by the Transfer of Tribunal Functions and Revenue and Customs Appeals Order, SI 2009/56 art 3, Sch 1 paras 196, 197 with effect from 1 April 2009.

VALUE ADDED TAX ACT 1994

(1994 Chapter 23)

ARRANGEMENT OF SECTIONS

PART I
THE CHARGE TO TAX

PART II
RELIEFS, EXEMPTIONS AND REPAYMENTS

Reliefs etc generally available

PART VI
SUPPLEMENTARY PROVISIONS

An Act to consolidate the enactments relating to value added tax, including certain enactments relating to VAT tribunals.

[5th July 1994]

PART I
THE CHARGE TO TAX

Cross reference—See Isle of Man Act 1979 s 6, VAT (Isle of Man) Orders, SI 1982/1067, SI 1982/1068 and VATA 1994 Sch 13 para 23 (treatment of UK and Isle of Man as a single area for the purposes of this Act).
F(No 2)A 2010 s 3 (standard rate of VAT increased to 20 per cent for supplies made on or after 4 January 2011).

F(No 2)A 2010 Sch 2 (supplementary charge to VAT where supply spans 4 January 2011).

Imposition and rate of VAT

1 Value added tax

(1) Value added tax shall be charged, in accordance with the provisions of this Act—

(*a*) on the supply of goods or services in the United Kingdom (including anything treated as such a supply),

(*b*) on the acquisition in the United Kingdom from other member States of any goods, and

(*c*) on the importation of goods from places outside the member States,

and references in this Act to VAT are references to value added tax.

(2) VAT on any supply of goods or services is a liability of the person making the supply and (subject to provisions about accounting and payment) becomes due at the time of supply.

(3) VAT on any acquisition of goods from another member State is a liability of the person who acquires the goods and (subject to provisions about accounting and payment) becomes due at the time of acquisition.

(4) VAT on the importation of goods from places outside the member States shall be charged and payable as if it were a duty of customs.

Commentary—*De Voil Indirect Tax Service* **V3.101**.

Simon's Tax Cases—s 1(1), *C&E Comrs v Fine Art Developments plc* [1989] STC 85*.

Definitions—"Acquisition of goods from another member State", s 11; "another member State", s 96(1); "importation of goods from places outside the member States", s 15; "other member States", s 96(1); "supply ", s 5, Sch 4; "time of acquisition", s 12; "time of supply", s 6; "United Kingdom", s 96(11); "VAT", s 96(1).

2 Rate of VAT

(1) Subject to the following provisions of this section [and to the provisions of section 29A][2] . . . [1], VAT shall be charged at the rate of [20 per cent][5] and shall be charged—

(*a*) on the supply of goods or services, by reference to the value of the supply as determined under this Act; and

(*b*) on the acquisition of goods from another member State, by reference to the value of the acquisition as determined under this Act; and

(*c*) on the importation of goods from a place outside the member States, by reference to the value of the goods as determined under this Act.

(1A)–(1C) . . . [2].

(2) The Treasury may by order increase or decrease the rate of VAT for the time being in force [under this section][3] by such percentage thereof not exceeding 25 per cent as may be specified in the order, but any such order [that has not previously expired or been revoked][4] shall cease to be in force at the expiration of a period of one year from the date on which it takes effect, unless continued in force by a further order under this subsection.

(3) In relation to an order made under subsection (2) above to continue, vary or replace a previous order, the reference in that subsection to the rate for the time being in force [under this section][3] is a reference to the rate which would be in force if no order under that subsection had been made.

Summer Finance Bill 2015 The Summer Finance Bill introduces a "VAT lock", restricting the standard and reduced rates of VAT to current rates. Please check the latest version of the Bill and subsequent Finance Act for details.

Commentary—*De Voil Indirect Tax Service* **V1.131, V3.151, V1.121**.

Definitions—"Acquisition of goods from another member State", s 11; "another member State", s 96(1); "importation of goods from a place outside the member States", s 15; "supply", s 5, Sch 4; "VAT", ss 1, 96(1); "value of the acquisition", s 20; "value of the goods", s 21; "value of the supply", s 19, Sch 6.

Cross references—See VATA 1994 s 50A (Treasury may by order provide an option for VAT to be charged by reference to profit margin rather than value in relation to certain supplies);

VATA 1994 s 88 (supplies spanning date of change in rate of VAT);

VAT Regulations, SI 1995/2518 reg 15 (credit note to be issued by supplier following change of rate, where an election is made under s 88).

F(No 2)A 2010 Sch 2 (supplementary charge to VAT where supply spans 4 January 2011).

FA 2009 Sch 3 (supplementary charge to VAT).

Note—The standard rate of tax was reduced to 15%, by the VAT (Change of Rate) Order, SI 2008/3020 arts 2, 3 with effect from 1 December 2008 to 31 December 2009 (extended from 30 November 2009 by FA 2009 s 9). On 1 January 2010 the standard rate reverted to 17.5% and was then increased to 20% on 4 January 2011.

Amendments—[1] Words omitted from sub-s (1) repealed by FA 1995 s 21(2), (6), with effect in relation to any supply made after 31 March 1995 and any acquisition or importation taking place after that date.

[2] Words in sub-s (1) inserted, and sub-s (1A), (1B) repealed by FA 2001 s 99(2), (3) with effect for supplies made, and acquisitions and importations taking place, after 31 October 2001. Sub-s (1C) repealed by FA 2001 s 99(2), (3) with effect from 1 November 2001.

[3] Words in sub-ss (2), (3) inserted by FA 2001 s 99(6), Sch 31 para 2 with effect for orders under sub-s (2) that make changes only in the rate of VAT that is in force at times after 31 October 2001.

[4] Words in sub-s (2) inserted by FA 2009 Sch 3 para 25(2) with effect from 21 July 2009.

[5] In sub-s (1), words substituted for words "17.5 per cent" by F(No 2)A 2010 s 3(1) with effect in relation to any supply made on or after 4 January 2011 and any acquisition or importation taking place on or after that date.

3 Taxable persons and registration

(1) A person is a taxable person for the purposes of this Act while he is, or is required to be, registered under this Act.

(2) [Schedules 1 to 3A][1] shall have effect with respect to registration.

(3) Persons registered under any of those Schedules shall be registered in a single register kept by the Commissioners for the purposes of this Act; and, accordingly, references in this Act to being registered under this Act are references to being registered under any of those Schedules.

(4) The Commissioners may by regulations make provision as to the inclusion and correction of information in that register with respect to the Schedule under which any person is registered.

Commentary—*De Voil Indirect Tax Service* **V3.513**.

Regulations—See VAT Regulations, SI 1995/2518 regs 5–7.

VAT (Amendment) (No 2) Regulations, SI 2012/1899.

Press releases etc—C&E News Release 22/96 4-4-96 (prohibition on disclosure of information on the VAT register continues).

Simon's Tax Cases—*R&C Comrs v Pal and others* [2008] STC 2442.

Definitions—"The Commissioners", s 96(1); "regulations", s 96(1).

Amendments—[1] Words in sub-s (2) substituted by FA 2000 s 136(1), with effect for supplies made after 20 March 2000.

[3A [Supplies of electronic, telecommunication and broadcasting services: special accounting schemes]

(1) Schedule 3B (scheme enabling persons who supply electronically supplied services[, telecommunication services or broadcasting services][3] in any member State, but who are not established in a member State, to account for and pay VAT in the United Kingdom on those supplies) has effect.

[(1A) Schedule 3BA—

(*a*) establishes a special accounting scheme for use by persons established in the UK and supplying electronically supplied services, telecommunication services or broadcasting services in other member States, and

(*b*) makes provision about corresponding schemes in other member States.][3]

(2) The Treasury may by order amend Schedule 3B [or 3BA][2].

(3) The power of the Treasury by order to amend [Schedules 3B and 3BA][2] includes power to make such incidental, supplemental, consequential and transitional provision in connection with any amendment of that Schedule as they think fit.][1]

Amendments—[1] This section inserted by FA 2003 s 23, Sch 2 paras 1, 2 in relation to qualifying supplies made after 30 June 2003, see FA 2003 s 23(2).

[2] In sub-s (2), words inserted, and in sub-s (3), words substituted for words "Schedule 3B", by FA 2014 s 103, Sch 22 para 2 with effect in relation to supplies made on or after 1 January 2015.

[3] In sub-s (1), words inserted, sub-s (1A) inserted, and in section heading words substituted for words "Supply of electronic services in member States: special accounting scheme" by FA 2014 s 103, Sch 22 paras 11, 12 with effect in relation to supplies made on or after 1 January 2015.

Supply of goods or services in the United Kingdom

4 Scope of VAT on taxable supplies

(1) VAT shall be charged on any supply of goods or services made in the United Kingdom, where it is a taxable supply made by a taxable person in the course or furtherance of any business carried on by him.

(2) A taxable supply is a supply of goods or services made in the United Kingdom other than an exempt supply.

Commentary—*De Voil Indirect Tax Service* **V3.421, V3.131, V3.122**.

HMRC Manuals—VAT Guidance V1-3: Supply and consideration para 2.1 (scope of VAT).

Simon's Tax Cases—*C&E Comrs v Professional Footballers' Association (Enterprises) Ltd* [1993] STC 86*; *R v Ryan* [1994] STC 446*; *B J Rice & Associates v C&E Comrs* [1996] STC 581*; *ICAEW v C&E Comrs* [1999] STC 398.

Press releases etc—C&E VAT Notes 1/95 (oath fees retained personally by associate or assistant solicitor not subject to VAT generally).

Definitions—"Business", s 96(1); "exempt supply", s 31, Sch 9; "supply", s 5, Sch 4; "taxable person", s 3; "United Kingdom", s 3; "VAT", ss 1, 96(1).

5 Meaning of supply: alteration by Treasury order

(1) Schedule 4 shall apply for determining what is, or is to be treated as, a supply of goods or a supply of services.

(2) Subject to any provision made by that Schedule and to Treasury orders under subsections (3) to (6) below—

(*a*) "supply" in this Act includes all forms of supply, but not anything done otherwise than for a consideration;

(*b*) anything which is not a supply of goods but is done for a consideration (including, if so done, the granting, assignment or surrender of any right) is a supply of services.

(3) The Treasury may by order provide with respect to any description of transaction—

(*a*) that it is to be treated as a supply of goods and not as a supply of services; or

(*b*) that it is to be treated as a supply of services and not as a supply of goods; or

(*c*) that it is to be treated as neither a supply of goods nor a supply of services;

and without prejudice to the foregoing, such an order may provide that paragraph 5(4) of Schedule 4 is not to apply, in relation to goods of any prescribed description used or made available for use in prescribed circumstances, so as to make that a supply of services under that paragraph and may provide that paragraph 6 of that Schedule shall not apply, in such circumstances as may be described in the order, so as to make a removal of assets a supply of goods under that paragraph.

(4) Without prejudice to subsection (3) above, the Treasury may by order make provision for securing, with respect to services of any description specified in the order, that where—

(*a*) a person carrying on a business does anything which is not a supply of services but would, if done for a consideration, be a supply of services of a description specified in the order; and

(*b*) such other conditions as may be specified in the order are satisfied,

such services are treated for the purposes of this Act as being supplied by him in the course or furtherance of that business.

(5) The Treasury may by order make provision for securing, subject to any exceptions provided for by or under the order, that where in such circumstances as may be specified in the order goods of a description so specified are taken possession of or produced by a person in the course or furtherance of a business carried on by him and—

(*a*) are neither supplied to another person nor incorporated in other goods produced in the course or furtherance of that business; but

(*b*) are used by him for the purpose of a business carried on by him,

the goods are treated for the purposes of this Act as being both supplied to him for the purpose of that business and supplied by him in the course or furtherance of it.

(6) The Treasury may by order make provision for securing, with respect to services of any description specified in the order, that where—

(*a*) a person, in the course or furtherance of a business carried on by him, does anything for the purpose of that business which is not a supply of services but would, if done for a consideration, be a supply of services of a description specified in the order; and

(*b*) such other conditions as may be specified in the order are satisfied,

such services are treated for the purposes of this Act as being both supplied to him for the purpose of that business and supplied by him in the course or furtherance of it.

(7) For the purposes of this section, where goods are manufactured or produced from any other goods, those other goods shall be treated as incorporated in the first-mentioned goods.

(8) An order under subsection (4) or (6) above may provide for the method by which the value of any supply of services which is treated as taking place by virtue of the order is to be calculated.

Commentary—*De Voil Indirect Tax Service* **V3.102**.

HMRC Manuals—VAT Guidance V1-3: Supply and consideration, para 2.2 (supply for consideration).

Para 2.8 (list of Orders made under this section).

Para 2.9–2.11 (definitions of supply of goods and supply of services).

Para 2.12 (self-supply).

Para 4.2 (supply of services for consideration).

Para 4.12 (sale of goodwill as taxable supply of services).

Para 15.3 (supply of services: sale of options).

Simon's Tax Cases—*C&E Comrs v Apple and Pear Development Council* [1985] STC 383*; *C&E Comrs v High Street Vouchers Ltd* [1990] STC 575*; *Phillip Drakard Trading Ltd v C&E Comrs* [1992] STC 568*; *Church of England Children's Society v Revenue and Customs Commissioners* [2005] STC 1644.

s 5(1), *Philips Exports Ltd v C&E Comrs* [1990] STC 508*.

s 5(2), *C&E Comrs v Professional Footballers' Association (Enterprises) Ltd* [1992] STC 294*; *Eastbourne Town Radio Cars Association v C&E Comrs* [2001] STC 606; *C&E Comrs v Church Schools Foundation Ltd* [2001] STC 1661.

s 5(2)(*b*), *C&E Comrs v Diners Club Ltd* [1989] STC 407*; *C&E Comrs v Battersea Leisure Ltd* [1992] STC 213*.

s 5(3), *C&E Comrs v Co-operative Wholesale Society Ltd* [1995] STC 983*; *WHA Ltd and another v C&E Comrs* [2004] STC 1081.

Orders—See VAT (Treatment of Transactions) (No 1) Order, SI 1973/325; VAT (Treatment of Transactions) Order, SI 1986/896; VAT (Tour Operators) Order, SI 1987/1806; VAT (Self-supply of Construction Services) Order, SI 1989/472; VAT (Water) Order, SI 1989/1114; VAT (Treatment of Transactions) Order, SI 1992/630; VAT (Removal of Goods) Order, SI 1992/3111; VAT (Cars) Order, SI 1992/3122; VAT (Supply of Temporarily Imported Goods) Order, SI 1992/3130; VAT (Supply of Services) Order, SI 1993/1507; VAT (Treatment of Transactions) Order, SI 1995/958; VAT (Special Provisions) Order, SI 1995/1268; VAT (Fiscal Warehousing) (Treatment of Transactions) Order, SI 1996/1255; VAT (Removal of Gas, Electricity, Heat and Cooling) Order, SI 2010/2925; VAT (Removal of Goods) (Amendment) Order, SI 2012/2953.

Press releases etc—C&E Business Brief 8/95 5-5-95 (Barter transactions subject to VAT).

Definitions—"Business", s 94; "prescribed", s 96(1).

Cross references—See VATA 1994 s 6(11) (goods treated as supplied by an order under sub-s (5) of this section: time of supply);

VATA 1994 s 43(2) (VAT groups: orders under sub-s (5) or (6) of this section may provide that certain goods or services may be treated as supplied to or by representative member of group);

VATA 1994 s 97(3), (4) (procedure for making orders under sub-s (4) of this section);

VATA 1994 Sch 6 para 6 (valuation of transactions treated as supplies of goods by virtue of an order under sub-s (5) of this section);

VATA 1994 Sch 6 para 7 (valuation of transactions treated as supplies of services by virtue of an order under sub-s (4) of this section).

VAT Regulations, SI 1995/2518 reg 81(2) (time of supply of services specified in orders made under sub-s (4) of this section).

6 Time of supply

(1) The provisions of this section shall apply, subject to [sections 18, 18B and 18C][1], for determining the time when a supply of goods or services is to be treated as taking place for the purposes of the charge to VAT.

(2) Subject to subsections (4) to (14) below, a supply of goods shall be treated as taking place—

(*a*) if the goods are to be removed, at the time of the removal;

(*b*) if the goods are not to be removed, at the time when they are made available to the person to whom they are supplied;

(*c*) if the goods (being sent or taken on approval or sale or return or similar terms) are removed before it is known whether a supply will take place, at the time when it becomes certain that the supply has taken place or, if sooner, 12 months after the removal.

(3) Subject to subsections (4) to (14) below, a supply of services shall be treated as taking place at the time when the services are performed.

(4) If, before the time applicable under subsection (2) or (3) above, the person making the supply issues a VAT invoice in respect of it or if, before the time applicable under subsection (2)(*a*) or (*b*) or (3) above, he receives a payment in respect of it, the supply shall, to the extent covered by the invoice or payment, be treated as taking place at the time the invoice is issued or the payment is received.

(5) If, within 14 days after the time applicable under subsection (2) or (3) above, the person making the supply issues a VAT invoice in respect of it, then, unless he has notified the Commissioners in writing that he elects not to avail himself of this subsection, the supply shall (to the extent that it is not treated as taking place at the time mentioned in subsection (4) above) be treated as taking place at the time the invoice is issued.

(6) The Commissioners may, at the request of a taxable person, direct that subsection (5) above shall apply in relation to supplies made by him (or such supplies made by him as may be specified in the direction) as if for the period of 14 days there were substituted such longer period as may be specified in the direction.

(7) Where any supply of goods involves both—

(*a*) the removal of the goods from the United Kingdom; and

(*b*) their acquisition in another member State by a person who is liable for VAT on the acquisition in accordance with provisions of the law of that member State corresponding, in relation to that member State, to the provisions of section 10,

subsections (2), (4) to (6) and (10) to (12) of this section shall not apply and the supply shall be treated for the purposes of this Act as taking place on whichever is the earlier of the days specified in subsection (8) below.

(8) The days mentioned in subsection (7) above are—

(*a*) the 15th day of the month following that in which the removal in question takes place; and

(*b*) the day of the issue, in respect of the supply, of a VAT invoice or of an invoice of such other description as the Commissioners may by regulations prescribe.

(9) . . . [3]

(10) The Commissioners may, at the request of a taxable person, by direction alter the time at which supplies made by him (or such supplies made by him as may be specified in the direction) are to be treated as taking place, either—

(*a*) by directing those supplies to be treated as taking place—

(i) at times or on dates determined by or by reference to the occurrence of some event described in the direction; or

(ii) at times or on dates determined by or by reference to the time when some event so described would in the ordinary course of events occur,

the resulting times or dates being in every case earlier than would otherwise apply; or

(*b*) by directing that, notwithstanding subsections (5) and (6) above, those supplies shall (to the extent that they are not treated as taking place at the time mentioned in subsection (4) above) be treated as taking place—

(i) at the beginning of the relevant working period (as defined in his case in and for the purposes of the direction); or

(ii) at the end of the relevant working period (as so defined).

(11) Where goods are treated as supplied by an order under section 5(5), the supply is treated as taking place when they are appropriated to the use mentioned in that section.

(12) Where there is a supply of goods by virtue only of paragraph 5(1) of Schedule 4, the supply is treated as taking place when the goods are transferred or disposed of as mentioned in that paragraph.

(13) Where there is a supply of services by virtue only of paragraph 5(4) of Schedule 4, the supply is treated as taking place when the goods are appropriated to the use mentioned in that paragraph.

(14) The Commissioners may by regulations make provision with respect to the time at which (notwithstanding subsections (2) to (8) and (11) to (13) above or section 55(4)) a supply is to be treated as taking place in cases where—

(*a*) it is a supply of goods or services for a consideration the whole or part of which is determined or payable periodically, or from time to time, or at the end of any period, or
(*b*) it is a supply of goods for a consideration the whole or part of which is determined at the time when the goods are appropriated for any purpose, or
(*c*) there is a supply to which section 55 applies, or
(*d*) there is a supply of services by virtue of paragraph 5(4) of Schedule 4 or an order under section 5(4);

and for any such case as is mentioned in this subsection the regulations may provide for goods or services to be treated as separately and successively supplied at prescribed times or intervals.

[(14A) . . .,[4] This section and any regulations under this section or section 8(4) shall have effect subject to section 97A.][2]

(15) In this Act "VAT invoice" means such an invoice as is required under [paragraph 2A][3] of Schedule 11, or would be so required if the person to whom the supply is made were a person to whom such an invoice should be issued.

Commentary—*De Voil Indirect Tax Service* **V3.131**.

Simon's Tax Cases—*Purshotam M Pattni & Sons v C&E Comrs* [1987] STC 1*; *BJ Rice & Associates v C&E Comrs* [1996] STC 581*; *C&E Comrs v BRS Automotive Ltd* [1997] STC 336; *C&E Comrs v Thorn Materials Supply Ltd and Thorn Resources Ltd* [1998] STC 725*.

s 6(2)(*c*), *R&C Comrs v Robertson's Electrical Ltd* [2007] STC 612.

s 6(4), *C&E Comrs v Richmond Theatre Management Ltd* [1995] STC 257*; *Higher Education Statistics Agency v C&E Comrs* [2000] STC 332; *Cumbernauld Development Corporation v C&E Comrs* [2002] STC 226.

Regulations—See VAT Regulations, SI 1995/2518 regs 81, 84–86, 88–95.

VAT (Amendment) (No 3) Regulations, SI 2012/2951.

Press releases etc—ICAEW 15/94 16-8-94 (guidance notes on supplies by accountants). VAT Information Sheet 13/95 1.9.95 (tax point will be time at which supplier keys details of transaction into the system where a corporate purchasing or procurement card is used).

Definitions—"Another member State", s 96(1); "the Commissioners", s 96(1); "document", s 96(1); "invoice", s 96(1); "law of that member State", s 92; "prescribed", s 96(1); "regulations", s 96(1); "supply", s 5, Sch 4; "taxable person", s 3; "VAT", ss 1, 96(1).

Cross references—See VATA 1994 s 17(5)(*b*) (supplies of free zone goods: provision for regulations to determine time of supply);

VATA 1994 s 55(4) (disapplication of sub-ss (4)–(10) of this section in relation to certain supplies of gold and other precious metals and stones);

VATA 1994 s 88 (supplies spanning date of change in rate of VAT),

VATA 1994 Sch 11 paras 2(9), 3(3) (provisions as to deemed date of issue of an invoice described in regulations made for purposes of sub-s (8)(*b*) of this section and VAT to be accounted for by reference to that date);

VATA 1994 Sch 13 para 4 (pre-21 April 1975 arrangements as to time of supplies: treatment for purposes of this section as if a direction had been issued by the Commissioners under sub-s (10)).

VAT Regulations, SI 1995/2518 reg 14(3) (consignment or delivery note: whether treated as a VAT invoice for the purposes of sub-ss (2)(*c*), (5) of this section);

VAT Regulations, SI 1995/2518 reg 84(1) (compulsory purchase of land: consideration not known at time of purchase);

VAT Regulations, SI 1995/2518 reg 84(2) (grant or assignment of fee simple in land: total consideration not determinable at time of grant etc);

VAT Regulations, SI 1995/2518 reg 85 (grant of tenancy or lease: consideration payable periodically: time of supply);

VAT Regulations, SI 1995/2518 reg 86 (supplies of water, gas and other forms of heat, power, ventilation or refrigeration: time of supply);

VAT Regulations, SI 1995/2518 reg 88 (agreements by which supplier retains property in goods pending appropriation by buyer: time of supply);

VAT Regulations, SI 1995/2518 reg 89 (retention of part of consideration pending performance of contract: time of supply);

VAT Regulations, SI 1995/2518 reg 90 (continuous supplies of services);

VAT Regulations, SI 1995/2518 reg 91 (royalties etc: time of supply);

VAT Regulations, SI 1995/2518 reg 92 (services of barristers and advocates: time of supply);

VAT Regulations, SI 1995/2518 reg 93 (construction industry supplies: consideration payable periodically: time of supply);

VAT (Tour Operators) Order, SI 1987/1806 art 4 (disapplication of this section to supplies of designated travel services).

Amendments—[1] Words in sub-s (1) substituted by FA 1996 Sch 3 para 1 with effect in relation to any supply taking place on or after 1 June 1996; see Finance Act 1996, Section 26, (Appointed Day) Order, SI 1996/1249.

[2] Sub-s (14A) inserted by FA 1998 s 22 with effect from 17 March 1998.

[3] Sub-s (9) repealed, and in sub-s (15), words substituted by FA 2002 ss 24(1)(a), (4)(a), (5), 139, Sch 40 Pt 2(2) with effect from 1 December 2003 (by virtue of SI 2003/3043).

[4] In sub-s (14A) words "In relation to any services of a description specified in an order under section 7(11)" repealed by FA 2009 s 76, Sch 36 para 2 with effect from 1 January 2010.

7 Place of supply [of goods][2]

(1) This section shall apply (subject to [sections 14, 18 and 18B][1]) for determining, for the purposes of this Act, whether goods . . . [2] are supplied in the United Kingdom.

(2) Subject to the following provisions of this section, if the supply of any goods does not involve their removal from or to the United Kingdom they shall be treated as supplied in the United Kingdom if they are in the United Kingdom and otherwise shall be treated as supplied outside the United Kingdom.

(3) Goods shall be treated—

(*a*) as supplied in the United Kingdom where their supply involves their installation or assembly at a place in the United Kingdom to which they are removed; and

(*b*) as supplied outside the United Kingdom where their supply involves their installation or assembly at a place outside the United Kingdom to which they are removed.

(4) Goods whose place of supply is not determined under any of the preceding provisions of this section shall be treated as supplied in the United Kingdom where—

(*a*) the supply involves the removal of the goods to the United Kingdom by or under the directions of the person who supplies them;

(*b*) the supply is a transaction in pursuance of which the goods are acquired in the United Kingdom from another member State by a person who is not a taxable person;

(*c*) the supplier—

(i) is liable to be registered under Schedule 2; or

(ii) would be so liable if he were not already registered under this Act or liable to be registered under Schedule 1 [or 1A][3]; and

(*d*) the supply is neither a supply of goods consisting in a new means of transport nor anything which is treated as a supply for the purposes of this Act by virtue only of paragraph 5(1) or 6 of Schedule 4.

(5) Goods whose place of supply is not determined under any of the preceding provisions of this section and which do not consist in a new means of transport shall be treated as supplied outside the United Kingdom where—

(*a*) the supply involves the removal of the goods, by or under the directions of the person who supplies them, to another member State;

(*b*) the person who makes the supply is taxable in another member State; and

(*c*) provisions of the law of that member State corresponding, in relation to that member State, to the provisions made by subsection (4) above make that person liable to VAT on the supply;

but this subsection shall not apply in relation to any supply in a case where the liability mentioned in paragraph (c) above depends on the exercise by any person of an option in the United Kingdom corresponding to such an option as is mentioned in paragraph 1(2) of Schedule 2 unless that person has given, and has not withdrawn, a notification to the Commissioners that he wishes his supplies to be treated as taking place outside the United Kingdom where they are supplies in relation to which the other requirements of this subsection are satisfied.

(6) Goods whose place of supply is not determined under any of the preceding provisions of this section shall be treated as supplied in the United Kingdom where—

(*a*) their supply involves their being imported from a place outside the member States; and

(*b*) the person who supplies them is the person by whom, or under whose directions, they are so imported.

(7) Goods whose place of supply is not determined under any of the preceding provisions of this section but whose supply involves their removal to or from the United Kingdom shall be treated—

(*a*) as supplied in the United Kingdom where their supply involves their removal from the United Kingdom without also involving their previous removal to the United Kingdom; and

(*b*) as supplied outside the United Kingdom in any other case.

(8) For the purposes of the preceding provisions of this section, where goods, in the course of their removal from a place in the United Kingdom to another place in the United Kingdom, leave and re-enter the United Kingdom the removal shall not be treated as a removal from or to the United Kingdom.

(9) The Commissioners may by regulations provide that a notification for the purposes of subsection (5) above is not to be given or withdrawn except in such circumstances, and in such form and manner, as may be prescribed.

(10) . . . [2]

(11) The Treasury may by order provide, in relation to goods . . . [2] generally or to particular goods . . . [2] specified in the order, for varying the rules for determining where a supply of goods . . . [2] is made.

Commentary—*De Voil Indirect Tax Service* **V3.172, V3.173**.

Simon's Tax Cases—s 7(1), *Purshotam M Pattni & Sons v C&E Comrs* [1987] STC 1*; *Tas-Stage Ltd v C&E Comrs* [1988] STC 436*; *Nevisbrook Ltd v C&E Comrs, Dormers Builders (London) Ltd v C&E Comrs, C&E Comrs v West Yorkshire Independent Hospital (Contract Services) Ltd C&E, Comrs v Faith Construction Ltd* [1989] STC 539*, [1992] STC 544*

Regulations—See VAT Regulations, SI 1995/2518 reg 98.

Orders—See VAT (Tour Operators) Order, SI 1987/1806; VAT (Place of Supply of Services) Order, SI 1992/3121; VAT (Place of Supply of Goods) (Amendment) Order, SI 2010/2923.

Press releases etc—ICAEW 15/94 16-8-94 (guidance note on supplies by accountants).

C&E Business Brief 26/96 19-12-96 (the service of carrying out of a statutory order of the accounts of a UK incorporated company trading entirely overseas is supplied in the UK and is standard-rated).

Definitions—"Acquisition of goods from another member State", s 11; "another member State", s 96(1); "belongs in the "United Kingdom"; belongs in that other country", s 9; "the Commissioners", s 96(1); "imported from a place outside the member States", s 15; "law of that member State", s 92; "new means of transport", s 95; "person . . . .taxable in another member State", s 92; "prescribed", s 96(1); "registered", s 3(3); "regulations", s 96(1); "supply ", s 5, Sch 4; "taxable person", s 3; "United Kingdom", s 96(11); "VAT", ss 1, 96(1).

Cross references—See VAT (Isle of Man) Order, SI 1982/1067 art 1(4) (treatment of UK and Isle of Man as a single area for VAT purposes);

VAT (Tour Operators) Order, SI 1987/1806 art 7 (modification of this section in relation to supplies of designated travel services).

Amendments—[1] Words in sub-s (1) substituted by FA 1996 Sch 3 para 2, with effect in relation to any supply taking place on or after 1 June 1996; see Finance Act 1996, Section 26, (Appointed Day) Order, SI 1996/1249.

[2] Words inserted in heading, and words "or services" in sub-ss (1), (11) and whole of sub-s (10) repealed, by FA 2009 s 76, Sch 36 paras 1, 3 with effect in relation to supplies made on or after 1 January 2010.

[3] In sub-s (4)(*c*)(ii), words inserted by FA 2012 s 203, Sch 28 paras 2, 3 with effect in relation to supplies made or to be made on or after 1 December 2012.

[7A Place of supply of services

(1) This section applies for determining, for the purposes of this Act, the country in which services are supplied.

(2) A supply of services is to be treated as made—

(*a*) in a case in which the person to whom the services are supplied is a relevant business person, in the country in which the recipient belongs, and

(*b*) otherwise, in the country in which the supplier belongs.

(3) The place of supply of a right to services is the same as that in which the supply of the services would be treated as made if made by the supplier of the right to the recipient of the right (whether or not the right is exercised); and for this purpose a right to services includes any right, option or priority with respect to the supply of services and an interest deriving from a right to services.

(4) For the purposes of this Act a person is a relevant business person in relation to a supply of services if the person—

(*a*) is a taxable person within the meaning of Article 9 of Council Directive 2006/112/EC,

(*b*) is registered under this Act,

(*c*) is identified for the purposes of VAT in accordance with the law of a member State other than the United Kingdom, or

(*d*) is registered under an Act of Tynwald for the purposes of any tax imposed by or under an Act of Tynwald which corresponds to value added tax,

and the services are received by the person otherwise than wholly for private purposes.

(5) Subsection (2) has effect subject to Schedule 4A.

(6) The Treasury may by order—

(*a*) amend subsection (4),

(*b*) amend Schedule 4A, or

(*c*) otherwise make provision for exceptions from either or both of the paragraphs of subsection (2).

(7) An order under subsection (6) may include incidental, supplemental, consequential and transitional provision.][1]

Orders—VAT (Exceptions Relating to Supplies not Made to Relevant Business Person) Order, SI 2010/3017.

VAT (Place of Supply of Services) (Transport of Goods) Order, SI 2012/2787.

VAT (Place of Supply of Services) (Exceptions Relating to Supplies Not Made to Relevant Business Person) Order, SI 2014/2726.

Amendments—[1] Section 7A inserted by FA 2009 s 76, Sch 3 paras 1, 4 with effect in relation to supplies made on or after 1 January 2010, except the powers contained in sub-s (6) which may be exercised at any time from 21 July 2009.

8 Reverse charge on supplies received from abroad

[(1) Where services are supplied by a person who belongs in a country other than the United Kingdom in circumstances in which this subsection applies, this Act has effect as if (instead of there being a supply of the services by that person)—

(*a*) there were a supply of the services by the recipient in the United Kingdom in the course or furtherance of a business carried on by the recipient, and

(*b*) that supply were a taxable supply.

(2) Subsection (1) above applies if—

(*a*) the recipient is a relevant business person who belongs in the United Kingdom, and

(*b*) the place of supply of the services is inside the United Kingdom,

and, where the supply of the services is one to which any paragraph of Part 1 or 2 of Schedule 4A applies, the recipient is registered under this Act.][2]

(3) Supplies which are treated as made by the recipient under subsection (1) above are not to be taken into account as supplies made by him when determining any allowance of input tax in his case under section 26(1).

(4) In applying subsection (1) above, the supply of services treated as made by the recipient shall be assumed to have been made at a time to be determined in accordance with regulations prescribing rules for attributing a time of supply in cases within that subsection.

[(4A) Subsection (1) does not apply to services of any of the descriptions specified in Schedule 9.][2]

(5) The Treasury may by order [amend subsection (4A) by altering the descriptions of services specified in that subsection][2].

(6) . . .[2]

[(7) The power of the Treasury by order to [amend subsection (4A)][2] shall include power to make such incidental, supplemental, consequential and transitional provision in connection with any [amendment of that subsection][2] as they think fit.][1]

[(8) Without prejudice to the generality of subsection (7) above, the provision that may be made under that subsection includes—

(*a*) provision making such modifications of section 43(2A) to (2E) as the Treasury may think fit in connection with any [amendment of subsection (4A)][2]; and

(*b*) provision modifying the effect of any regulations under subsection (4) above in relation to any services added to [that subsection][2].][1]

Commentary—*De Voil Indirect Tax Service* **V3.231**.

Regulations—See VAT Regulations, SI 1995/2518 reg 82.

VAT (Reverse Charge) (Anti-avoidance) Order, SI 1997/1523.

Simon's Tax Cases—*R (on the application of the Medical Protection Society Ltd) v R&C Comrs* [2010] STC 555.

Definitions—"Belongs in another country other than the United Kingdom", s 9; "business", s 94; "input tax", s 24; "regulations", s 96(1); "supply", s 5, Sch 4; "taxable person", s 3; "taxable supply", s 4(2); "time of supply", s 6; "United Kingdom", s 96(11); "VAT", ss 1, 96(1).

Cross references—See VATA 1994 Sch 5 para 10 (sub-s (1) of this section to apply to certain services which are supplied to registered persons and whose place of supply is determined by order to be in the UK as if the recipient belonged in the UK for the purposes of sub-s (1)(*b*));

VATA 1994 Sch 6 para 8 (valuation of supplies of services treated by virtue of this section as made by the recipient).

VAT Regulations, SI 1995/2518 reg 82 (time of deemed supplies under sub-s (1) of this section).

Press releases etc—Business Brief 6/02, 14-3-02 (VAT: clarification of the treatment of internet service packages).

Amendments—[1] Sub-s (7) and (8) inserted by FA 1997 s 42 with effect from 19 March 1997.

[2] Sub-ss (1), (2), words "add to or vary Schedule 5" in sub-ss (5), (7), "addition to or variation of that Schedule" in sub-ss (7), (8)(a), "the Schedule" in sub-s (8)(*b*) substituted, sub-s (4A) inserted and sub-s (6) repealed, by FA 2009 s 76, Sch 36 paras 1, 5 with effect in relation to supplies made on or after 1 January 2010.

[9 Place where supplier or recipient of services belongs

(1) This section has effect for determining for the purposes of section 7A (or Schedule 4A) or section 8, in relation to any supply of services, whether a person who is the supplier or recipient belongs in one country or another.

(2) A person who is a relevant business person is to be treated as belonging in the relevant country.

(3) In subsection (2) "the relevant country" means—

(*a*) if the person has a business establishment, or some other fixed establishment, in a country (and none in any other country), that country,

(*b*) if the person has a business establishment, or some other fixed establishment or establishments, in more than one country, the country in which the relevant establishment is, and

(*c*) otherwise, the country in which the person's usual place of residence [or permanent address][2] is.

(4) In subsection (3)(*b*) "relevant establishment" means whichever of the person's business establishment, or other fixed establishments, is most directly concerned with the supply.

(5) A person who is not a relevant business person is to be treated as [belonging—

(*a*) in the country in which the person's usual place of residence or permanent address is (except in the case of a body corporate or other legal person);

(*b*) in the case of a body corporate or other legal person, in the country in which the place where it is established is.][2]

[(6) The reference in subsection (5)(*b*) to the place where a body corporate or other legal person "is established" is to be read in accordance with Article 13a of Implementing Regulation (EU) No 282/2011 (which is inserted by Council Implementing Regulation (EU) No 1042/2013).][2]][1]

Commentary—*De Voil Indirect Tax Service* **V3.183**.

Simon's Tax Cases—*C&E Comrs v Chinese Channel (Hong Kong) Ltd* [1998] STC 347.

Definitions—"Business", s 94; "supply of services", s 5, Sch 4.

Cross reference—See VAT (Tour Operators) Order, SI 1987/1806 art 7 (modification of this section in relation to supplies of designated travel services).

Press releases etc—Business Brief 12/98 21-5-98 (Overseas businesses established in the UK through agencies).

VAT Information Sheet 3/01 April 2001 (guidance on the VAT treatment of digitised publications).

Amendments—[1] Section substituted by FA 2009 s 76, Sch 36 paras 1, 6 with effect in relation to supplies made on or after 1 January 2010.

[2] In sub-s (3)(*c*), words inserted, in sub-s (5), words substituted, and sub-s (6) substituted, by FA 2014 s 104 with effect in relation to supplies made on or after 1 January 2015.

[9A Reverse charge on gas[, electricity, heat or cooling][2] supplied by persons outside the United Kingdom

(1) This section applies if relevant goods are supplied—

(*a*) by a person who is outside the United Kingdom,

(*b*) to a person who is registered under this Act,

for the purposes of any business carried on by the recipient.

(2) The same consequences follow under this Act (and particularly so much as charges VAT on a supply and entitles a taxable person to credit for input tax) as if—

(*a*) the recipient had himself supplied the relevant goods in the course or furtherance of his business, and

(*b*) that supply were a taxable supply.

(3) But supplies which are treated as made by the recipient under subsection (2) are not to be taken into account as supplies made by him when determining any allowance of input tax in his case under section 26(1).

(4) In applying subsection (2) the supply of relevant goods treated as made by the recipient shall be assumed to have been made at a time to be determined in accordance with regulations prescribing rules for attributing a time of supply in cases to which this section applies.

[(5) "Relevant goods" means—

(*a*) gas supplied through a natural gas system situated within the territory of a member State or any network connected to such a system,

(*b*) electricity, and

(*c*) heat or cooling supplied through a network.][2]

(6) Whether a person is outside the United Kingdom is to be determined in accordance with an order made by the Treasury.][1]

Commentary—*De Voil Indirect Tax Service* **V3.232.**

Press releases—Budget Note BN40, 22 June 2010: VAT—place of supply of gas, heat and cooling.

Amendments—[1] This section inserted by FA 2004 s 21 with effect for supplies made after 31 December 2004.

[2] Sub-s (5) substituted, and words in heading substituted for words "and electricity", by F(No 3)A 2010 s 20(1) with effect in relation to supplies made on or after 1 January 2011.

Acquisition of goods from member States

10 Scope of VAT on acquisitions from member States

(1) VAT shall be charged on any acquisition from another member State of any goods where—

(*a*) the acquisition is a taxable acquisition and takes place in the United Kingdom;

(*b*) the acquisition is otherwise than in pursuance of a taxable supply; and

(*c*) the person who makes the acquisition is a taxable person or the goods are subject to a duty of excise or consist in a new means of transport.

(2) An acquisition of goods from another member State is a taxable acquisition if—

(*a*) it falls within subsection (3) below or the goods consist in a new means of transport; and

(*b*) it is not an exempt acquisition.

(3) An acquisition of goods from another member State falls within this subsection if—

(*a*) the goods are acquired in the course or furtherance of—

(i) any business carried on by any person; or

(ii) any activities carried on otherwise than by way of business by any body corporate or by any club, association, organisation or other unincorporated body;

(*b*) it is the person who carries on that business or, as the case may be, those activities who acquires the goods; and

(*c*) the supplier—

(i) is taxable in another member State at the time of the transaction in pursuance of which the goods are acquired; and

(ii) in participating in that transaction, acts in the course or furtherance of a business carried on by him.

Commentary—*De Voil Indirect Tax Service* **V3.368.**

Simon's Tax Cases—*C&E Comrs v Westmorland Motorway Services Ltd* [1998] STC 431.

Definitions—"Acquisition of goods from another member State", s 11; "another member State", s 96(1); "business", s 94; "exempt acquisition", s 31, Sch 9; "new means of transport", s 95; "taxable in another member State", s 92; "taxable person", s 3; "taxable supply", s 4(2); "United Kingdom", s 96(11); "VAT", ss 1, 96(1).

11 Meaning of acquisition of goods from another member State

(1) Subject to the following provisions of this section, references in this Act to the acquisition of goods from another member State shall be construed as references to any acquisition of goods in pursuance of a transaction in relation to which the following conditions are satisfied, that is to say—

(*a*) the transaction is a supply of goods (including anything treated for the purposes of this Act as a supply of goods); and

(*b*) the transaction involves the removal of the goods from another member State;

and references in this Act, in relation to such an acquisition, to the supplier shall be construed accordingly.

(2) It shall be immaterial for the purposes of subsection (1) above whether the removal of the goods from the other member State is by or under the directions of the supplier or by or under the directions of the person who acquires them or any other person.

(3) Where the person with the property in any goods does not change in consequence of anything which is treated for the purposes of this Act as a supply of goods, that supply shall be treated for the purposes of this Act as a transaction in pursuance of which there is an acquisition of goods by the person making it.

(4) The Treasury may by order provide with respect to any description of transaction that the acquisition of goods in pursuance of a transaction of that description is not to be treated for the purposes of this Act as the acquisition of goods from another member State.

Commentary—*De Voil Indirect Tax Service* **V2.181, V3.363**.

Orders—See VAT (Treatment of Transactions) (No 2) Order, SI 1992/3132; VAT (Special Provisions) Order, SI 1995/1268.

Definitions—"Another (other) member State", s 96(1); "supply", s 5, Sch 4.

12 Time of acquisition

(1) Subject to [sections 18 and 18B][1] and any regulations under subsection (3) below, where goods are acquired from another member State, the acquisition shall be treated for the purposes of this Act as taking place on whichever is the earlier of—

(*a*) the 15th day of the month following that in which the event occurs which, in relation to that acquisition, is the first relevant event for the purposes of taxing the acquisition; and

(*b*) the day of the issue, in respect of the transaction in pursuance of which the goods are acquired, of an invoice of such a description as the Commissioners may by regulations prescribe.

(2) For the purposes of this Act the event which, in relation to any acquisition of goods from another member State, is the first relevant event for the purposes of taxing the acquisition is the first removal of the goods which is involved in the transaction in pursuance of which they are acquired.

(3) The Commissioners may by regulations make provision with respect to the time at which an acquisition is to be treated as taking place in prescribed cases where the whole or part of any consideration comprised in the transaction in pursuance of which the goods are acquired is determined or payable periodically, or from time to time, or at the end of a period; and any such regulations may provide, in relation to any case to which they apply, for goods to be treated as separately and successively acquired at prescribed times or intervals.

Commentary—*De Voil Indirect Tax Service* **V3.388**.

Regulations—See VAT Regulations, SI 1995/2518 regs 83, 87.

VAT (Amendment) (No 3) Regulations, SI 2012/2951.

Definitions—"Acquisition of goods from another member State", s 11; "another member State", s 96(1); "the Commissioners", s 96(1); "invoice", s 96(1); "prescribed", s 96(1); "regulations", s 96(1).

Cross references—See VATA 1994 s 14(4) (modification of sub-s (1) of this section in relation to acquisitions from persons belonging in other member states);

VATA 1994 Sch 11 paras 2(9), 3(3) (provisions as to deemed date of issue of an invoice described in regulations made for purposes of sub-s (1)(*b*) of this section and VAT to be accounted for by reference to that date).

VAT Regulations, SI 1995/2518 reg 83 (description of invoice for purposes of sub-s(1)(*b*) of this section).

VAT Regulations, SI 1995/2518 reg 87 (acquisitions of water, gas and other forms of heat, power, ventilation or refrigeration from another member state: time of acquisition).

Amendments—[1] Words in sub-s (1) substituted by FA 1996 Sch 3 para 3, with effect in relation to any acquisition of goods from another member State taking place on or after 1 June 1996; see Finance Act 1996, Section 26, (Appointed Day) Order, SI 1996/1249.

13 Place of acquisition

(1) This section shall apply (subject to [sections 18 and 18B][1]) for determining for the purposes of this Act whether goods acquired from another member State are acquired in the United Kingdom.

(2) The goods shall be treated as acquired in the United Kingdom if they are acquired in pursuance of a transaction which involves their removal to the United Kingdom and does not involve their removal from the United Kingdom, and (subject to the following provisions of this section) shall otherwise be treated as acquired outside the United Kingdom.

(3) Subject to subsection (4) below, the goods shall be treated as acquired in the United Kingdom if they are acquired by a person who, for the purposes of their acquisition, makes use of a number assigned to him for the purposes of VAT in the United Kingdom.

(4) Subsection (3) above shall not require any goods to be treated as acquired in the United Kingdom where it is established, in accordance with regulations made by the Commissioners for the purposes of this section that VAT—

(*a*) has been paid in another member State on the acquisition of those goods; and

(*b*) fell to be paid by virtue of provisions of the law of that member State corresponding, in relation to that member State, to the provision made by subsection (2) above.

(5) The Commissioners may by regulations make provision for the purposes of this section—

(*a*) for the circumstances in which a person is to be treated as having been assigned a number for the purposes of VAT in the United Kingdom;

(*b*) for the circumstances in which a person is to be treated as having made use of such a number for the purposes of the acquisition of any goods; and (*c*) for the refund, in prescribed circumstances, of VAT paid in the United Kingdom on acquisitions of goods in relation to which the conditions specified in subsection (4)(*a*) and (*b*) above are satisfied.

Commentary—*De Voil Indirect Tax Service* **V3.377, V3.369**.

Definitions—"Acquisition of goods from another member State", s 81; "another member State", s 96(1); "the Commissioners", s 96(1); "law of that member State", s 92; "prescribed", s 96(1); "regulations", s 96(1); "VAT", ss 1, 96(1).

Cross references—See VATA 1994 s 60(1), (2) (civil penalty for evading VAT by dishonestly claiming a refund under regulations made under sub-s (5) of this section);

VATA 1994 s 72(1), (2) (criminal penalty for fraudulent evasion of VAT by falsely claiming a refund under regulations made under sub-s (5) of this section);

VATA 1994 s 83 (appeal to a tribunal with respect to a claim for a refund under regulations made under sub-s (5) of this section).

Amendments—[1] Words in sub-s (1) substituted by FA 1996 Sch 3 para 4, with effect in relation to any acquisition of goods from another member State taking place on or after 1 June 1996; see Finance Act 1996, Section 26, (Appointed Day) Order, SI 1996/1249.

14 Acquisitions from persons belonging in other member States

(1) Subject to subsection (3) below, where—

(*a*) a person ("the original supplier") makes a supply of goods to a person who belongs in another member State ("the intermediate supplier");

(*b*) that supply involves the removal of the goods from another member State and their removal to the United Kingdom but does not involve the removal of the goods from the United Kingdom;

(*c*) both that supply and the removal of the goods to the United Kingdom are for the purposes of the making of a supply by the intermediate supplier to another person ("the customer") who is registered under this Act;

(*d*) neither of those supplies involves the removal of the goods from a member State in which the intermediate supplier is taxable at the time of the removal without also involving the previous removal of the goods to that member State; and

(*e*) there would be a taxable acquisition by the customer if the supply to him involved the removal of goods from another member State to the United Kingdom,

the supply by the original supplier to the intermediate supplier shall be disregarded for the purposes of this Act and the supply by the intermediate supplier to the customer shall be treated for the purposes of this Act, other than Schedule 3, as if it did involve the removal of the goods from another member State to the United Kingdom.

(2) Subject to subsection (3) below, where—

(*a*) a person belonging in another member State makes such a supply of goods to a person who is registered under this Act as involves their installation or assembly at a place in the United Kingdom to which they are removed; and

(*b*) there would be a taxable acquisition by the registered person if that supply were treated as not being a taxable supply but as involving the removal of the goods from another member State to the United Kingdom,

that supply shall be so treated except for the purposes of Schedule 3.

(3) Neither subsection (1) nor subsection (2) above shall apply in relation to any supply unless the intermediate supplier or, as the case may be, the person making the supply complies with such requirements as to the furnishing (whether before or after the supply is made) of invoices and other documents, and of information, to—

(*a*) the Commissioners, and

(*b*) the person supplied,

as the Commissioners may by regulations prescribe; and regulations under this subsection may provide for the times at which, and the form and manner in which, any document or information is to be furnished and for the particulars which it is to contain.

(4) Where this section has the effect of treating a taxable acquisition as having been made, section 12(1) shall apply in relation to that acquisition with the omission of the words from "whichever" to "acquisition; and" at the end of paragraph (*a*).

(5) For the purposes of this section a person belongs in another member State if—

(*a*) he does not have any business establishment or other fixed establishment in the United Kingdom and does not have his usual place of residence in the United Kingdom;

(*b*) he is neither registered under this Act nor required to be so registered;

(*c*) he does not have a VAT representative and is not for the time being required to appoint one; and

(*d*) he is taxable in another member State;

but, in determining for the purposes of paragraph (b) above whether a person is required to be registered under this Act, there shall be disregarded any supplies which, if he did belong in another member State and complied with the requirements prescribed under subsection (3) above, would fall to be disregarded by virtue of this section.

(6) Without prejudice to section 13(4), where—

(*a*) any goods are acquired from another member State in a case which corresponds, in relation to another member State, to the case specified in relation to the United Kingdom in subsection (1) above; and

(*b*) the person who acquires the goods is registered under this Act and would be the intermediate supplier in relation to that corresponding case,

the supply to him of those goods and the supply by him of those goods to the person who would be the customer in that corresponding case shall both be disregarded for the purposes of this Act, other than the purposes of the information provisions referred to in section 92(7).

(7) References in this section to a person being taxable in another member State shall not include references to a person who is so taxable by virtue only of provisions of the law of another member State corresponding to the provisions of this Act by virtue of which a person who is not registered under this Act is a taxable person if he is required to be so registered.

(8) This section does not apply in relation to any supply of goods by an intermediate supplier to whom the goods were supplied before 1st August 1993.

Commentary—*De Voil Indirect Tax Service* **V3.380**.

Regulations—See VAT Regulations, SI 1995/2518 regs 11, 12, 17–19.

Definitions—"Another member State", s 96(1); "business", s 94; "the Commissioners", s 96(1); "document", s 96(1); "invoice", s 96(1); "law of that member State", s 92; "registered", s 3(3); "regulations", s 96(1); "supply", s 5, Sch 4; "taxable acquisition", s 10(2); "taxable in another member State", s 92; "taxable person", ss 3, 96(1); "taxable supply", s 4(2); "United Kingdom", s 96(11); "VAT", ss 1, 96(1); "VAT representative", s 48.

Cross references—See VATA 1994 Sch 13 para 6 (continued application of VATA 1983 s 32B (overseas suppliers accounting through their customers) in relation to supplies to which this section does not apply by virtue of sub-s (8)).

VAT Regulations, SI 1995/2518 reg 11 (notification of intended supplies by intermediate suppliers under sub-s (1) of this section).

VAT Regulations, SI 1995/2518 reg 12 (notification of intended supplies by persons belonging in other member States under sub-s (2) of this section);

VAT Regulations, SI 1995/2518 reg 17 (tax invoices for supplies under sub-s (6) of this section to persons belonging in other member States);

VAT Regulations, SI 1995/2518 reg 18 (tax invoices for supplies under sub-s (1) of this section by intermediate suppliers);

VAT Regulations, SI 1995/2518 reg 19 (tax invoices for supplies under sub-s (2) of this section by persons belonging in other member States).

Importation of goods from outside the member States

15 General provisions relating to imported goods

(1) For the purposes of this Act goods are imported from a place outside the member States where—

(*a*) having been removed from a place outside the member States, they enter the territory of the Community;

(*b*) they enter that territory by being removed to the United Kingdom or are removed to the United Kingdom after entering that territory; and

(*c*) the circumstances are such that it is on their removal to the United Kingdom or subsequently while they are in the United Kingdom that any Community customs debt in respect of duty on their entry into the territory of the Community would be incurred.

(2) Accordingly—

(*a*) goods shall not be treated for the purposes of this Act as imported at any time before a Community customs debt in respect of duty on their entry into the territory of the Community would be incurred, and

(*b*) the person who is to be treated for the purposes of this Act as importing any goods from a place outside the member States is the person who would be liable to discharge any such Community customs debt.

(3) Subsections (1) and (2) above shall not apply, except in so far as the context otherwise requires or provision to the contrary is contained in regulations under section 16(1), for construing any references to importation or to an importer in any enactment or subordinate legislation applied for the purposes of this Act by section 16(1).

Commentary—*De Voil Indirect Tax Service* **V3.302**.

Definitions—"Regulations", s 96(1); "subordinate legislation", s 96(1); "United Kingdom, s 96(11).

16 Application of customs enactments

(1) Subject to such exceptions and adaptations as the Commissioners may by regulations prescribe and except where the contrary intention appears—

(*a*) the provision made by or under the Customs and Excise Acts 1979 and the other enactments and subordinate legislation for the time being having effect generally in relation to duties of customs and excise charged on the importation of goods into the United Kingdom; and

(*b*) the Community legislation for the time being having effect in relation to Community customs duties charged on goods entering the territory of the Community,

shall apply (so far as relevant) in relation to any VAT chargeable on the importation of goods from places outside the member States as they apply in relation to any such duty of customs or excise or, as the case may be, Community customs duties.

(2) Regulations under [section 105 of the Postal Services Act 2000][1] (which provides for the application of customs enactments to postal packets) may make special provision in relation to VAT.

Commentary—*De Voil Indirect Tax Service* **V1.225, V1.227**.
Regulations—See Postal Packets (Customs and Excise) Regulations, SI 1986/260; VAT Regulations, SI 1995/2518 regs 118–121.
Definitions—"The Commissioners", s 96(1); "goods imported form a place outside the member States", s 15; "regulations", s 96(1); "subordinate legislation", s 96(1); "United Kingdom", s 96(11); "VAT", ss 1, 96(1).
Cross references—See VAT (Isle of Man) Order, SI 1982/1067 art 7 (references to VAT in this section to include references to VAT chargeable under Isle of Man legislation);
VAT Regulations, SI 1995/2518 regs 118–120 (prescribed exceptions for the purposes of sub-s (1) of this section);
VAT Regulations, SI 1995/2518 reg 121 (prescribed adaptations for the purposes of sub-s (1) of this section).
Amendments—[1] Words in sub-s (2) substituted by the Postal Services Act 2000 s 127(4), Sch 8 para 22(1), (2) as from 26 March 2001 (by virtue of SI 2000/2957).

17 Free zone regulations

(1) This section applies in relation to VAT chargeable on the importation of goods from places outside the member States; and in this section "free zone" has the meaning given by section 100A(2) of the Management Act.

(2) Subject to any contrary provision made by any directly applicable Community provision, goods which are chargeable with VAT may be moved into a free zone and may remain as free zone goods without payment of VAT.

(3) The Commissioners may by regulations ("free zone regulations") make provision with respect to the movement of goods into, and the removal of goods from, any free zone and the keeping, securing and treatment of goods which are within a free zone, and subject to any provision of the regulations, "free zone goods" means goods which are within a free zone.

(4) Without prejudice to the generality of subsection (3), free zone regulations may make provision—

(*a*) for enabling the Commissioners to allow goods to be removed from a free zone without payment of VAT in such circumstances and subject to such conditions as they may determine;

(*b*) for determining where any VAT becomes payable in respect of goods which cease to be free zone goods—

(i) the rates of any VAT applicable; and

(ii) the time at which those goods cease to be free zone goods;

(*c*) for determining for the purpose of enabling VAT to be charged in respect of free zone goods in a case where a person wishes to pay that VAT notwithstanding that the goods will continue to be free zone goods, the rate of VAT to be applied; and

(*d*) permitting free zone goods to be destroyed without payment of VAT in such circumstances and subject to such conditions as the Commissioners may determine.

(5) The Commissioners, with respect to free zone goods or the movement of goods into any free zone, may by regulations make provision—

(*a*) for relief from the whole or part of any VAT chargeable on the importation of goods into the United Kingdom in such circumstances as they may determine;

(*b*) in place of, or in addition to, any provision made by section 6 or any other enactment, for determining the time when a supply of goods which are or have been free zone goods is to be treated as taking place for the purposes of the charge to VAT; and

(*c*) as to the treatment, for the purposes of VAT, of goods which are manufactured or produced within a free zone from other goods or which have other goods incorporated in them while they are free zone goods.

Commentary—*De Voil Indirect Tax Service* **V3.331**.
Regulations—See Free Zone Regulations, SI 1984/1177; SI 1991/2727.
Definitions—"The Commissioners", s 96(1); "goods imported from a place outside the member States", s 15; "the Management Act", s 96(1); "regulations", s 96(1); "United Kingdom", s 96(11); "VAT", ss 1, 96(1).

Goods subject to a warehousing regime

18 Place and time of acquisition or supply

(1) Where—

(*a*) any goods have been removed from a place outside the member States and have entered the territory of the Community;

(*b*) the material time for any acquisition of those goods from another member State or for any supply of those goods is while they are subject to a warehousing regime and before the duty point; and

(*c*) those goods are not mixed with any dutiable goods which were produced or manufactured in the United Kingdom or acquired from another member State,

then the acquisition or supply mentioned in paragraph (b) above shall be treated for the purposes of this Act as taking place outside the United Kingdom.

[(1A) The Commissioners may by regulations prescribe circumstances in which subsection (1) above shall not apply.][2]

(2) Subsection (3) below applies where—

(*a*) any dutiable goods are acquired from another member State; or

(*b*) any person makes a supply of—

(i) any dutiable goods which were produced or manufactured in the United Kingdom or acquired from another member State; or

(ii) any goods comprising a mixture of goods falling within sub-paragraph (i) above and other goods.

(3) Where this subsection applies and the material time for the acquisition or supply mentioned in subsection (2) above is while the goods in question are subject to a warehousing regime and before the duty point, that acquisition or supply shall be treated for the purposes of this Act as taking place outside the United Kingdom if the material time for any subsequent supply of those goods is also while the goods are subject to the warehousing regime and before the duty point.

(4) Where the material time for any acquisition or supply of any goods in relation to which subsection (3) above applies is while the goods are subject to a warehousing regime and before the duty point but the acquisition or supply nevertheless falls, for the purposes of this Act, to be treated as taking place in the United Kingdom—

(*a*) that acquisition or supply shall be treated for the purposes of this Act as taking place at the earlier of the following times, that is to say, the time when the goods are removed from the warehousing regime and the duty point; and

(*b*) in the case of a supply, any VAT payable on the supply shall be paid (subject to any regulations under subsection (5) below)—

(i) at the time when the supply is treated as taking place under paragraph (*a*) above; and

(ii) by the person by whom the goods are so removed or, as the case may be, together with the duty or agricultural levy, by the person who is required to pay the duty or levy.

[(5) The Commissioners may by regulations make provision for enabling a taxable person to pay the VAT he is required to pay by virtue of paragraph (*b*) of subsection (4) above at a time later than that provided for by that paragraph.][1]

[(5A) Regulations under subsection (5) above may in particular make provision for either or both of the following—

(*a*) for the taxable person to pay the VAT together with the VAT chargeable on other supplies by him of goods and services;

(*b*) for the taxable person to pay the VAT together with any duty of excise deferment of which has been granted to him under section 127A of the Customs and Excise Management Act 1979;

and they may make different provision for different descriptions of taxable person and for different descriptions of goods.][1]

(6) In this section—

"dutiable goods" means any goods which are subject—

(*a*) to a duty of excise; or

(*b*) in accordance with any provision for the time being having effect for transitional purposes in connection with the accession of any State to the European Communities, to any Community customs duty or agricultural levy of the Economic Community;

"the duty point", in relation to any goods, means—

(*a*) in the case of goods which are subject to a duty of excise, the time when the requirement to pay the duty on those goods takes effect; and

(*b*) in the case of goods which are not so subject, the time when any Community customs debt in respect of duty on the entry of the goods into the territory of the Community would be incurred or, as the case may be, the corresponding time in relation to any such duty or levy as is mentioned in paragraph (*b*) of the definition of dutiable goods;

"material time"—

(*a*) in relation to any acquisition or supply the time of which is determined in accordance with regulations under section 6(14) or 12(3), means such time as may be prescribed for the purpose of this section by those regulations;

(*b*) in relation to any other acquisition, means the time of the event which, in relation to the acquisition, is the first relevant event for the purposes of taxing it; and

(*c*) in relation to any other supply, means the time when the supply would be treated as taking place in accordance with subsection (2) of section 6 if paragraph (*c*) of that subsection were omitted;

"warehouse" means any warehouse where goods may be stored in any member State without payment of any one or more of the following, that is to say—

(*a*) Community customs duty;

(*b*) any agricultural levy of the European Community;

(*c*) VAT on the importation of the goods into any member State;

(*d*) any duty of excise or any duty which is equivalent in another member State to a duty of excise.

(7) References in this section to goods being subject to a warehousing regime is a reference to goods being kept in a warehouse or being transported between warehouses (whether in the same or different member States) without the payment in a member State of any duty, levy or VAT; and references to the removal of goods from a warehousing regime shall be construed accordingly.

Commentary—*De Voil Indirect Tax Service* **V5.141, V3.173, V3.383**.

Regulations—VAT Regulations, SI 1995/2518 reg 43.

Definitions—"Acquisition of goods from another member State", s 11; "another member State", s 96(1); "the Commissioners ", s 96(1); "prescribed", s 96(1); "regulations", s 96(1); "supply", s 5, Sch 4; "taxable person", ss 3, 96(1); "United Kingdom", s 96(11); "VAT", ss 1, 96(1).

Cross reference—See VATA 1994 s 73(7B) (the Commissioners may assess VAT due to the best of their judgment where goods are removed from a warehouse without payment of VAT payable under sub-s (4) above).

VAT (Isle of Man) Order, SI 1982/1067 art 8 (taxable persons for the purposes of Isle of Man VAT legislation to be treated as taxable persons for the purposes of this section).

Amendments—[1] Sub-ss (5), (5A) substituted for original sub-s (5) by FA 1995 s 29.

[2] Sub-s (1A) inserted by F(No 2)A 2005 s 1 with effect from 20 July 2005.

[18A Fiscal warehousing

(1) The Commissioners may, if it appears to them proper, upon application approve any registered person as a fiscal warehouse keeper; and such approval shall be subject to such conditions as they shall impose.

(2) Subject to those conditions and to regulations made under section 18F such a person shall be entitled to keep a fiscal warehouse.

(3) "Fiscal warehouse" means such place in the United Kingdom in the occupation or under the control of the fiscal warehouse keeper, not being retail premises, as he shall notify to the Commissioners in writing; and such a place shall become a fiscal warehouse on receipt by the Commissioners of that notification or on the date stated in it as the date from which it is to have effect, whichever is the later, and, subject to subsection (6) below, shall remain a fiscal warehouse so long as it is in the occupation or under the control of the fiscal warehouse keeper or until he shall notify the Commissioners in writing that it is to cease to be a fiscal warehouse.

(4) The Commissioners may in considering an application by a person to be a fiscal warehousekeeper take into account any matter which they consider relevant, and may without prejudice to the generality of that provision take into account all or any one or more of the following—

(*a*) his record of compliance and ability to comply with the requirements of this Act and regulations made hereunder;

(*b*) his record of compliance and ability to comply with the requirements of the customs and excise Acts (as defined in the Management Act) and regulations made thereunder;

(*c*) his record of compliance and ability to comply with Community customs provisions;

(*d*) his record of compliance and ability to comply with the requirements of other member States relating to VAT and duties equivalent to duties of excise;

(*e*) if the applicant is a company the records of compliance and ability to comply with the matters set out at (*a*) to (*d*) above of its directors, persons connected with its directors, its managing officers, any shadow directors or any of those persons, and, if it is a close company, the records of compliance and ability to comply with the matters set out at (*a*) to (*d*) above of the beneficial owners of the shares of the company or any of them; and

(*f*) if the applicant is an individual the records of compliance and ability to comply with the matters set out at (*a*) to (*d*) above of any company of which he is or has been a director, managing officer or shadow director or, in the case of a close company, a shareholder or the beneficial owner of shares,

and for the purposes of paragraphs (e) and (f) "connected" shall have the meaning given by section 24(7), "managing officer" the meaning given by section 61(6), "shadow director" the meaning given by [section 251 of the Companies Act 2006][2] and "close company" the meaning given by the Taxes Act.

(5) Subject to subsection (6) below, a person approved under subsection (1) shall remain a fiscal warehouse keeper until he ceases to be a registered person or until he shall notify the Commissioners in writing that he is to cease to be a fiscal warehouse keeper.

(6) The Commissioners may if they consider it appropriate from time to time—

(*a*) impose conditions on a fiscal warehouse keeper in addition to those conditions, if any, which they imposed under subsection (1), and vary or revoke any conditions previously imposed;

(*b*) withdraw approval of any person as a fiscal warehouse keeper, and

(*c*) withdraw fiscal warehouse status from any premises.

(7) Any application by or on behalf of a person to be a fiscal warehousekeeper shall be in writing in such form as the Commissioners may direct and shall be accompanied by such information as they shall require.

(8) Any approval by the Commissioners under subsection (1) above, and any withdrawal of approval or other act by them under subsection (6) above, shall be notified by them to the fiscal warehousekeeper in writing and shall take effect on such notification being made or on any later date specified for the purpose in the notification.

(9) Without prejudice to the provisions of section 43 concerning liability for VAT, in subsections (1) and (2) above "registered person" includes any body corporate which under that section is for the time being treated as a member of a group.][1]

Commentary—*De Voil Indirect Tax Service* **V3.384**.

Definitions—"The Commissioners", s 96(1); "fiscal warehousekeeper", s 18F(1); "the Management Act", s 96(1); "other member States", s 96(1); "registered", s 96(2); "regulations", s 96(1); "the Taxes Act", s 96(1); "United Kingdom", s 96(11).

Cross references—See VATA 1994 s 18F (supplementary provisions).

VATA 1994 s 69(1)(*g*) (penalties for failure to comply with conditions imposed under sub-ss (1) or (6) above).

VATA 1994 ss 83, 84 (appeals relating to decisions of the Commissioners as to approval of fiscal warehousekeepers and fiscal warehouses).

Amendments—[1] This section, and ss 18B–18F, inserted by FA 1996 Sch 3 para 5, with effect from 1 June 1996; see Finance Act 1996, Section 26, (Appointed Day) Order, SI 1996/1249, and applying to any acquisition of goods from another member State and any supply taking place on or after that day, except in so far as these sections confer power to make regulations, when they come into force on 29 April 1996.

[2] Words in sub-s (4) substituted by the Companies Act 2006 (Commencement No 3, Consequential Amendments, Transitional Provisions and Savings) Order, SI 2007/2194 art 10(1), Sch 4 para 85 with effect from 1 October 2007.

[18B Fiscally warehoused goods: relief

(1) Subsections (3) and (4) below apply where—

(*a*) there is an acquisition of goods from another member State;

(*b*) those goods are eligible goods;

(*c*) either

(i) the acquisition takes place while the goods are subject to a fiscal warehousing regime; or

(ii) after the acquisition but before the supply, if any, of those goods which next occurs, the acquirer causes the goods to be placed in a fiscal warehousing regime; and

(*d*) the acquirer, not later than the time of the acquisition, prepares and keeps a certificate that the goods are subject to a fiscal warehousing regime, or (as the case may be) that he will cause paragraph (*c*)(ii) above to be satisfied; and the certificate shall . . . [2] be kept for such period as the Commissioners may by regulations specify.

(2) Subsections (3) and (4) below also apply where—

(*a*) there is a supply of goods;

(*b*) those goods are eligible goods;

(*c*) either—

(i) that supply takes place while the goods are subject to a fiscal warehousing regime; or

(ii) after that supply but before the supply, if any, of those goods which next occurs, the person to whom the former supply is made causes the goods to be placed in a fiscal warehousing regime;

(*d*) in a case falling within paragraph (*c*)(ii) above, the person to whom the supply is made gives the supplier, not later than the time of the supply, a certificate . . . [2] that he will cause paragraph (*c*)(ii) to be satisfied; and

(*e*) the supply is not a retail transaction.

[(2A) A certificate under subsection (1)(*d*) or (2)(*d*) must be in such form as may be specified by regulations or by the Commissioners in accordance with regulations.][2]

(3) The acquisition or supply in question shall be treated for the purposes of this Act as taking place outside the United Kingdom if any subsequent supply of those goods is while they are subject to the fiscal warehousing regime.

(4) Where subsection (3) does not apply and the acquisition or supply in question falls, for the purposes of this Act, to be treated as taking place in the United Kingdom, that acquisition or supply shall be treated for the purposes of this Act as taking place when the goods are removed from the fiscal warehousing regime.

(5) Where—

(*a*) subsection (4) above applies to an acquisition or a supply,

(*b*) the acquisition or supply is taxable and not zero-rated, and

(*c*) the acquirer or supplier is not a taxable person but would be were it not for paragraph 1(9) of Schedule 1, paragraph 1(7) of Schedule 2 and paragraph 1(6) of Schedule 3, or any of those provisions,

VAT shall be chargeable on that acquisition or supply notwithstanding that the acquirer or the supplier is not a taxable person.

(6) In this section "eligible goods" means goods—

(*a*) of a description falling within Schedule 5A;

(*b*) upon which any import duties, as defined in article 4(10) of the Community Customs Code of 12th October 1992 (Council Regulation (EEC) No 2913/92), either have been paid or have been deferred under article 224 of that Code or regulations made under section 45 of the Management Act;

(*c*) (in the case of goods imported from a place outside the member States) upon which any VAT chargeable under section 1(1)(*c*) has been either paid or deferred in accordance with Community customs provisions, and

(*d*) (in the case of goods subject to a duty of excise) upon which that duty has been either paid or deferred under section 127A of the Management Act.

(7) For the purposes of this section, apart from subsection (4), an acquisition or supply shall be treated as taking place at the material time for the acquisition or supply.

(8) The Treasury may by order vary Schedule 5A by adding to or deleting from it any goods or varying any description of any goods.][1]

Commentary—*De Voil Indirect Tax Service* **V3.384**.

Regulations—VAT (Amendment) (No 2) Regulations, SI 2012/1899.

Definitions—"Acquisition of goods from another member State", s 11; "another member State", s 96(1); "the Commissioners", s 96(1); "fiscal warehousing regime", s 18F(2); "the Management Act", s 96(1); "material time", s 18F(1); "regulations", s 96(1); "supply of goods", s 5, Sch 4; "taxable person", ss 3, 96(1); "taxable supply", ss 4(2), 96(1); "United Kingdom", s 96(11); "VAT", s 96(1).

Cross references—See VATA 1994 s 18D (payment of VAT on supplies within sub-s (4) and acquisitions within sub-s (5) above).

VATA 1994 s 18F (supplementary provisions).

VATA 1994 s 30(8A) (regulations may provide for the zero-rating of a supply of goods involving the removal of goods from a fiscal warehousing regime to an equivalent regime in another member State).

VATA 1994 s 62(1) (penalty for the preparation or giving of an incorrect certificate under sub-ss (1) and (2) above).

Amendments—[1] This section inserted by FA 1996 Sch 3 para 5, with effect from 1 June 1996; (see Finance Act 1996, Section 26, (Appointed Day) Order, SI 1996/1249), and applying to any acquisition of goods from another member State and any supply taking place on or after that day, except in so far as it confers power to make regulations, when it comes into force on 29 April 1996.

[2] In sub-s (1)(*d*), words "be in such form and" repealed, in sub-s (2)(*d*), words "in such form as the Commissioners may by regulations specify" repealed, and sub-s (2A) inserted, by FA 2012 s 204, Sch 29 paras 1, 2 with effect from 17 July 2012.

[18C Warehouses and fiscal warehouses: services

(1) Where—

(*a*) a taxable person makes a supply of specified services;

(*b*) those services are wholly performed on or in relation to goods while those goods are subject to a warehousing or fiscal warehousing regime;

(*c*) (except where the services are the supply by an occupier of a warehouse or a fiscal warehousekeeper of warehousing or fiscally warehousing the goods) the person to whom the supply is made gives the supplier a certificate . . . [2] that the services are so performed;

(*d*) the supply of services would (apart from this section) be taxable and not zero-rated; and

(*e*) the supplier issues to the person to whom the supply is made an invoice of such a description as the Commissioners may by regulations prescribe,

his supply shall be zero-rated.

[(1A) A certificate under subsection (1)(*c*) must be in such form as may be specified by regulations or by the Commissioners in accordance with regulations.][2]

(2) If a supply of services is zero-rated under subsection (1) above ("the zero-rated supply of services") then, unless there is a supply of the goods in question the material time for which is—

(*a*) while the goods are subject to a warehousing or fiscal warehousing regime, and

(*b*) after the material time for the zero-rated supply of services,

subsection (3) below shall apply.

(3) Where this subsection applies—

(*a*) a supply of services identical to the zero-rated supply of services shall be treated for the purposes of this Act as being, at the time the goods are removed from the warehousing or fiscal warehousing regime or (if earlier) at the duty point, both made (for the purposes of his business) to the person to whom the zero-rated supply of services was actually made and made by him in the course or furtherance of his business,

(*b*) that supply shall have the same value as the zero-rated supply of services,

(*c*) that supply shall be a taxable (and not a zero-rated) supply, and

(*d*) VAT shall be charged on that supply even if the person treated as making it is not a taxable person.

(4) In this section "specified services" means—

(*a*) services of an occupier of a warehouse or a fiscal warehousekeeper of keeping the goods in question in a warehousing or fiscal warehousing regime;

(*b*) in relation to goods subject to a warehousing regime, services of carrying out on the goods operations which are permitted to be carried out under Community customs provisions or warehousing regulations as the case may be; and (*c*) in relation to goods subject to a fiscal warehousing regime, services of carrying out on the goods any physical operations (other than any prohibited by regulations made under section 18F), for example, and without prejudice to the generality of the foregoing words, preservation and repacking operations.][1]

Commentary—*De Voil Indirect Tax Service* **V4.209**.

Regulations—VAT (Amendment) (No 2) Regulations, SI 2012/1899.

Definitions—"The Commissioners", s 96(1); "fiscal warehousekeeper", s 18F(1); "fiscal warehousing regime", s 18F(2); "the material time", s 18F(1); "regulations", s 96(1); "supply", s 5, Sch 4; "taxable person", ss 3, 96(1); "taxable supply", ss 4(2), 96(1); "warehouse", s 18F(1); "warehousing regime", s 18F(3); "warehousing regulations", s 18F(1).

Cross references—See VATA 1994 s 18D (payment of VAT on a supply within sub-s (3) above).

VATA 1994 s 18F (supplementary provisions).

VATA 1994 s 62(1) (penalty for the giving of an incorrect certificate under sub-s (1) above).

Amendments—[1] This section inserted by FA 1996 Sch 3 para 5, with effect from 1 June 1996; (see Finance Act 1996, Section 26, (Appointed Day) Order, SI 1996/1249), and applying to any acquisition of goods from another member State and any supply taking place on or after that day, except in so far as it confers power to make regulations, when it comes into force on 29 April 1996.

[2] In sub-s (1)(*c*), words ", in such a form as the Commissioners may by regulations specify," repealed, and sub-s (1A) inserted, by FA 2012 s 204, Sch 29 paras 1, 3 with effect from 17 July 2012.

[18D Removal from warehousing: accountability

(1) This section applies to any supply to which section 18B(4) or section 18C(3) applies (supply treated as taking place on removal or duty point) and any acquisition to which section 18B(5) applies (acquisition treated as taking place on removal where acquirer not a taxable person).

(2) Any VAT payable on the supply or acquisition shall (subject to any regulations under subsection (3) below) be paid—

(*a*) at the time when the supply or acquisition is treated as taking place under the section in question; and

(*b*) by the person by whom the goods are removed or, as the case may be, together with the excise duty, by the person who is required to pay that duty.

(3) The Commissioners may by regulations make provision for enabling a taxable person to pay the VAT he is required to pay by virtue of subsection (2) above at a time later than that provided by that subsection; and they may make different provisions for different descriptions of taxable persons and for different descriptions of goods and services.][1]

Commentary—*De Voil Indirect Tax Service* **V5.141A**.

Definitions—"The Commissioners", s 96(1); "regulations", s 96(1); "supply", s 5, Sch 4; "taxable person", ss 3, 96(1); "VAT", s 96(1).

Cross references—See VATA 1994 s 18F (supplementary provisions).

VATA 1994 s 30(8A) (regulations may provide for the zero-rating of a supply of goods involving their removal from a fiscal warehousing regime to an equivalent regime in another member State).

VATA 1994 s 73(7B) (Commissioners may assess VAT due to the best of their judgment where it appears to them that goods have been removed from a fiscal warehouse without payment of VAT payable under this section).

Amendments—[1] This section inserted by FA 1996 Sch 3 para 5, with effect from 1 June 1996 (see Finance Act 1996, Section 26, (Appointed Day) Order, SI 1996/1249), and applies to any acquisition of goods from another member State and any supply taking place on or after that day, except in so far as it confers power to make regulations, when it comes into force on 29 April 1996.

[18E Deficiency in fiscally warehoused goods

(1) This section applies where goods have been subject to a fiscal warehousing regime and, before being lawfully removed from the fiscal warehouse, they are found to be missing or deficient.

(2) In any case where this section applies, unless it is shown to the satisfaction of the Commissioners that the absence of or deficiency in the goods can be accounted for by natural waste or other legitimate cause, the Commissioners may require the fiscal warehousekeeper to pay immediately in respect of the missing goods or of the whole or any part of the deficiency, as they see fit, the VAT that would have been chargeable.

(3) In subsection (2) "VAT that would have been chargeable" means VAT that would have been chargeable on a supply of the missing goods, or the amount of goods by which the goods are deficient, taking place at the time immediately before the absence arose or the deficiency occurred, if the value of that supply were the open market value; but where that time cannot be ascertained to the Commissioners' satisfaction, that VAT shall be the greater of the amounts of VAT which would have been chargeable on a supply of those goods—

(*a*) if the value of that supply were the highest open market value during the period (the relevant period) commencing when the goods were placed in the fiscal warehousing regime and ending when the absence or deficiency came to the notice of the Commissioners, or

(*b*) if the rate of VAT chargeable on that supply were the highest rate chargeable on a supply of such goods during the relevant period and the value of that supply were the highest open market value while that rate prevailed.

(4) This section has effect without prejudice to any penalty incurred under any other provision of this Act or regulations made under it.]

Commentary—*De Voil Indirect Tax Service* **V5.141A**.

Definitions—"The Commissioners", s 96(1); "fiscal warehouse", ss 18A(3), 18F(1); "fiscal warehousekeeper", s 18F(1); "fiscal warehousing regime", s 18F(2); "open market value", s 19(5); "regulations", s 96(1); "VAT", s 96(1).

Cross references—See VATA 1994 s 18F (supplementary provisions).

VATA 1994 s 73(7A) (Commissioners may assess VAT due to the best of their judgment where fiscal warehousekeeper fails to pay VAT required under sub-s (2) above).

Amendments—This section inserted by FA 1996 Sch 3 para 5, with effect from 1 June 1996 (see Finance Act 1996, Section 26, (Appointed Day) Order, SI 1996/1249).

[18F Sections 18A to 18E: supplementary

(1) In sections 18A to 18E and this section—

"duty point" has the meaning given by section 18(6);

"eligible goods" has the meaning given by section 18B(6);

"fiscal warehouse" means a place notified to the Commissioners under section 18A(3) and from which such status has not been withdrawn;

"fiscal warehousekeeper" means a person approved under section 18A(1);

"material time"—

(*a*) in relation to any acquisition or supply the time of which is determined in accordance with regulations under section 6(14) or 12(3), means such time as may be prescribed for the purpose of this section by those regulations;

(*b*) in relation to any other acquisition, means the time when the goods reach the destination to which they are despatched from the member State in question;

(*c*) in relation to any other supply of goods, means the time when the supply would be treated as taking place in accordance with subsection (2) of section 6 if paragraph (*c*) of that subsection were omitted; and

(*d*) in relation to any other supply of services, means the time when the services are performed;

"warehouse", except in the expression "fiscal warehouse", has the meaning given by section 18(6);

"warehousing regulations" has the same meaning as in the Management Act.

(2) Any reference in sections 18A to 18E or this section to goods being subject to a fiscal warehousing regime is, subject to any regulations made under subsection (8)(*e*) below, a reference to eligible goods being kept in a fiscal warehouse or being transferred between fiscal warehouses in accordance with such regulations; and any reference to the removal of goods from a fiscal warehousing regime shall be construed accordingly.

(3) Subject to subsection (2) above, any reference in sections 18C and 18D to goods being subject to a warehousing regime or to the removal of goods from a warehousing regime shall have the same meaning as in section 18(7).

(4) Where as a result of an operation on eligible goods subject to a fiscal warehousing regime they change their nature but the resulting goods are also eligible goods, the provisions of sections 18B to 18E and this section shall apply as if the resulting goods were the original goods.

(5) Where as a result of an operation on eligible goods subject to a fiscal warehousing regime they cease to be eligible goods, on their ceasing to be so sections 18B to 18E shall apply as if they had at that time been removed from the fiscal warehousing regime; and for that purpose the proprietor of the goods shall be treated as if he were the person removing them.

(6) Where—

(*a*) any person ceases to be a fiscal warehouse keeper; or

(*b*) any premises cease to have fiscal warehouse status,

sections 18B to 18E and this section shall apply as if the goods of which he is the fiscal warehousekeeper, or the goods in the fiscal warehouse, as the case may be, had at that time been removed from the fiscal warehousing regime; and for that purpose the proprietor of the goods shall be treated as if he were the person removing them.

(7) The Commissioners may make regulations governing the deposit, keeping, securing and treatment of goods in a fiscal warehouse, and the removal of goods from a fiscal warehouse.

(8) Regulations may, without prejudice to the generality of subsection (7) above, include provisions—

(*a*) in relation to—

(i) goods which are, have been or are to be subject to a fiscal warehousing regime,

(ii) other goods which are, have been or are to be kept in fiscal warehouses,

(iii) fiscal warehouse premises, and

(iv) fiscal warehousekeepers and their businesses,

as to the keeping, preservation and production of records and the furnishing of returns and information by fiscal warehousekeepers and any other persons;

(*b*) requiring goods deposited in a fiscal warehouse to be produced to or made available for inspection by an authorised person on request by him;

(*c*) prohibiting the carrying out on fiscally warehoused goods of such operations as they may prescribe;

(*d*) regulating the transfer of goods from one fiscal warehouse to another;

(*e*) concerning goods which, though kept in a fiscal warehouse, are not eligible goods or are not intended by a relevant person to be goods in respect of which reliefs are to be enjoyed under sections 18A to 18E and this section;

(*f*) prohibiting the fiscal warehouse keeper from allowing goods to be removed from the fiscal warehousing regime without payment of any VAT payable under section 18D on or by reference to that removal and, if in breach of that prohibition he allows goods to be so removed, making him liable for the VAT jointly and severally with the remover,

and may contain such incidental or supplementary provisions as the Commissioners think necessary or expedient.

(9) Regulations may make different provision for different cases, including different provision for different fiscal warehousekeepers or descriptions of fiscal warehousekeeper, for fiscal warehouses of different descriptions or for goods of different classes or descriptions or of the same class or description in different circumstances.][1]

Commentary—*De Voil Indirect Tax Service* **V3.384**.

Definitions—"Authorised person", s 96(1); "the Commissioners", s 96(1); "the Management Act", s 96(1); "regulations", s 96(1); "supply", s 5, Sch 4; "VAT", ss 1, 96(1).

Amendments—[1] This section inserted by FA 1996 Sch 3 para 5, with effect from 1 June 1996; (see Finance Act 1996, Section 26, (Appointed Day) Order, SI 1996/1249)., and applying to any acquisition of goods from another member State and any supply taking place on or after that day, except in so far as it confers power to make regulations, when it comes into force on 29 April 1996.

Determination of value

19 Value of supply of goods or services

(1) For the purposes of this Act the value of any supply of goods or services shall, except as otherwise provided by or under this Act, be determined in accordance with this section and Schedule 6, and for those purposes subsections (2) to (4) below have effect subject to that Schedule.

(2) If the supply is for a consideration in money its value shall be taken to be such amount as, with the addition of the VAT chargeable, is equal to the consideration.

(3) If the supply is for a consideration not consisting or not wholly consisting of money, its value shall be taken to be such amount in money as, with the addition of the VAT chargeable, is equivalent to the consideration.

(4) Where a supply of any goods or services is not the only matter to which a consideration in money relates, the supply shall be deemed to be for such part of the consideration as is properly attributable to it.

(5) For the purposes of this Act the open market value of a supply of goods or services shall be taken to be the amount that would fall to be taken as its value under subsection (2) above if the supply were for such consideration in money as would be payable by a person standing in no such relationship with any person as would affect that consideration.

Commentary—*De Voil Indirect Tax Service* **V3.152, V3.161**.

Simon's Tax Cases—s 19, *Naturally Yours Cosmetics Ltd v C&E Comrs* [1988] STC 879*; *Fine Art Developments plc v C&E Comrs* [1993] STC 29*; *C&E Comrs v Thorn Materials Supply Ltd and Thorn Resources Ltd* [1998] STC 725*; *C&E Comrs v Euphony Communications Ltd* [2004] STC 301.

s 19(2), *Trafalgar Tours Ltd v C&E Comrs* [1990] STC 127*; *C&E Comrs v Tron Theatre Ltd* [1994] STC 177*; *C&E Comrs v British Telecommunications plc* [1999] STC 758; *Total UK Ltd v R&C Comrs* [2007] STC 564; *Simpson & Marwick (a firm) v R&C Comrs* [2011] UKUT 498 (TCC), [2012] STC 611.

s 19(3), *Boots Co plc v C&E Comrs* [1988] STC 138*; *C&E Comrs v Sai Jewellers* [1996] STC 269*; *C&E Comrs v Bugeja* [2000] STC 1; *Hartwell plc v C&E Comrs* [2002] STC 22.

s 19(4), *C&E Comrs v Tron Theatre Ltd* [1994] STC 177*; *C&E Comrs v Ping (Europe) Ltd* [2002] STC 1186, CA.

Press releases etc—C&E Business Brief 8/95 5-5-95 (Value of barter transactions).

C&E Business Brief 21/96 17-10-96 (a discount given by an MOT test centre to an unapproved garage is no longer treated as consideration for a taxable supply).

Definitions—"Money", s 96(1); "supply", s 5, Sch 4; "VAT", ss 1, 96(1).

Cross references—See VATA 1994 s 20(2) (valuation of acquisitions from other member states otherwise than through a taxable supply: disapplication of this section);

VATA 1994 s 52 (provision for regulations modifying this section in relation to the valuation of supplies of goods under trading stamp schemes);

VATA 1994 Sch 6 para 4 (valuation of supplies made on terms allowing discount for prompt payment);

VATA 1994 Sch 6 para 12 (treatment of money paid in respect of a supply by persons other than the person to whom the supply was made).

VAT Regulations, SI 1995/2518 reg 77 (modifications of sub-s (5) of this section in relation to goods supplied in exchange for trading stamps).

20 Valuation of acquisitions from other member States

(1) [Subject to section 18C,][1] For the purposes of this Act the value of any acquisition of goods from another member State shall be taken to be the value of the transaction in pursuance of which they are acquired.

(2) Where goods are acquired from another member State otherwise than in pursuance of a taxable supply, the value of the transaction in pursuance of which they are acquired shall be determined for the purposes of subsection (1) above in accordance with this section and Schedule 7, and for those purposes—

(*a*) subsections (3) to (5) below have effect subject to that Schedule; and

(*b*) section 19 and Schedule 6 shall not apply in relation to the transaction.

(3) If the transaction is for a consideration in money, its value shall be taken to be such amount as is equal to the consideration.

(4) If the transaction is for a consideration not consisting or not wholly consisting of money, its value shall be taken to be such amount in money as is equivalent to the consideration.

(5) Where a transaction in pursuance of which goods are acquired from another member State is not the only matter to which a consideration in money relates, the transaction shall be deemed to be for such part of the consideration as is properly attributable to it.

Commentary—*De Voil Indirect Tax Service* **V3.390.**

Definitions—"Acquisition of goods from another member State", s 11; "another member State", s 96(1); "money", s 96(1); "taxable supply", s 4(2).

Cross reference—See VATA 1994 s 52 (provision for regulations modifying this section in relation to the valuation of acquisitions of goods under trading stamp schemes).

Amendments—[1] Words in sub-s (1) inserted by FA 1996 Sch 3 para 6, with effect to any acquisition of goods from another member State taking place on or after 1 June 1996; (see Finance Act 1996, Section 26, (Appointed Day) Order, SI 1996/1249).

21 Value of imported goods

(1) For the purposes of this Act, the value of goods imported from a place outside the member States shall (subject to subsections (2) [to (4)][1] below) be determined according to the rules applicable in the case of Community customs duties, whether or not the goods' in question are subject to any such duties.

(2) For the purposes of this Act the value of any goods imported from a place outside the member States shall [(subject to subsection (2A) below)][5] be taken to include the following so far as they are not already included in that value in accordance with the rules mentioned in subsection (1) above, that is to say—

(*a*) all taxes, duties and other charges levied either outside or, by reason of importation, within the United Kingdom (except VAT); . . . [2]

[(*b*) all incidental expenses, such as commission, packing, transport and insurance costs, up to the goods' first destination in the United Kingdom; and

(*c*) if at the time of the importation of the goods from a place outside the member States a further destination for the goods is known, and that destination is within the United Kingdom or another member State, all such incidental expenses in so far as they result from the transport of the goods to that other destination;

and in this subsection "the goods' first destination" means the place mentioned on the consignment note or any other document by means of which the goods are imported into the United Kingdom, or in the absence of such documentation it means the place of the first transfer of cargo in the United Kingdom.][2]

[(2A) Where—

(*a*) any goods falling within subsection (5) below are sold by auction at a time when they are subject to the procedure specified in subsection (2B) below, and

(*b*) arrangements made by or on behalf of the purchaser of the goods following the sale by auction result in the importation of the goods from a place outside the member States,

the value of the goods shall not be taken for the purposes of this Act to include, in relation to that importation, any commission or premium payable to the auctioneer in connection with the sale of the goods.

(2B) That procedure is the customs procedure for temporary importation with total relief from import duties provided for in Articles 137 to 141 of Council Regulation 2913/92/EEC establishing the Community Customs Code.][5]

(3) Subject to subsection (2) above, where—

(*a*) goods are imported from a place outside the member States for a consideration which is or includes a price in money payable as on the transfer of property;

(*b*) the terms on which those goods are so imported allow a discount for prompt payment of that price;

(*c*) those terms do not include provision for payment of that price by instalments; and

(*d*) payment of that price is made in accordance with those terms so that the discount falls to be allowed,

the value of the goods shall be taken for the purposes of this Act to be reduced by the amount of the discount.

[(4) [Subject to subsection (6D) below,][3] for the purposes of this Act, the value of any goods falling within subsection (5) below which are imported from a place outside the member States shall be taken to be an amount equal to [25 per cent][7] of the amount which, apart from this subsection, would be their value for those purposes.][1]

[(5) The goods that fall within this subsection are—

(*a*) any work of art;

(*b*) any antique, not falling within paragraph (*a*) above or (*c*) below, that is more than one hundred years old;

(*c*) any collection or collector's piece that is of zoological, botanical, mineralogical, anatomical, historical, archaeological, palaeontological, ethnographic, numismatic or philatelic interest.

(6) In this section "work of art" means, subject to subsections (6A) and (6B) below—

(*a*) any mounted or unmounted painting, drawing, collage, decorative plaque or similar picture that was executed by hand;

(*b*) any original engraving, lithograph or other print which—

(i) was produced from one or more plates executed by hand by an individual who executed them without using any mechanical or photomechanical process; and

(ii) either is the only one produced from the plate or plates or is comprised in a limited edition;

(*c*) any original sculpture or statuary, in any material;

(*d*) any sculpture cast which—

(i) was produced by or under the supervision of the individual who made the mould or became entitled to it by succession on the death of that individual; and

(ii) either is the only cast produced from the mould or is comprised in a limited edition;

(*e*) any tapestry or other hanging which—

(i) was made by hand from an original design; and

(ii) either is the only one made from the design or is comprised in a limited edition;

(*f*) any ceramic executed by an individual and signed by him;

(*g*) any enamel on copper which—

(i) was executed by hand;

(ii) is signed either by the person who executed it or by someone on behalf of the studio where it was executed;

(iii) either is the only one made from the design in question or is comprised in a limited edition; and

(iv) is not comprised in an article of jewellery or an article of a kind produced by goldsmiths or silversmiths;

(*h*) any mounted or unmounted photograph which—

(i) was printed by or under the supervision of the photographer;

(ii) is signed by him; and

(iii) either is the only print made from the exposure in question or is comprised in a limited edition;

(6A) The following do not fall within subsection (5) above by virtue of subsection (6)(*a*) above, that is to say—

(*a*) any technical drawing, map or plan;

(*b*) any picture comprised in a manufactured article that has been hand-decorated; or

(*c*) anything in the nature of scenery, including a backcloth.

(6B) An item comprised in a limited edition shall be taken to be so comprised for the purposes of subsection (6)(*d*) to (*h*) above only if—

(*a*) in the case of sculpture casts—

(i) the edition is limited so that the number produced from the same mould does not exceed eight; or

(ii) the edition comprises a limited edition of nine or more casts made before 1st January 1989 which the Commissioners have directed should be treated, in the exceptional circumstances of the case, as a limited edition for the purposes of subsection (6)(*d*) above;

(*b*) in the case of tapestries and hangings, the edition is limited so that the number produced from the same design does not exceed eight;

(*c*) in the case of enamels on copper—

(i) the edition is limited so that the number produced from the same design does not exceed eight; and

(ii) each of the enamels in the edition is numbered and is signed as mentioned in subsection (6)(*g*)(ii) above;

(*d*) in the case of photographs—

(i) the edition is limited so that the number produced from the same exposure does not exceed thirty; and

(ii) each of the prints in the edition is numbered and is signed as mentioned in subsection (6)(*h*)(ii) above.

(6C) For the purposes of this section a collector's piece is of philatelic interest if—

(*a*) it is a postage or revenue stamp, a postmark, a first-day cover or an item of pre-stamped stationery; and

(*b*) it is franked or (if unfranked) it is not legal tender and is not intended for use as such.

(6D) Subsection (4) above does not apply in the case of any goods imported from outside the member States if—

(*a*) the whole of the VAT chargeable on their importation falls to be relieved by virtue of an order under section 37(1); or

(*b*) they were exported from the United Kingdom during the period of twelve months ending with the date of their importation [in circumstances where the exportation and subsequent importation were effected to obtain the benefit of that subsection][6].][4]

(7) An order under section 2(2) may contain provision making such alteration of the percentage for the time being specified in subsection (4) above as the Treasury consider appropriate in consequence of any increase or decrease by that order of the rate of VAT.][1]

Commentary—*De Voil Indirect Tax Service* **V1.298**.

Simon's Tax Cases—*R v Redmond* [2011] EWCA Crim 203,[2011] STC 1892.

Press releases etc—HC Official Report, Standing Committee D 2-2-95 (new sub-s (5)(*b*) restricts the reduced rate to first importation; glass crystal is covered by new sub-s (5)(*c*)).

C&E News Release 20/95 3-4-95 (implementation of charges to the valuation of imported works of art etc introduced by FA 1995 delayed until 1 June 1996).

VAT Information Sheet 9/95 1-5-95 (valuation of imported works of art, antiques and collectors' pieces from 1 June 1996).

C&E News Release 29/99 2-7-99 and VAT Information Sheet 9/99 July 1999 (increase in the reduced rate from 2.5% to 5% and extension of scope).

C&E News Release 15-4-02 (new concession: revocation of the rule denying the reduced rate where goods are exported from the UK within 12 months before the date of re-importation).

Definitions—"Another member State", s 96(1); "goods imported from a place outside the member States", s 15; "member States", s 15; "money", s 96(1); "United Kingdom", s 96(11); "VAT", ss 1, 96(1).

Amendments—[1] Words in sub-s (1) substituted, and sub-ss (4)–(7) added, by FA 1995 s 22 with effect in relation to goods imported at any time on or after 1 May 1995.

[2] Word omitted from sub-s (2)(a) repealed and sub-s (2)(b), (c) and words following substituted for sub-s (2)(b) by FA 1996 s 27, Sch 41 Pt IV(3) with effect in relation to goods imported after 31 December 1995.

[3] Words in sub-s (4) inserted, by FA 1999 s 12 in relation to goods imported at any time from 27 July 1999.

[4] Sub-ss (5), (6) substituted by (5)–(6D) by FA 1999 s 12 in relation to goods imported at any time from 27 July 1999.

[5] Words '(subject to subsection (2A) below)' in sub-s (2) and sub-ss (2A) and (2B) inserted by FA 2006 s 18 with effect from 1 September 2006 (by virtue of SI 2006/2149).

[6] In sub-s (6D)(b), words inserted by the Enactment of Extra-Statutory Concessions Order, SI 2009/730 art 17 with effect in relation to importations on or after 6 April 2009.

[7] In sub-s (4), words substituted for words "28.58 per cent" by F(No 2)A 2010 s 3(2) with effect in relation to goods imported on or after 4 January 2011.

22 Value of certain goods

Amendments—This section repealed by FA 1996 s 28, Sch 41 Pt IV(2) with effect in relation to supplies made after 31 December 1995.

[23 Value of supplies involving relevant machine games

(1) If a person plays a relevant machine game, then for the purposes of VAT the amount paid by the person is to be treated as consideration for a supply of services to that person.

(2) "Relevant machine game" is defined in section 23A.

(3) The value to be taken as the value of supplies made by a person ("the supplier") in the circumstances mentioned in subsection (1) in any period is to be determined as if the consideration for the supplies were reduced by an amount equal to X.

(4) X is the amount (if any) paid out in that period by way of winnings in respect of relevant machine games made available by the supplier (whether the games were played in the same period or an earlier one).

(5) X does not include any winnings paid out to the supplier or a person acting on the supplier's behalf.

(6) Inserting a token into a machine on which a relevant machine game is played is to be treated for the purposes of subsection (1) as the payment of an amount equal to that for which the token can be obtained.

(7) Providing a specified kind of token by way of winnings is to be treated for the purposes of subsection (4) as the payment out of an amount by way of winnings equal to the value of the token.

(8) A specified kind of token is—

(*a*) a token that can be inserted into the same machine to enable games to be played on the machine, or

(*b*) a token that is not of such a kind but can be exchanged for money.

(9) The value of a specified kind of token is—

(*a*) for a token within subsection (8)(*a*), an amount equal to that for which the token can be obtained, and

(*b*) for a token within subsection (8)(*b*), an amount equal to that for which the token can be exchanged.

(10) If it is not reasonably practicable to attribute payments and winnings to relevant machine games or to apportion them between relevant machine games and other games or other activities, any attribution or apportionment is to be done on a just and reasonable basis.

(11) For the purposes of this section, a person plays a game if the person participates in the game—

(*a*) whether or not there are other participants in the game, and

(*b*) whether or not a computer generates images or data taken to represent the actions of other participants in the game.][1]

Commentary—*De Voil Indirect Tax Service* **V3.264**.
Simon's Tax Cases—*Feehan v C&E Comrs* [1995] STC 75*.
Press releases etc—HMRC Brief 70/09, 19-11-09 (electronic lottery terminals)).
HMRC Brief 11/10, 16-3-10 (the decision of the VAT Tribunal in respect of Rank (gaming machines)).
Definitions—"Money", s 96(1); "supply of services", s 5, Sch 4; "VAT", ss 1, 96(1); "value of supply of services", s 19, Sch 6.
Cross reference—See VATA 1994 Sch 11 para 9 (power to require action necessary to ascertain value of supplies relating to gaming machines).
Amendments—[1] Sections 23, 23A substituted for former s 23 by FA 2012 s 191, Sch 24 para 63 with effect in relation to supplies made on or after 1 February 2013.

[23A Meaning of "relevant machine game"

(1) A "relevant machine game" is a game (whether of skill or chance or both) that—

(*a*)

(*b*)

(a) is played on a machine for a prize, and

(b) is not excluded by subsection (2).

(2) A game is excluded by this subsection if—

(*a*) takings and payouts in respect of it are taken into account in determining any charge to machine games duty,

(*b*) it involves betting on future real events,

(*c*) bingo duty is charged on the playing of it or would be so charged but for paragraphs 1 to 5 of Schedule 3 to the Betting and Gaming Duties Act 1981 (exemptions from bingo duty),

(*d*) lottery duty is charged on the taking of a ticket or chance in it or would be so charged but for an express exception,

(*e*) lottery duty is charged on the taking of a ticket or chance in it or would be so charged but for an express exception,

(*f*) playing it amounts to remote gaming within the meaning of [section 154(1) of the Finance Act 2014 (meaning of remote gaming)][2].

(3) In this section—

"game" does not include a sport;

"machine" means any apparatus that uses or applies mechanical power, electrical power or both;

"prize", in relation to a game, does not include the opportunity to play the game again;

"real game of chance" means a game of chance (within the meaning of [Part 3 of the Finance Act 2014 (see section 188(1)(*b*))][2]) that is non-virtual.

(4) The Treasury may by order amend this section.][1]

Amendments—[1] Sections 23, 23A substituted for former s 23 by FA 2012 s 191, Sch 24 para 63 with effect in relation to supplies made on or after 1 February 2013.

[2] In sub-s (2)(*f*), words substituted for words "section 26A of the Betting and Gaming Duties Act 1981 (remote gaming duty: interpretation)", and in sub-s (3), words substituted for words "the Betting and Gaming Duties Act 1981", by FA 2014 s 196, Sch 28 para 19 with effect from 1 December 2014 (FA 2014 s 198(2)), subject to transitional provisions and savings in FA 2014 Sch 29.

Payment of VAT by taxable persons

24 Input tax and output tax

(1) Subject to the following provisions of this section, "input tax", in relation to a taxable person, means the following tax, that is to say—

(*a*) VAT on the supply to him of any goods or services;

(*b*) VAT on the acquisition by him from another member State of any goods; and

(*c*) VAT paid or payable by him on the importation of any goods from a place outside the member States,

being (in each case) goods or services used or to be used for the purpose of any business carried on or to be carried on by him.

(2) Subject to the following provisions of this section, "output tax", in relation to a taxable person, means VAT on supplies which he makes or on the acquisition by him from another member State of goods (including VAT which is also to be counted as input tax by virtue of subsection (1)(*b*) above).

(3) . . . [3]

(4) The Treasury may by order provide with respect to any description of goods or services that, where goods or services of that description are supplied to a person who is not a taxable person, they shall, in such circumstances as may be specified in the order, be treated for the purposes of subsections (1) and (2) above as supplied to such other person as may be determined in accordance with the order.

(5) Where goods or services supplied to a taxable person, goods acquired by a taxable person from another member State or goods imported by a taxable person from a place outside the member States are used or to be used partly for the purposes of a business carried on or to be carried on by him and partly for other purposes[—

(*a*) VAT on supplies, acquisitions and importations shall be apportioned so that so much as is referable to the taxable person's business purposes is counted as that person's input tax, and

(*b*) the remainder of that VAT ("the non-business VAT") shall count as that person's input tax only to the extent (if any) provided for by regulations under subsection (6)(*e*).][2]

[(5A) For the purposes of subsections (1) and (5), a relevant asset held for the purposes of a business carried on or to be carried on by a taxable person is not, in any circumstances, to be regarded as used or to be used for the purposes of the business if, and to the extent that, it is used or to be used for that person's private use or the private use of that person's staff.

(5B) In subsection (5A) "relevant asset" means—

(*a*) any interest in land,

(*b*) any building or part of a building,

(*c*) any civil engineering work or part of such a work,

(*d*) any goods incorporated or to be incorporated in a building or civil engineering work (whether by being installed as fixtures or fittings or otherwise),

(*e*) any ship, boat or other vessel, or

(*f*) any aircraft.][3]

(6) Regulations may provide—

(*a*) for VAT on the supply of goods or services to a taxable person, VAT on the acquisition of goods by a taxable person from other member States and VAT paid or payable by a taxable person on the importation of goods from places outside the member States to be treated as his input tax only if and to the extent that the charge to VAT is evidenced and quantified by reference to such documents [or other information][1] as may be specified in the regulations or the Commissioners may direct either generally or in particular cases or classes of cases;

(*b*) for a taxable person to count as his input tax, in such circumstances, to such extent and subject to such conditions as may be prescribed, VAT on the supply to him of goods or services or on the acquisition of goods by him from another member State or paid by him on the importation of goods from places outside the member States notwithstanding that he was not a taxable person at the time of the supply, acquisition or payment;

(*c*) for a taxable person that is a body corporate to count as its input tax, in such circumstances, to such extent and subject to such conditions as may be prescribed, VAT on the supply, acquisition or importation of goods before the company's incorporation for appropriation to the company or its business or on the supply of services before that time for its benefit or in connection with its incorporation;

(*d*) in the case of a person who has been, but is no longer, a taxable person, for him to be paid by the Commissioners the amount of any VAT on a supply of services made to him for the purposes of the business carried on by him when he was a taxable person;

[(*e*) in cases where an apportionment is made under subsection (5), for the non-business VAT to be counted as the taxable person's input tax for the purposes of any provision made by or under section 26 in such circumstances, to such extent and subject to such conditions as may be prescribed.][2]

[(6A) Regulations under subsection (6) may contain such supplementary, incidental, consequential and transitional provisions as appear to the Commissioners to be necessary or expedient.][2]

(7) . . . [3]

Commentary—*De Voil Indirect Tax Service* **V3.421**.

HMRC Manuals—VAT Guidance V1-3: Supply and consideration, para 5.17 (business/non-business use: *Lennartz*).

Simon's Tax Cases—s 24(1), *Schemepanel Trading Ltd v C&E Comrs* [1996] STC 871; *WHA Ltd and another v C&E Comrs* [2003] STC 648, [2004] STC 1081; *BUPA Purchasing Ltd and others v C&E Comrs* [2003] STC 1203; *R&C Comrs v Jeancharm Ltd (trading as Beaver International)* [2005] STC 918; *R&C Comrs v Gracechurch Management Services Ltd* [2008] STC 795; *R&C Comrs v Airtours Holidays Transport Ltd* [2010] UKUT 404 (TCC), [2011] STC 239.

s 24(2), *C&E Comrs v Rosner* [1994] STC 228*.

s 24(3)(*a*), *Turner (T/A Turner Agricultural) v C&E Comrs* [1992] STC 621*.

s 24(5), *Victoria and Albert Museum Trustees v C&E Comrs* [1996] STC 1016*; *St Helen's School Northwood Ltd v R&C Comrs* [2007] STC 633.

Orders—See VAT Regulations, SI 1995/2518.

VAT (Input Tax) (Reimbursement by Employers of Employees' Business Use of Road Fuel) Regulations, SI 2005/3290.

VAT (Input Tax) (Person Supplied) Order, SI 2005/3291.

Press releases etc—HMRC Statement of Practice: VAT Strategy—Input tax deduction without a valid VAT invoice. 10 April 2007.

HMRC Brief 2/10 Lennartz Accounting–new policy following ECJ case. 22 January 2010.

Definitions—"Acquisition of goods from another member State", s 11; "another member State", s 96(1); "business", s 94; "the Commissioners", s 96(1); "document", s 96(1); "goods imported from a place outside the member States", s 15; "prescribed", s 96(1); "regulations", s 96(1); "supply ", s 5, Sch 4; "tax", s 96(1); "taxable person", s 3; "VAT", ss 1, 96(1).

Cross references—See VATA 1994 s 56(5) (no apportionment of VAT to be made under sub-s (5) of this section in respect of fuel for private use).

VAT (Tour Operators) Order, SI 1987/1806 art 12 (disallowance of credit for input tax on goods and services acquired by a tour operator for re-supply as designated travel services);

Amendments—[1] Words in sub-s (6)(a) inserted by FA 2003, s 17(2) with effect from 10 April 2003.

[2] In sub-s (5), words substituted for words ", VAT on supplies, acquisitions and importations shall be apportioned so that only so much as is referable to his business purposes is counted as his input tax.", and sub-ss (6)(*e*), (6A) inserted, by F(No 3)A 2010 s 19, Sch 8 para 1(1), (3), (5), (6) with effect from 16 December 2010.

[3] Sub-ss (3), (7) repealed and sub-ss (5A), (5B) inserted, by F(No 3)A 2010 s 19, Sch 8 para 1(1), (2), (4), (7) with effect in relation to VAT incurred by a taxable person on or after 1 January 2011. The VAT "incurred" by a person in respect of an asset is VAT on the supply to the person of the asset, VAT on the supply to the person of any goods or services the expenditure on which constitutes expenditure related to the asset, VAT on the acquisition by the person from another member State of the asset or anything comprised in it, and VAT paid or payable by the person on the importation of the asset or anything comprised in it from a place outside the member States, and such VAT is incurred at the time of the supply, acquisition or importation in question (F(No 3)A 2010 Sch 8 para 1(9)).

25 Payment by reference to accounting periods and credit for input tax against output tax

(1) A taxable person shall—

(*a*) in respect of supplies made by him, and

(*b*) in respect of the acquisition by him from other member States of any goods,

account for and pay VAT by reference to such periods (in this Act referred to as "prescribed accounting periods") at such time and in such manner as may be determined by or under regulations and regulations may make different provision for different circumstances.

(2) Subject to the provisions of this section, he is entitled at the end of each prescribed accounting period to credit for so much of his input tax as is allowable under section 26, and then to deduct that amount from any output tax that is due from him.

(3) If either no output tax is due at the end of the period, or the amount of the credit exceeds that of the output tax then, subject to subsections (4) and (5) below, the amount of the credit or, as the case may be, the amount of the excess shall be paid to the taxable person by the Commissioners; and an amount which is due under this subsection is referred to in this Act as a "VAT credit".

(4) The whole or any part of the credit may, subject to and in accordance with regulations, be held over to be credited in and for a subsequent period; and the regulations may allow for it to be so held over either on the taxable person's own application or in accordance with general or special directions given by the Commissioners from time to time.

(5) Where at the end of any period a VAT credit is due to a taxable person who has failed to submit returns for any earlier period as required by this Act, the Commissioners may withhold payment of the credit until he has complied with that requirement.

(6) A deduction under subsection (2) above and payment of a VAT credit shall not be made or paid except on a claim made in such manner and at such time as may be determined by or under regulations; and, in the case of a person who has made no taxable supplies in the period concerned or any previous period, payment of a VAT credit shall be made subject to such conditions (if any) as the Commissioners think fit to impose, including conditions as to repayment in specified circumstances.

(7) The Treasury may by order provide, in relation to such supplies, acquisitions and importations as the order may specify, that VAT charged on them is to be excluded from any credit under this section; and—

(*a*) any such provision may be framed by reference to the description of goods or services supplied or goods acquired or imported, the person by whom they are supplied, acquired or imported or to whom they are supplied, the purposes for which they are supplied, acquired or imported, or any circumstances whatsoever; and

(*b*) such an order may contain provision for consequential relief from output tax.

Commentary—*De Voil Indirect Tax Service* **V3.418, V3.401**.

Note—The reference in sub-s (2) to output tax due from the taxable person does not include any VAT that the taxable person is liable to pay to another member State under a non-UK special scheme (VATA 1994 Sch 3BA para 19(5)).

Simon's Tax Cases—*Betterware Products Ltd v C&E Comrs (No 2)* [1988] STC 6*; *C&E Comrs v Fine Art Developments plc* [1989] STC 85*; *Neuvale Ltd v C&E Comrs* [1989] STC 395*; *R v C&E Comrs, ex p Kay & Co Ltd* [1996] STC 1500.

s 25(2), (3), *R v Comrs of Customs and Excise, ex p Strangewood Ltd* [1987] STC 502*.

s 25(7), *Group Ltd v C&E Comrs* [1996] STC 898*; *R v C&E Comrs, ex p Greater Manchester Police Authority* [2000] STC 620, [2001] STC 406, CA.

Regulations—See VAT Regulations, SI 1995/2518.

VAT (Annual Accounting) Regulations, SI 1996/542.

VAT (Amendment) Regulations, SI 2012/33

VAT (Amendment) (No 2) Regulations, SI 2012/1899.

VAT (Amendment) (No 2) Regulations, SI 2014/1497.

Definitions—"Acquisition of goods from another member State", s 11; "another member State", s 96(1); "the Commissioners", s 96(1); "input tax", s 24; "output tax", s 24; "regulations", s 96(1); "supply", s 5, Sch 4; "taxable person", s 3; "taxable supply", s 4(2); "VAT", ss 1, 96(1).

Press releases etc—HMRC Statement of Practice: VAT Strategy—Input tax deduction without a valid VAT invoice. 10 April 2007.

VAT Guidance V1–13, para 6.3 (Deduction of input tax, the basic rule).

Cross references—See VATA 1994 s 27(1) (VAT payable by taxable person on importation of goods partly or wholly for private purposes is not to be treated as input tax eligible for deduction or credit under this section);

VATA 1994 s 34(1) (capital expenditure on supply of machinery or plant: relief for VAT which is not eligible for credit under this section);

VATA 1994 s 54(3) (supplies under flat rate scheme for farmers: treatment of percentage of consideration as VAT for purposes of determining entitlement to input tax credit of person supplied);

VATA 1994 s 69(1), (5) (penalty for failure to pay VAT within time limit imposed by regulations made under sub-s (1) of this section);

VATA 1994 s 80(5) (repayment supplement: treatment as credit due under sub-s (3) of this section);

VATA 1994 s 81(1) (interest payable by Commissioners: treatment as credit due under sub-s (3) of this section);

VATA 1994 s 90(3) (VAT repaid as a result of the failure of a resolution under PCTA 1968 may not be credited as input tax under this section);

VATA 1994 s 97(3), (4) (procedure for making orders for excluding any VAT from credit under this section).

VAT (Input Tax) Order, SI 1992/3222 (disallowance of credit for input tax on specified supplies, acquisitions and importations).

VAT Regulations, SI 1995/2518 reg 6(3) (business transferred as a going concern: repayment of input tax);

VAT Regulations, SI 1995/2518 reg 29 (claims for deduction of input tax: form and documentation);

VAT Regulations, SI 1995/2518 reg 34 (correction of over- and understatements of input tax credit);

VAT Regulations, SI 1995/2518 reg 101(3) (where a supply is excluded from output tax by an order under sub-s (7), its value is to be excluded in determining proportion of input tax attributable to taxable supplies under reg 101(2)(*d*)).

FA 2008 s 121(2) (the requirement in sub-s (6) that a claim for deduction of input tax be made at such time as may be determined by or under regulations does not apply to a claim that became chargeable, and in respect of which the claimant held the required evidence, in a prescribed accounting period ending before 1 May 1997 if the claim is made before 1 April 2009).

F(No 3)A 2010 Sch 8 para 4 (output tax charge where credit attributable to purported Sch 4 para 5(4) supply).

26 Input tax allowable under section 25

(1) The amount of input tax for which a taxable person is entitled to credit at the end of any period shall be so much of the input tax for the period (that is input tax on supplies, acquisitions and importations in the period) as is allowable by or under regulations as being attributable to supplies within subsection (2) below.

(2) The supplies within this subsection are the following supplies made or to be made by the taxable person in the course or furtherance of his business—

(*a*) taxable supplies;

(*b*) supplies outside the United Kingdom which would be taxable supplies if made in the United Kingdom;

(*c*) such other supplies outside the United Kingdom and such exempt supplies as the Treasury may by order specify for the purposes of this subsection.

(3) The Commissioners shall make regulations for securing a fair and reasonable attribution of input tax to supplies within subsection (2) above, and any such regulations may provide for—

(*a*) determining a proportion by reference to which input tax for any prescribed accounting period is to be provisionally attributed to those supplies;

(*b*) adjusting, in accordance with a proportion determined in like manner for any longer period comprising two or more prescribed accounting periods or parts thereof, the provisional attribution for any of those periods;

(*c*) the making of payments in respect of input tax, by the Commissioners to a taxable person (or a person who has been a taxable person) or by a taxable person (or a person who has been a taxable person) to the Commissioners, in cases where events prove inaccurate an estimate on the basis of which an attribution was made; and

(*d*) preventing input tax on a supply which, under or by virtue of any provision of this Act, a person makes to himself from being allowable as attributable to that supply.

(4) Regulations under subsection (3) above may make different provision for different circumstances and, in particular (but without prejudice to the generality of that subsection) for different descriptions of goods or services; and may contain such incidental[, supplementary, consequential and transitional][1] provisions as appear to the Commissioners necessary or expedient.

Commentary—*De Voil Indirect Tax Service* **V3.460**.

Simon's Tax Cases—*C&E Comrs v Apple and Pear Development Council* [1985] STC 383*; *Neuvale Ltd v C&E Comrs* [1989] STC 395*; *St Helen's School Northwood Ltd v R&C Comrs* [2007] STC 633.

s 26(2), *WHA Ltd and another v C&E Comrs* [2004] STC 1081.

s 26(3), *C&E Comrs v University of Wales College, Cardiff* [1995] STC 611*; *Kwik-Fit (GB) Ltd v C&E Comrs* [1998] STC 159; *Banbury Visionplus Ltd v R&C Comrs and other appeals* [2006] STC 1568.

Orders—VAT (Input Tax) (Specified Supplies) Order, SI 1999/3121.

Regulations—See VAT Regulations, SI 1995/2518 regs 99–111.

VAT (Amendment) (No 2) Regulations, SI 2012/1899.

Definitions—"Business", s 94; "the Commissioners", s 96(1); "exempt supply", s 31; "input tax", s 24; "prescribed accounting period", s 25(1); "regulations", s 96(1); "supply", s 5, Sch 4; "taxable person", s 3; "taxable supply", s 4(2); "United Kingdom", s 96(11).

Press releases etc—C&E Business Brief 6/95 28-3-95 (services of investigating accountants; rules determining the person to whom they are supplied). Business Brief 23/97, 10-10-97 (Input tax blocked goods—VAT changes on sales of input tax blocked goods).

C&E Business Brief 8/01 2-7-01 (Customs' policy on the deduction of input tax incurred on expenses relating to the transfer of part of a business as a going concern).

HMRC Brief 2/10 Lennartz Accounting–new policy following ECJ case. 22 January 2010.

Cross references—See VATA 1994 s 8(3) (supplies treated as made by recipient under reverse charge provisions are not to be taken into account as supplies made by him in determining his entitlement to input tax credit under sub-s (1) of this section);

VATA 1994 s 44(6) (deemed supply to and by representative member of VAT group where a business is transferred as a going concern to a group member: deemed supply by representative member not to be taken into account in determining allowance of input tax under this section);

VATA 1994 s 54(3) (supplies under flat rate scheme for farmers: treatment of percentage of consideration as VAT for purposes of determining entitlement to input tax credit of person supplied);

VATA 1994 ss 83, 84 (appeal to a tribunal as to the proportion of input tax allowable under this section).

VAT (Input Tax) (Specified Supplies) Order, SI 1999/3121 (supplies specified for the purposes of sub-s (2)(*c*) of this section).

VAT Regulations, SI 1995/2518 reg 103(1) (extent to which input tax used or to be used in making supplies within sub-s (2)(*b*) or (*c*) of this section is to be attributed to taxable supplies).

FA 1999 s 11(1) (regs made under s 26(3), in respect of exempt supplies relating to gold, may provide that input tax is allowable as being attributable to the supplies only in relation to specified matters).

F(No 3)A 2010 Sch 8 para 4 (output tax charge where credit attributable to purported Sch 4 para 5(4) supply).

Amendments—[1] In sub-s (4), words substituted for words "and supplementary" by F(No 3)A 2010 s 19, Sch 8 para 2 with effect from 16 December 2010.

[26A Disallowance of input tax where consideration not paid

(1) Where—

(*a*) a person has become entitled to credit for any input tax, and

(*b*) the consideration for the supply to which that input tax relates, or any part of it, is unpaid at the end of the period of six months following the relevant date,

he shall be taken, as from the end of that period, not to have been entitled to credit for input tax in respect of the VAT that is referable to the unpaid consideration or part.

(2) For the purposes of subsection (1) above "the relevant date", in relation to any sum representing consideration for a supply, is—

(*a*) the date of the supply; or

(*b*) if later, the date on which the sum became payable.

(3) Regulations may make such supplementary, incidental, consequential or transitional provisions as appear to the Commissioners to be necessary or expedient for the purposes of this section.

(4) Regulations under this section may in particular—

(*a*) make provision for restoring the whole or any part of an entitlement to credit for input tax where there is a payment after the end of the period mentioned in subsection (1) above;

(*b*) make rules for ascertaining whether anything paid is to be taken as paid by way of consideration for a particular supply;

(*c*) make rules dealing with particular cases, such as those involving payment of part of the consideration or mutual debts.

(5) Regulations under this section may make different provision for different circumstances.

(6) Section 6 shall apply for determining the time when a supply is to be treated as taking place for the purposes of construing this section.][1]

Commentary—*De Voil Indirect Tax Service* **V3.450**.

Amendments—[1] This section inserted by FA 2002 s 22(1), (3) with effect for supplies made after 31 December 2002 (by virtue of SI 2002/3028).

[26AB Adjustment of output tax in respect of supplies under section 55A

(1) This section applies if—

(*a*) a person is, as a result of section 26A, taken not to have been entitled to any credit for input tax in respect of any supply, and

(*b*) the supply is one in respect of which the person is required under section 55A(6) to account for and pay VAT.

(2) The person is entitled to make an adjustment to the amount of VAT which he is so required to account for and pay.

(3) The amount of the adjustment is to be equal to the amount of the credit for the input tax to which the person is taken not to be entitled.

(4) Regulations may make such supplementary, incidental, consequential or transitional provisions as appear to the Commissioners to be necessary or expedient for the purposes of this section.

(5) Regulations under this section may in particular—

(*a*) make provision for the manner in which, and the period for which, the adjustment is to be given effect, (*b*) require the adjustment to be evidenced and quantified by reference to such records and other documents as may be specified by or under the regulations,

(*c*) require the person entitled to the adjustment to keep, for such period and in such form and manner as may be so specified, those records and documents,

(*d*) make provision for readjustments if any credit for input tax is restored under section 26A.

(6) Regulations under this section may make different provision for different circumstances.][1]

Commentary—*De Voil Indirect Tax Service* **V3.450, V3.233**.

Press releases etc—HMRC Brief 24/07, 20-3-07 (Proposed reverse charge accounting for businesses trading in mobile telephones and computer chips: announcement of targeted implementation and details of how the rules will operate in practice; and exposure of draft legislation for comment).

Regulations—VAT (Amendment) (No 2) Regulations, SI 2012/1899.

Amendments—[1] Section inserted by FA 2006 s 19(2), (8) in relation to supplies made on or after 1 June 2007 (by virtue of the Finance Act 2006, section 19, (Appointed Day) Order, SI 2007/1419).

[26B Flat-rate scheme

(1) The Commissioners may by regulations make provision under which, where a taxable person so elects, the amount of his liability to VAT in respect of his relevant supplies in any prescribed accounting period shall be the appropriate percentage of his relevant turnover for that period.

A person whose liability to VAT is to any extent determined as mentioned above is referred to in this section as participating in the flat-rate scheme.

(2) For the purposes of this section—

(*a*) a person's "relevant supplies" are all supplies made by him except supplies made at such times or of such descriptions as may be specified in the regulations;

(*b*) the "appropriate percentage" is the percentage so specified for the category of business carried on by the person in question;

(*c*) a person's "relevant turnover" is the total of—

(i) the value of those of his relevant supplies that are taxable supplies, together with the VAT chargeable on them, and

(ii) the value of those of his relevant supplies that are exempt supplies.

(3) The regulations may designate certain categories of business as categories in relation to which the references in subsection (1) above to liability to VAT are to be read as references to entitlement to credit for VAT.

(4) The regulations may provide for persons to be eligible to participate in the flat-rate scheme only in such cases and subject to such conditions and exceptions as may be specified in, or determined by or under, the regulations.

(5) Subject to such exceptions as the regulations may provide for, a participant in the flat-rate scheme shall not be entitled to credit for input tax.

This is without prejudice to subsection (3) above.

(6) The regulations may—

(*a*) provide for the appropriate percentage to be determined by reference to the category of business that a person is expected, on reasonable grounds, to carry on in a particular period;

(*b*) provide, in such circumstances as may be prescribed, for different percentages to apply in relation to different parts of the same prescribed accounting period;

(*c*) make provision for determining the category of business to be regarded as carried on by a person carrying on businesses in more than one category.

(7) The regulations may provide for the following matters to be determined in accordance with notices published by the Commissioners—

(*a*) when supplies are to be treated as taking place for the purposes of ascertaining a person's relevant turnover for a particular period;

(*b*) the method of calculating any adjustments that fall to be made in accordance with the regulations in a case where a person begins or ceases to participate in the flat-rate scheme.

(8) The regulations may make provision enabling the Commissioners—

(*a*) to authorise a person to participate in the flat-rate scheme with effect from—

(i) a day before the date of his election to participate, or

(ii) a day that is not earlier than that date but is before the date of the authorisation;

(*b*) to direct that a person shall cease to be a participant in the scheme with effect from a day before the date of the direction.

The day mentioned in paragraph (*a*)(i) above may be a day before the date on which the regulations come into force.

(9) Regulations under this section—

(*a*) may make different provision for different circumstances;

(*b*) may make such incidental, supplemental, consequential or transitional provision as the Commissioners think fit, including provision disapplying or applying with modifications any provision contained in or made under this Act.][1]

Simon's Tax Cases—26B, *R&C Comrs v Burke* [2009] EWHC 2587 (Ch), [2011] STC 625.

Regulations—Value Added Tax (Amendment) (No 2) Regulations, SI 2010/2240.

Amendments—[1] This section inserted by FA 2002 s 23(1), (4) and deemed to have come into force on 24 April 2002.

27 Goods imported for private purposes

(1) Where goods are imported by a taxable person from a place outside the member States and—

(*a*) at the time of importation they belong wholly or partly to another person; and

(*b*) the purposes for which they are to be used include private purposes either of himself or of the other,

VAT paid or payable by the taxable person on the importation of the goods shall not be regarded as input tax to be deducted or credited under section 25; but he may make a separate claim to the Commissioners for it to be repaid.

(2) The Commissioners shall allow the claim if they are satisfied that to disallow it would result, in effect, in a double charge to VAT; and where they allow it they shall do so only to the extent necessary to avoid the double charge.

(3) In considering a claim under this section, the Commissioners shall have regard to the circumstances of the importation and, so far as appearing to them to be relevant, things done with, or occurring in relation to, the goods at any subsequent time.

(4) Any amount allowed by the Commissioners on the claim shall be paid by them to the taxable person.

(5) The reference above to a person's private purposes is to purposes which are not those of any business carried on by him.

Commentary—*De Voil Indirect Tax Service* **V5.153**.

Definitions—"Business", s 94; "the Commissioners", s 96(1); "goods imported from a place outside the member States", s 15; "input tax", s 24; "VAT", ss 1, 96(1).

Cross references—See VATA 1994 s 83 (appeal to a tribunal in respect of a claim by a taxable person under this section).

VAT (Isle of Man) Order, SI 1982/1067 art 7 (references to VAT in this section to include references to VAT chargeable under Isle of Man legislation);

VAT (Isle of Man) Order, SI 1982/1067 art 8 (taxable persons for the purposes of Isle of Man VAT legislation to be treated as taxable persons for the purposes of this section).

28 Payments on account of VAT

(1) The Treasury may make an order under this section if they consider it desirable to do so in the interests of the national economy.

(2) An order under this section may provide that a taxable person of a description specified in the order shall be under a duty—

(*a*) to pay, on account of any VAT he may become liable to pay in respect of a prescribed accounting period, amounts determined in accordance with the order, and

(*b*) to do so at such times as are so determined.

[(2AA) An order under this section may provide for the matters with respect to which an appeal under section 83 lies to a tribunal to include such decisions of the Commissioners under that or any other order under this section as may be specified in the order.][2]

[(2A) The Commissioners may give directions, to persons who are or may become liable by virtue of any order under this section to make payments on account of VAT, about the manner in which they are to make such payments; and where such a direction has been given to any person and has not subsequently been withdrawn, any duty of that person by virtue of such an order to make such a payment shall have effect as if it included a requirement for the payment to be made in the manner directed.][1]

(3) Where an order is made under this section, the Commissioners may make regulations containing such supplementary, incidental or consequential provisions as appear to the Commissioners to be necessary or expedient.

(4) A provision of an order or regulations under this section may be made in such way as the Treasury or, as the case may be, the Commissioners think fit (whether by amending provisions of or made under the enactments relating to VAT or otherwise).

(5) An order or regulations under this section may make different provision for different circumstances.

Commentary—*De Voil Indirect Tax Service* **V5.110**.

Regulations—See VAT Regulations, SI 1995/2518 regs 44–48.

Orders—See VAT (Payments on Account) Order, SI 1993/2001.

Definitions—"The Commissioners", s 96(1); "prescribed accounting period", s 25(1); "regulations", s 96(1); "taxable person", s 3; "VAT", ss 1, 96(1).

Cross reference—See VATA 1994 s 97(3), (4) (procedure for making orders under this section).

Amendments—[1] Sub-s (2A) inserted by FA 1996 s 34.

[2] Sub-s (2AA) inserted by FA 1997 s 43 with effect from 19 March 1997.

29 Invoices provided by recipients of goods or services

Where—

(*a*) a taxable person ("the recipient") provides a document to himself which purports to be an invoice in respect of a taxable supply of goods or services to him by another taxable person; and

(*b*) that document understates the VAT chargeable on the supply, the Commissioners may, by notice served on the recipient and on the supplier, elect that the amount of VAT understated by the document shall be regarded for all purposes as VAT due from the recipient and not from the supplier.

Definitions—"The Commissioners", s 96(1); "document", s 96(1); "invoice", s 96(1); "supply", s 5, Sch 4; "taxable person", s 3; "taxable supply", s 4(2); "VAT", ss 1, 96(1).

PART II
RELIEFS, EXEMPTIONS AND REPAYMENTS

Reliefs etc generally available

[29A Reduced rate

(1) VAT charged on—

(*a*) any supply that is of a description for the time being specified in Schedule 7A, or

(*b*) any equivalent acquisition or importation,

shall be charged at the rate of 5 per cent.

(2) The reference in subsection (1) above to an equivalent acquisition or importation, in relation to any supply that is of a description for the time being specified in Schedule 7A, is a reference (as the case may be) to—

(*a*) any acquisition from another member State of goods the supply of which would be such a supply; or

(*b*) any importation from a place outside the member States of any such goods.

(3) The Treasury may by order vary Schedule 7A by adding to or deleting from it any description of supply or by varying any description of supply for the time being specified in it.

(4) The power to vary Schedule 7A conferred by subsection (3) above may be exercised so as to describe a supply of goods or services by reference to matters unrelated to the characteristics of the goods or services themselves.

In the case of a supply of goods, those matters include, in particular, the use that has been made of the goods.][1]

Summer Finance Bill 2015 The Summer Finance Bill introduces a "VAT lock", restricting the standard and reduced rates of VAT to current rates. Please check the latest version of the Bill and subsequent Finance Act for details.

Commentary—*De Voil Indirect Tax Service* **V3.389**.

Orders—VAT (Reduced Rate) (Cable-Suspended Passenger Transport Systems) Order, SI 2013/430.

VAT (Independence Payment) Order, SI 2013/601.

Amendments—[1] This section inserted by FA 2001 s 99(4), (7)(*c*) with effect for sub-ss (1), (2) in relation to supplies made and acquisitions and importations taking place, after 31 October 2001.

30 Zero-rating

(1) Where a taxable person supplies goods or services and the supply is zero-rated, then, whether or not VAT would be chargeable on the supply apart from this section—

(*a*) no VAT shall be charged on the supply; but

(*b*) it shall in all other respects be treated as a taxable supply;

and accordingly the rate at which VAT is treated as charged on the supply shall be nil.

(2) A supply of goods or services is zero-rated by virtue of this subsection if the goods or services are of a description for the time being specified in Schedule 8 or the supply is of a description for the time being so specified.

[(2A) A supply by a person of services which consist of applying a treatment or process to another person's goods is zero-rated by virtue of this subsection if by doing so he produces goods, and either—

(*a*) those goods are of a description for the time being specified in Schedule 8; or

(*b*) a supply by him of those goods to the person to whom he supplies the services would be of a description so specified.][2]

(3) Where goods of a description for the time being specified in that Schedule, or of a description forming part of a description of supply for the time being so specified, are acquired in the United Kingdom from another member State or imported from a place outside the member States, no VAT shall be chargeable on their acquisition or importation, except as otherwise provided in that Schedule.

(4) The Treasury may by order vary Schedule 8 by adding to or deleting from it any description or by varying any description for the time being specified in it.

[(5) The export of any goods by a charity to a place outside the member States shall for the purposes of this Act be treated as a supply made by the charity—

(*a*) in the United Kingdom, and

(*b*) in the course or furtherance of a business carried on by the charity.][1]

(6) A supply of goods is zero-rated by virtue of this subsection if the Commissioners are satisfied that the person supplying the goods—

(*a*) has exported them to a place outside the member States; or

(*b*) has shipped them for use as stores on a voyage or flight to an eventual destination outside the United Kingdom, or as merchandise for sale by retail to persons carried on such a voyage or flight in a ship or aircraft, and in either case if such other conditions, if any, as may be specified in regulations or the Commissioners may impose are fulfilled.

(7) Subsection (6)(*b*) above shall not apply in the case of goods shipped for use as stores on a voyage or flight to be made by the person to whom the goods were supplied and to be made for a purpose which is private.

(8) Regulations may provide for the zero-rating of supplies of goods, or of such goods as may be specified in the regulations, in cases where—

(*a*) the Commissioners are satisfied that the goods have been or are to be exported to a place outside the member States or that the supply in question involves both—

(i) the removal of the goods from the United Kingdom; and

(ii) their acquisition in another member State by a person who is liable for VAT on the acquisition in accordance with provisions of the law of that member State corresponding, in relation to that member State, to the provisions of section 10; and

(*b*) such other conditions, if any, as may be specified in the regulations or the Commissioners may impose are fulfilled.

[(8A) Regulations may provide for the zero-rating of supplies of goods, or of such goods as may be specified in regulations, in cases where—

(*a*) the Commissioners are satisfied that the supply in question involves both—

(i) the removal of the goods from a fiscal warehousing regime within the meaning of section 18F(2); and

(ii) their being placed in a warehousing regime in another member State, or in such member State or States as may be prescribed, where that regime is established by provisions of the law of that member State corresponding, in relation to that member State, to the provisions of sections 18A and 18B; and

(*b*) such other conditions, if any, as may be specified in the regulations or the Commissioners may impose are fulfilled.][3]

(9) Regulations may provide for the zero-rating of a supply of services which is made where goods are let on hire and the Commissioners are satisfied that the goods have been or are to be removed from the United Kingdom during the period of the letting, and such other conditions, if any, as may be specified in the regulations or the Commissioners may impose are fulfilled.

(10) Where the supply of any goods has been zero-rated by virtue of subsection (6) above or in pursuance of regulations made under [subsection (8), (8A) or (9)][2] above and—

(*a*) the goods are found in the United Kingdom after the date on which they were alleged to have been or were to be exported or shipped or otherwise removed from the United Kingdom; or

(*b*) any condition specified in the relevant regulations under [subsection (6), (8), (8A) or (9)][3] above or imposed by the Commissioners is not complied with,

and the presence of the goods in the United Kingdom after that date or the non-observance of the condition has not been authorised for the purposes of this subsection by the Commissioners, the goods shall be liable to forfeiture under the Management Act and the VAT that would have been chargeable on the supply but for the zero-rating shall become payable forthwith by the person to whom the goods were supplied or by any person in whose possession the goods are found in the United Kingdom; but the Commissioners may, if they think fit, waive payment of the whole or part of that VAT.

Commentary—*De Voil Indirect Tax Service* **V4.201, V4.202.**

Simon's Tax Cases—*R&C Comrs v Roger Skinner Ltd* [2014] UKUT 204 (TCC), [2014] STC 2335.

s 30(6), *R&C Comrs v Arkeley Ltd (in liquidation)* [2014] STC 309, [2013] UKUT 393 (TCC).

Regulations—See VAT Regulations, SI 1995/2518 regs 127–135.

Orders—See VAT (Tour Operators) Order, SI 1987/1806.

VAT (Drugs and Medicines) Order, SI 2009/2972.

VAT (Relief for European Research Infrastructure Consortia) Order, SI 2012/2907.

VAT (Independence Payment) Order, SI 2013/601.

Value Added Tax (Amendment) (No 2) Regulations, SI 2013/2241.

Value Added Tax (Drugs and Medicines) Order, SI 2014/1111.

Definitions—"Acquisition of goods from another member State", s 11; "another member State", s 96(1); "business", s 94; "the Commissioners", s 96(1); "goods being acquired by a person in another member State", s 92; "goods imported from a place outside the member States", s 15; "law of that member State", s 92; "the Management Act", s 96(1); "regulations", s 96(10); "ship", s 96(1); "supply", s 5, Sch 4; "taxable person", s 3; "taxable supply", s 4(2); "United Kingdom", s 96(11); "VAT", ss 1, 96(1).

Cross references—See VATA 1994 s 35(5) (extension of the power of the Treasury to vary Sch 8 to matters relating to the refund of VAT to persons constructing certain residential or charitable buildings).

VATA 1994 Sch 8 Group 5 note (13) (sub-s (3) of this section does not apply to goods forming part of a description of a supply within Sch 8 Group 5 (zero rating: construction of buildings etc));

VATA 1994 Sch 8 Group 10 note (2) (sub-s (3) of this section does not apply to goods forming part of a description of a supply within Sch 8 Group 10 (zero rating: gold));

VATA 1994 Sch 8 Group 12 note (1) (sub-s (3) of this section does not apply to goods forming part of a description of certain supplies within Sch 8 Group 12 (zero rating: drugs, medicines, aids for the handicapped etc)).

VAT Regulations, SI 1995/2518 reg 123 (temporary importations).

Amendments—[1] Sub-s (5) substituted by FA 1995 s 28 with effect in relation to transactions occurring on or after 1 May 1995.
[2] Sub-s (2A) inserted by FA 1996 s 29(2), with effect in relation to supplies made after 31 December 1995.
[3] Sub-s (8A) inserted and words in sub-s (10) substituted by FA 1996 s 26(1), (3) Sch 3 para 7, with effect from 29 April 1996.

31 Exempt supplies and acquisitions

(1) A supply of goods or services is an exempt supply if it is of a description for the time being specified in Schedule 9 and an acquisition of goods from another member State is an exempt acquisition if the goods are acquired in pursuance of an exempt supply.
(2) The Treasury may by order vary that Schedule by adding to or deleting from it any description of supply or by varying any description of supply for the time being specified in it, and the Schedule may be varied so as to describe a supply of goods by reference to the use which has been made of them or to other matters unrelated to the characteristics of the goods themselves.
[(3) The Treasury may by regulations make an exemption of a group 16 supply of a description specified in the regulations subject to conditions.
(4) Regulations under subsection (3) may—
  (*a*) make different provision for different cases, and
  (*b*) make consequential or transitional provision (including provision amending this Act).
(5) In subsection (3) "group 16 supply" means a supply falling within Group 16 of Schedule 9.][1]

Commentary—*De Voil Indirect Tax Service* **V3.121, V3.368, V4.101**.
Simon's Tax Cases—*Cooper and Chapman (Builders) Ltd v C&E Comrs* [1993] STC 1*.
Definitions—"Acquisition of goods from another member State", s 11; "another member State", s 96(1); "supply", s 5, Sch 4.
Cross references—See FA 1999 s 13(2) (an order under 31(2), may provide that what would other wise be an exempt supply under the terms of the order shall be, if the supplier chooses, a taxable supplies. It may also make provision by reference to public notices).
Orders—Value Added Tax (Land Exemption) Order, SI 2012/58.
Value Added Tax (Education) Order, SI 2013/1897.
Value Added Tax (Sport) Order, SI 2014/3185.
Amendments—[1] Sub-ss (3)–(5) inserted by FA 2012 s 197(3) with effect from 17 July 2012.

32 Relief on supply of certain second-hand goods

. . .

Amendments—This section repealed by FA 1995 ss 24(2), 162, Sch 29 Pt VI(3) with effect from 1 June 1995 by virtue of SI 1995/1374.

33 Refunds of VAT in certain cases

(1) Subject to the following provisions of this section, where—
  (*a*) VAT is chargeable on the supply of goods or services to a body to which this section applies, on the acquisition of any goods by such a body from another member State or on the importation of any goods by such a body from a place outside the member States, and
  (*b*) the supply, acquisition or importation is not for the purpose of any business carried on by the body,

the Commissioners shall, on a claim made by the body at such time and in such form and manner as the Commissioners may determine, refund to it the amount of the VAT so chargeable.
(2) Where goods or services so supplied to or acquired or imported by the body cannot be conveniently distinguished from goods or services supplied to or acquired or imported by it for the purpose of a business carried on by it, the amount to be refunded under this section shall be such amount as remains after deducting from the whole of the VAT chargeable on any supply to or acquisition or importation by the body such proportion thereof as appears to the Commissioners to be attributable to the carrying on of the business; but where—
  (*a*) the VAT so attributable is or includes VAT attributable, in accordance with regulations under section 26, to exempt supplies by the body, and
  (*b*) the VAT attributable to the exempt supplies is in the opinion of the Commissioners an insignificant proportion of the VAT so chargeable,

they may include it in the VAT refunded under this section.
(3) The bodies to which this section applies are—
  (*a*) a local authority;
  (*b*) a river purification board established under section 135 of the Local Government (Scotland) Act 1973 and a water development board within the meaning of section 109 of the Water (Scotland) Act 1980;
  (*c*) an internal drainage board;
  [(*d*) an Integrated Transport Authority, Passenger Transport Authority or Passenger Transport Executive for the purposes of Part 2 of the Transport Act 1968;][3]
  (*e*) a port health authority within the meaning of the Public Health (Control of Disease) Act 1984 . . .[4];
  (*f*) [a police and crime commissioner, the Mayor's Office for Policing and Crime and][5] a police authority and the Receiver for the Metropolitan Police District;

(*g*) a development corporation within the meaning of the New Towns Act 1981 or the New Towns (Scotland) Act 1968 a new town commission within the meaning of the New Towns Act (Northern Ireland) 1965 and the Commission for the New Towns;

(*h*) a general lighthouse authority within the meaning of [Part VIII of the Merchant Shipping Act 1995][1];

(*i*) the British Broadcasting Corporation;

[(*j*) the appointed news provider referred to in section 280 of the Communications Act 2003; and][2]

(*k*) any body specified for the purposes of this section by an order made by the Treasury.

(4) No VAT shall be refunded under this section to a general lighthouse authority which in the opinion of the Commissioners is attributable to activities other than those concerned with the provision, maintenance or management of lights or other navigational aids.

(5) No VAT shall be refunded under this section to [an appointed][2] news provider which in the opinion of the Commissioners is attributable to activities other than the provision of news programmes for broadcasting by holders of regional Channel 3 licences (within the meaning of Part I of the Broadcasting Act 1990).

(6) References in this section to VAT chargeable do not include any VAT which, by virtue of any order under section 25(7), is excluded from credit under that section.

Commentary—*De Voil Indirect Tax Service* **V5.162**.

Simon's Tax Cases—*R v C&E Comrs, ex p Greater Manchester Police Authority* [2000] STC 620, [2001] STC 406, CA; *Ashfield District Council v C&E Comrs* [2001] STC 1706; *R (on the application of Cardiff County Council) v C&E Comrs* [2002] STC 1318, [2004] STC 356.

s 33(1), (2), *Haringey London Borough Council v C&E Comrs* [1995] STC 830*.

s 33(3)(*f*), (*k*), *R v HM Treasury, ex p Service Authority for the National Crime Squad and other* s [2000] STC 638.

Orders—See VAT (Refund of Tax) Orders, SI 1973/2121, SI 1976/2028, SI 1985/1101, SI 1986/336, SI 1986/532, SI 1989/1217, SI 1995/1978, SI 1995/2999, SI 1997/2558, SI 1999/2076, SI 2000/1046, SI 2001/3453, 2006/1793.

VAT (Refund of Tax to Charter Trustees and Conservators) Order, SI 2009/1177.

VAT (Refund of VAT to Chief Constables and the Commissioner of Police of the Metropolis) Order, SI 2012/2393.

VAT (Refund of Tax to the Natural Resources Body for Wales) Order, SI 2013/412.

Value Added Tax (Refund of Tax) Order, SI 2014/1112.

Value Added Tax (Refund of Tax to the London Legacy Development Corporation) Order, SI 2015/449.

Definitions—"Acquisition of goods from another member State", s 11; "another member State", s 96(1); "the Commissioners", s 96(1); "exempt supply", s 31; "goods imported from a place outside the member States", s 15; "local authority", s 96(1), (4); "regulations", s 96(1); "supply ", s 5, Sch 4; "VAT", ss 1, 96(1).

Press releases etc—C&E Business Brief 9/95 18-5-95 (services between local authorities).

HMRC Brief 53/09, 18-8-09 (VAT recovery on expenditure relating to capital works at voluntary aided schools).

Cross references—See VATA 1994 s 80(5) (repayment supplement: treatment as refund due under this section);

VATA 1994 s 90(3) (VAT repaid as a result of the failure of a resolution under PCTA 1968 may not be refunded under this section).

VAT (Isle of Man) Order, SI 1982/1067 art 7 (references to VAT in this section to include references to VAT chargeable under Isle of Man legislation).

Amendments—[1] Words in sub-s (3)(h) substituted by the Merchant Shipping Act 1995 Sch 13 para 95 with effect from 1 January 1996.

[2] Sub-s (3)(j) substituted, and words in sub-s (5) substituted, by the Communications Act 2003 s 406, Sch 17 para 129(1), (2) with effect from 29 December 2003 (by virtue of SI 2003/3142).

[3] Sub-s (3)(d) substituted, in relation to England and Wales, by the Local Transport Act 2008 s 77(5), Sch 4 para 59 with effect from 9 February 2009 (by virtue of SI 2009/107 art 2(1), Sch 1 Pt 1).

[4] In sub-s (3)(*e*), words "and a port local authority and joint port local authority constituted under Part X of the Public Health (Scotland) Act 1897" repealed by the Public Health etc (Scotland) Act 2008 s 126(1), Sch 3 Pt 1 with effect from 1 October 2009 (by virtue of SSI 2009/319 art 2(*a*), Sch 1).

[5] In sub-s (3)(*f*) words inserted by the Police Reform and Social Responsibility Act 2011, s 99, Sch 16, Pt 3, para 217 with effect from 16 January 2012 (by virtue of SI 2011/3019 art 3, Sch 1 para *nnn* (iii)).

Prospective amendments—In sub-s (3)(*f*), words "and the Receiver for the Metropolitan Police District" to be repealed by the Greater London Authority Act 1999, s 325, Sch 27 para 68 with effect from a day to be appointed.

[33A Refunds of VAT to museums and galleries

(1) Subsections (2) to (5) below apply where—

(*a*) VAT is chargeable on—

(i) the supply of goods or services to a body to which this section applies,

(ii) the acquisition of any goods by such a body from another member State, or

(iii) the importation of any goods by such a body from a place outside the member States,

(*b*) the supply, acquisition or importation is attributable to the provision by the body of free rights of admission to a relevant museum or gallery, and

(*c*) the supply is made, or the acquisition or importation takes place, on or after 1st April 2001.

(2) The Commissioners shall, on a claim made by the body in such form and manner as the Commissioners may determine, refund to the body the amount of VAT so chargeable.

(3) The claim must be made before the end of the claim period.

(4) Subject to subsection (5) below, "the claim period" is the period of [4 years][2] beginning with the day on which the supply is made or the acquisition or importation takes place.

(5) If the Commissioners so determine, the claim period is such shorter period beginning with that day as the Commissioners may determine.

(6) Subsection (7) below applies where goods or services supplied to, or acquired or imported by, a body to which this section applies that are attributable to free admissions cannot conveniently be distinguished from goods or services supplied to, or acquired or imported by, the body that are not attributable to free admissions.

(7) The amount to be refunded on a claim by the body under this section shall be such amount as remains after deducting from the VAT related to the claim such proportion of that VAT as appears to the Commissioners to be attributable otherwise than to free admissions.

(8) For the purposes of subsections (6) and (7) above—

(*a*) goods or services are, and VAT is, attributable to free admissions if they are, or it is, attributable to the provision by the body of free rights of admission to a relevant museum or gallery;

(*b*) the VAT related to a claim is the whole of the VAT chargeable on—

(i) the supplies to the body, and

(ii) the acquisitions and importations by the body,

to which the claim relates.

(9) The Treasury may by order—

(*a*) specify a body as being a body to which this section applies;

(*b*) when specifying a body under paragraph (*a*), specify any museum or gallery that, for the purposes of this section, is a "relevant" museum or gallery in relation to the body;

(*c*) specify an additional museum or gallery as being, for the purposes of this section, a "relevant" museum or gallery in relation to a body to which this section applies;

(*d*) when specifying a museum or gallery under paragraph (*b*) or (*c*), provide that this section shall have effect in the case of the museum or gallery as if in subsection (1)(*c*) there were substituted for 1st April 2001 a later date specified in the order.

(10) References in this section to VAT do not include any VAT which, by virtue of any order under section 25(7), is excluded from credit under that section.][1]

Commentary—*De Voil Indirect Tax Service* **V5.162A**.

Orders—See VAT (Refund of Tax to Museums and Galleries) Order, SI 2001/2879.

Press releases etc—Business Brief 16/01, 19-11-01, Concession for "section 33A" museums and galleries.

Amendments—[1] This section inserted by FA 2001 s 98(2), (10), (11) with effect from 11 May 2001 for the purpose only of the exercise of the power to make orders under sub-s (9). Subject to that, this section comes into force on 1 September 2001.

[2] In sub-s (4) words substituted for words "3 years" by FA 2008 s 118, Sch 39 paras 32, 33 with effect from 1 April 2009 (by virtue of SI 2009/403). FA 2008 Sch 39 para 33 is disregarded where, for the purposes of VATA 1994 s 33A, the day on which the supply was made or the acquisition or importation took place was on or before 31 March 2006 (SI 2009/403 art 3).

[33B Refunds of VAT to Academies

(1) This section applies where—

(*a*) VAT is chargeable on—

(i) the supply of goods or services to the proprietor of an Academy,

(ii) the acquisition of any goods from another member State by the proprietor of an Academy, or

(iii) the importation of any goods from a place outside the member States by the proprietor of an Academy, and

(*b*) the supply, acquisition or importation is not for the purposes of any business carried on by the proprietor of the Academy.

(2) The Commissioners shall, on a claim made by the proprietor of the Academy at such time and in such form and manner as the Commissioners may determine, refund to that proprietor the amount of VAT so chargeable.

(3) Subject to subsection (4), the claim must be made before the end of the period of 4 years beginning with the day on which the supply is made or the acquisition or importation takes place.

(4) If the Commissioners so determine, the claim period is such shorter period beginning with that day as the Commissioners may determine.

(5) Subsection (6) applies where goods or services supplied to, or acquired or imported by, the proprietor of the Academy cannot be conveniently distinguished from goods or services supplied to, or acquired or imported by, it for the purpose of a business carried on by that proprietor.

(6) The amount to be refunded under this section is such amount as remains after deducting from the whole of the VAT chargeable on any supply to, or acquisition or importation by, the proprietor of the Academy such proportion of that VAT as appears to the Commissioners to be attributable to the carrying on of the business.

(7) References in this section to VAT do not include any VAT which, by virtue of an order under section 25(7), is excluded from credit under section 25.

(8) In this section—

(*a*) references to the proprietor of an Academy are to the proprietor of the Academy acting in that capacity, and (*b*) "Academy" and "proprietor" have the same meaning as in the Education Act 1996 (see section 579 of that Act).][1]

Commentary—*De Voil Indirect Tax Service* **V5.162C**.

Amendments—[1] Section 33B inserted by FA 2011 s 76(1) with effect in relation to supplies made, and acquisitions and importations taking place, on or after 1 April 2011.

[33C Refunds of VAT to charities within section 33D

(1) This section applies to a charity that falls within any of the descriptions in section 33D. A charity to which this section applies is referred to in this section as a "qualifying charity".

(2) This section applies where—

(*a*) VAT is chargeable on—

(i) the supply of goods or services to a qualifying charity,

(ii) the acquisition of any goods from another member State by a qualifying charity, or

(iii) the importation of any goods from a place outside the member States by a qualifying charity, and

(*b*) the supply, acquisition or importation is not for the purpose of any business carried on by the qualifying charity.

(3) The Commissioners shall, on a claim made by the qualifying charity at such time and in such form and manner as the Commissioners may determine, refund to the qualifying charity the amount of the VAT so chargeable.

(4) A claim under subsection (3) above in respect of a supply, acquisition or importation must be made before the end of the period of 4 years beginning with the day on which the supply is made or the acquisition or importation takes place.

(5) Subsection (6) applies where goods or services supplied to, or acquired or imported by, a qualifying charity otherwise than for the purpose of any business carried on by the qualifying charity cannot be conveniently distinguished from goods or services supplied to, or acquired or imported by, the qualifying charity for the purpose of such a business.

(6) The amount to be refunded under this section is such amount as remains after deducting from the whole of the VAT chargeable on any supply to, or acquisition or importation by, the qualifying charity such proportion of that VAT as appears to the Commissioners to be attributable to the carrying on of the business.

(7) References in this section to VAT do not include any VAT which, by virtue of an order under section 25(7), is excluded from credit under section 25.][1]

Amendments—[1] Sections 33C, 33D inserted by FA 2015 s 66(1) with effect in relation to supplies made, and acquisitions and importations taking place, on or after 1 April 2015.

[33D Charities to which section 33C applies

Palliative care charities

(1) "Palliative care charity" means a charity the main purpose of which is the provision of palliative care at the direction of, or under the supervision of, a medical professional to persons who are in need of such care as a result of having a terminal illness.

(2) In subsection (1) "medical professional" means—

(*a*) a registered medical practitioner, or

(*b*) a registered nurse.

Air ambulance charities

(3) "Air ambulance charity" means a charity the main purpose of which is to provide an air ambulance service in pursuance of arrangements made by, or at the request of, a relevant NHS body.

(4) In subsection (3) "relevant NHS body" means a body the main purpose of which is to provide ambulance services and which is—

(*a*) an NHS foundation trust in England,

(*b*) an NHS trust in Wales,

(*c*) a Special Health Board constituted under section 2 of the National Health Service (Scotland) Act 1978, or

(*d*) a Health and Social Care trust established under the Health and Personal Social Services (Northern Ireland) Order 1991.

Search and rescue charities

(5) "Search and rescue charity" means a charity that meets condition A or B.

(6) Condition A is that—

(*a*) the main purpose of the charity is to carry out search and rescue activities in the United Kingdom or the UK marine area, and

(*b*) the search and rescue activities carried out by the charity are co-ordinated by a relevant authority.

(7) Condition B is that the main purpose of the charity is to support, develop and promote the activities of a charity which meets condition A.

(8) For the purposes of subsection (6)—

"search and rescue activities" means searching for, and rescuing, persons who are, or may be, at risk of death or serious injury;

"relevant authority" means—

(*a*) the Secretary of State;

(*b*) a police force;

(*c*) the Scottish Fire and Rescue Service;

(*d*) any other person or body specified for the purposes of subsection (6) by an order made by the Treasury;

"police force" means—

(*a*) a police force within the meaning of the Police Act 1996;

(*b*) the Police Service of Scotland;

(*c*) the Police Service of Northern Ireland;

(*d*) the Police Service of Northern Ireland Reserve;

(*e*) the British Transport Police Force;

(*f*) the Civil Nuclear Constabulary;

(*g*) the Ministry of Defence Police;

"UK marine area" has the meaning given by section 42(1) of the Marine and Coastal Access Act 2009.

Medical courier charities

(9) "Medical courier charity" means a charity that meets condition A or B.

(10) Condition A is that the main purpose of the charity is to provide services for the transportation of items intended for use for medical purposes, including in particular—

(*a*) blood;

(*b*) medicines and other medical supplies;

(*c*) items relating to people who are undergoing medical treatment.

(11) Condition B is that the main purpose of the charity is to support, develop and promote the activities of a charity which meets condition A.

(12) In subsection (10) "item" includes any substance.][1]

NoteUntil the Health and Social Care Act 2012 s 79 (which abolishes NHS trusts in England) is fully brought into force, references in this section to an NHS foundation trust in England include an NHS trust in England (FA 2015 s 66(6)).

Amendments—[1] Sections 33C, 33D inserted by FA 2015 s 66(1) with effect in relation to supplies made, and acquisitions and importations taking place, on or after 1 April 2015.

34 Capital goods

(1) The Treasury may by order make provision for the giving of relief, in such cases, to such extent and subject to such exceptions as may be specified in the order, from VAT paid on the supply, acquisition or importation for the purpose of a business carried on by any person of machinery or plant or any specified description of machinery or plant in cases where that VAT or part of that VAT cannot be credited under section 25 and such other conditions are satisfied as may be specified in the order.

(2) Without prejudice to the generality of subsection (1) above, an order under this section may provide for relief to be given by deduction or refunding of VAT and for aggregating or excluding the aggregation of value where goods of the same description are supplied, acquired or imported together.

Commentary—*De Voil Indirect Tax Service* **V5.166**.

35 Refund of VAT to persons constructing certain buildings

[(1) Where—

(*a*) a person carries out works to which this section applies,

(*b*) his carrying out of the works is lawful and otherwise than in the course or furtherance of any business, and

(*c*) VAT is chargeable on the supply, acquisition or importation of any goods used by him for the purposes of the works,

the Commissioners shall, on a claim made in that behalf, refund to that person the amount of VAT so chargeable.

(1A) The works to which this section applies are—

(*a*) the construction of a building designed as a dwelling or number of dwellings;

(*b*) the construction of a building for use solely for a relevant residential purpose or relevant charitable purpose; and

(*c*) a residential conversion.

(1B) For the purposes of this section goods shall be treated as used for the purposes of works to which this section applies by the person carrying out the works in so far only as they are building materials which, in the course of the works, are incorporated in the building in question or its site.

(1C) Where—

(*a*) a person ("the relevant person") carries out a residential conversion by arranging for any of the work of the conversion to be done by another ("a contractor"),

(*b*) the relevant person's carrying out of the conversion is lawful and otherwise than in the course or furtherance of any business,

(*c*) the contractor is not acting as an architect, surveyor or consultant or in a supervisory capacity, and

(*d*) VAT is chargeable on services consisting in the work done by the contractor,

the Commissioners shall, on a claim made in that behalf, refund to the relevant person the amount of VAT so chargeable.

(1D) For the purposes of this section works constitute a residential conversion to the extent that they consist in the conversion of a non-residential building, or a non-residential part of a building, into—

(*a*) a building designed as a dwelling or a number of dwellings;

(*b*) a building intended for use solely for a relevant residential purpose; or

(*c*) anything which would fall within paragraph (*a*) or (*b*) above if different parts of a building were treated as separate buildings.][1]

(2) The Commissioners shall not be required to entertain a claim for a refund of VAT under this section unless the claim—

(*a*) is made within such time and in such form and manner, and

(*b*) contains such information, and

(*c*) is accompanied by such documents, whether by way of evidence or otherwise,

[as may be specified by regulations or by the Commissioners in accordance with regulations.][3].

(3) This section shall have effect—

(*a*) as if the reference in subsection (1) above to the VAT chargeable on the supply of any goods included a reference to VAT chargeable on the supply in accordance with the law of another member State; and

(*b*) in relation to VAT chargeable in accordance with the law of another member State, as if references to refunding VAT to any person were references to paying that person an amount equal to the VAT chargeable in accordance with the law of that member State;

and the provisions of this Act and of any other enactment or subordinate legislation (whenever passed or made) so far as they relate to a refund under this section shall be construed accordingly.

[(4) The notes to Group 5 of Schedule 8 shall apply for construing this section as they apply for construing that Group [but this is subject to subsection (4A) below.][2]

[(4A) The meaning of "non-residential" given by Note (7A) of Group 5 of Schedule 8 (and not that given by Note (7) of that Group) applies for the purposes of this section but as if—

(*a*) references in that Note to item 3 of that Group were references to this section, and

(*b*) paragraph (*b*)(iii) of that Note were omitted.][2]

(5) The power of the Treasury by order under section 30 to vary Schedule 8 shall include—

(*a*) power to apply any variation made by the order for the purposes of this section; and

(*b*) power to make such consequential modifications of this section as they may think fit.][1]

Commentary—*De Voil Indirect Tax Service* **V5.164**.

Regulations—See VAT Regulations, SI 1995/2518 regs 200, 201.

VAT (Amendment) (No 2) Regulations, SI 2012/1899.

Press releases etc—News Release 15/96, 13-3-96 (C&E will consider making refunds of VAT under the DIY scheme to certain charitable organisations, even though they are in business, which are unable to sell the converted property).

Simon's Tax Cases—*C&E Comrs v Arnold* [1996] STC 1271*; *C&E Comrs v Blom-Cooper* [2002] STC 1061, [2003] STC 669; *C&E Comrs v Jacobs* [2005] STC 1518; *R&C Comrs v Patel* [2014] UKUT 361 (TCC), [2015] STC 148.

Definitions—"Acquisition of goods from another member State", s 11; "another member State", s 96(1); "building designed as a dwelling or number of dwellings", Sch 8 Group 5 note (2); "building materials", Sch 8 Group 5 note (22); "business", s 94; "the Commissioners", s 96(1); "document", s 96(1); "importation of goods from a place outside the member States", s 15; "law of another member State", s 92; "non-residential building", Sch 8 Group 5 note (7); "regulations", s 96(1); "relevant charitable purpose", Sch 8 Group 5 note (6); "relevant residential purpose", Sch 8 Group 5 note (4); "subordinate legislation", s 96(10); "supply", s 5, Sch 4; "VAT", ss 1, 96(1); "zero-rating", s 30.

Cross references—See VATA 1994 s 60(1), (2) (civil penalty for evading VAT by dishonestly claiming a refund under this section);

VATA 1994 s 72(1), (2) (criminal penalty for fraudulent evasion of VAT by falsely claiming a refund under this section);

VATA 1994 s 83 (appeal to a tribunal in respect of the amount of a refund under this section);

VATA 1994 s 90(3) (VAT repaid as a result of the failure of a resolution under PCTA 1968 may not be refunded under this section).

VAT (Isle of Man) Order, SI 1982/1067 art 9 (this section does not apply to the construction of dwellings in the Isle of Man).

VAT (Conversion of Buildings) Order, SI 2001/2305 art 4 (VATA 1994 Sch 8 Group 5 note (7A)shall apply for the purposes of this section).

Amendments—[1] Sub-ss (1), (1A)–(1D) substituted for sub-s (1), and sub-ss (4), (5) added by FA 1996 s 30, with effect in relation to any case in which a claim for repayment under this section is made at any time on or after 29 April 1996.

[2] Sub-s (4) amended, and sub-s (4A) inserted, by the VAT (Conversion of Buildings) Order, SI 2001/2305 arts 1, 4 with effect for supplies made after 31 July 2001.

[3] In sub-s (2), words substituted for words "as the Commissioners may by regulations prescribe or, in the case of documents, as the Commissioners may determine in accordance with the regulations.", by FA 2012 s 204, Sch 29 paras 1, 4 with effect from 17 July 2012.

36 Bad debts

(1) Subsection (2) below applies where—

(*a*) a person has supplied goods or services [. . .][2] and has accounted for and paid VAT on the supply,

(*b*) the whole or any part of the consideration for the supply has been written off in his accounts as a bad debt, and

(*c*) a period of 6 months (beginning with the date of the supply) has elapsed.

(2) Subject to the following provisions of this section and to regulations under it the person shall be entitled, on making a claim to the Commissioners, to a refund of the amount of VAT chargeable by reference to the outstanding amount.

[(3) In subsection (2) above "the outstanding amount" means—

(*a*) if at the time of the claim no part of the consideration written off in the claimant's accounts as a bad debt has been received, an amount equal to the amount of the consideration so written off;

(*b*) if at that time any part of the consideration so written off has been received, an amount by which that part is exceeded by the amount of the consideration written off;

and in this subsection "received" means received either by the claimant or by a person to whom has been assigned a right to receive the whole or any part of the consideration written off.][5]

[(3A) For the purposes of this section, where the whole or any part of the consideration for the supply does not consist of money, the amount in money that shall be taken to represent any non-monetary part of the consideration shall be so much of the amount made up of—

(*a*) the value of the supply, and

(*b*) the VAT charged on the supply,

as is attributable to the non-monetary consideration in question.][4]

(4) A person shall not be entitled to a refund under subsection (2) above unless—

(*a*) the value of the supply is equal to or less than its open market value, . . . [1]

(*b*) . . . [1]

(4A) . . . [7]

(5) Regulations under this section may—

(*a*) require a claim to be made at such time and in such form and manner as may be specified by or under the regulations;

(*b*) require a claim to be evidenced and quantified by reference to such records and other documents as may be so specified;

(*c*) require the claimant to keep, for such period and in such form and manner as may be so specified, those records and documents and a record of such information relating to the claim and to [anything subsequently received][3] by way of consideration as may be so specified;

(*d*) require the repayment of a refund allowed under this section where any requirement of the regulations is not complied with;

(*e*) require the repayment of the whole or, as the case may be, an appropriate part of a refund allowed under this section [where any part (or further part) of the consideration written off in the claimant's accounts as a bad debt is subsequently received either by the claimant or, except in such circumstances as may be prescribed, by a person to whom has been assigned a right to receive the whole or any part of that consideration;][6]

(*ea*) . . . [7]

(*f*) include such supplementary, incidental, consequential or transitional provisions as appear to the Commissioners to be necessary or expedient for the purposes of this section;

(*g*) make different provision for different circumstances.

(6) The provisions which may be included in regulations by virtue of subsection (5)(*f*) above may include rules for ascertaining—

(*a*) whether, when and to what extent consideration is to be taken to have been written off in accounts as a bad debt;

(*b*) whether [anything received][3] is to be taken as received by way of consideration for a particular supply;

(*c*) whether, and to what extent, [anything received][3] is to be taken as received by way of consideration written off in accounts as a bad debt.

(7) The provisions which may be included in regulations by virtue of subsection (5)(*f*) above may include rules dealing with particular cases, such as those involving [receipt of part of the consideration][3] or mutual debts; and in particular such rules may vary the way in which the following amounts are to be calculated—

(*a*) the outstanding amount mentioned in subsection (2) above, and

(*b*) the amount of any repayment where a refund has been allowed under this section.

(8) Section 6 shall apply for determining the time when a supply is to be treated as taking place for the purposes of construing this section.

Commentary—*De Voil Indirect Tax Service* **V5.156.**

Regulations—VAT Regulations, SI 1995/2518 regs 156–172.
VAT (Amendment) (No 3) Regulations, SI 2014/2430.
Press releases etc—Business Brief 9/97, 27-3-97 (changes to the VAT bad debt relief scheme). Business Brief 21/97, 3-10-97 (bad debt relief scheme changes for barter transactions). Business Brief 5/98 10.2.98 (VAT bad debt relief—insolvency practitioners). Business Brief 19/01, 6-12-01 (VAT—bad debt relief on goods supplied by hire purchase or conditional sale).
Simon's Tax Cases—*Goldsmiths (Jewellers) Ltd v C&E Comrs* (Case C-330/95) [1997] STC 1073*; *Simpson & Marwick (a firm) v R&C Comrs* [2011] UKUT 498 (TCC), [2012] STC 611.
Definitions—"The Commissioners", s 96(1); "document", s 96(1); "money", s 96(1); "open market value of a supply of goods or services", s 19(5); "regulations", s 96(1); "supply", s 5, Sch 4; "VAT", ss 1, 96(1); "value of supply of goods or services", s 19, Sch 6.
Cross references—See VATA 1994 s 60(1), (2) (civil penalty for evading VAT by dishonestly claiming a refund under this section);
VATA 1994 s 72(1), (2) (criminal penalty for fraudulent evasion of VAT by falsely claiming a refund under this section);
VATA 1994 s 83 (appeal to a tribunal in respect of a claim for a refund under this section);
VATA 1994 Sch 13 para 9 (claims for refunds of VAT relating to supplies made between 1 April 1989 and 31 August 1994).
VATA 1994 Sch 3B para 16L, Sch 3BA para 32 (amendment of return under special scheme/non-UK special scheme, to account for writing off of bad debt, treated as a refund claim under sub-s (2)).
Value Added Tax Regulations, SI 1995/2158 reg 6(3)(*d*) (rights to claims for refunds of VAT on transfer of going concern).
FA 1999 s 15(4) (Value Added Tax Regulations, SI 1995/2518 Part XIX, other than reg 171, shall, subject to provisions made under VATA 1994 s 36, be read as if a reference to a payment being received by the claimant includes a payment received by a person to whom a right to receive it has been assigned).
Amendments—[1] Sub-s (4)(b), and the word "and" immediately preceding it, repealed by FA 1997 s 39(1), Sch 18 Pt IV(3) in respect of any claim made under this section in relation to a supply of goods made after 19 March 1997.
[2] In sub-s (1)(a) the words "for a consideration in money" repealed by FA 1998 s 23(1), Sch 27 Part II with effect from 31 July 1998.
[3] Words in sub-ss (3)(a), (b), (5)(c), (6)(b), (c) and (7) substituted by FA 1998 s 23 with effect from 31 July 1998.
[4] Sub-s (3A) inserted by FA 1998 s 23 with effect from 31 July 1998.
[5] Sub-s (3) substituted by FA 1999 s 15 with effect for the purposes of the making of any refund or repayment after 9 March 1999, but do not have effect in relation to anything received on or before that day.
[6] Words in sub-s (5)(e) substituted by FA 1999 s 15 with effect from 27 July 1999.
[7] Sub-ss (4A) and (5)(ea) repealed by FA 2002 ss 22(2), (3), 139, Sch 40 Pt 2(1) with effect for supplies made after 31 December 2002 (by virtue of SI 2002/3028).

[Acquisitions

36A Relief from VAT on acquisition if importation would attract relief

(1) The Treasury may by order make provision for relieving from VAT the acquisition from another member State of any goods if, or to the extent that, relief from VAT would be given by an order under section 37 if the acquisition were an importation from a place outside the member States.
(2) An order under this section may provide for relief to be subject to such conditions as appear to the Treasury to be necessary or expedient.
These may—

(*a*) include conditions prohibiting or restricting the disposal of or dealing with the goods concerned;
(*b*) be framed by reference to the conditions to which, by virtue of any order under section 37 in force at the time of the acquisition, relief under such an order would be subject in the case of an importation of the goods concerned.

(3) Where relief from VAT given by an order under this section was subject to a condition that has been breached or not complied with, the VAT shall become payable at the time of the breach or, as the case may be, at the latest time allowed for compliance.][1]

Commentary—*De Voil Indirect Tax Service* **V3.398**.
Orders—See the VAT (Acquisitions) Relief Order, SI 2002/1935.
VAT (Relief for European Research Infrastructure Consortia) Order, SI 2012/2907.
Amendments—[1] This section inserted by FA 2002 s 25 with effect from 24 July 2002.

Imports, overseas businesses etc

37 Relief from VAT on importation of goods

(1) The Treasury may by order make provision for giving relief from the whole or part of the VAT chargeable on the importation of goods from places outside the member States, subject to such conditions (including conditions prohibiting or restricting the disposal of or dealing with the goods) as may be imposed by or under the order, if and so far as the relief appears to the Treasury to be necessary or expedient, having regard to any international agreement or arrangements.
(2) In any case where—

(*a*) it is proposed that goods which have been imported from a place outside the member States by any person ("the original importer") with the benefit of relief under subsection (1) above shall be transferred to another person ("the transferee"), and
(*b*) on an application made by the transferee, the Commissioners direct that this subsection shall apply,

this Act shall have effect as if, on the date of the transfer of the goods (and in place of the transfer), the goods were exported by the original importer and imported by the transferee and, accordingly, where appropriate, provision made under subsection (1) above shall have effect in relation to the VAT chargeable on the importation of the goods by the transferee.

(3) The Commissioners may by regulations make provision for remitting or repaying, if they think fit, the whole or part of the VAT chargeable on the importation of any goods from places outside the member States which are shown to their satisfaction to have been previously exported from the United Kingdom or removed from any member State.

(4) The Commissioners may by regulations make provision for remitting or repaying the whole or part of the VAT chargeable on the importation of any goods from places outside the member States if they are satisfied that the goods have been or are to be re-exported or otherwise removed from the United Kingdom and they think fit to do so in all the circumstances and having regard—

(*a*) to the VAT chargeable on the supply of like goods in the United Kingdom;

(*b*) to any VAT which may have become chargeable in another member State in respect of the goods

Commentary—*De Voil Indirect Tax Service* **V3.316**.

Regulations—See VAT Regulations, SI 1995/2518 regs 123–126.

VAT (Imported Gas, Electricity, Heat and Cooling) Relief Order, SI 2010/2924

Orders—See VAT (Imported Goods) Relief Order, SI 1984/746; VAT (Small Non-commercial Consignments) Relief Order, SI 1986/939; VAT (Imported Gold) Relief Order, SI 1992/3124; VAT (Importation of Investment Gold) Relief Order, SI 1999/3115; VAT (Relief for European Research Infrastructure Consortia) Order, SI 2012/2907; VAT (Imported Goods) Relief (Amendment) Order, SI 2014/2364.

Press releases etc—News Release 35/97, 12-12-97 (New VAT avoidance on property developments blocked).

Definitions—"Another member State", s 96(1); "the Commissioners", s 96(1); "importation of goods from places outside the member States", s 15; "regulations", s 96(1); "supply" s 5, Sch 4; "United Kingdom", s 96(11); "VAT", ss 1, 96(1).

Cross references—See FA 1999 s 13(3) (an order made under s 37(1) which gives relief from VAT on certain importations of gold may make provision by reference to public notices).

38 Importation of goods by taxable persons

The Commissioners may by regulations make provision for enabling goods imported from a place outside the member States by a taxable person in the course or furtherance of any business carried on by him to be delivered or removed, subject to such conditions or restrictions as the Commissioners may impose for the protection of the revenue, without payment of the VAT chargeable on the importation, and for that VAT to be accounted for together with the VAT chargeable on the supply of goods or services by him or on the acquisition of goods by him from other member States.

Commentary—*De Voil Indirect Tax Service* **V5.122**.

Regulations—See VAT Regulations, SI 1995/2518 reg 122.

Definitions—"Acquisition of goods from other member States", s 11; "business", s 94; "the Commissioners", s 96(1); "goods imported from a place outside the member States", s 15; "other member States", s 96(1); "regulations", s 96(1); "supply", s 5, Sch 4; "taxable person", s 3; "VAT", ss 1, 96(1).

Cross references—See VATA 1994 s 43(1) (VAT groups: goods imported by group companies to be treated as imported by representative member for purposes of this section).

VAT (Isle of Man) Order, SI 1982/1067 art 8 (taxable persons for the purposes of Isle of Man VAT legislation to be treated as taxable persons for the purposes of this section).

39 Repayment of VAT to those in business overseas

(1) The Commissioners may, by means of a scheme embodied in regulations, provide for the repayment, to persons to whom this section applies, of VAT on supplies to them in the United Kingdom or on the importation of goods by them from places outside the member States which would be input tax of theirs if they were taxable persons in the United Kingdom.

(2) This section—

(*a*) applies to persons carrying on business in another member State, and

(*b*) shall apply also to persons carrying on business in other countries, if, pursuant to any Community Directive, rules are adopted by the Council of the Communities about refunds of VAT to persons established elsewhere than in the member States,

but does not apply to persons carrying on business in the United Kingdom.

(3) Repayment shall be made in such cases [and to such extent][1] only, and subject to such conditions, as the scheme may prescribe (being conditions specified in the regulations or imposed by the Commissioners either generally or in particular cases); and the scheme may provide—

[(*za*) for claims to be made in such form and manner as may be specified in the scheme or by the Commissioners in accordance with the scheme;][2]

(*a*) for claims and repayments to be made only through agents in the United Kingdom;

(*b*) either generally or for specified purposes—

(i) for the agents to be treated under this Act as if they were taxable persons; and

(ii) for treating claims as if they were returns under this Act [in respect of such period as may be prescribed][1] and repayments as if they were repayments of input tax;

[(*ba*) for and in connection with the payment of interest to or by the Commissioners (including in relation to the repayment of interest wrongly paid), and][1]

[(*c*) for generally regulating—

(i) the time by which claims must be made, and

(ii) the methods by which the amount of any repayment is to be determined and the repayment is to be made.][2]

Commentary—*De Voil Indirect Tax Service* **V5.151, V5.152.**

Regulations—See VAT Regulations, SI 1995/2518 regs 173–197.

VAT (Amendment) (No 2) Regulations, SI 2012/1899.

VAT (Amendment) (No 3) Regulations, SI 2014/2430.

Definitions—"Another member State", s 96(1); "business", s 94; "the Commissioners", s 96(1); "importation of goods from places outside the member States", s 15; "input tax", s 24; "regulations", s 96(1); "supply", s 5, Sch 4; "taxable person", s 3; "United Kingdom", s 96(11); "VAT", ss 1, 96(1).

Cross references—See VATA 1994 s 54(5) (supplies under flat rate scheme for farmers: power to provide for repayment of percentage of consideration paid by persons carrying on business overseas as if it were VAT);

VATA 1994 s 60(1), (2) (civil penalty for evading VAT by dishonestly claiming a repayment under this section);

VATA 1994 s 72(1), (2) (criminal penalty for fraudulent evasion of VAT by falsely claiming a repayment under this section).

VAT (Isle of Man) Order, SI 1982/1067 art 7 (references to VAT in this section to include references to VAT chargeable under Isle of Man legislation).

VATA 1994 Sch 18 para 20 (power of Commissioners to make regulations under this section in relation to refund of VAT on certain supplies to participants in special accounting schemes under Directive 2008/9/EC (e-services)).

Amendments—[1] In sub-s (3) words inserted, and para (*ba*) inserted by FA 2009 s 77 with effect from 21 July 2009.

[2] In sub-s (3), para (*za*) inserted, and para (*c*) substituted, by FA 2012 s 204, Sch 29 paras 1, 5 with effect from 17 July 2012.

[39A Applications for forwarding of VAT repayment claims to other member States

The Commissioners must make arrangements for dealing with applications made to the Commissioners by taxable persons, in accordance with Council Directive 2008/9/EC, for the forwarding to the tax authorities of another member State of claims for refunds of VAT on—

(*a*) supplies to them in that member State, or

(*b*) the importation of goods by them into that member State from places outside the member States.][1]

Amendments—[1] Section 39A inserted by FA 2009 s 77 with effect from 21 July 2009.

40 Refunds in relation to new means of transport supplied to other member States

(1) Subject to subsection (2) below, where a person who is not a taxable person makes such a supply of goods consisting in a new means of transport as involves the removal of the goods to another member State, the Commissioners shall, on a claim made in that behalf, refund to that person, as the case may be—

(*a*) the amount of any VAT on the supply of that means of transport to that person, or

(*b*) the amount of any VAT paid by that person on the acquisition of that means of transport from another member State or on its importation from a place outside the member States.

(2) The amount of VAT refunded under this section shall not exceed the amount that would have been payable on the supply involving the removal if it had been a taxable supply by a taxable person and had not been zero-rated.

(3) The Commissioners shall not be entitled to entertain a claim for refund of VAT under this section unless the claim—

(*a*) is made within such time and in such form and manner;

(*b*) contains such information; and

(*c*) is accompanied by such documents, whether by way of evidence or otherwise,

as the Commissioners may by regulations prescribe.

Commentary—*De Voil Indirect Tax Service* **V5.154**.

Regulations—See VAT Regulations, SI 1995/2518 regs 146, 149–154.

Definitions—"Acquisition from another member State", s 11; "another member State", s 96(1); "the Commissioners", s 96(1); "document", s 96(1); "importation from a place outside the member States", s 15; "means of transport", s 95; "new means of transport", s 95; "regulations", s 96(1); "supply", s 5, Sch 4; "taxable person", s 3; "taxable supply", s 4(2); "VAT", ss 1, 96(1); "zero-rated", s 30.

Cross references—See VATA 1994 s 60(1), (2) (civil penalty for evading VAT by dishonestly claiming a refund under this section);

VATA 1994 s 72(1), (2) (criminal penalty for fraudulent evasion of VAT by falsely claiming a refund under this section);

VATA 1994 s 83 (appeal to a tribunal in respect of the amount of a refund under this section);

VATA 1994 s 90(3) (VAT repaid as a result of the failure of a resolution under PCTA 1968 may not be refunded under this section).

PART III

APPLICATION OF ACT IN PARTICULAR CASES

Cross reference—See VATA 1994 Sch 13 para 6 (VATA 1983 s 32B (overseas suppliers accounting through their customers) is to continue to apply in relation to supplies to which s 14 of this Act (acquisitions from persons belonging in other member states) does not apply by virtue of s 14(8) (supplies before 1 August 1993), and for that purpose s 32B is to be treated as if it were included in this Part of this Act).

41 Application to the Crown

(1) This Act shall apply in relation to taxable supplies by the Crown as it applies in relation to taxable supplies by taxable persons.

(2) Where the supply by a Government department of any goods or services does not amount to the carrying on of a business but it appears to the Treasury that similar goods or services are or might be supplied by taxable persons in the course or furtherance of any business, then, if and to the extent that the Treasury so direct, the supply of those goods or services by that department shall be treated for the purposes of this Act as a supply in the course or furtherance of any business carried on by it.[8]

(3) Where VAT is chargeable on the supply of goods or services to a Government department, on the acquisition of any goods by a Government department from another member State or on the importation of any goods by a Government department from a place outside the member States and the supply, acquisition or importation is not for the purpose—

(*a*) of any business carried on by the department, or

(*b*) of a supply by the department which, by virtue of [section 41A,][8] is treated as a supply in the course or furtherance of a business,

then, if and to the extent that the Treasury so direct and subject to subsection (4) below, the Commissioners shall, on a claim made by the department at such time and in such form and manner as the Commissioners may determine, refund to it the amount of the VAT so chargeable.

(4) The Commissioners may make the refunding of any amount due under subsection (3) above conditional upon compliance by the claimant with requirements with respect to the keeping, preservation and production of records relating to the supply, acquisition or importation in question.

(5) For the purposes of this section goods or services obtained by one Government department from another Government department shall be treated, if and to the extent that the Treasury so direct, as supplied by that other department and similarly as regards goods or services obtained by or from the Crown Estate Commissioners.

(6) In this section "Government department" includes [the Scottish Administration][2] [, the [Welsh Assembly Government][7]][1], a Northern Ireland department, a Northern Ireland health and social services body, any body of persons exercising functions on behalf of a Minister of the Crown, including . . . [4] and any part of a Government department (as defined in the foregoing) designated for the purposes of this subsection by a direction of the Treasury.

(7) For the purposes of subsection (6) [each of the following is to be regarded as a body of persons exercising functions on behalf of a Minister of the Crown][11][—

[(*a*)] a health service body as defined in section 60(7) of the National Health Service and Community Care Act 1990,

[(*b*)] a National Health Service trust established under Part I of that Act][4] or the National Health Service (Scotland) Act 1978[,

[(*c*)] [an NHS foundation trust][6][,

[(*d*)] [a Primary Care Trust][3][,

[(*e*)] [a Local Health Board[,

[(*f*)] [a clinical commissioning group,

[(*g*)] the Health and Social Care Information Centre,

[(*h*)] the National Health Service Commissioning Board[,

[(*i*)] the National Institute for Health and Care Excellence][9]][5][,

[(*j*)] [Health Education England (established by the Care Act 2014), . . . [11]

[(*k*)] the Health Research Authority (also established by that Act),][10]

[(*l*) a strategic highways company appointed under section 1 of the Infrastructure Act 2015.][11]

(8) In subsection (6) "a Northern Ireland health and social services body" means—

(*a*) a health and social services body as defined in Article 7(6) of the Health and Personal Social Services (Northern Ireland) Order 1991; and

(*b*) a Health and Social Services trust established under that Order.

Commentary—*De Voil Indirect Tax Service* **V5.161**.

Press releases etc—C&E Business Brief 18/03 (extent to which government departments and NHS bodies can recover VAT on two new types of PFI arrangement).

London Gazette 12-4-96 (Treasury direction dated 1 April 1996 under sub-ss (2), (5) and (6) above).

London Gazette 2-7-96 (amended Treasury direction dated 2 July 1996 under sub-s (3) above).

London Gazette 10-1-03 (amended Treasury direction dated 2 December 2002 under sub-s (3) above).

Definitions—"Acquisition of goods from another member State", s 11; "another member State", s 96(1); "business", s 94; "the Commissioners", s 96(1); "importation of goods from a place outside the member States", s 15; "supply", s 5, Sch 4; "taxable person", s 3; "taxable supply", s 4(2); "VAT", ss 1, 96(1).

Note—Note that National Health Service trusts are to be abolished by the Health and Social Care Act 2012 s 179 with effect from a date to be appointed. Primary Care Trusts are expected to be abolished in April 2013 (by the Health and Social Care Act 2012 s 34).

Reference to the Welsh Assembly Government is to be read as, or as including, a reference to the Welsh Government, unless the context requires otherwise (Wales Act 2014 s 4(4)(a)).

Amendments—[1] Words in sub-s (6) inserted by the Government of Wales Act 1998 Sch 12 para 35 with effect from 1 April 1999 by virtue of the Government of Wales Act 1998 (Commencement No 4) Order, SI 1999/782.

[2] Words in sub-s (6) inserted by the Scotland Act 1998 Sch 8 para 30, with effect from 6 May 1999 by virtue of by the Scotland Act 1998 (Commencement) Order SI 1998/3178.

[3] Words in sub-s (7) inserted by the Health Act 1999 s 65 Sch 8 para 86 with effect from 1 April 2000 (by virtue of the Health Act 1999 (Commencement No 2) Order, SI 1999/2342 art 2(4)(b)(iii)).

4 Words in sub-s (6) revoked and words in sub-s (7) substituted by the Health Act 1999 (Supplementary, Consequential etc Provisions) Order, SI 2000/90 art 3(1), Sch 1 para 29 with effect from 8 February 2000.

5 Words inserted by the National Health Service Reform and Health Care Professions Act 2002 s 6(2), Sch 5 para 40 with effect from 10 October 2002 (by virtue of SI 2002/2532).

6 Words in sub-s (7) inserted by the Health and Social Care (Community Health and Standards) Act 2003 s 33(3) with effect from 1 April 2004 (by virtue of SI 2004/759, art 2).

7 Words in sub-s (6) substituted by the Government of Wales Act 2006, s 160(1), Sch 10, para 39 with effect from 25 May 2007, being the date on which the initial period ended (following the appointment of the First Minister) (Government of Wales Act 2006, ss 46, 161(4), (5)).

8 Sub-s (2) repealed, and in sub-s (3)(*b*), words substituted for words "a direction under subsection (2) above,", by FA 2012 s 198(1), (2) with effect from 17 July 2012.

9 Words in sub-s (7) inserted by FA 2013 s 191. This amendment is treated as having come into force on 1 April 2013.

10 Sub-s (7) restructured into a list format, entries for "Health Education England" and "the Heath Research Authority" inserted, and in final sentence, words substituted for word "shall", by FA 2014 s 107 with effect from 17 July 2014.

11 In sub-s (7), words inserted, word at the end of para (*j*) repealed, and para (*l*) inserted by FA 2015 s 67 with effect from 1 April 2015.

Prospective amendments—In sub-s (7), words "section 18 of the National Health Service (Wales) Act 2006" to be substituted for words "Part I of that Act", by the Health and Social Care Act 2012 s 179, Sch 14 paras 65, 66 with effect from a date to be appointed.

[41A Supply of goods or services by public bodies

(1) This section applies where goods or services are supplied by a body mentioned in Article 13(1) of the VAT Directive (status of public bodies as taxable persons) in the course of activities or transactions in which it is engaged as a public authority.

(2) If the supply is in respect of an activity listed in Annex I to the VAT Directive (activities in respect of which public bodies are to be taxable persons), it is to be treated for the purposes of this Act as a supply in the course or furtherance of a business unless it is on such a small scale as to be negligible.

(3) If the supply is not in respect of such an activity, it is to be treated for the purposes of this Act as a supply in the course or furtherance of a business if (and only if) not charging VAT on the supply would lead to a significant distortion of competition.

(4) In this section "the VAT Directive" means Council Directive 2006/112/ EC on the common system of value added tax.][1]

Amendments—[1] Section 41A inserted by FA 2012 s 198(1), (3) with effect from 17 July 2012.

42 Local authorities

A local authority which makes taxable supplies is liable to be registered under this Act, whatever the value of the supplies; and accordingly Schedule 1 shall apply, in a case where the value of the taxable supplies made by a local authority in any period of one year does not exceed the sum for the time being specified in paragraph 1(1)(*a*) of that Schedule, as if that value exceeded that sum.

Commentary—*De Voil Indirect Tax Service* **V2.108, V2.138.**

Press releases etc—C&E Business Brief 9/95 18-5-95 (services between local authorities).

C&E Business Brief 9/95 18-5-95 (VAT standard rated on local authority sporting services).

C&E Business Brief 23/95 24-10-95 and 26/95, 11-12-95 (building regulation fees charged by local authorities are outside the scope of VAT except where there is competition to supply building regulation services).

New release 10/96, 16-2-96 (refunds of VAT incorrectly charged by local authorities on building regulation fees).

Definitions—"Local authority", s 96(1), (4); "registered", s 3(3); "taxable supply", s 4(2); "value of supply", s 19, Sch 6.

43 Groups of companies

(1) Where under [sections 43A to 43D][10] any bodies corporate are treated as members of a group, any business carried on by a member of the group shall be treated as carried on by the representative member, and—

(*a*) any supply of goods or services by a member of the group to another member of the group shall be disregarded; and

(*b*) any [supply which is a supply to which paragraph (*a*) above does not apply and is a supply][1] of goods or services by or to a member of the group shall be treated as a supply by or to the representative member; and

(*c*) any VAT paid or payable by a member of the group on the acquisition of goods from another member State or on the importation of goods from a place outside the member States shall be treated as paid or payable by the representative member and the goods shall be treated—

(i) in the case of goods acquired from another member State, for the purposes of section 73(7); and

(ii) in the case of goods imported from a place outside the member States, for those purposes and the purposes of section 38,

as acquired or, as the case may be, imported by the representative member;

and all members of the group shall be liable jointly and severally for any VAT due from the representative member.

[(1AA) Where—

(*a*) it is material, for the purposes of any provision made by or under this Act ('the relevant provision'), whether the person by or to whom a supply is made, or the person by whom goods are acquired or imported, is a person of a particular description,

(*b*) paragraph (*b*) or (*c*) of subsection (1) above applies to any supply, acquisition or importation, and

(*c*) there is a difference that would be material for the purposes of the relevant provision between—

(i) the description applicable to the representative member, and

(ii) the description applicable to the body which (apart from this section) would be regarded for the purposes of this Act as making the supply, acquisition or importation or, as the case may be, as being the person to whom the supply is made.

the relevant provision shall have effect in relation to that supply, acquisition or importation as if the only description applicable to the representative member were the description in fact applicable to that body.][5]

[(1AB) Subsection (1AA) above does not apply to the extent that what is material for the purposes of the relevant provision is whether a person is a taxable person."][5]

[(1A) . . .][4]

(2) An order under section 5(5) or (6) may make provision for securing that any goods or services which, if all the members of the group were one person, would fall to be treated under that section as supplied to and by that person, are treated as supplied to and by the representative member [and may provide for that purpose that the representative member is to be treated as a person of such description as may be determined under the order][6].

[(2A) A supply made by a member of a group ('the supplier') to another member of the group ('the UK member') shall not be disregarded under subsection (*1*)(*a*) above if—

(*a*) it would (if there were no group) be a supply of services [to which section 7A(2)(*a*) applies made][11] to a person belonging in the United Kingdom;

(*b*) those services are not within any of the descriptions specified in Schedule 9;

(*c*) the supplier has been supplied (whether or not by a person belonging in the United Kingdom) with [any services . . . [11] which do not fall within any of the descriptions specified in Schedule 9][8] [and section 7A(2)(*a*) applied to the supply][11];

(*d*) the supplier belonged outside the United Kingdom when it was supplied with the services mentioned in paragraph (*c*) above; and

(*e*) the services so mentioned have been used by the supplier for making the supply to the UK member.][7]

[(2B) Subject to subsection (2C) below, where a supply is excluded by virtue of subsection (2A) above from the supplies that are disregarded in pursuance of subsection (1)(*a*) above, all the same consequences shall follow under this Act as if that supply—

(*a*) were a taxable supply in the United Kingdom by the representative member to itself, and

(*b*) without prejudice to that, were made by the representative member in the course or furtherance of its business.][7]

[(2C) [Except in so far as the Commissioners may be regulations otherwise provide][9] a supply which is deemed by virtue of subsection (2B) above to be a supply by the representative member to itself—

(*a*) shall not be taken into account as a supply made by the representative member when determining any allowance of input tax under section 26(1) in the case of the representative member;

(*b*) shall be deemed for the purposes of paragraph 1 of Schedule 6 to be a supply in the case of which the person making the supply and the person supplied are connected within the meaning of [section 1122 of the Corporation Tax Act 2010][12] (connected persons); and

(*c*) subject to paragraph (*b*) above [and paragraph 8A of Schedule 6][13], shall be taken to be a supply the value and time of which are determined as if it were a supply of services which is treated by virtue of section 8 as made by the person by whom the services are received.][7]

[(2D) For the purposes of subsection (2A) above where—

(*a*) there has been a supply of the assets of a business of a person ('the transferor') to a person to whom the whole or any part of that business was transferred as a going concern ('the transferee'),

(*b*) that supply is either—

(i) a supply falling to be treated, in accordance with an order under section 5(3), as being neither a supply of goods nor a supply of services, or

(ii) a supply that would have fallen to be so treated if it had taken place in the United Kingdom,

and

(*c*) the transferor was supplied with services . . . [11] at a time before the transfer when the transferor belonged outside the United Kingdom [and section 7A(2)(*a*) applied to the supply][11], those services, so far as they are used by the transferee for making any supply [to which section 7A(2)(a) applies][11], shall be deemed to have been supplied to the transferee at a time when the transferee belonged outside the United Kingdom.][7]

[(2E) Where, in the case of a supply of assets falling within paragraphs (*a*) and (*b*) of subsection (2D) above—

(*a*) the transferor himself acquired any of the assets in question by way of a previous supply of assets falling within those paragraphs, and

(*b*) [there is a supply to which section 7A(2)(*a*) applies of services which, if used by the transferor for making such a supply][11], would be deemed by virtue of that subsection to have been supplied to the transferor at a time when he belonged outside the United Kingdom,

that subsection shall have effect, notwithstanding that the services have not been so used by the transferor, as if the transferor were a person to whom those services were supplied and as if he were a person belonging outside the United Kingdom at the time of their deemed supply to him; and this subsection shall apply accordingly through any number of successive supplies of assets falling within paragraphs (a) and (b) of that subsection.][7]

(3)–(8) . . . [2]

[(9) Schedule 9A (which makes provision for ensuring that this section is not used for tax avoidance) shall have effect.][3]

Commentary—*De Voil Indirect Tax Service* **V2.190**.

Orders—See VAT (Self-supply of Construction Services) Order, SI 1989/472; VAT (Cars) Order, SI 1992/3122; VAT (Special Provisions) Order, SI 1995/1268.

Press releases etc—C&E Business Brief 31/97 22.12.97 (Refusing applications for group treatment to protect the revenue). C&E Business Brief 15/9912/7/99 (New anti-avoidance provisions).

Simon's Tax Cases—*C&E Comrs v Kingfisher plc* [1994] STC 63*; *C&E Comrs v Thorn Materials Supply Ltd and Thorn Resources Ltd* [1998] STC 725*; *C&E Comrs v Barclays Bank plc* [2000] STC 665; *R&C Comrs v Gracechurch Management Services Ltd* [2008] STC 795.

Definitions—"Acquisition of goods from another member State", s 11; "another member State", s 96(1); "belonging", s 9(2), (3); "business", s 94; "the Commissioners", s 96(1); "importation of goods from a place outside the member States", s 15; "prescribed accounting period", s 25(1); "supply", s 5, Sch 4; "taxable person", s 3; "United Kingdom", s 96(11); "VAT", ss 1, 96(1).

Cross references—See VATA 1994 s 43(1)(*d*) (tour operators: provision for orders excluding a body corporate from the application of this section);

VATA 1994 s 83 (appeal to a tribunal in respect of the refusal of an application under this section);

VATA 1994 Sch 9A para 2(2) (assumption that supply does not fall within sub-s (1)(*a*) above to the extent that the Commissioners so direct);

VATA 1994 Sch 9A para 2(3) (assumption that a body corporate is (not) to be treated as a member of a group where the Commissioners so direct).

VAT (Isle of Man) Order, SI 1982/1067 art 10 (supplies made both in UK and in Isle of Man: determination of representative member of group);

VAT (Isle of Man) Order, SI 1982/1067 art 11(6) (group member acquiring an establishment in the Isle of Man: notification required);

VAT (Tour Operators) Order, SI 1987/1806 art 13 (tour operators: eligibility for treatment as group members);

VAT (Self-supply of Construction Services) Order, SI 1989/472 art 3(4) (construction supplies by group members otherwise than for consideration);

VAT (Cars) Order, SI 1992/3122 art 7 (deemed self-supplies of cars by group members);

VAT (Payments on Account) Order, SI 1993/2001 art 17 (payments on account by group members);

VAT (Special Provisions) Order, SI 1995/1268 art 11(4) (deemed self-supplies of printed matter by group members).

FA 1999 Sch 2 paras 6(1), (3), (4) (transitional provisions—VAT groups anti-avoidance legislation).

Amendments—[1] Words in sub-s (1)(b) substituted by FA 1995 s 25(2), (5), with effect in relation to any supply made on or after 1 March 1995 and any supply made before that date in the case of which both the body making the supply and the body supplied continued to be members of the group in question until at least that date.

[2] Words in sub-ss (3) to (8) repealed by FA 1999 s 16, Sch 2 para 1 with effect from 27 July 1999, subject to FA 1999 Sch 2 para 6.

[3] Sub-s (9) added by FA 1996 s 31(1) with effect from 29 April 1996.

[4] Sub-s (1A) (inserted by FA 1995 s 25(2)) repealed by FA 1996 s 31(5), Sch 41 Pt IV(5) with effect in relation to supplies on or after 29 April 1996.

[5] Sub-ss (1AA) and (1AB) inserted by FA 1997 s 40(1) in relation to any supply made after 26 November 1996 and in relation to any acquisition or importation taking place after that date.

[6] Words in sub-s (2) inserted by FA 1997 s 40(2) with effect from 19 March 1997.

[7] Sub-ss (2A)–(2E) inserted by FA 1997 s 41 in relation to supplies made on or after 26 November 1996.

[8] Words in sub-s (2A) (c) substituted by FA 1997 s 41(3), (4) in relation to supplies made after 19 March 1997. In relation to supplies made after 25 November 1996 and before 20 March 1997, the substituted words read 'services falling within any of paragraphs 1 to 8 of Schedule 5'.

[9] Words in sub-s (2C) inserted by FA 1997 s 41 (4)(5) in relation to supplies made after 19 March 1997.

[10] Words in sub-s (1) substituted by FA 2004 s 20(3) with effect from 22 July 2004.

[11] In sub-s (2A)(a) words "falling within Schedule 5", in sub-s (2D) "falling within that Schedule", in sub-s (2E)(b) "there are services falling within paragraphs 1 to 8 of Schedule 5 which, if used by the transferor for making supplies falling within that Schedule" substituted, in sub-ss (2A)(c), (2D)(c) words inserted and "falling within paragraphs 1 to 8 of Schedule 5" repealed, by FA 2009 s 76, Sch 36 paras 1, 7, 14, with effect from 1 January 2010. The references to a supply to which s 7A(2) applies include a supply of services falling within Sch 5 paras 1 to 8 made before that date.

12 In sub-s (2C)(*b*) words substituted for words "section 839 of the Taxes Act 1988" by CTA 2010 s 1177, Sch 1 para 285(a). CTA 2010 has effect for corporation tax purposes for accounting periods ending on or after 1 April 2010, and for income and capital gains tax purposes for the tax year 2010–11 and subsequent tax years.

13 Words in sub-s (2C)(*c*) inserted by FA 2012 s 200(1), (2) with effect in relation to supplies made on or after 17 July 2012.

[43A Groups: eligibility

(1) Two or more bodies corporate are eligible to be treated as members of a group if each is established or has a fixed establishment in the United Kingdom and—

(*a*) one of them controls each of the others,

(*b*) one person (whether a body corporate or an individual) controls all of them, or

(*c*) two or more individuals carrying on a business in partnership control all of them.

(2) For the purposes of this section a body corporate shall be taken to control another body corporate if it is empowered by statute to control that body's activities or if it is that body's holding company within the meaning of section [1159 of and Schedule 6 to][2] the Companies Act [2006][2].

(3) For the purposes of this section an individual or individuals shall be taken to control a body corporate if he or they, were he or they a company, would be that body's holding company within the meaning of [those provisions][2].][1]

Commentary—*De Voil Indirect Tax Service* **V2.189P**.

Cross references—See the VAT (Groups: eligibility) Order, SI 2004/1931 (modification regarding this section).

Press releases etc—C&E Business Brief 15/99 12/7/99 (New anti-avoidance provisions).

Amendments—[1] This section inserted by FA 1999 s 16, Sch 2 para 2 with effect from 27 July 1999, subject to FA 1999 Sch 2 para 6.

2 In sub-s (2), words substituted for words "736 of" and "1985", and in sub-s (3), words substituted for words "that section", by the Companies Act 2006 (Consequential Amendments) (Taxes and National Insurance) Order, SI 2009/1890 art 4(1)(j), (3) with effect from 1 October 2009.

[43AA Power to alter eligibility for grouping

(1) The Treasury may by order provide for section 43A to have effect with specified modifications in relation to a specified class of person.

(2) An order under subsection (1) may, in particular—

(*a*) make provision by reference to generally accepted accounting practice;

(*b*) define generally accepted accounting practice for that purpose by reference to a specified document or instrument (and may provide for the reference to be read as including a reference to any later document or instrument that amends or replaces the first);

(*c*) adopt any statutory or other definition of generally accepted accounting practice (with or without modification);

(*d*) make provision by reference to what would be required or permitted by generally accepted accounting practice if accounts, or accounts of a specified kind, were prepared for a person.

(3) An order under subsection (1) may also, in particular, make provision by reference to—

(*a*) the nature of a person;

(*b*) past or intended future activities of a person;

(*c*) the relationship between a number of persons;

(*d*) the effect of including a person within a group or of excluding a person from a group.

(4) An order under subsection (1) may—

(*a*) make provision which applies generally or only in specified circumstances;

(*b*) make different provision for different circumstances;

(*c*) include supplementary, incidental, consequential or transitional provision.][1]

Orders—See VAT (Groups: eligibility) Order, SI 2004/1931.

Amendments—[1] This section inserted by FA 2004 s 20(1) with effect from 22 July 2004.

[43B Groups: applications

(1) This section applies where an application is made to the Commissioners for two or more bodies corporate, which are eligible [by virtue of section 43A][2], to be treated as members of a group.

(2) This section also applies where two or more bodies corporate are treated as members of a group and an application is made to the Commissioners—

(*a*) for another body corporate, which is eligible [by virtue of section 43A][2] to be treated as a member of the group, to be treated as a member of the group,

(*b*) for a body corporate to cease to be treated as a member of the group,

(*c*) for a member to be substituted as the group's representative member, or

(*d*) for the bodies corporate no longer to be treated as members of a group.

(3) An application with respect to any bodies corporate—

(*a*) must be made by one of them or by the person controlling them, and

(*b*) in the case of an application for the bodies to be treated as a group, must appoint one of them as the representative member.

(4) Where this section applies in relation to an application it shall, subject to subsection (6) below, be taken to be granted with effect from—

(*a*) the day on which the application is received by the Commissioners, or

(*b*) such earlier or later time as the Commissioners may allow.

(5) The Commissioners may refuse an application, within the period of 90 days starting with the day on which it was received by them, if it appears to them—

(*a*) in the case of an application such as is mentioned in subsection (1) above, that the bodies corporate are not eligible [by virtue of section 43A][2] to be treated as members of a group,

(*b*) in the case of an application such as is mentioned in subsection (2)(*a*) above, that the body corporate is not eligible [by virtue of section 43A][2] to be treated as a member of the group, or

(*c*) in any case, that refusal of the application is necessary for the protection of the revenue.

(6) If the Commissioners refuse an application it shall be taken never to have been granted.][1]

Commentary—*De Voil Indirect Tax Service* **V2.190**.

Press releases etc—C&E Business Brief 15/9912/7/99 (New anti-avoidance provisions).

Amendments—[1] This section inserted by FA 1999 s 16, Sch 2 para 2 with effect from 27 July 1999, subject to FA 1999 Sch 2 para 6.

[2] Words in sub-ss (1), (2)(a), (5)(a) and (5)(b) substituted by FA 2004 s 20(4) with effect from 22 July 2004.

[43C Groups: termination of membership

(1) The Commissioners may, by notice given to a body corporate, terminate its treatment as a member of a group from a date—

(*a*) which is specified in the notice, and

(*b*) which is, or falls after, the date on which the notice is given.

(2) The Commissioners may give a notice under subsection (1) above only if it appears to them to be necessary for the protection of the revenue.

(3) Where—

(*a*) a body is treated as a member of a group, and

(*b*) it appears to the Commissioners that the body is not, or is no longer, eligible [by virtue of section 43A][2] to be treated as a member of the group,

the Commissioners shall, by notice given to the body, terminate its treatment as a member of the group from a date specified in the notice.

(4) The date specified in a notice under subsection (3) above may be earlier than the date on which the notice is given but shall not be earlier than—

(*a*) the first date on which, in the opinion of the Commissioners, the body was not eligible to be treated as a member of the group, or

(*b*) the date on which, in the opinion of the Commissioners, the body ceased to be eligible to be treated as a member of the group.][1]

Commentary—*De Voil Indirect Tax Service* **V2.190**.

Press releases etc—C&E Business Brief 15/9912/7/99 (New anti-avoidance provisions).

Amendments—[1] This section inserted by FA 1999 s 16, Sch 2 para 2 with effect from 27 July 1999 subject to FA 1999 Sch 2 para 6.

[2] Words in sub-s (3)(b) substituted by FA 2004 s 20(4) with effect from 22 July 2004.

[43D Groups: duplication

(1) A body corporate may not be treated as a member of more than one group at a time.

(2) A body which is a member of one group is not eligible by virtue of section 43A to be treated as a member of another group.

(3) If—

(*a*) an application under section 43B(1) would have effect from a time in accordance with section 43B(4), but

(*b*) at that time one or more of the bodies specified in the application is a member of a group (other than that to which the application relates),

the application shall have effect from that time, but with the exclusion of the body or bodies mentioned in paragraph (b).

(4) If—

(*a*) an application under section 43B(2)(*a*) would have effect from a time in accordance with section 43B(4), but

(*b*) at that time the body specified in the application is a member of a group (other than that to which the application relates),

the application shall have no effect.

(5) Where a body is a subject of two or more applications under section 43B(1) or (2)(*a*) that have not been granted or refused, the applications shall have no effect.][1]

Commentary—*De Voil Indirect Tax Service* **V2.190**.

Amendments—[1] This section inserted by FA 2004 s 20(2) with effect from 22 July 2004.

44 Supplies to groups

(1) Subject to subsections (2) to (4) below, subsection (5) below applies where—

(*a*) a business, or part of a business, carried on by a taxable person is transferred as a going concern to a body corporate treated as a member of a group under section 43;

(*b*) on the transfer of the business or part, chargeable assets of the business are transferred to the body corporate; and (*c*) the transfer of the assets is treated by virtue of section 5(3)(*c*) as neither a supply of goods nor a supply of services.

(2) Subsection (5) below shall not apply if the representative member of the group is entitled to credit for the whole of the input tax on supplies to it and acquisitions and importations by it—

(*a*) during the prescribed accounting period in which the assets are transferred, and

(*b*) during any longer period to which regulations under section 26(3)(*b*) relate and in which the assets are transferred.

(3) Subsection (5) below shall not apply if the Commissioners are satisfied that the assets were assets of the taxable person transferring them more than 3 years before the day on which they are transferred.

(4) Subsection (5) below shall not apply to the extent that the chargeable assets consist of capital items in respect of which regulations made under section 26(3) and (4), and in force when the assets are transferred, provide for adjustment to the deduction of input tax.

(5) The chargeable assets shall be treated for the purposes of this Act as being, on the day on which they are transferred, both supplied to the representative member of the group for the purpose of its business and supplied by that member in the course or furtherance of its business.

(6) A supply treated under subsection (5) above as made by a representative member shall not be taken into account as a supply made by him when determining the allowance of input tax in his case under section 26.

(7) The value of a supply treated under subsection (5) above as made to or by a representative member shall be taken to be the open market value of the chargeable assets.

(8) For the purposes of this section, the open market value of any chargeable assets shall be taken to be the price that would be paid on a sale (on which no VAT is payable) between a buyer and a seller who are not in such a relationship as to affect the price.

(9) The Commissioners may reduce the VAT chargeable by virtue of subsection (5) above in a case where they are satisfied that the person by whom the chargeable assets are transferred has not received credit for the full amount of input tax arising on the supply to or acquisition or importation by him of the chargeable assets.

(10) For the purposes of this section, assets are chargeable assets if their supply in the United Kingdom by a taxable person in the course or furtherance of his business would be a taxable supply (and not a zero-rated supply).

Commentary—*De Voil Indirect Tax Service* **V3.246**.

Definitions—"Business", s 94; "the Commissioners", s 96(1); "input tax", s 24; "prescribed accounting period", s 25(1); "regulations", s 96(1); "representative member", s 43(4); "supply", s 5, Sch 4; "taxable person", s 4(2); "taxable supply", s 4(2); "United Kingdom", s 96(11); "VAT", ss 1, 96(1).

Cross references—See VATA 1994 Sch 9A para 2(3) (assumption that a body corporate is (not) to be treated as a member of a group where the Commissioners so direct).

45 Partnerships

(1) The registration under this Act of persons—

(*a*) carrying on a business in partnership, or

(*b*) carrying on in partnership any other activities in the course or furtherance of which they acquire goods from other member States,

may be in the name of the firm; and no account shall be taken, in determining for any purpose of this Act whether goods or services are supplied to or by such persons or are acquired by such persons from another member State, of any change in the partnership.

(2) Without prejudice to section 36 of the Partnership Act 1890 (rights of persons dealing with firm against apparent members of firm), until the date on which a change in the partnership is notified to the Commissioners a person who has ceased to be a member of a partnership shall be regarded as continuing to be a partner for the purposes of this Act and, in particular, for the purpose of any liability for VAT on the supply of goods or services by the partnership or on the acquisition of goods by the partnership from another member State.

(3) Where a person ceases to be a member of a partnership during a prescribed accounting period (or is treated as so doing by virtue of subsection (2) above) any notice, whether of assessment or otherwise, which is served on the partnership and relates to, or to any matter arising in, that period or any earlier period during the whole or part of which he was a member of the partnership shall be treated as served also on him.

(4) Without prejudice to section 16 of the Partnership Act 1890 (notice to acting partner to be notice to the firm) any notice, whether of assessment or otherwise, which is addressed to a partnership by the name in which it is registered by virtue of subsection (1) above and is served in accordance with this Act shall be treated for the purposes of this Act as served on the partnership and, accordingly, where subsection (3) above applies, as served also on the former partner.

(5) Subsections (1) and (3) above shall not affect the extent to which, under section 9 of the Partnership Act 1890, a partner is liable for VAT owed by the firm; but where a person is a partner in a firm during part only of a prescribed accounting period, his liability for VAT on the supply by the

firm of goods or services during that accounting period or on the acquisition during that period by the firm of any goods from another member State shall be such proportion of the firm's liability as may be just.

Commentary—*De Voil Indirect Tax Service* **V2.110**.

Simon's Tax Cases—s 45(1), *Scrace v R&C Comrs* [2007] STC 269; *R&C Comrs v Pal and others* [2008] STC 2442. s 45(2), *C&E Comrs v Jamieson* [2002] STC 1418.

Definitions—"Acquisition of goods from other member States", s 11; "another member State", s 96(1); "business", s 94; "the Commissioners", s 96(1); "other member States", s 96(1); "prescribed accounting period", s 25(1); "registered", s 3(3); "supply", s 5, Sch 4; "VAT", ss 1, 96(1).

46 Business carried on in divisions or by unincorporated bodies, personal representatives etc

(1) The registration under this Act of a body corporate carrying on a business in several divisions may, if the body corporate so requests and the Commissioners see fit, be in the names of those divisions.

(2) The Commissioners may by regulations make provision for determining by what persons anything required by or under this Act to be done by a person carrying on a business is to be done where a business is carried on in partnership or by a club, association or organisation the affairs of which are managed by its members or a committee or committees of its members.

(3) The registration under this Act of any such club, association or organisation may be in the name of the club, association or organisation; and in determining whether goods or services are supplied to or by such a club, association or organisation or whether goods are acquired by such a club, association or organisation from another member State, no account shall be taken of any change in its members.

(4) The Commissioners may by regulations make provision for persons who carry on a business of a taxable person who has died or become bankrupt or has had his estate sequestrated or has become incapacitated to be treated for a limited time as taxable persons, and for securing continuity in the application of this Act in cases where persons are so treated.

(5) In relation to a company which is a taxable person, the reference in subsection (4) above to the taxable person having become bankrupt or having had his estate sequestrated or having become incapacitated shall be construed as a reference to its being in liquidation or receivership or [administration][1].

(6) References in this section to a business include references to any other activities in the course or furtherance of which any body corporate or any club, association, organisation or other unincorporated body acquires goods from another member State.

Commentary—*De Voil Indirect Tax Service* **V2.190A**.

Regulations—See VAT Regulations, SI 1995/2518 regs 8, 9.

Definitions—"Acquisition of goods from another member State", s 11; "another member State", s 96(1); "business", s 94; "the Commissioners", s 96(1); "registered", s 3(3); "regulations", s 96(1); "supply", s 5, Sch 4; "taxable person", s 3.

Cross reference—See VAT (Payments on Account) Order, SI 1993/2001 art 16 (payments on account: businesses carried on in divisions).

Amendments—[1] Word in sub-s (5) substituted by the Enterprise Act 2002 (Insolvency) Order, SI 2003/2096 art 4, Schedule paras 24, 25 with effect from 15 September 2003. However, this amendment does not apply in any case where a petition for an administration order was presented before that date: SI 2003/2096 arts 1, 6.

47 Agents etc

(1) Where—

(*a*) goods are acquired from another member State by a person who is not a taxable person and a taxable person acts in relation to the acquisition, and then supplies the goods as agent for the person by whom they are so acquired; or

(*b*) goods are imported from a place outside the member States by a taxable person who supplies them as agent for a person who is not a taxable person,

[then, if the taxable person acts in relation to the supply in his own name, the goods shall][1] be treated for the purposes of this Act as acquired and supplied or, as the case may be, imported and supplied by the taxable person as principal.

(2) For the purposes of subsection (1) above a person who is not resident in the United Kingdom and whose place or principal place of business is outside the United Kingdom may be treated as not being a taxable person if as a result he will not be required to be registered under this Act.

[(2A) Where, in the case of any supply of goods to which subsection (1) above does not apply, goods are supplied through an agent who acts in his own name, the supply shall be treated both as a supply to the agent and as a supply by the agent.][2]

(3) Where . . . [3] services[, other than electronically supplied services and telecommunication services,][4] are supplied through an agent who acts in his own name the Commissioners may, if they think fit, treat the supply both as a supply to the agent and as a supply by the agent.

[(4) Where electronically supplied services or telecommunication services are supplied through an agent, the supply is to be treated both as a supply to the agent and as a supply by the agent.

(5) For the purposes of subsection (4) "agent" means a person ("A") who acts in A's own name but on behalf of another person within the meaning of Article 28 of Council Directive 2006/112/EC on the common system of value added tax.

(6) In this section "electronically supplied services" and "telecommunication services" have the same meaning as in Schedule 4A (see paragraph 9(3) and (4) and paragraph 8(2) of that Schedule).][4]

Commentary—*De Voil Indirect Tax Service* **V3.221**.

Simon's Tax Cases—s 47(3), *Metropolitan Borough of Wirral v C&E Comrs* [1995] STC 597*.

Definitions—"Acquisition of goods from another member State", s 11; "another member State", s 96(1); "business", s 94; "the Commissioners", s 96(1); "goods imported from a place outside the member States", s 15; "registered", s 3(3); "supply", s 5, Sch 4; "taxable person", s 3; "United Kingdom", s 96(11).

Press releases etc—Business Brief 28/97, 12-12-97 (VAT treatment of debt collection revised).

Amendments—[1] Words in sub-s (1) substituted by FA 1995 s 23(1), (4)(a) with effect in relation to goods acquired or imported on or after 1 May 1995.

[2] Sub-s (2A) inserted by FA 1995 s 23(2), (4)(b) with effect in relation to any supply taking place on or after 1 May 1995.

[3] Words repealed by FA 1995 s 23(3), (4)(b), Sch 29 Pt VI(2) with effect in relation to any supply taking place on or after 1 May 1995.

[4] In sub-s (3), words inserted, and sub-ss (4)–(6) inserted, by FA 2014 s 106 with effect in relation to supplies made on or after 1 January 2015.

48 VAT representatives

(1) Where any person—

(*a*) is a taxable person for the purposes of this Act or, without being a taxable person, is a person who makes taxable supplies or who acquires goods in the United Kingdom from one or more other member States;

[(*b*) is not established, and does not have any fixed establishment, in the United Kingdom;][2]

[(*ba*) is established in a country or territory in respect of which it appears to the Commissioners that the condition specified in subsection (1A) below is satisfied; and][2]

(*c*) in the case of an individual, does not have his usual place of residence in the United Kingdom,

the Commissioners may direct that person to appoint another person (in this Act referred to as a "VAT representative") to act on his behalf in relation to VAT.

[(1A) The condition mentioned in subsection (1)(*ba*) above is that—

(*a*) the country or territory is neither a member State nor a part of a member State, and

(*b*) there is no provision for mutual assistance between the United Kingdom and the country or territory similar in scope to the assistance provided for between the United Kingdom and each other member State by the mutual assistance provisions.][2]

[(1B) In subsection (1A) above "the mutual assistance provisions" means—

[(*a*) section 134 of the Finance Act 2002 and Schedule 39 to that Act (recovery of taxes etc due in other member States);][3]

(*b*) section 197 of the Finance Act 2003 (exchange of information between tax authorities of member States);][3]

[(*c*) Council Regulation (EC) No 904/2010 of 7 October 2010 on administrative cooperation and combating fraud in the field of value added tax.][4]

[(2) With the agreement of the Commissioners, a person—

(*a*) who has not been required under subsection (1) above to appoint another person to act on his behalf in relation to VAT, and

(*b*) in relation to whom the conditions specified in paragraphs (*a*), (*b*) and (*c*) of that subsection are satisfied,

may appoint another person to act on his behalf in relation to VAT.][2]

[(2A) In this Act "VAT representative" means a person appointed under subsection (1) or (2) above.][2]

(3) Where any person is appointed by virtue of this section to be the VAT representative of another ("his principal"), then, subject to subsections (4) to (6) below, the VAT representative—

(*a*) shall be entitled to act on his principal's behalf for any of the purposes of this Act, of any other enactment (whenever passed) relating to VAT or of any subordinate legislation made under this Act or any such enactment;

(*b*) shall, subject to such provisions as may be made by the Commissioners by regulations, secure (where appropriate by acting on his principal's behalf) his principal's compliance with and discharge of the obligations and liabilities to which his principal is subject by virtue of this Act, any such other enactment or any such subordinate legislation; and

(*c*) shall be personally liable in respect of—

(i) any failure to secure his principal's compliance with or discharge of any such obligation or liability; and

(ii) anything done for purposes connected with acting on his principal's behalf,

as if the obligations and liabilities imposed on his principal were imposed jointly and severally on the VAT representative and his principal.

(4) A VAT representative shall not be liable by virtue of subsection (3) above himself to be registered under this Act, but regulations made by the Commissioners may—

(*a*) require the registration of the names of VAT representatives against the names of their principals in any register kept for the purposes of this Act; and

(*b*) make it the duty of a VAT representative, for the purposes of registration, to notify the Commissioners, within such period as may be prescribed, that his appointment has taken effect or has ceased to have effect.

[(4A) Regulations under subsection (4) may require a notification under that subsection to be made in such form and manner, and to contain such particulars, as may be specified in the regulations or by the Commissioners in accordance with the regulations.][4]

(5) A VAT representative shall not by virtue of subsection (3) above be guilty of any offence except in so far as—

(*a*) the VAT representative has consented to, or connived in, the commission of the offence by his principal;

(*b*) the commission of the offence by his principal is attributable to any neglect on the part of the VAT representative; or

(*c*) the offence consists in a contravention by the VAT representative of an obligation which, by virtue of that subsection, is imposed both on the VAT representative and on his principal.

(6) The Commissioners may by regulations make provision as to the manner and circumstances in which a person is to be appointed, or is to be treated as having ceased to be, another's VAT representative; and regulations under this subsection may include such provision as the Commissioners think fit for the purposes of subsection (4) above with respect to the making or deletion of entries in any register.

(7) Where a person fails to appoint a VAT representative in accordance with any direction under subsection (1) above, the Commissioners may require him to provide such security, or further security, as they may think appropriate for the payment of any VAT which is or may become due from him.

[(7A) A sum required by way of security under subsection (7) above shall be deemed for the purposes of—

(*a*) section 51 of the Finance Act 1997 (enforcement [by taking control of goods or, in Northern Ireland,][5] by distress) and any regulations under that section, and

(*b*) section 52 of that Act (enforcement [by taking control of goods or, in Northern Ireland,][5] by diligence),

to be recoverable as if it were VAT due from the person who is required to provide it.][1]

(8) For the purposes of this Act a person shall not be treated as having been directed to appoint a VAT representative, or as having been required to provide security under subsection (7) above, unless the Commissioners have either—

(*a*) served notice of the direction or requirement on him; or

(*b*) taken all such other steps as appear to them to be reasonable for bringing the direction or requirement to his attention.

[(9) The Treasury may by order amend the definition of "the mutual assistance provisions" in subsection (1B) above.][3]

Regulations—See VAT Regulations, SI 1995/2518 reg 10.
VAT (Amendment) (No 2) Regulations, SI 2012/1899.

Definitions—"Acquisition of goods from another member State", s 11; "business", s 94; "the Commissioners", s 96(1); "other member States", s 96(1); "prescribed", s 96(1); "registered", s 3(3); "regulations", s 96(1); "subordinate legislation", s 96(1); "taxable person", s 3; "taxable supply", s 4(2); "United Kingdom", s 96(11); "VAT", ss 1, 96(1).

Cross references—See VATA 1994 s 69(1) (penalty for breach of regulations made under this section requiring a VAT representative to notify the Commissioners of his appointment or of the cessation of his appointment);
VATA 1994 ss 83, 84 (appeal to a tribunal in respect of a requirement for security under sub-s (7) of this section);
VATA 1994 Sch 11 para 5(10) (recovery of sums required by way of security under sub-s (7) of this section).
VAT Regulations, SI 1995/2518 reg 10(1), Sch 1, form 8 (form of notification of appointment as VAT representative);
VAT Regulations, SI 1995/2518 reg 10(3) (registration of VAT representatives);
VAT Regulations, SI 1995/2518 reg 10(5) (cessation of appointment as VAT representative).

Amendments—[1] Sub-s (7A) inserted by FA 1997 s 53 (6) with effect from 1 July 1997 (see SI 1997/1432).
[2] Sub-s (1)(b), (ba) substituted for original sub-s (1)(b), sub-ss (1A), (1B) inserted, and sub-ss (2), (2A) substituted for original sub-s (2) by FA 2001 s 100 with effect from 31 December 2001.
[3] Sub-s (1B)(a), (b) substituted, and sub-s (9) inserted, by FA 2003 s 197(7) with effect from 10 July 2003.
[4] Sub-s (1B)(*c*) substituted, and sub-s (4A) inserted, by FA 2012 s 204, Sch 29 paras 1, 6 with effect from 17 July 2012.
[5] In sub-s (7A) words inserted by the Tribunals, Courts and Enforcement Act 2007 s 62(3), Sch 13 paras 117, 118 with effect from 6 April 2014 (the date appointed by virtue of the Tribunals, Courts and Enforcement Act 2007 (Commencement No 11) Order, SI 2014/768 art 2(1)(*b*)).

49 Transfers of going concerns

(1) Where a business[, or part of a business,][1] carried on by a taxable person is transferred to another person as a going concern, then—

(*a*) for the purpose of determining whether the transferee is liable to be registered under this Act he shall be treated as having carried on the business [or part of the business][1] before as well as after the transfer and supplies by the transferor shall be treated accordingly; . . . [1]

(*b*) . . . [1]

(2) Without prejudice to subsection (1) above, the Commissioners may by regulations make provision for securing continuity in the application of this Act in cases where a business[, or part of a business,][1] carried on by a taxable person is transferred to another person as a going concern and the transferee is registered under this Act in substitution for the transferor.

[(2A) Regulations under subsection (2) above may, in particular, provide for the duties under this Act of the transferor to preserve records relating to the business or part of the business for any period after the transfer to become duties of the transferee unless the Commissioners, at the request of the transferor, otherwise direct.][1]

(3) Regulations under subsection (2) above may, in particular, provide—

(*a*) for liabilities and duties under this Act (excluding sections 59 to 70) of the transferor [(other than the duties mentioned in subsection (2A) above)][1] to become, to such extent as may be provided by the regulations, liabilities and duties of the transferee; and

(*b*) for any right of either of them to repayment or credit in respect of VAT to be satisfied by making a repayment or allowing a credit to the other;

but no such provision as is mentioned in paragraph (a) or (b) of this subsection shall have effect in relation to any transferor and transferee unless an application in that behalf has been made by them under the regulations.

[(4) Subsection (5) below applies where—

(*a*) a business, or part of a business, carried on by a taxable person is transferred to another person as a going concern, and

(*b*) the transferor continues to be required under this Act to preserve for any period after the transfer any records relating to the business or part of the business.

(5) So far as is necessary for the purpose of complying with the transferee's duties under this Act, the transferee ("E") may require the transferor—

(*a*) to give to E, within such time and in such form as E may reasonably require, such information contained in the records as E may reasonably specify,

(*b*) to give to E, within such time and in such form as E may reasonably require, such copies of documents forming part of the records as E may reasonably specify, and

(*c*) to make the records available for E's inspection at such time and place as E may reasonably require (and permit E to take copies of, or make extracts from, them).

(6) Where a business, or part of a business, carried on by a taxable person is transferred to another person as a going concern, the Commissioners may disclose to the transferee any information relating to the business when it was carried on by the transferor for the purpose of enabling the transferee to comply with the transferee's duties under this Act.][1]

Commentary—*De Voil Indirect Tax Service* **V2.226.**

Regulations—See VAT Regulations, SI 1995/2518 reg 6.

VAT (Amendment) (No 2) Regulations, SI 2012/1899.

Definitions—"Business", s 94; "the Commissioners", s 96(1); "registered", s 3(3); "regulations", s 96(1); "supply", s 5, Sch 4; "taxable person", s 3; "VAT", ss 1, 96(1).

Cross reference—See VAT (Special Provisions) Order, SI 1995/1268 art 5 (certain transfers of going concerns treated as neither a supply of goods or services).

Amendments—[1] Words in sub-s (1) inserted and repealed, words in sub-ss (2), (3) and whole of sub-ss (2A), (4)–(6) inserted, by FA 2007 ss 100(1)–(6), 114, Sch 27 Pt 6(2) with effect in relation to transfers pursuant to contracts entered into on or after 1 September 2007.

50 Terminal markets

(1) The Treasury may by order make provision for modifying the provisions of this Act in their application to dealings on terminal markets and such persons ordinarily engaged in such dealings as may be specified in the order, subject to such conditions as may be so specified.

(2) Without prejudice to the generality of subsection (1) above, an order under this section may include provision—

(*a*) for zero-rating the supply of any goods or services or for treating the supply of any goods or services as exempt;

(*b*) for the registration under this Act of any body of persons representing persons ordinarily engaged in dealing on a terminal market and for disregarding such dealings by persons so represented in determining liability to be registered under this Act, and for disregarding such dealings between persons so represented for all the purposes of this Act;

(*c*) for refunding, to such persons as may be specified by or under the order, input tax attributable to such dealings on a terminal market as may be so specified,

and may contain such incidental and supplementary provisions as appear to the Treasury to be necessary or expedient.

(3) An order under this section may make different provision with respect to different terminal markets and with respect to different commodities.

Commentary—*De Voil Indirect Tax Service* **V2.116.**

Orders—See VAT (Terminal Markets) Order, SI 1973/173.

Definitions—"Exempt supply", s 31; "input tax", s 24; "registered", s 3(3); "supply", s 5, Sch 4; "zero-rating", s 30.

[50A Margin schemes

(1) The Treasury may by order provide, in relation to any such description of supplies to which this section applies as may be specified in the order, for a taxable person to be entitled to opt that, where he makes supplies of that description, VAT is to be charged by reference to the profit margin on the supplies, instead of by reference to their value.

(2) This section applies to the following supplies, that is to say—

(*a*) supplies of works of art, antiques or collectors' items;

(*b*) supplies of motor vehicles;

(*c*) supplies of second-hand goods; and

(*d*) any supply of goods through a person who acts as an agent, but in his own name, in relation to the supply.

(3) An option for the purposes of an order under this section shall be exercisable, and may be withdrawn, in such manner as may be required by such an order.

(4) Subject to subsection (7) below, the profit margin on a supply to which this section applies shall be taken, for the purposes of an order under this section, to be equal to the amount (if any) by which the price at which the person making the supply obtained the goods in question is exceeded by the price at which he supplies them.

(5) For the purposes of this section the price at which a person has obtained any goods and the price at which he supplies them shall each be calculated in accordance with the provisions contained in an order under this section; and such an order may, in particular, make provision stipulating the extent to which any VAT charged on a supply, acquisition or importation of any goods is to be treated as included in the price at which those goods have been obtained or are supplied.

(6) An order under this section may provide that the consideration for any services supplied in connection with a supply of goods by a person who acts as an agent, but in his own name, in relation to the supply of the goods is to be treated for the purposes of any such order as an amount to be taken into account in computing the profit margin on the supply of the goods, instead of being separately chargeable to VAT as comprised in the value of the services supplied.

(7) An order under this section may provide for the total profit margin on all the goods of a particular description supplied by a person in any prescribed accounting period to be calculated by—

(*a*) aggregating all the prices at which that person obtained goods of that description in that period together with any amount carried forward to that period in pursuance of paragraph (*d*) below;

(*b*) aggregating all the prices at which he supplies goods of that description in that period;

(*c*) treating the total profit margin on goods supplied in that period as being equal to the amount (if any) by which, for that period, the aggregate calculated in pursuance of paragraph (*a*) above is exceeded by the aggregate calculated in pursuance of paragraph (*b*) above; and

(*d*) treating any amount by which, for that period, the aggregate calculated in pursuance of paragraph (*b*) above is exceeded by the aggregate calculated in pursuance of paragraph (*a*) above as an amount to be carried forward to the following prescribed accounting period so as to be included, for the period to which it is carried forward, in any aggregate falling to be calculated in pursuance of paragraph (*a*) above.

(8) An order under this section may—

(*a*) make different provision for different cases; and

(*b*) make provisions of the order subject to such general or special directions as may, in accordance with the order, be given by the Commissioners with respect to any matter to which the order relates.][1]

Commentary—*De Voil Indirect Tax Service* **V3.531, V3.532, V3.534**.

Order—VAT (Special Provisions) Order, SI 1995/1268.

Press releases etc—VAT Information Sheet 6/01 (December 2001) (changes to the VAT second-hand margin scheme).

Definitions—"Acquisition of goods from another member state", s 11; "the Commissioners", s 96(1); "prescribed accounting period", s 25(1); "supply", s 5, Sch 4; "taxable person", s 3; "VAT", s 96(1).

Cross references—See Value Added Tax Regulations, SI 1995/2518 reg 172A (bad debt relief under margin schemes).

Amendments—[1] Section inserted by FA 1995 s 24(1).

51 Buildings and land

(1) Schedule 10 shall have effect with respect to buildings and land.

(2) The Treasury may by order amend Schedule 10.

Commentary—*De Voil Indirect Tax Service* **V4.111–V4.115**.

Orders—VAT (Buildings and Land) Order, SI 2011/86.

Cross reference—See VATA 1994 s 97(3), (4) (procedure for making certain orders under this section).

[51A Co-owners etc of buildings and land

(1) This section applies to a supply consisting in the grant, assignment or surrender of any interest in or right over land in a case where there is more than one person by whom the grant, assignment or surrender is made or treated as made; and for this purpose—

(a) a licence to occupy land, and

(b) in relation to land in Scotland, a personal right to call for or be granted any interest or right in or over land,

shall be taken to be a right over land.

(2) The persons who make or are treated as making a supply to which this section applies ("the grantors") shall be treated, in relation to that supply and in relation to any other such supply with respect to which the grantors are the same, as a single person ("the property-owner") who is distinct from each of the grantors individually.

(3) Registration under this Act of the property-owner shall be in the name of the grantors acting together as a property-owner.

(4) The grantors shall be jointly and severally liable in respect of the obligations falling by virtue of this section on the property-owner.

(5) Any notice, whether of assessment or otherwise, which is addressed to the property-owner by the name in which the property-owner is registered and is served on any of the grantors in accordance with this Act shall be treated for the purposes of this Act as served on the property-owner.

(6) Where there is any change in some, but not all, of the persons who are for the time being to be treated as the grantors in relation to any supply to which this section applies—

(a) that change shall be disregarded for the purposes of this section in relation to any prescribed accounting period beginning before the change is notified in the prescribed manner to the Commissioners; and

(b) any notice (whether of assessment or otherwise) which is served, at any time after such a notification, on the property-owner for the time being shall, so far as it relates to, or to any matter arising in, such a period, be treated for the purposes of this Act as served on whoever was the property-owner in that period.][1, 2]

Commentary—*De Voil Indirect Tax Service* **V2.117**.

Definitions—"Assignment", s 96(1); "the Commissioners", s 96(1); "prescribed", s 96(1); "prescribed accounting period", s 25(1); "registered", s 3(3); "supply", s 5.

Amendments—[1] Section inserted by FA 1995 s 26(1), (4) with effect from a day to be appointed by order made by the Commissioners of Customs and Excise.

[2] This section repealed by the Value Added Tax (Buildings and Land) Order, SI 2008/1146 art 5(2) with effect in relation to supplies made on or after 1 June 2008, subject to savings in Sch 2 of the Order.

[51B Face-value vouchers

Schedule 10A shall have effect with respect to face-value vouchers.][1]

[1] Section inserted by FA 2003 s 19, Sch 1 para 1 with effect for supplies of tokens, stamps or vouchers issued after 8 April 2003.

52 Trading stamp schemes

The Commissioners may by regulations modify sections 19 and 20 and Schedules 6 and 7 for the purpose of providing (in place of the provision for the time being contained in those sections and Schedules) for the manner of determining for the purposes of this Act the value of—

(*a*) a supply of goods, or

(*b*) a transaction in pursuance of which goods are acquired from another member State,

in a case where the goods are supplied or acquired under a trading stamp scheme (within the meaning of the Trading Stamps Act 1964 or the Trading Stamps Act (Northern Ireland) 1965) or under any scheme of an equivalent description which is in operation in another member State.

Commentary—*De Voil Indirect Tax Service* **V3.392**.

Regulations—See VAT Regulations, SI 1995/2518 regs 76–80.

Definitions—"Acquisition of goods from another member State", s 11; "another member State", s 96(1); "the Commissioners", s 96(1); "regulations", s 96(1); "supply", s 5, Sch 4; "value of supply of goods", s 19, Sch 6; "value of goods acquired from another member State", s 20.

53 Tour operators

(1) The Treasury may by order modify the application of this Act in relation to supplies of goods or services by tour operators or in relation to such of those supplies as may be determined by or under the order.

(2) Without prejudice to the generality of subsection (1) above, an order under this section may make provision—

(*a*) for two or more supplies of goods or services by a tour operator to be treated as a single supply of services;

(*b*) for the value of that supply to be ascertained, in such manner as may be determined by or under the order, by reference to the difference between sums paid or payable to and sums paid or payable by the tour operator;

(*c*) for account to be taken, in determining the VAT chargeable on that supply, of the different rates of VAT that would have been applicable apart from this section;

(*d*) excluding any body corporate from the application of section 43;

(*e*) as to the time when a supply is to be treated as taking place.

(3) In this section "tour operator" includes a travel agent acting as principal and any other person providing for the benefit of travellers services of any kind commonly provided by tour operators or travel agents.

(4) Section 97(3) shall not apply to an order under this section, notwithstanding that it makes provision for excluding any VAT from credit under section 25.

Commentary—*De Voil Indirect Tax Service* **V6.373**.

Orders—See VAT (Tour Operators) Order, SI 1987/1806.

Press releases etc—VAT Information Sheet 5/95 1-4-95 (guidance on new rules from 1 January 1996).

VAT Information Sheet 2/96, 3/96, 4/96 1-7-96 (practical implementation of "trader to trader options", "airline charter option" and "agency option").

VAT Information Sheet 6/96 1-11-96 (guidance on "seat only" sales).

VAT Information Sheet 1/97 (practical implementation of the "trader to trader (wholesale) option").

Business Brief 14/97, 30-6-97 (treatment of tour operators making supplies to other businesses).

HMRC Brief 27/09, 8-4-09 (changes to TOMS taking effect from 1 January 2010).

HMRC Brief 21/10 25-5-10 (TOMS: invoicing for supplies under the arrangement known as "hotel billback")

Simon's Tax Cases—*Madgett and Baldwin (T/A Howden Court Hotel) v C&E Comrs* [1998] STC 1189*; *Secret Hotels2 Ltd (formerly Med Hotels Ltd) v R&C Comrs* [2012] EWCA Civ 1571, [2013] STC 452.

Definitions—"Supply", s 5, Sch 4; "value of supply of goods or services", s 19, Sch 6; "VAT", ss 1, 96(1).

Cross references—See Value Added Tax Regulations, SI 1995/2518 reg 172B (bad debt relief under tour operators margin scheme).

54 Farmers etc

(1) The Commissioners may, in accordance with such provision as may be contained in regulations made by them, certify for the purposes of this section any person who satisfies them—

(*a*) that he is carrying on a business involving one or more designated activities;

(*b*) that he is of such a description and has complied with such requirements as may be prescribed; and

(*c*) where an earlier certification of that person has been cancelled, that more than the prescribed period has elapsed since the cancellation or that such other conditions as may be prescribed are satisfied.

(2) Where a person is for the time being certified under this section, then (whether or not that person is a taxable person) so much of any supply by him of any goods or services as, in accordance with provision contained in regulations, is allocated to the relevant part of his business shall be disregarded for the purpose of determining whether he is, has become or has ceased to be liable or entitled to be registered under Schedule 1 [or is, has become or has ceased to be liable to be registered under Schedule 1A][1].

(3) The Commissioners may by regulations provide for an amount included in the consideration for any taxable supply which is made—

(*a*) in the course or furtherance of the relevant part of his business by a person who is for the time being certified under this section;

(*b*) at a time when that person is not a taxable person; and

(*c*) to a taxable person,

to be treated, for the purpose of determining the entitlement of the person supplied to credit under sections 25 and 26, as VAT on a supply to that person.

(4) The amount which, for the purposes of any provision made under subsection (3) above, may be included in the consideration for any supply shall be an amount equal to such percentage as the Treasury may by order specify of the sum which, with the addition of that amount, is equal to the consideration for the supply.

(5) The Commissioners' power by regulations under section 39 to provide for the repayment to persons to whom that section applies of VAT which would be input tax of theirs if they were taxable persons in the United Kingdom includes power to provide for the payment to persons to whom that section applies of sums equal to the amounts which, if they were taxable persons in the United Kingdom, would be input tax of theirs by virtue of regulations under this section; and references in that section, or in any other enactment, to a repayment of VAT shall be construed accordingly.

(6) Regulations under this section may provide—

(*a*) for . . . [2] an application for certification under this section, or for the cancellation of any such certification, [to be made in the form and manner specified in the regulations or by the Commissioners in accordance with the regulations][2];

(*b*) for the cases and manner in which the Commissioners may cancel a person's certification;

(*c*) for entitlement to a credit such as is mentioned in subsection (3) above to depend on the issue of an invoice containing such particulars as may be prescribed, or as may be notified by the Commissioners in accordance with provision contained in regulations; and

(*d*) for the imposition on certified persons of obligations with respect to the keeping, preservation and production of such records as may be prescribed and of obligations to comply with such requirements with respect to any of those matters as may be so notified;

and regulations made by virtue of paragraph (b) above may confer on the Commissioners power, if they think fit, to refuse to cancel a person's certification, and to refuse to give effect to any entitlement of that person to be registered, until the end of such period after the grant of certification as may be prescribed.

(7) In this section references, in relation to any person, to the relevant part of his business are references—

(*a*) where the whole of his business relates to the carrying on of one or more designated activities, to that business; and

(*b*) in any other case, to so much of his business as does so relate.

(8) In this section "designated activities" means such activities, being activities carried on by a person who, by virtue of carrying them on, falls to be treated as a farmer for the purposes of Article 25 of the directive of the Council of the European Communities dated 17th May 1977 No 77/388/EEC (common flat-rate scheme for farmers), as the Treasury may by order designate.

Commentary—*De Voil Indirect Tax Service* **V2.191**.

Regulations—See VAT Regulations, SI 1995/2518 regs 202–211.

VAT (Amendment) (No 2) Regulations, SI 2012/1899.

Orders—See VAT (Flat-rate Scheme for Farmers) (Designated Activities) Order, SI 1992/3220; VAT (Flat-rate Scheme for Farmers) (Percentage Addition) Order, SI 1992/3221.

Definitions—"Business", s 94; "the Commissioners", s 96(1); "input tax", s 24; "invoice", s 96(1); "prescribed", s 96(1); "registered", s 3(3); "regulations", s 96(1); "supply", s 5, Sch 4; "taxable person", s 3; "taxable supply", s 4(2); "United Kingdom", s 96(11); "VAT", ss 1, 96(1).

Cross references—See VATA 1994 s 83 (appeal to a tribunal in respect of a refusal of, cancellation of, or refusal to cancel certification under this section);

VATA 1994 s 97(3), (4) (procedure for making orders under sub-s (4) or (8) of this section).

VAT (Flat-rate Scheme for Farmers) (Designated Activities) Order, SI 1992/3220 (designated activities for the purposes of this section).

VAT (Flat-rate Scheme for Farmers) (Percentage Addition) Order, SI 1992/3221 (the percentage specified for the purposes of sub-s (4) of this section is 4 per cent).

VAT Regulations, SI 1995/2518 reg 209(1) (treatment of amounts within sub-s (4) of this section as VAT on a supply for purposes of determining entitlement to input tax credit).

Amendments—[1] In sub-s (2), words inserted by FA 2012 s 203, Sch 28 paras 2, 4 with effect in relation to supplies made or to be made on or after 1 December 2012.

[2] In sub-s (6)(*a*), words "the form and manner in which" repealed, and words substituted for words "is to be made", by FA 2012 s 204, Sch 29 paras 1, 7 with effect from 17 July 2012.

55 Customers to account for tax on supplies of gold etc

(1) Where any person makes a supply of gold to another person and that supply is a taxable supply but not a zero rated supply, the supply shall be treated for purposes of [Schedules 1 and 1A][3]—

(*a*) as a taxable supply of that other person (as well as a taxable supply of the person who makes it); and

(*b*) in so far as that other person is supplied in connection with the carrying on by him of any business, as a supply made by him in the course or furtherance of that business;

but nothing in paragraph (b) above shall require any supply to be disregarded for the purposes of [Schedule 1][3] on the grounds that it is a supply of capital assets of that other person's business.

(2) Where a taxable person makes a supply of gold to a person who—

(*a*) is himself a taxable person at the time when the supply is made; and

(*b*) is supplied in connection with the carrying on by him of any business,

it shall be for the person supplied, on the supplier's behalf, to account for and pay tax on the supply, and not for the supplier.

(3) So much of this Act and of any other enactment or any subordinate legislation as has effect for the purposes of or in connection with, the enforcement of any obligation to account for and pay VAT shall apply for the purposes of this section in relation to any person who is required under subsection (2) above to account for and pay any VAT as if that VAT were VAT on a supply made by him.

(4) Section 6(4) to (10) shall not apply for determining when any supply of gold is to be treated as taking place.

(5) References in this section to a supply of gold are references to—

[(*a*) any supply of goods consisting in fine gold, in gold grain of any purity or in gold coins of any purity; . . . [2]][1]

(*b*) any supply of goods containing gold where the consideration for the supply (apart from any VAT) is, or is equivalent to, an amount which does not exceed, or exceeds by no more than a negligible amount, the open market value of the gold contained in the goods [; or

(*c*) any supply of services consisting in the application to another person's goods of a treatment or process which produces goods a supply of which would fall within paragraph (*a*) above.][2]

(6) The Treasury may by order provide for this section to apply, as it applies to the supplies specified in subsection (5) above, to such other supplies of—

(*a*) goods consisting in or containing any precious or semi-precious metal or stones; or

(*b*) services relating to, or to anything containing, any precious or semi-precious metal or stones,

as may be specified or described in the order.

Commentary—*De Voil Indirect Tax Service* **V5.143**.

Definitions—"Business", s 94; "open market value", s 19(5); "subordinate legislation", s 96(1); "supply", s 5, Sch 4; "tax", s 96(1); "taxable person", s 3; "taxable supply", s 4(2); "VAT", ss 1, 96(1); "zero-rating", s 30.

Cross reference—See VATA 1994 s 6(14) (provision for regulations to determine the time of a supply under this section).
Amendments—[1] Sub-s (5)(a) substituted by FA 1996 s 32 in relation to any supply after 28 November 1995.
[2] Word omitted from sub-s (5) repealed and sub-s (5)(c) and word "; or" preceding it inserted by FA 1996 s 29(3), Sch 41 Pt IV(2), with effect in relation to supplies made after 31 December 1995.
[3] In sub-s (1), words substituted for words "Schedule 1" and "that Schedule", by FA 2012 s 203, Sch 28 paras 2, 5 with effect in relation to supplies made or to be made on or after 1 December 2012.

[55A Customers to account for tax on supplies of goods [or services][2] of a kind used in missing trader intra-community fraud

(1) Subsection (3) applies if—
(*a*) a taxable (but not a zero-rated) supply of goods [or services][2] ("the relevant supply") is made to a person ("the recipient"),
(*b*) the relevant supply is of goods [or services][2] to which this section applies (see subsection (9)),
(*c*) the relevant supply is not an excepted supply (see subsection (10)), and
(*d*) the total value of the relevant supply, and of corresponding supplies made to the recipient in the month in which the relevant supply is made, exceeds £1,000 ("the disregarded amount").

(2) For this purpose a "corresponding supply" means a taxable (but not a zero-rated) supply of goods [or services][2] which—
(*a*) is a supply of goods [or services][2] to which this section applies, and
(*b*) is not an excepted supply.

(3) The relevant supply, and the corresponding supplies made to the recipient in the month in which the relevant supply is made, are to be treated for the purposes of [Schedules 1 and 1A][3]—
(*a*) as taxable supplies of the recipient (as well as taxable supplies of the person making them), and
(*b*) in so far as the recipient is supplied in connection with the carrying on by him of any business, as supplies made by him in the course or furtherance of that business,
but the relevant supply, and those corresponding supplies, are to be so treated only in so far as their total value exceeds the disregarded amount.

(4) Nothing in subsection (3)(*b*) requires any supply to be disregarded for the purposes of Schedule 1 on the grounds that it is a supply of capital assets of the recipient's business.

(5) For the purposes of subsections (1) and (3), the value of a supply is determined on the basis that no VAT is chargeable on the supply.

(6) If—
(*a*) a taxable person makes a supply of goods [or services][2] to a person ("the recipient") at any time,
(*b*) the supply is of goods [or services][2] to which this section applies and is not an excepted supply, and
(*c*) the recipient is a taxable person at that time and is supplied in connection with the carrying on by him of any business,
it is for the recipient, on the supplier's behalf, to account for and pay tax on the supply and not for the supplier.

(7) The relevant enforcement provisions apply for the purposes of this section, in relation to any person required under subsection (6) to account for and pay any VAT, as if that VAT were VAT on a supply made by him.

(8) For this purpose "the relevant enforcement provisions" means so much of—
(*a*) this Act and any other enactment, and
(*b*) any subordinate legislation,
as has effect for the purposes of, or in connection with the enforcement of, any obligation to account for and pay VAT.

(9) For the purposes of this section, goods [or services][2] are goods [or services][2] to which this section applies if they are of a description specified in an order made by the Treasury.

(10) For the purposes of this section, an "excepted supply" means a supply which is of a description specified in, or determined in accordance with, provision contained in an order made by the Treasury.

(11) Any order made under subsection (10) may describe a supply of goods [or services][2] by reference to—
(*a*) the use which has been made of the goods [or services][2], or
(*b*) other matters unrelated to the characteristics of the goods [or services][2] themselves.

(12) The Treasury may by order substitute for the sum for the time being specified in subsection (1)(*d*) such greater sum as they think fit.

(13) The Treasury may by order make such amendments of any provision of this Act as they consider necessary or expedient for the purposes of this section or in connection with this section.

An order under this subsection may confer power on the Commissioners to make regulations or exercise any other function, but no order may be made under this subsection on or after 22nd March 2009.

(14) Any order made under this section (other than one under subsection (12)) may—

(*a*) make different provision for different cases, and
(*b*) contain supplementary, incidental, consequential or transitional provisions.][1]

Commentary—*De Voil Indirect Tax Service* **V3.233, V5.273.**

Press releases etc—HMRC Brief 24/07, 20-3-07 (Proposed reverse charge accounting for businesses trading in mobile telephones and computer chips: announcement of targeted implementation and details of how the rules will operate in practice; and exposure of draft legislation for comment).

Orders—Value Added Tax (Section 55A) (Specified Goods and Services and Excepted Supplies) Order, SI 2010/2239 (specifies goods and services to which VATA 1994 s 55A applies, and excepted supplies).

Value Added Tax (Section 55A) (Specified Goods and Excepted Supplies) Order, SI 2014/1458 (specifies goods to which this section applies, and excepted supplies; this Order relates to various supplies of gas and electricity).

Amendments—[1] This section inserted by FA 2006 s 19(1), (8) in relation to supplies made on or after 1 June 2007 (by virtue of the Finance Act 2006, section 19, (Appointed Day) Order, SI 2007/1419).

[2] Words inserted in each place by FA 2010 s 50(1) with effect from 8 April 2010.

[3] In sub-s (3), words substituted for words "Schedule 1" by FA 2012 s 203, Sch 28 paras 2, 6 with effect in relation to supplies made or to be made on or after 1 December 2012.

56 Fuel for private use

(1) The provisions of this section apply where, in any prescribed accounting period, fuel which is or has previously been supplied to or imported or manufactured by a taxable person in the course of his business—

(a) is provided or to be provided by the taxable person to an individual for private use in his own vehicle or a vehicle allocated to him and is so provided by reason of that individual's employment; or

(b) where the taxable person is an individual, is appropriated or to be appropriated by him for private use in his own vehicle; or

(c) where the taxable person is a partnership, is provided or to be provided to any of the individual partners for private use in his own vehicle.

(2) For the purposes of this section fuel shall not be regarded as provided to any person for his private use if it is supplied at a price which—

(a) in the case of fuel supplied to or imported by the taxable person, is not less than the price at which it was so supplied or imported; and

(b) in the case of fuel manufactured by the taxable person, is not less than the aggregate of the cost of the raw material and of manufacturing together with any excise duty thereon.

(3) For the purposes of this section and section 57—

(a) "fuel for private use" means fuel which, having been supplied to or imported or manufactured by a taxable person in the course of his business, is or is to be provided or appropriated for private use as mentioned in subsection (1) above;

(b) any reference to fuel supplied to a taxable person shall include a reference to fuel acquired by a taxable person from another member State and any reference to fuel imported by a taxable person shall be confined to a reference to fuel imported by that person from a place outside the member States;

(c) any reference to an individual's own vehicle shall be construed as including any vehicle of which for the time being he has the use, other than a vehicle allocated to him;

(d) subject to subsection (9) below, a vehicle shall at any time be taken to be allocated to an individual if at that time it is made available (without any transfer of the property in it) either to the individual himself or to any other person, and is so made available by reason of the individual's employment and for private use; and

(e) fuel provided by an employer to an employee and fuel provided to any person for private use in a vehicle which, by virtue of paragraph (d) above, is for the time being taken to be allocated to the employee shall be taken to be provided to the employee by reason of his employment.

(4) Where under section 43 any bodies corporate are treated as members of a group, any provision of fuel by a member of the group to an individual shall be treated for the purposes of this section as provision by the representative member.

(5) In relation to the taxable person, tax on the supply, acquisition or importation of fuel for private use shall be treated for the purposes of this Act as input tax, notwithstanding that the fuel is not used or to be used for the purposes of a business carried on by the taxable person (and, accordingly, no apportionment of VAT shall fall to be made under section 24(5) by reference to fuel for private use).

(6) At the time at which fuel for private use is put into the fuel tank of an individual's own vehicle or of a vehicle allocated to him, the fuel shall be treated for the purposes of this Act as supplied to him by the taxable person in the course or furtherance of his business for a consideration determined in accordance with subsection (7) below (and, accordingly, where the fuel is appropriated by the taxable person to his own private use, he shall be treated as supplying it to himself in his private capacity).

(7) In any prescribed accounting period of the taxable person in which, by virtue of subsection (6) above, he is treated as supplying fuel for private use to an individual, the consideration for all the supplies made to that individual in that period in respect of any one vehicle shall be that which, by virtue of section 57, is appropriate to a vehicle of that description, and that consideration shall be taken to be inclusive of VAT.

(8) In any case where—

(a) in any prescribed accounting period, fuel for private use is, by virtue of subsection (6) above, treated as supplied to an individual in respect of one vehicle for a part of the period and in respect of another vehicle for another part of the period; and

(b) at the end of that period one of those vehicles neither belongs to him nor is allocated to him,

subsection (7) above shall have effect as if the supplies made to the individual during those parts of the period were in respect of only one vehicle.

(9) In any prescribed accounting period a vehicle shall not be regarded as allocated to an individual by reason of his employment if—

(a) in that period it was made available to, and actually used by, more than one of the employees of one or more employers and, in the case of each of them, it was made available to him by reason of his employment but was not in that period ordinarily used by any one of them to the exclusion of the others; and

(b) in the case of each of the employees, any private use of the vehicle made by him in that period was merely incidental to his other use of it in that period; and

(c) it was in that period not normally kept overnight on or in the vicinity of any residential premises where any of the employees was residing, except while being kept overnight on premises occupied by the person making the vehicle available to them.

(10) In this section and section 57—

"employment" includes any office; and related expressions shall be construed accordingly;

"vehicle" means a mechanically propelled road vehicle other than—

(a) a motor cycle as defined in section 185(1) of the Road Traffic Act 1988 or, for Northern Ireland, in Article 37(1)(f) of the Road Traffic (Northern Ireland) Order 1981, or

(b) an invalid carriage as defined in that section or, for Northern Ireland, in Article 37(1)(g) of that Order.[1]

Note—HMRC's VAT fuel scale charge pages are available at: www.gov.uk/fuel-scale-charge.

Commentary—*De Voil Indirect Tax Service* **V3.266**.

Sub-ss (6)–(10): FA 1986 s 9(6)–(10), Road Traffic (Consequential Provisions) Act 1988 Sch 3 para 32.

Definitions—"acquired from another member State", s 11; "another member State", s 96(1); "business", s 94; "excise duty", s 96(5); "importation from a place outside the member States", s 15; "input tax", s 24; "prescribed accounting period", s 25(1); "representative member", s 43(4); "supply", s 5, Sch 4; "tax", s 96(1); "taxable person", s 3; "VAT", ss 1, 96(1).

Cross-reference—See FA 2013 Sch 38 para 7(2) (this section has effect on and after 11 December 2012 as if in sub-s (2) for the words after "it is supplied" there were substituted "for consideration.").

See the VAT (Flat-rate Valuation of Supplies of Fuel for Private Use) Order, SI 2013/2911 and the revalorised table made under art 7 of that Order.

Amendments—[1] Sections 56, 57 repealed by FA 2013 s 192, Sch 38 paras 1, 4 with effect in relation to prescribed accounting periods beginning on or after 1 February 2014.

57 Determination of consideration for fuel supplied for private use

(1) This section has effect to determine the consideration referred to in section 56(7) in respect of any one vehicle; and in this section—

"the prescribed accounting period" means that in respect of supplies in which the consideration is to be determined; and

"the individual" means the individual to whom those supplies are treated as made.

[(1A) Where the prescribed accounting period is a period of 12 months, the consideration appropriate to any vehicle is that specified in relation to a vehicle of the appropriate description in the second column of Table A below.][1]

(2) Where the prescribed accounting period is a period of 3 months, the consideration appropriate to any vehicle is that specified in relation to a vehicle of the appropriate description in the [third][1] *column of Table A below.*

(3) Where the prescribed accounting period is a period of one month, the consideration appropriate to any vehicle is that specified in relation to a vehicle of the appropriate description in the [fourth][1] *column of Table A below.*

[Table A

Description of vehicle:	*12 month period*	*3 month period*	*1 month period*
vehicle's CO_2 emissions figure	£	£	£
120 or less	675.00	168.00	56.00

Description of vehicle: *vehicle's CO2 emissions figure*	*12 month period* £	*3 month period* £	*1 month period* £
125	1,010.00	253.00	84.00
130	1,080.00	269.00	89.00
135	1,145.00	286.00	95.00
140	1,215.00	303.00	101.00
145	1,280.00	320.00	106.00
150	1,350.00	337.00	112.00
155	1,415.00	354.00	118.00
160	1,485.00	371.00	123.00
165	1,550.00	388.00	129.00
170	1,620.00	404.00	134.00
175	1,685.00	421.00	140.00
180	1,755.00	438.00	146.00
185	1,820.00	455.00	151.00
190	1,890.00	472.00	157.00
195	1,955.00	489.00	163.00
200	2,025.00	506.00	168.00
205	2,090.00	523.00	174.00
210	2,160.00	539.00	179.00
215	2,225.00	556.00	185.00
220	2,295.00	573.00	191.00
225 or more	2,360.00	590.00	196.00][6]

[Notes

(1) *If a CO_2 emissions figure is specified in relation to a vehicle in an EC certificate of conformity or a UK approval certificate, the vehicle's CO_2 emissions figure for the purposes of Table A is determined as follows.*

(2) *If only one figure is specified in the certificate, that figure is the vehicle's CO_2 emissions figure for those purposes.*

(3) *If more than one figure is specified in the certificate, the figure specified as the CO2 (combined) emissions figure is the vehicle's CO_2 emissions figure for those purposes.*

(4) *If separate CO_2 emissions figures are specified for different fuels, the lowest figure specified or, in a case within note (3), the lowest CO_2 emissions (combined) figure specified is the vehicle's CO_2 emissions figure for those purposes.*

(5) *If the vehicle's CO_2 emissions figure (determined in accordance with notes (2) to (4)) is not a multiple of 5, it is rounded down to the nearest multiple of 5 for those purposes.*

(6) *If no EC certificate of conformity or UK approval certificate is issued in relation to a vehicle or no emissions figure is specified in relation to it in any such certificate, the vehicle's CO_2 emissions figure for those purposes is—*

(a) *140 . . .* [4] *(if its cylinder capacity is 1,400 cubic centimetres or less),*

(b) *175 (if its cylinder capacity exceeds 1,400 cubic centimetres but does not exceed 2,000 cubic centimetres), and*

(c) *[225]*[5] *or more (if its cylinder capacity exceeds 2,000 cubic centimetres).]*[3]

(4) The Treasury may by order taking effect from the beginning of any prescribed accounting period beginning after the order is made substitute a different Table for Table A for the time being set out above.

[(4A) The power conferred by subsection (4) above includes power to substitute for Table A a Table (whether or not of the same or a similar configuration) where any description of vehicle may be by reference to any one or more of the following—

(a) *the CO_2 emissions figure for the vehicle;*

(b) *the type or types of fuel or power by which the vehicle is, or is capable of being, propelled;*

(c) *the cylinder capacity of the engine in cubic centimetres.*

(4B) The provision that may be included in any such Table includes provision for the purpose of enabling the consideration to be determined by reference to the Table—

(a) *by applying a percentage specified in the Table to a monetary amount specified in the Table, or*

(b) by any other method.
(4C) Table A, as from time to time substituted by virtue of subsection (4A) above, may be implemented or supplemented by either or both of the following—
(a) provision in Rules inserted before the Table, prescribing how the consideration is to be determined by reference to the Table;
(b) provision in Notes inserted after the Table in accordance with the following provisions of this section.
(4D) The provision that may be made in Notes includes provision—
(a) with respect to the interpretation or application of the Table or any Rules or Notes;
(b) with respect to the figure that is to be regarded as the CO_2 emissions figure for any vehicle or any particular description of vehicle;
(c) for treating a vehicle as a vehicle with a particular CO_2 emissions figure;
(d) for treating a vehicle with a CO_2 emissions figure as a vehicle with a different CO_2 emissions figure;
(e) for or in connection with determining the consideration appropriate to vehicles of any particular description (in particular, vehicles falling within any one or more of the descriptions in subsection (4E) below).
(4E) The descriptions are—
(a) vehicles capable of being propelled by any particular type or types of fuel or power;
(b) vehicles first registered before 1st January 1998;
(c) vehicles first registered on or after that date which satisfy the condition in subsection (4F) below (registration without a CO_2 emissions figure).
(4F) The condition is that the vehicle is not one which, when it is first registered, is so registered on the basis of—
(a) an EC certificate of conformity that specifies a CO_2 emissions figure, or
(b) a UK approval certificate that specifies such a figure
(4G) Any Rules or Notes do not form part of the Table, but the Treasury, by order taking effect from the beginning of any prescribed accounting period beginning after the order is made, may—
(a) insert Rules or Notes,
(b) vary or remove Rules or Notes, or
(c) substitute any or all Rules or Notes.][2]
(5) Where, by virtue of section 56(8), subsection (7) of that section has effect as if, in the prescribed accounting period, supplies of fuel for private use made in respect of 2 or more vehicles were made in respect of only one vehicle, the consideration appropriate shall be determined as follows—
(a) if each of the 2 or more vehicles falls within the same description of vehicle specified in [Table A above or any Notes, that Table and those Notes][2] *shall apply as if only one of the vehicles were to be considered throughout the whole period, and*
(b) if one of those vehicles falls within a description of vehicle specified in that Table [or those Notes][2] *which is different from the other or others, the consideration shall be the aggregate of the relevant fractions of the consideration appropriate for each description of vehicle under that Table [or those Notes]*[2].
(6) For the purposes of subsection (5)(b) above, the relevant fraction in relation to any vehicle is that which the part of the prescribed accounting period in which fuel for private use was supplied in respect of that vehicle bears to the whole of that period.
(7) In the case of a vehicle having an internal combustion engine with one or more reciprocating pistons, its cubic capacity for the purposes of Table A above [and any Notes][2] *is the capacity of its engine as calculated for the purposes of the Vehicle Excise and Registration Act 1994.*
(8) In the case of a vehicle not falling within subsection (7) above, its cubic capacity shall be such as may be determined for the purposes of Table A above [and any Notes][2] *by order by the Treasury.*
[(9) In this section—
"CO_2 emissions figure" means a CO_2 emissions figure expressed in grams per kilometre driven;
"EC certificate of conformity" means a certificate of conformity issued by a manufacturer under any provision of the law of a Member State implementing Article 6 of Council Directive 70/ 156/ EEC, as from time to time amended;
"Notes" means Notes inserted by virtue of subsection (4C)(b) above;
"Rules" means Rules inserted by virtue of subsection (4C)(a) above;
"UK approval certificate" means a certificate issued under—
(a) section 58(1) or (4) of the Road Traffic Act 1988, or
(b) Article 31A(4) or (5) of the Road Traffic (Northern Ireland) Order 1981.
(10) If the Treasury consider it necessary or expedient to do so in consequence of—
(a) the form or content of any Table substituted or to be substituted by virtue of subsection (4A) above, or
(b) any provision included or to be included in Rules or Notes,
they may by order amend, repeal or replace so much of this section as for the time being follows subsection (1) and precedes Table A and relates to the use of that Table.][2, 7]

Note—The following valuation table, published under art 7 of SI 2013/2911, provides the flat-rate amounts, as revalorised, for prescribed accounting periods beginning on or after **1 May 2015**—

Description of vehicle: vehicle's CO_2 emissions figure	VAT inclusive consideration for a 12 month prescribed accounting period £	VAT inclusive consideration for a 3 month prescribed accounting period £	VAT inclusive consideration for a 1 month prescribed accounting period £
120 or less	536.00	133.00	44.00
125	802.00	200.00	66.00
130	857.00	213.00	70.00
135	909.00	227.00	75.00
140	965.00	240.00	80.00
145	1,016.00	254.00	84.00
150	1,072.00	267.00	88.00
155	1,123.00	281.00	93.00
160	1,179.00	294.00	97.00
165	1,231.00	308.00	102.00
170	1,286.00	320.00	106.00
175	1,338.00	334.00	111.00
180	1,393.00	347.00	115.00
185	1,445.00	361.00	119.00
190	1,501.00	374.00	124.00
195	1,552.00	388.00	129.00
200	1,608.00	401.00	133.00
205	1,660.00	415.00	138.00
210	1,715.00	428.00	142.00
215	1,767.00	441.00	146.00
220	1,822.00	455.00	151.00
225 or more	1,874.00	468.00	155.00

HMRC's VAT fuel scale charge pages are available at: www.gov.uk/fuel-scale-charge.

Commentary—*De Voil Indirect Tax Service* **V3.266**.

Orders—Value Added Tax (Consideration for Fuel Provided for Private Use) Order, SI 2013/659.

Value Added Tax (Flat-rate Valuation of Supplies of Fuel for Private Use) Order, 2013/2911.

Definitions—"Fuel for private use", s 56(3)(*a*); "supply", s 5, Sch 4; "vehicle", s 56(10).

Amendments—

1 Sub-s (1A) inserted and words in sub-ss (2), (3) substituted by FA 1995 s 30 with effect in relation to prescribed accounting periods beginning after 5 April 1995 (but not so as to be taken to prejudice any practice by which the consideration appropriate to a vehicle is arrived at where a prescribed accounting period beginning before 6 April 1995 is a period of 12 months).

2 Sub-ss (4A)–(4G), (9), (10) inserted; in sub-s (5)(a) words substituted; in sub-s (5)(b) words inserted; and in sub-ss (7), (8) words inserted; by F(No 2)A 2005 s 2 with effect from 22 March 2007 (by virtue of SI 2007/946, art 2).

3 Notes inserted by the Value Added Tax (Consideration for Fuel Provided for Private Use) Order 2007, SI 2007/966 art 4 with effect from the beginning of prescribed accounting periods beginning on or after 1 May 2007.

4 In sub-s (3), in Note (6)(a), words repealed by the VAT (Consideration for Fuel Provided for Private Use) Order, SI 2008/722 art 3 with effect from the beginning of prescribed accounting periods beginning on or after 1 May 2008.

5 Figure in Note (6)(*c*) substituted for figure "230", by the VAT (Consideration for Fuel Provided for Private Use) Order, SI 2011/898 art 2 with effect from the beginning of prescribed accounting periods beginning on or after 1 May 2011.

6 Table A substituted by the Value Added Tax (Consideration for Fuel Provided for Private Use) Order, SI 2013/659 art 2 with effect from the beginning of prescribed accounting periods beginning on or after 1 May 2013.

7 Sections 56, 57 repealed by FA 2013 s 192, Sch 38 paras 1, 4 with effect in relation to prescribed accounting periods beginning on or after 1 February 2014.

PART IV
ADMINISTRATION, COLLECTION AND ENFORCEMENT

Cross reference—See VATA 1994 Sch 13 para 12 (this Part of this Act, except s 72, does not apply in relation to any act or omission before 25 July 1985).

General administrative provisions

58 General provisions relating to the administration and collection of VAT

Schedule 11 shall have effect, subject to section 92(6), with respect to the administration, collection and enforcement of VAT.

Definition—"VAT", ss 1, 96(1).
Regulations—Value Added Tax (Amendment) (No 2) Regulations, SI 2010/2240.

Disclosure of avoidance schemes

[58A Disclosure of avoidance schemes

Schedule 11A (which imposes disclosure requirements relating to the use of schemes for avoiding VAT) shall have effect.][1]

Commentary—*De Voil Indirect Tax Service* **V5.213, 358**.
Definition—"VAT", ss 1, 96(1).
Amendments—[1] This section inserted by FA 2004 s 19, Sch 2 para 1 with effect from the passing of FA 2004, so far as is necessary for enabling the making of any orders or regulations by virtue of FA 2004 Sch 2, and otherwise with effect from 1 August 2004 (by virtue of SI 2004/1934).

[58B Payment by cheque

Regulations under section 95(1) of the Finance Act 2007 (payment by cheque) may, in particular, provide for a payment which is made by cheque in contravention of regulations under section 25(1) above to be treated as made when the cheque clears, as defined in the regulations under section 95(1) of that Act.][1]

Commentary—*De Voil Indirect Tax Service* **V5.109A**.
Press releases etc—HMRC Brief 14/10, 17-3-10 (From 1 April 2010 all cheque payments sent by post will be treated as being received on the date when cleared funds reach the HMRC bank account).
Amendments—[1] This section inserted by FA 2007 s 95(8) with effect from 19 July 2007.

Default surcharges and other penalties and criminal offences

59 The default surcharge

(1) [Subject to subsection (1A) below][1] If, by the last day on which a taxable person is required in accordance with regulations under this Act to furnish a return for a prescribed accounting period—

(*a*) the Commissioners have not received that return, or
(*b*) the Commissioners have received that return but have not received the amount of VAT shown on the return as payable by him in respect of that period,

then that person shall be regarded for the purposes of this section as being in default in respect of that period.

[(1A) A person shall not be regarded for the purposes of this section as being in default in respect of any prescribed accounting period if that period is one in respect of which he is required by virtue of any order under section 28 to make any payment on account of VAT.][1]

(2) Subject to subsections (9) and (10) below, subsection (4) below applies in any case where—

(*a*) a taxable person is in default in respect of a prescribed accounting period; and
(*b*) the Commissioners serve notice on the taxable person (a "surcharge liability notice") specifying as a surcharge period for the purposes of this section a period ending on the first anniversary of the last day of the period referred to in paragraph (*a*) above and beginning, subject to subsection (3) below, on the date of the notice.

(3) If a surcharge liability notice is served by reason of a default in respect of a prescribed accounting period and that period ends at or before the expiry of an existing surcharge period already notified to the taxable person concerned, the surcharge period specified in that notice shall be expressed as a continuation of the existing surcharge period and, accordingly, for the purposes of this section, that existing period and its extension shall be regarded as a single surcharge period.

(4) Subject to subsections (7) to (10) below, if a taxable person on whom a surcharge liability notice has been served—

(*a*) is in default in respect of a prescribed accounting period ending within the surcharge period specified in (or extended by) that notice, and
(*b*) has outstanding VAT for that prescribed accounting period,

he shall be liable to a surcharge equal to whichever is the greater of the following, namely, the specified percentage of his outstanding VAT for that prescribed accounting period and £30.

(5) Subject to subsections (7) to (10) below, the specified percentage referred to in subsection (4) above shall be determined in relation to a prescribed accounting period by reference to the number of such periods in respect of which the taxable person is in default during the surcharge period and for which he has outstanding VAT, so that—

(*a*) in relation to the first such prescribed accounting period, the specified percentage is 2 per cent;
(*b*) in relation to the second such period, the specified percentage is 5 per cent;
(*c*) in relation to the third such period, the specified percentage is 10 per cent; and
(*d*) in relation to each such period after the third, the specified percentage is 15 per cent.

(6) For the purposes of subsections (4) and (5) above a person has outstanding VAT for a prescribed accounting period if some or all of the VAT for which he is liable in respect of that period has not been paid by the last day on which he is required (as mentioned in subsection (1) above) to make a return for that period; and the reference in subsection (4) above to a person's outstanding VAT for a prescribed accounting period is to so much of the VAT for which he is so liable as has not been paid by that day.

(7) If a person who, apart from this subsection, would be liable to a surcharge under subsection (4) above satisfies the Commissioners or, on appeal, a tribunal that, in the case of a default which is material to the surcharge—

(*a*) the return or, as the case may be, the VAT shown on the return was despatched at such a time and in such a manner that it was reasonable to expect that it would be received by the Commissioners within the appropriate time limit, or

(*b*) there is a reasonable excuse for the return or VAT not having been so despatched,

he shall not be liable to the surcharge and for the purposes of the preceding provisions of this section he shall be treated as not having been in default in respect of the prescribed accounting period in question (and, accordingly, any surcharge liability notice the service of which depended upon that default shall be deemed not to have been served).

(8) For the purposes of subsection (7) above, a default is material to a surcharge if—

(*a*) it is the default which, by virtue of subsection (4) above, gives rise to the surcharge; or

(*b*) it is a default which was taken into account in the service of the surcharge liability notice upon which the surcharge depends and the person concerned has not previously been liable to a surcharge in respect of a prescribed accounting period ending within the surcharge period specified in or extended by that notice.

(9) In any case where—

(*a*) the conduct by virtue of which a person is in default in respect of a prescribed accounting period is also conduct falling within section 69(1), and

(*b*) by reason of that conduct, the person concerned is assessed to a penalty under that section,

the default shall be left out of account for the purposes of subsections (2) to (5) above.

(10) If the Commissioners, after consultation with the Treasury, so direct, a default in respect of a prescribed accounting period specified in the direction shall be left out of account for the purposes of subsections (2) to (5) above.

[(11) For the purposes of this section references to a thing's being done by any day include references to its being done on that day.][1]

Commentary—*De Voil Indirect Tax Service* **V5.371–V5.376**.

Press releases etc—C&E Press Notice 23/95 10-4-95 (Customs error in imposing penalties).

Simon's Tax Cases—s 59, *R&C Comrs v Total Technology* [2013] STC 681, [2012] UKUT 418 (TCC).

s 59(7), *T E Davey Photo Service Ltd v C&E Comrs* [1997] STC 889*; *CMS Peripherals Ltd v R&C Comrs* [2008] STC 985.

Definitions—"The Commissioners", s 96(1); "prescribed accounting period", s 25(1); "reasonable excuse", s 71(1); "regulations", s 96(1); "taxable person", s 3; "tribunal", s 82; "VAT", ss 1, 96(1).

Cross references—See VATA 1994 s 59B(1)(*b*), (3) (application of this section where a prescribed accounting period in respect of which a person is not liable to make a payment on account ends within a surcharge period under s 59A).

VATA 1994 s 66(7) (failure to submit EC sales statement within time limit: circumstances in which person is not to be treated as in default);

VATA 1994 s 69(4)(*a*), (9) (avoidance of double penalty for same conduct);

VATA 1994 s 71(1) (reasonable excuse for conduct within this section);

VATA 1994 s 71(2) (meaning of "credit for input tax");

VATA 1994 ss 76, 77 (assessment of surcharges under this section);

VATA 1994 ss 83, 84 (appeal to a tribunal in respect of a surcharge under this section);

VATA 1994 Sch 13 para 14 (modification of this section in its application to certain periods before the commencement of VATA 1994).

FA 2009 s 108 (suspension of penalties during currency of agreement for deferred payment).

Amendments—[1] Words in sub-s (1), and sub-ss (1A), (11), inserted by FA 1996 s 35(3), (4), with effect in relation to any prescribed accounting period ending on or after 1 June 1996, but a liability to make a payment on account of VAT shall be disregarded for the purposes of the amendments made by FA 1996 s 35 if the payment is one becoming due before that date.

[59A Default surcharge: payments on account

(1) For the purposes of this section a taxable person shall be regarded as in default in respect of any prescribed accounting period if the period is one in respect of which he is required, by virtue of an order under section 28, to make any payment on account of VAT and either—

(*a*) a payment which he is so required to make in respect of that period has not been received in full by the Commissioners by the day on which it became due; or

(*b*) he would, but for section 59(1A), be in default in respect of that period for the purposes of section 59.

(2) Subject to subsections (10) and (11) below, subsection (4) below applies in any case where—

(*a*) a taxable person is in default in respect of a prescribed accounting period; and

(*b*) the Commissioners serve notice on the taxable person (a "surcharge liability notice") specifying as a surcharge period for the purposes of this section a period which—

(i) begins, subject to subsection (3) below, on the date of the notice; and

(ii) ends on the first anniversary of the last day of the period referred to in paragraph (*a*) above.

(3) If—

(*a*) a surcharge liability notice is served by reason of a default in respect of a prescribed accounting period, and

(*b*) that period ends at or before the expiry of an existing surcharge period already notified to the taxable person concerned,

the surcharge period specified in that notice shall be expressed as a continuation of the existing surcharge period; and, accordingly, the existing period and its extension shall be regarded as a single surcharge period.

(4) Subject to subsections (7) to (11) below, if—

(*a*) a taxable person on whom a surcharge liability notice has been served is in default in respect of a prescribed accounting period,

(*b*) that prescribed accounting period is one ending within the surcharge period specified in (or extended by) that notice, and

(*c*) the aggregate value of his defaults in respect of that prescribed accounting period is more than nil,

that person shall be liable to a surcharge equal to whichever is the greater of £30 and the specified percentage of the aggregate value of his defaults in respect of that prescribed accounting period.

(5) Subject to subsections (7) to (11) below, the specified percentage referred to in subsection (4) above shall be determined in relation to a prescribed accounting period by reference to the number of such periods during the surcharge period which are periods in respect of which the taxable person is in default and in respect of which the value of his defaults is more than nil, so that—

(*a*) in relation to the first such prescribed accounting period, the specified percentage is 2 per cent;

(*b*) in relation to the second such period, the specified percentage is 5 per cent;

(*c*) in relation to the third such period, the specified percentage is 10 per cent; and

(*d*) in relation to each such period after the third, the specified percentage is 15 per cent.

(6) For the purposes of this section the aggregate value of a person's defaults in respect of a prescribed accounting period shall be calculated as follows—

(*a*) where the whole or any part of a payment in respect of that period on account of VAT was not received by the Commissioners by the day on which it became due, an amount equal to that payment or, as the case may be, to that part of it shall be taken to be the value of the default relating to that payment;

(*b*) if there is more than one default with a value given by paragraph (*a*) above, those values shall be aggregated;

(*c*) the total given by paragraph (*b*) above, or (where there is only one default) the value of the default under paragraph (*a*) above, shall be taken to be the value for that period of that person's defaults on payments on account;

(*d*) the value of any default by that person which is a default falling within subsection (1)(*b*) above shall be taken to be equal to the amount of any outstanding VAT less the amount of unpaid payments on account; and

(*e*) the aggregate value of a person's defaults in respect of that period shall be taken to be the aggregate of—

(i) the value for that period of that person's defaults (if any) on payments on account; and

(ii) the value of any default of his in respect of that period that falls within subsection (1)(*b*) above.

(7) In the application of subsection (6) above for the calculation of the aggregate value of a person's defaults in respect of a prescribed accounting period—

(*a*) the amount of outstanding VAT referred to in paragraph (*d*) of that subsection is the amount (if any) which would be the amount of that person's outstanding VAT for that period for the purposes of section 59(4); and

(*b*) the amount of unpaid payments on account referred to in that paragraph is the amount (if any) equal to so much of any payments on account of VAT (being payments in respect of that period) as has not been received by the Commissioners by the last day on which that person is required (as mentioned in section 59(1)) to make a return for that period.

(8) If a person who, apart from this subsection, would be liable to a surcharge under subsection (4) above satisfies the Commissioners or, on appeal, a tribunal—

(*a*) in the case of a default that is material for the purposes of the surcharge and falls within subsection (1)(*a*) above—

(i) that the payment on account of VAT was despatched at such a time and in such a manner that it was reasonable to expect that it would be received by the Commissioners by the day on which it became due, or

(ii) that there is a reasonable excuse for the payment not having been so despatched, or

(*b*) in the case of a default that is material for the purposes of the surcharge and falls within subsection (1)(*b*) above, that the condition specified in section 59(7)(*a*) or (*b*) is satisfied as respects the default,

he shall not be liable to the surcharge and for the purposes of the preceding provisions of this section he shall be treated as not having been in default in respect of the prescribed accounting period in question (and, accordingly, any surcharge liability notice the service of which depended upon that default shall be deemed not to have been served).

(9) For the purposes of subsection (8) above, a default is material to a surcharge if—

(*a*) it is the default which, by virtue of subsection (4) above, gives rise to the surcharge; or

(*b*) it is a default which was taken into account in the service of the surcharge liability notice upon which the surcharge depends and the person concerned has not previously been liable to a surcharge in respect of a prescribed accounting period ending within the surcharge period specified in or extended by that notice.

10) In any case where—

(*a*) the conduct by virtue of which a person is in default in respect of a prescribed accounting period is also conduct falling within section 69(1), and

(*b*) by reason of that conduct, the person concerned is assessed to a penalty under section 69,

the default shall be left out of account for the purposes of subsections (2) to (5) above.

(11) If the Commissioners, after consultation with the Treasury, so direct, a default in respect of a prescribed accounting period specified in the direction shall be left out of account for the purposes of subsections (2) to (5) above.

(12) For the purposes of this section the Commissioners shall be taken not to receive a payment by the day on which it becomes due unless it is made in such a manner as secures (in a case where the payment is made otherwise than in cash) that, by the last day for the payment of that amount, all the transactions can be completed that need to be completed before the whole amount of the payment becomes available to the Commissioners.

(13) In determining for the purposes of this section whether any person would, but for section 59(1A), be in default in respect of any period for the purposes of section 59, subsection (12) above shall be deemed to apply for the purposes of section 59 as it applies for the purposes of this section.

(14) For the purposes of this section references to a thing's being done by any day include references to its being done on that day.][1]

Commentary—*De Voil Indirect Tax Service* **V5.381**.

Simon's Tax Cases—s 59A(1), *CMS Peripherals Ltd v R&C Comrs* [2008] STC 985.

Definitions—"The Commissioners", s 96(1); "prescribed accounting period", s 25(1); "reasonable excuse", s 71(1); "taxable person", ss 3, 96(1); "tribunal", ss 82, 96(1); "VAT", s 96(1).

Cross references—See VATA 1994 s 59B(1)(*a*), (2) (application of this section where a prescribed accounting period in respect of which a person is liable to make a payment on account ends within a surcharge period under s 59).

VATA 1994 s 66(7) (failure to submit EC sales statement within time limit: circumstances in which a person is not to be treated as in default).

VATA 1994 s 69(4)(*a*), (9) (avoidance of double penalty for the same conduct).

VATA 1994 ss 76, 77 (assessment of surcharges under this section).

FA 2009 s 108 (suspension of penalties during currency of agreement for deferred payment).

Amendments—[1] Section inserted by FA 1996 s 35(2), with effect in relation to any prescribed accounting period ending on or after 1 June 1996, but a liability to make a payment on account of VAT shall be disregarded for the purposes of the amendments made by FA 1996 s 35 if the payment is one becoming due before that date.

[59B Relationship between sections 59 and 59A

(1) This section applies in each of the following cases, namely—

(*a*) where a section 28 accounting period ends within a surcharge period begun or extended by the service on a taxable person (whether before or after the coming into force of section 59A) of a surcharge liability notice under section 59; and

(*b*) where a prescribed accounting period which is not a section 28 accounting period ends within a surcharge period begun or extended by the service on a taxable person of a surcharge liability notice under section 59A.

(2) In a case falling within subsection (1)(*a*) above section 59A shall have effect as if—

(*a*) subject to paragraph (*b*) below, the section 28 accounting period were deemed to be a period ending within a surcharge period begun or, as the case may be, extended by a notice served under section 59A; but

(*b*) any question—

(i) whether a surcharge period was begun or extended by the notice, or

(ii) whether the taxable person was in default in respect of any prescribed accounting period which was not a section 28 accounting period but ended within the surcharge period begun or extended by that notice,

were to be determined as it would be determined for the purposes of section 59.

(3) In a case falling within subsection (1)(*b*) above section 59 shall have effect as if—

(*a*) subject to paragraph (*b*) below, the prescribed accounting period that is not a section 28 accounting period were deemed to be a period ending within a surcharge period begun or, as the case may be, extended by a notice served under section 59;

(*b*) any question—

(i) whether a surcharge period was begun or extended by the notice, or

(ii) whether the taxable person was in default in respect of any prescribed accounting period which was a section 28 accounting period but ended within the surcharge period begun or extended by that notice,

were to be determined as it would be determined for the purposes of section 59A; and

(*c*) that person were to be treated as having had outstanding VAT for a section 28 accounting period in any case where the aggregate value of his defaults in respect of that period was, for the purposes of section 59A, more than nil.

(4) In this section "a section 28 accounting period", in relation to a taxable person, means any prescribed accounting period ending on or after the day on which the Finance Act 1996 was passed in respect of which that person is liable by virtue of an order under section 28 to make any payment on account of VAT.][1]

Commentary—*De Voil Indirect Tax Service* **V5.381**.

Definitions—"Prescribed accounting period", s 25(1); "surcharge liability notice", s 59(2); "taxable person", ss 3, 96(1).

Amendments—[1] Section inserted by FA 1996 s 35(5), with effect in relation to any prescribed accounting period ending on or after 1 June 1996, but a liability to make a payment on account of VAT shall be disregarded for the purposes of the amendments made by FA 1996 s 35 if the payment is one becoming due before that date.

60 VAT evasion: conduct involving dishonesty

(1) In any case where—

(a) for the purpose of evading VAT, a person does any act or omits to take any action, and

(b) his conduct involves dishonesty (whether or not it is such as to give rise to criminal liability),

he shall be liable, subject to subsection (6) below, to a penalty equal to the amount of VAT evaded or, as the case may be, sought to be evaded, by his conduct.

(2) The reference in subsection (1)(a) above to evading VAT includes a reference to obtaining any of the following sums—

(a) a refund under any regulations made by virtue of section 13(5);

(b) a VAT credit;

(c) a refund under section 35, 36 or 40 of this Act or section 22 of the 1983 Act; and

(d) a repayment under section 39,

in circumstances where the person concerned is not entitled to that sum.

(3) The reference in subsection (1) above to the amount of the VAT evaded or sought to be evaded by a person's conduct shall be construed—

(a) in relation to VAT itself or a VAT credit as a reference to the aggregate of the amount (if any) falsely claimed by way of credit for input tax and the amount (if any) by which output tax was falsely understated; and

(b) in relation to the sums referred to in subsection (2)(a), (c) and (e) above, as a reference to the amount falsely claimed by way of refund or repayment.

(4) Statements made or documents produced by or on behalf of a person shall not be inadmissible in any such proceedings as are mentioned in subsection (5) below by reason only that it has been drawn to his attention—

(a) that, in relation to VAT, the Commissioners may assess an amount due by way of a civil penalty instead of instituting criminal proceedings and, though no undertaking can be given as to whether the Commissioners will make such an assessment in the case of any person, it is their practice to be influenced by the fact that a person has made a full confession of any dishonest conduct to which he has been a party and has given full facilities for investigation, and

(b) that the Commissioners or, on appeal, a tribunal have power under section 70 to reduce a penalty under this section,

and that he was or may have been induced thereby to make the statements or produce the documents.

(5) The proceedings mentioned in subsection (4) above are—

(a) any criminal proceedings against the person concerned in respect of any offence in connection with or in relation to VAT, and

(b) any proceedings against him for the recovery of any sum due from him in connection with or in relation to VAT.

(6) Where, by reason of conduct falling within subsection (1) above, a person is convicted of an offence (whether under this Act or otherwise), that conduct shall not also give rise to liability to a penalty under this section.

(7) On an appeal against an assessment to a penalty under this section, the burden of proof as to the matters specified in subsection (1)(a) and (b) above shall lie upon the Commissioners.[1]

Commentary—*De Voil Indirect Tax Service* **V5.341**.
Simon's Tax Cases—*Nidderdale Building Ltd v C&E Comrs* [1997] STC 800; *1st Indian Cavalry Club Ltd and Chowdhury v C&E Comrs* [1998] STC 293; *Ali (T/A Vakas Balti) v R&C Comrs* [2007] STC 618.
s 60(1), *Stuttarrd and anor v C&E Comrs* [2000] STC 342; *McNicholas Construction Limited v C&E Comrs* [2000] STC 553, *C&E Comrs v Han* [2001] STC 1188; *Khan (t/a Greyhound Dry Cleaners) v C&E Comrs* [2006] STC 1167.
s 60(2), *Stevenson and Telford Building & Design Ltd v C&E Comrs* [1996] STC 1096*.
s 60(3), *C&E Comrs v Stevenson* [1995] STC 667*; *Stevenson and Telford Building & Design Ltd v C&E Comrs* [1996] STC 1096*.
Definitions—"The 1983 Act", s 96(1); "the Commissioners", s 96(1); "credit for input tax", s 71(2); "document", s 96(1); "input tax", s 24; "output tax", s 24; "tribunal", s 82; "VAT", ss 1, 96(1); "VAT credit", s 25(3).
Cross references—See VATA 1994 ss 63(11), 64(6), 67(8), 69(9) (avoidance of double penalty for the same conduct);
VATA 1994 s 66(7) (failure to submit EC sales statement within time limit: circumstances in which person is not to be treated as in default);
VATA 1994 s 70(1) (mitigation of penalties imposed under this section);
VATA 1994 s 71(1) (reasonable excuse for conduct within this section);
VATA 1994 s 71(2) (meaning of "credit for input tax");
VATA 1994 ss 76, 77 (assessment of penalties under this section);
VATA 1994 ss 83, 84 (appeal to a tribunal in respect of a penalty under this section);
VATA 1994 Sch 13 para 17 (modification of this section in relation to penalties assessed before 27 July 1993).
VAT Tribunals Rules, SI 1986/590 reg 7 (statement of case, defence and reply in appeals under this section);
VAT Tribunals Rules, SI 1986/590 reg 20(2) (time limit for service of documents in appeals under this section);
VAT Tribunals Rules, SI 1986/590 reg 21(6) (time limit for witness statements in appeals under this section);
VAT Tribunals Rules, SI 1986/590 reg 27(2) (procedure for hearing of appeals under this section).
Amendments—[1] This section repealed by FA 2007 ss 97, 114, Sch 24 para 29(d), Sch 27 Pt 5(5) with effect as follows (by virtue of SI 2008/568 art 2, and subject to transitional provisions and savings in arts 3, 4)—

- 1 April 2008 in relation to relevant documents relating to tax periods commencing on or after that date;
- 1 April 2008 in relation to assessments falling within Sch 24 para 2 for tax periods commencing on or after that date;
- 1 July 2008 in relation to relevant documents relating to claims under the Thirteenth Council Directive (arrangements for the refund of value added tax to persons not established in Community territory) for years commencing on or after that date;
- 1 January 2009 in relation to relevant documents relating to claims under the Eighth Council Directive (arrangements for the refund of value added tax to taxable persons not established in the territory of the country) for years commencing on or after that date;
- 1 April 2009 in relation to documents relating to all other claims for repayments of relevant tax made on or after 1 April 2009 which are not related to a tax period; and
- in any other case, 1 April 2009 in relation to documents given where a person's liability to pay relevant tax arises on or after that date.

Sections 60, 61 shall continue to have effect with respect to conduct involving dishonesty which does not relate to an inaccuracy in a document or a failure to notify HMRC of an under-assessment by HMRC (SI 2008/568 art 4).
Notwithstanding FA 2007 Sch 24 para 29(d), ss 60 and 61 shall continue to have effect with respect to conduct involving dishonesty which does not relate to an inaccuracy in a document or a failure to notify HMRC of an under-assessment by HMRC (SI 2009/571 art 7).

61 VAT evasion: liability of directors etc

(1) Where it appears to the Commissioners—

(a) that a body corporate is liable to a penalty under section 60, and

(b) that the conduct giving rise to that penalty is, in whole or in part, attributable to the dishonesty of a person who is, or at the material time was, a director or managing officer of the body corporate (a "named officer"),

the Commissioners may serve a notice under this section on the body corporate and on the named officer.

(2) A notice under this section shall state—

(a) the amount of the penalty referred to in subsection (1)(a) above ("the basic penalty"), and

(b) that the Commissioners propose, in accordance with this section, to recover from the named officer such portion (which may be the whole) of the basic penalty as is specified in the notice.

(3) Where a notice is served under this section, the portion of the basic penalty specified in the notice shall be recoverable from the named officer as if he were personally liable under section 60 to a penalty which corresponds to that portion; and the amount of that penalty may be assessed and notified to him accordingly under section 76.

(4) Where a notice is served under this section—

(a) the amount which, under section 76, may be assessed as the amount due by way of penalty from the body corporate shall be only so much (if any) of the basic penalty as is not assessed on and notified to a named officer by virtue of subsection (3) above; and

(b) the body corporate shall be treated as discharged from liability for so much of the basic penalty as is so assessed and notified.

(5) No appeal shall lie against a notice under this section as such but—

(a) where a body corporate is assessed as mentioned in subsection (4)(a) above, the body corporate may appeal against the Commissioners' decision as to its liability to a penalty and against the amount of the basic penalty as if it were specified in the assessment; and

(b) where an assessment is made on a named officer by virtue of subsection (3) above, the named officer may appeal against the Commissioners' decision that the conduct of the body corporate referred to in subsection (1)(b) above is, in whole or part, attributable to his dishonesty and against their decision as to the portion of the penalty which the Commissioners propose to recover from him.

(6) In this section a "managing officer", in relation to a body corporate, means any manager, secretary or other similar officer of the body corporate or any person purporting to act in any such capacity or as a director; and where the affairs of a body corporate are managed by its members, this section shall apply in relation to the conduct of a member in connection with his functions of management as if he were a director of the body corporate.[1]

Commentary—*De Voil Indirect Tax Service* **V5.341**.

Simon's Tax Cases—*C&E Comrs v Bassimeh* [1997] STC 33*; *Nidderdale Building Ltd v C&E Comrs*; *Lofthouse v C&E Comrs* [1997] STC 800.

s 61(1), (6), *McNicholas Construction Limited v C&E Comrs* [2000] STC 553.

Definitions—"The Commissioners", s 96(1).

Cross references—See VATA 1994 ss 64(6), 69(9) (avoidance of double penalty for the same conduct);

VATA 1994 s 66(7) (failure to submit EC sales statement within time limit: circumstances in which person is not to be treated as in default);

VATA 1994 s 71(1) (reasonable excuse for conduct within this section);

VATA 1994 s 71(2) (meaning of "credit for input tax");

VATA 1994 ss 76, 77 (assessment of penalties under this section);

VATA 1994 ss 83, 84 (appeal to a tribunal in respect of a penalty or a decision of the Commissioners under this section);

VATA 1994 Sch 13 para 17 (modification of sub-s (6) of this section in relation to penalties assessed before 27 July 1993).

VAT Tribunals Rules, SI 1986/590 reg 7 (statement of case, defence and reply in appeals under this section);

VAT Tribunals Rules, SI 1986/590 reg 20(2) (time limit for service of documents in appeals under this section);

VAT Tribunals Rules, SI 1986/590 reg 21(6) (time limit for witness statements in appeals under this section);

VAT Tribunals Rules, SI 1986/590 reg 27(2) (procedure for hearing of appeals under this section).

Amendments—[1] This section repealed by FA 2007 ss 97, 114, Sch 24 para 29(d), Sch 27 Pt 5(5) with effect as follows (by virtue of SI 2008/568 art 2, and subject to transitional provisions and savings in arts 3, 4)—

- 1 April 2008 in relation to relevant documents relating to tax periods commencing on or after that date;
- 1 April 2008 in relation to assessments falling within Sch 24 para 2 for tax periods commencing on or after that date;
- 1 July 2008 in relation to relevant documents relating to claims under the Thirteenth Council Directive (arrangements for the refund of value added tax to persons not established in Community territory) for years commencing on or after that date;
- 1 January 2009 in relation to relevant documents relating to claims under the Eighth Council Directive (arrangements for the refund of value added tax to taxable persons not established in the territory of the country) for years commencing on or after that date;
- 1 April 2009 in relation to documents relating to all other claims for repayments of relevant tax made on or after 1 April 2009 which are not related to a tax period; and
- in any other case, 1 April 2009 in relation to documents given where a person's liability to pay relevant tax arises on or after that date.

Sections 60, 61 shall continue to have effect with respect to conduct involving dishonesty which does not relate to an inaccuracy in a document or a failure to notify HMRC of an under-assessment by HMRC (SI 2008/568 art 4).

Notwithstanding FA 2007 Sch 24 para 29(d), ss 60 and 61 shall continue to have effect with respect to conduct involving dishonesty which does not relate to an inaccuracy in a document or a failure to notify HMRC of an under-assessment by HMRC (SI 2009/571 art 7).

62 Incorrect certificates as to zero-rating etc

[(1) Subject to subsections (3) and (4) below, where—

(*a*) a person to whom one or more supplies are, or are to be, made—

(i) gives to the supplier a certificate that the supply or supplies fall, or will fall, wholly or partly within [any of the Groups of Schedule 7A][3], Group 5 or 6 of Schedule 8 or Group 1 of Schedule 9, or

(ii) gives to the supplier a certificate for the purposes of section 18B(2)(*d*) or 18C(1)(*c*),

and

(*b*) the certificate is incorrect,

the person giving the certificate shall be liable to a penalty.

(1A) Subject to subsections (3) and (4) below, where—

(*a*) a person who makes, or is to make, an acquisition of goods from another member State prepares a certificate for the purposes of section 18B(1)(*d*), and

(*b*) the certificate is incorrect,

the person preparing the certificate shall be liable to a penalty.

(2) The amount of the penalty shall be equal to—

(*a*) in a case where the penalty is imposed by virtue of subsection (1) above, the difference between—

(i) the amount of the VAT which would have been chargeable on the supply or supplies if the certificate had been correct; and

(ii) the amount of VAT actually chargeable;

(*b*) in a case where it is imposed by virtue of subsection (1A) above, the amount of VAT actually chargeable on the acquisition.][2]

(3) The giving [or preparing][1] of a certificate shall not give rise to a penalty under this section if the person who gave [or prepared][1] it satisfies the Commissioners or, on appeal, a tribunal that there is a reasonable excuse for his having given [or prepared][1] it.

(4) Where by reason of giving [or preparing][1] a certificate a person is convicted of an offence (whether under this Act or otherwise), the giving [or preparing][1] of the certificate shall not also give rise to a penalty under this section.

Commentary—*De Voil Indirect Tax Service* **V5.340**.

Definitions—"The 1983 Act", s 96(1); "acquisition of goods from another member State", s 11; "the Commissioners", s 96(1); "reasonable excuse", s 71(1); "supply", s 5, Sch 4; "tribunal", s 82; "VAT", ss 1, 96(1).

Cross references—See VATA 1994 ss 64(6), 69(9) (avoidance of double penalty for the same conduct);

VATA 1994 s 66(7) (failure to submit EC sales statement within time limit: circumstances in which person is not to be treated as in default);

VATA 1994 s 71(1) (reasonable excuse for conduct within this section);

VATA 1994 s 71(2) (meaning of "credit for input tax");

VATA 1994 ss 76, 77 (assessment of penalties under this section);

VATA 1994 ss 83, 84 (appeal to a tribunal in respect of a penalty under this section).

Amendments—[1] Words in sub-ss (3) and (4) inserted and word "or" at the end of sub-para (i) and word "and" at the end of sub-para (ii) of sub-s (1)(a) repealed by FA 1996 Sch 3 para 8, Sch 41 Pt IV(1), with effect from 1 June 1996 (see Finance Act 1996, Section 26, (Appointed Day) Order, SI 1996/1249), and applying to any acquisition of goods from another member State and any supply taking place on or after that day.

[2] Sub-ss (1) and (2) substituted and sub-s (1A) inserted by FA 1999 s 17 with effect in relation to certificates given or, as the case may be, prepared on or after 27 July 1999.

[3] Words substituted for "paragraph 1 of Schedule A1" by FA 2001 s 99(6), Sch 31 para 3 with effect for supplies made, or to be made, after 31 October 2001.

63 Penalty for misdeclaration or neglect resulting in VAT loss for one accounting period equalling or exceeding certain amounts

(1) In any case where, for a prescribed accounting period—

(a) a return is made which understates a person's liability to VAT or overstates his entitlement to a VAT credit, or

(b) an assessment is made which understates a person's liability to VAT and, at the end of the period of 30 days beginning on the date of the assessment, he has not taken all such steps as are reasonable to draw the understatement to the attention of the Commissioners,

and the circumstances are as set out in subsection (2) below, the person concerned shall be liable, subject to subsections (10) and (11) below, to a penalty equal to 15 per cent of the VAT which would have been lost if the inaccuracy had not been discovered.

(2) The circumstances referred to in subsection (1) above are that the VAT for the period concerned which would have been lost if the inaccuracy had not been discovered equals or exceeds whichever is the lesser of £1,000,000 and 30 per cent of the relevant amount for that period.

(3) Any reference in this section to the VAT for a prescribed accounting period which would have been lost if an inaccuracy had not been discovered is a reference to the amount of the understatement of liability or, as the case may be, overstatement of entitlement referred to, in relation to that period, in subsection (1) above.

(4) In this section "the relevant amount", in relation to a prescribed accounting period, means—

(a) for the purposes of a case falling within subsection (1)(a) above, the gross amount of VAT for that period; and

(b) for the purposes of a case falling within subsection (1)(b) above, the true amount of VAT for that period.

(5) In this section "the gross amount of tax", in relation to a prescribed accounting period, means the aggregate of the following amounts, that is to say—

(a) the amount of credit for input tax which (subject to subsection (8) below) should have been stated on the return for that period, and

(b) the amount of output tax which (subject to that subsection) should have been so stated.

(6) In relation to any return which, in accordance with prescribed requirements, includes a single amount as the aggregate for the prescribed accounting period to which the return relates of—

(a) the amount representing credit for input tax, and

(b) any other amounts representing refunds or repayments of VAT to which there is an entitlement,

references in this section to the amount of credit for input tax shall have effect (so far as they would not so have effect by virtue of subsection (9) below) as references to the amount of that aggregate.

(7) In this section "the true amount of VAT", in relation to a prescribed accounting period, means the amount of VAT which was due from the person concerned for that period or, as the case may be, the amount of the VAT credit (if any) to which he was entitled for that period.

(8) Where—

(a) a return for any prescribed accounting period overstates or understates to any extent a person's liability to VAT or his entitlement to a VAT credit, and

(b) that return is corrected, in such circumstances and in accordance with such conditions as may be prescribed, by a return for a later such period which understates or overstates, to the corresponding extent, that liability or entitlement,

it shall be assumed for the purposes of this section that the statements made by each of those returns (so far as they are not inaccurate in any other respect) are correct statements for the accounting period to which it relates.

(9) This section shall have effect in relation to a body which is registered and to which section 33 applies as if—

(a) any reference to a VAT credit included a reference to a refund under that section, and

(b) any reference to credit for input tax included a reference to VAT chargeable on supplies, acquisitions or importations which were not for the purposes of any business carried on by the body.

[(9A) This section shall have effect in relation to a body which is registered and to which section 33A applies as if—

(a) any reference to a VAT credit included a reference to a refund under that section, and

(b) any reference to credit for input tax included a reference to VAT chargeable on supplies, acquisitions or importations which were attributable to the provision by the body of free rights of admission to a museum or gallery that in relation to the body was a relevant museum or gallery for the purposes of section 33A.][1]

(10) Conduct falling within subsection (1) above shall not give rise to liability to a penalty under this section if—

(a) the person concerned satisfies the Commissioners or, on appeal, a tribunal that there is a reasonable excuse for the conduct, or

(b) at a time when he had no reason to believe that enquiries were being made by the Commissioners into his affairs, so far as they relate to VAT, the person concerned furnished to the Commissioners full information with respect to the inaccuracy concerned.

(11) Where, by reason of conduct falling within subsection (1) above—

(a) a person is convicted of an offence (whether under this Act or otherwise), or

(b) a person is assessed to a penalty under section 60,

that conduct shall not also give rise to liability to a penalty under this section.[2]

Commentary—*De Voil Indirect Tax Service* **V5.343, V5.344**.

Definitions—"Business", s 94; "the Commissioners", s 96(1); "credit for input tax", s 71(2); "input tax", s 24; "output tax", s 24; "prescribed", s 96(1); "prescribed accounting period", s 25(1); "reasonable excuse", s 71(1); "registered", s 3(3); "supply", s 5, Sch 4; "tribunal", s 82; "VAT", ss 1, 96(1); "VAT credit", s 25(3).

Cross references—See VATA 1994 ss 64(6), 69(9) (avoidance of double penalty for the same conduct);

VATA 1994 s 66(7) (failure to submit EC sales statement within time limit: circumstances in which person is not to be treated as in default);

VATA 1994 s 70(1) (mitigation of penalties imposed under this section);

VATA 1994 s 71(1) (reasonable excuse for conduct within this section);

VATA 1994 s 71(2) (meaning of "credit for input tax");

VATA 1994 ss 76, 77 (assessment of penalties under this section);

VATA 1994 ss 83, 84 (appeal to a tribunal in respect of a penalty under this section);

VATA 1994 Sch 13 para 15 (this section does not apply to returns and assessments made for prescribed accounting periods beginning before 1 April 1990 and applies with modifications in relation to periods beginning after that date but before 1 June 1994).

Amendments—[1] Sub-s (9A) inserted by FA 2001 s 98(1), (3) with effect from 1 September 2001.

[2] This section repealed by FA 2007 ss 97, 114, Sch 24 para 29(d), Sch 27 Pt 5(5) with effect as follows (by virtue of SI 2008/568 art 2, and subject to transitional provisions and savings in arts 3, 4)—

- 1 April 2008 in relation to relevant documents relating to tax periods commencing on or after that date;
- 1 April 2008 in relation to assessments falling within Sch 24 para 2 for tax periods commencing on or after that date;
- 1 July 2008 in relation to relevant documents relating to claims under the Thirteenth Council Directive (arrangements for the refund of value added tax to persons not established in Community territory) for years commencing on or after that date;
- 1 January 2009 in relation to relevant documents relating to claims under the Eighth Council Directive (arrangements for the refund of value added tax to taxable persons not established in the territory of the country) for years commencing on or after that date;
- 1 April 2009 in relation to documents relating to all other claims for repayments of relevant tax made on or after 1 April 2009 which are not related to a tax period; and
- in any other case, 1 April 2009 in relation to documents given where a person's liability to pay relevant tax arises on or after that date.

64 Repeated misdeclarations

(1) In any case where—

(a) for a prescribed accounting period (including one beginning before the commencement of this section), a return has been made which understates a person's liability to VAT or overstates his entitlement to a VAT credit; and

(b) the VAT for that period which would have been lost if the inaccuracy had not been discovered equals or exceeds whichever is the lesser of £500,000 and 10 per cent of the gross amount of tax for that period,

the inaccuracy shall be regarded, subject to subsections (5) and (6) below, as material for the purposes of this section.

(2) Subsection (3) below applies in any case where—

(a) there is a material inaccuracy in respect of any prescribed accounting period;

(b) the Commissioners serve notice on the person concerned (a "penalty liability notice") specifying a penalty period for the purposes of this section;

(c) that notice is served before the end of 5 consecutive prescribed accounting periods beginning with the period in respect of which there was the material inaccuracy; and

(d) the period specified in the penalty liability notice as the penalty period is the period of 8 consecutive prescribed accounting periods beginning with that in which the date of the notice falls.

(3) If, where a penalty liability notice has been served on any person, there is a material inaccuracy in respect of any of the prescribed accounting periods falling within the penalty period specified in the notice, that person shall be liable, except in relation to the first of those periods in respect of which there is a material inaccuracy, to a penalty equal to 15 per cent of the VAT for the prescribed accounting period in question which would have been lost if the inaccuracy had not been discovered.

(4) Subsections (3), (5), (8) and (9) of section 63 shall apply for the purposes of this section as they apply for the purposes of that section.

(5) An inaccuracy shall not be regarded as material for the purposes of this section if—

(a) the person concerned satisfies the Commissioners or, on appeal, a tribunal that there is a reasonable excuse for the inaccuracy; or

(b) at a time when he had no reason to believe that enquiries were being made by the Commissioners into his affairs, so far as they relate to VAT, the person concerned furnished to the Commissioners full information with respect to the inaccuracy.

[(6) Subject to subsection (6A) below, where by reason of conduct falling within subsection (1) above—

(a) a person is convicted of an offence (whether under this Act or otherwise), or

(b) a person is assessed to a penalty under section 60 or 63,

the inaccuracy concerned shall not be regarded as material for the purposes of this section.][1]

[(6A) Subsection (6) above shall not prevent an inaccuracy by reason of which a person has been assessed to a penalty under section 63—

(a) from being regarded as a material inaccuracy in respect of which the Commissioners may serve a penalty liability notice under subsection (2) above; or

(b) from being regarded for the purposes of subsection (3) above as a material inaccuracy by reference to which any prescribed accounting period falling within the penalty period is to be treated as the first prescribed accounting period so falling in respect of which there is a material inaccuracy.][1]

[(7) Where subsection (5) or (6) above requires any inaccuracy to be regarded as not material for the purposes of the serving of a penalty liability notice, any such notice served in respect of that inaccuracy shall be deemed not to have been served.][1, 2]

Commentary—*De Voil Indirect Tax Service* **V5.344**.

Definitions—"The Commissioners", s 96(1); "prescribed accounting period", s 25(1); "reasonable excuse", s 71(1); "tribunal", s 82; "VAT", ss 1, 96(1); "VAT credit", s 25(3); "VAT which would have been lost if the inaccuracy had not been discovered", s 64(3).

Cross references—See VATA 1994 s 66(7) (failure to submit EC sales statement within time limit: circumstances in which person is not to be treated as in default);

VATA 1994 s 70(1) (mitigation of penalties imposed under this section);

VATA 1994 s 71(1) (reasonable excuse for conduct within this section);

VATA 1994 s 71(2) (meaning of "credit for input tax");

VATA 1994 ss 76, 77 (assessment of penalties under this section);

VATA 1994 ss 83, 84 (appeal to a tribunal in respect of a penalty under this section);

VATA 1994 Sch 13 para 16 (this section applies with modifications in relation to prescribed accounting periods beginning before 1 December 1993; a penalty liability notice cannot be served under this section by reference to a material inaccuracy for a period beginning before that date).

Amendments—[1] Sub-ss (6), (6A), (7) substituted for sub-ss (6), (7) by FA 1996 s 36, with effect in relation to inaccuracies contained in returns made on or after 29 April 1996.

[2] This section repealed by FA 2007 ss 97, 114, Sch 24 para 29(d), Sch 27 Pt 5(5) with effect as follows (by virtue of SI 2008/568 art 2, and subject to transitional provisions and savings in arts 3, 4)—

– 1 April 2008 in relation to relevant documents relating to tax periods commencing on or after that date;
– 1 April 2008 in relation to assessments falling within Sch 24 para 2 for tax periods commencing on or after that date;
– 1 July 2008 in relation to relevant documents relating to claims under the Thirteenth Council Directive (arrangements for the refund of value added tax to persons not established in Community territory) for years commencing on or after that date;

– 1 January 2009 in relation to relevant documents relating to claims under the Eighth Council Directive (arrangements for the refund of value added tax to taxable persons not established in the territory of the country) for years commencing on or after that date;
– 1 April 2009 in relation to documents relating to all other claims for repayments of relevant tax made on or after 1 April 2009 which are not related to a tax period; and
– in any other case, 1 April 2009 in relation to documents given where a person's liability to pay relevant tax arises on or after that date.

65 Inaccuracies in EC sales statements [or in statements relating to section 55A][1]

(1) Where—

(*a*) an EC sales statement containing a material inaccuracy has been submitted by any person to the Commissioners;

(*b*) the Commissioners have, within 6 months of discovering the inaccuracy, issued that person with a written warning identifying that statement and stating that future inaccuracies might result in the service of a notice for the purposes of this section;

(*c*) another EC sales statement containing a material inaccuracy ("the second inaccurate statement") has been submitted by that person to the Commissioners;

(*d*) the submission date for the second inaccurate statement fell within the period of 2 years beginning with the day after the warning was issued;

(*e*) the Commissioners have, within 6 months of discovering the inaccuracy in the second inaccurate statement, served that person with a notice identifying that statement and stating that future inaccuracies will attract a penalty under this section;

(*f*) yet another EC sales statement containing a material inaccuracy is submitted by that person to the Commissioners; and

(*g*) the submission date for the statement falling within paragraph (*f*) above is not more than 2 years after the service of the notice or the date on which any previous statement attracting a penalty was submitted by that person to the Commissioners,

that person shall be liable to a penalty of £100 in respect of the statement so falling.

(2) Subject to subsections (3) and (4) below, an EC sales statement shall be regarded for the purposes of this section as containing a material inaccuracy if, having regard to the matters required to be included in the statement, the inclusion or omission of any information from the statement is misleading in any material respect.

(3) An inaccuracy contained in an EC sales statement shall not be regarded as material for the purposes of this section if—

(*a*) the person who submitted the statement satisfies the Commissioners or, on appeal, a tribunal that there is a reasonable excuse for the inaccuracy; or

(*b*) at a time when he had no reason to believe that enquiries were being made by the Commissioners into his affairs, that person furnished the Commissioners with full information with respect to the inaccuracy.

(4) Where, by reason of the submission of a statement containing a material inaccuracy by any person, that person is convicted of an offence (whether under this Act or otherwise), the inaccuracy to which the conviction relates shall be regarded for the purposes of this section as not being material.

(5) Where the only statement identified in a warning or notice served for the purposes of subsection (1)(*b*) or (*e*) above is one which (whether by virtue of either or both of subsections (3) and (4) above or otherwise) is regarded as containing no material inaccuracies, that warning or notice shall be deemed not to have been issued or served for those purposes.

(6) In this section—

"EC sales statement" means any statement which is required to be submitted to the Commissioners in accordance with regulations under paragraph 2(3) of Schedule 11; and

"submission date", in relation to such a statement, means whichever is the earlier of the last day for the submission of the statement to the Commissioners in accordance with those regulations and the day on which it was in fact submitted to the Commissioners.

[(7) This section applies in relation to a statement which is required to be submitted to the Commissioners in accordance with regulations under paragraph 2(3A) of Schedule 11 as it applies in relation to an EC sales statement.][1]

Commentary—*De Voil Indirect Tax Service* **V5.346**.

Definitions—"The Commissioners", s 96(1); "reasonable excuse", s 71(1); "tribunal", s 82.

Cross references—See VATA 1994 s 66(7) (failure to submit EC sales statement within time limit: circumstances in which person is not to be treated as in default);

VATA 1994 s 71(1) (reasonable excuse for conduct within this section);

VATA 1994 s 71(2) (meaning of "credit for input tax");

VATA 1994 ss 76, 77 (assessment of penalties under this section);

VATA 1994 ss 83, 84 (appeal to a tribunal in respect of a penalty under this section).

Amendments—[1] Heading amended and sub-s (7) inserted by FA 2006 s 19(3), (8) with effect for supplies made on or after 1 June 2007 (by virtue of the Finance Act 2006, section 19, (Appointed Day) Order, SI 2007/1419).

66 Failure to submit EC sales statement [or statement relating to section 55A][1]

(1) If, by the last day on which a person is required in accordance with regulations under this Act to submit an EC sales statement for any prescribed period to the Commissioners, the Commissioners have not received that statement, that person shall be regarded for the purposes of this section as being in default in relation to that statement until it is submitted.

(2) Where any person is in default in respect of any EC sales statement the Commissioners may serve notice on him stating—

(*a*) that he is in default in relation to the statement specified in the notice;

(*b*) that (subject to the liability mentioned in paragraph (*d*) below) no action will be taken if he remedies the default before the end of the period of 14 days beginning with the day after the service of the notice;

(*c*) that if the default is not so remedied, that person will become liable in respect of his default to penalties calculated on a daily basis from the end of that period in accordance with the following provisions of this section; and

(*d*) that that person will become liable, without any further notices being served under this section, to penalties under this section if he commits any more defaults before a period of 12 months has elapsed without his being in default.

(3) Where a person has been served with a notice under subsection (2) above, he shall become liable under this section—

(*a*) if the statement to which the notice relates is not submitted before the end of the period of 14 days beginning with the day after the service of the notice, to a penalty in respect of that statement; and

(*b*) whether or not that statement is so submitted, to a penalty in respect of any EC sales statement the last day for the submission of which is after the service and before the expiry of the notice and in relation to which he is in default.

(4) For the purposes of this section a notice served on any person under subsection (2) above shall continue in force—

(*a*) except in a case falling within paragraph (*b*) below, until the end of the period of 12 months beginning with the day after the service of the notice; and

(*b*) where at any time in that period of 12 months that person is in default in relation to any EC sales statement other than one in relation to which he was in default when the notice was served, until a period of 12 months has elapsed without that person becoming liable to a penalty under this section in respect of any EC sales statement.

(5) The amount of any penalty to which a person who has been served with a notice under subsection (2) above is liable under this section shall be whichever is the greater of £50 and—

(*a*) in the case of a liability in respect of the statement to which the notice relates, a penalty of £5 for every day for which the default continues after the end of the period of 14 days mentioned in subsection (3)(*a*) above, up to a maximum of 100 days; and

(*b*) in the case of a liability in respect of any other statement, a penalty of the relevant amount for every day for which the default continues, up to a maximum of 100 days.

(6) In subsection (5)(*b*) above "the relevant amount", in relation to a person served with a notice under subsection (2) above, means—

(*a*) £5, where (that person not having been liable to a penalty under this section in respect of the statement to which the notice relates) the statement in question is the first statement in respect of which that person has become liable to a penalty while the notice has been in force;

(*b*) £10 where the statement in question is the second statement in respect of which he has become so liable while the notice has been in force (counting the statement to which the notice relates where he has become liable in respect of that statement); and

(*c*) £15 in any other case.

(7) If a person who, apart from this subsection, would be liable to a penalty under this section satisfies the Commissioners or, on appeal a tribunal, that—

(*a*) an EC sales statement has been submitted at such a time and in such a manner that it was reasonable to expect that it would be received by the Commissioners within the appropriate time limit; or

(*b*) there is a reasonable excuse for such a statement not having been dispatched,

he shall be treated for the purposes of this section and sections 59 to 65 and 67 to 71, 73, 75 and 76 [and Schedule 24 to the Finance Act 2007][2] as not having been in default in relation to that statement and, accordingly, he shall not be liable to any penalty under this section [or that Schedule][2] in respect of that statement and any notice served under subsection (2) above exclusively in relation to the failure to submit that statement shall have no effect for the purposes of this section.

(8) If it appears to the Treasury that there has been a change in the value of money since 1st January 1993 or, as the case may be, the last occasion when the sums specified in subsections (5) and (6) above were varied, they may by order substitute for the sums for the time being specified in those

subsections such other sums as appear to them to be justified by the change; but an order under this section shall not apply to any default in relation to a statement the last day for the submission of which was before the order comes into force.

(9) In this section "EC sales statement" means any statement which is required to be submitted to the Commissioners in accordance with regulations under paragraph 2(3) of Schedule 11.

[(10) This section applies in relation to a statement which is required to be submitted to the Commissioners in accordance with regulations under paragraph 2(3A) of Schedule 11 as it applies in relation to an EC sales statement.][1]

Commentary—*De Voil Indirect Tax Service* **V5.355**.

Definitions—"The Commissioners", s 96(1); "prescribed", s 96(1); "reasonable excuse", s 71(1); "regulations", s 96(1); "tribunal", s 82.

Cross references—See VATA 1994 s 71(1) (reasonable excuse for conduct within this section);
VATA 1994 s 71(2) (meaning of "credit for input tax");
VATA 1994 ss 76, 77 (assessment of penalties under this section).

Amendments—[1] Heading amended and sub-s (10) inserted by FA 2006 s 19(3), (8) with effect for supplies on or after 1 June 2007 (by virtue of the Finance Act 2006, section 19, (Appointed Day) Order, SI 2007/1419).

[2] Words in sub-s (7) inserted by the Finance Act 2008, Schedule 40 (Appointed Day, Transitional Provisions and Consequential Amendments) Order, SI 2009/571 art 8, Sch 1 paras 12, 13 with effect from 1 April 2009.

67 Failure to notify and unauthorised issue of invoices

. . .

Amendments—Section 67 repealed by FA 2008 Sch 41 para 25(*f*) with effect from 1 April 2010 (by virtue of SI 2009/511 art 2).

67A Breach of controlled goods agreement

. . .

Amendments—Section 67A was to have been inserted by the Tribunals, Courts and Enforcement Act 2007 s 62(3), Sch 13 paras 117, 119 with effect from a date to be appointed, but was repealed by FA 2008 s 129, Sch 43 para 4 with effect from 6 April 2014 (by virtue of SI 2014/906 art 2) without having come into force.

68 Breaches of walking possession agreements

(1) This section applies where—

(*a*) in accordance with regulations under [section 51 of the Finance Act 1997 (enforcement by distress)][1], a distress is authorised to be levied on the goods and chattels of a person (a "person in default") who has refused or neglected to pay any VAT due or any amount recoverable as if it were VAT due, and

(*b*) the person levying the distress and the person in default have entered into a walking possession agreement, as defined in subsection (2) below.

(2) In this section a "walking possession agreement" means an agreement under which, in consideration of the property distrained upon being allowed to remain in the custody of the person in default and of the delaying of its sale, the person in default—

(*a*) acknowledges that the property specified in the agreement is under distraint and held in walking possession; and

(*b*) undertakes that, except with the consent of the Commissioners and subject to such conditions as they may impose, he will not remove or allow the removal of any of the specified property from the premises named in the agreement.

(3) Subject to subsection (4) below, if the person in default is in breach of the undertaking contained in a walking possession agreement, he shall be liable to a penalty equal to half of the VAT or other amount referred to in subsection (1)(*a*) above.

(4) The person in default shall not be liable to a penalty under subsection (3) above if he satisfies the Commissioners or, on appeal, a tribunal that there is a reasonable excuse for the breach in question.

[(5) This section extends only to Northern Ireland.][2]

Commentary—*De Voil Indirect Tax Service* **V5.351**.

Definitions—"The Commissioners", s 96(1); "reasonable excuse", s 71(1); "regulations", s 96(1); "tribunal", s 82; "VAT", ss 1, 96(1).

Cross references—See VATA 1994 s 66(7) (failure to submit EC sales statement within time limit: circumstances in which person is not to be treated as in default);
VATA 1994 s 71(1) (reasonable excuse for conduct within this section);
VATA 1994 s 71(2) (meaning of "credit for input tax");
VATA 1994 ss 76, 77 (assessment of penalties under this section);
VATA 1994 ss 83, 84 (appeal to a tribunal in respect of a penalty under this section).

Amendments—[1] Words in sub-s (1)(a) substituted for the words "paragraph 5(4) of Schedule 11" by FA 1997 s 53(7) with effect from 1 July 1997 (see SI 1997/1432).

[2] Sub-s (5) substituted by the Tribunals, Courts and Enforcement Act 2007 s 62(3), Sch 13 paras 117, 120 with effect from 6 April 2014 (the date appointed by virtue of the Tribunals, Courts and Enforcement Act 2007 (Commencement No 11) Order, SI 2014/768 art 2(1)(*b*)).

69 Breaches of regulatory provisions

(1) If any person fails to comply with a regulatory requirement, that is to say, a requirement imposed under—

(*a*) paragraph 11 or 12 of Schedule 1, [paragraph 7 of Schedule 1A,][6] paragraph 5 of Schedule 2[, paragraph 5 of Schedule 3 or paragraph 5 of Schedule 3A][3]; or

(*b*) any regulations made under section 48 requiring a VAT representative, for the purposes of registration, to notify the Commissioners that his appointment has taken effect or has ceased to have effect; or

[(*ba*) paragraph 2(3B) of Schedule 11; or][4]

(*c*) paragraph 6(1) or 7 of Schedule 11; or

(*d*) any regulations or rules made under this Act, other than rules made under paragraph 9 of Schedule 12; or

(*e*) any order made by the Treasury under this Act; or

(*f*) any regulations made under the European Communities Act 1972 and relating to VAT [; or

(*g*) section 18A in the form of a condition imposed by the Commissioners under subsection (1) or (6) of that section,][1]

he shall be liable, subject to subsections (8) and (9) below and section 76(6), to a penalty equal to the prescribed rate multiplied by the number of days on which the failure continues (up to a maximum of 100) or, if it is greater, to a penalty of £50.

(2) If any person fails to comply with a requirement to preserve records imposed under paragraph 6(3) of Schedule 11, he shall be liable, subject to the following provisions of this section, to a penalty of £500.

(3) Subject to subsection (4) below, in relation to a failure to comply with any regulatory requirement, the prescribed rate shall be determined by reference to the number of occasions in the period of 2 years preceding the beginning of the failure in question on which the person concerned has previously failed to comply with that requirement and, subject to the following provisions of this section, the prescribed rate shall be—

(*a*) if there has been no such previous occasion in that period, £5;

(*b*) if there has been only one such occasion in that period, £10; and

(*c*) in any other case, £15.

(4) For the purposes of subsection (3) above—

(*a*) a failure to comply with any regulatory requirement shall be disregarded if, as a result of the failure, the person concerned became liable for a surcharge under section 59 [or 59A][2];

(*b*) a continuing failure to comply with any such requirement shall be regarded as one occasion of failure occurring on the date on which the failure began;

(*c*) if the same omission gives rise to a failure to comply with more than one such requirement, it shall nevertheless be regarded as the occasion of only one failure; and

(*d*) in relation to a failure to comply with a requirement imposed by regulations as to the furnishing of a return or as to the payment of VAT, a previous failure to comply with such a requirement as to either of those matters shall be regarded as a previous failure to comply with the requirement in question.

(5) Where the failure referred to in subsection (1) above consists—

(*a*) in not paying the VAT due in respect of any period within the time required by regulations under section 25(1), or

(*b*) in not furnishing a return in respect of any period within the time required by regulations under paragraph 2(1) of Schedule 11,

the prescribed rate shall be whichever is the greater of that which is appropriate under subsection (3)(a) to (c) above and an amount equal to one-sixth, one-third or one-half of 1 per cent of the VAT due in respect of that period, the appropriate fraction being determined according to whether subsection (3)(a), (b) or (c) above is applicable.

(6) For the purposes of subsection (5) above, the VAT due—

(*a*) if the person concerned has furnished a return, shall be taken to be the VAT shown in the return as that for which he is accountable in respect of the period in question, and

(*b*) in any other case, shall be taken to be such VAT as has been assessed for that period and notified to him under section 73(1).

(7) If it appears to the Treasury that there has been a change in the value of money since 25th July 1985 or, as the case may be, the last occasion when the power conferred by this subsection was exercised, they may by order substitute for the sums for the time being specified in subsections (2) and (3)(*a*) to (*c*) above such other sums as appear to them to be justified by the change; but an order under this subsection shall not apply to a failure which began before the date on which the order comes into force.

(8) A failure by any person to comply with any regulatory requirement or the requirement referred to in subsection (2) above shall not give rise to liability to a penalty under this section if the person concerned satisfies the Commissioners or, on appeal, a tribunal that there is a reasonable excuse for the failure; and a failure in respect of which the Commissioners or tribunal have been so satisfied shall be disregarded for the purposes of subsection (3) above.

(9) Where, by reason of conduct falling within subsection (1) or (2) above—

(*a*) a person is convicted of an offence (whether under this Act or otherwise), or (*b*) a person is assessed to a surcharge under section 59 [or 59A][2], or

(*c*) a person is assessed to a penalty under section 60 or 63 [or a penalty under Schedule 24 to the Finance Act 2007][5],

that conduct shall not also give rise to liability to a penalty under this section.

(10) This section applies in relation to failures occurring before as well as after the commencement of this Act, and for that purpose any reference to any provision of this Act includes a reference to the corresponding provision of the enactments repealed by this Act.

Commentary—*De Voil Indirect Tax Service* **V5.352, V5.354**.

Definitions—"The Commissioners", s 96(1); "prescribed", s 96(1); "reasonable excuse", s 71(1); "regulations", s 96(1); "tribunal", s 82; "VAT", ss 1, 96(1); "VAT representative", s 48.

Cross references—See VATA 1994 s 59(9) (avoidance of double penalty for same conduct);

VATA 1994 s 66(7) (failure to submit EC sales statement within time limit: circumstances in which person is not to be treated as in default);

VATA 1994 s 71(1) (reasonable excuse for conduct within this section);

VATA 1994 s 71(2) (meaning of "credit for input tax");

VATA 1994 ss 76, 77 (assessment of penalties under this section);

VATA 1994 ss 83, 84 (appeal to a tribunal in respect of a penalty under this section).

Amendments—[1] Words in sub-s (1) added by FA 1996 Sch 3 para 9, with effect from 1 June 1996 (see Finance Act 1996, Section 26, (Appointed Day) Order, SI 1996/1249), and applying to any acquisition of goods from another member State and any supply taking place on or after that day.

[2] Words in sub-ss (4), (9) inserted by FA 1996 s 35(6), with effect in relation to any prescribed accounting period ending on or after 1 June 1996, but a liability to make a payment on account of VAT shall be disregarded for the purposes of the amendments made by FA 1996 s 35 if the payment is one becoming due before that date.

[3] Words in sub-s (1)(a) substituted by FA 2000 s 136(3), with effect for supplies made after 20 March 2000.

[4] Sub-s (1)(ba) inserted by FA 2006 s 19(5), (8) with effect for supplies made on or after 1 June 2007 (by virtue of the Finance Act 2006, section 19, (Appointed Day) Order, SI 2007/1419).

[5] Words in sub-s (9)(c) inserted by the Finance Act 2008, Schedule 40 (Appointed Day, Transitional Provisions and Consequential Amendments) Order, SI 2009/571 art 8, Sch 1 paras 12, 14 with effect from 1 April 2009.

[6] In sub-s (1)(*a*), words inserted by FA 2012 s 203, Sch 28 paras 2, 7 with effect in relation to supplies made or to be made on or after 1 December 2012.

[69A Breach of record-keeping requirements etc in relation to transactions in gold

(1) This section applies where a person fails to comply with a requirement of regulations under section 13(5)(*a*) or (*b*) of the Finance Act 1999 (gold: duties to keep records or provide information). Where this section applies, the provisions of section 69 do not apply.

(2) A person who fails to comply with any such requirement is liable to a penalty not exceeding 17.5% of the value of the transactions to which the failure relates.

(3) For the purposes of assessing the amount of any such penalty, the value of the transactions to which the failure relates shall be determined by the Commissioners to the best of their judgement and notified by them to the person liable.

(4) No assessment of a penalty under this section shall be made more than 2 years after evidence of facts sufficient in the opinion of the Commissioners to justify the making of the assessment comes to their knowledge.

(5) The reference in subsection (4) above to facts sufficient to justify the making of the assessment is to facts sufficient—

(*a*) to indicate that there had been a failure to comply with any such requirement as is referred to in subsection (1) above, and

(*b*) to determine the value of the transactions to which the failure relates.

(6) A failure by any person to comply with any such requirement as is mentioned in subsection (1) above shall not give rise to a liability to a penalty under this section if the person concerned satisfies the Commissioners or, on appeal, a tribunal, that there is a reasonable excuse for the failure.

(7) Where by reason of conduct falling within subsection (1) above a person—

(*a*) is assessed to a penalty under section 60 [or a penalty for a deliberate inaccuracy under Schedule 24 to the Finance Act 2007][2], or

(*b*) is convicted of an offence (whether under this Act or otherwise),

that conduct shall not also give rise to a penalty under this section.][1]

Commentary—*De Voil Indirect Tax Service* **V5.356**.

Amendments—[1] This section inserted by FA 2000 s 137(1), (2), with effect from 28 July 2000.

[2] Words in sub-s (7)(*b*) inserted by the Finance Act 2008, Schedule 40 (Appointed Day, Transitional Provisions and Consequential Amendments) Order, SI 2009/571 art 8, Sch 1 paras 12, 15 with effect from 1 April 2009.

[69B Breach of record-keeping requirements imposed by directions

(1) If any person fails to comply with a requirement imposed under paragraph 6A(1) of Schedule 11, the person is liable to a penalty.

(2) The amount of the penalty is equal to £200 multiplied by the number of days on which the failure continues (up to a maximum of 30 days).

(3) If any person fails to comply with a requirement to preserve records imposed under paragraph 6A(6) of Schedule 11, the person is liable to a penalty of £500.

(4) If it appears to the Treasury that there has been a change in the value of money since—

(*a*) the day on which the Finance Act 2006 is passed, or

(*b*) (if later) the last occasion when the power conferred by this subsection was exercised,

they may by order substitute for the sums for the time being specified in subsections (2) and (3) such other sums as appear to them to be justified by the change.

(5) But any such order does not apply to a failure which began before the date on which the order comes into force.

(6) A failure by any person to comply with any requirement mentioned in subsection (1) or (3) does not give rise to a liability to a penalty under this section if the person concerned satisfies—

(*a*) the Commissioners, or

(*b*) on appeal, a tribunal,

that there is a reasonable excuse for the failure.

(7) If by reason of conduct falling within subsection (1) or (3) a person—

(*a*) is assessed to a penalty under section 60 [or a penalty for a deliberate inaccuracy under Schedule 24 to the Finance Act 2007][2], or

(*b*) is convicted of an offence (whether under this Act or otherwise),

that conduct does not also give rise to a penalty under this section.][1]

Commentary—*De Voil Indirect Tax Service* **V5.356A**.

Amendments—[1] Inserted by FA 2006 s 21(2) with effect from 19 July 2006.

[2] Words in sub-s (7)(*a*) inserted by the Finance Act 2008, Schedule 40 (Appointed Day, Transitional Provisions and Consequential Amendments) Order, SI 2009/571 art 8, Sch 1 paras 12, 16 with effect from 1 April 2009.

70 Mitigation of penalties under sections 60, 63, 64 and 67

(1) Where a person is liable to a penalty under section 60, 63, 64[, 67 or 69A][1] [or under paragraph 10 of Schedule 11A][2], the Commissioners or, on appeal, a tribunal may reduce the penalty to such amount (including nil) as they think proper.

(2) In the case of a penalty reduced by the Commissioners under subsection (1) above, a tribunal, on an appeal relating to the penalty, may cancel the whole or any part of the reduction made by the Commissioners.

(3) None of the matters specified in subsection (4) below shall be matters which the Commissioners or any tribunal shall be entitled to take into account in exercising their powers under this section.

(4) Those matters are—

(*a*) the insufficiency of the funds available to any person for paying any VAT due or for paying the amount of the penalty;

(*b*) the fact that there has, in the case in question or in that case taken with any other cases, been no or no significant loss of VAT;

(*c*) the fact that the person liable to the penalty or a person acting on his behalf has acted in good faith.

Commentary—*De Voil Indirect Tax Service* **V5.334**.

Definitions—"The Commissioners", s 96(1); "tribunal", s 82; "VAT", ss 1, 96(1).

Cross references—See VATA 1994 s 66(7) (failure to submit EC sales statement within time limit: circumstances in which person is not to be treated as in default);

VATA 1994 s 71(1) (reasonable excuse for conduct within this section);

VATA 1994 Sch 13 para 17 (this section does not apply in relation to a penalty assessed before 27 July 1993).

Amendments—[1] Words in sub-s (1) substituted for "or 67" by FA 2000 s 137(1), (3), with effect from 28 July 2000.

[2] Words in sub-s (1) inserted by FA 2004 s 19, Sch 2 para 3 with effect from the passing of FA 2004, so far as is necessary for enabling the making of any orders or regulations by virtue of FA 2004 Sch 2, and otherwise with effect from such day as the Treasury may by order made by statutory instrument appoint.

71 Construction of sections 59 to 70

(1) For the purpose of any provision of sections 59 to 70 which refers to a reasonable excuse for any conduct—

(*a*) an insufficiency of funds to pay any VAT due is not a reasonable excuse; and

(*b*) where reliance is placed on any other person to perform any task, neither the fact of that reliance nor any dilatoriness or inaccuracy on the part of the person relied upon is a reasonable excuse.

(2) In relation to a prescribed accounting period, any reference in sections 59 to 69 to credit for input tax includes a reference to any sum which, in a return for that period, is claimed as a deduction from VAT due.

Commentary—*De Voil Indirect Tax Service* **V5.335**.

Simon's Tax Cases—s 71(1), *Profile Security Services Ltd v C&E Comrs* [1996] STC 808*; *T E Davey Photo Service Ltd v C&E Comrs* [1997] STC 889*.

Definitions—"Input tax", ss 24, 96(1); "prescribed accounting period", s 25(1); "VAT", ss 1, 96(1).

Cross reference—See VATA 1994 s 66(7) (failure to submit EC sales statement within time limit: circumstances in which person is not to be treated as in default).

72 Offences

(1) If any person is knowingly concerned in, or in the taking of steps with a view to, the fraudulent evasion of VAT by him or any other person, he shall be liable—

(*a*) on summary conviction, to a penalty of the statutory maximum or of three times the amount of the VAT, whichever is the greater, or to imprisonment for a term not exceeding 6 months or to both; or

(*b*) on conviction on indictment, to a penalty of any amount or to imprisonment for a term not exceeding 7 years or to both.

(2) Any reference in subsection (1) above or subsection (8) below to the evasion of VAT includes a reference to the obtaining of—

(*a*) the payment of a VAT credit; or

(*b*) a refund under section 35, 36 or 40 of this Act or section 22 of the 1983 Act; or

(*c*) a refund under any regulations made by virtue of section 13(5); or

(*d*) a repayment under section 39;

and any reference in those subsections to the amount of the VAT shall be construed—

(i) in relation to VAT itself or a VAT credit, as a reference to the aggregate of the amount (if any) falsely claimed by way of credit for input tax and the amount (if any) by which output tax was falsely understated, and

(ii) in relation to a refund or repayment falling within paragraph (*b*), (*c*) or (*d*) above, as a reference to the amount falsely claimed by way of refund or repayment.

(3) If any person—

(*a*) with intent to deceive produces, furnishes or sends for the purposes of this Act or otherwise makes use for those purposes of any document which is false in a material particular; or

(*b*) in furnishing any information for the purposes of this Act makes any statement which he knows to be false in a material particular or recklessly makes a statement which is false in a material particular,

he shall be liable—

(i) on summary conviction, to a penalty of the statutory maximum or, where subsection (4) or (5) below applies, to the alternative penalty specified in that subsection if it is greater, or to imprisonment for a term not exceeding 6 months or to both; or

(ii) on conviction on indictment, to a penalty of any amount or to imprisonment for a term not exceeding 7 years or to both.

(4) In any case where—

(*a*) the document referred to in subsection (3)(*a*) above is a return required under this Act, or

(*b*) the information referred to in subsection (3)(*b*) above is contained in or otherwise relevant to such a return,

the alternative penalty referred to in subsection (3)(i) above is a penalty equal to three times the aggregate of the amount (if any) falsely claimed by way of credit for input tax and the amount (if any) by which output tax was falsely understated.

(5) In any case where—

(*a*) the document referred to in subsection (3)(*a*) above is a claim for a refund under section 35, 36 or 40 of this Act or section 22 of the 1983 Act, for a refund under any regulations made by virtue of section 13(5) or for a repayment under section 39, or

(*b*) the information referred to in subsection (3)(*b*) above is contained in or otherwise relevant to such a claim,

the alternative penalty referred to in subsection (3)(i) above is a penalty equal to 3 times the amount falsely claimed.

(6) The reference in subsection (3)(*a*) above to furnishing, sending or otherwise making use of a document which is false in a material particular, with intent to deceive, includes a reference to furnishing, sending or otherwise making use of such a document, with intent to secure that a machine will respond to the document as if it were a true document.

(7) Any reference in subsection (3)(*a*) or (6) above to producing, furnishing or sending a document includes a reference to causing a document to be produced, furnished or sent.

(8) Where a person's conduct during any specified period must have involved the commission by him of one or more offences under the preceding provisions of this section, then, whether or not the particulars of that offence or those offences are known, he shall, by virtue of this subsection, be guilty of an offence and liable—

(*a*) on summary conviction, to a penalty of the statutory maximum or, if greater, 3 times the amount of any VAT that was or was intended to be evaded by his conduct, or to imprisonment for a term not exceeding 6 months or to both, or

(*b*) on conviction on indictment to a penalty of any amount or to imprisonment for a term not exceeding 7 years or to both.

(9) . . . [2]

(10) If any person acquires possession of or deals with any goods, or accepts the supply of any services, having reason to believe that VAT on the supply of the goods or services, on the acquisition of the goods from another member State or on the importation of the goods from a place outside the member States has been or will be evaded, he shall be liable on summary conviction to a penalty of level 5 on the standard scale or three times the amount of the VAT, whichever is the greater.

(11) If any person supplies [or is supplied with][1] goods or services in contravention of paragraph 4(2) of Schedule 11, he shall be liable on summary conviction to a penalty of level 5 on the standard scale.
(12) Subject to subsection (13) below, sections 145 to 155 of the Management Act (proceedings for offences, mitigation of penalties and certain other matters) shall apply in relation to offences under this Act (which include any act or omission in respect of which a penalty is imposed) and penalties imposed under this Act as they apply in relation to offences and penalties under the customs and excise Acts as defined in that Act; and accordingly in section 154(2) as it applies by virtue of this subsection the reference to duty shall be construed as a reference to VAT.
(13) In subsection (12) above the references to penalties do not include references to penalties under sections 60 to 70.

Commentary—*De Voil Indirect Tax Service* **V5.311, 312**.
Simon's Tax Cases—*R v Dealy* [1995] STC 217*; *R v Ike* [1996] STC 391.
s 72(1), (3), (8), *R v Choudhury; R v Uddin* [1996] STC 1163*; *Coudrat v Revenue and Customs Commissioners* [2005] STC 1006.
s 72(11), *Chaudhry v R&C Prosecution Office* [2008] STC 2357.
Definitions—"The 1983 Act", s 96(1); "acquisition of goods from another member State", s 11; "another member State", s 96(1); "authorised person", s 96(1); "credit for input tax", s 71(2); "document", s 96(1); "importation of goods from a place outside the member States", s 15; "input tax", s 24; "the Management Act", s 96(1); "output tax", s 24; "regulations", s 96(1); "supply", s 5, Sch 4; "VAT", ss 1, 96(1); "VAT Credit", s 25(3).
Cross references—See VATA 1994 Sch 11 para 10(3), (4) (power to issue search warrants in respect of premises where an offence under sub-s (1)–(8) of this section is suspected to have taken place);
VATA 1994 Sch 13 para 13 (modification of this section in relation to offences committed or allegedly committed between 25 July 1983 and 26 July 1985).
FA 2014 Sch 34 para 6(4)(*g*) (application of sub-sections (1), (3), (8) in relation to the issue of conduct notices to promoters of tax avoidance schemes).
Amendments—[1] Words in sub-s (11) inserted by FA 2003 s 17(5) with effect from 10 April 2003.
[2] Sub-s (9) repealed by FA 2007 ss 84, 114, Sch 22 paras 3, 8(a), Sch 27 Pt 5(1) with effect from 1 December 2007 (by virtue of SI 2007/3166 art 3(a)).

Assessments of VAT and other payments due

73 Failure to make returns etc

(1) Where a person has failed to make any returns required under this Act (or under any provision repealed by this Act) or to keep any documents and afford the facilities necessary to verify such returns or where it appears to the Commissioners that such returns are incomplete or incorrect, they may assess the amount of VAT due from him to the best of their judgment and notify it to him.
(2) In any case where, for any prescribed accounting period, there has been paid or credited to any person—
(*a*) as being a repayment or refund of VAT, or
(*b*) as being due to him as a VAT credit,
an amount which ought not to have been so paid or credited, or which would not have been so paid or credited had the facts been known or been as they later turn out to be, the Commissioners may assess that amount as being VAT due from him for that period and notify it to him accordingly.
(3) An amount—
(*a*) which has been paid to any person as being due to him as a VAT credit, and
(*b*) which, by reason of the cancellation of that person's registration under paragraph 13(2) to (6) of Schedule 1, [paragraph 9 or 11 of Schedule 1A,][4] paragraph 6(2) of Schedule 2[, paragraph 6(2) or (3) of Schedule 3 or paragraph 6(1) or (2) of Schedule 3A][2] ought not to have been so paid,
may be assessed under subsection (2) above notwithstanding that cancellation.
(4) Where a person is assessed under subsections (1) and (2) above in respect of the same prescribed accounting period the assessments may be combined and notified to him as one assessment.
(5) Where the person failing to make a return, or making a return which appears to the Commissioners to be incomplete or incorrect, was required to make the return as a personal representative, trustee in bankruptcy, interim or permanent trustee, receiver, liquidator or person otherwise acting in a representative capacity in relation to another person, subsection (1) above shall apply as if the reference to VAT due from him included a reference to VAT due from that other person.
(6) An assessment under subsection (1), (2) or (3) above of an amount of VAT due for any prescribed accounting period must be made within the time limits provided for in section 77 and shall not be made after the later of the following—
(*a*) 2 years after the end of the prescribed accounting period; or
(*b*) one year after evidence of facts, sufficient in the opinion of the Commissioners to justify the making of the assessment, comes to their knowledge,
but (subject to that section) where further such evidence comes to the Commissioners' knowledge after the making of an assessment under subsection (1), (2) or (3) above, another assessment may be made under that subsection, in addition to any earlier assessment.

[(6A) In the case of an assessment under subsection (2), the prescribed accounting period referred to in subsection (6)(*a*) and in section 77(1)(*a*) is the prescribed accounting period in which the repayment or refund of VAT, or the VAT credit, was paid or credited.][3]

(7) Where a taxable person—

(*a*) has in the course or furtherance of a business carried on by him, been supplied with any goods, acquired any goods from another member State or otherwise obtained possession or control of any goods, or

(*b*) has, in the course or furtherance of such a business, imported any goods from a place outside the member States,

the Commissioners may require him from time to time to account for the goods; and if he fails to prove that the goods have been or are available to be supplied by him or have been exported or otherwise removed from the United Kingdom without being exported or so removed by way of supply or have been lost or destroyed, they may assess to the best of their judgment and notify to him the amount of VAT that would have been chargeable in respect of the supply of the goods if they had been supplied by him.

[(7A) Where a fiscal warehousekeeper has failed to pay VAT required by the Commissioners under section 18E(2), the Commissioners may assess to the best of their judgment the amount of that VAT due from him and notify it to him.

(7B) Where it appears to the Commissioners that goods have been removed from a warehouse or fiscal warehouse without payment of the VAT payable under section 18(4) or section 18D on that removal, they may assess to the best of their judgment the amount of VAT due from the person removing the goods or other person liable and notify it to him][1].

(8) In any case where—

(*a*) as a result of a person's failure to make a return for a prescribed accounting period, the Commissioners have made an assessment under subsection (1) above for that period,

(*b*) the VAT assessed has been paid but no proper return has been made for the period to which the assessment related, and

(*c*) as a result of a failure to make a return for a later prescribed accounting period, being a failure by a person referred to in paragraph (*a*) above or a person acting in a representative capacity in relation to him, as mentioned in subsection (5) above, the Commissioners find it necessary to make another assessment under subsection (1) above,

then, if the Commissioners think fit, having regard to the failure referred to in paragraph (a) above, they may specify in the assessment referred to in paragraph (c) above an amount of VAT greater than that which they would otherwise have considered to be appropriate.

(9) Where an amount has been assessed and notified to any person under subsection (1), (2), (3) [, (7), (7A) or (7B)][1] above it shall, subject to the provisions of this Act as to appeals, be deemed to be an amount of VAT due from him and may be recovered accordingly, unless, or except to the extent that, the assessment has subsequently been withdrawn or reduced.

(10) For the purposes of this section notification to a personal representative, trustee in bankruptcy, interim or permanent trustee, receiver, liquidator or person otherwise acting as aforesaid shall be treated as notification to the person in relation to whom he so acts.

Commentary—*De Voil Indirect Tax Service* **V5.131**.

Modifications—VATA 1994 Sch 3BA para 20 (for the purposes of Sch 3BA, modification of this section so that sub-s (1) reads as if reference to returns required under this Act includes relevant non-UK returns, and references in this section to a prescribed accounting period include a tax period).

VATA 1994 Sch 3BA para 21(1)–(3): for the purposes of Sch 3BA, modification of this section as follows—

- sub-ss (3A)–(3C) inserted, and
- reference in sub-s (9) to sub-s (1) of this section includes a reference to sub-s (3A).

Sub-ss (3A)–(3C), for the purposes of this modification, read as follows—

"(3A) Where a person has failed to make an amendment or notification that the person is required to make under paragraph 31 of Schedule 3BA in respect of an increase in the consideration for a UK supply (as defined in paragraph 31(7)), the Commissioners may assess the amount of VAT due from the person as a result of the increase to the best of their judgement and notify it to the person.

(3B) An assessment under subsection (3A)—

(a) is of VAT due for the tax period mentioned in paragraph 31(1)(a) of Schedule 3BA;

(b) must be made within the time limits provided for in section 77, and must not be made after the later of—

(i) 2 years after the end of the tax period referred to in paragraph 31(1)(a);

(ii) one year after evidence of facts sufficient in the opinion of the Commissioners to justify making the assessment comes to their knowledge.

(3C) Subject to section 77, where further evidence such as is mentioned in subsection (3B)(b)(ii) comes to the Commissioners' knowledge after they have made an assessment under subsection (3A), another assessment may be made under that subsection, in addition to any earlier assessment.".

VATA 1994 Sch 3B para 16 (for the purposes of Sch 3B, modification of this section so that sub-s (1) reads as if reference to returns required under this Act includes relevant special scheme returns, and references in this section to a prescribed accounting period include a tax period).

VATA 1994 Sch 3B para 16A(1)–(3): for the purposes of Sch 3B, modification of this section as follows—

- sub-ss (3A)–(3C) inserted, and

– reference in sub-s (9) to sub-s (1) of this section includes a reference to sub-s (3A).

Sub-ss (3A)–(3C), for the purposes of this modification, read as follows—

"(3A) Where a person has failed to make an amendment or notification that the person is required to make under paragraph 16K of Schedule 3B in respect of an increase in the consideration for a UK supply (as defined in paragraph 16K(7)), the Commissioners may assess the amount of VAT due from the person as a result of the increase to the best of their judgement and notify it to the person.

(3B) An assessment under subsection (3A)—

(a) is of VAT due for the tax period mentioned in paragraph 16K(1)(a) of Schedule 3B;

(b) must be made within the time limits provided for in section 77, and must not be made after the later of—

(i) 2 years after the end of the tax period referred to in paragraph 16K(1)(a);

(ii) one year after evidence of facts sufficient in the opinion of the Commissioners to justify making the assessment comes to their knowledge.

(3C) Subject to section 77, where further evidence such as is mentioned in subsection (3B)(b)(ii) comes to the Commissioners' knowledge after they have made an assessment under subsection (3A), another assessment may be made under that subsection, in addition to any earlier assessment.".

Simon's Tax Cases—*C&E Comrs v Pegasus Birds Ltd* [2004] STC 262; *Courts plc v C&E Comrs* [2004] STC 690, [2005] STC 27; *Hossain v C&E Comrs* [2004] STC 1572; *BUPA Purchasing Ltd and others v C&E Comrs* (No 2) [2008] STC 101.

s 73(1), *Bennett v C&E Comrs (No 2)* [2001] STC 137; *Rahman (T/A Khayam Restaurant) v C&E Comrs (No 2)* [2003] STC 150, CA; *Hindle and another (trading as D J Baker Bar) v C&E Comrs* [2004] STC 412; *C&E Comrs v Pegasus Birds Ltd* [2004] STC 1509; *Westone Wholesale Ltd v R&C Comrs* [2008] STC 828; *R&C Comrs v Raj Restaurant (a firm) and others* [2009] STC 729, *Mithras (Wine Bars) Ltd v HM R&C Comrs* [2010] UKUT 115 (TCC), *Queenspice Ltd v R&C Comrs* [2010] UKUT 111 (TCC), [2011] STC1457.

s 73(2), *Mr Wishmore Ltd v Customs and Excise* [1988] STC 723*; *C&E Comrs v Croydon Hotel & Leisure Co Ltd* [1996] STC 1105*; *C&E Comrs v Laura Ashley Ltd* [2004] STC 635.

s 73(6), *Lord Advocate v Shanks (T/A Shanks & Co)* [1992] STC 928*, *C&E Comrs v Croydon Hotel & Leisure Co Ltd* [1996] STC 1105*; *Cheeseman (T/A Well in Tune) v C&E Comrs* [2000] STC 1119.

s 73(6)(*b*), *Cutts v C&E Comrs* [1989] STC 201*; *Spillane v C&E Comrs* [1990] STC 212*; *C&E Comrs v Post Office* [1995] STC 749*; *Pegasus Birds Ltd v C&E Comrs* [2000] STC 91; *McNicholas Construction Limited v C&E Comrs* [2000] STC 553; *LRF Ltd v R&C Comrs* [2012] UKUT 105 (TCC), [2012] STC 1738.

s 73(9), *Lord Advocate v Shanks (T/A Shanks & Co)* [1992] STC 928*; *Elias Gale Racing v C&E Comrs* [1999] STC 66; *Bennett v C&E Comrs (No 2)* [2001] STC 137; *Infinity Distribution Ltd v R&C Comrs* [2010] STC 2258.

Definitions—"Acquisition of goods from another member State", s 11; "another member State", s 96(1); "business", s 94; "the Commissioners", s 96(1); "document", s 96(1); "fiscal warehouse", ss 18A(3), 18F(1); "fiscal warehouse keeper", s 18F(1); "importation of goods from a place outside the member States", s 15; "interim trustee", s 96(1); "permanent trustee", s 96(1); "prescribed accounting period", s 25(1); "registered", s 3(3); "supply", s 5, Sch 4; "taxable person", s 3; "United Kingdom", s 96(11); "VAT", ss 1, 96(1); "VAT credit", s 25(3); "warehouse", s 18(6); "relevant non-UK return", Sch 3BA para 20(3); "relevant special scheme return", Sch 3B para 16(3).

Press releases etc—C&E Business Brief 5/01 13-3-01 (changes to Customs' practice of making and notifying assessments for under-declared VAT, with effect from 1 March 2001).

Cross references—See VATA 1994 s 43(1) (VAT groups: goods acquired from another member state or imported by group companies to be treated as acquired or imported by representative member for purposes of sub-s (7) of this section);

VATA 1994 s 66(7) (failure to submit EC sales statement within time limit: circumstances in which person is not to be treated as in default);

VATA 1994 s 76(5) (ability to combine assessments under s 76(3) and sub-ss (1), (2), (7), (7A) and (7B) above).

VATA 1994 ss 83, 84 (appeal to a tribunal in respect of an assessment under sub-s (1), (2), (7), (7A) or (7B) of this section);

VATA 1994 s 92(6), (7) (exercise of information powers under sub-s (7) of this section in relation to matters relevant to a charge to VAT under the law of another member state),

VATA 1994 Sch 13 para 20 (modification of this section in its application to amounts paid or credited before the commencement of VATA 1994).

VAT Regulations, SI 1995/2518 reg 181 (claim for repayment by Community trader: treatment as return required under Sch 11 para 2);

VAT Regulations, SI 1995/2518 reg 194 (claim for repayment by third country trader: treatment as return required under Sch 11 para 2);

VAT Regulations, SI 1995/2518 reg 212 (recovery of amounts due under sub-s (9) of this section: distress).

Distress for Customs and Excise Duties and Other Indirect Taxes Regulations, SI 1997/1431 reg 5 (levying distress where tax due under s 73(9) above).

Amendments—[1] Sub-ss (7A), (7B) inserted and words in sub-s (9) substituted by FA 1996 Sch 3 paras 10, 11, with effect from 1 June 1996 (see Finance Act 1996, Section 26, (Appointed Day) Order, SI 1996/1249), and applying to any acquisition of goods from another member State and any supply taking place on or after that day.

[2] Words in sub-s (3)(b) substituted by FA 2000 s 136(4), with effect for supplies made after 20 March 2000.

[3] Sub-s (6A) inserted by FA 2008 s 120(1). This amendment is treated as having come into force on 19 March 2008.

[4] In sub-s (3)(*b*), words inserted by FA 2012 s 203, Sch 28 paras 2, 8 with effect in relation to supplies made or to be made on or after 1 December 2012.

74 Interest on VAT recovered or recoverable by assessment

(1) Subject to section 76(8), where an assessment is made under any provision of section 73 and, in the case of an assessment under section 73(1) at least one of the following conditions is fulfilled, namely—

(*a*) the assessment relates to a prescribed accounting period in respect of which either—

(i) a return has previously been made, or

(ii) an earlier assessment has already been notified to the person concerned, (*b*) the assessment relates to a prescribed accounting period which exceeds 3 months and begins on the date with effect from which the person concerned was, or was required to be, registered,

(*c*) the assessment relates to a prescribed accounting period at the beginning of which the person concerned was, but should no longer have been, exempted from registration under paragraph 14(1) of Schedule 1[, [under paragraph 13 of Schedule 1A,][4] under paragraph 8 of Schedule 3 or under paragraph 7 of Schedule 3A][2],

the whole of the amount assessed shall, subject to subsection (3) below, carry interest at [the rate applicable under section 197 of the Finance Act 1996][1] from the reckonable date until payment.

(2) In any case where—

(*a*) the circumstances are such that an assessment falling within subsection (1) above could have been made, but

(*b*) before such an assessment was made the VAT due or other amount concerned was paid (so that no such assessment was necessary),

the whole of the amount paid shall, subject to subsection (3) below, carry interest at [the rate applicable under section 197 of the Finance Act 1996][1] from the reckonable date until the date on which it was paid.

(3) Where (apart from this subsection)—

(*a*) the period before the assessment in question for which any amount would carry interest under subsection (1) above; or

(*b*) the period for which any amount would carry interest under subsection (2) above,

would exceed 3 years, the part of that period for which that amount shall carry interest under that subsection shall be confined to the last 3 years of that period.

(4) Where an unauthorised person, as defined in [paragraph 2(3) of Schedule 41 to the Finance Act 2008][3], issues an invoice showing an amount as being VAT or as including an amount attributable to VAT, the amount which is shown as VAT or, as the case may be, is to be taken as representing VAT shall carry interest at [the rate applicable under section 197 of the Finance Act 1996][1] from the date of the invoice until payment.

(5) The references in subsections (1) and (2) above to the reckonable date shall be construed as follows—

(*a*) where the amount assessed or paid is such an amount as is referred to in section 73(2)(*a*) or (*b*), the reckonable date is the seventh day after the day on which a written instruction was issued by the Commissioners directing the making of the payment of the amount which ought not to have been repaid or paid to the person concerned; and

(*b*) in all other cases the reckonable date is the latest date on which (in accordance with regulations under this Act) a return is required to be made for the prescribed accounting period to which the amount assessed or paid relates; and

(*c*) in the case of an amount assessed under section 73(7) the sum assessed shall be taken for the purposes of paragraph (*b*) above to relate to the period for which the assessment was made;

and interest under this section shall run from the reckonable date even if that date is a non-business day, within the meaning of section 92 of the Bills of Exchange Act 1882.

(6) . . .[1]

(7) Interest under this section shall be paid without any deduction of income tax.

Commentary—*De Voil Indirect Tax Service* **V5.361**.

Modifications—References to prescribed accounting periods in this section are to be read in accordance with the modifications made by VATA 1994 Sch 3BA paras 20 and 21, in relation to the use of non-UK special accounting schemes for supplies of e-services from 1 January 2015 (VATA 1994 Sch 3BA para 22).

References to prescribed accounting periods in this section are to be read in accordance with the modifications made by VATA 1994 Sch 3B paras 16 and 16A, in relation to returns under the non-Union scheme from 1 January 2015 (VATA 1994 Sch 3B para 16B).

Press releases etc—C&E Press Notice 34/94 7-9-94 (interest will not be assessed unless it represents commercial restitution).

C&E News Release 9/95 31-1-95 (interest no longer to be assessed on underdeclaration voluntary disclosures where the net amount of the errors is £2000 or less).

Simon's Tax Cases—*C&E Comrs v Musashi Autoparts Europe Ltd (formerly TAP Manufacturing Ltd)* [2004] STC 220.

Definitions—"The Commissioners", s 96(1); "invoice", s 96(1); "prescribed", s 96(1); "prescribed accounting period", s 25(1); "registered", s 3(3); "regulations", s 96(1); "VAT", ss 1, 96(1).

Cross references—See VATA 1994 ss 76, 77 (assessment of interest under this section);

VATA 1994 Sch 9A para 5(8) (limitation on amount of interest which may be assessed resulting from a direction under Sch 9A (anti-avoidance provisions: groups)).

VATA 1994 Sch 13 para 18 (this section does not apply to prescribed accounting periods beginning before 1 April 1990 and sub-s (3) does not apply to interest on amounts assessed or paid before 1 October 1993).

VATA 1994 Sch 3BA para 24 (definition of "reckonable date" for the purposes of sub-ss (1) and (2) in relation to the use of non-UK special accounting schemes).

VATA 1994 Sch 3B para 16D (definition of "reckonable date" for the purposes of sub-ss (1) and (2) in relation to the returns under the non-Union scheme).

Amendments—[1] Words in sub-ss (1), (2), (4) substituted for words "the prescribed rate" and sub-s (6) repealed by FA 1996 s 197(6)(d), (7), Sch 41 Pt VIII(1) with effect for periods beginning on or after 1 April 1997 (see SI 1997/1015) and with effect in relation to interest running from before that day, as well as in relation to interest running from, or from after, that day.
[2] Words in sub-s (1)(c) substituted by FA 2000 s 136(5), with effect for supplies made after 20 March 2000.
[3] In sub-s (4), words substituted for words "section 67(2)" by the Finance Act 2008 (Penalties for Errors and Failure to Notify etc) (Consequential Amendments) Order, SI 2010/530 art 2, Schedule para 5 with effect from 1 April 2010.
[4] In sub-s (1)(*c*), words inserted by FA 2012 s 203, Sch 28 paras 2, 9 with effect in relation to supplies made or to be made on or after 1 December 2012.

75 Assessments in cases of acquisitions of certain goods by non-taxable persons

(1) Where a person who has, at a time when he was not a taxable person, acquired in the United Kingdom from another member State any goods subject to a duty of excise or consisting in a new means of transport and—

(*a*) notification of that acquisition has not been given to the Commissioners by the person who is required to give one by regulations under paragraph 2(4) of Schedule 11 (whether before or after the commencement of this Act);

(*b*) the Commissioners are not satisfied that the particulars relating to the acquisition in any notification given to them are accurate and complete; or

(*c*) there has been a failure to supply the Commissioners with the information necessary to verify the particulars contained in any such notification,

they may assess the amount of VAT due on the acquisition to the best of their judgment and notify their assessment to that person.

(2) An assessment under this section must be made within the time limits provided for in section 77 and shall not be made after whichever is the later of the following—

(*a*) 2 years after the time when a notification of the acquisition of the goods in question is given to the Commissioners by the person who is required to give one by regulations under paragraph 2(4) of Schedule 11;

(*b*) one year after evidence of the facts, sufficient in the opinion of the Commissioners to justify the making of the assessment, comes to their knowledge,

but (subject to section 77) where further such evidence comes to the Commissioners' knowledge after the making of an assessment under this section, another assessment may be made under this section, in addition to any earlier assessment.

(3) Where an amount has been assessed and notified to any person under this section, it shall, subject to the provisions of this Act as to appeals, be deemed to be an amount of VAT due from him and may be recovered accordingly, unless, or except to the extent that, the assessment has subsequently been withdrawn or reduced.

(4) For the purposes of this section, notification to a personal representative, trustee in bankruptcy, interim or permanent trustee, receiver, liquidator or person otherwise acting in a representative capacity in relation to the person who made the acquisition in question shall be treated as notification to the person in relation to whom he so acts.

Commentary—*De Voil Indirect Tax Service* **V5.132B**.

Definitions—"Acquisition of goods from another member State", s 11; "another member State", s 96(1); "the Commissioners", s 96(1); "interim trustee", s 96(1); "means of transport", s 95; "new means of transport", s 95; "permanent trustee", s 96(1); "regulations", s 96(1); "taxable person", s 3; "United Kingdom", s 96(11); "VAT", ss 1, 96(1).

Cross references—See VATA 1994 s 66(7) (failure to submit EC sales statement within time limit: circumstances in which person is not to be treated as in default);
VATA 1994 ss 83, 84 (appeal to a tribunal in respect of an assessment under this section).

76 Assessment of amounts due by way of penalty, interest or surcharge

(1) Where any person is liable—

(*a*) to a surcharge under section 59 [, section 59A, paragraph 16F of Schedule 3B or paragraph 26 of Schedule 3BA,][7] or

(*b*) to a penalty under any of sections 60 [to [69B][5]][4], or

(*c*) for interest under section 74, [or

(*d*) a penalty under regulations made under section 135 of the Finance Act 2002 (mandatory electronic filing of returns) in connection with VAT,][6]

the Commissioners may, subject to subsection (2) below, assess the amount due by way of penalty, interest or surcharge, as the case may be, and notify it to him accordingly; and the fact that any conduct giving rise to a penalty under any of sections 60 [to [69B][5]][4] [or the regulations][6] may have ceased before an assessment is made under this section shall not affect the power of the Commissioners to make such an assessment.

(2) Where a person is liable to a penalty under section 69 for any failure to comply with such a requirement as is referred to in subsection (1)(*c*) to (*f*) of that section, no assessment shall be made under this section of the amount due from him by way of such penalty unless, within the period of 2 years preceding the assessment, the Commissioners have issued him with a written warning of the consequences of a continuing failure to comply with that requirement.

(3) In the case of the penalties, interest and surcharge referred to in the following paragraphs, the assessment under this section shall be of an amount due in respect of the prescribed accounting period which in the paragraph concerned is referred to as "the relevant period"—

(*a*) in the case of a surcharge under section 59 [or 59A][1], the relevant period is the prescribed accounting period in respect of which the taxable person is in default and in respect of which the surcharge arises;

(*b*) in the case of a penalty under section 60 relating to the evasion of VAT, the relevant period is the prescribed accounting period for which the VAT evaded was due;

(*c*) in the case of a penalty under section 60 relating to the obtaining of the payment of a VAT credit, the relevant period is the prescribed accounting period in respect of which the payment was obtained;

(*d*) in the case of a penalty under section 63, the relevant period is the prescribed accounting period for which liability to VAT was understated or, as the case may be, for which entitlement to a VAT credit was overstated; . . . [6]

(*e*) in the case of interest under section 74, the relevant period is the prescribed accounting period in respect of which the VAT (or amount assessed as VAT) was due[; and

(*f*) in the case of a penalty under regulations made under section 135 of the Finance Act 2002, the relevant period is the prescribed accounting period in respect of which the contravention of, or failure to comply with, the regulations occurred.][6]

[(3A) In the case of a surcharge under paragraph 16F of Schedule 3B or paragraph 26 of Schedule 3BA, the assessment under this section is of an amount due in respect of "the relevant period", that is to say, the tax period (see section 76A) in respect of which the person is in default and in respect of which the surcharge arises.][7]

(4) In any case where the amount of any penalty, interest or surcharge falls to be calculated by reference to VAT which was not paid at the time it should have been and that VAT (or the supply which gives rise to it) cannot be readily attributed to any one or more prescribed accounting periods, it shall be treated for the purposes of this Act as VAT due for such period or periods as the Commissioners may determine to the best of their judgement and notify to the person liable for the VAT and penalty, interest or surcharge.

(5) Where a person is assessed under this section to an amount due by way of any penalty, interest or surcharge falling within subsection (3) [or (3A)][7] above and is also assessed under section 73(1), (2)[, (7), (7A) or (7B)][2] for the prescribed accounting period which is the relevant period under subsection (3) [or (3A)][7] above, the assessments may be combined and notified to him as one assessment, but the amount of the penalty, interest or surcharge shall be separately identified in the notice.

(6) An assessment to a penalty under section 67 by virtue of subsection (1)(*b*) of that section may be combined with an assessment under section 75 and the 2 assessments notified together but the amount of the penalty shall be separately identified in the notice.

(7) In the case of an amount due by way of penalty under section 66 or 69 or interest under section 74—

(*a*) a notice of assessment under this section shall specify a date, being not later than the date of the notice, to which the aggregate amount of the penalty which is assessed or, as the case may be, the amount of interest is calculated; and

(*b*) if the penalty or interest continues to accrue after that date, a further assessment or assessments may be made under this section in respect of amounts which so accrue.

(8) If, within such period as may be notified by the Commissioners to the person liable to a penalty under section 66 or 69 or for interest under section 74—

(*a*) a failure or default falling within section 66(1) or 69(1) is remedied, or

(*b*) the VAT or other amount referred to in section 74(1) is paid,

it shall be treated for the purposes of section 66 or 69 or, as the case may be, section 74 as paid or remedied on the date specified as mentioned in subsection (7)(a) above.

(9) If an amount is assessed and notified to any person under this section, then unless, or except to the extent that, the assessment is withdrawn or reduced, that amount shall be recoverable as if it were VAT due from him.

(10) For the purposes of this section, notification to a personal representative, trustee in bankruptcy, interim or permanent trustee, receiver, liquidator or person otherwise acting in a representative capacity in relation to [another][3] shall be treated as notification to the person in relation to whom he so acts.

Commentary—*De Voil Indirect Tax Service* **V5.333, V5.336, V5.379**.

Simon's Tax Cases—*Georgiou (T/A Marios Chippery) v C&E Comrs* [1996] STC 463*; *C&E Comrs v Bassimeh* [1997] STC 33*; *R&C Comrs v Raj Restaurant (a firm) and others* [2009] STC 729; *LRF Ltd v R&C Comrs* [2012] UKUT 105 (TCC), [2012] STC 1738.

Modifications—Recovery of Duties and Taxes Etc Due on Other Member States (Corresponding UK Claims, Procedure and Supplementary) (adaptation of this section with respect to VAT interest).

VATA 1994 Sch 3BA para 21(4) (for the purposes of Sch 3BA, modification of this section so that reference in sub-s (5) to s 73(1) includes a reference to s 73(3A)).

References to prescribed accounting periods in this section are to be read in accordance with the modifications made by VATA 1994 Sch 3BA paras 20 and 21, in relation to the use of non-UK special accounting schemes for supplies of e-services (VATA 1994 Sch 3BA para 22).

VATA 1994 Sch 3B para 16A(4) (for the purposes of Sch 3B, modification of this section so that reference in sub-s (5) to s 73(1) includes a reference to s 73(3A)).

References to prescribed accounting periods in this section are to be read in accordance with the modifications made by VATA 1994 Sch 3B paras 16 and 16A, in relation to returns under the non-Union scheme from 1 January 2015 (VATA 1994 Sch 3B para 16B).

Definitions—"The Commissioners", s 96(1); "interim trustee", s 96(1); "permanent trustee", s 96(1); "prescribed accounting period", s 25(1); "supply", s 5, Sch 4; "taxable person", s 3; "VAT", ss 1, 96(1); "VAT credit", s 25(3).

Cross references—See VATA 1994 s 61(3), (4) (liability of body corporate to penalty for evasion of VAT: assessment of part of penalty on director);

VATA 1994 s 66(7) (failure to submit EC sales statement within time limit: circumstances in which person is not to be treated as in default);

VATA 1994 s 76A (cases involving special accounting schemes).

VATA 1994 ss 83, 84 (appeal to a tribunal in respect of the amount of any penalty, interest or surcharge specified in an assessment under this section).

VATA 1994 Sch 9A para 5(8) (modification of the application of this section to interest under s 74 resulting from a direction under Sch 9A (anti-avoidance provisions: groups)).

Amendments—[1] Words in sub-s (3) inserted by FA 1996 s 35(7), with effect in relation to any prescribed accounting period ending on or after 1 June 1996, but a liability to make a payment on account of VAT shall be disregarded for the purposes of the amendments made by FA 1996 s 35 if the payment is one becoming due before that date.

[2] Words in sub-s (5) substituted by FA 1996 Sch 3 para 11, with effect from 1 June 1996 (see Finance Act 1996, Section 26, (Appointed Day) Order, SI 1996/1249), and applying to any acquisition of goods from another member State and any supply taking place on or after that day.

[3] Word "another" in sub-s(10) substituted by FA 1997 s 45(6) and deemed always to have had effect.

[4] Words in sub-s (1) substituted for "to 69" by FA 2000 s 137(1), (4), with effect from 28 July 2000.

[5] Words "69B" in both places substituted by FA 2006 s 21(3) with effect from 19 July 2006.

[6] Sub-s (1)(d) and preceding word "or", words in sub-s (1), and sub-s (3)(f) and preceding word "and", inserted, and in sub-s (3)(d) word "and" repealed, by FA 2007 ss 93(4)–(7), 114, Sch 27 Pt 5(4) with effect from 19 July 2007.

[7] In sub-s (1)(*a*), words substituted for words "or 59A,", sub-s (3A) inserted, and in sub-s (5), words inserted, by FA 2014 s 103, Sch 22 paras 11, 13 with effect in relation to supplies made on or after 1 January 2015.

[76A Section 76: cases involving special accounting schemes

(1) References in section 76 to a prescribed accounting period are to be read as including a tax period so far as that is necessary for the purposes of the references in section 76(1)(*a*) to paragraph 16F of Schedule 3B and paragraph 26 of Schedule 3BA (assessment of surcharge in certain cases involving special accounting schemes).

(2) References in section 77 to a prescribed accounting period are to be read accordingly.

(3) In this section and section 76 "tax period" means a tax period as defined in paragraph 23(1) of Schedule 3B or paragraph 38(1) of Schedule 3BA, as the case requires.][1]

Amendments—[1] Section 76A inserted by FA 2014 s 103, Sch 22 paras 11, 14 with effect in relation to supplies made on or after 1 January 2015.

77 Assessments: time limits and supplementary assessments

(1) Subject to the following provisions of this section, an assessment under section 73, 75 or 76, shall not be made—

(*a*) more than [4 years][2] after the end of the prescribed accounting period or importation or acquisition concerned, or

(*b*) in the case of an assessment under section 76 of an amount due by way of a penalty which is not among those referred to in subsection (3) of that section, [4 years][2] after the event giving rise to the penalty.

[(2) Subject to subsection (5) below, an assessment under section 76 of an amount due by way of any penalty, interest or surcharge referred to in subsection (3) [or (3A)][4] of that section may be made at any time before the expiry of the period of 2 years beginning with the time when the amount of VAT due for the prescribed accounting period concerned has been finally determined.][1]

[(2A) Subject to subsection (5) below, an assessment under section 76 of a penalty under section 65 or 66 may be made at any time before the expiry of the period of 2 years beginning with the time when facts sufficient in the opinion of the Commissioners to indicate, as the case may be—

(*a*) that the statement in question contained a material inaccuracy, or

(*b*) that there had been a default within the meaning of section 66(1),

came to the Commissioners' knowledge.][1]

(3) In relation to an assessment under section 76, any reference in subsection (1) or (2) above to the prescribed accounting period concerned is a reference to that period which, in the case of the penalty, interest or surcharge concerned, is the relevant period referred to in subsection (3) [or (3A)][4] of that section.

[(4) In any case falling within subsection (4A), an assessment of a person ("P"), or of an amount payable by P, may be made at any time not more than 20 years after the end of the prescribed accounting period or the importation, acquisition or event giving rise to the penalty, as appropriate (subject to subsection (5)).

(4A) Those cases are—

(*a*) a case involving a loss of VAT brought about deliberately by P (or by another person acting on P's behalf),

(*b*) a case in which P has participated in a transaction knowing that it was part of arrangements of any kind (whether or not legally enforceable) intended to bring about a loss of VAT,

(*c*) a case involving a loss of VAT attributable to a failure by P to comply with a notification obligation, and

(*d*) a case involving a loss of VAT attributable to a scheme in respect of which P has failed to comply with an obligation under paragraph 6 of Schedule 11A.

(4B) In subsection (4A) the references to a loss of tax brought about deliberately by P or another person include a loss that arises as a result of a deliberate inaccuracy in a document given to Her Majesty's Revenue and Customs by that person.

(4C) In subsection (4A)(*c*) "notification obligation" means an obligation under—

(*a*) paragraph 5, 6, 7 or 14(2) or (3) of Schedule 1,

[(*aa*) paragraph 5, 6 or 13(3) of Schedule 1A,][3]

(*b*) paragraph 3 of Schedule 2,

(*c*) paragraph 3 or 8(2) of Schedule 3,

(*d*) paragraph 3, 4 or 7(2) or (3) of Schedule 3A, or

(*e*) regulations under paragraph 2(4) of Schedule 11.][2]

(5) Where, after a person's death, the Commissioners propose to assess a sum as due by reason of some conduct (howsoever described) of the deceased, including a sum due by way of penalty, interest or surcharge—

(*a*) the assessment shall not be made more than [4 years][2] after the death; *and*[2]

(b) if the circumstances are as set out in subsection (4) above, the modification of subsection (1) above contained in that subsection shall not apply but any assessment which (from the point of view of time limits) could have been made immediately after the death may be made at any time within 3 years after it.[2]

(6) If, otherwise than in circumstances falling within section 73(6)(*b*) or 75(2)(*b*), it appears to the Commissioners that the amount which ought to have been assessed in an assessment under that section or under section 76 exceeds the amount which was so assessed, then—

(*a*) under the like provision as that assessment was made, and

(*b*) on or before the last day on which that assessment could have been made,

the Commissioners may make a supplementary assessment of the amount of the excess and shall notify the person concerned accordingly.

Commentary—*De Voil Indirect Tax Service* **V5.134, V5.136**.

Modifications—References to prescribed accounting periods in this section are to be read in accordance with the modifications made by VATA 1994 Sch 3BA paras 20 and 21, in relation to the use of non-UK special accounting schemes for supplies of e-services (VATA 1994 Sch 3BA para 22).

References to prescribed accounting periods in this section are to be read in accordance with the modifications made by VATA 1994 Sch 3B paras 16 and 16A, in relation to returns under the non-Union scheme from 1 January 2015 (VATA 1994 Sch 3B para 16B).

Simon's Tax Cases—*C&E Comrs v Post Office* [1995] STC 749*.

S 77(1)(*a*), *R&C Comrs v Dunwood Travel Ltd* [2008] STC 959.

s 77(2), *Ali (T/A Vakas Balti) v R&C Comrs* [2007] STC 618.

s 77(4), *McNicholas Construction Limited v C&E Comrs* [2000] STC 553.

Definitions—"The Commissioners", s 96(1); "prescribed accounting period", s 25(1); "VAT", ss 1, 96(1).

Cross reference—See VATA 1994 s 76A (cases involving special accounting schemes).

VATA 1994 ss 83, 84 (appeal to a tribunal in respect of an assessment under sub-s (4) of this section).

VATA 1994 Sch 9A para 5(8) (this section, except sub-s (6) does not apply to an assessment for interest under s 74 resulting from a direction under Sch 9A (anti-avoidance provisions: groups)).

Amendments—[1] Sub-s (2) substituted and sub-s (2A) inserted by FA 1999 s 18 with effect in relation to any amount by way of penalty, interest or surcharge which becomes due on or after 27 July 1999.

[2] In sub-ss (1)(*a*), (*b*), (5)(*a*), words substituted, sub-ss (4)–(4C) substituted for previous sub-s (4), and sub-s (5)(*b*) and preceding word "and" repealed, by FA 2008 Sch 39 para 34 with effect from 1 April 2009 (by virtue of SI 2009/403 art 2(2)). FA 2008 Sch 39 para 34 is disregarded where—

- for the purposes of VATA 1994 s 77, the end of the prescribed accounting period or the importation, acquisition or event giving rise to the penalty, as appropriate, occurred on or before 31 March 2006; and
- after a person's death, a sum is assessed as due by reason of some conduct (however described) of the deceased, including a sum due by way of penalty, interest or surcharge, and the date of the death is on or before 31 March 2006 (SI 2009/403 art 4).Sub-s (4A)(*c*), (*d*) shall not apply where the end of the prescribed accounting period or the importation, acquisition or event giving rise to the penalty, as appropriate, occurred on or before 31 March 2010, except where VAT has been lost in circumstances giving rise to a penalty under VATA 1994 s 67 (SI 2009/403 art 9).

[3] Sub-s (4C)(*aa*) inserted by FA 2012 s 203, Sch 28 paras 2, 10 with effect in relation to supplies made or to be made on or after 1 December 2012.

[4] In sub-ss (2), (3), words inserted by FA 2014 s 103, Sch 22 paras 11, 15 with effect in relation to supplies made on or after 1 January 2015.

[Liability for unpaid VAT of another

77A Joint and several liability of traders in supply chain where tax unpaid

(1) This section applies to goods [which fall within any one or more][2] of the following descriptions—

[(*a*) any equipment made or adapted for use as a telephone and any other equipment made or adapted for use in connection with telephones or telecommunication;

(*b*) any equipment made or adapted for use as a computer and any other equipment made or adapted for use in connection with computers or computer systems (including, in particular, positional determination devices for use with satellite navigation systems);

(*c*) any other electronic equipment made or adapted for use by individuals for the purposes of leisure, amusement or entertainment and any other equipment made or adapted for use in connection with any such electronic equipment;

and in this subsection "other equipment" includes parts, accessories and software.][2]

(2) Where—

(*a*) a taxable supply of goods to which this section applies has been made to a taxable person, and

(*b*) at the time of the supply the person knew or had reasonable grounds to suspect that some or all of the VAT payable in respect of that supply, or on any previous or subsequent supply of those goods, would go unpaid,

the Commissioners may serve on him a notice specifying the amount of the VAT so payable that is unpaid, and stating the effect of the notice.

(3) The effect of a notice under this section is that—

(*a*) the person served with the notice, and

(*b*) the person liable, apart from this section, for the amount specified in the notice,

are jointly and severally liable to the Commissioners for that amount.

(4) For the purposes of subsection (2) above the amount of VAT that is payable in respect of a supply is the lesser of—

(*a*) the amount chargeable on the supply, and

(*b*) the amount shown as due on the supplier's return for the prescribed accounting period in question (if he has made one) together with any amount assessed as due from him for that period (subject to any appeal by him).

(5) The reference in subsection (4)(*b*) above to assessing an amount as due from a person includes a reference to the case where, because it is impracticable to do so, the amount is not notified to him.

(6) For the purposes of subsection (2) above, a person shall be presumed to have reasonable grounds for suspecting matters to be as mentioned in paragraph (*b*) of that subsection if the price payable by him for the goods in question—

(*a*) was less than the lowest price that might reasonably be expected to be payable for them on the open market, or

(*b*) was less than the price payable on any previous supply of those goods.

(7) The presumption provided for by subsection (6) above is rebuttable on proof that the low price payable for the goods was due to circumstances unconnected with failure to pay VAT.

(8) Subsection (6) above is without prejudice to any other way of establishing reasonable grounds for suspicion.

[(9) The Treasury may by order amend subsection (1) above.

(9A) The Treasury may by order amend this section in order to extend or otherwise alter the circumstances in which a person shall be presumed to have reasonable grounds for suspecting matters to be as mentioned in subsection (2)(*b*) above.

(9B) Any order under this section may make such incidental, supplemental, consequential or transitional provision as the Treasury think fit.][3]

(10) For the purposes of this section—

(*a*) "goods" includes services;

(*b*) an amount of VAT counts as unpaid only to the extent that it exceeds the amount of any refund due.][1]

Simon's Tax Cases—*R (on the application of Federation of Technological Industries and others) v C&E Comrs and another* [2004] STC 1424; *C&E Comrs and another v Federation of Technological Industries and others* [2006] STC 1483.

Amendments—[1] This section inserted by FA 2003 s 18(1) with effect from 10 April 2003.

[2] In sub-s (1) words substituted, and paras (*a*)–(*c*) substituted for original paras (*a*), (*b*), by the VAT (Amendment of section 77A of the VATA 1994) Order, SI 2007/939 reg 2 with effect from 1 May 2007.

[3] Sub-ss (9)–(9B) substituted for original sub-s (9) by FA 2007 s 98(1) with effect from 19 July 2007.

Interest, repayment supplements etc payable by Commissioners

78 Interest in certain cases of official error

(1) Where, due to an error on the part of the Commissioners, a person has—

(*a*) accounted to them for an amount by way of output tax which was not output tax due from him [and, as a result, they are liable under section 80(2A) to pay (or repay) an amount to him,][5] or

(*b*) failed to claim credit under section 25 for an amount for which he was entitled so to claim credit and which they are in consequence liable to pay to him, or

(*c*) (otherwise than in a case falling within paragraph (*a*) or (*b*) above) paid to them by way of VAT an amount that was not VAT due and which they are in consequence liable to repay to him, or

(*d*) suffered delay in receiving payment of an amount due to him from them in connection with VAT,

then, if and to the extent that they would not be liable to do so apart from this section, they shall pay interest to him on that amount for the applicable period, but subject to the following provisions of this section.

[(1A) In subsection (1) above—

(*a*) references to an amount which the Commissioners are liable in consequence of any matter to pay or repay to any person are references, where a claim for the payment or repayment has to be made, to only so much of that amount as is the subject of a claim that the Commissioners are required to satisfy or have satisfied; and

(*b*) the amounts referred to in paragraph (*d*) do not include any amount payable under this section.][2]

(2) Nothing in subsection (1) above requires the Commissioners to pay interest—

(*a*) on any amount which falls to be increased by a supplement under section 79; or

(*b*) where an amount is increased under that section, on so much of the increased amount as represents the supplement.

(3) Interest under this section shall be payable at [the rate applicable under section 197 of the Finance Act 1996][1].

(4) The "applicable period" in a case falling within subsection (1)(*a*) or (*b*) above is the period—

(*a*) beginning with the appropriate commencement date, and

(*b*) ending with the date on which the Commissioners authorise payment of the amount on which the interest is payable.

(5) In subsection (4) above, the "appropriate commencement date"—

(*a*) in a case where an amount would have been due from the person by way of VAT in connection with the relevant return, had his input tax and output tax been as stated in that return, means the date on which the Commissioners received payment of that amount; and

(*b*) in a case where no such payment would have been due from him in connection with that return, means the date on which the Commissioners would, apart from the error, have authorised payment of the amount on which the interest is payable;

and in this subsection "the relevant return" means the return in which the person accounted for, or (as the case may be) ought to have claimed credit for, the amount on which the interest is payable.

(6) The "applicable period" in a case falling within subsection (1)(*c*) above is the period—

(*a*) beginning with the date on which the payment is received by the Commissioners, and

(*b*) ending with the date on which they authorise payment of the amount on which the interest is payable.

(7) The "applicable period" in a case falling within subsection (1)(*d*) above is the period—

(*a*) beginning with the date on which, apart from the error, the Commissioners might reasonably have been expected to authorise payment of the amount on which the interest is payable, and

(*b*) ending with the date on which they in fact authorise payment of that amount.

[(8) In determining in accordance with subsection (4), (6) or (7) above the applicable period for the purposes of subsection (1) above, there shall be left out of account any period by which the Commissioners' authorisation of the payment of interest is delayed by the conduct of the person who claims the interest.][4]

[(8A) The reference in subsection (8) above to a period by which the Commissioners' authorisation of the payment of interest is delayed by the conduct of the person who claims it includes, in particular, any period which is referable to—

(*a*) any unreasonable delay in the making of the claim for interest or in the making of any claim for the payment or repayment of the amount on which interest is claimed;

(*b*) any failure by that person or a person acting on his behalf or under his influence to provide the Commissioners—

(i) at or before the time of the making of a claim, or

(ii) subsequently in response to a request for information by the Commissioners,

with all the information required by them to enable the existence and amount of the claimant's entitlement to a payment or repayment, and to interest on that payment or repayment, to be determined; and

(*c*) the making, as part of or in association with either—

(i) the claim for interest, or

(ii) any claim for the payment or repayment of the amount on which interest is claimed,

of a claim to anything to which the claimant was not entitled.][4]

[(9) In determining for the purposes of subsection (8A) above whether any period of delay is referable to a failure by any person to provide information in response to a request by the Commissioners, there shall be taken to be so referable, except so far as may be prescribed, any period which—

(*a*) begins with the date on which the Commissioners require that person to provide information which they reasonably consider relevant to the matter to be determined; and

(*b*) ends with the earliest date on which it would be reasonable for the Commissioners to conclude—

(i) that they have received a complete answer to their request for information;

(ii) that they have received all that they need in answer to that request; or

(iii) that it is unnecessary for them to be provided with any information in answer to that request.][4]

(10) The Commissioners shall only be liable to pay interest under this section on a claim made in writing for that purpose.

[(11) A claim under this section shall not be made more than [4 years][6] after the end of the applicable period to which it relates.][3]

(12) In this section—

(*a*) references to the authorisation by the Commissioners of the payment of any amount include references to the discharge by way of set-off (whether under section 81(3) or otherwise) of the Commissioners' liability to pay that amount; and][2]

(*b*) any reference to a return is a reference to a return required to be made in accordance with paragraph 2 of Schedule 11.

Commentary—*De Voil Indirect Tax Service* **V5.196**.

Modifications—VATA 1994 Sch 3BA para 28 (in relation to cases where, because of an error on the part of the Commissioners, a person has accounted under a non-UK special scheme for UK VAT that was not due, this section applies as if the condition in sub-s (1)(a) were met in relation to that person).

VATA 1994 Sch 3B para 16H (in relation to cases where, because of an error on the part of the Commissioners, a person has accounted under a special scheme for UK VAT that was not due, this section applies as if the condition in sub-s (1)(a) were met in relation to that person).

Orders—See VATA 1983 (Interest on Overpayments etc) (Prescribed Rate) Order, SI 1991/1754.

Simon's Tax Cases—s 78, *R (on the application of Elite Mobile plc) v Customs and Excise Commissioners* [2005] STC 275; *R (on the application of Mobile Export 365 Ltd and another) v R&C Comrs* [2006] STC 1069; *R&C Comrs v RSPCA and another, R&C Comrs v ToTel Ltd* [2008] STC 885; *John Wilkins (Motor Engineers) Ltd v R&C Comrs and other appeals* [2009] STC 2485; *FJ Chalke Ltd and anor v R&C Comrs* [2010] STC 1640; *Littlewoods Retail Ltd and anor v R&C Comrs* [2010] STC 2072; *Littlewoods Retail Ltd and others v R&C Comrs* [2011] STC 171; *Littlewoods Ltd v R&C Comrs* [2010] EWHC 2771 (Ch), [2011] STC 171; *Littlewoods Retail Ltd and others v R&C Comrs* (Case C-591/10) [2012] STC 1714; *Littlewoods Retail Ltd and others v R&C Comrs* [2014] EWHC 868 (Ch), [2014] STC 1761.

s 78(1)(*a*), *Mathieson v C&E Comrs* [1999] STC 835.

Definitions—"Authorised person", s 96(1); "the Commissioners", s 96(1); "input tax", s 24; "output tax", s 24 and, in relation to non-UK special schemes, Sch 3BA para 28(4), Sch 3B para 16H(4); "VAT", ss 1, 96(1).

Cross references—See VATA 1994 s 83 (appeal to a tribunal in respect of any liability of the Commissioners to pay interest under this section);

VATA 1994 s 101(2) (this section to have effect generally to the exclusion of VATA 1983 s 39).

FA 1997 s 44(6) (corresponding amendments in earlier enactments).

Amendments—[1] Words in sub-s (3) substituted by FA 1996 s 197(6)(d) with effect for periods beginning or after 1 April 1997 (see SI 1997/1015) and with effect in relation to interest running from before that day, as well as in relation to interest running from, or from after, that day.

[2] Sub-s (1A) inserted, and sub-s (12)(a) substituted, by FA 1997 s 44 (1), (3) and deemed always to have had effect.

[3] Sub-s (11) substituted by FA 1997 s 44 (2) in relation to claims made on or after 18 July 1996 and deemed always to have had effect in relation to such claims.

[4] Sub-s (8), (8A) and (9) substituted by FA 1997 s 44 (4), (5) for the purposes of determining whether any period beginning on or after 19 March 1997 is left out of account.

[5] In sub-s (1)(a), words substituted for the words "and which they are in consequence liable to repay to him" by F(No 2)A 2005 s 4(1), (2) with effect in any case where a claim under VATA 1994 s 80(2) is made on or after 26 May 2005, whenever the event occurred in respect of which the claim is made: F(No 2)A 2005 s 4(6).

[6] In sub-s (11), words substituted for words "three years" by FA 2008 Sch 39 para 35 with effect from 1 April 2009 (by virtue of SI 2009/403 art 2(2)). FA 2008 Sch 39 para 35 is disregarded where, for the purposes of a claim under VATA 1994 s 78, the end of the applicable period to which the claim relates was on or before 31 March 2006 (SI 2009/403 art 5).

[78A Assessment for interest overpayments

(1) Where—

(*a*) any amount has been paid to any person by way of interest under section 78, but

(*b*) that person was not entitled to that amount under that section,

the Commissioners may, to the best of their judgement, assess the amount so paid to which that person was not entitled and notify it to him.

(2) An assessment made under subsection (1) above shall not be made more than two years after the time when evidence of facts sufficient in the opinion of the Commissioners to justify the making of the assessment comes to the knowledge of the Commissioners.

(3) Where an amount has been assessed and notified to any person under subsection (1) above, that amount shall be deemed (subject to the provisions of this Act as to appeals) to be an amount of VAT due from him and may be recovered accordingly.

(4) Subsection (3) above does not have effect if or to the extent that the assessment in question has been withdrawn or reduced.

(5) An assessment under subsection (1) above shall be a recovery assessment for the purposes of section 84(3A).

(6) Sections 74 and 77(6) apply in relation to assessments under subsection (1) above as they apply in relation to assessments under section 73 but as if the reference in subsection (1) of section 74 to the reckonable date were a reference to the date on which the assessment is notified.

(7) Where by virtue of subsection (6) above any person is liable to interest under section 74—

(*a*) section 76 shall have effect in relation to that liability with the omission of subsections (2) to (6); and

(*b*) section 77, except subsection (6), shall not apply to an assessment of the amount due by way of interest;

and (without prejudice to the power to make assessments for interest for later periods) the interest to which any assessment made under section 76 by virtue of paragraph (a) above may relate shall be confined to interest for a period of no more than two years ending with the time when the assessment to interest is made.

(8) For the purposes of this section notification to a personal representative, trustee in bankruptcy, interim or permanent trustee, receiver, liquidator or person otherwise acting in a representative capacity in relation to another shall be treated as notification to the person in relation to whom he so acts.][1]

Commentary—*De Voil Indirect Tax Service* **V5.196**.

Simon's Tax Cases—*R v C&E Comrs, ex p Building Societies Ombudsman Co Ltd* [2000] STC 892; *C&E Comrs v DFS Furniture Co plc* [2004] STC 559, CA.

Definitions—"The Commissioners", s 96(1).

Amendments—[1] Inserted by FA 1997 s 45(1) and deemed to have come into force on 4 December 1996 in relation to amounts paid by way of interest on or after 18 July 1996.

79 Repayment supplement in respect of certain delayed payments or refunds

(1) In any case where—

(*a*) a person is entitled to a VAT credit, or

(*b*) a body which is registered and to which section 33 applies is entitled to a refund under that section, [or

(*c*) a body which is registered and to which section 33A applies is entitled to a refund under that section,][2] [or

(*d*) the proprietor of an Academy who is registered is entitled to a refund under section 33B, [or][3]

(*e*) a charity which is registered is entitled to a refund under section 33C,][4]

and the conditions mentioned in subsection (2) below are satisfied, the amount which, apart from this section, would be due by way of that payment or refund shall be increased by the addition of a supplement equal to 5 per cent of that amount or £50, whichever is the greater.

(2) The said conditions are—

(*a*) that the requisite return or claim is received by the Commissioners not later than the last day on which it is required to be furnished or made, and

(*b*) that a written instruction directing the making of the payment or refund is not issued by the Commissioners within [the relevant period][1], and

(*c*) that the amount shown on that return or claim as due by way of payment or refund does not exceed the payment or refund which was in fact due by more than 5 per cent of that payment or refund or £250, whichever is the greater.

[(2A) The relevant period in relation to a return or claim is the period of 30 days beginning with the later of—

(*a*) the day after the last day of the prescribed accounting period to which the return or claim relates, and

(*b*) the date of the receipt by the Commissioners of the return or claim.][1]

(3) Regulations may provide that, in computing the period of 30 days referred to in [subsection (2A)][1] above, there shall be left out of account periods determined in accordance with the regulations and referable to—

(*a*) the raising and answering of any reasonable inquiry relating to the requisite return or claim,

(*b*) the correction by the Commissioners of any errors or omissions in that return or claim, and

(*c*) in the case of a payment, the following matters, namely—

(i) any such continuing failure to submit returns as is referred to in section 25(5), and

(ii) compliance with any such condition as is referred to in paragraph 4(1) of Schedule 11.

(4) In determining for the purposes of regulations under subsection (3) above whether any period is referable to the raising and answering of such an inquiry as is mentioned in that subsection, there shall be taken to be so referable any period which—

(*a*) begins with the date on which the Commissioners first consider it necessary to make such an inquiry, and

(*b*) ends with the date on which the Commissioners—

(i) satisfy themselves that they have received a complete answer to the inquiry, or

(ii) determine not to make the inquiry or, if they have made it, not to pursue it further,

but excluding so much of that period as may be prescribed; and it is immaterial whether any inquiry is in fact made or whether it is or might have been made of the person or body making the requisite return or claim or of an authorised person or of some other person.

(5) Except for the purpose of determining the amount of the supplement—

(*a*) a supplement paid to any person under subsection (1)(*a*) above shall be treated as an amount due to him by way of credit under section 25(3), and

(*b*) a supplement paid to any body under subsection (1)(*b*) above shall be treated as an amount due to it by way of refund under section 33[, and

(*c*) a supplement paid to any body under subsection (1)(*c*) shall be treated as an amount due to it by way of refund under section 33A][2][, and

(*d*) a supplement paid to the proprietor of an Academy under subsection (1)(*d*) shall be treated as an amount due to that proprietor by way of refund under section 33B[, and][3]

(*e*) a supplement paid to a charity under subsection (1)(*e*) shall be treated as an amount due to the charity by way of refund under section 33C.][4]

(6) In this section "requisite return or claim" means—

(*a*) in relation to a payment, the return for the prescribed accounting period concerned which is required to be furnished in accordance with regulations under this Act, and

(*b*) in relation to a refund, the claim for that refund which is required to be made in accordance with the Commissioners' determination under section 33 [or (as the case may be) the Commissioners' determination under, and the provisions of, section 33A[, 33B or 33C][4].][2]

(7) If the Treasury by order so direct, any period specified in the order shall be disregarded for the purpose of calculating the period of 30 days referred to in [subsection (2A)][1] above.

Commentary—*De Voil Indirect Tax Service* **V5.191, V5.192**.

Regulations—See VAT Regulations, SI 1995/2518 regs 198, 199.

Simon's Tax Cases—*R&C Comrs v RSPCA and another, R&C Comrs v ToTel Ltd* [2008] STC 885; *Our Communications Ltd v R&C Comrs* [2013] UKUT 595 (TCC), [2014] STC 608.

Definitions—"Authorised person", s 96(1); "the Commissioners", s 96(1); "prescribed", s 96(1); "prescribed accounting period", s 25(1); "registered", s 3(3); "regulations", s 96(1); "VAT credit", s 25(3).

Cross reference—See VAT Regulations, SI 1995/2518 reg 198 (computation of 30-day period for purposes of sub-s (2)(*b*) of this section).

Amendments—[1] Words in sub-s (2)(*b*), (3) and (7) substituted, and sub-s (2A) inserted by FA 1999 s 19 with effect in relation to returns and claims received by the Commissioners on or after 9 March 1999.

[2] Sub-ss (1)(*c*), (5)(*c*) inserted by FA 2001 s 98(4)–(7) with effect from 1 September 2001.

[3] Sub-s (1)(*d*) and preceding word "or", and sub-s (5)(*d*) and preceding word "and", and words in sub-s (6)(*b*), inserted, by FA 2011 s 76(2) with effect in relation to supplies made, and acquisitions and importations taking place, on or after 1 April 2011. Words "or 33C" inserted by FA 2015 s 66(2)(c) with effect in relation to supplies made, and acquisitions and importations taking place, on or after 1 April 2015.

[4] Sub-ss (1)(*e*), (5)(*e*) and preceding word in each case inserted, and in sub-s (6)(*b*), words substituted, by FA 2015 s 66(1), (2) with effect in relation to supplies made, and acquisitions and importations taking place, on or after 1 April 2015.

80 [Credit for, or repayment of, overstated or overpaid VAT][4]

[(1) Where a person—

(*a*) has accounted to the Commissioners for VAT for a prescribed accounting period (whenever ended), and

(*b*) in doing so, has brought into account as output tax an amount that was not output tax due,

the Commissioners shall be liable to credit the person with that amount.][4]

[(1A) Where the Commissioners—

(*a*) have assessed a person to VAT for a prescribed accounting period (whenever ended), and

(*b*) in doing so, have brought into account as output tax an amount that was not output tax due,

they shall be liable to credit the person with that amount.][4]

[(1B) Where a person has for a prescribed accounting period (whenever ended) paid to the Commissioners an amount by way of VAT that was not VAT due to them, otherwise than as a result of—

(*a*) an amount that was not output tax due being brought into account as output tax, or

(*b*) an amount of input tax allowable under section 26 not being brought into account,

the Commissioners shall be liable to repay to that person the amount so paid.][4]

(2) The Commissioners shall only be liable to [credit or][4] repay an amount under this section on a claim being made for the purpose.

[(2A) Where—

(*a*) as a result of a claim under this section by virtue of subsection (1) or (1A) above an amount falls to be credited to a person, and

(*b*) after setting any sums against it under or by virtue of this Act, some or all of that amount remains to his credit,

the Commissioners shall be liable to pay (or repay) to him so much of that amount as so remains.][4]

(3) It shall be a defence, in relation to a claim [under this section by virtue of subsection (1) or (1A) above, that the crediting][4] of an amount would unjustly enrich the claimant.

[(3A) Subsection (3B) below applies for the purposes of subsection (3) above where—

(*a*) an amount would (apart from subsection (3) above) fall to be credited under subsection (1) or (1A) above to any person ("the taxpayer"), and

(*b*) the whole or a part of the amount brought into account as mentioned in paragraph (*b*) of that subsection has, for practical purposes, been borne by a person other than the taxpayer.][4]

[(3B) Where, in a case to which this subsection applies, loss or damage has been or may be incurred by the taxpayer as a result of mistaken assumptions made in his case about the operation of any VAT provisions, that loss or damage shall be disregarded, except to the extent of the quantified amount, in the making of any determination—

(*a*) of whether or to what extent the [crediting][4] of an amount to the taxpayer would enrich him; or

(*b*) of whether or to what extent any enrichment of the taxpayer would be unjust.][1]

[(3C) In subsection (3B) above —

"the quantified amount" means the amount (if any) which is shown by the taxpayer to constitute the amount that would appropriately compensate him for loss or damage shown by him to have resulted, for any business carried on by him, from the making of the mistaken assumptions; and

"VAT provisions" means the provisions of—

(*a*) any enactment, subordinate legislation or Community legislation (whether or not still in force) which relates to VAT or to any matter connected with VAT; or

(*b*) any notice published by the Commissioners under or for the purposes of any such enactment or subordinate legislation.][1]

[(4) The Commissioners shall not be liable on a claim under this section—

(*a*) to credit an amount to a person under subsection (1) or (1A) above, or

(*b*) to repay an amount to a person under subsection (1B) above,

if the claim is made more than [4 years][6] after the relevant date.][4]

[(4ZA) The relevant date is—

(*a*) in the case of a claim by virtue of subsection (1) above, the end of the prescribed accounting period mentioned in that subsection, unless paragraph (*b*) below applies;

(*b*) in the case of a claim by virtue of subsection (1) above in respect of an erroneous voluntary disclosure, the end of the prescribed accounting period in which the disclosure was made;

(*c*) in the case of a claim by virtue of subsection (1A) above in respect of an assessment issued on the basis of an erroneous voluntary disclosure, the end of the prescribed accounting period in which the disclosure was made;

(*d*) in the case of a claim by virtue of subsection (1A) above in any other case, the end of the prescribed accounting period in which the assessment was made;

(*e*) in the case of a claim by virtue of subsection (1B) above, the date on which the payment was made.

In the case of a person who has ceased to be registered under this Act, any reference in paragraphs (*b*) to (*d*) above to a prescribed accounting period includes a reference to a period that would have been a prescribed accounting period had the person continued to be registered under this Act.][4]

[(4ZB) For the purposes of this section the cases where there is an erroneous voluntary disclosure are those cases where—

(*a*) a person discloses to the Commissioners that he has not brought into account for a prescribed accounting period (whenever ended) an amount of output tax due for the period;

(*b*) the disclosure is made in a later prescribed accounting period (whenever ended); and

(*c*) some or all of the amount is not output tax due.][4]

[(4A) Where—

(*a*) an amount has been credited under subsection (1) or (1A) above to any person at any time on or after 26th May 2005, and

(*b*) the amount so credited exceeded the amount which the Commissioners were liable at that time to credit to that person,

the Commissioners may, to the best of their judgement, assess the excess credited to that person and notify it to him.][4]

[(4AA) An assessment under subsection (4A) shall not be made more than 2 years after the later of—

(a) the end of the prescribed accounting period in which the amount was credited to the person, and

(b) the time when evidence of facts sufficient in the opinion of the Commissioners to justify the making of the assessment comes to the knowledge of the Commissioners.][5]

(4B) . . . [4]

[(4C) Subsections [(3)][5] to (8) of section 78A apply in the case of an assessment under subsection (4A) above as they apply in the case of an assessment under section 78A(1).][3]

(5) . . . [2]

(6) A claim under this section shall be made in such form and manner and shall be supported by such documentary evidence as the Commissioners prescribe by regulations; and regulations under this subsection may make different provision for different cases.

[(7) Except as provided by this section [(and paragraph 16I of Schedule 3B and paragraph 29 of Schedule 3BA)][7], the Commissioners shall not be liable to credit or repay any amount accounted for or paid to them by way of VAT that was not VAT due to them.][4]

Commentary—*De Voil Indirect Tax Service* **V5.159**.

Modifications—VATA 1994 Sch 3BA para 30 (modification of this section in relation to claims for overpayments regarding the use of non-UK special accounting schemes).

VATA 1994 Sch 3B para 16J (modification of this section in relation to overpayment claims by participants in special schemes).

Regulations—See VAT Regulations, SI 1995/2518 reg 37.

VAT (Amendment) (No 3) Regulations, SI 2014/2430.

Simon's Tax Cases—*Hawthorn v Smallcorn* [1998] STC 591*; *R (on the application of Cardiff County Council) v C&E Comrs* [2002] STC 1318; *Midlands Co-operative Society Ltd v R&C Comrs* [2008] STC 1803; *Marks & Spencer plc v R&C Comrs* [2009] STC 452; *FJ Chalke Ltd and anor v R&C Comrs* [2010] STC 1640; *Littlewoods Retail Ltd and anor v R&C Comrs* [2010] STC 2072; *R&C Comrs v Moorbury Ltd* [2010] STC 2715; *Littlewoods Retail Ltd and others v R&C Comrs* [2011] STC 171; *Littlewoods Ltd v R&C Comrs* [2010] EWHC 2771 (Ch), [2011] STC 171; *Littlewoods Retail Ltd and others v R&C Comrs* (Case C-591/10) [2012] STC 1714; *R (on the application of Capital Accommodation (London) Ltd v R&C Comrs* [2012] UKUT 276 (TCC), [2013] STC 303; *Leeds City Council v R&C Comrs* [2013] UKUT 596 (TCC), [2014] STC 789; *Littlewoods Retail Ltd and others v R&C Comrs* [2014] EWHC 868 (Ch), [2014] STC 1761; *British Telecommunications plc v R&C Comrs* [2014] EWCA Civ 433, [2014] STC 1926; *Taylor Clark Leisure plc v R&C Comrs* [2014] UKUT 396 (TCC), [2015] STC 223.

s 80(1), *Marks and Spencer plc v C&E Comrs, University of Sussex v C&E Comrs* [2004] STC 1; *R (on the application of Cardiff County Council) v C&E Comrs* [2004] STC 356.

s 80(3), *C&E Comrs v McMaster Stores (Scotland) Ltd (in receivership)* [1995] STC 846*; *C&E Comrs v National Westminster Bank plc* [2003] STC 1072; *Marks and Spencer plc v C&E Comrs, University of Sussex v C&E Comrs* [2004] STC 1; *Baines & Ernst Ltd v C&E Comrs* [2006] STC 1632.

s 80(4), (4A), (4B), *R (oao DFS Furniture Co plc) v C&E Comrs* [2003] STC 1, CA; *C&E Comrs v DFS Furniture Co plc* [2003] STC 739; *Marks and Spencer plc v C&E Comrs, University of Sussex v C&E Comrs* [2004] STC 1; *R (on the application of Cardiff County Council) v C&E Comrs* [2004] STC 356.

s 80(7), *Investment Trust Companies (in liquidation) v R&C Comrs* [2012] EWHC 458 (Ch), [2012] STC 1150.

Definitions—"The Commissioners", s 96(1); "prescribed", s 96(1); "regulations", s 96(1); "VAT", ss 1, 96(1).

Cross reference—See VATA 1994 s 83 (appeal to a tribunal in respect of a repayment claim under this section).

VAT Regulations, SI 1995/2518 reg 37 (form of repayment claim).

FA 1997 s 47(3)–(5) (repayments after 17 July 1996 where legal proceedings previously brought).

FA 1997 s 47(12) (references to a claim in sub-s (4)).

FA 2008 s 121(1) (disapplication of requirement that a claim under this section be made within three years of the relevant date in respect of an amount brought into account or paid for a prescribed accounting period ending before 4 December 1996 if the claim is made before 1 April 2009).

Press releases etc—Business Brief 2/98, 27-1-98 (three year time limit for refunds).

Business Brief 4/02, 22-2-02 (late claims to input tax submitted before 1 May 1997).

Business Brief 13/06, 24-8-06 (Court of Appeal Judgment in Michael Fleming t/a Bodycraft).

HMRC Brief 14/09, 20-3-09 (VAT repayment claims and statutory interest: treatment for the purposes of direct tax).

Amendments—[1] Sub-ss (3A)–(3C) inserted by FA 1997 s 46(1) with effect for the purposes of making any repayment on or after 19 March 1997, even if the claim for that repayment was made before that date.

[2] Sub-s (4) substituted for sub-ss (4), (5) by FA 1997 s 47(1) with effect from 18 July 1996, subject to transitional provisions in FA 1997 s 47(3)–(5).

[3] Sub-ss (4A)–(4C) inserted by FA 1997 s 47(6) and deemed to have come into force on 4 December 1996.

[4] Sub-s (1)–(1B) substituted for sub-s (1); words inserted in sub-s (2); sub-s (2A) inserted; in sub-s (3), words substituted for the words "under this section, that repayment"; sub-ss (3A), (7) substituted; in sub-s (3B)(a), word substituted for the word "repayment"; sub-ss (4)–(4ZB) substituted for sub-s (4); sub-s (4A) substituted for sub-ss (4A), (4B); and Heading substituted; by F(No 2)A 2005 s 3 with effect in any case where a claim under sub-s (2) above is made on or after 26 May 2005, whenever the event occurred in respect of which the claim is made: F(No 2)A 2005 s 4(6).

[5] Sub-s (4AA) inserted, and reference in sub-s (4C) substituted by FA 2008 s 120(2)–(4). These amendments are treated as having come into force on 19 March 2008.

[6] In sub-s (4) words substituted for words "3 years" by FA 2008 Sch 39 para 36 with effect from 1 April 2009 (by virtue of SI 2009/403 art 2(2)). FA 2008 Sch 39 para 36 is disregarded where, for the purposes of VATA 1994 s 80, the relevant date is on or before 31 March 2006 (SI 2009/403 art 6).

[7] In sub-s (7), words inserted by FA 2014 s 103, Sch 22 paras 11, 16 with effect in relation to supplies made on or after 1 January 2015.

[80A Arrangements for reimbursing customers

(1) The Commissioners may by regulations make provision for reimbursement arrangements made by any person to be disregarded for the purposes of section 80(3) except where the arrangements—

(*a*) contain such provision as may be required by the regulations; and

(*b*) are supported by such undertakings to comply with the provisions of the arrangements as may be required by the regulations to be given to the Commissioners.

(2) In this section 'reimbursement arrangements' means any arrangements for the purposes of a claim under section 80 which—

(*a*) are made by any person for the purpose of securing that he is not unjustly enriched by the [crediting][2] of any amount in pursuance of the claim; and

(*b*) provide for the reimbursement of persons who have for practical purposes borne the whole or any part of [the amount brought into account as mentioned in paragraph (*b*) of subsection (1) or (1A) of that section][2].

(3) Without prejudice to the generality of subsection (1) above, the provision that may be required by regulations under this section to be contained in reimbursement arrangements includes—

(*a*) provision requiring a reimbursement for which the arrangements provide to be made within such period after the [crediting of the amount][2] to which it relates as may be specified in the regulations;

[(*b*) provision for cases where an amount is credited but an equal amount is not reimbursed in accordance with the arrangements;][2]

(*c*) provision requiring interest paid by the Commissioners on any amount [paid (or repaid)][2] by them to be treated in the same way as that amount for the purposes of any requirement under the arrangements to make reimbursement or to repay the Commissioners;

(*d*) provision requiring such records relating to the carrying out of the arrangements as may be described in the regulations to be kept and produced to the Commissioners, or to an officer of theirs.

(4) Regulations under this section may impose obligations on such persons as may be specified in the regulations—

(*a*) [to make the repayments, or give the notifications, to the Commissioners that they are required to make or give][2] in pursuance of any provisions contained in any reimbursement arrangements by virtue of subsection (3)(*b*) or (*c*) above;

(*b*) to comply with any requirements contained in any such arrangements by virtue of subsection (3)(*d*) above.

(5) Regulations under this section may make provision for the form and manner in which, and the times at which, undertakings are to be given to the Commissioners in accordance with the regulations; and any such provision may allow for those matters to be determined by the Commissioners in accordance with the regulations.

(6) Regulations under this section may—

(*a*) contain any such incidental, supplementary, consequential or transitional provision as appears to the Commissioners to be necessary or expedient; and

(*b*) make different provision for different circumstances.

(7) Regulations under this section may have effect (irrespective of when the claim for [credit][2] was made) for the purposes of [the crediting of any amount][2] by the Commissioners after the time when the regulations are made; and, accordingly, such regulations may apply to arrangements made before that time.][1]

Commentary—*De Voil Indirect Tax Service* **V5.159B**.
Regulations—VAT (Amendment) (No 3) Regulations, SI 2014/2430.
Definitions—"The Commissioners", s 96(1); "regulations", s 96(1).
Amendments—[1] This section inserted by FA 1997 s 46(2).
[2] In sub-s (2)(a), (3)(a), (7), words substituted for the word "repayment"; in sub-s (2)(b), words substituted for the words "the cost of the original payment of that amount to the Commissioners"; sub-s (3)(b) substituted; in sub-s (3)(c), words substituted for the word "repaid"; in sub-s (4)(a), words substituted for the words "to make the repayments to the Commissioners that they are required to make"; in sub-s (7), words substituted for the words "the making of any repayment"; by F(No 2)A 2005 s 4(1), (3) with effect in any case where a claim under VATA 1994 s 80(2) is made on or after 26 May 2005, whenever the event occurred in respect of which the claim is made: F(No 2)A 2005 s 4(6).

[80B Assessments of amounts due under section 80A arrangements

(1) Where any person is liable to pay any amount to the Commissioners in pursuance of an obligation imposed by virtue of section 80A(4)(*a*), the Commissioners may, to the best of their judgement, assess the amount due from that person and notify it to him.

[(1A) Where—

(*a*) an amount ("the gross credit") has been credited to any person under subsection (1) or (1A) of section 80,

(*b*) any sums were set against that amount, in accordance with subsection (2A) of that section, and

(*c*) the amount reimbursed in accordance with the reimbursement arrangements was less than the gross credit,

subsection (1B) below applies.][2]

[(1B) In any such case—

(*a*) the person shall cease to be entitled to so much of the gross credit as exceeds the amount so reimbursed, and

(*b*) the Commissioners may, to the best of their judgement, assess the amount due from that person and notify it to him,

but an amount shall not be assessed under this subsection to the extent that the person is liable to pay it to the Commissioners as mentioned in subsection (1) above.][2]

[(1C) In determining the amount that a person is liable to pay as mentioned in subsection (1) above, any amount reimbursed in accordance with the reimbursement arrangements shall be regarded as first reducing so far as possible the amount that he would have been liable so to pay, but for the reimbursement of that amount.][2]

[(1D) For the purposes of this section, nil is an amount.][2]

[(1E) Any reference in any other provision of this Act to an assessment under subsection (1) above includes, if the context so admits, a reference to an assessment under subsection (1B) above.][2]

(2) Subsections (2) to (8) of section 78A apply in the case of an assessment under subsection (1) above as they apply in the case of an assessment under section 78A(1).][1]

Commentary—*De Voil Indirect Tax Service* **V5.132B**.

Definitions—"The Commissioners", s 96(1).

Simon's Tax Cases—*R&C Comrs v Earlsferry Thistle Golf Club* [2014] UKUT 250 (TCC), [2014] STC 2498.

Amendments—[1] This section inserted by FA 1997 s 46(2).

[2] Sub-ss (1A)–(1E) inserted by F(No 2)A 2005 s 4(1), (4) with effect in any case where a claim under VATA 1994 s 80(2) is made on or after 26 May 2005, whenever the event occurred in respect of which the claim is made: F(No 2)A 2005 s 4(6).

81 Interest given by way of credit and set-off of credits

(1) Any interest payable by the Commissioners (whether under an enactment or instrument or otherwise) to a person on a sum due to him under or by virtue of any provision of this Act shall be treated as an amount due by way of credit under section 25(3).

(2) Subsection (1) above shall be disregarded for the purpose of determining a person's entitlement to interest or the amount of interest to which he is entitled.

(3) Subject to subsection (1) above, in any case where—

(*a*) an amount is due from the Commissioners to any person under any provision of this Act, and

(*b*) that person is liable to pay a sum by way of VAT, penalty, interest or surcharge,

the amount referred to in paragraph (a) above shall be set against the sum referred to in paragraph (b) above and, accordingly, to the extent of the set-off, the obligations of the Commissioners and the person concerned shall be discharged.

[(3A) Where—

(*a*) the Commissioners are liable to pay or repay any amount to any person under this Act,

(*b*) that amount falls to be paid or repaid in consequence of a mistake previously made about whether or to what extent amounts were payable under this Act to or by that person, and

(*c*) by reason of that mistake a liability of that person to pay a sum by way of VAT, penalty, interest or surcharge was not assessed, was not enforced or was not satisfied,

any limitation on the time within which the Commissioners are entitled to take steps for recovering that sum shall be disregarded in determining whether that sum is required by subsection (3) above to be set against the amount mentioned in paragraph (a) above.][2]

[(4A) Subsection (3) above shall not require any such amount as is mentioned in paragraph (*a*) of that subsection ("the credit") to be set against any such sum as is mentioned in paragraph (*b*) of that subsection ("the debit") in any case where—

(*a*) an insolvency procedure has been applied to the person entitled to the credit;

(*b*) the credit became due after that procedure was so applied; and

(*c*) the liability to pay the debit either arose before that procedure was so applied or (having arisen afterwards) relates to, or to matters occurring in the course of, the carrying on of any business at times before the procedure was so applied.][1]

[(4B) Subject to subsection (4C) below, the following are the times when an insolvency procedure is to be taken, for the purposes of this section, to be applied to any person, that is to say—

[(*a*) when a bankruptcy order or winding-up order or award of sequestration is made or an administrator is appointed in relation to that person;][3]

(*b*) when that person is put into administrative receivership;

(*c*) when that person, being a corporation, passes a resolution for voluntary winding up;

(*d*) when any voluntary arrangement approved in accordance with Part I or VIII of the Insolvency Act 1986 or Part II or Chapter II of Part VIII of the Insolvency (Northern Ireland) Order 1989 comes into force in relation to that person;

(*e*) when a deed of arrangement registered in accordance with the Deeds of Arrangement Act 1914 or Chapter I of Part VIII of that Order of 1989 takes effect in relation to that person;

(*f*) when that person's estate becomes vested in any other person as that person's trustee under a trust deed.][1]

[(4C) In this section, references to the application of an insolvency procedure to a person do not include—

(*a*) the application of an insolvency procedure to a person at a time when another insolvency procedure applies to the person, or

(*b*) the application of an insolvency procedure to a person immediately upon another insolvency procedure ceasing to have effect.][4]

[(4D) For the purposes of this section a person shall be regarded as being in administrative receivership throughout any continuous period for which (disregarding any temporary vacancy in the office of receiver) there is an administrative receiver of that person, and the reference in subsection (4B) above to a person being put into administrative receivership shall be construed accordingly.][1]

(5) In [this section][1]—

(*a*) *"administration order" means an administration order under Part II of the Insolvency Act 1986 or an administration order within the meaning of Article 5(1) of the Insolvency (Northern Ireland) Order 1989;* [4]

(*b*) "administrative receiver" means an administrative receiver within the meaning of section 251 of [the Insolvency Act 1986][4] or Article 5(1) of [the Insolvency (Northern Ireland) Order 1989][4];

[(*ba*) "administrator" means a person appointed to manage the affairs, business and property of another person under Schedule B1 to that Act or to that Order;][4] and

(*c*) "trust deed" has the same meaning as in the Bankruptcy (Scotland) Act 1985.

Commentary—*De Voil Indirect Tax Service* **V5.196**.

Definitions—"The Commissioners", s 96(1); "interim trustee", s 96(1); "permanent trustee", s 96(1); "VAT", ss 1, 96(1).

Cross references—See VATA 1994 Sch 13 para 21 (modification of this section in its application to amounts becoming due before 10 May 1994).

VAT Regulations, SI 1995/2518 reg 48(3) (this section cannot require overpayments on account in respect of one division of a business to be set against liabilities of another division).

Press releases etc—Business Brief 5/98 10-2-98 (VAT bad debt relief—insolvency practitioners).

Simon's Tax Cases—s 81(3A), *Birmingham Hippodrome Theatre Ltd v R&C Comrs* [2014] EWCA Civ 684, [2014] STC 2222.

Amendments—[1] Sub-ss (4A)–(4D) substituted for sub-s (4) as originally enacted, and words in sub-s (5) substituted by FA 1995 s 27 with effect in relation to amounts becoming due from the Commissioners of Customs and Excise at times on or after 1 May 1995.

[2] Sub-s (3A) inserted by FA 1997 s 48(1) and deemed to have come into force on 18 July 1996 for determining the amount of any payment or repayment by C&E on or after that date.

[3] Sub-ss (4B)(*a*) substituted, by the Enterprise Act 2002 (Insolvency) Order, SI 2003/2096 art 4, Schedule, paras 24, 26 with effect from 15 September 2003. However, this amendment does not apply in any case where a petition for an administration order was presented before that date: SI 2003/2096 arts 1, 6.

[4] Sub-s (4C) substituted, sub-s (5)(*a*) repealed, in sub-s (5)(*b*), words substituted for words "that Act of 1986", and "that Order of 1989", and sub-s (5)(ba) inserted, by FA 2008 s 132 with effect from 21 July 2008.

Prospective amendments—In sub-s (4B)(*e*), words "the Deeds of Arrangement Act 1914 or" to be repealed by the Deregulation Act 2015 s 19, Sch 6 para 2(1), (13) with effect from a day to be appointed. This repeal has no effect in relation to a deed of arrangement registered under the Deeds of Arrangement Act 1914 s 5 before the date on which the Deregulation Act Sch 6 para 1 comes into force if, immediately before that date, the estate of the debtor who executed the deed of arrangement has not been finally wound up (Deregulation Act Sch 6 para 3).

PART V
[REVIEWS AND APPEALS]

Cross reference—See VATA 1994 Sch 13 para 22 (references in this Part to any provision of VATA 1994 include a reference to the corresponding provision of the enactments repealed by that Act).

VAT Tribunals Rules, SI 1986/590 (procedure for appeals before tribunals).

Amendments—Heading substituted for previous heading "Appeals" by the Transfer of Tribunal Functions and Revenue and Customs Appeals Order, SI 2009/56 art 3, Sch 1 para 217 with effect from 1 April 2009, subject to transitional and savings provisions in Sch 3 para 4.

[82 Meaning of "tribunal"

In this Act "tribunal" means the First-tier Tribunal or, where determined by or under Tribunal Procedure Rules, the Upper Tribunal.][1]

Commentary—*De Voil Indirect Tax Service* **V1.288**.

Definitions—"VAT", ss 1, 96(1).

Amendments—[1] This section substituted by the Transfer of Tribunal Functions and Revenue and Customs Appeals Order, SI 2009/56 art 3, Sch 1 para 218 with effect from 1 April 2009, subject to transitional and savings provisions in Sch 3 para 4.

83 Appeals

[(1)] [21]Subject to [sections 83G and 84][21], an appeal shall lie to [the tribunal][21] with respect to any of the following matters—

(*a*) the registration or cancellation of registration of any person under this Act;

(*b*) the VAT chargeable on the supply of any goods or services, on the acquisition of goods from another member State or, subject to section 84(9), on the importation of goods from a place outside the member States;

(*c*) the amount of any input tax which may be credited to a person;

(*d*) any claim for a refund under any regulations made by virtue of section 13(5);

[(*da*) a decision of the Commissioners under section 18A—

(i) as to whether or not a person is to be approved as a fiscal warehouse keeper or the conditions from time to time subject to which he is so approved;
(ii) for the withdrawal of any such approval; or
(iii) for the withdrawal of fiscal warehouse status from any premises;][1]

(*e*) the proportion of input tax allowable under section 26;
(*f*) a claim by a taxable person under section 27;
[(*fza*) a decision of the Commissioners—
(i) refusing or withdrawing authorisation for a person's liability to pay VAT (or entitlement to credit for VAT) to be determined as mentioned in subsection (1) of section 26B;
(ii) as to the appropriate percentage or percentages (within the meaning of that section) applicable in a person's case.][10]

[(*fa*) a decision contained in a notification under paragraph (4) of article 12A of the Value Added Tax (Payments on Account) Order 1993 that an election under paragraph (1) of that article shall cease to have effect;][6]
(*g*) the amount of any refunds under section 35;
(*h*) a claim for a refund under section 36 or section 22 of the 1983 Act;
[(*ha*) any decision of the Commissioners to refuse to make a repayment under a scheme under section 39;][22]
(*j*) the amount of any refunds under section 40;
[(*k*) the refusal of an application such as is mentioned in section 43B(1) or (2);
(*ka*) the giving of a notice under section 43C(1) or (3);][7]
(*l*) the requirement of any security under section 48(7) or [paragraph 4(1A) or (2)][11] of Schedule 11;
(*m*) any refusal or cancellation of certification under section 54 or any refusal to cancel such certification;
(*n*) any liability to a penalty or surcharge by virtue of any of sections [59 to [69B][17]][8];
(*o*) a decision of the Commissioners under section 61 (in accordance with section 61(5));
(*p*) an assessment—
(i) under section 73(1) or (2) in respect of a period for which the appellant has made a return under this Act; or
(ii) under [subsections (7), (7A) or (7B)][1] of that section; or
(iii) under section 75;

or the amount of such an assessment;
(*q*) the amount of any penalty, interest or surcharge specified in an assessment under section 76;
(*r*) the making of an assessment on the basis set out in section 77(4);
[(*ra*) any liability arising by virtue of section 77A;][12]
(*s*) any liability of the Commissioners to pay interest under section 78 or the amount of interest so payable;
[(*sa*) an assessment under section 78A(1) or the amount of such an assessment;][3]
(*t*) a claim for the [crediting or][16] repayment of an amount under section 80[, an assessment under subsection (4A) of that section or the amount of such an assessment;][5]
[(*ta*) an assessment under section 80B(1) [or (1B)][16] or the amount of such an assessment;][4]
(*u*) any direction or supplementary direction made under paragraph 2 of Schedule 1;
(*v*) any direction under paragraph 1[, 1A][15][, 2 or 8A][23] of Schedule 6 or under paragraph 2 of Schedule 4 to the 1983 Act;
(*w*) any direction under paragraph 1 of Schedule 7;
[(*wa*) any direction or assessment under Schedule 9A;][2]
[(*wb*) any refusal of the Commissioners to grant any permission under, or otherwise to exercise in favour of a particular person any power conferred by, any provision of Part 1 of Schedule 10;][20]
(*x*) any refusal to permit the value of supplies to be determined by a method described in a notice published under paragraph 2(6) of Schedule 11;
(*y*) any refusal of authorisation or termination of authorisation in connection with the scheme made under paragraph 2(7) of Schedule 11;
[(*z*) any conditions imposed by the Commissioners in a particular case by virtue of paragraph 2B(2)(*c*) or 3(1) of Schedule 11][13]
[(*zza*) a direction under paragraph 6A of Schedule 11;][18]
[(*za*) a direction under paragraph 8 of Schedule 11A;][14]
[(*zb*) any liability to a penalty under paragraph 10(1) of Schedule 11A, any assessment under paragraph 12(1) of that Schedule or the amount of such an assessment;][14]
[(*zc*) a decision of the Commissioners about the application of regulations under section 135 of the Finance Act 2002 (mandatory electronic filing of returns) in connection with VAT (including, in particular, a decision as to whether a requirement of the regulations applies and a decision to impose a penalty);][19]

(*zz*) . . . [9]

[(2) In the following provisions of this Part, a reference to a decision with respect to which an appeal under this section lies, or has been made, includes any matter listed in subsection (1) whether or not described there as a decision.][21]

Commentary—*De Voil Indirect Tax Service* **V5.404**.

Modifications—VATA 1994 Sch 3BA para 37 (where the Commissioners have made an assessment under s 73 in relation to a relevant non-UK return, sub-s (1)(*p*)(i) applies as if that return were a return under this Act).

Simon's Tax Cases—*Odhams Leisure Group Ltd v C&E Comrs* [1992] STC 332*; *C&E Comrs v Pegasus Birds Ltd* [2004] STC 262; *Benridge Care Homes Ltd and others v R&C Comrs* [2012] UKUT 132 (TCC), [2012] STC 1714.

Simon's Tax Cases—s 83(1), *R&C Comrs v Earlsferry Thistle Golf Club* [2014] UKUT 250 (TCC), [2014] STC 2498.

s 83(*b*), *Don Pasquale (a firm) v C&E Comrs* [1990] STC 556*.

s 83(*c*), *Touchwood Services Ltd v R&C Comrs* [2007] STC 1425; *R&C Comrs v Mobilx Ltd* [2008] STC 3071.

s 83(*e*), *Banbury Visionplus Ltd v R&C Comrs and other appeals* [2006] STC 1568.

s 83(*l*), *John Dee Ltd v C&E Comrs* [1995] STC 941*.

s 83(*n*), (*q*), *Dollar Land (Feltham) Ltd, Dollar Land (Cumbernauld) Ltd and Dollar Land (Calthorpe House) Ltd v C&E Comrs* [1995] STC 414*.

s 83(*p*), *Don Pasquale (a firm) v C&E Comrs* [1990] STC 556*; *Murat v C&E Comrs* [1998] STC 923; *Touchwood Services Ltd v R&C Comrs* [2007] STC 1425.

s 83(*t*), *C&E Comrs v National Westminster Bank plc* [2003] STC 1072.

Definitions—"The 1983 Act", s 96(1); "acquisition of goods from another member State", s 11; "another member State", s 96(1); "the Commissioners", s 96(1); "fiscal warehouse", ss 18A(3), 18F(1); "fiscal warehouse keeper", s 18F(1); "importation of goods from a place outside the member States", s 15; "input tax", s 24; "registered", s 3(3); "regulations", s 96(1); "supply", s 5, Sch 4; "taxable person", s 3; "tribunal", s 82; "VAT", ss 1, 96(1).

Cross references—See VATA 1994 Sch 13 para 22 (application of this section to acts and omissions before the coming into force of VATA 1994).

VAT (Isle of Man) Order, SI 1982/1067 art 8 (taxable persons for the purposes of Isle of Man VAT legislation to be treated as taxable persons for the purposes of sub-s(1)(*g*) of this section);

VAT Regulations, SI 1995/2518 reg 182 (repayment claimed by Community trader: treatment as an amount of input tax for the purposes of para (*c*) of this section).

VAT Regulations, SI 1995/2518 reg 195 (repayment claimed by third country trader: treatment as an amount of input tax for the purposes of para (*c*) of this section).

Amendments—[1] Para (da) inserted and words in para (p)(ii) substituted by FA 1996 Sch 3 para 12, with effect from 1 June 1996 (see Finance Act 1996, Section 26, (Appointed Day) Order SI 1996/1249), and applying to any acquisition of goods from another member State and any supply taking place on or after that day.

[2] Para (wa) inserted by FA 1996 s 31(3).

[3] Para (sa) inserted by FA 1997 s 45(2) and deemed to have come into force on 4 December 1996 in relation to assessments made on or after that date.

[4] Para (ta) inserted by FA 1997 s 46 (3).

[5] Words in para (t) inserted by FA 1997 s 47 (7) with effect from 4 December 1996.

[6] Para (fa) inserted by the VAT (Payments on Account) (Appeals) Order, SI 1997/2542 with effect from 1 December 1997.

[7] Para (k) substituted and para (ka) inserted by FA 1999 s 16, Sch 2 para 3 with effect from 27 July 1999 subject to FA 1999 Sch 2 para 6.

[8] Words in para (n) substituted for "59 to 69" by FA 2000 s 137(1), (5), with effect from 28 July 2000.

[9] Para (zz) (originally added by the Money Laundering Regulations 2001) repealed by the Money Laundering Regulations, SI 2007/2157 reg 51, Sch 6 para 1 with effect from 15 December 2007.

[10] Para (fza) inserted by FA 2002 s 23(2), (4) and deemed to have come into force on 24 April 2002.

[11] Words in para (l) substituted for the words "paragraph 4(2)" by FA 2003 s 17(6) with effect from 10 April 2003.

[12] Para (ra) inserted by FA 2003 s 18(2) with effect from 10 April 2003.

[13] Para (z) substituted by FA 2002 s 24(4)(b), (5), with effect from 1 December 2003 (by virtue of SI 2003/3043).

[14] Paras (za) and (zb) inserted by FA 2004 s 19, Sch 2 para 4 with effect from the passing of FA 2004, so far as is necessary for enabling the making of any orders or regulations by virtue of FA 2004 Sch 2, and otherwise with effect from such day as the Treasury may by order made by statutory instrument appoint.

[15] Words in para (v) inserted by FA 2004 s 22(3) with effect from 22 July 2004.

[16] Words in paras (t), (ta) inserted by F(No 2)A 2005 s 4(1), (5) with effect in any case where a claim under VATA 1994 s 80(2) is made on or after 26 May 2005, whenever the event occurred in respect of which the claim is made: F(No 2)A 2005 s 4(6).

[17] Words "69B" in para (n) substituted by FA 2006 s 21(4) with effect from 19 July 2006.

[18] Para (zza) inserted by FA 2006 s 21(4) with effect from 19 July 2006.

[19] Para (zc) inserted by FA 2007 s 93(8) with effect from 19 July 2007.

[20] Para (wb) inserted by the Value Added Tax (Buildings and Land) Order, SI 2008/1146, art 3(1), (2) with effect in relation to supplies made on or after 1 June 2008, subject to savings in Sch 2 of the Order.

[21] Sub-s (1) numbered as such; in new sub-s (1) words in the first place substituted for the words "section 84" and in the second place substituted for the words "a tribunal"; sub-s (2) inserted by the Transfer of Tribunal Functions and Revenue and Customs Appeals Order, SI 2009/56 art 3, Sch 1 para 219 with effect from 1 April 2009, subject to transitional and savings provisions in Sch 3 para 4.

[22] Para (ha) inserted by FA 2009 s 77 with effect from 21 July 2009.

[23] In sub-s (1)(v), words substituted for words "or 2" by FA 2012 s 200(1), (3) with effect in relation to supplies made on or after 17 July 2012.

[83A Offer of review

(1) HMRC must offer a person (P) a review of a decision that has been notified to P if an appeal lies under section 83 in respect of the decision.

(2) The offer of the review must be made by notice given to P at the same time as the decision is notified to P.

(3) This section does not apply to the notification of the conclusions of a review.][1]

Commentary—*De Voil Indirect Tax Service* **V5.407**.

Amendments—[1] Sections 83A–83G inserted by the Transfer of Tribunal Functions and Revenue and Customs Appeals Order, SI 2009/56 art 3, Sch 1 para 220 with effect from 1 April 2009, subject to transitional and savings provisions in Sch 3 para 4.

[83B Right to require review

(1) Any person (other than P) who has the right of appeal under section 83 against a decision may require HMRC to review that decision if that person has not appealed to the tribunal under section 83G.

(2) A notification that such a person requires a review must be made within 30 days of that person becoming aware of the decision.][1]

Commentary—*De Voil Indirect Tax Service* **V5.407**.

Amendments—[1] Sections 83A–83G inserted by the Transfer of Tribunal Functions and Revenue and Customs Appeals Order, SI 2009/56 art 3, Sch 1 para 220 with effect from 1 April 2009, subject to transitional and savings provisions in Sch 3 para 4.

[83C Review by HMRC

(1) HMRC must review a decision if—

(*a*) they have offered a review of the decision under section 83A, and

(*b*) P notifies HMRC accepting the offer within 30 days from the date of the document containing the notification of the offer.

(2) But P may not notify acceptance of the offer if P has already appealed to the tribunal under section 83G.

(3) HMRC must review a decision if a person other than P notifies them under section 83B.

(4) HMRC shall not review a decision if P, or another person, has appealed to the tribunal under section 83G in respect of the decision.][1]

Commentary—*De Voil Indirect Tax Service* **V5.407**.

Amendments—[1] Sections 83A–83G inserted by the Transfer of Tribunal Functions and Revenue and Customs Appeals Order, SI 2009/56 art 3, Sch 1 para 220 with effect from 1 April 2009, subject to transitional and savings provisions in Sch 3 para 4.

[83D Extensions of time

(1) If under section 83A HMRC have offered P a review of a decision, HMRC may within the relevant period notify P that the relevant period is extended.

(2) If under section 83B another person may require HMRC to review a matter, HMRC may within the relevant period notify the other person that the relevant period is extended.

(3) If notice is given the relevant period is extended to the end of 30 days from—

(*a*) the date of the notice, or

(*b*) any other date set out in the notice or a further notice.

(4) In this section "relevant period" means—

(*a*) the period of 30 days referred to in—

(i) section 83C(1)(*b*) (in a case falling within subsection (1)), or

(ii) section 83B(2) (in a case falling within subsection (2)), or

(*b*) if notice has been given under subsection (1) or (2), that period as extended (or as most recently extended) in accordance with subsection (3).][1]

Commentary—*De Voil Indirect Tax Service* **V5.407**.

Amendments—[1] Sections 83A–83G inserted by the Transfer of Tribunal Functions and Revenue and Customs Appeals Order, SI 2009/56 art 3, Sch 1 para 220 with effect from 1 April 2009, subject to transitional and savings provisions in Sch 3 para 4.

[83E Review out of time

(1) This section applies if—

(*a*) HMRC have offered a review of a decision under section 83A and P does not accept the offer within the time allowed under section 83C(1)(*b*) or 83D(3); or

(*b*) a person who requires a review under section 83B does not notify HMRC within the time allowed under that section or section 83D(3).

(2) HMRC must review the decision under section 83C if—

(*a*) after the time allowed, P, or the other person, notifies HMRC in writing requesting a review out of time,

(*b*) HMRC are satisfied that P, or the other person, had a reasonable excuse for not accepting the offer or requiring review within the time allowed, and

(*c*) HMRC are satisfied that P, or the other person, made the request without unreasonable delay after the excuse had ceased to apply.

(3) HMRC shall not review a decision if P, or another person, has appealed to the tribunal under section 83G in respect of the decision.][1]

Commentary—*De Voil Indirect Tax Service* **V5.407**.

Amendments—[1] Sections 83A–83G inserted by the Transfer of Tribunal Functions and Revenue and Customs Appeals Order, SI 2009/56 art 3, Sch 1 para 220 with effect from 1 April 2009, subject to transitional and savings provisions in Sch 3 para 4.

[83F Nature of review etc

(1) This section applies if HMRC are required to undertake a review under section 83C or 83E.

(2) The nature and extent of the review are to be such as appear appropriate to HMRC in the circumstances.
(3) For the purpose of subsection (2), HMRC must, in particular, have regard to steps taken before the beginning of the review—
 (*a*) by HMRC in reaching the decision, and
 (*b*) by any person in seeking to resolve disagreement about the decision.
(4) The review must take account of any representations made by P, or the other person, at a stage which gives HMRC a reasonable opportunity to consider them.
(5) The review may conclude that the decision is to be—
 (*a*) upheld,
 (*b*) varied, or
 (*c*) cancelled.
(6) HMRC must give P, or the other person, notice of the conclusions of the review and their reasoning within—
 (*a*) a period of 45 days beginning with the relevant date, or
 (*b*) such other period as HMRC and P, or the other person, may agree.
(7) In subsection (6) "relevant date" means—
 (*a*) the date HMRC received P's notification accepting the offer of a review (in a case falling within section 83A), or
 (*b*) the date HMRC received notification from another person requiring review (in a case falling within section 83B), or
 (*c*) the date on which HMRC decided to undertake the review (in a case falling within section 83E).
(8) Where HMRC are required to undertake a review but do not give notice of the conclusions within the time period specified in subsection (6), the review is to be treated as having concluded that the decision is upheld.
(9) If subsection (8) applies, HMRC must notify P or the other person of the conclusion which the review is treated as having reached.][1]

Commentary—*De Voil Indirect Tax Service* **V5.407**.
Amendments—[1] Sections 83A–83G inserted by the Transfer of Tribunal Functions and Revenue and Customs Appeals Order, SI 2009/56 art 3, Sch 1 para 220 with effect from 1 April 2009, subject to transitional and savings provisions in Sch 3 para 4.

[83G Bringing of appeals

(1) An appeal under section 83 is to be made to the tribunal before—
 (*a*) the end of the period of 30 days beginning with—
  (i) in a case where P is the appellant, the date of the document notifying the decision to which the appeal relates, or
  (ii) in a case where a person other than P is the appellant, the date that person becomes aware of the decision, or
 (*b*) if later, the end of the relevant period (within the meaning of section 83D).
(2) But that is subject to subsections (3) to (5).
(3) In a case where HMRC are required to undertake a review under section 83C—
 (*a*) an appeal may not be made until the conclusion date, and
 (*b*) any appeal is to be made within the period of 30 days beginning with the conclusion date.
[(4) In a case where HMRC are requested to undertake a review by virtue of section 83E—
 (*a*) an appeal may not be made—
  (i) unless HMRC have notified P, or the other person, as to whether or not a review will be undertaken, and
  (ii) if HMRC have notified P, or the other person, that a review will be undertaken, until the conclusion date;
 (*b*) any appeal where paragraph (*a*)(ii) applies is to be made within the period of 30 days beginning with the conclusion date;
 (*c*) if HMRC have notified P, or the other person, that a review will not be undertaken, an appeal may be made only if the tribunal gives permission to do so.][2]
(5) In a case where section 83F(8) applies, an appeal may be made at any time from the end of the period specified in section 83F(6) to the date 30 days after the conclusion date.
(6) An appeal may be made after the end of the period specified in subsection (1), (3)(*b*), (4)(b) or (5) if the tribunal gives permission to do so.
(7) In this section "conclusion date" means the date of the document notifying the conclusions of the review.][1]

Commentary—*De Voil Indirect Tax Service* **V5.411**.
Amendments—[1] Sections 83A–83G inserted by the Transfer of Tribunal Functions and Revenue and Customs Appeals Order, SI 2009/56 art 3, Sch 1 para 220 with effect from 1 April 2009, subject to transitional and savings provisions in Sch 3 para 4.
[2] Sub-s (4) substituted by the Revenue and Customs (Amendment of Appeal Provisions for Out of Time Reviews) Order, SI 2014/1264 art 4 with effect in relation to requests for a review out of time notified to HMRC on or after 14 May 2014.

84 Further provisions relating to appeals

(1) References in this section to an appeal are references to an appeal under section 83.

(2) . . .[10]

[(3) Subject to subsections (3B) and (3C), where the appeal is against a decision with respect to any of the matters mentioned in section 83(1)(*b*), (*n*), (*p*), (*q*), (*ra*) or (*zb*), it shall not be entertained unless the amount which HMRC have determined to be payable as VAT has been paid or deposited with them.][10]

[(3A) Subject to subsections (3B) and (3C), where the appeal is against an assessment which is a recovery assessment for the purposes of this subsection, or against the amount of such an assessment, it shall not be entertained unless the amount notified by the assessment has been paid or deposited with HMRC.][10]

[(3B) In a case where the amount determined to be payable as VAT or the amount notified by the recovery assessment has not been paid or deposited an appeal shall be entertained if—

(*a*) HMRC are satisfied (on the application of the appellant), or

(*b*) the tribunal decides (HMRC not being so satisfied and on the application of the appellant),

that the requirement to pay or deposit the amount determined would cause the appellant to suffer hardship.

(3C) Notwithstanding the provisions of sections 11 and 13 of the Tribunals, Courts and Enforcement Act 2007, the decision of the tribunal as to the issue of hardship is final.][10]

(4) Subject to subsection (11) below, where—

(*a*) there is an appeal against a decision of [HMRC][10] with respect to, or to so much of any assessment as concerns, the amount of input tax that may be credited to any person or the proportion of input tax allowable under section 26, and

(*b*) that appeal relates, in whole or in part, to any determination by [HMRC][10]—

(i) as to the purposes for which any goods or services were or were to be used by any person, or

(ii) as to whether or to what extent the matters to which any input tax was attributable were or included matters other than the making of supplies within section 26(2), and

(*c*) VAT for which, in pursuance of that determination, there is no entitlement to a credit is VAT on the supply, acquisition or importation of something in the nature of a luxury, amusement or entertainment,

the tribunal shall not allow the appeal or, as the case may be, so much of it as relates to that determination unless it considers that the determination is one which it was unreasonable to make or which it would have been unreasonable to make if information brought to the attention of the tribunal that could not have been brought to the attention of [HMRC][10] had been available to be taken into account when the determination was made.

[(4ZA) Where an appeal is brought—

(*a*) against such a decision as is mentioned in section [83(1)][10](*fza*), or

(*b*) to the extent that it is based on such a decision, against an assessment,

the tribunal shall not allow the appeal unless it considers that [HMRC][10] could not reasonably have been satisfied that there were grounds for the decision.][4]

[(4A) Where an appeal is brought against the refusal of an application such as is mentioned in section 43B(1) or (2) on the grounds stated in section 43B(5)(*c*)—

(*a*) the tribunal shall not allow the appeal unless it considers that [HMRC][10] could not reasonably have been satisfied that there were grounds for refusing the application,

(*b*) the refusal shall have effect pending the determination of the appeal, and

(*c*) if the appeal is allowed, the refusal shall be deemed not to have occurred.

(4B) Where an appeal is brought against the giving of a notice under section 43C(1) or (3)—

(*a*) the notice shall have effect pending the determination of the appeal, and

(*b*) if the appeal is allowed, the notice shall be deemed never to have had effect.

(4C) Where an appeal is brought against the giving of a notice under section 43C(1), the tribunal shall not allow the appeal unless it considers that [HMRC][10] could not reasonably have been satisfied that there were grounds for giving the notice.

(4D) Where—

(*a*) an appeal is brought against the giving of a notice under section 43C(3), and

(*b*) the grounds of appeal relate wholly or partly to the date specified in the notice,

the tribunal shall not allow the appeal in respect of the date unless it considers that [HMRC][10] could not reasonably have been satisfied that it was appropriate.][3]

[(4E) Where an appeal is brought against a requirement imposed under paragraph 4(2)(*b*) of Schedule 11 that a person give security, the tribunal shall allow the appeal unless [HMRC satisfies][10] the tribunal that—

(*a*) there has been an evasion of, or an attempt to evade, VAT in relation to goods or services supplied to or by that person, or (*b*) it is likely, or without the requirement for security it is likely, that VAT in relation to such goods or services will be evaded.

(4F)A reference in subsection (4E) above to evading VAT includes a reference to obtaining a VAT credit that is not due or a VAT credit in excess of what is due.][5]

(5) Where, on an appeal against a decision with respect to any of the matters mentioned in section [83(1)][10](*p*)—

(*a*) it is found that the amount specified in the assessment is less than it ought to have been, and

(*b*) the tribunal gives a direction specifying the correct amount,

the assessment shall have effect as an assessment of the amount specified in the direction, and that amount shall be deemed to have been notified to the appellant.

(6) Without prejudice to section 70, [or (as the case requires) paragraph 26 of Schedule 3BA or paragraph 16F of Schedule 3B][11] nothing in section[83(1)][10](*q*) shall be taken to confer on a tribunal any power to vary an amount assessed by way of penalty, interest or surcharge except in so far as it is necessary to reduce it to the amount which is appropriate under sections 59 to 70; and in this subsection "penalty" includes an amount assessed by virtue of section 61(3) or (4)(*a*).

[(6A) Without prejudice to section 70, nothing in section [83(1)][10](*zb*) shall be taken to confer on a tribunal any power to vary an amount assessed by way of penalty except in so far as it is necessary to reduce it to the amount which is appropriate under paragraph 11 of Schedule 11A.][6]

[(6B) Nothing in section [83(1)][10](*zc*) shall be taken to confer on a tribunal any power to vary an amount assessed by way of penalty except in so far as it is necessary to reduce it to the amount which is appropriate under regulations made under section 135 of the Finance Act 2002.][8]

(7) Where there is an appeal against a decision to make such a direction as is mentioned in section [83(1)][10](*u*), the tribunal shall not allow the appeal unless it considers that [HMRC][10] could not reasonably have been satisfied [that there were grounds for making the direction][2].

[(7A) Where there is an appeal against a decision to make such a direction as is mentioned in section [83(1)][10](*wa*), the cases in which the tribunal shall allow the appeal shall include (in addition to the case where the conditions for the making of the direction were not fulfilled) the case where the tribunal are satisfied in relation to the relevant event by reference to which the direction was given, that—

(*a*) the change in the treatment of the body corporate, or

(*b*) the transaction in question,

had as its main purpose or, as the case may be, as each of its main purposes a genuine commercial purpose unconnected with the fulfilment of the condition specified in paragraph 1(3) of Schedule 9A.][1]

[(7ZA) Where there is an appeal against such a refusal as is mentioned in section [83(1)][10](*wb*)—

(*a*) the tribunal shall not allow the appeal unless it considers that [HMRC][10] could not reasonably have been satisfied that there were grounds for the refusal, and

(*b*) the refusal shall have effect pending the determination of the appeal.][9]

[(7B) Where there is an appeal against a decision to make such a direction as is mentioned in section [83(1)][10](*zza*)—

(*a*) the tribunal shall not allow the appeal unless it considers that [HMRC][10] could not reasonably have been satisfied that there were grounds for making the direction;

(*b*) the direction shall have effect pending the determination of the appeal.][7]

(8) . . . [10]

(9) No appeal shall lie under this section with respect to the subject-matter of any decision which by virtue of section 16 is a decision to which section 14 [or 15A][10] of the Finance Act 1994 (decisions subject to review) applies unless the decision—

(*a*) relates exclusively to one or both of the following matters, namely whether or not section 30(3) applies in relation to the importation of the goods in question and (if it does not) the rate of tax charged on those goods; and

(*b*) is not one in respect of which notice has been given to [HMRC][10] under section 14 of that Act requiring them to review it[; and

(*c*) a review is not being undertaken following a request under section 14A of that Act; and

(*d*) a review is not being undertaken under section 15 of that Act as a consequence of section 15B(3), 15C(3) or 15E(3) of that Act.][10]

(10) Where an appeal is against [an HMRC decision][10] which depended upon a prior decision taken . . . [10] in relation to the appellant, the fact that the prior decision is not within section 83 shall not prevent the tribunal from allowing the appeal on the ground that it would have allowed an appeal against the prior decision.

(11) Subsection (4) above shall not apply in relation to any appeal relating to the input tax that may be credited to any person at the end of a prescribed accounting period beginning before 27th July 1993.

Simon's Tax Cases—s 84(2), *R v Value Added Tax Tribunal, ex p Minster Associates* [1988] STC 386*; *R v C&E Comrs, ex p Menzies* [1989] STC 40*; *R v London Value Added Tax Tribunal and C&E Comrs, ex p Theodorou* [1989] STC 292*.

the preceding provisions of this section shall have effect as if, at the date of the appellant's notification, the appellant and [HMRC][1] had come to an agreement, orally or in writing, as the case may be, that the decision under appeal should be upheld without variation.

(5) References in this section to an agreement being come to with an appellant and the giving of notice or notification to or by an appellant include references to an agreement being come to with, and the giving of notice or notification to or by, a person acting on behalf of the appellant in relation to the appeal.

Note—In sub-s (2), the word "for" after "resile" appears to be an error. In the previous enactment, FA 1985 s 25(2), the grammatically correct word "from" is used.

Commentary—*De Voil Indirect Tax Service* **V5.443.**

Simon's Tax Cases—*R (oao DFS Furniture Co plc) v C&E Comrs* [2003] STC 1, CA.

Definitions—"HMRC", s 96(1); "tribunal", s 82.

Amendments—[1] Word substituted in each place for the words "the Commissioners" and in sub-s (1) words "(including any terms as to costs)" at the end repealed by the Transfer of Tribunal Functions and Revenue and Customs Appeals Order, SI 2009/56 art 3, Sch 1 para 222 with effect from 1 April 2009, subject to transitional and savings provisions in Sch 3 para 4.

[85A Payment of tax on determination of appeal

(1) This section applies where the tribunal has determined an appeal under section 83.

(2) Where on the appeal the tribunal has determined that—

(*a*) the whole or part of any disputed amount paid or deposited is not due, or

(*b*) the whole or part of any VAT credit due to the appellant has not been paid,

so much of that amount, or of that credit, as the tribunal determines not to be due or not to have been paid shall be paid or repaid with interest at the rate applicable under section 197 of the Finance Act 1996.

(3) Where on the appeal the tribunal has determined that—

(*a*) the whole or part of any disputed amount not paid or deposited is due, or

(*b*) the whole or part of any VAT credit paid was not payable,

so much of that amount, or of that credit, as the tribunal determines to be due or not payable shall be paid or repaid to HMRC with interest at the rate applicable under section 197 of the Finance Act 1996.

(4) Interest under subsection (3) shall be paid without any deduction of income tax.

(5) Nothing in this section requires HMRC to pay interest—

(*a*) on any amount which falls to be increased by a supplement under section 79 (repayment supplement in respect of certain delayed payments or refunds); or

(*b*) where an amount is increased under that section, on so much of the increased amount as represents the supplement.][1]

Commentary—*De Voil Indirect Tax Service* **V5.467.**

Amendments—[1] Sections 85A–85B inserted by the Transfer of Tribunal Functions and Revenue and Customs Appeals Order, SI 2009/56 art 3, Sch 1 para 223 with effect from 1 April 2009, subject to transitional and savings provisions in Sch 3 para 4.

[85B Payment of tax where there is a further appeal

(1) Where a party makes a further appeal, notwithstanding that the further appeal is pending, value added tax or VAT credits, or a credit of overstated or overpaid value added tax shall be payable or repayable in accordance with the determination of the tribunal or court against which the further appeal is made.

(2) But if the amount payable or repayable is altered by the order or judgment of the tribunal or court on the further appeal—

(*a*) if too much value added tax has been paid or the whole or part of any VAT credit due to the appellant has not been paid the amount overpaid or not paid shall be refunded with such interest, if any, as the tribunal or court may allow; and

(*b*) if too little value added tax has been charged or the whole or part of any VAT credit paid was not payable so much of the amount as the tribunal or court determines to be due or not payable shall be due or repayable, as appropriate, at the expiration of a period of thirty days beginning with the date on which HMRC issue to the other party a notice of the total amount payable in accordance with the order or judgment of that tribunal or court.

(3) If, on the application of HMRC, the relevant tribunal or court considers it necessary for the protection of the revenue, subsection (1) shall not apply and the relevant tribunal or court may—

(*a*) give permission to withhold any payment or repayment; or

(*b*) require the provision of adequate security before payment or repayment is made.

(4) If, on the application of the original appellant, HMRC are satisfied that financial extremity might be reasonably expected to result if payment or repayment is required or withheld as appropriate, HMRC may do one or more of the things listed in subsection (6).

(5) If on the application of the original appellant, the relevant tribunal or court decides that—

(*a*) the original appellant has applied to HMRC under subsection (4),

(*b*) HMRC have decided that application,

(*c*) financial extremity might be reasonably expected to result from that decision by HMRC,

s 84(3), *Don Pasquale (a firm) v C&E Comrs* [1990] STC 556*; *Infinity Distribution Ltd v R&C Comrs* [2010] STC 2258; *R (on the application of ToTel Ltd) v First-tier Tribunal (Tax Chamber) and another (HM Treasury, interested party)* [2011] EWHC 652 (Admin), [2011] STC 1485.
s 84(5), *Elias Gale Racing v C&E Comrs* [1999] STC 66; *BUPA Purchasing Ltd and others v C&E Comrs* [2008] STC 101.
S 84(8), *R&C Comrs v RSPCA and another, R&C Comrs v ToTel Ltd* [2008] STC 885.
s 84(10), *C&E Comrs v Arnold* [1996] STC 1271.

Definitions—"The Commissioners", s 96(1); "input tax", s 24; "prescribed accounting period", s 25(1); "recovery assessment", s 78A(5); "supply", s 5, Sch 4; "tax", s 96(1); "tribunal", s 82; "VAT", ss 1, 96(1); "VAT credit", s 25(3).

Cross reference—See VATA 1994 Sch 13 para 22 (modification of this section in its application before the day appointed for the purposes of FA 1994 s 18(3)).
VATA 1994 Sch 3B para 20(3) (assessments relating to special scheme returns).
VATA 1994 Sch 3BA para 37 (assessments relating to relevant non-UK returns).

Modifications—Money Laundering Regulations, SI 2007/2157 reg 44(3), Sch 5 para 1 (repeal of this section in relation to appeals to a VAT and duties tribunal made under SI 2007/2157 reg 44).
Transfer of Funds (Information on the Payer) Regulations, SI 2007/3298 reg 13(4), Sch 2 para 2 (repeal of this section in relation to appeals to a VAT and duties tribunal made under SI 2007/3298 reg 13).

Amendments—[1] Sub-s (7A) inserted by FA 1996 s 31(4).
[2] Words in sub-s (7) substituted for the words 'as to the matters in sub-paragraph (2)(a) to (d) of paragraph 2 of Schedule 1 or, as the case may be, as to the matters in sub-paragraph (4) of that paragraph" by FA 1997 s 31 in relation to directions made on or after the date of passing of FA 1997.
[3] Sub-ss (4A)–(4D) inserted by FA 1999 s 16, Sch 2 para 4 with effect from 27 July 1999 subject to FA 1999 Sch 2 para 6.
[4] Sub-s (4ZA) inserted by FA 2002 s 23(3), (4) and deemed to have come into force on 24 April 2002.
[5] Sub-ss (4E), (4F) inserted by FA 2003 s 17(7) with effect from 10 April 2003.
[6] Sub-s (6A) inserted, by FA 2004 s 19, Sch 2 para 5 with effect from the passing of FA 2004, so far as is necessary for enabling the making of any orders or regulations by virtue of FA 2004 Sch 2, and otherwise with effect from such day as the Treasury may by order made by statutory instrument appoint.
[7] Sub-ss (7B) inserted by FA 2006 s 21(5) with effect from 19 July 2006.
[8] Sub-s (6B) inserted by FA 2007 s 93(9) with effect from 19 July 2007.
[9] Sub-s (7ZA) inserted by the Value Added Tax (Buildings and Land) Order, SI 2008/1146, art 3(1), (3) with effect in relation to supplies made on or after 1 June 2008, subject to savings in Sch 2 of the Order.
[10] The following amendments made by the Transfer of Tribunal Functions and Revenue and Customs Appeals Order, SI 2009/56 art 3, Sch 1 para 221 with effect from 1 April 2009, subject to transitional and savings provisions in Sch 3 para 4—
– sub-ss (2), (8) repealed;
– sub-ss (3), (3A) substituted;
– sub-ss (3B), (3C) inserted;
– in sub-ss (4)(a), (b) and words at the end, (4ZA), (4A)(a), (4C), (4D), (7), (7ZA) and (7B), words substituted for the words "the Commissioners";
– in sub-ss (4ZA)(a), (5), (6), (6A), (6B), (7), (7A), (7ZA) and (7B) words substituted for the words "83";
– in sub-s (4E) words substituted for the words "the Commissioners satisfy";
– in sub-s (9) words at the beginning inserted; words in (9)(b) substituted for "the Commissioners"; sub-(9);
– in sub-s (10) words in the first place substituted for the words "a decision of the Commissioners" and words "by them" in the second place repealed.
[11] In sub-s (6), words inserted by FA 2014 s 103, Sch 22 para 17 with effect in relation to supplies made on or after 1 January 2015.

85 Settling appeals by agreement

(1) Subject to the provisions of this section, where a person gives notice of appeal under section 83 and, before the appeal is determined by a tribunal, [HMRC][1] and the appellant come to an agreement (whether in writing or otherwise) under the terms of which the decision under appeal is to be treated—

(*a*) as upheld without variation, or

(*b*) as varied in a particular manner, or

(*c*) as discharged or cancelled,

the like consequences shall ensue for all purposes as would have ensued if, at the time when the agreement was come to, a tribunal had determined the appeal in accordance with the terms of the agreement . . . [1].

(2) Subsection (1) above shall not apply where, within 30 days from the date when the agreement was come to, the appellant gives notice in writing to [HMRC][1] that he desires to repudiate or resile for the agreement.

(3) Where an agreement is not in writing—

(*a*) the preceding provisions of this section shall not apply unless the fact that an agreement was come to, and the terms agreed, are confirmed by notice in writing given by [HMRC][1] to the appellant or by the appellant to [HMRC][1], and

(*b*) references in those provisions to the time when the agreement was come to shall be construed as references to the time of the giving of that notice of confirmation.

(4) Where—

(*a*) a person who has given a notice of appeal notifies [HMRC][1], whether orally or in writing, that he desires not to proceed with the appeal; and

(*b*) 30 days have elapsed since the giving of the notification without [HMRC][1] giving to the appellant notice in writing indicating that they are unwilling that the appeal should be treated as withdrawn, the relevant tribunal or court may replace, vary or supplement the decision by HMRC by doing one or more of the things listed in subsection (6).

(6) These are the things which HMRC or the relevant tribunal or court may do under subsection (4) or (5)—

(*a*) decide how much, if any, of the amount under appeal should be paid or repaid as appropriate,

(*b*) require the provision of adequate security from the original appellant,

(*c*) stay the requirement to pay or repay under subsection (1).

(7) Subsections (3) to (6) cease to have effect when the further appeal has been determined.

(8) In this section—

"adequate security" means security that is of such amount and given in such manner—

(*a*) as the tribunal or court may determine (in a case falling within subsection (3) or (5)), or

(*b*) as HMRC consider adequate to protect the revenue (in a case falling within subsection (4));

"further appeal" means an appeal against—

(*a*) the tribunal's determination of an appeal under section 83, or

(*b*) a decision of the Upper Tribunal or a court that arises (directly or indirectly) from that determination;

"original appellant" means the person who made the appeal to the tribunal under section 83;

"relevant tribunal or court" means the tribunal or court from which permission or leave to appeal is sought.][1]

Commentary—*De Voil Indirect Tax Service* **V5.467**.

Amendments—[1] Sections 85A–85B inserted by the Transfer of Tribunal Functions and Revenue and Customs Appeals Order, SI 2009/56 art 3, Sch 1 para 223 with effect from 1 April 2009, subject to transitional and savings provisions in Sch 3 para 4. If an appeal from a decision of a VAT and duties tribunal, or from a court, is made before 1 April 2009, this section does not apply in relation to that decision (SI 2009/56 Sch 3 para 10).

[86 Appeals to Court of Appeal

(1) The Lord Chancellor may by order provide that—

(a) in such classes of appeal as may be prescribed by the order, and

(b) subject to the consent of the parties and to such other conditions as may be so prescribed,

an appeal from a tribunal shall lie to the Court of Appeal.

(2) An order under this section may provide that section 11 of the Tribunals and Inquiries Act 1992 (which provides for appeals to the High Court from a tribunal) shall have effect, in relation to any appeal to which the order applies, with such modifications as may be specified in the order.

[(2A) Before making an order under this section that relates to England and Wales, the Lord Chancellor must consult the Lord Chief Justice of England and Wales.

(2B) Before making an order under this section that relates to Northern Ireland, the Lord Chancellor must consult the Lord Chief Justice of Northern Ireland.

(2C) The Lord Chief Justice of England and Wales may nominate a judicial office holder (as defined in section 109(4) of the Constitutional Reform Act 2005) to exercise his functions under this section.

(2D) The Lord Chief Justice of Northern Ireland may nominate any of the following to exercise his functions under this section—

(a) the holder of one of the offices listed in Schedule 1 to the Justice (Northern Ireland) Act 2002;

(b) a Lord Justice of Appeal (as defined in section 88 of that Act).][1]

(3) This section does not extend to Scotland.][2]

Commentary—*De Voil Indirect Tax Service* **V5.400**.

Orders—See VAT Tribunals Appeals Order, SI 1986/2288; VAT Tribunals Appeals (Northern Ireland) Order, SI 1994/1978.

Definition—"Tribunal", s 82.

Cross reference—See VATA 1994 s 97(2) (a statutory instrument containing an order under this section is subject to annulment in pursuance of a resolution of either House of Parliament).

Amendments—[1] Sub-ss (2A)–(2D) inserted by Constitutional Reform Act 2005 s 15, Sch 4 paras 235, 236 with effect from 3 April 2006 by virtue of SI 2006/1014 art 2(a), Sch 1 para 11.

[2] This section repealed by the Transfer of Tribunal Functions and Revenue and Customs Appeals Order, SI 2009/56 art 3, Sch 1 para 224 with effect from 1 April 2009, subject to transitional and savings provisions in Sch 3 para 4.

[87 Enforcement of registered or recorded tribunal decisions etc

(1) If the decision of a tribunal in England and Wales on an appeal under section 83 is registered by the Commissioners in accordance with rules of court, payment of—

(a) any amount which, as a result of the decision, is, or is recoverable as, VAT due from any person, and

(b) any costs awarded to the Commissioners by the decision,

may be enforced by the High Court as if that amount or, as the case may be, the amount of those costs were an amount due to the Commissioners in pursuance of a judgment or order of the High Court.

(2) If the decision of a tribunal in Scotland on an appeal under section 83—

(a) confirms or varies an amount which is, or is recoverable as, VAT due from any person, or

(b) awards costs to the Commissioners,

the decision may be recorded for execution in the Books of Council and Session and shall be enforceable accordingly.

(3) Subsection (4) below shall apply in relation to the decision of a tribunal in Northern Ireland on an appeal under section 83 where—

(a) any amount is, or is recoverable as, VAT due from any person, as a result of the decision, whether with or without an award of costs to the Commissioners; or

(b) any costs are awarded to the Commissioners by the decision.

(4) Where this subsection applies—

(a) payment of the amount mentioned in paragraph (a) of subsection (3) above or, as the case may be, the amount of the costs mentioned in paragraph (b) of that subsection may be enforced by the Enforcement of Judgments Office; and

(b) a sum equal to any such amount shall be deemed to be payable under a money judgment within the meaning of Article 2(2) of the Judgments Enforcement (Northern Ireland) Order 1981, and the provisions of that Order shall apply accordingly.

(5) Any reference in this section to a decision of a tribunal includes a reference to an order (however described) made by a tribunal for giving effect to a decision.][1]

Definitions—"The Commissioners", s 96(1); "tribunal", s 82; "VAT", ss 1, 96(1).

Modifications—Money Laundering Regulations, SI 2007/2157 reg 44(3), Sch 5 para 1 (in sub-ss (1)(*a*), (2)(*a*), (3)(*a*), words ", or is recoverable as, VAT" repealed, in relation to appeals to a VAT and duties tribunal made under SI 2007/2157 reg 44).

Amendments—[1] This section repealed by the Transfer of Tribunal Functions and Revenue and Customs Appeals Order, SI 2009/56 art 3, Sch 1 para 224 with effect from 1 April 2009, subject to transitional and savings provisions in Sch 3 para 4.

PART VI
SUPPLEMENTARY PROVISIONS

Change in rate of VAT etc and disclosure of information

88 Supplies spanning change of rate etc

(1) This section applies where there is a change in the rate of VAT in force under section 2 [or 29A][1] or in the descriptions of exempt[, zero-rated or reduced-rate][1] supplies or exempt[, zero-rated or reduced-rate][1] acquisitions.

(2) Where—

(*a*) a supply affected by the change would, apart from section 6(4), (5), (6) or (10), be treated under section 6(2) or (3) as made wholly or partly at a time when it would not have been affected by the change; or

(*b*) a supply not so affected would apart from section 6(4), (5), (6) or (10) be treated under section 6(2) or (3) as made wholly or partly at a time when it would have been so affected,

the rate at which VAT is chargeable on the supply, or any question whether it is zero-rated or exempt [or a reduced-rate supply][1], shall if the person making it so elects be determined without regard to section 6(4), (5), (6) or (10).

(3) Any power to make regulations under this Act with respect to the time when a supply is to be treated as taking place shall include power to provide for this section to apply as if the references in subsection (2) above to section 6(4), (5), (6) or (10) included references to specified provisions of the regulations.

(4) Where—

(*a*) any acquisition of goods from another member State which is affected by the change would not have been affected (in whole or in part) if it had been treated as taking place at the time of the event which, in relation to that acquisition, is the first relevant event for the purposes of taxing the acquisition; or

(*b*) any acquisition of goods from another member State which is not so affected would have been affected (in whole or in part) if it had been treated as taking place at the time of that event,

the rate at which VAT is chargeable on the acquisition, or any question whether it is zero-rated or exempt [or a reduced-rate acquisition][1], shall, if the person making the acquisition so elects, be determined as at the time of that event.

(5) Regulations under [paragraph 2A][2] of Schedule 11 may make provision for the replacement or correction of any VAT invoice which—

(*a*) relates to a supply in respect of which an election is made under this section, but

(*b*) was issued before the election was made.

(6) No election may be made under this section in respect of a supply to which [paragraph 7 of Schedule 4 or paragraph 2B(4) of Schedule 11][2] applies.

(7) References in this section to an acquisition being zero-rated are references to an acquisition of goods from another member State being one in relation to which section 30(3) provides for no VAT to be chargeable.

[(8) References in this section—

(*a*) to a supply being a reduced-rate supply, or

(*b*) to an acquisition being a reduced-rate acquisition,

are references to a supply, or (as the case may be) an acquisition, being one on which VAT is charged at the rate in force under section 29A.][1]

Commentary—*De Voil Indirect Tax Service* **V3.141**.

Regulations—See VAT Regulations, SI 1995/2518 reg 95.

Press releases etc—Business Brief 21/95 8-10-95 (operation of retail scheme spanning rate change).

Definitions—"Acquisition of goods from another member State", s 11; "another member State", s 96(1); "exempt acquisition", s 31; "exempt supply", s 31; "regulations", s 96(1); "supply", s 5, Sch 4; "VAT", ss 1, 96(1); "VAT invoice", s 6(15); "zero-rating", s 30.

Cross references—See VAT Regulations, SI 1995/2518 reg 15 (credit note to be issued by supplier following change of rate, where an election is made under this section).

VAT Regulations, SI 1995/2518 reg 95 (supplies spanning change in rate of VAT: deemed time of supply: extension of sub-s (2) of this section).

Amendments—[1] In sub-s (1), "or 29A" inserted, and words substituted for "or zero-rated"; words in sub-ss (2), (4) inserted; and sub-s (8) added, by FA 2001 s 99(6), Sch 31 para 4 with effect from 11 May 2001.

[2] Words in sub-ss (5), (6) substituted by FA 2002 s 24(4)(c), (5) with effect from 1 December 2003 (by virtue of SI 2003/3043).

89 Adjustments of contracts on changes in VAT

(1) Where, after the making of a contract for the supply of goods or services and before the goods or services are supplied, there is a change in the VAT charged on the supply, then, unless the contract otherwise provided, there shall be added to or deducted from the consideration for the supply an amount equal to the change.

(2) Subsection (1) above shall apply in relation to a tenancy or lease as it applies in relation to a contract except that a term of a tenancy or lease shall not be taken to provide that the rule contained in that subsection is not to apply in the case of the tenancy or lease if the term does not [refer][1] specifically to VAT or this section.

(3) References in this section to a change in the VAT charged on a supply include references to a change to or from no VAT being charged on the supply (including a change attributable to the making of an [option to tax any land under Part 1 of Schedule 10][2]).

Commentary—*De Voil Indirect Tax Service* **V3.151**.

Definitions—"Supply", s 5, Sch 4; "VAT", ss 1, 96(1).

Amendments—[1] The Commissioners have confirmed that the word "refer" has been accidentally omitted from s 89(2).

[2] In sub-s (3) words substituted by the Value Added Tax (Buildings and Land) Order, SI 2008/1146, art 6, Sch 1 paras 1, 2 with effect in relation to supplies made on or after 1 June 2008, subject to savings in Sch 2 of the Order.

90 Failure of resolution under Provisional Collection of Taxes Act 1968

(1) Where—

(*a*) by virtue of a resolution having effect under the Provisional Collection of Taxes Act 1968 VAT has been paid at a rate specified in the resolution on the supply of any goods or services by reference to a value determined under section 19(2) or on the acquisition of goods from another member State by reference to a value determined under section 20(3), and

(*b*) by virtue of section 1(6) or (7) or 5(3) of that Act any of that VAT is repayable in consequence of the restoration in relation to that supply or acquisition of a lower rate,

the amount repayable shall be the difference between the VAT paid by reference to that value at the rate specified in the resolution and the VAT that would have been payable by reference to that value at the lower rate.

(2) Where—

(*a*) by virtue of such a resolution VAT is chargeable at a rate specified in the resolution on the supply of any goods or services by reference to a value determined under section 19(2) or on the acquisition of goods from another member State by reference to a value determined under section 20(3), but

(*b*) before the VAT is paid it ceases to be chargeable at that rate in consequence of the restoration in relation to that supply or acquisition of a lower rate,

the VAT chargeable at the lower rate shall be charged by reference to the same value as that by reference to which VAT would have been chargeable at the rate specified in the resolution.

(3) The VAT that may be credited as input tax under section 25 or refunded under section 33, [or 33A,][1] [33B,][2] [33C,][3] 35 or 40 does not include VAT that has been repaid by virtue of any of the provisions mentioned in subsection (1)(*b*) above or that would be repayable by virtue of any of those provisions if it had been paid.

Commentary—*De Voil Indirect Tax Service* **V1.131**.

Definitions—"Acquisition of goods from another member State", s 11; "another member State", s 96(1); "input tax", s 24; "supply", s 5, Sch 4; "VAT", ss 1, 96(1).

Amendments—[1] Words in sub-s (3) inserted by FA 2001 s 98(8) with effect from 1 September 2001.

[2] Words in sub-s (3) inserted by FA 2011 s 76(3) with effect in relation to supplies made, and acquisitions and importations taking place, on or after 1 April 2011.

[3] Words in sub-s (3)" inserted by FA 2015 s 66(1), (3) with effect in relation to supplies made, and acquisitions and importations taking place, on or after 1 April 2015.

91 Disclosure of information for statistical purposes

(1) For the purpose of the compilation or maintenance by the Department of Trade and Industry or the [Statistics Board][1] of a central register of businesses, or for the purpose of any statistical survey conducted or to be conducted by that Department [or Board][1], the Commissioners or an authorised officer of the Commissioners may disclose to an authorised officer of that Department [or Board][1] particulars of the following descriptions obtained or recorded by them in pursuance of this Act—

(*a*) numbers allocated by the Commissioners on the registration of persons under this Act and reference numbers for members of a group;

(*b*) names, trading styles and addresses of persons so registered or of members of groups and status and trade classifications of businesses; and

(*c*) actual or estimated value of supplies.

(2) Subject to subsection (3) below, no information obtained by virtue of this section by an officer of the Department of Trade and Industry or the [Statistics Board][1] may be disclosed except to an officer of a Government department (including a Northern Ireland department [or to a member of the staff of the Scottish Administration][2]) for the purpose for which the information was obtained, or for a like purpose.

(3) Subsection (2) above does not prevent the disclosure—

(*a*) of any information in the form of a summary so framed as not to enable particulars to be identified as particulars relating to a particular person or to the business carried on by a particular person; or

(*b*) with the consent of any person, of any information enabling particulars to be identified as particulars relating only to him or to a business carried on by him.

(4) If any person who has obtained any information by virtue of this section discloses it in contravention of this section he shall be liable—

(*a*) on summary conviction to a fine not exceeding the statutory maximum; and

(*b*) on conviction on indictment to imprisonment for a term not exceeding 2 years or to a fine of any amount or to both.

(5) In this section, references to the Department of Trade and Industry or the [Statistics Board][1] include references to any Northern Ireland department [or to any part of the Scottish Administration][2] carrying out similar functions.

Commentary—*De Voil Indirect Tax Service* **V1.270**.

Definitions—"The Commissioners", s 96(1); "business", s 94; "registered", s 3(3); "supply", s 5, Sch 4.

Amendments—[1] Words in sub-ss (1), (2), (5) substituted by Statistics and Registration Service Act 2007 s 46, Sch 2 para 6 with effect from 1 April 2008, by virtue of SI 2008/839, art 2.

[2] Words in sub-ss (2), (5) inserted by The Scotland Act 1998 (Consequential Modifications) (No 2) Order, SI 1999/1820 s 114(2), which comes into force on the "principle appointed day", currently 1 July 1999, by virtue of the Scotland Act 1998 (Commencement) Order 1998/3178.

Interpretative provisions

92 Taxation under the laws of other member States etc

(1) Subject to the following provisions of this section, references in this Act, in relation to another member State, to the law of that member State shall be construed as confined to so much of the law of that member State as for the time being has effect for the purposes of any Community instrument relating to VAT.

(2) Subject to the following provisions of this section—

(*a*) references in this Act to a person being taxable in another member State are references to that person being taxable under so much of the law of that member State as makes provision for purposes corresponding, in relation to that member State, to the purposes of so much of this Act as makes provision as to whether a person is a taxable person; and

(*b*) references in this Act to goods being acquired by a person in another member State are references to goods being treated as so acquired in accordance with provisions of the law of that member State corresponding, in relation to that member State, to so much of this Act as makes provision for treating goods as acquired in the United Kingdom from another member State.

(3) Without prejudice to subsection (5) below, the Commissioners may by regulations make provision for the manner in which any of the following are to be or may be proved for any of the purposes of this Act, that is to say—

(*a*) the effect of any provisions of the law of any other member State;

(*b*) that provisions of any such law correspond or have a purpose corresponding, in relation to any member State, to or to the purpose of any provision of this Act.

(4) The Commissioners may by regulations provide—

(*a*) for a person to be treated for prescribed purposes of this Act as taxable in another member State only where he has given such notification, and furnished such other information, to the Commissioners as may be prescribed;

(*b*) for the form and manner in which any notification or information is to be given or furnished under the regulations and the particulars which it is to contain;

(*c*) for the proportion of any consideration for any transaction which is to be taken for the purposes of this Act as representing a liability, under the law of another member State, for VAT to be conclusively determined by reference to such invoices or in such other manner as may be prescribed.

(5) In any proceedings (whether civil or criminal), a certificate of the Commissioners—

(*a*) that a person was or was not, at any date, taxable in another member State; or

(*b*) that any VAT payable under the law of another member State has or has not been paid,

shall be sufficient evidence of that fact until the contrary is proved, and any document purporting to be a certificate under this subsection shall be deemed to be such a certificate until the contrary is proved.

(6) Without prejudice to the generality of any of the powers of the Commissioners under the relevant information provisions, those powers shall, for the purpose of facilitating compliance with any Community obligations, be exercisable with respect to matters that are relevant to a charge to VAT under the law of another member State, as they are exercisable with respect to matters that are relevant for any of the purposes of this Act.

(7) The reference in subsection (6) above to the relevant information provisions is a reference to the provisions of section 73(7) and Schedule 11 relating to—

(*a*) the keeping of accounts;

(*b*) the making of returns and the submission of other documents to the Commissioners;

(*c*) the production, use and contents of invoices;

(*d*) the keeping and preservation of records; and

(*e*) the furnishing of information and the production of documents.

Commentary—*De Voil Indirect Tax Service* **V1.244**.

Definitions—"Acquisition of goods from another member State", s 11; "another member State", s 96(1); "the Commissioners", s 96(1); "document", s 96(1); "invoice", s 96(1); "prescribed", s 96(1); "regulations", s 96(1); "taxable person", s 3; "United Kingdom", s 96(11); "VAT", ss 1, 96(1).

93 Territories included in references to other member States etc

(1) The Commissioners may by regulations provide for the territory of the Community, or for the member States, to be treated for any of the purposes of this Act as including or excluding such territories as may be prescribed.

(2) Without prejudice to the generality of the powers conferred by subsection (1) and section 16, the Commissioners may, for any of the purposes of this Act, by regulations provide for prescribed provisions of any customs and excise legislation to apply in relation to cases where any territory is treated under subsection (1) above as excluded from the territory of the Community, with such exceptions and adaptations as may be prescribed.

(3) In subsection (2) above the reference to customs and excise legislation is a reference to any enactment or subordinate or Community legislation (whenever passed, made or adopted) which has effect in relation to, or to any assigned matter connected with, the importation or exportation of goods.

(4) In subsection (3) above "assigned matter" has the same meaning as in the Management Act.

Commentary—*De Voil Indirect Tax Service* **V1.213**.

Regulations—See VAT Regulations, SI 1995/2518 regs 118–121, 136–145.

Value Added Tax (Amendment) (No 3) Regulations 2013/3211.

Definitions—"The Commissioners", s 96(1); "subordinate legislation", s 96(1).

94 Meaning of "business" etc

(1) In this Act "business" includes any trade, profession or vocation.

(2) Without prejudice to the generality of anything else in this Act, the following are deemed to be the carrying on of a business—

(*a*) the provision by a club, association or organisation (for a subscription or other consideration) of the facilities or advantages available to its members; and

(*b*) the admission, for a consideration, of persons to any premises.

(3) . . . [1]

(4) Where a person, in the course or furtherance of a trade, profession or vocation, accepts any office, services supplied by him as the holder of that office are treated as supplied in the course or furtherance of the trade, profession or vocation.

(5) Anything done in connection with the termination or intended termination of a business is treated as being done in the course or furtherance of that business.

(6) The disposition of a business[, or part of a business,][2] as a going concern, or of [the assets or liabilities of the business or part of the business][2] (whether or not in connection with its reorganisation or winding up), is a supply made in the course or furtherance of the business.

Commentary—*De Voil Indirect Tax Service* **V2.202**.

HMRC Manuals—VAT Guidance V1-3: Supply and consideration, para 4.9 (office holders: services supplied in the course of trade).

Simon's Tax Cases—*C&E Comrs v Apple and Pear Development Council* [1984] STC 296*; *Lord Advocate v Largs Golf Club* [1985] STC 226*.

s 94(2), *Eastbourne Town Radio Cars Association v C&E Comrs* [2001] STC 606.
s 94(2)(*a*), *C&E Comrs v British Field Sports Society* [1998] STC 315*.
s 94(3), *C&E Comrs v British Field Sports Society* [1997] STC 746*.
Definition—"Supply", s 5, Sch 4.
Amendments—[1] Sub-s (3) repealed by FA 1999 s 20 Sch 20 Pt II with effect from 1 December 1999 (by virtue of the Finance Act 1999, Section 20, (Appointed Day) Order, SI 1999/2769, art 2).
[2] In sub-s (6) words inserted and substituted by FA 2007 s 100(7), (10) with effect in relation to transfers pursuant to contracts entered into on or after 1 September 2007.

95 Meaning of "new means of transport"

(1) In this Act "means of transport" in the expression "new means of transport" means, subject to subsection (2) below, any of the following, that is to say—

(*a*) any ship exceeding 7.5 metres in length;
(*b*) any aircraft the take-off weight of which exceeds 1550 kilograms;
(*c*) any motorised land vehicle which—
(i) has an engine with a displacement or cylinder capacity exceeding 48 cubic centimetres; or
(ii) is constructed or adapted to be electrically propelled using more than 7.2 kilowatts.

(2) A ship, aircraft or motorised land vehicle does not fall within subsection (1) above unless it is intended for the transport of persons or goods.

[(3) For the purposes of this Act a means of transport shall be treated as new, in relation to any supply or any acquisition from another member State, at any time unless at that time—

(*a*) the period that has elapsed since its first entry into service is—
(i) in the case of a ship or aircraft, a period of more than 3 months; and
(ii) in the case of a land vehicle, a period of more than 6 months;

and][1]

(*b*) it has, since its first entry into service, travelled under its own power—
(i) in the case of a ship, for more than 100 hours;
(ii) in the case of an aircraft, for more than 40 hours; and
(iii) in the case of a land vehicle, for more than [6000 kilometres][1].

(4) The Treasury may by order vary this section—

(*a*) by adding or deleting any ship, aircraft or vehicle of a description specified in the order to or from those which are for the time being specified in subsection (1) above; and
(*b*) by altering, omitting or adding to the provisions of subsection (3) above for determining whether a means of transport is new.

(5) The Commissioners may by regulations make provision specifying the circumstances in which a means of transport is to be treated for the purposes of this section as having first entered into service.

Commentary—*De Voil Indirect Tax Service* **V1.294**.
Regulations—See VAT Regulations, SI 1995/2518 reg 147.
Definitions—"The Commissioners", s 96(1); "regulations", s 96(1); "ship", s 96(1).
Cross reference—See VAT Regulations, SI 1995/2518 reg 147 (time when a means of transport is treated as having first entered into service).
Amendments—[1] Words in sub-s (3) substituted by the Value Added Tax (Means of Transport) Order, SI 1994/3128 with effect in relation to means of transport whose first entry into service is on or after 1 January 1995.

96 Other interpretative provisions

(1) In this Act—

"the 1983 Act" means the Value Added Tax Act 1983;
"another member State" means, subject to section 93(1), any member State other than the United Kingdom, and "other member States" shall be construed accordingly;
"assignment", in relation to Scotland, means assignation;
"authorised person" means any person acting under the authority of the Commissioners;
"the Commissioners" means the Commissioners of Customs and Excise;
["document" means anything in which information of any description is recorded; and][2]
["copy", in relation to a document, means anything onto which information recorded in the document has been copied, by whatever means and whether directly or indirectly;][2]
"fee simple"—
(*a*) in relation to Scotland, means the . . . [8] interest of the owner;
(*b*) in relation to Northern Ireland, includes the estate of a person who holds land under a fee farm grant;
["HMRC" means Her Majesty's Revenue and Customs;][10]
"invoice" includes any document similar to an invoice;
"input tax" has the meaning given by section 24;
"interim trustee" has the same meaning as in the Bankruptcy (Scotland) Act 1985;
"local authority" has the meaning given by subsection (4) below;

"major interest", in relation to land, means the fee simple or a tenancy for a term certain exceeding 21 years, and in relation to Scotland means [the][8] interest of the owner, or the lessee's interest under a lease for a period [of not less than 20 years][5];
"the Management Act" means the Customs and Excise Management Act 1979;
"money" includes currencies other than sterling;
"output tax" has the meaning given by section 24;
"permanent trustee" has the same meaning as in the Bankruptcy (Scotland) Act 1985;
. . . [12]
"prescribed" means prescribed by regulations;
"prescribed accounting period" has the meaning given by section 25(1);
"quarter" means a period of 3 months ending at the end of March, June, September or December;
"regulations" means regulations made by the Commissioners under this Act;
["relevant business person" has the meaning given by section 7A(4)][11];
"ship" includes hovercraft;
"subordinate legislation" has the same meaning as in the Interpretation Act 1978;
"tax" means VAT;
"taxable acquisition" has the meaning given by section 10(2);
"taxable person" means a person who is a taxable person under section 3;
"taxable supply" has the meaning given by section 4(2);
"the Taxes Act" means the Income and Corporation Taxes Act 1988;
"tribunal" has the meaning given by section 82;
"VAT" means value added tax charged in accordance with this Act or, where the context requires, with the law of another member State;
"VAT credit" has the meaning given by section 25(3);
"VAT invoice" has the meaning given by section 6(15);
"VAT representative" has the meaning given by section 48;

and any reference to a particular section, Part or Schedule is a reference to that section or Part of, or Schedule to, this Act.

(2) Any reference in this Act to being registered shall be construed in accordance with section 3(3).

(3) Subject to section 93—

(*a*) the question whether or not goods have entered the territory of the Community;
(*b*) the time when any Community customs debt in respect of duty on the entry of any goods into the territory of the Community would be incurred; and
(*c*) the person by whom any such debt would fall to be discharged,

shall for the purposes of this Act be determined (whether or not the goods in question are themselves subject to any such duties) according to the Community legislation applicable to goods which are in fact subject to such duties.

(4) In this Act "local authority" means the council of a county, [county borough,][1] district, London borough, parish or group of parishes (or, in Wales, community or group of communities), the Common Council of the City of London, the Council of the Isles of Scilly, and any joint committee or joint board established by two or more of the foregoing and, in relation to Scotland, a regional, islands or district council within the meaning of the Local Government (Scotland) Act 1973 any combination and any joint committee or joint board established by two or more of the foregoing and any joint board to which section 226 of that Act applies.

(5) Any reference in this Act to the amount of any duty of excise on any goods shall be taken to be a reference to the amount of duty charged on those goods with any addition or deduction falling to be made under section 1 of the Excise Duties (Surcharges or Rebates) Act 1979.

(6), (7) . . . [3]

(8) The question whether, in relation to any supply of services, the supplier or the recipient of the supply belongs in one country or another shall be determined . . . [11] in accordance with section 9.

(9) Schedules [7A,][6] 8 and 9 shall be interpreted in accordance with the notes contained in those Schedules; and accordingly the powers conferred by this Act to vary those Schedules include a power to add to, delete or vary those notes.

(10) The descriptions of Groups in those Schedules are for ease of reference only and shall not affect the interpretation of the descriptions of items in those Groups.

[(10A) Where—

(*a*) the grant of any interest, right, licence or facilities gives rise for the purposes of this Act to supplies made at different times after the making of the grant, and
(*b*) a question whether any of those supplies is zero-rated or exempt falls to be determined according to whether or not the grant is a grant of a description specified in Schedule 8 or 9 or [any of paragraphs 5 to 11 of Schedule 10][9],

that question shall be determined according to whether the description is applicable as at the time of supply, rather than by reference to the time of the grant.][4]

[(10B) Notwithstanding subsection (10A) above—

(*a*) item 1 of Group 1 of Schedule 9 does not make exempt any supply that arises for the purposes of this Act from the prior grant of a fee simple falling within paragraph (*a*) of that item; and

(*b*) that paragraph does not prevent the exemption of a supply that arises for the purposes of this Act from the prior grant of a fee simple not falling within that paragraph.][7]

(11) References in this Act to the United Kingdom include the territorial sea of the United Kingdom.

Commentary—*De Voil Indirect Tax Service* **V1.241**.

Definition—"Supply", s 5, Sch 4.

Orders—Value Added Tax (Drugs and Medicines) Order, SI 2009/2972.
VAT (Relief for European Research Infrastructure Consortia) Order, SI 2012/2907.
Value Added Tax (Reduced Rate) (Cable-Suspended Passenger Transport Systems) Order, SI 2013/430.
Value Added Tax (Drugs and Medicines) Order, SI 2014/1111.
Value Added Tax (Sport) Order, SI 2014/3185.

Amendments—[1] Words in sub-s (4) inserted by the Local Government Reorganisation (Wales) (Consequential Amendments No 2) Order, SI 1995/1510 art 2 with effect from 16 June 1995.

[2] Definitions "document" and "copy" in sub-s (1) inserted by the Civil Evidence Act 1995 Sch 1 para 20 with effect from 31 January 1997 (see SI 1996/3217).

[3] Sub-ss (6), (7) repealed by the Civil Evidence Act 1995 Sch 2 with effect from 31 January 1997 (see SI 1996/3217).

[4] Sub-s (10A) inserted by FA 1997 s 35 and deemed always to have had effect.

[5] Words in the definition of "major interest" in para (b) substituted by FA 1998 s 24 with effect from 31 July 1998.

[6] In sub-s (9), "7A" inserted by FA 2001 s 99(6), Sch 31 para 5 with effect from 11 May 2001.

[7] Sub-s (10B) inserted by FA 2003 s 20 with effect for any supply that arises for the purposes of VATA 1994 from the prior grant of a fee simple made after 8 April 2003.

[8] In sub-s (1), words in definition of "fee simple" repealed and words in definition of "major interest" substituted by the Abolition of Feudal Tenure etc (Scotland) Act 2000 s 76(1), (2), Sch 12 Pt I para 57, Sch 13 Pt 1 with effect from 28 November 2004 (by virtue of SI 2003/456).

[9] In sub-s (10A)(b), words substituted by the Value Added Tax (Buildings and Land) Order, SI 2008/1146, art 6, Sch 1 paras 1, 3 with effect in relation to supplies made on or after 1 June 2008, subject to savings in Sch 2 of the Order.

[10] In sub-s (1) definition of "HMRC" inserted by the Transfer of Tribunal Functions and Revenue and Customs Appeals Order, SI 2009/56 art 3, Sch 1 para 225 with effect from 1 April 2009, subject to transitional and savings provisions in Sch 3 para 4.

[11] In sub-s (1) words inserted, in sub-s (8) words "(subject to any provision made under section 8(6))" repealed by FA 2009 s 76, Sch 36 paras 1, 8 with effect in relation to supplies made on or after 1 January 2010.

[12] In sub-s (1), definition of "the Post Office company" repealed by F(No 3)A 2010 s 22(3)(*a*) with effect in relation to supplies made on or after 31 January 2011.

Supplementary provisions

97 Orders, rules and regulations

(1) Any order made by the Treasury . . .[12] under this Act and any regulations or rules under this Act shall be made by statutory instrument.

(2) . . .[12]

(3) An order to which this subsection applies shall be laid before the House of Commons; and unless it is approved by that House before the expiration of a period of 28 days beginning with the date on which it was made, it shall cease to have effect on the expiration of that period, but without prejudice to anything previously done thereunder or to the making of a new order.

In reckoning any such period no account shall be taken of any time during which Parliament is dissolved or prorogued or during which the House of Commons is adjourned for more than 4 days.

(4) Subject to section 53(4), subsection (3) above applies to—

(*aa*) . . .[1]

(*a*) an order under section 5(4)[, 7A(6)][14] or 28;

[(*ab*) an order under paragraph 5(7) of Schedule 4 substituting a lesser sum for the sum for the time being specified in paragraph 5(2)(*a*) of that Schedule;][2]

(*b*) . . .[3]

(*c*) an order under this Act making provision—

(i) for increasing the rate of VAT in force [under section 2][4] at the time of the making of the order;

(ii) for excluding any VAT from credit under section 25;

[(iia) for varying Schedule 7A so as to cause VAT to be charged on a supply at the rate in force under section 2 instead of that in force under section 29A;][5]

(iii) for varying Schedule 8 or 9 so as to abolish the zero-rating of a supply or to abolish the exemption of a supply without zero-rating it;

[(*ca*) an order under section 43AA(1) if as a result of the order any bodies would cease to be eligible to be treated as members of a group;][8]

(*d*) an order under section 51, except one making only such amendments as are necessary or expedient in consequence of provisions of an order under this Act which—

(i) vary Schedule [7A,][5] 8 or 9; but

(ii) are not within paragraph (*c*) above;

(*e*) an order under section 54(4) or (8);

[(*ea*) an order under section 55A(13);][10]

[(*eb*) an order under section 77A(9) or (9A);][11]
[(*f*) an order under paragraph [B1, C1(4),][16] 1A(7)[, 2A(4)][16] [or 8A(7)][15] of Schedule 6;][6]
[(*fa*) an order under paragraph 3(4) of Schedule 10A);][9]
[(*g*) an order under paragraph 3 or 4 of Schedule 11A][7].

[(4A) Where an order under section 2(2) is in force, the reference in subsection (4)(*c*)(i) of this section to the rate of VAT in force under section 2 at the time of the making of an order is a reference to the rate which would be in force at that time if no such order had been made.][13]

(5) A statutory instrument made under any provision of this Act except—

(*a*) an order made under section 79, or

(*b*) an instrument as respects which any other Parliamentary procedure is expressly provided, or

(*c*) an instrument containing an order appointing a day for the purposes of any provision of this Act, being a day as from which the provision will have effect, with or without amendments, or will cease to have effect,

shall be subject to annulment in pursuance of a resolution of the House of Commons.

Commentary—*De Voil Indirect Tax Service* **V1.236**.

Definitions—"Exempt supply", s 31; "regulations", s 96(1); "supply", s 5, Sch 4; "VAT", ss 1, 96(1); "zero-rating", s 30.

Cross references—See VATA 1994 s 53(4) (sub-s (3) of this section disapplied in relation to orders under s 53 (tour operators)).
VAT (Isle of Man) Order, SI 1982/1067 art 7 (references to VAT in this section to include references to VAT chargeable under Isle of Man legislation).

Amendments—[1] Sub-s (4)(aa) inserted by FA 1995 s 21(4), (6), with effect in relation to any supply made after 31 March 1995 and any acquisition or importation taking place after that date, and repealed by FA 2001 s 110, Sch 33 Pt 3(1) with effect from 1 November 2001.

[2] Sub-s (4)(ab) inserted by FA 1996 s 33(3).

[3] Sub-s (4)(b) repealed by FA 1996 Sch 41 Pt IV(2).

[4] Words in sub-s (4)(c)(i) inserted by FA 2001 s 99(6), Sch 31 para 6(2) with effect in relation to orders under VATA 1994 s 2(2) that make changes only in the rate of VAT that is in force at times after 31 October 2001.

[5] Sub-s (4)(c)(iia) inserted, and words in sub-s (4)(d)(i) inserted, by FA 2001 s 99(6), Sch 31 para 6(3), (4) with effect from 11 May 2001.

[6] Sub-s (4)(f) inserted by FA 2004 s 22(4) with effect from 22 July 2004.

[7] Sub-s (4)(g) inserted by FA 2004 s 19, Sch 2 para 6 with effect from the passing of FA 2004, so far as is necessary for enabling the making of any orders or regulations by virtue of FA 2004 Sch 2, and otherwise with effect from such day as the Treasury may by order made by statutory instrument appoint.

[8] Sub-s (ca) inserted by FA 2004 s 20(5) with effect from 22 July 2004.

[9] Sub-s (4)(fa) inserted by FA 2006 s 22(2) with effect from 19 July 2006.

[10] Sub-s (4)(ea) inserted by FA 2006 s 19(6), (8) with effect for supplies made on or after 1 June 2007 (by virtue of the Finance Act 2006, Section 19, (Appointed Day) Order, SI 2007/1419).

[11] Sub-s (4)(eb) inserted by FA 2007 s 98(2) with effect from 19 July 2007.

[12] In sub-s (1) words "or the Lord Chancellor" repealed; sub-(2) repealed by the Transfer of Tribunal Functions and Revenue and Customs Appeals Order, SI 2009/56 art 3, Sch 1 para 226 with effect from 1 April 2009, subject to transitional and savings provisions in Sch 3 para 4.

[13] Sub-s (4A) inserted by FA 2009 Sch 3 para 25(3) with effect from 21 July 2009.

[14] Words in sub-s (4)(a) inserted by FA 2009 s 76, Sch 36 paras 1, 9 with effect in relation to supplies made on or after 1 January 2010.

[15] In sub-s (4)(f), words inserted by FA 2012 s 200(1), (4) with effect in relation to supplies made on or after 17 July 2012.

[16] Words inserted in sub-s (4)(*f*) by FA 2013 s 192, Sch 38 paras 1, 5 with effect from 17 July 2013.

[97A Place of supply orders: transitional provision.

(1) This section shall have effect for the purpose of giving effect to any order made [under section 7A(6)][2], if—

(*a*) the order provides for services of a description specified in the order to be treated as supplied in the United Kingdom;

(*b*) the services would not have fallen to be so treated apart from the order;

(*c*) the services are not services that would have fallen to be so treated under any provision re-enacted in the order; and

(*d*) the order is expressed to come into force in relation to services supplied on or after a date specified in the order ("the commencement date").

(2) Invoices and other documents provided to any person before the commencement date shall be disregarded in determining the time of the supply of any services which, if their time of supply were on or after the commencement date, would be treated by virtue of the order as supplied in the United Kingdom.

(3) If there is a payment in respect of any services of the specified description that was received by the supplier before the commencement date, so much (if any) of that payment as relates to times on or after that date shall be treated as if it were a payment received on the commencement date.

(4) If there is a payment in respect of services of the specified description that is or has been received by the supplier on or after the commencement date, so much (if any) of that payment as relates to times before that date shall be treated as if it were a payment received before that date.

(5) Subject to subsection (6) below, a payment in respect of any services shall be taken for the purposes of this section to relate to the time of the performance of those services.

(6) Where a payment is received in respect of any services the performance of which takes place over a period a part of which falls before the commencement date and a part of which does not—

(*a*) an apportionment shall be made, on a just and reasonable basis, of the extent to which the payment is attributable to so much of the performance of those services as took place before that date;

(*b*) the payment shall, to that extent, be taken for the purposes of this section to relate to a time before that date; and

(*c*) the remainder, if any, of the payment shall be taken for those purposes to relate to times on or after that date.][1]

Note—Section 97A is to be ignored for the purpose of giving effect to any order under s 7A(6), made on or after 17 July 2014, which is expressed as having effect in relation to supplies made on or after 1 January 2015 and makes provision about the place of supply of electronically supplied services, telecommunications services and radio and television broadcasting services. This applies only so far as the order makes provision about supplies to which Art 2 of Council Implementing Regulation 1042/2013/EU applies (FA 2014 s 105).

Amendments—[1] This section inserted by FA 1998 s 22 with effect from 17 March 1998.

[2] In sub-s (1) words "on or after 17th March 1998 under section 7(11)" substituted by FA 2009 s 76, Sch 36 paras 1, 10 with effect in relation to supplies made on or after 1 January 2010.

98 Service of notices

Any notice, notification, requirement or demand to be served on, given to or made of any person for the purposes of this Act may be served, given or made by sending it by post in a letter addressed to that person or his VAT representative at the last or usual residence or place of business of that person or representative.

Commentary—*De Voil Indirect Tax Service* **V2.110**.

Definitions—"Business", s 94; "VAT representative", s 48.

99 Refund of VAT to Government of Northern Ireland

The Commissioners shall refund to the Government of Northern Ireland the amount of the VAT charged on the supply of goods or services to that Government, on the acquisition of any goods by that Government from another member State or on the importation of any goods by that Government from a place outside the member States, after deducting therefrom so much of that amount as may be agreed between them and the Department of Finance and Personnel for Northern Ireland as attributable to supplies, acquisitions and importations for the purpose of a business carried on by the Government of Northern Ireland.

Commentary—*De Voil Indirect Tax Service* **V1.215**.

Definitions—"Acquisition of goods from another member State", s 11; "another member State", s 96(1); "business", s 94; "the Commissioners", s 96(1); "importation of goods from a place outside the member States", s 15; "supply", s 5, Sch 4; "VAT", ss 1, 96(1).

Cross reference—See VAT (Isle of Man) Order, SI 1982/1067 art 7 (references to VAT in this section to include references to VAT chargeable under Isle of Man legislation).

100 Savings and transitional provisions, consequential amendments and repeals

(1) Schedule 13 (savings and transitional provisions) and Schedule 14 (consequential amendments) shall have effect.

(2) The enactments and Orders specified in Schedule 15 are hereby repealed to the extent mentioned in the third column of that Schedule.

(3) This section is without prejudice to the operation of sections 15 to 17 of the Interpretation Act 1978 (which relate to the effect of repeals).

101 Commencement and extent

(1) This Act shall come into force on 1st September 1994 and Part I shall have effect in relation to the charge to VAT on supplies, acquisitions and importations in prescribed accounting periods ending on or after that date.

(2) Without prejudice to section 16 of the Interpretation Act 1978 (continuation of proceedings under repealed enactments) except in so far as it enables proceedings to be continued under repealed enactments, section 72 shall have effect on the commencement of this Act to the exclusion of section 39 of the 1983 Act.

(3) This Act extends to Northern Ireland.

(4) Paragraph 23 of Schedule 13 and paragraph 7 of Schedule 14 shall extend to the Isle of Man but no other provision of this Act shall extend there.

Definitions—"Prescribed accounting period", s 25(1); "supply", s 5, Sch 4; "VAT", ss 1, 96(1).

102 Short title

This Act may be cited as the Value Added Tax Act 1994.

SCHEDULES

[SCHEDULE A1

CHARGE AT REDUCED RATE]

Section 2

Amendments—Sch A1 inserted by FA 1995 s 21(3), (6), with effect in relation to any supply made after 31 March 1995 and any acquisition or importation taking place after that date, and repealed by FA 2001 s 99(3) with effect for supplies made, and acquisitions and importations taking place, after 31 October 2001. See VATA 1994 Sch 7A for supplies, etc after 31 October 2001.

SCHEDULE 1

REGISTRATION IN RESPECT OF TAXABLE SUPPLIES[: UK ESTABLISHMENT]

Section 3(2)

Cross references—See VATA 1994 s 54(2) (flat rate scheme for farmers: exclusion of supplies within scheme in determining liability for registration under this Schedule);

VATA 1994 s 55(1), (5) (supplies of gold and other precious metals and stones).

Liability to be registered

1—(1) Subject to sub-paragraphs (3) to (7) below, a person who makes taxable supplies but is not registered under this Act becomes liable to be registered under this Schedule—

(*a*) at the end of any month, if [the person is UK-established and][5] the value of his taxable supplies in the period of one year then ending has exceeded [£82,000][6]; or

(*b*) at any time, if [the person is UK-established and][5] there are reasonable grounds for believing that the value of his taxable supplies in the period of 30 days then beginning will exceed [£82,000][6].

(2) Where a business[, or part of a business,][4] carried on by a taxable person is transferred to another person as a going concern[, the transferee is UK-established at the time of the transfer and the transferee is not registered under this Act at that time][5], then, subject to sub-paragraphs (3) to (7) below, the transferee becomes liable to be registered under this Schedule at that time if—

(*a*) the value of his taxable supplies in the period of one year ending at the time of the transfer has exceeded [£82,000][6]; or

(*b*) there are reasonable grounds for believing that the value of his taxable supplies in the period of 30 days beginning at the time of the transfer will exceed [£82,000][6].

[(2A) In determining the value of a person's supplies for the purposes of sub-paragraph (1)(*a*) or (2)(*a*), supplies are to be taken into account (subject to sub-paragraphs (3) to (7)) whether or not the person was UK-established when they were made.][5]

(3) A person does not become liable to be registered by virtue of sub-paragraph (1)(*a*) or (2)(*a*) above if the Commissioners are satisfied that the value of his taxable supplies in the period of one year beginning at the time at which, apart from this sub-paragraph, he would become liable to be registered will not exceed [£80,000][6].

(4) In determining the value of a person's supplies for the purposes of sub-paragraph (1)(*a*) or (2)(*a*) above, supplies made at a time when he was previously registered under this Act shall be disregarded if—

(*a*) his registration was cancelled otherwise than under paragraph 13(3) below, [paragraph 11 of Schedule 1A,][5] paragraph 6(2) of Schedule 2[, paragraph 6(3) of Schedule 3 or paragraph 6(2) of Schedule 3A][3], and

(*b*) the Commissioners are satisfied that before his registration was cancelled he had given them all the information they needed in order to determine whether to cancel the registration.

(5) A person shall be treated as having become liable to be registered under this Schedule at any time when he would have become so liable under the preceding provisions of this paragraph but for any registration which is subsequently cancelled under paragraph 13(3) below, [paragraph 11 of Schedule 1A,][5] paragraph 6(2) of Schedule 2[, paragraph 6(3) of Schedule 3 or paragraph 6(2) of Schedule 3A][3].

(6) A person shall not cease to be liable to be registered under this Schedule except in accordance with paragraph 2(5), 3 or 4 below.

(7) In determining the value of a person's supplies for the purposes of sub-paragraph (1) or (2) above, supplies of goods or services that are capital assets of the business in the course or furtherance of which they are supplied and any taxable supplies which would not be taxable supplies apart from section 7(4) shall be disregarded.

(8) Where, apart from this sub-paragraph, an interest in, right over or licence to occupy any land would under sub-paragraph (7) above be disregarded for the purposes of sub-paragraph (1) or (2) above, it shall not be if it is supplied on a taxable supply which is not zero-rated.

[(9) In determining the value of a person's supplies for the purposes of sub-paragraph (1) or (2) above, supplies to which section 18B(4) (last acquisition or supply of goods before removal from fiscal warehousing) applies and supplies treated as made by him under section 18C(3) (self-supply of services on removal of goods from warehousing) shall be disregarded.][1]

[(10) A person is "UK-established" if the person has a business establishment, or some other fixed establishment, in the United Kingdom in relation to a business carried on by the person.][5]

Commentary—*De Voil Indirect Tax Service* **V2.134**, **V2.135**, **V2.136**.

Simon's Tax Cases—*Bennett v C&E Comrs* [1999] STC 248*; *Dyer v C&E Comrs* [2005] STC 715.

Sub-para (1)(*a*)(i), *Neal v C&E Comrs* [1988] STC 131*.

Definitions—"Business", s 94; "the Commissioners", s 96(1); "registered", s 3(3); "supplies", Sch 1 para 19; "taxable person", s 3; "taxable supply", s 4(2); "zero-rating", s 30.

Amendments—[1] Sub-para (9) added by FA 1996 Sch 3 para 13, with effect from 1 June 1996 (see Finance Act 1996, Section 26, (Appointed Day) Order, SI 1996/1249), and applying to any acquisition of goods from another member State and any supply taking place on or after that day.

[3] Words in sub-paras (4)(*a*), (5) substituted by FA 2000 s 136(6), with effect for supplies made after 20 March 2000.

[4] Words in sub-para (2) inserted by FA 2007 s 100(8), (10) with effect in relation to transfers pursuant to contracts entered into on or after 1 September 2007.

[5] In sub-paras (1)(*a*), (*b*), (4)(*a*), (5) words inserted, in sub-para (2) words substituted for words "and the transferee is not registered under this Act at the time of the transfer", sub-paras (2A), (10) inserted, and words in Schedule heading inserted, by FA 2012 s 203, Sch 28 paras 2, 11, 13 with effect in relation to supplies made or to be made on or after 1 December 2012.

[6] Sums in sub-paras (1)(*a*), (*b*), (2)(*a*), (*b*), (3)substituted by the VAT (Increase of Registration Limits) Order, SI 2015/750 arts 2, 3(*a*), (*b*) with effect from 1 April 2015. The VAT registration limit figure was previously £81,000 and the cancellation of registration figure £79,000 from 1 April 2014 to 31 March 2015.

[1A—(1) Paragraph 2 below is for the purpose of preventing the maintenance or creation of any artificial separation of business activities carried on by two or more persons from resulting in an avoidance of VAT.

(2) In determining for the purposes of sub-paragraph (1) above whether any separation of business activities is artificial, regard shall be had to the extent to which the different persons carrying on those activities are closely bound to one another by financial, economic and organisational links.][1]

Amendments—[1] This paragraph inserted by FA 1997 s 31(1) in relation to directions made on or after 19 March 1997.

2—(1) Without prejudice to paragraph 1 above, if the Commissioners make a direction under this paragraph, the persons named in the direction shall be treated as a single taxable person carrying on the activities of a business described in the direction and that taxable person shall be liable to be registered under this Schedule with effect from the date of the direction or, if the direction so provides, from such later date as may be specified therein.

(2) The Commissioners shall not make a direction under this paragraph naming any person unless they are satisfied—

(*a*) that he is making or has made taxable supplies; and

(*b*) that the activities in the course of which he makes or made those taxable supplies form only part of certain activities . . . [1], the other activities being carried on concurrently or previously (or both) by one or more other persons; and

(*c*) that, if all the taxable supplies [the business described in the direction][1] were taken into account, a person carrying on that business would at the time of the direction be liable to be registered by virtue of paragraph 1 above; . . . [1]

(*d*) . . . [1]

(3) A direction made under this paragraph shall be served on each of the persons named in it.

(4) Where, after a direction has been given under this paragraph specifying a description of business, it appears to the Commissioners that a person who was not named in that direction is making taxable supplies in the course of activities which should . . . [1] be regarded as part of the activities of that business, the Commissioners may make and serve on him a supplementary direction referring to the earlier direction and the description of business specified in it and adding that person's name to those of the persons named in the earlier direction with effect from—

(*a*) the date on which he began to make those taxable supplies, or

(*b*) if it was later, the date with effect from which the single taxable person referred to in the earlier direction became liable to be registered under this Schedule.

(5) If, immediately before a direction (including a supplementary direction) is made under this paragraph, any person named in the direction is registered in respect of the taxable supplies made by him as mentioned in sub-paragraph (2) or (4) above, he shall cease to be liable to be so registered with effect from whichever is the later of—

(*a*) the date with effect from which the single taxable person concerned became liable to be registered; and

(*b*) the date of the direction.

(6) In relation to a business specified in a direction under this paragraph, the persons named in the direction, together with any person named in a supplementary direction relating to that business (being the persons who together are to be treated as the taxable person), are in sub-paragraphs (7) and (8) below referred to as "the constituent members".

(7) Where a direction is made under this paragraph then, for the purposes of this Act—

(*a*) the taxable person carrying on the business specified in the direction shall be registrable in such name as the persons named in the direction may jointly nominate by notice in writing given to the Commissioners not later than 14 days after the date of the direction or, in default of such a nomination, in such name as may be specified in the direction;

(*b*) any supply of goods or services by or to one of the constituent members in the course of the activities of the taxable person shall be treated as a supply by or to that person;

(*c*) any acquisition of goods from another member State by one of the constituent members in the course of the activities of the taxable person shall be treated as an acquisition by that person;

(*d*) each of the constituent members shall be jointly and severally liable for any VAT due from the taxable person;

(*e*) without prejudice to paragraph (*d*) above, any failure by the taxable person to comply with any requirement imposed by or under this Act shall be treated as a failure by each of the constituent members severally; and

(*f*) subject to paragraphs (*a*) to (*e*) above, the constituent members shall be treated as a partnership carrying on the business of the taxable person and any question as to the scope of the activities of that business at any time shall be determined accordingly.

(8) If it appears to the Commissioners that any person who is one of the constituent members should no longer be regarded as such for the purposes of paragraphs (*d*) and (*e*) of sub-paragraph (7) above and they give notice to that effect, he shall not have any liability by virtue of those paragraphs for anything done after the date specified in that notice and, accordingly, on that date he shall be treated as having ceased to be a member of the partnership referred to in paragraph (*f*) of that sub-paragraph.

Commentary—*De Voil Indirect Tax Service* **V2.190C**.
Simon's Tax Cases—Sub-para (1), *Chamberlain v C&E Comrs* [1989] STC 505*.
Sub-para (2), *Chamberlain v C&E Comrs* [1989] STC 505*; *Osman v C&E Comrs* [1989] STC 596*.
Definitions—"Acquisition of goods from another member State", s 11; "business", s 94; "the Commissioners", s 96(1); "registrable", Sch 1 para 18; "registered", s 3(3); "supply", s 5, Sch 4; "taxable person", s 3; "taxable supply", s 4(2);
Cross reference—See VATA 1994 ss 83, 84 (appeal to a tribunal in respect of a direction under this para).
Amendments—[1] Word in sub-para (2)(b), (4) and whole of sub-para (2)(d) and the word "and " preceding it repealed, and words in sub-para (2)(c) substituted by FA 1997 s 31(2), (4), Sch 18 Pt IV(1) with effect in relation to directions made after 18 March 1997.

3 A person who has become liable to be registered under this Schedule shall cease to be so liable at any time if the Commissioners are satisfied in relation to that time that he—

(*a*) has ceased to make taxable supplies; or

(*b*) is not at that time a person in relation to whom any of the conditions specified in paragraphs 1(1)(*a*) and (*b*) and (2)(*a*) and (*b*) above is satisfied[; or

(*c*) is not at that time UK-established (see paragraph 1(10)).][1]

Commentary—*De Voil Indirect Tax Service* **V2.151**.
Definitions—"The Commissioners", s 96(1); "registered", s 3(3); "taxable supply", s 4(2);
Cross reference—See VATA 1994 ss 83, 84 (appeal to a tribunal in respect of a direction under this para).
Amendments—[1] Para (*c*) inserted, by FA 2012 s 203, Sch 28 paras 2, 12 with effect in relation to supplies made or to be made on or after 1 December 2012.

4—(1) Subject to sub-paragraph (2) below, a person who has become liable to be registered under this Schedule shall cease to be so liable at any time after being registered if the Commissioners are satisfied that the value of his taxable supplies in the period of one year then beginning will not exceed [£80,000][1].

(2) A person shall not cease to be liable to be registered under this Schedule by virtue of sub-paragraph (1) above if the Commissioners are satisfied that the reason the value of his taxable supplies will not exceed [£80,000][1] is that in the period in question he will cease making taxable supplies, or will suspend making them for a period of 30 days or more.

(3) In determining the value of a person's supplies for the purposes of sub-paragraph (1) above, supplies of goods or services that are capital assets of the business in the course or furtherance of which they are supplied and any taxable supplies which would not be taxable supplies apart from section 7(4) shall be disregarded.

(4) Where, apart from this sub-paragraph, an interest in, right over or licence to occupy any land would under sub-paragraph (3) above be disregarded for the purposes of sub-paragraph (1) above, it shall not be if it is supplied on a taxable supply which is not zero-rated.

Commentary—*De Voil Indirect Tax Service* **V2.151**.
Definitions—"Business", s 94; "the Commissioners", s 96(1); "registered", s 3(3); "supplies", Sch 1 para 19; "taxable supply", s 4(2); "zero-rating", s 30.
Cross reference—See VATA 1994 ss 83, 84 (appeal to a tribunal in respect of a direction under this para).

Amendments—[1] Sums in sub-paras (1), (2) substituted by the VAT (Increase of Registration Limits) Order, SI 2015/750 arts 2, 3(*c*) with effect from 1 April 2015. Figures were previously £79,000 from 1 April 2014 to 31 March 2015.

Notification of liability and registration

5—(1) A person who becomes liable to be registered by virtue of paragraph 1(1)(*a*) above shall notify the Commissioners of the liability within 30 days of the end of the relevant month.

(2) The Commissioners shall register any such person (whether or not he so notifies them) with effect from the end of the month following the relevant month or from such earlier date as may be agreed between them and him.

(3) In this paragraph "the relevant month", in relation to a person who becomes liable to be registered by virtue of paragraph 1(1)(*a*) above, means the month at the end of which he becomes liable to be so registered.

Commentary—*De Voil Indirect Tax Service* **V2.135**.
Simon's Tax Cases—*Neal v C&E Comrs* [1988] STC 131*.
Sub-para (3), *Henderson and anor (T/A Tony's Fish and Chip Shop) v C&E Comrs* [2001] STC 47; *Dyer v C&E Comrs* [2005] STC 715.
Definitions—"The Commissioners", s 96(1); "registered", s 3(3).
Cross references—See VATA 1994 s 67(1) (penalty for failure to comply with this para).
VAT (Isle of Man) Order, SI 1982/1067 art 11(3), (4) (persons registrable under Isle of Man VAT legislation);
VAT (Isle of Man) Order, SI 1982/1067 art 11(5) (notification required from persons having an establishment in the Isle of Man);
VAT Regulations, SI 1995/2518 reg 5(1), Sch 1 forms 1, 2 (form of application for VAT registration).

6—(1) A person who becomes liable to be registered by virtue of paragraph 1(1)(*b*) above shall notify the Commissioners of the liability before the end of the period by reference to which the liability arises.

(2) The Commissioners shall register any such person (whether or not he so notifies them) with effect from the beginning of the period by reference to which the liability arises.

Commentary—*De Voil Indirect Tax Service* **V2.136**.
Definitions—"The Commissioners", s 96(1); "registered", s 3(3).
Cross references—See VATA 1994 s 67(1) (penalty for failure to comply with this para).
VAT (Isle of Man) Order, SI 1982/1067 art 11(3), (4) (persons registrable under Isle of Man VAT legislation);
VAT (Isle of Man) Order, SI 1982/1067 art 11(5) (notification required from persons having an establishment in the Isle of Man);
VAT Regulations, SI 1995/2518 reg 5(1), Sch 1 forms 1, 2 (form of application for VAT registration).

7—(1) A person who becomes liable to be registered by virtue of paragraph 1(2) above shall notify the Commissioners of the liability within 30 days of the time when the business is transferred.

(2) The Commissioners shall register any such person (whether or not he so notifies them) with effect from the time when the business is transferred.

Commentary—*De Voil Indirect Tax Service* **V5.352**.
Definitions—"Business", s 94; "the Commissioners", s 96(1); "registered", s 3(3).
Cross reference—VAT Regulations, SI 1995/2518 reg 5(4), (5), Sch 1, form 3 (form of application for VAT registration).

8 Where a person becomes liable to be registered by virtue of paragraph 1(1)(*a*) above and by virtue of paragraph 1(1)(*b*) or 1(2) above at the same time, the Commissioners shall register him in accordance with paragraph 6(2) or 7(2) above, as the case may be, rather than paragraph 5(2) above.

Definitions—"The Commissioners", s 96(1); "registered", s 3(3).

Entitlement to be registered

9 Where a person who is not liable to be registered under this Act and is not already so registered satisfies the Commissioners that he—

(*a*) makes taxable supplies; or

(*b*) is carrying on a business and intends to make such supplies in the course or furtherance of that business,

they shall, if he so requests, register him with effect from the day on which the request is made or from such earlier date as may be agreed between them and him.

Commentary—*De Voil Indirect Tax Service* **V2.144**.
Press releases etc—Business Brief 8/97, 25 March 1997 (retrospective voluntary registration).
Simon's Tax Cases—*C&E Comrs v Eastwood Care Homes (Ilkeston) Ltd and others* [2001] STC 1629.
Definitions—"Business", s 94; "the Commissioners", s 96(1); "registered", s 3(3); "supplies", Sch 1 para 19; "taxable supply", s 4(2);
Cross references—See VATA 1994 Sch 2 para 4(3) (a person who is entitled to be registered under this para but requests registration under Sch 2 para 4 (registration in respect of supplies from other member states) must instead be registered under this para);
VATA 1994 Sch 3 para 4(4) (a person who is entitled to be registered under this para but requests registration under Sch 3 para 4 (registration in respect of acquisitions from other member states) must instead be registered under this para).

10—(1) Where a person who is not liable to be registered under this Act and is not already so registered satisfies the Commissioners that he—

(*a*) makes supplies within sub-paragraph (2) below; or

(*b*) is carrying on a business and intends to make such supplies in the course or furtherance of that business,

and (in either case) is within sub-paragraph (3) below, they shall, if he so requests, register him with effect from the day on which the request is made or from such earlier date as may be agreed between them and him.

[(2) A supply is within this sub-paragraph if—

(*a*) it is made outside the United Kingdom but would be a taxable supply if made in the United Kingdom; or

(*b*) it is specified for the purposes of subsection (2) of section 26 in an order made under paragraph (*c*) of that subsection.][1]

(3) A person is within this sub-paragraph if—

(*a*) he has a business establishment in the United Kingdom or his usual place of residence is in the United Kingdom; and

(*b*) he does not make and does not intend to make taxable supplies.

(4) For the purposes of this paragraph—

(*a*) a person carrying on a business through a branch or agency in the United Kingdom shall be treated as having a business establishment in the United Kingdom, and

(*b*) "usual place of residence", in relation to a body corporate, means the place where it is legally constituted.

Commentary—*De Voil Indirect Tax Service* **V2.146**.

Definitions—"Business", s 94; "the Commissioners", s 96(1); "registered", s 3(3); "supplies", Sch 1 para 19; "supply", s 5, Sch 4; "taxable supply", s 4(2); "United Kingdom", s 96(11).

Cross references—See VATA 1994 Sch 2 para 4(3) (a person who is entitled to be registered under this para but requests registration under Sch 2 para 4 (registration in respect of supplies from other member states) must instead be registered under this para);

VATA 1994 Sch 3 para 4(4) (a person who is entitled to be registered under this para but requests registration under Sch 3 para 4 (registration in respect of acquisitions from other member states) must instead be registered under this para).

Amendments—[1] Sub-para (2) substituted by FA 1997 s 32 with effect from 19 March 1997.

Notification of end of liability or entitlement etc

11 A person registered under paragraph 5, 6 or 9 above who ceases to make or have the intention of making taxable supplies shall notify the Commissioners of that fact within 30 days of the day on which he does so unless he would, when he so ceases, be otherwise liable or entitled to be registered under this Act if his registration and any enactment preventing a person from being liable to be registered under different provisions at the same time were disregarded.

Commentary—*De Voil Indirect Tax Service* **V2.151**.

Definitions—"The Commissioners", s 96(1); "registered", s 3(3); "taxable supplies", s 4(2).

Cross references—See VATA 1994 s 69(1) (penalty for breach of a requirement imposed under this para).

VAT Regulations, SI 1995/2518 reg 5(3) (form of notification under this para);

VAT Regulations, SI 1995/2518 reg 6(2) (notification of transfer of business as a going concern).

12 A person registered under paragraph 10 above who—

(*a*) ceases to make or have the intention of making supplies within sub-paragraph (2) of that paragraph; or

(*b*) makes or forms the intention of making taxable supplies,

shall notify the Commissioners of that fact within 30 days of the day on which he does so unless, in the case of a person ceasing as mentioned in sub-paragraph (a) above, he would, when he so ceases, be otherwise liable or entitled to be registered under this Act if his registration and any enactment preventing a person from being liable to be registered under different provisions at the same time were disregarded.

Commentary—*De Voil Indirect Tax Service* **V2.153**.

Definitions—"The Commissioners", s 96(1); "registered", s 3(3); "taxable supplies", s 4(2).

Cross references—See VATA 1994 s 69(1) (penalty for breach of a requirement imposed under this para).

VAT Regulations, SI 1995/2518 reg 5(3) (form of notification under this para).

Cancellation of registration

13—(1) Subject to sub-paragraph (4) below, where a registered person satisfies the Commissioners that he is not liable to be registered under this Schedule, they shall, if he so requests, cancel his registration with effect from the day on which the request is made or from such later date as may be agreed between them and him.

(2) Subject to sub-paragraph (5) below, where the Commissioners are satisfied that a registered person has ceased to be registrable, they may cancel his registration with effect from the day on which he so ceased or from such later date as may be agreed between them and him.

(3) Where the Commissioners are satisfied that on the day on which a registered person was registered he was not registrable, they may cancel his registration with effect from that day.
(4) The Commissioners shall not under sub-paragraph (1) above cancel a person's registration with effect from any time unless they are satisfied that it is not a time when that person would be subject to a requirement to be registered under this Act.
(5) The Commissioners shall not under sub-paragraph (2) above cancel a person's registration with effect from any time unless they are satisfied that it is not a time when that person would be subject to a requirement, or entitled, to be registered under this Act.
(6) In determining for the purposes of sub-paragraph (4) or (5) above whether a person would be subject to a requirement, or entitled, to be registered at any time, so much of any provision of this Act as prevents a person from becoming liable or entitled to be registered when he is already registered or when he is so liable under any other provision shall be disregarded.
(7) In this paragraph, any reference to a registered person is a reference to a person who is registered under this Schedule.
[(8) This paragraph is subject to paragraph 18 of Schedule 3B (cancellation of registration under this Schedule of persons seeking to be registered under that Schedule, etc).][1]

Commentary—*De Voil Indirect Tax Service* **V2.151, V2.152**.
Definitions—"The Commissioners", s 96(1); "registrable", Sch 1, para 18; "registered", s 3(3).
Amendments—[1] Sub-para (8) inserted by FA 2003 s 23, Sch 2 paras 1, 3 with effect for qualifying supplies made after 30 June 2003.

Exemption from registration

14—(1) Notwithstanding the preceding provisions of this Schedule, where a person who makes or intends to make taxable supplies satisfies the Commissioners that any such supply is zero-rated or would be zero-rated if he were a taxable person, they may, if he so requests and they think fit, exempt him from registration under this Schedule until it appears to them that the request should no longer be acted upon or is withdrawn.
(2) Where there is a material change in the nature of the supplies made by a person exempted under this paragraph from registration under this Schedule, he shall notify the Commissioners of the change—

(*a*) within 30 days of the date on which it occurred; or
(*b*) if no particular day is identifiable as the day on which it occurred, within 30 days of the end of the quarter in which it occurred.

(3) Where there is a material alteration in any quarter in the proportion of taxable supplies of such a person that are zero-rated, he shall notify the Commissioners of the alteration within 30 days of the end of the quarter.

Commentary—*De Voil Indirect Tax Service* **V2.147**.
Definitions—"The Commissioners", s 96(1); "quarter", s 96(1); "registered", s 3(3); "supplies", Sch 1 para 19; "supply", s 6, Sch 4; "taxable person", s 3; "taxable supply", s 4(2); "zero-rating", s 30.
Cross reference—See VATA 1994 s 67(1) (penalty for failure to comply with sub-para (2) or (3) of this para).

Power to vary specified sums by order

15 The Treasury may by order substitute for any of the sums for the time being specified in this Schedule such greater sums as they think fit.

Orders—VAT (Increase of Registration Limits) Order, SI 2014/703.
VAT (Increase of Registration Limits) Order, SI 2015/750.

Supplementary

16 The value of a supply of goods or services shall be determined for the purposes of this Schedule on the basis that no VAT is chargeable on the supply.

Definitions—"Supply", s 5, Sch 4; "VAT", ss 1, 96(1).

17 Any notification required under this Schedule shall be made in such form [and manner][1] and shall contain such particulars [as may be specified in regulations or by the Commissioners in accordance with regulations.][1]

Regulations—See VAT Regulations, SI 1995/2518 reg 5 Sch 1.
VAT (Amendment) (No 2) Regulations, SI 2012/1899.
Definitions—"The Commissioners", s 96(1); "regulations", s 96(1).
Amendments—[1] Words inserted, and words substituted for words "as the Commissioners may by regulations prescribe", by FA 2012 s 204, Sch 29 paras 1, 8 with effect from 17 July 2012.

18 In this Schedule "registrable" means liable or entitled to be registered under this Schedule.

Definitions—"Registered", s 3(3);

19 References in this Schedule to supplies are references to supplies made in the course or furtherance of a business.

Definitions—"Business", s 94.

[SCHEDULE 1A
REGISTRATION IN RESPECT OF TAXABLE SUPPLIES: NON-UK ESTABLISHMENT]

Cross-references—See VATA 1994 Sch 3BA para 16 (power for HMRC Commissioners to deregister a person who has registered in the UK in relation to e-services where that person intends to use a non-UK scheme).

Amendments—Schedule 1A inserted by FA 2012 s 203, Sch 28 para 1 with effect in relation to supplies made or to be made on or after 1 December 2012.

[Liability to be registered

1—(1) A person becomes liable to be registered under this Schedule at any time if conditions A to D are met.

(2) Condition A is that—

(*a*) the person makes taxable supplies, or

(*b*) there are reasonable grounds for believing that the person will make taxable supplies in the period of 30 days then beginning.

(3) Condition B is that those supplies (or any of them) are or will be made in the course or furtherance of a business carried on by the person.

(4) Condition C is that the person has no business establishment, or other fixed establishment, in the United Kingdom in relation to any business carried on by the person.

(5) Condition D is that the person is not registered under this Act.][1]

Amendments—[1] Schedule 1A inserted by FA 2012 s 203, Sch 28 para 1 with effect in relation to supplies made or to be made on or after 1 December 2012.

[2—(1) A person does not become liable to be registered by virtue of paragraph 1(2)(*b*) if the reason for believing that taxable supplies will be made in the 30-day period mentioned there is that a business, or part of a business, carried on by a taxable person is to be transferred to the person as a going concern in that period.

(2) But if the transfer takes place, the transferee becomes liable to be registered under this Schedule at the time of the transfer if conditions A to D in paragraph 1 are met in relation to the transferee at that time.

(3) In determining for the purposes of sub-paragraph (2) whether condition B is met, the reference in paragraph 1(3) to a business is to be read as a reference to the business, or part of the business, that is transferred to the transferee.][1]

Amendments—[1] Schedule 1A inserted by FA 2012 s 203, Sch 28 para 1 with effect in relation to supplies made or to be made on or after 1 December 2012.

[3 A person is treated as having become liable to be registered under this Schedule at any time when the person would have become so liable under paragraph 1 or 2 but for any registration that is subsequently cancelled under—

(*a*) paragraph 11,

(*b*) paragraph 13(3) of Schedule 1,

(*c*) paragraph 6(2) of Schedule 2,

(*d*) paragraph 6(3) of Schedule 3, or

(*e*) paragraph 6(2) of Schedule 3A.][1]

Amendments—[1] Schedule 1A inserted by FA 2012 s 203, Sch 28 para 1 with effect in relation to supplies made or to be made on or after 1 December 2012.

[4—(1) A person does not cease to be liable to be registered under this Schedule except in accordance with sub-paragraph (2).

(2) A person who has become liable to be registered under this Schedule ceases to be so liable at any time if the Commissioners are satisfied that—

(*a*) the person has ceased to make taxable supplies in the course or furtherance of a business carried on by the person, or

(*b*) the person is no longer a person in relation to whom condition C in paragraph 1 is met.][1]

Amendments—[1] Schedule 1A inserted by FA 2012 s 203, Sch 28 para 1 with effect in relation to supplies made or to be made on or after 1 December 2012.

[Notification of liability and registration

5—(1) A person who becomes liable to be registered by virtue of paragraph 1(2)(*a*) or 2(2) must notify the Commissioners of the liability before the end of the period of 30 days beginning with the day on which the liability arises.

(2) The Commissioners must register any such person (whether or not the person so notifies them) with effect from the beginning of the day on which the liability arises.][1]

Amendments—[1] Schedule 1A inserted by FA 2012 s 203, Sch 28 para 1 with effect in relation to supplies made or to be made on or after 1 December 2012.

[6—(1) A person who becomes liable to be registered by virtue of paragraph 1(2)(*b*) must notify the Commissioners of the liability before the end of the period by reference to which the liability arises.
(2) The Commissioners must register any such person (whether or not the person so notifies them) with effect from the beginning of the period by reference to which the liability arises.][1]

Amendments—[1] Schedule 1A inserted by FA 2012 s 203, Sch 28 para 1 with effect in relation to supplies made or to be made on or after 1 December 2012.

[Notification of end of liability

7—(1) A person registered under paragraph 5 or 6 who, on any day, ceases to make or have the intention of making taxable supplies in the course or furtherance of a business carried on by that person must notify the Commissioners of that fact within 30 days beginning with that day.
(2) But the person need not notify the Commissioners if on that day the person would otherwise be liable or entitled to be registered under this Act (disregarding for this purpose the person's registration under this Schedule and any enactment that prevents a person from being liable to be registered under different provisions at the same time).][1]

Amendments—[1] Schedule 1A inserted by FA 2012 s 203, Sch 28 para 1 with effect in relation to supplies made or to be made on or after 1 December 2012.

[Cancellation of registration

8—(1) The Commissioners must cancel a person's registration under this Schedule if—
(*a*) the person satisfies them that the person is not liable to be registered under this Schedule, and
(*b*) the person requests the cancellation.
(2) The cancellation is to be made with effect from—
(*a*) the day on which the request is made, or
(*b*) such later day as may be agreed between the Commissioners and the person.
(3) But the Commissioners must not cancel the registration with effect from any time unless they are satisfied that it is not a time when the person would be subject to a requirement to be registered under this Act.][1]

Amendments—[1] Schedule 1A inserted by FA 2012 s 203, Sch 28 para 1 with effect in relation to supplies made or to be made on or after 1 December 2012.

[9—(1) The Commissioners may cancel a person's registration under this Schedule if they are satisfied that the person has ceased to be liable to be registered under this Schedule.
(2) The cancellation is to be made with effect from—
(*a*) the day on which the person ceased to be so liable, or
(*b*) such later day as may be agreed between the Commissioners and the person.
(3) But the Commissioners must not cancel the registration with effect from any time unless they are satisfied that it is not a time when the person would be subject to a requirement, or entitled, to be registered under this Act.][1]

Amendments—[1] Schedule 1A inserted by FA 2012 s 203, Sch 28 para 1 with effect in relation to supplies made or to be made on or after 1 December 2012.

[10 In determining for the purposes of paragraphs 8 and 9 whether a time is a time when a person would be subject to a requirement, or entitled, to be registered under this Act, so much of any provision of this Act as prevents a person from becoming liable or entitled to be registered when the person is already registered or when the person is so liable under any other provision must be disregarded.][1]

Amendments—[1] Schedule 1A inserted by FA 2012 s 203, Sch 28 para 1 with effect in relation to supplies made or to be made on or after 1 December 2012.

[11—(1) The Commissioners may cancel a person's registration under this Schedule if they are satisfied that the person was not liable to be registered under this Schedule on the day on which the person was registered.
(2) The cancellation is to be made with effect from the day on which the person was registered.][1]

Amendments—[1] Schedule 1A inserted by FA 2012 s 203, Sch 28 para 1 with effect in relation to supplies made or to be made on or after 1 December 2012.

[12 Paragraphs 8 to 11 are subject to paragraph 18 of Schedule 3B [and paragraph 16 of Schedule 3BA][2] (cancellation of registration under this Schedule of persons seeking to be registered under [the Schedule concerned][2]).][1]

Amendments—[1] Schedule 1A inserted by FA 2012 s 203, Sch 28 para 1 with effect in relation to supplies made or to be made on or after 1 December 2012.

[2] Words inserted, and words substituted for words "that Schedule etc", by FA 2014 s 103, Sch 22 para 18 with effect in relation to supplies made on or after 1 January 2015.

[Exemption from registration

13—(1) The Commissioners may exempt a person from registration under this Schedule if the person satisfies them that the taxable supplies that the person makes or intends to make—

(*a*) are all zero-rated, or

(*b*) would all be zero-rated if the person were a taxable person.

(2) The power in sub-paragraph (1) is exercisable only if the person so requests and the Commissioners think fit.

(3) If there is a material change in the nature of the supplies made by a person exempted under this paragraph, the person must notify the Commissioners of the change—

(*a*) within 30 days beginning with the day on which the change occurred, or

(*b*) if no particular day is identifiable as that day, within 30 days of the end of the quarter in which the change occurred.

(4) If it appears to the Commissioners that a request under this paragraph should no longer be acted upon on or after any day or has been withdrawn on any day, they must register the person who made the request with effect from that day.

(5) A reference in this paragraph to supplies is to supplies made in the course or furtherance of a business carried on by the person.][1]

Amendments—[1] Schedule 1A inserted by FA 2012 s 203, Sch 28 para 1 with effect in relation to supplies made or to be made on or after 1 December 2012.

[Supplementary

14 Any notification required under this Schedule must be made in such form and manner and must contain such particulars as may be specified in regulations or by the Commissioners in accordance with regulations.][1]

Regulations—VAT (Amendment) (No 2) Regulations, SI 2012/1899.

Amendments—[1] Schedule 1A inserted by FA 2012 s 203, Sch 28 para 1 with effect in relation to supplies made or to be made on or after 1 December 2012.

SCHEDULE 2

REGISTRATION IN RESPECT OF SUPPLIES FROM OTHER MEMBER STATES

Section 3(2)

Liability to be registered

1—(1) A person who—

(*a*) is not registered under this Act; and

(*b*) is not liable to be registered under Schedule 1 [or 1A][3],

becomes liable to be registered under this Schedule on any day if, in the period beginning with 1st January of the year in which that day falls, that person has made relevant supplies whose value exceeds £70,000.

(2) A person who is not registered or liable to be registered as mentioned in sub-paragraph (1)(*a*) and (*b*) above becomes liable to be registered under this Schedule where—

(*a*) that person has exercised any option, in accordance with the law of any other member State where he is taxable, for treating relevant supplies made by him as taking place outside that member State;

(*b*) the supplies to which the option relates involve the removal of goods from that member State and, apart from the exercise of the option, would be treated, in accordance with the law of that member State, as taking place in that member State; and

(*c*) that person makes a relevant supply at a time when the option is in force in relation to him.

(3) A person who is not registered or liable to be registered as mentioned in sub-paragraph (1)(*a*) and (*b*) above becomes liable to be registered under this Schedule if he makes a supply in relation to which the following conditions are satisfied, that is to say—

(*a*) it is a supply of goods subject to a duty of excise;

(*b*) it involves the removal of the goods to the United Kingdom by or under the directions of the person making the supply;

(*c*) it is a transaction in pursuance of which the goods are acquired in the United Kingdom from another member State by a person who is not a taxable person;

(*d*) it is made on or after 1st January 1993 and in the course or furtherance of a business carried on by the supplier; and

(*e*) it is not anything which is treated as a supply for the purposes of this Act by virtue only of paragraph 5(1) or 6 of Schedule 4.

(4) A person shall be treated as having become liable to be registered under this Schedule at any time when he would have become so liable under the preceding provisions of this paragraph but for any registration which is subsequently cancelled under paragraph 6(2) below, paragraph 13(3) of Schedule 1[, [paragraph 11 of Schedule 1A,][3] paragraph 6(3) of Schedule 3 or paragraph 6(2) of Schedule 3A][2].

(5) A person shall not cease to be liable to be registered under this Schedule except in accordance with paragraph 2 below.

(6) In determining for the purposes of this paragraph the value of any relevant supplies, so much of the consideration for any supply as represents any liability of the supplier, under the law of another member State, for VAT on that supply shall be disregarded.

[(7) For the purposes of sub-paragraphs (1) and (2) above supplies to which section 18B(4) (last acquisition or supply of goods before removal from fiscal warehousing) applies shall be disregarded.][1]

Commentary—*De Voil Indirect Tax Service* **V2.171**.

Definitions—"Another member State", s 96(1); "business", s 94; "other member State", s 96(1); "registered", s 3(3); "relevant supply", Sch 2 para 10; "supply", s 5, Sch 4; "United Kingdom", s 96(11); "VAT", ss 1, 96(1).

Amendments—[1] Sub-para (7) added by FA 1996 Sch 3 para 14, with effect for any supply taking place on or after 1 June 1996 (see Finance Act 1996, Section 26, (Appointed Day) Order, SI 1996/1249).

[2] Words in sub-para (4) substituted by FA 2000 s 136(6), with effect for supplies made after 20 March 2000.

[3] In sub-paras (1)(*b*), (4), words inserted by FA 2012 s 203, Sch 28 paras 2, 14 with effect in relation to supplies made or to be made on or after 1 December 2012.

2—(1) Subject to sub-paragraph (2) below, a person who has become liable to be registered under this Schedule shall cease to be so liable if at any time—

(*a*) the relevant supplies made by him in the year ending with 31st December last before that time did not have a value exceeding £70,000 and did not include any supply in relation to which the conditions mentioned in paragraph 1(3) above were satisfied, and

(*b*) the Commissioners are satisfied that the value of his relevant supplies in the year immediately following that year will not exceed £70,000 and that those supplies will not include a supply in relation to which those conditions are satisfied.

(2) A person shall not cease to be liable to be registered under this Schedule at any time when such an option as is mentioned in paragraph 1(2) above is in force in relation to him.

Commentary—*De Voil Indirect Tax Service* **V2.151**.

Definitions—"The Commissioners", s 96(1); "registered", s 3(3); "relevant supply", Sch 2 para 10; "supply", s 5, Sch 4.

Notification of liability and registration

3—(1) A person who becomes liable to be registered under this Schedule shall notify the Commissioners of the liability within the period of 30 days after the day on which the liability arises.

(2) The Commissioners shall register any such person (whether or not he so notifies them) with effect from the day on which the liability arose or from such earlier time as may be agreed between them and him.

Commentary—*De Voil Indirect Tax Service* **V2.173**.

Definitions—"The Commissioners", s 96(1); "registered", s 3(3).

Cross references—See VATA 1994 s 67(1) (penalty for failure to comply with this para).

VAT Regulations, SI 1995/2518 reg 5(1), Sch 1 forms 2, 6 (form of application for VAT registration: distance sales).

Request to be registered

4—(1) Where a person who is not liable to be registered under this Act and is not already so registered—

(*a*) satisfies the Commissioners that he intends—

(i) to exercise an option such as is mentioned in paragraph 1(2) above and, from a specified date, to make relevant supplies to which that option will relate;

(ii) from a specified date to make relevant supplies to which any such option that he has exercised will relate; or

(iii) from a specified date to make supplies in relation to which the conditions mentioned in paragraph 1(3) above will be satisfied; and

(*b*) requests to be registered under this Schedule,

the Commissioners may, subject to such conditions as they think fit to impose, register him with effect from such date as may be agreed between them and him.

(2) Conditions imposed under sub-paragraph (1) above—

(*a*) may be so imposed wholly or partly by reference to, or without reference to, any conditions prescribed for the purposes of this paragraph; and

(*b*) may, whenever imposed, be subsequently varied by the Commissioners.

(3) Where a person who is entitled to be registered under paragraph 9 or 10 of Schedule 1 requests registration under this paragraph, he shall be registered under that Schedule, and not under this Schedule.

Commentary—*De Voil Indirect Tax Service* **V2.174**.

Press releases etc—C&E Business Brief 8/96 17-5-96 (following abolition of the self-supply charge for developers, VAT offices require detailed information before allowing intending trader registration).

Definitions—"The Commissioners", s 96(1); "prescribed", s 96(1); "registered", s 3(3); "relevant supplies", Sch 2 para 10; "supply", s 5, Sch 4.

Notification of matters affecting continuance of registration

5—(1) Any person registered under this Schedule who ceases to be registrable under this Act shall notify the Commissioners of that fact within 30 days of the day on which he does so.

(2) A person registered under paragraph 4 above by reference to any intention of his to exercise any option or to make supplies of any description shall notify the Commissioners within 30 days of exercising that option or, as the case may be, of the first occasion after his registration when he makes such a supply, that he has exercised the option or made such a supply.

(3) A person who has exercised such an option as is mentioned in paragraph 1(2) above which, as a consequence of its revocation or otherwise, ceases to have effect in relation to any relevant supplies by him shall notify the Commissioners, within 30 days of the option's ceasing so to have effect, that it has done so.

(4) For the purposes of this paragraph, a person ceases to be registrable under this Act where—

(*a*) he ceases to be a person who would be liable or entitled to be registered under this Act if his registration and any enactment preventing a person from being liable to be registered under different provisions at the same time were disregarded; or

(*b*) in the case of a person who (having been registered under paragraph 4 above) has not been such a person during the period of his registration, he ceases to have any such intention as is mentioned in sub-paragraph (1)(*a*) of that paragraph.

Commentary—*De Voil Indirect Tax Service* **V2.176**.

Definitions—"The Commissioners", s 96(1); "registered", s 3(3); "relevant supplies", Sch 2 para 10; "supply", s 5, Sch 4.

Cross reference—See VATA 1994 s 69(1) (penalty for breach of a requirement imposed under this para).
VAT Regulations, SI 1995/2518 reg 5(3) (form of notification under this para).

Cancellation of registration

6—(1) Subject to paragraph 7 below, where a person registered under this Schedule satisfies the Commissioners that he is not liable to be so registered, they shall, if he so requests, cancel his registration with effect from the day on which the request is made or from such later date as may be agreed between them and him.

(2) Where the Commissioners are satisfied that, on the day on which a person was registered under this Schedule, he—

(*a*) was not liable to be registered under this Schedule; and

(*b*) in the case of a person registered under paragraph 4 above, did not have the intention by reference to which he was registered,

they may cancel his registration with effect from that day.

(3) Subject to paragraph 7 below, where the Commissioners are satisfied that a person who has been registered under paragraph 4 above and is not for the time being liable to be registered under this Schedule—

(*a*) has not, by the date specified in his request to be registered, begun to make relevant supplies, exercised the option in question or, as the case may be, begun to make supplies in relation to which the conditions mentioned in paragraph 1(3) above are satisfied; or

(*b*) has contravened any condition of his registration,

they may cancel his registration with effect from the date so specified or, as the case may be, the date of the contravention or from such later date as may be agreed between them and him.

Commentary—*De Voil Indirect Tax Service* **V2.177**.

Definitions—"The Commissioners", s 96(1); "registered", s 3(3); "relevant supplies", Sch 2 para 10; "supply", s 5, Sch 4.

Conditions of cancellation

7—(1) The Commissioners shall not, under paragraph 6(1) above, cancel a person's registration with effect from any time unless they are satisfied that it is not a time when that person would be subject to a requirement to be registered under this Act.

(2) The Commissioners shall not, under paragraph 6(3) above, cancel a person's registration with effect from any time unless they are satisfied that it is not a time when that person would be subject to a requirement, or entitled, to be registered under this Act.

(3) The registration of a person who has exercised such an option as is mentioned in paragraph 1(2) above shall not be cancelled with effect from any time before the 1st January which is, or next follows, the second anniversary of the date on which his registration took effect.
(4) In determining for the purposes of this paragraph whether a person would be subject to a requirement, or entitled, to be registered at any time, so much of any provision of this Act as prevents a person from becoming liable or entitled to be registered when he is already registered or when he is so liable under any other provision shall be disregarded.

Commentary—*De Voil Indirect Tax Service* **V2.177**.
Definitions—"The Commissioners", s 96(1); "registered", s 3(3).

Power to vary specified sums by order

8 The Treasury may by order substitute for any of the sums for the time being specified in this Schedule such greater sums as they think fit.

Supplementary

9 Any notification required under this Schedule shall be made in such form [and manner][1] and shall contain such particulars [as may be specified in regulations or by the Commissioners in accordance with regulations.][1]

Regulations—VAT Regulations, SI 1995/2518 reg 5, Sch 1.
VAT (Amendment) (No 2) Regulations, SI 2012/1899.
Definitions—"The Commissioners", s 96(1); "regulations", s 96(1);
Amendments—[1] Words inserted, and words substituted for words "as the Commissioners may by regulations prescribe", by FA 2012 s 204, Sch 29 paras 1, 9 with effect from 17 July 2012.

10 For the purposes of this Schedule a supply of goods is a relevant supply where—
(*a*) the supply involves the removal of the goods to the United Kingdom by or under the directions of the person making the supply;
(*b*) the supply does not involve the installation or assembly of the goods at a place in the United Kingdom;
(*c*) the supply is a transaction in pursuance of which goods are acquired in the United Kingdom from another member State by a person who is not a taxable person;
(*d*) the supply is made on or after 1st January 1993 and in the course or furtherance of a business carried on by the supplier; and
(*e*) the supply is neither an exempt supply nor a supply of goods which are subject to a duty of excise or consist in a new means of transport and is not anything which is treated as a supply for the purposes of this Act by virtue only of paragraph 5(1) or 6 of Schedule 4.

Commentary—*De Voil Indirect Tax Service* **V3.172**.
Definitions—"Another member State", s 96(1); "business", s 94; "exempt supply", s 31; "new means of transport", s 95; "supply", s 5, Sch 4; "United Kingdom", s 96(11).

SCHEDULE 3

REGISTRATION IN RESPECT OF ACQUISITIONS FROM OTHER MEMBER STATES

Section 3(2)

Liability to be registered

1—(1) A person who—
(*a*) is not registered under this Act; and
(*b*) is not liable to be registered under Schedule 1[, 1A][4] or 2,
becomes liable to be registered under this Schedule at the end of any month if, in the period beginning with 1st January of the year in which that month falls, that person had made relevant acquisitions whose value exceeds [£82,000][5].
(2) A person who is not registered or liable to be registered as mentioned in sub-paragraph (1)(*a*) and (*b*) above becomes liable to be registered under this Schedule at any time if there are reasonable grounds for believing that the value of his relevant acquisitions in the period of 30 days then beginning will exceed [£82,000][5].
(3) A person shall be treated as having become liable to be registered under this Schedule at any time when he would have become so liable under the preceding provisions of this paragraph but for any registration which is subsequently cancelled under paragraph 6(3) below, paragraph 13(3) of Schedule 1[, [paragraph 11 of Schedule 1A,][4] paragraph 6(2) of Schedule 2 or paragraph 6(2) of Schedule 3A][3].
(4) A person shall not cease to be liable to be registered under this Schedule except in accordance with paragraph 2 below.

(5) In determining the value of any person's relevant acquisitions for the purposes of this paragraph, so much of the consideration for any acquisition as represents any liability of the supplier, under the law of another member State, for VAT on the transaction in pursuance of which the acquisition is made, shall be disregarded.

[(6) In determining the value of a person's acquisitions for the purposes of sub-paragraph (1) or (2) above, acquisitions to which section 18B(4) (last acquisition or supply of goods before removal from fiscal warehousing) applies shall be disregarded.][1]

Commentary—*De Voil Indirect Tax Service* **V2.181**.

Definitions—"Another member State", s 96(1); "registered", s 3(3); "relevant acquisition", Sch 3 para 11; "VAT", ss 1, 96(1).

Amendments—[1] Sub-para (6) inserted by FA 1996 Sch 3 para 15, with effect for any acquisition of goods from another member State taking place on or after 1 June 1996 (see Finance Act 1996, Section 26, (Appointed Day) Order, SI 1996/1249).

[3] Words in sub-para (3) substituted by FA 2000 s 136(7), with effect for supplies made after 20 March 2000.

[4] In sub-paras (1)(*b*), (3), words inserted by FA 2012 s 203, Sch 28 paras 2, 15 with effect in relation to supplies made or to be made on or after 1 December 2012.

[5] Sums in sub-paras (1), (2) substituted by the VAT (Increase of Registration Limits) Order, SI 2014/750 arts 2, 4(*a*) with effect from 1 April 2015. Figures were previously £81,000 from 1 April 2014 to 31 March 2015.

2—(1) Subject to sub-paragraph (2) below, a person who has become liable to be registered under this Schedule shall cease to be so liable if at any time—

(*a*) his relevant acquisitions in the year ending with 31st December last before that time did not have a value exceeding [£82,000][1]; and

(*b*) the Commissioners are satisfied that the value of his relevant acquisitions in the year immediately following that year will not exceed [£82,000][1].

(2) A person shall not cease to be liable to be registered under this Schedule at any time if there are reasonable grounds for believing that the value of that person's relevant acquisitions in the period of 30 days then beginning will exceed [£82,000][1].

Commentary—*De Voil Indirect Tax Service* **V2.188**.

Definitions—"The Commissioners", s 96(1); "registered", s 3(3); "relevant acquisition", Sch 3 para 11.

Amendments—[1] Sums in sub-paras (1)(*a*), (*b*), (2) substituted by the VAT (Increase of Registration Limits) Order, SI 2014/750 arts 2, 4(*b*) with effect from 1 April 2015. Figures were previously £81,000 from 1 April 2014 to 31 March 2015.

Notification of liability and registration

3—(1) A person who becomes liable to be registered under this Schedule shall notify the Commissioners of the liability—

(*a*) in the case of a liability under sub-paragraph (1) of paragraph 1 above, within 30 days of the end of the month when he becomes so liable; and

(*b*) in the case of a liability under sub-paragraph (2) of that paragraph, before the end of the period by reference to which the liability arises.

(2) The Commissioners shall register any such person (whether or not he so notifies them) with effect from the relevant time or from such earlier time as may be agreed between them and him.

(3) In this paragraph "the relevant time"—

(*a*) in a case falling within sub-paragraph (1)(*a*) above, means the end of the month following the month at the end of which the liability arose; and

(*b*) in a case falling within sub-paragraph (1)(*b*), means the beginning of the period by reference to which the liability arose.

Commentary—*De Voil Indirect Tax Service* **V2.184**.

Definitions—"The Commissioners", s 96(1); "registered", s 3(3);

Cross references—See VATA 1994 s 67(1) (penalty for failure to comply with this para).

VAT Regulations, SI 1995/2518 reg 5(1), Sch 1 forms 2, 7 (form of application for VAT registration: acquisitions).

Entitlement to be registered etc

4—(1) Where a person who is not liable to be registered under this Act and is not already so registered satisfies the Commissioners that he makes relevant acquisitions, they shall, if he so requests, register him with effect from the day on which the request is made or from such earlier date as may be agreed between them and him.

(2) Where a person who is not liable to be registered under this Act and is not already so registered—

(*a*) satisfies the Commissioners that he intends to make relevant acquisitions from a specified date; and

(*b*) requests to be registered under this Schedule,

the Commissioners may, subject to such conditions as they think fit to impose, register him with effect from such date as may be agreed between them and him.

(3) Conditions imposed under sub-paragraph (2) above—

(*a*) may be so imposed wholly or partly by reference to, or without reference to, any conditions prescribed for the purposes of this paragraph, and

(*b*) may, whenever imposed, be subsequently varied by the Commissioners.

(4) Where a person who is entitled to be registered under paragraph 9 or 10 of Schedule 1 requests registration under this paragraph, he shall be registered under that Schedule, and not under this Schedule.

Commentary—*De Voil Indirect Tax Service* **V2.181**.
Definitions—"The Commissioners", s 96(1); "registered", s 3(3); "relevant acquisition", Sch 3 para 11.

Notification of matters affecting continuance of registration

5—(1) Any person registered under this Schedule who ceases to be registrable under this Act shall notify the Commissioners of that fact within 30 days of the day on which he does so.
(2) A person registered under paragraph 4(2) above shall notify the Commissioners, within 30 days of the first occasion after his registration when he makes a relevant acquisition, that he has done so.
(3) For the purposes of this paragraph a person ceases to be registrable under this Act where—
(*a*) he ceases to be a person who would be liable or entitled to be registered under this Act if his registration and any enactment preventing a person from being liable to be registered under different provisions at the same time were disregarded; or
(*b*) in the case of a person who (having been registered under paragraph 4(2) above) has not been such a person during the period of his registration, he ceases to have any intention of making relevant acquisitions.

Commentary—*De Voil Indirect Tax Service* **V2.187.**
Definitions—"The Commissioners", s 96(1); "registered", s 3(3); "relevant acquisition", Sch 3 para 11.
Cross references—See VATA 1994 s 69(1) (penalty for breach of a requirement imposed under this para).
VAT Regulations, SI 1995/2518 reg 5(3) (form of notification under this para).

Cancellation of registration

6—(1) Subject to paragraph 7 below, where a person registered under this Schedule satisfies the Commissioners that he is not liable to be so registered, they shall, if he so requests, cancel his registration with effect from the day on which the request is made or from such later date as may be agreed between them and him.
(2) Subject to paragraph 7 below, where the Commissioners are satisfied that a person registered under this Schedule has ceased since his registration to be registrable under this Schedule, they may cancel his registration with effect from the day on which he so ceased or from such later date as may be agreed between them and him.
(3) Where the Commissioners are satisfied that, on the day on which a person was registered under this Schedule, he—
(*a*) was not registrable under this Schedule; and
(*b*) in the case of a person registered under paragraph 4(2) above, did not have the intention by reference to which he was registered,
they may cancel his registration with effect from that day.
(4) Subject to paragraph 7 below, where the Commissioners are satisfied that a person who has been registered under paragraph 4(2) above and is not for the time being liable to be registered under this Schedule—
(*a*) has not begun, by the date specified in his request to be registered, to make relevant acquisitions; or
(*b*) has contravened any condition of his registration,
they may cancel his registration with effect from the date so specified or, as the case may be, the date of the contravention or from such later date as may be agreed between them and him.
(5) For the purposes of this paragraph a person is registrable under this Schedule at any time when he is liable to be registered under this Schedule or is a person who makes relevant acquisitions.

Commentary—*De Voil Indirect Tax Service* **V2.188**.
Definitions—"The Commissioners", s 96(1); "registered", s 3(3); "relevant acquisition", Sch 3 para 11.

Conditions of cancellation

7—(1) The Commissioners shall not, under paragraph 6(1) above, cancel a person's registration with effect from any time unless they are satisfied that it is not a time when that person would be subject to a requirement to be registered under this Act.
(2) The Commissioners shall not, under paragraph 6(2) or (4) above, cancel a person's registration with effect from any time unless they are satisfied that it is not a time when that person would be subject to a requirement, or entitled, to be registered under this Act.
(3) Subject to sub-paragraph (4) below, the registration of a person who—
(*a*) is registered under paragraph 4 above; or
(*b*) would not, if he were not registered, be liable or entitled to be registered under any provision of this Act except paragraph 4 above,
shall not be cancelled with effect from any time before the 1st January which is, or next follows, the second anniversary of the date on which his registration took effect.

(4) Sub-paragraph (3) above does not apply to cancellation under paragraph 6(3) or (4) above.
(5) In determining for the purposes of this paragraph whether a person would be subject to a requirement, or entitled, to be registered at any time, so much of any provision of this Act as prevents a person from becoming liable or entitled to be registered when he is already registered or when he is so liable under any other provision shall be disregarded.

Commentary—*De Voil Indirect Tax Service* **V2.188**.
Definitions—"The Commissioners", s 96(1); "registered", s 3(3).

Exemption from registration

8—(1) Notwithstanding the preceding provisions of this Schedule, where a person who makes or intends to make relevant acquisitions satisfies the Commissioners that any such acquisition would be an acquisition in pursuance of a transaction which would be zero-rated if it were a taxable supply by a taxable person, they may, if he so requests and they think fit, exempt him from registration under this Schedule until it appears to them that the request should no longer be acted upon or is withdrawn.
(2) Where a person who is exempted under this paragraph from registration under this Schedule makes any relevant acquisition in pursuance of any transaction which would, if it were a taxable supply by a taxable person, be chargeable to VAT otherwise than as a zero-rated supply, he shall notify the Commissioners of the change within 30 days of the date on which he made the acquisition.

Commentary—*De Voil Indirect Tax Service* **V2.183**.
Definitions—"The Commissioners", s 96(1); "registration", s 3(3); "relevant acquisition", Sch 3 para 11; "taxable person", s 3; "taxable supply", s 4(2); "VAT", ss 1, 96(1); "zero-rated", s 30.
Cross reference—See VATA 1994 s 67(1) (penalty for failure to comply with sub-para (2) of this para).

Power to vary specified sums by order

9 The Treasury may by order substitute for any of the sums for the time being specified in this Schedule such greater sums as they think fit.

Orders—VAT (Increase of Registration Limits) Order, SI 2014/703.
VAT (Increase of Registration Limits) Order, SI 2015/750.

Supplementary

10 Any notification required under this Schedule shall be made in such form [and manner][1] and shall contain such particulars [as may be specified in regulations or by the Commissioners in accordance with regulations.][1]

Regulations—See VAT Regulations, SI 1995/2518 reg 5, Sch 1.
VAT (Amendment) (No 2) Regulations, SI 2012/1899.
Definitions—"The Commissioners", s 96(1); "prescribe", s 96(1); "regulations", s 96(1);
Amendments—[1] Words inserted, and words substituted for words "as the Commissioners may by regulations prescribe", by FA 2012 s 204, Sch 29 paras 1, 10 with effect from 17 July 2012.

11 For the purposes of this Schedule an acquisition of goods from another member State is a relevant acquisition where—

(*a*) it is a taxable acquisition of goods other than goods which are subject to a duty of excise or consist in a new means of transport;
(*b*) it is an acquisition otherwise than in pursuance of a taxable supply and is treated, for the purposes of this Act, as taking place in the United Kingdom; and
(*c*) the event which, in relation to that acquisition, is the first relevant event for the purposes of taxing that acquisition occurs on or after 1st January 1993.

Definitions—"Acquisition of goods from another member State", s 11; "new means of transport", s 95; "taxable acquisition", s 10(2); "taxable supply", s 4(2); "United Kingdom", s 96(11).

[SCHEDULE 3A
REGISTRATION IN RESPECT OF DISPOSALS OF ASSETS FOR WHICH A VAT REPAYMENT IS CLAIMED][1]

Section 3(2)

[1] Sch 3A inserted by FA 2000 s 136(8), Sch 36, with effect for relevant supplies (within the meaning of this Schedule) made after 20 March 2000.

Liability to be registered

[1—(1) A person who is not registered under this Act, and is not liable to be registered under Schedule 1, [1A,][2] 2 or 3, becomes liable to be registered under this Schedule at any time—

(*a*) if he makes relevant supplies; or
(*b*) if there are reasonable grounds for believing that he will make such supplies in the period of 30 days then beginning.

(2) A person shall be treated as having become liable to be registered under this Schedule at any time when he would have become so liable under sub-paragraph (1) above but for any registration which is subsequently cancelled under paragraph 6(2) below, paragraph 13(3) of Schedule 1, [paragraph 11 of Schedule 1A,][2] paragraph 6(2) of Schedule 2 or paragraph 6(3) of Schedule 3.
(3) A person shall not cease to be liable to be registered under this Schedule except in accordance with paragraph 2 below.][1]

Amendments—[1] Sch 3A inserted by FA 2000 s 136(8), Sch 36, with effect for relevant supplies (within the meaning of this Schedule) made after 20 March 2000.

[2] In sub-paras (1), (2), words inserted by FA 2012 s 203, Sch 28 paras 2, 16 with effect in relation to supplies made or to be made on or after 1 December 2012.

[2 A person who has become liable to be registered under this Schedule shall cease to be so liable at any time if the Commissioners are satisfied that he has ceased to make relevant supplies.][1]

Amendments—[1] Sch 3A inserted by FA 2000 s 136(8), Sch 36, with effect for relevant supplies (within the meaning of this Schedule) made after 20 March 2000.

Notification of liability and registration

[3—(1) A person who becomes liable to be registered by virtue of paragraph 1(1)(*a*) above shall notify the Commissioners of the liability before the end of the period of 30 days beginning with the day on which the liability arises.
(2) The Commissioners shall register any such person (whether or not he so notifies them) with effect from the beginning of the day on which the liability arises.][1]

Amendments—[1] Sch 3A inserted by FA 2000 s 136(8), Sch 36, with effect for relevant supplies (within the meaning of this Schedule) made after 20 March 2000.

[4—(1) A person who becomes liable to be registered by virtue of paragraph 1(1)(*b*) above shall notify the Commissioners of the liability before the end of the period by reference to which the liability arises.
(2) The Commissioners shall register any such person (whether or not he so notifies them) with effect from the beginning of the period by reference to which the liability arises.][1]

Amendments—[1] Sch 3A inserted by FA 2000 s 136(8), Sch 36, with effect for relevant supplies (within the meaning of this Schedule) made after 20 March 2000.

Notification of end of liability

[5—(1) Subject to sub-paragraph (2) below, a person registered under paragraph 3 or 4 above who ceases to make or have the intention of making relevant supplies shall notify the Commissioners of that fact within 30 days of the day on which he does so.
(2) Sub-paragraph (1) above does not apply if the person would, when he so ceases, be otherwise liable or entitled to be registered under this Act if his registration and any enactment preventing a person from being liable to be registered under different provisions at the same time were disregarded.][1]

Amendments—[1] Sch 3A inserted by FA 2000 s 136(8), Sch 36, with effect for relevant supplies (within the meaning of this Schedule) made after 20 March 2000.

Cancellation of registration

[6—(1) Subject to sub-paragraph (3) below, where the Commissioners are satisfied that a registered person has ceased to be liable to be registered under this Schedule, they may cancel his registration with effect from the day on which he so ceased or from such later date as may be agreed between them and him.
(2) Where the Commissioners are satisfied that on the day on which a registered person was registered he was not registrable, they may cancel his registration with effect from that day.
(3) The Commissioners shall not under sub-paragraph (1) above cancel a person's registration with effect from any time unless they are satisfied that it is not a time when that person would be subject to a requirement, or entitled, to be registered under this Act.
(4) In determining for the purposes of sub-paragraph (3) above whether a person would be subject to a requirement, or entitled, to be registered at any time, so much of any provision of this Act as prevents a person from becoming liable or entitled to be registered when he is already registered or when he is so liable under any other provision shall be disregarded.][1]

Amendments—[1] Sch 3A inserted by FA 2000 s 136(8), Sch 36, with effect for relevant supplies (within the meaning of this Schedule) made after 20 March 2000.

Exemption from registration

[7—(1) Notwithstanding the preceding provisions of this Schedule, where a person who makes or intends to make relevant supplies satisfies the Commissioners that any such supply is zero-rated or would be zero-rated if he were a taxable person, they may, if he so requests and they think fit, exempt him from registration under this Schedule.

(2) Where there is a material change in the nature of the supplies made by a person exempted under this paragraph from registration under this Schedule, he shall notify the Commissioners of the change—

(*a*) within 30 days of the date on which the change occurred; or

(*b*) if no particular date is identifiable as the day on which it occurred, within 30 days of the end of the quarter in which it occurred.

(3) Where there is a material alteration in any quarter in the proportion of relevant supplies of such a person that are zero-rated, he shall notify the Commissioners of the alteration within 30 days of the end of the quarter.

(4) If it appears to the Commissioners that a request under sub-paragraph (1) above should no longer have been acted upon on or after any day, or has been withdrawn on any day, they shall register the person who made the request with effect from that day.][1]

Commentary—*De Voil Indirect Tax Service* **V2.189A**.

Amendments—[1] Sch 3A inserted by FA 2000 s 136(8), Sch 36, with effect for relevant supplies (within the meaning of this Schedule) made after 20 March 2000.

Supplementary

[**8** Any notification required under this Schedule shall be made in such form [and manner][2] and shall contain such particulars [as may be specified in regulations or by the Commissioners in accordance with regulations.][2]][1]

Regulations—VAT (Amendment) (No 2) Regulations, SI 2012/1899.

Amendments—[1] Sch 3A inserted by FA 2000 s 136(8), Sch 36, with effect for relevant supplies (within the meaning of this Schedule) made after 20 March 2000.

[2] Words inserted, and words substituted for words "as the Commissioners may by regulations prescribe", by FA 2012 s 204, Sch 29 paras 1, 11 with effect from 17 July 2012.

[**9**—(1) For the purposes of this Schedule a supply of goods is a relevant supply where—

(*a*) the supply is a taxable supply;

(*b*) the goods are assets of the business in the course or furtherance of which they are supplied; and

(*c*) the person by whom they are supplied, or a predecessor of his, has received or claimed, or is intending to claim, a repayment of VAT on the supply to him, or the importation by him, of the goods or of anything comprised in them.

(2) In relation to any goods, a person is the predecessor of another for the purposes of this paragraph if—

(*a*) that other person is a person to whom he has transferred assets of his business by a transfer of that business, or part of it, as a going concern;

(*b*) those assets consisted of or included those goods; and

(*c*) the transfer of the assets is one falling by virtue of an order under section 5(3) (or under an enactment re-enacted in section 5(3)) to be treated as neither a supply of goods nor a supply of services;

and the reference in this paragraph to a person's predecessor includes references to the predecessors of his predecessor through any number of transfers.

(3) The reference in this paragraph to a repayment of VAT is a reference to such a repayment under a scheme embodied in regulations made under section 39.][1]

Amendments—[1] Sch 3A inserted by FA 2000 s 136(8), Sch 36, with effect for relevant supplies (within the meaning of this Schedule) made after 20 March 2000.

[SCHEDULE 3B

[ELECTRONIC, TELECOMMUNICATION AND BROADCASTING SERVICES: NON-UNION SCHEME]]

Section 3A

Amendments—Sch 3B inserted by FA 2003 s 23, Sch 2 paras 1, 4 with effect for qualifying supplies made after 30 June 2003, see FA 2003 s 23(2).

In Schedule heading, words substituted for words "Supply of electronic services in member states: special accounting scheme" by FA 2014 s 103, Sch 22 paras 3, 5 with effect in relation to supplies made on or after 1 January 2015.

PART 1

[NON-UNION SCHEME: REGISTRATION]

Amendments—In heading for Part 1, words substituted for word "Registration" by FA 2014 s 103, Sch 22 paras 3, 6(8) with effect in relation to supplies made on or after 1 January 2015.

The register

[1 Persons registered under this Schedule are to be registered in a single register kept by the Commissioners for the purposes of this Schedule.][1]

Commentary—*De Voil Indirect Tax Service* **V2.121**.

Amendments—[1] Sch 3B inserted by FA 2003 s 23, Sch 2 paras 1, 4 with effect for qualifying supplies made after 30 June 2003, see FA 2003 s 23(2).

Persons who may be registered

[2—(1) A person may be registered under this Schedule if he satisfies the following conditions.

(2) Condition 1 is that the person makes or intends to make qualifying supplies in the course of a business carried on by him.

(3) Condition 2 is that the person has neither his business establishment nor a fixed establishment in the United Kingdom or in another member State in relation to any supply of goods or services.

(4) Condition 3 is that the person is not—

(*a*) registered under this Act,

(*b*) identified for the purposes of VAT in accordance with the law of another member State, or

(*c*) registered under an Act of Tynwald for the purposes of any tax imposed by or under an Act of Tynwald which corresponds to VAT.

(5) Condition 4 is that the person—

(*a*) is not required to be registered or identified as mentioned in condition 3, or

(*b*) is required to be so registered or identified, but solely by virtue of the fact that he makes or intends to make qualifying supplies.

(6) Condition 5 is that the person is not identified under any provision of the law of another member State which implements [Section 2 of Chapter 6 of Title XII of the VAT Directive][2].

[(7) In this Schedule "the VAT Directive" means Directive 2006/112/EC (Title XII of which is amended by Council Directive 2008/8/EC).][2]

(8) References in this Schedule to a person's being registered under this Act do not include a reference to that person's being registered under this Schedule.][1]

Amendments—[1] Sch 3B inserted by FA 2003 s 23, Sch 2 paras 1, 4 with effect for qualifying supplies made after 30 June 2003, see FA 2003 s 23(2).

[2] In sub-para (6), words substituted for words "Article 26c", and sub-para (7) substituted, by FA 2014 s 103, Sch 22 paras 3, 6(1), (2) with effect in relation to supplies made on or after 1 January 2015.

Qualifying supplies

[3—(1) In this Schedule "qualifying supply" means a supply of electronically supplied services, telecommunication services or broadcasting services to a person who—

(*a*) belongs in the United Kingdom or another member State, and

(*b*) is not a relevant business person.

(2) In sub-paragraph (1)—

"broadcasting services" means radio and television broadcasting services;

"electronically supplied services" has the same meaning as in Schedule 4A (see paragraph 9(3) and (4) of that Schedule);

"telecommunication services" has the same meaning as in Schedule 4A (see paragraph 8(2) of that Schedule).][1]

Amendments—[1] Sch 3B inserted by FA 2003 s 23, Sch 2 paras 1, 4 with effect for qualifying supplies made after 30 June 2003, see FA 2003 s 23(2).

Registration request

[4—(1) If a person—

(*a*) satisfies the Commissioners that the conditions in paragraph 2 above are satisfied in his case, and

(*b*) makes a request in accordance with this paragraph (a "registration request"),

the Commissioners must register him under this Schedule.

(2) Sub-paragraph (1) above is subject to [Article 58b of Implementing Regulation (EU) No 282/2011][3].

(3) A registration request must contain the following particulars—

(*a*) the name of the person making the request;

(*b*) his postal address;

(*c*) his electronic addresses (including any websites);

(*d*) where he has been allocated a number by the tax authorities in the country in which he belongs, that number;

(*e*) the date on which he began, or intends to begin, making qualifying supplies.

(4) A registration request must include a statement that the person making the request is not—

(*a*) registered under this Act,

(*b*) identified for the purposes of VAT in accordance with the law of another member State, or

(*c*) registered under an Act of Tynwald for the purposes of any tax imposed by or under an Act of Tynwald which corresponds to VAT.][1]

[(5) A registration request—

(*a*) must contain any further information, and any declaration about its contents, that the Commissioners may by regulations require;

(*b*) must be made by such electronic means, and in such manner, as the Commissioners may direct or may by regulations require.][2]

Commentary—*De Voil Indirect Tax Service* **V2.189G.**

Regulations—VAT (Amendment) (No 3) Regulations, SI 2014/2430.

Amendments—[1] Sch 3B inserted by FA 2003 s 23, Sch 2 paras 1, 4 with effect for qualifying supplies made after 30 June 2003, see FA 2003 s 23(2).

[2] Sub-para (5) substituted by FA 2014 s 103, Sch 22 para 6(1), (3)(*b*) with effect from 17 July 2014.

[3] In sub-para (2), words substituted for words "paragraph 9 below" by FA 2014 s 103, Sch 22 para 6(1), (3)(*a*) with effect in relation to supplies made on or after 1 January 2015.

[5—

Amendments—Para 5 and preceding heading repealed by FA 2014 s 103, Sch 22 para 6(1), (4) with effect in relation to supplies made on or after 1 January 2015.

Registration number

[6 On registering a person under this Schedule, the Commissioners must—

(*a*) allocate a registration number to him, and

(*b*) notify him electronically of the number.][1]

Amendments—[1] Sch 3B inserted by FA 2003 s 23, Sch 2 paras 1, 4 with effect for qualifying supplies made after 30 June 2003, see FA 2003 s 23(2).

Obligation to notify changes

[7—(1) . . . [2]

(2) . . . [2]

(3) A notification under [Article 57h of Implementing Regulation (EU) No 282/2011][2] must be given by such electronic means, and in such manner, as the Commissioners may direct or may by regulations prescribe.][1]

Regulations—VAT (Amendment) (No 3) Regulations, SI 2014/2430.

Amendments—[1] Sch 3B inserted by FA 2003 s 23, Sch 2 paras 1, 4 with effect for qualifying supplies made after 30 June 2003, see FA 2003 s 23(2).

[2] Sub-paras (1), (2) repealed, and in sub-para (3), words substituted for words "this paragraph", by FA 2014 s 103, Sch 22 para 6(1), (5) with effect in relation to supplies made on or after 1 January 2015.

Cancellation of registration

[8—(1) The Commissioners must cancel a person's registration under this Schedule if—

(*a*) he notifies them that he has ceased to make, or to have the intention of making, qualifying supplies,

(*b*) they otherwise determine that he has ceased to make, or to have the intention of making, qualifying supplies,

(*c*) he notifies them that he has ceased to satisfy the conditions in any of sub-paragraphs (3) to (6) of paragraph 2 above,

(*d*) they otherwise determine that he has ceased to satisfy any of those conditions, or

(*e*) they determine that he has persistently failed to comply with his obligations under this Schedule [or Implementing Regulation (EU) No 282/2011][2].

(2), (3) . . . [2]][1]

Commentary—*De Voil Indirect Tax Service* **V2.189J.**

Amendments—[1] Sch 3B inserted by FA 2003 s 23, Sch 2 paras 1, 4 with effect for qualifying supplies made after 30 June 2003, see FA 2003 s 23(2).

[2] In sub-para (1)(*e*), words inserted, and sub-paras (2), (3) repealed, by FA 2014 s 103, Sch 22 para 6(1), (6) with effect in relation to supplies made on or after 1 January 2015.

. . .

9—

Amendments—Para 9 and preceding heading repealed by FA 2014 s 103, Sch 22 para 6(1), (7) with effect in relation to supplies made on or after 1 January 2015.

PART 2

[NON-UNION SCHEME: LIABILITY, RETURNS, PAYMENT ETC]

Amendments—In heading to Part 2, words substituted for words "Obligations following registration, etc" by FA 2014 s 103, Sch 22 paras 3, 7(1), (8) with effect in relation to supplies made on or after 1 January 2015.

Liability for VAT

[10—(1) A person is liable to pay VAT under and in accordance with this Schedule if—

(*a*) he makes a qualifying supply, and

(*b*) he is registered under this Schedule when he makes the supply.

(2) The amount of VAT which a person is liable to pay by virtue of this Schedule on any qualifying supply is to be determined in accordance with sub-paragraphs (3) and (4) below [(and the VAT is to be paid without any deduction of VAT pursuant to Article 168 of Directive 2006/112/EC)][2].

(3) If the qualifying supply is treated as made in the United Kingdom, the amount is the amount of VAT . . . [2] charged on the supply under this Act [(see paragraph 17(2))][2].

(4) If the qualifying supply is treated as made in another member State, the amount is the amount of VAT . . . [2] charged on the supply in accordance with the law of that member State . . . [2].

(5) Where a person is liable to pay VAT by virtue of this Schedule—

(*a*) any amount falling to be determined in accordance with sub-paragraph (3) above is to be regarded for the purposes of this Act as VAT charged in accordance with this Act, . . . [2]

(*b*) . . . [2]][1]

Amendments—[1] Sch 3B inserted by FA 2003 s 23, Sch 2 paras 1, 4 with effect for qualifying supplies made after 30 June 2003, see FA 2003 s 23(2).

[2] In sub-para (2), words inserted, in sub-para (3), words "that would have been" repealed and words substituted for words "if the person had been registered under this Act when he made the supply", in sub-para (4), words "that would have been" repealed and words "if the person had been identified for the purposes of VAT in that member State when he made the supply" repealed, and in sub-para (5), para (*b*) and preceding word "and" repealed, by FA 2014 s 103, Sch 22 paras 3, 7(1), (2) with effect in relation to supplies made on or after 1 January 2015.

Obligation to submit special accounting returns

[11—(1) A person who is, or has been, registered under this Schedule must submit a return (a "special accounting return") to the [Commissioners][2] for each reporting period.

(2) Each quarter for the whole or any part of which a person is registered under this Schedule is a "reporting period" in the case of that person.

(3)–(7) . . . [2]][1]

Amendments—[1] Sch 3B inserted by FA 2003 s 23, Sch 2 paras 1, 4 with effect for qualifying supplies made after 30 June 2003, see FA 2003 s 23(2).

[2] In sub-para (1), word substituted for word "Controller", and sub-paras (3)–(7) repealed, by FA 2014 s 103, Sch 22 paras 3, 7(1), (3) with effect in relation to supplies made on or after 1 January 2015.

Further obligations with respect to special accounting returns

[12—(1) A special accounting return [is to be made out in sterling][2].

(2) Any conversion from one currency into another for the purposes of sub-paragraph (1) above shall be made by using the exchange rates published by the European Central Bank—

(*a*) for the last day of the reporting period to which the special accounting return relates, or

(*b*) if no such rate is published for that day, for the next day for which such a rate is published.

(3) A special accounting return must be submitted to the [Commissioners][2] within the period of 20 days after the last day of the reporting period to which it relates.

(4) A special accounting return must be submitted by such electronic means, and in such manner, as the Commissioners may direct or may by regulations prescribe.][1]

Regulations—VAT (Amendment) (No 3) Regulations, SI 2014/2430.

Amendments—[1] Sch 3B inserted by FA 2003 s 23, Sch 2 paras 1, 4 with effect for qualifying supplies made after 30 June 2003, see FA 2003 s 23(2).

[2] In sub-para (1), words substituted for words "must set out in sterling the amounts referred to in paragraph 11 above", and in sub-para (3), word substituted for word "Controller", by FA 2014 s 103, Sch 22 paras 3, 7(1), (4) with effect in relation to supplies made on or after 1 January 2015.

Payment of VAT

[13—(1) A person who is required to submit a special accounting return must, [by the deadline for submitting the return, pay to the Commissioners the amount of VAT that the person is liable, in accordance with paragraph 10, to pay on qualifying supplies treated as made by the person in][2] the reporting period to which the return relates.

(2) A payment under this paragraph must be made in such manner as the Commissioners may direct or may by regulations prescribe.][1]

Amendments—[1] Sch 3B inserted by FA 2003 s 23, Sch 2 paras 1, 4 with effect for qualifying supplies made after 30 June 2003, see FA 2003 s 23(2).

[2] In sub-para (1), words substituted for words "at the same time as he submits the return, pay to the Controller in sterling the amount referred to in paragraph 11(5) above in respect of", by FA 2014 s 103, Sch 22 paras 3, 7(1), (5) with effect in relation to supplies made on or after 1 January 2015.

Obligations to keep and produce records

[14—(1) A person must keep records of the transactions which he enters into for the purposes of, or in connection with, qualifying supplies made by him at any time when he is registered under this Schedule.

(2) The records to be kept must be such as will enable the tax authorities for the member State in which a qualifying supply is treated as made to determine whether any special accounting return which is submitted in respect of that supply is correct.

(3) Any records required to be kept must be made available—

(*a*) to the tax authorities for the member State in which the qualifying supply to which the records relate was treated as made, if they so request, or

(*b*) to the Commissioners, if they so request.

(4) Records must be made available electronically under sub-paragraph (3) above.

(5) The records relating to a transaction must be maintained for a period of ten years beginning with the 1st January following the date on which the transaction was entered into.][1]

Commentary—*De Voil Indirect Tax Service* **V5.201**.

Amendments—[1] Sch 3B inserted by FA 2003 s 23, Sch 2 paras 1, 4 with effect for qualifying supplies made after 30 June 2003, see FA 2003 s 23(2).

Commissioners' power to request production of records

[15—(1) The Commissioners may request a person to make available to them electronically records of the transactions entered into by him for the purposes of, or in connection with, qualifying supplies to which this paragraph applies.

(2) This paragraph applies to qualifying supplies which—

(*a*) are treated as made in the United Kingdom, and

(*b*) are made by the person while he is identified under any provision of the law of another member State which implements [Section 2 of Chapter 6 of Title XII of the VAT Directive][2].][1]

Amendments—[1] Sch 3B inserted by FA 2003 s 23, Sch 2 paras 1, 4 with effect for qualifying supplies made after 30 June 2003, see FA 2003 s 23(2).

[2] In sub-para (2)(*b*), words substituted for words "Article 26c" by FA 2014 s 103, Sch 22 paras 3, 7(1), (6) with effect in relation to supplies made on or after 1 January 2015.

[15A—Section 44 of the Commissioners for Revenue and Customs Act 2005 (requirement to pay receipts into the Consolidated Fund) does not apply to any money received for or on account of VAT that is required to be paid to another member State under Article 46 of Council Regulation (EU) No 904/2010.][1]

Amendments—[1] Para 15A inserted by FA 2014 s 103, Sch 22 paras 3, 7(1), (7) with effect in relation to supplies made on or after 1 January 2015.

[PART 3

SPECIAL SCHEMES: COLLECTION ETC OF UK VAT

Assessments: general modifications of section 73

16—(1) For the purposes of this Schedule, section 73 (assessments: incorrect returns etc) is to be read as if—

(*a*) the reference in subsection (1) of that section to returns required under this Act included relevant special scheme returns, and

(*b*) references in that section to a prescribed accounting period included a tax period.

(2) See also the modifications in paragraph 16A.

(3) In this Schedule "relevant special scheme return" means a special scheme return that is required to be made (wholly or partly) in respect of supplies of scheme services that are treated as made in the United Kingdom.][1]

Commentary—*De Voil Indirect Tax Service* **V2.189L**.

Amendments—[1] Part 3 (paras 16–16N) substituted by FA 2014 s 103, Sch 22 paras 3, 8 with effect in relation to supplies made on or after 1 January 2015. Any amendment made by FA 2014 Sch 22 so far as it confers power to make regulations has effect from 17 July 2014 (FA 2014 Sch 22 para 23(2)(*b*)). Part 3, as it applied in relation to supplies made before 1 January 2015, is reproduced below after para 16N.

[Assessment in connection with increase in consideration

16A—(1) Sub-paragraphs (2) to (4) make modifications of sections 73 and 76 which—

(*a*) have effect for the purposes of this Schedule, and

(*b*) are in addition to any other modifications of those sections made by this Schedule.

(2) Section 73 has effect as if the following were inserted after subsection (3) of that section—

"(3A) Where a person has failed to make an amendment or notification that the person is required to make under paragraph 16K of Schedule 3B in respect of an increase in the consideration for a UK supply (as defined in paragraph 16K(7)), the Commissioners may assess the amount of VAT due from the person as a result of the increase to the best of their judgement and notify it to the person.

(3B) An assessment under subsection (3A)—

(*a*) is of VAT due for the tax period mentioned in paragraph 16K(1)(*a*) of Schedule 3B;

(*b*) must be made within the time limits provided for in section 77, and must not be made after the later of—

(i) 2 years after the end of the tax period referred to in paragraph 16K(1)(*a*);

(ii) one year after evidence of facts sufficient in the opinion of the Commissioners to justify making the assessment comes to their knowledge.

(3C) Subject to section 77, where further evidence such as is mentioned in subsection (3B)(*b*)(ii) comes to the Commissioners' knowledge after they have made an assessment under subsection (3A), another assessment may be made under that subsection, in addition to any earlier assessment."

(3) The reference in section 73(9) to subsection (1) of that section is taken to include a reference to section 73(3A) (as inserted by sub-paragraph (2)).

(4) Section 76 (assessment of amounts due by way of interest etc) is to be read as if the reference in subsection (5) of that section to section 73(1) included a reference to section 73(3A) (as inserted by sub-paragraph (2)).][1]

Commentary—*De Voil Indirect Tax Service* **V2.189L**.

Amendments—[1] Part 3 (paras 16–16N) substituted by FA 2014 s 103, Sch 22 paras 3, 8 with effect in relation to supplies made on or after 1 January 2015. Any amendment made by FA 2014 Sch 22 so far as it confers power to make regulations has effect from 17 July 2014 (FA 2014 Sch 22 para 23(2)(*b*)). Part 3, as it applied in relation to supplies made before 1 January 2015, is reproduced below after para 16N.

[Assessments: consequential modifications

16B References to prescribed accounting periods in the following provisions are to be read in accordance with the modifications made by paragraphs 16 and 16A—

(*a*) section 74 (interest on VAT recovered or recoverable by assessment);

(*b*) section 76 (assessment of amounts due by way of penalty, interest or surcharge);

(*c*) section 77 (assessment: time limits).][1]

Commentary—*De Voil Indirect Tax Service* **V2.189L**.

Amendments—[1] Part 3 (paras 16–16N) substituted by FA 2014 s 103, Sch 22 paras 3, 8 with effect in relation to supplies made on or after 1 January 2015. Any amendment made by FA 2014 Sch 22 so far as it confers power to make regulations has effect from 17 July 2014 (FA 2014 Sch 22 para 23(2)(*b*)). Part 3, as it applied in relation to supplies made before 1 January 2015, is reproduced below after para 16N.

[Deemed amendments of relevant special scheme returns

16C—(1) Where a person who has made a relevant special scheme return makes a claim under paragraph 16I(7)(*b*) (overpayments) in relation to an error in the return, the relevant special scheme return is taken for the purposes of this Act to have been amended by the information in the claim.

(2) Where a person who has made a relevant special scheme return gives the Commissioners a notice relating to the return under paragraph 16K(2)(*b*) (increase or decrease in consideration), the relevant special scheme return is taken for the purposes of this Act to have been amended by that information.

(3) Where (in a case not falling within sub-paragraph (1) or (2)) a person who has made a relevant special scheme return notifies the Commissioners (after the expiry of the period during which the non-UK return may be amended under Article 61 of the Implementing Regulation) of a change that needs to be made to the return to correct an error, or rectify an omission, in it, the relevant special scheme return is taken for the purposes of this Act to have been amended by that information.

(4) The Commissioners may by regulations—

(*a*) specify within what period and in what form and manner notice may be given under sub-paragraph (3);

(*b*) require notices to be supported by documentary evidence described in the regulations.][1]

Commentary—*De Voil Indirect Tax Service* **V2.189L**.

Regulations—VAT (Amendment) (No 3) Regulations, SI 2014/2430.

Amendments—[1] Part 3 (paras 16–16N) substituted by FA 2014 s 103, Sch 22 paras 3, 8 with effect in relation to supplies made on or after 1 January 2015. Any amendment made by FA 2014 Sch 22 so far as it confers power to make regulations has effect from 17 July 2014 (FA 2014 Sch 22 para 23(2)(*b*)). Part 3, as it applied in relation to supplies made before 1 January 2015, is reproduced below after para 16N.

[Interest on VAT: "reckonable date"

16D—(1) Sub-paragraph (2) states the "reckonable date" for the purposes of section 74(1) and (2) for any case where an amount carrying interest under that section—

(*a*) is an amount assessed under section 73(2) (refunds etc) in reliance on paragraph 16, or that could have been so assessed, and

(*b*) was correctly paid or credited to the person, but would not have been paid or credited to the person had the facts been as they later turn out to be.

(2) The "reckonable date" is the first day after the end of the tax period in which the events occurred as a result of which the Commissioners were authorised to make the assessment (that was or could have been made) under section 73(2).

(3) Sub-paragraph (4) states the "reckonable date", for any other case where an amount carrying interest under section 74 is assessed under section 74(1) or (2) in reliance on paragraph 16, or could have been so assessed.

(4) The "reckonable date" is taken to be the latest date by which a non-UK return was required to be made for the tax period to which the amount assessed relates.

(5) Where section 74(1) or (2) (interest on VAT recovered or recoverable by assessment) applies in relation to an amount assessed under section 73(3A) (as inserted by paragraph 16A(2)), the "reckonable date" for the purposes of section 74(1) or (2) is taken to be the day after the end of the tax period referred to in paragraph 16K(2).][1]

Commentary—*De Voil Indirect Tax Service* **V2.189L**.

Amendments—[1] Part 3 (paras 16–16N) substituted by FA 2014 s 103, Sch 22 paras 3, 8 with effect in relation to supplies made on or after 1 January 2015. Any amendment made by FA 2014 Sch 22 so far as it confers power to make regulations has effect from 17 July 2014 (FA 2014 Sch 22 para 23(2)(*b*)). Part 3, as it applied in relation to supplies made before 1 January 2015, is reproduced below after para 16N.

[Default surcharge: notice of special surcharge period

16E—(1) A person who is required to make a relevant special scheme return for a tax period is regarded for the purposes of this paragraph and paragraph 16F as being in default in respect of that period if either—

(*a*) conditions 1A and 2A are met, or

(*b*) conditions 1B and 2B are met;

(but see also paragraph 16G).

(2) For the purposes of sub-paragraph (1)(*a*)—

(*a*) condition 1A is that the tax authorities for the administering member State have not received the return by the deadline for submitting it;

(*b*) condition 2A is that those tax authorities have, in accordance with Article 60a of the Implementing Regulation, issued a reminder of the obligation to submit the return.

(3) For the purposes of sub-paragraph (1)(*b*)—

(*a*) condition 1B is that, by the deadline for submitting the return, the tax authorities for the administering member State have received the return but have not received the amount of VAT shown on the return as payable by the person in respect of the tax period;

(*b*) condition 2B is that those tax authorities have, in accordance with Article 60a of the Implementing Regulation, issued a reminder of the VAT outstanding.

(4) The Commissioners may serve on a person who is in default in respect of a tax period a notice (a "special surcharge liability notice") specifying a period—

(*a*) ending on the first anniversary of the last day of that tax period, and

(*b*) beginning on the date of the notice.

(5) A period specified under sub-paragraph (4) is a "special surcharge period".

(6) If a special surcharge liability notice is served in respect of a tax period which ends at or before the end of an existing special surcharge period, the special surcharge period specified in that notice must be expressed as a continuation of the existing special surcharge period (so that the existing period and its extension are regarded as a single special surcharge period).][1]

Commentary—*De Voil Indirect Tax Service* **V2.189L**.

Amendments—[1] Part 3 (paras 16–16N) substituted by FA 2014 s 103, Sch 22 paras 3, 8 with effect in relation to supplies made on or after 1 January 2015. Any amendment made by FA 2014 Sch 22 so far as it confers power to make regulations has effect from 17 July 2014 (FA 2014 Sch 22 para 23(2)(*b*)). Part 3, as it applied in relation to supplies made before 1 January 2015, is reproduced below after para 16N.

[Further default after service of notice

16F—(1) If a person on whom a special surcharge liability notice has been served—

(*a*) is in default in respect of a tax period ending within the special surcharge period specified in (or extended by) that notice, and

(*b*) has outstanding special scheme VAT for that tax period,

the person is to be liable to a surcharge of the amount given by sub-paragraph (2).

(2) The surcharge is equal to whichever is the greater of—

(*a*) £30, and

(*b*) the specified percentage of the person's outstanding special scheme VAT for the tax period.

(3) The specified percentage depends on whether the tax period is the first, second or third etc in the default period in respect of which the person is in default and has outstanding special scheme VAT, and is—

(*a*) for the first such tax period, 2%;

(*b*) for the second such tax period, 5%;

(*c*) for the third such tax period, 10%;

(*d*) for each such tax period after the third, 15%.

(4) "Special scheme VAT", in relation to a person, means VAT that the person is liable to pay to the tax authorities for the administering member State under a special scheme in respect of supplies of scheme services treated as made in the United Kingdom.

(5) A person has "outstanding special scheme VAT" for a tax period if some or all of the special scheme VAT for which the person is liable in respect of that period has not been paid by the deadline for the person to submit a special scheme return for that period (and the amount unpaid is referred to in sub-paragraph (2)(*b*) as "the person's outstanding special scheme VAT" for the tax period).][1]

Commentary—*De Voil Indirect Tax Service* **V2.189L**.

Amendments—[1] Part 3 (paras 16–16N) substituted by FA 2014 s 103, Sch 22 paras 3, 8 with effect in relation to supplies made on or after 1 January 2015. Any amendment made by FA 2014 Sch 22 so far as it confers power to make regulations has effect from 17 July 2014 (FA 2014 Sch 22 para 23(2)(*b*)). Part 3, as it applied in relation to supplies made before 1 January 2015, is reproduced below after para 16N.

[Default surcharge: exceptions for reasonable excuse etc

16G—(1) A person who would otherwise have been liable to a surcharge under paragraph 16F(1) is not to be liable to the surcharge if the person satisfies the Commissioners or, on appeal, the tribunal that, in the case of a default which is material to the surcharge—

(*a*) the special scheme return or, as the case may be, the VAT shown on that return, was despatched at such a time and in such manner that it was reasonable to expect that it would be received by the tax authorities for the administering member State within the appropriate time limit, or

(*b*) there is a reasonable excuse for the return or the VAT not having been so despatched.

(2) Where sub-paragraph (1) applies to a person—

(*a*) the person is treated as not having been in default in respect of the tax period in question, and

(*b*) accordingly, any special surcharge liability notice the service of which depended on that default is regarded as not having been served.

(3) A default is "material" to a surcharge if—

(*a*) it is the default which gives rise to the surcharge, under paragraph 16F(1), or

(*b*) it is a default which was taken into account in the service of the special surcharge liability notice on which the surcharge depends and the person concerned has not previously been liable to a surcharge in respect of a tax period ending within the special surcharge period specified in or extended by that notice.

(4) A default is left out of account for the purposes of paragraphs 16E(4) and 16F(1) if—

(*a*) the conduct by virtue of which the person is in default is also conduct falling within section 69(1) (breaches of regulatory provisions), and

(*b*) by reason of that conduct the person concerned is assessed to a penalty under that section.

(5) If the Commissioners, after consultation with the Treasury, so direct, a default in respect of a tax period specified in the direction is to be left out of account for the purposes of paragraphs 16E(4) and 16F(1).

(6) Section 71(1) (meaning of "reasonable excuse") applies for the purposes of this paragraph as it applies for the purposes of sections 59 to 70.][1]

Commentary—*De Voil Indirect Tax Service* **V2.189L**.

Amendments—[1] Part 3 (paras 16–16N) substituted by FA 2014 s 103, Sch 22 paras 3, 8 with effect in relation to supplies made on or after 1 January 2015. Any amendment made by FA 2014 Sch 22 so far as it confers power to make regulations has effect from 17 July 2014 (FA 2014 Sch 22 para 23(2)(*b*)). Part 3, as it applied in relation to supplies made before 1 January 2015, is reproduced below after para 16N.

[Interest in certain cases of official error

16H—(1) Section 78 (interest in certain cases of official error) applies as follows in relation to a case where, due to an error on the part of the Commissioners—

(*a*) a person has accounted, under a special scheme, for an amount by way of UK VAT that was not UK VAT due from the person, and as a result the Commissioners are liable under paragraph 16I to pay (or repay) an amount to the person, or

(*b*) (in a case not falling within paragraph (*a*)), a person has paid, in accordance with an obligation under a special scheme, an amount by way of UK VAT that was not UK VAT due from the person and which the Commissioners are in consequence liable to repay to the person.

(2) Section 78 has effect as if the condition in section 78(1)(*a*) were met in relation to that person.

(3) In the application of section 78 as a result of this paragraph, section 78(12)(*b*) is read as providing that any reference in that section to a return is to a return required to be made under a special scheme.

(4) In section 78 in its application as a result of this section, "output tax" has the meaning that that expression would have if the reference in section 24(2) to a "taxable person" were to a "person".][1]

Commentary—*De Voil Indirect Tax Service* **V2.189L**.

Amendments—[1] Part 3 (paras 16–16N) substituted by FA 2014 s 103, Sch 22 paras 3, 8 with effect in relation to supplies made on or after 1 January 2015. Any amendment made by FA 2014 Sch 22 so far as it confers power to make regulations has effect from 17 July 2014 (FA 2014 Sch 22 para 23(2)(*b*)). Part 3, as it applied in relation to supplies made before 1 January 2015, is reproduced below after para 16N.

[Overpayments

16I—(1) A person may make a claim if the person—

(*a*) has made a special scheme return for a tax period relating wholly or partly to supplies of scheme services treated as made in the United Kingdom,

(*b*) has accounted to the tax authorities for the administering member State (whether that is the United Kingdom or another member State) for VAT in respect of those supplies, and

(*c*) in doing so has brought into account as UK VAT due to those authorities an amount ("the overpaid amount") that was not UK VAT due to them.

(2) A person may make a claim if the person has, as a participant in a special scheme, paid (to the tax authorities for the administering member State or to the Commissioners) an amount by way of UK VAT that was not UK VAT due ("the overpaid amount"), otherwise than in the circumstances mentioned in sub-paragraph (1)(*c*).

(3) A person who is or has been a participant in a special scheme may make a claim if the Commissioners—

(*a*) have assessed the person to VAT for a tax period, and

(*b*) in doing so, have brought into account as VAT an amount ("the amount not due") that was not VAT due.

(4) Where a person makes a claim under sub-paragraph (1) or (2), the Commissioners must repay the overpaid amount to the person.

(5) Where a person makes a claim under sub-paragraph (3), the Commissioners must credit the person with the amount not due.

(6) Where—

(a) as a result of a claim under sub-paragraph (3) an amount is to be credited to a person, and

(b) after setting any sums against that amount under or by virtue of this Act, some or all of the amount remains to the person's credit,

the Commissioners must pay (or repay) to the person so much of the amount as remains to the person's credit.

(7) The reference in sub-paragraph (1) to a claim is to a claim made—

(*a*) by correcting, in accordance with Article 61 of the Implementing Regulation, the error in the non-UK return mentioned in sub-paragraph (1)(*a*), or (*b*) (after the expiry of the period during which the non-UK return may be amended under Article 61) to the Commissioners.

(8) Sub-paragraphs (1) and (2) do not require any amount to be repaid except so far as that is required by Article 63 of the Implementing Regulation.][1]

Commentary—*De Voil Indirect Tax Service* **V2.189L.**

Amendments—[1] Part 3 (paras 16–16N) substituted by FA 2014 s 103, Sch 22 paras 3, 8 with effect in relation to supplies made on or after 1 January 2015. Any amendment made by FA 2014 Sch 22 so far as it confers power to make regulations has effect from 17 July 2014 (FA 2014 Sch 22 para 23(2)(*b*)). Part 3, as it applied in relation to supplies made before 1 January 2015, is reproduced below after para 16N.

[Overpayments: supplementary

16J—(1) In section 80—

(*a*) subsections (3) to (3C) (unjust enrichment), and

(*b*) subsections (4A), (4C) and (6) (recovery by assessment of amounts wrongly credited),

have effect as if a claim under paragraph 16I(1) were a claim under section 80(1), a claim under paragraph 16I(2) were a claim under section 80(1B) and a claim under paragraph 16I(3) were a claim under section 80(1A).

(2) In section 80(3) to (3C), (4A), (4C) and (6), as applied by sub-paragraph (1)—

(*a*) references to the crediting of amounts are to be read as including the payment of amounts;

(*b*) references to a prescribed accounting period include a tax period.

(3) The Commissioners are not liable to repay the overpaid amount on a claim made—

(*a*) under paragraph 16I(2),or

(*b*) as mentioned in paragraph 16I(7)(*b*),

if the claim is made more than 4 years after the relevant date.

(4) On a claim made under paragraph 16I(3), the Commissioners are not liable to credit the amount not due if the claim is made more than 4 years after the relevant date.

(5) The "relevant date" is—

(*a*) in the case of a claim under paragraph 16I(1), the end of the tax period mentioned in paragraph 16I(1)(*a*), except in the case of a claim resulting from an incorrect disclosure;

(*b*) in the case of a claim under paragraph 16I(1) resulting from an incorrect disclosure, the end of the tax period in which the disclosure was made;

(*c*) in the case of a claim under paragraph 16I(2), the date on which the payment was made;

(*d*) in the case of a claim under paragraph 16I(3), the end of the quarter in which the assessment was made.

(6) A person makes an "incorrect disclosure" where—

(*a*) the person discloses to the tax authorities in question (whether the Commissioners or the tax authorities for the administering member State) that the person has not brought into account for a tax period an amount of UK VAT due for the period ("the disclosed amount"),

(*b*) the disclosure is made in a later tax period, and

(*c*) some or all of the disclosed amount is not in fact VAT due.][1]

Commentary—*De Voil Indirect Tax Service* **V2.189L.**

Regulations—VAT (Amendment) (No 3) Regulations, SI 2014/2430.

Amendments—[1] Part 3 (paras 16–16N) substituted by FA 2014 s 103, Sch 22 paras 3, 8 with effect in relation to supplies made on or after 1 January 2015. Any amendment made by FA 2014 Sch 22 so far as it confers power to make regulations has effect from 17 July 2014 (FA 2014 Sch 22 para 23(2)(*b*)). Part 3, as it applied in relation to supplies made before 1 January 2015, is reproduced below after para 16N.

[Increase or decrease in consideration for a supply

16K—(1) This paragraph applies where—

(*a*) a person makes a special scheme return for a tax period ("the affected tax period") relating (wholly or partly) to a UK supply, and

(*b*) after the return has been made the amount of the consideration for the UK supply increases or decreases.

(2) The person must, in the tax period in which the increase or decrease is accounted for in the person's business accounts—

(*a*) amend the special scheme return to take account of the increase or decrease, or

(*b*) (if the period during which the person is entitled under Article 61 of the Implementing Regulation to amend the special scheme return has expired) notify the Commissioners of the adjustment needed to the figures in the special scheme return because of the increase or decrease.

(3) Where the change to which an amendment or notice under sub-paragraph (2) relates is an increase in the consideration for a UK supply, the person must pay to the tax authorities for the administering member State (in accordance with Article 62 of the Implementing Regulation) or, in a case falling within sub-paragraph (2)(*b*), the Commissioners, the difference between—

(*a*) the amount of VAT that was chargeable on the supply before the increase in consideration, and

(*b*) the amount of VAT that is chargeable in respect of the whole of the increased consideration for the supply.

(4) Where the change to which an amendment or notice under sub-paragraph (2) relates is a decrease in the consideration for a UK supply, the amendment or notice has effect as a claim; and where a claim is made the Commissioners must repay any VAT paid by the person that would not have been VAT due from the person had the consideration for the supply always been the decreased amount.

(5) The Commissioners may by regulations specify—

(*a*) the latest time by which, and the form and manner in which, a claim or other notice under sub-paragraph (2)(*b*) must be given;

(*b*) the latest time by which, and the form in which, a payment under sub-paragraph (3) must be made in a case within sub-paragraph (2)(*b*).

(6) A payment made under sub-paragraph (3) in a case within sub-paragraph (2)(*a*) must be made before the end of the tax period referred to in sub-paragraph (2).

(7) In this paragraph "UK supply" means a supply of scheme services that is treated as made in the United Kingdom.][1]

Commentary—*De Voil Indirect Tax Service* **V2.189L**.

Regulations—VAT (Amendment) (No 3) Regulations, SI 2014/2430.

Amendments—[1] Part 3 (paras 16–16N) substituted by FA 2014 s 103, Sch 22 paras 3, 8 with effect in relation to supplies made on or after 1 January 2015. Any amendment made by FA 2014 Sch 22 so far as it confers power to make regulations has effect from 17 July 2014 (FA 2014 Sch 22 para 23(2)(*b*)). Part 3, as it applied in relation to supplies made before 1 January 2015, is reproduced below after para 16N.

[Bad debts

16L Where a participant in a special scheme—

(*a*) has submitted a special scheme return to the tax authorities for the administering member State, and

(*b*) amends the return to take account of the writing-off as a bad debt of the whole or part of the consideration for a supply of scheme services that is treated as made in the United Kingdom,

the amending of the return may be treated as the making of a claim to the Commissioners for the purposes of section 36(2) (bad debts: claim for refund of VAT).][1]

Commentary—*De Voil Indirect Tax Service* **V2.189L**.

Regulations—VAT (Amendment) (No 3) Regulations, SI 2014/2430.

Amendments—[1] Part 3 (paras 16–16N) substituted by FA 2014 s 103, Sch 22 paras 3, 8 with effect in relation to supplies made on or after 1 January 2015. Any amendment made by FA 2014 Sch 22 so far as it confers power to make regulations has effect from 17 July 2014 (FA 2014 Sch 22 para 23(2)(*b*)). Part 3, as it applied in relation to supplies made before 1 January 2015, is reproduced below after para 16N.

[Penalties for errors: disclosure

16M Where a person corrects a special scheme return in a way that constitutes telling the tax authorities for the administering member State about—

(*a*) an inaccuracy in the return,

(*b*) a supply of false information, or

(*c*) a withholding of information,

the person is regarded as telling HMRC about that for the purposes of paragraph 9 of Schedule 24 to the Finance Act 2007.][1]

Commentary—*De Voil Indirect Tax Service* **V2.189L**.

Amendments—[1] Part 3 (paras 16–16N) substituted by FA 2014 s 103, Sch 22 paras 3, 8 with effect in relation to supplies made on or after 1 January 2015. Any amendment made by FA 2014 Sch 22 so far as it confers power to make regulations has effect from 17 July 2014 (FA 2014 Sch 22 para 23(2)(*b*)). Part 3, as it applied in relation to supplies made before 1 January 2015, is reproduced below after para 16N.

[Set-offs

16N Where a participant in a special scheme is liable to pay UK VAT to the tax authorities for the administering member State in accordance with the scheme, the UK VAT is regarded for the purposes of section 130(6) of the Finance Act 2008 (set-off: England, Wales and Northern Ireland) as payable to the Commissioners.][1]

Commentary—*De Voil Indirect Tax Service* **V2.189L**.

Amendments—[1] Part 3 (paras 16–16N) substituted by FA 2014 s 103, Sch 22 paras 3, 8 with effect in relation to supplies made on or after 1 January 2015. Any amendment made by FA 2014 Sch 22 so far as it confers power to make regulations has effect from 17 July 2014 (FA 2014 Sch 22 para 23(2)(*b*)). Part 3, as it applied in relation to supplies made before 1 January 2015, read as follows—

"Part 3

Understatements and overstatements of UK VAT

Understatement or overstatement of UK VAT in special scheme return

16—

(1) If the Commissioners consider that a person who is or has been a participant in the special scheme has submitted a special scheme return which understates his liability to UK VAT, they may give him a notice—

identifying the return in which they consider that the understatement was made,

specifying the amount by which they consider that the person's liability to UK VAT has been understated, and

requesting him to pay that amount to the Controller within the period of 30 days beginning with the date on which the notice is given.

(2) If the Commissioners consider that a person who is or has been a participant in the special scheme has submitted a special scheme return which overstates his liability to UK VAT, they may give him a notice—

identifying the return in which they consider that the overstatement was made, and

specifying the amount by which they consider that the person's liability to UK VAT has been overstated.

(3) Where the Commissioners give a person a notice under sub-paragraph (2) above, they are liable to pay him the amount specified in the notice.

(4) No notice under this paragraph may be given more than 3 years after the end of the period for which the special scheme return in question was made.

(5) In this Schedule, "participant in the special scheme" means a person who—

is registered under this Schedule, or

is identified under any provision of the law of another member State which implements Article 26c.

(6) In this paragraph—

"special scheme return" means—

a special accounting return; or

a value added tax return submitted to the tax authorities of another member State;

"UK VAT" means VAT which a person is liable to pay (whether in the United Kingdom or another member State) in respect of qualifying supplies treated as made in the United Kingdom at a time when he is or was a participant in the special scheme;

"value added tax return", in relation to another member State, means any value added tax return required to be submitted under any provision of the law of that member State which implements Article 26c(*B*)(5) of the 1977 VAT Directive.".

PART 4
[OTHER PROVISIONS ABOUT SPECIAL SCHEMES]

Amendments—In heading to Part 4, words substituted for words "Application of provisions relating to VAT", by FA 2014 s 103, Sch 22 paras 3, 9(1), (8) with effect in relation to supplies made on or after 1 January 2015.

Registration under this Act

[17 [(1)] [2]Notwithstanding any provision in this Act to the contrary, a participant in the special scheme is not required to be registered under this Act by virtue of making qualifying supplies.

[(2) Where a participant in the special scheme ("the scheme participant") makes relevant supplies, it is to be assumed for all purposes of this Act relating to the determination of—

(*a*) whether or not VAT is chargeable under this Act on those supplies,

(*b*) how much VAT is chargeable under this Act on those supplies,

(*c*) the time at which those supplies are treated as taking place, and

(*d*) any other matter that the Commissioners may specify by regulations,

that the scheme participant is registered under this Act.

(3) Supplies of scheme services made by the scheme participant are "relevant supplies" if—

(*a*) the value of the supplies must be accounted for in a special scheme return, and

(*b*) the supplies are treated as made in the United Kingdom.]²]¹

Amendments—¹ Sch 3B inserted by FA 2003 s 23, Sch 2 paras 1, 4 with effect for qualifying supplies made after 30 June 2003, see FA 2003 s 23(2).

² Sub-para (1) numbered as such, and sub-paras (2), (3) inserted, by FA 2014 s 103, Sch 22 paras 3, 9(1)–(3) with effect in relation to supplies made on or after 1 January 2015.

De-registration

[18 Where a person who is registered under Schedule 1 [or 1A]² satisfies the Commissioners that he intends to apply for—

(*a*) registration under this Schedule, or

(*b*) identification under any provision of the law of another member State which implements [Section 2 of Chapter 6 of Title XII of the VAT Directive,]³ they may, if he so requests, cancel his registration under Schedule 1[or, as the case may be, 1A][2] with effect from the day on which the request is made or from such later date as may be agreed between him and the Commissioners.][1]

Amendments—[1] Sch 3B inserted by FA 2003 s 23, Sch 2 paras 1, 4 with effect for qualifying supplies made after 30 June 2003, see FA 2003 s 23(2).

[2] Words inserted by FA 2012 s 203, Sch 28 paras 2, 17 with effect in relation to supplies made or to be made on or after 1 December 2012.

[3] In para (*b*), words substituted for words "Article 26c," by FA 2014 s 103, Sch 22 paras 3, 9(1), (4) with effect in relation to supplies made on or after 1 January 2015.

[Value of supplies to connected persons

18A In paragraph 1 of Schedule 6 (valuation: supply to connected person at less than market value) the reference to a supply made by a taxable person is to be read as including a supply of scheme services that is made by a participant in the special scheme (and is treated as made in the United Kingdom).][1]

Amendments—[1] Para 18A inserted by FA 2014 s 103, Sch 22 paras 3, 9(1), (5) with effect in relation to supplies made on or after 1 January 2015.

VAT representatives

[19 Section 48(1) (VAT representatives) does not permit the Commissioners to direct a participant in the special scheme to appoint a VAT representative.][1]

Amendments—[1] Sch 3B inserted by FA 2003 s 23, Sch 2 paras 1, 4 with effect for qualifying supplies made after 30 June 2003, see FA 2003 s 23(2).

Appeals

[20—(1) An appeal shall lie to a tribunal with respect to any of the following—

(*a*) the registration or cancellation of the registration of any person under this Schedule;

[(*b*) a refusal to make a repayment under paragraph 16I (overpayments), or a decision by the Commissioners as to the amount of the repayment due under that provision;

(*c*) a refusal to make a repayment under paragraph 16K(4) (decrease in consideration);

(*d*) any liability to a surcharge under paragraph 16F (default surcharge).][3]

[(2) Part 5 (appeals), and any order or regulations under that Part, have effect as if an appeal under this paragraph were an appeal which lies to the tribunal under section 83(1) (but not under any particular paragraph of that subsection).][2]][1]

[(3) Where the Commissioners have made an assessment under section 73 in reliance on paragraph 16 or 16A—

(*a*) section 83(1)(*p*)(i): (appeals against assessments under section 73(1) etc) applies as if the relevant special scheme return were a return under this Act, and

(*b*) the references in section 84(3) and (5) to the matters mentioned in section 83(1)(*p*) are to be read accordingly.][3]

Amendments—[1] Sch 3B inserted by FA 2003 Sch 2 para 4 with effect in relation to qualifying supplies made after 30 June 2003, see FA 2003 s 23(2).

[2] Sub-para (2) substituted by the Transfer of Tribunal Functions and Revenue and Customs Appeals Order, SI 2009/56 art 3, Sch 1 para 227 with effect from 1 April 2009, subject to transitional and savings provisions in Sch 3 para 4.

[3] In sub-para (1), paras (*b*)–(*d*) substituted for previous paras (*b*), (*c*), and sub-para (3) inserted, by FA 2014 s 103, Sch 22 paras 3, 9(1), (6) with effect in relation to supplies made on or after 1 January 2015.

Payments on account of non-UK VAT to other member States

[21—(1) Neither—

(a) paragraph 1(2) of Schedule 11, nor

[(b) section 44 of the Commissioners for Revenue and Customs Act 2005,][2]

applies to money or securities for money collected or received for or on account of VAT if required to be paid to another member State by virtue of the VAT Co-operation Regulation.

(2) In sub-paragraph (1) above, "the VAT Co-operation Regulation" means the Council Regulation of 27 January 1992 on administrative co-operation in the field of indirect taxation (VAT) (218/92/EEC), as amended by the Council Regulation of 7 May 2002 (792/2002/EC) (which temporarily amends the VAT Co-operation Regulation as regards additional measures regarding electronic commerce).][1], [3]

Amendments—[1] Sch 3B inserted by FA 2003 Sch 2 para 4 with effect in relation to qualifying supplies made after 30 June 2003, see FA 2003 s 23(2).

[2] Sub-para (1)(b) substituted by Commissioners for Revenue and Customs Act 2005 s 50, Sch 4 para 55 with effect from 18 April 2005 by virtue of the Commissioners for Revenue and Customs Act 2005 (Commencement) Order, SI 2005/1126, art 2(2).

[3] Para 21 and preceding heading repealed by FA 2014 s 103, Sch 22 paras 3, 9(1), (7) with effect in relation to supplies made on or after 1 January 2015. See also para 15A above as inserted by FA 2014 Sch 22 para 7(7)).

Refund of UK VAT

[22—(1) The provisions which give effect to the 1986 VAT Refund Directive in the United Kingdom have effect in relation to a participant in the special scheme, but with the following modifications.

(2) The provision which gives effect to Article 2(1) of the 1986 VAT Refund Directive (as at 9th April 2003, see regulation 186 of the Value Added Tax Regulations 1995) shall apply in relation to a participant in the special scheme, but only so as to entitle him to a refund of VAT charged on—

(*a*) goods imported by him into the United Kingdom, and

(*b*) supplies made to him in the United Kingdom,

in connection with the making by him of qualifying supplies while he is a participant in the special scheme.

(3) The following provisions shall be omitted.

(4) The first provision is that which gives effect to Article 1(1) of the 1986 VAT Refund Directive, so far as it requires a member State to prevent a person who is deemed to have supplied services in that member State during a period from being granted a refund of VAT for that period (as at 9th April 2003, see regulation 188(2)(*b*) of the Value Added Tax Regulations 1995).

(5) The second provision is that which gives effect to Article 2(2) of the 1986 VAT Refund Directive (which permits member States to make refunds conditional upon the granting by third States of comparable advantages regarding turnover taxes: as at 9th April 2003, see regulation 188(1) of the Value Added Tax Regulations 1995).

(6) The third provision is that which gives effect to Article 2(3) of the 1986 VAT Refund Directive (which permits member States to require the appointment of a tax representative: as at 9th April 2003, see regulation 187 of the Value Added Tax Regulations 1995).

(7) The fourth provision is that which gives effect to Article 4(2) of the 1986 VAT Refund Directive (which permits member States to provide for the exclusion of certain expenditure and to make refunds subject to additional conditions).

(8) In this paragraph "the 1986 VAT Refund Directive" means the Thirteenth Council Directive of 17th November 1986 on the harmonisation of the laws of the member States relating to turnover taxes—arrangements for the refund of value added tax to taxable persons not established in Community territory (86/560/EEC).][1]

Amendments—[1] Sch 3B inserted by FA 2003 s 23, Sch 2 paras 1, 4 with effect for qualifying supplies made after 30 June 2003, see FA 2003 s 23(2).

PART 5
SUPPLEMENTARY

Interpretation

[23—(1) In this Schedule—

"the 1977 VAT Directive" means the Sixth Council Directive of 17 May 1977 on the harmonisation of the laws of the member States relating to turnover taxes—common system of value added tax: uniform basis of assessment (77/388/EEC);

"the 2002 VAT Directive" means the Council Directive of 7 May 2002 amending and amending temporarily the 1977 VAT Directive as regards the value added tax arrangements applicable to radio and television broadcasting services and certain electronically supplied services (2002/38/EC);

["administering member State", in relation to a special scheme, means the member State under whose law the scheme is established (whether that is the United Kingdom or another member State);

"the Implementing Regulation" means Implementing Regulation (EU) No 282/2011;][2]

["participant in the special scheme" means a person who—

(*a*) is registered under this Schedule, or

(*b*) is identified under any provision of the law of another member State which implements Section 2 of Chapter 6 of Title XII of the VAT Directive;][2]

"qualifying supply" has the meaning given by paragraph 3 above;

"registration number" means the number allocated to a person on his registration under this Schedule in accordance with paragraph 6(*a*) above;

"registration request" is to be construed in accordance with paragraph 4(1)(*b*) above;

["relevant special scheme return" has the meaning given by paragraph 16(3);][2]

"reporting period" is to be construed in accordance with paragraph 11(2) above;

["scheme services" means electronically supplied services, broadcasting services or telecommunication services (and in this definition "electronically supplied services", "broadcasting services" and
"telecommunication services" have the meaning given by paragraph 3(2));][2]

"special accounting return" is to be construed in accordance with paragraph 11(1) above.

["special scheme" means—

(*a*) the accounting scheme under this Schedule, or

(*b*) any other scheme, under the law of another member State, implementing Section 2 of Title XII of Directive 2006/112/EC;

"special scheme return" means—

(*a*) a special accounting return, or

(*b*) a value added tax return submitted to the tax authorities of another member State;

"tax period" means—

(*a*) a reporting period (under the accounting scheme under this Schedule), or

(*b*) any other period for which a person is required to make a return under a special scheme;

"UK VAT" means VAT which a person is liable to pay (whether in the United Kingdom or another member State) in respect of qualifying supplies treated as made in the United Kingdom at a time when the person is or was a participant in the special scheme;

"value added tax return", in relation to another member State, means any value added tax return required to be submitted under any provision of the law of that member State which implements Article 364 of the VAT Directive (as substituted by Article 5(11) of Council Directive 2008/8/EC);

"the VAT Directive" has the meaning given by paragraph 2(7);][2]

(2) References in this Schedule to a qualifying supply being "treated as made" in a member State are references to its being treated as made—

(*a*) in the United Kingdom, by [paragraph 15 of Schedule 4A (place of supply of electronic, telecommunication and broadcasting services),][2] or

(*b*) in another member State, by virtue of any provision of the law of that member State which gives effect to that Article.

(3) The provision which, as at 9th April 2003, is to give effect in the United Kingdom to Article 9(2)(*f*) of the 1977 VAT Directive (as mentioned in sub-paragraph (2)(*a*) above) is article 16A of the Value Added Tax (Place of Supply of Services) Order 1992 (which is prospectively inserted by article 3 of the Value Added Tax (Place of Supply of Services) (Amendment) Order 2003).][1]

Amendments—[1] Sch 3B inserted by FA 2003 s 23, Sch 2 paras 1, 4 with effect for qualifying supplies made after 30 June 2003, see FA 2003 s 23(2).

[2] In sub-para (1) definitions substituted and inserted, in sub-para (2)(*a*), words substituted for words "virtue of any provision which gives effect in the United Kingdom to Article 9(2)(*f*) of the 1977 VAT Directive (which is inserted by Article 1(1)(*b*) of the 2002 VAT Directive),", and sub-para (3) repealed, by FA 2014 s 103, Sch 22 paras 3, 10 with effect in relation to supplies made on or after 1 January 2015.

[SCHEDULE 3BA

ELECTRONIC, TELECOMMUNICATION AND BROADCASTING SERVICES: UNION SCHEME

Amendments—Sch 3BA inserted by FA 2014 s 103, Sch 22 para 1 with effect in relation to supplies made on or after 1 January 2015, except in so far as it confers power to make regulations in which case it has effect from 17 July 2014.

No registration under Sch 3BA may take effect before 1 January 2015. A request for registration under Sch 3BA that is made before 1 October 2014 is to be treated for the purposes of Article 57d of Implementing Regulation (EU) No 282/2011 (registration to have effect from first day of subsequent quarter) as if it were made on that date (FA 2014 Sch 22 para 24).

PART 1
INTRODUCTION

Overview

1 In this Schedule—

(*a*) Parts 2 and 3 establish a special accounting scheme (called the "Union scheme") which may be used by certain persons established in the United Kingdom who make supplies of electronically supplied, telecommunication or broadcasting services that are treated as made in other member States;

(*b*) Part 4 is about persons participating in schemes in other member States that correspond to the Union scheme;

(*c*) Part 5 is about appeals;

(*d*) Part 6 contains definitions for the Schedule.][1]

Amendments—[1] Sch 3BA inserted by FA 2014 s 103, Sch 22 para 1 with effect in relation to supplies made on or after 1 January 2015, except in so far as it confers power to make regulations in which case it has effect from 17 July 2014. No registration under Sch 3BA may take effect before 1 January 2015. A request for registration under Sch 3BA that is made before 1 October 2014 is to be treated for the purposes of Article 57d of Implementing Regulation (EU) No 282/2011 (registration to have effect from first day of subsequent quarter) as if it were made on that date (FA 2014 Sch 22 para 24).

[Meaning of "scheme services"

2—(1) In this Schedule "scheme services" means electronically supplied services, broadcasting services or telecommunication services.

(2) In sub-paragraph (1)—

"broadcasting services" means radio and television broadcasting services;

"electronically supplied services" has the same meaning as in Schedule 4A (see paragraph 9(3) and (4) of that Schedule);

"telecommunication services" has the same meaning as in Schedule 4A (see paragraph 8(2) of that Schedule).][1]

Amendments—[1] Sch 3BA inserted by FA 2014 s 103, Sch 22 para 1 with effect in relation to supplies made on or after 1 January 2015, except in so far as it confers power to make regulations in which case it has effect from 17 July 2014. No registration under Sch 3BA may take effect before 1 January 2015. A request for registration under Sch 3BA that is made before 1 October 2014 is to be treated for the purposes of Article 57d of Implementing Regulation (EU) No 282/2011 (registration to have effect from first day of subsequent quarter) as if it were made on that date (FA 2014 Sch 22 para 24).

[PART 2
UNION SCHEME: REGISTRATION

The register

3 Persons registered under the scheme provided for by this Schedule ("the Union scheme") are to be registered in a single register kept by the Commissioners for the purposes of the scheme.][1]

Amendments—[1] Sch 3BA inserted by FA 2014 s 103, Sch 22 para 1 with effect in relation to supplies made on or after 1 January 2015, except in so far as it confers power to make regulations in which case it has effect from 17 July 2014. No registration under Sch 3BA may take effect before 1 January 2015. A request for registration under Sch 3BA that is made before 1 October 2014 is to be treated for the purposes of Article 57d of Implementing Regulation (EU) No 282/2011 (registration to have effect from first day of subsequent quarter) as if it were made on that date (FA 2014 Sch 22 para 24).

[Persons who may be registered

4 (1) A person may register under the Union scheme if all the following conditions are met—

(*a*) the person makes or intends to make one or more qualifying supplies of scheme services in the course of a business that the person carries on;

(*b*) either the person's business is established in the United Kingdom or (if the person's business is not established in any member State) the person has a fixed establishment in the United Kingdom;

(*c*) the person is not barred from registering by sub-paragraph (3), by the second paragraph of Article 369a(2) of Directive 2006/112/EC or by any provision of the Implementing Regulation;

(*d*) the person is registered under Schedule 1.

(2) A supply of scheme services is a "qualifying supply of scheme services" if the following conditions are met.

1. The recipient of the services must belong in a member State other than the United Kingdom and must not be a relevant business person.
2. The person making the supply must not have a fixed establishment in the member State in which the recipient belongs.

(3) A person may not be registered under the Union scheme if the person is a participant in a non-UK special scheme (see paragraph 38(1)).][1]

Amendments—[1] Sch 3BA inserted by FA 2014 s 103, Sch 22 para 1 with effect in relation to supplies made on or after 1 January 2015, except in so far as it confers power to make regulations in which case it has effect from 17 July 2014. No registration under Sch 3BA may take effect before 1 January 2015. A request for registration under Sch 3BA that is made before 1 October 2014 is to be treated for the purposes of Article 57d of Implementing Regulation (EU) No 282/2011 (registration to have effect from first day of subsequent quarter) as if it were made on that date (FA 2014 Sch 22 para 24).

Becoming registered

5—(1) The Commissioners must register under the Union scheme any person who—

(*a*) satisfies them that the requirements for registration are met, and

(*b*) makes a request in accordance with this paragraph (a "registration request").

(2) A registration request made by a person must state the person's—

(*a*) name and postal address, and

(*b*) electronic addresses (including any websites).

(3) A registration request made by a person must also state—

(*a*) whether or not the person has begun to make qualifying supplies of scheme services, and

(*b*) (if applicable) the date on which the person began to do so.

(4) A registration request made by a person must also state—

(*a*) whether or not the person has previously been identified under a non-UK special scheme, and

(*b*) (if applicable) the date on which the person was first identified under the scheme concerned.

(5) A registration request—

(*a*) must contain any further information, and any declaration about its contents, that the Commissioners may by regulations require;

(*b*) must be made by such electronic means, and in such manner, as the Commissioners may direct or may by regulations require.][1]

Regulations—VAT (Amendment) (No 3) Regulations, SI 2014/2430.

Amendments—[1] Sch 3BA inserted by FA 2014 s 103, Sch 22 para 1 with effect in relation to supplies made on or after 1 January 2015, except in so far as it confers power to make regulations in which case it has effect from 17 July 2014. No registration under Sch 3BA may take effect before 1 January 2015. A request for registration under Sch 3BA that is made before 1 October 2014 is to be treated for the purposes of Article 57d of Implementing Regulation (EU) No 282/2011 (registration to have effect from first day of subsequent quarter) as if it were made on that date (FA 2014 Sch 22 para 24).

[Notification of changes etc

6—(1) A person registered under the Union scheme must inform the Commissioners of the date when the person first makes qualifying supplies of scheme services (unless the person has already given the Commissioners the information mentioned in paragraph 5(3)(*b*)).

(2) That information, and any information a person is required to give under Article 57h of the Implementing Regulation (notification of certain changes), must be communicated by such electronic means, and in such manner, as the Commissioners may direct or may by regulations require.][1]

Regulations—VAT (Amendment) (No 3) Regulations, SI 2014/2430.

Amendments—[1] Sch 3BA inserted by FA 2014 s 103, Sch 22 para 1 with effect in relation to supplies made on or after 1 January 2015, except in so far as it confers power to make regulations in which case it has effect from 17 July 2014. No registration under Sch 3BA may take effect before 1 January 2015. A request for registration under Sch 3BA that is made before 1 October 2014 is to be treated for the purposes of Article 57d of Implementing Regulation (EU) No 282/2011 (registration to have effect from first day of subsequent quarter) as if it were made on that date (FA 2014 Sch 22 para 24).

[Cancellation of registration

7 The Commissioners must cancel the registration under the Union scheme of a person if—

(*a*) the person has ceased to make, or no longer intends to make, supplies of scheme services and has notified them of that fact;

(*b*) they otherwise determine that the person has ceased to make, or no longer intends to make, supplies of scheme services;

(*c*) the person has ceased to satisfy any of the other conditions for registration in paragraph 4(1) and has notified them of that fact,

(*d*) they otherwise determine that the person has ceased to satisfy any of those conditions, or

(*e*) they determine that the person has persistently failed to comply with the person's obligations under this Schedule or the Implementing Regulation.][1]

Amendments—[1] Sch 3BA inserted by FA 2014 s 103, Sch 22 para 1 with effect in relation to supplies made on or after 1 January 2015, except in so far as it confers power to make regulations in which case it has effect from 17 July 2014. No registration under Sch 3BA may take effect before 1 January 2015. A request for registration under Sch 3BA that is made before 1 October 2014 is to be treated for the purposes of Article 57d of Implementing Regulation (EU) No 282/2011 (registration to have effect from first day of subsequent quarter) as if it were made on that date (FA 2014 Sch 22 para 24).

[PART 3
UNION SCHEME : LIABILITY, RETURNS, PAYMENT ETC

Liability to pay non-UK VAT to Commissioners

8—(1) This paragraph applies where a person—

(*a*) makes a qualifying supply of scheme services, and

(*b*) is registered under the Union scheme when the supply is made.

(2) The person is liable to pay to the Commissioners the gross amount of VAT on the supply.

(3) The reference in sub-paragraph (2) to the gross amount of VAT on the supply is to the amount of VAT charged on the supply in accordance with the law of the member State in which the supply is treated as made, without any deduction of VAT pursuant to Article 168 of Directive 2006/112/EC.][1]

Amendments—[1] Sch 3BA inserted by FA 2014 s 103, Sch 22 para 1 with effect in relation to supplies made on or after 1 January 2015, except in so far as it confers power to make regulations in which case it has effect from 17 July 2014. No registration under Sch 3BA may take effect before 1 January 2015. A request for registration under Sch 3BA that is made before 1 October 2014 is to be treated for the purposes of Article 57d of Implementing Regulation (EU) No 282/2011 (registration to have effect from first day of subsequent quarter) as if it were made on that date (FA 2014 Sch 22 para 24).

[Union scheme returns

9—(1) A person who is or has been registered under the Union scheme must submit a return (a "Union scheme return") to the Commissioners for each reporting period.
(2) Each quarter for the whole or part of which a person is registered under the Union scheme is a "reporting period" for that person.][1]

Amendments—[1] Sch 3BA inserted by FA 2014 s 103, Sch 22 para 1 with effect in relation to supplies made on or after 1 January 2015, except in so far as it confers power to make regulations in which case it has effect from 17 July 2014. No registration under Sch 3BA may take effect before 1 January 2015. A request for registration under Sch 3BA that is made before 1 October 2014 is to be treated for the purposes of Article 57d of Implementing Regulation (EU) No 282/2011 (registration to have effect from first day of subsequent quarter) as if it were made on that date (FA 2014 Sch 22 para 24).

[Union scheme returns: further requirements

10—(1) A Union scheme return is to be made out in sterling.
(2) Any conversion from one currency into another for the purposes of sub-paragraph (1) is to be made using the exchange rates published by the European Central Bank—
(*a*) for the last day of the reporting period to which the Union scheme return relates, or
(*b*) if no such rate is published for that day, for the next day for which such a rate is published.
(3) A Union scheme return—
(*a*) must be submitted to the Commissioners within the 20 days after the last day of the reporting period to which it relates;
(*b*) must be submitted by such electronic means, and in such manner, as the Commissioners may direct or may by regulations require.][1]

Regulations—VAT (Amendment) (No 3) Regulations, SI 2014/2430.
Amendments—[1] Sch 3BA inserted by FA 2014 s 103, Sch 22 para 1 with effect in relation to supplies made on or after 1 January 2015, except in so far as it confers power to make regulations in which case it has effect from 17 July 2014. No registration under Sch 3BA may take effect before 1 January 2015. A request for registration under Sch 3BA that is made before 1 October 2014 is to be treated for the purposes of Article 57d of Implementing Regulation (EU) No 282/2011 (registration to have effect from first day of subsequent quarter) as if it were made on that date (FA 2014 Sch 22 para 24).

[Payment

11—(1) A person who is required to submit a Union scheme return must pay, by the deadline for submitting the return, the amounts required in accordance with paragraph 8 in respect of qualifying supplies of scheme services made in the reporting period to which the return relates.
(2) A payment under this paragraph must be made in such manner as the Commissioners may direct or may by regulations require.][1]

Amendments—[1] Sch 3BA inserted by FA 2014 s 103, Sch 22 para 1 with effect in relation to supplies made on or after 1 January 2015, except in so far as it confers power to make regulations in which case it has effect from 17 July 2014. No registration under Sch 3BA may take effect before 1 January 2015. A request for registration under Sch 3BA that is made before 1 October 2014 is to be treated for the purposes of Article 57d of Implementing Regulation (EU) No 282/2011 (registration to have effect from first day of subsequent quarter) as if it were made on that date (FA 2014 Sch 22 para 24).

[Availability of records

12 (1) A person who is registered under the Union scheme must make available to the Commissioners, on request, any obligatory records the person is keeping of transactions entered into by the person while registered under the scheme.
(2) The records must be made available by electronic means.
(3) In sub-paragraph (1) "obligatory records" means records kept in accordance with an obligation imposed in accordance with Article 369k of Directive 2006/112/EC.][1]

Amendments—[1] Sch 3BA inserted by FA 2014 s 103, Sch 22 para 1 with effect in relation to supplies made on or after 1 January 2015, except in so far as it confers power to make regulations in which case it has effect from 17 July 2014. No registration under Sch 3BA may take effect before 1 January 2015. A request for registration under Sch 3BA that is made before 1 October 2014 is to be treated for the purposes of Article 57d of Implementing Regulation (EU) No 282/2011 (registration to have effect from first day of subsequent quarter) as if it were made on that date (FA 2014 Sch 22 para 24).

[Amounts required to be paid to other member States

13 Section 44 of the Commissioners for Revenue and Customs Act 2005 (requirement to pay receipts into the Consolidated Fund) does not apply to any money received for or on account of VAT that is required to be paid to another member State under Article 46 of Council Regulation (EU) No 904/2010.][1]

Amendments—[1] Sch 3BA inserted by FA 2014 s 103, Sch 22 para 1 with effect in relation to supplies made on or after 1 January 2015, except in so far as it confers power to make regulations in which case it has effect from 17 July 2014. No registration under Sch 3BA may take effect before 1 January 2015. A request for registration under Sch 3BA that is made before 1 October 2014 is to be treated for the purposes of Article 57d of Implementing Regulation (EU) No 282/2011 (registration to have effect from first day of subsequent quarter) as if it were made on that date (FA 2014 Sch 22 para 24).

[PART 4
PERSONS REGISTERED UNDER NON-UK SPECIAL SCHEMES

Meaning of "non-UK special scheme"

14—(1) In this Schedule "non-UK special scheme" means any provision of the law of a member State other than the United Kingdom which implements Section 3 of Chapter 6 of Title XII of Directive 2006/ 112/EC.

(2) In relation to a non-UK special scheme, references to the "administering member State" are to the member State under whose law the scheme is established.][1]

Amendments—[1] Sch 3BA inserted by FA 2014 s 103, Sch 22 para 1 with effect in relation to supplies made on or after 1 January 2015, except in so far as it confers power to make regulations in which case it has effect from 17 July 2014. No registration under Sch 3BA may take effect before 1 January 2015. A request for registration under Sch 3BA that is made before 1 October 2014 is to be treated for the purposes of Article 57d of Implementing Regulation (EU) No 282/2011 (registration to have effect from first day of subsequent quarter) as if it were made on that date (FA 2014 Sch 22 para 24).

[Exemption from requirement to register under this Act

15—(1) A participant in a non-UK special scheme is not required to be registered under this Act by virtue of making supplies of scheme services in respect of which the participant is required to make returns under that scheme.

(2) Sub-paragraph (1) overrides any contrary provision in this Act.

(3) Where a participant in a non-UK special scheme who is not registered under this Act ("the unregistered person") makes relevant supplies, it is to be assumed for all purposes of this Act relating to the determination of—

(*a*) whether or not VAT is chargeable under this Act on those supplies,

(*b*) how much VAT is chargeable under this Act on those supplies,

(*c*) the time at which those supplies are treated as taking place, and

(*d*) any other matter that the Commissioners may specify by regulations,

that the unregistered person is registered under this Act.

(4) Supplies of scheme services made by the unregistered person are "relevant supplies" if—

(*a*) the value of the supplies must be accounted for in a return required to be made by the unregistered person under the non-UK special scheme, and

(*b*) the supplies are treated as made in the United Kingdom.][1]

Amendments—[1] Sch 3BA inserted by FA 2014 s 103, Sch 22 para 1 with effect in relation to supplies made on or after 1 January 2015, except in so far as it confers power to make regulations in which case it has effect from 17 July 2014. No registration under Sch 3BA may take effect before 1 January 2015. A request for registration under Sch 3BA that is made before 1 October 2014 is to be treated for the purposes of Article 57d of Implementing Regulation (EU) No 282/2011 (registration to have effect from first day of subsequent quarter) as if it were made on that date (FA 2014 Sch 22 para 24).

[De-registration

16—(1) Sub-paragraph (2) applies where a person who is registered under Schedule 1A—

(*a*) satisfies the Commissioners that the person intends to apply for identification under a non-UK special scheme, and

(*b*) asks the Commissioners to cancel the person's registration under Schedule 1A.

(2) The Commissioners may cancel the person's registration under Schedule 1A with effect from—

(*a*) the day on which the request is made, or

(*b*) a later date agreed between the person and the Commissioners.][1]

Amendments—[1] Sch 3BA inserted by FA 2014 s 103, Sch 22 para 1 with effect in relation to supplies made on or after 1 January 2015, except in so far as it confers power to make regulations in which case it has effect from 17 July 2014. No registration under Sch 3BA may take effect before 1 January 2015. A request for registration under Sch 3BA that is made before 1 October 2014 is to be treated for the purposes of Article 57d of Implementing Regulation (EU) No 282/2011 (registration to have effect from first day of subsequent quarter) as if it were made on that date (FA 2014 Sch 22 para 24).

[Scheme participants who are also registered under this Act

17—(1) A person who—

(*a*) is a participant in a non-UK special scheme, and

(*b*) is also registered, or required to be registered, under this Act,

is not required to discharge any obligation placed on the person as a taxable person, so far as the obligation relates to relevant supplies.

(2) The reference in sub-paragraph (1) to an obligation placed on the person as a taxable person is to an obligation—

(*a*) to which the person is subject under or by virtue of this Act, and

(*b*) to which the person would not be subject if the person were neither registered nor required to be registered under this Act.

(3) A supply made by a participant in a non-UK special scheme is a "relevant supply" if—

(*a*) the value of the supply must be accounted for in a return required to be made by the participant under the non-UK special scheme, and

(*b*) the supply is treated as made in the United Kingdom.

(4) The Commissioners may by regulations specify cases in relation to which sub-paragraph (1) is not to apply.

(5) In section 25(2) (deduction of input tax from output tax by taxable person) the reference to output tax that is due from the taxable person does not include any VAT that the taxable person is liable under a non-UK special scheme to pay to the tax authorities for the administering member State.][1]

Regulations—VAT (Amendment) (No 3) Regulations, SI 2014/2430.

Amendments—[1] Sch 3BA inserted by FA 2014 s 103, Sch 22 para 1 with effect in relation to supplies made on or after 1 January 2015, except in so far as it confers power to make regulations in which case it has effect from 17 July 2014. No registration under Sch 3BA may take effect before 1 January 2015. A request for registration under Sch 3BA that is made before 1 October 2014 is to be treated for the purposes of Article 57d of Implementing Regulation (EU) No 282/2011 (registration to have effect from first day of subsequent quarter) as if it were made on that date (FA 2014 Sch 22 para 24).

[Value of supplies to connected persons

18 In paragraph 1 of Schedule 6 (valuation: supply to connected person at less than market value) the reference to a supply made by a taxable person is to be read as including a supply of scheme services that is made by a participant in a non-UK special scheme (and is treated as made in the United Kingdom).][1]

Amendments—[1] Sch 3BA inserted by FA 2014 s 103, Sch 22 para 1 with effect in relation to supplies made on or after 1 January 2015, except in so far as it confers power to make regulations in which case it has effect from 17 July 2014. No registration under Sch 3BA may take effect before 1 January 2015. A request for registration under Sch 3BA that is made before 1 October 2014 is to be treated for the purposes of Article 57d of Implementing Regulation (EU) No 282/2011 (registration to have effect from first day of subsequent quarter) as if it were made on that date (FA 2014 Sch 22 para 24).

[Refund of VAT on supplies of goods and services supplied to scheme participant

19 The power of the Commissioners to make regulations under section 39 (repayment of VAT to those in business overseas) includes power to make provision for giving effect to the second sentence of Article 369j of Directive 2006/112/EC (which provides for VAT on certain supplies to participants in special accounting schemes to be refunded in accordance with Directive 2008/9/EC).][1]

Regulations—VAT (Amendment) (No 3) Regulations, SI 2014/2430.

Amendments—[1] Sch 3BA inserted by FA 2014 s 103, Sch 22 para 1 with effect in relation to supplies made on or after 1 January 2015, except in so far as it confers power to make regulations in which case it has effect from 17 July 2014. No registration under Sch 3BA may take effect before 1 January 2015. A request for registration under Sch 3BA that is made before 1 October 2014 is to be treated for the purposes of Article 57d of Implementing Regulation (EU) No 282/2011 (registration to have effect from first day of subsequent quarter) as if it were made on that date (FA 2014 Sch 22 para 24).

[Assessments: general modifications of section 73

20—(1) For the purposes of this Schedule, section 73 (assessments: incorrect returns etc) is to be read as if—

(*a*) the reference in subsection (1) of that section to returns required under this Act included relevant non-UK returns, and

(*b*) references in that section to a prescribed accounting period included a tax period.

(2) See also the modifications in paragraph 21.

(3) In this Schedule "relevant non-UK return" means a non-UK return (see paragraph 38(1)) that is required to be made (wholly or partly) in respect of supplies of scheme services that are treated as made in the United Kingdom.][1]

Amendments—[1] Sch 3BA inserted by FA 2014 s 103, Sch 22 para 1 with effect in relation to supplies made on or after 1 January 2015, except in so far as it confers power to make regulations in which case it has effect from 17 July 2014. No registration under Sch 3BA may take effect before 1 January 2015. A request for registration under Sch 3BA that is made before 1 October 2014 is to be treated for the purposes of Article 57d of Implementing Regulation (EU) No 282/2011 (registration to have effect from first day of subsequent quarter) as if it were made on that date (FA 2014 Sch 22 para 24).

[Assessment in connection with increase in consideration

21—(1) Sub-paragraphs (2) to (4) make modifications of sections 73 and 76 which—

(*a*) have effect for the purposes of this Schedule, and

(*b*) are in addition to any other modifications of those sections made by this Schedule.

(2) Section 73 has effect as if the following were inserted after subsection (3) of that section—

"(3A) Where a person has failed to make an amendment or notification that the person is required to make under paragraph 31 of Schedule 3BA in respect of an increase in the consideration for a UK supply (as defined in paragraph 31(7)), the Commissioners may assess the amount of VAT due from the person as a result of the increase to the best of their judgement and notify it to the person.

(3B) An assessment under subsection (3A)—

(*a*) is of VAT due for the tax period mentioned in paragraph 31(1)(*a*) of Schedule 3BA;

(*b*) must be made within the time limits provided for in section 77, and must not be made after the later of—

(i) 2 years after the end of the tax period referred to in paragraph 31(1)(*a*);

(ii) one year after evidence of facts sufficient in the opinion of the Commissioners to justify making the assessment comes to their knowledge.

(3C) Subject to section 77, where further evidence such as is mentioned in subsection (3B)(*b*)(ii) comes to the Commissioners' knowledge after they have made an assessment under subsection (3A), another assessment may be made under that subsection, in addition to any earlier assessment."

(3) The reference in section 73(9) to subsection (1) of that section is taken to include a reference to section 73(3A) (as inserted by sub-paragraph (2)).

(4) Section 76 (assessment of amounts due by way of interest etc) is to be read as if the reference in subsection (5) of that section to section 73(1) included a reference to section 73(3A) (as inserted by sub-paragraph (2)).][1]

Amendments—[1] Sch 3BA inserted by FA 2014 s 103, Sch 22 para 1 with effect in relation to supplies made on or after 1 January 2015, except in so far as it confers power to make regulations in which case it has effect from 17 July 2014. No registration under Sch 3BA may take effect before 1 January 2015. A request for registration under Sch 3BA that is made before 1 October 2014 is to be treated for the purposes of Article 57d of Implementing Regulation (EU) No 282/2011 (registration to have effect from first day of subsequent quarter) as if it were made on that date (FA 2014 Sch 22 para 24).

[Assessments: consequential modifications

22 References to prescribed accounting periods in the following provisions are to be read in accordance with the modifications made by paragraphs 20 and 21—

(*a*) section 74 (interest on VAT recovered or recoverable by assessment);

(*b*) section 76 (assessment of amounts due by way of penalty, interest or surcharge);

(*c*) section 77 (assessment: time limits).][1]

Amendments—[1] Sch 3BA inserted by FA 2014 s 103, Sch 22 para 1 with effect in relation to supplies made on or after 1 January 2015, except in so far as it confers power to make regulations in which case it has effect from 17 July 2014. No registration under Sch 3BA may take effect before 1 January 2015. A request for registration under Sch 3BA that is made before 1 October 2014 is to be treated for the purposes of Article 57d of Implementing Regulation (EU) No 282/2011 (registration to have effect from first day of subsequent quarter) as if it were made on that date (FA 2014 Sch 22 para 24).

[Deemed amendments of relevant non-UK returns

23 (1) Where a person who has made a relevant non-UK return makes a claim under paragraph 29(7)(*b*) (overpayments) in relation to an error in the return, the relevant non-UK return is taken for the purposes of this Act to have been amended by the information in the claim.

(2) Where a person who has made a relevant non-UK return gives the Commissioners a notice relating to the return under paragraph 31(2)(*b*) (increase or decrease in consideration), the relevant non- UK return is taken for the purposes of this Act to have been amended by that information.

(3) Where (in a case not falling within sub-paragraph (1) or (2)) a person who has made a relevant non-UK return notifies the Commissioners (after the expiry of the period during which the non-UK return may be amended under Article 61 of the Implementing Regulation) of a change that needs to be made to the return to correct an error, or rectify an omission, in it, the relevant non-UK return is taken for the purposes of this Act to have been amended by that information.

(4) The Commissioners may by regulations—

(*a*) specify within what period and in what form and manner notice is to be given under sub-paragraph (3);

(*b*) require notices to be supported by documentary evidence described in the regulations.][1]

Regulations—VAT (Amendment) (No 3) Regulations, SI 2014/2430.

Amendments—[1] Sch 3BA inserted by FA 2014 s 103, Sch 22 para 1 with effect in relation to supplies made on or after 1 January 2015, except in so far as it confers power to make regulations in which case it has effect from 17 July 2014. No registration under Sch 3BA may take effect before 1 January 2015. A request for registration under Sch 3BA that is made before 1 October 2014 is to be treated for the purposes of Article 57d of Implementing Regulation (EU) No 282/2011 (registration to have effect from first day of subsequent quarter) as if it were made on that date (FA 2014 Sch 22 para 24).

[Interest on VAT: "reckonable date"

24—(1) Sub-paragraph (2) states the "reckonable date" for the purposes of section 74(1) and (2) for any case where an amount carrying interest under that section—

(*a*) is an amount assessed under section 73(2) (refunds etc) in reliance on paragraph 20, or that could have been so assessed, and

(*b*) was correctly paid or credited to the person, but would not have been paid or credited to the person had the facts been as they later turn out to be.

(2) The "reckonable date" is the first day after the end of the tax period in which the events occurred as a result of which the Commissioners were authorised to make the assessment (that was or could have been made) under section 73(2).

(3) Sub-paragraph (4) states the "reckonable date" for any other case where an amount carrying interest under section 74 is assessed under section 74(1) or (2) in reliance on paragraph 20, or could have been so assessed.

(4) The "reckonable date" is taken to be the latest date by which a non- UK return was required to be made for the tax period to which the amount assessed relates.

(5) Where section 74(1) or (2) (interest on VAT recovered or recoverable by assessment) applies in relation to an amount assessed under section 73(3A) (as inserted by paragraph 21(2)), the "reckonable date" for the purposes of section 74(1) or (2) is taken to be the day after the end of the tax period referred to in paragraph 31(2).][1]

Amendments—[1] Sch 3BA inserted by FA 2014 s 103, Sch 22 para 1 with effect in relation to supplies made on or after 1 January 2015, except in so far as it confers power to make regulations in which case it has effect from 17 July 2014. No registration under Sch 3BA may take effect before 1 January 2015. A request for registration under Sch 3BA that is made before 1 October 2014 is to be treated for the purposes of Article 57d of Implementing Regulation (EU) No 282/2011 (registration to have effect from first day of subsequent quarter) as if it were made on that date (FA 2014 Sch 22 para 24).

Default surcharge: notice of special surcharge period

25 (1) A person who is required to make a relevant non-UK return for a tax period is regarded for the purposes of this paragraph and paragraph 26 as being in default in respect of that period if either—

(*a*) conditions 1A and 2A are met, or

(*b*) conditions 1B and 2B are met;

(but see also paragraph 27).

(2) For the purposes of sub-paragraph (1)(*a*)—

(*a*) condition 1A is that the tax authorities for the administering member State have not received the return by the deadline for submitting it;

(*b*) condition 2A is that those tax authorities have, in accordance with Article 60a of the Implementing Regulation, issued a reminder of the obligation to submit the return.

(3) For the purposes of sub-paragraph (1)(*b*)—

(*a*) condition 1B is that, by the deadline for submitting the return, the tax authorities for the administering member State have received the return but have not received the amount of VAT shown on the return as payable by the person in respect of the tax period;

(*b*) condition 2B is that those tax authorities have, in accordance with Article 60a of the Implementing Regulation, issued a reminder of the VAT outstanding.

(4) The Commissioners may serve on a person who is in default in respect of a tax period a notice (a "special surcharge liability notice") specifying a period—

(*a*) ending on the first anniversary of the last day of that tax period, and

(*b*) beginning on the date of the notice.

(5) A period specified under sub-paragraph (4) is a "special surcharge period".

(6) If a special surcharge liability notice is served in respect of a tax period which ends at or before the end of an existing special surcharge period, the special surcharge period specified in that notice must be expressed as a continuation of the existing special surcharge period (so that the existing period and its extension are regarded as a single special surcharge period).][1]

Amendments—[1] Sch 3BA inserted by FA 2014 s 103, Sch 22 para 1 with effect in relation to supplies made on or after 1 January 2015, except in so far as it confers power to make regulations in which case it has effect from 17 July 2014. No registration under Sch 3BA may take effect before 1 January 2015. A request for registration under Sch 3BA that is made before 1 October 2014 is to be treated for the purposes of Article 57d of Implementing Regulation (EU) No 282/2011 (registration to have effect from first day of subsequent quarter) as if it were made on that date (FA 2014 Sch 22 para 24).

[Further default after service of notice

26—(1) If a person on whom a special surcharge liability notice has been served—

(*a*) is in default in respect of a tax period ending within the special surcharge period specified in (or extended by) that notice, and

(*b*) has outstanding special scheme VAT for that tax period, the person is to be liable to a surcharge of the amount given by sub-paragraph (2).

(2) The surcharge is equal to whichever is the greater of—

(*a*) £30, and

(*b*) the specified percentage of the person's outstanding special scheme VAT for the tax period.

(3) The specified percentage depends on whether the tax period is the first, second or third etc in the default period in respect of which the person is in default and has outstanding special scheme VAT, and is—

(*a*) for the first such tax period, 2%;

(*b*) for the second such tax period, 5%;

(*c*) for the third such tax period, 10%;

(*d*) for each such tax period after the third, 15%.

(4) "Special scheme VAT", in relation to a person, means VAT that the person is liable to pay to the tax authorities for the administering member State under a non-UK special scheme in respect of supplies of scheme services treated as made in the United Kingdom.

(5) A person has "outstanding special scheme VAT" for a tax period if some or all of the special scheme VAT for which the person is liable in respect of that period has not been paid by the deadline for the person to submit a non-UK return for that period (and the amount unpaid is referred to in sub-paragraph (2)(*b*) as "the person's outstanding special scheme VAT" for the tax period).][1]

Amendments—[1] Sch 3BA inserted by FA 2014 s 103, Sch 22 para 1 with effect in relation to supplies made on or after 1 January 2015, except in so far as it confers power to make regulations in which case it has effect from 17 July 2014. No registration under Sch 3BA may take effect before 1 January 2015. A request for registration under Sch 3BA that is made before 1 October 2014 is to be treated for the purposes of Article 57d of Implementing Regulation (EU) No 282/2011 (registration to have effect from first day of subsequent quarter) as if it were made on that date (FA 2014 Sch 22 para 24).

[Default surcharge: exceptions for reasonable excuse etc

27—(1) A person who would otherwise have been liable to a surcharge under paragraph 26(1) is not to be liable to the surcharge if the person satisfies the Commissioners or, on appeal, the tribunal that, in the case of a default which is material to the surcharge—

(*a*) the non-UK return or, as the case may be, the VAT shown on that return, was despatched at such a time and in such manner that it was reasonable to expect that it would be received by the tax authorities for the administering member State within the appropriate time limit, or

(*b*) there is a reasonable excuse for the return or the VAT not having been so despatched.

(2) Where sub-paragraph (1) applies to a person—

(*a*) the person is treated as not having been in default in respect of the tax period in question, and

(*b*) accordingly, any special surcharge liability notice the service of which depended on that default is regarded as not having been served.

(3) A default is "material" to a surcharge if—

(*a*) it is the default which gives rise to the surcharge, under paragraph 26(1), or

(*b*) it is a default which was taken into account in the service of the special surcharge liability notice on which the surcharge depends and the person concerned has not previously been liable to a surcharge in respect of a tax period ending within the special surcharge period specified in or extended by that notice.

(4) A default is left out of account for the purposes of paragraphs 25(4) and 26(1) if—

(*a*) the conduct by virtue of which the person is in default is also conduct falling within section 69(1) (breaches of regulatory provisions), and

(*b*) by reason of that conduct the person concerned is assessed to a penalty under that section.

(5) If the Commissioners, after consultation with the Treasury, so direct, a default in respect of a tax period specified in the direction is to be left out of account for the purposes of paragraphs 25(4) and 26(1).

(6) Section 71(1) (meaning of "reasonable excuse") applies for the purposes of this paragraph as it applies for the purposes of sections 59 to 70.][1]

Amendments—[1] Sch 3BA inserted by FA 2014 s 103, Sch 22 para 1 with effect in relation to supplies made on or after 1 January 2015, except in so far as it confers power to make regulations in which case it has effect from 17 July 2014. No registration under Sch 3BA may take effect before 1 January 2015. A request for registration under Sch 3BA that is made before 1 October 2014 is to be treated for the purposes of Article 57d of Implementing Regulation (EU) No 282/2011 (registration to have effect from first day of subsequent quarter) as if it were made on that date (FA 2014 Sch 22 para 24).

[Interest in certain cases of official error

28—(1) Section 78 (interest in certain cases of official error) applies as follows in relation to a case where, due to an error on the part of the Commissioners—

(*a*) a person has accounted under a non-UK special scheme for an amount by way of UK VAT that was not UK VAT due from the person, and as a result the Commissioners are liable under paragraph 29 to pay (or repay) an amount to the person, or (*b*) (in a case not falling within paragraph (*a*)), a person has paid, in accordance with an obligation under a non-UK special scheme, an amount by way of UK VAT that was not UK VAT due from the person and which the Commissioners are in consequence liable to repay to the person.

(2) Section 78 has effect as if the condition in section 78(1)(*a*) were met in relation to that person.

(3) In the application of section 78 as a result of this paragraph, section 78(12)(*b*) is read as providing that any reference in that section to a return is to a return required to be made under a non-UK special scheme.

(4) In section 78, as it applies as a result of this section, "output tax" has the meaning that that expression would have if the reference in section 24(2) to a "taxable person" were to a "person".][1]

Amendments—[1] Sch 3BA inserted by FA 2014 s 103, Sch 22 para 1 with effect in relation to supplies made on or after 1 January 2015, except in so far as it confers power to make regulations in which case it has effect from 17 July 2014. No registration under Sch 3BA may take effect before 1 January 2015. A request for registration under Sch 3BA that is made before 1 October 2014 is to be treated for the purposes of Article 57d of Implementing Regulation (EU) No 282/2011 (registration to have effect from first day of subsequent quarter) as if it were made on that date (FA 2014 Sch 22 para 24).

[Overpayments

29—(1) A person may make a claim if the person—

(*a*) has made a non-UK return for a tax period relating wholly or partly to supplies of scheme services treated as made in the United Kingdom,

(*b*) has accounted to the tax authorities for the administering member State for VAT in respect of those supplies, and

(*c*) in doing so has brought into account as UK VAT due to those authorities an amount ("the overpaid amount") that was not UK VAT due to them.

(2) A person may make a claim if the person has, as a participant in a non-UK special scheme, paid (to the tax authorities for the administering member State or to the Commissioners) an amount by way of UK VAT that was not UK VAT due ("the overpaid amount"), otherwise than in the circumstances mentioned in sub-paragraph (1)(*c*).

(3) A person who is or has been a participant in a non-UK special scheme may make a claim if the Commissioners—

(*a*) have assessed the person to VAT for a tax period, and

(*b*) in doing so, have brought into account as VAT an amount ("the amount not due") that was not VAT due.

(4) Where a person makes a claim under sub-paragraph (1) or (2), the Commissioners must repay the overpaid amount to the person.

(5) Where a person makes a claim under sub-paragraph (3), the Commissioners must credit the person with the amount not due.

(6) Where—

(*a*) as a result of a claim under sub-paragraph (3) an amount is to be credited to a person, and

(*b*) after setting any sums against that amount under or by virtue of this Act, some or all of the amount remains to the person's credit,

the Commissioners must pay (or repay) to the person so much of the amount as remains to the person's credit.

(7) The reference in sub-paragraph (1) to a claim is to a claim made—

(*a*) by correcting, in accordance with Article 61 of the Implementing Regulation, the error in the non-UK return mentioned in sub-paragraph (1)(*a*), or

(*b*) (after the expiry of the period during which the non-UK return may be amended under Article 61) to the Commissioners.

(8) Sub-paragraphs (1) and (2) do not require any amount to be repaid except so far as that is required by Article 63 of the Implementing Regulation.][1]

Amendments—[1] Sch 3BA inserted by FA 2014 s 103, Sch 22 para 1 with effect in relation to supplies made on or after 1 January 2015, except in so far as it confers power to make regulations in which case it has effect from 17 July 2014. No registration under Sch 3BA may take effect before 1 January 2015. A request for registration under Sch 3BA that is made before 1 October 2014 is to be treated for the purposes of Article 57d of Implementing Regulation (EU) No 282/2011 (registration to have effect from first day of subsequent quarter) as if it were made on that date (FA 2014 Sch 22 para 24).

[Overpayments: supplementary

30—(1) In section 80—

(*a*) subsections (3) to (3C) (unjust enrichment), and

(*b*) subsections (4A), (4C) and (6) (recovery by assessment of amounts wrongly credited),

have effect as if a claim under paragraph 29(1) were a claim under section 80(1), a claim under paragraph 29(2) were a claim under section 80(1B) and a claim under paragraph 29(3) were a claim under section 80(1A).

(2) In section 80(3) to (3C), (4A), (4C) and (6), as applied by sub-paragraph (1)—

(*a*) references to the crediting of amounts are to be read as including the payment of amounts;

(*b*) references to a prescribed accounting period include a tax period.

(3) The Commissioners are not liable to repay the overpaid amount on a claim made—

(*a*) under paragraph 29(2),or

(*b*) as mentioned in paragraph 29(7)(*b*),

if the claim is made more than 4 years after the relevant date.

(4) On a claim made under paragraph 29(3), the Commissioners are not liable to credit the amount not due if the claim is made more than 4 years after the relevant date.

(5) The "relevant date" is—

(*a*) in the case of a claim under paragraph 29(1), the end of the tax period mentioned in paragraph 29(1)(*a*), except in the case of a claim resulting from an incorrect disclosure;

(*b*) in the case of a claim under paragraph 29(1) resulting from an incorrect disclosure, the end of the tax period in which the disclosure was made;

(*c*) in the case of a claim under paragraph 29(2), the date on which the payment was made;

(*d*) in the case of a claim under paragraph 29(3), the end of the quarter in which the assessment was made.

(6) A person makes an "incorrect disclosure" where—

(*a*) the person discloses to the tax authorities in question (whether the Commissioners or the tax authorities for the administering member State) that the person has not brought into account for a tax period an amount of UK VAT due for the period ("the disclosed amount"),

(*b*) the disclosure is made in a later tax period, and

(*c*) some or all of the disclosed amount is not in fact VAT due.][1]

Regulations—VAT (Amendment) (No 3) Regulations, SI 2014/2430.

Amendments—[1] Sch 3BA inserted by FA 2014 s 103, Sch 22 para 1 with effect in relation to supplies made on or after 1 January 2015, except in so far as it confers power to make regulations in which case it has effect from 17 July 2014. No registration under Sch 3BA may take effect before 1 January 2015. A request for registration under Sch 3BA that is made before 1 October 2014 is to be treated for the purposes of Article 57d of Implementing Regulation (EU) No 282/2011 (registration to have effect from first day of subsequent quarter) as if it were made on that date (FA 2014 Sch 22 para 24).

[Increase or decrease in consideration for a supply

31—(1) This paragraph applies where—

(*a*) a person makes a non-UK return for a tax period ("the affected tax period") relating (wholly or partly) to a UK supply, and

(*b*) after the return has been made the amount of the consideration for the UK supply increases or decreases.

(2) The person must, in the tax period in which the increase or decrease is accounted for in the person's business accounts—

(*a*) amend the non-UK return to take account of the increase or decrease, or

(*b*) (if the period during which the person is entitled under Article 61 of the Implementing Regulation to amend the non-UK return has expired) notify the Commissioners of the adjustment needed to the figures in the non-UK return because of the increase or decrease.

(3) Where the change to which an amendment or notice under sub-paragraph (2) relates is an increase in the consideration for a UK supply, the person must pay to the tax authorities for the administering member State (in accordance with Article 62 of the Implementing Regulation) or, in a case falling within sub-paragraph (2)(*b*), the Commissioners, the difference between—

(*a*) the amount of VAT that was chargeable on the supply before the increase in consideration, and

(*b*) the amount of VAT that is chargeable in respect of the whole of the increased consideration for the supply.

(4) Where the change to which an amendment or notice under sub-paragraph (2) relates is a decrease in the consideration for a UK supply, the amendment or notice has effect as a claim; and where a claim is made the Commissioners must repay any VAT paid by the person that would not have been VAT due from the person had the consideration for the supply always been the decreased amount.

(5) The Commissioners may by regulations specify—

(*a*) the latest time by which, and the form and manner in which, a claim or other notice under sub-paragraph (2)(b) must be given;

(*b*) the latest time by which, and the form in which, a payment under sub-paragraph (3) must be made in a case within sub-paragraph (2)(*b*).

(6) A payment made under sub-paragraph (3) in a case within sub-paragraph (2)(*a*) must be made before the end of the tax period referred to in sub-paragraph (2).

(7) In this paragraph "UK supply" means a supply of scheme services that is treated as made in the United Kingdom.][1]

Regulations—VAT (Amendment) (No 3) Regulations, SI 2014/2430.

Amendments—[1] Sch 3BA inserted by FA 2014 s 103, Sch 22 para 1 with effect in relation to supplies made on or after 1 January 2015, except in so far as it confers power to make regulations in which case it has effect from 17 July 2014. No registration under Sch 3BA may take effect before 1 January 2015. A request for registration under Sch 3BA that is made before 1 October 2014 is to be treated for the purposes of Article 57d of Implementing Regulation (EU) No 282/2011 (registration to have effect from first day of subsequent quarter) as if it were made on that date (FA 2014 Sch 22 para 24).

[Bad debts

32 Where a participant in a non-UK special scheme—

(*a*) has submitted a non-UK return to the tax authorities for the administering member State, and

(*b*) amends the return to take account of the writing-off as a bad debt of the whole or part of the consideration for a supply of scheme services that is treated as made in the United Kingdom,

the amending of the return may be treated as the making of a claim to the Commissioners for the purposes of section 36(2) (bad debts: claim for refund of VAT).][1]

Regulations—VAT (Amendment) (No 3) Regulations, SI 2014/2430.

Amendments—[1] Sch 3BA inserted by FA 2014 s 103, Sch 22 para 1 with effect in relation to supplies made on or after 1 January 2015, except in so far as it confers power to make regulations in which case it has effect from 17 July 2014. No registration under Sch 3BA may take effect before 1 January 2015. A request for registration under Sch 3BA that is made before 1 October 2014 is to be treated for the purposes of Article 57d of Implementing Regulation (EU) No 282/2011 (registration to have effect from first day of subsequent quarter) as if it were made on that date (FA 2014 Sch 22 para 24).

[Records relating to supplies in UK

33—(1) A person who is a participant in a non-UK special scheme must keep records of the transactions which the person enters into for the purposes of, or in connection with, relevant supplies.

(2) A supply made by a participant in a non-UK special scheme is a "relevant supply" if—

(*a*) the value of the supply must be accounted for in a return required to be made by the participant under the non-UK special scheme, and

(*b*) the supply is treated as made in the United Kingdom.

(3) The records must be sufficiently detailed to enable the Commissioners to determine whether any special scheme return submitted in respect of the supplies is correct.

(4) The records must be made available on request to the Commissioners by electronic means.

(5) Records must be kept for 10 years beginning with the 1 January following the date on which the transaction was entered into.][1]

Amendments—[1] Sch 3BA inserted by FA 2014 s 103, Sch 22 para 1 with effect in relation to supplies made on or after 1 January 2015, except in so far as it confers power to make regulations in which case it has effect from 17 July 2014. No registration under Sch 3BA may take effect before 1 January 2015. A request for registration under Sch 3BA that is made before 1 October 2014 is to be treated for the purposes of Article 57d of Implementing Regulation (EU) No 282/2011 (registration to have effect from first day of subsequent quarter) as if it were made on that date (FA 2014 Sch 22 para 24).

[Penalties for errors: disclosure

34 Where a person corrects a non-UK return in a way that constitutes telling the tax authorities for the administering member State about—

(*a*) an inaccuracy in the return,

(*b*) a supply of false information, or

(*c*) a withholding of information,

the person is regarded as telling HMRC about that for the purposes of paragraph 9 of Schedule 24 to the Finance Act 2007.][1]

Amendments—[1] Sch 3BA inserted by FA 2014 s 103, Sch 22 para 1 with effect in relation to supplies made on or after 1 January 2015, except in so far as it confers power to make regulations in which case it has effect from 17 July 2014. No registration under Sch 3BA may take effect before 1 January 2015. A request for registration under Sch 3BA that is made before 1 October 2014 is to be treated for the purposes of Article 57d of Implementing Regulation (EU) No 282/2011 (registration to have effect from first day of subsequent quarter) as if it were made on that date (FA 2014 Sch 22 para 24).

[Set-offs

35 Where a participant in a non-UK special scheme is liable to pay UK VAT to the tax authorities for the administering member State in accordance with the scheme, the UK VAT is regarded for the purposes of section 130(6) of the Finance Act 2008 (set-off: England, Wales and Northern Ireland) as payable to the Commissioners.][1]

Amendments—[1] Sch 3BA inserted by FA 2014 s 103, Sch 22 para 1 with effect in relation to supplies made on or after 1 January 2015, except in so far as it confers power to make regulations in which case it has effect from 17 July 2014. No registration under Sch 3BA may take effect before 1 January 2015. A request for registration under Sch 3BA that is made before 1 October 2014 is to be treated for the purposes of Article 57d of Implementing Regulation (EU) No 282/2011 (registration to have effect from first day of subsequent quarter) as if it were made on that date (FA 2014 Sch 22 para 24).

[PART 5

APPEALS

36—(1) An appeal lies to the tribunal with respect to any of the following—

(*a*) a refusal to register a person under the Union scheme;

(*b*) the cancellation of the registration of any person under the Union scheme;

(*c*) a refusal to make a repayment under paragraph 29 (overpayments), or a decision by the Commissioners as to the amount of the repayment due under that provision;

(*d*) a refusal to make a repayment under paragraph 31(4) (decrease in consideration);

(*e*) any liability to a surcharge under paragraph 26 (default surcharge).

(2) Part 5 of this Act (appeals), and any order or regulations under that Part, have effect as if an appeal under this paragraph were an appeal which lies to the tribunal under section 83(1) (but not under any particular paragraph of that subsection).][1]

Amendments—[1] Sch 3BA inserted by FA 2014 s 103, Sch 22 para 1 with effect in relation to supplies made on or after 1 January 2015, except in so far as it confers power to make regulations in which case it has effect from 17 July 2014. No registration under Sch 3BA may take effect before 1 January 2015. A request for registration under Sch 3BA that is made before 1 October 2014 is to be treated for the purposes of Article 57d of Implementing Regulation (EU) No 282/2011 (registration to have effect from first day of subsequent quarter) as if it were made on that date (FA 2014 Sch 22 para 24).

[37 Where the Commissioners have made an assessment under section 73 in reliance on paragraph 20 or 21—

(*a*) section 83(1)(*p*)(i): (appeals against assessments under section 73(1) etc) applies as if the relevant non-UK return were a return under this Act, and

(*b*) the references in section 84(3) and (5) to the matters mentioned in section 83(1)(*p*) are to be read accordingly.][1]

Amendments—[1] Sch 3BA inserted by FA 2014 s 103, Sch 22 para 1 with effect in relation to supplies made on or after 1 January 2015, except in so far as it confers power to make regulations in which case it has effect from 17 July 2014. No registration under Sch 3BA may take effect before 1 January 2015. A request for registration under Sch 3BA that is made before 1 October 2014 is to be treated for the purposes of Article 57d of Implementing Regulation (EU) No 282/2011 (registration to have effect from first day of subsequent quarter) as if it were made on that date (FA 2014 Sch 22 para 24).

[PART 6

INTERPRETATION OF SCHEDULE

38—(1) In this Schedule—

"administering member State", in relation to a non-UK special scheme, has the meaning given by paragraph 14(2);

"the Implementing Regulation" means Council Implementing Regulation (EU) No 282/2011;

"non-UK return" means a return required to be made, for a tax period, under a non-UK special scheme;

"non-UK special scheme" has the meaning given by paragraph 14(1);

"participant", in relation to a non-UK special scheme, means a person who is identified under that scheme;

"qualifying supply of scheme services" has the meaning given by paragraph 4(2);

"relevant non-UK return" has the meaning given by paragraph 20(3);

"reporting period" is to be read in accordance with paragraph 9(2);

"scheme services" has the meaning given by paragraph 2;

"tax period" means a period for which a person is required to make a return under a non-UK special scheme;

"UK VAT" means VAT in respect of supplies of scheme services treated as made in the United Kingdom;

"Union scheme" has the meaning given by paragraph 3;

"Union scheme return" has the meaning given by paragraph 9(1).

(2) In relation to a non-UK special scheme (or a non-UK return), references in this Schedule to "the tax authorities" are to the tax authorities for the member State under whose law the non-UK special scheme is established.

(3) References in this Schedule to a supply of scheme services being "treated as made" in the United Kingdom are to its being treated as made in the United Kingdom by paragraph 15 of Schedule 4A.][1]

Amendments—[1] Sch 3BA inserted by FA 2014 s 103, Sch 22 para 1 with effect in relation to supplies made on or after 1 January 2015, except in so far as it confers power to make regulations in which case it has effect from 17 July 2014. No registration under Sch 3BA may take effect before 1 January 2015. A request for registration under Sch 3BA that is made before 1 October 2014 is to be treated for the purposes of Article 57d of Implementing Regulation (EU) No 282/2011 (registration to have effect from first day of subsequent quarter) as if it were made on that date (FA 2014 Sch 22 para 24).

SCHEDULE 4

MATTERS TO BE TREATED AS SUPPLY OF GOODS OR SERVICES

Section 5

HMRC Manuals—VAT Guidance V1-3: Supply and consideration, para 2.7 (supplies of goods or services).
Simon's Tax Cases—*Philips Exports Ltd v C&E Comrs* [1990] STC 508*.

1—(1) Any transfer of the whole property in goods is a supply of goods; but, subject to sub-paragraph (2) below, the transfer—

(*a*) of any undivided share of the property, or

(*b*) of the possession of goods,

is a supply of services.

(2) If the possession of goods is transferred—

(*a*) under an agreement for the sale of the goods, or

(*b*) under agreements which expressly contemplate that the property also will pass at some time in the future (determined by, or ascertainable from, the agreements but in any case not later than when the goods are fully paid for),

it is then in either case a supply of the goods.

Commentary—*De Voil Indirect Tax Service* **V3.112, V3.113**.
HMRC Manuals—VAT Guidance V1-3: Supply and consideration, para 2.9 (definition of supply of goods).
Paras 2.11, 4.2 (supply of services).
Para 15.7 (distinguishing between an outright supply of goods or a lease hire (supply of services).
Press releases etc—C&E Business Brief 17/94 12-9-94 (transfer of milk quota without land is a supply of services).
Simon's Tax Cases—*Phillip Drakard Trading Ltd v C&E Comrs* [1992] STC 568*; *British Airways plc v C&E Comrs* [1996] STC 1127*, *Stewart (t/a GT Shooting) v C&E Comrs* [2002] STC 255.
Definitions—"Supply", s 5, Sch 4.

2 . . . [1]

Amendments—[1] Paragraph repealed by FA 1996 s 29(4), Sch 41 Pt IV(2), with effect in relation to supplies made after 31 December 1995.

3 The supply of any form of power, heat, refrigeration [or other cooling,][1] or ventilation is a supply of goods.

Commentary—*De Voil Indirect Tax Service* **V3.178**.
Definitions—"Supply", s 5, Sch 4.
Amendments—[1] Words inserted by F(No 3)A 2010 s 20(2) with effect in relation to supplies made on or after 1 January 2011.

4 The grant, assignment or surrender of a major interest in land is a supply of goods.

Commentary—*De Voil Indirect Tax Service* **V3.140A**.
Definitions—"Assignment", s 96(1); "major interest", s 96(1); "supply", s 5, Sch 4;
Cross reference—See VAT Regulations, SI 1995/2518 reg 85 (grant of tenancy or lease: consideration payable periodically: time of supply).

5—(1) Subject to sub-paragraph (2) below, where goods forming part of the assets of a business are transferred or disposed of by or under the directions of the person carrying on the business so as no longer to form part of those assets, whether or not for a consideration, that is a supply by him of goods.

(2) Sub-paragraph (1) above does not apply where the transfer or disposal is—

[(*a*) a business gift the cost of which, together with the cost of any other business gifts made to the same person in the same year, was not more than £50;][6]

[(*b*) the provision to a person, otherwise than for a consideration, of a sample of goods.][9]

[(2ZA) In sub-paragraph (2) above—

"business gift" means a gift of goods that is made in the course or furtherance of the business in question;

"cost", in relation to a gift of goods, means the cost to the donor of acquiring or, as the case may be, producing the goods;

"the same year", in relation to a gift, means any period of twelve months that includes the day on which the gift is made.][7]

[(2A) For the purposes of determining the cost to the donor of acquiring or producing goods of which he has made a gift, where—

(*a*) the acquisition by the donor of the goods, or anything comprised in the goods, was by means of a transfer of a business, or a part of a business, as a going concern,

(*b*) the assets transferred by that transfer included those goods or that thing, and

(*c*) the transfer of those assets is one falling by virtue of an order under section 5(3) (or under an enactment re-enacted in section 5(3)) to be treated as neither a supply of goods nor a supply of services, the donor and his predecessor or, as the case may be, all of his predecessors shall be treated as if they were the same person.][4]

(3) . . . [9]

(4) Where by or under the directions of a person carrying on a business goods held or used for the purposes of the business are put to any private use or are used, or made available to any person for use, for any purpose other than a purpose of the business, whether or not for a consideration, that is a supply of services.

[(4A) Sub-paragraph (4) does not apply (despite paragraph 9(1)) to—

(*a*) any interest in land,

(*b*) any building or part of a building,

(*c*) any civil engineering work or part of such a work,

(*d*) any goods incorporated or to be incorporated in a building or civil engineering work (whether by being installed as fixtures or fittings or otherwise),

(*e*) any ship, boat or other vessel, or

(*f*) any aircraft.][8]

(5) Neither sub-paragraph (1) nor [sub-paragraph (4) above][1] shall require anything which a person carrying on a business does otherwise than for a consideration in relation to any goods to be treated as a supply except in a case where that person [or any of his predecessors is a person who (disregarding this paragraph) has or will become][3] entitled—

[(*a*) under sections 25 and 26, to credit for the whole or any part of the VAT on the supply, acquisition or importation of those goods or of anything comprised in them; or

(*b*) under a scheme embodied in regulations made under section 39, to a repayment of VAT on the supply or importation of those goods or of anything comprised in them.][5]

[(5A) In relation to any goods or anything comprised in any goods, a person is the predecessor of another for the purposes of this paragraph if—

(*a*) that other person is a person to whom he has transferred assets of his business by a transfer of that business, or a part of it, as a going concern;

(*b*) those assets consisted of or included those goods or that thing; and

(*c*) the transfer of the assets is one falling by virtue of an order under section 5(3) (or under an enactment re-enacted in section 5(3)) to be treated as neither a supply of goods nor a supply of services;

and references in this paragraph to a person's predecessors include references to the predecessors of his predecessors through any number of transfers.][4]

(6) Anything which is a supply of goods or services by virtue of sub-paragraph (1) or (4) above is to be treated as made in the course or furtherance of the business (if it would not otherwise be so treated); and in the case of a business carried on by an individual—

(*a*) sub-paragraph (1) above applies to any transfer or disposition of goods in favour of himself personally; and

(*b*) [sub-paragraph (4) above][1] applies to goods used, or made available for use, by himself personally.

[(7) The Treasury may by order substitute for the sum for the time being specified in sub-paragraph (2)(*a*) above such sum, not being less than £10, as they think fit.][2]

Commentary—*De Voil Indirect Tax Service* **V3.211, V3.212**.

HMRC Manuals—VAT Guidance V1-3: Supply and consideration, para 2.4 (supply for no consideration).
Para 4.2 (supply of services for consideration).
Para 5.1 (assets used for business purposes).
Para 5.5 (supply of samples: first sample exempt).
Para 6.2 (free loan of business assets).

Simon's Tax Cases—Sub-para (1), *C&E Comrs v Professional Footballers' Association (Enterprises) Ltd* [1993] STC 86*; *Church of England Children's Society v Revenue and Customs Commissioners* [2005] STC 1644.

Definitions—"Supply", s 5, Sch 4; "VAT", ss 1, 96(1).

Cross references—See VATA 1994 s 5(3) (orders providing that sub-para (4) of this para is not to apply to make the use of prescribed goods in prescribed circumstances a supply of services);
VATA 1994 s 6(12) (supplies treated as taking place by virtue of sub-para (1) of this para: time of supply);
VATA 1994 s 6(13), (14) (supplies treated as taking place by virtue of sub-para (4) of this para: time of supply);
VATA 1994 s 97(3), (4) (procedure for making an order under sub-s (7) above specifying a lesser sum than in sub-s (2)(*a*)).
VATA 1994 Sch 6 para 6 (valuation of supplies made otherwise than for consideration which are treated as supplies of goods by virtue of sub-para (1) of this para);
VATA 1994 Sch 6 para 7 (valuation of supplies made otherwise than for consideration which are treated as supplies of services by virtue of sub-para (3) of this para);
VATA 1994 Sch 7 para 3 (valuation of transactions involving the acquisition of goods from another member state otherwise than for consideration which are treated as supplies by virtue of sub-para (1) of this para).
VAT Regulations, SI 1995/2518 reg 81(1) (supplies treated as taking place by virtue of sub-para (4) of this para: time of supply).
F(No 3)A 2010 Sch 8 para 4 (output tax charge where credit attributable to purported para 5(4) supply).

VATA 1994 Sch 6 Part 1 (valuation of supplies of fuel for private use).

Amendments—[1] Words in sub-paras (5), (6)(b) substituted by FA 1995 s 33(1), (3)(a) and are deemed to have always had effect.

[2] Sub-para (7) added by FA 1996 s 33(2).

[3] Words in sub-paras (2)(a), (5) inserted by FA 1998 s 21 with effect for goods transferred or disposed of, or put to use, used or made available for use after 16 March 1998.

[4] Sub-paras (2A), (5A) inserted by FA 1998 s 21 with effect for goods transferred or disposed of, or put to use, used or made available for use after 16 March 1998.

[5] Words in sub-para (5) substituted by FA 2000 s 136(9), with effect for supplies made after 20 March 2000.

[6] Words in sub-para (2)(a) substituted by FA 2003 s 21(2) with effect for gifts made after 30 September 2003.

[7] Sub-para (2ZA) inserted by FA 2003 s 21(3) with effect for gifts made after 30 September 2003.

[8] Sub-para (4A) inserted by F(No 3)A 2010 s 19, Sch 8 para 3(1) with effect from 1 January 2011. Note that this amendment does not apply in relation to an asset in respect of which the person in question or any of that person's predecessors incurred VAT before 1 January 2011 but, where VAT is incurred by such a person before that date in respect of the asset, VAT incurred by such a person on or after that date in respect of the asset is not to be treated as referable to that person's business purposes by virtue of sub-paras (4) and (6) if, and to the extent that, the asset is used or to be used for that person's private use or the private use of that person's staff, or more generally for purposes other than those of that person's business (F(No 3)A 2010 Sch 8 para 3(3), (4)). See also definitions in relation to this note in F(No 3)A 2010 Sch 8 para 3(5).

[9] Sub-para (2)(*b*) substituted and sub-para (3) repealed, by FA 2011 s 74(1)–(3) with effect from 19 July 2011.

6—(1) Where, in a case not falling within paragraph 5(1) above, goods forming part of the assets of any business—

(*a*) are removed from any member State by or under the directions of the person carrying on the business; and

(*b*) are so removed in the course or furtherance of that business for the purpose of being taken to a place in a member State other than that from which they are removed,

then, whether or not the removal is or is connected with a transaction for a consideration, that is a supply of goods by that person.

(2) Sub-paragraph (1) above does not apply—

(*a*) to the removal of goods from any member State in the course of their removal from one part of that member State to another part of the same member State; or

(*b*) to goods which have been removed from a place outside the member States for entry into the territory of the Community and are removed from a member State before the time when any Community customs debt in respect of any Community customs duty on their entry into that territory would be incurred.

Commentary—*De Voil Indirect Tax Service* **V3.213**.

Definitions—"Business", s 94.

Cross references—See VATA 1994 s 5(3) (orders providing that this para is not to apply to make a removal of assets a supply of goods in prescribed circumstances);

VATA 1994 Sch 6 para 6 (valuation of supplies made otherwise than for consideration which are treated as supplies of goods by virtue of this para);

VATA 1994 Sch 7 para 3 (valuation of transactions involving the acquisition of goods from another member state otherwise than for consideration which are treated as supplies by virtue of this para).

VAT (Removal of Goods) Order, SI 1992/3111 (this paragraph not to apply to removals of goods between member states in specified circumstances).

VAT (Removal of Gas, Electricity, Heat and Cooling Order, SI 2010/2925 art 3 (sub-para (1) shall not apply to the removal of gas through a natural gas system situated within the territory of a member state or any network connected to such system, electricity, or heat or cooling supplied through a network).

7 Where in the case of a business carried on by a taxable person goods forming part of the assets of the business are, under any power exercisable by another person, sold by the other in or towards satisfaction of a debt owed by the taxable person, they shall be deemed to be supplied by the taxable person in the course or furtherance of his business.

Commentary—*De Voil Indirect Tax Service* **V3.226**.

Definitions—"Business", s 94; "taxable person", s 3;

Cross references—See VATA 1994 Sch 11 para 2(12) (provision for regulations as to payment of VAT chargeable on deemed supply under this para).

VAT Regulations, SI 1995/2518 reg 13(2), (5) (VAT invoices in respect of deemed supplies under this para);

VAT Regulations, SI 1995/2518 reg 27 (returns in respect of deemed supplies under this para).

8—(1) Where a person ceases to be a taxable person, any goods then forming part of the assets of a business carried on by him shall be deemed to be supplied by him in the course or furtherance of his business immediately before he ceases to be a taxable person, unless—

(*a*) the business is transferred as a going concern to another taxable person; or

(*b*) the business is carried on by another person who, under regulations made under section 46(4), is treated as a taxable person; or

(*c*) the VAT on the deemed supply would not be more than [£1,000][1].

(2) This paragraph does not apply to any goods in the case of which the taxable person can show to the satisfaction of the Commissioners—

(*a*) that no credit for input tax has been allowed to him in respect of the supply of the goods, their acquisition from another member State or their importation from a place outside the member States;

(*b*) that the goods did not become his as part of the assets of a business[, or part of a business,][2] which was transferred to him as a going concern by another taxable person; and

(*c*) that he has not obtained relief in respect of the goods under section 4 of the Finance Act 1973.

(3) This paragraph does not apply where a person ceases to be a taxable person in consequence of having been certified under section 54.

(4) The Treasury may by order increase or further increase the sum specified in sub-paragraph (1)(*c*) above.

Commentary—*De Voil Indirect Tax Service* **V3.261**.

HMRC Manuals—VAT Guidance V1-3: Supply and consideration, para 5.6 (deemed supply of goods where a person ceases to be a taxable person, with business assets on hand).

Press releases etc—HMRC Brief 1/2012 23 January 2012. VAT—Pre-registration claims following de-registration of the same legal entity.

Definitions—"Acquisition of goods from another member State", s 11; "another member State", s 96(1); "business", s 94; "the Commissioners", s 96(1); "importation of goods from a place outside the member States", s 15; "input tax", s 24; "regulations", s 96(1); "taxable person", s 3; "VAT", ss 1, 96(1).

Cross references—See VATA 1994 Sch 6 para 6 (valuation of supplies which are treated as supplies of goods by virtue of this para).

VAT (Isle of Man) Order, SI 1982/1067 art 11(8) (persons who become registered under Isle of Man VAT legislation remain taxable persons for the purposes of this para).

Amendments—[1] Figure in para (1)(c) substituted by the VAT (Deemed Supply of Goods) Order, SI 2000/266, art 2 with effect from 1 April 2000.

[2] Words in sub-para (2)(b) inserted by FA 2007 s 100(9), (10) with effect in relation to transfers pursuant to contracts entered into on or after 1 September 2007.

9—(1) Subject to sub-paragraphs (2) and (3) below, paragraphs 5 to 8 above have effect in relation to land forming part of the assets of, or held or used for the purposes of, a business as if it were goods forming part of the assets of, or held or used for the purposes of, a business.

(2) In the application of those paragraphs by virtue of sub-paragraph (1) above, references to transfer, disposition or sale shall have effect as references to the grant or assignment of any interest in, right over or licence to occupy the land concerned.

(3) Except in relation to—

(*a*) the grant or assignment of a major interest; or

(*b*) a grant or assignment otherwise than for a consideration,

in the application of paragraph 5(1) above by virtue of sub-paragraph (1) above the reference to a supply of goods shall have effect as a reference to a supply of services.

[(4) In this paragraph "grant" includes surrender.][1]

Commentary—*De Voil Indirect Tax Service* **V3.211**.

Definitions—"Assignment", s 96(1); "business", s 94; "major interest", s 96(1); "supply", s 5, Sch 4.

Amendments—[1] Sub-para (4) inserted by FA 2007 s 99(1), (3), (7) with effect for surrenders on or after 21 March 2007.

[SCHEDULE 4A

PLACE OF SUPPLY OF SERVICES: SPECIAL RULES][1]

Section 7A

Amendments—[1] Sch 4A inserted by FA 2009 s 76, Sch 36 paras 1, 11 with effect in relation to supplies made on or after 1 January 2010.

PART 1
GENERAL EXCEPTIONS

Services relating to land

1—(1) A supply of services to which this paragraph applies is to be treated as made in the country in which the land in connection with which the supply is made is situated.

(2) This paragraph applies to—

(*a*) the grant, assignment or surrender of any interest in or right over land,

(*b*) the grant, assignment or surrender of a personal right to call for or be granted any interest in or right over land,

(*c*) the grant, assignment or surrender of a licence to occupy land or any other contractual right exercisable over or in relation to land (including the provision of holiday accommodation, seasonal pitches for caravans and facilities at caravan parks for persons for whom such pitches are provided and pitches for tents and camping facilities), (*d*) the provision in an hotel, inn, boarding house or similar establishment of sleeping accommodation or of accommodation in rooms which are provided in conjunction with sleeping accommodation or for the purpose of a supply of catering,

(*e*) any works of construction, demolition, conversion, reconstruction, alteration, enlargement, repair or maintenance of a building or civil engineering work, and

(*f*) services such as are supplied by estate agents, auctioneers, architects, surveyors, engineers and others involved in matters relating to land.

(3) In sub-paragraph (2)(*c*) "holiday accommodation" includes any accommodation in a building, hut (including a beach hut or chalet), caravan, houseboat or tent which is advertised or held out as holiday accommodation or as suitable for holiday or leisure use.

(4) In sub-paragraph (2)(*d*) "similar establishment" includes premises in which there is provided furnished sleeping accommodation, whether with or without the provision of board or facilities for the preparation of food, which are used by, or held out as being suitable for use by, visitors or travellers.][1]

Commentary—*De Voil Indirect Tax Service* **V3.188**.

Amendments—[1] Sch 4A inserted by FA 2009 s 76, Sch 36 paras 1, 11 with effect in relation to supplies made on or after 1 January 2010.

[Passenger transport

2—(1) A supply of services consisting of the transportation of passengers (or of any luggage or motor vehicles accompanying passengers) is to be treated as made in the country in which the transportation takes place, and (in a case where it takes place in more than one country) in proportion to the distances covered in each.

(2) For the purposes of sub-paragraph (1) transportation which takes place partly outside the territorial jurisdiction of a country is to be treated as taking place wholly in the country if—

(*a*) it takes place in the course of a journey between two points in the country (whether or not as part of a longer journey involving travel to or from another country), and

(*b*) the means of transport used does not (except in an emergency or involuntarily) stop, put in or land in another country in the course of the journey between those two points.

(3) For the purposes of sub-paragraph (1) a pleasure cruise is to be regarded as the transportation of passengers (so that services provided as part of a pleasure cruise are to be treated as supplied in the same place as the transportation of the passengers).

(4) In sub-paragraph (3) "pleasure cruise" includes a cruise wholly or partly for education or training.][1]

Commentary—*De Voil Indirect Tax Service* **V3.189**.

Amendments—[1] Sch 4A inserted by FA 2009 s 76, Sch 36 paras 1, 11 with effect in relation to supplies made on or after 1 January 2010.

[Hiring of means of transport

3—(1) A supply of services consisting of the short-term hiring of a means of transport is to be treated as made in the country in which the means of transport is actually put at the disposal of the person by whom it is hired.

But this is subject to sub-paragraphs (3) and (4).

(2) For the purposes of this Schedule the hiring of a means of transport is "short-term" if it is hired for a continuous period not exceeding—

(*a*) if the means of transport is a vessel, 90 days, and

(*b*) otherwise, 30 days.

(3) Where—

(*a*) a supply of services consisting of the hiring of a means of transport would otherwise be treated as made in the United Kingdom, and

(*b*) the services are to any extent effectively used and enjoyed in a country which is not a member State,

the supply is to be treated to that extent as made in that country.

(4) Where—

(*a*) a supply of services consisting of the hiring of a means of transport would otherwise be treated as made in a country which is not a member State, and

(*b*) the services are to any extent effectively used and enjoyed in the United Kingdom,

the supply is to be treated to that extent as made in the United Kingdom.][1]

Commentary—*De Voil Indirect Tax Service* **V3.194**.

Amendments—[1] Sch 4A inserted by FA 2009 s 76, Sch 36 paras 1, 11 with effect in relation to supplies made on or after 1 January 2010.

[Cultural, educational and entertainment services etc

4—(1) A supply of services to which this paragraph applies is to be treated as made in the country in which the services are physically carried out.
(2) This paragraph applies to the provision of—
(a) services relating to cultural, artistic, sporting, scientific, educational, entertainment or similar activities (including fairs and exhibitions), and
(b) ancillary services relating to such activities, including services of organisers of such activities.][1], [2]

Commentary—*De Voil Indirect Tax Service* **V3.192.**
Amendments—[1] Sch 4A inserted by FA 2009 s 76, Sch 36 paras 1, 11 with effect in relation to supplies made on or after 1 January 2010.
[2] Para 4 repealed by FA 2009 s 76, Sch 36 paras 1, 15(2) with effect in relation to supplies made on or after 1 January 2011.

[Restaurant and catering services: general

5—(1) A supply of services to which this paragraph applies is to be treated as made in the country in which the services are physically carried out.
(2) This paragraph applies to the provision of restaurant services and the provision of catering services, other than the provision of services to which paragraph 6 applies.][1]

Commentary—*De Voil Indirect Tax Service* **V3.198.**
Amendments—[1] Sch 4A inserted by FA 2009 s 76, Sch 36 paras 1, 11 with effect in relation to supplies made on or after 1 January 2010.

[EC on-board restaurant and catering services

6—(1) A supply of services consisting of
(*a*) the provision of restaurant services, or
(*b*) the provision of catering services,
on board a ship, aircraft or train in connection with the transportation of passengers during an intra-EC passenger transport operation is to be treated as made in the country in which the relevant point of departure is located.
(2) An intra-EC passenger transport operation is a passenger transport operation which, or so much of a passenger transport operation as,—
(*a*) has as the first place at which passengers can embark a place which is within the EC,
(*b*) has as the last place at which passengers who embarked in a member State can disembark a place which is within the EC, and
(*c*) does not include a stop at a place which is not within the EC and at which passengers can embark or passengers who embarked in a member State can disembark.
(3) "Relevant point of departure", in relation to an intra-EC passenger transport operation, is the first place in the intra-EC passenger transport operation at which passengers can embark.
(4) A place is within the EC if it is within any member State.
(5) For the purposes of this paragraph the return stage of a return passenger transport operation is to be regarded as a separate passenger transport operation; and for this purpose—
(*a*) a return passenger transport operation is one which takes place in more than one country but is expected to end in the country in which it begins, and
(*b*) the return stage of a return passenger transport operation is the part of it which ends in the country in which it began and begins with the last stop at a place at which there has not been a previous stop during it.][1]

Commentary—*De Voil Indirect Tax Service* **V3.198.**
Amendments—[1] Sch 4A inserted by FA 2009 s 76, Sch 36 paras 1, 11 with effect in relation to supplies made on or after 1 January 2010.

[Hiring of goods

7—(1) Where—
(*a*) a supply of services consisting of the hiring of any goods other than a means of transport would otherwise be treated as made in the United Kingdom, and
(*b*) the services are to any extent effectively used and enjoyed in a country which is not a member State,
the supply is to be treated to that extent as made in that country.
(2) Where—
(*a*) a supply of services consisting of the hiring of any goods other than a means of transport would otherwise be treated as made in a country which is not a member State, and
(*b*) the services are to any extent effectively used and enjoyed in the United Kingdom,
the supply is to be treated to that extent as made in the United Kingdom.][1]

Amendments—[1] Sch 4A inserted by FA 2009 s 76, Sch 36 paras 1, 11 with effect in relation to supplies made on or after 1 January 2010.

[Telecommunication and broadcasting services

8—(1) This paragraph applies to a supply of services consisting of the provision of—

(*a*) telecommunication services, or

(*b*) radio or television broadcasting services.

(2) In this Schedule "telecommunication services" means services relating to the transmission, emission or reception of signals, writing, images and sounds or information of any nature by wire, radio, optical or other electromagnetic systems, including—

(*a*) the related transfer or assignment of the right to use capacity for such transmission, emission or reception, and

(*b*) the provision of access to global information networks.

(3) Where—

(*a*) a supply of services to which this paragraph applies would otherwise be treated as made in the United Kingdom, and

(*b*) the services are to any extent effectively used and enjoyed in a country which is not a member State,

the supply is to be treated to that extent as made in that country.

(4) Where—

(*a*) a supply of services to which this paragraph applies would otherwise be treated as made in a country which is not a member State, and

(*b*) the services are to any extent effectively used and enjoyed in the United Kingdom,

the supply is to be treated to that extent as made in the United Kingdom.][1]

Amendments—[1] Sch 4A inserted by FA 2009 s 76, Sch 36 paras 1, 11 with effect in relation to supplies made on or after 1 January 2010.

[PART 2

EXCEPTIONS RELATING TO SUPPLIES MADE TO RELEVANT BUSINESS PERSON

Electronically-supplied services

9—(1) Where—

(*a*) a supply of services consisting of the provision of electronically supplied services to a relevant business person would otherwise be treated as made in the United Kingdom, and

(*b*) the services are to any extent effectively used and enjoyed in a country which is not a member State,

the supply is to be treated to that extent as made in that country.

(2) Where—

(*a*) a supply of services consisting of the provision of electronically supplied services to a relevant business person would otherwise be treated as made in a country which is not a member State, and

(*b*) the services are to any extent effectively used and enjoyed in the United Kingdom,

the supply is to be treated to that extent as made in the United Kingdom.

(3) Examples of what are electronically supplied services for the purposes of this Schedule include—

(*a*) website supply, web-hosting and distance maintenance of programmes and equipment,

(*b*) the supply of software and the updating of software,

(*c*) the supply of images, text and information, and the making available of databases,

(*d*) the supply of music, films and games (including games of chance and gambling games),

(*e*) the supply of political, cultural, artistic, sporting, scientific, educational or entertainment broadcasts (including broadcasts of events), and

(*f*) the supply of distance teaching.

(4) But where the supplier of a service and the supplier's customer communicate via electronic mail, this does not of itself mean that the service provided is an electronically supplied service for the purposes of this Schedule.][1]

Amendments—[1] Sch 4A inserted by FA 2009 s 76, Sch 36 paras 1, 11 with effect in relation to supplies made on or after 1 January 2010.

[Admission to cultural, educational and entertainment activities etc

9A—(1) A supply to a relevant business person of services to which this paragraph applies is to be treated as made in the country in which the events in question actually take place.

(2) This paragraph applies to the provision of—

(*a*) services in respect of admission to cultural, artistic, sporting, scientific, educational, entertainment or similar events (including fairs and exhibitions), and

(*b*) ancillary services relating to admission to such events.][1]

Amendments—[1] Para 9A inserted by FA 2009 s 76, Sch 36 paras 1, 15(3) with effect in relation to supplies made on or after 1 January 2011.

[Transport of goods

9B Where—

(*a*) a supply of services to a relevant business person consisting of the transportation of goods would otherwise be treated as made in the United Kingdom, and

(*b*) the transportation takes place wholly outside the member States,

the supply is to be treated as made wholly outside the member States.][1]

Amendments—[1] Paras 9B, 9C inserted by the Value Added Tax (Place of Supply of Services) (Transport of Goods) Order, SI 2012/2787 art 2 with effect in relation to supplies made on or after 20 December 2012.

[Ancillary transport services

9C—(1) Where—

(*a*) a supply of services to a relevant business person consisting of ancillary transport services would otherwise be treated as made in the United Kingdom, and

(*b*) the services are physically performed wholly outside the member States,

the supply is to be treated as made wholly outside the member States.

(2) In sub-paragraph (1)(*a*) "ancillary transport services" means loading, unloading, handling and similar activities.][1]

Amendments—[1] Paras 9B, 9C inserted by the Value Added Tax (Place of Supply of Services) (Transport of Goods) Order, SI 2012/2787 art 2 with effect in relation to supplies made on or after 20 December 2012.

[PART 3
EXCEPTIONS RELATING TO SUPPLIES NOT MADE TO RELEVANT BUSINESS PERSON

Intermediaries

10—(1) A supply of services to which this paragraph applies is to be treated as made in the same country as the supply to which it relates.

(2) This paragraph applies to a supply to a person who is not a relevant business person consisting of the making of arrangements for a supply by or to another person or of any other activity intended to facilitate the making of such a supply.][1]

Commentary—*De Voil Indirect Tax Service* **V3.195**.

Amendments—[1] Sch 4A inserted by FA 2009 s 76, Sch 36 paras 1, 11 with effect in relation to supplies made on or after 1 January 2010.

[Transport of goods: general

11—(1) A supply of services to a person who is not a relevant business person consisting of the transportation of goods is to be treated as made in the country in which the transportation takes place, and (in a case where it takes place in more than one country) in proportion to the distances covered in each.

(2) For the purposes of sub-paragraph (1) transportation which takes place partly outside the territorial jurisdiction of a country is to be treated as taking place wholly in the country if—

(*a*) it takes place in the course of a journey between two points in the country (whether or not as part of a longer journey involving travel to or from another country), and

(*b*) the means of transport used does not (except in an emergency or involuntarily) stop, put in or land in another country in the course of the journey between those two points.

(3) This paragraph does not apply to a transportation of goods beginning in one member State and ending in another (see paragraph 12).][1]

Amendments—[1] Sch 4A inserted by FA 2009 s 76, Sch 36 paras 1, 11 with effect in relation to supplies made on or after 1 January 2010.

[Intra-Community transport of goods

12—A supply of services to a person who is not a relevant business person consisting of the transportation of goods which begins in one member State and ends in another is to be treated as made in the member State in which the transportation begins.][1]

Commentary—*De Voil Indirect Tax Service* **V3.190**.

Amendments—[1] Sch 4A inserted by FA 2009 s 76, Sch 36 paras 1, 11 with effect in relation to supplies made on or after 1 January 2010.

[Ancillary transport services

13—(1) A supply to a person who is not a relevant business person of ancillary transport services is to be treated as made where the services are physically performed.
(2) "Ancillary transport services" means loading, unloading handling and similar activities.][1]

Commentary—*De Voil Indirect Tax Service* **V3.191**.
Amendments—[1] Sch 4A inserted by FA 2009 s 76, Sch 36 paras 1, 11 with effect in relation to supplies made on or after 1 January 2010.

[Long-term hiring of means of transport

13A—(1) A supply to a person who is not a relevant business person ("the recipient") of services consisting of the long-term hiring of a means of transport is to be treated as made in the country in which the recipient belongs.
But this is subject to sub-paragraph (2) and paragraph 3(3) and (4).
(2) A supply to a person who is not a relevant business person ("the recipient") of services consisting of the long-term hiring of a pleasure boat which is actually put at the disposal of the recipient at the supplier's business establishment, or some other fixed establishment of the supplier, is to be treated as made in the country where the pleasure boat is actually put at the disposal of the recipient.
(3) For the purposes of this Schedule, the hiring of a means of transport is "long-term" if it is not short-term (as to the meaning of which see paragraph 3(2)).][1]

Amendments—[1] This para inserted by FA 2009 s 76, Sch 36 paras 1, 17 with effect in relation to supplies made on or after 1 January 2013.

[Valuation services etc

14 A supply to a person who is not a relevant business person of services consisting of the valuation of, or carrying out of work on, goods is to be treated as made where the services are physically performed.][1]

Amendments—[1] Sch 4A inserted by FA 2009 s 76, Sch 36 paras 1, 11 with effect in relation to supplies made on or after 1 January 2010.

[Cultural, educational and entertainment services etc

14A—(1) A supply to a person who is not a relevant business person of services to which this paragraph applies is to be treated as made in the country in which the activities concerned actually take place.
(2) This paragraph applies to the provision of—

(*a*) services relating to cultural, artistic, sporting, scientific, educational, entertainment or similar activities (including fairs and exhibitions), and
(*b*) ancillary services relating to such activities, including services of organisers of such activities.][1]

Amendments—[1] Para 14A inserted by FA 2009 s 76, Sch 36 paras 1, 15(4) with effect in relation to supplies made on or after 1 January 2011.

[[Electronically supplied, telecommunication and broadcasting services]

[15—(1) A supply to a person who is not a relevant business person of services to which this paragraph applies is to be treated as made in the country in which the recipient belongs (but see paragraph 8).
(2) This paragraph applies to-

(*a*) electronically supplied services (as to the meaning of which see paragraph 9(3) and (4)),
(*b*) telecommunication services (as to the meaning of which see paragraph 8(2)), and
(*c*) radio and television broadcasting services.][2]][1]

Commentary—*De Voil Indirect Tax Service* **V3.193B**.
Press releases etc—HMRC Guidance Note: "HMRC guide to place of supply of digital services and VAT 'mini one-stop-shop' ", 16 May 2014 (*SWTI 2014, Issue 20*).
Amendments—[1] Sch 4A inserted by FA 2009 s 76, Sch 36 paras 1, 11 with effect in relation to supplies made on or after 1 January 2010.
[2] Para 15 and preceding heading substituted by the VAT (Place of Supply of Services) (Exceptions Relating to Supplies Not Made to Relevant Business Person) Order, SI 2014/2726 arts 2, 3 with effect in relation to supplies made on or after 1 January 2015.

[Other services provided to recipient belonging outside EC

16—(1) A supply consisting of the provision to a person ("the recipient") who—

(*a*) is not a relevant business person, and
(*b*) belongs in a country which is not a member State (other than the Isle of Man),

of services to which this paragraph applies is to be treated as made in the country in which the recipient belongs.

(2) This paragraph applies to—

(*a*) transfers and assignments of copyright, patents, licences, trademarks and similar rights,

(*b*) the acceptance of any obligation to refrain from pursuing or exercising (in whole or in part) any business activity or any rights within paragraph (*a*),

(*c*) advertising services,

(*d*) services of consultants, engineers, consultancy bureaux, lawyers, accountants, and similar services, data processing and provision of information, other than any services relating to land,

(*e*) banking, financial and insurance services (including reinsurance), other than the provision of safe deposit facilities,

[(*f*) the provision of access to, or transmission or distribution through—

(i) a natural gas system situated within the territory of a member State or any network connected to such a system, or

(ii) an electricity system, or

(iii) a network through which heat or cooling is supplied,

and the provision of other directly linked services,][2]

(*g*) the supply of staff, [and][3]

(*h*) the letting on hire of goods other than means of transport,

(*i*) . . . [3]

(*j*) . . . [3]

(*k*) . . . [3]][1]

Commentary—*De Voil Indirect Tax Service* **V3.193A**.

Amendments—[1] Sch 4A inserted by FA 2009 s 76, Sch 36 paras 1, 11 with effect in relation to supplies made on or after 1 January 2010.

[2] Sub-para (2)(*f*) substituted by the VAT (Exceptions Relating to Supplies not Made to Relevant Business Person) Order, SI 2010/3017 art 2 with effect in relation to supplies made on or after 1 January 2011.

[3] In sub-para (2), paras (*i*), (*j*), (*k*) repealed, and word inserted at end of para (*g*), by the VAT (Place of Supply of Services) (Exceptions Relating to Supplies Not Made to Relevant Business Person) Order, SI 2014/2726 arts 2, 4 with effect in relation to supplies made on or after 1 January 2015.

SCHEDULE 5

SERVICES SUPPLIED WHERE RECEIVED

Section 8

Amendments—Sch 5 repealed by FA 2009 s 76, Sch 36 paras 1, 12 with effect in relation to supplies made on or after 1 January 2010.

[SCHEDULE 5A

GOODS ELIGIBLE TO BE FISCALLY WAREHOUSED

Section 18B

Description of goods	*Combined nomenclature code of the European Communities*
Tin	8001
Copper	7402
	7403
	7405
	7408
Zinc	7901
Nickel	7502
Aluminium	7601
Lead	7801
Indium	ex 811291
	ex 811299
Cereals	1001 to 1005
	1006: unprocessed rice only
	1007 to 1008
Oil seeds and oleaginous fruit	1201 to 1207

Description of goods	*Combined nomenclature code of the European Communities*
Coconuts, Brazil nuts and cashew nuts	0801
Other nuts	0502
Olives	071120
Grains and seeds (including soya beans)	1201 to 1207
Coffee, not roasted	0901 11 00
	0901 12 00
Tea	0902
Cocoa beans, whole or broken, raw or roasted	1801
Raw sugar	1701 11
	1701 12
Rubber, in primary forms or in plates, sheets or strip	4001
	4002
Wool	5101
Chemicals in bulk	Chapters 28 and 29
Mineral oils (including propane and butane; also including crude petroleum oils)	2709
	2710
	2711 12
	2711 13
Silver	7106
Platinum (palladium, rhodium)	7110 11 00
	7110 21 00
	7110 31 00
Potatoes	0701
Vegetable oils and fats and their fractions, whether or not refined, but not chemically modified	1507 to 1515][1]

Commentary—*De Voil Indirect Tax Service* **V3.176**.
Cross reference—VATA 1994 s 18B(8) (Treasury may by order vary this Schedule).
Amendments—

[1] Schedule inserted by FA 1996 Sch 3 para 18, with effect from 1 June 1996 (see Finance Act 1996, Section 26, (Appointed Day) Order, SI 1996/1249).

SCHEDULE 6
VALUATION: SPECIAL CASES
Section 19

Cross references—See VATA 1994 s 20(2) (valuation of acquisitions from other member states otherwise than through a taxable supply: disapplication of this Schedule);

VATA 1994 s 52 (provision for regulations modifying this Schedule in relation to the valuation of supplies of goods under trading stamp schemes).

[PART 1
VALUATION OF SUPPLIES OF FUEL FOR PRIVATE USE

Option for valuation on flat-rate basis

A1— (1) This paragraph applies if, in a prescribed accounting period, supplies of goods by a taxable person ("P") arise by virtue of paragraph 5(1) of Schedule 4 (but otherwise than for a consideration) where road fuel which is or has previously been supplied to or imported or manufactured by P in the course of P's business is provided for, or appropriated to, private use.

(2) For this purpose "road fuel is provided for, or appropriated to, private use" if—

(*a*) it is provided or to be provided by P—

(i) to an individual for private use in the individual's own car or a car allocated to the individual, and

(ii) by reason of the individual's employment,

(*b*) where P is an individual, it is appropriated or to be appropriated by P for private use in P's own car, or (*c*) where P is a partnership, it is provided or to be provided to any of the individual partners for private use in that partner's own car.

(3) P may opt for all supplies of goods within sub-paragraph (1) made by P in the prescribed accounting period to be valued on the flat-rate basis.

(4) On the flat-rate basis, the value of all supplies made to any one individual in respect of any one car is that determined in accordance with an order under paragraph B1.]

Amendments—Part 1 (paras A1–C1), and heading to Part 2, inserted by FA 2013 s 192, Sch 38 paras 1, 2 with effect in relation to prescribed accounting periods beginning on or after 1 February 2014.

[B1—(1) The Treasury must, by order, make provision about the valuation of supplies on the flat-rate basis.

(2) In particular, an order under this paragraph must—

(*a*) set out a table ("the base valuation table") by reference to which the value of supplies is to be determined until such time as the base valuation table is replaced under paragraph (*b*),

(*b*) provide that at regular intervals—

(i) the amounts specified in the base valuation table are to be revalorised by the Commissioners in accordance with the order, and

(ii) a table (an "updated valuation table") containing the revalorised amounts is to take effect (and replace any existing table) in accordance with the order, and

(*c*) require the Commissioners to publish any updated valuation table before it takes effect, together with a statement specifying the date from which it has effect.

(3) An order under this paragraph may provide for the base valuation table and any updated valuation table to be implemented or supplemented by either or both of the following—

(*a*) rules set out in the order which explain how the value is to be determined by reference to any table;

(*b*) notes set out in the order with respect to the interpretation or application of any table or any rules or notes.

(4) Rules or notes may make different provision for different circumstances or cases.]

Orders—Value Added Tax (Flat-rate Valuation of Supplies of Fuel for Private Use) Order, SI 2013/2911.

Amendments—Part 1 (paras A1–C1), and heading to Part 2, inserted by FA 2013 s 192, Sch 38 paras 1, 2 with effect in relation to prescribed accounting periods beginning on or after 1 February 2014.

[Interpretation

C1—(1) For the purposes of this Part of this Schedule—

(*a*) any reference to an individual's own car is to be construed as including any car of which for the time being the individual has the use, other than a car allocated to the individual,

(*b*) subject to sub-paragraph (2), a car is at any time to be taken to be allocated to an individual if at that time it is made available (without any transfer of the property in it) either to the individual or to any other person, and is so made available by reason of the individual's employment and for private use, and

(*c*) fuel provided by an employer to an employee and fuel provided to any person for private use in a car which, by virtue of paragraph (*b*), is for the time being taken to be allocated to the employee is to be taken to be provided to the employee by reason of the employee's employment.

(2) For the purposes of this Part of this Schedule, in any prescribed accounting period a car is not regarded as allocated to an individual by reason of the individual's employment if—

(*a*) in that period it was made available to, and actually used by, more than one of the employees of one or more employers and, in the case of each of them, it—

(i) was made available to that employee by reason of the employment, but

(ii) was not in that period ordinarily used by any one of them to the exclusion of the others,

(*b*) in the case of each of the employees, any private use of the car made by the employee in that period was merely incidental to the employee's other use of it in that period, and

(*c*) in that period it was not normally kept overnight on or in the vicinity of any residential premises where any of the employees was residing, except while being kept overnight on premises occupied by the person making the car available to them.

(3) In this Part of this Schedule—

"employment" includes any office, and related expressions are to be construed accordingly;

"car" means a motor car as defined by paragraph 1A(4) and (5);

"road fuel" means hydrocarbon oil as defined by the Hydrocarbon Oil Duties Act 1979 (see section 1(2) of that Act) on which duty has been or is required to be paid in accordance with that Act.

(4) The Treasury may, by order, amend the definition of "road fuel" in sub-paragraph (3).]

Amendments—Part 1 (paras A1–C1), and heading to Part 2, inserted by FA 2013 s 192, Sch 38 paras 1, 2 with effect in relation to prescribed accounting periods beginning on or after 1 February 2014.

[PART 2
OTHER PROVISIONS]

Amendments—Part 1 (paras A1–C1), and heading to Part 2, inserted by FA 2013 s 192, Sch 38 paras 1, 2 with effect in relation to prescribed accounting periods beginning on or after 1 February 2014.

1—(1) Where—

(*a*) the value of a supply made by a taxable person for a consideration in money is (apart from this paragraph) less than its open market value, and

(*b*) the person making the supply and the person to whom it is made are connected, and

(*c*) if the supply is a taxable supply, the person to whom the supply is made is not entitled under sections 25 and 26 to credit for all the VAT on the supply,

the Commissioners may direct that the value of the supply shall be taken to be its open market value.

(2) A direction under this paragraph shall be given by notice in writing to the person making the supply, but no direction may be given more than 3 years after the time of the supply.

(3) A direction given to a person under this paragraph in respect of a supply made by him may include a direction that the value of any supply—

(*a*) which is made by him after the giving of the notice, or after such later date as may be specified in the notice, and

(*b*) as to which the conditions in paragraphs (*a*) to (*c*) of sub-paragraph (1) above are satisfied,

shall be taken to be its open market value.

(4) For the purposes of this paragraph any question whether a person is connected with another shall be determined in accordance with [section 1122 of the Corporation Tax Act 2010][1].

(5) This paragraph does not apply to a supply to which paragraph [8A or][2] 10 below applies.

Commentary—*De Voil Indirect Tax Service* **V3.162**.

Definitions—"The Commissioners", s 96(10); "money", s 96(1); "open market value", s 19(5); "prescribed", s 96(1); "supply", s 5, Sch 4; "taxable person", s 3, "taxable supply", s 4(2); "the Taxes Act", s 96(1); "VAT", ss 1, 96(1).

Cross reference—See VATA 1994 s 83 (appeal to a tribunal in respect of a direction under this para).

VATA 1994 Sch 3B para 18A (reference in this para to a supply made by a taxable person is to be read as including a supply of scheme services that is made by a participant in the special scheme, and is treated as made in the UK).

VATA 1994 Sch 3BA para 19 (power of Commissioners under this section includes power to make provision in relation to refunds of VAT on certain supplies to participants in special accounting schemes under Directive 2008/9/EC (e-services)).

Amendments—[1] In sub-para (4) words substituted for words "section 839 of the Taxes Act 1988" by CTA 2010 s 1177, Sch 1 para 285(b). CTA 2010 has effect for corporation tax purposes for accounting periods ending on or after 1 April 2010, and for income and capital gains tax purposes for the tax year 2010–11 and subsequent tax years.

[2] Words in sub-para (5) inserted by FA 2012 s 200(1), (5), (6) with effect in relation to supplies made on or after 17 July 2012.

[1A—(1) Where—

(*a*) the value of a supply made by a taxable person for a consideration is (apart from this sub-paragraph) less than its open market value,

(*b*) the taxable person is a motor manufacturer or motor dealer,

(*c*) the person to whom the supply is made is—

(i) an employee of the taxable person,

(ii) a person who, under the terms of his employment, provides services to the taxable person, or

(iii) a relative of a person falling within sub-paragraph (i) or (ii) above,

(*d*) the supply is a supply of services by virtue of sub-paragraph (4) of paragraph 5 of Schedule 4 (business goods put to private use etc),

(*e*) the goods mentioned in that sub-paragraph consist of a motor car (whether or not any particular motor car) that forms part of the stock in trade of the taxable person, and

(*f*) the supply is not one to which paragraph 1 above applies,

the Commissioners may direct that the value of the supply shall be taken to be its open market value.

(2) A direction under this paragraph shall be given by notice in writing to the person making the supply, but no direction may be given more than 3 years after the time of the supply.

(3) A direction given to a person under this paragraph in respect of a supply made by him may include a direction that the value of any supply—

(*a*) which is made by him after the giving of the notice, or after such later date as may be specified in the notice, and

(*b*) as to which the conditions in paragraphs (*a*) to (*f*) of sub-paragraph (1) above are satisfied,

shall be taken to be its open market value.

(4) In this paragraph—

"motor car" means any motor vehicle of a kind normally used on public roads which has three or more wheels and either—

(*a*) is constructed or adapted solely or mainly for the carriage of passengers, or

(*b*) has to the rear of the driver's seat roofed accommodation which is fitted with side windows or which is constructed or adapted for the fitting of side windows, but does not include any vehicle excluded by sub-paragraph (5) below;

"motor dealer" means a person whose business consists in whole or in part of obtaining supplies of, or acquiring from another member State or importing, new or second-hand motor cars for resale with a view to making an overall profit on the sale of them (whether or not a profit is made on each sale);

"motor manufacturer" means a person whose business consists in whole or part of producing motor cars including producing motor cars by conversion of a vehicle (whether a motor car or not);

"relative" means husband, wife, brother, sister, ancestor or lineal descendant;

"stock in trade" means new or second-hand motor cars (other than second-hand motor cars which are not qualifying motor cars within sub-paragraph (6) below) which are—

(*a*) produced by a motor manufacturer or, as the case may require, supplied to or acquired from another member State or imported by a motor dealer, for the purpose of resale, and

(*b*) intended to be sold—

(i) by a motor manufacturer within 12 months of their production, or

(ii) by a motor dealer within 12 months of their supply, acquisition from another member State or importation, as the case may require,

and such motor cars shall not cease to be stock in trade where they are temporarily put to a use in the motor manufacturer's or, as the case may be, the motor dealer's business which involves making them available for private use.

(5) The vehicles excluded by this sub-paragraph are—

(*a*) vehicles capable of accommodating only one person;

(*b*) vehicles which meet the requirements of Schedule 6 to the Road Vehicles (Construction and Use) Regulations 1986 and are capable of carrying twelve or more seated persons;

(*c*) vehicles of not less than three tonnes unladen weight (as defined in the Table to regulation 3(2) of the Road Vehicles (Construction and Use) Regulations 1986);

(*d*) vehicles constructed to carry a payload (the difference between—

(i) a vehicle's kerb weight (as defined in the Table to regulation 3(2) of the Road Vehicles (Construction and Use) Regulations 1986), and

(ii) its maximum gross weight (as defined in that Table)),

of one tonne or more;

(*e*) caravans, ambulances and prison vans;

(*f*) vehicles constructed for a special purpose other than the carriage of persons and having no other accommodation for carrying persons than such as is incidental to that purpose.

(6) For the purposes of this paragraph a motor car is a "qualifying motor car" if—

(*a*) it has never been supplied, acquired from another member State, or imported in circumstances in which the VAT on that supply, acquisition or importation was wholly excluded from credit as input tax by virtue of an order under section 25(7) (as at 17th March 2004 see article 7 of the Value Added Tax (Input Tax) Order 1992); or

(*b*) a taxable person has elected under such an order for it to be treated as such.

(7) The Treasury may by order amend any of the definitions in this paragraph.][1]

Commentary—*De Voil Indirect Tax Service* **V3.162A**.

Amendments—[1] This paragraph inserted by FA 2004 s 22(1), (2), (5), (6) in relation to any use or availability for use on or after such day as the Treasury may by order made by statutory instrument appoint, whatever the date of the directions mentioned in VATA 1994 Sch 4 para 5(4). The appointed date is 1 January 2005 (by virtue of SI 2004/3104).

2 Where—

(*a*) the whole or part of a business carried on by a taxable person consists in supplying to a number of persons goods to be sold, whether by them or others, by retail, and

(*b*) those persons are not taxable persons,

the Commissioners may by notice in writing to the taxable person direct that the value of any such supply by him after the giving of the notice or after such later date as may be specified in the notice shall be taken to be its open market value on a sale by retail.

Commentary—*De Voil Indirect Tax Service* **V3.163**.

Simon's Tax Cases—*Direct Cosmetics Ltd and Laughtons Photographs Ltd v C&E Comrs* [1988] STC 540*; *Gold Star Publications Ltd v C&E Comrs* [1992] STC 365*; *Fine Art Developments plc v C&E Comrs* [1996] STC 246*.

Definitions—"Business", s 94; "the Commissioners", s 96(10); "open market value", s 19(5);

Cross reference—See VATA 1994 s 83 (appeal to a tribunal in respect of a direction under this para).

[2A—(1) This paragraph applies if—

(*a*) a taxable person ("P") makes a supply of road fuel for a consideration,

(*b*) the recipient of the supply is—

(i) connected with P, or

(ii) an employee or partner of P or a person who is connected with such an employee or partner,

(*c*) the value of the supply would (in the absence of this paragraph) be less than its open market value, and

(*d*) the recipient of the supply is not entitled to credit for the whole of the input tax arising on the supply.

(2) The value of the supply is to be taken to be an amount equal to its open market value.

(3) For the purposes of this paragraph—

(*a*) "road fuel" means hydrocarbon oil as defined by the Hydrocarbon Oil Duties Act 1979 (see section 1(2) of that Act) on which duty has been or is required to be paid in accordance with that Act, and

(*b*) any question whether a person is connected with another is to be determined in accordance with section 1122 of the Corporation Tax Act 2010.

(4) The Treasury may, by order, amend the definition of "road fuel" in sub-paragraph (3)(*a*).][1]

Amendments—[1] Para 2A inserted by FA 2013 s 192, Sch 38 paras 1, 6. This amendment is to be treated as coming into force on 11 December 2012 and has effect in relation to—

(a) supplies of goods on or after the commencement day, and

(b) supplies of goods in the period beginning with 11 December 2012 and ending immediately before the commencement day, if and to the extent that the goods are not made available before the end of that period to the person to whom they are supplied.

The commencement day means 17 July 2013 (FA 2013 Sch 38 para 8(2)).

3—(1) Where—

(*a*) any goods whose supply involves their removal to the United Kingdom—

(i) are charged in connection with their removal to the United Kingdom with a duty of excise; or

(ii) on that removal are subject, in accordance with any provision for the time being having effect for transitional purposes in connection with the accession of any State to the European Communities, to any Community customs duty or agricultural levy of the Economic Community; or

(*b*) the time of supply of any dutiable goods, or of any goods which comprise a mixture of dutiable goods and other goods, is determined under section 18(4) to be the duty point,

then the value of the supply shall be taken for the purposes of this Act to be the sum of its value apart from this paragraph and the amount, so far as not already included in that value, of the duty or, as the case may be, agricultural levy which has been or is to be paid in respect of the goods.

(2) In this paragraph "dutiable goods" and "duty point" have the same meanings as in section 18.

Commentary—*De Voil Indirect Tax Service* **V5.141**.

Definitions—"Supply", s 5, Sch 4; "United Kingdom", s 96(11).

[**4**—(1) Sub-paragraph (2) applies where—

(*a*) goods or services are supplied for a consideration which is a price in money,

(*b*) the terms on which those goods or services are so supplied allow a discount for prompt payment of that price,

(*c*) payment of that price is not made by instalments, and

(*d*) payment of that price is made in accordance with those terms so that the discount is realised in relation to that payment.

(2) For the purposes of section 19 (value of supply of goods or services) the consideration is the discounted price paid.][1]

Commentary—*De Voil Indirect Tax Service* **V3.157**.

Simon's Tax Cases—*Gold Star Publications Ltd v C&E Comrs* [1992] STC 365*.

Definitions—"Money", s 96(1); "relevant supply", FA 2014 s 108(5); telecommunication services, VATA 1994 Sch 4A para 8(2).

Amendments—[1] Paragraph substituted by FA 2014 s 108 with effect in relation to relevant supplies made on or after 1 May 2014.

Note that the Treasury may by order made by statutory instrument provide that the amendment has effect in relation to supplies of a description specified in the order made on or after a date so specified (being a date before 1 April 2015) (FA 2014 s 108(3). Subject to that, the amendment has effect in relation to supplies made on or after 1 April 2015.

5 . . .

Amendments—Paragraph repealed by FA 2003 ss 19, 216, Sch 1 para 3, Sch 43 Pt 2 with effect for supplies of tokens, stamps or vouchers issued after 8 April 2003.

6—(1) Where there is a supply of goods by virtue of—

(*a*) a Treasury order under section 5(5); or

(*b*) paragraph 5(1) or 6 of Schedule 4 but otherwise than for a consideration); or

(*c*) paragraph 8 of that Schedule,

then, except where [the person making the supply opts under paragraph A1(3) above for valuation on the flat-rate basis or][1] paragraph 10 below applies, the value of the supply shall be determined as follows.

(2) The value of the supply shall be taken to be—

(*a*) such consideration in money as would be payable by the person making the supply if he were, at the time of the supply, to purchase goods identical in every respect (including age and condition) to the goods concerned; or

(*b*) where the value cannot be ascertained in accordance with paragraph (*a*) above, such consideration in money as would be payable by that person if he were, at that time, to purchase goods similar to, and of the same age and condition as, the goods concerned; or

(*c*) where the value can be ascertained in accordance with neither paragraph (*a*) nor paragraph (*b*) above, the cost of producing the goods concerned if they were produced at that time.

(3) For the purposes of sub-paragraph (2) above the amount of consideration in money that would be payable by any person if he were to purchase any goods shall be taken to be the amount that would be so payable after the deduction of any amount included in the purchase price in respect of VAT on the supply of the goods to that person.

Commentary—*De Voil Indirect Tax Service* **V3.211, V3.213, V3.242.**

Simon's Tax Cases—*C&E Comrs v Telemed Ltd* [1992] STC 89*; *C&E Comrs v Professional Footballers' Association (Enterprises) Ltd* [1993] STC 86*; *Church of England Children's Society v Revenue and Customs Commissioners* [2005] STC 1644.

Definitions—"Supply", s 5, Sch 4; "VAT", ss 1, 96(1).

Amendments—[1] In sub-para (1) words inserted by FA 2013 s 192, Sch 38 paras 1, 3 with effect in relation to prescribed accounting periods beginning on or after 1 February 2014.

7—[(1)] [2] Where there is a supply of services by virtue of—

(*a*) a Treasury order under section 5(4); or

(*b*) [paragraph 5(4)][1] of Schedule 4 (but otherwise than for a consideration),

the value of the supply shall be taken to be the full cost to the taxable person of providing the services except where paragraph 10 below applies.

[(2) Regulations may, in relation to a supply of services by virtue of paragraph 5(4) of Schedule 4 (but otherwise than for a consideration), make provision for determining how the full cost to the taxable person of providing the services is to be calculated.

(3) The regulations may, in particular, make provision for the calculation to be made by reference to any prescribed period.

(4) The regulations may make—

(*a*) different provision for different circumstances;

(*b*) such incidental, supplementary, consequential or transitional provision as the Commissioners think fit.][2]

Commentary—*De Voil Indirect Tax Service* **V3.212.**

Simon's Tax Cases—*Comrs of Customs and Excise v Teknequip Ltd* [1987] STC 664*.

Definitions—"Supply", s 5, Sch 4; "taxable person", s 3;

Amendments—[1] Words in sub-para (b) substituted by FA 1995 s 33(1), (3)(b) and are deemed to have always had effect.

[2] Sub-s (1) numbered as such, and sub-ss (2)–(4) inserted by FA 2007 s 99(4), (5) with effect from 19 July 2007.

8 Where any supply of services is treated by virtue of section 8[, or any supply of goods is treated by virtue of section 9A,][1] as made by the person by whom they are received, the value of the supply shall be taken—

(*a*) in a case where the consideration for which the services [or goods][1] were in fact supplied to him was a consideration in money, to be such amount as is equal to that consideration; and

(*b*) in a case where that consideration did not consist or not wholly consist of money, to be such amount in money as is equivalent to that consideration.

Commentary—*De Voil Indirect Tax Service* **V3.231.**

Definitions—"Money", s 96(1); "supply", s 5, Sch 4.

Cross reference—See VAT (Reverse Charge) (Anti-avoidance) Order, SI 1997/1523 arts 7, 8 (modification of Sch 6 para 8 in relation to telecommunication services).

Amendments—[1] Words inserted by F(No 2)A 2005 s 5 with effect in relation to supplies made on or after 17 March 2005.

[8A—(1) This paragraph applies where—

(*a*) a supply ("the intra-group supply") made by a member of a group ("the supplier") to another member of the group is, by virtue of section 43(2A), excluded from the supplies disregarded under section 43(1)(*a*), and

(*b*) the representative member of the group satisfies the Commissioners as to the value of each bought-in supply.

(2) "Bought-in supply", in relation to the intra-group supply, means a supply of services to the supplier to which section 43(2A)(*c*) to (*e*) refers, so far as that supply is used by the supplier for making the intra-group supply.

(3) The value of the intra-group supply shall be taken to be the total of the relevant amounts in relation to the bought-in supplies.
(4) The relevant amount in relation to a bought-in supply is the value of the bought-in supply, unless a direction is made under subparagraph (5).
(5) If the value of a bought-in supply is less than its open market value, the Commissioners may direct that the relevant amount in relation to that supply is its open market value.
(6) A direction under this paragraph must be given by notice in writing to the representative member, but no direction may be given more than 3 years after the time of the intra-group supply.
(7) The Treasury may by order vary the provision made by this Schedule about the value of supplies of the kind mentioned in subparagraph (1)(*a*).
(8) An order under sub-paragraph (7) may include incidental, supplemental, consequential or transitional provision (including provision amending section 43 or 83).][1]

Amendments—[1] Para 8A inserted by FA 2012 s 200(1), (5), (7) with effect in relation to supplies made on or after 17 July 2012.

9—(1) This paragraph applies where a supply of services consists in the provision of accommodation falling within paragraph (*d*) of Item 1 of Group 1 in Schedule 9 and—

(*a*) that provision is made to an individual for a period exceeding 4 weeks; and
(*b*) throughout that period the accommodation is provided for the use of the individual either alone or together with one or more other persons who occupy the accommodation with him otherwise than at their own expense (whether incurred directly or indirectly).

(2) Where this paragraph applies—

(*a*) the value of so much of the supply as is in excess of 4 weeks shall be taken to be reduced to such part thereof as is attributable to facilities other than the right to occupy the accommodation; and
(*b*) that part shall be taken to be not less than 20 per cent.

Commentary—*De Voil Indirect Tax Service* **V3.166**.
Definitions—"Supply", s 5, Sch 4.

10—(1) This paragraph applies to a supply of goods or services, whether or not for consideration, which is made by an employer and consists of—

(*a*) the provision in the course of catering of food or beverages to his employees, or
(*b*) the provision of accommodation for his employees in a hotel, inn, boarding house or similar establishment.

(2) The value of a supply to which this paragraph applies shall be taken to be nil unless the supply is for a consideration consisting wholly or partly of money, and in that case its value shall be determined without regard to any consideration other than money.

Commentary—*De Voil Indirect Tax Service* **V3.166**.
HMRC Manuals—VAT Guidance V1-3: Supply and consideration, para 5.3 (supplies by employer to employees).
Definitions—"Money", s 96(1); "supply", s 5, Sch 4.

11—(1) Subject to the following provisions of this paragraph, where—

(*a*) there is a supply of goods or services; and
(*b*) any sum relevant for determining the value of the supply is expressed in a currency other than sterling,

then, for the purpose of valuing the supply, that sum is to be converted into sterling at the market rate which, on the relevant day, would apply in the United Kingdom to a purchase with sterling by the person to whom they are supplied of that sum in the currency in question.
(2) Where the Commissioners have published a notice which, for the purposes of this paragraph, specifies—

(*a*) rates of exchange; or
(*b*) methods of determining rates of exchange,

a rate specified in or determined in accordance with the notice, as for the time being in force, shall apply (instead of the rate for which sub-paragraph (1) above provides) in the case of any supply by a person who opts, in such manner as may be allowed by the Commissioners, for the use of that rate in relation to that supply.
(3) An option for the purposes of sub-paragraph (2) above for the use of a particular rate or method of determining a rate—

(*a*) shall not be exercised by any person except in relation to all such supplies by him as are of a particular description or after a particular date; and
(*b*) shall not be withdrawn or varied except with the consent of the Commissioners and in such manner as they may require.

(4) In specifying a method of determining a rate of exchange a notice published by the Commissioners under sub-paragraph (2) above may allow a person to apply to the Commissioners for the use, for the purpose of valuing some or all of his supplies, of a rate of exchange which is different from any which would otherwise apply.

(5) On an application made in accordance with provision contained in a notice under sub-paragraph (4) above, the Commissioners may authorise the use with respect to the applicant of such a rate of exchange, in such circumstances, in relation to such supplies and subject to such conditions as they think fit.

(6) A notice published by the Commissioners for the purposes of this paragraph may be withdrawn or varied by a subsequent notice published by the Commissioners.

(7) The time by reference to which the appropriate rate of exchange is to be determined for the purpose of valuing any supply is the time when the supply takes place; and, accordingly, the day on which it takes place is the relevant day for the purposes of sub-paragraph (1) above.

Commentary—*De Voil Indirect Tax Service* **V3.164**.

Customs and Excise Notices—Notice 700: The VAT Guide, para 7.7 (values expressed in foreign currency).

Definitions—"The Commissioners", s 96(10); "supply", s 5, Sch 4; "United Kingdom", s 96(11).

12 Regulations may require that in prescribed circumstances there is to be taken into account, as constituting part of the consideration for the purposes of section 19(2) (where it would not otherwise be so taken into account), money paid in respect of the supply by persons other than those to whom the supply is made.

Commentary—*De Voil Indirect Tax Service* **V3.153**.

Definitions—"Supply", s 5, Sch 4.

13 A direction under paragraph 1 or 2 above may be varied or withdrawn by the Commissioners by a further direction given by notice in writing.

Commentary—*De Voil Indirect Tax Service* **V3.162, V3.163**.

Definitions—"The Commissioners", s 96(10).

SCHEDULE 7

VALUATION OF ACQUISITIONS FROM OTHER MEMBER STATES: SPECIAL CASES

Section 20

Cross reference—See VATA 1994 s 52 (provision for regulations modifying this Schedule in relation to the valuation of acquisitions of goods under trading stamp schemes).

1—(1) Where, in the case of the acquisition of any goods from another member State—

(*a*) the relevant transaction is for a consideration in money;

(*b*) the value of the relevant transaction is (apart from this paragraph) less than the transaction's open market value;

(*c*) the supplier and the person who acquires the goods are connected; and

(*d*) that person is not entitled under sections 25 and 26 to credit for all the VAT on the acquisition,

the Commissioners may direct that the value of the relevant transaction shall be taken to be its open market value.

(2) A direction under this paragraph shall be given by notice in writing to the person by whom the acquisition in question is made; but no direction may be given more than 3 years after the relevant time.

(3) A direction given to a person under this paragraph in respect of a transaction may include a direction that the value of any transaction—

(*a*) in pursuance of which goods are acquired by him from another member State after the giving of the notice, or after such later date as may be specified in the notice; and

(*b*) as to which the conditions in paragraphs (*a*) to (*d*) of sub-paragraph (1) above are satisfied,

shall be taken to be its open market value.

(4) For the purposes of this paragraph the open market value of a transaction in pursuance of which goods are acquired from another member State shall be taken to be the amount which would fall to be taken as its value under section 20(3) if it were for such consideration in money as would be payable by a person standing in no such relationship with any person as would affect that consideration.

(5) For the purposes of this paragraph any question whether a person is connected with another shall be determined in accordance with [section 1122 of the Corporation Tax Act 2010][1].

(6) A direction under this paragraph may be varied or withdrawn by the Commissioners by a further direction given by notice in writing.

Commentary—*De Voil Indirect Tax Service* **V3.391**.

Definitions—"Acquisition of goods from another member State", s 11; "another member State", s 96(1); "the Commissioners", s 96(1); "money", s 96(1); "open market value", s 19(5); "prescribed", s 96(1); "the Taxes Act", s 96(1); "VAT", ss 1, 96(1).
Cross reference—See VATA 1994 s 83 (appeal to a tribunal in respect of a direction under this para).
Amendments—[1] In sub-para (5) words substituted for words "section 839 of the Taxes Act 1988" by CTA 2010 s 1177, Sch 1 para 285(c). CTA 2010 has effect for corporation tax purposes for accounting periods ending on or after 1 April 2010, and for income and capital gains tax purposes for the tax year 2010–11 and subsequent tax years.

2—(1) Where, in such cases as the Commissioners may by regulations prescribe, goods acquired in the United Kingdom from another member State—

(*a*) are charged in connection with their removal to the United Kingdom with a duty of excise; or

(*b*) on that removal are subject, in accordance with any provision for the time being having effect for transitional purposes in connection with the accession of any State to the European Communities, to any Community customs duty or agricultural levy of the Economic Community,

then the value of the relevant transaction shall be taken for the purposes of this Act to be the sum of its value apart from this paragraph and the amount, so far as not already included in that value, of the duty or, as the case may be, agricultural levy which has been or is to be paid in respect of those goods.

(2) Sub-paragraph (1) above shall not require the inclusion of any amount of duty or agricultural levy in the value of a transaction in pursuance of which there is an acquisition of goods which, under subsection (4) of section 18, is treated as taking place before the time which is the duty point within the meaning of that section.

Commentary—*De Voil Indirect Tax Service* **V3.390**.
Regulations—See VAT Regulations, SI 1995/2518 regs 96, 97.
Definitions—"Amount of any duty of excise", s 96(5); "the Commissioners", s 96(1).
Cross reference—See VAT Regulations, SI 1995/2518 reg 97 (cases to which this para applies).

3—(1) Where goods are acquired from another member State in pursuance of anything which is treated as a supply for the purposes of this Act by virtue of paragraph 5(1) or 6 of Schedule 4, the value of the relevant transaction shall be determined, in a case where there is no consideration, as follows.

(2) The value of the transaction shall be taken to be—

(*a*) such consideration in money as would be payable by the supplier if he were, at the time of the acquisition, to purchase goods identical in every respect (including age and condition) to the goods concerned; or

(*b*) where the value cannot be ascertained in accordance with paragraph (*a*) above, such consideration in money as would be payable by the supplier if he were, at that time, to purchase goods similar to, and of the same age and condition as, the goods concerned; or

(*c*) where the value can be ascertained in accordance with neither paragraph (*a*) nor paragraph (*b*) above, the cost of producing the goods concerned if they were produced at that time.

(3) For the purposes of sub-paragraph (2) above the amount of consideration in money that would be payable by any person if he were to purchase any goods shall be taken to be the amount that would be so payable after the deduction of any amount included in the purchase price in respect of VAT on the supply of the goods to that person.

Commentary—*De Voil Indirect Tax Service* **V3.390**.
Definitions—"Acquisition of goods from another member State", s 11; "another member State", s 11; "VAT", ss 1, 96(1).

4—(1) Subject to the following provisions of this paragraph, where—

(*a*) goods are acquired from another member State; and

(*b*) any sum relevant for determining the value of the relevant transaction is expressed in a currency other than sterling,

then, for the purpose of valuing the relevant transaction, that sum is to be converted into sterling at the market rate which, on the relevant day, would apply in the United Kingdom to a purchase with sterling by the person making the acquisition of that sum in the currency in question.

(2) Where the Commissioners have published a notice which, for the purposes of this paragraph, specifies—

(*a*) rates of exchange; or

(*b*) methods of determining rates of exchange,

a rate specified in or determined in accordance with the notice, as for the time being in force, shall apply (instead of the rate for which sub-paragraph (1) above provides) in the case of any transaction in pursuance of which goods are acquired by a person who opts, in such manner as may be allowed by the Commissioners, for the use of that rate in relation to that transaction.

(3) An option for the purposes of sub-paragraph (2) above for the use of a particular rate or method of determining a rate—

(*a*) shall not be exercised by any person except in relation to all such transactions in pursuance of which goods are acquired by him from another member State as are of a particular description or after a particular date; and

(*b*) shall not be withdrawn or varied except with the consent of the Commissioners and in such manner as they may require.

(4) In specifying a method of determining a rate of exchange a notice published by the Commissioners under sub-paragraph (2) above may allow a person to apply to the Commissioners for the use, for the purpose of valuing some or all of the transactions in pursuance of which goods are acquired by him from another member State, of a rate of exchange which is different from any which would otherwise apply.

(5) On an application made in accordance with provision contained in a notice under sub-paragraph (4) above, the Commissioners may authorise the use with respect to the applicant of such a rate of exchange, in such circumstances, in relation to such transactions and subject to such conditions as they think fit.

(6) A notice published by the Commissioners for the purposes of this paragraph may be withdrawn or varied by a subsequent notice published by the Commissioners.

(7) Where goods are acquired from another member State, the appropriate rate of exchange is to be determined for the purpose of valuing the relevant transaction by reference to the relevant time; and, accordingly, the day on which that time falls is the relevant day for the purposes of sub-paragraph (1) above.

Commentary—*De Voil Indirect Tax Service* **V3.393**.

Definitions—"Acquisition of goods from another member State", s 11; "amount of any duty of excise", s 96(5); "another member State", s 96(1); "the Commissioners", s 96(1); "United Kingdom", s 96(11).

5 In this Schedule—

"relevant transaction", in relation to any acquisition of goods from another member State, means the transaction in pursuance of which the goods are acquired;

"the relevant time", in relation to any such acquisition, means—

(*a*) if the person by whom the goods are acquired is not a taxable person and the time of acquisition does not fall to be determined in accordance with regulations made under section 12(3), the time of the event which, in relation to that acquisition, is the first relevant event for the purposes of taxing the acquisition; and

(*b*) in any other case, the time of acquisition.

[SCHEDULE 7A
CHARGE AT REDUCED RATE]

Section 29A

Summer Finance Bill 2015 The Summer Finance Bill introduces a "VAT lock", restricting the standard and reduced rates of VAT to current rates. The Bill also provides that no supply specified in this Schedule at the beginning of the VAT lock period may be removed from this Schedule under s 29A(3) during that period. Please check the latest version of the Bill and subsequent Finance Act for details.

Amendments—This Schedule inserted by FA 2001 s 99(5), Sch 31 with effect for supplies made, and acquisitions and importations taking place, after 31 October 2001.

[PART I
INDEX TO REDUCED-RATE SUPPLIES OF GOODS AND SERVICES

[Cable-suspended passenger transport systems	Group 13][4]
[Caravans	Group 12][5]
Children's car seats	Group 5
[Contraceptive products	Group 8][2]
Domestic fuel or power	Group 1
Energy-saving materials: installation	Group 2
Heating equipment, security goods and gas supplies: grant-funded installation or connection	Group 3
[Installation of mobility aids for the elderly	Group 10][3]
Residential renovations and alterations	Group 7
Residential conversions	Group 6
[Smoking cessation products	Group 11][3]
[Welfare advice or information	Group 9][2]
Women's sanitary products][1]	Group 4

Amendments—[1] This Schedule inserted by FA 2001 s 99(5), Sch 31 with effect for supplies made, and acquisitions and importations taking place, after 31 October 2001.
[2] Entries inserted by the Value Added Tax (Reduced Rate) Order, SI 2006/1472 arts 2, 3 with effect from 1 July 2006.
[3] Entries inserted by the Value Added Tax (Reduced Rate) Order, SI 2007/1601 arts 2, 3. Entry "Installation of mobility aids for the elderly" has effect in relation to supplies made on or after 1 July 2007. Entry "Smoking cessation products" has effect in relation to supplies made on or after 1 July 2007 but before 1 July 2008.
[4] Entry for "Cable-suspended passenger transport systems" (Group 13) inserted by the Value Added Tax (Reduced Rate) (Cable-Suspended Passenger Transport Systems) Order, SI 2013/430 art 2(1), (2) with effect from 1 April 2013.
[5] Entry for Caravans (Group 12) inserted by FA 2012 s 196, Sch 26 para 6(1), (2) with effect from 6 April 2013.

[PART II
THE GROUPS

GROUP 1
SUPPLIES OF DOMESTIC FUEL OR POWER

Item No.

1 Supplies for qualifying use of—
(*a*) coal, coke or other solid substances held out for sale solely as fuel;
(*b*) coal gas, water gas, producer gases or similar gases;
(*c*) petroleum gases, or other gaseous hydrocarbons, whether in a gaseous or liquid state;
(*d*) fuel oil, gas oil or kerosene; or
(*e*) electricity, heat or air-conditioning.

NOTES:

Matters included or not included in the supplies

1—(1) Item 1(*a*) shall be deemed to include combustible materials put up for sale for kindling fires but shall not include matches.
(2) Item 1(*b*) and (*c*) shall not include any road fuel gas (within the meaning of the Hydrocarbon Oil Duties Act 1979) on which a duty of excise has been charged or is chargeable.
(3) Item 1(*d*) shall not include hydrocarbon oil on which a duty of excise has been or is to be charged without relief from, or rebate of, such duty by virtue of the provisions of the Hydrocarbon Oil Duties Act 1979[, unless the oil is—
(*a*) kerosene in respect of which a relevant declaration has been made under section 13AC(3) of that Act (use of rebated kerosene for private pleasure-flying); or
(*b*) oil in respect of which a relevant declaration has been made under section 14E(3) of that Act (use of rebated heavy oil for private pleasure craft)][1].

Amendments—[1] In Note 1 para (3), words inserted at end by the Value Added Tax (Reduced Rate) (Supplies of Domestic Fuel or Power) Order, SI 2008/2676 art 2 with effect from 1 November 2008.

Meaning of "fuel oil", "gas oil" and "kerosene"

2—(1) In this Group "fuel oil" means heavy oil which contains in solution an amount of asphaltenes of not less than 0.5 per cent. or which contains less than 0.5 per cent. but not less than 0.1 per cent. of asphaltenes and has a closed flash point not exceeding 150°C.
(2) In this Group "gas oil" means heavy oil of which not more than 50 per cent. by volume distils at a temperature not exceeding 240°C and of which more than 50 per cent. by volume distils at a temperature not exceeding 340°C.
(3) In this Group "kerosene" means heavy oil of which more than 50 per cent. by volume distils at a temperature not exceeding 240°C.
(4) In this paragraph "heavy oil" has the same meaning as in the Hydrocarbon Oil Duties Act 1979.

Meaning of "qualifying use"

3 In this Group "qualifying use" means—
(*a*) domestic use; or
(*b*) use by a charity otherwise than in the course or furtherance of a business.

Supplies only partly for qualifying use

4 For the purposes of this Group, where there is a supply of goods partly for qualifying use and partly not—
(*a*) if at least 60 per cent. of the goods are supplied for qualifying use, the whole supply shall be treated as a supply for qualifying use; and
(*b*) in any other case, an apportionment shall be made to determine the extent to which the supply is a supply for qualifying use.

Supplies deemed to be for domestic use

5 For the purposes of this Group the following supplies are always for domestic use—

(*a*) a supply of not more than one tonne of coal or coke held out for sale as domestic fuel;

(*b* a supply of wood, peat or charcoal not intended for sale by the recipient;

(*c*) a supply to a person at any premises of piped gas (that is, gas within item 1(*b*), or petroleum gas in a gaseous state, provided through pipes) where the gas (together with any other piped gas provided to him at the premises by the same supplier) was not provided at a rate exceeding 150 therms a month or, if the supplier charges for the gas by reference to the number of kilowatt hours supplied, 4397 kilowatt hours a month;

(*d*) a supply of petroleum gas in a liquid state where the gas is supplied in cylinders the net weight of each of which is less than 50 kilogrammes and either the number of cylinders supplied is 20 or fewer or the gas is not intended for sale by the recipient;

(*e*) a supply of petroleum gas in a liquid state, otherwise than in cylinders, to a person at any premises at which he is not able to store more than two tonnes of such gas;

(*f*) a supply of not more than 2,300 litres of fuel oil, gas oil or kerosene;

(*g*) a supply of electricity to a person at any premises where the electricity (together with any other electricity provided to him at the premises by the same supplier) was not provided at a rate exceeding 1000 kilowatt hours a month.

Other supplies that are for domestic use

6 For the purposes of this Group supplies not within paragraph 5 are for domestic use if and only if the goods supplied are for use in—

(*a*) a building, or part of a building, that consists of a dwelling or number of dwellings;

(*b*) a building, or part of a building, used for a relevant residential purpose;

(*c*) self-catering holiday accommodation;

(*d*) a caravan; or

(*e*) a houseboat.

Interpretation of paragraph 6

7—(1) For the purposes of this Group, "use for a relevant residential purpose" means use as—

(*a*) a home or other institution providing residential accommodation for children,

(*b*) a home or other institution providing residential accommodation with personal care for persons in need of personal care by reason of old age, disablement, past or present dependence on alcohol or drugs or past or present mental disorder,

(*c*) a hospice,

(*d*) residential accommodation for students or school pupils,

(*e*) residential accommodation for members of any of the armed forces,

(*f*) a monastery, nunnery or similar establishment, or

(*g*) an institution which is the sole or main residence of at least 90 per cent. of its residents,

except use as a hospital, a prison or similar institution or an hotel or inn or similar establishment.

(2) For the purposes of this Group "self-catering holiday accommodation" includes any accommodation advertised or held out as such.

(3) In paragraph 6 "houseboat" means a boat or other floating decked structure designed or adapted for use solely as a place of permanent habitation and not having means of, or capable of being readily adapted for, self-propulsion.][1]

Amendments—[1] This Schedule inserted by FA 2001 s 99(5), Sch 31 with effect for supplies made, and acquisitions and importations taking place, after 31 October 2001.

[GROUP 2

INSTALLATION OF ENERGY-SAVING MATERIALS

Item No.

[**1** Supplies of services of installing energy-saving materials in residential accommodation.

2 Supplies of energy-saving materials by a person who installs those materials in residential accommodation.][4]

NOTES:

Meaning of "energy-saving materials"

1 For the purposes of this Group "energy-saving materials" means any of the following—

(*a*) insulation for walls, floors, ceilings, roofs or lofts or for water tanks, pipes or other plumbing fittings;
(*b*) draught stripping for windows and doors;
(*c*) central heating system controls (including thermostatic radiator valves);
(*d*) hot water system controls;
(*e*) solar panels;
(*f*) wind turbines;
(*g*) water turbines;
[(*h*) ground source heat pumps][1].
[(*i*) air source heat pumps;
(*j*) micro combined heat and power units;][2]
[(*k*) boilers designed to be fuelled solely by wood, straw or similar vegetal matter.][3]

Simon's Tax Cases—Item 2, note 1(a), *R&C Comrs v Pinevale Ltd* [2014] UKUT 204 (TCC), [2014] STC 2217.

Amendments—[1] Note (1)(*h*) inserted by the VAT (Reduced Rate) Order, SI 2004/777 with effect from 1 June 2004.
[2] Note (1)(*i*), (*j*) inserted by the VAT (Reduced Rate) Order, SI 2005/726 with effect from 7 April 2005.
[3] Note (1)(*k*) inserted by the VAT (Reduced Rate) (No 2) Order, SI 2005/3329 with effect from 1 January 2006.
[4] Items 1, 2 substituted by FA 2013 s 193(1), (2) with effect in relation to supplies made on or after 1 August 2013.

Meaning of "residential accommodation"

2—(1) For the purposes of this Group "residential accommodation" means—
(*a*) a building, or part of a building, that consists of a dwelling or a number of dwellings;
(*b*) a building, or part of a building, used for a relevant residential purpose;
(*c*) a caravan used as a place of permanent habitation; or
(*d*) a houseboat.

(2) For the purposes of this Group "use for a relevant residential purpose" has the same meaning as it has for the purposes of Group 1 (see paragraph 7(1) of the Notes to that Group).

(3) In sub-paragraph (1)(*d*) "houseboat" has the meaning given by paragraph 7(3) of the Notes to Group 1.

Meaning of "use for a relevant charitable purpose"

3 For the purposes of this Group "use for a relevant charitable purpose" means use by a charity in either or both of the following ways, namely—
(*a*) otherwise than in the course or furtherance of a business;
(*b*) as a village hall or similarly in providing social or recreational facilities for a local community.][1], [2]

Amendments—[1] This Schedule inserted by FA 2001 s 99(5), Sch 31 with effect for supplies made, and acquisitions and importations taking place, after 31 October 2001.
[2] Note 3 repealed by FA 2013 s 193(1), (3) with effect in relation to supplies made on or after 1 August 2013.

[GROUP 3

GRANT-FUNDED INSTALLATION OF HEATING EQUIPMENT OR SECURITY GOODS OR CONNECTION OF GAS SUPPLY

Item No.

1 Supplies to a qualifying person of any services of installing heating appliances in the qualifying person's sole or main residence.

2 Supplies of heating appliances made to a qualifying person by a person who installs those appliances in the qualifying person's sole or main residence.

3 Supplies to a qualifying person of services of connecting, or reconnecting, a mains gas supply to the qualifying person's sole or main residence.

4 Supplies of goods made to a qualifying person by a person connecting, or reconnecting, a mains gas supply to the qualifying person's sole or main residence, being goods whose installation is necessary for the connection, or reconnection, of the mains gas supply.

5 Supplies to a qualifying person of services of installing, maintaining or repairing a central heating system in the qualifying person's sole or main residence.

6 Supplies of goods made to a qualifying person by a person installing, maintaining or repairing a central heating system in the qualifying person's sole or main residence, being goods whose installation is necessary for the installation, maintenance or repair of the central heating system.

7 Supplies consisting in the leasing of goods that form the whole or part of a central heating system installed in the sole or main residence of a qualifying person.

8 Supplies of goods that form the whole or part of a central heating system installed in a qualifying person's sole or main residence and that, immediately before being supplied, were goods leased under arrangements such that the consideration for the supplies consisting in the leasing of the goods was, in whole or in part, funded by a grant made under a relevant scheme.

[8A Supplies to a qualifying person of services of installing, maintaining or repairing a renewable source heating system in the qualifying person's sole or main residence.][1]

Amendments—[1] Items 8A, 8B inserted, words in Notes (1), (4) substituted, and Notes (4A), (4B) inserted, by the VAT (Reduced Rate) Order, SI 2002/1100 arts 2, 3 with effect from 1 June 2002.

[8B Supplies of goods made to a qualifying person by a person installing, maintaining or repairing a renewable source heating system in the qualifying person's sole or main residence, being goods whose installation is necessary for the installation, maintenance or repair of the system.][1]

Amendments—[1] Items 8A, 8B inserted, words in Notes (1), (4) substituted, and Notes (4A), (4B) inserted, by the VAT (Reduced Rate) Order, SI 2002/1100 arts 2, 3 with effect from 1 June 2002.

9 Supplies to a qualifying person of services of installing qualifying security goods in the qualifying person's sole or main residence.

10 Supplies of qualifying security goods made to a qualifying person by a person who installs those goods in the qualifying person's sole or main residence.

NOTES:

Supply only included so far as grant-funded

1—(1) Each of [items 1 to 7 and 8A to 10][1] applies to a supply only to the extent that the consideration for the supply is, or is to be, funded by a grant made under a relevant scheme.

(2) Item 8 applies to a supply only to the extent that the consideration for the supply—

(*a*) is, or is to be, funded by a grant made under a relevant scheme; or

(*b*) is a payment becoming due only by reason of the termination (whether by the passage of time or otherwise) of the leasing of the goods in question.

Amendments—[1] Words in Notes (1), (4) substituted by the VAT (Reduced Rate) Order, SI 2002/1100 arts 2, 3 with effect from 1 June 2002.

Meaning of "relevant scheme"

2—(1) For the purposes of this Group a scheme is a "relevant scheme" if it is one which satisfies the conditions specified in this paragraph.

(2) The first condition is that the scheme has as one of its objectives the funding of the installation of energy-saving materials in the homes of any persons who are qualifying persons.

(3) The second condition is that the scheme disburses, whether directly or indirectly, its grants in whole or in part out of funds made available to it in order to achieve that objective—

(*a*) by the Secretary of State,

(*b*) by the Scottish Ministers,

(*c*) by the National Assembly for Wales,

(*d*) by a Minister (within the meaning given by section 7(3) of the Northern Ireland Act 1998) or a Northern Ireland department,

(*e*) by the European Community,

(*f*) under an arrangement approved by the Gas and Electricity Markets Authority,

(*g*) under an arrangement approved by the Director General of Electricity Supply for Northern Ireland, or

(*h*) by a local authority.

(4) The reference in sub-paragraph (3)(*f*) to an arrangement approved by the Gas and Electricity Markets Authority includes a reference to an arrangement approved by the Director General of Electricity Supply, or the Director General of Gas Supply, before the transfer (under the Utilities Act 2000) of his functions to the Authority.

Apportionment of grants that also cover other supplies

3 Where a grant is made under a relevant scheme in order—

(*a*) to fund a supply of a description to which any of items 1 to 10 applies ("the relevant supply"), and

(*b*) also to fund a supply to which none of those items applies ("the non-relevant supply"),

the proportion of the grant that is to be attributed, for the purposes of paragraph 1, to the relevant supply shall be the same proportion as the consideration reasonably attributable to that supply bears to the consideration for that supply and for the non-relevant supply.

Meaning of "heating appliances"

4 For the purposes of items 1 and 2 "heating appliances" means any of the following—

(*a*) gas-fired room heaters that are fitted with thermostatic controls;

(*b*) electric storage heaters;

(*c*) closed solid fuel fire cassettes;

(*d*) electric dual immersion water heaters with [factory-insulated][1] hot water tanks;

(*e*) gas-fired boilers;

(*f*) oil-fired boilers;

(*g*) radiators.

Amendments—[1] Words in Notes (1), (4) substituted by the VAT (Reduced Rate) Order, SI 2002/1100 arts 2, 3 with effect from 1 June 2002.

[Meaning of "central heating system"

4A For the purposes of items 5 to 8 "central heating system" includes a system which generates electricity.][1]

Amendments—[1] Notes (4A), (4B) inserted, by the VAT (Reduced Rate) Order, SI 2002/1100 arts 2, 3 with effect from 1 June 2002.

[Meaning of "renewable source heating system"

4B For the purposes of items 8A and 8B "renewable source heating system" means a space or water heating system which uses energy from

(*a*) renewable sources, including solar, wind and hydroelectric power; or

(*b*) near renewable resources, including ground and air heat.][1]

Amendments—[1] Notes (4A), (4B) inserted, by the VAT (Reduced Rate) Order, SI 2002/1100 arts 2, 3 with effect from 1 June 2002.

Meaning of "qualifying security goods"

5 For the purposes of items 9 and 10 "qualifying security goods" means any of the following—

(*a*) locks or bolts for windows;

(*b*) locks, bolts or security chains for doors;

(*c*) spy holes;

(*d*) smoke alarms.

Meaning of "qualifying person"

6—(1) For the purposes of this Group, a person to whom a supply is made is "a qualifying person" if at the time of the supply he—

(*a*) is aged 60 or over; or

(*b*) is in receipt of one or more of the benefits mentioned in sub-paragraph (2).

(2) Those benefits are—

(*a*) council tax benefit under Part VII of the Contributions and Benefits Act;

(*b*) disability living allowance under Part III of the Contributions and Benefits Act or Part III of the Northern Ireland Act;

(*c*) [any element of child tax credit other than the family element, working tax credit,][2] housing benefit or income support under Part VII of the Contributions and Benefits Act or Part VII of the Northern Ireland Act;

(*d*) an income-based jobseeker's allowance within the meaning of section 1(4) of the Jobseekers Act 1995 or Article 3(4) of the Jobseekers (Northern Ireland) Order 1995;

(*e*) disablement pension under Part V of the Contributions and Benefits Act, or Part V of the Northern Ireland Act, that is payable at the increased rate provided for under section 104 (constant attendance allowance) of the Act concerned;

(*f*) war disablement pension under the Naval, Military and Air Forces Etc. (Disablement and Death) Service Pensions Order 1983 that is payable at the increased rate provided for under article 14 (constant attendance allowance) or article 26A (mobility supplement) of that Order.

[(*g*) personal independence payment under Part 4 of the Welfare Reform Act 2012 or the corresponding provision having effect in Northern Ireland;

(*h*) armed forces independence payment under a scheme established under section 1 of the Armed Forces (Pensions and Compensation) Act 2004.][3]

[(*i*) universal credit under Part 1 of the Welfare Reform Act 2012.][4]

(3) In sub-paragraph (2)—

(*a*) "the Contributions and Benefits Act" means the Social Security Contributions and Benefits Act 1992; and

(*b*) "the Northern Ireland Act" means the Social Security Contributions and Benefits (Northern Ireland) Act 1992.][1]

Amendments—[1] This Schedule inserted by FA 2001 s 99(5), Sch 31 with effect for supplies made, and acquisitions and importations taking place, after 31 October 2001.

[2] Words substituted by TCA 2002 s 47, Sch 3 paras 47, 48 with effect from 6 April 2003 (by virtue of SI 2003/962).

[3] Paras (6)(*g*), (*h*) inserted by the Value Added Tax (Independence Payment) Order, SI 2013/601 art 2 with effect from 8 April 2013.

[4] Para (2)(*i*) inserted by the Universal Credit (Consequential, Supplementary, Incidental and Miscellaneous Provisions) Regulations, SI 2013/630 reg 9 with effect from 29 April 2013.

Prospective amendments—In Note 6(2)(*b*), words "Part III of the Contributions and Benefits Act or" to be repealed by the Welfare Reform Act 2012 s 147, Sch 14 Part 9 with effect from a date to be appointed.

[GROUP 4

WOMEN'S SANITARY PRODUCTS

Item No.

1 Supplies of women's sanitary products.

NOTES:

Meaning of "women's sanitary products"

1—(1) In this Group "women's sanitary products" means women's sanitary products of any of the following descriptions—

(*a*) subject to sub-paragraph (2), products that are designed, and marketed, as being solely for use for absorbing, or otherwise collecting, lochia or menstrual flow;

(*b*) panty liners, other than panty liners that are designed as being primarily for use as incontinence products;

(*c*) sanitary belts.

(2) Sub-paragraph (1)(*a*) does not include protective briefs or any other form of clothing.][1]

Amendments—[1] This Schedule inserted by FA 2001 s 99(5), Sch 31 with effect for supplies made, and acquisitions and importations taking place, after 31 October 2001.

[GROUP 5

CHILDREN'S CAR SEATS

Item No.

1 Supplies of children's car seats.

NOTES:

Meaning of "children's car seats"

1—(1) For the purposes of this Group, the following are "children's car seats"—

(*a*) a safety seat;

[(*aa*) a related base unit for a safety seat;][1]

(*b*) the combination of a safety seat and a related wheeled framework;

(*c*) a booster seat;

(*d*) a booster cushion.

(2) In this Group "child" means a person aged under 14 years.

Amendments—[1] In Note 1, para (1)(*aa*) inserted by the Value Added Tax (Reduced Rate) (Children's Car Seats) Order, SI 2009/1359 arts 2, 3 with effect in relation to supplies made, and acquisitions and importations taking place, on or after 1 July 2009.

Meaning of "safety seat"

2 In this Group "safety seat" means a seat—

(*a*) designed to be sat in by a child in a road vehicle,

[(*b*) designed so that, when in use in a road vehicle, it can be restrained in one or more of the following ways—

(i) by a seat belt fitted in the vehicle, or

(ii) by belts, or anchorages, that form part of the seat being attached to the vehicle, or

(iii) by a related base unit, and][1]

(*c*) incorporating an integral harness, or integral impact shield, for restraining a child seated in it.

Amendments—[1] Note 2 para (*b*) substituted, by the Value Added Tax (Reduced Rate) (Children's Car Seats) Order, SI 2009/1359 arts 2, 3 with effect in relation to supplies made, and acquisitions and importations taking place, on or after 1 July 2009.

[Meaning of "related base unit"

2A In this Group "related base unit" means a base unit which is designed solely for the purpose of attaching a safety seat securely in a road vehicle by means of anchorages that form part of the base unit and which, when in use in a road vehicle, can be restrained in one or more of the following ways—

(*a*) by a seat belt fitted in the vehicle, or
(*b*) by permanent anchorage points in the vehicle, or
(*c*) by belts attached to permanent anchorage points in the vehicle.][1]

Amendments—[1] Note 2A inserted, by the Value Added Tax (Reduced Rate) (Children's Car Seats) Order, SI 2009/1359 arts 2, 3 with effect in relation to supplies made, and acquisitions and importations taking place, on or after 1 July 2009.

Meaning of "related wheeled framework"

3 For the purposes of this Group, a wheeled framework is "related" to a safety seat if the framework and the seat are each designed so that—

(*a*) when the seat is not in use in a road vehicle it can be attached to the framework, and
(*b*) when the seat is so attached, the combination of the seat and the framework can be used as a child's pushchair.

Meaning of "booster seat"

4 In this Group "booster seat" means a seat designed—

(*a*) to be sat in by a child in a road vehicle, and
(*b*) so that, when in use in a road vehicle, it and a child seated in it can be restrained by a seat belt fitted in the vehicle.

Meaning of "booster cushion"

5 In this Group "booster cushion" means a cushion designed—

(*a*) to be sat on by a child in a road vehicle, and
(*b*) so that a child seated on it can be restrained by a seat belt fitted in the vehicle.][1]

Amendments—[1] This Schedule inserted by FA 2001 s 99(5), Sch 31 with effect for supplies made, and acquisitions and importations taking place, after 31 October 2001.

[GROUP 6

RESIDENTIAL CONVERSIONS

Item No.

1 The supply, in the course of a qualifying conversion, of qualifying services related to the conversion.

2 The supply of building materials if—

(*a*) the materials are supplied by a person who, in the course of a qualifying conversion, is supplying qualifying services related to the conversion, and
(*b*) those services include the incorporation of the materials in the building concerned or its immediate site.

NOTES:

Supplies only partly within item 1

1—(1) Sub-paragraph (2) applies where a supply of services is only in part a supply to which item 1 applies.
(2) The supply, to the extent that it is one to which item 1 applies, is to be taken to be a supply to which item 1 applies.
(3) An apportionment may be made to determine that extent.

Meaning of "qualifying conversion"

2—(1) A "qualifying conversion" means—

(*a*) a changed number of dwellings conversion (see paragraph 3);
(*b*) a house in multiple occupation conversion (see paragraph 5); or
(*c*) a special residential conversion (see paragraph 7).

(2) Sub-paragraph (1) is subject to paragraphs 9 and 10.

Meaning of "changed number of dwellings conversion"

3—(1) A "changed number of dwellings conversion" is—

(*a*) a conversion of premises consisting of a building where the conditions specified in this paragraph are satisfied, or

(*b*) a conversion of premises consisting of a part of a building where those conditions are satisfied.

(2) The first condition is that after the conversion the premises being converted contain a number of single household dwellings that is—

(*a*) different from the number (if any) that the premises contain before the conversion, and

(*b*) greater than, or equal to, one.

(3) The second condition is that there is no part of the premises being converted that is a part that after the conversion contains the same number of single household dwellings (whether zero, one or two or more) as before the conversion.

Meaning of "single household dwelling" and "multiple occupancy dwelling"

4—(1) For the purposes of this Group "single household dwelling" means a dwelling—

(*a*) that is designed for occupation by a single household, and

(*b*) in relation to which the conditions set out in sub-paragraph (3) are satisfied.

(2) For the purposes of this Group "multiple occupancy dwelling" means a dwelling—

(*a*) that is designed for occupation by persons not forming a single household, . . .

[(*aa*) that is not to any extent used for a relevant residential purpose, and][1]

(*b*) in relation to which the conditions set out in sub-paragraph (3) are satisfied.

(3) The conditions are—

(*a*) that the dwelling consists of self-contained living accommodation,

(*b*) that there is no provision for direct internal access from the dwelling to any other dwelling or part of a dwelling,

(*c*) that the separate use of the dwelling is not prohibited by the terms of any covenant, statutory planning consent or similar provision, and

(*d*) that the separate disposal of the dwelling is not prohibited by any such terms.

(4) For the purposes of this paragraph, a dwelling "is designed" for occupation of a particular kind if it is so designed—

(*a*) as a result of having been originally constructed for occupation of that kind and not having been subsequently adapted for occupation of any other kind, or

(*b*) as a result of adaptation.

Amendments—[1] Note (4)(2)(*aa*) inserted by the VAT (Reduced Rate) Order, SI 2002/1100 arts 2, 4 with effect from 1 June 2002.

Meaning of "house in multiple occupation conversion"

5—(1) A "house in multiple occupation conversion" is—

(*a*) a conversion of premises consisting of a building where the condition specified in sub-paragraph (2) below is satisfied, or

(*b*) a conversion of premises consisting of a part of a building where that condition is satisfied.

(2) The condition is that—

[(*a*) before the conversion the premises being converted do not contain any multiple occupancy dwellings,][1]

(*b*) after the conversion those premises contain only a multiple occupancy dwelling or two or more such dwellings, and

(*c*) the use to which those premises are intended to be put after the conversion is not to any extent use for a relevant residential purpose.

Amendments—[1] Note 5(2)(*a*) substituted by the VAT (Reduced Rate) Order, SI 2002/1100 arts 2, 4 with effect from 1 June 2002.

Meaning of "use for a relevant residential purpose"

6 For the purposes of this Group "use for a relevant residential purpose" means use as—

(*a*) a home or other institution providing residential accommodation for children,

(*b*) a home or other institution providing residential accommodation with personal care for persons in need of personal care by reason of old age, disablement, past or present dependence on alcohol or drugs or past or present mental disorder,

(*c*) a hospice,

(*d*) residential accommodation for students or school pupils,

(*e*) residential accommodation for members of any of the armed forces,

(*f*) a monastery, nunnery or similar establishment, or

(*g*) an institution which is the sole or main residence of at least 90 per cent. of its residents,

except use as a hospital, prison or similar institution or an hotel, inn or similar establishment.

Meaning of "special residential conversion"

7—(1) A "special residential conversion" is a conversion of premises consisting of—

(*a*) a building or two or more buildings,

(*b*) a part of a building or two or more parts of buildings, or

(*c*) a combination of—

(i) a building or two or more buildings, and

(ii) a part of a building or two or more parts of buildings,

where the conditions specified in this paragraph are satisfied.

[(2) The first condition is that—

(*a*) the use to which the premises being converted were last put before the conversion was not to any extent use for a relevant residential purpose, and

(*b*) those premises are intended to be used solely for a relevant residential purpose after the conversion.][1]

(3)–(5) . . . [1]

(6) The [second][1] condition is that, where the relevant residential purpose [for which the premises are intended to be used][1] is an institutional purpose, the premises being converted must be intended to form after the conversion the entirety of an institution used for that purpose.

(7) In sub-paragraph (6) "institutional purpose" means a purpose within paragraph 6(*a*) to (*c*), (*f*) or (*g*).

Amendments—[1] Note 7(2) and words in Note 7(6) substituted, Notes 7(3)–(5) repealed, by the VAT (Reduced Rate) Order, SI 2002/1100 arts 2, 4 with effect from 1 June 2002.

Special residential conversions: reduced rate only for supplies made to intended user of converted accommodation

8—(1) This paragraph applies where the qualifying conversion concerned is a special residential conversion.

(2) Item 1 or 2 does not apply to a supply unless—

(*a*) it is made to a person who intends to use the premises being converted for the relevant residential purpose, and

(*b*) before it is made, the person to whom it is made has given to the person making it a certificate that satisfies the requirements in sub-paragraph (3).

(3) Those requirements are that the certificate—

(*a*) is in such form as may be specified in a notice published by the Commissioners, and

(*b*) states that the conversion is a special residential conversion.

(4) In sub-paragraph (2)(*a*) "the relevant residential purpose" means the purpose within paragraph 6 for which the premises being converted are intended to be used after the conversion.

"Qualifying conversion" includes related garage works

9—(1) A qualifying conversion includes any garage works related to the—

(*a*) changed number of dwellings conversion,

(*b*) house in multiple occupation conversion, or

(*c*) special residential conversion,

concerned.

(2) In this paragraph "garage works" means—

(*a*) the construction of a garage, or

(*b*) a conversion of a non-residential building, or of a non-residential part of a building, that results in a garage.

(3) For the purposes of sub-paragraph (1), garage works are "related" to a conversion if—

(*a*) they are carried out at the same time as the conversion, and

(*b*) the resulting garage is intended to be occupied with—

(i) where the conversion concerned is a changed number of dwellings conversion, a single household dwelling that will after the conversion be contained in the building, or part of a building, being converted,

(ii) where the conversion concerned is a house in multiple occupation conversion, a multiple occupancy dwelling that will after the conversion be contained in the building, or part of a building, being converted, or

(iii) where the conversion concerned is a special residential conversion, the institution or other accommodation resulting from the conversion.

(4) In sub-paragraph (2) "non-residential" means neither designed, nor adapted, for use—

(*a*) as a dwelling or two or more dwellings, or

(*b*) for a relevant residential purpose.

Conversion not "qualifying" if planning consent and building control approval not obtained

10—(1) A conversion is not a qualifying conversion if any statutory planning consent needed for the conversion has not been granted.

(2) A conversion is not a qualifying conversion if any statutory building control approval needed for the conversion has not been granted.

Meaning of "supply of qualifying services"

11—(1) In the case of a conversion of a building, "supply of qualifying services" means a supply of services that consists in—

(*a*) the carrying out of works to the fabric of the building, or

(*b*) the carrying out of works within the immediate site of the building that are in connection with—

(i) the means of providing water, power, heat or access to the building,

(ii) the means of providing drainage or security for the building, or

(iii) the provision of means of waste disposal for the building.

(2) In the case of a conversion of part of a building, "supply of qualifying services" means a supply of services that consists in—

(*a*) the carrying out of works to the fabric of the part, or

(*b*) the carrying out of works to the fabric of the building, or within the immediate site of the building, that are in connection with—

(i) the means of providing water, power, heat or access to the part,

(ii) the means of providing drainage or security for the part, or

(iii) the provision of means of waste disposal for the part.

(3) In this paragraph—

(*a*) references to the carrying out of works to the fabric of a building do not include the incorporation, or installation as fittings, in the building of any goods that are not building materials;

(*b*) references to the carrying out of works to the fabric of a part of a building do not include the incorporation, or installation as fittings, in the part of any goods that are not building materials.

Meaning of "building materials"

12 In this Group "building materials" has the meaning given by Notes (22) and (23) of Group 5 to Schedule 8 (zero-rating of construction and conversion of buildings).][1]

Amendments—[1] This Schedule inserted by FA 2001 s 99(5), Sch 31 with effect for supplies made, and acquisitions and importations taking place, after 31 October 2001.

[GROUP 7

[RESIDENTIAL RENOVATIONS AND ALTERATIONS]

Amendments—Title substituted, words in Items 1 and 2, Note (2) substituted, Notes (3) and (5) amended, and Notes (3A), (4A) inserted, by the VAT (Reduced Rate) Order, SI 2002/1100 arts 2, 5 with effect from 1 June 2002.

Item No.

1 The supply, in the course of the renovation or alteration of [qualifying residential premises][1], of qualifying services related to the renovation or alteration.

Amendments—[1] Words in Items 1 and 2 substituted by the VAT (Reduced Rate) Order, SI 2002/1100 arts 2, 5 with effect from 1 June 2002.

2 The supply of building materials if—

(*a*) the materials are supplied by a person who, in the course of the renovation or alteration of a [qualifying residential premises], is supplying qualifying services related to the renovation or alteration, and

(*b*) those services include the incorporation of the materials in [the premises concerned or their immediate site][1].

Amendments—[1] Words in Items 1 and 2 substituted by the VAT (Reduced Rate) Order, SI 2002/1100 arts 2, 5 with effect from 1 June 2002.

NOTES:

Supplies only partly within item 1

1—(1) Sub-paragraph (2) applies where a supply of services is only in part a supply to which item 1 applies.

(2) The supply, to the extent that it is one to which item 1 applies, is to be taken to be a supply to which item 1 applies.

(3) An apportionment may be made to determine that extent.

Meaning of "alteration" and "single household dwelling"

2—(1) For the purposes of this Group—

"alteration" includes extension;

"qualifying residential premises" means—

(*a*) a single household dwelling,

(*b*) a multiple occupancy dwelling, or

(*c*) a building, or part of a building, which, when it was last lived in, was used for a relevant residential purpose.

(2) Where a building, when it was last lived in, formed part of a relevant residential unit then, to the extent that it would not be so regarded otherwise, the building shall be treated as having been used for a relevant residential purpose.

(3) A building forms part of a relevant residential unit at any time when—

(*a*) it is one of a number of buildings on the same site, and

(*b*) the buildings are used together as a unit for a relevant residential purpose.

(4) The following expressions have the same meaning in this Group as they have in Group 6—

"multiple occupancy dwelling" (paragraph 4(2) of the Notes to that Group);

"single household dwelling" (paragraph 4(1) of the Notes);

"use for a relevant residential purpose" (paragraph 6 of the Notes).]

Items 1 and 2 only apply where [premises have] been empty for at least [2 years]

3—[(1) Item 1 or 2 does not apply to a supply unless—

(*a*) the first empty home condition is satisfied, or

(*b*) if the premises are a single household dwelling, either of the empty home conditions is satisfied.]

[(2) The first "empty home condition" is that neither—

(*a*) the premises concerned, nor

(*b*) where those premises are a building, or part of a building, which, when it was last lived in, formed part of a relevant residential unit, any of the other buildings that formed part of the unit,

have been lived in during the period of [2 years] ending with the commencement of the relevant works.]

(3) The second "empty home condition" is that—

(*a*) the dwelling was not lived in during a period of at least [2 years];

(*b*) the person, or one the persons, whose beginning to live in the dwelling brought that period to an end was a person who (whether alone or jointly with another or others) acquired the dwelling at a time—

(i) no later than the end of that period, and

(ii) when the dwelling had been not lived in for at least [2 years];

(*c*) no works by way of renovation or alteration were carried out to the dwelling during the period of [2 years] ending with the acquisition;

(*d*) the supply is made to a person who is—

(i) the person, or one of the persons, whose beginning to live in the property brought to an end the period mentioned in paragraph (*a*), and

(ii) the person, or one of the persons, who acquired the dwelling as mentioned in paragraph (*b*); and

(*e*) the relevant works are carried out during the period of one year beginning with the day of the acquisition.

(4) In this paragraph "the relevant works" means—

(*a*) where the supply is of the description set out in item 1, the works that constitute the services supplied;

(*b*) where the supply is of the description set out in item 2, the works by which the materials concerned are incorporated in [the premises concerned or their immediate site].

(5) In sub-paragraph (3), references to a person acquiring a dwelling are to that person having a major interest in the dwelling granted, or assigned, to him for a consideration.

[Items 1 and 2 apply to related garage works

3A—(1) For the purposes of this Group a renovation or alteration of any premises includes any garage works related to the renovation or alteration.
(2) In this paragraph "garage works" means—
(*a*) the construction of a garage,
(*b*) the conversion of a building, or of a part of a building, that results in a garage, or
(*c*) the renovation or alteration of a garage.
(3) For the purposes of sub-paragraph (1), garage works are "related" to a renovation or alteration if—
(*a*) they are carried out at the same time as the renovation or alteration of the premises concerned, and
(*b*) the garage is intended to be occupied with the premises.]

Items 1 and 2 only apply if planning consent and building control approval obtained

4—(1) Item 1 or 2 does not apply to a supply unless any statutory planning consent needed for the renovation or alteration has been granted.
(2) Item 1 or 2 does not apply to a supply unless any statutory building control approval needed for the renovation or alteration has been granted.

[Items 1 and 2 only apply if building used for relevant residential purpose is subsequently used solely for that purpose

4A—(1) Item 1 or 2 does not apply to a supply if the premises in question are a building, or part of a building, which, when it was last lived in, was used for a relevant residential purpose unless—
(*a*) the building or part is intended to be used solely for such a purpose after the renovation or alteration, and
(*b*) before the supply is made the person to whom it is made has given to the person making it a certificate stating that intention.
(2) Where a number of buildings on the same site are—
(*a*) renovated or altered at the same time, and
(*b*) intended to be used together as a unit solely for a relevant residential purpose,
then each of those buildings, to the extent that it would not be so regarded otherwise, shall be treated as intended for use solely for a relevant residential purpose.]

Meaning of "supply of qualifying services"

5—(1) "Supply of qualifying services" means a supply of services that consists in—
(*a*) the carrying out of works to the fabric of the [premises], or
(*b*) the carrying out of works within the immediate site of the [premises] that are in connection with—
(i) the means of providing water, power, heat or access to the [premises],
(ii) the means of providing drainage or security for the [premises], or
(iii) the provision of means of waste disposal for the [premises].
(2) In sub-paragraph (1)(*a*), the reference to the carrying out of works to the fabric of the [premises] does not include the incorporation, or installation as fittings, in the [premises] of any goods that are not building materials.

Meaning of "building materials"

6 In this Group "building materials" has the meaning given by Notes (22) and (23) of Group 5 to Schedule 8 (zero-rating of construction and conversion of buildings).]

Commentary—*De Voil Indirect Tax Service* **V4.413**.

Amendments—This Schedule inserted by FA 2001 s 99(5), Sch 31 with effect for supplies made, and acquisitions and importations taking place, after 31 October 2001.

Note (2) substituted, Notes (3) and (5) amended, and Notes (3A), (4A) inserted, by the VAT (Reduced Rate) Order, SI 2002/1100 arts 2, 5 with effect from 1 June 2002.

Words "2 years" in Note (3), and in heading to Note (3), substituted by the VAT (Reduced Rate) (No 2) Order, SI 2007/3448 regs 2–4 with effect from 1 January 2008: SI 2007/3448 reg 1.

[GROUP 8

CONTRACEPTIVE PRODUCTS

Item No

1 Supplies of contraceptive products, other than relevant exempt supplies.

NOTES:

Meaning of "contraceptive products"

1 In this Group "contraceptive product" means any product designed for the purposes of human contraception, but does not include any product designed for the purpose of monitoring fertility.

Meaning of "relevant exempt supplies"

2 In this Group "relevant exempt supplies" means supplies which fall within item 4 of Group 7 of Schedule 9 (exempt supplies of goods in any hospital etc in connection with medical or surgical treatment etc).][1]

Amendments—[1] This Group inserted by the Value Added Tax (Reduced Rate) Order, SI 2006/1472 arts 2, 4, Schedule with effect from 1 July 2006.

[GROUP 9

WELFARE ADVICE OR INFORMATION

Item No

1 Supplies of welfare advice or information by—

(*a*) a charity, or

(*b*) a state-regulated private welfare institution or agency.

NOTES:

Meaning of "welfare advice or information"

1 In this Group "welfare advice or information" means advice or information which directly relates to—

(*a*) the physical or mental welfare of elderly, sick, distressed or disabled persons, or

(*b*) the care or protection of children and young persons.

Meaning of "state-regulated"

2 For the purposes of this Group "state-regulated" has the same meaning as in Group 7 (health and welfare) of Schedule 9 (see Note (8) of that Group).

Supplies not included in item 1

3 Item 1 does not include—

(*a*) supplies that would be exempt by virtue of Group 6 of Schedule 9 (education) if they were made by an eligible body within the meaning of that Group,

(*b*) supplies of goods, unless the goods are supplied wholly or almost wholly for the purpose of conveying the advice or information, or

(*c*) supplies of advice or information provided solely for the benefit of a particular individual or according to his personal circumstances.][1]

Amendments—[1] This Group inserted by the Value Added Tax (Reduced Rate) Order, SI 2006/1472 arts 2, 4, Schedule with effect from 1 July 2006.

[GROUP 10

INSTALLATION OF MOBILITY AIDS FOR THE ELDERLY

Item No

1 The supply of services of installing mobility aids for use in domestic accommodation by a person who, at the time of the supply, is aged 60 or over.

2 The supply of mobility aids by a person installing them for use in domestic accommodation by a person who, at the time of the supply, is aged 60 or over.

NOTES:

Meaning of "mobility aids"

1 For the purposes of this Group "mobility aids" means any of the following—

(*a*) grab rails;

(*b*) ramps;

(*c*) stair lifts;

(*d*) bath lifts;

(*e*) built-in shower seats or showers containing built-in shower seats;
(*f*) walk-in baths fitted with sealable doors.

Meaning of "domestic accommodation"

2 For the purposes of this Group "domestic accommodation" means a building, or part of a building, that consists of a dwelling or a number of dwellings.][1]

Amendments—[1] This Group inserted by the Value Added Tax (Reduced Rate) Order, SI 2007/1601 arts 2, 4, with effect in relation to supplies made on or after 1 July 2007.

[GROUP 11

SMOKING CESSATION PRODUCTS

Item No.

1 Supplies of pharmaceutical products designed to help people to stop smoking tobacco.][1]

Order—The Value Added Tax (Reduced Rate) (Smoking Cessation Products) Order, SI 2008/1410 arts 2, 3 (the reduced rate provided for in Group 11 shall have effect in relation to supplies made on or after 1 July 2008).

Amendments—[1] This Group inserted by the Value Added Tax (Reduced Rate) Order, SI 2007/1601 arts 2, 5, with effect in relation to supplies made on or after 1 July 2007 but before 1 July 2008. The reduced rate for smoking cessation products continues in relation to supplies made on or after 1 July 2008: see note above.

[GROUP 12

CARAVANS

Item No

1 Supplies of caravans which exceed the limits of size of a trailer for the time being permitted to be towed on roads by a motor vehicle having a maximum gross weight of 3,500 kilogrammes.

2 The supply of such services as are described in paragraph 1(1) or 5(4) of Schedule 4 in respect of a caravan within item 1.

NOTE:

This Group does not include—

(*a*) removable contents other than goods of a kind mentioned in item 4 of Group 5 of Schedule 8, or
(*b*) the supply of accommodation in a caravan.][1]

Amendments—[1] Group 12 inserted by FA 2012 s 196, Sch 26 para 6(1), (3) with effect from 6 April 2013.

[GROUP 13

CABLE-SUSPENDED PASSENGER TRANSPORT SYSTEMS

Item No

1 Transport of passengers by means of a cable-suspended chair, bar, gondola or similar vehicle designed or adapted to carry not more than 9 passengers.

NOTES:

Supplies not within item 1

1. Item 1 does not include the transport of passengers to, from or within—

(i) a place of entertainment, recreation or amusement; or
(ii) a place of cultural, scientific, historical or similar interest,

by the person, or a person connected with that person, who supplies a right of admission to, or a right to use facilities at, such a place.

2. For the purposes of Note 1 any question as to whether a person is connected with another shall be determined in accordance with section 1122 of the Corporation Tax Act 2010.][1]

Amendments—[1] Group 13 inserted by the Value Added Tax (Reduced Rate) (Cable-Suspended Passenger Transport Systems) Order, SI 2013/430 art 2(1), (3) with effect from 1 April 2013.

SCHEDULE 8

ZERO-RATING

Section 30

Summer Finance Bill 2015 The Summer Finance Bill introduces a "VAT lock", restricting the standard and reduced rates of VAT to current rates. The Bill also provides that no goods, services or supply specified in this Schedule at the beginning of the VAT lock period may be removed from this Schedule under s 30(4) during that period. Please check the latest version of the Bill and subsequent Finance Act for details.

Simon's Tax Cases—*Home Protection Co v C&E Comrs* [1984] STC 278*; *C&E Comrs v Sutton Housing Trust* [1984] STC 352*.

Cross references—See VATA 1994 s 97(3), (4) (procedure for making orders for varying this Schedule so as to abolish the zero rating of a supply);

VATA 1994 Sch 13 para 8 (preservation of zero rating for certain supplies in the course of an approved alteration of a protected building made pursuant to an obligation incurred before 21 June 1988).

PART I
INDEX TO ZERO-RATED SUPPLIES OF GOODS AND SERVICES

Subject matter	*Group Number*
Bank notes	Group 11
Books etc	Group 3
Caravans and houseboats	Group 9
Charities etc	Group 15
Clothing and footwear	Group 16
Construction of buildings etc	Group 5
Drugs, medicines, aids for the handicapped etc	Group 12
. . .	. . . [2]
[European Research Infrastructure Consortia	Group 18][3]
Food	Group 1
Gold	Group 10
Imports, exports etc	Group 13
International services	Group 7
Protected buildings	Group 6
Sewerage services and water	Group 2
Talking books for the blind and handicapped and wireless sets for the blind	Group 4
[. . .][1]	
Transport	Group 8

Amendments—

[1] Group 14 deleted by the Value Added Tax (Abolition of Zero-Rating for Tax Free Shops) Order, SI 1999/1642, with effect from 1 July 1999.

[2] Entry for "Emissions allowances" repealed by the Value Added Tax (Emissions Allowances) Order, SI 2010/2549 art 2(1), (2) with effect from 1 November 2010.

[3] Group 18 inserted by the Value Added Tax (Relief for European Research Infrastructure Consortia) Order, SI 2012/2907 art 3(1) with effect in relation to importations, acquisitions or supplies made on or after 1 January 2013.

PART II
THE GROUPS

GROUP 1 — FOOD

The supply of anything comprised in the general items set out below, except—

(*a*) a supply in the course of catering; and

(*b*) a supply of anything comprised in any of the excepted items set out below, unless it is also comprised in any of the items overriding the exceptions set out below which relates to that excepted item.

General items

Item No

1 Food of a kind used for human consumption.

2 Animal feeding stuffs.

3 Seeds or other means of propagation of plants comprised in item 1 or 2.

4 Live animals of a kind generally used as, or yielding or producing, food for human consumption.

Excepted items

Item No

1 Ice cream, ice lollies, frozen yoghurt, water ices and similar frozen products, and prepared mixes and powders for making such products.

2 Confectionery, not including cakes or biscuits other than biscuits wholly or partly covered with chocolate or some product similar in taste and appearance.

3 Beverages chargeable with any duty of excise specifically charged on spirits, beer, wine or made-wine and preparations thereof.

4 Other beverages (including fruit juices and bottled waters) and syrups, concentrates, essences, powders, crystals or other products for the preparation of beverages.

[4A Sports drinks that are advertised or marketed as products designed to enhance physical performance, accelerate recovery after exercise or build bulk, and other similar drinks, including (in either case) syrups, concentrates, essences, powders, crystals or other products for the preparation of such drinks.][2]

5 Any of the following when packaged for human consumption without further preparation, namely, potato crisps, potato sticks, potato puffs, and similar products made from the potato, or from potato flour, or from potato starch, and savoury food products obtained by the swelling of cereals or cereal products; and salted or roasted nuts other than nuts in shell.

6 Pet foods, canned, packaged or prepared; packaged foods (not being pet foods) for birds other than poultry or game; and biscuits and meal for cats and dogs.

7 Goods described in items 1, 2 and 3 of the general items which are canned, bottled, packaged or prepared for use—

(*a*) in the domestic brewing of any beer;

(*b*) in the domestic making of any cider or perry;

(*c*) in the domestic production of any wine or made-wine.

Items overriding the exceptions

Item No

1 Yoghurt unsuitable for immediate consumption when frozen.

2 Drained cherries.

3 Candied peels.

4 Tea, maté, herbal teas and similar products, and preparations and extracts thereof.

5 Cocoa, coffee and chicory and other roasted coffee substitutes, and preparations and extracts thereof.

6 Milk and preparations and extracts thereof.

7 Preparations and extracts of meat, yeast or egg.

NOTES:

(1) "Food" includes drink.

(2) "Animal" includes bird, fish, crustacean and mollusc.

(3) A supply of anything in the course of catering includes—

(*a*) any supply of it for consumption on the premises on which it is supplied; and

(*b*) any supply of hot food for consumption off those premises;

. . . [2]

[(3A) For the purposes of Note (3), in the case of any supplier, the premises on which food is supplied include any area set aside for the consumption of food by that supplier's customers, whether or not the area may also be used by the customers of other suppliers.

(3B) "Hot food" means food which (or any part of which) is hot at the time it is provided to the customer and—

(*a*) has been heated for the purposes of enabling it to be consumed hot,

(*b*) has been heated to order,

(*c*) has been kept hot after being heated,

(*d*) is provided to a customer in packaging that retains heat (whether or not the packaging was primarily designed for that purpose) or in any other packaging that is specifically designed for hot food, or

(*e*) is advertised or marketed in a way that indicates that it is supplied hot.

(3C) For the purposes of Note (3B)—

(*a*) something is "hot" if it is at a temperature above the ambient air temperature, and (*b*) something is "kept hot" after being heated if the supplier stores it in an environment which provides, applies or retains heat, or takes other steps to ensure it remains hot or to slow down the natural cooling process.

(3D) In Notes (3B) and (3C), references to food being heated include references to it being cooked or reheated.][2]

(4) Item 1 of the items overriding the exceptions relates to item 1 of the excepted items.

(5) Items 2 and 3 of the items overriding the exceptions relate to item 2 of the excepted items; and for the purposes of item 2 of the excepted items "confectionery" includes chocolates, sweets and biscuits; drained, glacé or crystallised fruits; and any item of sweetened prepared food which is normally eaten with the fingers.

(6) Items 4 to 6 of the items overriding the exceptions relate to item 4 of the excepted items.

(7) Any supply described in this Group shall include a supply of services described in paragraph 1(1) of Schedule 4.

Commentary—*De Voil Indirect Tax Service* **V4.221, V4.226, V4.227.**

Press releases etc—C&E Business Brief 18/94 6-10-94 (scope of item 4 overriding the exceptions).

C&E Business Brief 6/95 28-3-95 (ostriches and fertilised ostrich eggs zero-rated from 1-4-95).

C&E Business Brief 12/95 19-6-95 (pre-germinated grass seed standard rated with effect from 1 October 1995).

Simon's Tax Cases—*R v C&E Comrs, ex p Sims (T/A Supersonic Snacks)* [1988] STC 210*; *C&E Comrs v Lawson Tancred* [1988] STC 326*; *John Pimblett & Sons Ltd v C&E Comrs* [1988] STC 358*, *EC Commission v United Kingdom* [1988] STC 456*; *R&C Comrs v Compass Contract Services UK Ltd* [2006] STC 1999; *R&C Comrs v Roger Skinner Ltd* [2014] UKUT 204 (TCC), [2014] STC 2335.

Sub-para (*a*), *British Airways plc v C&E Comrs* [1990] STC 643*; *C&E Comrs v Safeway Stores plc* [1997] STC 163.

Item 1, Note (3)(*b*), *Deliverance Ltd v R&C Comrs* [2011] UKUT 58 (TCC), [2011] STC 1049; *Sub One Ltd (t/a Subway) v R&C Comrs* [2014] EWCA Civ 773, [2014] STC 508.

Item 1, Note (3)(*b*)(i), *British Airways plc v C&E Comrs* [1990] STC 643*, *C&E Comrs v Safeway Stores plc* [1997] STC 163; *Malik (T/A Hotline Foods) v C&E Comrs* [1998] STC 537; *Sub One Ltd (t/a Subway) v R&C Comrs* [2012] UKUT 34 (TCC), [2012] STC 318.

Item 1, Note (3)(*b*)(ii), *Sub One Ltd (t/a Subway) v R&C Comrs* [2012] UKUT 34 (TCC), [2012] STC 318.

Item 1, *C&E Comrs v Macphie & Co (Glenbervie) Ltd* [1992] STC 886*.

Item 2, *Fluff Ltd (T/A Mag-it) v C&E Comrs* [2001] STC 674.

Excepted item 1, *Meschia's Frozen Foods v C&E Comrs* [2001] STC 1.

Excepted item 2, *C&E Comrs v Ferrero UK Ltd* [1997] STC 881*; *R&C Comrs v Premier Foods Ltd* [2008] STC 176.

Excepted item 4, *Kalron Foods Ltd v R&C Comrs* [2007] STC 1100; *GlaxoSmithKline Services Unlimited v R&C Comrs* [2011] UKUT 432 (TCC), [2012] STC 10.

Excepted item 5, *Procter & Gamble UK v R&C Comrs* [2009] STC 1990.

Definitions—"Supply", s 5, Sch 4.

Cross reference—See VAT Regulations, SI 1995/2518 reg 73 (retailers making both zero-rated supplies of food and supplies in course of catering: method of accounting).

Note—VATA 1994 Sch 8 Group 1 shall, in respect of preparations of meat, yeast or egg, shall be deemed to have and to always have had effect as if for Items "4 to 6" in Note (6) there were substituted "Items 4 to 7", FA 1999 s 14.

Amendments—[1] In Note (3), para (ii) substituted by the VAT (Food) Order, SI 2004/3343 with effect from 1 January 2005.

[2] Excepted item 4A inserted, in Note (3) words repealed, and Notes (3A)–(3D) inserted, by FA 2012 s 196, Sch 26 paras 1, 2 with effect from 1 October 2012.

GROUP 2 — SEWERAGE SERVICES AND WATER

Item No

1 Services of—

(*a*) reception, disposal or treatment of foul water or sewage in bulk, and

(*b*) emptying of cesspools, septic tanks or similar receptacles which are used otherwise than in connection with the carrying on in the course of a business of a relevant industrial activity.

2 The supply, for use otherwise than in connection with the carrying on in the course of a business of a relevant industrial activity, of water other than—

(*a*) distilled water, deionised water and water of similar purity, . . . [1]

(*b*) water comprised in any of the excepted items set out in Group 1 [and

(*c*) water which has been heated so that it is supplied at a temperature higher than that at which it was before it was heated][1].

Note: "Relevant industrial activity" means any activity described in any of Divisions 1 to 5 of the 1980 edition of the publication prepared by the Central Statistical Office and known as the Standard Industrial Classification.

Commentary—*De Voil Indirect Tax Service* **V4.271.**

Press releases etc—C&E Business Brief 15/94 19-7-94 (VAT treatment of connection charges to caravans and mobile homes by caravan park owner to follow treatment of rent).

Simon's Tax Cases—*EC Commission v United Kingdom* [1988] STC 456*.

Definitions—"Business", s 94; "Supply", s 5, Sch 4.

Amendments—[1] Word revoked from para (a) of item 2 and para (c) added to item 2 by the Value Added Tax (Anti-avoidance (Heating)) Order, SI 1996/1661 with effect from 27 June 1996.

GROUP 3 — BOOKS, ETC

Item No

1 Books, booklets, brochures, pamphlets and leaflets.

2 Newspapers, journals and periodicals.

3 Children's picture books and painting books.

4 Music (printed, duplicated or manuscript).

5 Maps, charts and topographical plans.

6 Covers, cases and other articles supplied with items 1 to 5 and not separately accounted for.

[Notes:

(1) Items 1 to 6—][1]

(*a*) do not include plans or drawings for industrial, architectural, engineering, commercial or similar purposes; but

(*b*) include the supply of the services described in paragraph 1(1) of Schedule 4 in respect of goods comprised in the items.

[(2) Items 1 to 6 do not include goods in circumstances where—

(*a*) the supply of the goods is connected with a supply of services, and

(*b*) those connected supplies are made by different suppliers.

(3) For the purposes of Note (2) a supply of goods is connected with a supply of services if, had those two supplies been made by a single supplier—

(*a*) they would have been treated as a single supply of services, and

(*b*) that single supply would have been a taxable supply (other than a zero-rated supply) or an exempt supply.][1]

Commentary—*De Voil Indirect Tax Service* **V4.273.**

Simon's Tax Cases—*Odhams Leisure Group Ltd v C&E Comrs* [1992] STC 332*.

Item 1, *C&E Comrs v Colour Offset Ltd* [1995] STC 85*; *R&C Comrs v Weight Watchers (UK) Ltd* [2008] STC 301.

Item 2, *Telewest Communications v C&E Comrs* [2004] STC 517; *R&C Comrs v Weight Watchers (UK) Ltd* [2008] STC 301.

Definition—"Supply", s 5, Sch 4.

Amendment—[1] Words substituted for words "*Note: Items 1 to 6*—", and words inserted, by FA 2011 s 75(1)–(3) with effect in relation to supplies made on or after 19 July 2011.

GROUP 4 — TALKING BOOKS FOR THE BLIND AND HANDICAPPED AND WIRELESS SETS FOR THE BLIND

Item No

1 The supply to the Royal National Institute for the Blind, the National Listening Library or other similar charities of—

(*a*) magnetic tape specially adapted for the recording and reproduction of speech for the blind or severely handicapped;

(*b*) apparatus designed or specially adapted for the making on a magnetic tape, by way of the transfer of recorded speech from another magnetic tape, of a recording described in paragraph (*f*) below;

(*c*) apparatus designed or specially adapted for transfer to magnetic tapes of a recording made by apparatus described in paragraph (*b*) above;

(*d*) apparatus for re-winding magnetic tape described in paragraph (*f*) below;

(*e*) apparatus designed or specially adapted for the reproduction from recorded magnetic tape of speech for the blind or severely handicapped which is not available for use otherwise than by the blind or severely handicapped;

(*f*) magnetic tape upon which has been recorded speech for the blind or severely handicapped, such recording being suitable for reproduction only in the apparatus mentioned in paragraph (*e*) above;

(*g*) apparatus solely for the making on a magnetic tape of a sound recording which is for use by the blind or severely handicapped;

(*h*) parts and accessories (other than a magnetic tape for use with apparatus described in paragraph (*g*) above) for goods comprised in paragraphs (*a*) to (*g*) above;

(*i*) the supply of a service of repair or maintenance of any goods comprised in paragraphs (*a*) to (*h*) above.

2 The supply to a charity of—

(*a*) wireless receiving sets; or

(*b*) apparatus solely for the making and reproduction of a sound recording on a magnetic tape permanently contained in a cassette, being goods solely for gratuitous loan to the blind.

Note: The supply mentioned in items 1 and 2 includes the letting on hire of goods comprised in the items.

Commentary—*De Voil Indirect Tax Service* **V4.262.**
Definition—"Supply", s 5, Sch 4.

[GROUP 5—CONSTRUCTION OF BUILDINGS, ETC

Item No

1 The first grant by a person—
(*a*) constructing a building—
(i) designed as a dwelling or number of dwellings; or
(ii) intended for use solely for a relevant residential or a relevant charitable purpose; or
(*b*) converting a non-residential building or a non-residential part of a building into a building designed as a dwelling or number of dwellings or a building intended for use solely for a relevant residential purpose,

of a major interest in, or in any part of, the building, dwelling or its site.

2 The supply in the course of the construction of—
(*a*) a building designed as a dwelling or number of dwellings or intended for use solely for a relevant residential purpose or a relevant charitable purpose; or
(*b*) any civil engineering work necessary for the development of a permanent park for residential caravans,

of any services related to the construction other than the services of an architect, surveyor or any person acting as a consultant or in a supervisory capacity.

3 The supply to a [relevant housing association][1] in the course of conversion of a non-residential building or a non-residential part of a building into—
(*a*) a building or part of a building designed as a dwelling or number of dwellings; or
(*b*) a building or part of a building intended for use solely for a relevant residential purpose,

of any services related to the conversion other than the services of an architect, surveyor or any person acting as a consultant or in a supervisory capacity.

Amendments—[1] Words in Item No 3 substituted by the VAT (Registered Social Landlords) (No 1) Order, SI 1997/50 with effect from 1 March 1997.

4 The supply of building materials to a person to whom the supplier is supplying services within item 2 or 3 of this Group which include the incorporation of the materials into the building (or its site) in question.

NOTES

(1) "Grant" includes an assignment or surrender.

(2) A building is designed as a dwelling or a number of dwellings where in relation to each dwelling the following conditions are satisfied—
(*a*) the dwelling consists of self-contained living accommodation;
(*b*) there is no provision for direct internal access from the dwelling to any other dwelling or part of a dwelling;
(*c*) the separate use, or disposal of the dwelling is not prohibited by the term of any covenant, statutory planning consent or similar provision; and
(*d*) statutory planning consent has been granted in respect of that dwelling and its construction or conversion has been carried out in accordance with that consent.

(3) The construction of, or conversion of a non-residential building to, a building designed as a dwelling or a number of dwellings includes the construction of, or conversion of a non-residential building to, a garage provided that—
(*a*) the dwelling and the garage are constructed or converted at the same time; and
(*b*) the garage is intended to be occupied with the dwelling or one of the dwellings.

(4) Use for a relevant residential purpose means use as—
(*a*) a home or other institution providing residential accommodation for children;
(*b*) a home or other institution providing residential accommodation with personal care for persons in need of personal care by reason of old age, disablement, past or present dependence on alcohol or drugs or past or present mental disorder;
(*c*) a hospice;
(*d*) residential accommodation for students or school pupils;
(*e*) residential accommodation for members of any of the armed forces;
(*f*) a monastery, nunnery or similar establishment; or
(*g*) an institution which is the sole or main residence of at least 90 per cent of its residents,

except use as a hospital, prison or similar institution or an hotel, inn or similar establishment.

(5) Where a number of buildings are—

(*a*) constructed at the same time and on the same site; and

(*b*) are intended to be used together as a unit solely for a relevant residential purpose;

then each of those buildings, to the extent that they would not be so regarded but for this Note, are to be treated as intended for use solely for a relevant residential purpose.

(6) Use for a relevant charitable purpose means use by a charity in either or both the following ways, namely—

(*a*) otherwise than in the course or furtherance of a business;

(*b*) as a village hall or similarly in providing social or recreational facilities for a local community.

[(7) For the purposes of item 1(*b*), and for the purposes of these Notes so far as having effect for the purposes of item 1(*b*), a building or part of a building is "non-residential" if—

(*a*) it is neither designed, nor adapted, for use—

(i) as a dwelling or number of dwellings, or

(ii) for a relevant residential purpose; or

(*b*) it is designed, or adapted, for such use but—

(i) it was constructed more than 10 years before the grant of the major interest; and

(ii) no part of it has, in the period of 10 years immediately preceding the grant, been used as a dwelling or for a relevant residential purpose.][3]

[(7A) For the purposes of item 3, and for the purposes of these Notes so far as having effect for the purposes of item 3, a building or part of a building is "non-residential" if—

(*a*) it is neither designed, nor adapted, for use—

(i) as a dwelling or number of dwellings, or

(ii) for a relevant residential purpose; or

(*b*) it is designed, or adapted, for such use but—

(i) it was constructed more than 10 years before the commencement of the works of conversion, and

(ii) no part of it has, in the period of 10 years immediately preceding the commencement of those works, been used as a dwelling or for a relevant residential purpose, and

(iii) no part of it is being so used.][3]

(8) References to a non-residential building or a non-residential part of a building do not include a reference to a garage occupied together with a dwelling.

(9) The conversion, other than to a building designed for a relevant residential purpose, of a non-residential part of a building which already contains a residential part is not included within items 1(*b*) or 3 unless the result of that conversion is to create an additional dwelling or dwellings.

(10) Where—

(*a*) part of a building that is constructed is designed as a dwelling or number of dwellings or is intended for use solely for a relevant residential purpose or relevant charitable purpose (and part is not); or

(*b*) part of a building that is converted is designed as a dwelling or number of dwellings or is used solely for a relevant residential purpose (and part is not)—

then in the case of—

(i) a grant or other supply relating only to the part so designed or intended for that use (or its site) shall be treated as relating to a building so designed or intended for such use;

(ii) a grant or other supply relating only to the part neither so designed nor intended for such use (or its site) shall not be so treated; and

(ii) any other grant or other supply relating to, or to any part of, the building (or its site), an apportionment shall be made to determine the extent to which it is to be so treated.

(11) Where, a service falling within the description in items 2 or 3 is supplied in part in relation to the construction or conversion of a building and in part for other purposes, an apportionment may be made to determine the extent to which the supply is to be treated as falling within items 2 or 3.

(12) Where all or part of a building is intended for use solely for a relevant residential purpose or a relevant charitable purpose—

(*a*) a supply relating to the building (or any part of it) shall not be taken for the purposes of items 2 and 4 as relating to a building intended for such use unless it is made to a person who intends to use the building (or part) for such a purpose; and

(*b*) a grant or other supply relating to the building (or any part of it) shall not be taken as relating to a building intended for such use unless before it is made the person to whom it is made has given to the person making it a certificate in such form as may be specified in a notice published by the Commissioners stating that the grant or other supply (or a specified part of it) so relates.

(13) The grant of an interest in, or in any part of—

(*a*) a building designed as a dwelling or number of dwellings; or

(*b*) the site of such a building,

is not within item 1 if—

(i) the interest granted is such that the grantee is not entitled to reside in the building or part, throughout the year; or

(ii) residence there throughout the year, or the use of the building or part as the grantee's principal private residence, is prevented by the terms of a covenant, statutory planning consent or similar permission.

(14) Where the major interest referred to in item l is a tenancy or lease—

(*a*) if a premium is payable, the grant falls within that item-only to the extent that it is made for consideration in the form of the premium; and

(*b*) if a premium is not payable, the grant falls within that item only to the extent that it is made for consideration in the form of the first payment of rent due under the tenancy or lease.

(15) The reference in item 2(*b*) of this Group to the construction of a civil engineering work does not include a reference to the conversion, reconstruction, alteration or enlargement of a work.

(16) For the purpose of this Group, the construction of a building does not include—

(*a*) the conversion, reconstruction or alteration of an existing building; or

(*b*) any enlargement of, or extension to, an existing building except to the extent the enlargement or extension creates an additional dwelling or dwellings; or

(*c*) subject to Note (17) below, the construction of an annexe to an existing building.

(17) Note 16(*c*) above shall not apply [where the whole or a part of an annexe is intended for use solely for a relevant charitable purpose and][4]—

(*a*) [the annexe][4] is capable of functioning independently from the existing building; and

(*b*) the only access or where there is more than one means of access, the main access to:

(i) the annexe is not via the existing building; and

(ii) the existing building is not via the annexe.

(18) A building only ceases to be an existing building when:

(*a*) demolished completely to ground level; or

(*b*) the part remaining above ground level consists of no more than a single facade or where a corner site, a double facade, the retention of which is a condition or requirement of statutory planning consent or similar permission.

(19) A caravan is not a residential caravan if residence in it throughout the year is prevented by the terms of a covenant, statutory planning consent or similar permission.

(20) Item 2 and Item 3 do not include the supply of services described in paragraph 1(1) or 5(4) of Schedule 4.

[(21) In Item 3 "relevant housing association" means—

[(*za*) a private registered provider of social housing,][5]

(*a*) a registered social landlord within the meaning of Part 1 of the Housing Act 1996 [(Welsh registered social landlords)][5],

[(*b*) a registered social landlord within the meaning of the Housing (Scotland) Act 2010 (asp 17) which is either—

(i) a society registered under the Co-operative and Community Benefit Societies and Credit Unions Act 1965 (c 12), or

(ii) a company within the meaning of the Companies Act 2006 (c 46), or][6]

(*c*) a registered housing association within the meaning of Part II of the Housing (Northern Ireland) Order 1992 (Northern Irish registered housing association).][2]

(22) "Building materials", in relation to any description of building, means goods of a description ordinarily incorporated by builders in a building of that description, (or its site), but does not include—

(*a*) finished or prefabricated furniture, other than furniture designed to be fitted in kitchens;

(*b*) materials for the construction of fitted furniture, other than kitchen furniture;

(*c*) electrical or gas appliances, unless the appliance is an appliance which is—

(i) designed to heat space or water (or both) or to provide ventilation, air cooling, air purification, or dust extraction; or

(ii) intended for use in a building designed as a number of dwellings and is a door-entry system, a waste disposal unit or a machine for compacting waste; or

(iii) a burglar alarm, a fire alarm, or fire safety equipment or designed solely for the purpose of enabling aid to be summoned in an emergency; or

(iv) a lift or hoist;

(*d*) carpets or carpeting material.

(23) For the purposes of Note (22) above the incorporation of goods in a building includes their installation as fittings.

(24) Section 30(3) does not apply to goods forming part of a description of supply in this Group.][1]

Press releases etc—VAT Information Sheet 10/95 11-4-95 (guidance on the changes to the liability of supplies in connection with buildings with effect from 1 March 1995).

Business Brief 12/97, 5 June 1997 (Fitted Furniture in new buildings).

VAT Information Sheet 5/01 July 2001 (guidance on the adjustment to the zero rate for the sale of houses that are renovated after having been empty for at least 10 years).

HMRC Brief 66/07, 5-11-07 (treatment of the construction of houses or flats in the grounds of existing care homes, nursing homes or similar buildings).

HMRC Brief 39/09, 1-7-09 (revised interpretation of legal provisions that apply the zero rate to new buildings used for a relevant charitable purpose).

HMRC Brief 8/10, 15-3-10 (Changes to the operation of the option to tax and updated definitions of housing associations).

Simon's Tax Cases—*EC Commission v United Kingdom* [1988] STC 456*.

Item 1, *C&E Comrs v Link Housing Association Ltd* [1992] STC 718*.

Item 1(*a*)(ii), note (4), *R (on the application of Greenwich Property Ltd) v C&E Comrs* [2001] STC 618.

Item 2, *C&E Comrs v Rannoch School Ltd* [1993] STC 389*; *C&E Comrs v Lewis* [1994] STC 739*; *C&E Comrs v Marchday Holdings Ltd* [1995] STC 898*; *C&E Comrs v St Mary's RC High School* [1996] STC 1091*; *C&E Comrs v St Paul's Community Project Ltd* [2005] STC 95; *Riverside Housing Association Ltd v R&C Comrs* [2006] STC 2072; *Wakefield College v R&C Comrs* [2011] UKUT 495 (TCC), [2012] STC 642..

Item 2(*a*), Notes 4(*b*), (6)(*a*), (*b*), *Jubilee Hall Recreation Centre Ltd v C&E Comrs* [1999] STC 381; *C&E Comrs v Yarburgh Children's Trust* [2002] STC 207.

Item 3, *C&E Comrs v John Willmott Housing Ltd* [1987] STC 692*; *C&E Comrs v Arbib* [1995] STC 490*; *C&E Comrs v Jeffs (T/A J & J Joinery)* [1995] STC 759*.

Note (4)(*b*), *R&C Comrs v Fenwood Developments Ltd* [2006] STC 644.

Note (9), *C&E Comrs v Lewis* [1994] STC 739*; *C&E Comrs v Marchday Holdings Ltd* [1997] STC 272*; *C&E Comrs v Jacobs* [2005] STC 1518.

Note (16) *Cantrell v C&E Comrs* [2000] STC 100; *Colchester v R&C Comrs* [2014] UKUT 83 (TCC); [2014] STC 2078.

Note (22) *Colaingrove Ltd v R&C Comrs* [2014] UKUT 132 (TCC), [2014] STC 1457.

Definitions—"Assignment", s 96(1); "business", s 94; "the Commissioners", s 96(1); "major interest", s 96(1); "supply", s 5, Sch 4.

Cross references—See VATA 1994 s 62(1) (penalty for incorrect certificate that a supply is eligible for zero rating within this Group);

VATA 1994 Sch 9 Group 1 note (11) (any grant of a major interest which is excluded from item 1 of this Group by note (7) is included in Sch 9 Group 1 item 1(*e*) (exemption: land);

VAT Regulations, SI 1995/2518 reg 101(3) (exclusion of supplies within item 1 of this Group in determining proportion of input tax attributable to taxable supplies under reg 101(2)(*d*)).

VATA 1994 s 35 (note (7A) above shall apply for the purposes of that section).

Amendments—[1] Group 5 substituted by the Value Added Tax (Construction of Buildings) Order, SI 1995/280 with effect from 1 March 1995.

[2] Words in Note (21) substituted by the VAT (Registered Social Landlords) (No 1) Order, SI 1997/50 with effect from 1 March 1997.

[3] Notes (7), (7A) substituted for Note (7) by the VAT (Conversion of Buildings) Order, SI 2001/2305 arts 1–3 with effect for supplies made after 31 July 2001.

[4] Words in Note (17) substituted and inserted by the VAT (Construction of Buildings) Order, SI 2002/1101 art 2 with effect from 1 June 2002.

[5] In Note (21), whole of para (*za*), and words in para (*a*), inserted by the VAT (Construction of Buildings) Order, SI 2010/486 art 2(1) with effect from 1 April 2010.

Note that until the coming into force of provision defining "private registered provider of social housing" in enactments and instruments generally, that expression in Note 21 means persons listed in the register of providers of social housing maintained under the Housing and Regeneration Act 2008 Part 2, Chapter 3 who are not local authorities within the meaning of the Housing Associations Act 1985.

[6] In Note (21) para (*b*) substituted by the Housing (Scotland) Act 2010 (Consequential Provisions and Modifications) Order, SI 2012/700 art 4, Schedule para 5(1), (2) with effect from 1 April 2012.

[GROUP 6—PROTECTED BUILDINGS

Item No

1 The first grant by a person substantially reconstructing a protected building, of a major interest in, or in any part of, the building or its site.

2 The supply, in the course of an approved alteration of a protected building, of any services other than the services of an architect, surveyor or any person acting as consultant or in a supervisory capacity.[4]

3 The supply of building materials to a person to whom the supplier is supplying services within item 2 of this Group which include the incorporation of the materials into the building (or its site) in question.[4]

NOTES

(1) "Protected building" means a building which is designed to remain as or become a dwelling or number of dwellings (as defined in Note (2) below) or is intended for use solely for a relevant residential purpose or a relevant charitable purpose after the reconstruction or alteration and which, in either case, is—

(*a*) *a listed building, within the meaning of—*

(i) *the Planning (Listed Buildings and Conservation Areas) Act 1990; or*

(ii) *[the Planning (Listed Buildings and Conservation Areas) (Scotland) Act 1997][3]; or*

(iii) *the Planning (Northern Ireland) Order 1991; or*

(*b*) *a scheduled monument, within the meaning of—*

(i) *the Ancient Monuments and Archaeological Areas Act 1979; or*

(ii) *[the Historic Monuments and Archaeological Objects (Northern Ireland) Order 1995.][2]*

(2) A building is designed to remain as or become a dwelling or number of dwellings where in relation to each dwelling the following conditions are satisfied—

(*a*) *the dwelling consists of self-contained living accommodation;*

(*b*) *there is no provision for direct internal access from the dwelling to any other dwelling or part of a dwelling;*

(*c*) *the separate use, or disposal of the dwelling is not prohibited by the terms of any covenant, statutory planning consent or similar provision,*

and includes a garage (occupied together with a dwelling) either constructed at the same time as the building or where the building has been substantially reconstructed at the same time as that reconstruction.

(3) Notes (1), (4), (6), [and (12) to (14)][5] of Group 5 apply in relation to this Group as they apply in relation to that Group but subject to any appropriate modifications.

[(4) For the purposes of item 1, a protected building is not to be regarded as substantially reconstructed unless, when the reconstruction is completed, the reconstructed building incorporates no more of the original building (that is to say, the building as it was before the reconstruction began) than the external walls, together with other external features of architectural or historic interest.][4]

(5) Where part of a protected building that is substantially reconstructed is designed to remain as or become a dwelling or a number of dwellings or is intended for use solely for a relevant residential or relevant charitable purpose (and part is not)—

(*a*) *a grant . . .* [4] *relating only to the part so designed or intended for such use (or its site) shall be treated as relating to a building so designed or intended for such use;*

(*b*) *a grant . . .* [4] *relating only to the part neither so designed nor intended for such use (or its site) shall not be so treated; and*

(*c*) *in the case of any other grant . . .* [4] *relating to, or to any part of, the building (or its site), an apportionment shall be made to determine the extent to which it is to be so treated.*

(6) "Approved alteration" means—

(*a*) *in the case of a protected building which is an ecclesiastical building to which section 60 of the Planning (Listed Buildings and Conservation Areas) Act 1990 applies, any works of alteration; and*

(*b*) *in the case of a protected building which is a scheduled monument within the meaning of the Historic Monuments Act (Northern Ireland) 1971 and in respect of which a protection order, within the meaning of that Act, is in force, works of alteration for which consent has been given under section 10 of that Act; and*

(*c*) *in any other case, works of alteration which may not, or but for the existence of a Crown interest or Duchy interest could not, be carried out unless authorised under, or under any provision of—*

(i) *Part I of the Planning (Listed Buildings and Conservation Areas) Act 1990,*

(ii) *[Part I of the Planning (Listed Buildings and Conservation Areas) (Scotland) Act 1997][3],*

(iii) *Part V of the Planning (Northern Ireland) Order 1991,*

(iv) *Part I of the Ancient Monuments and Archaeological Areas Act 1979,*

and for which, except in the case of a Crown interest or Duchy interest, consent has been obtained under any provision of that Part,

but does not include any works of repair or maintenance, or any incidental alteration to the fabric of a building which results from the carrying out of repairs, or maintenance work.[4]

(7) For the purposes of paragraph (a) of Note (6), a building used or available for use by a minister of religion wholly or mainly as a residence from which to perform the duties of his office shall be treated as not being an ecclesiastical building.[4]

(8) For the purposes of paragraph (c) of Note (6) "Crown interest" and "Duchy interest" have the same meaning as in section 50 of the Ancient Monuments and Archaeological Areas Act 1979.[4]

(9) Where a service is supplied in part in relation to an approved alteration of a building, and in part for other purposes, an apportionment may be made to determine the extent to which the supply is to be treated as falling within item 2.[4]

(10) For the purposes of item 2 the construction of a building separate from, but in the curtilage of, a protected building does not constitute an alteration of the protected building.[4]

(11) Item 2 does not include the supply of services described in paragraph 1(1) or 5(4) of Schedule 4.[4]*]*[1]

Commentary—*De Voil Indirect Tax Service* **V4.232C, V4.235, V4.239.**

Simon's Tax Cases—Item 2, *C&E Comrs v Arbib* [1995] STC 490*; *C&E Comrs v Windflower Housing Association* [1995] STC 860*; *Jubilee Hall Recreation Centre Ltd v C&E Comrs* [1998] STC 954*.

Item 2, note (1), *Jubilee Hall Recreation Centre Ltd v C&E Comrs* [1999] STC 381; *C&E Comrs v Zielinski Baker & Partners Ltd* [2004] STC 456, UKHL; *C&E Comrs v Tinsley* [2005] STC 1612.

Item 2, note (2), *C&E Comrs v Zielinski Baker & Partners Ltd* [2002] STC 829; *R&C Comrs v Lunn* [2010] STC 486.

Notes (1), (2), *Jubilee Hall Recreation Centre Ltd v C&E Comrs* [1997] STC 414.

Note (6), *C&E Comrs v Windflower Housing Association* [1995] STC 860*; *C&E Comrs v Morrish* [1998] 954.

Note (10), *C&E Comrs v Arbib* [1995] STC 490*.

Definitions—"Building materials", Sch 8 Group 5 note (22); "grant", Sch 8 Group 5 note (1); "major interest", s 96(1); "use for a relevant charitable purpose", Sch 8 Group 5 note (6); "use for a relevant residential purpose", Sch 8 Group 5 note (4); "supply", s 5, Sch 4; "taxable person", s 3.

Cross reference—See VATA 1994 s 62(1) (penalty for incorrect certificate that a supply is eligible for zero rating within this Group).

VAT Regulations, SI 1995/2518 reg 101(3) (exclusion of supplies within item 1 of this Group in determining proportion of input tax attributable to taxable supplies under reg 101(2)(*d*)).

Amendments—[1] Group 6 substituted by the Value Added Tax (Protected Buildings) Order, SI 1995/283 with effect from 1 March 1995.

[2] Words in Note (1)(b)(ii) substituted by the Historic Monuments and Archaeological Objects (Northern Ireland) Order, SI 1995/1625 (NI 9) Sch 3 para 4 with effect from 29 August 1995.

[3] Words in notes (1)(a)(ii) and (6)(c)(ii) substituted by the Planning (Consequential Provisions) (Scotland) Act 1997, s 4, Sch 2, para 57(a).

[4] Items 2, 3 and Notes (6)–(11) repealed, in Note (3), words substituted for words "(12) to (14) and (22) to (24)", Note (4) substituted, and in Note (5), in paras (*a*), (*b*), (*c*), words "or other supply" repealed, by FA 2012 s 196, Sch 26 paras 1, 3 with effect, in relation to relevant supplies, from 1 October 2015, subject to transitional provisions in FA 2012 Sch 26 para 7(4)–(10). Note (4) previously read as follows—

> (4) For the purposes of item 1, a protected building shall not be regarded as substantially reconstructed unless the reconstruction is such that at least one of the following conditions is fulfilled when the reconstruction is completed—
> that, of the works carried out to effect the reconstruction, at least three-fifths, measured by reference to cost, are of such a nature that the supply of services (other than excluded services), materials and other items to carry out the works, would, if supplied by a taxable person, be within either item 2 or item 3 of this Group; and
> that the reconstructed building incorporates no more of the original building (that is to say, the building as it was before the reconstruction began) than the external walls, together with other external features of architectural or historic interest;
> and in paragraph (*a*) above "excluded services" means the services of an architect, surveyor or other person acting as consultant or in a supervisory capacity.".

Purported amendments—The following amendments were purportedly made to Note (4): para (*b*) and the word "or" at the end of para (*c*)(iii) are repealed, and in para (*c*), sub-para (*v*) and the word "or" immediately preceding it are inserted as follows by the Historic Objects (Northern Ireland) Order, SI 1995/1625 (NI 9) Sch 3 para 4, Sch 4, with effect from 29 August 1995:

> "(*v*) Part II of the Historic Monuments and Archaeological Objects (Northern Ireland) Order 1995,".

This amendment relates to the text of this Group prior to its substitution by SI 1995/283 (see footnote 1 above) and it is submitted that Note (6), as so substituted, should be considered in the light of these amendments.

GROUP 7 — INTERNATIONAL SERVICES

Item No

1 The supply of services of work carried out on goods which, for that purpose, have been obtained or acquired in, or imported into, any of the member States and which are intended to be, and in fact are, subsequently exported to a place outside the member States—

(*a*) by or on behalf of the supplier; or

(*b*) where the recipient of the services belongs in a place outside the member States, by or on behalf of the recipient.

2 The supply of services consisting of the making of arrangements for—

(*a*) the export of any goods to a place outside the member States;

(*b*) a supply of services of the description specified in item 1 of this Group; or

(*c*) any supply of services which is made outside the member States.

NOTE

This Group does not include any services of a description specified in Group 2 or Group 5 of Schedule 9.

Commentary—*De Voil Indirect Tax Service* **V4.246.**

Simon's Tax Cases—*Bophuthatswana National Commercial Corp Ltd v C&E Comrs* [1992] STC 741*.
Definition—"Supply", s 5, Sch 4.

GROUP 8 — TRANSPORT

Item No

[1 The supply, repair or maintenance of a qualifying ship or the modification or conversion of any such ship provided that when so modified or converted it will remain a qualifying ship.][1]

Amendments—[1] Items 1 and 2 substituted, by the Value Added Tax (Ships and Aircraft) Order, SI 1995/3039 with effect from 1 January 1996.

[2 The supply, repair or maintenance of a qualifying aircraft or the modification or conversion of any such aircraft provided that when so modified or converted it will remain a qualifying aircraft.][1]

Amendments—[1] Items 1 and 2 substituted, by the Value Added Tax (Ships and Aircraft) Order, SI 1995/3039 with effect from 1 January 1996.

[2A The supply of parts and equipment, of a kind ordinarily installed or incorporated in, and to be installed, or incorporated in,—

(*a*) the propulsion, navigation or communication systems; or
(*b*) the general structure,

of a qualifying ship or, as the case may be, aircraft.][1]

Amendments—[1] Items 2A, 2B inserted by the Value Added Tax (Ships and Aircraft) Order, SI 1995/3039 with effect from 1 January 1996.

[2B The supply of life jackets, life rafts, smoke hoods and similar safety equipment for use in a qualifying ship or, as the case may be, aircraft.][1]

Amendments—[1] Items 2A, 2B inserted by the Value Added Tax (Ships and Aircraft) Order, SI 1995/3039 with effect from 1 January 1996.

3

(*a*) The supply to and repair or maintenance for a charity providing rescue or assistance at sea of—
(i) any lifeboat;
(ii) carriage equipment designed solely for the launching and recovery of lifeboats;
(iii) tractors for the sole use of the launching and recovery of lifeboats;
(iv) winches and hauling equipment for the sole use of the recovery of lifeboats.

(*b*) The construction, modification, repair or maintenance for a charity providing rescue or assistance at sea of slipways used solely for the launching and recovery of lifeboats.

(*c*) The supply of spare parts or accessories to a charity providing rescue or assistance at sea for use in or with goods comprised in paragraph (*a*) above or slipways comprised in paragraph (*b*) above.

[(*d*) The supply to a charity providing rescue or assistance at sea of equipment that is to be installed, incorporated or used in a lifeboat and is of a kind ordinarily installed, incorporated or used in a lifeboat.][1]

[(*e*) The supply of fuel to a charity providing rescue or assistance at sea where the fuel is for use in a lifeboat.][2]

Amendments—[1] Para (*d*) in item 3 added by the VAT (Equipment in Lifeboats) Order, SI 2002/456 with effect from 1 April 2002.

[2] Para (*e*) of item 3 inserted by the Value Added Tax (Lifeboats) Order, SI 2006/1750 arts 1, 2 with effect from 1 August 2006.

4 Transport of passengers—

(*a*) in any vehicle, ship or aircraft designed or adapted to carry not less than [10][1] passengers;
(*b*) by [a universal service provider][2];
(*c*) on any scheduled flight; or
(*d*) from a place within to a place outside the United Kingdom or vice versa, to the extent that those services are supplied in the United Kingdom.

Amendments—[1] Figure in item 4 substituted inserted by the Value Added Tax (Passenger Vehicles) Order, SI 2001/753 arts 2, 3 with effect for supplies made after 31 March 2001.

[2] In item 4, words substituted for words "the Post Office company", by F(No 3)A 2010 s 22(1) with effect in relation to supplies made on or after 31 January 2011.

5 The transport of goods from a place within to a place outside the member States or vice versa, to the extent that those services are supplied within the United Kingdom.

6 Any services provided for—

(*a*) the handling of ships or aircraft in a port, customs and excise airport or outside the United Kingdom; or

[(*b*) the handling or storage—
  (i) in a port,
  (ii) on land adjacent to a port,
  (iii) in a customs and excise airport, or
  (iv) in a transit shed,
of goods carried in a ship or aircraft.][1]

Amendments—[1] Para (*b*) of item 6 substituted by the Value Added Tax (Transport) Order, SI 2002/1173 art 2 with effect from 1 June 2002.

[6A Air navigation services.][1]

Amendments—[1] Item 6A inserted by the Value Added Tax (Transport) Order, SI 1995/653 with effect from 1 April 1995.

7 Pilotage services.

8 Salvage or towage services.

9 Any services supplied for or in connection with the surveying of any ship or aircraft or the classification of any ship or aircraft for the purposes of any register.

10 The making of arrangements for—
(*a*) the supply of, or of space in, any ship or aircraft; . . .
(*b*) the supply of any service included in [items 1 and 2, 3 to 9 and 11; or][1]
[(*c*) the supply of any goods of a description falling within items 2A or 2B][1][, or paragraph (*d*) of item 3.][2]

Amendments—[1] Words in item 10 substituted by the Value Added Tax (Ships and Aircraft) Order, SI 1995/3039 with effect from 1 January 1996.
[2] Words in item 10 added by the VAT (Equipment in Lifeboats) Order, SI 2002/456 with effect from 1 April 2002.

11 The supply—
(*a*) of services consisting of
  (i) the handling or storage of goods at, or their transport to or from, a place at which they are to be exported to or have been imported from a place outside the member States; or
  (ii) the handling or storage of such goods in connection with such transport; or
(*b*) to a person who receives the supply for the purpose of a business carried on by him and who belongs outside the United Kingdom, of services of a description specified in paragraph (*a*) of item 6, [item 6A,][1] item 9 or paragraph (*a*) of item 10 of this Group.

Amendments—[1] Words in item 11(*b*) inserted by the Value Added Tax (Transport) Order, SI 1995/653 with effect from 1 April 1995.

12 The supply of a designated travel service to be enjoyed outside the European Community, to the extent to which the supply is so enjoyed.

13 Intra-Community transport services supplied in connection with the transport of goods to or from the Azores or Madeira or between those places, to the extent that the services are treated as supplied in the United Kingdom.

NOTES

[(A1) In this Group—
(*a*) a "qualifying ship" is any ship of a gross tonnage of not less than 15 tons which is neither designed nor adapted for use for recreation or pleasure; and
[(*b*) a "qualifying aircraft" is any aircraft which—
  (i) is used by an airline operating for reward chiefly on international routes, or
  (ii) is used by a State institution and meets the condition in Note (B1).][9]][3]

[(B1) The condition is that the aircraft—
(*a*) is of a weight of not less than 8,000 kilograms, and
(*b*) is neither designed nor adapted for use for recreation or pleasure.

(C1) In Note (A1)(*b*)—
"airline" means an undertaking which provides services for the carriage by air of passengers or cargo (or both);
"State institution" has the same meaning as in Part B of Annex X to the Council Directive 2006/112/EC on the common system of value added tax (transactions which member States may continue to exempt).][9]

(1) In items 1 and 2 the supply of a [qualifying][3] ship or, as the case may be, aircraft includes the supply of services under a charter of that ship or aircraft except where the services supplied under such a charter consist wholly of any one or more of the following—
(*a*) transport of passengers;
(*b*) accommodation;

(*c*) entertainment;

(*d*) education;

being services wholly performed in the United Kingdom.

(2) Items 1, 2 [, 2A, 2B][3] and 3 include the letting on hire of the goods specified in the items.

[(2A) Items 2A and 2B do not include the supply of parts and equipment to a Government department [or any part of the Scottish Administration][4] unless—

(*a*) they are installed or incorporated in the course of a supply which is treated as being made in the course of furtherance of a business carried on by the department; or

(*b*) the parts and equipment are to be installed or incorporated in ships or aircraft used for the purpose of providing rescue or assistance at sea.][3]

(3) Item 3 shall not apply unless, before the supply is made, the recipient of the supply gives to the person making the supply a certificate stating—

(*a*) the name and address of the recipient;

(*b*) that the supply is of a description specified in item 3 of this Group.

(4) "Lifeboat" means any vessel used or to be used solely for rescue or assistance at sea.

[(4A) Item 4 does not include the transport of passengers—

(*a*) in any vehicle to, from or within—

(i) a place of entertainment, recreation or amusement; or

(ii) a place of cultural, scientific, historical or similar interest,

by the person, or a person connected with him, who supplies a right of admission to, or a right to use facilities at, such a place;

(*b*) in any motor vehicle between a car park (or land adjacent thereto) and an airport passenger terminal (or land adjacent thereto) by the person, or a person connected with him, who supplies facilities for the parking of vehicles in that car park; or

(*c*) in an aircraft where the flight is advertised or held out to be for the purpose of—

(i) providing entertainment, recreation or amusement; or

(ii) the experience of flying, or the experience of flying in that particular aircraft,

and not primarily for the purpose of transporting passengers from one place to another.][1]

[(4B) For the purposes of Note (4A) any question whether a person is connected with another shall be determined in accordance with [section 1122 of the Corporation Tax Act 2010][8].][1]

[(4C) In Note (4A)(*b*) "motor vehicle" means a mechanically propelled vehicle intended or adapted for use on the roads.][1]

[(4D) Item 4(*a*) includes the transport of passengers in a vehicle—

(*a*) which is designed, or substantially and permanently adapted, for the safe carriage of a person in a wheelchair or two or more such persons, and

(*b*) which, if it were not so designed or adapted, would be capable of carrying no less than 10 persons.][6]

[(4E) "Universal service provider" means a person who provides a universal postal service (within the meaning of [Part 3 of the Postal Services Act 2011][11]), or part of such a service, in the United Kingdom.][10]

(5) Item 6 does not include the letting on hire of goods.

(6) "Port"[,"customs and excise airport" and "transit shed"][7] have the same meanings as in the Management Act.

[(6A) "Air navigation services" has the same meaning as in the Civil Aviation Act 1982.][2]

(7) Except for the purposes of item 11, paragraph (*a*) of item 6, [item 6A,][2] item 9 and paragraph (*a*) of item 10 [only include supplies of services where the ships or aircraft referred to in those paragraphs are qualifying ships or, as the case may be, aircraft.][3]

(8) "Designated travel service" has the same meaning as in the Value Added Tax Tour Operators) Order 1987.

(9) "Intra-Community transport services" means—

(*a*) the intra-Community transport of goods within the meaning of the Value Added Tax (Place of Supply of Services) Order 1992;

(*b*) ancillary transport services within the meaning of the Value Added Tax (Place of Supply of Services) Order 1992 which are provided in connection with the intra-Community transport of goods; or

(*c*) the making of arrangements for the supply by or to another person of a supply within (*a*) or (*b*) above or any other activity which is intended to facilitate the making of such a supply,

and, for the purpose of this Note only, the Azores and Madeira shall each be treated as a separate member State.

Commentary—*De Voil Indirect Tax Service* **V4.251, V6.377**.

Press releases etc—C&E Business Brief 27/95 18-12-95 (a holiday cruise is a single supply of passenger transport zero-rated under item 4; C&E to appeal decision).

C&E Business Brief 2/96 9-2-96 (guidance on the VAT treatment of commission for transport only sales by travel agents).

C&E Business Brief 4/96 13-3-96 (conditions for treatment of airline passenger perks as part of air passenger transport).
C&E Business Brief 14/96 15-7-96 (VAT treatment of holiday and other cruises).
HMRC Brief 38/09 VAT—"Dutch barges" and similar vessels designed for and used as permanent residential accommodation by owners.

Simon's Tax Cases—Item 1, *R&C Comrs v Stone; The Kei* [2008] STC 2501.
Item 4, *Virgin Atlantic Airways v C&E Comrs* [1995] STC 341*.
Item 4(*a*), *British Airways plc v C&E Comrs* [1990] STC 643*; *C&E Comrs v Peninsular and Oriental Steam Navigation Co Ltd* [1996] STC 698; *Cirdan Sailing Trust v C&E Comrs* [2006] STC 185; *Davies (trading as Special Occasions/2XL Limos) v R&C Comrs* [2012] UKUT 130 (TCC), [2012] STC 1978.
Item 4(*c*), *British Airways plc v C&E Comrs* [1990] STC 643*.
Item 6, *R&C Comrs v EB Central Services Ltd and another* [2008] STC 2209.
Item 10, *Société Internationale de Télécommunications Aéronautiques v C&E Comrs* [2004] STC 950.
Item 11(*a*), *R&C Comrs v EB Central Services Ltd and another* [2008] STC 2209.
Note 4A(*b*), *Purple Parking Ltd and another v R&C Comrs* (Case C-117/11) [2012] STC 1680.

Definitions—"Business", s 94; "the Management Act", s 96(1); "ship", s 96(1); "supply", s 5, Sch 4; "United Kingdom", s 96(11).

Amendments—[1] Notes (4A)–(4C) inserted by the Value Added Tax (Transport) Order, SI 1994/3014 with effect from 1 April 1995.
[2] Item 6A and Note (6A) inserted, and words in item 11(b) and Note (7) inserted, by the Value Added Tax (Transport) Order, SI 1995/653 with effect from 1 April 1995.
[3] Items 1 and 2 substituted, items 2A, 2B inserted, words in item 10 substituted, Notes (A1), (2A) and words in Notes (1), (2) inserted and words in Note (7) substituted by the Value Added Tax (Ships and Aircraft) Order, SI 1995/3039 with effect from 1 January 1996.
[4] Words in Note (2A) inserted by The Scotland Act 1998 (Consequential Modifications) (No 2) Order, SI 1999/1820 s 114(2), which comes into force on the "principle appointed day", currently 1 July 1999, by virtue of the Scotland Act 1998 (Commencement) Order 1998/3178.
[6] Figure in item 4 substituted, and Note (4D) inserted by the Value Added Tax (Passenger Vehicles) Order, SI 2001/753 arts 2, 3 with effect for supplies made after 31 March 2001.
[7] Para (b) of item 6, and words in Note (6) substituted by the Value Added Tax (Transport) Order, SI 2002/1173 art 2 with effect from 1 June 2002.
[8] In Note (4B) words substituted for words "section 839 of the Taxes Act 1988" by CTA 2010 s 1177, Sch 1 para 285(d). CTA 2010 has effect for corporation tax purposes for accounting periods ending on or after 1 April 2010, and for income and capital gains tax purposes for the tax year 2010–11 and subsequent tax years.
[9] In Note (A1), para (*b*) substituted, and Notes (B1), (C1) inserted, by F(No 3)A 2010 s 21(1)–(3) with effect in relation to supplies made, and acquisitions and importations taking place, on or after 1 January 2011.
[10] Note (4E) inserted by F(No 3)A 2010 s 22(1) with effect in relation to supplies made on or after 31 January 2011.
[11] In Note (4E) words substituted by the Postal Services Act 2011 (Consequential Modifications and Amendments) Order, SI 2011/2085 art 5(1), Schedule para 28(1), (2) with effect from 1 October 2011.

GROUP 9 — CARAVANS AND HOUSEBOATS

Item No

[1 **1** Caravans which exceed the limits of size of a trailer for the time being permitted to be towed on roads by a motor vehicle having a maximum gross weight of 3,500 kilogrammes and which—

(*a*) were manufactured to standard BS 3632:2005 approved by the British Standards Institution, or

(*b*) are second hand, were manufactured to a previous version of standard BS 3632 approved by that Institution and were occupied before 6 April 2013.][1]

2 Houseboats being boats or other floating decked structures designed or adapted for use solely as places of permanent habitation and not having means of, or capable of being readily adapted for, self-propulsion.

3 The supply of such services as are described in paragraph 1(1) or [5(4)][1] of Schedule 4 in respect of a caravan comprised in item 1 or a houseboat comprised in item 2.

Note: This Group does not include—

(*a*) removable contents other than goods of a kind mentioned in [item 4][1] of Group 5; or

(*b*) the supply of accommodation in a caravan or houseboat.

Commentary—*De Voil Indirect Tax Service* **V4.275**.

Simon's Tax Cases—Item 1, Note (a) *Colaingrove Ltd v R&C Comrs* [2014] UKUT 132 (TCC), [2014] STC 1457.
Talacre Beach Caravan Sales Ltd v C&E Comrs [2006] STC 1671.

Press releases etc—HMRC Brief 38/09, 9-7-09 ("Dutch barges" and similar vessels designed for and used as permanent residential accommodation by owners: change of policy).
HMRC Brief 20/10 15-4-10 (change to the dimensions of caravan that will be eligible to be zero-rated).

Definition—"Supply", s 5, Sch 4.

Amendments—[1] Item 1 substituted, and in item (3) and in the Note words substituted, by FA 2012 s 196, Sch 26 paras 1, 4 with effect from 6 April 2013.

GROUP 10 — GOLD

Item No

1 The supply, by a Central Bank to another Central Bank or a member of the London Gold Market, of gold held in the United Kingdom.

2 The supply, by a member of the London Gold Market to a Central Bank, of gold held in the United Kingdom.

NOTES

(1) "Gold" includes gold coins.

(2) Section 30(3) does not apply to goods forming part of a description of supply in this Group.

(3) Items 1 and 2 include—

(*a*) the granting of a right to acquire a quantity of gold; and

(*b*) any supply described in those items which by virtue of paragraph 1 of Schedule 4 is a supply of services.

Commentary—*De Voil Indirect Tax Service* **V4.277**.
Definitions—"Supply", s 5, Sch 4; "United Kingdom", s 96(11).

GROUP 11 — BANK NOTES

Item No

1 The issue by a bank of a note payable to bearer on demand.

Simon's Tax Cases—Item 1 *Royal Bank of Scotland Group plc v C & E Comrs* [2002] STC 575.
Commentary—*De Voil Indirect Tax Service* **V4.279**.

GROUP 12 — DRUGS, MEDICINES, AIDS FOR THE HANDICAPPED, ETC

Item No

[1 The supply of any qualifying goods dispensed to an individual for that individual's personal use on the prescription of an appropriate practitioner where the dispensing is—

(*a*) by a registered pharmacist, or

(*b*) in accordance with a requirement or authorisation under a relevant provision.][1]

Amendments—[1] Item 1 substituted for previous Items 1, 1A, by the Value Added Tax (Drugs and Medicines) Order, SI 2009/2972 arts 2–7 with effect in relation to supplies made on or after 2 December 2009.

Note that Item 1 is purported to be amended further by the Pharmacy Order, SI 2010/231 art 68, Sch 4 para 5(2) with effect from 27 September 2010 (by virtue of SI 2010/1621). However, the amendment made by Sch 4 para 5(2) appears to refer to the text of Item 1 prior to substitution by SI 2009/2972. This amendment has therefore not been carried through in the text.

2 The supply to a handicapped person for domestic or his personal use, or to a charity for making available to handicapped persons by sale or otherwise, for domestic or their personal use, of—

(*a*) medical or surgical appliances designed solely for the relief of a severe abnormality or severe injury;

(*b*) electrically or mechanically adjustable beds designed for invalids;

(*c*) commode chairs, commode stools, devices incorporating a bidet jet and warm air drier and frames or other devices for sitting over or rising from a sanitary appliance;

(*d*) chair lifts or stair lifts designed for use in connection with invalid wheelchairs;

(*e*) hoists and lifters designed for use by invalids;

(*f*) motor vehicles designed or substantially and permanently adapted for the carriage of a person in a wheelchair or on a stretcher and of no more than [11][1] other persons;

(*g*) equipment and appliances not included in paragraphs (*a*) to (*f*) above designed solely for use by a handicapped person;

(*h*) parts and accessories designed solely for use in or with goods described in paragraphs (*a*) to (*g*) above;

(*i*) boats designed or substantially and permanently adapted for use by handicapped persons.

Amendments—[1] Figure substituted in Item 2(*f*) by SI 2001/754 arts 2, 4 and 5 with effect for supplies, acquisitions or importations made after 31 March 2001.

[2A The supply of a qualifying motor vehicle—

(*a*) to a handicapped person—

(i) who usually uses a wheelchair, or

(ii) who is usually carried on a stretcher, for domestic or his personal use; or

(*b*) to a charity for making available to such a handicapped person by sale or otherwise, for domestic or his personal use.][1]

Amendments—[1] Item 2A inserted by the Value Added Tax (Vehicles Designed or Adapted for Handicapped Persons) Order, SI 2001/754 arts 3, 6 with effect for supplies, acquisitions or importations made after 31 March 2001.

3 The supply to a handicapped person of services of adapting goods to suit his condition.

4 The supply to a charity of services of adapting goods to suit the condition of a handicapped person to whom the goods are to be made available, by sale or otherwise, by the charity.

5 The supply to a handicapped person or to a charity of a service of repair or maintenance of any goods specified in item 2, [2A,][1] 6, 18 or 19 and supplied as described in that item.

Amendments—[1] Figure added in Item 5 by SI 2001/754 arts 2, 4 and 5 with effect for supplies, acquisitions or importations made after 31 March 2001.

6 The supply of goods in connection with a supply described in item 3, 4 or 5.

7 The supply to a handicapped person or to a charity of services necessarily performed in the installation of equipment or appliances (including parts and accessories therefor) specified in item 2 and supplied as described in that item.

8 The supply to a handicapped person of a service of constructing ramps or widening doorways or passages for the purpose of facilitating his entry to or movement within his private residence.

9 The supply to a charity of a service described in item 8 for the purpose of facilitating a handicapped person's entry to or movement within any building.

10 The supply to a handicapped person of a service of providing, extending or adapting a bathroom, washroom or lavatory in his private residence where such provision, extension or adaptation is necessary by reason of his condition.

[**11** The supply to a charity of a service of providing, extending or adapting a bathroom, washroom or lavatory for use by handicapped persons—

(*a*) in residential accommodation, or

(*b*) in a day-centre where at least 20 per cent of the individuals using the centre are handicapped persons,

where such provision, extension or adaptation is necessary by reason of the condition of the handicapped persons.][1]

Amendments—[1] Item 11 substituted by the VAT (Charities and Aids for the Handicapped) Order, SI 2000/805 arts 2, 3 with effect from 1 April 2000.

12 The supply to a charity of a service of providing, extending or adapting a washroom or lavatory for use by handicapped persons in a building, or any part of a building, used principally by a charity for charitable purposes where such provision, extension or adaptation is necessary to facilitate the use of the washroom or lavatory by handicapped persons.

13 The supply of goods in connection with a supply described in items 8, 9, 10 or 11.

14 The letting on hire of a motor vehicle for a period of not less than 3 years to a handicapped person in receipt of a disability living allowance by virtue of entitlement to the mobility component[, of a personal independence payment by virtue of entitlement to the mobility component, of an armed forces independence payment][1] or of mobility supplement where the lessor's business consists predominantly of the provision of motor vehicles to such persons.

Amendments—[1] Words inserted by the Value Added Tax (Independence Payment) Order, SI 2013/601 art 3(*a*) with effect from 8 April 2013.

15 The sale of a motor vehicle which had been let on hire in the circumstances described in item 14, where such sale constitutes the first supply of the vehicle after the end of the period of such letting.

16 The supply to a handicapped person of services necessarily performed in the installation of a lift for the purpose of facilitating his movement between floors within his private residence.

17 The supply to a charity providing a permanent or temporary residence or day-centre for handicapped persons of services necessarily performed in the installation of a lift for the purpose of facilitating the movement of handicapped persons between floors within that building.

18 The supply of goods in connection with a supply described in item 16 or 17.

19 The supply to a handicapped person for domestic or his personal use, or to a charity for making available to handicapped persons by sale or otherwise for domestic or their personal use, of an alarm system designed to be capable of operation by a handicapped person, and to enable him to alert directly a specified person or a control centre.

20 The supply of services necessarily performed by a control centre in receiving and responding to calls from an alarm system specified in item 19.

NOTES

(1) Section 30(3) does not apply to goods forming part of a description of supply in item 1 . . . [14], nor to other goods forming part of a description of supply in this Group, except where those other goods are acquired from another member State or imported from a place outside the member States by a handicapped person for domestic or his personal use, or by a charity for making available to handicapped persons, by sale or otherwise, for domestic or their personal use.

(2) . . . [13]

[(2A) In [item 1][14], 'qualifying goods' means any goods designed or adapted for use in connection with any medical or surgical treatment except—

(*a*) hearing aids;

(*b*) dentures; and

(*c*) spectacles and contact lenses.][3]

[(2B) In item 1 "appropriate practitioner" means—

(*a*) a registered medical practitioner;

(*b*) a person registered in the dentists' register under the Dentists Act 1984;

(*c*) a community practitioner nurse prescriber;

(*d*) a nurse independent prescriber;

(*e*) an optometrist independent prescriber;

(*f*) a pharmacist independent prescriber;

[(*fa*) a physiotherapist independent prescriber;

(*fb*) a podiatrist independent prescriber;][17]

(*g*) a supplementary prescriber.

For the purposes of this Note "community practitioner nurse prescriber", "nurse independent prescriber", "optometrist independent prescriber", "pharmacist independent prescriber"[, "physiotherapist independent prescriber", "podiatrist independent prescriber"][17] and "supplementary prescriber" have the meanings given in [regulation 8(1) of the Human Medicines Regulations 2012][14].

(2C) In item 1 "registered pharmacist" means a person who is—

(*a*) registered in the Register of Pharmacists maintained under the Pharmacists and Pharmacy Technicians Order 2007, or

(*b*) registered in the register of pharmaceutical chemists kept under the Pharmacy (Northern Ireland) Order 1976.

(2D) In item 1 "relevant provision" means—

(*a*) article 57 of the Health and Personal Social Services (Northern Ireland) Order 1972;

(*b*) regulation 20 of the National Health Service (Pharmaceutical Services) Regulations 1992;

(*c*) regulation 12 of the Pharmaceutical Services Regulations (Northern Ireland) 1997;

(*d*) paragraph 44 of Schedule 5 to the National Health Service (General Medical Services Contracts) (Scotland) Regulations 2004;

(*e*) paragraph 15 of Schedule 1 to the National Health Service (Primary Medical Services Section 17C Agreements) (Scotland) Regulations 2004;

(*f*) paragraphs 47 and 49 of Schedule 6 to the National Health Service (General Medical Services Contracts) Regulations 2004;

(*g*) paragraph 44 of Schedule 5 to the Health and Personal Social Services (General Medical Services Contracts) Regulations (Northern Ireland) 2004;

(*h*) paragraphs 46, 48 and 49 of Schedule 5 to the National Health Service (Personal Medical Services Agreements) Regulations 2004;

(*i*) paragraph 47 of Schedule 6 to the National Health Service (General Medical Services Contracts) (Wales) Regulations 2004;

(*j*) regulation 60 of the National Health Service (Pharmaceutical Services) Regulations 2005.][14]

(3) "Handicapped" means chronically sick or disabled.

(4) Item 2 shall not include hearing aids (except hearing aids designed for the auditory training of deaf children), dentures, spectacles and contact lenses but shall be deemed to include—

(*a*) clothing, footwear and wigs;

(*b*) invalid wheelchairs, and invalid carriages [. . .][4]; and

(*c*) renal haemodialysis units, oxygen concentrators, artificial respirators and other similar apparatus.

(5) The supplies described in Items 1[, 1A][1] [, 2 and 2A][8] include supplies of services of letting on hire of the goods respectively comprised in those items.

[(5A) In item 1 the reference to personal use does not include any use which is, or involves, a use by or in relation to an individual while that individual, for the purposes of being provided (whether or not by the person making the supply) with medical or surgical treatment, or with any form of care—

(*a*) is an in-patient or resident in a relevant institution which is a hospital or nursing home; or

(*b*) is attending at the premises of a relevant institution which is a hospital or nursing home.

(5B) Subject to Notes (5C) and (5D), in item 2 the reference to domestic or personal use does not include any use which is, or involves, a use by or in relation to a handicapped person while that person, for the purposes of being provided (whether or not by the person making the supply) with medical or surgical treatment, or with any form of care—

(*a*) is an in-patient or resident in a relevant institution; or

(*b*) is attending at the premises of a relevant institution.

(5C) Note (5B) does not apply for the purpose of determining whether any of the following supplies falls within item 2, that is to say—

(*a*) a supply to a charity;

(*b*) a supply by a person mentioned in any of paragraphs (*a*) to (*g*) of Note (5H) of an invalid wheelchair or invalid carriage;

(*c*) a supply by a person so mentioned of any parts or accessories designed solely for use in or with an invalid wheelchair or invalid carriage.

(5D) Note (5B) applies for the purpose of determining whether a supply of goods by a person not mentioned in any of paragraphs (*a*) to (*g*) of Note (5H) falls within item 2 only if those goods are—

(*a*) goods falling within paragraph (*a*) of that item;

(*b*) incontinence products and wound dressings; or

(*c*) parts and accessories designed solely for use in or with goods falling within paragraph (*a*) of this Note.

(5E) Subject to Note (5F), item 2 does not include—

(*a*) a supply made in accordance with any agreement, arrangement or understanding (whether or not legally enforceable) to which any of the persons mentioned in paragraphs (*a*) to (*g*) of Note (5H) is or has been a party otherwise than as the supplier; or

(*b*) any supply the whole or any part of the consideration for which is provided (whether directly or indirectly) by a person so mentioned.

(5F) A supply to a handicapped person of an invalid wheelchair or invalid carriage is excluded from item 2 by Note (5E) only if—

(*a*) that Note applies in relation to that supply by reference to a person falling within paragraph (*g*) of Note (5H); or

(*b*) the whole of the consideration for the supply is provided (whether directly or indirectly) by a person falling within any of paragraphs (*a*) to (*f*) of Note (5H).

(5G) In Notes (4), (5C) and (5F), the references to an invalid wheelchair and to an invalid carriage do not include references to any mechanically propelled vehicle which is intended or adapted for use on roads.

(5H) The persons referred to in Notes (5C) to (5F) are—

[(*a*) a Strategic Health Authority or Special Health Authority in England;][10]

[(*aa*) a Health Authority, Special Health Authority or Local Health Board in Wales;][10]

(*b*) a Health Board or Special Health Board in Scotland;

(*c*) a Health and Social Services Board in Northern Ireland;

(*d*) the Common Services Agency for the Scottish Health Service, the Northern Ireland Central Services Agency for Health and Social Services and the Isle of Man Health Services Board;

(*e*) a National Health Service trust established under Part I of the National Health Service and Community Care Act 1990 or the National Health Service (Scotland) Act 1978;

[(*eaa*) an NHS foundation trust;][11]

[(*ea*) a Primary Care Trust established under section 16A of the National Health Service Act 1977;][5]

(*f*) a Health and Social Services trust established under Article 10 of the Health and Personal Social Services (Northern Ireland) Order 1991; or

(*g*) any person not falling within any of paragraphs (*a*) to (*f*) above who is engaged in the carrying on of any activity in respect of which a relevant institution is required to be approved, licensed or registered or as the case may be, would be so required if not exempt.

(5I) In Notes (5A), (5B) and (5H), 'relevant institution' means any institution (whether a hospital, nursing home or other institution) which provides care or medical or surgical treatment and is either—

(*a*) approved, licensed or registered in accordance with the provisions of any enactment or Northern Ireland legislation; or

(*b*) exempted by or under the provisions of any enactment or Northern Ireland legislation from any requirement to be approved, licensed or registered;

and in this Note the references to the provisions of any enactment or Northern Ireland legislation include references only to provisions which, so far as relating to England, Wales, Scotland or Northern Ireland, have the same effect in every locality within that part of the United Kingdom.][3]

[(5J) For the purposes of item 11 "residential accommodation" means—

(*a*) a residential home, or

(*b*) self-contained living accommodation,

provided as a residence (whether on a permanent or temporary basis or both) for handicapped persons, but does not include an inn, hotel, boarding house or similar establishment or accommodation in any such type of establishment.

(5K) In this Group "washroom" means a room that contains a lavatory or washbasin (or both) but does not contain a bath or a shower or cooking, sleeping or laundry facilities.][6]

[(5L) A "qualifying motor vehicle" for the purposes of item 2A is a motor vehicle (other than a motor vehicle capable of carrying more than 12 persons including the driver)—

(*a*) that is designed or substantially and permanently adapted to enable a handicapped person—

(i) who usually uses a wheelchair, or

(ii) who is usually carried on a stretcher,

to enter, and drive or be otherwise carried in, the motor vehicle; or

(*b*) that by reason of its design, or being substantially and permanently adapted, includes features whose design is such that their sole purpose is to allow a wheelchair used by a handicapped person to be carried in or on the motor vehicle.][7]

(6) Item 14 applies only—

(*a*) where the vehicle is unused at the commencement of the period of letting; and

(*b*) where the consideration for the letting consists wholly or partly of sums paid to the lessor by [the Department for Work and Pensions][9] or the Ministry of Defence on behalf of the lessee in respect of the mobility component of the disability living allowance[, the mobility component of the personal independence payment, armed forces independence payment][16] or mobility supplement to which he is entitled.

(7) In item 14—

(*a*) "disability living allowance" is a disability living allowance within the meaning of section 71 of the Social Security Contributions and Benefits Act 1992 or section 71 of the Social Security Contributions and Benefits (Northern Ireland) Act 1992; . . .[16]

[(*aa*) "personal independence payment" means a personal independence payment under Part 4 of the Welfare Reform Act 2012 or the corresponding provision having effect in Northern Ireland;

(*ab*) "armed forces independence payment" means an armed forces independence payment under a scheme established under section 1 of the Armed Forces (Pensions and Compensation) Act 2004; and][16]

(*b*) "mobility supplement" is a mobility supplement within the meaning of Article 26A of the Naval, Military and Air Forces etc (Disablement and Death Service Pensions Order 1983, Article 25A of the Personal Injuries (Civilians) Scheme 1983, Article 3 of the Motor Vehicles (Exemption from Vehicles Excise Duty) Order 1985 or Article 3 of the Motor Vehicles (Exemption from Vehicles Excise Duty) (Northern Ireland) Order 1985.

(8) Where in item 3 or 4 the goods are adapted in accordance with that item prior to their supply to the handicapped person or the charity, an apportionment shall be made to determine the supply of services which falls within item 3 or 4.

(9) In item 19 or 20, a specified person or control centre is a person or centre who or which—

(*a*) is appointed to receive directly calls activated by an alarm system described in that item, and

(*b*) retains information about the handicapped person to assist him in the event of illness, injury or similar emergency.

Commentary—*see De Voil Indirect Tax Service* **V4.281**.

Press releases etc—C&E Business Brief 12/95 19-6-95 (supplies of drugs, prostheses etc by hospitals as part of an exempt supply of hospital services under Sch 9 Group 7 cannot be separately zero-rated).

C&E Business Brief 18/95 6-9-95 (end of concessionary treatment for supplies of dispensed medicines on prescription by doctors).

C&E Business Brief 23/95 24-10-95 (supplies of incontinence products to commercial nursing homes and NHS Trusts).

C&E Business Brief 16/96 30-7-96 (allergy relief products will be liable to VAT at the standard rate irrespective of to whom supplied).

C&E Business Brief 16/96 30-7-96 (zero rated supplies of incontinence products can no longer be made by NHS or non-charitable nursing homes).

C&E Business Brief 5/97 5-3-97 (supplies of incontinence products to patients residing at home are zero rated).

VAT Information Sheet 7/01 June 2001 (guidance on when a supplier is entitled to zero rate the supply of an eligible adapted motor vehicle to a disabled person, a charitable institution and certain other eligible bodies. Also details the necessary documentation with regard to the relief).

Simon's Tax Cases—Item 1, *British United Provident Association Ltd v C&E Comrs* [1995] STC 628*; *Provident Association Ltd* [1997] STC 445*.

Items 2, 7, *British United Provident Association Ltd v C&E Comrs* [1995] STC 628*; *Provident Association Ltd* [1997] STC 445*; *Dr Beynon and Partners v C&E Comrs* [2003] STC 169, CA.

Definitions—"Acquisition of goods from another member State", s 11; "another member State", s 96(1); "business", s 94; "importation of goods from a place outside the member States", s 15; "supply", s 5, Sch 4.

Cross reference—See VAT Regulations, SI 1995/2518 reg 74 (retail schemes: adjustment of calculations for supplies within this Group).

Modification—Pending amendment of Group 12 to take account of the repeal of the National Health Service (Pharmaceutical Services) Regulations 2005, the definition of "relevant provision" in Note (2D) shall apply in relation to supplies on or after 1 October 2010 as if for paragraph (j) there were substituted: "(j) Part 8 of the National Health Service (Pharmaceutical Services) Regulations 2012." (National Health Service (Pharmaceutical Services) Regulations, SI 2012/1909 reg 103, Sch 7 para 15 with effect from 1 September 2012).

Amendments—[1] Words in Notes (1), (5), inserted by the VAT (Supply of Pharmaceutical Goods) Order, SI 1995/652 with effect from 1 April 1995.

3 Notes (2A), (5A), (5B), (5C), (5D), (5E), (5F), (5G), (5H), (5I), inserted by the VAT (Drugs, Medicines and Aids for the Handicapped) Order, SI 1997/2744 with effect from 1 January 1998.

4 Words in Note (4)(b) deleted by the VAT (Drugs, Medicines and Aids for the Handicapped) Order, SI 1997/2744 with effect from 1 January 1998.

5 Para (*ea*) in Note (5H) inserted by the VAT (Drugs, Medicines, Aids for the Handicapped and Charities Etc) Order, SI 2000/503 arts 2, 3 with effect from 1 April 2000.

6 Notes (5J), (5K) inserted by the VAT (Charities and Aids for the Handicapped) Order, SI 2000/805 arts 2, 3 with effect from 1 April 2000.

7 Note (5L) inserted by the Value Added Tax (Vehicles Designed or Adapted for Handicapped Persons) Order, SI 2001/754 arts 3, 6 with effect for supplies, acquisitions or importations made after 31 March 2001.

8 Figure substituted in Item 2(*f*); "2A" added in Item 5, and words substituted in Note (5) by SI 2001/754 arts 2, 4 and 5 with effect for supplies, acquisitions or importations made after 31 March 2001.

9 Words in Note (6)(*b*) substituted by the Secretaries of State for Education and Skills and for Work and Pensions Order, SI 2002/1397 art 12, Schedule para 11 with effect from 27 June 2002.

10 Note (5H)(*a*), (*aa*) substituted for Note (5H)(a) as originally enacted, by the VAT (Drugs, Medicines, Aids for the Handicapped and Charities etc) Order, SI 2002/2813 arts 2, 3 with effect from 5 December 2002.

11 In Note (5H), para (*eaa*) inserted by the Health and Social Care (Community Health and Standards) Act 2003 s 34, Sch 4 paras 97, 98 with effect, in relation to England and Wales, from 1 April 2004 (by virtue of SI 2004/759) and in relation to Scotland, from a date to be appointed.

13 Note 2 repealed by the European Qualifications (Health and Social Care Professions) Regulations, SI 2007/3101 reg 65(a) with effect from 3 December 2007.

14 In Note (1), words "or item 1A" repealed, in Note (2A), words substituted for words "items 1 and 1A", Notes (2B)–(2D) inserted, and in Note (5), reference "1A," repealed, by the Value Added Tax (Drugs and Medicines) Order, SI 2009/2972 arts 2–7 with effect in relation to supplies made on or after 2 December 2009.

15 In Note (2B), words substituted for words "article 1(2) of the Prescription Only Medicines (Human Use) Order 1997" by the Human Medicines Regulations, SI 2012/1916 reg 348, Sch 34 para 42(*a*) with effect from 14 August 2012.

16 In Note (6), words in para (*b*) inserted; in Note (7), word "and" at end of para (*a*) repealed, and paras (*aa*), (*ab*) inserted, by the Value Added Tax (Independence Payment) Order, SI 2013/601 art 3(*b*), (*c*) with effect from 8 April 2013.

17 In note (2B), paras (*fa*), (*fb*) inserted, and words in second sentence inserted, by the Value Added Tax (Drugs and Medicines) Order, SI 2014/1111 art 2 with effect in relation to supplies made on or after 21 May 2014.

Prospective amendments—In Note (5H)(*e*), words "the National Health Service Act 2006 or" to be repealed by the Health and Social Care Act 2012 s 179, Sch 14 paras 65, 67(*a*) with effect from a date to be appointed.

In Note (7)(*a*) words "section 71 of the Social Security Contributions and Benefits Act 1992, or" to be repealed by the Welfare Reform Act 2012 s 147, Sch 14 Part 9 with effect from a date to be appointed.

In Note (2D) (*j*) "Part 8 of the National Health Service (Pharmaceutical and Local Pharmaceutical Services) Regulations 2013.'' to be substituted by the National Health Service (Pharmaceutical and Local Pharmaceutical Services) Regulations, SI 2013/349, Sch 9 para 17 in relation to supplies on or after the appointed day. Note (2D) (*j*) as substituted to read as follows—

"(*j*) Part 8 of the National Health Service (Pharmaceutical and Local Pharmaceutical Services) Regulations 2013.".

GROUP 13 — IMPORTS, EXPORTS ETC

Item No

1 The supply before the delivery of an entry (within the meaning of regulation 5 of the Customs Controls on Importation of Goods Regulations 1991)) under an agreement requiring the purchaser to make such entry of goods imported from a place outside the member States.

2 The supply to or by an overseas authority, overseas body or overseas trader, charged with the management of any defence project which is the subject of an international collaboration arrangement or under direct contract with any government or government-sponsored international body participating in a defence project under such an arrangement, of goods or services in the course of giving effect to that arrangement.

3 The supply to an overseas authority, overseas body or overseas trader of jigs, patterns, templates, dies, punches and similar machine tools used in the United Kingdom solely for the manufacture of goods for export to places outside the member States.

Notes

(1) An "international collaboration arrangement" means any arrangement which—

(*a*) is made between the United Kingdom Government and the government of one or more other countries, or any government-sponsored international body for collaboration in a joint project of research, development or production; and

(*b*) includes provision for participating governments to relieve the cost of the project from taxation.

(2) "Overseas authority" means any country other than the United Kingdom or any part of or place in such a country or the government of any such country, part or place.
(3) "Overseas body" means a body established outside the United Kingdom.
(4) "Overseas trader" means a person who carries on a business and has his principal place of business outside the United Kingdom.
(5) Item 3 does not apply where the overseas authority, overseas body or overseas trader is a taxable person, another member State, any part of or place in another member State, the government of any such member State, part or place, a body established in another member State or a person who carries on business, or has a place of business, in another member State.

Commentary—*De Voil Indirect Tax Service* **V.283**.

Definitions—"Another member State", s 96(1); "business", s 94; "importation of goods from a place outside the member States", s 15; "supply", s 5, Sch 4; "taxable person", s 3; "United Kingdom", s 96(11).

GROUP 14 — TAX-FREE SHOPS

. . .

Amendments—Group 14 deleted by the Value Added Tax (Abolition of Zero-Rating for Tax Free Shops) Order, SI 1999/1642, with effect from 1 July 1999.

GROUP 15 — CHARITIES ETC

Item No

[1 The sale, or letting on hire, by a charity of any goods donated to it for—
(*a*) sale,
(*b*) letting,
(*c*) sale or letting,
(*d*) sale or export,
(*e*) letting or export, or
(*f*) sale, letting or export.

1A The sale, or letting on hire, by a taxable person of any goods donated to him for—
(*a*) sale,
(*b*) letting,
(*c*) sale or letting,
(*d*) sale or export,
(*e*) letting or export, or
(*f*) sale, letting or export,
if he is a profits-to-charity person in respect of the goods.

2 The donation of any goods for any one or more of the following purposes—
(*a*) sale by a charity or a taxable person who is a profits-to-charity person in respect of the goods;
(*b*) export by a charity or such a taxable person;
(*c*) letting by a charity or such a taxable person.][1]

Amendments—[1] Items 1, 1A and 2 substituted for original items 1, 2 by the VAT (Charities and Aids for the Handicapped) Order, SI 2000/805 arts 5–9 with effect from 1 April 2000.

3 The export of any goods by a charity to a place outside the member States.

4 The supply of any relevant goods for donation to a nominated eligible body where the goods are purchased with funds provided by a charity or from voluntary contributions.

5 The supply of any relevant goods to an eligible body which pays for them with funds provided by a charity or from voluntary contributions or to an eligible body which is a charitable institution providing care or medical or surgical treatment for handicapped persons.

6 Repair and maintenance of relevant goods owned by an eligible body.

7 The supply of goods in connection with the supply described in item 6.

[8 The supply to a charity of a right to promulgate an advertisement by means of a medium of communication with the public.

8A A supply to a charity that consists in the promulgation of an advertisement by means of such a medium.

8B The supply to a charity of services of design or production of an advertisement that is, or was intended to be, promulgated by means of such a medium.

8C The supply to a charity of goods closely related to a supply within item 8B.][1]

Amendments—[1] Items 8, 8A, 8B, 8C substituted for original item 8 by the VAT (Charities and Aids for the Handicapped) Order, SI 2000/805 arts 5–9 with effect from 1 April 2000.

9 The supply to a charity, providing care or medical or surgical treatment for human beings or animals, or engaging in medical or veterinary research, of a medicinal product [or veterinary medicinal product][1] where the supply is solely for use by the charity in such care, treatment or research.

Amendments—[1] Words in item 9 inserted by the Veterinary Medicines Regulations, SI 2006/2407, reg 44(3), Sch 9 para 10(*a*), (*b*) with effect from 1 October 2006.

10 The supply to a charity of a substance directly used for synthesis or testing in the course of medical or veterinary research.

NOTES

[(1) Item 1 or 1A does not apply unless the sale or letting—

(*a*) takes place as a result of the goods having been made available—

(i) to two or more specified persons, or

(ii) to the general public,

for purchase or hire (whether so made available in a shop or elsewhere), and

(*b*) does not take place as a result of any arrangements (whether legally binding or not) relating to the goods and entered into, before the goods were made so available, by—

(i) each of the parties to the sale or letting, or

(ii) the donor of the goods and either or both of those parties.

(1A) For the purposes of items 1, 1A and 2, goods are donated for letting only if they are donated for—

(*a*) letting, and

(*b*) re-letting after the end of any first or subsequent letting, and

(*c*) all or any of—

(i) sale,

(ii) export, or

(iii) disposal as waste,

if not, or when no longer, used for letting.

(1B) Items 1 and 1A do not include (and shall be treated as having not included) any sale, or letting on hire, of particular donated goods if the goods, at any time after they are donated but before they are sold, exported or disposed of as waste, are whilst unlet used for any purpose other than, or in addition to, that of being available for purchase, hire or export.

(1C) In Note (1) "specified person" means a person who—

(*a*) is handicapped, or

(*b*) is entitled to any one or more of the specified benefits, or

(*c*) is both handicapped and so entitled.

(1D) For the purposes of Note (1C) the specified benefits are—

(*a*) income support under Part VII of the Social Security Contributions and Benefits Act 1992 or Part VII of the Social Security Contributions and Benefits (Northern Ireland) Act 1992;

(*b*) housing benefit under Part VII of the Social Security Contributions and Benefits Act 1992 or Part VII of the Social Security Contributions and Benefits (Northern Ireland) Act 1992;

(*c*) council tax benefit under Part VII of the Social Security Contributions and Benefits Act 1992;

(*d*) an income-based jobseeker's allowance within the meaning of section 1(4) of the Jobseekers Act 1995 or article 3(4) of the Jobseekers (Northern Ireland) Order 1995;

[(*e*) any element of child tax credit other than the family element; . . . [8]][5]

[(*f*) working tax credit.][5] [and

(*g*) universal credit under Part 1 of the Welfare Reform Act 2012.][8]

(1E) For the purposes of items 1A and 2 a taxable person is a "profits-to-charity" person in respect of any goods if—

(*a*) he has agreed in writing (whether or not contained in a deed) to transfer to a charity his profits from supplies and lettings of the goods, or

(*b*) his profits from supplies and lettings of the goods are otherwise payable to a charity.

(1F) In items 1, 1A and 2, and any Notes relating to any of those items, "goods" means goods (and, in particular, does not include anything that is not goods even though provision made by or under an enactment provides for a supply of that thing to be, or be treated as, a supply of goods).][3]

(2) "Animals" includes any species of the animal kingdom.

(3) "Relevant goods" means—

(*a*) medical, scientific, computer, video, sterilising, laboratory or refrigeration equipment for use in medical or veterinary research, training, diagnosis or treatment;

(*b*) ambulances;

(*c*) parts or accessories for use in or with goods described in paragraph (*a*) or (*b*) above;
(*d*) goods of a kind described in item 2 of Group 12 of this Schedule;
(*e*) motor vehicles (other than vehicles with more than 50 seats) designed or substantially and permanently adapted for the safe carriage of a handicapped person in a wheelchair provided that—
(i) in the case of vehicles with more than 16 but fewer than 27 seats, the number of persons for which such provision shall exist shall be at least 2;
(ii) in the case of vehicles with more than 26 but fewer than 37 seats, the number of persons for which such provision shall exist shall be at least 3;
(iii) in the case of vehicles with more than 36 but fewer than 47 seats, the number of persons for which such provision shall exist shall be at least 4;
(iv) in the case of vehicles with more than 46 seats, the number of persons for which such provision shall exist shall be at least 5;
(v) there is either a fitted electrically or hydraulically operated lift or, in the case of vehicles with fewer than 17 seats, a fitted ramp to provide access for a passenger in a wheelchair;
(*f*) motor vehicles (with more than 6 but fewer than 51 seats) for use by an eligible body providing care for blind, deaf, mentally handicapped or terminally sick persons mainly to transport such persons;
(*g*) telecommunication, aural, visual, light enhancing or heat detecting equipment (not being equipment ordinarily supplied for private or recreational use) solely for use for the purpose of rescue or first aid services undertaken by a charitable institution providing such services.

(4) "Eligible body" means—
[(*a*) a Strategic Health Authority or Special Health Authority in England;][4]
[(*aa*) a Health Authority, Special Health Authority or Local Health Board in Wales;][4]
(*b*) a Health Board in Scotland;
(*c*) a Health and Social Services Board in Northern Ireland;
(*d*) a hospital whose activities are not carried on for profit;
(*e*) a research institution whose activities are not carried on for profit;
(*f*) a charitable institution providing care or medical or surgical treatment for handicapped persons;
(*g*) the Common Services Agency for the Scottish Health Service, the Northern Ireland Central Services Agency for Health and Social Services or the Isle of Man Health Services Board;
(*h*) a charitable institution providing rescue or first-aid services;
(*i*) a National Health Service trust established under Part I of the National Health Service and Community Care Act 1990 or the National Health Service (Scotland) Act 1978;
[(*j*) a Primary Care Trust established under section 16A of the National Health Service Act 1977][2].

[(4A) Subject to Note (5B), a charitable institution shall not be regarded as providing care or medical or surgical treatment for handicapped persons unless—
(*a*) it provides care or medical or surgical treatment in a relevant establishment; and
(*b*) the majority of the persons who receive care or medical or surgical treatment in that establishment are handicapped persons.][1]

[(4B) "Relevant establishment" means—
(*a*) a day-centre, other than a day-centre which exists primarily as a place for activities that are social or recreational or both; or
(*b*) an institution which is—
(i) approved, licensed or registered in accordance with the provisions of any enactment or Northern Ireland legislation; or
(ii) exempted by or under the provisions of any enactment or Northern Ireland legislation from any requirement to be approved, licensed or registered;

and in paragraph (b) above the references to the provisions of any enactment or Northern Ireland legislation are references only to provisions which, so far as relating to England, Wales, Scotland or Northern Ireland, have the same effect in every locality within that part of the United Kingdom.][1]

(5) "Handicapped" means chronically sick or disabled.

[(5A) Subject to Note (5B), items 4 to 7 do not apply where the eligible body falls within Note (4)(*f*) unless the relevant goods are or are to be used in a relevant establishment in which that body provides care or medical or surgical treatment to persons the majority of whom are handicapped.][1]

[(5B) Nothing in Note (4A) or (5A) shall prevent a supply from falling within items 4 to 7 where—
(*a*) the eligible body provides medical care to handicapped persons in their own homes;
(*b*) the relevant goods fall within Note (3)(*a*) or are parts or accessories for use in or with goods described in Note (3)(*a*); and

(*c*) those goods are or are to be used in or in connection with the provision of that care.][1]

(6) Item 4 does not apply where the donee of the goods is not a charity and has contributed in whole or in part to the funds for the purchase of the goods.

(7) Item 5 does not apply where the body to whom the goods are supplied is not a charity and has contributed in whole or in part to the funds for the purchase of the goods.

(8) Items 6 and 7 do not apply unless—

(*a*) the supply is paid for with funds which have been provided by a charity or from voluntary contributions, and

(*b*) in a case where the owner of the goods repaired or maintained is not a charity, it has not contributed in whole or in part to those funds.

(9) Items 4 and 5 include the letting on hire of relevant goods; accordingly in items 4, 5 and 6 and the notes relating thereto, references to the purchase or ownership of goods shall be deemed to include references respectively to their hiring and possession.

(10) Item 5 includes computer services by way of the provision of computer software solely for use in medical research, diagnosis or treatment.

[(10A) Neither of items 8 and 8A includes a supply where any of the members of the public (whether individuals or other persons) who are reached through the medium are selected by or on behalf of the charity.

For this purpose "selected" includes selected by address (whether postal address or telephone number, e-mail address or other address for electronic communications purposes) or at random.

(10B) None of items 8 to 8C includes a supply used to create, or contribute to, a website that is the charity's own.

For this purpose a website is a charity's own even though hosted by another person.

(10C) Neither of items 8B and 8C includes a supply to a charity that is used directly by the charity to design or produce an advertisement.][3]

(11) In item 9—

[(*a*) "medicinal product" has the meaning assigned to it by regulation 2(1) of the Human Medicines Regulations 2012;][7]

(*b*) . . . [7]

(*c*) . . . [7]

[(*d*) "veterinary medicinal product" has the meaning assigned to it by regulation 2 of the Veterinary Medicines Regulations 2006.][6]

(12) In items 9 and 10 "substance" and "ingredient" have the meanings assigned to them by section 132 of the Medicines Act 1968.

Commentary—*De Voil Indirect Tax Service* **V4.266**.

Concession ESC 3.22—Charities: sale of poor quality donated goods. Supplies of "relevant goods" to charities.

Press releases etc—C&E Business Brief 9/96 24-5-96 (zero-rating of job recruitment advertising by charities).

C&E Business Brief 18/96 27-8-96 ("eligible body" in relation to supplies of community transport vehicles for the disabled is defined).

C&E Business Brief 18/96 27-8-96 (zero-rating no longer applies to certain supplies of stationery to charities).

C&E Business Brief 21/96 17-10-96 (confirmation that share dealing by charities is outside the scope of VAT).

HMRC Brief 25/10 7-6-10 (PPC-sponsored links appearing on search engine websites qualify for zero-rating when supplied to a charity).

Simon's Tax Cases—Item 5, *C&E Comrs v David Lewis Centre* [1995] STC 485*; *C&E Comrs v Help The Aged* [1997] STC 406.

Item 5, note (3)(*c*), *Royal Midland Counties Home for Disabled People v C&E Comrs* [2002] STC 395.

Item 8(*c*), *C&E Comrs v Royal Society for the Encouragement of Arts Manufacture and Commerce* [1997] STC 437.

Note (3), *C&E Comrs v David Lewis Centre* [1995] STC 485*.

Notes (3)(*e*), (4)(*f*), *C&E Comrs v Help The Aged* [1997] STC 406.

Definitions—"Computer", s 96(1); "supply", s 5, Sch 4; "taxable person", s 3.

Note—Note that National Health Service trusts are to be abolished by the Health and Social Care Act 2012 s 179 with effect from a date to be appointed. Primary Care Trusts are expected to be abolished in April 2013 (by the Health and Social Care Act 2012 s 34).

Amendments—[1] Notes (4A), (4B), (5A) and (5B) inserted by FA 1997 s 34 in relation to supplies made on or after 26 November 1996.

[2] Para (*j*) in Note (4) added by the VAT (Drugs, Medicines, Aids for the Handicapped and Charities Etc) Order, SI 2000/503 arts 2, 4 with effect from 1 April 2000.

[3] Notes (1)–(1F) substituted for original Note (1) and Notes (10A)–(10C) inserted by the VAT (Charities and Aids for the Handicapped) Order, SI 2000/805 arts 5–9 with effect from 1 April 2000.

[4] Note (4)(*a*), (*aa*) substituted for Note (4)(*a*) by the VAT (Drugs, Medicines, Aids for the Handicapped and Charities Etc) Order, SI 2002/2813 arts 2, 4 with effect from 5 December 2002.

[5] Note (1D)(*e*), (*f*) substituted by TCA 2002 s 47, Sch 3 paras 47, 49 with effect from 6 April 2003 (by virtue of SI 2003/962).

[6] Words in Note (11)(*a*), and Note (11)(*d*) inserted by the Veterinary Medicines Regulations, SI 2006/2407, reg 44(3), Sch 9 para 10(*a*), (*b*) with effect from 1 October 2006.

[7] In note (11), para (*a*) substituted and paras (*b*), (*c*) repealed, by the Human Medicines Regulations, SI 2012/1916 reg 348, Sch 34 para 42(*b*) with effect from 14 August 2012.

8 In Note (1D), word "and" at the end of para (*e*) repealed, and para (*g*) and preceding word "and" inserted, by the Universal Credit (Consequential, Supplementary, Incidental and Miscellaneous Provisions) Regulations, SI 2013/630 reg 9 with effect from 29 April 2013.

Prospective amendments—In Note (4)(i), words "section 18 of the National Health Service (Wales) Act 2006" to be substituted for words "Part I of the National Health Service and Community Care Act 1990" by the Health and Social Care Act 2012 s 179, Sch 14 paras 65, 67(*b*) with effect from a date to be appointed.

GROUP 16 — CLOTHING AND FOOTWEAR

Item No

1 Articles designed as clothing or footwear for young children and not suitable for older persons.

2 The supply to a person for use otherwise than by employees of his of protective boots and helmets for industrial use.

3 Protective helmets for wear by a person driving or riding a motor bicycle [or riding a pedal cycle][2].

NOTES

(1) "Clothing" includes hats and other headgear.

(2) Item 1 does not include articles of clothing made wholly or partly of fur skin, except—

(*a*) headgear;

(*b*) gloves;

(*c*) buttons, belts and buckles;

(*d*) any garment merely trimmed with fur skin unless the trimming has an area greater than one fifth of the area of the outside material or, in the case of a new garment, represents a cost to the manufacturer greater than the cost to him of the other components.

(3) "Fur skin" means any skin with fur, hair or wool attached except—

(*a*) rabbit skin;

(*b*) woolled sheep or lamb skin; and

(*c*) the skin, if neither tanned nor dressed, of bovine cattle (including buffalo), equine animals, goats or kids (other than Yemen, Mongolian and Tibetan goats or kids), swine (including peccary), chamois, gazelles, deer or dogs.

(4) [Item 2 applies only where the goods to which it refers are—][1]

(*a*) goods which—

(i) are manufactured to standards approved by the British Standards Institution; and

(ii) bear a marking indicating compliance with the specification relating to such goods; or

(*b*) goods which—

(i) are manufactured to standards which satisfy requirements imposed (whether under the law of the United Kingdom or the law of any other member State) for giving effect to the directive of the Council of the European Communities dated 21st December 1989 No 89/686/EEC [or to that directive as amended by Council Directives 93/68/EEC of 22nd July 1993, 93/95/EEC of 29th October 1993 and 96/58/EC of 3rd September 1996][3]; and

(ii) bear any mark of conformity provided for by virtue of that directive[, or (as the case may be) that directive as so amended,][3] in relation to those goods.

[(4A) Item 3 does not apply to a protective helmet unless—

(*a*) it is of a type that on 30th June 2000 is prescribed by regulations made under section 17 of the Road Traffic Act 1988 (types of helmet recommended as affording protection to persons on or in motor cycles from injury in the event of accident); or

(*b*) it is of a type that—

(i) is manufactured to a standard which satisfies requirements imposed (whether under the law of the United Kingdom or the law of any other member State) for giving effect to Council Directive 89/686/EEC of 21st December 1989 as amended by Council Directives 93/68/EEC of 22nd July 1993, 93/95/EEC of 29th October 1993 and 96/58/EC of 3rd September 1996; and

(ii) bears any mark of conformity required by virtue of those directives.][3]

(5) Items 1, 2 and 3 include the supply of the services described in paragraphs 1(1) and [5(4)][1] of Schedule 4 in respect of goods comprised in the items, but, in the case of goods comprised in item 2, only if the goods are for use otherwise than by employees of the person to whom the services are supplied.

Commentary—*De Voil Indirect Tax Service* **V4.287**.

Press releases etc—C&E Business Brief 8/96 17-5-96 (maximum size for zero-rating boys' footwear is UK size 6½, equivalent to continental size 40).

Simon's Tax Cases—*EC Commission v United Kingdom* [1988] STC 456*.

Item 1, *C&E Comrs v Ali Baba Tex Ltd* [1992] STC 590*; *H&M Hennes Ltd v C&E Comrs* [2005] STC 1749.

Definitions—"Law of any member State", s 92; "other member States", s 96(1); "supply", s 5, Sch 4; "United Kingdom", s 96(11).

Amendments—[1] Words in Note (4), (5) substituted by the VAT (Protective Helmets) Order, SI 2000/1517 arts 2–5 with effect in relation to supplies made after 29 June 2000.

[2] Words in Item 3 inserted by the Value Added Tax (Protective Helmets) Order, SI 2001/732 art 3 with effect for supplies made after 31 March 2001

[3] Words in Notes (4)(b)(i) and (4)(b)(ii) inserted; and Note (4A) substituted by SI 2001/732 arts 4–6 with effect for supplies made after 31 March 2001.

[GROUP 17—EMISSIONS ALLOWANCES

Amendments—Group 17 repealed by the Value Added Tax (Emissions Allowances) Order, SI 2010/2549 art 2(1), (32) with effect from 1 November 2010.

[GROUP 18—EUROPEAN RESEARCH INFRASTRUCTURE CONSORTIA

Item No

1 The supply of goods or services to an ERIC.

NOTES

(1) "ERIC" means a body set up as a European Research Infrastructure Consortium by a decision under Article 6(1)(*a*) of Council Regulation (EC) No 723/2009 on the Community legal framework for a European Research Infrastructure Consortium.

(2) Item 1 applies only where the following requirements are met—

(*a*) the statutory seat of the ERIC referred to in Article 8(1) of Council Regulation (EC) No 723/2009 is located in a member State;

(*b*) the goods or services are for the official use of the ERIC;

(*c*) a certificate in writing has been given to the supplier on behalf of the ERIC that—

(i) the requirements in paragraphs (*a*) and (*b*) are met in relation to the supply, and

(ii) the relief is not precluded by the limitations and conditions referred to in Note (3); and

(*d*) VAT would have been chargeable on the supply but for item 1.

(3) Item 1 is subject to the limitations and conditions laid down in the agreement between the members of the ERIC referred to in Article 5(1)(d) of Council Regulation (EC) No 723/2009.][1]

Amendments—[1] Group 18 inserted by the Value Added Tax (Relief for European Research Infrastructure Consortia) Order, SI 2012/2907 art 3(2) with effect in relation to importations, acquisitions or supplies made on or after 1 January 2013.

SCHEDULE 9
EXEMPTIONS

Sections 8 and 31

PART I
INDEX TO EXEMPT SUPPLIES OF GOODS AND SERVICES

Cross reference—See VATA 1994 s 97(3), (4) (procedure for making orders for varying this Schedule so as to abolish the exemption of a supply without zero rating it).

[Betting, gaming, dutiable machine games and lotteries][5]	Group 4
Burial and cremation	Group 8
[Cultural services etc	Group 13][1]
Education	Group 6
Finance	Group 5
Fund raising events by charities and other qualifying bodies	Group 12
Health and welfare	Group 7
Insurance	Group 2
[Investment gold	Group 15][2]
Land	Group 1
Postal services	Group 3
Sport, sports competitions and physical education	Group 10
[Subscriptions to trade unions, professional and other public interest bodies	Group 9][1]
[Supplies of goods where input tax cannot be recovered	Group 14][3]
[Supplies of services by groups involving cost sharing	Group 16][4]
Works of art etc	Group 11

Amendments—[1] Entry inserted and words substituted by the Value Added Tax (Subscriptions to Trade Unions, Professional and Other Public Interest Bodies) Order, SI 1999/2834, arts 2, 3, with effect from 1 December 1999.

[2] Entry inserted by the Value Added Tax (Investment Gold) Order, SI 1999/3116, art 2(1), (2), with effect from 1 January 2000.

[3] Entry inserted by the Value Added Tax (Supplies of Goods where Input Tax cannot be recovered) Order, SI 1999/2833, art 2(1), (2), with effect from 1 March 2000.

[4] Entry inserted by FA 2012 s 197(1) with effect from 17 July 2012.

[5] In entry for "Betting, gaming and lotteries", words substituted by FA 2012 s 191, Sch 24 para 64(1), (5)(*b*) with effect in relation to supplies made on or after 1 February 2013.

PART II
THE GROUPS
GROUP 1 — LAND

Item No

1 The grant of any interest in or right over land or of any licence to occupy land, or, in relation to land in Scotland, any personal right to call for or be granted any such interest or right, other than—

(*a*) the grant of the fee simple in—

(i) a building which has not been completed and which is neither designed as a dwelling or number of dwellings nor intended for use solely for a relevant residential purpose or a relevant charitable purpose;

(ii) a new building which is neither designed as a dwelling or number of dwellings nor intended for use solely for a relevant residential purpose or a relevant charitable purpose after the grant;

(iii) a civil engineering work which has not been completed;

(iv) a new civil engineering work;

(*b*) a supply made pursuant to a developmental tenancy, developmental lease or developmental licence;

(*c*) the grant of any interest, right or licence consisting of a right to take game or fish unless at the time of the grant the grantor grants to the grantee the fee simple of the land over which the right to take game or fish is exercisable;

(*d*) the provision in an hotel, inn, boarding house or similar establishment of sleeping accommodation or of accommodation in rooms which are provided in conjunction with sleeping accommodation or for the purpose of a supply of catering;

(*e*) the grant of any interest in, right over or licence to occupy holiday accommodation;

(*f*) the provision of seasonal pitches for caravans, and the grant of facilities at caravan parks to persons for whom such pitches are provided;

(*g*) the provision of pitches for tents or of camping facilities;

(*h*) the grant of facilities for parking a vehicle;

(*j*) the grant of any right to fell and remove standing timber;

(*k*) the grant of facilities for housing, or storage of, an aircraft or for mooring, or storage of, a ship, boat or other vessel;

[(*ka*) the grant of facilities for the self storage of goods;][3]

(*l*) the grant of any right to occupy a box, seat or other accommodation at a sports ground, theatre, concert hall or other place of entertainment;

(*m*) the grant of facilities for playing any sport or participating in any physical recreation; . . . [3]

[(*ma*) the grant of facilities to a person who uses the facilities wholly or mainly to supply hairdressing services; and][3]

(*n*) the grant of any right, including—

(i) an equitable right,

(ii) a right under an option or right of pre-emption, or

(iii) in relation to land in Scotland, a personal right,

to call for or be granted an interest or right which would fall within any of paragraphs (*a*) or (*c*) to [(*ma*)][3] above.

NOTES

[(1) "Grant" includes an assignment or surrender and the supply made by the person to whom an interest is surrendered when there is a reverse surrender.][1]

[(1A) A "reverse surrender" is one in which the person to whom the interest is surrendered is paid by the person by whom the interest is being surrendered to accept the surrender.][1]

(2) A building shall be taken to be completed when an architect issues a certificate of practical completion in relation to it or it is first fully occupied, whichever happens first; and a civil engineering work shall be taken to be completed when an engineer issues a certificate of completion in relation to it or it is first fully used, whichever happens first.

(3) [Notes (2) to (10) and (12)][1] to Group 5 of Schedule 8 apply in relation to this Group as they apply in relation to that Group.

(4) A building or civil engineering work is new if it was completed less than three years before the grant.

(5) Subject to Note (6), the grant of the fee simple in a building or work completed before 1st April 1989 is not excluded from this Group by paragraph (*a*) (ii) or (iv).

(6) Note (5) does not apply where the grant is the first grant of the fee simple made on or after 1st April 1989 and the building was not fully occupied, or the work not fully used, before that date.

(7) A tenancy of, lease of or licence to occupy a building or work is treated as becoming a developmental tenancy, developmental lease or developmental licence (as the case may be) when a tenancy of, lease of or licence to occupy a building or work, whose construction, reconstruction, enlargement or extension commenced on or after 1st January 1992, is treated as being supplied to and by the developer under paragraph 6(1) of Schedule 10 [(except where that paragraph applies by virtue of paragraph 5(1)(*b*) of that Schedule)][1].

(8) Where a grant of an interest in, right over or licence to occupy land includes a valuable right to take game or fish, an apportionment shall be made to determine the supply falling outside this Group by virtue of paragraph (*c*).

(9) "Similar establishment" includes premises in which there is provided furnished sleeping accommodation, whether with or without the provision of board or facilities for the preparation of food, which are used by or held out as being suitable for use by visitors or travellers.

(10) "Houseboat" includes a houseboat within the meaning of Group 9 of Schedule 8.

(11) Paragraph (*e*) includes—

(*a*) any grant excluded from item 1 of Group 5 of Schedule 8 by [Note (13)][1] in that Group;

(*b*) any supply made pursuant to a tenancy, lease or licence under which the grantee is or has been permitted to erect and occupy holiday accommodation.

(12) Paragraph (*e*) does not include a grant in respect of a building or part which is not a new building of—

(*a*) the fee simple, or

(*b*) a tenancy, lease or licence to the extent that the grant is made for a consideration in the form of a premium.

(13) "Holiday accommodation" includes any accommodation in a building, hut (including a beach hut or chalet), caravan, houseboat or tent which is advertised or held out as holiday accommodation or as suitable for holiday or leisure use, but excludes any accommodation within paragraph (*d*).

[(14) A seasonal pitch for a caravan is—

(a) a pitch on a holiday site other than an employee pitch, or

(b) a non-residential pitch on any other site.

(14A) In this Note and in Note (14)—

"employee pitch" means a pitch occupied by an employee of the site operator as that person's principal place of residence during the period of occupancy;

"holiday site" means a site or part of a site which is operated as a holiday or leisure site;

"non-residential pitch" means a pitch which—

(a) is provided for less than a year, or

(b) is provided for a year or more and is subject to an occupation restriction,

and which is not intended to be used as the occupant's principal place of residence during the period of occupancy;

"occupation restriction" means any covenant, statutory planning consent or similar permission, the terms of which prevent the person to whom the pitch is provided from occupying it by living in a caravan at all times throughout the period for which the pitch is provided.][2]

(15) "Mooring" includes anchoring or berthing.

[(15A) In paragraph (*ka*)—

"facilities for the self storage of goods" means the use of a relevant structure for the storage of goods by the person (or persons) to whom the grant of facilities is made, and "goods" does not include live animals.

(15B) For the purposes of Note (15A), use by a person with the permission of the person (or any of the persons) to whom the grant of facilities is made counts as use by the person (or persons) to whom that grant is made.

(15C) A grant of facilities for the self storage of goods does not fall within paragraph (*ka*) if—

(*a*) the person making the grant ("P")—

(i) is doing so in circumstances where the relevant structure used is, or forms part of, a relevant capital item, and

(ii) is connected with any person who uses that relevant structure for the self storage of goods, (*b*) the grant is made to a charity which uses the relevant structure solely otherwise than in the course of a business, or

(*c*) in a case where the relevant structure is part of a building, its use for the storage of goods by the person (or persons) to whom the grant is made is ancillary to other use of the building by that person (or those persons).

(15D) In Notes (15A) and (15C) "relevant structure" means the whole or part of—

(*a*) a container or other structure that is fully enclosed, or

(*b*) a unit or building.

(15E) In Note (15C)(*a*)(i) "relevant capital item" means a capital item which—

(*a*) is subject to adjustments of input tax deduction by P under regulations made under section 26(3), and

(*b*) has not yet reached the end of its prescribed period of adjustment.][3]

(16) Paragraph (*m*) shall not apply where the grant of the facilities is for—

(*a*) a continuous period of use exceeding 24 hours; or

(*b*) a series of 10 or more periods, whether or not exceeding 24 hours in total, where the following conditions are satisfied—

(i) each period is in respect of the same activity carried on at the same place;

(ii) the interval between each period is not less than one day and not more than 14 days;

(iii) consideration is payable by reference to the whole series and is evidenced by written agreement;

(iv) the grantee has exclusive use of the facilities; and

(v) the grantee is a school, a club, an association or an organisation representing affiliated clubs or constituent associations.

[(17) Paragraph (*ma*) does not apply to a grant of facilities which provides for the exclusive use, by the person to whom the grant is made, of a whole building, a whole floor, a separate room or a clearly defined area, unless the person making the grant or a person connected with that person provides or makes available (directly or indirectly) services related to hairdressing for use by the person to whom the grant is made.

(18) For the purposes of Note (17)—

(*a*) "services related to hairdressing" means the services of a hairdresser's assistant or cashier, the booking of appointments, the laundering of towels, the cleaning of the facilities subject to the grant, the making of refreshments and other similar services typically used in connection with hairdressing, but does not include the provision of utilities or the cleaning of shared areas in a building, and

(*b*) it does not matter if the services related to hairdressing are shared with other persons.

(19) For the purposes of Notes (15C) and (17) any question whether a person is connected with any other person is to be determined in accordance with section 1122 of the Corporation Tax Act 2010 (connected person).][3]

Commentary—*De Voil Indirect Tax Service* **V3.140A**.

Press releases etc—C&E Business Brief 17/94 12-9-94 (supply of milk quota with land follows VAT liability of the land).

C&E Business Brief 4/03 27-5-03 (VAT on property – clarification of recent judgments).

Simon's Tax Cases—*C & E Comrs v Mirror Group plc* (Case C-409/98) [2001] STC 1453), ECJ.

C&E Comrs v Sinclair Collis Ltd [2001] STC 989.

Item 1, *Billingham v Myers* [1994] STC 101*; *Nell Gwynn House Maintenance Fund Trustees v C&E Comrs* [1999] STC 79*; *C&E Comrs v Latchmere Properties Ltd* [2005] STC 731; *Byrom and others (t/a Salon 24) v R&C Comrs* [2006] STC 992; *R&C Comrs v Denyer* [2008] STC 633; *Holland (t/a The Studio Hair Company) v R&C Comrs* [2009] STC 150; *Grimsby College Enterprises Ltd v R&C Comrs* [2010] STC 2009; *Finnamore (trading as Hanbidge Storage Services) v R&C Comrs* [2014] UKUT 336 (TCC), [2014] STC 2754.

Item 1(*b*), *Cooper and Chapman (Builders) Ltd v C&E Comrs* [1993] STC 1*.

Item 1(*e*), *C&E Comrs v Parkinson* [1989] STC 51*.

Item 1(*f*), *Colaingrove Ltd v C&E Comrs* [2003] STC 680; [2004] STC 712; *R&C Comrs v Tallington Lakes Ltd* [2008] STC 2734.

Item 1(*h*), *C&E Comrs v Trinity Factoring Services Ltd* [1994] STC 504*.

Note (1), *Cooper and Chapman (Builders) Ltd v C&E Comrs* [1993] STC 1*; *Lubbock Fine & Co v C&E Comrs* (Case C-63/92) [1994] STC 101*.

Definitions—"Assignment", s 96(1); "building designed as a dwelling or number of dwellings", Sch 8 Group 5 note (2); "dwelling", Sch 8 Group 5 note (2); "fee simple", s 96(1); "ship", s 96(1); "supply", s 5, Sch 4; "use for a relevant charitable purpose", Sch 8 Group 5 note (6); "use for a relevant residential purpose", Sch 8 Group 5 note (4).

Cross references—See VATA 1994 s 62(1) (penalty for incorrect certificate that a supply is eligible for exemption within this Group);

VATA 1994 Sch 6 para 9 (valuation of certain supplies of accommodation within item 1 para (*d*) of this Group);

VAT Regulations, SI 1995/2518 reg 101(3) (exclusion of grants within item 1 or 1(*a*) of this Group in determining proportion of input tax attributable to taxable supplies under reg 101(2)(*d*)).

Amendments—[1] Note (1) and words in Notes (3), (11) substituted, Note (1A) inserted, and words in Note (7) added, by the Value Added Tax (Land) Order, SI 1995/282 with effect from 1 March 1995.

[2] Notes (14), (14A) substituted for previous Note (14) by the Value Added Tax (Land Exemption) Order, SI 2012/58 arts 2, 3 with effect from 1 March 2012.

[3] Item 1(*ka*), (*ma*) and Notes (15A)–(15E), (17)–(19) inserted; in Item 1, word "and" at the end of para (*m*) repealed, and in para (*n*), reference substituted for previous reference "(*m*)", by FA 2012 s 196, Sch 26 para 5 with effect from 1 October 2012.

Prospective amendments—Item 1(*b*), and Note (7), to be repealed by the Value Added Tax (Buildings and Land) Order, SI 2008/1146 art 4 with effect in relation to supplies made on or after 1 June 2020. The fact that former VATA 1994 Sch 10 paras 5–7 are not rewritten by SI 2008/1146 art 2 is not to affect the continued operation of Sch 9 Group 1 item 1(*b*), as read with Note (7), in relation to supplies made before 1 June 2020.

[GROUP 2—INSURANCE

Item No.

[1 Insurance transactions and reinsurance transactions.][1]

Amendments—[1] Item 1 substituted for Items 1–3 by the VAT (Insurance) Order, SI 2004/3083 with effect from 1 January 2005.

4 The provision by an insurance broker or insurance agent of any of the services of an insurance intermediary in a case in which those services—

(*a*) are related (whether or not [a contract of insurance][2] [or reinsurance][3] is finally concluded) to [an insurance transaction or a reinsurance transaction][3]; and

(*b*) are provided by that broker or agent in the course of his acting in an intermediary capacity.

NOTES

(A1)–(C1) . . . [3]

(1) For the purposes of item 4 services are services of an insurance intermediary if they fall within any of the following paragraphs—

(*a*) the bringing together, with a view to the insurance or reinsurance of risks, of—

(i) persons who are or may be seeking insurance or reinsurance, and

(ii) persons who provide insurance or reinsurance;

(*b*) the carrying out of work preparatory to the conclusion of contracts of insurance or reinsurance;

(*c*) the provision of assistance in the administration and performance of such contracts, including the handling of claims;

(*d*) the collection of premiums.

(2) For the purposes of item 4 an insurance broker or insurance agent is acting 'in an intermediary capacity' wherever he is acting as an intermediary, or one of the intermediaries, between—

(*a*) a person who provides [insurance or reinsurance][3], and

(*b*) a person who is or may be seeking insurance or reinsurance or is an insured person.

(3) Where—

(*a*) a person ('the supplier') makes a supply of goods or services to another ('the customer'),

(*b*) the supply of the goods or services is a taxable supply and is not a zero-rated supply,

(*c*) a transaction under which insurance is to be or may be arranged for the customer is entered into in connection with the supply of the goods or services,

(*d*) a supply of services which are related (whether or not a contract of insurance is finally concluded) to the provision of insurance in pursuance of that transaction is made by—

(i) the person by whom the supply of the goods or services is made, or

(ii) a person who is connected with that person and, in connection with the provision of that insurance, deals directly with the customer,

and

(*e*) the related services do not consist in the handling of claims under the contract for that insurance,

those related services do not fall within item 4 unless the relevant requirements are fulfilled.

(4) For the purposes of Note (3) the relevant requirements are—

(*a*) that a document containing the statements specified in Note (5) is prepared;

(*b*) that the matters that must be stated in the document have been disclosed to the customer at or before the time when the transaction mentioned in Note (3)(*c*) is entered into; and

(*c*) that there is compliance with all such requirements (if any) as to—

(i) the preparation and form of the document,

(ii) the manner of disclosing to the customer the matters that must be stated in the document, and

(iii) the delivery of a copy of the document to the customer,

as may be set out in a notice that has been published by the Commissioners and has not been withdrawn.

(5) The statements referred to in Note (4) are—

(*a*) a statement setting out the amount of the premium under any contract of insurance that is to be or may be entered into in pursuance of the transaction in question; and (*b*) a statement setting out every amount that the customer is, is to be or has been required to pay, otherwise than by way of such a premium, in connection with that transaction or anything that is to be, may be or has been done in pursuance of that transaction.

(6) For the purposes of Note (3) any question whether a person is connected with another shall be determined in accordance with [section 1122 of the Corporation Tax Act 2010][4].

(7) Item 4 does not include—

(*a*) the supply of any market research, product design, advertising, promotional or similar services; or

(*b*) the collection, collation and provision of information for use in connection with market research, product design, advertising, promotional or similar activities.

(8) Item 4 does not include the supply of any valuation or inspection services.

(9) Item 4 does not include the supply of any services by loss adjusters, average adjusters, motor assessors, surveyors or other experts except where—

(*a*) the services consist in the handling of a claim under a contract of insurance or reinsurance;

(*b*) the person handling the claim is authorised when doing so to act on behalf of the insurer or reinsurer; and

(*c*) that person's authority so to act includes written authority to determine whether to accept or reject the claim and, where accepting it in whole or in part, to settle the amount to be paid on the claim.

(10) Item 4 does not include the supply of any services which—

(*a*) are supplied in pursuance of a contract of insurance or reinsurance or of any arrangements made in connection with such a contract; and

(*b*) are so supplied either—

(i) instead of the payment of the whole or any part of any indemnity for which the contract provides, or

(ii) for the purpose, in any other manner, of satisfying any claim under that contract, whether in whole or in part.][1]

Commentary—*De Voil Indirect Tax Service* **V4.122, V4.123**.

Press releases etc—C&E Business Brief 6/95 28-3-95 (VAT on costs of settling insurance claims should be attributed to the supply which gives rise to the item).

Simon's Tax Cases—Item 1, *Card Protection Plan Ltd v C&E Comrs* [1999] STC 270*; *Ford Motor Co Ltd v R&C Comrs* [2007] STC 1783.

Item 3, *Card Protection Plan Ltd v C&E Comrs* [1999] STC 270*; *Peugeot Motor Company plc and another v C&E Comrs* [2003] STC 1438.

Item 4, *Century Life plc v C&E Comrs* [2001] STC 38, CA; *WHA Ltd and another v C&E Comrs* [2004] STC 1081; *Ford Motor Co Ltd v R&C Comrs* [2007] STC 1783; *InsuranceWide.com Services Ltd v R&C Comrs* [2010] STC 1572; *Westinsure Group Ltd v R&C Comrs* [2014] UKUT 452 (TCC), [2015] STC 238.

Note 5(*b*), *C R Smith Glaziers (Dunfermline) Ltd v C&E Comrs* [2001] STC 770, [2203] STC 419.

Definitions—"Belongs", s 9(2)(3); "supply", s 5, Sch 4; "United Kingdom", s 96(11).

Cross reference—See VAT Regulations, SI 1995/2518 reg 105(1) (treatment of certain exempt input tax attributable to a supply within item 3 of this Group as attributable to taxable supplies).

Amendments—[1] This Group substituted by FA 1997 s 38 with effect in relation to supplies made on or after 19 March 1997.

[2] Item 2 substituted, words in Item 4 substituted by the Financial Services and Markets Act 2000 (Consequential Amendments and Repeals) Order, SI 2001/3649 art 347 with effect from 1 December 2001.

[3] Item 1 substituted for Items 1–3, words in Item 4(*a*) substituted and inserted, Notes (A1)–(C1) repealed, and words in Note (2)(*a*) substituted, by the VAT (Insurance) Order, SI 2004/3083 with effect from 1 January 2005.

[4] In Note (6) words substituted for words "section 839 of the Taxes Act 1988" by CTA 2010 s 1177, Sch 1 para 285(e)(*i*). CTA 2010 has effect for corporation tax purposes for accounting periods ending on or after 1 April 2010, and for income and capital gains tax purposes for the tax year 2010–11 and subsequent tax years.

[GROUP 3—POSTAL SERVICES

Item No

1 The supply of public postal services by a universal service provider.

2 The supply of goods by a universal service provider which is incidental to the supply of public postal services by that provider.

NOTES:

(1) . . . [2]

(2) Subject to the following Notes, "public postal services", in relation to a universal service provider, means any postal services which the provider is required to provide in the discharge of [a specified condition][2].

(3) Public postal services include postal services which a universal service provider provides to allow a person access to the provider's [postal network (within the meaning of section 38 of the Postal Services Act 2011) and which are required to be provided by a specified condition][2].

(4) Services are not "public postal services" if—

(*a*) the price is not controlled by or under [a specified condition][2], or (*b*) any of the other terms on which the services are provided are freely negotiated.

(5) But Note (4) does not apply if [a specified condition][2] requires the universal service provider to make the services available to persons generally—

(*a*) where the price is not controlled by or under [the condition][2], at the same price, or

(*b*) where terms are freely negotiated as mentioned in Note (4)(*b*), on those terms.

[(6) In this Group "specified condition" means a designated USP condition, a USP access condition or a transitory condition under paragraph 5 of Schedule 9 to the Postal Services Act 2011 which is imposed only on a universal service provider.][1]

(7) Any expression which is used in this Group and in Part 3 of the Postal Services Act 2011 has the same meaning in this Group as in that Part.][2]

Commentary—*De Voil Indirect Tax Service* **V4.126**.

Press releases—HMRC Brief 64/09: VAT treatment of postal services: ECJ decision in *TNT Post UK Ltd*.

HMRC Brief 19/10: Postal services—claims for Input Tax.

Amendments—[1] Group 3 substituted by F(No 3)A 2010 s 22(2) with effect in relation to supplies made on or after 31 January 2011.

[2] Note (1) repealed, in Notes (2)–(5) words substituted, and Notes (6), (7) substituted for previous Note (6) by the Postal Services Act 2011 (Consequential Modifications and Amendments) Order, SI 2011/2085 art 5(1), Sch 1 para 28(1), (3), art 5(2) Sch 2 with effect from 1 October 2011.

GROUP 4 — BETTING, GAMING[, DUTIABLE MACHINE GAMES] AND LOTTERIES

Amendments—In heading to Group 4, words inserted by FA 2012 s 191, Sch 24 para 64(1), (5) with effect in relation to supplies made on or after 1 February 2013.

Item No

1 The provision of any facilities for the placing of bets [or for the playing of any games of chance for a prize][1].

Amendments—[1] Words in item 1 substituted by the Value Added Tax (Betting, Gaming and Lotteries) Order, SI 2006/2685 art 2, with effect from 1 November 2006.

[**1A** The provision of any facilities for the playing of dutiable machine games (as defined in Part 1 of Schedule 24 to the Finance Act 2012) but only to the extent that—

(a) the facilities are used to play such games, and

(b) the takings and payouts in respect of those games are taken into account in determining the charge to machine games duty.][1]

Amendments—[1] Item 1A inserted by FA 2012 s 191, Sch 24 para 64(1), (2) with effect in relation to supplies made on or after 1 February 2013.

2 The granting of a right to take part in a lottery.

NOTES

(1) [Items 1 and 1A do][3] not include—

(*a*) admission to any premises; or

(*b*) . . . [2]

(*c*) the provision by a club of such facilities to its members as are available to them on payment of their subscription but without further charge; . . . [3]

(*d*) . . . [3]

[(1A) Item 1 does not apply to the provision of facilities to the extent that the facilities are used to play a relevant machine game (as defined in section 23A).][3]

[(2) "Game of chance"—

(*a*) includes—

(i) a game that involves both an element of chance and an element of skill,

(ii) a game that involves an element of chance that can be eliminated by superlative skill, and

(iii) a game that is presented as involving an element of chance, but

(*b*) does not include a sport.

(3) A person plays a game of chance if he participates in a game of chance—

(*a*) whether or not there are other participants in the game, and

(*b*) whether or not a computer generates images or data taken to represent the actions of other participants in the game.

(4) "Prize" does not include the opportunity to play the game again.][1]

(5)–(11) . . . [2]

Commentary—*De Voil Indirect Tax Service* **V4.131**.

Press releases etc—Business Brief 16/06, 13-10-06 (new definitions of "gambling" and "game of chance").

Simon's Tax Cases—Item 1, *C&E Comrs v Annabel's Casino Ltd* [1995] STC 225*; *United Utilities plc v C&E Comrs*, [2003] STC 223.

Simon's Tax Cases—Item 1, Note (3), *R&C Comrs v Rank Group plc* [2013] EWCA Civ 1289, [2014] STC 470.

Note (1)(*d*), *R v Ryan* [1994] STC 446*; *C&E Comrs v Feehan* [1995] STC 75*.

Amendments—[1] Notes (2)–(4) substituted for Notes (2)–(8) as previously enacted, by the Value Added Tax (Betting, Gaming and Lotteries) Order, SI 2006/2685 art 2, with effect from 1 November 2006.

[2] Note (1)(*b*) and Notes (5)–(11) repealed by FA 2009 s 113 with effect from 27 April 2009.

[3] In Note (1), words substituted for words "Item 1 does", and para (d) and preceding word "or" repealed, and Note (1A) inserted, by FA 2012 s 191, Sch 24 para 64(1), (3), (4) with effect in relation to supplies made on or after 1 February 2013.

GROUP 5 — FINANCE

Item No

1 The issue, transfer or receipt of, or any dealing with, money, any security for money or any note or order for the payment of money.

2 The making of any advance or the granting of any credit.

[2A The management of credit by the person granting it.][1]

Amendments—[1] Item 2A by the VAT (Finance) (No 2) Order, SI 2003/1569 with effect for any services performed after 31 July 2003.

3 The provision of the facility of instalment credit finance in a hire-purchase, conditional sale or credit sale agreement for which facility a separate charge is made and disclosed to the recipient of the supply of goods.

4 The provision of administrative arrangements and documentation and the transfer of title to the goods in connection with the supply described in item 3 if the total consideration therefor is specified in the agreement and does not exceed £10.

5 [The provision of intermediary services in relation to any transaction comprised in item 1, 2, 3, 4 or 6 (whether or not any such transaction is finally concluded) by a person acting in an intermediary capacity.][1]

Amendments—[1] Item 5 substituted and Item 5A inserted by the VAT (Finance) Order, SI 1999/594 art 3, with effect from 10 March 1999.

[5A—The underwriting of an issue within item 1 or any transaction within item 6.][1]

Amendments—[1] Item 5 substituted and Item 5A inserted by the VAT (Finance) Order, SI 1999/594 art 3, with effect from 10 March 1999.

6 The issue, transfer or receipt of, or any dealing with, any security or secondary security being—

(*a*) shares, stocks, bonds, notes (other than promissory notes), debentures, debenture stock or shares in an oil royalty; or

(*b*) any document relating to money, in any currency, which has been deposited with the issuer or some other person, being a document which recognises an obligation to pay a stated amount to bearer or to order, with or without interest, and being a document by the delivery of which, with or without endorsement, the right to receive that stated amount, with or without interest, is transferable; or

(*c*) any bill, note or other obligation of the Treasury or of a Government in any part of the world, being a document by the delivery of which, with or without endorsement, title is transferable, and not being an obligation which is or has been legal tender in any part of the world; or

(*d*) any letter of allotment or rights, any warrant conferring an option to acquire a security included in this item, any renounceable or scrip certificates, rights coupons, coupons representing dividends or interest on such a security, bond mandates or other documents conferring or containing evidence of title to or rights in respect of such a security; or

(*e*) units or other documents conferring rights under any trust established for the purpose, or having the effect of providing, for persons having funds available for investment, facilities for the participation by them as beneficiaries under the trust, in any profits or income arising from the acquisition, holding, management or disposal of any property whatsoever.

7 [. . . .][1]

Amendments—[1] Item 7 repealed by the VAT (Finance) Order, SI 1999/594 arts 4, 5 and 6 respectively, with effect from 10 March 1999.

8 The operation of any current, deposit or savings account.

[9 The management of—

(*a*) an authorised open-ended investment company; or

[(*aa*) an authorised contractual scheme; or][2]

(*b*) an authorised unit trust scheme; or

(*c*) a Gibraltar collective investment scheme that is not an umbrella scheme; or

(*d*) a sub-fund of any other Gibraltar collective investment scheme; or

(*e*) an individually recognised overseas scheme that is not an umbrella scheme; or (*f*) a sub-fund of any other individually recognised overseas scheme; or

(*g*) *a recognised collective investment scheme authorised in a designated country or territory that is not an umbrella scheme; or*

(*h*) *a sub-fund of any other recognised collective investment scheme authorised in a designated country or territory; or*[3]

(*i*) a recognised collective investment scheme constituted in another EEA state that is not an umbrella scheme; or

(*j*) a sub-fund of any other recognised collective investment scheme constituted in another EEA state.][1]

Amendments—[1] Item 9 substituted by the Value Added Tax (Finance) (No 2) Order, SI 2008/2547 art 3 with effect from 1 October 2008.

Note that Item 9 was to be substituted, by the Value Added Tax (Finance) Order, SI 2008/1892 art 2(1), (2) with effect from 1 October 2008. However, this Order was revoked, following further consultation, by the Value Added Tax (Finance) (No 2) Order, SI 2008/2547 art 2 with effect from 30 September 2008 and was therefore revoked before it was due to take effect.

[2] Para (*aa*) inserted by the Value Added Tax (Finance) Order, SI 2013/1402 art 2(2) with effect from 28 June 2013.

[3] Paras (*g*), (*h*) repealed by the Alternative Investment Fund Managers Regulations, SI 2013/1773 reg 80, Sch 1 para 40 with effect from 22 July 2013.

[10 The management of a closed-ended collective investment undertaking.][8]

NOTES

(1) Item 1 does not include anything included in item 6.

[(1A) Item 1 does not include a supply of services which is preparatory to the carrying out of a transaction falling within that item.][5]

(2) This Group does not include the supply of a coin or a banknote as a collectors' piece or as an investment article.

(2A) . . .[7]

(2B) . . . [6]

(3) Item 2 includes the supply of credit by a person, in connection with a supply of goods or services by him, for which a separate charge is made and disclosed to the recipient of the supply of goods or services.

(4) This Group includes any supply by a person carrying on a credit card, charge card or similar payment card operation made in connection with that operation to a person who accepts the card used in the operation when presented to him in payment for goods or services.

[(5) For the purposes of item 5 "intermediary services" consist of bringing together, with a view to the provision of financial services—

(*a*) persons who are or may be seeking to receive financial services, and

(*b*) persons who provide financial services,

together with (in the case of financial services falling within item 1, 2, 3 or 4) the performance of work preparatory to the conclusion of contracts for the provision of those financial services, but do not include the supply of any market research, product design, advertising, promotional or similar services or the collection, collation and provision of information in connection with such activities.

(5A) For the purposes of item 5 a person is "acting in an intermediary capacity" wherever he is acting as an intermediary, or one of the intermediaries, between—

(*a*) a person who provides financial services, and

(*b*) a person who is or may be seeking to receive financial services . . . [7]

(5B) For the purposes of notes 5 and 5A "financial services" means the carrying out of any transaction falling within item 1, 2, 3, 4 or 6.][4]

[(6) For the purposes of this Group—

"authorised open-ended investment company"[, "authorised contractual scheme"][9] and "authorised unit trust scheme" have the meaning given in section 237(3) of the Financial Services and Markets Act 2000;

"closed-ended collective investment undertaking" means an undertaking in relation to which the following conditions are satisfied—

(*a*) its sole object is the investment of capital, raised from the public, wholly or mainly in securities; and

(*b*) it manages its assets on the principle of spreading investment risk; and

(*c*) all of its ordinary shares (of each class if there is more than one) or equivalent units are included in the official list maintained by the [Financial Conduct Authority][10] pursuant to section 74(1) of the Financial Services and Markets Act 2000; and

(*d*) all of its ordinary shares (of each class if there is more than one) or equivalent units are admitted to trading on a regulated market situated or operating in the United Kingdom;

"collective investment scheme" has the meaning given in section 235 of the Financial Services and Markets Act 2000;

"Gibraltar collective investment scheme" means—

(*a*) a collective investment scheme to which section 264 of the Financial Services and Markets Act 2000 applies pursuant to an order made under section 409(1)(*d*) of that Act; or

(*b*) a collective investment scheme to which the Financial Services and Markets Act 2000 applies pursuant to an order made under section 409(1)(*f*) of that Act;

"individually recognised overseas scheme" means a collective investment scheme declared by the [Financial Conduct Authority][10] Financial Services Authority to be a recognised scheme pursuant to section 272 of the Financial Services and Markets Act 2000;

"recognised collective investment scheme authorised in a designated country or territory" means a collective investment scheme recognised pursuant to section 270 of the Financial Services and Markets Act 2000;[11]

"recognised collective investment scheme constituted in another EEA state" means a collective investment scheme which is recognised pursuant to section 264 of the Financial Services and Markets Act 2000;

"regulated market" has the meaning given in section 103(1) of the Financial Services and Markets Act 2000;

"sub-fund" means a separate part of the property of an umbrella scheme that is pooled separately;

"umbrella scheme" means a collective investment scheme under which the contributions of the participants in the scheme and the profits or income out of which payments are to be made to them are pooled separately in relation to separate parts of the scheme property.][8]

[(6A) A collective investment scheme, or sub-fund, that is not for the time being marketed in the United Kingdom is to be treated as not falling within item 9(*c*) to (*j*) if—

(*a*) it has never been marketed in the United Kingdom, or

(*b*) less than 5% of its shares or units are held by, or on behalf of, investors who are in the United Kingdom.][8]

(7) . . .[7]

(8) For the purposes of item 10 . . .[7]*, an open-ended investment company's scheme property is the property subject to the collective investment scheme constituted by that company.*[8]

(9) . . .[7]

[(10) For the purposes of this Group—

"collective investment scheme" has the meaning given in section 235 of the Financial Services and Markets Act 2000; and

"open-ended investment company" has the meaning given in section 236 of that Act.][5]][1, 8]

Commentary—*De Voil Indirect Tax Service* **V4.136–V4.136F**.

HMRC Manuals—VAT Guidance V1-3: Supply and consideration, para 4.11 (agreements with finance companies at non-standard rates of interest).

Press releases etc—C&E Business Brief 10/03 25-7-03 (VAT – changes to finance exemptions)

C&E Business Brief 25/94 16-12-94 (restocking of cash point machines by supermarket does not fall within this group).

C&E Business Brief 25/95 20-11-95 (all issues of, or dealings in, securities falling within item 1 will be treated as a supply of services.)

C&E Business Brief 15/96 22-7-96 (VAT treatment of goods sold on interest-free credit).

C&E News Releases 12/97 13-3-97 (the investment management of open-ended investment companies by their authorised corporate directors is VAT exempt from 24 March 1997).

VAT Information Sheet 10/99 August 1999 (notes on changes introduced by SI 1999/594).

Simon's Tax Cases—Item 1, *Kingfisher plc v C&E Comrs* [2000] STC 992; *R&C Comrs v Axa UK plc* [2008] STC 2091.

Item 2, *C&E Comrs v BAA plc* [2002] STC 327; *HBOS plc v R&C Comrs* [2009] STC 486.

Item 5, *Primback Ltd v C&E Comrs* [1996] STC 757*; *C&E Comrs v Civil Service Motoring Association Ltd* [1998] STC 111*; *C&E Comrs v BAA plc; Institute of Directors v C&E Comrs* [2003] STC 35, CA; *Bookit Ltd v R&C Comrs* [2006] STC 1367; *HBOS plc v R&C Comrs* [2009] STC 486.

Items 6(*a*), 7, *Ivory & Sime Trustlink Ltd v C&E Comrs* [1998] STC 597.

Note (3), *Primback Ltd v C&E Comrs* [1996] STC 757*

Definitions—"Document", s 96(1); "money", s 96(1); "supply", s 5, Sch 4.

Cross references—See VAT Regulations, SI 1995/2518 reg 101(3) (exclusion of supplies within this Group in determining proportion of input tax attributable to taxable supplies under reg 101(2)(*d*));

VAT Regulations, SI 1995/2518 reg 103(2) (attribution of certain input tax used in making both supplies within item 1 or 6 of this Group and any other supply).

Amendments—[1] Notes (7)–(10) inserted by the VAT (Finance) Order, SI 1997/510 art 2 with effect from 24 March 1997.

[3] Notes (1A), (2A), (2B) inserted by the VAT (Finance) Order, SI 1999/594 arts 4, 5 and 6 respectively, with effect from 10 March 1999.

[4] Note (5) substituted and Notes (5A), (5B) inserted by the VAT (Finance) Order, SI 1999/594 art 7, with effect from 10 March 1999.

[5] Note (10) substituted by the Financial Services and Markets Act 2000 (Consequential Amendments and Repeals) Order, SI 2001/3649 art 348 with effect from 1 December 2001.

[6] Note (2B) (inserted by SI 1999/594) repealed by the VAT (Finance) Order, SI 2003/1568 with effect for any services performed after 31 July 2003.

[7] Notes (2A), (7) and (9), words in Note (5A), and words in Note (8) repealed, by the VAT (Finance) (No 2) Order, SI 2003/1569 with effect for any services performed after 31 July 2003.

8 Item 10 and Note (6) substituted, Note (6A) inserted, and Notes (8), (9) repealed, by the Value Added Tax (Finance) (No 2) Order, SI 2008/2547 art 3 with effect from 1 October 2008.
Note that the intention appears to have been to repeal Note (10) rather than Note (9) which was already repealed as per footnote 7 above.
Note that Item 10, and Note (6) were to be substituted, and Notes (8), (10) were to be repealed, by the Value Added Tax (Finance) Order, SI 2008/1892 art 2(1), (2) with effect from 1 October 2008. However, this Order was revoked, following further consultation, by the Value Added Tax (Finance) (No 2) Order, SI 2008/2547 art 2 with effect from 30 September 2008 and was therefore revoked before it was due to take effect.
9 In Note (6) words inserted by the Value Added Tax (Finance) Order, SI 2013/1402 art 2 with effect from 28 June 2013.
10 In Note (6), in definitions of "closed-ended collective investment undertaking" and "individually-recognised overseas scheme", words substituted by the Financial Services Act 2012, s 114(1), Sch 18 para 81 with effect from 1 April 2013 (the appointed day for the coming into force of Sch 18 by virtue of SI 2013/423 art 3).
11 In Note (6), definition of "recognised collective investment scheme authorised in a designated country or territory" repealed by the Alternative Fund Managers Regulations, SI 2013/1773 reg 80, Sch 1 para 40 with effect from 22 July 2013.

GROUP 6 — EDUCATION

Item No

1 The provision by an eligible body of—
(*a*) education;
(*b*) *research, where supplied to an eligible body*[2]; or
(*c*) vocational training.

2 The supply of private tuition, in a subject ordinarily taught in a school or university, by an individual teacher acting independently of an employer.

3 The provision of examination services—
(*a*) by or to an eligible body; or
(*b*) to a person receiving education or vocational training which is—
(i) exempt by virtue of items 1, 2[, 5 or 5A][1]; or
(ii) provided otherwise than in the course or furtherance of a business.

Simon's Tax Cases—Item 1, *London College of Computing Ltd v R&C Comrs* [2013] UKUT 404 (TCC), [2014] STC 404.
Item 1, note (1), *Finance and Business Training Ltd v R&C Comrs* [2013] UKUT 594 (TCC), [2014] STC 900.

Amendments—[1] Words in Item 3(*b*)(i) substituted by the Learning and Skills Act 2000 Sch 9 para 47 with effect from 1 April 2001 (by virtue of SI 2001/654).
2 In item 1, para (*b*) repealed by the Value Added Tax (Education) Order, SI 2013/1897 art 2 with effect from 1 August 2013. Note that this amendment does not apply in relation to a supply of services made pursuant to a written contract entered into before 1 August 2013 if the supply is within the scope of that contract as it stood immediately before that date (SI 2013/1897 art 1(2), (3)).

4 The supply of any goods or services (other than examination services) which are closely related to a supply of a description falling within item 1 (the principal supply) by or to the eligible body making the principal supply provided—
(*a*) the goods or services are for the direct use of the pupil, student or trainee (as the case may be) receiving the principal supply; and
(*b*) where the supply is to the eligible body making the principal supply, it is made by another eligible body.

Simon's Tax Cases—*R&C Comrs v Brockenhurst College* [2014] UKUT 46 (TCC), [2014] STC 1332.

5 The provision of vocational training, and the supply of any goods or services essential thereto by the person providing the vocational training, to the extent that the consideration payable is ultimately a charge to funds provided pursuant to arrangements made under section 2 of the Employment and Training Act 1973, section 1A of the Employment and Training Act (Northern Ireland) 1950 or section 2 of the Enterprise and New Towns (Scotland) Act 1990.

[5A The provision of education or vocational training and the supply, by the person providing that education or training, of any goods or services essential to that provision, to the extent that the consideration payable is ultimately a charge to funds provided by—
[(a) . . . [3]
(*b*) . . . [4]
(*c*)][2] the National Council for Education and Training for Wales under . . . [2] Part II of the Learning and Skills Act 2000.][1]

Amendments—[1] Item 5A and Note (5A) inserted by the Learning and Skills Act 2000 Sch 9 para 47 with effect from 1 April 2001 (by virtue of SI 2001/654).
2 In Item 5A, words substituted for words "the Learning and Skills Council for England or", and words "Part 1 or" repealed, by the Apprenticeships, Skills, Children and Learning Act 2009 (Consequential Amendments) (England and Wales) Order, SI 2010/1080 art 2(1), Sch 1 paras 26, 94, Sch 2 Pt 1, with effect from 1 April 2010.
3 In Item 5A, para (*a*) repealed and words in para (*b*) substituted by the Education Act 2011 s 67, Sch 16 para 9(1), (2) with effect from 1 April 2012 (by virtue of SI 2012/924, art 2).

[4] In Item 5A, para (*b*) repealed by the Deregulation Act 2015 s 64(3), Sch 14 paras 41(1), (2) with effect from 26 May 2015. Para (*b*) previously read as follows—

"(*b*) the Chief Executive of Skills Funding under Part 4 of the Apprenticeships, Skills, Children and Learning Act 2009; or".

[5B The provision of education or vocational training and the supply, by the person providing that education or training, of any goods or services essential to that provision, to persons who are—

(*a*) aged under 19,

(*b*) aged 19 or over, in respect of education or training begun by them when they were aged under 19,

[(*ba*) aged 19 or over and for whom an EHC plan is maintained,][2]

(*c*) aged 19 or over but under 25 and subject to learning difficulty assessment, or

(*d*) aged 25 or over, in respect of education or training begun by them when they were within paragraph [(*ba*) or][2] (*c*),

to the extent that the consideration payable is ultimately a charge to funds provided by the Secretary of State.][1]

Amendments—[1] Item 5B inserted by the Education Act 2011 s 67, Sch 16 para 9(1), (3) with effect from 1 April 2012 (by virtue of SI 2012/924, art 2).

[2] Para (*ba*), and words in para (*d*), inserted, by the Children and Families Act 2014 s 82, Sch 3 para 66 with effect from 1 September 2014 (by virtue of SI 2014/889 art 7(*a*))..

[5C The provision of education or vocational training and the supply, by the person providing that education or training, of any goods or services essential to that provision, to persons who are aged 19 or over, to the extent that the consideration payable is ultimately a charge to funds provided by the Secretary of State in exercise of functions under Part 4 of the Apprenticeships, Skills, Children and Learning Act 2009.][1]

Amendments—[1] Item 5C inserted by the Deregulation Act 2015 s 64(3), Sch 14 paras 41(1), (3) with effect from 26 May 2015.

6 The provision of facilities by—

(*a*) a youth club or an association of youth clubs to its members; or

(*b*) an association of youth clubs to members of a youth club which is a member of that association.

NOTES

(1) For the purposes of this Group an "eligible body" is—

(*a*) a school within the meaning of [The Education Act 1996][2], the Education (Scotland) Act 1980 the Education and Libraries (Northern Ireland) Order 1986 or the Education Reform (Northern Ireland) Order 1989, which is—

(i) provisionally or finally registered or deemed to be registered as a school within the meaning of the aforesaid legislation in a register of independent schools; or

(ii) a school in respect of which grants are made by the Secretary of State to the proprietor or managers; or

(iii) [[a community, foundation or voluntary school within the meaning of the School Standards and Framework Act 1998, a special school within the meaning of section 337 of the Education Act 1996][3] or a maintained school within the meaning of][2] the Education and Libraries (Northern Ireland) Order 1986; or

(iv) a public school within the meaning of section 135(1) of the Education (Scotland) Act 1980; or

(v) . . .[3]; or

(vi) . . .[5]

(vii) . . .[3]; or

(viii) a grant-maintained integrated school within the meaning of Article 65 of the Education Reform (Northern Ireland) Order 1989;

(*b*) a United Kingdom university, and any college, institution, school or hall of such a university;

(*c*) an institution—

(i) falling within section 91(3)(*a*)[, (*b*) or (*c*)][6] or section 91(5)(*b*) or (*c*) of the Further and Higher Education Act 1992; or

(ii) which is a designated institution as defined in section 44(2) of the Further and Higher Education (Scotland) Act 1992; or

(iii) managed by a board of management as defined in section 36(1) of the Further and Higher Education (Scotland) Act 1992; or

(iv) to which grants are paid by the Department of Education for Northern Ireland under Article 66(2) of the Education and Libraries (Northern Ireland) Order 1986;

(*d*) a public body of a description in Note (5) to Group 7 below;

[(*e*) a body which—

(i) is precluded from distributing and does not distribute any profit it makes; and

(ii) applies any profits made from supplies of a description within this Group to the continuance or improvement of such supplies;][1]

[(*f*) a body not falling within paragraphs (*a*) to (*e*) above which provides the teaching of English as a foreign language.][1]

(2) A supply by a body, which is an eligible body only by virtue of falling within Note [(1)(*f*)][1], shall not fall within this Group insofar as it consists of the provision of anything other than the teaching of English as a foreign language.

[(3) "Vocational training" means—

training, re-training or the provision of work experience for—

(*a*) any trade, profession or employment; or

(*b*) any voluntary work connected with—

(i) education, health, safety, or welfare; or

(ii) the carrying out of activities of a charitable nature.][1]

(4) "Examination services" include the setting and marking of examinations, the setting of educational or training standards, the making of assessments and other services provided with a view to ensuring educational and training standards are maintained.

(5) For the purposes of item 5 a supply of any goods or services shall not be taken to be essential to the provision of vocational training unless the goods or services in question are provided directly to the trainee.

[(5A) For the purposes of [items 5A [to 5C][9]][7] a supply of any goods or services shall not be taken to be essential to the provision of education or vocational training unless—

(*a*) in the case of the provision of education, the goods or services are provided directly to the person receiving the education;

(*b*) in the case of the provision of vocational training, the goods or services are provided directly to the person receiving the training.][4]

[(5B) In item 5B, ["EHC plan" and][8] "subject to learning difficulty assessment" [have the same meanings][8] as in the Education Act 1996.][7]

(6) For the purposes of item 6 a club is a "youth club" if—

(*a*) it is established to promote the social, physical, educational or spiritual development of its members;

(*b*) its members are mainly under 21 years of age; and

(*c*) it satisfies the requirements of Note (1)(*f*)(i) and (ii).

Note—The reference in Note (6)(*c*) to "Note 1(*f*)(i) and (ii)" appears to be an error. It appears that the reference should instead be to "Note 1(*e*)(i) and (ii)".

Commentary—*De Voil Indirect Tax Service* **V4.141**.

Press releases etc—VAT Information Sheet 5/94 (1-12-94 as amended 1-1-95) (school photographers).

C&E Business Brief 13/96 1-7-96 (supplies of training, re-training or work experience paid for using Further Education Funding Council funds is exempt under item 5 of this Group).

C&E Business Brief 18/99 18-8-99 (extent of exemption for providers of the teaching of English as a foreign language).

HMRC Brief 9/10, 12-3-10 (HMRC revised policy on supply of education by a university subsidiary trading company).

Simon's Tax Cases—*C&E Comrs v Zinn* [1988] STC 57*; *C&E Comrs v Bell Concord Educational Trust Ltd* [1988] STC 143*.

Item 1, *C&E Comrs v Bell Concord Educational Trust Ltd* [1999] STC 1027; *R&C Comrs v Board of Governors of the Robert Gordon University* [2008] STC 1890; *Birkdale School, Sheffield v R&C Comrs* [2008] STC 2002.

Item 1, note (1), *C&E Comrs v School of Finance and Management (London) Ltd* [2002] STC 1690.

Items 1, 4, notes (1)(*f*), (2), *Pilgrims Language Courses Ltd v C&E Comrs* [1999] STC 874

Item 2, *Marcus Webb Golf Professional v R&C Comrs* [2012] UKUT 378 (TCC), [2013] STC 574.

Item 2(*a*), *C&E Comrs v Bell Concord Educational Trust Ltd* [1989] STC 264*.

Item 4, notes (1)(*b*), (*e*), *C&E Comrs v University of Leicester Student's Union, CA* [2002] STC 147; *College of Estate Management v C&E Comrs* [2004] STC 235; [2004] STC 1471; *College of Estate Management v C&E Comrs* [2005] STC 1597.

Definitions—"Business ", s 94; "supply", s 5, Sch 4; "United Kingdom", s 96(11).

Amendments—[1] Notes (1)(*e*), (*f*), (3) and the figure in note (2) substituted by the Value Added Tax (Education) (No 2) Order, SI 1994/2969 with effect from 1 January 1995.

[2] Words in Note (1)(*a*) substituted by Education Act 1996 s 582(1), Sch 37 Part I para 125.

[3] Words in Note (1)(*a*)(iii) substituted and sub-paras (v) and (vii) omitted by School Standards and Framework Act 1998 Sch 30 para 51, with effect from 1 September 1999, by the School Standards and Framework Act 1998 (Commencement No 7 and Saving and Transitional Provisions) Order SI 1999/2323 para 2(1), Sch 1.

[4] Note (5A) inserted by the Learning and Skills Act 2000 Sch 9 para 47 with effect from 1 April 2001 (by virtue of SI 2001/654).

[5] Note (1)(*a*)(vi) repealed by the Standards in Scotland's Schools etc Act 2000 s 60(2), Sch 3 with effect from 31 December 2004 (by virtue of SSI 2004/528).

[6] In Note (1)(*c*)(i) words substituted for words "or (*b*)", by the Apprenticeships, Skills, Children and Learning Act 2009 (Consequential Amendments) (England and Wales) Order, SI 2010/1080 art 2(1), Sch 1 paras 26, 94, Sch 2 Pt 1, with effect from 1 April 2010.

[7] In Note (5A) words substituted and Note 5B inserted by the Education Act 2011 s 67, Sch 16 para 9(1), (4), (5) with effect from 1 April 2012 (by virtue of SI 2012/924, art 2).

8 In Note (5B), words inserted and substituted by the Children and Families Act 2014 s 82, Sch 3 para 66 with effect from 1 September 2014 (by virtue of SI 2014/889 art 7(*a*))..

9 In Note (5A) words substituted by the Deregulation Act 2015 s 64(3), Sch 14 paras 41(1), (4) with effect from 26 May 2015.

GROUP 7 — HEALTH AND WELFARE

Item No

1 The supply of services [consisting in the provision of medical care][5] by a person registered or enrolled in any of the following—

(*a*) the register of medical practitioners or the register of medical practitioners with limited registration;

(*b*) either of the registers of ophthalmic opticians or the register of dispensing opticians kept under the Opticians Act 1989 or either of the lists kept under section 9 of that Act of bodies corporate carrying on business as ophthalmic opticians or as dispensing opticians;

[(*c*) the register kept under [the Health and Social Work Professions Order 2001][7];][4]

[(*ca*) the register of osteopaths maintained in accordance with the provisions of the Osteopaths Act 1993;][2]

[(*cb*) the register of chiropractors maintained in accordance with the provisions of the Chiropractors Act 1994;][3]

[(*d*) the register of qualified nurses and midwives maintained under article 5 of the Nursing and Midwifery Order 2001][1]

(*e*) *the register of dispensers of hearing aids or the register of persons employing such dispensers maintained under section 2 of the Hearing Aid Council Act 1968.*[6]

Amendments—[1] Words in Item 1(*d*) substituted by the Nursing and Midwifery Order, SI 2002/253 art 54, Sch 5 para 12 with effect from 1 August 2004 (see the London Gazette, 21 July 2004).

2 Item 1(*ca*) inserted by Value Added Tax (Osteopaths) Order, SI 1998/1294 with effect from 12 June 1998.

3 Item 1 (*cb*) inserted by Value Added Tax (Chiropractors) Order, SI 1999/1575 with effect from 29 June 1999 (implements art 13A(1)(c) of the Sixth Council Directive, 77/388/EEC (OJ L145, 17.05.1977, p1)).

4 Item 1(*c*) substituted by the Health Professions Order, SI 2002/254 art 48, Sch 4 para 6 with effect from 9 July 2003 (see the London Gazette, 27 June 2003).

5 Words in item 1 inserted by the VAT (Health and Welfare) Order, SI 2007/206 arts 2–6 with effect from 1 May 2007.

6 Item 1(*e*) repealed by the Health and Social Care Act 2008 s 166, Sch 15 Pt 2 with effect from 1 April 2010 (by virtue of SI 2010/708 art 4(2)(*d*)(vi)).

7 Words in item 1(*c*) substituted for words "the Health Professions Order 2001" by the Health and Social Care Act 2012 s 213(7)(*g*) with effect from 1 August 2012 (SI 2012/1319, art 2(1), (4)).

2 [The supply of any services consisting in the provision of medical care, or the supply of dental prostheses, by][1] —

(*a*) a person registered in the dentists' register;

[(*b*) a person registered in the dental care professionals register established under section 36B of the Dentists Act 1984;][2] . . .[1]

Simon's Tax Cases—Item 2, *Moher (trading as Premier Dental Agency) v R&C Comrs* [2012] STC 1356.

Amendments—[1] Words in items 1, 3 inserted, words in item 2 substituted, item 2(c) and preceding word "or" repealed, and item 2A inserted, by the VAT (Health and Welfare) Order, SI 2007/206 arts 2–6 with effect from 1 May 2007.

2 Item 2(*b*) substituted by the Dentists Act 1984 (Amendment) Order, SI 2005/2011 art 49, Sch 6 para 3 with effect from 31 July 2006.

[2A The supply of any services or dental prostheses by a dental technician.][1]

Amendments—[1] Item 2A inserted by the VAT (Health and Welfare) Order, SI 2007/206 arts 2–6 with effect from 1 May 2007.

3 The supply of any services [consisting in the provision of medical care][1] by a person registered in the register of pharmaceutical chemists kept under the Pharmacy Act 1954 or the Pharmacy (Northern Ireland) Order 1976.

Amendments—[1] Words in item 3 inserted by the VAT (Health and Welfare) Order, SI 2007/206 arts 2–6 with effect from 1 May 2007.

4 The provision of care or medical or surgical treatment and, in connection with it, the supply of any goods, in any hospital [or state regulated institution][1].

Amendments—[1] Words in Item 4 substituted by the Value Added Tax (Health and Welfare) Order, SI 2002/762 with effect from 21 March 2002.

5 The provision of a deputy for a person registered in the register of medical practitioners or the register of medical practitioners with limited registration.

6 Human blood.

7 Products for therapeutic purposes, derived from human blood.

8 Human (including foetal) organs or tissue for diagnostic or therapeutic purposes or medical research.

[9 The supply by—
(*a*) a charity,
(*b*) a state-regulated private welfare institution [or agency][2], or
(*c*) a public body,
of welfare services and of goods supplied in connection with those welfare services.][1]

Amendments—[1] Item 9 and Note (6) substituted by the Value Added Tax (Health and Welfare) Order, SI 2002/762 with effect from 21 March 2002.
[2] Words in Item 9(*b*) inserted by the VAT (Health and Welfare) Order, SI 2003/24 with effect from 31 January 2003.

10 The supply, otherwise than for profit, of goods and services incidental to the provision of spiritual welfare by a religious community to a resident member of that community in return for a subscription or other consideration paid as a condition of membership.

11 The supply of transport services for sick or injured persons in vehicles specially designed for that purpose.

NOTES

(1) Item 1 does not include the letting on hire of goods except where the letting is in connection with a supply of other services comprised in the item.

(2) Paragraphs (*a*) to (*d*) of item 1 and paragraphs (*a*) and (*b*) of item 2 include supplies of services made by a person who is not registered or enrolled in any of the registers or rolls specified in those paragraphs where the services are wholly performed or directly supervised by a person who is so registered or enrolled.

[(2ZA) Paragraph (*c*) of item 1 does not include supplies of services made by a person in the capacity of a registered member of the social work profession in England (within the meaning of section 60 of the Health Act 1999).][4]

[(2A Item 3 includes supplies of services made by a person who is not registered in either of the registers specified in that item where the services are wholly performed by a person who is so registered.][1]

(3) Item 3 does not include the letting on hire of goods.

(4) . . .[3]

(5) In item 9 "public body" means—
(*a*) a Government department within the meaning of section 41(6);
(*b*) a local authority;
(*c*) a body which acts under any enactment or instrument for public purposes and not for its own profit and which performs functions similar to those of a Government department or local authority.

[(6) In item 9 "welfare services" means services which are directly connected with—
(*a*) the provision of care, treatment or instruction designed to promote the physical or mental welfare of elderly, sick, distressed or disabled persons,
(*b*) the care or protection of children and young persons, or
(*c*) the provision of spiritual welfare by a religious institution as part of a course of instruction or a retreat, not being a course or a retreat designed primarily to provide recreation or a holiday,
and, in the case of services supplied by a state-regulated private welfare institution, includes only those services in respect of which the institution is so regulated.][2]

(7) Item 9 does not include the supply of accommodation or catering except where it is ancillary to the provision of care, treatment or instruction.

[(8) In this Group "state-regulated" means approved, licensed, registered or exempted from registration by any Minister or other authority pursuant to a provision of a public general Act, other than a provision that is capable of being brought into effect at different times in relation to different local authority areas.

Here "Act" means—
(*a*) an Act of Parliament;
(*b*) an Act of the Scottish Parliament;
(*c*) an Act of the Northern Ireland Assembly;
(*d*) an Order in Council under Schedule 1 to the Northern Ireland Act 1974;
(*e*) a Measure of the Northern Ireland Assembly established under section 1 of the Northern Ireland Assembly Act 1973;
(*f*) an Order in Council under section 1(3) of the Northern Ireland (Temporary Provisions) Act 1972;
(*g*) an Act of the Parliament of Northern Ireland.][2]

Commentary—*De Voil Indirect Tax Service* **V4.146.**

Press releases etc—C&E Business Brief 8/95 5-5-95 (clarification for opticians on VAT treatment of corrective spectacles).
C&E Business Brief 12/95 19-6-95 (drugs and prostheses provided in course of hospital care are an exempt supply).
C&E Business Brief 19/95 13-9-95 (procedures for opticians claiming overpaid VAT).

C&E Press Notice 48/95 9-10-95 (commercial agencies providing homecare services without charging VAT).
C&E News Release 23/96, 11-4-96 (item 1, note 2: healthcare services of unqualified staff "directly supervised" by qualified professionals: guidance on when services are "directly supervised" when the qualified professional is not physically present).
C&E Business Brief 8/96 (Customs now accept that General Practitioners and General Dental Practitioners were in business for their supplies to the NHS prior to 19 March 1993).
C&E VAT Information sheet 5/96 1-5-96 (clarification of the VAT treatment of supplies by dentists).
C&E Business Brief 26/96 19-12-96 (Customs have changed the liability of certain medico-legal services provided by doctors from exempt to taxable when made to third parties).
C&E Business Brief 1/97 24-1-97 (item above limited to activities of 'legal' persons).
C&E Business Brief 2/97 7-2-97 (medico-legal services clarified).
C&E Business Brief 3/02 12-2-02 (single and multiple supplies—sale of spectacles and contact lenses—Customs' policy clarified).
C&E Business Brief 7/02 21-3-02 (while commercially provided residential care (other than nursing or medical care) does not qualify for exemption as care in a hospital or similar establishment, it qualifies for the exemption that applies to residential accommodation).
HMRC Brief 43/09, 23-7-09 (VAT exemption for psychologists' services).
HMRC Brief 12/10 18-3-10 (Provision of health professionals, nursing auxiliaries, care assistants and support workers by employment businesses: clarification of policy).
Simon's Tax Cases—*EC Commission v United Kingdom* [1988] STC 251*; *Barkworth v C&E Comrs* [1988] STC 771*.
Item 1(*a*), *Dr Beynon and Partners v C&E Comrs* [2003] STC 169, CA, [2005] STC 55, HL.
Item 1(*b*), *C&E Comrs v Leightons Ltd* [1995] STC 458*.
Item 2, *d'Ambrumenil and another v C&E Comrs* (Case C-307/01) [2005] STC 650.
Item 4, *C&E Comrs v St Martins Hospital Ltd* [1995] STC 628*; *Gregg v Comrs of Customs and Excise* (Case C-216/97) [1999] STC 934; *C&E Comrs v Kingscrest Associates Ltd (t/a Kingscrest Residential Care Homes)* [2002] STC 490.
Item 8, *Future Health Technologies v R&C Comrs* [2010] STC 1836.
Item 9, *Kingscrest Associates Ltd and another v C&E Comrs* [2005] STC 1547; *Revenue and Customs Commissioners v K & L Childcare Service Ltd* [2006] STC 18.
Definitions—"Local authority", s 96(4); "supply", s 5, Sch 4.
Note—Note that Item 3 is purported to be amended by the Pharmacy Order, SI 2010/231 art 68, Sch 4 para 5(3) with effect from 27 September 2010 (by virtue of SI 2010/1621). However, the amendment appears to be erroneous. The text of Sch 4 para 5(3) reads as follows—

> "In Part 2 of Schedule 9 (exemptions—the Groups), in group 7, in item 3, for "the Register of Pharmacists maintained under the Pharmacists and Pharmacy Technicians Order 2007 or in the register of pharmaceutical chemists kept under" substitute "the register maintained under article 19 of the Pharmacy Order 2010 or in the register of pharmaceutical chemists kept under".

Amendments—[1] Note (2A) inserted by the VAT (Pharmaceutical Chemists) Order, SI 1996/2949 with effect from 1 January 1997.
[2] Note (6) substituted, and Note (8) added, by the Value Added Tax (Health and Welfare) Order, SI 2002/762 with effect from 21 March 2002.
[3] Note 4 repealed by the European Qualifications (Health and Social Care Professions) Regulations, SI 2007/3101 reg 65(b) with effect from 3 December 2007.
[4] Note (2ZA) inserted by the Health and Social Care Act 2012 s 220(4) with effect from 1 August 2012 (SI 2012/1319, art 2(1), (4)).

GROUP 8 — BURIAL AND CREMATION

Item No

1 The disposal of the remains of the dead.

2 The making of arrangements for or in connection with the disposal of the remains of the dead.

Commentary—*De Voil Indirect Tax Service* **V4.151**.
Simon's Tax Cases—Item 2, *Network Insurance Brokers Ltd v C&E Comrs* [1998] STC 742; *Co-operative Wholesale Society Ltd v C&E Comrs* [1999] STC 1096; *Co-operative Wholesale Society Ltd v C&E Comrs* [2000] STC 727.

[GROUP 9— SUBSCRIPTIONS TO TRADE UNIONS, PROFESSIONAL AND OTHER PUBLIC INTEREST BODIES][1]

Item No

1 The supply to its members of such services and, in connection with those services, of such goods as are both referable only to its aims and available without payment other than a membership subscription by any of the following non-profit-making organisations—

(*a*) a trade union or other organisation of persons having as its main object the negotiation on behalf of its members of the terms and conditions of their employment;

(*b*) a professional association, membership of which is wholly or mainly restricted to individuals who have or are seeking a qualification appropriate to the practice of the profession concerned;

(*c*) an association, the primary purpose of which is the advancement of a particular branch of knowledge, or the fostering of professional expertise, connected with the past or present professions or employments of its members;

(*d*) an association, the primary purpose of which is to make representations to the Government on legislation and other public matters which affect the business or professional interests of its members.

[(*e*) a body which has objects which are in the public domain and are of a political, religious, patriotic, philosophical, philanthropic or civic nature.][1]

NOTES

(1) Item 1 does not include any right of admission to any premises, event or performance, to which non-members are admitted for a consideration.

(2) "Trade union" has the meaning assigned to it by section 1 of the Trade Union and Labour Relations (Consolidation) Act 1992.

(3) Item 1 shall include organisations and associations the membership of which consists wholly or mainly of constituent or affiliated associations which as individual associations would be comprised in the item; and "member" shall be construed as including such an association and "membership subscription" shall include an affiliation fee or similar levy.

(4) Paragraph (*c*) does not apply unless the association restricts its membership wholly or mainly to individuals whose present or previous professions or employments are directly connected with the purposes of the association.

(5) Paragraph (*d*) does not apply unless the association restricts its membership wholly or mainly to individuals or corporate bodies whose business or professional interests are directly connected with the purposes of the association.

Commentary—*De Voil Indirect Tax Service* **V4.156**.

Simon's Tax Cases—*Institute of Leisure and Amenity Management v C&E Comrs* [1988] STC 602*.

Item 1(*b*), (*c*), *Committee of Directors of Polytechnics v C&E Comrs* [1992] STC 873*.

Item 1(*e*), *Expert Witness Institute v C&E Comrs, CA* [2002] STC 42.

Definitions—"Business", s 94; "supply", s 5, Sch 4.

Amendments—[1] Group title substituted, and Item 1, para (e) inserted by the Value Added Tax (Subscriptions to Trade Unions, Professional and Other Public Interest Bodies) Order, SI 1999/2834, arts 2, 4.

GROUP 10 — SPORT, SPORTS COMPETITIONS AND PHYSICAL EDUCATION

Item No

1 The grant of a right to enter a competition in sport or physical recreation where the consideration for the grant consists in money which is to be allocated wholly towards the provision of a prize or prizes awarded in that competition.

2 The grant, by a [an eligible body][1] established for the purposes of sport or physical recreation, of a right to enter a competition in such an activity.

Amendments—[1] Words in Items 2 and 3 substituted by the VAT (Sport, Sports Competitions and Physical Education) Order, SI 1999/1994, arts 2–5, with effect from 1 January 2000.

3 The supply by a [an eligible body][1] to an individual . . . [3] of services closely linked with and essential to sport or physical education in which the individual is taking part.

NOTES

(1) Item 3 does not include the supply of any services by a [an eligible body][1] of residential accommodation, catering or transport.

(2) . . . [3]

[(2A) Subject to Notes (2C) and (3), in this Group "eligible body" means a non-profit making body which—

(*a*) is precluded from distributing any profit it makes, or is allowed to distribute any such profit by means only of distributions to a non-profit making body;

(*b*) applies in accordance with Note (2B) any profits it makes from supplies of a description within Item 2 or 3; and

(*c*) is not subject to commercial influence.

(2B) For the purposes of Note (2A)(*b*) the application of profits made by any body from supplies of a description within Item 2 or 3 is in accordance with this Note only if those profits are applied for one or more of the following purposes, namely—

(*a*) the continuance or improvement of any facilities made available in or in connection with the making of the supplies of those descriptions made by that body;

(*b*) the purposes of a non-profit making body.

(2C) In determining whether the requirements of Note (2A) for being an eligible body are satisfied in the case of any body, there shall be disregarded any distribution of amounts representing unapplied or undistributed profits that falls to be made to the body's members on its winding-up or dissolution.][1]

(3) In Item 3 a "[an eligible body][1]" does not include—

(*a*) a local authority;

(*b*) a Government department within the meaning of section 41(6); or (*c*) a non-departmental public body which is listed in the 1993 edition of the publication prepared by the Office of Public Service and Science and known as Public Bodies.

[(4) For the purposes of this Group a body shall be taken, in relation to a sports supply, to be subject to commercial influence if, and only if, there is a time in the relevant period when—

(*a*) a relevant supply was made to that body by a person associated with it at that time;

(*b*) an emolument was paid by that body to such a person;

(*c*) an agreement existed for either or both of the following to take place after the end of that period, namely—

(i) the making of a relevant supply to that body by such a person; or

(ii) the payment by that body to such a person of any emoluments.

(5) In this Group "the relevant period", in relation to a sports supply, means—

(*a*) where that supply is one made before 1st January 2003, the period beginning with 14th January 1999 and ending with the making of that sports supply; and

(*b*) where that supply is one made on or after 1st January 2003, the period of three years ending with the making of that sports supply.

(6) Subject to Note (7), in this Group "relevant supply", in relation to any body, means a supply falling within any of the following paragraphs—

(*a*) the grant of any interest in or right over land which at any time in the relevant period was or was expected to become sports land;

(*b*) the grant of any licence to occupy any land which at any such time was or was expected to become sports land;

(*c*) the grant, in the case of land in Scotland, of any personal right to call for or be granted any such interest or right as is mentioned in paragraph (*a*) above;

(*d*) a supply arising from a grant falling within paragraph (*a*), (*b*) or (*c*) above, other than a grant made before 1st April 1996;

(*e*) the supply of any services consisting in the management or administration of any facilities provided by that body;

(*f*) the supply of any goods or services for a consideration in excess of what would have been agreed between parties entering into a commercial transaction at arm's length.

(7) A supply which has been, or is to be or may be, made by any person shall not be taken, in relation to a sports supply made by any body, to be a relevant supply for the purposes of this Group if—

(*a*) the principal purpose of that body is confined, at the time when the sports supply is made, to the provision for employees of that person of facilities for use for or in connection with sport or physical recreation, or both;

(*b*) the supply in question is one made by a charity or local authority or one which (if it is made) will be made by a person who is a charity or local authority at the time when the sports supply is made;

(*c*) the supply in question is a grant falling within Note (6)(*a*) to (*c*) which has been made, or (if it is made) will be made, for a nominal consideration;

(*d*) the supply in question is one arising from such a grant as is mentioned in paragraph (*c*) above and is not itself a supply the consideration for which was, or will or may be, more than a nominal consideration; or

(*e*) the supply in question—

(i) is a grant falling within Note (6)(*a*) to (*c*) which is made for no consideration; but

(ii) falls to be treated as a supply of goods or services, or (if it is made) will fall to be so treated, by reason only of the application, in accordance with paragraph 9 of Schedule 4, of paragraph 5 of that Schedule.

(8) Subject to Note (10), a person shall be taken, for the purposes of this Group, to have been associated with a body at any of the following times, that is to say—

(*a*) the time when a supply was made to that body by that person;

(*b*) the time when an emolument was paid by that body to that person; or

(*c*) the time when an agreement was in existence for the making of a relevant supply or the payment of emoluments,

if, at that time, or at another time (whether before or after that time) in the relevant period, that person was an officer or shadow officer of that body or an intermediary for supplies to that body.

(9) Subject to Note (10), a person shall also be taken, for the purposes of this Group, to have been associated with a body at a time mentioned in paragraph (*a*), (*b*) or (*c*) of Note (8) if, at that time, he was connected with another person who in accordance with that Note—

(*a*) is to be taken to have been so associated at that time; or

(*b*) would be taken to have been so associated were that time the time of a supply by the other person to that body.

(10) Subject to Note (11), a person shall not be taken for the purposes of this Group to have been associated with a body at a time mentioned in paragraph (*a*), (*b*) or (*c*) of Note (8) if the only times in the relevant period when that person or the person connected with him was an officer or shadow officer of the body are times before 1st January 2000.

(11) Note (10) does not apply where (but for that Note) the body would be treated as subject to commercial influence at any time in the relevant period by virtue of—

(*a*) the existence of any agreement entered into on or after 14th January 1999 and before 1st January 2000; or

(*b*) anything done in pursuance of any such agreement.

(12) For the purposes of this Group a person shall be taken, in relation to a sports supply, to have been at all times in the relevant period an intermediary for supplies to the body making that supply if—

(*a*) at any time in that period either a supply was made to him by another person or an agreement for the making of a supply to him by another was in existence; and

(*b*) the circumstances were such that, if—

(i) that body had been the person to whom the supply was made or (in the case of an agreement) the person to whom it was to be or might be made; and

(ii) Note (7) above were to be disregarded to the extent (if at all) that it would prevent the supply from being a relevant supply, the body would have fallen to be regarded in relation to the sports supply as subject to commercial influence.

(13) In determining for the purposes of Note (12) or this Note whether there are such circumstances as are mentioned in paragraph (*b*) of that Note in the case of any supply, that Note and this Note shall be applied first for determining whether the person by whom the supply was made, or was to be or might be made, was himself an intermediary for supplies to the body in question, and so on through any number of other supplies or agreements.

(14) In determining for the purposes of this Group whether a supply made by any person was made by an intermediary for supplies to a body, it shall be immaterial that the supply by that person was made before the making of the supply or agreement by reference to which that person falls to be regarded as such an intermediary.

(15) Without prejudice to the generality of subsection (1AA) of section 43, for the purpose of determining—

(*a*) whether a relevant supply has at any time been made to any person;

(*b*) whether there has at any time been an agreement for the making of a relevant supply to any person; and

(*c*) whether a person falls to be treated as an intermediary for the supplies to any body by reference to supplies that have been, were to be or might have been made to him,

references in the preceding Notes to a supply shall be deemed to include references to a supply falling for other purposes to be disregarded in accordance with section 43(1)(a).

(16) In this Group—

"agreement" includes any arrangement or understanding (whether or not legally enforceable);

"emolument" means any emolument (within the meaning of the Income Tax Acts) the amount of which falls or may fall, in accordance with the agreement under which it is payable, to be determined or varied wholly or partly by reference—

(i) to the profits from some or all of the activities of the body paying the emolument; or

(ii) to the level of that body's gross income from some or all of its activities;

"employees", in relation to a person, includes retired employees of that person;

"grant" includes an assignment or surrender;

"officer", in relation to a body, includes—

(i) a director of a body corporate; and

(ii) any committee member or trustee concerned in the general control and management of the administration of the body;

"shadow officer", in relation to a body, means a person in accordance with whose directions or instructions the members or officers of the body are accustomed to act;

"sports land", in relation to any body, means any land used or held for use for or in connection with the provision by that body of facilities for use for or in connection with sport or physical recreation, or both;

"sports supply" means a supply which, if made by an eligible body, would fall within Item 2 or 3.

(17) For the purposes of this Group any question whether a person is connected with another shall be determined in accordance with [section 1122 of the Corporation Tax Act 2010][2] (connected persons).][1]

Commentary—*De Voil Indirect Tax Service* **V4.161.**

Definitions—"Local authority", s 96(4); "money", s 96(1); "supply", s 5, Sch 4.
Simon's Tax Cases—*Messenger Leisure Developments Ltd v Revenue and Customs Commissioners* [2005] STC 1078.
Item 3, *R&C Comrs v Atrium Club Ltd* [2010] STC 1494.
Press releases etc—HMRC Brief 13/09, 19-3-09 (Leisure Trusts providing all-inclusive membership schemes).
Cross references—Council Directive (EEC) 77/388, Article 13A(1)(*m*).
Amendments—[1] Words in Items 2 and 3 and words in Notes (1) and (3) substituted, and Notes (2A)–(2C) and (4)–(17) inserted, by the VAT (Sport, Sports Competitions and Physical Education) Order, SI 1999/1994, arts 2–5, with effect from 1 January 2000.
[2] In Note (17) words substituted for words "section 839 of the Taxes Act 1988" by CTA 2010 s 1177, Sch 1 para 285(e)(*ii*). CTA 2010 has effect for corporation tax purposes for accounting periods ending on or after 1 April 2010, and for income and capital gains tax purposes for the tax year 2010–11 and subsequent tax years.
[3] In Item 3, words ", except, where the body operates a membership scheme, an individual who is not a member," repealed, and Note (2) repealed, by the Value Added Tax (Sport) Order, SI 2014/3185 art 2 with effect from 1 January 2015.

GROUP 11 — WORKS OF ART ETC

Item No

1 The disposal of an object with respect to which estate duty is not chargeable by virtue of section 30(3) of the Finance Act 1953, section 34(1) of the Finance Act 1956 or the proviso to section 40(2) of the Finance Act 1930.

2 The disposal of an object with respect to which inheritance tax is not chargeable by virtue of paragraph 1(3)(*a*) or (4), paragraph 3(4)(*a*), or the words following paragraph 3(4), of Schedule 5 to the Inheritance Tax Act 1984.

3 The disposal of property with respect to which inheritance tax is not chargeable by virtue of section 32(4) or 32A(5) or (7) of the Inheritance Tax Act 1984.

4 The disposal of an asset in a case in which any gain accruing on that disposal is not a chargeable gain by virtue of section 258(2) of the Taxation of Chargeable Gains Act 1992.
Commentary—*De Voil Indirect Tax Service* **V4.166**.

[GROUP 12—FUND-RAISING EVENTS BY CHARITIES AND OTHER QUALIFYING BODIES

Item No.

1 The supply of goods and services by a charity in connection with an event—
(*a*) that is organised for charitable purposes by a charity or jointly by more than one charity,
(*b*) whose primary purpose is the raising of money, and
(*c*) that is promoted as being primarily for the raising of money.

2 The supply of goods and services by a qualifying body in connection with an event—
(*a*) that is organised exclusively for the body's own benefit,
(*b*) whose primary purpose is the raising of money, and
(*c*) that is promoted as being primarily for the raising of money.

3 The supply of goods and services by a charity or a qualifying body in connection with an event—
(*a*) that is organised jointly by a charity, or two or more charities, and the qualifying body,
(*b*) that is so organised exclusively for charitable purposes or exclusively for the body's own benefit or exclusively for a combination of those purposes and that benefit,
(*c*) whose primary purpose is the raising of money, and
(*d*) that is promoted as being primarily for the raising of money.

NOTES

(1) For the purposes of this Group "event" includes an event accessed (wholly or partly) by means of electronic communications.
For this purpose "electronic communications" includes any communications by means of [an electronic communications network][2].
(2) For the purposes of this Group "charity" includes a body corporate that is wholly owned by a charity if—
(*a*) the body has agreed in writing (whether or not contained in a deed) to transfer its profits (from whatever source) to a charity, or
(*b*) the body's profits (from whatever source) are otherwise payable to a charity.
(3) For the purposes of this Group "qualifying body means—
(*a*) any non-profit making organisation mentioned in item 1 of Group 9;
(*b*) any body that is an eligible body for the purposes of Group 10 and whose principal purpose is the provision of facilities for persons to take part in sport or physical education; or
(*c*) any body that is an eligible body for the purposes of item 2 of Group 13.

(4) Where in a financial year of a charity or qualifying body there are held at the same location more than 15 events involving the charity or body that are of the same kind, items 1 to 3 do not apply (or shall be treated as having not applied) to a supply in connection with any event involving the charity or body that is of that kind and is held in that financial year at that location.

(5) In determining whether the limit of 15 events mentioned in Note (4) has been exceeded in the case of events of any one kind held at the same location, disregard any event of that kind held at that location in a week during which the aggregate gross takings from events involving the charity or body that are of that kind and are held in that location do not exceed £1,000.

(6) In the case of a financial year that is longer or shorter than a year, Notes (4) and (5) have effect as if for "15" there were substituted the whole number nearest to the number obtained by—

(*a*) first multiplying the number of days in the financial year by 15, and

(*b*) then dividing the result by 365.

(7) For the purposes of Notes (4) and (5)—

(*a*) an event involves a charity if the event is organised by the charity or a connected charity;

(*b*) an event involves a qualifying body if the event is organised by the body.

In this Note "organised" means organised alone or jointly in any combination, and "organising" in Note (8) shall be construed accordingly.

(8) Items 1 to 3 do not include any supply in connection with an event if—

(*a*) accommodation in connection with the event is provided to a person by means of a supply, or in pursuance of arrangements, made by—

(i) the charity or any of the charities, or the qualifying body, organising the event, or

(ii) a charity connected with any charity organising the event,

and

(*b*) the provision of the accommodation is not incidental to the event.

(9) For the purposes of Note (8) the provision of accommodation is incidental to the event only if accommodation provided to the person by such means, or in pursuance of such arrangements, as are mentioned in paragraph (*a*) of that Note—

(*a*) does not exceed two nights in total (whether or not consecutive), and

(*b*) is not to any extent provided by means of a supply to which an order under section 53 applies.

(10) For the purposes of Notes (7)(*a*) and (8), two charities are connected if—

(*a*) one is a charity for the purposes of this Group only by virtue of Note (2) and the other is the charity that owns it, or

(*b*) each is a charity for the purposes of this Group only by virtue of Note (2) and the two of them are owned by the same charity.

(11) Items 1 to 3 do not include any supply the exemption of which would be likely to create distortions of competition such as to place a commercial enterprise carried on by a taxable person at a disadvantage.][1]

Commentary—*De Voil Indirect Tax Service* **V4.171.**

Simon's Tax Cases—item 1, *Loughborough Students Union v R&C Comrs* [2014] STC 357, [2013] UKUT 517 (TCC).

Definition—"Supply", s 5, Sch 4.

Amendments—[1] Group substituted by the Value Added Tax (Fund-Raising Events by Charities and Other Qualifying Bodies) Order, SI 2000/802 arts 2, 3 with effect in the case of supplies made from 1 April 2000.

[2] Words in Note (1) substituted by the Communications Act 2003 s 406, Sch 17 para 129(1), (3) with effect from 25 July 2003 to 29 December 2003 for certain purposes (see SI 2003/1900), 29 December 2003 for other purposes (see SI 2003/3142), and from a date to be appointed for remaining purposes.

[GROUP 13—CULTURAL SERVICES ETC

Item No

1 The supply by a public body of a right of admission to—

(*a*) a museum, gallery, art exhibition or zoo; or

(*b*) a theatrical, musical or choreographic performance of a cultural nature.

2 The supply by an eligible body of a right of admission to—

(*a*) a museum, gallery, art exhibition or zoo; or

(*b*) a theatrical, musical or choreographic performance of a cultural nature.

NOTES

(1) For the purposes of this Group "public body" means—

(*a*) a local authority;

(*b*) a government department within the meaning of section 41(6); or

(*c*) a non-departmental public body which is listed in the 1995 edition of the publication prepared by the Office of Public Service and known as "Public Bodies".

(2) For the purposes of item 2 "eligible body" means any body (other than a public body) which—

(*a*) is precluded from distributing, and does not distribute, any profit it makes;

(*b*) applies any profits made from supplies of a description falling within item 2 to the continuance or improvement of the facilities made available by means of the supplies; and

(*c*) is managed and administered on a voluntary basis by persons who have no direct or indirect financial interest in its activities.

(3) Item 1 does not include any supply the exemption of which would be likely to create distortions of competition such as to place a commercial enterprise carried on by a taxable person at a disadvantage

(4) Item 1(*b*) includes the supply of a right of admission to a performance only if the performance is provided exclusively by one or more public bodies, one or more eligible bodies or any combination of public bodies and eligible bodies.][1]

Commentary—*De Voil Indirect Tax Service* **V4.176**.

Simon's Tax Cases—*Bournemouth Symphony Orchestra v C&E Comrs, Longborough Festival Opera v R&C Comrs* [2007] STC 198.

Definitions—"Supply", s 5, Sch 4.

Press releases etc—HMRC Brief 27/07, 22-3-07 (Cultural exemption – clarification of "direct or indirect financial interest" following recent CA Judgments in *Bournemouth Symphony Orchestra* (C3/2005/1681) and *Longborough Festival Opera* (C3/2006/0369)).

Amendments—[1] This group inserted by the VAT (Cultural Services) Order, SI 1996/1256, with effect from 1 June 1996.

[GROUP 14—SUPPLIES OF GOODS WHERE INPUT TAX CANNOT BE RECOVERED

Item No

1 A supply of goods in relation to which each of the following conditions is satisfied, that is to say—

(*a*) there is input tax of the person making the supply ('the relevant supplier'), or of any predecessor of his, that has arisen or will arise on the supply to, or acquisition or importation by, the relevant supplier or any such predecessor of goods used for the supply made by the relevant supplier;

(*b*) the only such input tax is non-deductible input tax; and

(*c*) the supply made by the relevant supplier is not a supply which would be exempt under Item 1 of Group 1 of Schedule 9 but for an [option to tax any land under Part 1 of Schedule 10][3].

NOTES

(1) Subject to Note (2) below, in relation to any supply of goods by the relevant supplier, the goods used for that supply are—

(*a*) the goods supplied, and

(*b*) any goods used in the process of producing the supplied goods so as to be comprised in them.

(2) In relation to a supply by any person consisting in or arising from the grant of a major interest in land ('the relevant supply')—

(*a*) any supply consisting in or arising from a previous grant of a major interest in the land is a supply of goods used for the relevant supply, and

(*b*) subject to paragraph (*a*) above, the goods used for the relevant supply are any goods used in the construction of a building or civil engineering work so as to become part of the land.

(3) Subject to Notes (7) to (10) below, non-deductible input tax is input tax to which Note (4) or (5) below applies.

(4) This Note applies to input tax which (disregarding this Group and regulation 106 of the Value Added Tax Regulations 1995 (*de minimis* rule)) is not, and will not become, attributable to supplies to which section 26(2) applies.

(5) This Note applies to input tax if—

(*a*) disregarding this Group and the provisions mentioned in Note (6) below, the relevant supplier or a predecessor of his has or will become entitled to credit for the whole or a part of the amount of that input tax; and

(*b*) the effect (disregarding this Group) of one or more of those provisions is that neither the relevant supplier nor any predecessor of his has or will become entitled to credit for any part of that amount.

(6) The provisions mentioned in Note (5) above are—

(*a*) Article 5 of the Value Added Tax (Input Tax) Order 1992 (no credit for input tax on goods or services used for business entertainment);

(*b*) Article 6 of that Order (no credit for input tax on non-building materials incorporated in building or site);

(*c*) Article 7 of that Order (no credit for input tax on motor cars);

(*d*) any provision directly or indirectly re-enacted (with or without modification) in a provision mentioned in paragraphs (*a*) to (*c*) above.

(7) For the purposes of this Group the input tax of a person shall be deemed to include any VAT which—

(*a*) has arisen or will arise on a supply to, or acquisition or importation by, that person; and (*b*) would fall to be treated as input tax of that person but for its arising when that person is not a taxable person.

(8) Subject to Note (9) below, the input tax that is taken to be non-deductible input tax shall include any VAT which—

(*a*) is deemed to be input tax of any person by virtue of Note (7) above; and

(*b*) would be input tax to which Note (4) or (5) above would apply if it were input tax of that person and, in the case of a person to whom section 39 applies, if his business were carried on in the United Kingdom.

(9) Non-deductible input tax does not include any VAT that has arisen or will arise on a supply to, or acquisition or importation by, any person of any goods used for a supply of goods ('the relevant supply') if—

(*a*) that VAT; or

(*b*) any other VAT arising on the supply to, or acquisition or importation by, that person or any predecessor of his of any goods used for the relevant supply,

has been or will be refunded under section 33, [33A,][2] [33B,][4] [33C,][5] 39 or 41.

(10) Input tax arising on a supply, acquisition or importation of goods shall be disregarded for the purposes of determining whether the conditions in Item No 1(*a*) and (*b*) are satisfied if, at a time after that supply, acquisition or importation but before the supply by the relevant supplier, a supply of the goods or of anything in which they are comprised is treated under or by virtue of any provision of this Act as having been made by the relevant supplier or any predecessor of his to himself.

(11) In relation to any goods or anything comprised in any goods, a person is a predecessor of another ('the putative successor') only if Note (12) or (13) below applies to him in relation to those goods or that thing; and references in this Group to a person's predecessors include references to the predecessors of his predecessors through any number of transfers and events such as are mentioned in Notes (12) and (13).

(12) This Note applies to a person in relation to any goods or thing if—

(*a*) the putative successor is a person to whom he has transferred assets of his business by a transfer of that business, or a part of it, as a going concern;

(*b*) those assets consisted of or included those goods or that thing; and

(*c*) the transfer of the assets is one falling by virtue of an Order under section 5(3) (or under an enactment re-enacted in section 5(3)) to be treated as neither a supply of goods nor a supply of services.

(13) This Note applies to a body corporate in relation to any goods or thing if—

(*a*) those goods or that thing formed part of the assets of the business of that body at a time when it became a member of a group of which the putative successor was at that time the representative member;

(*b*) those goods or that thing formed part of the assets of the business of that body corporate, or of any other body corporate which was a member of the same group as that body, at a time when that body was succeeded as the representative member of the group by the putative successor; or

(*c*) those goods or that thing formed part of the assets of the putative successor at a time when it ceased to be a member of a group of which the body corporate in question was at the time the representative member.

(14) References in Note (13) above to a body corporate's being or becoming or ceasing to be a member of a group or the representative member of a group are references to its falling to be so treated for the purposes of section 43.

(15) In Notes (11) to (13) above the references to anything comprised in other goods shall be taken, in relation to any supply consisting in or arising from the grant of a major interest in land, to include anything the supply, acquisition or importation of which is, by virtue of Note (2) above, taken to be a supply, acquisition or importation of goods used for making the supply so consisting or arising.

(16) Notes (1) and (1A) to Group 1 shall apply for the purposes of this Group as they apply for the purposes of that Group.][1]

Commentary—*De Voil Indirect Tax Service* **V4.181.**

Amendments—[1] This group inserted by the Value Added Tax (Supplies of Goods where Input Tax cannot be recovered) Order, SI 1999/2833, art 2(1), (3), with effect from 1 March 2000.

[2] In Note (9), "33A," inserted after "33," by FA 2001 s 98(9) with effect from 1 September 2001.

[3] In Item 1(c) words substituted by the Value Added Tax (Buildings and Land) Order, SI 2008/1146, art 6, Sch 1 paras 1, 4 with effect in relation to supplies made on or after 1 June 2008, subject to savings in Sch 2 of the Order.

[4] In Note (9), "33B," inserted after "33A," by FA 2011 s 76(4) with effect in relation to supplies made, and acquisitions and importations taking place, on or after 1 April 2011.

[5] In Note (9), words inserted by FA 2015 s 66(1), (4) with effect in relation to supplies made, and acquisitions and importations taking place, on or after 1 April 2015.

[GROUP 15—INVESTMENT GOLD

Item no:

1 The supply of investment gold.

2 The grant, assignment or surrender of any right, interest, or claim in, over or to investment gold if the right, interest or claim is or confers a right to the transfer of the possession of investment gold.

3 The supply, by a person acting as agent for a disclosed principal, of services consisting of—

(*a*) the effecting of a supply falling within item 1 or 2 that is made by or to his principal, or

(*b*) attempting to effect a supply falling within item 1 or 2 that is intended to be made by or to his principal but is not in fact made.

NOTES:

(1) For the purposes of this Group "investment gold" means—

(*a*) gold of a purity not less than 995 thousandths that is in the form of a bar, or a wafer, of a weight accepted by the bullion markets;

(*b*) a gold coin minted after 1800 that—

(i) is of a purity of not less than 900 thousandths,

(ii) is, or has been, legal tender in its country of origin, and

(iii) is of a description of coin that is normally sold at a price that does not exceed 180% of the open market value of the gold contained in the coin; or

(*c*) a gold coin of a description specified in a notice that has been published by the Commissioners for the purposes of this Group and has not been withdrawn.

(2) A notice under Note (1)(*c*) may provide that a description specified in the notice has effect only for the purposes of supplies made at times falling within a period specified in the notice.

(3) Item 2 does not include—

(*a*) the grant of an option, or

(*b*) the assignment or surrender of a right under an option at a time before the option is exercised.

(4) This Group does not include a supply—

(*a*) between members of the London Bullion Market Association, or

(*b*) by a member of that Association to a taxable person who is not a member or by such a person to a member.][1]

Commentary—*De Voil Indirect Tax Service* **V4.186**.

Amendments—[1] This group inserted by the Value Added Tax (Investment Gold) Order, SI 1999/3116, art 2(1), (3), with effect from 1 January 2000.

GROUP 16—SUPPLIES OF SERVICES BY GROUPS INVOLVING COST SHARING

Item No

1 The supply of services by an independent group of persons where each of the following conditions is satisfied—

(*a*) each of those persons is a person who is carrying on an activity ("the relevant activity") which is exempt from VAT or in relation to which the person is not a taxable person within the meaning of Article 9 of Council Directive 2006/112/EC,

(*b*) the supply of services is made for the purpose of rendering the members of the group the services directly necessary for the exercise of the relevant activity,

(*c*) the group merely claims from its members exact reimbursement of their share of the joint expenses, and

(*d*) the exemption of the supply is not likely to cause distortion of competition.][1]

Amendments—[1] Group 16 inserted by FA 2012 s 197(2) with effect from 17 July 2012.

[SCHEDULE 9A

ANTI-AVOIDANCE PROVISIONS: GROUPS]

Section 43(9)

Commentary—*De Voil Indirect Tax Service* **V2.190B**.

Cross references—See VATA 1994 ss 83, 84 (appeals against directions or assessments under this Schedule).

Amendments—This Schedule inserted by FA 1996 s 31(2), Sch 4.

Power to give directions

[1—(1) Subject to paragraph 2 below, the Commissioners may give a direction under this Schedule if, in any case—

(*a*) a relevant event has occurred;

(*b*) the condition specified in sub-paragraph (3) below is fulfilled;

(*c*) that condition would not be fulfilled apart from the occurrence of that event; and

(*d*) in the case of an event falling within sub-paragraph (2)(*b*) below, the transaction in question is not a supply which is the only supply by reference to which the case falls within paragraphs (*a*) to (*c*) above.

(2) For the purposes of this Schedule, a relevant event occurs when a body corporate—

(*a*) begins to be, or ceases to be, treated as a member of a group; or

(*b*) enters into any transaction.

(3) The condition mentioned in sub-paragraph (1) above is that—

(*a*) there has been, or will or may be, a taxable supply on which VAT has been, or will or may be, charged otherwise than by reference to the supply's full value;

(*b*) there is at least a part of the supply which is not or, as the case may be, would not be zero-rated; and

(*c*) the charging of VAT on the supply otherwise than by reference to its full value gives rise or, as the case may be, would give rise to a tax advantage.

(4) For the purposes of this paragraph the charging of VAT on a supply ("the undercharged supply") otherwise than by reference to its full value shall be taken to give rise to a tax advantage if, and only if, a person has become entitled—

(*a*) to credit for input tax allowable as attributable to that supply or any part of it, or

(*b*) in accordance with regulations under section 39, to any repayment in respect of that supply or any part of it.

(5) The case where a person shall be taken for the purposes of sub-paragraph (4) above to have become entitled to a credit for input tax allowable as attributable to the undercharged supply, or to a part of it, shall include any case where—

(*a*) a person has become entitled to a credit for any input tax on the supply to him, or the acquisition or importation by him, of any goods or services; and

(*b*) whatever the supplies to which the credit was treated as attributable when the entitlement to it arose, those goods or services are used by him in making the undercharged supply, or a part of it.

(6) For the purposes of sub-paragraphs (4) and (5) above where—

(*a*) there is a supply of any of the assets of a business of a person ("the transferor") to a person to whom the whole or any part of that business is transferred as a going concern ("the transferee"), and

(*b*) that supply is treated, in accordance with an order under section 5(3), as being neither a supply of goods nor a supply of services,

the question, so far as it falls to be determined by reference to those assets, whether a credit for input tax to which any person has become entitled is one allowable as attributable to the whole or any part of a supply shall be determined as if the transferor and the transferee were the same person.

(7) Where, in a case to which sub-paragraph (6) above applies, the transferor himself acquired any of the assets in question by way of a supply falling within paragraphs (*a*) and (*b*) of that sub-paragraph, that sub-paragraph shall have the effect, as respects the assets so acquired, of requiring the person from whom those assets were acquired to be treated for the purposes of sub-paragraphs (4) and (5) above as the same person as the transferor and the transferee, and so on in the case of any number of successive supplies falling within those paragraphs.

(8) For the purposes of this paragraph any question—

(*a*) whether any credit for input tax to which a person has become entitled was, or is to be taken to have been, a credit allowable as attributable to the whole or any part of a supply, or

(*b*) whether any repayment is a repayment in respect of the whole or any part of a supply,

shall be determined, in relation to a supply of a right to goods or services or to a supply of goods or services by virtue of such a right, as if the supply of the right and supplies made by virtue of the right were a single supply of which the supply of the right and each of those supplies constituted different parts.

(9) References in this paragraph to the full value of a supply are references to the amount which (having regard to any direction under paragraph 1 of Schedule 6) would be the full value of that supply for the purposes of the charge to VAT if that supply were not a supply falling to be disregarded, to any extent, in pursuance of section 43(1)(*a*).

(10) References in this paragraph to the supply of a right to goods or services include references to the supply of any right, option or priority with respect to the supply of goods or services, and to the supply of an interest deriving from any right to goods or services.][1]

Definitions—"The Commissioners", s 96(1); "input tax", ss 24, 96(1); "supply", s 5, Sch 4; "taxable supply", ss 4(2), 96(1); "VAT", ss 1, 96(1).

Amendments—[1] This Schedule inserted by FA 1996 s 31(2), Sch 4.

Restrictions on giving directions

2—[(1)] [2] The Commissioners shall not give a direction under this Schedule by reference to a relevant event if they are satisfied that—

(*a*) the change in the treatment of the body corporate, or

(*b*) the transaction in question,

had as its main purpose or, as the case may be, as each of its main purposes a genuine commercial purpose unconnected with the fulfilment of the condition specified in paragraph 1(3) above.][1]
[(2) This paragraph shall not apply where the relevant event is the termination of a body corporate's treatment as a member of a group by a notice under section 43C(1) or (3).][2]

Definitions—"The Commissioners", s 96(1); "relevant event", Sch 9A para 1(2).
Amendments—[1] This Schedule inserted by FA 1996 s 31(2), Sch 4.
[2] Para 2 amended to renumber existing text as sub-para (1), and sub-para (2) inserted by FA 1999 s 16, Sch 2 para 5 with effect from 27 July 1999 subject to FA 1999 Sch 2 para 6.

Form of directions under Schedule

[3—(1) The directions that may be given by the Commissioners under this Schedule are either—
(*a*) a direction relating to any supply of goods or services that has been made, in whole or in part, by one body corporate to another; or
(*b*) a direction relating to a particular body corporate.
(2) A direction under this Schedule relating to a supply shall require it to be assumed (where it would not otherwise be the case) that, to the extent described in the direction, the supply was not a supply falling to be disregarded in pursuance of section 43(1)(*a*).
(3) A direction under this Schedule relating to a body corporate shall require it to be assumed (where it would not otherwise be the case) that, for such period (comprising times before the giving of the direction or times afterwards or both) as may be described in the direction, the body corporate—
(*a*) did not fall to be treated, or is not to be treated, as a member of a group, or of a particular group so described; or
(*b*) fell to be treated, or is to be treated, as a member of any group so described of which, for that period, it was or is eligible to be a member.
(4) Where a direction under this Schedule requires any assumptions to be made, then—
(*a*) so far as the assumptions relate to times on or after the day on which the direction is given, this Act shall have effect in relation to such times in accordance with those assumptions; and
(*b*) paragraph 6 below shall apply for giving effect to those assumptions in so far as they relate to earlier times.
(5) A direction falling within sub-paragraph (3)(*b*) above may identify in relation to any times or period the body corporate which is to be assumed to have been, or to be, the representative member of the group at those times or for that period.
(6) A direction under this Schedule may vary the effect of a previous direction under this Schedule.
(7) The Commissioners may at any time, by notice in writing to the person to whom it was given, withdraw a direction under this Schedule.
(8) The refusal or non-refusal by the Commissioners of an application [such as is mentioned in section 43B][2] shall not prejudice the power of the Commissioners to give a direction under this Schedule requiring any case to be assumed to be what it would have been had the application not been refused or, as the case may be, had it been refused.][1]

Definitions—"The Commissioners", s 96(1); "representative member", s 43(4); "supply", s 5, Sch 4.
Amendments—[1] This Schedule inserted by FA 1996 s 31(2), Sch 4.
[2] Words in sub-para (8) substituted by FA 1999 s 16, Sch 2 para 5 with effect from 27 July 1999 subject to FA 1999 Sch 2 para 6.

Time limit on directions

[4—(1) A direction under this Schedule shall not be given more than six years after whichever is the later of—
(*a*) the occurrence of the relevant event by reference to which it is given; and
(*b*) the time when the relevant entitlement arose.
(2) A direction under this Schedule shall not be given by reference to a relevant event occurring on or before 28th November 1995.
(3) Subject to sub-paragraphs (1) and (2) above, a direction under this Schedule—
(*a*) may be given by reference to a relevant event occurring before the coming into force of this Schedule; and
(*b*) may require assumptions to be made in relation to times (including times before 29th November 1995) falling before the occurrence of the relevant event by reference to which the direction is given, or before the relevant entitlement arose.
(4) For the purposes of this paragraph the reference, in relation to the giving of a direction, to the relevant entitlement is a reference to the entitlement by reference to which the requirements of paragraph 1(4) above are taken to be satisfied for the purposes of that direction.][1]

Press releases etc—Hansard 6-2-96 (scope for retrospective directions under this paragraph).
Definitions—"Input tax", ss 24, 96(1); "prescribed accounting period", s 25(1).
Amendments—[1] This Schedule inserted by FA 1996 s 31(2), Sch 4.

Manner of giving directions

[5—(1) A direction under this Schedule relating to a supply may be given to—

(*a*) the person who made the supply to which the direction relates; or

(*b*) any body corporate which, at the time when the direction is given, is the representative member of a group of which that person was treated as being a member at the time of the supply.

(2) A direction under this Schedule relating to a body corporate ("the relevant body") may be given to that body or to any body corporate which at the time when the direction is given is, or in pursuance of the direction is to be treated as, the representative member of a group of which the relevant body—

(*a*) is treated as being a member;

(*b*) was treated as being a member at a time to which the direction relates; or

(*c*) is to be treated as being, or having been, a member at any such time.

(3) A direction given to any person under this Schedule shall be given to him by notice in writing.

(4) A direction under this Schedule must specify the relevant event by reference to which it is given.][1]

Definitions—"The Commissioners", s 96(1); "representative member", s 43(4).

Amendments—[1] This Schedule inserted by FA 1996 s 31(2), Sch 4.

Assessment in consequence of a direction

[6—(1) Subject to sub-paragraph (3) below, where—

(*a*) a direction is given under this Schedule, and

(*b*) there is an amount of VAT ("the unpaid tax") for which a relevant person would have been liable before the giving of the direction if the facts had accorded with the assumptions specified in the direction,

the Commissioners may, to the best of their judgment, assess the amount of unpaid tax as tax due from the person to whom the direction was given or another relevant person and notify their assessment to that person.

(2) In sub-paragraph (1) above the reference to an amount of VAT for which a person would, on particular assumptions, have been liable before the giving of a direction under this Schedule is a reference to the aggregate of the following—

(*a*) any amount of output tax which, on those assumptions but not otherwise, would have been due from a relevant person at the end of a prescribed accounting period ending before the giving of the direction;

(*b*) the amount of any credit for input tax to which a relevant person is treated as having been entitled at the end of such an accounting period but to which he would not have been entitled on those assumptions; and

(*c*) the amount of any repayment of tax made to a relevant person in accordance with regulations under section 39 but to which he would not have been entitled on those assumptions.

(3) Where any assessment falls to be made under this paragraph in a case in which the Commissioners are satisfied that the actual revenue loss is less than the unpaid tax, the total amount to be assessed under this paragraph shall not exceed what appears to them, to the best of their judgement, to be the amount of that loss.

(4) For the purposes of the making of an assessment under this paragraph in relation to any direction, the actual revenue loss shall be taken to be equal to the amount of the unpaid tax less the amount given by aggregating the amounts of every entitlement—

(*a*) to credit for input tax, or

(*b*) to a repayment in accordance with regulations under section 39,

which (whether as an entitlement of the person in relation to whom the assessment is made or as an entitlement of any other person) would have arisen on the assumptions contained in the direction, but not otherwise.

(5) An assessment under this paragraph relating to a direction may be notified to the person to whom that direction is given by being incorporated in the same notice as that direction.

(6) An assessment under this paragraph shall not be made—

(*a*) more than one year after the day on which the direction to which it relates was given, or

(*b*) in the case of any direction that has been withdrawn.

(7) Where an amount has been assessed on any person under this paragraph and notified to him—

(*a*) that amount shall be deemed (subject to the provisions of this Act as to appeals) to be an amount of VAT due from him;

(*b*) that amount may be recovered accordingly, either from that person or, in the case of a body corporate that is for the time being treated as a member of a group, from the representative member of that group; and (*c*) to the extent that more than one person is liable by virtue of any assessment under this paragraph in respect of the same amount of unpaid tax, those persons shall be treated as jointly and severally liable for that amount.

(8) Sub-paragraph (7) above does not have effect if or to the extent that the assessment in question has been withdrawn or reduced.

(9) Sections 74 and 77(6) apply in relation to assessments under this paragraph as they apply in relation to assessments under section 73 but as if the reference in subsection (1) of section 74 to the reckonable date were a reference to the date on which the assessment is notified.

(10) Where by virtue of sub-paragraph (9) above any person is liable to interest under section 74—

(*a*) section 76 shall have effect in relation to that liability with the omission of subsections (2) to (6); and

(*b*) section 77, except subsection (6), shall not apply to an assessment of the amount due by way of interest;

and (without prejudice to the power to make assessments for interest for later periods) the interest to which any assessment made under section 76 by virtue of paragraph (a) above may relate shall be confined to interest for a period of no more than two years ending with the time when the assessment to interest is made.

(11) In this paragraph "a relevant person", in relation to a direction, means—

(*a*) the person to whom the direction is given;

(*b*) the body corporate which was the representative member of any group of which that person was treated as being, or in pursuance of the direction is to be treated as having been, a member at a time to which the assumption specified in the direction relates; or

(*c*) any body corporate which, in pursuance of the direction, is to be treated as having been the representative member of such a group.][1]

Definitions—"The Commissioners", s 96(1); "input tax", ss 24, 96(1); "prescribed accounting period", s 25(1); "VAT", ss 1, 96(1).

Amendments—[1] This Schedule inserted by FA 1996 s 31(2), Sch 4.

Interpretation of Schedule etc

[7—(1) References in this Schedule to being treated as a member of a group and to being eligible to be treated as a member of a group shall be construed in accordance with [sections 43 to 43C][2].

(2) For the purposes of this Schedule the giving of any notice or notification to any receiver, liquidator or person otherwise acting in a representative capacity in relation to another shall be treated as the giving of a notice or, as the case may be, notification to the person in relation to whom he so acts.][1]

[1] This Schedule inserted by FA 1996 s 31(2), Sch 4.

[2] Words in sub-para (1) substituted by FA 1999 s 16, Sch 2 para 5 with effect from 27 July 1999 subject to FA 1999 Sch 2 para 6.

[SCHEDULE 10
BUILDINGS AND LAND

Section 51]

Press releases etc—HMRC Brief 28/08, 30-5-08 (Land & buildings – announcing a new revised Notice 742A "Opting to tax land and buildings and associated forms and certificates" (see *VAT Notices* section ante.))

HMRC Brief 8/10, 15-3-10 (Changes to the operation of the option to tax and updated definitions of housing associations).

Commentary—De Voil Indirect Tax Service **V4.116**.

Simon's Tax Cases—*Enterprise Inns Plc and another v R&C Comrs* [2012] UKUT 240 (TCC), [2012] STC 2313.

Amendment—Schedule 10 substituted by the Value Added Tax (Buildings and Land) Order, SI 2008/1146, art 2 with effect in relation to supplies made on or after 1 June 2008, subject to savings in Sch 2 of the Order.

[PART 1
THE OPTION TO TAX LAND

INTRODUCTION

Overview of the option to tax

1—(1) This Part of the Schedule makes provision for a person to opt to tax any land.

(2) The effect of the option to tax is dealt with in paragraph 2 (exempt supplies become taxable), as read with paragraph 3.

(3) Grants are excluded from the effect of paragraph 2 by—

(*a*) paragraph 5 (dwellings designed or adapted, and intended for use, as dwelling etc),

(*b*) paragraph 6 (conversion of buildings for use as dwelling etc),

(*c*) paragraph 7 (charities),

(*d*) paragraph 8 (residential caravans),

(*e*) paragraph 9 (residential houseboats),

(*f*) paragraph 10 (relevant housing associations), and

(*g*) paragraph 11 (grant to individual for construction of dwelling).

(4) Paragraphs 12 to 17 (anti-avoidance: developers of land etc) provide for certain supplies to which any grant gives rise to be excluded from the effect of paragraph 2.

(5) Paragraphs 18 to 30 deal with—

(*a*) the scope of the option to tax,

(*b*) the day from which the option to tax has effect,

(*c*) notification requirements,

(*d*) elections to opt to tax land subsequently acquired,

(*e*) the revocation of the option,

(*f*) the effect of the option to tax in relation to new buildings, and

(*g*) requirements for prior permission in the case of exempt grants made before the exercise of an option to tax.

(6) Paragraphs 31 to 34 deal with definitions which apply for the purposes of this Part, as well as other supplemental matters.][1]

Commentary—*De Voil Indirect Tax Service* **V3.248, V4.113**.

Cross reference—See VATA 1994 Sch 13 para 8 (preservation of zero rating for certain supplies in the course of an approved alteration of a protected building made pursuant to an obligation incurred before 21 June 1988: such supplies are not "relevant zero rated supplies" for the purposes of this para).

Amendments—[1] Schedule 10 substituted by the Value Added Tax (Buildings and Land) Order, SI 2008/1146, art 2 with effect in relation to supplies made on or after 1 June 2008, subject to savings in Sch 2 of the Order.

[THE OPTION TO TAX

Effect of the option to tax: exempt supplies become taxable

2—(1) This paragraph applies if—

(*a*) a person exercises the option to tax any land under this Part of this Schedule, and

(*b*) a grant is made in relation to the land at any time when the option to tax it has effect.

(2) If the grant is made—

(*a*) by the person exercising that option, or

(*b*) by a relevant associate (if that person is a body corporate),

the grant does not fall within Group 1 of Schedule 9 (exemptions for land).

(3) For the meaning of "relevant associate", see paragraph 3.][1]

Commentary—*De Voil Indirect Tax Service* **V4.115**.

Simon's Tax Cases—*Marlow Gardner & Cooke Ltd Directors' Pension Scheme v R&C Comrs* [2006] STC 2014*; *R&C Comrs v Principal and Fellows of Newnham College in the University of Cambridge* [2008] STC 1225*, *Mason v Boscawen* [2009] STC 624.

Press releases etc—C&E Business Brief 8/01 2-7-01 (from 1 August 2001, where vendor of building has opted to tax, and immediate purchaser does not intend to use building himself as a dwelling, nor to convert it into dwellings for sale or rent, the vendor must account for the VAT on the sale).

Amendments—[1] Schedule 10 substituted by the Value Added Tax (Buildings and Land) Order, SI 2008/1146, art 2 with effect in relation to supplies made on or after 1 June 2008, subject to savings in Sch 2 of the Order.

[Meaning of "relevant associate"

3—(1) This paragraph explains for the purposes of this Part of this Schedule what is meant by a "relevant associate" in a case where a body corporate ("the opter") exercises an option to tax in relation to any building or land.

(2) A body corporate is a relevant associate of the opter if under sections 43A to 43D (groups of companies) the body corporate—

(*a*) was treated as a member of the same group as the opter at the time when the option first had effect,

(*b*) has been so treated at any later time when the opter had a relevant interest in the building or land, or

(*c*) has been treated as a member of the same group as a body corporate within paragraph (*a*) or (*b*) or this paragraph at a time when that body had a relevant interest in the building or land.

(3) But a body corporate ceases to be a relevant associate of the opter in relation to the building or land in the following circumstances.

(4) The body corporate ceases to be a relevant associate of the opter in relation to the building or land at the time when all of the following conditions are first met—

(*a*) the body corporate has no relevant interest in the building or land [,

(*aa*) where the body corporate has disposed of such an interest, it is not the case that a supply for the purposes of the charge to VAT in respect of the disposal—

(i) is yet to take place, or

(ii) would be yet to take place if one or more conditions (such as the happening of an event or the doing of an act) were to be met,][2]

(*b*) the body corporate or the opter is not treated under sections 43A to 43D as a member of the group mentioned above, and

(*c*) the body corporate is not connected with any person who has a relevant interest in the building or land where that person is the opter or another relevant associate of the opter.

(5) The body corporate also ceases to be a relevant associate of the opter in relation to the building or land if the body corporate—

(*a*) meets conditions specified in a public notice (see paragraph 4), or

(*b*) gets the prior permission of the Commissioners (also, see that paragraph).

The time when the body corporate ceases to be a relevant associate of the opter is determined in accordance with that paragraph.

(6) In this paragraph "relevant interest in the building or land" means an interest in, right over or licence to occupy the building or land (or any part of it).][1]

Commentary—*De Voil Indirect Tax Service* **V4.115**.

Simon's Tax Cases—Sub-para (9), *C&E Comrs v R & R Pension Fund Trustees* [1996] STC 889*; *Marlow Gardner & Cooke Ltd Directors' Pension Scheme v R&C Comrs* [2006] STC 2014*.

Amendments—[1] Schedule 10 substituted by the Value Added Tax (Buildings and Land) Order, SI 2008/1146, art 2 with effect in relation to supplies made on or after 1 June 2008, subject to savings in Sch 2 of the Order.

[2] In sub-para (4), words substituted for words "and no part of any consideration payable in respect of any disposal by the body corporate of such a interest is unpaid,", by the Value Added Tax (Buildings and Land) Order, SI 2009/1966 arts 2, 3 with effect in relation to supplies made on or after 1 August 2009.

[Permission for a body corporate to cease to be a relevant associate of the opter

4—(1) This paragraph applies for the purposes of paragraph 3(5) in relation to a body corporate which has been a relevant associate of the opter.

(2) If the conditions specified in the public notice under paragraph 3(5)(*a*) are met in relation to the body corporate, it ceases to be a relevant associate of the opter only if notification of those conditions being met is given to the Commissioners.

(3) The notification must—

(*a*) be made in a form specified in a public notice,

(*b*) state the day from which the body corporate is to cease to be a relevant associate of the opter (which may not be before the day on which the notification is given),

(*c*) contain a statement by the body corporate certifying that, on that day, the conditions specified in the public notice under paragraph 3(5)(*a*) are met in relation to it, and

(*d*) contain other information specified in a public notice.

(4) An application for the prior permission of the Commissioners must—

(*a*) be made in a form specified in a public notice,

(*b*) contain a statement by the body corporate certifying which (if any) of the conditions specified in the public notice under paragraph 3(5)(*a*) are met in relation to it, and

(*c*) contain other information specified in a public notice.

(5) If the body corporate gets the prior permission of the Commissioners, it ceases to be a relevant associate of the opter from—

(*a*) the day on which the Commissioners give their permission, or

(*b*) such earlier or later day as they specify in their permission.

(6) The Commissioners may specify an earlier day only if—

(*a*) the body corporate has purported to give a notification of its ceasing to be a relevant associate of the opter,

(*b*) the conditions specified in the public notice are not, in the event, met in relation to the body corporate, and

(*c*) the Commissioners consider that the grounds on which those conditions are not so met are insignificant.

(7) The day specified may be the day from which the body corporate would have ceased to be a relevant associate of the opter if those conditions had been so met.

(8) The Commissioners may specify conditions subject to which their permission is given and, if any of those conditions are broken, they may treat the application as if it had not been made.][1]

Simon's Tax Cases—Sub-para (9), *C&E Comrs v R & R Pension Fund Trustees* [1996] STC 889*; *Marlow Gardner & Cooke Ltd Directors' Pension Scheme v R&C Comrs* [2006] STC 2014*.

Amendments—[1] Schedule 10 substituted by the Value Added Tax (Buildings and Land) Order, SI 2008/1146, art 2 with effect in relation to supplies made on or after 1 June 2008, subject to savings in Sch 2 of the Order.

[EXCLUSIONS FROM EFFECT OF OPTION TO TAX

Dwellings designed or adapted, and intended for use, as dwelling etc

5—(1) An option to tax has no effect in relation to any grant in relation to a building or part of a building if the building or part of the building is designed or adapted, and is intended, for use—

(*a*) as a dwelling or number of dwellings, or

(*b*) solely for a relevant residential purpose.

(2) In relation to the expression "relevant residential purpose", see the certification requirement imposed as a result of the application of Note (12) of Group 5 of Schedule 8 by paragraph 33 of this Schedule.][1]

Commentary—*De Voil Indirect Tax Service* **V4.116**.

Simon's Tax Cases—*Principal and Fellows of Newnham College in the University of Cambridge v R&C Comrs* [2006] STC 1010*; *Marlow Gardner & Cooke Ltd Directors' Pension Scheme v R&C Comrs* [2006] STC 2014*.

Amendments—[1] Schedule 10 substituted by the Value Added Tax (Buildings and Land) Order, SI 2008/1146, art 2 with effect in relation to supplies made on or after 1 June 2008, subject to savings in Sch 2 of the Order.

[Conversion of buildings for use as dwelling etc

6—(1) An option to tax has no effect in relation to any grant made to a person ("the recipient") in relation to a building or part of a building if the recipient certifies that the building or part of the building is intended for use—

(*a*) as a dwelling or number of dwellings, or

(*b*) solely for a relevant residential purpose.

(2) The recipient must give the certificate to the person making the grant ("the seller")—

(*a*) within the period specified in a public notice, or

(*b*) if the seller agrees, at any later time before the seller makes a supply to which the grant gives rise.

(3) The recipient may give the certificate to the seller only if the recipient—

(*a*) intends to use the building or part of the building as mentioned above,

(*b*) has the relevant conversion intention, or

(*c*) is a relevant intermediary.

(4) The recipient is a relevant intermediary if—

(*a*) the recipient intends to dispose of the relevant interest to another person, and

(*b*) that other person gives the recipient a certificate stating that the other person has the relevant conversion intention or the relevant disposal intention.

(5) For this purpose a person has the relevant disposal intention if—

(*a*) the person intends to dispose of the relevant interest to a third person, and

(*b*) the third person gives a qualifying certificate to the person.

(6) A person (P) gives a qualifying certificate to another if P gives a certificate to that other person stating that P has the relevant conversion intention or intends to dispose of the relevant interest to another person (Q) who has given a certificate to P stating—

(*a*) that Q has the relevant conversion intention, or

(*b*) that Q intends to dispose of the relevant interest to another person who has given a qualifying certificate to Q,

and so on (in the case of further disposals of the relevant interest).

(7) In this paragraph—

"the relevant conversion intention", in relation to a person, means an intention of the person to convert the building or part of the building with a view to its being used as mentioned above, and

"the relevant interest", in relation to any interest in the building or part of the building to which the grant gives rise, means the whole of that interest.

(8) For the purposes of this paragraph a building or part of a building is not to be regarded as intended for use as a dwelling or number of dwellings at any time if there is intended to be a period before that time during which it will not be so used (but disregarding use for incidental or other minor purposes).

(9) For the purposes of this paragraph the reference to use solely for a relevant residential purpose is to be read without regard to Note (12) of Group 5 of Schedule 8 (which would otherwise apply as a result of paragraph 33 of this Schedule).

(10) The Commissioners may publish a notice for the purposes of this paragraph—

(*a*) preventing a person from giving any certificate under this paragraph unless the person meets conditions specified in the notice,

(*b*) specifying the form in which any certificate under this paragraph must be made, and

(*c*) specifying any information which any certificate under this paragraph must contain.][1]

Commentary—*De Voil Indirect Tax Service* **V4.116**.

Simon's Tax Cases—*Principal and Fellows of Newnham College in the University of Cambridge v R&C Comrs* [2006] STC 1010*; *Marlow Gardner & Cooke Ltd Directors' Pension Scheme v R&C Comrs* [2006] STC 2014*.

Amendments—[1] Schedule 10 substituted by the Value Added Tax (Buildings and Land) Order, SI 2008/1146, art 2 with effect in relation to supplies made on or after 1 June 2008, subject to savings in Sch 2 of the Order.

[Charities

7—(1) An option to tax has no effect in relation to any grant made to a person in relation to a building or part of a building intended by the person for use—

(*a*) solely for a relevant charitable purpose, but

(*b*) not as an office.

(2) In relation to the expression "relevant charitable purpose", see the certification requirement imposed as a result of the application of Note (12) of Group 5 of Schedule 8 by paragraph 33 of this Schedule.][1]

Commentary—*De Voil Indirect Tax Service* **V4.113**.

Simon's Tax Cases—*Principal and Fellows of Newnham College in the University of Cambridge v R&C Comrs* [2006] STC 1010*; *Marlow Gardner & Cooke Ltd Directors' Pension Scheme v R&C Comrs* [2006] STC 2014*.

Amendments—[1] Schedule 10 substituted by the Value Added Tax (Buildings and Land) Order, SI 2008/1146, art 2 with effect in relation to supplies made on or after 1 June 2008, subject to savings in Sch 2 of the Order.

Residential caravans

8—(1) An option to tax has no effect in relation to any grant made in relation to a pitch for a residential caravan.

(2) A caravan is not a residential caravan if residence in it throughout the year is prevented by the terms of a covenant, statutory planning consent or similar permission.][1]

Simon's Tax Cases—*Principal and Fellows of Newnham College in the University of Cambridge v R&C Comrs* [2006] STC 1010*; *Marlow Gardner & Cooke Ltd Directors' Pension Scheme v R&C Comrs* [2006] STC 2014*.

Amendments—[1] Schedule 10 substituted by the Value Added Tax (Buildings and Land) Order, SI 2008/1146, art 2 with effect in relation to supplies made on or after 1 June 2008, subject to savings in Sch 2 of the Order.

[Residential houseboats

9—(1) An option to tax has no effect in relation to any grant made in relation to facilities for the mooring of a residential houseboat.

"Mooring" includes anchoring or berthing.

(2) In this paragraph—

(*a*) "houseboat" means a houseboat within the meaning of Group 9 of Schedule 8, and

(*b*) a houseboat is not a residential houseboat if residence in it throughout the year is prevented by the terms of a covenant, statutory planning consent or similar permission.][1]

Simon's Tax Cases—*Principal and Fellows of Newnham College in the University of Cambridge v R&C Comrs* [2006] STC 1010*; *Marlow Gardner & Cooke Ltd Directors' Pension Scheme v R&C Comrs* [2006] STC 2014*.

Amendments—[1] Schedule 10 substituted by the Value Added Tax (Buildings and Land) Order, SI 2008/1146, art 2 with effect in relation to supplies made on or after 1 June 2008, subject to savings in Sch 2 of the Order.

[Relevant housing associations

10—(1) An option to tax has no effect in relation to any grant made to a relevant housing association in relation to any land if the association certifies that the land is to be used (after any necessary demolition work) for the construction of a building or buildings intended for use—

(*a*) as a dwelling or number of dwellings, or

(*b*) solely for a relevant residential purpose.

(2) The association must give the certificate to the person making the grant ("the seller")—

(*a*) within the period specified in a public notice, or

(*b*) if the seller agrees, at any later time before the seller makes a supply to which the grant gives rise.

(3) In this paragraph "relevant housing association" means—

[(*za*) a private registered provider of social housing,][2]

(*a*) a registered social landlord within the meaning of Part 1 of the Housing Act 1996 (. . . [2] Welsh registered social landlords),

[(*b*) a registered social landlord within the meaning of the Housing (Scotland) Act 2010 (asp 17) which is either—

(i) a society registered under the Co-operative and Community Benefit Societies and Credit Unions Act 1965 (c 12), or

(ii) a company within the meaning of the Companies Act 2006 (c 46), or][3]

(*c*) a registered housing association within the meaning of Part 2 of the Housing (Northern Ireland) Order 1992 (Northern Irish registered housing associations).

(4) For the purposes of this paragraph the reference to use solely for a relevant residential purpose is to be read without regard to Note (12) of Group 5 of Schedule 8 (which would otherwise apply as a result of paragraph 33 of this Schedule).

(5) The Commissioners may publish a notice for the purposes of this paragraph—

(*a*) specifying the form in which any certificate under this paragraph must be made, and

(*b*) specifying any information which any certificate under this paragraph must contain.][1]

Simon's Tax Cases—*Principal and Fellows of Newnham College in the University of Cambridge v R&C Comrs* [2006] STC 1010*; *Marlow Gardner & Cooke Ltd Directors' Pension Scheme v R&C Comrs* [2006] STC 2014*.

Amendments—[1] Schedule 10 substituted by the Value Added Tax (Buildings and Land) Order, SI 2008/1146, art 2 with effect in relation to supplies made on or after 1 June 2008, subject to savings in Sch 2 of the Order.

[2] In sub-para (3), para (*za*) inserted, and in para (*a*) words "English or" repealed, by the VAT (Buildings and Land) Order, SI 2010/485 arts 3, 4(1) with effect from 1 April 2010. Note that until the coming into force of provision defining "private registered provider of social housing" in enactments and instruments generally, that expression in para 10(3) means persons listed in the register of providers of social housing maintained under the Housing and Regeneration Act 2008 Part 2, Chapter 3 who are not local authorities within the meaning of the Housing Associations Act 1985 (SI 2010/485 art 4(2)).

[3] Sub-para (3)(*b*) substituted by the Housing (Scotland) Act 2010 (Consequential Provisions and Modifications) Order, SI 2012/700 art 4, Schedule para 5(1), (3) with effect from 1 April 2012.

[Grant to individual for construction of dwelling

11 An option to tax has no effect in relation to any grant made to an individual if—

(*a*) the land is to be used for the construction of a building intended for use by the individual as a dwelling, and

(*b*) the construction is not carried out in the course or furtherance of a business carried on by the individual.][1]

Simon's Tax Cases—*Principal and Fellows of Newnham College in the University of Cambridge v R&C Comrs* [2006] STC 1010*; *Marlow Gardner & Cooke Ltd Directors' Pension Scheme v R&C Comrs* [2006] STC 2014*.

Amendments—[1] Schedule 10 substituted by the Value Added Tax (Buildings and Land) Order, SI 2008/1146, art 2 with effect in relation to supplies made on or after 1 June 2008, subject to savings in Sch 2 of the Order.

[ANTI-AVOIDANCE

Developers of exempt land

12—(1) A supply is not, as a result of an option to tax, a taxable supply if—

(*a*) the grant giving rise to the supply was made by a person ("the grantor") who was a developer of the land, and

(*b*) the exempt land test is met.

(2) The exempt land test is met if, at the time when the grant was made (or treated for the purposes of this paragraph as made), the relevant person intended or expected that the land—

(*a*) would become exempt land (whether immediately or eventually and whether or not as a result of the grant), or

(*b*) would continue, for a period at least, to be exempt land.

(3) "The relevant person" means—

(*a*) the grantor, or

(*b*) a development financier.

(4) For the meaning of a development financier, see paragraph 14.

(5) For the meaning of "exempt land", see paragraphs 15 and 16.

(6) If a supply is made by a person other than the person who made the grant giving rise to it—

(*a*) the person making the supply is treated for the purposes of this paragraph as the person who made the grant giving rise to it, and

(*b*) the grant is treated for the purposes of this paragraph as made at the time when that person made the first supply arising from the grant.

(7) For a special rule in the case of a grant made on or after 19th March 1997 and before 10th March 1999, see paragraph 17.

(8) Nothing in this paragraph applies in relation to a supply arising from—

(*a*) a grant made before 26th November 1996, or

(*b*) a grant made on or after that date but before 30th November 1999, in pursuance of a written agreement entered into before 26th November 1996, on terms which (as terms for which provision was made by that agreement) were fixed before 26th November 1996.][1]

Commentary—*De Voil Indirect Tax Service* **V4.116.**

Amendments—[1] Schedule 10 substituted by the Value Added Tax (Buildings and Land) Order, SI 2008/1146, art 2 with effect in relation to supplies made on or after 1 June 2008, subject to savings in Sch 2 of the Order.

[Meaning of grants made by a developer

13—(1) This paragraph applies for the purposes of paragraph 12.

(2) A grant made by any person ("the grantor") in relation to any land is made by a developer of the land if—

(*a*) the land is, or was intended or expected to be, a relevant capital item (see sub-paragraphs (3) to (5)), and

(*b*) the grant is made at an eligible time as respects that capital item (see sub-paragraph (6)).

(3) The land is a relevant capital item if—

(*a*) the land, or

(*b*) the building or part of a building on the land,

is a capital item in relation to the grantor.

(4) The land was intended or expected to be a relevant capital item if the grantor, or a development financier, intended or expected that—

(*a*) the land, or

(*b*) a building or part of a building on, or to be constructed on, the land,

would become a capital item in relation to the grantor or any relevant transferee.

(5) A person is a relevant transferee if the person is someone to whom the land, building or part of a building was to be transferred—

(*a*) in the course of a supply, or

(*b*) in the course of a transfer of a business or part of a business as a going concern.

(6) A grant is made at an eligible time as respects a capital item if it is made before the end of the period provided in the relevant regulations for the making of adjustments relating to the deduction of input tax as respects the capital item.

(7) But if—

(*a*) a person other than the grantor is treated by paragraph 12(6) as making the grant of the land, and

(*b*) the grant is consequently treated as made at what would otherwise be an ineligible time,

the grant is treated instead as if were not made at an ineligible time.

(8) In this paragraph a "capital item", in relation to any person, means an asset falling, in relation to the person, to be treated as a capital item for the purposes of the relevant regulations.

(9) In this paragraph "the relevant regulations", as respects any item, means regulations under section 26(3) and (4) providing for adjustments relating to the deduction of input tax to be made as respects that item.][1]

Amendments—[1] Schedule 10 substituted by the Value Added Tax (Buildings and Land) Order, SI 2008/1146, art 2 with effect in relation to supplies made on or after 1 June 2008, subject to savings in Sch 2 of the Order.

[Meaning of "development financier"

14—(1) This paragraph explains for the purposes of paragraphs 12 to 17 what is meant, in relation to the grantor of any land, by a development financier.

(2) A "development financier" means a person who—

(*a*) has provided finance for the grantor's development of the land, or

(*b*) has entered into any arrangement to provide finance for the grantor's development of the land,

with the intention or in the expectation that the land will become exempt land or continue (for a period at least) to be exempt land.

(3) For the purposes of this paragraph references to finance being provided for the grantor's development of the land are to doing (directly or indirectly) any one or more of the following—

(*a*) providing funds for meeting the whole or any part of the cost of the grantor's development of the land,

(*b*) procuring the provision of such funds by another,

(*c*) providing funds for discharging (in whole or in part) any liability that has been or may be incurred by any person for or in connection with the raising of funds to meet the cost of the grantor's development of the land, and

(*d*) procuring that any such liability is or will be discharged (in whole or in part) by another.

(4) For the purposes of this paragraph references to providing funds for a particular purpose are to—

(*a*) the making of a loan of funds that are or are to be used for that purpose,

(*b*) the provision of any guarantee or other security in relation to such a loan,

(*c*) the provision of any of the consideration for the issue of any shares or other securities issued wholly or partly for raising those funds,

(*d*) the provision of any consideration for the acquisition by any person of any shares or other securities issued wholly or partly for raising those funds, or

(*e*) any other transfer of assets or value as a consequence of which any of those funds are made available for that purpose.

(5) For the purposes of this paragraph references to the grantor's development of the land are to the acquisition by the grantor of the asset which—

(*a*) consists in the land or a building or part of a building on the land, and

(*b*) is, or (as the case may be) was intended or expected to be, a relevant capital item in relation to the grantor (within the meaning of paragraph 13).

(6) For this purpose the reference to the acquisition of the asset includes—

(*a*) its construction or reconstruction, and

(*b*) the carrying out in relation to it of any other works by reference to which it is, or was intended or expected to be, a relevant capital item (within the meaning of paragraph 13).

(7) In this paragraph "arrangement" means any agreement, arrangement or understanding (whether or not legally enforceable).][1]

Amendments—[1] Schedule 10 substituted by the Value Added Tax (Buildings and Land) Order, SI 2008/1146, art 2 with effect in relation to supplies made on or after 1 June 2008, subject to savings in Sch 2 of the Order.

[Meaning of "exempt land": basic definition

15—(1) This paragraph explains for the purposes of paragraphs 12 to 17 what is meant by exempt land.

(2) Land is exempt land if, at any time before the end of the relevant adjustment period as respects that land—

(*a*) a relevant person is in occupation of the land, and

(*b*) that occupation is not wholly, or substantially wholly, for eligible purposes.

(3) Each of the following is a relevant person—

(*a*) the grantor,

(*b*) a person connected with the grantor,

(*c*) a development financier, and

(*d*) a person connected with a development financier.

[(3A) Where a person ("P") is in occupation of the land at any time before the end of the relevant adjustment period as respects that land, P is treated for the purposes of sub-paragraph (2) as not in occupation of the land at that time if—

(*a*) the building occupation conditions are met at that time, or

(*b*) P's occupation of the land arises solely by reference to any automatic teller machine of P.][2]

(4) The relevant adjustment period as respects any land is the period provided in the relevant regulations (within the meaning of paragraph 13) for the making of adjustments relating to the deduction of input tax as respects the land.

(5) For the purposes of this paragraph any question whether a person's occupation of any land is "wholly, or substantially wholly," for eligible purposes is to be decided by reference to criteria specified in a public notice.][1]

Commentary—*De Voil Indirect Tax Service* **V4.116**.

Amendments—[1] Schedule 10 substituted by the Value Added Tax (Buildings and Land) Order, SI 2008/1146, art 2 with effect in relation to supplies made on or after 1 June 2008, subject to savings in Sch 2 of the Order.

[2] Sub-para (3A) substituted by the VAT (Buildings and Land) Order, SI 2011/86 arts 4, 5 with effect in relation to supplies made on or after 1 March 2011 other than a supply arising from a grant made before 1 March 2011 (SI 2011/86 art 2). Sub-para (3A) was originally inserted by SI 2010/485 arts 3, 5 with effect in relation to supplies made on or after 1 April 2010 other than a supply arising from a grant made before 1 April 2010.

[Meaning of "exempt land": the building occupation conditions

15A (1) For the purposes of paragraph 15(3A), the building occupation conditions are met at any time ("the time in question") if—

(*a*) the grant consists of or includes the grant of a relevant interest in a building, and

(*b*) P does not, at the time in question, occupy—

(i) any part of the land that is not a building, or

(ii) more than [the maximum allowable percentage][2] of any relevant building.

(2) For the purposes of sub-paragraph (1)(*b*)(i) and (ii) occupation by a person connected with P is treated as occupation by P [if that occupation is not wholly, or substantially wholly, for eligible purposes][2].

(3) For the purposes of sub-paragraph (1)(*b*)(i) occupation by a person of—

(*a*) land used for the parking of cars or other vehicles, or

(*b*) land that is within the curtilage of a building,

is disregarded if the occupation is ancillary to the occupation by that person of a building.

[(4) In sub-paragraph (1)(*b*)(ii)—

"the maximum allowable percentage" means—

(*a*) 2% where P is the grantor or a person connected with the grantor, and (*b*) 10% where P is a development financier or a person connected with a development financier (but not also the grantor or a person connected with the grantor), and

"relevant building"—

(*a*) means a building any relevant interest in which is included in the grant, other than any part of such a building in which, immediately before the grant, neither the grantor nor any person connected with the grantor held a relevant interest, but

(*b*) does not include any building P's occupation of which arises solely by reference to any automatic teller machine of P.][2]

(5) The way in which occupation by a person of a building is measured for the purposes of sub-paragraph (1)(*b*)(ii) is to be determined in accordance with conditions specified in a public notice.

(6) In this paragraph "relevant interest", in relation to a building or part of a building, means any interest in, right over or licence to occupy the building or part.

[(6A) Sub-paragraph (5) of paragraph 15 (determination of whether occupation "wholly, or substantially wholly" for eligible purposes to be by reference to criteria in public notice) applies for the purposes of this paragraph.][2]

(7) Sub-paragraphs (4) to (7) of paragraph 18 (meaning of "building") apply for the purposes of this paragraph.][1]

Amendments—[1] Para 15A inserted by the VAT (Buildings and Land) Order, SI 2010/485 arts 3, 6 with effect in relation to supplies made on or after 1 April 2010 other than a supply arising from a grant made before 1 April 2010.

[2] In sub-para (1)(*b*)(ii) words substituted for figure "10%", in sub-para (2) words inserted, sub-para (4) substituted, and sub-para (6A) inserted, by the VAT (Buildings and Land) Order, SI 2011/86 arts 4, 6 with effect in relation to supplies made on or after 1 March 2011 other than a supply arising from a grant made before 1 March 2011 (SI 2011/86 art 2). Sub-para (4) previously read as follows—

"(4) In sub-paragraph (1)(*b*)(ii) "relevant building"—

means a building any relevant interest in which is included in the grant, but

does not include any part of such a building in which, immediately before the grant, neither the grantor nor any person connected with the grantor held a relevant interest.".

[Meaning of "exempt land": eligible purposes

16—(1) This paragraph explains what is meant for the purposes of paragraph 15 by a person occupying land for eligible purposes.

(2) A person cannot occupy land at any time for eligible purposes unless the person is a taxable person at that time (but this rule is qualified by sub-paragraphs (5) and (6)).

(3) A taxable person occupies land for eligible purposes so far as the occupation is for the purpose of making creditable supplies (but this rule is qualified by sub-paragraphs (5) to (7)).

(4) "Creditable supplies" means supplies which—

(*a*) are or are to be made in the course or furtherance of a business carried on by the person, and

(*b*) are supplies of such a description that the person would be entitled to a credit for any input tax wholly attributable to those supplies.

(5) Any occupation of land by a body to which section 33 applies (local authorities etc) is occupation of the land for eligible purposes so far as the occupation is for purposes other than those of a business carried on by the body.

(6) Any occupation of land by a Government department (within the meaning of section 41) is occupation of the land for eligible purposes.

(7) . . . [2]

(8) If a person occupying land—

(*a*) holds the land in order to put it to use for particular purposes, and

(*b*) does not occupy it for any other purpose,

the person is treated for the purposes of this paragraph, for so long as the conditions in paragraphs (a) and (b) continue to be met, as occupying the land for the purposes for which the person proposes to use it.

(9) If land is in the occupation of a person ("A") who—

(*a*) is not a taxable person, but

(*b*) is a person whose supplies are treated for the purposes of this Act as made by another person ("B") who is a taxable person,

the land is treated for the purposes of this paragraph as if A and B were a single taxable person.

(10) For the purposes of this paragraph a person occupies land—

(*a*) whether the person occupies it alone or together with one or more other persons, and

(*b*) whether the person occupies all of the land or only part of it.][1]

Commentary—*De Voil Indirect Tax Service* **V4.116**.

Press releases etc—HMRC Brief 33/09, 9-6-09 (HMRC's policy following the judgment in *Newnham College*).

Amendments—[1] Schedule 10 substituted by the Value Added Tax (Buildings and Land) Order, SI 2008/1146, art 2 with effect in relation to supplies made on or after 1 June 2008, subject to savings in Sch 2 of the Order.

[2] Sub-para (7) revoked by the VAT (Buildings and Land) Order, SI 2011/86 arts 4, 7 with effect in relation to supplies made on or after 1 March 2011 other than a supply arising from a grant made before 1 March 2011 (SI 2011/86 art 2). Sub-para (7) previously read as follows—

"(7) Any occupation of land by a person is occupation of the land for eligible purposes in so far as the occupation arises merely by reference to any automatic teller machine of the person which is fixed to the land.".

[Paragraph 12: grants made on or after 19th March 1997 and before 10th March 1999

17—(1) A grant in relation to land which was made—

(*a*) on or after 19th March 1997, and

(*b*) before 10th March 1999,

is treated for the purposes of paragraph 12 as made on 10th March 1999 if, at the time of the grant, the capital item test was met.

(2) The capital item test was met if the person making the grant, or a development financier, intended or expected that—

(*a*) the land, or

(*b*) a building or part of a building on, or to be constructed on, the land,

would become a capital item in relation to the grantor or any relevant transferee but it had not become such an item.

(3) For the purposes of that test "capital item" and "relevant transferee" have the meaning given by paragraph 13.][1]

Simon's Tax Cases—*Principal and Fellows of Newnham College in the University of Cambridge v R&C Comrs* [2006] STC 1010*; *Marlow Gardner & Cooke Ltd Directors' Pension Scheme v R&C Comrs* [2006] STC 2014*.

Press releases etc—HMRC Brief 33/09, 9-6-09 (HMRC's policy following the judgment in *Newnham College*).

Amendments—[1] Schedule 10 substituted by the Value Added Tax (Buildings and Land) Order, SI 2008/1146, art 2 with effect in relation to supplies made on or after 1 June 2008, subject to savings in Sch 2 of the Order.

[SCOPE OF THE OPTION, ITS DURATION, NOTIFICATION ETC

Scope of the option

18—(1) An option to tax has effect in relation to the particular land specified in the option.

(2) If an option to tax is exercised in relation to—

(*a*) a building, or

(*b*) part of a building,

the option has effect in relation to the whole of the building and all the land within its curtilage.

(3) If an option to tax—

(*a*) is exercised in relation to any land, but

(*b*) is not exercised by reference to a building or part of a building,

the option is nonetheless taken to have effect in relation to any building which is (or is to be) constructed on the land (as well as in relation to land on which no building is constructed).

(4) For the purposes of this paragraph—

(*a*) buildings linked internally or by a covered walkway, and

(*b*) complexes consisting of a number of units grouped around a fully enclosed concourse,

are treated as a single building.

(5) But for those purposes—

(*a*) buildings which are linked internally are not treated as a single building if the internal link is created after the buildings are completed, and

(*b*) buildings which are linked by a covered walkway are not treated as a single building if the walkway starts to be constructed after the buildings are completed.

(6) In this paragraph a "building" includes—

(*a*) an enlarged or extended building,

(*b*) an annexe to a building, and

(*c*) a planned building.

(7) In this paragraph "covered walkway" does not include a covered walkway to which the general public has reasonable access.][1]

Commentary—*De Voil Indirect Tax Service* **V4.116**.

Amendments—[1] Schedule 10 substituted by the Value Added Tax (Buildings and Land) Order, SI 2008/1146, art 2 with effect in relation to supplies made on or after 1 June 2008, subject to savings in Sch 2 of the Order.

[The day from which the option has effect

19—(1) An option to tax has effect from—

(*a*) the start of the day on which it is exercised, or

(*b*) the start of any later day specified in the option.

(2) But if, when an option to tax is exercised, the person exercising the option intends to revoke it in accordance with paragraph 23 (revocation of option: the "cooling off" period), the option is treated for the purposes of this Act as if it had never been exercised.
(3) An option to tax may be revoked in accordance with paragraph 22(2) or (3) and any of paragraphs 23 to 25, but not otherwise.
(4) This paragraph needs to be read with—
(*a*) paragraph 20 (requirement to notify the option), and
(*b*) paragraph 29(3) (application for prior permission in the case of an exempt grant before the exercise of an option to tax).][1]

Amendments—[1] Schedule 10 substituted by the Value Added Tax (Buildings and Land) Order, SI 2008/1146, art 2 with effect in relation to supplies made on or after 1 June 2008, subject to savings in Sch 2 of the Order.

[Requirement to notify the option

20—(1) An option to tax has effect only if—
(*a*) notification of the option is given to the Commissioners within the allowed time, and
(*b*) that notification is given together with such information as the Commissioners may require.
(2) Notification of an option is given within the allowed time if (and only if) it is given—
(*a*) before the end of the period of 30 days beginning with the day on which the option was exercised, or
(*b*) before the end of such longer period beginning with that day as the Commissioners may in any particular case allow.
(3) The Commissioners may publish a notice for the purposes of this paragraph specifying—
(*a*) the form in which a notification under this paragraph must be made, and
(*b*) the information which a notification under this paragraph must contain.
(4) Notification of an option to tax does not need to be given under this paragraph if the option is treated as exercised in accordance with paragraph 29(3).][1]

Commentary—*De Voil Indirect Tax Service* **V4.116**.
Amendments—[1] Schedule 10 substituted by the Value Added Tax (Buildings and Land) Order, SI 2008/1146, art 2 with effect in relation to supplies made on or after 1 June 2008, subject to savings in Sch 2 of the Order.

[Real estate elections: elections to opt to tax land subsequently acquired

21—(1) A person (E) may make an election (a "real estate election") for this paragraph to have effect in relation to—
(*a*) relevant interests in any building or land which E acquires after the election is made, and
(*b*) relevant interests in any building or land which a body corporate acquires after the election is made at a time when the body is a relevant group member.
(2) If E makes a real estate election—
(*a*) E is treated for the purposes of this Part of this Schedule as if E had exercised an option to tax in relation to the building or land in which the relevant interest is acquired,
(*b*) that option is treated for those purposes as if it had been exercised on the day on which the acquisition was made and as if it had effect from the start of that day, and
(*c*) paragraph 20 does not apply in relation to that option,
but this sub-paragraph is subject to sub-paragraphs (3) to (5).
(3) A person (P) is not to be treated as a result of this paragraph as exercising an option to tax in relation to any building or land where at any time—
(*a*) P, or any body corporate which was a relevant group member at that time, exercises an option to tax in relation to the building (or part of the building) or land apart from this paragraph, and
(*b*) that option has effect from a time earlier than the time from which an option to tax exercised by P in relation to the building or land would otherwise have been treated as having effect as a result of this paragraph.
(4) A person (P) is not to be treated as a result of this paragraph as exercising an option to tax in relation to any building or land in which a relevant interest is acquired ("the later interest") if—
(*a*) the person making the acquisition in question held another relevant interest in that building or land before P makes a real estate election, and
(*b*) the person making the acquisition in question continues to hold that other relevant interest at the time when the later interest is acquired.
(5) A person is not to be treated as a result of this paragraph as exercising an option to tax in relation to any building or land if—
(*a*) a relevant interest in the building or land is acquired as mentioned in sub-paragraph (1), and
(*b*) on the relevant assumptions the case would fall within paragraph 28 (pre-option exempt grants: requirement for prior permission before exercise of option to tax).
(6) The relevant assumptions are that—

(*a*) the effect of this paragraph is disregarded, and

(*b*) the day from which the person would want the option to tax to have effect for the purposes of paragraphs 28 or 29(3) is the day on which the relevant interest is acquired.

(7) A real estate election has effect only if—

(*a*) notification of the election is given to the Commissioners before the end of the period of 30 days beginning with the day on which it was made or such longer period as the Commissioners may in any particular case allow,

(*b*) the notification is made in a form specified in a public notice, and

(*c*) the notification contains information so specified.

(8) The Commissioners may at any time require a person who has made a real estate election to give to the Commissioners information specified in a public notice before the end of—

(*a*) the period of 30 days beginning with that time, or

(*b*) such longer period as the Commissioners may in any particular case allow.

(9) If a person (P) does not comply with that requirement—

(*a*) the Commissioners may revoke the election, and

(*b*) that revocation has effect in relation to relevant interests in any building or land acquired after the notified time by P or a body corporate which is a relevant group member at the time of acquisition.

"The notified time" means the time specified in a notification given by the Commissioners to P (which may not be before the notification is given).

(10) A real estate election may not be revoked except in accordance with sub-paragraph (9).

(11) If a real estate election made by a person (P) is revoked in accordance with that sub-paragraph, another real estate election may be made at any subsequent time by—

(*a*) P, or

(*b*) any body corporate which is a relevant group member at that subsequent time,

but only with the prior permission of the Commissioners.

(12) In this paragraph—

"relevant group member", in relation to any person making a real estate election and any time, means a body corporate which is treated under sections 43A to 43D as a member of the same group as that person at that time, and

"relevant interest", in relation to any building or land, means any interest in, right over or licence to occupy the building or land (or any part of it).][1]

[(13) For the purposes of this paragraph, the time at which a relevant interest in any building or land is acquired is—

(*a*) the time at which a supply is treated as taking place for the purposes of the charge to VAT in respect of the acquisition, or

(*b*) if there is more than one such time, the earliest of them.

(14) For the purposes of sub-paragraph (13)(*a*), any order under section 5(3)(*c*) that would otherwise have the effect that the acquisition in question is to be treated as neither a supply of goods nor a supply of services is to be disregarded.][2]

Amendments—[1] Schedule 10 substituted by the Value Added Tax (Buildings and Land) Order, SI 2008/1146, art 2 with effect in relation to supplies made on or after 1 June 2008, subject to savings in Sch 2 of the Order.

[2] Sub-paras (13), (14) inserted by the Value Added Tax (Buildings and Land) Order, SI 2009/1966 arts 2, 4 with effect in relation to supplies made on or after 1 August 2009.

[Real estate elections: supplementary

22—(1) This paragraph applies if, at any time ("the relevant time"), a person (*e*) makes a real estate election under paragraph 21.

(2) An option to tax exercised in relation to any building or part of any building before the relevant time by—

(*a*) E, or

(*b*) any relevant group member,

is treated for the purposes of this Part of this Schedule as if it had been revoked from the relevant time if, at that time, neither E nor any relevant group member has a relevant interest in that building.

(3) An option to tax exercised in relation to any land (otherwise than by reference to any building or part of a building) before the relevant time by—

(*a*) E, or

(*b*) any relevant group member,

is treated for the purposes of this Part of this Schedule as if it had been revoked in accordance with sub-paragraph (4) from the relevant time if, at that time, neither E nor any relevant group member has a relevant interest in that land, or E or any relevant group member has a relevant interest in only some of it.

(4) The option is treated for the purposes of this Part of this Schedule as if it had been revoked in relation to—

(*a*) that land, or

(*b*) the parts of that land in which neither E nor any relevant group member has a relevant interest at the relevant time,

as the case may be.

(5) Sub-paragraphs (2) and (3) are subject to paragraph 26 (anti-avoidance).

(6) An option to tax ("the original option") exercised in relation to any land (otherwise than by reference to any building or part of a building) before the relevant time by—

(*a*) E, or

(*b*) any relevant group member,

may, in circumstances specified in a public notice, be converted by E into separate options to tax if, at the relevant time, E or any relevant group member has a relevant interest in the land or any part of it.

(7) The original option is converted into separate options to tax different parcels of land comprised in that land or part.

(8) Those separate options to tax are treated for the purposes of this Part of this Schedule—

(*a*) as if they had been exercised by E, and

(*b*) as if they had effect from the time from which the original option had effect.

(9) But—

(*a*) those separate options to tax are treated for the purposes of paragraph 3(2) as if they had effect from the relevant time, and

(*b*) paragraph 23 (revocation of an option: the "cooling off" period) does not apply to those separate options to tax.

(10) The notification of the election given by E must identify—

(*a*) the separate options to tax treated as exercised by E as a result of sub-paragraphs (6) to (8), and

(*b*) the different parcels of land in relation to which those separate options to tax are treated as having effect.

(11) In this paragraph—

(*a*) any reference to any relevant group member is to a body corporate which is a relevant group member at the relevant time, and

(*b*) any reference to any relevant group member, in relation to any relevant interest in any building or land (or any part of it), is to any relevant group member regardless of whether it has exercised an option to tax the building or land (or any part of it).

(12) In this paragraph "relevant group member" and "relevant interest", have the meaning given by paragraph 21.

(13) In this paragraph any reference to a real estate election under paragraph 21 does not include an election which is made under sub-paragraph (11) of that paragraph.][1]

Amendments—[1] Schedule 10 substituted by the Value Added Tax (Buildings and Land) Order, SI 2008/1146, art 2 with effect in relation to supplies made on or after 1 June 2008, subject to savings in Sch 2 of the Order.

[Revocation of option: the "cooling off" period

23—(1) An option to tax any land exercised by any person ("the taxpayer") may be revoked with effect from the day on which it was exercised if—

(*a*) the time that has lapsed since the day on which the option had effect is less than 6 months,

(*b*) *the taxpayer has not used the land since the option had effect,*[2]

(*c*) no tax has become chargeable as a result of the option,

(*d*) there is no relevant transfer of a business as a going concern (see sub-paragraph (2)), and

(*e*) notification of the revocation is given to the Commissioners (see sub-paragraph (3)).

(2) There is no relevant transfer of a business as a going concern if, since the option had effect, no grant in relation to the land has been made which is treated as neither a supply of goods nor a supply of services because—

(*a*) the supply is a supply of the assets of a business by the taxpayer to a person to whom the business (or part of it) is transferred as a going concern, or

(*b*) the supply is a supply of assets of a business by a person to the taxpayer to whom the business (or part of it) is so transferred.

(3) The notification of the revocation must—

(*a*) be made in a form specified in a public notice, and

(*b*) contain information so specified.

(4) The Commissioners may publish a notice for the purposes of this paragraph providing that a revocation under this paragraph is effective only if—

(*a*) the conditions specified in the notice are met in relation to the option, or (*b*) the taxpayer gets the prior permission of the Commissioners on an application made to them before the end of the 6 month period mentioned above.

(5) A notice under sub-paragraph (4) may—

(*a*) provide that, in a case falling with paragraph (*a*) of that sub-paragraph, the taxpayer must certify that the conditions specified under that paragraph are met in relation to the option,

(*b*) specify the form in which an application under paragraph (*b*) of that sub-paragraph must be made,

(*c*) provide that an application under that paragraph must contain a statement by the taxpayer certifying which (if any) of the conditions specified under sub-paragraph (4)(*a*) are met in relation to the option,

(*d*) specify other information which an application under sub-paragraph (4)(*a*) must contain, and

(*e*) provide that the Commissioners may specify conditions subject to which their permission is given and, if any of those conditions are broken, the Commissioners may treat the revocation as if it had not been made.][1]

Amendments—[1] Schedule 10 substituted by the Value Added Tax (Buildings and Land) Order, SI 2008/1146, art 2 with effect in relation to supplies made on or after 1 June 2008, subject to savings in Sch 2 of the Order.

[2] Sub-para (1)(*b*) repealed by the VAT (Buildings and Land) Order, SI 2010/485 arts 3, 7 with effect from 1 April 2010.

[Revocation of option: lapse of 6 years since having a relevant interest

24—(1) An option to tax exercised by any person in relation to any building or land is treated for the purposes of this Part of this Schedule as revoked if the person does not have a relevant interest in the building or land throughout any continuous period of 6 years beginning at any time after the option has effect.

(2) The option to tax is treated for the purposes of this Part of this Schedule as revoked from the end of that period.

(3) In this paragraph "a relevant interest in the building or land" means an interest in, right over or licence to occupy the building or land (or any part of it).

(4) This paragraph is subject to paragraph 26 (anti-avoidance).][1]

Amendments—[1] Schedule 10 substituted by the Value Added Tax (Buildings and Land) Order, SI 2008/1146, art 2 with effect in relation to supplies made on or after 1 June 2008, subject to savings in Sch 2 of the Order.

[Revocation of option: lapse of more than 20 years since option had effect

25—(1) An option to tax any land exercised by any person ("the taxpayer") may be revoked if the time that has lapsed since the day on which the option had effect is more than 20 years and—

(*a*) at the time when the option is to be revoked the conditions specified in a public notice are met in relation to the option (in which case, see sub-paragraphs (2) to (4)), or

(*b*) the taxpayer gets the prior permission of the Commissioners (in which case, see the remaining sub-paragraphs).

(2) If the conditions specified in the public notice are met in relation to the option, the revocation has effect only if notification of the revocation is given to the Commissioners.

(3) The notification must—

(*a*) be made in the specified form,

(*b*) state the day from which the option is to be revoked (which may not be before the day on which the notification is given),

(*c*) contain a statement by the taxpayer certifying that, on that day, the conditions specified in the public notice are met in relation to the option, and

(*d*) contain other information specified in a public notice.

(4) If—

(*a*) notification of the revocation of an option is given to the Commissioners on the basis that the conditions specified in the public notice were met in relation to the option, but

(*b*) it is subsequently discovered that those conditions were not met in relation to the option,

the Commissioners may nonetheless treat the option as if it had been validly revoked in accordance with this paragraph.

(5) An application for the prior permission of the Commissioners must—

(*a*) be made in a form specified in a public notice,

(*b*) contain a statement by the taxpayer certifying which (if any) of the conditions specified in the public notice under sub-paragraph (1)(*a*) are met in relation to the option, and

(*c*) contain other information specified in a public notice.

(6) If the taxpayer gets the prior permission of the Commissioners for the revocation of an option, the option is revoked from—

(*a*) the day on which the Commissioners give their permission, or

(*b*) such earlier or later day [or time as they may][2] specify in their permission.

(7) The Commissioners may specify an earlier day [or time][2] only if—

(*a*) the taxpayer has purported to give a notification of the revocation of the option,

(*b*) the conditions specified in the public notice are not, in the event, met in relation to the option, and

(*c*) the Commissioners consider that the grounds on which those conditions are not so met are insignificant.

[(8) The Commissioners may specify a day or time under sub-paragraph (6)(*b*) by reference to the happening of an event or the meeting of a condition.][2]

(9) The Commissioners may specify conditions subject to which their permission is given and, if any of those conditions are broken, they may treat the revocation as if it had not been made.][1]

Amendments—[1] Schedule 10 substituted by the Value Added Tax (Buildings and Land) Order, SI 2008/1146, art 2 with effect in relation to supplies made on or after 1 June 2008, subject to savings in Sch 2 of the Order.

[2] In sub-para (6)(b), words substituted for words "as they", in sub-para (7), words inserted, and sub-para (8) substituted, by the Value Added Tax (Buildings and Land) Order, SI 2009/1966 arts 2, 4 with effect in relation to supplies made on or after 1 August 2009.

[26—(1) Sub-paragraphs (2) and (3) of paragraph 22 (revocation of option to tax where a real estate election is made) do not apply if condition A or B is met.

(2) Paragraph 24 (lapse of option to tax) does not apply if condition A, B or C is met.

(3) Condition A is that—

(*a*) the opter, or a relevant associate of the opter, disposes of a relevant interest in the building or land before the relevant time, and

(*b*) at the relevant time, a supply for the purposes of the charge to VAT in respect of the disposal—

(i) is yet to take place, or

(ii) would be yet to take place if one or more conditions (such as the happening of an event or the doing of an act) were to be met.

(4) Condition B is that—

(*a*) the opter is a body corporate that was, at any time before the relevant time, treated under sections 43A to 43D as a member of a group ("the group"), and

(*b*) before the relevant time, a relevant associate of the opter in relation to the building or land ceased to be treated under those sections as a member of the group without at the same time meeting the conditions in sub-paragraph (5).

(5) A person ("A") meets the conditions in this sub-paragraph if—

(*a*) A has no relevant interest in the building or land,

(*b*) where A has disposed of such an interest, it is not the case that a supply for the purposes of the charge to VAT in respect of the disposal—

(i) is yet to take place, or

(ii) would be yet to take place if one or more conditions (such as the happening of an event or the doing of an act) were to be met, and

(*c*) A is not connected with any person who has a relevant interest in the building or land where that person is the opter or another relevant associate of the opter.

(6) Condition C is that the opter is a body corporate and, at the relevant time, a relevant associate of the opter in relation to the building or land—

(*a*) is treated under sections 43A to 43D as a member of the same group as the opter, and

(*b*) holds a relevant interest in the building or land or has held such an interest at any time within the previous 6 years.

(7) In this paragraph—

"relevant interest in the building or land" means an interest in, right over or license to occupy the building or land (or any part of it);

"the relevant time", in relation to any option to tax, means the time from which the option would (but for this paragraph) have been treated as revoked as a result of paragraph 22(2) or (3) or 24;

"opter" means the person who exercised the option to tax in question.][1]

Amendments—[1] This para substituted, by the Value Added Tax (Buildings and Land) Order, SI 2009/1966 arts 2, 6 with effect in relation to supplies made on or after 1 August 2009.

[Exclusion of new building from effect of an option

27—(1) This paragraph applies if—

(*a*) a person ("the taxpayer") has at any time opted to tax any land,

(*b*) at any subsequent time the construction of a building ("the new building") on the land begins, and

(*c*) no land within the curtilage of the new building is within the curtilage of an existing building.

(2) The taxpayer may exclude—

(*a*) the whole of the new building, and

(*b*) all the land within its curtilage,
from the effect of the option if notification of that exclusion is given to the Commissioners.
(3) The exclusion has effect from the earliest of the following times—
(*a*) the time when a grant of an interest in, or in any part of, the new building is first made,
(*b*) the time when the new building, or any part of it, is first used,
(*c*) the time when the new building is completed.
(4) The notification of the exclusion must—
[(*za*) be given before the end of the period of 30 days beginning with the day on which it is to have effect or such longer period as the Commissioners may in any case allow,][2]
(*a*) be made in a form specified in a public notice,
[(*b*) state the time from which it is to have effect, and][2]
(*c*) contain other information so specified.
(5) Sub-paragraphs (4) to (6) of paragraph 18 (meaning of "building") apply for the purposes of this paragraph as they apply for the purposes of that paragraph.
(6) For the purposes of this paragraph the reference to the construction of a building is to be read without regard to Note (17) or (18)(*b*) of Group 5 of Schedule 8 (which would otherwise apply as a result of paragraph 33 of this Schedule).
(7) The Commissioners may publish a notice for determining the time at which the construction of a building on any land is to be taken to begin for the purposes of this paragraph.][1]

Amendments—[1] Schedule 10 substituted by the Value Added Tax (Buildings and Land) Order, SI 2008/1146, art 2 with effect in relation to supplies made on or after 1 June 2008, subject to savings in Sch 2 of the Order.
[2] In sub-para (4), para (za) inserted and para (b) substituted, by the Value Added Tax (Buildings and Land) Order, SI 2009/1966 arts 2, 7 with effect in relation to supplies made on or after 1 August 2009.

[Pre-option exempt grants: requirement for prior permission before exercise of option to tax

28—(1) This paragraph applies if—
(*a*) a person wants to exercise an option to tax any land with effect from a particular day,
(*b*) at any time ("the relevant time") before that day the person has made, makes or intends to make an exempt supply to which any grant in relation to the land gives rise, and
(*c*) the relevant time is within the period of 10 years ending with that day.
(2) The person may exercise the option to tax the land only if—
(*a*) the conditions specified in a public notice are met in relation to the land, or
(*b*) the person gets the prior permission of the Commissioners (but see also paragraph 30).
(3) The Commissioners must refuse their permission if they are not satisfied that there would be a fair and reasonable attribution of relevant input tax to relevant supplies.
(4) For this purpose—
"relevant input tax" means input tax incurred, or likely to be incurred, in relation to the land, and
"relevant supplies" means supplies to which any grant in relation to the land gives rise which would be taxable (if the option has effect).
(5) In deciding whether there would be a fair and reasonable attribution of relevant input tax to relevant supplies, the Commissioners must have regard to all the circumstances of the case.
(6) But they must have regard in particular to—
(*a*) the total value of any exempt supply to which any grant in relation to the land gives rise and which is made or to be made before the day from which the person wants the option to have effect,
(*b*) the expected total value of any supply to which any grant in relation to the land gives rise that would be taxable (if the option has effect), and
(*c*) the total amount of input tax incurred, or likely to be incurred, in relation to the land.][1]

Amendments—[1] Schedule 10 substituted by the Value Added Tax (Buildings and Land) Order, SI 2008/1146, art 2 with effect in relation to supplies made on or after 1 June 2008, subject to savings in Sch 2 of the Order.

[Paragraph 28: application for prior permission

29—(1) An application for the prior permission of the Commissioners under paragraph 28 must—
(*a*) be made in a form specified in a public notice,
(*b*) contain a statement by the applicant certifying which (if any) of the conditions specified in the public notice under paragraph 28(2)(*a*) are met in relation to the land, and
(*c*) contain other information specified in a public notice.
(2) The Commissioners may specify conditions subject to which their permission is given and, if any of those conditions are broken, they may treat the application as if it had not been made.
(3) If the applicant (*a*) gets the prior permission of the Commissioners, A is, as a result of this sub-paragraph, treated for the purposes of this Part of this Schedule as if A had exercised the option to tax the land with effect from—
(*a*) the start of the day on which the application was made, or

(*b*) the start of any later day specified in the application.][1]

Amendments—[1] Schedule 10 substituted by the Value Added Tax (Buildings and Land) Order, SI 2008/1146, art 2 with effect in relation to supplies made on or after 1 June 2008, subject to savings in Sch 2 of the Order.

[Paragraph 28: purported exercise where prior permission not obtained

30—(1) This paragraph applies if—

(*a*) an option to tax was purportedly exercised in a case where, before the option could be exercised, the prior permission of the Commissioners was required under paragraph 28, and

(*b*) notification of the purported option was purportedly given to the Commissioners in accordance with paragraph 20.

(2) The Commissioners may, in the case of any such option, subsequently dispense with the requirement for their prior permission to be given under paragraph 28.

(3) If the Commissioners dispense with that requirement, a purported option—

(*a*) is treated for the purposes of this Part of this Schedule as if it had instead been validly exercised, and

(*b*) has effect in accordance with paragraph 19.][1]

Amendments—[1] Schedule 10 substituted by the Value Added Tax (Buildings and Land) Order, SI 2008/1146, art 2 with effect in relation to supplies made on or after 1 June 2008, subject to savings in Sch 2 of the Order.

[SUPPLEMENTARY PROVISIONS

Timing of grant and supplies

31—(1) This paragraph applies if—

(*a*) an option to tax is exercised in relation to any land,

(*b*) a grant in relation to the land would otherwise be taken to have been made (whether in whole or in part) before the time when the option has effect, and

(*c*) the grant gives rise to supplies which are treated for the purposes of this Act as taking place after that time.

(2) For the purposes of this Part of this Schedule, the option to tax has effect, in relation to those supplies, as if the grant had been made after that time.][1]

Amendments—[1] Schedule 10 substituted by the Value Added Tax (Buildings and Land) Order, SI 2008/1146, art 2 with effect in relation to supplies made on or after 1 June 2008, subject to savings in Sch 2 of the Order.

[Supplies in relation to a building where part designed or intended for residential or charitable use and part designed or intended for other uses

32 Note (10) of Group 5 of Schedule 8 applies for the purposes of this Part of this Schedule.][1]

Amendments—[1] Schedule 10 substituted by the Value Added Tax (Buildings and Land) Order, SI 2008/1146, art 2 with effect in relation to supplies made on or after 1 June 2008, subject to savings in Sch 2 of the Order.

[Definitions in Schedules 8 or 9 that are applied for the purposes of this Schedule

33 In this Part of this Schedule, references to the expressions listed in the first column are to be read in accordance with the provisions listed in the second column—

Expression	*Provision*
building designed or adapted for use as a dwelling or a number of dwellings	Note (2) to Group 5 of Schedule 8
completion of a building	Note (2) to Group 1 of Schedule 9
Construction of a building	Notes (16) to (18) to Group 5 of Schedule 8 (but see paragraph 27(6) of this Schedule)
Construction of a building intended for use as a dwelling or a number of dwellings	Note (3) to Group 5 of Schedule 8
Grant	Note (1) to Group 5 of Schedule 8/ Notes (1) and (1A) to Group 1 of Schedule 9
use for a relevant charitable purpose	Notes (6) and (12) to Group 5 of Schedule 8
use for a relevant residential purpose	Notes (4), (5) and (12) to Group 5 of Schedule 8 (but see paragraphs 6(9) and 10(4) of this Schedule)][1]

Amendments—

[1] Schedule 10 substituted by the Value Added Tax (Buildings and Land) Order, SI 2008/1146, art 2 with effect in relation to supplies made on or after 1 June 2008, subject to savings in Sch 2 of the Order.

[Other definitions etc

34—(1) In this Part of this Schedule—

"notification" means written notification, and

"permission" means written permission.

(2) For the purposes of this Part of this Schedule any question whether a person is connected with another person is to be decided in accordance with [section 1122 of the Corporation Tax Act 2010][3][; but this is subject to sub-paragraph (2A)][2].

[(2A) For the purposes of this Part of this Schedule, a company is not connected with another company only because both are under the control of—

(*a*) the Crown,

(*b*) a Minister of the Crown,

(*c*) a government department, or

(*d*) a Northern Ireland department.

(2B) In sub-paragraph (2A) "company" and "control" have the same meaning as in section 839 of the Taxes Act.][2]

(3) Any reference in any provision of this Part of this Schedule to a public notice is to a notice published by the Commissioners for the purposes of that provision.][1]

Amendments—[1] Schedule 10 substituted by the Value Added Tax (Buildings and Land) Order, SI 2008/1146, art 2 with effect in relation to supplies made on or after 1 June 2008, subject to savings in Sch 2 of the Order.

[2] In sub-para (2), words inserted and sub-paras (2A), (2B) inserted, by the Value Added Tax (Buildings and Land) Order, SI 2009/1966 arts 2, 8 with effect in relation to supplies made on or after 1 August 2009.

[3] In sub-para (2) words substituted for words "section 839 of the Taxes Act 1988" by CTA 2010 s 1177, Sch 1 para 285(f). CTA 2010 has effect for corporation tax purposes for accounting periods ending on or after 1 April 2010, and for income and capital gains tax purposes for the tax year 2010–11 and subsequent tax years. Note that the reference to TA 1988 s 839 in sub-para (2B) is not expressly substituted by CTA 2010.

[PART 2

RESIDENTIAL AND CHARITABLE BUILDINGS: CHANGE OF USE ETC

[Introductory

35—(1) This Part of this Schedule applies where one or more relevant zero-rated supplies relating to a building (or part of a building) have been made to a person ("P").

(2) In this Part of this Schedule—

"relevant zero-rated supply" means a grant or other supply which relates to a building (or part of a building) intended for use solely for—

(*a*) a relevant residential purpose, or

(*b*) a relevant charitable purpose,

and which, as a result of Group 5 of Schedule 8, is zero-rated (in whole or in part);

"relevant premises" means the building (or part of a building) in relation to which a relevant zero-rated supply has been made to P;

"relevant period", in relation to relevant premises, means 10 years beginning with the day on which the relevant premises are completed.

(3) Where P is a body corporate treated as a member of a group under sections 43A to 43D, any reference in this Part of this Schedule to P includes a reference to any member of that group.][1]

Commentary—*De Voil Indirect Tax Service* **V3.248, V4.113**.

Amendments—[1] Paras 35–37 substituted by the VAT (Buildings and Land) Order, SI 2011/86 arts 4, 8 with effect in relation to buildings that are completed on or after 1 March 2011.

[Disposal of interest or change of use following relevant zero-rated supply

36—(1) Paragraph 37 applies on each occasion during the relevant period when—

(*a*) there is an increase in the proportion of the relevant premises falling within sub-paragraph (2) or (3), and

(*b*) as a result, the proportion of the relevant premises so falling ("R2") exceeds the maximum proportion of those premises so falling at any earlier time in the relevant period ("R1").

(2) The relevant premises fall (or part of the relevant premises falls) within this sub-paragraph if P has, since the beginning of the relevant period, disposed of P's entire interest in the relevant premises (or part).

(3) The relevant premises fall (or a part of the relevant premises falls) within this sub-paragraph if—

(*a*) those premises do not (or that part does not) fall within sub-paragraph (2), and

(*b*) those premises are (or that part is) being used for a purpose that is neither a relevant residential purpose nor a relevant charitable purpose.

(4) Sub-paragraph (5) applies where—

(*a*) only a proportion of the use of the relevant premises (or the use of a part of those premises) is for a relevant residential purpose or a relevant charitable purpose, and

(*b*) that use is not confined to a part of those premises (or of that part) which is used solely for a relevant residential purpose or a relevant charitable purpose.

(5) Where this sub-paragraph applies, sub-paragraph (3) applies as if—

(*a*) the same proportion of the relevant premises (or part) were being used for a relevant residential purpose or a relevant charitable purpose, and

(*b*) the remainder of the relevant premises (or part) were being used for a purpose that is neither a relevant residential purpose nor a relevant charitable purpose.

(6) Where P is a charity using the relevant premises (or a part of the relevant premises) as a village hall or similarly in providing social or recreational facilities for a local community the premises are (or the part is) treated as being used for a relevant charitable purpose whether or not any person in occupation is using the premises (or part) for a relevant charitable purpose.][1]

Commentary—*De Voil Indirect Tax Service* **V3.248, V4.113**.

Amendments—[1] Paras 35–37 substituted by the VAT (Buildings and Land) Order, SI 2011/86 arts 4, 8 with effect in relation to buildings that are completed on or after 1 March 2011.

[Charge to VAT

37—(1) Where this paragraph applies, P's interest, right or licence in the relevant premises held immediately prior to the time when the increase referred to in paragraph 36(1) occurs is treated for the purposes of this Part of this Schedule as—

(*a*) supplied to P for the purposes of a business which P carries on, and

(*b*) supplied by P in the course or furtherance of that business

immediately prior to the time of that increase.

(2) The supply is taken to be a taxable supply which is not zero-rated as a result of Group 5 of Schedule 8.

(3) The value of the supply is taken to be—

(*a*) in the case of the first deemed supply under this paragraph, the amount obtained by the formula—

$R2 \times Y \times ((120 - Z) / 120)$, and

(*b*) in the case of any subsequent deemed supply under this paragraph, the amount obtained by the formula—

$(R2 - R1) \times Y \times ((120 - Z) / 120)$

(4) For the purpose of sub-paragraph (3)—

(*a*) R1 and R2 have the meaning given by paragraph 36(1)(*b*),

(*b*) Y is the amount that yields an amount of VAT chargeable on it equal to—

(i) the VAT which would have been chargeable on the relevant zero-rated supply, or

(ii) if there was more than one supply, the aggregate amount of the VAT which would have been chargeable on the supplies,

had the relevant premises not been intended for use solely for a relevant residential purpose or a relevant charitable purpose, and

(*c*) Z is the number of whole months since the day on which the relevant premises were completed.][1]

Commentary—*De Voil Indirect Tax Service* **V3.248**.

Amendments—[1] Paras 35–37 substituted by the VAT (Buildings and Land) Order, SI 2011/86 arts 4, 8 with effect in relation to buildings that are completed on or after 1 March 2011.

[Supplies in relation to a building where part designed for residential or charitable use and part designed for other uses

38 Note (10) of Group 5 of Schedule 8 applies for the purposes of this Part of this Schedule.][1]

Amendments—[1] Schedule 10 substituted by the Value Added Tax (Buildings and Land) Order, SI 2008/1146, art 2 with effect in relation to supplies made on or after 1 June 2008, subject to savings in Sch 2 of the Order.

[Definitions

39 In this Part of this Schedule, references to the expressions listed in the first column are to be read in accordance with the provisions listed in the second column—

Expression	*Provision*
completion of a building	Note (2) to Group 1 of Schedule 9
Grant	Note (1) to Group 5 of Schedule 8/ Notes (1) and (1A) to Group 1 of Schedule 9
use for a relevant charitable purpose	Notes (6) and (12) to Group 5 of Schedule 8

Expression	Provision
use for a relevant residential purpose	Notes (4), (5) and (12) to Group 5 of Schedule 8][1]

Amendments—

[1] Schedule 10 substituted by the Value Added Tax (Buildings and Land) Order, SI 2008/1146, art 2 with effect in relation to supplies made on or after 1 June 2008, subject to savings in Sch 2 of the Order.

[PART 3
GENERAL

Benefit of consideration for grant accruing to a person other than the grantor

40—(1) This paragraph applies if the benefit of the consideration for the grant of an interest in, right over or licence to occupy land accrues to a person ("the beneficiary") other than the person making the grant.
(2) The beneficiary is to be treated for the purposes of this Act as the person making the grant.
(3) So far as any input tax of the person actually making the grant is attributable to the grant, it is to be treated for the purposes of this Act as input tax of the beneficiary.][1]

Amendments—[1] Schedule 10 substituted by the Value Added Tax (Buildings and Land) Order, SI 2008/1146, art 2 with effect in relation to supplies made on or after 1 June 2008, subject to savings in Sch 2 of the Order.

[SCHEDULE 10A

FACE-VALUE VOUCHERS]

Section 51B

Amendments—This Schedule inserted by FA 2003 s 19, Sch 1 para 2 with effect for supplies of tokens, stamps or vouchers issued after 8 April 2003.

Meaning of "face-value voucher" etc

[1—(1) In this Schedule "face-value voucher" means a token, stamp or voucher (whether in physical or electronic form) that represents a right to receive goods or services to the value of an amount stated on it or recorded in it.
(2) References in this Schedule to the "face value" of a voucher are to the amount referred to in sub-paragraph (1) above.][1]

Simon's Tax Cases—*Leisure Pass Group Ltd v R&C Comrs* [2008] STC 3340.

Amendments—[1] Schedule inserted by FA 2003 Sch 1 para 2 in relation to supplies of tokens, stamps or vouchers issued after 8 April 2003.

Nature of supply

[2 The issue of a face-value voucher, or any subsequent supply of it, is a supply of services for the purposes of this Act.][1]

[1] Schedule inserted by FA 2003 Sch 1 para 2 in relation to supplies of tokens, stamps or vouchers issued after 8 April 2003.

Treatment of credit vouchers

[3—(1) This paragraph applies to a face-value voucher issued by a person who—
(*a*) is not a person from whom goods or services may be obtained by the use of the voucher, and
(*b*) undertakes to give complete or partial reimbursement to any such person from whom goods or services are so obtained.

Such a voucher is referred to in this Schedule as a "credit voucher".
(2) The consideration for any supply of a credit voucher shall be disregarded for the purposes of this Act except to the extent (if any) that it exceeds the face value of the voucher.
(3) Sub-paragraph (2) above does not apply if any of the persons from whom goods or services are obtained by the use of the voucher fails to account for any of the VAT due on the supply of those goods or services to the person using the voucher to obtain them.][1]
[(4) The Treasury may by order specify other circumstances in which sub-paragraph (2) above does not apply.][2]

Simon's Tax Cases—para 3, *R (on the application of IDT Card Services Ireland Ltd) v Customs and Excise Commissioners* [2005] STC 314; *R&C Comrs v IDT Card Service Ireland Ltd* [2006] STC 1252.

Amendments—[1] Schedule inserted by FA 2003 Sch 1 para 2 in relation to supplies of tokens, stamps or vouchers issued after 8 April 2003.
[2] Sub-para (4) inserted by FA 2006 s 22(3) with effect from 19 July 2006.

Treatment of retailer vouchers

[4—(1) This paragraph applies to a face-value voucher issued by a person who—

(*a*) is a person from whom goods or services may be obtained by the use of the voucher, and

(*b*) if there are other such persons, undertakes to give complete or partial reimbursement to those from whom goods or services are so obtained.

Such a voucher is referred to in this Schedule as a "retailer voucher".

(2) The consideration for the issue of a retailer voucher shall be disregarded for the purposes of this Act except to the extent (if any) that it exceeds the face value of the voucher.

(3) Sub-paragraph (2) above does not apply if—

(*a*) the voucher is used to obtain goods or services from a person other than the issuer, and

(*b*) that person fails to account for any of the VAT due on the supply of those goods or services to the person using the voucher to obtain them.

(4) Any supply of a retailer voucher subsequent to the issue of it shall be treated in the same way as the supply of a voucher to which paragraph 6 applies.][1]

Amendments—[1] Schedule inserted by FA 2003 Sch 1 para 2 in relation to supplies of tokens, stamps or vouchers issued after 8 April 2003.

Treatment of postage stamps

[**5**—The consideration for the supply of a face-value voucher that is a postage stamp shall be disregarded for the purposes of this Act except to the extent (if any) that it exceeds the face value of the stamp.][1]

Amendments—[1] Schedule inserted by FA 2003 Sch 1 para 2 in relation to supplies of tokens, stamps or vouchers issued after 8 April 2003.

Treatment of other kinds of face-value voucher

[**6**—(1) This paragraph applies to a face-value voucher that is not a credit voucher, a retailer voucher or a postage stamp.

(2) A supply of such a voucher is chargeable at the rate in force under section 2(1) (standard rate) except where sub-paragraph (3), (4) or (5) below applies.

(3) Where the voucher is one that can only be used to obtain goods or services in one particular non-standard rate category, the supply of the voucher falls in that category.

(4) Where the voucher is used to obtain goods or services all of which fall in one particular non-standard rate category, the supply of the voucher falls in that category.

(5) Where the voucher is used to obtain goods or services in a number of different rate categories—

(*a*) the supply of the voucher shall be treated as that many different supplies, each falling in the category in question, and

(*b*) the value of each of those supplies shall be determined on a just and reasonable basis.][1]

Amendments—[1] Schedule inserted by FA 2003 Sch 1 para 2 in relation to supplies of tokens, stamps or vouchers issued after 8 April 2003.

Vouchers supplied free with other goods or services

[**7** Where—

(*a*) a face-value voucher (other than a postage stamp) and other goods or services are supplied to the same person in a composite transaction, and

(*b*) the total consideration for the supplies is no different, or not significantly different, from what it would be if the voucher were not supplied, the supply of the voucher shall be treated as being made for no consideration.][1]

Amendments—[1] Schedule inserted by FA 2003 Sch 1 para 2 in relation to supplies of tokens, stamps or vouchers issued after 8 April 2003.

[Exclusion of single purpose vouchers

7A Paragraphs 2 to 4, 6 and 7 do not apply in relation to the issue, or any subsequent supply, of a face-value voucher that represents a right to receive goods or services of one type which are subject to a single rate of VAT.][1]

Amendments—[1] This para inserted by FA 2012 s 201 with effect in relation to supplies of face-value vouchers issued on or after 10 May 2012, subject to provisions relating to vouchers issued before 10 May 2012 and used after that date: see FA 2012 s 201(3), (4).

Interpretation

[**8**— (1) In this Schedule—

"credit voucher" has the meaning given by paragraph 3(1) above;

"face value" has the meaning given by paragraph 1(2) above;

"face value voucher" has the meaning given by paragraph 1(1) above;

"retailer voucher" has the meaning given by paragraph 4(1) above.

(2) For the purposes of this Schedule—

(*a*) the "rate categories" of supplies are—

(i) supplies chargeable at the rate in force under section 2(1) (standard rate),

(ii) supplies chargeable at the rate in force under section 29A (reduced rate),

(iii) zero-rated supplies, and

(iv) exempt supplies and other supplies that are not taxable supplies;

(*b*) the "non-standard rate categories" of supplies are those in sub-paragraphs (ii), (iii) and (iv) of paragraph (*a*) above;

(*c*) goods or services are in a particular rate category if a supply of those goods or services falls in that category.

(3) A reference in this Schedule to a voucher being used to obtain goods or services includes a reference to the case where it is used as part-payment for those goods or services.][1]

Amendments—[1] Schedule inserted by FA 2003 Sch 1 para 2 in relation to supplies of tokens, stamps or vouchers issued after 8 April 2003.

SCHEDULE 11

ADMINISTRATION, COLLECTION AND ENFORCEMENT

Section 58

Cross reference—See VATA 1994 s 92(6), (7) (exercise of certain information powers under this Schedule in relation to matters relevant to a charge to VAT under the law of another member state).

See FA 2008 s 127 (Enforcement by taking control of goods: England and Wales).

See FA 2008 s 128 (Summary warrant: Scotland).

General

[1—The Commissioners for Her Majesty's Revenue and Customs shall be responsible for the collection and management of VAT.][1]

Definitions—"The Commissioners", s 96(1); "VAT", ss 1, 96(1).

Amendments—[1] Para substituted by the Commissioners for Revenue and Customs Act 2005 s 50, Sch 4 para 56 with effect from 18 April 2005 by virtue of the Commissioners for Revenue and Customs Act 2005 (Commencement) Order, SI 2005/1126, art 2(2).

Accounting for VAT . . . and payment of VAT

2—(1) Regulations under this paragraph may require the keeping of accounts and the making of returns in such form and manner as may be specified in the regulations . . . [2] [or by the Commissioners in accordance with the regulations.][8]

(2), (2A) . . . [2]

(3) Regulations under this paragraph may require the submission to the Commissioners by taxable persons, at such times and intervals, in such cases and in such form and manner as may be—

(*a*) specified in the regulations; or

[(*b*) specified by the Commissioners in accordance with the regulations,][8]

of statements containing such particulars of transactions in which the taxable persons are concerned and [to which this sub-paragraph applies][5], and of the persons concerned in those transactions, as may be [so specified][8].

[(3ZA) Sub-paragraph (3) above applies to—

(*a*) transactions involving the movement of goods between member States, and

(*b*) transactions involving the supply of services to a person in a member State other than the United Kingdom who is required to pay VAT on the supply in accordance with provisions of the law of that other member State giving effect to Article 196 of Council Directive 2006/112/EC.][5]

[(3A) Regulations under this paragraph may require the submission to the Commissioners by taxable persons, at such times and intervals, in such cases and in such form and manner as may be—

(*a*) specified in the regulations, or

(*b*) determined by the Commissioners in accordance with powers conferred by the regulations,

of statements containing such particulars of supplies to which section 55A(6) applies in which the taxable persons are concerned, and of the persons concerned in those supplies, as may be [so specified][8].

[(3B) Regulations under this paragraph may make provision for requiring—

(*a*) a person who first makes a supply of goods [or services][6] to which section 55A(6) applies (a "reverse charge supply"), (*b*) a person who ceases making reverse charge supplies without intending subsequently to make such supplies, or

(*c*) a person who has fallen within paragraph (*b*) above but who nonetheless starts to make reverse charge supplies again,

to give to the Commissioners such notification of that fact at such time and in such form and manner as may be specified in the regulations or [by the Commissioners in accordance with the regulations][8].][4].][3]

(4) Regulations under this paragraph may make provision in relation to cases where—

(*a*) any goods which are subject to a duty of excise or consist in a new means of transport are acquired in the United Kingdom from another member State by any person;

(*b*) the acquisition of the goods is a taxable acquisition and is not in pursuance of a taxable supply; and

(*c*) that person is not a taxable person at the time of the acquisition,

for requiring the person who acquires the goods to give to the Commissioners such notification of the acquisition, and for requiring any VAT on the acquisition to be paid, at such time and in such form or manner as may be specified in the regulations [or (in the case of the notification requirement) by the Commissioners in accordance with the regulations][8].

(5) Regulations under this paragraph may provide for a notification required by virtue of sub-paragraph (4) above—

(*a*) to contain such particulars relating to the notified acquisition and any VAT chargeable thereon as may be specified in the regulations [or by the Commissioners in accordance with the regulations][8]; and

(*b*) to be given, in prescribed cases, by the personal representative, trustee in bankruptcy, interim or permanent trustee, receiver, liquidator or person otherwise acting in a representative capacity in relation to the person who makes that acquisition.

[(5A) Regulations under this paragraph may make provision—

(*a*) for requiring the relevant person to give to the Commissioners such notification of the arrival in the United Kingdom of goods consisting of a means of transport, at such time and in such form and manner, as may be specified in the regulations or by the Commissioners in accordance with the regulations, and

(*b*) where notification of the arrival of a means of transport acquired from another member State, or imported from a place outside the member States, is required by virtue of paragraph (*a*), for requiring any VAT on the acquisition or importation to be paid at such time and in such manner as may be specified in the regulations.

(5B) The provision that may be made by regulations made by virtue of sub-paragraph (5A) includes—

(*a*) provision for a notification required by virtue of that subparagraph to contain such particulars relating to the notified arrival of the means of transport and any VAT chargeable on its acquisition or importation as may be specified in the regulations or by the Commissioners in accordance with the regulations,

(*b*) provision for such a notification to be given by a person who is not the relevant person and is so specified, or is of a description so specified,

(*c*) provision for such a notification to contain a declaration, given in such form and by such person as may be so specified, as to the information contained in the notification, and

(*d*) supplementary, incidental, consequential or transitional provision (including provision amending any provision made by or under this Act or any other enactment).

(5C) Subsection (3) of section 97 (orders subject to Commons approval) applies to a statutory instrument containing any regulations made by virtue of sub-paragraph (5A) which amend an enactment as it applies to an order within subsection (4) of that section.

(5D) For the purposes of sub-paragraph (5A)—

"means of transport" has the same meaning as it has in this Act in the expression "new means of transport" (see section 95);

"relevant person", in relation to the arrival of a means of transport in the United Kingdom, means—

(*a*) where the means of transport has been acquired in the United Kingdom from another member State, the person who so acquires it,

(*b*) where it has been imported from a place outside the member States, the person liable to pay VAT on the importation, and

(*c*) in any other case—

(i) the owner of the means of transport at the time of its arrival in the United Kingdom, or

(ii) where it is subject to a lease or hire agreement, the lessee or hirer of the means of transport at that time.][7]

(6) Regulations under this paragraph may make special provision for such taxable supplies by retailers of any goods or of any description of goods or of services or any description of services as may be determined by or under the regulations and, in particular—

(*a*) for permitting the value which is to be taken as the value of the supplies in any prescribed accounting period or part thereof to be determined, subject to any limitations or restrictions, by such method or one of such methods as may have been described in any notice published by the Commissioners in pursuance of the regulations and not withdrawn by a further notice or as may be agreed with the Commissioners; and

(*b*) for determining the proportion of the value of the supplies which is to be attributed to any description of supplies; and

(*c*) for adjusting that value and proportion for periods comprising two or more prescribed accounting periods or parts thereof.

(7) Regulations under this paragraph may make provision whereby, in such cases and subject to such conditions as may be determined by or under the regulations, VAT in respect of a supply may be accounted for and paid by reference to the time when consideration for the supply is received; and any such regulations may make such modifications of the provisions of this Act (including in particular, but without prejudice to the generality of the power, the provisions as to the time when, and the circumstances in which, credit for input tax is to be allowed) as appear to the Commissioners necessary or expedient.

(8) Regulations under this paragraph may make provision whereby, in such cases and subject to such conditions as may be determined by or under the regulations—

(*a*) VAT in respect of any supply by a taxable person of dutiable goods, or

(*b*) VAT in respect of an acquisition by any person from another member State of dutiable goods,

may be accounted for and paid, and any question as to the inclusion of any duty or agricultural levy in the value of the supply or acquisition determined, by reference to the duty point or by reference to such later time as the Commissioners may allow.

In this sub-paragraph "dutiable goods" and "duty point" have the same meanings as in section 18.

(9) Regulations under this paragraph may provide for the time when any invoice described in regulations made for the purposes of section 6(8)(*b*) or 12(1)(*b*) is to be treated as having been issued and provide for VAT accounted for and paid by reference to the date of issue of such an invoice to be confined to VAT on so much of the value of the supply or acquisition as is shown on the invoice.

(10) Regulations under this paragraph may make provision—

(*a*) for treating VAT chargeable in one prescribed accounting period as chargeable in another such period; and

(*b*) with respect to the making of entries in accounts for the purpose of making adjustments, whether for the correction of errors or otherwise; and

(*c*) for the making of financial adjustments in connection with the making of entries in accounts for the purpose mentioned in paragraph (*b*) above [and

(*d*) for a person, for purposes connected with the making of any such entry or financial adjustment, to be required to provide to any prescribed person, or to retain, a document in the prescribed form containing prescribed particulars of the matters to which the entry or adjustment relates; and

(*e*) for enabling the Commissioners, in such cases as they may think fit, to dispense with or relax a requirement imposed by regulations made by virtue of paragraph (*d*) above.][1]

(11) Regulations under this paragraph may make different provision for different circumstances and may provide for different dates as the commencement of prescribed accounting periods applicable to different persons.

(12) The provisions made by regulations under this paragraph for cases where goods are treated as supplied by a taxable person by virtue of paragraph 7 of Schedule 4 may require VAT chargeable on the supply to be accounted for and paid, and particulars thereof to be provided, by such other person and in such manner as may be specified by the regulations.

(13) Where, at the end of a prescribed accounting period, the amount of VAT due from any person or the amount of any VAT credit would be less than £1, that amount shall be treated as nil.

Simon's Tax Cases—Sub-para (6), *C&E Comrs v Kingfisher plc* [1994] STC 63*.

Definitions—"Acquisition of goods from another member State", s 11; "another member State", s 96(1); "the Commissioners", s 96(1); "document", s 96(1); "input tax", s 24; "interim trustee", s 96(1); "invoice", s 96(1); "law of another member State", s 92; "new means of transport", s 95; "permanent trustee", s 96(1); "place of supply", s 7; "prescribed", s 96(1); "prescribed accounting period", s 25(1); "regulations", s 96(1); "supply", s 5, Sch 4; "taxable acquisition", s 10(2); "taxable person", s 3; "taxable supply", s 4(2); "time of acquisition", s 12; "time of supply", s 6; "United Kingdom", s 96(11); "VAT", ss 1, 96(1); "VAT credit", s 25(3); "VAT invoice", s 6(15); "value of acquisition", s 20; "value of supply", s 19, Sch 6.

Regulations—See VAT Regulations, SI 1995/2518 regs 13–20 (VAT and other invoices); regs 21–23 (EC sales statements); regs 24–42 (accounting and records); regs 49–55 (annual accounting scheme); regs 56–65 (cash accounting scheme); regs 66–75 (retail schemes); regs 146–155 (new means of transport).

Value Added Tax (Amendment) (No 2) Regulations, SI 2010/2240.

VAT (Amendment) Regulations, SI 2012/33

VAT (Amendment) (No 2) Regulations, SI 2012/1899.
VAT (Amendment) Regulations, SI 2013/701.
Value Added Tax (Amendment) Regulations, SI 2014/548.
Value Added Tax (Amendment) (No 2) Regulations, SI 2014/1497.

Cross references—See VATA 1994 s 67(1) (penalty for failure to comply with regulations under sub-para (4) of this para);
VATA 1994 s 69(1), (5) (penalty for failure to comply with time limit for submission of return imposed by regulations under sub-para (1) of this para);
VATA 1994 s 75 (assessment of VAT where notification of an acquisition has not been given as required by regulations under sub-para (4) of this para);
VATA 1994 s 83 (appeals to a tribunal against a refusal to allow the use of a retail scheme under sub-para (6) of this para and against a refusal of authorisation to use a cash accounting scheme under sub-para (7) of this para);
VATA 1994 s 88(5) (supplies spanning date of change in rate of VAT: power to make regulations under this para providing for replacement or correction of VAT invoices).
VAT (Isle of Man) Order, SI 1982/1067 art 8 (taxable persons for the purposes of Isle of Man VAT legislation to be treated as taxable persons for the purposes of this para).

Amendments—[1] Sub-para (2A) and sub-para (10)(*d*), (*e*) inserted by FA 1996 s 38.
[2] Words in Heading and sub-para (1) repealed, and sub-paras (2), (2A) repealed by FA 2002 ss 24(1)(*b*), (5), 139, Sch 40 Pt 2(2) with effect 1 December 2003 (by virtue of SI 2003/3043).
[3] Sub-paras (3A), (3B) inserted by FA 2006 s 19(7), (8) with effect for supplies made on or after 1 June 2007 (by virtue of the Finance Act 2006, Section 19, (Appointed Day) Order, SI 2007/1419).
[4] Sub-para (3B) substituted by the VAT (Administration, Collection and Enforcement) Order, SI 2007/1421 art 2 with effect from 1 June 2007.
[5] Words "which involve the movement of goods between member States" in sub-para (3) substituted, and sub-para (3ZA) inserted, by FA 2009 s 78 with effect from 21 July 2009.
[6] Words in sub-para (3B) inserted by FA 2010 s 50(2) with effect from 8 April 2010.
[7] Sub-paras (5A)–(5D) inserted by FA 2012 s 202 with effect from 17 July 2012.
[8] In sub-paras (1), (4), (5)(*a*), words inserted; in sub-paras (3), (3A), para (*b*) substituted and words substituted for word "prescribed"; and in sub-para (3B), words substituted for words "determined by the Commissioners in accordance with powers conferred by the regulations"; by FA 2012 s 204, Sch 29 paras 1, 12 with effect from 17 July 2012.

[VAT invoices

2A—(1) Regulations may require a taxable person supplying goods or services to provide an invoice (a "VAT invoice") to the person supplied.

(2) A VAT invoice must give—

(*a*) such particulars as may be prescribed of the supply, the supplier and the person supplied;

(*b*) such an indication as may be prescribed of whether VAT is chargeable on the supply under this Act or the law of another member State;

(*c*) such particulars of any VAT that is so chargeable as may be prescribed.

(3) Regulations may confer power on the Commissioners to allow the requirements of any regulations as to the information to be given in a VAT invoice to be relaxed or dispensed with.

(4) Regulations may—

(*a*) provide that the VAT invoice that is required to be provided in connection with a particular description of supply must be provided within a prescribed time after the supply is treated as taking place, or at such time before the supply is treated as taking place as may be prescribed;

(*b*) allow for the invoice to be issued later than required by the regulations where it is issued in accordance with general or special directions given by the Commissioners.

(5) Regulations may—

(*a*) make provision about the manner in which a VAT invoice may be provided, including provision prescribing conditions that must be complied with in the case of an invoice issued by a third party on behalf of the supplier;

(*b*) prescribe conditions that must be complied with in the case of a VAT invoice that relates to more than one supply;

(*c*) make, in relation to a document that refers to a VAT invoice and is intended to amend it, such provision corresponding to that which may be made in relation to a VAT invoice as appears to the Commissioners to be appropriate.

(6) Regulations may confer power on the Commissioners to require a person who has received in the United Kingdom a VAT invoice that is (or part of which is) in a language other than English to provide them with an English translation of the invoice (or part).

(7) Regulations under this paragraph—

(*a*) may be framed so as to apply only in prescribed cases or only in relation to supplies made to persons of prescribed descriptions;

(*b*) may make different provision for different circumstances.][1]

Regulations—VAT (Amendment) (No 2) Regulations, SI 2012/1899.
VAT (Amendment) (No 3) Regulations, SI 2012/2951.

Amendments—[1] Para 2A inserted by FA 2002 s 24(2), (5) with effect from 1 December 2003 (by virtue of SI 2003/3043).

[Self-billed invoices

2B—(1) This paragraph applies where a taxable person provides to himself a document (a "self-billed invoice") that purports to be a VAT invoice in respect of a supply of goods or services to him by another taxable person.

(2) Subject to compliance with such conditions as may be—

(*a*) prescribed,

(*b*) specified in a notice published by the Commissioners, or

(*c*) imposed in a particular case in accordance with regulations,

a self-billed invoice shall be treated as the VAT invoice required by regulations under paragraph 2A above to be provided by the supplier.

(3) For the purposes of section 6(4) (under which the time of supply can be determined by the prior issue of an invoice) a self-billed invoice shall not be treated as issued by the supplier.

(4) For the purposes of section 6(5) and (6) (under which the time of supply can be determined by the subsequent issue of an invoice) a self-billed invoice in relation to which the conditions mentioned in sub-paragraph (2) are complied with shall, subject to compliance with such further conditions as may be prescribed, be treated as issued by the supplier.

In such a case, any notice of election given or request made for the purposes of section 6(5) or (6) by the person providing the self-billed invoice shall be treated for those purposes as given or made by the supplier.

(5) Regulations under this paragraph—

(*a*) may be framed so as to apply only in prescribed cases or only in relation to supplies made to persons of prescribed descriptions;

(*b*) may make different provision for different circumstances.][1]

Regulations—VAT (Amendment) (No 3) Regulations, SI 2012/2951.

Amendments—[1] Para 2B inserted by FA 2002 s 24(2), (5) with effect 1 December 2003 (by virtue of SI 2003/3043).

[Electronic communication and storage of VAT invoices etc

3—(1) Regulations may prescribe, or provide for the Commissioners to impose in a particular case, conditions that must be complied with in relation to—

(*a*) the provision by electronic means of any item to which this paragraph applies;

(*b*) the preservation by electronic means of any such item or of information contained in any such item.

(2) The items to which this paragraph applies are—

(*a*) any VAT invoice;

(*b*) any document that refers to a VAT invoice and is intended to amend it;

(*c*) any invoice described in regulations made for the purposes of section 6(8)(*b*) or 12(1)(*b*).

(3) Regulations under this paragraph may make different provision for different circumstances.][1]

Regulations—VAT (Amendment) (No 3) Regulations, SI 2012/2951.

Amendments—[1] This paragraph substituted by FA 2002 s 24(3), (5) with effect from 1 December 2003 (by virtue of SI 2003/3043).

Power to require security and production of evidence

4—[(1) The Commissioners may, as a condition of allowing or repaying input tax to any person, require the production of such evidence relating to VAT as they may specify.

(1A) If they think it necessary for the protection of the revenue, the Commissioners may require, as a condition of making any VAT credit, the giving of such security for the amount of the payment as appears to them appropriate.][1]

[(2) If they think it necessary for the protection of the revenue, the Commissioners may require a taxable person, as a condition of his supplying or being supplied with goods or services under a taxable supply, to give security, or further security, for the payment of any VAT that is or may become due from—

(*a*) the taxable person, or

(*b*) any person by or to whom relevant goods or services are supplied.

(3) In sub-paragraph (2) above "relevant goods or services" means goods or services supplied by or to the taxable person.

(4) Security under sub-paragraph (2) above shall be of such amount, and shall be given in such manner, as the Commissioners may determine.

(5) The powers conferred on the Commissioners by sub-paragraph (2) above are without prejudice to their powers under section 48(7).][2]

Simon's Tax Cases—Sub-para (1), *Garage Molenheide BVBA and ors v Belgian State* (Joined cases C-286/94, C-340/95, C-401/95 and C-47/96) [1998] STC 126, ECJ.

Sub-para (2), *C&E Comrs v Peachtree Enterprises Ltd* [1994] STC 747; *C&E Comrs and another v Federation of Technological Industries and others* [2006] STC 1483, *Chaudhry v R&C Prosecution Office* [2008] STC 2357.

Definitions—"The Commissioners", s 96(1); "document", s 96(1); "input tax", s 24; "supply", s 5, Sch 4; "taxable person", s 3; "taxable supply", s 4(2); "VAT", ss 1, 96(1); "VAT credit", s 25(3).

Cross references—See VATA 1994 s 72(11) (penalty for making supplies in contravention of sub-para (2) of this para);
VATA 1994 ss 83, 84 (appeal to a tribunal in respect of a requirement for security under sub-para (2) of this para).
VAT (Isle of Man) Order, SI 1982/1067 art 7 (references to VAT in this para to include references to VAT chargeable under Isle of Man legislation).

Amendments—[1] Sub-paras (1), (1A) substituted for sub-para (1) by FA 2003 s 17(3) with effect from 10 April 2003.
[2] Sub-paras (2)–(5) substituted for sub-s (2) by FA 2003 s 17(4) with effect from 10 April 2003.

Recovery of VAT, etc

5—(1) VAT due from any person shall be recoverable as a debt due to the Crown.

(2) Where an invoice shows a supply of goods or services as taking place with VAT chargeable on it, there shall be recoverable from the person who issued the invoice an amount equal to that which is shown on the invoice as VAT or, if VAT is not separately shown, to so much of the total amount shown as payable as is to be taken as representing VAT on the supply.

(3) Sub-paragraph (2) above applies whether or not—

(*a*) the invoice is a VAT invoice issued in pursuance of paragraph 2(1) above; or

(*b*) the supply shown on the invoice actually takes or has taken place, or the amount shown as VAT, or any amount of VAT, is or was chargeable on the supply; or

(*c*) the person issuing the invoice is a taxable person;

and any sum recoverable from a person under the sub-paragraph shall, if it is in any case VAT be recoverable as such and shall otherwise be recoverable as a debt due to the Crown.

(4)–(10) . . . [1]

Regulations—See VAT Regulations, SI 1995/2518 regs 212, 213.

Simon's Tax Cases—*C&E Comrs v International Language Centres Ltd* [1986] STC 279*.

Definitions—"The Commissioners", s 96(1); "invoice", s 96(1); "regulations", s 96(1); "supply", s 5, Sch 4; "taxable person", s 3; "VAT", ss 1, 96(1); "VAT invoice", s 6(15).

Cross reference—See VAT (Isle of Man) Order, SI 1982/1067 art 7 (references to VAT in this para to include references to VAT chargeable under Isle of Man legislation).
FA 2012 Sch 36 para 26 (references to VAT in this para to include VAT due as part of the one-off payment under the agreement between UK and Switzerland).

Amendments—[1] Sub-paras (4)–(10) repealed by FA 1997 Sch 18(2) Part V(2) with effect from 1 July 1997 (see SI 1997/1433).

Duty to keep records

6—(1) Every taxable person shall keep such records as the Commissioners may by regulations require, and every person who, at a time when he is not a taxable person, acquires in the United Kingdom from another member State any goods which are subject to a duty of excise or consist in a new means of transport shall keep such records with respect to the acquisition (if it is a taxable acquisition and is not in pursuance of a taxable supply) as the Commissioners may so require.

(2) Regulations under sub-paragraph (1) above may make different provision for different cases and may be framed by reference to such records as may be specified in any notice published by the Commissioners in pursuance of the regulations and not withdrawn by a further notice.

(3) The Commissioners may require any records kept in pursuance of this paragraph to be preserved for such period not exceeding 6 years as they may [specify in writing (and different periods may be specified for different cases)][1].

[(4) The duty under this paragraph to preserve records may be discharged—

(*a*) by preserving them in any form and by any means, or

(*b*) by preserving the information contained in them in any form and by any means,

subject to any conditions or exceptions specified in writing by the Commissioners for Her Majesty's Revenue and Customs.][1]

Regulations—See VAT Regulations, SI 1995/2518 regs 31, 33.
VAT (Amendment) (No 3) Regulations, SI 2012/2951.

Definitions—"Acquisition of goods from another member State", s 11; "another member State", s 96(1); "the Commissioners", s 96(1); "copy", s 96(1); "document", s 96(1); "new means of transport", s 95; "regulations", s 96(1); "taxable acquisition", s 10(2); "taxable person", s 3; "taxable supply", s 4(2); "United Kingdom", s 96(11).

Cross references—See VATA 1994 s 49(1) (transfer of going concerns: preservation of records by transferee);
VATA 1994 s 69(1) (penalty for breach of a requirement imposed under sub-para (1) of this para);
VATA 1994 s 69(2) (penalty for breach of a requirement to keep records imposed under sub-para (3) of this para).
VAT (Isle of Man) Order, SI 1982/1067 art 8 (taxable persons for the purposes of Isle of Man VAT legislation to be treated as taxable persons for the purposes of this para).

Amendments—[1] In sub-para (3), words substituted for word "require", and sub-para (4) substituted for previous sub-para (4), by FA 2008 s 115, Sch 37 paras 4, 5 with effect from 1 April 2009 (by virtue of SI 2009/402).

[6A—(1) The Commissioners may direct any taxable person named in the direction to keep such records as they specify in the direction in relation to such goods as they so specify.

(2) A direction under this paragraph may require the records to be compiled by reference to VAT invoices or any other matter.

(3) The Commissioners may not make a direction under this paragraph unless they have reasonable grounds for believing that the records specified in the direction might assist in identifying taxable supplies in respect of which the VAT chargeable might not be paid.

(4) The taxable supplies in question may be supplies made by—

(*a*) the person named in the direction, or

(*b*) any other person.

(5) A direction under this paragraph—

(*a*) must be given by notice in writing to the person named in it,

(*b*) must warn that person of the consequences under section 69B of failing to comply with it, and

(*c*) remains in force until it is revoked or replaced by a further direction.

(6) The Commissioners may require any records kept in pursuance of this paragraph to be preserved for such period not exceeding 6 years as they may require.

(7) [Sub-paragraph (4) of paragraph 6 (preservation of information) applies][2] for the purposes of this paragraph as [it applies][2] for the purposes of that paragraph.

(8) This paragraph is without prejudice to the power conferred by paragraph 6(1) to make regulations requiring records to be kept.

(9) Any records required to be kept by virtue of this paragraph are in addition to any records required to be kept by virtue of paragraph 6.][1]

1 Para 6A inserted by FA 2006 s 21(6) with effect from 19 July 2006.

2 Words in sub-para (7) substituted by FA 2008 Sch 37 paras 4, 6 with effect from 1 April 2009 (by virtue of SI 2009/402).

Furnishing of information and production of documents

7—(1) The Commissioners may by regulations make provision for requiring taxable persons to notify to the Commissioners such particulars of changes in circumstances relating to those persons or any business carried on by them as appear to the Commissioners required for the purpose of keeping the register kept under this Act up to date.

(2)–(9) . . .[2]

Regulations—See VAT Regulations, SI 1995/2518 regs 31, 33.

VAT (Amendment) (No 2) Regulations, SI 2012/1899.

Simon's Tax Cases—*EMI Records Ltd v Spillane* [1986] STC 374*, *Singh v HM Advocate* [2001] STC 790*.

Definitions—"Acquisition of goods from another member State", s 11; "another member State", s 96(1); "authorised person", s 96(1); "business", s 94; "the Commissioners", s 96(1); "copy", s 96(1); "document", s 96(1); "importation of goods from a place outside the member States" s 15; "regulations", s 96(1); "supply", s 5, Sch 4; "taxable person", s 3.

Cross reference—See VATA 1994 s 69(1) (penalty for breach of a requirement imposed under this para).

Amendments—[1] Sub-para (9) inserted by FA 1999 s 15 with effect from 27 July 1999.

[2] Sub-paras (2)–(9) repealed by FA 2008 s 113, Sch 36 para 87 with effect from 1 April 2009 (by virtue of SI 2009/404 art 2).

Power to take samples

8—(1) An authorised person, if it appears to him necessary for the protection of the revenue against mistake or fraud, may at any time take, from the goods in the possession of any person who supplies goods or acquires goods from another member State [, or in the possession of a fiscal warehouse keeper,][1] such samples as the authorised person may require with a view to determining how the goods or the materials of which they are made ought to be or to have been treated for the purposes of VAT.

(2) Any sample taken under this paragraph shall be disposed of and accounted for in such manner as the Commissioners may direct.

(3) Where a sample is taken under this paragraph from the goods in any person's possession and is not returned to him within a reasonable time and in good condition the Commissioners shall pay him by way of compensation a sum equal to the cost of the sample to him or such larger sum as they may determine.

Definitions—"Acquires goods from another member State", s 11; "another member State", s 96(1); "authorised person", s 96(1); "the Commissioners", s 96(1); "fiscal warehouse keeper", s 18F(1); "supply", s 5, Sch 4; "VAT", ss 1, 96(1).

Cross reference—See VAT (Isle of Man) Order, SI 1982/1067 art 7 (references to VAT in this para to include references to VAT chargeable under Isle of Man legislation).

Amendments—[1] Words in sub-para (1) inserted by FA 1996 Sch 3 para 16, with effect from 1 June 1996 (see Finance Act 1996, Section 26, (Appointed Day) Order, SI 1996/1249).

Power to require opening of [machines on which relevant machine games are played][1]

9 An authorised person may at any reasonable time require a person making such a supply as is referred to in section 23(1) or any person acting on his behalf—

[(*a*) to open any machine on which relevant machine games (as defined in section 23A) are capable of being played; and][1] (*b*) to carry out any other operation which may be necessary to enable the authorised person to ascertain the amount which, in accordance with [section 23(3)][1], is to be taken as the value of supplies made in the circumstances mentioned in subsection (1) of that section in any period.

Definitions—"Authorised person", s 96(1); "supply", s 5, Sch 4; "value of supply", s 19, Sch 6.

Amendments—[1] Para (*a*) substituted, and in para (*b*) and in italic heading, words substituted by FA 2012 s 191, Sch 24 para 64(1), (5)(*b*) with effect in relation to supplies made on or after 1 February 2013.

Entry and search of premises and persons

***10**—(1)–(2A)* . . . [5]
(3)–(6) . . . [4]

Simon's Tax Cases—*R v C&E Comrs and IRC, ex p X Ltd* [1997] STC 1197.
Sub-para (5)(*a*), *Singh v HM Advocate* [2001] STC 790*.
R (oao Paul Da Costa & Co (a firm) v Thames Magistrates Court [2002] STC 267.

Cross references—Criminal Justice and Police Act 2001 s 50, Sch 1 Pt 1 (s 50 of that Act which provides additional powers of seizure from premises applies to the power of seizure conferred under sub-para (3) above).

Definitions—"Acquisition of goods from other member States", s 11; "authorised person", s 96(1); "business", s 94; "copy", s 96(1); "document", s 96(1); "fiscal warehouse", ss 18A(3), 18F(1); "other member State", s 96(1); "supply", s 5, Sch 4; "taxable acquisition", s 10(2); "taxable supply", s 4(2).

Amendments—[1] Words in sub-para (2) inserted by FA 1996 Sch 3 para 17, with effect from 1 June 1996 (see Finance Act 1996, Section 26, (Appointed Day) Order, SI 1996/1249).
[2] Words in sub-para (3) substituted, subject to transitional provisions and savings, by Criminal Procedure (Consequential Provisions)(Scotland) Act 1995 Sch 3, Sch 4 para 91(a).
[3] Sub-para (2A) inserted by FA 2006 s 20 with effect from 19 July 2006.
[4] Sub-paras (3)–(6) repealed by FA 2007 ss 84, 114, Sch 22 paras 3, 8(b), Sch 27 Pt 5(1) with effect from 1 December 2007 (by virtue of SI 2007/3166 art 3(a)).
[5] Sub-paras (1)–(2A) repealed by FA 2008 s 113, Sch 36 para 87 with effect from 1 April 2009 (by virtue of SI 2009/404 art 2).

Order for access to recorded information etc

11—(1) Where, on an application by an authorised person, a justice of the peace or, in Scotland, a justice (within the meaning of [section 308 of the Criminal Procedure (Scotland) Act 1975][1]) is satisfied that there are reasonable grounds for believing—

(*a*) that an offence in connection with VAT is being, has been or is about to be committed, and

(*b*) that any recorded information (including any document of any nature whatsoever) which may be required as evidence for the purpose of any proceedings in respect of such an offence is in the possession of any person,

he may make an order under this paragraph.

(2) An order under this paragraph is an order that the person who appears to the justice to be in possession of the recorded information to which the application relates shall—

(*a*) give an authorised person access to it, and

(*b*) permit an authorised person to remove and take away any of it which he reasonably considers necessary,

not later than the end of the period of 7 days beginning on the date of the order or the end of such longer period as the order may specify.

(3) The reference in sub-paragraph (2)(*a*) above to giving an authorised person access to the recorded information to which the application relates includes a reference to permitting the authorised person to take copies of it or to make extracts from it.

(4) Where the recorded information consists of information [stored in any electronic form][2], an order under this paragraph shall have effect as an order to produce the information in a form in which it is visible and legible [or from which it can readily be produced in a visible and legible form][2] and, if the authorised person wishes to remove it, in a form in which it can be removed.

(5) This paragraph is without prejudice to paragraphs 7 and 10 above.

Simon's Tax Cases—*R v Epsom Justices, ex p Bell* [1989] STC 169*; *R v City of London Magistrates, ex p Asif* [1997] STC 141; *C&E Comrs v City of London Magistrates' Court* [2000] STC 447.
Sub-para (1)(*a*), *Singh v HM Advocate* [2001] STC 790*.

Definitions—"Authorised person", s 96(1); "copy", s 96(1); "document", s 96(1); "VAT", ss 1, 96(1).

Amendments—[1] Words in sub-para (1) substituted, subject to transitional provisions and savings by Criminal Procedure (Consequential Provisions) (Scotland) Act 1995 Sch 3, Sch 4 para 91(b).
[2] Words in sub-para (4) substituted and inserted by Criminal Justice and Police Act 2001 ss 70, 138, Sch 2 Pt 2 para 13 with effect from 1 April 2003 (by virtue of SI 2003/708).

Procedure where documents etc are removed

12—(1) An authorised person who removes anything in the exercise of a power conferred by or under paragraph 10 or 11 above shall, if so requested by a person showing himself—

(*a*) to be the occupier of premises from which it was removed, or

(*b*) to have had custody or control of it immediately before the removal, provide that person with a record of what he removed.

(2) The authorised person shall provide the record within a reasonable time from the making of the request for it.

(3) Subject to sub-paragraph (7) below, if a request for permission to be granted access to anything which—

(*a*) has been removed by an authorised person, and

(*b*) is retained by the Commissioners for the purposes of investigating an offence,

is made to the officer in overall charge of the investigation by a person who had custody or control of the thing immediately before it was so removed or by someone acting on behalf of such a person, the officer shall allow the person who made the request access to it under the supervision of an authorised person.

(4) Subject to sub-paragraph (7) below, if a request for a photograph or copy of any such thing is made to the officer in overall charge of the investigation by a person who had custody or control of the thing immediately before it was so removed, or by someone acting on behalf of such a person, the officer shall—

(*a*) allow the person who made the request access to it under the supervision of an authorised person for the purpose of photographing it or copying it, or

(*b*) photograph or copy it, or cause it to be photographed or copied.

(5) Where anything is photographed or copied under sub-paragraph (4)(*b*) above the photograph or copy shall be supplied to the person who made the request.

(6) The photograph or copy shall be supplied within a reasonable time from the making of the request.

(7) There is no duty under this paragraph to grant access to, or to supply a photograph or copy of, anything if the officer in overall charge of the investigation for the purposes of which it was removed has reasonable grounds for believing that to do so would prejudice—

(*a*) that investigation;

(*b*) the investigation of an offence other than the offence for the purposes of the investigation of which the thing was removed; or

(*c*) any criminal proceedings which may be brought as a result of—

(i) the investigation of which he is in charge, or

(ii) any such investigation as is mentioned in paragraph (*b*) above.

(8) Any reference in this paragraph to the officer in overall charge of the investigation is a reference to the person whose name and address are endorsed on the warrant or order concerned as being the officer so in charge.

Definitions—"Authorised person", s 96(1); "the Commissioners", s 96(1); "copy", s 96(1).

13—(1) Where, on an application made as mentioned in sub-paragraph (2) below, the appropriate judicial authority is satisfied that a person has failed to comply with a requirement imposed by paragraph 12 above, the authority may order that person to comply with the requirement within such time and in such manner as may be specified in the order.

(2) An application under sub-paragraph (1) above shall be made—

(*a*) in the case of a failure to comply with any of the requirements imposed by paragraph 12(1) and (2) above, by the occupier of the premises from which the thing in question was removed or by the person who had custody or control of it immediately before it was so removed, and

(*b*) in any other case, by the person who had such custody or control.

(3) In this paragraph "the appropriate judicial authority" means—

(*a*) in England and Wales, a magistrates' court;

(*b*) in Scotland, the sheriff; and

(*c*) in Northern Ireland, a court of summary jurisdiction.

(4) In England and Wales and Northern Ireland, an application for an order under this paragraph shall be made by way of complaint; and sections 21 and 42(2) of the Interpretation Act (Northern Ireland) 1954 shall apply as if any reference in those provisions to any enactment included a reference to this paragraph.

Evidence by certificate, etc

14—(1) A certificate of the Commissioners—

(*a*) that a person was or was not, at any date, registered under this Act; or

(*b*) that any return required by or under this Act has not been made or had not been made at any date; or

(*c*) that any statement or notification required to be submitted or given to the Commissioners in accordance with any regulations under paragraph 2(3) or (4) above has not been submitted or given or had not been submitted or given at any date; [. . .][1]

(*d*) . . . [1]

shall be sufficient evidence of that fact until the contrary is proved.

(2) A photograph of any document furnished to the Commissioners for the purposes of this Act and certified by them to be such a photograph shall be admissible in any proceedings, whether civil or criminal, to the same extent as the document itself.

(3) Any document purporting to be a certificate under sub-paragraph (1) or (2) above shall be deemed to be such a certificate until the contrary is proved.

Definitions—"The Commissioners", s 96(1); "document", s 96(1); "registered", s 3(3); "regulations", s 96(1); "VAT", ss 1, 96(1).

Amendments—[1] Sub-para (1)(d) and preceding word "or" repealed by FA 2008 s 138, Sch 44 para 6 with effect from 21 July 2008.

[SCHEDULE 11A

DISCLOSURE OF AVOIDANCE SCHEMES][1]

Section 58A

Commentary—*De Voil Indirect Tax Service* **V5.213, 358**.

Amendments—[1] Schedule inserted by FA 2004 s 19, Sch 2 para 2 with effect from the passing of FA 2004 so far as is necessary for enabling the making of any orders or regulations by virtue of FA 2004 Sch 2, and otherwise with effect from 1 August 2004 (by virtue of SI 2004/1934).

[Interpretation

1 In this Schedule—

"designated scheme" has the meaning given by paragraph 3(4);

["non-deductible tax", in relation to a taxable person, has the meaning given by paragraph 2A,][2]

"notifiable scheme" has the meaning given by paragraph 5(1);

"scheme" includes any arrangements, transaction or series of transactions;

"tax advantage" is to be read in accordance with paragraph 2.][1]

Amendments—[1] Schedule inserted by FA 2004 s 19, Sch 2 para 2 with effect from the passing of FA 2004, so far as is necessary for enabling the making of any orders or regulations by virtue of FA 2004 Sch 2, and otherwise with effect from 1 August 2004 (by virtue of SI 2004/1934).

[2] Definition of "non-deductible tax" inserted by F(No 2)A 2005 s 6, Sch 1 paras 1, 2 with effect from 1 August 2005, by virtue of SI 2005/2010 art 2, subject to savings in arts 3, 4.

[Obtaining a tax advantage

[2—(1) For the purposes of this Schedule, a taxable person obtains a tax advantage if—

(*a*) in any prescribed accounting period, the amount by which the output tax accounted for by him exceeds the input tax deducted by him is less than it would otherwise be,

(*b*) he obtains a VAT credit when he would not otherwise do so, or obtains a larger VAT credit or obtains a VAT credit earlier than would otherwise be the case,

(*c*) in a case where he recovers input tax as a recipient of a supply before the supplier accounts for the output tax, the period between the time when the input tax is recovered and the time when the output tax is accounted for is greater than would otherwise be the case, or

(*d*) in any prescribed accounting period, the amount of his non-deductible tax is less than it would otherwise be.

(2) For the purposes of this Schedule, a person who is not a taxable person obtains a tax advantage if his non-refundable tax is less than it would otherwise be.

(3) In sub-paragraph (2), "non-refundable tax", in relation to a person who is not a taxable person, means—

(*a*) VAT on the supply to him of any goods or services,

(*b*) VAT on the acquisition by him from another member State of any goods, and

(*c*) VAT paid or payable by him on the importation of any goods from a place outside the member States,

but excluding (in each case) any VAT in respect of which he is entitled to a refund from the Commissioners by virtue of any provision of this Act.][2]][1]

Amendments—[1] Schedule inserted by FA 2004 s 19, Sch 2 para 2 with effect from the passing of FA 2004, so far as is necessary for enabling the making of any orders or regulations by virtue of FA 2004 Sch 2, and otherwise with effect from 1 August 2004 (by virtue of SI 2004/1934).

[2] This paragraph substituted by F(No 2)A 2005 s 6, Sch 1 paras 1, 3 with effect from 1 August 2005 (by virtue of SI 2005/2010 art 2, subject to savings in arts 3, 4).

[Meaning of "non-deductible tax"

2A—(1) In this Schedule "non-deductible tax", in relation to a taxable person, means—

(*a*) input tax for which he is not entitled to credit under section 25, and

(*b*) any VAT incurred by him which is not input tax and in respect of which he is not entitled to a refund from the Commissioners by virtue of any provision of this Act.

(2) For the purposes of sub-paragraph (1)(*b*), the VAT "incurred" by a taxable person is—

(*a*) VAT on the supply to him of any goods or services,

(*b*) VAT on the acquisition by him from another member State of any goods, and

(*c*) VAT paid or payable by him on the importation of any goods from a place outside the member States.][1]

Amendments—[1] Paragraph 2A inserted by F(No 2)A 2005 s 6, Sch 1 paras 1, 4 with effect from 1 August 2005 (by virtue of SI 2005/2010 art 2, subject to savings in arts 3, 4).

[Designation by order of avoidance schemes

3—(1) If it appears to the Treasury—

(*a*) that a scheme of a particular description has been, or might be, entered into for the purpose of enabling any person to obtain a tax advantage, and

(*b*) that it is unlikely that persons would enter into a scheme of that description unless the main purpose, or one of the main purposes, of doing so was the obtaining by any person of a tax advantage,

the Treasury may by order designate that scheme for the purposes of this paragraph.

(2) A scheme may be designated for the purposes of this paragraph even though the Treasury are of the opinion that no scheme of that description could as a matter of law result in the obtaining by any person of a tax advantage.

(3) The order must allocate a reference number to each scheme.

(4) In this Schedule "designated scheme" means a scheme of a description designated for the purposes of this paragraph.][1]

Orders—See VAT (Disclosure of Avoidance Schemes) (Designations) Order, SI 2004/1933.

Amendments—[1] Schedule inserted by FA 2004 s 19, Sch 2 para 2 with effect from the passing of FA 2004, so far as is necessary for enabling the making of any orders or regulations by virtue of FA 2004 Sch 2, and otherwise with effect from 1 August 2004 (by virtue of SI 2004/1934).

[Designation by order of provisions included in or associated with avoidance schemes

4—(1) If it appears to the Treasury that a provision of a particular description is, or is likely to be, included in or associated with schemes that are entered into for the purpose of enabling any person to obtain a tax advantage, the Treasury may by order designate that provision for the purposes of this paragraph.

(2) A provision may be designated under this paragraph even though it also appears to the Treasury that the provision is, or is likely to be, included in or associated with schemes that are not entered into for the purpose of obtaining a tax advantage.

(3) In this paragraph "provision" includes any agreement, transaction, act or course of conduct.][1]

Orders—See VAT (Disclosure of Avoidance Schemes) (Designations) Order, SI 2004/1933.

Amendments—[1] Schedule inserted by FA 2004 s 19, Sch 2 para 2 with effect from the passing of FA 2004, so far as is necessary for enabling the making of any orders or regulations by virtue of FA 2004 Sch 2, and otherwise with effect from 1 August 2004 (by virtue of SI 2004/1934).

[Meaning of "notifiable scheme"

5—(1) For the purposes of this Schedule, a scheme is a "notifiable scheme" if—

(*a*) it is a designated scheme, or

(*b*) although it is not a designated scheme, conditions A and B below are met in relation to it.

(2) Condition A is that the scheme includes, or is associated with, a provision of a description designated under paragraph 4.

(3) Condition B is that the scheme has as its main purpose, or one of its main purposes, the obtaining of a tax advantage by any person.][1]

Amendments—[1] Schedule inserted by FA 2004 s 19, Sch 2 para 2 with effect from the passing of FA 2004, so far as is necessary for enabling the making of any orders or regulations by virtue of FA 2004 Sch 2, and otherwise with effect from 1 August 2004 (by virtue of SI 2004/1934).

[Duty to notify Commissioners

6—(1) This paragraph applies in relation to a taxable person where—

(*a*) the amount of VAT shown in a return in respect of a prescribed accounting period as payable by or to him is less than or greater than it would be but for any notifiable scheme to which he is party, . . . [2]

(*b*) he makes a claim for the repayment of output tax or an increase in credit for input tax in respect of any prescribed accounting period in respect of which he has previously delivered a return and the amount claimed is greater than it would be but for such a scheme[, or

(*c*) the amount of his non-deductible tax in respect of any prescribed accounting period is less than it would be but for such a scheme.][2]

(2) Where the scheme is a designated scheme, the taxable person must notify the Commissioners within the prescribed time, and in such form and manner as may be required by or under regulations, of the reference number allocated to the scheme under paragraph 3(3).

[(2A) Sub-paragraph (2) does not apply to a taxable person in relation to any scheme if he has on a previous occasion—

(*a*) notified the Commissioners under that sub-paragraph in relation to the scheme, or

(*b*) provided the Commissioners with prescribed information under sub-paragraph (3) (as it applied before the scheme became a designated scheme) in relation to the scheme.][2]

(3) Where the scheme is not a designated scheme, the taxable person must, subject to sub-paragraph (4), provide the Commissioners within the prescribed time, and in such form and manner as may be required by or under regulations, with prescribed information relating to the scheme.

(4) Sub-paragraph (3) does not apply where the scheme is one in respect of which any person has previously—

(*a*) provided the Commissioners with prescribed information under paragraph 9, and

(*b*) provided the taxable person with a reference number notified to him by the Commissioners under paragraph 9(2)(*b*).

[(5) Sub-paragraph (3) also does not apply where the scheme is one in respect of which the taxable person has on a previous occasion provided the Commissioners with prescribed information under that sub-paragraph.][2]

(6) This paragraph has effect subject to paragraph 7.][1]

Orders—See VAT (Disclosure of Avoidance Schemes) Regulations, SI 2004/1929.

Amendments—[1] Schedule inserted by FA 2004 s 19, Sch 2 para 2 with effect from the passing of FA 2004, so far as is necessary for enabling the making of any orders or regulations by virtue of FA 2004 Sch 2, and otherwise with effect from 1 August 2004 (by virtue of SI 2004/1934).

[2] Word "or" in sub-para (1)(a) repealed; sub-paras (1)(c), (2A) inserted; and sub-para (5) substituted; by F(No 2)A 2005 ss 6, 70, Sch 1 paras 1, 5, Sch 11 Pt 1 with effect from 1 August 2005 (by virtue of SI 2005/2010 art 2, subject to savings in arts 3, 4). Paragraph 6(1)(c) shall not apply in relation to any prescribed accounting period beginning before 1 August 2005.

[Exemptions from duty to notify under paragraph 6

7—(1) Paragraph 6 does not apply to a taxable person in relation to a scheme—

(*a*) where the taxable person is not a group undertaking in relation to any other undertaking and conditions A and B below, as they have effect in relation to the scheme, are met in relation to the taxable person, or

(*b*) where the taxable person is a group undertaking in relation to any other undertaking and conditions A and B below, as they have effect in relation to the scheme, are met in relation to the taxable person and every other group undertaking.

(2) Condition A is that the total value of the person's taxable supplies and exempt supplies in the period of twelve months ending immediately before the beginning of the relevant period is less than the minimum turnover.

(3) Condition B is that the total value of the person's taxable supplies and exempt supplies in the prescribed accounting period immediately preceding the relevant period is less than the appropriate proportion of the minimum turnover.

(4) In sub-paragraphs (2) and (3) "the minimum turnover" means—

(*a*) in relation to a designated scheme, £600,000, and

(*b*) in relation to any other notifiable scheme, £10,000,000.

(5) In sub-paragraph (3) "the appropriate proportion" means the proportion which the length of the prescribed accounting period bears to twelve months.

(6) The value of a supply of goods or services shall be determined for the purposes of this paragraph on the basis that no VAT is chargeable on the supply.

(7) The Treasury may by order substitute for the sum for the time being specified in sub-paragraph (4)(*a*) or (*b*) such other sum as they think fit.

(8) This paragraph has effect subject to paragraph 8.

(9) In this paragraph—

"relevant period" means the prescribed accounting period referred to in paragraph [6(1)(*a*), (*b*) or (*c*)][2];

"undertaking" and "group undertaking" have the same meanings as in [section 1161 of the Companies Act 2006][3].][1]

Amendments—[1] Schedule inserted by FA 2004 s 19, Sch 2 para 2 with effect from the passing of FA 2004, so far as is necessary for enabling the making of any orders or regulations by virtue of FA 2004 Sch 2, and otherwise with effect from 1 August 2004 (by virtue of SI 2004/1934).

[2] In the definition of "relevant period", words substituted for the words "6(1)(a) or (b)" by F(No 2)A 2005 s 6, Sch 1 paras 1, 6 with effect from 1 August 2005 (by virtue of SI 2005/2010 art 2, subject to savings in arts 3, 4).

[3] Words in sub-para (9) substituted by the Companies Act 2006 (Consequential Amendments) (Taxes and National Insurance) Order, SI 2008/954 art 20 with effect from 6 April 2008.

[Power to exclude exemption

8—(1) The purpose of this paragraph is to prevent the maintenance or creation of any artificial separation of business activities carried on by two or more persons from resulting in an avoidance of the obligations imposed by paragraph 6.

(2) In determining for the purposes of sub-paragraph (1) whether any separation of business activities is artificial, regard shall be had to the extent to which the different persons carrying on those activities are closely bound to one another by financial, economic and organisational links.

(3) If the Commissioners make a direction under this section—

(*a*) the persons named in the direction shall be treated for the purposes of paragraph 7 as a single taxable person carrying on the activities of a business described in the direction with effect from the date of the direction or, if the direction so provides, from such later date as may be specified in the direction, and

(*b*) if paragraph 7 would not exclude the application of paragraph 6, in respect of any notifiable scheme, to that single taxable person, it shall not exclude the application of paragraph 6, in respect of that scheme, to the persons named in the direction.

(4) The Commissioners shall not make a direction under this section naming any person unless they are satisfied—

(*a*) that he is making or has made taxable or exempt supplies,

(*b*) that the activities in the course of which he makes those supplies form only part of certain activities, the other activities being carried on concurrently or previously (or both) by one or more other persons, and

(*c*) that, if all the taxable and exempt supplies of the business described in the direction were taken into account, conditions A and B in paragraph 7(2) and (3), as those conditions have effect in relation to designated schemes, would not be met in relation to that business.

(5) A direction under this paragraph shall be served on each of the persons named in it.

(6) A direction under this paragraph remains in force until it is revoked or replaced by a further direction.][1]

Amendments—[1] Schedule inserted by FA 2004 s 19, Sch 2 para 2 with effect from the passing of FA 2004, so far as is necessary for enabling the making of any orders or regulations by virtue of FA 2004 Sch 2, and otherwise with effect from 1 August 2004 (by virtue of SI 2004/1934).

[Voluntary notification of avoidance scheme that is not designated scheme

9—(1) Any person may, at any time, provide the Commissioners with prescribed information relating to a scheme or proposed scheme of a particular description which is (or, if implemented, would be) a notifiable scheme by virtue of paragraph 5(1)(*b*).

(2) On receiving the prescribed information, the Commissioners may—

(*a*) allocate a reference number to the scheme (if they have not previously done so under this paragraph), and

(*b*) notify the person who provided the information of the number allocated.][1]

Orders—See VAT (Disclosure of Avoidance Schemes) Regulations, SI 2004/1929.

Amendments—[1] Schedule inserted by FA 2004 s 19, Sch 2 para 2 with effect from the passing of FA 2004, so far as is necessary for enabling the making of any orders or regulations by virtue of FA 2004 Sch 2, and otherwise with effect from 1 August 2004 (by virtue of SI 2004/1934).

[Penalty for failure to notify use of notifiable scheme

10—(1) A person who fails to comply with paragraph 6 shall be liable, subject to sub-paragraphs (2) and (3), to a penalty of an amount determined under paragraph 11.

(2) Conduct falling within sub-paragraph (1) shall not give rise to liability to a penalty under this paragraph if the person concerned satisfies the Commissioners or, on appeal, a tribunal that there is a reasonable excuse for the failure.

(3) Where, by reason of conduct falling within sub-paragraph (1)—

(*a*) a person is convicted of an offence (whether under this Act or otherwise), or

(*b*) a person is assessed to a penalty under section 60 [or a penalty for a deliberate inaccuracy under Schedule 24 to the Finance Act 2007][2],

that conduct shall not give rise to a penalty under this paragraph.][1]

Amendments—[1] Schedule inserted by FA 2004 s 19, Sch 2 para 2 with effect from the passing of FA 2004, so far as is necessary for enabling the making of any orders or regulations by virtue of FA 2004 Sch 2, and otherwise with effect from 1 August 2004 (by virtue of SI 2004/1934).

[2] Words in sub-para (3)(b) inserted by the Finance Act 2008, Schedule 40 (Appointed Day, Transitional Provisions and Consequential Amendments) Order, SI 2009/571 art 8, Sch 1 paras 12, 17 with effect from 1 April 2009.

[Amount of penalty

11—(1) Where the failure mentioned in paragraph 10(1) relates to a notifiable scheme that is not a designated scheme, the amount of the penalty is £5,000.

(2) Where the failure mentioned in paragraph 10(1) relates to a designated scheme, the amount of the penalty is 15 per cent. of the VAT saving (as determined under sub-paragraph (3)).

(3) For this purpose the VAT saving is—

(*a*) to the extent that the case falls within paragraph 6(1)(*a*), the aggregate of—

(i) the amount by which the amount of VAT that would, but for the scheme, have been shown in returns in respect of the relevant periods as payable by the taxable person exceeds the amount of VAT that was shown in those returns as payable by him, and

(ii) the amount by which the amount of VAT that was shown in such returns as payable to the taxable person exceeds the amount of VAT that would, but for the scheme, have been shown in those returns as payable to him, . . . [2]

(*b*) to the extent that the case falls within paragraph 6(1)(*b*), the amount by which the amount claimed exceeds the amount which the taxable person would, but for the scheme, have claimed[, and

(*c*) to the extent that—

(i) the case falls within paragraph 6(1)(*c*), and

(ii) the excess of the notional non-deductible tax of the taxable person for the relevant periods over his non-deductible tax for those periods is not represented by a corresponding amount which by virtue of paragraph (*a*) or (*b*) is part of the VAT saving,

the amount of the excess.][2]

(4) In sub-paragraph (3)(*a*) [and (*c*)][2] "the relevant periods" means the prescribed accounting periods beginning with that in respect of which the duty to comply with paragraph 6 first arose and ending with the earlier of the following—

(*a*) the prescribed accounting period in which the taxable person complied with that paragraph, and

(*b*) the prescribed accounting period immediately preceding the notification by the Commissioners of the penalty assessment.][1]

[(5) In sub-paragraph (3)(*c*), "notional non-deductible tax", in relation to a taxable person, means the amount that would, but for the scheme, have been the amount of his non-deductible tax.][2]

Amendments—[1] Schedule inserted by FA 2004 s 19, Sch 2 para 2 with effect from the passing of FA 2004, so far as is necessary for enabling the making of any orders or regulations by virtue of FA 2004 Sch 2, and otherwise with effect from 1 August 2004 (by virtue of SI 2004/1934).

[2] Word "and" in sub-para (3)(a) repealed; sub-para (3)(c) inserted; words in sub-para (4) inserted; and sub-para (5) inserted; by F(No 2)A 2005 ss 6, 70, Sch 1 paras 1, 7, Sch 11 Pt 1 with effect from 1 August 2005 (by virtue of SI 2005/2010 art 2, subject to savings in arts 3, 4).

[Penalty assessments

12—(1) Where any person is liable under paragraph 10 to a penalty of an amount determined under paragraph 11, the Commissioners may, subject to sub-paragraph (3), assess the amount due by way of penalty and notify it to him accordingly.

(2) The fact that any conduct giving rise to a penalty under paragraph 10 may have ceased before an assessment is made under this paragraph shall not affect the power of the Commissioners to make such an assessment.

[(3) In a case where—

(*a*) the penalty falls to be calculated by reference to the VAT saving as determined under paragraph 11(3), and

(*b*) the notional tax cannot readily be attributed to any one or more prescribed accounting periods,

the notional tax shall be treated for the purposes of this Schedule as attributable to such period or periods as the Commissioners may determine to the best of their judgment and notify to the person liable for the penalty.][2]

[(3A) In sub-paragraph (3) "the notional tax" means—

(*a*) the VAT that would, but for the scheme, have been shown in returns as payable by or to the taxable person, or

(*b*) any amount that would, but for the scheme, have been the amount of the non-deductible tax of the taxable person.][2]

(4) No assessment to a penalty under this paragraph shall be made more than two years from the time when facts sufficient, in the opinion of the Commissioners, to indicate that there has been a failure to comply with paragraph 6 in relation to a notifiable scheme came to the Commissioners' knowledge.

(5) Where the Commissioners notify a person of a penalty in accordance with sub-paragraph (1), the notice of assessment shall specify—

(*a*) the amount of the penalty,

(*b*) the reasons for the imposition of the penalty,

(*c*) how the penalty has been calculated, and

(*d*) any reduction of the penalty in accordance with section 70.

(6) Where a person is assessed under this paragraph to an amount due by way of penalty and is also assessed under section 73(1), (2), (7), (7A) or (7B) for any of the prescribed accounting periods to which the assessment under this paragraph relates, the assessments may be combined and notified to him as one assessment, but the amount of the penalty shall be separately identified in the notice.

(7) If an amount is assessed and notified to any person under this paragraph, then unless, or except to the extent that, the assessment is withdrawn or reduced, that amount shall be recoverable as if it were VAT due from him.

(8) Subsection (10) of section 76 (notification to certain persons acting for others) applies for the purposes of this paragraph as it applies for the purposes of that section.][1]

Amendments—[1] Schedule inserted by FA 2004 s 19, Sch 2 para 2 with effect from the passing of FA 2004, so far as is necessary for enabling the making of any orders or regulations by virtue of FA 2004 Sch 2, and otherwise with effect from 1 August 2004 (by virtue of SI 2004/1934).

[2] Sub-paras (3), (3A) substituted for sub-para (3) by F(No 2)A 2005 s 6, Sch 1 paras 1, 8 with effect from 1 August 2005 (by virtue of SI 2005/2010 art 2, subject to savings in arts 3, 4).

[13—Regulations under this Schedule—

(*a*) may make different provision for different circumstances, and

(*b*) may include transitional provisions or savings.] [1]

Orders—See VAT (Disclosure of Avoidance Schemes) Regulations, SI 2004/1929.

Amendments—[1] Schedule inserted by FA 2004 s 19, Sch 2 para 2 with effect from the passing of FA 2004, so far as is necessary for enabling the making of any orders or regulations by virtue of FA 2004 Sch 2, and otherwise with effect from 1 August 2004 (by virtue of SI 2004/1934).

SCHEDULE 12

CONSTITUTION AND PROCEDURE OF TRIBUNALS

Section 61

Note—The term "VAT and duties tribunals" substituted for "VAT tribunals" throughout Schedule 12, from 1 September 1994, by virtue of Sch 12 para 1(2).

Amendments—This schedule repealed by the Transfer of Tribunal Functions and Revenue and Customs Appeals Order, SI 2009/56 art 3, Sch 1 para 228 with effect from 1 April 2009, subject to transitional and savings provisions in Sch 3 para 4.

Establishment of tribunals

1—(1) There shall continue to be tribunals for England and Wales, Scotland and Northern Ireland respectively known as [VAT and duties tribunals].

(2) If section 7(1) and (2) of the Finance Act 1994 have come into force before this Schedule comes into force then for any reference in this Schedule to VAT tribunals there shall, as from the commencement of this Schedule, be substituted a reference to VAT and duties tribunals.

(3) If sub-paragraph (2) above does not apply, then, as from a day to be appointed by order made by the Commissioners by statutory instrument for the purposes of this paragraph, for any reference in this Schedule to VAT tribunals there shall be substituted a reference to VAT and duties tribunals.

(4) Any reference in any enactment or any subordinate legislation to a value added tax tribunal (or to a [VAT and duties tribunal]) shall be construed in accordance with paragraphs (1) to (3) above, and cognate expressions shall be construed similarly.[1]

Commentary—*De Voil Indirect Tax Service* **V1.288**.

Definitions—"The Commissioners", s 96(1); "subordinate legislation", s 96(1); "tribunal", s 82; "VAT", ss 1, 96(1).

Amendments—[1] This schedule repealed by the Transfer of Tribunal Functions and Revenue and Customs Appeals Order, SI 2009/56 art 3, Sch 1 para 228 with effect from 1 April 2009, subject to transitional and savings provisions in Sch 3 para 4.

The President

2—(1) There shall continue to be a President of [VAT and duties tribunals], who shall perform the functions conferred on him by the following provisions of this Schedule in relation to [VAT and duties tribunals] in any part of the United Kingdom.

(2) The President shall be appointed by the Lord Chancellor after consultation with the [Secretary of State][1] *and shall be—*

[(a) a person who satisfies the judicial-appointment eligibility condition on a 7-year basis;][2]

(b) an advocate or solicitor in Scotland of at least [7][2] *years' standing; or*

(c) a member of the Bar of Northern Ireland or solicitor of the Supreme Court of Northern Ireland of at least [7][2] *years' standing.*

(3) Subject to paragraph 3 below, the appointment of the President shall be for such term and subject to such conditions as may be determined by the Lord Chancellor, after consultation with the [Secretary of State][1]*, and a person who ceases to hold the office of President shall be eligible for re-appointment thereto.*[3]

Definitions—"Tribunal", s 82; "United Kingdom", s 96(11); "VAT", ss 1, 96(1).

Amendments—[1] Words substituted by the Transfer of Functions (Lord Advocate and Secretary of State) Order, SI 1999/678 with effect from 19 May 1999.

[2] Sub-para (2)(a) substituted, and in sub-para (2)(b), (c) figure "7" substituted for figure "10", by the Tribunals, Courts and Enforcement Act 2007 s 50, Sch 10 para 24 with effect from 21 July 2008 (by virtue of SI 2008/1653 art 2(d)).

[3] This schedule repealed by the Transfer of Tribunal Functions and Revenue and Customs Appeals Order, SI 2009/56 art 3, Sch 1 para 228 with effect from 1 April 2009, subject to transitional and savings provisions in Sch 3 para 4.

3—(1) The President may resign his office at any time and shall vacate his office—

(a) at the end of the completed year of service in which he attains the age of 72, or

(b) if sub-paragraph (2) below applies, on the date on which he attains the age of 75.

This sub-paragraph shall cease to have effect on the day appointed under section 31 of the Judicial Pensions and Retirement Act 1993 ("the 1993 Act") for the coming into force of section 26 of that Act.

(2) If the Lord Chancellor, after consultation with the [Secretary of State][1]*, considers it desirable in the public interest to do so he may authorise the President to continue in office after the end of the completed year of service mentioned in sub-paragraph (1)(a) above.*

(3) The President—

(a) may resign his office at any time; and

(b) shall vacate his office on the day on which he attains the age of 70;

but sub-paragraph (b) above is subject to section 26(4) to (6) of the 1993 Act (power to authorise continuance in office up to the age of 75).

This sub-paragraph shall come into force on the day appointed under section 31 of the 1993 Act for the coming into force of section 26 of that Act.

(4) The Lord Chancellor may, if he thinks fit and after consultation with the [Secretary of State][1]*, remove the President from office on the ground of incapacity or misbehaviour.*

(5) The functions of the President may, if he is for any reason unable to act or his office is vacant, be discharged by a person nominated for the purpose by the Lord Chancellor after consultation with the [Secretary of State][1]*.*

[(5A) The Lord Chancellor may remove a person from office under sub-paragraph (4), or nominate a person under sub-paragraph (5), only with the concurrence of all of the following—

(a) the Lord Chief Justice of England and Wales;

(b) the Lord President of the Court of Session;

(c) the Lord Chief Justice of Northern Ireland.][2]

(6) There shall be paid to the President such salary or fees and there may be paid to or in respect of a former President such pension, allowance or gratuity as the Lord Chancellor may with the approval of the Treasury determine.

(7) Sub-paragraph (6) above, so far as relating to pensions allowances and gratuities, shall not have effect in relation to a person to whom Part I of the 1993 Act applies, except to the extent provided under or by that Act.

(8) If a person ceases to be President of [VAT and duties tribunals] and it appears to the Lord Chancellor that there are special circumstances which make it right that he should receive compensation, there may be paid to that person a sum of such amount as the Lord Chancellor may with the approval of the Treasury determine.

[(9) The Lord Chief Justice of England and Wales may nominate a judicial office holder (as defined in section 109(4) of the Constitutional Reform Act 2005) to exercise his functions under sub-paragraph (5A) in relation to the nomination of a person under sub-paragraph (5).

(10) The Lord President of the Court of Session may nominate a judge of the Court of Session who is a member of the First or Second Division of the Inner House of that Court to exercise his functions under sub-paragraph (5A) in relation to the nomination of a person under sub-paragraph (5).

(11) The Lord Chief Justice of Northern Ireland may nominate any of the following to exercise his functions under sub-paragraph (5A) in relation to the nomination of a person under sub-paragraph (5)—

(a) the holder of one of the offices listed in Schedule 1 to the Justice (Northern Ireland) Act 2002;

(b) a Lord Justice of Appeal (as defined in section 88 of that Act)][2] [3]

Definitions—"Tribunal", s 82; "VAT", ss 1, 96(1).

Amendments—[1] Words substituted by the Transfer of Functions (Lord Advocate and Secretary of State) Order, SI 1999/678 with effect from 19 May 1999.

[2] Sub-paras (5A), (9)–(11) inserted by the Constitutional Reform Act 2005 s 15, Sch 4 paras 235, 237(1), (2) with effect from 3 April 2006 by virtue of SI 2006/1014 art 2(a), Sch 1 para 11.

[3] This schedule repealed by the Transfer of Tribunal Functions and Revenue and Customs Appeals Order, SI 2009/56 art 3, Sch 1 para 228 with effect from 1 April 2009, subject to transitional and savings provisions in Sch 3 para 4.

Sittings of tribunals

4—[(1)] Such number of [VAT and duties tribunals] shall be established as the Lord Chancellor or, in relation to Scotland, the Secretary of State may from time to time determine, and they shall sit at such times and at such places as the Lord Chancellor or, as the case may be, the Secretary of State may from time to time determine.

[(2) The powers of the Lord Chancellor under sub-paragraph (1) may be exercised—

(a) in relation to England and Wales only after consulting the Lord Chief Justice of England and Wales;

(b) in relation to Northern Ireland only after consulting the Lord Chief Justice of Northern Ireland.

(3) The Lord Chief Justice of England and Wales may nominate a judicial office holder (as defined in section 109(4) of the Constitutional Reform Act 2005) to exercise his functions under this paragraph.

(4) The Lord Chief Justice of Northern Ireland may nominate any of the following to exercise his functions under this paragraph—

(a) the holder of one of the offices listed in Schedule 1 to the Justice (Northern Ireland) Act 2002;

(b) a Lord Justice of Appeal (as defined in section 88 of that Act).][1], [2]

Definitions—"Tribunal", s 82; "VAT", ss 1, 96(1).

Amendments—[1] Paragraph renumbered as sub-para (1), and sub-paras (2)–(4) inserted, by the Constitutional Reform Act 2005 s 15, Sch 4 paras 235, 237(1), (3) with effect from 3 April 2006, by virtue of SI 2006/1014 art 2(a), Sch 1 para 11.

[2] This schedule repealed by the Transfer of Tribunal Functions and Revenue and Customs Appeals Order, SI 2009/56 art 3, Sch 1 para 228 with effect from 1 April 2009, subject to transitional and savings provisions in Sch 3 para 4.

Composition of tribunals

5—(1) A [VAT and duties tribunal] shall consist of a chairman sitting either with two other members or with one other member or alone.

(2) If the tribunal does not consist of the chairman sitting alone, its decisions may be taken by a majority of votes and the chairman, if sitting with one other member, shall have a casting vote.[1]

Simon's Tax Cases—Sub-para (2), *Rahman (T/A Khayam Restaurant) v C&E Comrs* [1998] STC 826.

Definitions—"Tribunal", s 82; "VAT", ss 1, 96(1).

Amendments—[1] This schedule repealed by the Transfer of Tribunal Functions and Revenue and Customs Appeals Order, SI 2009/56 art 3, Sch 1 para 228 with effect from 1 April 2009, subject to transitional and savings provisions in Sch 3 para 4.

Membership of tribunals

6 For each sitting of a [VAT and duties tribunal] the chairman shall be either the President or if so authorised by the President, a member of the appropriate panel of chairmen constituted in accordance with paragraph 7 below; and any other member of the tribunal shall be a person selected from the appropriate panel of other members so constituted, the selection being made either by the President or by a member of the panel of chairmen, authorised by the President to make it.[1]

Definitions—"Document", s 96(1); "subordinate legislation", s 96(1); "tribunal", s 82; "VAT", ss 1, 96(1).

Amendments—[1] This schedule repealed by the Transfer of Tribunal Functions and Revenue and Customs Appeals Order, SI 2009/56 art 3, Sch 1 para 228 with effect from 1 April 2009, subject to transitional and savings provisions in Sch 3 para 4.

7—(1) There shall be a panel of chairmen and a panel of other members of [VAT and duties tribunals] for England and Wales, Scotland and Northern Ireland respectively.

(2) One member of each panel of chairmen shall be known as Vice-President of [VAT and duties tribunals].

(3) Appointments to a panel of chairmen shall be made by the appropriate authority, that is to say—

(a) for England and Wales, the Lord Chancellor;

(b) for Scotland, the Lord President of the Court of Session; and

(c) for Northern Ireland, the [Lord Chancellor][1]*;*

and appointments to a panel of other members shall be made by the Treasury.

(4) No person may be appointed to a panel of chairmen of tribunals for England and Wales or Northern Ireland unless he is—

[(a) a person who satisfies the judicial-appointment eligibility condition on a 5-year basis; or][2]

(b) a member of the Bar of Northern Ireland or solicitor of the Supreme Court of Northern Ireland of at least [5][2] *years' standing,*

and no person may be appointed to a panel of chairmen of tribunals for Scotland unless he is an advocate or solicitor of not less than [5][2] *years' standing.*

(5) Subject to the following provisions of this paragraph, the appointment of a chairman of [VAT and duties tribunals] shall be for such term and subject to such conditions as may be determined by the appropriate authority, and a person who ceases to hold the office of chairman shall be eligible for re-appointment thereto.

(6) A chairman of [VAT and duties tribunals]—

(a) may resign his office at any time; and

(b) shall vacate his office on the day on which he attains the age of 70 years;

but paragraph (b) above is subject to section 26(4) to (6) of the Judicial Pensions and Retirement Act 1993 (power to authorise continuance in office up to the age of 75).

(7) The appropriate authority may, if he thinks fit, remove a chairman of [VAT and duties tribunals] from office on the ground of incapacity or misbehaviour.

[(7A) The Lord Chancellor may, with the concurrence of the Lord Chief Justice of England and Wales, remove from office on the ground of incapacity or misbehaviour a chairman of VAT Tribunals appointed under sub-paragraph (3)(a).

(7B) The Lord President of the Court of Session may remove from office on the ground of incapacity or misbehaviour a chairman of VAT Tribunals appointed under sub-paragraph (3)(b).][1]

(8) There shall be paid to a chairman of [VAT and duties tribunals] such salary or fees, and to other members such fees, as the Lord Chancellor may with the approval of the Treasury determine; and there may be paid to or in respect of a former chairman of [VAT and duties tribunals] such pension, allowance or gratuity as the Lord Chancellor may with the approval of the Treasury determine.

(9) Sub-paragraph (8) above, so far as relating to pensions allowances and gratuities, shall not have effect in relation to a person to whom Part I of the Judicial Pensions and Retirement Act 1993 applies, except to the extent provided under or by that Act.

(10) If a person ceases to be a chairman of [VAT and duties tribunals] and it appears to the Lord Chancellor that there are special circumstances which make it right that he should receive compensation, there may be paid to that person a sum of such amount as the Lord Chancellor may with the approval of the Treasury determine.[3]

Definitions—"Tribunal", s 82; "VAT", ss 1, 96(1).

Amendments—[1] In sub-para (3)(c), words substituted for words "Lord Chief Justice of Northern Ireland"; and sub-paras (7A), (7B) substituted for former sub-para (7); by the Constitutional Reform Act 2005 s 15, Sch 4 paras 235, 237(1), (4) with from 3 April 2006, by virtue of SI 2006/1014 art 2(a), Sch 1 para 11.

[2] Sub-para (4)(a) substituted, and in sub-para (4)(b) and in the words following that para, figure "5" substituted for figure "7", by the Tribunals, Courts and Enforcement Act 2007 s 50, Sch 10 para 24(1), (3) with effect from 21 July 2008 (by virtue of SI 2008/1653 art 2(d)).

[3] This schedule repealed by the Transfer of Tribunal Functions and Revenue and Customs Appeals Order, SI 2009/56 art 3, Sch 1 para 228 with effect from 1 April 2009, subject to transitional and savings provisions in Sch 3 para 4.

Exemption from jury service

8 No member of a [VAT and duties tribunal] shall be compelled to serve on any jury in Scotland or Northern Ireland.[1]

Definitions—"Tribunal", s 82; "VAT", ss 1, 96(1).

Amendments—[1] This schedule repealed by the Transfer of Tribunal Functions and Revenue and Customs Appeals Order, SI 2009/56 art 3, Sch 1 para 228 with effect from 1 April 2009, subject to transitional and savings provisions in Sch 3 para 4.

Rules of procedure

9 The Lord Chancellor after consultation with the [Secretary of State][1] may make rules with respect to the procedure to be followed on appeals to and in other proceedings before [VAT and duties tribunals] and such rules may include provisions—

(a) for limiting the time within which appeals may be brought;

(b) for enabling hearings to be held in private in such circumstances as may be determined by or under the rules;

(c) for parties to proceedings to be represented by such persons as may be determined by or under the rules;

(d) for requiring persons to attend to give evidence;

(e) for discovery and for requiring persons to produce documents;

(f) for the payment of expenses and allowances to persons attending as witnesses or producing documents;

(g) for the award and recovery of costs;

(h) for authorising the administration of oaths to witnesses; and

(j) with respect to the joinder of appeals brought by different persons where a notice is served under section 61 and the appeals relate to, or to different portions of, the basic penalty referred to in the notice.[2]

Rules—See VAT Tribunals Rules, SI 1986/590.

Definitions—"Document", s 96(1); "tribunal", s 82; "VAT", ss 1, 96(1).

Cross reference—See VATA 1994 s 97(2) (a statutory instrument containing rules under this para is subject to annulment in pursuance of a resolution of either House of Parliament).

Amendments—[1] Words substituted by the Transfer of Functions (Lord Advocate and Secretary of State) Order, SI 1999/678 with effect from 19 May 1999.

[2] This schedule repealed by the Transfer of Tribunal Functions and Revenue and Customs Appeals Order, SI 2009/56 art 3, Sch 1 para 228 with effect from 1 April 2009, subject to transitional and savings provisions in Sch 3 para 4.

10—(1) A person who fails to comply with a direction or summons issued by a [VAT and duties tribunal] under rules made under paragraph 9 above shall be liable to a penalty not exceeding £1,000.

(2) A penalty for which a person is liable by virtue of sub-paragraph (1) above may be awarded summarily by a tribunal notwithstanding that no proceedings for its recovery have been commenced.

(3) An appeal shall lie to the High Court or, in Scotland, the Court of Session as the Court of Exchequer in Scotland, from the award of a penalty under this paragraph, and on such an appeal the court may either confirm or reverse the decision of the tribunal or reduce or increase the sum awarded.

(4) A penalty awarded by virtue of this paragraph shall be recoverable as if it were VAT due from the person liable for the penalty.[1]

Definitions—"Tribunal", s 82; "VAT", ss 1, 96(1).

Amendments—[1] This schedule repealed by the Transfer of Tribunal Functions and Revenue and Customs Appeals Order, SI 2009/56 art 3, Sch 1 para 228 with effect from 1 April 2009, subject to transitional and savings provisions in Sch 3 para 4.

SCHEDULE 13

TRANSITIONAL PROVISIONS AND SAVINGS

Section 100

General provisions

1—(1) The continuity of the law relating to VAT shall not be affected by the substitution of this Act for the enactments repealed by this Act and earlier enactments repealed by and corresponding to any of those enactments ("the repealed enactments").

(2) Any reference, whether express or implied, in any enactment, instrument or document (including this Act or any Act amended by this Act) to, or to things done falling to be done under or for the purposes of, any provision of this Act shall, if and so far as the nature of the reference permits, be construed as including, in relation to the times, years or periods, circumstances or purposes in relation to which the corresponding provision in the repealed enactments has or had effect, a reference to, or as the case may be, to things done or falling to be done under or for the purposes of, that corresponding provision.

(3) Any reference, whether express or implied, in any enactment, instrument or document (including the repealed enactments and enactments, instruments and documents passed or made or otherwise coming into existence after the commencement of this Act) to, or to things done or falling to be done under or for the purposes of, any of the repealed enactments shall, if and so far as the nature of the reference permits, be construed as including, in relation to the times, years or periods, circumstances or purposes in relation to which the corresponding provision of this Act has effect, a reference to, or as the case may be to things done or falling to be done under or for the purposes of, that corresponding provision.

(4) Without prejudice to paragraphs (1) to (3) above, in any case where as respects the charge to VAT on any supply, acquisition or importation made at a time before 1st September 1994 but falling in a prescribed accounting period to which Part I applies

(*a*) an enactment applicable to that charge to VAT is not re-enacted in this Act or is re-enacted with amendments which came into force after that time, or

(*b*) a repealed enactment corresponding to an enactment in this Act did not apply to that charge to VAT,

any question arising under Part I and relating to that charge to VAT shall continue to be determined in accordance with the law in force at that time.

Definitions—"Document", s 96(1); "supply", s 5, Sch 4; "VAT", ss 1, 96(1).

Validity of subordinate legislation

2 So far as this Act re-enacts any provision contained in a statutory instrument made in exercise of powers conferred by any Act, it shall be without prejudice to the validity of that provision, and any question as to its validity shall be determined as if the re-enacted provision were contained in a statutory instrument made under those powers.

Provisions related to the introduction of VAT

3 Where a vehicle in respect of which purchase tax was remitted under section 23 of the Purchase Tax Act 1963 (vehicles for use outside the United Kingdom) is brought back to the United Kingdom the vehicle shall not, when brought back, be treated as imported for the purpose of VAT chargeable on the importation of goods.

Definitions—"United Kingdom", s 96(11); "VAT", ss 1, 96(1).

Supply in accordance with pre-21.4.75 arrangements

4 Where there were in force immediately before 21st April 1975 arrangements between the Commissioners and any taxable person for supplies made by him (or such supplies made by him as were specified in the arrangements) to be treated as taking place at times or on dates which, had section 6(10) been in force when the arrangements were made, could have been provided for by a direction under that section, he shall be treated for the purposes of that section as having requested the Commissioners to give a direction thereunder to the like effect, and the Commissioners may give a direction (or a general direction applying to cases of any class or description specified in the direction) accordingly.

Definitions—"The Commissioners", s 96(1); "supply", s 5, Sch 4; "taxable person", s 82.

President, chairmen etc of tribunals

5—(1) Any appointment to a panel of chairmen of the tribunals current at the commencement of this Act and made by the Treasury before the passing of the 1983 Act shall not be affected by the repeal by this Act of paragraph 8 of Schedule 10 to that Act.

(2) The terms of appointment of any person who was appointed to the office of President of the tribunal or chairman or other member of the tribunals before 1st April 1986 and holds that office on the coming into force of this Act shall continue to have effect notwithstanding the re-enactment, as Schedule 12 to this Act, of Schedule 8 to the 1983 Act as amended by Schedule 8 to the Finance Act 1985.

Overseas suppliers accounting through their customers

6 Notwithstanding the repeal by this Act of section 32B of the 1983 Act, that section shall continue to apply in relation to any supply in relation to which section 14 does not apply by virtue of section 14(8), and for the purposes to this paragraph section 32B shall have effect as if it were included in Part III of this Act, any reference in section 32B to any enactment repealed by this Act being read as a reference to the corresponding provision of this Act.

Supplies of fuel and power for domestic or charity use

7 . . . [1]

Amendments—[1] Para 7 repealed by FA 1995 s 21(5), (6), Sch 29 Pt VI(1), with effect in relation to any supply made after 31 March 1995 and any acquisition or importation taking place after that date.

Zero-rated supplies of goods and services

8—(1) A supply of services made after the commencement of this Act in pursuance of a legally binding obligation incurred before 21st June 1988 shall if—

(*a*) the supply fell within item 2 of Group 8A of Schedule 5 to the 1983 Act immediately before 1st April 1989, and

(*b*) it was by virtue of paragraph 13(1) of Schedule 3 to the Finance Act 1989 a zero-rated supply,

be a zero-rated supply for the purposes of this Act.

(2) Where a grant, assignment or other supply is zero-rated by virtue of this paragraph, it is not a relevant zero-rated supply for the purposes of [Part 2 of Schedule 10][1].

Definitions—"Supply", s 5, Sch 4.

Amendments—[1] In sub-para (2), words substituted by the Value Added Tax (Buildings and Land) Order, SI 2008/1146, art 6, Sch 1 paras 1, 5(a) with effect in relation to supplies made on or after 1 June 2008, subject to savings in Sch 2 of the Order.

Bad debt relief

9—(1) . . . [2]

[(2) Claims for refunds of VAT shall not be made in accordance with section 36 of this Act in relation to—

(*a*) any supply made before 1st April 1989; or

(*b*) any supply as respects which a claim is or has been made under section 22 of the 1983 Act.][1]

Commentary—*De Voil Indirect Tax Service* **V5.156**.

Definitions—"Supply", s 5, Sch 4; "VAT", ss 1, 96(1);

Amendments—[1] Sub-para (2) substituted by FA 1995 s 33(1), (4) and is deemed to have always had effect.

[2] Sub-para (1) repealed by FA 1997 Sch 18 Part IV(3) in relation to claims made after 19 March 1997.

Supplies during construction of buildings and works

***10**—(1) Nothing in paragraphs 5 and 6 of Schedule 10 shall apply—*

(a) in relation to a person who has constructed a building if he incurred before 21st June 1988 a legally binding obligation to make a grant or assignment of a major interest in, or in any part of, the building or its site;

(b) in relation to a building or work if there was incurred before that date a legally binding obligation to make in relation to the building or work a supply within item 2 of Group 8 of Schedule 5 to the 1983 Act;

(c) in relation to a person who has constructed a building if—

(i) he incurred before that date a legally binding obligation to construct the building or any development of which it forms part, and

(ii) planning permission for the construction of the building was granted before that date, and

(iii) he has made a grant or assignment of a major interest in, or in any part of, the building or its site before 21st June 1993.

(2) Sub-paragraph (1) above shall not apply in any case where the Commissioners required proof of any of the matters specified in paragraph (a), (b) or (c)(i) above to be given to their satisfaction by the production of documents made before 21st June 1988 and that requirement was not complied with.[1]

Definitions—"Assignment", s 96(1); "the Commissioners", s 96(1).

Amendments—[1] Para 10 repealed by the Value Added Tax (Buildings and Land) Order, SI 2008/1146, art 6, Sch 1 paras 1, 5(b) with effect in relation to supplies made on or after 1 June 2008, subject to savings in Sch 2 of the Order.

Offences and Penalties

11 Where an offence for the continuation of which a penalty was provided has been committed under an enactment repealed by this Act, proceedings may be taken under this Act in respect of the continuance of the offence after the commencement of this Act in the same manner as if the offence had been committed under the corresponding provision of this Act.

12 Part IV of this Act, except section 72, shall not apply in relation to any act done or omitted to be done before 25th July 1985, and the following provision of this Schedule shall have effect accordingly.

13—(1) Section 72 shall have effect in relation to any offence committed or alleged to have been committed at any time ("the relevant time") before the commencement of this Act subject to the following provisions of this paragraph.

(2) Where the relevant time falls between 25th July 1983 and 26th July 1985 (the dates of passing of the 1983 and 1985 Finance Acts respectively), section 72 shall apply—

(*a*) with the substitution in subsection (1)(*b*), (3)(ii) and (8)(*b*) of "2 years" for "7 years";

(*b*) with the omission of subsections (2) and (4) to (7).

14—(1) The provisions of this paragraph have effect in relation to section 59.

(2) Section 59 shall apply in any case where a person is in default in respect of a prescribed accounting period which has ended before the commencement of this Act, but shall have effect in any case where the last day referred to in subsection (1) of that section falls before 1st October 1993 subject to the following modifications—

(*a*) for the words "a prescribed accounting period" in subsection (2)(*a*) there shall be substituted "any two prescribed accounting periods";

(*b*) with the addition of the following paragraph in subsection (2)—

"(*aa*) the last day of the later one of those periods falls on or before the first anniversary of the last day of the earlier one; and";

(*c*) for the words "period referred to in paragraph (*a*)" in subsection (2)(*b*) there shall be substituted "later period referred to in paragraph (aa)"; and

(*d*) for the words "a default in respect of a prescribed accounting period and that period" in subsection (3) there shall be substituted "defaults in respect of two prescribed accounting periods and the second of those periods".

(3) Section 59 shall have effect, in any case where a person has been served with a surcharge liability notice and that person is in default in respect of a prescribed accounting period because of a failure of the Commissioners to receive a return or an amount of VAT on or before a day falling before 30th September 1993 with the omission of—

(*a*) subsection (4)(*b*);

(*b*) the words in subsection (5) "and for which he has outstanding VAT"; and

(*c*) subsection (6).

15—(1) Section 63 does not apply in relation to returns and assessments made for prescribed accounting periods beginning before 1st April 1990 but subject to that shall have effect in relation to the cases referred to in the following sub-paragraphs subject to the modifications there specified.

(2) Subsection (1) shall have effect in a case falling within paragraph (*b*) of that subsection where the assessment was made on or before 10th March 1992 with the substitution of "20 per cent" for "15 per cent".

(3) In relation to any prescribed accounting period beginning before 1st December 1993 section 63 shall have effect with the substitution—

(*a*) for the words in subsection (2) following "exceeds" of "either 30 per cent of the true amount of the VAT for that period or whichever is the greater of £10,000 and 5 per cent of the true amount of VAT for that period." and with the omission of subsections (4) to (6); and

(*b*) for the words in subsection (8) from "subsections" to "statements" of "subsection (7) that the statement by each of those returns is a correct statement".

(4) In relation to any prescribed accounting period beginning before 1st June 1994 section 63 shall have effect with the substitution for subsection (3) of the following subsection—

"(3) Any reference in this section to the VAT for a prescribed accounting period which would have been lost if an inaccuracy had not been discovered is a reference to the aggregate of—

(*a*) the amount (if any) by which credit for input tax for that period was overstated; and

(*b*) the amount (if any) by which output tax for that period was understated;

but if for any period there is an understatement of credit for input tax or an overstatement of output tax, allowance shall be made for that error in determining the VAT for that period which would have been so lost."

and in subsection (8) for "this section" there shall be substituted "subsections (5) and (7) above".

Definitions—"Input tax", s 24; "output tax", s 24; "VAT", ss 1, 96(1).

16—(1) In relation to any prescribed accounting period beginning before 1st December 1993 section 64 shall have effect subject to the following modifications—

(*a*) in subsection (1)(*b*) for the words from "whichever" to "period" there shall be substituted "whichever is the greater of £100 and 1 per cent of the true amount of VAT for that period";

(*b*) for subsections (2) and (3) there shall be substituted—

"(2) Subsection (3) below applies in any case where—

(*a*) there is a material inaccuracy in respect of any two prescribed accounting periods, and

(*b*) the last day of the later one of those periods falls on or before the second anniversary of the last day of the earlier one, and

(*c*) after 29th July 1988 the Commissioners serve notice on the person concerned ("a penalty liability notice") specifying as a penalty period for the purposes of this section a period beginning on the date of the notice and ending on the second anniversary of that date.

(3) If there is a material inaccuracy in respect of a prescribed accounting period ending within the penalty period specified in a penalty liability notice served on the person concerned that person shall be liable to a penalty equal to 15 per cent of the VAT for that period which would have been lost if the inaccuracy had not been discovered.";

(*c*) in subsection (4) for "(5)" there shall be substituted "(7)"; and

(*d*) in subsection (6) the words from "except" to the end shall be omitted.

(2) A penalty liability notice shall not be served under section 64 by reference to any material inaccuracy in respect of a prescribed accounting period beginning before 1st December 1993, and the penalty period specified in any penalty liability notice served before that day shall be deemed to end with the day before that day.

Definitions—"The Commissioners", s 96(1); "prescribed accounting period", s 25(1); "VAT", ss 1, 96(1).

17 Section 70 shall not apply in relation to any penalty to which a person has been assessed before 27th July 1993 and in the case of any penalty in relation to which that section does not apply by virtue of this paragraph, section 60 shall have effect subject to the following modifications—

(*a*) in subsection (1) for "subsection (6)" there shall be substituted "subsections (3A) and (6)";

(*b*) after subsection (3) there shall be inserted—

"(3A) If a person liable to a penalty under this section has co-operated with the Commissioners in the investigation of his true liability to tax or, as the case may be, of his true entitlement to any payment, refund or repayment, the Commissioners or, on appeal, a tribunal may reduce the penalty to an amount which is not less than half what it would have been apart from this subsection; and in determining the extent of any reduction under this subsection, the Commissioners or tribunal shall have regard to the extent of the co-operation which the person concerned has given to the Commissioners in their investigation.";

(*c*) in subsection (4)(*b*) for the words from "under" to "this section" there shall be substituted "to reduce a penalty under this section, as provided in subsection (4) above, and, in determining the extent of such a reduction in the case of any person, the Commissioners or tribunal will have regard to the extent of the co-operation which he has given to the Commissioners in their investigation";

and in section 61(6) for "70" there shall be substituted "60(3A)".

Commentary—*De Voil Indirect Tax Service* **V5.334**.
Definitions—"The Commissioners", s 96(1); "tribunal", s 82.

18 Section 74 shall not apply in relation to prescribed accounting periods beginning before 1st April 1990 and subsection (3) of that section shall not apply in relation to interest on amounts assessed or, as the case may be, paid before 1st October 1993.

Importation of goods

19 Nothing in this Act shall prejudice the effect of the Finance (No 2) Act 1992 (Commencement No 4 and Transitional Provisions) Order 1992 and accordingly—

(*a*) where Article 4 of that Order applies immediately before the commencement of this Act in relation to any importation of goods, that Article and the legislation repealed by this Act shall continue to apply in relation to that importation as if this Act had not been enacted, and

(*b*) where Article 5 of that Order applies in relation to any goods, this Act shall apply in relation to those goods in accordance with that Article and Article 6 of that Order.

Assessments

20 An assessment may be made under section 73 in relation to amounts paid or credited before the commencement of this Act but—

(*a*) in relation to an amount paid or credited before 30th July 1990 section 73(2) shall have effect with the omission of the words from "or which" to "out to be", and

(*b*) in relation to amounts repaid or paid to any person before the passing of the Finance Act 1982 section 73 shall have effect with the omission of subsection (2).

Set-off of credits

21 Section 81 shall have effect in relation to amounts becoming due before 10th May 1994 with the omission of subsections (4) and (5).

VAT tribunals

22—(1) Without prejudice to paragraph 1 above, section 83 applies to things done or omitted to be done before the coming into force of this Act and accordingly references in Part V to any provision of this Act includes a reference to the corresponding provision of the enactments repealed by this Act or by any enactment repealed by such an enactment.

(2) Section 84 shall have effect before such day as may be appointed for the purposes of section 18(3) of the Finance Act 1994 with the substitution for subsection (5) of the following subsection—

"(5) No appeal shall lie with respect to any matter that has been or could have been referred to arbitration under section 127 of the Management Act as applied by section 16."

Isle of Man

23 Nothing in paragraph 7 of Schedule 14 shall affect the validity of any Order made under section 6 of the Isle of Man Act 1979 and, without prejudice to section 17 of the Interpretation Act 1978 for any reference in any such Order to any enactment repealed by this Act there shall be substituted a reference to the corresponding provision of this Act.

SCHEDULE 14

CONSEQUENTIAL AMENDMENTS

1–5 (*amend* provisions outside the scope of this Publication).

Customs and Excise Management Act 1979 c 2

6 (*amends* CEMA 1979 s 1(1)).

Isle of Man Act 1979 c 58

7 (*amends* IOM 1979 ss 1(1), 6(1), 14(4)).

Cross references—See VATA 1994 s 101(4) (this para to extend to the Isle of Man);
VATA 1994 Sch 13 para 23 (this para does not affect the validity of any order made under Isle of Man Act 1979 s 6).

Insolvency Act 1986 c 45

8 (*amended* Sch 6, *repealed by* the Enterprise Act 2002 s 278, Sch 26).

Bankruptcy (Scotland) Act 1985 c 66

9 (*amends* Sch 3 para 8).

Income and Corporation Taxes Act 1988 c 1

10 (*amends* TA 1988 s 827).

Capital Allowances Act 1990 c 1

11 (*amended* s 159A, *repealed by* CAA 2001 s 580, Sch 4 with effect in accordance with CAA 2001 s 579).

Tribunals and Inquiries Act 1992 c 53

[**12** *(amends Sch 1).*][1]

1 This para repealed by the Transfer of Tribunal Functions and Revenue and Customs Appeals Order, SI 2009/56 art 3, Sch 1 para 229 with effect from 1 April 2009, subject to transitional and savings provisions in Sch 3 para 4.

Finance Act 1994 c 9

13 (*amends* s 7(4), (5) (and is *amended* by FA 1995 s 33(1), (5), this amendment being deemed to have always had effect)).

Vehicle Excise and Registration Act 1994 c 22

14 (*amends* Sch 2 para 23).

VATA 1994: Destination table

This table shows in column (1) the enactments and instruments repealed or revoked by VATA 1994 and in column (2) the provisions of that Act corresponding thereto.

In certain cases the enactment or instrument in column (1), though having a corresponding provision in column (2), is not, or not wholly, repealed or revoked as it is still required, or partly required, for the purposes of other legislation.

A "dash" adjacent to a repealed or revoked provision indicates that that provision is spent, unnecessary or for some other reason not specifically reproduced.

Subsequent amendments to VATA 1994 after its date of Royal Assent are not accounted for in the table below.

(1)	(2)
Customs and Excise Management Act 1979 (c 2)	Value Added Tax Act 1994 (c 23)
s 100B	s 17(3)
s 100C(1)	s 17(2)
s 100C(2)	Rep SI 1991/2727, reg 3(1)
s 100C(3)	s 17(4)
s 100C(4)(*a*)–(*c*)	s 17(5)
s 100C(4)(*d*)	s 17(3)
Value Added Tax Act 1983 (c 55)	Value Added Tax Act 1994 (c 23)
s 1	s 1(1)
s 2(1)	s 4(1)
s 2(2)	s 4(2)
s 2(3)	s 1(2)
s 2(4), (5)	Rep 1992 c 48, s 82, Sch 18 Pt V(1)
s 2A(1)–(3)	s 10(1)–(3)
s 2A(4)	s 1(3)
s 2B(1)	s 1(4)
s 2B(2)–(4)	s 15(1)–(3)
s 2C	s 3
s 3	s 5
s 4	s 6(1)–(3)
s 5(1)–(3)	s 6(4)–(6)
s 5(3A), (3B)	s 6(7), (8)
s 5(4)–(10)	s 6(9)–(15)
s 6(1), (2)	s 7(1), (2)
s 6(2A)–(2D)	s 7(3)–(6)
s 6(3), (4)	s 7(7), (8)
s 6(4A)	s 7(9)
s 6(5), (6)	s 7(10), (11)
s 7	s 8
s 8	s 9
s 8A	s 11
s 8B	s 12
s 8C	s 13
s 8D	s 14(1)–(7)
s 9	s 2
s 10(1)–(5)	s 19(1)–(5)
s 10(6)	Rep 1992 c 48, s 82, Sch 18 Pt V(1)

(1)	(2)
Value Added Tax Act 1983 (c 55)	Value Added Tax Act 1994 (c 23)
s 14(10)	s 25(7)
s 14(11)	s 24(7)
s 15	s 26
s 16(1)–(6)	s 30(1)–(6)
s 16(6A)	s 30(7)
s 16(7)–(9)	s 30(8)–(10)
s 17	s 31
s 18	s 32
s 19(1)	s 37(1)
s 19(1A)	s 37(2)
s 19(2), (3)	s 37(3), (4)
s 20(1)–(4)	s 33(1)–(4)
s 20(4A)	s 33(5)
s 20(5)	s 33(6)
s 20(6)	s 96(4)
s 20A	s 40
s 21(1), (2)	s 35(1), (2)
s 21(2A)	s 35(3)
s 22	Rep 1990 c 29, ss 11(9), 132, Sch 19 Pt III
s 23	s 39
s 24(1)	s 16(1)
s 24(2), (3)	—
s 24(4)	s 16(2)
s 25	s 38
s 26	s 27
s 27(1), (2)	s 41(1), (2)
s 27(2A), (2B)	s 41(3), (4)
s 27(3)–(6)	s 41(5)–(8)
s 28(1)	s 42
s 28(2)	—
s 29(1), (2)	s 43(1), (2)
s 29(3), (3A)	s 43(3)
s 29(4)–(8)	s 43(4)–(8)
s 29A(1)–(3)	s 44(1)–(3)
s 29A(3A)	s 44(4)
s 29A(4)–(9)	s 44(5)–(10)

(1) Customs and Excise Management Act 1979 (c 2)	(2) Value Added Tax Act 1994 (c 23)	(1) Value Added Tax Act 1983 (c 55)	(2) Value Added Tax Act 1994 (c 23)
s 10A	s 20	s 30	s 45
s 11(1), (2)	s 21(1), (2)	s 31	s 46
s 11(2A)	s 21(3)	s 32(1)	Rep 1992 c 48, s 82, Sch 18 Pt V(1)
s 11(3), (4)	Rep 1992 c 48, s 82, Sch 18 Pt V(1)	s 32(2)–(4)	s 47
s 12	s 22	s 32A	s 48
s 13	s 23	s 32B	Rep 1993 c 34, ss 44(2), 213, Sch 23 Pt II(3)
s 14(1), (2)	s 25(1), (2)	s 33(1)	s 49(1)
s 14(3)	s 24(1), (2)	s 33(1A)	Rep 1990 c 29, ss 10(7), 132, Sch 19 Pt III
s 14(3A), (3B)	s 24(3), (4)	s 33(2), (3)	s 49(2), (3)
s 14(4)	s 24(5)	s 34	s 50
s 14(5)–(8)	s 25(3)–(6)	s 35	s 18
s 14(9)	s 24(6)	s 35A	s 51

(1) Value Added Tax Act 1983 (c 55)	(2) Value Added Tax Act 1994 (c 23)	(1) Value Added Tax Act 1983 (c 55)	(2) Value Added Tax Act 1994 (c 23)
s 36(1), (2)	s 34(1), (2)	para 1B	Sch 1, para 3
s 36(3)	Rep 1992 c 48, s 82, Sch 18 Pt V(1)	para 2	Sch 1, para 4
s 37	s 52	paras 3, 4	Sch 1, paras 5, 6
s 37A	s 53	paras 4A, 4B	Sch 1, paras 7, 8
s 37B	s 54	para 5	Sch 1, para 9
s 37C	s 55	para 5A	Sch 1, para 10
s 38	s 58	para 6	Rep 1987 c 16, ss 14(6), 72, Sch 16 Pt IV
s 38A(1)–(8)	s 78(1)–(8)	para 7	Sch 1, para 11
s 38A(8A)	s 78(9)	para 7A	Sch 1, para 12
s 38A(9)–(11)	s 78(10)–(12)	para 8	Rep 1987 c 16, s 72, Sch 16 Pt IV
s 38A(12)	—	para 8A(1)	Sch 1, para 13(1)
s 38B	s 81(1), (2)	para 8A(1A)	Sch 1, para 13(4)
s 38C	s 28	para 8A(1B)	Sch 1, para 13(6)
s 39(1)	s 72(1)	para 8A(2)	Sch 1, para 13(7)
s 39(1A)	s 72(2)	para 9(1)	Sch 1, para 13(2)
s 39(2)	s 72(3)	para 9(1A)	Sch 1, para 13(5)
s 39(2A)–(2D)	s 72(4)–(7)	para 9(1B)	Sch 1, para 13(6)
s 39(3)	s 72(8)	para 9(2)	Sch 1, para 18
s 39(3A)	s 72(9)	para 10	Sch 1, para 13(3)
s 39(4), (5)	s 72(10), (11)	paras 11, 12	Sch 1, paras 14, 15

(1) Value Added Tax Act 1983 (c 55)	(2) Value Added Tax Act 1994 (c 23)
s 39(6)–(8)	Rep 1985 c 54, ss 12(7), 98(6), Sch 27 Pt IV
s 39(9)	s 72(12)
s 40(1)	s 83
s 40(1A)	s 84(6)
s 40(2), (3)	s 84(2), (3)
s 40(3A)	s 84(7)
s 40(3ZA)	s 84(4)
s 40(3B)	s 84(5)
s 40(4)–(6)	s 84(8)–(10)
s 41(1)–(3)	s 88(1)–(3)
s 41(3A)	s 88(4)
s 41(4)–(6)	s 88(5)–(7)
s 42(1)	s 89(1)
s 42(1A)	s 89(2)
s 42(2)	s 89(3)
s 43	s 90
s 44	s 91
s 45(1)	s 97(1)
s 45(2)	s 97(5)
s 45(3), (4)	s 97(3), (4)
s 46	s 98
s 46A	s 92
s 46B	s 93
s 47	s 94
s 47A(1)	s 95(1)
s 47A(1A)	s 95(2)
s 47A(2)–(4)	s 95(3)–(5)
s 48(1)	s 96(1)
s 48(1A), (1B)	s 96(3), (5)
s 48(2), (3)	Rep 1993 c 50, s 1(1), Sch 1 Pt XIV
s 48(4)	s 96(6)
s 48(5)–(8)	s 96(8)–(11)
s 48(9)	s 96(2)

(1) Value Added Tax Act 1983 (c 55)	(2) Value Added Tax Act 1994 (c 23)
para 13	Sch 1, para 16
para 14	Sch 1, para 17
para 15	Sch 1, para 19
Sch 1A	Sch 2
Sch 1B	Sch 3
Sch 2, paras 1–4	Sch 4, paras 1–4
para 5(1), (2)	Sch 4, para 5(1),(2)
para 5(2A)	Sch 4, para 5(3)
para 5(3)	Sch 4, para 5(4)
para 5(3A)	Sch 4, para 5(5)
para 5(4)	Sch 4, para 5(6)
para 5A	Sch 4, para 6
para 6	Sch 4, para 7
para 7(1), (2)	Sch 4, para 8(1),(2)
para 7(2A)	Sch 4, para 8(3)
para 7(3)	Sch 4, para 8(4)
para 8	Sch 4, para 9
Sch 3, paras 1–6	Sch 5, paras 1–6
para 6A	Sch 5, para 7
paras 7, 8	Sch 5, paras 8, 9
Sch 4, para 1	Sch 6, para 1
para 2	Rep 1992 c 48, ss 14, 82, Sch 3 Pt I para 61(1), Sch 18, Pt V(1)
para 3	Sch 6, para 2
para 3A	Sch 6, para 3
para 4	Sch 6, para 4
para 5	Rep 1992 c 48, ss 14, 82, Sch 3 Pt I para 61(1), Sch 18, Pt V(1)
paras 6–8	Sch 6, paras 5–7
para 8A	Sch 6, para 8
paras 9–13	Sch 6, paras 9–13
Sch 4A	Sch 7
Sch 5, Groups 1–4	Sch 8, Pt II, Groups 1–4
Group 5	Rep 1985 c 54, ss 11, 98(6), Sch 27 Pt IV
Group 6	Rep 1989 c 26, ss 20, 187(1), Sch 17 Pt III

(1) Value Added Tax Act 1983 (c 55)	(2) Value Added Tax Act 1994 (c 23)
s 49	s 99
ss 50, 51	—
Sch 1, para 1(1)–(4)	Sch 1, para 1(1)–(4)
para 1(4A), (4B)	Sch 1, para 1(5),(6)
para 1(5), (6)	Sch 1, para 1(7),(8)
para 1A	Sch 1, para 2

(1) Value Added Tax Act 1983 (c 55)	(2) Value Added Tax Act 1994 (c 23)
Group 7	Rep 1993 c 34, s 213, Sch 23 Pt II(1)
Group 8	Sch 8, Pt II, Group 5
Group 8A	Sch 8, Pt II, Group 6
Groups 9–15	Sch 8, Pt II, Groups 7–13
Group 15A	Sch 8, Pt II, Group 14
Groups 16, 17	Sch 8, Pt II, Groups 15, 16

(1) Value Added Tax Act 1983 (c 55)	(2) Value Added Tax Act 1994 (c 23)
Sch 6, Groups 1–12	Sch 9, Pt II, Groups 1–12
Sch 6A, paras 1, 2	Sch 10, paras 1, 2
para 3(1)–(6)	Sch 10, para 3(1)–(6)
para 3(7)	Rep SI 1991/2560, art 4(*c*)
para 3(8)–(10)	Sch 10, para 3(7)–(9)
paras 4, 5	Sch 10, paras 4, 5
para 6(1), (2)	Sch 10, para 6(1),(2)
para 6(2A), (2B)	Sch 10, para 6(3),(4)
para 6(3)–(6)	Sch 10, para 6(5)–(8)
para 6A	Sch 10, para 7
paras 7, 8	Sch 10, paras 8, 9
Sch 7, para 1	Sch 11, para 1
para 2(1), (2)	Sch 11, para 2(1),(2)
para 2(2A)–(2C)	Sch 11, para 2(3)–(5)
para 2(3)	Sch 11, para 2(6)
para 2(3A)	Sch 11, para 2(7)
para 2(3B), (3C)	Sch 11, para 2(8),(9)
para 2(4)–(7)	Sch 11, para 2(10)–(13)
para 3(1), (2)	Sch 11, para 3(1),(2)
para 3(2A)	Sch 11, para 3(3)
para 3(3), (4)	Rep 1985 c 54, s 98(6), Sch 27 Pt IV
para 4(1), (2)	s 73(1), (2)
para 4(2A)	s 73(3)
para 4(3)–(6)	s 73(4)–(7)

(1) Value Added Tax Act 1983 (c 55)	(2) Value Added Tax Act 1994 (c 23)
para 7(1)–(3)	Sch 12, para 7(1)–(3)
para 7(3A), (3B)	Sch 12, para 7(4),(5)
para 7(3C)	Sch 12, para 7(6)
para 7(3D)	—
para 7(3E)	Sch 12, para 7(7)
para 7(4)	Sch 12, para 7(8)
para 7(4A)	Sch 12, para 7(9)
para 7(5)	Sch 12, para 7(10)
paras 8–10	Sch 12, paras 8–10
Sch 10	Cf Sch 13
Sch 11	—

Finance Act 1984 (c 43)	Value Added Tax Act 1994 (c 23)
s 10	—
s 11	s 41(3), (4)
s 12	Rep 1989 c 39, s 148, Sch 14 Pt III
s 13	—
Sch 6, Pt I	Sch 8, Pt II, Group I
Pt II	Rep 1989 c 26, s 187(1), Sch 17 Pt III
Pt III	Sch 8, Pt II, Group 6

Inheritance Act 1984 (c 51)	Value Added Tax Act 1994 (c 23)
Sch 8, para 24	Sch 9, Pt II, Group 11

Finance Act 1985 (c 54)	Value Added Tax Act 1994 (c 23)
s 11	—
s 12(1)	—

(1) Value Added Tax Act 1983 (c 55)	(2) Value Added Tax Act 1994 (c 23)	(1) Value Added Tax Act 1983 (c 55)	(2) Value Added Tax Act 1994 (c 23)
para 4(6A)	s 73(8)	s 12(2)	s 72(1), (3), (8)
para 4(7), (8)	Rep 1985 c 54, ss 22(6), 98(6), Sch 27 Pt IV	s 12(3)	s 72(2)
para 4(9), (10)	s 73(9), (10)	s 12(4)	s 73(3)
para 4A	s 75	s 12(5)	s 72(4)–(7)
para 5	Sch 11, para 4	s 12(6)	s 72(9)
para 6(1)–(3)	Sch 11, para 5(1)–(3)	s 12(7)	—
para 6(4)(*a*)	Sch 11, para 5(4)	s 12(8)	—
para 6(4)(*b*)	Applies to Scotland	s 12(9)	—
para 6(5)–(9)	Apply to Scotland	s 13(1)–(3)	s 60(1)–(3)
para 6(10)	Sch 11, para 5(10)	s 13(4)	Rep 1993 c 34, ss 49, 213, Sch 2 para 3(2), Sch 23, Pt II(4)
para 7(1)	Sch 11, para 6(1)	s 13(5)–(7)	s 60(4)–(6)
para 7(1A)	Sch 11, para 6(2)	s 13A	s 62
para 7(2)–(5)	Sch 11, para 6(3)–(6)	s 14(1), (2)	s 63(1), (2)
para 7(6)–(8)	Rep 1984 c 60, s 119(2), Sch 7 Pt III	s 14(3)	—
para 8(1)–(4)	Sch 11, para 7(1)–(4)	s 14(4)	s 63(3)
para 8(4A)–(4C)	Sch 11, para 7(5)–(7)	s 14(4A)–(4C)	s 63(4)–(6)
para 8(5)	Sch 11, para 7(8)	s 14(5)	s 63(7)
para 9	Sch 11, para 8	s 14(5A), (5B)	s 63(8), (9)
para 9A	Sch 11, para 9	s 14(6), (7)	s 63(10), (11)
para 10	Sch 11, para 10	s 14(8)	—
paras 10A–10C	Sch 11, paras 11–13	s 14A	s 64
para 11	Sch 11, para 14	s 14B	s 65
para 12	Rep 1985 c 65, s 235(3), Sch 10 Pt IV	s 15(1)–(3)	s 67(1)–(3)
Sch 8, paras 1, 2	Sch 12, paras 1, 2	s 15(3A)–(3D)	s 67(4)–(7)
para 3(1)	Sch 12, para 3(1),(3)	s 15(4)–(7)	s 67(8)–(11)
para 3(1A)	Sch 12, para 3(2)	s 15(8)	s 97(5)
para 3(2)–(4)	Sch 12, para 3(4)–(6)	s 15A	s 70
para 3(4A)	Sch 12, para 3(7)	s 16	s 68
para 3(5)	Sch 12, para 3(8)	s 17(1)–(3)	s 69(1)–(3)
paras 4–6	Sch 12, paras 4–6	s 17(4)(*a*), (*c*)–(*e*)	s 69(4)

(1) Finance Act 1985 (c 54)	(2) Value Added Tax Act 1994 (c 23)	(1) Finance Act 1985 (c 54)	(2) Value Added Tax Act 1994 (c 23)
s 17(4)(*b*)	—	s 33(5)(*b*)	—

(1) Finance Act 1985 (c 54)	(2) Value Added Tax Act 1994 (c 23)
s 17(5)	s 69(5)
s 17(6), (7)	s 69(6), (7)
s 17(8)	s 97(5)
s 17(9), (10)	s 69(8), (9)
s 17A(1)–(8)	s 66(1)–(8)
s 17A(9)	s 97(5)
s 17A(10)	s 66(9)
s 18(1)	s 74(1)
s 18(2)	Rep 1988 c 39, ss 18(4), 148, Sch 14 Pt III
s 18(3)	s 74(2)
s 18(3A)	s 74(3)
s 18(4), (5)	Rep 1990 c 29, ss 16(4), 132, Sch 19 Pt III
s 18(6), (7)	s 74(4), (5)
s 18(8)(*a*), (*b*)	s 74(6)
s 18(8)(*c*)	s 97(1), (5)
s 18(9)	s 74(7)
s 18(10)	—
s 19(1)–(5)	s 59(1)–(5)
s 19(5A)	s 59(6)
s 19(6)–(9)	s 59(7)–(10)
s 19(10)	—
s 20(1)–(3)	s 79(1)–(3)
s 20(3A)	s 79(4)
s 20(4), (5)	s 79(5), (6)
s 20(6)	—
s 20(7)	s 79(7)
s 21(1)	s 76(1)
s 21(1A)	s 76(2)
s 21(2)–(4)	s 76(3)–(5)
s 21(4A)	s 76(6)
s 21(5)–(8)	s 76(7)–(10)
s 22(1)–(5)	s 77(1)–(5)
s 22(6)	—

(1) Finance Act 1985 (c 54)	(2) Value Added Tax Act 1994 (c 23)
s 75(11)†	s 73(10)
Sch 6	—
Sch 7, para 1(1)	Rep 1988 c 39, s 148, Sch 14 Pt III
para 1(2)	s 73(7)
para 1(3)	s 73(8)
para 2	Sch 11, para 6(3)
para 3(1)	Sch 11, para 7(2),(3)
para 3(2)	Sch 11, para 7(4)
para 3(3)	Sch 11, para 7(5)–(7)
para 4	Sch 11, para 9
para 5(1)	Sch 11, para 10(3)
para 5(2)	Sch 11, para 10(4)–(6)
para 6	Sch 11, paras 11–13
Sch 8, para 1	—
para 2(1)	Sch 12, para 2(2)
para 2(2)	Sch 12, para 2(3)
para 3(1)	Sch 12, para 3(1)
para 3(2)	Sch 12, para 3(2)
para 3(3)	Sch 12, para 3(4)
para 3(4)	Sch 12, para 3(5)
para 3(5)	Sch 12, para 3(6)
para 3(6)	Sch 12, para 3(8)
para 4	Sch 12, para 4
para 5(1)	Sch 12, para 7(3)
para 5(2)	Sch 12, para 7(4),(5), (7)
para 5(3)	Sch 12, para 7(8)
para 5(4)	Sch 12, para 7(10)
para 6	—
Sch 26, para 14	Sch 9, Pt II, Group 11

Finance Act 1986 (c 41)	Value Added Tax Act 1994 (c 23)
s 9(1), (2)	s 56(1), (2)
s 9(3)(*a*)	s 56(3)(*a*)
s 9(3)(aa)	s 56(3)(*b*)

(1)	(2)	(1)	(2)
Finance Act 1985 (c 54)	Value Added Tax Act 1994 (c 23)	Finance Act 1985 (c 54)	Value Added Tax Act 1994 (c 23)
s 22(7)	s 77(6)	s 9(3)(*b*)–(*d*)	s 56(3)(*c*)–(*e*)
s 23	—	s 9(4)–(9)	s 56(4)–(9)
s 24(1)	s 83(*n*), (*q*), (*r*)	s 9(10)	s 56(10)
s 24(2)	s 84(6)	s 9(11)	—
s 24(3)	s 84(2)	s 10(1)	Sch 1, para 2
s 24(4)	s 84(3)	s 10(2)	s 83(4)
s 24(5)	s 84(5)	s 10(3)	s 84(5), (7)
s 25	s 85	s 11(1)	Sch 6, para 9
s 26(1)	s 86(1)	s 11(2)	—
s 26(2)(*a*)	s 86(2)	s 12(1)	s 30(6)
s 26(2)(*b*)	s 97(1), (2)	s 12(2)	s 30(10)
s 26(3)	s 86(3)	s 13	s 37(2)
s 27(1)	s 60(7)	s 14(1)–(5)	s 61(1)–(5)
s 27(2), (3)(*a*)	Sch 12, para 9	s 14(6)	ss 83(*o*), 84(6)
s 27(3)(*b*)	—	s 14(7)	Sch 12, para 9
s 27(3)(*c*)	s 97(1), (2)	s 14(8)	s 61(6)
s 27(4)	s 97(5)	s 14(9)	—
s 28	Sch 12, para 10	s 15(1)	s 69(1)
s 29	s 84	s 15(2)	—
s 30(1)	s 82(1)	Sch 6, para 1	s 57(1)
s 30(2), (3)	—	para 2	s 57(2), (3)
s 31	s 46(5)	para 3	Rep 1993 c 34, ss 43(1), 213, Sch 23 Pt II(2)
s 32	Rep 1990 c 29, s 132, Sch 19 Pt III	para 4	s 57(4)
s 33(1)	—	para 5(1)	s 57(5)
s 33(2), (3)	s 71(1), (2)	para 5(2)	s 57(6)
s 33(4)	Rep 1988 c 39, s 148, Sch 14 Pt III	para 6(1)	s 57(7)
s 33(5)(*a*)	s 72(13)	para 6(2)	s 57(8)

† Not repealed

(1)	(2)	(1)	(2)
Finance Act 1987 (c 16)	Value Added Tax Act 1994 (c 23)	Finance Act 1988 (c 39)	Value Added Tax Act 1994 (c 23)
s 11(1)	s 25(1)	s 17	s 64
s 11(2)	Sch 11, para 2(7)	s 18(1)	s 67(1)
s 12(1)	s 26(1)–(3)	s 18(2)	s 67(3)
s 12(2)	s 7(1)	s 18(3)	s 67(4)
s 12(3)	Rep 1992 c 48, s 82, Sch 18 Pt V(1)	s 18(4)(*a*)	—

(1)	(2)
Finance Act 1987 (c 16)	Value Added Tax Act 1994 (c 23)
s 12(4)	—
s 13(1)	—
s 13(2), (3)	Rep 1992 c 48, s 82, Sch 18 Pt V(1)
s 13(4)	Rep 1988 c 39, s 148, Sch 14 Pt III
s 13(5)	—
s 14(1)	—
s 14(2)	Sch 1, para 1(4),(7)
s 14(3)	Sch 1, para 4(1)–(3)
s 14(4), (5)	Rep 1990 c 29, s 132, Sch 19 Pt III
s 14(7)–(9)	Rep 1988 c 39, s 148, Sch 14 Pt III
s 14(10)	Sch 1, paras 16, 17, 19
s 15(1)	s 44(1)–(3), (5)–(10)
s 15(2)	—
s 16(1)	s 53
s 16(2)	s 97(4)
s 17(1)	Sch 6, para 1(1)
s 17(2)	—
s 18(1)	Sch 9, Pt II, Group 5
s 18(2)	—
s 19	—
Sch 2, para 1	s 8(1), (3), (4)
para 2	s 39(1)
para 3	Rep 1990 c 29, s 132, Sch 19 Pt III
para 4	s 80(*e*)

(1)	(2)
Debtors (Scotland) Act 1987 (c 18)	Value Added Tax Act 1994 (c 23)
Sch 4, para 4	Applies to Scotland

(1)	(2)
Finance Act 1988 (c 39)	Value Added Tax Act 1994 (c 23)
s 13(1)	—
s 13(2), (3)	Sch 9, Pt II, Group 7
s 13(4)	—
s 14(1)	—
s 14(2)	Sch 1, paras 1(7), 4(3)
s 14(3)	—
s 14(4)	Sch 1, paras 9, 10
s 14(5)	Sch 1, paras 11, 12
s 14(6)	Sch 1, paras 13, 18
s 14(7)	Sch 1, paras 14, 15
s 14(8)(*a*)	Rep 1992 c 48, s 82, Sch 18 Pt V(1)
s 14(8)(*b*)	s 74(1)
s 15(1)	—
s 18(4)(*b*)	s 74(2)
s 18(5)*	
s 18(6)	—
s 19(1)	s 69(1)
s 19(2)	s 69(3)
s 19(3)	s 76(1), (2)
s 19(4)	—
s 19(5)	—
s 20	s 79(1)–(3), (5)–(7)
s 21(1)	s 81(3)
s 21(2)	s 81(4)
s 21(3)	s 81(5)
s 22	s 29

(1)	(2)
Road Traffic (Consequential Provisions) Act 1988 (c 54)	Value Added Tax Act 1994 (c 23)
Sch 3, para 32	s 56(10)

(1)	(2)
Finance Act 1989 (c 26)	Value Added Tax Act 1994 (c 23)
s 10	—
s 19(1)–(4)	Sch 8, Pt II, Group 2
s 19(5)	—
ss 20, 21	—
s 22(1), (2)	Sch 8, Pt II, Group 16
s 22(3)	—
s 23(1)	s 62
s 23(2)	—
s 24(1)–(7)	s 80(1)–(7)
s 24(8)	s 80(1)
s 24(9)	s 83(*t*)
s 24(10), (11)	—
s 25(1)	—
s 25(2)	Sch 11, para 2(10)(*b*), (*c*)
s 25(3)	Sch 11, para 6(1)
s 25(4)	Sch 11, para 6(2)
s 25(5), (6)	—
s 26	s 26(3)(*d*)
Sch 3, para 1	Sch 8, Pt II, Group 5
para 2	Sch 8, Pt II, Group 6
para 3	Sch 8, Pt II, Group 9
para 4(1)	Sch 9, Pt II, Group 1
para 4(2)	Sch 6, para 9
para 5	s 35(1), (2)

(1)	(2)
Finance Act 1987 (c 16)	Value Added Tax Act 1994 (c 23)
s 15(2)	s 73(2), (3)
s 15(3)	s 73(6)
s 15(4)	s 73(9)
s 16(1)	—
s 16(2)	s 63(2)
s 16(3)	s 63(3)
s 16(4)	s 63(7)
s 16(5)	s 63(8), (9)

(1)	(2)
Finance Act 1988 (c 39)	Value Added Tax Act 1994 (c 23)
para 6(1)	s 51
para 6(2)	Sch 10
para 7(*a*)	s 89(2)
para 7(*b*)	s 89(3)
para 8	s 97(4)(*d*)
para 9	s 96(1)
para 10(*a*)	Sch 1, para 1(8)
para 10(*b*)	Sch 1, para 4(4)

* Repealed in part

(1)	(2)
Finance Act 1989 (c 26)	Value Added Tax Act 1994 (c 23)
para 11(*a*)	Sch 4, para 4
para 11(*b*)	Sch 4, para 5(1)
para 11(*c*)	Sch 4, para 9
paras 12, 13	—
Companies Act 1989 (c 40)	Value Added Tax Act 1994 (c 23)
Sch 18, para 27	s 43(8)
Opticians Act 1989 (c 44)	Value Added Tax Act 1994 (c 23)
s 37(3)	Sch 9, Pt II, Group 7
Planning (Consequential Provisions) Act 1990 (c 11)	Value Added Tax Act 1994 (c 23)
Sch 2, para 61	Sch 8, Pt II, Group 6
National Health Service and Community Care Act 1990 (c 19)	Value Added Tax Act 1994 (c 23)
s 61(4)	s 41(7)
Sch 8, para 9	s 41(6)
Finance Act 1990 (c 29)	Value Added Tax Act 1994 (c 23)
s 10(1)	—
s 10(2)	Sch 1, para 1(1)–(3)
s 10(3)	Sch 1, para 1(4)
s 10(4)	Sch 1, para 1(7)
s 10(5)	Sch 1, para 1(8)
s 10(6)	Sch 1, paras 5–8
s 10(7)	—
s 10(8)	s 42
s 10(9), (10)	—
s 11(1)–(7)	s 36(1)–(7)

(1)	(2)
Finance Act 1990 (c 29)	Value Added Tax Act 1994 (c 23)
s 14(4)	—
s 15(1)	s 73(2)
s 15(2)	—
s 16(1)	—
s 16(2)	s 74(1)
s 16(3)	s 74(2)
s 16(4)	—
s 16(5)	s 74(5)
s 16(6)	—
Courts and Legal Services Act 1990 (c 41)	Value Added Tax Act 1994 (c 23)
Sch 10, para 52(1)	Sch 12, para 2(2)
para 52(2)	Sch 12, para 7(4)
Broadcasting Act 1990 (c 42)	Value Added Tax Act 1994 (c 23)
Sch 20, para 37(*a*)	s 33(3)
para 37(*b*)	s 33(5)
Disability Living Allowance and Disability Working Allowance Act 1991 (c 21)	Value Added Tax Act 1994 (c 23)
Sch 2, para 13	Sch 8, Pt II, Group 12
Finance Act 1991 (c 31)	Value Added Tax Act 1994 (c 23)
s 13(1)	s 2(1)
s 13(2)	—
s 14	s 24(4)
s 15	—
s 16(1)	—
s 16(2), (3)	s 43(3)

(1)	(2)
Finance Act 1989 (c 26)	Value Added Tax Act 1994 (c 23)
s 11(8)	—
s 11(9)	—
s 11(10)	s 36(8)
s 11(11)(*a*)	s 72(2)(*b*)
s 11(11)(*b*)	s 83(*h*)
s 11(12)	s 60(2)(*c*)
s 12(1)	—
s 12(2)	s 24(3)
s 12(3)	s 24(7)
s 12(4)	—
s 13(1)	s 30(7)
s 13(2)	—
s 14(1)	—
s 14(2)	s 44(1)
s 14(3)	s 44(4)

(1)	(2)
Finance Act 1990 (c 29)	Value Added Tax Act 1994 (c 23)
s 17(1)	ss 78(1)–(8), (10)–(12), 81(1), (2)
s 17(2)	s 83(*s*)
s 18	—
Taxation of Chargeable Gains Act 1992 (c 12)	Value Added Tax Act 1994 (c 23)
Sch 10, para 6	Sch 9, Pt II, Group 11
Finance Act 1992 (c 20)	Value Added Tax Act 1994 (c 23)
s 6(1)	s 28
s 6(2)	s 97(4)(*a*)
s 7(1)	s 63(1)
s 7(2)–(5)	—
Finance (No 2) Act 1992 (c 48)	Value Added Tax Act 1994 (c 23)
s 14	—
s 15(1)	s 79(4)
s 15(2)	s 78(9)
s 15(3), (4)	—

(1)	(2)
Finance (No 2) Act 1992 (c 48)	Value Added Tax Act 1994 (c 23)
s 16(1)	s 54
s 16(2)	s 83(*m*)
s 16(3)	s 97(4)(*e*)
s 16(4)	Sch 4, para 8(3)
s 16(5)	s 67(7)
s 16(6)	—
s 17	—
Sch 3, Pt I	
para 1	—
para 2	s 1(1)
para 3	ss 1(3), (4), 3, 10, 15
para 4(1)	s 5(3)
para 4(2)	s 5(5)
para 5	s 6(1)
para 6(1)	s 6(7), (8)
para 6(2)(*a*)	s 6(14)
para 6(2)(*b*)	Rep 1993 c 34, s 213, Sch 23 Pt II(3)
para 6(3)	s 6(15)
para 7(1)	s 7(1)

(1)	(2)
Finance (No 2) Act 1992 (c 48)	Value Added Tax Act 1994 (c 23)
para 28(1)	s 41(3)
para 28(2)	s 41(4)
para 29	s 43(1)
para 30(1)	s 44(2)
para 30(2)	s 44(3)
para 30(3)	s 44(8)
para 31(1)	s 45(1)
para 31(2)	s 45(2)
para 31(3)	s 45(5)
para 32(1)	s 46(3)
para 32(2)	s 46(6)
para 33	s 47(1)
para 34	s 48
para 35	s 18
para 36(1)	s 34(1)
para 36(2)	s 34(2)
para 37	s 52
para 38	s 58
para 39(1)	s 72(2)

(1) Finance (No 2) Act 1992 (c 48)	(2) Value Added Tax Act 1994 (c 23)
para 7(2)	s 7(2)
para 7(3)	s 7(3)–(7)
para 7(4)	s 7(8)
para 7(5)	s 7(9)
para 7(6)	s 7(11)
para 8	s 8(6)
para 9	s 9(1)
para 10	ss 11, 12, 13
para 11	s 2(1)
para 12(1)	s 19(1)
para 12(2)	s 19(3)
para 13	s 20
para 14(1)	s 21(1)
para 14(2)	s 21(2)
para 14(3)	s 21(3)
para 15(1)	s 25(1)
para 15(2)	s 24(1), (2)
para 15(3)	s 24(3)
para 15(4)	s 24(5)
para 15(5)	s 24(6)
para 15(6)	s 25(7)
para 16(1)	s 26(1)
para 16(2)	s 26(2)(*c*)
para 17(1)	s 30(3)
para 17(2)	s 30(6)
para 17(3)	s 30(8)
para 17(4)	s 30(9)
para 17(5)	s 30(10)
para 18	s 31(1)
para 19(1)	s 32(3)
para 19(2)	s 32(4)
para 20(1)	s 37(1)
para 20(2)	s 37(2)

(1) Finance (No 2) Act 1992 (c 48)	(2) Value Added Tax Act 1994 (c 23)
para 39(2)	s 72(5)(*a*)
para 39(3)	s 72(10)
para 40(*a*)	s 83(*b*)
para 40(*b*)	s 83(*j*)
para 40(*c*)	s 83(*d*)
para 40(*d*)	s 83(*w*)
para 40(*e*)	s 83(*p*)
para 40(*f*)	s 83(*l*)
para 40(*g*)	s 83(*n*)
para 41(1)	s 88(1)
para 41(2)	s 88(4)
para 41(3)	s 88(7)
para 42(1)	s 90(1)
para 42(2)	s 90(2)
para 42(3)	s 90(3)
para 43	s 98
para 44	ss 92, 93
para 45	s 95(1), (3)–(5)
para 46(1)	s 96(1)
para 46(2)	s 96(3), (5)
para 46(3)	s 96(8)
para 46(4)	s 96(2)
para 47	s 99
para 48(1)	Sch 1, para 1(1)
para 48(2)	Sch 1, para 1(2)
para 48(3)	Sch 1, para 1(4)
para 48(4)	Sch 1, para 1(5),(6)
para 48(5)	Sch 1, para 1(7)
para 49(1)	Sch 1, para 2(1),(4)(*b*)
para 49(2)	Sch 1, para 2(7)(*c*)
para 50	Sch 1, para 3
para 51(1)	Sch 1, para 4(1)
para 51(2)	Sch 1, para 4(2)

(1)	(2)
Finance (No 2) Act 1992 (c 48)	Value Added Tax Act 1994 (c 23)
para 20(3)	s 37(3)
para 20(4)	s 37(4)
para 21(1)	s 33(1)
para 21(2)	s 33(2)
para 22	s 40
para 23(1)	s 35(1)
para 23(2)	s 35(3)
para 24(1)	s 39(1)
para 24(2)	s 39(2)
para 25	s 16(1)
para 26	s 38
para 27	s 27(1)

(1)	(2)
Finance (No 2) Act 1992 (c 48)	Value Added Tax Act 1994 (c 23)
para 51(3)	Sch 1, para 4(3)
para 52	Sch 1, para 5(3)
para 53	Sch 1, paras 9, 10(1)
para 54	Sch 1, para 11
para 55	Sch 1, para 12
para 56(1)	Sch 1, para 13(1)
para 56(2)	Sch 1, para 13(4)
para 56(3)	Sch 1, para 13(7)
para 57(1)	Sch 1, para 13(2)
para 57(2)	Sch 1, para 13(5)
para 57(3)	Sch 1, para 18
para 58(1)	Sch 1, para 14(1)

(1)	(2)
Finance (No 2) Act 1992 (c 48)	Value Added Tax Act 1994 (c 23)
para 58(2)	Sch 1, para 14(2)
para 59	Schs 2, 3
para 60(1)	Sch 4, para 6
para 60(2)	Sch 4, para 8(2)
para 61(1)	—
para 61(2)	Sch 6, para 3
para 61(3)	Sch 6, para 6
para 61(4)	Sch 6, para 8
para 61(5)	Sch 6, para 11
para 62	Sch 7
para 63(1)	Sch 8, Pt II, Group 12
para 63(2), (3)	Sch 8, Pt II, Group 13
para 63(4)	Sch 8, Pt II, Group 15
para 64(1)	Sch 11, para 2(1)
para 64(2)	Sch 11, para 2(2)
para 64(3)	Sch 11, para 2(3)–(5)
para 64(4)	Sch 11, para 2(8),(9)
para 65	Sch 11, para 3(3)

(1)	(2)
Finance (No 2) Act 1992 (c 48)	Value Added Tax Act 1994 (c 23)
para 92	Cf Sch 14, para 5
para 93	—
para 94(*a*)	s 56(3)(*b*)
para 94(*b*)	s 56(5)
para 95	Cf Sch 14, para 10

Trade Union and Labour Relations (Consolidation) Act 1992 (c 52)	Value Added Tax Act 1994 (c 23)
Sch 2, para 32	Sch 9, Pt II, Group 9

Tribunals and Inquiries Act 1992 (c 53)	Value Added Tax Act 1994 (c 23)
Sch 3, para 17	s 86(2)

Judicial Pensions and Retirement Act 1993 (c 8)	Value Added Tax Act 1994 (c 23)
Sch 6, para 35(1)	Sch 12, para 3(3)
para 35(2)	Sch 12, para 7(6)
Sch 8, para 16(1)	Sch 12, para 3(7)
para 16(2)	Sch 12, para 7(9)

Finance Act 1993 (c 34)	Value Added Tax Act 1994 (c 23)
s 42	—
s 43(1)	—
s 43(2)(*a*)	s 57(5)(*a*)

(1) Finance (No 2) Act 1992 (c 48)	(2) Value Added Tax Act 1994 (c 23)	(1) Finance (No 2) Act 1992 (c 48)	(2) Value Added Tax Act 1994 (c 23)
para 66(1)	s 73(3)	s 43(2)(*b*)	s 57(5)(*b*)
para 66(2)	s 73(6)	s 43(2)(*c*)	s 57(7)
para 66(3)	s 73(7)	s 43(2)(*d*)	s 57(8)
para 67	s 75	s 43(3)	s 57(4)
para 68	Sch 11, para 4(2)	s 44(1)	s 14(1)–(7)
para 69	Sch 11, para 5(10)	s 44(2)	—
para 70	Sch 11, para 6(1)	s 44(3)(*a*)	s 7(1)
para 71(1)	Sch 11, para 7(2)	s 44(3)(*b*)	s 13(1)
para 71(2)	Sch 11, para 7(4)	s 44(4)	s 14(8)
para 72	Sch 11, para 8(1)	s 45(1)	s 55
para 73	Sch 11, para 10(2)	s 45(2)	s 6(14)
para 74	Sch 11, para 14(1)(*c*)	s 45(3)	—
para 75	—	s 46(1)	s 84(4)
Pt II		s 46(2)	s 84(11)
para 76	—	s 47(1)	—
para 77(1)	s 60(2)(*a*), (*c*)	s 47(2)	Sch 4, para 5(2)
para 77(2)	s 60(3)	s 47(3)	Sch 4, para 5(3)
para 78	s 63(9)	s 47(4)	Sch 4, para 5(5)
para 79	s 65	s 48(1)	s 36(1)(*c*)
para 80(1)	s 67(1)(*a*), (*b*)	s 48(2)	—
para 80(2)	s 67(3)(*a*)–(*c*)	s 49	—
para 80(3)	s 67(4)	s 50(1)–(3)	—
para 80(4)	s 67(5), (6)	s 50(4)	Sch 11, para 2(8)
para 81	s 69(1)(*a*), (*b*)	Sch 2, para 1(1)	s 63(2)
para 82	ss 66, 97(5)	para 1(2)	s 63(4)–(6)
para 83	s 74(1)(*c*)	para 1(3)	s 63(8)
para 84(1)	s 76(1)	para 1(4)	—
para 84(2)	s 76(6)	para 2(1)	s 64(1)
para 84(3)	s 76(7)	para 2(2)	s 64(2), (3)
para 84(4)	s 76(8)	para 2(3)	s 64(4)
para 85(1)	s 77(1)	para 2(4)	s 64(6)
para 85(2)	s 77(2)	para 2(5), (6)	—
para 85(3)	s 77(6)	para 3(1)	s 70

(1)	(2)
Finance (No 2) Act 1992 (c 48)	Value Added Tax Act 1994 (c 23)
para 86	s 72(13)
Pt III	
para 87	Cf Sch 14, para 1
para 88	Cf Sch 14, para 2
para 89	Cf Sch 14, para 3
para 90	Cf Sch 14, para 4
para 91	Rep 1994 c 22, s 65, Sch 5 Pt I

(1)	(2)
Finance (No 2) Act 1992 (c 48)	Value Added Tax Act 1994 (c 23)
para 3(2)(*a*)	s 60(1)
para 3(2)(*b*)	s 60(4)
para 3(2)(*c*)	s 84(6)
para 3(3)	—
para 4(1)	s 74(1), (2)
para 4(2)	s 74(3)
para 4(3)	—

(1)	(2)
Finance Act 1993 (c 34)	Value Added Tax Act 1994 (c 23)
para 5(1)	s 59(2)
para 5(2)	s 59(3)
para 5(3)	—
para 6(1)	s 59(4)
para 6(2)	s 59(5)
para 6(3)	s 59(6)
para 6(4)	—
para 7(1), (2)	—
para 7(3)	s 59(5)
para 7(4)	—
para 8	—
Finance Act 1994 (c 9)	Value Added Tax Act 1994 (c 23)
s 7(1), (2)	s 82(1), (2), Sch 12, para 1
s 18(3)*	s 84(9)
s 45(1)	—
s 45(2)	s 63(3)
s 45(3)	s 63(8)
s 45(4)	—
s 46(1)	—
s 46(2)	s 79(1)
s 46(3)	s 79(2)
s 46(4)	—
s 47(1)	s 81(4), (5)
s 47(2)	—

(1)	(2)
Vehicle Excise and Registration Act 1994 (c 22)	Value Added Tax Act 1994 (c 23)
Sch 3, para 21	s 57(7)
Value Added Tax (Fuel and Power) Order 1980 (SI 1980/440)	Value Added Tax Act 1994 (c 23)
. . . .	—
Value Added Tax (Charities, Etc) Order 1983 (SI 1983/1717)	Value Added Tax Act 1994 (c 23)
. . . .	Sch 8, Pt II, Group 15
Value Added Tax (Handicapped Persons) Order 1984 (SI 1984/489)	Value Added Tax Act 1994 (c 23)
. . . .	Sch 8, Pt II, Group 12
Value Added Tax (Lifeboats) Order 1984 (SI 1984/631)	Value Added Tax Act 1994 (c 23)
. . . .	Sch 8, Pt II, Group 8
Value Added Tax (Charities, Etc) Order 1984 (SI 1984/766)	Value Added Tax Act 1994 (c 23)
. . . .	Sch 8, Pt II, Group 15
Value Added Tax (Marine etc Insurance) Order 1984 (SI 1984/767)	Value Added Tax Act 1994 (c 23)
. . . .	—
Value Added Tax (Handicapped Persons) (No 2) Order 1984 (SI 1984/959)	Value Added Tax Act 1994 (c 23)
. . . .	Sch 8, Pt II, Group 12
Value Added Tax (Optical Appliances) Order 1984 (SI 1984/1784)	Value Added Tax Act 1994 (c 23)
. . . .	—
Value Added Tax (Protected Buildings) Order 1985 (SI 1985/18)	Value Added Tax Act 1994 (c 23)
. . . .	Sch 8, Pt II, Group 6
Value Added Tax (Charities, Etc) Order 1985 (SI 1985/431)	Value Added Tax Act 1994 (c 23)
. . . .	—
Value Added Tax (Finance) Order 1985 (SI 1985/432)	Value Added Tax Act 1994 (c 23)
. . . .	Sch 9, Pt II, Group 5

* Repealed in part

(1)	(2)
Value Added Tax (Hiring of Goods) Order 1985 (SI 1985/799)	Value Added Tax Act 1994 (c 23)
arts 1, 2	—

(1)	(2)
Value Added Tax (Finance) Order 1987 (SI 1987/860)	Value Added Tax Act 1994 (c 23)
. . . .	Sch 9, Pt II, Group 5

(1)	(2)
Value Added Tax (Hiring of Goods) Order 1985 (SI 1985/799)	Value Added Tax Act 1994 (c 23)
art 3.	Sch 5, paras 7, 8
art 4.	—
Value Added Tax (Handicapped Persons) Order 1985 (SI 1985/919)	Value Added Tax Act 1994 (c 23)
art 3.	Sch 8, Pt II, Group 12
Value Added Tax (Welfare) Order 1985 (SI 1985/1900)	Value Added Tax Act 1994 (c 23)
. . . .	Sch 9, Pt II, Group 7
Value Added Tax (Handicapped Persons and Charities) Order 1986 (SI 1986/530)	Value Added Tax Act 1994 (c 23)
art 1.	—
art 2.	Sch 8, Pt II, Group 4
art 3.	Sch 8, Pt II, Group 12
art 4.	Sch 8, Pt II, Group 15
Value Added Tax (Charities) Order 1987 (SI 1987/437)	Value Added Tax Act 1994 (c 23)
art 1.	—
art 2.	Sch 8, Pt II, Group 12
art 3.	Sch 8, Pt II, Group 15
Value Added Tax (Betting, Gaming and Lotteries) Order 1987 (SI 1987/517)	Value Added Tax Act 1994 (c 23)
. . . .	Sch 9, Pt II, Group 4
Value Added Tax (International Services) Order 1987 (SI 1987/518)	Value Added Tax Act 1994 (c 23)
. . . .	—
Value Added Tax (Construction of Buildings) (No 2) Order 1987 (SI 1987/1072)	Value Added Tax Act 1994 (c 23)
art 2.	—

(1)	(2)
Value Added Tax (Finance) Order 1987 (SI 1987/860)	Value Added Tax Act 1994 (c 23)
Value Added Tax (Education) Order 1987 (SI 1987/1259)	Value Added Tax Act 1994 (c 23)
. . . .	—
Value Added Tax (Tour Operators) Order 1987 (SI 1987/1806)	Value Added Tax Act 1994 (c 23)
art 11.	Sch 8, Pt II, Group 8
Value Added Tax (Cash Accounting) Regulations 1987 (SI 1987/1427)	Value Added Tax Act 1994 (c 23)
reg 11†	s 83(*y*)
Value Added Tax (Confectionery) Order 1988 (SI 1988/507)	Value Added Tax Act 1994 (c 23)
. . . .	Sch 8, Pt II, Group 1
Value Added Tax (Training) Order 1988 (SI 1988/1282)	Value Added Tax Act 1994 (c 23)
. . . .	—
Value Added Tax (Education) Order 1989 (SI 1989/267)	Value Added Tax Act 1994 (c 23)
. . . .	—
Value Added Tax (Fund-Raising Events and Charities) Order 1989 (SI 1989/470)	Value Added Tax Act 1994 (c 23)
art 1.	—
art 2.	Sch 8, Pt II, Group 15
art 3.	Sch 9, Pt II, Group 12
Value Added Tax (Finance, Health and Welfare) Order 1989 (SI 1989/2272)	Value Added Tax Act 1994 (c 23)
art 1.	—
art 2.	Sch 9, Pt II, Group 5
art 3.	Sch 9, Pt II, Group 7

† Not repealed

(1)	(2)
Value Added Tax (Increase of Registration Limits) Order 1990 (SI 1990/682)	Value Added Tax Act 1994 (c 23)
. . . .	—
Value Added Tax (Charities) Order 1990 (SI 1990/750)	Value Added Tax Act 1994 (c 23)
. . . .	Sch 8, Pt II, Group 15
Value Added Tax (Transport) Order 1990 (SI 1990/752)	Value Added Tax Act 1994 (c 23)
. . . .	Sch 8, Pt II, Group 8
Value Added Tax (Insurance) Order 1990 (SI 1990/2037)	Value Added Tax Act 1994 (c 23)
. . . .	Sch 9, Pt II, Group 2
Value Added Tax (Charities) (No 2) Order 1990 (SI 1990/2129)	Value Added Tax Act 1994 (c 23)
. . . .	Sch 8, Pt II, Group 15
Value Added Tax (Construction of Dwellings and Land) Order 1990 (SI 1990/2553)	Value Added Tax Act 1994 (c 23)
art 1.	—
art 2.	Sch 8, Pt II, Group 5
art 3.	Sch 9, Pt II, Group 1

(1)	(2)
Value Added Tax (Piped Gas) (Metrication) Order 1991 (SI 1991/2534)	Value Added Tax Act 1994 (c 23)
. . . .	—
Value Added Tax (Buildings and Land) Order 1991 (SI 1991/2569)	Value Added Tax Act 1994 (c 23)
art 1.	—
art 2.	Sch 9, Pt II, Group 1
art 3.	Sch 10, para 2(8),(9)
art 4.	Sch 10, para 3(1),(6), (9)
art 5.	Sch 10, para 5(8)–(10)
art 6.	Sch 10, para 6(2)–(4), (6)–(8)
art 7.	Sch 10, para 7
art 8.	Sch 10, para 9
Value Added Tax (Charities and Aids for Handicapped Persons) Order 1992 (SI 1992/628)	Value Added Tax Act 1994 (c 23)
art 1.	—
art 2.	Sch 8, Pt II, Group 4

(1)	(2)
Value Added Tax (Charities) Order 1991 (SI 1991/737)	Value Added Tax Act 1994 (c 23)
arts 1, 2.	—
arts 3–6.	Sch 8, Pt II, Group 15
art 7.	—
art 8.	Sch 8, Pt II, Group 15
art 9.	Sch 9, Pt II, Group 12
Value Added Tax (Increase of Registration Limits) Order 1991 (SI 1991/738)	Value Added Tax Act 1994 (c 23)
. . . .	—

(1)	(2)
art 3.	Sch 8, Pt II, Group 8
art 4.	Sch 8, Pt II, Group 12
Value Added Tax (Increase of Registration Limits) Order 1992 (SI 1992/629)	Value Added Tax Act 1994 (c 23)
. . . .	—
Value Added Tax (Increase of Consideration for Fuel) Order 1992 (SI 1992/733)	Value Added Tax Act 1994 (c 23)
. . . .	—
Value Added Tax (Motor Vehicles for the Handicapped) Order 1992 (SI 1992/3065)	Value Added Tax Act 1994 (c 23)
. . . .	Sch 8, Pt II, Group 12
Customs and Excise (Single Market etc) Regulations 1992 (SI 1992/3095)	Value Added Tax Act 1994 (c 23)
Sch 1, para 8†	Sch 8, Pt II, Group 13

† Not repealed

(1)	(2)
Value Added Tax (Transport) Order 1992 (SI 1992/3126)	Value Added Tax Act 1994 (c 23)
. . . .	Sch 8, Pt II, Group 8
Value Added Tax (Means of Transport) Order 1992 (SI 1992/3127)	Value Added Tax Act 1994 (c 23)
. . . .	s 95(1), (2)
Value Added Tax (Tax Free Shops) Order 1992 (SI 1992/3131)	Value Added Tax Act 1994 (c 23)
. . . .	Sch 8, Pt II, Group 14
Value Added Tax (International Services and Transport) Order 1992 (SI 1992/3223)	Value Added Tax Act 1994 (c 23)
art 1.	—
art 2.	Sch 8, Pt II, Group 7
art 3.	Sch 8, Pt II, Group 8
art 4.	—
Value Added Tax (Increase of Consideration for Fuel) Order 1993 (SI 1993/765)	Value Added Tax Act 1994 (c 23)
. . . .	—
Value Added Tax (Increase of Registration Limits) Order 1993 (SI 1993/766)	Value Added Tax Act 1994 (c 23)
. . . .	—
Value Added Tax (Protective Boots and Helmets) Order 1993 (SI 1993/767)	Value Added Tax Act 1994 (c 23)
. . . .	Sch 8, Pt II, Group 16
Value Added Tax (Education) (No 2) Order 1993 (SI 1993/1124)	Value Added Tax Act 1994 (c 23)
. . . .	—
Finance Act 1993 (Appointed Day) Order 1993 (SI 1993/2214)	Value Added Tax Act 1994 (c 23)
. . . .	—

(1)	(2)
Value Added Tax (Revenue Charge) Order 1993 (SI 1993/2328)	Value Added Tax Act 1994 (c 23)
arts 1, 2	—
art 3.	Sch 5, para 9
art 4.	Sch 5, para 10
art 5.	—
Value Added Tax (Beverages) Order 1993 (SI 1993/2498)	Value Added Tax Act 1994 (c 23)
. . . .	Sch 8, Pt II, Group I
Value Added Tax (Increase of Consideration for Fuel) (No 2) Order 1993 (SI 1993/2952)	Value Added Tax Act 1994 (c 23)
. . . .	s 57(3), Table A
Value Added Tax (Increase of Registration Limits) (No 2) Order 1993 (SI 1993/2953)	Value Added Tax Act 1994 (c 23)
art 1.	—
art 2.	Sch 1, paras 1(1)–(3), 4(1), (2)
art 3.	Sch 3, paras 1(1), (2), 2
Value Added Tax (Tax Free Shops) Order 1994 (SI 1994/686)	Value Added Tax Act 1994 (c 23)
. . . .	Sch 8, Pt II, Group 14
Value Added Tax (Sport, Physical Education and Fund-Raising Events) Order 1994 (SI 1994/687)	Value Added Tax Act 1994 (c 23)
art 1.	—
art 2.	Sch 9, Pt II, Group 10
art 3.	Sch 9, Pt II, Group 12
Value Added Tax (Education) Order 1994 (SI 1994/1188)	Value Added Tax Act 1994 (c 23)
. . . .	Sch 9, Pt II, Group 6

FINANCE ACT 1995

(1995 Chapter 4)

An Act to grant certain duties, to alter other duties, and to amend the law relating to the National Debt and the Public Revenue, and to make further provision in connection with Finance.

[1 May 1995]

PART II
VALUE ADDED TAX AND INSURANCE PREMIUM TAX

Value added tax

21 Fuel and power for domestic or charity use

Amendments—This section repealed by FA 2001 s 110, Sch 33 Pt 3(1) with effect for supplies made, and acquisitions and importations taking place, after 31 October 2001 (by virtue of FA 2001 s 99(7)(*b*)).

22 Imported works of art, antiques, etc

(1) (*amends* VATA 1994 s 21).

(2) This section shall have effect in relation to goods imported at any time on or after the day on which this Act is passed.

Commentary—*De Voil Indirect Tax service* **V3.355.**

23 Agent acting in their own names

(1)–(3) (*amend* VATA 1994 s 47).

(4) This section shall have effect—

(*a*) so far as it amends section 47(1) of that Act, in relation to goods acquired or imported on or after the day on which this Act is passed; and

(*b*) for other purposes, in relation to any supply taking place on or after that day.

24 Margin schemes

(1) (*inserts* VATA 1994 s 50A).

(2) Section 32 of that Act (relief on supply of certain second-hand goods) shall cease to have effect on such day as the Commissioners of Customs and Excise may by order made by statutory instrument appoint.

Commentary—*De Voil Indirect Tax service* **V3.351.**

Notes—"That Act" in sub-s (2) is VATA 1994.

25 Groups of companies

(1) Section 43 of the Value Added Tax Act 1994 (groups of companies) shall be amended as follows.

(2) (*amends* VATA 1994 s 43).

(*3*) , (4) . . . [1]

(5) Subsection (2) above has effect in relation to—

(*a*) any supply made on or after 1st March 1995, and

(*b*) any supply made before that date in the case of which both the body making the supply and the body supplied continued to be members of the group in question until at least that date,

and subsections (3) and (4) above have effect in relation to applications made on or after the day on which this Act is passed.

Commentary—*De Voil Indirect Tax service* **V2.113.**

Amendments—[1] Sub-ss (3), (4) repealed by FA 1999 Sch 20 Pt II with effect from 27 July 1999 subject to FA 1999 s 16, Sch 2 para 6.

26 Co-owners etc of buildings and land

Repeal—This section repealed by the Value Added Tax (Buildings and Land) Order, SI 2008/1146 art 5(1) with effect in relation to supplies in relation to supplies made on or after 1 June 2008, subject to savings in Sch 2 of the Order.

27 Set-off of credits

(1) Section 81 of the Value Added Tax Act 1994 (which includes provision as to the setting off of credits) shall be amended as follows.

(2) (3) (*amends* VATA 1994 s 81).

(4) This section shall have effect in relation to amounts becoming due from the Commissioners of Customs and Excise at times on or after the day on which this Act is passed.

28 Transactions treated as supplies for purposes of zero-rating etc

(1) (*amends* VATA 1994 s 30).

(2) This section shall have effect in relation to transactions occurring on or after the day on which this Act is passed.

Commentary—*De Voil Indirect Tax Service* **V4.266.**

29 Goods removed from warehousing regime

(*amends* VATA 1994 s 18).

Commentary—*De Voil Indirect Tax Service* **V3.138.**

30 Fuel supplied for private use

(1) Section 57 of the Value Added Tax Act 1994 (determination of consideration for fuel supplied for private use) shall be amended as follows.
(2)–(5) (*amends* VATA 1994 s 57).
(6) This section shall apply in relation to prescribed accounting periods beginning on or after 6th April 1995.
(7) Nothing in this section shall be taken to prejudice any practice by which the consideration appropriate to a vehicle is arrived at where a prescribed accounting period beginning before 6th April 1995 is a period of 12 months.

Commentary—*De Voil Indirect Tax Service* **V3.176.**

31 Appeals: payment of amounts shown in returns

(1) (*amends* VATA 1994 s 84).
(2) This section shall apply in relation to appeals brought after the day on which this Act is passed.

32 Penalties for failure to notify etc

(1) (amends VATA 1994 s 67).
(2) Section 15(3A) of the Finance Act 1985 (provision which is repealed by the 1994 Act and which corresponds to section 67(4)) shall have effect subject to the amendments made by subsection (1) above.
(3) Subject to subsection (4) below, subsections (1) and (2) above shall apply where a penalty is assessed on or after 1st January 1995.
(4) Subsections (1) and (2) above shall not apply in the case of a supplementary assessment if the original assessment was made before 1st January 1995.

Commentary—*De Voil Indirect Tax Service* **V5.347–5.350.**
Amendments—This section repealed by FA 2008 s 123, Sch 41 para 25(*g*) with effect from 1 April 2010 (by virtue of SI 2009/511 art 2).

33 Correction of consolidation errors

(1) The Value Added Tax Act 1994 shall have effect, and be deemed always to have had effect, as if it had been enacted as follows.
(2)–(5) (*amends* VATA 1994 s 35, Sch 4 para 5, Sch 6 para 7, Sch 13 para 9, Sch 14 para 13).

FINANCE ACT 1996

(1996 Chapter 8)

ARRANGEMENT OF SECTIONS

PART II

VALUE ADDED TAX

EC Second VAT Simplification Directive

Schedule 3—Value added tax: fiscal and other warehousing.
Schedule 4—Value added tax: anti-avoidance provisions.

An Act to grant certain duties, to alter other duties, and to amend the law relating to the National Debt and the Public Revenue, and to make further provision in connection with Finance.

[29 April 1996]

PART II

VALUE ADDED TAX

EC Second VAT Simplification Directive

25 EC Second VAT Simplification Directive

Sections 26 to 29 of and Schedule 3 to this Act are for the purpose of giving effect to requirements of the directive of the Council of the European Communities dated 17th May 1977 No 77/388/EEC and the amendments of that directive by the directive of that Council dated 10th April 1995 No 95/7/EC (amendments with a view to introducing new simplification measures with regard to value added tax).

Commentary—*De Voil Indirect Tax Service* **V1.227.**

26 Fiscal and other warehousing

(1) The provisions of Schedule 3 to this Act shall have effect.

(2) Subject to subsection (3) below, this section and Schedule 3 to this Act shall come into force on such day as the Commissioners of Customs and Excise may by order made by statutory instrument appoint, and shall apply to any acquisition of goods from another member State and any supply taking place on or after that day.

(3) In so far as the provisions inserted by Schedule 3 to this Act confer power to make regulations they shall come into force on the day this Act is passed.

Commentary—*De Voil Indirect Tax Service* **V3.176, V3.332.**

27 Value of imported goods

(1) Section 21 of the Value Added Tax Act 1994 (value of imported goods) shall be amended as follows.

(2), (3) (*amends* VATA 1994 s 21(2)(*a*), (*b*)).

(4) This section shall have effect in relation to goods imported on or after 1st January 1996.

Commentary—*De Voil Indirect Tax Service* **V3.323.**

28 Adaptation of aircraft and hovercraft

(1) Section 22 of the Value Added Tax Act 1994 shall be omitted.

(2) This section shall apply to supplies made on or after 1st January 1996.

29 Work on materials

(1) The Value Added Tax Act 1994 shall be amended as follows.

(2), (3) (*insert* VATA 1994 ss 30(2A), 55(5)(*c*)).

(4) Paragraph 2 of Schedule 4 (which provides that the treatment or processing of another person's goods shall in certain circumstances be a supply of goods) shall be omitted.

(5) This section shall apply to supplies made on or after 1st January 1996.

Commentary—*De Voil Indirect Tax Service* **V3.112; V4.206; V5.143.**

Other provisions relating to charges to VAT

30 Refunds in connection with construction and conversion

(1)–(3) (*substitute* VATA 1994 s 35(1), (1A)–(1D), *amended* s 35(2) and *insert* s 34(4), (5)).

(4) This section applies in relation to any case in which a claim for repayment under section 35 of the Value Added Tax Act 1994 is made at any time on or after the day on which this Act is passed.

Commentary—*De Voil Indirect Tax Service* **V5.164.**

Amendments—Sub-s (2) repealed by FA 2012 s 204, Sch 29 para 13(*a*) with effect from 17 July 2012.

31 Groups: anti-avoidance

(1) (*inserts* VATA 1994 s 43(9)).

(2) After Schedule 9 to that Act there shall be inserted the Schedule set out in Schedule 4 to this Act.

(3), (4) (*amend* VATA 1994 s 83(*ab*) and *insert* VATA 1994 s 84(7A)).

(5) Subsection (1A) of section 43 of that Act shall not have effect in relation to supplies on or after the day on which this Act is passed.

Commentary—*De Voil Indirect Tax Service* **V2.104, V2.113.**

32 Supplies of gold etc

(1) (*substitutes* VATA 1994 s 55(5) (*a*)).

(2) This section applies in relation to any supply after 28th November 1995.

Commentary—*De Voil Indirect Tax Service* **V3.502, V5.143.**

33 Small gifts

(1)–(3) (*amend* VATA 1994 Sch 4 para 5(2)(*a*) and *insert* s 97(4)(*ab*), Sch 4, para 5(7)).

(4) Subsection (1) above shall apply where a gift is made after 28th November 1995.

Commentary—*De Voil Indirect Tax Service* **V3.211.**

Payment and enforcement

34

Method of making payments on account

(*inserts* VATA 1994 s 28(2A)).

35 Default surcharges

(1) The Value Added Tax Act 1994 shall be amended as follows.

(2)–(7) (*insert* VATA 1994 s 59(11), 59A, 59B and *amend* ss 59(1), 69(4)(*a*), (9)(*b*), 76(1), (3)(*a*)).

(8) This section applies in relation to any prescribed accounting period ending on or after 1st June 1996, but a liability to make a payment on account of VAT shall be disregarded for the purposes of the amendments made by this section if the payment is one becoming due before that date.

Commentary—*De Voil Indirect Tax Service* **V5.371–5.380.**

36 Repeated misdeclaration penalty

(1) (substitutes VATA 1994 s 64(6), (6A), (7) *for* s 64(6), (7)).

(2) This section has effect in relation to inaccuracies contained in returns made on or after the day on which this Act is passed.

Commentary—*De Voil Indirect Tax Service* **V5.344.**

Amendments—This section repealed by FA 2007 ss 97, 114, Sch 27 Pt 5(5) with effect as follows (by virtue of SI 2008/568 art 2)—

- 1 April 2008 in relation to relevant documents relating to tax periods commencing on or after that date;
- 1 April 2008 in relation to assessments falling within FA 2007 Sch 24 para 2 for tax periods commencing on or after that date;
- 1 July 2008 in relation to relevant documents relating to claims under the Thirteenth Council Directive (arrangements for the refund of value added tax to persons not established in Community territory) for years commencing on or after that date;
- 1 January 2009 in relation to relevant documents relating to claims under the Eighth Council Directive (arrangements for the refund of value added tax to taxable persons not established in the territory of the country) for years commencing on or after that date;
- 1 April 2009 in relation to documents relating to all other claims for repayments of relevant tax made on or after 1 April 2009 which are not related to a tax period; and
- in any other case, 1 April 2009 in relation to documents given where a person's liability to pay relevant tax arises on or after that date.

37 Penalties for failure to notify

Amendments—This section repealed by FA 2008 s 123, Sch 41 para 25 with effect from 1 April 2010 (by virtue of SI 2009/511 art 2).

38 VAT invoices and accounting

(1) Paragraph 2 of Schedule 11 to the Value Added Tax Act 1994 (regulations about accounting for VAT, VAT invoices etc) shall be amended as follows.

(2), (3) (*insert* VATA 1994 Sch 11, para 2(2A), 10(*d*), (*e*)); *repealed in part* by FA 2002 s 139(2), Sch 40 Pt 2(2) with effect from 1 December 2003 (by virtue of SI 2003/3043)).

Commentary—De Voil Indirect Tax Service **V3.514**, **V3.518–3.520.**

PART VII

MISCELLANEOUS AND SUPPLEMENTAL

Miscellaneous: indirect taxation

197 Setting of rates of interest

(1) The rate of interest applicable for the purposes of an enactment to which this section applies shall be the rate which for the purposes of that enactment is provided for by regulations made by the Treasury under this section.

(2) This section applies to—

(*a*), (*b*) . . .

(*c*) sections 74 and 78 of the Value Added Tax Act 1994 (interest on VAT recovered or recoverable by assessment and interest payable in cases of official error); . . .

(*d*)–(*h*) . . .

(3) Regulations under this section may—

(*a*) make different provision for different enactments or for different purposes of the same enactment,

(*b*) either themselves specify a rate of interest for the purposes of an enactment or make provision for any such rate to be determined, and to change from time to time, by reference to such rate or the average of such rates as may be referred to in the regulations, (*c*) provide for rates to be reduced below, or increased above, what they otherwise would be by specified amounts or by reference to specified formulae,

(*d*) provide for rates arrived at by reference to averages or formulae to be rounded up or down,

(*e*) provide for circumstances in which changes of rates of interest are or are not to take place, and

(*f*) provide that changes of rates are to have effect for periods beginning on or after a day determined in accordance with the regulations in relation to interest running from before that day, as well as in relation to interest running from, or from after, that day.

(4) The power to make regulations under this section shall be exercisable by statutory instrument subject to annulment in pursuance of a resolution of the House of Commons.

(5) . . . [1]

(6) The words "the rate applicable under section 197 of the Finance Act 1996" shall be substituted—

(*a*)–(*c*) . . .

(*d*) in the Value Added Tax Act 1994—

(i), (ii) (*amends* VATA 1994 s 74(1), (2), (4), 78(3)).

(7) Subsections (1) and (6) above shall have effect for periods beginning on or after such day as the Treasury may by order made by statutory instrument appoint and shall have effect in relation to interest running from before that day, as well as in relation to interest running from, or from after, that day; and different days may be appointed under this subsection for different purposes.

Commentary—*De Voil Indirect Tax Service* **V5.196**, **V5.361–5.365.**

Note—Sub-ss (2)(*a*), (*b*), (*d*)–(*h*), (6)(*a*)–(*c*) are not relevant to VAT.

Sub-ss (1), (6) have effect for periods beginning on or after 1 April 1997 (see FA 1996 s 197 (Appointed Day) Order, SI 1997/1015).

Amendment—[1] Sub-s (5) repealed by FA 2009 s 105(6)(*b*) with effect from 21 July 2009.

SCHEDULES

SCHEDULE 3

VALUE ADDED TAX: FISCAL AND OTHER WAREHOUSING

Section 26

1–18(*amend* VATA 1994 ss 6(1), 7(1), 12(1), 13(1), 20(1), 30(10), 62(1), (3), (4), 73(9), 76(5), 83(*p*)(ii), Sch 11 para 8(1), 10(2), and *insert* ss 18A–18F, 30(8A), 69(1)(*g*), 73(7A), (7B), 83(*da*), Sch 2 para 1(7), Sch 3, para 1(6), Sch 5A).

Commentary—*De Voil Indirect Tax Service* **V3.176**, **V3.332.**

Amendment—Para 17 repealed by FA 2008 s 113, Sch 36 para 92(*e*), (*f*) with effect from 1 April 2009 (by virtue of SI 2009/404 art 2).

In consequence of SI 2009/404 arts 1–11, the amendments made by FA 2008 Sch 36 para 92 shall be disregarded so far as they affect any notice referred to in those provisions, given on or before 31 March 2009.

SCHEDULE 4

VALUE ADDED TAX: ANTI-AVOIDANCE PROVISIONS

Section 31

(*Inserts VATA 1994 Sch 9A.*)

Commentary—*De Voil Indirect Tax Service* **V2.104**, **V2.113.**

FINANCE ACT 1997

(1997 Chapter 16)

ARRANGEMENT OF SECTIONS

PART I

EXCISE DUTIES

Gaming duty

PART III

VALUE ADDED TAX

Registration

An Act to grant certain duties, to alter other duties, and to amend the law relating to the National Debt and the Public Revenue, and to make further provision in connection with Finance.

[19 March 1997]

PART I
EXCISE DUTIES

Gaming duty

13 Supplemental provisions relating to gaming duty

(2) Schedule 2 to this Act (which amends the Customs and Excise Management Act 1979 and contains other amendments) shall have effect.

PART III
VALUE ADDED TAX

Registration

31 Aggregation of businesses

(1) (*inserts* VATA 1994 Sch 1 para 1A).

(2), (3) (*amend* VATA 1994 s 84(7) Sch 1 para 2(2)(4)).

(4) This section has effect in relation to the making of directions on or after the day on which this Act is passed.

Commentary—*De Voil Indirect Tax Service* **V2.223.**

32 Voluntary registration

(*substitutes* VATA 1994 Sch 1 para 10(2)).

Commentary—*De Voil Indirect Tax Service* **V4.136.**

Zero-rating

33 Sale of goods donated to charity

(1) (*substitutes* VATA 1994 Sch 8 Group 15 Note (1)).

(2) This section has effect in relation to supplies made on or after 26th November 1996.

Commentary—*De Voil Indirect Tax Service* **V4.266.**

34 Charitable institutions providing care etc

(1), (2) (*inserts* VATA 1994 Sch 8 Group 15 Notes (4A) and (4B), (5A) and (5B)).

(3) This section has effect in relation to supplies made on or after 26th November 1996.

Commentary—*De Voil Indirect Tax Service* **V4.266.**

Buildings and land

35 References to grants

(1), (2) (*insert* VATA 1994 s 96(10A), Sch 10 para 3(5A) and (5B); sub-s (2) *repealed* by SI 2008/1146 with effect in relation to supplies made on or after 1 June 2008).

(3) Amendments corresponding to those made by subsections (1) and (2) above shall be deemed to have had effect, for the purposes of the cases to which it applied, in relation to the Value Added Tax Act 1983; and any provisions about the coming into force of any amendment of that Act shall be deemed to have had effect accordingly.

(4) Nothing in this section shall be taken to affect the operation, in relation to times before its repeal took effect, of paragraph 4 of Schedule 10 to the Value Added Tax Act 1994 or of any enactment re-enacted in that paragraph.

Commentary—*De Voil Indirect Tax Service* **V4.115.**

36 Buildings intended to be used as dwellings

Repeal—Section 36 repealed by the Value Added Tax (Buildings and Land) Order, SI 2008/1146, art 6, Sch 1 paras 6, 8 with effect in relation to supplies made on or after 1 June 2008, subject to savings in Sch 2 of the Order.

37 Supplies to non-taxable persons etc

(1) Paragraphs 2(3A) and 3(8A) of Schedule 10 to the Value Added Tax Act 1994 (which relate to grants of land made to connected persons where they are not fully taxable) shall not have effect in relation to any supply made after 26th November 1996.

(2)–(6) . . . [1]

Commentary—*De Voil Indirect Tax Service* **V4.115.**

Amendment—[1] Sub-ss (2)–(6) repealed by the Value Added Tax (Buildings and Land) Order, SI 2008/1146, art 6, Sch 1 paras 6, 9 with effect in relation to supplies made on or after 1 June 2008, subject to savings in Sch 2 of the Order.

Exempt insurance supplies

38 Exempt insurance supplies

(1) (*substitutes* VATA 1994 Sch 9 Group 2).

(2) This section has effect in relation to supplies made on or after the day on which this Act is passed.

Commentary—*De Voil Indirect Tax Service* **V4.121.**

Bad debt relief

39 Bad debt relief

(1) In section 36 of the Value Added Tax Act 1994, paragraph (*b*) of subsection (4) (condition of bad debt relief that property in goods supplied has passed) shall not apply in the case of any claim made under that section in relation to a supply of goods made after the day on which this Act is passed.

(2) (*inserts* VATA 1994 s 36(4A)).

(3) Subsection (2) above has effect in relation to any entitlement under section 36 of that Act of 1994 to a refund of VAT charged on a supply made after 26th November 1996.

(4) (*inserts* VATA 1994 s 36(5)(*ea*)).

(5) No claim for a refund may be made in accordance with section 22 of the Value Added Tax Act 1983 (old scheme for bad debt relief) at any time after the day on which this Act is passed.

Commentary—*De Voil Indirect Tax Service* **V5.156.**

Simon's Tax Cases—s 39(5), *GMAC UK plc v R&C Comrs*; *BT plc v R&C Comrs* [2012] UKUT 279 (TCC), [2012] STC 2349; *BT plc v R&C Comrs* [2014] EWCA Civ 433, [2014] STC 1926.

Amendments—Sub-s (2)–(4) repealed by FA 2002 s 139, Sch 40 Pt 2(1) with effect for supplies made on or after such day as the Commissioners appoint by statutory instrument.

Groups of companies

40 Groups containing bodies of different descriptions

(1), (2) (*inserts* VATA 1994 s 43(1AA) and (1AB) and amends s 43(2)).

(3) Subsection (1) above has effect in relation to any supply made after 26th November 1996 and in relation to any acquisition or importation taking place after that date.

Commentary—*De Voil Indirect Tax Service* **V2.104.**

41 Group supplies using an overseas member

(1) (*inserts* VATA 1994 s 43(2A), (2B), (2C), ((2D) and (2E)).

(2) Subject to subsection (3) below, subsection (1) above has effect in relation to supplies made on or after 26th November 1996.

(3) Section 43 of the Value Added Tax Act 1994 shall have effect in relation to supplies made after the day on which this Act is passed with the provisions inserted by subsection (1) above modified in accordance with subsections (4) and (5) below.

(4) In subsection (2A), in paragraph (*c*) for the words from "services" to the end of the paragraph there shall be substituted "any services falling within paragraphs 1 to 8 of Schedule 5 which do not fall within any of the descriptions specified in Schedule 9;".

(5) In subsection (2C), at the beginning there shall be inserted "Except in so far as the Commissioners may by regulations otherwise provide,".

Commentary—*De Voil Indirect Tax Service* **V2.104.**

Incidental and supplemental provisions etc

42 Services subject to the reverse charge

(*inserts* VATA 1994 s 8(7) and (8)).

Commentary—*De Voil Indirect Tax Service* **V3.181–V3.183.**

43 Payments on account: appeals

(*inserts* VATA 1994 s 28(2AA)).

Commentary—*De Voil Indirect Tax Service* **V5.110.**

PART IV

PAYMENTS AND OVERPAYMENTS IN RESPECT OF INDIRECT TAXES

Value added tax

44 Liability of Commissioners to interest

(1) (*inserts* VATA 1994 s 78(1A)).

(2)–(4) (*substitute* VATA 1994 ss 74(8), (9), (12)(*a*), 78(11)).

(5) Subsection (4) above shall have effect for the purposes of determining whether any period beginning on or after the day on which this Act is passed is left out of account.

(6) Amendments corresponding to those made by subsections (1) and (3) above shall be deemed to have had effect, for the purposes of the cases to which the enactments applied, in relation to the enactments directly or indirectly re-enacted in section 78 of the Value Added Tax Act 1994.

Commentary—*De Voil Indirect Tax Service* **V5.151–V5.166.**

45 Assessment for overpayments of interest

(1)–(3) (*insert* VATA 1994 s 78A, 83(*sa*), 84(3A).)

(4) Subsection (1) above shall be deemed to have come into force on 4th December 1996 in relation to amounts paid by way of interest at any time on or after 18th July 1996.

(5) Subsections (2) and (3) above shall be deemed to have come into force on 4th December 1996 in relation to assessments made on or after that date.

(6) (*amends* VATA 1994 s 76(10)).

Commentary—*De Voil Indirect Tax Service* **V5.151–V5.166.**

46 Repayments of overpayments: unjust enrichment

(1)–(3) (*insert* VATA 1994 ss 80(3A), (3B), (3C), 80A, 80B, 83(*ta*)).

(4) Subsection (1) above has effect for the purposes of making any repayment on or after the day on which this Act is passed, even if the claim for that repayment was made before that day.

Commentary—*De Voil Indirect Tax Service* **V5.151–V5.166.**

47 Repayments and assessments: time limits

(1) (*substitutes* VATA 1994 s 80(4) and (5)).

(2) Subject to subsections (3) and (4) below, subsection (1) above shall be deemed to have come into force on 18th July 1996 as a provision applying, for the purposes of the making of any repayment on or after that date, to all claims under section 80 of the Value Added Tax Act 1994, including claims made before that date and claims relating to payments made before that date.

(3) Subsection (4) below applies as respects the making of any repayment on or after 18th July 1996 on a claim under section 80 of the Value Added Tax Act 1994 if—

(*a*) legal proceedings for questioning any decision ("the disputed decision") of the Commissioners, or of an officer of the Commissioners, were brought by any person at any time before that date,

(*b*) a determination has been or is made in those proceedings that the disputed decision was wrong or should be set aside,

(*c*) the claim is one made by that person at a time after the proceedings were brought (whether before or after the making of the determination), and

(*d*) the claim relates to—

(i) an amount paid by that person to the Commissioners on the basis of the disputed decision, or

(ii) an amount paid by that person to the Commissioners before the relevant date (including an amount paid before the making of the disputed decision) on grounds which, in all material respects, correspond to those on which that decision was made.

(4) Where this subsection applies in the case of any claim—

(*a*) subsection (4) of section 80 of the Value Added Tax Act 1994 (as inserted by this section) shall not apply, and shall be taken never to have applied, in relation to so much of that claim as relates to an amount falling within subsection (3)(*d*)(i) or (ii) above, but

(*b*) the Commissioners shall not be liable on that claim, and shall be taken never to have been liable on that claim, to repay any amount so falling which was paid to them more than three years before the proceedings mentioned in subsection (3)(*a*) above were brought.

(5) In subsection (3)(*d*) above—

(*a*) the reference to the relevant date is a reference to whichever is the earlier of 18th July 1996 and the date of the making of the determination in question; and

(*b*) the reference to an amount paid on the basis of a decision, or on any grounds, includes an amount so paid on terms (however expressed) which questioned the correctness of the decision or, as the case may be, of those grounds.

(6), (7) (*insert* VATA 1994 s 80(4A), (4B) and (4C), and *amend* s 83(*t*)).

(8) Nothing contained in—

(*a*) any regulations under section 25(1) of, or paragraph 2 of Schedule 11 to, that Act relating to the correction of errors or the making of adjustments, or

(*b*) any requirement imposed under any such regulations,

shall be taken, in relation to any time on or after 18th July 1996, to have conferred an entitlement on any person to receive, by way of repayment, any amount to which he would not have had any entitlement on a claim under section 80 of that Act.

(9) Subsections (6) to (8) above shall be deemed to have come into force on 4th December 1996.

(10) (amends VATA 1994 s 77(1) and (4)).

(11) In this section—

"the Commissioners" means the Commissioners of Customs and Excise; and

"legal proceedings" means any proceedings before a court or tribunal.

(12) Without prejudice to the generality of paragraph 1(2) of Schedule 13 to the Value Added Tax Act 1994 (transitional provisions), the references in this section, and in subsection (4) of section 80 of that Act (as inserted by this section), to a claim under that section include references to a claim first made under section 24 of the Finance Act 1989 which was re-enacted in section 80.

Commentary—*De Voil Indirect Tax Service* **V5.151–V5.166.**

Simon's Tax Cases—*Leeds City Council v R&C Comrs* [2014] UKUT 596 (TCC), [2014] STC 789.

Amendments—Sub-s (10) repealed by FA 2008 Sch 39 para 65(*c*) with effect from 1 April 2010 (by virtue of SI 2009/403 art 2(2)), subject to transitional provisions in SI 2009/403 art 10(2) (where art 10 applies the appointed day is 1 April 2012).

48 Set-off of credits and debits

(1) (*inserts* VATA 1994 s 81(3A)).

(2) Subsection (1) above shall be deemed to have come into force on 18th July 1996 as a provision applying for determining the amount of any payment or repayment by the Commissioners on or after that date, including a payment or repayment in respect of a liability arising before that date.

Commentary—*De Voil Indirect Tax Service* **V5.151–V5.166.**

49 Transitional provision for set-offs etc

(1) Where—

(*a*) at any time before 4th December 1996, any person ("the taxpayer") became liable to pay any sum ("the relevant sum") to the Commissioners by way of VAT, penalty, interest or surcharge, (*b*) at any time on or after 18th July 1996 and before 4th December 1996 an amount was set against the whole or any part of the relevant sum,

(*c*) the amount set against that sum was an amount which is treated under section 47 above as not having been due from the Commissioners at the time when it was set against that sum, and

(*d*) as a consequence, the taxpayer's liability to pay the whole or a part of the relevant sum falls to be treated as not having been discharged in accordance with section 81(3) of the 1994 Act,

the Commissioners may, to the best of their judgement, assess the amount of the continuing liability of the taxpayer and notify it to him.

(2) In subsection (1) above the reference to the continuing liability of the taxpayer is a reference to so much of the liability to pay the relevant sum as—

(*a*) would have been discharged if the amount mentioned in subsection (1)(*b*) above had been required to be set against the relevant sum in accordance with section 81(3) of the 1994 Act, but

(*b*) falls, by virtue of section 47 above, to be treated as not having been discharged in accordance with section 81(3) of that Act.

(3) The taxpayer's only liabilities under the 1994 Act in respect of his failure, on or after the time mentioned in subsection (1)(*b*) above, to pay an amount assessable under this section shall be—

(*a*) his liability to be assessed for that amount under this section; and

(*b*) liabilities arising under the following provisions of this section.

(4) Subsections (2) to (8) of section 78A of the 1994 Act apply in the case of an assessment under subsection (1) above as they apply in the case of an assessment under section 78A(1) of that Act.

(5) The 1994 Act shall have effect as if the matters specified in section 83 of that Act (matters subject to appeal) included an assessment under this section and the amount of such an assessment.

(6) Nothing contained in—

(*a*) any regulations under section 25(1) of, or paragraph 2 of Schedule 11 to, the 1994 Act relating to the correction of errors or the making of adjustments, or

(*b*) any requirement imposed under any such regulations,

shall be taken, in relation to any time on or after 18th July 1996, to have conferred on any person any entitlement, otherwise than in accordance with section 81(3) of that Act, to set any amount, as an amount due from the Commissioners, against any sum which that person was liable to pay to the Commissioners by way of VAT, penalty, interest or surcharge.

(7) In this section—

"the 1994 Act" means the Value Added Tax Act 1994; and

"the Commissioners" means the Commissioners of Customs and Excise.

(8) This section shall be deemed to have come into force on 4th December 1996.

(9) Where at any time on or after 4th December 1996 and before the day on which this Act is passed any assessment corresponding to an assessment under this section was made under a resolution of the House of Commons having effect in accordance with the provisions of the Provisional Collection of Taxes Act 1968, this section has effect, on and after the day on which this Act is passed, as if that assessment were an assessment under this section and as if any appeal brought under that resolution had been brought under this section.

Commentary—*De Voil Indirect Tax Service* **V5.151–V5.166**

Excise duties and other indirect taxes

50 Overpayments, interest, assessments, etc

. . .

(2) Schedule 6 to this Act (which makes further provision for the assessment of amounts payable under enactments relating to excise duty) shall also have effect.

Notes—Words omitted are not relevant for the purposes of VAT.

Enforcement of payment

51 Enforcement by distress

(1) The Commissioners may by regulations [not having effect in England and Wales or Scotland][1] make provision—

(*a*) for authorising distress to be levied on the goods and chattels of any person refusing or neglecting to pay—

(i) any amount of relevant tax due from him, or

(ii) any amount recoverable as if it were relevant tax due from him;

(*b*) for the disposal of any goods or chattels on which distress is levied in pursuance of the regulations; and

(*c*) for the imposition and recovery of costs, charges, expenses and fees in connection with anything done under the regulations.

(2) The provision that may be contained in regulations under this section shall include, in particular—

(*a*) provision for the levying of distress, by any person authorised to do so under the regulations, on goods or chattels located at any place whatever (including on a public highway); and
(*b*) provision authorising distress to be levied at any such time of the day or night, and on any such day of the week, as may be specified or described in the regulations.

(3) Regulations under this section may—
(*a*) make different provision for different cases, and
(*b*) contain any such incidental, supplemental, consequential or transitional provision as the Commissioners think fit;

and the transitional provision that may be contained in regulations under this section shall include transitional provision in connection with the coming into force of the repeal by this Act of any other power by regulations to make provision for or in connection with the levying of distress.

(4) The power to make regulations under this section shall be exercisable by statutory instrument subject to annulment in pursuance of a resolution of the House of Commons.

(5) The following are relevant taxes for the purposes of this section, that is to say—
(*a*) . . .
(*b*) value added tax;
(*c*)–(*f*) . . .

(6) In this section "the Commissioners" means the Commissioners of Customs and Excise.

(7) Regulations made under this section shall not have effect in Scotland.[1]

Commentary—De Voil Indirect Tax Service **V5.173.**

Note—Sub-ss (5)(*a*), (*c*)–(*f*) are not relevant to VAT.

Sub-s (A1) was to have been inserted by the Tribunals, Courts and Enforcement Act 2007 ss 62(3), 146, Sch 13 para 126(2), but the inserting provision was repealed by FA 2008 s 129, Sch 43 para 11(*d*) with effect from 5 April 2014 (the date appointed by virtue of the Finance Act 2008, Section 127 and Part 1 of Schedule 43) Appointed Day) Order, SI 2014/906 art 3) prior to bringing sub-s (A1) into effect.

Regulations—See Distress for Customs and Excise Duties and other Indirect Taxes Regulations, SI 1997/1431.

AMENDMENTS—

1 In sub-s (1) words inserted and sub-s (7) repealed by the Tribunals, Courts and Enforcement Act 2007 ss 62(3), 146, Sch 13 para 126(3), (4) and Sch 23 Pt 3 with effect from 6 April 2014 (the date appointed by virtue of the Tribunals, Courts and Enforcement Act 2007 (Commencement No 11) Order, SI 2014/768 art 2(1)(*b*)).

52 Enforcement by diligence

(1) Where any amount of relevant tax or any amount recoverable as if it were relevant tax is due and has not been paid, the sheriff, on an application by the Commissioners accompanied by a certificate by them—
(a) stating that none of the persons specified in the application has paid the amount due from him;
(b) stating that payment of the amount due from each such person has been demanded from him; and
(c) specifying the amount due from and unpaid by each such person,

shall grant a summary warrant in a form prescribed by Act of Sederunt authorising the recovery, by any of the diligences mentioned in subsection (2) below, of the amount remaining due and unpaid.

(2) The diligences referred to in subsection (1) above are—
[(a) an attachment;][1]
(b) an earnings arrestment;
(c) an arrestment and action of furthcoming or sale.

(3) Subject to subsection (4) below and without prejudice to [section 39(1) of the Debt Arrangement and Attachment (Scotland) Act 2002 (asp 17) (expenses of attachment)][1] *the sheriff officer's fees, together with the outlays necessarily incurred by him, in connection with the execution of a summary warrant shall be chargeable against the debtor.*

(4) No fees shall be chargeable by the sheriff officer against the debtor for collecting, and accounting to the Commissioners for, sums paid to him by the debtor in respect of the amount owing.

(5) The following are relevant taxes for the purposes of this section, that is to say—
(a) . . .
(b) value added tax;
(c)–(f) . . .

(6) In this section "the Commissioners" means the Commissioners of Customs and Excise.

(7) This section shall come into force on such day as the Commissioners of Customs and Excise may by order made by statutory instrument appoint, and different days may be appointed under this subsection for different purposes.

(8) This section extends only to Scotland.[2]

Commentary—*De Voil Indirect Tax Service* **V5.173.**

Notes—Sub-ss (5)(*a*), (*c*)–(*f*) are not relevant to VAT.

The appointed day under sub-s (7) above is 1 July 1997 (see SI 1997/1432).

Amendments—[1] Sub-s (2)(*a*) and words in sub-s (3) substituted by the Debt Arrangement and Attachment (Scotland) Act 2002, s 61, Sch 3, Pt 1, para 26 with effect from 30 December 2002.

[2] This section repealed by FA 2008 s 129, Sch 43 para 15 with effect from 23 November 2009 (by virtue of SI 2009/3024 art 3). Note that if before the commencement date a warrant has been granted under this section, that warrant shall continue to have effect according to the provisions under which it was granted (SI 2009/3024 art 4(1)(*c*)). See also FA 2008 ss 127,128.

53 Amendments consequential on sections 51 and 52

. . .

(6) (*inserts* VATA 1994 s 48(7A)).

(7) (*amends* VATA 1994 s 68(1)(*a*)).

. . .

(9) This section shall come into force on such day as the Commissioners of Customs and Excise may by order made by statutory instrument appoint, and different days may be appointed under this subsection for different purposes.

Commentary—*De Voil Indirect Tax Service* **V5.171.**

Notes—Words omitted are not relevant for the purposes of VAT.

The appointed day under sub-s (9) above is 1 July 1997 (see SI 1997/1432).

Miscellaneous

110 Obtaining information from social security authorities

Amendments—This section repealed by the Welfare Reform Act 2012 s 147, Sch 14 Pt 13 with effect from 8 May 2012 (two months after Royal Asset to the Welfare Reform Act 2012 (see s 150(2)(*f*) to that Act).

111 Report on VAT on energy saving materials

. . .

Amendments—This section repealed by Statute Law (Repeals) Act 1998 Sch 1 Group 5, with effect from 19 November 1998.

Supplemental

113 Repeals

(1) The enactments mentioned in Schedule 18 to this Act (which include spent provisions) are hereby repealed to the extent specified in the third column of that Schedule.

(2) The repeals specified in that Schedule have effect subject to the commencement provisions and savings contained or referred to in the notes set out in that Schedule.

114 Short title

This Act may be cited as the Finance Act 1997.

SCHEDULES

SCHEDULE 2

GAMING DUTY: CONSEQUENTIAL AND INCIDENTAL AMENDMENTS

Section 13

PART I

AMENDMENTS OF THE CUSTOMS AND EXCISE MANAGEMENT ACT 1979

Introductory

1 The Customs and Excise Management Act 1979 shall be amended in accordance with the provisions of this Part of this Schedule.

Meaning of "revenue trade provisions" and "revenue trader"

2—(1) This paragraph amends section 1(1) (interpretation).

(2)–(4) (*amends* CEMA 1979 s 1(1)).

SCHEDULE 6

ASSESSMENTS FOR EXCISE DUTY PURPOSES

Section 50

Assessments in cases of untrue declarations etc

5 (*inserts* CEMA 1979 s 167(5)).

FINANCE ACT 1998

(1998 Chapter 36)

An Act to grant certain duties, to alter other duties, and to amend the law relating to the National Debt and the Public Revenue, and to make further provision in connection with Finance.

[31 July 1998]

PART II
VALUE ADDED TAX

21 Deemed supplies.

(1) Paragraph 5 of Schedule 4 to the Value Added Tax Act 1994 (disposal of business assets) shall be amended as follows.

(2) (*amends* VATA 1994 Sch 4 para 5(2)(*a*)).

(3) (*inserts* VATA 1994 Sch 4 para 5(2A)).

(4) (*amends* VATA 1994 Sch 4 para 5(5)).

(5) (*inserts* VATA 1994 Sch 4 para 5(5A)).

(6) The preceding provisions of this section apply to any case where the time when the goods are transferred or disposed of or, as the case may be, put to use, used or made available for use is on or after 17th March 1998.

22 Changes of place of supply: transitional.

(1) (*inserts* VATA 1994 s 97A).

(2) (*inserts* VATA 1994 s 6(14A)).

(3) This section shall be deemed to have come into force on 17th March 1998.

23 Bad debt relief.

(1) (*amends* VATA 1994 s 36(1)(*a*)).

(2) (*amends* VATA 1994 s 36(3)).

(3) (*inserts* VATA 1994 s 36(3A)).

(4) In subsection (5) of that section—

(*a*) (*amends* VATA 1994 s 36(5)(*c*)).

(*b*) (*amends* VATA 1994 s 36(5)(*e*)).

(5) (*amends* VATA 1994 s 36(6)(*b*), (*c*)).

(6) (*amends* VATA 1994 s 36(7)).

(7) Subsections (1) to (3) above have effect in relation to claims made on or after the day on which this Act is passed.

24 Long leases in Scotland.

(*amends* VATA 1994 s 96(1) definition of "major interest").

HUMAN RIGHTS ACT 1998

(1998 Chapter 42)

An Act to give further effect to rights and freedoms guaranteed under the European Convention on Human Rights; to make provision with respect to holders of certain judicial offices who become judges of the European Court of Human Rights; and for connected purposes.

[9 November 1998]

Note—This Act was brought into force as follows—

ss 1–17 on 2 October 2000 (by the Human Rights Act 1998 (Commencement No 2) Order, SI 2000/1851 art 2).

s 19 on 24 November 1998 (by the Human Rights Act 1998 (Commencement) Order, SI 1998/2882 art 2).

s 20 on 9 November 1998 (RA).

s 21(1)–(4) (by the Human Rights Act 1998 (Commencement) Order, SI 1998/2882 art 2).

s 21(5) on 9 November 1998 (RA).

s 22 on 9 November 1998 (RA).

Schs 1, 2 (by the Human Rights Act 1998 (Commencement) Order, SI 1998/2882 art 2).

ARRANGEMENT OF SECTIONS

Introduction

Legislation

Introduction

1 The Convention Rights

(1) In this Act "the Convention rights" means the rights and fundamental freedoms set out in—

(*a*) Articles 2 to 12 and 14 of the Convention,
(*b*) Articles 1 to 3 of the First Protocol, and
(*c*) [Article 1 of the Thirteenth Protocol][2],

as read with Articles 16 to 18 of the Convention.

(2) Those Articles are to have effect for the purposes of this Act subject to any designated derogation or reservation (as to which see sections 14 and 15).

(3) The Articles are set out in Schedule 1.

(4) The [Secretary of State][1] may by order make such amendments to this Act as he considers appropriate to reflect the effect, in relation to the United Kingdom, of a protocol.

(5) In subsection (4) "protocol" means a protocol to the Convention—

(*a*) which the United Kingdom has ratified; or
(*b*) which the United Kingdom has signed with a view to ratification.

(6) No amendment may be made by an order under subsection (4) so as to come into force before the protocol concerned is in force in relation to the United Kingdom.

Simon's Tax Cases—*Holland (executor of Holland, dec'd) v IRC* [2003] STC (SCD) 43.

Amendments—[1] Words in square brackets substituted by the Secretary of State for Constitutional Affairs Order, SI 2003/1887 art 9, Sch 2 para 10(1) with effect from 19 August 2003.

[2] Sub-s (1)(*c*) substituted by Human Rights Act 1998 (Amendment) Order, SI 2004/1574, art 1, 2(1) with effect from 22 June 2004.

2 Interpretation of Convention rights

(1) A court or tribunal determining a question which has arisen in connection with a Convention right must take into account any—

(*a*) judgment, decision, declaration or advisory opinion of the European Court of Human Rights,
(*b*) opinion of the Commission given in a report adopted under Article 31 of the Convention,
(*c*) decision of the Commission in connection with Article 26 or 27(2) of the Convention, or
(*d*) decision of the Committee of Ministers taken under Article 46 of the Convention,

whenever made or given, so far as, in the opinion of the court or tribunal, it is relevant to the proceedings in which that question has arisen.

(2) Evidence of any judgment, decision, declaration or opinion of which account may have to be taken under this section is to be given in proceedings before any court or tribunal in such manner as may be provided by rules.

(3) In this section "rules" means rules of court or, in the case of proceedings before a tribunal, rules made for the purposes of this section—

(*a*) by . . . [1] [the Lord Chancellor or][2] the Secretary of State, in relation to any proceedings outside Scotland;

(*b*) by the Secretary of State, in relation to proceedings in Scotland; or

(*c*) by a Northern Ireland department, in relation to proceedings before a tribunal in Northern Ireland—

(i) which deals with transferred matters; and

(ii) for which no rules made under paragraph (*a*) are in force.

Amendments—[1] Words revoked by the Secretary of State for Constitutional Affairs Order, SI 2003/1887 art 9, Sch 2 para 10(2) with effect from 19 August 2003.

[2] Words in sub-s (3)(*a*) inserted by Transfer of Functions (Lord Chancellor and Secretary of State) Order, SI 2005/3429 art 8, Schedule para 3 with effect from 12 January 2006.

Legislation

3 Interpretation of legislation

(1) So far as it is possible to do so, primary legislation and subordinate legislation must be read and given effect in a way which is compatible with the Convention rights.

(2) This section—

(*a*) applies to primary legislation and subordinate legislation whenever enacted;

(*b*) does not affect the validity, continuing operation or enforcement of any incompatible primary legislation; and

(*c*) does not affect the validity, continuing operation or enforcement of any incompatible subordinate legislation if (disregarding any possibility of revocation) primary legislation prevents removal of the incompatibility.

Simon's Tax Cases—*Bancroft and anor v Crutchfield (Insp of Taxes)* [2002] STC 347; *Carney v Nathan (Insp of Taxes)* [2003] STC (SCD) 28; *Holland (executor of Holland, dec'd) v IRC* [2003] STC (SCD) 43.

4 Declaration of incompatibility

(1) Subsection (2) applies in any proceedings in which a court determines whether a provision of primary legislation is compatible with a Convention right.

(2) If the court is satisfied that the provision is incompatible with a Convention right, it may make a declaration of that incompatibility.

(3) Subsection (4) applies in any proceedings in which a court determines whether a provision of subordinate legislation, made in the exercise of a power conferred by primary legislation, is compatible with a Convention right.

(4) If the court is satisfied—

(*a*) that the provision is incompatible with a Convention right, and

(*b*) that (disregarding any possibility of revocation) the primary legislation concerned prevents removal of the incompatibility,

it may make a declaration of that incompatibility.

(5) In this section "court" means—

(*a*) [the Supreme Court;][2];

(*b*) the Judicial Committee of the Privy Council;

(*c*) the [Court Martial Appeal Court][3];

(*d*) in Scotland, the High Court of Justiciary sitting otherwise than as a trial court or the Court of Session;

(*e*) in England and Wales or Northern Ireland, the High Court or the Court of Appeal.

[(*f*) the Court of Protection, in any matter being dealt with by the President of the Family Division, the Vice-Chancellor or a puisne judge of the High Court.][1]

(6) A declaration under this section ("a declaration of incompatibility")—

(*a*) does not affect the validity, continuing operation or enforcement of the provision in respect of which it is given; and

(*b*) is not binding on the parties to the proceedings in which it is made.

Simon's Tax Cases—*Holland (executor of Holland, dec'd) v IRC* [2003] STC (SCD) 43.

Amendments—[1] Sub-s (5)(*f*) inserted by the Mental Capacity Act 2005 s 67(1), Sch 6 para 43 with effect from 1 October 2007 (by virtue of SI 2007/1897 art 2).

[2] Sub-s (5)(*a*) substituted by the Constitutional Reform Act 2005 s 40, Sch 9 para 66(1), (2) with effect from 1 October 2009 (by virtue of SI 2009/1604 art 2(*d*)).

[3] In sub-s (5)(*c*), words substituted for words "Courts-Martial Appeal Court" by the Armed Forces Act 2006 s 378(1), Sch 16 para 156 with effect, for certain purposes from 28 March 2009 (by virtue of SI 2009/812 art 3(*a*), (*b*)) and for remaining purposes from 31 October 2009 (by virtue of SI 2009/1167 art 4).

5 Right of Crown to intervene

(1) Where a court is considering whether to make a declaration of incompatibility, the Crown is entitled to notice in accordance with rules of court.

(2) In any case to which subsection (1) applies—

(*a*) a Minister of the Crown (or a person nominated by him),

(*b*) a member of the Scottish Executive,

(*c*) a Northern Ireland Minister,

(*d*) a Northern Ireland department,

is entitled, on giving notice in accordance with rules of court, to be joined as a party to the proceedings.

(3) Notice under subsection (2) may be given at any time during the proceedings.

(4) A person who has been made a party to criminal proceedings (other than in Scotland) as the result of a notice under subsection (2) may, with leave, appeal to the [Supreme Court][2] against any declaration of incompatibility made in the proceedings.

(5) In subsection (4)—

"criminal proceedings" includes all proceedings before the [Court Martial Appeal Court][1]; and "leave" means leave granted by the court making the declaration of incompatibility or by the [Supreme Court][2].

Amendment—[1] In sub-s (5) words in definition of "criminal proceedings" substituted for words "Courts-Martial Appeal Court" by the Armed Forces Act 2006, s 378(1), Sch 16, para 157 with effect for certain purposes from 28 March 2009 (by virtue of SI 2009/812 art 3(*a*), (*b*)) and for remaining purposes from 31 October 2009 (by virtue of SI 2009/1167 art 4).

[2] In sub-ss (4), (5), words substituted for words "House of Lords" by the Constitutional Reform Act 2005 s 40, Sch 9 para 66(1)–(3) with effect from 1 October 2009 (by virtue of SI 2009/1604 art 2(*d*)).

Public authorities

6 Acts of public authorities

(1) It is unlawful for a public authority to act in a way which is incompatible with a Convention right.

(2) Subsection (1) does not apply to an act if—

(*a*) as the result of one or more provisions of primary legislation, the authority could not have acted differently; or

(*b*) in the case of one or more provisions of, or made under, primary legislation which cannot be read or given effect in a way which is compatible with the Convention rights, the authority was acting so as to give effect to or enforce those provisions.

(3) In this section "public authority" includes—

(*a*) a court or tribunal, and

(*b*) any person certain of whose functions are functions of a public nature,

but does not include either House of Parliament or a person exercising functions in connection with proceedings in Parliament.

(4) In subsection (3) "Parliament" does not include the House of Lords in its judicial capacity.

(5) In relation to a particular act, a person is not a public authority by virtue only of subsection (3)(*b*) if the nature of the act is private.

(6) "An act" includes a failure to act but does not include a failure to—

(*a*) introduce in, or lay before, Parliament a proposal for legislation; or

(*b*) make any primary legislation or remedial order.

Simon's Tax Cases—*R (oao Wilkinson) v IRC* [2002] STC 347; *Holland (executor of Holland, decd) v IRC* [2003] STC (SCD) 43; *R (on the application of Wilkinson) v IRC* [2003] STC 1113, [2006] STC 270.

Amendments—Sub-s (4) repealed by the Constitutional Reform Act 2005 ss 40, 146, Sch 9 para 66(1), (4), Sch 18 with effect from 1 October 2009 (by virtue of SI 2009/1604, art 2(*d*)).

7 Proceedings

(1) A person who claims that a public authority has acted (or proposes to act) in a way which is made unlawful by section 6(1) may—

(*a*) bring proceedings against the authority under this Act in the appropriate court or tribunal, or

(*b*) rely on the Convention right or rights concerned in any legal proceedings,

but only if he is (or would be) a victim of the unlawful act.

(2) In subsection (1)(*a*) "appropriate court or tribunal" means such court or tribunal as may be determined in accordance with rules; and proceedings against an authority include a counterclaim or similar proceeding.

(3) If the proceedings are brought on an application for judicial review, the applicant is to be taken to have a sufficient interest in relation to the unlawful act only if he is, or would be, a victim of that act.

(4) If the proceedings are made by way of a petition for judicial review in Scotland, the applicant shall be taken to have title and interest to sue in relation to the unlawful act only if he is, or would be, a victim of that act.

(5) Proceedings under subsection (1)(*a*) must be brought before the end of—

(*a*) the period of one year beginning with the date on which the act complained of took place; or
(*b*) such longer period as the court or tribunal considers equitable having regard to all the circumstances,

but that is subject to any rule imposing a stricter time limit in relation to the procedure in question.
(6) In subsection (1)(*b*) "legal proceedings" includes—
(*a*) proceedings brought by or at the instigation of a public authority; and
(*b*) an appeal against the decision of a court or tribunal.
(7) For the purposes of this section, a person is a victim of an unlawful act only if he would be a victim for the purposes of Article 34 of the Convention if proceedings were brought in the European Court of Human Rights in respect of that act.
(8) Nothing in this Act creates a criminal offence.
(9) In this section "rules" means—
(*a*) in relation to proceedings before a court or tribunal outside Scotland, rules made by . . . [1][the Lord Chancellor or][2]the Secretary of State for the purposes of this section or rules of court,
(*b*) in relation to proceedings before a court or tribunal in Scotland, rules made by the Secretary of State for those purposes,
(*c*) in relation to proceedings before a tribunal in Northern Ireland—
(i) which deals with transferred matters; and
(ii) for which no rules made under paragraph (*a*) are in force,

rules made by a Northern Ireland department for those purposes,

and includes provision made by order under section 1 of the Courts and Legal Services Act 1990.
(10) In making rules, regard must be had to section 9.
(11) The Minister who has power to make rules in relation to a particular tribunal may, to the extent he considers it necessary to ensure that the tribunal can provide an appropriate remedy in relation to an act (or proposed act) of a public authority which is (or would be) unlawful as a result of section 6(1), by order add to—
(*a*) the relief or remedies which the tribunal may grant; or
(*b*) the grounds on which it may grant any of them.
(12) An order made under subsection (11) may contain such incidental, supplemental, consequential or transitional provision as the Minister making it considers appropriate.
(13) "The Minister" includes the Northern Ireland department concerned.

Simon's Tax Cases—*Holland (executor of Holland, decd) v IRC* [2003] STC (SCD) 43.

Amendments—[1] Words revoked by the Secretary of State for Constitutional Affairs Order, SI 2003/1887 art 9, Sch 2 para 10(2) with effect from 19 August 2003.

[2] Words in sub-s (9)(*a*) inserted by Transfer of Functions (Lord Chancellor and Secretary of State) Order, SI 2005/3429 art 8, Schedule para 3 with effect from 12 January 2006.

8 Judicial remedies

(1) In relation to any act (or proposed act) of a public authority which the court finds is (or would be) unlawful, it may grant such relief or remedy, or make such order, within its powers as it considers just and appropriate.
(2) But damages may be awarded only by a court which has power to award damages, or to order the payment of compensation, in civil proceedings.
(3) No award of damages is to be made unless, taking account of all the circumstances of the case, including—
(*a*) any other relief or remedy granted, or order made, in relation to the act in question (by that or any other court), and
(*b*) the consequences of any decision (of that or any other court) in respect of that act,

the court is satisfied that the award is necessary to afford just satisfaction to the person in whose favour it is made.
(4) In determining—
(*a*) whether to award damages, or
(*b*) the amount of an award,

the court must take into account the principles applied by the European Court of Human Rights in relation to the award of compensation under Article 41 of the Convention.
(5) A public authority against which damages are awarded is to be treated—
(*a*) in Scotland, for the purposes of section 3 of the Law Reform (Miscellaneous Provisions) (Scotland) Act 1940 as if the award were made in an action of damages in which the authority has been found liable in respect of loss or damage to the person to whom the award is made;
(*b*) for the purposes of the Civil Liability (Contribution) Act 1978 as liable in respect of damage suffered by the person to whom the award is made.
(6) In this section—
"court" includes a tribunal;
"damages" means damages for an unlawful act of a public authority; and

"unlawful" means unlawful under section 6(1).

Simon's Tax Cases—*R (on the application of Wilkinson) v IRC* [2003] STC 1113.

9 Judicial acts

(1) Proceedings under section 7(1)(*a*) in respect of a judicial act may be brought only—

(*a*) by exercising a right of appeal;

(*b*) on an application (in Scotland a petition) for judicial review; or

(*c*) in such other forum as may be prescribed by rules.

(2) That does not affect any rule of law which prevents a court from being the subject of judicial review.

(3) In proceedings under this Act in respect of a judicial act done in good faith, damages may not be awarded otherwise than to compensate a person to the extent required by Article 5(5) of the Convention.

(4) An award of damages permitted by subsection (3) is to be made against the Crown; but no award may be made unless the appropriate person, if not a party to the proceedings, is joined.

(5) In this section—

"appropriate person" means the Minister responsible for the court concerned, or a person or government department nominated by him;

"court" includes a tribunal;

"judge" includes a member of a tribunal, a justice of the peace [(or, in Northern Ireland, a lay magistrate)][1]and a clerk or other officer entitled to exercise the jurisdiction of a court;

"judicial act" means a judicial act of a court and includes an act done on the instructions, or on behalf, of a judge; and

"rules" has the same meaning as in section 7(9).

Amendments—[1] In sub s (5), words inserted in the definition of "judge" by the Justice (Northern Ireland) Act 2002 s 10, Sch 4 para 39 with effect 1 April 2005 (by virtue of the Justice (Northern Ireland) Act 2002 (Commencement No 8) Order 2005, SR 2005/109 art 2, Schedule).

Remedial action

10 Power to take remedial action

(1) This section applies if—

(*a*) a provision of legislation has been declared under section 4 to be incompatible with a Convention right and, if an appeal lies—

(i) all persons who may appeal have stated in writing that they do not intend to do so;

(ii) the time for bringing an appeal has expired and no appeal has been brought within that time; or

(iii) an appeal brought within that time has been determined or abandoned; or

(*b*) it appears to a Minister of the Crown or Her Majesty in Council that, having regard to a finding of the European Court of Human Rights made after the coming into force of this section in proceedings against the United Kingdom, a provision of legislation is incompatible with an obligation of the United Kingdom arising from the Convention.

(2) If a Minister of the Crown considers that there are compelling reasons for proceeding under this section, he may by order make such amendments to the legislation as he considers necessary to remove the incompatibility.

(3) If, in the case of subordinate legislation, a Minister of the Crown considers—

(*a*) that it is necessary to amend the primary legislation under which the subordinate legislation in question was made, in order to enable the incompatibility to be removed, and

(*b*) that there are compelling reasons for proceeding under this section,

he may by order make such amendments to the primary legislation as he considers necessary.

(4) This section also applies where the provision in question is in subordinate legislation and has been quashed, or declared invalid, by reason of incompatibility with a Convention right and the Minister proposes to proceed under paragraph 2(*b*) of Schedule 2.

(5) If the legislation is an Order in Council, the power conferred by subsection (2) or (3) is exercisable by Her Majesty in Council.

(6) In this section "legislation" does not include a Measure of the Church Assembly or of the General Synod of the Church of England.

(7) Schedule 2 makes further provision about remedial orders.

Other rights and proceedings

11 Safeguard for existing human rights

A person's reliance on a Convention right does not restrict—

(*a*) any other right or freedom conferred on him by or under any law having effect in any part of the United Kingdom; or

(*b*) his right to make any claim or bring any proceedings which he could make or bring apart from sections 7 to 9.

12 Freedom of expression

(1) This section applies if a court is considering whether to grant any relief which, if granted, might affect the exercise of the Convention right to freedom of expression.

(2) If the person against whom the application for relief is made ("the respondent") is neither present nor represented, no such relief is to be granted unless the court is satisfied—

(*a*) that the applicant has taken all practicable steps to notify the respondent; or

(*b*) that there are compelling reasons why the respondent should not be notified.

(3) No such relief is to be granted so as to restrain publication before trial unless the court is satisfied that the applicant is likely to establish that publication should not be allowed.

(4) The court must have particular regard to the importance of the Convention right to freedom of expression and, where the proceedings relate to material which the respondent claims, or which appears to the court, to be journalistic, literary or artistic material (or to conduct connected with such material), to—

(*a*) the extent to which—

(i) the material has, or is about to, become available to the public; or

(ii) it is, or would be, in the public interest for the material to be published;

(*b*) any relevant privacy code.

(5) In this section—

"court" includes a tribunal; and

"relief" includes any remedy or order (other than in criminal proceedings).

13 Freedom of thought, conscience and religion

(1) If a court's determination of any question arising under this Act might affect the exercise by a religious organisation (itself or its members collectively) of the Convention right to freedom of thought, conscience and religion, it must have particular regard to the importance of that right.

(2) In this section "court" includes a tribunal.

Derogations and reservations

14 Derogations

(1) In this Act "designated derogation" means—

. . . [1]any derogation by the United Kingdom from an Article of the Convention, or of any protocol to the Convention, which is designated for the purposes of this Act in an order made by the [Secretary of State][2].

(2) . . . [1].

(3) If a designated derogation is amended or replaced it ceases to be a designated derogation.

(4) But subsection (3) does not prevent the [Secretary of State][2]from exercising his power under subsection (1) . . . [1]to make a fresh designation order in respect of the Article concerned.

(5) The [Secretary of State][2]must by order make such amendments to Schedule 3 as he considers appropriate to reflect—

(*a*) any designation order; or

(*b*) the effect of subsection (3).

(6) A designation order may be made in anticipation of the making by the United Kingdom of a proposed derogation.

Amendments—[1] In sub-s (1), para (*a*), and letter "(*b*)" revoked, sub-s (2) revoked, and letter "(b)" in sub-s (4) revoked, by the Human Rights Act (Amendment) Order, SI 2001/1216 art 2 with effect from 1 April 2001.

[2] Words in square brackets substituted by the Secretary of State for Constitutional Affairs Order, SI 2003/1887 art 9, Sch 2 para 10(1) with effect from 19 August 2003.

15 Reservations

(1) In this Act "designated reservation" means—

(*a*) the United Kingdom's reservation to Article 2 of the First Protocol to the Convention; and

(*b*) any other reservation by the United Kingdom to an Article of the Convention, or of any protocol to the Convention, which is designated for the purposes of this Act in an order made by the [Secretary of State][1].

(2) The text of the reservation referred to in subsection (1)(*a*) is set out in Part II of Schedule 3.

(3) If a designated reservation is withdrawn wholly or in part it ceases to be a designated reservation.

(4) But subsection (3) does not prevent the [Secretary of State][1] from exercising his power under subsection (1)(*b*) to make a fresh designation order in respect of the Article concerned.

(5) The [Secretary of State][1] must by order make such amendments to this Act as he considers appropriate to reflect—

(*a*) any designation order; or

(*b*) the effect of subsection (3).

Amendments—[1] Words in square brackets substituted by the Secretary of State for Constitutional Affairs Order, SI 2003/1887 art 9, Sch 2 para 10(1) with effect from 19 August 2003.

16 Period for which designated derogations have effect

(1) If it has not already been withdrawn by the United Kingdom, a designated derogation ceases to have effect for the purposes of this Act—

. . . [1]at the end of the period of five years beginning with the date on which the order designating it was made.

(2) At any time before the period—

(*a*) fixed by subsection (1) . . . [1], or

(*b*) extended by an order under this subsection,

comes to an end, the [Secretary of State][2]may by order extend it by a further period of five years.

(3) An order under section 14(1) . . . [1]ceases to have effect at the end of the period for consideration, unless a resolution has been passed by each House approving the order.

(4) Subsection (3) does not affect—

(*a*) anything done in reliance on the order; or

(*b*) the power to make a fresh order under section 14(1) . . . [1].

(5) In subsection (3) "period for consideration" means the period of forty days beginning with the day on which the order was made.

(6) In calculating the period for consideration, no account is to be taken of any time during which—

(*a*) Parliament is dissolved or prorogued; or

(*b*) both Houses are adjourned for more than four days.

(7) If a designated derogation is withdrawn by the United Kingdom, the [Secretary of State][2] must by order make such amendments to this Act as he considers are required to reflect that withdrawal.

Amendments—[1] Words in sub-ss (1), (2)(*a*) revoked, and the letter "(b)" in sub-ss (3), (4) revoked, by the Human Rights Act (Amendment) Order, SI 2001/1216 art 3 with effect from 1 April 2001.

[2] Words in square brackets substituted by the Secretary of State for Constitutional Affairs Order, SI 2003/1887 art 9, Sch 2 para 10(1) with effect from 19 August 2003.

17 Periodic review of designated reservations

(1) The appropriate Minister must review the designated reservation referred to in section 15(1)(*a*)—

(*a*) before the end of the period of five years beginning with the date on which section 1(2) came into force; and

(*b*) if that designation is still in force, before the end of the period of five years beginning with the date on which the last report relating to it was laid under subsection (3).

(2) The appropriate Minister must review each of the other designated reservations (if any)—

(*a*) before the end of the period of five years beginning with the date on which the order designating the reservation first came into force; and

(*b*) if the designation is still in force, before the end of the period of five years beginning with the date on which the last report relating to it was laid under subsection (3).

(3) The Minister conducting a review under this section must prepare a report on the result of the review and lay a copy of it before each House of Parliament.

Judges of the European Court of Human Rights

18 Appointment to European Court of Human Rights

[not reproduced: see *Halsbury's Statutes* (4th edn) CIVIL RIGHTS and LIBERTIES].

Parliamentary procedure

19 Statements of compatibility

(1) A Minister of the Crown in charge of a Bill in either House of Parliament must, before Second Reading of the Bill—

(*a*) make a statement to the effect that in his view the provisions of the Bill are compatible with the Convention rights ("a statement of compatibility"); or

(*b*) make a statement to the effect that although he is unable to make a statement of compatibility the government nevertheless wishes the House to proceed with the Bill.

(2) The statement must be in writing and be published in such manner as the Minister making it considers appropriate.

Note—This section was brought into force on 24 November 1998 by the Human Rights Act 1998 (Commencement) Order, SI 1998/2882 art 2.

Supplemental

20 Orders etc under this Act

(1) Any power of a Minister of the Crown to make an order under this Act is exercisable by statutory instrument.

(2) The power of . . . [1][the Lord Chancellor or][2]the Secretary of State to make rules (other than rules of court) under section 2(3) or 7(9) is exercisable by statutory instrument.

(3) Any statutory instrument made under section 14, 15 or 16(7) must be laid before Parliament.

(4) No order may be made by . . . [1][the Lord Chancellor or][2] the Secretary of State under section 1(4), 7(11) or 16(2) unless a draft of the order has been laid before, and approved by, each House of Parliament.

(5) Any statutory instrument made under section 18(7) or Schedule 4, or to which subsection (2) applies, shall be subject to annulment in pursuance of a resolution of either House of Parliament.

(6) The power of a Northern Ireland department to make—

(*a*) rules under section 2(3)(*c*) or 7(9)(*c*), or

(*b*) an order under section 7(11),

is exercisable by statutory rule for the purposes of the Statutory Rules (Northern Ireland) Order 1979.

(7) Any rules made under section 2(3)(*c*) or 7(9)(*c*) shall be subject to negative resolution; and section 41(6) of the Interpretation Act (Northern Ireland) 1954 (meaning of "subject to negative resolution") shall apply as if the power to make the rules were conferred by an Act of the Northern Ireland Assembly.

(8) No order may be made by a Northern Ireland department under section 7(11) unless a draft of the order has been laid before, and approved by, the Northern Ireland Assembly.

Amendments—[1] Words revoked by the Secretary of State for Constitutional Affairs Order, SI 2003/1887 art 9, Sch 2 para 10(2) with effect from 19 August 2003.

[2] Words in sub-ss (2), (4) inserted by Transfer of Functions (Lord Chancellor and Secretary of State) Order, SI 2005/3429 art 8, Schedule para 3 with effect from 12 January 2006.

21 Interpretation, etc

(1) In this Act—

"amend" includes repeal and apply (with or without modifications);

"the appropriate Minister" means the Minister of the Crown having charge of the appropriate authorised government department (within the meaning of the Crown Proceedings Act 1947);

"the Commission" means the European Commission of Human Rights;

"the Convention" means the Convention for the Protection of Human Rights and Fundamental Freedoms, agreed by the Council of Europe at Rome on 4th November 1950 as it has effect for the time being in relation to the United Kingdom;

"declaration of incompatibility" means a declaration under section 4;

"Minister of the Crown" has the same meaning as in the Ministers of the Crown Act 1975;

"Northern Ireland Minister" includes the First Minister and the deputy First Minister in Northern Ireland;

"primary legislation" means any—

(*a*) public general Act;

(*b*) local and personal Act;

(*c*) private Act;

(*d*) Measure of the Church Assembly;

(*e*) Measure of the General Synod of the Church of England;

(*f*) Order in Council—

(i) made in exercise of Her Majesty's Royal Prerogative;

(ii) made under section 38(1)(*a*) of the Northern Ireland Constitution Act 1973 or the corresponding provision of the Northern Ireland Act 1998; or

(iii) amending an Act of a kind mentioned in paragraph (*a*), (*b*) or (*c*);

and includes an order or other instrument made under primary legislation (otherwise than by the [Welsh Ministers, the First Minister for Wales, the Counsel General to the Welsh Assembly Government][2], a member of the Scottish Executive, a Northern Ireland Minister or a Northern Ireland department) to the extent to which it operates to bring one or more provisions of that legislation into force or amends any primary legislation;

"the First Protocol" means the protocol to the Convention agreed at Paris on 20th March 1952;

. . .[1]

"the Eleventh Protocol" means the protocol to the Convention (restructuring the control machinery established by the Convention) agreed at Strasbourg on 11th May 1994;

["the Thirteenth Protocol" means the protocol to the Convention (concerning the abolition of the death penalty in all circumstances) agreed at Vilnius on 3rd May 2002;][1]

"remedial order" means an order under section 10;

"subordinate legislation" means any—

(*a*) Order in Council other than one—

(i) made in exercise of Her Majesty's Royal Prerogative;

(ii) made under section 38(1)(*a*) of the Northern Ireland Constitution Act 1973 or the corresponding provision of the Northern Ireland Act 1998; or

(iii) amending an Act of a kind mentioned in the definition of primary legislation;

(*b*) Act of the Scottish Parliament;

[(*ba*) Measure of the National Assembly for Wales;

(*bb*) Act of the National Assembly for Wales;][2]

(*c*) Act of the Parliament of Northern Ireland;

(*d*) Measure of the Assembly established under section 1 of the Northern Ireland Assembly Act 1973;

(*e*) Act of the Northern Ireland Assembly;

(*f*) order, rules, regulations, scheme, warrant, byelaw or other instrument made under primary legislation (except to the extent to which it operates to bring one or more provisions of that legislation into force or amends any primary legislation);

(*g*) order, rules, regulations, scheme, warrant, byelaw or other instrument made under legislation mentioned in paragraph (*b*), (*c*), (*d*) or (*e*) or made under an Order in Council applying only to Northern Ireland;

(*h*) order, rules, regulations, scheme, warrant, byelaw or other instrument made by a member of the Scottish Executive[, Welsh Ministers, the First Minister for Wales, the Counsel General to the Welsh Assembly Government][2], a Northern Ireland Minister or a Northern Ireland department in exercise of prerogative or other executive functions of Her Majesty which are exercisable by such a person on behalf of Her Majesty;

"transferred matters" has the same meaning as in the Northern Ireland Act 1998; and

"tribunal" means any tribunal in which legal proceedings may be brought.

(2) The references in paragraphs (*b*) and (*c*) of section 2(1) to Articles are to Articles of the Convention as they had effect immediately before the coming into force of the Eleventh Protocol.

(3) The reference in paragraph (*d*) of section 2(1) to Article 46 includes a reference to Articles 32 and 54 of the Convention as they had effect immediately before the coming into force of the Eleventh Protocol.

(4) The references in section 2(1) to a report or decision of the Commission or a decision of the Committee of Ministers include references to a report or decision made as provided by paragraphs 3, 4 and 6 of Article 5 of the Eleventh Protocol (transitional provisions).

(5) Any liability under the Army Act 1955, the Air Force Act 1955 or the Naval Discipline Act 1957 to suffer death for an offence is replaced by a liability to imprisonment for life or any less punishment authorised by those Acts; and those Acts shall accordingly have effect with the necessary modifications.[3]

Note—Reference to the Welsh Assembly Government is to be read as, or as including, a reference to the Welsh Government, unless the context requires otherwise (Wales Act 2014 s 4(4)(a)).

Amendments—[1] Definition of "the Sixth Protocol" revoked, and definition of "the Thirteenth Protocol" inserted by Human Rights Act 1998 (Amendment) Order, SI 2004/1574, art 1, 2(2) with effect from 22 June 2004.

[2] In sub-s (1), in definition of "primary legislation", words substituted; and in definition of "subordinate legislation" paras (*ba*), (*bb*) and words in para (h) inserted; by the Government of Wales Act 2006 s 160(1), Sch 10 para 56(1)–(3) with effect from 25 May 2007, being the date on which the initial period ended (following the appointment of the First Minister).

[3] Sub-s (5) repealed by the Armed Forces Act 2006 s 378(2), Sch 17 with effect for certain purposes from 28 March 2009 (by virtue of SI 2009/812, art 3(*a*), (*b*)) and for remaining purposes from 31 October 2009 (by virtue of SI 2009/1167 art 4).

22 Short title, commencement, application and extent

(1) This Act may be cited as the Human Rights Act 1998.

(2) Sections 18, 20 and 21(5) and this section come into force on the passing of this Act.

(3) The other provisions of this Act come into force on such day as the Secretary of State may by order appoint; and different days may be appointed for different purposes.

(4) Paragraph (*b*) of subsection (1) of section 7 applies to proceedings brought by or at the instigation of a public authority whenever the act in question took place; but otherwise that subsection does not apply to an act taking place before the coming into force of that section.

(5) This Act binds the Crown.

(6) This Act extends to Northern Ireland.

(7) Section 21(5), so far as it relates to any provision contained in the Army Act 1955, the Air Force Act 1955 or the Naval Discipline Act 1957, extends to any place to which that provision extends.[1]

Amendments—[1] Sub-s (7) repealed by the Armed Forces Act 2006 s 378(2), Sch 17 with effect for certain purposes from 28 March 2009 (by virtue of SI 2009/812, art 3(*a*), (*b*)) and for remaining purposes from 31 October 2009 (by virtue of SI 2009/1167 art 4).

SCHEDULES

SCHEDULE 1

THE ARTICLES

Section 1(3)

PART I

THE CONVENTION

RIGHTS AND FREEDOMS

[Article 2 (Right to life), Article 3 (Prohibition of torture), Article 4 and Article 5 (Right to liberty and security) (Prohibition of slavery and forced labour) are not reproduced here: see *Halsbury's Statutes* (4th edn) CIVIL RIGHTS and LIBERTIES].

ARTICLE 6

Right to a fair trial

1 In the determination of his civil rights and obligations or of any criminal charge against him, everyone is entitled to a fair and public hearing within a reasonable time by an independent and impartial tribunal established by law. Judgment shall be pronounced publicly but the press and public may be excluded from all or part of the trial in the interest of morals, public order or national security in a democratic society, where the interests of juveniles or the protection of the private life of the parties so require, or to the extent strictly necessary in the opinion of the court in special circumstances where publicity would prejudice the interests of justice.

2 Everyone charged with a criminal offence shall be presumed innocent until proved guilty according to law.

3 Everyone charged with a criminal offence has the following minimum rights:

(*a*) to be informed promptly, in a language which he understands and in detail, of the nature and cause of the accusation against him;

(*b*) to have adequate time and facilities for the preparation of his defence;

(*c*) to defend himself in person or through legal assistance of his own choosing or, if he has not sufficient means to pay for legal assistance, to be given it free when the interests of justice so require;

(*d*) to examine or have examined witnesses against him and to obtain the attendance and examination of witnesses on his behalf under the same conditions as witnesses against him;

(*e*) to have the free assistance of an interpreter if he cannot understand or speak the language used in court.

Simon's Tax Cases—*Bancroft and anor v Crutchfield* (Insp of Taxes) [2002] STC 347; *Khan (trading as Greyhound Dry Cleaners) v C&E Comrs* [2005] STC 1271; *Significant Ltd v Farrel (Insp of Taxes)* [2006] STC 1626; *Sharkey v R&C Comrs* [2006] STC 2026; *R (on the application of ToTel Ltd) v First-tier Tribunal (Tax Chamber) and another (HM Treasury, interested party)* [2011] EWHC 652 (Admin), [2011] STC 1485.

ARTICLE 7

No punishment without law

[not reproduced: see *Halsbury's Statutes* (4th edn) CIVIL RIGHTS and LIBERTIES].

ARTICLE 8

Right to respect for private and family life

1 Everyone has the right to respect for his private and family life, his home and his correspondence.

2 There shall be no interference by a public authority with the exercise of this right except such as is in accordance with the law and is necessary in a democratic society in the interests of national security, public safety or the economic well-being of the country, for the prevention of disorder or crime, for the protection of health or morals, or for the protection of the rights and freedoms of others.

[Article 9 (Freedom of thought, conscience and religion), Article 10 (Freedom of expression), Article 11 (Freedom of assembly and association) and Article 12 (Right to marry) not reproduced here: see *Halsbury's Statutes* (4th edn) CIVIL RIGHTS and LIBERTIES].

ARTICLE 14

Prohibition of discrimination

The enjoyment of the rights and freedoms set forth in this Convention shall be secured without discrimination on any ground such as sex, race, colour, language, religion, political or other opinion, national or social origin, association with a national minority, property, birth or other status.

Simon's Tax Cases—*Aston Cantlow and Wilmcote with Billesley Parochial Church Council v Wallbank* [2002] STC 313; *R (oao Wilkinson) v IRC* [2002] STC 347; *Burden and another v UK* [2007] STC 252; *Walker v United Kingdom* [2008] STC 786; *Burden and another v UK* [2008] STC 1305; *Hobbs and others v UK* [2008] STC 1469.

[Article 16 (Restrictions on political activity of aliens) not reproduced here: see *Halsbury's Statutes* (4th edn) CIVIL RIGHTS and LIBERTIES].

ARTICLE 17

Prohibition of abuse of rights

Nothing in this Convention may be interpreted as implying for any State, group or person any right to engage in any activity or perform any act aimed at the destruction of any of the rights and freedoms set forth herein or at their limitation to a greater extent than is provided for in the Convention.

ARTICLE 18

Limitation on use of restrictions on rights

The restrictions permitted under this Convention to the said rights and freedoms shall not be applied for any purpose other than those for which they have been prescribed.

PART II

THE FIRST PROTOCOL

ARTICLE 1

Protection of property

Every natural or legal person is entitled to the peaceful enjoyment of his possessions. No one shall be deprived of his possessions except in the public interest and subject to the conditions provided for by law and by the general principles of international law.

The preceding provisions shall not, however, in any way impair the right of a State to enforce such laws as it deems necessary to control the use of property in accordance with the general interest or to secure the payment of taxes or other contributions or penalties.

[Article 2 (Right to education) and Article 3 (Right to free elections) not reproduced.

Simon's Tax Cases—*R (oao Wilkinson) v IRC* [2002] STC 347; *R (oao Carvill) v IRC (No 2)* [2003] STC 1539; *C&E Comrs v Pegasus Birds Ltd* [2004] STC 262; *Burden and another v UK* [2007] STC 252; *Walker v UK* [2008] STC 786; *Hobbs and others v UK* [2008] STC 1469; *R (oao the Federation of Tour Operators and others) v HM Treasury* [2008] STC 2524; *Monro v R&C Comrs* [2008] STC 1815; *R&C Comrs v Smith* [2008] STC 1941; *R (on the application of Huitson) v R&C Comrs* [2011] EWCA Civ 893, [2011] STC 1860.

[PART III

ARTICLE 1 OF THE THIRTEENTH PROTOCOL]

(not reproduced)

SCHEDULE 2

REMEDIAL ORDERS

Section 10

Orders

1 (1) A remedial order may—

(*a*) contain such incidental, supplemental, consequential or transitional provision as the person making it considers appropriate;

(*b*) be made so as to have effect from a date earlier than that on which it is made;

(*c*) make provision for the delegation of specific functions;

(*d*) make different provision for different cases.

(2) The power conferred by sub-paragraph (1)(*a*) includes—

(*a*) power to amend primary legislation (including primary legislation other than that which contains the incompatible provision); and

(*b*) power to amend or revoke subordinate legislation (including subordinate legislation other than that which contains the incompatible provision).

(3) A remedial order may be made so as to have the same extent as the legislation which it affects.

(4) No person is to be guilty of an offence solely as a result of the retrospective effect of a remedial order.

Procedure

2 No remedial order may be made unless—

(*a*) a draft of the order has been approved by a resolution of each House of Parliament made after the end of the period of 60 days beginning with the day on which the draft was laid; or

(*b*) it is declared in the order that it appears to the person making it that, because of the urgency of the matter, it is necessary to make the order without a draft being so approved.

Orders laid in draft

3—(1) No draft may be laid under paragraph 2(*a*) unless—

(*a*) the person proposing to make the order has laid before Parliament a document which contains a draft of the proposed order and the required information; and

(*b*) the period of 60 days, beginning with the day on which the document required by this sub-paragraph was laid, has ended.

(2) If representations have been made during that period, the draft laid under paragraph 2(*a*) must be accompanied by a statement containing—

(*a*) a summary of the representations; and

(*b*) if, as a result of the representations, the proposed order has been changed, details of the changes.

Urgent cases

4—(1) If a remedial order ("the original order") is made without being approved in draft, the person making it must lay it before Parliament, accompanied by the required information, after it is made.

(2) If representations have been made during the period of 60 days beginning with the day on which the original order was made, the person making it must (after the end of that period) lay before Parliament a statement containing—

(*a*) a summary of the representations; and

(*b*) if, as a result of the representations, he considers it appropriate to make changes to the original order, details of the changes.

(3) If sub-paragraph (2)(*b*) applies, the person making the statement must—

(*a*) make a further remedial order replacing the original order; and

(*b*) lay the replacement order before Parliament.

(4) If, at the end of the period of 120 days beginning with the day on which the original order was made, a resolution has not been passed by each House approving the original or replacement order, the order ceases to have effect (but without that affecting anything previously done under either order or the power to make a fresh remedial order).

Definitions

5 In this Schedule—

"representations" means representations about a remedial order (or proposed remedial order) made to the person making (or proposing to make) it and includes any relevant Parliamentary report or resolution; and

"required information" means—

(*a*) an explanation of the incompatibility which the order (or proposed order) seeks to remove, including particulars of the relevant declaration, finding or order; and

(*b*) a statement of the reasons for proceeding under section 10 and for making an order in those terms.

Calculating periods

6 In calculating any period for the purposes of this Schedule, no account is to be taken of any time during which—

(*a*) Parliament is dissolved or prorogued; or

(*b*) both Houses are adjourned for more than four days.

[**7**—(1) This paragraph applies in relation to—

(*a*) any remedial order made, and any draft of such an order proposed to be made—

(i) by the Scottish Ministers; or

(ii) within devolved competence (within the meaning of the Scotland Act 1998) by Her Majesty in Council; and (*b*) any document or statement to be laid in connection with such an order (or proposed order).

(2) This Schedule has effect in relation to any such order (or proposed order), document or statement subject to the following modifications.

(3) Any reference to Parliament, each House of Parliament or both Houses of Parliament shall be construed as a reference to the Scottish Parliament.

(4) Paragraph 6 does not apply and instead, in calculating any period for the purposes of this Schedule, no account is to be taken of any time during which the Scottish Parliament is dissolved or is in recess for more than four days.]

Amendments—Para 7 inserted by the Scotland Act 1998 (Consequential Modifications) Order, SI 2000/2040 art 2, Schedule para 21 with effect from 27 July 2000.

SCHEDULE 3

DEROGATION AND RESERVATION

(not reproduced)

SCHEDULE 4

JUDICIAL PENSIONS

(not reproduced)

FINANCE ACT 1999

(1999 Chapter 16)

An Act to grant certain duties, to alter other duties, and to amend the law relating to the National Debt and the Public Revenue, and to make further provision in connection with Finance.

[27 July 1999]

PART II

VALUE ADDED TAX

12 Works of art, antiques, etc

(1), (2) (*Amend* VATA 1994 s 21(4) and *substitute* 21(5), (6)).

(3) This section has effect in relation to goods imported at any time on or after the day on which this Act is passed.

Commentary—*De Voil Indirect Tax Service* **V3.325.**

13 Gold

(1) Notwithstanding the words preceding paragraph (*a*) in section 26(3) of the Value Added Tax Act 1994 (input tax allowable against output tax), regulations which—

(*a*) are made under section 26(3), and

(*b*) have effect in respect of exempt supplies which relate to gold,

may provide that input tax is allowable, as being attributable to the supplies, only in relation to specified matters.

(2) An order under section 31(2) of that Act (exempt supplies and acquisitions) which provides for certain supplies which relate to gold to be exempt supplies may—

(*a*) provide that a supply which would be an exempt supply by virtue of the order shall, if the supplier so chooses, be a taxable supply;

(*b*) make provision by reference to notices to be published by the Commissioners.

(3) An order under section 37(1) of that Act (relief on importation of goods) which gives relief from VAT on certain importations of gold may make provision by reference to notices to be published by the Commissioners.

(4) Provision made by virtue of subsection (2) or (3) above may be expressed—

(*a*) to apply only in specified circumstances;

(*b*) to apply subject to compliance with specified conditions (which may include conditions relating to general or specific approval of the Commissioners).

(5) Regulations may—

(*a*) require specified persons to keep specified records in relation to specified transactions concerning gold;

(*b*) require specified persons to give specified information to the Commissioners about specified transactions concerning gold;

(*c*) *provide for paragraph 10(2) of Schedule 11 to that Act (entry and inspection of premises) to apply in relation to specified transactions concerning gold as it applies in relation to the supply of goods under taxable supplies.*[2]

(6) The provisions of that Act (including, in particular, section 97 and paragraph 6(2) to [(4)][1] of Schedule 11) shall apply in relation to regulations under subsection (5) above[, and to records kept in pursuance of such regulations,][1] as they apply in relation to regulations under paragraph 6(1) of Schedule 11 to that Act [and to records kept in pursuance of that paragraph][1].

(7) In this section "the Commissioners" means the Commissioners of Customs and Excise.

Commentary—*De Voil Indirect Tax Service* **V5.143, V6.151.**

Amendments—[1] In sub-s (6), figure substituted for figure "(6)", and words inserted, by FA 2008 s 115, Sch 37 para 10 with effect from 1 April 2009 (by virtue of SI 2009/402).

[2] Sub-s (5)(*c*) repealed by FA 2008 Sch 36 para 89 with effect from 1 April 2009 (by virtue of SI 2009/404 art 2).

14 Preparations etc of meat, yeast or egg

(*Amends* VATA 1994 Sch 8).

15 Assignment of debts

(1)–(3) [2] (*Substitute* VATA 1994 s 36(3) and *amend* (5)(*e*), Sch 11, para 7).

(4) . . . [1]

(5) Subsections (1) and (4) above have effect for the purposes of the making of any refund or repayment after 9th March 1999, but do not have effect in relation to anything received on or before that day.

Commentary—*De Voil Indirect Tax Service* **V3.140, V5.156.**

Amendments—[1] Sub-s (4) repealed by the Value Added Tax Regulations, SI 1999/3029, regs 2, 5 with effect from 1 December 1999.

[2] Sub-s (3) repealed by FA 2008 s 113, Sch 36 para 92(h) with effect from 1 April 2009 (by virtue of SI 2009/404 art 2). In consequence of SI 2009/404 arts 1–11, the amendments made by FA 2008 Sch 36 para 92 shall be disregarded so far as they affect any notice referred to in those provisions, given on or before 31 March 2009.

16 Groups of companies

Schedule 2 to this Act (which makes changes to provisions about the treatment of bodies corporate as members of a group) shall have effect.

Commentary—*De Voil Indirect Tax Service* **V2.104.**

17 Penalties for incorrect certificates

(1) (*Substitutes* VATA 1994 s 62(1), (2)).

(2) Subsection (1) above has effect in relation to certificates given or, as the case may be, prepared on or after the day on which this Act is passed.

Commentary—*De Voil Indirect Tax Service* **V5.342.**

18 EC sales statements: time limits for assessments to penalties

(1) (*Substitutes* VATA 1994 s 77(2)).

(2) Subsection (1) above has effect in relation to any amount by way of penalty, interest or surcharge which becomes due on or after the day on which this Act is passed.

Commentary—*De Voil Indirect Tax Service* **V5.346, 355.**

19 Period before repayment supplement payable

(1)–(4) (*Amend* VATA 1994 s 79(2)(*b*), (3), (7) and *insert* s 79(2A)).

(5) This section has effect in relation to returns and claims received by the Commissioners on or after 9th March 1999.

Commentary—*De Voil Indirect Tax Service* **V5.191, 192.**

20 Meaning of "business"

(1) (*Repeals* VATA 1994 s 94(3)).

(2) This section shall come into force in accordance with such provision as the Commissioners of Customs and Excise may make by order made by statutory instrument.

Commentary—*De Voil Indirect Tax Service* **V2.241, V4.156.**

21 Accounting for VAT by Government departments

Amendment—This section repealed by the Government Resources and Accounts Act 2000 ss 21, 29(2), Sch 2 with effect from 1 April 2001 (by virtue of SI 2000/3349 art 3).

PART VIII

MISCELLANEOUS AND SUPPLEMENTAL

General administration of tax

132 Power to provide for use of electronic communications

(1) Regulations may be made, in accordance with this section, for facilitating the use of electronic communications for—

(*a*) the delivery of information the delivery of which is authorised or required by or under any legislation relating to a taxation matter;

(*b*) the making of payments under any such legislation.

(2) The power to make regulations under this section is conferred—

(*a*) on the Commissioners of Inland Revenue in relation to matters which are under their care and management; and (*b*) on the Commissioners of Customs and Excise in relation to matters which are under their care and management.

(3) For the purposes of this section provision for facilitating the use of electronic communications includes any of the following—

(*a*) provision authorising persons to use electronic communications for the delivery of information to tax authorities, or for the making of payments to tax authorities;

(*b*) provision requiring electronic communications to be used for the making to tax authorities of payments due from persons using such communications for the delivery of information to those authorities;

(*c*) provision authorising tax authorities to use electronic communications for the delivery of information to other persons or for the making of any payments;

(*d*) provision as to the electronic form to be taken by any information that is delivered to any tax authorities using electronic communications;

(*e*) provision requiring persons to prepare and keep records of information delivered to tax authorities by means of electronic communications, and of payments made to any such authorities by any such means;

(*f*) provision for the production of the contents of records kept in accordance with any regulations under this section;

(*g*) provision imposing conditions that must be complied with in connection with any use of electronic communications for the delivery of information or the making of any payment;

(*h*) provision, in relation to cases where use is made of electronic communications, for treating information as not having been delivered, or a payment as not having been made, unless conditions imposed by any such regulations are satisfied;

(*i*) provision, in relation to such cases, for determining the time when information is delivered or a payment is made;

(*j*) provision, in relation to such cases, for determining the person by whom information is to be taken to have been delivered or by whom a payment is to be taken to have been made;

(*k*) provision, in relation to cases where information is delivered by means of electronic communications, for authenticating whatever is delivered.

(4) The power to make provision under this section for facilitating the use of electronic communications shall also include power to make such provision as the persons exercising the power think fit (including provision for the application of conclusive or other presumptions) as to the manner of proving for any purpose—

(*a*) whether any use of electronic communications is to be taken as having resulted in the delivery of information or the making of a payment;

(*b*) the time of delivery of any information for the delivery of which electronic communications have been used;

(*c*) the time of the making of any payment for the making of which electronic communications have been used;

(*d*) the person by whom information delivered by means of electronic communications was delivered;

(*e*) the contents of anything so delivered;

(*f*) the contents of any records;

(*g*) any other matter for which provision may be made by regulations under this section.

(5) Regulations under this section may—

(*a*) allow any authorisation or requirement for which such regulations may provide to be given or imposed by means of a specific or general direction given by the Commissioners of Inland Revenue or the Commissioners of Customs and Excise;

(*b*) provide that the conditions of any such authorisation or requirement are to be taken to be satisfied only where such tax authorities as may be determined under the regulations are satisfied as to specified matters;

(*c*) allow a person to refuse to accept delivery of information in an electronic form or by means of electronic communications except in such circumstances as may be specified in or determined under the regulations;

(*d*) allow or require use to be made of intermediaries in connection with—

(i) the delivery of information, or the making of payments, by means of electronic communications; or

(ii) the authentication or security of anything transmitted by any such means.

(6) Power to make provision by regulations under this section shall include power—

(*a*) to provide for a contravention of, or any failure to comply with, a specified provision of any such regulations to attract a penalty of a specified amount not exceeding £1,000;

(*b*) to provide that specified enactments relating to penalties imposed for the purposes of any taxation matter (including enactments relating to assessments, review and appeal) are to apply, with or without modifications, in relation to penalties under such regulations;

(*c*) to make different provision for different cases;

(*d*) to make such incidental, supplemental, consequential and transitional provision in connection with any provision contained in any such regulations as the persons exercising the power think fit.

(7) The power to make regulations under this section shall be exercisable by statutory instrument subject to annulment in pursuance of a resolution of the House of Commons.

(8) References in this section to the delivery of information include references to any of the following (however referred to)—

(*a*) the production or furnishing to a person of any information, account, record or document;

(*b*) the giving, making, issue or surrender to, or service on, any person of any notice, notification, statement, declaration, certificate or direction;

(*c*) the imposition on any person of any requirement or the issue to any person of any request;

(*d*) the making of any return, claim, election or application;

(*e*) the amendment or withdrawal of anything mentioned in paragraphs (*a*) to (*d*) above.

(9) References in this section to a taxation matter are references to any of the matters which are under the care and management of the Commissioners of Inland Revenue or of the Commissioners of Customs and Excise.

(10) In this section—

"electronic communications" includes any communications by means of [an electronic communications service][1];

"legislation" means any enactment, Community legislation or subordinate legislation;

"payment" includes a repayment;

"records" includes records in electronic form;

"subordinate legislation" has the same meaning as in the Interpretation Act 1978;

"tax authorities" means—

(*a*) the Commissioners of Inland Revenue or the Commissioners of Customs and Excise,

(*b*) any officer of either body of Commissioners; or

(*c*) any other person who for the purposes of electronic communications is acting under the authority of either body of Commissioners.

Cross references—See Income Tax (Electronic Communications) Regulations, SI 2000/945 (delivery by electronic means of information in respect of income tax assessments).

FA 2000 Sch 38 para 1(1) (regulations may be made in accordance with FA 2000 Sch 38 for providing incentives to use electronic communications the purposes of mention in sub-s (1) above).

Regulations—VAT (Amendment) Regulations, SI 2012/33.

VAT (Amendment) Regulations, SI 2013/701.

VAT (Amendment) Regulations, SI 2014/548.

VAT (Amendment) (No 2) Regulations, SI 2014/1497.

Amendments—[1] In sub-s (10), words in definition of "electronic communications" substituted by the Communications Act 2003 s 406, Sch 17 para 156 with effect from 25 July 2003 to 29 December 2003 for certain purposes (see SI 2003/1900), 29 December 2003 for other purposes (see SI 2003/3142), and from a date to be appointed for remaining purposes.

133 Use of electronic communications under other provisions

(1) Without prejudice to section 132 above, where any power to make subordinate legislation for or in connection with the delivery of information or the making of payments is conferred in relation to any taxation matter on—

(*a*) the Commissioners of Inland Revenue,

(*b*) the Commissioners of Customs and Excise, or

(*c*) the Treasury,

that power shall be taken (to the extent that it would not otherwise be so taken) to include power to make any such provision in relation to the delivery of that information or the making of those payments as could be made by any person by regulations in exercise of a power conferred by that section.

(2) Provision made in exercise of the powers conferred by section 132 above or subsection (1) above shall have effect notwithstanding so much of any enactment or subordinate legislation as (apart from the provision so made) would require—

(*a*) any information to be delivered, or

(*b*) any amount to be paid,

in a form or manner that would preclude the use of electronic communications for its delivery or payment, or the use in connection with its delivery or payment of an intermediary.

(3) Schedule 3A to the Taxes Management Act 1970 (electronic lodgement of tax returns etc) shall cease to have effect.

(4) Subsection (3) above shall come into force on such day as the Treasury may by order made by statutory instrument appoint; and different days may be appointed under this subsection for different purposes.

(5) Expressions used in this section and section 132 above have the same meanings in this section as in that section.

Cross references—See Income Tax (Electronic Communications) Regulations, SI 2000/945 (delivery by electronic means of information in respect of income tax assessments).

Regulations—Registered Pension Schemes and Overseas Pension Schemes (Electronic Communication of Returns and Information) Regulations, SI 2006/570.

Employee Share Schemes (Electronic Communication of Returns and Information) Regulations, SI 2007/792.
VAT (Amendment) Regulations, SI 2012/33.
Income Tax (Pay As You Earn) (Amendments) Regulations, SI 2012/822.
Registered Pension Schemes and Overseas Pension Schemes (Miscellaneous Amendments) Regulations, SI 2012/884.
Income Tax (Pay As You Earn) (Amendment) Regulations, SI 2013/521.
VAT (Amendment) Regulations, SI 2013/701.
Income Tax (Pay As You Earn) and the Income Tax (Construction Industry Scheme) (Amendment) Regulations, SI 2014/472.
VAT (Amendment) Regulations, SI 2014/548.
VAT (Amendment) (No 2) Regulations, SI 2014/1497.
Income Tax (Pay As You Earn) (Amendment) Regulations, SI 2015/2.

Supplemental

139 Repeals

(1) The enactments mentioned in Schedule 20 to this Act (which include provisions that are spent or of no practical utility) are hereby repealed to the extent specified in the third column of that Schedule.
(2) The repeals specified in that Schedule have effect subject to the commencement provisions and savings contained or referred to in the notes set out in that Schedule.

140 Short title

This Act may be cited as the Finance Act 1999.

SCHEDULES

SCHEDULE 2

VAT: GROUPS OF COMPANIES

Section 16

Commentary—*De Voil Indirect Tax Service* **V2.104.**

Amendment of Value Added Tax Act 1994

1, 2 (*amend* VATA 1994 s 43(1), *repeal* s 43(3)–(8) and *insert* ss 43A–43C).

3 (*amends* VATA 1994 s 83(*k*)).

4 (*inserts* VATA 1994 s 84(4A)–(4D)).

5 (*amends* VATA 1994 Sch 9A).

Transitional provisions

6 (1) In this paragraph—
"the old law" means sections 43, 83 and 84 of, and Schedule 9A to, the Value Added Tax Act 1994 as they have effect without the amendments in paragraphs 1 to 5 of this Schedule, and
"the new law" means sections 43 to 43C, 83 and 84 of, and Schedule 9A to, that Act as they have effect by virtue of paragraphs 1 to 5 of this Schedule.
(2) Where, immediately before this Schedule comes into force, two or more bodies corporate are treated as members of a group by virtue of the old law—
(*a*) they shall continue to be treated as members of a group, and
(*b*) in their treatment as members of a group after this Schedule comes into force, they shall be treated as if any application under the old law by virtue of which they are treated as members of a group had been an equivalent application under the new law.
(3) Where an application under section 43 of the Value Added Tax Act 1994 is received by the Commissioners, and has neither taken effect nor been refused before the day on which this Act is passed, the old law shall apply to determine whether the application is to take effect; but where it is determined under this sub-paragraph that an application is to take effect—
(*a*) it shall be treated as if it were an equivalent application under the new law, and
(*b*) it shall be taken to have been granted under the new law at the time when it would have taken effect in accordance with the old law.
(4) In a case to which sub-paragraph (2) or (3) above applies, the power under section 43C(3) shall not be used to terminate the treatment of a body corporate as a member of a group—
(*a*) on the ground that the body corporate is not established, and does not have a fixed establishment, in the United Kingdom, and
(*b*) from a date before 1st January 2000.
(5) Where an application which purports to be an application under the old law is received by the Commissioners after the day on which this Act is passed—

(*a*) it shall be treated as if it were an application under the new law, and
(*b*) section 43B of the new law shall apply notwithstanding any provision in the application for a date from which it is to take effect.

FINANCE ACT 2000

(2000 Chapter 17)

An act to grant certain duties, to alter other duties, and to amend the law relating to the National Debt and the Public Revenue, and to make further provision in connection with finance.

[28 July 2000]

PART V
OTHER TAXES

Value added tax

135 Supplies to which reduced rate applies

Amendments—This section repealed by FA 2001 s 110, Sch 33 Pt 3(1) with effect for supplies made, and acquisitions and importations taking place, after 31 October 2001 (by virtue of FA 2001 s 99(7)(*b*)).

136 Disposals of assets for which a VAT repayment is claimed

(1) (*amends* VATA 1994 s 3(2)).
(2) (*amends VATA 1994 s 67*).
(3) (*amends* VATA 1994 s 69(1)).
(4) (*amends* VATA 199A s 73(3)).
(5) (*amends* VATA 1994 s 74(1)).
(6) (*amends* VATA 1994 Sch 1 para 1, Sch 2 para 1).
(7) (*amends* VATA 1994 Sch 3 para 1).
(8) (*inserts* VATA 1994 Sch 3A).
(9) (*amends* VATA 1994 Sch 4 para 5).
(10) Subsections (1) to (7) and (9) above have effect in relation to supplies made on or after 21st March 2000; and subsection (8) above and Schedule 36 to this Act have effect in relation to relevant supplies (within the meaning of Schedule 3A to that Act) made on or after that date.

Commentary—*De Voil Indirect Tax Service* **V2.171, V5.151, V5.152.**

Amendments—Sub-s (2) repealed by FA 2008 s 123, Sch 41 para 25(*k*) with effect from 1 April 2010 (by virtue of SI 2009/511 art 2).

137 Gold: penalty for failure to comply with record-keeping requirements etc

(1) Part IV of the Value Added Tax Act 1994 (administration, collection and enforcement) is amended as follows.
(2) (*inserts* VATA 1994 s 69A).
(3) (*amends* VATA 1994 s 70(1)).
(4) (*amends* VATA 1994 s 76(1)).
(5) (*amends* VATA 1994 s 83).

Commentary—*De Voil Indirect Tax Service* **V5.143.**

PART VI
MISCELLANEOUS AND SUPPLEMENTARY PROVISIONS

Incentives for electronic communications

143 Power to provide incentives to use electronic communications

(1) Regulations may be made in accordance with Schedule 38 to this Act for providing incentives to use electronic communications.
(2) . . . [1]

Commentary—*Simon's Taxes* **A4.101.**

Amendments—[1] Sub-s (2) repealed by CTA 2009 ss 1322, 1326, Sch 1 paras 462, 466. CTA 2009 applies for accounting periods ending on or after 1 April 2009 (for corporation tax purposes) and for tax years 2009–10 onwards (for income and capital gains tax purposes).

Supplementary provisions

156 Repeals

(1) The enactments mentioned in Schedule 40 to this Act (which include provisions that are spent or of no practical utility) are repealed to the extent specified in the third column of that Schedule.
(2) The repeals specified in that Schedule have effect subject to the commencement provisions and savings contained or referred to in the notes set out in that Schedule.

157 Short title

This Act may be cited as the Finance Act 2000.

SCHEDULES

SCHEDULE 35

VALUE ADDED TAX: CHARGE AT REDUCED RATE

Section 135

Amendment—This Schedule repealed by FA 2001 s 110, Sch 33 Pt III(1) with effect for supplies made, and acquisitions and importations taking place, after 31 October 2001 (by virtue of FA 2001 s 99(7)(*b*)).

SCHEDULE 36

NEW SCHEDULE 3A TO THE VALUE ADDED TAX ACT 1994

Section 136(8)

Commentary—*De Voil Indirect Tax Service* **V2.171, V5.151, 152.**

Note—This Schedule sets out VATA 1994 Sch 3A as inserted by FA 2000 s 136(8).

SCHEDULE 38

REGULATIONS FOR PROVIDING INCENTIVES FOR ELECTRONIC COMMUNICATIONS

Section 143(1)

Commentary—*Simon's Taxes* **A4.101.**

Regulations—See the Value Added Tax (Electronic Communications) (Incentives) Regulations, SI 2001/759.

Introduction

1—(1) Regulations may be made in accordance with this Schedule for providing incentives to use electronic communications—

(*a*) for the purposes mentioned in section 132(1) of the Finance Act 1999 (power to provide for use of electronic communications for delivery of information and making of payments), or

(*b*) for any other communications with the tax authorities or in connection with taxation matters.

(2) The power to make regulations under this Schedule is conferred—

(*a*) on the Commissioners of Inland Revenue in relation to matters which are under their care and management, and

(*b*) on the Commissioners of Customs and Excise in relation to matters which are under their care and management.

Kinds of incentive

2—(1) The incentives shall be of such description as may be provided for in the regulations.

(2) They may, in particular, take the form of—

(*a*) discounts;

(*b*) the allowing of additional time to comply with any obligations under tax legislation (including obligations relating to the payment of tax or other amounts); or

(*c*) the facility to deliver information or make payments at more convenient intervals.

Conditions of entitlement

3—(1) The regulations may make provision as to the conditions of entitlement to an incentive.

(2) They may, in particular, make entitlement conditional—

(*a*) on the use of electronic communications for all communications or payments (or all communications and payments of a specified description) with, to or from the tax authority concerned, and

(*b*) on the use of specified means of electronic communication or payment acceptable to the tax authority concerned.

(3) The regulations may make provision for an appeal against a decision that the conditions of entitlement are not met.

Withdrawal of entitlement

4—(1) The regulations may make provision for the withdrawal of an incentive in specified circumstances.

(2) If they do, they may make provision—

(*a*) for giving notice of the withdrawal,

(*b*) for an appeal, and

(*c*) for the recovery of an amount not exceeding the value of the incentive.

(3) The regulations may provide that specified enactments relating to assessments, [reviews,][1] appeals and recovery of tax are to apply, with such adaptations as may be specified, in relation to the withdrawal of an incentive.

Amendments—[1] In sub-para (3), word inserted by the Transfer of Tribunal Functions and Revenue and Customs Appeals Order, SI 2009/56 art 3, Sch 1 para 295 with effect from 1 April 2009.

Power to authorise provision by directions

5 The regulations may authorise the making of any such provision as is mentioned in paragraph 3 or 4 by means of a specific or general direction given by the Commissioners of Inland Revenue or the Commissioners of Customs and Excise.

Power to provide for penalties

6—(1) The regulations may provide for contravention of, or failure to comply with, a specified provision of any such regulations to attract a penalty of a specified amount not exceeding £1,000.
(2) If they do, they may provide that specified enactments relating to penalties imposed in relation to any taxation matter (including enactments relating to assessments, review and appeals) are to apply, with or without modifications, in relation to penalties under the regulations.

General supplementary provisions

7—(1) Power to make provision by regulations under this Schedule includes power—
(*a*) to make different provision for different cases; and
(*b*) to make such incidental, supplemental, consequential and transitional provision in connection with any provision contained in any such regulations as the persons exercising the power think fit.
(2) The power to make regulations under this Schedule is exercisable by statutory instrument subject to annulment in pursuance of a resolution of the House of Commons.

Interpretation

8—(1) In this Schedule—
"discount" includes payment;
"electronic communications" includes any communications by means of [an electronic communications service][1];
"legislation" means any enactment, Community legislation or subordinate legislation;
"payment" includes a repayment;
"subordinate legislation" has the same meaning as in the Interpretation Act 1978;
"taxation matter" means any of the matters under the care and management of the Commissioners of Inland Revenue or the Commissioners of Customs and Excise;
"tax authorities" means—
(*a*) the Commissioners of Inland Revenue or the Commissioners of Customs and Excise,
(*b*) any officer of either body of Commissioners; or
(*c*) any other person who for the purposes of electronic communications is acting under the authority of either body of Commissioners;
"tax legislation" means legislation relating to any taxation matter.
(2) References in this Schedule to the delivery of information have the same meaning as in section 132 of the Finance Act 1999.

Amendments—[1] Words in definition of "electronic communications" substituted by the Communications Act 2003 s 406, Sch 17 para 160 with effect from 25 July 2003 to 29 December 2003 for certain purposes (see SI 2003/1900), 29 December 2003 for other purposes (see SI 2003/3142), and from a date to be appointed for remaining purposes.

GOVERNMENT RESOURCES AND ACCOUNTS ACT 2000

(2000 Chapter 20)

Value Added Tax

21 Supplies by government departments

(1) This section applies where a government department makes supplies of goods or services which are taxable supplies for the purposes of the Value Added Tax Act 1994.
(2) The Treasury may make arrangements—
(*a*) about the treatment of receipts and payments in respect of value added tax in accounts under section 5 or 7;
(*b*) for the exemption of receipts in respect of value added tax, to such extent and on such conditions as may be specified, from any requirement for payment into the Consolidated Fund.
(3) For the purposes of this section "government department" has the same meaning as it has for the purposes of section 41 of the Value Added Tax Act 1994 (application to the Crown).
(4) . . .[1]

Amendments—[1] Sub-s (4) repealed by Statute Law (Repeals) Act 2004 s 1(1), Sch 1 Part 9 Group 6.

POSTAL SERVICES ACT 2000

(2000 Chapter 26)

[28 July 2000]

PART VII
MISCELLANEOUS AND SUPPLEMENTARY

Inviolability of mails etc

105 Application of customs and excise enactments to certain postal packets

(1) Subject as follows, the enactments for the time being in force in relation to customs or excise shall apply in relation to goods contained in postal packets to which this section applies which are brought into or sent out of the United Kingdom by post from or to any place outside the United Kingdom as they apply in relation to goods otherwise imported, exported or removed into or out of the United Kingdom from or to any such place.

(2) The Treasury, on the recommendation of the Commissioners of Customs and Excise and the Secretary of State, may make regulations for—

(*a*) specifying the postal packets to which this section applies,

(*b*) making modifications or exceptions in the application of the enactments mentioned in subsection (1) to such packets,

(*c*) enabling persons engaged in the business of a postal operator to perform for the purposes of those enactments and otherwise all or any of the duties of the importer, exporter or person removing the goods,

(*d*) carrying into effect any arrangement with the government or postal administration of any country or territory outside the United Kingdom with respect to foreign postal packets,

(*e*) securing the observance of the enactments mentioned in subsection (1),

(*f*) without prejudice to any liability of any person under those enactments, punishing any contravention of the regulations.

(3) Duties (whether of customs or excise) charged on imported goods or other charges payable in respect of postal packets to which this section applies (whether payable to a postal operator or to a foreign administration) may be recovered by the postal operator concerned and in England and Wales and Northern Ireland may be so recovered as a civil debt due to him.

(4) In any proceedings for the recovery of any charges payable as mentioned in subsection (3), a certificate of the postal operator concerned of the amount of the charges shall be evidence (and, in Scotland, sufficient evidence) of that fact.

[(4A) A postal operator may detain a postal packet to which this section applies until any duties and charges in respect of the packet that are recoverable by virtue of subsection (3) have been paid.][2]

(5) In this section "foreign postal packet" means any postal packet either posted in the United Kingdom and sent to a place outside the United Kingdom, or posted in a place outside the United Kingdom and sent to a place within the United Kingdom, or in transit through the United Kingdom to a place outside the United Kingdom.

[(6) And in this section "goods" includes cash (within the meaning of section 289(6) and (7) of the Proceeds of Crime Act 2002).][1]

Amendments—[1] Sub-s (6) inserted by the Policing and Crime Act 2009 s 99(4) with effect from 25 January 2010 (by virtue of SI 2010/52 art 2).

[2] Sub-s (4A) inserted by the Postal Services Act 2011 s 91, Sch 12 para 36 with effect from 1 October 2011 (by virtue of SI 2011/2329 art 3(1)).

[105A Section 105: limit on handling charges etc

(1) OFCOM may give a direction to a postal operator—

(*a*) limiting the amount of any handling charge, and

(*b*) limiting the length of time for which a postal packet may be detained under section 105(4A) (and, if a direction is given under this paragraph, that subsection has effect subject to the direction).

(2) Where a direction is given to an operator limiting the amount of a handling charge, section 105(3) to (4A) have effect in relation to the operator (in any case where the charge would otherwise exceed the amount specified in the direction) as if the charge were equal to the amount specified in the direction.

(3) Before giving a direction to a postal operator under this section, OFCOM must—

(*a*) inform the operator that they propose to give it a direction, and

(*b*) allow the operator an opportunity to make representations about the proposal.

(4) In this section "handling charge" means a charge payable to a postal operator, in respect of a postal packet, for the performance by the operator of all or any of the duties mentioned in section 105(2)(c).][1]

Amendments—[1] Section 105A inserted by the Postal Services Act 2011 s 91, Sch 12 para 37 with effect from 1 October 2011 (by virtue of SI 2011/2329 art 3(1)).

FINANCE ACT 2001

(2001 Chapter 9)

An Act to grant certain duties, to alter other duties, and to amend the law relating to the National Debt and the Public Revenue, and to make further provision in connection with Finance.

[11 May 2001]

PART 4
OTHER TAXES

Value added tax

96 VAT: children's car seats

(1) (*inserts* VATA 1994 Sch A1 para 1(5)).
(2) (*inserts* VATA 1994 Sch A1 para 7).
(3) The amendments made by this section have effect in relation to supplies made after the day on which this Act is passed.

Commentary—*De Voil Indirect Tax Service* **V4.4.**

97 VAT: residential conversions and renovations

(1) (*inserts* VATA 1994 Sch A1 para 1(6)–(9)).
(2) (*inserts* VATA 1994 Sch A1 paras 8–22).
(3) The amendments made by this section have effect in relation to supplies made after the day on which this Act is passed.

Commentary—*De Voil Indirect Tax Service* **V4.4.**

98 VAT: museums and galleries

(1) The Value Added Tax Act 1994 is amended as follows.
(2) (*inserts* VATA 1994 s 33A).
(3) (*inserted* VATA 1994 s 63(9A)).
(4)–(7) (*amend* VATA 1994 s 79).
(8) (*amends* VATA 1994 s 90(3)).
(9) (*amends* VATA 1994 Sch 9 Group 14 Note (9))
(10) Subject to subsection (11), this section comes into force on 1st September 2001.
(11) For the purpose only of the exercise of the power to make orders under the section 33A(9) inserted by this section, this section comes into force on the day on which this Act is passed.

Commentary—*De Voil Indirect Tax Service* **V5.162.**

Amendments—Sub-s (3) repealed by FA 2007 ss 97, 114, Sch 27 Pt 5(5) with effect as follows (by virtue of SI 2008/568 art 2).

- 1 April 2008 in relation to relevant documents relating to tax periods commencing on or after that date;
- 1 April 2008 in relation to assessments falling within FA 2007 Sch 24 para 2 for tax periods commencing on or after that date;
- 1 July 2008 in relation to relevant documents relating to claims under the Thirteenth Council Directive (arrangements for the refund of value added tax to persons not established in Community territory) for years commencing on or after that date;
- 1 January 2009 in relation to relevant documents relating to claims under the Eighth Council Directive (arrangements for the refund of value added tax to taxable persons not established in the territory of the country) for years commencing on or after that date;
- 1 April 2009 in relation to documents relating to all other claims for repayments of relevant tax made on or after 1 April 2009 which are not related to a tax period; and
- in any other case, 1 April 2009 in relation to documents given where a person's liability to pay relevant tax arises on or after that date.

99 VAT: re-enactment of reduced-rate provisions

(1) For the purpose of re-enacting the provisions of the Value Added Tax Act 1994 that provide for VAT on certain supplies, acquisitions and importations to be charged at a reduced rate of 5 per cent, that Act is amended as follows.
(2) (*amends* VATA 1994 s 2(1)).
(3) (*repeals* VATA 1994 s 2(1A)–(1C)).
(4) (*inserts* VATA 1994 s 29A).
(5) (*inserts* VATA 1994 Sch 7A).
(6) The consequential amendments in Part II of Schedule 31 to this Act have effect.
(7) The following provisions have effect in relation to supplies made, and acquisitions and importations taking place, on or after 1st November 2001—

(*a*) subsections (2) and (5),
(*b*) subsection (3) so far as providing for section 2(1A) and (1B), and Schedule A1, to cease to have effect, and
(*c*) subsection (4) so far as inserting subsections (1) and (2) of the new section 29A.

(8) Subsection (3), so far as providing for section 2(1C) to cease to have effect, comes into force on 1st November 2001.
(9) Subsection (6)—

(*a*) so far as relating to the amendments made by paragraphs 2 and 6(2) of Schedule 31 to this Act, has effect in relation to orders under section 2(2) of the Value Added Tax Act 1994 that make changes only in the rate of VAT that is in force at times on or after 1st November 2001;

(*b*) so far as relating to the amendment made by paragraph 3 of Schedule 31 to this Act, has effect in relation to supplies made, or to be made, on or after 1st November 2001.

Commentary—*De Voil Indirect Tax Service* **V4.4.**

100 VAT representatives

(1)–(3) (*substitutes* VATA 1994 s 48(1)(*b*), (*ba*) for sub-s (1)(*b*), *inserts* sub-ss (1A), (1B), and *substitutes* sub-ss (2), (2)(A) for sub-s (2)).

(4) The amendments made by this section come into force on 31st December 2001.

Commentary—*De Voil Indirect Tax Service* **V2.106.**

PART 5

MISCELLANEOUS AND SUPPLEMENTARY PROVISIONS

Supplementary

. . .

110 Repeals and revocations

(1) The enactments mentioned in Schedule 33 to this Act (which include provisions that are spent or of no practical utility) are repealed or revoked to the extent specified.

(2) The repeals and revocations specified in that Schedule have effect subject to the commencement provisions and savings contained or referred to in the notes set out in that Schedule.

111 Short title

This Act may be cited as the Finance Act 2001.

SCHEDULES

SCHEDULE 31

VALUE ADDED TAX: RE-ENACTMENT OF REDUCED RATE PROVISIONS

Section 99

Commentary—*De Voil Indirect Tax Service* **V4.4.**

PART 1

NEW SCHEDULE 7A TO THE VALUE ADDED TAX ACT 1994

1 (*sets out* VATA 1994 Sch 7A *as inserted by* FA 2001 s 99(5)).

PART 2

CONSEQUENTIAL AMENDMENTS

Value Added Tax Act 1994 (c 23)

2–6 (*amend* VATA 1994 ss 2, 62, 88, 96, and 97).

Finance Act 2000 (c 17)

7 (*inserts* FA 2000 Sch 6 para 9(5)).

CRIMINAL JUSTICE AND POLICE ACT 2001

(2001 Chapter 16)

ARRANGEMENT OF SECTIONS

PART 2

POWERS OF SEIZURE

Additional powers of seizure

An Act to make provision for combatting crime and disorder; to make provision about the disclosure of information relating to criminal matters and about powers of search and seizure; to amend the Police and Criminal Evidence Act 1984, the Police and Criminal Evidence (Northern Ireland) Order 1989 and the Terrorism Act 2000; to make provision about the police, the National Criminal Intelligence Service and the National Crime Squad; to make provision about the powers of the courts in relation to criminal matters; and for connected purposes.

[11 May 2001]

PART 2
POWERS OF SEIZURE

Additional powers of seizure

50 Additional powers of seizure from premises

(1) Where—

(*a*) a person who is lawfully on any premises finds anything on those premises that he has reasonable grounds for believing may be or may contain something for which he is authorised to search on those premises,

(*b*) a power of seizure to which this section applies or the power conferred by subsection (2) would entitle him, if he found it, to seize whatever it is that he has grounds for believing that thing to be or to contain, and

(*c*) in all the circumstances, it is not reasonably practicable for it to be determined, on those premises—

(i) whether what he has found is something that he is entitled to seize, or

(ii) the extent to which what he has found contains something that he is entitled to seize,

that person's powers of seizure shall include power under this section to seize so much of what he has found as it is necessary to remove from the premises to enable that to be determined.

(2) Where—

(*a*) a person who is lawfully on any premises finds anything on those premises ("the seizable property") which he would be entitled to seize but for its being comprised in something else that he has (apart from this subsection) no power to seize,

(*b*) the power under which that person would have power to seize the seizable property is a power to which this section applies, and (*c*) in all the circumstances it is not reasonably practicable for the seizable property to be separated, on those premises, from that in which it is comprised,

that person's powers of seizure shall include power under this section to seize both the seizable property and that from which it is not reasonably practicable to separate it.

(3) The factors to be taken into account in considering, for the purposes of this section, whether or not it is reasonably practicable on particular premises for something to be determined, or for something to be separated from something else, shall be confined to the following—

(*a*) how long it would take to carry out the determination or separation on those premises;

(*b*) the number of persons that would be required to carry out that determination or separation on those premises within a reasonable period;

(*c*) whether the determination or separation would (or would if carried out on those premises) involve damage to property;

(*d*) the apparatus or equipment that it would be necessary or appropriate to use for the carrying out of the determination or separation; and

(*e*) in the case of separation, whether the separation—

(i) would be likely, or

(ii) if carried out by the only means that are reasonably practicable on those premises, would be likely,

to prejudice the use of some or all of the separated seizable property for a purpose for which something seized under the power in question is capable of being used.

(4) Section 19(6) of the 1984 Act and Article 21(6) of the Police and Criminal Evidence (Northern Ireland) Order 1989 (SI 1989/1341 (NI 12)) (powers of seizure not to include power to seize anything that a person has reasonable grounds for believing is legally privileged) shall not apply to the power of seizure conferred by subsection (2).

(5) This section applies to each of the powers of seizure specified in Part 1 of Schedule 1.

(6) Without prejudice to any power conferred by this section to take a copy of any document, nothing in this section, so far as it has effect by reference to the power to take copies of documents under section 28(2)(*b*) of the Competition Act 1998 (c 41), shall be taken to confer any power to seize any document.

51 Additional powers of seizure from the person

(1) Where—

(*a*) a person carrying out a lawful search of any person finds something that he has reasonable grounds for believing may be or may contain something for which he is authorised to search,

(*b*) a power of seizure to which this section applies or the power conferred by subsection (2) would entitle him, if he found it, to seize whatever it is that he has grounds for believing that thing to be or to contain, and

(*c*) in all the circumstances it is not reasonably practicable for it to be determined, at the time and place of the search—

(i) whether what he has found is something that he is entitled to seize, or

(ii) the extent to which what he has found contains something that he is entitled to seize,

that person's powers of seizure shall include power under this section to seize so much of what he has found as it is necessary to remove from that place to enable that to be determined.

(2) Where—

(*a*) a person carrying out a lawful search of any person finds something ("the seizable property") which he would be entitled to seize but for its being comprised in something else that he has (apart from this subsection) no power to seize,

(*b*) the power under which that person would have power to seize the seizable property is a power to which this section applies, and

(*c*) in all the circumstances it is not reasonably practicable for the seizable property to be separated, at the time and place of the search, from that in which it is comprised,

that person's powers of seizure shall include power under this section to seize both the seizable property and that from which it is not reasonably practicable to separate it.

(3) The factors to be taken into account in considering, for the purposes of this section, whether or not it is reasonably practicable, at the time and place of a search, for something to be determined, or for something to be separated from something else, shall be confined to the following—

(*a*) how long it would take to carry out the determination or separation at that time and place;

(*b*) the number of persons that would be required to carry out that determination or separation at that time and place within a reasonable period;

(*c*) whether the determination or separation would (or would if carried out at that time and place) involve damage to property;

(*d*) the apparatus or equipment that it would be necessary or appropriate to use for the carrying out of the determination or separation; and (*e*) in the case of separation, whether the separation—

(i) would be likely, or

(ii) if carried out by the only means that are reasonably practicable at that time and place, would be likely,

to prejudice the use of some or all of the separated seizable property for a purpose for which something seized under the power in question is capable of being used.

(4) Section 19(6) of the 1984 Act and Article 21(6) of the Police and Criminal Evidence (Northern Ireland) Order 1989 (SI 1989/1341 (NI 12)) (powers of seizure not to include power to seize anything a person has reasonable grounds for believing is legally privileged) shall not apply to the power of seizure conferred by subsection (2).

(5) This section applies to each of the powers of seizure specified in Part 2 of Schedule 1.

52 Notice of exercise of power under s. 50 or 51

(1) Where a person exercises a power of seizure conferred by section 50, it shall (subject to subsections (2) and (3)) be his duty, on doing so, to give to the occupier of the premises a written notice—

(*a*) specifying what has been seized in reliance on the powers conferred by that section;

(*b*) specifying the grounds on which those powers have been exercised;

(*c*) setting out the effect of sections 59 to 61;

(*d*) specifying the name and address of the person to whom notice of an application under section 59(2) to the appropriate judicial authority in respect of any of the seized property must be given; and

(*e*) specifying the name and address of the person to whom an application may be made to be allowed to attend the initial examination required by any arrangements made for the purposes of section 53(2).

(2) Where it appears to the person exercising on any premises a power of seizure conferred by section 50—

(*a*) that the occupier of the premises is not present on the premises at the time of the exercise of the power, but

(*b*) that there is some other person present on the premises who is in charge of the premises,

subsection (1) of this section shall have effect as if it required the notice under that subsection to be given to that other person.

(3) Where it appears to the person exercising a power of seizure conferred by section 50 that there is no one present on the premises to whom he may give a notice for the purposes of complying with subsection (1) of this section, he shall, before leaving the premises, instead of complying with that subsection, attach a notice such as is mentioned in that subsection in a prominent place to the premises.

(4) Where a person exercises a power of seizure conferred by section 51 it shall be his duty, on doing so, to give a written notice to the person from whom the seizure is made—

(*a*) specifying what has been seized in reliance on the powers conferred by that section;

(*b*) specifying the grounds on which those powers have been exercised;

(*c*) setting out the effect of sections 59 to 61;

(*d*) specifying the name and address of the person to whom notice of any application under section 59(2) to the appropriate judicial authority in respect of any of the seized property must be given; and

(*e*) specifying the name and address of the person to whom an application may be made to be allowed to attend the initial examination required by any arrangements made for the purposes of section 53(2).

(5) The Secretary of State may by regulations made by statutory instrument, after consultation with the Scottish Ministers [and the Department of Justice in Northern Ireland][1], provide that a person who exercises a power of seizure conferred by section 50 shall be required to give a notice such as is mentioned in subsection (1) of this section to any person, or send it to any place, described in the regulations.

(6) Regulations under subsection (5) may make different provision for different cases.

(7) A statutory instrument containing regulations under subsection (5) shall be subject to annulment in pursuance of a resolution of either House of Parliament.

Amendments—[1] In sub-s (5), words inserted by the Northern Ireland Act 1998 (Devolution of Policing and Justice Functions) Order, SI 2010/976 art 12, Sch 14 para 46(1), (2) with effect from 12 April 2010.

Return or retention of seized property

53 Examination and return of property seized under s. 50 or 51

(1) This section applies where anything has been seized under a power conferred by section 50 or 51.

(2) It shall be the duty of the person for the time being in possession of the seized property in consequence of the exercise of that power to secure that there are arrangements in force which (subject to section 61) ensure—

(*a*) that an initial examination of the property is carried out as soon as reasonably practicable after the seizure;

(*b*) that that examination is confined to whatever is necessary for determining how much of the property falls within subsection (3);

(*c*) that anything which is found, on that examination, not to fall within subsection (3) is separated from the rest of the seized property and is returned as soon as reasonably practicable after the examination of an the seized property has been completed; and

(*d*) that, until the initial examination of all the seized property has been completed and anything which does not fall within subsection (3) has been returned, the seized property is kept separate from anything seized under any other power.

(3) The seized property falls within this subsection to the extent only—

(*a*) that it is property for which the person seizing it had power to search when he made the seizure but is not property the return of which is required by section 54;

(*b*) that it is property the retention of which is authorised by section 56; or

(*c*) that it is something which, in all the circumstances, it will not be reasonably practicable, following the examination, to separate from property falling within paragraph (*a*) or (*b*).

(4) In determining for the purposes of this section the earliest practicable time for the carrying out of an initial examination of the seized property, due regard shall be had to the desirability of allowing the person from whom it was seized, or a person with an interest in that property, an opportunity of being present or (if he chooses) of being represented at the examination.

(5) In this section, references to whether or not it is reasonably practicable to separate part of the seized property from the rest of it are references to whether or not it is reasonably practicable to do so without prejudicing the use of the rest of that property, or a part of it, for purposes for which (disregarding the part to be separated) the use of the whole or of a part of the rest of the property, if retained, would be lawful.

54 Obligation to return items subject to legal privilege

(1) If, at any time after a seizure of anything has been made in exercise of a power of seizure to which this section applies—

(*a*) it appears to the person for the time being having possession of the seized property in consequence of the seizure that the property—

(i) is an item subject to legal privilege, or

(ii) has such an item comprised in it,

and

(*b*) in a case where the item is comprised in something else which has been lawfully seized, it is not comprised in property falling within subsection (2),

it shall be the duty of that person to secure that the item is returned as soon as reasonably practicable after the seizure.

(2) Property in which an item subject to legal privilege is comprised falls within this subsection if—

(*a*) the whole or a part of the rest of the property is property falling within subsection (3) or property the retention of which is authorised by section 56; and

(*b*) in all the circumstances, it is not reasonably practicable for that item to be separated from the rest of that property (or, as the case may be, from that part of it) without prejudicing the use of the rest of that property, or that part of it, for purposes for which (disregarding that item) its use, if retained, would be lawful.

(3) Property falls within this subsection to the extent that it is property for which the person seizing it had power to search when he made the seizure, but is not property which is required to be returned under this section or section 55.

(4) This section applies—

(*a*) to the powers of seizure conferred by sections 50 and 51;

(*b*) to each of the powers of seizure specified in Parts 1 and 2 of Schedule 1; and

(*c*) to any power of seizure (not falling within paragraph (*a*) or (*b*)) conferred on a constable by or under any enactment, including an enactment passed after this Act.

55 Obligation to return excluded and special procedure material

(1) If, at any time after a seizure of anything has been made in exercise of a power to which this section applies—

(*a*) it appears to the person for the time being having possession of the seized property in consequence of the seizure that the property—

(i) is excluded material or special procedure material, or

(ii) has any excluded material or any special procedure material comprised in it,

(*b*) its retention is not authorised by section 56, and

(*c*) in a case where the material is comprised in something else which has been lawfully seized, it is not comprised in property falling within subsection (2) or (3), it shall be the duty of that person to secure that the item is returned as soon as reasonably practicable after the seizure.

(2) Property in which any excluded material or special procedure material is comprised falls within this subsection if—

(*a*) the whole or a part of the rest of the property is property for which the person seizing it had power to search when he made the seizure but is not property the return of which is required by this section or section 54; and

(*b*) in all the circumstances, it is not reasonably practicable for that material to be separated from the rest of that property (or, as the case may be, from that part of it) without prejudicing the use of the rest of that property, or that part of it, for purposes for which (disregarding that material) its use, if retained, would be lawful.

(3) Property in which any excluded material or special procedure material is comprised falls within this subsection if—

(*a*) the whole or a part of the rest of the property is property the retention of which is authorised by section 56; and

(*b*) in all the circumstances, it is not reasonably practicable for that material to be separated from the rest of that property (or, as the case may be, from that part of it) without prejudicing the use of the rest of that property, or that part of it, for purposes for which (disregarding that material) its use, if retained, would be lawful.

(4) This section applies (subject to subsection (5)) to each of the powers of seizure specified in Part 3 of Schedule 1.

(5) In its application to the powers of seizure conferred by—

(*a*) . . . [2]

(*b*) section 56(5) of the Drug Trafficking Act 1994 (c 37), . . . [1]

(*c*) Article 51(5) of the Proceeds of Crime (Northern Ireland) Order 1996 (SI 1996/1299 (NI 6)), [and

(*d*) section 352(4) of the Proceeds of Crime Act 2002,][1]

this section shall have effect with the omission of every reference to special procedure material.

(6) In this section, except in its application to—

(*a*) the power of seizure conferred by section 8(2) of the 1984 Act,

(*b*) the power of seizure conferred by Article 10(2) of the Police and Criminal Evidence (Northern Ireland) Order 1989 (SI 1989/1341 (NI 12)),

(*c*) each of the powers of seizure conferred by the provisions of paragraphs 1 and 3 of Schedule 5 to the Terrorism Act 2000 (c 11), and

(*d*) the power of seizure conferred by paragraphs 15 and 19 of Schedule 5 to that Act of 2000, so far only as the power in question is conferred by reference to paragraph 1 of that Schedule,

"special procedure material" means special procedure material consisting of documents or records other than documents.

Amendments—[1] Word in sub-s (5)(*b*) repealed, and sub-s (5)(*d*) and word preceding it inserted, by the Proceeds of Crime Act 2002 ss 456, 457, Sch 11 paras 1, 40(1), (2), Sch 12 with effect from 24 February 2003 (by virtue of SI 2003/120).

[2] Sub-s (5)(*a*) repealed by the Proceeds of Crime Act 2002 s 457, Sch 12 with effect from 24 March 2003 (by virtue of SI 2003/333).

56 Property seized by constables etc

(1) The retention of—

(*a*) property seized on any premises by a constable who was lawfully on the premises,

(*b*) property seized on any premises by a relevant person who was on the premises accompanied by a constable, and

(*c*) property seized by a constable carrying out a lawful search of any person,

is authorised by this section if the property falls within subsection (2) or (3).

(2) Property falls within this subsection to the extent that there are reasonable grounds for believing—

(*a*) that it is property obtained in consequence of the commission of an offence; and

(*b*) that it is necessary for it to be retained in order to prevent its being concealed, lost, damaged, altered or destroyed.

(3) Property falls within this subsection to the extent that there are reasonable grounds for believing—

(*a*) that it is evidence in relation to any offence; and

(*b*) that it is necessary for it to be retained in order to prevent its being concealed, lost, altered or destroyed.

(4) Nothing in this section authorises the retention (except in pursuance of section 54(2)) of anything at any time when its return is required by section 54.

[(4A) Subsection (1)(*a*) includes property seized on any premises—

(*a*) by a person authorised under section 16(2) of the 1984 Act to accompany a constable executing a warrant, or (*b*) by a person accompanying a constable under section 2(6) of the Criminal Justice Act 1987 in the execution of a warrant under section 2(4) of that Act.][2]

(5) In subsection (1)(*b*) the reference to a relevant person's being on any premises accompanied by a constable is a reference only to a person who was so on the premises under the authority of—

(*a*) a warrant under section 448 of the Companies Act 1985 (c 6) authorising him to exercise together with a constable the powers conferred by subsection (3) of that section;

(*b*) . . . [3]

(*c*)–(*e*) . . . [1]

Amendments—[1] Sub-s (5)(*c*)–(*e*) repealed by the Financial Services and Markets Act 2000 (Consequential Amendments and Repeals) Order, SI 2001/3649 art 364(*a*) with effect from 1 December 2001.

[2] Sub-s (4A) inserted by the Criminal Justice Act 2003 s 12, Sch 1 para 14 with effect from 20 January 2004 (by virtue of SI 2004/81).

[3] Sub-s (5)(b) repealed by the Companies Act 2006 (Consequential Amendments, Transitional Provisions and Savings) Order, SI 2009/1941 art 2(1), Sch 1 para 189(1), (2) with effect from 1 October 2009.

57 Retention of seized items

(1) This section has effect in relation to the following provisions (which are about the retention of items which have been seized and are referred to in this section as "the relevant provisions")—

(*a*) section 22 of the 1984 Act;

(*b*) Article 24 of the Police and Criminal Evidence (Northern Ireland) Order 1989 (SI 1989/1341 (NI 12));

(*c*) *section 20CC(3) of the Taxes Management Act 1970 (c 9);*[6]

(*d*) paragraph 4 of Schedule 9 to the Weights and Measures (Northern Ireland) Order 1981 (SI 1981/231 (NI 10));

(*e*) . . . [1];

(*f*) section 448(6) of the Companies Act 1985 (c 6);

(*g*) paragraph 4 of [Schedule 7 to the Weights and Measures (Packaged Goods) Regulations 2006][3];

(*h*) . . . [1];

(*i*) . . . [7];

(*j*) . . . [1];

(*k*) [paragraph 7(4) of Schedule 3B to][8] the Human Fertilisation and Embryology Act 1990 (c 37);

(*l*) section 5(4) of the Knives Act 1997 (c 21);

(*m*) paragraph 7(2) of Schedule 9 to the Data Protection Act 1998 (c 29);

(*n*) section 28(7) of the Competition Act 1998 (c 41);

(*o*) [section 176A][9] of the Financial Services and Markets Act 2000 (c 8);

(*p*) paragraph 7(2) of Schedule 3 to the Freedom of Information Act 2000 (c 36).

[(*pa*) section 227F of the Enterprise Act 2002;][4]

[(*q*) paragraph 5(4) of Schedule 5 to the Human Tissue Act 2004.][2]

[(*r*) paragraph 12(3) of Schedule 2 to the Animal Welfare Act 2006.][5]

(2) The relevant provisions shall apply in relation to any property seized in exercise of a power conferred by section 50 or 51 as if the property had been seized under the power of seizure by reference to which the power under that section was exercised in relation to that property.

(3) Nothing in any of sections 53 to 56 authorises the retention of any property at any time when its retention would not (apart from the provisions of this Part) be authorised by the relevant provisions.

(4) Nothing in any of the relevant provisions authorises the retention of anything after an obligation to return it has arisen under this Part.

Amendments—[1] Sub-s (1)(*e*), (*h*), (*j*) repealed by the Financial Services and Markets Act 2000 (Consequential Amendments and Repeals) Order, SI 2001/3649 art 364(*b*) with effect from 1 December 2001.

[2] Sub-s (1)(*q*) inserted by the Human Tissue Act 2004 s 56, Sch 56 para 5(1), (2) with effect, for certain purposes, from 1 March 2006, and for other purposes from 6 April 2006. For commencement provisions, see the Human Tissue Act 2004 (Commencement No 4 and Transitional Provisions) Order, SI 2006/404 arts 2–4.

[3] Words in sub-s (1)(*g*) substituted by Weights and Measures (Packaged Goods) Regulations, SI 2006/659 reg 1(2), Sch 1 Pt2(24), (25) with effect from 6 April 2006.

[4] Sub-s (1)(*pa*) inserted by the Enterprise Act 2002 (Amendment) Regulations, SI 2006/3363 regs 24, 25 with effect from 8 January 2007.

[5] Sub-s (1)(*r*) inserted by the Animal Welfare Act 2006 s 64, Sch 3 para 14(1) with effect as follows—

- in relation to Wales, from 27 March 2007 (by virtue of SI 2007/1030 art 2(1)(*j*), (*l*));
- in relation to England, from 6 April 2007 (by virtue of SI 2007/499 art 2(2)(*l*));
- in relation to Scotland and Northern Ireland, from a date to be appointed.

[6] Sub-s (1)(*c*) repealed by FA 2007 ss 84, 114, Sch 22 para 13(1)(*a*), Sch 27 Pt 5(1) with effect from 1 December 2007 (by virtue of SI 2007/3166 art 3(*a*)).

[7] Sub-s (1)(i) repealed by the Companies Act 2006 (Consequential Amendments, Transitional Provisions and Savings) Order, SI 2009/1941 art 2(1), Sch 1 para 189(1), (3) with effect from 1 October 2009.

[8] In sub-s (1)(*k*), words substituted for words "section 40(4) of" by the Human Fertilisation and Embryology Act 2008 s 65, Sch 7 para 19 with effect from 1 October 2009 (by virtue of SI 2009/2232, art 2(*t*), (*y*)).

[9] In sub-s(1)(*o*), words substituted by the Financial Services Act 2012 s 114(1), Sch 18 para 92 with effect from 1 April 2013 (the appointed day for the purposes of Sch 18 by virtue of SI 2013/423 art 3, Schedule).

Prospective amendments—Sub-s (1)(*d*), (*g*), (*pa*) to be repealed and sub-s (1)(*s*) to be inserted by the Consumer Rights Act 2015 s 77(2), Sch 6 paras 61, 62 with effect from a date to be appointed. Sub-s (1)(*s*) as inserted to read as follows—

"(*s*) paragraphs 28(7) and 29(8) of Schedule 5 to the Consumer Rights Act 2015."

58 Person to whom seized property is to be returned

(1) Where—

(*a*) anything has been seized in exercise of any power of seizure, and

(*b*) there is an obligation under this Part for the whole or any part of the seized property to be returned,

the obligation to return it shall (subject to the following provisions of this section) be an obligation to return it to the person from whom it was seized.

(2) Where—

(*a*) any person is obliged under this Part to return anything that has been seized to the person from whom it was seized, and

(*b*) the person under that obligation is satisfied that some other person has a better right to that thing than the person from whom it was seized,

his duty to return it shall, instead, be a duty to return it to that other person or, as the case may be, to the person appearing to him to have the best right to the thing in question.

(3) Where different persons claim to be entitled to the return of anything that is required to be returned under this Part, that thing may be retained for as long as is reasonably necessary for the determination in accordance with subsection (2) of the person to whom it must be returned.

(4) References in this Part to the person from whom something has been seized, in relation to a case in which the power of seizure was exercisable by reason of that thing's having been found on any premises, are references to the occupier of the premises at the time of the seizure.

(5) References in this section to the occupier of any premises at the time of a seizure, in relation to a case in which—

(*a*) a notice in connection with the entry or search of the premises in question, or with the seizure, was given to a person appearing in the occupier's absence to be in charge of the premises, and

(*b*) it is practicable, for the purpose of returning something that has been seized, to identify that person but not to identify the occupier of the premises,

are references to that person.

Remedies and safeguards

59 Application to the appropriate judicial authority

(1) This section applies where anything has been seized in exercise, or purported exercise, of a relevant power of seizure.

(2) Any person with a relevant interest in the seized property may apply to the appropriate judicial authority, on one or more of the grounds mentioned in subsection (3), for the return of the whole or a part of the seized property.

(3) Those grounds are—

(*a*) that there was no power to make the seizure;

(*b*) that the seized property is or contains an item subject to legal privilege that is not comprised in property falling within section 54(2);

(*c*) that the seized property is or contains any excluded material or special procedure material which—

(i) has been seized under a power to which section 55 applies;

(ii) is not comprised in property falling within section 55(2) or (3); and

(iii) is not property the retention of which is authorised by section 56;

(*d*) that the seized property is or contains something seized under section 50 or 51 which does not fall within section 53(3);

and subsections (5) and (6) of section 55 shall apply for the purposes of paragraph (*c*) as they apply for the purposes of that section.

(4) Subject to subsection (6), the appropriate judicial authority, on an application under subsection (2), shall—

(*a*) if satisfied as to any of the matters mentioned in subsection (3), order the return of so much of the seized property as is property in relation to which the authority is so satisfied; and

(*b*) to the extent that that authority is not so satisfied, dismiss the application.

(5) The appropriate judicial authority—

(*a*) on an application under subsection (2),

(*b*) on an application made by the person for the time being having possession of anything in consequence of its seizure under a relevant power of seizure, or

(*c*) on an application made—

(i) by a person with a relevant interest in anything seized under section 50 or 51, and

(ii) on the grounds that the requirements of section 53(2) have not been or are not being complied with,

may give such directions as the authority thinks fit as to the examination, retention, separation or return of the whole or any part of the seized property.

(6) On any application under this section, the appropriate judicial authority may authorise the retention of any property which—

(*a*) has been seized in exercise, or purported exercise, of a relevant power of seizure, and

(*b*) would otherwise fall to be returned,

if that authority is satisfied that the retention of the property is justified on grounds falling within subsection (7).

(7) Those grounds are that (if the property were returned) it would immediately become appropriate—

(*a*) to issue, on the application of the person who is in possession of the property at the time of the application under this section, a warrant in pursuance of which, or of the exercise of which, it would be lawful to seize the property; or

(*b*) to make an order under—

(i) paragraph 4 of Schedule 1 to the 1984 Act,

(ii) paragraph 4 of Schedule 1 to the Police and Criminal Evidence (Northern Ireland) Order 1989 (SI 1989/1341 (NI 12)),

(iii) section 20BA of the Taxes Management Act 1970 (c 9), or

(iv) paragraph 5 of Schedule 5 to the Terrorism Act 2000 (c 11), under which the property would fall to be delivered up or produced to the person mentioned in paragraph (*a*).

(8) Where any property which has been seized in exercise, or purported exercise, of a relevant power of seizure has parts ("part A" and "part B") comprised in it such that—

(*a*) it would be inappropriate, if the property were returned, to take any action such as is mentioned in subsection (7) in relation to part A,

(*b*) it would (or would but for the facts mentioned in paragraph (*a*)) be appropriate, if the property were returned, to take such action in relation to part B, and

(*c*) in all the circumstances, it is not reasonably practicable to separate part A from part B without prejudicing the use of part B for purposes for which it is lawful to use property seized under the power in question,

the facts mentioned in paragraph (*a*) shall not be taken into account by the appropriate judicial authority in deciding whether the retention of the property is justified on grounds falling within subsection (7).

(9) If a person fails to comply with any order or direction made or given by a judge of the Crown Court in exercise of any jurisdiction under this section—

(*a*) the authority may deal with him as if he had committed a contempt of the Crown Court; and

(*b*) any enactment relating to contempt of the Crown Court shall have effect in relation to the failure as if it were such a contempt.

(10) The relevant powers of seizure for the purposes of this section are—

(*a*) the powers of seizure conferred by sections 50 and 51;

(*b*) each of the powers of seizure specified in Parts 1 and 2 of Schedule 1; and

(*c*) any power of seizure (not falling within paragraph (*a*) or (*b*)) conferred on a constable by or under any enactment, including an enactment passed after this Act.

(11) References in this section to a person with a relevant interest in seized property are references to—

(*a*) the person from whom it was seized;

(*b*) any person with an interest in the property; or

(*c*) any person, not falling within paragraph (*a*) or (*b*), who had custody or control of the property immediately before the seizure.

(12) For the purposes of subsection (11)(*b*), the persons who have an interest in seized property shall, in the case of property which is or contains an item subject to legal privilege, be taken to include the person in whose favour that privilege is conferred.

[(13) Criminal Procedure Rules may make provision about proceedings under this section on an application to a judge of the Crown Court in England and Wales.][1]

Amendments—[1] Sub-s (13) inserted by the Deregulation Act 2015 s 82(5) with effect from 26 May 2015 (by virtue of SI 2015/994).

60 Cases where duty to secure arises

(1) Where property has been seized in exercise, or purported exercise, of any power of seizure conferred by section 50 or 51, a duty to secure arises under section 61 in relation to the seized property if—

(*a*) a person entitled to do so makes an application under section 59 for the return of the property;

(*b*) in relation to England, Wales and Northern Ireland, at least one of the conditions set out in subsections (2) and (3) is satisfied;

(*c*) in relation to Scotland, the condition set out in subsection (2) is satisfied; and

(*d*) notice of the application is given to a relevant person.

(2) The first condition is that the application is made on the grounds that the seized property is or contains an item subject to legal privilege that is not comprised in property falling within section 54(2).

(3) The second condition is that—

(*a*) the seized property was seized by a person who had, or purported to have, power under this Part to seize it by virtue only of one or more of the powers specified in subsection (6); and

(*b*) the application—

(i) is made on the ground that the seized property is or contains something which does not fall within section 53(3); and

(ii) states that the seized property is or contains special procedure material or excluded material.

(4) In relation to property seized by a person who had. or purported to have, power under this Part to seize it by virtue only of one or more of the powers of seizure conferred by—

(*a*) . . . [1]

(*b*) section 56(5) of the Drug Trafficking Act 1994 (c 37), . . . [2]

(*c*) Article 51(5) of the Proceeds of Crime (Northern Ireland) Order 1996 (SI 1996/1299 (NI 6)), [or

(*d*) section 352(4) of the Proceeds of Crime Act 2002,][2]

the second condition is satisfied only if the application states that the seized property is or contains excluded material.

(5) In relation to property seized by a person who had, or purported to have, power under this Part to seize it by virtue only of one or more of the powers of seizure specified in Part 3 of Schedule 1 but not by virtue of—

(*a*) the power of seizure conferred by section 8(2) of the 1984 Act,

(*b*) the power of seizure conferred by Article 10(2) of the Police and Criminal Evidence (Northern Ireland) Order 1989 (SI 1989/1341 (NI 12)),

(*c*) either of the powers of seizure conferred by paragraphs 1 and 3 of Schedule 5 to the Terrorism Act 2000 (c 11), or

(*d*) either of the powers of seizure conferred by paragraphs 15 and 19 of Schedule 5 to that Act of 2000 so far as they are conferred by reference to paragraph 1 of that Schedule,

the second condition is satisfied only if the application states that the seized property is or contains excluded material or special procedure material consisting of documents or records other than documents.

(6) The powers mentioned in subsection (3) are—

(*a*) the powers of seizure specified in Part 3 of Schedule 1;

(*b*) the powers of seizure conferred by the provisions of Parts 2 and 3 of the 1984 Act (except section 8(2) of that Act);

(*c*) the powers of seizure conferred by the provisions of Parts 3 and 4 of the Police and Criminal Evidence (Northern Ireland) Order 1989 (except Article 10(2) of that Order);

(*d*) the powers of seizure conferred by the provisions of paragraph 11 of Schedule 5 to the Terrorism Act 2000; and

(*e*) the powers of seizure conferred by the provisions of paragraphs 15 and 19 of that Schedule so far as they are conferred by reference to paragraph 11 of that Schedule.

(7) In this section "a relevant person" means any one of the following—

(*a*) the person who made the seizure;

(*b*) the person for the time being having possession, in consequence of the seizure, of the seized property;

(*c*) the person named for the purposes of subsection (1)(*d*) or (4)(*d*) of section 52 in any notice given under that section with respect to the seizure.

Amendments—[1] Sub-s (4)(*a*) repealed by the Proceeds of Crime Act 2002 s 457, Sch 12 with effect from 24 March 2003 (by virtue of SI 2003/333).

[2] Word in sub-s (4)(*b*) repealed, and sub-s (4)(*d*) and word preceding it inserted, by the Proceeds of Crime Act 2002 ss 456, 457, Sch 11 paras 1, 40(1), (3), Sch 12 with effect from 24 February 2003 (by virtue of SI 2003/120).

61 The duty to secure

(1) The duty to secure that arises under this section is a duty of the person for the time being having possession, in consequence of the seizure, of the seized property to secure that arrangements are in force that ensure that the seized property (without being returned) is not, at any time after the giving of the notice of the application under section 60(1), either—

(*a*) examined or copied, or

(*b*) put to any use to which its seizure would, apart from this subsection, entitle it to be put,

except with the consent of the applicant or in accordance with the directions of the appropriate judicial authority.

(2) Subsection (1) shall not have effect in relation to any time after the withdrawal of the application to which the notice relates.
(3) Nothing in any arrangements for the purposes of this section shall be taken to prevent the giving of a notice under section 49 of the Regulation of Investigatory Powers Act 2000 (c 23) (notices for the disclosure of material protected by encryption etc) in respect of any information contained in the seized material; but subsection (1) of this section shall apply to anything disclosed for the purpose of complying with such a notice as it applies to the seized material in which the information in question is contained.
(4) Subsection (9) of section 59 shall apply in relation to any jurisdiction conferred on the appropriate judicial authority by this section as it applies in relation to the jurisdiction conferred by that section.

62 Use of inextricably linked property

(1) This section applies to property, other than property which is for the time being required to be secured in pursuance of section 61, if—
(*a*) it has been seized under any power conferred by section 50 or 51 or specified in Part 1 or 2 of Schedule 1, and
(*b*) it is inextricably linked property.
(2) Subject to subsection (3), it shall be the duty of the person for the time being having possession, in consequence of the seizure, of the inextricably linked property to ensure that arrangements are in force which secure that that property (without being returned) is not at any time, except with the consent of the person from whom it was seized, either—
(*a*) examined or copied, or
(*b*) put to any other use.
(3) Subsection (2) does not require that arrangements under that subsection should prevent inextricably linked property from being put to any use falling within subsection (4).
(4) A use falls within this subsection to the extent that it is use which is necessary for facilitating the use, in any investigation or proceedings, of property in which the inextricably linked property is comprised.
(5) Property is inextricably linked property for the purposes of this section if it falls within any of subsections (6) to (8).
(6) Property falls within this subsection if—
(*a*) it has been seized under a power conferred by section 50 or 51; and
(*b*) but for subsection (3)(*c*) of section 53, arrangements under subsection (2) of that section in relation to the property would be required to ensure the return of the property as mentioned in subsection (2)(*c*) of that section.
(7) Property falls within this subsection if—
(*a*) it has been seized under a power to which section 54 applies; and
(*b*) but for paragraph (*b*) of subsection (1) of that section, the person for the time being having possession of the property would be under a duty to secure its return as mentioned in that subsection.
(8) Property falls within this subsection if—
(*a*) it has been seized under a power of seizure to which section 55 applies; and
(*b*) but for paragraph (*c*) of subsection (1) of that section, the person for the time being having possession of the property would be under a duty to secure its return as mentioned in that subsection.

Construction of Part 2

63 Copies

(1) Subject to subsection (3)—
(*a*) in this Part, "seize" includes "take a copy of", and cognate expressions shall be construed accordingly;
(*b*) this Part shall apply as if any copy taken under any power to which any provision of this Part applies were the original of that of which it is a copy; and
(*c*) for the purposes of this Part, except sections 50 and 51, the powers mentioned in subsection (2) (which are powers to obtain hard copies etc of information which is stored in electronic form) shall be treated as powers of seizure, and references to seizure and to seized property shall be construed accordingly.
(2) The powers mentioned in subsection (1)(*c*) are any powers which are conferred by—
(*a*) section 19(4) or 20 of the 1984 Act;
(*b*) Article 21(4) or 22 of the Police and Criminal Evidence (Northern Ireland) Order 1989 (SI 1989/1341 (NI 12));
(*c*) section 46(3) of the Firearms Act 1968 (c 27);
[(*d*) *section 43(5)(aa) of the Gaming Act 1968 (c 65);*][1]
(*e*) *section 20C(3A) of the Taxes Management Act 1970 (c 9);*[2]
(*f*) section 32(6)(*b*) of the Food Safety Act 1990 (c 16);

(*g*) Article 34(6)(*b*) of the Food Safety (Northern Ireland) Order 1991 (SI 1991/762 (NI 7));

[(*ga*) section 23E(5)(*b*) (as read with section 23K(2)) of the Criminal Law (Consolidation) (Scotland) Act 1995;][3]

(*h*) section 28(2)(*f*) of the Competition Act 1998 (c 41); or

(*i*) section 8(2)(*c*) of the Nuclear Safeguards Act 2000 (c 5).

(3) Subsection (1) does not apply to section 50(6) or 57.

Amendments—[1] Sub-s (2)(*d*) repealed by the Gambling Act 2005 s 356(4), Sch 17 with effect from 1 September 2007 (by virtue of SI 2006/3272, art 2(4)).

[2] Sub-s (2)(*e*) repealed by FA 2007 ss 84, 114, Sch 22 para 13(1)(*b*), Sch 27 Pt 5(1) with effect from 1 December 2007 (by virtue of SI 2007/3166 art 3(*a*)).

[3] Sub-s (2)(*ga*) inserted by FA 2007 s 85, Sch 23 paras 11, 12, 14 with effect from 1 December 2007 (by virtue of SI 2007/3166 art 3(*b*)).

64 Meaning of "appropriate judicial authority"

(1) Subject to subsection (2), in this Part "appropriate judicial authority" means—

(*a*) in relation to England and Wales and Northern Ireland, a judge of the Crown Court;

(*b*) in relation to Scotland, a sheriff.

(2) In this Part "appropriate judicial authority", in relation to the seizure of items under any power mentioned in subsection (3) and in relation to items seized under any such power, means—

(*a*) in relation to England and Wales and Northern Ireland, the High Court;

(*b*) in relation to Scotland, the Court of Session.

(3) Those powers are—

(*a*) the powers of seizure conferred by—

(i) section 448(3) of the Companies Act 1985 (c 6);

(ii) . . . [3]; and

(iii) section 28(2) of the Competition Act 1998; . . . [1]

[(*aa*) the power of seizure conferred by section 352(4) of the Proceeds of Crime Act 2002, if the power is exercisable for the purposes of a civil recovery investigation . . . [4] (within the meaning of Part 8 of that Act);][1]

(*b*) any power of seizure conferred by section 50, so far as that power is exercisable by reference to any power mentioned in paragraph (*a*).

Amendments—[1] Word in sub-s (3)(*a*)(iii) repealed, and sub-s (3)(*aa*) and word preceding it inserted, by the Proceeds of Crime Act 2002 ss 456, 457, Sch 11 paras 1, 40(1), (4), Sch 12 with effect from 24 February 2003 (by virtue of SI 2003/120).

[2] Words in sub-s (3)(*aa*) inserted by the Serious Crime Act 2007 s 77, Sch 10 para 27 with effect from 6 April 2008 (by virtue of SI 2008/755 art 17(1)(*d*)(iv).

[3] Sub-s (3)(*a*)(ii) repealed by the Companies Act 2006 (Consequential Amendments, Transitional Provisions and Savings) Order, SI 2009/1941 art 2(1), Sch 1 para 189(1), (4) with effect from 1 October 2009.

[4] In sub-s (3)(*aa*), words "or a detained cash investigation" repealed by the Policing and Crime Act 2009 s 112(1), (2), Sch 7 Pt 8, para 115, Sch 8 Pt 5 with effect from 1 June 2015 (by virtue of SI 2015/983).

65 Meaning of "legal privilege"

(1) Subject to the following provisions of this section, references in this Part to an item subject to legal privilege shall be construed—

(*a*) for the purposes of the application of this Part to England and Wales, in accordance with section 10 of the 1984 Act (meaning of legal privilege");

(*b*) for the purposes of the application of this Part to Scotland, in accordance with section [412 of the Proceeds of Crime Act 2002][1] (interpretation); and

(*c*) for the purposes of the application of this Part to Northern Ireland, in accordance with Article 12 of the Police and Criminal Evidence (Northern Ireland) Order 1989 (meaning of "legal privilege").

(2) In relation to property which has been seized in exercise, or purported exercise, of—

(*a*) the power of seizure conferred by section 28(2) of the Competition Act 1998, or

(*b*) so much of any power of seizure conferred by section 50 as is exercisable by reference to that power,

references in this Part to an item subject to legal privilege shall be read as references to a privileged communication within the meaning of section 30 of that Act.

(3) . . . [3]

[(3A) In relation to property which has been seized in exercise, or purported exercise, of—

(*a*) the power of seizure conferred by section 352(4) of the Proceeds of Crime Act 2002, or

(*b*) so much of any power of seizure conferred by section 50 as is exercisable by reference to that power,

references in this Part to an item subject to legal privilege shall be read as references to privileged material within the meaning of section 354(2) of that Act.][1]

(4) An item which is, or is comprised in, property which has been seized in exercise, or purported exercise, of the power of seizure conferred by section 448(3) of the Companies Act 1985 (c 6) shall be taken for the purposes of this Part to be an item subject to legal privilege if, and only if, the seizure of that item was in contravention of section 452(2) of that Act (privileged information).

(5) . . .[4]
(6) An item which is, or is comprised in, property which has been seized in exercise, or purported exercise, of the power of seizure conferred by [[regulation 33(3)][6] of the Timeshare, Holiday Products, Resale and Exchange Contracts Regulations 2010][5] shall be taken for the purposes of this Part to be an item subject to legal privilege if, and only if, the seizure of that item was in contravention of [[regulation 33(8)][6] of those Regulations][5] (privileged documents).
(7) An item which is, or is comprised in, property which has been seized in exercise, or purported exercise, of the power of seizure conferred by paragraph 1 of Schedule 9 to the Data Protection Act 1998 (c 29) shall be taken for the purposes of this Part to be an item subject to legal privilege if, and only if, the seizure of that item was in contravention of paragraph 9 of that Schedule (privileged communications).
(8) An item which is, or is comprised in, property which has been seized in exercise, or purported exercise, of the power of seizure conferred by paragraph 1 of Schedule 3 to the Freedom of Information Act 2000 (c 36) shall be taken for the purposes of this Part to be an item subject to legal privilege if, and only if, the seizure of that item was in contravention of paragraph 9 of that Schedule (privileged communications).
[(8A) An item which is, or is comprised in, property which has been seized in exercise, or purported exercise, of the power of seizure conferred by section 227C of the Enterprise Act 2002 (c 40) shall be taken for the purposes of this Part to be an item subject to legal privilege if, and only if, the seizure of that item was in contravention of section 227B(4) of that Act (privileged items).][2]
(9) An item which is, or is comprised in, property which has been seized in exercise, or purported exercise, of so much of any power of seizure conferred by section 50 as is exercisable by reference to a power of seizure conferred by—

(*a*) section 448(3) of the Companies Act 1985,
(*b*) Article 441(3) of the Companies (Northern Ireland) Order 1986,
[(*c*) [regulation 33(3)][6] of the Timeshare, Holiday Products, Resale and Exchange Contracts Regulations 2010,][5]
(*d*) paragraph 1 of Schedule 9 to the Data Protection Act 1998, . . .[2]
(*e*) paragraph 1 of Schedule 3 to the Freedom of Information Act 2000, [or
(*f*) section 227C of the Enterprise Act 2002,][2]

shall be taken for the purposes of this Part to be an item subject to legal privilege if, and only if, the item would have been taken for the purposes of this Part to be an item subject to legal privilege had it been seized under the power of seizure by reference to which the power conferred by section 50 was exercised.

Amendments—[1] Words in sub-s (1)(*b*) substituted, and sub-s (3A) inserted, by the Proceeds of Crime Act 2002 ss 456, Sch 11 paras 1, 40(1), (5) with effect from 24 February 2003 (by virtue of SI 2003/120).
[2] Sub-ss (8A), (9)(*f*) and preceding word "or", inserted; and word in sub-s (9)(*d*) repealed, by the Enterprise Act 2002 (Amendment) Regulations, SI 2006/3363 regs 24, 26(1)–(3) with effect from 8 January 2007.
[3] Sub-s (3) repealed by FA 2007 ss 84, 114, Sch 22 para 13(1)(*c*), Sch 27 Pt 5(1) with effect from 1 December 2007 (by virtue of SI 2007/3166 art 3(*a*)).
[4] Sub-s (5) repealed by the Companies Act 2006 (Consequential Amendments, Transitional Provisions and Savings) Order, SI 2009/1941 art 2(1), Sch 1 para 189(1), (5) with effect from 1 October 2009.
[5] Words in sub-s (6), and whole of sub-s (9)(*c*), substituted, by the Timeshare, Holiday Products, Resale and Exchange Contracts Regulations, SI 2010/2960 reg 36(3), Sch 6 para 2(1), (2)(*a*), (*b*) with effect from 23 February 2011.
[6] Words in sub-s (6) and sub-s (9)(*c*) substituted by the Timeshare (Amendment) Regulations, SI 2011/1065 reg 2(1), (2)(*a*), (*b*) with effect from 28 April 2011.

Prospective amendments—Sub-ss (6), (8A) (9)(*c*) to be repealed, sub-s (8B) to be inserted, in sub-s (9)(*d*), word "or" at the end to be repealed, and sub-s (9)(*f*) and preceding word "or" to be repealed by the Consumer Rights Act 2015 s 77(2), Sch 6 paras 61, 63 with effect from a date to be appointed. Sub-s (8B) as inserted to read as follows—

> "(8B) An item which is, or is comprised in, property which has been seized in exercise or purported exercise of the power of seizure conferred by paragraph 27(1)(*b*) or 29(1) of Schedule 5 to the Consumer Rights Act 2015 shall be taken for the purposes of this Part to be an item subject to legal privilege if, and only if, the seizure of that item was in contravention of paragraph 27(6) or (as the case may be) 29(6) of that Schedule (privileged documents).".

66 General interpretation of Part 2

(1) In this Part—

"appropriate judicial authority" has the meaning given by section 64;
"documents" includes information recorded in any form;
"item subject to legal privilege" shall be construed in accordance with section 65;
"premises" includes any vehicle, stall or moveable structure (including an offshore installation) and any other place whatever, whether or not occupied as land;
"offshore installation" has the same meaning as in the Mineral Workings (Offshore Installations) Act 1971 (c 61);
"return", in relation to seized property, shall be construed in accordance with section 58, and cognate expressions shall be construed accordingly;
"seize", and cognate expressions, shall be construed in accordance with section 63(1) and subsection (5) below;

"seized property" in relation to any exercise of a power of seizure, means (subject to subsection (5)) anything seized in exercise of that power; and

"vehicle" includes any vessel, aircraft or hovercraft.

(2) In this Part references, in relation to a time when seized property is in any person's possession in consequence of a seizure ("the relevant time"), to something for which the person making the seizure had power to search shall be construed—

(*a*) where the seizure was made on the occasion of a search carried out on the authority of a warrant, as including anything of the description of things the presence or suspected presence of which provided grounds for the issue of the warrant;

(*b*) where the property was seized in the course of a search on the occasion of which it would have been lawful for the person carrying out the search to seize anything which on that occasion was believed by him to be, or appeared to him to be, of a particular description, as including—

(i) anything which at the relevant time is believed by the person in possession of the seized property, or (as the case may be) appears to him, to be of that description; and

(ii) anything which is in fact of that description;

(*c*) where the property was seized in the course of a search on the occasion of which it would have been lawful for the person carrying out the search to seize anything which there were on that occasion reasonable grounds for believing was of a particular description, as including—

(i) anything which there are at the relevant time reasonable grounds for believing is of that description; and

(ii) anything which is in fact of that description;

(*d*) where the property was seized in the course of a search to which neither paragraph (*b*) nor paragraph (*c*) applies, as including anything which is of a description of things which, on the occasion of the search, it would have been lawful for the person carrying it out to seize otherwise than under section 50 and 51; and

(*e*) where the property was seized on the occasion of a search authorised under section 82 of the Terrorism Act 2000 (c 11) (seizure of items suspected to have been, or to be intended to be, used in commission of certain offences), as including anything—

(i) which is or has been, or is or was intended to be, used in the commission of an offence such as is mentioned in subsection (3)(*a*) or (*b*) of that section; or

(ii) which at the relevant time the person who is in possession of the seized property reasonably suspects is something falling within sub-paragraph (*i*).

(3) For the purpose of determining in accordance with subsection (2), in relation to any time, whether or to what extent property seized on the occasion of a search authorised under section 9 of the Official Secrets Act 1911 (c 28) (seizure of evidence of offences under that Act having been or being about to be committed) is something for which the person making the seizure had power to search, subsection (1) of that section shall be construed—

(*a*) as if the reference in that subsection to evidence of an offence under that Act being about to be committed were a reference to evidence of such an offence having been, at the time of the seizure, about to be committed; and

(*b*) as if the reference in that subsection to reasonable ground for suspecting that such an offence is about to be committed were a reference to reasonable ground for suspecting that at the time of the seizure such an offence was about to be committed.

(4) References in subsection (2) to a search include references to any activities authorised by virtue of any of the following—

(*a*) section 28(1) of the Trade Descriptions Act 1968 (c 29) (power to enter premises and to inspect and seize goods and documents);

(*b*) section 29(1) of the Fair Trading Act 1973 (c 41) (power to enter premises and to inspect and seize goods and documents);

(*c*) paragraph 9 of the Schedule to the Prices Act 1974 (c 24) (powers of entry and inspection);

(*d*) section 162(1) of the Consumer Credit Act 1974 (c 39) (powers of entry and inspection);

(*e*) [section 11(1) to (1C) of the Estate Agents Act 1979][8](c 38) (powers of entry and inspection);

(*f*) Schedule 9 to the Weights and Measures (Northern Ireland) Order 1981 (SI 1981/231 (NI 10));

[(*g*) section 79 of the Weights and Measures Act 1985 (c 72) or Schedule 7 to the Weights and Measures (Packaged Goods) Regulations 2006 (powers of entry and inspection etc);][4];

(*h*) section 29 of the Consumer Protection Act 1987 (c 43) (powers of search etc);

(*i*) . . . [7]

(*j*) section 32(5) of the Food Safety Act 1990 (c 16) (power to inspect records relating to a food business);

[(*ja*) paragraph 5 of Schedule 3B to the Human Fertilisation and Embryology Act 1990;][10]

(*k*) . . . [13]

(*l*) Article 33(6) of the Food Safety (Northern Ireland) Order 1991 (SI 1991/762 (NI 7));

(*m*) . . . [11]

[(*ma*) section 227C of the Enterprise Act 2002 (power to enter premises with warrant)][5]

[(*n*) paragraph 2 of Schedule 5 to the Human Tissue Act 2004 (entry and inspection of licensed premises).][2]

[(*o*) regulation 22 of the General Product Safety Regulations 2005 (powers of entry and search etc)][3]

[(*p*) sections 26(1), 27(1), 28(1) and 29(1) of the Animal Welfare Act 2006 (inspection in connection with licences, inspection in connection with registration, inspection of farm premises and inspection relating to Community obligations)][6]

[(*q*) regulation 23 of the Business Protection from Misleading Marketing Regulations 2008 (power of entry and investigation, etc);

(*r*) regulation 21 of the Consumer Protection from Unfair Trading Regulations 2008 (power of entry and investigation, etc);][7]

[(*s*) [regulation 33][12] of the Timeshare, Holiday Products, Resale and Exchange Contracts Regulations 2010 (powers of officers of enforcement authorities)][11].

(5) References in this Part to a power of seizure include references to each of the powers to take possession of items under—

(*a*) . . .[1];

(*b*) section 448(3) of the Companies Act 1985 (c 6);

(*c*) . . .[1];

(*d*) . . .[9]

(*e*) . . .[1];

(*f*) section 2(5) of the Criminal Justice Act 1987 (c 38);

(*g*) *section 40(2) of the Human Fertilisation and Embryology Act 1990 (c 37);*[10]

(*h*) section 28(2)(*c*) of the Competition Act 1998 (c 41); and

(*i*) section 176(5) of the Financial Services and Markets Act 2000 (c 8);

and references in this Part to seizure and to seized property shall be construed accordingly.

(6) In this Part, so far as it applies to England and Wales—

(*a*) references to excluded material shall be construed in accordance with section 11 of the 1984 Act (meaning of "excluded material"); and

(*b*) references to special procedure material shall be construed in accordance with section 14 of that Act (meaning of "special procedure material").

(7) In this Part, so far as it applies to Northern Ireland—

(*a*) references to excluded material shall be construed in accordance with Article 13 of the Police and Criminal Evidence (Northern Ireland) Order 1989 (SI 1989/1341 (NI 12)) (meaning of "excluded material"); and

(*b*) references to special procedure material shall be construed in accordance with Article 16 of that Order (meaning of "special procedure material").

(8) References in this Part to any item or material being comprised in other property include references to its being mixed with that other property.

(9) In this Part "enactment" includes an enactment contained in Northern Ireland legislation.

Amendments—[1] Sub-s (5)(*a*), (*c*), (*e*) repealed by the Financial Services and Markets Act 2000 (Consequential Amendments and Repeals) Order, SI 2001/3649 art 364(*c*) with effect from 1 December 2001.

[2] Sub-s (4)(*n*) inserted by the Human Tissue Act 2004 s 56, Sch 6 para 5(1), (3) with effect, for certain purposes, from 1 March 2006, for certain purposes, from 7 April 2006, and for other purposes from 1 September 2006. For commencement provisions, see the Human Tissue Act 2004 (Commencement No 4 and Transitional Provisions) Order, SI 2006/404 arts 2–4.

[3] Sub-s (4)(*n*) inserted by the General Product Safety Regulations, SI 2005/1803 reg 47 with effect from 1 October 2005 (reg 1(1)).

[4] Sub-s (4)(*g*) substituted by Weights and Measures (Packaged Goods) Regulations, SI 2006/659 reg 1(2), Sch 1 Pt2(24), (26) with effect from 6 April 2006.

[5] Sub-s (4)(*ma*) inserted by the Enterprise Act 2002 (Amendment) Regulations, SI 2006/3363 regs 24, 27 with effect from 8 January 2007.

[6] Sub-s (4)(*p*) inserted by the Animal Welfare Act 2006 s 64, Sch 3 para 14(2) with effect as follows—

– in relation to Wales, from 27 March 2007 (by virtue of SI 2007/1030 art 2(1)(*j*), (*l*));

– in relation to England, from 6 April 2007 (by virtue of SI 2007/499 art 2(2)(*l*));

– in relation to Scotland and Northern Ireland, from a date to be appointed.

[7] Sub-s (4)(*q*), (*r*) inserted, and sub-s (4)(i) repealed, by the Consumer Protection from Unfair Trading Regulations, SI 2008/1277 reg 30(*1*), (3), Sch 2 para 63, Sch 4 Pt 1 with effect from 26 May 2008.

[8] In sub-s (4)(*e*), words substituted for words "section 11(1) of the Estate Agents Act 1979", by the Consumers, Estate Agents and Redress Act 2007 s 63, Sch 7 para 22 with effect from 1 October 2008 (by virtue of SI 2008/2550 art 2, Schedule).

[9] Sub-s (5)(d) repealed by the Companies Act 2006 (Consequential Amendments, Transitional Provisions and Savings) Order, SI 2009/1941 art 2(1), Sch 1 para 189(1), (6) with effect from 1 October 2009.

[10] Sub-s (4)(*ja*) inserted, and sub-s (5)(*g*) repealed by the Human Fertilisation and Embryology Act 2008 s 65, Sch 7 para 20 with effect from 1 October 2009 (by virtue of SI 2009/2232, art 2(*t*), (*y*)).

[11] Sub-s (4)(*m*) repealed and sub-s (4)(*s*) inserted, by the Timeshare, Holiday Products, Resale and Exchange Contracts Regulations, SI 2010/2960 reg 36(3), (5), Sch 6 para 2(1), (3)(*a*), (*b*), Sch 8 Pt 1 with effect from 23 February 2011.

[12] Words in sub-s (4)(*s*) substituted by the Timeshare (Amendment) Regulations, SI 2011/1065 reg 2(1), (3) with effect from 28 April 2011.

13 Sub-s (4)(*k*) repealed by the Property Misdescription Act 1991 (Repeal) Order, SI 2013/1575 art 3, Schedule para 5 with effect from 1 October 2013.

Prospective amendments—Definition of "marine installation" to be inserted, and in definition of "premises", words "or other marine installation" to be inserted after word "installation", by the Marine and Coastal Access Act 2009 s 253(6) with effect from a date to be appointed. That definition to read as follows—

" 'marine installation' has the meaning given by section 262 of the Marine and Coastal Access Act 2009".

In sub-s (4), paras (*a*), (*c*)–(*g*), (*ma*), (*q*)–(*s*) to be repealed, in para (*h*), reference "29" to be substituted for "29(4)", in para (*o*), reference "22" to be substituted for "22(4)", and para (*t*) to be inserted by the Consumer Rights Act 2015 s 77(2), Sch 6 paras 61, 64 with effect from a date to be appointed. Sub-s (4)(*t*) as inserted to read as follows—

"(*t*) Part 4 of Schedule 5 to the Consumer Rights Act 2015".

Supplemental provisions of Part 2

67 Application to [officers of Revenue and Customs][1]

The powers conferred by section 114(2) of the 1984 Act and Article 85(1) of the Police and Criminal Evidence (Northern Ireland) Order 1989 (application of provisions relating to police officers to [officers of Revenue and Customs][1]) shall have effect in relation to the provisions of this Part as they have effect in relation to the provisions of that Act or, as the case may be, that Order.

Amendments—[1] In s 67 and heading to s 67, words substituted for words "customs officers" by FA 2007 s 84, Sch 22 para 2 with effect from 1 December 2007 (by virtue of SI 2007/3166 art 3(*a*)).

68 Application to Scotland

(1) In the application of this Part to Scotland—

(*a*) subsection (4) of section 54 and subsection (10) of section 59 shall each have effect with the omission of paragraph (*c*) of that subsection;

(*b*) section 55 and subsection (3)(*c*) of section 59 shall be omitted; and

(*c*) Schedule 1 shall have effect as if the powers specified in that Schedule did not include any power of seizure under any enactment mentioned in that Schedule, so far as it is exercisable in Scotland by a constable, except a power conferred by an enactment mentioned in subsection (2).

(2) Those enactments are—

(*a*) section 43(5) of the Gaming Act 1968 (c 65);

(*b*) . . . [1]

(*c*) section 448(3) of the Companies Act 1985 (c 6);

(*d*) . . . [1]

(*e*) . . . [1] and

(*f*) section 176(5) of the Financial Services and Markets Act 2000 (c 8).

[(*g*) regulation 39(6) of the Money Laundering Regulations 2007; and

(*h*) regulation 9(6) of the Transfer of Funds (Information on the Payer) Regulations 2007.][2]

Amendments—[1] Sub-s (2)(*b*), (*d*), (*e*) repealed by the Financial Services and Markets Act 2000 (Consequential Amendments and Repeals) Order, SI 2001/3649 art 364(*d*) with effect from 1 December 2001.

2 Sub-s (2)(*g*), (*h*) inserted by the Transfer of Funds (Information on the Payer) Regulations, SI 2007/3298 reg 19, Sch 3 para 2 with effect from 15 December 2007.

69 Application to powers designated by order

(1) The Secretary of State may by order—

(*a*) provide for any power designated by the order to be added to those specified in Schedule 1 or section 63(2);

(*b*) make any modification of the provisions of this Part which the Secretary of State considers appropriate in consequence of any provision made by virtue of paragraph (*a*);

(*c*) make any modification of any enactment making provision in relation to seizures, or things seized, under a power designated by an order under this subsection which the Secretary of State considers appropriate in consequence of any provision made by virtue of that paragraph.

(2) Where the power designated by the order made under subsection (1) is a power conferred in relation to Scotland, the Secretary of State shall consult the Scottish Ministers before making the order.

[(2A) Where the power designated by the order made under subsection (1) is a power conferred in relation to Northern Ireland, the Secretary of State shall consult the Department of Justice in Northern Ireland before making the order.][1]

(3) The power to make an order under subsection (1) shall be exercisable by statutory instrument; and no such order shall be made unless a draft of it has been laid before Parliament and approved by a resolution of each House.

(4) In this section "modification" includes any exclusion, extension or application.

Orders—Criminal Justice and Police Act 2001 (Powers of Seizure) Order, SI 2003/934.

Amendments—[1] Sub-s (2A) inserted by the Northern Ireland Act 1998 (Devolution of Policing and Justice Functions) Order, SI 2010/976 art 12, Sch 14 para 46(1), (3) with effect from 12 April 2010.

70 Consequential applications and amendments of enactments

Schedule 2 (which applies enactments in relation to provision made by this Part and contains minor and consequential amendments) shall have effect.

PART 6

MISCELLANEOUS AND SUPPLEMENTAL

Supplemental

136 General interpretation

In this Act—

"the 1984 Act" means the Police and Criminal Evidence Act 1984 (c 60);
"the 1996 Act" means the Police Act 1996 (c 16); and
"the 1997 Act" means the Police Act 1997 (c 50).

137 Repeals

The enactments and instruments mentioned in Schedule 7 (which include spent provisions) are hereby repealed or (as the case may be) revoked to the extent specified in the third column of that Schedule.

138 Short title, commencement and extent

(1) This Act may be cited as the Criminal Justice and Police Act 2001.
(2) The provisions of this Act, other than this section and sections 42 and 43, 81 to 85, 109, 116(7) and 119(7), shall come into force on such day as the Secretary of State may by order made by statutory instrument appoint; and different days may be appointed under this subsection for different purposes.
(3) An order under subsection (2) may contain such savings as the Secretary of State thinks fit.
(4) Section 85 comes into force at the end of the period of two months beginning with the day on which this Act is passed.
(5) Subject to subsections (6) to (12), this Act extends to England and Wales only.
(6) The following provisions of this Act extend to the United Kingdom—

(*a*) sections 33 to 38;
(*b*) Part 2;
(*c*) section 86(1) and (2);
(*d*) . . . [1]
(*e*) section 127; and
(*f*) section 136 and this section.

(7) . . . [2]
(8) Section 126 extends to Great Britain only.
(9) Sections 29, 39 to 41, 72, 75, 84 and 134 extend to England and Wales and Northern Ireland only.
(10) Section 83 extends to Northern Ireland only.
(11) Section 86(3) has the same extent as section 27 of the Petty Sessions (Ireland) Act 1851 (c 93).
(12) An amendment, repeal or revocation contained in Schedule 4, 6 or 7 has the same extent as the enactment or instrument to which it relates.

Amendments—[1] Sub-s (6)(*d*) repealed by the Serious Organised Crime and Police Act 2005 ss 59, 174(2), Sch 4 paras 162, 167, Sch 17 Pt 2 with effect from 1 April 2006 (by virtue of SI 2006/378 art 4(1), Schedule para 10).
[2] Sub-s (7) repealed by the Companies Act 2006 (Consequential Amendments, Transitional Provisions and Savings) Order, SI 2009/1941 art 2(2), Sch 2 with effect from 1 October 2009.

SCHEDULES

SCHEDULE 2

APPLICATIONS AND MINOR AND CONSEQUENTIAL AMENDMENTS

PART 1

APPLICATION OF ENACTMENTS

. . .

Disclosure of information

11 Any provision which—

(*a*) restricts the disclosure, or permits the disclosure only for limited purposes or in limited circumstances, of information obtained through the exercise of a power of seizure specified in Part 1 or 2 of Schedule 1, or

(*b*) confers power to make provision which does either or both of those things,

shall apply in relation to information obtained under section 50 or 51 in reliance on the power in question as it applies in relation to information obtained through the exercise of that power.

Interpretation

12 For the purposes of this Part of this Schedule, an item is seized, or information is obtained, under section 50 or 51 in reliance on a power of seizure if the item is seized, or the information obtained, in exercise of so much of any power conferred by that section as is exercisable by reference to that power of seizure.

PART 2

MINOR AND CONSEQUENTIAL AMENDMENTS

13 (1) In each of the provisions mentioned in sub-paragraph (2) (which confer powers to require the production of information contained in a computer in a visible and legible form)—

(*a*) for "contained in a computer" there shall be substituted "stored in any electronic form"; and

(*b*) after "in which it is visible and legible" there shall be inserted "or from which it can readily be produced in a visible and legible form".

(2) Those provisions are—

. . .

(*f*) paragraph 11(4) of Schedule 11 to the Value Added Tax Act 1994 (c. 23);

(*g*) paragraph 4A(4) of Schedule 7 to the Finance Act 1994 (c. 9);

(*h*) paragraph 7(4) of Schedule 5 to the Finance Act 1996 (c. 8);

(*i*) paragraph 131(4) of Schedule 6 to the Finance Act 2000 (c. 17).

Note—Words omitted from this Schedule are not relevant to this publication.

ANTI-TERRORISM, CRIME AND SECURITY ACT 2001

(2001 Chapter 24)

An Act to amend the Terrorism Act 2000; to make further provision about terrorism and security; . . . ; and for connected purposes.

[14 December 2001]

PART 3

DISCLOSURE OF INFORMATION

17 Extension of existing disclosure powers

(1) This section applies to the provisions listed in Schedule 4, so far as they authorise the disclosure of information.

(2) Each of the provisions to which this section applies shall have effect, in relation to the disclosure of information by or on behalf of a public authority, as if the purposes for which the disclosure of information is authorised by that provision included each of the following—

(*a*) the purposes of any criminal investigation whatever which is being or may be carried out, whether in the United Kingdom or elsewhere;

(*b*) the purposes of any criminal proceedings whatever which have been or may be initiated, whether in the United Kingdom or elsewhere;

(*c*) the purposes of the initiation or bringing to an end of any such investigation or proceedings;

(*d*) the purpose of facilitating a determination of whether any such investigation or proceedings should be initiated or brought to an end.

(3) The Treasury may by order made by statutory instrument add any provision contained in any subordinate legislation to the provisions to which this section applies.

(4) The Treasury shall not make an order under subsection (3) unless a draft of it has been laid before Parliament and approved by a resolution of each House.

(5) No disclosure of information shall be made by virtue of this section unless the public authority by which the disclosure is made is satisfied that the making of the disclosure is proportionate to what is sought to be achieved by it.

(6) Nothing in this section shall be taken to prejudice any power to disclose information which exists apart from this section.

(7) The information that may be disclosed by virtue of this section includes information obtained before the commencement of this section.

18 Restriction on disclosure of information for overseas purposes

(1) Subject to subsections (2) and (3), the Secretary of State may give a direction which—

(*a*) specifies any overseas proceedings or any description of overseas proceedings; and

(*b*) prohibits the making of any relevant disclosure for the purposes of those proceedings or, as the case may be, of proceedings of that description.

(2) In subsection (1) the reference, in relation to a direction, to a relevant disclosure is a reference to a disclosure authorised by any of the provisions to which section 17 applies which—

(*a*) is made for a purpose mentioned in subsection (2)(*a*) to (*d*) of that section; and
(*b*) is a disclosure of any such information as is described in the direction.

(3) The Secretary of State shall not give a direction under this section unless it appears to him that the overseas proceedings in question, or that overseas proceedings of the description in question, relate or would relate—
(*a*) to a matter in respect of which it would be more appropriate for any jurisdiction or investigation to be exercised or carried out by a court or other authority of the United Kingdom, or of a particular part of the United Kingdom;
(*b*) to a matter in respect of which it would be more appropriate for any jurisdiction or investigation to be exercised or carried out by a court or other authority of a third country; or
(*c*) to a matter that would fall within paragraph (*a*) or (*b*)—
(i) if it were appropriate for there to be any exercise of jurisdiction or investigation at all; and
(ii) if (where one does not exist) a court or other authority with the necessary jurisdiction or functions existed in the United Kingdom, in the part of the United Kingdom in question or, as the case may be, in the third country in question.

(4) A direction under this section shall not have the effect of prohibiting—
(*a*) the making of any disclosure by a Minister of the Crown or by the Treasury; or
(*b*) the making of any disclosure in pursuance of a Community obligation.

(5) A direction under this section—
(*a*) may prohibit the making of disclosures absolutely or in such cases, or subject to such conditions as to consent or otherwise, as may be specified in it; and
(*b*) must be published or otherwise issued by the Secretary of State in such manner as he considers appropriate for bringing it to the attention of persons likely to be affected by it.

(6) A person who, knowing of any direction under this section, discloses any information in contravention of that direction shall be guilty of an offence and liable—
(*a*) on conviction on indictment, to imprisonment for a term not exceeding two years or to a fine or to both;
(*b*) on summary conviction, to imprisonment for a term not exceeding three months or to a fine not exceeding the statutory maximum or to both.

(7) The following are overseas proceedings for the purposes of this section—
(*a*) criminal proceedings which are taking place, or will or may take place, in a country or territory outside the United Kingdom;
(*b*) a criminal investigation which is being, or will or may be, conducted by an authority of any such country or territory.

(8) References in this section, in relation to any proceedings or investigation, to a third country are references to any country or territory outside the United Kingdom which is not the country or territory where the proceedings are taking place, or will or may take place or, as the case may be, is not the country or territory of the authority which is conducting the investigation, or which will or may conduct it.

(9) In this section "court" includes a tribunal of any description.

19 Disclosure of information held by revenue departments

(1) This section applies to information which is held by or on behalf of the Commissioners of Inland Revenue or by or on behalf of the Commissioners of Customs and Excise, including information obtained before the coming into force of this section.

(2) No obligation of secrecy imposed by statute or otherwise prevents the disclosure, in accordance with the following provisions of this section, of information to which this section applies if the disclosure is made—
(*a*) . . . [1]
(*b*) for the purposes of any criminal investigation whatever which is being or may be carried out, whether in the United Kingdom or elsewhere;
(*c*) for the purposes of any criminal proceedings whatever which have been or may be initiated, whether in the United Kingdom or elsewhere;
(*d*) for the purposes of the initiation or bringing to an end of any such investigation or proceedings; or
(*e*) for the purpose of facilitating a determination of whether any such investigation or proceedings should be initiated or brought to an end.

(3) No disclosure of information to which this section applies shall be made by virtue of this section unless the person by whom the disclosure is made is satisfied that the making of the disclosure is proportionate to what is sought to be achieved by it.

(4) Information to which this section applies shall not be disclosed by virtue of this section except by the Commissioners by or on whose behalf it is held or with their authority.

(5) Information obtained by means of a disclosure authorised by subsection (2) shall not be further disclosed except—
(*a*) for a purpose mentioned in that subsection; and

(*b*) with the consent of the Commissioners by whom or with whose authority it was initially disclosed;

and information so obtained otherwise than by or on behalf of any of the intelligence services shall not be further disclosed (with or without such consent) to any of those services, or to any person acting on behalf of any of those services, except for a purpose mentioned in paragraphs (*b*) to (*e*) of that subsection.

(6) A consent for the purposes of subsection (5) may be given either in relation to a particular disclosure or in relation to disclosures made in such circumstances as may be specified or described in the consent.

(7) Nothing in this section authorises the making of any disclosure which is prohibited by any provision of the Data Protection Act 1998.

(8) References in this section to information which is held on behalf of the Commissioners of Inland Revenue or of the Commissioners of Customs & Excise include references to information which—

(*a*) is held by a person who provides services to the Commissioners of Inland Revenue or, as the case may be, to the Commissioners of Customs and Excise; and

(*b*) is held by that person in connection with the provision of those services.

(9) In this section "intelligence service" has the same meaning as in the Regulation of Investigatory Powers Act 2000.

(10) Nothing in this section shall be taken to prejudice any power to disclose information which exists apart from this section.

Amendments—[1] Sub-s (2)(*a*) repealed by the Counter-Terrorism Act 2008 ss 20(4), 99, Sch 1 para 1, Sch 9 Pt 2 with effect from 24 December 2008 (by virtue of SI 2008/3296 art 2).

20 Interpretation of Part 3

Amendments—This para repealed by the Property Misdescriptions Act 1991 (Repeal) Order, SI 2013/1575 art 3, Schedule para 7 with effect from 1 October 2013.

PART 14

SUPPLEMENTAL

127 Commencement

(1) Except as provided in subsections (2) to (4), this Act comes into force on such day as the Secretary of State may appoint by order.

(2) The following provisions come into force on the day on which this Act is passed—

(*a*) Parts 2 to 6,

(*b*)–(*h*) . . .

(*i*) this Part, except section 125 and Schedule 8 so far as they relate to the entries—

(i) in Part 1 of Schedule 8,

(ii) in Part 5 of Schedule 8, in respect of the Nuclear Installations Act 1965,

(iii) in Part 6 of Schedule 8, in respect of the British Transport Commission Act 1962 and the Ministry of Defence Police Act 1987, so far as those entries extend to Scotland,

(iv) in Part 7 of Schedule 8, in respect of Schedule 5 to the Terrorism Act 2000.

(3), (4) . . .

(5) Different days may be appointed for different provisions and for different purposes.

(6) An order under this section—

(*a*) must be made by statutory instrument, and

(*b*) may contain incidental, supplemental, consequential or transitional provision.

Note—Sub-ss (2)(*b*)–(*h*), (3), (4) are outside the scope of this work.

129 Short title

This Act may be cited as the Anti-terrorism, Crime and Security Act 2001.

FINANCE ACT 2002

(2002 Chapter 23)

An Act to grant certain duties, to alter other duties, and to amend the law relating to the National Debt and the Public Revenue, and to make further provision in connection with Finance.

[24 July 2002]

PART 2

VALUE ADDED TAX

22 Disallowance of input tax where consideration not paid

(1) (*inserts* VATA 1994 s 26A).

(2) (*repeals* VATA 1994 s 36(4A), (5)(*ea*)).

(3) This section has effect in relation to supplies made on or after such day as the Commissioners of Customs and Excise may appoint by order made by statutory instrument.

Commentary—*De Voil Indirect Tax Service* **V5.157.**
Orders—Finance Act 2002, section 22, (Appointed Day) Order, SI 2002/3028 (the appointed day is 1 January 2003).

23 Flat-rate scheme

(1) (*inserts* VATA 1994 s 26B).
(2) (*inserts* VATA 1994 s 83(*fza*)).
(3) (*inserts* VATA 1994 s 84(4ZA)).
(4) This section shall be deemed to have come into force on 24th April 2002.

Commentary—*De Voil Indirect Tax Service* **V2.199B.**

24 Invoices

(1) (*repeals* VATA 1994 s 6(9) and *amends* VATA 1994 Sch 11 para 2).
(2) (*inserts* VATA 1994 Sch 11 paras 2A, 2B)
(3) (*substitutes* VATA 1994 Sch 11 para 3)
(4) The following amendments to the Value Added Tax Act 1994 (c 23) are consequential on other amendments made by this section—

(*a*) (*amends* VATA 1994 s 6(15))
(*b*) (*substitutes* VATA 1994 s 83(*z*))
(*c*) (*amends* VATA 1994 s 88(5), (6))

(5) This section comes into force on such day as the Treasury may by order made by statutory instrument appoint, and different days may be appointed for different provisions or different purposes.
(6) An order under subsection (5) may contain such transitional provisions and savings as appear to the Treasury necessary or expedient in connection with the provisions brought into force.

Commentary—*De Voil Indirect Tax Service* **V3.513–516**, **V3.523.**
Orders—Finance Act 2002, section 24, (Appointed Day) Order 2003, SI 2003/3043 (the appointed day is 1 December 2003).

25 Relief from VAT on acquisition if importation would attract relief

(*inserts* VATA 1994 s 36A).

PART 6
MISCELLANEOUS AND SUPPLEMENTARY PROVISIONS

Recovery of taxes etc due in other member States

134 Recovery of taxes etc due in other member States

Amendments—Section 134, Schedule 39 repealed by FA 2011 s 87, Sch 25 para 17(1) with effect from 1 January 2012. Note that any outstanding request for assistance made in accordance with Council Directive 2008/55/EC before that date is to be treated on and after that date for the purposes of FA 2011 Sch 25 as if it had been made in accordance with Council Directive 2010/24/EU.

Mandatory e-filing

135 Mandatory e-filing

(1) [The Commissioners for Her Majesty's Revenue and Customs][2] ("the Commissioners") may make regulations requiring the use of electronic communications for the delivery by specified persons of specified information required or authorised to be delivered by or under legislation relating to a taxation matter.
(2) Regulations under this section may make provision—

(*a*) as to the electronic form to be taken by information delivered to the [Revenue and Customs][1] using electronic communications;
(*b*) requiring persons to prepare and keep records of information delivered to [Revenue and Customs][1] by means of electronic communications;
(*c*) for the production of the contents of records kept in accordance with the regulations;
(*d*) as to conditions that must be complied with in connection with the use of electronic communications for the delivery of information;
(*e*) for treating information as not having been delivered unless conditions imposed by any of the regulations are satisfied;
(*f*) for determining the time at which and person by whom information is to be taken to have been delivered;
(*g*) for authenticating whatever is delivered.

(3) Regulations under this section may also make provision (which may include provision for the application of conclusive or other presumptions) as to the manner of proving for any purpose—

(*a*) whether any use of electronic communications is to be taken as having resulted in the delivery of information;
(*b*) the time of delivery of any information for the delivery of which electronic communications have been used;
(*c*) the person by whom information delivered by means of electronic communications was delivered;
(*d*) the contents of anything so delivered;
(*e*) the contents of any records;

(*f*) any other matter for which provision may be made by regulations under this section.

(4) Regulations under this section may—

(*a*) allow any authorisation or requirement for which the regulations may provide to be given or imposed by means of a specific or general direction given by the Commissioners;

(*b*) provide that the conditions of any such authorisation or requirement are to be taken to be satisfied only where the [Revenue and Customs][1]are satisfied as to specified matters;

(*c*) allow a person to refuse to accept delivery of information in an electronic form or by means of electronic communications except in such circumstances as may be specified in or determined under the regulations;

(*d*) allow or require use to be made of intermediaries in connection with—

(i) the delivery of information by means of electronic communications; or

(ii) the authentication or security of anything transmitted by any such means.

(5) Regulations under this section may contain provision—

(*a*) requiring the [Revenue and Customs][1]to notify persons appearing to them to be, or to have become, a person of a specified description and accordingly required to use electronic communications for any purpose in accordance with the regulations,

(*b*) enabling a person so notified to have the question whether he is a person of such a description determined in the same way as an appeal.

(6) Regulations under this section may provide—

(*a*) that information delivered by means of electronic communications must meet standards of accuracy and completeness set by specific or general directions given by the Commissioners, and

(*b*) that failure to meet those standards may be treated—

(i) as a failure to deliver the information, or

(ii) as a failure to comply with the requirements of the regulations.

(7) The power to make provision by regulations under this section includes power—

(*a*) to provide for a contravention of, or any failure to comply with, the regulations to attract a penalty of a specified amount not exceeding £3,000;

(*b*) to provide that specified enactments relating to penalties imposed for the purposes of any taxation matter (including enactments relating to assessments, review and appeal) apply, with or without modifications, in relation to penalties under the regulations;

[(*ba*) to specify other consequences of contravention of, or failure to comply with, the regulations (which may include disregarding a return delivered otherwise than by the use of electronic communications);][2]

(*c*) to make different provision for different cases;

(*d*) to make such incidental, supplemental, consequential and transitional provision in connection with any provision contained in any of the regulations as the Commissioners think fit.

(8) References in this section to the delivery of information include references to any of the following (however referred to)—

(*a*) the production or furnishing to a person of any information, account, record or document;

(*b*) the giving, making, issue or surrender to, or service on, any person of any notice, notification, statement, declaration, certificate or direction;

(*c*) the imposition on any person of any requirement or the issue to any person of any request;

(*d*) the making of any return, claim, election or application;

(*e*) the amendment or withdrawal of anything mentioned in paragraphs (*a*) to (*d*) above.

(9) Regulations under this section shall be made by statutory instrument subject to annulment in pursuance of a resolution of the House of Commons.

(10) In this section—

["the Revenue and Customs" means—

(*a*) the Commissioners,

(*b*) any officer of Revenue and Customs, and

(*c*) any other person who for the purposes of electronic communications is acting under the authority of the Commissioners;][1]

"legislation" means any enactment, Community legislation or subordinate legislation;

"specified" means specified by or under regulations under this section;

"subordinate legislation" has the same meaning as in the Interpretation Act 1978 (c 30);

["taxation matter" means any matter relating to a tax (or duty) for which the Commissioners are responsible.][2]

Regulations—Tax Avoidance Schemes (Information) Regulations, SI 2004/1864.

Registered Pension Schemes and Overseas Pension Schemes (Electronic Communication of Returns and Information) Regulations, SI 2006/570.

VAT (Amendment) Regulations, SI 2012/33

VAT (Amendment) (No 2) Regulations, SI 2014/1497.

Amendments—[1] Words substituted and definition in sub-s (10) substituted by CRCA 2005 s 50, Sch 4 paras 94, 95 with effect from 18 April 2005 (by virtue of SI 2005/1126).

[2] Sub-s (7)(ba) inserted, and in sub-s (10), definition of "taxation matter" substituted, by FA 2007 s 93(1)–(3) with effect from 19 July 2007.

136 Use of electronic communications under other provisions

(1) Any power to make subordinate legislation for or in connection with the delivery of information conferred in relation to a taxation matter on—

(*a*) the Commissioners of Inland Revenue, or

(*b*) the Treasury,

includes power to make any such provision in relation to the delivery of that information as could be made in exercise of the power conferred by section 135.

(2) Provision made in exercise of the powers conferred by section 135 or subsection (1) above has effect notwithstanding so much of any enactment or subordinate legislation as would otherwise—

(*a*) allow information to be delivered otherwise than by means of electronic communications, or

(*b*) preclude the use of an intermediary in connection with its delivery.

(3) Expressions used in this section and section 135 have the same meaning in this section as in that section.

(4) Nothing in this section shall be read as restricting the generality of the power conferred by section 135.

Regulations—VAT (Amendment) Regulations, SI 2012/33
VAT (Amendment) (No 2) Regulations, SI 2014/1497.

Supplementary

141 Repeals

(1) The enactments mentioned in Schedule 40 to this Act (which include provisions that are spent or of no practical utility) are repealed to the extent specified.

(2) The repeals specified in that Schedule have effect subject to the commencement provisions and savings contained or referred to in the notes set out in that Schedule.

143 Short title

This Act may be cited as the Finance Act 2002.

SCHEDULES

SCHEDULE 39

RECOVERY OF TAXES ETC DUE IN OTHER MEMBER STATES

Section 134(1)

Amendments—Schedule 39 repealed by FA 2011 s 87, Sch 25 para 17(1) with effect from 1 January 2012. Note that any outstanding request for assistance made in accordance with Council Directive 2008/55/EC before that date is to be treated on and after that date for the purposes of FA 2011 Sch 25 as if it had been made in accordance with Council Directive 2010/24/EU.

POLICE REFORM ACT 2002

(2002 c 30)

An Act to make new provision about the supervision, administration, functions and conduct of police forces, police officers and other persons serving with, or carrying out functions in relation to, the police; to amend police powers and to provide for the exercise of police powers by persons who are not police officers; to amend the law relating to anti-social behaviour orders; to amend the law relating to sex offender orders; and for connected purposes.

[24 July 2002]

Note—For the text of this legislation as modified to apply to Her Majesty's Revenue and Customs, please refer to Part 1 of *Tolley's Yellow Tax Handbook*.

FINANCE ACT 2003

(2003 Chapter 14)

ARRANGEMENT OF SECTIONS

PART 2

VALUE ADDED TAX

An Act to grant certain duties, to alter other duties, and to amend the law relating to the National Debt and the Public Revenue, and to make further provision in connection with finance.

[10 July 2003]

PART 2

VALUE ADDED TAX

17 Requirement of evidence or security

(1) The Value Added Tax Act 1994 (c 23) is amended as follows.

(2)–(7) (*amend* ss 24(6), 72(11), 83(*l*), 84, Sch 11 para 4)

(8) This section shall be deemed to have come into force on 10th April 2003.

Commentary—*De Voil Indirect Tax Service* **V3.415, V5.186.**

18 Joint and several liability for unpaid VAT of another trader

(1)–(3) (*insert* VATA 1994 ss 77A(1), 83(*ra*), *amend* s 84(3))

(4) This section shall be deemed to have come into force on 10th April 2003 except subsection (3) which applies in relation to any appeal notice of which is given on or after the day on which this Act is passed.

Commentary—*De Voil Indirect Tax Service* **V5.171.**

19 Face-value vouchers

Schedule 1 to this Act (VAT: face-value vouchers) has effect.

Commentary—*De Voil Indirect Tax Service* **V3.166.**

20 Supplies arising from prior grant of fee simple

(1) (*inserts* VATA 1994 s 96(10B))

(2) This section applies in relation to any supply that arises for the purposes of the Value Added Tax Act 1994 (c 23) from the prior grant of a fee simple made on or after 9th April 2003.

Commentary—*De Voil Indirect Tax Service* **V3.140, V4.113.**

21 Business gifts

(1) In Schedule 4 to the Value Added Tax Act 1994 (matters to be treated as supply of goods or services), paragraph 5 (business gifts etc) is amended as follows.

(2), (3) (*amend* sub-paras (2), *insert* sub-para 2ZA)

(4) This section applies in relation to gifts made on or after 1st October 2003.

Commentary—*De Voil Indirect Tax Service* **V3.211, V6.120A.**

22 Non-business use of business property

(*inserted* VATA 1994 Sch 4 para 5(4A); *repealed by* FA 2007 s 114, Sch 27 Pt 6(1) in accordance with FA 2007 s 99)

23 Supply of electronic services in member States: special accounting scheme

(1) Schedule 2 to this Act (scheme enabling persons who supply certain electronic services in any member State, but who are not established in a member State, to account for and pay VAT in the United Kingdom on those supplies) has effect.

(2) The amendments made by that Schedule have effect in relation to qualifying supplies made on or after 1st July 2003.

Commentary—*De Voil Indirect Tax Service* **V3.196, V2.106.**

PART 3

TAXES AND DUTIES ON IMPORTATION AND EXPORTATION: PENALTIES

Commentary—*De Voil Indirect Tax Service* **V3.311, V5.301, V5.331.**

Note—The appointed day for the purposes of this Part is 27 November 2003 (by virtue of SI 2003/2985).

Preliminary

24 Introductory

(1) This Part makes provision for and in connection with the imposition of liability to a penalty where a person—

(*a*) engages in any conduct for the purpose of evading any relevant tax or duty, or

(*b*) engages in any conduct by which he contravenes a duty, obligation, requirement or condition imposed by or under legislation relating to any relevant tax or duty.

(2) For the purposes of this Part "relevant tax or duty" means any of the following—

(*a*) customs duty;

(*b*) Community export duty;

(*c*) Community import duty;

(*d*) import VAT;

(*e*) customs duty of a preferential tariff country.

(3) In this Part—

"appeal tribunal" means [the First-tier Tribunal or, where determined by or under Tribunal Procedure Rules, the Upper Tribunal][1];

"the Commissioners" means the Commissioners of Customs and Excise;
"the Community Customs Code" means Council Regulation 2913/92/EEC establishing the Community Customs Code;
"Community export duty" means any of the duties, charges or levies which are export duties within the meaning of the Community Customs Code (as at 9th April 2003, see the definition of "export duties" in Article 4(11) of that Code);
"Community import duty" means any of the duties, charges or levies which are import duties within the meaning of the Community Customs Code (as at 9th April 2003, see the definition of "import duties" in Article 4(10) of that Code);
"contravene" includes fail to comply with;
"customs duty of a preferential tariff country" includes a reference to any charge imposed by a preferential tariff country and having an equivalent effect to customs duty payable on the importation of goods into the territory of that country;
"demand notice" means a demand notice within the meaning of section 30;
["HMRC" means "Her Majesty's Revenue and Customs.][1]
"import VAT" means value added tax chargeable by virtue of section 1(1)(*c*) of the Value Added Tax Act 1994 (c 23) (importation of goods from places outside the member States);
"notice" means notice in writing;
"preferential tariff country" means a country outside the European Community which is, or is a member of a group of countries which is, party to an agreement falling within Article 20(3)(*d*) of the Community Customs Code (preferential tariff agreements with the Community);
"prescribed" means specified in, or determined in accordance with, regulations made by the Treasury;
"relevant rule", in relation to any relevant tax or duty, has the meaning given by subsection (8) of section 26 (as read with subsection (9) of that section);
"representative", in relation to any person, means—

(*a*) his personal representative,
(*b*) his trustee in bankruptcy or interim or permanent trustee,
(*c*) any receiver or liquidator appointed in relation to that person or any of his property,

or any other person acting in a representative capacity in relation to that person.

(4) References in this Part to the Community Customs Code are references to that Code as from time to time amended, whether before or after the coming into force of this Part.

(5) The Treasury may by order amend this Part for the purpose of replacing any reference to, or to a provision of,—

(*a*) the Community Customs Code, or
(*b*) any instrument referred to in this Part by virtue of an order under this subsection,

with a reference to, or (as the case may be) to a provision of, a different instrument.

(6) A statutory instrument containing an order under subsection (5) may not be made unless a draft of the instrument has been laid before, and approved by a resolution of, the House of Commons.

(7) Except for this subsection and section 41 (which accordingly come into force on the passing of this Act), this Part comes into force on such day as the Treasury may by order appoint.

Regulations—Finance Act 2003, Part 3, (Appointed Day) Order 2003, SI 2003/2985 (appoints 27 November 2003 as the date for Part 3 to come into force).
Customs (Contravention of a Relevant Rule) (Amendment) Regulations, SI 2015/636.

Amendment—[1] In sub-s (3) words in the definition of "appeal tribunal" substituted for the words "VAT and duties tribunal"; definition of "HMRC" inserted by the Transfer of Tribunal Functions and Revenue and Customs Appeals Order, SI 2009/56 art 3, Sch 1 para 360 with effect from 1 April 2009.

The penalties

25 Penalty for evasion

(1) In any case where—

(*a*) a person engages in any conduct for the purpose of evading any relevant tax or duty, and
(*b*) his conduct involves dishonesty (whether or not such as to give rise to any criminal liability),

that person is liable to a penalty of an amount equal to the amount of the tax or duty evaded or, as the case may be, sought to be evaded.

(2) Subsection (1) is subject to the following provisions of this Part.

(3) Nothing in this section applies in relation to any customs duty of a preferential tariff country.

(4) Any reference in this section to a person's "evading" any relevant tax or duty includes a reference to his obtaining or securing, without his being entitled to it,—

(*a*) any repayment, rebate or drawback of any relevant tax or duty,
(*b*) any relief or exemption from, or any allowance against, any relevant tax or duty, or
(*c*) any deferral or other postponement of his liability to pay any relevant tax or duty or of the discharge by payment of any such liability,

and also includes a reference to his evading the cancellation of any entitlement to, or the withdrawal of, any such repayment, rebate, drawback, relief, exemption or allowance.

(5) In relation to any such evasion of any relevant tax or duty as is mentioned in subsection (4), the reference in subsection (1) to the amount of the tax or duty evaded or sought to be evaded is a reference to the amount of—

(*a*) the repayment, rebate or drawback,

(*b*) the relief, exemption or allowance, or

(*c*) the payment which, or the liability to make which, is deferred or otherwise postponed,

as the case may be.

(6) Where, by reason of conduct falling within subsection (1) in the case of any relevant tax or duty, a person—

(*a*) is convicted of an offence,

(*b*) is given, and has not had withdrawn, a demand notice in respect of a penalty to which he is liable under section 26, or

(*c*) is liable to a penalty imposed upon him under any other provision of the law relating to that relevant tax or duty,

that conduct does not also give rise to liability to a penalty under this section in respect of that relevant tax or duty.

26 Penalty for contravention of relevant rule

(1) If, in the case of any relevant tax or duty, a person of a prescribed description engages in any conduct by which he contravenes—

(*a*) a prescribed relevant rule, or

(*b*) a relevant rule of a prescribed description,

he is liable to a penalty under this section of a prescribed amount.

(2) Subsection (1) is subject to the following provisions of this Part.

(3) The power conferred by subsection (1) to prescribe a description of person includes power to prescribe any person (without further qualification) as such a description.

(4) Different penalties may be prescribed under subsection (1) for different cases or different circumstances.

(5) Any amount prescribed under subsection (1) as the amount of a penalty must not be more than £2,500.

(6) The Treasury may by order amend subsection (5) by substituting a different amount for the amount for the time being specified in that subsection.

(7) A statutory instrument containing an order under subsection (6) may not be made unless a draft of the instrument has been laid before, and approved by a resolution of, the House of Commons.

(8) In this Part "relevant rule", in relation to any relevant tax or duty, means any duty, obligation, requirement or condition imposed by or under any of the following—

(*a*) the Customs and Excise Management Act 1979 (c 2), as it applies in relation to the relevant tax or duty;

(*b*) any other Act, or any statutory instrument, as it applies in relation to the relevant tax or duty;

(*c*) in the case of customs duty, Community export duty or Community import duty, Community customs rules;

(*d*) in the case of import VAT, Community customs rules as they apply in relation to import VAT;

(*e*) any directly applicable Community legislation relating to the relevant tax or duty;

(*f*) any relevant international rules applying in relation to the relevant tax or duty.

(9) In subsection (8)—

"Community customs rules" means customs rules, as defined in Article 1 of the Community Customs Code;

"relevant international rules" means international agreements so far as applying in relation to a relevant tax or duty and having effect as part of the law of any part of the United Kingdom by virtue of—

(*a*) any Act or statutory instrument, or

(*b*) any directly applicable Community legislation.

Cross-references—See FA 2014 s 102 (application of FA 2003 ss 26, 27 and 29–41 in relation to excise duty).
Regulations—Customs (Contravention of a Relevant Rule) Regulations, SI 2003/3113.
Customs (Contravention of a Relevant Rule) (Amendment) Regulations, SI 2015/636.

27 Exceptions from section 26

(1) A person is not liable to a penalty under section 26 if he satisfies—

(*a*) the Commissioners, or

(*b*) on appeal, an appeal tribunal,

that there is a reasonable excuse for his conduct.

(2) For the purposes of subsection (1) none of the following is a reasonable excuse—

(*a*) an insufficiency of funds available to any person for paying any relevant tax or duty or any penalty due;

(*b*) that reliance was placed by any person on another to perform any task;

(*c*) that the contravention is attributable, in whole or in part, to the conduct of a person on whom reliance to perform any task was so placed.

(3) Where, by reason of conduct falling within subsection (1) of section 26 in the case of any relevant tax or duty, a person—

(*a*) is prosecuted for an offence,

(*b*) is given, and has not had withdrawn, a demand notice in respect of a penalty to which he is liable under section 25, or

(*c*) is liable to a penalty imposed upon him under any other provision of the law relating to that relevant tax or duty,

that conduct does not also give rise to liability to a penalty under section 26 in respect of that relevant tax or duty.

(4) A person is not liable to a penalty under section 26 in respect of any conduct, so far as relating to import VAT, if in respect of that conduct—

(*a*) he is liable to a penalty under any of sections 62 to 69A of the Value Added Tax Act 1994 (c 23) (penalty for contravention of statutory requirements as to VAT), or

(*b*) he would be so liable but for section 62(4), 63(11), 64(6), 67(9), 69(9) or 69A(7) of that Act (conduct resulting in conviction, different penalty etc).

Cross-references—See FA 2014 s 102 (application of FA 2003 ss 26, 27 and 29–41 in relation to excise duty).

28 Liability of directors etc where body corporate liable to penalty for evasion

(1) Where it appears to the Commissioners—

(*a*) that a body corporate is liable to a penalty under section 25, and

(*b*) that the conduct giving rise to the penalty is, in whole or in part, attributable to the dishonesty of a person who is, or at the material time was, a director or managing officer of the body corporate (a "relevant officer"),

the Commissioners may give a notice under this section to the body corporate (or its representative) and to the relevant officer (or his representative).

(2) A notice under this section must state—

(*a*) the amount of the penalty referred to in subsection (1)(*a*) (the "basic penalty"), and

(*b*) that the Commissioners propose, in accordance with this section, to recover from the relevant officer such portion (which may be the whole) of the basic penalty as is specified in the notice.

(3) If a notice is given under this section, this Part shall apply in relation to the relevant officer as if he were personally liable under section 25 to a penalty which corresponds to that portion of the basic penalty specified in the notice.

(4) If a notice is given under this section—

(*a*) the amount which may be recovered from the body corporate under this Part is limited to so much (if any) of the basic penalty as is not recoverable from the relevant officer by virtue of subsection (3), and

(*b*) the body corporate is to be treated as discharged from liability for so much of the basic penalty as is so recoverable from the relevant officer.

(5) In this section "managing officer", in relation to a body corporate, means—

(*a*) a manager, secretary or other similar officer of the body corporate, or

(*b*) a person purporting to act in any such capacity or as a director.

(6) Where the affairs of a body corporate are managed by its members, this section applies in relation to the conduct of a member in connection with his functions of management as if he were a director of the body corporate.

Reduction of amount of penalty

29 Reduction of penalty under section 25 or 26

(1) Where a person is liable to a penalty under section 25 or 26—

(*a*) the Commissioners (whether originally or on review) or, on appeal, an appeal tribunal may reduce the penalty to such amount (including nil) as they think proper; and

(*b*) the Commissioners on a review, or an appeal tribunal on an appeal, relating to a penalty reduced by the Commissioners under this subsection may cancel the whole or any part of the reduction previously made by the Commissioners.

(2) In exercising their powers under subsection (1), neither the Commissioners nor an appeal tribunal are entitled to take into account any of the matters specified in subsection (3).

(3) Those matters are—

(*a*) the insufficiency of the funds available to any person for paying any relevant tax or duty or the amount of the penalty,

(*b*) the fact that there has, in the case in question or in that case taken with any other cases, been no or no significant loss of any relevant tax or duty,

(*c*) the fact that the person liable to the penalty, or a person acting on his behalf, has acted in good faith.

Cross-references—See FA 2014 s 102 (application of FA 2003 ss 26, 27 and 29–41 in relation to excise duty).

Demand notices

30 Demands for penalties

(1) Where a person is liable to a penalty under this Part, the Commissioners may give to that person or his representative a notice in writing (a "demand notice") demanding payment of the amount due by way of penalty.

(2) An amount demanded as due from a person or his representative in accordance with subsection (1) is recoverable as if it were an amount due from the person or, as the case may be, the representative as an amount of customs duty.

This subsection is subject to—

(*a*) any appeal under section [33][1] (appeals to tribunal); and

(*b*) subsection (3).

(3) An amount so demanded is not recoverable if or to the extent that—

(*a*) the demand has subsequently been withdrawn; or

(*b*) the amount has been reduced under section 29.

Cross-references—See FA 2014 s 102 (application of FA 2003 ss 26, 27 and 29–41 in relation to excise duty).

Amendments—[1] In sub-s (2) figure substituted for the figure "36"; definition of "HMRC" inserted by the Transfer of Tribunal Functions and Revenue and Customs Appeals Order, SI 2009/56 art 3, Sch 1 para 361 with effect from 1 April 2009.

31 Time limits for demands for penalties

(1) A demand notice may not be given—

(*a*) in the case of a penalty under section 25, more than 20 years after the conduct giving rise to the liability to the penalty ceased, or

(*b*) in the case of a penalty under section 26, more than 3 years after the conduct giving rise to the liability to the penalty ceased.

(2) A demand notice may not be given more than 2 years after there has come to the knowledge of the Commissioners evidence of facts sufficient in the opinion of the Commissioners to justify the giving of the demand notice.

(3) A demand notice—

(*a*) may be given in respect of a penalty to which a person was liable under section 25 or 26 immediately before his death, but

(*b*) in the case of a penalty to which the deceased was so liable under section 25, may not be given more than 3 years after his death.

Cross-references—See FA 2014 s 102 (application of FA 2003 ss 26, 27 and 29–41 in relation to excise duty).

32 No prosecution after demand notice for penalty under section 26

Where a demand notice is given demanding payment of an amount due by way of penalty under section 26 in respect of any conduct of a person, no proceedings may be brought against that person for any offence constituted by that conduct (whether or not the demand notice is subsequently withdrawn).

[Appeals and reviews][1]

Cross-references—See FA 2014 s 102 (application of FA 2003 ss 26, 27 and 29–41 in relation to excise duty).

Amendments—[1] Cross-head substituted for "Reviews" by the Transfer of Tribunal Functions and Revenue and Customs Appeals Order, SI 2009/56 art 3, Sch 1 para 363 with effect from 1 April 2009, subject to transitional and savings provisions in Sch 3 paras 2, 3.

33 [Right to appeal against certain decisions][1]

(1) If, in the case of any relevant tax or duty, [HMRC][1] give a person or his representative a notice informing him—

(*a*) that they have decided that the person has engaged in conduct by which he contravenes a relevant rule, and

(*b*) that the person is, in consequence, liable to a penalty under section 26, but

(*c*) that they do not propose to give a demand notice in respect of the penalty,

the person or his representative may [make an appeal to an appeal tribunal in respect of][1] the decision mentioned in paragraph (a).

(2) Where [HMRC][1] give a demand notice to a person or his representative, the person or his representative may [make an appeal to an appeal tribunal in respect of][1]—

(*a*) their decision that the person is liable to a penalty under section 25 or 26, or

(*b*) their decision as to the amount of the liability.

(3) Where [HMRC][1]give a notice under section 28 to a body corporate and to a relevant officer—

(*a*) subsection (2) does not apply to any demand notice given in respect of the liability of either of them to a penalty under this Part in respect of the conduct in question, but

(*b*) subsections (4) and (5) have effect instead in relation to any such demand notice.

(4) Where [HMRC][1]give a demand notice to the relevant officer or his representative for a penalty which corresponds to the portion of the basic penalty specified in the notice under section 28, the relevant officer or his representative may make an appeal to an appeal tribunal in respect of][1]—

(*a*) their decision that the conduct of the body corporate referred to in section 28(1)(*b*) is, in whole or in part, attributable to the relevant officer's dishonesty, or (*b*) their decision as to the portion of the basic penalty which [HMRC][1]are seeking to recover from the relevant officer or his representative.

(5) Where [HMRC][1] give a demand notice to the body corporate or its representative for so much of the basic penalty as is not recoverable from the relevant officer by virtue of section 28(3), the body corporate or its representative may make an appeal to an appeal tribunal in respect of][1]—

(*a*) their decision that the body corporate is liable to a penalty under section 25, or

(*b*) their decision as to amount of the basic penalty as if it were the amount specified in the demand notice.

[(6) The powers of an appeal tribunal on an appeal under this section include—

(*a*) power to quash or vary a decision; and

(*b*) power to substitute the tribunal's own decision for any decision so quashed.

(7) On an appeal under this section—

(*a*) the burden of proof as to the matters mentioned in section 25(1) or 26(1) lies on HMRC; but

(*b*) it is otherwise for the appellant to show that the grounds on which any such appeal is brought have been established.][1]

Cross-references—See FA 2014 s 102 (application of FA 2003 ss 26, 27 and 29–41 in relation to excise duty).

Amendments—[1] The following amendments made by the Transfer of Tribunal Functions and Revenue and Customs Appeals Order, SI 2009/56 art 3, Sch 1 para 363 with effect from 1 April 2009, subject to transitional and savings provisions in Sch 3 paras 2, 3—

- cross-head substituted for "Reviews";
- heading substituted for the former heading "Right to review of certain decisions";
- in sub-ss (1)–(5) words in the first place and in sub-s (4)(*b*) words substituted for the words "the Commissioners";
- in sub-s (1) words in the second place substituted for the words "give a notice to the Commissioners requiring them to review";
- in sub-ss (2), (4), (5) words in the second place substituted for the words "by notice require the Commissioners to review";
- sub-ss (6), (7) substituted for former sub-s (6).

33A Offer of review

(1) HMRC must offer a person (P) a review of a decision that has been notified to P if an appeal lies under section 33 in respect of the decision.

(2) The offer of the review must be made by notice given to P at the same time as the decision is notified to P.

(3) This section does not apply to the notification of the conclusions of a review.][1]

Cross-references—See FA 2014 s 102 (application of FA 2003 ss 26, 27 and 29–41 in relation to excise duty).

Amendments—[1] Sections 33A–33F inserted by the Transfer of Tribunal Functions and Revenue and Customs Appeals Order, SI 2009/56 art 3, Sch 1 para 364 with effect from 1 April 2009.

33B Review by HMRC

(1) HMRC must review a decision if—

(*a*) they have offered a review of the decision under section 33A, and

(*b*) P notifies HMRC accepting the offer within 30 days from the date of the document containing the notification of the offer.

(2) But P may not notify acceptance of the offer if P has already appealed to the appeal tribunal under section 33F.

(3) HMRC shall not review a decision if P has appealed to the appeal tribunal under section 33F in respect of the decision.[1]

Cross-references—See FA 2014 s 102 (application of FA 2003 ss 26, 27 and 29–41 in relation to excise duty).

Amendments—[1] Sections 33A–33F inserted by the Transfer of Tribunal Functions and Revenue and Customs Appeals Order, SI 2009/56 art 3, Sch 1 para 364 with effect from 1 April 2009.

33C Extensions of time

(1) If under section 33A, HMRC have offered P a review of a decision, HMRC may within the relevant period notify P that the relevant period is extended.

(2) If notice is given the relevant period is extended to the end of 30 days from—

(*a*) the date of the notice, or

(*b*) any other date set out in the notice or a further notice.

(3) In this section "relevant period" means—

(*a*) the period of 30 days referred to in section 33B(1)(*b*), or

(*b*) if notice has been given under subsection (1) that period as extended (or as most recently extended) in accordance with subsection (2).][1]

Cross-references—See FA 2014 s 102 (application of FA 2003 ss 26, 27 and 29–41 in relation to excise duty).

Amendments—[1] Sections 33A–33F inserted by the Transfer of Tribunal Functions and Revenue and Customs Appeals Order, SI 2009/56 art 3, Sch 1 para 364 with effect from 1 April 2009.

33D Review out of time

(1) This section applies if—

(*a*) HMRC have offered a review of a decision under section 33A, and

(*b*) P does not accept the offer within the time allowed under section 33B(1)(*b*) or 33C(2).

(2) HMRC must review the decision under section 33B if—

(*a*) after the time allowed, P notifies HMRC in writing requesting a review out of time,

(*b*) HMRC are satisfied that P had a reasonable excuse for not accepting the offer or requiring review within the time allowed, and

(*c*) HMRC are satisfied that P made the request without unreasonable delay after the excuse had ceased to apply.

(3) HMRC shall not review a decision if P has appealed to the appeal tribunal under section 33F in respect of the decision.][1]

Cross-references—See FA 2014 s 102 (application of FA 2003 ss 26, 27 and 29–41 in relation to excise duty).

Amendments—[1] Sections 33A–33F inserted by the Transfer of Tribunal Functions and Revenue and Customs Appeals Order, SI 2009/56 art 3, Sch 1 para 364 with effect from 1 April 2009.

33E Nature of review etc

(1) This section applies if HMRC are required to undertake a review under section 33B or 33D.

(2) The nature and extent of the review are to be such as appear appropriate to HMRC in the circumstances.

(3) For the purpose of subsection (2), HMRC must, in particular, have regard to steps taken before the beginning of the review—

(*a*) by HMRC in reaching the decision, and

(*b*) by any person in seeking to resolve disagreement about the decision.

(4) The review must take account of any representations made by P at a stage which gives HMRC a reasonable opportunity to consider them.

(5) The review may conclude that the decision is to be—

(*a*) upheld,

(*b*) varied, or

(*c*) cancelled.

(6) HMRC must give P notice of the conclusions of the review and their reasoning within—

(*a*) a period of 45 days beginning with the relevant date, or

(*b*) such other period as HMRC and P may agree.

(7) In subsection (6) "relevant date" means—

(*a*) the date HMRC received P's notification accepting the offer of a review (in a case falling within section 33A), or

(*b*) the date on which HMRC decided to undertake the review (in a case falling within section 33D).

(8) Where HMRC are required to undertake a review but do not give notice of the conclusions within the period specified in subsection (6), the review is to be treated as having concluded that the decision is upheld.

(9) If subsection (8) applies, HMRC must notify P of the conclusions which the review is treated as having reached.][1]

Cross-references—See FA 2014 s 102 (application of FA 2003 ss 26, 27 and 29–41 in relation to excise duty).

Amendments—[1] Sections 33A–33F inserted by the Transfer of Tribunal Functions and Revenue and Customs Appeals Order, SI 2009/56 art 3, Sch 1 para 364 with effect from 1 April 2009.

33F Bringing of appeals

(1) An appeal under section 33 is to be made to the appeal tribunal before—

(*a*) the end of the period of 30 days beginning with the date of the document notifying the decision to which the appeal relates, or

(*b*) if later, the end of the relevant period (within the meaning of section 33C).

(2) But that is subject to subsections (3) to (5).

(3) In a case where HMRC are required to undertake a review under section 33C—

(*a*) an appeal may not be made until the conclusion date, and

(*b*) any appeal is to be made within the period of 30 days beginning with the conclusion date.

(4) In a case where HMRC are requested to undertake a review in accordance with section 33D—

(*a*) an appeal may not be made—

(i) unless HMRC have decided whether or not to undertake a review, and

(ii) if HMRC decide to undertake a review, until the conclusion date; and

(*b*) any appeal is to be made within the period of 30 days beginning with—

(i) the conclusion date (if HMRC decide to undertake a review), or

(ii) the date on which HMRC decide not to undertake a review.

(5) In a case where section 33E(8) applies, an appeal may be made at any time from the end of the period specified in section 33E(6) to the date 30 days after the conclusion date.

(6) An appeal may be made after the end of the period specified in subsection (1), (3)(*b*), (4)(*b*) or (5) if an appeal tribunal gives permission to do so.

(7) In this section "conclusion date" means the date of the document notifying the conclusions of the review.][1]

Cross-references—See FA 2014 s 102 (application of FA 2003 ss 26, 27 and 29–41 in relation to excise duty).

Amendments—[1] Sections 33A–33F inserted by the Transfer of Tribunal Functions and Revenue and Customs Appeals Order, SI 2009/56 art 3, Sch 1 para 364 with effect from 1 April 2009.

34 Time limit and right to further review

(1) The Commissioners are not required under section 33 to review any decision unless the notice requiring the review is given before the end of the permitted period.

(2) For the purposes of this section the "permitted period" is the period of 45 days beginning with the day on which the relevant notice is given.

(3) For the purposes of subsection (2) the "relevant notice" is—

(a) in the case of a review by virtue of subsection (1) of section 33, the notice mentioned in that subsection; or

(b) in any other case, the demand notice in question.

(4) Nothing in subsection (1) prevents the Commissioners from agreeing on request to review a decision in a case where the notice required by that subsection is not given within the permitted period.

(5) A person may give notice under section 33 requiring a decision to be reviewed a second or subsequent time only if—

(a) the grounds on which he requires the further review are that the Commissioners did not, on any previous review, have the opportunity to consider any particular facts or matters; and

(b) he does not, on the further review, require the Commissioners to consider any facts or matters which were considered on a previous review of the decision, except in so far as they are relevant to any issue to which the facts or matters not previously considered relate.[1]

Amendments—[1] Sections 34–36 and the crosshead before s 36 repealed by the Transfer of Tribunal Functions and Revenue and Customs Appeals Order, SI 2009/56 art 3, Sch 1 para 365 with effect from 1 April 2009, subject to transitional and savings provisions in Sch 3 paras 2, 3.

35 Powers of Commissioners on a review

(1) Where the Commissioners—

(a) are required in accordance with section 33 to review a decision, or

(b) agree to do so on such a request as is mentioned in section 34(4),

the following provisions of this section apply.

(2) On any such review, the Commissioners may—

(a) confirm the decision,

(b) withdraw the decision, or

(c) vary the decision.

(3) Where the Commissioners withdraw or vary the decision, they may also take such further steps (if any) in consequence of the withdrawal or variation as they may consider appropriate.

(4) If the Commissioners do not within the permitted period give notice of their determination on the review to the person who required the review or his representative, they shall be taken for the purposes of this Part to have confirmed the decision.

(5) For the purposes of subsection (4), the "permitted period" is the period of 45 days beginning with the day on which the review—

(a) is required by the person or his representative in accordance with section 33, or

(b) is agreed to by the Commissioners as mentioned in section 34(4).[1]

Amendments—[1] Sections 34–36 and the crosshead before s 36 repealed by the Transfer of Tribunal Functions and Revenue and Customs Appeals Order, SI 2009/56 art 3, Sch 1 para 365 with effect from 1 April 2009, subject to transitional and savings provisions in Sch 3 paras 2, 3.

Appeals

36 Appeals to a tribunal

(1) Where the Commissioners—

(a) are required in accordance with section 33 to review a decision, or

(b) agree to do so on such a request as is mentioned in section 34(4),

an appeal lies to an appeal tribunal against any decision by the Commissioners on the review (including any confirmation under section 35(4)).

(2) An appeal lies under this section only if the appellant is one of the following persons—

(a) the person who required the review in question,

(b) where the person who required the review in question did so as representative of another person, that other person, or

(c) a representative of a person falling within paragraph (a) or (b.

(3) The powers of an appeal tribunal on an appeal under this section include—

(a) power to quash or vary a decision; and

(b) power to substitute the tribunal's own decision for any decision so quashed.

(4) On an appeal under this section—

(a) the burden of proof as to the matters mentioned in section 25(1) or 26(1) lies on the Commissioners; but

(*b*) *it is otherwise for the appellant to show that the grounds on which any such appeal is brought have been established.*[1]

Amendments—[1] Sections 34–36 and the cross-head before s 36 repealed by the Transfer of Tribunal Functions and Revenue and Customs Appeals Order, SI 2009/56 art 3, Sch 1 para 365 with effect from 1 April 2009, subject to transitional and savings provisions in Sch 3 paras 2, 3.

[37 Appeal tribunals

Section 85 of the Value Added Tax Act 1994 (settling appeals by agreement) has effect as if the reference to section 83 of that Act included a reference to section 33 above.][1]

Cross-references—See FA 2014 s 102 (application of FA 2003 ss 26, 27 and 29–41 in relation to excise duty).

Amendments—[1] Sections 37 substituted by the Transfer of Tribunal Functions and Revenue and Customs Appeals Order, SI 2009/56 art 3, Sch 1 para 366 with effect from 1 April 2009, subject to transitional and savings provisions in Sch 3 paras 2, 3.

Evidence

38 Admissibility of certain statements and documents

(1) Statements made or documents produced by or on behalf of a person are not inadmissible in—

(*a*) any criminal proceedings against that person in respect of any offence in connection with or in relation to any relevant tax or duty, or

(*b*) any proceedings against that person for the recovery of any sum due from him in connection with or in relation to any relevant tax or duty,

by reason only that any of the matters specified in subsection (2) has been drawn to his attention and that he was, or may have been, induced by that matter having been brought to his attention to make the statements or produce the documents.

(2) The matters mentioned in subsection (1) are—

(*a*) that the Commissioners have power, in relation to any relevant tax or duty, to demand by means of a written notice an amount by way of a civil penalty, instead of instituting criminal proceedings;

(*b*) that it is the Commissioners' practice, without being able to give an undertaking as to whether they will make such a demand in any case, to be influenced in determining whether to make such a demand by the fact (where it is the case) that a person has made a full confession of any dishonest conduct to which he has been a party and has given full facilities for an investigation;

(*c*) that the Commissioners or, on appeal, an appeal tribunal have power to reduce a penalty under section 25, as provided in subsection (1) of section 29; and

(*d*) that, in determining the extent of such a reduction in the case of any person, the Commissioners or tribunal will have regard to the extent of the co-operation which he has given to the Commissioners in their investigation.

(3) References in this section to a relevant tax or duty do not include a reference to customs duty of a preferential tariff country.

Miscellaneous and supplementary

39 Service of notices

Any notice to be given to any person for the purposes of this Part may be given by sending it by post in a letter addressed to that person or his representative at the last or usual residence or place of business of that person or representative.

Cross-references—See FA 2014 s 102 (application of FA 2003 ss 26, 27 and 29–41 in relation to excise duty).

40 Penalties not to be deducted for income tax or corporation tax purposes

(*inserts* TA 1988 s 827(1E); *repealed* by CTA 2009 s 1326, Sch 3 Pt 1).

41 Regulations and orders

(1) Any power conferred on the Treasury by this Part to make regulations or an order includes power—

(*a*) to make different provision for different cases, and

(*b*) to make incidental, consequential, supplemental or transitional provision or savings.

(2) Any power conferred on the Treasury by this Part to make regulations or an order shall be exercisable by statutory instrument.

(3) Any statutory instrument containing regulations under this Part shall be subject to annulment in pursuance of a resolution of the House of Commons.

Cross-references—See FA 2014 s 102 (application of FA 2003 ss 26, 27 and 29–41 in relation to excise duty).

Regulations—Customs (Contravention of a Relevant Rule) Regulations, SI 2003/3113.

Customs (Contravention of a Relevant Rule) (Amendment) Regulations, SI 2015/636.

Order—Finance Act 2003, Part 3 (Appointed Day) Order, SI 2003/2985.

PART 9
MISCELLANEOUS AND SUPPLEMENTARY PROVISIONS

International matters

197 Exchange of information between tax authorities of member States

(1) No obligation as to secrecy imposed by statute or otherwise precludes the Commissioners or an authorised officer of the Commissioners from disclosing to the competent authorities of another member State any information required to be so disclosed by virtue of the Mutual Assistance Directive.

(2) Neither the Commissioners nor an authorised officer shall disclose any information in pursuance of the Mutual Assistance Directive unless satisfied that the competent authorities of the other State are bound by, or have undertaken to observe, rules of confidentiality with respect to the information that are not less strict than those applying to it in the United Kingdom.

(3) Nothing in this section permits the Commissioners or an authorised officer of the Commissioners to authorise the use of information disclosed by virtue of the Mutual Assistance Directive otherwise than for the purposes of taxation or to facilitate legal proceedings for failure to observe the tax laws of the receiving State.

(4) In this section—

"the Commissioners" means the Commissioners of Inland Revenue or the Commissioners of Customs and Excise;

the "Mutual Assistance Directive" means Council Directive 77/799/EEC, [as amended by Council Directives 92/12/EEC[, 2003/93/EC[, 2004/56/EC, 2004/106/EC and 2006/98/EC][3]][2]][1].

(5) The Treasury may by order make such provision amending the definition of the "Mutual Assurance Directive" in subsection (4) as appears to them appropriate for the purpose of giving effect to any Council Directive adopted after 16th April 2003 amending or replacing the Mutual Assistance Directive.

(6) An order under subsection (5) shall be made by statutory instrument which shall be subject to annulment in pursuance of a resolution of the House of Commons.

(7) (*amends* VATA 1994 s 48)[4]

Commentary—*De Voil Indirect Tax Service* **V1.270, V5.234.**

Amendments—[1] In sub-s (4), words in the definition of the "Mutual Assistance Directive" substituted by the Mutual Assistance Provisions Order, SI 2003/3092 art 3 with effect from 1 January 2004.

[2] In sub-s (4), words in the definition of "the Mutual Assistance Directive" substituted by the Mutual Assistance Provisions Order, SI 2004/3207 with effect from 1 January 2005.

[3] In sub-s (4), words in definition of the "Mutual Assistance Directive" substituted by the Mutual Assistance Provisions Order, SI 2006/3283 art 2 with effect from 1 January 2007.

[4] This section repealed by the European Administrative Co-Operation (Taxation) Regulations, SI 2012/3062 reg 7, Schedule with effect from 1 January 2013.

Administrative matters

204 Mandatory electronic payment . . . [1]

[(1) The Commissioners for Her Majesty's Revenue and Customs may make regulations requiring a person to use electronic means in making specified payments under legislation relating to a tax (or duty) for which the Commissioners are responsible.

(2) The regulations may provide for exceptions.][1]

(3) Regulations under this section may make provision—

(*a*) as to conditions that must be complied with in connection with the use of electronic means for the making of any payment;

(*b*) for treating a payment as not having been made unless conditions imposed by any of the regulations are satisfied;

(*c*) for determining the time when payment is to be taken to have been made.

(4) Regulations under this section may also make provision (which may include provision for the application of conclusive or other presumptions) as to the manner of proving for any purpose—

(*a*) whether any use of electronic means for making a payment is to be taken as having resulted in the payment being made;

(*b*) the time of the making of any payment for the making of which electronic means have been used;

(*c*) any other matter for which provision may be made by regulations under this section.

(5) Regulations under this section may—

(*a*) allow any authorisation or requirement for which the regulations may provide to be given or imposed by means of a specific or general direction given by the Commissioners;

(*b*) provide that the conditions of any such authorisation or requirement are to be taken to be satisfied only where [Her Majesty's Revenue and Customs][1]are satisfied as to specified matters.

(6) Regulations under this section may contain provision—

(*a*) requiring [Her Majesty's Revenue and Customs][1]to notify persons appearing to them to be, or to have become, a person required to use electronic means for the making of any payments in accordance with the regulations;

(*b*) enabling a person so notified to have the question whether he is such a person determined in the same way as an appeal.

(7) Regulations under this section may confer power on the Commissioners to give specific or general directions—

(*a*) suspending, for any period during which the use of electronic means for the making of payments is impossible or impractical, any requirements imposed by the regulations relating to the use of such means;

(*b*) substituting alternative requirements for the suspended ones;

(*c*) making any provision that is necessary in consequence of the imposition of the substituted requirements.

(8) The power to make provision by regulations under this section includes power—

(*a*) to provide for [a contravention by a large employer of, or any failure by a large employer to comply with,][1]the regulations (a "default") to attract a surcharge of a specified amount;

(*b*) to provide that specified enactments relating to penalties imposed for the purposes of any [matter relating to a tax (or duty) for which the Commissioners are responsible][1](including enactments relating to assessments, review and appeal) apply, with or without modifications, in relation to surcharges under the regulations.

(9) The regulations may specify the surcharge for each default as—

(*a*) a specified percentage, depending on the circumstances but not exceeding 10%, of the amount of the payment to which the default relates, or

(*b*) a specified percentage, depending on the circumstances but not exceeding 0.83%, of the total amount of tax due for the accounting period, year of assessment or other specified period of twelve months during which the default occurred;

but, in either case, they may specify £30 if it is more.

(10) Regulations under this section may—

(*a*) make different provision for different cases;

(*b*) make such incidental, supplemental, consequential and transitional provision in connection with any provision contained in any of the regulations as the Commissioners think fit.

(11) Regulations under this section shall be made by statutory instrument subject to annulment in pursuance of a resolution of the House of Commons.

(12) In this section—

["Her Majesty's Revenue and Customs" includes a person acting under the authority of the Commissioners in relation to payment by electronic means;][1]

["large employer" means a person paying PAYE income to 250 or more recipients (and regulations under this section may make provision as to the date or period by reference to which this is to be determined and the circumstances in which a person is to be treated as paying PAYE income to a recipient);][1]

"legislation" means any enactment, Community legislation or subordinate legislation;

"specified" means specified by or under regulations under this section;

"subordinate legislation" has the same meaning as in the Interpretation Act 1978 (c 30).

[(13) Regulations under section 95(1) of the Finance Act 2007 (payment by cheque) may, in particular, provide for a payment which is made by cheque in contravention of regulations under this section to be treated as made when the cheque clears, as defined in the regulations under that section.][2]

Regulations—VAT (Amendment) Regulations, SI 2013/701.

Amendments—[1] Sub-ss (1), (2), words in sub-ss (5)(*b*), (6)(*a*), (8)(*a*), (*b*), substituted; in sub-s (12) definition of "Her Majesty's Revenue and Customs" substituted for definition of "the Inland Revenue", and definition of "large employer" inserted; and words in heading repealed; by FA 2007 s 94(1)–(7) with effect from 19 July 2007.

[2] Sub-s (13) inserted by FA 2007 s 95(6) with effect from 19 July 2007.

205 Use of electronic means of payment under other provisions

(1) Any power to make subordinate legislation for or in connection with the making of payments conferred in relation to a taxation [(or duty)][1]matter on—

(*a*) [the Commissioners for Her Majesty's Revenue and Customs][1], or

(*b*) the Treasury,

includes power to make any such provision in relation to the making of those payments as could be made in exercise of the power conferred by section 204.

(2) Provision as to means of payment made in exercise of the powers conferred by section 204 or subsection (1) above has effect notwithstanding so much of any enactment or subordinate legislation as would otherwise allow payment to be made by any other means.

(3) Expressions used in this section and section 204 have the same meaning in this section as in that section.

(4) Nothing in this section shall be read as restricting the generality of the power conferred by section 204.

Amendments—[1] Words in sub-s (1) inserted and substituted by FA 2007 s 94(8) with effect from 19 July 2007.

SCHEDULES

SCHEDULE 1

VAT: FACE-VALUE VOUCHERS

Section 19

Commentary—*De Voil Indirect Tax Service* **V3.166.**

1–3 (*insert* VATA 1994 s 51B, Sch 10A and Sch 6 para 5)

4 The amendments made by this Schedule apply to supplies of tokens, stamps or vouchers issued on or after 9th April 2003.

SCHEDULE 2

SUPPLY OF ELECTRONIC SERVICES IN MEMBER STATES: VAT SPECIAL ACCOUNTING SCHEME

Section 23

Commentary—*De Voil Indirect Tax Service* **V3.196, V2.106.**

Introductory

1 The Value Added Tax Act 1994 is amended as follows.

Insertion of new section 3A

2 (*inserts* VATA 1994 s 3A)

Persons registered under Schedule 1

3 (*inserts* VATA 1994 Sch 1 para 13(8))

The special accounting scheme

4 (*inserts* VATA 1994 Sch 3B)

FINANCE ACT 2004

(2004 Chapter 12)

An Act to Grant certain duties, to alter other duties, and to amend the law relating to the National Debt and the Public Revenue, and to make further provision in connection with finance.

[22 July 2004]

PART 2

VALUE ADDED TAX

19 Disclosure of VAT avoidance schemes

(1) Schedule 2 (which relates to the disclosure of schemes for the avoidance of value added tax) has effect.

(2) Subsection (1) and that Schedule—

(*a*) come into force on the passing of this Act, so far as is necessary for enabling the making of any orders or regulations by virtue of that Schedule, and

(*b*) otherwise, come into force on such day as the Treasury may by order made by statutory instrument appoint.

Orders—See Finance Act 2004, section 19(1) and Schedule 2, (Appointed Day) Order, SI 2004/1934 (the appointed day under sub-s (2)(*b*) above, insofar as this section and FA 2004 Sch 2 are not already in force, is 1 August 2004).

20 Groups

(1) (*inserts* VATA 1994 s 43AA)

(2) (*inserts* VATA 1994 s 43D)

(3) (*amends* VATA 1994 s 43(1))

(4) (*amends* VATA 1994 s 43B)

(5) (*inserts* VATA 1994 s 97(4)(*ca*))

VAT Statutes

21 Reverse charge on gas and electricity supplied by persons outside UK
(1) (*inserts* VATA 1994 s 9A)
(2) This section has effect in relation to supplies made on or after 1st January 2005.

22 Use of stock in trade cars for consideration less than market value
(1) The Value Added Tax Act 1994 (c. 23) is amended as follows.
(2) (*inserts* VATA 1994 Sch 6 para 1A)
(3) (*amends* VATA 1994 s 83(v))
(4) (*inserts* VATA 1994 s 97(4)(*f*))
(5) The amendment made by subsection (2) applies in relation to any use or availability for use on or after the appointed day (whatever the date of the directions mentioned in paragraph 5(4) of Schedule 4 to the Value Added Tax Act 1994 (c. 23)).
(6) In subsection (5) "the appointed day" means such day as the Treasury may by order made by statutory instrument appoint.

Note—Section 22(2) has effect in relation to any use or availability for use on or after 1 January 2005, by virtue of Finance Act 2004, section 22(2), (Appointed Day) Order, SI 2004/3104, art 2.

PART 8
MISCELLANEOUS MATTERS

322 Mutual assistance: customs union with the Principality of Andorra
(1) The UK mutual assistance provisions have effect for the purposes of giving effect to the EC-Andorra Mutual Assistance Recovery Decision as they have effect for the purposes of giving effect to the Mutual Assistance Recovery Directive.
(2) In this section—
"the EC-Andorra Mutual Assistance Recovery Decision" means Chapter 2 of Title 1 of, and Annex 1 to, Decision No 1/2003 of the EC-Andorra Joint Committee of 3 September 2003 (on the laws, regulations and administrative provisions necessary for the proper functioning of the Customs Union between the European Community and the Principality of Andorra);
"the Mutual Assistance Recovery Directive" has the same meaning as [MARD has][1] in the UK mutual assistance provisions;
["the UK mutual assistance provisions" means the provisions of section 87 of the Finance Act 2011 (mutual assistance for recovery of taxes etc) and Schedule 25 to that Act.][1]
[(3) In the UK mutual assistance provisions as they have effect in accordance with subsection (1)—
(*a*) references (except for the one in paragraph 1 of Schedule 25) to MARD are to be read as references to the EC-Andorra Mutual Assistance Recovery Decision,
(*b*) references to another member State are to be read as references to the Principality of Andorra,
(*c*) references to an applicant authority of another member State are to be read as references to the competent authority of the Principality of Andorra,
(*d*) references to a MARD-related instrument are to be disregarded, and
(*e*) paragraph 10 of Schedule 25 (power to make further provision) is to be treated as omitted.][1]
(4) The powers in [section 87(2) of the Finance Act 2011 and paragraph 9 of Schedule 25][1] to that Act may be exercised so as to make provision for the purposes of giving effect to the EC-Andorra Mutual Assistance Recovery Decision (or amendments of the Decision) which is different to that made for the purposes of giving effect to the Mutual Assistance Recovery Directive (or amendments of the Directive).

Cross references—See FA 2011 Sch 25 (mutual assistance for recovery of taxes).
Amendments—[1] In sub-s (2), in definition of "the Mutual Assistance Recovery Directive", words inserted, definition of "the UK mutual assistance provisions" substituted, sub-s (3) substituted, and in sub-s (4), words substituted for words "section 134(6) of the Finance Act 2002 and paragraph 3 of Schedule 39", by FA 2011 s 87, Sch 25 para 18(1)–(5) with effect from 1 January 2012. Note that any regulations made by virtue of FA 2004 s 322(4) and in force immediately before 1 January 2012 are to have effect on and after that date as if made by virtue of that subsection as amended by FA 2011 Sch 25 para 18(5).

PART 9
SUPPLEMENTARY PROVISIONS

328 Short title
This Act may be cited as the Finance Act 2004.

SCHEDULES

SCHEDULE 2
DISCLOSURE OF VALUE ADDED TAX AVOIDANCE SCHEMES

Section 19

PART 1
PRINCIPAL AMENDMENTS OF VALUE ADDED TAX ACT 1994

1 (*inserts* VATA 1994 s 58A)

2 (*inserts* VATA 1994 Sch 11A)

PART 2
CONSEQUENTIAL AMENDMENTS

3 (*amends* VATA 1994 s 70(1))

4 (*inserts* VATA 1994 s 83(*za*), (*zb*))

5 (*amends* VATA 1994 s 83)

6 (*inserts* VATA 1994 s 97(4)(*g*))

COMMISSIONERS FOR REVENUE AND CUSTOMS ACT 2005

(2005 Chapter 11)

ARRANGEMENT OF SECTIONS

An Act to make provision for the appointment of Commissioners to exercise functions presently vested in the Commissioners of Inland Revenue and the Commissioners of Customs and Excise; for the establishment of a Revenue and Customs Prosecutions Office; and for connected purposes.

[7th April 2005]

Commissioners and officers

1 The Commissioners

(1) Her Majesty may by Letters Patent appoint Commissioners for Her Majesty's Revenue and Customs.

(2) The Welsh title of the Commissioners shall be Comisynwyr Cyllid a Thollau Ei Mawrhydi.

(3) A Commissioner—

(*a*) may resign by notice in writing to the Treasury, and

(*b*) otherwise, shall hold office in accordance with the terms and conditions of his appointment (which may include provision for dismissal).

(4) In exercising their functions, the Commissioners act on behalf of the Crown.

(5) Service as a Commissioner is service in the civil service of the State.

2 Officers of Revenue and Customs

(1) The Commissioners may appoint staff, to be known as officers of Revenue and Customs.

(2) A person shall hold and vacate office as an officer of Revenue and Customs in accordance with the terms of his appointment (which may include provision for dismissal).

(3) An officer of Revenue and Customs shall comply with directions of the Commissioners (whether he is exercising a function conferred on officers of Revenue and Customs or exercising a function on behalf of the Commissioners).

(4) Anything (including anything in relation to legal proceedings) begun by or in relation to one officer of Revenue and Customs may be continued by or in relation to another.

(5) Appointments under subsection (1) may be made only with the approval of the Minister for the Civil Service as to terms and conditions of service.

(6) Service in the employment of the Commissioners is service in the civil service of the State.

(7) (*amends* IA 1978 Sch 1).

3 Declaration of confidentiality

(1) Each person who is appointed under this Act as a Commissioner or officer of Revenue and Customs shall make a declaration acknowledging his obligation of confidentiality under section 18.

(2) A declaration under subsection (1) shall be made—

(*a*) as soon as is reasonably practicable following the person's appointment, and

(*b*) in such form, and before such a person, as the Commissioners may direct.

(3) For the purposes of this section, the renewal of a fixed term appointment shall not be treated as an appointment.

4 "Her Majesty's Revenue and Customs"

(1) The Commissioners and the officers of Revenue and Customs may together be referred to as Her Majesty's Revenue and Customs.

(2) The Welsh title of the Commissioners and the officers of Revenue and Customs together shall be Cyllid a Thollau Ei Mawrhydi.

(3) (*amends* Interpretation Act 1978 Sch 1).

Functions

5 Commissioners' initial functions

(1) The Commissioners shall be responsible for—

(*a*) the collection and management of revenue for which the Commissioners of Inland Revenue were responsible before the commencement of this section,

(*b*) the collection and management of revenue for which the Commissioners of Customs and Excise were responsible before the commencement of this section, and

(*c*) the payment and management of tax credits for which the Commissioners of Inland Revenue were responsible before the commencement of this section.

(2) The Commissioners shall also have all the other functions which before the commencement of this section vested in—

(*a*) the Commissioners of Inland Revenue (or in a Commissioner), or

(*b*) the Commissioners of Customs and Excise (or in a Commissioner).

(3) This section is subject to section 35.

(4) In this Act "revenue" includes taxes, duties and national insurance contributions.

Order—See the Commissioners for Revenue and Customs Act 2005 (Commencement) Order, SI 2005/1126, art 2(2) (this section came into force on 18 April 2005).

Prospective amendments—In sub-s (1)(*a*), word "and" to be inserted at the end by WRA 2012 s 33, Sch 3 paras 19, 20 with effect from a date to be appointed.

Sub-s (3)(*c*) and preceding word "and" to be repealed by WRA 2012 s 147, Sch 14 Pt 1 with effect from a date to be appointed.

6 Officers' initial functions

(1) A function conferred by an enactment (in whatever terms) on any of the persons listed in subsection (2) shall by virtue of this subsection vest in an officer of Revenue and Customs.

(2) Those persons are—

(*a*) an officer as defined by section 1(1) of the Customs and Excise Management Act 1979 (c 2),

(*b*) a person acting under the authority of the Commissioners of Customs and Excise,

(*c*) an officer of the Commissioners of Customs and Excise,

(*d*) a customs officer,

(*e*) an officer of customs,

(*f*) a customs and excise officer,

(*g*) an officer of customs and excise, and

(*h*) a collector of customs and excise.

(3) This section is subject to sections 7 and 35.

Order—See the Commissioners for Revenue and Customs Act 2005 (Commencement) Order, SI 2005/1126, art 2(2) (this section came into force on 18 April 2005).

Cross reference—FA 2007 s 84(2) (nothing in this section restricts the functions in connection with which officers of Revenue and Customs may exercise a power under PACE 1984 s 114 (as amended by FA 2007 s 83)).

Serious Crime Act 2007 s 88, Sch 12 para 31 (nothing in this section restricts the functions in connection with which HMRC may exercise a power under an enactment amended by SCA 2007 Sch 12).

FA 2013 Sch 48 para 22 (nothing in this section restricts the functions in connection with which officers of Revenue and Customs may exercise a power under PCA 2002 Pt 5, Ch 3 or Pt 8 Chs 2, 3 (as amended by FA 2013 Sch 48)).

7 Former Inland Revenue matters

(1) This section applies to the matters listed in Schedule 1.

(2) A function conferred by an enactment (in whatever terms) on any of the persons specified in subsection (3) shall by virtue of this subsection vest in an officer of Revenue and Customs—

(*a*) if or in so far as it relates to a matter to which this section applies, and

(*b*) in so far as the officer is exercising a function (whether or not by virtue of paragraph (*a*)) which relates to a matter to which this section applies.

(3) Those persons are—

(*a*) an officer of the Commissioners of Inland Revenue,

(*b*) an officer of the Board of Inland Revenue,

(*c*) an officer of inland revenue,

(*d*) a collector of Inland Revenue,

(*e*) an inspector of taxes,

(*f*) a collector of taxes,

(*g*) a person authorised to act as an inspector of taxes or collector of taxes for specific purposes,

(*h*) an officer having powers in relation to tax,

(*i*) a revenue official,

(*j*) a person employed in relation to Inland Revenue (or "the Inland Revenue"), and (*k*) an Inland Revenue official.

(4) In so far as an officer of Revenue and Customs is exercising a function which relates to a matter to which this section applies, section 6(1) shall not apply.

(5) This section is subject to section 35.

Order—See the Commissioners for Revenue and Customs Act 2005 (Commencement) Order, SI 2005/1126, art 2(2) (this section and Sch 1 came into force on 18 April 2005).

Cross reference—FA 2007 s 84(2) (nothing in this section restricts the functions in connection with which officers of Revenue and Customs may exercise a power under PACE 1984 s 114 (as amended by FA 2007 s 83)).

Serious Crime Act 2007 s 88, Sch 12 para 31 (nothing in this section restricts the functions in connection with which HMRC may exercise a power under an enactment amended by SCA 2007 Sch 12).

FA 2013 Sch 48 para 22 (nothing in this section restricts the functions in connection with which officers of Revenue and Customs may exercise a power under PCA 2002 Pt 5, Ch 3 or Pt 8 Chs 2, 3 (as amended by FA 2013 Sch 48).

8 Power to transfer functions

(1) (*inserts* Ministers of the Crown Act 1975 s 5A).

(2) For the purposes of sections 63 and 108 of the Scotland Act 1998 (c 46) (transfer of functions)—

(*a*) the Commissioners shall be treated as a Minister of the Crown, and

(*b*) the officers of Revenue and Customs shall be treated as a Minister of the Crown.

(3) An Order in Council under section 63 or 108 of that Act—

(*a*) may not make provision about a function specified in section 5(1) of this Act, and

(*b*) if it transfers a function to the Commissioners or to officers of Revenue and Customs—

(i) may restrict or prohibit the exercise of specified powers in relation to that function, and

(ii) may provide that the function may be exercised only with the consent of a specified member of the Scottish Executive.

(4) For the purposes of section 22 of and Schedule 3 to the Government of Wales Act 1998 (c 38) (transfer of functions)—

(*a*) the Commissioners shall be treated as a Minister of the Crown, and

(*b*) the officers of Revenue and Customs shall be treated as a Minister of the Crown.

(5) An Order in Council under section 22 of that Act may not make provision about a function specified in section 5(1) of this Act.

Order—See the Commissioners for Revenue and Customs Act 2005 (Commencement) Order, SI 2005/1126, art 2(2) (this section came into force on 18 April 2005).

[8A The Extractive Industries Transparency Initiative

(1) The Commissioners may do anything which they think necessary or expedient in connection with the Extractive Industries Transparency Initiative in so far as it relates to taxes the collection and management of which is the responsibility of the Commissioners.

(2) In this section "the Extractive Industries Transparency Initiative" means the international initiative of that name which has the aim of promoting openness in the management of revenues from natural resources.][1]

Amendments—[1] Section 8A inserted by the Infrastructure Act 2015 s 40 with effect from 12 April 2015.

9 Ancillary powers

(1) The Commissioners may do anything which they think—

(*a*) necessary or expedient in connection with the exercise of their functions, or

(*b*) incidental or conducive to the exercise of their functions.

(2) This section is subject to section 35.

10 The Valuation Office

(1) An officer of Revenue and Customs may provide a valuation of property—

(*a*) for a purpose relating to the functions of Her Majesty's Revenue and Customs, or

(*b*) at the request of any person who appears to the officer to be a public authority, or

(*c*) at the request of any other person if the officer is satisfied that the valuation is necessary or expedient in connection with—

(i) the exercise of a function of a public nature, or

(ii) the management of money or assets received from a person exercising functions of a public nature.

(2) The Commissioners may charge a fee for the provision of a valuation under subsection (1)(*b*) or (*c*).

(3) In this section a reference to providing valuations of property includes a reference to advising about matters appearing to an officer of Revenue and Customs to be connected to the valuation of property.

Exercise of functions

11 Treasury directions

In the exercise of their functions the Commissioners shall comply with any directions of a general nature given to them by the Treasury.

12 Commissioners' arrangements

(1) The Commissioners shall make arrangements for—

(*a*) the conduct of their proceedings, and

(*b*) the conduct of the proceedings of any committee established by them.

(2) Arrangements under subsection (1) may, in particular—

(*a*) make provision for a quorum at meetings;

(*b*) provide that a function of the Commissioners—

(i) may be exercised by two Commissioners, or

(ii) may be exercised by a specified number of Commissioners (greater than two).

(3) A decision to make arrangements under subsection (1) must be taken with the agreement of more than half of the Commissioners holding office at the time.

13 Exercise of Commissioners' functions by officers

(1) An officer of Revenue and Customs may exercise any function of the Commissioners.

(2) But subsection (1)—

(*a*) does not apply to the functions specified in subsection (3), and

(*b*) is subject to directions under section 2(3) and arrangements under section 12.

(3) The non-delegable functions mentioned in subsection (2)(*a*) are—

(*a*) making, by statutory instrument, regulations, rules or an order,

(*b*) . . . [1]

(*c*) . . . [1]

(*d*) giving instructions for the disclosure of information under section 20(1)(*a*), except that an officer of Revenue and Customs may give an instruction under section 20(1)(*a*) authorising disclosure of specified information relating to—

(i) one or more specified persons,

(ii) one or more specified transactions, or

(iii) specified goods.

Amendments—[1] Sub-s (3)(*b*), (*c*) repealed by FA 2007 ss 84, 114, Sch 22 paras 3, 17(*a*), Sch 27 Pt 5(1) with effect from 1 December 2007 (by virtue of SI 2007/3166 art 3(*a*)).

14 Delegation

(1) Arrangements under section 12 may, in particular, enable the Commissioners, or a number of Commissioners acting in accordance with arrangements by virtue of section 12(2)(*b*), to delegate a function of the Commissioners, other than a function specified in subsection (2) below—

(*a*) to a single Commissioner,

(*b*) to a committee established by the Commissioners (which may include persons who are neither Commissioners nor staff of the Commissioners nor officers of Revenue and Customs), or

(*c*) to any other person.

(2) The non-delegable functions mentioned in subsection (1) are—

(*a*) making, by statutory instrument, regulations, rules or an order,

(*b*) . . . [1]

(*c*) . . . [1]

(3) The Commissioners may not delegate the function under section 20(1)(*a*) except to a single Commissioner.

(4) The delegation of a function by virtue of subsection (1) by the Commissioners or a number of Commissioners—

(*a*) shall not prevent the exercise of the function by the Commissioners or those Commissioners, and

(*b*) shall not, subject to express provision to the contrary in directions under section 2(3) or arrangements under section 12, prevent the exercise of the function by an officer of Revenue and Customs.

(5) Where the Commissioners or a number of Commissioners delegate a function to a person by virtue of subsection (1)(*c*)—

(*a*) the Commissioners or those Commissioners shall monitor the exercise of the function by that person, and

(*b*) in the exercise of the function the delegate shall comply with any directions of the Commissioners or of those Commissioners.

Amendments—[1] Sub-s (2)(*b*), (*c*) repealed by FA 2007 ss 84, 114, Sch 22 paras 3, 17(*b*), Sch 27 Pt 5(1) with effect from 1 December 2007 (by virtue of SI 2007/3166 art 3(*a*)).

15 [Agency: Scotland, Northern Ireland and Wales]

(1) For the purposes of section 93 of the Scotland Act 1998 (c 46) (agency)—

(*a*) the Commissioners shall be treated as a Minister of the Crown, and

(*b*) the officers of Revenue and Customs shall be treated as a Minister of the Crown.

(2) For the purposes of section 28 of the Northern Ireland Act 1998 (c 47) (agency)—

(*a*) the Commissioners shall be treated as a Minister of the Crown, and (*b*) the officers of Revenue and Customs shall be treated as a Minister of the Crown.

[(3) For the purposes of section 83 of the Government of Wales Act 2006 (agency arrangements)—

(*a*) the Commissioners are to be treated as a relevant authority, and

(*b*) the officers of Revenue and Customs are to be treated as a relevant authority.][1]

Amendments—[1] Sub-s (3) inserted, and heading substituted, by the Wales Act 2014 s 7(2)–(4) with effect from 17 February 2015.

16 Restrictions, &c

Part 1 of Schedule 2 (which restricts, or makes other provision in connection with, the exercise of certain functions) shall have effect.

Order—See the Commissioners for Revenue and Customs Act 2005 (Commencement) Order, SI 2005/1126, art 2(2) (this section and Sch 2 Pt 1 came into force on 18 April 2005).

[16A Charter of standards and values

(1) The Commissioners must prepare a Charter.

(2) The Charter must include standards of behaviour and values to which Her Majesty's Revenue and Customs will aspire when dealing with people in the exercise of their functions.

(3) The Commissioners must—

(*a*) regularly review the Charter, and

(*b*) publish revisions, or revised versions, of it when they consider it appropriate to do so.

(4) The Commissioners must, at least once every year, make a report reviewing the extent to which Her Majesty's Revenue and Customs have demonstrated the standards of behaviour and values included in the Charter.][1]

Amendments—[1] This section inserted by FA 2009 s 92(1) with effect from 21 July 2009.

Information

17 Use of information

(1) Information acquired by the Revenue and Customs in connection with a function may be used by them in connection with any other function.

(2) Subsection (1) is subject to any provision which restricts or prohibits the use of information and which is contained in—

(*a*) this Act,

(*b*) any other enactment, or

(*c*) an international or other agreement to which the United Kingdom or Her Majesty's Government is party.

(3) In subsection (1) "the Revenue and Customs" means—

(*a*) the Commissioners,

(*b*) an officer of Revenue and Customs,

(*c*) a person acting on behalf of the Commissioners or an officer of Revenue and Customs,

(*d*) a committee established by the Commissioners,

(*e*) a member of a committee established by the Commissioners,

(*f*) the Commissioners of Inland Revenue (or any committee or staff of theirs or anyone acting on their behalf),

(*g*) the Commissioners of Customs and Excise (or any committee or staff of theirs or anyone acting on their behalf), and

(*h*) a person specified in section 6(2) or 7(3).

(4) In subsection (1) "function" means a function of any of the persons listed in subsection (3).

(5) In subsection (2) the reference to an enactment does not include—

(*a*) an Act of the Scottish Parliament or an instrument made under such an Act,

[(*aa*) an Act of the National Assembly for Wales or an instrument made under such an Act,][1]

(*b*) an Act of the Northern Ireland Assembly or an instrument made under such an Act.

(6) Part 2 of Schedule 2 (which makes provision about the supply and other use of information in specified circumstances) shall have effect.

Amendments—[1] Sub-s (5)(*aa*) inserted by the Wales Act 2014 s 7(2), (5) with effect from 17 February 2015.

18 Confidentiality

(1) Revenue and Customs officials may not disclose information which is held by the Revenue and Customs in connection with a function of the Revenue and Customs.

(2) But subsection (1) does not apply to a disclosure—

(*a*) which—

(i) is made for the purposes of a function of the Revenue and Customs, and

(ii) does not contravene any restriction imposed by the Commissioners,

(*b*) which is made in accordance with section 20 or 21,

(*c*) which is made for the purposes of civil proceedings (whether or not within the United Kingdom) relating to a matter in respect of which the Revenue and Customs have functions, (*d*) which is made for the purposes of a criminal investigation or criminal proceedings (whether or not within the United Kingdom) relating to a matter in respect of which the Revenue and Customs have functions,

(*e*) which is made in pursuance of an order of a court,

(*f*) which is made to Her Majesty's Inspectors of Constabulary, the Scottish inspectors or the Northern Ireland inspectors for the purpose of an inspection by virtue of section 27,

(*g*) which is made to the Independent Police Complaints Commission, or a person acting on its behalf, for the purpose of the exercise of a function by virtue of section 28, . . .[1]

(*h*) which is made with the consent of each person to whom the information relates[, . . .[3]

(*i*) which is made to [Revenue Scotland][2] in connection with the collection and management of a devolved tax within the meaning of the Scotland Act 1998[, or

(*j*) which is made to the Welsh Ministers in connection with the collection and management of a devolved tax within the meaning of the Government of Wales Act 2006][3].][1]

(2A) [2]

(3) Subsection (1) is subject to any other enactment permitting disclosure.

(4) In this section—

(*a*) a reference to Revenue and Customs officials is a reference to any person who is or was—

(i) a Commissioner,

(ii) an officer of Revenue and Customs,

(iii) a person acting on behalf of the Commissioners or an officer of Revenue and Customs, or

(iv) a member of a committee established by the Commissioners,

(*b*) a reference to the Revenue and Customs has the same meaning as in section 17,

(*c*) a reference to a function of the Revenue and Customs is a reference to a function of—

(i) the Commissioners, or

(ii) an officer of Revenue and Customs,

(*d*) a reference to the Scottish inspectors or the Northern Ireland inspectors has the same meaning as in section 27, and

(*e*) a reference to an enactment does not include—

(i) an Act of the Scottish Parliament or an instrument made under such an Act,

[(*ia*) an Act of the National Assembly for Wales or an instrument made under such an Act,][3] or

(ii) an Act of the Northern Ireland Assembly or an instrument made under such an Act.

Cross references—FA 2006 Sch 5 para 24 (sub-s (1) above does not prevent disclosure to the Secretary of State for the purposes of his functions under FiA 1985 Sch 1; other provisions relating to disclosure of confidential information).

ITA 2007 s 257SI(1) (in relation to social investment ("SI") relief, sub-s (1) does not prevent an officer of Revenue and Customs from disclosing to the social enterprise that SI relief has been obtained or claimed in respect of a particular number or proportion of any investments in it).

ITA 2007 s 257SI(2) (in relation to social investment ("SI") relief, sub-s (1) does not prevent disclosure to the Regulator of Community Interest Companies for the purposes of the Regulator's functions).

Serious Crime Act 2007 s 85 (disclosure of information by HMRC).

FA 2013 s 80(6) (sub-s (1) above does not prevent disclosure to a Minister of the Crown for the purpose of enabling the Minister of the Crown to determine the extent of any liability under a decommissioning relief agreement, or disclosure to a company that has rights under a decommissioning relief agreement for the purpose of enabling the company to determine the reference amount).

FA 2014 s 287(16) (application of this section in relation to breaches of the Code of Practice on Taxation for Banks).

Simon's Tax Cases—*R (on the appn of Ingenious Media Holdings plc and anor) R&C Comrs* [2013] EWHC 3258 (Admin), [2014] STC 673.

Amendments—[1] In sub-s (2), word "or" at end of para (*g*) repealed, and para (*i*) and preceding word "or" inserted by the Scotland Act 2012 s 24(1)–(4) with effect from 1 July 2012.

[2] In sub-s (2)(*i*), words substituted for words "the Scottish Ministers", and sub-s (2A) repealed, by the Revenue Scotland and Tax Powers Act 2014 (Consequential Provisions and Modifications) Order, SI 2014/3294 art 4(1)(*a*) with effect from 1 January 2015. Sub-s (2A) previously read as follows—

> "(2A) Information disclosed in reliance on subsection (2)(i) may not be further disclosed without the consent of the Commissioners (which may be general or specific).".

[3] In sub-s (2), word "or" at end of para (*h*) repealed, and para (*j*) inserted, and sub-s (4)(*e*)(ia) inserted, by the Wales Act 2014 s 7(2), (6)–(9) with effect from 17 February 2015. Note that s 7(8) also purports to amend the wording of sub-s (2A) (inserting words "or (*j*)" after words "(2)(*i*)"), although sub-s (2A) was repealed with effect from 1 January 2015.

19 Wrongful disclosure

(1) A person commits an offence if he contravenes section 18(1) . . .[3] or 20(9) by disclosing revenue and customs information relating to a person whose identity—

(*a*) is specified in the disclosure, or

(*b*) can be deduced from it.

(2) In subsection (1) "revenue and customs information relating to a person" means information about, acquired as a result of, or held in connection with the exercise of a function of the Revenue and Customs (within the meaning given by section 18(4)(*c*)) in respect of the person; but it does not include information about internal administrative arrangements of Her Majesty's Revenue and Customs (whether relating to Commissioners, officers or others).

(3) It is a defence for a person charged with an offence under this section of disclosing information to prove that he reasonably believed—

(*a*) that the disclosure was lawful, or

(*b*) that the information had already and lawfully been made available to the public.

(4) A person guilty of an offence under this section shall be liable—

(*a*) on conviction on indictment, to imprisonment for a term not exceeding two years, to a fine or to both, or

(*b*) on summary conviction, to imprisonment for a term not exceeding 12 months, to a fine not exceeding the statutory maximum or to both.

(5) A prosecution for an offence under this section may be instituted in England and Wales [only by or with the consent of the Director of Public Prosecutions][2]

(6) A prosecution for an offence under this section may be instituted in Northern Ireland only—

(*a*) by the Commissioners, or

(*b*) with the consent of the Director of Public Prosecutions for Northern Ireland.

(7) In the application of this section to Scotland or Northern Ireland the reference in subsection (4)(*b*) to 12 months shall be taken as a reference to six months.

(8) This section is without prejudice to the pursuit of any remedy or the taking of any action in relation to a contravention of section 18(1) . . . [3] or 20(9) (whether or not this section applies to the contravention).

Amendments—[1] In sub-ss (1), (8) words inserted by the Scotland Act 2012 s 24(1), (2), (5) with effect from 1 July 2012.

[2] In sub-s (5), words substituted by the Public Bodies (Merger of the Director of Public Prosecutions and the Director of Revenue and Customs Prosecutions) Order, SI 2014/834 art 3(3), Sch 1 paras 5, 6 with effect from 27 March 2014.

[3] In sub-ss (1), (8) words "or (2A)" repealed by the Revenue Scotland and Tax Powers Act 2014 (Consequential Provisions and Modifications) Order, SI 2014/3294 art 4(1)(*b*) with effect from 1 January 2015.

20 Public interest disclosure

(1) Disclosure is in accordance with this section (as mentioned in section 18(2)(*b*)) if—

(*a*) it is made on the instructions of the Commissioners (which may be general or specific),

(*b*) it is of a kind—

(i) to which any of subsections (2) to (7) applies, or

(ii) specified in regulations made by the Treasury, and

(*c*) the Commissioners are satisfied that it is in the public interest.

(2) This subsection applies to a disclosure made—

(*a*) to a person exercising public functions (whether or not within the United Kingdom),

(*b*) for the purposes of the prevention or detection of crime, and

(*c*) in order to comply with an obligation of the United Kingdom, or Her Majesty's Government, under an international or other agreement relating to the movement of persons, goods or services.

(3) This subsection applies to a disclosure if—

(*a*) it is made to a body which has responsibility for the regulation of a profession,

(*b*) it relates to misconduct on the part of a member of the profession, and

(*c*) the misconduct relates to a function of the Revenue and Customs.

(4) This subsection applies to a disclosure if—

(*a*) it is made to a constable, and

(*b*) either—

(i) the constable is exercising functions which relate to the movement of persons or goods into or out of the United Kingdom, or

(ii) the disclosure is made for the purposes of the prevention or detection of crime.

(5) This subsection applies to a disclosure if it is made—

(*a*) to the National Criminal Intelligence Service, and

(*b*) for a purpose connected with its functions under section 2(2) of the Police Act 1997 (c 50) (criminal intelligence).

(6) This subsection applies to a disclosure if it is made—

(*a*) to a person exercising public functions in relation to public safety or public health, and

(*b*) for the purposes of those functions.

(7) This subsection applies to a disclosure if it—

(*a*) is made to the [Secretary of State][1] for the purpose of enabling information to be entered in a computerised database, and

(*b*) relates to—

(i) a person suspected of an offence,

(ii) a person arrested for an offence,

(iii) the results of an investigation, or

(iv) anything seized.

(8) Regulations under subsection (1)(*b*)(ii)—

(*a*) may specify a kind of disclosure only if the Treasury are satisfied that it relates to—

(i) national security,

(ii) public safety,

(iii) public health, or

(iv) the prevention or detection of crime;

(*b*) may make provision limiting or restricting the disclosures that may be made in reliance on the regulations; and that provision may, in particular, operate by reference to—

(i) the nature of information,

(ii) the person or class of person to whom the disclosure is made,

(iii) the person or class of person by whom the disclosure is made,

(iv) any other factor, or

(v) a combination of factors;

(*c*) shall be made by statutory instrument;

(*d*) may not be made unless a draft has been laid before and approved by resolution of each House of Parliament.

(9) Information disclosed in reliance on this section may not be further disclosed without the consent of the Commissioners (which may be general or specific); (but the Commissioners shall be taken to have consented to further disclosure by use of the computerised database of information disclosed by virtue of subsection (7)).

Amendments—[1] In sub-s (7)(*a*,) words substituted for words "national Policing Improvement Agency" by the Crime and Courts Act 2013 s 15, Sch 8 para 156 with effect from 7 October 2013 by virtue of SI 2013/1682, art 3(*v*).

21 Disclosure to prosecuting authority

(1) Disclosure is in accordance with this section (as mentioned in section 18(2)(*b*)) if made—

(*a*) to a prosecuting authority, and

(*b*) for the purpose of enabling the authority—

(i) to consider whether to institute criminal proceedings in respect of a matter considered in the course of an investigation conducted by or on behalf of Her Majesty's Revenue and Customs, . . .

(ii) to give advice in connection with a criminal investigation . . .[2] or criminal proceedings [or

(iii) in the case of [the Director of Public Prosecutions][2], to exercise his functions under, or in relation to, Part 5 or 8 of the Proceeds of Crime Act 2002 (c 29)][1].

(2) In subsection (1) "prosecuting authority" means—

(*a*) [the Director of Public Prosecutions][2],

(*b*) in Scotland, the Lord Advocate or a procurator fiscal, and

(*c*) in Northern Ireland, the Director of Public Prosecutions for Northern Ireland.

[(2A) In subsection (1) "criminal investigation" means any process—

(i) for considering whether an offence has been committed,

(ii) for discovering by whom an offence has been committed, or

(iii) as a result of which an offence is alleged to have been committed.][2]

(3) Information disclosed to a prosecuting authority in accordance with this section may not be further disclosed except—

(*a*) for a purpose connected with the exercise of the prosecuting authority's functions, or

(*b*) with the consent of the Commissioners (which may be general or specific).

(4) A person commits an offence if he contravenes subsection (3).

(5) It is a defence for a person charged with an offence under this section to prove that he reasonably believed—

(*a*) that the disclosure was lawful, or

(*b*) that the information had already and lawfully been made available to the public.

(6) A person guilty of an offence under this section shall be liable—

(*a*) on conviction on indictment, to imprisonment for a term not exceeding two years, to a fine or to both, or

(*b*) on summary conviction, to imprisonment for a term not exceeding 12 months, to a fine not exceeding the statutory maximum or to both.

(7) A prosecution for an offence under this section may be instituted in England and Wales [only by or with the consent of the Director of Public Prosecutions][2]

(8) A prosecution for an offence under this section may be instituted in Northern Ireland only—

(*a*) by the Commissioners, or

(*b*) with the consent of the Director of Public Prosecutions for Northern Ireland.

(9) In the application of this section to Scotland or Northern Ireland the reference in subsection (6)(*b*) to 12 months shall be taken as a reference to six months.

Cross reference—Serious Crime Act 2007 s 37, Sch 2 para 10 (this section has effect as if the purpose mentioned in sub-s (1)(*b*) included the purpose of enabling the Director to exercise his functions under this Part).

Amendments—[1] In sub-s (1)(*b*)(i), word "or" repealed, and sub-s (1)(*b*)(iii) and preceding word "or" inserted, by the Serious Crime Act 2007 ss 74(2), 92, Sch 8 para 164, Sch 14 with effect from 1 April 2008: SI 2008/755 art 2(1)(*a*), subject to transitional provisions and savings in art 3.

[2] In sub-s (1)(*b*)(ii), words repealed, in sub-ss (1)(*b*)(iii), (2)(*a*), (7), words substituted, and sub-s (2A) inserted, by the Public Bodies (Merger of the Director of Public Prosecutions and the Director of Revenue and Customs Prosecutions) Order, SI 2014/834 art 3(3), Sch 1 paras 5, 7 with effect from 27 March 2014.

22 Data protection, &c

Nothing in sections 17 to 21 authorises the making of a disclosure which—

(*a*) contravenes the Data Protection Act 1998 (c 29), or

(*b*) is prohibited by Part 1 of the Regulation of Investigatory Powers Act 2000 (c 23).

23 Freedom of information

(1) Revenue and customs information relating to a person, the disclosure of which is prohibited by section 18(1), is exempt information by virtue of section 44(1)(*a*) of the Freedom of Information Act 2000 (c 36) (prohibitions on disclosure) if its disclosure—

(*a*) would specify the identity of the person to whom the information relates, or

(*b*) would enable the identity of such a person to be deduced.

[(1A) Subsections (2) and (3) of section 18 are to be disregarded in determining for the purposes of subsection (1) of this section whether the disclosure of revenue and customs information relating to a person is prohibited by subsection (1) of that section.][1]

(2) Except as specified in subsection (1), information the disclosure of which is prohibited by section 18(1) is not exempt information for the purposes of section 44(1)(*a*) of the Freedom of Information Act 2000.

(3) In subsection (1) "revenue and customs information relating to a person" has the same meaning as in section 19.

Amendments—[1] Sub-s (1A) inserted by the Borders, Citizenship and Immigration Act 2009 s 19(4) with effect from 12 November 2009.

Proceedings

24 Evidence

(1) A document that purports to have been issued or signed by or with the authority of the Commissioners—

(*a*) shall be treated as having been so issued or signed unless the contrary is proved, and

(*b*) shall be admissible in any legal proceedings.

(2) A document that purports to have been issued by the Commissioners and which certifies any of the matters specified in subsection (3) shall (in addition to the matters provided for by subsection (1)(*a*) and (*b*)) be treated as accurate unless the contrary is proved.

(3) The matters mentioned in subsection (2) are—

(*a*) that a specified person was appointed as a commissioner on a specified date,

(*b*) that a specified person was appointed as an officer of Revenue and Customs on a specified date,

(*c*) that at a specified time or for a specified purpose (or both) a function was delegated to a specified Commissioner,

(*d*) that at a specified time or for a specified purpose (or both) a function was delegated to a specified committee, and

(*e*) that at a specified time or for a specified purpose (or both) a function was delegated to another specified person.

(4) A photographic or other copy of a document acquired by the Commissioners shall, if certified by them to be an accurate copy, be admissible in any legal proceedings to the same extent as the document itself.

(5) Section 2 of the Documentary Evidence Act 1868 (c 37) (proof of documents) shall apply to a Revenue and Customs document as it applies in relation to the documents mentioned in that section.

(6) In the application of that section to a Revenue and Customs document the Schedule to that Act shall be treated as if—

(*a*) the first column contained a reference to the Commissioners, and

(*b*) the second column contained a reference to a Commissioner or a person acting on his authority.

(7) In this section—

(*a*) "Revenue and Customs document" means a document issued by or on behalf of the Commissioners, and

(*b*) a reference to the Commissioners includes a reference to the Commissioners of Inland Revenue and to the Commissioners of Customs and Excise.

25 Conduct of civil proceedings

(1) An officer of Revenue and Customs or a person authorised by the Commissioners may conduct civil proceedings, in a magistrates' court or in the sheriff court, relating to a function of the Revenue and Customs.

[(1A) An officer of Revenue and Customs or a person authorised by the Commissioners may conduct county court proceedings for the recovery of an amount payable to the Commissioners under or by virtue of an enactment or under a contract settlement.][1]

(2) A solicitor member of the Commissioners' staff may act as a solicitor in connection with civil proceedings relating to a function of the Revenue and Customs.

(3) A legally qualified member of the Commissioners' staff may conduct county court proceedings relating to a matter specified in section 7.

(4) A court shall grant any rights of audience necessary to enable a person to exercise a function under this section.

(5) In this section—

(*a*) a reference to a function of the Revenue and Customs is a reference to a function of—

(i) the Commissioners, or

(ii) an officer of Revenue and Customs,

(*b*) a reference to civil proceedings is a reference to proceedings other than proceedings in respect of an offence,

(*c*) a reference to county court proceedings is a reference to civil proceedings [in England and Wales in the county court or in Northern Ireland][2] in a county court,

(*d*) the reference to a legally qualified member of the Commissioners' staff is a reference to a member of staff who has been admitted as a solicitor, or called to the Bar, whether or not he holds a practising certificate, and

(*e*) the reference to a solicitor member of the Commissioners' staff—

(i) except in relation to Scotland, is a reference to a member of staff who has been admitted as a solicitor, whether or not he holds a practising certificate,

(ii) in relation to Scotland, is a reference to a member of staff who has been admitted as a solicitor and who holds a practising certificate.

[(6) In this section "contract settlement" means an agreement made in connection with any person's liability to make a payment to the Commissioners under or by virtue of an enactment.][1]

Amendments—[1] Sub-ss (1A), (6) inserted by FA 2008 s 137(1) with effect from 21 July 2008.

[2] In sub-s (5)(*c*), words inserted by the Crime and Courts Act 2013 s 17, Sch 9 para 68 with effect from 22 April 2014, by virtue of SI 2014/954 art 2.

[25A Certificates of debt

(1) A certificate of an officer of Revenue and Customs that, to the best of that officer's knowledge and belief, a relevant sum has not been paid is sufficient evidence that the sum mentioned in the certificate is unpaid.

(2) In subsection (1) "relevant sum" means a sum payable to the Commissioners under or by virtue of an enactment or under a contract settlement (within the meaning of section 25).

(3) Any document purporting to be such a certificate shall be treated as if it were such a certificate until the contrary is proved.

(4) Subsection (1) has effect subject to any provision treating the certificate as conclusive evidence.][1]

Amendments—[1] This section inserted by FA 2008 s 138(1) with effect from 21 July 2008.

26 Rewards

The Commissioners may pay a reward to a person in return for a service which relates to a function of—

(*a*) the Commissioners, or

(*b*) an officer of Revenue and Customs.

Inspection and complaints

27 Inspection

(1) The Treasury may make regulations conferring functions on Her Majesty's Inspectors of Constabulary, the Scottish inspectors or the Northern Ireland inspectors in relation to—

(*a*) the Commissioners for Her Majesty's Revenue and Customs, and

(*b*) officers of Revenue and Customs.

(2) Regulations under subsection (1)—

(*a*) may—

(i) in relation to Her Majesty's Inspectors of Constabulary, apply (with or without modification) or make provision similar to any provision of sections 54 to 56 of the Police Act 1996 (c 16) (inspection);

(ii) in relation to the Scottish inspectors, apply (with or without modification) or make provision similar to any provision of section 33 or 34 of the Police (Scotland) Act 1967 (c 77) (inspection);

(iii) in relation to the Northern Ireland inspectors, apply (with or without modification) or make provision similar to any provision of section 41 or 42 of the Police (Northern Ireland) Act 1998 (c 32) (inspection);

(*b*) may enable a Minister of the Crown or the Commissioners to require an inspection to be carried out;

(*c*) shall provide for a report of an inspection to be made and, subject to any exceptions required or permitted by the regulations, published;

(*d*) shall provide for an annual report by Her Majesty's Inspectors of Constabulary;

(*e*) may make provision for payment by the Commissioners to or in respect of Her Majesty's Inspectors of Constabulary, the Scottish inspectors or the Northern Ireland inspectors.

(3) An inspection carried out by virtue of this section may not address a matter of a kind which the Comptroller and Auditor General may examine under section 6 of the National Audit Act 1983 (c 44).

(4) An inspection carried out by virtue of this section shall be carried out jointly by Her Majesty's Inspectors of Constabulary and the Scottish inspectors—

(*a*) if it is carried out wholly in Scotland, or

(*b*) in a case where it is carried out partly in Scotland, to the extent that it is carried out there.

(5) Regulations under subsection (1)—

(*a*) shall be made by statutory instrument, and

(*b*) shall be subject to annulment in pursuance of a resolution of either House of Parliament.

(6) In this section—

(*a*) "the Scottish inspectors" means the inspectors of constabulary appointed under section 33(1) of the Police (Scotland) Act 1967, and

(*b*) "the Northern Ireland inspectors" means the inspectors of constabulary appointed under section 41(1) of the Police (Northern Ireland) Act 1998.

Regulations—See the Revenue and Customs (Inspections) Regulations, SI 2005/1133.

28 Complaints and misconduct: England and Wales

(1) The Treasury may make regulations conferring functions on the Independent Police Complaints Commission in relation to—

(*a*) the Commissioners for Her Majesty's Revenue and Customs, and

(*b*) officers of Revenue and Customs.

(2) Regulations under subsection (1)—

(*a*) may apply (with or without modification) or make provision similar to any provision of or made under Part 2 of the Police Reform Act 2002 (c 30) (complaints);

(*b*) may confer on the Independent Police Complaints Commission, or on a person acting on its behalf, a power of a kind conferred by this Act or another enactment on an officer of Revenue and Customs;

(*c*) may make provision for payment by the Commissioners to or in respect of the Independent Police Complaints Commission.

(3) The Independent Police Complaints Commission and the Parliamentary Commissioner for Administration may disclose information to each other for the purposes of the exercise of a function—

(*a*) by virtue of this section, or

(*b*) under the Parliamentary Commissioner Act 1967 (c 13).

(4) The Independent Police Complaints Commission and the Parliamentary Commissioner for Administration may jointly investigate a matter in relation to which—

(*a*) the Independent Police Complaints Commission has functions by virtue of this section, and

(*b*) the Parliamentary Commissioner for Administration has functions by virtue of the Parliamentary Commissioner Act 1967.

(5) Regulations under subsection (1)—

(*a*) shall be made by statutory instrument, and

(*b*) shall be subject to annulment in pursuance of a resolution of either House of Parliament.

(6) Regulations under subsection (1) shall relate to the Commissioners or officers of Revenue and Customs only in so far as their functions are exercised in or in relation to England and Wales.

Commentary—*Simon's Taxes* **A5.403**.

Regulations—Revenue and Customs (Complaints and Misconduct) (Amendment) Regulations, SI 2011/3061.

29 Confidentiality, &c

(1) Where Her Majesty's Inspectors of Constabulary, the Scottish inspectors or the Northern Ireland inspectors obtain information in the course of exercising a function by virtue of section 27—

(*a*) they may not disclose it without the consent of the Commissioners, and

(*b*) they may not use it for any purpose other than the exercise of the function by virtue of section 27.

(2) A report of an inspection by virtue of section 27 may not include information relating to a specified person without his consent.

(3) Where the Independent Police Complaints Commission or a person acting on its behalf obtains information from the Commissioners or an officer of Revenue and Customs, or from the Parliamentary Commissioner for Administration, in the course of exercising a function by virtue of section 28—

(*a*) the Commission or person shall comply with any restriction on disclosure imposed by regulations under that section (and those regulations may, in particular, prohibit disclosure generally or only in specified circumstances or only without the consent of the Commissioners), and

(*b*) the Commission or person may not use the information for any purpose other than the exercise of the function by virtue of that section.

(4) A person commits an offence if he contravenes a provision of this section.

(5) It is a defence for a person charged with an offence under this section of disclosing or using information to prove that he reasonably believed—

(*a*) that the disclosure or use was lawful, or

(*b*) that the information had already and lawfully been made available to the public.

(6) A person guilty of an offence under this section shall be liable—

(*a*) on conviction on indictment, to imprisonment for a term not exceeding two years, to a fine or to both, or

(*b*) on summary conviction, to imprisonment for a term not exceeding 12 months, to a fine not exceeding the statutory maximum or to both.

(7) A prosecution for an offence under this section may be instituted in England and Wales [only by or with the consent of the Director of Public Prosecutions.][1]

(8) A prosecution for an offence under this section may be instituted in Northern Ireland only—

(*a*) by the Commissioners, or

(*b*) with the consent of the Director of Public Prosecutions for Northern Ireland.

(9) In the application of this section to Scotland or Northern Ireland the reference in subsection (6)(*b*) to 12 months shall be taken as a reference to six months.

(10) In this section a reference to the Scottish inspectors or the Northern Ireland inspectors has the same meaning as in section 27.

Amendments—[1] In sub-s (7), words substituted by the Public Bodies (Merger of the Director of Public Prosecutions and the Director of Revenue and Customs Prosecutions) Order, SI 2014/834 art 3(3), Sch 1 paras 5, 8 with effect from 27 March 2014.

Offences

30 Impersonation

(1) A person commits an offence if he pretends to be a Commissioner or an officer of Revenue and Customs with a view to obtaining—

(*a*) admission to premises,

(*b*) information, or

(*c*) any other benefit.

(2) A person guilty of an offence under this section shall be liable on summary conviction to—

(*a*) imprisonment for a period not exceeding 51 weeks,

(*b*) a fine not exceeding level 5 on the standard scale, or

(*c*) both.

(3) In the application of this section to Scotland or Northern Ireland the reference in subsection (2)(*a*) to 51 weeks shall be taken as a reference to six months.

Cross references—FA 2014 Sch 34 para 6(4)(*i*) (application of this section in relation to the issue of conduct notices to promoters of tax avoidance schemes).

31 Obstruction

(1) A person commits an offence if without reasonable excuse he obstructs—

(*a*) an officer of Revenue and Customs,

(*b*) a person acting on behalf of the Commissioners or an officer of Revenue and Customs, or

(*c*) a person assisting an officer of Revenue and Customs.

(2) A person guilty of an offence under this section shall be liable on summary conviction to—

(*a*) imprisonment for a period not exceeding 51 weeks,

(*b*) a fine not exceeding level 3 on the standard scale, or

(*c*) both.

(3) In the application of this section to Scotland or Northern Ireland the reference in subsection (2)(*a*) to 51 weeks shall be taken as a reference to six months.

Cross references—FA 2014 Sch 34 para 6(4)(*i*) (application of this section in relation to the issue of conduct notices to promoters of tax avoidance schemes).

32 Assault

(1) A person commits an offence if he assaults an officer of Revenue and Customs.

(2) A person guilty of an offence under this section shall be liable on summary conviction to—

(*a*) imprisonment for a period not exceeding 51 weeks,

(*b*) a fine not exceeding level 5 on the standard scale, or (*c*) both.

(3) In the application of this section to Scotland or Northern Ireland the reference in subsection (2)(*a*) to 51 weeks shall be taken as a reference to six months.

Cross references—FA 2014 Sch 34 para 6(4)(*i*) (application of this section in relation to the issue of conduct notices to promoters of tax avoidance schemes).

33 Power of arrest

(1) An authorised officer of Revenue and Customs may arrest a person without warrant if the officer reasonably suspects that the person—

(*a*) has committed an offence under section 30, 31 or 32,

(*b*) is committing an offence under any of those sections, or

(*c*) is about to commit an offence under any of those sections.

(2) In subsection (1) "authorised" means authorised by the Commissioners.

(3) Authorisation for the purposes of this section may be specific or general.

(4) In Scotland or Northern Ireland, a constable may arrest a person without warrant if the constable reasonably suspects that the person—

(*a*) has committed an offence under this Act,

(*b*) is committing an offence under this Act, or

(*c*) is about to commit an offence under this Act.

Prosecutions

34–39 The Revenue and Customs Prosecutions Office

Amendments— Sections 34–39 repealed by the Public Bodies (Merger of the Director of Public Prosecutions and the Director of Revenue and Customs Prosecutions) Order, SI 2014/834 art 3(3), Sch 1 paras 5, 9 with effect from 27 March 2014.

40 Confidentiality

(1) [The Crown Prosecution Service][4] may not disclose information which—

(*a*) is held by [the Service in connection with any of the Director of Public Prosecution's functions][4], . . .[4]

(*b*) relates to a person whose identity is specified in the disclosure or can be deduced from it[, and

(*c*) was disclosed to the Director of Public Prosecutions by Her Majesty's Revenue and Customs for use in connection with a Revenue and Customs function of the Director of Public Prosecutions.][4]

(2) But subsection (1)—

(*a*) does not apply to a disclosure which—

(i) is made for the purposes of a function of [the Director of Public Prosecutions][4], and

(ii) does not contravene any restriction imposed by the Director [of Public Prosecutions][4],

(*b*) does not apply to a disclosure made to Her Majesty's Revenue and Customs in connection with a function of the Revenue and Customs (within the meaning of section 25),

(*c*) does not apply to a disclosure made for the purposes of a criminal investigation or criminal proceedings (whether or not within the United Kingdom),

[(*ca*) does not apply to a disclosure made for the purposes of—

(i) the exercise of any functions of the prosecutor under Parts 2, 3 and 4 of the Proceeds of Crime Act 2002 (c 29),

(ii) the exercise of any functions of the [National Crime Agency][3] under that Act,

(iii) the exercise of any functions of . . .[4] the Director of the Serious Fraud Office, the Director of Public Prosecutions for Northern Ireland or the Scottish Ministers under, or in relation to, Part 5 or 8 of that Act,

(iv) the exercise of any functions of an officer of Revenue and Customs[, an accredited financial investigator][2] or a constable under Chapter 3 of Part 5 of that Act, or

(v) investigations or proceedings outside the United Kingdom which have led or may lead to the making of an external order within the meaning of section 447 of that Act,][1]

(*cb*) . . .[4]

(*d*) does not apply to a disclosure which in the opinion of the Director [of Public Prosecutions][4] is desirable for the purpose of safeguarding national security,

(*e*) does not apply to a disclosure made in pursuance of an order of a court,

[(*ea*) does not apply to a disclosure made with the consent of the Commissioners (which may be general or specific),][4]

(*f*) does not apply to a disclosure made with the consent of each person to whom the information relates, and

(*g*) is subject to any other enactment.

(3) A person commits an offence if he contravenes subsection (1).

(4) Subsection (3) does not apply to the disclosure of information about internal administrative arrangements of [the Crown Prosecution Service][4] (whether relating to a member of [the service][2] or to another person).

(5) It is a defence for a person charged with an offence under this section of disclosing information to prove that he reasonably believed—

(*a*) that the disclosure was lawful, or

(*b*) that the information had already and lawfully been made available to the public.

(6) In this section a reference to [the Crown Prosecution Service][4] includes a reference to—

[(*za*) former members of the Crown Prosecution Service,

(*zb*) persons who hold or have held appointment under section 5 of the Prosecution of Offences Act 1985,][4]

(*a*) former members of [the Revenue and Customs Prosecutions Office][4], and

(*b*) persons who . . . [4] have held appointment under section 38.

[(6A) In this section "Revenue and Customs function of the Director of Public Prosecutions" means—

(*a*) a function of the Director of Public Prosecutions under section 3(2)(*ab*), (*bb*) or (*ee*) of the Prosecution of Offences Act 1985, or

(*b*) a function of the Director of Public Prosecutions under the Proceeds of Crime Act 2002 that relates to a function of the Commissioners for Her Majesty's Revenue and Customs or an officer of Revenue and Customs.][4]

(7) A person guilty of an offence under this section shall be liable—

(*a*) on conviction on indictment, to imprisonment for a term not exceeding two years, to a fine or to both, or

(*b*) on summary conviction, to imprisonment for a term not exceeding 12 months, to a fine not exceeding the statutory maximum or to both.

(8) A prosecution for an offence under this section may be instituted in England and Wales [only by or with the consent of the Director of Public Prosecutions.][4]

(9) A prosecution for an offence under this section may be instituted in Northern Ireland only—

(*a*) by the Commissioners, or

(*b*) with the consent of the Director of Public Prosecutions for Northern Ireland.

(10) In the application of this section to Scotland or Northern Ireland the reference in subsection (7)(*b*) to 12 months shall be taken as a reference to six months.

(10A) . . . [4]

(11) In subsection (2) the reference to an enactment does not include—

(*a*) an Act of the Scottish Parliament or an instrument made under such an Act,

[(*aa*) an Act of the National Assembly for Wales or an instrument made under such an Act,][5] or

(*b*) an Act of the Northern Ireland Assembly or an instrument made under such an Act.

Amendments—[1] Sub-s (2)(*ca*) inserted by the Serious Crime Act 2007 s 74(2), Sch 8 para 167 with effect from 1 April 2008: SI 2008/755 art 2(1)(a), subject to transitional provisions and savings in art 3.

[2] Words in sub-s (2)(*ca*)(iv) inserted by the Serious Crime Act 2007 s 79, Sch 11 para 16 with effect from 6 April 2008: SI 2008/755 art 17(1)(f) subject to transitional provisions and savings in SI 2008/755 art 3.

[3] In sub-s (2)(*ca*)(ii), words substituted for words "Serious Organised Crime Agency" by the Crime and Courts Act 2013 s 15, Sch 8 para 156 with effect from 7 October 2013 by virtue of SI 2013/1682, art 3(*v*).

[4] The following amendments made by the Public Bodies (Merger of the Director of Public Prosecutions and the Director of Revenue and Customs Prosecutions) Order, SI 2014/834 art 3(3), Sch 1 paras 5, 10 with effect from 27 March 2014—

- in sub-s (1), words substituted and repealed, and para (*c*) and preceding word "and" inserted;
- in sub-s (2), words substituted, inserted and repealed, and para (*ea*) inserted;
- in sub-s (4), words substituted;
- in sub-s (6), words substituted and repealed, and paras (*za*), (*zb*) inserted;
- sub-s (6A) inserted;
- in sub-s (8), words substituted; and
- sub-s (10A) repealed.

[5] Sub-s (11)(*aa*) inserted by the Wales Act 2014 s 7(2), (10) with effect from 17 February 2015.

41

Amendments—Section 41 repealed by the Public Bodies (Merger of the Director of Public Prosecutions and the Director of Revenue and Customs Prosecutions) Order, SI 2014/834 art 3(3), Sch 1 paras 5, 11 with effect from 27 March 2014.

42

Amendments—Section 42 repealed by the Public Bodies (Merger of the Director of Public Prosecutions and the Director of Revenue and Customs Prosecutions) Order, SI 2014/834 art 3(3), Sch 1 paras 5, 12 with effect from 27 March 2014.

Money and property

43 Expenditure

Expenditure of the Commissioners in connection with the exercise of their functions shall be paid out of money provided by Parliament.

44 Payment into Consolidated Fund

(1) The Commissioners shall pay money received in the exercise of their functions into the Consolidated Fund—

(*a*) at such times and in such manner as the Treasury directs,

(*b*) with the exception of receipts specified in subsection (2), and

(*c*) after deduction of the disbursements specified in subsection (3).

(2) The exceptions mentioned in subsection (1)(*b*) are—

(*a*) contributions under Part I of the Social Security Contributions and Benefits Act 1992 (c 4),

(*b*) contributions under Part I of the Social Security Contributions and Benefits (Northern Ireland) Act 1992 (c 7),

(*c*) any other sums payable, under or by virtue of an enactment, into the National Insurance Fund or the Northern Ireland National Insurance Fund,

[(*ca*) sums required by section 30A(15) of the Finance Act 1994 (air passenger duty: Northern Ireland long haul rates of duty) to be paid into the Consolidated Fund of Northern Ireland,][3]

(*d*) sums required under or by virtue of an enactment to be paid into the National Loans Fund,

(*e*) sums required to be paid to a Minister of the Crown [or other person][1] by virtue of an enactment relating to financial support for students,

(f) penalties under section 21 of the National Minimum Wage Act 1998 (c 39) (non-compliance), and[2]

(*g*) sums required under or by virtue of an enactment to be paid into the Scottish Consolidated Fund.

(3) The disbursements mentioned in subsection (1)(*c*) are—

(*a*) payments in connection with drawback, repayments and discounts,

(*b*) payments under section 77 of the Scotland Act 1998 (c 46) (additional tax),

(*c*) payments under section 2 of the Isle of Man Act 1979 (c 58) (Isle of Man share of common duties), and

(*d*) tax credits.

(4) In subsection (3)(*a*) "repayments" includes—

(*a*) payments in respect of actual or deemed credits relating to any tax or duty, and

(*b*) payments of interest (or repayment supplement) on—

(i) repayments, or

(ii) payments treated as repayments.

Cross-references—See VATA 1994 Sch 3BA para 13 (s 44 does not apply to any money received for or on account of VAT that is required to be paid to another member State under Art 46 of Council Regulation 904/2010/EU).

Amendments—[1] In sub-s (2)(*e*), words inserted, in relation to England and Wales, by the Sale of Student Loans Act 2008 s 6(5) with effect from 21 July 2008 (by virtue of the Sale of Student Loans Act 2008 s 14).

[2] Sub-s (2)(*f*) repealed by the Employment Act 2008, ss 9(5), 20, Schedule Pt 2 with effect from 6 April 2009 (by virtue of SI 2009/603 arts 2, 3 and subject to savings in relation to the enforcement of the agricultural minimum wage in Scotland and Northern Ireland in s 9(7) thereof).

[3] Sub-s (2)(*ca*) inserted by FA 2012 s 190, Sch 23 para 14 with effect from 17 July 2012.

Prospective amendments—Sub-s (3)(*b*) to be repealed by the Scotland Act 2012 s 25, Sch 2 para 3(1), (2) with effect from a date to be appointed.

In sub-s (3)(*b*), word "and" to be inserted at the end by WRA 2012 s 33, Sch 3 paras 19, 21 with effect from a date to be appointed.

Sub-s (3)(*d*) and preceding word "and" to be repealed by WRA 2012 s 147, Sch 14 Pt 1 with effect from a date to be appointed.

45 Remuneration, &c

(1) The Commissioners shall be paid, out of money provided by Parliament, such remuneration, expenses and other allowances as may be determined by the Minister for the Civil Service.

(2) The Commissioners may incur expenditure in respect of staff (whether in respect of remuneration, allowances, pensions, gratuities or otherwise).

(3) The Commissioners shall pay to the Minister for the Civil Service, at such times as the Minister may direct, such sums as the Minister may determine in respect of any increase attributable to this Act in the sums payable under the Superannuation Act 1972 (c 11) out of money provided by Parliament.

46 Accounts

(1) The Commissioners shall provide to the Comptroller and Auditor General, in such form as the Treasury shall direct, a daily account of—

(*a*) the amount of revenue received, and

(*b*) the disposal of revenue received.

(2) The Commissioners shall provide to the Comptroller and Auditor General, in such form and at such times as the Treasury shall direct, an account of liabilities satisfied by the acceptance of property in satisfaction of tax under—

(*a*) section 230 of the Inheritance Tax Act 1984 (c 51), or

(*b*) any other enactment.

47 Payment out of Consolidated Fund

(1) This section applies if the Treasury think that the funds available to the Commissioners may be insufficient to make, under or by virtue of an enactment—

(*a*) a payment into the National Insurance Fund,

(*b*) a payment into the Northern Ireland National Insurance Fund,

(*c*) a payment of a kind specified in section 44(2)(*c*) to (*g*), or

(*d*) a disbursement of a kind specified in section 44(3).

(2) Where this section applies the Treasury may pay money to the Commissioners out of the Consolidated Fund to enable them to make a payment or disbursement.

(3) This section applies whether or not the reason for a deficiency is or may be that an amount has been paid or retained on the basis of an estimate that has proved or may prove to be inaccurate.

48 Transfer of property, &c: general

(1) Upon commencement the property, rights and liabilities of any of the old commissioners shall by virtue of this section vest in the new commissioners.

(2) Anything done by, on behalf of or in relation to any of the old commissioners which has effect immediately before commencement shall continue to have effect as if done by, on behalf of or in relation to the new commissioners.

(3) Anything (including any legal proceedings) which immediately before commencement is in the process of being done by, on behalf of or in relation to any of the old commissioners may be continued by, on behalf of or in relation to the new commissioners.

(4) Upon commencement the property, rights and liabilities of any of the old officers shall by virtue of this section vest in the officers of Revenue and Customs.

(5) Anything done by, on behalf of or in relation to any of the old officers which has effect immediately before commencement shall continue to have effect as if done by, on behalf of or in relation to an officer of Revenue and Customs.

(6) Anything (including any legal proceedings) which immediately before commencement is in the process of being done by, on behalf of or in relation to any of the old officers may be continued by, on behalf of or in relation to an officer of Revenue and Customs.

(7) So far as is necessary or appropriate in consequence of section 5 or the preceding provisions of this section, on and after commencement—

(*a*) a reference to any of the old commissioners in an agreement (whether written or not), instrument or other document shall be treated as a reference to the new commissioners, and

(*b*) a reference in an agreement (whether written or not), instrument or other document to any of the old officers shall be treated as a reference to an officer of Revenue and Customs.

(8) This section shall operate in relation to property, rights or liabilities—

(*a*) whether or not they would otherwise be capable of being transferred,

(*b*) without any instrument or other formality being required, and

(*c*) irrespective of any requirement for consent that would otherwise apply.

(9) In this section—

"commencement" means the time appointed under section 53 for the commencement of section 5,

"rights and liabilities" includes rights and liabilities relating to employment,

"the old commissioners" means—

(*a*) the Commissioners of Inland Revenue, and

(*b*) the Commissioners of Customs and Excise,

"the old officers" means any of the persons listed in section 6(2) or 7(3), and

"the new commissioners" means the Commissioners for Her Majesty's Revenue and Customs.

(10) This section is subject to section 49.

49

Amendments—Section 49 repealed by the Public Bodies (Merger of the Director of Public Prosecutions and the Director of Revenue and Customs Prosecutions) Order, SI 2014/834 art 3(3), Sch 1 paras 5, 13 with effect from 27 March 2014.

General

50 Consequential amendments, &c

(1) In so far as is appropriate in consequence of section 5 a reference in an enactment, instrument or other document to the Commissioners of Customs and Excise, to customs and excise or to the Commissioners of Inland Revenue (however expressed) shall be taken as a reference to the Commissioners for Her Majesty's Revenue and Customs.

(2) In so far as is appropriate in consequence of sections 6 and 7 a reference in an enactment, instrument or other document to any of the persons specified in section 6(2) or 7(3) (however expressed) shall be taken as a reference to an officer of Revenue and Customs.

(3) In so far as is appropriate in consequence of this Act a reference in an enactment, instrument or other document to the Valuation Office of the Inland Revenue (however expressed) shall be taken as a reference to the Valuation Office of Her Majesty's Revenue and Customs.

(4) The Treasury may by regulations make such provision as they think appropriate in consequence of section 5, 6 or 7 in respect of a reference in an enactment (however expressed) to—

(*a*) the Commissioners of Inland Revenue (or to a Commissioner),

(*b*) the Commissioners of Customs and Excise (or to a Commissioner),

(*c*) customs,

(*d*) customs and excise,

(*e*) Inland Revenue, or

(*f*) any of the persons specified in section 6(2) or 7(3).

(5) Regulations under subsection (4) in respect of a reference in an enactment—

(*a*) may amend an enactment,

(*b*) may make incidental and consequential provision,

(*c*) shall be made by statutory instrument, and

(*d*) shall not be made unless a draft has first been laid before, and approved by resolution of, each House of Parliament.

(6) Schedule 4 (consequential amendments, &c) shall have effect (and is without prejudice to the generality of subsections (1) to (4)).

(7) Subsections (1) to (4) shall, subject to any express provision to the contrary, have effect in relation to enactments passed or made, and instruments and documents issued, whether before or after the passing of this Act.

Order—See the Commissioners for Revenue and Customs Act 2005 (Commencement) Order, SI 2005/1126, art 2(2) (this section and Sch 4 came into force on 18 April 2005).

51 Interpretation

(1) In this Act—

except where otherwise expressly provided, "enactment" includes—

(*a*) an Act of the Scottish Parliament,

(*b*) an instrument made under an Act of the Scottish Parliament,

[(*ba*) an Act of the National Assembly for Wales,

[(*bb*) an instrument made under an Act of the National Assembly for Wales,][2]

(*c*) Northern Ireland legislation, and

(*d*) an instrument made under Northern Ireland legislation,

"officer of Revenue and Customs" means a person appointed under section 2, and

"revenue" has the meaning given by section 5(4).

(2) In this Act—

(*a*) "function" means any power or duty (including a power or duty that is ancillary to another power or duty), and

(*b*) a reference to the functions of the Commissioners or of officers of Revenue and Customs is a reference to the functions conferred—

(i) by or by virtue of this Act, or

(ii) by or by virtue of any enactment passed or made after the commencement of this Act.

[(2A) But a reference to the functions of the Commissioners or of officers of Revenue and Customs does not include a function which—

(*a*) is conferred on them by or by virtue of an Act of the Scottish Parliament or an instrument made under such an Act, and

(*b*) relates to a devolved tax within the meaning of the Scotland Act 1998.][1]

[(2B) Nor does such a reference include a function which—

(*a*) is conferred on the Commissioners or on officers of Revenue and Customs by or by virtue of an Act of the National Assembly for Wales or an instrument made under such an Act, and

(*b*) relates to a devolved tax within the meaning of the Government of Wales Act 2006.][2]

(3) A reference in this Act, in an enactment amended by this Act or, subject to express provision to the contrary, in any future enactment, to responsibility for collection and management of revenue has the same meaning as references to responsibility for care and management of revenue in enactments passed before this Act.

(4) In this Act a reference to information acquired in connection with a matter includes a reference to information held in connection with that matter.

Amendments—[1] Sub-s (2A) inserted by the Scotland Act 2012 s 24(1), (2), (6) with effect from 1 July 2012.

[2] Sub-ss (1)(*ba*), (*bb*), (2B) inserted by the Wales Act 2014 s 7(2), (11)–(13) with effect from 17 February 2015.

52 Repeals

(1) The following shall cease to have effect—

(*a*) (*repeals* CEMA 1979 ss 12, 15, 32, 84, 86, 152(*c*), (*d*), 169).

(*b*) (*repeals* TMA 1970 s 111(2)).

(2) The enactments specified in Schedule 5 are hereby repealed to the extent specified.

Order—See the Commissioners for Revenue and Customs Act 2005 (Commencement) Order, SI 2005/1126, art 2(2) (this section and Sch 5 came into force on 18 April 2005).

53 Commencement

(1) This Act shall come into force in accordance with provision made by order of the Treasury.

(2) An order under subsection (1)—

(*a*) may make provision generally or only in relation to specified provisions or purposes,

(*b*) may include transitional, consequential or incidental provision or savings, and

(*c*) shall be made by statutory instrument.

Orders—See the Commissioners for Revenue and Customs Act 2005 (Commencement) Order, SI 2005/1126 (the Act came into force on 7 April 2005 at 5.45pm, subject to the provisions specified in SI 2005/1126 art 2(2) which came into force on 18 April 2005).

54 Transitional: general

(1) In the application of section 5—

(*a*) a reference to responsibility before commencement of that section includes a reference to responsibility under an enactment passed or made, but not yet in force, before commencement, and

(*b*) a reference to a function vesting includes a reference to a function which is to vest under an enactment passed or made, but not yet in force, before commencement of that section.

(2) In the application of section 6 or 7 a reference to a function conferred by an enactment includes a reference to a function conferred by an enactment passed or made, but not yet in force, before commencement of that section.

(3) Where immediately before the commencement of section 6 a person holds appointment as a member of the staff of the Commissioners of Inland Revenue or of the Commissioners of Customs and Excise, his appointment shall have effect on commencement as if made by the Commissioners for Her Majesty's Revenue and Customs under section 2.

(4) The following shall be treated as being included in the list in Schedule 1—

(*a*) development land tax,

(*b*) disabled person's tax credit,

(*c*) estate duty,

(*d*) the national defence contribution under Part III of the Finance Act 1937 (c 54),

(*e*) the special tax on banking deposits under section 134 of the Finance Act 1981 (c 35), and

(*f*) working families tax credit.

(5) The Treasury may by order made by statutory instrument add to the list in subsection (4) an item relating to a matter for which the Commissioners of Inland Revenue or a person listed in section 7(3) had responsibility before the commencement of section 5, if it appears to the Treasury that the law relating to that matter has lapsed or ceased to have effect but that transitional matters may continue to arise in respect of it.

(6) An order under subsection (5)—

(*a*) may include consequential, transitional or incidental provision,

(*b*) shall be made by statutory instrument, and

(*c*) shall be subject to annulment in pursuance of a resolution of either House of Parliament.

(7) A reference in this Act to anything done by, on behalf of or in relation to a specified person or class of person includes a reference to anything treated as if done by, on behalf of or in relation to that person by virtue of transitional provision of an enactment passed or made before this Act.

Order—See the Commissioners for Revenue and Customs Act 2005 (Commencement) Order, SI 2005/1126, art 2(2) (this section came into force on 18 April 2005).

Prospective amendments—Sub-s (4)(*f*), and preceding word "and" to be repealed by WRA 2012 s 147, Sch 14 Pt 1 with effect from a date to be appointed.

55 Transitional: penalties

(1) In relation to an offence under section 19 committed before the commencement of section 282 of the Criminal Justice Act 2003 (c 44) (short sentences) the reference in section 19(4)(*b*) to 12 months shall have effect as if it were a reference to six months.

(2) In relation to an offence under section 21 committed before the commencement of section 282 of the Criminal Justice Act (short sentences), the reference in section 21(6)(*b*) to 12 months shall have effect as if it were a reference to six months.

(3) In relation to an offence under section 29 committed before the commencement of section 282 of the Criminal Justice Act 2003 (c 44) (short sentences) the reference in section 29(6)(*b*) to 12 months shall have effect as if it were a reference to six months.

(4) In relation to an offence under section 30 committed before the commencement of section 281(4) and (5) of the Criminal Justice Act 2003 (51 week maximum term of sentences) the reference in section 30(2)(*a*) to 51 weeks shall have effect as if it were a reference to six months.

(5) In relation to an offence under section 31 committed before the commencement of section 281(4) and (5) of the Criminal Justice Act 2003 (51 week maximum term of sentences) the reference in section 31(2)(*a*) to 51 weeks shall have effect as if it were a reference to one month.

(6) In relation to an offence under section 32 committed before the commencement of section 281(4) and (5) of the Criminal Justice Act 2003 (51 week maximum term of sentences) the reference in section 32(2)(*a*) to 51 weeks shall have effect as if it were a reference to six months.

(7) In relation to an offence under section 40 committed before the commencement of section 282 of the Criminal Justice Act 2003 (short sentences) the reference in section 40(7)(*b*) to 12 months shall have effect as if it were a reference to six months.

56 Extent

(1) This Act extends to the United Kingdom.

(2) But an amendment, modification or repeal effected by this Act has the same extent as the enactment (or the relevant part of the enactment) to which it relates.

57 Short title

This Act may be cited as the Commissioners for Revenue and Customs Act 2005.

SCHEDULES

SCHEDULE 1

FORMER INLAND REVENUE MATTERS

Section 7

Order—See the Commissioners for Revenue and Customs Act 2005 (Commencement) Order, SI 2005/1126, art 2(2) (this Schedule and s 7 came into force on 18 April 2005).

1 Capital gains tax.

2 Charities.

3 Child benefit.

4 Child tax credit.

Prospective amendments—This para to be repealed by WRA 2012 s 147, Sch 14 Pt 1 with effect from a date to be appointed.

5 Child trust funds.

6 Corporation tax (and amounts assessable or chargeable as if they were corporation tax).

7 Guardian's allowance.

8 Income tax.

9 Inheritance tax.

10 The issue of bank notes.

11 National insurance contributions.

12 The National Insurance Fund.

13 The national minimum wage.

14 Oil and gas royalties.

15 Payment of or in lieu of rates.

16 Payment in lieu of tax reliefs, in so far as the Commissioners of Inland Revenue were responsible before the commencement of section 5.

17 Pension schemes.

18 Petroleum revenue tax.

19 Rating lists.

20 Recovery of taxes due in other member States, in relation to matters corresponding to those for which the Commissioners of Inland Revenue were responsible before the commencement of section 5.

21 Stamp duty.

22 Stamp duty land tax.

23 Stamp duty reserve tax.

24 Statutory adoption pay.

25 Statutory maternity pay.

[26 [Statutory][2] paternity pay.][1]

Amendments—[1] Paragraphs 26, 26A substituted for previous para 26 by the Work and Families Act 2006 s 11(1), Sch 1 para 61 with effect from 6 April 2010 (by virtue of SI 2010/495).

[2] Word substituted by the Children and Families Act 2014 s 126, Sch 7 para 64(1), (2) with effect from 5 April 2015 (by virtue of SI 2014/1640 art 7(*kk*));

Prospective amendments—This para to be repealed by WRA 2012 s 147, Sch 14 Pt 1 with effect from a date to be appointed.

26A . . . [1]

Amendments—[1] Para 26A (additional statutory paternity pay) repealed by the Children and Families Act 2014 s 126, Sch 7 para 64(1), (3) with effect from 5 April 2015 (by virtue of SI 2014/1640 art 7(*kk*));

[26B Statutory shared parental pay.][1]

Amendments—[1] Para 26B inserted by the Children and Families Act 2014 s 126, Sch 7 para 64(1), (4) with effect from 1 December 2014 (by virtue of see SI 2014/1640 art 5(2)).

27 Statutory sick pay.

28 Student loans.

29 Valuation lists in relation to council tax.

30 Valuation of property.

31 Working tax credit.

Prospective amendments—This para to be repealed by WRA 2012 s 147, Sch 14 Pt 1 with effect from a date to be appointed.

SCHEDULE 2

FUNCTIONS OF COMMISSIONERS AND OFFICERS: RESTRICTIONS, &C

Sections 16 and 17

PART 1

GENERAL

Order—See the Commissioners for Revenue and Customs Act 2005 (Commencement) Order, SI 2005/1126, art 2(2) (Part 1 of this Schedule and s 16 came into force on 18 April 2005).

[Wireless Telegraphy Act 2006 (c 36)

1

Amendments—Para 1 repealed by the Serious Crime Act 2007 ss 88, 92, Sch 12 para 30, Sch 14 with effect from 15 February 2008: SI 2008/219 art 2(b).

Taxes Management Act 1970 (c 9)

2

Amendments—This para repealed by FA 2011 s 86(1), Sch 23 para 59 with effect from 1 April 2012 in relation to relevant data with a bearing on any period (whether before, on or after 1 April 2012) subject to FA 2011 Sch 23 para 3(2). This para will continue to have effect in relation to notices given, or requests made, under any of the provisions repealed by FA 2011 Sch 23 Pt 6 before 1 April 2012 as if the repeal had not been made (FA 2011 Sch 23 para 65(2)).

3 Section 113(3) of that Act (form of documents) shall have effect only in connection with functions relating to matters to which section 7 above applies.

Customs and Excise Management Act 1979 (c 2)

4 Section 8(2) and (3) of the Customs and Excise Management Act 1979 (person acting deemed to be proper officer) shall not apply to a person engaged in connection with a function relating to a matter to which section 7 above applies.

5—(1) Section 11 of that Act (assistance to be rendered by police, &c) shall not apply in connection with a function relating to a matter to which section 7 above applies.

(2) A person may rely for the purposes of section 11 of that Act on a statement (written or oral) of an officer of Revenue and Customs that a function does not relate to a matter to which section 7 above applies.

6 Sections 167 (untrue declarations, &c) and 168 (counterfeiting documents, &c) of that Act shall not apply in relation to a declaration, document or statement in respect of a function relating to a matter to which section 7 above applies.

Police and Criminal Evidence Act 1984 (c 60)

7—

Amendments—This paragraph repealed by FA 2007 ss 84(1)(*a*), (5), 114, Sch 27 Pt 5(1) with effect from 8 November 2007: SI 2007/3166 art 2(*c*).

Finance Act 1985 (c 54)

8 Section 10 of the Finance Act 1985 (computer records &c) shall not apply in connection with a function relating to a matter to which section 7 above applies.

Police and Criminal Evidence (Northern Ireland) Order 1989 (SI 1989/1341 (NI 12))

9—

Amendments—This paragraph repealed by FA 2007 ss 84(1)(*b*), (5), 114, Sch 27 Pt 5(1) with effect from 8 November 2007: SI 2007/3166 art 2(*c*).

Finance Act 1998 (c 36)

10 (*amends* FA 1998 s 163(1)).

Regulation of Investigatory Powers Act 2000 (c 23)

11—

Amendments—Para 11 repealed by the Serious Crime Act 2007 ss 88, 92, Sch 12 para 30, Sch 14 with effect from 15 February 2008: SI 2008/219 art 2(b).

Finance Act 2002 (c 23)

12—(*amended* FA 2002 s 135(10); *repealed by* FA 2007 s 14, Sch 7 Pt 5(4)).

. . .

13, 13A

Amendments—Paragraphs 13, 13A and preceding cross-head repealed by FA 2013 s 224, Sch 48 para 21 with effect from 17 July 2013.

Crime (International Co-operation) Act 2003 (c 32)

14

Amendments—This para repealed by the Criminal Justice and Immigration Act 2008 ss 97(2), 149, Sch 28 Pt 6 with effect from 14 July 2008 (by virtue of SI 2008/1586 art 2(1), Sch 1 paras 41, 50(1), (6)).

PART 2
USE OF INFORMATION

Teaching and Higher Education Act 1998 (c 30)

15 The Commissioners may supply information in accordance with section 24 of the Teaching and Higher Education Act 1998 (supply of information in connection with the student loan scheme) only if the information was obtained or is held in the exercise of a function relating to matters to which section 7 above applies.

Employment Relations Act 1999 (c 26)

16 The Commissioners may supply information in accordance with section 39 of the Employment Relations Act 1999 (supply of information in connection with the national minimum wage and agricultural wages) only if the information was obtained or is held in the exercise of a function relating to matters to which section 7 above applies.

Immigration and Asylum Act 1999 (c 33)

17

Amendments—Para 17 repealed by the UK Borders Act 2007 ss 40(6)(*c*), 58, Schedule, with effect from 31 January 2008 (by virtue of SI 2008/99 art 2(*m*)).

Financial Services and Markets Act 2000 (c 8)

18 The Commissioners may supply information in accordance with section 350 of the Financial Services and Markets Act 2000 (supply of information to assist with an investigation under section 168 of that Act) only if the information was obtained or is held in the exercise of a function relating to matters to which section 7 above applies.

Terrorism Act 2000 (c 11)

19 Information may be supplied in accordance with paragraph 4(2) of Schedule 14 to the Terrorism Act 2000 (exercise of officers' powers) only if the information has not been held solely in the exercise of functions relating to matters to which section 7 above applies.

Nationality, Immigration and Asylum Act 2002 (c 41)

20

Amendments—Para 20 repealed by the UK Borders Act 2007 ss 40(6)(*c*), 58, Schedule, with effect from 31 January 2008 (by virtue of SI 2008/99 art 2(*m*)).

SCHEDULE 3
REVENUE AND CUSTOMS PROSECUTIONS OFFICE

Section 34

Amendments—Schedule 3 repealed by the Public Bodies (Merger of the Director of Public Prosecutions and the Director of Revenue and Customs Prosecutions) Order, SI 2014/834 art 3(3), Sch 1 paras 5, 14 with effect from 27 March 2014.

SCHEDULE 4
CONSEQUENTIAL AMENDMENTS, &C

Section 50

Order—See the Commissioners for Revenue and Customs Act 2005 (Commencement) Order, SI 2005/1126, art 2(2) (this Schedule and s 50 came into force on 18 April 2005).

Harbours, Docks, and Piers Clauses Act 1847 (c 27)

1 (*amends* Harbours, Docks and Piers Clauses Act 1847 s 14).

Public Revenue and Consolidated Fund Charges Act 1854 (c 94)

2 (*amends* Public Revenue and Consolidated Fund Charges Act Sch (*b*)).

Exchequer and Audit Departments Act 1866 (c 39)

3 (*amends* Exchequer and Audit Departments Act 1866 s 10).

Game Laws Amendment (Scotland) Act 1877 (c 28)

4 (*amends* Game Laws Amendment (Scotland) Act 1877 s 11).

Inland Revenue Regulation Act 1890 (c 21)

5 (*repeals* Inland Revenue Regulation Act 1890).

Public Accounts and Charges Act 1891 (c 24)

6 (*repeals* Public Accounts and Charges Act 1891)

Judicial Pensions Act (Northern Ireland) 1951 (c 20 (N.I))

7 (*amends* Judicial Pensions Act (Northern Ireland) 1951 Sch 2Apara 6(3) (as inserted by Judicial Pensions (Northern Ireland) Order, SI 1991/2631, Sch 2)).

County Courts Act (Northern Ireland) 1959 (c 25 (NI))

8 (*amends* County Courts Act (Northern Ireland) 1959 Sch 2A para 6(3) (as inserted by Judicial Pensions (Northern Ireland) Order, SI 1991/2631, Sch 2)).

Resident Magistrates' Pensions Act (Northern Ireland) 1960 (c 2 (NI))

9 (*amends* Resident Magistrates' Pensions Act (Northern Ireland) 1960 Sch 3 para 6(3) (as inserted by Judicial Pensions (Northern Ireland) Order, SI 1991/2631, Sch 2)).

Parliamentary Commissioner Act 1967 (c 13)

10 (*amends* Parliamentary Commissioner Act 1967 Sch 2).

Taxes Management Act 1970 (c 9)

11 The Taxes Management Act 1970 shall be amended as follows.

12 (*substitutes* TMA 1970 s 1).

13 (*repeals* TMA 1970 s 6(3), (4)).

14 (*repeals* TMA 1970 s 111(2)).

15 (*amends* TMA 1970 Sch 1 Part 1).

Finance Act 1972 (c 41)

16 (*repeals* FA 1972 s 127).

Biological Weapons Act 1974 (c 6)

17 (*amends* Biological Weapons Act 1974 s 1B).

Health and Safety at Work etc Act 1974 (c 37)

18—(1) Section 27A of the Health and Safety at Work etc Act 1974 (disclosure by Commissioners of Customs and Excise) shall be amended as follows.
(2)–(4) (*amend* Health and Safety at Work etc Act 1974 s 27A(1), (3) and section heading).

Health and Safety at Work (Northern Ireland) Order 1978 (SI 1978/1039 (NI 9))

19—(1) Article 29A of the Health and Safety at Work (Northern Ireland) Order 1978 (disclosure by Commissioners of Customs and Excise) shall be amended as follows.
(2)–(4) (*amend* Health and Safety at Work (Northern Ireland) Order 1978 art 29A(1), (3) and section heading).

Customs and Excise Management Act 1979 (c 2)

20 The Customs and Excise Management Act 1979 shall be amended as follows.

21 (*repeals* CEMA 1979 ss 6, 7, 8(1), 13, 14, 16, 17, 18, 153, 155(2), 165).

22 (*amends* CEMA 1979 s 1(1)).

23 (*amends* CEMA 1979 s 145(1), (2), (4), (6)).

24 (*amends* CEMA 1979 s 146A(7)).

25 (*amends* CEMA 1979 s 150(1)).

26 (*amends* CEMA 1979 s 152(*a*)).

27 (*substitutes* CEMA 1979 s 155(1)).

28 (*inserts* CEMA 1979 s 171(4A)).

Judicial Pensions Act 1981 (c 20)

29 (*amends* Judicial Pensions Act 1981 Sch 1A para 6(3)).

Police and Criminal Evidence Act 1984 (c 60)

30

Amendments—Paras 30, 41, 69, 77, 97 repealed by the Public Bodies (Merger of the Director of Public Prosecutions and the Director of Revenue and Customs Prosecutions) Order, SI 2014/834 art 3(3), Sch 1 paras 5, 15 with effect from 27 March 2014.

31 (*repeals* PACE 1984 s114(4)).

Debtors (Scotland) Act 1987 (c 18)

32 The Debtors (Scotland) Act 1987 shall be amended as follows.

33 (*amends* Debtors (Scotland) Act 1987 s 1(5)(*d*)).

34 (*amends* Debtors (Scotland) Act 1987 s 5(4)(*d*)).

Criminal Justice Act 1987 (c 38)

35—(1) (*amends* CJA 1987 s 3(1), (2)).
(2) (*inserts* CJA 1987 s 3(8)).

Consumer Protection Act 1987 (c 43)

36—(1) Section 37 of the Consumer Protection Act 1987 (disclosure by Commissioners of Customs and Excise) shall be amended as follows.

(2)–(4) (*amend* Consumer Protection Act 1987 s 37(1), (3) and section heading).

Income and Corporation Taxes Act 1988 (c 1)

37

Amendments—This para repealed by TIOPA 2010 s 378, Sch 10 Pt 1.

Copyright, Designs and Patents Act 1988 (c 48)

38 (*repeals* Copyright, Designs and Patents Act 1988 s 112(5)).

Finance Act 1989 (c 26)

39 (*inserts* FA 1989 s 182(10A)).

Police and Criminal Evidence (Northern Ireland) Order 1989 (SI 1989/1341 (NI 12))

40 (*repeals* Police and Criminal Evidence (Northern Ireland) Order 1989 art 85(3)).

Criminal Justice (International Co-operation) Act 1990 (c 5)

41

Amendments—Paras 30, 41, 69, 77, 97 repealed by the Public Bodies (Merger of the Director of Public Prosecutions and the Director of Revenue and Customs Prosecutions) Order, SI 2014/834 art 3(3), Sch 1 paras 5, 15 with effect from 27 March 2014.

Child Support Act 1991 (c 48)

42 (*amends* Child Support Act 1991 Sch 2).

Social Security Contributions and Benefits Act 1992 (c 4)

43 (*amends* Social Security Contributions and Benefits Act 1992 s 171).

Social Security Administration Act 1992 (c 5)

44 The Social Security Administration Act 1992 shall be amended as follows.

45 (*amended* Social Security Administration Act 1992 s 122ZA; *repealed by* WRA 2012 s 147, Sch 14 Pt 13).

46 (*amends* Social Security Administration Act 1992 s 122AA).

47 (*substitutes* Social Security Administration Act 1992 s 161(1)).

Social Security Contributions and Benefits (Northern Ireland) Act 1992 (c 7)

48 (*amends* Social Security Contributions and Benefits (Northern Ireland) Act 1992 s 167(1)).

Social Security Administration (Northern Ireland) Act 1992 (c 8)

49 (*amends* Social Security Administration (Northern Ireland) Act 1992 s 116ZA).

50 (*amends* Social Security Administration (Northern Ireland) Act 1992 s 116AA).

Pension Schemes Act 1993 (c 48)

51 (*amends* Pension Schemes Act 1993 s 158).

Pension Schemes (Northern Ireland) Act 1993 (c 49)

52 (*amends* Pension Schemes (Northern Ireland) Act 1993 s 154).

Finance Act 1994 (c 9)

53 (*repeals* FA 1994 Sch 7 para 32).

Value Added Tax Act 1994 (c 23)

54 The Value Added Tax Act 1994 shall be amended as follows.

55 (*substitutes* VATA 1994 Sch 3B para 21(1)(*b*)).

56 (*substitutes* VATA 1994 Sch 11 para 1).

Trade Marks Act 1994 (c 26)

57 (*repeals* Trade Marks Act 1994 s 90(5)).

58 (*amends* Trade Marks Act 1994 s 91 and section heading).

Drug Trafficking Act 1994 (c 37)

59 (*amends* Drug Trafficking Act 1994 s 60).

Finance Act 1995 (c 4)

60 (*repeals* FA 1995 s 158).

Merchant Shipping Act 1995 (c 21)

61 (*repeals* Merchant Shipping Act 1995 s 303).

Criminal Appeal Act 1995 (c 35)

62 (*substitutes* Criminal Appeal Act 1995 s 22(4)(*e*), (*f*)).

Criminal Law (Consolidation) (Scotland) Act 1995 (c 39)

63—(1) Section 30 of the Criminal Law (Consolidation) (Scotland) Act 1995 (disclosure of information) shall be amended as follows.
(2)–(4) (*amend* Criminal Law (Consolidation) (Scotland) Act 1995 s 30(1), (2), (7)).

Chemical Weapons Act 1996 (c 6)

64 (*amends* Chemical Weapons Act 1996 s 30A).

Finance Act 1996 (c 8)

65 (*repeals* FA 1996 Sch 5 para 41).

Landmines Act 1998 (c 33)

66 (*amends* Landmines Act 1998 s 21).

Finance Act 1998 (c 36)

67 (*repeals* FA 1998 s 145).

68 Schedule 18 to that Act (company tax returns &c) shall have effect—
(*a*) with the substitution for "the Inland Revenue", in each place, of "an officer of Revenue and Customs",
(*b*) with the omission of paragraph 95 (meaning of references to Inland Revenue), and
(*c*) with any other necessary consequential modifications.

Crime and Disorder Act 1998 (c 37)

69

Amendments—Paras 30, 41, 69, 77, 97 repealed by the Public Bodies (Merger of the Director of Public Prosecutions and the Director of Revenue and Customs Prosecutions) Order, SI 2014/834 art 3(3), Sch 1 paras 5, 15 with effect from 27 March 2014.

Scotland Act 1998 (c 46)

70 The Scotland Act 1998 shall be amended as follows.

Prospective amendments—Paras 70–72 to be repealed by the Scotland Act 2012 s 25, Sch 2 para 3(1), (3) with effect from a date to be appointed.

71 (*amends* Scotland Act 1988 s 77).

Prospective amendments—Paras 70–72 to be repealed by the Scotland Act 2012 s 25, Sch 2 para 3(1), (3) with effect from a date to be appointed.

72 (*repeals* Scotland Act 1998 s 78(8)).

Prospective amendments—Paras 70–72 to be repealed by the Scotland Act 2012 s 25, Sch 2 para 3(1), (3) with effect from a date to be appointed.

Social Security Contributions (Transfer of Functions, etc) Act 1999 (c 2)

73 The Social Security Contributions (Transfer of Functions etc) Act 1999 shall be amended as follows.

74 (*substitutes* Social Security Contributions (Transfer of Functions etc) Act 1999 s 3(1)).

75 (*repeals* Social Security Contributions (Transfer of Functions etc) Act 1999 s 7).

Finance Act 1999 (c 16)

76 (*amends* FA 1999 s 135(2)).

Crown Prosecution Service Inspectorate Act 2000 (c 10)

77

Amendments—Paras 30, 41, 69, 77, 97 repealed by the Public Bodies (Merger of the Director of Public Prosecutions and the Director of Revenue and Customs Prosecutions) Order, SI 2014/834 art 3(3), Sch 1 paras 5, 15 with effect from 27 March 2014.

Terrorism Act 2000 (c 11)

78 (*amends* Terrorism Act 2000 s 121).

Finance Act 2000 (c 17)

79 The Finance Act 2000 shall be amended as follows.

80 (*repeals* FA 2000 s 148(2)).

81 (*repeals* FA 2000 Sch 6 para 140).

Capital Allowances Act 2001 (c 2)

82 The Capital Allowances Act 2001 shall be amended as follows.

83—(1) For "the Inland Revenue", wherever that expression appears, substitute "an officer of Revenue and Customs" (except as provided in paragraph 84).
(2) For "the Board of Inland Revenue", wherever that expression appears, substitute "the Commissioners for Her Majesty's Revenue and Customs".

84 (*amended* CAA 2001 s 51; *repealed* by FA 2008 s 76(6)).

85 (*repeals* CAA 2001 s 576).

86 (*amends* CAA 2001 Sch 1 Part 2).

Anti-terrorism, Crime and Security Act 2001 (c 24)

87 (*amends* Anti-terrorism, Crime and Security Act s 53).

Tax Credits Act 2002 (c 21)

88 (*substitutes* TCA 2002 s 2).

89 (*repeals* TCA 2002 s 40(1)(*a*)).

90 (*substitutes* TCA 2002 s 53).

91 (*repeals* TCA 2002 Sch 5 para 2).

92 To the extent that the Tax Credits Act 1999 (c 10) is saved by the Tax Credits Act 2002 (Commencement No 4, Transitional and Savings) Order 2003 (SI 2003/962), the modifications made by paragraphs 88 to 91 shall have effect in relation to the relevant provisions of that Act as they have effect in relation to the Tax Credits Act 2002 (c 21).

Employment Act 2002 (c 22)

93 (*repeals* Employment Act 2002 s 5).

Finance Act 2002 (c 23)

94 The Finance Act 2002 shall be amended as follows.

95—(1) (*amends* FA 2002 s 135).
(2) (*amended* FA 2002 s 135(1); *repealed by* FA 2007 s 114, Sch 27 Pt 5(4)).

96 (*repeals* FA 2002 Sch 13 para 26).

Proceeds of Crime Act 2002 (c 29)

97

Amendments—Paras 30, 41, 69, 77, 97 repealed by the Public Bodies (Merger of the Director of Public Prosecutions and the Director of Revenue and Customs Prosecutions) Order, SI 2014/834 art 3(3), Sch 1 paras 5, 15 with effect from 27 March 2014.

98 (*inserted* Proceeds of Crime Act 2002 s 436(5)(*ga*); repealed by the Serious Crime Act 2007 Sch 14).

99 (*amends* Proceeds of Crime Act 2002 s 451).

100 In Schedule 8 to that Act (declarations) for "an offence relating to inland revenue,", in each place, substitute "an offence relating to a former Inland Revenue matter (being a matter listed in Schedule 1 to the Commissioners for Revenue and Customs Act 2005 except for paragraphs 2, 10, 13, 14, 15, 17, 19, 28, 29 and 30),".

Income Tax (Earnings and Pensions) Act 2003 (c 1)

101 The Income Tax (Earnings and Pensions) Act 2003 shall be amended as follows.

102—(1) For the expression "the Inland Revenue", wherever it appears, substitute "an officer of Revenue and Customs" (except as provided in paragraphs 109, 117 and 118).
(2) For the expression "the Board of Inland Revenue", wherever it appears, substitute "the Commissioners for Her Majesty's Revenue and Customs".
(3) In the following provisions for "Board" substitute "Commissioners" and for "Board's" substitute "Commissioners'"—
(*a*) section 28(6),
(*b*) –(*d*)(*amended* ITEPA 2003 ss 42, 43; *repealed by* FA 2008 s 25, Sch 7 para 79(*c*)
(*e*) section 343,
(*f*) section 355,
(*g*) section 591,
(*h*) section 647,
(*i*) section 691,
(*j*) section 703,
(*k*) section 704, and
(*l*) the title of section 717.

103—(1) In the following provisions for "they" or "them" in each place substitute "the officer"—
(*a*) section 58(3),
(*b*) section 65(3),
(*c*) section 79(2),
(*d*) section 96(2),
(*e*) section 179(3),
(*f*) section 312(5),
(*g*) section 344(3),
(*h*) section 392(4) and (5),
(*i*) section 421J(4),
(*j*) paragraph 81(1) and (3) of Schedule 2,
(*k*) paragraph 84(2) of Schedule 2,
(*l*) paragraph 85(1) of Schedule 2,
(*m*) paragraph 93(1) of Schedule 2,
(*n*) paragraph 40(1) and (3) of Schedule 3,
(*o*) paragraph 42(2A) of Schedule 3,
(*p*) paragraph 43 of Schedule 3,
(*q*) paragraph 44(1) of Schedule 3,
(*r*) paragraph 45(1) of Schedule 3,
(*s*) paragraph 28(1) and (3) of Schedule 4,
(*t*) paragraph 30(3) of Schedule 4,
(*u*) paragraph 31 of Schedule 4,
(*v*) paragraph 32(1) of Schedule 4,
(*w*) paragraph 33(1) of Schedule 4,
(*x*) paragraph 46(2) of Schedule 5,
(*y*) paragraph 46(3) of Schedule 5,
(*z*) paragraph 47 of Schedule 5, and
(*aa*) paragraph 51(1) of Schedule 5.
(2) In the following provisions for "their" in each place substitute "the officer's"—
(*a*) section 715(3)(*b*),
(*b*) paragraph 85(3) of Schedule 2,
(*c*) paragraph 93(1)(*a*) of Schedule 2,

(*d*) paragraph 41(2) of Schedule 3,
(*e*) paragraph 44(3) of Schedule 3,
(*f*) paragraph 45(1) of Schedule 3,
(*g*) paragraph 29(2) of Schedule 4,
(*h*) paragraph 32(3) of Schedule 4,
(*i*) paragraph 33(1) of Schedule 4,
(*j*) paragraph 46(2) and (3) of Schedule 5,
(*k*) paragraph 47(1)(*b*) and (3)(*b*) of Schedule 5,
(*l*) paragraph 49(2) and (3) of Schedule 5, and
(*m*) paragraph 51(1) of Schedule 5.

(3) In the following provisions in each place for "their" substitute "the"—
(*a*) paragraph 81(3) of Schedule 2,
(*b*) paragraph 82(2) of Schedule 2,
(*c*) paragraph 85(3) of Schedule 2,
(*d*) paragraph 40(3) of Schedule 3,
(*e*) paragraph 43 of Schedule 3,
(*f*) paragraph 28(3) of Schedule 4,
(*g*) paragraph 31 of Schedule 4, and
(*h*) paragraph 47(1)(*a*) and (3)(*a*) of Schedule 5.

(4) In the following provisions omit "their"—
(*a*) paragraph 84(2) of Schedule 2,
(*b*) paragraph 42(2A) of Schedule 3, and
(*c*) paragraph 30(3) of Schedule 4.

104 (*amended* ITEPA 2003 s 43(1); *repealed by* FA 2008 s 25, Sch 7 para 79(*c*)).

105 (*amends* ITEPA 2003 s 58(3)).

106 (*amends* ITEPA 2003 s 65(3), (4)).

107 (*amends* ITEPA 2003 s 79(2)).

108 (*amends* ITEPA 2003 s 96(2), (3)).

109 (*amends* ITEPA 2003 s 79(3)).

110 (*amends* ITEPA 2003 s 183(1)(*a*)).

111 (*amends* ITEPA 2003 s 312(5)).

112 (*amends* ITEPA 2003 s (3)).

113 (*amends* ITEPA 2003 s 392(4), (5)).

114 (*amends* ITEPA 2003 s 511(2)(*a*), (*b*)).

115 (*amends* ITEPA 2003 s 514(2)(*a*), (*b*))

116 (*amends* ITEPA 2003 s 647(3)(*b*)).

117 (*amends* ITEPA 2003 s 684).

118 (*amends* ITEPA 2003 s 715(3)(*b*)).

119 (*repeals* ITEPA 2003 s 720).

120 (*amends* ITEPA 2003 Sch 1, Pt 2).

121 In Schedule 2—
(*a*) (*amends* ITEPA 2003 Sch 2 para 81(1), (3)).
(*b*) (*amends* ITEPA 2003 Sch 2 para 82(1)).
(*c*) (*amends* ITEPA 2003 Sch 2 para 85(1)).
(*d*) (*amends* ITEPA 2003 Sch 2 para 93(1)(*a*)).
(*e*) (*amends* ITEPA 2003 Sch 2 para 100).

122 In Schedule 3—
(*a*) (*amends* ITEPA 2003 Sch 3 para 40(1), (3)).
(*b*) (*amends* ITEPA 2003 Sch 3 para 41(1)).
(*c*) (*amends* ITEPA 2003 Sch 3 para 43).
(*d*) (*amends* ITEPA 2003 Sch 3 para 44(1)).

(*e*) (*amends* ITEPA 2003 Sch 3 para 45(1)).
(*f*) (*amends* ITEPA 2003 Sch 3 para 49).

123 In Schedule 4—
(*a*) (*amends* ITEPA 2003 Sch 4 para 28(1), (3)).
(*b*) (*amends* ITEPA 2003 Sch 4 para 29(1)).
(*c*) (*amends* ITEPA 2003 Sch 4 para 31).
(*d*) (*amends* ITEPA 2003 Sch 4 para 32(1)).
(*e*) (*amends* ITEPA 2003 Sch 4 para 33(1)(*a*)).
(*f*) (*amends* ITEPA 2003 Sch 4 para 37).

124 In Schedule 5—
(*a*) (*amends* ITEPA 2003 Sch 5 para 46(2), (3), (6)).
(*b*) (*amends* ITEPA 2003 Sch 5 para 47(1)–(3)).
(*c*) (*amends* ITEPA 2003 Sch 5 para 48(5)).
(*d*) (*amends* ITEPA 2003 Sch 5 para 49(1), (2)).
(*e*) (*amends* ITEPA 2003 Sch 5 para 51(1)(*a*)).
(*f*) (*amends* ITEPA 2003 Sch 5 para 59).

Finance Act 2003 (c 14)

125–127 (*amended* ITEPA 2003 ss 129(6), 130(6); *repealed by* FA 2012 s 227, Sch 39 para 9(2)).

Dealing in Cultural Objects (Offences) Act 2003 (c 27)

128 (*amends* Dealing in Cultural Objects (Offences) Act 2003 s 4).

Criminal Justice Act 2003 (c 44)

129 (*amends* Criminal Justice Act 2003 s 27).

130 (*inserts* Criminal Justice Act 2003 s 29(5)(*ca*)).

Income Tax (Trading and Other Income) Act 2005 (c 5)

131 The Income Tax (Trading and Other Income) Act 2005 shall be amended as follows.

132—(1) For the expression "the Inland Revenue", wherever it appears, substitute "an officer of Revenue and Customs" (except as provided by paragraph 133(2)(*b*) and (5)).
(2) For the expression "the Board of Inland Revenue", wherever it appears, substitute "the Commissioners for Her Majesty's Revenue and Customs".
(3) In the following provisions, for "Board" substitute "Commissioners" and for "Board's" substitute "Commissioners'"—
(*a*) *the title of section 343,*[2]
(*b*) section 695(4),
(*c*) section 698(3) and (4),
(*d*) section 699(2),
(*e*) *section 700(1)(b)*, (2) and (5),[1]
(*f*) section 757(3),
(*g*) section 762(2),
(*h*) the title of section 873, and

Amendments—[1] Sub-para (3)(*e*) repealed by the Finance Act 2009, Section 96 and Schedule 48 (Appointed Day, Savings and Consequential Amendments) Order, SI 2009/3054 art 3, Schedule para 16(*e*) with effect from 1 April 2010.
[2] Sub-para (3)(*a*) repealed by FA 2012 s 227, Sch 39 para 43(2)(*b*) with effect in relation to mineral royalties which a person is entitled to receive on or after 6 April 2013.

(*i*) section 883(3).

133—*(1) In section 75(5)*—
(*a*) for "have" substitute "has", and
(*b*) in each place for "they" substitute "the officer".[2]
(2) In section 218—
(*a*) in subsections (1) and (2) for "do" substitute "does", and
(*b*) in subsection (3)(*a*) for "the Inland Revenue are not" substitute "the officer is not".
(3) In section 305(1) for "have" substitute "has".[2]
(4) In section 647(1)
(*a*) for "them" substitute "the officer",
(*b*) for "they" in each place substitute "the officer", and

(*c*) for "consider" substitute "considers".

(5) . . . [1]

(6) In section 758(5) for "has" substitute "have" '.

Amendments—[1] Sub-para (5) repealed by FA 2007 s 114, Sch 27 Pt 2(13) with effect from 6 April 2008 (by virtue of FA 2007, ss 46(9), 114, Sch 27, Pt 2(13), SI 2008/561 art 2).

[2] Sub-paras (1), (3) repealed by Finance Act 2009 Schedule 47 (Consequential Amendments) Order, SI 2009/2035, Art 2 Schedule, para 60(*k*) with effect from 13 August 2009.

134—(1) In section 878(1), omit the definitions of "the Board of Inland Revenue" and "the Inland Revenue".

(2) In Part 2 of Schedule 4, omit the entries for "the Board of Inland Revenue" and "the Inland Revenue".

SCHEDULE 5
REPEALS

Section 52

Note—The repeals made under this Schedule are already in force and have therefore been omitted.

FINANCE (NO 2) ACT 2005

(2005 Chapter 22)

An Act to Grant certain duties, to alter other duties, and to amend the law relating to the National Debt and the Public Revenue, and to make further provision in connection with finance.

[20 July 2005]

PART 1
VALUE ADDED TAX

1 Goods subject to warehousing regime: place of acquisition or supply

(*inserts* VATA 1994 s 18(1A)).

2 Cars: determination of consideration for fuel supplied for private use

(1) Section 57 of VATA 1994 (determination of consideration for fuel supplied for private use) is amended as follows.

(2) (*inserts* VATA 1994 s 57(4A)–(4G)).

(3)–(5) (*amend* VATA 1994 s 57(5), (7), (8)).

(6) (*inserts* VATA 1994 s 57(9), (10)).

(7) The amendments made by this section come into force on such day or days as the Treasury may appoint by order made by statutory instrument; and different days may be so appointed for different purposes.

Orders—Finance (No 2) Act 2005, Section 2(7), (Appointed Day) Order, SI 2007/946 art 2 (appointed day is 22 March 2007).

3 Credit for, or repayment of, overstated or overpaid VAT

(1) Section 80 of VATA 1994 (recovery of overpaid VAT) is amended as follows.

(2) (*substitutes* VATA 1994 s 80(1)–(1B)).

(3) (*amends* VATA 1994 s 80(2)).

(4) (*inserts* VATA 1994 s 80(2A)).

(5) (*amends* VATA 1994 s 80(3)).

(6) (*substitutes* VATA 1994 s 80(3A)).

(7) (*amends* VATA 1994 s 80(3B)).

(8) (*substitutes* VATA 1994 s 80(4)–(4ZB)).

(9) (*substitutes* VATA 1994 s 80(4A)).

(10) (*substitutes* VATA 1994 s 80(7)).

(11) The side-note to the section accordingly becomes "Credit for, or repayment of, overstated or overpaid VAT".

(12) Section 4 contains consequential and supplementary provision.

4 Section 3: consequential and supplementary provision

(1) In consequence of the amendments made by section 3, VATA 1994 is amended as follows.

(2) (*amends* VATA 1994 s 78(1)(*a*)).

(3) (*amends* VATA 1994 s 80A).

(4) (*inserts* VATA 1994 s 80B(1A)–(1E)).

(5) (*amends* VATA 1994 s 83).

(6) The amendments made by section 3 and this section have effect in any case where a claim under section 80(2) of VATA 1994 is made on or after 26th May 2005, whenever the event occurred in respect of which the claim is made.

5 Reverse charge: gas and electricity valuation
(1) (*amends* VATA 1994 Sch 6 para 8).
(2) This section has effect in relation to supplies made on or after 17th March 2005.

6 Disclosure of value added tax avoidance schemes
(1) Schedule 1 (which contains amendments of Schedule 11A to VATA 1994) has effect.
(2) Subsection (1) and Schedule 1 shall come into force on such day as the Treasury may by order made by statutory instrument appoint.
(3) An order under subsection (2) may—
(*a*) appoint different days for different purposes, and
(*b*) contain transitional provisions and savings.

Orders—See the Finance (No 2) Act 2005, section 6, (Appointed Day and Savings Provisions) Order, SI 2005/2010.

PART 6
SUPPLEMENTARY PROVISIONS

70 Repeals
(1) The enactments mentioned in Schedule 11 (which include provisions that are spent or of no practical utility) are repealed to the extent specified.
(2) The repeals specified in that Schedule have effect subject to the commencement provisions and savings contained or referred to in the notes set out in that Schedule.

71 Interpretation
In this Act—
"CAA 2001" means the Capital Allowances Act 2001 (c. 2);
"FA", followed by a year, means the Finance Act of that year;
"ICTA" means the Income and Corporation Taxes Act 1988 (c. 1);
"ITEPA 2003" means the Income Tax (Earnings and Pensions) Act 2003 (c. 1);
"ITTOIA 2005" means the Income Tax (Trading and Other Income) Act 2005 (c. 5);
"TCGA 1992" means the Taxation of Chargeable Gains Act 1992 (c. 12);
"VATA 1994" means the Value Added Tax Act 1994 (c. 23);
"VERA 1994" means the Vehicle Excise and Registration Act 1994 (c. 22).

72 Short title
This Act may be cited as the Finance (No 2) Act 2005.

SCHEDULES

SCHEDULE 1

DISCLOSURE OF VALUE ADDED TAX AVOIDANCE SCHEMES

Section 6

Orders—Finance (No 2) Act 2005, section 6, (Appointed Day and Savings Provisions) Order 2005, SI 2005/2010.

Introduction

1 Schedule 11A to VATA 1994 (disclosure of avoidance schemes) is amended in accordance with this Schedule.

Interpretative provisions

2 (*amends* VATA 1994 Sch 11A para 1).

3 (*substitutes* VATA 1994 Sch 11A para 2).

4 (*inserts* VATA 1994 Sch 11A para 2A).

Duty to notify Commissioners

5—(1) Paragraph 6 (duty to notify Commissioners) is amended as follows.
(2) (*amends* VATA 1994 Sch 11A para 6(1)).
(3) (*inserts* VATA 1994 Sch 11A para 6(2A)).
(4) (*substitutes* VATA 1994 Sch 11A para 6(5)).

6 (*amends* VATA 1994 Sch 11A para 7(9)).

Amount of penalty

7—(1) Paragraph 11 (amount of penalty) is amended as follows.
(2) (*amends* VATA 1994 Sch 11A para 11(3)).
(3) (*amends* VATA 1994 Sch 11A para 11(4)).

(4) (*inserts* VATA 1994 Sch 11A para 11(5)).

Penalty assessments

8 (*substitutes* VATA 1994 Sch 11A para 12(3), (3A)).

SCHEDULE 11

REPEALS

Section 70

PART 1

VALUE ADDED TAX

Note—The repeals made under this Part are already in force and are therefore omitted.

FINANCE ACT 2006

(2006 Chapter 25)

An Act to Grant certain duties, to alter other duties, and to amend the law relating to the National Debt and the Public Revenue, and to make further provision in connection with finance.

[19 July 2006]

PART 2

VALUE ADDED TAX

Gaming machines

16 Gaming machines

(1) Section 23 of VATA 1994 (gaming machines) shall be amended as follows.

(2) (*amends* VATA 1994 s 23(1))

(3) (*amends* VATA 1994 s 23(2))

(4) (*amends* VATA 1994 s 23(3))

(5) (*substitutes* VATA 1994 s 23(4)–(7))

(6) This section shall have effect in relation to anything done on or after 6th December 2005.

(7) In the application of section 23(5)(*c*) of VATA 1994 as substituted by this section in relation to anything done before 1st November 2006, "game of chance" shall have the same meaning as in the Gaming Act 1968 (c 65).

Land

17 Buildings and land

(1) The Treasury may by order—

(*a*) make provision for substituting Schedule 10 to VATA 1994 (buildings and land) for the purpose of rewriting that Schedule with amendments;

(*b*) make provision amending sections 83 and 84 of that Act (appeals) in connection with any provision of that Schedule as so rewritten.

(2) The Treasury may by order make provision repealing—

(*a*) paragraph (*b*) of item 1 in Group 1 of Schedule 9 to VATA 1994 (exempt supplies of land not to include supplies made pursuant to a developmental tenancy, developmental lease or developmental licence), and

(*b*) Note (7) in that Group (meaning of developmental tenancy, developmental lease or developmental licence).

The power conferred by this subsection is not to be regarded as affecting in any way the power to vary Schedule 9 to that Act conferred by section 31(2) of that Act.

(3) The Treasury may by order make provision repealing—

(*a*) section 26 of FA 1995 (co-owners etc of buildings and land), and

(*b*) the enactments inserted by that section (section 51A of VATA 1994 and paragraph 8(2) and (3) of Schedule 10 to that Act).

(4) Any power to make an order under this section includes power—

(*a*) to make any provision that might be made by an Act, and

(*b*) to make incidental, consequential, supplemental, or transitional provision or savings.

(5) The consequential provision that may be made under subsection (4)(*b*) includes provision amending any Act or any instrument made under any Act.

(6) Any order under this section—

(*a*) is to be made by statutory instrument,

(*b*) must be laid before the House of Commons, and

(*c*) unless approved by that House before the end of the period of 28 days beginning with the date on which it is made, ceases to have effect at the end of that period.

(7) But, if an order so ceases to have effect, this does not affect—
(*a*) anything previously done under the order, or
(*b*) the making of a new order.
(8) In reckoning the period of 28 days no account is to be taken of any time—
(*a*) during which Parliament is dissolved or prorogued, or
(*b*) during which the House of Commons is adjourned for more than 4 days.

Orders—VAT (Buildings and Land) Order, SI 2008/1146 (made under sub-ss (1)–(5)).

Imported works of art etc

18 Value of imported works of art etc: auctioneer's commission

(1) Section 21 of VATA 1994 (value of imported goods) is amended as follows.
(2) (*amends* VATA 1994 s 21(2))
(3) (*inserts* VATA 1994 s 21(2A), (2B))
(4) Subsections (1) to (3) come into force on such day as the Treasury may by order made by statutory instrument appoint.

Notes—The appointed day for the purposes of sub-ss (1)–(3) above is 1 September 2006 by virtue of the Finance Act 2006, Section 18, (Appointed Day) Order, SI 2006/2149, art 2.

Avoidance and fraud

19 Missing trader intra-community fraud

(1) (*inserts* VATA 1994 s 55A)
(2) (*inserts* VATA 1994 s 26A)
(3) In section 65 of VATA 1994 (inaccuracies in EC sales statements)—
(*a*) (*inserts* VATA 1994 s 65(7))
(*b*) (*amends* VATA 1994 s 65 heading)
(4) In section 66 of VATA 1994 (failure to submit EC sales statements)—
(*a*) (*inserts* VATA 1994 s 66(10))
(*b*) (*amends* VATA 1994 s 66 heading)
(5) (*inserts* VATA 1994 s 69(1)(*ba*))
(6) (*inserts* VATA 1994 s 97(4)(*ea*))
(7) (*inserts* VATA 1994 Sch 11 para 2(3A), (3B))
(8) The amendments made by this section have effect in relation to supplies made on or after such day as the Treasury may by order made by statutory instrument appoint.
But no order may be made under this subsection on or after 22nd March 2009.
(9) An order under subsection (8) may contain transitional provision and savings.

Order—Finance Act 2006, section 19, (Appointed Day) Order, SI 2007/1419 (appointed day for amendments made by s 19 is 1 June 2007).

20 Power to inspect goods

(1) In Schedule 11 to VATA 1994 (administration, collection and enforcement), paragraph 10 (entry and search of premises and persons) is amended as follows.
(2) (inserts VATA 1994 Sch 11 para 10(2A))

Amendments—This section repealed by FA 2008 s 113, Sch 36 para 92(*i*) with effect from 1 April 2009 (by virtue of SI 2009/404 art 2).

In consequence of SI 2009/404 arts 1–11, the amendments made by FA 2008 Sch 36 para 92 shall be disregarded so far as they affect any notice referred to in those provisions, given on or before 31 March 2009.

21 Directions to keep records where belief VAT might not be paid

(1) VATA 1994 is amended as follows.
(2) (*inserts* VATA 1994 s 69B)
(3) (*amends* VATA 1994 s 76(1))
(4) In section 83 (appeals)—
(*a*) (*amends* VATA 1994 s 83(*n*))
(*b*) (*inserts* VATA 1994 s 83(*zza*))
(5) (*inserts* VATA 1994 s 84(7B))
(6) (*inserts* VATA 1994 Sch 11 para 6A)

22 Treatment of credit vouchers

(1) VATA 1994 is amended as follows.
(2) (*inserts* VATA 1994 s 97(4)(*fa*))
(3) (*inserts* VATA 1994 Sch 10A para 3(4))

PART 9
MISCELLANEOUS PROVISIONS

Disclosure of information

177 Disclosure of information

(1) (*inserts* Gambling Act 2005 s 352A)

(2) Section 352A of the Gambling Act 2005 as inserted by subsection (1) above shall come into force on the passing of this Act.

PART 10

SUPPLEMENTARY PROVISIONS

178 Repeals

(1) The enactments mentioned in Schedule 26 (which include provisions that are spent or of no practical utility) are repealed to the extent specified.

(2) The repeals specified in that Schedule have effect subject to the commencement provisions and savings contained or referred to in the notes set out in that Schedule.

179 Interpretation

In this Act—

. . .

"FA", followed by a year, means the Finance Act of that year;

. . .

"VATA 1994" means the Value Added Tax Act 1994 (c 23);

. . .

SCHEDULES

SCHEDULE 26

REPEALS

Section 178

PART 2

VALUE ADDED TAX

Note—The repeals made under this Part are already in force and are therefore omitted.

COMPANIES ACT 2006

(2006 Chapter 46)

PART 38

COMPANIES: INTERPRETATION

Meaning of "UK-registered company"

1158 Meaning of "UK-registered company"

In the Companies Acts "UK-registered company" means a company registered under this Act. The expression does not include an overseas company that has registered particulars under section 1046.

Meaning of "subsidiary" and related expressions

1159 Meaning of "subsidiary" etc

(1) A company is a "subsidiary" of another company, its "holding company", if that other company—

(a) holds a majority of the voting rights in it, or

(b) is a member of it and has the right to appoint or remove a majority of its board of directors, or

(c) is a member of it and controls alone, pursuant to an agreement with other members, a majority of the voting rights in it,

or if it is a subsidiary of a company that is itself a subsidiary of that other company.

(2) A company is a "wholly-owned subsidiary" of another company if it has no members except that other and that other's wholly-owned subsidiaries or persons acting on behalf of that other or its wholly-owned subsidiaries.

(3) Schedule 6 contains provisions explaining expressions used in this section and otherwise supplementing this section.

(3) In this section and that Schedule "company" includes any body corporate.

Derivation—This section was derived from Companies Act 1985 s 736.

Cross references—See VATA 1994 s 43A (Groups: eligibility).

FINANCE ACT 2007

(2007 Chapter 11)

CONTENTS

An Act to Grant certain duties, to alter other duties, and to amend the law relating to the National Debt and the Public Revenue, and to make further provision in connection with finance.

[19 July 2007]

PART 1
CHARGES, RATES, THRESHOLDS ETC

Environment

16 Emissions trading: charges for allocations

(1) The Treasury may impose charges by providing for Community tradeable emissions allowances to be allocated in return for payment.

(2) The Treasury must by regulations make provision for and in connection with allocations of allowances in return for payment.

(3) . . . [2]

(4) The regulations may make any other provision about allocations which the Treasury consider appropriate, including (in particular)—

(*a*) provision as to the imposition of fees, and as to the making and forfeiting of deposits, in connection with participation in allocations,

(*b*) provision as to the persons by whom allocations are to be conducted,

(*c*) provision for the [creation of criminal offences, or for the imposition and recovery of civil penalties,][1] for failure to comply with the terms of a scheme made under subsection (5),

(*d*) provision for and in connection with the recovery of payments due in respect of allowances allocated (including provision as to the imposition and recovery of interest and penalties), and

(*e*) provision conferring rights of appeal against decisions made in allocations, the forfeiting of deposits and the imposition of penalties (including provision specifying the person, court or tribunal to hear and determine appeals).

(5) The Treasury may make schemes about the conduct and terms of allocations (to have effect subject to any regulations under this section); and schemes may in particular include provision about—

(*a*) who may participate in allocations,

(*b*) the allowances to be allocated, and

(*c*) where and when allocations are to take place.

(6) "Community tradeable emissions allowances" are transferable allowances which—

(*a*) relate to the making of emissions of greenhouse gases, and

(*b*) are allocated as part of a system made for the purpose of implementing any Community obligation of the United Kingdom relating to such emissions;

and "greenhouse gases" means carbon dioxide, methane, nitrous oxide, hydrofluorocarbons, perfluorocarbons and sulphur hexafluoride.

[(6A) Subsection (4)(*c*) does not permit the creation of a criminal offence with maximum penalties in excess of the maximum penalties which an instrument under section 2(2) of the European Communities Act 1972 may provide in respect of an offence created by such an instrument.][1]

(7) Regulations under this section are to be made by statutory instrument.

(8) A statutory instrument containing regulations under this section is subject to annulment in pursuance of a resolution of the House of Commons unless a draft of the regulations has been laid before, and approved by a resolution of, that House.

Amendments—[1] Sub-s (6A) inserted, and in sub-s (4)(*c*) words substituted for words "imposition and recovery of penalties", by FA 2008 s 164 with effect from 21 July 2008.

[2] Sub-s (3) repealed by the Community Emissions Trading Scheme (Allocation of Allowances for Payment) Regulations, SI 2012/2661 reg 6(1)(*a*) with effect from 14 November 2012, subject to the savings in reg 6(2) in respect of auctioning of Phase II allowances, Sub-s (3) previously read as follows—

"(3) The regulations must provide for allocations to be overseen by an independent person appointed by the Treasury.".

PART 6

INVESTIGATION, ADMINISTRATION ETC

Investigation etc

82 Criminal investigations: powers of Revenue and Customs

(1) Section 114 of the Police and Criminal Evidence Act 1984 (c 60) (application of Act to customs and excise) is amended as follows.

(2) In paragraph (*a*) of subsection (2)—

(*a*) for "investigations conducted by officers of Customs and Excise of offences which relate to assigned matters, as defined in section 1 of the Customs and Excise Management Act 1979," substitute "investigations conducted by officers of Revenue and Customs", and

(*b*) for "persons detained by officers of Customs and Excise;" substitute "persons detained by officers of Revenue and Customs;".

(3) In the opening words of paragraph (*b*) of that subsection, for "investigations of offences conducted by officers of Customs and Excise" substitute "investigations of offences conducted by officers of Revenue and Customs".

(4) In sub-paragraph (i) of that paragraph, for "section" substitute "sections".

(5) In the section 14A deemed to be inserted by that sub-paragraph—

(*a*) for "and which relates to an assigned matter, as defined in section 1 of the Customs and Excise Management Act 1979," substitute "and which relates to a matter in relation to which Her Majesty's Revenue and Customs have functions," and

(*b*) in the heading, for "**Customs and Excise**" substitute "**Revenue and Customs**".

(6) After that section insert—

"14B Revenue and Customs: restriction on other powers to apply for production of documents

(1) An officer of Revenue and Customs may make an application for the delivery of, or access to, documents under a provision specified in subsection (3) only if the condition in subsection (2) is satisfied.

(2) The condition is that the officer thinks that an application under Schedule 1 would not succeed because the material required does not consist of or include special procedure material.

(3) The provisions are—

(*a*) section 20BA of, and Schedule 1AA to, the Taxes Management Act 1970 (serious tax fraud);

(*b*) paragraph 11 of Schedule 11 to the Value Added Tax Act 1994 (VAT);

(*c*) paragraph 4A of Schedule 7 to the Finance Act 1994 (insurance premium tax);

(*d*) paragraph 7 of Schedule 5 to the Finance Act 1996 (landfill tax);

(*e*) paragraph 131 of Schedule 6 to the Finance Act 2000 (climate change levy);

(*f*) paragraph 8 of Schedule 7 to the Finance Act 2001 (aggregates levy);

(*g*) Part 6 of Schedule 13 to the Finance Act 2003 (stamp duty land tax)."

(7) In paragraph (*c*) of subsection (2)—

(*a*) for "customs detention" substitute "Revenue and Customs detention", and

(*b*) for "an officer of Customs and Excise" substitute "an officer of Revenue and Customs".

(8) After that paragraph (*c*) insert—

"(*d*) that where an officer of Revenue and Customs searches premises in reliance on a warrant under section 8 of, or paragraph 12 of Schedule 1 to, this Act (as applied by an order under this subsection) the officer shall have the power to search persons found on the premises—

(i) in such cases and circumstances as are specified in the order, and

(ii) subject to any conditions specified in the order; and

(*e*) that powers and functions conferred by a provision of this Act (as applied by an order under this subsection) may be exercised only by officers of Revenue and Customs acting with the authority (which may be general or specific) of the Commissioners for Her Majesty's Revenue and Customs."

(9) After that subsection insert—

"(2A) A certificate of the Commissioners that an officer of Revenue and Customs had authority under subsection (2)(*e*) to exercise a power or function conferred by a provision of this Act shall be conclusive evidence of that fact."

(10) For subsection (3) substitute—

"(3) An order under subsection (2)—

(*a*) may make provision that applies generally or only in specified cases or circumstances,

(*b*) may make different provision for different cases or circumstances,

(*c*) may, in modifying a provision, in particular impose conditions on the exercise of a function, and

(*d*) shall not be taken to limit a power under section 164 of the Customs and Excise Management Act 1979."

(11) The heading of section 114 accordingly becomes "**Application of Act to Revenue and Customs**".

Orders—Finance Act 2007 (Sections 82 to 84 and Schedule 23) (Commencement) Order 2007, SI 2007/3166 (this section comes into force on 8 November 2007).

83 Northern Ireland criminal investigations

(1) Article 85 of the Police and Criminal Evidence (Northern Ireland) Order 1989 (SI 1989/1341 (NI 12)) (application of Order to customs and excise) is amended as follows.

(2) In sub-paragraph (*a*) of paragraph (1)—

(*a*) for "investigations conducted by officers of Customs and Excise of offences which relate to assigned matters, as defined in section 1 of the Customs and Excise Management Act 1979," substitute "investigations conducted by officers of Revenue and Customs", and

(*b*) for "persons detained by officers of Customs and Excise;" substitute "persons detained by officers of Revenue and Customs;".

(3) In the opening words of sub-paragraph (*b*) of that paragraph, for "investigations of offences conducted by officers of Customs and Excise" substitute "investigations of offences conducted by officers of Revenue and Customs".

(4) In paragraph (i) of that sub-paragraph, for "Article" substitute "Articles".

(5) In the Article 16A deemed to be inserted by that paragraph—

(*a*) for "and which relates to an assigned matter, as defined in section 1 of the Customs and Excise Management Act 1979," substitute "and which relates to a matter in relation to which Her Majesty's Revenue and Customs have functions," and

(*b*) in the heading, for "**Customs and Excise**" substitute "**Revenue and Customs**".

(6) After that Article insert—

"16B Revenue and Customs: restriction on other powers to apply for production of documents

(1) An officer of Revenue and Customs may make an application for the delivery of, or access to, documents under a provision specified in paragraph (3) only if the condition in paragraph (2) is satisfied.

(2) The condition is that the officer thinks that an application under Schedule 1 would not succeed because the material required does not consist of or include special procedure material.

(3) The provisions are—

(*a*) section 20BA of, and Schedule 1AA to, the Taxes Management Act 1970 (serious tax fraud);

(*b*) paragraph 11 of Schedule 11 to the Value Added Tax Act 1994 (VAT);

(*c*) paragraph 4A of Schedule 7 to the Finance Act 1994 (insurance premium tax);

(*d*) paragraph 7 of Schedule 5 to the Finance Act 1996 (landfill tax);

(*e*) paragraph 131 of Schedule 6 to the Finance Act 2000 (climate change levy);

(*f*) paragraph 8 of Schedule 7 to the Finance Act 2001 (aggregates levy);

(*g*) Part 6 of Schedule 13 to the Finance Act 2003 (stamp duty land tax)."

(7) After sub-paragraph (*b*) of paragraph (1) insert—

"(*c*) that where an officer of Revenue and Customs searches premises in reliance on a warrant under Article 10 of, or paragraph 9 of Schedule 1 to, this Order (as applied by an order under this paragraph) the officer shall have the power to search persons found on the premises—

(i) in such cases and circumstances as are specified in the order, and

(ii) subject to any conditions specified in the order; and

(*d*) that powers and functions conferred by a provision of this Order (as applied by an order under this paragraph) may be exercised only by officers of Revenue and Customs acting with the authority (which may be general or specific) of the Commissioners for Her Majesty's Revenue and Customs."

(8) After that paragraph insert—

"(1A) A certificate of the Commissioners that an officer of Revenue and Customs had authority under paragraph (1)(*d*) to exercise a power or function conferred by a provision of this Order shall be conclusive evidence of that fact."

(9) For paragraph (2) substitute—

"(2) An order under paragraph (1)—

(*a*) may, in modifying a provision, in particular impose conditions on the exercise of a function, and

(*b*) shall not be taken to limit a power under section 164 of the Customs and Excise Management Act 1979."

(10) The heading of Article 85 accordingly becomes "**Application of Order to Revenue and Customs**".

Orders—Finance Act 2007 (Sections 82 to 84 and Schedule 23) (Commencement) Order 2007, SI 2007/3166 (this section comes into force on 8 November 2007).

84 Sections 82 and 83: supplementary

(1) In Schedule 2 to CRCA 2005 (restrictions on the exercise of functions), omit—

(*a*) (*repeals* CRCA 2005 Sch 2 para 7)

(*b*) paragraph 9 (Police and Criminal Evidence (Northern Ireland) Order 1989 (SI 1989/1341 (NI 12))).

(2) Nothing in section 6 or 7 of CRCA 2005 (initial functions) restricts the functions in connection with which officers of Revenue and Customs may exercise a power under—

(*a*) the Police and Criminal Evidence Act 1984 by virtue of section 114 of that Act (as amended by section 82 above), or

(*b*) the Police and Criminal Evidence (Northern Ireland) Order 1989 by virtue of Article 85 of that Order (as amended by section 83 above).

(3) But neither an order under section 114 of the Police and Criminal Evidence Act 1984 nor an order under Article 85 of the Police and Criminal Evidence (Northern Ireland) Order 1989 has effect in relation to a matter specified in section 54(4)(*b*) or (*f*) of, or in paragraphs 3, 7, 10, [14,][1] 19 or 24 to 29 of Schedule 1 to, CRCA 2005 (former Inland Revenue matters).

(4) Schedule 22 contains amendments and repeals consequential on extension of police powers to Revenue and Customs.

(5) Sections 82 and 83 and this section come into force in accordance with provision made by the Treasury by order.

(6) The power to make an order under subsection (5) is exercisable by statutory instrument.

Orders—Finance Act 2007 (Sections 82 to 84 and Schedule 23) (Commencement) Order 2007, SI 2007/3166 (this section comes into force on 8 November 2007, except for sub-s (4), which comes into force on 1 December 2007).

Amendments—[1] In sub-s (3), reference substituted by the Employment Act 2008 s 12(1) with effect from 6 April 2009 (by virtue of SI 2009/603 arts 2, 3).

85 Criminal investigations: Scotland

Schedule 23 contains provision for Scotland about the investigation of offences by Her Majesty's Revenue and Customs.

Orders—Finance Act 2007 (Sections 82 to 84 and Schedule 23) (Commencement) Order 2007, SI 2007/3166 (Schedule 23 comes into force on 1 December 2007).

86 Search warrants

In section 8 of the Police and Criminal Evidence Act 1984, after subsection (6) insert—

"(7) Section 4 of the Summary Jurisdiction (Process) Act 1881 (execution of process of English courts in Scotland) shall apply to a warrant issued on the application of an officer of Revenue and Customs under this section by virtue of section 114 below."

87 Cross-border exercise of powers

(1) This section relates to the Criminal Justice and Public Order Act 1994 (c 33).

(2) Sections 136 to 139 (execution of warrants and powers of arrest and search) shall apply to an officer of Revenue and Customs as they apply to a constable; and for that purpose—

(*a*) a reference to a constable (including a reference to a constable of a police force in England and Wales, a constable of a police force in Scotland or a constable of a police force in Northern Ireland) shall be treated as a reference to an officer of Revenue and Customs, and

(*b*) a reference to a police station, or a designated police station, includes a reference to an office of Revenue and Customs or (in England and Wales and Northern Ireland) a designated office of Revenue and Customs.

[(3) In the application of section 138 to an officer of Revenue and Customs—

(*a*) subsection (1B) shall be treated as if it provided as follows—

"(1B) Where a person is arrested under subsection (2) of the principal section but not charged in connection with an offence, subsections (2) to (9) of section 25A of the Criminal Law (Consolidation) (Scotland) Act 1995 (right of suspects to have access to a solicitor) apply with the following modifications—

(*a*) omit the references to "other premises or place" in subsections (2) and (6);

(*b*) the right under subsection (2) arises when the person is arrested;

(*c*) the reference in subsection (2)(*b*) to the office of Revenue and Customs where the person is being detained is to be read as a reference to the police station to which the person is to be taken; and

(*d*) subsection (6) is to be read as requiring that the person be informed of the rights under section 25A(2) and (3) on being arrested."

(*b*) in subsection (2), the references to the 1995 Act and to section 14(1) of that Act are to be treated as references to the Criminal Law (Consolidation) (Scotland) Act 1995 ("the Consolidation Act") and to section 24(1) of that Act;

(*c*) subsection (2A) is to be treated as if it provided as follows—

"(2A) Those provisions are—

(*a*) section 24(2) to (8A) (detention and questioning at office of Revenue and Customs);

(*b*) sections 24A and 24B (extension of period of detention under section 24);

(*c*) section 25 (right to have someone informed when detained);

(*d*) section 25A(2) to (9) (right of access to solicitor)"

(*d*) in subsection (6) the reference to the 1995 Act is to be treated as a reference to the Consolidation Act;

(*e*) in subsection 7—

(i) the reference to section 14 is to be treated as a reference to section 24 of the Consolidation Act; and

(ii) the reference to subsections (6) and (9) of section 14 is to be treated as a reference to subsections (5) and (8) of section 24;

(*f*) in subsection 8—

(i) the reference to section 15 is to be treated as a reference to section 25 of the Consolidation Act;

(ii) paragraph (*a*) is to be treated as if it provided as follows—

(*a*) "in subsection (1)—

(i) the words "other premises or place" (in both places) are to be treated as if they referred to a police station;

(ii) the reference in paragraph (*a*) to other premises is to be treated as a reference to a police station:"

(iii) paragraph (*b*) does not apply;

(iv) the references in paragraph (*c*)(i) and (iii) to the right under subsection (1)(*b*) are to be treated as references to the right under section 25(1) to have someone informed when detained;

(v) the reference in paragraph (*c*)(ii) to subsection (1)(*b*) is to be treated as a reference to section 25(1);

(vi) the reference in paragraph (*c*)(iii) to subsection (2) is to be treated as a reference to the words in section 25(1) beginning "and the person shall be informed";

(vii) the reference to subsection (4) is to be treated as a reference to section 25(2); and

(*g*) in subsection 9—

(i) the reference to section 15A is to be treated as a reference to section 25A;

(ii) paragraph (*a*) is to be treated as if it provided as follows—

(*a*) "the words "other premises or place" in subsections (2) and (6) are to be treated as referring to a police station;"

; and

(iii) in paragraph (*b*)(iii) the reference to section 15A(2) and (3) is to be treated as a reference to section 25A(2) and (3).][1]

(4) An officer of Revenue and Customs may exercise a power under sections 136 to 139 only in the exercise of a function relating to tax (including duties and tax credits).

(5) In subsection (2)—

"office of Revenue and Customs" means premises wholly or partly occupied by Her Majesty's Revenue and Customs, and

"designated office of Revenue and Customs" has the meaning given by an order under section 114 of the Police and Criminal Evidence Act 1984 (c 60) (power to extend provisions to HMRC) or, in Northern Ireland, by an order under Article 85 of the Police and Criminal Evidence (Northern Ireland) Order 1989 (SI 1989/1341 (NI 12)) (power to extend Order to HMRC).

(6) In section 136, after subsection (8) insert—

"(9) Powers under this section and sections 137 to 139 may be exercised by an officer of Revenue and Customs in accordance with section 87 of the Finance Act 2007."

Amendments—[1] Sub-s (3) substituted by the Criminal Procedure (Legal Assistance, Detention and Appeals) (Scotland) Act 2010 (Consequential Provisions) Order, SI 2011/1739 art 7 with effect from 15 July 2011. Note that this amendment does not affect the operation of CJPO 1994 ss 136–139 (as they apply to HMRC officers by virtue of FA 1987 s 87 as it has effect immediately before 15 July 2011) in relation to a person arrested or detained under s 137(2) of that Act (as it applies to such officers,) where the arrest occurred or the period of detention began before that time.

Other administration

93 Mandatory electronic filing of returns

(1) Section 135 of FA 2002 (mandatory electronic filing) is amended as follows.
(2) (*inserts* FA 2002 s 135(7)(*ba*))
(3) (*amends* FA 2002 s 135(10))
(4) Section 76 of VATA 1994 (assessment) is amended as follows.
(5) (*inserts* VATA 1994 s 76(1)(*d*))
(6) (*amends* VATA 1994 s 76(1))
(7) (*inserts* VATA 1994 s 76(3)(*f*))
(8) (*inserts* VATA 1994 s 83(*zc*))
(9) (*inserts* VATA 1994 s 84(6B))

94 Mandatory electronic payment

(1) Section 204 of FA 2003 (mandatory electronic payment by large employers) is amended as follows.
(2) (*substitutes* FA 2003 s 204(1), (2))
(3) (*amends* FA 2003 s 204(5)(*b*))
(4) (*amends* FA 2003 s 204(6)(*a*))
(5) (*amends* FA 2003 s 204(8)(*a*), (*b*))
(6) (*amends* FA 2003 s 204(12))
(7) (*amends* FA 2003 s 204 heading)
(8) (*amends* FA 2003 s 205(1))

95 Payment by cheque

(1) The Commissioners may make regulations providing for a payment to HMRC made by cheque to be treated as made when the cheque clears, as defined in the regulations.

(2) Section 70A of TMA 1970 (payment by cheque treated as made on receipt by HMRC) is subject to regulations under subsection (1).

(3) Regulations under subsection (1)—

(*a*) may make provision generally or only for specified purposes,

(*b*) may make different provision for different purposes, and

(*c*) may include incidental, consequential or transitional provision.

(4) Regulations under subsection (1)—

(*a*) shall be made by statutory instrument, and

(*b*) shall be subject to annulment in pursuance of a resolution of the House of Commons.

(5) In this section—

(*a*) "the Commissioners" means the Commissioners for Her Majesty's Revenue and Customs, and

(*b*) "HMRC" means Her Majesty's Revenue and Customs.

(6) (*inserts* FA 2003 s 204(13))

(7) (*inserts* TMA 1970 s 70A(3))

(8) (*inserts* VATA 1994 s 58B)

97 Penalties for errors

(1) Schedule 24 contains provisions imposing penalties on taxpayers who—

(*a*) make errors in certain documents sent to HMRC, or

(*b*) unreasonably fail to report errors in assessments by HMRC.

(2) That Schedule comes into force in accordance with provision made by the Treasury by order.

(3) An order—

(*a*) may commence a provision generally or only for specified purposes,

(*b*) may make different provision for different purposes, and

(*c*) may include incidental, consequential or transitional provision.

(4) The power to make an order is exercisable by statutory instrument.

Orders—Finance Act 2007, Schedule 24 (Commencement and Transitional Provisions) Order 2008, SI 2008/568.

PART 7

MISCELLANEOUS

Value added tax and insurance premium tax

98 VAT: joint and several liability of traders in supply chain where tax unpaid

(1) (*substitutes* VATA 1994 s 77A(9)–(9B))

(2) (*inserts* VATA 1994 s 97(4)(*eb*))

99 VAT: non-business use etc of business goods

(1) Schedule 4 to VATA 1994 (matters to be treated as supply of goods or services) is amended as follows.

(2) (*repeals* VATA 1994 Sch 4 para 5(4A))

(3) (*inserts* VATA 1994 Sch 4 para 9(4))

(4) Paragraph 7 of Schedule 6 to VATA 1994 (valuation of supply of services otherwise than for consideration by virtue of paragraph 5(4) of Schedule 4 etc) is amended as follows.

(5) (*inserts* VATA 1994 Sch 6 para 7(2)–(4))

(6) The amendment made by subsection (2) comes into force on 1st September 2007.

(7) The amendment made by subsection (3) has effect in relation to surrenders on or after 21st March 2007.

100 VAT: transfers of going concerns

(1) Section 49 of VATA 1994 (transfers of going concern) is amended as follows.

(2) (*amends* VATA 1994 s 49(1))

(3) (*amends* VATA 1994 s 49(2))

(4) (*inserts* VATA 1994 s 49(2A))

(5) (*amends* VATA 1994 s 49(3))

(6) (*inserts* VATA 1994 s 49(4)–(6))

(7) (*amends* VATA 1994 s 94(6))

(8) (*amends* VATA 1994 Sch 1 para 1(2))

(9) (*amends* VATA 1994 Sch 4 para 8(2)(*b*))

(10) The amendments made by this section have effect in relation to transfers pursuant to contracts entered into on or after 1st September 2007.

112 Updating references to Standing Committees

(1) (*amends* PCTA 1968 s 1(4)(*b*))

(2) (*amends* FA 1973 s 50(2)(*a*))

PART 8

FINAL PROVISIONS

113 Interpretation

(1) In this Act—

"BGDA 1981" means the Betting and Gaming Duties Act 1981 (c 63),
"CAA 2001" means the Capital Allowances Act 2001 (c 2),
"CEMA 1979" means the Customs and Excise Management Act 1979 (c 2),
"CRCA 2005" means the Commissioners for Revenue and Customs Act 2005 (c 11),
"ICTA" means the Income and Corporation Taxes Act 1988 (c 1),
"IHTA 1984" means the Inheritance Tax Act 1984 (c 51),
"ITA 2007" means the Income Tax Act 2007 (c 3),
"ITEPA 2003" means the Income Tax (Earnings and Pensions) Act 2003 (c 1),
"ITTOIA 2005" means the Income Tax (Trading and Other Income) Act 2005 (c 5),
"TCGA 1992" means the Taxation of Chargeable Gains Act 1992 (c 12),
"TMA 1970" means the Taxes Management Act 1970 (c 9),
"VATA 1994" means the Value Added Tax Act 1994 (c 23), and
"VERA 1994" means the Vehicle Excise and Registration Act 1994 (c 22).

(2) In this Act—

"FA", followed by a year, means the Finance Act of that year, and
"F(No 2)A", followed by a year, means the Finance (No 2) Act of that year.

114 Repeals

Schedule 27 contains repeals.

115 Short title

This Act may be cited as the Finance Act 2007.

SCHEDULES

SCHEDULE 22

AMENDMENTS AND REPEALS CONSEQUENTIAL ON EXTENSION OF HMRC POWERS

Section 84

Order—Finance Act 2007 (Sections 82 to 84 and Schedule 23) (Commencement) Order, SI 2007/3166 art 3(*a*) (FA 2007 s 84(4) comes into force on 1 December 2007).

PART 1

AMENDMENTS

1 (*amends* TMA 1970 s 20D(1))

2 (*amends* CJPA 2001 s 67)

PART 2

REPEALS

3 The provisions listed below are omitted.

4 (*repeals* TMA 1970 ss 20C, 20CC, and *amends* TMA 1970 s 118)

5 (*repeals* CEMA 1979 118C(3)(*c*), and *amends* CEMA 1979 s 118C(4)(*b*) and (5))

6 (*repeals* BGDA 1981 Sch 1 para 16, Sch 3 para 17, Sch 4 para 17)

7 (*repeals* FA 1989 s 148(4))

8 (*repeals* VATA 1994 s 72(9), Sch 11 para 10(3)–(6))

9 (*repeals* FA 1994 Sch 7 para 4(2)–(7))

10 (*repeals* FA 1996 Sch 5 paras 5, 6)

11 (*repeals* FA 2000 Sch 6 paras 97, 130)

12 (*repeals* FA 2001 Sch 6 para 6, Sch 7 para 7)

13—(1) (*repeals* CJPA 2001 ss 57(1)(*c*), 63(2)(*e*), 65(3))

(2) (*repeals* CJPA 2001 Sch 1 paras 13, 28, 29, 57, 58, 61, 72)

14 (*repeals* TCA 2002 s 36(2), (3))

15 (*repeals* PCA 2002 s 323(3)(*e*), (*f*))

16 (*repeals* FA 2003 Sch 13 Pt 7)

17 (*repeals* CRCA 2005 13(3)(*b*), (*c*), 14(2)(*b*), (*c*))

SCHEDULE 23

EXTENSION OF HMRC POWERS: SCOTLAND

Section 85

Orders—Finance Act 2007 (Sections 82 to 84 and Schedule 23) (Commencement) Order 2007, SI 2007/3166 (this Schedule comes into force on 1 December 2007).

Criminal Law (Consolidation) (Scotland) Act 1995 (c 39)

1–7 (amend provisions outside the scope of this publication)

Criminal Procedure (Scotland) Act 1995 (c 46)

8–10 (amend provisions outside the scope of this publication)

Criminal Justice and Police Act 2001 (c 16)

11 The Criminal Justice and Police Act 2001 is amended as follows.

12 (*inserts* CJPA 2001 s 63(2)(*ga*))

13 (amends provisions outside the scope of this publication)

14—(1) The amendments made by this Schedule come into force in accordance with provision made by the Treasury by order.
(2) The power to make an order under this paragraph is exercisable by statutory instrument.

SCHEDULE 24

PENALTIES FOR ERRORS

Section 97

HMRC Manuals—Compliance Handbook Manual, CH81000–84974 (HMRC Compliance Handbook Manual chapter on penalties for inaccuracies).

Orders—The Finance Act 2007, Schedule 24 (Commencement And Transitional Provisions) Order, SI 2008/568: this Schedule has effect as follows—

(a) 1 April 2008 in relation to relevant documents relating to tax periods commencing on or after that date;

(b) 1 April 2008 in relation to assessments falling within Sch 24 para 2 for tax periods commencing on or after that date;

(c) 1 July 2008 in relation to relevant documents relating to claims under the Thirteenth Council Directive (arrangements for the refund of value added tax to persons not established in Community territory) for years commencing on or after that date;

(d) 1 January 2009 in relation to relevant documents relating to claims under the Eighth Council Directive (arrangements for the refund of value added tax to taxable persons not established in the territory of the country) for years commencing on or after that date;

(e) 1 April 2009 in relation to documents relating to all other claims for repayments of relevant tax made on or after 1 April 2009 which are not related to a tax period; and

(f) in any other case, 1 April 2009 in relation to documents given where a person's liability to pay relevant tax arises on or after that date.

Press releases etc—HMRC Compliance Checks Factsheet CC/FS7a—Compliance checks series—Penalties for inaccuracies in returns or documents.

HMRC Compliance Checks Factsheet CC/FS7b—Compliance checks series—Penalties for not telling us about an under-assessment.

HMRC Compliance Checks Factsheet CC/FS19—Compliance checks—Employer and Contractor returns and "old" penalty rules.

Cross-references—Small Charitable Donations Regulations, SI 2013/938 reg 15 (application of this Schedule, with modifications, in relation to small charitable donations under the Small Charitable Donations Act 2012).

FA 2014 ss 208–214, Sch 30 (follower notices: penalties).

FA 2014 Sch 35 para 13(*a*) (a person is not liable to a penalty under this Schedule by reason of any failure to include in any return or account a reference number required by FA 2014 s 253).

SSCBA 1992 s 11A (this Schedule applies with the necessary modifications, in relation to Class 2 contributions under SSCBA 1992 s 11(2) as if those contributions were income tax chargeable under ITTOIA 2005 Pt 2 Ch 2 in respect of profits of a trade, profession or vocation which is not carried on wholly outside the United Kingdom).

PART 1
LIABILITY FOR PENALTY
Error in taxpayer's document

1—(1) A penalty is payable by a person (P) where—

(*a*) P gives HMRC a document of a kind listed in the Table below, and

(*b*) Conditions 1 and 2 are satisfied.

(2) Condition 1 is that the document contains an inaccuracy which amounts to, or leads to—

(*a*) an understatement of [a][1] liability to tax,

(*b*) a false or inflated statement of a loss . . . [1], or

(*c*) a false or inflated claim to repayment of tax.

(3) Condition 2 is that the inaccuracy was [careless (within the meaning of paragraph 3) or deliberate on P's part][1].

(4) Where a document contains more than one inaccuracy, a penalty is payable for each inaccuracy.

Tax	*Document*
Income tax or capital gains tax	Return under section 8 of TMA 1970 (personal return).
Income tax or capital gains tax	Return under section 8A of TMA 1970 (trustee's return).
Income tax or capital gains tax	Return, statement or declaration in connection with a claim for an allowance, deduction or relief.
Income tax or capital gains tax	Accounts in connection with ascertaining liability to tax.
Income tax or capital gains tax	Partnership return.
Income tax or capital gains tax	Statement or declaration in connection with a partnership return.
Income tax or capital gains tax	Accounts in connection with a partnership return.
[Capital gains tax	Return under section 12ZB of TMA 1970 (NRCGT return).][6]
[Income tax	Return under section 254 of FA 2004.][1]
Income tax	Return for the purposes of PAYE regulations.
Construction industry deductions	Return for the purposes of regulations under section 70(1)(a) of FA 2004 in connection with deductions on account of tax under the Construction Industry Scheme.
Corporation tax	Company tax return under paragraph 3 of Schedule 18 to FA 1998.
Corporation tax	Return, statement or declaration in connection with a claim for an allowance, deduction or relief.
Corporation tax	Accounts in connection with ascertaining liability to tax.
VAT	VAT return under regulations made under paragraph 2 of Schedule 11 to VATA 1994.
VAT	Return, statement or declaration in connection with a claim.
[VAT	Return under a special scheme.][5]
[Insurance premium tax	Return under regulations under section 54 of FA 1994.
Insurance premium tax	Return, statement or declaration in connection with a claim.
Inheritance tax	Account under section 216 or 217 of IHTA 1984.
Inheritance tax	Information or document under regulations under section 256 of IHTA 1984.
Inheritance tax	Statement or declaration in connection with a deduction, exemption or relief.
Stamp duty land tax	Return under section 76 of FA 2003.

Tax	*Document*
Stamp duty reserve tax	Return under regulations under section 98 of FA 1986.
[Annual tax on enveloped dwellings	Annual tax on enveloped dwellings return.
Annual tax on enveloped dwellings	Return of adjusted chargeable amount.][4]
Petroleum revenue tax	Return under paragraph 2 of Schedule 2 to the Oil Taxation Act 1975.
[Petroleum revenue tax	Statement or declaration in connection with a claim under paragraph 13A of Schedule 2 to the Oil Taxation Act 1975.][2]
Petroleum revenue tax	Statement or declaration in connection with a claim under Schedule 5, 6, 7 or 8 to the Oil Taxation Act 1975.
Petroleum revenue tax	Statement under section 1(1)(*a*) of the Petroleum Revenue Tax Act 1980.
Aggregates levy	Return under regulations under section 25 of FA 2001.
Climate change levy	Return under regulations under paragraph 41 of Schedule 6 to FA 2000.
Landfill tax	Return under regulations under section 49 of FA 1996.
Air passenger duty	Return under section 38 of FA 1994.
Alcoholic liquor duties	Return under regulations under section 13, 49, 56 or 62 of the Alcoholic Liquor Duties Act 1979.
Alcoholic liquor duties	Statement or declaration in connection with a claim for repayment of duty under section 4(4) of FA 1995.
Tobacco products duty	Return under regulations under section 7 of the Tobacco Products Duties Act 1979.
Hydrocarbon oil duties	Return under regulations under section 21 of the Hydrocarbon Oil Duties Act 1979.
Excise duties	Return under regulations under section 93 of CEMA 1979.
Excise duties	Return under regulations under section 100G or 100H of CEMA 1979.
Excise duties	Statement or declaration in connection with a claim.
General betting duty	Return under regulations under paragraph 2 of Schedule 1 to BGDA 1981.
Pool betting duty	Return under regulations under paragraph 2A of Schedule 1 to BGDA 1981.
Bingo duty	Return under regulations under paragraph 9 of Schedule 3 to BGDA 1981.
Lottery duty	Return under regulations under section 28(2) of FA 1993.
Gaming duty	Return under directions under paragraph 10 of Schedule 1 to FA 1997.
Remote gaming duty	Return under regulations under section 26K of BGDA 1981.][1]
[Machine games duty	Return under regulations under paragraph 18 of Schedule 24 to FA 2012.][3]
[Any of the taxes mentioned above][1]	Any document which is likely to be relied upon by HMRC to determine, without further inquiry, a question about— (a) P's liability to tax, (b) payments by P by way of or in connection with tax, (c) any other payment by P (including penalties), or

Tax	*Document*
	(d) repayments, or any other kind of payment or credit, to P.

[(4A) In this paragraph "return under a special scheme" means any of the following, so far as relating to supplies of services treated as made in the United Kingdom—

(*a*) a special accounting return under paragraph 11 of Schedule 3B;

(*b*) a value added tax return submitted under any provision of the law of a member State other than the United Kingdom which implements Article 364 of the VAT Directive (as substituted by Article 5(11) of the Amending Directive);

(*c*) a value added tax return submitted under any provision of the law of a member State other than the United Kingdom which implements Article 369f of the VAT Directive (as inserted by Article 5(15) of the Amending Directive).

(4B) A value added tax return mentioned in paragraph (*b*) or (*c*) of subparagraph (4A) is regarded for the purposes of sub-paragraph (1) as given to HMRC when it is submitted to the authority to whom it is required to be submitted.

(4C) In sub-paragraph (4A)—

"the VAT Directive" means Directive 2006/112/EC;

"the Amending Directive" means Council Directive 2008/8/EC.][5]

(5) In relation to a return under paragraph 2 of Schedule 2 to the Oil Taxation Act 1975 [or a statement or declaration under paragraph 13A of that Schedule][2], references in this Schedule to P include any person who, after the giving of the return for a taxable field (within the meaning of that Act), becomes the responsible person for the field (within the meaning of that Act).][1]

HMRC Manuals—Compliance Handbook Manual, CH81011–81013 (penalties for inaccuracies: commencement date for penalties).

CH81060 (penalties for inaccuracies: which documents do penalties for inaccuracies apply to).

CH81070 (conditions for penalty for inaccuracy).

Cross reference—FA 2009 s 94 (Publishing details of deliberate tax defaulters).

FA 2015 Sch 21 (penalties in connection with offshore asset moves).

Modifications—FA 2007 Sch 24 has effect as if, in the Table in this para, the list of taxes included bank payroll tax and the list of documents included a bank payroll tax return (FA 2010 s 22, Sch 1 para 37(1)).

Simon's Tax Cases—*Harding v R&C Comrs* [2013] UKUT 575 (TCC), [2014] STC 891.

Amendments—

1 In sub-para (2), word substituted for word "P's" and words "by P" repealed, in sub-para (3), words substituted for words "careless or deliberate (within the meaning of paragraph 3)", in the table, entries inserted, in the last entry in column 1 words substituted for words "Income tax, capital gains tax, corporation tax or VAT", and sub-para (5) inserted, by FA 2008 s 122, Sch 40 paras 1, 2 with effect from 1 April 2009 (by virtue of SI 2009/571 art 2). In their application in relation to penalties payable under paras 1, 1A of this Schedule, the entries inserted in the table (by FA 2008 Sch 40 para 2(4), (5)) shall have effect in relation to—

(a) relevant documents—

(i) which relate to tax periods commencing on or after 1 April 2009, and

(ii) for which the filing date is on or after 1 April 2010;

(b) relevant documents relating to all claims for repayments of relevant tax made on or after 1 April 2010 which are not related to a tax period;

(c) relevant documents produced under regulations under IHTA 1984 s 256 where the date of death is on or after 1 April 2009; and

(d) in any other case, relevant documents given where a person's liability to pay relevant tax arises on or after 1 April 2010 (SI 2009/571 arts 3, 4).

In their application in relation to assessments falling within para 2 of this Schedule, the entries inserted in the table (by FA 2008 Sch 40 para 2(4), (5)) shall have effect in relation to tax periods commencing on or after 1 April 2009, where the filing date for the relevant document is on or after 1 April 2010 (SI 2009/571 art 5).

2 In table, entry inserted, and in sub-para (5) words inserted, by F(No 3)A 2010 s 28, Sch 12 Pt 2 para 12 with effect in relation to claims made on or after 1 April 2011.

3 In table, entry inserted by FA 2012 s 191, Sch 24 para 29 with effect in relation to the playing of machine games on or after 1 February 2013

4 In table, entries inserted by FA 2013 s 164, Sch 34 para 6 with effect from 17 July 2013.

5 In para 1, third entry for VAT inserted, and sub-paras (4A)–(4C) inserted, by FA 2014 s 103, Sch 22 para 19 with effect in relation to supplies made on or after 1 January 2015.

6 In table, entry inserted by FA 2015 s 37, Sch 7 para 56(1), (2) with effect in relation to disposals made on or after 6 April 2015.

[Error in taxpayer's document attributable to another person

1A—(1) A penalty is payable by a person (T) where—

(*a*) another person (P) gives HMRC a document of a kind listed in the Table in paragraph 1,

(*b*) the document contains a relevant inaccuracy, and

(*c*) the inaccuracy was attributable to T deliberately supplying false information to P (whether directly or indirectly), or to T deliberately withholding information from P, with the intention of the document containing the inaccuracy.

(2) A "relevant inaccuracy" is an inaccuracy which amounts to, or leads to—

(*a*) an understatement of a liability to tax,

(*b*) a false or inflated statement of a loss, or

(*c*) a false or inflated claim to repayment of tax.

(3) A penalty is payable under this paragraph in respect of an inaccuracy whether or not P is liable to a penalty under paragraph 1 in respect of the same inaccuracy.][1]

HMRC Manuals—Compliance Handbook Manual, CH81011–81013 (penalties for inaccuracies: commencement date for penalties).

CH84545 (other penalty issues: agent acting – inaccuracy attributable to another person).

CH81075 (penalties for inaccuracies: inaccuracy due to another person).

CH81165–81166 (inaccuracy attributable to another person).

CH81167–81168 (intentions of another person, with examples).

CH81110 (penalties for inaccuracies: the four types of inaccuracy).

Cross reference—FA 2009 s 94 (Publishing details of deliberate tax defaulters).

Amendment—[1] Paragraph 1A inserted by FA 2008 s 122, Sch 40 paras 1, 3 with effect from 1 April 2009 (by virtue of SI 2009/571 art 2).

Under-assessment by HMRC

2—(1) A penalty is payable by a person (P) where—

(*a*) an assessment issued to P by HMRC understates P's liability to [a relevant tax][1], and

(*b*) P has failed to take reasonable steps to notify HMRC, within the period of 30 days beginning with the date of the assessment, that it is an under-assessment.

(2) In deciding what steps (if any) were reasonable HMRC must consider—

(*a*) whether P knew, or should have known, about the under-assessment, and

(*b*) what steps would have been reasonable to take to notify HMRC.

[(3) In sub-paragraph (1) "relevant tax" means any tax mentioned in the Table in paragraph 1.][1]

[(4) In this paragraph (and in Part 2 of this Schedule so far as relating to this paragraph)—

(*a*) "assessment" includes determination, and

(*b*) accordingly, references to an under-assessment include an under-determination.][2]

HMRC Manuals—Compliance Handbook Manual, CH81011–81013 (penalties for inaccuracies: commencement date for penalties).

CH81090 (penalties for inaccuracies: under assessment by HMRC).

CH81170 (under assessment by HMRC).

Amendments—[1] In sub-para (1), words substituted for word "tax", and sub-para (3) substituted, by FA 2008 s 122, Sch 40 paras 1, 4 with effect from 1 April 2009 (by virtue of SI 2009/571 art 2).

[2] Sub-para (4) inserted by FA 2009 s 109, Sch 57 para 2 with effect from 21 July 2009.

Degrees of culpability

3—(1) [For the purposes of a penalty under paragraph 1, inaccuracy in][1] a document given by P to HMRC is—

(*a*) "careless" if the inaccuracy is due to failure by P to take reasonable care,

(*b*) "deliberate but not concealed" if the inaccuracy is deliberate [on P's part][1] but P does not make arrangements to conceal it, and

(*c*) "deliberate and concealed" if the inaccuracy is deliberate [on P's part][1] and P makes arrangements to conceal it (for example, by submitting false evidence in support of an inaccurate figure).

(2) An inaccuracy in a document given by P to HMRC, which was neither careless nor deliberate [on P's part][1] when the document was given, is to be treated as careless if P—

(*a*) discovered the inaccuracy at some later time, and

(*b*) did not take reasonable steps to inform HMRC.

HMRC Manuals—Compliance Handbook Manual, CH81080 (penalties for inaccuracies: inaccuracy discovered after document sent to HMRC).

CH81120–81140 (what is reasonable care, with examples at CH81131).

CH81141–81142 (correction of errors for indirect taxes).

CH81145 (examples of careless inaccuracy).

CH81150–81151 (deliberate but not concealed inaccuracy, with examples).

CH81160–81161 (deliberate and concealed inaccuracy, with examples).

CH81110 (penalties for inaccuracies: the four types of inaccuracy).

Cross references—FA 2014 s 276 (for the purposes of sub-para (1)(*a*) above, reliance on legal advice provided by monitored promoter not to be regarded as taking reasonable care).

Simon's Tax Cases—*Harding v R&C Comrs* [2013] UKUT 575 (TCC), [2014] STC 891.

Amendments—[1] In sub-para (1), words substituted for words "Inaccuracy in", and in sub-paras (1), (2), words inserted, by FA 2008 s 122, Sch 40 paras 1, 5 with effect from 1 April 2009 (by virtue of SI 2009/571 art 2).

PART 2
AMOUNT OF PENALTY

Standard amount

[4 (1) This paragraph sets out the penalty payable under paragraph 1.

(2) If the inaccuracy is in category 1, the penalty is—

(*a*) for careless action, 30% of the potential lost revenue,

(*b*) for deliberate but not concealed action, 70% of the potential lost revenue, and

(*c*) for deliberate and concealed action, 100% of the potential lost revenue.

(3) If the inaccuracy is in category 2, the penalty is—

(*a*) for careless action, 45% of the potential lost revenue,

(*b*) for deliberate but not concealed action, 105% of the potential lost revenue, and

(*c*) for deliberate and concealed action, 150% of the potential lost revenue.

(4) If the inaccuracy is in category 3, the penalty is—

(*a*) for careless action, 60% of the potential lost revenue,

(*b*) for deliberate but not concealed action, 140% of the potential lost revenue, and

(*c*) for deliberate and concealed action, 200% of the potential lost revenue.

(5) Paragraph 4A explains the 3 categories of inaccuracy.][1]

HMRC Manuals—Compliance Handbook Manual, CH82120 (penalties for inaccuracies: introduction to amount of penalty).

Cross references—FA 2014 s 212 (application of this paragraph in calculation of aggregate penalties for failure to take corrective action in response to a follower notice).

Amendments—[1] Paras 4–4D substituted for previous para 4 by FA 2010 s 35 Sch 10 paras 1, 2 with effect from 6 April 2011 (by virtue of SI 2011/975 art 2(1)). Note that these changes do not have effect in relation to documents given to HMRC, and assessments issued by HMRC, in relation to a tax period commencing on or before 5 April 2011 (SI 2011/975 art 3).

Prospective amendments—Sub-para (1A) to be inserted, in sub-para (2), figures "37.5%" to be substituted for "30%", "87.5%" to be substituted for "70%" and "125%" to be substituted for "100%", and in sub-para (5), figure "4" to be substituted for figure "3", by FA 2015 s 120, Sch 20 paras 1, 2 with effect from a day to be appointed. Sub-para (1A) as inserted to read as follows—

"(1A) If the inaccuracy is in category 0, the penalty is—

for careless action, 30% of the potential lost revenue,

for deliberate but not concealed action, 70% of the potential lost revenue, and

for deliberate and concealed action, 100% of the potential lost revenue.".

[4A (1) An inaccuracy is in category 1 if—

(*a*) it involves a domestic matter, or

(*b*) it involves an offshore matter and—

(i) the territory in question is a category 1 territory, or

(ii) the tax at stake is a tax other than income tax or capital gains tax.

(2) An inaccuracy is in category 2 if—

(*a*) it involves an offshore matter,

(*b*) the territory in question is a category 2 territory, and

(*c*) the tax at stake is income tax or capital gains tax.

(3) An inaccuracy is in category 3 if—

(*a*) it involves an offshore matter,

(*b*) the territory in question is a category 3 territory, and

(*c*) the tax at stake is income tax or capital gains tax.

(4) An inaccuracy "involves an offshore matter" if it results in a potential loss of revenue that is charged on or by reference to—

(*a*) income arising from a source in a territory outside the UK,

(*b*) assets situated or held in a territory outside the UK,

(*c*) activities carried on wholly or mainly in a territory outside the UK, or

(*d*) anything having effect as if it were income, assets or activities of a kind described above.

(5) An inaccuracy "involves a domestic matter" if it results in a potential loss of revenue that is charged on or by reference to anything not mentioned in sub-paragraph (4)(*a*) to (*d*).

(6) If a single inaccuracy is in more than one category (each referred to as a "relevant category")—

(*a*) it is to be treated for the purposes of this Schedule as if it were separate inaccuracies, one in each relevant category according to the matters that it involves, and

(*b*) the potential lost revenue is to be calculated separately in respect of each separate inaccuracy.

(7) "Category 1 territory", "category 2 territory" and "category 3 territory" are defined in paragraph 21A.

(8) "Assets" has the meaning given in section 21(1) of TCGA 1992, but also includes sterling.][1]

Amendments—[1] Paras 4–4D substituted for previous para 4 by FA 2010 s 35 Sch 10 paras 1, 2 with effect from 6 April 2011 (by virtue of SI 2011/975 art 2(1)). Note that these changes do not have effect in relation to documents given to HMRC, and assessments issued by HMRC, in relation to a tax period commencing on or before 5 April 2011 (SI 2011/975 art 3).

Prospective amendments—The following amendments to be made by FA 2015 s 120, Sch 20 paras 1, 3 with effect from a day to be appointed—

- sub-paras (A1), (1) to be substituted for sub-para (1);
- in sub-paras (2)(*a*), (3)(*a*), words "or an offshore transfer" to be inserted after word "matter", and in sub-paras (2)(*c*), (3)(*c*), words ", capital gains tax or inheritance tax" to be substituted for words "or capital gains tax";
- sub-paras (4A), (4B) to be inserted;
- in sub-para (5), words "and does not involve either an offshore matter or an offshore transfer" to be substituted for words following word "revenue";
- in sub-para (6)(*a*), words "or transfers" to be inserted after word "matters"; and
- in sub-para (7), words ""Category 0 territory", "category 1" to be substituted for words ""Category 1".

Sub-paragraphs (A1), (1) as substituted to read as follows—

"(A1) An inaccuracy is in category 0 if—

it involves a domestic matter,

it involves an offshore matter or an offshore transfer, the territory in question is a category 0 territory and the tax at stake is income tax, capital gains tax or inheritance tax, or

it involves an offshore matter and the tax at stake is a tax other than income tax, capital gains tax or inheritance tax.

(1) An inaccuracy is in category 1 if—

it involves an offshore matter or an offshore transfer,

the territory in question is a category 1 territory, and

the tax at stake is income tax, capital gains tax or inheritance tax.".

Sub-paragraphs (4A), (4B) as inserted to read as follows—

"(4A) Where the tax at stake is inheritance tax, assets are treated for the purposes of sub-paragraph (4) as situated or held in a territory outside the UK if they are so situated or held immediately after the transfer of value by reason of which inheritance tax becomes chargeable.

(4B) An inaccuracy "involves an offshore transfer" if—

it does not involve an offshore matter,

it is deliberate (whether or not concealed) and results in a potential loss of revenue,

the tax at stake is income tax, capital gains tax or inheritance tax, and

the applicable condition in paragraph 4AA is satisfied.".

[4AA (1) This paragraph makes provision in relation to offshore transfers.

(2) Where the tax at stake is income tax, the applicable condition is satisfied if the income on or by reference to which the tax is charged, or any part of the income—

(*a*) is received in a territory outside the UK, or

(*b*) is transferred before the filing date to a territory outside the UK.

(3) Where the tax at stake is capital gains tax, the applicable condition is satisfied if the proceeds of the disposal on or by reference to which the tax is charged, or any part of the proceeds—

(*a*) are received in a territory outside the UK, or

(*b*) are transferred before the filing date to a territory outside the UK.

(4) Where the tax at stake is inheritance tax, the applicable condition is satisfied if—

(*a*) the disposition that gives rise to the transfer of value by reason of which the tax becomes chargeable involves a transfer of assets, and

(*b*) after that disposition but before the filing date the assets, or any part of the assets, are transferred to a territory outside the UK.

(5) In the case of a transfer falling within sub-paragraph (2)(*b*), (3)(*b*) or (4)(*b*), references to the income, proceeds or assets transferred are to be read as including references to any assets derived from or representing the income, proceeds or assets.

(6) In relation to an offshore transfer, the territory in question for the purposes of paragraph 4A is the highest category of territory by virtue of which the inaccuracy involves an offshore transfer.

(7) "Filing date" means the date when the document containing the inaccuracy is given to HMRC.

(8) "Assets" has the same meaning as in paragraph 4A.]

Prospective amendments—Paragraph 4AA to be inserted by FA 2015 s 120, Sch 20 paras 1, 4 with effect from a day to be appointed.

[4B The penalty payable under paragraph 1A is 100% of the potential lost revenue.][1]

Amendments—[1] Paras 4–4D substituted for previous para 4 by FA 2010 s 35 Sch 10 paras 1, 2 with effect from 6 April 2011 (by virtue of SI 2011/975 art 2(1)). Note that these changes do not have effect in relation to documents given to HMRC, and assessments issued by HMRC, in relation to a tax period commencing on or before 5 April 2011 (SI 2011/975 art 3).

[4C The penalty payable under paragraph 2 is 30% of the potential lost revenue.][1]

Amendments—[1] Paras 4–4D substituted for previous para 4 by FA 2010 s 35 Sch 10 paras 1, 2 with effect from 6 April 2011 (by virtue of SI 2011/975 art 2(1)). Note that these changes do not have effect in relation to documents given to HMRC, and assessments issued by HMRC, in relation to a tax period commencing on or before 5 April 2011 (SI 2011/975 art 3).

[4D Paragraphs 5 to 8 define "potential lost revenue".][1]

Amendments—[1] Paras 4–4D substituted for previous para 4 by FA 2010 s 35 Sch 10 paras 1, 2 with effect from 6 April 2011 (by virtue of SI 2011/975 art 2(1)). Note that these changes do not have effect in relation to documents given to HMRC, and assessments issued by HMRC, in relation to a tax period commencing on or before 5 April 2011 (SI 2011/975 art 3).

Potential lost revenue: normal rule

5—(1) "The potential lost revenue" in respect of an inaccuracy in a document [(including an inaccuracy attributable to a supply of false information or withholding of information)][1] or a failure to notify an under-assessment is the additional amount due or payable in respect of tax as a result of correcting the inaccuracy or assessment.

(2) The reference in sub-paragraph (1) to the additional amount due or payable includes a reference to—

(*a*) an amount payable to HMRC having been erroneously paid by way of repayment of tax, and

(*b*) an amount which would have been repayable by HMRC had the inaccuracy or assessment not been corrected.

(3) In sub-paragraph (1) "tax" includes national insurance contributions.

(4) The following shall be ignored in calculating potential lost revenue under this paragraph—

(*a*) group relief, and

[(*b*) any relief under [section 458 of CTA 2010][3] (relief in respect of repayment etc of loan) which is deferred under [subsection (5)][3] of that section;][2]

(but this sub-paragraph does not prevent a penalty being charged in respect of an inaccurate claim for relief).

HMRC Manuals—Compliance Handbook Manual, CH82160–82161 (penalties for inaccuracies: single inaccuracy with examples of potential lost revenue).

CH82162 (examples of potential lost revenue for an under assessment).

Cross reference—FA 2009 s 94 (Publishing details of deliberate tax defaulters).

Amendments—[1] In sub-para (1), words inserted by FA 2008 s 122, Sch 40 paras 1, 7 with effect from 1 April 2009 (by virtue of SI 2009/571 art 2).

[2] Sub-para (4)(*b*) substituted by FA 2009 s 109, Sch 57 para 3 with effect from 21 July 2009.

[3] In sub-para (4)(*b*) words "subsection (4) of section 419 of ICTA" and "subsection (4A)" substituted by CTA 2010 s 1177, Sch 1 paras 573, 575. CTA 2010 has effect for corporation tax purposes for accounting periods ending on or after 1 April 2010, and for income and capital gains tax purposes for the tax year 2010–11 and subsequent tax years.

Potential lost revenue: multiple errors

6—(1) Where P is liable to a penalty [under paragraph 1][1] in respect of more than one inaccuracy, and the calculation of potential lost revenue under paragraph 5 in respect of each inaccuracy depends on the order in which they are corrected—

(*a*) careless inaccuracies shall be taken to be corrected before deliberate inaccuracies, and

(*b*) deliberate but not concealed inaccuracies shall be taken to be corrected before deliberate and concealed inaccuracies.

(2) In calculating potential lost revenue where P is liable to a penalty [under paragraph 1][1] in respect of one or more understatements in one or more documents relating to a tax period, account shall be taken of any overstatement in any document given by P which relates to the same tax period.

(3) In sub-paragraph (2)—

(*a*) "understatement" means an inaccuracy that satisfies Condition 1 of paragraph 1, and

(*b*) "overstatement" means an inaccuracy that does not satisfy that condition.

(4) For the purposes of sub-paragraph (2) overstatements shall be set against understatements in the following order—

(*a*) understatements in respect of which P is not liable to a penalty,

(*b*) careless understatements,

(*c*) deliberate but not concealed understatements, and

(*d*) deliberate and concealed understatements.

(5) In calculating [for the purposes of a penalty under paragraph 1][1] potential lost revenue in respect of a document given by or on behalf of P no account shall be taken of the fact that a potential loss of revenue from P is or may be balanced by a potential over-payment by another person (except to the extent that an enactment requires or permits a person's tax liability to be adjusted by reference to P's).

HMRC Manuals—Compliance Handbook Manual, CH82180–82250 (penalties for inaccuracies: more than one inaccuracy and when inaccuracies should or should not be grouped).

CH82260 (overstatements, with a worked example).

CH82270 (calculating potential lost revenue for multiple inaccuracies).

CH82271 (calculating potential lost revenue for multiple inaccuracies – employer and contractor issues).

CH82272 (example of allocating overstatements to potential lost revenue).

Cross reference—FA 2009 s 94 (Publishing details of deliberate tax defaulters).

Amendments—[1] In sub-paras (1), (2), (5) words inserted, by FA 2008 s 122, Sch 40 paras 1, 8 with effect from 1 April 2009 (by virtue of SI 2009/571 art 2).

Potential lost revenue: losses

7—(1) Where an inaccuracy has the result that a loss is wrongly recorded for purposes of direct tax and the loss has been wholly used to reduce the amount due or payable in respect of tax, the potential lost revenue is calculated in accordance with paragraph 5.

(2) Where an inaccuracy has the result that a loss is wrongly recorded for purposes of direct tax and the loss has not been wholly used to reduce the amount due or payable in respect of tax, the potential lost revenue is—

(*a*) the potential lost revenue calculated in accordance with paragraph 5 in respect of any part of the loss that has been used to reduce the amount due or payable in respect of tax, plus

(*b*) 10% of any part that has not.

(3) Sub-paragraphs (1) and (2) apply both—

(*a*) to a case where no loss would have been recorded but for the inaccuracy, and

(*b*) to a case where a loss of a different amount would have been recorded (but in that case sub-paragraphs (1) and (2) apply only to the difference between the amount recorded and the true amount).

(4) Where an inaccuracy has the effect of creating or increasing an aggregate loss recorded for a group of companies—

(*a*) the potential lost revenue shall be calculated in accordance with this paragraph, and

(*b*) in applying paragraph 5 in accordance with sub-paragraphs (1) and (2) above, group relief may be taken into account (despite paragraph 5(4)(*a*)).

(5) The potential lost revenue in respect of a loss is nil where, because of the nature of the loss or P's circumstances, there is no reasonable prospect of the loss being used to support a claim to reduce a tax liability (of any person).

HMRC Manuals—Compliance Handbook Manual, CH82310–82320 (calculating the penalty: losses used and not used)
CH82330 (losses available for potential lost revenue calculation).
CH82331 (losses available – income tax example).
CH82332 (losses available – capital gains tax example).
CH82333 (losses available – corporation tax example).
CH82340–82341 (aggregate group profits).
CH82342–82345 (worked examples of understatements and overstatements of profits creating or increasing and aggregate loss).
CH82350 (losses and when to assess a penalty).
CH82370–82371 (losses where there is no reasonable prospect of use, with example).
Cross reference—FA 2009 s 94 (Publishing details of deliberate tax defaulters).

Potential lost revenue: delayed tax

8—(1) Where an inaccuracy resulted in an amount of tax being declared later than it should have been ("the delayed tax"), the potential lost revenue is—

(*a*) 5% of the delayed tax for each year of the delay, or

(*b*) a percentage of the delayed tax, for each separate period of delay of less than a year, equating to 5% per year.

(2) This paragraph does not apply to a case to which paragraph 7 applies.

HMRC Manuals—Compliance Handbook Manual, CH82390 (calculating the penalty: delayed tax and potential lost revenue).
CH82395 and 82396 (examples of tax declared late).
CH82397 (capital allowances example of delayed tax).
Cross reference—FA 2009 s 94 (Publishing details of deliberate tax defaulters).

Reductions for disclosure

9—[(A1) Paragraph 10 provides for reductions in penalties under paragraphs 1, 1A and 2 where a person discloses an inaccuracy, a supply of false information or withholding of information, or a failure to disclose an under-assessment.][1]

(1) A person discloses an inaccuracy[, a supply of false information or withholding of information,][1] or a failure to disclose an under-assessment by—

(*a*) telling HMRC about it,

(*b*) giving HMRC reasonable help in quantifying the inaccuracy[, the inaccuracy attributable to the [supply of false information][2] or withholding of information, or the][1] under-assessment, and

(*c*) allowing HMRC access to records for the purpose of ensuring that the inaccuracy[, the inaccuracy attributable to the [supply of false information][2] or withholding of information, or the][1] under-assessment is fully corrected.

(2) Disclosure—

(*a*) is "unprompted" if made at a time when the person making it has no reason to believe that HMRC have discovered or are about to discover the inaccuracy[, the supply of false information or withholding of information, or the under-assessment][1], and

(*b*) otherwise, is "prompted".

(3) In relation to disclosure "quality" includes timing, nature and extent.

Cross-references—See VATA 1994 Sch 3B para 16M (correction of special scheme return which involves disclosure of inaccuracy, supply of false information or a withholding of information to the tax authority for the administering member State, regarded as disclosure to HMRC for the purposes of this para).

VATA 1994 Sch 3BA para 34 (correction of non-UK return which involves disclosure of inaccuracy, supply of false information or a withholding of information to the tax authority for the administering member State, regarded as disclosure to HMRC for the purposes of this para).

HMRC Manuals—Compliance Handbook Manual, CH82410 (calculating the penalty: penalty reductions for disclosure).
CH82420–82422 (unprompted and prompted disclosure, with examples).
CH82430–82431 (quality of disclosure).
CH82432 (calculating the reduction for disclosure example).
CH82440–82460 (quality of disclosure: telling, helping and giving access),
CH82470 (maximum and minimum penalties for each type of behaviour).

Amendments—[1] Sub-para (A1) to be inserted, and in sub-para (1), words inserted, in paras (*b*), (*c*), words substituted for word "or", and in sub-para (2)(*a*), words substituted for words "or under-assessment", by FA 2008 s 122, Sch 40 paras 1, 9 with effect from 1 April 2009 (by virtue of SI 2009/571 art 2).

[2] In sub-para (1)(*b*), (*c*), words "supply of false information" substituted for words "supply or false information" by FA 2009 s 109, Sch 57 para 4 with effect from 21 July 2009.

[10—(1) If a person who would otherwise be liable to a penalty of a percentage shown in column 1 of the Table (a "standard percentage") has made a disclosure, HMRC must reduce the standard percentage to one that reflects the quality of the disclosure.

(2) But the standard percentage may not be reduced to a percentage that is below the minimum shown for it—

(*a*) in the case of a prompted disclosure, in column 2 of the Table, and

(*b*) in the case of an unprompted disclosure, in column 3 of the Table.

Standard %	*Minimum % for prompted disclosure*	*Minimum % for unprompted disclosure*
30%	15%	0%
45%	22.5%	0%
60%	30%	0%
70%	35%	20%
105%	52.5%	30%
140%	70%	40%
100%	50%	30%
150%	75%	45%
200%	100%	60%.][1]

HMRC Manuals—Compliance Handbook Manual, CH82500–82512 (calculating the penalty: how to calculate the penalty with examples).

Cross reference—FA 2009 s 94 (Publishing details of deliberate tax defaulters).

Amendments—

[1] This para substituted by FA 2010 s 35 Sch 10 paras 1, 3 with effect from 6 April 2011 (by virtue of SI 2011/975 art 2(1)). Note that these changes do not have effect in relation to documents given to HMRC, and assessments issued by HMRC, in relation to a tax period commencing on or before 5 April 2011 (SI 2011/975 art 3).

Prospective amendments—In sub-para (2), the following Table entries to be inserted at the appropriate places by FA 2015 s 120, Sch 20 paras 1, 5 with effect from a day to be appointed—

"37.5%	18.75%	0%"
"87.5%	43.75%	25%"
"125%	62.5%	40%".

Special reduction

11—(1) If they think it right because of special circumstances, HMRC may reduce a penalty under paragraph 1[, 1A][1] or 2.

(2) In sub-paragraph (1) "special circumstances" does not include—

(*a*) ability to pay, or

(*b*) the fact that a potential loss of revenue from one taxpayer is balanced by a potential over-payment by another.

(3) In sub-paragraph (1) the reference to reducing a penalty includes a reference to—

(*a*) staying a penalty, and

(*b*) agreeing a compromise in relation to proceedings for a penalty.

HMRC Manuals—Compliance Handbook Manual, CH82490 (calculating the penalty: guidance regarding special reduction).

Amendments—[1] In sub-para (1) reference inserted, by FA 2008 s 122, Sch 40 paras 1, 10 with effect from 1 April 2009 (by virtue of SI 2009/571 art 2).

Interaction with other penalties [and late payment surcharges]

12—(1) The final entry in the Table in paragraph 1 excludes a document in respect of which a penalty is payable under section 98 of TMA 1970 (special returns).

(2) The amount of a penalty for which P is liable under paragraph 1 or 2 in respect of a document relating to a tax period shall be reduced by the amount of any other penalty [incurred by P, or any surcharge for late payment of tax imposed on P, if the amount of the penalty or surcharge is determined by reference to the same tax liability.][1]

[(2A) In sub-paragraph (2) "any other penalty" does not include a penalty under Part 4 of FA 2014 (penalty where corrective action not taken after follower notice etc).][3]

(3) In the application of section 97A of TMA 1970 (multiple penalties) no account shall be taken of a penalty under paragraph 1 or 2.

[(4) Where penalties are imposed under paragraphs 1 and 1A in respect of the same inaccuracy, the aggregate of the amounts of the penalties must not exceed the relevant percentage of the potential lost revenue.

(5) The relevant percentage is—

(*a*) if the penalty imposed under paragraph 1 is for an inaccuracy in category 1, 100%,

(*b*) if the penalty imposed under paragraph 1 is for an inaccuracy in category 2, 150%, and

(*c*) if the penalty imposed under paragraph 1 is for an inaccuracy in category 3, 200%.][2]

HMRC Manuals—Compliance Handbook Manual, CH84960 (interaction with other penalties: penalties for inaccurate documents other than returns).

CH84970–84972 (more than one penalty/surcharge on the same tax with examples).

Amendments—[1] In sub-para (2), words substituted for words "which P has incurred and the amount of which is determined by reference to P's tax liability for that period.", and words inserted at end of heading, by FA 2008 s 122, Sch 40 paras 1, 11 with effect from 1 April 2009 (by virtue of SI 2009/571 art 2).

[2] Sub-paras (4), (5) substituted for previous sub-para (4) by FA 2010 s 35 Sch 10 paras 1, 4 with effect from 6 April 2011 (by virtue of SI 2011/975 art 2(1)). Note that these changes do not have effect in relation to documents given to HMRC, and assessments issued by HMRC, in relation to a tax period commencing on or before 5 April 2011 (SI 2011/975 art 3). Sub-para (4) previously read as follows—

"(4) Where penalties are imposed under paragraphs 1 and 1A in respect of the same inaccuracy, the aggregate of the amounts of the penalties must not exceed 100% of the potential lost revenue.".

[3] Sub-para (2A) inserted by FA 2014 s 233, Sch 33 para 3 with effect from 17 July 2014.

Prospective amendments—Sub-para (5)(*za*) to be inserted before sub-para (*a*), and in sub-para (5)(*a*), figure "125%" to be substituted for "100%", by FA 2015 s 120, Sch 20 paras 1, 6 with effect from a day to be appointed. Sub-para (5)(*za*) as inserted to read as follows—

"(*za*) if the penalty imposed under paragraph 1 is for an inaccuracy in category 0, 100%,".

PART 3
PROCEDURE

Assessment

13—(1) [Where a person][1] becomes liable for a penalty under paragraph 1[, 1A][1] or 2 HMRC shall—

(*a*) assess the penalty,

(*b*) [notify the person][1], and

(*c*) state in the notice a tax period in respect of which the penalty is assessed [(subject to sub-paragraph (1ZB))][3].

[(1ZA) Sub-paragraph (1ZB) applies where—

(*a*) a person is at any time liable for two or more penalties relating to PAYE returns, or for two or more penalties relating to CIS returns, and

(*b*) the penalties ("the relevant penalties") are assessed in respect of more than one tax period ("the relevant tax periods").

(1ZB) A notice under sub-paragraph (1) in respect of any of the relevant penalties may, instead of stating the tax period in respect of which the penalty is assessed, state the tax year or the part of a tax year to which the penalty relates.

(1ZC) For that purpose, a relevant penalty relates to the tax year or the part of a tax year in which the relevant tax periods fall.
(1ZD) For the purposes of sub-paragraph (1ZA)—

"a PAYE return" means a return for the purposes of PAYE regulations;

"a CIS return" means a return for the purposes of regulations under section 70(1)(*a*) of FA 2004 in connection with deductions on account of tax under the Construction Industry Scheme.][3]

[(1A) A penalty under paragraph 1, 1A or 2 must be paid before the end of the period of 30 days beginning with the day on which notification of the penalty is issued.][1]
(2) An assessment—

(*a*) shall be treated for procedural purposes in the same way as an assessment to tax (except in respect of a matter expressly provided for by this Act),

(*b*) may be enforced as if it were an assessment to tax, and

(*c*) may be combined with an assessment to tax.

(3) An assessment of a penalty under paragraph 1[or 1A][1] must be made [before the end of the][1] period of 12 months beginning with—

(*a*) the end of the appeal period for the decision correcting the inaccuracy, or

(*b*) if there is no assessment [to the tax concerned][1] within paragraph (*a*), the date on which the inaccuracy is corrected.

(4) An assessment of a penalty under paragraph 2 must be made [before the end of the period of 12 months beginning with—

(*a*) the end of the appeal period for the assessment of tax which corrected the understatement, or

(*b*) if there is no assessment within paragraph (*a*), the date on which the understatement is corrected.][1]

(5) For the purpose of sub-paragraphs (3) and (4) a reference to an appeal period is a reference to the period during which—

(*a*) an appeal could be brought, or

(*b*) an appeal that has been brought has not been determined or withdrawn.

(6) Subject to sub-paragraphs (3) and (4), a supplementary assessment may be made in respect of a penalty if an earlier assessment operated by reference to an underestimate of potential lost revenue.
[(7) In this Part of this Schedule references to an assessment to tax, in relation to inheritance tax and stamp duty reserve tax, are to a determination.][2]

HMRC Manuals—Compliance Handbook Manual, CH83020–83030 (processing the penalty: penalty assessments and what they must include).
CH83040 (when you should assess a penalty).
CH83050 (supplementary penalties).
CH83060 (enforcement of penalties).

Amendments—[1] In sub-para (1), words substituted for words "Where P" and "notify P" respectively, and words inserted, sub-para (1A) inserted, in sub-para (3), words inserted and words substituted for words "within the", and in sub-para (4), words substituted for words "within the period of 12 months beginning with the end of the appeal period for the assessment of tax which corrected the understatement.", by FA 2008 s 122, Sch 40 paras 1, 12 with effect from 1 April 2009 (by virtue of SI 2009/571 art 2).

[2] Sub-s (7) inserted by FA 2009 s 109, Sch 57 para 5 with effect from 21 July 2009.

[3] Words in sub-para (1)(*c*) inserted, and sub-paras (1ZA)–(1ZD) inserted, by FA 2013 s 230, Sch 50 para 1 with effect in relation to any assessment of a penalty under this Schedule made on or after 17 July 2013.

Suspension

14—(1) HMRC may suspend all or part of a penalty for a careless inaccuracy under paragraph 1 by notice in writing to P.
(2) A notice must specify—

(*a*) what part of the penalty is to be suspended,

(*b*) a period of suspension not exceeding two years, and

(*c*) conditions of suspension to be complied with by P.

(3) HMRC may suspend all or part of a penalty only if compliance with a condition of suspension would help P to avoid becoming liable to further penalties under paragraph 1 for careless inaccuracy.
(4) A condition of suspension may specify—

(*a*) action to be taken, and

(*b*) a period within which it must be taken.

(5) On the expiry of the period of suspension—

(*a*) if P satisfies HMRC that the conditions of suspension have been complied with, the suspended penalty or part is cancelled, and

(*b*) otherwise, the suspended penalty or part becomes payable.

(6) If, during the period of suspension of all or part of a penalty under paragraph 1, P becomes liable for another penalty under that paragraph, the suspended penalty or part becomes payable.

HMRC Manuals—Compliance Handbook Manual, CH83110–83120 (suspension of a penalty).

Appeal

15—(1) [A person may][1] appeal against a decision of HMRC that a penalty is payable [by the person][1].

(2) [A person may][1] appeal against a decision of HMRC as to the amount of a penalty payable [by the person][1].

(3) [A person may][1] appeal against a decision of HMRC not to suspend a penalty payable [by the person][1].

(4) [A person may][1] appeal against a decision of HMRC setting conditions of suspension of a penalty payable [by the person][1].

HMRC Manuals—Compliance Handbook Manual, CH84010–84020 (appeals against a penalty: types of appeal and entitlement to appeal).

Amendments—[1] Words substituted for words "P may" and words "by P", in each place, by FA 2008 s 122, Sch 40 paras 1, 13 with effect from 1 April 2009 (by virtue of SI 2009/571 art 2).

[16—(1) An appeal under this Part of this Schedule shall be treated in the same way as an appeal against an assessment to the tax concerned (including by the application of any provision about bringing the appeal by notice to HMRC, about HMRC review of the decision or about determination of the appeal by the First-tier Tribunal or Upper Tribunal).

[(2) Sub-paragraph (1) does not apply—

(*a*) so as to require P to pay a penalty before an appeal against the assessment of the penalty is determined, or

(*b*) in respect of any other matter expressly provided for by this Act.][2]][1]

HMRC Manuals—Compliance Handbook Manual, CH84070 (appeals against a penalty: which Tribunal will hear the appeal and procedures).

Amendments—[1] Paragraph 16 substituted by the Transfer of Tribunal Functions and Revenue and Customs Appeals Order, SI 2009/56 art 3, Sch 1 para 466 with effect from 1 April 2009. The previous substitution made by FA 2008 therefore effectively never took place.

[2] Sub-para (2) substituted by FA 2009 s 109, Sch 57 para 6 with effect from 21 July 2009.

17—(1) On an appeal under paragraph 15(1) the . . . [1] tribunal may affirm or cancel HMRC's decision.

(2) On an appeal under paragraph 15(2) the . . . [1] tribunal may—

(*a*) affirm HMRC's decision, or

(*b*) substitute for HMRC's decision another decision that HMRC had power to make.

(3) If the . . . [1] tribunal substitutes its decision for HMRC's, the . . . [1] tribunal may rely on paragraph 11—

(*a*) to the same extent as HMRC (which may mean applying the same percentage reduction as HMRC to a different starting point), or

(*b*) to a different extent, but only if the . . . [1] tribunal thinks that HMRC's decision in respect of the application of paragraph 11 was flawed.

(4) On an appeal under paragraph 15(3)—

(*a*) the . . . [1] tribunal may order HMRC to suspend the penalty only if it thinks that HMRC's decision not to suspend was flawed, and

(*b*) if the . . . [1] tribunal orders HMRC to suspend the penalty—

(i) P may appeal [1] against a provision of the notice of suspension, and

(ii) the . . . [1] tribunal may order HMRC to amend the notice.

(5) On an appeal under paragraph 15(4) the . . . [1] tribunal—

(*a*) may affirm the conditions of suspension, or

(*b*) may vary the conditions of suspension, but only if the . . . [1] tribunal thinks that HMRC's decision in respect of the conditions was flawed.

[(5A) In this paragraph "tribunal" means the First-tier Tribunal or Upper Tribunal (as appropriate by virtue of paragraph 16(1)).][1]

(6) In sub-paragraphs (3)(*b*), (4)(*a*) and (5)(*b*) "flawed" means flawed when considered in the light of the principles applicable in proceedings for judicial review.

(7) Paragraph 14 (see in particular paragraph 14(3)) is subject to the possibility of an order under this paragraph.

HMRC Manuals—Compliance Handbook Manual, CH84030–84040 (appeals against a penalty: appeals against the imposition or amount of a penalty).

CH84050 (appeals against the decision not to suspend a penalty).

CH84060 (appeals against the conditions set for penalty suspension).

CH84080 (flawed decision).

Amendment—[1] In sub-paras (1), (2), (3), (4)(*a*), (4)(*b*) in the first place, (4)(*b*)(ii), (5) in each place, word "appellate" repealed, in para (4)(*b*) (i) words "to the appellate tribunal" repealed; sub-para (5A) inserted by the Transfer of Tribunal Functions and Revenue and Customs Appeals Order, SI 2009/56 art 3, Sch 1 para 467 with effect from 1 April 2009.

PART 4
MISCELLANEOUS
Agency

18—(1) P is liable under paragraph 1(1)(*a*) where a document which contains a careless inaccuracy (within the meaning of paragraph 3) is given to HMRC on P's behalf.
(2) In paragraph 2(1)(*b*) and (2)(*a*) a reference to P includes a reference to a person who acts on P's behalf in relation to tax.
(3) Despite sub-paragraphs (1) and (2), P is not liable to a penalty [under paragraph 1 or 2][1] in respect of anything done or omitted by P's agent where P satisfies HMRC that P took reasonable care to avoid inaccuracy (in relation to paragraph 1) or unreasonable failure (in relation to paragraph 2).
(4) In paragraph 3(1)(*a*) (whether in its application to a document given by P or, by virtue of sub-paragraph (1) above, in its application to a document given on P's behalf) a reference to P includes a reference to a person who acts on P's behalf in relation to tax.
(5) In paragraph 3(2) a reference to P includes a reference to a person who acts on P's behalf in relation to tax.

HMRC Manuals—Compliance Handbook Manual, CH84520–84530 (other penalty issues: agent acting).
CH84540 (reliance on use of an agent to avoid an inaccuracy).
CH84545 (agent acting – inaccuracy attributable to another person).
Amendments—[1] In sub-para (3), words inserted by FA 2008 s 122, Sch 40 paras 1, 15 with effect from 1 April 2009 (by virtue of SI 2009/571 art 2).

Companies: officers' liability

19—(1) Where a penalty under paragraph 1 is payable by a company for a deliberate inaccuracy which was attributable to an officer [of the company, the officer is liable to pay such portion of the penalty (which may be 100%) as HMRC][1] may specify by written notice to the officer.
(2) Sub-paragraph (1) does not allow HMRC to recover more than 100% of a penalty.
(3) In the application of sub-paragraph (1) to a body corporate [other than a limited liability partnership][2] "officer" means—

(*a*) a director (including a shadow director within the meaning of section 251 of the Companies Act 2006 (c 46)), . . . [2]
[(*aa*) a manager, and][2]
(*b*) a secretary.

[(3A) In the application of sub-paragraph (1) to a limited liability partnership, "officer" means a member.][2]
(4) In the application of sub-paragraph (1) in any other case "officer" means—

(*a*) a director,
(*b*) a manager,
(*c*) a secretary, and
(*d*) any other person managing or purporting to manage any of the company's affairs.

[(5) Where HMRC have specified a portion of a penalty in a notice given to an officer under sub-paragraph (1)—

(*a*) paragraph 11 applies to the specified portion as to a penalty,
(*b*) the officer must pay the specified portion before the end of the period of 30 days beginning with the day on which the notice is given,
(*c*) paragraph 13(2), (3) and (5) apply as if the notice were an assessment of a penalty,
(*d*) a further notice may be given in respect of a portion of any additional amount assessed in a supplementary assessment in respect of the penalty under paragraph 13(6),
(*e*) paragraphs 15(1) and (2), 16 and 17(1) to (3) and (6) apply as if HMRC had decided that a penalty of the amount of the specified portion is payable by the officer, and
(*f*) paragraph 21 applies as if the officer were liable to a penalty.][1]

[(6) In this paragraph "company" means any body corporate or unincorporated association, but does not include a partnership, a local authority or a local authority association.][2]

HMRC Manuals—Compliance Handbook Manual, CH84610 (company penalties: officer of a company liable to a penalty).
CH84611 (deliberate action by officer of the company).
CH84620 (what is a company).
CH84625 (who is an officer of the company).
CH84630 (notice of liability).
CH84640 (amount of officer's liability).
CH84650 (personal gain).
CH84660 (insolvency or imminent insolvency).
Amendments—[1] In sub-para (1), words substituted, and sub-para (5) substituted, by FA 2008 s 122, Sch 40 paras 1, 16 with effect from 1 April 2009 (by virtue of SI 2009/571 art 2).
[2] In sub-para (3) words inserted; word "or" repealed and para (*aa*) inserted; sub-paras (3A), (6) inserted, by FA 2009 s 109, Sch 57 para 7 with effect from 21 July 2009.

Partnerships

20—(1) This paragraph applies where P is liable to a penalty under paragraph 1 for an inaccuracy in or in connection with a partnership return.
(2) Where the inaccuracy affects the amount of tax due or payable by a partner of P, the partner is also liable to a penalty ("a partner's penalty").
(3) Paragraphs 4 to 13 and 19 shall apply in relation to a partner's penalty (for which purpose a reference to P shall be taken as a reference to the partner).
(4) Potential lost revenue shall be calculated separately for the purpose of P's penalty and any partner's penalty, by reference to the proportions of any tax liability that would be borne by each partner.
(5) Paragraph 14 shall apply jointly to P's penalty and any partner's penalties.
(6) P may bring an appeal under paragraph 15 in respect of a partner's penalty (in addition to any appeal that P may bring in connection with the penalty for which P is liable).

HMRC Manuals—Compliance Handbook Manual, CH84720 (partnership penalties: partnerships and self assessment).
CH84730 (liable partners).
CH84740–84741 (calculating potential lost revenue, with example for partnerships).
CH84750–84760 (suspended penalties and appeals against penalties).

Double jeopardy

21 [A person is][1] not liable to a penalty under paragraph 1[, 1A][1] or 2 in respect of an inaccuracy or failure in respect of which [the person has][1] been convicted of an offence.

HMRC Manuals—Compliance Handbook Manual, CH84900 (partnership penalties: double jeopardy).
Amendments—[1] Words substituted for words "P is" and "the person has" respectively, and reference inserted, by FA 2008 s 122, Sch 40 paras 1, 17 with effect from 1 April 2009 (by virtue of SI 2009/571 art 2).

PART 5
GENERAL

[Classification of territories

21A—(1) A category 1 territory is a territory designated as a category 1 territory by order made by the Treasury.
(2) A category 2 territory is a territory that is neither—
(*a*) a category 1 territory, nor
(*b*) a category 3 territory.
(3) A category 3 territory is a territory designated as a category 3 territory by order made by the Treasury.
(4) In considering how to classify a territory for the purposes of this paragraph, the Treasury must have regard to—
(*a*) the existence of any arrangements between the UK and that territory for the exchange of information for tax enforcement purposes,
(*b*) the quality of any such arrangements (in particular, whether they provide for information to be exchanged automatically or on request), . . .[2]
(*c*) the benefit that the UK would be likely to obtain from receiving information from that territory, were such arrangements to exist with it,
(*d*) the existence of any other arrangements between the UK and that territory for co-operation in the area of taxation, and
(*e*) the quality of any such other arrangements (in particular, the extent to which the co-operation provided for in them assists or is likely to assist in the protection of revenue raised from taxation in the UK).][2]
(5) An order under this paragraph is to be made by statutory instrument.
(6) Subject to sub-paragraph (7), an instrument containing an order under this paragraph is subject to annulment in pursuance of a resolution of the House of Commons.
(7) If the order is—
(*a*) the first order to be made under sub-paragraph (1), or
(*b*) the first order to be made under sub-paragraph (3),
it may not be made unless a draft of the instrument containing it has been laid before, and approved by a resolution of, the House of Commons.
(8) An order under this paragraph does not apply to inaccuracies in a document given to HMRC (or, in a case within paragraph 3(2), inaccuracies discovered by P) before the date on which the order comes into force.][1]

Orders—Penalties, Offshore Income etc. (Designation of Territories) Order, SI 2011/976.
Penalties, Offshore Income etc. (Designation of Territories) (Amendment) Order, SI 2013/1618.

Amendments—[1] Paras 21A, 21B inserted by FA 2010 s 35 Sch 10 paras 1, 5 with effect from 6 April 2011 (by virtue of SI 2011/975 art 2(1)). Note that these changes do not have effect in relation to documents given to HMRC, and assessments issued by HMRC, in relation to a tax period commencing on or before 5 April 2011 (SI 2011/975 art 3).

[2] Word "and" at the end of sub-para (4)(*b*) repealed, and sub-para (4)(*d*), (*e*) inserted, by FA 2012 s 219 with effect from 17 July 2012.

Prospective amendments—Sub-para (A1) to be inserted before sub-para (1), and sub-paras (2), (7) to be substituted, by FA 2015 s 120, Sch 20 paras 1, 7 with effect from a day to be appointed. Sub-para (A1) as inserted to read as follows—

"(A1) A category 0 territory is a territory designated as a category 0 territory by order made by the Treasury.".

Sub-para (2) as substituted to read as follows—

"(2) A category 2 territory is a territory that is not any of the following—
a category 0 territory;
a category 1 territory;
a category 3 territory.".

Sub-para (7) as substituted to read as follows—

"(7) An instrument containing (whether alone or with other provisions) the first order to be made under sub-paragraph (A1) may not be made unless a draft of the instrument has been laid before, and approved by a resolution of, the House of Commons.".

[Location of assets etc

21B—(1) The Treasury may by regulations make provision for determining for the purposes of paragraph 4A where—
(*a*) a source of income is located,
(*b*) an asset is situated or held, or
(*c*) activities are wholly or mainly carried on.
(2) Different provision may be made for different cases and for income tax and capital gains tax.
(3) Regulations under this paragraph are to be made by statutory instrument.
(4) An instrument containing regulations under this paragraph is subject to annulment in pursuance of a resolution of the House of Commons.][1]

Amendments—[1] Paras 21A, 21B inserted by FA 2010 s 35 Sch 10 paras 1, 5 with effect from 6 April 2011 (by virtue of SI 2011/975 art 2(1)). Note that these changes do not have effect in relation to documents given to HMRC, and assessments issued by HMRC, in relation to a tax period commencing on or before 5 April 2011 (SI 2011/975 art 3).

Prospective amendments—Sub-para (1A) to be inserted, and in sub-para (2), words ", capital gains tax and inheritance tax" to be substituted for words "and capital gains tax", by FA 2015 s 120, Sch 20 paras 1, 8 with effect from a day to be appointed. Sub-para (1A) as inserted to read as follows—

"(1A) The Treasury may by regulations make provision for determining for the purposes of paragraph 4AA where—
income is received or transferred,
the proceeds of a disposal are received or transferred, or
assets are transferred.".

[Treatment of certain payments on account of tax

21C In paragraphs 1(2) and 5 references to "tax" are to be interpreted as if amounts payable under section 59AA(2) of TMA 1970 (non-resident CGT disposals: payments on account of capital gains tax) were tax.][1]

Amendments—[1] Paragraph 21C inserted by FA 2015 s 37, Sch 7 para 56(1), (3) with effect in relation to disposals made on or after 6 April 2015.

Interpretation

22 Paragraphs 23 to [27][1] apply for the construction of this Schedule.

Amendments—[1] Reference substituted for reference "26", by FA 2008 s 122, Sch 40 paras 1, 18 with effect from 1 April 2009 (by virtue of SI 2009/571 art 2).

23 HMRC means Her Majesty's Revenue and Customs.

[23A "Tax", without more, includes duty.][1]

Amendments—[1] Paragraph 23A inserted by FA 2008 s 122, Sch 40 paras 1, 19 with effect from 1 April 2009 (by virtue of SI 2009/571 art 2).

[23B "UK" means the United Kingdom, including the territorial sea of the United Kingdom.][1]

Amendments—[1] This para inserted by FA 2010 s 35 Sch 10 paras 1, 6 with effect from 6 April 2011 (by virtue of SI 2011/975 art 2(1)). Note that these changes do not have effect in relation to documents given to HMRC, and assessments issued by HMRC, in relation to a tax period commencing on or before 5 April 2011 (SI 2011/975 art 3).

24 An expression used in relation to income tax has the same meaning as in the Income Tax Acts.

25 An expression used in relation to corporation tax has the same meaning as in the Corporation Tax Acts.

26 An expression used in relation to capital gains tax has the same meaning as in the enactments relating to that tax.

27 An expression used in relation to VAT has the same meaning as in VATA 1994.

28 In this Schedule—

(*a*) a reference to corporation tax includes a reference to tax or duty which by virtue of an enactment is assessable or chargeable as if it were corporation tax,

(*b*) a reference to tax includes a reference to construction industry deductions under Chapter 3 of Part 3 of FA 2004,

(*c*) "direct tax" means—

(i) income tax,

(ii) capital gains tax, . . . [1]

(iii) corporation tax, [and

(iv) petroleum revenue tax,][1]

(*d*) a reference to understating liability to VAT includes a reference to overstating entitlement to a VAT credit,

[*(da) references to an assessment to tax, in relation to inheritance tax, means a determination,*][1,3]

(*e*) a reference to a loss includes a reference to a charge, expense, deficit and any other amount which may be available for, or relied on to claim, a deduction or relief,

(*f*) a reference to repayment of tax includes a reference to allowing a credit [against tax or to a payment of a corporation tax credit][1],

[(*fa*) "corporation tax credit" means—

(i) an R&D tax credit under [Chapter 2 or 7 of Part 13 of CTA 2009][2],

[(ia) an R&D expenditure credit under Chapter 6A of Part 3 of CTA 2009,][4]

(ii) a land remediation tax credit or life assurance company tax credit under [Chapter 3 or 4 respectively of Part 14 of CTA 2009][2],

(iii) *a tax credit under Schedule 13 to FA 2002 (vaccine research etc),*[2]

(iv) a film tax credit under [Chapter 3 of Part 15 of CTA 2009][2], . . .[5]

[(iva) a television tax credit under Chapter 3 of Part 15A of that Act,

(ivb) a video game tax credit under Chapter 3 of Part 15B of that Act, . . . [6]][5]

[(ivc) a theatre tax credit under section 1217K of that Act, or][6]

(v) a first-year tax credit under Schedule A1 to CAA 2001,][1]

(*g*) "tax period" means a tax year, accounting period or other period in respect of which tax is charged,

(*h*) a reference to giving a document to HMRC includes a reference to communicating information to HMRC in any form and by any method (whether by post, fax, email, telephone or otherwise),

(*i*) a reference to giving a document to HMRC includes a reference to making a statement or declaration in a document,

(*j*) a reference to making a return or doing anything in relation to a return includes a reference to amending a return or doing anything in relation to an amended return, and

(*k*) a reference to action includes a reference to omission.

HMRC Manuals—Compliance Handbook Manual, CH81050 (penalties for inaccuracies: what is meant by "giving a document").

CH81071 (what is a "repayment of tax").

Amendments—[1] In sub-para (*c*), word "and" after para (ii) repealed, after para (iii) word "and" inserted, and para (iv) inserted, sub-paras (*da*), (*fa*) inserted, and in sub-para (*f*), words inserted, by FA 2008 s 122, Sch 40 para 20 with effect from 1 April 2009 (by virtue of SI 2009/571 art 2).

[2] In sub-para (*fa*)(i) words substituted for words "Schedule 20 to FA 2000"; in sub-para (*fa*)(ii) words substituted for words "Schedule 22 to FA 2001"; sub-para (*fa*)(iii) repealed; and in sub-para (*fa*)(iv) words substituted for words "Schedule 5 to FA 2006"; by CTA 2009 ss 1322, 1326, Sch 1 paras 722, 727, Sch 3 Part 1. CTA 2009 applies for accounting periods ending on or after 1 April 2009 (for corporation tax purposes) and for tax years 2009–10 onwards (for income and capital gains tax purposes).

[3] Sub-para (*da*) repealed by FA 2009 s 109, Sch 57 para 8 with effect from 21 July 2009.

[4] Sub-para (*fa*)(ia) inserted by FA 2013 s 35, Sch 15 para 8 with effect in relation to expenditure incurred on or after 1 April 2013.

[5] In sub-para (*fa*), word "or" at end of para (iv) repealed and paras (iva), (ivb) inserted, by FA 2013 s 36, Sch 18 para 7. The amendments made by Sch 18 come into force as follows—

- so far as relating to television tax relief on 19 July 2013 (by virtue of SI 2013/1817 art 2(2)); and
- so far as relating to video game development, with effect from 1 April 2014 (by virtue of SI 2014/1962 art 2(3)).

Those amendments have effect in relation to accounting periods beginning on or after the "relevant day", subject to transitional provisions. The "Relevant day" is defined as follows—

- in the case of amendments relating to CTA 2009 Part 15A (as inserted by FA 2013 Sch 16), 1 April 2013, and
- in the case of amendments relating to CTA 2009 Part 15B (as inserted by FA 2013 Sch 17), 1 April 2014 (by virtue of SI 2014/1962 art 2(3)).).

See FA 2013 Sch 18 paras 22, 23 for commencement provisions.

6 In sub-para (*fa*), word "or" at the end of para (ivb) repealed, and para (ivc) inserted, by FA 2014 s 36, Sch 4 para 8 with effect in relation to accounting periods beginning on or after 1 September 2014, subject to transitional provisions for accounting periods straddling that date (FA 2014 Sch 4 para 17). SI 2014/2228 reg 2 provides that the amendments made by FA 2014 Sch 4 come into force on 22 August 2014 (other than the power to make regulations under Sch 4 para 16(1) which came into force on 17 July 2014).

Consequential amendments

29 The following provisions are omitted—

(*a*) sections 95, 95A, 97 and 98A(4) of TMA 1970 (incorrect returns and accounts),

(*b*) sections 100A(1) and 103(2) of TMA 1970 (deceased persons),

(*c*) in Schedule 18 to FA 1998 (company tax returns), paragraphs 20 and 89 (company tax returns), and

(*d*) sections 60, 61, 63 and 64 of VATA 1994 (evasion).

Note—Notwithstanding sub-para (*d*), VATA 1994 ss 60, 61 shall continue to have effect with respect to conduct involving dishonesty which does not relate to an inaccuracy in a document or a failure to notify HMRC of an under-assessment by HMRC (SI 2009/571 art 7).

30 In [paragraphs 7 and 7B][1] of Schedule 1 to the Social Security Contributions and Benefits Act 1992 (c 4) (penalties) a reference to a provision of TMA 1970 shall be construed as a reference to this Schedule so far as is necessary to preserve its effect.

Amendments—[1] Words substituted for words "paragraph 7" by FA 2009 s 109, Sch 57 para 9 with effect from 21 July 2009.

31 In [paragraphs 7 and 7B][1] of Schedule 1 to the Social Security Contributions and Benefits (Northern Ireland) Act 1992 (c 7) (penalties) a reference to a provision of TMA 1970 shall be construed as a reference to this Schedule so far as is necessary to preserve its effect.

Amendments—[1] Words substituted for words "paragraph 7" by FA 2009 s 109, Sch 57 para 9 with effect from 21 July 2009.

SCHEDULE 27

REPEALS

Section 114

PART 5

INVESTIGATION, ADMINISTRATION ETC

Note—The repeals made under this Part are already in force and are therefore omitted.

PART 6

MISCELLANEOUS

Note—The repeals made under this Part are already in force and are therefore omitted.

TRIBUNALS, COURTS AND ENFORCEMENT ACT 2007

(2007 Chapter 15)

ARRANGEMENT OF SECTIONS

PART 1
TRIBUNALS AND INQUIRIES

CHAPTER 1
TRIBUNAL JUDICIARY: INDEPENDENCE AND SENIOR PRESIDENT

CHAPTER 2
FIRST-TIER TRIBUNAL AND UPPER TRIBUNAL

Establishment

Schedule 23—Repeals

An Act to make provision about tribunals and inquiries; to establish an Administrative Justice and Tribunals Council; to amend the law relating to judicial appointments and appointments to the Law Commission; to amend the law relating to the enforcement of judgments and debts; to make further provision about the management and relief of debt; to make provision protecting cultural objects from seizure or forfeiture in certain circumstances; to amend the law relating to the taking of possession of land affected by compulsory purchase; to alter the powers of the High Court in judicial review applications; and for connected purposes.

[19th July 2007]

PART 1
TRIBUNALS AND INQUIRIES

CHAPTER 1
TRIBUNAL JUDICIARY: INDEPENDENCE AND SENIOR PRESIDENT

1 Independence of tribunal judiciary

(*Inserts* Constitutional Reform Act 2005 s 3(7A), (7B) with effect from 19 September 2007: SI 2007/2709 art 2)

2 Senior President of Tribunals

(1) Her Majesty may, on the recommendation of the Lord Chancellor, appoint a person to the office of Senior President of Tribunals.

(2) Schedule 1 makes further provision about the Senior President of Tribunals and about recommendations for appointment under subsection (1).

(3) A holder of the office of Senior President of Tribunals must, in carrying out the functions of that office, have regard to—

(*a*) the need for tribunals to be accessible,

(*b*) the need for proceedings before tribunals—

(i) to be fair, and

(ii) to be handled quickly and efficiently,

(*c*) the need for members of tribunals to be experts in the subject-matter of, or the law to be applied in, cases in which they decide matters, and

(*d*) the need to develop innovative methods of resolving disputes that are of a type that may be brought before tribunals.

(4) In subsection (3) "tribunals" means—

(*a*) the First-tier Tribunal,

(*b*) the Upper Tribunal,

(*c*) employment tribunals,

(*d*) the Employment Appeal Tribunal, and

(*e*) the Asylum and Immigration Tribunal.

Commencement—Tribunals, Courts and Enforcement Act 2007 (Commencement No 1) Order, SI 2007/2709 art 2(a) (this section comes into force on 19 September 2007).

CHAPTER 2

FIRST-TIER TRIBUNAL AND UPPER TRIBUNAL

Establishment

3 The First-tier Tribunal and the Upper Tribunal

(1) There is to be a tribunal, known as the First-tier Tribunal, for the purpose of exercising the functions conferred on it under or by virtue of this Act or any other Act.

(2) There is to be a tribunal, known as the Upper Tribunal, for the purpose of exercising the functions conferred on it under or by virtue of this Act or any other Act.

(3) Each of the First-tier Tribunal, and the Upper Tribunal, is to consist of its judges and other members.

(4) The Senior President of Tribunals is to preside over both of the First-tier Tribunal and the Upper Tribunal.

(5) The Upper Tribunal is to be a superior court of record.

Commencement—Tribunals, Courts and Enforcement Act 2007 (Commencement No 6 and Transitional Provisions) Order, SI 2008/2696 art 5(a) (this section comes into force on 3 November 2008).

Simon's Tax Cases—*R (Cart) v Upper Tribunal* [2010] STC 2556.

Members and composition of tribunals

4 Judges and other members of the First-tier Tribunal

(1) A person is a judge of the First-tier Tribunal if the person—

(*a*) is a judge of the First-tier Tribunal by virtue of appointment under paragraph 1(1) of Schedule 2,

(*b*) is a transferred-in judge of the First-tier Tribunal (see section 31(2)),

(*c*) is a judge of the Upper Tribunal,

[(*ca*) is within section 6A,][1]

(*d*) is a member of the Asylum and Immigration Tribunal appointed under paragraph 2(1)(*a*) to (*d*) of Schedule 4 to the Nationality, Immigration and Asylum Act 2002 (c 41) (legally qualified members) and is not a judge of the Upper Tribunal, or

(*e*) is a member of a panel of [Employment Judges][1] of employment tribunals.

(2) A person is also a judge of the First-tier Tribunal, but only as regards functions of the tribunal in relation to appeals such as are mentioned in subsection (1) of section 5 of the Criminal Injuries Compensation Act 1995 (c 53), if the person is an adjudicator appointed under that section by the Scottish Ministers.

(3) A person is one of the other members of the First-tier Tribunal if the person—

(*a*) is a member of the First-tier Tribunal by virtue of appointment under paragraph 2(1) of Schedule 2,

(*b*) is a transferred-in other member of the First-tier Tribunal (see section 31(2)),

(*c*) is one of the other members of the Upper Tribunal, or

(*d*) is a member of a panel of members of employment tribunals that is not a panel of [Employment Judges][1] of employment tribunals.

(4) Schedule 2—

contains provision for the appointment of persons to be judges or other members of the First-tier Tribunal, and

makes further provision in connection with judges and other members of the First-tier Tribunal.

Commencement—Tribunals, Courts and Enforcement Act 2007 (Commencement No 6 and Transitional Provisions) Order, SI 2008/2696 art 5(a) (this section comes into force on 3 November 2008).

Amendments—[1] Sub-s (1)(*ca*) inserted, and in sub-ss (1)(*e*), (3)(*d*), words substituted for word "chairmen" by the Crime and Courts Act 2013 s 21, Sch 14 paras 6, 7 with effect from 1 October 2013 (by virtue of SI 2013/2200).

5 Judges and other members of the Upper Tribunal

(1) A person is a judge of the Upper Tribunal if the person—

(*a*) is the Senior President of Tribunals,

(*b*) is a judge of the Upper Tribunal by virtue of appointment under paragraph 1(1) of Schedule 3,

(*c*) is a transferred-in judge of the Upper Tribunal (see section 31(2)),

(*d*) is a member of the Asylum and Immigration Tribunal appointed under paragraph 2(1)(*a*) to (*d*) of Schedule 4 to the Nationality, Immigration and Asylum Act 2002 (c 41) (legally qualified members) who—

(i) is the President or a Deputy President of that tribunal, or

(ii) has the title Senior Immigration Judge but is neither the President nor a Deputy President of that tribunal,

(*e*) is the Chief Social Security Commissioner, or any other Social Security Commissioner, appointed under section 50(1) of the Social Security Administration (Northern Ireland) Act 1992 (c 8),

(*f*) is a Social Security Commissioner appointed under section 50(2) of that Act (deputy Commissioners),

(*g*) is within section 6(1),

(*h*) is a deputy judge of the Upper Tribunal (whether under paragraph 7 of Schedule 3 or under section 31(2)), or

(*i*) is a Chamber President or a Deputy Chamber President, whether of a chamber of the Upper Tribunal or of a chamber of the First-tier Tribunal, and does not fall within any of paragraphs (*a*) to (*h*).

(2) A person is one of the other members of the Upper Tribunal if the person—

(*a*) is a member of the Upper Tribunal by virtue of appointment under paragraph 2(1) of Schedule 3,

(*b*) is a transferred-in other member of the Upper Tribunal (see section 31(2)),

(*c*) is a member of the Employment Appeal Tribunal appointed under section 22(1)(*c*) of the Employment Tribunals Act 1996 (c 17), or

(*d*) is a member of the Asylum and Immigration Tribunal appointed under paragraph 2(1)(*e*) of Schedule 4 to the Nationality, Immigration and Asylum Act 2002 (members other than "legally qualified members").

(3) Schedule 3—

contains provision for the appointment of persons to be judges (including deputy judges), or other members, of the Upper Tribunal, and

makes further provision in connection with judges and other members of the Upper Tribunal.

Commencement—Tribunals, Courts and Enforcement Act 2007 (Commencement No 6 and Transitional Provisions) Order, SI 2008/2696 art 5(a) (this section comes into force on 3 November 2008).

6 Certain judges who are also judges of First-tier Tribunal and Upper Tribunal

(1) A person is within this subsection (and so, by virtue of sections 4(1)(*c*) and 5(1)(*g*), is a judge of the First-tier Tribunal and of the Upper Tribunal) if the person—

[(*za*) is the Lord Chief Justice of England and Wales,

(*zb*) is the Master of the Rolls,

(*zc*) is the President of the Queen's Bench Division of the High Court in England and Wales,

(*zd*) is the President of the Family Division of the High Court in England and Wales,

(*ze*) is the Chancellor of the High Court in England and Wales,][1]

(*a*) is an ordinary judge of the Court of Appeal in England and Wales (including the vice-president, if any, of either division of that Court),

(*b*) is a Lord Justice of Appeal in Northern Ireland,

(*c*) is a judge of the Court of Session,

[(*da*) is a deputy judge of the High Court in England and Wales,

(*db*) is the Judge Advocate General,][1]

(*d*) is a puisne judge of the High Court in England and Wales or Northern Ireland,

(*e*) is a circuit judge,

(*f*) is a sheriff in Scotland,

(*g*) is a county court judge in Northern Ireland,

(*h*) is a district judge in England and Wales or Northern Ireland, or

(*i*) is a District Judge (Magistrates' Courts).

(2) References in subsection (1)(*c*) to (*i*) to office-holders do not include deputies or temporary office holders.

Commencement—Tribunals, Courts and Enforcement Act 2007 (Commencement No 6 and Transitional Provisions) Order, SI 2008/2696 art 5(a) (this section comes into force on 3 November 2008).

Amendments—[1] Sub-s (1)(*za*)–(*ze*), (*da*), (*db*) inserted by the Crime and Courts Act 2013 s 21, Sch 14 paras 6, 8 with effect from 1 October 2013 (by virtue of SI 2013/2200).

[6A Certain judges who are also judges of the First-tier Tribunal

A person is within this section (and so, by virtue of section 4(1)(ca), is a judge of the First-tier Tribunal) if the person—

(*a*) is a deputy Circuit judge,

(*b*) is a Recorder,

(*c*) is a person who holds an office listed—

(i) in the first column of the table in section 89(3C) of the Senior Courts Act 1981 (senior High Court Masters etc), or

(ii) in column 1 of Part 2 of Schedule 2 to that Act (High Court Masters etc),

(*d*) is a deputy district judge appointed under section 102 of that Act or section 8 of the County Courts Act 1984,

(*e*) is a Deputy District Judge (Magistrates' Courts), or

(*f*) is a person appointed under section 30(1)(*a*) or (*b*) of the Courts-Martial (Appeals) Act 1951 (assistants to the Judge Advocate General).][1]

Amendments—[1] Section 6A inserted by the Crime and Courts Act 2013 s 21, Sch 14 paras 6, 9 with effect from 1 October 2013 (by virtue of SI 2013/2200).

7 Chambers: jurisdiction and Presidents

(1) The Lord Chancellor may, with the concurrence of the Senior President of Tribunals, by order make provision for the organisation of each of the First-tier Tribunal and the Upper Tribunal into a number of chambers.

(2) There is—

(*a*) for each chamber of the First-tier Tribunal, and

(*b*) for each chamber of the Upper Tribunal,

to be a person, or two persons, to preside over that chamber.

(3) A person may not at any particular time preside over more than one chamber of the First-tier Tribunal and may not at any particular time preside over more than one chamber of the Upper Tribunal (but may at the same time preside over one chamber of the First-tier Tribunal and over one chamber of the Upper Tribunal).

(4) A person appointed under this section to preside over a chamber is to be known as a Chamber President.

(5) Where two persons are appointed under this section to preside over the same chamber, any reference in an enactment to the Chamber President of the chamber is a reference to a person appointed under this section to preside over the chamber.

(6) The Senior President of Tribunals may (consistently with subsections (2) and (3)) appoint a person who is the Chamber President of a chamber to preside instead, or to preside also, over another chamber.

(7) The [Senior President of Tribunals][1] may (consistently with subsections (2) and (3)) appoint a person who is not a Chamber President to preside over a chamber.
(8) Schedule 4 (eligibility for appointment under subsection (7), appointment of Deputy Chamber Presidents and Acting Chamber Presidents, assignment of judges and other members of the First-tier Tribunal and Upper Tribunal, and further provision about Chamber Presidents and chambers) has effect.
(9) Each of the Lord Chancellor and the Senior President of Tribunals may, with the concurrence of the other, by order—

(*a*) make provision for the allocation of the First-tier Tribunal's functions between its chambers;
(*b*) make provision for the allocation of the Upper Tribunal's functions between its chambers;
(*c*) amend or revoke any order made under this subsection.

Commencement—Tribunals, Courts and Enforcement Act 2007 (Commencement No 1) Order, SI 2007/2709 art 2(a) (sub-ss (1), (9) come into force on 19 September 2007).
Tribunals, Courts and Enforcement Act 2007 (Commencement No 6 and Transitional Provisions) Order, SI 2008/2696 art 5(a) (sub-ss (2)–(8) come into force on 3 November 2008).
Orders—First-tier Tribunal and Upper Tribunal (Chambers) (Amendment) Order, SI 2009/196 (*note: revoked except for art 9 transitional provisions*).
First-tier Tribunal and Upper Tribunal (Chambers) Order, SI 2010/2655.
First-tier Tribunal and Upper Tribunal (Chambers) (Amendment) Order, SI 2012/1673.
First-tier Tribunal and Upper Tribunal (Chambers) (Amendment) Order, SI 2013/1187.
First-tier Tribunal and Upper Tribunal (Chambers) (Amendment No 2) Order, SI 2013/2068.
First-tier Tribunal and Upper Tribunal (Chambers) (Amendment) Order, SI 2014/1901.
First-tier Tribunal and Upper Tribunal (Chambers) (Amendment) Order, SI 2015/1563.
Amendments—[1] In sub-s (7), words substituted for words "Lord Chancellor" by the Crime and Courts Act 2013 s 20, Sch 13 paras 42, 43 with effect from 1 October 2013 (by virtue of SI 2013/2200).

8 Senior President of Tribunals: power to delegate

(1) The Senior President of Tribunals may delegate any function he has in his capacity as Senior President of Tribunals—

(*a*) to any judge, or other member, of the Upper Tribunal or First-tier Tribunal;
(*b*) to staff appointed under section 40(1).

[(1A) A function under paragraph 1(1) or 2(1) of Schedule 2 may be delegated under subsection (1) only to a Chamber President of a chamber of the Upper Tribunal.][1]
(2) Subsection (1) does not apply to functions of the Senior President of Tribunals [under any of the following—

section 7(7);
section 7(9);
paragraph 2(1) of Schedule 3;
paragraph 7(1) of Schedule 3;
paragraph 2 of Schedule 4;
paragraph 5(1) and (3) of Schedule 4;
paragraph 5(5) to (8) of Schedule 4;
paragraph 5A(2)(a) of Schedule 4;
paragraph 5A(3)(a) of Schedule 4.][1]

(3) A delegation under subsection (1) is not revoked by the delegator's becoming incapacitated.
(4) Any delegation under subsection (1) that is in force immediately before a person ceases to be Senior President of Tribunals continues in force until varied or revoked by a subsequent holder of the office of Senior President of Tribunals.
(5) The delegation under this section of a function shall not prevent the exercise of the function by the Senior President of Tribunals.

Commencement—Tribunals, Courts and Enforcement Act 2007 (Commencement No 6 and Transitional Provisions) Order, SI 2008/2696 art 5(a) (this section comes into force on 3 November 2008).
Amendments—[1] Sub-s (1A) inserted, and in sub-s (2), words substituted for words "under section 7(9)" by the Crime and Courts Act 2013 s 20, Sch 13 paras 42, 44(1), (2) with effect from 1 October 2013 (by virtue of SI 2013/2200).

Review of decisions and appeals

9 Review of decision of First-tier Tribunal

(1) The First-tier Tribunal may review a decision made by it on a matter in a case, other than a decision that is an excluded decision for the purposes of section 11(1) (but see subsection (9)).
(2) The First-tier Tribunal's power under subsection (1) in relation to a decision is exercisable—

(*a*) of its own initiative, or
(*b*) on application by a person who for the purposes of section 11(2) has a right of appeal in respect of the decision.

(3) Tribunal Procedure Rules may—

(*a*) provide that the First-tier Tribunal may not under subsection (1) review (whether of its own initiative or on application under subsection (2)(*b*)) a decision of a description specified for the purposes of this paragraph in Tribunal Procedure Rules;

(*b*) provide that the First-tier Tribunal's power under subsection (1) to review a decision of a description specified for the purposes of this paragraph in Tribunal Procedure Rules is exercisable only of the tribunal's own initiative;

(*c*) provide that an application under subsection (2)(*b*) that is of a description specified for the purposes of this paragraph in Tribunal Procedure Rules may be made only on grounds specified for the purposes of this paragraph in Tribunal Procedure Rules;

(*d*) provide, in relation to a decision of a description specified for the purposes of this paragraph in Tribunal Procedure Rules, that the First-tier Tribunal's power under subsection (1) to review the decision of its own initiative is exercisable only on grounds specified for the purposes of this paragraph in Tribunal Procedure Rules.

(4) Where the First-tier Tribunal has under subsection (1) reviewed a decision, the First-tier Tribunal may in the light of the review do any of the following—

(*a*) correct accidental errors in the decision or in a record of the decision;

(*b*) amend reasons given for the decision;

(*c*) set the decision aside.

(5) Where under subsection (4)(*c*) the First-tier Tribunal sets a decision aside, the First-tier Tribunal must either—

(*a*) re-decide the matter concerned, or

(*b*) refer that matter to the Upper Tribunal.

(6) Where a matter is referred to the Upper Tribunal under subsection (5)(*b*), the Upper Tribunal must re-decide the matter.

(7) Where the Upper Tribunal is under subsection (6) re-deciding a matter, it may make any decision which the First-tier Tribunal could make if the First-tier Tribunal were re-deciding the matter.

(8) Where a tribunal is acting under subsection (5)(*a*) or (6), it may make such findings of fact as it considers appropriate.

(9) This section has effect as if a decision under subsection (4)(*c*) to set aside an earlier decision were not an excluded decision for the purposes of section 11(1), but the First-tier Tribunal's only power in the light of a review under subsection (1) of a decision under subsection (4)(*c*) is the power under subsection (4)(*a*).

(10) A decision of the First-tier Tribunal may not be reviewed under subsection (1) more than once, and once the First-tier Tribunal has decided that an earlier decision should not be reviewed under subsection (1) it may not then decide to review that earlier decision under that subsection.

(11) Where under this section a decision is set aside and the matter concerned is then re-decided, the decision set aside and the decision made in re-deciding the matter are for the purposes of subsection (10) to be taken to be different decisions.

Commencement—Tribunals, Courts and Enforcement Act 2007 (Commencement No 1) Order, SI 2007/2709 art 2(*a*) (sub-s (3) comes into force on 19 September 2007).

Tribunals, Courts and Enforcement Act 2007 (Commencement No 6 and Transitional Provisions) Order, SI 2008/2696 art 5(a) (sub-ss (1), (2), (4)–(11) come into force on 3 November 2008).

Orders—Tribunal Procedure (First-tier Tribunal) (Social Entitlement Chamber) Rules, SI 2008/2685 (made under sub-s (3)).

Tribunal Procedure (First-tier Tribunal) (War Pensions and Armed Forces Compensation Chamber) Rules, SI 2008/2686 (made under sub-para (3)).

Tribunal Procedure (First-tier Tribunal) (Health, Education and Social Care Chamber) Rules, SI 2008/2699 (made under sub-s (3)).

Tribunal Procedure (First-tier Tribunal) (Tax Chamber) Rules, SI 2009/273 (made under sub-s (3)).

10 Review of decision of Upper Tribunal

(1) The Upper Tribunal may review a decision made by it on a matter in a case, other than a decision that is an excluded decision for the purposes of section 13(1) (but see subsection (7)).

(2) The Upper Tribunal's power under subsection (1) in relation to a decision is exercisable—

(*a*) of its own initiative, or

(*b*) on application by a person who for the purposes of section 13(2) has a right of appeal in respect of the decision.

(3) Tribunal Procedure Rules may—

(*a*) provide that the Upper Tribunal may not under subsection (1) review (whether of its own initiative or on application under subsection (2)(*b*)) a decision of a description specified for the purposes of this paragraph in Tribunal Procedure Rules;

(*b*) provide that the Upper Tribunal's power under subsection (1) to review a decision of a description specified for the purposes of this paragraph in Tribunal Procedure Rules is exercisable only of the tribunal's own initiative;

(*c*) provide that an application under subsection (2)(*b*) that is of a description specified for the purposes of this paragraph in Tribunal Procedure Rules may be made only on grounds specified for the purposes of this paragraph in Tribunal Procedure Rules;

(*d*) provide, in relation to a decision of a description specified for the purposes of this paragraph in Tribunal Procedure Rules, that the Upper Tribunal's power under subsection (1) to review the decision of its own initiative is exercisable only on grounds specified for the purposes of this paragraph in Tribunal Procedure Rules.

(4) Where the Upper Tribunal has under subsection (1) reviewed a decision, the Upper Tribunal may in the light of the review do any of the following—

(*a*) correct accidental errors in the decision or in a record of the decision;

(*b*) amend reasons given for the decision;

(*c*) set the decision aside.

(5) Where under subsection (4)(*c*) the Upper Tribunal sets a decision aside, the Upper Tribunal must re-decide the matter concerned.

(6) Where the Upper Tribunal is acting under subsection (5), it may make such findings of fact as it considers appropriate.

(7) This section has effect as if a decision under subsection (4)(*c*) to set aside an earlier decision were not an excluded decision for the purposes of section 13(1), but the Upper Tribunal's only power in the light of a review under subsection (1) of a decision under subsection (4)(*c*) is the power under subsection (4)(*a*).

(8) A decision of the Upper Tribunal may not be reviewed under subsection (1) more than once, and once the Upper Tribunal has decided that an earlier decision should not be reviewed under subsection (1) it may not then decide to review that earlier decision under that subsection.

(9) Where under this section a decision is set aside and the matter concerned is then re-decided, the decision set aside and the decision made in re-deciding the matter are for the purposes of subsection (8) to be taken to be different decisions.

Commencement—Tribunals, Courts and Enforcement Act 2007 (Commencement No 1) Order, SI 2007/2709 art 2(*a*) (sub-s (3) comes into force on 19 September 2007).

Tribunals, Courts and Enforcement Act 2007 (Commencement No 6 and Transitional Provisions) Order, SI 2008/2696 art 5(a) (sub-ss (1), (2), (4)–(9) come into force on 3 November 2008).

11 Right to appeal to Upper Tribunal

(1) For the purposes of subsection (2), the reference to a right of appeal is to a right to appeal to the Upper Tribunal on any point of law arising from a decision made by the First-tier Tribunal other than an excluded decision.

(2) Any party to a case has a right of appeal, subject to subsection (8).

(3) That right may be exercised only with permission (or, in Northern Ireland, leave).

(4) Permission (or leave) may be given by—

(*a*) the First-tier Tribunal, or

(*b*) the Upper Tribunal,

on an application by the party.

(5) For the purposes of subsection (1), an "excluded decision" is—

(*a*) any decision of the First-tier Tribunal on an appeal made in exercise of a right conferred by the Criminal Injuries Compensation Scheme in compliance with section 5(1)(*a*) of the Criminal Injuries Compensation Act 1995 (c 53) (appeals against decisions on reviews),

[(*aa*) any decision of the First-tier Tribunal on an appeal made in exercise of a right conferred by the Victims of Overseas Terrorism Compensation Scheme in compliance with section 52(3) of the Crime and Security Act 2010,][1]

(*b*) any decision of the First-tier Tribunal on an appeal under section 28(4) or (6) of the Data Protection Act 1998 (c 29) (appeals against national security certificate),

(*c*) any decision of the First-tier Tribunal on an appeal under section 60(1) or (4) of the Freedom of Information Act 2000 (c 36) (appeals against national security certificate),

(*d*) a decision of the First-tier Tribunal under section 9—

(i) to review, or not to review, an earlier decision of the tribunal,

(ii) to take no action, or not to take any particular action, in the light of a review of an earlier decision of the tribunal,

(iii) to set aside an earlier decision of the tribunal, or

(iv) to refer, or not to refer, a matter to the Upper Tribunal,

(*e*) a decision of the First-tier Tribunal that is set aside under section 9 (including a decision set aside after proceedings on an appeal under this section have been begun), or

(*f*) any decision of the First-tier Tribunal that is of a description specified in an order made by the Lord Chancellor.

(6) A description may be specified under subsection (5)(*f*) only if—

(*a*) in the case of a decision of that description, there is a right to appeal to a court, the Upper Tribunal or any other tribunal from the decision and that right is, or includes, something other than a right (however expressed) to appeal on any point of law arising from the decision, or

(*b*) decisions of that description are made in carrying out a function transferred under section 30 and prior to the transfer of the function under section 30(1) there was no right to appeal from decisions of that description.

(7) Where—

(*a*) an order under subsection (5)(*f*) specifies a description of decisions, and

(*b*) decisions of that description are made in carrying out a function transferred under section 30, the order must be framed so as to come into force no later than the time when the transfer under section 30 of the function takes effect (but power to revoke the order continues to be exercisable after that time, and power to amend the order continues to be exercisable after that time for the purpose of narrowing the description for the time being specified).

(8) The Lord Chancellor may by order make provision for a person to be treated as being, or to be treated as not being, a party to a case for the purposes of subsection (2).

Commencement—Tribunals, Courts and Enforcement Act 2007 (Commencement No 1) Order, SI 2007/2709 art 2(*a*) (sub-ss (5)(*f*), (6)–(8) come into force on 19 September 2007).

Tribunals, Courts and Enforcement Act 2007 (Commencement No 6 and Transitional Provisions) Order, SI 2008/2696 art 5(*a*) (sub-ss (1)–(4), (5)(*a*)–(*e*) come into force on 3 November 2008).

Cross references—See Tribunals, Courts and Enforcement Act 2007 (Transitional and Consequential Provisions) Order, SI 2008/2683, art 5 (transitional provisions).

Charities Act 2011 s 317 (appeals from the Tribunal involving the Charity Commission).

FA 2014 s 256(7) (tribunal decisions in connection with the giving of an information notice under FA 2014 s 255 to a monitored promoter (or relevant intermediary) are final).

FA 2014 s 266(10) (tribunal decisions in connection with appeals against requirements of information notice to a monitored promoter (or relevant intermediary) are final).

Orders—Appeals (Excluded Decisions) Order, SI 2009/275 (made under sub-s (5)(*f*)).

Amendments—[1] Sub-s (5)(*aa*) inserted by the Crime and Security Act 2010 s 48(4), Sch 2 para 5 with effect from 8 April 2010 (Crime and Security Act 2010 s 59(2)(*b*)).

12 Proceedings on appeal to Upper Tribunal

(1) Subsection (2) applies if the Upper Tribunal, in deciding an appeal under section 11, finds that the making of the decision concerned involved the making of an error on a point of law.

(2) The Upper Tribunal—

(*a*) may (but need not) set aside the decision of the First-tier Tribunal, and

(*b*) if it does, must either—

(i) remit the case to the First-tier Tribunal with directions for its reconsideration, or

(ii) re-make the decision.

(3) In acting under subsection (2)(*b*)(i), the Upper Tribunal may also—

(*a*) direct that the members of the First-tier Tribunal who are chosen to reconsider the case are not to be the same as those who made the decision that has been set aside;

(*b*) give procedural directions in connection with the reconsideration of the case by the First-tier Tribunal.

(4) In acting under subsection (2)(*b*)(ii), the Upper Tribunal—

(*a*) may make any decision which the First-tier Tribunal could make if the First-tier Tribunal were re-making the decision, and

(*b*) may make such findings of fact as it considers appropriate.

Commencement—Tribunals, Courts and Enforcement Act 2007 (Commencement No 6 and Transitional Provisions) Order, SI 2008/2696 art 5(*a*) (this section comes into force on 3 November 2008).

Simon's Tax Cases—12(2)(*b*)(ii), *Capital Air Services Ltd v R&C Comrs* [2011] STC 617.

Modification—See the Mental Health Act 1983, s 78A (as inserted by SI 2008/2833, art 9(1), Sch 3, paras 39, 60) (in relation to the application with modifications of this section to appeals from the Mental Health Review Tribunal for Wales).

13 Right to appeal to Court of Appeal etc

(1) For the purposes of subsection (2), the reference to a right of appeal is to a right to appeal to the relevant appellate court on any point of law arising from a decision made by the Upper Tribunal other than an excluded decision.

(2) Any party to a case has a right of appeal, subject to subsection (14).

(3) That right may be exercised only with permission (or, in Northern Ireland, leave).

(4) Permission (or leave) may be given by—

(*a*) the Upper Tribunal, or

(*b*) the relevant appellate court,

on an application by the party.

(5) An application may be made under subsection (4) to the relevant appellate court only if permission (or leave) has been refused by the Upper Tribunal.

(6) The Lord Chancellor may, as respects an application under subsection (4) that falls within subsection (7) and for which the relevant appellate court is the Court of Appeal in England and Wales or the Court of Appeal in Northern Ireland, by order make provision for permission (or leave) not to be granted on the application unless the Upper Tribunal or (as the case may be) the relevant appellate court considers—

(*a*) that the proposed appeal would raise some important point of principle or practice, or

(*b*) that there is some other compelling reason for the relevant appellate court to hear the appeal.

[(6A) Rules of court may make provision for permission not to be granted on an application under subsection (4) to the Court of Session that falls within subsection (7) unless the court considers—

(*a*) that the proposed appeal would raise some important point of principle [or practice][2], or

(*b*) that there is some other compelling reason for the court to hear the appeal.][1]

(7) An application falls within this subsection if the application is for permission (or leave) to appeal from any decision of the Upper Tribunal on an appeal under section 11.

(8) For the purposes of subsection (1), an "excluded decision" is—

(*a*) any decision of the Upper Tribunal on an appeal under section 28(4) or (6) of the Data Protection Act 1998 (c 29) (appeals against national security certificate),

(*b*) any decision of the Upper Tribunal on an appeal under section 60(1) or (4) of the Freedom of Information Act 2000 (c 36) (appeals against national security certificate),

(*c*) any decision of the Upper Tribunal on an application under section 11(4)(*b*) (application for permission or leave to appeal),

(*d*) a decision of the Upper Tribunal under section 10—

(i) to review, or not to review, an earlier decision of the tribunal,

(ii) to take no action, or not to take any particular action, in the light of a review of an earlier decision of the tribunal, or

(iii) to set aside an earlier decision of the tribunal,

(*e*) a decision of the Upper Tribunal that is set aside under section 10 (including a decision set aside after proceedings on an appeal under this section have been begun), or

(*f*) any decision of the Upper Tribunal that is of a description specified in an order made by the Lord Chancellor.

(9) A description may be specified under subsection (8)(*f*) only if—

(*a*) in the case of a decision of that description, there is a right to appeal to a court from the decision and that right is, or includes, something other than a right (however expressed) to appeal on any point of law arising from the decision, or

(*b*) decisions of that description are made in carrying out a function transferred under section 30 and prior to the transfer of the function under section 30(1) there was no right to appeal from decisions of that description.

(10) Where—

(*a*) an order under subsection (8)(*f*) specifies a description of decisions, and

(*b*) decisions of that description are made in carrying out a function transferred under section 30,

the order must be framed so as to come into force no later than the time when the transfer under section 30 of the function takes effect (but power to revoke the order continues to be exercisable after that time, and power to amend the order continues to be exercisable after that time for the purpose of narrowing the description for the time being specified).

(11) Before the Upper Tribunal decides an application made to it under subsection (4), the Upper Tribunal must specify the court that is to be the relevant appellate court as respects the proposed appeal.

(12) The court to be specified under subsection (11) in relation to a proposed appeal is whichever of the following courts appears to the Upper Tribunal to be the most appropriate—

(*a*) the Court of Appeal in England and Wales;

(*b*) the Court of Session;

(*c*) the Court of Appeal in Northern Ireland.

(13) In this section except subsection (11), "the relevant appellate court", as respects an appeal, means the court specified as respects that appeal by the Upper Tribunal under subsection (11).

(14) The Lord Chancellor may by order make provision for a person to be treated as being, or to be treated as not being, a party to a case for the purposes of subsection (2).

(15) Rules of court may make provision as to the time within which an application under subsection (4) to the relevant appellate court must be made.

Commencement—Tribunals, Courts and Enforcement Act 2007 (Commencement No 1) Order, SI 2007/2709 art 2(*a*) (sub-ss (6), (8)(*f*), (9), (10), (14), (15) come into force on 19 September 2007).

Tribunals, Courts and Enforcement Act 2007 (Commencement No 6 and Transitional Provisions) Order, SI 2008/2696 art 5(*a*) (sub-ss (1)–(5), (7), (8)(*a*)–(*e*), (11)–(13) come into force on 3 November 2008).

Cross references—Charities Act 2011 s 317 (appeals from the Tribunal involving the Charity Commission).

FA 2014 s 256(7) (tribunal decisions in connection with the giving of an information notice under FA 2014 s 255 to a monitored promoter (or relevant intermediary) are final).

FA 2014 s 266(10) (tribunal decisions in connection with appeals against requirements of information notice to a monitored promoter (or relevant intermediary) are final).

Orders—Appeals from the Upper Tribunal to the Court of Appeal Order, SI 2008/2834 (made under sub-s (6)).

Appeals (Excluded Decisions) Order, SI 2009/275 (made under sub-s (8)(*f*)).

Amendments—[1] Sub-s (6A) inserted by the Crime and Courts Act 2013 s 23 with effect from 7 October 2013 (by virtue of SI 2013/1725, art 3(*b*)).

[2] In sub-s (6A)(*a*), words inserted by the Criminal Justice and Courts Act 2015 s 83(2)with effect from 13 April 2015 (by virtue of SI 2015/778).

14 Proceedings on appeal to Court of Appeal etc

(1) Subsection (2) applies if the relevant appellate court, in deciding an appeal under section 13, finds that the making of the decision concerned involved the making of an error on a point of law.

(2) The relevant appellate court—

(*a*) may (but need not) set aside the decision of the Upper Tribunal, and (*b*) if it does, must either—

(i) remit the case to the Upper Tribunal or, where the decision of the Upper Tribunal was on an appeal or reference from another tribunal or some other person, to the Upper Tribunal or that other tribunal or person, with directions for its reconsideration, or

(ii) re-make the decision.

(3) In acting under subsection (2)(*b*)(i), the relevant appellate court may also—

(*a*) direct that the persons who are chosen to reconsider the case are not to be the same as those who—

(i) where the case is remitted to the Upper Tribunal, made the decision of the Upper Tribunal that has been set aside, or

(ii) where the case is remitted to another tribunal or person, made the decision in respect of which the appeal or reference to the Upper Tribunal was made;

(*b*) give procedural directions in connection with the reconsideration of the case by the Upper Tribunal or other tribunal or person.

(4) In acting under subsection (2)(*b*)(ii), the relevant appellate court—

(*a*) may make any decision which the Upper Tribunal could make if the Upper Tribunal were re-making the decision or (as the case may be) which the other tribunal or person could make if that other tribunal or person were re-making the decision, and

(*b*) may make such findings of fact as it considers appropriate.

(5) Where—

(*a*) under subsection (2)(*b*)(i) the relevant appellate court remits a case to the Upper Tribunal, and

(*b*) the decision set aside under subsection (2)(*a*) was made by the Upper Tribunal on an appeal or reference from another tribunal or some other person,

the Upper Tribunal may (instead of reconsidering the case itself) remit the case to that other tribunal or person, with the directions given by the relevant appellate court for its reconsideration.

(6) In acting under subsection (5), the Upper Tribunal may also—

(*a*) direct that the persons who are chosen to reconsider the case are not to be the same as those who made the decision in respect of which the appeal or reference to the Upper Tribunal was made;

(*b*) give procedural directions in connection with the reconsideration of the case by the other tribunal or person.

(7) In this section "the relevant appellate court", as respects an appeal under section 13, means the court specified as respects that appeal by the Upper Tribunal under section 13(11).

Commencement—Tribunals, Courts and Enforcement Act 2007 (Commencement No 6 and Transitional Provisions) Order, SI 2008/2696 art 5(*a*) (this section comes into force on 3 November 2008).

[14A Appeal to Supreme Court: grant of certificate by Upper Tribunal

(1) If the Upper Tribunal is satisfied that—

(*a*) the conditions in subsection (4) or (5) are fulfilled in relation to the Upper Tribunal's decision in any proceedings, and

(*b*) as regards that decision, a sufficient case for an appeal to the Supreme Court has been made out to justify an application under section 14B,

the Upper Tribunal may grant a certificate to that effect.

(2) The Upper Tribunal may grant a certificate under this section only on an application made by a party to the proceedings.

(3) The Upper Tribunal may grant a certificate under this section only if the relevant appellate court as regards the proceedings is—

(*a*) the Court of Appeal in England and Wales, or

(*b*) Court of Appeal in Northern Ireland.

(4) The conditions in this subsection are that a point of law of general public importance is involved in the decision of the Upper Tribunal and that point of law is—

(*a*) a point of law that—

(i) relates wholly or mainly to the construction of an enactment or statutory instrument, and

(ii) has been fully argued in the proceedings and fully considered in the judgment of the Upper Tribunal in the proceedings, or

(*b*) a point of law—

(i) in respect of which the Upper Tribunal is bound by a decision of the relevant appellate court or the Supreme Court in previous proceedings, and

(ii) that was fully considered in the judgments given by the relevant appellate court or, as the case may be, the Supreme Court in those previous proceedings.

(5) The conditions in this subsection are that a point of law of general public importance is involved in the decision of the Upper Tribunal and that—

(*a*) the proceedings entail a decision relating to a matter of national importance or consideration of such a matter, (*b*) the result of the proceedings is so significant (whether considered on its own or together with other proceedings or likely proceedings) that, in the opinion of the Upper Tribunal, a hearing by the Supreme Court is justified, or

(*c*) the Upper Tribunal is satisfied that the benefits of earlier consideration by the Supreme Court outweigh the benefits of consideration by the Court of Appeal.

(6) Before the Upper Tribunal decides an application made to it under this section, the Upper Tribunal must specify the court that would be the relevant appellate court if the application were an application for permission (or leave) under section 13.

(7) In this section except subsection (6) and in sections 14B and 14C, "the relevant appellate court", as respects an application, means the court specified as respects that application by the Upper Tribunal under subsection (6).

(8) No appeal lies against the grant or refusal of a certificate under subsection (1).

Prospective amendments—Sections 14A–14C to be inserted by the Criminal Justice and Courts Act 2015 s 64 with effect from a date to be appointed.

[14B Appeal to Supreme Court: permission to appeal

(1) If the Upper Tribunal grants a certificate under section 14A in relation to any proceedings, a party to those proceedings may apply to the Supreme Court for permission to appeal directly to the Supreme Court.

(2) An application under subsection (1) must be made—

(*a*) within one month from the date on which that certificate is granted, or

(*b*) within such time as the Supreme Court may allow in a particular case.

(3) If on such an application it appears to the Supreme Court to be expedient to do so, the Supreme Court may grant permission for such an appeal.

(4) If permission is granted under this section—

(*a*) no appeal from the decision to which the certificate relates lies to the relevant appellate court, but

(*b*) an appeal lies from that decision to the Supreme Court.

(5) An application under subsection (1) is to be determined without a hearing.

(6) Subject to subsection (4), no appeal lies to the relevant appellate court from a decision of the Upper Tribunal in respect of which a certificate is granted under section 14A until—

(*a*) the time within which an application can be made under subsection (1) has expired, and

(*b*) where such an application is made, that application has been determined in accordance with this section.

Prospective amendments—Sections 14A–14C to be inserted by the Criminal Justice and Courts Act 2015 s 64 with effect from a date to be appointed.

[14C Appeal to Supreme Court: exclusions

(1) No certificate may be granted under section 14A in respect of a decision of the Upper Tribunal in any proceedings where, by virtue of any enactment (other than sections 14A and 14B), no appeal would lie from that decision of the Upper Tribunal to the relevant appellate court, with or without the permission (or leave) of the Upper Tribunal or the relevant appellate court.

(2) No certificate may be granted under section 14A in respect of a decision of the Upper Tribunal in any proceedings where, by virtue of any enactment, no appeal would lie from a decision of the relevant appellate court on that decision of the Upper Tribunal to the Supreme Court, with or without the permission (or leave) of the relevant appellate court or the Supreme Court.

(3) Where no appeal would lie to the relevant appellate court from the decision of the Upper Tribunal except with the permission (or leave) of the Upper Tribunal or the relevant appellate court, no certificate may be granted under section 14A in respect of a decision of the Upper Tribunal unless it appears to the Upper Tribunal that it would be a proper case for giving permission (or leave) to appeal to the relevant appellate court.

(4) No certificate may be granted under section 14A in respect of a decision or order of the Upper Tribunal made by it in the exercise of its jurisdiction to punish for contempt."

Prospective amendments—Sections 14A–14C to be inserted by the Criminal Justice and Courts Act 2015 s 64 with effect from a date to be appointed.

"Judicial review"

15 Upper Tribunal's "judicial review" jurisdiction

(1) The Upper Tribunal has power, in cases arising under the law of England and Wales or under the law of Northern Ireland, to grant the following kinds of relief—

(*a*) a mandatory order;

(*b*) a prohibiting order;

(*c*) a quashing order;

(*d*) a declaration;

(*e*) an injunction.

(2) The power under subsection (1) may be exercised by the Upper Tribunal if—

(*a*) certain conditions are met (see section 18), or

(*b*) the tribunal is authorised to proceed even though not all of those conditions are met (see section 19(3) and (4)).

(3) Relief under subsection (1) granted by the Upper Tribunal—

(*a*) has the same effect as the corresponding relief granted by the High Court on an application for judicial review, and

(*b*) is enforceable as if it were relief granted by the High Court on an application for judicial review.

(4) In deciding whether to grant relief under subsection (1)(*a*), (*b*) or (*c*), the Upper Tribunal must apply the principles that the High Court would apply in deciding whether to grant that relief on an application for judicial review.

(5) In deciding whether to grant relief under subsection (1)(*d*) or (*e*), the Upper Tribunal must—

(*a*) in cases arising under the law of England and Wales apply the principles that the High Court would apply in deciding whether to grant that relief under section 31(2) of the Supreme Court Act 1981 (c 54) on an application for judicial review, and

(*b*) in cases arising under the law of Northern Ireland apply the principles that the High Court would apply in deciding whether to grant that relief on an application for judicial review.

(6) For the purposes of the application of subsection (3)(*a*) in relation to cases arising under the law of Northern Ireland—

(*a*) a mandatory order under subsection (1)(*a*) shall be taken to correspond to an order of mandamus,

(*b*) a prohibiting order under subsection (1)(*b*) shall be taken to correspond to an order of prohibition, and

(*c*) a quashing order under subsection (1)(*c*) shall be taken to correspond to an order of certiorari.

Commencement—Tribunals, Courts and Enforcement Act 2007 (Commencement No 6 and Transitional Provisions) Order, SI 2008/2696 art 5(*a*) (this section comes into force on 3 November 2008).

Prospective amendments—Sub-ss (5A), (5B) to be inserted by the Criminal Justice and Courts Act 2015 s 84(4) with effect from a date to be appointed. Sub-ss (5A), (5B) as inserted to read as follows—

"(5A) In cases arising under the law of England and Wales, subsections (2A) and (2B) of section 31 of the Senior Courts Act 1981 apply to the Upper Tribunal when deciding whether to grant relief under subsection (1) as they apply to the High Court when deciding whether to grant relief on an application for judicial review.

(5B) If the tribunal grants relief in reliance on section 31(2B) of the Senior Courts Act 1981 as applied by subsection (5A), the tribunal must certify that the condition in section 31(2B) as so applied is satisfied.".

16 Application for relief under section 15(1)

(1) This section applies in relation to an application to the Upper Tribunal for relief under section 15(1).

(2) The application may be made only if permission (or, in a case arising under the law of Northern Ireland, leave) to make it has been obtained from the tribunal.

(3) The tribunal may not grant permission (or leave) to make the application unless it considers that the applicant has a sufficient interest in the matter to which the application relates.

(4) Subsection (5) applies where the tribunal considers—

(*a*) that there has been undue delay in making the application, and

(*b*) that granting the relief sought on the application would be likely to cause substantial hardship to, or substantially prejudice the rights of, any person or would be detrimental to good administration.

(5) The tribunal may—

(*a*) refuse to grant permission (or leave) for the making of the application;

(*b*) refuse to grant any relief sought on the application.

(6) The tribunal may award to the applicant damages, restitution or the recovery of a sum due if—

(*a*) the application includes a claim for such an award arising from any matter to which the application relates, and

(*b*) the tribunal is satisfied that such an award would have been made by the High Court if the claim had been made in an action begun in the High Court by the applicant at the time of making the application.

(7) An award under subsection (6) may be enforced as if it were an award of the High Court.

(8) Where—

(*a*) the tribunal refuses to grant permission (or leave) to apply for relief under section 15(1),

(*b*) the applicant appeals against that refusal, and

(*c*) the Court of Appeal grants the permission (or leave),

the Court of Appeal may go on to decide the application for relief under section 15(1).

(9) Subsections (4) and (5) do not prevent Tribunal Procedure Rules from limiting the time within which applications may be made.

Commencement—Tribunals, Courts and Enforcement Act 2007 (Commencement No 6 and Transitional Provisions) Order, SI 2008/2696 art 5(*a*) (this section comes into force on 3 November 2008).

Orders—Tribunal Procedure (Upper Tribunal) Rules, SI 2008/2698 (made under sub-s (9)).
Tribunal Procedure (Amendment) Rules, SI 2009/274 (made under sub-s (9)).

Prospective amendments—In sub-s (3), text following the word "unless" to be designated para (*a*), para (*b*) and preceding words ", and" to be inserted, and sub-ss (3C)–(3G), (6A), (6B) to be inserted, by the Criminal Justice and Courts Act 2015 s 85(3), (4) with effect from a date to be appointed. Para (*b*) as inserted to read as follows—

"(*b*) in cases arising under the law of England and Wales, the applicant has provided the tribunal with any information about the financing of the application that is specified in Tribunal Procedure Rules for the purposes of this paragraph.".

Sub-ss (3C)–(3G) as inserted to read as follows—

"(3C) In cases arising under the law of England and Wales, when considering whether to grant permission to make the application, the tribunal—

may of its own initiative consider whether the outcome for the applicant would have been substantially different if the conduct complained of had not occurred, and

must consider that question if the respondent asks it to do so.

(3D) In subsection (3C) "the conduct complained of" means the conduct (or alleged conduct) of the respondent that the applicant claims justifies the tribunal in granting relief.

(3E) If, on considering the question mentioned in subsection (3C)(*a*) and (b), it appears to the tribunal to be highly likely that the outcome for the applicant would not have been substantially different, the tribunal must refuse to grant permission.

(3F) The tribunal may disregard the requirement in subsection (3E) if it considers that it is appropriate to do so for reasons of exceptional public interest.

(3G) If the tribunal grants permission in reliance on subsection (3F), the tribunal must certify that the condition in subsection (3F) is satisfied.".

Sub-ss (6A), (6B) as inserted to read as follows—

"(6A) In cases arising under the law of England and Wales, subsections (2A) and (2B) of section 31 of the Senior Courts Act 1981 apply to the Upper Tribunal as regards the making of an award under subsection (6) as they apply to the High Court as regards the making of an award under section 31(4) of the Senior Courts Act 1981.

(6B) If the tribunal makes an award in reliance on section 31(2B) of the Senior Courts Act 1981 as applied by subsection (6A), the tribunal must certify that the condition in section 31(2B) as so applied is satisfied.".

17 Quashing orders under section 15(1): supplementary provision

(1) If the Upper Tribunal makes a quashing order under section 15(1)(*c*) in respect of a decision, it may in addition—

(*a*) remit the matter concerned to the court, tribunal or authority that made the decision, with a direction to reconsider the matter and reach a decision in accordance with the findings of the Upper Tribunal, or

(*b*) substitute its own decision for the decision in question.

(2) The power conferred by subsection (1)(*b*) is exercisable only if—

(*a*) the decision in question was made by a court or tribunal,

(*b*) the decision is quashed on the ground that there has been an error of law, and

(*c*) without the error, there would have been only one decision that the court or tribunal could have reached.

(3) Unless the Upper Tribunal otherwise directs, a decision substituted by it under subsection (1)(*b*) has effect as if it were a decision of the relevant court or tribunal.

Commencement—Tribunals, Courts and Enforcement Act 2007 (Commencement No 6 and Transitional Provisions) Order, SI 2008/2696 art 5(*a*) (this section comes into force on 3 November 2008).

18 Limits of jurisdiction under section 15(1)

(1) This section applies where an application made to the Upper Tribunal seeks (whether or not alone)—

(*a*) relief under section 15(1), or

(*b*) permission (or, in a case arising under the law of Northern Ireland, leave) to apply for relief under section 15(1).

(2) If Conditions 1 to 4 are met, the tribunal has the function of deciding the application.

(3) If the tribunal does not have the function of deciding the application, it must by order transfer the application to the High Court.

(4) Condition 1 is that the application does not seek anything other than—

(*a*) relief under section 15(1);

(*b*) permission (or, in a case arising under the law of Northern Ireland, leave) to apply for relief under section 15(1);

(*c*) an award under section 16(6);

(*d*) interest;

(*e*) costs.

(5) Condition 2 is that the application does not call into question anything done by the Crown Court.

(6) Condition 3 is that the application falls within a class specified for the purposes of this subsection in a direction given in accordance with Part 1 of Schedule 2 to the Constitutional Reform Act 2005 (c 4).

VAT Statutes

(7) The power to give directions under subsection (6) includes—

(*a*) power to vary or revoke directions made in exercise of the power, and

(*b*) power to make different provision for different purposes.

(8) Condition 4 is that the judge presiding at the hearing of the application is either—

(*a*) a judge of the High Court or the Court of Appeal in England and Wales or Northern Ireland, or a judge of the Court of Session, or

(*b*) such other persons as may be agreed from time to time between the Lord Chief Justice, the Lord President, or the Lord Chief Justice of Northern Ireland, as the case may be, and the Senior President of Tribunals.

(9) Where the application is transferred to the High Court under subsection (3)—

(*a*) the application is to be treated for all purposes as if it—

(i) had been made to the High Court, and

(ii) sought things corresponding to those sought from the tribunal, and

(*b*) any steps taken, permission (or leave) given or orders made by the tribunal in relation to the application are to be treated as taken, given or made by the High Court.

(10) Rules of court may make provision for the purpose of supplementing subsection (9).

(11) The provision that may be made by Tribunal Procedure Rules about amendment of an application for relief under section 15(1) includes, in particular, provision about amendments that would cause the application to become transferable under subsection (3).

(12) For the purposes of subsection (9)(*a*)(ii), in relation to an application transferred to the High Court in Northern Ireland—

(*a*) an order of mandamus shall be taken to correspond to a mandatory order under section 15(1)(*a*),

(*b*) an order of prohibition shall be taken to correspond to a prohibiting order under section 15(1)(*b*), and

(*c*) an order of certiorari shall be taken to correspond to a quashing order under section 15(1)(*c*).

Commencement—Tribunals, Courts and Enforcement Act 2007 (Commencement No 1) Order, SI 2007/2709 art 2(*a*) (sub-ss (10), (11) come into force on 19 September 2007).

Tribunals, Courts and Enforcement Act 2007 (Commencement No 6 and Transitional Provisions) Order, SI 2008/2696 art 5(*a*) (this section comes into force on 3 November 2008).

19 Transfer of judicial review applications from High Court

(1) In the Supreme Court Act 1981 (c 54), after section 31 insert—

"31A Transfer of judicial review applications to Upper Tribunal

(1) This section applies where an application is made to the High Court—

(*a*) for judicial review, or

(*b*) for permission to apply for judicial review.

(2) If Conditions 1, 2, 3 and 4 are met, the High Court must by order transfer the application to the Upper Tribunal.

(3) If Conditions 1, 2 and 4 are met, but Condition 3 is not, the High Court may by order transfer the application to the Upper Tribunal if it appears to the High Court to be just and convenient to do so.

(4) Condition 1 is that the application does not seek anything other than—

(*a*) relief under section 31(1)(*a*) and (*b*);

(*b*) permission to apply for relief under section 31(1)(*a*) and (*b*);

(*c*) an award under section 31(4);

(*d*) interest;

(*e*) costs.

(5) Condition 2 is that the application does not call into question anything done by the Crown Court.

(6) Condition 3 is that the application falls within a class specified under section 18(6) of the Tribunals, Courts and Enforcement Act 2007.

(7) Condition 4 is that the application does not call into question any decision made under—

(*a*) the Immigration Acts,

(*b*) the British Nationality Act 1981 (c 61),

(*c*) any instrument having effect under an enactment within paragraph (*a*) or (*b*), or

(*d*) any other provision of law for the time being in force which determines British citizenship, British overseas territories citizenship, the status of a British National (Overseas) or British Overseas citizenship."

(2) In the Judicature (Northern Ireland) Act 1978 (c 23), after section 25 insert—

"25A Transfer of judicial review applications to Upper Tribunal

(1) This section applies where an application is made to the High Court—

(*a*) for judicial review, or
(*b*) for leave to apply for judicial review.

(2) If Conditions 1, 2, 3 and 4 are met, the High Court must by order transfer the application to the Upper Tribunal.

(3) If Conditions 1, 2 and 4 are met, but Condition 3 is not, the High Court may by order transfer the application to the Upper Tribunal if it appears to the High Court to be just and convenient to do so.

(4) Condition 1 is that the application does not seek anything other than—
(*a*) relief under section 18(1)(*a*) to (*e*);
(*b*) leave to apply for relief under section 18(1)(*a*) to (*e*);
(*c*) an award under section 20;
(*d*) interest;
(*e*) costs.

(5) Condition 2 is that the application does not call into question anything done by the Crown Court.

(6) Condition 3 is that the application falls within a class specified under section 18(6) of the Tribunals, Courts and Enforcement Act 2007.

(7) Condition 4 is that the application does not call into question any decision made under—
(*a*) the Immigration Acts,
(*b*) the British Nationality Act 1981,
(*c*) any instrument having effect under an enactment within paragraph (*a*) or (*b*), or
(*d*) any other provision of law for the time being in force which determines British citizenship, British overseas territories citizenship, the status of a British National (Overseas) or British Overseas citizenship."

(3) Where an application is transferred to the Upper Tribunal under 31A of the Supreme Court Act 1981 (c 54) or section 25A of the Judicature (Northern Ireland) Act 1978 (transfer from the High Court of judicial review applications)—
(*a*) the application is to be treated for all purposes as if it—
(i) had been made to the tribunal, and
(ii) sought things corresponding to those sought from the High Court,
(*b*) the tribunal has the function of deciding the application, even if it does not fall within a class specified under section 18(6), and
(*c*) any steps taken, permission given, leave given or orders made by the High Court in relation to the application are to be treated as taken, given or made by the tribunal.

(4) Where—
(*a*) an application for permission is transferred to the Upper Tribunal under section 31A of the Supreme Court Act 1981 (c 54) and the tribunal grants permission, or
(*b*) an application for leave is transferred to the Upper Tribunal under section 25A of the Judicature (Northern Ireland) Act 1978 (c 23) and the tribunal grants leave,

the tribunal has the function of deciding any subsequent application brought under the permission or leave, even if the subsequent application does not fall within a class specified under section 18(6).

(5) Tribunal Procedure Rules may make further provision for the purposes of supplementing subsections (3) and (4).

(6) For the purposes of subsection (3)(*a*)(ii), in relation to an application transferred to the Upper Tribunal under section 25A of the Judicature (Northern Ireland) Act 1978—
(*a*) a mandatory order under section 15(1)(*a*) shall be taken to correspond to an order of mandamus,
(*b*) a prohibiting order under section 15(1)(*b*) shall be taken to correspond to an order of prohibition, and
(*c*) a quashing order under section 15(1)(*c*) shall be taken to correspond to an order of certiorari.

Commencement—Tribunals, Courts and Enforcement Act 2007 (Commencement No 6 and Transitional Provisions) Order, SI 2008/2696 art 5(*a*) (this section comes into force on 3 November 2008).

20 Transfer of judicial review applications from the Court of Session

(1) Where an application is made to the supervisory jurisdiction of the Court of Session, the Court—
(*a*) must, if Conditions 1 [and 2 are met, and][2][. . .
(*aa*) . . . [2]
(*b*) may, if Conditions 1 [and 3][3] are met, but Condition 2 is not,

by order transfer the application to the Upper Tribunal.

(2) Condition 1 is that the application does not seek anything other than an exercise of the supervisory jurisdiction of the Court of Session.

(3) Condition 2 is that the application falls within a class specified for the purposes of this subsection by act of sederunt made with the consent of the Lord Chancellor.

(4) Condition 3 is that the subject matter of the application is not a devolved Scottish matter.

(5) . . . [2]

(5A) . . . [2]

(6) There may not be specified under subsection (3) any class of application which includes an application the subject matter of which is a devolved Scottish matter.

(7) For the purposes of this section, the subject matter of an application is a devolved Scottish matter if it—

(*a*) concerns the exercise of functions in or as regards Scotland, and

(*b*) does not relate to a reserved matter within the meaning of the Scotland Act 1998 (c 46).

(8) In subsection (2), the reference to the exercise of the supervisory jurisdiction of the Court of Session includes a reference to the making of any order in connection with or in consequence of the exercise of that jurisdiction.

Commencement—Tribunals, Courts and Enforcement Act 2007 (Commencement No 1) Order, SI 2007/2709 art 2(*a*) (sub-ss (3), (6), (7) come into force on 19 September 2007).

Tribunals, Courts and Enforcement Act 2007 (Commencement No 6 and Transitional Provisions) Order, SI 2008/2696 art 5(*a*) (this section comes into force on 3 November 2008).

Amendments—[1] Sub-s (1)(*aa*) substituted for word "and" at the end of sub-s (1)(*a*), sub-s 5A inserted by the Borders, Citizenship and Immigration Act 2007 s 53(3) with effect from 8 August 2011 (by virtue of SI 2011/1741

[2] In sub-s (1)(*a*), words substituted for words ", 2 and 4 are met", sub-ss (1)(*aa*), (5), (5A) repealed, and in sub-s (1)(*b*), words substituted for words ", 3 and 4" by the Crime and Courts Act 2013 s 22(2) with effect from 7 October 2013 (by virtue of SI 2013/1725, art 3(*b*)).

[20A Procedural steps where application transferred

(1) This section applies where the Court of Session transfers an application under section 20(1).

(2) It is for the Upper Tribunal to determine—

(*a*) whether the application has been made timeously, and

(*b*) whether to grant permission for the application to proceed under section 27B of the Court of Session Act 1988 ("the 1988 Act") (requirement for permission).

(3) Accordingly—

(*a*) the Upper Tribunal has the same powers in relation to the application as the Court of Session would have had in relation to it under sections 27A to 27C of the 1988 Act,

(*b*) sections 27C and 27D of that Act apply in relation to a decision of the Upper Tribunal under section 27B(1) of that Act as they apply in relation to such a decision of the Court of Session.

(4) The references in section 27C(3) and (4) of the 1988 Act (oral hearings where permission refused) to a different Lord Ordinary from the one who granted or refused permission are to be read as references to different members of the Tribunal from those of whom it was composed when it refused or granted permission.]

Prospective amendments—Section 20A to be inserted by the Courts Reform (Scotland) Act 2014 (Consequential Provisions and Modifications) Order, SI 2015/700 art 7 with effect from a date to be appointed (being the same day as the Courts Reform (Scotland) Act 2014 s 89 comes into force: see SI 2015/700 arts 1, 8.

21 Upper Tribunal's "judicial review" jurisdiction: Scotland

(1) The Upper Tribunal has the function of deciding applications transferred to it from the Court of Session under section 20(1).

(2) The powers of review of the Upper Tribunal in relation to such applications are the same as the powers of review of the Court of Session in an application to the supervisory jurisdiction of that Court.

(3) In deciding an application by virtue of subsection (1), the Upper Tribunal must apply principles that the Court of Session would apply in deciding an application to the supervisory jurisdiction of that Court.

(4) An order of the Upper Tribunal by virtue of subsection (1)—

(*a*) has the same effect as the corresponding order granted by the Court of Session on an application to the supervisory jurisdiction of that Court, and

(*b*) is enforceable as if it were an order so granted by that Court.

(5) Where an application is transferred to the Upper Tribunal by virtue of section 20(1), any steps taken or orders made by the Court of Session in relation to the application (other than the order to transfer the application under section 20(1)) are to be treated as taken or made by the tribunal.

(6) Tribunal Procedure Rules may make further provision for the purposes of supplementing subsection (5).

Commencement—Tribunals, Courts and Enforcement Act 2007 (Commencement No 1) Order, SI 2007/2709 art 2(*a*) (sub-s (6) comes into force on 19 September 2007).

Tribunals, Courts and Enforcement Act 2007 (Commencement No 6 and Transitional Provisions) Order, SI 2008/2696 art 5(*a*) (sub-ss (1)–(5) come into force on 3 November 2008).

Miscellaneous

22 Tribunal Procedure Rules

(1) There are to be rules, to be called "Tribunal Procedure Rules", governing—

(*a*) the practice and procedure to be followed in the First-tier Tribunal, and (*b*) the practice and procedure to be followed in the Upper Tribunal.

(2) Tribunal Procedure Rules are to be made by the Tribunal Procedure Committee.

(3) In Schedule 5—

Part 1 makes further provision about the content of Tribunal Procedure Rules,

Part 2 makes provision about the membership of the Tribunal Procedure Committee,

Part 3 makes provision about the making of Tribunal Procedure Rules by the Committee, and

Part 4 confers power to amend legislation in connection with Tribunal Procedure Rules.

(4) Power to make Tribunal Procedure Rules is to be exercised with a view to securing—

(*a*) that, in proceedings before the First-tier Tribunal and Upper Tribunal, justice is done,

(*b*) that the tribunal system is accessible and fair,

(*c*) that proceedings before the First-tier Tribunal or Upper Tribunal are handled quickly and efficiently,

(*d*) that the rules are both simple and simply expressed, and

(*e*) that the rules where appropriate confer on members of the First-tier Tribunal, or Upper Tribunal, responsibility for ensuring that proceedings before the tribunal are handled quickly and efficiently.

(5) In subsection (4)(*b*) "the tribunal system" means the system for deciding matters within the jurisdiction of the First-tier Tribunal or the Upper Tribunal.

Commencement—Tribunals, Courts and Enforcement Act 2007 (Commencement No 1) Order, SI 2007/2709 art 2(*a*) (this section comes into force on 19 September 2007).

Rules—Tribunal Procedure (First-tier Tribunal) (Social Entitlement Chamber) Rules, SI 2008/2685.

Tribunal Procedure (First-tier Tribunal) (War Pensions and Armed Forces Compensation Chamber) Rules, SI 2008/2686.

Tribunal Procedure (Upper Tribunal) Rules, SI 2008/2698.

Tribunal Procedure (First-tier Tribunal) (Tax Chamber) Rules, SI 2009/273.

Tribunal Procedure (Amendment) Rules, SI 2009/274.

Tribunal Procedure (Amendment) Rules, SI 2012/500.

Tribunal Procedure (Amendment No 2) Rules, SI 2012/1363.

Tribunal Procedure (Upper Tribunal) (Amendment) Rules, SI 2012/2890.

Tribunal Procedure (Amendment) Rules, SI 2013/477.

Tribunal Procedure (Amendment No 2) Rules 2013/606.

Tribunal Procedure (Amendment No 3) Rules, SI 2013/1188 (amendments to the Tribunal Procedure (Upper Tribunal) (Lands Chamber) Rules, SI 2010/2600 only).

Tribunal Procedure (Amendment No 4) Rules, SI 2013/2067.

Tribunal Procedure (Amendment) Rules, SI 2014/514.

Tribunal Procedure (Amendment No 2) Rules, SI 2014/1505.

Tribunal Procedure (Amendment No 3) Rules, SI 2014/2128.

Tribunal Procedure (Amendment) Rules, SI 2015/1510.

23 Practice directions

(1) The Senior President of Tribunals may give directions—

(*a*) as to the practice and procedure of the First-tier Tribunal;

(*b*) as to the practice and procedure of the Upper Tribunal.

(2) A Chamber President may give directions as to the practice and procedure of the chamber over which he presides.

(3) A power under this section to give directions includes—

(*a*) power to vary or revoke directions made in exercise of the power, and

(*b*) power to make different provision for different purposes (including different provision for different areas).

(4) Directions under subsection (1) may not be given without the approval of the Lord Chancellor.

(5) Directions under subsection (2) may not be given without the approval of—

(*a*) the Senior President of Tribunals, and

(*b*) the Lord Chancellor.

(6) Subsections (4) and (5)(*b*) do not apply to directions to the extent that they consist of guidance about any of the following—

(*a*) the application or interpretation of the law;

(*b*) the making of decisions by members of the First-tier Tribunal or Upper Tribunal.

(7) Subsections (4) and (5)(*b*) do not apply to directions to the extent that they consist of criteria for determining which members of the First-tier Tribunal or Upper Tribunal may be chosen to decide particular categories of matter; but the directions may, to that extent, be given only after consulting the Lord Chancellor.

Commencement—Tribunals, Courts and Enforcement Act 2007 (Commencement No 6 and Transitional Provisions) Order, SI 2008/2696 art 5(*a*) (this section comes into force on 3 November 2008).

24 Mediation

(1) A person exercising power to make Tribunal Procedure Rules or give practice directions must, when making provision in relation to mediation, have regard to the following principles—

(*a*) mediation of matters in dispute between parties to proceedings is to take place only by agreement between those parties;

(*b*) where parties to proceedings fail to mediate, or where mediation between parties to proceedings fails to resolve disputed matters, the failure is not to affect the outcome of the proceedings.

(2) Practice directions may provide for members to act as mediators in relation to disputed matters in a case that is the subject of proceedings.

(3) The provision that may be made by virtue of subsection (2) includes provision for a member to act as a mediator in relation to disputed matters in a case even though the member has been chosen to decide matters in the case.

(4) Once a member has begun to act as a mediator in relation to a disputed matter in a case that is the subject of proceedings, the member may decide matters in the case only with the consent of the parties.

(5) Staff appointed under section 40(1) may, subject to their terms of appointment, act as mediators in relation to disputed matters in a case that is the subject of proceedings.

(6) In this section—

"member" means a judge or other member of the First-tier Tribunal or a judge or other member of the Upper Tribunal;

"practice direction" means a direction under section 23(1) or (2);

"proceedings" means proceedings before the First-tier Tribunal or proceedings before the Upper Tribunal.

Commencement—Tribunals, Courts and Enforcement Act 2007 (Commencement No 6 and Transitional Provisions) Order, SI 2008/2696 art 5(*a*) (this section comes into force on 3 November 2008).

25 Supplementary powers of Upper Tribunal

(1) In relation to the matters mentioned in subsection (2), the Upper Tribunal—

(*a*) has, in England and Wales or in Northern Ireland, the same powers, rights, privileges and authority as the High Court, and

(*b*) has, in Scotland, the same powers, rights, privileges and authority as the Court of Session.

(2) The matters are—

(*a*) the attendance and examination of witnesses,

(*b*) the production and inspection of documents, and

(*c*) all other matters incidental to the Upper Tribunal's functions.

(3) Subsection (1) shall not be taken—

(*a*) to limit any power to make Tribunal Procedure Rules;

(*b*) to be limited by anything in Tribunal Procedure Rules other than an express limitation.

(4) A power, right, privilege or authority conferred in a territory by subsection (1) is available for purposes of proceedings in the Upper Tribunal that take place outside that territory (as well as for purposes of proceedings in the tribunal that take place within that territory).

Commencement—Tribunals, Courts and Enforcement Act 2007 (Commencement No 6 and Transitional Provisions) Order, SI 2008/2696 art 5(*a*) (this section comes into force on 3 November 2008).

Simon's Tax Cases—*R (Cart) v Upper Tribunal* [2010] STC 2556.

Cross-references—Tribunal Procedure (First-tier Tribunal) (Tax Chamber) Rules, SI 2009/273 rule 7 (reference to Upper Tribunal in case of failure to comply with Rules).

26 First-tier Tribunal and Upper Tribunal: sitting places

Each of the First-tier Tribunal and the Upper Tribunal may decide a case—

(*a*) in England and Wales,

(*b*) in Scotland, or

(*c*) in Northern Ireland,

even though the case arises under the law of a territory other than the one in which the case is decided.

Commencement—Tribunals, Courts and Enforcement Act 2007 (Commencement No 6 and Transitional Provisions) Order, SI 2008/2696 art 5(*a*) (this section comes into force on 3 November 2008).

27 Enforcement

(1) A sum payable in pursuance of a decision of the First-tier Tribunal or Upper Tribunal made in England and Wales—

(*a*) shall be recoverable as if it were payable under an order of [the county court][1] in England and Wales;

(*b*) shall be recoverable as if it were payable under an order of the High Court in England and Wales.

(2) An order for the payment of a sum payable in pursuance of a decision of the First-tier Tribunal or Upper Tribunal made in Scotland (or a copy of such an order certified in accordance with Tribunal Procedure Rules) may be enforced as if it were an extract registered decree arbitral bearing a warrant for execution issued by the sheriff court of any sheriffdom in Scotland.

(3) A sum payable in pursuance of a decision of the First-tier Tribunal or Upper Tribunal made in Northern Ireland—

(*a*) shall be recoverable as if it were payable under an order of [the county court][1] in Northern Ireland;

(*b*) shall be recoverable as if it were payable under an order of the High Court in Northern Ireland.

(4) This section does not apply to a sum payable in pursuance of—

(*a*) an award under section 16(6), or

(*b*) an order by virtue of section 21(1).

(5) The Lord Chancellor may by order make provision for subsection (1) or (3) to apply in relation to a sum of a description specified in the order with the omission of one (but not both) of paragraphs (*a*) and (*b*).

(6) Tribunal Procedure Rules—

(*a*) may make provision as to where, for purposes of this section, a decision is to be taken to be made;

(*b*) may provide for all or any of subsections (1) to (3) to apply only, or not to apply except, in relation to sums of a description specified in Tribunal Procedure Rules.

Commencement—Tribunals, Courts and Enforcement Act 2007 (Commencement No 1) Order, SI 2007/2709 art 2(*a*) (sub-ss (5), (6) come into force on 19 September 2007).

Tribunals, Courts and Enforcement Act 2007 (Commencement No 6 and Transitional Provisions) Order, SI 2008/2696 art 6(*a*) (sub-ss (1)–(4) come into force on 1 April 2009).

Amendments—[1] In sub-s (1)(*a*), words substituted for words "a county court" by the Crime and Courts Act 2013 s 17, Sch 9 para 52 with effect from 22 April 2014 (by virtue of SI 2014/954 art 2(*c*)).

28 Assessors

(1) If it appears to the First-tier Tribunal or the Upper Tribunal that a matter before it requires special expertise not otherwise available to it, it may direct that in dealing with that matter it shall have the assistance of a person or persons appearing to it to have relevant knowledge or experience.

(2) The remuneration of a person who gives assistance to either tribunal as mentioned in subsection (1) shall be determined and paid by the Lord Chancellor.

(3) The Lord Chancellor may—

(*a*) establish panels of persons from which either tribunal may (but need not) select persons to give it assistance as mentioned in subsection (1);

(*b*) under paragraph (*a*) establish different panels for different purposes;

(*c*) after carrying out such consultation as he considers appropriate, appoint persons to a panel established under paragraph (*a*);

(*d*) remove a person from such a panel.

Commencement—Tribunals, Courts and Enforcement Act 2007 (Commencement No 6 and Transitional Provisions) Order, SI 2008/2696 art 5(*a*) (this section comes into force on 3 November 2008).

29 Costs or expenses

(1) The costs of and incidental to—

(*a*) all proceedings in the First-tier Tribunal, and

(*b*) all proceedings in the Upper Tribunal,

shall be in the discretion of the Tribunal in which the proceedings take place.

(2) The relevant Tribunal shall have full power to determine by whom and to what extent the costs are to be paid.

(3) Subsections (1) and (2) have effect subject to Tribunal Procedure Rules.

(4) In any proceedings mentioned in subsection (1), the relevant Tribunal may—

(*a*) disallow, or

(*b*) (as the case may be) order the legal or other representative concerned to meet,

the whole of any wasted costs or such part of them as may be determined in accordance with Tribunal Procedure Rules.

(5) In subsection (4) "wasted costs" means any costs incurred by a party—

(*a*) as a result of any improper, unreasonable or negligent act or omission on the part of any legal or other representative or any employee of such a representative, or

(*b*) which, in the light of any such act or omission occurring after they were incurred, the relevant Tribunal considers it is unreasonable to expect that party to pay.

(6) In this section "legal or other representative", in relation to a party to proceedings, means any person exercising a right of audience or right to conduct the proceedings on his behalf.

(7) In the application of this section in relation to Scotland, any reference in this section to costs is to be read as a reference to expenses.

Commencement—Tribunals, Courts and Enforcement Act 2007 (Commencement No 6 and Transitional Provisions) Order, SI 2008/2696 art 5(*a*) (this section comes into force on 3 November 2008).

Simon's Tax Cases—29, *Capital Air Services Ltd v R&C Comrs* [2011] STC 617.

Orders/Rules—Tribunal Procedure (First-tier Tribunal) (Social Entitlement Chamber) Rules, SI 2008/2685 (made under sub-s (3)).

Tribunal Procedure (First-tier Tribunal) (War Pensions and Armed Forces Compensation Chamber) Rules, SI 2008/2686 (made under sub-para (3)).

Tribunal Procedure (Upper Tribunal) Rules, SI 2008/2698 (made under sub-ss (3), (4)).

Tribunal Procedure (First-tier Tribunal) (Health, Education and Social Care Chamber) Rules, SI 2008/2699 (made under sub-ss (2), (3)).

Tribunal Procedure (First-tier Tribunal) (Tax Chamber) Rules, SI 2009/273 (made under sub-s (3)).
Tribunal Procedure (Amendment) Rules, SI 2009/274 (made under sub-ss (3), (4)).
Tribunal Procedure (Amendment) Rules, SI 2013/477.
Tribunal Procedure (Amendment No 3) Rules, SI 2013/1188 (amendments to the Tribunal Procedure (Upper Tribunal) (Lands Chamber) Rules, SI 2010/2600 only).
Tribunal Procedure (Amendment) Rules, SI 2014/514.
Cross-references—Tribunal Procedure (First-tier Tribunal) (Tax Chamber) Rules, SI 2009/273 rule 10 (order for costs).

CHAPTER 3

TRANSFER OF TRIBUNAL FUNCTIONS

30 Transfer of functions of certain tribunals

(1) The Lord Chancellor may by order provide for a function of a scheduled tribunal to be transferred—

(*a*) to the First-tier Tribunal,
(*b*) to the Upper Tribunal,
(*c*) to the First-tier Tribunal and the Upper Tribunal with the question as to which of them is to exercise the function in a particular case being determined by a person under provisions of the order,
(*d*) to the First-tier Tribunal to the extent specified in the order and to the Upper Tribunal to the extent so specified,
(*e*) to the First-tier Tribunal and the Upper Tribunal with the question as to which of them is to exercise the function in a particular case being determined by, or under, Tribunal Procedure Rules,
(*f*) to an employment tribunal,
(*g*) to the Employment Appeal Tribunal,
(*h*) to an employment tribunal and the Employment Appeal Tribunal with the question as to which of them is to exercise the function in a particular case being determined by a person under provisions of the order, or
(*i*) to an employment tribunal to the extent specified in the order and to the Employment Appeal Tribunal to the extent so specified.

(2) In subsection (1) "scheduled tribunal" means a tribunal in a list in Schedule 6 that has effect for the purposes of this section.

(3) The Lord Chancellor may, as respects a function transferred under subsection (1) or this subsection, by order provide for the function to be further transferred as mentioned in any of paragraphs (*a*) to (*i*) of subsection (1).

(4) An order under subsection (1) or (3) may include provision for the purposes of or in consequence of, or for giving full effect to, a transfer under that subsection.

(5) A function of a tribunal may not be transferred under subsection (1) or (3) if, or to the extent that, the provision conferring the function—

(*a*) would be within the legislative competence of the Scottish Parliament if it were included in an Act of that Parliament, or
(*b*) would be within the legislative competence of the Northern Ireland Assembly if it were included in an Act of that Assembly.

(6) Subsection (5) does not apply to—

(*a*) the Secretary of State's function of deciding appeals under section 41 of the Consumer Credit Act 1974 (c 39),
(*b*) functions of the Consumer Credit Appeals Tribunal,
(*c*) the Secretary of State's function of deciding appeals under section 7(1) of the Estate Agents Act 1979 (c 38), or
(*d*) functions of an adjudicator under section 5 of the Criminal Injuries Compensation Act 1995 (c 53) (but see subsection (7)).

(7) Functions of an adjudicator under section 5 of the Criminal Injuries Compensation Act 1995 (c 53), so far as they relate to Scotland, may be transferred under subsection (1) or (3) only with the consent of the Scottish Ministers.

(8) A function of a tribunal may be transferred under subsection (1) or (3) only with the consent of the Welsh Ministers if any relevant function is exercisable in relation to the tribunal by the Welsh Ministers (whether by the Welsh Ministers alone, or by the Welsh Ministers jointly or concurrently with any other person).

(9) In subsection (8) "relevant function", in relation to a tribunal, means a function which relates—

(*a*) to the operation of the tribunal (including, in particular, its membership, administration, staff, accommodation and funding, and payments to its members or staff), or
(*b*) to the provision of expenses and allowances to persons attending the tribunal or attending elsewhere in connection with proceedings before the tribunal.

Commencement—Tribunals, Courts and Enforcement Act 2007 (Commencement No 1) Order, SI 2007/2709 art 2(*a*) (this section comes into force on 19 September 2007).

Orders—Transfer of Tribunal Functions Order, SI 2008/2833 (made under sub-ss (1), (4)).
Transfer of Tribunal Functions and Revenue and Customs Appeals Order, SI 2009/56 (made under sub-ss (1), (4)).
Transfer of Functions of the Asylum and Immigration Tribunal Order 2010, SI 2010/21 (made under sub-ss (1), (4)).
Transfer of Tribunal Functions (Lands Tribunal and Miscellaneous Amendments) Order 2009, SI 2009/1307 (made under sub-ss (1), (4)).

31 Transfers under section 30: supplementary powers

(1) The Lord Chancellor may by order make provision for abolishing the tribunal by whom a function transferred under section 30(1) is exercisable immediately before its transfer.

(2) The Lord Chancellor may by order make provision, where functions of a tribunal are transferred under section 30(1), for a person—

(*a*) who is the tribunal (but is not the Secretary of State), or

(*b*) who is a member of the tribunal, or

(*c*) who is an authorised decision-maker for the tribunal,

to (instead or in addition) be the holder of an office specified in subsection (3).

(3) Those offices are—

(*a*) transferred-in judge of the First-tier Tribunal,

(*b*) transferred-in other member of the First-tier Tribunal,

(*c*) transferred-in judge of the Upper Tribunal,

(*d*) transferred-in other member of the Upper Tribunal, and

(*e*) deputy judge of the Upper Tribunal.

(4) Where functions of a tribunal are transferred under section 30(1), the Lord Chancellor must exercise the power under subsection (2) so as to secure that each person who immediately before the end of the tribunal's life—

(*a*) is the tribunal,

(*b*) is a member of the tribunal, or

(*c*) is an authorised decision-maker for the tribunal,

becomes the holder of an office specified in subsection (3) with effect from the end of the tribunal's life (if the person is not then already the holder of such an office).

(5) Subsection (4) does not apply in relation to a person—

(*a*) by virtue of the person's being the Secretary of State, or

(*b*) by virtue of the person's being a Commissioner for the general purposes of the income tax;

and a reference in subsection (4) to the end of a tribunal's life is to when the tribunal is abolished or (without being abolished) comes to have no functions.

(6) For the purposes of this section, a person is an "authorised decision-maker" for a tribunal if—

(*a*) the tribunal is listed in column 1 of an entry in the following Table, and

(*b*) the person is of the description specified in column 2 of that entry.

(1) *Tribunal*	*(2)* *Authorised decision-maker*
Adjudicator to Her Majesty's Land Registry	Member of the Adjudicator's staff who is authorised by the Adjudicator to carry out functions of the Adjudicator which are not of an administrative character
The Secretary of State as respects his function of deciding appeals under section 41 of the Consumer Credit Act 1974 (c 39)	Person who is a member of a panel under regulation 24 of the Consumer Credit Licensing (Appeals) Regulations 1998 (SI 1998/1203)
The Secretary of State as respects his function of deciding appeals under section 7(1) of the Estate Agents Act 1979 (c 38)	Person appointed, at any time after 2005, under regulation 19(1) of the Estate Agents (Appeals) Regulations 1981 (SI 1981/1518) to hear an appeal on behalf of the Secretary of State

(7) Where a function of a tribunal is transferred under section 30(1), the Lord Chancellor may by order provide for procedural rules in force immediately before the transfer to have effect, or to have effect with appropriate modifications, after the transfer (and, accordingly, to be capable of being varied or revoked) as if they were—

(*a*) Tribunal Procedure Rules, or

(*b*) employment tribunal procedure regulations, or Appeal Tribunal procedure rules, within the meaning given by section 42(1) of the Employment Tribunals Act 1996 (c 17).

(8) In subsection (7)—

"procedural rules" means provision (whether called rules or not)—

(*a*) regulating practice or procedure before the tribunal, and

(*b*) applying for purposes connected with the exercise of the function;

"appropriate modifications" means modifications (including additions and omissions) that appear to the Lord Chancellor to be necessary to secure, or expedient in connection with securing, that the procedural rules apply in relation to the exercise of the function after the transfer.

(9) The Lord Chancellor may, in connection with provision made by order under section 30 or the preceding provisions of this section, make by order such incidental, supplemental, transitional or consequential provision, or provision for savings, as the Lord Chancellor thinks fit, including provision applying only in relation to cases selected by a member—

(*a*) of the First-tier Tribunal,

(*b*) of the Upper Tribunal,

(*c*) of the Employment Appeal Tribunal, or

(*d*) of a panel of members of employment tribunals.

(10) Subsections (1), (2) and (7) are not to be taken as prejudicing the generality of subsection (9).

Commencement—Tribunals, Courts and Enforcement Act 2007 (Commencement No 1) Order, SI 2007/2709 art 2(*a*) (this section comes into force on 19 September 2007).

Orders—Tribunals, Courts and Enforcement Act 2007 (Transitional and Consequential Provisions) Order, SI 2008/2683 (made under sub-s (9)).

Tribunals, Courts and Enforcement Act 2007 (Commencement No 6 and Transitional Provisions) Order, SI 2008/2696 (made under sub-s (9)).

Transfer of Tribunal Functions Order, SI 2008/2833 (made under sub-ss (1), (2), (9)).

Transfer of Tribunal Functions and Revenue and Customs Appeals Order, SI 2009/56 (made under sub-ss (1), (2), (9)).

Transfer of Functions of the Asylum and Immigration Tribunal Order 2010, SI 2010/21 (made under sub-ss (1), (2), (7), (9)).

Transfer of Tribunal Functions (Lands Tribunal and Miscellaneous Amendments) Order 2009, SI 2009/1307 (made under sub-ss (1), (2), (7), (9)).

32 Power to provide for appeal to Upper Tribunal from tribunals in Wales

(1) Subsection (2) applies if—

(*a*) a function is transferred under section 30(1)(*a*), (*c*), (*d*) or (*e*) in relation to England but is not transferred under section 30(1) in relation to Wales, or

(*b*) a function that is not exercisable in relation to Wales is transferred under section 30(1)(*a*), (*c*), (*d*) or (*e*) in relation to England and, although there is a corresponding function that is exercisable in relation to Wales, that corresponding function is not transferred under section 30(1) in relation to Wales.

(2) The Lord Chancellor may by order—

(*a*) provide for an appeal against a decision to be made to the Upper Tribunal instead of to the court to which an appeal would otherwise fall to be made where the decision is made in exercising, in relation to Wales, the function mentioned in subsection (1)(*a*) or (as the case may be) the corresponding function mentioned in subsection (1)(*b*);

(*b*) provide for a reference of any matter to be made to the Upper Tribunal instead of to the court to which a reference would otherwise fall to be made where the matter arises in exercising, in relation to Wales, the function mentioned in subsection (1)(*a*) or (as the case may be) the corresponding function mentioned in subsection (1)(*b*).

(3) The Lord Chancellor may by order provide for an appeal against a decision of a scheduled tribunal to be made to the Upper Tribunal, instead of to the court to which an appeal would otherwise fall to be made, where the decision is made by the tribunal in exercising a function in relation to Wales.

(4) In subsection (3) "scheduled tribunal" means a tribunal in a list in Schedule 6 that has effect for the purposes of that subsection.

(5) An order under subsection (2) or (3)—

(*a*) may include provision for the purposes of or in consequence of, or for giving full effect to, provision made by the order;

(*b*) may include such incidental, supplemental, transitional or consequential provision or savings as the Lord Chancellor thinks fit.

Commencement—Tribunals, Courts and Enforcement Act 2007 (Commencement No 1) Order, SI 2007/2709 art 2(*a*) (this section comes into force on 19 September 2007).

Orders—Transfer of Tribunal Functions Order, SI 2008/2833 (made under sub-ss (3), (5)).

33 Power to provide for appeal to Upper Tribunal from tribunals in Scotland

(1) Subsection (2) applies if—

(*a*) a function is transferred under section 30(1)(*a*), (*c*), (*d*) or (*e*) in relation to England (whether or not also in relation to Wales) but is not transferred under section 30(1) in relation to Scotland,

(*b*) an appeal may be made to the Upper Tribunal against any decision, or any decision of a particular description, made in exercising the transferred function in relation to England, and

(*c*) no appeal may be made against a corresponding decision made in exercising the function in relation to Scotland.

(2) The Lord Chancellor may by order provide for an appeal against any such corresponding decision to be made to the Upper Tribunal.

(3) An order under subsection (2)—

(*a*) may include provision for the purposes of or in consequence of, or for giving full effect to, provision made by the order;

(*b*) may include such incidental, supplemental, transitional or consequential provision or savings as the Lord Chancellor thinks fit.

(4) An order under subsection (2) does not cease to have effect, and power to vary or revoke the order does not cease to be exercisable, just because either or each of the conditions in subsection (1)(*b*) and (*c*) ceases to be satisfied in relation to the function and decisions concerned.

Commencement—Tribunals, Courts and Enforcement Act 2007 (Commencement No 1) Order, SI 2007/2709 art 2(*a*) (this section comes into force on 19 September 2007).

Orders—Transfer of Tribunal Functions Order, SI 2008/2833 (made under sub-ss (2), (3)).

34 Power to provide for appeal to Upper Tribunal from tribunals in Northern Ireland

(1) Subsection (2) applies if—

(*a*) a function is transferred under section 30(1)(*a*), (*c*), (*d*) or (*e*) in relation to England (whether or not also in relation to Wales) but is not transferred under section 30(1) in relation to Northern Ireland,

(*b*) an appeal may be made to the Upper Tribunal against any decision, or any decision of a particular description, made in exercising the transferred function in relation to England, and

(*c*) no appeal may be made against a corresponding decision made in exercising the function in relation to Northern Ireland.

(2) The Lord Chancellor may by order provide for an appeal against any such corresponding decision to be made to the Upper Tribunal.

(3) An order under subsection (2)—

(*a*) may include provision for the purposes of or in consequence of, or for giving full effect to, provision made by the order;

(*b*) may include such incidental, supplemental, transitional or consequential provision or savings as the Lord Chancellor thinks fit.

(4) An order under subsection (2) does not cease to have effect, and power to vary or revoke the order does not cease to be exercisable, just because either or each of the conditions in subsection (1)(*b*) and (*c*) ceases to be satisfied in relation to the function and decisions concerned.

Commencement—Tribunals, Courts and Enforcement Act 2007 (Commencement No 1) Order, SI 2007/2709 art 2(*a*) (this section comes into force on 19 September 2007).

Orders—Transfer of Tribunal Functions Order, SI 2008/2833 (made under sub-ss (2), (3)).

35 Transfer of Ministerial responsibilities for certain tribunals

(1) The Lord Chancellor may by order—

(*a*) transfer any relevant function, so far as that function is exercisable by a Minister of the Crown—

(i) to the Lord Chancellor, or

(ii) to two (or more) Ministers of the Crown of whom one is the Lord Chancellor;

(*b*) provide for any relevant function that is exercisable by a Minister of the Crown other than the Lord Chancellor to be exercisable by the other Minister of the Crown concurrently with the Lord Chancellor;

(*c*) provide for any relevant function that is exercisable by the Lord Chancellor concurrently with another Minister of the Crown to cease to be exercisable by the other Minister of the Crown.

(2) In this section "relevant function" means a function, in relation to a scheduled tribunal, which relates—

(*a*) to the operation of the tribunal (including, in particular, its membership, administration, staff, accommodation and funding, and payments to its members or staff), or

(*b*) to the provision of expenses and allowances to persons attending the tribunal or attending elsewhere in connection with proceedings before the tribunal.

(3) In subsection (2) "scheduled tribunal" means a tribunal in a list in Schedule 6 that has effect for the purposes of this section.

(4) A relevant function may not be transferred under subsection (1) if, or to the extent that, the provision conferring the function—

(*a*) would be within the legislative competence of the Scottish Parliament if it were included in an Act of that Parliament, or

(*b*) would be within the legislative competence of the Northern Ireland Assembly if it were included in an Act of that Assembly.

(5) Subsection (4) does not apply to any relevant function of the Secretary of State—

(*a*) under section 41 of the Consumer Credit Act 1974 (c 39) (appeals), or

(*b*) under section 7 of the Estate Agents Act 1979 (c 38) (appeals).

(6) Any reference in subsection (1) to a Minister of the Crown includes a reference to a Minister of the Crown acting jointly.

(7) An order under subsection (1)—

(*a*) may relate to a function either wholly or in cases (including cases framed by reference to areas) specified in the order;
(*b*) may include provision for the purposes of, or in consequence of, or for giving full effect to, the transfer or (as the case may be) other change as regards exercise;
(*c*) may include such incidental, supplementary, transitional or consequential provision or savings as the Lord Chancellor thinks fit;
(*d*) may include provision for the transfer of any property, rights or liabilities of the person who loses functions or whose functions become shared with the Lord Chancellor.

(8) An order under subsection (1), so far as it—
(*a*) provides under paragraph (*a*) for the transfer of a function, or
(*b*) provides under paragraph (*b*) for a function to become exercisable by the Lord Chancellor, or
(*c*) provides under paragraph (*c*) for a function to cease to be exercisable by a Minister of the Crown other than the Lord Chancellor,

may not, after that transfer or other change has taken place, be revoked by another order under that subsection.

(9) Section 1 of the 1975 Act (power to transfer Ministerial functions) does not apply to a function of the Lord Chancellor—
(*a*) so far as it is a function transferred to the Lord Chancellor under subsection (1)(*a*),
(*b*) so far as it is a function exercisable by the Lord Chancellor as a result of provision under subsection (1)(*b*), or
(*c*) so far as it is a function that has become exercisable by the Lord Chancellor alone as a result of provision under subsection (1)(*c*).

(10) In this section—
"Minister of the Crown" has the meaning given by section 8(1) of the 1975 Act but includes the Commissioners for Her Majesty's Revenue and Customs;
"the 1975 Act" means the Ministers of the Crown Act 1975 (c 26).

Commencement—Tribunals, Courts and Enforcement Act 2007 (Commencement No 1) Order, SI 2007/2709 art 2(*a*) (this section comes into force on 19 September 2007).

36 Transfer of powers to make procedural rules for certain tribunals

(1) The Lord Chancellor may by order transfer any power to make procedural rules for a scheduled tribunal to—
(*a*) himself, or
(*b*) the Tribunal Procedure Committee.

(2) A power may not be transferred under subsection (1) if, or to the extent that, the provision conferring the power—
(*a*) would be within the legislative competence of the Scottish Parliament if it were included in an Act of that Parliament, or
(*b*) would be within the legislative competence of the Northern Ireland Assembly if it were included in an Act of that Assembly.

(3) Subsection (2) does not apply to—
(*a*) power conferred by section 40A(3) . . . [1] of the Consumer Credit Act 1974 (c 39) (power to make provision with respect to appeals), or
(*b*) power conferred by section 7(3) of the Estate Agents Act 1979 (c 38) (duty of Secretary of State to make regulations with respect to appeals under section 7(1) of that Act).

(4) An order under subsection (1)(*b*)—
(*a*) may not alter any parliamentary procedure relating to the making of the procedural rules concerned, but
(*b*) may otherwise include provision for the purpose of assimilating the procedure for making them to the procedure for making Tribunal Procedure Rules.

(5) An order under subsection (1)(*b*) may include provision requiring the Tribunal Procedure Committee to make procedural rules for purposes notified to it by the Lord Chancellor.

(6) An order under this section—
(*a*) may relate to a power either wholly or in cases (including cases framed by reference to areas) specified in the order;
(*b*) may include provision for the purposes of or in consequence of, or for giving full effect to, the transfer;
(*c*) may include such incidental, supplementary, transitional or consequential provision or savings as the Lord Chancellor thinks fit.

(7) A power to make procedural rules for a tribunal that is exercisable by the Tribunal Procedure Committee by virtue of an order under this section must be exercised by the committee with a view to securing—
(*a*) that the system for deciding matters within the jurisdiction of that tribunal is accessible and fair,
(*b*) that proceedings before that tribunal are handled quickly and efficiently,
(*c*) that the rules are both simple and simply expressed, and

(*d*) that the rules where appropriate confer on persons who are, or who are members of, that tribunal responsibility for ensuring that proceedings before that tribunal are handled quickly and efficiently.

(8) In this section—

"procedural rules", in relation to a tribunal, means provision (whether called rules or not) regulating practice or procedure before the tribunal;

"scheduled tribunal" means a tribunal in a list in Schedule 6 that has effect for the purposes of this section.

Commencement—Tribunals, Courts and Enforcement Act 2007 (Commencement No 1) Order, SI 2007/2709 art 2(*a*) (this section comes into force on 19 September 2007).

Amendments—[1] Words "or 41(2)" repealed by TCEA 2007 s 146, Sch 23 Pt 1 with effect from 3 November 2008 (by virtue of SI 2008/2696 art 5(i), (vii)).

37 Power to amend lists of tribunals in Schedule 6

(1) The Lord Chancellor may by order amend Schedule 6—

(*a*) for the purpose of adding a tribunal to a list in the Schedule;

(*b*) for the purpose of removing a tribunal from a list in the Schedule;

(*c*) for the purpose of removing a list from the Schedule;

(*d*) for the purpose of adding to the Schedule a list of tribunals that has effect for the purposes of any one or more of sections 30, 32(3), 35 and 36.

(2) The following rules apply to the exercise of power under subsection (1)—

(*a*) a tribunal may not be added to a list, or be in an added list, if the tribunal is established otherwise than by or under an enactment;

(*b*) a tribunal established by an enactment passed or made after the last day of the Session in which this Act is passed must not be added to a list, or be in an added list, that has effect for the purposes of section 30;

(*c*) if any relevant function is exercisable in relation to a tribunal by the Welsh Ministers (whether by the Welsh Ministers alone, or by the Welsh Ministers jointly or concurrently with any other person), the tribunal may be added to a list, or be in an added list, only with the consent of the Welsh Ministers;

(*d*) a tribunal may be in more than one list.

(3) In subsection (2)(*c*) "relevant function", in relation to a tribunal, means a function which relates—

(*a*) to the operation of the tribunal (including, in particular, its membership, administration, staff, accommodation and funding, and payments to its members or staff), or

(*b*) to the provision of expenses and allowances to persons attending the tribunal or attending elsewhere in connection with proceedings before the tribunal.

(4) In subsection (1) "tribunal" does not include an ordinary court of law.

(5) In this section "enactment" means any enactment whenever passed or made, including an enactment comprised in subordinate legislation (within the meaning of the Interpretation Act 1978 (c 30)).

Commencement—Tribunals, Courts and Enforcement Act 2007 (Commencement No 1) Order, SI 2007/2709 art 2(*a*) (this section comes into force on 19 September 2007).

Orders—Transfer of Tribunal Functions Order, SI 2008/2833 (made under sub-s (1)).

Amendments to Schedule 6 to the Tribunals, Courts and Enforcement Act 2007 Order, SI 2013/1034.

38 Orders under sections 30 to 36: supplementary

(1) Provision in an order under any of sections 30 to 36 may take the form of amendments, repeals or revocations of enactments.

(2) In this section "enactment" means any enactment whenever passed or made, including an enactment comprised in subordinate legislation (within the meaning of the Interpretation Act 1978).

(3) Any power to extend enactments to a territory outside the United Kingdom shall have effect as if it included—

(*a*) power to extend those enactments as they have effect with any amendments and repeals made in them by orders under any of sections 30 to 36, and

(*b*) power to extend those enactments as if any amendments and repeals made in them under those sections had not been made.

Commencement—Tribunals, Courts and Enforcement Act 2007 (Commencement No 1) Order, SI 2007/2709 art 2(*a*) (this section comes into force on 19 September 2007).

Orders—Transfer of Functions of the Asylum and Immigration Tribunal Order 2010, SI 2010/21.

Transfer of Tribunal Functions (Lands Tribunal and Miscellaneous Amendments) Order 2009, SI 2009/1307.

CHAPTER 4
ADMINISTRATIVE MATTERS IN RESPECT OF CERTAIN TRIBUNALS

39 The general duty

(1) The Lord Chancellor is under a duty to ensure that there is an efficient and effective system to support the carrying on of the business of—

(*a*) the First-tier Tribunal,
(*b*) the Upper Tribunal,
(*c*) employment tribunals,
(*d*) the Employment Appeal Tribunal, and
(*e*) the Asylum and Immigration Tribunal,

and that appropriate services are provided for those tribunals (referred to in this section and in sections 40 and 41 as "the tribunals").

(2) Any reference in this section, or in section 40 or 41, to the Lord Chancellor's general duty in relation to the tribunals is to his duty under subsection (1).

(3) The Lord Chancellor must annually prepare and lay before each House of Parliament a report as to the way in which he has discharged his general duty in relation to the tribunals.

Commencement—Tribunals, Courts and Enforcement Act 2007 (Commencement No 1) Order, SI 2007/2709 art 2(*a*) (this section comes into force on 19 September 2007).

40 Tribunal staff and services

(1) The Lord Chancellor may appoint such staff as appear to him appropriate for the purpose of discharging his general duty in relation to the tribunals.

(2) Subject to subsections (3) and (4), the Lord Chancellor may enter into such contracts with other persons for the provision, by them or their sub-contractors, of staff or services as appear to him appropriate for the purpose of discharging his general duty in relation to the tribunals.

(3) The Lord Chancellor may not enter into contracts for the provision of staff to discharge functions which involve making judicial decisions or exercising any judicial discretion.

(4) The Lord Chancellor may not enter into contracts for the provision of staff to carry out the administrative work of the tribunals unless an order made by the Lord Chancellor authorises him to do so.

(5) Before making an order under subsection (4) the Lord Chancellor must consult the Senior President of Tribunals as to what effect (if any) the order might have on the proper and efficient administration of justice.

(6) An order under subsection (4) may authorise the Lord Chancellor to enter into contracts for the provision of staff to discharge functions—

(*a*) wholly or to the extent specified in the order,
(*b*) generally or in cases or areas specified in the order, and
(*c*) unconditionally or subject to the fulfilment of conditions specified in the order.

Commencement—Tribunals, Courts and Enforcement Act 2007 (Commencement No 1) Order, SI 2007/2709 art 2(*a*) (this section comes into force on 19 September 2007).

Orders—Contracting Out (Administrative Work of Tribunals) Order, SI 2009/121 (made under sub-s (4)).

Cross-references—Tribunal Procedure (First-tier Tribunal) (Tax Chamber) Rules, SI 2009/273 rule 4 (delegation to staff).
Transfer of Tribunal Functions and Revenue and Customs Appeals Order, SI 2009/56 art 6, Sch 3 para 12 (staff appointed to existing tribunals before 1 April 2009 are, from that date, to be treated as if they had been appointed under sub-s (1)).

41 Provision of accommodation

(1) The Lord Chancellor may provide, equip, maintain and manage such tribunal buildings, offices and other accommodation as appear to him appropriate for the purpose of discharging his general duty in relation to the tribunals.

(2) The Lord Chancellor may enter into such arrangements for the provision, equipment, maintenance or management of tribunal buildings, offices or other accommodation as appear to him appropriate for the purpose of discharging his general duty in relation to the tribunals.

(3) The powers under—

(*a*) section 2 of the Commissioners of Works Act 1852 (c 28) (acquisition by agreement), and
(*b*) section 228(1) of the Town and Country Planning Act 1990 (c 8) (compulsory acquisition),

to acquire land necessary for the public service are to be treated as including power to acquire land for the purpose of its provision under arrangements entered into under subsection (2).

(4) In this section "tribunal building" means any place where any of the tribunals sits, including the precincts of any building in which it sits.

Commencement—Tribunals, Courts and Enforcement Act 2007 (Commencement No 1) Order, SI 2007/2709 art 2(*a*) (this section comes into force on 19 September 2007).

42 Fees

(1) The Lord Chancellor may by order prescribe fees payable in respect of—

(*a*) anything dealt with by the First-tier Tribunal,
(*b*) anything dealt with by the Upper Tribunal,

(c) anything dealt with by the Asylum and Immigration Tribunal,
(d) anything dealt with by an added tribunal, and
(e) mediation conducted by staff appointed under section 40(1).

(2) An order under subsection (1) may, in particular, contain provision as to—
(a) scales or rates of fees;
(b) exemptions from or reductions in fees;
(c) remission of fees in whole or in part.

(3) In subsection (1)(d) "added tribunal" means a tribunal specified in an order made by the Lord Chancellor.

(4) A tribunal may be specified in an order under subsection (3) only if—
(a) it is established by or under an enactment, whenever passed or made, and
(b) is not an ordinary court of law.

(5) Before making an order under this section, the Lord Chancellor must consult—
(a) the Senior President of Tribunals, ...[1]
(b) . . . [1]

(6) The making of an order under subsection (1) requires the consent of the Treasury except where the order contains provision only for the purpose of altering amounts payable by way of fees already prescribed under that subsection.

(7) The Lord Chancellor must take such steps as are reasonably practicable to bring information about fees under subsection (1) to the attention of persons likely to have to pay them.

(8) Fees payable under subsection (1) are recoverable summarily as a civil debt.

(9) Subsection (8) does not apply to the recovery in Scotland of fees payable under this section.

(10) . . . [1]

Commencement—Tribunals, Courts and Enforcement Act 2007 (Commencement No 1) Order, SI 2007/2709 art 2(a) (this section comes into force on 19 September 2007).

Orders—Added Tribunals (Employment Tribunals and Employment Appeal Tribunal) Order, SI 2013/1892.
Employment Tribunals and the Employment Appeal Tribunal Fees Order, SI 2013/1893.

Amendments—[1] Sub-ss (5)(b) and word preceding it, (10) repealed by Public Bodies (Abolition of Administrative Justice and Tribunals Council) Order, Si 2013/2042 art 2(2), Schedule para 32 with effect from 19 August 2013.

43 Report by Senior President of Tribunals

(1) Each year the Senior President of Tribunals must give the Lord Chancellor a report covering, in relation to relevant tribunal cases—
(a) matters that the Senior President of Tribunals wishes to bring to the attention of the Lord Chancellor, and
(b) matters that the Lord Chancellor has asked the Senior President of Tribunals to cover in the report.

(2) The Lord Chancellor must publish each report given to him under subsection (1).

(3) In this section "relevant tribunal cases" means—
(a) cases coming before the First-tier Tribunal,
(b) cases coming before the Upper Tribunal,
(c) cases coming before the Employment Appeal Tribunal, . . . [1]
(d) cases coming before employment tribunals[, and
(e) cases coming before the Asylum and Immigration Tribunal.][1]

Commencement—Tribunals, Courts and Enforcement Act 2007 (Commencement No 6 and Transitional Provisions) Order, SI 2008/2696 art 5(a) (this section comes into force on 3 November 2008).

Amendments—[1] Word "and" in sub-s (3)(c) repealed, and sub-s (3)(e) and preceding word "and" inserted, by the UK Borders Act 2007 ss 56, 58, Schedule, with effect from 1 April 2008: SI 2008/309, art 4(g).

CHAPTER 5

OVERSIGHT OF ADMINISTRATIVE JUSTICE SYSTEM, TRIBUNALS AND INQUIRIES

44 The Administrative Justice and Tribunals Council

. . .

Amendments—This section repealed by the Public Bodies (Abolition of Administrative Justice and Tribunals Council) Order, SI 2013/2042 art 2(2), Schedule para 33 with effect from 19 August 2013.

45 Abolition of the Council on Tribunals

. . .

Amendments—This section repealed by the Public Bodies (Abolition of Administrative Justice and Tribunals Council) Order, SI 2013/2042 art 2(2), Schedule para 34 with effect from 19 August 2013.

CHAPTER 6
SUPPLEMENTARY

46 Delegation of functions by Lord Chief Justice etc

(1) The Lord Chief Justice of England and Wales may nominate a judicial office holder (as defined in section 109(4) of the Constitutional Reform Act 2005) to exercise any of his functions under the provisions listed in subsection (2).

(2) The provisions are—

paragraphs 3(4) and 6(3)(*a*) of Schedule 2;
paragraphs 3(4) and 6(3)(*a*) of Schedule 3;
paragraphs 2(2) and 5(5) of Schedule 4;
paragraphs 21(2), 22, 24 and 25(2)(*a*) of Schedule 5.

(3) The Lord President of the Court of Session may nominate any of the following to exercise any of his functions under the provisions listed in subsection (4)—

(*a*) a judge who is a member of the First or Second Division of the Inner House of the Court of Session;
(*b*) the Senior President of Tribunals.

(4) The provisions are—

paragraphs 3(2) and 6(3)(*b*) of Schedule 2;
paragraphs 3(2) and 6(3)(*b*) of Schedule 3;
paragraphs 2(3) and 5(6) of Schedule 4;
paragraphs 23, 24, 25(2)(*b*) and (*c*) and 28(1)(*b*) of Schedule 5.

(5) The Lord Chief Justice of Northern Ireland may nominate any of the following to exercise any of his functions under the provisions listed in subsection (6)—

(*a*) the holder of one of the offices listed in Schedule 1 to the Justice (Northern Ireland) Act 2002 (c 26);
(*b*) a Lord Justice of Appeal (as defined in section 88 of that Act);
(*c*) the Senior President of Tribunals.

(6) The provisions are—

paragraphs 3(3) and 6(3)(*c*) of Schedule 2;
paragraphs 3(3) and 6(3)(*c*) of Schedule 3;
paragraphs 2(4) and 5(7) of Schedule 4;
paragraphs 24 and 25(2)(*c*) of Schedule 5.

[(7) In Schedules 2 to 4 "senior judge" means—

(*a*) the Lord Chief Justice of England and Wales,
(*b*) the Lord President of the Court of Session,
(*c*) the Lord Chief Justice of Northern Ireland, or
(*d*) the Senior President of Tribunals.][1]

Commencement—Tribunals, Courts and Enforcement Act 2007 (Commencement No 1) Order, SI 2007/2709 art 2(*b*) (this section, to the extent that it relates to Sch 5, comes into force on 19 September 2007).

Tribunals, Courts and Enforcement Act 2007 (Commencement No 6 and Transitional Provisions) Order, SI 2008/2696 art 5(*a*) (for remaining purposes, this section comes into force on 3 November 2008).

Amendments—[1] Sub-s (7) inserted by the Crime and Courts Act 2013 s 20, Sch 13 paras 42, 44(3) with effect from 1 October 2013 (by virtue of SI 2013/2200).

47 Co-operation in relation to judicial training, guidance and welfare

(1) Persons with responsibilities in connection with a courts-related activity, and persons with responsibilities in connection with the corresponding tribunals activity, must co-operate with each other in relation to the carrying-on of those activities.

(2) In this section "courts-related activity" and "corresponding tribunals activity" are to be read as follows—

(*a*) making arrangements for training of judiciary of a territory is a courts-related activity, and the corresponding tribunals activity is making arrangements for training of tribunal members;
(*b*) making arrangements for guidance of judiciary of a territory is a courts-related activity, and the corresponding tribunals activity is making arrangements for guidance of tribunal members;
(*c*) making arrangements for the welfare of judiciary of a territory is a courts-related activity, and the corresponding tribunals activity is making arrangements for the welfare of tribunal members.

(3) Subsection (1) applies to a person who has responsibilities in connection with a courts-related activity only if—

(*a*) the person is the chief justice of the territory concerned, or
(*b*) what the person does in discharging those responsibilities is done (directly or indirectly) on behalf of the chief justice of that territory.

(4) Subsection (1) applies to a person who has responsibilities in connection with a corresponding tribunals activity only if—

(*a*) the person is the Senior President of Tribunals, or

(*b*) what the person does in discharging those responsibilities is done (directly or indirectly) on behalf of the Senior President of Tribunals.

(5) For the purposes of this section—

(*a*) "territory" means—

(i) England and Wales,

(ii) Scotland, or

(iii) Northern Ireland;

(*b*) the "chief justice"—

(i) of England and Wales is the Lord Chief Justice of England and Wales,

(ii) of Scotland is the Lord President of the Court of Session, and

(iii) of Northern Ireland is the Lord Chief Justice of Northern Ireland;

(*c*) a person is a "tribunal member" if the person is—

(i) a judge, or other member, of the First-tier Tribunal or Upper Tribunal,

(ii) a judge, or other member, of the Employment Appeal Tribunal,

(iii) a member of a panel of members of employment tribunals (whether or not a panel of [Employment Judges][1]), or

(iv) any member of the Asylum and Immigration Tribunal.

Commencement—Tribunals, Courts and Enforcement Act 2007 (Commencement No 6 and Transitional Provisions) Order, SI 2008/2696 art 5(*a*) (this section comes into force on 3 November 2008).

Amendments—[1] In sub-s (5)(*c*)(iii), words substituted for word "chairmen" by the Crime and Courts Act 2013 s 21, Sch 14 para 13(1) with effect from 1 October 2013 (by virtue of SI 2013/2200).

48 Consequential and other amendments, and transitional provisions

(1) Schedule 8, which makes—

amendments consequential on provisions of this Part, and

other amendments in connection with tribunals and inquiries,

has effect.

(2) Schedule 9, which contains transitional provisions, has effect.

Commencement—Tribunals, Courts and Enforcement Act 2007 (Commencement No 1) Order, SI 2007/2709 art 2(*c*), (*d*) (sub-s (1) comes into force on 19 September 2007, to the extent that it relates to Sch 8 paras 31(1)–(3), 62, 63, 65(1), (2) and para 65(3) to the extent that it relates to the Senior President of Tribunals; sub-s (2) comes into force on 19 September 2007 to the extent that it relates to Sch 9 paras 1, 2, 12(2)).

Tribunals, Courts and Enforcement Act 2007 (Commencement No 1) Order, SI 2007/2709 art 3(*b*) (sub-s (1) comes into force on 1 November 2007, to the extent that it relates to the following paras of Sch 8—

(a) paras 2, 3, 8–12, 14, 15, 17, 19–23, 30(*a*)–(*c*), 32, 33(1), (2), 49–52, 56–61;

(b) paras 4, 5, 7, 53 to the extent that the relate to the Administrative Justice and Tribunals Council and to the Scottish Committee of the Administrative Justice and Tribunals Council; and

(c) para 18 to the extent that it relates to the Administrative Justice and Tribunals Council.).

Tribunals, Courts and Enforcement Act 2007 (Commencement No 1) Order, SI 2007/2709 art 4 (sub-s (1) comes into force on 1 December 2007, to the extent that it relates to Sch 8 paras 35–39).

Tribunals, Courts and Enforcement Act 2007 (Commencement No 1) Order, SI 2007/2709 art 6(*a*) (sub-s (1) comes into force on 1 June 2008, to the extent that it relates to the following paras of Sch 8—

(a) paras 4, 5 to the extent that they relate to the Welsh Committee of the Administrative Justice and Tribunals Council;

(b) paras 7, 18, 53 to the extent that they are not already in force; and

(c) para 30(*d*).).

Tribunals, Courts and Enforcement Act 2007 (Commencement No 5 and Transitional Provisions) Order, SI 2008/1653 art 2(*a*) (sub-s (1) comes into force on 21 July 2008 in relation to the repeal made by Sch 8 para 27 in so far as it applies to the powers of a minister).

Tribunals, Courts and Enforcement Act 2007 (Commencement No 6 and Transitional Provisions) Order, SI 2008/2696—

(a) art 5(*c*) (sub-s (1) comes into force on 3 November 2008 to the extent that it relates to the following provisions of Sch 8—

– paras 6, 16, 28, 31(4)–(6), 33(3), 40–42, 44–48, 54, 64(*b*), and 66;

– para 25 to the extent that it relates to the Tribunals and Inquiries Act 1992 Sch 1 para 7(*b*);

– paras 4 and 5 to the extent that they are not already in force; and

– para 65(3) to the extent that it is not already in force);

(b) art 5(*d*) (sub-s (2) comes into force on 3 November 2008 to the extent that it relates to Sch 9 paras 3–11, 12(1), (3)–(7), 13–19); and

(c) art 6(*b*) (sub-s (1) comes into force on 1 April 2009 to the extent that it related to Sch 8 paras 1, 43, 45).

Tribunals, Courts and Enforcement Act 2007 (Commencement No 10) Order, SI 2013/2043 (sub-s (1) comes into force on 9 August 2013 to the extent that it relates to—

(a) Sch 8 para 24;

(b) Sch 8 para 27 to the extent that it is not already in force, and

(c) the entries in Sch 23 Pt 1 relating to the Tribunals and Inquiries Act 1992 ss 5, 8).

49 Orders and regulations under Part 1: supplemental and procedural provisions

(1) Power—

(*a*) of the Lord Chancellor to make an order, or regulations, under this Part,

(*b*) of the Senior President of Tribunals to make an order under section 7(9), or (*c*) of the Scottish Ministers, or the Welsh Ministers, to make an order under paragraph 25(2) of Schedule 7,

is exercisable by statutory instrument.

(2) The Statutory Instruments Act 1946 (c 36) shall apply in relation to the power to make orders conferred on the Senior President of Tribunals by section 7(9) as if the Senior President of Tribunals were a Minister of the Crown.

(3) Any power mentioned in subsection (1) includes power to make different provision for different purposes.

(4) Without prejudice to the generality of subsection (3), power to make an order under section 30 or 31 includes power to make different provision in relation to England, Scotland, Wales and Northern Ireland respectively.

(5) No order mentioned in subsection (6) is to be made unless a draft of the statutory instrument containing it (whether alone or with other provision) has been laid before, and approved by a resolution of, each House of Parliament.

(6) Those orders are—

(*a*) an order under section 11(8), 13(6) or (14), 30, 31(1), 32, 33, 34, 35, 36, 37 or 42(3);

(*b*) an order under paragraph 15 of Schedule 4;

(*c*) an order under section 42(1)(*a*) to (*d*) that provides for fees to be payable in respect of things for which fees have never been payable;

(*d*) an order under section 31(2), (7) or (9), or paragraph 30(1) of Schedule 5, that contains provision taking the form of an amendment or repeal of an enactment comprised in an Act.

(7) A statutory instrument that—

(*a*) contains—

(i) an order mentioned in subsection (8), or

(ii) regulations under Part 3 of Schedule 9, and

(*b*) is not subject to any requirement that a draft of the instrument be laid before, and approved by a resolution of, each House of Parliament,

is subject to annulment in pursuance of a resolution of either House of Parliament.

(8) Those orders are—

(*a*) an order made by the Lord Chancellor under this Part;

(*b*) an order made by the Senior President of Tribunals under section 7(9).

(9) A statutory instrument that contains an order made by the Scottish Ministers under paragraph 25(2) of Schedule 7 is subject to annulment in pursuance of a resolution of the Scottish Parliament.

(10) A statutory instrument that contains an order made by the Welsh Ministers under paragraph 25(2) of Schedule 7 is subject to annulment in pursuance of a resolution of the National Assembly for Wales.

Commencement—Tribunals, Courts and Enforcement Act 2007 (Commencement No 1) Order, SI 2007/2709 art 2(*a*) (this section comes into force on 19 September 2007).

Orders—Employment Tribunals and the Employment Appeal Tribunal Fees Order, SI 2013/1893.

PART 3

ENFORCEMENT BY TAKING CONTROL OF GOODS

CHAPTER 1

PROCEDURE

62 Enforcement by taking control of goods

(1) Schedule 12 applies where an enactment, writ or warrant confers power to use the procedure in that Schedule (taking control of goods and selling them to recover a sum of money).

(2) The power conferred by a writ or warrant of control to recover a sum of money, and any power conferred by a writ or warrant of possession or delivery to take control of goods and sell them to recover a sum of money, is exercisable only by using that procedure.

(3) Schedule 13—

(*a*) amends some powers previously called powers to distrain, so that they become powers to use that procedure;

(*b*) makes other amendments relating to Schedule 12 and to distress or execution.

(4) The following are renamed—

(*a*) writs of fieri facias, except writs of fieri facias de bonis ecclesiasticis, are renamed writs of control;

(*b*) warrants of execution are renamed warrants of control;

(*c*) warrants of distress, unless the power they confer is exercisable only against specific goods, are renamed warrants of control.

Note—This section does not extend to Scotland (s 147(2)).

Commencement—Tribunals, Courts and Enforcement Act 2007 (Commencement No 9) Order, SI 2013/1739 art 3 (s 62(1) comes into force on 15 July 2013 for the purpose only of exercising any power to make regulations).

Tribunals, Courts and Enforcement Act 2007 (Commencement No 11) Order, SI 2014/768 art 2(1)(*a*) (s 62 comes into force for all remaining purposes on 6 April 2014).

63 Enforcement agents

(1) This section and section 64 apply for the purposes of Schedule 12.

(2) An individual may act as an enforcement agent only if one of these applies—

(*a*) he acts under a certificate under section 64;

(*b*) he is exempt;

(*c*) he acts in the presence and under the direction of a person to whom paragraph (*a*) or (*b*) applies.

(3) An individual is exempt if he acts in the course of his duty as one of these—

(*a*) a constable;

(*b*) an officer of Revenue and Customs;

(*c*) a person appointed under section 2(1) of the Courts Act 2003 (c 39) (court officers and staff).

(4) An individual is exempt if he acts in the course of his duty as an officer of a government department.

(5) For the purposes of an enforcement power conferred by a warrant, an individual is exempt if in relation to the warrant he is a civilian enforcement officer, as defined in section 125A of the Magistrates' Courts Act 1980 (c 43).

(6) A person is guilty of an offence if, knowingly or recklessly, he purports to act as an enforcement agent without being authorised to do so by subsection (2).

(7) A person guilty of an offence under this section is liable on summary conviction to a fine not exceeding level 5 on the standard scale.

Commencement—Tribunals, Courts and Enforcement Act 2007 (Commencement No 11) Order, SI 2014/768 art 2(1)(*a*) (s 63 comes into force on 6 April 2014).

Note—This section does not extend to Scotland (s 147(2)).

64 Certificates to act as an enforcement agent

(1) A certificate may be issued under this [section by a judge of the county court][1]

(2) The Lord Chancellor must make regulations about certificates under this section.

(3) The regulations may in particular include provision—

(*a*) for fees to be charged for applications;

(*b*) for certificates to be issued subject to conditions, including the giving of security;

(*c*) for certificates to be limited to purposes specified by or under the regulations;

(*d*) about complaints against holders of certificates;

(*e*) about suspension and cancellation of certificates;

(*f*) to modify or supplement Schedule 12 for cases where a certificate is suspended or cancelled or expires;

(*g*) requiring courts to make information available relating to certificates.

(4) A certificate under section 7 of the Law of Distress Amendment Act 1888 (c 21) which is in force on the coming into force of this section has effect as a certificate under this section, subject to any provision made by regulations.

Note—This section does not extend to Scotland (s 147(2)).

Commencement—Tribunals, Courts and Enforcement Act 2007 (Commencement No 9) Order, SI 2013/1739 art 3 (s 64(2), (3), (4) comes into force on 15 July 2013 for the purpose only of exercising any power to make regulations).

Tribunals, Courts and Enforcement Act 2007 (Commencement No 11) Order, SI 2014/768 art 2(1)(*a*) (s 64 comes into force on 6 April 2014 for all remaining purposes).

Amendments—[1] In sub-s (1), words substituted by the Crime and Courts Act 2013 s 17, Sch 9 paras 45, 46 with effect from 22 April 2014 (by virtue of SI 2014/954 art 2(*c*)).

65 Common law rules replaced

(1) This Chapter replaces the common law rules about the exercise of the powers which under it become powers to use the procedure in Schedule 12.

(2) The rules replaced include—

(*a*) rules distinguishing between an illegal, an irregular and an excessive exercise of a power;

(*b*) rules that would entitle a person to bring proceedings of a kind for which paragraph 66 of Schedule 12 provides (remedies available to the debtor);

(*c*) rules of replevin;

(*d*) rules about rescuing goods.

Commencement—Tribunals, Courts and Enforcement Act 2007 (Commencement No 11) Order, SI 2014/768 art 2(1)(*a*) (s 65 comes into force on 6 April 2014).

Note—This section does not extend to Scotland (s 147(2)).

66 Pre-commencement enforcement not affected

Where—

(*a*) by any provision of this Part a power becomes a power to use the procedure in Schedule 12, and

(*b*) before the commencement of that provision, goods have been distrained or executed against, or made subject to a walking possession agreement, under the power, this Part does not affect the continuing exercise of the power in relation to those goods.

Commencement—Tribunals, Courts and Enforcement Act 2007 (Commencement No 11) Order, SI 2014/768 art 2(1)(*a*) (s 66 comes into force on 6 April 2014).

Note—This section does not extend to Scotland (s 147(2)).

67 Transfer of county court enforcement

In section 85(2) of the County Courts Act 1984 (c 28) (under which writs of control give the district judge, formerly called the registrar, power to execute judgments or orders for payment of money) for "the registrar shall be" substitute "any person authorised by or on behalf of the Lord Chancellor is".

Commencement—Tribunals, Courts and Enforcement Act 2007 (Commencement No 11) Order, SI 2014/768 art 2(1)(*a*) (s 67 comes into force on 6 April 2014).

Note—This section does not extend to Scotland (s 147(2)).

68 Magistrates' courts warrants of control

In the Magistrates' Courts Act 1980 (c 43) after section 125 insert—

"125ZA Warrants of control

(1) This section applies to a warrant of control issued by a justice of the peace.

(2) The person to whom it is directed must endorse the warrant as soon as possible after receiving it.

(3) For the purposes of this section a person endorses a warrant by inserting on the back the date and time when he received it.

(4) No fee may be charged for endorsing a warrant under this section."

Commencement—Tribunals, Courts and Enforcement Act 2007 (Commencement No 11) Order, SI 2014/768 art 2(1)(*a*) (s 68 comes into force on 6 April 2014).

Note—This section does not extend to Scotland (s 147(2)).

69 County court warrants of control etc

For section 99 of the County Courts Act 1984 substitute—

"99 Endorsement of warrants of control etc

(1) This section applies to—

(*a*) a warrant of control issued under section 85(2);

(*b*) a warrant of delivery or of possession, but only if it includes a power to take control of and sell goods to recover a sum of money and only for the purposes of exercising that power.

(2) The person to whom the warrant is directed must, as soon as possible after receiving it, endorse it by inserting on the back the date and time when he received it.

(3) No fee may be charged for endorsing a warrant under this section."

Commencement—Tribunals, Courts and Enforcement Act 2007 (Commencement No 11) Order, SI 2014/768 art 2(1)(*a*) (s 69 comes into force on 6 April 2014).

Note—This section does not extend to Scotland (s 147(2)).

70 Power of High Court to stay execution

(1) If, at any time, the High Court is satisfied that a party to proceedings is unable to pay—

(*a*) a sum recovered against him (by way of satisfaction of the claim or counterclaim in the proceedings or by way of costs or otherwise), or

(*b*) any instalment of such a sum,

the court may stay the execution of any writ of control issued in the proceedings, for whatever period and on whatever terms it thinks fit.

(2) The court may act under subsection (1) from time to time until it appears that the cause of the inability to pay has ceased.

(3) In this section a party to proceedings includes every person, whether or not named as a party, who is served with notice of the proceedings or attends them.

Commencement—Tribunals, Courts and Enforcement Act 2007 (Commencement No 11) Order, SI 2014/768 art 2(1)(*a*) (s 70 comes into force on 6 April 2014).

Note—This section does not extend to Scotland (s 147(2)).

CHAPTER 2

RENT ARREARS RECOVERY

(not reproduced)

CHAPTER 3
GENERAL

88 Abolition of Crown preference

Crown preference for the purposes of execution against goods is abolished.

Commencment—Tribunals, Courts and Enforcement Act 2007 (Commencement No 11) Order, SI 2014/768 art 2(1)(*a*) (s 88 comes into force on 6 April 2014).

Note—This section does not extend to Scotland (s 147(2)).

89 Application to the Crown

(1) This Part binds the Crown.

(2) But the procedure in Schedule 12 may not be used—

(*a*) to recover debts due from the Crown,

(*b*) to take control of or sell goods of the Crown (including goods owned by the Crown jointly or in common with another person), or

(*c*) to enter premises occupied by the Crown.

Commencement—Tribunals, Courts and Enforcement Act 2007 (Commencement No 11) Order, SI 2014/768 art 2(1)(*a*) (s 89 comes into force on 6 April 2014).

Note—This section does not extend to Scotland (s 147(2)).

90 Regulations

(1) In this Part—

"prescribed" means prescribed by regulations;

"regulations" means regulations made by the Lord Chancellor.

(2) The following apply to regulations under this Part.

(3) Any power to make regulations is exercisable by statutory instrument.

(4) . . . [1]

(5) . . . [1] a statutory instrument containing regulations is subject to annulment in pursuance of a resolution of either House of Parliament.

(6) Regulations may include any of these that the Lord Chancellor considers necessary or expedient—

(*a*) supplementary, incidental or consequential provision;

(*b*) transitory, transitional or saving provision.

(7) Regulations may make different provision for different cases.

Note—This section does not extend to Scotland (s 147(2)).

Commencement—Tribunals, Courts and Enforcement Act 2007 (Commencement No 9) Order, SI 2013/1739 (s 90 comes into force on 15 July 2013).

Amendments—[1] Sub-s (4) repealed, and in sub-s (5), words "In any other case" repealed by the Crime and Courts Act 2013 s 25(1), (8) with effect from 15 July 2013 (by virtue of SI 2013/1725 art 2(*d*)).

PART 4
ENFORCEMENT OF JUDGMENTS AND ORDERS

Attachment of earnings orders

91 Attachment of earnings orders: deductions at fixed rates

(1) Schedule 15 makes amendments to the Attachment of Earnings Act 1971 (c 32).

(2) Those amendments are about the basis on which periodical deductions are to be made under an attachment of earnings order.

(3) In particular, they provide that deductions under certain orders are to be made in accordance with a fixed deductions scheme made by the Lord Chancellor (rather than in accordance with Part I of Schedule 3 to the 1971 Act).

92 Attachment of earnings orders: finding the debtor's current employer

(1) After section 15 of the Attachment of Earnings Act 1971 insert—

"15A Finding the debtor's current employer

(1) If an attachment of earnings order lapses under section 9(4), the proper authority may request the Commissioners—

(*a*) to disclose whether it appears to the Commissioners that the debtor has a current employer, and

(*b*) if it appears to the Commissioners that the debtor has a current employer, to disclose the name and address of that employer.

(2) The proper authority may make a request under subsection (1) only for the purpose of enabling the lapsed order to be directed to the debtor's current employer.

(3) The proper authority may not make a request under subsection (1) unless regulations under section 15B(5) and (8) are in force.

(4) The proper authority may disclose such information (including information identifying the debtor) as it considers necessary to assist the Commissioners to comply with a request under subsection (1).

(5) The Commissioners may disclose to the proper authority any information (whether held by the Commissioners or on their behalf) that the Commissioners consider is necessary to comply with a request under subsection (1).

(6) A disclosure under subsection (4) or (5) is not to be taken to breach any restriction on the disclosure of information (however imposed).

(7) Nothing in this section is to be taken to prejudice any power to request or disclose information that exists apart from this section.

(8) The reference in subsection (5) to information held on behalf of the Commissioners includes a reference to any information which—

(*a*) is held by a person who provides services to the Commissioners, and

(*b*) is held by that person in connection with the provision of those services.

15B Offence of unauthorised use or disclosure

(1) This section applies if the Commissioners make a disclosure of information ("debtor information") under section 15A(5).

(2) A person to whom the debtor information is disclosed commits an offence if—

(*a*) he uses or discloses the debtor information, and

(*b*) the use or disclosure is not authorised by subsection (3), (5), (6) or (7).

(3) The use or disclosure of the debtor information is authorised if it is—

(*a*) for a purpose connected with the enforcement of the lapsed order (including the direction of the order to the debtor's current employer), and

(*b*) with the consent of the Commissioners.

(4) Consent for the purposes of subsection (3) may be given—

(*a*) in relation to particular use or a particular disclosure, or

(*b*) in relation to use, or a disclosure made, in such circumstances as may be specified or described in the consent.

(5) The use or disclosure of the debtor information is authorised if it is—

(*a*) in accordance with an enactment or an order of court, or

(*b*) for the purposes of any proceedings before a court,

and it is in accordance with regulations.

(6) The use or disclosure of the debtor information is authorised if the information has previously been lawfully disclosed to the public.

(7) The use or disclosure of the debtor information is authorised if it is in accordance with rules of court that comply with regulations under subsection (8).

(8) Regulations may make provision about the circumstances, if any, in which rules of court may allow any of the following—

(*a*) access to, or the supply of, debtor information;

(*b*) access to, or the supply of copies of, any attachment of earnings order which has been directed to an employer using debtor information.

(9) It is a defence for a person charged with an offence under subsection (2) to prove that he reasonably believed that the disclosure was lawful.

(10) A person guilty of an offence under subsection (2) is liable—

(*a*) on conviction on indictment, to imprisonment for a term not exceeding two years, to a fine, or to both;

(*b*) on summary conviction, to imprisonment for a term not exceeding twelve months, to a fine not exceeding the statutory maximum, or to both.

15C Regulations

(1) It is for the Lord Chancellor to make regulations under section 15B.

(2) But the Lord Chancellor may make regulations under section 15B only with the agreement of the Commissioners.

(3) Regulations under section 15B are to be made by statutory instrument.

(4) A statutory instrument containing regulations under section 15B may not be made unless a draft of the instrument has been laid before and approved by a resolution of each House of Parliament.

15D Interpretation

(1) For the purposes of sections 15A to 15C (and this section)—

"the Commissioners" means the Commissioners for Her Majesty's Revenue and Customs;

"information" means information held in any form;

"the lapsed order" means the attachment of earnings order referred to in section 15A(1);

"the proper authority" is determined in accordance with subsections (2) to (5).

(2) If the lapsed order was made by the High Court, the proper authority is the High Court.

(3) If the lapsed order was made by a county court, the proper authority is a county court.

(4) If the lapsed order was made by a magistrates' court under this Act, the proper authority is—

(*a*) a magistrates' court, or

(*b*) the designated officer for a magistrates' court.

(5) If the lapsed order was made by a magistrates' court or a fines officer under Schedule 5 to the Courts Act 2003, the proper authority is—

(*a*) a magistrates' court, or

(*b*) a fines officer."

(2) This section applies in relation to any attachment of earnings order, whether made before or after the commencement of this section.

(3) In relation to an offence committed before the commencement of section 154(1) of the Criminal Justice Act 2003 (c 44), the reference in section 15B(10)(*b*) of the Attachment of Earnings Act 1971 (c 32) to 12 months is to be read as a reference to 6 months.

Note—This section does not extend to Scotland (s 147(2)).

Charging orders

93 Payment by instalments: making and enforcing charging orders

(1) Subsections (2), (3) and (4) make amendments to the Charging Orders Act 1979 (c 53).

(2) In section 1 (charging orders), after subsection (5) insert—

"(6) Subsections (7) and (8) apply where, under a judgment or order of the High Court or a county court, a debtor is required to pay a sum of money by instalments.

(7) The fact that there has been no default in payment of the instalments does not prevent a charging order from being made in respect of that sum.

(8) But if there has been no default, the court must take that into account when considering the circumstances of the case under subsection (5)."

(3) In section 3 (provisions supplementing sections 1 and 2), after subsection (4) insert—

"(4A) Subsections (4C) to (4E) apply where—

(*a*) a debtor is required to pay a sum of money in instalments under a judgment or order of the High Court or a county court (an "instalments order"), and

(*b*) a charge has been imposed by a charging order in respect of that sum.

(4B) In subsections (4C) to (4E) references to the enforcement of a charge are to the making of an order for the enforcement of the charge.

(4C) The charge may not be enforced unless there has been default in payment of an instalment under the instalments order.

(4D) Rules of court may—

(*a*) provide that, if there has been default in payment of an instalment, the charge may be enforced only in prescribed cases, and

(*b*) limit the amounts for which, and the times at which, the charge may be enforced.

(4E) Except so far as otherwise provided by rules of court under subsection (4D)—

(*a*) the charge may be enforced, if there has been default in payment of an instalment, for the whole of the sum of money secured by the charge and the costs then remaining unpaid, or for such part as the court may order, but

(*b*) the charge may not be enforced unless, at the time of enforcement, the whole or part of an instalment which has become due under the instalments order remains unpaid."

(4) In section 6(2) (meaning of references to judgment or order of High Court or county court), for "section 1" substitute "sections 1 and 3".

(5) In section 313(4) of the Insolvency Act 1986 (c 45) (charge on bankrupt's home: certain provisions of section 3 of Charging Orders Act 1979 to apply), for the words before "section 3" substitute "Subsection (1), (2), (4), (5) and (6) of".

(6) This section does not apply in a case where a judgment or order of the High Court or a county court under which a debtor is required to pay a sum of money by instalments was made, or applied for, before the coming into force of this section.

Note—This section does not extend to Scotland (s 147(2)).

Commencement—Tribunals, Courts and Enforcement Act 2007 (Commencement No 8) Order, SI 2012/1312 (section 93 comes into force on 1 October 2012).

94 Charging orders: power to set financial thresholds

In the Charging Orders Act 1979 (c 53), after section 3 there is inserted—

"3A Power to set financial thresholds

(1) The Lord Chancellor may by regulations provide that a charge may not be imposed by a charging order for securing the payment of money of an amount below that determined in accordance with the regulations.

(2) The Lord Chancellor may by regulations provide that a charge imposed by a charging order may not be enforced by way of order for sale to recover money of an amount below that determined in accordance with the regulations.

(3) Regulations under this section may—

(*a*) make different provision for different cases;

(*b*) include such transitional provision as the Lord Chancellor thinks fit.

(4) The power to make regulations under this section is exercisable by statutory instrument.

(5) The Lord Chancellor may not make the first regulations under subsection (1) or (2) unless (in each case) a draft of the statutory instrument containing the regulations has been laid before, and approved by a resolution of, each House of Parliament.

(6) A statutory instrument containing any subsequent regulations under those subsections is subject to annulment in pursuance of a resolution of either House of Parliament."

Note—This section does not extend to Scotland (s 147(2)).

Commencement—Tribunals, Courts and Enforcement Act 2007 (Commencement No 8) Order, SI 2012/1312 (section 94 comes into force on 17 May 2012).

Information requests and orders

95 Application for information about action to recover judgment debt

(1) A person who is the creditor in relation to a judgment debt may apply to the High Court[, the family court][1] or a county court for information about what kind of action it would be appropriate to take in court to recover that particular debt.

(2) An application under subsection (1) must comply with any provision made in regulations about the making of such applications.

Note This section does not extend to Scotland (s 147(2)).

Amendments—[1] In sub-s (1), words inserted by the Crime and Courts Act 2013 (Family Court: Consequential Provision) Order, SI 2014/605 arts 22, 23 with effect from 22 April 2014 (being the date on which the Crime and Courts Act 2013, s 17(3) is brought fully into force by virtue of SI 2014/954, art 2(*a*), see SI 2014/605, art 1).

96 Action by the court

(1) This section applies if the creditor in relation to a judgment debt makes an application for information under section 95.

(2) The relevant court may make one or more of the following in relation to the debtor—

(*a*) a departmental information request;

(*b*) an information order.

(3) The relevant court may exercise its powers under subsection (2) only if it is satisfied that to do so will help it to deal with the creditor's application.

(4) Before exercising its powers under subsection (2), the relevant court must give notice to the debtor that the court intends to make a request or order.

(5) The relevant court may not make a departmental information request to the Commissioners unless regulations are in force that have been made under section 102(4) and (7) and relate to the use or disclosure of debtor information disclosed by the Commissioners.

(6) The relevant court may disclose such information (including information identifying the debtor) as it considers necessary to assist the recipient of a request or order to comply with the request or order.

(7) A disclosure under subsection (6) is not to be taken to breach any restriction on the disclosure of information (however imposed).

(8) Nothing in this section is to be taken to prejudice any power that exists apart from this section to request or order the disclosure of information.

Note—This section does not extend to Scotland (s 147(2)).

97 Departmental information requests

(1) A departmental information request is a request for the disclosure of information held by, or on behalf of, a government department.

(2) The request is to be made to the Minister of the Crown, or other person, who is in charge of the department.

(3) In the case of a request made to the designated Secretary of State, the disclosure of some or all of the following information may be requested—

(*a*) the full name of the debtor;

(*b*) the address of the debtor;

(*c*) the date of birth of the debtor;

(*d*) the national insurance number of the debtor;

(*e*) prescribed information.

(4) In the case of a request made to the Commissioners, the disclosure of some or all of the following information may be requested—

(*a*) whether or not the debtor is employed;

(*b*) the name and address of the employer (if the debtor is employed);

(*c*) the national insurance number of the debtor;
(*d*) prescribed information.

(5) In the case of any other request, the disclosure of prescribed information may be requested.

(6) In this section—

"designated Secretary of State" means the Secretary of State designated for the purpose of this section by regulations;

"government department" does not include the following—

(*a*) any part of the Scottish Administration;
(*b*) a Northern Ireland department;
(*c*) the Welsh Assembly Government or any member of staff appointed under section 52 of the Government of Wales Act 2006 (c 32);

"prescribed information", in relation to a departmental information request, means information that falls within the category or categories of information (if any) prescribed by regulations in relation to the department to which the request relates.

Note—This section does not extend to Scotland (s 147(2)).
Reference to the Welsh Assembly Government is to be read as, or as including, a reference to the Welsh Government, unless the context requires otherwise (Wales Act 2014 s 4(4)(a)).

98 Information orders

(1) An information order is an order of the relevant court which—

(*a*) specifies a prescribed person ("the information discloser"),
(*b*) specifies prescribed information relating to the debtor ("the required information"), and
(*c*) orders the information discloser to disclose the required information to the relevant court.

(2) In subsection (1) "prescribed" means prescribed in regulations.

(3) Regulations under this section may be made by reference to—

(*a*) particular persons or particular descriptions of person (or both);
(*b*) particular information or particular descriptions of information (or both).

(4) Regulations may, in particular, be made under this section so as to ensure that—

(*a*) an information order made against a particular person, or a person of a particular description, may order that person to disclose only particular information, or information of a particular description;
(*b*) an information order that orders the disclosure of particular information, or information of a particular description, may only be made against a particular person, or a person of a particular description.

(5) Regulations under this section must not make provision that would allow the relevant court to order—

(*a*) the disclosure of information by the debtor, or
(*b*) the disclosure of information held by, or on behalf of, a government department.

Note—This section does not extend to Scotland (s 147(2)).

99 Responding to a departmental information request

(1) This section applies if the relevant court makes a departmental information request.

(2) The recipient of the request may disclose to the relevant court any information (whether held by the department or on its behalf) that the recipient considers is necessary to comply with the request.

(3) A disclosure under subsection (2) is not to be taken to breach any restriction on the disclosure of information (however imposed).

(4) Nothing in this section is to be taken to prejudice any power that exists apart from this section to disclose information.

Note—This section does not extend to Scotland (s 147(2)).

100 Information order: required information not held etc

(1) An information discloser is not to be regarded as having breached an information order because of a failure to disclose some or all of the required information, if that failure is for one of the permitted reasons.

(2) These are the permitted reasons—

(*a*) the information provider does not hold the information;
(*b*) the information provider is unable to ascertain whether the information is held, because of the way in which the information order identifies the debtor;
(*c*) the disclosure of the information would involve the information discloser in unreasonable effort or expense.

(3) It is to be presumed that a failure to disclose required information is for a permitted reason if—

(*a*) the information discloser gives the relevant court a certificate that complies with subsection (4), and
(*b*) there is no evidence that the failure is not for a permitted reason.

(4) The certificate must state—

(*a*) which of the required information is not being disclosed;

(*b*) what the permitted reason is, or permitted reasons are, for the failure to disclose that information.

(5) Any reference in this section to the information discloser holding, or not holding, information includes a reference to the information being held, or not being held, on the information discloser's behalf.

Note—This section does not extend to Scotland (s 147(2)).

101 Using the information about the debtor

(1) This section applies if—

(*a*) the creditor in relation to a judgment debt makes an application for information under section 95, and

(*b*) information ("debtor information") is disclosed to the relevant court in compliance with a request or order made under section 96.

(2) The relevant court may use the debtor information for the purpose of making another request or order under section 96 in relation to the debtor.

(3) The relevant court may use the debtor information for the purpose of providing the creditor with information about what kind of action (if any) it would be appropriate to take in court (whether the relevant court or another court) to recover the judgment debt.

(4) If the creditor takes any action in the relevant court to recover the judgment debt, the relevant court may use the debtor information in carrying out functions in relation to that action.

(5) If the creditor takes any action in another court to recover the judgment debt—

(*a*) the relevant court may disclose the debtor information to the other court, and

(*b*) the other court may use that information in carrying out functions in relation to that action.

(6) Debtor information may be used or disclosed under any of subsections (3) to (5) only if—

(*a*) regulations about such use or disclosure of information are in force, and

(*b*) the use or disclosure complies with those regulations.

(7) In addition, if the debtor information was disclosed by the Commissioners, the information may be used or disclosed under any of subsections (3) to (5) only with the consent of the Commissioners.

(8) Consent for the purposes of subsection (7) may be given—

(*a*) in relation to particular use or a particular disclosure, or

(*b*) in relation to use, or a disclosure made, in such circumstances as may be specified or described in the consent.

(9) The use or disclosure of information in accordance with this section is not to be taken to breach any restriction on the use or disclosure of information (however imposed).

(10) Nothing in this section is to be taken to prejudice any power that exists apart from this section to use or disclose information.

Note—This section does not extend to Scotland (s 147(2)).

102 Offence of unauthorised use or disclosure

(1) This section applies if—

(*a*) an application is made under section 95 in relation to recovery of a judgment debt ("the relevant judgment debt"),

(*b*) a departmental information request or an information order is made in consequence of that application, and

(*c*) information ("debtor information") is disclosed in accordance with the request or order.

(2) A person to whom the debtor information is disclosed commits an offence if he—

(*a*) uses or discloses the debtor information, and

(*b*) the use or disclosure is not authorised by any of subsections (3) to (6).

(3) The use or disclosure of the debtor information is authorised if it is in accordance with section 101.

(4) The use or disclosure of the debtor information is authorised if it is—

(*a*) in accordance with an enactment or order of court, or

(*b*) for the purposes of any proceedings before a court,

and it is in accordance with regulations.

(5) The use or disclosure of the debtor information is authorised if the information has previously been lawfully disclosed to the public.

(6) The use or disclosure of the debtor information is authorised if it is in accordance with rules of court that comply with regulations under subsection (7).

(7) Regulations may make provision about the circumstances, if any, in which rules of court may allow access to, or the supply of, information disclosed in accordance with a department information request or an information order.

(8) It is a defence for a person charged with an offence under subsection (2) to prove that he reasonably believed that the use or disclosure was lawful.

(9) A person guilty of an offence under subsection (2) is liable—

(*a*) on conviction on indictment, to imprisonment for a term not exceeding two years, to a fine or to both;

(*b*) on summary conviction, to imprisonment for a term not exceeding twelve months, to a fine not exceeding the statutory maximum, or to both.

Note—This section does not extend to Scotland (s 147(2)).

103 Regulations

(1) It is for the Lord Chancellor to make information regulations.

(2) But the Lord Chancellor may make the following regulations only with the agreement of the Commissioners—

(*a*) regulations under section 97(4)(*d*);

(*b*) regulations under section 102(4) or (7) so far as the regulations relate to the use or disclosure of debtor information disclosed by the Commissioners.

(3) Information regulations are to be made by statutory instrument.

(4) A statutory instrument containing information regulations may not be made unless a draft of the instrument has been laid before and approved by a resolution of each House of Parliament.

(5) But subsection (4) does not apply in the case of a statutory instrument that contains only—

(*a*) regulations under section 95, or

(*b*) regulations under section 97 which designate a Secretary of State for the purpose of that section.

(6) In such a case, the statutory instrument is subject to annulment in pursuance of a resolution of either House of Parliament.

(7) In this section "information regulations" means regulations under any of sections 95 to 102.

Note—This section does not extend to Scotland (s 147(2)).

104 Interpretation

(1) This section applies for the purposes of sections 95 to 103.

(2) In those provisions—

"Commissioners" means the Commissioners for Her Majesty's Revenue and Customs;

"creditor", in relation to a judgment debt, means—

(*a*) the person to whom the debt is payable (whether directly or through [any court,][1] an officer of any court or another person);

(*b*) where the debt is payable under an administration order (within the meaning of Part 6 of the County Courts Act 1984 (c 28)), any one of the creditors scheduled to the order;

"debtor", in relation to a judgment debt, means the person by whom the debt is payable;

"departmental information request" has the meaning given by section 97;

"information" means information held in any form;

"information discloser", in relation to an information order, has the meaning given by section 98(1)(*a*);

"information order" has the meaning given by section 98;

"judgment debt" means either of the following—

(*a*) a sum which is payable under a judgment or order enforceable by the High Court[, the family court][1] or a county court;

(*b*) a sum which, by virtue of an enactment, is recoverable as if it were payable under a judgment or order of the High Court[, the family court][1] or of a county court (including a sum which is so recoverable because a court so orders);

"required information", in relation to an information order, has the meaning given by section 98(1)(*b*);

"relevant court", in relation to an application under section 95, means the court to which the application is made.

(3) Any reference to information held on behalf of a government department, or on behalf of an information discloser, includes a reference to any information which—

(*a*) is held by a person who provides services to the department or to the information discloser, and

(*b*) is held by that person in connection with the provision of those services.

Note—This section does not extend to Scotland (s 147(2)).

Amendments—[1] In sub-s (2), words in definitions of "creditor" and "judgment debt", inserted by the Crime and Courts Act 2013 (Family Court: Consequential Provision) Order, SI 2014/605 arts 22, 24 with effect from 22 April 2014 (being the date on which the Crime and Courts Act 2013, s 17(3) is brought fully into force by virtue of SI 2014/954, art 2(*a*), see SI 2014/605, art 1).

105 Application and transitional provision

(1) Sections 95 to 104 apply in relation to any judgment debt, whether it became payable, or recoverable, before or after the commencement of those sections.

(2) In relation to an offence committed before the commencement of section 154(1) of the Criminal Justice Act 2003 (c 44), the reference in section 102(9)(*b*) to 12 months is to be read as a reference to 6 months.

Note—This section does not extend to Scotland (s 147(2)).

PART 8
GENERAL

. . .

146 Repeals

Schedule 23 contains repeals.

Commencement—Tribunals, Courts and Enforcement Act 2007 (Commencement No 1) Order, SI 2007/2709 art 3(*a*) (this section comes into force on 1 November 2007).

Tribunals, Courts and Enforcement Act 2007 (Commencement No 10) Order, SI 2013/2043 (this section comes into force on 9 August 2013 to the extent that it relates to—

(a) Sch 8 para 24;
(b) Sch 8 para 27 to the extent that it is not already in force, and
(c) the entries in Sch 23 Pt 1).

147 Extent

(1) Parts 1, 2 and 6 and this Part extend to England and Wales, Scotland and Northern Ireland.

(2) The other provisions of this Act extend only to England and Wales.

(3) Subsections (1) and (2) are subject to subsections (4) and (5).

(4) Unless provided otherwise, amendments, repeals and revocations in this Act extend to any part of the United Kingdom to which the provisions amended, repealed or revoked extend.

(5) The following extend also to the Isle of Man—

(*a*) section 143(1) and (2),

(*b*) the repeal by this Act of any provision specified in Part 6 of Schedule 23 that extends to the Isle of Man,

(*c*) sections 145 and 148(5) to (7) so far as relating to—

(i) section 143(1) and (2), and

(ii) the provisions of this Act by which the repeals mentioned in paragraph (*b*) are effected, and

(*d*) this section and section 149.

148 Commencement

(1) Section 60 comes into force at the end of the period of two months beginning with the day on which this Act is passed.

(2) The provisions of Chapter 3 of Part 5 come into force in accordance with provision made by the Lord Chancellor or the Secretary of State by order.

(3) The provisions of Part 6 come into force, except as provided by subsection (4), in accordance with provision made by the Secretary of State by order.

(4) The provisions of Part 6 come into force, in so far as they extend to Scotland, in accordance with provision made by the Scottish Ministers by order.

(5) The remaining provisions of this Act, except sections 53, 55, 56, 57, 145, 147, 149, this section and Schedule 11, come into force in accordance with provision made by the Lord Chancellor by order.

(6) An order under this section may make different provision for different purposes.

(7) The power to make an order under this section is exercisable by statutory instrument.

Orders—Tribunals, Courts and Enforcement Act 2007 (Commencement No 1) Order, SI 2007/2709.

Tribunals, Courts and Enforcement Act 2007 (Commencement No 2) Order, SI 2007/3613.

Tribunals, Courts and Enforcement Act 2007 (Commencement) (Scotland) Order, SSI 2008/150 (in relation to Scotland only).

Tribunals, Courts and Enforcement Act 2007 (Commencement No 3) Order, SI 2008/749.

Tribunals, Courts and Enforcement Act 2007 (Commencement No 4) Order, SI 2008/1158.

Tribunals, Courts and Enforcement Act 2007 (Commencement No 5 and Transitional Provisions) Order, SI 2008/1653.

Tribunals, Courts and Enforcement Act 2007 (Commencement No 6 and Transitional Provisions) Order, SI 2008/2696.

Tribunals, Courts and Enforcement Act 2007 (Commencement No 7) Order, SI 2009/382.

Tribunals, Courts and Enforcement Act 2007 (Commencement No 8) Order, SI 2012/1312.

Tribunals, Courts and Enforcement Act 2007 (Commencement No 9) Order, SI 2013/1739.

Tribunals, Courts and Enforcement Act 2007 (Commencement No 10) Order, SI 2013/2043.

Tribunals, Courts and Enforcement Act 2007 (Commencement No 11) Order, SI 2014/768.

149 Short title

This Act may be cited as the Tribunals, Courts and Enforcement Act 2007.

SCHEDULES

SCHEDULE 1
SENIOR PRESIDENT OF TRIBUNALS

Section 2

PART 1
RECOMMENDATIONS FOR APPOINTMENT

Duty to fill vacancies

1—(1) If there is a vacancy in the office of Senior President of Tribunals, the Lord Chancellor must recommend a person for appointment to that office.

(2) Sub-paragraph (1) does not apply to a vacancy while the Lord Chief Justice of England and Wales agrees that it may remain unfilled.

Commencement—Tribunals, Courts and Enforcement Act 2007 (Commencement No 1) Order, SI 2007/2709 art 2(*g*) (paras 1–11 come into force on 19 September 2007).

The two routes to a recommendation: agreement under this paragraph or selection under Part 2

2—(1) Before the Lord Chancellor may recommend a person for appointment to the office of Senior President of Tribunals, the Lord Chancellor must consult—

(*a*) the Lord Chief Justice of England and Wales,
(*b*) the Lord President of the Court of Session, and
(*c*) the Lord Chief Justice of Northern Ireland.

(2) Sub-paragraphs (3) and (4) apply if—

(*a*) the outcome of consultation under sub-paragraph (1) is agreement between—
   (i) the Lord Chancellor,
   (ii) the Lord Chief Justice of England and Wales,
   (iii) the Lord President of the Court of Session, and
   (iv) the Lord Chief Justice of Northern Ireland,

   as to the person to be recommended, and

(*b*) the person is—
   (i) an ordinary judge of the Court of Appeal in England and Wales,
   (ii) a judge of the Court of Session who is a member of the First or Second Division of the Inner House of that Court, or
   (iii) a Lord Justice of Appeal in Northern Ireland.

(3) The Lord Chancellor must recommend the person for appointment to the office of Senior President of Tribunals, subject to sub-paragraph (4).

(4) Where the person—

(*a*) declines to be recommended, or does not agree within a time specified to him for that purpose, or
(*b*) is otherwise not available within a reasonable time to be recommended,

the Lord Chancellor must, instead of recommending the person for appointment, consult afresh under sub-paragraph (1).

(5) If the Lord Chancellor has consulted under sub-paragraph (1) but sub-paragraphs (3) and (4) do not apply following that consultation, the Lord Chancellor must make a request to the Judicial Appointments Commission for a person to be selected for recommendation for appointment to the office of Senior President of Tribunals.

Commencement—Tribunals, Courts and Enforcement Act 2007 (Commencement No 1) Order, SI 2007/2709 art 2(*g*) (paras 1–11 come into force on 19 September 2007).

PART 2
SELECTION BY THE JUDICIAL APPOINTMENTS COMMISSION

Eligibility for selection

3 A person is eligible for selection in pursuance of a request under paragraph 2(5) only if—

(*a*) he satisfies the judicial-appointment eligibility condition on a 7-year basis,
(*b*) he is an advocate or solicitor in Scotland of at least seven years' standing, or
(*c*) he is a barrister or solicitor in Northern Ireland of at least seven years' standing.

Commencement—Tribunals, Courts and Enforcement Act 2007 (Commencement No 1) Order, SI 2007/2709 art 2(*g*) (paras 1–11 come into force on 19 September 2007).

The selection process

4 In Chapter 2 of Part 4 of the Constitutional Reform Act 2005 (c 4) (appointments), after section 75 insert—

"Senior President of Tribunals

"75A Sections 75B to 75G apply where request made for selection

(1) Sections 75B to 75G apply where the Lord Chancellor makes a request to the Commission under paragraph 2(5) of Schedule 1 to the Tribunals, Courts and Enforcement Act 2007 (request for person to be selected for recommendation for appointment to the office of Senior President of Tribunals).

(2) Those sections are subject to section 95 (withdrawal and modification of requests).

75B Selection process

(1) On receiving a request the Commission must appoint a selection panel.

(2) The panel must—

(*a*) determine the selection process to be applied,

(*b*) apply the selection process, and

(*c*) make a selection accordingly.

(3) As part of the selection process the panel must consult—

(*a*) the Lord Chief Justice, if not a member of the panel,

(*b*) the Lord President of the Court of Session, if not a member of the panel, and

(*c*) the Lord Chief Justice of Northern Ireland, if not a member of the panel.

(4) One person only must be selected for the recommendation to which a request relates.

(5) Subsection (4) applies to selection under this section and to selection under section 75G.

(6) A selection panel is a committee of the Commission.

75C Selection panel

(1) The selection panel must consist of four members.

(2) The first member is the Lord Chief Justice, or his nominee.

(3) The second member is a person designated by the Lord Chief Justice.

(4) Unless subsection (7) applies, the third member is the chairman of the Commission or his nominee.

(5) The fourth member is a lay member of the Commission designated by the third member.

(6) Subsection (7) applies if—

(*a*) there is no chairman of the Commission, or

(*b*) the chairman of the Commission is unavailable and has not nominated a person under subsection (4).

(7) In those cases the third member is a lay member of the Commission selected by the lay members of the Commission other than the chairman.

(8) A nominee of the Lord Chief Justice must be a Head of Division or a Lord Justice of Appeal.

(9) The person designated under subsection (3) must be—

(*a*) a person who holds, or has held, the office of Senior President of Tribunals,

(*b*) a person who holds, or has held, office as a Chamber President of a chamber of the First-tier Tribunal or of a chamber of the Upper Tribunal, or

(*c*) a person who holds, or has held, an office that, in the opinion of the Lord Chief Justice, is such that a holder of it would acquire knowledge or experience of tribunals broadly similar to that which would be acquired by—

(i) a person who holds the office of Senior President of Tribunals, or

(ii) a person who holds office as a Chamber President of a chamber of the First-tier Tribunal, or

(iii) a person who holds office as a Chamber President of a chamber of the Upper Tribunal.

(10) Before designating a person under subsection (3), the Lord Chief Justice must consult—

(*a*) the Lord President of the Court of Session, and

(*b*) the Lord Chief Justice of Northern Ireland.

(11) A person may not be appointed to the panel if he is willing to be considered for selection.

(12) A person may not be appointed to the panel as the nominee of more than one person.

(13) A person appointed to the panel otherwise than as a nominee may not be a nominee.

(14) The first member is the chairman of the panel.

(15) On any vote by the panel the chairman of the panel has an additional, casting vote in the event of a tie.

75D Report

(1) After complying with section 75B(2) the selection panel must submit a report to the Lord Chancellor.

(2) The report must—

(*a*) state who has been selected;

(*b*) contain any other information required by the Lord Chancellor.

(3) The report must be in a form approved by the Lord Chancellor.

(4) After submitting the report the panel must provide any further information the Lord Chancellor may require.

75E The Lord Chancellor's options

(1) This section refers to the following stages—

Stage 1:	where a person has been selected under section 75B
Stage 2:	where a person has been selected following a rejection or reconsideration at stage 1
Stage 3:	where a person has been selected following a rejection or reconsideration at stage 2

(2) At stage 1 the Lord Chancellor must do one of the following—

(*a*) accept the selection;

(*b*) reject the selection;

(*c*) require the selection panel to reconsider the selection.

(3) At stage 2 the Lord Chancellor must do one of the following—

(*a*) accept the selection;

(*b*) reject the selection, but only if it was made following a reconsideration at stage 1;

(*c*) require the selection panel to reconsider the selection, but only if it was made following a rejection at stage 1.

(4) At stage 3 the Lord Chancellor must accept the selection, unless subsection (5) applies and he accepts a selection under it.

(5) If a person whose selection the Lord Chancellor required to be reconsidered at stage 1 or 2 was not selected again at the next stage, the Lord Chancellor may, at stage 3, accept the selection made at that earlier stage.

75F Exercise of powers to reject or require reconsideration

(1) The power of the Lord Chancellor under section 75E to reject a selection at stage 1 or 2 is exercisable only on the grounds that, in the Lord Chancellor's opinion, the person selected is not suitable for the office of Senior President of Tribunals.

(2) The power of the Lord Chancellor under section 75E to require the selection panel to reconsider a selection at stage 1 or 2 is exercisable only on the grounds that, in the Lord Chancellor's opinion—

(*a*) there is not enough evidence that the person is suitable for the office of Senior President of Tribunals, or

(*b*) there is evidence that the person is not the best candidate on merit.

(3) The Lord Chancellor must give the selection panel reasons in writing for rejecting or requiring reconsideration of a selection.

75G Selection following rejection or requirement to reconsider

(1) If under section 75F the Lord Chancellor rejects or requires reconsideration of a selection at stage 1 or 2, the selection panel must select a person in accordance with this section.

(2) If the Lord Chancellor rejects a selection, the selection panel—

(*a*) may not select the person rejected, and

(*b*) where the rejection is following reconsideration of a selection, may not select the person (if different) whose selection it reconsidered.

(3) If the Lord Chancellor requires a selection to be reconsidered, the selection panel—

(*a*) may select the same person or a different person, but

(*b*) where the requirement is following a rejection, may not select the person rejected.

(4) The selection panel must inform the Lord Chancellor of the person selected following a rejection or a requirement to reconsider.

(5) Subsections (2) and (3) do not prevent a person being selected on a subsequent request under paragraph 2(5) of Schedule 1 to the Tribunals, Courts and Enforcement Act 2007."

Commencement—Tribunals, Courts and Enforcement Act 2007 (Commencement No 1) Order, SI 2007/2709 art 2(*g*) (paras 1–11 come into force on 19 September 2007).

Withdrawal and modification of requests under paragraph 2(5)

5—(1) Section 95 of the Constitutional Reform Act 2005 (c 4) (withdrawal and modification of requests) is amended as follows.

(2) In subsection (1) (application of section), after "87" insert "or paragraph 2(5) of Schedule 1 to the Tribunals, Courts and Enforcement Act 2007".

(3) In subsection (4) (limitation on withdrawal of request under subsection (2)(*c*)), after "73(2)," insert "75E(2),".

Commencement—Tribunals, Courts and Enforcement Act 2007 (Commencement No 1) Order, SI 2007/2709 art 2(*g*) (paras 1–11 come into force on 19 September 2007).

PART 3
TERMS OF OFFICE

Tenure, removal, resignation etc

6—(1) If—

(*a*) a person appointed to the office of Senior President of Tribunals is appointed on terms that provide for him to retire from the office at a particular time specified in those terms ("the end of the fixed-term"), and

(*b*) the end of the fixed-term is earlier than the time at which the person is required by the 1993 Act to retire from the office,

the person shall, if still holding the office at the end of the fixed-term, vacate the office at the end of the fixed-term.

(2) Subject to sub-paragraph (1) (and to the 1993 Act), a person appointed to the office of Senior President of Tribunals shall hold that office during good behaviour, subject to a power of removal by Her Majesty on an address presented to Her by both Houses of Parliament.

(3) It is for the Lord Chancellor to recommend to Her Majesty the exercise of the power of removal under sub-paragraph (2).

(4) In this paragraph "the 1993 Act" means the Judicial Pensions and Retirement Act 1993 (c 8).

Commencement—Tribunals, Courts and Enforcement Act 2007 (Commencement No 1) Order, SI 2007/2709 art 2(*g*) (paras 1–11 come into force on 19 September 2007).

7—(1) Sub-paragraph (2) applies to a person appointed to the office of Senior President of Tribunals on a recommendation made under paragraph 2(3).

(2) The person ceases to be Senior President of Tribunals if he ceases to fall within paragraph 2(2)(*b*).

Commencement—Tribunals, Courts and Enforcement Act 2007 (Commencement No 1) Order, SI 2007/2709 art 2(*g*) (paras 1–11 come into force on 19 September 2007).

8 A person who holds the office of Senior President of Tribunals may at any time resign that office by giving the Lord Chancellor notice in writing to that effect.

Commencement—Tribunals, Courts and Enforcement Act 2007 (Commencement No 1) Order, SI 2007/2709 art 2(*g*) (paras 1–11 come into force on 19 September 2007).

9—(1) The Lord Chancellor, if satisfied by means of a medical certificate that a person holding the office of Senior President of Tribunals—

(*a*) is disabled by permanent infirmity from the performance of the duties of the office, and

(*b*) is for the time being incapacitated from resigning the office,

may, subject to sub-paragraph (2), by instrument under his hand declare the person to have vacated the office; and the instrument shall have the like effect for all purposes as if the person had on the date of the instrument resigned the office.

(2) A declaration under sub-paragraph (1) with respect to a person shall be of no effect unless it is made with the concurrence of—

(*a*) the Lord Chief Justice of England and Wales,

(*b*) the Lord President of the Court of Session, and

(*c*) the Lord Chief Justice of Northern Ireland.

Commencement—Tribunals, Courts and Enforcement Act 2007 (Commencement No 1) Order, SI 2007/2709 art 2(*g*) (paras 1–11 come into force on 19 September 2007).

Remuneration, allowances and expenses

10 The Lord Chancellor may pay to the Senior President of Tribunals such amounts (if any) as the Lord Chancellor may determine by way of—

(*a*) remuneration;

(*b*) allowances;

(*c*) expenses.

Commencement—Tribunals, Courts and Enforcement Act 2007 (Commencement No 1) Order, SI 2007/2709 art 2(*g*) (paras 1–11 come into force on 19 September 2007).

Oaths

11—(1) A person appointed to the office of Senior President of Tribunals must take the required oaths in the presence of—

(*a*) the Lord Chief Justice of England and Wales, or

(*b*) another holder of high judicial office (as defined in section 60(2) of the Constitutional Reform Act 2005 (c 4)) who is nominated by the Lord Chief Justice of England and Wales for the purpose of taking the oaths from the person.

(2) Sub-paragraph (1) applies whether or not the person has previously taken the required oaths after accepting another office.

(3) In this paragraph "the required oaths" means—

(*a*) the oath of allegiance, and

(*b*) the judicial oath,

as set out in the Promissory Oaths Act 1868 (c 72).

Commencement—Tribunals, Courts and Enforcement Act 2007 (Commencement No 1) Order, SI 2007/2709 art 2(*g*) (paras 1–11 come into force on 19 September 2007).

PART 4
CERTAIN FUNCTIONS OF THE SENIOR PRESIDENT

Meaning of "tribunal member"

12—(1) For the purposes of this Part of this Schedule, each of the following is a "tribunal member"—

(*a*) a judge, or other member, of the First-tier Tribunal or Upper Tribunal,

(*b*) any member of the Asylum and Immigration Tribunal,

(*c*) a member of a panel of members of employment tribunals (whether or not a panel of [Employment Judges][1]),

(*d*) a judge, or other member, of the Employment Appeal Tribunal, and

(*e*) a person who is, or is a member of, a tribunal in a list in Schedule 6 that has effect for the purposes of section 30.

(2) In this Part of this Schedule "tribunals" means—

(*a*) the First-tier Tribunal,

(*b*) the Upper Tribunal,

(*c*) the Asylum and Immigration Tribunal,

(*d*) employment tribunals,

(*e*) the Employment Appeal Tribunal, and

(*f*) any tribunal in a list in Schedule 6 that has effect for the purposes of section 30.

Commencement—Tribunals, Courts and Enforcement Act 2007 (Commencement No 6 and Transitional Provisions) Order, SI 2008/2696 art 5(*e*) (paras 12–14 come into force on 3 November 2008).

Amendments—

[1] In sub-para (1)(*c*), words substituted for word "chairmen" by the Crime and Courts Act 2013 s 21, Sch 14 para 13(1) with effect from 1 October 2013 (by virtue of SI 2013/2200).

Representations to Parliament

13 The Senior President of Tribunals may lay before Parliament written representations on matters that appear to him to be matters of importance relating—

(*a*) to tribunal members, or

(*b*) otherwise to the administration of justice by tribunals.

Commencement—Tribunals, Courts and Enforcement Act 2007 (Commencement No 6 and Transitional Provisions) Order, SI 2008/2696 art 5(*e*) (paras 12–14 come into force on 3 November 2008).

Representation of views of tribunal members

14 The Senior President of Tribunals is responsible for representing the views of tribunal members to Parliament, to the Lord Chancellor and to Ministers of the Crown generally.

Commencement—Tribunals, Courts and Enforcement Act 2007 (Commencement No 6 and Transitional Provisions) Order, SI 2008/2696 art 5(*e*) (paras 12–14 come into force on 3 November 2008).

SCHEDULE 2

JUDGES AND OTHER MEMBERS OF THE FIRST-TIER TRIBUNAL

Section 4

Power to appoint judges of First-tier Tribunal

1—(1) The [Senior President of Tribunals][1] may appoint a person to be one of the judges of the First-tier Tribunal.

(2) A person is eligible for appointment under sub-paragraph (1) only if the person—

(*a*) satisfies the judicial-appointment eligibility condition on a 5-year basis,

(*b*) is an advocate or solicitor in Scotland of at least five years' standing,

(*c*) is a barrister or solicitor in Northern Ireland of at least five years' standing, or

(*d*) in the [opinion of the Senior President of Tribunals][1], has gained experience in law which makes the person as suitable for appointment as if the person satisfied any of paragraphs (*a*) to (*c*).

(3) Section 52(2) to (5) (meaning of "gain experience in law") apply for the purposes of sub-paragraph (2)(*d*), but as if section 52(4)(*i*) referred to the [Senior President of Tribunals][1] instead of to the relevant decision-maker.

Commencement—Tribunals, Courts and Enforcement Act 2007 (Commencement No 6 and Transitional Provisions) Order, SI 2008/2696 art 5(*f*) (Sch 2 comes into force on 3 November 2008).

Amendments—[1] In sub-paras (1), (3), words substituted for words "Lord Chancellor", and in sub-para (2)(*d*), words substituted for words "Lord Chancellor's opinion" by the Crime and Courts Act 2013 s 20, Sch 13 paras 42, 45(1)–(4) with effect from 1 October 2013 (by virtue of SI 2013/2200).

Power to appoint other members of First-tier Tribunal

2—(1) The [Senior President of Tribunals][1] may appoint a person to be one of the members of the First-tier Tribunal who are not judges of the tribunal.

(2) A person is eligible for appointment under sub-paragraph (1) only if the person has qualifications prescribed in an order made by the Lord Chancellor with the concurrence of the Senior President of Tribunals.

Commencement—Tribunals, Courts and Enforcement Act 2007 (Commencement No 6 and Transitional Provisions) Order, SI 2008/2696 art 5(*f*) (Sch 2 comes into force on 3 November 2008).

Orders—Qualifications for Appointment of Members to the First-tier Tribunal and Upper Tribunal Order, SI 2008/2692 (made under para 2(2)).

Qualifications for Appointment of Members to the First-tier Tribunal and Upper Tribunal (Amendment) Order, SI 2012/897.

Qualifications for Appointment of Members to the First-tier Tribunal and Upper Tribunal (Amendment) Order, SI 2013/1185.

Amendments—[1] In sub-para (1), words substituted for words "Lord Chancellor" by the Crime and Courts Act 2013 s 20, Sch 13 paras 42, 45(1), (2) with effect from 1 October 2013 (by virtue of SI 2013/2200).

Appointed and transferred-in judges and other members: removal from office

3—(1) This paragraph applies to any power by which—

(*a*) a person appointed under paragraph 1(1) or 2(1),

(*b*) a transferred-in judge of the First-tier Tribunal, or

(*c*) a transferred-in other member of the First-tier Tribunal,

may be removed from office.

(2) If the person exercises functions wholly or mainly in Scotland, the power may be exercised only with the concurrence of the Lord President of the Court of Session.

(3) If the person exercises functions wholly or mainly in Northern Ireland, the power may be exercised only with the concurrence of the Lord Chief Justice of Northern Ireland.

(4) If neither of sub-paragraphs (2) and (3) applies, the power may be exercised only with the concurrence of the Lord Chief Justice of England and Wales.

Commencement—Tribunals, Courts and Enforcement Act 2007 (Commencement No 6 and Transitional Provisions) Order, SI 2008/2696 art 5(*f*) (Sch 2 comes into force on 3 November 2008).

Terms of appointment

4—(1) This paragraph applies—

(*a*) to a person appointed under paragraph 1(1) or 2(1),

(*b*) to a transferred-in judge of the First-tier Tribunal, and

(*c*) to a transferred-in other member of the First-tier Tribunal.

(2) If the terms of the person's appointment provide that he is appointed on a salaried (as opposed to fee-paid) basis, the person may be removed from office—

(*a*) only by the Lord Chancellor (and in accordance with paragraph 3), and

(*b*) only on the ground of inability or misbehaviour.

[(2A) If the terms of the person's appointment provide that the person is appointed on a fee-paid basis, the person may be removed from office—

(*a*) only by the Lord Chancellor (and in accordance with paragraph 3), and

(*b*) only on—

(i) the ground of inability or misbehaviour, or

(ii) a ground specified in the person's terms of appointment.

(2B) If the period (or extended period) for which the person is appointed ends before—

(*a*) the day on which the person attains the age of 70, or

(*b*) if different, the day that for the purposes of section 26 of the Judicial Pensions and Retirement Act 1993 is the compulsory retirement date for the office concerned in the person's case,

then, subject to sub-paragraph (2C), the Lord Chancellor must extend the period of the person's appointment (including a period already extended under this sub-paragraph) before it ends.

(2C) Extension under sub-paragraph (2B)—

(*a*) requires the person's agreement,

(*b*) is to be for such period as the Lord Chancellor considers appropriate, and

(*c*) may be refused on—

(i) the ground of inability or misbehaviour, or

(ii) a ground specified in the person's terms of appointment,

but only with any agreement of a senior judge (see section 46(7)), or a nominee of a senior judge, that may be required by those terms.][1]

(3) Subject to [the preceding provisions of this paragraph (but subject in the first place][1] to the Judicial Pensions and Retirement Act 1993 (c 8)), the person is to hold and vacate office in accordance with the terms of his appointment[, which are to be such as the Lord Chancellor may determine][1].

Commencement—Tribunals, Courts and Enforcement Act 2007 (Commencement No 6 and Transitional Provisions) Order, SI 2008/2696 art 5(*f*) (Sch 2 comes into force on 3 November 2008).

Amendments—[1] Sub-paras (2A)–(2C) inserted, and in sub-para (3), words substituted for words "sub-paragraph (2) (and" and words inserted by the Crime and Courts Act 2013 s 20, Sch 13 paras 42, 45(1), (5), (6) with effect from 1 October 2013 (by virtue of SI 2013/2200).

Remuneration, allowances and expenses

5—(1) Sub-paragraph (2) applies—

(*a*) to a person appointed under paragraph 1(1) or 2(1),

(*b*) to a transferred-in judge of the First-tier Tribunal, and

(*c*) to a transferred-in other member of the First-tier Tribunal.

(2) The Lord Chancellor may pay to a person to whom this sub-paragraph applies such amounts (if any) as the Lord Chancellor may determine by way of—

(*a*) remuneration;

(*b*) allowances;

(*c*) expenses.

Commencement—Tribunals, Courts and Enforcement Act 2007 (Commencement No 6 and Transitional Provisions) Order, SI 2008/2696 art 5(*f*) (Sch 2 comes into force on 3 November 2008).

Certain judges neither appointed under paragraph 1(1) nor transferred in

6—(1) In this paragraph "judge by request of the First-tier Tribunal" means a person who is a judge of the First-tier Tribunal but who—

(*a*) is not the Senior President of Tribunals,

(*b*) is not a judge of the First-tier Tribunal appointed under paragraph 1(1),

(*c*) is not a transferred-in judge of the First-tier Tribunal,

(*d*) is not a Chamber President, or Acting Chamber President or Deputy Chamber President, of a chamber of the First-tier Tribunal,

(*e*) is not a judge of the First-tier Tribunal by virtue of section 4(1)(*e*) (chairman of employment tribunal), (*f*) is not a judge of the First-tier Tribunal by virtue of section 4(1)(*d*) or by virtue of the combination of sections 4(1)(*c*) and 5(1)(*d*) (legally qualified member of Asylum and Immigration Tribunal), and

(*g*) is not a judge of the First-tier tribunal by virtue of section 4(2) (criminal injuries compensation adjudicator appointed by the Scottish Ministers).

(2) A judge by request of the First-tier Tribunal may act as a judge of the First-tier Tribunal only if requested to do so by the Senior President of Tribunals.

(3) Such a request made to a person who is a judge of the First-tier Tribunal by virtue of the combination of sections 4(1)(*c*) and 5(1)(*g*) may be made only with—

(*a*) the concurrence of the Lord Chief Justice of England and Wales where the person is—

(i) an ordinary judge of the Court of Appeal in England and Wales,

(ii) a puisne judge of the High Court in England and Wales,

(iii) a circuit judge,

(iv) a district judge in England and Wales, . . . [1]

(v) a District Judge (Magistrates' Courts);

[(vi) the Master of the Rolls,

(vii) the President of the Queen's Bench Division of the High Court of England and Wales,

(viii) the President of the Family Division of that court,

(ix) the Chancellor of that court,

(x) a deputy judge of that court, or

(xi) the Judge Advocate General;][1]

(*b*) the concurrence of the Lord President of the Court of Session where the person is—

(i) a judge of the Court of Session, or

(ii) a sheriff;

(*c*) the concurrence of the Lord Chief Justice of Northern Ireland where the person is—

(i) a Lord Justice of Appeal in Northern Ireland,

(ii) a puisne judge of the High Court in Northern Ireland,

(iii) a county court judge in Northern Ireland, or

(iv) a district judge in Northern Ireland.

[(3A) A request made under sub-paragraph (2) to a person who is a judge of the First-tier Tribunal by virtue of section 4(1)(ca) may be made only with the concurrence of the Lord Chief Justice of England and Wales.][1]

(4) Sub-paragraph (5) applies—

(*a*) to a judge by request of the First-tier Tribunal,

(*b*) to a person who is a judge of the First-tier Tribunal by virtue of section 4(1)(*e*) (chairman of employment tribunal), and

(*c*) to a person who is a judge of the First-tier Tribunal by virtue of section 4(1)(*d*) or by virtue of the combination of sections 4(1)(*c*) and 5(1)(*d*) (legally qualified member of Asylum and Immigration Tribunal).

(5) The Lord Chancellor may pay to a person to whom this sub-paragraph applies such amounts (if any) as the Lord Chancellor may determine by way of—

(*a*) remuneration;

(*b*) allowances;

(*c*) expenses.

Commencement—Tribunals, Courts and Enforcement Act 2007 (Commencement No 6 and Transitional Provisions) Order, SI 2008/2696 art 5(*f*) (Sch 2 comes into force on 3 November 2008).

Amendments—[1] In sub-para (3)(*a*)(iv), word "or" at the end repealed, and sub-paras (3)(*a*)(vi)–(xi), (3A) inserted by the Crime and Courts Act 2013 s 21, Sch 14 paras 6, 10 with effect from 1 October 2013 (by virtue of SI 2013/2200).

Other members neither appointed under paragraph 2(1) nor transferred in

7—(1) In this paragraph "ex officio member of the First-tier Tribunal" means a person who is a member of the First-tier Tribunal by virtue of—

(*a*) section 4(3)(*d*) (members of employment tribunals who are not [Employment Judges][1]),

(*b*) the combination of sections 4(3)(*c*) and 5(2)(*c*) (members of Employment Appeal Tribunal appointed under section 22(1)(*c*) of the Employment Tribunals Act 1996), or

(*c*) the combination of sections 4(3)(*c*) and 5(2)(*d*) (members of Asylum and Immigration Tribunal who are not legally qualified members).

(2) The Lord Chancellor may pay to an ex officio member of the First-tier Tribunal such amounts (if any) as the Lord Chancellor may determine by way of—

(*a*) remuneration;

(*b*) allowances;

(*c*) expenses.

Commencement—Tribunals, Courts and Enforcement Act 2007 (Commencement No 6 and Transitional Provisions) Order, SI 2008/2696 art 5(*f*) (Sch 2 comes into force on 3 November 2008).

Amendments—[1] In sub-para (1)(*a*), words substituted for word "chairmen" by the Crime and Courts Act 2013 s 21, Sch 14 para 13(1) with effect from 1 October 2013 (by virtue of SI 2013/2200).

Training etc

8 The Senior President of Tribunals is responsible, within the resources made available by the Lord Chancellor, for the maintenance of appropriate arrangements for the training, guidance and welfare of judges and other members of the First-tier Tribunal (in their capacities as such judges and other members).

Commencement—Tribunals, Courts and Enforcement Act 2007 (Commencement No 6 and Transitional Provisions) Order, SI 2008/2696 art 5(*f*) (Sch 2 comes into force on 3 November 2008).

Oaths

9—(1) Sub-paragraph (2) applies to a person ("J")—

(*a*) who is appointed under paragraph 1(1) or 2(1), or

(*b*) who becomes a transferred-in judge, or a transferred-in other member, of the First-tier Tribunal and has not previously taken the required oaths after accepting another office.

(2) J must take the required oaths before—

(*a*) the Senior President of Tribunals, or

(*b*) an eligible person who is nominated by the Senior President of Tribunals for the purpose of taking the oaths from J.

(3) A person is eligible for the purposes of sub-paragraph (2)(*b*) if any one or more of the following paragraphs applies to him—

(*a*) he holds high judicial office (as defined in section 60(2) of the Constitutional Reform Act 2005 (c 4));

(*b*) he holds judicial office (as defined in section 109(4) of that Act);

(*c*) he holds (in Scotland) the office of sheriff.

(4) In this paragraph "the required oaths" means (subject to sub-paragraph (5))—

(*a*) the oath of allegiance, and

(*b*) the judicial oath,

as set out in the Promissory Oaths Act 1868 (c 72).

(5) Where it appears to the Lord Chancellor that J will carry out functions as a judge or other member of the First-tier Tribunal wholly or mainly in Northern Ireland, the Lord Chancellor may direct that in relation to J "the required oaths" means—

(*a*) the oath as set out in section 19(2) of the Justice (Northern Ireland) Act 2002 (c 26), or

(*b*) the affirmation and declaration as set out in section 19(3) of that Act.

Commencement—Tribunals, Courts and Enforcement Act 2007 (Commencement No 6 and Transitional Provisions) Order, SI 2008/2696 art 5(*f*) (Sch 2 comes into force on 3 November 2008).

SCHEDULE 3

JUDGES AND OTHER MEMBERS OF THE UPPER TRIBUNAL

Section 5

Power to appoint judges of Upper Tribunal

1—(1) Her Majesty, on the recommendation of the Lord Chancellor, may appoint a person to be one of the judges of the Upper Tribunal.

(2) A person is eligible for appointment under sub-paragraph (1) only if the person—

(*a*) satisfies the judicial-appointment eligibility condition on a 7-year basis,

(*b*) is an advocate or solicitor in Scotland of at least seven years' standing,

(*c*) is a barrister or solicitor in Northern Ireland of at least seven years' standing, or

(*d*) in the [opinion of the Senior President of Tribunals][1], has gained experience in law which makes the person as suitable for appointment as if the person satisfied any of paragraphs (*a*) to (*c*).

(3) Section 52(2) to (5) (meaning of "gain experience in law") apply for the purposes of sub-paragraph (2)(*d*), but as if section 52(4)(*i*) referred to the [Senior President of Tribunals][1] instead of to the relevant decision-maker.

Commencement—Tribunals, Courts and Enforcement Act 2007 (Commencement No 6 and Transitional Provisions) Order, SI 2008/2696 art 5(*f*) (Sch 3 comes into force on 3 November 2008).

Amendments—[1] In sub-para (2)(*d*), words substituted for words "Lord Chancellor's opinion", and in sub-para (3), words substituted for words "Lord Chancellor" by the Crime and Courts Act 2013 s 20, Sch 13 para 30 with effect from 1 October 2013 (by virtue of SI 2013/2200).

Power to appoint other members of Upper Tribunal

2—(1) The [Senior President of Tribunals][1] may appoint a person to be one of the members of the Upper Tribunal who are not judges of the tribunal.
(2) A person is eligible for appointment under sub-paragraph (1) only if the person has qualifications prescribed in an order made by the Lord Chancellor with the concurrence of the Senior President of Tribunals.

Commencement—Tribunals, Courts and Enforcement Act 2007 (Commencement No 6 and Transitional Provisions) Order, SI 2008/2696 art 5(*f*) (Sch 3 comes into force on 3 November 2008).

Orders—Qualifications for Appointment of Members to the First-tier Tribunal and Upper Tribunal Order, SI 2008/2692 (made under para 2(2)).

Qualifications for Appointment of Members to the First-tier Tribunal and Upper Tribunal (Amendment) Order, SI 2012/897.

Qualifications for Appointment of Members to the First-tier Tribunal and Upper Tribunal (Amendment) Order, SI 2013/1185.

Amendments—[1] In sub-para (1), words substituted for words "Lord Chancellor" by the Crime and Courts Act 2013 s 20, Sch 13 paras 42, 46(1), (2) with effect from 1 October 2013 (by virtue of SI 2013/2200).

Appointed and transferred-in judges and other members: removal from office

3—(1) This paragraph applies to any power by which—
(*a*) a person appointed under paragraph 1(1) or 2(1),
(*b*) a transferred-in judge of the Upper Tribunal,
[(*ba*) a person who is a deputy judge of the Upper Tribunal (whether by appointment under paragraph 7(1) or as a result of provision under section 31(2)), or][1]
(*c*) a transferred-in other member of the Upper Tribunal,
may be removed from office.
(2) If the person exercises functions wholly or mainly in Scotland, the power may be exercised only with the concurrence of the Lord President of the Court of Session.
(3) If the person exercises functions wholly or mainly in Northern Ireland, the power may be exercised only with the concurrence of the Lord Chief Justice of Northern Ireland.
(4) If neither of sub-paragraphs (2) and (3) applies, the power may be exercised only with the concurrence of the Lord Chief Justice of England and Wales.

Commencement—Tribunals, Courts and Enforcement Act 2007 (Commencement No 6 and Transitional Provisions) Order, SI 2008/2696 art 5(*f*) (Sch 3 comes into force on 3 November 2008).

Amendments—[1] Sub-para (1)(*ba*) inserted by the Crime and Courts Act 2013 s 20, Sch 13 paras 42, 46(1), (3) with effect from 1 October 2013 (by virtue of SI 2013/2200).

Terms of appointment

4—(1) This paragraph applies—
(*a*) to a person appointed under paragraph 1(1) or 2(1),
(*b*) to a transferred-in judge of the Upper Tribunal, and
(*c*) to a transferred-in other member of the Upper Tribunal.
(2) If the terms of the person's appointment provide that he is appointed on a salaried (as opposed to fee-paid) basis, the person may be removed from office—
(*a*) only by the Lord Chancellor (and in accordance with paragraph 3), and
(*b*) only on the ground of inability or misbehaviour.
[(2A) If the terms of the person's appointment provide that the person is appointed on a fee-paid basis, the person may be removed from office—
(*a*) only by the Lord Chancellor (and in accordance with paragraph 3), and
(*b*) only on—
(i) the ground of inability or misbehaviour, or
(ii) a ground specified in the person's terms of appointment.
(2B) If the period (or extended period) for which the person is appointed ends before—
(*a*) the day on which the person attains the age of 70, or
(*b*) if different, the day that for the purposes of section 26 of the Judicial Pensions and Retirement Act 1993 is the compulsory retirement date for the office concerned in the person's case,
then, subject to sub-paragraph (2C), the Lord Chancellor must extend the period of the person's appointment (including a period already extended under this sub-paragraph) before it ends.
(2C) Extension under sub-paragraph (2B)—
(*a*) requires the person's agreement,
(*b*) is to be for such period as the Lord Chancellor considers appropriate, and
(*c*) may be refused on—
(i) the ground of inability or misbehaviour, or
(ii) a ground specified in the person's terms of appointment,

but only with any agreement of a senior judge (see section 46(7)), or a nominee of a senior judge, that may be required by those terms.][1]

(3) Subject to [the preceding provisions of this paragraph (but subject in the first place][1] to the Judicial Pensions and Retirement Act 1993 (c 8)), the person is to hold and vacate office as a judge, or other member, of the Upper Tribunal in accordance with the terms of his appointment[, which are to be such as the Lord Chancellor may determine][1].

Commencement—Tribunals, Courts and Enforcement Act 2007 (Commencement No 6 and Transitional Provisions) Order, SI 2008/2696 art 5(*f*) (Sch 3 comes into force on 3 November 2008).

Amendments—[1] Sub-paras (2A)–(2C) inserted, and in sub-para (3), words substituted for words "sub-paragraph (2) (and" and words inserted by the Crime and Courts Act 2013 s 20, Sch 13 paras 42, 46(1), (4), (5) with effect from 1 October 2013 (by virtue of SI 2013/2200).

Remuneration, allowances and expenses

5—(1) Sub-paragraph (2) applies—

(*a*) to a person appointed under paragraph 1(1) or 2(1),

(*b*) to a transferred-in judge of the Upper Tribunal, and

(*c*) to a transferred-in other member of the Upper Tribunal.

(2) The Lord Chancellor may pay to a person to whom this sub-paragraph applies such amounts (if any) as the Lord Chancellor may determine by way of—

(*a*) remuneration;

(*b*) allowances;

(*c*) expenses.

Commencement—Tribunals, Courts and Enforcement Act 2007 (Commencement No 6 and Transitional Provisions) Order, SI 2008/2696 art 5(*f*) (Sch 3 comes into force on 3 November 2008).

Certain judges neither appointed under paragraph 1(1) nor transferred in

6—(1) In this paragraph "judge by request of the Upper Tribunal" means a person who is a judge of the Upper Tribunal but—

(*a*) is not the Senior President of Tribunals,

(*b*) is not a judge of the Upper Tribunal appointed under paragraph 1(1),

(*c*) is not a transferred-in judge of the Upper Tribunal,

(*d*) is not a judge of the Upper Tribunal by virtue of section 5(1)(*d*) (legally qualified member of Asylum and Immigration Tribunal),

(*e*) is not a deputy judge of the Upper Tribunal, and

(*f*) is not a Chamber President, or Acting Chamber President or Deputy Chamber President, of a chamber of the Upper Tribunal.

(2) A judge by request of the Upper Tribunal may act as a judge of the Upper Tribunal only if requested to do so by the Senior President of Tribunals.

(3) Such a request made to a person who is a judge of the Upper Tribunal by virtue of section 5(1)(*g*) may be made only with—

(*a*) the concurrence of the Lord Chief Justice of England and Wales where the person is—

(i) an ordinary judge of the Court of Appeal in England and Wales,

(ii) a puisne judge of the High Court in England and Wales,

(iii) a circuit judge,

(iv) a district judge in England and Wales, . . . [1]

[(vi) the Master of the Rolls,

(vii) the President of the Queen's Bench Division of the High Court of England and Wales,

(viii) the President of the Family Division of that court,

(ix) the Chancellor of that court,

(x) a deputy judge of that court, or

(xi) the Judge Advocate General;][1]

(v) a District Judge (Magistrates' Courts);

(*b*) the concurrence of the Lord President of the Court of Session where the person is—

(i) a judge of the Court of Session, or

(ii) a sheriff;

(*c*) the concurrence of the Lord Chief Justice of Northern Ireland where the person is—

(i) a Lord Justice of Appeal in Northern Ireland,

(ii) a puisne judge of the High Court in Northern Ireland,

(iii) a county court judge in Northern Ireland, or

(iv) a district judge in Northern Ireland.

(4) The Lord Chancellor may pay to a judge by request of the Upper Tribunal, or a person who is a judge of the Upper Tribunal by virtue of section 5(1)(*d*), such amounts (if any) as the Lord Chancellor may determine by way of—

(*a*) remuneration;
(*b*) allowances;
(*c*) expenses.

Commencement—Tribunals, Courts and Enforcement Act 2007 (Commencement No 6 and Transitional Provisions) Order, SI 2008/2696 art 5(*f*) (Sch 3 comes into force on 3 November 2008).

Amendments—[1] In sub-para (3)(*a*)(iv), word "or" at the end repealed, and sub-para (3)(*a*)(vi)–(xi) inserted by the Crime and Courts Act 2013 s 21, Sch 14 paras 6, 10(1) with effect from 1 October 2013 (by virtue of SI 2013/2200).

Deputy judges of the Upper Tribunal

7—(1) The [Senior President of Tribunals][1] may appoint a person to be a deputy judge of the Upper Tribunal for such period as the Lord Chancellor considers appropriate.

(2) A person is eligible for appointment under sub-paragraph (1) only if he is eligible to be appointed under paragraph 1(1) (see paragraph 1(2)).

(3) [The following provisions of this paragraph][1] apply—

(*a*) to a person appointed under sub-paragraph (1), and
(*b*) to a person who becomes a deputy judge of the Upper Tribunal as a result of provision under section 31(2).

[(3A) The person may be removed from office—

(a) only by the Lord Chancellor (and in accordance with paragraph 3), and
(b) only on—
(i) the ground of inability or misbehaviour, or
(ii) a ground specified in the person's terms of appointment.

(3B) If the period (or extended period) for which the person is appointed ends before—

(a) the day on which the person attains the age of 70, or
(b) if different, the day that for the purposes of section 26 of the Judicial Pensions and Retirement Act 1993 is the compulsory retirement date for the office concerned in the person's case,

then, subject to sub-paragraph (3C), the Lord Chancellor must extend the period of the person's appointment (including a period already extended under this sub-paragraph) before it ends.

(3C) Extension under sub-paragraph (3B)—

(a) requires the person's agreement,
(b) is to be for such period as the Lord Chancellor considers appropriate, and
(c) may be refused on—
(i) the ground of inability or misbehaviour, or
(ii) a ground specified in the person's terms of appointment,

but only with any agreement of a senior judge (see section 46(7)), or a nominee of a senior judge, that may be required by those terms.

(4) Subject to the previous provisions of this paragraph (but subject in the first place to the Judicial Pensions and Retirement Act 1993), a person is to hold and vacate office as a deputy judge of the Upper Tribunal in accordance with the person's terms of appointment, which are to be such as the Lord Chancellor may determine.][1]

(5) The Lord Chancellor may pay to a person to whom this sub-paragraph applies such amounts (if any) as the Lord Chancellor may determine by way of—

(*a*) remuneration;
(*b*) allowances;
(*c*) expenses.

Commencement—Tribunals, Courts and Enforcement Act 2007 (Commencement No 6 and Transitional Provisions) Order, SI 2008/2696 art 5(*f*) (Sch 3 comes into force on 3 November 2008).

Amendments—[1] In sub-para (1), words substituted for words "Lord Chancellor" in the first place; in sub-para (3), words substituted for words "Subparagraphs (4) and (5)"; and sub-paras (3A)–(4) substituted for former sub-para (4) by the Crime and Courts Act 2013 s 20, Sch 13 paras 42, 46(1), (6)–(8) with effect from 1 October 2013 (by virtue of SI 2013/2200).

Other members neither appointed under paragraph 2(1) nor transferred in

8—(1) In this paragraph "ex officio member of the Upper Tribunal" means—

(*a*) a person who is a member of the Upper Tribunal by virtue of section 5(2)(*c*) (member of Employment Appeal Tribunal appointed under section 22(1)(*c*) of the Employment Tribunals Act 1996 (c 17)), or
(*b*) a person who is a member of the Upper Tribunal by virtue of section 5(2)(*d*) (member of the Asylum and Immigration Tribunal who is not a legally qualified member).

(2) The Lord Chancellor may pay to an ex officio member of the Upper Tribunal such amounts (if any) as the Lord Chancellor may determine by way of—

(*a*) remuneration;

(*b*) allowances;

(*c*) expenses.

Commencement—Tribunals, Courts and Enforcement Act 2007 (Commencement No 6 and Transitional Provisions) Order, SI 2008/2696 art 5(*f*) (Sch 3 comes into force on 3 November 2008).

Training etc

9 The Senior President of Tribunals is responsible, within the resources made available by the Lord Chancellor, for the maintenance of appropriate arrangements for the training, guidance and welfare of judges and other members of the Upper Tribunal (in their capacities as such judges and other members).

Commencement—Tribunals, Courts and Enforcement Act 2007 (Commencement No 6 and Transitional Provisions) Order, SI 2008/2696 art 5(*f*) (Sch 3 comes into force on 3 November 2008).

Oaths

10—(1) Sub-paragraph (2) applies to a person ("J")—

(*a*) who is appointed under paragraph 1(1), 2(1) or 7(1), or

(*b*) who—

(i) becomes a transferred-in judge, or a transferred-in other member, of the Upper Tribunal, or

(ii) becomes a deputy judge of the Upper Tribunal as a result of provision under section 31(2),

and has not previously taken the required oaths after accepting another office.

(2) J must take the required oaths before—

(*a*) the Senior President of Tribunals, or

(*b*) an eligible person who is nominated by the Senior President of Tribunals for the purpose of taking the oaths from J.

(3) A person is eligible for the purposes of sub-paragraph (2)(*b*) if any one or more of the following paragraphs applies to him—

(*a*) he holds high judicial office (as defined in section 60(2) of the Constitutional Reform Act 2005 (c 4));

(*b*) he holds judicial office (as defined in section 109(4) of that Act);

(*c*) he holds (in Scotland) the office of sheriff.

(4) In this paragraph "the required oaths" means (subject to sub-paragraph (5))—

(*a*) the oath of allegiance, and

(*b*) the judicial oath,

as set out in the Promissory Oaths Act 1868 (c 72).

(5) Where it appears to the Lord Chancellor that J will carry out functions as a judge or other member of the Upper Tribunal wholly or mainly in Northern Ireland, the Lord Chancellor may direct that in relation to J "the required oaths" means—

(*a*) the oath as set out in section 19(2) of the Justice (Northern Ireland) Act 2002 (c 26), or

(*b*) the affirmation and declaration as set out in section 19(3) of that Act.

Commencement—Tribunals, Courts and Enforcement Act 2007 (Commencement No 6 and Transitional Provisions) Order, SI 2008/2696 art 5(*f*) (Sch 3 comes into force on 3 November 2008).

SCHEDULE 4

CHAMBERS AND CHAMBER PRESIDENTS: FURTHER PROVISION

Section 7

PART 1

CHAMBER PRESIDENTS: APPOINTMENT, DELEGATION, DEPUTIES AND FURTHER PROVISION

Eligibility for appointment as Chamber President [under section 7(7)][1]

1 A person is eligible for appointment under section 7(7) only if—

(*a*) he is a judge of the Upper Tribunal, or

(*b*) he does not fall within paragraph (*a*) but is eligible to be appointed under paragraph 1(1) of Schedule 3 as a judge of the Upper Tribunal (see paragraph 1(2) of that Schedule).

Commencement—Tribunals, Courts and Enforcement Act 2007 (Commencement No 6 and Transitional Provisions) Order, SI 2008/2696 art 5(*h*) (paras 1–8 come into force on 3 November 2008).

Amendments—[1] In cross-head preceding this para, words substituted for words " by Lord Chancellor" by the Crime and Courts Act 2013 s 20, Sch 13 paras 42, 47(1), (2) with effect from 1 October 2013 (by virtue of SI 2013/2200).

Appointment as Chamber President [under section 7(7)][1]: consultation and nomination

2—(1) The [Senior President of Tribunals must consult the Lord Chancellor before the Senior President of Tribunals][1] appoints under section 7(7) a person within—

section 6(1)(*a*) (ordinary judge of Court of Appeal in England and Wales),

section 6(1)(*b*) (Lord Justice of Appeal in Northern Ireland),

section 6(1)(*c*) (judge of the Court of Session), or

section 6(1)(*d*) (puisne judge of the High Court in England and Wales or Northern Ireland).

(2) If the [Senior President of Tribunals][1], in exercise of his power under section 7(7) in a particular case, wishes that the person appointed should be drawn from among the ordinary judges of the Court of Appeal in England and Wales or the puisne judges of the High Court in England and Wales, the [Senior President of Tribunals][1] must first ask the Lord Chief Justice of England and Wales to nominate one of those judges for the purpose.

(3) If the [Senior President of Tribunals][1], in exercise of his power under section 7(7) in a particular case, wishes that the person appointed should be drawn from among the judges of the Court of Session, the [Senior President of Tribunals][1] must first ask the Lord President of the Court of Session to nominate one of those judges for the purpose.

(4) If the [Senior President of Tribunals][1], in exercise of his power under section 7(7) in a particular case, wishes that the person appointed should be drawn from among the Lords Justices of Appeal in Northern Ireland or the puisne judges of the High Court in Northern Ireland, the [Senior President of Tribunals][1] must first ask the Lord Chief Justice of Northern Ireland to nominate one of those judges for the purpose.

[(4A) The Senior President of Tribunals may make a request under subparagraph (2), (3) or (4) only with the Lord Chancellor's concurrence.][1]

(5) If a judge is nominated under sub-paragraph (2), (3) or (4) in response to a request under that sub-paragraph, the [Senior President of Tribunals][1] must appoint the nominated judge as Chamber President of the chamber concerned.

Commencement—Tribunals, Courts and Enforcement Act 2007 (Commencement No 6 and Transitional Provisions) Order, SI 2008/2696 art 5(*h*) (paras 1–8 come into force on 3 November 2008).

Amendments—[1] In cross-head preceding this para, words substituted for words "by Lord Chancellor", in sub-para (1), words substituted for words "Lord Chancellor must consult the Senior President of Tribunals before the Lord Chancellor", in sub-paras (2)–(5) in each place, words substituted for words "Lord Chancellor", and sub-para (4A) inserted by the Crime and Courts Act 2013 s 20, Sch 13 paras 42, 47(1)–(6) with effect from 1 October 2013 (by virtue of SI 2013/2200).

Chamber Presidents: duration of appointment, remuneration etc

3—(1) A Chamber President is to hold and vacate office as a Chamber President in accordance with the terms of his appointment as a Chamber President [but subject to paragraph 5A (and subject in the first place][1] to the Judicial Pensions and Retirement Act 1993 (c 8))[, and those terms are to be such as the Lord Chancellor may determine][1].

(2) The Lord Chancellor may pay to a Chamber President such amounts (if any) as the Lord Chancellor may determine by way of—

(*a*) remuneration;

(*b*) allowances;

(*c*) expenses.

Commencement—Tribunals, Courts and Enforcement Act 2007 (Commencement No 6 and Transitional Provisions) Order, SI 2008/2696 art 5(*h*) (paras 1–8 come into force on 3 November 2008).

Amendments—[1] In sub-para (1), words substituted for words "(subject", and words inserted by the Crime and Courts Act 2013 s 20, Sch 13 paras 42, 47(1), (7) with effect from 1 October 2013 (by virtue of SI 2013/2200).

Delegation of functions by Chamber Presidents

4—(1) The Chamber President of a chamber of the First-tier Tribunal or Upper Tribunal may delegate any function he has in his capacity as the Chamber President of the chamber—

(*a*) to any judge, or other member, of either of those tribunals;

(*b*) to staff appointed under section 40(1).

(2) A delegation under sub-paragraph (1) is not revoked by the delegator's becoming incapacitated.

(3) Any delegation made by a person under sub-paragraph (1) that is in force immediately before the person ceases to be the Chamber President of a chamber continues in force until subsequently varied or revoked by another holder of the office of Chamber President of that chamber.

(4) The delegation under sub-paragraph (1) of a function shall not prevent the exercise of the function by the Chamber President of the chamber concerned.

(5) In this paragraph "delegate" includes further delegate.

Commencement—Tribunals, Courts and Enforcement Act 2007 (Commencement No 6 and Transitional Provisions) Order, SI 2008/2696 art 5(*h*) (paras 1–8 come into force on 3 November 2008).

Deputy Chamber Presidents

5—(1) The [Senior President of Tribunals][1] may appoint a person who is not a Deputy Chamber President of a chamber to be a Deputy Chamber President of a chamber.

(2) The Senior President of Tribunals may appoint a person who is a Deputy Chamber President of a chamber to be instead, or to be also, a Deputy Chamber President of another chamber.

(3) The power under sub-paragraph (1) is exercisable in any particular case only if the [Senior President of Tribunals][1]—

(*a*) has consulted the [Lord Chancellor][1] about whether a Deputy Chamber President should be appointed for the chamber concerned, and

(*b*) considers, in the light of the consultation, that a Deputy Chamber President of the chamber should be appointed.

(4) A person is eligible for appointment under sub-paragraph (1) only if—

(*a*) he is a judge of the Upper Tribunal by virtue of appointment under paragraph 1(1) of Schedule 3,

(*b*) he is a transferred-in judge of the Upper Tribunal (see section 31(2)),

(*c*) he is a judge of the Upper Tribunal by virtue of—

section 5(1)(*d*) (legally qualified member of Asylum and Immigration Tribunal),

section 5(1)(*e*) (Social Security Commissioner for Northern Ireland),

section 5(1)(*g*) (certain judges of courts in the United Kingdom), or

section 5(1)(*h*) (deputy judge of the Upper Tribunal), or

(*d*) he falls within none of paragraphs (*a*) to (*c*) but is eligible to be appointed under paragraph 1(1) of Schedule 3 as a judge of the Upper Tribunal (see paragraph 1(2) of that Schedule).

(5) If the [Senior President of Tribunals][1], in exercise of his power under sub-paragraph (1) in a particular case, wishes that the person appointed should be drawn from among the ordinary judges of the Court of Appeal in England and Wales or the puisne judges of the High Court in England and Wales, the [Senior President of Tribunals][1] must first ask the Lord Chief Justice of England and Wales to nominate one of those judges for the purpose.

(6) If the [Senior President of Tribunals][1], in exercise of his power under sub-paragraph (1) in a particular case, wishes that the person appointed should be drawn from among the judges of the Court of Session, the Lord Chancellor must first ask the Lord President of the Court of Session to nominate one of those judges for the purpose.

(7) If the [Senior President of Tribunals][1], in exercise of his power under sub-paragraph (1) in a particular case, wishes that the person appointed should be drawn from among the Lords Justices of Appeal in Northern Ireland or the puisne judges of the High Court in Northern Ireland, the [Senior President of Tribunals][1] must first ask the Lord Chief Justice of Northern Ireland to nominate one of those judges for the purpose.

[(7A) The Senior President of Tribunals may make a request under sub-paragraph (5), (6) or (7) only with the Lord Chancellor's concurrence.][1]

(8) If a judge is nominated under sub-paragraph (5), (6) or (7) in response to a request under that sub-paragraph, the [Senior President of Tribunals][1] must appoint the nominated judge as a Deputy Chamber President of the chamber concerned.

(9) A Deputy Chamber President is to hold and vacate office as a Deputy Chamber President in accordance with the terms of his appointment [but subject to paragraph 5A (and subject in the first place)][1] to the Judicial Pensions and Retirement Act 1993 (c 8))[, and those terms are to be such as the Lord Chancellor may determine][1].

(10) The Lord Chancellor may pay to a Deputy Chamber President such amounts (if any) as the Lord Chancellor may determine by way of—

(*a*) remuneration;

(*b*) allowances;

(*c*) expenses.

(11) In sub-paragraphs (1) and (2) "chamber" means chamber of the First-tier Tribunal or chamber of the Upper Tribunal.

Commencement—Tribunals, Courts and Enforcement Act 2007 (Commencement No 6 and Transitional Provisions) Order, SI 2008/2696 art 5(*h*) (paras 1–8 come into force on 3 November 2008).

Amendments—[1] In sub-paras (1), (3), (5)–(8), words substituted in each place for words "Lord Chancellor"; in sub-para (3)(*a*), words substituted for words "Senior President of Tribunals"; sub-para (7A) inserted; and in sub-para (9), words substituted for word "(subject" and words inserted by the Crime and Courts Act 2013 s 20, Sch 13 paras 42, 47(1), (8)–(13) with effect from 1 October 2013 (by virtue of SI 2013/2200).

[Chamber Presidents and Deputies: removal from office and extension of appointment

5A—(1) This paragraph applies to a person—

(*a*) appointed under section 7(6) or (7) as a Chamber President, or

(*b*) appointed under paragraph 5(1) or (2) as a Deputy Chamber President of a chamber.

(2) If the terms of the person's appointment provide that the person is appointed otherwise than on a fee-paid basis, the person may be removed from office—

(*a*) only by the Lord Chancellor with the concurrence of the Senior President of Tribunals, and

(*b*) only on the ground of inability or misbehaviour.

(3) If the terms of the person's appointment provide that the person is appointed on a fee-paid basis, the person may be removed from office—

(*a*) only by the Lord Chancellor with the concurrence of the Senior President of Tribunals, and

(*b*) only on—

(i) the ground of inability or misbehaviour, or

(ii) a ground specified in the person's terms of appointment.

(4) If the period (or extended period) for which the person is appointed ends before—

(*a*) the day on which the person attains the age of 70, or

(*b*) if different, the day that for the purposes of section 26 of the Judicial Pensions and Retirement Act 1993 is the compulsory retirement date for the office concerned in the person's case,

then, subject to sub-paragraph (5), the Lord Chancellor must extend the period of the person's appointment (including a period already extended under this sub-paragraph) before it ends.

(5) Extension under sub-paragraph (4)—

(*a*) requires the person's agreement,

(*b*) is to be for such period as the Lord Chancellor considers appropriate, and

(*c*) may be refused on—

(i) the ground of inability or misbehaviour, or

(ii) a ground specified in the person's terms of appointment,

but only with any agreement of a senior judge (see section 46(7)), or a nominee of a senior judge, that may be required by those terms.][1]

Amendments—[1] Para 5A inserted by the Crime and Courts Act 2013 s 20, Sch 13 paras 42, 47(1), (14) with effect from 1 October 2013 (by virtue of SI 2013/2200).

Acting Chamber Presidents

6—(1) If in the case of a particular chamber of the First-tier Tribunal or Upper Tribunal there is no-one appointed under section 7 to preside over the chamber, the Senior President of Tribunals may appoint a person to preside over the chamber during the vacancy.

(2) A person appointed under sub-paragraph (1) is to be known as an Acting Chamber President.

(3) A person who is the Acting Chamber President of a chamber is to be treated as the Chamber President of the chamber for all purposes other than—

(*a*) the purposes of this paragraph of this Schedule, and

(*b*) the purposes of the Judicial Pensions and Retirement Act 1993 (c 8).

(4) A person is eligible for appointment under sub-paragraph (1) only if he is eligible for appointment as a Chamber President.

(5) An Acting Chamber President is to hold and vacate office as an Acting Chamber President in accordance with the terms of his appointment.

(6) The Lord Chancellor may pay to an Acting Chamber President such amounts (if any) as the Lord Chancellor may determine by way of—

(*a*) remuneration;

(*b*) allowances;

(*c*) expenses.

Commencement—Tribunals, Courts and Enforcement Act 2007 (Commencement No 6 and Transitional Provisions) Order, SI 2008/2696 art 5(*h*) (paras 1–8 come into force on 3 November 2008).

Guidance

7 The Chamber President of a chamber of the First-tier Tribunal or the Upper Tribunal is to make arrangements for the issuing of guidance on changes in the law and practice as they relate to the functions allocated to the chamber.

Commencement—Tribunals, Courts and Enforcement Act 2007 (Commencement No 6 and Transitional Provisions) Order, SI 2008/2696 art 5(*h*) (paras 1–8 come into force on 3 November 2008).

Oaths

8—(1) Sub-paragraph (2) applies to a person ("the appointee")—

(*a*) appointed under section 7(7) as a Chamber President,

(*b*) appointed under paragraph 5(1) as a Deputy Chamber President of a chamber, or

(*c*) appointed as an Acting Chamber President.

(2) The appointee must take the required oaths before—

(*a*) the Senior President of Tribunals, or

(*b*) an eligible person who is nominated by the Senior President of Tribunals for the purpose of taking the oaths from the appointee.

(3) A person is eligible for the purposes of sub-paragraph (2)(*b*) if any one or more of the following paragraphs applies to him—

(*a*) he holds high judicial office (as defined in section 60(2) of the Constitutional Reform Act 2005 (c 4));

(*b*) he holds judicial office (as defined in section 109(4) of that Act);

(*c*) he holds (in Scotland) the office of sheriff.

(4) Sub-paragraph (2) does not apply to the appointee if he has previously taken the required oaths in compliance with a requirement imposed on him under paragraph 9 of Schedule 2 or paragraph 10 of Schedule 3.

(5) In this paragraph "the required oaths" means (subject to sub-paragraph (6))—

(*a*) the oath of allegiance, and

(*b*) the judicial oath,

as set out in the Promissory Oaths Act 1868 (c 72).

(6) Where it appears to the Lord Chancellor that the appointee will carry out functions under his appointment wholly or mainly in Northern Ireland, the Lord Chancellor may direct that in relation to the appointee "the required oaths" means—

(*a*) the oath as set out in section 19(2) of the Justice (Northern Ireland) Act 2002 (c 26), or

(*b*) the affirmation and declaration as set out in section 19(3) of that Act.

Commencement—Tribunals, Courts and Enforcement Act 2007 (Commencement No 6 and Transitional Provisions) Order, SI 2008/2696 art 5(*h*) (paras 1–8 come into force on 3 November 2008).

PART 2
JUDGES AND OTHER MEMBERS OF CHAMBERS: ASSIGNMENT AND JURISDICTION

Assignment is function of Senior President of Tribunals

9—(1) The Senior President of Tribunals has—

(*a*) the function of assigning judges and other members of the First-tier Tribunal (including himself) to chambers of the First-tier Tribunal, and

(*b*) the function of assigning judges and other members of the Upper Tribunal (including himself) to chambers of the Upper Tribunal.

(2) The functions under sub-paragraph (1) are to be exercised in accordance with the following provisions of this Part of this Schedule.

Commencement—Tribunals, Courts and Enforcement Act 2007 (Commencement No 6 and Transitional Provisions) Order, SI 2008/2696 art 5(*h*) (paras 9–14 come into force on 3 November 2008).

Deemed assignment of Chamber Presidents and Deputy Chamber Presidents

10—(1) The Chamber President, or a Deputy Chamber President, of a chamber—

(*a*) is to be taken to be assigned to that chamber;

(*b*) may be assigned additionally to one or more of the other chambers;

(*c*) may be assigned under paragraph (*b*) to different chambers at different times.

(2) Paragraphs 11(1) and (2) and 12(2) and (3) do not apply to assignment of a person who is a Chamber President or a Deputy Chamber President.

(3) In sub-paragraph (1) "chamber" means chamber of the First-tier Tribunal or the Upper Tribunal.

Commencement—Tribunals, Courts and Enforcement Act 2007 (Commencement No 6 and Transitional Provisions) Order, SI 2008/2696 art 5(*h*) (paras 9–14 come into force on 3 November 2008).

Assigning members of First-tier Tribunal to its chambers

11—(1) Each person who is a judge or other member of the First-tier Tribunal by virtue of appointment under paragraph 1(1) or 2(1) of Schedule 2 or who is a transferred-in judge, or transferred-in other member, of the First-tier Tribunal—

(*a*) is to be assigned to at least one of the chambers of the First-tier Tribunal, and

(*b*) may be assigned to different chambers of the First-tier Tribunal at different times.

(2) A judge or other member of the First-tier Tribunal to whom sub-paragraph (1) does not apply—

(*a*) may be assigned to one or more of the chambers of the First-tier Tribunal, and

(*b*) may be assigned to different chambers of the First-tier Tribunal at different times.

(3) The Senior President of Tribunals may assign a judge or other member of the First-tier Tribunal to a particular chamber of the First-tier Tribunal only with the concurrence—

(*a*) of the Chamber President of the chamber, and

(*b*) of the judge or other member.

(4) The Senior President of Tribunals may end the assignment of a judge or other member of the First-tier Tribunal to a particular chamber of the First-tier Tribunal only with the concurrence of the Chamber President of the chamber.

(5) Sub-paragraph (3)(*a*) does not apply where the judge, or other member, concerned is not assigned to any of the chambers of the First-tier Tribunal.

(6) Sub-paragraphs (3)(*a*) and (4) do not apply where the judge concerned is within section 6(1)(*a*) to (*d*) (judges of Courts of Appeal, Court of Session and High Courts).

(7) Sub-paragraphs (3) and (4) do not apply where the judge concerned is the Senior President of Tribunals himself.

Commencement—Tribunals, Courts and Enforcement Act 2007 (Commencement No 6 and Transitional Provisions) Order, SI 2008/2696 art 5(*h*) (paras 9–14 come into force on 3 November 2008).

Assigning members of Upper Tribunal to its chambers

12—(1) Sub-paragraph (2) applies to a person if—

(*a*) he is a judge of the Upper Tribunal by virtue of appointment under paragraph 1(1) of Schedule 3, or

(*b*) he is a transferred-in judge of the Upper Tribunal, or

(*c*) he is a deputy judge of the Upper Tribunal, or

(*d*) he is a member of the Upper Tribunal by virtue of appointment under paragraph 2(1) of Schedule 3, or

(*e*) he is a transferred-in other member of the Upper Tribunal.

(2) Each person to whom this sub-paragraph applies—

(*a*) is to be assigned to at least one of the chambers of the Upper Tribunal, and

(*b*) may be assigned to different chambers of the Upper Tribunal at different times.

(3) A judge or other member of the Upper Tribunal to whom sub-paragraph (2) does not apply—

(*a*) may be assigned to one or more of the chambers of the Upper Tribunal, and

(*b*) may be assigned to different chambers of the Upper Tribunal at different times.

(4) The Senior President of Tribunals may assign a judge or other member of the Upper Tribunal to a particular chamber of the Upper Tribunal only with the concurrence—

(*a*) of the Chamber President of the chamber, and

(*b*) of the judge or other member.

(5) The Senior President of Tribunals may end the assignment of a judge or other member of the Upper Tribunal to a particular chamber of the Upper Tribunal only with the concurrence of the Chamber President of the chamber.

(6) Sub-paragraph (4)(*a*) does not apply where the judge, or other member, concerned is not assigned to any of the chambers of the Upper Tribunal.

(7) Sub-paragraphs (4)(*a*) and (5) do not apply where the judge concerned is within section 6(1)(*a*) to (*d*) (judges of Courts of Appeal, Court of Session and High Courts).

(8) Sub-paragraphs (4) and (5) do not apply where the judge concerned is the Senior President of Tribunals himself.

Commencement—Tribunals, Courts and Enforcement Act 2007 (Commencement No 6 and Transitional Provisions) Order, SI 2008/2696 art 5(*h*) (paras 9–14 come into force on 3 November 2008).

Policy of Senior President of Tribunals as respects assigning members to chambers etc

13—(1) The Senior President of Tribunals must publish a document recording the policy adopted by him in relation to—

(*a*) the assigning of persons to chambers in exercise of his functions under paragraph 9,

(*b*) the assigning of persons to act as members of the Asylum and Immigration Tribunal in exercise of his functions under paragraphs 5A and 5B of Schedule 4 to the Nationality, Immigration and Asylum Act 2002 (c 41), and

(*c*) the nominating of persons to act as members of panels of members of employment tribunals in exercise of his functions under any such provision as is mentioned in section 5D(1) of the Employment Tribunals Act 1996 (c 17).

(2) That policy must be such as to secure—

(*a*) that appropriate use is made of the knowledge and experience of the judges and other members of the First-tier Tribunal and Upper Tribunal, and (*b*) that, in the case of a chamber (of the First-tier Tribunal or Upper Tribunal) whose business consists of, or includes, cases likely to involve the application of the law of Scotland or Northern Ireland, sufficient knowledge and experience of that law is to be found among persons assigned to the chamber.

(3) No policy may be adopted by the Senior President of Tribunals for the purposes of sub-paragraph (1) unless the Lord Chancellor concurs in the policy.

(4) The Senior President of Tribunals must keep any policy adopted for the purposes of sub-paragraph (1) under review.

Commencement—Tribunals, Courts and Enforcement Act 2007 (Commencement No 6 and Transitional Provisions) Order, SI 2008/2696 art 5(*h*) (paras 9–14 come into force on 3 November 2008).

Choosing members to decide cases

14—(1) The First-tier Tribunal's function, or the Upper Tribunal's function, of deciding any matter in a case before the tribunal is to be exercised by a member or members of the chamber of the tribunal to which the case is allocated.

(2) The member or members must be chosen by the Senior President of Tribunals.

(3) A person choosing under sub-paragraph (2)—

(*a*) must act in accordance with any provision under paragraph 15;

(*b*) may choose himself.

(4) In this paragraph "member", in relation to a chamber of a tribunal, means a judge or other member of the tribunal who is assigned to the chamber.

Commencement—Tribunals, Courts and Enforcement Act 2007 (Commencement No 6 and Transitional Provisions) Order, SI 2008/2696 art 5(*h*) (paras 9–14 come into force on 3 November 2008).

Composition of tribunals

15—(1) The Lord Chancellor must by order make provision, in relation to every matter that may fall to be decided by the First-tier Tribunal or the Upper Tribunal, for determining the number of members of the tribunal who are to decide the matter.

(2) Where an order under sub-paragraph (1) provides for a matter to be decided by a single member of a tribunal, the order—

(*a*) must make provision for determining whether the matter is to be decided by one of the judges, or by one of the other members, of the tribunal, and

(*b*) may make provision for determining, if the matter is to be decided by one of the other members of the tribunal, what qualifications (if any) that other member must have.

(3) Where an order under sub-paragraph (1) provides for a matter to be decided by two or more members of a tribunal, the order—

(*a*) must make provision for determining how many (if any) of those members are to be judges of the tribunal and how many (if any) are to be other members of the tribunal, and

(*b*) may make provision for determining—

(i) if the matter is to be decided by persons who include one or more of the other members of the tribunal, or

(ii) if the matter is to be decided by two or more of the other members of the tribunal,

what qualifications (if any) that other member or any of those other members must have.

(4) A duty under sub-paragraph (1), (2) or (3) to provide for the determination of anything may be discharged by providing for the thing to be determined by the Senior President of Tribunals, or a Chamber President, in accordance with any provision made under that sub-paragraph.

(5) Power under paragraph (*b*) of sub-paragraph (2) or (3) to provide for the determination of anything may be exercised by giving, to the Senior President of Tribunals or a Chamber President, power to determine that thing in accordance with any provision made under that paragraph.

(6) Where under sub-paragraphs (1) to (4) a matter is to be decided by two or more members of a tribunal, the matter may, if the parties to the case agree, be decided in the absence of one or more (but not all) of the members chosen to decide the matter.

(7) Where the member, or any of the members, of a tribunal chosen to decide a matter does not have any qualification that he is required to have under sub-paragraphs (2)(*b*), or (3)(*b*), and (5), the matter may despite that, if the parties to the case agree, be decided by the chosen member or members.

(8) Before making an order under this paragraph, the Lord Chancellor must consult the Senior President of Tribunals.

(9) In this paragraph "qualification" includes experience.

Commencement—Tribunals, Courts and Enforcement Act 2007 (Commencement No 1) Order, SI 2007/2709 art 2(*h*) (para 15 comes into force on 19 September 2007).

Orders—First-tier Tribunal and Upper Tribunal (Composition of Tribunal) Order, SI 2008/2835.

SCHEDULE 5

PROCEDURE IN FIRST-TIER TRIBUNAL AND UPPER TRIBUNAL

Section 22

Commencement—Tribunals, Courts and Enforcement Act 2007 (Commencement No 1) Order, SI 2007/2709 art 2(*i*) (Sch 5 comes into force on 19 September 2007).

Rules—Tribunals, Courts and Enforcement Act 2007 (Transitional and Consequential Provisions) Order, SI 2008/2683.

Tribunal Procedure (First-tier Tribunal) (Social Entitlement Chamber) Rules, SI 2008/2685.

Tribunal Procedure (First-tier Tribunal) (War Pensions and Armed Forces Compensation Chamber) Rules, SI 2008/2686.

Tribunal Procedure (Upper Tribunal) Rules, SI 2008/2698.

Tribunal Procedure (First-tier Tribunal) (Health, Education and Social Care Chamber) Rules, SI 2008/2699.

Transfer of Tribunal Functions Order, SI 2008/2833.

Transfer of Tribunal Functions and Revenue and Customs Appeals Order, SI 2009/56.

Tribunal Procedure (First-tier Tribunal) (Tax Chamber) Rules, SI 2009/273.

Tribunal Procedure (Amendment) Rules, SI 2009/274.

Tribunal Procedure (Amendment) Rules, SI 2012/500.

Tribunal Procedure (Amendment No 2) Rules, SI 2012/1363.

Tribunal Procedure (Upper Tribunal) (Amendment) Rules, SI 2012/2890.

Tribunal Procedure (Amendment) Rules, SI 2013/477.

Tribunal Procedure (Amendment No 2) Rules 2013/606.

Tribunal Procedure (Amendment No 3) Rules, SI 2013/1188 (amendments to the Tribunal Procedure (Upper Tribunal) (Lands Chamber) Rules, SI 2010/2600 only).

Tribunal Procedure (Amendment No 4) Rules, SI 2013/2067.

Tribunal Procedure (Amendment No 2) Rules, SI 2014/1505.

Tribunal Procedure (Amendment No 3) Rules, SI 2014/2128.

Tribunal Procedure (Amendment) Rules, SI 2015/1510.

PART 1

TRIBUNAL PROCEDURE RULES

Introductory

1—(1) This Part of this Schedule makes further provision about the content of Tribunal Procedure Rules.

(2) The generality of section 22(1) is not to be taken to be prejudiced by—

(*a*) the following paragraphs of this Part of this Schedule, or

(*b*) any other provision (including future provision) authorising or requiring the making of provision by Tribunal Procedure Rules.

(3) In the following paragraphs of this Part of this Schedule "Rules" means Tribunal Procedure Rules.

Commencement—Tribunals, Courts and Enforcement Act 2007 (Commencement No 1) Order, SI 2007/2709 art 2(*i*) (Sch 5 comes into force on 19 September 2007).

Concurrent functions

2 Rules may make provision as to who is to decide, or as to how to decide, which of the First-tier Tribunal and Upper Tribunal is to exercise, in relation to any particular matter, a function that is exercisable by the two tribunals on the basis that the question as to which of them is to exercise the function is to be determined by, or under, Rules.

Commencement—Tribunals, Courts and Enforcement Act 2007 (Commencement No 1) Order, SI 2007/2709 art 2(*i*) (Sch 5 comes into force on 19 September 2007).

Delegation of functions to staff

3—(1) Rules may provide for functions—

(*a*) of the First-tier Tribunal, or
(*b*) of the Upper Tribunal,
to be exercised by staff appointed under section 40(1).

(2) In making provision of the kind mentioned in sub-paragraph (1) in relation to a function, Rules may (in particular)—
(*a*) provide for the function to be exercisable by a member of staff only if the member of staff is, or is of a description, specified in exercise of a discretion conferred by Rules;
(*b*) provide for the function to be exercisable by a member of staff only if the member of staff is approved, or is of a description approved, for the purpose by a person specified in Rules.

Commencement—Tribunals, Courts and Enforcement Act 2007 (Commencement No 1) Order, SI 2007/2709 art 2(*i*) (Sch 5 comes into force on 19 September 2007).

Time limits

4 Rules may make provision for time limits as respects initiating, or taking any step in, proceedings before the First-tier Tribunal or the Upper Tribunal.

Commencement—Tribunals, Courts and Enforcement Act 2007 (Commencement No 1) Order, SI 2007/2709 art 2(*i*) (Sch 5 comes into force on 19 September 2007).

Repeat applications

5 Rules may make provision restricting the making of fresh applications where a previous application in relation to the same matter has been made.

Commencement—Tribunals, Courts and Enforcement Act 2007 (Commencement No 1) Order, SI 2007/2709 art 2(*i*) (Sch 5 comes into force on 19 September 2007).

Tribunal acting of its own initiative

6 Rules may make provision about the circumstances in which the First-tier Tribunal, or the Upper Tribunal, may exercise its powers of its own initiative.

Commencement—Tribunals, Courts and Enforcement Act 2007 (Commencement No 1) Order, SI 2007/2709 art 2(*i*) (Sch 5 comes into force on 19 September 2007).

Hearings

7 Rules may—
(*a*) make provision for dealing with matters without a hearing;
(*b*) make provision as respects allowing or requiring a hearing to be in private or as respects allowing or requiring a hearing to be in public.

Commencement—Tribunals, Courts and Enforcement Act 2007 (Commencement No 1) Order, SI 2007/2709 art 2(*i*) (Sch 5 comes into force on 19 September 2007).

Proceedings without notice

8 Rules may make provision for proceedings to take place, in circumstances described in Rules, at the request of one party even though the other, or another, party has had no notice.

Commencement—Tribunals, Courts and Enforcement Act 2007 (Commencement No 1) Order, SI 2007/2709 art 2(*i*) (Sch 5 comes into force on 19 September 2007).

Representation

9 Rules may make provision conferring additional rights of audience before the First-tier Tribunal or the Upper Tribunal.

Commencement—Tribunals, Courts and Enforcement Act 2007 (Commencement No 1) Order, SI 2007/2709 art 2(*i*) (Sch 5 comes into force on 19 September 2007).

Evidence, witnesses and attendance

10—(1) Rules may make provision about evidence (including evidence on oath and administration of oaths).

(2) Rules may modify any rules of evidence provided for elsewhere, so far as they would apply to proceedings before the First-tier Tribunal or Upper Tribunal.

(3) Rules may make provision, where the First-tier Tribunal has required a person—
(*a*) to attend at any place for the purpose of giving evidence,
(*b*) otherwise to make himself available to give evidence,
(*c*) to swear an oath in connection with the giving of evidence,
(*d*) to give evidence as a witness,

(*e*) to produce a document, or

(*f*) to facilitate the inspection of a document or any other thing (including any premises),

for the Upper Tribunal to deal with non-compliance with the requirement as though the requirement had been imposed by the Upper Tribunal.

(4) Rules may make provision for the payment of expenses and allowances to persons giving evidence, producing documents, attending proceedings or required to attend proceedings.

Commencement—Tribunals, Courts and Enforcement Act 2007 (Commencement No 1) Order, SI 2007/2709 art 2(*i*) (Sch 5 comes into force on 19 September 2007).

Use of information

11—(1) Rules may make provision for the disclosure or non-disclosure of information received during the course of proceedings before the First-tier Tribunal or Upper Tribunal.

(2) Rules may make provision for imposing reporting restrictions in circumstances described in Rules.

Commencement—Tribunals, Courts and Enforcement Act 2007 (Commencement No 1) Order, SI 2007/2709 art 2(*i*) (Sch 5 comes into force on 19 September 2007).

Costs and expenses

12—(1) Rules may make provision for regulating matters relating to costs, or (in Scotland) expenses, of proceedings before the First-tier Tribunal or Upper Tribunal.

(2) The provision mentioned in sub-paragraph (1) includes (in particular)—

(*a*) provision prescribing scales of costs or expenses;

(*b*) provision for enabling costs to undergo detailed assessment in England and Wales by a county court or the High Court;

(*c*) provision for taxation in Scotland of accounts of expenses by an Auditor of Court;

(*d*) provision for enabling costs to be taxed in Northern Ireland in a county court or the High Court;

(*e*) provision for costs or expenses—

(i) not to be allowed in respect of items of a description specified in Rules;

(ii) not to be allowed in proceedings of a description so specified;

(*f*) provision for other exceptions to either or both of subsections (1) and (2) of section 29.

Commencement—Tribunals, Courts and Enforcement Act 2007 (Commencement No 1) Order, SI 2007/2709 art 2(*i*) (Sch 5 comes into force on 19 September 2007).

Set-off and interest

13—(1) Rules may make provision for a party to proceedings to deduct, from amounts payable by him, amounts payable to him.

(2) Rules may make provision for interest on sums awarded (including provision conferring a discretion or provision in accordance with which interest is to be calculated).

Commencement—Tribunals, Courts and Enforcement Act 2007 (Commencement No 1) Order, SI 2007/2709 art 2(*i*) (Sch 5 comes into force on 19 September 2007).

Arbitration

14 Rules may provide for [any of the provisions of sections 1 to 15 of and schedule 1 to the Arbitration (Scotland) Act 2010 (which extends to Scotland) or][1] Part 1 of the Arbitration Act 1996 (c 23) (which extends to England and Wales, and Northern Ireland, but not Scotland) not to apply, or not to apply except so far as is specified in Rules, where the First-tier Tribunal, or Upper Tribunal, acts as arbitrator.

Commencement—Tribunals, Courts and Enforcement Act 2007 (Commencement No 1) Order, SI 2007/2709 art 2(*i*) (Sch 5 comes into force on 19 September 2007).

Amendments—[1] Words inserted by the Arbitration (Scotland) Act 2010 (Consequential Amendments) Order 2010, SI 2010/220 Schedule, para 8 with effect from 1 June 2010.

Correction of errors and setting-aside of decisions on procedural grounds

15—(1) Rules may make provision for the correction of accidental errors in a decision or record of a decision.

(2) Rules may make provision for the setting aside of a decision in proceedings before the First-tier Tribunal or Upper Tribunal—

(*a*) where a document relating to the proceedings was not sent to, or was not received at an appropriate time by, a party to the proceedings or a party's representative,

(*b*) where a document relating to the proceedings was not sent to the First-tier Tribunal or Upper Tribunal at an appropriate time, (*c*) where a party to the proceedings, or a party's representative, was not present at a hearing related to the proceedings, or

(*d*) where there has been any other procedural irregularity in the proceedings.

(3) Sub-paragraphs (1) and (2) shall not be taken to prejudice, or to be prejudiced by, any power to correct errors or set aside decisions that is exercisable apart from rules made by virtue of those sub-paragraphs.

Commencement—Tribunals, Courts and Enforcement Act 2007 (Commencement No 1) Order, SI 2007/2709 art 2(*i*) (Sch 5 comes into force on 19 September 2007).

Ancillary powers

16 Rules may confer on the First-tier Tribunal, or the Upper Tribunal, such ancillary powers as are necessary for the proper discharge of its functions.

Commencement—Tribunals, Courts and Enforcement Act 2007 (Commencement No 1) Order, SI 2007/2709 art 2(*i*) (Sch 5 comes into force on 19 September 2007).

Rules may refer to practice directions

17 Rules may, instead of providing for any matter, refer to provision made or to be made about that matter by directions under section 23.

Commencement—Tribunals, Courts and Enforcement Act 2007 (Commencement No 1) Order, SI 2007/2709 art 2(*i*) (Sch 5 comes into force on 19 September 2007).

Presumptions

18 Rules may make provision in the form of presumptions (including, in particular, presumptions as to service or notification).

Commencement—Tribunals, Courts and Enforcement Act 2007 (Commencement No 1) Order, SI 2007/2709 art 2(*i*) (Sch 5 comes into force on 19 September 2007).

Differential provision

19 Rules may make different provision for different purposes or different areas.

Commencement—Tribunals, Courts and Enforcement Act 2007 (Commencement No 1) Order, SI 2007/2709 art 2(*i*) (Sch 5 comes into force on 19 September 2007).

PART 2
TRIBUNAL PROCEDURE COMMITTEE

Membership

20 The Tribunal Procedure Committee is to consist of—

(*a*) the Senior President of Tribunals or a person nominated by him,

(*b*) the persons currently appointed by the Lord Chancellor under paragraph 21,

(*c*) the persons currently appointed by the Lord Chief Justice of England and Wales under paragraph 22,

(*d*) the person currently appointed by the Lord President of the Court of Session under paragraph 23, and

(*e*) any person currently appointed under paragraph 24 at the request of the Senior President of Tribunals.

Commencement—Tribunals, Courts and Enforcement Act 2007 (Commencement No 1) Order, SI 2007/2709 art 2(*i*) (Sch 5 comes into force on 19 September 2007).

Lord Chancellor's appointees

21—(1) The Lord Chancellor must appoint—

(*a*) three persons each of whom must be a person with experience of—

(i) practice in tribunals, or

(ii) advising persons involved in tribunal proceedings, ...[1]

(*b*) . . . [1]

(2) Before making an appointment under sub-paragraph (1), the Lord Chancellor must consult the Lord Chief Justice of England and Wales.

(3) . . . [1]

Commencement—Tribunals, Courts and Enforcement Act 2007 (Commencement No 1) Order, SI 2007/2709 art 2(*i*) (Sch 5 comes into force on 19 September 2007).

Amendments—[1] Sub-para (1)(*b*) and preceding word repealed, and sub-para(3) repealed by the Public Bodies (Abolition of Administrative Justice and Tribunals Council) Order, SI 2013/2042 art 2(2), Schedule para 35 with effect from 19 August 2013.

Lord Chief Justice's appointees

22—(1) The Lord Chief Justice of England and Wales must appoint—

(*a*) one of the judges of the First-tier Tribunal,

(*b*) one of the judges of the Upper Tribunal, and

(*c*) one person who is a member of the First-tier Tribunal, or is a member of the Upper Tribunal, but is not a judge of the First-tier Tribunal and is not a judge of the Upper Tribunal.

(2) Before making an appointment under sub-paragraph (1), the Lord Chief Justice of England and Wales must consult the Lord Chancellor.

Commencement—Tribunals, Courts and Enforcement Act 2007 (Commencement No 1) Order, SI 2007/2709 art 2(*i*) (Sch 5 comes into force on 19 September 2007).

Lord President's appointee

23—(1) The Lord President of the Court of Session must appoint one person with experience in and knowledge of the Scottish legal system.

(2) Before making an appointment under sub-paragraph (1), the Lord President of the Court of Session must consult the Lord Chancellor.

Commencement—Tribunals, Courts and Enforcement Act 2007 (Commencement No 1) Order, SI 2007/2709 art 2(*i*) (Sch 5 comes into force on 19 September 2007).

Persons appointed at request of Senior President of Tribunals

24—(1) At the request of the Senior President of Tribunals, an appropriate senior judge may appoint a person or persons with experience in and knowledge of—

(*a*) a particular issue, or

(*b*) a particular subject area in relation to which the First-tier Tribunal or the Upper Tribunal has, or is likely to have, jurisdiction,

for the purpose of assisting the Committee with regard to that issue or subject area.

(2) In sub-paragraph (1) "an appropriate senior judge" means any of—

(*a*) the Lord Chief Justice of England and Wales,

(*b*) the Lord President of the Court of Session, and

(*c*) the Lord Chief Justice of Northern Ireland.

(3) The total number of persons appointed at any time under sub-paragraph (1) must not exceed four.

(4) Before making an appointment under sub-paragraph (1), the person making the appointment must consult the Lord Chancellor.

(5) The terms of appointment of a person appointed under sub-paragraph (1) may (in particular) authorise him to act as a member of the Committee only in relation to matters specified by those terms.

Commencement—Tribunals, Courts and Enforcement Act 2007 (Commencement No 1) Order, SI 2007/2709 art 2(*i*) (Sch 5 comes into force on 19 September 2007).

Power to amend paragraphs 20 to 24

25—(1) The Lord Chancellor may by order—

(*a*) amend any of paragraphs 20, 21(1), 22(1), 23(1) and 24(1), and

(*b*) make consequential amendments in any other provision of paragraphs 21 to 24 or in paragraph 28(7).

(2) The making of an order under this paragraph—

(*a*) requires the concurrence of the Lord Chief Justice of England and Wales,

(*b*) if the order amends paragraph 23(1), requires also the concurrence of the Lord President of the Court of Session, and

(*c*) if the order amends paragraph 24(1), requires also the concurrence of the Lord President of the Court of Session and the Lord Chief Justice of Northern Ireland.

Commencement—Tribunals, Courts and Enforcement Act 2007 (Commencement No 1) Order, SI 2007/2709 art 2(*i*) (Sch 5 comes into force on 19 September 2007).

Committee members' expenses

26 The Lord Chancellor may reimburse members of the Tribunal Procedure Committee their travelling and out-of-pocket expenses.

Commencement—Tribunals, Courts and Enforcement Act 2007 (Commencement No 1) Order, SI 2007/2709 art 2(*i*) (Sch 5 comes into force on 19 September 2007).

PART 3
MAKING OF TRIBUNAL PROCEDURE RULES BY TRIBUNAL PROCEDURE COMMITTEE

Meaning of "Rules" and "the Committee"

27 In the following provisions of this Part of this Schedule—
"the Committee" means the Tribunal Procedure Committee;
"Rules" means Tribunal Procedure Rules.

Commencement—Tribunals, Courts and Enforcement Act 2007 (Commencement No 1) Order, SI 2007/2709 art 2(*i*) (Sch 5 comes into force on 19 September 2007).

Process for making Rules

28—(1) Before the Committee makes Rules, the Committee must—
(*a*) consult such persons (including such of the Chamber Presidents) as it considers appropriate,
(*b*) consult the Lord President of the Court of Session if the Rules contain provision relating to proceedings in Scotland, and
(*c*) meet (unless it is inexpedient to do so).
(2) Rules made by the Committee must be—
(*a*) signed by a majority of the members of the Committee, and
(*b*) submitted to the Lord Chancellor.
(3) The Lord Chancellor may allow or disallow Rules so made.
(4) If the Lord Chancellor disallows Rules so made, he must give the Committee written reasons for doing so.
(5) Rules so made and allowed—
(*a*) come into force on such day as the Lord Chancellor directs, and
(*b*) are to be contained in a statutory instrument to which the Statutory Instruments Act 1946 (c 36) applies as if the instrument contained rules made by a Minister of the Crown.
(6) A statutory instrument containing Rules made by the Committee is subject to annulment in pursuance of a resolution of either House of Parliament.
(7) In the case of a member of the Committee appointed under paragraph 24, the terms of his appointment may (in particular) provide that, for the purposes of sub-paragraph (2)(*a*), he is to count as a member of the Committee only in relation to matters specified in those terms.

Commencement—Tribunals, Courts and Enforcement Act 2007 (Commencement No 1) Order, SI 2007/2709 art 2(*i*) (Sch 5 comes into force on 19 September 2007).
Rules—Tribunal Procedure (Amendment) Rules, SI 2010/43.
Tribunal Procedure (Amendment No 4) Rules, SI 2013/2067.

Power of Lord Chancellor to require Rules to be made

29—(1) This paragraph applies if the Lord Chancellor gives the Committee written notice that he thinks it is expedient for Rules to include provision that would achieve a purpose specified in the notice.
(2) The Committee must make such Rules, in accordance with paragraph 28, as it considers necessary to achieve the specified purpose.
(3) Those Rules must be made—
(*a*) within such period as may be specified by the Lord Chancellor in the notice, or
(*b*) if no period is so specified, within a reasonable period after the Lord Chancellor gives the notice to the Committee.

Commencement—Tribunals, Courts and Enforcement Act 2007 (Commencement No 1) Order, SI 2007/2709 art 2(*i*) (Sch 5 comes into force on 19 September 2007).

PART 4
POWER TO AMEND LEGISLATION IN CONNECTION WITH TRIBUNAL PROCEDURE RULES

Lord Chancellor's power

30—(1) The Lord Chancellor may by order amend, repeal or revoke any enactment to the extent he considers necessary or desirable—
(*a*) in order to facilitate the making of Tribunal Procedure Rules, or
(*b*) in consequence of—
(i) section 22,
(ii) Part 1 or 3 of this Schedule, or
(iii) Tribunal Procedure Rules.

(2) In this paragraph "enactment" means any enactment whenever passed or made, including an enactment comprised in subordinate legislation (within the meaning of the Interpretation Act 1978 (c 30)).

Commencement—Tribunals, Courts and Enforcement Act 2007 (Commencement No 1) Order, SI 2007/2709 art 2(*i*) (Sch 5 comes into force on 19 September 2007).

Orders—Tribunals, Courts and Enforcement Act 2007 (Transitional and Consequential Provisions) Order, SI 2008/2683.
Transfer of Tribunal Functions Order, SI 2008/2833.
Transfer of Tribunal Functions and Revenue and Customs Appeals Order, SI 2009/56.

SCHEDULE 6

TRIBUNALS FOR THE PURPOSES OF SECTIONS 30 TO 36

Sections 30 to 37

Commencement—Tribunals, Courts and Enforcement Act 2007 (Commencement No 1) Order, SI 2007/2709 art 2(*j*) (Sch 6 comes into force on 19 September 2007).

PART 1

TRIBUNALS FOR THE PURPOSES OF SECTIONS 30, 35 AND 36

Tribunal	*Enactment*
[Agricultural Land Tribunals for areas in England	Section 73 of the Agriculture Act 1947 (c.48)][2]
Appeal tribunal	Chapter 1 of Part 1 of the Social Security Act 1998 (c 14)
Child Support Commissioner	Section 22 of the Child Support Act 1991 (c 48)
[Claims Management Services Tribunal	Section 12 of the Compensation Act 2006 (c 29)][1]
The Secretary of State as respects his function of deciding appeals under:	Section 41 of the Consumer Credit Act 1974 (c 39)
The Secretary of State as respects his function of deciding appeals under:	Section 7(1) of the Estate Agents Act 1979 (c 38)
Foreign Compensation Commission	Section 1 of the Foreign Compensation Act 1950 (c 12)
[Gender Recognition Panel	Section 1(3) of the Gender Recognition Act 2004 (c 7)][1]
Commissioner for the general purposes of the income tax	Section 2 of the Taxes Management Act 1970 (c 9)
Information Tribunal	Section 6 of the Data Protection Act 1998 (c 29)
Meat Hygiene Appeals Tribunal	Regulation 6 of the Fresh Meat (Hygiene and Inspection) Regulations 1995 (SI 1995/539)
Meat Hygiene Appeals Tribunal	Regulation 6 of the Poultry Meat, Farmed Game Bird Meat and Rabbit Meat (Hygiene and Inspection) Regulations 1995 (SI 1995/540)
Meat Hygiene Appeals Tribunal	Regulation 5 of the Wild Game Meat (Hygiene and Inspection) Regulations 1995 (SI 1995/2148)
Mental Health Review Tribunal for a region of England	Section 65(1) and (1A)(a) of the Mental Health Act 1983 (c 20)
Reinstatement Committee	Paragraph 1 of Schedule 2 to the Reserve Forces (Safeguard of Employment) Act 1985 (c 17)
[Rent assessment committees for areas in England	Section 65 of, and Schedule 10 to, the Rent Act 1977 (c. 42)][2]
Reserve forces appeal tribunal	Section 88 of the Reserve Forces Act 1996 (c 14)
Sea Fish Licence Tribunal	Section 4AA of the Sea Fish (Conservation) Act 1967 (c 84)
Social Security Commissioner	Schedule 4 to the Social Security Act 1998 (c 14)

Tribunal	*Enactment*
Special Educational Needs and Disability Tribunal	Section 333 of the Education Act 1996 (c 56)
Transport Tribunal	Schedule 4 to the Transport Act 1985 (c 67)
[Tribunal	Section 704 of the Income Tax Act 2007 (c 3)][1]
Umpire or deputy umpire	Paragraph 5 of Schedule 2 to the Reserve Forces (Safeguard of Employment) Act 1985
VAT and duties tribunal	Schedule 12 to the Value Added Tax Act 1994 (c 23)

Commencement—Tribunals, Courts and Enforcement Act 2007 (Commencement No 1) Order, SI 2007/2709 art 2(*j*) (Sch 6 comes into force on 19 September 2007).

Amendments—

1 Entries inserted by the Transfer of Tribunal Functions Order, SI 2008/2833 art 2 with effect from 3 November 2008.

2 Entries inserted by the Amendments to Schedule 6 to the Tribunals, Courts and Enforcement Act 2007 Order, SI 2013/1034 art 2.

PART 2
TRIBUNALS FOR THE PURPOSES OF SECTIONS 30 AND 35

Tribunal	*Enactment*
Adjudicator	Section 5 of the Criminal Injuries Compensation Act 1995 (c 53)

Commencement—Tribunals, Courts and Enforcement Act 2007 (Commencement No 1) Order, SI 2007/2709 art 2(*j*) (Sch 6 comes into force on 19 September 2007).

PART 3
TRIBUNALS FOR THE PURPOSES OF SECTIONS 30 AND 36

Tribunal	*Enactment*
Adjudicator to Her Majesty's Land Registry	Section 107 of the Land Registration Act 2002 (c 9)
Charity Tribunal	Section 2A of the Charities Act 1993 (c 10)
Consumer Credit Appeals Tribunal	Section 40A of the Consumer Credit Act 1974 (c 39)
Financial Services and Markets Tribunal	Section 132 of the Financial Services and Markets Act 2000 (c 8)
Gambling Appeals Tribunal	Section 140 of the Gambling Act 2005 (c 19)
Immigration Services Tribunal	Section 87 of the Immigration and Asylum Act 1999 (c 33)
Lands Tribunal	Section 1(1)(b) of the Lands Tribunal Act 1949 (c 42)
Pensions Appeal Tribunal in England and Wales	Paragraph 1(1) of the Schedule to the Pensions Appeal Tribunals Act 1943 (c 39)
Pensions Regulator Tribunal	Section 102 of the Pensions Act 2004 (c 35)
Commissioner for the special purposes of the Income Tax Acts	Section 4 of the Taxes Management Act 1970 (c 9)

Commencement—Tribunals, Courts and Enforcement Act 2007 (Commencement No 1) Order, SI 2007/2709 art 2(*j*) (Sch 6 comes into force on 19 September 2007).

PART 4
TRIBUNALS FOR THE PURPOSES OF SECTION 30

Tribunal	*Enactment*
. . .[3]	. . .[3]

Tribunal	*Enactment*
. . . [4]	. . . [4]
Antarctic Act Tribunal	Regulation 11 of the Antarctic Regulations 1995 (SI 1995/490)
Appeal tribunal	Part 2 of Schedule 9 to the Scheme set out in Schedule 2 to the Firefighters' Pension Scheme Order 1992 (SI 1992/129)
[Asylum and Immigration Tribunal	Section 81 of the Nationality, Immigration and Asylum Act 2002(b)][2]
Asylum Support Adjudicator	Section 102 of the Immigration and Asylum Act 1999
Case tribunal, or interim case tribunal, drawn from the Adjudication Panel for England	Section 76 of the Local Government Act 2000 (c 22)
Family Health Services Appeal Authority	Section 49S of the National Health Service Act 1977 (c 49)
Insolvency Practitioners Tribunal	Section 396(1) of the Insolvency Act 1986 (c 45)
Appeals Tribunal	Part 3 of the Local Authorities (Code of Conduct) (Local Determination) Regulations 2003 (SI 2003/1483)
[Panel	Section 189(6) of the Greater London Authority Act 1999][1]
Plant Varieties and Seeds Tribunal	Section 42 of the Plant Varieties Act 1997 (c 66)
Tribunal	Rule 6 of the model provisions with respect to appeals as applied with modifications by the Chemical Weapons (Licence Appeal Provisions) Order 1996 (SI 1996/3030)
Tribunal	Health Service Medicines (Price Control Appeals) Regulations 2000 (SI 2000/124)
Tribunal	Section 706 of the Income and Corporation Taxes Act 1988 (c 1)
Tribunal	Section 150 of the Mines and Quarries Act 1954 (c 70)
Tribunal	Part 1 of Schedule 3 to the Misuse of Drugs Act 1971 (c 38)
Tribunal	Regulation H6(3) of the Police Pensions Regulations 1987 (SI 1987/257)
Tribunal	Section 9 of the Protection of Children Act 1999 (c 14)

Commencement—Tribunals, Courts and Enforcement Act 2007 (Commencement No 1) Order, SI 2007/2709 art 2(*j*) (Sch 6 comes into force on 19 September 2007).

Amendments—

1 Entry for "panel" inserted by the Transfer of Functions (Estate Agents Appeals and Additional Scheduled Tribunal) Order, SI 2009/1836 art 4 with effect from 8 July 2009.

2 Entry inserted by the Amendment to Schedule 6 to the Tribunals, Courts and Enforcement Act 2007 Order 2010, SI 2010/21 art 2 with effect from 14 February 2010.

3 Entry relating to "Agricultural Land Tribunal" repealed by the Amendments to Schedule 6 to the Tribunals, Courts and Enforcement Act 2007 Order, SI 2013/1034 art 3.

4 Entry relating to "Aircraft and Shipbuilding Industries Arbitration Tribunal" repealed by the Public Bodies (Abolition of the Aircraft and Shipbuilding Industries Arbitration Tribunal) Order, SI 2013/686 art 3, Sch 1, para 9 with effect from 22 March 2013.

Prospective amendments—Entry relating to "Insolvency Practitioners Tribunal" to be repealed by the Deregulation Act 2015 s 19, Sch 6, para 22(1), (16)(*a*) with effect from a date to be appointed.

PART 5

TRIBUNALS FOR THE PURPOSES OF SECTIONS 35 AND 36

Tribunal	*Enactment*
Employment Appeal Tribunal	Section 20 of the Employment Tribunals Act 1996 (c 17)

Commencement—Tribunals, Courts and Enforcement Act 2007 (Commencement No 1) Order, SI 2007/2709 art 2(*j*) (Sch 6 comes into force on 19 September 2007).

PART 6

TRIBUNALS FOR THE PURPOSES OF SECTION 35

Tribunal	*Enactment*
Employment tribunal	Section 1 of the Employment Tribunals Act 1996

Commencement—Tribunals, Courts and Enforcement Act 2007 (Commencement No 1) Order, SI 2007/2709 art 2(*j*) (Sch 6 comes into force on 19 September 2007).

PART 7

TRIBUNALS FOR THE PURPOSES OF SECTION 32(3)

Tribunal	*Enactment*
Case tribunal, or interim case tribunal, drawn from the Adjudication Panel for Wales	Section 76 of the Local Government Act 2000 (c 22)
[Agricultural Land Tribunal for Wales	Section 73 of the Agriculture Act 1947 (c. 48)][1]
Appeals Tribunal	Local Government Investigations (Functions of Monitoring Officers and Standards Committees) (Wales) Regulations 2001 (SI 2001/2281)
Mental Health Review Tribunal for Wales	Section 65(1) and (1A)(b) of the Mental Health Act 1983 (c 20)
[Rent assessment committees for areas in Wales	Section 65 of, and Schedule 10 to, the Rent Act 1977 (c. 42)][1]
Special Educational Needs Tribunal for Wales	Section 336ZA of the Education Act 1996 (c 56)
Tribunal	Section 27 of, and Schedule 3 to, the Education Act 2005 (c 18)

Commencement—Tribunals, Courts and Enforcement Act 2007 (Commencement No 1) Order, SI 2007/2709 art 2(*j*) (Sch 6 comes into force on 19 September 2007).

Amendments—

[1] Entries inserted by the Amendments to Schedule 6 to the Tribunals, Courts and Enforcement Act 2007 Order, SI 2013/1034 art 4.

SCHEDULE 10

AMENDMENTS RELATING TO JUDICIAL APPOINTMENTS

Section 50

Note—Provisions omitted are not relevant to this work.

Commencement—Tribunals, Courts and Enforcement Act 2007 (Commencement No 5 and Transitional Provisions) Order, SI 2008/1653 art 2(*d*) (Sch 10 comes into force on 21 July 2008).

PART 1

AMENDMENTS

. . .

8—(1) Section 4(2) of the Taxes Management Act 1970 (c 9) (Special Commissioners) is amended as follows.

(2) For paragraph (*a*) substitute—

"(*a*) he satisfies the judicial-appointment eligibility condition on a 7-year basis;".

(3) In paragraphs (*b*) and (*c*), for "10" substitute "7".

. . .

19—(1) Paragraph 1(1)(*a*) of Schedule 7 to the Insolvency Act 1986 (c 45) (members of Insolvency Practitioners Tribunal) is amended as follows.

(2) For sub-paragraph (i) substitute—

"(i) satisfy the judicial-appointment eligibility condition on a 5-year basis;".

(3) In sub-paragraph (ii), for "7" substitute "5".

Prospective amendments—Para 19 to be repealed by the Deregulation Act 2015 s 19, Sch 6, para 22(1), (16)(*b*) with effect from a date to be appointed.

23

Amendments—This para repealed by the Transfer of Functions of the Charity Tribunal Order, SI 2009/1834 art 4(1), Sch 3 with effect from 1 September 2009.

24—(1) Schedule 12 to the Value Added Tax Act 1994 (c 23) is amended as follows.

(2) In paragraph 2(2) (President of VAT and duties tribunals)—

(*a*) for paragraph (*a*) substitute—

"(*a*) a person who satisfies the judicial-appointment eligibility condition on a 7-year basis;", and

(*b*) in paragraphs (*b*) and (*c*), for "10" substitute "7".

(3) In paragraph 7(4) (panel of chairmen)—

(*a*) for paragraph (*a*) substitute—

"(*a*) a person who satisfies the judicial-appointment eligibility condition on a 5-year basis; or", and

(*b*) in paragraph (*b*) and in the words after that paragraph, for "7" substitute "5".

. . .

29 . . .

Amendments—Para 29 repealed by the Transfer of Tribunal Functions Order, SI 2008/2833 art 6, Sch 3 para 228(*r*) with effect from 3 November 2008.

. . .

34—(1) Schedule 13 to the Financial Services and Markets Act 2000 (c 8) is amended as follows.

(2) In paragraph 2(5) (President of Financial Services and Markets Tribunal)—

(*a*) *for paragraph* (*a*) substitute—

"(*a*) *satisfies the judicial-appointment eligibility condition on a 7-year basis;", and*

(*b*) *in paragraphs* (*b*) and (*c*)(i) and (ii), for "ten" substitute "7".

(3) In paragraph 3(2) (panel of chairmen)—

(*a*) *for paragraph* (*a*) substitute—

"(*a*) *he satisfies the judicial-appointment eligibility condition on a 5-year basis;", and*

(*b*) *in paragraphs* (*b*) and (*c*)(i) and (ii), for "seven" substitute "5".[1]

Amendments—[1] Para 34 repealed by the Transfer of Tribunal Functions Order, SI 2010/22 art 5(3), Sch 4 Pt 2 with effect from 6 April 2010.

35—(1) The Land Registration Act 2002 (c 9) is amended as follows.

(2) In section 107(2) (Adjudicator to Her Majesty's Land Registry), for the words from "have" to the end substitute "satisfy the judicial-appointment eligibility condition on a 7-year basis."

(3) In paragraph 4(2) of Schedule 9 (delegation by adjudicator of non-administrative functions to staff), for the words from "has" to the end substitute "satisfies the judicial-appointment eligibility condition on a 7-year basis."

36—(1) Paragraph 1 of Schedule 2 to the Enterprise Act 2002 (c 40) is amended as follows.

(2) In sub-paragraph (1) (President of Competition Appeal Tribunal)—

(*a*) for paragraph (*a*) substitute—

"(*a*) he satisfies the judicial-appointment eligibility condition on a 7-year basis;", and

(*b*) in paragraphs (*b*) and (*c*), for "10" substitute "7".

(3) In sub-paragraph (2) (chairmen)—

(*a*) for paragraph (*a*) substitute—

"(*a*) he satisfies the judicial-appointment eligibility condition on a 5-year basis;", and

(*b*) in paragraphs (*b*) and (*c*), for "7" substitute "5".

. . .

40—(1) Schedule 4 to the Pensions Act 2004 (c 35) is amended as follows.

(2) In paragraph 1(2) (panel of chairmen of Pensions Regulator Tribunal)—

(*a*) *for paragraph* (*a*) substitute—

"(*a*) *he satisfies the judicial-appointment eligibility condition on a 5-year basis," and* (*b*) *in paragraphs (b), (c) and (d), for "7" substitute "5".*

(3) In paragraph 2(5) (President or Deputy President)—

(*a*) *for paragraph (a) substitute—*

"(*a*) *satisfies the judicial-appointment eligibility condition on a 7-year basis," and*

(*b*) *in paragraphs (b), (c) and (d), for "10" substitute "7".*[1]

Amendments—[1] Para 40 repealed by the Transfer of Tribunal Functions Order, SI 2010/22 art 5(3), Sch 4 Pt 2 with effect from 6 April 2010.

41—(1) Section 25 of the Constitutional Reform Act 2005 (c 4) (judges of the Supreme Court) is amended as follows.

(2) In subsection (1), for paragraph (*b*) and the word "or" immediately preceding it substitute—

"(*b*) satisfied the judicial-appointment eligibility condition on a 15-year basis, or

(*c*) been a qualifying practitioner for a period of at least 15 years."

(3) In subsection (2), omit paragraph (*a*).

42 In paragraph 1(2) of Schedule 3 to the Education Act 2005 (c 18) (Chairman of tribunal hearing appeals under section 27 of that Act), for the words from "have a" to the end substitute "satisfy the judicial-appointment eligibility condition on a 5-year basis."

43—(1) Paragraph 2 of Schedule 8 to the Gambling Act 2005 (c 19) (President and members of Gambling Appeals Tribunal) is amended as follows.

(2) For paragraph (a) substitute—

"(*a*) *he satisfies the judicial-appointment eligibility condition on a 5-year basis,".*

(3) In paragraphs (b) and (c), for "seven" substitute "5".

. . .

Amendments—[1] Para 43 repealed by the Transfer of Tribunal Functions Order, SI 2010/22 art 5(3), Sch 4 Pt 1 with effect from 18 January 2010.

SCHEDULE 12

TAKING CONTROL OF GOODS

Section 62(1)

Commencement—Tribunals, Courts and Enforcement Act 2007 (Commencement No 11) Order, SI 2014/768 art 2(1)(*b*) (Sch 12 comes into force on 6 April 2014 (to the extent that it is not already in force)).

Note—This Schedule does not extend to Scotland (s 147(2)).

PART 1

INTRODUCTORY

The procedure

1—(1) Using the procedure in this Schedule to recover a sum means taking control of goods and selling them to recover that sum in accordance with this Schedule and regulations under it.

(2) In this Schedule a power to use the procedure to recover a particular sum is called an "enforcement power".

(3) The following apply in relation to an enforcement power.

(4) "Debt" means the sum recoverable.

(5) "Debtor" means the person liable to pay the debt or, if two or more persons are jointly or jointly and severally liable, any one or more of them.

(6) "Creditor" means the person for whom the debt is recoverable.

Commencement—Tribunals, Courts and Enforcement Act 2007 (Commencement No 11) Order, SI 2014/768 art 2(1)(*b*) (Sch 12 comes into force on 6 April 2014).

Enforcement agents

2—(1) In this Schedule "enforcement agent" means an individual authorised by section 63(2) to act as an enforcement agent.

(2) Only an enforcement agent may take control of goods and sell them under an enforcement power.

(3) An enforcement agent, if he is not the person on whom an enforcement power is conferred, may act under the power only if authorised by that person.

(4) In relation to goods taken control of by an enforcement agent under an enforcement power, references to the enforcement agent are references to any person for the time being acting as an enforcement agent under the power.

Commencement—Tribunals, Courts and Enforcement Act 2007 (Commencement No, 11) Order, SI 2014/768 art 2(1)(*b*) (Sch 12 comes into force on 6 April 2014).

General interpretation

3—(1) In this Schedule—

"amount outstanding" is defined in paragraph 50(3);

"control" (except in paragraph 5(4)(*a*)) means control under an enforcement power;

"controlled goods" means goods taken control of that—

(*a*) have not been sold or abandoned,

(*b*) if they have been removed, have not been returned to the debtor (unless subject to a controlled goods agreement), and

(*c*) if they are goods of another person, have not been returned to that person;

"controlled goods agreement" has the meaning given by paragraph 13(4);

"co-owner" in relation to goods of the debtor means a person other than the debtor who has an interest in the goods, but only if the enforcement agent—

(*a*) knows that the person has an interest in the particular goods, or

(*b*) would know, if he made reasonable enquiries;

"the court", unless otherwise stated, and subject to rules of court, means—

(*a*) the High Court, in relation to an enforcement power under a writ of the High Court;

(*b*) a county court, in relation to an enforcement power under a warrant issued by a county court;

(*c*) in any other case, a magistrates' court;

"disposal" and related expressions, in relation to securities, are to be read in accordance with paragraph 48(2);

"exempt goods" means goods that regulations exempt by description or circumstances or both;

"goods" means property of any description, other than land;

"interest" means a beneficial interest;

"money" means money in sterling or another currency;

"premises" means any place, and in particular includes—

(*a*) a vehicle, vessel, aircraft or hovercraft;

(*b*) a tent or movable structure;

"securities" includes bills of exchange, promissory notes, bonds, specialties and securities for money.

(2) In this Schedule—

(*a*) references to goods of the debtor or another person are references to goods in which the debtor or that person has an interest, but

(*b*) references to goods of the debtor do not include references to trust property in which either the debtor or a co-owner has an interest not vested in possession.

Commencement—Tribunals, Courts and Enforcement Act 2007 (Commencement No 9) Order, SI 2013/1739 art 3 (para 3(1) comes into force on 15 July 2013 for the purpose only of exercising any power to make regulations).

Tribunals, Courts and Enforcement Act 2007 (Commencement No 11) Order, SI 2014/768 art 2(1)(*b*) (para 3 comes into force on 6 April 2014 for all other purposes).

PART 2
THE PROCEDURE

Binding property in the debtor's goods

4—(1) For the purposes of any enforcement power, the property in all goods of the debtor, except goods that are exempt goods for the purposes of this Schedule or are protected under any other enactment, becomes bound in accordance with this paragraph.

(2) Where the power is conferred by a writ issued from the High Court the writ binds the property in the goods from the time when it is received by the person who is under a duty to endorse it.

(3) Where the power is conferred by a warrant to which section 99 of the County Courts Act 1984 (c 28) or section 125ZA of the Magistrates' Courts Act 1980 (c 43) applies, the warrant binds the property in the goods from the time when it is received by the person who is under a duty to endorse it under that section.

(4) Where sub-paragraphs (2) and (3) do not apply but notice is given to the debtor under paragraph 7(1), the notice binds the property in the goods from the time when the notice is given.

Commencement—Tribunals, Courts and Enforcement Act 2007 (Commencement No 11) Order, SI 2014/768 art 2(1)(*b*) (Sch 12 comes into force on 6 April 2014).

Effect of property in goods being bound

5—(1) An assignment or transfer of any interest of the debtor's in goods while the property in them is bound for the purposes of an enforcement power—

(*a*) is subject to that power, and

(*b*) does not affect the operation of this Schedule in relation to the goods, except as provided by paragraph 61 (application to assignee or transferee).

(2) Sub-paragraph (1) does not prejudice the title to any of the debtor's goods that a person acquires—

(*a*) in good faith,

(*b*) for valuable consideration, and

(*c*) without notice.

(3) For the purposes of sub-paragraph (2)(*a*), a thing is to be treated as done in good faith if it is in fact done honestly (whether it is done negligently or not).

(4) In sub-paragraph (2)(*c*) "notice" means—

(*a*) where the property in the goods is bound by a writ or warrant, notice that the writ or warrant, or any other writ or warrant by virtue of which the goods of the debtor might be seized or otherwise taken control of, had been received by the person who was under a duty to endorse it and that goods remained bound under it;

(*b*) where the property in the goods is bound by notice under paragraph 7(1), notice that that notice had been given and that goods remained bound under it.

(5) In sub-paragraph (4)(*a*) "endorse" in relation to a warrant to which section 99 of the County Courts Act 1984 (c 28) or section 125ZA of the Magistrates' Courts Act 1980 (c 43) applies, means endorse under that section.

Commencement—Tribunals, Courts and Enforcement Act 2007 (Commencement No 11) Order, SI 2014/768 art 2(1)(*b*) (Sch 12 comes into force on 6 April 2014).

Time when property ceases to be bound

6—(1) For the purposes of any enforcement power the property in goods of the debtor ceases to be bound in accordance with this paragraph.

(2) The property in any goods ceases to be bound—

(*a*) when the goods are sold;

(*b*) in the case of money used to pay any of the amount outstanding, when it is used.

(3) The property in all goods ceases to be bound when any of these happens—

(*a*) the amount outstanding is paid, out of the proceeds of sale or otherwise;

(*b*) the instrument under which the power is exercisable ceases to have effect;

(*c*) the power ceases to be exercisable for any other reason.

Commencement—Tribunals, Courts and Enforcement Act 2007 (Commencement No 11) Order, SI 2014/768 art 2(1)(*b*) (Sch 12 comes into force on 6 April 2014).

Notice of enforcement

7—(1) An enforcement agent may not take control of goods unless the debtor has been given notice.

(2) Regulations must state—

(*a*) the minimum period of notice;

(*b*) the form of the notice;

(*c*) what it must contain;

(*d*) how it must be given;

(*e*) who must give it.

(3) The enforcement agent must keep a record of the time when the notice is given.

(4) If regulations authorise it, the court may order in prescribed circumstances that the notice given may be less than the minimum period.

(5) The order may be subject to conditions.

Commencement—Tribunals, Courts and Enforcement Act 2007 (Commencement No 9) Order, SI 2013/1739 art 3 (para 7(2), (4) comes into force on 15 July 2013 for the purpose only of exercising any power to make regulations).
Tribunals, Courts and Enforcement Act 2007 (Commencement No 11) Order, SI 2014/768 art 2(1)(*b*) (this para comes into force on 6 April 2014 for all other purposes).

Time limit for taking control

8—(1) An enforcement agent may not take control of goods after the prescribed period.

(2) The period may be prescribed by reference to the date of notice of enforcement or of any writ or warrant conferring the enforcement power or any other date.

(3) Regulations may provide for the period to be extended or further extended by the court in accordance with the regulations.

Commencement—Tribunals, Courts and Enforcement Act 2007 (Commencement No 9) Order, SI 2013/1739 art 3 (para 8 comes into force on 15 July 2013 for the purpose only of exercising any power to make regulations).
Tribunals, Courts and Enforcement Act 2007 (Commencement No 11) Order, SI 2014/768 art 2(1)(*b*) (this para comes into force on 6 April 2014 for all other purposes).

Goods which may be taken

9 An enforcement agent may take control of goods only if they are—

(*a*) on premises that he has power to enter under this Schedule, or

(*b*) on a highway.

Commencement—Tribunals, Courts and Enforcement Act 2007 (Commencement No 11) Order, SI 2014/768 art 2(1)(*b*) (Sch 12 comes into force on 6 April 2014).

10 An enforcement agent may take control of goods only if they are goods of the debtor.

Commencement—Tribunals, Courts and Enforcement Act 2007 (Commencement No 11) Order, SI 2014/768 art 2(1)(*b*) (Sch 12 comes into force on 6 April 2014).

11—(1) Subject to paragraphs 9 and 10 and to any other enactment under which goods are protected, an enforcement agent—

(*a*) may take control of goods anywhere in England and Wales;

(*b*) may take control of any goods that are not exempt.

(2) Regulations may authorise him to take control of exempt goods in prescribed circumstances, if he provides the debtor with replacements in accordance with the regulations.

Commencement—Tribunals, Courts and Enforcement Act 2007 (Commencement No 9) Order, SI 2013/1739 art 3 (para 11(2) comes into force on 15 July 2013 for the purpose only of exercising any power to make regulations).
Tribunals, Courts and Enforcement Act 2007 (Commencement No 11) Order, SI 2014/768 art 2(1)(*b*) (this para comes into force on 6 April 2014 for all other purposes).

Value of goods taken

12 (1) Unless sub-paragraph (2) applies, an enforcement agent may not take control of goods whose aggregate value is more than—

(*a*) the amount outstanding, and

(*b*) an amount in respect of future costs, calculated in accordance with regulations.

(2) An enforcement agent may take control of goods of higher value on premises or on a highway, only to the extent necessary, if there are not enough goods of a lower value within a reasonable distance—

(*a*) on a highway, or

(*b*) on premises that he has power to enter under this Schedule, either under paragraph 14 or under an existing warrant.

(3) For the purposes of this paragraph goods are above a given value only if it is or ought to be clear to the enforcement agent that they are.

(4) Sub-paragraph (1) does not affect the power to keep control of goods if they rise in value once they have been taken.

Commencement—Tribunals, Courts and Enforcement Act 2007 (Commencement No 9) Order, SI 2013/1739 art 3 (para 12(1) comes into force on 15 July 2013 for the purpose only of exercising any power to make regulations).
Tribunals, Courts and Enforcement Act 2007 (Commencement No 11) Order, SI 2014/768 art 2(1)(*b*) (this para comes into force on 6 April 2014 for all other purposes).

Ways of taking control

13—(1) To take control of goods an enforcement agent must do one of the following—

(*a*) secure the goods on the premises on which he finds them;

(*b*) if he finds them on a highway, secure them on a highway, where he finds them or within a reasonable distance;

(*c*) remove them and secure them elsewhere;

(*d*) enter into a controlled goods agreement with the debtor.

(2) Any liability of an enforcement agent (including criminal liability) arising out of his securing goods on a highway under this paragraph is excluded to the extent that he acted with reasonable care.

(3) Regulations may make further provision about taking control in any of the ways listed in sub-paragraph (1), including provision—

(*a*) determining the time when control is taken;

(*b*) prohibiting use of any of those ways for goods by description or circumstances or both.

(4) A controlled goods agreement is an agreement under which the debtor—

(*a*) is permitted to retain custody of the goods,

(*b*) acknowledges that the enforcement agent is taking control of them, and

(*c*) agrees not to remove or dispose of them, nor to permit anyone else to, before the debt is paid.

Commencement—Tribunals, Courts and Enforcement Act 2007 (Commencement No 9) Order, SI 2013/1739 art 3 (para 13(3) comes into force on 15 July 2013 for the purpose only of exercising any power to make regulations).
Tribunals, Courts and Enforcement Act 2007 (Commencement No 11) Order, SI 2014/768 art 2(1)(*b*) (this para comes into force on 6 April 2014 for all other purposes).

Entry without warrant

14—(1) An enforcement agent may enter relevant premises to search for and take control of goods.

(2) Where there are different relevant premises this paragraph authorises entry to each of them.

(3) This paragraph authorises repeated entry to the same premises, subject to any restriction in regulations.

(4) If the enforcement agent is acting under section 72(1) (CRAR), the only relevant premises are the demised premises.

(5) . . . [1]

(6) Otherwise premises are relevant if the enforcement agent reasonably believes that they are the place, or one of the places, where the debtor—

(*a*) usually lives, or

(*b*) carries on a trade or business.

Commencement—Tribunals, Courts and Enforcement Act 2007 (Commencement No 9) Order, SI 2013/1739 art 3 (para 14(3) comes into force on 15 July 2013 for the purpose only of exercising any power to make regulations).

Tribunals, Courts and Enforcement Act 2007 (Commencement No 11) Order, SI 2014/768 art 2(1)(*b*) (this para comes into force on 6 April 2014 for all other purposes).

Amendments—[1] Sub-s (5) repealed by FA 2008 s 129, Sch 43 para 10(2) with effect from 6 April 2014 (by virtue of SI 2014/906 art 2).

Entry under warrant

15—(1) If an enforcement agent applies to the court it may issue a warrant authorising him to enter specified premises to search for and take control of goods.

(2) Before issuing the warrant the court must be satisfied that all these conditions are met—

(*a*) an enforcement power has become exercisable;

(*b*) there is reason to believe that there are goods on the premises that the enforcement power will be exercisable to take control of if the warrant is issued;

(*c*) it is reasonable in all the circumstances to issue the warrant.

(3) The warrant authorises repeated entry to the same premises, subject to any restriction in regulations.

Commencement—Tribunals, Courts and Enforcement Act 2007 (Commencement No 9) Order, SI 2013/1739 art 3 (para 15(3) comes into force on 15 July 2013 for the purpose only of exercising any power to make regulations).

Tribunals, Courts and Enforcement Act 2007 (Commencement No 11) Order, SI 2014/768 art 2(1)(*b*) (this para comes into force on 6 April 2014 for all other purposes).

Re-entry

16—(1) This paragraph applies where goods on any premises have been taken control of and have not been removed by the enforcement agent.

(2) The enforcement agent may enter the premises to inspect the goods or to remove them for storage or sale.

(3) This paragraph authorises repeated entry to the same premises.

General powers to use reasonable force

17 Where paragraph 18 [, 18A, 19 or 19A][1] applies, an enforcement agent may if necessary use reasonable force to enter premises or to do anything for which the entry is authorised.

Commencement—Tribunals, Courts and Enforcement Act 2007 (Commencement No 11) Order, SI 2014/768 art 2(1)(*b*) (Sch 12 comes into force on 6 April 2014).

Amendments—[1] Words substituted by the Crime and Courts Act 2013 s 25(1), (2) with effect from 6 April 2014 (by virtue of SI 2014/830 art 2).

18 This paragraph applies if these conditions are met—

(*a*) the enforcement agent has power to enter the premises under paragraph 14 or 16 or under a warrant under paragraph 15;

(*b*) he is acting under an enforcement power conferred by a warrant of control under section 76(1) of the Magistrates' Courts Act 1980 (c 43) for the recovery of a sum adjudged to be paid by a conviction;

(*c*) he is entitled to execute the warrant by virtue of section 125A (civilian enforcement officers) or 125B (approved enforcement agencies) of that Act.

Commencement—Tribunals, Courts and Enforcement Act 2007 (Commencement No. 11) Order, SI 2014/768 art 2(1)(*b*) (Sch 12 comes into force on 6 April 2014).

[18A (1) This paragraph applies if these conditions are met—

(*a*) the enforcement agent has power to enter the premises under paragraph 14;

(*b*) the enforcement agent reasonably believes that the debtor carries on a trade or business on the premises;

(*c*) the enforcement agent is acting under a writ or warrant of control issued for the purpose of recovering a sum payable under a High Court or county court judgment;

(*d*) the sum so payable is not a traffic contravention debt.

(2) "Traffic contravention debt" has the meaning given by section 82(2) of the Traffic Management Act 2004.][1]

Commencement—Tribunals, Courts and Enforcement Act 2007 (Commencement No 11) Order, SI 2014/768 art 2(1)(*b*) (Sch 12 comes into force on 6 April 2014).

Amendments—[1] This para inserted by the Crime and Courts Act 2013 s 25(1), (3) with effect from 6 April 2014 (by virtue of SI 2014/830 art 2).

19—(1) This paragraph applies if these conditions are met—

(*a*) the enforcement agent has power to enter the premises under paragraph 16;

(*b*) he reasonably believes that the debtor carries on a trade or business on the premises;

(*c*) he is acting under an enforcement power within sub-paragraph (2).

(2) The enforcement powers are those under any of the following—

(*a*) a writ or warrant of control issued for the purpose of recovering a sum payable under a High Court or county court judgment;

[(*b*) section 127 of the Finance Act 2008.][1]

Commencement—Tribunals, Courts and Enforcement Act 2007 (Commencement No 11) Order, SI 2014/768 art 2(1)(*b*) (Sch 12 comes into force on 6 April 2014).

Amendments—[1] Sub-para (2)(*b*) substituted for former paras (*b*)–(*e*) by FA 2008 s 129, Sch 43 para 10(3) with effect from 6 April 2014 (by virtue of SI 2014/906 art 2).

[19A (1) This paragraph applies if these conditions are met

(a) the enforcement agent has power to enter the premises under paragraph 16;

(b) the enforcement agent has taken control of the goods by entering into a controlled goods agreement with the debtor;

(c) the debtor has failed to comply with any provision of the controlled goods agreement relating to the payment by the debtor of the debt;

(d) the debtor has been given notice of the intention of the enforcement agent to enter the premises to inspect the goods or to remove them for storage or sale;

(e) neither paragraph 18 nor paragraph 19 applies.

(2) For the purposes of a notice under sub-paragraph (1)(d), regulations must state—

(a) the minimum period of notice;

(b) the form of the notice;

(c) what it must contain;

(d) how it must be given;

(e) who must give it.

(3) The enforcement agent must keep a record of the time when a notice under sub-paragraph (1)(d) is given.

(4) If regulations authorise it, the court may order in prescribed circumstances that the notice given may be less than the minimum period.

(5) The order may be subject to conditions.][1]

Commencement—Tribunals, Courts and Enforcement Act 2007 (Commencement No 11) Order, SI 2014/768 art 2(1)(*b*) (Sch 12 comes into force on 6 April 2014).

Amendments—[1] Para 19A inserted by the Crime and Courts Act 2013 s 25(1), (4)—

– for the purposes of making regulations, with effect from 15 July 2013 (by virtue of SI 2013/1725 art 2(*c*)); and

– for all other purposes, with effect from a date to be appointed.

Application for power to use reasonable force

20—(1) This paragraph applies if an enforcement agent has power to enter premises under paragraph 14 or 16 or under a warrant under paragraph 15.

(2) If the enforcement agent applies to the court it may issue a warrant which authorises him to use, if necessary, reasonable force to enter the premises or to do anything for which entry is authorised.

Commencement—Tribunals, Courts and Enforcement Act 2007 (Commencement No 11) Order, SI 2014/768 art 2(1)(*b*) (Sch 12 comes into force on 6 April 2014).

21—(1) This paragraph applies if an enforcement agent is applying for power to enter premises under a warrant under paragraph 15.

(2) If the enforcement agent applies to the court it may include in the warrant provision authorising him to use, if necessary, reasonable force to enter the premises or to do anything for which entry is authorised.

Commencement—Tribunals, Courts and Enforcement Act 2007 (Commencement No 11) Order, SI 2014/768 art 2(1)(*b*) (Sch 12 comes into force on 6 April 2014 for all other purposes).

22—(1) The court may not issue a warrant under paragraph 20 or include provision under paragraph 21 unless it is satisfied that prescribed conditions are met.

(2) A warrant under paragraph 20 or provision included under paragraph 21 may require any constable to assist the enforcement agent to execute the warrant.

Commencement—Tribunals, Courts and Enforcement Act 2007 (Commencement No 9) Order, SI 2013/1739 art 3 (para 22(1) comes into force on 15 July 2013 for the purpose only of exercising any power to make regulations).

Tribunals, Courts and Enforcement Act 2007 (Commencement No 11) Order, SI 2014/768 art 2(1)(*b*) (this para comes into force on 6 April 2014 for all other purposes).

Other provisions about powers of entry

23 Paragraphs 24 to 30 apply where an enforcement agent has power to enter premises under paragraph 14 or 16 or under a warrant under paragraph 15.

24—(1) The power to enter and any power to use force are subject to any restriction imposed by or under regulations.

(2) A power to use force does not include power to use force against persons . . . [1].

Commencement—Tribunals, Courts and Enforcement Act 2007 (Commencement No 9) Order, SI 2013/1739 art 3 (para 24(1) comes into force on 15 July 2013 for the purpose only of exercising any power to make regulations).

Tribunals, Courts and Enforcement Act 2007 (Commencement No 11) Order, SI 2014/768 art 2(1)(*b*) (this para comes into force on 6 April 2014 for all other purposes).

Amendments—[1] In sub-para (2), words ", except to the extent that regulations provide that it does" repealed by the Crime and Courts Act 2013 s 25(1), (5) with effect from 15 July 2013 (by virtue of SI 2013/1725 art 2(*d*)).

25—(1) The enforcement agent may enter and remain on the premises only within prescribed times of day.

(2) Regulations may give the court power in prescribed circumstances to authorise him to enter or remain on the premises at other times.

(3) The authorisation—

(*a*) may be by order or in a warrant under paragraph 15;

(*b*) may be subject to conditions.

Commencement—Tribunals, Courts and Enforcement Act 2007 (Commencement No 9) Order, SI 2013/1739 art 3 (para 25(1), (2) comes into force on 15 July 2013 for the purpose only of exercising any power to make regulations).

Tribunals, Courts and Enforcement Act 2007 (Commencement No 11) Order, SI 2014/768 art 2(1)(*b*) (this para comes into force on 6 April 2014 for all other purposes).

26—(1) The enforcement agent must on request show the debtor and any person who appears to him to be in charge of the premises evidence of—

(*a*) his identity, and

(*b*) his authority to enter the premises.

(2) The request may be made before the enforcement agent enters the premises or while he is there.

Commencement—Tribunals, Courts and Enforcement Act 2007 (Commencement No 11) Order, SI 2014/768 art 2(1)(*b*) (Sch 12 comes into force on 6 April 2014).

27—(1) The enforcement agent may take other people onto the premises.

(2) They may assist him in exercising any power, including a power to use force.

(3) They must not remain on the premises without the enforcement agent.

(4) The enforcement agent may take any equipment onto the premises.

(5) He may leave equipment on the premises if he leaves controlled goods there.

Commencement—Tribunals, Courts and Enforcement Act 2007 (Commencement No 11) Order, SI 2014/768 art 2(1)(*b*) (Sch 12 comes into force on 6 April 2014).

28—(1) After entering the premises the enforcement agent must provide a notice for the debtor giving information about what the enforcement agent is doing.

(2) Regulations must state—

(*a*) the form of the notice;

(*b*) what information it must give.

(3) Regulations may prescribe circumstances in which a notice need not be provided after re-entry to premises.

(4) If the debtor is on the premises when the enforcement agent is there, the enforcement agent must give him the notice then.

(5) If the debtor is not there, the enforcement agent must leave the notice in a conspicuous place on the premises.

(6) If the enforcement agent knows that there is someone else there or that there are other occupiers, a notice he leaves under sub-paragraph (5) must be in a sealed envelope addressed to the debtor.

Commencement—Tribunals, Courts and Enforcement Act 2007 (Commencement No 9) Order, SI 2013/1739 art 3 (para 28(2), (3) comes into force on 15 July 2013 for the purpose only of exercising any power to make regulations).

Tribunals, Courts and Enforcement Act 2007 (Commencement No 11) Order, SI 2014/768 art 2(1)(*b*) (this para comes into force on 6 April 2014 for all other purposes).

29 If the premises are occupied by any person apart from the debtor, the enforcement agent must leave at the premises a list of any goods he takes away.

Commencement—Tribunals, Courts and Enforcement Act 2007 (Commencement No 11) Order, SI 2014/768 art 2(1)(*b*) (Sch 12 comes into force on 6 April 2014).

30 The enforcement agent must leave the premises as effectively secured as he finds them.

Commencement—Tribunals, Courts and Enforcement Act 2007 (Commencement No 11) Order, SI 2014/768 art 2(1)(*b*) (Sch 12 comes into force on 6 April 2014).

Goods on a highway

31—(1) If the enforcement agent applies to the court it may issue a warrant which authorises him to use, if necessary, reasonable force to take control of goods on a highway.

(2) The court may not issue a warrant unless it is satisfied that prescribed conditions are met.

(3) The warrant may require any constable to assist the enforcement agent to execute it.

(4) The power to use force is subject to any restriction imposed by or under regulations.

(5) The power to use force does not include power to use force against persons . . . [1]

Commencement—Tribunals, Courts and Enforcement Act 2007 (Commencement No 9) Order, SI 2013/1739 art 3 (para 31(2), (4) comes into force on 15 July 2013 for the purpose only of exercising any power to make regulations).
Tribunals, Courts and Enforcement Act 2007 (Commencement No 11) Order, SI 2014/768 art 2(1)(*b*) (this para comes into force on 6 April 2014 for all other purposes).

Amendments—[1] In sub-para (5), words ", except to the extent that regulations provide that it does" repealed by the Crime and Courts Act 2013 s 25(1), (5) with effect from 15 July 2013 (by virtue of SI 2013/1725 art 2(*d*)).

32—(1) The enforcement agent may not exercise any power under this Schedule on a highway except within prescribed times of day.

(2) Regulations may give the court power in prescribed circumstances to authorise him to exercise a power at other times.

(3) The authorisation may be subject to conditions.

Commencement—Tribunals, Courts and Enforcement Act 2007 (Commencement No 9) Order, SI 2013/1739 art 3 (para 31(1), (2) comes into force on 15 July 2013 for the purpose only of exercising any power to make regulations).
Tribunals, Courts and Enforcement Act 2007 (Commencement No 11) Order, SI 2014/768 art 2(1)(*b*) (this para comes into force on 6 April 2014 for all remaining purposes).

33—(1) If the enforcement agent takes control of goods on a highway or enters a vehicle on a highway with the intention of taking control of goods, he must provide a notice for the debtor giving information about what he is doing.

(2) Regulations must state—

(*a*) the form of the notice;

(*b*) what information it must give.

(3) If the debtor is present when the enforcement agent is there, the enforcement agent must give him the notice then.

(4) Otherwise the enforcement agent must deliver the notice to any relevant premises (as defined by paragraph 14) in a sealed envelope addressed to the debtor.

Commencement—Tribunals, Courts and Enforcement Act 2007 (Commencement No 9) Order, SI 2013/1739 art 3 (para 33(2) comes into force on 15 July 2013 for the purpose only of exercising any power to make regulations).
Tribunals, Courts and Enforcement Act 2007 (Commencement No 11) Order, SI 2014/768 art 2(1)(*b*) (this para comes into force on 6 April 2014 for all other purposes).

Inventory

34—(1) If an enforcement agent takes control of goods he must provide the debtor with an inventory of them as soon as reasonably practicable.

(2) But if there are co-owners of any of the goods, the enforcement agent must instead provide the debtor as soon as reasonably practicable with separate inventories of goods owned by the debtor and each co-owner and an inventory of the goods without a co-owner.

(3) The enforcement agent must as soon as reasonably practicable provide the co-owner of any of the goods with—

(*a*) the inventory of those goods, and

(*b*) a copy of the notice under paragraph 28.

(4) Regulations must state—

(*a*) the form of an inventory, and

(*b*) what it must contain.

Commencement—Tribunals, Courts and Enforcement Act 2007 (Commencement No 9) Order, SI 2013/1739 art 3 (para 34(4) comes into force on 15 July 2013 for the purpose only of exercising any power to make regulations).
Tribunals, Courts and Enforcement Act 2007 (Commencement No 11) Order, SI 2014/768 art 2(1)(*b*) (this para comes into force on 6 April 2014 for all remaining purposes).

Care of goods removed

35—(1) An enforcement agent must take reasonable care of controlled goods that he removes from the premises or highway where he finds them.
(2) He must comply with any provision of regulations about their care while they remain controlled goods.

Commencement—Tribunals, Courts and Enforcement Act 2007 (Commencement No 9) Order, SI 2013/1739 art 3 (para 35(2) comes into force on 15 July 2013 for the purpose only of exercising any power to make regulations).
Tribunals, Courts and Enforcement Act 2007 (Commencement No 11) Order, SI 2014/768 art 2(1)(*b*) (this para comes into force on 6 April 2014 for all remaining purposes).

Valuation

36—(1) Before the end of the minimum period, the enforcement agent must—
(*a*) make or obtain a valuation of the controlled goods in accordance with regulations;
(*b*) give the debtor, and separately any co-owner, an opportunity to obtain an independent valuation of the goods.
(2) In this paragraph "minimum period" means the period specified by regulations under—
(*a*) paragraph 49, in the case of securities;
(*b*) paragraph 39, in any other case.

Commencement—Tribunals, Courts and Enforcement Act 2007 (Commencement No 9) Order, SI 2013/1739 art 3 (para 36 comes into force on 15 July 2013 for the purpose only of exercising any power to make regulations).
Tribunals, Courts and Enforcement Act 2007 (Commencement No 11) Order, SI 2014/768 art 2(1)(*b*) (this para comes into force on 6 April 2014).

Best price

37—(1) An enforcement agent must sell or dispose of controlled goods for the best price that can reasonably be obtained in accordance with this Schedule.
(2) That does not apply to money that can be used for paying any of the outstanding amount, unless the best price is more than its value if used in that way.

Commencement—Tribunals, Courts and Enforcement Act 2007 (Commencement No 11) Order, SI 2014/768 art 2(1)(*b*) (Sch 12 comes into force on 6 April 2014).

Sale

38 Paragraphs 39 to 42 apply to the sale of controlled goods, except where—
(*a*) the controlled goods are securities, or
(*b*) the sale is by exchange of one currency for another.

Commencement—Tribunals, Courts and Enforcement Act 2007 (Commencement No 11) Order, SI 2014/768 art 2(1)(*b*) (Sch 12 comes into force on 6 April 2014).

39—(1) The sale must not be before the end of the minimum period except with the agreement of the debtor and any co-owner.
(2) Regulations must specify the minimum period.

Commencement—Tribunals, Courts and Enforcement Act 2007 (Commencement No 9) Order, SI 2013/1739 art 3 (para 39(2) comes into force on 15 July 2013 for the purpose only of exercising any power to make regulations).
Tribunals, Courts and Enforcement Act 2007 (Commencement No 11) Order, SI 2014/768 art 2(1)(*b*) (this para comes into force on 6 April 2014 for all remaining purposes).

40—(1) Before the sale, the enforcement agent must give notice of the date, time and place of the sale to the debtor and any co-owner.
(2) Regulations must state—
(*a*) the minimum period of notice;
(*b*) the form of the notice;
(*c*) what it must contain (besides the date, time and place of sale);
(*d*) how it must be given.
(3) The enforcement agent may replace a notice with a new notice, subject to any restriction in regulations.
(4) Any notice must be given within the permitted period.
(5) Unless extended the permitted period is 12 months beginning with the day on which the enforcement agent takes control of the goods.
(6) Any extension must be by agreement in writing between the creditor and debtor before the end of the period.
(7) They may extend the period more than once.

Commencement—Tribunals, Courts and Enforcement Act 2007 (Commencement No 9) Order, SI 2013/1739 art 3 (para 40(2), (3) comes into force on 15 July 2013 for the purpose only of exercising any power to make regulations).

Tribunals, Courts and Enforcement Act 2007 (Commencement No 11) Order, SI 2014/768 art 2(1)(*b*) (this para comes into force on 6 April 2014 for all remaining purposes).

41—(1) The sale must be by public auction unless the court orders otherwise.
(2) The court may make an order only on an application by the enforcement agent.
(3) Regulations may make provision about the types of sale the court may order.
(4) In an application for an order under sub-paragraph (2) the enforcement agent must state whether he has reason to believe that an enforcement power has become exercisable by another creditor against the debtor or a co-owner.
(5) If the enforcement agent states that he does, the court may not consider the application until notice of it has been given to the other creditor in accordance with regulations (or until the court is satisfied that an enforcement power is not exercisable by the other creditor against the debtor or a co-owner).

Commencement—Tribunals, Courts and Enforcement Act 2007 (Commencement No 9) Order, SI 2013/1739 art 3 (para 41(3), (5) comes into force on 15 July 2013 for the purpose only of exercising any power to make regulations).
Tribunals, Courts and Enforcement Act 2007 (Commencement No 11) Order, SI 2014/768 art 2(1)(*b*) (this para comes into force on 6 April 2014 for all remaining purposes).

42 Regulations may make further provision about the sale of controlled goods, including in particular—

(*a*) requirements for advertising;
(*b*) provision about the conduct of a sale.

Commencement—Tribunals, Courts and Enforcement Act 2007 (Commencement No 9) Order, SI 2013/1739 art 3 (para 42 comes into force on 15 July 2013 for the purpose only of exercising any power to make regulations).
Tribunals, Courts and Enforcement Act 2007 (Commencement No 11) Order, SI 2014/768 art 2(1)(*b*) (this para comes into force on 6 April 2014 for all remaining purposes).

Place of sale

43—(1) Regulations may make provision about the place of sale of controlled goods.
(2) They may prescribe circumstances in which the sale may be held on premises where goods were found by the enforcement agent.
(3) Except where the regulations provide otherwise, the sale may not be held on those premises without the consent of the occupier.
(4) Paragraphs 44 to 46 apply if the sale may be held on those premises.

Commencement—Tribunals, Courts and Enforcement Act 2007 (Commencement No 9) Order, SI 2013/1739 art 3 (para 43(1)–(3) comes into force on 15 July 2013 for the purpose only of exercising any power to make regulations).
Tribunals, Courts and Enforcement Act 2007 (Commencement No 11) Order, SI 2014/768 art 2(1)(*b*) (this para comes into force on 6 April 2014 for all remaining purposes).

44—(1) The enforcement agent and any person permitted by him—

(*a*) may enter the premises to conduct or attend the sale;
(*b*) may bring equipment onto the premises for the purposes of the sale.

(2) This paragraph authorises repeated entry to the premises.
(3) If necessary the enforcement agent may use reasonable force to enable the sale to be conducted and any person to enter under this paragraph.

Commencement—Tribunals, Courts and Enforcement Act 2007 (Commencement No 11) Order, SI 2014/768 art 2(1)(*b*) (Sch 12 comes into force on 6 April 2014).

45—(1) The enforcement agent must on request show the debtor and any person who appears to him to be in charge of the premises evidence of—

(*a*) his identity, and
(*b*) his authority to enter and hold the sale on the premises.

(2) The request may be made before the enforcement agent enters the premises or while he is there.

Commencement—Tribunals, Courts and Enforcement Act 2007 (Commencement No 11) Order, SI 2014/768 art 2(1)(*b*) (Sch 12 comes into force on 6 April 2014).

46 The enforcement agent must leave the premises as effectively secured as he finds them.

Commencement—Tribunals, Courts and Enforcement Act 2007 (Commencement No 11) Order, SI 2014/768 art 2(1)(*b*) (Sch 12 comes into force on 6 April 2014).

Holding and disposal of securities

47 Paragraphs 48 and 49 apply to securities as controlled goods.

Commencement—Tribunals, Courts and Enforcement Act 2007 (Commencement No 11) Order, SI 2014/768 art 2(1)(*b*) (Sch 12 comes into force on 6 April 2014).

48—(1) Regulations may make provision about how securities are to be held and disposed of.

(2) In this Schedule, references to disposal include, in relation to securities, realising the sums secured or made payable by them, suing for the recovery of those sums or assigning the right to sue for their recovery.

(3) Regulations may in particular make provision for purposes corresponding to those for which provision is made in this Schedule in relation to the disposal of other controlled goods.

(4) The power to make regulations under this paragraph is subject to paragraph 49.

Commencement—Tribunals, Courts and Enforcement Act 2007 (Commencement No 9) Order, SI 2013/1739 art 3 (para 48 comes into force on 15 July 2013 for the purpose only of exercising any power to make regulations).
Tribunals, Courts and Enforcement Act 2007 (Commencement No 11) Order, SI 2014/768 art 2(1)(*b*) (this para comes into force on 6 April 2014 for all remaining purposes).

49—(1) The creditor may sue in the name of the debtor, or in the name of any person in whose name the debtor might have sued, for the recovery of any sum secured or made payable by securities, when the time of payment arrives.

(2) Before any proceedings under sub-paragraph (1) are commenced or the securities are otherwise disposed of, the enforcement agent must give notice of the disposal to the debtor and any co-owner.

(3) Regulations must state—

(*a*) the minimum period of notice;

(*b*) the form of the notice;

(*c*) what it must contain;

(*d*) how it must be given.

(4) The enforcement agent may replace a notice with a new notice, subject to any restriction in regulations.

(5) Any notice must be given within the permitted period.

(6) Unless extended the permitted period is 12 months beginning with the time of payment.

(7) Any extension must be by agreement in writing between the creditor and debtor before the end of the period.

(8) They may extend the period more than once.

Commencement—Tribunals, Courts and Enforcement Act 2007 (Commencement No 9) Order, SI 2013/1739 art 3 (para 49(3), (4) comes into force on 15 July 2013 for the purpose only of exercising any power to make regulations).
Tribunals, Courts and Enforcement Act 2007 (Commencement No 11) Order, SI 2014/768 art 2(1)(*b*) (this para comes into force on 6 April 2014 for all remaining purposes).

Application of proceeds

50—(1) Proceeds from the exercise of an enforcement power must be used to pay the amount outstanding.

(2) Proceeds are any of these—

(*a*) proceeds of sale or disposal of controlled goods;

(*b*) money taken in exercise of the power, if paragraph 37(1) does not apply to it.

(3) The amount outstanding is the sum of these—

(*a*) the amount of the debt which remains unpaid (or an amount that the creditor agrees to accept in full satisfaction of the debt);

(*b*) any amounts recoverable out of proceeds in accordance with regulations under paragraph 62 (costs).

(4) If the proceeds are less than the amount outstanding, which amounts in sub-paragraph (3)(*a*) and (*b*) must be paid, and how much of any amount, is to be determined in accordance with regulations.

(5) If the proceeds are more than the amount outstanding, the surplus must be paid to the debtor.

(6) If there is a co-owner of any of the goods, the enforcement agent must—

(*a*) first pay the co-owner a share of the proceeds of those goods proportionate to his interest;

(*b*) then deal with the rest of the proceeds under sub-paragraphs (1) to (5).

(7) Regulations may make provision for resolving disputes about what share is due under sub-paragraph (6)(*a*).

Commencement—Tribunals, Courts and Enforcement Act 2007 (Commencement No 9) Order, SI 2013/1739 art 3 (para 50(3), (4), (7) comes into force on 15 July 2013 for the purpose only of exercising any power to make regulations).
Tribunals, Courts and Enforcement Act 2007 (Commencement No 11) Order, SI 2014/768 art 2(1)(*b*) (this para comes into force on 6 April 2014 for all remaining purposes).

Passing of title

51—(1) A purchaser of controlled goods acquires good title, with two exceptions.

(2) The exceptions apply only if the goods are not the debtor's at the time of sale.

(3) The first exception is where the purchaser, the creditor, the enforcement agent or a related party has notice that the goods are not the debtor's.

(4) The second exception is where a lawful claimant has already made an application to the court claiming an interest in the goods.

(5) A lawful claimant in relation to goods is a person who has an interest in them at the time of sale, other than an interest that was assigned or transferred to him while the property in the goods was bound for the purposes of the enforcement power.
(6) A related party is any person who acts in exercise of an enforcement power, other than the creditor or enforcement agent.
(7) "The court" has the same meaning as in paragraph 60.

Commencement—Tribunals, Courts and Enforcement Act 2007 (Commencement No 11) Order, SI 2014/768 art 2(1)(*b*) (Sch 12 comes into force on 6 April 2014).

Orders—Transfer of Tribunal Functions (Lands Tribunal and Miscellaneous Amendments) Order 2009, SI 2009/1307 (made under sub-s (1)).

Abandonment of goods other than securities

52 Paragraphs 53 and 54 apply to controlled goods other than—
(*a*) securities;
(*b*) money to which paragraph 37(1) does not apply.

Commencement—Tribunals, Courts and Enforcement Act 2007 (Commencement No 11) Order, SI 2014/768 art 2(1)(*b*) (Sch 12 comes into force on 6 April 2014).

53—(1) Controlled goods are abandoned if the enforcement agent does not give the debtor or any co-owner notice under paragraph 40 (notice of sale) within the permitted period.
(2) . . . [1]

Commencement—Tribunals, Courts and Enforcement Act 2007 (Commencement No 9) Order, SI 2013/1739 art 3 (para 53(3) comes into force on 15 July 2013 for the purpose only of exercising any power to make regulations).
Tribunals, Courts and Enforcement Act 2007 (Commencement No 11) Order, SI 2014/768 art 2(1)(*b*) (this para comes into force on 6 April 2014 for all remaining purposes).

Amendments—[1] Sub-para (2) repealed by the Crime and Courts Act 2013 s 25(1), (6) with effect from 6 April 2014 (by virtue of SI 2014/830 art 2).

(3) Regulations may prescribe other circumstances in which controlled goods are abandoned.

54—(1) If controlled goods are abandoned then, in relation to the enforcement power concerned, the following apply—
(*a*) the enforcement power ceases to be exercisable;
(*b*) as soon as reasonably practicable the enforcement agent must make the goods available for collection by the debtor, if he removed them from where he found them.
(2) Regulations may make further provision about arrangements under sub-paragraph (1)(*b*), including in particular provision about the disposal of goods uncollected after a prescribed period.
(3) Where the enforcement power was under a writ or warrant, sub-paragraph (1) does not affect any power to issue another writ or warrant.

Commencement—Tribunals, Courts and Enforcement Act 2007 (Commencement No 9) Order, SI 2013/1739 art 3 (para 54(2) comes into force on 15 July 2013 for the purpose only of exercising any power to make regulations).
Tribunals, Courts and Enforcement Act 2007 (Commencement No 11) Order, SI 2014/768 art 2(1)(*b*) (this para comes into force on 6 April 2014 for all remaining purposes).

Abandonment of securities

55 Paragraphs 56 and 57 apply to securities as controlled goods.

Commencement—Tribunals, Courts and Enforcement Act 2007 (Commencement No 11) Order, SI 2014/768 art 2(1)(*b*) (Sch 12 comes into force on 6 April 2014).

56—(1) Securities are abandoned if the enforcement agent does not give the debtor or any co-owner notice under paragraph 49 (notice of disposal) within the permitted period.
(2) . . . [1].
(3) Regulations may prescribe other circumstances in which securities are abandoned.

Commencement—Tribunals, Courts and Enforcement Act 2007 (Commencement No 9) Order, SI 2013/1739 art 3 (para 56(3) comes into force on 15 July 2013 for the purpose only of exercising any power to make regulations).
Tribunals, Courts and Enforcement Act 2007 (Commencement No. 11) Order, SI 2014/768 art 2(1)(*b*) (this para comes into force on 6 April 2014 for all remaining purposes).

Amendments—[1] Sub-para (2) repealed by the Crime and Courts Act 2013 s 25(1), (7) with effect from 6 April 2014 (by virtue of SI 2014/830 art 2).

57—(1) If securities are abandoned then, in relation to the enforcement power concerned, the following apply—
(*a*) the enforcement power ceases to be exercisable;
(*b*) as soon as reasonably practicable the enforcement agent must make the securities available for collection by the debtor, if he removed them from where he found them.
(2) Where the enforcement power was under a writ or warrant, sub-paragraph (1) does not affect any power to issue another writ or warrant.

Commencement—Tribunals, Courts and Enforcement Act 2007 (Commencement No 11) Order, SI 2014/768 art 2(1)(*b*) (Sch 12 comes into force on 6 April 2014).

Payment of amount outstanding

58—(1) This paragraph applies where the debtor pays the amount outstanding in full—

(*a*) after the enforcement agent has taken control of goods, and

(*b*) before they are sold or abandoned.

(2) If the enforcement agent has removed the goods he must as soon as reasonably practicable make them available for collection by the debtor.

(3) No further step may be taken under the enforcement power concerned.

(4) For the purposes of this paragraph the amount outstanding is reduced by the value of any controlled goods consisting of money required to be used to pay that amount, and sub-paragraph (2) does not apply to that money.

Commencement—Tribunals, Courts and Enforcement Act 2007 (Commencement No 11) Order, SI 2014/768 art 2(1)(*b*) (Sch 12 comes into force on 6 April 2014).

59—(1) This paragraph applies if a further step is taken despite paragraph 58(3).

(2) The enforcement agent is not liable unless he had notice, when the step was taken, that the amount outstanding had been paid in full.

(3) Sub-paragraph (2) applies to a related party as to the enforcement agent.

(4) If the step taken is sale of any of the goods the purchaser acquires good title unless, at the time of sale, he or the enforcement agent had notice that the amount outstanding had been paid in full.

(5) A person has notice that the amount outstanding has been paid in full if he would have found it out if he had made reasonable enquiries.

(6) Sub-paragraphs (2) to (4) do not affect any right of the debtor or a co-owner to a remedy against any person other than the enforcement agent or a related party.

(7) In this paragraph, "related party" has the meaning given by paragraph 65(4).

Commencement—Tribunals, Courts and Enforcement Act 2007 (Commencement No 11) Order, SI 2014/768 art 2(1)(*b*) (Sch 12 comes into force on 6 April 2014).

Third party claiming goods

60—(1) This paragraph applies where a person makes an application to the court claiming that goods taken control of are his and not the debtor's.

(2) After receiving notice of the application the enforcement agent must not sell the goods, or dispose of them (in the case of securities), unless directed by the court under this paragraph.

(3) The court may direct the enforcement agent to sell or dispose of the goods if the applicant fails to make, or to continue to make, the required payments into court.

(4) The required payments are—

(*a*) payment on making the application (subject to sub-paragraph (5)) of an amount equal to the value of the goods, or to a proportion of it directed by the court;

(*b*) payment, at prescribed times (on making the application or later), of any amounts prescribed in respect of the enforcement agent's costs of retaining the goods.

(5) If the applicant makes a payment under sub-paragraph (4)(*a*) but the enforcement agent disputes the value of the goods, any underpayment is to be—

(*a*) determined by reference to an independent valuation carried out in accordance with regulations, and

(*b*) paid at the prescribed time.

(6) If sub-paragraph (3) does not apply the court may still direct the enforcement agent to sell or dispose of the goods before the court determines the applicant's claim, if it considers it appropriate.

(7) If the court makes a direction under sub-paragraph (3) or (6)—

(*a*) paragraphs 38 to 49, and regulations under them, apply subject to any modification directed by the court;

(*b*) the enforcement agent must pay the proceeds of sale or disposal into court.

(8) In this paragraph "the court", subject to rules of court, means—

(*a*) the High Court, in relation to an enforcement power under a writ of the High Court;

(*b*) a county court, in relation to an enforcement power under a warrant issued by a county court;

(*c*) in any other case, the High Court or a county court.

Commencement—Tribunals, Courts and Enforcement Act 2007 (Commencement No 9) Order, SI 2013/1739 art 3 (para 60(4), (5) comes into force on 15 July 2013 for the purpose only of exercising any power to make regulations).
Tribunals, Courts and Enforcement Act 2007 (Commencement No 11) Order, SI 2014/768 art 2(1)(*b*) (this para comes into force on 6 April 2014 for all remaining purposes).

Application to assignee or transferee

61—(1) This Schedule applies as follows where an interest of the debtor's in goods is assigned or transferred while the property in the goods is bound for the purposes of an enforcement power, and the enforcement agent—

(*a*) knows that the assignee or transferee has an interest in the particular goods, or

(*b*) would know, if he made reasonable enquiries.

(2) These apply as if the assignee or transferee were a co-owner of the goods with the debtor—

(*a*) paragraph 34 (inventory);

(*b*) paragraph 36 (valuation);

(*c*) paragraphs 39 to 41 (sale);

(*d*) paragraph 59(6) (remedies after payment of amount outstanding).

(3) If the interest of the assignee or transferee was acquired in good faith, for valuable consideration and without notice, paragraph 50(6) applies as if "co-owner" included the assignee or transferee.

(4) If the interest of the assignee or transferee was not acquired in good faith, for valuable consideration and without notice, the enforcement agent must pay any surplus under paragraph 50(5) to the assignee or transferee and to the debtor (if he retains an interest).

(5) If the surplus is payable to two or more persons it must be paid in shares proportionate to their interests.

(6) Paragraph 5(3) and (4) ("good faith" and "notice") apply for the purposes of this paragraph.

Commencement—Tribunals, Courts and Enforcement Act 2007 (Commencement No 11) Order, SI 2014/768 art 2(1)(*b*) (Sch 12 comes into force on 6 April 2014).

Costs

62—(1) Regulations may make provision for the recovery by any person from the debtor of amounts in respect of costs of enforcement-related services.

(2) The regulations may provide for recovery to be out of proceeds or otherwise.

(3) The amount recoverable under the regulations in any case is to be determined by or under the regulations.

(4) The regulations may in particular provide for the amount, if disputed, to be assessed in accordance with rules of court.

(5) "Enforcement-related services" means anything done under or in connection with an enforcement power, or in connection with obtaining an enforcement power, or any services used for the purposes of a provision of this Schedule or regulations under it.

Commencement—Tribunals, Courts and Enforcement Act 2007 (Commencement No 9) Order, SI 2013/1739 art 3 (para 62 comes into force on 15 July 2013 for the purpose only of exercising any power to make regulations).

Tribunals, Courts and Enforcement Act 2007 (Commencement No 11) Order, SI 2014/768 art 2(1)(*b*) (this para comes into force on 6 April 2014 for all remaining purposes).

Limitation of liability for sale or payment of proceeds

63—(1) Any liability of an enforcement agent or related party to a lawful claimant for the sale of controlled goods is excluded except in two cases.

(2) The first exception is where at the time of the sale the enforcement agent had notice that the goods were not the debtor's, or not his alone.

(3) The second exception is where before sale the lawful claimant had made an application to the court claiming an interest in the goods.

(4) A lawful claimant in relation to goods is a person who has an interest in them at the time of sale, other than an interest that was assigned or transferred to him while the property in the goods was bound for the purposes of the enforcement power.

64—(1) Any liability of an enforcement agent or related party to a lawful claimant for paying over proceeds is excluded except in two cases.

(2) The first exception is where at the time of the payment he had notice that the goods were not the debtor's, or not his alone.

(3) The second exception is where before that time the lawful claimant had made an application to the court claiming an interest in the goods.

(4) A lawful claimant in relation to goods is a person who has an interest in them at the time of sale.

Commencement—Tribunals, Courts and Enforcement Act 2007 (Commencement No 11) Order, SI 2014/768 art 2(1)(*b*) (Sch 12 comes into force on 6 April 2014).

65—(1) Paragraphs 63 and 64—

(*a*) do not affect the liability of a person other than the enforcement agent or a related party;

(*b*) do not apply to the creditor if he is the enforcement agent.

(2) The following apply for the purposes of those paragraphs.

(3) The enforcement agent or a related party has notice of something if he would have found it out if he had made reasonable enquiries.
(4) A related party is any person who acts in exercise of an enforcement power, other than the creditor or enforcement agent.
(5) "The court" has the same meaning as in paragraph 60.

Commencement—Tribunals, Courts and Enforcement Act 2007 (Commencement No 11) Order, SI 2014/768 art 2(1)(*b*) (Sch 12 comes into force on 6 April 2014).

Remedies available to the debtor

66—(1) This paragraph applies where an enforcement agent—
(*a*) breaches a provision of this Schedule, or
(*b*) acts under an enforcement power under a writ, warrant, liability order or other instrument that is defective.
(2) The breach or defect does not make the enforcement agent, or a person he is acting for, a trespasser.
(3) But the debtor may bring proceedings under this paragraph.
(4) Subject to rules of court, the proceedings may be brought—
(*a*) in the High Court, in relation to an enforcement power under a writ of the High Court;
(*b*) in a county court, in relation to an enforcement power under a warrant issued by a county court;
(*c*) in any other case, in the High Court or a county court.
(5) In the proceedings the court may—
(*a*) order goods to be returned to the debtor;
(*b*) order the enforcement agent or a related party to pay damages in respect of loss suffered by the debtor as a result of the breach or of anything done under the defective instrument.
(6) A related party is either of the following (if different from the enforcement agent)—
(*a*) the person on whom the enforcement power is conferred,
(*b*) the creditor.
(7) Sub-paragraph (5) is without prejudice to any other powers of the court.
(8) Sub-paragraph (5)(*b*) does not apply where the enforcement agent acted in the reasonable belief—
(*a*) that he was not breaching a provision of this Schedule, or
(*b*) (as the case may be) that the instrument was not defective.
(9) This paragraph is subject to paragraph 59 in the case of a breach of paragraph 58(3).

Commencement—Tribunals, Courts and Enforcement Act 2007 (Commencement No 11) Order, SI 2014/768 art 2(1)(*b*) (Sch 12 comes into force on 6 April 2014).

Remedies available to the creditor

67 If a debtor wrongfully interferes with controlled goods and the creditor suffers loss as a result, the creditor may bring a claim against the debtor in respect of the loss.

Commencement—Tribunals, Courts and Enforcement Act 2007 (Commencement No 11) Order, SI 2014/768 art 2(1)(*b*) (Sch 12 comes into force on 6 April 2014).

Offences

68—(1) A person is guilty of an offence if he intentionally obstructs a person lawfully acting as an enforcement agent.
(2) A person is guilty of an offence if he intentionally interferes with controlled goods without lawful excuse.
(3) A person guilty of an offence under this paragraph is liable on summary conviction to—
(*a*) imprisonment for a term not exceeding 51 weeks, or
(*b*) a fine not exceeding level 4 on the standard scale, or
(*c*) both.
(4) In relation to an offence committed before the commencement of section 281(5) of the Criminal Justice Act 2003 (c 44), the reference in sub-paragraph (3)(*a*) to 51 weeks is to be read as a reference to 6 months.

Commencement—Tribunals, Courts and Enforcement Act 2007 (Commencement No 11) Order, SI 2014/768 art 2(1)(*b*) (Sch 12 comes into force on 6 April 2014).

Relation to insolvency provisions

69 This Schedule is subject to sections 183, 184 and 346 of the Insolvency Act 1986 (c 45).

Commencement—Tribunals, Courts and Enforcement Act 2007 (Commencement No 11) Order, SI 2014/768 art 2(1)(*b*) (Sch 12 comes into force on 6 April 2014).

SCHEDULE 13

TAKING CONTROL OF GOODS: AMENDMENTS

Section 62(3)

Commencement—Tribunals, Courts and Enforcement Act 2007 (Commencement No 11) Order, SI 2014/768 art 2(1)(*b*) (Sch 13 comes into force on 6 April 2014).

. . .

Taxes Management Act 1970 (c 9)

32 The Taxes Management Act 1970 is amended as follows.

33—*(1) Section 61 (distraint by collectors) is amended as follows.*
*(2) (inserted*TMA 1970 s 61(1)(*a*), (*b*))
(3) (inserts TMA 1970 s 61(1A)).[1]

Note—Sch 13 was brought into effect by the Tribunals, Courts and Enforcement Act 2007 (Commencement No 11) Order, SI 2014/768 art 2(1)(*b* with effect from 6 April 2014. However this para was repealed prior to this date without ever coming into effect.

Amendments—This para repealed by FA 2008 s 129, Sch 43 para 11(*d*) with effect from 5 April 2014 (by virtue of SI 2014/906, art 3).

34 (*inserts* TMA 1970 s 62(4))

. . .

Commencement—Tribunals, Courts and Enforcement Act 2007 (Commencement No 11) Order, SI 2014/768 art 2(1)(*b*) (Sch 13 comes into force on 6 April 2014).

Social Security Administration Act 1992 (c 5)

101 The Social Security Administration Act 1992 is amended as follows.

Commencement—Tribunals Courts and Enforcement Act 2007 (Commencement No 11) Order, SI 2014/768 art 2(1)(*b*) (Sch 13 comes into force on 6 April 2014).

104—*(1) Section 121A (recovery of contributions etc in England and Wales) is amended as follows.*
(2) (amended SSAA 1992 s 121A(1)(*b*); *repealed by* FA 2008 s 129, Sch 43 para 11(*d*))
*(3) (repeals*SSAA1992 s 121A(2)–(8), (10)).

Note—Sch 13 was brought into effect by the Tribunals, Courts and Enforcement Act 2007 (Commencement No 11) Order, SI 2014/768 art 2(1)(*b* with effect from 6 April 2014. However this para was repealed prior to this date without ever coming into effect.

Value Added Tax Act 1994 (c 23)

117 The Value Added Tax Act 1994 is amended as follows.

118 (*amends*VATA 1994 s 48(7A))Ireland,".

119 (*inserted* VATA 1994 s 67A; *repealed by* FA 2008 s 129, Sch 43 para 11(*d*))

Note—Sch 13 was brought into effect by the Tribunals, Courts and Enforcement Act 2007 (Commencement No 11) Order, SI 2014/768 art 2(1)(*b* with effect from 6 April 2014. However this para was repealed prior to this date without ever coming into effect.

120 (*substitutes* VATA 1994 s 68(5))

Finance Act 1996 (c 8)

122 Schedule 5 to the Finance Act 1996 (landfill tax) is amended as follows.

123 (*inserted* FA 1996 s 23A; *repealed by* FA 2008 s 129, Sch 43 para 11(*d*))

Note—Sch 13 was brought into effect by the Tribunals, Courts and Enforcement Act 2007 (Commencement No 11) Order, SI 2014/768 art 2(1)(*b* with effect from 6 April 2014. However this para was repealed prior to this date without ever coming into effect.

124 (*substitutes* FA 1996 Sch 5 para 24(4))

Commencement—Tribunals, Courts and Enforcement Act 2007 (Commencement No 11) Order, SI 2014/768 art 2(1)(*b*) (Sch 13 comes into force on 6 April 2014).

Finance Act 1997 (c 16)

126—(1) Section 51 of the Finance Act 1997 (enforcement by distress) is amended as follows.
(2) (inserted FA 1997 s 51(A1); *repealed by* FA 2008 s 129, Sch 43 para 11(*d*))
(3) (*amends* FA 1997 s 51(1)).
(4) (*repeals* FA 1997 s 51(7))

Commencement—Tribunals, Courts and Enforcement Act 2007 (Commencement No 11) Order, SI 2014/768 art 2(1)(*b*) (Sch 13 comes into force on 6 April 2014).

Finance Act 2000 (c 17)

135 Schedule 6 to the Finance Act 2000 (climate change levy) is amended as follows.

136 *(inserted* FA 2000 s 89A; *repealed by* FA 2008 s 129, Sch 43 para 11(*d*))

Note—Sch 13 was brought into effect by the Tribunals, Courts and Enforcement Act 2007 (Commencement No 11) Order, SI 2014/768 art 2(1)(*b* with effect from 6 April 2014. However this para was repealed prior to this date without ever coming into effect.

137 (*substitutes* FA 2000 Sch 6 para 90(5))

Commencement—Tribunals, Courts and Enforcement Act 2007 (Commencement No 11) Order, SI 2014/768 art 2(1)(*b*) (Sch 13 comes into force on 6 April 2014).

Finance Act 2001 (c 9)

139 Schedule 5 to the Finance Act 2001 (aggregates levy: recovery and interest) is amended as follows.

140 *(inserted* FA 2001 s 14A; *repealed by* FA 2008 s 129, Sch 43 para 11(*d*))

Note—Sch 13 was brought into effect by the Tribunals, Courts and Enforcement Act 2007 (Commencement No 11) Order, SI 2014/768 art 2(1)(*b* with effect from 6 April 2014. However this para was repealed prior to this date without ever coming into effect.

141 (substitutes FA 2000 Sch 5 para 15(5))

Commencement—Tribunals, Courts and Enforcement Act 2007 (Commencement No 11) Order, SI 2014/768 art 2(1)(*b*) (Sch 13 comes into force on 6 April 2014).

Finance Act 2003 (c 14)

147—(1) Schedule 12 to the Finance Act 2003 (stamp duty land tax: collection and recovery of tax) is amended as follows.

(2) (amended FA 2003 Sch 12 para 1A; *repealed by* FA 2008 s 129, Sch 43 para 11(*d*)))

(3) (*amended* FA 2003 Sch 12 para 2(1); *repealed by* FA 2008 s 129 Sch 43 para 11(*d*)))[1]

Note—Sch 13 was brought into effect by the Tribunals, Courts and Enforcement Act 2007 (Commencement No 11) Order, SI 2014/768 art 2(1)(*b* with effect from 6 April 2014. However this para was repealed prior to this date without ever coming into effect.

Income Tax Act 2007 (c 3)

157 (*amends* ITA 2007 s 955(4)).

Commencement—Tribunals, Courts and Enforcement Act 2007 (Commencement No 11) Order, SI 2014/768 art 2(1)(*b*) (Sch 13 comes into force on 6 April 2014).

SCHEDULE 23

REPEALS

Section 146

PART 1

TRIBUNALS AND INQUIRIES

Reference	*Extent of repeal or revocation*
Taxes Management Act 1970 (c 9)	Sections 2 to 3A.
	In section 5(1), the words "General Commissioner or".
	In section 6—
	(a) in subsection (1), the words "a General Commissioner or" and the words ", or before a General Commissioner", and
	(b) subsection (2).
	In section 56(3), the words "the clerk to".
	Section 115(4).
Superannuation Act 1972 (c 11)	In Schedule 6, paragraph 77.
Finance Act 1972 (c 41)	Section 130.
Consumer Credit Act 1974 (c 39)	In Schedule A1, paragraph 11.
House of Commons Disqualification Act 1975 (c 24)	In Schedule 1, in Part 2—

Reference	*Extent of repeal or revocation*
	(a) the entry relating to the Council on Tribunals, and
	(b) the entry relating to the Scottish Committee of the Council on Tribunals.
Northern Ireland Assembly Disqualification Act 1975 (c 25)	In Schedule 1, in Part 2—
	(a) the entry relating to the Council on Tribunals, and
	(b) the entry relating to the Scottish Committee of the Council on Tribunals.
Race Relations Act 1976 (c 74)	In Schedule 1A, in Part 2, the entry relating to the Council on Tribunals.
Estate Agents Act 1979 (c 38)	Section 24(2).
Finance Act 1988 (c 39)	Section 134(1).
Food Safety Act 1990 (c 16)	In section 26(2)—
	(a) in paragraph (e), the words "or to a tribunal constituted in accordance with the regulations," and
	(b) paragraph (f).
	Section 37(2)(a).
	Section 47.
Finance (No 2) Act 1992 (c 48)	In section 75(1), paragraph (a).
	In Schedule 16, paragraph 2.
Tribunals and Inquiries Act 1992 (c 53)	Sections 1 to 5, 6(1) to (3), (6) and (7) and 8.
	In section 13—
	(a) subsection (2), and
	(b) in subsection (5)(c), the words "the reference in section 8(1) to the Foreign Compensation Commission and".
	Section 14(1A).
	In section 16(1), in the definition of "decision", "procedural rules" and "working", the words ", "procedural rules" and "working"".
	In Schedule 1, paragraph 19.
Judicial Pensions and Retirement Act 1993 (c 8)	In section 1(1), the word "and" at the end of paragraph (c).
	Section 12(1)(b).
Employment Tribunals Act 1996 (c 17)	Section 26.
	In section 27(1)—
	(a) in paragraph (b), the word "and" at the end,
	(b) paragraph (c), and
	(c) the words after "persons within paragraph (a) or (b)".
Social Security Act 1998 (c 14)	In Schedule 7, in paragraph 118(1), "subsection (3) of" and the words after "1992".
Social Security Contributions (Transfer of Functions, Etc.) Act 1999 (c 2)	In Schedule 7, paragraph 1.
Access to Justice Act 1999 (c 22)	Sections 101 to 103.
Social Security Contributions (Transfer of Functions, etc) (Northern Ireland) Order 1999 (SI 1999/671)	In Schedule 6, in paragraph 1, the words "section 2(1) (appointment of General Commissioners),".
Scotland Act 1998 (Cross-Border Public Authorities) (Adaptation of Functions etc) Order 1999 (SI 1999/1747)	Schedule 9.

Reference	*Extent of repeal or revocation*
Scotland Act 1998 (Transfer of Functions to the Scottish Ministers etc) Order 1999 (SI 1999/1750)	In Schedule 1, the entry in respect of sections 2(3), 2(6) and 3(4) of the Taxes Management Act 1970.
Freedom of Information Act 2000 (c 36)	In Schedule 1, in Part 6, the entry relating to the Council on Tribunals and the entry relating to the Scottish Committee of the Council on Tribunals.
Financial Services and Markets Act 2000 (Consequential Amendments and Repeals) Order 2001 (SI 2001/3649)	Article 335(3).
Justice (Northern Ireland) Act 2002 (c 26)	In each of Schedules 1 and 6, the entry relating to the panel of persons appointed under section 6(1) of the Tribunals and Inquiries Act 1992 to act as chairmen of tribunals that sit in Northern Ireland.
Nationality, Immigration and Asylum Act 2002 (c 41)	In Schedule 4, paragraphs 9 and 10(b) and (c).
Scottish Public Services Ombudsman Act 2002 (Consequential Provisions and Modifications) Order 2004 (SI 2004/1823)	Article 14.
Constitutional Reform Act 2005 (c 4)	In Schedule 4, paragraph 64.
	In Schedule 5, in the amendment made by paragraph 122(5), and in the amendment made by paragraph 126(5), the entry relating to the panel of persons appointed under section 6(1) of the Tribunals and Inquiries Act 1992 to act as chairmen of tribunals that sit in Northern Ireland.
	In Schedule 7, in Part A of the list in paragraph 4—
	(a) the entry for section 6(2), (8) and (9) of the Tribunals and Inquiries Act 1992, and
	(b) the entry for paragraph 7(4) of Schedule 5 to that Act.
	In Schedule 12, in paragraph 4(4)(a), the words "or no other except that of General Commissioner,".
	In Schedule 14, in Part 2, the entry relating to General Commissioner for a division in England and Wales.
	In Schedule 14, in Part 3, the entry relating to members of panels appointed under section 6(1) of the Tribunals and Inquiries Act 1992.
Tribunals, Courts and Enforcement Act 2007 (c 15)	In section 36(3)(a), the words "or 41(2)".
	In Schedule 8, paragraph 26.

Commencement—Tribunals, Courts and Enforcement Act 2007 (Commencement No 1) Order, SI 2007/2709 art 3(*d*) (entries relating to the following, come into force on 1 November 2007—

(a) House of Commons Disqualification Act 1975;
(b) Northern Ireland Assembly Disqualification Act 1975;
(c) Race Relations Act 1976;
(d) Estate Agents Act 1979;
(e) Tribunals and Inquiries Act 1992 ss 1, 2, 3, 4 and 13(5)(*c*);
(f) Scotland Act 1998 (Cross-Border Public Authorities) (Adaptation of Functions etc) Order 1999 to the extent that Schedule 9 applies to Tribunals and Inquiries Act 1992 ss 2, 4;
(g) Freedom of Information Act 2000; and
(h) Scottish Public Services Ombudsman Act 2002 (Consequential Provisions and Modifications) Order 2004.).

Tribunals, Courts and Enforcement Act 2007 (Commencement No 6 and Transitional Provisions) Order, SI 2008/2696 art 5(*j*) (entries relating to the following come into force on 3 November 2008—

(a) Consumer Credit Act 1974;
(b) Judicial Pensions and Retirement Act 1993;
(c) Employment Tribunals Act 1996;

(d) Justice (Northern Ireland) Act 2002;
(e) Nationality, Immigration and Asylum Act 2002;
(f) Constitutional Reform Act 2005 Sch 4; and
(g) Tribunals, Courts and Enforcement Act 2007.).

Tribunals, Courts and Enforcement Act 2007 (Commencement No 6 and Transitional Provisions) Order, SI 2008/2696 art 6(*c*) (entries relating to the following come into force on 1 April 2009—

(a) Taxes Management Act 1970;
(b) Superannuation Act 1972;
(c) Finance Act 1972;
(d) Finance Act 1988;
(e) Finance (No 2) Act 1992;
(f) Social Security Contributions (Transfer of Functions, etc) Act 1999;
(g) Access to Justice Act 1999;
(h) Social Security Contributions (Transfer of Functions, etc) (Northern Ireland) Order, SI 1999/671;
(i) Scotland Act 1998 (Transfer of Functions to the Scottish Ministers etc) Order, SI 1999/1750; and
(j) Constitutional Reform Act 2005 Sch 12, Sch 14 Pt 2.).

Tribunals, Courts and Enforcement Act 2007 (Commencement No 10) Order, SI 2013/2043 art 2(*c*) (entries relating to the Tribunals and Inquiries Act 1992 ss 5, 8 come into force on 19 August 2013).

PART 2
JUDICIAL APPOINTMENTS

Reference	*Extent of repeal*
Courts and Legal Services Act 1990 (c 41)	In Schedule 10—
	(a) paragraph 4,
	(b) in paragraph 6(1), the words "paragraph 13(1) of" and the words after "1947", and
	(c) paragraphs 24, 26, 32, 49, 50(2)(b) and 57.
Judicial Pensions and Retirement Act 1993 (c 8)	In Schedule 5—
	(a) in the entry for a deputy district judge appointed under section 102 of the Supreme Court Act 1981, the words "for a district registry", and
	(b) in the entry for a deputy district judge appointed under section 8 of the County Courts Act 1984, the words "for a county court district".
Child Support Act 1991 (c 48)	In section 54, the definition of "general qualification".
Social Security Act 1998 (c 14)	In Schedule 4, paragraph 1(3).
Enterprise Act 2002 (c 40)	In Schedule 2, paragraph 1(4).
Constitutional Reform Act 2005 (c 4)	Section 25(2)(a).
	In Schedule 3, paragraph 2(3).
	In Schedule 14, in Part 2—
	(a) in the entry relating to a deputy district judge in a district registry of the High Court, the words "in a district registry of the High Court", and
	(b) in the entry relating to a deputy district judge for a county court district, the words "for a county court district".
	In Schedule 14, in Part 3, the entries relating to—
	(a) Member of the Special Immigration Appeals Commission;
	(b) Chairman of the Special Immigration Appeals Commission;
	(c) Member of the Proscribed Organisations Appeal Commission;

Reference	*Extent of repeal*
	(d) Chairman of the Proscribed Organisations Appeal Commission;
	(e) Member of the Pathogens Access Appeal Commission; and
	(f) Chairman of the Pathogens Access Appeal Commission.

Commencement—Tribunals, Courts and Enforcement Act 2007 (Commencement No 6 and Transitional Provisions) Order, SI 2008/2696 art 5(*j*) (Part 2 comes into force on 3 November 2008).

PART 3
ENFORCEMENT BY TAKING CONTROL OF GOODS

COMMENCEMENT—

This part comes into effect on 6 April 2014 by virtue of the Tribunal, Courts and Enforcement Act 2007 (Commencement No 11) Order, SI 2014/768 art 2(1)(*b*).

Reference	*Extent of repeal*
Inclosure Act 1773 (c 81)	In section 4, the words from "rendering" to the end.
	In section 16, the words from "rendering" to the end.
Sale of Farming Stock Act 1816 (c 50)	The whole Act.
Judgments Act 1838 (c 110)	Section 12.
Compulsory Purchase Act 1965 (c 56)	Section 13(5).
	Section 29.
Sea Fisheries Act 1968 (c 77)	In section 12(3), the words from "as they apply" to the end.
Criminal Justice Act 1972 (c 71)	In section 66(2), the words from ""sentence of imprisonment"" to the end.
Magistrates' Courts Act 1980 (c 43)	In section 125(2), the words from "This subsection" to the end.
	Section 125D(3)(c).
	Section 151.
	In Schedule 4A, paragraph 3.
British Fishing Boats Act 1983 (c 8)	In section 5(3), the words from "as they apply" to the end.
County Courts Act 1984 (c 28)	Section 85(3).
	Section 87(2).
	Sections 89 to 91.
	Sections 93 to 100.
	Sections 102 and 103.
	Section 123.
	In section 126—
	(a) in subsection (3) the words from "but" to the end;
	(b) in subsection (4) ""bailiff"".
	In section 147(1) the definition of "bailiff".
Finance Act 1984 (c 43)	Section 16.
Local Government Finance Act 1988 (c 41)	In Schedule 9, paragraph 3(2)(b).
Child Support Act 1991 (c 48)	Section 35(2) to (8).
Social Security Administration Act 1992 (c 5)	Section 121A(2) to (8) and (10).
Local Government Finance Act 1992 (c 14)	In Schedule 4—
	(a) paragraph 7;
	(b) in paragraph 8(1)(a) the words from "an authority" to "paragraph 7 above";

Reference	*Extent of repeal*
	(c) paragraph 12(1)(c);
	(d) paragraph 19(3).
Finance Act 1997 (c 16)	Section 51(7).
Courts Act 2003 (c 39)	In Schedule 7, paragraph 8(5).
Traffic Management Act 2004 (c 18)	Section 82(3)(a).
	Section 83.

FINANCE ACT 2008

(2008 Chapter 9)

CONTENTS

An Act to Grant certain duties, to alter other duties, and to amend the law relating to the National Debt and the Public Revenue, and to make further provision in connection with finance.

[21 July 2008]

PART 7
ADMINISTRATION

Press releases—HMRC Guidance Note, 18 July 2008 (HMRC set-off across taxes following Finance Bill 2008).

CHAPTER 1

INFORMATION ETC

New information etc powers

113 Information and inspection powers

(1) Schedule 36 contains provision about the powers of officers of Revenue and Customs to obtain information and to inspect businesses.

(2) That Schedule comes into force on such day as the Treasury may by order made by statutory instrument appoint.

(3) An order under subsection (2) may contain transitional provision and savings.

Orders—Finance Act 2008, Schedule 36 (Appointed Day and Savings) Order, SI 2009/404 (made under sub-ss (2), (3)).

114 Computer records etc

(1) This section applies to any enactment that, in connection with an HMRC matter—

(*a*) requires a person to produce a document or cause a document to be produced,
(*b*) requires a person to permit the Commissioners or an officer of Revenue and Customs—
(i) to inspect a document, or
(ii) to make or take copies of or extracts from or remove a document,
(*c*) makes provision about penalties or offences in connection with the production or inspection of documents, including in connection with the falsification of or failure to produce or permit the inspection of documents, or
(*d*) makes any other provision in connection with a requirement mentioned in paragraph (*a*) or (*b*).

(2) An enactment to which this section applies has effect as if—
(*a*) any reference in the enactment to a document were a reference to anything in which information of any description is recorded, and
(*b*) any reference in the enactment to a copy of a document were a reference to anything onto which information recorded in the document has been copied, by whatever means and whether directly or indirectly.

(3) An authorised person may, at any reasonable time, obtain access to, and inspect and check the operation of, any computer and any associated apparatus or material which is or has been used in connection with a relevant document.

(4) In subsection (3) "relevant document" means a document that a person has been, or may be, required pursuant to an enactment to which this section applies—
(*a*) to produce or cause to be produced, or
(*b*) to permit the Commissioners or an officer of Revenue and Customs to inspect, to make or take copies of or extracts from or to remove.

(5) An authorised person may require—
(*a*) the person by whom or on whose behalf the computer is or has been so used, or
(*b*) any person having charge of, or otherwise concerned with the operation of, the computer, apparatus or material,

to provide the authorised person with such reasonable assistance as may be required for the purposes of subsection (3).

(6) Any person who—
(*a*) obstructs the exercise of a power conferred by this section, or
(*b*) fails to comply within a reasonable time with a requirement under subsection (5),

is liable to a penalty of £300.

(7) Paragraphs 45 to 49 and 52 of Schedule 36 (assessment of and appeals against penalties) apply in relation to a penalty under this section as they apply in relation to a penalty under paragraph 39 of that Schedule.

(8) Omit the following—
(*a*) (*repeals* FA 1985 s 10)
(*b*) (*repeals* FA 1988 s 127)
(*c*) (*repeals* Civil Evidence Act 1995 Sch 1 paras 11(2)–(4), 13(2), (3))

(9) In this section—
"authorised person" means a person who is, or is a member of a class of persons who are, authorised by the Commissioners to exercise the powers under subsection (3),
"the Commissioners" means the Commissioners for Her Majesty's Revenue and Customs,
"enactment" includes an enactment contained in subordinate legislation (within the meaning of the Interpretation Act 1978 (c 30)),
"HMRC matter" means a matter in relation to which the Commissioners, or officers of Revenue and Customs, have a power or duty, and
"produce", in relation to a document, includes furnish, deliver and any other equivalent expression.

Other measures

115 Record-keeping

(1) Schedule 37 contains provision about the obligations to keep records for the purposes of income tax, capital gains tax, corporation tax and value added tax.

(2) The amendments made by that Schedule come into force on such day as the Treasury may by order made by statutory instrument appoint.

Orders—Finance Act 2008, Schedule 37 (Appointed Day) Order, SI 2009/402 (made under sub-s (2)).

116 Disclosure of tax avoidance schemes

(1) Schedule 38 contains amendments relating to the disclosure of tax avoidance schemes.

(2) The amendments made by that Schedule come into force on such day as the Treasury may by order made by statutory instrument appoint; and different days may be appointed for different purposes.

Orders—Finance Act 2008, Schedule 38, (Appointed Day) Order, SI 2008/1935 (made under sub-s (2)).

Finance Act 2008, Schedule 38 (Appointed Day) Order, SI 2010/409 (day appointed as the day on which the amendments made by Sch 38 come into force for the purposes of stamp duty land tax is 1 April 2010).

117 Power to open or unpack containers

(1) CEMA 1979 is amended as follows.

(2) (*amends* CEMA 1979 s 1(1))

(3) Section 159 (power to examine and take account of goods) is amended as follows.

(4) (*amends* CEMA 1979 s 159(1))

(5) (*amends* CEMA 1979 s 159(4))

CHAPTER 2

TIME LIMITS FOR CLAIMS AND ASSESSMENTS ETC

General

118 Time limits for assessments, claims etc

(1) Schedule 39 contains provision about time limits for assessments, claims etc

(2) The amendments and saving made by that Schedule come into force on such day as the Treasury may by order made by statutory instrument appoint.

(3) An order under subsection (2)—

(*a*) may make different provision for different purposes, and

(*b*) may include transitional provision and further savings.

Orders—Finance Act 2008, Schedule 39 (Appointed Day, Transitional Provision and Savings) Order, SI 2009/403 (made under sub-ss (2), (3)).

Income tax and corporation tax

119 Correction and amendment of tax returns

(1) (*amends* TMA 1970 s 9ZB(1))

(2) (*amends* TMA 1970 s 12ABB(1))

(3)–(11) (*amend* FA 1998 Sch 18)

(12) (*amends* TMA 1970 ss 46B–46D, 55; TA 1988 s 754)

(13) The amendments made by this section come into force on such day as the Treasury may by order appoint.

Orders—Finance Act 2008, Section 119 (Appointed Day) Order, SI 2009/405 (made under sub-s (13)).

Amendments—Sub-s (12)(*a*)(i), (ii) repealed by the Transfer of Tribunal Functions and Revenue and Customs Appeals Order, SI 2009/56 art 3(1), Sch 1 paras 468, 469 with effect from 1 April 2009.

VAT

120 VAT: time limits for assessments of excess credits etc

(1) (*inserts* VATA 1994 s 73(6A))

(2) Section 80 of that Act (credit for, or repayment of, overstated or overpaid VAT) is amended as follows.

(3) (*inserts* VATA 1994 s 80(4AA))

(4) (*amends* VATA 1994 s 80(4C))

(5) The amendments made by this section are treated as having come into force on 19 March 2008.

121 Old VAT claims: extended time limits

(1) The requirement in section 80(4) of VATA 1994 that a claim under that section be made within 3 years of the relevant date does not apply to a claim in respect of an amount brought into account, or paid, for a prescribed accounting period ending before 4 December 1996 if the claim is made before 1 April 2009.

(2) The requirement in section 25(6) of VATA 1994 that a claim for deduction of input tax be made at such time as may be determined by or under regulations does not apply to a claim for deduction of input tax that became chargeable, and in respect of which the claimant held the required evidence, in a prescribed accounting period ending before 1 May 1997 if the claim is made before 1 April 2009.

(3) In this section—

"input tax" and "prescribed accounting period" have the same meaning as in VATA 1994 (see section 96 of that Act), and

"the required evidence" means the evidence of the charge to value added tax specified in or under regulation 29(2) of the Value Added Tax Regulations 1995 (SI 1995/2518).

(4) This section is treated as having come into force on 19 March 2008.

CHAPTER 3
PENALTIES

122 Penalties for errors

(1) Schedule 40 contains provisions amending Schedule 24 to FA 2007 (penalties for errors in returns etc).

(2) That Schedule comes into force on such day as the Treasury may by order appoint.
(3) An order under subsection (2)—
(*a*) may commence a provision generally or only for specified purposes, and
(*b*) may appoint different days for different provisions or for different purposes.
(4) The Treasury may by order make any incidental, supplemental, consequential, transitional, transitory or saving provision which may appear appropriate in consequence of, or otherwise in connection with, Schedule 24 to FA 2007 or Schedule 40.
(5) An order under subsection (4) may include provision amending, repealing or revoking any provision of any Act or subordinate legislation whenever passed or made (including this Act and any Act amended by it).
(6) An order under subsection (4) may make different provision for different purposes.
(7) The power to make an order under this section is exercisable by statutory instrument.
(8) A statutory instrument containing an order under subsection (4) which includes provision amending or repealing any provision of an Act is subject to annulment in pursuance of a resolution of the House of Commons.

Orders—Finance Act 2008, Schedule 41 (Appointed Day and Transitional Provisions) Order, SI 2009/511.
Finance Act 2008, Schedule 40 (Appointed Day, Transitional Provisions and Consequential Amendments) Order, SI 2009/571.

123 Penalties for failure to notify etc

(1) Schedule 41 contains provisions for imposing penalties on persons in respect of failures to notify HMRC that they are chargeable to tax etc and certain wrongdoings relating to invoices showing VAT and excise duties.
(2) That Schedule comes into force on such day as the Treasury may by order appoint.
(3) An order under subsection (2)—
(*a*) may commence a provision generally or only for specified purposes, and
(*b*) may appoint different days for different provisions or for different purposes.
(4) The Treasury may by order make any incidental, supplemental, consequential, transitional, transitory or saving provision which may appear appropriate in consequence of, or otherwise in connection with, Schedule 41.
(5) An order under subsection (4) may include provision amending, repealing or revoking any provision of any Act or subordinate legislation whenever passed or made (including this Act and any Act amended by it).
(6) An order under subsection (4) may make different provision for different purposes.
(7) The power to make an order under this section is exercisable by statutory instrument.
(8) A statutory instrument containing an order under subsection (4) which includes provision amending or repealing any provision of an Act is subject to annulment in pursuance of a resolution of the House of Commons.

Orders—Finance Act 2008, Schedule 41 (Appointed Day and Transitional Provisions) Order, SI 2009/511.
Finance Act 2008 (Penalties for Errors and Failure to Notify etc) (Consequential Amendments) Order 2010, SI 2010/530.

CHAPTER 4

APPEALS ETC

Reviews and appeals etc: general

124 HMRC decisions etc: reviews and appeals

(1) The Treasury may by order made by statutory instrument make provision—
(*a*) for and in connection with reviews by the Commissioners, or by an officer of Revenue and Customs, of HMRC decisions, and
(*b*) in connection with appeals against HMRC decisions.
(2) An order under subsection (1) may, in particular, contain provision about—
(*a*) the circumstances in which, or the time within which—
(i) a right to a review may be exercised, or
(ii) an appeal may be made, and
(*b*) the circumstances in which, or the time at which, an appeal or review is, or may be treated as, concluded.
(3) An order under subsection (1) may, in particular, contain provision about the payment of sums by, or to, the Commissioners in cases where—
(*a*) a right to a review is exercised, or
(*b*) an appeal is made or determined.
(4) That includes provision about payment of sums where an appeal has been determined, but a further appeal may be or has been made, including provision—
(*a*) requiring payments to be made,
(*b*) enabling payments to be postponed, or
(*c*) imposing conditions in connection with the making or postponement of payments.

(5) An order under subsection (1) may, in particular, contain provision about interest on any sum that is payable by, or to, the Commissioners in accordance with a decision made on the determination of an appeal.

(6) Provision under subsection (1) may be made by amending, repealing or revoking any provision of any Act or subordinate legislation (whenever passed or made, including this Act and any Act amended by it).

(7) An order under subsection (1) may—

(*a*) provide that any provision contained in the order comes into force on a day appointed by an order of the Treasury made by statutory instrument (and may provide that different days may be appointed for different purposes),

(*b*) contain incidental, supplemental, consequential, transitional, transitory and saving provision, and

(*c*) make different provision for different purposes.

(8) A statutory instrument containing an order under subsection (1) may not be made unless a draft of it has been laid before and approved by resolution of the House of Commons.

(9) But if the order, or any other order under subsection (1) contained in the statutory instrument, is made in connection with a transfer of functions carried out under the Tribunals, Courts and Enforcement Act 2007 (c 15), the statutory instrument may only be made if a draft of it has been laid before and approved by resolution of each House of Parliament.

(10) In this section—

(*a*) references to appeals against HMRC decisions include any other kind of proceedings relating to an HMRC matter, and

(*b*) references to the making, determination or conclusion of appeals are to be read accordingly.

(11) In this section—

"the Commissioners" means the Commissioners for Her Majesty's Revenue and Customs;

"HMRC decision" means—

(*a*) any decision of the Commissioners relating to an HMRC matter, or

(*b*) any decision of an officer of Revenue and Customs relating to an HMRC matter,

and references to an HMRC decision include references to anything done by such a person in connection with making such a decision or in consequence of such a decision;

"HMRC matter" means any matter connected with a function of the Commissioners or an officer of Revenue and Customs.

Simon's Tax Cases—*R (on the application of ToTel Ltd) v First-tier Tribunal (Tax Chamber) and another (HM Treasury, interested party)* [2011] EWHC 652 (Admin), [2011] STC 1485.

Orders—Transfer of Tribunal Functions and Revenue and Customs Appeals Order, SI 2009/56 (made under sub-ss (1)–(7)).
Revenue and Customs Appeals Order, SI 2009/777 (made under sub-ss (1)–(7)).
Revenue and Customs (Amendment of Appeal Provisions for Out of Time Reviews) Order, SI 2014/1264.

Customs and excise decisions subject to review and appeal

126 Security under CEMA 1979

(1) (*amends* FA 1994 Sch 5 para 2(1)(*s*))

(2) The amendments made by subsection (1) have effect in relation to decisions made on or after the day on which this Act is passed.

CHAPTER 5
PAYMENT AND ENFORCEMENT

Taking control of goods etc

127 Enforcement by taking control of goods: England and Wales

(1) This section applies if a person does not pay a sum that is payable by that person to the Commissioners under or by virtue of an enactment or under a contract settlement.

(2) The Commissioners may use the procedure in Schedule 12 to the Tribunals, Courts and Enforcement Act 2007 (c 15) (taking control of goods) to recover that sum.

(3) This section extends to England and Wales only.

Commencement—Finance Act 2008, Section 127 and Part 1 of Schedule 43 (Appointed Day) Order, SI 2014/906 (the appointed day for the coming into force of this section is 6 April 2014).

128 Summary warrant: Scotland

(1) This section applies if a person does not pay a sum that is payable by that person to the Commissioners under or by virtue of any enactment or under a contract settlement.

(2) An officer of Revenue and Customs may apply to the sheriff for a summary warrant.

(3) An application under subsection (2) must be accompanied by a certificate which—

(*a*) complies with subsection (4), and

(*b*) is signed by the officer.

(4) A certificate complies with this subsection if—

(*a*) it states that—

(i) none of the persons specified in the application has paid the sum payable by that person,
(ii) the officer has demanded payment from each such person of the sum payable by that person, and
(iii) the period of 14 days beginning with the day on which the demand is made has expired without payment being made, and
(*b*) it specifies the sum payable by each person specified in the application.

(5) Subsection (4)(*a*)(iii) does not apply to an application under subsection (2) insofar as it relates to—
(*a*) sums payable in respect of value added tax,
(*b*) sums payable in respect of deductions required to be made under section 61 of FA 2004 (sub-contractors in the construction industry), and
(*c*) sums payable by a person in that person's capacity as an employer.

(6) The sheriff must, on an application by an officer of Revenue and Customs under subsection (2), grant a summary warrant in, or as nearly as may be in, the form prescribed by Act of Sederunt.

(7) A summary warrant granted under subsection (6) authorises the recovery of the sum payable by—
(*a*) attachment,
(*b*) money attachment,
(*c*) earnings arrestment,
(*d*) arrestment and action of furthcoming or sale.

(8) Subject to subsection (9) and without prejudice to section 39(1) of the Debt Arrangement and Attachment (Scotland) Act 2002 (asp 17) (expenses of attachment)—
(*a*) the sheriff officer's fees, and
(*b*) any outlays necessarily incurred by that officer,
in connection with the execution of a summary warrant are to be chargeable against the person in relation to whom the warrant was granted.

(9) No fees are to be chargeable by the sheriff officer against the person in relation to whom the summary warrant was granted for collecting, and accounting to the Commissioners for, sums paid to that officer by that person in respect of the sum payable.

(10) This section extends to Scotland only.

Orders—Finance Act 2008, Section 128 and Part 2 of Schedule 43 (Appointed Day, Transitional Provision and Savings) Order, SI 2009/3024 (day appointed for the coming into force of s 128 and Sch 43 Part 2 is 23 November 2009).

129 Consequential provision and commencement

(1) Part 1 of Schedule 43 contains provision consequential on section 127.

(2) Part 2 of that Schedule contains provision consequential on section 128.

(3) The extent of the amendments and repeals in Schedule 43 is the same as the provision amended or repealed.

(4) Sections 127 and 128 and Schedule 43 come into force on such day as the Commissioners may by order made by statutory instrument appoint.

(5) An order under subsection (4) may—
(*a*) make different provision for different purposes, and
(*b*) contain transitional provision and savings.

Commencement—Finance Act 2008, Section 128 and Part 2 of Schedule 43 (Appointed Day, Transitional Provision and Savings) Order, SI 2009/3024.
Finance Act 2008, Section 127 and Part 1 of Schedule 43 (Appointed Day) Order, SI 2014/906.

Set off

130 Set-off: England and Wales and Northern Ireland

(1) This section applies where there is both a credit and a debit in relation to a person.

(2) The Commissioners may set the credit against the debit (subject to section 131 and any obligation of the Commissioners to set the credit against another sum).

(3) The obligations of the Commissioners and the person concerned are discharged to the extent of any set-off under subsection (2).

(4) "Credit", in relation to a person, means—
(*a*) a sum that is payable by the Commissioners to the person under or by virtue of an enactment, or
(*b*) a relevant sum that may be repaid to the person by the Commissioners.

(5) For the purposes of subsection (4), in relation to a person, "relevant sum" means a sum that was paid in connection with any liability (including any purported or anticipated liability) of that person to make a payment to the Commissioners under or by virtue of an enactment or under a contract settlement.

(6) "Debit", in relation to a person, means a sum that is payable by the person to the Commissioners under or by virtue of an enactment or under a contract settlement.

(7) In this section references to sums paid, repaid or payable by or to a person (however expressed) include sums that have been or are to be credited by or to a person.

(8) This section has effect without prejudice to any other power of the Commissioners to set off amounts.

(9) (*amends* ITA 2007 s 429(5))

(10) Subsections (1) to (8) extend to England and Wales and Northern Ireland only.

CROSS-REFERENCES—

See VATA 1994 Sch 3B para 16N (where a participant in a special scheme is liable to pay UK VAT to the tax authorities for the administering member State in accordance with the scheme, the UK VAT is regarded for the purposes of sub-s (6) as payable to the Commissioners).

VATA 1994 Sch 3BA para 35 (where a participant in a non-UK special scheme is liable to pay UK VAT to the tax authorities for the administering member State in accordance with the scheme, the UK VAT is regarded for the purposes of sub-s (6) as payable to the Commissioners).

131 No set-off where insolvency procedure has been applied

(1) This section applies where—

(*a*) an insolvency procedure has been applied to a person, and

(*b*) there is a post-insolvency credit in relation to that person.

(2) The Commissioners may not use the power under section 130 to set that post-insolvency credit against a pre-insolvency debit in relation to the person.

(3) "Post-insolvency credit" means a credit that—

(*a*) became due after the insolvency procedure was applied to the person, and

(*b*) relates to, or to matters occurring at, times after it was so applied.

(4) "Pre-insolvency debit" means a debit that—

(*a*) arose before the insolvency procedure was applied to the person, or

(*b*) arose after that procedure was so applied but relates to, or to matters occurring at, times before it was so applied.

(5) Subject to subsection (6), an insolvency procedure is to be taken, for the purposes of this section, to be applied to a person when—

(*a*) a bankruptcy order or winding up order is made or an administrator is appointed in relation to that person,

(*b*) that person is put into administrative receivership,

(*c*) if the person is a corporation, that person passes a resolution for voluntary winding up,

(*d*) a voluntary arrangement comes into force in relation to that person, or

(*e*) a deed of arrangement takes effect in relation to that person.

(6) In this section references to the application of an insolvency procedure to a person do not include—

(*a*) the application of an insolvency procedure to a person at a time when another insolvency procedure applies to the person, or

(*b*) the application of an insolvency procedure to a person immediately upon another insolvency procedure ceasing to have effect.

(7) For the purposes of this section—

(*a*) a person shall be treated as being in administrative receivership throughout any continuous period for which there is an administrative receiver of that person (disregarding any temporary vacancy in the office of receiver), and

(*b*) the reference in subsection (5) to a person being put into administrative receivership shall be interpreted accordingly.

(8) In this section—

"administrative receiver" means an administrative receiver within the meaning of section 251 of the Insolvency Act 1986 (c 45) or Article 5(1) of the Insolvency (Northern Ireland) Order 1989 (SI 1989/2405 (NI 19)),

"administrator" means a person appointed to manage the affairs, business and property of another person under Schedule B1 to that Act or to that Order,

"credit" and "debit" have the same meaning as in section 130,

"deed of arrangement" means a deed of arrangement registered in accordance with the Deeds of Arrangement Act 1914 (c 47) or Chapter 1 of Part 8 the Insolvency (Northern Ireland) Order 1989 (SI 1989/2405 (NI 19)), and

"voluntary arrangement" means a voluntary arrangement approved in accordance with Part 1 or Part 8 of the Insolvency Act 1986 (c 45) or Part 2 or Chapter 2 of Part 8 of the Insolvency (Northern Ireland) Order 1989.

(9) This section extends to England and Wales and Northern Ireland only.

132 VAT: requirement to set-off

(1) Section 81 of VATA 1994 (set-off of credits etc) is amended as follows.

(2) (*substitutes* VATA 1994 s 81(4C))

(3) In subsection (5)—

(*a*) (*repeals* VATA 1994 s 81(5)(*a*))

(*b*) (*amends* VATA 1994 s 81(5)(*b*))

(*c*) (*inserts* VATA 1994 s 81(5)(*ba*))

133 Set-off etc where right to be paid a sum has been transferred

(1) This section applies where there has been a transfer from one person ("the original creditor") to another person ("the current creditor") of a right to be paid a sum ("the transferred sum") by the Commissioners.

(2) The Commissioners—

(*a*) must set the transferred sum against a sum payable to them by the original creditor if they would have had an obligation to do so under or by virtue of an enactment had the original creditor retained the right, and

(*b*) may do so if they would have had a power to do so under or by virtue of an enactment or under a rule of law had the original creditor retained the right.

(3) Subsection (2) applies whether the sum payable by the original creditor to the Commissioners first became payable before or after the transfer (but not if it only became payable after the Commissioners discharged their obligation to pay the transferred sum to the current creditor).

(4) The following are discharged to the extent of any set-off under this section—

(*a*) the obligations of the Commissioners in relation to the current creditor, and

(*b*) the obligations of the original creditor.

(5) An obligation under or by virtue of an enactment (other than this section) to set the transferred sum against a sum payable to the Commissioners by a person other than the original creditor has effect subject to the obligation under subsection (2)(*a*) and to any exercise of the power under subsection (2)(*b*).

(6) A power under or by virtue of an enactment (other than this section) or under a rule of law to set the transferred sum against a sum payable to the Commissioners by a person other than the original creditor has effect subject to the obligation under subsection (2)(*a*).

(7) In determining the sum (if any) to be paid, the Commissioners may make any reduction that they could have made if the original creditor had retained the right to be paid the transferred sum (in addition to any other reduction that they are entitled to make), including a reduction arising from any defence to a claim for the sum.

(8) In this section—

(*a*) references to the transfer of a right are to its transfer by assignment, assignation or any other means, . . . [1]

(*b*) references to a sum that is payable by or to a person are to a sum that is to be paid, repaid or credited by or to that person and references to the payment of the sum (however expressed) are to be interpreted accordingly, and

(*c*) where a right in relation to a sum has been transferred more than once, references to the original creditor are to the person from whom the right was first transferred (except in subsection (1)).

(9) Where the right to be paid the transferred sum is dependent on the making of a claim—

(*a*) subsection (2) does not apply unless a claim in respect of the transferred sum has been made, and

(*b*) the references in subsections (2) and (7) to the obligations or powers that the Commissioners would have had if the original creditor had retained the right are references to those that they would have had if the original creditor had also made the claim in respect of the transferred sum.

(10) This section has effect where the right to be paid the transferred sum was transferred from the original creditor on or after 25 June 2008.

Amendments—

[1] Words in sub-s (8)(a) repealed by FA 2012 s 50(2)(c). This amendment is treated as having come into force on 6 April 2012.

134 Retained funding bonds: tender by Commissioners

(1)–(4) (*amend* ITA 2007 s 939)

(5) The amendments made by this section have effect in relation to funding bonds issued on or after 12 March 2008.

Other measures

135 Interest on unpaid tax in case of disaster etc of national significance

(1) This section applies in any case where the Commissioners agree that the payment of a relevant sum may be deferred by reason of circumstances arising as a result of a disaster or emergency specified in an order under this section (an "agreement for deferred payment").

(2) In subsection (1) "relevant sum" means a sum to meet any liability to the Commissioners arising under or by virtue of an enactment or a contract settlement.

(3) No interest on the amount deferred is chargeable in respect of the relief period and no liability to a surcharge on the deferred amount arises during that period.

(4) The relief period is the period—

(*a*) beginning with a date specified in the order or, if the Commissioners so direct, a later date from which the agreement for deferred payment has effect, and

(*b*) ending with the date on which the agreement for deferred payment ceases to have effect or, if earlier, the date on which the order is revoked.

(5) The agreement for deferred payment ceases to have effect at the end of the period of deferment specified in the agreement or, if the Commissioners agree to extend (or further extend) that period by reason of circumstances arising as a result of the disaster or emergency, with the end of that extended (or further extended) period.

(6) If the agreement for deferred payment is an agreement for payment by instalments, the period of deferment in relation to each instalment ends with the date on or before which that instalment is to be paid; but if an instalment is not paid by the agreed date and the Commissioners do not agree to extend the period of deferment, the whole of the agreement for deferred payment is to be treated as ceasing to have effect on that date.

(7) This section applies whether the agreement for deferred payment was made—

(*a*) before or after the amount to which it relates becomes due and payable, or

(*b*) before or after the making of the order concerned.

(8) If in any case the Commissioners are satisfied that, although no agreement for deferred payment was made, one could have been made, this section applies as if one had been made; and the terms of the notional agreement for deferred payment are to be assumed to be such as the Commissioners are satisfied would have been agreed in the circumstances.

(9) An order under this section may be made only in relation to a disaster or emergency which the Treasury consider to be of national significance.

(10) Such an order—

(*a*) may specify a disaster or emergency which has begun (or both begun and ended) before it is made (including one which has begun, or both begun and ended, before the passing of this Act), and

(*b*) may specify a date before the date on which it is made (including a date before the passing of this Act).

(11) The power to make an order under this section is exercisable by the Treasury by statutory instrument.

(12) A statutory instrument containing such an order is subject to annulment in pursuance of a resolution of the House of Commons.

(13) In FA 2001, omit section 107 (interest on unpaid tax etc: foot and mouth disease); but the repeal of that section does not affect any agreement for deferred payment made before this Act is passed.

136 Fee for payment

(1) The Commissioners may by regulations provide that, where a person makes a payment to the Commissioners or a person authorised by the Commissioners using a method of payment specified in the regulations, the person must also pay a fee specified in, or determined in accordance with, the regulations.

(2) A method of payment may only be specified in regulations made under this section if the Commissioners expect that they, or the person authorised by them, will be required to pay a fee or charge (however described) in connection with amounts paid using that method of payment.

(3) Regulations under this section—

(*a*) may make provision about the time and manner in which the fee must or may be paid,

(*b*) may make provision generally or only for specified purposes, and

(*c*) may make different provision for different purposes.

(4) Regulations under this section are to be made by statutory instrument.

(5) A statutory instrument containing regulations under this section is subject to annulment in pursuance of a resolution of the House of Commons.

Orders—The Taxes, etc (Fees for Payment by Internet) Regulations, SI 2011/711.
Taxes, etc (Fees for Payment by Telephone) Regulations, SI 2012/689.

137 County court proceedings

(1) (*inserts* CRCA 2005 s 25(1A), (6))

(2) (*amends* TMA 1970 s 66)

(3) (*repeals* FA 1984 s 57(2))

(4) (*amends* IHTA 1984 s 244)

(5) (*amends* Social Security Contributions (Transfer of Functions, etc) Act 1999)

(6) (*amends* FA 2003 Sch 12 para 5)

(7) Nothing in subsections (2) to (6) affects proceedings commenced or brought in the name of a collector or authorised officer before this Act is passed.

138 Certificates of debt

(1) (*inserts* CRCA 2005 s 25A)

(2) Schedule 44 contains provisions consequential on this section.

Supplementary

139 Interpretation of Chapter

In this Chapter—

"the Commissioners" means the Commissioners for Her Majesty's Revenue and Customs, and "contract settlement" means an agreement made in connection with any person's liability to make a payment to the Commissioners under or by virtue of an enactment.

PART 8
MISCELLANEOUS

Payments from Exchequer accounts

158 Power of Treasury to make payments

(1) This section applies if a person makes a claim which, in the Treasury's opinion, is a financial claim that concerns an Exchequer account.

(2) The Treasury may pay money from any Exchequer account—

(*a*) to satisfy the claim (in whole or in part), or

(*b*) to enable the claim to be satisfied (in whole or in part) from another government account.

(3) The reference in this section to a financial claim that concerns an Exchequer account includes, in particular, either of the following cases.

(4) The first case is where a financial claim relates to—

(*a*) a case where money is paid into a government account, but the money should not have, or need not have, been paid into that account, or

(*b*) a case where money should have been, or needed to be, paid out of a government account, but the money—

(i) was not paid out of that account, or

(ii) was paid out of that account, but not as it should have been, or needed to be, paid.

(5) The second case is where a financial claim relates to the exercise of functions that relate to an Exchequer account (whether the functions are exercisable by the Treasury or another person).

(6) In this section—

"Exchequer account" means—

(*a*) the Consolidated Fund,

(*b*) the Debt Management Account,

(*c*) the Exchange Equalisation Account, or

(*d*) the National Loans Fund;

and a reference to an Exchequer account includes a reference to the assets or liabilities of the account;

"financial claim" means a claim (whether or not legally enforceable) for the payment of an amount of money, including a claim in respect of—

(*a*) money paid or not paid by any person,

(*b*) interest earned or not earned by any person, or

(*c*) loss, costs or expenses incurred by any person;

"government account" means—

(*a*) an Exchequer account, or

(*b*) any other account in which money is held by or on behalf of Her Majesty's Government in the United Kingdom.

159 Payments from certain Exchequer accounts: mechanism

(1) This section applies to money to be paid under section 158 from—

(*a*) the Consolidated Fund, or

(*b*) the National Loans Fund.

(2) In the case of the Consolidated Fund—

(*a*) the Comptroller and Auditor General shall on receipt of a requisition from the Treasury grant a credit on the Exchequer Account at the Bank of England (or on its growing balance), and

(*b*) an issue shall be made on orders given to the Bank by the Treasury in accordance with a credit granted under paragraph (*a*).

(3) An issue made under subsection (2) shall be recorded in the daily account under section 15(5) of the Exchequer and Audit Departments Act 1866 (c 39).

(4) In the case of the National Loans Fund—

(*a*) the Comptroller and Auditor General shall at the request of the Treasury grant a credit on the National Loans Fund, and

(*b*) a payment out of the Fund shall be made by the Treasury in accordance with a credit granted under paragraph (*a*).

(5) A payment made under subsection (4) shall be recorded in the daily account under section 1(2) of the National Loans Act 1968 (c 13).

Other matters

160 Power to give statutory effect to concessions

(1) The Treasury may by order make provision for and in connection with giving effect to any existing HMRC concession.

(2) "Existing HMRC concession" means a statement made by the Commissioners for Her Majesty's Revenue and Customs before the passing of this Act, and having effect at that time, that they will treat persons as if they were entitled to—

(*a*) a reduction in a liability to a tax or duty, or

(*b*) any other concession relating to a tax or duty,

to which they are not, or may not be, entitled in accordance with the law.

(3) For this purpose "statement" means a statement of any sort, whether it was described as an extra-statutory concession, a statement of practice, an interpretation, a decision or a press release or in any other way.

(4) The reference in subsection (2) to the Commissioners for Her Majesty's Revenue and Customs includes the Commissioners of Inland Revenue and the Commissioners of Customs and Excise.

(5) An order under this section—

(*a*) may give effect to an existing HMRC concession with or without modification,

(*b*) may include supplementary, incidental, consequential or transitional provision, and

(*c*) may include provisions amending (or repealing or revoking) any enactment or instrument (whenever passed or made).

(6) The power to make an order under this section is exercisable by statutory instrument.

(7) No order is to be made under this section unless a draft of the order has been laid before, and approved by a resolution of, the House of Commons.

Orders—Enactment of Extra-Statutory Concessions Order, SI 2009/730.

Enactment of Extra-Statutory Concessions Order, SI 2010/157.

Enactment of Extra-Statutory Concessions Order, SI 2012/266.

Enactment of Extra-Statutory Concessions Order, SI 2013/234.

PART 9

FINAL PROVISIONS

165 Interpretation

(1) In this Act—

"ALDA 1979" means the Alcoholic Liquor Duties Act 1979 (c 4),

"BGDA 1981" means the Betting and Gaming Duties Act 1981 (c 63),

"CAA 2001" means the Capital Allowances Act 2001 (c 2),

"CEMA 1979" means the Customs and Excise Management Act 1979 (c 2),

"CRCA 2005" means the Commissioners for Revenue and Customs Act 2005 (c 11),

"CTTA 1984" means the Capital Transfer Tax Act 1984 (c 51),

"HODA 1979" means the Hydrocarbon Oil Duties Act 1979 (c 5),

"ICTA" means the Income and Corporation Taxes Act 1988 (c 1),

"IHTA 1984" means the Inheritance Tax Act 1984 (c 51),

"ITA 2007" means the Income Tax Act 2007 (c 3),

"ITEPA 2003" means the Income Tax (Earnings and Pensions) Act 2003 (c 1),

"ITTOIA 2005" means the Income Tax (Trading and Other Income) Act 2005 (c 5),

"OTA 1975" means the Oil Taxation Act 1975 (c 22),

"TCGA 1992" means the Taxation of Chargeable Gains Act 1992 (c 12),

"TMA 1970" means the Taxes Management Act 1970 (c 9),

"TPDA 1979" means the Tobacco Products Duty Act 1979 (c 7),

"VATA 1994" means the Value Added Tax Act 1994 (c 23), and

"VERA 1994" means the Vehicle Excise and Registration Act 1994 (c 22).

(2) In this Act—

"FA", followed by a year, means the Finance Act of that year, and

"F(No 2)A", followed by a year, means the Finance (No 2) Act of that year.

166 Short title

This Act may be cited as the Finance Act 2008.

SCHEDULES

SCHEDULE 36

INFORMATION AND INSPECTION POWERS

Section 113

Commentary—*Simon's Taxes* **A6.301A.**

Commencement—Finance Act 2008, Schedule 36 (Appointed Day and Savings) Order, SI 2009/404 art 2 (appointed day for the coming into force of Sch 36 is 1 April 2009).
HMRC Manuals—Compliance Handbook Manual, CH275000–285000 (HMRC inspection powers – compliance check).

CH20150–27200 (HMRC information and inspection powers).
Cross-references—See the Small Charitable Donations Regulations, SI 2013/938 reg 5 (application of this Schedule regarding checking a charity's position in relation to a top-up claim or an overpayment for the purposes of small charitable donations).

PART 1
POWERS TO OBTAIN INFORMATION AND DOCUMENTS

Power to obtain information and documents from taxpayer

1—(1) An officer of Revenue and Customs may by notice in writing require a person ("the taxpayer")—

(*a*) to provide information, or

(*b*) to produce a document,

if the information or document is reasonably required by the officer for the purpose of checking the taxpayer's tax position.
(2) In this Schedule, "taxpayer notice" means a notice under this paragraph.

Commentary—*Simon's Taxes* **A6.301A**.
Commencement—Finance Act 2008, Schedule 36 (Appointed Day and Savings) Order, SI 2009/404 art 2 (appointed day for the coming into force of Sch 36 is 1 April 2009).
HMRC Manuals—Compliance Handbook Manual, CH23060 and 23080 (HMRC inspection powers: three types of information notice and approval thereof).
CH23520 (HMRC inspection powers: specific rules regarding taxpayer notice).
CH221000–223200 (HMRC inspection powers – how to do a compliance check: taxpayer notice).
CH223400 (tribunal approval).
Cross references—FA 2014 Sch 34 para 10 (failure to comply with a notice under this section triggers threshold condition leading to consideration for a conduct notice).

Power to obtain information and documents from third party

2—(1) An officer of Revenue and Customs may by notice in writing require a person—

(*a*) to provide information, or

(*b*) to produce a document,

if the information or document is reasonably required by the officer for the purpose of checking the tax position of another person whose identity is known to the officer ("the taxpayer").
(2) A third party notice must name the taxpayer to whom it relates, unless the [tribunal][1] has approved the giving of the notice and disapplied this requirement under paragraph 3.
(3) In this Schedule, "third party notice" means a notice under this paragraph.

Commentary—*Simon's Taxes* **A6.301A**.
Commencement—Finance Act 2008, Schedule 36 (Appointed Day and Savings) Order, SI 2009/404 art 2 (appointed day for the coming into force of Sch 36 is 1 April 2009).
HMRC Manuals—Compliance Handbook Manual, CH23060 and 23080 (HMRC inspection powers: three types of information notice and approval thereof).
CH23620 (HMRC inspection powers: specific rules regarding third party notice).
CH225050 (HMRC inspection powers – how to do a compliance check: what is a third party notice).
CH225100 (persons on whom a third party notice can be served).
CH225150 (considerations prior to issue).
CH225200 (restrictions on third party notices).
Cross references—FA 2014 Sch 34 para 10 (failure to comply with a notice under this section triggers threshold condition leading to consideration for a conduct notice).
Amendments—[1] In sub-para (2) word substituted for the words "First-tier Tribunal" by the Transfer of Tribunal Functions and Revenue and Customs Appeals Order, SI 2009/56 art 3, Sch 1 para 471 with effect from 1 April 2009.

Approval etc of taxpayer notices and third party notices

3—(1) An officer of Revenue and Customs may not give a third party notice without—

(*a*) the agreement of the taxpayer, or

(*b*) the approval of the [tribunal][1].

(2) An officer of Revenue and Customs may ask for the approval of the [tribunal][1] to the giving of any taxpayer notice or third party notice (and for the effect of obtaining such approval see paragraphs 29, 30 and 53 (appeals against notices and offence)).
[(2A) An application for approval under this paragraph may be made without notice (except as required under sub-paragraph (3)).][2]
(3) The [tribunal][1] may not approve the giving of a taxpayer notice or third party notice unless—

(*a*) an application for approval is made by, or with the agreement of, an authorised officer of Revenue and Customs,

(*b*) the [tribunal][1] is satisfied that, in the circumstances, the officer giving the notice is justified in doing so,

(*c*) the person to whom the notice is [to be][2] addressed has been told that the information or documents referred to in the notice are required and given a reasonable opportunity to make representations to an officer of Revenue and Customs,

(*d*) the [tribunal][1] has been given a summary of any representations made by that person, and

(*e*) in the case of a third party notice, the taxpayer has been given a summary of the reasons why an officer of Revenue and Customs requires the information and documents.

(4) Paragraphs (*c*) to (*e*) of sub-paragraph (3) do not apply to the extent that the [tribunal][1] is satisfied that taking the action specified in those paragraphs might prejudice the assessment or collection of tax.

(5) Where the [tribunal][1] approves the giving of a third party notice under this paragraph, it may also disapply the requirement to name the taxpayer in the notice if it is satisfied that the officer has reasonable grounds for believing that naming the taxpayer might seriously prejudice the assessment or collection of tax.

Commentary—*Simon's Taxes* **A6.301A**.

Commencement—Finance Act 2008, Schedule 36 (Appointed Day and Savings) Order, SI 2009/404 art 2 (appointed day for the coming into force of Sch 36 is 1 April 2009).

HMRC Manuals—Compliance Handbook Manual, CH23060 and 23080 (HMRC inspection powers: three types of information notice and approval thereof).

CH23520 (HMRC inspection powers: specific rules regarding taxpayer notice).

CH23620 (HMRC inspection powers: specific rules regarding third party notice).

CH24100 (HMRC inspection powers: the Tribunal).

CH24120–24180 (taxpayer and third party notices).

CH25450 (Tribunal approval).

CH225310–225320 (where no approval is required).

CH225410 (where approval is required).

CH225420 (taxpayer agreement).

CH225430–225440 (summary of reasons and reasons not be given).

CH225460 (opportunity letter requirements).

Amendments—[1] Word substituted for the words "First-tier Tribunal" in each place; in sub-para (4) word substituted for the word "Tribunal" by the Transfer of Tribunal Functions and Revenue and Customs Appeals Order, SI 2009/56 art 3, Sch 1 para 471 with effect from 1 April 2009.

[2] Sub-para (2A), and words in sub-para (3)(*c*), inserted, by FA 2009 s 95, Sch 47 para 2 with effect from 21 July 2009.

Copying third party notice to taxpayer

4—(1) An officer of Revenue and Customs who gives a third party notice must give a copy of the notice to the taxpayer to whom it relates, unless the [tribunal][1] has disapplied this requirement.

(2) The [tribunal][1] may not disapply that requirement unless—

(*a*) an application for approval is made by, or with the agreement of, an authorised officer of Revenue and Customs, and

(*b*) the [tribunal][1] is satisfied that the officer has reasonable grounds for believing that giving a copy of the notice to the taxpayer might prejudice the assessment or collection of tax.

Commentary—*Simon's Taxes* **A6.301A**.

Commencement—Finance Act 2008, Schedule 36 (Appointed Day and Savings) Order, SI 2009/404 art 2 (appointed day for the coming into force of Sch 36 is 1 April 2009).

HMRC Manuals—Compliance Handbook Manual, CH23620 (HMRC inspection powers: specific rules regarding third party notice).

CH23640–23660 (HMRC inspection powers: copy of the notice to the named person).

CH225250 (HMRC inspection powers – how to do a compliance check: copying notice to taxpayer).

Amendments—[1] Word substituted for the words "First-tier Tribunal" in each place; in sub-para (2)(*b*) word substituted for the word "Tribunal" by the Transfer of Tribunal Functions and Revenue and Customs Appeals Order, SI 2009/56 art 3, Sch 1 para 471 with effect from 1 April 2009.

Power to obtain information and documents about persons whose identity is not known

5—(1) An authorised officer of Revenue and Customs may by notice in writing require a person—

(*a*) to provide information, or

(*b*) to produce a document,

if the condition in sub-paragraph (2) is met.

(2) That condition is that the information or document is reasonably required by the officer for the purpose of checking the . . . [4] tax position of—

(*a*) a person whose identity is not known to the officer, or

(*b*) a class of persons whose individual identities are not known to the officer.

(3) An officer of Revenue and Customs may not give a notice under this paragraph without the approval of the [tribunal][1].

[(3A) An application for approval under this paragraph may be made without notice.][2]

(4) The [tribunal][1] may not [approve the giving of a notice under][2] this paragraph unless it is satisfied that—

(*a*) the notice would meet the condition in sub-paragraph (2),

(*b*) there are reasonable grounds for believing that the person or any of the class of persons to whom the notice relates may have failed or may fail to comply with any provision of [the law (including the law of a territory outside the United Kingdom) relating to tax,][4][3],

(*c*) any such failure is likely to have led or to lead to serious prejudice to the assessment or collection of . . . [4] tax, and

(*d*) the information or document to which the notice relates is not readily available from another source.

(5) . . . [4]

Commentary—*Simon's Taxes* **A6.301A.**

Commencement—Finance Act 2008, Schedule 36 (Appointed Day and Savings) Order, SI 2009/404 art 2 (appointed day for the coming into force of Sch 36 is 1 April 2009).

HMRC Manuals—Compliance Handbook Manual, CH23900 (HMRC inspection powers: identity unknown notice).
CH24200 (HMRC inspection powers: Tribunal approval of identity unknown notice).
CH227100–227200 (HMRC inspection powers – how to do a compliance check: identity unknown notice).

Cross references—FA 2014 Sch 34 para 10 (failure to comply with a notice under this section triggers threshold condition leading to consideration for a conduct notice).

Amendments—[1] In sub-paras (3), (4) word substituted for the words "First-tier Tribunal" by the Transfer of Tribunal Functions and Revenue and Customs Appeals Order, SI 2009/56 art 3, Sch 1 para 471 with effect from 1 April 2009.

[2] Sub-para (3A) inserted, in sub-para (4) words substituted for words "give its approval for the purpose of", by FA 2009 s 95, Sch 47 para 3 with effect from 21 July 2009.

[3] In sub-para (4)(*b*) words substituted for words ", VATA 1994 or any other enactment relating to value added tax charged in accordance with that Act", by FA 2009 s 96, Sch 48 para 2 with effect from 1 April 2010 (by virtue of SI 2009/3054 art 2.

[4] In sub-paras (2), (4)*c*), word repealed, in sub-para (4)(*b*) words substituted, and sub-para (5) repealed, by FA 2011 s 86(2), Sch 24 paras 1, 2 with effect from 1 April 2012 and from then on in relation to tax regardless of when the tax became due (whether before, on or after that date).

[Power to obtain information about persons whose identity can be ascertained

5A—(1) An authorised officer of Revenue and Customs may by notice in writing require a person to provide relevant information about another person ("the taxpayer") if conditions A to D are met.

(2) Condition A is that the information is reasonably required by the officer for the purpose of checking the tax position of the taxpayer.

(3) Condition B is that—

(*a*) the taxpayer's identity is not known to the officer, but

(*b*) the officer holds information from which the taxpayer's identity can be ascertained.

(4) Condition C is that the officer has reason to believe that—

(*a*) the person will be able to ascertain the taxpayer's identity from the information held by the officer, and

(*b*) the person obtained relevant information about the taxpayer in the course of carrying on a business.

(5) Condition D is that the taxpayer's identity cannot readily be ascertained by other means from the information held by the officer.

(6) "Relevant information" means all or any of the following—

(*a*) name,

(*b*) last known address, and

(*c*) date of birth (in the case of an individual).

(7) This paragraph applies for the purpose of checking the tax position of a class of persons as for the purpose of checking the tax position of a single person (and references to "the taxpayer" are to be read accordingly).][1]

Cross references—FA 2014 Sch 34 para 10 (failure to comply with a notice under this section triggers threshold condition leading to consideration for a conduct notice).

Amendments—[1] This para inserted by FA 2012 s 224(1), (2) with effect for the purpose of checking the tax position of a taxpayer as regards periods or tax liabilities whenever arising (whether before, on or after 17 July 2012).

Notices

6—(1) In this Schedule, "information notice" means a notice under paragraph 1, 2[, 5 or 5A][3].

(2) An information notice may specify or describe the information or documents to be provided or produced.

(3) If an information notice is given with the approval of the [tribunal][1], it must state that it is given with that approval.

[(4) A decision of the tribunal under paragraph 3, 4 or 5 is final (despite the provisions of sections 11 and 13 of the Tribunals, Courts and Enforcement Act 2007).][2]

Commentary—*Simon's Taxes* **A6.301A**.

Commencement—Finance Act 2008, Schedule 36 (Appointed Day and Savings) Order, SI 2009/404 art 2 (appointed day for the coming into force of Sch 36 is 1 April 2009).

HMRC Manuals—Compliance Handbook Manual, CH229300–229900 (HMRC inspection powers – how to do a compliance check: rules that apply to all notices).

Amendments—[1] In sub-para (3) word substituted for the words "First-tier Tribunal" by the Transfer of Tribunal Functions and Revenue and Customs Appeals Order, SI 2009/56 art 3, Sch 1 para 471 with effect from 1 April 2009.

[2] Sub-para (4) inserted by FA 2009 s 95, Sch 47 para 4 with effect from 21 July 2009.

[3] In sub-para (1) words substituted by FA 2012 s 224(1), (3) with effect for the purpose of checking the tax position of a taxpayer as regards periods or tax liabilities whenever arising (whether before, on or after 17 July 2012).

Complying with notices

7—(1) Where a person is required by an information notice to provide information or produce a document, the person must do so—

(*a*) within such period, and

(*b*) at such time, by such means and in such form (if any),

as is reasonably specified or described in the notice.

(2) Where an information notice requires a person to produce a document, it must be produced for inspection—

(*a*) at a place agreed to by that person and an officer of Revenue and Customs, or

(*b*) at such place as an officer of Revenue and Customs may reasonably specify.

(3) An officer of Revenue and Customs must not specify a place that is used solely as a dwelling.

(4) The production of a document in compliance with an information notice is not to be regarded as breaking any lien claimed on the document.

Commencement—Finance Act 2008, Schedule 36 (Appointed Day and Savings) Order, SI 2009/404 art 2 (appointed day for the coming into force of Sch 36 is 1 April 2009).

HMRC Manuals—Compliance Handbook Manual, CH23220 (HMRC inspection powers: meaning of "provide information", with example).

CH23260 (meaning of "produce documents").

CH23420 (date by which information required).

CH23480 (complying with a notice).

Producing copies of documents

8—(1) Where an information notice requires a person to produce a document, the person may comply with the notice by producing a copy of the document, subject to any conditions or exceptions set out in regulations made by the Commissioners.

(2) Sub-paragraph (1) does not apply where—

(*a*) the notice requires the person to produce the original document, or

(*b*) an officer of Revenue and Customs subsequently makes a request in writing to the person for the original document.

(3) Where an officer of Revenue and Customs requests a document under sub-paragraph (2)(*b*), the person to whom the request is made must produce the document—

(*a*) within such period, and

(*b*) at such time and by such means (if any),

as is reasonably requested by the officer.

Commencement—Finance Act 2008, Schedule 36 (Appointed Day and Savings) Order, SI 2009/404 art 2 (appointed day for the coming into force of Sch 36 is 1 April 2009).

Restrictions and special cases

9 This Part of this Schedule has effect subject to Parts 4 and 6 of this Schedule.

Commencement—Finance Act 2008, Schedule 36 (Appointed Day and Savings) Order, SI 2009/404 art 2 (appointed day for the coming into force of Sch 36 is 1 April 2009).

PART 2
POWERS TO INSPECT [PREMISES AND OTHER PROPERTY][1]

Amendments—[1] Words in heading substituted for words "Businesses etc" by the Finance Act 2009, Section 96 and Schedule 48 (Appointed Day, Savings and Consequential Amendments) Order, SI 2009/3054 art 3, Schedule para 15 with effect from 1 April 2010.

Power to inspect business premises etc

10—(1) An officer of Revenue and Customs may enter a person's business premises and inspect—

(*a*) the premises,

(*b*) business assets that are on the premises, and

(*c*) business documents that are on the premises,

if the inspection is reasonably required for the purpose of checking that person's tax position.

(2) The powers under this paragraph do not include power to enter or inspect any part of the premises that is used solely as a dwelling.

(3) In this Schedule—

"business assets" means assets that an officer of Revenue and Customs has reason to believe are owned, leased or used in connection with the carrying on of a business by any person [(but see sub-paragraph (4))][1],

"business documents" means documents (or copies of documents)—

(*a*) that relate to the carrying on of a business by any person, and

(*b*) that form part of any person's statutory records, and

"business premises", in relation to a person, means premises (or any part of premises) that an officer of Revenue and Customs has reason to believe are (or is) used in connection with the carrying on of a business by or on behalf of the person.

[(4) For the purposes of this Schedule, "business assets" does not include documents, other than—

(*a*) documents that are trading stock for the purposes of Chapter 11A of Part 2 of ITTOIA 2005 (see section 172A of that Act), and

(*b*) documents that are plant for the purposes of Part 2 of CAA 2001.][1]

Commentary—*Simon's Taxes* **A6.301A**.

Commencement—Finance Act 2008, Schedule 36 (Appointed Day and Savings) Order, SI 2009/404 art 2 (appointed day for the coming into force of Sch 36 is 1 April 2009).

HMRC Manuals—Compliance Handbook Manual, CH25120 (HMRC inspection powers: meaning of "enter").

CH25140–25160 (meaning of "inspect" with examples).

CH25180 (meaning of "business premises").

CH25220–25240 (inspecting business premises that are a home).

CH25260 and 25280 (meaning of "business assets" and "business documents").

CH25420 (HMRC inspection powers: start and end of an inspection).

CH25460 (when to carry out an inspection).

CH25480 (HMRC inspection powers: announced and unannounced inspection).

CH25540 (Tribunal approval).

CH25560 (wording of inspection notices).

Amendments—[1] In sub-para (3) in the definition of "business assets" words substituted for words ", excluding documents", and sub-para (4) inserted by FA 2009 s 95, Sch 47 para 5 with effect from 21 July 2009.

[Power to inspect business premises etc of involved third parties

10A—(1) An officer of Revenue and Customs may enter business premises of an involved third party (see paragraph 61A) and inspect—

(*a*) the premises,

(*b*) business assets that are on the premises, and

(*c*) relevant documents that are on the premises,

if the inspection is reasonably required by the officer for the purpose of checking the position of any person or class of persons as regards a relevant tax.

(2) The powers under this paragraph may be exercised whether or not the identity of that person is, or the individual identities of those persons are, known to the officer.

(3) The powers under this paragraph do not include power to enter or inspect any part of the premises that is used solely as a dwelling.

(4) In relation to an involved third party, "relevant documents" and "relevant tax" are defined in paragraph 61A.]

Amendments—Para 10A inserted by FA 2009 s 96, Sch 48 para 3 with effect from 1 April 2010 (by virtue of SI 2009/3054 art 2).

Power to inspect premises used in connection with taxable supplies etc

11—(1) This paragraph applies where an officer of Revenue and Customs has reason to believe that—

(*a*) premises are used in connection with the supply of goods under taxable supplies and goods to be so supplied [or documents relating to such goods][1] are on those premises,

(*b*) premises are used in connection with the acquisition of goods from other member States under taxable acquisitions and goods to be so acquired [or documents relating to such goods][1] are on those premises, or

(*c*) premises are used as [or in connection with][1] a fiscal warehouse.

(2) An officer of Revenue and Customs may enter the premises and inspect—

(*a*) the premises,

(*b*) any goods that are on the premises, and

(*c*) any documents on the premises that appear to the officer to relate to [the supply of goods under taxable supplies, the acquisition of goods from other member States under taxable acquisitions or fiscal warehousing][1].

(3) The powers under this paragraph do not include power to enter or inspect any part of the premises that is used solely as a dwelling.

(4) Terms used both in [this paragraph][1] and in VATA 1994 have the same meaning [here][1] as they have in that Act.

Commentary—*Simon's Taxes* **A6.301A**.

Commencement—Finance Act 2008, Schedule 36 (Appointed Day and Savings) Order, SI 2009/404 art 2 (appointed day for the coming into force of Sch 36 is 1 April 2009).

HMRC Manuals—Compliance Handbook Manual, CH25420 (HMRC inspection powers: start and end of an inspection).
CH25460 (when to carry out an inspection).
CH25480 (HMRC inspection powers: announced and unannounced inspection).
CH25540 (Tribunal approval).
CH25560 (wording of inspection notices).

Amendments—[1] In sub-para (1)(*a*), (*b*), (*c*) words inserted; in sub-para (2)(*c*) words substituted for words "such goods"; in sub-para (4) words substituted in the first place for words "sub-paragraph (1)" and in the second place for words "in that sub-paragraph", by FA 2009 s 95, Sch 47 para 6 with effect from 21 July 2009.

Carrying out inspections [under paragraph 10, 10A or 11]

12—(1) An inspection under [paragraph 10, 10A or 11][3] may be carried out only—

(*a*) at a time agreed to by the occupier of the premises, or

(*b*) if sub-paragraph (2) is satisfied, at any reasonable time.

(2) This sub-paragraph is satisfied if—

(*a*) the occupier of the premises has been given at least 7 days' notice of the time of the inspection (whether in writing or otherwise), or

(*b*) the inspection is carried out by, or with the agreement of, an authorised officer of Revenue and Customs.

(3) An officer of Revenue and Customs seeking to carry out an inspection under sub-paragraph (2)(*b*) must provide a notice in writing as follows—

(*a*) if the occupier of the premises is present at the time the inspection is to begin, the notice must be provided to the occupier,

(*b*) if the occupier of the premises is not present but a person who appears to the officer to be in charge of the premises is present, the notice must be provided to that person, and

(*c*) in any other case, the notice must be left in a prominent place on the premises.

(4) The notice referred to in sub-paragraph (3) must state the possible consequences of obstructing the officer in the exercise of the power.

(5) If a notice referred to in sub-paragraph (3) is given [in respect of an inspection approved by][2] the [tribunal][1] (see paragraph 13), it must state that [the inspection has been so approved][2].

Commencement—Finance Act 2008, Schedule 36 (Appointed Day and Savings) Order, SI 2009/404 art 2 (appointed day for the coming into force of Sch 36 is 1 April 2009).

HMRC Manuals—Compliance Handbook Manual, CH25480 (HMRC inspection powers: announced and unannounced inspection).
CH25540 (Tribunal approval).
CH25560 (wording of inspection notices).
CH250000 (HMRC inspection powers – how to do a compliance check: visits to business premises).
CH254000 (how to do a compliance check: unannounced visits).
CH255500 (how to do a compliance check: during a visit).
CH255520 (how to do a compliance check: what to do if entry is refused).

Amendments—[1] In sub-para (5) word substituted for the words "First-tier Tribunal" by the Transfer of Tribunal Functions and Revenue and Customs Appeals Order, SI 2009/56 art 3, Sch 1 para 471 with effect from 1 April 2009.

[2] In sub-para (5) words substituted in the first place for the words "with the approval of" and in the second place for the words "it is given with that approval", by FA 2009 s 95, Sch 47 para 7 with effect from 21 July 2009.

[3] In heading words inserted, in sub-para (1) words substituted for words "this Part of this Schedule", by FA 2009 s 96, Sch 48 para 4 with effect from 1 April 2010 (by virtue of SI 2009/3054 art 2).

[Powers to inspect property for valuation etc

12A—(1) An officer of Revenue and Customs may enter and inspect premises for the purpose of valuing the premises if the valuation is reasonably required for the purpose of checking any person's position as regards income tax or corporation tax.

(2) An officer of Revenue and Customs may enter premises and inspect—

(*a*) the premises, and

(*b*) any other property on the premises,

for the purpose of valuing, measuring or determining the character of the premises or property.

(3) Sub-paragraph (2) only applies if the valuation, measurement or determination is reasonably required for the purpose of checking any person's position as regards—

(*a*) capital gains tax,
(*b*) corporation tax in respect of chargeable gains,
(*c*) inheritance tax,
(*d*) stamp duty land tax, . . . [2]
(*e*) stamp duty reserve tax[, or
(*f*) annual tax on enveloped dwellings.][2]

(4) A person who the officer considers is needed to assist with the valuation, measurement or determination may enter and inspect the premises or property with the officer.][1]

Amendments—[1] Paras 12A, 12B inserted by FA 2009 s 96, Sch 48 para 5 with effect from 1 April 2010 (by virtue of SI 2009/3054 art 2).

[2] In sub-para (3), word "or" in para (*d*) repealed, and para (*f*) and preceding word "or" inserted by FA 2013 s 164, Sch 34 paras 1, 2 with effect from 17 July 2013.

[Carrying out inspections under paragraph 12A

12B—(1) An inspection under paragraph 12A may be carried out only if condition A or B is satisfied.

(2) Condition A is that—
(*a*) the inspection is carried out at a time agreed to by a relevant person, and
(*b*) the relevant person has been given notice in writing of the agreed time of the inspection.

(3) "Relevant person" means—
(*a*) the occupier of the premises, or
(*b*) if the occupier cannot be identified or the premises are vacant, a person who controls the premises.

(4) Condition B is that—
(*a*) the inspection has been approved by the tribunal, and
(*b*) any relevant person specified by the tribunal has been given at least 7 days' notice in writing of the time of the inspection.

(5) A notice under sub-paragraph (4)(*b*) must state the possible consequences of obstructing the officer in the exercise of the power.

(6) If a notice is given under this paragraph in respect of an inspection approved by the tribunal (see paragraph 13), it must state that the inspection has been so approved.

(7) An officer of Revenue and Customs seeking to carry out an inspection under paragraph 12A must produce evidence of authority to carry out the inspection if asked to do so by—
(*a*) the occupier of the premises, or
(*b*) any other person who appears to the officer to be in charge of the premises or property.]

Amendments—Paras 12A, 12B inserted by FA 2009 s 96, Sch 48 para 5 with effect from 1 April 2010 (by virtue of SI 2009/3054 art 2).

Approval of [tribunal]

13—(1) An officer of Revenue and Customs may ask the [tribunal][1] to approve an inspection under this Part of this Schedule [(and for the effect of obtaining such approval see paragraph 39 (penalties))][3].

[(1A) An application for approval under this paragraph may be made without notice [(except as required under sub-paragraph (2A))][3].][2]

(2) The [tribunal][1] may not approve an inspection [under paragraph 10, 10A or 11][3] unless—
(*a*) an application for approval is made by, or with the agreement of, an authorised officer of Revenue and Customs, and
(*b*) the [tribunal][1] is satisfied that, in the circumstances, the inspection is justified.

[(2A) The tribunal may not approve an inspection under paragraph 12A unless—
(*a*) an application for approval is made by, or with the agreement of, an authorised officer of Revenue and Customs,
(*b*) the person whose tax position is the subject of the proposed inspection has been given a reasonable opportunity to make representations to the officer of Revenue and Customs about that inspection,
(*c*) the occupier of the premises has been given a reasonable opportunity to make such representations,
(*d*) the tribunal has been given a summary of any representations made, and
(*e*) the tribunal is satisfied that, in the circumstances, the inspection is justified.

(2B) Paragraph (*c*) of sub-paragraph (2A) does not apply if the tribunal is satisfied that the occupier of the premises cannot be identified.][3]

[(3) A decision of the tribunal under this paragraph is final (despite the provisions of sections 11 and 13 of the Tribunals, Courts and Enforcement Act 2007).][2]

Commencement—Finance Act 2008, Schedule 36 (Appointed Day and Savings) Order, SI 2009/404 art 2 (appointed day for the coming into force of Sch 36 is 1 April 2009).

Amendments—[1] Word substituted for the words "First-tier Tribunal" in the heading and in each place; in sub-para (2)(*b*) word substituted for the word "Tribunal" by the Transfer of Tribunal Functions and Revenue and Customs Appeals Order, SI 2009/56 art 3, Sch 1 para 471 with effect from 1 April 2009.

[2] Sub-paras (1A), (3) inserted by FA 2009 s 95, Sch 47 para 8 with effect from 21 July 2009.

[3] In sub-paras (1), (1A), (2), words inserted, and whole of sub-paras (2A), (2B) inserted, by FA 2009 s 96, Sch 48 para 6 with effect from 1 April 2010 (by virtue of SI 2009/3054 art 2).

Restrictions and special cases

14 This Part of this Schedule has effect subject to Parts 4 and 6 of this Schedule.

Commencement—Finance Act 2008, Schedule 36 (Appointed Day and Savings) Order, SI 2009/404 art 2 (appointed day for the coming into force of Sch 36 is 1 April 2009).

HMRC Manuals—Compliance Handbook Manual, CH25300 (HMRC inspection powers: documents you cannot inspect).

PART 3
FURTHER POWERS

Power to copy documents

15 Where a document (or a copy of a document) is produced to, or inspected by, an officer of Revenue and Customs, such an officer may take copies of, or make extracts from, the document.

Commencement—Finance Act 2008, Schedule 36 (Appointed Day and Savings) Order, SI 2009/404 art 2 (appointed day for the coming into force of Sch 36 is 1 April 2009).

HMRC Manuals—Compliance Handbook Manual, CH23300 (HMRC inspection powers: copying or removing documents).
CH25320 (HMRC inspection powers: obtaining and recording information and copying documents).
CH255540 (HMRC inspection powers – how to do a compliance check: copying records).

Power to remove documents

16—(1) Where a document is produced to, or inspected by, an officer of Revenue and Customs, such an officer may—

(*a*) remove the document at a reasonable time, and

(*b*) retain it for a reasonable period,

if it appears to the officer to be necessary to do so.

(2) Where a document is removed in accordance with sub-paragraph (1), the person who produced the document may request—

(*a*) a receipt for the document, and

(*b*) if the document is reasonably required for any purpose, a copy of the document,

and an officer of Revenue and Customs must comply with such a request without charge.

(3) The removal of a document under this paragraph is not to be regarded as breaking any lien claimed on the document.

(4) Where a document removed under this paragraph is lost or damaged, the Commissioners are liable to compensate the owner of the document for any expenses reasonably incurred in replacing or repairing the document.

(5) In this paragraph references to a document include a copy of a document.

Commencement—Finance Act 2008, Schedule 36 (Appointed Day and Savings) Order, SI 2009/404 art 2 (appointed day for the coming into force of Sch 36 is 1 April 2009).

HMRC Manuals—Compliance Handbook Manual, CH23300 (HMRC inspection powers: copying or removing documents).
CH25320 (HMRC inspection powers: obtaining and recording information and copying documents).
CH255545–255555 (inspection powers – how to do a compliance check: removing, storing and returning records).

Power to mark assets and to record information

17 The powers under Part 2 of this Schedule include—

(*a*) power to mark business assets, and anything containing business assets, for the purpose of indicating that they have been inspected, and

(*b*) power to obtain and record information (whether electronically or otherwise) relating to the premises, [property, goods,][1] assets and documents that have been inspected.

Commencement—Finance Act 2008, Schedule 36 (Appointed Day and Savings) Order, SI 2009/404 art 2 (appointed day for the coming into force of Sch 36 is 1 April 2009).

HMRC Manuals—Compliance Handbook Manual, CH25320 (HMRC inspection powers: obtaining and recording information and copying documents).
CH25340 (HMRC inspection powers: marking goods or assets).

Amendments—[1] In para (*b*) words inserted by FA 2009 s 96, Sch 48 para 7 with effect from 1 April 2010 (by virtue of SI 2009/3054 art 2).

PART 4
RESTRICTIONS ON POWERS

Documents not in person's possession or power

18 An information notice only requires a person to produce a document if it is in the person's possession or power.

Commentary—*Simon's Taxes* **A6.301A**.

Commencement—Finance Act 2008, Schedule 36 (Appointed Day and Savings) Order, SI 2009/404 art 2 (appointed day for the coming into force of Sch 36 is 1 April 2009).

HMRC Manuals—Compliance Handbook Manual, CH22120 (HMRC inspection powers: meaning of possession and power).

Types of information

19—(1) An information notice does not require a person to provide or produce—

(*a*) information that relates to the conduct of a pending appeal relating to tax or any part of a document containing such information, or

(*b*) journalistic material (as defined in section 13 of the Police and Criminal Evidence Act 1984 (c 60)) or information contained in such material.

(2) An information notice does not require a person to provide or produce personal records (as defined in section 12 of the Police and Criminal Evidence Act 1984) or information contained in such records, subject to sub-paragraph (3).

(3) An information notice may require a person—

(*a*) to produce documents, or copies of documents, that are personal records, omitting any information whose inclusion (whether alone or with other information) makes the original documents personal records ("personal information"), and

(*b*) to provide any information contained in such records that is not personal information.

Commentary—*Simon's Taxes* **A6.301A**.

Commencement—Finance Act 2008, Schedule 36 (Appointed Day and Savings) Order, SI 2009/404 art 2 (appointed day for the coming into force of Sch 36 is 1 April 2009).

HMRC Manuals—Compliance Handbook Manual, CH22160 (HMRC inspection powers: appeal material, with example). CH22180 and 22200 (personal records, with example).

Old documents

20 An information notice may not require a person to produce a document if the whole of the document originates more than 6 years before the date of the notice, unless the notice is given by, or with the agreement of, an authorised officer.

Commentary—*Simon's Taxes* **A6.301A**.

Commencement—Finance Act 2008, Schedule 36 (Appointed Day and Savings) Order, SI 2009/404 art 2 (appointed day for the coming into force of Sch 36 is 1 April 2009).

HMRC Manuals—Compliance Handbook Manual, CH22140 (HMRC inspection powers: old documents).

Taxpayer notices [following tax return]

21—(1) Where a person has made a tax return in respect of a chargeable period under section 8, 8A or 12AA of TMA 1970 (returns for purpose of income tax and capital gains tax), a taxpayer notice may not be given for the purpose of checking that person's income tax position or capital gains tax position in relation to the chargeable period.

(2) Where a person has made a tax return in respect of a chargeable period under paragraph 3 of Schedule 18 to FA 1998 (company tax returns), a taxpayer notice may not be given for the purpose of checking that person's corporation tax position in relation to the chargeable period.

(3) Sub-paragraphs (1) and (2) do not apply where, or to the extent that, any of conditions A to D is met.

(4) Condition A is that a notice of enquiry has been given in respect of—

(*a*) the return, or

(*b*) a claim or election (or an amendment of a claim or election) made by the person in relation to the chargeable period in respect of the tax (or one of the taxes) to which the return relates ("relevant tax"),

and the enquiry has not been completed.

(5) In sub-paragraph (4), "notice of enquiry" means a notice under—

(*a*) section 9A or 12AC of, or paragraph 5 of Schedule 1A to, TMA 1970, or

(*b*) paragraph 24 of Schedule 18 to FA 1998.

(6) Condition B is that an officer of Revenue and Customs has reason to suspect that[, as regards the person,][1]—

(*a*) an amount that ought to have been assessed to relevant tax for the chargeable period may not have been assessed, (*b*) an assessment to relevant tax for the chargeable period may be or have become insufficient, or

(*c*) relief from relevant tax given for the chargeable period may be or have become excessive.

(7) Condition C is that the notice is given for the purpose of obtaining any information or document that is also required for the purpose of checking [the][1] person's [position as regards any tax other than income tax, capital gains tax or corporation tax][2].

(8) Condition D is that the notice is given for the purpose of obtaining any information or document that is required (or also required) for the purpose of checking the person's position as regards any deductions or repayments [of tax or withholding of income][1] referred to in paragraph 64(2) [or (2A)][1] (PAYE etc).

[(9) In this paragraph, references to the person who made the return are only to that person in the capacity in which the return was made.][1]

Commencement—Finance Act 2008, Schedule 36 (Appointed Day and Savings) Order, SI 2009/404 art 2 (appointed day for the coming into force of Sch 36 is 1 April 2009).

Modification—See FA 2010 Sch 1 para 36 (modification of this para in relation to bank payroll tax).

HMRC Manuals—Compliance Handbook Manual, CH23520 (HMRC inspection powers: specific rules regarding taxpayer notice).

CH23540 (HMRC inspection powers: where self assessment return made).

CH23560 (meaning of "reason to suspect").

Amendments—[1] In sub-paras (6), (8) in both places, words inserted; in sub-para (7) word substituted for the word "that"; and sub-para (9) inserted, by FA 2009 s 95, Sch 47 para 9 with effect from 21 July 2009.

[2] In the cross-heading words inserted, and in sub-para (7) words substituted for words "VAT position", by FA 2009 s 95, Sch 48 para 8 with effect from 1 April 2010 (by virtue of SI 2009/3054 art 2).

[Taxpayer notices following NRCGT return

21ZA (1) Where a person has delivered an NRCGT return with respect to a non-resident CGT disposal, a taxpayer notice may not be given for the purpose of checking the person's capital gains tax position as regards the matters dealt with in that return.

(2) Sub-paragraph (1) does not apply where, or to the extent that, any of conditions A to C is met.

(3) Condition A is that notice of enquiry has been given in respect of—

(*a*) the return, or

(*b*) a claim (or an amendment of a claim) made by the person in relation to the chargeable period,

and the enquiry has not been completed.

(4) In sub-paragraph (3) "notice of enquiry" means a notice under section 12ZM of TMA 1970.

(5) Condition B is that an officer of Revenue and Customs has reason to suspect that—

(*a*) an amount that ought to have been assessed under section 12ZE of TMA 1970 as payable on account of the person's liability to capital gains tax for the tax year to which the return relates has not been so assessed by the filing date for the return, or

(*b*) an assessment under section 12ZE of TMA 1970 of the amount payable on account of P's liability to capital gains tax for the tax year to which the return relates has become insufficient.

(6) Condition C is that the notice is given for the purpose of obtaining any information or document that is also required for the purpose of checking that person's position as regards a tax other than capital gains tax.

(7) In this paragraph—

"NRCGT return" has the meaning given by section 12ZB of TMA 1970;

"non-resident CGT disposal" has the meaning given by section 14B of TCGA 1992.][1]

Amendments—[1] Paragraph 21ZA inserted by FA 2015 s 37, Sch 7 para 57 with effect in relation to disposals made on or after 6 April 2015.

[Taxpayer notices following land transaction return

21A—(1) Where a person has delivered a land transaction return under section 76 of FA 2003 (returns for purposes of stamp duty land tax) in respect of a transaction, a taxpayer notice may not be given for the purpose of checking that person's stamp duty land tax position in relation to that transaction.

(2) Sub-paragraph (1) does not apply where, or to the extent that, any of conditions A to C is met.

(3) Condition A is that a notice of enquiry has been given in respect of—

(*a*) the return, or

(*b*) a claim (or an amendment of a claim) made by the person in connection with the transaction,

and the enquiry has not been completed.

(4) In sub-paragraph (3) "notice of enquiry" means a notice under paragraph 12 of Schedule 10, or paragraph 7 of Schedule 11A, to FA 2003.

(5) Condition B is that, as regards the person, an officer of Revenue and Customs has reason to suspect that—

(*a*) an amount that ought to have been assessed to stamp duty land tax in respect of the transaction may not have been assessed,

(*b*) an assessment to stamp duty land tax in respect of the transaction may be or have become insufficient, or

(*c*) relief from stamp duty land tax in respect of the transaction may be or have become excessive.

(6) Condition C is that the notice is given for the purpose of obtaining any information or document that is also required for the purpose of checking that person's position as regards a tax other than stamp duty land tax.]

Amendments—Para 21A inserted by FA 2009 s 96, Sch 48 para 9 with effect from 1 April 2010 (by virtue of SI 2009/3054 art 2).

[Annual tax on enveloped dwellings: taxpayer notices following return

21B—(1) Where a person has delivered, for a chargeable period with respect to a single-dwelling interest—

(*a*) an annual tax on enveloped dwellings return, or

(*b*) a return of the adjusted chargeable amount,

a taxpayer notice may not be given for the purpose of checking the person's annual tax on enveloped dwellings position as regards the matters dealt with in that return.

(2) Sub-paragraph (1) does not apply where, or to the extent that, any of conditions A to C is met.

(3) Condition A is that notice of enquiry has been given in respect of—

(*a*) the return, or

(*b*) a claim (or an amendment of a claim) made by the person in relation to the chargeable period,

and the enquiry has not been completed.

(4) In sub-paragraph (3) "notice of enquiry" means a notice under paragraph 8 of Schedule 33 to FA 2013 or paragraph 7 of Schedule 11A to FA 2003 (as applied by paragraphs 28(2) and 31(3) of Schedule 33 to FA 2013).

(5) Condition B is that, as regards the person, an officer of Revenue and Customs has reason to suspect that—

(*a*) an amount that ought to have been assessed to annual tax on enveloped dwellings for the chargeable period may not have been assessed,

(*b*) an assessment to annual tax on enveloped dwellings for the chargeable period may be or have become insufficient, or

(*c*) relief from annual tax on enveloped dwellings for the chargeable period may be or have become excessive.

(6) Condition C is that the notice is given for the purpose of obtaining any information or document that is also required for the purpose of checking that person's position as regards a tax other than annual tax on enveloped dwellings.

(7) In this Schedule references to a "single-dwelling interest" are to be read in accordance with section 108 of FA 2013.][1]

Amendments—[1] Para 21B inserted by FA 2013 s 164, Sch 34 paras 1, 3 with effect from 17 July 2013.

Deceased persons

22 An information notice given for the purpose of checking the tax position of a person who has died may not be given more than 4 years after the person's death.

Commencement—Finance Act 2008, Schedule 36 (Appointed Day and Savings) Order, SI 2009/404 art 2 (appointed day for the coming into force of Sch 36 is 1 April 2009).

HMRC Manuals—Compliance Handbook Manual, CH23620 (HMRC inspection powers: specific rules regarding third party notice).

Privileged communications between professional legal advisers and clients

23—(1) An information notice does not require a person—

(*a*) to provide privileged information, or

(*b*) to produce any part of a document that is privileged.

(2) For the purpose of this Schedule, information or a document is privileged if it is information or a document in respect of which a claim to legal professional privilege, or (in Scotland) to confidentiality of communications as between client and professional legal adviser, could be maintained in legal proceedings.

(3) The Commissioners may by regulations make provision for the resolution by the [tribunal][1] of disputes as to whether any information or document is privileged.

(4) The regulations may, in particular, make provision as to—

(*a*) the custody of a document while its status is being decided, . . . [1]

(*b*) . . . [1]

Commentary—*Simon's Taxes* **A6.301A**.

Commencement—Finance Act 2008, Schedule 36 (Appointed Day and Savings) Order, SI 2009/404 art 2 (appointed day for the coming into force of Sch 36 is 1 April 2009).

HMRC Manuals—Compliance Handbook Manual, CH22240 (HMRC restrictions on inspection powers: legal professional privilege).

Regulations—Information Notice: Resolution of Disputes as to Privileged Communications Regulations, SI 2009/1916.

Cross references—See FA 2012 Sch 38 para 17 (application of regulations made under this para to disputes as to whether a document is privileged).

Amendments—[1] In sub-para (3) word substituted for the words "First-tier Tribunal"; sub-para (4)(*b*) and the word "and" immediately preceding it repealed by the Transfer of Tribunal Functions and Revenue and Customs Appeals Order, SI 2009/56 art 3, Sch 1 para 471 with effect from 1 April 2009.

Auditors

24—(1) An information notice does not require a person who has been appointed as an auditor for the purpose of an enactment—

(*a*) to provide information held in connection with the performance of the person's functions under that enactment, or

(*b*) to produce documents which are that person's property and which were created by that person or on that person's behalf for or in connection with the performance of those functions.

(2) Sub-paragraph (1) has effect subject to paragraph 26.

Commentary—*Simon's Taxes* **A6.301A, A6.310**.

Commencement—Finance Act 2008, Schedule 36 (Appointed Day and Savings) Order, SI 2009/404 art 2 (appointed day for the coming into force of Sch 36 is 1 April 2009).

Tax advisers

25—(1) An information notice does not require a tax adviser—

(*a*) to provide information about relevant communications, or

(*b*) to produce documents which are the tax adviser's property and consist of relevant communications.

(2) Sub-paragraph (1) has effect subject to paragraph 26.

(3) In this paragraph—

"relevant communications" means communications between the tax adviser and—

(*a*) a person in relation to whose tax affairs he has been appointed, or

(*b*) any other tax adviser of such a person,

the purpose of which is the giving or obtaining of advice about any of those tax affairs, and

"tax adviser" means a person appointed to give advice about the tax affairs of another person (whether appointed directly by that person or by another tax adviser of that person).

Commentary—*Simon's Taxes* **A6.301A, A6.310**.

Commencement—Finance Act 2008, Schedule 36 (Appointed Day and Savings) Order, SI 2009/404 art 2 (appointed day for the coming into force of Sch 36 is 1 April 2009).

HMRC Manuals—Compliance Handbook Manual, CH22240 and 22320 (HMRC restrictions on inspection powers: tax advisers' papers).

Auditors and tax advisers: supplementary

26—(1) Paragraphs 24(1) and 25(1) do not have effect in relation to—

(*a*) information explaining any information or document which the person to whom the notice is given has, as tax accountant, assisted any client in preparing for, or delivering to, HMRC, or

(*b*) a document which contains such information.

(2) In the case of a notice given under paragraph 5, paragraphs 24(1) and 25(1) do not have effect in relation to—

(*a*) any information giving the identity or address of a person to whom the notice relates or of a person who has acted on behalf of such a person, or

(*b*) a document which contains such information.

(3) Paragraphs 24(1) and 25(1) are not disapplied by sub-paragraph (1) or (2) if the information in question has already been provided, or a document containing the information in question has already been produced, to an officer of Revenue and Customs.

Commentary—*Simon's Taxes* **A6.301A, A6.310**.

Commencement—Finance Act 2008, Schedule 36 (Appointed Day and Savings) Order, SI 2009/404 art 2 (appointed day for the coming into force of Sch 36 is 1 April 2009).

HMRC Manuals—Compliance Handbook Manual, CH22340 (HMRC restrictions on inspection powers: exceptions for auditors' and tax advisers' papers).

27—(1) This paragraph applies where paragraph 24(1) or 25(1) is disapplied in relation to a document by paragraph 26(1) or (2).

(2) An information notice that requires the document to be produced has effect as if it required any part or parts of the document containing the information mentioned in paragraph 26(1) or (2) to be produced.

Commencement—Finance Act 2008, Schedule 36 (Appointed Day and Savings) Order, SI 2009/404 art 2 (appointed day for the coming into force of Sch 36 is 1 April 2009).

HMRC Manuals—Compliance Handbook Manual, CH22340 (HMRC restrictions on inspection powers: exceptions for auditors' and tax advisers' papers).

Corresponding restrictions on inspection of . . . documents[1]

28 An officer of Revenue and Customs may not inspect a business document under Part 2 of this Schedule if or to the extent that, by virtue of this Part of this Schedule, an information notice given at the time of the inspection to the occupier of the premises could not require the occupier to produce the document.

Commencement—Finance Act 2008, Schedule 36 (Appointed Day and Savings) Order, SI 2009/404 art 2 (appointed day for the coming into force of Sch 36 is 1 April 2009).

Amendments—[1] In the heading, word "business" repealed by FA 2009 s 96, Sch 48 para 10 with effect from 1 April 2010 (by virtue of SI 2009/3054 art 2).

PART 5
APPEALS AGAINST INFORMATION NOTICES

Right to appeal against taxpayer notice

29—(1) Where a taxpayer is given a taxpayer notice, the taxpayer may appeal . . . [1] against the notice or any requirement in the notice.

(2) Sub-paragraph (1) does not apply to a requirement in a taxpayer notice to provide any information, or produce any document, that forms part of the taxpayer's statutory records.

(3) Sub-paragraph (1) does not apply if the [tribunal][1] approved the giving of the notice in accordance with paragraph 3.

Commentary—*Simon's Taxes* **A6.301A**.

Commencement—Finance Act 2008, Schedule 36 (Appointed Day and Savings) Order, SI 2009/404 art 2 (appointed day for the coming into force of Sch 36 is 1 April 2009).

HMRC Manuals—Compliance Handbook Manual, CH23520 (HMRC inspection powers: specific rules regarding taxpayer notice).

CH24100 (HMRC inspection powers: appealing against a taxpayer notice).

Amendments—[1] In sub-para (1) words "to the First-tier Tribunal" repealed; in sub-para (3) word substituted for the words "First-tier Tribunal" by the Transfer of Tribunal Functions and Revenue and Customs Appeals Order, SI 2009/56 art 3, Sch 1 para 471 with effect from 1 April 2009.

Right to appeal against third party notice

30—(1) Where a person is given a third party notice, the person may appeal . . . [1] against the notice or any requirement in the notice on the ground that it would be unduly onerous to comply with the notice or requirement.

(2) Sub-paragraph (1) does not apply to a requirement in a third party notice to provide any information, or produce any document, that forms part of the taxpayer's statutory records.

(3) Sub-paragraph (1) does not apply if the [tribunal][1] approved the giving of the notice in accordance with paragraph 3.

Commentary—*Simon's Taxes* **A6.301A**.

Commencement—Finance Act 2008, Schedule 36 (Appointed Day and Savings) Order, SI 2009/404 art 2 (appointed day for the coming into force of Sch 36 is 1 April 2009).

HMRC Manuals—Compliance Handbook Manual, CH23620 (HMRC inspection powers: specific rules regarding third party notice).

CH24100 (HMRC inspection powers: appealing against a third party notice).

CH24420 (meaning of "unduly onerous").

Amendments—[1] In sub-para (1) words "to the First-tier Tribunal" repealed; in sub-para (3) word substituted for the words "First-tier Tribunal" by the Transfer of Tribunal Functions and Revenue and Customs Appeals Order, SI 2009/56 art 3, Sch 1 para 471 with effect from 1 April 2009.

Right to appeal against notice given under paragraph 5 [or 5A]

31 Where a person is given a notice under paragraph 5 [or 5A][2], the person may appeal . . . [1] against the notice or any requirement in the notice on the ground that it would be unduly onerous to comply with the notice or requirement.

Commencement—Finance Act 2008, Schedule 36 (Appointed Day and Savings) Order, SI 2009/404 art 2 (appointed day for the coming into force of Sch 36 is 1 April 2009).

HMRC Manuals—Compliance Handbook Manual, CH23900 (HMRC inspection powers: identity unknown notice).

CH24100 (HMRC inspection powers: appealing against an identity unknown notice).

Amendments—[1] In sub-para (1) words "to the First-tier Tribunal" repealed by the Transfer of Tribunal Functions and Revenue and Customs Appeals Order, SI 2009/56 art 3, Sch 1 para 471 with effect from 1 April 2009.

[2] Words inserted by FA 2012 s 224(1), (4), (5) with effect for the purpose of checking the tax position of a taxpayer as regards periods or tax liabilities whenever arising (whether before, on or after 17 July 2012).

Procedure

32—(1) Notice of an appeal under this Part of this Schedule must be given—

(*a*) in writing,

(*b*) before the end of the period of 30 days beginning with the date on which the information notice is given, and

(*c*) to the officer of Revenue and Customs by whom the information notice was given.

(2) Notice of an appeal under this Part of this Schedule must state the grounds of appeal.

(3) On an appeal the [that is notified to the tribunal, the tribunal][1] may—

(*a*) confirm the information notice or a requirement in the information notice,

(*b*) vary the information notice or such a requirement, or

(*c*) set aside the information notice or such a requirement.

(4) Where the [tribunal][1] confirms or varies the information notice or a requirement, the person to whom the information notice was given must comply with the notice or requirement—

(*a*) within such period as is specified by the [tribunal][1], or

(*b*) if the [tribunal][1] does not specify a period, within such period as is reasonably specified in writing by an officer of Revenue and Customs following the [tribunal's][1] decision.

[(5) Notwithstanding the provisions of sections 11 and 13 of the Tribunals, Courts and Enforcement Act 2007 a decision of the tribunal on an appeal under this Part of this Schedule is final.][1]

(6) Subject to this paragraph, the provisions of Part 5 of TMA 1970 relating to appeals have effect in relation to appeals under this Part of this Schedule as they have effect in relation to an appeal against an assessment to income tax.

Commentary—*Simon's Taxes* **A6.301A**.

Commencement—Finance Act 2008, Schedule 36 (Appointed Day and Savings) Order, SI 2009/404 art 2 (appointed day for the coming into force of Sch 36 is 1 April 2009).

HMRC Manuals—Compliance Handbook Manual, CH24340 (HMRC inspection powers: appeal procedures).

CH24440 (what the first-tier Tribunal can decide).

Amendments—[1] In sub-paras (3), (4) word substituted for the words "First-tier Tribunal"; in sub-para (4)(*a*), (*b*) word substituted for word "Tribunal" and "Tribunal's"; sub-para (5) substituted by the Transfer of Tribunal Functions and Revenue and Customs Appeals Order, SI 2009/56 art 3, Sch 1 para 471 with effect from 1 April 2009.

Special cases

33 This Part of this Schedule has effect subject to Part 6 of this Schedule.

Commencement—Finance Act 2008, Schedule 36 (Appointed Day and Savings) Order, SI 2009/404 art 2 (appointed day for the coming into force of Sch 36 is 1 April 2009).

PART 6
SPECIAL CASES

Supply of goods or services etc

34—(1) This paragraph applies to a taxpayer notice or third party notice that refers only to information or documents that form part of any person's statutory records and relate to—

(*a*) the supply of goods or services,

(*b*) the acquisition of goods from another member State, or

(*c*) the importation of goods from a place outside the member States in the course of carrying on a business.

(2) Paragraph 3(1) (requirement for consent to, or approval of, third party notice) does not apply to such a notice.

(3) Where a person is given such a notice, the person may not appeal . . . [1] against the notice or any requirement in the notice.

(4) Sections 5, 11 and 15 of, and Schedule 4 to, VATA 1994, and any orders made under those provisions, apply for the purposes of this paragraph as if it were part of that Act.

Commencement—Finance Act 2008, Schedule 36 (Appointed Day and Savings) Order, SI 2009/404 art 2 (appointed day for the coming into force of Sch 36 is 1 April 2009).

HMRC Manuals—Compliance Handbook Manual, CH23520 (HMRC inspection powers: specific rules regarding taxpayer notice).

CH23620 (HMRC inspection powers: specific rules regarding third party notice).

Amendments—[1] In sub-para (3) words "to the First-tier Tribunal" repealed by the Transfer of Tribunal Functions and Revenue and Customs Appeals Order, SI 2009/56 art 3, Sch 1 para 471 with effect from 1 April 2009.

[Involved third parties

***34A**—(1) This paragraph applies to a third party notice or a notice under paragraph 5 if—*

(a) it is given to an involved third party (see paragraph 61A),

(b) it is given for the purpose of checking the position of a person, or a class of persons, as regards the relevant tax, and

(c) it refers only to relevant information or relevant documents.

(2) In relation to such a third party notice—

(a) paragraph 3(1) (approval etc of third party notices) does not apply,

(b) paragraph 4(1) (copying third party notices to taxpayer) does not apply, and

(c) paragraph 30(1) (appeal) has effect as if it permitted an appeal on any grounds.

(3) In relation to such a notice under paragraph 5—

(a) sub-paragraphs (3) and (4) of that paragraph (approval of tribunal) have effect as if they permitted, but did not require, an authorised officer of Revenue and Customs to obtain the approval of the tribunal, and

(b) paragraph 31 (appeal) has effect as if it permitted an appeal on any grounds.

(4) The involved third party may not appeal against a requirement in the notice to provide any information, or produce any document, that forms part of the involved third party's statutory records.

(5) In relation to an involved third party, "relevant documents", "relevant information" and "relevant tax" are defined in paragraph 61A.][1], [2]

Amendments—[1] Paras 34A–34C inserted by FA 2009 s 96, Sch 48 para 11 with effect from 1 April 2010 (by virtue of SI 2009/3054 art 2).

[2] This para repealed by FA 2011 s 86(1), Sch 23 paras 60, 62(1), (2) with effect from 1 April 2012 in relation to relevant data with a bearing on any period (whether before, on or after 1 April 2012) subject to FA 2011 Sch 23 para 3(2). This para will continue to have effect in relation to notices given, or requests made, under any of the provisions repealed by FA 2011 Sch 23 Pt 6 before 1 April 2012 as if the repeal had not been made (FA 2011 Sch 23 para 65(2)).

[Registered pension schemes etc

34B—(1) This paragraph applies to a third party notice or a notice under paragraph 5 if it refers only to information or documents that relate to any pensions matter.

(2) "Pensions matter" means any matter relating to—

(*a*) a registered pension scheme,

(*b*) an annuity purchased with sums or assets held for the purposes of a registered pension scheme or a pre-2006 pension scheme, . . . [2]

(*c*) an employer-financed retirement benefits scheme,

[(*d*) a QROPS or former QROPS, or

(*e*) an annuity purchased with sums or assets held for the purposes of a QROPS or former QROPS.][2]

(3) In relation to such a third party notice—

(*a*) paragraph 3(1) (approval etc of third party notices) does not apply,

(*b*) paragraph 4(1) (copying third party notices to taxpayer) does not apply, and

(*c*) paragraph 30(1) (appeal) has effect as if it permitted an appeal on any grounds.

(4) In relation to such a notice under paragraph 5—

(*a*) sub-paragraphs (3) and (4) of that paragraph (approval of tribunal) have effect as if they permitted, but did not require, an authorised officer of Revenue and Customs to obtain the approval of the tribunal, and

(*b*) paragraph 31 (appeal) has effect as if it permitted an appeal on any grounds.

[(4A) In relation to a notice to which this paragraph applies that refers only to information or documents relating to a matter within sub-paragraph (2)(*d*) or (*e*), paragraph 20 (old documents) has effect as if the reference to 6 years were to 10 years.][2]

(5) A person may not appeal against a requirement in the notice to provide any information, or produce any document, that forms part of any person's statutory records.

(6) Where the notice relates to a matter within sub-paragraph (2)(*a*) or (*b*), the officer of Revenue and Customs who gives the notice must give a copy of the notice to the scheme administrator in relation to the pension scheme.

(7) Where the notice relates to a matter within sub-paragraph (2)(*c*), the officer of Revenue and Customs who gives the notice must give a copy of the notice to the responsible person in relation to the employer-financed retirement benefits scheme.

[(7A) Where the notice relates to a matter within sub-paragraph (2)(*d*) or (*e*), the officer of Revenue and Customs who gives the notice must give a copy of the notice to the scheme manager in relation to the pension scheme.][2]

(8) Sub-paragraphs (6) [to (7A)][2] do not apply if the notice is given to a person who, in relation to the scheme or annuity to which the notice relates, is a prescribed description of person.][1]

RegulationsRegistered Pension Schemes and Overseas Pension Schemes (Miscellaneous Amendments) Regulations 2013, SI 2013/2259.

Note—References in this para to a former QROPS include a scheme that ceased to be a QROPS before FA 2013 was passed (17 July 2013) (FA 2013 s 54(4)).

Amendments—[1] Paras 34A–34C inserted by FA 2009 s 96, Sch 48 para 11 with effect from 1 April 2010 (by virtue of SI 2009/3054 art 2).

[2] In sub-para (2), word "or" at end of para (*b*) repealed, and paras (*d*), (*e*) inserted; sub-paras (4A), (7A) inserted; and in sub-para (8), words substituted for words "and (7)"; by FA 2013 s 54(1), (2) with effect from 17 July 2013.

[Registered pension schemes etc: interpretation

34C In paragraph 34B—

"employer-financed retirement benefits scheme" has the same meaning as in Chapter 2 of Part 6 of ITEPA 2003 (see sections 393A and 393B of that Act);

"pension scheme" has the same meaning as in Part 4 of FA 2004;

"pre-2006 pension scheme" means a scheme that, at or in respect of any time before 6 April 2006, was—

(*a*) a retirement benefits scheme approved for the purposes of Chapter 1 of Part 14 of ICTA,

(*b*) a former approved superannuation fund (as defined in paragraph 1(3) of Schedule 36 to FA 2004),

(*c*) a relevant statutory scheme (as defined in section 611A of ICTA) or a pension scheme treated as if it were such a scheme, or

(*d*) a personal pension scheme approved under Chapter 4 of Part 14 of ICTA;

"prescribed" means prescribed by regulations made by the Commissioners;

["QROPS" and "former QROPS" have the meanings given by section 169(8) of FA 2004;][2]

"registered pension scheme" means a pension scheme that is or has been a registered pension scheme within the meaning of Part 4 of FA 2004 or in relation to which an application for registration under that Part of that Act has been made;

"responsible person", in relation to an employer-financed retirement benefits scheme, has the same meaning as in Chapter 2 of Part 6 of ITEPA 2003 (see section 399A of that Act);

"scheme administrator", in relation to a pension scheme, has the same meaning as in Part 4 of FA 2004 (see section 270 of that Act).

["scheme manager", in relation to a pension scheme, has the meaning given by section 169(3) of FA 2004.][2]][1]

Note—References in this para to a former QROPS include a scheme that ceased to be a QROPS before FA 2013 was passed (17 July 2013) (FA 2013 s 54(4)).

Amendments—[1] Paras 34A–34C inserted by FA 2009 s 96, Sch 48 para 11 with effect from 1 April 2010 (by virtue of SI 2009/3054 art 2).

[2] Definitions of "QROPS" and "former QROPS", and "scheme manager", inserted by FA 2013 s 54(1), (3) with effect from 17 July 2013.

Groups of undertakings

35—(1) This paragraph applies where an undertaking is a parent undertaking in relation to another undertaking (a subsidiary undertaking).

(2) Where a third party notice is given to any person for the purpose of checking the tax position of the parent undertaking and any of its subsidiary undertakings, [—

(*a*) paragraph 2(2)][1] only requires the notice to state this and name the parent undertaking[, and

(*b*) the references in paragraph 3(5) to naming the taxpayer are to making that statement and naming the parent undertaking][1].

(3) In relation to such a notice—

(*a*) in paragraphs 3 and 4 (approval etc of notices and copying third party notices to taxpayer), the references to the taxpayer have effect as if they were references to the parent undertaking, but

(*b*) in paragraph 30(2) (no appeal in relation to taxpayer's statutory records), the reference to the taxpayer has effect as if it were a reference to the parent undertaking and each of its subsidiary undertakings.

[(4) Where a third party notice is given to the parent undertaking for the purpose of checking the tax position of more than one subsidiary undertaking—

(*a*) paragraph 2(2) only requires the notice to state this, and

(*b*) the references in paragraph 3(5) to naming the taxpayer are to making that statement.

(4A) In relation to such a notice—

(*a*) in paragraph 3 (approval etc of notices), sub-paragraphs (1) and (3)(*e*) do not apply,

(*b*) paragraph 4(1) (copying third party notices to taxpayer) does not apply, (*c*) [paragraphs 21 and 21A][2] (restrictions on giving taxpayer notice where taxpayer has made return) [apply][2] as if the notice was a taxpayer notice or taxpayer notices given to each subsidiary undertaking (or, if the notice names the subsidiary undertakings to which it relates, to each of those undertakings),

(*d*) paragraph 30(1) (appeal) has effect as if it permitted an appeal on any grounds, and

(*e*) in paragraph 30(2) (no appeal in relation to taxpayer's statutory records), the reference to the taxpayer has effect as if it were a reference to the parent undertaking or any of its subsidiary undertakings.][1]

(5) Where a notice is given under paragraph 5 to the parent undertaking for the purpose of checking the tax position of one or more subsidiary undertakings whose identities are not known to the officer giving the notice[—

(*a*) sub-paragraphs (3) and (4) of that paragraph (approval of tribunal) have effect as if they permitted, but did not require, the officer to obtain the approval of the tribunal, and

(*b*) paragraph 31 (appeal) has effect as if it permitted an appeal on any grounds, but the parent undertaking may not appeal against a requirement in the notice to produce any document that forms part of the statutory records of the parent undertaking or any of its subsidiary undertakings][1].

(6) Where a third party notice or a notice under paragraph 5 is given to the parent undertaking for the purpose of checking the tax position of one or more subsidiary undertakings, the parent undertaking may not appeal against a requirement in the notice to produce any document that forms part of the statutory records of the parent undertaking or any of its subsidiary undertakings.[1]

(7) In this paragraph "parent undertaking", "subsidiary undertaking" and "undertaking" have the same meaning as in the Companies Acts (see sections 1161 and 1162 of, and Schedule 7 to, the Companies Act 2006 (c 46)).

Commencement—Finance Act 2008, Schedule 36 (Appointed Day and Savings) Order, SI 2009/404 art 2 (appointed day for the coming into force of Sch 36 is 1 April 2009).

HMRC Manuals—Compliance Handbook Manual, CH23740 (HMRC inspection powers: groups of undertakings).
CH23760–23780 (notice about the parent and its subsidiaries).
CH23900 (HMRC inspection powers: identity unknown notice).
CH225510–225530 (HMRC inspection powers – how to do a compliance check: guidance on groups of undertakings).

Amendments—[1] In sub-para (2), words substituted for the words "paragraph 2" and words at the end inserted; sub-paras (4), (4A) substituted for previous sub-para (4); words in sub-para (5) substituted for the words ", sub-paragraph (3) of that paragraph (approval of tribunal) does not apply"; and sub-para (6) repealed, by FA 2009 s 95, Sch 47 para 10 with effect from 21 July 2009.

[2] In sub-para (4A)(*c*), words substituted for words "paragraph 21", and word substituted for word "applies", by FA 2009 s 96, Sch 48 para 12 with effect from 1 April 2010 (by virtue of SI 2009/3054 art 2).

Change of ownership of companies

36—(1) Sub-paragraph (2) applies where it appears to the Commissioners that—

(*a*) there has been a change in the ownership of a company, and

(*b*) in connection with that change a person ("the seller") may be or become liable to be assessed and charged to corporation tax under [section 710 or 713 of CTA 2010][1].

(2) Paragraph 21 (restrictions on giving taxpayer notice where taxpayer has made tax return) does not apply in relation to a taxpayer notice given to the seller.

(3) [Chapter 7 of Part 14 of CTA 2010][1] applies for the purposes of determining when there has been a change in the ownership of a company.

HMRC Manuals—Compliance Handbook Manual, CH23520 (HMRC inspection powers: specific rules regarding taxpayer notice).

Amendments—[1] In sub-para (1)(*b*) words "section 767A or 767AA of ICTA" substituted and in sub-para (3) words "Section 769 of ICTA" substituted by CTA 2010 s 1177, Sch 1 paras 576, 582(1), (2). CTA 2010 has effect for corporation tax purposes for accounting periods ending on or after 1 April 2010, and for income and capital gains tax purposes for the tax year 2010–11 and subsequent tax years.

Partnerships

37—(1) This paragraph applies where a business is carried on by two or more persons in partnership.

[(2) Where, in respect of a chargeable period, any of the partners has—

(*a*) made a tax return under section 12AA of TMA 1970 (partnership returns), or

(*b*) made a claim or election in accordance with section 42(6)(*b*) of TMA 1970 (partnership claims and elections),

paragraph 21 (restrictions where taxpayer has made tax return) has effect as if that return, claim or election had been made by each of the partners.][1]

[(2A) Where, in respect of a transaction entered into as purchaser by or on behalf of the members of the partnership, any of the partners has—

(*a*) delivered a land transaction return under Part 4 of FA 2003 (stamp duty land tax), or (*b*) made a claim under that Part of that Act, paragraph 21A (restrictions where taxpayer has delivered land transaction return) has effect as if that return had been delivered, or that claim had been made, by each of the partners.][2]

[(2B) Where, in respect of a single-dwelling interest (see paragraph 21B(7)) to which one or more companies are or were entitled as members of a partnership, any member of the partnership has—

(*a*) delivered an annual tax on enveloped dwellings return or a return of the adjusted chargeable amount under Part 3 of FA 2013, or

(*b*) made a claim under that Part of that Act,

paragraph 21B (restrictions where taxpayer has delivered return) has effect as if that return had been delivered, or that claim had been made, by each member of the partnership.][4]

(3) Where a third party notice is given . . . [1] for the purpose of checking the tax position of more than one of the partners (in their capacity as such), [—

(*a*) ...[3]

(*b*) the references in paragraph 3(5) to naming the taxpayer are to making that statement and naming the partnership][1].

(4) In relation to such a notice [given to a person other than one of the partners][1]—

(*a*) in paragraphs 3 and 4 (approval etc of notices and copying third party notices to taxpayer), the references to the taxpayer have effect as if they were references to at least one of the partners, and

(*b*) in paragraph 30(2) (no appeal in relation to taxpayer's statutory records), the reference to the taxpayer has effect as if it were a reference to [any of the partners in the partnership][1] [, or

(*c*) section 733 of CTA 2010 (company liable to counteraction of corporation tax advantage).][3]

[(5) In relation to a third party notice given to one of the partners for the purpose of checking the tax position of one or more of the other partners (in their capacity as such)—

(*a*) in paragraph 3 (approval etc of notices), sub-paragraphs (1) and (3)(*e*) do not apply,

(*b*) paragraph 4(1) (copying third party notices to taxpayer) does not apply,

(*c*) paragraph 30(1) (appeal) has effect as if it permitted an appeal on any grounds, and

(*d*) in paragraph 30(2) (no appeal in relation to taxpayer's statutory records), the reference to the taxpayer has effect as if it were a reference to any of the partners in the partnership.][1]

(6) Where a notice is given under paragraph 5 to one of the partners for the purpose of checking the tax position of one or more of the other partners whose identities are not known to the officer giving the notice[—

(*a*) sub-paragraphs (3) and (4) of that paragraph (approval of tribunal) have effect as if they permitted, but did not require, the officer to obtain the approval of the tribunal, and

(*b*) paragraph 31 (appeal) has effect as if it permitted an appeal on any grounds, but the partner to whom the notice is given may not appeal against a requirement in the notice to produce any document that forms part of that partner's statutory records.][1]

(7) Where a third party notice or a notice under paragraph 5 is given to one of the partners for the purpose of checking the tax position of one or more of the other partners, that partner may not appeal against a requirement in the notice to produce any document that forms part of that partner's statutory records.[1]

Commencement—Finance Act 2008, Schedule 36 (Appointed Day and Savings) Order, SI 2009/404 art 2 (appointed day for the coming into force of Sch 36 is 1 April 2009).

HMRC Manuals—Compliance Handbook Manual, CH23520 (HMRC inspection powers: specific rules regarding taxpayer notice).

CH23620 (HMRC inspection powers: specific rules regarding third party notice).

CH23680–23720 (HMRC inspection powers: notices given to partners).

CH23900 (HMRC inspection powers: identity unknown notice).

Amendments—[1] The following amendments made by FA 2009 s 95, Sch 47 para 11 with effect from 21 July 2009—

– sub-paras (2), (5) substituted;
– in sub-para (3) words "to any person (other than one of the partners)" repealed, words substituted for the words "paragraph 2", and para (*b*) and the preceding word "and" inserted;
– in sub-para (4) words inserted, and words substituted for the words "each of the partners";
– in sub-para (6) words substituted for the words ", sub-paragraph (3) of that paragraph (approval of tribunal) does not apply";
– sub-para (7) repealed.

[2] Sub-para (2A) inserted by FA 2009 s 96, Sch 48 para 13 with effect from 1 April 2010 (by virtue of SI 2009/3054 art 2).

[3] Sub-para (3)(*a*) repealed and (3)(*c*) inserted by CTA 2010 s 1177, Sch 1 paras 576, 582(1),(3), Sch 3 Pt 1. CTA 2010 has effect for corporation tax purposes for accounting periods ending on or after 1 April 2010, and for income and capital gains tax purposes for the tax year 2010–11 and subsequent tax years.

[4] Sub-para (2B) inserted by FA 2013 s 164, Sch 34 paras 1, 4 with effect from 17 July 2013.

[Information in connection with herd basis election

37A—(1) This paragraph applies to a taxpayer notice given to a person carrying on a trade in relation to which a herd basis election is made if the notice refers only to information or documents that relate to—

(*a*) the animals kept for the purposes of the trade, or
(*b*) the products of those animals.

(2) Paragraph 21 (restrictions on giving taxpayer notice where taxpayer has made tax return) does not apply in relation to the notice.

(3) "Herd basis election" means an election under Chapter 8 of Part 2 of ITTOIA 2005 or Chapter 8 of Part 3 of CTA 2009.][1]

Amendments—[1] Paras 37A, 37B inserted by FA 2009 s 95, Sch 47 para 12 with effect from 21 July 2009.

[Information from persons liable to counteraction of tax advantage

37B—(1) This paragraph applies to a taxpayer notice given to a person if—
(*a*) it appears to an officer of Revenue and Customs that a counteraction provision may apply to the person by reason of one or more transactions, and
(*b*) the notice refers only to information or documents relating to the transaction (or, if there are two or more transactions, any of them).

(2) Paragraph 21 (restrictions on giving taxpayer notice where taxpayer has made tax return) does not apply in relation to the notice.

(3) "Counteraction provision" means—
(*a*) *section 703 of ICTA (company liable to counteraction of corporation tax advantage), or*[2]
(*b*) section 684 of ITA 2007 (person liable to counteraction of income tax advantage)][1] [, or
(*c*) section 733 of CTA 2010 (company liable to counteraction of corporation tax advantage).][2]

Amendments—[1] Paras 37A, 37B inserted by FA 2009 s 94, Sch 47 para 12 with effect from 21 July 2009.
[2] Sub-s (3)(*a*) repealed and sub-para (3)(*c*) inserted by CTA 2010 ss 1177, 1181, Sch 1 paras 576, 582 (1) ,(3), Sch 3 Pt 1. CTA 2010 has effect for corporation tax purposes for accounting periods ending on or after 1 April 2010, and for income and capital gains tax purposes for the tax year 2010–11 and subsequent tax years.

Application to the Crown

38 This Schedule (other than Part 8) applies to the Crown, but not to Her Majesty in Her private capacity (within the meaning of the Crown Proceedings Act 1947 (c 44)).

Commencement—Finance Act 2008, Schedule 36 (Appointed Day and Savings) Order, SI 2009/404 art 2 (appointed day for the coming into force of Sch 36 is 1 April 2009).
HMRC Manuals—Compliance Handbook Manual, CH21580 (HMRC inspection powers: meaning of "person").

PART 7
PENALTIES

. . . *Penalties [for failure to comply or obstruction]*

39—(1) This paragraph applies to a person who—
(*a*) fails to comply with an information notice, or
(*b*) deliberately obstructs an officer of Revenue and Customs in the course of an inspection under Part 2 of this Schedule that has been approved by the [tribunal][1].

(2) [The person][2] is liable to a penalty of £300.

(3) The reference in this paragraph to a person who fails to comply with an information notice includes a person who conceals, destroys or otherwise disposes of, or arranges for the concealment, destruction or disposal of, a document in breach of paragraph 42 or 43.

Commentary—*Simon's Taxes* **A6.301A**.
Commencement—Finance Act 2008, Schedule 36 (Appointed Day and Savings) Order, SI 2009/404 art 2 (appointed day for the coming into force of Sch 36 is 1 April 2009).
HMRC Manuals—Compliance Handbook Manual, CH25700 (HMRC inspection powers: information and deliberate obstruction of an inspection).
CH26220 (penalties: failure to comply with an information notice).
CH26240 (deliberate obstruction of a Tribunal approved inspection).
CH26260 (concealing, destroying or disposing of a document).
CH26640 (details of standard penalty).
CH26760 (HMRC inspection powers: two examples relating to penalties).
Cross-references—Recognised Overseas Pensions Schemes and Corresponding Relief) Regulations, SI 2006/208 reg 5 (application and modification of the penalty provisions in FA 2008 Sch 36 Pt 7 in respect of QROPS).
Amendments—[1] In sub-para (1)(*b*) word substituted for the words "First-tier Tribunal" by the Transfer of Tribunal Functions and Revenue and Customs Appeals Order, SI 2009/56 art 3, Sch 1 para 471 with effect from 1 April 2009.
[2] In heading, word "Standard" at the start repealed and words at the end inserted, and in sub-para (2) words substituted for the words "A person to whom this paragraph applies", by FA 2009 s 95, Sch 47 para 13 with effect from 21 July 2009.

Daily default penalties [for failure to comply or obstruction]

40—(1) This paragraph applies if the failure or obstruction mentioned in paragraph 39(1) continues after the date on which a penalty is imposed under that paragraph in respect of the failure or obstruction.

(2) The person is liable to a further penalty or penalties not exceeding £60 for each subsequent day on which the failure or obstruction continues.

Commentary—*Simon's Taxes* **A6.301A**.

Commencement—Finance Act 2008, Schedule 36 (Appointed Day and Savings) Order, SI 2009/404 art 2 (appointed day for the coming into force of Sch 36 is 1 April 2009).

HMRC Manuals—Compliance Handbook Manual, CH26660–26680 (HMRC inspection powers: details regarding daily penalties).

CH26760 (HMRC inspection powers: two examples relating to penalties).

Cross-references—Recognised Overseas Pensions Schemes and Corresponding Relief) Regulations, SI 2006/208 reg 5 (application and modification of the penalty provisions in FA 2008 Sch 36 Pt 7 in respect of QROPS).

Amendments—In heading words at the end inserted by FA 2009 s 95, Sch 47 para 14 with effect from 21 July 2009.

[Penalties for inaccurate information and documents

40A—(1) This paragraph applies if—

(*a*) in complying with an information notice, a person provides inaccurate information or produces a document that contains an inaccuracy, and

(*b*) condition [A, B or C][2] is met.

(2) Condition A is that the inaccuracy is careless or deliberate.

(3) An inaccuracy is careless if it is due to a failure by the person to take reasonable care.

[(3A) Condition B is that the person knows of the inaccuracy at the time the information is provided or the document produced but does not inform HMRC at that time.][2]

(4) Condition [C][2] is that the person—

(*a*) discovers the inaccuracy some time later, and

(*b*) fails to take reasonable steps to inform HMRC.

(5) The person is liable to a penalty not exceeding £3,000.

(6) Where the information or document contains more than one inaccuracy, a penalty is payable for each inaccuracy.][1]

Cross-references—Recognised Overseas Pensions Schemes and Corresponding Relief) Regulations, SI 2006/208 reg 5 (application and modification of the penalty provisions in FA 2008 Sch 36 Pt 7 in respect of QROPS).

Amendments—[1] Para 40A inserted by FA 2009 s 95, Sch 47 para 15 with effect from 21 July 2009.

[2] In sub-para (1)(*b*), words substituted, sub-para (3A) inserted, and in sub-para (4), letter substituted, by FA 2011 s 86(2), Sch 24 paras 1, 3 with effect in relation to any inaccuracy in information provided, or in documents produced, on or after 1 April 2012.

Power to change amount of . . . penalties

41—(1) If it appears to the Treasury that there has been a change in the value of money since the last relevant date, they may by regulations substitute for the sums for the time being specified in paragraphs 39(2)[, 40(2) and 40A(5)][1] such other sums as appear to them to be justified by the change.

(2) In sub-paragraph (1)[, in relation to a specified sum,][1] "relevant date" means—

(*a*) the date on which this Act is passed, and

(*b*) each date on which the power conferred by that sub-paragraph has been exercised [in relation to that sum][1].

(3) Regulations under this paragraph do not apply to[—

(*a*)] [1]any failure or obstruction which began before the date on which they come into force[, or

(*b*) an inaccuracy in any information or document provided to HMRC before that date.][1]

Commencement—Finance Act 2008, Schedule 36 (Appointed Day and Savings) Order, SI 2009/404 art 2 (appointed day for the coming into force of Sch 36 is 1 April 2009).

Cross-references—Recognised Overseas Pensions Schemes and Corresponding Relief) Regulations, SI 2006/208 reg 5 (application and modification of the penalty provisions in FA 2008 Sch 36 Pt 7 in respect of QROPS).

Amendments—[1] In cross-heading words "standard and daily default" repealed; in sub-para (1) words substituted for the words "and 40(2)"; in sub-para (2) words inserted in both places; in sub-para (3) words inserted, and para (*b*) and the preceding word "or" inserted; by FA 2009 s 95, Sch 47 para 16 with effect from 21 July 2009.

Concealing, destroying etc documents following information notice

42—(1) A person must not conceal, destroy or otherwise dispose of, or arrange for the concealment, destruction or disposal of, a document that is the subject of an information notice addressed to the person (subject to sub-paragraphs (2) and (3)).

(2) Sub-paragraph (1) does not apply if the person acts after the document has been produced to an officer of Revenue and Customs in accordance with the information notice, unless an officer of Revenue and Customs has notified the person in writing that the document must continue to be available for inspection (and has not withdrawn the notification).

(3) Sub-paragraph (1) does not apply, in a case to which paragraph 8(1) applies, if the person acts after the expiry of the period of 6 months beginning with the day on which a copy of the document was produced in accordance with that paragraph unless, before the expiry of that period, an officer of Revenue and Customs made a request for the original document under paragraph 8(2)(*b*).

Commencement—Finance Act 2008, Schedule 36 (Appointed Day and Savings) Order, SI 2009/404 art 2 (appointed day for the coming into force of Sch 36 is 1 April 2009).

Cross-references—Recognised Overseas Pensions Schemes and Corresponding Relief) Regulations, SI 2006/208 reg 5 (application and modification of the penalty provisions in FA 2008 Sch 36 Pt 7 in respect of QROPS).

Concealing, destroying etc documents following informal notification

43—(1) A person must not conceal, destroy or otherwise dispose of, or arrange for the concealment, destruction or disposal of, a document if an officer of Revenue and Customs has informed the person that the document is, or is likely, to be the subject of an information notice addressed to that person (subject to sub-paragraph (2)).

(2) Sub-paragraph (1) does not apply if the person acts after—

(*a*) at least 6 months has expired since the person was, or was last, so informed, or

(*b*) an information notice has been given to the person requiring the document to be produced.

Commencement—Finance Act 2008, Schedule 36 (Appointed Day and Savings) Order, SI 2009/404 art 2 (appointed day for the coming into force of Sch 36 is 1 April 2009).

Cross-references—Recognised Overseas Pensions Schemes and Corresponding Relief) Regulations, SI 2006/208 reg 5 (application and modification of the penalty provisions in FA 2008 Sch 36 Pt 7 in respect of QROPS).

Failure to comply with time limit

44 A failure by a person to do anything required to be done within a limited period of time does not give rise to liability to a penalty under paragraph 39 or 40 if the person did it within such further time, if any, as an officer of Revenue and Customs may have allowed.

Commencement—Finance Act 2008, Schedule 36 (Appointed Day and Savings) Order, SI 2009/404 art 2 (appointed day for the coming into force of Sch 36 is 1 April 2009).

Commentary—*Simon's Taxes* **A6.301A**.

Cross-references—Recognised Overseas Pensions Schemes and Corresponding Relief) Regulations, SI 2006/208 reg 5 (application and modification of the penalty provisions in FA 2008 Sch 36 Pt 7 in respect of QROPS).

Reasonable excuse

45—(1) Liability to a penalty under paragraph 39 or 40 does not arise if the person satisfies HMRC or [(on an appeal notified to the tribunal) the tribunal][1] that there is a reasonable excuse for the failure or the obstruction of an officer of Revenue and Customs.

(2) For the purposes of this paragraph—

(*a*) an insufficiency of funds is not a reasonable excuse unless attributable to events outside the person's control,

(*b*) where the person relies on any other person to do anything, that is not a reasonable excuse unless the first person took reasonable care to avoid the failure or obstruction, and

(*c*) where the person had a reasonable excuse for the failure or obstruction but the excuse has ceased, the person is to be treated as having continued to have the excuse if the failure is remedied, or the obstruction stops, without unreasonable delay after the excuse ceased.

Commentary—*Simon's Taxes* **A6.301A**.

Commencement—Finance Act 2008, Schedule 36 (Appointed Day and Savings) Order, SI 2009/404 art 2 (appointed day for the coming into force of Sch 36 is 1 April 2009).

HMRC Manuals—Compliance Handbook Manual, CH26320–26440 (HMRC inspection powers: what is and is not a reasonable excuse, with example at CH26420).

Cross-references—Recognised Overseas Pensions Schemes and Corresponding Relief) Regulations, SI 2006/208 reg 5 (application and modification of the penalty provisions in FA 2008 Sch 36 Pt 7 in respect of QROPS).

Amendments—[1] In sub-para (1) words substituted for the words "(on appeal) the First-tier Tribunal" by the Transfer of Tribunal Functions and Revenue and Customs Appeals Order, SI 2009/56 art 3, Sch 1 para 471 with effect from 1 April 2009.

Assessment of . . . penalty

46—(1) Where a person becomes liable for a penalty under paragraph 39[, 40 or 40A][1], . . . [1]—

(*a*) [HMRC may][1] assess the penalty, and

(*b*) [if they do so, they must][1] notify the person.

(2) An assessment of a penalty under paragraph 39 or 40 must be made [within the period of 12 months beginning with the date on which the person became liable to the penalty, subject to sub-paragraph (3)][1].

[(3) In a case involving an information notice against which a person may appeal, an assessment of a penalty under paragraph 39 or 40 must be made within the period of 12 months beginning with the latest of the following—

(*a*) the date on which the person became liable to the penalty,

(*b*) the end of the period in which notice of an appeal against the information notice could have been given, and

(*c*) if notice of such an appeal is given, the date on which the appeal is determined or withdrawn.

(4) An assessment of a penalty under paragraph 40A must be made—

(*a*) within the period of 12 months beginning with the date on which the inaccuracy first came to the attention of an officer of Revenue and Customs, and

(*b*) within the period of 6 years beginning with the date on which the person became liable to the penalty.][1]

Commencement—Finance Act 2008, Schedule 36 (Appointed Day and Savings) Order, SI 2009/404 art 2 (appointed day for the coming into force of Sch 36 is 1 April 2009).

HMRC Manuals—Compliance Handbook Manual, CH26840 (HMRC inspection powers: what the penalty assessment must include).

CH26860 (when to issue a penalty assessment).

Cross-references—Recognised Overseas Pensions Schemes and Corresponding Relief) Regulations, SI 2006/208 reg 5 (application and modification of the penalty provisions in FA 2008 Sch 36 Pt 7 in respect of QROPS).

Amendments—[1] In the cross-heading, words "standard penalty or daily default" repealed; in sub-para (1) words substituted for the words "or 40"; words "HMRC may" repealed and words at the beginning of paras (*a*), (*b*) inserted; in sub-para (2), words substituted for the words "within 12 months of the relevant date"; and sub-paras (3), (4) substituted for previous sub-para (3), by FA 2009 s 95, Sch 47 para 17 with effect from 21 July 2009.

Right to appeal against . . . penalty

47 A person may appeal . . . [1] against any of the following decisions of an officer of Revenue and Customs—

(*a*) a decision that a penalty is payable by that person under paragraph 39[, 40 or 40A][2], or

(*b*) a decision as to the amount of such a penalty.

Commentary—*Simon's Taxes* **A6.301A**.

Commencement—Finance Act 2008, Schedule 36 (Appointed Day and Savings) Order, SI 2009/404 art 2 (appointed day for the coming into force of Sch 36 is 1 April 2009).

HMRC Manuals—Compliance Handbook Manual, CH26900 (HMRC inspection powers (penalties): types of appeal and procedures).

Cross-references—Recognised Overseas Pensions Schemes and Corresponding Relief) Regulations, SI 2006/208 reg 5 (application and modification of the penalty provisions in FA 2008 Sch 36 Pt 7 in respect of QROPS).

Amendments—[1] Words "to the First-tier Tribunal" repealed by the Transfer of Tribunal Functions and Revenue and Customs Appeals Order, SI 2009/56 art 3, Sch 1 para 471 with effect from 1 April 2009.

[2] In the cross-heading, words "standard penalty or daily default" repealed, in sub-para (*a*) words substituted for the words "or 40", by FA 2009 s 95, Sch 47 para 18 with effect from 21 July 2009.

Procedure on appeal against . . . penalty

48—(1) Notice of an appeal under paragraph 47 must be given—

(*a*) in writing,

(*b*) before the end of the period of 30 days beginning with the date on which the notification under paragraph 46 was issued, and

(*c*) to HMRC.

(2) Notice of an appeal under paragraph 47 must state the grounds of appeal.

(3) On an appeal under paragraph 47(*a*), [that is notified to the tribunal, the tribunal][1] may confirm or cancel the decision.

(4) On an appeal under paragraph 47(*b*), [that is notified to the tribunal, the tribunal][1] may—

(*a*) confirm the decision, or

(*b*) substitute for the decision another decision that the officer of Revenue and Customs had power to make.

(5) Subject to this paragraph and paragraph 49, the provisions of Part 5 of TMA 1970 relating to appeals have effect in relation to appeals under this Part of this Schedule as they have effect in relation to an appeal against an assessment to income tax.

Commencement—Finance Act 2008, Schedule 36 (Appointed Day and Savings) Order, SI 2009/404 art 2 (appointed day for the coming into force of Sch 36 is 1 April 2009).

HMRC Manuals—Compliance Handbook Manual, CH26900 (HMRC inspection powers (penalties): types of appeal and procedures).

Cross-references—Recognised Overseas Pensions Schemes and Corresponding Relief) Regulations, SI 2006/208 reg 5 (application and modification of the penalty provisions in FA 2008 Sch 36 Pt 7 in respect of QROPS).

Amendments—In the heading, words "standard penalty or daily default" repealed by FA 2009 s 95, Sch 47 para 19 with effect from 21 July 2009.

[1] In sub-paras (3), 4) words substituted for the words "First-tier Tribunal" by the Transfer of Tribunal Functions and Revenue and Customs Appeals Order, SI 2009/56 art 3, Sch 1 para 471 with effect from 1 April 2009.

Enforcement of . . . penalty

49—(1) A penalty under paragraph 39[, 40 or 40A][1] must be paid—

(*a*) before the end of the period of 30 days beginning with the date on which the notification under paragraph 46 was issued, or (*b*) if a notice of an appeal against the penalty is given, before the end of the period of 30 days beginning with the date on which the appeal is determined or withdrawn.

(2) A penalty under paragraph 39[, 40 or 40A][1] may be enforced as if it were income tax charged in an assessment and due and payable.

Commentary—*Simon's Taxes* **A6.301A**.

Commencement—Finance Act 2008, Schedule 36 (Appointed Day and Savings) Order, SI 2009/404 art 2 (appointed day for the coming into force of Sch 36 is 1 April 2009).

HMRC Manuals—Compliance Handbook Manual, CH26880 (HMRC inspection powers: when is the penalty payable).

Cross-references—Recognised Overseas Pensions Schemes and Corresponding Relief) Regulations, SI 2006/208 reg 5 (application and modification of the penalty provisions in FA 2008 Sch 36 Pt 7 in respect of QROPS).

Amendments—[1] In the heading, words "standard penalty or daily default" repealed, in sub-paras (1), (2) words substituted for the words "or 40", by FA 2009 s 95, Sch 47 para 20 with effect from 21 July 2009.

[Increased daily default penalty

49A (1) This paragraph applies if—

(*a*) a penalty under paragraph 40 is assessed under paragraph 46 in respect of a person's failure to comply with a notice under paragraph 5,

(*b*) the failure continues for more than 30 days beginning with the date on which notification of that assessment was issued, and

(*c*) the person has been told that an application may be made under this paragraph for an increased daily penalty to be imposed.

(2) If this paragraph applies, an officer of Revenue and Customs may make an application to the tribunal for an increased daily penalty to be imposed on the person.

(3) If the tribunal decides that an increased daily penalty should be imposed, then for each applicable day (see paragraph 49B) on which the failure continues—

(*a*) the person is not liable to a penalty under paragraph 40 in respect of the failure, and

(*b*) the person is liable instead to a penalty under this paragraph of an amount determined by the tribunal.

(4) The tribunal may not determine an amount exceeding £1,000 for each applicable day.

(5) But subject to that, in determining the amount the tribunal must have regard to—

(*a*) the likely cost to the person of complying with the notice,

(*b*) any benefits to the person of not complying with it, and

(*c*) any benefits to anyone else resulting from the person's non-compliance.

(6) Paragraph 41 applies in relation to the sum specified in sub-paragraph (4) as it applies in relation to the sums mentioned in paragraph 41(1).][1]

Cross-references—Recognised Overseas Pensions Schemes and Corresponding Relief) Regulations, SI 2006/208 reg 5 (application and modification of the penalty provisions in FA 2008 Sch 36 Pt 7 in respect of QROPS).

Amendments—[1] Paras 49A–49C inserted by FA 2011 s 86(2), Sch 24 paras 1, 4 with effect in relation to failures to comply with a notice under FA 2008 Sch 36 para 5 that begin on or after 1 April 2012.

[49B (1) If a person becomes liable to a penalty under paragraph 49A, HMRC must notify the person.

(2) The notification must specify the day from which the increased penalty is to apply.

(3) That day and any subsequent day is an "applicable day" for the purposes of paragraph 49A(3).][1]

Cross-references—Recognised Overseas Pensions Schemes and Corresponding Relief) Regulations, SI 2006/208 reg 5 (application and modification of the penalty provisions in FA 2008 Sch 36 Pt 7 in respect of QROPS).

Amendments—[1] Paras 49A–49C inserted by FA 2011 s 86(2), Sch 24 paras 1, 4 with effect in relation to failures to comply with a notice under FA 2008 Sch 36 para 5 that begin on or after 1 April 2012.

[49C (1) A penalty under paragraph 49A must be paid before the end of the period of 30 days beginning with the date on which the notification under paragraph 49B is issued.

(2) A penalty under paragraph 49A may be enforced as if it were income tax charged in an assessment and due and payable.][1]

Cross-references—Recognised Overseas Pensions Schemes and Corresponding Relief) Regulations, SI 2006/208 reg 5 (application and modification of the penalty provisions in FA 2008 Sch 36 Pt 7 in respect of QROPS).

Amendments—[1] Paras 49A–49C inserted by FA 2011 s 86(2), Sch 24 paras 1, 4 with effect in relation to failures to comply with a notice under FA 2008 Sch 36 para 5 that begin on or after 1 April 2012.

Tax-related penalty

50—(1) This paragraph applies where—

(*a*) a person becomes liable to a penalty under paragraph 39,

(*b*) the failure or obstruction continues after a penalty is imposed under that paragraph,

(*c*) an officer of Revenue and Customs has reason to believe that, as a result of the failure or obstruction, the amount of tax that the person has paid, or is likely to pay, is significantly less than it would otherwise have been, (*d*) before the end of the period of 12 months beginning with the relevant date . . . [1], an officer of Revenue and Customs makes an application to the Upper Tribunal for an additional penalty to be imposed on the person, and

(*e*) the Upper Tribunal decides that it is appropriate for an additional penalty to be imposed.

(2) The person is liable to a penalty of an amount decided by the Upper Tribunal.

(3) In deciding the amount of the penalty, the Upper Tribunal must have regard to the amount of tax which has not been, or is not likely to be, paid by the person.

(4) Where a person becomes liable to a penalty under this paragraph, HMRC must notify the person.

(5) Any penalty under this paragraph is in addition to the penalty or penalties under paragraph 39 or 40.

(6) In the application of the following provisions, no account shall be taken of a penalty under this paragraph—

(*a*) section 97A of TMA 1970 (multiple penalties),

(*b*) paragraph 12(2) of Schedule 24 to FA 2007 (interaction with other penalties), and

(*c*) paragraph 15(1) of Schedule 41 (interaction with other penalties).

[(7) In sub-paragraph (1)(*d*) "the relevant date" means—

(*a*) in a case involving an information notice against which a person may appeal, the latest of—

(i) the date on which the person became liable to the penalty under paragraph 39,

(ii) the end of the period in which notice of an appeal against the information notice could have been given, and

(iii) if notice of such an appeal is given, the date on which the appeal is determined or withdrawn, and

(*b*) in any other case, the date on which the person became liable to the penalty under paragraph 39.][1]

Commentary—*Simon's Taxes* **A6.301A**.

Commencement—Finance Act 2008, Schedule 36 (Appointed Day and Savings) Order, SI 2009/404 art 2 (appointed day for the coming into force of Sch 36 is 1 April 2009).

HMRC Manuals—Compliance Handbook Manual, CH26720 (HMRC inspection powers: details regarding tax related penalty). CH26760 (HMRC inspection powers: two examples relating to penalties).

Cross-references—Recognised Overseas Pensions Schemes and Corresponding Relief) Regulations, SI 2006/208 reg 5 (application and modification of the penalty provisions in FA 2008 Sch 36 Pt 7 in respect of QROPS).

Amendments—[1] In sub-para (1)(*d*) words "(within the meaning of paragraph 46)" repealed, and sub-para (7) inserted, by FA 2011 s 86(2), Sch 24 paras 1, 5(1)–(3) with effect where a person becomes liable to a penalty under FA 2008 Sch 36 para 39 on or after 19 July 2011.

Enforcement of tax-related penalty

51—(1) A penalty under paragraph 50 must be paid before the end of the period of 30 days beginning with the date on which the notification of the penalty is issued.

(2) A penalty under paragraph 50 may be enforced as if it were income tax charged in an assessment and due and payable.

Commentary—*Simon's Taxes* **A6.301A**.

Commencement—Finance Act 2008, Schedule 36 (Appointed Day and Savings) Order, SI 2009/404 art 2 (appointed day for the coming into force of Sch 36 is 1 April 2009).

Cross-references—Recognised Overseas Pensions Schemes and Corresponding Relief) Regulations, SI 2006/208 reg 5 (application and modification of the penalty provisions in FA 2008 Sch 36 Pt 7 in respect of QROPS).

Double jeopardy

52 A person is not liable to a penalty under this Schedule in respect of anything in respect of which the person has been convicted of an offence.

Commentary—*Simon's Taxes* **A6.301A**.

Commencement—Finance Act 2008, Schedule 36 (Appointed Day and Savings) Order, SI 2009/404 art 2 (appointed day for the coming into force of Sch 36 is 1 April 2009).

Cross-references—Recognised Overseas Pensions Schemes and Corresponding Relief) Regulations, SI 2006/208 reg 5 (application and modification of the penalty provisions in FA 2008 Sch 36 Pt 7 in respect of QROPS).

PART 8
OFFENCE

Concealing etc documents following information notice

53—(1) A person is guilty of an offence (subject to sub-paragraphs (2) and (3)) if—

(*a*) the person is required to produce a document by an information notice,

(*b*) the [tribunal][1] approved the giving of the notice in accordance with paragraph 3 or 5, and

(*c*) the person conceals, destroys or otherwise disposes of, or arranges for the concealment, destruction or disposal of, that document.

(2) Sub-paragraph (1) does not apply if the person acts after the document has been produced to an officer of Revenue and Customs in accordance with the information notice, unless an officer of Revenue and Customs has notified the person in writing that the document must continue to be available for inspection (and has not withdrawn the notification).
(3) Sub-paragraph (1) does not apply, in a case to which paragraph 8(1) applies, if the person acts after the expiry of the period of 6 months beginning with the day on which a copy of the document was so produced unless, before the expiry of that period, an officer of Revenue and Customs made a request for the original document under paragraph 8(2)(*b*).

Commencement—Finance Act 2008, Schedule 36 (Appointed Day and Savings) Order, SI 2009/404 art 2 (appointed day for the coming into force of Sch 36 is 1 April 2009).

HMRC Manuals—Compliance Handbook Manual, CH27200 (HMRC inspection powers (penalties): criminal proceedings for concealing, destroying or disposing of a document).

Amendments—[1] In sub-para (1)(*b*) word substituted for the words "First-tier Tribunal" by the Transfer of Tribunal Functions and Revenue and Customs Appeals Order, SI 2009/56 art 3, Sch 1 para 471 with effect from 1 April 2009.

Concealing etc documents following informal notification

54—(1) A person is also guilty of an offence (subject to sub-paragraph (2)) if the person conceals, destroys or otherwise disposes of, or arranges for the concealment, destruction or disposal of a document after the person has been informed by an officer of Revenue and Customs in writing that—

(*a*) the document is, or is likely, to be the subject of an information notice addressed to that person, and

(*b*) an officer of Revenue and Customs intends to seek the approval of the [tribunal][1] to the giving of the notice under paragraph 3 or 5 in respect of the document.

(2) A person is not guilty of an offence under this paragraph if the person acts after—

(*a*) at least 6 months has expired since the person was, or was last, so informed, or

(*b*) an information notice has been given to the person requiring the document to be produced.

Commencement—Finance Act 2008, Schedule 36 (Appointed Day and Savings) Order, SI 2009/404 art 2 (appointed day for the coming into force of Sch 36 is 1 April 2009).

Amendments—[1] In sub-para (1)(*b*) word substituted for the words "First-tier Tribunal" by the Transfer of Tribunal Functions and Revenue and Customs Appeals Order, SI 2009/56 art 3, Sch 1 para 471 with effect from 1 April 2009.

Fine or imprisonment

55 A person who is guilty of an offence under this Part of this Schedule is liable—

(*a*) on summary conviction, to a fine not exceeding the statutory maximum, and

(*b*) on conviction on indictment, to imprisonment for a term not exceeding 2 years or to a fine, or both.

Commencement—Finance Act 2008, Schedule 36 (Appointed Day and Savings) Order, SI 2009/404 art 2 (appointed day for the coming into force of Sch 36 is 1 April 2009).

PART 9

MISCELLANEOUS PROVISIONS AND INTERPRETATION

Application of provisions of TMA 1970

56 Subject to the provisions of this Schedule, the following provisions of TMA 1970 apply for the purposes of this Schedule as they apply for the purposes of the Taxes Acts—

(*a*) section 108 (responsibility of company officers),

(*b*) section 114 (want of form), and

(*c*) section 115 (delivery and service of documents).

Commencement—Finance Act 2008, Schedule 36 (Appointed Day and Savings) Order, SI 2009/404 art 2 (appointed day for the coming into force of Sch 36 is 1 April 2009).

HMRC Manuals—Compliance Handbook Manual, CH23440 (HMRC inspection powers: serving notices). CH23460 (mistakes in a notice).

Regulations under this Schedule

57—(1) Regulations made by the Commissioners or the Treasury under this Schedule are to be made by statutory instrument.
(2) A statutory instrument containing regulations under this Schedule is subject to annulment in pursuance of a resolution of the House of Commons.

Commencement—Finance Act 2008, Schedule 36 (Appointed Day and Savings) Order, SI 2009/404 art 2 (appointed day for the coming into force of Sch 36 is 1 April 2009).

General interpretation

58 In this Schedule—

"checking" includes carrying out an investigation or enquiry of any kind, "the Commissioners" means the Commissioners for Her Majesty's Revenue and Customs,

"document" includes a part of a document (except where the context otherwise requires),

"enactment" includes subordinate legislation (within the meaning of the Interpretation Act 1978 (c 30)),

"HMRC" means Her Majesty's Revenue and Customs,

"premises" includes—

(*a*) any building or structure,

(*b*) any land, and

(*c*) any means of transport,

"the Taxes Acts" means—

(*a*) TMA 1970,

(*b*) the Tax Acts, and

(*c*) TCGA 1992 and all other enactments relating to capital gains tax, . . . [1]

"taxpayer", in relation to a taxpayer notice or a third party notice, has the meaning given in paragraph 1(1) or 2(1) (as appropriate) [and][1]

["tribunal" means the First-tier Tribunal or, where determined by or under Tribunal Procedure Rules, the Upper Tribunal.][1]

Commencement—Finance Act 2008, Schedule 36 (Appointed Day and Savings) Order, SI 2009/404 art 2 (appointed day for the coming into force of Sch 36 is 1 April 2009).

HMRC Manuals—Compliance Handbook Manual, CH21660 (HMRC inspection powers: checks).

CH23320–23360 (HMRC inspection powers: what is a "document", part of a document or electronic document).

Amendments—[1] In sub-para (*c*) in the definition of "the Taxes Acts" word "and" at the end repealed; definition of "tribunal" and the preceding word "and" inserted by the Transfer of Tribunal Functions and Revenue and Customs Appeals Order, SI 2009/56 art 3, Sch 1 para 471 with effect from 1 April 2009.

Authorised officer of Revenue and Customs

59 A reference in a provision of this Schedule to an authorised officer of Revenue and Customs is a reference to an officer of Revenue and Customs who is, or is a member of a class of officers who are, authorised by the Commissioners for the purpose of that provision.

Commencement—Finance Act 2008, Schedule 36 (Appointed Day and Savings) Order, SI 2009/404 art 2 (appointed day for the coming into force of Sch 36 is 1 April 2009).

HMRC Manuals—Compliance Handbook Manual, CH260000 (HMRC inspection powers – how to do a compliance check: authorisation levels).

CH21720 (HMRC inspection powers: authorised officer).

Business

60—(1) In this Schedule (subject to regulations under this paragraph), references to carrying on a business include—

(*a*) the letting of property,

(*b*) the activities of a charity, and

(*c*) the activities of a government department, a local authority, a local authority association and any other public authority.

(2) In sub-paragraph (1)—

. . . [1]

"local authority" has the meaning given in section 999 of ITA 2007, and

"local authority association" has the meaning given in section 1000 of that Act.

(3) The Commissioners may by regulations provide that for the purposes of this Schedule—

(*a*) the carrying on of an activity specified in the regulations, or

(*b*) the carrying on of such an activity (or any activity) by a person specified in the regulations,

is or is not to be treated as the carrying on of a business.

Commencement—Finance Act 2008, Schedule 36 (Appointed Day and Savings) Order, SI 2009/404 art 2 (appointed day for the coming into force of Sch 36 is 1 April 2009).

HMRC Manuals—Compliance Handbook Manual, CH25200 (HMRC inspection powers: meaning of "carrying on a business").

Amendments—[1] In sub-s (2) definition of "charity" repealed by FA 2010 s 30, Sch 6 para 24 with effect from 1 April 2012 (SI 2012/736 art 19).

Chargeable period

61 In this Schedule "chargeable period" means—

(*a*) in relation to income tax or capital gains tax, a tax year, and

(*b*) in relation to corporation tax, an accounting period.

Commencement—Finance Act 2008, Schedule 36 (Appointed Day and Savings) Order, SI 2009/404 art 2 (appointed day for the coming into force of Sch 36 is 1 April 2009).

[Involved third parties

61A—(1) In this Schedule, "involved third party" means a person described in the first column of the Table below.

(2) In this Schedule, in relation to an involved third party, . . . [3] "relevant document" and "relevant tax" have the meaning given in the corresponding entries in that Table.

	Involved third party	*Relevant . . . [3] documents*	*Relevant tax*
1	A body approved by an officer of Revenue and Customs for the purpose of paying donations within the meaning of Part 12 of ITEPA 2003 (donations to charity: payroll giving) (see section 714 of that Act)	[Documents][3] relating to the donations	Income tax
2	A plan manager (see section 696 of ITTOIA 2005 (managers of individual investment plans))	[Documents][3] relating to the plan, including investments which are or have been held under the plan	Income tax
3	An account provider in relation to a child trust fund (as defined in section 3 of the Child Trust Funds Act 2004)	[Documents][3] relating to the fund, including investments which are or have been held under the fund	Income tax
4	A person who is or has been registered as a managing agent at Lloyd's in relation to a syndicate of underwriting members of Lloyd's	[Documents][3] relating to, and to the activities of, the syndicate	Income tax Capital gains tax Corporation tax
5	A person involved (in any capacity) in an insurance business (as defined for the purposes of Part 3 of FA 1994)	[Documents][3] relating to contracts of insurance entered into in the course of the business	Insurance premium tax
6	A person who makes arrangements for persons to enter into contracts of insurance	[Documents][3] relating to the contracts	Insurance premium tax
7	A person who— (*a*) is concerned in a business that is not an insurance business (as defined for the purposes of Part 3 of FA 1994), and (*b*) has been involved in the entry into a contract of insurance providing cover for any matter associated with that business	[Documents][3] relating to the contracts	Insurance premium tax
8	A person who, in relation to a charge to stamp duty reserve tax on an agreement, transfer, issue, appropriation or surrender, is an accountable person (as defined in regulation 2 of the Stamp Duty Reserve Tax Regulations SI 1986/1711 (as amended from time to time))	[Documents][3] relating to the agreement, transfer, issue, appropriation or surrender	Stamp duty reserve tax
9	A responsible person in relation to an oil field (as defined for the purposes of Part 1 of OTA 1975)	[Documents][3] relating to the oil field	Petroleum revenue tax

	Involved third party	*Relevant . . .* [3] *documents*	*Relevant tax*
10	A person involved (in any capacity) in subjecting aggregate to exploitation in the United Kingdom (as defined for the purposes of Part 2 of FA 2001) or in connected activities	[Documents][3] relating to matters in which the person is or has been involved	Aggregates levy
11	A person involved (in any capacity) in making or receiving [supplies of][2] taxable commodities (as defined for the purposes of Schedule 6 to FA 2000) or in connected activities	[Documents][3] relating to matters in which the person is or has been involved	Climate change levy
12	A person involved (in any capacity) with any landfill disposal (as defined for the purposes of Part 3 of FA 1996)	[Documents][3] relating to the disposal	Landfill tax][1]

Amendments—

[1] Para 61A inserted by FA 2009 s 96, Sch 48 para 14 with effect from 1 April 2010 (by virtue of SI 2009/3054 art 2).

[2] In Table, words in item 11 inserted by FA 2011 s 86(2), Sch 24 paras 1, 6 with effect from 19 July 2011.

[3] In sub-para (2) words ""relevant information"," repealed, in each in entry in second column of the Table word substituted for words "Information and documents", and in heading of that column words "information and relevant" repealed, by FA 2011 s 86(1), Sch 23 paras 60, 62(1), (3) with effect from 1 April 2012 in relation to relevant data with a bearing on any period (whether before, on or after 1 April 2012) subject to FA 2011 Sch 23 para 3(2). This para will continue to have effect in relation to notices given, or requests made, under any of the provisions repealed by FA 2011 Sch 23 Pt 6 before 1 April 2012 as if the amendments had not been made (FA 2011 Sch 23 para 65(2)).

Statutory records

62— (1) For the purposes of this Schedule, information or a document forms part of a person's statutory records if it is information or a document which the person is required to keep and preserve under or by virtue of—

(*a*) the Taxes Acts, or

[(*b*) any other enactment relating to a tax,][1]

subject to the following provisions of this paragraph.

(2) To the extent that any information or document that is required to be kept and preserved under or by virtue of the Taxes Acts—

(*a*) does not relate to the carrying on of a business, and

(*b*) is not also required to be kept or preserved under or by virtue of [any other enactment relating to a tax][1],

it only forms part of a person's statutory records to the extent that the chargeable period or periods to which it relates has or have ended.

(3) Information and documents cease to form part of a person's statutory records when the period for which they are required to be preserved by the enactments mentioned in sub-paragraph (1) has expired.

Commencement—Finance Act 2008, Schedule 36 (Appointed Day and Savings) Order, SI 2009/404 art 2 (appointed day for the coming into force of Sch 36 is 1 April 2009).

HMRC Manuals—Compliance Handbook Manual, CH21700 (HMRC inspection powers: statutory records).

Amendments—[1] Sub-para (1)(*b*) substituted, and in sub-para (2) words substituted for words "VATA 1994 or any other enactment relating to value added tax", by FA 2009 s 95, Sch 48 para 15 with effect from 1 April 2010 (by virtue of SI 2009/3054 art 2).

Tax

63—(1) In this Schedule, except where the context otherwise requires, "tax" means all or any of the following—

(*a*) income tax,

(*b*) capital gains tax,

(*c*) corporation tax,

[(*ca*) diverted profits tax,][5]

(*d*) VAT, and

[(*e*) insurance premium tax,
(*f*) inheritance tax,
(*g*) stamp duty land tax,
(*h*) stamp duty reserve tax,
[(*ha*) annual tax on enveloped dwellings,][3]
(*i*) petroleum revenue tax,
(*j*) aggregates levy,
(*k*) climate change levy,
(*l*) landfill tax, and
(*m*) relevant foreign tax,][2]

and references to "a tax" are to be interpreted accordingly.

(2) In this Schedule "corporation tax" includes any amount assessable or chargeable as if it were corporation tax.

(3) In this Schedule "VAT" means—

(*a*) value added tax charged in accordance with VATA 1994, . . . [1]
(*b*) value added tax charged in accordance with the law of another member State, [and
(*c*) amounts listed in sub-paragraph (3A).][1]

[(3A) Those amounts are—

(*a*) any amount that is recoverable under paragraph 5(2) of Schedule 11 to VATA 1994 (amounts shown on invoices as VAT), and
(*b*) any amount that is treated as VAT by virtue of regulations under section 54 of VATA 1994 (farmers etc).][1]

(4) In this Schedule "relevant foreign tax" means—

(*a*) a tax of a member State, other than the United Kingdom, which is covered by the provisions for the exchange of information under [Council Directive 2011/16/EU of 15 February 2011 on administrative cooperation in the field of taxation][4] (as amended from time to time), and
(*b*) any tax or duty which is imposed under the law of a territory in relation to which arrangements having effect by virtue of section 173 of FA 2006 (international tax enforcement arrangements) have been made and which is covered by the arrangements.

Commencement—Finance Act 2008, Schedule 36 (Appointed Day and Savings) Order, SI 2009/404 art 2 (appointed day for the coming into force of Sch 36 is 1 April 2009).

Modification—See FA 2010 Sch 1 para 36 (modification of this para in relation to bank payroll tax).

HMRC Manuals—Compliance Handbook Manual, CH21540 (HMRC inspection powers: tax position).
CH21560 (meaning of relevant foreign tax).

Amendments—[1] In sub-para (3)(*a*) word "and" repealed, sub-para (3)(*c*) and the preceding word "and" substituted for the words "and includes any amount that is recoverable under paragraph 5(2) of Schedule 11 to VATA 1994 (amounts shown on invoices as VAT)", and sub-para (3A) inserted, by FA 2009 s 95, Sch 47 para 21 with effect from 21 July 2009.

[2] In sub-para (1), paras (*e*)–(*m*) substituted for previous para (*e*) and preceding word "and" by FA 2009 s 96(1) with effect from 1 April 2010 (by virtue of SI 2009/3054 art 2).

[3] Sub-para (1)(*ha*) inserted by FA 2013 s 164, Sch 34 paras 1, 5 with effect from 17 July 2013.

[4] In sub-para (4)(*a*), words substituted by the European Administrative Co-operation (Taxation) Regulations, SI 2012/3062 reg 6 with effect from 1 January 2013.

[5] Sub-para (1)(*ca*) inserted by FA 2015 s 105(2) with effect in relation to accounting periods beginning on or after 1 April 2015. For accounting periods that straddle that date, see FA 2015 s 116(2).

Tax position

64—(1) In this Schedule, except as otherwise provided, "tax position", in relation to a person, means the person's position as regards any tax, including the person's position as regards—

(*a*) past, present and future liability to pay any tax,
(*b*) penalties and other amounts that have been paid, or are or may be payable, by or to the person in connection with any tax, and
(*c*) claims, elections, applications and notices that have been or may be made or given in connection with [the person's liability to pay][1] any tax,

and references to a person's position as regards a particular tax (however expressed) are to be interpreted accordingly.

(2) References in this Schedule to a person's tax position include, where appropriate, a reference to the person's position as regards any deductions or repayments of tax, or of sums representing tax, that the person is required to make—

(*a*) under PAYE regulations,
(*b*) under Chapter 3 of Part 3 of FA 2004 or regulations made under that Chapter (construction industry scheme), or
(*c*) by or under any other provision of the Taxes Acts.

[(2A) References in this Schedule to a person's tax position also include, where appropriate, a reference to the person's position as regards the withholding by the person of another person's PAYE income (as defined in section 683 of ITEPA 2003).][1]

(3) References in this Schedule to the tax position of a person include the tax position of—

(*a*) a company that has ceased to exist, and

(*b*) an individual who has died.

(4) References in this Schedule to a person's tax position are to the person's tax position at any time or in relation to any period, unless otherwise stated.

Commencement—Finance Act 2008, Schedule 36 (Appointed Day and Savings) Order, SI 2009/404 art 2 (appointed day for the coming into force of Sch 36 is 1 April 2009).

Amendments—[1] In sub-para (1)(*c*) words inserted, and sub-para (2A) inserted, by FA 2009 s 95, Sch 47 para 22 with effect from 21 July 2009.

PART 10
CONSEQUENTIAL PROVISIONS

Commencement—Finance Act 2008, Schedule 36 (Appointed Day and Savings) Order, SI 2009/404 art 2 (appointed day for the coming into force of Sch 36 is 1 April 2009).

TMA 1970

65 TMA 1970 is amended as follows.

66 Omit section 19A (power to call for documents for purposes of enquiries).

67 Omit section 20 (power to call for documents of taxpayer and others).

68—(1) Section 20B (restrictions on powers to call for documents under ss 20 and 20A) is amended as follows.

(2) In the heading, for "**ss 20 and**" substitute "**section**".

(3) In subsection (1)—

(*a*) omit "under section 20(1), (3) or (8A), or",

(*b*) omit "(or, in the case of section 20(3), to deliver or make available)",

(*c*) omit ", or to furnish the particulars in question", and

(*d*) omit "section 20(7) or (8A) or, as the case may be,".

(4) Omit subsections (1A) and (1B).

(5) In subsection (2), omit from the beginning to "taxpayer; and".

(6) In subsection (3)—

(*a*) omit "under section 20(1) or (3) or", and

(*b*) omit "section 20(3) and (4) and".

(7) In subsection (4)—

(*a*) omit "section 20(1) or", and

(*b*) omit ", and as an alternative to delivering documents to comply with a notice under section 20(3) or (8A)".

(8) Omit subsections (5), (6) and (7).

(9) In subsection (8), omit "section 20(3) or (8A) or".

(10) Omit subsections (9) to (14).

69—(1) Section 20BB (falsification etc of documents) is amended as follows.

(2) In subsection (1)(*a*), omit "20 or".

(3) In subsection (2)(*b*), omit "or, in a case within section 20(3) or (8A) above, inspected".

70—(1) Section 20D (interpretation) is amended as follows.

(2) In subsection (2), for "sections 20 and" substitute "section".

(3) Omit subsection (3).

71 In section 29(6)(*c*) (assessment where loss of tax discovered), omit ", whether in pursuance of a notice under section 19A of this Act or otherwise".

72 Omit section 97AA (failure to produce documents under section 19A).

73 In section 98 (penalties), in the Table—

(*a*) in the first column, omit the entry for section 767C of ICTA, and

(*b*) in the second column, omit the entry for section 28(2) of F(No 2)A 1992.

74 *In section 100(2) (exclusions from provisions relating to determination of penalties under the Taxes Acts), insert at the end "or*

(g) Schedule 36 to the Finance Act 2008."

Amendments—Para 74 repealed by FA 2009 s 109, Sch 57 para 14(*a*) with effect from 21 July 2009.

75 (1) Section 107A (relevant trustees) is amended as follows.
(2) In subsection (2)(*a*), for ", 95 or 97AA" substitute 'or 95'.
(3) In subsection (3)(*a*), omit "or 97AA(1)(*b*)".

76 In section 118 (interpretation), in the definition of "tax", omit "20,".

77 In Schedule 1A (claims etc not included in returns), omit paragraphs 6 and 6A (power to call for documents for purposes of enquiries and power to appeal against notice to produce documents).

National Savings Bank Act 1971 (c 29)

78 In section 12(3) (secrecy), for the words from "and of section 20(3)" to the end substitute "and of Schedule 36 to the Finance Act 2008 (powers of officers of Revenue and Customs to obtain information and documents and inspect business premises)".

ICTA

79 ICTA is amended as follows.

80 In section 767B (change of company ownership: supplementary), in subsection (4), for "767AA and 767C" substitute "and 767AA".[1]

Amendments—[1] This para repealed by CTA 2010 s 1181, Sch 3 Pt 1. CTA 2010 has effect for corporation tax purposes for accounting periods ending on or after 1 April 2010, and for income and capital gains tax purposes for the tax year 2010–11 and subsequent tax years.

81 Omit section 767C (change in company ownership: information).

82 In section 769 (rules for ascertaining change in ownership of company)—

(*a*) *in subsections (1) and (5), omit ", 767C", and*

(*b*) *in subsections (2A) and (9), for "767AA or 767C" substitute "or 767AA".*[1]

Amendments—[1] This para repealed by CTA 2010 s 1181, Sch 3 Pt 1. CTA 2010 has effect for corporation tax purposes for accounting periods ending on or after 1 April 2010, and for income and capital gains tax purposes for the tax year 2010–11 and subsequent tax years.

FA 1990

83 In section 125 of FA 1990 (information for tax authorities in other member States)—

(*a*) omit subsections (1) and (2),

(*b*) *in subsection (3), for "the Directive mentioned in subsection (1) above" substitute "the Directive of the Council of the European Communities dated 19 December 1977 No 77/799/EEC (the "1977 Directive")",*[1]

(*c*) *in subsection (4), for "such as is mentioned in subsection (1) above" substitute "which is covered by the provisions for the exchange of information under the 1977 Directive", and*[1]

(*d*) *in subsection (6), omit the words from the beginning to "passed,".*[1]

Amendments—[1] Sub-paras (*b*)–(*d*) repealed by Finance Act 2009 Schedule 47 (Consequential Amendments) Order, SI 2009/2035, Art 2 Schedule, para 60(*p*) with effect from 13 August 2009.

Social Security Administration Act 1992 (c 5)

84 In section 110ZA of the Social Security Administration Act 1992 (Class 1, 1A, 1B or 2 contributions: powers to call for documents etc), for subsections (1) and (2) substitute—

"(1) Schedule 36 to the Finance Act 2008 (information and inspection powers) applies for the purpose of checking a person's position as regards relevant contributions as it applies for the purpose of checking a person's tax position, subject to the modifications in subsection (2).

(2) That Schedule applies as if—

(*a*) references to any provision of the Taxes Acts were to any provision of this Act or the Contributions and Benefits Act relating to relevant contributions,

(*b*) references to prejudice to the assessment or collection of tax were to prejudice to the assessment of liability for, and payment of, relevant contributions,

(*c*) the reference to information relating to the conduct of a pending appeal relating to tax were a reference to information relating to the conduct of a pending appeal relating to relevant contributions, and

(*d*) paragraphs 21, 35(4)(*b*), 36 and 37(2) of that Schedule (restrictions on giving taxpayer notice where taxpayer has made tax return) were omitted."

Social Security Administration (Northern Ireland) Act 1992 (c 8)

85 In section 104ZA of the Social Security Administration (Northern Ireland) Act 1992 (Class 1, 1A, 1B or 2 contributions: powers to call for documents etc), for subsections (1) and (2) substitute—

"(1) Schedule 36 to the Finance Act 2008 (information and inspection powers) applies for the purpose of checking a person's position as regards relevant contributions as it applies for the purpose of checking a person's tax position, subject to the modifications in subsection (2).

(2) That Schedule applies as if—

(*a*) references to any provision of the Taxes Acts were to any provision of this Act or the Contributions and Benefits Act relating to relevant contributions,

(*b*) references to prejudice to the assessment or collection of tax were to prejudice to the assessment of liability for, and payment of, relevant contributions,

(*c*) the reference to information relating to the conduct of a pending appeal relating to tax were a reference to information relating to the conduct of a pending appeal relating to relevant contributions, and

(*d*) paragraphs 21, 35(4)(*b*), 36 and 37(2) of that Schedule (restrictions on giving taxpayer notice where taxpayer has made tax return) were omitted."

F(No 2)A 1992

86 Omit section 28(1) to (3) (powers of inspection).

VATA 1994

87 (*amends* VATA 1994 Sch 11)

FA 1998

88 In Schedule 18 to FA 1998 (company tax returns), omit paragraphs 27, 28 and 29 (notice to produce documents etc for purposes of enquiry into company tax return, power to appeal against such notices and penalty for failure to produce documents etc).

FA 1999

89 In section 13(5) (gold), omit paragraph (*c*).

Tax Credits Act 2002 (c 21)

90 In section 25 of the Tax Credits Act 2002 (payments of working tax credit by employers), omit subsections (3) and (4).

FA 2006

91 Omit section 174 of FA 2006 (international tax enforcement arrangements: information powers).

Other repeals

92 In consequence of the preceding provisions of this Part of this Schedule, omit the following—

(*a*) section 126 of FA 1988,

(*b*) sections 142(2), (3), (4), (6)(*a*), (7), (8) and (9) and 144(3), (5) and (7) of FA 1989,

(*c*) sections 187 and 255 of, and paragraph 29 of Schedule 19 to, FA 1994,

(*d*) paragraph 6 of Schedule 1 to the Civil Evidence Act 1995 (c 38),

(*e*) paragraph 17 of Schedule 3, paragraph 3 of Schedule 19 and paragraph 2 of Schedule 22 to FA 1996,

(*f*) paragraph 17 of Schedule 3, paragraph 3 of Schedule 19 and paragraph 2 of Schedule 22 to FA 1996,

(*g*) section 115 of, and paragraphs 36 and 42(6) and (7) of Schedule 19 to, FA 1998,

(*h*) section 15(3) of FA 1999,

(*i*) paragraphs 21 and 38(4) of Schedule 29 to FA 2001,

(*j*) section 20 of FA 2006, and

(*k*) paragraph 350 of Schedule 1 to ITA 2007.

SCHEDULE 37

RECORD-KEEPING

Section 115

Commencement—Finance Act 2008, Schedule 37 (Appointed Day) Order, SI 2009/402 (Sch 37 comes into force on 1 April 2009).

TMA 1970

1–3 (See the *Yellow Tax Handbook* for amendments made to TMA 1970)

Commencement—Finance Act 2008, Schedule 37 (Appointed Day) Order, SI 2009/402 (Sch 37 comes into force on 1 April 2009).

VATA 1994

4 Schedule 11 to VATA 1994 (administration, collection and enforcement) is amended as follows.

Commencement—Finance Act 2008, Schedule 37 (Appointed Day) Order, SI 2009/402 (Sch 37 comes into force on 1 April 2009).

5—(1) Paragraph 6 (duty to keep records) is amended as follows.
(2) (*amends* VATA 1994 Sch 11 para 6(3))
(3) (*substitutes* VATA 1994 Sch 11 para 6(4))

Commencement—Finance Act 2008, Schedule 37 (Appointed Day) Order, SI 2009/402 (Sch 37 comes into force on 1 April 2009).

6 (*amends* VATA 1994 Sch 11 para 6A(7))

Commencement—Finance Act 2008, Schedule 37 (Appointed Day) Order, SI 2009/402 (Sch 37 comes into force on 1 April 2009).

FA 1998

7–9 (See the *Yellow Tax Handbook* for amendments made to FA 1998)

Consequential provisions

10 (*amends* FA 1999 s 13(6))

Commencement—Finance Act 2008, Schedule 37 (Appointed Day) Order, SI 2009/402 (Sch 37 comes into force on 1 April 2009).

11 (See the *Yellow Tax Handbook* for amendments made to FA 1995, FA 1996)

SCHEDULE 39

TIME LIMITS FOR ASSESSMENTS, CLAIMS ETC

Section 118

Commencement—Finance Act 2008, Schedule 39 (Appointed Day, Transitional Provision and Savings) Order, SI 2009/403 art 2(2). The appointed day for the coming into force of paras 1–31, 37–66 is 1 April 2010, subject to transitional provisions in SI 2009/403 art 10(2): where art 10 applies the appointed day is 1 April 2012.

TMA 1970

1–15 (See the *Yellow Tax Handbook* for amendments made to TMA 1970)

ICTA

16–26 (See the *Yellow Tax Handbook* for amendments made to TA 1988)

FA 1991

27 (See the *Yellow Tax Handbook* for amendments made to FA 1991)

TCGA 1992

28–31 (See the *Yellow Tax Handbook* for amendments made to TCGA 1992)

VATA 1994

32 VATA 1994 is amended as follows.

Commencement—Finance Act 2008, Schedule 39 (Appointed Day, Transitional Provision and Savings) Order, SI 2009/403 art 2(2). The appointed day for the coming into force of paras 32–36 is 1 April 2009.

33 (*amends* VATA 1994 s 33A(4))

Commencement—Finance Act 2008, Schedule 39 (Appointed Day, Transitional Provision and Savings) Order, SI 2009/403 art 2(2). The appointed day for the coming into force of paras 32–36 is 1 April 2009.
Paragraph 33 is disregarded where, for the purposes of VATA 1994 s 33A, the day on which the supply was made or the acquisition or importation took place was on or before 31 March 2006.

34—(1) Section 77 (assessments: time limits and supplementary assessments) is amended as follows.
(2) (*amends* VATA 1994 s 77(1)(*a*), (*b*))
(3) (*substitutes* VATA 1994 s 77(4)–(4C))
(4) (*amends* VATA 1994 s 77(5))

Commencement—Finance Act 2008, Schedule 39 (Appointed Day, Transitional Provision and Savings) Order, SI 2009/403 art 2(2). The appointed day for the coming into force of paras 32–36 is 1 April 2009.

Paragraph 34 is disregarded where—

– for the purposes of VATA 1994 s 77, the end of the prescribed accounting period or the importation, acquisition or event giving rise to the penalty, as appropriate, occurred on or before 31 March 2006; and

– after a person's death, a sum is assessed as due by reason of some conduct (however described) of the deceased, including a sum due by way of penalty, interest or surcharge, and the date of the death is on or before 31 March 2006 (SI 2009/403 art 4).

35 (*amends* VATA 1994 s 78(11))

Commencement—Finance Act 2008, Schedule 39 (Appointed Day, Transitional Provision and Savings) Order, SI 2009/403 art 2(2). The appointed day for the coming into force of paras 32–36 is 1 April 2009.

Paragraph 35 is disregarded where, for the purposes of a claim under VATA 1994 s 78, the end of the applicable period to which the claim relates was on or before 31 March 2006 (SI 2009/403 art 5).

36 (*amends* VATA 1994 s 80(4))

Commencement—Finance Act 2008, Schedule 39 (Appointed Day, Transitional Provision and Savings) Order, SI 2009/403 art 2(2). The appointed day for the coming into force of paras 32–36 is 1 April 2009.

Paragraph 36 is disregarded where, for the purposes of VATA 1994 s 80, the relevant date is on or before 31 March 2006 (SI 2009/403 art 6).

FA 1998

37–47 (See the *Yellow Tax Handbook* for amendments made to FA 1998)

FA 2002

48 (See the *Yellow Tax Handbook* for amendments made to FA 2002)

ITEPA 2003

49 (See the *Yellow Tax Handbook* for amendments made to ITEPA 2003)

ITTOIA 2005

50–53 (See the *Yellow Tax Handbook* for amendments made to ITTOIA 2005)

ITA 2007

54–62 (See the *Yellow Tax Handbook* for amendments made to ITA 2007)

Consequential amendments

63 (See the *Yellow Tax Handbook* for amendments made to FA 1993 s 178(3))

64 (See the *Yellow Tax Handbook* for amendments made to FA 1994 s 225(3)(*b*))

65 In consequence of the preceding provisions of this Schedule, omit—

(*a*) section 149(4)(*a*)(i) and (ii) of FA 1989,

(*b*) paragraphs 4 and 6 of Schedule 21 to FA 1996,

(*c*) section 47(10) of FA 1997,

(*d*) paragraph 18 of Schedule 19 to FA 1998, and

(*e*) section 91(6)(*b*) of FA 2007.

Saving

66 (See the *Yellow Tax Handbook*)

SCHEDULE 40

PENALTIES: AMENDMENTS OF SCHEDULE 24 TO FA 2007

Section 122

Commencement—Finance Act 2008, Schedule 40 (Appointed Day, Transitional Provisions and Consequential Amendments) Order, SI 2009/571 art 2 (the appointed day for the purposes of this Schedule is 1 April 2009).

1 Schedule 24 to FA 2007 (penalties for errors) is amended as follows.

Commencement—Finance Act 2008, Schedule 40 (Appointed Day, Transitional Provisions and Consequential Amendments) Order, SI 2009/571 art 2 (the appointed day for the purposes of this Schedule is 1 April 2009).

2—(1) Paragraph 1 (error in taxpayer's document) is amended as follows.

(2) (*amends* FA 2007 Sch 24 para 1(2))

(3) (*amends* FA 2007 Sch 24 para 1(3))

(4)–(6) (*amend* FA 2007 Sch 24 para 1 Table)
(7) (*inserts* FA 2007 Sch 24 para 1(5))

Commencement—Finance Act 2008, Schedule 40 (Appointed Day, Transitional Provisions and Consequential Amendments) Order, SI 2009/571 art 2 (the appointed day for the purposes of this Schedule is 1 April 2009).

3 (*inserts* FA 2007 Sch 24 para 1A)

Commencement—Finance Act 2008, Schedule 40 (Appointed Day, Transitional Provisions and Consequential Amendments) Order, SI 2009/571 art 2 (the appointed day for the purposes of this Schedule is 1 April 2009).

4—(1) Paragraph 2 (under-assessment by HMRC) is amended as follows.
(2) (*amends* FA 2007 Sch 24 para 2(1))
(3) (*substitutes* FA 2007 Sch 24 para 2(3))

Commencement—Finance Act 2008, Schedule 40 (Appointed Day, Transitional Provisions and Consequential Amendments) Order, SI 2009/571 art 2 (the appointed day for the purposes of this Schedule is 1 April 2009).

5—(1) Paragraph 3 (degrees of culpability) is amended as follows
(2) (*amends* FA 2007 Sch 24 para 3(1))
(3) (*amends* FA 2007 Sch 24 para 3(2))

Commencement—Finance Act 2008, Schedule 40 (Appointed Day, Transitional Provisions and Consequential Amendments) Order, SI 2009/571 art 2 (the appointed day for the purposes of this Schedule is 1 April 2009).

6 (*inserts* FA 2007 Sch 24 para 4(1A))

Commencement—Finance Act 2008, Schedule 40 (Appointed Day, Transitional Provisions and Consequential Amendments) Order, SI 2009/571 art 2 (the appointed day for the purposes of this Schedule is 1 April 2009).

7 (*amends* FA 2007 Sch 24 para 5(1))

Commencement—Finance Act 2008, Schedule 40 (Appointed Day, Transitional Provisions and Consequential Amendments) Order, SI 2009/571 art 2 (the appointed day for the purposes of this Schedule is 1 April 2009).

8—(1) Paragraph 6 (potential lost revenue: multiple errors) is amended as follows.
(2) (*amends* FA 2007 Sch 24 para 6(1), (2))
(3) (*amends* FA 2007 Sch 24 para 6(5))

Commencement—Finance Act 2008, Schedule 40 (Appointed Day, Transitional Provisions and Consequential Amendments) Order, SI 2009/571 art 2 (the appointed day for the purposes of this Schedule is 1 April 2009).

9—(1) Paragraph 9 (reductions for disclosure) is amended as follows.
(2) (*inserts* FA 2007 Sch 24 para 9(A1))
(3) (*amends* FA 2007 Sch 24 para 9(1))
(4) (*amends* FA 2007 Sch 24 para 9(2)(*a*))

Commencement—Finance Act 2008, Schedule 40 (Appointed Day, Transitional Provisions and Consequential Amendments) Order, SI 2009/571 art 2 (the appointed day for the purposes of this Schedule is 1 April 2009).

10 (*amends* FA 2007 Sch 24 para 11(1))

Commencement—Finance Act 2008, Schedule 40 (Appointed Day, Transitional Provisions and Consequential Amendments) Order, SI 2009/571 art 2 (the appointed day for the purposes of this Schedule is 1 April 2009).

11—(1) Paragraph 12 (interaction with other penalties) is amended as follows.
(2) (*amends* FA 2007 Sch 24 para 12(2))
(3) (*inserts* FA 2007 Sch 24 para 12(4))
(4) (*amends* FA 2007 Sch 24 para 12 heading)

Commencement—Finance Act 2008, Schedule 40 (Appointed Day, Transitional Provisions and Consequential Amendments) Order, SI 2009/571 art 2 (the appointed day for the purposes of this Schedule is 1 April 2009).

12—(1) Paragraph 13 (assessment) is amended as follows.
(2) (*amends* FA 2007 Sch 24 para 13(1))
(3) (*inserts* FA 2007 Sch 24 para 13(1A))
(4) (*amends* FA 2007 Sch 24 para 13(3))
(5) (*amends* FA 2007 Sch 24 para 13(4))

Commencement—Finance Act 2008, Schedule 40 (Appointed Day, Transitional Provisions and Consequential Amendments) Order, SI 2009/571 art 2 (the appointed day for the purposes of this Schedule is 1 April 2009).

13 (*amends* FA 2007 Sch 24 para 15)

Commencement—Finance Act 2008, Schedule 40 (Appointed Day, Transitional Provisions and Consequential Amendments) Order, SI 2009/571 art 2 (the appointed day for the purposes of this Schedule is 1 April 2009).

14 (*substitutes* FA 2007 Sch 24 para 16; subsequently *repealed* by SI 2009/56 art 3, Sch 1 para 472 with effect from April 2009)

Commencement—Finance Act 2008, Schedule 40 (Appointed Day, Transitional Provisions and Consequential Amendments) Order, SI 2009/571 art 2 (the appointed day for the purposes of this Schedule is 1 April 2009).

15 (*amends* FA 2007 Sch 24 para 18(3))

Commencement—Finance Act 2008, Schedule 40 (Appointed Day, Transitional Provisions and Consequential Amendments) Order, SI 2009/571 art 2 (the appointed day for the purposes of this Schedule is 1 April 2009).

16—(1) Paragraph 19 (companies: officers' liability) is amended as follows.
(2) (*amends* FA 2007 Sch 24 para 19(1))
(3) (*substitutes* FA 2007 Sch 24 para 19(5))

Commencement—Finance Act 2008, Schedule 40 (Appointed Day, Transitional Provisions and Consequential Amendments) Order, SI 2009/571 art 2 (the appointed day for the purposes of this Schedule is 1 April 2009).

17 (*amends* FA 2007 Sch 24 para 21)

Commencement—Finance Act 2008, Schedule 40 (Appointed Day, Transitional Provisions and Consequential Amendments) Order, SI 2009/571 art 2 (the appointed day for the purposes of this Schedule is 1 April 2009).

18 (*amends* FA 2007 Sch 24 para 22)

Commencement—Finance Act 2008, Schedule 40 (Appointed Day, Transitional Provisions and Consequential Amendments) Order, SI 2009/571 art 2 (the appointed day for the purposes of this Schedule is 1 April 2009).

19 (*inserts* FA 2007 Sch 24 para 23A)

Commencement—Finance Act 2008, Schedule 40 (Appointed Day, Transitional Provisions and Consequential Amendments) Order, SI 2009/571 art 2 (the appointed day for the purposes of this Schedule is 1 April 2009).

20—(1) Paragraph 28 (interpretation) is amended as follows.
(2) (*inserts* FA 2007 Sch 24 para 28(*c*)(iv))
(3) (*inserted* FA 2007 Sch 24 para 28(*da*); repealed by FA 2009 s 109, Sch 57 para 14(*b*).)
(4) (*amends* FA 2007 Sch 24 para 28(*f*))
(5) (*inserts* FA 2007 Sch 24 para 28(*fa*))

Commencement—Finance Act 2008, Schedule 40 (Appointed Day, Transitional Provisions and Consequential Amendments) Order, SI 2009/571 art 2 (the appointed day for the purposes of this Schedule is 1 April 2009).

21 In consequence of this Schedule the following provisions are omitted—

(*a*) –(*g*) . . .
(*h*) paragraphs 98 to 100 of Schedule 6 to FA 2000,
(*i*) in Schedule 6 to FA 2001, paragraphs 7 to 9, and in paragraph 9A(5), paragraph (*b*) and the "or" before it,
(*j*) section 133(2) to (4) of FA 2002,
(*k*) in FA 2003—
  (i) section 192(8), and
  (ii) paragraph 8 of Schedule 10 to FA 2003, and
(*l*) section 295(4)(*a*) of FA 2004.

Note—Omitted paras not relevant to this work.

Commencement—Finance Act 2008, Schedule 40 (Appointed Day, Transitional Provisions and Consequential Amendments) Order, SI 2009/571 art 2 (the appointed day for the purposes of this Schedule is 1 April 2009). This para repeals the provisions listed below only in so far as those provisions relate to conduct involving dishonesty which relates to—

(a) an inaccuracy in a document, or
(b) a failure to notify HMRC of an under-assessment by HMRC.

Those provisions referred to above are—

(a) in FA 1994—
  (i) section 8; and
  (ii) Sch 7 paras 12, 13;
(b) FA 1996 Sch 5 paras 18, 19;
(c) FA 2000 Sch 6 paras 98, 99;
(d) in FA 2001 Sch 6—
  (i) paras 7, 8; and
  (ii) para 9A(5)(*b*);
(e) FA 2002 s 133(2)–(4).

SCHEDULE 41

PENALTIES: FAILURE TO NOTIFY AND CERTAIN VAT AND EXCISE WRONGDOING

Section 123

Commentary—*Simon's Taxes* **Division A4.5**.

Commencement—Finance Act 2008, Schedule 41 (Appointed Day and Transitional Provisions) Order, SI 2009/511 art 2 (the appointed day for the purposes of this Schedule is 1 April 2010).

This Schedule has effect (by virtue of SI 2009/511 art 3)—

(a) in relation to any relevant obligation arising on or after 1 April 2010;
(b) in relation to any unauthorised issue of an invoice taking place on or after 1 April 2010;

(c) in relation to any act which enables HMRC to assess an amount as duty under a relevant excise provision and which is done on or after 1 April 2010; and

(d) in relation to any act giving rise to a penalty under para 4 which is done on or after 1 April 2010.

Cross-references—See FA 2014 ss 208–214, Sch 30 (follower notices: penalties).

Failure to notify etc

1 A penalty is payable by a person (P) where P fails to comply with an obligation specified in the Table below (a "relevant obligation").

Tax to which obligation relates	*Obligation*
Income tax and capital gains tax	Obligation under section 7 of TMA 1970 (obligation to give notice of liability to income tax or capital gains tax).
Corporation tax	Obligation under paragraph 2 of Schedule 18 to FA 1998 (obligation to give notice of chargeability to corporation tax).
[Diverted profits tax	Obligation under section 92 of FA 2015 (duty to notify if within scope of diverted profits tax).][7]
Value added tax	Obligations under paragraphs 5, 6, 7 and 14(2) and (3) of Schedule 1 to VATA 1994 (obligations to notify liability to register and notify material change in nature of supplies made by person exempted from registration).
[Value added tax	Obligations under paragraphs 5, 6 and 13(3) of Schedule 1A to VATA 1994 (obligations to notify liability to register and notify material change in nature of supplies made by person exempted from registration).][1]
Value added tax	Obligation under paragraph 3 of Schedule 2 to VATA 1994 (obligation to notify liability to register).
Value added tax	Obligations under paragraphs 3 and 8(2) of Schedule 3 to VATA 1994 (obligations to notify liability to register and notify acquisition affecting exemption from registration).
Value added tax	Obligations under paragraphs 3, 4 and 7(2) and (3) of Schedule 3A to VATA 1994 (obligations to notify liability to register and notify relevant change in supplies made by person exempted from registration).
Value added tax	Obligation under regulations under paragraph 2(4) of Schedule 11 to VATA 1994 (obligation to give notification of acquisition of goods from another member State).
Insurance premium tax	Obligations under section 53(1) and (2) of FA 1994 (obligations to register in respect of receipt of premiums in course of taxable business and notify intended receipt of premiums in course of taxable business).
Insurance premium tax	Obligations under section 53AA(1) and (3) of FA 1994 (obligations to register as taxable intermediary and notify intention to charge taxable intermediary's fees).
Aggregates levy	Obligations under section 24(2) of, and paragraph 1 of Schedule 4 to, FA 2001 (obligations to register in respect of carrying out of taxable activities and notify intention of carrying out such activities).
Climate change levy	Obligations under paragraphs 53 and 55 of Schedule 6 to FA 2000 (obligations to register in respect of taxable supplies and notify intention to make, or have made, taxable supply).
Landfill tax	Obligations under section 47(2) and (3) of FA 1996 (obligations to register in respect of carrying out of taxable activities and notify intention of carrying out such activities).
Air passenger duty	Obligation under section 33(4) [or 33A(4)][2] of FA 1994 (obligation to give notice of liability to register to operate chargeable aircraft).
[Alcohol liquor duties	Obligation to be authorised and registered to obtain and use duty stamps under regulations under paragraph 4 of Schedule 2A to ALDA 1979 (duty stamps).

Tax to which obligation relates	*Obligation*
Alcohol liquor duties	Obligations under sections 12(1), 47(1), 54(2), 55(2) and 62(2) of ALDA 1979 (obligations to hold licence to manufacture spirits, register to brew beer, hold licence to produce wine or made-wine and register to make cider).
Alcohol liquor duties	Obligation to have plant and processes approved for the manufacture of spirits under regulations under section 15(6) of ALDA 1979 (distillers' warehouses).
Tobacco products duty	Obligation to manufacture tobacco products only on premises registered under regulations under section 7 of TPDA 1979 (management of tobacco products duty).
Hydrocarbon oil duties	Obligation to make entry of premises intended to be used for production of oil under regulations under section 21 of HODA 1979 (administration and enforcement).
Excise duties	Obligation to receive, deposit or hold duty suspended excise goods only in premises approved under regulations under section 92 of CEMA 1979 (approval of warehouses).
Excise duties	Obligation to receive duty suspended excise goods only if approved or registered (or approved and registered) as a REDS or an Occasional Importer under regulations under section 100G or 100H of CEMA 1979 (registered excise dealers and shippers etc).
Excise duties	Obligation to receive, deposit or hold duty suspended excise goods only if approved or registered (or approved and registered) as a registered owner, a duty representative, a registered mobile operator or a fiscal representative of a registered mobile operator or an authorised warehousekeeper under regulations under section 100G or 100H of CEMA 1979 (registered excise dealers and shippers etc).
[General betting duty	Obligation to register under section 164(2) of FA 2014 (registration of persons liable etc for general betting duty).
Pool betting duty	Obligation to register under section 164(2) of FA 2014 (registration of persons liable etc for pool betting duty).][6]
Bingo duty	Obligations under paragraph 10(1) and (1A) of Schedule 3 to BGDA 1981 (obligation to notify and register in respect of bingo-promotion).
Lottery duty	Obligation under section 29(1) of FA 1993 (obligation to register in respect of promotion of lotteries).
Gaming duty	Obligations under paragraphs 3 and 6 of Schedule 1 to FA 1997 (obligations to register in respect of gaming and to notify premises).
[Remote gaming duty	Obligation to register under section 164(2) of FA 2014 (registration of persons liable etc for remote gaming duty).][6]
[Machine games duty	Obligation under paragraph 20(3) of Schedule 24 to FA 2012 (obligation to register in respect of premises).][4]
. . .	. . .][5]

Commencement—Finance Act 2008, Schedule 41 (Appointed Day and Transitional Provisions) Order, SI 2009/511 art 2 (the appointed day for the purposes of this Schedule is 1 April 2010).

Cross reference—FA 2009 s 94 (Publishing details of deliberate tax defaulters).

FA 2015 Sch 21 (penalties in connection with offshore asset moves).

Amendments—

1 Entry inserted by FA 2012 s 203, Sch 28 para 18 with effect in relation to supplies made or to be made on or after 1 December 2012.

2 In entry for air passenger duty, words in column 2 inserted by FA 2012 s 190, Sch 23 para 15 with effect from 17 July 2012.

3 Words in entries for "general betting duty", "pool betting duty" and "remote gaming duty" substituted by FA 2012 s 194, Sch 25 para 11 with effect in relation to accounting periods ending on or after 1 April 2012 (and, accordingly, the first reconciliation period begins with the first accounting period in relation to which the amendments have effect) (FA 2012 Sch 25 para 12).

4 Entry inserted by FA 2012 s 191, Sch 24 para 30 with effect in relation to the playing of machine games on or after 1 February 2013.

5 Entry relating to amusement machine licence duty repealed by FA 2012 s 191, Sch 24 para 57 with effect in relation to the provision of amusement machines on or after 1 February 2013. That definition to continue to have effect (with necessary

modifications) on and after that date in relation to the provision of amusement machines before that date (FA 2012 Sch 24 para 62). That definition read as follows—

"Amusement machine licence duty	Obligation under section 21 of BGDA 1981 (obligation to licence amusement machine or premises on which amusement machine is provided for play).".

6 Entries for general betting duty, pool betting duty and remote gaming duty substituted by FA 2014 s 196, Sch 28 para 27 with effect from 1 December 2014 (FA 2014 s 198(2)), subject to the transitional provisions and savings in FA 2014 Sch 29. Those entries previously read as follows—

"General betting duty	Obligations under paragraph 8(2) of Schedule A1 to BGDA 1981 (obligation to notify reduction etc in qualifying foreign tax) or paragraph 4(1) to (3) of Schedule 1 to that Act (obligation to notify intention to carry on general betting business and make entry of, or notify, premises).
Pool betting duty	Obligations under paragraph 8(2) of Schedule A1 to BGDA 1981 (obligation to notify reduction etc in qualifying foreign tax) or paragraphs 4(2) and 5(1) of Schedule 1 to that Act (obligation to make entry and hold permit for carrying on pool betting business).".
"Remote gaming duty	Obligation to notify under paragraph 8(2) of Schedule 4B to BGDA 1981 (reduction etc in qualifying foreign tax) and obligation to register under regulations under section 26J of that Act (facilities for remote gaming).".

7 Entry for diverted profits tax inserted by FA 2015 s 104(4), (5) with effect in relation to accounting periods beginning on or after 1 April 2015. For accounting periods that straddle that date, see FA 2015 s 116(2).

Issue of invoice showing VAT by unauthorised person

2—(1) A penalty is payable by a person (P) where P makes an unauthorised issue of an invoice showing VAT.

(2) P makes an unauthorised issue of an invoice showing VAT if P—

(*a*) is an unauthorised person, and

(*b*) issues an invoice showing an amount as being value added tax or as including an amount attributable to value added tax.

(3) In sub-paragraph (2)(*a*) "an unauthorised person" means anyone other than—

(*a*) a person registered under VATA 1994,

(*b*) a body corporate treated for the purposes of section 43 of that Act as a member of a group,

(*c*) a person treated as a taxable person under regulations under section 46(4) of that Act,

(*d*) a person authorised to issue an invoice under regulations under paragraph 2(12) of Schedule 11 to that Act, or

(*e*) a person acting on behalf of the Crown.

(4) This paragraph has effect in relation to any invoice which—

(*a*) for the purposes of any provision made under subsection (3) of section 54 of VATA 1994 shows an amount as included in the consideration for any supply, and

(*b*) either fails to comply with the requirements of any regulations under that section or is issued by a person who is not for the time being authorised to do so for the purposes of that section,

as if the person issuing the invoice were an unauthorised person and that amount were shown on the invoice as an amount attributable to value added tax.

Commencement—Finance Act 2008, Schedule 41 (Appointed Day and Transitional Provisions) Order, SI 2009/511 art 2 (the appointed day for the purposes of this Schedule is 1 April 2010).

Cross reference—FA 2009 s 94 (Publishing details of deliberate tax defaulters).

Putting product to use that attracts higher duty

3—(1) A penalty is payable by a person ("P") where P does an act which enables HMRC to assess an amount as duty due from P under any of the provisions in the Table below (a "relevant excise provision").

Provision under which assessment may be made	*Subject-matter of provision*
ALDA 1979 section 8(4)	Spirits for use for medical or scientific purposes.
ALDA 1979 section 10(4)	Spirits for use in art or manufacture.
ALDA 1979 section 11(3)	Imported goods not for human consumption containing spirits.
HODA 1979 section 10(3)	Duty-free oil.

Provision under which assessment may be made	*Subject-matter of provision*
HODA 1979 section 13(1A)	Rebated heavy oil.
HODA 1979 section 13AB(1)(a) or (2)(a)	Kerosene.
HODA 1979 section 13AD(2)	Kerosene.
HODA 1979 section 13ZB(1)	Heating oil etc
HODA 1979 section 14(4)	Light oil for use as furnace oil.
HODA 1979 section 14D(1)	Rebated biodiesel or bioblend.
HODA 1979 section 14F(2)	Rebated heavy oil or bioblend.
HODA 1979 section 23(1B)	Road fuel gas on which no duty paid.
HODA 1979 section 24(4A)	Duty-free and rebated oil.

(2) A penalty is payable by a person ("P") where P supplies a product knowing that it will be used in a way which enables HMRC to assess an amount as duty due from another person under a relevant excise provision.

Commencement—Finance Act 2008, Schedule 41 (Appointed Day and Transitional Provisions) Order, SI 2009/511 art 2 (the appointed day for the purposes of this Schedule is 1 April 2010).

Cross reference—FA 2009 s 94 (Publishing details of deliberate tax defaulters).

Handling goods subject to unpaid excise duty

4—(1) A penalty is payable by a person (P) where—

(*a*) after the excise duty point for any goods which are chargeable with a duty of excise, P acquires possession of the goods or is concerned in carrying, removing, depositing, keeping or otherwise dealing with the goods, and

(*b*) at the time when P acquires possession of the goods or is so concerned, a payment of duty on the goods is outstanding and has not been deferred.

(2) In sub-paragraph (1)—

"excise duty point" has the meaning given by section 1 of F(No 2)A 1992, and

"goods" has the meaning given by section 1(1) of CEMA 1979.

Commencement—Finance Act 2008, Schedule 41 (Appointed Day and Transitional Provisions) Order, SI 2009/511 art 2 (the appointed day for the purposes of this Schedule is 1 April 2010).

Cross reference—FA 2009 s 94 (Publishing details of deliberate tax defaulters).

Degrees of culpability

5—(1) A failure by P to comply with a relevant obligation is—

(*a*) "deliberate and concealed" if the failure is deliberate and P makes arrangements to conceal the situation giving rise to the obligation, and

(*b*) "deliberate but not concealed" if the failure is deliberate but P does not make arrangements to conceal the situation giving rise to the obligation.

(2) The making by P of an unauthorised issue of an invoice showing VAT is—

(*a*) "deliberate and concealed" if it is done deliberately and P makes arrangements to conceal it, and

(*b*) "deliberate but not concealed" if it is done deliberately but P does not make arrangements to conceal it.

(3) The doing by P of an act which enables HMRC to assess an amount of duty as due from P under a relevant excise provision is—

(*a*) "deliberate and concealed" if it is done deliberately and P makes arrangements to conceal it, and

(*b*) "deliberate but not concealed" if it is done deliberately but P does not make arrangements to conceal it.

(4) P's acquiring possession of, or being concerned in dealing with, goods on which a payment of duty is outstanding and has not been deferred is—

(*a*) "deliberate and concealed" if it is done deliberately and P makes arrangements to conceal it, and

(*b*) "deliberate but not concealed" if it is done deliberately but P does not make arrangements to conceal it.

Commencement—Finance Act 2008, Schedule 41 (Appointed Day and Transitional Provisions) Order, SI 2009/511 art 2 (the appointed day for the purposes of this Schedule is 1 April 2010).

Amount of penalty: standard amount

[6—(1) This paragraph sets out the penalty payable under paragraph 1.

(2) If the failure is in category 1, the penalty is—

(*a*) for a deliberate and concealed failure, 100% of the potential lost revenue,

(*b*) for a deliberate but not concealed failure, 70% of the potential lost revenue, and

(*c*) for any other case, 30% of the potential lost revenue.

(3) If the failure is in category 2, the penalty is—

(*a*) for a deliberate and concealed failure, 150% of the potential lost revenue,

(*b*) for a deliberate but not concealed failure, 105% of the potential lost revenue, and

(*c*) for any other case, 45% of the potential lost revenue.

(4) If the failure is in category 3, the penalty is—

(*a*) for a deliberate and concealed failure, 200% of the potential lost revenue,

(*b*) for a deliberate but not concealed failure, 140% of the potential lost revenue, and

(*c*) for any other case, 60% of the potential lost revenue.

(5) Paragraph 6A explains the 3 categories of failure.][1]

Commencement—Finance Act 2008, Schedule 41 (Appointed Day and Transitional Provisions) Order, SI 2009/511 art 2 (the appointed day for the purposes of this Schedule is 1 April 2010).

Cross references—FA 2014 s 212 (application of this paragraph in calculation of aggregate penalties for failure to take corrective action in response to a follower notice).

Amendments—

[1] Paras 6–6D substituted for previous para 6 by FA 2010 s 35 Sch 10 paras 7, 8 with effect from 6 April 2011 (by virtue of SI 2011/975 art 2(1)). Note that (by virtue of SI 2011/975 art 4) these changes do not have effect in relation to—

- any relevant obligation arising under TMA 1970 s 7, FA 1990 Sch 18 para 2, and VATA 1994 Sch 1 paras 5, 6, 14(2), (3), Sch 3 para 3, Sch 3A paras 4, 7(2), (3), in relation to a tax period commencing on or before 5 April 2011;
- all other relevant obligations arising on or before 5 April 2011;
- any unauthorised issue of an invoice taking place on or before 5 April 2011;
- any act which enables HMRC to assess an amount as duty under a relevant excise provision and which is done on or before 5 April 2011; and
- any act giving rise to a penalty under FA 2008 Sch 41 para 4 which is done on or before 5 April 2011.

Prospective amendments—Sub-para (1A) to be inserted, in sub-para (2), "125%" to be substituted for "100%", "87.5%" to be substituted for "70%" and "37.5%" to be substituted for "30%", and in sub-para (5), figure "4" to be substituted for figure "3", by FA 2015 s 120, Sch 20 paras 9, 10 with effect from a day to be appointed. Sub-para (1A) as inserted to read as follows—

"(1A) If the failure is in category 0, the penalty is—

for a deliberate and concealed failure, 100% of the potential lost revenue,

for a deliberate but not concealed failure, 70% of the potential lost revenue, and

for any other case, 30% of the potential lost revenue.".

[6A—(1) A failure is in category 1 if—

(*a*) it involves a domestic matter, or

(*b*) it involves an offshore matter and—

(i) the territory in question is a category 1 territory, or

(ii) the tax at stake is a tax other than income tax or capital gains tax.

(2) A failure is in category 2 if—

(*a*) it involves an offshore matter,

(*b*) the territory in question is a category 2 territory, and

(*c*) the tax at stake is income tax or capital gains tax.

(3) A failure is in category 3 if—

(*a*) it involves an offshore matter,

(*b*) the territory in question is a category 3 territory, and

(*c*) the tax at stake is income tax or capital gains tax.

(4) A failure "involves an offshore matter" if it results in a potential loss of revenue that is charged on or by reference to—

(*a*) income arising from a source in a territory outside the UK,

(*b*) assets situated or held in a territory outside the UK,

(*c*) activities carried on wholly or mainly in a territory outside the UK, or

(*d*) anything having effect as if it were income, assets or activities of a kind described above.

(5) A failure "involves a domestic matter" if it results in a potential loss of revenue that is charged on or by reference to anything not mentioned in sub-paragraph (4)(*a*) to (*d*).

(6) If a single failure is in more than one category (each referred to as a "relevant category")—

(*a*) it is to be treated for the purposes of this Schedule as if it were separate failures, one in each relevant category according to the matters that it involves, and (*b*) the potential lost revenue in respect of each separate failure is taken to be such share of the potential lost revenue in respect of the single failure (see paragraphs 7 and 11) as is just and reasonable.

(7) For the purposes of this Schedule—

(*a*) paragraph 21A of Schedule 24 to FA 2007 (classification of territories) has effect, but

(*b*) an order under that paragraph does not apply to relevant obligations that are to be complied with by a date before the date on which the order comes into force.

(8) Regulations under paragraph 21B of Schedule 24 to FA 2007 (location of assets etc) apply for the purposes of paragraph 6A of this Schedule as they apply for the purposes of paragraph 4A of that Schedule.

(9) In this paragraph—

"assets" has the meaning given in section 21(1) of TCGA 1992, but also includes sterling;

"UK" means the United Kingdom, including the territorial sea of the United Kingdom.][1]

Commencement—Finance Act 2008, Schedule 41 (Appointed Day and Transitional Provisions) Order, SI 2009/511 art 2 (the appointed day for the purposes of this Schedule is 1 April 2010).

Amendments—[1] Paras 6–6D substituted for previous para 6 by FA 2010 s 35 Sch 10 paras 7, 8 with effect from 6 April 2011 (by virtue of SI 2011/975 art 2(1)). Note that (by virtue of SI 2011/975 art 4) these changes do not have effect in relation to—

- any relevant obligation arising under TMA 1970 s 7, FA 1998 Sch 18 para 2, and VATA 1994 Sch 1 paras 5, 6, 14(2), (3), Sch 3 para 3, Sch 3A paras 4, 7(2), (3), in relation to a tax period commencing on or before 5 April 2011;
- all other relevant obligations arising on or before 5 April 2011;
- any unauthorised issue of an invoice taking place on or before 5 April 2011;
- any act which enables HMRC to assess an amount as duty under a relevant excise provision and which is done on or before 5 April 2011; and
- any act giving rise to a penalty under FA 2008 Sch 41 para 4 which is done on or before 5 April 2011.

Prospective amendments—The following amendments to be made by FA 2015 s 120, Sch 20 paras 9, 11 with effect from a day to be appointed—

- sub-paras (A1), (1) to be substituted for sub-para (1);
- in sub-paras (2)(*a*), (3)(*a*), words "or an offshore transfer" to be inserted after word "matter";
- sub-para (4A) to be inserted and sub-para (8) to be repealed;
- in sub-para (5), words "and does not involve either an offshore matter or an offshore transfer" to be substituted for words following word "revenue"; and
- in sub-para (6)(*a*), words "or transfers" to be inserted after word "matters", and
- in sub-para (9), words "and paragraph 6AA" to be inserted after word "paragraph".

Sub-paragraphs (A1), (1) as substituted to read as follows—

"(A1) A failure is in category 0 if—

it involves a domestic matter,

it involves an offshore matter or an offshore transfer, the territory in question is a category 0 territory and the tax at stake is income tax or capital gains tax, or

it involves an offshore matter and the tax at stake is a tax other than income tax or capital gains tax.

(1) A failure is in category 1 if—

it involves an offshore matter or an offshore transfer,

the territory in question is a category 1 territory, and

the tax at stake is income tax or capital gains tax.".

Sub-paragraph (4A) as inserted to read as follows—

"(4A) A failure "involves an offshore transfer" if—

it does not involve an offshore matter,

it is deliberate (whether or not concealed) and results in a potential loss of revenue,

the tax at stake is income tax or capital gains tax, and

the applicable condition in paragraph 6AA is satisfied.".

[6AA (1) This paragraph makes provision in relation to offshore transfers.

(2) Where the tax at stake is income tax, the applicable condition is satisfied if the income on or by reference to which the tax is charged, or any part of the income—

(*a*) is received in a territory outside the UK, or

(*b*) is transferred before the calculation date to a territory outside the UK.

(3) Where the tax at stake is capital gains tax, the applicable condition is satisfied if the proceeds of the disposal on or by reference to which the tax is charged, or any part of the proceeds—

(*a*) are received in a territory outside the UK, or

(*b*) are transferred before the calculation date to a territory outside the UK.

(4) In the case of a transfer falling within sub-paragraph (2)(*b*) or (3)(*b*), references to the income or proceeds transferred are to be read as including references to any assets derived from or representing the income or proceeds.

(5) In relation to an offshore transfer, the territory in question for the purposes of paragraph 6A is the highest category of territory by virtue of which the failure involves an offshore transfer.

(6) In this paragraph "calculation date" means the date by reference to which the potential lost revenue is to be calculated (see paragraph 7).]

Prospective amendments—Paragraphs 6AA, 6AB to be inserted by FA 2015 s 120, Sch 20 paras 9, 12 with effect from a day to be appointed.

[6AB Regulations under paragraph 21B of Schedule 24 to FA 2007 (location of assets etc) apply for the purposes of paragraphs 6A and 6AA of this Schedule as they apply for the purposes of paragraphs 4A and 4AA of that Schedule.]

Prospective amendments—Paragraphs 6AA, 6AB to be inserted by FA 2015 s 120, Sch 20 paras 9, 12 with effect from a day to be appointed.

[6B The penalty payable under any of paragraphs 2, 3(1) and 4 is—

(*a*) for a deliberate and concealed act or failure, 100% of the potential lost revenue,

(*b*) for a deliberate but not concealed act or failure, 70% of the potential lost revenue, and

(*c*) for any other case, 30% of the potential lost revenue.][1]

Commencement—Finance Act 2008, Schedule 41 (Appointed Day and Transitional Provisions) Order, SI 2009/511 art 2 (the appointed day for the purposes of this Schedule is 1 April 2010).

Amendments—[1] Paras 6–6D substituted for previous para 6 by FA 2010 s 35 Sch 10 paras 7, 8 with effect from 6 April 2011 (by virtue of SI 2011/975 art 2(1)). Note that (by virtue of SI 2011/975 art 4) these changes do not have effect in relation to—

- any relevant obligation arising under TMA 1970 s 7, FA 1998 Sch 18 para 2, and VATA 1994 Sch 1 paras 5, 6, 14(2), (3), Sch 3 para 3, Sch 3A paras 4, 7(2), (3), in relation to a tax period commencing on or before 5 April 2011;
- all other relevant obligations arising on or before 5 April 2011;
- any unauthorised issue of an invoice taking place on or before 5 April 2011;
- any act which enables HMRC to assess an amount as duty under a relevant excise provision and which is done on or before 5 April 2011; and
- any act giving rise to a penalty under FA 2008 Sch 41 para 4 which is done on or before 5 April 2011.

[6C The penalty payable under paragraph 3(2) is 100% of the potential lost revenue.][1]

Commencement—Finance Act 2008, Schedule 41 (Appointed Day and Transitional Provisions) Order, SI 2009/511 art 2 (the appointed day for the purposes of this Schedule is 1 April 2010).

Amendments—[1] Paras 6–6D substituted for previous para 6 by FA 2010 s 35 Sch 10 paras 7, 8 with effect from 6 April 2011 (by virtue of SI 2011/975 art 2(1)). Note that (by virtue of SI 2011/975 art 4) these changes do not have effect in relation to—

- any relevant obligation arising under TMA 1970 s 7, FA 1998 Sch 18 para 2, and VATA 1994 Sch 1 paras 5, 6, 14(2), (3), Sch 3 para 3, Sch 3A paras 4, 7(2), (3), in relation to a tax period commencing on or before 5 April 2011;
- all other relevant obligations arising on or before 5 April 2011;
- any unauthorised issue of an invoice taking place on or before 5 April 2011;
- any act which enables HMRC to assess an amount as duty under a relevant excise provision and which is done on or before 5 April 2011; and
- any act giving rise to a penalty under FA 2008 Sch 41 para 4 which is done on or before 5 April 2011.

[6D Paragraphs 7 to 11 define "potential lost revenue".][1]

Commencement—Finance Act 2008, Schedule 41 (Appointed Day and Transitional Provisions) Order, SI 2009/511 art 2 (the appointed day for the purposes of this Schedule is 1 April 2010).

Amendments—[1] Paras 6–6D substituted for previous para 6 by FA 2010 s 35 Sch 10 paras 7, 8 with effect from 6 April 2011 (by virtue of SI 2011/975 art 2(1)). Note that (by virtue of SI 2011/975 art 4) these changes do not have effect in relation to—

- any relevant obligation arising under TMA 1970 s 7, FA 1998 Sch 18 para 2, and VATA 1994 Sch 1 paras 5, 6, 14(2), (3), Sch 3 para 3, Sch 3A paras 4, 7(2), (3), in relation to a tax period commencing on or before 5 April 2011;
- all other relevant obligations arising on or before 5 April 2011;
- any unauthorised issue of an invoice taking place on or before 5 April 2011;
- any act which enables HMRC to assess an amount as duty under a relevant excise provision and which is done on or before 5 April 2011; and
- any act giving rise to a penalty under FA 2008 Sch 41 para 4 which is done on or before 5 April 2011.

Potential lost revenue

7—(1) "The potential lost revenue" in respect of a failure to comply with a relevant obligation is as follows.

[(1A) In the case of an obligation under section 7 of TMA 1970 which arises by virtue of subsection (1B) of that section, the potential lost revenue is so much of any income tax or capital gains tax to which P is liable in respect of the tax year in question as is, by reason of the failure to comply with the obligation—

(*a*) where the period specified in subsection (1C)(*b*)(ii) of that section applies and ends after the relevant date, unpaid at the end of that period, or

(*b*) in any other case, unpaid on the relevant date.

(1B) For the purposes of sub-paragraph (1A) the relevant date is—

(*a*) 31 January following the tax year, or

(*b*) if, after that date, HMRC refund a payment on account in respect of the tax year to P, the day after the refund is issued.][2]

(2) In the case of a relevant obligation relating to income tax or capital gains tax and a tax year [(not falling within subparagraph (1A))][2], the potential lost revenue is so much of any income tax or capital gains tax to which P is liable in respect of the tax year as by reason of the failure is unpaid on 31 January following the tax year.

(3) In the case of a relevant obligation relating to corporation tax and an accounting period, the potential lost revenue is (subject to sub-paragraph (4)) so much of any corporation tax to which P is liable in respect of the accounting period as by reason of the failure is unpaid 12 months after the end of the accounting period.

(4) In computing the amount of that tax no account shall be taken of any relief under [section 458 of CTA 2010][1] (relief in respect of repayment etc of loan) which is deferred under [subsection (5)][1] of that section.

[(4A) In the case of a relevant obligation relating to diverted profits tax, the potential lost revenue is the amount of diverted profits tax for which P would be liable at the end of the period of 6 months beginning immediately after the accounting period assuming—

(*a*) a charge to diverted profits tax had been imposed on P on the taxable diverted profits arising to P for the accounting period, and

(*b*) that tax was required to be paid before the end of that period of 6 months.][3]

(5) In any case where the failure is a failure to comply with the obligation under paragraph 2(4) of Schedule 11 to VATA 1994, the potential lost revenue is the value added tax on the acquisition to which the failure relates.

(6) In the case of any other relevant obligation relating to value added tax, the potential lost revenue is the amount of the value added tax (if any) for which P is, or but for any exemption from registration would be, liable for the relevant period (see sub-paragraph (7)), but subject to sub-paragraph (8).

(7) "The relevant period" is—

(*a*) in relation to a failure to comply with paragraph 14(2) or (3) of Schedule 1 to VATA 1994, paragraph 8(2) of Schedule 3 to that Act or paragraph 7(2) or (3) of Schedule 3A to that Act, the period beginning on the date of the change or alteration concerned and ending on the date on which HMRC received notification of, or otherwise became fully aware of, that change or alteration, and

(*b*) in relation to a failure to comply with an obligation under any other provision, the period beginning on the date with effect from which P is required in accordance with that provision to be registered and ending on the date on which HMRC received notification of, or otherwise became fully aware of, P's liability to be registered.

(8) But the amount mentioned in sub-paragraph (6) is reduced—

(*a*) if the amount of the tax mentioned in that sub-paragraph includes tax on an acquisition of goods from another member State, by the amount of any VAT which HMRC are satisfied has been paid on the supply in pursuance of which the goods were acquired under the law of that member State, and

(*b*) if the amount of that tax includes tax chargeable by virtue of section 7(4) of VATA 1994 on a supply, by the amount of any VAT which HMRC are satisfied has been paid on that supply under the law of another member State.

(9) In the case of a relevant obligation under any provision relating to insurance premium tax, aggregates levy, climate change levy, landfill tax or air passenger duty, the potential lost revenue is the amount of the tax (if any) for which P is liable for the period—

(*a*) beginning on the date with effect from which P is required in accordance with that provision to be registered, and

(*b*) ending on the date on which HMRC received notification of, or otherwise became fully aware of, P's liability to be registered.

(10) In the case of a failure to comply with a relevant obligation relating to any other tax, the potential lost revenue is the amount of any tax which is unpaid by reason of the failure.

Commencement—Finance Act 2008, Schedule 41 (Appointed Day and Transitional Provisions) Order, SI 2009/511 art 2 (the appointed day for the purposes of this Schedule is 1 April 2010).

Cross reference—FA 2009 s 94 (Publishing details of deliberate tax defaulters).

Amendments—[1] In sub-para (4) words "subsection (4) of section 419 of ICTA" and "subsection (4A)" substituted by CTA 2010 s 1177, Sch 1 paras 576, 583. CTA 2010 has effect for corporation tax purposes for accounting periods ending on or after 1 April 2010, and for income and capital gains tax purposes for the tax year 2010–11 and subsequent tax years.

[2] Sub-paras (1A), (1B) inserted, and words in sub-s (2) inserted, by FA 2013 s 233, Sch 51 paras 1, 6 with effect in relation to a return—

(a) under TMA 1970 s 12AA for a partnership which includes one or more companies, for a relevant period beginning on or after 6 April 2012; and

(b) under TMA 1970 s 12AA for any other partnership, or a return under TMA 1970 s 8 or s 8A, for a year of assessment beginning on or after 6 April 2012.

A "relevant period" means a period in respect of which a return is required: FA 2013 Sch 51 para 9(2).

[3] Sub-para (4A) inserted by FA 2015 s 104(4), (6) with effect in relation to accounting periods beginning on or after 1 April 2015. For accounting periods that straddle that date, see FA 2015 s 116(2).

8 In the case of the making of an unauthorised issue of an invoice showing VAT, the potential lost revenue is the amount shown on the invoice as value added tax or the amount to be taken as representing value added tax.

Commencement—Finance Act 2008, Schedule 41 (Appointed Day and Transitional Provisions) Order, SI 2009/511 art 2 (the appointed day for the purposes of this Schedule is 1 April 2010).
Cross reference—FA 2009 s 94 (Publishing details of deliberate tax defaulters).

9 In the case of—

(*a*) the doing of an act which enables HMRC to assess an amount of duty as due under a relevant excise provision, or

(*b*) supplying a product knowing that it will be used in a way which enables HMRC to assess an amount as duty due from another person under a relevant excise provision,

the potential lost revenue is the amount of the duty which may be assessed as due.

Commencement—Finance Act 2008, Schedule 41 (Appointed Day and Transitional Provisions) Order, SI 2009/511 art 2 (the appointed day for the purposes of this Schedule is 1 April 2010).
Cross reference—FA 2009 s 94 (Publishing details of deliberate tax defaulters).

10 In the case of acquiring possession of, or being concerned in dealing with, goods the payment of duty on which is outstanding and has not been deferred, the potential lost revenue is an amount equal to the amount of duty due on the goods.

Commencement—Finance Act 2008, Schedule 41 (Appointed Day and Transitional Provisions) Order, SI 2009/511 art 2 (the appointed day for the purposes of this Schedule is 1 April 2010).
Cross reference—FA 2009 s 94 (Publishing details of deliberate tax defaulters).

11—(1) In calculating potential lost revenue in respect of a relevant act or failure on the part of P no account is to be taken of the fact that a potential loss of revenue from P is or may be balanced by a potential over-payment by another person (except to the extent that an enactment requires or permits a person's tax liability to be adjusted by reference to P's).

(2) In this Schedule "a relevant act or failure" means—

(*a*) a failure to comply with a relevant obligation,

(*b*) the making of an unauthorised issue of an invoice showing VAT,

(*c*) the doing of an act which enables HMRC to assess an amount of duty as due under a relevant excise provision or supplying a product knowing that it will be used in a way which enables HMRC to assess an amount as duty due from another person under a relevant excise provision, or

(*d*) acquiring possession of, or being concerned in dealing with, goods the payment of duty on which is outstanding and has not been deferred.

Commencement—Finance Act 2008, Schedule 41 (Appointed Day and Transitional Provisions) Order, SI 2009/511 art 2 (the appointed day for the purposes of this Schedule is 1 April 2010).
Cross reference—FA 2009 s 94 (Publishing details of deliberate tax defaulters).

Reductions for disclosure

12—(1) Paragraph 13 provides for reductions in penalties under paragraphs 1 to 4 where P discloses a relevant act or failure

(2) P discloses a relevant act or failure by—

(*a*) telling HMRC about it,

(*b*) giving HMRC reasonable help in quantifying the tax unpaid by reason of it, and

(*c*) allowing HMRC access to records for the purpose of checking how much tax is so unpaid.

(3) Disclosure of a relevant act or failure—

(*a*) is "unprompted" if made at a time when the person making it has no reason to believe that HMRC have discovered or are about to discover the relevant act or failure, and

(*b*) otherwise, is "prompted".

(4) In relation to disclosure "quality" includes timing, nature and extent.

Commencement—Finance Act 2008, Schedule 41 (Appointed Day and Transitional Provisions) Order, SI 2009/511 art 2 (the appointed day for the purposes of this Schedule is 1 April 2010).

[13 (1) If a person who would otherwise be liable to a penalty of a percentage shown in column 1 of the Table (a "standard percentage") has made a disclosure, HMRC must reduce the standard percentage to one that reflects the quality of the disclosure.

(2) But the standard percentage may not be reduced to a percentage that is below the minimum shown for it—

(*a*) for a prompted disclosure, in column 2 of the Table, and

(*b*) for an unprompted disclosure, in column 3 of the Table.

(3) Where the Table shows a different minimum for case A and case B—

(*a*) the case A minimum applies if—

(i) the penalty is one under paragraph 1, and

(ii) HMRC become aware of the failure less than 12 months after the time when the tax first becomes unpaid by reason of the failure, and

(*b*) otherwise, the case B minimum applies.

Standard %	*Minimum % for prompted disclosure*	*Minimum % for unprompted disclosure*
30%	case A: 10% case B: 20%	case A: 0% case B: 10%
45%	case A: 15% case B: 30%	case A: 0% case B: 15%
60%	case A: 20% case B: 40%	case A: 0% case B: 20%
70%	35%	20%
105%	52.5%	30%
140%	70%	40%
100%	50%	30%
150%	75%	45%
200%	100%	60%][1]

Commencement—Finance Act 2008, Schedule 41 (Appointed Day and Transitional Provisions) Order, SI 2009/511 art 2 (the appointed day for the purposes of this Schedule is 1 April 2010).

Cross reference—FA 2009 s 94 (Publishing details of deliberate tax defaulters).

Amendments—

[1] This para substituted by FA 2010 s 35 Sch 10 paras 7, 9 with effect from 6 April 2011 (by virtue of SI 2011/975 art 2(1)). Note that (by virtue of SI 2011/975 art 4) these changes do not have effect in relation to—

– any relevant obligation arising under TMA 1970 s 7, FA 1998 Sch 18 para 2, and VATA 1994 Sch 1 paras 5, 6, 14(2), (3), Sch 3 para 3, Sch 3A paras 4, 7(2), (3), in relation to a tax period commencing on or before 5 April 2011;

– all other relevant obligations arising on or before 5 April 2011;

– any unauthorised issue of an invoice taking place on or before 5 April 2011;

– any act which enables HMRC to assess an amount as duty under a relevant excise provision and which is done on or before 5 April 2011; and

– any act giving rise to a penalty under FA 2008 Sch 41 para 4 which is done on or before 5 April 2011.

Prospective amendments—In sub-para (3), the following Table entries to be inserted at the appropriate places by FA 2015 s 120, Sch 20 paras 9, 13 with effect from a day to be appointed—

"37.5%	case A: 12.5% case B: 25%	case A: 0% case B: 12.5%"
"87.5%	43.75%	25%"
"125%	62.5%	40%"

Special reduction

14—(1) If HMRC think it right because of special circumstances, they may reduce a penalty under any of paragraphs 1 to 4.

(2) In sub-paragraph (1) "special circumstances" does not include—

(*a*) ability to pay, or

(*b*) the fact that a potential loss of revenue from one taxpayer is balanced by a potential overpayment by another.

(3) In sub-paragraph (1) the reference to reducing a penalty includes a reference to—

(*a*) staying a penalty, and

(*b*) agreeing a compromise in relation to proceedings for a penalty.

Commencement—Finance Act 2008, Schedule 41 (Appointed Day and Transitional Provisions) Order, SI 2009/511 art 2 (the appointed day for the purposes of this Schedule is 1 April 2010).

Interaction with other penalties and late payment surcharges

15—(1) The amount of a penalty for which P is liable under any of paragraphs 1 to 4 shall be reduced by the amount of any other penalty incurred by P, or any surcharge for late payment of tax imposed on P, if the amount of the penalty or surcharge is determined by reference to the same tax liability.
[(1A) In sub-paragraph (2) "any other penalty" does not include a penalty under Part 4 of FA 2014 (penalty where corrective action not taken after follower notice etc).][1]
(2) If P is liable to a penalty under section 9 of FA 1994 in respect of a failure to comply with a relevant obligation, the amount of any penalty payable under paragraph 1 in respect of the failure is to be reduced by the amount of the penalty under that section.
(3) Where penalties are imposed under paragraph 3(1) and (2) in respect of the same act or use, the aggregate of the amounts of the penalties must not exceed 100% of the potential lost revenue.

Commencement—Finance Act 2008, Schedule 41 (Appointed Day and Transitional Provisions) Order, SI 2009/511 art 2 (the appointed day for the purposes of this Schedule is 1 April 2010).
Amendments—[1] Sub-para (1A) inserted by FA 2014 s 233, Sch 33 para 4 with effect from 17 July 2014.

Assessment

16—(1) Where P becomes liable for a penalty under any of paragraphs 1 to 4 HMRC shall—
(*a*) assess the penalty,
(*b*) notify P, and
(*c*) state in the notice the period in respect of which the penalty is assessed.
(2) A penalty under any of paragraphs 1 to 4 must be paid before the end of the period of 30 days beginning with the day on which notification of the penalty is issued.
(3) An assessment—
(*a*) shall be treated for procedural purposes in the same way as an assessment to tax (except in respect of a matter expressly provided for by this Act),
(*b*) may be enforced as if it were an assessment to tax, and
(*c*) may be combined with an assessment to tax.
(4) An assessment of a penalty under any of paragraphs 1 to 4 must be made before the end of the period of 12 months beginning with—
(*a*) the end of the appeal period for the assessment of tax unpaid by reason of the relevant act or failure in respect of which the penalty is imposed, or
(*b*) if there is no such assessment, the date on which the amount of tax unpaid by reason of the relevant act or failure is ascertained.
(5) In sub-paragraph (4)(*a*) "appeal period" means the period during which—
(*a*) an appeal could be brought, or
(*b*) an appeal that has been brought has not been determined or withdrawn.
(6) Subject to sub-paragraph (4), a supplementary assessment may be made in respect of a penalty if an earlier assessment operated by reference to an underestimate of potential lost revenue.
(7) The references in this paragraph to "an assessment to tax" are, in relation to a penalty under paragraph 2, a demand for recovery.

Commencement—Finance Act 2008, Schedule 41 (Appointed Day and Transitional Provisions) Order, SI 2009/511 art 2 (the appointed day for the purposes of this Schedule is 1 April 2010).

Appeal

17—(1) P may appeal against a decision of HMRC that a penalty is payable by P.
(2) P may appeal against a decision of HMRC as to the amount of a penalty payable by P.

Commencement—Finance Act 2008, Schedule 41 (Appointed Day and Transitional Provisions) Order, SI 2009/511 art 2 (the appointed day for the purposes of this Schedule is 1 April 2010).
Commentary—*Simon's Taxes* **A1.414**.

[18—(1) An appeal shall be treated in the same way as an appeal against an assessment to the tax concerned (including by the application of any provision about bringing the appeal by notice to HMRC, about HMRC review of the decision or about determination of the appeal by the First-tier Tribunal or the Upper Tribunal).
[(2) Sub-paragraph (1) does not apply—
(*a*) so as to require P to pay a penalty before an appeal against the assessment of the penalty is determined, or
(*b*) in respect of any other matter expressly provided for by this Act.][2]][1]

Commencement—Finance Act 2008, Schedule 41 (Appointed Day and Transitional Provisions) Order, SI 2009/511 art 2 (the appointed day for the purposes of this Schedule is 1 April 2010).

Commentary—*Simon's Taxes* **A1.414**.

Amendments—[1] This para substituted by the Transfer of Tribunal Functions and Revenue and Customs Appeals Order, SI 2009/56 art 3, Sch 1 para 473 with effect from 1 April 2009.

[2] Sub-para (2) substituted by FA 2009 s 109, Sch 57 para 11 with effect from 21 July 2009.

19—(1) On an appeal under paragraph 17(1) the [tribunal][1] may affirm or cancel HMRC's decision.

(2) On an appeal under paragraph 17(2) the [tribunal][1] may—

(*a*) affirm HMRC's decision, or

(*b*) substitute for HMRC's decision another decision that HMRC had power to make.

(3) If the First-tier [tribunal][1] substitutes its decision for HMRC's, the [tribunal][1] may rely on paragraph 14—

(*a*) to the same extent as HMRC (which may mean applying the same percentage reduction as HMRC to a different starting point), or

(*b*) to a different extent, but only if the [tribunal][1] thinks that HMRC's decision in respect of the application of paragraph 14 was flawed.

(4) In sub-paragraph (3)(*b*) "flawed" means flawed when considered in the light of the principles applicable in proceedings for judicial review.

[(5) In this paragraph, "tribunal" means the First-tier Tribunal or Upper Tribunal (as appropriate by virtue of paragraph 18(1)).][1]

Commencement—Finance Act 2008, Schedule 41 (Appointed Day and Transitional Provisions) Order, SI 2009/511 art 2 (the appointed day for the purposes of this Schedule is 1 April 2010).

Amendments—[1] In sub-paras (1), (2) word substituted for the words "First-tier Tribunal"; in sub-para (3) word substituted for the word "Tribunal" in each place; sub-para (5) inserted by the Transfer of Tribunal Functions and Revenue and Customs Appeals Order, SI 2009/56 art 3, Sch 1 para 473 with effect from 1 April 2009.

Reasonable excuse

20—(1) Liability to a penalty under any of paragraphs 1, 2, 3(1) and 4 does not arise in relation to an act or failure which is not deliberate if P satisfies HMRC or [(on an appeal notified to the tribunal) the tribunal][1] that there is a reasonable excuse for the act or failure.

(2) For the purposes of sub-paragraph (1)—

(*a*) an insufficiency of funds is not a reasonable excuse unless attributable to events outside P's control,

(*b*) where P relies on any other person to do anything, that is not a reasonable excuse unless P took reasonable care to avoid the relevant act or failure, and

(*c*) where P had a reasonable excuse for the relevant act or failure but the excuse has ceased, P is to be treated as having continued to have the excuse if the relevant act or failure is remedied without unreasonable delay after the excuse ceased.

Commencement—Finance Act 2008, Schedule 41 (Appointed Day and Transitional Provisions) Order, SI 2009/511 art 2 (the appointed day for the purposes of this Schedule is 1 April 2010).

Amendments—[1] In sub-para (1) words substituted for the words "[on appeal) the First-tier Tribunal" by the Transfer of Tribunal Functions and Revenue and Customs Appeals Order, SI 2009/56 art 3, Sch 1 para 473 with effect from 1 April 2009.

Agency

21—(1) In paragraph 1 the reference to a failure by P includes a failure by a person who acts on P's behalf; but P is not liable to a penalty in respect of any failure by P's agent where P satisfies HMRC or [(on an appeal notified to the tribunal) the tribunal][1] that P took reasonable care to avoid the failure.

(2) In paragraph 2 the reference to the making by P of an unauthorised issue of an invoice showing VAT includes the making of such an unauthorised issue by a person who acts on P's behalf; but P is not liable to a penalty in respect of any action by P's agent where P satisfies HMRC or (on appeal) the First-tier Tribunal that P took reasonable care to avoid it.

(3) In paragraph 3(1) the reference to the doing by P of an act which enables HMRC to assess an amount as duty due from P under a relevant excise provision includes the doing of such an act by a person who acts on P's behalf; but P is not liable to a penalty in respect of any action by P's agent where P satisfies HMRC or (on appeal) the First-tier Tribunal that P took reasonable care to avoid it.

(4) In paragraph 4 the reference to P acquiring possession of, or being concerned in dealing with, goods the payment of duty on which is outstanding and has not been deferred includes a person who acts on P's behalf doing so; but P is not liable to a penalty in respect of any action by P's agent where P satisfies HMRC or (on appeal) the First-tier Tribunal that P took reasonable care to avoid it.

Commencement—Finance Act 2008, Schedule 41 (Appointed Day and Transitional Provisions) Order, SI 2009/511 art 2 (the appointed day for the purposes of this Schedule is 1 April 2010).

Amendments—[1] In sub-para (1) words substituted for the words "[on appeal) the First-tier Tribunal" by the Transfer of Tribunal Functions and Revenue and Customs Appeals Order, SI 2009/56 art 3, Sch 1 para 473 with effect from 1 April 2009.

Companies: officers' liability

22—(1) Where a penalty under any of paragraphs 1, 2, 3(1) and 4 is payable by a company for a deliberate act or failure which was attributable to an officer of the company, the officer is liable to pay such portion of the penalty (which may be 100%) as HMRC may specify by written notice to the officer.

(2) Sub-paragraph (1) does not allow HMRC to recover more than 100% of a penalty.

(3) In the application of sub-paragraph (1) to a body corporate [other than a limited liability partnership][1] "officer" means—

(*a*) a director (including a shadow director within the meaning of section 251 of the Companies Act 2006 (c 46)), . . . [1]

[(*aa*) a manager, and][1]

(*b*) a secretary.

[(3A) In the application of sub-paragraph (1) to a limited liability partnership, "officer" means a member.][1]

(4) In the application of sub-paragraph (1) in any other case "officer" means—

(*a*) a director,

(*b*) a manager,

(*c*) a secretary, and

(*d*) any other person managing or purporting to manage any of the company's affairs.

(5) Where HMRC have specified a portion of a penalty in a notice given to an officer under sub-paragraph (1)—

(*a*) paragraph 14 applies to the specified portion as to a penalty,

(*b*) the officer must pay the specified portion before the end of the period of 30 days beginning with the day on which the notice is given,

(*c*) paragraph 16(3) to (5) and (7) apply as if the notice were an assessment of a penalty,

(*d*) a further notice may be given in respect of a portion of any additional amount assessed in a supplementary assessment in respect of the penalty under paragraph 16(6),

(*e*) paragraphs 17 to 19 apply as if HMRC had decided that a penalty of the amount of the specified portion is payable by the officer, and

(*f*) paragraph 23 applies as if the officer were liable to a penalty.

[(6) In this paragraph "company" means any body corporate or unincorporated association, but does not include a partnership, a local authority or a local authority association.][1]

Commencement—Finance Act 2008, Schedule 41 (Appointed Day and Transitional Provisions) Order, SI 2009/511 art 2 (the appointed day for the purposes of this Schedule is 1 April 2010).

Amendments—[1] In sub-para (3) words inserted, word "or" repealed and para (*aa*) inserted, sub-paras (3A), (6) inserted, by FA 2009 s 109, Sch 57 para 12 with effect from 21 July 2009.

Double jeopardy

23 P is not liable to a penalty under any of paragraphs 1 to 4 in respect of a failure or action in respect of which P has been convicted of an offence.

Commencement—Finance Act 2008, Schedule 41 (Appointed Day and Transitional Provisions) Order, SI 2009/511 art 2 (the appointed day for the purposes of this Schedule is 1 April 2010).

Commentary—*Simon's Taxes* **A4.530**.

Interpretation

24—(1) This paragraph applies for the construction of this Schedule

(2) "HMRC" means Her Majesty's Revenue and Customs.

(3) "Tax", without more, includes duty.

(4) An expression used in relation to value added tax has the same meaning as in VATA 1994.

Commencement—Finance Act 2008, Schedule 41 (Appointed Day and Transitional Provisions) Order, SI 2009/511 art 2 (the appointed day for the purposes of this Schedule is 1 April 2010).

Consequential repeals

25 In consequence of this Schedule the following provisions are omitted—

(*a*) in TMA 1970—

(i) section 7(8), and

(ii) in the table in section 98, in the second column, the entry relating to section 55 of FA 2004,

(*b*) section 170A of CEMA 1979,

(*c*) in ALDA 1979—

(i) in section 47(5), "which shall be calculated by reference to the amount of duty charged on the beer produced",

(ii) in section 54(5), "which shall be calculated by reference to the amount of duty charged on the wine produced",
(iii) in section 55(6), "which shall be calculated by reference to the amount of duty charged on the made-wine produced", and
(iv) in section 62(4), "which shall be calculated by reference to the amount of duty charged on the cider made",

(*d*) in HODA 1979—
(i) section 13AD(4)(*a*) and (*b*), and
(ii) section 14F(4)(*a*) and (*b*),

(*e*) in FA 1994—
(i) section 33(6),
(ii) paragraph 13 of Schedule 4, and
(iii) paragraph 14 of Schedule 7,

(*f*) section 67 of VATA 1994,
(*g*) section 32 of FA 1995,
(*h*) in FA 1996—
(i) section 37, and
(ii) paragraph 21(1), (2) and (4) of Schedule 5,

(*i*) section 27(11) of FA 1997,
(*j*) paragraph 2(3) and (4) of Schedule 18 to FA 1998,
(*k*) in FA 2000—
(i) section 136(2), and
(ii) paragraph 55(2) to (6) of Schedule 6, and

(*l*) paragraph 1(2) to (6) of Schedule 4 to FA 2001.

Commencement—Finance Act 2008, Schedule 41 (Appointed Day and Transitional Provisions) Order, SI 2009/511 art 2 (the appointed day for the purposes of this Schedule is 1 April 2010).

SCHEDULE 43

TAKING CONTROL OF GOODS ETC: CONSEQUENTIAL PROVISION

Section 129

PART 1

CONSEQUENTIAL PROVISION: TAKING CONTROL OF GOODS

TMA 1970

(see *Yellow Tax Handbook* for amendments to TMA 1970)

Social Security Administration Act 1992 (c 5)

2 (see *Yellow Tax Handbook* for amendments to SSAA 1992)

FA 1994

3—(1) FA 1994 is amended as follows.
(2) Omit section 10A (breaches of controlled goods agreements).
(3) In Schedule 7 (insurance premium tax), omit paragraph 18A (breaches of controlled goods agreements).

VATA 1994

4 In VATA 1994, omit section 67A (breach of controlled goods agreement).

FA 1996

5 In Schedule 5 to FA 1996 (landfill tax), omit paragraph 23A (controlled goods agreements).

FA 1997

6 In section 51 of FA 1997 (enforcement by distress), omit subsection (A1).

FA 2000

7 In Schedule 6 to FA 2000 (climate change levy), omit paragraph 89A (controlled goods agreements).

FA 2001

8 In Schedule 5 to FA 2001 (aggregates levy: recovery and interest), omit paragraph 14A (controlled goods agreements).

FA 2003

9 In Schedule 12 to FA 2003 (stamp duty land tax: collection and recovery), omit paragraph 1A (recovery of tax in England and Wales).

Tribunals, Courts and Enforcement Act 2007 (c 15)

10—(1) Schedule 12 of the Tribunals, Courts and Enforcement Act 2007 (taking control of goods) is amended as follows.
(2) Omit paragraph 14(5) (relevant premises where enforcement agent acting under section 121A of Social Security Administration Act 1992).
(3) In paragraph 19(2) (powers to use reasonable force), for paragraphs (*b*) to (*e*) substitute—
"(*b*) section 127 of the Finance Act 2008."

Other repeals

11 In consequence of the preceding provisions of this Schedule, omit—
(*a*) paragraph 8 of Schedule 5 to the Social Security Contributions (Transfer of Functions, etc) Act 1999 (c 2),
(*b*) paragraph 6 of Schedule 11 to the Welfare Reform and Pensions Act 1999 (c 30),
(*c*) section 5(1) of the National Insurance Contributions and Statutory Payments Act 2004 (c 3), and
(*d*) paragraphs 33, 104(2), 114, 116(2), 119, 123, 126(2), 136, 140 and 147(2) of Schedule 13 to the Tribunals, Courts and Enforcement Act 2007 (c 15).

PART 2
CONSEQUENTIAL PROVISION: SUMMARY WARRANT

Commencement—Finance Act 2008, Section 128 and Part 2 of Schedule 43 (Appointed Day, Transitional Provision and Savings) Order, SI 2009/3024 (day appointed for the coming into force of s 128 and Sch 43 Part 2 is 23 November 2009).

TMA 1970

12 (see *Yellow Tax Handbook* for amendments to TMA 1970)

Commencement—Finance Act 2008, Section 128 and Part 2 of Schedule 43 (Appointed Day, Transitional Provision and Savings) Order, SI 2009/3024 (day appointed for the coming into force of s 128 and Sch 43 Part 2 is 23 November 2009).

Debtors (Scotland) Act 1987 (c 18)

13—(1) (*amends*) DSA 1987 s 1
(2) (*amends*) DSA 1987 s 5
(3) (*amends*) DSA 1987 s 106

Commencement—Finance Act 2008, Section 128 and Part 2 of Schedule 43 (Appointed Day, Transitional Provision and Savings) Order, SI 2009/3024 (day appointed for the coming into force of s 128 and Sch 43 Part 2 is 23 November 2009).

Social Security Administration Act 1992 (c 5)

14 (see *Yellow Tax Handbook* for amendments to SSAA 1992)

Commencement—Finance Act 2008, Section 128 and Part 2 of Schedule 43 (Appointed Day, Transitional Provision and Savings) Order, SI 2009/3024 (day appointed for the coming into force of s 128 and Sch 43 Part 2 is 23 November 2009).

FA 1997

15 In FA 1997, omit section 52 (recovery of relevant tax in Scotland).

Commencement—Finance Act 2008, Section 128 and Part 2 of Schedule 43 (Appointed Day, Transitional Provision and Savings) Order, SI 2009/3024 (day appointed for the coming into force of s 128 and Sch 43 Part 2 is 23 November 2009).

FA 2003

16 In Schedule 12 to FA 2003 (stamp duty land tax: collection and recovery), omit paragraph 3 (recovery of tax in Scotland).

Commencement—Finance Act 2008, Section 128 and Part 2 of Schedule 43 (Appointed Day, Transitional Provision and Savings) Order, SI 2009/3024 (day appointed for the coming into force of s 128 and Sch 43 Part 2 is 23 November 2009).

SCHEDULE 44

CERTIFICATES OF DEBT: CONSEQUENTIAL PROVISION

Section 138

TMA 1970

1 (see *Yellow Tax Handbook* for amendments to TMA 1970)

OTA 1975

2 (see *Yellow Tax Handbook* for amendments to OTA 1975)

IHTA 1984

3 (see *Yellow Tax Handbook* for amendments to IHTA 1984)

Social Security Administration Act 1992 (c 5)

4 (see *Yellow Tax Handbook* for amendments to SSAA 1992)

FA 1994

5 In Schedule 7 to FA 1994 (insurance premium tax), in paragraph 29(1) (evidence by certificate)—

(*a*) in paragraph (*a*), after "Act," insert "or", and
(*b*) omit paragraph (*c*) (and the "or" before it).

VATA 1994

6 In Schedule 11 to VATA 1994 (administration, collection and enforcement of VAT), in paragraph 14(1) (evidence by certificate), omit paragraph (*d*) (and the "or" before it).

FA 1996

7 In Schedule 5 to FA 1996 (landfill tax), in paragraph 37(1) (evidence by certificate)—

(*a*) in paragraph (*a*), after "Act," insert "or", and
(*b*) omit paragraph (*c*) (and the "or" before it).

FA 2000

8 In Schedule 6 to FA 2000 (climate change levy), in paragraph 135(1) (evidence by certificate)—

(*a*) in paragraph (*a*), after "levy," insert "or", and
(*b*) omit paragraphs (*c*) and (*d*).

FA 2001

9 In Schedule 7 to FA 2001 (aggregates levy: information and evidence etc), in paragraph 12(1)—

(*a*) in paragraph (*a*), after "registered," insert "or", and
(*b*) omit paragraphs (*c*) and (*d*).

FA 2003

10 In Schedule 12 to FA 2003 (stamp duty land tax: collection and recovery of tax), omit paragraph 7 (evidence of unpaid debt) and the heading before it.

Other repeals

11 In consequence of the preceding provisions of this Schedule, omit—

(*a*) paragraph 21 of Schedule 19 to FA 1994,
(*b*) section 62(1) of the Social Security Act 1998 (c 14),
(*c*) paragraph 32 of Schedule 19 to FA 1998,
(*d*) paragraph 7(2) and (6) of Schedule 5 to the Social Security (Transfer of Functions, etc) Act 1999 (c 2),
(*e*) section 89(3) of FA 2001, and
(*f*) paragraph 135(2) of Schedule 6 to ITEPA 2003.

FINANCE ACT 2009

(2009 Chapter 10)

PART 1
CHARGES, RATES, ALLOWANCES, ETC

Value added tax

9 Extension of reduced standard rate and anti-avoidance provision

PART 7
ADMINISTRATION

Standards and values

92 HMRC Charter
93 Duties of senior accounting officers of qualifying companies
94 Publishing details of deliberate tax defaulters

Information etc

95 Amendment of information and inspection powers
96 Extension of information and inspection powers to further taxes
97 Powers to obtain contact details for debtors

Interest

101 Late payment interest on sums due to HMRC
102 Repayment interest on sums to be paid by HMRC

Penalties

109 Miscellaneous amendments

PART 9
FINAL PROVISIONS

126 Interpretation
127 Short title

Schedules
Schedule 3—VAT: Supplementary Charge and Orders Changing Rate
Part 1—Supplementary Charge to VAT
Part 2—Exceptions
Part 3—Liability and Amount
Part 4—Listed Supplies
Part 5—Administration and Interpretation
Part 6—Amendments of VATA 1994
Schedule 36—VAT: Place of Supply of Services etc
Part 1—Amendments Coming into Force in 2010
Part 2—Amendments Coming into Force in 2011
Part 3—Amendments Coming into Force in 2013
Part 4—Transitional Provisions
Schedule 46—Duties of Senior Accounting Officers of Qualifying Companies
Schedule 47—Amendment of Information and Inspection Powers
Schedule 48—Extension of Information and Inspection Powers
Schedule 49—Powers to Obtain Contact Details for Debtors
Schedule 53—Late Payment Interest
Schedule 54—Repayment Interest
Part 1—Repayment Interest Start Date: General Rule
Schedule 55—Penalty for Failure to Make Returns etc
Schedule 56—Penalty for Failure to Make Payments on Time
Schedule 57—Amendments Relating to Penalties
Part 1—Amendments of Schedule 24 to FA 2007
Part 2—Amendments of Schedule 41 to FA 2008
Part 3—Other Amendments

An Act to Grant certain duties, to alter other duties, and to amend the law relating to the National Debt and the Public Revenue, and to make further provision in connection with finance.

[21 July 2009]

PART 1
CHARGES, RATES, ALLOWANCES, ETC

Value added tax

9 Extension of reduced standard rate and anti-avoidance provision

(1) The Value Added Tax (Change of Rate) Order 2008 (SI 2008/3020) (reducing standard rate of value added tax to 15 per cent) is to cease to be in force on 1 January 2010 (rather than ceasing to be in force on 1 December 2009 in accordance with section 2(2) of VATA 1994).

(2) Schedule 3 contains—

(*a*) provision for a supplementary charge to value added tax on supplies spanning the date of the VAT change (see Parts 1 to 5), and

(*b*) minor amendments of provisions about orders changing the standard rate of value added tax (see Part 6).

PART 4
VALUE ADDED TAX

76 Place of supply of services etc

Schedule 36 contains provisions about the place of supply of services for the purposes of value added tax and related matters.

77 Repayment to those in business in other States

(1) VATA 1994 is amended as follows.

(2) (*amends* VATA 1994 s 39)

(3) (*inserts* VATA 1994 s 39A)

(4) (*amends* VATA 1994 s section 83(1))

Amendments—Sub-s (2)(*d*), which amended VATA 1994 s 39(3)(*c*), repealed by FA 2012 s 204, Sch 29 para 13(*b*) with effect from 17 July 2012.

78 Information relating to cross-border supplies of services to taxable recipients

(1) Paragraph 2 of Schedule 11 to VATA 1994 (accounting for VAT and submission of particulars of transactions etc) is amended as follows.

(2), (3) (*amend* VATA 1994 Sch 11 para 2)

79 Effect of VAT changes on arbitration of rent for agricultural holdings

(1), (2) (*amend* Agricultural Holdings Act 1986 Sch 2 para 4)

(3) The references in that provision and in subsection (2) to an option to tax, or to the exercise or revocation of such an option, under Schedule 10 to VATA 1994 include a reference to an election to waive exemption, or to the making or revocation of such an election, under that Schedule (as it had effect before 1 June 2008).

PART 7
ADMINISTRATION

Standards and values

92 HMRC Charter

(1) (*inserts* CRCA 2005 s 16A)

(2) The duty imposed by section 16A(1) of CRCA 2005 must be complied with before the end of 2009.

93 Duties of senior accounting officers of qualifying companies

(1) Schedule 46 contains provision about the duties of senior accounting officers of qualifying companies.

(2) That Schedule has effect in relation to financial years (within the meaning of the Companies Act 2006) beginning on or after the day on which this Act is passed.

94 Publishing details of deliberate tax defaulters

(1) The Commissioners may publish information about any person if—

(*a*) in consequence of an investigation conducted by the Commissioners, one or more relevant tax penalties is found to have been incurred by the person, and

(*b*) the potential lost revenue in relation to the penalty (or the aggregate of the potential lost revenue in relation to each of the penalties) exceeds £25,000.

(2) A "relevant tax penalty" is—

(*a*) a penalty under paragraph 1 of Schedule 24 to FA 2007 (inaccuracy in taxpayer's document) in respect of a deliberate inaccuracy on the part of the person, (*b*) a penalty under paragraph 1A of that Schedule (inaccuracy in taxpayer's document attributable to deliberate supply of false information or deliberate withholding of information by person),

(*c*) a penalty under paragraph 1 of Schedule 41 to FA 2008 (failure to notify) in respect of a deliberate failure on the part of the person, or

(*d*) a penalty under paragraph 2 (unauthorised VAT invoice), 3 (putting product to use attracting higher duty etc) or 4 (handling goods subject to unpaid excise duty) of that Schedule in respect of deliberate action by the person.

(3) "Potential lost revenue", in relation to a penalty, has the meaning given by—

(*a*) paragraphs 5 to 8 of Schedule 24 to FA 2007, or

(*b*) paragraphs 7 to 11 of Schedule 41 to FA 2008,

in relation to the inaccuracy, failure or action to which the penalty relates.

(4) The information that may be published is—

(*a*) the person's name (including any trading name, previous name or pseudonym),

(*b*) the person's address (or registered office),

(*c*) the nature of any business carried on by the person,

(*d*) the amount of the penalty or penalties and the potential lost revenue in relation to the penalty (or the aggregate of the potential lost revenue in relation to each of the penalties),

(*e*) the periods or times to which the inaccuracy, failure or action giving rise to the penalty (or any of the penalties) relates, and

(*f*) any such other information as the Commissioners consider it appropriate to publish in order to make clear the person's identity.

(5) The information may be published in any manner that the Commissioners consider appropriate.

(6) Before publishing any information the Commissioners—

(*a*) must inform the person that they are considering doing so, and

(*b*) afford the person reasonable opportunity to make representations about whether it should be published.

(7) No information may be published before the day when the penalty becomes final (or the latest day when any of the penalties becomes final).

(8) No information may be published for the first time after the end of the period of one year beginning with that day (or that latest day).

(9) No information may be published (or continue to be published) after the end of the period of one year beginning with the day on which it is first published.

(10) No information may be published if the amount of the penalty is reduced under—

(*a*) paragraph 10 of Schedule 24 to FA 2007, or

(*b*) paragraph 13 of Schedule 41 to FA 2008, (reductions for disclosure) to the full extent permitted.

(11) For the purposes of this section, a penalty becomes final—

(*a*) if it has been assessed, when the time for any appeal or further appeal relating to it expires or, if later, any appeal or final appeal relating to it is finally determined, or

(*b*) if a contract is made between the Commissioners and the person under which the Commissioners undertake not to assess the penalty or (if it has been assessed) not to take proceedings to recover it, at the time when the contract is made.

(12) The Treasury may by order vary the amount for the time being specified in subsection (1).

(13) This section comes into force on a day appointed by order made by the Treasury.

(14) Orders under this section are to be made by statutory instrument.

(15) A statutory instrument containing an order under subsection (12) is subject to annulment in pursuance of a resolution of the House of Commons.

(16) In this section "the Commissioners" means the Commissioners for Her Majesty's Revenue and Customs.

Commencement—Finance Act 2009, Section 94 (Appointed Day) Order, SI 2010/574 art 2 (1 April 2010 is the day appointed for the coming into force of s 94).

Modification—Small Charitable Donations Regulations, SI 2013/938 reg 16 (this section modified where a charity and its managers have incurred one or more penalties in relation to a top-up claim).

Cross-references—See FA 2012 Sch 38 (tax agents: dishonest conduct).

FA 2014 Sch 34 para 2 (application of this section in relation to the issue of conduct notices to promoters of tax avoidance schemes).

Information etc

95 Amendment of information and inspection powers

(1) Schedule 47 contains amendments of Schedule 36 to FA 2008 (information and inspection powers).

(2) The Treasury may by order make any incidental, supplemental, consequential, transitional or transitory provision or saving which appears appropriate in consequence of, or otherwise in connection with, Schedule 36 to FA 2008 or Schedule 47.

(3) An order under this section may—

(*a*) make different provision for different purposes, and
(*b*) make provision amending, repealing or revoking an enactment or instrument (whenever passed or made).

(4) An order under this section is to be made by statutory instrument.

(5) A statutory instrument containing an order under this section is subject to annulment in pursuance of a resolution of the House of Commons.

Orders—Finance Act 2009, Schedule 47 (Consequential Amendments) Order 2009, SI 2009/2035 (this Order comes into force on 13 August 2009).

96 Extension of information and inspection powers to further taxes

(1) In paragraph 63(1) of Schedule 36 to FA 2008 (information and inspection powers: meaning of "tax"), for paragraph (*e*) (and the "and" before it) substitute—

"(*e*) insurance premium tax,
(*f*) inheritance tax,
(*g*) stamp duty land tax,
(*h*) stamp duty reserve tax,
(*i*) petroleum revenue tax,
(*j*) aggregates levy,
(*k*) climate change levy,
(*l*) landfill tax, and
(*m*) relevant foreign tax,".

(2) Schedule 48 contains further amendments of that Schedule.

(3) The amendments made by this section and Schedule 48 come into force on such day as the Treasury may by order appoint.

(4) An order under subsection (3) may—
(*a*) appoint different days for different purposes, and
(*b*) contain transitional provision and savings.

(5) The Treasury may by order make any incidental, supplemental, consequential, transitional or transitory provision or saving which appears appropriate in consequence of, or otherwise in connection with, this section and Schedule 48.

(6) An order under subsection (5) may—
(*a*) make different provision for different purposes, and
(*b*) make provision amending, repealing or revoking an enactment or instrument (whenever passed or made).

(7) An order under this section is to be made by statutory instrument.

(8) A statutory instrument containing an order under subsection (5) is subject to annulment in pursuance of a resolution of the House of Commons.

Commencement—Finance Act 2009, Section 96 and Schedule 48 (Appointed Day, Savings and Consequential Amendments) Order, SI 2009/3054 (day appointed as the day on which the amendments made by s 96 and Sch 48 come into force is 1 April 2010).

97 Powers to obtain contact details for debtors

Schedule 49 contains provision about the powers of officers of Revenue and Customs to obtain contact details of debtors.

Interest

101 Late payment interest on sums due to HMRC

(1) This section applies to any amount that is payable by a person to HMRC under or by virtue of an enactment.

(2) But this section does not apply to—
(*a*) an amount of corporation tax,
(*b*) an amount of petroleum revenue tax, or
(*c*) an amount of any description specified in an order made by the Treasury.

(3) An amount to which this section applies carries interest at the late payment interest rate from the late payment interest start date until the date of payment.

(4) The late payment interest start date in respect of any amount is the date on which that amount becomes due and payable.

(5) In Schedule 53—
(*a*) Part 1 makes special provision as to the amount on which late payment interest is calculated,
(*b*) Part 2 makes special provision as to the late payment interest start date,
(*c*) Part 3 makes special provision as to the date to which late payment interest runs, and
(*d*) Part 4 makes provision about the effect that the giving of a relief has on late payment interest.

(6) Subsection (3) applies even if the late payment interest start date is a non-business day within the meaning of section 92 of the Bills of Exchange Act 1882.

(7) Late payment interest is to be paid without any deduction of income tax.

(8) Late payment interest is not payable on late payment interest.

(9) For the purposes of this section any reference to the payment of an amount to HMRC includes a reference to its being set off against an amount payable by HMRC (and, accordingly, the reference to the date on which an amount is paid includes a reference to the date from which the set-off takes effect).

[(10) The reference in subsection (1) to amounts payable to HMRC includes—

(*a*) amounts of UK VAT payable under a non-UK special scheme;

(*b*) amounts of UK VAT payable under a special scheme;

and references in Schedule 53 to amounts due or payable to HMRC are to be read accordingly.

(11) In subsection (10)—

(*a*) expressions used in paragraph (a) have the meaning given by paragraph 23(1) of Schedule 3B to VATA 1994 (non- Union scheme);

(*b*) expressions used in paragraph (b) have the meaning given by paragraph 38(1) of Schedule 3BA to VATA 1994 (Union scheme).][1]

Commencement—Finance Act 2009, Sections 101 to 103 (Appointed Day and Supplemental Provision) Order, SI 2010/1878 (day appointed as the day on which FA 2009 ss 101–103 come into force for the purposes of bank payroll tax (including any penalties assessed in relation to that tax) is 31 August 2010).

Finance Act 2009, Sections 101 to 103 (Income Tax Self Assessment) (Appointed Days and Transitional and Consequential Provisions) Order, SI 2011/701 (for the purposes of any self-assessment amount payable by a person to HMRC, ss 101 and 103 come into force on 31 October 2011; for the purposes of any self-assessment amount payable or repayable by HMRC to any person, ss 102 and 103 come into force on 31 October 2011).

Finance (No 3) Act 2010, Schedule 10 and the Finance Act 2009, Schedule 55 and Sections 101 to 103 (Appointed Day, etc) (Construction Industry Scheme) Order, SI 2011/2391 (the day appointed for the coming into force of ss 101–103 is 6 October 2011, but only in relation to a penalty under Sch 55 paras 7–13 (Construction Industry Scheme).

Finance Act 2009, Sections 101 and 102 (Machine Games Duty) (Appointed Day) Order, SI 2013/67 (the day appointed for the coming into force of ss 101 and 102 is 1 February 2013 for the purposes of machine games duty, including any penalties assessed in relation to that duty).

Finance Act 2009, Section 101 (Tax Agents: Dishonest Conduct) (Appointed Day) Order, SI 2013/280 art 2 (the day appointed for coming into force of s 101 for the purposes of penalties assessed under FA 2012 Sch 38 Pts 3–5 (penalties for dishonest conduct or for failure to comply with a file access notice) is 1 April 2013).

Finance Act 2009, Schedules 55 and 56 and Sections 101 and 102 (Stamp Duty Reserve Tax) (Appointed Days, Consequential and Transitional Provision) Order, SI 2014/3269 art 4 (the day appointed as the day on which ss 101 and 102 come into force for the purposes of stamp duty reserve tax (including any penalties assessed in relation to that tax) is 1 January 2015. This only applies to a charge with a due and payable date falling after 31 December 2014.).

Finance Act 2009, Sections 101 and 102 (Remote Gambling Taxes) (Appointed Day) Order, SI 2014/3324 art 3 (the day appointed as the day on which ss 101 and 102 come into force for the purposes of remote gambling taxes is 1 January 2015).

Finance Act 2009, Sections 101 and 102 (Diverted Profits Tax) (Appointed Day) Order, SI 2015/974 (the day appointed for the coming into force of ss 101, 102 for the purposes of diverted profits tax and penalties assessed in relation to that tax is 1 April 2015).

Cross-references—See FA 2014 s 176 in relation to interest charged under s 101 in relation to general betting duty, pool betting duty and remote gaming duty (outside the scope of this work).

Regulations—Taxes and Duties (Interest Rate) Regulations, SI 2010/1879 (formula for calculating late payment interest rate for the purposes of this section).

Amendments—[1] Sub-ss (10), (11) inserted by FA 2014 s 103, Sch 22 para 20(1), (2) with effect from 17 July 2014.

Prospective amendment—Sub-s (2)(*a*), (*b*) to be repealed by F(No 3)A 2010 s 25, Sch 9 Pt 1 paras 1, 2, Pt 2 paras 13, 14 with effect from a day to be appointed (F(No 3)A 2010 s 25).

102 Repayment interest on sums to be paid by HMRC

(1) This section applies to—

(*a*) any amount that is payable by HMRC to any person under or by virtue of an enactment, and

(*b*) a relevant amount paid by a person to HMRC that is repaid by HMRC to that person or to another person.

(2) But this section does not apply to—

(*a*) an amount constituting a repayment of corporation tax,

(*b*) an amount constituting a repayment of petroleum revenue tax, or

(*c*) an amount of any description specified in an order made by the Treasury.

(3) An amount to which this section applies carries interest at the repayment interest rate from the repayment interest start date until the date on which the payment or repayment is made.

(4) In Schedule 54—

(*a*) Parts 1 and 2 define the repayment interest start date, and

(*b*) Part 3 makes supplementary provision.

(5) Subsection (3) applies even if the repayment interest start date is a non-business day within the meaning of section 92 of the Bills of Exchange Act 1882.

(6) Repayment interest is not payable on an amount payable in consequence of an order or judgment of a court having power to allow interest on the amount.

(7) Repayment interest is not payable on repayment interest.

(8) For the purposes of this section—

(*a*) "relevant amount" means any sum that was paid in connection with any liability (including any purported or anticipated liability) to make a payment to HMRC under or by virtue of an enactment, and (*b*) any reference to the payment or repayment of an amount by HMRC includes a reference to its being set off against an amount owed to HMRC (and, accordingly, the reference to the date on which an amount is paid or repaid by HMRC includes a reference to the date from which the set-off takes effect).

Commentary—*Simon's Taxes* **A4.629.**

Commencement—Finance Act 2009, Sections 101 to 103 (Appointed Day and Supplemental Provision) Order, SI 2010/1878 (day appointed as the day on which FA 2009 ss 101–103 come into force for the purposes of bank payroll tax (including any penalties assessed in relation to that tax) is 31 August 2010).

Finance Act 2009, Sections 101 to 103 (Income Tax Self Assessment) (Appointed Days and Transitional and Consequential Provisions) Order, SI 2011/701 (for the purposes of any self-assessment amount payable by a person to HMRC, ss 101 and 103 come into force on 31 October 2011; for the purposes of any self-assessment amount payable or repayable by HMRC to any person, ss 102 and 103 come into force on 31 October 2011).

Finance (No 3) Act 2010, Schedule 10 and the Finance Act 2009, Schedule 55 and Sections 101 to 103 (Appointed Day, etc) (Construction Industry Scheme) Order, SI 2011/2391 (the day appointed for the coming into force of ss 101–103 is 6 October 2011, but only in relation to a penalty under Sch 55 paras 7–13 (Construction Industry Scheme).

Finance Act 2009, Sections 101 and 102 (Machine Games Duty) (Appointed Day) Order, SI 2013/67 (the day appointed for the coming into force of ss 101 and 102 is 1 February 2013 for the purposes of machine games duty, including any penalties assessed in relation to that duty).

Finance Act 2009, Schedules 55 and 56 and Sections 101 and 102 (Stamp Duty Reserve Tax) (Appointed Days, Consequential and Transitional Provision) Order, SI 2014/3269 art 4 (the day appointed as the day on which ss 101 and 102 come into force for the purposes of stamp duty reserve tax (including any penalties assessed in relation to that tax) is 1 January 2015. This only applies to a charge with a due and payable date falling after 31 December 2014.).

Finance Act 2009, Sections 101 and 102 (Remote Gambling Taxes) (Appointed Day) Order, SI 2014/3324 art 3 (the day appointed as the day on which ss 101 and 102 come into force for the purposes of remote gambling taxes is 1 January 2015).

Finance Act 2009, Sections 101 and 102 (Diverted Profits Tax) (Appointed Day) Order, SI 2015/974 (the day appointed for the coming into force of ss 101, 102 for the purposes of diverted profits tax and penalties assessed in relation to that tax is 1 April 2015).

Regulations—Taxes and Duties (Interest Rate) Regulations, SI 2010/1879 (formula for calculating repayment payment interest rate for the purposes of this section).

Prospective amendment—Sub-s (2)(*a*), (*b*) to be repealed, and sub-s (4)(*za*) to be inserted before sub-s (4)(*a*), by F(No 3)A 2010 s 25, Sch 9 Pt 1 paras 1, 3, Pt 2 paras 13, 15 with effect from a day to be appointed (F(No 3)A 2010 s 25). Sub-s (4)(*za*) as inserted to read—

"(*za*) Part A1 makes special provision as to the amount of corporation tax on which repayment interest is calculated,".

Penalties

108 Suspension of penalties during currency of agreement for deferred payment

(1) This section applies if—

(*a*) a person ("P") fails to pay an amount of tax falling within the Table in subsection (5) when it becomes due and payable,

(*b*) P makes a request to an officer of Revenue and Customs that payment of the amount of tax be deferred, and

(*c*) an officer of Revenue and Customs agrees that payment of that amount may be deferred for a period ("the deferral period").

(2) P is not liable to a penalty for failing to pay the amount mentioned in subsection (1) if—

(*a*) the penalty falls within the Table, and

(*b*) P would (apart from this subsection) become liable to it between the date on which P makes the request and the end of the deferral period.

(3) But if—

(*a*) P breaks the agreement (see subsection (4)), and

(*b*) an officer of Revenue and Customs serves on P a notice specifying any penalty to which P would become liable apart from subsection (2),

P becomes liable, at the date of the notice, to that penalty.

(4) P breaks an agreement if—

(*a*) P fails to pay the amount of tax in question when the deferral period ends, or

(*b*) the deferral is subject to P complying with a condition (including a condition that part of the amount be paid during the deferral period) and P fails to comply with it.

(5) The taxes and penalties referred to in subsections (1) and (2) are—

Tax	*Penalty*
Income tax or capital gains tax	*Surcharge under section 59C(2) or (3) of TMA 1970*[1]
Value added tax	Surcharge under section 59(4) or 59A(4) of VATA 1994 [or under paragraph 16F of Schedule 3B, or paragraph 26 of Schedule 3BA, to that Act][2]
Aggregates levy	Penalty interest under paragraph 5 of Schedule 5 to FA 2001

Climate change levy	Penalty interest under paragraph 82 of Schedule 6 to FA 2000
Landfill tax	Penalty interest under paragraph 27(2) of Schedule 5 to FA 1996
Insurance premium tax	Penalty under paragraph 15(2) or (3) of Schedule 7 to FA 1994 which is payable by virtue of paragraph 15(1)(a) of that Schedule.
Any duty of excise	Penalty under section 9(2) or (3) of FA 1994 which is imposed for a failure to pay an amount of any duty of excise or an amount payable on account of any such duty.

(6) If the agreement mentioned in subsection (1)(*c*) is varied at any time by a further agreement between P and an officer of Revenue and Customs, this section applies from that time to the agreement as varied.

(7) The Treasury may by order amend the Table by adding or removing a tax or a penalty.

(8) An order under subsection (7) is to be made by statutory instrument.

(9) A statutory instrument containing an order under subsection (7) is subject to annulment in pursuance of a resolution of the House of Commons.

(10) In this section, except in the entries in the Table, "penalty" includes surcharge and penalty interest.

(11) This section has effect where the agreement mentioned in subsection (1)(*c*) is made on or after 24 November 2008.

Modification—Social Security (Contributions) Regulations, SI 2001/1004 reg 90K(8) (this section modified in relation to a surcharge payable under SI 2001/1004 reg 90K).

Income Tax (Pay As You Earn) Regulations, SI 2003/2682 reg 203(8) (this section modified in relation to a surcharge payable under SI 2003/2682 reg 203).

Income Tax (Construction Industry Scheme) (Amendment) Regulations, SI 2009/2030 reg 2 (this section modified in relation to a surcharge payable under SI 2009/2030 reg 2).

Amendments—

1 In sub-s (5), first row of Table repealed by the Finance Act 2009, Schedules 55 and 56 (Income Tax Self Assessment and Pension Schemes) (Appointed Days and Consequential and Savings Provisions) Order, SI 2011/702 art 15(*b*) with effect from 1 April 2011. This amendment has no effect in relation to a return or other document which is required to be made or delivered to HMRC or an amount of tax which is payable in relation to the tax year 2009–10 or any previous tax year (SI 2011/702 art 20).

2 In sub-s (5), in Table, in second column of entry relating to VAT, words inserted by FA 2014 s 103, Sch 22 para 20(1), (3) with effect in relation to supplies made on or after 1 January 2015.

109 Miscellaneous amendments

Schedule 57 contains amendments of Schedule 24 to FA 2007 (penalties for errors), Schedule 41 to FA 2008 (penalties for failure to notify and certain other wrongdoing) and certain other enactments relating to penalties.

PART 9
FINAL PROVISIONS

126 Interpretation

(1) In this Act—

"ALDA 1979" means the Alcoholic Liquor Duties Act 1979,
"BGDA 1981" means the Betting and Gaming Duties Act 1981,
"CAA 2001" means the Capital Allowances Act 2001,
"CRCA 2005" means the Commissioners for Revenue and Customs Act 2005,
"CTA 2009" means the Corporation Tax Act 2009,
"FISMA 2000" means the Financial Services and Markets Act 2000,
"HODA 1979" means the Hydrocarbon Oil Duties Act 1979,
"ICTA" means the Income and Corporation Taxes Act 1988,
"IHTA 1984" means the Inheritance Tax Act 1984,
"ITA 2007" means the Income Tax Act 2007,
"ITEPA 2003" means the Income Tax (Earnings and Pensions) Act 2003,
"ITTOIA 2005" means the Income Tax (Trading and Other Income) Act 2005,
"OTA 1975" means the Oil Taxation Act 1975,
"OTA 1983" means the Oil Taxation Act 1983,
"PRTA 1980" means the Petroleum Revenue Tax Act 1980,
"TCGA 1992" means the Taxation of Chargeable Gains Act 1992,
"TMA 1970" means the Taxes Management Act 1970,
"TPDA 1979" means the Tobacco Products Duty Act 1979,
"VATA 1994" means the Value Added Tax Act 1994, and

"VERA 1994" means the Vehicle Excise and Registration Act 1994.

(2) In this Act—

"FA", followed by a year, means the Finance Act of that year, and "F(No 2)A", followed by a year, means the Finance (No 2) Act of that year.

(3)–(5) (*amend* CAA 2001, ITEPA 2003, ITTOIA 2005)

(6) Accordingly, omit—

(*a*) in FA 2004, in Schedule 35, paragraphs 49 and 65(2),

(*b*) in F(No 2)A 2005, section 10(7),

(*c*) in FA 2006, section 84(4), and

(*d*) in FA 2008, in Schedule 25, paragraph 6.

127 Short title

This Act may be cited as the Finance Act 2009.

SCHEDULES

SCHEDULE 3

VAT: SUPPLEMENTARY CHARGE AND ORDERS CHANGING RATE

Section 9

PART 1

SUPPLEMENTARY CHARGE TO VAT

The charge

1—(1) There is a supplementary charge on a supply of goods or services that is treated as taking place on or after 25 November 2008 if—

(*a*) the supply spans the date of the VAT change,

(*b*) it is subject to VAT at the rate in force under section 2 of VATA 1994,

(*c*) the person to whom the supply is made is not entitled under VATA 1994 to credit for, or the repayment or refund of, all of the VAT on the supply, and

(*d*) a relevant condition is met.

(2) In this Schedule "the date of the VAT change" means 1 January 2010.

(3) For the cases in which a supply, other than the grant of a right to goods or services, spans the date of the VAT change and the relevant conditions in relation to such a supply, see paragraph 2.

(4) For the cases in which a supply consisting of the grant of a right to goods or services spans the date of the VAT change and the relevant conditions in relation to such a supply, see paragraph 3.

(5) Sub-paragraph (1) has effect subject to the exceptions made by or under Part 2 of this Schedule.

(6) In this Schedule—

Part 3 contains provision about liability for, and the amount of, a supplementary charge under this Schedule,

Part 4 contains special provision about listed supplies, and

Part 5 contains provision about administration and interpretation.

(7) A supplementary charge under this Schedule is to be treated for all purposes as if it were value added tax charged in accordance with VATA 1994.

Supply spanning the date of the VAT change

2—(1) For the purposes of this Schedule, a supply of goods or services spans the date of the VAT change where—

(*a*) by virtue of the issue of a VAT invoice or the receipt of a payment by the person making the supply ("the supplier"), the supply is treated as taking place before the date of the VAT change, but

(*b*) the basic time of supply (see paragraph 4) is on or after the date of the VAT change.

(2) The relevant conditions are—

(*a*) in relation to a supply that is within sub-paragraph (1)(*a*) by virtue of the issue of a VAT invoice, conditions A to D, and

(*b*) in relation to a supply that is within sub-paragraph (1)(*a*) by virtue of the receipt of a payment, conditions A to C.

(3) Condition A is that the supplier and the person to whom the supply is made are connected with each other at any time in the period—

(*a*) beginning with the day on which the supply is treated as taking place, and

(*b*) ending on the date of the VAT change.

(4) Paragraph 5 modifies condition A in cases involving a series of supplies.

(5) Condition B is that the aggregate of the following is more than £100,000—

(*a*) the relevant consideration for the supply, and

(*b*) the relevant consideration for every related supply of goods or services (including every related grant of a right to goods or services) that spans the date of the VAT change (see paragraph 6).

(6) Condition C is that a prepayment in respect of the supply is financed by the supplier or a person connected with the supplier (see paragraph 7).

(7) In sub-paragraph (6) "prepayment", in respect of a supply, means a payment that is received by the supplier before the basic time of supply.

(8) Condition D is that full payment of the amount shown on the VAT invoice referred to in sub-paragraph (1)(*a*) is not due before the end of the period of 6 months beginning with the date on which the invoice is issued.

(9) This paragraph does not apply in relation to a supply consisting of the grant of a right to goods or services (see paragraph 3).

Modification—This para modified by the VAT (Supplementary Charge) Order, SI 2009/3127 art 2 with effect from 31 December 2009 so that there is no supplementary charge on a supply of goods within this para if—

(a) the only relevant condition met is condition D,

(b) the VAT invoice—

(i) relates to a supply of goods made under a hire-purchase, conditional sale or credit sale agreement,

(ii) forms part of that agreement, and

(iii) is issued in accordance with normal commercial practice in relation to a supply made under such an agreement, and

(c) the basic time of supply of the goods is intended and expected to be within six months of the date of the VAT invoice which relates to the supply.

Grant of right spanning the date of the VAT change

3—(1) For the purposes of this Schedule, a supply consisting of the grant by a person ("the grantor") of a right to goods or services spans the date of the VAT change where—

(*a*) that supply is treated as taking place before the date of the VAT change,

(*b*) the goods or services are to be supplied at a discount or free of charge, and

(*c*) the basic time of supply for the supply of some or all of the goods or services (see paragraph 4) is on or after the date of the VAT change.

(2) In relation to the grant of the right, the relevant conditions are conditions A to C.

(3) Condition A is that the grantor and the person to whom the right is granted are connected with each other at any time in the period—

(*a*) beginning with the day on which the supply consisting of the grant of the right is treated as taking place, and

(*b*) ending on the date of the VAT change or, if the right is exercised (entirely or partly) on a later date, that date (or, if more than one, the first of those dates).

(4) Paragraph 5 modifies condition A in cases involving a series of supplies.

(5) Condition B is that the aggregate of the following is more than £100,000—

(*a*) the relevant consideration for the grant of the right, and

(*b*) the relevant consideration for every related supply of goods or services (including every related grant of a right to goods or services) that spans the date of the VAT change (see paragraph 6).

(6) Condition C is that the payment made in respect of the grant of the right is financed by the grantor or a person connected with the grantor (see paragraph 7).

(7) In this Schedule references to a right to goods or services include—

(*a*) any right or option with respect to such goods or services, and

(*b*) any interest deriving from such a right or option.

"Basic time of supply"

4—(1) In this Schedule the "basic time of supply" is the time given by subsection (2) or (3) of section 6 of VATA 1994 (disregarding subsections (4) to (14) of that section).

(2) Sub-paragraph (1) does not apply in relation to listed supplies (see Part 4 of this Schedule).

Series of supplies

5—(1) This paragraph applies where—

(*a*) the supply or grant of a right referred to in paragraph 2 or 3 ("the affected supply or grant") is one of a series of supplies of, or grants of a right to, the same or substantially the same goods or services, and

(*b*) each of the supplies, and the grants of a right, in the series was or will be made in the expectation that the affected supply or grant would or will take place.

(2) In condition A in paragraphs 2 and 3, the references to the supplier and the grantor include any person who makes one of the supplies or grants one of the rights in the series.

"Relevant consideration" and "related" supplies

6—(1) This paragraph applies for the purposes of condition B in paragraphs 2 and 3.
(2) "Relevant consideration" means—
- (*a*) in relation to a supply that is within paragraph 2(1) by virtue of the issue of a VAT invoice, the amount shown on that invoice,
- (*b*) in relation to a supply that is within paragraph 2(1) by virtue of the receipt of a payment, the amount of that payment, and
- (*c*) in relation to a grant of a right to goods or services within paragraph 3(1), the consideration for the grant of the right,

but does not include any amount in respect of VAT.
(3) A supply within paragraph 2(1), or a grant of a right within paragraph 3(1), is related to another such supply or grant if they are both made as part of the same scheme.
(4) "Scheme" includes any arrangements, transaction or series of transactions.

Financing

7—(1) This paragraph applies for the purposes of condition C in paragraphs 2 and 3.
(2) A payment is financed by a person if, directly or indirectly, the person—
- (*a*) provides funds to enable the person to whom the supply is made to make the whole or part of the payment (whether the funds are provided before or after the payment is made),
- (*b*) procures the provision of such funds by another person,
- (*c*) provides funds for discharging (in whole or in part) any liability that has been or may be incurred by any person for or in connection with raising funds to enable the person to whom the supply is made to make the payment, or
- (*d*) procures that any such liability is or will be discharged (in whole or in part) by another person.

(3) In sub-paragraph (2) the references to providing funds for a purpose are to—
- (*a*) making a loan of funds that are or are to be used for that purpose,
- (*b*) providing a guarantee or other security in relation to such a loan,
- (*c*) providing consideration for the issue of shares or other securities issued wholly or partly for raising those funds,
- (*d*) providing consideration for the acquisition by any person of any such shares or securities, or
- (*e*) any other transfer of assets or value as a consequence of which any of those funds are made available for that purpose.

Connected persons

8 [Section 1122 of CTA 2010][1] (connected persons) applies for the purposes of this Schedule.

Amendments—[1] Words substituted for words "Section 839 of ICTA" by CTA 2010 s 1177, Sch 1 para 713.CTA 2010 has effect for corporation tax purposes for accounting periods ending on or after 1 April 2010, and for income and capital gains tax purposes for the tax year 2010–11 and subsequent tax years.

Receipt of payments

9 In this Schedule a reference to receipt of a payment by the person making a supply or granting a right (however expressed) includes a reference to receipt by a person to whom a right to receive it has been assigned.

Power to change relevant conditions

10—(1) The Treasury may by order amend this Part of this Schedule by adding, modifying or omitting relevant conditions.
(2) An order under this paragraph—
- (*a*) may make different provision for different cases, and
- (*b*) may make incidental or consequential amendments of this Schedule.

Supplies treated as taking place before 31 March 2009

11 In relation to supplies treated as taking place before 31 March 2009, this Schedule has effect as if—
- (*a*) paragraphs 2(5), 3(5) and 6 (condition B) and all references to condition B were omitted,
- (*b*) in paragraph 2(6) (condition C), the words "or a person connected with the supplier" were omitted, and

(*c*) in paragraph 3(6) (condition C), the words "or a person connected with the grantor" were omitted.

PART 2
EXCEPTIONS

Letting etc of assets

12—(1) This paragraph applies in relation to a supply within paragraph 2 which arises from the letting, hiring or rental of assets.
(2) There is no supplementary charge under this Schedule if—

(*a*) the period to which the VAT invoice or payment referred to in paragraph 2(1) relates does not exceed 12 months, and

(*b*) the VAT invoice is issued, or the payment is received, in accordance with normal commercial practice in relation to the letting, hiring or rental of such assets.

Condition B cases involving normal commercial practice

13 There is no supplementary charge under this Schedule on a supply of goods or services within paragraph 2 or a grant of a right to goods or services within paragraph 3 if—

(*a*) the only relevant condition met is condition B, and

(*b*) the supply is made, or the right is granted, in accordance with normal commercial practice in relation to the supply of, or the grant of a right to, such goods or services.

Normal commercial practice

14 In this Part of this Schedule "normal commercial practice" means normal commercial practice at a time when an increase in the rate of VAT in force under section 2 of VATA 1994 is not expected.

Further exceptions

15—(1) The Treasury may by order provide that there is no supplementary charge under this Schedule on supplies (including grants of rights to goods or services) of a description specified in the order.
(2) An order under this paragraph may make provision having effect in relation to supplies of goods or services that are treated as taking place on or after 25 November 2008 or a later date.

Order—Value Added Tax (Supplementary Charge) Order, SI 2009/3127.

PART 3
LIABILITY AND AMOUNT

Liability

16—(1) A supplementary charge under this Schedule on a supply within paragraph 2—

(*a*) is a liability of the supplier (subject to sub-paragraph (3)), and

(*b*) becomes due on the date of the VAT change (rather than at the time of supply).

(2) A supplementary charge under this Schedule on a supply consisting of the grant of a right to goods or services within paragraph 3—

(*a*) is a liability of the grantor (subject to sub-paragraph (3)), and

(*b*) becomes due on the first occasion on or after the date of the VAT change on which the right is exercised (rather than at the time the right is granted).

(3) If, on the date on which the supplementary charge becomes due, the person who would be liable to pay the charge under sub-paragraph (1) or (2)—

(*a*) is not a taxable person, but

(*b*) is treated as a member of a group under sections 43A to 43D of VATA 1994,

the supplementary charge is a liability of the representative member of the group.

Amount

17—(1) The amount of the supplementary charge on a supply within paragraph 2 is equal to the difference between—

(*a*) the amount of VAT chargeable on the supply apart from this Schedule, and

(*b*) the amount of VAT that would be chargeable on the supply if it were subject to VAT at the rate of 17.5%.

(2) The amount of the supplementary charge on a grant of a right to goods or services within paragraph 3 is equal to the difference between—

(*a*) the amount of VAT chargeable on the grant of the right apart from this Schedule, and (*b*) the amount of VAT that would be chargeable on the grant of the right if it were subject to VAT at the rate of 17.5%,

(but see sub-paragraph (3)).

(3) If the basic time of supply for some of those goods and services is before the date of the VAT change, sub-paragraph (2) has effect as if the references to the amount of VAT chargeable and to the amount of VAT that would be chargeable were references to the relevant proportion of each of those amounts.

(4) "The relevant proportion" is—

$$P / W$$

where—

P is so much of the consideration for the grant of the right as is attributable on a just and reasonable basis to a right to the goods and services for which the basic time of supply is on or after the date of the VAT change, and

W is the whole of the consideration for the grant of the right.

PART 4
LISTED SUPPLIES

"Listed supply"

18—(1) In this Schedule "listed supply" means a supply falling within sub-paragraph (2)—

(*a*) which is made for a consideration the whole or part of which is determined or payable periodically or from time to time, and

(*b*) which is treated as taking place by virtue of the issue of a VAT invoice or the receipt of a payment by the person making the supply.

(2) The following supplies fall within this sub-paragraph—

(*a*) a supply of services,

(*b*) a supply arising from the grant of a major interest in land,

(*c*) a supply of water other than—

(i) distilled water, deionised water or water of similar purity, or

(ii) bottled water,

(*d*) a supply of—

(i) coal gas, water gas, producer gases or similar gases, or

(ii) petroleum gases, or other gaseous hydrocarbons, in a gaseous state,

(*e*) a supply of power, heat, refrigeration or ventilation, and

(*f*) a supply of goods together with services in the course of the construction, alteration, demolition, repair or maintenance of a building or civil engineering work.

(3) The Treasury may by order amend sub-paragraph (2) by—

(*a*) adding or omitting any description of supply, or

(*b*) varying any description of supply for the time being listed in that sub-paragraph.

"Basic time of supply": listed supplies

19—(1) For the purposes of this Schedule, in relation to a listed supply, "the basic time of supply" is the end of the period to which the VAT invoice or payment mentioned in paragraph 18(1) relates, except as provided in sub-paragraphs (2) and (4).

(2) Where the person making the supply issues an invoice—

(*a*) in respect of part of the listed supply to which the VAT invoice or payment mentioned in paragraph 18(1) relates, and

(*b*) for a period (a "billing period") ending before the end of the period to which that VAT invoice or payment relates,

"the basic time of supply", in relation to that part of the supply, is the end of the billing period.

(3) For the purposes of sub-paragraph (2), the listed supply (and the consideration for the supply) must be apportioned between periods on a just and reasonable basis.

(4) Where a listed supply is treated as taking place by virtue of—

(*a*) the issue by the person making the supply of a VAT invoice relating to a premium for the grant of a tenancy or lease, or

(*b*) the receipt by the person making the supply of such a premium, "the basic time of supply" is the date of the grant of the tenancy or lease.

PART 5
ADMINISTRATION AND INTERPRETATION

Person ceasing to be taxable person before supplementary charge due

20—(1) This paragraph applies if, on the date on which a supplementary charge under this Schedule becomes due ("the due date"), the person who is liable to pay the charge under paragraph 16 is not a taxable person.

(2) The supplementary charge must be accounted for by that person in accordance with VATA 1994 (and regulations made under that Act) as if it were VAT due in the last period for which the person was required to make a return by or under VATA 1994.

(3) If an amount assessed as due by way of supplementary charge under this Schedule would (in the absence of this sub-paragraph) carry interest from a date earlier than the due date, it is to be treated as only carrying interest from the due date.

Adjustment of contracts following the VAT change

21—(1) This paragraph applies where—

(*a*) a contract for the supply of goods or services is made before the date of the VAT change, and

(*b*) there is a supplementary charge under this Schedule on the supply.

(2) The consideration for the supply is to be increased by an amount equal to the supplementary charge, unless the contract provides otherwise.

Invoices

22 Regulations under paragraph 2A of Schedule 11 to VATA 1994 (VAT invoices) may make provision about the provision, replacement or correction of invoices in connection with a supplementary charge under this Schedule.

Orders under this Schedule

23—(1) An order under this Schedule is to be made by statutory instrument.

(2) A statutory instrument containing an order under this Schedule is subject to annulment in pursuance of a resolution of the House of Commons, unless it is an instrument to which sub-paragraph (4) applies.

(3) Sub-paragraph (4) applies to a statutory instrument containing an order made under paragraph 10 (or under that paragraph and under other provisions) which extends the supplies that are subject to a supplementary charge under this Schedule.

(4) An instrument to which this sub-paragraph applies—

(*a*) must be laid before the House of Commons, and

(*b*) ceases to have effect at the end of the period of 28 days beginning with the day on which it was made unless it is approved during that period by a resolution of the House of Commons.

(5) In reckoning the period of 28 days no account is to be taken of any time during which Parliament is dissolved or prorogued or during which the House of Commons is adjourned for more than 4 days.

(6) The order ceasing to have effect does not affect—

(*a*) anything previously done under it, or

(*b*) the making of a new order.

Interpretation: general

24—(1) Expressions used in this Schedule and in VATA 1994 have the same meaning in this Schedule as in that Act.

(2) In this Schedule—

(*a*) "treated as taking place" means treated as taking place for the purposes of the charge to VAT, and

(*b*) references to the person by or to whom a supply is made (however expressed) are to the person by or to whom the supply is treated as being made for the purposes of VATA 1994.

PART 6
AMENDMENTS OF VATA 1994

25—(1) VATA 1994 is amended as follows.

(2) In section 2(2) (orders increasing or decreasing rate of VAT), after "such order" insert "that has not previously expired or been revoked".

(3) (*inserts* VATA 1994 s 97(4A))

SCHEDULE 36

VAT: PLACE OF SUPPLY OF SERVICES ETC

Section 76

PART 1

AMENDMENTS COMING INTO FORCE IN 2010

1 VATA 1994 is amended as follows.

2 In section 6(14A) (time of supply), omit "In relation to any services of a description specified in an order under section 7(11),".

3—(1) Section 7 (place of supply) is amended as follows.
(2) In subsection (1), omit "or services".
(3) Omit subsection (10).
(4) In subsection (11), omit "or services" (in each place).
(5) In the heading, insert at the end "of goods".

4 (*inserts* VATA 1994 s 7A)

5—(1) Section 8 (reverse charge on supplies received from abroad) is amended as follows.
(2) (*substitutes* VATA 1994 s 8(1), (2))
(3) (*inserts* VATA 1994 s 8(4A))
(4) In subsection (5), for "add to, or vary, Schedule 5" substitute "amend subsection (4A) by altering the descriptions of services specified in that subsection".
(5) Omit subsection (6).
(6) In subsection (7)—
(*a*) for "add to or vary Schedule 5" substitute "amend subsection (4A)", and
(*b*) for "addition to or variation of that Schedule" substitute "amendment of that subsection".
(7) In subsection (8)—
(*a*) for "addition to or variation of that Schedule" substitute "amendment of subsection (4A)", and
(*b*) for "the Schedule" substitute "that subsection".

6 (*substitutes* VATA 1994 s 9)

7—(1) Section 43 (groups of companies) is amended as follows.
(2) In subsection (2A)—
(*a*) in paragraph (*a*), for "falling within Schedule 5" substitute "to which section 7A(2)(*a*) applies made", and
(*b*) in paragraph (*c*)—
(i) omit "falling within paragraphs 1 to 8 of Schedule 5", and
(ii) insert at the end "and section 7A(2)(*a*) applied to the supply".
(3) In subsection (2D)—
(*a*) in paragraph (*c*)—
(i) omit "falling within paragraphs 1 to 8 of Schedule 5", and
(ii) insert at the end "and section 7A(2)(*a*) applied to the supply", and
(*b*) in the words after the paragraphs, for "falling within that Schedule," substitute "to which section 7A(2)(*a*) applies,".
(4) In subsection (2E)(*b*), for "there are services falling within paragraphs 1 to 8 of Schedule 5 which, if used by the transferor for making supplies falling within that Schedule," substitute "there is a supply to which section 7A(2)(*a*) applies of services which, if used by the transferor for making such a supply,".

8—(1) Section 96 (interpretation) is amended as follows.
(2) In subsection (1), after the definition of "regulations" insert—
""relevant business person" has the meaning given by section 7A(4);".
(3) In subsection (8), omit "(subject to any provision made under section 8(6))".

9 Section 97(4)(*a*) (orders subject to requirement of Parliamentary approval after making), after "5(4)" insert ", 7A(6)".

10 Section 97A(1) (place of supply orders: transitional provision), for "on or after 17th March 1998 under section 7(11)" substitute "under section 7A(6)".

11 (*inserts* VATA 1994 Sch 4A)

12 Omit Schedule 5 (services supplied where received).

13 In Article 5 of the Value Added Tax (Tour Operators) Order 1987 (SI 1987/1806)—

(*a*) omit paragraph (1), and

(*b*) in paragraph (2) after "treated" insert "for the purposes of this Act", and treat that article as made under section 7A(6)(*c*) of VATA 1994 (inserted by paragraph 4).

14—(1) The powers contained in section 7A(6) of VATA 1994 (inserted by paragraph 4) may be exercised at any time on or after the day on which this Act is passed.

(2) The amendments made by paragraph 7 come into force on 1 January 2010; but the references in section 43 of VATA 1994 (as amended by that paragraph) to a supply to which section 7A(2) of that Act applies includes a supply of services falling within paragraphs 1 to 8 of Schedule 5 made before that date.

(3) Subject to that, the amendments made by this Part have effect in relation to supplies made on or after 1 January 2010.

PART 2
AMENDMENTS COMING INTO FORCE IN 2011

Admission to cultural, educational and entertainment activities etc

15—(1) Schedule 4A to VATA 1994 (inserted by paragraph 11) is amended as follows.

(2) Omit paragraph 4.

(3) After paragraph 9 insert—

"Admission to cultural, educational and entertainment activities etc

9A—

(1) A supply to a relevant business person of services to which this paragraph applies is to be treated as made in the country in which the events in question actually take place.

(2) This paragraph applies to the provision of—

(*a*) services in respect of admission to cultural, artistic, sporting, scientific, educational, entertainment or similar events (including fairs and exhibitions), and

(*b*) ancillary services relating to admission to such events."

(4) After paragraph 14 insert—

"Cultural, educational and entertainment services etc

14A—

(1) A supply to a person who is not a relevant business person of services to which this paragraph applies is to be treated as made in the country in which the activities concerned actually take place.

(2) This paragraph applies to the provision of—

(*a*) services relating to cultural, artistic, sporting, scientific, educational, entertainment or similar activities (including fairs and exhibitions), and

(*b*) ancillary services relating to such activities, including services of organisers of such activities."

16 The amendments made by this Part have effect in relation to supplies made on or after 1 January 2011.

PART 3
AMENDMENTS COMING INTO FORCE IN 2013

17 In Schedule 4A to VATA 1994 (inserted by paragraph 11), after paragraph 13 insert—

"Long-term hiring of means of transport

13A—

(1) A supply to a person who is not a relevant business person ("the recipient") of services consisting of the long-term hiring of a means of transport is to be treated as made in the country in which the recipient belongs.

But this is subject to sub-paragraph (2) and paragraph 3(3) and (4).

(2) A supply to a person who is not a relevant business person ("the recipient") of services consisting of the long-term hiring of a pleasure boat which is actually put at the disposal of the recipient at the supplier's business establishment, or some other fixed establishment of the

supplier, is to be treated as made in the country where the pleasure boat is actually put at the disposal of the recipient.

(3) For the purposes of this Schedule, the hiring of a means of transport is "long-term" if it is not short-term (as to the meaning of which see paragraph 3(2))."

18 The amendment made by this Part has effect in relation to supplies made on or after 1 January 2013.

PART 4
TRANSITIONAL PROVISIONS

19—(1) This paragraph applies where—

(*a*) amendments made by this Schedule provide for a supply of services to be treated as made in the United Kingdom,

(*b*) the supply would not have fallen to be so treated apart from the amendments, and

(*c*) the services are treated under the law of a member State other than the United Kingdom as supplied in that member State before the commencement date.

(2) The supply is not to be treated as made in the United Kingdom.

(3) "The commencement date" means the date specified by this Schedule as that on or after which a supply must be made if it is to be treated as made in the United Kingdom by virtue of the amendments.

SCHEDULE 46
DUTIES OF SENIOR ACCOUNTING OFFICERS OF QUALIFYING COMPANIES

Section 93

Main duty of senior accounting officer

1—(1) The senior accounting officer of a qualifying company must take reasonable steps to ensure that the company establishes and maintains appropriate tax accounting arrangements.

(2) The senior accounting officer of a qualifying company must, in particular, take reasonable steps—

(*a*) to monitor the accounting arrangements of the company, and

(*b*) to identify any respects in which those arrangements are not appropriate tax accounting arrangements.

Certificate for Commissioners

2—(1) The senior accounting officer of a qualifying company must provide the Commissioners with a certificate for each financial year of the company.

(2) The certificate must—

(*a*) state whether the company had appropriate tax accounting arrangements throughout the financial year, and

(*b*) if it did not, give an explanation of the respects in which the accounting arrangements of the company were not appropriate tax accounting arrangements.

(3) The certificate must be provided—

(*a*) by such means and in such form as is reasonably specified by an officer of Revenue and Customs, and

(*b*) not later than the end of the period for filing the company's accounts for the financial year (or such later time as an officer of Revenue and Customs may have allowed).

(4) A certificate may relate to more than one qualifying company.

Notifying Commissioners of name of senior accounting officer

3—(1) For each financial year a qualifying company must ensure that the Commissioners are notified of the name of each person who was its senior accounting officer at any time during the year.

(2) The notification must be given—

(*a*) by such means and in such form as is reasonably specified by an officer of Revenue and Customs, and

(*b*) not later than the end of the period for filing the company's accounts for the financial year (or such later time as an officer of Revenue and Customs may have allowed for providing the certificate for the financial year under paragraph 2).

(3) A notification may relate to more than one qualifying company.

Penalty for failure to comply with main duty

4—(1) This paragraph applies if a senior accounting officer fails to comply with paragraph 1 at any time in a financial year.

(2) The senior accounting officer is liable to a penalty of £5,000.
(3) A person is not liable to more than one penalty under this paragraph in respect of the same company and the same financial year.

Penalties for failure to provide certificate etc

5—(1) This paragraph applies if a senior accounting officer—
(*a*) fails to provide a certificate in accordance with paragraph 2, or
(*b*) provides a certificate in accordance with that paragraph that contains a careless or deliberate inaccuracy.
(2) The senior accounting officer is liable to a penalty of £5,000.
(3) For the purposes of this Schedule, an inaccuracy is careless if the inaccuracy is due to a failure by the senior accounting officer to take reasonable care.
(4) An inaccuracy in a certificate that was neither careless nor deliberate when the certificate was given is to be treated as careless if the senior accounting officer—
(*a*) discovered the inaccuracy some time later, and
(*b*) did not take reasonable steps to inform HMRC.

More than one senior accounting officer

6—(1) This paragraph applies if the identity of the senior accounting officer of a company changes.
(2) If (but for this sub-paragraph) more than one person would be liable to a penalty under paragraph 4 in respect of a financial year of the company, only the one who became the senior accounting officer latest in the year is liable to such a penalty.
(3) If a person who is or has been the senior accounting officer of the company complies, or purports to comply, with paragraph 2 in respect of a financial year, no other person is liable to a penalty under paragraph 5 in respect of that company and that financial year.
(4) A person who is replaced as the senior accounting officer of the company before the last day for compliance with paragraph 2 in respect of a financial year is not liable to a penalty under paragraph 5(1)(*a*) for failing to comply with that paragraph in respect of that company and that financial year.

Penalty for failure to notify Commissioners of name of senior accounting officer

7 A qualifying company is liable to a penalty of £5,000 if, for a financial year, the Commissioners are not notified of the name or names of its senior accounting officer or officers in accordance with paragraph 3.

Reasonable excuse

8—(1) Liability to a penalty for a failure to comply with this Schedule does not arise if the senior accounting officer or qualifying company satisfies HMRC or (on an appeal notified to the tribunal) the tribunal that there is a reasonable excuse for the failure.
(2) For the purposes of this paragraph—
(*a*) an insufficiency of funds is not a reasonable excuse unless attributable to events outside the person's control,
(*b*) where the person relies on any other person to do anything, that is not a reasonable excuse unless the first person took reasonable care to avoid the failure, and
(*c*) where the person had a reasonable excuse for the failure but the excuse has ceased, the person is to be treated as having continued to have the excuse if the failure is remedied without unreasonable delay after the excuse ceased.

Assessment of penalties

9—(1) Where a senior accounting officer or a qualifying company becomes liable for a penalty under this Schedule—
(*a*) HMRC may assess the penalty, and
(*b*) if they do so, they must notify the officer or company liable for the penalty.
(2) An assessment of a penalty under this Schedule for a failure in respect of a financial year, or an inaccuracy in a certificate for a financial year, may not be made—
(*a*) more than 6 months after the failure or inaccuracy first comes to the attention of an officer of Revenue and Customs, or
(*b*) more than 6 years after the end of the period for filing the company's accounts for the financial year.
(3) HMRC may not assess a person who is the senior accounting officer of a company ("C") as liable to a penalty under paragraph 4 or 5 for a financial year ("the relevant financial year") if—

(*a*) at any time in the relevant financial year the person was the senior accounting officer of another company that was a member of the same group as C, and

(*b*) HMRC has assessed the person as liable, as the senior accounting officer of the other company, to a penalty under that paragraph for a financial year that ends on a day in the relevant financial year.

(4) HMRC may not assess a company ("C") as liable to a penalty under paragraph 7 for a financial year ("the relevant financial year") if—

(*a*) C was a member of a group at the end of that year, and

(*b*) HMRC has assessed another company that was a member of the same group as C at that time as liable to a penalty under that paragraph—

(i) for its financial year ending on the same day as the relevant financial year, or

(ii) if its financial year does not end on that day, for its financial year ending last before that day.

Appeal

10—(1) A person may appeal against a decision of HMRC that a penalty is payable by that person.

(2) Notice of an appeal must be given—

(*a*) in writing,

(*b*) before the end of the period of 30 days beginning with the date on which the notification under paragraph 9 was issued, and

(*c*) to HMRC.

(3) Notice of an appeal must state the grounds of appeal.

(4) On an appeal that is notified to the tribunal, the tribunal may confirm or cancel the decision.

(5) Subject to this paragraph and paragraph 11, the provisions of Part 5 of TMA 1970 relating to appeals have effect in relation to appeals under this Schedule as they have effect in relation to an appeal against an assessment to income tax.

Enforcement of penalties

11—(1) A penalty under this Schedule must be paid—

(*a*) before the end of the period of 30 days beginning with the date on which the notification under paragraph 9 was issued, or

(*b*) if a notice of appeal against the penalty is given, before the end of the period of 30 days beginning with the date on which the appeal is determined or withdrawn.

(2) A penalty under this Schedule may be enforced as if it were income tax charged in an assessment and due and payable.

Power to change amount of penalties

12—(1) If it appears to the Treasury that there has been a change in the value of money since the last relevant date, they may by regulations substitute for the sums for the time being specified in paragraphs 4, 5 and 7 such other sums as appear to them to be justified by the change.

(2) In sub-paragraph (1), in relation to a specified sum, "relevant date" means—

(*a*) the date on which this Act is passed, and

(*b*) in relation to that sum, each date on which the power conferred by that sub-paragraph has been exercised.

(3) Regulations under this paragraph do not apply to—

(*a*) a failure that occurs in respect of a financial year of a company that begins before the date on which they come into force, or

(*b*) an inaccuracy in a certificate that was provided to HMRC in respect of such a financial year.

Application of provisions of TMA 1970

13 Subject to the provisions of this Schedule, the following provisions of TMA 1970 apply for the purposes of this Schedule as they apply for the purposes of the Taxes Acts—

(*a*) section 108 (responsibility of company officers),

(*b*) section 114 (want of form), and

(*c*) section 115 (delivery and service of documents).

Meaning of "appropriate tax accounting arrangements"

14—(1) "Appropriate tax accounting arrangements" means accounting arrangements that enable the company's relevant liabilities to be calculated accurately in all material respects.

(2) "Accounting arrangements" includes arrangements for keeping accounting records.

(3) "Relevant liabilities", in relation to a company, means liabilities in respect of—

(*a*) corporation tax (including any amount assessable or chargeable as if it were corporation tax),
(*b*) value added tax,
(*c*) amounts for which the company is accountable under PAYE regulations,
(*d*) insurance premium tax,
(*e*) stamp duty land tax,
(*f*) stamp duty reserve tax,
(*g*) petroleum revenue tax,
(*h*) customs duties, and
(*i*) excise duties.

Meaning of "qualifying company"

15—(1) A company is a qualifying company in relation to a financial year if the qualification test was satisfied in the previous financial year (subject to any regulations under sub-paragraph (8)).
(2) The qualification test is that the company satisfied either or both of the following requirements—

1 Relevant turnover	More than £200 million
2 Relevant balance sheet total	More than £2 billion.

(3) If the company was not a member of a group at the end of the previous financial year—
(*a*) "relevant turnover" means the company's turnover, and
(*b*) "relevant balance sheet total" means the company's balance sheet total.
(4) If the company was a member of a group at the end of the previous financial year—
(*a*) "relevant turnover" means the aggregate turnover of the company ("C") and any other company that was a member of the same group as C at the end of C's previous financial year, and
(*b*) "relevant balance sheet total" means the aggregate balance sheet totals of C and any such company.
(5) If the financial year of a company that was a member of the same group as C does not end on the same day as C's previous financial year, the figures for that company that are to be included in the aggregate figures are the figures for that company's financial year ending last before the end of C's previous financial year.
(6) "Turnover", in relation to a company, has the same meaning as in Part 15 of the Companies Act 2006 (see section 474 of that Act).
(7) "Balance sheet total", in relation to a company and a financial year, means the aggregate of the amounts shown as assets in the company's balance sheet as at the end of the financial year.
(8) The Treasury may by regulations provide that a company of a description specified in the regulations is not a qualifying company for the purposes of this Schedule.

Meaning of "senior accounting officer"

16—(1) "Senior accounting officer", in relation to a company that is not a member of a group, means the director or officer who, in the company's reasonable opinion, has overall responsibility for the company's financial accounting arrangements.
(2) "Senior accounting officer", in relation to a company that is a member of a group, means the group director or officer who, in the company's reasonable opinion, has overall responsibility for the company's financial accounting arrangements.
(3) "Group director or officer", in relation to a company, means a director or officer of the company or of a relevant body that is a member of the same group as the company.
(4) A person may be the senior accounting officer of more than one company.

Regulations

17—(1) Regulations under this Schedule are to be made by statutory instrument.
(2) A statutory instrument containing regulations under this Schedule is subject to annulment in pursuance of a resolution of the House of Commons.

Other definitions

18—(1) In this Schedule—
"the Commissioners" means the Commissioners for Her Majesty's Revenue and Customs;
"company" has the same meaning as in the Companies Acts (see section 1(1) of the Companies Act 2006) but does not include a company that is an open-ended investment company (within the meaning of [section 613 of CTA 2010][1]) or an investment trust (within the meaning of [section 1158 of CTA 2010][1]);

"financial year", in relation to a company, has the same meaning as in the Companies Act 2006 (see section 390 of that Act);

"HMRC" means Her Majesty's Revenue and Customs;

"period for filing", in relation to accounts, has the same meaning as in the Companies Acts (see section 442 of the Companies Act 2006);

"relevant body" means a company or other body corporate but does not include a limited liability partnership;

"tribunal" means the First-tier Tribunal or, where determined by or under Tribunal Procedure Rules, the Upper Tribunal.

(2) For the purposes of this Schedule—

(*a*) a relevant body is a member of a group if—

(i) another relevant body is its 51 per cent subsidiary, or

(ii) it is a 51 per cent subsidiary of another relevant body, and

(*b*) two relevant bodies are members of the same group if—

(i) one is a 51 per cent subsidiary of the other, or

(ii) both are 51 per cent subsidiaries of a third relevant body.

(3) [Chapter 3 of Part 24 of CTA 2010][1] (meaning of "51 per cent subsidiary") applies for the purposes of this Schedule as it applies for the purposes of the Corporation Tax Acts (subject to the modification in sub-paragraph (4)).

(4) It applies as if references in that [Chapter][1] to a body corporate were to a relevant body.

Amendments—

[1] In sub-para (1) words in definition of "company" substituted for words "section 468A of ICTA" and "section 842 of ICTA" , in sub-para (3) words substituted for words "Section 838 of ICTA" and in sub-para (4) word substituted for words "section" by CTA 2010 s 1177, Sch 1 paras 706, 721. CTA 2010 has effect for corporation tax purposes for accounting periods ending on or after 1 April 2010, and for income and capital gains tax purposes for the tax year 2010–11 and subsequent tax years.

SCHEDULE 47

AMENDMENT OF INFORMATION AND INSPECTION POWERS

Section 95

1 Schedule 36 to FA 2008 (information and inspection powers) is amended as follows.

2—(1) Paragraph 3 (approval etc of taxpayer notices and third party notices) is amended as follows.

(2) After sub-paragraph (2) insert—

"(2A) An application for approval under this paragraph may be made without notice (except as required under sub-paragraph (3))."

(3) In sub-paragraph (3)(*c*), after "is" insert "to be".

3—(1) Paragraph 5 (power to obtain information and documents about persons whose identity is not known) is amended as follows.

(2) After sub-paragraph (3) insert—

"(3A) An application for approval under this paragraph may be made without notice."

(3) In sub-paragraph (4), for "give its approval for the purpose of" substitute "approve the giving of a notice under".

4 In paragraph 6 (notices), insert at the end—

"(4) A decision of the tribunal under paragraph 3, 4 or 5 is final (despite the provisions of sections 11 and 13 of the Tribunals, Courts and Enforcement Act 2007)."

5—(1) Paragraph 10 (power to inspect business premises etc) is amended as follows.

(2) In sub-paragraph (3), in the definition of "business assets", for ", excluding documents" substitute "(but see sub-paragraph (4))".

(3) After that sub-paragraph insert—

"(4) For the purposes of this Schedule, "business assets" does not include documents, other than—

(*a*) documents that are trading stock for the purposes of Chapter 11A of Part 2 of ITTOIA 2005 (see section 172A of that Act), and

(*b*) documents that are plant for the purposes of Part 2 of CAA 2001."

6—(1) Paragraph 11 (power to inspect premises used in connection with taxable supplies etc) is amended as follows.

(2) In sub-paragraph (1)—

(*a*) in paragraph (*a*), after "supplied" insert "or documents relating to such goods",

(*b*) in paragraph (*b*), after "acquired" insert "or documents relating to such goods", and (*c*) in paragraph (*c*), after "as" insert "or in connection with".

(3) In sub-paragraph (2)(*c*), for "such goods" substitute "the supply of goods under taxable supplies, the acquisition of goods from other member States under taxable acquisitions or fiscal warehousing".

(4) In sub-paragraph (4)—

(*a*) for "sub-paragraph (1)" substitute "this paragraph", and

(*b*) for "in that sub-paragraph" substitute "here".

7 In paragraph 12(5) (carrying out inspections)—

(*a*) for "with the approval of" substitute "in respect of an inspection approved by", and

(*b*) for "it is given with that approval" substitute "the inspection has been so approved".

8—(1) Paragraph 13 (approval of inspections) is amended as follows.

(2) After sub-paragraph (1) insert—

"(1A) An application for approval under this paragraph may be made without notice."

(3) Insert at the end—

"(3) A decision of the tribunal under this paragraph is final (despite the provisions of sections 11 and 13 of the Tribunals, Courts and Enforcement Act 2007)."

9—(1) Paragraph 21 (taxpayer notices) is amended as follows.

(2) In sub-paragraph (6), after "that" (in the first place) insert ", as regards the person,".

(3) In sub-paragraph (7), for "that" (in the third place) substitute "the".

(4) In sub-paragraph (8)—

(*a*) after "repayments" insert "of tax or withholding of income", and

(*b*) after "64(2)" insert "or (2A)".

(5) After sub-paragraph (8) insert—

"(9) In this paragraph, references to the person who made the return are only to that person in the capacity in which the return was made."

10—(1) Paragraph 35 (special cases: groups of undertakings) is amended as follows.

(2) In sub-paragraph (2)—

(*a*) for "paragraph 2" substitute "—

(*a*) paragraph 2(2)", and

(*b*) insert at the end ", and

(*b*) the references in paragraph 3(5) to naming the taxpayer are to making that statement and naming the parent undertaking."

(3) For sub-paragraph (4) substitute—

"(4) Where a third party notice is given to the parent undertaking for the purpose of checking the tax position of more than one subsidiary undertaking—

(*a*) paragraph 2(2) only requires the notice to state this, and

(*b*) the references in paragraph 3(5) to naming the taxpayer are to making that statement.

(4A) In relation to such a notice—

(*a*) in paragraph 3 (approval etc of notices), sub-paragraphs (1) and (3)(*e*) do not apply,

(*b*) paragraph 4(1) (copying third party notices to taxpayer) does not apply,

(*c*) paragraph 21 (restrictions on giving taxpayer notice where taxpayer has made return) applies as if the notice was a taxpayer notice or taxpayer notices given to each subsidiary undertaking (or, if the notice names the subsidiary undertakings to which it relates, to each of those undertakings),

(*d*) paragraph 30(1) (appeal) has effect as if it permitted an appeal on any grounds, and

(*e*) in paragraph 30(2) (no appeal in relation to taxpayer's statutory records), the reference to the taxpayer has effect as if it were a reference to the parent undertaking or any of its subsidiary undertakings."

(4) In sub-paragraph (5), for the words after "the notice" substitute "—

(*a*) sub-paragraphs (3) and (4) of that paragraph (approval of tribunal) have effect as if they permitted, but did not require, the officer to obtain the approval of the tribunal, and

(*b*) paragraph 31 (appeal) has effect as if it permitted an appeal on any grounds, but the parent undertaking may not appeal against a requirement in the notice to produce any document that forms part of the statutory records of the parent undertaking or any of its subsidiary undertakings."

(5) Omit sub-paragraph (6).

11—(1) Paragraph 37 (special cases: partnerships) is amended as follows.
(2) For sub-paragraph (2) substitute—

"(2) Where, in respect of a chargeable period, any of the partners has—

(*a*) made a tax return under section 12AA of TMA 1970 (partnership returns), or

(*b*) made a claim or election in accordance with section 42(6)(*b*) of TMA 1970 (partnership claims and elections),

paragraph 21 (restrictions where taxpayer has made tax return) has effect as if that return, claim or election had been made by each of the partners."

(3) In sub-paragraph (3)—

(*a*) omit "to any person (other than one of the partners)",

(*b*) for "paragraph 2" substitute

"—

(*a*) paragraph 2(2)", and

(*c*) insert at the end

", and

(*b*) the references in paragraph 3(5) to naming the taxpayer are to making that statement and naming the partnership."

(4) In sub-paragraph (4)—

(*a*) after "notice" insert "given to a person other than one of the partners", and

(*b*) in paragraph (*b*), for "each of the partners" substitute "any of the partners in the partnership".

(5) For sub-paragraph (5) substitute—

"(5) In relation to a third party notice given to one of the partners for the purpose of checking the tax position of one or more of the other partners (in their capacity as such)—

(*a*) in paragraph 3 (approval etc of notices), sub-paragraphs (1) and (3)(*e*) do not apply,

(*b*) paragraph 4(1) (copying third party notices to taxpayer) does not apply,

(*c*) paragraph 30(1) (appeal) has effect as if it permitted an appeal on any grounds, and

(*d*) in paragraph 30(2) (no appeal in relation to taxpayer's statutory records), the reference to the taxpayer has effect as if it were a reference to any of the partners in the partnership."

(6) In sub-paragraph (6) for the words after "the notice" substitute

"—

(*a*) sub-paragraphs (3) and (4) of that paragraph (approval of tribunal) have effect as if they permitted, but did not require, the officer to obtain the approval of the tribunal, and

(*b*) paragraph 31 (appeal) has effect as if it permitted an appeal on any grounds, but the partner to whom the notice is given may not appeal against a requirement in the notice to produce any document that forms part of that partner's statutory records."

(7) Omit sub-paragraph (7).

12 (*inserts* FA 2008 Sch 36 paras 37A, 37B)

13—(1) Paragraph 39 (standard penalties) is amended as follows.
(2) In sub-paragraph (2), for "A person to whom this paragraph applies" substitute "The person".
(3) In the heading—

(*a*) omit "*Standard*", and

(*b*) insert at the end "*for failure to comply or obstruction*".

14 In the heading before paragraph 40 (daily default penalties), insert at the end "*for failure to comply or obstruction*".

15 (*inserts* FA 2008 Sch 36 para 40A)

16—(1) Paragraph 41 (power to change amount of penalties) is amended as follows.
(2) In sub-paragraph (1), for "and 40(2)" substitute ", 40(2) and 40A(5)".
(3) In sub-paragraph (2)—

(*a*) after "(1)" insert ", in relation to a specified sum,", and

(*b*) in paragraph (*b*), insert at the end "in relation to that sum".

(4) In sub-paragraph (3)—

(*a*) after "to" insert

"—

(*a*) ", and

(*b*) insert at the end

", or

(*b*) an inaccuracy in any information or document provided to HMRC before that date."

(5) Accordingly, in the heading omit "*standard and daily default*".

17—(1) Paragraph 46 (assessment of penalty) is amended as follows.

(2) In sub-paragraph (1)—

(*a*) for "or 40" substitute ", 40 or 40A",

(*b*) omit "HMRC may",

(*c*) at the beginning of paragraph (*a*), insert "HMRC may", and

(*d*) at the beginning of paragraph (*b*), insert "if they do so, they must".

(3) In sub-paragraph (2), for "within 12 months of the relevant date" substitute "within the period of 12 months beginning with the date on which the person became liable to the penalty, subject to sub-paragraph (3)".

(4) For sub-paragraph (3) substitute—

"(3) In a case involving an information notice against which a person may appeal, an assessment of a penalty under paragraph 39 or 40 must be made within the period of 12 months beginning with the latest of the following—

(*a*) the date on which the person became liable to the penalty,

(*b*) the end of the period in which notice of an appeal against the information notice could have been given, and

(*c*) if notice of such an appeal is given, the date on which the appeal is determined or withdrawn.

(4) An assessment of a penalty under paragraph 40A must be made—

(*a*) within the period of 12 months beginning with the date on which the inaccuracy first came to the attention of an officer of Revenue and Customs, and

(*b*) within the period of 6 years beginning with the date on which the person became liable to the penalty."

(5) Accordingly, in the heading omit "*standard penalty or daily default*".

18—(1) Paragraph 47 (right to appeal) is amended as follows.

(2) In paragraph (*a*), for "or 40" substitute ", 40 or 40A".

(3) Accordingly, in the heading, omit "*standard penalty or daily default*".

19 In the heading before paragraph 48 (procedure on appeal), omit "*standard or daily default*".

20—(1) Paragraph 49 (enforcement) is amended as follows.

(2) In sub-paragraph (1), for "or 40" substitute ", 40 or 40A".

(3) In sub-paragraph (2), for "or 40" substitute ", 40 or 40A".

(4) Accordingly, in the heading, omit "*standard penalty or daily default*".

21—(1) Paragraph 63 (tax) is amended as follows.

(2) In sub-paragraph (3)—

(*a*) omit the "and" at the end of paragraph (*a*), and

(*b*) for the words following paragraph (*b*) substitute ", and

(*c*) amounts listed in sub-paragraph (3A)."

(3) After that sub-paragraph insert—

"(3A) Those amounts are—

(*a*) any amount that is recoverable under paragraph 5(2) of Schedule 11 to VATA 1994 (amounts shown on invoices as VAT), and

(*b*) any amount that is treated as VAT by virtue of regulations under section 54 of VATA 1994 (farmers etc)."

22—(1) Paragraph 64 (tax position) is amended as follows.

(2) In sub-paragraph (1)(*c*), after "with" insert "the person's liability to pay".

(3) After sub-paragraph (2) insert—

"(2A) References in this Schedule to a person's tax position also include, where appropriate, a reference to the person's position as regards the withholding by the person of another person's PAYE income (as defined in section 683 of ITEPA 2003)."

SCHEDULE 48

EXTENSION OF INFORMATION AND INSPECTION POWERS

Section 96

Commencement—Finance Act 2009, Section 96 and Schedule 48 (Appointed Day, Savings and Consequential Amendments) Order, SI 2009/3054 art 2 (day appointed as the day on which the amendments made by s 96 and Sch 48 come into force is 1 April 2010).

1 Schedule 36 to FA 2008 (information and inspection powers) is amended as follows.

Commencement—Finance Act 2009, Section 96 and Schedule 48 (Appointed Day, Savings and Consequential Amendments) Order, SI 2009/3054 art 2 (day appointed as the day on which the amendments made by s 96 and Sch 48 come into force is 1 April 2010).

2 In paragraph 5(4)(*b*) (power to obtain information and documents about persons whose identity is not known), for the words from ", VATA 1994" to the end substitute "or any other enactment relating to UK tax".

Commencement—Finance Act 2009, Section 96 and Schedule 48 (Appointed Day, Savings and Consequential Amendments) Order, SI 2009/3054 art 2 (day appointed as the day on which the amendments made by s 96 and Sch 48 come into force is 1 April 2010).

3 After paragraph 10 insert—

"Power to inspect business premises etc of involved third parties

10A—

(1) An officer of Revenue and Customs may enter business premises of an involved third party (see paragraph 61A) and inspect—

(*a*) the premises,

(*b*) business assets that are on the premises, and

(*c*) relevant documents that are on the premises,

if the inspection is reasonably required by the officer for the purpose of checking the position of any person or class of persons as regards a relevant tax.

(2) The powers under this paragraph may be exercised whether or not the identity of that person is, or the individual identities of those persons are, known to the officer.

(3) The powers under this paragraph do not include power to enter or inspect any part of the premises that is used solely as a dwelling.

(4) In relation to an involved third party, "relevant documents" and "relevant tax" are defined in paragraph 61A."

Commencement—Finance Act 2009, Section 96 and Schedule 48 (Appointed Day, Savings and Consequential Amendments) Order, SI 2009/3054 art 2 (day appointed as the day on which the amendments made by s 96 and Sch 48 come into force is 1 April 2010).

4—(1) Paragraph 12 (carrying out inspections) is amended as follows.

(2) In sub-paragraph (1), for "this Part of this Schedule" substitute "paragraph 10, 10A or 11".

(3) Accordingly, in the heading, insert at the end "*under paragraph 10, 10A or 11*".

Commencement—Finance Act 2009, Section 96 and Schedule 48 (Appointed Day, Savings and Consequential Amendments) Order, SI 2009/3054 art 2 (day appointed as the day on which the amendments made by s 96 and Sch 48 come into force is 1 April 2010).

5 After that paragraph insert—

"Powers to inspect property for valuation etc

12A—

(1) An officer of Revenue and Customs may enter and inspect premises for the purpose of valuing the premises if the valuation is reasonably required for the purpose of checking any person's position as regards income tax or corporation tax.

(2) An officer of Revenue and Customs may enter premises and inspect—

(*a*) the premises, and

(*b*) any other property on the premises,

for the purpose of valuing, measuring or determining the character of the premises or property.

(3) Sub-paragraph (2) only applies if the valuation, measurement or determination is reasonably required for the purpose of checking any person's position as regards—

(*a*) capital gains tax,

(*b*) corporation tax in respect of chargeable gains,

(*c*) inheritance tax,

(*d*) stamp duty land tax, or

(*e*) stamp duty reserve tax.

(4) A person who the officer considers is needed to assist with the valuation, measurement or determination may enter and inspect the premises or property with the officer.

Carrying out inspections under paragraph 12A

12B—

(1) An inspection under paragraph 12A may be carried out only if condition A or B is satisfied.

(2) Condition A is that—

(*a*) the inspection is carried out at a time agreed to by a relevant person, and

(*b*) the relevant person has been given notice in writing of the agreed time of the inspection.

(3) "Relevant person" means—

(*a*) the occupier of the premises, or

(*b*) if the occupier cannot be identified or the premises are vacant, a person who controls the premises.

(4) Condition B is that—

(*a*) the inspection has been approved by the tribunal, and

(*b*) any relevant person specified by the tribunal has been given at least 7 days' notice in writing of the time of the inspection.

(5) A notice under sub-paragraph (4)(*b*) must state the possible consequences of obstructing the officer in the exercise of the power.

(6) If a notice is given under this paragraph in respect of an inspection approved by the tribunal (see paragraph 13), it must state that the inspection has been so approved.

(7) An officer of Revenue and Customs seeking to carry out an inspection under paragraph 12A must produce evidence of authority to carry out the inspection if asked to do so by—

(*a*) the occupier of the premises, or

(*b*) any other person who appears to the officer to be in charge of the premises or property."

Commencement—Finance Act 2009, Section 96 and Schedule 48 (Appointed Day, Savings and Consequential Amendments) Order, SI 2009/3054 art 2 (day appointed as the day on which the amendments made by s 96 and Sch 48 come into force is 1 April 2010).

6—(1) Paragraph 13 (approval of tribunal) is amended as follows.

(2) In sub-paragraph (1), insert at the end "(and for the effect of obtaining such approval see paragraph 39 (penalties))".

(3) In sub-paragraph (1A) (inserted by Schedule 47), insert at the end "(except as required under sub-paragraph (2A))".

(4) In sub-paragraph (2), after "an inspection" insert "under paragraph 10, 10A or 11".

(5) After that sub-paragraph insert—

"(2A) The tribunal may not approve an inspection under paragraph 12A unless—

(*a*) an application for approval is made by, or with the agreement of, an authorised officer of Revenue and Customs,

(*b*) the person whose tax position is the subject of the proposed inspection has been given a reasonable opportunity to make representations to the officer of Revenue and Customs about that inspection,

(*c*) the occupier of the premises has been given a reasonable opportunity to make such representations,

(*d*) the tribunal has been given a summary of any representations made, and

(*e*) the tribunal is satisfied that, in the circumstances, the inspection is justified.

(2B) Paragraph (*c*) of sub-paragraph (2A) does not apply if the tribunal is satisfied that the occupier of the premises cannot be identified."

Commencement—Finance Act 2009, Section 96 and Schedule 48 (Appointed Day, Savings and Consequential Amendments) Order, SI 2009/3054 art 2 (day appointed as the day on which the amendments made by s 96 and Sch 48 come into force is 1 April 2010).

7 In paragraph 17(*b*) (power to record information), after "premises," insert "property, goods,".

Commencement—Finance Act 2009, Section 96 and Schedule 48 (Appointed Day, Savings and Consequential Amendments) Order, SI 2009/3054 art 2 (day appointed as the day on which the amendments made by s 96 and Sch 48 come into force is 1 April 2010).

8—(1) Paragraph 21 (restrictions on giving taxpayer notices) is amended as follows.

(2) In sub-paragraph (7), for "VAT position" substitute "position as regards any tax other than income tax, capital gains tax or corporation tax".

(3) In the heading, insert at the end "*following tax return*".

Commencement—Finance Act 2009, Section 96 and Schedule 48 (Appointed Day, Savings and Consequential Amendments) Order, SI 2009/3054 art 2 (day appointed as the day on which the amendments made by s 96 and Sch 48 come into force is 1 April 2010).

9 After that paragraph insert—

"Taxpayer notices following land transaction return

21A—

(1) Where a person has delivered a land transaction return under section 76 of FA 2003 (returns for purposes of stamp duty land tax) in respect of a transaction, a taxpayer notice may not be given for the purpose of checking that person's stamp duty land tax position in relation to that transaction.

(2) Sub-paragraph (1) does not apply where, or to the extent that, any of conditions A to C is met.

(3) Condition A is that a notice of enquiry has been given in respect of—

(*a*) the return, or

(*b*) a claim (or an amendment of a claim) made by the person in connection with the transaction,

and the enquiry has not been completed.

(4) In sub-paragraph (3) "notice of enquiry" means a notice under paragraph 12 of Schedule 10, or paragraph 7 of Schedule 11A, to FA 2003.

(5) Condition B is that, as regards the person, an officer of Revenue and Customs has reason to suspect that—

(*a*) an amount that ought to have been assessed to stamp duty land tax in respect of the transaction may not have been assessed,

(*b*) an assessment to stamp duty land tax in respect of the transaction may be or have become insufficient, or

(*c*) relief from stamp duty land tax in respect of the transaction may be or have become excessive.

(6) Condition C is that the notice is given for the purpose of obtaining any information or document that is also required for the purpose of checking that person's position as regards a tax other than stamp duty land tax."

Commencement—Finance Act 2009, Section 96 and Schedule 48 (Appointed Day, Savings and Consequential Amendments) Order, SI 2009/3054 art 2 (day appointed as the day on which the amendments made by s 96 and Sch 48 come into force is 1 April 2010).

10 In paragraph 28 (restrictions on inspection of business documents), and in the heading before that paragraph, omit "*business*".

Commencement—Finance Act 2009, Section 96 and Schedule 48 (Appointed Day, Savings and Consequential Amendments) Order, SI 2009/3054 art 2 (day appointed as the day on which the amendments made by s 96 and Sch 48 come into force is 1 April 2010).

11 After paragraph 34 insert—

"Involved third parties

34A—

(1) This paragraph applies to a third party notice or a notice under paragraph 5 if—

(*a*) it is given to an involved third party (see paragraph 61A),

(*b*) it is given for the purpose of checking the position of a person, or a class of persons, as regards the relevant tax, and

(*c*) it refers only to relevant information or relevant documents.

(2) In relation to such a third party notice—

(*a*) paragraph 3(1) (approval etc of third party notices) does not apply,

(*b*) paragraph 4(1) (copying third party notices to taxpayer) does not apply, and

(*c*) paragraph 30(1) (appeal) has effect as if it permitted an appeal on any grounds.

(3) In relation to such a notice under paragraph 5—

(*a*) sub-paragraphs (3) and (4) of that paragraph (approval of tribunal) have effect as if they permitted, but did not require, an authorised officer of Revenue and Customs to obtain the approval of the tribunal, and

(*b*) paragraph 31 (appeal) has effect as if it permitted an appeal on any grounds.

(4) The involved third party may not appeal against a requirement in the notice to provide any information, or produce any document, that forms part of the involved third party's statutory records.

(5) In relation to an involved third party, "relevant documents", "relevant information" and "relevant tax" are defined in paragraph 61A.

Registered pension schemes etc

34B—

(1) This paragraph applies to a third party notice or a notice under paragraph 5 if it refers only to information or documents that relate to any pensions matter.

(2) "Pensions matter" means any matter relating to—

(*a*) a registered pension scheme,

(*b*) an annuity purchased with sums or assets held for the purposes of a registered pension scheme or a pre-2006 pension scheme, or

(*c*) an employer-financed retirement benefits scheme.

(3) In relation to such a third party notice—

(*a*) paragraph 3(1) (approval etc of third party notices) does not apply,

(*b*) paragraph 4(1) (copying third party notices to taxpayer) does not apply, and

(*c*) paragraph 30(1) (appeal) has effect as if it permitted an appeal on any grounds.

(4) In relation to such a notice under paragraph 5—

(*a*) sub-paragraphs (3) and (4) of that paragraph (approval of tribunal) have effect as if they permitted, but did not require, an authorised officer of Revenue and Customs to obtain the approval of the tribunal, and

(*b*) paragraph 31 (appeal) has effect as if it permitted an appeal on any grounds.

(5) A person may not appeal against a requirement in the notice to provide any information, or produce any document, that forms part of any person's statutory records.

(6) Where the notice relates to a matter within sub-paragraph (2)(*a*) or (*b*), the officer of Revenue and Customs who gives the notice must give a copy of the notice to the scheme administrator in relation to the pension scheme.

(7) Where the notice relates to a matter within sub-paragraph (2)(*c*), the officer of Revenue and Customs who gives the notice must give a copy of the notice to the responsible person in relation to the employer-financed retirement benefits scheme.

(8) Sub-paragraphs (6) and (7) do not apply if the notice is given to a person who, in relation to the scheme or annuity to which the notice relates, is a prescribed description of person.

Registered pension schemes etc: interpretation

34C

In paragraph 34B—

"employer-financed retirement benefits scheme" has the same meaning as in Chapter 2 of Part 6 of ITEPA 2003 (see sections 393A and 393B of that Act);

"pension scheme" has the same meaning as in Part 4 of FA 2004;

"pre-2006 pension scheme" means a scheme that, at or in respect of any time before 6 April 2006, was—

(*a*) a retirement benefits scheme approved for the purposes of Chapter 1 of Part 14 of ICTA,

(*b*) a former approved superannuation fund (as defined in paragraph 1(3) of Schedule 36 to FA 2004),

(*c*) a relevant statutory scheme (as defined in section 611A of ICTA) or a pension scheme treated as if it were such a scheme, or

(*d*) a personal pension scheme approved under Chapter 4 of Part 14 of ICTA;

"prescribed" means prescribed by regulations made by the Commissioners;

"registered pension scheme" means a pension scheme that is or has been a registered pension scheme within the meaning of Part 4 of FA 2004 or in relation to which an application for registration under that Part of that Act has been made;

"responsible person", in relation to an employer-financed retirement benefits scheme, has the same meaning as in Chapter 2 of Part 6 of ITEPA 2003 (see section 399A of that Act);

"scheme administrator", in relation to a pension scheme, has the same meaning as in Part 4 of FA 2004 (see section 270 of that Act)."

Commencement—Finance Act 2009, Section 96 and Schedule 48 (Appointed Day, Savings and Consequential Amendments) Order, SI 2009/3054 art 2 (day appointed as the day on which the amendments made by s 96 and Sch 48 come into force is 1 April 2010).

12 In paragraph 35 (special cases: groups of undertakings), in sub-paragraph (4A)(*c*) (inserted by Schedule 47)—

(*a*) for "paragraph 21" substitute "paragraphs 21 and 21A", and

(*b*) for "applies" substitute "apply".

Commencement—Finance Act 2009, Section 96 and Schedule 48 (Appointed Day, Savings and Consequential Amendments) Order, SI 2009/3054 art 2 (day appointed as the day on which the amendments made by s 96 and Sch 48 come into force is 1 April 2010).

13 In paragraph 37 (special cases: partnerships), after sub-paragraph (2) insert—

"(2A) Where, in respect of a transaction entered into as purchaser by or on behalf of the members of the partnership, any of the partners has—

(*a*) delivered a land transaction return under Part 4 of FA 2003 (stamp duty land tax), or

(*b*) made a claim under that Part of that Act, paragraph 21A (restrictions where taxpayer has delivered land transaction return) has effect as if that return had been delivered, or that claim had been made, by each of the partners."

Commencement—Finance Act 2009, Section 96 and Schedule 48 (Appointed Day, Savings and Consequential Amendments) Order, SI 2009/3054 art 2 (day appointed as the day on which the amendments made by s 96 and Sch 48 come into force is 1 April 2010).

14 After paragraph 61 insert—

"Involved third parties

61A—

(1) In this Schedule, "involved third party" means a person described in the first column of the Table below.

(2) In this Schedule, in relation to an involved third party, "relevant information", "relevant document" and "relevant tax" have the meaning given in the corresponding entries in that Table.

	Involved third party	*Relevant information and relevant documents*	*Relevant tax*
1	A body approved by an officer of Revenue and Customs for the purpose of paying donations within the meaning of Part 12 of ITEPA 2003 (donations to charity: payroll giving) (see section 714 of that Act)	Information and documents relating to the donations	Income tax
2	A plan manager (see section 696 of ITTOIA 2005 (managers of individual investment plans))	Information and documents relating to the plan, including investments which are or have been held under the plan	Income tax
3	An account provider in relation to a child trust fund (as defined in section 3 of the Child Trust Funds Act 2004)	Information and documents relating to the fund, including investments which are or have been held under the fund	Income tax
4	A person who is or has been registered as a managing agent at Lloyd's in relation to a syndicate of underwriting members of Lloyd's	Information and documents relating to, and to the activities of, the syndicate	Income tax Capital gains tax Corporation tax
5	A person involved (in any capacity) in an insurance business (as defined for the purposes of Part 3 of FA 1994)	Information and documents relating to contracts of insurance entered into in the course of the business	Insurance premium tax
6	A person who makes arrangements for persons to enter into contracts of insurance	Information and documents relating to the contracts	Insurance premium tax
7	A person who—	Information and documents relating to the contracts	Insurance premium tax

	(*a*) is concerned in a business that is not an insurance business (as defined for the purposes of Part 3 of FA 1994), and		
	(*b*) has been involved in the entry into a contract of insurance providing cover for any matter associated with that business		
8	A person who, in relation to a charge to stamp duty reserve tax on an agreement, transfer, issue, appropriation or surrender, is an accountable person (as defined in regulation 2 of the Stamp Duty Reserve Tax Regulations SI 1986/1711 (as amended from time to time))	Information and documents relating to the agreement, transfer, issue, appropriation or surrender	Stamp duty reserve tax
9	A responsible person in relation to an oil field (as defined for the purposes of Part 1 of OTA 1975)	Information and documents relating to the oil field	Petroleum revenue tax
10	A person involved (in any capacity) in subjecting aggregate to exploitation in the United Kingdom (as defined for the purposes of Part 2 of FA 2001) or in connected activities	Information and documents relating to matters in which the person is or has been involved	Aggregates levy
11	A person involved (in any capacity) in making or receiving taxable commodities (as defined for the purposes of Schedule 6 to FA 2000) or in connected activities	Information and documents relating to matters in which the person is or has been involved	Climate change levy
12	A person involved (in any capacity) with any landfill disposal (as defined for the purposes of Part 3 of FA 1996)	Information and documents relating to the disposal	Landfill tax".

Commencement—Finance Act 2009, Section 96 and Schedule 48 (Appointed Day, Savings and Consequential Amendments) Order, SI 2009/3054 art 2 (day appointed as the day on which the amendments made by s 96 and Sch 48 come into force is 1 April 2010).

15— (1) Paragraph 62 (meaning of "statutory records") is amended as follows.

(2) In sub-paragraph (1), for paragraph (*b*) substitute—

"(*b*) any other enactment relating to a tax,".

(3) In sub-paragraph (2)(*b*), for "VATA 1994 or any other enactment relating to value added tax" substitute "any other enactment relating to a tax".

Commencement—Finance Act 2009, Section 96 and Schedule 48 (Appointed Day, Savings and Consequential Amendments) Order, SI 2009/3054 art 2 (day appointed as the day on which the amendments made by s 96 and Sch 48 come into force is 1 April 2010).

SCHEDULE 49

POWERS TO OBTAIN CONTACT DETAILS FOR DEBTORS

Section 97

Requirement for contact details for debtor

1—(1) This Schedule applies where—

(*a*) a sum is payable by a person ("the debtor") to the Commissioners under or by virtue of an enactment or under a contract settlement,

(*b*) an officer of Revenue and Customs reasonably requires contact details for the debtor for the purpose of collecting that sum,

(*c*) the officer has reasonable grounds to believe that a person ("the third party") has any such details, and

(*d*) the condition in sub-paragraph (2) is met.

(2) That condition is that—

(*a*) the third party is a company, a local authority or a local authority association, or (*b*) the officer has reasonable grounds to believe that the third party obtained the details in the course of carrying on a business.

(3) This Schedule does not apply if—

(*a*) the third party is a charity and obtained the details in the course of providing services free of charge, or

(*b*) the third party is not a charity but obtained the details in the course of providing services on behalf of a charity that are free of charge to the recipient of the service.

Power to obtain details

2—(1) An officer of Revenue and Customs may by notice in writing require the third party to provide the details.

(2) The notice must name the debtor.

Complying with notices

3 If a notice is given to the third party under this Schedule, the third party must provide the details—

(*a*) within such period, and

(*b*) at such time, by such means and in such form (if any), as is reasonably specified or described in the notice.

Right to appeal

4—(1) The third party may appeal against the notice or any requirement in the notice on the ground that it would be unduly onerous to comply with the notice or requirement.

(2) Paragraph 32 of Schedule 36 to FA 2008 (procedure on appeal to tribunal) applies to an appeal under this paragraph as it applies to an appeal relating to a notice under that Schedule.

Penalty

5—(1) This paragraph applies if the third party fails to comply with the notice.

(2) The third party is liable to a penalty of £300.

(3) Paragraphs 44 to 49 and 52 of Schedule 36 to FA 2008 (assessment and enforcement of penalties etc) apply in relation to a penalty under this paragraph as they apply in relation to a penalty under paragraph 39(1)(*a*) of that Schedule (and references in those provisions to an information notice include a notice under this Schedule).

Power to change amount of penalty

6—(1) If it appears to the Treasury that there has been a change in the value of money since the last relevant date, they may by regulations substitute for the sum for the time being specified in paragraph 5 such other sum as appears to them to be justified by the change.

(2) In sub-paragraph (1), "relevant date" means—

(*a*) the date on which this Act is passed, and

(*b*) each date on which the power conferred by that sub-paragraph has been exercised.

(3) Regulations under this paragraph do not apply to any failure which began before the date on which they come into force.

(4) Regulations made by the Treasury under this paragraph are to be made by statutory instrument.

(5) A statutory instrument containing regulations under this paragraph is subject to annulment in pursuance of a resolution of the House of Commons.

Application of provisions of TMA 1970

7 Subject to the provisions of this Schedule, the following provisions of TMA 1970 apply for the purposes of this Schedule as they apply for the purposes of the Taxes Acts—

(*a*) section 108 (responsibility of company officers),

(*b*) section 114 (want of form), and

(*c*) section 115 (delivery and service of documents).

General interpretation

8 In this Schedule—

"business" includes—

(*a*) a profession, and

(*b*) a property business;

. . . [1]

"the Commissioners" means the Commissioners for Her Majesty's Revenue and Customs;

"contact details", in relation to a person, means the person's address and any other information about how the person may be contacted;

"contract settlement" means an agreement made in connection with any person's liability to make a payment to the Commissioners under or by virtue of an enactment;

"enactment" includes subordinate legislation (within the meaning of the Interpretation Act 1978);

"local authority" has the meaning given in section 999 of ITA 2007;

"local authority association" has the meaning given in section 1000 of that Act;

"property business" has the same meaning as in ITTOIA 2005 (see section 263(6) of that Act).

Amendments—[1] Definition of "charity" repealed by FA 2010 s 30, Sch 6 para 26 with effect from 1 April 2012 (SI 2012/736 art 20).

SCHEDULE 53

LATE PAYMENT INTEREST

Section 101

PART 2
SPECIAL PROVISION: LATE PAYMENT INTEREST START DATE

Amendments and discovery assessments etc

3—(1) This paragraph applies to any amount which is due and payable as a result of—

(*a*) an amendment or correction to an assessment or self-assessment ("assessment A"),

(*b*) an assessment made by HMRC in place of or in addition to an assessment ("assessment A") which was made by a taxpayer, or

(*c*) an assessment made by HMRC in place of an assessment ("assessment A") which ought to have been made by a taxpayer.

(2) The late payment interest start date in respect of that amount is the date which would have been the late payment interest start date if—

(*a*) assessment A had been complete and accurate and had been made on the date (if any) by which it was required to be made, and

(*b*) accordingly, the amount had been due and payable as a result of assessment A.

(3) In the case of a person ("P") who failed to give notice [in accordance with a requirement][1] under section 7 of TMA 1970 (notice of liability to tax) [that arose by virtue of subsection (1A) of that section][1], the reference in sub-paragraph (1)(*c*) to an assessment which ought to have been made by P is a reference to the assessment which P would have been required to make if an officer of Revenue and Customs had given notice under section 8 of that Act.

[(3A) In the case of a person ("P") who failed to give notice in accordance with a requirement under section 7 of TMA 1970 that arose by virtue of subsection (1B) of that section, the reference in subparagraph (1)(*c*) to an assessment which ought to have been made by P is a reference to the assessment which P would have been required to make if no notice relating to the year of assessment concerned had been withdrawn under section 8B of that Act.][1]

(4) In this paragraph "assessment" means any assessment or determination (however described) of any amount due and payable to HMRC.

Amendments—[1] In sub-para (3) words substituted for words "as required" and words inserted, and sub-para (3A) inserted, by FA 2013 s 233, Sch 51 paras 1, 7 with effect in relation to a return—

(a) under TMA 1970 s 12AA for a partnership which includes one or more companies, for a relevant period beginning on or after 6 April 2012; and

(b) under TMA 1970 s 12AA for any other partnership, or a return under TMA 1970 s 8 or s 8A, for a year of assessment beginning on or after 6 April 2012.

A "relevant period" means a period in respect of which a return is required: FA 2013 Sch 51 para 9(2).

VAT due from persons not registered as required

10—(1) This paragraph applies where an amount of value added tax is due from a person ("P") in respect of a period during which P was liable to be registered under VATA 1994 but was not registered.

(2) The late payment interest start date in respect of the amount is the date which would have been the late payment interest date in respect of that amount if P had become registered when P had first become liable to be so.

Unauthorised VAT invoices

11—(1) This paragraph applies where an unauthorised person issues an invoice showing an amount as being value added tax or as including an amount attributable to value added tax.

(2) The late payment interest start date in respect of the amount which is shown as being value added tax, or which is to be taken as representing value added tax, is the date of the invoice.
(3) In this paragraph "unauthorised person" has the meaning given in paragraph 2 of Schedule 41 to FA 2008.

Death of taxpayer

12—(1) This paragraph applies if—
(*a*) a person chargeable to an amount of revenue dies before the amount becomes due and payable, and
(*b*) the executor or administrator is unable to pay the amount before obtaining probate or letters of administration or (in Scotland) the executor is unable to pay the amount before obtaining confirmation.
(2) The late payment interest start date in respect of that amount is the later of the following—
(*a*) the date which would be the late payment interest start date apart from this paragraph, and
(*b*) the day after the end of the period of 30 days beginning with the grant of probate or letters of administration or (in Scotland) the grant of confirmation.

SCHEDULE 55
PENALTY FOR FAILURE TO MAKE RETURNS ETC

Section 106

Commencement—Finance Act 2009, Schedules 55 and 56 (Income Tax Self Assessment and Pension Schemes) (Appointed Days and Consequential and Savings Provisions) Order, SI 2011/702 art 2 (appointed day for the coming into force of Sch 55 is 6 April 2011 in relation to a return or other document which is required to be made or delivered to HMRC in relation to the tax year 2010–11 or any subsequent tax year and falls within item 1, 2 or 3 of the Table in para 1).

Finance (No 3) Act 2010, Schedule 10 and the Finance Act 2009, Schedule 55 and Sections 101 to 103 (Appointed Day, etc) (Construction Industry Scheme) Order, SI 2011/2391 (the day appointed for the coming into force of the following paras of Sch 55 is 6 October 2011, with effect only in relation to a return within item 6 of Sch 55 para 1(5), and for which the filing date for the purposes of Sch 55 is after 19 October 2011—
– para 1 (but only in relation to item 6 in the Table in para 1(5);
– paras 7–13; and
– 14–24, 26, and 27(1)–(4) but only as relevant to paras 7–13).

FA 2013 Sch 34 para 7(2) (Sch 55, as amended by FA 2013 Sch 34 para 7(1), is taken to have come into force for the purposes of annual tax on enveloped dwellings on 17 July 2013).

Finance Act 2009, Schedule 55 (Penalties for failure to make returns) (Appointed Days and Consequential Provision) Order, SI 2014/2395 (appoints various days for the coming into force of Sch 55 in relation to a return falling within item 4 of the Table in para 1). The effect of SI 2014/2395, along with SI 2014/2396, is to bring into force the penalties for late returns of in-year PAYE information under the real time information regime with effect from 6 October 2014 for existing large RTI employers (50 or more employees), and 6 March 2015 for remaining employers.

Finance Act 2009, Schedules 55 and 56 and Sections 101 and 102 (Stamp Duty Reserve Tax) (Appointed Days, Consequential and Transitional Provision) Order, SI 2014/3269 art 2 (the day appointed for the coming into force of Sch 55 is 1 January 2015 in relation to a charge to tax which is specified in item 11 of the Table in para 1 (SDRT)).

FA 2015 Sch 7 para 59 (Sch 55, as amended by FA 2015 Sch 7 para 59(2), is taken to have come into force for the purposes of NRCGT returns on 26 March 2015).

Cross-references—See FA 2014 ss 208–214, Sch 30 (follower notices: penalties).

SSCBA 1992 s 11A (this Schedule applies with the necessary modifications, in relation to Class 2 contributions under SSCBA 1992 s 11(2) as if those contributions were income tax chargeable under ITTOIA 2005 Pt 2 Ch 2 in respect of profits of a trade, profession or vocation which is not carried on wholly outside the United Kingdom).

Penalty for failure to make returns etc

1—(1) A penalty is payable by a person ("P") where P fails to make or deliver a return, or to deliver any other document, specified in the Table below on or before the filing date.
(2) Paragraphs 2 to 13 set out—
(*a*) the circumstances in which a penalty is payable, and
(*b*) subject to paragraphs 14 to 17, the amount of the penalty.
(3) If P's failure falls within more than one paragraph of this Schedule, P is liable to a penalty under each of those paragraphs (but this is subject to paragraph 17(3)).
(4) In this Schedule—

"filing date", in relation to a return or other document, means the date by which it is required to be made or delivered to HMRC;

"penalty date", in relation to a return or other document [falling within any of items 1 to 3 and 5 to 13 in the Table][3], means the date on which a penalty is first payable for failing to make or deliver it (that is to say, the day after the filing date).

[(4A) The Treasury may by order make such amendments to item 4 in the Table as they think fit in consequence of any amendment, revocation or re-enactment of the regulations mentioned in that item.][3]

(5) In the provisions of this Schedule which follow the Table—

(*a*) any reference to a return includes a reference to any other document specified in the Table, and

(*b*) any reference to making a return includes a reference to delivering a return or to delivering any such document.

	Tax to which return etc relates	*Return or other document*
1	Income tax or capital gains tax	(a) Return under section 8(1)(a) of TMA 1970 (b) Accounts, statement or document required under section 8(1)(b) of TMA 1970
2	Income tax or capital gains tax	(a) Return under section 8A(1)(a) of TMA 1970 (b) Accounts, statement or document required under section 8A(1)(b) of TMA 1970
[2A	Capital gains tax	NRCGT return under section 12ZB of TMA 1970][4]
3	Income tax or corporation tax	(a) Return under section 12AA(2)(a) or (3)(a) of TMA 1970 (b) Accounts, statement or document required under section 12AA(2)(b) or (3)(b) of TMA 1970
4	Income tax	[Return under any of the following provisions of the Income Tax (PAYE) Regulations 2003 (SI 2003/2682)— (a) regulation 67B (real time returns) (b) regulation 67D (exceptions to regulation 67B)][3]
5	Income tax	Return under section 254 of FA 2004 (pension schemes)
6	Deductions on account of tax under Chapter 3 of Part 3 of FA 2004 (construction industry scheme)	Return under regulations under section 70 of FA 2004
7	Corporation tax	Company tax return under paragraph 3 of Schedule 18 to FA 1998
8	Inheritance tax	Account under section 216 or 217 of IHTA 1984
9	Stamp duty land tax	Land transaction return under section 76 of FA 2003 or further return under section 81 of that Act
10	Stamp duty land tax	Return under paragraph 3, 4 or 8 of Schedule 17A to FA 2003
11	Stamp duty reserve tax	Notice of charge to tax under regulations under section 98 of FA 1986
[11A	Annual tax on enveloped dwellings	Annual tax on enveloped dwellings return under section 157 of FA 2013
11B	Annual tax on enveloped dwellings	Return of adjusted chargeable amount under section 158 of FA 2013][2]
12	Petroleum revenue tax	Return under paragraph 2 of Schedule 2 to OTA 1975
13	Petroleum revenue tax	Statement under section 1(1)(a) of PRTA 1980
[20A	Excise duties	Return under regulations under section 60A of the Customs and Excise Management Act 1979][5]
[29	Machine games duty	Return under regulations under paragraph 18 of Schedule 24 to FA 2012][1]

Commencement—Finance Act 2009, Schedules 55 and 56 (Income Tax Self Assessment and Pension Schemes) (Appointed Days and Consequential and Savings Provisions) Order, SI 2011/702 art 2 (appointed day for the coming into force of Sch 55 is

6 April 2011 in relation to a return or other document which is required to be made or delivered to HMRC in relation to the tax year 2010–11 or any subsequent tax year and falls within item 1, 2 or 3 of the Table in para 1).

Finance (No 3) Act 2010, Schedule 10 and the Finance Act 2009, Schedule 55 and Sections 101 to 103 (Appointed Day, etc) (Construction Industry Scheme) Order, SI 2011/2391 (the day appointed for the coming into force of the following paras of Sch 55 is 6 October 2011, with effect only in relation to a return within item 6 of Sch 55 para 1(5), and for which the filing date for the purposes of Sch 55 is after 19 October 2011—

- para 1 (but only in relation to item 6 in the Table in para 1(5);
- paras 7–13; and
- 14–24, 26, and 27(1)–(4) but only as relevant to paras 7–13).

Finance Act 2009, Schedule 55 (Penalties for failure to make returns) (Appointed Days and Consequential Provision) Order, SI 2014/2395 provides dates for the coming into force of Sch 55 in relation to returns falling within item 4 of the table (PAYE returns), as follows—

- **11 September 2014:** powers to make regulations in relation to quanta of RTI late-filing penalties in para 6C(5), (7), (8), (9), (11) (see also SI 2014/2396).
- **6 October 2014:** provisions of Sch 55 relating to failures to make returns under the PAYE Regulations (SI 2003/2682) regs 67B and 67D where the employer is a large existing employer (an employer which as at 6 October 2014 employs at least 50 employees). Affected returns are those required to be made or delivered to HMRC on or after 6 October 2014.
- **6 March 2015:** provisions of Sch 55 relating to failures to make returns under regs 67B and 67D where the employer is a small existing employer (an employer which as at 6 October 2014 employs no more than 49 employees) or is a new employer. Affected returns are those required to be made or delivered to HMRC on or after 6 March 2015.

Modifications—FA 2009 Sch 55 has effect as if a bank payroll tax return were specified in the Table in this para (and bank payroll tax were specified in relation to it) (FA 2010 s 22, Sch 1 para 38(1)(*a*)).

Amendments—

[1] Item 29 inserted by FA 2012 s 191, Sch 24 para 31 with effect in relation to the playing of machine games on or after 1 February 2013 (and Schs 55, 56, as amended by FA 2012 Sch 24 Part 1, are taken to have come into force for the purposes of machine games duty on that date).

[2] In table, entries inserted by FA 2013 s 164, Sch 34 para 7 with effect from 17 July 2013. Note that Sch 55 is taken to have come into force for the purposes of annual tax on enveloped dwellings on 17 July 2013 (FA 2013 Sch 34 para 7(2)).

[3] In sub-para (4), in definition of "penalty date" words inserted, sub-para (4A) inserted, and in Table, in item 4, words in the third column substituted, by FA 2013 s 230, Sch 50 paras 2–4, with effect for the tax year 2014–15 and subsequent tax years in relation to failures to make returns with a filing date (as defined in FA 2009 Sch 55 para 1(4)) on or after 6 April 2014.

[4] In table, entry inserted by FA 2015 s 37, Sch 7 para 59 with effect for the purposes of NRCGT returns from 26 March 2015.

[5] In Table, item 20A inserted by FA 2014 s 101, Sch 21 para 7 with effect from 1 April 2015 (by virtue of SI 2015/812 art 2).

Prospective amendments—In sub-para (2), figure"13J" to be substituted for figure "13", in sub-para (4), in the definition of "filing date" at the end, words "(or, in the case of a return mentioned in item 7AA or 7AB of the Table, to the tax authorities to whom the return is required to be delivered)" to be inserted, and in the table, entries to be inserted after item 7, by F(No 3)A 2010 s 26, Sch 10 paras 1, 2 (as amended by FA 2014 s 103, Sch 22 para 21) with effect from a day to be appointed by Treasury order. Note that entries 23, 24 and 28 are amended by FA 2014 s 196, Sch 28 paras 28, 29 with effect from a date to be appointed). Entries as inserted to read as follows—

"7A	Value added tax	Return under regulations under paragraph 2 of Schedule 11 to VATA 1994
7AA	Value added tax	Relevant non-UK return (as defined in paragraph 20(3) of Schedule 3BA to VATA 1994)
7AB	Value added tax	Relevant special scheme return (as defined in paragraph 16(3) of Schedule 3B to VATA 1994)
7B	Insurance premium tax	Return under regulations under section 54 of FA 1994".

and

"14	Aggregates levy	Return under regulations under section 25 of FA 2001
15	Climate change levy	Return under regulations under paragraph 41 of Schedule 6 to FA 2000
16	Landfill tax	Return under regulations under section 49 of FA 1996
17	Air passenger duty	Return under regulations under section 38 of FA 1994
18	Alcoholic liquor duties	Return under regulations under section 13, 49, 56 or 62 of ALDA 1979
19	Tobacco products duty	Return under regulations under section 7 of TPDA 1979
20	Hydrocarbon oil duties	Return under regulations under section 21 of HODA 1979

21	Excise duties	Return under regulations under section 93 of the Customs and Excise Management Act 1979
22	Excise duties	Return under regulations under section 100G or 100H of the Customs and Excise Management Act 1979
23	General betting duty	Return under regulations under [section 166 of FA 2014]
24	Pool betting duty	Return under regulations under [section 166 of FA 2014]
25	Bingo duty	Return under regulations under paragraph 9 of Schedule 3 to BGDA 1981
26	Lottery duty	Return under regulations under section 28(2) of FA 1993
27	Gaming duty	Return under directions under paragraph 10 of Schedule 1 to FA 1997
28	Remote gaming duty	Return under regulations under [166 of FA 2014]".

Amount of penalty: occasional returns and annual returns

2 Paragraphs 3 to 6 apply in the case of a return falling within any of items [1 to 3, 5][1] and 7 to 13 in the Table.

Commencement Finance Act 2009, Schedules 55 and 56 (Income Tax Self Assessment and Pension Schemes) (Appointed Days and Consequential and Savings Provisions) Order, SI 2011/702 art 2 (appointed day for the coming into force of Sch 55 is 6 April 2011 in relation to a return or other document which is required to be made or delivered to HMRC in relation to the tax year 2010–11 or any subsequent tax year and falls within item 1, 2 or 3 of the Table in para 1).

Modifications—FA 2009 Sch 55 has effect as if the reference in this para to a return falling within certain items in the Table included a reference to a bank payroll tax return (FA 2010 s 22, Sch 1 para 38(1)(*b*)).

Amendments—

[1] Words substituted by FA 2013 s 230, Sch 50 paras 2, 5, with effect for the tax year 2014–15 and subsequent tax years in relation to failures to make returns with a filing date (as defined in FA 2009 Sch 55 para 1(4)) on or after 6 April 2014.

Prospective amendments—This para and preceding cross-head to be substituted by F(No 3)A 2010 s 26, Sch 10 paras 1, 3 with effect from a day to be appointed by Treasury order. This para as substituted to read—

"*Amount of penalty: occasional returns and returns for periods of 6 months or more*

(1) Paragraphs 3 to 6 apply in the case of—

a return falling within any of items 1 to 5, 7 and 8 to 13 in the Table,

a return falling within any of items 7A, 7B and 14 to 28 which relates to a period of 6 months or more, and

a return falling within item 7A which relates to a transitional period for the purposes of the annual accounting scheme.

(2) In sub-paragraph (1)(*c*), a transitional period for the purposes of the annual accounting scheme is a prescribed accounting period (within the meaning of section 25(1) of VATA 1994) which—

ends on the day immediately preceding the date indicated by the Commissioners for Her Majesty's Revenue and Customs in a notification of authorisation under regulation 50 of the Value Added Tax Regulations 1995 (SI 1995/2518) (admission to annual accounting scheme), or

begins on the day immediately following the end of the last period of 12 months for which such an authorisation has effect.".

In sub-para (1)(*b*) (as substituted), "29" to be substituted for "28", by FA 2012 s 191, Sch 24 para 32(*a*), with effect in relation to the playing of machine games on or after 1 February 2013 (and Schs 55, 56, as amended by FA 2012 Sch 24 Part 1, are taken to have come into force for the purposes of machine games duty on that date).

3 P is liable to a penalty under this paragraph of £100.

Commencement—Finance Act 2009, Schedules 55 and 56 (Income Tax Self Assessment and Pension Schemes) (Appointed Days and Consequential and Savings Provisions) Order, SI 2011/702 art 2 (appointed day for the coming into force of Sch 55 is 6 April 2011 in relation to a return or other document which is required to be made or delivered to HMRC in relation to the tax year 2010–11 or any subsequent tax year and falls within item 1, 2 or 3 of the Table in para 1).

4— (1) P is liable to a penalty under this paragraph if (and only if)—

(*a*) P's failure continues after the end of the period of 3 months beginning with the penalty date,

(*b*) HMRC decide that such a penalty should be payable, and

(*c*) HMRC give notice to P specifying the date from which the penalty is payable.

(2) The penalty under this paragraph is £10 for each day that the failure continues during the period of 90 days beginning with the date specified in the notice given under sub-paragraph (1)(*c*).

(3) The date specified in the notice under sub-paragraph (1)(*c*)—

(*a*) may be earlier than the date on which the notice is given, but (*b*) may not be earlier than the end of the period mentioned in sub-paragraph (1)(*a*).

Commencement—Finance Act 2009, Schedules 55 and 56 (Income Tax Self Assessment and Pension Schemes) (Appointed Days and Consequential and Savings Provisions) Order, SI 2011/702 art 2 (appointed day for the coming into force of Sch 55 is 6 April 2011 in relation to a return or other document which is required to be made or delivered to HMRC in relation to the tax year 2010–11 or any subsequent tax year and falls within item 1, 2 or 3 of the Table in para 1).

5—(1) P is liable to a penalty under this paragraph if (and only if) P's failure continues after the end of the period of 6 months beginning with the penalty date.

(2) The penalty under this paragraph is the greater of—

(*a*) 5% of any liability to tax which would have been shown in the return in question, and

(*b*) £300.

Commencement—Finance Act 2009, Schedules 55 and 56 (Income Tax Self Assessment and Pension Schemes) (Appointed Days and Consequential and Savings Provisions) Order, SI 2011/702 art 2 (appointed day for the coming into force of Sch 55 is 6 April 2011 in relation to a return or other document which is required to be made or delivered to HMRC in relation to the tax year 2010–11 or any subsequent tax year and falls within item 1, 2 or 3 of the Table in para 1).

Cross references—FA 2014 s 212 (application of this paragraph in calculation of aggregate penalties for failure to take corrective action in response to a follower notice).

6—(1) P is liable to a penalty under this paragraph if (and only if) P's failure continues after the end of the period of 12 months beginning with the penalty date.

(2) Where, by failing to make the return, P [deliberately][1] withholds information which would enable or assist HMRC to assess P's liability to tax, the penalty under this paragraph is determined in accordance with sub-paragraphs (3) and (4).

(3) If the withholding of the information is deliberate and concealed, the penalty is the greater of—

(*a*) [the relevant percentage][2] of any liability to tax which would have been shown in the return in question, and

(*b*) £300.

[(3A) For the purposes of sub-paragraph (3)(*a*), the relevant percentage is—

(*a*) for the withholding of category 1 information, 100%,

(*b*) for the withholding of category 2 information, 150%, and

(*c*) for the withholding of category 3 information, 200%.][2]

(4) If the withholding of the information is deliberate but not concealed, the penalty is the greater of—

(*a*) [the relevant percentage][2] of any liability to tax which would have been shown in the return in question, and

(*b*) £300.

[(4A) For the purposes of sub-paragraph (4)(*a*), the relevant percentage is—

(*a*) for the withholding of category 1 information, 70%,

(*b*) for the withholding of category 2 information, 105%, and

(*c*) for the withholding of category 3 information, 140%.][2]

(5) In [any case not falling within sub-paragraph (2)][1], the penalty under this paragraph is the greater of—

(*a*) 5% of any liability to tax which would have been shown in the return in question, and

(*b*) £300.

[(6) Paragraph 6A explains the 3 categories of information.][2]

Commencement—Finance Act 2009, Schedules 55 and 56 (Income Tax Self Assessment and Pension Schemes) (Appointed Days and Consequential and Savings Provisions) Order, SI 2011/702 art 2 (appointed day for the coming into force of Sch 55 is 6 April 2011 in relation to a return or other document which is required to be made or delivered to HMRC in relation to the tax year 2010–11 or any subsequent tax year and falls within item 1, 2 or 3 of the Table in para 1).

Cross references—FA 2014 s 212 (application of this paragraph in calculation of aggregate penalties for failure to take corrective action in response to a follower notice).

FA 2015 Sch 21 (penalties in connection with offshore asset moves).

Amendments—[1] In sub-para (2) word "deliberately" inserted, and in sub-para (5) words substituted for words "any other case", by F(No 3)A 2010 s 26, Sch 10 paras 1, 4 with effect as follows (by virtue of SI 2011/703)—

– from 6 April 2011 in relation to a return or other document which is required to be made or delivered to HMRC in relation to the tax year 2010–11 or any subsequent tax year, and falls within item 1, 2 or 3 of the Table in Sch 55 para 1; and

– from 1 April 2011 in relation to a return under FA 2004 s 254 to be made in respect of a return period ending on or after 31 March 2011.

[2] In sub-para (3)(*a*), words substituted for figure "100%", in sub-para (4)(*a*), words substituted for figure "70%", and sub-paras (3A), (4A), (6) inserted, by FA 2010 s 35, Sch 10 paras 10, 11 with effect from 6 April 2011 in relation to a return or other document which is required to be made or delivered to HMRC in relation to the tax year 2011–12 or any subsequent tax year, and falls within item 1, 2 or 3 of the Table in FA 2009 Sch 55 para 1. Note that these changes do not have effect in relation to Sch 55 in relation to a return or other document which is required to be made or delivered to HMRC in relation to the tax year 2010–11 or any previous tax year (SI 2011/975 art 5).

Prospective amendments—Sub-paras (3A)(*za*), (4A)(*za*) to be inserted before sub-paras (3A)(*a*), (4A)(*a*), in sub-para (3A)(*a*), figure "125%" to be substituted for "100%", in sub-para (4A)(*a*), figure "87.5%" to be substituted for "70%", and in sub-para (6), figure "4" to be substituted for figure "3" by FA 2015 s 120, Sch 20 paras 14, 15 with effect from a day to be appointed. Sub-para (3A)(*za*) as inserted to read as follows—

"(za) for the withholding of category 0 information, 100%,".

Sub-para (4A)(*za*) as inserted to read as follows—

"(za) for the withholding of category 0 information, 70%,".

[6A (1) Information is category 1 information if—

(*a*) it involves a domestic matter, or

(*b*) it involves an offshore matter and—

(i) the territory in question is a category 1 territory, or

(ii) it is information which would enable or assist HMRC to assess P's liability to a tax other than income tax or capital gains tax.

(2) Information is category 2 information if—

(*a*) it involves an offshore matter,

(*b*) the territory in question is a category 2 territory, and

(*c*) it is information which would enable or assist HMRC to assess P's liability to income tax or capital gains tax.

(3) Information is category 3 information if—

(*a*) it involves an offshore matter,

(*b*) the territory in question is a category 3 territory, and

(*c*) it is information which would enable or assist HMRC to assess P's liability to income tax or capital gains tax.

(4) Information "involves an offshore matter" if the liability to tax which would have been shown in the return includes a liability to tax charged on or by reference to—

(*a*) income arising from a source in a territory outside the UK,

(*b*) assets situated or held in a territory outside the UK,

(*c*) activities carried on wholly or mainly in a territory outside the UK, or

(*d*) anything having effect as if it were income, assets or activities of a kind described above.

(5) Information "involves a domestic matter" if the liability to tax which would have been shown in the return includes a liability to tax charged on or by reference to anything not mentioned in sub-paragraph (4)(*a*) to (*d*).

(6) If the information which P withholds falls into more than one category—

(*a*) P's failure to make the return is to be treated for the purposes of this Schedule as if it were separate failures, one for each category of information according to the matters which the information involves, and

(*b*) for each separate failure, the liability to tax which would have been shown in the return in question is taken to be such share of the liability to tax which would have been shown in the return mentioned in paragraph (*a*) as is just and reasonable.

(7) For the purposes of this Schedule—

(*a*) paragraph 21A of Schedule 24 to FA 2007 (classification of territories) has effect, but

(*b*) an order under that paragraph does not apply to a failure if the filing date is before the date on which the order comes into force.

(8) Regulations under paragraph 21B of Schedule 24 to FA 2007 (location of assets etc) apply for the purposes of paragraph 6A of this Schedule as they apply for the purposes of paragraph 4A of that Schedule.

(9) In this paragraph—

"assets" has the meaning given in section 21(1) of TCGA 1992, but also includes sterling;

"UK" means the United Kingdom, including the territorial sea of the United Kingdom.][1]

Commencement—Finance Act 2009, Schedules 55 and 56 (Income Tax Self Assessment and Pension Schemes) (Appointed Days and Consequential and Savings Provisions) Order, SI 2011/702 art 2 (appointed day for the coming into force of Sch 55 is 6 April 2011 in relation to a return or other document which is required to be made or delivered to HMRC in relation to the tax year 2010–11 or any subsequent tax year and falls within item 1, 2 or 3 of the Table in para 1).

Amendments—[1] Para 6A inserted by FA 2010 s 35, Sch 10 paras 10, 12 with effect from 6 April 2011 in relation to a return or other document which is required to be made or delivered to HMRC in relation to the tax year 2011–12 or any subsequent tax year, and falls within item 1, 2 or 3 of the Table in FA 2009 Sch 55 para 1. Note that these changes do not have effect in relation to Sch 55 in relation to a return or other document which is required to be made or delivered to HMRC in relation to the tax year 2010–11 or any previous tax year (SI 2011/975 art 5).

Prospective amendments—The following amendments to be made by FA 2015 s 120, Sch 20 paras 14, 16 with effect from a day to be appointed—

- sub-paras (A1), (1) to be substituted for sub-para (1);
- in sub-paras (2)(*a*), (3)(*a*), words "or an offshore transfer" to be inserted after word "matter", and in sub-paras (2)(*c*), (3)(*c*), words ", capital gains tax or inheritance tax" to be substituted for words "or capital gains tax";

– sub-paras (4A), (4B) to be inserted and sub-para (8) to be repealed;
– in sub-para (5), words "it does not involve an offshore matter or an offshore transfer" to be substituted for words following word "if";
– in sub-para (6)(*a*), words "or transfers" to be inserted after word "matters"; and
– in sub-para (9), words "and paragraph 6AA" to be inserted after word "paragraph".

Sub-paragraphs (A1), (1) as substituted to read as follows—

"(A1) Information is category 0 information if—

it involves a domestic matter,

it involves an offshore matter or an offshore transfer, the territory in question is a category 0 territory and it is information which would enable or assist HMRC to assess P's liability to income tax, capital gains tax or inheritance tax, or

it involves an offshore matter and it is information which would enable or assist HMRC to assess P's liability to a tax other than income tax, capital gains tax or inheritance tax.

(1) Information is category 1 information if—

it involves an offshore matter or an offshore transfer,

the territory in question is a category 1 territory, and

it is information which would enable or assist HMRC to assess P's liability to income tax, capital gains tax or inheritance tax.".

Sub-paragraphs (4A), (4B) as inserted to read as follows—

"(4A) If the liability to tax which would have been shown in the return is a liability to inheritance tax, assets are treated for the purposes of sub-paragraph (4) as situated or held in a territory outside the UK if they are so situated or held immediately after the transfer of value by reason of which inheritance tax becomes chargeable.

(4B) Information "involves an offshore transfer" if—

it does not involve an offshore matter,

it is information which would enable or assist HMRC to assess P's liability to income tax, capital gains tax or inheritance tax,

by failing to make the return, P deliberately withholds the information (whether or not the withholding of the information is also concealed), and

the applicable condition in paragraph 6AA is satisfied.".

[6AA (1) This paragraph makes provision in relation to offshore transfers.

(2) Where the liability to tax which would have been shown in the return is a liability to income tax, the applicable condition is satisfied if the income on or by reference to which the tax is charged, or any part of the income—

(*a*) is received in a territory outside the UK, or

(*b*) is transferred before the relevant date to a territory outside the UK.

(3) Where the liability to tax which would have been shown in the return is a liability to capital gains tax, the applicable condition is satisfied if the proceeds of the disposal on or by reference to which the tax is charged, or any part of the proceeds—

(*a*) are received in a territory outside the UK, or

(*b*) are transferred before the relevant date to a territory outside the UK.

(4) Where the liability to tax which would have been shown in the return is a liability to inheritance tax, the applicable condition is satisfied if—

(*a*) the disposition that gives rise to the transfer of value by reason of which the tax becomes chargeable involves a transfer of assets, and

(*b*) after that disposition but before the relevant date the assets, or any part of the assets, are transferred to a territory outside the UK.

(5) In the case of a transfer falling within sub-paragraph (2)(*b*), (3)(*b*) or (4)(*b*), references to the income, proceeds or assets transferred are to be read as including references to any assets derived from or representing the income, proceeds or assets.

(6) In relation to an offshore transfer, the territory in question for the purposes of paragraph 6A is the highest category of territory by virtue of which the information involves an offshore transfer.

(7) "Relevant date" means the date on which P becomes liable to a penalty under paragraph 6.]

Prospective amendments—Paragraphs 6AA, 6AB to be inserted by FA 2015 s 120, Sch 20 paras 14, 17 with effect from a day to be appointed.

[6AB Regulations under paragraph 21B of Schedule 24 to FA 2007 (location of assets etc) apply for the purposes of paragraphs 6A and 6AA of this Schedule as they apply for the purposes of paragraphs 4A and 4AA of that Schedule.]

Prospective amendments—Paragraphs 6AA, 6AB to be inserted by FA 2015 s 120, Sch 20 paras 14, 17 with effect from a day to be appointed.

[Amount of penalty: real time information for PAYE

6B Paragraphs 6C and 6D apply in the case of a return falling within item 4 in the Table.][1]

Commencement—Finance Act 2009, Schedule 55 (Penalties for failure to make returns) (Appointed Days and Consequential Provision) Order, SI 2014/2395 provides dates for the coming into force of Sch 55 in relation to returns falling within item 4 of the table in para 1 above (PAYE returns), as follows—

- **11 September 2014:** powers to make regulations in relation to quanta of RTI late-filing penalties in para 6C(5), (7), (8), (9), (11) (see also SI 2014/2396).
- for paras 1, 6B, 6C(1)–(4), (6), (10), 6D, 16–24, 26, 27 (relating to failures to make returns under the PAYE Regulations (SI 2003/2682) regs 67B and 67D):
  - (a) **6 October 2014:** where the employer is a large existing employer (an employer which as at 6 October 2014 employs at least 50 employees). Affected returns are those required to be made or delivered to HMRC on or after 6 October 2014.
  - (b) **6 March 2015:** where the employer is a small existing employer (an employer which as at 6 October 2014 employs no more than 49 employees) or is a new employer. Affected returns are those required to be made or delivered to HMRC on or after 6 March 2015.

Amendments—[1] Paragraphs 6B–6D and preceding cross-head inserted by FA 2013 s 230, Sch 50 paras 2, 6 with effect for the tax year 2014–15 and subsequent tax years in relation to failures to make returns with a filing date (as defined in FA 2009 Sch 55 para 1(4)) on or after 6 April 2014.

[6C—(1) If P fails during a tax month to make a return on or before the filing date, P is liable to a penalty under this paragraph in respect of that month.

(2) But this is subject to sub-paragraphs (3) and (4).

(3) P is not liable to a penalty under this paragraph in respect of a tax month as a result of any failure to make a return on or before the filing date which occurs during the initial period.

(4) P is not liable to a penalty under this paragraph in respect of a tax month falling in a tax year if the month is the first tax month in that tax year during which P fails to make a return on or before the filing date (disregarding for this purpose any failure which occurs during the initial period).

(5) In sub-paragraphs (3) and (4) "the initial period" means the period which—

(*a*) begins with the day in the first tax year on which P is first required to make a return, and

(*b*) is of such duration as is specified in regulations made by the Commissioners,

and for this purpose "the first tax year" means the first tax year in which P is required to make returns.

(6) P may be liable under this paragraph to no more than one penalty in respect of each tax month.

(7) The penalty under this paragraph is to be calculated in accordance with regulations made by the Commissioners.

(8) Regulations under sub-paragraph (7) may provide for a penalty under this paragraph in respect of a tax month to be calculated by reference to either or both of the following matters—

(*a*) the number of persons employed by P, or treated as employed by P for the purposes of PAYE regulations;

(*b*) the number of previous penalties incurred by P under this paragraph in the same tax year.

(9) The Commissioners may by regulations disapply sub-paragraph (3) or (4) in such circumstances as are specified in the regulations.

(10) If P has elected under PAYE regulations to be treated as different employers in relation to different groups of employees, this paragraph applies to P as if—

(*a*) in respect of each group P were a different person, and

(*b*) each group constituted all of P's employees.

(11) Regulations made by the Commissioners under this paragraph may—

(*a*) make different provision for different cases, and

(*b*) include incidental, consequential and supplementary provision.][1]

Commencement—Finance Act 2009, Schedule 55 (Penalties for failure to make returns) (Appointed Days and Consequential Provision) Order, SI 2014/2395 provides dates for the coming into force of Sch 55 in relation to returns falling within item 4 of the table in para 1 above (PAYE returns), as follows—

- **11 September 2014:** powers to make regulations in relation to quanta of RTI late-filing penalties in para 6C(5), (7), (8), (9), (11) (see also SI 2014/2396).
- for paras 1, 6B, 6C(1)–(4), (6), (10), 6D, 16–24, 26, 27 (relating to failures to make returns under the PAYE Regulations (SI 2003/2682) regs 67B and 67D):
  - (a) **6 October 2014:** where the employer is a large existing employer (an employer which as at 6 October 2014 employs at least 50 employees). Affected returns are those required to be made or delivered to HMRC on or after 6 October 2014.
  - (b) **6 March 2015:** where the employer is a small existing employer (an employer which as at 6 October 2014 employs no more than 49 employees) or is a new employer. Affected returns are those required to be made or delivered to HMRC on or after 6 March 2015.

Regulations—Income Tax (Pay As You Earn) (Amendment No 3) Regulations, SI 2014/2396.

Amendments—[1] Paragraphs 6B–6D and preceding cross-head inserted by FA 2013 s 230, Sch 50 paras 2, 6 with effect for the tax year 2014–15 and subsequent tax years in relation to failures to make returns with a filing date (as defined in FA 2009 Sch 55 para 1(4)) on or after 6 April 2014.

[6D—(1) P may be liable to one or more penalties under this paragraph in respect of extended failures.

(2) In this paragraph an "extended failure" means a failure to make a return on or before the filing date which continues after the end of the period of 3 months beginning with the day after the filing date.

(3) P is liable to a penalty or penalties under this paragraph if (and only if)—

(*a*) HMRC decide at any time that such a penalty or penalties should be payable in accordance with sub-paragraph (4) or (6), and

(*b*) HMRC give notice to P specifying the date from which the penalty, or each penalty, is payable.

(4) HMRC may decide under sub-paragraph (3)(*a*) that a separate penalty should be payable in respect of each unpenalised extended failure in the tax year to date.

(5) In that case the amount of the penalty in respect of each failure is 5% of any liability to make payments which would have been shown in the return in question.

(6) HMRC may decide under sub-paragraph (3)(*a*) that a single penalty should be payable in respect of all the unpenalised extended failures in the tax year to date.

(7) In that case the amount of the penalty in respect of those failures is 5% of the sum of the liabilities to make payments which would have been shown in each of the returns in question.

(8) For the purposes of this paragraph, an extended failure is unpenalised if a penalty has not already been imposed in respect of it under this paragraph (whether in accordance with subparagraph (4) or (6)).

(9) The date specified in the notice under sub-paragraph (3)(*b*) in relation to a penalty—

(*a*) may be earlier than the date on which the notice is given, but

(*b*) may not be earlier than the end of the period mentioned in sub-paragraph (2) in relation to the relevant extended failure.

(10) In sub-paragraph (9)(*b*) "the relevant extended failure" means—

(*a*) the extended failure in respect of which the penalty is payable, or

(*b*) if the penalty is payable in respect of more than one extended failure (in accordance with sub-paragraph (6)), the extended failure with the latest filing date.][1]

Commencement—Finance Act 2009, Schedule 55 (Penalties for failure to make returns) (Appointed Days and Consequential Provision) Order, SI 2014/2395 provides dates for the coming into force of Sch 55 in relation to returns falling within item 4 of the table in para 1 above (PAYE returns), as follows—

– **11 September 2014:** powers to make regulations in relation to quanta of RTI late-filing penalties in para 6C(5), (7), (8), (9), (11) (see also SI 2014/2396).

– for paras 1, 6B, 6C(1)–(4), (6), (10), 6D, 16–24, 26, 27 (relating to failures to make returns under the PAYE Regulations (SI 2003/2682) regs 67B and 67D):

(a) **6 October 2014:** where the employer is a large existing employer (an employer which as at 6 October 2014 employs at least 50 employees). Affected returns are those required to be made or delivered to HMRC on or after 6 October 2014.

(b) **6 March 2015:** where the employer is a small existing employer (an employer which as at 6 October 2014 employs no more than 49 employees) or is a new employer. Affected returns are those required to be made or delivered to HMRC on or after 6 March 2015.

Amendments—[1] Paragraphs 6B–6D and preceding cross-head inserted by FA 2013 s 230, Sch 50 paras 2, 6 with effect for the tax year 2014–15 and subsequent tax years in relation to failures to make returns with a filing date (as defined in FA 2009 Sch 55 para 1(4)) on or after 6 April 2014.

Amount of penalty: CIS returns

7 Paragraphs 8 to 13 apply in the case of a return falling within item 6 in the Table.

Commencement—Finance Act 2009, Schedules 55 and 56 (Income Tax Self Assessment and Pension Schemes) (Appointed Days and Consequential and Savings Provisions) Order, SI 2011/702 art 2 (appointed day for the coming into force of Sch 55 is 6 April 2011 in relation to a return or other document which is required to be made or delivered to HMRC in relation to the tax year 2010–11 or any subsequent tax year and falls within item 1, 2 or 3 of the Table in para 1).

Finance (No 3) Act 2010, Schedule 10 and the Finance Act 2009, Schedule 55 and Sections 101 to 103 (Appointed Day, etc) (Construction Industry Scheme) Order, SI 2011/2391 (the day appointed for the coming into force of the following paras of Sch 55 is 6 October 2011, with effect only in relation to a return within item 6 of Sch 55 para 1(5), and for which the filing date for the purposes of Sch 55 is after 19 October 2011—

– para 1 (but only in relation to item 6 in the Table in para 1(5);
– paras 7–13; and
– 14–24, 26, and 27(1)–(4) but only as relevant to paras 7–13).

8 P is liable to a penalty under this paragraph of £100.

Commencement—Finance Act 2009, Schedules 55 and 56 (Income Tax Self Assessment and Pension Schemes) (Appointed Days and Consequential and Savings Provisions) Order, SI 2011/702 art 2 (appointed day for the coming into force of Sch 55 is 6 April 2011 in relation to a return or other document which is required to be made or delivered to HMRC in relation to the tax year 2010–11 or any subsequent tax year and falls within item 1, 2 or 3 of the Table in para 1).

Finance (No 3) Act 2010, Schedule 10 and the Finance Act 2009, Schedule 55 and Sections 101 to 103 (Appointed Day, etc) (Construction Industry Scheme) Order, SI 2011/2391 (the day appointed for the coming into force of the following paras of Sch 55 is 6 October 2011, with effect only in relation to a return within item 6 of Sch 55 para 1(5), and for which the filing date for the purposes of Sch 55 is after 19 October 2011—

- para 1 (but only in relation to item 6 in the Table in para 1(5);
- paras 7–13; and
- 14–24, 26, and 27(1)–(4) but only as relevant to paras 7–13).

9—(1) P is liable to a penalty under this paragraph if (and only if) P's failure continues after the end of the period of 2 months beginning with the penalty date.
(2) The penalty under this paragraph is £200.

Commencement—Finance Act 2009, Schedules 55 and 56 (Income Tax Self Assessment and Pension Schemes) (Appointed Days and Consequential and Savings Provisions) Order, SI 2011/702 art 2 (appointed day for the coming into force of Sch 55 is 6 April 2011 in relation to a return or other document which is required to be made or delivered to HMRC in relation to the tax year 2010–11 or any subsequent tax year and falls within item 1, 2 or 3 of the Table in para 1).
Finance (No 3) Act 2010, Schedule 10 and the Finance Act 2009, Schedule 55 and Sections 101 to 103 (Appointed Day, etc) (Construction Industry Scheme) Order, SI 2011/2391 (the day appointed for the coming into force of the following paras of Sch 55 is 6 October 2011, with effect only in relation to a return within item 6 of Sch 55 para 1(5), and for which the filing date for the purposes of Sch 55 is after 19 October 2011—

- para 1 (but only in relation to item 6 in the Table in para 1(5);
- paras 7–13; and
- 14–24, 26, and 27(1)–(4) but only as relevant to paras 7–13).

10—(1) P is liable to a penalty under this paragraph if (and only if) P's failure continues after the end of the period of 6 months beginning with the penalty date.
(2) The penalty under this paragraph is the greater of—
(*a*) 5% of any liability to make payments which would have been shown in the return in question, and
(*b*) £300.

Commencement—Finance Act 2009, Schedules 55 and 56 (Income Tax Self Assessment and Pension Schemes) (Appointed Days and Consequential and Savings Provisions) Order, SI 2011/702 art 2 (appointed day for the coming into force of Sch 55 is 6 April 2011 in relation to a return or other document which is required to be made or delivered to HMRC in relation to the tax year 2010–11 or any subsequent tax year and falls within item 1, 2 or 3 of the Table in para 1).
Finance (No 3) Act 2010, Schedule 10 and the Finance Act 2009, Schedule 55 and Sections 101 to 103 (Appointed Day, etc) (Construction Industry Scheme) Order, SI 2011/2391 (the day appointed for the coming into force of the following paras of Sch 55 is 6 October 2011, with effect only in relation to a return within item 6 of Sch 55 para 1(5), and for which the filing date for the purposes of Sch 55 is after 19 October 2011—

- para 1 (but only in relation to item 6 in the Table in para 1(5);
- paras 7–13; and
- 14–24, 26, and 27(1)–(4) but only as relevant to paras 7–13).

11—(1) P is liable to a penalty under this paragraph if (and only if) P's failure continues after the end of the period of 12 months beginning with the penalty date.
(2) Where, by failing to make the return, P [deliberately][1] withholds information which would enable or assist HMRC to assess the amount that P is liable to pay to HMRC in accordance with Chapter 3 of Part 3 of FA 2004, the penalty under this paragraph is determined in accordance with sub-paragraphs (3) and (4).
(3) If the withholding of the information is deliberate and concealed, the penalty is the greater of—
(*a*) 100% of any liability to make payments which would have been shown in the return in question, and
(*b*) £3,000.
(4) If the withholding of the information is deliberate but not concealed, the penalty is the greater of—
(*a*) 70% of any liability to make payments which would have been shown in the return in question, and
(*b*) £1,500.
(5) In [any case not falling within sub-paragraph (2)][1], the penalty under this paragraph is the greater of—
(*a*) 5% of any liability to make payments which would have been shown in the return in question, and
(*b*) £300.

Commencement—Finance Act 2009, Schedules 55 and 56 (Income Tax Self Assessment and Pension Schemes) (Appointed Days and Consequential and Savings Provisions) Order, SI 2011/702 art 2 (appointed day for the coming into force of Sch 55 is 6 April 2011 in relation to a return or other document which is required to be made or delivered to HMRC in relation to the tax year 2010–11 or any subsequent tax year and falls within item 1, 2 or 3 of the Table in para 1).
Finance (No 3) Act 2010, Schedule 10 and the Finance Act 2009, Schedule 55 and Sections 101 to 103 (Appointed Day, etc) (Construction Industry Scheme) Order, SI 2011/2391 (the day appointed for the coming into force of the following paras of Sch 55 is 6 October 2011, with effect only in relation to a return within item 6 of Sch 55 para 1(5), and for which the filing date for the purposes of Sch 55 is after 19 October 2011—

- para 1 (but only in relation to item 6 in the Table in para 1(5);
- paras 7–13; and
- 14–24, 26, and 27(1)–(4) but only as relevant to paras 7–13).

Amendments—[1] In sub-para (2) word inserted, and in sub-para (5) words substituted for words "any other case", by F(No 3)A 2010 s 26, Sch 10 paras 1, 5 with effect from 6 October 2011 (by virtue of SI 2011/2391). These amendments have effect in relation to a return within item 6 of Sch 55 para 1(5), and for which the filing date for the purposes of Sch 55 is after 19 October 2011 (SI 2011/2391 art 3(1)).

12—(1) P is liable to a penalty under this paragraph if (and only if)—

(*a*) P's failure continues after the end of the period of 12 months beginning with the penalty date, and

(*b*) the information required in the return relates only to persons registered for gross payment (within the meaning of Chapter 3 of Part 3 of FA 2004).

(2) Where, by failing to make the return, P [deliberately][1] withholds information which relates to such persons, the penalty under this paragraph is—

(*a*) if the withholding of the information is deliberate and concealed, £3,000, and

(*b*) if the withholding of the information is deliberate but not concealed, £1,500.

Commencement—Finance Act 2009, Schedules 55 and 56 (Income Tax Self Assessment and Pension Schemes) (Appointed Days and Consequential and Savings Provisions) Order, SI 2011/702 art 2 (appointed day for the coming into force of Sch 55 is 6 April 2011 in relation to a return or other document which is required to be made or delivered to HMRC in relation to the tax year 2010–11 or any subsequent tax year and falls within item 1, 2 or 3 of the Table in para 1).

Finance (No 3) Act 2010, Schedule 10 and the Finance Act 2009, Schedule 55 and Sections 101 to 103 (Appointed Day, etc) (Construction Industry Scheme) Order, SI 2011/2391 (the day appointed for the coming into force of the following paras of Sch 55 is 6 October 2011, with effect only in relation to a return within item 6 of Sch 55 para 1(5), and for which the filing date for the purposes of Sch 55 is after 19 October 2011—

- para 1 (but only in relation to item 6 in the Table in para 1(5);
- paras 7–13; and
- 14–24, 26, and 27(1)–(4) but only as relevant to paras 7–13).

Amendments—[1] In sub-para (2) word inserted by F(No 3)A 2010 s 26, Sch 10 paras 1, 6 with effect from 6 October 2011 (by virtue of SI 2011/2391). This amendment has effect in relation to a return within item 6 of Sch 55 para 1(5), and for which the filing date for the purposes of Sch 55 is after 19 October 2011 (SI 2011/2391 art 3(1)).

13—(1) This paragraph applies—

(*a*) at any time before P first makes a return falling within item 6 in the Table, to any return falling within that item, and

(*b*) at any time after P first makes a return falling within that item, to that return and any earlier return.

(2) In respect of any return or returns to which this paragraph applies—

(*a*) paragraphs 10(2)(*b*) and 11(5)(*b*) do not apply, and

(*b*) P is not liable to penalties under paragraphs 8 and 9 which exceed, in total, £3,000.

(3) In sub-paragraph (1)(*b*) "earlier return" means any return falling within item 6 which has a filing date earlier than the date on which P first made a return.

Commencement—Finance Act 2009, Schedules 55 and 56 (Income Tax Self Assessment and Pension Schemes) (Appointed Days and Consequential and Savings Provisions) Order, SI 2011/702 art 2 (appointed day for the coming into force of Sch 55 is 6 April 2011 in relation to a return or other document which is required to be made or delivered to HMRC in relation to the tax year 2010–11 or any subsequent tax year and falls within item 1, 2 or 3 of the Table in para 1).

Finance (No 3) Act 2010, Schedule 10 and the Finance Act 2009, Schedule 55 and Sections 101 to 103 (Appointed Day, etc) (Construction Industry Scheme) Order, SI 2011/2391 (the day appointed for the coming into force of the following paras of Sch 55 is 6 October 2011, with effect only in relation to a return within item 6 of Sch 55 para 1(5), and for which the filing date for the purposes of Sch 55 is after 19 October 2011—

- para 1 (but only in relation to item 6 in the Table in para 1(5);
- paras 7–13; and
- 14–24, 26, and 27(1)-(4) but only as relevant to paras 7–13).

[Amount of penalty: returns for periods of between 2 and 6 months

13A—*(1) Paragraphs 13B to 13E apply in the case of a return falling within any of items 7A to 7B and 14 to [29][1] in the Table which relates to a period of less than 6 months but more than 2 months.*

(2) But those paragraphs do not apply in the case of a return mentioned in paragraph 2(1)(c).]

Commencement—Finance Act 2009, Schedules 55 and 56 (Income Tax Self Assessment and Pension Schemes) (Appointed Days and Consequential and Savings Provisions) Order, SI 2011/702 art 2 (appointed day for the coming into force of Sch 55 is 6 April 2011 in relation to a return or other document which is required to be made or delivered to HMRC in relation to the tax year 2010–11 or any subsequent tax year and falls within item 1, 2 or 3 of the Table in para 1).

Amendments—[1] In sub-para (1) figure substituted by FA 2012 s 191, Sch 24 para 32(*b*), with effect in relation to the playing of machine games on or after 1 February 2013 (and Schs 55, 56, as amended by FA 2012 Sch 24 Part 1, are taken to have come into force for the purposes of machine games duty on that date).

Prospective amendments—Paras 13A–13J and preceding cross-heads to be inserted by F(No 3)A 2010 s 26, Sch 10 paras 1, 7 (as amended by FA 2014 s 103, Sch 22 para 21) with effect from a day to be appointed by Treasury order.

[13B—*(1) P is liable to a penalty under this paragraph of £100.*

(2) In addition, a penalty period begins to run on the penalty date for the return.

(3) The penalty period ends with the day 12 months after the filing date for the return, unless it is extended under paragraph 13C(2)(c) or 13H(2)(c).]

Commencement—Finance Act 2009, Schedules 55 and 56 (Income Tax Self Assessment and Pension Schemes) (Appointed Days and Consequential and Savings Provisions) Order, SI 2011/702 art 2 (appointed day for the coming into force of Sch 55 is 6 April 2011 in relation to a return or other document which is required to be made or delivered to HMRC in relation to the tax year 2010–11 or any subsequent tax year and falls within item 1, 2 or 3 of the Table in para 1).
Prospective amendment—Paras 13A–13J and preceding cross-heads to be inserted by F(No 3)A 2010 s 26, Sch 10 paras 1, 7 with effect from a day to be appointed by Treasury order.

[**13C**—(1) This paragraph applies if—
(*a*) a penalty period has begun under paragraph 13B or 13G because P has failed to make a return ("return A"), and
(*b*) before the end of the period, P fails to make another return ("return B") falling within the same item in the Table as return A.
(2) In such a case—
(*a*) paragraph 13B(1) and (2) do not apply to the failure to make return B, but
(*b*) P is liable to a penalty under this paragraph for that failure, and
(*c*) the penalty period that has begun is extended so that it ends with the day 12 months after the filing date for return B.
(3) The amount of the penalty under this paragraph is determined by reference to the number of returns that P has failed to make during the penalty period.
(4) If the failure to make return B is P's first failure to make a return during the penalty period, P is liable, at the time of the failure, to a penalty of £200.
(5) If the failure to make return B is P's second failure to make a return during the penalty period, P is liable, at the time of the failure, to a penalty of £300.
(6) If the failure to make return B is P's third or a subsequent failure to make a return during the penalty period, P is liable, at the time of the failure, to a penalty of £400.
(7) For the purposes of this paragraph—
(*a*) in accordance with sub-paragraph (1)(*b*), the references in sub-paragraphs (3) to (6) to a return are references to a return falling within the same item in the Table as returns A and B, and
(*b*) a failure to make a return counts for the purposes of those sub-paragraphs if (but only if) the return relates to a period of less than 6 months.
(8) A penalty period may be extended more than once under sub-paragraph (2)(*c*).

Commencement—Finance Act 2009, Schedules 55 and 56 (Income Tax Self Assessment and Pension Schemes) (Appointed Days and Consequential and Savings Provisions) Order, SI 2011/702 art 2 (appointed day for the coming into force of Sch 55 is 6 April 2011 in relation to a return or other document which is required to be made or delivered to HMRC in relation to the tax year 2010–11 or any subsequent tax year and falls within item 1, 2 or 3 of the Table in para 1).
Prospective amendment—Paras 13A–13J and preceding cross-heads to be inserted by F(No 3)A 2010 s 26, Sch 10 paras 1, 7 with effect from a day to be appointed by Treasury order.

[**13D**—(1) P is liable to a penalty under this paragraph if (and only if) P's failure continues after the end of the period of 6 months beginning with the penalty date.
(2) The penalty under this paragraph is the greater of—
(*a*) 5% of any liability to tax which would have been shown in the return in question, and
(*b*) £300.]

Commencement—Finance Act 2009, Schedules 55 and 56 (Income Tax Self Assessment and Pension Schemes) (Appointed Days and Consequential and Savings Provisions) Order, SI 2011/702 art 2 (appointed day for the coming into force of Sch 55 is 6 April 2011 in relation to a return or other document which is required to be made or delivered to HMRC in relation to the tax year 2010–11 or any subsequent tax year and falls within item 1, 2 or 3 of the Table in para 1).
Prospective amendment—Paras 13A–13J and preceding cross-heads to be inserted by F(No 3)A 2010 s 26, Sch 10 paras 1, 7 with effect from a day to be appointed by Treasury order.

[**13E**—(1) P is liable to a penalty under this paragraph if (and only if) P's failure continues after the end of the period of 12 months beginning with the penalty date.
(2) Where, by failing to make the return, P deliberately withholds information which would enable or assist HMRC to assess P's liability to tax, the penalty under this paragraph is determined in accordance with sub-paragraphs (3) and (4).
(3) If the withholding of the information is deliberate and concealed, the penalty is the greater of—
(*a*) 100% of any liability to tax which would have been shown in the return in question, and
(*b*) £300.
(4) If the withholding of the information is deliberate but not concealed, the penalty is the greater of—
(*a*) 70% of any liability to tax which would have been shown in the return in question, and
(*b*) £300.
(5) In any case not falling within sub-paragraph (2), the penalty under this paragraph is the greater of—
(*a*) 5% of any liability to tax which would have been shown in the return in question, and
(*b*) £300.]

Commencement—Finance Act 2009, Schedules 55 and 56 (Income Tax Self Assessment and Pension Schemes) (Appointed Days and Consequential and Savings Provisions) Order, SI 2011/702 art 2 (appointed day for the coming into force of Sch 55 is 6 April 2011 in relation to a return or other document which is required to be made or delivered to HMRC in relation to the tax year 2010–11 or any subsequent tax year and falls within item 1, 2 or 3 of the Table in para 1).

Prospective amendment—Paras 13A–13J and preceding cross-heads to be inserted by F(No 3)A 2010 s 26, Sch 10 paras 1, 7 with effect from a day to be appointed by Treasury order.

[Amount of penalty: returns for periods of 2 months or less

13F (1) Paragraphs 13G to 13J apply in the case of a return falling within any of items 7A, 7B and 14 to [29][1] in the Table which relates to a period of 2 months or less.

(2) But those paragraphs do not apply in the case of a return mentioned in paragraph 2(1)(*c*).]

Commencement—Finance Act 2009, Schedules 55 and 56 (Income Tax Self Assessment and Pension Schemes) (Appointed Days and Consequential and Savings Provisions) Order, SI 2011/702 art 2 (appointed day for the coming into force of Sch 55 is 6 April 2011 in relation to a return or other document which is required to be made or delivered to HMRC in relation to the tax year 2010–11 or any subsequent tax year and falls within item 1, 2 or 3 of the Table in para 1).

Amendments—[1] In sub-para (1), "29" substituted for "28", by FA 2012 s 191, Sch 24 para 32(*a*), with effect in relation to the playing of machine games on or after 1 February 2013 (and Schs 55, 56, as amended by FA 2012 Sch 24 Part 1, are taken to have come into force for the purposes of machine games duty on that date).

Prospective amendments—Paras 13A–13J and preceding cross-heads to be inserted by F(No 3)A 2010 s 26, Sch 10 paras 1, 7 with effect from a day to be appointed by Treasury order.

[13G—(1) P is liable to a penalty under this paragraph of £100.

(2) In addition, a penalty period begins to run on the penalty date for the return.

(3) The penalty period ends with the day 12 months after the filing date for the return, unless it is extended under paragraph 13C(2)(*c*) or 13H(2)(*c*).]

Commencement—Finance Act 2009, Schedules 55 and 56 (Income Tax Self Assessment and Pension Schemes) (Appointed Days and Consequential and Savings Provisions) Order, SI 2011/702 art 2 (appointed day for the coming into force of Sch 55 is 6 April 2011 in relation to a return or other document which is required to be made or delivered to HMRC in relation to the tax year 2010–11 or any subsequent tax year and falls within item 1, 2 or 3 of the Table in para 1).

Prospective amendment—Paras 13A–13J and preceding cross-heads to be inserted by F(No 3)A 2010 s 26, Sch 10 paras 1, 7 with effect from a day to be appointed by Treasury order.

[13H—(1) This paragraph applies if—

- (*a*) a penalty period has begun under paragraph 13B or 13G because P has failed to make a return ("return A"), and
- (*b*) before the end of the period, P fails to make another return ("return B") falling within the same item in the Table as return A.

(2) In such a case—

- (*a*) paragraph 13G(1) and (2) do not apply to the failure to make return B, but
- (*b*) P is liable to a penalty under this paragraph for that failure, and
- (*c*) the penalty period that has begun is extended so that it ends with the day 12 months after the filing date for return B.

(3) The amount of the penalty under this paragraph is determined by reference to the number of returns that P has failed to make during the penalty period.

(4) If the failure to make return B is P's first, second, third, fourth or fifth failure to make a return during the penalty period, P is liable, at the time of the failure, to a penalty of £100.

(5) If the failure to make return B is P's sixth or a subsequent failure to make a return during the penalty period, P is liable, at the time of the failure, to a penalty of £200.

(6) For the purposes of this paragraph—

- (*a*) in accordance with sub-paragraph (1)(*b*), the references in sub-paragraphs (3) to (5) to a return are references to a return falling within the same item in the Table as returns A and B, and
- (*b*) a failure to make a return counts for the purposes of those sub-paragraphs if (but only if) the return relates to a period of less than 6 months.

(7) A penalty period may be extended more than once under sub-paragraph (2)(*c*).]

Commencement—Finance Act 2009, Schedules 55 and 56 (Income Tax Self Assessment and Pension Schemes) (Appointed Days and Consequential and Savings Provisions) Order, SI 2011/702 art 2 (appointed day for the coming into force of Sch 55 is 6 April 2011 in relation to a return or other document which is required to be made or delivered to HMRC in relation to the tax year 2010–11 or any subsequent tax year and falls within item 1, 2 or 3 of the Table in para 1).

Prospective amendment—Paras 13A–13J and preceding cross-heads to be inserted by F(No 3)A 2010 s 26, Sch 10 paras 1, 7 with effect from a day to be appointed by Treasury order.

[13I—(1) P is liable to a penalty under this paragraph if (and only if) P's failure continues after the end of the period of 6 months beginning with the penalty date.

(2) The penalty under this paragraph is the greater of—

- (*a*) 5% of any liability to tax which would have been shown in the return in question, and
- (*b*) £300.]

Commencement—Finance Act 2009, Schedules 55 and 56 (Income Tax Self Assessment and Pension Schemes) (Appointed Days and Consequential and Savings Provisions) Order, SI 2011/702 art 2 (appointed day for the coming into force of Sch 55 is 6 April 2011 in relation to a return or other document which is required to be made or delivered to HMRC in relation to the tax year 2010–11 or any subsequent tax year and falls within item 1, 2 or 3 of the Table in para 1).

Prospective amendment—Paras 13A–13J and preceding cross-heads to be inserted by F(No 3)A 2010 s 26, Sch 10 paras 1, 7 with effect from a day to be appointed by Treasury order.

[13J—(1) P is liable to a penalty under this paragraph if (and only if) P's failure continues after the end of the period of 12 months beginning with the penalty date.

(2) Where, by failing to make the return, P deliberately withholds information which would enable or assist HMRC to assess P's liability to tax, the penalty under this paragraph is determined in accordance with sub-paragraphs (3) and (4).

(3) If the withholding of the information is deliberate and concealed, the penalty is the greater of—

(*a*) 100% of any liability to tax which would have been shown in the return in question, and

(*b*) £300.

(4) If the withholding of the information is deliberate but not concealed, the penalty is the greater of—

(*a*) 70% of any liability to tax which would have been shown in the return in question, and

(*b*) £300.

(5) In any case not falling within sub-paragraph (2), the penalty under this paragraph is the greater of—

(*a*) 5% of any liability to tax which would have been shown in the return in question, and

(*b*) £300.]

Commencement—Finance Act 2009, Schedules 55 and 56 (Income Tax Self Assessment and Pension Schemes) (Appointed Days and Consequential and Savings Provisions) Order, SI 2011/702 art 2 (appointed day for the coming into force of Sch 55 is 6 April 2011 in relation to a return or other document which is required to be made or delivered to HMRC in relation to the tax year 2010–11 or any subsequent tax year and falls within item 1, 2 or 3 of the Table in para 1).

Prospective amendment—Paras 13A–13J and preceding cross-heads to be inserted by F(No 3)A 2010 s 26, Sch 10 paras 1, 7 with effect from a day to be appointed by Treasury order.

Reductions for disclosure

14—(1) Paragraph 15 provides for reductions in the penalty under paragraph 6(3) or (4) or 11(3) or (4) where P discloses information which has been withheld by a failure to make a return ("relevant information").

(2) P discloses relevant information by—

(*a*) telling HMRC about it,

(*b*) giving HMRC reasonable help in quantifying any tax unpaid by reason of its having been withheld, and

(*c*) allowing HMRC access to records for the purpose of checking how much tax is so unpaid.

(3) Disclosure of relevant information—

(*a*) is "unprompted" if made at a time when P has no reason to believe that HMRC have discovered or are about to discover the relevant information, and

(*b*) otherwise, is "prompted".

(4) In relation to disclosure "quality" includes timing, nature and extent.

Commencement—Finance Act 2009, Schedules 55 and 56 (Income Tax Self Assessment and Pension Schemes) (Appointed Days and Consequential and Savings Provisions) Order, SI 2011/702 art 2 (appointed day for the coming into force of Sch 55 is 6 April 2011 in relation to a return or other document which is required to be made or delivered to HMRC in relation to the tax year 2010–11 or any subsequent tax year and falls within item 1, 2 or 3 of the Table in para 1).

Finance (No 3) Act 2010, Schedule 10 and the Finance Act 2009, Schedule 55 and Sections 101 to 103 (Appointed Day, etc) (Construction Industry Scheme) Order, SI 2011/2391 (the day appointed for the coming into force of the following paras of Sch 55 is 6 October 2011, with effect only in relation to a return within item 6 of Sch 55 para 1(5), and for which the filing date for the purposes of Sch 55 is after 19 October 2011—

- para 1 (but only in relation to item 6 in the Table in para 1(5);
- paras 7–13; and
- 14–24, 26, and 27(1)-(4) but only as relevant to paras 7–13).

Prospective amendment—In sub-para (1), words ", 11(3) or (4), 13E(3) or (4) or 13J(3) or (4)" to be substituted for words "or 11(3) or (4)" by F(No 3)A 2010 s 26, Sch 10 paras 1, 8 with effect from a day to be appointed by Treasury order.

15—[(1) If a person who would otherwise be liable to a penalty of a percentage shown in column 1 of the Table (a "standard percentage") has made a disclosure, HMRC must reduce the standard percentage to one that reflects the quality of the disclosure.

(2) But the standard percentage may not be reduced to a percentage that is below the minimum shown for it—

(*a*) in the case of a prompted disclosure, in column 2 of the Table, and

(*b*) in the case of an unprompted disclosure, in column 3 of the Table.

Standard %	*Minimum % for prompted disclosure*	*Minimum % for unprompted disclosure*
70%	35%	20%
105%	52.5%	30%
140%	70%	40%
100%	50%	30%
150%	75%	45%
200%	100%	60%][1]

(3) . . .[1]

(4) . . .[1]

(5) But HMRC must not under this paragraph—

(*a*) reduce a penalty under paragraph 6(3) or (4) below £300, or

(*b*) reduce a penalty under paragraph 11(3) or (4) below the amount set by paragraph 11(3)(*b*) or (4)(*b*) (as the case may be).

Commencement—Finance Act 2009, Schedules 55 and 56 (Income Tax Self Assessment and Pension Schemes) (Appointed Days and Consequential and Savings Provisions) Order, SI 2011/702 art 2 (appointed day for the coming into force of Sch 55 is 6 April 2011 in relation to a return or other document which is required to be made or delivered to HMRC in relation to the tax year 2010–11 or any subsequent tax year and falls within item 1, 2 or 3 of the Table in para 1).

Finance (No 3) Act 2010, Schedule 10 and the Finance Act 2009, Schedule 55 and Sections 101 to 103 (Appointed Day, etc) (Construction Industry Scheme) Order, SI 2011/2391 (the day appointed for the coming into force of the following paras of Sch 55 is 6 October 2011, with effect only in relation to a return within item 6 of Sch 55 para 1(5), and for which the filing date for the purposes of Sch 55 is after 19 October 2011—

– para 1 (but only in relation to item 6 in the Table in para 1(5);
– paras 7–13; and
– 14–24, 26, and 27(1)-(4) but only as relevant to paras 7–13).

Amendments—

[1] Sub-paras (1), (2) substituted, and sub-paras (3), (4) repealed, by FA 2010 s 35, Sch 10 paras 10, 13 with effect from 6 April 2011 in relation to a return or other document which is required to be made or delivered to HMRC in relation to the tax year 2011–12 or any subsequent tax year, and falls within item 1, 2 or 3 of the Table in FA 2009 Sch 55 para 1. Note that these changes do not have effect in relation to Sch 55 in relation to a return or other document which is required to be made or delivered to HMRC in relation to the tax year 2010–11 or any previous tax year (SI 2011/975 art 5).

Prospective amendments—In sub-para (5), words "sub-paragraph (3) or (4) of any of paragraphs 11, 13E and 13J" to be substituted for words "paragraph 11(3) or (4)", and words "paragraph (*b*) of that sub-paragraph" to be substituted for words "paragraph 11(3)(*b*) or (4)(*b*) (as the case may be)", by F(No 3)A 2010 s 26, Sch 10 paras 1, 9 with effect from a day to be appointed by Treasury order.

In sub-para (2), the following Table entries to be inserted at the appropriate places by FA 2015 s 120, Sch 20 paras 14, 18 with effect from a day to be appointed—

"87.5%	43.75%	25%"
"125%	62.5%	40%".

Special reduction

16—(1) If HMRC think it right because of special circumstances, they may reduce a penalty under any paragraph of this Schedule.

(2) In sub-paragraph (1) "special circumstances" does not include—

(*a*) ability to pay, or

(*b*) the fact that a potential loss of revenue from one taxpayer is balanced by a potential over-payment by another.

(3) In sub-paragraph (1) the reference to reducing a penalty includes a reference to—

(*a*) staying a penalty, and

(*b*) agreeing a compromise in relation to proceedings for a penalty.

Commencement—Finance Act 2009, Schedules 55 and 56 (Income Tax Self Assessment and Pension Schemes) (Appointed Days and Consequential and Savings Provisions) Order, SI 2011/702 art 2 (appointed day for the coming into force of Sch 55 is 6 April 2011 in relation to a return or other document which is required to be made or delivered to HMRC in relation to the tax year 2010–11 or any subsequent tax year and falls within item 1, 2 or 3 of the Table in para 1).

Finance (No 3) Act 2010, Schedule 10 and the Finance Act 2009, Schedule 55 and Sections 101 to 103 (Appointed Day, etc) (Construction Industry Scheme) Order, SI 2011/2391 (the day appointed for the coming into force of the following paras of Sch 55 is 6 October 2011, with effect only in relation to a return within item 6 of Sch 55 para 1(5), and for which the filing date for the purposes of Sch 55 is after 19 October 2011—

– para 1 (but only in relation to item 6 in the Table in para 1(5);

- paras 7–13; and
- 14–24, 26, and 27(1)–(4) but only as relevant to paras 7–13).

Finance Act 2009, Schedule 55 (Penalties for failure to make returns) (Appointed Days and Consequential Provision) Order, SI 2014/2395 provides dates for the coming into force of Sch 55 in relation to returns falling within item 4 of the table in para 1 above (PAYE returns), as follows—

- **11 September 2014:** powers to make regulations in relation to quanta of RTI late-filing penalties in para 6C(5), (7), (8), (9), (11) (see also SI 2014/2396).
- for paras 1, 6B, 6C(1)–(4), (6), (10), 6D, 16–24, 26, 27 (relating to failures to make returns under the PAYE Regulations (SI 2003/2682) regs 67B and 67D):
  - (a) **6 October 2014:** where the employer is a large existing employer (an employer which as at 6 October 2014 employs at least 50 employees). Affected returns are those required to be made or delivered to HMRC on or after 6 October 2014.
  - (b) **6 March 2015:** where the employer is a small existing employer (an employer which as at 6 October 2014 employs no more than 49 employees) or is a new employer. Affected returns are those required to be made or delivered to HMRC on or after 6 March 2015.

Interaction with other penalties and late payment surcharges

17—(1) Where P is liable for a penalty under any paragraph of this Schedule which is determined by reference to a liability to tax, the amount of that penalty is to be reduced by the amount of any other penalty incurred by P, if the amount of the penalty is determined by reference to the same liability to tax.

(2) In sub-paragraph (1) the reference to "any other penalty" does not include—

(*a*) a penalty under any other paragraph of this Schedule, or

(*b*) a penalty under Schedule 56 (penalty for late payment of tax)[, or

(*c*) a penalty under Part 4 of FA 2014 (penalty where corrective action not taken after follower notice etc).][2]

(3) Where P is liable for a penalty under more than one paragraph of this Schedule which is determined by reference to a liability to tax, the aggregate of the amounts of those penalties must not exceed [the relevant percentage][1] of the liability to tax.

[(4) The relevant percentage is—

(*a*) if one of the penalties is a penalty under paragraph 6(3) or (4) and the information withheld is category 3 information, 200%,

(*b*) if one of the penalties is a penalty under paragraph 6(3) or (4) and the information withheld is category 2 information, 150%, and

(*c*) in all other cases, 100%.][1]

Commencement—Finance Act 2009, Schedules 55 and 56 (Income Tax Self Assessment and Pension Schemes) (Appointed Days and Consequential and Savings Provisions) Order, SI 2011/702 art 2 (appointed day for the coming into force of Sch 55 is 6 April 2011 in relation to a return or other document which is required to be made or delivered to HMRC in relation to the tax year 2010–11 or any subsequent tax year and falls within item 1, 2 or 3 of the Table in para 1).

Finance (No 3) Act 2010, Schedule 10 and the Finance Act 2009, Schedule 55 and Sections 101 to 103 (Appointed Day, etc) (Construction Industry Scheme) Order, SI 2011/2391 (the day appointed for the coming into force of the following paras of Sch 55 is 6 October 2011, with effect only in relation to a return within item 6 of Sch 55 para 1(5), and for which the filing date for the purposes of Sch 55 is after 19 October 2011—

- para 1 (but only in relation to item 6 in the Table in para 1(5);

- paras 7–13; and
- 14–24, 26, and 27(1)–(4) but only as relevant to paras 7–13).

Finance Act 2009, Schedule 55 (Penalties for failure to make returns) (Appointed Days and Consequential Provision) Order, SI 2014/2395 provides dates for the coming into force of Sch 55 in relation to returns falling within item 4 of the table in para 1 above (PAYE returns), as follows—

- **11 September 2014:** powers to make regulations in relation to quanta of RTI late-filing penalties in para 6C(5), (7), (8), (9), (11) (see also SI 2014/2396).
- for paras 1, 6B, 6C(1)–(4), (6), (10), 6D, 16–24, 26, 27 (relating to failures to make returns under the PAYE Regulations (SI 2003/2682) regs 67B and 67D):
  - (a) **6 October 2014:** where the employer is a large existing employer (an employer which as at 6 October 2014 employs at least 50 employees). Affected returns are those required to be made or delivered to HMRC on or after 6 October 2014.
  - (b) **6 March 2015:** where the employer is a small existing employer (an employer which as at 6 October 2014 employs no more than 49 employees) or is a new employer. Affected returns are those required to be made or delivered to HMRC on or after 6 March 2015.

Amendments—

1 In sub-para (3) words substituted for figure "100%", and sub-s (4) inserted, by FA 2010 s 35, Sch 10 paras 10, 14 with effect from 6 April 2011 in relation to a return or other document which is required to be made or delivered to HMRC in relation to the tax year 2011–12 or any subsequent tax year, and falls within item 1, 2 or 3 of the Table in FA 2009 Sch 55 para 1. Note that these changes do not have effect in relation to Sch 55 in relation to a return or other document which is required to be made or delivered to HMRC in relation to the tax year 2010–11 or any previous tax year (SI 2011/975 art 5).

2 Sub-para (2)(*c*) and preceding word "or" inserted by FA 2014 s 233, Sch 33 para 5 with effect from 17 July 2014.

Prospective amendments—Para 17(4)(*ba*) to be inserted by FA 2015 s 120, Sch 20 paras 14, 19 with effect from a day to be appointed. Para 17(4)(*ba*) as inserted to read as follows—

"(*ba*) if one of the penalties is a penalty under paragraph 6(3) or (4) and the information withheld is category 1 information, 125%, and".

[Cancellation of penalty

17A—(1) This paragraph applies where—

(*a*) P is liable for a penalty under any paragraph of this Schedule in relation to a failure to make a return falling within item 1 or 2 in the Table, and

(*b*) P makes a request under section 8B of TMA 1970 for HMRC to withdraw a notice under section 8 or 8A of that Act.

(2) The notice under section 8B of TMA 1970 may include provision under this paragraph cancelling liability to the penalty from the date specified in the notice.][1]

Commencement—Finance Act 2009, Schedule 55 (Penalties for failure to make returns) (Appointed Days and Consequential Provision) Order, SI 2014/2395 provides dates for the coming into force of Sch 55 in relation to returns falling within item 4 of the table in para 1 above (PAYE returns), as follows—

– **11 September 2014:** powers to make regulations in relation to quanta of RTI late-filing penalties in para 6C(5), (7), (8), (9), (11) (see also SI 2014/2396).

– for paras 1, 6B, 6C(1)–(4), (6), (10), 6D, 16–24, 26, 27 (relating to failures to make returns under the PAYE Regulations (SI 2003/2682) regs 67B and 67D):

(a) **6 October 2014:** where the employer is a large existing employer (an employer which as at 6 October 2014 employs at least 50 employees). Affected returns are those required to be made or delivered to HMRC on or after 6 October 2014.

(b) **6 March 2015:** where the employer is a small existing employer (an employer which as at 6 October 2014 employs no more than 49 employees) or is a new employer. Affected returns are those required to be made or delivered to HMRC on or after 6 March 2015.

Amendments—[1] Paragraphs 17A, 17B and preceding cross-head inserted by FA 2013 s 233, Sch 51 para 8 with effect in relation to a return—

(a) under TMA 1970 s 12AA for a partnership which includes one or more companies, for a relevant period beginning on or after 6 April 2012; and

(b) under TMA 1970 s 12AA for any other partnership, or a return under TMA 1970 s 8 or s 8A, for a year of assessment beginning on or after 6 April 2012.

A "relevant period" means a period in respect of which a return is required: FA 2013 Sch 51 para 9(2).

[17B—(1) This paragraph applies where—

(*a*) P is liable for a penalty under any paragraph of this Schedule in relation to a failure to make a return falling within item 3 in the Table, and

(*b*) a request is made under section 12AAA of TMA 1970 for HMRC to withdraw a notice under section 12AA of that Act.

(2) The notice under section 12AAA of TMA 1970 may include provision under this paragraph cancelling liability to the penalty from the date specified in the notice.][1]

Commencement—Finance Act 2009, Schedule 55 (Penalties for failure to make returns) (Appointed Days and Consequential Provision) Order, SI 2014/2395 provides dates for the coming into force of Sch 55 in relation to returns falling within item 4 of the table in para 1 above (PAYE returns), as follows—

– **11 September 2014:** powers to make regulations in relation to quanta of RTI late-filing penalties in para 6C(5), (7), (8), (9), (11) (see also SI 2014/2396).

– for paras 1, 6B, 6C(1)–(4), (6), (10), 6D, 16–24, 26, 27 (relating to failures to make returns under the PAYE Regulations (SI 2003/2682) regs 67B and 67D):

(a) **6 October 2014:** where the employer is a large existing employer (an employer which as at 6 October 2014 employs at least 50 employees). Affected returns are those required to be made or delivered to HMRC on or after 6 October 2014.

(b) **6 March 2015:** where the employer is a small existing employer (an employer which as at 6 October 2014 employs no more than 49 employees) or is a new employer. Affected returns are those required to be made or delivered to HMRC on or after 6 March 2015.

Amendments—[1] Paragraphs 17A, 17B and preceding cross-head inserted by FA 2013 s 233, Sch 51 para 8 with effect in relation to a return—

(a) under TMA 1970 s 12AA for a partnership which includes one or more companies, for a relevant period beginning on or after 6 April 2012; and

(b) under TMA 1970 s 12AA for any other partnership, or a return under TMA 1970 s 8 or s 8A, for a year of assessment beginning on or after 6 April 2012.

A "relevant period" means a period in respect of which a return is required: FA 2013 Sch 51 para 9(2).

Assessment

18—(1) Where P is liable for a penalty under any paragraph of this Schedule HMRC must—

(*a*) assess the penalty,

(*b*) notify P, and

(*c*) state in the notice the period in respect of which the penalty is assessed.

(2) A penalty under any paragraph of this Schedule must be paid before the end of the period of 30 days beginning with the day on which notification of the penalty is issued.

VAT Statutes

(3) An assessment of a penalty under any paragraph of this Schedule—

(*a*) is to be treated for procedural purposes in the same way as an assessment to tax (except in respect of a matter expressly provided for by this Schedule),

(*b*) may be enforced as if it were an assessment to tax, and

(*c*) may be combined with an assessment to tax.

(4) A supplementary assessment may be made in respect of a penalty if an earlier assessment operated by reference to an underestimate of the liability to tax which would have been shown in a return.

[(5) Sub-paragraph (6) applies if—

(*a*) an assessment in respect of a penalty is based on a liability to tax that would have been shown in a return, and

(*b*) that liability is found by HMRC to be excessive.

(6) HMRC may by notice to P amend the assessment so that it is based upon the correct amount.

(7) An amendment under sub-paragraph (6)—

(*a*) does not affect when the penalty must be paid;

(*b*) may be made after the last day on which the assessment in question could have been made under paragraph 19.][1]

Commencement—Finance Act 2009, Schedules 55 and 56 (Income Tax Self Assessment and Pension Schemes) (Appointed Days and Consequential and Savings Provisions) Order, SI 2011/702 art 2 (appointed day for the coming into force of Sch 55 is 6 April 2011 in relation to a return or other document which is required to be made or delivered to HMRC in relation to the tax year 2010–11 or any subsequent tax year and falls within item 1, 2 or 3 of the Table in para 1).

Finance (No 3) Act 2010, Schedule 10 and the Finance Act 2009, Schedule 55 and Sections 101 to 103 (Appointed Day, etc) (Construction Industry Scheme) Order, SI 2011/2391 (the day appointed for the coming into force of the following paras of Sch 55 is 6 October 2011, with effect only in relation to a return within item 6 of Sch 55 para 1(5), and for which the filing date for the purposes of Sch 55 is after 19 October 2011—

– para 1 (but only in relation to item 6 in the Table in para 1(5);
– paras 7–13; and
– 14–24, 26, and 27(1)–(4) but only as relevant to paras 7–13).

Finance Act 2009, Schedule 55 (Penalties for failure to make returns) (Appointed Days and Consequential Provision) Order, SI 2014/2395 provides dates for the coming into force of Sch 55 in relation to returns falling within item 4 of the table in para 1 above (PAYE returns), as follows—

– **11 September 2014:** powers to make regulations in relation to quanta of RTI late-filing penalties in para 6C(5), (7), (8), (9), (11) (see also SI 2014/2396).
– for paras 1, 6B, 6C(1)–(4), (6), (10), 6D, 16–24, 26, 27 (relating to failures to make returns under the PAYE Regulations (SI 2003/2682) regs 67B and 67D):
  (a) **6 October 2014:** where the employer is a large existing employer (an employer which as at 6 October 2014 employs at least 50 employees). Affected returns are those required to be made or delivered to HMRC on or after 6 October 2014.
  (b) **6 March 2015:** where the employer is a small existing employer (an employer which as at 6 October 2014 employs no more than 49 employees) or is a new employer. Affected returns are those required to be made or delivered to HMRC on or after 6 March 2015.

Amendments—[1] Sub-paras (5)–(7) substituted for sub-para (5) by FA 2013 s 230, Sch 50 paras 2, 7 with effect for the tax year 2014–15 and subsequent tax years in relation to failures to make returns with a filing date (as defined in FA 2009 Sch 55 para 1(4)) on or after 6 April 2014.

19—(1) An assessment of a penalty under any paragraph of this Schedule in respect of any amount must be made on or before the later of date A and (where it applies) date B.

(2) Date A is[—

(*a*) in the case of an assessment of a penalty under paragraph 6C, the last day of the period of 2 years beginning with the end of the tax month in respect of which the penalty is payable,

(*b*) in the case of an assessment of a penalty under paragraph 6D, the last day of the period of 2 years beginning with the filing date for the relevant extended failure (as defined in paragraph 6D(10)), and

(*c*) in any other case,][1]

the last day of the period of 2 years beginning with the filing date.

(3) Date B is the last day of the period of 12 months beginning with—

(*a*) the end of the appeal period for the assessment of the liability to tax which would have been shown in the return, [or returns (as the case may be in relation to penalties under section 6C or 6D)][1] or

(*b*) if there is no such assessment, the date on which that liability is ascertained or it is ascertained that the liability is nil.

(4) In sub-paragraph (3)(*a*) "appeal period" means the period during which—

(*a*) an appeal could be brought, or

(*b*) an appeal that has been brought has not been determined or withdrawn.

(5) Sub-paragraph (1) does not apply to a re-assessment under paragraph 24(2)(*b*).

Commencement—Finance Act 2009, Schedules 55 and 56 (Income Tax Self Assessment and Pension Schemes) (Appointed Days and Consequential and Savings Provisions) Order, SI 2011/702 art 2 (appointed day for the coming into force of Sch 55 is

6 April 2011 in relation to a return or other document which is required to be made or delivered to HMRC in relation to the tax year 2010–11 or any subsequent tax year and falls within item 1, 2 or 3 of the Table in para 1).

Finance (No 3) Act 2010, Schedule 10 and the Finance Act 2009, Schedule 55 and Sections 101 to 103 (Appointed Day, etc) (Construction Industry Scheme) Order, SI 2011/2391 (the day appointed for the coming into force of the following paras of Sch 55 is 6 October 2011, with effect only in relation to a return within item 6 of Sch 55 para 1(5), and for which the filing date for the purposes of Sch 55 is after 19 October 2011—

– para 1 (but only in relation to item 6 in the Table in para 1(5);
– paras 7–13; and
– 14–24, 26, and 27(1)–(4) but only as relevant to paras 7–13).

Finance Act 2009, Schedule 55 (Penalties for failure to make returns) (Appointed Days and Consequential Provision) Order, SI 2014/2395 provides dates for the coming into force of Sch 55 in relation to returns falling within item 4 of the table in para 1 above (PAYE returns), as follows—

– **11 September 2014:** powers to make regulations in relation to quanta of RTI late-filing penalties in para 6C(5), (7), (8), (9), (11) (see also SI 2014/2396).
– for paras 1, 6B, 6C(1)–(4), (6), (10), 6D, 16–24, 26, 27 (relating to failures to make returns under the PAYE Regulations (SI 2003/2682) regs 67B and 67D):
  (a) **6 October 2014:** where the employer is a large existing employer (an employer which as at 6 October 2014 employs at least 50 employees). Affected returns are those required to be made or delivered to HMRC on or after 6 October 2014.
  (b) **6 March 2015:** where the employer is a small existing employer (an employer which as at 6 October 2014 employs no more than 49 employees) or is a new employer. Affected returns are those required to be made or delivered to HMRC on or after 6 March 2015.

Amendments—[1] In sub-paras (2), (3)(*a*) words inserted by FA 2013 s 230, Sch 50 paras 2, 8 with effect for the tax year 2014–15 and subsequent tax years in relation to failures to make returns with a filing date (as defined in FA 2009 Sch 55 para 1(4)) on or after 6 April 2014.

Appeal

20—(1) P may appeal against a decision of HMRC that a penalty is payable by P.

(2) P may appeal against a decision of HMRC as to the amount of a penalty payable by P.

Commencement—Finance Act 2009, Schedules 55 and 56 (Income Tax Self Assessment and Pension Schemes) (Appointed Days and Consequential and Savings Provisions) Order, SI 2011/702 art 2 (appointed day for the coming into force of Sch 55 is 6 April 2011 in relation to a return or other document which is required to be made or delivered to HMRC in relation to the tax year 2010–11 or any subsequent tax year and falls within item 1, 2 or 3 of the Table in para 1).

Finance (No 3) Act 2010, Schedule 10 and the Finance Act 2009, Schedule 55 and Sections 101 to 103 (Appointed Day, etc) (Construction Industry Scheme) Order, SI 2011/2391 (the day appointed for the coming into force of the following paras of Sch 55 is 6 October 2011, with effect only in relation to a return within item 6 of Sch 55 para 1(5), and for which the filing date for the purposes of Sch 55 is after 19 October 2011—

– para 1 (but only in relation to item 6 in the Table in para 1(5);
– paras 7–13; and
– 14–24, 26, and 27(1)–(4) but only as relevant to paras 7–13).

Finance Act 2009, Schedule 55 (Penalties for failure to make returns) (Appointed Days and Consequential Provision) Order, SI 2014/2395 provides dates for the coming into force of Sch 55 in relation to returns falling within item 4 of the table in para 1 above (PAYE returns), as follows—

– **11 September 2014:** powers to make regulations in relation to quanta of RTI late-filing penalties in para 6C(5), (7), (8), (9), (11) (see also SI 2014/2396).
– for paras 1, 6B, 6C(1)–(4), (6), (10), 6D, 16–24, 26, 27 (relating to failures to make returns under the PAYE Regulations (SI 2003/2682) regs 67B and 67D):
  (a) **6 October 2014:** where the employer is a large existing employer (an employer which as at 6 October 2014 employs at least 50 employees). Affected returns are those required to be made or delivered to HMRC on or after 6 October 2014.
  (b) **6 March 2015:** where the employer is a small existing employer (an employer which as at 6 October 2014 employs no more than 49 employees) or is a new employer. Affected returns are those required to be made or delivered to HMRC on or after 6 March 2015.

21—(1) An appeal under paragraph 20 is to be treated in the same way as an appeal against an assessment to the tax concerned (including by the application of any provision about bringing the appeal by notice to HMRC, about HMRC review of the decision or about determination of the appeal by the First-tier Tribunal or Upper Tribunal).

(2) Sub-paragraph (1) does not apply—

(*a*) so as to require P to pay a penalty before an appeal against the assessment of the penalty is determined, or

(*b*) in respect of any other matter expressly provided for by this Act.

Commencement—Finance Act 2009, Schedules 55 and 56 (Income Tax Self Assessment and Pension Schemes) (Appointed Days and Consequential and Savings Provisions) Order, SI 2011/702 art 2 (appointed day for the coming into force of Sch 55 is 6 April 2011 in relation to a return or other document which is required to be made or delivered to HMRC in relation to the tax year 2010–11 or any subsequent tax year and falls within item 1, 2 or 3 of the Table in para 1).

Finance (No 3) Act 2010, Schedule 10 and the Finance Act 2009, Schedule 55 and Sections 101 to 103 (Appointed Day, etc) (Construction Industry Scheme) Order, SI 2011/2391 (the day appointed for the coming into force of the following paras of Sch 55 is 6 October 2011, with effect only in relation to a return within item 6 of Sch 55 para 1(5), and for which the filing date for the purposes of Sch 55 is after 19 October 2011—

– para 1 (but only in relation to item 6 in the Table in para 1(5);
– paras 7–13; and
– 14–24, 26, and 27(1)–(4) but only as relevant to paras 7–13).

Finance Act 2009, Schedule 55 (Penalties for failure to make returns) (Appointed Days and Consequential Provision) Order, SI 2014/2395 provides dates for the coming into force of Sch 55 in relation to returns falling within item 4 of the table in para 1 above (PAYE returns), as follows—

– **11 September 2014:** powers to make regulations in relation to quanta of RTI late-filing penalties in para 6C(5), (7), (8), (9), (11) (see also SI 2014/2396).
– for paras 1, 6B, 6C(1)–(4), (6), (10), 6D, 16–24, 26, 27 (relating to failures to make returns under the PAYE Regulations (SI 2003/2682) regs 67B and 67D):
  (a) **6 October 2014:** where the employer is a large existing employer (an employer which as at 6 October 2014 employs at least 50 employees). Affected returns are those required to be made or delivered to HMRC on or after 6 October 2014.
  (b) **6 March 2015:** where the employer is a small existing employer (an employer which as at 6 October 2014 employs no more than 49 employees) or is a new employer. Affected returns are those required to be made or delivered to HMRC on or after 6 March 2015.

22—(1) On an appeal under paragraph 20(1) that is notified to the tribunal, the tribunal may affirm or cancel HMRC's decision.

(2) On an appeal under paragraph 20(2) that is notified to the tribunal, the tribunal may—

(*a*) affirm HMRC's decision, or

(*b*) substitute for HMRC's decision another decision that HMRC had power to make.

(3) If the tribunal substitutes its decision for HMRC's, the tribunal may rely on paragraph 16—

(*a*) to the same extent as HMRC (which may mean applying the same percentage reduction as HMRC to a different starting point), or

(*b*) to a different extent, but only if the tribunal thinks that HMRC's decision in respect of the application of paragraph 16 was flawed.

(4) In sub-paragraph (3)(*b*) "flawed" means flawed when considered in the light of the principles applicable in proceedings for judicial review.

(5) In this paragraph "tribunal" means the First-tier Tribunal or Upper Tribunal (as appropriate by virtue of paragraph 21(1)).

Commencement—Finance Act 2009, Schedules 55 and 56 (Income Tax Self Assessment and Pension Schemes) (Appointed Days and Consequential and Savings Provisions) Order, SI 2011/702 art 2 (appointed day for the coming into force of Sch 55 is 6 April 2011 in relation to a return or other document which is required to be made or delivered to HMRC in relation to the tax year 2010–11 or any subsequent tax year and falls within item 1, 2 or 3 of the Table in para 1).

Finance (No 3) Act 2010, Schedule 10 and the Finance Act 2009, Schedule 55 and Sections 101 to 103 (Appointed Day, etc) (Construction Industry Scheme) Order, SI 2011/2391 (the day appointed for the coming into force of the following paras of Sch 55 is 6 October 2011, with effect only in relation to a return within item 6 of Sch 55 para 1(5), and for which the filing date for the purposes of Sch 55 is after 19 October 2011—

– para 1 (but only in relation to item 6 in the Table in para 1(5);
– paras 7–13; and
– 14–24, 26, and 27(1)–(4) but only as relevant to paras 7–13).

Finance Act 2009, Schedule 55 (Penalties for failure to make returns) (Appointed Days and Consequential Provision) Order, SI 2014/2395 provides dates for the coming into force of Sch 55 in relation to returns falling within item 4 of the table in para 1 above (PAYE returns), as follows—

– **11 September 2014:** powers to make regulations in relation to quanta of RTI late-filing penalties in para 6C(5), (7), (8), (9), (11) (see also SI 2014/2396).
– for paras 1, 6B, 6C(1)–(4), (6), (10), 6D, 16–24, 26, 27 (relating to failures to make returns under the PAYE Regulations (SI 2003/2682) regs 67B and 67D):
  (a) **6 October 2014:** where the employer is a large existing employer (an employer which as at 6 October 2014 employs at least 50 employees). Affected returns are those required to be made or delivered to HMRC on or after 6 October 2014.
  (b) **6 March 2015:** where the employer is a small existing employer (an employer which as at 6 October 2014 employs no more than 49 employees) or is a new employer. Affected returns are those required to be made or delivered to HMRC on or after 6 March 2015.

Reasonable excuse

23—(1) Liability to a penalty under any paragraph of this Schedule does not arise in relation to a failure to make a return if P satisfies HMRC or (on appeal) the First-tier Tribunal or Upper Tribunal that there is a reasonable excuse for the failure.

(2) For the purposes of sub-paragraph (1)—

(*a*) an insufficiency of funds is not a reasonable excuse, unless attributable to events outside P's control,

(*b*) where P relies on any other person to do anything, that is not a reasonable excuse unless P took reasonable care to avoid the failure, and

(*c*) where P had a reasonable excuse for the failure but the excuse has ceased, P is to be treated as having continued to have the excuse if the failure is remedied without unreasonable delay after the excuse ceased.

Commencement—Finance Act 2009, Schedules 55 and 56 (Income Tax Self Assessment and Pension Schemes) (Appointed Days and Consequential and Savings Provisions) Order, SI 2011/702 art 2 (appointed day for the coming into force of Sch 55 is 6 April 2011 in relation to a return or other document which is required to be made or delivered to HMRC in relation to the tax year 2010–11 or any subsequent tax year and falls within item 1, 2 or 3 of the Table in para 1).

Finance (No 3) Act 2010, Schedule 10 and the Finance Act 2009, Schedule 55 and Sections 101 to 103 (Appointed Day, etc) (Construction Industry Scheme) Order, SI 2011/2391 (the day appointed for the coming into force of the following paras of Sch 55 is 6 October 2011, with effect only in relation to a return within item 6 of Sch 55 para 1(5), and for which the filing date for the purposes of Sch 55 is after 19 October 2011—

- para 1 (but only in relation to item 6 in the Table in para 1(5);
- paras 7–13; and
- 14–24, 26, and 27(1)–(4) but only as relevant to paras 7–13).

Finance Act 2009, Schedule 55 (Penalties for failure to make returns) (Appointed Days and Consequential Provision) Order, SI 2014/2395 provides dates for the coming into force of Sch 55 in relation to returns falling within item 4 of the table in para 1 above (PAYE returns), as follows—

- **11 September 2014:** powers to make regulations in relation to quanta of RTI late-filing penalties in para 6C(5), (7), (8), (9), (11) (see also SI 2014/2396).
- for paras 1, 6B, 6C(1)–(4), (6), (10), 6D, 16–24, 26, 27 (relating to failures to make returns under the PAYE Regulations (SI 2003/2682) regs 67B and 67D):
  - (a) **6 October 2014:** where the employer is a large existing employer (an employer which as at 6 October 2014 employs at least 50 employees). Affected returns are those required to be made or delivered to HMRC on or after 6 October 2014.
  - (b) **6 March 2015:** where the employer is a small existing employer (an employer which as at 6 October 2014 employs no more than 49 employees) or is a new employer. Affected returns are those required to be made or delivered to HMRC on or after 6 March 2015.

Prospective amendment—Sub-para (1) to be substituted by F(No 3)A 2010 s 26, Sch 10 paras 1, 11 with effect from a day to be appointed by Treasury order. Sub-para (1) as substituted to read as follows—

"(1) If P satisfies HMRC or (on appeal) the First-tier Tribunal or Upper Tribunal that there is a reasonable excuse for a failure to make a return—

liability to a penalty under any paragraph of this Schedule does not arise in relation to that failure, and

the failure does not count for the purposes of paragraphs 13B(2), 13C, 13G(2) and 13H.".

Determination of penalty geared to tax liability where no return made

24—(1) References to a liability to tax which would have been shown in a return are references to the amount which, if a complete and accurate return had been delivered on the filing date, would have been shown to be due or payable by the taxpayer in respect of the tax concerned for the period to which the return relates.

(2) In the case of a penalty which is assessed at a time before P makes the return to which the penalty relates—

(*a*) HMRC is to determine the amount mentioned in sub-paragraph (1) to the best of HMRC's information and belief, and

(*b*) if P subsequently makes a return, the penalty must be re-assessed by reference to the amount of tax shown to be due and payable in that return (but subject to any amendments or corrections to the return).

(3) In calculating a liability to tax which would have been shown in a return, no account is to be taken of any relief under [section 458 of CTA 2010][1] (relief in respect of repayment etc of loan) which is deferred under [subsection (5)][1] of that section.

Commencement—Finance Act 2009, Schedules 55 and 56 (Income Tax Self Assessment and Pension Schemes) (Appointed Days and Consequential and Savings Provisions) Order, SI 2011/702 art 2 (appointed day for the coming into force of Sch 55 is 6 April 2011 in relation to a return or other document which is required to be made or delivered to HMRC in relation to the tax year 2010–11 or any subsequent tax year and falls within item 1, 2 or 3 of the Table in para 1).

Finance (No 3) Act 2010, Schedule 10 and the Finance Act 2009, Schedule 55 and Sections 101 to 103 (Appointed Day, etc) (Construction Industry Scheme) Order, SI 2011/2391 (the day appointed for the coming into force of the following paras of Sch 55 is 6 October 2011, with effect only in relation to a return within item 6 of Sch 55 para 1(5), and for which the filing date for the purposes of Sch 55 is after 19 October 2011—

- para 1 (but only in relation to item 6 in the Table in para 1(5);
- paras 7–13; and
- 14–24, 26, and 27(1)–(4) but only as relevant to paras 7–13).

Finance Act 2009, Schedule 55 (Penalties for failure to make returns) (Appointed Days and Consequential Provision) Order, SI 2014/2395 provides dates for the coming into force of Sch 55 in relation to returns falling within item 4 of the table in para 1 above (PAYE returns), as follows—

- **11 September 2014:** powers to make regulations in relation to quanta of RTI late-filing penalties in para 6C(5), (7), (8), (9), (11) (see also SI 2014/2396).
- for paras 1, 6B, 6C(1)–(4), (6), (10), 6D, 16–24, 26, 27 (relating to failures to make returns under the PAYE Regulations (SI 2003/2682) regs 67B and 67D):
  - (a) **6 October 2014:** where the employer is a large existing employer (an employer which as at 6 October 2014 employs at least 50 employees). Affected returns are those required to be made or delivered to HMRC on or after 6 October 2014.

(b) **6 March 2015:** where the employer is a small existing employer (an employer which as at 6 October 2014 employs no more than 49 employees) or is a new employer. Affected returns are those required to be made or delivered to HMRC on or after 6 March 2015.

Amendments—[1] In sub-para (3) words substituted for words "subsection (4) of section 419 of ICTA" and "subsection (4A)" by CTA 2010 s 1177, Sch 1 paras 706, 723. CTA 2010 has effect for corporation tax purposes for accounting periods ending on or after 1 April 2010, and for income and capital gains tax purposes for the tax year 2010–11 and subsequent tax years.

Partnerships

25—(1) This paragraph applies where—

(*a*) the representative partner, or

(*b*) a successor of the representative partner,

fails to make a return falling within item 3 in the Table (partnership returns).

(2) A penalty in respect of the failure is payable by every relevant partner.

(3) In accordance with sub-paragraph (2), any reference in this Schedule to P is to be read as including a reference to a relevant partner.

(4) An appeal under paragraph 20 in connection with a penalty payable by virtue of this paragraph may be brought only by—

(*a*) the representative partner, or

(*b*) a successor of the representative partner.

(5) Where such an appeal is brought in connection with a penalty payable in respect of a failure, the appeal is to treated as if it were an appeal in connection with every penalty payable in respect of that failure.

(6) In this paragraph—

"relevant partner" means a person who was a partner in the partnership to which the return relates at any time during the period in respect of which the return was required;

"representative partner" means a person who has been required by a notice served under or for the purposes of section 12AA(2) or (3) of TMA 1970 to deliver any return;

"successor" has the meaning given by section 12AA(11) of TMA 1970.

Commencement—Finance Act 2009, Schedules 55 and 56 (Income Tax Self Assessment and Pension Schemes) (Appointed Days and Consequential and Savings Provisions) Order, SI 2011/702 art 2 (appointed day for the coming into force of Sch 55 is 6 April 2011 in relation to a return or other document which is required to be made or delivered to HMRC in relation to the tax year 2010–11 or any subsequent tax year and falls within item 1, 2 or 3 of the Table in para 1).

Double jeopardy

26 P is not liable to a penalty under any paragraph of this Schedule in respect of a failure or action in respect of which P has been convicted of an offence.

Commencement—Finance Act 2009, Schedules 55 and 56 (Income Tax Self Assessment and Pension Schemes) (Appointed Days and Consequential and Savings Provisions) Order, SI 2011/702 art 2 (appointed day for the coming into force of Sch 55 is 6 April 2011 in relation to a return or other document which is required to be made or delivered to HMRC in relation to the tax year 2010–11 or any subsequent tax year and falls within item 1, 2 or 3 of the Table in para 1).

Finance (No 3) Act 2010, Schedule 10 and the Finance Act 2009, Schedule 55 and Sections 101 to 103 (Appointed Day, etc) (Construction Industry Scheme) Order, SI 2011/2391 (the day appointed for the coming into force of the following paras of Sch 55 is 6 October 2011, with effect only in relation to a return within item 6 of Sch 55 para 1(5), and for which the filing date for the purposes of Sch 55 is after 19 October 2011—

- para 1 (but only in relation to item 6 in the Table in para 1(5);
- paras 7–13; and
- 14–24, 26, and 27(1)–(4) but only as relevant to paras 7–13).

Finance Act 2009, Schedule 55 (Penalties for failure to make returns) (Appointed Days and Consequential Provision) Order, SI 2014/2395 provides dates for the coming into force of Sch 55 in relation to returns falling within item 4 of the table in para 1 above (PAYE returns), as follows—

- **11 September 2014:** powers to make regulations in relation to quanta of RTI late-filing penalties in para 6C(5), (7), (8), (9), (11) (see also SI 2014/2396).
- for paras 1, 6B, 6C(1)–(4), (6), (10), 6D, 16–24, 26, 27 (relating to failures to make returns under the PAYE Regulations (SI 2003/2682) regs 67B and 67D):

(a) **6 October 2014:** where the employer is a large existing employer (an employer which as at 6 October 2014 employs at least 50 employees). Affected returns are those required to be made or delivered to HMRC on or after 6 October 2014.

(b) **6 March 2015:** where the employer is a small existing employer (an employer which as at 6 October 2014 employs no more than 49 employees) or is a new employer. Affected returns are those required to be made or delivered to HMRC on or after 6 March 2015.

Interpretation

27—(1) This paragraph applies for the construction of this Schedule.

(2) The withholding of information by P is—

(*a*) "deliberate and concealed" if P deliberately withholds the information and makes arrangements to conceal the fact that the information has been withheld, and (*b*) "deliberate but not concealed" if P deliberately withholds the information but does not make arrangements to conceal the fact that the information has been withheld.

[(2A) "The Commissioners" means the Commissioners for Her Majesty's Revenue and Customs.][1]

(3) "HMRC" means Her Majesty's Revenue and Customs.

[(3A) "Tax month" means the period beginning with the 6th day of a month and ending with the 5th day of the following month.][1]

(4) References to a liability to tax, in relation to a return falling within item 6 in the Table (construction industry scheme), are to a liability to make payments in accordance with Chapter 3 of Part 3 of FA 2004.

(5) References to an assessment to tax, in relation to inheritance tax and stamp duty reserve tax, are to a determination.

Commencement—Finance Act 2009, Schedules 55 and 56 (Income Tax Self Assessment and Pension Schemes) (Appointed Days and Consequential and Savings Provisions) Order, SI 2011/702 art 2 (appointed day for the coming into force of Sch 55 is 6 April 2011 in relation to a return or other document which is required to be made or delivered to HMRC in relation to the tax year 2010–11 or any subsequent tax year and falls within item 1, 2 or 3 of the Table in para 1).

Finance (No 3) Act 2010, Schedule 10 and the Finance Act 2009, Schedule 55 and Sections 101 to 103 (Appointed Day, etc) (Construction Industry Scheme) Order, SI 2011/2391 (the day appointed for the coming into force of the following paras of Sch 55 is 6 October 2011, with effect only in relation to a return within item 6 of Sch 55 para 1(5), and for which the filing date for the purposes of Sch 55 is after 19 October 2011—

- para 1 (but only in relation to item 6 in the Table in para 1(5);
- paras 7–13; and
- 14–24, 26, and 27(1)–(4) but only as relevant to paras 7–13).

Finance Act 2009, Schedule 55 (Penalties for failure to make returns) (Appointed Days and Consequential Provision) Order, SI 2014/2395 provides dates for the coming into force of Sch 55 in relation to returns falling within item 4 of the table in para 1 above (PAYE returns), as follows—

- **11 September 2014:** powers to make regulations in relation to quanta of RTI late-filing penalties in para 6C(5), (7), (8), (9), (11) (see also SI 2014/2396).
- for paras 1, 6B, 6C(1)–(4), (6), (10), 6D, 16–24, 26, 27 (relating to failures to make returns under the PAYE Regulations (SI 2003/2682) regs 67B and 67D):
  (a) **6 October 2014:** where the employer is a large existing employer (an employer which as at 6 October 2014 employs at least 50 employees). Affected returns are those required to be made or delivered to HMRC on or after 6 October 2014.
  (b) **6 March 2015:** where the employer is a small existing employer (an employer which as at 6 October 2014 employs no more than 49 employees) or is a new employer. Affected returns are those required to be made or delivered to HMRC on or after 6 March 2015.

Amendments—[1] Sub-paras (2A), (3A) inserted by FA 2013 s 230, Sch 50 paras 2, 9 with effect for the tax year 2014–15 and subsequent tax years in relation to failures to make returns with a filing date (as defined in FA 2009 Sch 55 para 1(4)) on or after 6 April 2014.

SCHEDULE 56

PENALTY FOR FAILURE TO MAKE PAYMENTS ON TIME

Section 107

Commencement—Finance Act 2009, Schedule 56 (Appointed Day and Consequential Provisions) Order, SI 2010/466 (6 April 2010 appointed as day on which Sch 56 comes into force for certain purposes).

Finance Act 2009, Schedules 55 and 56 (Income Tax Self Assessment and Pension Schemes) (Appointed Days and Consequential and Savings Provisions) Order, SI 2011/702 art 2 (appointed day for the coming into force of Sch 56 is 6 April 2011 in relation to an amount of tax which is payable in relation to the tax year 2010–11 or any subsequent tax year and falls within item 1, 12, 18 or 19 of the Table in para 1, or in so far as the tax falls within item 1 of that Table, item 17, 23 or 24 of that Table).

FA 2013 Sch 34 para 12 (Sch 56, as amended by FA 2013 Sch 34 para 9, is taken to have come into force for the purposes of the annual tax on enveloped dwellings on 17 July 2013).

Finance Act 2009, Schedules 55 and 56 and Sections 101 and 102 (Stamp Duty Reserve Tax) (Appointed Days, Consequential and Transitional Provision) Order, SI 2014/3269 art 3 (the day appointed for the coming into force of Sch 56 is 1 January 2015 in relation to an amount of SDRT which is in item 10, 17, 23 or 24 of the Table in para 1).

Cross-references—See SSCBA 1992 s 11A (this Schedule applies with the necessary modifications, in relation to Class 2 contributions under SSCBA 1992 s 11(2) as if those contributions were income tax chargeable under ITTOIA 2005 Pt 2 Ch 2 in respect of profits of a trade, profession or vocation which is not carried on wholly outside the United Kingdom).

Penalty for failure to pay tax

1—(1) A penalty is payable by a person ("P") where P fails to pay an amount of tax specified in column 3 of the Table below on or before the date specified in column 4.

(2) Paragraphs 3 to 8 set out—

(*a*) the circumstances in which a penalty is payable, and

(*b*) subject to paragraph 9, the amount of the penalty.

(3) If P's failure falls within more than one provision of this Schedule, P is liable to a penalty under each of those provisions.

(4) In the following provisions of this Schedule, the "penalty date", in relation to an amount of tax, means [the day after the date specified in or for the purposes of column 4 of the Table in relation to that amount.][5]

	Tax to which payment relates	*Amount of tax payable*	*Date after which penalty is incurred*
PRINCIPAL AMOUNTS			
1	Income tax or capital gains tax	Amount payable under section 59B(3) or (4) of TMA 1970	The date falling 30 days after the date specified in section 59B(3) or (4) of TMA 1970 as the date by which the amount must be paid
2	Income tax	Amount payable under PAYE regulations . . .[1]	The date determined by or under PAYE regulations as the date by which the amount must be paid
3	Income tax	Amount shown in return under section 254(1) of FA 2004	The date falling 30 days after the date specified in section 254(5) of FA 2004 as the date by which the amount must be paid
4	Deductions on account of tax under Chapter 3 of Part 3 of FA 2004 (construction industry scheme)	Amount payable under section 62 of FA 2004 (except an amount falling within item 17, 23 or 24)	The date determined by or under regulations under [section 71][1] of FA 2004 as the date by which the amount must be paid
5	Corporation tax	Amount shown in company tax return under paragraph 3 of Schedule 18 to FA 1998	The filing date for the company tax return for the accounting period for which the tax is due (see paragraph 14 of Schedule 18 to FA 1998)
6	Corporation tax	Amount payable under regulations under section 59E of TMA 1970 (except an amount falling within item 17, 23 or 24)	The filing date for the company tax return for the accounting period for which the tax is due (see paragraph 14 of Schedule 18 to FA 1998)
[6ZA	Corporation tax	Amount payable under an exit charge payment plan entered into in accordance with Schedule 3ZB to TMA 1970	The later of— (*a*) the first day after the period of 12 months beginning immediately after the migration accounting period (as defined in Part 1 or 2 of Schedule 3ZB to TMA 1970, as the case may be), and (*b*) the date on which the amount is payable under the plan.][3]
[6ZB	Diverted profits tax	Amount of diverted profits tax payable under Part 3 of FA 2015	The date when, in accordance with section 98(2) of FA 2015, the amount must be paid][7]
7	Inheritance tax	Amount payable under section 226 of IHTA 1984 (except an amount falling within item 14 or 21)	The filing date (determined under section 216 of IHTA 1984) for the account in respect of the liability for that amount
8	Inheritance tax	Amount payable under section 227 or 229 of IHTA 1984 (except an amount falling within item 14 or 21)	For the first instalment, the filing date (determined under section 216 of IHTA 1984) for the account in respect of the liability for that amount For any later instalment, the date falling 30 days after the date determined under section 227 or 229 of IHTA 1984 as the date by which the instalment must be paid

	Tax to which payment relates	*Amount of tax payable*	*Date after which penalty is incurred*
9	Stamp duty land tax	Amount payable under section 86(1) or (2) of FA 2003	The date falling 30 days after the date specified in section 86(1) or (2) of FA 2003 as the date by which the amount must be paid
10	Stamp duty reserve tax	Amount payable under section 87, 93 or 96 of FA 1986 or Schedule 19 to FA 1999 (except an amount falling within item 17, 23 or 24)	The date falling 30 days after the date determined by or under regulations under section 98 of FA 1986 as the date by which the amount must be paid
[10A	Annual tax on enveloped dwellings	Amount payable under section 161(1) or (2) of FA 2013 (except an amount falling within item 23).	The date falling 30 days after the date specified in section 161(1) or (2) of FA 2013 as the date by which the amount must be paid][4]
11	Petroleum revenue tax	Amount charged in an assessment under paragraph 11(1) of Schedule 2 to OTA 1975	The date falling 30 days after the date determined in accordance with paragraph 13 of Schedule 2 to OTA 1975 as the date by which the amount must be paid
[11GA	Excise duties	Amount payable under regulations under section 60A of the Customs and Excise Management Act 1979 (except an amount falling within item 17A, 23 or 24).	The date determined by or under regulations under section 60A of the Customs and Excise Management Act 1979 as the date by which the amount must be paid][7]
[11N	Machine games duty	Amount payable under paragraph 6 of Schedule 24 to FA 2012 (except an amount falling within item 17A, 23 or 24)	The date determined by or under regulations under paragraph 19 of Schedule 24 to FA 2012 as the date by which the amount must be paid][2]
AMOUNTS PAYABLE IN DEFAULT OF A RETURN BEING MADE			
12	Income tax or capital gains tax	Amount payable under section 59B(5A) of TMA 1970	The date falling 30 days after the date specified in section 59B(5A) of TMA 1970 as the date by which the amount must be paid
13	Corporation tax	Amount shown in determination under paragraph 36 or 37 of Schedule 18 to FA 1998	The filing date for the company tax return for the accounting period for which the tax is due (see paragraph 14 of Schedule 18 to FA 1998)
14	Inheritance tax	Amount shown in a determination made by HMRC in the circumstances set out in paragraph 2	The filing date (determined under section 216 of IHTA 1984) for the account in respect of the liability for that amount
15	Stamp duty land tax	Amount shown in determination under paragraph 25 of Schedule 10 to FA 2003 (including that paragraph as applied by section 81(3) of that Act)	The date falling 30 days after the filing date for the return in question
[15A	Annual tax on enveloped dwellings	Amount shown in determination under paragraph 18 of Schedule 31 to FA 2013	The date falling 30 days after the filing date for the return in question][4]
16	Petroleum revenue tax	Amount charged in an assessment made where participator fails to deliver return for a chargeable period	The date falling 6 months and 30 days after the end of the chargeable period

	Tax to which payment relates	*Amount of tax payable*	*Date after which penalty is incurred*
17	Tax falling within any of items 1 to 6, 9[, 10 or 10A][3]	Amount (not falling within any of items 12 to [15A][3]) which is shown in an assessment or determination made by HMRC in the circumstances set out in paragraph 2	The date falling 30 days after the date by which the amount would have been required to be paid if it had been shown in the return in question
AMOUNT SHOWN TO BE DUE IN OTHER ASSESSMENTS, DETERMINATIONS, ETC			
18	Income tax or capital gains tax	Amount payable under section 55 of TMA 1970	The date falling 30 days after the date determined in accordance with section 55(3), (4), (6) or (9) of TMA 1970 as the date by which the amount must be paid
19	Income tax or capital gains tax	Amount payable under section 59B(5) or (6) of TMA 1970	The date falling 30 days after the date specified in section 59B(5) or (6) of TMA 1970 as the date by which the amount must be paid
20	. . . [1]		
21	Inheritance tax	Amount shown in— (*a*) an amendment or correction of a return showing an amount falling within item 7 or 8, or (*b*) a determination made by HMRC in circumstances other than those set out in paragraph 2	The later of— (*a*) the filing date (determined under section 216 of IHTA 1984) for the account in respect of the liability for that amount, and (*b*) the date falling 30 days after the date on which the amendment, correction, assessment or determination is made
22	Petroleum revenue tax	Amount charged in an assessment, or an amendment of an assessment, made in circumstances other than those set out in items 11 and 16	The date falling 30 days after— (*a*) the date by which the amount must be paid, or (*b*) the date on which the assessment or amendment is made, whichever is later
23	Tax falling within any of items 1 to 6, 9 or 10	Amount (not falling within any of items 18 to 20) shown in an amendment or correction of a return showing an amount falling within any of items 1 to 6, 9 or 10	The date falling 30 days after— (*a*) the date by which the amount must be paid, or (*b*) the date on which the amendment or correction is made, whichever is later
24	Tax falling within any of items 1 to 6, 9 or 10	Amount (not falling within any of items 18 to 20) shown in an assessment or determination made by HMRC in circumstances other than those set out in paragraph 2	The date falling 30 days after— (*a*) the date by which the amount must be paid, or

	Tax to which payment relates	*Amount of tax payable*	*Date after which penalty is incurred*
			(*b*) the date on which the assessment or determination is made, whichever is later

[(5) Sub-paragraph (4) is subject to paragraph 2A.][1]

Modifications—FA 2009 Sch 56 has effect as if the Table in this para included references to bank payroll tax (FA 2010 s 22, Sch 1 para 39 (1)–(4)).

FA 2013 Sch 34 para 10(1) (until F(No 3)A 2010 Sch 11 para 2(13)(*a*), (14)(*a*) come into force, this para has effect as if—

- in item 23 the references in the second and third columns to items 1 to 6, 9 or 10 included item 10A, and
- in item 24 the reference in the second column to items 1 to 6, 9 or 10 included item 10A.

Commencement—Finance Act 2009, Schedule 56 (Appointed Day and Consequential Provisions) Order, SI 2010/466: 6 April 2010 appointed as day on which Sch 56 comes into force for the following amounts specified in column 3 of the Table—items 2–4, and items 17, 23 and 24 but only in so far as the tax falls within any of items 2, 3 or 4 (see SI 2010/466 art 3).

Finance Act 2009, Schedules 55 and 56 (Income Tax Self Assessment and Pension Schemes) (Appointed Days and Consequential and Savings Provisions) Order, SI 2011/702 art 2 (appointed day for the coming into force of Sch 56 is 6 April 2011 in relation to an amount of tax which is payable in relation to the tax year 2010–11 or any subsequent tax year and falls within item 1, 12, 18 or 19 of the Table in para 1, or in so far as the tax falls within item 1 of that Table, item 17, 23 or 24 of that Table).

FA 2009 Sch 56, as amended by FA 2013 Sch 34 para 9, is taken to have come into force for the purposes of the annual tax on enveloped dwellings on 17 July 2013 (FA 2013 Sch 34 para 12).

Amendments—

[1] Sub-para (5) inserted; in Table, in item 2 column 3, words "(except an amount falling within item 20)" repealed, in item 4 column 4, words substituted for words "section 62", and item 20 repealed, by F(No 3)A 2010 s 27, Sch 11 paras 1, 2(1), (3), (5), (6), (12) with effect from 25 January 2011 (by virtue of SI 2011/132 art 2(*a*)).

[2] Item 11N inserted, and in items 17A, 23, 24 (as to be inserted by F(No 3)A 2010: see prospective amendment note below) reference "11N" to be substituted for reference "11M" by FA 2012 s 191, Sch 24 paras 33, 34 with effect in relation to the playing of machine games on or after 1 February 2013 (and Schs 55, 56, as amended by FA 2012 Sch 24 Part 1, are taken to have come into force for the purposes of machine games duty on that date).

[3] In sub-para (4), in Table, item 6ZA inserted by FA 2013 s 229, Sch 49 paras 1, 7. This amendment is treated as having come into force on 11 December 2012 in relation to an accounting period if the relevant day in relation to that period falls on or after 11 December 2012, subject to transitional provisions where the relevant day falls between 11 December 2012 and 31 March 2013 (inclusive): FA 2013 Sch 49 para 8(3).

The relevant day, in relation to an accounting period, means the first day after the period of 9 months beginning immediately after the accounting period: FA 2013 Sch 49 para 8(2).

[4] In table, items 10A, 15A inserted, and in item 17, in second column words substituted for words "or 10", and in third column reference substituted for reference "15", by FA 2013 s 164, Sch 34 paras 8, 9 with effect from 17 July 2013.

[5] In sub-para (4), words substituted by FA 2013 s 230, Sch 50 paras 10, 11 with effect for defaults made in relation to the tax year 2014–15 and subsequent tax years (see FA 2009 Sch 56 para 6(2), as amended by FA 2013 Sch 50 para 12(3), as to when a default is made in relation to a tax year).

[6] In Table, item 11GA inserted by FA 2014 s 101, Sch 21 para 8 with effect from 1 April 2015 (by virtue of SI 2015/812).

[7] In table, item 6ZB inserted by FA 2015 s 104(1), (2) with effect in relation to accounting periods beginning on or after 1 April 2015. For accounting periods that straddle that date, see FA 2015 s 116(2).

Prospective amendments—The following amendments are to be made by F(No 3)A 2010 s 27, Sch 11 paras 1, 2 (as amended by FA 2014 s 103, Sch 22 para 22(1)–(5)) with effect from a date to be appointed by Treasury order.

Note that the inserted text is amended by FA 2012 Sch 24 para 34 with effect in relation to the playing of machine games on or after 1 February 2013, as per the above footnote. See also the modification note above in relation to the application of this para until the coming into force of F(No 3)A 2010 Sch 11 para 2(13)(*a*), (14)(*a*)

Note that the inserted text is also amended by FA 2014 s 196, Sch 28 paras 28, 30 with effect from a date to be appointed. The FA 2014 amendments substitute items 11H, 11I and 11M; these changes are accounted for in the text below—

- in sub-para (2) figure "8J" to be substituted for figure "8";
- in Table—
  - entries to be inserted after items 6, 11, 13, 16 and 17;
  - item 20 to be repealed;
  - in item 23 columns 2, 3, item 24 column 2, words "items 1 to 6A, 6BA, 6BB, 6C, 9, 10 or 11A to 11M" to be substituted for words "items 1 to 6, 9 or 10";
  - in items 23, 24 column 3, words "item 18 or 19" to be substituted for words "any of items 18 to 20".

Table entries as inserted to read as follows—

"6A	Value added tax	Amount payable under section 25(1) of VATA 1994 (except an amount falling within item 6B, 13A, 23 or 24)	The date determined— (*a*) by or under regulations under section 25 of VATA 1994, or

			(*b*) in accordance with an order under section 28 of that Act, as the date by which the amount must be paid
6B	Value added tax	Amount payable under section 25(1) of VATA 1994 which is an instalment of an amount due in respect of a period of 9 months or more ("amount A")	The date on or before which P must pay any balancing payment or other outstanding payment due in respect of amount A
6BA	Value added tax	Amount payable under relevant special scheme return (as defined in paragraph 16(3) of Schedule 3B to VATA 1994) (except an amount falling within item 13A, 13AA, 13AB, 23 or 24)	The date by which the amount must be paid under the law of the member State which has established the special scheme
6BB	Value added tax	Amount payable under relevant non-UK return (as defined in paragraph 20(3) of Schedule 3BA to VATA 1994) (except an amount falling within item 13A, 13AA, 13AB, 23 or 24)	The date by which the amount must be paid under the law of the member State which has established the non-UK special scheme
6C	Insurance premium tax	Amount payable under regulations under section 54 of FA 1994 (except an amount falling within item 13B, 23 or 24)	The date determined by or under regulations under section 54 of FA 1994 as the date by which the amount must be paid".

"11A	Aggregates levy	Amount payable under regulations under section 25 of FA 2001 (except an amount falling within item 16A, 23 or 24)	The date determined by or under regulations under section 25 of FA 2001 as the date by which the amount must be paid
11B	Climate change levy	Amount payable under regulations under paragraph 41 of Schedule 6 to FA 2000 (except an amount falling within item 16B, 23 or 24)	The date determined by or under regulations under paragraph 41 of Schedule 6 to FA 2000 as the date by which the amount must be paid
11C	Landfill tax	Amount payable under regulations under section 49 of FA 1996 (except an amount falling within item 16C, 23 or 24)	The date determined by or under regulations under section 49 of FA 1996 as the date by which the amount must be paid
11D	Air passenger duty	Amount payable under regulations under section 38 of FA 1994 (except an amount falling within item 17A, 23 or 24)	The date determined by or under regulations under section 38 of FA 1994 as the date by which the amount must be paid
11E	Alcoholic liquor duties	Amount payable under regulations under section 13, 49, 56 or 62 of ALDA 1979 (except an amount falling within item 17A, 23 or 24)	The date determined by or under regulations under section 13, 49, 56 or 62 of ALDA 1979 as the date by which the amount must be paid
11F	Tobacco products duty	Amount payable under regulations under section 7 of TPDA 1979 (except an amount falling within item 17A, 23 or 24)	The date determined by or under regulations under section 7 of TPDA 1979 as the date by which the amount must be paid

11G	Hydrocarbon oil duties	Amount payable under regulations under section 21 or 24 of HODA 1979 (except an amount falling within item 17A, 23 or 24)	The date determined by or under regulations under section 21 or 24 of HODA 1979 as the date by which the amount must be paid
[11H	General betting duty	Amount payable under section 142 of FA 2014	The date determined— (*a*) under section 142 of FA 2014, or (*b*) by or under regulations under section 163 or 167 of that Act, as the date by which the amount must be paid
11I	Pool betting duty	Amount payable under section 151 of FA 2014	The date determined— (*a*) under section 151 of FA 2014, or (*b*) by or under regulations under section 163 or 167 of that Act, as the date by which the amount must be paid]
11J	Bingo duty	Amount payable under regulations under paragraph 9 of Schedule 3 to BGDA 1981 (except an amount falling within item 17A, 23 or 24)	The date determined by or under regulations under paragraph 9 of Schedule 3 to BGDA 1981 as the date by which the amount must be paid
11K	Lottery duty	Amount payable under section 26 of FA 1993 (except an amount falling within item 17A, 23 or 24)	The date determined — (*a*) by section 26 of FA 1993, or (*b*) by or under regulations under that section, as the date by which the amount must be paid
11L	Gaming duty	Amount payable under section 12 of FA 1997 (except an amount falling within item 17A, 23 or 24)	The date determined by or under regulations under — (*a*) section 12 of FA 1997, or (*b*) paragraph 11 of Schedule 1 to that Act, as the date by which the amount must be paid
[11M	Remote gaming duty	Amount payable under section 162 of FA 2014	The date determined by or under regulations under section 163 or 167 of FA 2014 as the date by which the amount must be paid]".

"13A	Value added tax	Amount assessed under section 73(1) of VATA 1994 in the absence of a return	The date by which the amount would have been required to be paid if it had been shown in the return

13AA	Value added tax	Amount assessed under section 73(1) of VATA 1994, by virtue of paragraph 16 of Schedule 3B to that Act, in the absence of a value added tax return (as defined in paragraph 23(1) of that Schedule)	The date by which the amount would have been required to be paid under the law of the member State under whose law the return was required
13AB	Value added tax	Amount assessed under section 73(1) of VATA 1994, by virtue of paragraph 20 of Schedule 3BA to that Act, in the absence of a relevant non-UK return (as defined in paragraph 38(1) of that Schedule)	The date by which the amount would have been required to be paid under the law of the member State under whose law the return was required
13B	Insurance premium tax	Amount assessed under section 56(1) of FA 1994 in the absence of a return	The date by which the amount would have been required to be paid if it had been shown in the return".

"16A	Aggregates levy	Amount assessed under paragraph 2 or 3 of Schedule 5 to FA 2001 in the absence of a return	The date by which the amount would have been required to be paid if it had been shown in the return
16B	Climate change levy	Amount assessed under paragraph 78 or 79 of Schedule 6 to FA 2000 in the absence of a return	The date by which the amount would have been required to be paid if it had been shown in the return
16C	Landfill tax	Amount assessed under section 50(1) of FA 1996 in the absence of a return	The date by which the amount would have been required to be paid if it had been shown in the return".

"17A	Tax falling within any of items 11D to 11M	Amount assessed under section 12(1) of FA 1994 in the absence of a return	The date by which the amount would have been required to be paid if it had been shown in the return".

In items 17A, 23 and 24 (as inserted), "11N" to be substituted for "11M" by FA 2012 s 191, Sch 24 para 34(*a*) with effect in relation to the playing of machine games on or after 1 February 2013 (and Schs 55, 56, as amended by FA 2012 Sch 24 Part 1, are taken to have come into force for the purposes of machine games duty on that date).

The following amendments to be made by FA 2013 Sch 34 para 10(2) with effect from the coming into force of F(No 3)A 2010 Sch 11 para 2(13)(*a*), (14)(*a*)—

- in item 23, in the second and third columns, for "9, 10" substitute "9 to 10A"; and
- in item 24, in the second column, for "9, 10" substitute "9 to 10A".

Assessments and determinations in default of return

2 The circumstances referred to in items 14, 17, 21 and 24 are where—

(*a*) P or another person is required to make or deliver a return falling within any item in the Table in Schedule 55,

(*b*) that person fails to make or deliver the return on or before the date by which it is required to be made or delivered, and

(*c*) if the return had been made or delivered as required, the return would have shown that an amount falling within any of items 1 to 10 was due and payable.

Modifications—FA 2009 Sch 56 has effect as if the reference to a return in this para included a reference to a bank payroll tax return (FA 2010 s 22, Sch 1 para 39(1), (5)).

Until F(No 3)A 2010 Sch 11 para 3 comes into force, para 2(*c*) has effect as if the reference in that para to items 1 to 10 were to items 1 to 10A (FA 2013 Sch 34 para 11).

Commencement—Finance Act 2009, Schedule 56 (Appointed Day and Consequential Provisions) Order, SI 2010/466: 6 April 2010 appointed as day on which Sch 56 comes into force for the following amounts specified in column 3 of the Table—items 2–4, and items 17, 23 and 24 but only in so far as the tax falls within any of items 2, 3 or 4 (see SI 2010/466 art 3).

Finance Act 2009, Schedules 55 and 56 (Income Tax Self Assessment and Pension Schemes) (Appointed Days and Consequential and Savings Provisions) Order, SI 2011/702 art 2 (appointed day for the coming into force of Sch 56 is 6 April 2011 in relation to an amount of tax which is payable in relation to the tax year 2010–11 or any subsequent tax year and falls within item 1, 12, 18 or 19 of the Table in para 1, or in so far as the tax falls within item 1 of that Table, item 17, 23 or 24 of that Table).

Prospective amendments—In sub-para (*c*) figure "11M" to be substituted for figure "10" by F(No 3)A 2010 s 27, Sch 11 paras 1, 3 with effect from a date to be appointed by Treasury order. Also see Modification note above.

In sub-para (*c*) "11N" substituted for "11M" (as prospectively substituted by F(No 3)A 2010) by FA 2012 s 191, Sch 24 para 34(*b*) with effect in relation to the playing of machine games on or after 1 February 2013 (and Schs 55, 56, as amended by FA 2012 Sch 24 Part 1, are taken to have come into force for the purposes of machine games duty on that date).

[Different penalty date for certain PAYE payments

2A—(1) PAYE regulations may provide that, in relation to specified payments of tax falling within item 2, the penalty date is a specified date later than that determined in accordance with column 4 of the Table.

(2) In sub-paragraph (1) "specified" means specified in the regulations.][1]

Commencement—Finance Act 2009, Schedules 55 and 56 (Income Tax Self Assessment and Pension Schemes) (Appointed Days and Consequential and Savings Provisions) Order, SI 2011/702 art 2 (appointed day for the coming into force of Sch 56 is 6 April 2011 in relation to an amount of tax which is payable in relation to the tax year 2010–11 or any subsequent tax year and falls within item 1, 12, 18 or 19 of the Table in para 1, or in so far as the tax falls within item 1 of that Table, item 17, 23 or 24 of that Table).

Amendments—

[1] This para and preceding cross-head inserted by F(No 3)A 2010 s 27, Sch 11 paras 1, 4 with effect from 25 January 2011 (by virtue of SI 2011/132 art 2(*b*)).

Amount of penalty: occasional amounts and amounts in respect of periods of 6 months or more

3—(1) This paragraph applies in the case of—

(*a*) a payment of tax falling within any of items 1, 3 and 7 to 24 in the Table,

[(*aa*) a payment of tax falling within item 6ZB in the Table,][1]

(*b*) a payment of tax falling within item 2 or 4 which relates to a period of 6 months or more, and

(*c*) a payment of tax falling within item 2 which is payable under regulations under section 688A of ITEPA 2003 (recovery from other persons of amounts due from managed service companies).

(2) P is liable to a penalty of 5% of the unpaid tax.

(3) If any amount of the tax is unpaid after the end of the period of 5 months beginning with the penalty date, P is liable to a penalty of 5% of that amount.

(4) If any amount of the tax is unpaid after the end of the period of 11 months beginning with the penalty date, P is liable to a penalty of 5% of that amount.

Modifications—FA 2009 Sch 56 has effect as if sub-para (1)(*a*) included a reference to a payment of bank payroll tax (FA 2010 s 22, Sch 1 para 39(1), (6)).

Commencement—Finance Act 2009, Schedule 56 (Appointed Day and Consequential Provisions) Order, SI 2010/466: 6 April 2010 appointed as day on which Sch 56 comes into force for the following amounts specified in column 3 of the Table—items 2–4, and items 17, 23 and 24 but only in so far as the tax falls within any of items 2, 3 or 4 (see SI 2010/466 art 3).

Finance Act 2009, Schedules 55 and 56 (Income Tax Self Assessment and Pension Schemes) (Appointed Days and Consequential and Savings Provisions) Order, SI 2011/702 art 2 (appointed day for the coming into force of Sch 56 is 6 April 2011 in relation to an amount of tax which is payable in relation to the tax year 2010–11 or any subsequent tax year and falls within item 1, 12, 18 or 19 of the Table in para 1, or in so far as the tax falls within item 1 of that Table, item 17, 23 or 24 of that Table).

Amendments—[1] Sub-para (1)(*aa*) inserted by FA 2015 s 104(1), (3) with effect in relation to accounting periods beginning on or after 1 April 2015. For accounting periods that straddle that date, see FA 2015 s 116(2).

Prospective amendments—In sub-para (1)(*a*) words "items 1, 3, 6B, 7 to 11 and 12 to 24" to be substituted for words "items 1, 3 and 7 to 24", in sub-para (1)(*b*) words "any of items 2, 4, 6A, 6C and 11A to 11M" to be substituted for words "item 2 or 4" and word "and" at the end to be repealed, and sub-paras (1)(*d*) and preceding word "and", and (1A) to be inserted, by F(No 3)A 2010 s 27, Sch 11 paras 1, 5 with effect from a date to be appointed by Treasury order. Sub-paras (1)(*d*), (1A) as inserted to read—

"(*d*) a payment of tax falling within item 6A which relates to a transitional period for the purposes of the annual accounting scheme.".

"(1A) In sub-paragraph (1)(*d*), a transitional period for the purposes of the annual accounting scheme is a prescribed accounting period (within the meaning of section 25(1) of VATA 1994) which—

ends on the day immediately preceding the date indicated by the Commissioners for Her Majesty's Revenue and Customs in a notification of authorisation under regulation 50 of the Value Added Tax Regulations 1995 (SI 1995/2518) (admission to annual accounting scheme), or

begins on the day immediately following the end of the last period of 12 months for which such an authorisation has effect.".

In sub-para (1)(*b*) "11N" to be substituted for "11M" by FA 2012 s 191, Sch 24 para 34(*c*) with effect in relation to the playing of machine games on or after 1 February 2013 (and Schs 55, 56, as amended by FA 2012 Sch 24 Part 1, are taken to have come into force for the purposes of machine games duty on that date).

4—(1) This paragraph applies in the case of a payment of tax falling within item 5 or 6 in the Table.
(2) P is liable to a penalty of 5% of the unpaid tax.
(3) If any amount of the tax is unpaid after the end of the period of 3 months beginning with the penalty date, P is liable to a penalty of 5% of that amount.
(4) If any amount of the tax is unpaid after the end of the period of 9 months beginning with the penalty date, P is liable to a penalty of 5% of that amount.

Commencement—Finance Act 2009, Schedules 55 and 56 (Income Tax Self Assessment and Pension Schemes) (Appointed Days and Consequential and Savings Provisions) Order, SI 2011/702 art 2 (appointed day for the coming into force of Sch 56 is 6 April 2011 in relation to an amount of tax which is payable in relation to the tax year 2010–11 or any subsequent tax year and falls within item 1, 12, 18 or 19 of the Table in para 1, or in so far as the tax falls within item 1 of that Table, item 17, 23 or 24 of that Table).

Amount of penalty: PAYE and CIS amounts

5—(1) Paragraphs 6 to 8 apply in the case of a payment of tax falling within item 2 or 4 in the Table.
(2) But those paragraphs do not apply in the case of a payment mentioned in paragraph 3(1)(*b*) or (*c*).

Commencement—Finance Act 2009, Schedule 56 (Appointed Day and Consequential Provisions) Order, SI 2010/466: 6 April 2010 appointed as day on which Sch 56 comes into force for the following amounts specified in column 3 of the Table—items 2–4, and items 17, 23 and 24 but only in so far as the tax falls within any of items 2, 3 or 4 (see SI 2010/466 art 3).
Finance Act 2009, Schedules 55 and 56 (Income Tax Self Assessment and Pension Schemes) (Appointed Days and Consequential and Savings Provisions) Order, SI 2011/702 art 2 (appointed day for the coming into force of Sch 56 is 6 April 2011 in relation to an amount of tax which is payable in relation to the tax year 2010–11 or any subsequent tax year and falls within item 1, 12, 18 or 19 of the Table in para 1, or in so far as the tax falls within item 1 of that Table, item 17, 23 or 24 of that Table).

[6—[(1) P is liable to a penalty under this paragraph, in relation to each tax, each time that P makes a default in relation to a tax year.][2]
(2) For the purposes of this paragraph, P makes a default [in relation to a tax year][2] when P fails to make one of the following payments (or to pay an amount comprising two or more of those payments) in full on or before the date on which it becomes due and payable—

(*a*) a payment under PAYE regulations [of tax payable in relation to the tax year][2];
(*b*) a payment of earnings-related contributions within the meaning of the Social Security (Contributions) Regulations 2001 (SI 2001/1004) [payable in relation to the tax year][2];
(*c*) a payment due under the Income Tax (Construction Industry Scheme) Regulations 2005 (SI 2005/2045) [payable in relation to the tax year][2];
(*d*) a repayment in respect of a student loan due under the Education (Student Loans) (Repayments) Regulations 2009 (SI 2009/470) or the Education (Student Loans) (Repayments) Regulations (Northern Ireland) 2000 (S.R. 2000 No 121) [and due for the tax year][2].

[(3) But where a failure to make one of those payments (or to pay an amount comprising two or more of those payments) would, apart from this sub-paragraph, constitute the first default in relation to a tax year, that failure does not count as a default in relation to that year for the purposes of a penalty under this paragraph.
(4) The amount of the penalty for a default made in relation to a tax year is determined by reference to—

(*a*) the amount of the tax comprised in the default, and
(*b*) the number of previous defaults that P has made in relation to the same tax year.

(5) If the default is P's 1st, 2nd or 3rd default in relation to the tax year, P is liable, at the time of the default, to a penalty of 1% of the amount of tax comprised in the default.
(6) If the default is P's 4th, 5th or 6th default in relation to the tax year, P is liable, at the time of the default, to a penalty of 2% of the amount of tax comprised in the default.
(7) If the default is P's 7th, 8th or 9th default in relation to the tax year, P is liable, at the time of the default, to a penalty of 3% of the amount of tax comprised in the default.
(7A) If the default is P's 10th or subsequent default in relation to the tax year, P is liable, at the time of the default, to a penalty of 4% of the amount of tax comprised in the default.][2]
(8) For the purposes of this paragraph—

(*a*) the amount of a tax comprised in a default is the amount of that tax comprised in the payment which P fails to make;
[(*b*) a previous default counts for the purposes of subparagraphs (5) to (7A) even if it is remedied before the time of the default giving rise to the penalty.][2]

[(8A) Regulations made by the Commissioners for Her Majesty's Revenue and Customs may specify—

(*a*) circumstances in which, for the purposes of sub-paragraph (2), a payment of less than the full amount may be treated as a payment in full;

(*b*) circumstances in which sub-paragraph (3) is not to apply.

(8B) Regulations under sub-paragraph (8A) may—

(*a*) make different provision for different cases, and

(*b*) include incidental, consequential and supplementary provision.][2]

(9) The Treasury may by order made by statutory instrument make such amendments to sub-paragraph (2) as they think fit in consequence of any amendment, revocation or re-enactment of the regulations mentioned in that sub-paragraph.][1]

Commencement—Finance Act 2009, Schedule 56 (Appointed Day and Consequential Provisions) Order, SI 2010/466: 6 April 2010 appointed as day on which Sch 56 comes into force for the following amounts specified in column 3 of the Table—items 2–4, and items 17, 23 and 24 but only in so far as the tax falls within any of items 2, 3 or 4 (see SI 2010/466 art 3).

Finance Act 2009, Schedules 55 and 56 (Income Tax Self Assessment and Pension Schemes) (Appointed Days and Consequential and Savings Provisions) Order, SI 2011/702 art 2 (appointed day for the coming into force of Sch 56 is 6 April 2011 in relation to an amount of tax which is payable in relation to the tax year 2010–11 or any subsequent tax year and falls within item 1, 12, 18 or 19 of the Table in para 1, or in so far as the tax falls within item 1 of that Table, item 17, 23 or 24 of that Table).

Regulations—Income Tax (Pay As You Earn) and the Income Tax (Construction Industry Scheme) (Amendment) Regulations, SI 2014/472.

Amendments—[1] This para substituted by F(No 3)A 2010 s 27, Sch 11 paras 1, 6 with effect from 25 January 2011 (by virtue of SI 2011/132 art 2(*b*)).

[2] Sub-paras (1), (8)(*b*) substituted, sub-paras (3)–(7A) substituted for sub-paras (3)–(7), in sub-para (2), (2)(*a*)–(*d*), words inserted, and sub-paras (8A), (8B) inserted, by FA 2013 s 230, Sch 50 paras 10, 12 with effect for defaults made in relation to the tax year 2014–15 and subsequent tax years (see FA 2009 Sch 56 para 6(2), as amended by FA 2013 Sch 50 para 12(3), as to when a default is made in relation to a tax year)—

7 If any amount of the tax is unpaid after the end of the period of 6 months beginning with the penalty date, P is liable to a penalty of 5% of that amount.

Commencement—Finance Act 2009, Schedule 56 (Appointed Day and Consequential Provisions) Order, SI 2010/466: 6 April 2010 appointed as day on which Sch 56 comes into force for the following amounts specified in column 3 of the Table—items 2–4, and items 17, 23 and 24 but only in so far as the tax falls within any of items 2, 3 or 4 (see SI 2010/466 art 3).

Finance Act 2009, Schedules 55 and 56 (Income Tax Self Assessment and Pension Schemes) (Appointed Days and Consequential and Savings Provisions) Order, SI 2011/702 art 2 (appointed day for the coming into force of Sch 56 is 6 April 2011 in relation to an amount of tax which is payable in relation to the tax year 2010–11 or any subsequent tax year and falls within item 1, 12, 18 or 19 of the Table in para 1, or in so far as the tax falls within item 1 of that Table, item 17, 23 or 24 of that Table).

8 If any amount of the tax is unpaid after the end of the period of 12 months beginning with the penalty date, P is liable to a penalty of 5% of that amount.

Commencement—Finance Act 2009, Schedule 56 (Appointed Day and Consequential Provisions) Order, SI 2010/466: 6 April 2010 appointed as day on which Sch 56 comes into force for the following amounts specified in column 3 of the Table—items 2–4, and items 17, 23 and 24 but only in so far as the tax falls within any of items 2, 3 or 4 (see SI 2010/466 art 3).

Finance Act 2009, Schedules 55 and 56 (Income Tax Self Assessment and Pension Schemes) (Appointed Days and Consequential and Savings Provisions) Order, SI 2011/702 art 2 (appointed day for the coming into force of Sch 56 is 6 April 2011 in relation to an amount of tax which is payable in relation to the tax year 2010–11 or any subsequent tax year and falls within item 1, 12, 18 or 19 of the Table in para 1, or in so far as the tax falls within item 1 of that Table, item 17, 23 or 24 of that Table).

[Amount of penalty: amounts in respect of periods of between 2 and 6 months

8A—(1) Paragraphs 8B to 8E apply in the case of a payment of tax falling within any of items 6A, 6BA, 6BB, 6C and 11A to [11N] in the Table which relates to a period of less than 6 months but more than 2 months.

(2) But those paragraphs do not apply in the case of a payment mentioned in paragraph 3(1)(*d*).

(3) Paragraph 8K sets out how payments on account of VAT (item 6A) are to be treated for the purposes of paragraphs 8B to 8E.]

Commencement—Finance Act 2009, Schedules 55 and 56 (Income Tax Self Assessment and Pension Schemes) (Appointed Days and Consequential and Savings Provisions) Order, SI 2011/702 art 2 (appointed day for the coming into force of Sch 56 is 6 April 2011 in relation to an amount of tax which is payable in relation to the tax year 2010–11 or any subsequent tax year and falls within item 1, 12, 18 or 19 of the Table in para 1, or in so far as the tax falls within item 1 of that Table, item 17, 23 or 24 of that Table).

Prospective amendments—Paras 8A–8J and preceding cross-heads to be inserted by F(No 3)A 2010 s 27, Sch 11 paras 1, 7 (as amended by FA 2014 s 103, Sch 22 para 22(6)) with effect from a date to be appointed by Treasury order.

In sub-para (1) "11N" substituted for "11M" by FA 2012 s 191, Sch 24 para 34(*d*) with effect in relation to the playing of machine games on or after 1 February 2013 (and Schs 55, 56, as amended by FA 2012 Sch 24 Part 1, are taken to have come into force for the purposes of machine games duty on that date).

[8B—(1) A penalty period begins to run on the penalty date for the payment of tax.

(2) The penalty period ends with the day 12 months after the date specified in or for the purposes of column 4 for the payment, unless it is extended under paragraph 8C(2)(*c*) or 8H(2)(*c*).]

Commencement—Finance Act 2009, Schedules 55 and 56 (Income Tax Self Assessment and Pension Schemes) (Appointed Days and Consequential and Savings Provisions) Order, SI 2011/702 art 2 (appointed day for the coming into force of Sch 56 is

6 April 2011 in relation to an amount of tax which is payable in relation to the tax year 2010–11 or any subsequent tax year and falls within item 1, 12, 18 or 19 of the Table in para 1, or in so far as the tax falls within item 1 of that Table, item 17, 23 or 24 of that Table).

Prospective amendments—Paras 8A–8J and preceding cross-heads to be inserted by F(No 3)A 2010 s 27, Sch 11 paras 1, 7 with effect from a date to be appointed by Treasury order.

[8C—(1) This paragraph applies if—

(*a*) a penalty period has begun under paragraph 8B or 8G because P has failed to make a payment ("payment A"), and

(*b*) before the end of the period, P fails to make another payment ("payment B") falling within the same item in the Table as payment A.

(2) In such a case—

(*a*) paragraph 8B(1) does not apply to the failure to make payment B,

(*b*) P is liable to a penalty under this paragraph for that failure, And

(*c*) the penalty period that has begun is extended so that it ends with the day 12 months after the date specified in or for the purposes of column 4 for payment B.

(3) The amount of the penalty under this paragraph is determined by reference to the number of defaults that P has made during the penalty period.

(4) If the default is P's first default during the penalty period, P is liable, at the time of the default, to a penalty of 2% of the amount of the default.

(5) If the default is P's second default during the penalty period, P is liable, at the time of the default, to a penalty of 3% of the amount of the default.

(6) If the default is P's third or a subsequent default during the penalty period, P is liable, at the time of the default, to a penalty of 4% of the amount of the default.

(7) For the purposes of this paragraph—

(*a*) P makes a default when P fails to pay an amount of tax in full on or before the date on which it becomes due and payable;

(*b*) in accordance with sub-paragraph (1)(*b*), the references in sub-paragraphs (3) to (6) to a default are references to a default in relation to the tax to which payments A and B relate;

(*c*) a default counts for the purposes of those sub-paragraphs if (but only if) the period to which the payment relates is less than 6 months;

(*d*) the amount of a default is the amount which P fails to pay.

(8) A penalty period may be extended more than once under subparagraph (2)(*c*).]

Commencement—Finance Act 2009, Schedules 55 and 56 (Income Tax Self Assessment and Pension Schemes) (Appointed Days and Consequential and Savings Provisions) Order, SI 2011/702 art 2 (appointed day for the coming into force of Sch 56 is 6 April 2011 in relation to an amount of tax which is payable in relation to the tax year 2010–11 or any subsequent tax year and falls within item 1, 12, 18 or 19 of the Table in para 1, or in so far as the tax falls within item 1 of that Table, item 17, 23 or 24 of that Table).

Prospective amendments—Paras 8A–8J and preceding cross-heads to be inserted by F(No 3)A 2010 s 27, Sch 11 paras 1, 7 with effect from a date to be appointed by Treasury order.

[8D If any amount of the tax is unpaid after the end of the period of 6 months beginning with the penalty date, P is liable to a penalty of 5% of that amount.]

Commencement—Finance Act 2009, Schedules 55 and 56 (Income Tax Self Assessment and Pension Schemes) (Appointed Days and Consequential and Savings Provisions) Order, SI 2011/702 art 2 (appointed day for the coming into force of Sch 56 is 6 April 2011 in relation to an amount of tax which is payable in relation to the tax year 2010–11 or any subsequent tax year and falls within item 1, 12, 18 or 19 of the Table in para 1, or in so far as the tax falls within item 1 of that Table, item 17, 23 or 24 of that Table).

Prospective amendments—Paras 8A–8J and preceding cross-heads to be inserted by F(No 3)A 2010 s 27, Sch 11 paras 1, 7 with effect from a date to be appointed by Treasury order.

[8E If any amount of the tax is unpaid after the end of the period of 12 months beginning with the penalty date, P is liable to a penalty of 5% of that amount.]

Commencement—Finance Act 2009, Schedules 55 and 56 (Income Tax Self Assessment and Pension Schemes) (Appointed Days and Consequential and Savings Provisions) Order, SI 2011/702 art 2 (appointed day for the coming into force of Sch 56 is 6 April 2011 in relation to an amount of tax which is payable in relation to the tax year 2010–11 or any subsequent tax year and falls within item 1, 12, 18 or 19 of the Table in para 1, or in so far as the tax falls within item 1 of that Table, item 17, 23 or 24 of that Table).

Prospective amendments—Paras 8A–8J and preceding cross-heads to be inserted by F(No 3)A 2010 s 27, Sch 11 paras 1, 7 with effect from a date to be appointed by Treasury order.

[Amount of penalty: amounts in respect of periods of 2 months or less

8F—(1) Paragraphs 8G to 8J apply in the case of a payment of tax falling within any of items 6A, 6C and 11A to [11N] in the Table which relates to a period of 2 months or less.

(2) But those paragraphs do not apply in the case of a payment mentioned in paragraph 3(1)(*d*).]

Commencement—Finance Act 2009, Schedules 55 and 56 (Income Tax Self Assessment and Pension Schemes) (Appointed Days and Consequential and Savings Provisions) Order, SI 2011/702 art 2 (appointed day for the coming into force of Sch 56 is

6 April 2011 in relation to an amount of tax which is payable in relation to the tax year 2010–11 or any subsequent tax year and falls within item 1, 12, 18 or 19 of the Table in para 1, or in so far as the tax falls within item 1 of that Table, item 17, 23 or 24 of that Table).

Prospective amendments—Paras 8A–8J and preceding cross-heads to be inserted by F(No 3)A 2010 s 27, Sch 11 paras 1, 7 with effect from a date to be appointed by Treasury order.

In sub-para (1) "11N" substituted for "11M" by FA 2012 s 191, Sch 24 para 34(*e*) with effect in relation to the playing of machine games on or after 1 February 2013 (and Schs 55, 56, as amended by FA 2012 Sch 24 Part 1, are taken to have come into force for the purposes of machine games duty on that date).

[8G—(1) A penalty period begins to run on the penalty date for the payment of tax.

(2) The penalty period ends with the day 12 months after the date specified in or for the purposes of column 4 for the payment, unless it is extended under paragraph 8C(2)(*c*) or 8H(2)(*c*).]

Commencement—Finance Act 2009, Schedules 55 and 56 (Income Tax Self Assessment and Pension Schemes) (Appointed Days and Consequential and Savings Provisions) Order, SI 2011/702 art 2 (appointed day for the coming into force of Sch 56 is 6 April 2011 in relation to an amount of tax which is payable in relation to the tax year 2010–11 or any subsequent tax year and falls within item 1, 12, 18 or 19 of the Table in para 1, or in so far as the tax falls within item 1 of that Table, item 17, 23 or 24 of that Table).

Prospective amendments—Paras 8A–8J and preceding cross-heads to be inserted by F(No 3)A 2010 s 27, Sch 11 paras 1, 7 with effect from a date to be appointed by Treasury order.

[8H—(1) This paragraph applies if—

(*a*) a penalty period has begun under paragraph 8B or 8G because P has failed to make a payment ("payment A"), and

(*b*) before the end of the period, P fails to make another payment ("payment B") falling within the same item in the Table as payment A.

(2) In such a case—

(*a*) paragraph 8G(1) does not apply to the failure to make payment B,

(*b*) P is liable to a penalty under this paragraph for that failure, and

(*c*) the penalty period that has begun is extended so that it ends with the day 12 months after the date specified in or for the purposes of column 4 for payment B.

(3) The amount of the penalty under this paragraph is determined by reference to the number of defaults that P has made during the penalty period.

(4) If the default is P's first, second or third default during the penalty period, P is liable, at the time of the default, to a penalty of 1% of the amount of the default.

(5) If the default is P's fourth, fifth or sixth default during the penalty period, P is liable, at the time of the default, to a penalty of 2% of the amount of the default.

(6) If the default is P's seventh, eighth or ninth default during the penalty period, P is liable, at the time of the default, to a penalty of 3% of the amount of the default.

(7) If the default is P's tenth or a subsequent default during the penalty period, P is liable, at the time of the default, to a penalty of 4% of the amount of the default.

(8) For the purposes of this paragraph—

(*a*) P makes a default when P fails to pay an amount of tax in full on or before the date on which it becomes due and payable;

(*b*) in accordance with sub-paragraph (1)(*b*), the references in sub-paragraphs (3) to (7) to a default are references to a default in relation to the tax to which payments A and B relate;

(*c*) a default counts for the purposes of those sub-paragraphs if (but only if) the period to which the payment relates is less than 6 months;

(*d*) the amount of a default is the amount which P fails to pay.

(9) A penalty period may be extended more than once under subparagraph (2)(*c*).]

Commencement—Finance Act 2009, Schedules 55 and 56 (Income Tax Self Assessment and Pension Schemes) (Appointed Days and Consequential and Savings Provisions) Order, SI 2011/702 art 2 (appointed day for the coming into force of Sch 56 is 6 April 2011 in relation to an amount of tax which is payable in relation to the tax year 2010–11 or any subsequent tax year and falls within item 1, 12, 18 or 19 of the Table in para 1, or in so far as the tax falls within item 1 of that Table, item 17, 23 or 24 of that Table).

Prospective amendments—Paras 8A–8J and preceding cross-heads to be inserted by F(No 3)A 2010 s 27, Sch 11 paras 1, 7 with effect from a date to be appointed by Treasury order.

[8I If any amount of the tax is unpaid after the end of the period of 6 months beginning with the penalty date, P is liable to a penalty of 5% of that amount.]

Commencement—Finance Act 2009, Schedules 55 and 56 (Income Tax Self Assessment and Pension Schemes) (Appointed Days and Consequential and Savings Provisions) Order, SI 2011/702 art 2 (appointed day for the coming into force of Sch 56 is 6 April 2011 in relation to an amount of tax which is payable in relation to the tax year 2010–11 or any subsequent tax year and falls within item 1, 12, 18 or 19 of the Table in para 1, or in so far as the tax falls within item 1 of that Table, item 17, 23 or 24 of that Table).

Prospective amendments—Paras 8A–8J and preceding cross-heads to be inserted by F(No 3)A 2010 s 27, Sch 11 paras 1, 7 with effect from a date to be appointed by Treasury order.

[8J If any amount of the tax is unpaid after the end of the period of 12 months beginning with the penalty date, P is liable to a penalty of 5% of that amount.]

Commencement—Finance Act 2009, Schedules 55 and 56 (Income Tax Self Assessment and Pension Schemes) (Appointed Days and Consequential and Savings Provisions) Order, SI 2011/702 art 2 (appointed day for the coming into force of Sch 56 is 6 April 2011 in relation to an amount of tax which is payable in relation to the tax year 2010–11 or any subsequent tax year and falls within item 1, 12, 18 or 19 of the Table in para 1, or in so far as the tax falls within item 1 of that Table, item 17, 23 or 24 of that Table).

Prospective amendments—Paras 8A–8J and preceding cross-heads to be inserted by F(No 3)A 2010 s 27, Sch 11 paras 1, 7 with effect from a date to be appointed by Treasury order.

[Calculation of unpaid VAT: treatment of payments on account

8K—(1) Where P is required, by virtue of an order under section 28 of VATA 1994, to make any payment on account of VAT—

(*a*) each payment is to be treated for the purposes of this Schedule as relating to the prescribed accounting period in respect of which it is to be paid (and not as relating to the interval between the dates on which payments on account are required to be made), and

(*b*) the amount of tax unpaid in respect of the prescribed accounting period is the total of the amounts produced by paragraphs (*a*) and (*b*) of sub-paragraph (3).

(2) In determining that total—

(*a*) if there is more than one amount of POAD or POAT, those amounts are to be added together, and

(*b*) if the amount produced by sub-paragraph (3)(*b*) is less than zero, that amount is to be disregarded.

(3) The amounts are—

(*a*) POAD – POAT, and

(*b*) BPD – BPT.

(4) In this paragraph—

POAD is the amount of any payment on account due in respect of the prescribed accounting period,

POAT is the amount of any payment on account paid on time (that is, on or before the date on which it was required to be made),

BPD (which is the balancing payment due in respect of the prescribed accounting period) is equal to PAPD – POAD, and

BPT (which is the amount paid on time in satisfaction of any liability to pay BPD) is equal to PAPP – POAP.

(5) In sub-paragraph (4)—

PAPD is the amount of VAT due in respect of the prescribed accounting period,

PAPP is the total amount paid, on or before the last day on which P is required to make payments in respect of that period, in satisfaction of any liability to pay PAPD, and

POAP is the total amount paid, on or before that day (but whether or not paid on time), in satisfaction of any liability to pay POAD.]

Commencement—Finance Act 2009, Schedules 55 and 56 (Income Tax Self Assessment and Pension Schemes) (Appointed Days and Consequential and Savings Provisions) Order, SI 2011/702 art 2 (appointed day for the coming into force of Sch 56 is 6 April 2011 in relation to an amount of tax which is payable in relation to the tax year 2010–11 or any subsequent tax year and falls within item 1, 12, 18 or 19 of the Table in para 1, or in so far as the tax falls within item 1 of that Table, item 17, 23 or 24 of that Table).

Prospective amendments—Para 8K and preceding cross-head to be inserted by F(No 3)A 2010 s 27, Sch 11 paras 1, 8 with effect from a date to be appointed by Treasury order.

Special reduction

9—(1) If HMRC think it right because of special circumstances, they may reduce a penalty under any paragraph of this Schedule.

(2) In sub-paragraph (1) "special circumstances" does not include—

(*a*) ability to pay, or

(*b*) the fact that a potential loss of revenue from one taxpayer is balanced by a potential over-payment by another.

(3) In sub-paragraph (1) the reference to reducing a penalty includes a reference to—

(*a*) staying a penalty, and

(*b*) agreeing a compromise in relation to proceedings for a penalty.

Commencement—Finance Act 2009, Schedule 56 (Appointed Day and Consequential Provisions) Order, SI 2010/466: 6 April 2010 appointed as day on which Sch 56 comes into force for the following amounts specified in column 3 of the Table—items 2–4, and items 17, 23 and 24 but only in so far as the tax falls within any of items 2, 3 or 4 (see SI 2010/466 art 3).

Finance Act 2009, Schedules 55 and 56 (Income Tax Self Assessment and Pension Schemes) (Appointed Days and Consequential and Savings Provisions) Order, SI 2011/702 art 2 (appointed day for the coming into force of Sch 56 is 6 April 2011 in relation to an amount of tax which is payable in relation to the tax year 2010–11 or any subsequent tax year and falls within item 1, 12, 18 or 19 of the Table in para 1, or in so far as the tax falls within item 1 of that Table, item 17, 23 or 24 of that Table).

Cross-references—See FA 2014 s 226(7) (application of paras 9–18 of this Schedule, with any necessary modifications, to penalties for failure to pay accelerated payment).

[Interaction with other penalties and late payment surcharges

9A In the application of the following provisions, no account shall be taken of a penalty under this Schedule—

(*a*) section 97A of TMA 1970 (multiple penalties),

(*b*) paragraph 12(2) of Schedule 24 to FA 2007 (interaction with other penalties), and

(*c*) paragraph 15(1) of Schedule 41 to FA 2008 (interaction with other penalties).][1]

Cross-references—See FA 2014 s 226(7) (application of paras 9–18 of this Schedule, with any necessary modifications, to penalties for failure to pay accelerated payment).

Amendments—[1] Paragraph 9A and preceding cross-head inserted by FA 2013 s 230, Sch 50 paras 10, 13 with effect for defaults made in relation to the tax year 2014–15 and subsequent tax years (see FA 2009 Sch 56 para 6(2), as amended by FA 2013 Sch 50 para 12(3), as to when a default is made in relation to a tax year).

Suspension of penalty during currency of agreement for deferred payment

10—(1) This paragraph applies if—

(*a*) P fails to pay an amount of tax when it becomes due and payable,

(*b*) P makes a request to HMRC that payment of the amount of tax be deferred, and

(*c*) HMRC agrees that payment of that amount may be deferred for a period ("the deferral period").

(2) If P would (apart from this sub-paragraph) become liable, between the date on which P makes the request and the end of the deferral period, to a penalty under any paragraph of this Schedule for failing to pay that amount, P is not liable to that penalty.

(3) But if—

(*a*) P breaks the agreement (see sub-paragraph (4)), and

(*b*) HMRC serves on P a notice specifying any penalty to which P would become liable apart from sub-paragraph (2),

P becomes liable, at the date of the notice, to that penalty.

(4) P breaks an agreement if—

(*a*) P fails to pay the amount of tax in question when the deferral period ends, or

(*b*) the deferral is subject to P complying with a condition (including a condition that part of the amount be paid during the deferral period) and P fails to comply with it.

(5) If the agreement mentioned in sub-paragraph (1)(*c*) is varied at any time by a further agreement between P and HMRC, this paragraph applies from that time to the agreement as varied.

Commencement—Finance Act 2009, Schedule 56 (Appointed Day and Consequential Provisions) Order, SI 2010/466: 6 April 2010 appointed as day on which Sch 56 comes into force for the following amounts specified in column 3 of the Table—items 2–4, and items 17, 23 and 24 but only in so far as the tax falls within any of items 2, 3 or 4 (see SI 2010/466 art 3).

Finance Act 2009, Schedules 55 and 56 (Income Tax Self Assessment and Pension Schemes) (Appointed Days and Consequential and Savings Provisions) Order, SI 2011/702 art 2 (appointed day for the coming into force of Sch 56 is 6 April 2011 in relation to an amount of tax which is payable in relation to the tax year 2010–11 or any subsequent tax year and falls within item 1, 12, 18 or 19 of the Table in para 1, or in so far as the tax falls within item 1 of that Table, item 17, 23 or 24 of that Table).

Cross-references—See FA 2014 s 226(7) (application of paras 9–18 of this Schedule, with any necessary modifications, to penalties for failure to pay accelerated payment).

Assessment

11—(1) Where P is liable for a penalty under any paragraph of this Schedule HMRC must—

(*a*) assess the penalty,

(*b*) notify P, and

(*c*) state in the notice the period in respect of which the penalty is assessed.

(2) A penalty under any paragraph of this Schedule must be paid before the end of the period of 30 days beginning with the day on which notice of the assessment of the penalty is issued.

(3) An assessment of a penalty under any paragraph of this Schedule—

(*a*) is to be treated for procedural purposes in the same way as an assessment to tax (except in respect of a matter expressly provided for by this Schedule),

(*b*) may be enforced as if it were an assessment to tax, and

(*c*) may be combined with an assessment to tax.

(4) A supplementary assessment may be made in respect of a penalty if an earlier assessment operated by reference to an underestimate of an amount of [tax which was due or payable][1].

[(4A) If an assessment in respect of a penalty is based on an amount of tax due or payable that is found by HMRC to be excessive, HMRC may by notice to P amend the assessment so that it is based upon the correct amount.

(4B) An amendment made under sub-paragraph (4A)—

(*a*) does not affect when the penalty must be paid;

(*b*) may be made after the last day on which the assessment in question could have been made under paragraph 12.][2]

(5) . . . [2]

Commencement—Finance Act 2009, Schedule 56 (Appointed Day and Consequential Provisions) Order, SI 2010/466: 6 April 2010 appointed as day on which Sch 56 comes into force for the following amounts specified in column 3 of the Table—items 2–4, and items 17, 23 and 24 but only in so far as the tax falls within any of items 2, 3 or 4 (see SI 2010/466 art 3).

Finance Act 2009, Schedules 55 and 56 (Income Tax Self Assessment and Pension Schemes) (Appointed Days and Consequential and Savings Provisions) Order, SI 2011/702 art 2 (appointed day for the coming into force of Sch 56 is 6 April 2011 in relation to an amount of tax which is payable in relation to the tax year 2010–11 or any subsequent tax year and falls within item 1, 12, 18 or 19 of the Table in para 1, or in so far as the tax falls within item 1 of that Table, item 17, 23 or 24 of that Table).

Cross-references—See FA 2014 s 226(7) (application of paras 9–18 of this Schedule, with any necessary modifications, to penalties for failure to pay accelerated payment).

Amendments—[1] In sub-para (4) words substituted for words "unpaid tax", and sub-para (4A) inserted, by (F(No 3)A 2010 s 27, Sch 11 paras 1, 9 with effect from 6 April 2011 in relation to an amount of tax which is payable in relation to the tax year 2010–11 or any subsequent tax year, and falls within item 1, 12, 18 or 19 of the Table in FA 2009 Sch 56 para 1, or insofar as the tax falls within item 1 of that Table, item 17, 23 or 24 of that Table (by virtue of SI 2011/703 art 3).

[2] Sub-paras (4A), (4B) substituted for sub-para (4A), and sub-para (5) repealed, by FA 2013 s 230, Sch 50 paras 10, 14 with effect for defaults made in relation to the tax year 2014–15 and subsequent tax years (see FA 2009 Sch 56 para 6(2), as amended by FA 2013 Sch 50 para 12(3), as to when a default is made in relation to a tax year).

12—(1) An assessment of a penalty under any paragraph of this Schedule in respect of any amount must be made on or before the later of date A and (where it applies) date B.

(2) Date A is the last day of the period of 2 years beginning with the date specified in or for the purposes of column 4 of the Table (that is to say, the last date on which payment may be made without incurring a penalty).

(3) Date B is the last day of the period of 12 months beginning with—

(*a*) the end of the appeal period for the assessment of the amount of tax in respect of which the penalty is assessed, or

(*b*) if there is no such assessment, the date on which that amount of tax is ascertained.

(4) In sub-paragraph (3)(*a*) "appeal period" means the period during which—

(*a*) an appeal could be brought, or

(*b*) an appeal that has been brought has not been determined or withdrawn.

Commencement—Finance Act 2009, Schedule 56 (Appointed Day and Consequential Provisions) Order, SI 2010/466: 6 April 2010 appointed as day on which Sch 56 comes into force for the following amounts specified in column 3 of the Table—items 2–4, and items 17, 23 and 24 but only in so far as the tax falls within any of items 2, 3 or 4 (see SI 2010/466 art 3).

Finance Act 2009, Schedules 55 and 56 (Income Tax Self Assessment and Pension Schemes) (Appointed Days and Consequential and Savings Provisions) Order, SI 2011/702 art 2 (appointed day for the coming into force of Sch 56 is 6 April 2011 in relation to an amount of tax which is payable in relation to the tax year 2010–11 or any subsequent tax year and falls within item 1, 12, 18 or 19 of the Table in para 1, or in so far as the tax falls within item 1 of that Table, item 17, 23 or 24 of that Table).

Cross-references—See FA 2014 s 226(7) (application of paras 9–18 of this Schedule, with any necessary modifications, to penalties for failure to pay accelerated payment).

Appeal

13—(1) P may appeal against a decision of HMRC that a penalty is payable by P.

(2) P may appeal against a decision of HMRC as to the amount of a penalty payable by P.

Commencement—Finance Act 2009, Schedule 56 (Appointed Day and Consequential Provisions) Order, SI 2010/466: 6 April 2010 appointed as day on which Sch 56 comes into force for the following amounts specified in column 3 of the Table—items 2–4, and items 17, 23 and 24 but only in so far as the tax falls within any of items 2, 3 or 4 (see SI 2010/466 art 3).

Finance Act 2009, Schedules 55 and 56 (Income Tax Self Assessment and Pension Schemes) (Appointed Days and Consequential and Savings Provisions) Order, SI 2011/702 art 2 (appointed day for the coming into force of Sch 56 is 6 April 2011 in relation to an amount of tax which is payable in relation to the tax year 2010–11 or any subsequent tax year and falls within item 1, 12, 18 or 19 of the Table in para 1, or in so far as the tax falls within item 1 of that Table, item 17, 23 or 24 of that Table).

Cross-references—See FA 2014 s 226(7) (application of paras 9–18 of this Schedule, with any necessary modifications, to penalties for failure to pay accelerated payment).

14—(1) An appeal under paragraph 13 is to be treated in the same way as an appeal against an assessment to the tax concerned (including by the application of any provision about bringing the appeal by notice to HMRC, about HMRC review of the decision or about determination of the appeal by the First-tier Tribunal or Upper Tribunal).

(2) Sub-paragraph (1) does not apply—

(*a*) so as to require P to pay a penalty before an appeal against the assessment of the penalty is determined, or

(*b*) in respect of any other matter expressly provided for by this Act.

Commencement—Finance Act 2009, Schedule 56 (Appointed Day and Consequential Provisions) Order, SI 2010/466: 6 April 2010 appointed as day on which Sch 56 comes into force for the following amounts specified in column 3 of the Table—items 2–4, and items 17, 23 and 24 but only in so far as the tax falls within any of items 2, 3 or 4 (see SI 2010/466 art 3).

Finance Act 2009, Schedules 55 and 56 (Income Tax Self Assessment and Pension Schemes) (Appointed Days and Consequential and Savings Provisions) Order, SI 2011/702 art 2 (appointed day for the coming into force of Sch 56 is 6 April 2011 in relation to an amount of tax which is payable in relation to the tax year 2010–11 or any subsequent tax year and falls within item 1, 12, 18 or 19 of the Table in para 1, or in so far as the tax falls within item 1 of that Table, item 17, 23 or 24 of that Table).

Cross-references—See FA 2014 s 226(7) (application of paras 9–18 of this Schedule, with any necessary modifications, to penalties for failure to pay accelerated payment).

15—(1) On an appeal under paragraph 13(1) that is notified to the tribunal, the tribunal may affirm or cancel HMRC's decision.

(2) On an appeal under paragraph 13(2) that is notified to the tribunal, the tribunal may—

(*a*) affirm HMRC's decision, or

(*b*) substitute for HMRC's decision another decision that HMRC had power to make.

(3) If the tribunal substitutes its decision for HMRC's, the tribunal may rely on paragraph 9—

(*a*) to the same extent as HMRC (which may mean applying the same percentage reduction as HMRC to a different starting point), or

(*b*) to a different extent, but only if the tribunal thinks that HMRC's decision in respect of the application of paragraph 9 was flawed.

(4) In sub-paragraph (3)(*b*) "flawed" means flawed when considered in the light of the principles applicable in proceedings for judicial review.

(5) In this paragraph "tribunal" means the First-tier Tribunal or Upper Tribunal (as appropriate by virtue of paragraph 14(1)).

Commencement—Finance Act 2009, Schedule 56 (Appointed Day and Consequential Provisions) Order, SI 2010/466: 6 April 2010 appointed as day on which Sch 56 comes into force for the following amounts specified in column 3 of the Table—items 2–4, and items 17, 23 and 24 but only in so far as the tax falls within any of items 2, 3 or 4 (see SI 2010/466 art 3).

Finance Act 2009, Schedules 55 and 56 (Income Tax Self Assessment and Pension Schemes) (Appointed Days and Consequential and Savings Provisions) Order, SI 2011/702 art 2 (appointed day for the coming into force of Sch 56 is 6 April 2011 in relation to an amount of tax which is payable in relation to the tax year 2010–11 or any subsequent tax year and falls within item 1, 12, 18 or 19 of the Table in para 1, or in so far as the tax falls within item 1 of that Table, item 17, 23 or 24 of that Table).

Cross-references—See FA 2014 s 226(7) (application of paras 9–18 of this Schedule, with any necessary modifications, to penalties for failure to pay accelerated payment).

Reasonable excuse

16—(1) Liability to a penalty under any paragraph of this Schedule does not arise in relation to a failure to make a payment if P satisfies HMRC or (on appeal) the First-tier Tribunal or Upper Tribunal that there is a reasonable excuse for the failure.

(2) For the purposes of sub-paragraph (1)—

(*a*) an insufficiency of funds is not a reasonable excuse unless attributable to events outside P's control,

(*b*) where P relies on any other person to do anything, that is not a reasonable excuse unless P took reasonable care to avoid the failure, and

(*c*) where P had a reasonable excuse for the failure but the excuse has ceased, P is to be treated as having continued to have the excuse if the failure is remedied without unreasonable delay after the excuse ceased.

Commencement—Finance Act 2009, Schedule 56 (Appointed Day and Consequential Provisions) Order, SI 2010/466: 6 April 2010 appointed as day on which Sch 56 comes into force for the following amounts specified in column 3 of the Table—items 2–4, and items 17, 23 and 24 but only in so far as the tax falls within any of items 2, 3 or 4 (see SI 2010/466 art 3).

Finance Act 2009, Schedules 55 and 56 (Income Tax Self Assessment and Pension Schemes) (Appointed Days and Consequential and Savings Provisions) Order, SI 2011/702 art 2 (appointed day for the coming into force of Sch 56 is 6 April 2011 in relation to an amount of tax which is payable in relation to the tax year 2010–11 or any subsequent tax year and falls within item 1, 12, 18 or 19 of the Table in para 1, or in so far as the tax falls within item 1 of that Table, item 17, 23 or 24 of that Table).

Cross-references—See FA 2014 s 226(7) (application of paras 9–18 of this Schedule, with any necessary modifications, to penalties for failure to pay accelerated payment).

Amendments—Sub-para (1) substituted by F(No 3)A 2010 s 27, Sch 11 paras 1, 10 with effect as follows—

- from 25 January 2011 in respect of the following amounts of tax specified in column 3 of the Table in Sch 56 para 1—
  - item 2 (PAYE regulations);
  - item 3 (returns under FA 2004 s 254(1));
  - item 4 (FA 2004 s 62); and
  - items 17, 23 and 24 but only insofar as the tax falls within any of items 2, 3 or 4.
-

for remaining purposes from a date to be appointed by Treasury order.

Sub-para (1) as substituted reads as follows—

"(1) If P satisfies HMRC or (on appeal) the First-tier Tribunal or Upper Tribunal that there is a reasonable excuse for a failure to make a payment—

liability to a penalty under any paragraph of this Schedule does not arise in relation to that failure, and

the failure does not count as a default for the purposes of paragraphs 6, 8B, 8C, 8G and 8H.".

Double jeopardy

17 P is not liable to a penalty under any paragraph of this Schedule in respect of a failure or action in respect of which P has been convicted of an offence.

Commencement—Finance Act 2009, Schedule 56 (Appointed Day and Consequential Provisions) Order, SI 2010/466: 6 April 2010 appointed as day on which Sch 56 comes into force for the following amounts specified in column 3 of the Table—items 2–4, and items 17, 23 and 24 but only in so far as the tax falls within any of items 2, 3 or 4 (see SI 2010/466 art 3).
Finance Act 2009, Schedules 55 and 56 (Income Tax Self Assessment and Pension Schemes) (Appointed Days and Consequential and Savings Provisions) Order, SI 2011/702 art 2 (appointed day for the coming into force of Sch 56 is 6 April 2011 in relation to an amount of tax which is payable in relation to the tax year 2010–11 or any subsequent tax year and falls within item 1, 12, 18 or 19 of the Table in para 1, or in so far as the tax falls within item 1 of that Table, item 17, 23 or 24 of that Table).
Cross-references—See FA 2014 s 226(7) (application of paras 9–18 of this Schedule, with any necessary modifications, to penalties for failure to pay accelerated payment).

Interpretation

18—(1) This paragraph applies for the construction of this Schedule.
(2) "HMRC" means Her Majesty's Revenue and Customs.
(3) References to tax include construction industry deductions under Chapter 3 of Part 3 of FA 2004.
(4) References to a determination, in relation to an amount payable under PAYE regulations or under Chapter 3 of Part 3 of FA 2004, include a certificate.
(5) References to an assessment to tax, in relation to inheritance tax and stamp duty reserve tax, are to a determination.

Commencement—Finance Act 2009, Schedule 56 (Appointed Day and Consequential Provisions) Order, SI 2010/466: 6 April 2010 appointed as day on which Sch 56 comes into force for the following amounts specified in column 3 of the Table—items 2–4, and items 17, 23 and 24 but only in so far as the tax falls within any of items 2, 3 or 4 (see SI 2010/466 art 3).
Finance Act 2009, Schedules 55 and 56 (Income Tax Self Assessment and Pension Schemes) (Appointed Days and Consequential and Savings Provisions) Order, SI 2011/702 art 2 (appointed day for the coming into force of Sch 56 is 6 April 2011 in relation to an amount of tax which is payable in relation to the tax year 2010–11 or any subsequent tax year and falls within item 1, 12, 18 or 19 of the Table in para 1, or in so far as the tax falls within item 1 of that Table, item 17, 23 or 24 of that Table).
Cross-references—See FA 2014 s 226(7) (application of paras 9–18 of this Schedule, with any necessary modifications, to penalties for failure to pay accelerated payment).

SCHEDULE 57

AMENDMENTS RELATING TO PENALTIES

Section 109

PART 1

AMENDMENTS OF SCHEDULE 24 TO FA 2007

1 Schedule 24 to FA 2007 (penalties for errors) is amended as follows.

2 (*inserts* FA 2007 Sch 24 para 2(4))

3 In paragraph 5 (normal rule for calculating potential lost revenue), for sub-paragraph (4)(*b*) substitute—

"(*b*) any relief under subsection (4) of section 419 of ICTA (relief in respect of repayment etc of loan) which is deferred under subsection (4A) of that section;".

4 In paragraph 9(1)(*b*) and (*c*) (reductions for disclosure), for "supply or false information" substitute "supply of false information".

5 (*inserts* FA 2007 Sch 24 para 13(7))

6 (*substitutes* FA 2007 Sch 24 para 16(2))

7—(1) Paragraph 19 (companies: officers' liability) is amended as follows.
(2) (*inserts* FA 2007 Sch 24 para
(*a*) after "a body corporate" insert "other than a limited liability partnership",
(*b*) in paragraph (*a*), omit the "or" at the end, and
(*c*) after that paragraph insert—
"(*aa*) a manager, and".
(3), (4) (*insert* FA 2007 Sch 24 para 19(3A), (6))

8 Omit paragraph 28(*da*) (interpretation of references to assessment).

9 In paragraphs 30 and 31 (consequential amendments) for "paragraph 7" substitute "paragraphs 7 and 7B".

PART 2

AMENDMENTS OF SCHEDULE 41 TO FA 2008

10 Schedule 41 to FA 2008 (penalties for failure to notify and certain other wrongdoing) is amended as follows.

11 (*substitutes* FA 2008 Sch 41 para 18(2))

12—(1) Paragraph 22 (companies: officers' liability) is amended as follows.
(2) In sub-paragraph (3)—
(*a*) after "a body corporate" insert "other than a limited liability partnership",
(*b*) in paragraph (*a*), omit the "or" at the end,
(*c*) after that paragraph insert—
"(*aa*) a manager, and".
(3), (4) (*insert* FA 2008 Sch 41 para 22(3A), (6))

PART 3
OTHER AMENDMENTS

13—(1) TMA 1970 is amended as follows.
(2) (*amends* TMA s 100(2))
(3) (*inserts* TMA 1970 s 103ZA)

14 In FA 2008 omit—
(*a*) paragraph 74 of Schedule 36 (information and inspection powers);
(*b*) paragraph 20(3) of Schedule 40 (amendment of Schedule 24 to FA 2007).

FINANCE ACT 2010

(2010 Chapter 13)

[8 April 2010]

PART 2
ANTI-AVOIDANCE AND REVENUE PROTECTION

Other international matters

35 Penalties: offshore income etc

(1) Schedule 10 contains provision about penalties in respect of offshore income etc.
(2) Schedule 10 comes into force on such day as the Treasury may by order appoint.
(3) An order under subsection (2)—
(*a*) may make different provision for different purposes, and
(*b*) may include transitional provisions and savings.
(4) The Treasury may by order make any incidental, supplemental, consequential, transitional or transitory provision or saving that appears appropriate in consequence of, or otherwise in connection with, Schedule 10.
(5) An order under subsection (4) may—
(*a*) make different provision for different purposes, and
(*b*) make provision amending, repealing or revoking an enactment or instrument (whenever passed or made).
(6) An order under this section is to be made by statutory instrument.
(7) A statutory instrument containing an order under subsection (4) is subject to annulment in pursuance of a resolution of the House of Commons.

Commencement—Finance Act 2010, Schedule 10 (Appointed Days and Transitional Provisions) Order, SI 2011/975 (6 April 2011 is the day appointed for the coming into force of Schedule 10, subject to transitional provisions in arts 3–5; the coming into force of paras 10–14 is subject to certain conditions in art 2(2)).

Value added tax and insurance premium tax

50 Extension of reverse charge provisions to supplies of services

(1) In section 55A of VATA 1994 (customers to account for tax on supplies of goods of a kind used in missing trader intra-community fraud), after "goods" (in each place, including the heading) insert "or services".
(2) In paragraph 2(3B) of Schedule 11 to that Act (power to require notifications relating to supplies to which section 55A(6) applies), after "goods" insert "or services".

SCHEDULE 6

CHARITIES AND COMMUNITY AMATEUR SPORTS CLUBS: DEFINITIONS

Section 30

PART 1

DEFINITION OF "CHARITY", "CHARITABLE COMPANY" AND "CHARITABLE TRUST"

Definition of "charity" etc

1 (1) For the purposes of the enactments to which this Part applies "charity" means a body of persons or trust that—

(*a*) is established for charitable purposes only,
(*b*) meets the jurisdiction condition (see paragraph 2),
(*c*) meets the registration condition (see paragraph 3), and
(*d*) meets the management condition (see paragraph 4).

(2) For the purposes of the enactments to which this Part applies—
"charitable company" means a charity that is a body of persons;
"charitable trust" means a charity that is a trust.

(3) Sub-paragraphs (1) and (2) are subject to any express provision to the contrary.

(4) For the meaning of "charitable purpose", see [section 2 of the Charities Act 2011][1] (which—
(*a*) applies regardless of where the body of persons or trust in question is established, and
(*b*) for this purpose forms part of the law of each part of the United Kingdom [(see sections 7 and 8 of that Act)][1]).

Cross-reference—Finance Act 2010, Schedule 6, Part 1 (Further Consequential and Incidental Provision etc) Order, SI 2012/735, arts 5, 6 (definition of "charity" in Part 1 of this Schedule applies for the purposes of enactments relating to value added tax, and capital gains tax).
FA 2015 s 123 (in the enactments to which FA 2010 Sch 6 Part 1 applies, any reference to a charity includes —
(a) the Commonwealth War Graves Commission, and
(b) the Imperial War Graves Endowment Fund Trustees.)

Amendments—[1] In sub-para (4) words substituted by the Charities Act 2011 s 354, Sch 7 para 143(1), (2) with effect from 14 March 2012.

Jurisdiction condition

2 (1) A body of persons or trust meets the jurisdiction condition if it falls to be subject to the control of—
(*a*) a relevant UK court in the exercise of its jurisdiction with respect to charities, or
(*b*) any other court in the exercise of a corresponding jurisdiction under the law of a relevant territory.

(2) In sub-paragraph (1)(*a*) "a relevant UK court" means—
(*a*) the High Court,
(*b*) the Court of Session, or
(*c*) the High Court in Northern Ireland.

(3) In sub-paragraph (1)(*b*) "a relevant territory" means—
(*a*) a member State other than the United Kingdom, or
(*b*) a territory specified in regulations made by the Commissioners for Her Majesty's Revenue and Customs.

(4) Regulations under this paragraph are to be made by statutory instrument.

(5) A statutory instrument containing regulations under this paragraph is subject to annulment in pursuance of a resolution of the House of Commons.

Regulations—Taxes (Definition of Charity) (Relevant Territories) Regulations, SI 2010/1904 (the Republic of Iceland and the Kingdom of Norway specified as "relevant territories" for the purposes of the meaning of a relevant territory in sub-para (3)).
Taxes (Definition of Charity) (Relevant Territories) Regulations, SI 2014/1807 (the Principality of Liechtenstein specified as a "relevant territory" for the purposes of the meaning of a relevant territory in sub-para (3)).

Cross-reference—Finance Act 2010, Schedule 6, Part 1 (Further Consequential and Incidental Provision etc) Order, SI 2012/735, arts 5, 6 (definition of "charity" in Part 1 of this Schedule applies for the purposes of enactments relating to value added tax, and capital gains tax).
FA 2015 s 123 (in the enactments to which FA 2010 Sch 6 Part 1 applies, any reference to a charity includes —
(a) the Commonwealth War Graves Commission, and
(b) the Imperial War Graves Endowment Fund Trustees.)

Registration condition

3 (1) A body of persons or trust meets the registration condition if—
(*a*) in the case of a body of persons or trust that is a charity [within the meaning of section 10 the Charities Act 2011][1], condition A is met, and
(*b*) in the case of any other body of persons or trust, condition B is met.

(2) Condition A is that the body of persons or trust has complied with any requirement to be registered in the register of charities kept under [section 29 of the Charities Act 2011][1].

(3) Condition B is that the body of persons or trust has complied with any requirement under the law of a territory outside England and Wales to be registered in a register corresponding to that mentioned in sub-paragraph (2).

Cross-reference—Finance Act 2010, Schedule 6, Part 1 (Further Consequential and Incidental Provision etc) Order, SI 2012/735, arts 5, 6 (definition of "charity" in Part 1 of this Schedule applies for the purposes of enactments relating to value added tax, and capital gains tax).
FA 2015 s 123 (in the enactments to which FA 2010 Sch 6 Part 1 applies, any reference to a charity includes —
(a) the Commonwealth War Graves Commission, and

(b) the Imperial War Graves Endowment Fund Trustees.)

Amendments—[1] In sub-paras (1)(*a*), (2) words substituted by the Charities Act 2011 s 354, Sch 7 para 143(1), (3), (4) with effect from 14 March 2012.

Management condition

4 (1) A body of persons or trust meets the management condition if its managers are fit and proper persons to be managers of the body or trust.

(2) In this paragraph "managers", in relation to a body of persons or trust, means the persons having the general control and management of the administration of the body or trust.

Cross-reference—Finance Act 2010, Schedule 6, Part 1 (Further Consequential and Incidental Provision etc) Order, SI 2012/735, arts 5, 6 (definition of "charity" in Part 1 of this Schedule applies for the purposes of enactments relating to value added tax, and capital gains tax).

FA 2015 s 123 (in the enactments to which FA 2010 Sch 6 Part 1 applies, any reference to a charity includes —

(a) the Commonwealth War Graves Commission, and
(b) the Imperial War Graves Endowment Fund Trustees.)

Periods over which management condition treated as met

5 (1) This paragraph applies in relation to any period throughout which the management condition is not met.

(2) The management condition is treated as met throughout the period if the Commissioners for Her Majesty's Revenue and Customs consider that—

(*a*) the failure to meet the management condition has not prejudiced the charitable purposes of the body or trust, or
(*b*) it is just and reasonable in all the circumstances for the condition to be treated as met throughout the period.

Cross-reference—Finance Act 2010, Schedule 6, Part 1 (Further Consequential and Incidental Provision etc) Order, SI 2012/735, arts 5, 6 (definition of "charity" in Part 1 of this Schedule applies for the purposes of enactments relating to value added tax, and capital gains tax).

FA 2015 s 123 (in the enactments to which FA 2010 Sch 6 Part 1 applies, any reference to a charity includes —

(a) the Commonwealth War Graves Commission, and
(b) the Imperial War Graves Endowment Fund Trustees.)

Publication of names and addresses of bodies or trusts regarded by HMRC as charities

6 Her Majesty's Revenue and Customs may publish the name and address of any body of persons or trust that appears to them to meet, or at any time to have met, the definition of a charity in paragraph 1.

Cross-reference—Finance Act 2010, Schedule 6, Part 1 (Further Consequential and Incidental Provision etc) Order, SI 2012/735, arts 5, 6 (definition of "charity" in Part 1 of this Schedule applies for the purposes of enactments relating to value added tax, and capital gains tax).

FA 2015 s 123 (in the enactments to which FA 2010 Sch 6 Part 1 applies, any reference to a charity includes —

(a) the Commonwealth War Graves Commission, and
(b) the Imperial War Graves Endowment Fund Trustees.)

Enactments to which this Part applies

7 The enactments to which this Part applies are the enactments relating to—

(*a*) income tax
(*b*) capital gains tax,
(*c*) corporation tax,
(*d*) value added tax,
(*e*) inheritance tax,
(*f*) stamp duty,
(*g*) stamp duty land tax, . . . [1]
(*h*) stamp duty reserve tax[, . . . [2]
(*i*) annual tax on enveloped dwellings][1][, and
[(*j*) diverted profits tax.][2]

Amendments—[1] Word "and" in para (*g*) repealed, and para (*i*) inserted, by FA 2013 s 168, Sch 35 para 3 with effect from 17 July 2013.

[2] Word "and" in para (*h*) repealed, and para (*j*) inserted, by FA 2015 s 115(2) with effect in relation to accounting periods beginning on or after 1 April 2015. For accounting periods that straddle that date, see FA 2015 s 116(2), (3).

Cross-reference—Finance Act 2010, Schedule 6, Part 1 (Further Consequential and Incidental Provision etc) Order, SI 2012/735, arts 5, 6 (definition of "charity" in Part 1 of this Schedule applies for the purposes of enactments relating to value added tax, and capital gains tax).

FA 2015 s 123 (in the enactments to which FA 2010 Sch 6 Part 1 applies, any reference to a charity includes —

(a) the Commonwealth War Graves Commission, and
(b) the Imperial War Graves Endowment Fund Trustees.)

PART 2
REPEALS OF SUPERSEDED DEFINITIONS AND OTHER CONSEQUENTIAL AMENDMENTS

FA 1982

8 (*amends* FA 1982 s 129(1))

Commencement—Finance Act 2010, Schedule 6, Part 2 (Commencement) Order, SI 2012/736 art 3 (para 8 comes into force in relation to any conveyance, transfer or lease made or agreed to be made on or after 1 April 2012).

FA 1983

9 (*amends* FA 1983 s 46(3))

Commencement—Finance Act 2010, Schedule 6, Part 2 (Commencement) Order, SI 2012/736 art 4 (para 9 comes into force on 1 April 2012).

IHTA 1984

10 (*amends* IHTA 1984 s 272)

Commencement—Finance Act 2010, Schedule 6, Part 2 (Commencement) Order, SI 2012/736 art 5 (para 10 comes into force in respect of transfers of value made on or after 1 April 2012).

FA 1986

11 (*amends* FA 1986 s 90(7))

Commencement—Finance Act 2010, Schedule 6, Part 2 (Commencement) Order, SI 2012/736 art 6 (para 11 comes into force in relation to any agreement to transfer securities made on or after 1 April 2012).

FA 1989

12 (*repeals* FA 1989 Sch 5 para 4(10)).

Commencement—Finance Act 2010, Schedule 6, Part 2 (Commencement) Order, SI 2012/736 art 7 (para 12 comes into force in relation to trusts established on or after 1 April 2012).

TCGA 1992

13 (1) TCGA 1992 is amended as follows.
(2) (*amends* TCGA 1992 s 222(8B)(*b*)(*iii*).
(3) (*repeals* TCGA 1992 s 256(6), (8))
(4) (*repeals* TCGA 1992 s 256C(6))
(5) (*repeals*TCGA 1992 s 256D(7)).

Commencement—Finance Act 2010, Schedule 6, Part 2 (Commencement) Order, SI 2012/736 arts 8, 9 (the amendments made by para 13 come into force as follows:

– sub-para (2): in relation to living accommodation provided for a director on or after 6 April 2012 if that accommodation was not already provided for the director immediately before that date;
– sub-paras (3)–(5): for corporation tax purposes, for accounting periods beginning on or after 1 April 2012 and, for capital gains tax purposes, for the tax year 2012–13 and subsequent tax years.

F(No 2)A 1997

14 …

Amendments—This para repealed by FA 2011 s 91, Sch 26 para 1(1), (2)(*b*)(ii) with effect from 19 July 2011.

FA 1999

15 (1) Schedule 19 to FA 1999 (stamp duty and stamp duty reserve tax: unit trusts) is amended as follows.
(2) (*amends* para 6(3))
(3) (*amends* para 15(*c*))

Commencement—Finance Act 2010, Schedule 6, Part 2 (Commencement) Order, SI 2012/736 arts 10, 11 (para 15(2) comes into force in relation to surrenders occurring on or after 1 April 2012; para 15(3) comes into force on 1 April 2012).

CAA 2001

16 (*amends* CAA 2001 s 63(2))

Commencement—Finance Act 2010, Schedule 6, Part 2 (Commencement) Order, SI 2012/736 art 12 (para 16 comes into force, for corporation tax purposes, for accounting periods beginning on or after 1 April 2012 and, for income tax purposes, for 2012–13 and subsequent tax years).

ITEPA 2003

17 (1) ITEPA 2003 is amended as follows.
(2) (*amends* ITEPA 2003 s 99(3)(*b*)(ii))
(3) (*amends* ITEPA 2003 s 216(3)(*b*))
(4) (*amends*ITEPA 2003 s 223(7)(*b*)(ii))
(5) I(*amends*ITEPA 2003 s 290(5))
(6) (*repeals* ITEPA 2003 s 351(5))
(7) (*amends* ITEPA 2003 s 714(2))

Commencement—Finance Act 2010, Schedule 6, Part 2 (Commencement) Order, SI 2012/736 art 13 (para 17 comes into effect for the tax year 2012–13 and subsequent tax years).

FA 2003

18 Schedule 8 to FA 2003 (SDLT: charities relief) is amended as follows.

Commencement—Finance Act 2010, Schedule 6, Part 2 (Commencement) Order, SI 2012/736 art 14 (para 18 comes into force in relation to a land transaction of which the effective date is on or after 1 April 2012).

19 (*repeals* FA 2003 Sch 8 para 1(4))

Commencement—Finance Act 2010, Schedule 6, Part 2 (Commencement) Order, SI 2012/736 art 14 (para 19 comes into force in relation to a land transaction of which the effective date is on or after 1 April 2012).

20 (*amends* FA 2003 Sch 8 para 4(2))

Commencement—Finance Act 2010, Schedule 6, Part 2 (Commencement) Order, SI 2012/736 art 14 (para 20 comes into force in relation to a land transaction of which the effective date is on or after 1 April 2012).

ITTOIA 2005

21 (1) ITTOIA 2005 is amended as follows.
(2) (*amends* ITTOIA 2005 s 410(3)(*b*))
(3) (*amends* ITTOIA 2005 s 545(1))
(4) (*amended*ITTOIA 2005 s 568(3); *repealed* by FA 2013 s 28, Sch 12 para 17)
(5) (*amends* ITTOIA 2005 Sch 4 Pt 2)

Commencement—Finance Act 2010, Schedule 6, Part 2 (Commencement) Order, SI 2012/736 art 15 (these amendments come into force for the tax year 2012–13 and subsequent tax years, subject to the following:

– the amendment made by sub-para (3) comes into force in relation to insurances and contracts made on or after 6 April 2012; and
– the amendment made by sub-para (5) comes into force in relation to insurances and contracts made on or after 6 April 2012, so far as the amendment applies in relation to ITTOIA 2005 Part 4 Chapter 9).

F(No 2)A 2005

22 (*amends* F(No 2)A s 18(3)(*b*)(i))

Commencement—Finance Act 2010, Schedule 6, Part 2 (Commencement) Order, SI 2012/736 art 16 (para 22 comes into force on 1 April 2012).

ITA 2007

23 (1) ITA 2007 is amended as follows.
(2) (*amends* ITA 2007 s 479(1)(*b*))
(3) (*amends* ITA 2007 s 481(1)(*c*))
(4) (*repeals* ITA 2007 s 519)
(5) (*amends*ITA 2007, s 873(2)(*a*), (*b*))
(6) (*amends* ITA 2007 s 989)
(7) (*amends* ITA 2007 Sch 4)

Commencement—Finance Act 2010, Schedule 6, Part 2 (Commencement) Order, SI 2012/736 arts 17, 18 (sub-paras (2)–(5), (7) come into force for the tax year 2012–13 and subsequent tax years; sub-para (6), so far as it applies for purposes other than those of ITA 2007 Part 8 Chapter 2, comes into force for the tax year 2012–13 and subsequent tax years).

FA 2008

24 (*amends* FA 2008 Sch 36 para 60(2))

Commencement—Finance Act 2010, Schedule 6, Part 2 (Commencement) Order, SI 2012/736 art 19 (para 24 comes into force on 1 April 2012).

CTA 2009

25 (1) CTA 2009 is amended as follows.
(2) In section 1319 (other definitions), omit the definition of "charity".

(3) In Schedule 4 (index of defined expressions), in the entry for "charity", for "section 1319" substitute "paragraph 1 of Schedule 6 to FA 2010".

FA 2009

26 (*amends* FA 2009 Sch 49 para 8)

Commencement—Finance Act 2010, Schedule 6, Part 2 (Commencement) Order, SI 2012/736 art 20 (para 26 comes into force on 1 April 2012).

CTA 2010

27 (1) CTA 2010 is amended as follows.
(2) (*amends* CTA 2010 s 202)
(3) (*amends* CTA 2010 s 217)
(4) (*repeals* CTA 2010 s 467)
(5) (*amends*CTA 2010 s 610(2)(*a*))
(6) (*amends* CTA 2010 s 1119)
(7) (*amends* CTA 2010 Sch 4)

Commencement—Finance Act 2010, Schedule 6, Part 2 (Commencement) Order, SI 2012/736 art 21 (para 27 comes into force as follows: for corporation tax purposes, for accounting periods beginning on or after 1 April 2012 and, for income tax purposes, for the tax year 2012-13 and subsequent tax years).

TIOPA 2010

28 (*amends* TIOPA 2010 s 326(3))

Commencement—Finance Act 2010, Schedule 6, Part 2 (Commencement) Order, SI 2012/736 art 22 (para 28 comes into force for accounting periods beginning on or after 1 April 2012).

Power to make further consequential provision

29 (1) The Commissioners for Her Majesty's Revenue and Customs may by order make such further consequential, incidental, supplemental, transitional or transitory provision or saving as appears appropriate in consequence of, or otherwise in connection with, Part 1.
(2) An order under this paragraph may—
(*a*) make different provision for different purposes, and
(*b*) make provision repealing, revoking or otherwise amending any enactment or instrument (whenever passed or made).
(3) An order under this paragraph is to be made by statutory instrument.
(4) A statutory instrument containing an order under this paragraph is subject to annulment in pursuance of an order of the House of Commons.

Regulations—Finance Act 2010, Schedule 6, Part 1 (Further Consequential and Incidental Provision etc) Order, SI 2012/735.

PART 3
MEANING OF "COMMUNITY AMATEUR SPORTS CLUB"

30 Chapter 9 of Part 13 of CTA 2010 (community amateur sports clubs) is amended as follows.

31 (*amended* CTA 2010 s 658; *repealed by* FA 2012 s 52(2))

32 (*inserts* CTA 2010 s 661A–661C)

PART 4
COMMENCEMENT

Commencement of Part 1

33 (1) Part 1 is treated as having come into force on 6 April 2010.
(2) But the definitions of "charity", "charitable company" and "charitable trust" in that Part do not apply for the purposes of an enactment in relation to which, on that date, another definition applies until such time as that other definition ceases to have effect on the coming into force of provision made by or under Part 2.
(3) For provision about the coming into force of provision made by that Part, see paragraph 34.

Cross-reference—Finance Act 2010, Schedule 6, Part 1 (Further Consequential and Incidental Provision etc) Order, SI 2012/735, arts 5, 6 (definition of "charity" in Part 1 of this Schedule applies for the purposes of enactments relating to value added tax, and capital gains tax).

FA 2015 s 123 (in the enactments to which FA 2010 Sch 6 Part 1 applies, any reference to a charity includes —

(a) the Commonwealth War Graves Commission, and
(b) the Imperial War Graves Endowment Fund Trustees.)

Commencement of Part 2

34 (1) The repeal of the definition of "charity" in section 989 of ITA 2007 made by paragraph 23(6) above has effect—

(*a*) so far as it applies for the purposes of Chapter 2 of Part 8 of that Act (gift aid), in relation to gifts made on or after 6 April 2010, and

(*b*) so far as it applies for other purposes, in accordance with such provision as the Treasury may make by order.

(2) The other amendments made by Part 2 come into force in accordance with such provision as the Treasury may make by order.

(3) An order under this paragraph may—

(*a*) make different provision for different purposes, and

(*b*) include transitional provision and savings.

(4) An order under this paragraph is to be made by statutory instrument.

Orders—Finance Act 2010, Schedule 6, Part 2 (Commencement) Order, SI 2012/736.

Commencement of Part 3

35 The amendments made by Part 3 are treated as having come into force on 6 April 2010.

SCHEDULE 10

PENALTIES: OFFSHORE INCOME ETC

Section 35

Commencement—Finance Act 2010, Schedule 10 (Appointed Days and Transitional Provisions) Order, SI 2011/975 (6 April 2011 is the day appointed for the coming into force of this Schedule, subject to transitional provisions in arts 3–5; the coming into force of paras 10–14 is subject to certain conditions in art 2(2)).

Schedule 24 to FA 2007

1 Schedule 24 to FA 2007 (penalties for errors) is amended as follows.

Commencement—Finance Act 2010, Schedule 10 (Appointed Days and Transitional Provisions) Order, SI 2011/975 (paras 1–9 come into force on 6 April 2011, subject to transitional provisions).

2 For paragraph 4 substitute—

"4

(1) This paragraph sets out the penalty payable under paragraph 1.

(2) If the inaccuracy is in category 1, the penalty is—

(*a*) for careless action, 30% of the potential lost revenue,

(*b*) for deliberate but not concealed action, 70% of the potential lost revenue, and

(*c*) for deliberate and concealed action, 100% of the potential lost revenue.

(3) If the inaccuracy is in category 2, the penalty is—

(*a*) for careless action, 45% of the potential lost revenue,

(*b*) for deliberate but not concealed action, 105% of the potential lost revenue, and

(*c*) for deliberate and concealed action, 150% of the potential lost revenue.

(4) If the inaccuracy is in category 3, the penalty is—

(*a*) for careless action, 60% of the potential lost revenue,

(*b*) for deliberate but not concealed action, 140% of the potential lost revenue, and

(*c*) for deliberate and concealed action, 200% of the potential lost revenue.

(5) Paragraph 4A explains the 3 categories of inaccuracy.

4A

(1) An inaccuracy is in category 1 if—

(*a*) it involves a domestic matter, or

(*b*) it involves an offshore matter and—

(i) the territory in question is a category 1 territory, or

(ii) the tax at stake is a tax other than income tax or capital gains tax.

(2) An inaccuracy is in category 2 if—

(*a*) it involves an offshore matter,

(*b*) the territory in question is a category 2 territory, and

(*c*) the tax at stake is income tax or capital gains tax.

(3) An inaccuracy is in category 3 if—

(*a*) it involves an offshore matter,

(*b*) the territory in question is a category 3 territory, and (*c*) the tax at stake is income tax or capital gains tax.

(4) An inaccuracy "involves an offshore matter" if it results in a potential loss of revenue that is charged on or by reference to—

(*a*) income arising from a source in a territory outside the UK,

(*b*) assets situated or held in a territory outside the UK,

(*c*) activities carried on wholly or mainly in a territory outside the UK, or

(*d*) anything having effect as if it were income, assets or activities of a kind described above.

(5) An inaccuracy "involves a domestic matter" if it results in a potential loss of revenue that is charged on or by reference to anything not mentioned in sub-paragraph (4)(*a*) to (*d*).

(6) If a single inaccuracy is in more than one category (each referred to as a "relevant category")—

(*a*) it is to be treated for the purposes of this Schedule as if it were separate inaccuracies, one in each relevant category according to the matters that it involves, and

(*b*) the potential lost revenue is to be calculated separately in respect of each separate inaccuracy.

(7) "Category 1 territory", "category 2 territory" and "category 3 territory" are defined in paragraph 21A.

(8) "Assets" has the meaning given in section 21(1) of TCGA 1992, but also includes sterling.

4B

The penalty payable under paragraph 1A is 100% of the potential lost revenue.

4C

The penalty payable under paragraph 2 is 30% of the potential lost revenue.

4D

Paragraphs 5 to 8 define "potential lost revenue"."

Commencement—Finance Act 2010, Schedule 10 (Appointed Days and Transitional Provisions) Order, SI 2011/975 (paras 1–9 come into force on 6 April 2011, subject to transitional provisions).

3 For paragraph 10 substitute—

"10

(1) If a person who would otherwise be liable to a penalty of a percentage shown in column 1 of the Table (a "standard percentage") has made a disclosure, HMRC must reduce the standard percentage to one that reflects the quality of the disclosure.

(2) But the standard percentage may not be reduced to a percentage that is below the minimum shown for it—

(*a*) in the case of a prompted disclosure, in column 2 of the Table, and

(*b*) in the case of an unprompted disclosure, in column 3 of the Table.

Standard %	*Minimum % for prompted disclosure*	*Minimum % for unprompted disclosure*
30%	15%	0%
45%	22.5%	0%
60%	30%	0%
70%	35%	20%
105%	52.5%	30%
140%	70%	40%
100%	50%	30%
150%	75%	45%
200%	100%	60%".

Commencement—Finance Act 2010, Schedule 10 (Appointed Days and Transitional Provisions) Order, SI 2011/975 (paras 1–9 come into force on 6 April 2011, subject to transitional provisions).

4 In paragraph 12 (interaction with other penalties), for sub-paragraph (4) substitute—

"(4) Where penalties are imposed under paragraphs 1 and 1A in respect of the same inaccuracy, the aggregate of the amounts of the penalties must not exceed the relevant percentage of the potential lost revenue.

(5) The relevant percentage is—

(*a*) if the penalty imposed under paragraph 1 is for an inaccuracy in category 1, 100%,

(*b*) if the penalty imposed under paragraph 1 is for an inaccuracy in category 2, 150%, and

(*c*) if the penalty imposed under paragraph 1 is for an inaccuracy in category 3, 200%."

Commencement—Finance Act 2010, Schedule 10 (Appointed Days and Transitional Provisions) Order, SI 2011/975 (paras 1–9 come into force on 6 April 2011, subject to transitional provisions).

5 In Part 5 (general), before the heading "Interpretation" insert—

"*Classification of territories*

21A

(1) A category 1 territory is a territory designated as a category 1 territory by order made by the Treasury.

(2) A category 2 territory is a territory that is neither—

(*a*) a category 1 territory, nor

(*b*) a category 3 territory.

(3) A category 3 territory is a territory designated as a category 3 territory by order made by the Treasury.

(4) In considering how to classify a territory for the purposes of this paragraph, the Treasury must have regard to—

(*a*) the existence of any arrangements between the UK and that territory for the exchange of information for tax enforcement purposes,

(*b*) the quality of any such arrangements (in particular, whether they provide for information to be exchanged automatically or on request), and

(*c*) the benefit that the UK would be likely to obtain from receiving information from that territory, were such arrangements to exist with it.

(5) An order under this paragraph is to be made by statutory instrument.

(6) Subject to sub-paragraph (7), an instrument containing an order under this paragraph is subject to annulment in pursuance of a resolution of the House of Commons.

(7) If the order is—

(*a*) the first order to be made under sub-paragraph (1), or

(*b*) the first order to be made under sub-paragraph (3),

it may not be made unless a draft of the instrument containing it has been laid before, and approved by a resolution of, the House of Commons.

(8) An order under this paragraph does not apply to inaccuracies in a document given to HMRC (or, in a case within paragraph 3(2), inaccuracies discovered by P) before the date on which the order comes into force.

Location of assets etc

21B

(1) The Treasury may by regulations make provision for determining for the purposes of paragraph 4A where—

(*a*) a source of income is located,

(*b*) an asset is situated or held, or

(*c*) activities are wholly or mainly carried on.

(2) Different provision may be made for different cases and for income tax and capital gains tax.

(3) Regulations under this paragraph are to be made by statutory instrument.

(4) An instrument containing regulations under this paragraph is subject to annulment in pursuance of a resolution of the House of Commons."

Commencement—Finance Act 2010, Schedule 10 (Appointed Days and Transitional Provisions) Order, SI 2011/975 (paras 1–9 come into force on 6 April 2011, subject to transitional provisions).

6 After paragraph 23A insert—

"23B

"UK" means the United Kingdom, including the territorial sea of the United Kingdom."

Commencement—Finance Act 2010, Schedule 10 (Appointed Days and Transitional Provisions) Order, SI 2011/975 (paras 1–9 come into force on 6 April 2011, subject to transitional provisions).

Schedule 41 to FA 2008

7 Schedule 41 to FA 2008 (penalties: failure to notify and certain VAT and excise wrongdoing) is amended as follows.

Commencement—Finance Act 2010, Schedule 10 (Appointed Days and Transitional Provisions) Order, SI 2011/975 (paras 1–9 come into force on 6 April 2011, subject to transitional provisions).

8 For paragraph 6 substitute—

"6

(1) This paragraph sets out the penalty payable under paragraph 1.

(2) If the failure is in category 1, the penalty is—

(*a*) for a deliberate and concealed failure, 100% of the potential lost revenue,

(*b*) for a deliberate but not concealed failure, 70% of the potential lost revenue, and

(*c*) for any other case, 30% of the potential lost revenue.

(3) If the failure is in category 2, the penalty is—

(*a*) for a deliberate and concealed failure, 150% of the potential lost revenue,

(*b*) for a deliberate but not concealed failure, 105% of the potential lost revenue, and

(*c*) for any other case, 45% of the potential lost revenue.

(4) If the failure is in category 3, the penalty is—

(*a*) for a deliberate and concealed failure, 200% of the potential lost revenue,

(*b*) for a deliberate but not concealed failure, 140% of the potential lost revenue, and

(*c*) for any other case, 60% of the potential lost revenue.

(5) Paragraph 6A explains the 3 categories of failure.

6A

(1) A failure is in category 1 if—

(*a*) it involves a domestic matter, or

(*b*) it involves an offshore matter and—

(i) the territory in question is a category 1 territory, or

(ii) the tax at stake is a tax other than income tax or capital gains tax.

(2) A failure is in category 2 if—

(*a*) it involves an offshore matter,

(*b*) the territory in question is a category 2 territory, and

(*c*) the tax at stake is income tax or capital gains tax.

(3) A failure is in category 3 if—

(*a*) it involves an offshore matter,

(*b*) the territory in question is a category 3 territory, and

(*c*) the tax at stake is income tax or capital gains tax.

(4) A failure "involves an offshore matter" if it results in a potential loss of revenue that is charged on or by reference to—

(*a*) income arising from a source in a territory outside the UK,

(*b*) assets situated or held in a territory outside the UK,

(*c*) activities carried on wholly or mainly in a territory outside the UK, or

(*d*) anything having effect as if it were income, assets or activities of a kind described above.

(5) A failure "involves a domestic matter" if it results in a potential loss of revenue that is charged on or by reference to anything not mentioned in sub-paragraph (4)(*a*) to (*d*).

(6) If a single failure is in more than one category (each referred to as a "relevant category")—

(*a*) it is to be treated for the purposes of this Schedule as if it were separate failures, one in each relevant category according to the matters that it involves, and

(*b*) the potential lost revenue in respect of each separate failure is taken to be such share of the potential lost revenue in respect of the single failure (see paragraphs 7 and 11) as is just and reasonable.

(7) For the purposes of this Schedule—

(*a*) paragraph 21A of Schedule 24 to FA 2007 (classification of territories) has effect, but

(*b*) an order under that paragraph does not apply to relevant obligations that are to be complied with by a date before the date on which the order comes into force.

(8) Regulations under paragraph 21B of Schedule 24 to FA 2007 (location of assets etc) apply for the purposes of paragraph 6A of this Schedule as they apply for the purposes of paragraph 4A of that Schedule.

(9) In this paragraph—

"assets" has the meaning given in section 21(1) of TCGA 1992, but also includes sterling;

"UK" means the United Kingdom, including the territorial sea of the United Kingdom.

6B

The penalty payable under any of paragraphs 2, 3(1) and 4 is—

(*a*) for a deliberate and concealed act or failure, 100% of the potential lost revenue,

(*b*) for a deliberate but not concealed act or failure, 70% of the potential lost revenue, and

(*c*) for any other case, 30% of the potential lost revenue.

6C

The penalty payable under paragraph 3(2) is 100% of the potential lost revenue.

6D

Paragraphs 7 to 11 define "potential lost revenue"."

Commencement—Finance Act 2010, Schedule 10 (Appointed Days and Transitional Provisions) Order, SI 2011/975 (paras 1–9 come into force on 6 April 2011, subject to transitional provisions).

9 For paragraph 13 substitute—

"13

(1) If a person who would otherwise be liable to a penalty of a percentage shown in column 1 of the Table (a "standard percentage") has made a disclosure, HMRC must reduce the standard percentage to one that reflects the quality of the disclosure.

(2) But the standard percentage may not be reduced to a percentage that is below the minimum shown for it—

(*a*) for a prompted disclosure, in column 2 of the Table, and

(*b*) for an unprompted disclosure, in column 3 of the Table.

(3) Where the Table shows a different minimum for case A and case B—

(*a*) the case A minimum applies if—

(i) the penalty is one under paragraph 1, and

(ii) HMRC become aware of the failure less than 12 months after the time when the tax first becomes unpaid by reason of the failure, and

(*b*) otherwise, the case B minimum applies.

Standard %	*Minimum % for prompted disclosure*	*Minimum % for unprompted disclosure*
30%	case A: 10% case B: 20%	case A: 0% case B: 10%
45%	case A: 15% case B: 30%	case A: 0% case B: 15%
60%	case A: 20% case B: 40%	case A: 0% case B: 20%
70%	35%	20%
105%	52.5%	30%
140%	70%	40%
100%	50%	30%
150%	75%	45%
200%	100%	60%".

Commencement—Finance Act 2010, Schedule 10 (Appointed Days and Transitional Provisions) Order, SI 2011/975 (paras 1–9 come into force on 6 April 2011, subject to transitional provisions).

Schedule 55 to FA 2009

10 Schedule 55 to FA 2009 (penalties for failure to make returns etc) is amended as follows.

Commencement—Finance Act 2010, Schedule 10 (Appointed Days and Transitional Provisions) Order, SI 2011/975 (paras 10–14 come into force on 6 April 2011 in relation to a return or other document which is required to be made or delivered to HMRC in relation to the tax year 2011–12 or any subsequent tax year, and falls within item 1, 2 or 3 of the Table in FA 2009 Sch 55 para 1, subject to transitional provisions).

11 (1) Paragraph 6 (amount of penalty if failure continues more than 12 months) is amended as follows.

(2) In sub-paragraph (3)(*a*), for "100%" substitute "the relevant percentage".

(3) After sub-paragraph (3) insert—

"(3A) For the purposes of sub-paragraph (3)(*a*), the relevant percentage is—

(*a*) for the withholding of category 1 information, 100%,

(*b*) for the withholding of category 2 information, 150%, and

(*c*) for the withholding of category 3 information, 200%."

(4) In sub-paragraph (4)(*a*), for "70%" substitute "the relevant percentage".

(5) After sub-paragraph (4) insert—

"(4A) For the purposes of sub-paragraph (4)(*a*), the relevant percentage is—

(*a*) for the withholding of category 1 information, 70%,

(*b*) for the withholding of category 2 information, 105%, and

(*c*) for the withholding of category 3 information, 140%."

(6) After sub-paragraph (5) insert—

"(6) Paragraph 6A explains the 3 categories of information."

Commencement—Finance Act 2010, Schedule 10 (Appointed Days and Transitional Provisions) Order, SI 2011/975 (paras 10–14 come into force on 6 April 2011 in relation to a return or other document which is required to be made or delivered to HMRC in relation to the tax year 2011–12 or any subsequent tax year, and falls within item 1, 2 or 3 of the Table in FA 2009 Sch 55 para 1, subject to transitional provisions).

12 After paragraph 6 insert—

"6A

(1) Information is category 1 information if—

(*a*) it involves a domestic matter, or

(*b*) it involves an offshore matter and—

(i) the territory in question is a category 1 territory, or

(ii) it is information which would enable or assist HMRC to assess P's liability to a tax other than income tax or capital gains tax.

(2) Information is category 2 information if—

(*a*) it involves an offshore matter,

(*b*) the territory in question is a category 2 territory, and

(*c*) it is information which would enable or assist HMRC to assess P's liability to income tax or capital gains tax.

(3) Information is category 3 information if—

(*a*) it involves an offshore matter,

(*b*) the territory in question is a category 3 territory, and

(*c*) it is information which would enable or assist HMRC to assess P's liability to income tax or capital gains tax.

(4) Information "involves an offshore matter" if the liability to tax which would have been shown in the return includes a liability to tax charged on or by reference to—

(*a*) income arising from a source in a territory outside the UK,

(*b*) assets situated or held in a territory outside the UK,

(*c*) activities carried on wholly or mainly in a territory outside the UK, or

(*d*) anything having effect as if it were income, assets or activities of a kind described above.

(5) Information "involves a domestic matter" if the liability to tax which would have been shown in the return includes a liability to tax charged on or by reference to anything not mentioned in sub-paragraph (4)(*a*) to (*d*).

(6) If the information which P withholds falls into more than one category—

(*a*) P's failure to make the return is to be treated for the purposes of this Schedule as if it were separate failures, one for each category of information according to the matters which the information involves, and

(*b*) for each separate failure, the liability to tax which would have been shown in the return in question is taken to be such share of the liability to tax which would have been shown in the return mentioned in paragraph (*a*) as is just and reasonable.

(7) For the purposes of this Schedule—

(*a*) paragraph 21A of Schedule 24 to FA 2007 (classification of territories) has effect, but

(*b*) an order under that paragraph does not apply to a failure if the filing date is before the date on which the order comes into force.

(8) Regulations under paragraph 21B of Schedule 24 to FA 2007 (location of assets etc) apply for the purposes of paragraph 6A of this Schedule as they apply for the purposes of paragraph 4A of that Schedule.

(9) In this paragraph—

"assets" has the meaning given in section 21(1) of TCGA 1992, but also includes sterling;

"UK" means the United Kingdom, including the territorial sea of the United Kingdom."

Commencement—Finance Act 2010, Schedule 10 (Appointed Days and Transitional Provisions) Order, SI 2011/975 (paras 10–14 come into force on 6 April 2011 in relation to a return or other document which is required to be made or delivered to HMRC in relation to the tax year 2011–12 or any subsequent tax year, and falls within item 1, 2 or 3 of the Table in FA 2009 Sch 55 para 1, subject to transitional provisions).

13 (1) Paragraph 15 (reductions for disclosure) is amended as follows.

(2) For sub-paragraphs (1) and (2) substitute—

"(1) If a person who would otherwise be liable to a penalty of a percentage shown in column 1 of the Table (a "standard percentage") has made a disclosure, HMRC must reduce the standard percentage to one that reflects the quality of the disclosure.

(2) But the standard percentage may not be reduced to a percentage that is below the minimum shown for it—

(*a*) in the case of a prompted disclosure, in column 2 of the Table, and

(*b*) in the case of an unprompted disclosure, in column 3 of the Table.

Standard %	*Minimum % for prompted disclosure*	*Minimum % for unprompted disclosure*
70%	35%	20%
105%	52.5%	30%
140%	70%	40%
100%	50%	30%
150%	75%	45%
200%	100%	60%".

(3) Omit sub-paragraphs (3) and (4).

Commencement—Finance Act 2010, Schedule 10 (Appointed Days and Transitional Provisions) Order, SI 2011/975 (paras 10–14 come into force on 6 April 2011 in relation to a return or other document which is required to be made or delivered to HMRC in relation to the tax year 2011–12 or any subsequent tax year, and falls within item 1, 2 or 3 of the Table in FA 2009 Sch 55 para 1, subject to transitional provisions).

14 In paragraph 17 (interaction with other penalties)—

(*a*) in sub-paragraph (3), for "100%" substitute "the relevant percentage", and

(*b*) after that sub-paragraph insert—

"(4) The relevant percentage is—

(*a*) if one of the penalties is a penalty under paragraph 6(3) or (4) and the information withheld is category 3 information, 200%,

(*b*) if one of the penalties is a penalty under paragraph 6(3) or (4) and the information withheld is category 2 information, 150%, and

(*c*) in all other cases, 100%."

Commencement—Finance Act 2010, Schedule 10 (Appointed Days and Transitional Provisions) Order, SI 2011/975 (paras 10–14 come into force on 6 April 2011 in relation to a return or other document which is required to be made or delivered to HMRC in relation to the tax year 2011–12 or any subsequent tax year, and falls within item 1, 2 or 3 of the Table in FA 2009 Sch 55 para 1, subject to transitional provisions).

FINANCE (NO 2) ACT 2010

(2010 Chapter 31)

[27 July 2010]

PART 1
RATES, ETC

Value added tax

3 Rate of value added tax

(1) In section 2(1) of VATA 1994 (rate of VAT), for "17.5 per cent" substitute "20 per cent".

(2) In section 21(4) of that Act (restriction on value of imported goods), for "28.58 per cent" substitute "25 per cent".

(3) The amendment made by subsection (1) has effect in relation to any supply made on or after 4 January 2011 and any acquisition or importation taking place on or after that date.

(4) The amendment made by subsection (2) has effect in relation to goods imported on or after 4 January 2011.

(5) Schedule 2 contains provision for a supplementary charge to value added tax on supplies spanning the date of the VAT change.

SCHEDULE 2
SUPPLEMENTARY CHARGE TO VAT

Section 2

PART 1
SUPPLEMENTARY CHARGE TO VAT

The charge

1—(1) There is a supplementary charge to value added tax on a supply of goods or services that is treated as taking place on or after 22 June 2010 if—

(*a*) the supply spans the date of the VAT change,

(*b*) it is subject to VAT at the rate in force under section 2 of VATA 1994,

(*c*) the person to whom the supply is made is not entitled under VATA 1994 to credit for, or the repayment or refund of, all of the VAT on the supply, and

(*d*) a relevant condition is met.

(2) In this Schedule "the date of the VAT change" means 4 January 2011.

(3) For the cases in which a supply, other than the grant of a right to goods or services, spans the date of the VAT change and the relevant conditions in relation to such a supply, see paragraph 2.

(4) For the cases in which a supply consisting of the grant of a right to goods or services spans the date of the VAT change and the relevant conditions in relation to such a supply, see paragraph 3.

(5) Sub-paragraph (1) has effect subject to the exceptions made by or under Part 2 of this Schedule.

(6) In this Schedule—

Part 3 contains provision about liability for, and the amount of, a supplementary charge under this Schedule,

Part 4 contains special provision about listed supplies, and

Part 5 contains provision about administration and interpretation.

(7) A supplementary charge to value added tax under this Schedule is to be treated for all purposes as if it were value added tax charged in accordance with VATA 1994.

Supply spanning the date of the VAT change

2—(1) For the purposes of this Schedule, a supply of goods or services spans the date of the VAT change where—

(*a*) by virtue of the issue of a VAT invoice or the receipt of a payment by the person making the supply ("the supplier"), the supply is treated as taking place before the date of the VAT change, but

(*b*) the basic time of supply (see paragraph 4) is on or after the date of the VAT change.

(2) The relevant conditions are—

(*a*) in relation to a supply that is within sub-paragraph (1)(*a*) by virtue of the issue of a VAT invoice, conditions A to D, and

(*b*) in relation to a supply that is within sub-paragraph (1)(*a*) by virtue of the receipt of a payment, conditions A to C.

(3) Condition A is that the supplier and the person to whom the supply is made are connected with each other at any time in the period—

(*a*) beginning with the day on which the supply is treated as taking place, and (*b*) ending on the date of the VAT change.

(4) Paragraph 5 modifies condition A in cases involving a series of supplies.

(5) Condition B is that the aggregate of the following is more than £100,000—

(*a*) the relevant consideration for the supply, and

(*b*) the relevant consideration for every related supply of goods or services (including every related grant of a right to goods or services) that spans the date of the VAT change (see paragraph 6).

(6) Condition C is that a prepayment in respect of the supply is financed by the supplier or a person connected with the supplier (see paragraph 7).

(7) In sub-paragraph (6) "prepayment", in respect of a supply, means a payment that is received by the supplier before the basic time of supply.

(8) Condition D is that full payment of the amount shown on the VAT invoice referred to in sub-paragraph (1)(*a*) is not due before the end of the period of 6 months beginning with the date on which the invoice is issued.

(9) This paragraph does not apply in relation to a supply consisting of the grant of a right to goods or services (see paragraph 3).

Grant of right spanning the date of the VAT change

3—(1) For the purposes of this Schedule, a supply consisting of the grant by a person ("the grantor") of a right to goods or services spans the date of the VAT change where—

(*a*) that supply is treated as taking place before the date of the VAT change,

(*b*) the goods or services are to be supplied at a discount or free of charge, and

(*c*) the basic time of supply for the supply of some or all of the goods or services (see paragraph 4) is on or after the date of the VAT change.

(2) In relation to the grant of the right, the relevant conditions are conditions A to C.

(3) Condition A is that the grantor and the person to whom the right is granted are connected with each other at any time in the period—

(*a*) beginning with the day on which the supply consisting of the grant of the right is treated as taking place, and

(*b*) ending on the date of the VAT change or, if the right is exercised (entirely or partly) on a later date, that date (or, if more than one, the first of those dates).

(4) Paragraph 5 modifies condition A in cases involving a series of supplies.

(5) Condition B is that the aggregate of the following is more than £100,000—

(*a*) the relevant consideration for the grant of the right, and

(*b*) the relevant consideration for every related supply of goods or services (including every related grant of a right to goods or services) that spans the date of the VAT change (see paragraph 6).

(6) Condition C is that the payment made in respect of the grant of the right is financed by the grantor or a person connected with the grantor (see paragraph 7).

(7) In this Schedule references to a right to goods or services include—

(*a*) any right or option with respect to such goods or services, and

(*b*) any interest deriving from such a right or option.

"Basic time of supply"

4—(1) In this Schedule the "basic time of supply" is the time given by subsection (2) or (3) of section 6 of VATA 1994 (disregarding subsections (4) to (14) of that section).

(2) Sub-paragraph (1) does not apply in relation to listed supplies (see Part 4 of this Schedule).

Series of supplies

5—(1) This paragraph applies where—

(*a*) the supply or grant of a right referred to in paragraph 2 or 3 ("the affected supply or grant") is one of a series of supplies of, or grants of a right to, the same or substantially the same goods or services, and

(*b*) each of the supplies, and the grants of a right, in the series was or will be made in the expectation that the affected supply or grant would or will take place.

(2) In condition A in paragraphs 2 and 3, the references to the supplier and the grantor include any person who makes one of the supplies or grants one of the rights in the series.

"Relevant consideration" and "related" supplies

6—(1) This paragraph applies for the purposes of condition B in paragraphs 2 and 3.

(2) "Relevant consideration" means—

(*a*) in relation to a supply that is within paragraph 2(1) by virtue of the issue of a VAT invoice, the amount shown on that invoice, (*b*) in relation to a supply that is within paragraph 2(1) by virtue of the receipt of a payment, the amount of that payment, and

(*c*) in relation to a grant of a right to goods or services within paragraph 3(1), the consideration for the grant of the right,

but does not include any amount in respect of VAT.

(3) A supply within paragraph 2(1), or a grant of a right within paragraph 3(1), is related to another such supply or grant if they are both made as part of the same scheme.

(4) "Scheme" includes any arrangements, transaction or series of transactions.

Financing

7—(1) This paragraph applies for the purposes of condition C in paragraphs 2 and 3.

(2) A payment is financed by a person if, directly or indirectly, the person—

(*a*) provides funds to enable the person to whom the supply is made to make the whole or part of the payment (whether the funds are provided before or after the payment is made),

(*b*) procures the provision of such funds by another person,

(*c*) provides funds for discharging (in whole or in part) any liability that has been or may be incurred by any person for or in connection with raising funds to enable the person to whom the supply is made to make the payment, or

(*d*) procures that any such liability is or will be discharged (in whole or in part) by another person.

(3) In sub-paragraph (2) the references to providing funds for a purpose are to—

(*a*) making a loan of funds that are or are to be used for that purpose,

(*b*) providing a guarantee or other security in relation to such a loan,

(*c*) providing consideration for the issue of shares or other securities issued wholly or partly for raising those funds,

(*d*) providing consideration for the acquisition by any person of any such shares or securities, or

(*e*) any other transfer of assets or value as a consequence of which any of those funds are made available for that purpose.

Connected persons

8 Section 1122 of CTA 2010 (connected persons) applies for the purposes of this Schedule.

Receipt of payments

9 In this Schedule a reference to receipt of a payment by the person making a supply or granting a right (however expressed) includes a reference to receipt by a person to whom a right to receive it has been assigned.

Power to change relevant conditions

10—(1) The Treasury may by order amend this Part of this Schedule by adding, modifying or omitting relevant conditions.

(2) An order under this paragraph—

(*a*) may make different provision for different cases, and

(*b*) may make incidental or consequential amendments of this Schedule.

PART 2

EXCEPTIONS

Letting etc of assets

11—(1) This paragraph applies in relation to a supply within paragraph 2 which arises from the letting, hiring or rental of assets.

(2) There is no supplementary charge under this Schedule if—

(*a*) the period to which the VAT invoice or payment referred to in paragraph 2(1) relates does not exceed 12 months, and

(*b*) the VAT invoice is issued, or the payment is received, in accordance with normal commercial practice in relation to the letting, hiring or rental of such assets.

Condition B cases involving normal commercial practice

12 There is no supplementary charge under this Schedule on a supply of goods or services within paragraph 2 or a grant of a right to goods or services within paragraph 3 if—

(*a*) the only relevant condition met is condition B, and

(*b*) the supply is made, or the right is granted, in accordance with normal commercial practice in relation to the supply of, or the grant of a right to, such goods or services.

Condition D cases involving hire purchase, conditional sale or credit sale of goods

13 There is no supplementary charge under this Schedule on a supply of goods within paragraph 2 if—

(*a*) the only relevant condition met is condition D,

(*b*) the VAT invoice—

(i) relates to a supply of goods made under a hire-purchase, conditional sale or credit sale agreement,

(ii) forms part of that agreement, and

(iii) is issued in accordance with normal commercial practice in relation to a supply made under such an agreement, and

(*c*) the basic time of supply of the goods is intended and expected to be within 6 months of the date of the VAT invoice which relates to the supply.

Normal commercial practice

14 In this Part of this Schedule, "normal commercial practice", in relation to a supply or grant of a right, means—

(*a*) normal commercial practice of the supplier or grantor at a time when an increase in the rate of VAT in force under section 2 of VATA 1994 is not expected, or

(*b*) if the supplier or grantor has no such practice, the normal commercial practice of suppliers making similar supplies, or granters granting similar rights, in the United Kingdom at such a time.

Further exceptions

15—(1) The Treasury may by order provide that there is no supplementary charge under this Schedule on supplies (including grants of rights to goods or services) of a description specified in the order.

(2) An order under this paragraph—

(*a*) may make provision having effect in relation to supplies of goods or services that are treated as taking place on or after 22 June 2010 or a later date, and

(*b*) may have effect in relation to a supplementary charge which has become due before the order is made.

PART 3
LIABILITY AND AMOUNT

Liability

16—(1) A supplementary charge under this Schedule on a supply within paragraph 2—

(*a*) is a liability of the supplier (subject to sub-paragraph (3)), and

(*b*) becomes due on the date of the VAT change (rather than at the time of supply).

(2) A supplementary charge under this Schedule on a supply consisting of the grant of a right to goods or services within paragraph 3—

(*a*) is a liability of the grantor (subject to sub-paragraph (3)), and

(*b*) becomes due on the first occasion on or after the date of the VAT change on which the right is exercised (rather than at the time the right is granted).

(3) If, on the date on which the supplementary charge becomes due, the person who would be liable to pay the charge under sub-paragraph (1) or (2)—

(*a*) is not a taxable person, but

(*b*) is treated as a member of a group under sections 43A to 43D of VATA 1994,

the supplementary charge is a liability of the representative member of the group.

Amount

17—(1) The amount of the supplementary charge on a supply within paragraph 2 is equal to the difference between—

(*a*) the amount of VAT chargeable on the supply apart from this Schedule, and

(*b*) the amount of VAT that would be chargeable on the supply if it were subject to VAT at the rate of 20%.

(2) The amount of the supplementary charge on a grant of a right to goods or services within paragraph 3 is equal to the difference between—

(*a*) the amount of VAT chargeable on the grant of the right apart from this Schedule, and

(*b*) the amount of VAT that would be chargeable on the grant of the right if it were subject to VAT at the rate of 20%,

(but see sub-paragraph (3)).

(3) If the basic time of supply for some of those goods and services is before the date of the VAT change, sub-paragraph (2) has effect as if the references to the amount of VAT chargeable and to the amount of VAT that would be chargeable were references to the relevant proportion of each of those amounts.

(4) "The relevant proportion" is—

P / W

where—

P is so much of the consideration for the grant of the right as is attributable on a just and reasonable basis to a right to the goods and services for which the basic time of supply is on or after the date of the VAT change, and

W is the whole of the consideration for the grant of the right.

PART 4

LISTED SUPPLIES

"Listed supply"

18—(1) In this Schedule "listed supply" means a supply falling within subparagraph (2)—

(*a*) which is made for a consideration the whole or part of which is determined or payable periodically or from time to time, and

(*b*) which is treated as taking place by virtue of the issue of a VAT invoice or the receipt of a payment by the person making the supply.

(2) The following supplies fall within this sub-paragraph—

(*a*) a supply of services,

(*b*) a supply arising from the grant of a major interest in land,

(*c*) a supply of water other than—

(i) distilled water, deionised water or water of similar purity, or

(ii) bottled water,

(*d*) a supply of—

(i) coal gas, water gas, producer gases or similar gases, or

(ii) petroleum gases, or other gaseous hydrocarbons, in a gaseous state,

(*e*) a supply of power, heat, refrigeration or ventilation, and

(*f*) a supply of goods together with services in the course of the construction, alteration, demolition, repair or maintenance of a building or civil engineering work.

(3) The Treasury may by order amend sub-paragraph (2) by—

(*a*) adding or omitting any description of supply, or

(*b*) varying any description of supply for the time being listed in that sub-paragraph.

"Basic time of supply": listed supplies

19—(1) For the purposes of this Schedule, in relation to a listed supply, "the basic time of supply" is the end of the period to which the VAT invoice or payment mentioned in paragraph 18(1) relates, except as provided in subparagraphs (2) and (4).

(2) Where the person making the supply issues an invoice—

(*a*) in respect of part of the listed supply to which the VAT invoice or payment mentioned in paragraph 18(1) relates, and

(*b*) for a period (a "billing period") ending before the end of the period to which that VAT invoice or payment relates,

"the basic time of supply", in relation to that part of the supply, is the end of the billing period.

(3) For the purposes of sub-paragraph (2), the listed supply (and the consideration for the supply) must be apportioned between periods on a just and reasonable basis.

(4) Where a listed supply is treated as taking place by virtue of—

(*a*) the issue by the person making the supply of a VAT invoice relating to a premium for the grant of a tenancy or lease, or

(*b*) the receipt by the person making the supply of such a premium,

"the basic time of supply" is the date of the grant of the tenancy or lease.

PART 5
ADMINISTRATION AND INTERPRETATION

Person ceasing to be taxable person before supplementary charge due

20—(1) This paragraph applies if, on the date on which a supplementary charge under this Schedule becomes due ("the due date"), the person who is liable to pay the charge under paragraph 16 is not a taxable person.

(2) The supplementary charge must be accounted for by that person in accordance with VATA 1994 (and regulations made under that Act) as if it were VAT due in the last period for which the person was required to make a return by or under VATA 1994.

(3) If an amount assessed as due by way of supplementary charge under this Schedule would (in the absence of this sub-paragraph) carry interest from a date earlier than the due date, it is to be treated as only carrying interest from the due date.

Adjustment of contracts following the VAT change

21—(1) This paragraph applies where—

(*a*) a contract for the supply of goods or services is made before the date of the VAT change, and

(*b*) there is a supplementary charge under this Schedule on the supply.

(2) The consideration for the supply is to be increased by an amount equal to the supplementary charge, unless the contract provides otherwise.

Invoices

22 Regulations under paragraph 2A of Schedule 11 to VATA 1994 (VAT invoices) may make provision about the provision, replacement or correction of invoices in connection with a supplementary charge under this Schedule.

Orders under this Schedule

23—(1) An order under this Schedule is to be made by statutory instrument.

(2) A statutory instrument containing an order under this Schedule is subject to annulment in pursuance of a resolution of the House of Commons, unless it is an instrument to which sub-paragraph (4) applies.

(3) Sub-paragraph (4) applies to a statutory instrument containing an order made under paragraph 10 (or under that paragraph and under other provisions) which extends the supplies that are subject to a supplementary charge under this Schedule.

(4) An instrument to which this sub-paragraph applies—

(*a*) must be laid before the House of Commons, and

(*b*) ceases to have effect at the end of the period of 28 days beginning with the day on which it was made unless it is approved during that period by a resolution of the House of Commons.

(5) In reckoning the period of 28 days no account is to be taken of any time during which Parliament is dissolved or prorogued or during which the House of Commons is adjourned for more than 4 days.

(6) The order ceasing to have effect does not affect—

(*a*) anything previously done under it, or

(*b*) the making of a new order.

Interpretation: general

24—(1) Expressions used in this Schedule and in VATA 1994 have the same meaning in this Schedule as in that Act.

(2) In this Schedule—

(*a*) "treated as taking place" means treated as taking place for the purposes of the charge to VAT, and

(*b*) references to the person by or to whom a supply is made (however expressed) are to the person by or to whom the supply is treated as being made for the purposes of VATA 1994.

FINANCE (NO 3) ACT 2010

(2010 Chapter 33)

ARRANGEMENT OF SECTIONS

An ACT TO Grant certain duties, to alter other duties, and to amend the law relating to the National Debt and the Public Revenue, and to make further provision in connection with finance.

[16 December 2010]

PART 2
OTHER TAXES AND DUTIES

Value added tax

19 Non-business use of business assets etc

Schedule 8 contains—

(*a*) provision about input tax, and

(*b*) provision about supplies under paragraph 5(4) of Schedule 4 to VATA 1994.

20 Supplies of gas, heat or cooling

(1) In section 9A of VATA 1994 (reverse charge on gas and electricity supplied by persons outside the United Kingdom)—

(*a*) for subsection (5) substitute—

"(5) "Relevant goods" means—

(*a*) gas supplied through a natural gas system situated within the territory of a member State or any network connected to such a system,

(*b*) electricity, and

(*c*) heat or cooling supplied through a network.", and

(*b*) in the heading, for "and electricity" substitute ", electricity, heat or cooling".

(2) In Schedule 4 to VATA 1994 (matters to be treated as supply of goods or services), in paragraph 3 after "refrigeration" insert "or other cooling,".

(3) The amendments made by this section have effect in relation to supplies made on or after 1 January 2011.

21 Supplies of aircraft etc

(1) Schedule 8 to VATA 1994 (zero-rating) is amended as follows.

(2) In Note (A1) of Group 8 (transport: definition of "qualifying aircraft" etc), for paragraph (*b*) substitute—

"(*b*) a "qualifying aircraft" is any aircraft which—

(i) is used by an airline operating for reward chiefly on international routes, or

(ii) is used by a State institution and meets the condition in Note (B1)."

(3) After that Note insert—

"(B1) The condition is that the aircraft—

(*a*) is of a weight of not less than 8,000 kilograms, and

(*b*) is neither designed nor adapted for use for recreation or pleasure.

(C1) In Note (A1)(*b*)—

"airline" means an undertaking which provides services for the carriage by air of passengers or cargo (or both);

"State institution" has the same meaning as in Part B of Annex X to the Council Directive 2006/112/EC on the common system of value added tax (transactions which member States may continue to exempt)."

(4) The amendments made by this section have effect in relation to supplies made, and acquisitions and importations taking place, on or after 1 January 2011.

22 Postal services etc

(1) In Schedule 8 to VATA 1994 (zero-rating), in Group 8—

(*a*) in item 4 (transport of passengers), for "the Post Office company" substitute "a universal service provider", and

(*b*) after Note (4D) insert—

"(4E) "Universal service provider" means a person who provides a universal postal service (within the meaning of the Postal Services Act 2000), or part of such a service, in the United Kingdom."

(2) In Schedule 9 to that Act (exemptions), for Group 3 (postal services) substitute—

"GROUP 3—POSTAL SERVICES

Item No

1

The supply of public postal services by a universal service provider.

2

The supply of goods by a universal service provider which is incidental to the supply of public postal services by that provider.

NOTES:

(1) "Universal service provider" means a person who provides a universal postal service, or part of such a service, in the United Kingdom.

(2) Subject to the following Notes, "public postal services", in relation to a universal service provider, means any postal services which the provider is required to provide in the discharge of a licence duty.

(3) Public postal services include postal services which a universal service provider provides to allow a person access to the provider's postal facilities, where such services are provided pursuant to a licence duty.

(4) Services are not "public postal services" if—

(*a*) the price is not controlled by or under a licence, or

(*b*) any of the other terms on which the services are provided are freely negotiated.

(5) But Note (4) does not apply if a licence duty requires the universal service provider to make the services available to persons generally—

(*a*) where the price is not controlled by or under the licence, at the same price, or

(*b*) where terms are freely negotiated as mentioned in Note (4)(*b*), on those terms.

(6) In this Group—

"licence" means a licence under Part 2 of the Postal Services Act 2000;

"licence duty" means a duty imposed as a condition of a licence;

"postal facilities", in relation to a universal service provider, means the resources and systems deployed by the provider, for the purpose of discharging any licence duty to provide a universal postal service or part of such a service;

"postal services" and "universal postal service" have the same meaning as in the Postal Services Act 2000."

(3) The following provisions are omitted—

(*a*) in section 96(1) of VATA 1994, the definition of "the Post Office company", and

(*b*) paragraph 22(3) and (4) of Schedule 8 to the Postal Services Act 2000.

(4) The amendments made by this section have effect in relation to supplies made on or after 31 January 2011.

PART 3

ADMINISTRATION

26 Penalties for failure to make returns etc

(1) Schedule 10 contains provision amending Schedule 55 to FA 2009 (penalties in respect of failures to make returns and other documents relating to liabilities for tax).

(2) Schedule 10 comes into force on such day as the Treasury may by order appoint.

(3) An order under subsection (2)—

(*a*) may commence a provision generally or only for specified purposes, and

(*b*) may appoint different days for different provisions or for different purposes.

(4) The Treasury may by order make any incidental, supplemental, consequential, transitional, transitory or saving provision which appears appropriate in consequence of, or otherwise in connection with, that Schedule.

(5) An order under subsection (4) may—

(*a*) make different provision for different purposes, and

(*b*) make provision amending, repealing or revoking any Act or subordinate legislation whenever passed or made (including this Act and any Act amended by it).

(6) An order under this section is to be made by statutory instrument.

(7) A statutory instrument containing an order under subsection (4) which includes provision amending or repealing any provision of an Act is subject to annulment in pursuance of a resolution of the House of Commons.

27 Penalties for failure to pay tax

(1) Schedule 11 contains provision amending Schedule 56 to FA 2009 (penalties in respect of failures to comply with obligations to pay tax).

(2) Schedule 11 comes into force on such day as the Treasury may by order appoint.

(3) An order under subsection (2)—

(*a*) may commence a provision generally or only for specified purposes, and

(*b*) may appoint different days for different provisions or for different purposes.

(4) The Treasury may by order make any incidental, supplemental, consequential, transitional, transitory or saving provision which appears appropriate in consequence of, or otherwise in connection with, that Schedule.

(5) An order under subsection (4) may—

(*a*) make different provision for different purposes, and

(*b*) make provision amending, repealing or revoking any Act or subordinate legislation whenever passed or made (including this Act and any Act amended by it).

(6) An order under this section is to be made by statutory instrument.

(7) A statutory instrument containing an order under subsection (4) which includes provision amending or repealing any provision of an Act is subject to annulment in pursuance of a resolution of the House of Commons.

Orders—Finance (No 3) Act 2010, Schedule 11 (Appointed Day) Order, SI 2011/132 (25 January 2011 appointed for the coming into force of—

- F(No 3)A 2010 Sch 11 paras 2(3), (5), (6), (12), 4, 6;
- F(No 3)A 2010 Sch 11 para 10 for the purposes of the following amounts of tax specified in column 3 of the Table in FA 2009 Sch 56 para 1—
  - item 2 (PAYE Regulations);
  - item 3 (returns under FA 2004 s 254(1));
  - item 4 (FA 2004 s 62); and
  - items 17, 23 and 24 but only insofar as the tax falls within any of items 2, 3 or 4.).

PART 5
FINAL PROVISIONS

32 Interpretation

(1) In this Act—

"BGDA 1981" means the Betting and Gaming Duties Act 1981;
"CAA 2001" means the Capital Allowances Act 2001;
"CTA 2009" means the Corporation Tax Act 2009;
"CTA 2010" means the Corporation Tax Act 2010;
"HODA 1979" means the Hydrocarbon Oil Duties Act 1979;
"ICTA" means the Income and Corporation Taxes Act 1988;
"IHTA 1984" means the Inheritance Tax Act 1984;
"ITA 2007" means the Income Tax Act 2007;
"ITEPA 2003" means the Income Tax (Earnings and Pensions) Act 2003;
"ITTOIA 2005" means the Income Tax (Trading and Other Income) Act 2005;
"OTA 1975" means the Oil Taxation Act 1975;
"TCGA 1992" means the Taxation of Chargeable Gains Act 1992;
"TIOPA 2010" means the Taxation (International and Other Provisions) Act 2010;
"TMA 1970" means the Taxes Management Act 1970;
"TPDA 1979" means the Tobacco Products Duty Act 1979;
"VATA 1994" means the Value Added Tax Act 1994;
"VERA 1994" means the Vehicle Excise and Registration Act 1994.

(2) In this Act—

"FA", followed by a year, means the Finance Act of that year;

"F(No 2)A", followed by a year, means the Finance (No 2) Act of that year.

33 Short title

This Act may be cited as the Finance (No 3) Act 2010.

SCHEDULE 8

VALUE ADDED TAX: NON-BUSINESS USE OF BUSINESS ASSETS ETC

Section 19

Input tax

1 (1) Section 24 of VATA 1994 (input tax and output tax) is amended as follows.

(2) Omit subsection (3) (accommodation used for domestic purposes by company director etc).

(3) In subsection (5) (goods or services used partly for business purposes), for the words after "other purposes" substitute "—

(*a*) VAT on supplies, acquisitions and importations shall be apportioned so that so much as is referable to the taxable person's business purposes is counted as that person's input tax, and

(*b*) the remainder of that VAT ("the non-business VAT") shall count as that person's input tax only to the extent (if any) provided for by regulations under subsection (6)(*e*)."

(4) After that subsection insert—

"(5A) For the purposes of subsections (1) and (5), a relevant asset held for the purposes of a business carried on or to be carried on by a taxable person is not, in any circumstances, to be regarded as used or to be used for the purposes of the business if, and to the extent that, it is used or to be used for that person's private use or the private use of that person's staff.

(5B) In subsection (5A) "relevant asset" means—

(*a*) any interest in land,

(*b*) any building or part of a building,

(*c*) any civil engineering work or part of such a work,

(*d*) any goods incorporated or to be incorporated in a building or civil engineering work (whether by being installed as fixtures or fittings or otherwise),

(*e*) any ship, boat or other vessel, or

(*f*) any aircraft."

(5) In subsection (6) (powers to make regulations), after paragraph (*d*) insert—

"(*e*) in cases where an apportionment is made under subsection (5), for the non-business VAT to be counted as the taxable person's input tax for the purposes of any provision made by or under section 26 in such circumstances, to such extent and subject to such conditions as may be prescribed."

(6) After that subsection insert—

"(6A) Regulations under subsection (6) may contain such supplementary, incidental, consequential and transitional provisions as appear to the Commissioners to be necessary or expedient."

(7) Omit subsection (7) (definition of "director" etc).

(8) The amendments made by sub-paragraphs (2), (4) and (7) come into force on 1 January 2011 and apply in relation to VAT incurred by a taxable person on or after that date.

(9) For the purposes of sub-paragraph (8), the VAT "incurred" by a person in respect of an asset is—

(*a*) VAT on the supply to the person of the asset,

(*b*) VAT on the supply to the person of any goods or services the expenditure on which constitutes expenditure related to the asset,

(*c*) VAT on the acquisition by the person from another member State of the asset or anything comprised in it, and

(*d*) VAT paid or payable by the person on the importation of the asset or anything comprised in it from a place outside the member States;

and VAT within paragraphs (*a*) to (*d*) is incurred at the time of the supply, acquisition or importation in question.

2 In section 26 of VATA 1994 (input tax allowable under section 25), in subsection (4) for "and supplementary" substitute ", supplementary, consequential and transitional".

Non-business use of certain assets not to be treated as supply of services

3 (1) In paragraph 5 of Schedule 4 to VATA 1994 (matters to be treated as supply of goods or services), after sub-paragraph (4) (non-business use of business asset treated as supply of services) insert—

"(4A) Sub-paragraph (4) does not apply (despite paragraph 9(1)) to—

(*a*) any interest in land,

(*b*) any building or part of a building,

(*c*) any civil engineering work or part of such a work,

(*d*) any goods incorporated or to be incorporated in a building or civil engineering work (whether by being installed as fixtures or fittings or otherwise),

(*e*) any ship, boat or other vessel, or

(*f*) any aircraft."

(2) This paragraph comes into force on 1 January 2011.

(3) This paragraph does not apply in relation to an asset in respect of which the person in question or any of that person's predecessors incurred VAT before 1 January 2011.

(4) But, where VAT is incurred by such a person before that date in respect of the asset, VAT incurred by such a person on or after that date in respect of the asset is not to be treated as referable to that person's business purposes by virtue of paragraph 5(4) and (6) of Schedule 4 to VATA 1994 if, and to the extent that, the asset is used or to be used for that person's private use or the private use of that person's staff, or more generally for purposes other than those of that person's business.

(5) For the purposes of this paragraph—

"asset" means anything falling within any of paragraphs (*a*) to (*f*) of paragraph 5(4A) of Schedule 4 to VATA 1994 (as inserted by subparagraph (1) above);

"the person in question" means the person carrying on the business referred to in paragraph 5(4) of that Schedule;

"predecessor" has the same meaning as in paragraph 5 of that Schedule;

and references to the VAT "incurred" by a person in respect of an asset are to be construed in accordance with paragraph 1(9).

Output tax charge where credit attributable to purported paragraph 5(4) supply

4 (1) Sub-paragraph (2) applies where—

(*a*) a person carrying on a business or any of that person's predecessors has been allowed credit under sections 25 and 26 of VATA 1994 for input tax on the basis that the input tax is attributable to a thing done or to be done which is or would be a paragraph 5(4) supply,

(*b*) some or all of that credit was allowed before 22 January 2010,

(*c*) disregarding sub-paragraph (2), the thing done or to be done is not or would not be a paragraph 5(4) supply, and

(*d*) the credit allowed as mentioned in paragraph (*a*) is not reversed in full.

(2) The thing done or to be done is to be treated for the purposes of VATA 1994 as if it were or would be a paragraph 5(4) supply.

(3) But sub-paragraph (2) does not confer on the person allowed credit as mentioned in sub-paragraph (1)(*a*) any entitlement to that credit under sections 25 and 26 of that Act.

(4) For the purposes of sub-paragraph (1) credit for input tax is "allowed" under sections 25 and 26 of VATA 1994 to the extent that the credit is claimed, and the claim is satisfied by one or more of the following—

(*a*) the deduction of input tax under section 25(2) of that Act from any output tax that is due to the Commissioners;

(*b*) a payment by the Commissioners in respect of the credit under section 25(3) of that Act;

(*c*) the setting off of the credit against a sum payable to the Commissioners, whether under section 81(3) of that Act or section 130 of FA 2008 or otherwise.

(5) In this paragraph—

"paragraph 5(4) supply" means a supply under paragraph 5(4) of Schedule 4 to VATA 1994 (goods held or used for the purposes of a business which are put to private use etc);

"predecessor" has the same meaning as in paragraph 5 of that Schedule.

(6) This paragraph is to be treated as having always had effect.

SCHEDULE 10
PENALTY FOR FAILURE TO MAKE RETURNS ETC

Section 26

Commencement—Finance (No 3) Act 2010, Schedules 10 and 11 (Income Tax Self Assessment and Pension Schemes) (Appointed Days) Order, SI 2011/703 (the day appointed for the coming into force of Sch 10 paras 1, 4 and 10 is—

- 6 April 2011 in relation to a return or other document which is required to be made or delivered to HMRC in relation to the tax year 2010–11 or any subsequent tax year, and falls within item 1, 2 or 3 of the Table in Sch 55 para 1; and
- 1 April 2011 in relation to a return under FA 2004 s 254 to be made un respect of a return period ending on or after 31 March 2011.

Finance (No 3) Act 2010, Schedule 10 and the Finance Act 2009, Schedule 55 and Sections 101 to 103 (Appointed Day, etc) (Construction Industry Scheme) Order, SI 2011/2391 (the day appointed for the coming into force of para 1, in so far as it is relevant to paras 5, 6 and 10 below, is 6 October 2011, with effect only in relation to a return within item 6 in FA 2009 Sch 55 para 1(5), and for which the filing date for the purposes of Sch 55 is after 19 October 2011).

1 Schedule 55 to FA 2009 (penalty for failure to make returns etc) is amended as follows.

Commencement—Finance (No 3) Act 2010, Schedules 10 and 11 (Income Tax Self Assessment and Pension Schemes) (Appointed Days) Order, SI 2011/703 (the day appointed for the coming into force of Sch 10 paras 1, 4 and 10 is—

- 6 April 2011 in relation to a return or other document which is required to be made or delivered to HMRC in relation to the tax year 2010–11 or any subsequent tax year, and falls within item 1, 2 or 3 of the Table in Sch 55 para 1; and
- 1 April 2011 in relation to a return under FA 2004 s 254 to be made un respect of a return period ending on or after 31 March 2011.

Finance (No 3) Act 2010, Schedule 10 and the Finance Act 2009, Schedule 55 and Sections 101 to 103 (Appointed Day, etc) (Construction Industry Scheme) Order, SI 2011/2391 (the day appointed for the coming into force of para 1, in so far as it is relevant to paras 5, 6 and 10 below, is 6 October 2011, with effect only in relation to a return within item 6 in FA 2009 Sch 55 para 1(5), and for which the filing date for the purposes of Sch 55 is after 19 October 2011).

2 (1) Paragraph 1 (penalty for failure) is amended as follows.
(2) In sub-paragraph (2), for "13" substitute "13J".
[(2A) In sub-paragraph (4), in the definition of "filing date", at the end insert "(or, in the case of a return mentioned in item 7AA or 7AB of the Table, to the tax authorities to whom the return is required to be delivered)".][1]
(3) The Table is amended as follows.
(4) After item 7 insert—

"7A	Value added tax	Return under regulations under paragraph 2 of Schedule 11 to VATA 1994
[7AA	Value added tax	Relevant non-UK return (as defined in paragraph 20(3) of Schedule 3BA to VATA 1994)
7AB	Value added tax	Relevant special scheme return (as defined in paragraph 16(3) of Schedule 3B to VATA 1994).][1]
7B	Insurance premium tax	Return under regulations under section 54 of FA 1994".

(5) Insert at the end—

"14	Aggregates levy	Return under regulations under section 25 of FA 2001
15	Climate change levy	Return under regulations under paragraph 41 of Schedule 6 to FA 2000
16	Landfill tax	Return under regulations under section 49 of FA 1996
17	Air passenger duty	Return under regulations under section 38 of FA 1994
18	Alcoholic liquor duties	Return under regulations under section 13, 49, 56 or 62 of ALDA 1979
19	Tobacco products duty	Return under regulations under section 7 of TPDA 1979

20	Hydrocarbon oil duties	Return under regulations under section 21 of HODA 1979
21	Excise duties	Return under regulations under section 93 of the Customs and Excise Management Act 1979
22	Excise duties	Return under regulations under section 100G or 100H of the Customs and Excise Management Act 1979
23	General betting duty	Return under regulations under paragraph 2 of Schedule 1 to BGDA 1981
24	Pool betting duty	Return under regulations under paragraph 2A of Schedule 1 to BGDA 1981
25	Bingo duty	Return under regulations under paragraph 9 of Schedule 3 to BGDA 1981
26	Lottery duty	Return under regulations under section 28(2) of FA 1993
27	Gaming duty	Return under directions under paragraph 10 of Schedule 1 to FA 1997
28	Remote gaming duty	Return under regulations under section 26K of BGDA 1981".

Amendments—

[1] Sub para (2A) inserted, and in sub-para (4) items 7AA, 7AB inserted, by FA 2014 s 103, Sch 22 para 21(1), (2) with effect from 17 July 2014.

3 For paragraph 2 (amount of penalty for occasional or annual returns) and the italic heading preceding it substitute—

"*Amount of penalty: occasional returns and returns for periods of 6 months or more*

2

(1) Paragraphs 3 to 6 apply in the case of—

(*a*) a return falling within any of items 1 to 5, 7 and 8 to 13 in the Table,

(*b*) a return falling within any of items 7A, 7B and 14 to 28 which relates to a period of 6 months or more, and

(*c*) a return falling within item 7A which relates to a transitional period for the purposes of the annual accounting scheme.

(2) In sub-paragraph (1)(*c*), a transitional period for the purposes of the annual accounting scheme is a prescribed accounting period (within the meaning of section 25(1) of VATA 1994) which—

(*a*) ends on the day immediately preceding the date indicated by the Commissioners for Her Majesty's Revenue and Customs in a notification of authorisation under regulation 50 of the Value Added Tax Regulations 1995 (SI 1995/2518) (admission to annual accounting scheme), or

(*b*) begins on the day immediately following the end of the last period of 12 months for which such an authorisation has effect."

4 (1) Paragraph 6 (amount of penalty for occasional returns and annual returns) is amended as follows.

(2) In sub-paragraph (2), after "P" in the first place it occurs insert "deliberately".

(3) In sub-paragraph (5), for "any other case" substitute "any case not falling within sub-paragraph (2)".

Commencement—Finance (No 3) Act 2010, Schedules 10 and 11 (Income Tax Self Assessment and Pension Schemes) (Appointed Days) Order, SI 2011/703 (the day appointed for the coming into force of Sch 10 paras 1, 4 and 10 is—

– 6 April 2011 in relation to a return or other document which is required to be made or delivered to HMRC in relation to the tax year 2010–11 or any subsequent tax year, and falls within item 1, 2 or 3 of the Table in Sch 55 para 1; and

– 1 April 2011 in relation to a return under FA 2004 s 254 to be made un respect of a return period ending on or after 31 March 2011.

5 (1) Paragraph 11 (amount of penalty for certain CIS returns after 12 months) is amended as follows.

(2) In sub-paragraph (2), after "P" in the first place it occurs insert "deliberately".

(3) In sub-paragraph (5), for "any other case" substitute "any case not falling within sub-paragraph (2)".

Commencement—Finance (No 3) Act 2010, Schedule 10 and the Finance Act 2009, Schedule 55 and Sections 101 to 103 (Appointed Day, etc) (Construction Industry Scheme) Order, SI 2011/2391 (the day appointed for the coming into force of Sch 10 paras 5, 6 and 10 (and, but only as relevant to those provisions, para 1) is 6 October 2011, with effect only in relation to a return within item 6 in FA 2009 Sch 55 para 1(5), and for which the filing date for the purposes of Sch 55 is after 19 October 2011).

6 (1) Paragraph 12 (amount of penalty for other CIS returns after 12 months) is amended as follows.
(2) In sub-paragraph (2), after "P" insert "deliberately".

Commencement—Finance (No 3) Act 2010, Schedule 10 and the Finance Act 2009, Schedule 55 and Sections 101 to 103 (Appointed Day, etc) (Construction Industry Scheme) Order, SI 2011/2391 (the day appointed for the coming into force of Sch 10 paras 5, 6 and 10 (and, but only as relevant to those provisions, para 1) is 6 October 2011, with effect only in relation to a return within item 6 in FA 2009 Sch 55 para 1(5), and for which the filing date for the purposes of Sch 55 is after 19 October 2011).

7 After paragraph 13 insert—

"Amount of penalty: returns for periods of between 2 and 6 months

13A

(1) Paragraphs 13B to 13E apply in the case of a return falling within any of items [7A to 7B][1] and 14 to 28 in the Table which relates to a period of less than 6 months but more than 2 months.
(2) But those paragraphs do not apply in the case of a return mentioned in paragraph 2(1)(*c*).

13B

(1) P is liable to a penalty under this paragraph of £100.
(2) In addition, a penalty period begins to run on the penalty date for the return.
(3) The penalty period ends with the day 12 months after the filing date for the return, unless it is extended under paragraph 13C(2)(*c*) or 13H(2)(*c*).

13C

(1) This paragraph applies if—
 (*a*) a penalty period has begun under paragraph 13B or 13G because P has failed to make a return ("return A"), and
 (*b*) before the end of the period, P fails to make another return ("return B") falling within the same item in the Table as return A.
(2) In such a case—
 (*a*) paragraph 13B(1) and (2) do not apply to the failure to make return B, but
 (*b*) P is liable to a penalty under this paragraph for that failure, and
 (*c*) the penalty period that has begun is extended so that it ends with the day 12 months after the filing date for return B.
(3) The amount of the penalty under this paragraph is determined by reference to the number of returns that P has failed to make during the penalty period.
(4) If the failure to make return B is P's first failure to make a return during the penalty period, P is liable, at the time of the failure, to a penalty of £200.
(5) If the failure to make return B is P's second failure to make a return during the penalty period, P is liable, at the time of the failure, to a penalty of £300.
(6) If the failure to make return B is P's third or a subsequent failure to make a return during the penalty period, P is liable, at the time of the failure, to a penalty of £400.
(7) For the purposes of this paragraph—
 (*a*) in accordance with sub-paragraph (1)(*b*), the references in sub-paragraphs (3) to (6) to a return are references to a return falling within the same item in the Table as returns A and B, and
 (*b*) a failure to make a return counts for the purposes of those sub-paragraphs if (but only if) the return relates to a period of less than 6 months.
(8) A penalty period may be extended more than once under subparagraph (2)(*c*).

13D

(1) P is liable to a penalty under this paragraph if (and only if) P's failure continues after the end of the period of 6 months beginning with the penalty date.
(2) The penalty under this paragraph is the greater of—
 (*a*) 5% of any liability to tax which would have been shown in the return in question, and

(*b*) £300.

13E

(1) P is liable to a penalty under this paragraph if (and only if) P's failure continues after the end of the period of 12 months beginning with the penalty date.

(2) Where, by failing to make the return, P deliberately withholds information which would enable or assist HMRC to assess P's liability to tax, the penalty under this paragraph is determined in accordance with sub-paragraphs (3) and (4).

(3) If the withholding of the information is deliberate and concealed, the penalty is the greater of—

(*a*) 100% of any liability to tax which would have been shown in the return in question, and

(*b*) £300.

(4) If the withholding of the information is deliberate but not concealed, the penalty is the greater of—

(*a*) 70% of any liability to tax which would have been shown in the return in question, and

(*b*) £300.

(5) In any case not falling within sub-paragraph (2), the penalty under this paragraph is the greater of—

(*a*) 5% of any liability to tax which would have been shown in the return in question, and

(*b*) £300.

Amount of penalty: returns for periods of 2 months or less

13F

(1) Paragraphs 13G to 13J apply in the case of a return falling within any of items 7A, 7B and 14 to 28 in the Table which relates to a period of 2 months or less.

(2) But those paragraphs do not apply in the case of a return mentioned in paragraph 2(1)(*c*).

13G

(1) P is liable to a penalty under this paragraph of £100.

(2) In addition, a penalty period begins to run on the penalty date for the return.

(3) The penalty period ends with the day 12 months after the filing date for the return, unless it is extended under paragraph 13C(2)(*c*) or 13H(2)(*c*).

13H

(1) This paragraph applies if—

(*a*) a penalty period has begun under paragraph 13B or 13G because P has failed to make a return ("return A"), and

(*b*) before the end of the period, P fails to make another return ("return B") falling within the same item in the Table as return A.

(2) In such a case—

(*a*) paragraph 13G(1) and (2) do not apply to the failure to make return B, but

(*b*) P is liable to a penalty under this paragraph for that failure, and

(*c*) the penalty period that has begun is extended so that it ends with the day 12 months after the filing date for return B.

(3) The amount of the penalty under this paragraph is determined by reference to the number of returns that P has failed to make during the penalty period.

(4) If the failure to make return B is P's first, second, third, fourth or fifth failure to make a return during the penalty period, P is liable, at the time of the failure, to a penalty of £100.

(5) If the failure to make return B is P's sixth or a subsequent failure to make a return during the penalty period, P is liable, at the time of the failure, to a penalty of £200.

(6) For the purposes of this paragraph—

(*a*) in accordance with sub-paragraph (1)(*b*), the references in sub-paragraphs (3) to (5) to a return are references to a return falling within the same item in the Table as returns A and B, and

(*b*) a failure to make a return counts for the purposes of those sub-paragraphs if (but only if) the return relates to a period of less than 6 months.

(7) A penalty period may be extended more than once under subparagraph (2)(*c*).

13I

(1) P is liable to a penalty under this paragraph if (and only if) P's failure continues after the end of the period of 6 months beginning with the penalty date.

(2) The penalty under this paragraph is the greater of—

(*a*) 5% of any liability to tax which would have been shown in the return in question, and

(*b*) £300.

13J

(1) P is liable to a penalty under this paragraph if (and only if) P's failure continues after the end of the period of 12 months beginning with the penalty date.

(2) Where, by failing to make the return, P deliberately withholds information which would enable or assist HMRC to assess P's liability to tax, the penalty under this paragraph is determined in accordance with sub-paragraphs (3) and (4).

(3) If the withholding of the information is deliberate and concealed, the penalty is the greater of—

(*a*) 100% of any liability to tax which would have been shown in the return in question, and

(*b*) £300.

(4) If the withholding of the information is deliberate but not concealed, the penalty is the greater of—

(*a*) 70% of any liability to tax which would have been shown in the return in question, and

(*b*) £300.

(5) In any case not falling within sub-paragraph (2), the penalty under this paragraph is the greater of—

(*a*) 5% of any liability to tax which would have been shown in the return in question, and

(*b*) £300."

Amendments—[1] In the inserted para 13A(1), words substituted for words "7A, 7B" by FA 2014 s 103, Sch 22 para 21(1), (3) with effect from 17 July 2014.

8 In paragraph 14(1) (reductions for disclosure), for "or 11(3) or (4)" substitute ", 11(3) or (4), 13E(3) or (4) or 13J(3) or (4)".

9 In paragraph 15(5) (reductions for disclosure not below certain amounts)—

(*a*) for "paragraph 11(3) or (4)" substitute "sub-paragraph (3) or (4) of any of paragraphs 11, 13E and 13J", and

(*b*) for "paragraph 11(3)(*b*) or (4)(*b*) (as the case may be)" substitute "paragraph (*b*) of that sub-paragraph".

10 In paragraph 18 (assessment), after sub-paragraph (4) insert—

"(5) A replacement assessment may be made in respect of a penalty if an earlier assessment operated by reference to an overestimate of the liability to tax which would have been shown in a return."

Commencement—Finance (No 3) Act 2010, Schedules 10 and 11 (Income Tax Self Assessment and Pension Schemes) (Appointed Days) Order, SI 2011/703 (the day appointed for the coming into force of Sch 10 paras 1, 4 and 10 is—

– 6 April 2011 in relation to a return or other document which is required to be made or delivered to HMRC in relation to the tax year 2010–11 or any subsequent tax year, and falls within item 1, 2 or 3 of the Table in Sch 55 para 1; and
– 1 April 2011 in relation to a return under FA 2004 s 254 to be made in respect of a return period ending on or after 31 March 2011.

Finance (No 3) Act 2010, Schedule 10 and the Finance Act 2009, Schedule 55 and Sections 101 to 103 (Appointed Day, etc) (Construction Industry Scheme) Order, SI 2011/2391 (the day appointed for the coming into force of Sch 10 paras 5, 6 and 10 (and, but only as relevant to those provisions, para 1) is 6 October 2011, with effect only in relation to a return within item 6 in FA 2009 Sch 55 para 1(5), and for which the filing date for the purposes of Sch 55 is after 19 October 2011).

11 For paragraph 23(1) (no liability where there is reasonable excuse for failure) substitute—

"(1) If P satisfies HMRC or (on appeal) the First-tier Tribunal or Upper Tribunal that there is a reasonable excuse for a failure to make a return—

(*a*) liability to a penalty under any paragraph of this Schedule does not arise in relation to that failure, and

(*b*) the failure does not count for the purposes of paragraphs 13B(2), 13C, 13G(2) and 13H."

SCHEDULE 11

PENALTY FOR FAILURE TO MAKE PAYMENTS ON TIME

Section 27

Commencement—Finance (No 3) Act 2010, Schedule 11 (Appointed Day) Order, SI 2011/132 (25 January 2011 appointed for the coming into force of—

- F(No 3)A 2010 Sch 11 paras 2(3), (5), (6), (12), 4, 6;
- F(No 3)A 2010 Sch 11 para 10 for the purposes of the following amounts of tax specified in column 3 of the Table in FA 2009 Sch 56 para 1—
  - item 2 (PAYE Regulations);
  - item 3 (returns under FA 2004 s 254(1));
  - item 4 (FA 2004 s 62); and
  - items 17, 23 and 24 but only insofar as the tax falls within any of items 2, 3 or 4.).

Finance (No 3) Act 2010, Schedules 10 and 11 (Income Tax Self Assessment and Pension Schemes) (Appointed Days) Order, SI 2011/703 art 3 (the day appointed for the coming into force of Sch 11 paras 1 and 9 is 6 April 2011 in relation to an amount of tax which is payable in relation to the tax year 2010–11 or any subsequent tax year, and falls within item 1, 12, 18 or 19 of the Table in FA 2009 Sch 56 para 1, or insofar as the tax falls within item 1 of that Table, item 17, 23 or 24 of that Table).

1 Schedule 56 to FA 2009 (penalty for failure to make payments on time) is amended as follows.

Commencement—Finance (No 3) Act 2010, Schedules 10 and 11 (Income Tax Self Assessment and Pension Schemes) (Appointed Days) Order, SI 2011/703 art 3 (the day appointed for the coming into force of Sch 11 paras 1 and 9 is 6 April 2011 in relation to an amount of tax which is payable in relation to the tax year 2010–11 or any subsequent tax year, and falls within item 1, 12, 18 or 19 of the Table in FA 2009 Sch 56 para 1, or insofar as the tax falls within item 1 of that Table, item 17, 23 or 24 of that Table).

2 (1) Paragraph 1 (penalty for failure) is amended as follows.

(2) In sub-paragraph (2), for "8" substitute "8J".

(3) After sub-paragraph (4) insert—

"(5) Sub-paragraph (4) is subject to paragraph 2A."

(4) The Table is amended as follows.

(5) In item 2, in column 3, omit "(except an amount falling within item 20)".

(6) In item 4, in column 4, for "section 62" substitute "section 71".

(7) After item 6 insert—

"6A	Value added tax	Amount payable under section 25(1) of VATA 1994 (except an amount falling within item 6B, 13A, 23 or 24)	The date determined— (*a*) by or under regulations under section 25 of VATA 1994, or (*b*) in accordance with an order under section 28 of that Act, as the date by which the amount must be paid
6B	Value added tax	Amount payable under section 25(1) of VATA 1994 which is an instalment of an amount due in respect of a period of 9 months or more ("amount A")	The date on or before which P must pay any balancing payment or other outstanding payment due in respect of amount A
[6BA	Value added tax	Amount payable under relevant special scheme return (as defined in paragraph 16(3) of Schedule 3B to VATA 1994) (except an amount falling within item 13A, 13AA, 13AB, 23 or 24)	The date by which the amount must be paid under the law of the member State which has established the special scheme

6BB	Value added tax	Amount payable under relevant non-UK return (as defined in paragraph 20(3) of Schedule 3BA to VATA 1994) (except an amount falling within item 13A, 13AA, 13AB, 23 or 24)	The date by which the amount must be paid under the law of the member State which has established the non-UK special scheme][1]
6C	Insurance premium tax	Amount payable under regulations under section 54 of FA 1994 (except an amount falling within item 13B, 23 or 24)	The date determined by or under regulations under section 54 of FA 1994 as the date by which the amount must be paid".

(8) After item 11 insert—

"11A	Aggregates levy	Amount payable under regulations under section 25 of FA 2001 (except an amount falling within item 16A, 23 or 24)	The date determined by or under regulations under section 25 of FA 2001 as the date by which the amount must be paid
11B	Climate change levy	Amount payable under regulations under paragraph 41 of Schedule 6 to FA 2000 (except an amount falling within item 16B, 23 or 24)	The date determined by or under regulations under paragraph 41 of Schedule 6 to FA 2000 as the date by which the amount must be paid
11C	Landfill tax	Amount payable under regulations under section 49 of FA 1996 (except an amount falling within item 16C, 23 or 24)	The date determined by or under regulations under section 49 of FA 1996 as the date by which the amount must be paid
11D	Air passenger duty	Amount payable under regulations under section 38 of FA 1994 (except an amount falling within item 17A, 23 or 24)	The date determined by or under regulations under section 38 of FA 1994 as the date by which the amount must be paid
11E	Alcoholic liquor duties	Amount payable under regulations under section 13, 49, 56 or 62 of ALDA 1979 (except an amount falling within item 17A, 23 or 24)	The date determined by or under regulations under section 13, 49, 56 or 62 of ALDA 1979 as the date by which the amount must be paid
11F	Tobacco products duty	Amount payable under regulations under section 7 of TPDA 1979 (except an amount falling within item 17A, 23 or 24)	The date determined by or under regulations under section 7 of TPDA 1979 as the date by which the amount must be paid
11G	Hydrocarbon oil duties	Amount payable under regulations under section 21 or 24 of HODA 1979 (except an amount falling within item 17A, 23 or 24)	The date determined by or under regulations under section 21 or 24 of HODA 1979 as the date by which the amount must be paid
11H	General betting duty	Amount payable under section 5B of BGDA 1981 (except an amount falling within item 17A, 23 or 24)	The date determined — (*a*) under section 5B of BGDA 1981, or (*b*) by or under regulations under paragraph 2 of Schedule 1 to that Act, as the date by which the amount must be paid

11I	Pool betting duty	Amount payable under section 8 of BGDA 1981 (except an amount falling within item 17A, 23 or 24)	The date determined — (*a*) under section 8 of BGDA 1981, or (*b*) by or under regulations under that section or directions under paragraph 3 of Schedule 1 to that Act, as the date by which the amount must be paid
11J	Bingo duty	Amount payable under regulations under paragraph 9 of Schedule 3 to BGDA 1981 (except an amount falling within item 17A, 23 or 24)	The date determined by or under regulations under paragraph 9 of Schedule 3 to BGDA 1981 as the date by which the amount must be paid
11K	Lottery duty	Amount payable under section 26 of FA 1993 (except an amount falling within item 17A, 23 or 24)	The date determined — (*a*) by section 26 of FA 1993, or (*b*) by or under regulations under that section, as the date by which the amount must be paid
11L	Gaming duty	Amount payable under section 12 of FA 1997 (except an amount falling within item 17A, 23 or 24)	The date determined by or under regulations under — (*a*) section 12 of FA 1997, or (*b*) paragraph 11 of Schedule 1 to that Act, as the date by which the amount must be paid
11M	Remote gaming duty	Amount payable under section 26I of BGDA 1981 (except an amount falling within item 17A, 23 or 24)	The date determined by or under regulations under section 26I of BGDA 1981 as the date by which the amount must be paid".

(9) After item 13 insert—

"13A	Value added tax	Amount assessed under section 73(1) of VATA 1994 in the absence of a return	The date by which the amount would have been required to be paid if it had been shown in the return
[13AA	Value added tax	Amount assessed under section 73(1) of VATA 1994, by virtue of paragraph 16 of Schedule 3B to that Act, in the absence of a value added tax return (as defined in paragraph 23(1) of that Schedule)	The date by which the amount would have been required to be paid under the law of the member State under whose law the return was required

13AB	Value added tax	Amount assessed under section 73(1) of VATA 1994, by virtue of paragraph 20 of Schedule 3BA to that Act, in the absence of a relevant non- UK return (as defined in paragraph 38(1) of that Schedule)	The date by which the amount would have been required to be paid under the law of the member State under whose law the return was required][1]
13B	Insurance premium tax	Amount assessed under section 56(1) of FA 1994 in the absence of a return	The date by which the amount would have been required to be paid if it had been shown in the return".

(10) After item 16 insert—

"16A	Aggregates levy	Amount assessed under paragraph 2 or 3 of Schedule 5 to FA 2001 in the absence of a return	The date by which the amount would have been required to be paid if it had been shown in the return
16B	Climate change levy	Amount assessed under paragraph 78 or 79 of Schedule 6 to FA 2000 in the absence of a return	The date by which the amount would have been required to be paid if it had been shown in the return
16C	Landfill tax	Amount assessed under section 50(1) of FA 1996 in the absence of a return	The date by which the amount would have been required to be paid if it had been shown in the return".

(11) After item 17 insert—

"17A	Tax falling within any of items 11D to 11M	Amount assessed under section 12(1) of FA 1994 in the absence of a return	The date by which the amount would have been required to be paid if it had been shown in the return".

(12) Omit item 20.

(13) In item 23—

(*a*) in columns 2 and 3, for "items 1 to 6, 9 or 10" substitute "items 1 to 6A, [6BA, 6BB,][1] 6C, 9, 10 or 11A to 11M", and

(*b*) in column 3, for "any of items 18 to 20" substitute "item 18 or 19".

(14) In item 24—

(*a*) in column 2, for "items 1 to 6, 9 or 10" substitute "items 1 to 6A, [6BA, 6BB,][1] 6C, 9, 10 or 11A to 11M", and

(*b*) in column 3, for "any of items 18 to 20" substitute "item 18 or 19".

Commencement—Finance (No 3) Act 2010, Schedule 11 (Appointed Day) Order, SI 2011/132 (25 January 2011 appointed for the coming into force of—

- F(No 3)A 2010 Sch 11 paras 2(3), (5), (6), (12), 4, 6;
- F(No 3)A 2010 Sch 11 para 10 for the purposes of the following amounts of tax specified in column 3 of the Table in FA 2009 Sch 56 para 1—
  - item 2 (PAYE Regulations);
  - item 3 (returns under FA 2004 s 254(1));
  - item 4 (FA 2004 s 62); and
  - items 17, 23 and 24 but only insofar as the tax falls within any of items 2, 3 or 4.).

Amendments—

[1] In sub-para (7), items 6BA, 6BB inserted, in sub-para (9), items 13AA, 13AB inserted, and in sub-paras (13)(*a*), (14)(*a*), words inserted, by FA 2014 s 103, Sch 22 para 22(1)–(5) with effect from 17 July 2014.

3 In paragraph 2 (assessments and determinations in default of return), in paragraph (*c*), for "10" substitute "11M".

4 *(inserts FA 2009 Sch 56 para 2A)*

Commencement—Finance (No 3) Act 2010, Schedule 11 (Appointed Day) Order, SI 2011/132 (25 January 2011 appointed for the coming into force of—

- F(No 3)A 2010 Sch 11 paras 2(3), (5), (6), (12), 4, 6;
- F(No 3)A 2010 Sch 11 para 10 for the purposes of the following amounts of tax specified in column 3 of the Table in FA 2009 Sch 56 para 1—
  - item 2 (PAYE Regulations);
  - item 3 (returns under FA 2004 s 254(1));
  - item 4 (FA 2004 s 62); and
  - items 17, 23 and 24 but only insofar as the tax falls within any of items 2, 3 or 4.).

5 (1) Paragraph 3 (amount of penalty for occasional amounts and amounts due for periods of 6 months or more) is amended as follows.

(2) Sub-paragraph (1) is amended as follows.

(3) In paragraph (*a*), for "items 1, 3 and 7 to 24" substitute "items 1, 3, 6B, 7 to 11 and 12 to 24".

(4) In paragraph (*b*)—

(*a*) for "item 2 or 4" substitute "any of items 2, 4, 6A, 6C and 11A to 11M", and

(*b*) omit the "and" at the end.

(5) After paragraph (*c*) insert ", and

(*d*) a payment of tax falling within item 6A which relates to a transitional period for the purposes of the annual accounting scheme."

(6) After sub-paragraph (1) insert—

"(1A) In sub-paragraph (1)(*d*), a transitional period for the purposes of the annual accounting scheme is a prescribed accounting period (within the meaning of section 25(1) of VATA 1994) which—

(*a*) ends on the day immediately preceding the date indicated by the Commissioners for Her Majesty's Revenue and Customs in a notification of authorisation under regulation 50 of the Value Added Tax Regulations 1995 (SI 1995/2518) (admission to annual accounting scheme), or

(*b*) begins on the day immediately following the end of the last period of 12 months for which such an authorisation has effect."

6 *(substitutes FA 2009 Sch 56 para 6)*

Commencement—Finance (No 3) Act 2010, Schedule 11 (Appointed Day) Order, SI 2011/132 (25 January 2011 appointed for the coming into force of—

- F(No 3)A 2010 Sch 11 paras 2(3), (5), (6), (12), 4, 6;
- F(No 3)A 2010 Sch 11 para 10 for the purposes of the following amounts of tax specified in column 3 of the Table in FA 2009 Sch 56 para 1—
  - item 2 (PAYE Regulations);
  - item 3 (returns under FA 2004 s 254(1));
  - item 4 (FA 2004 s 62); and
  - items 17, 23 and 24 but only insofar as the tax falls within any of items 2, 3 or 4.).

7 After paragraph 8 insert—

"Amount of penalty: amounts in respect of periods of between 2 and 6 months

8A

(1) Paragraphs 8B to 8E apply in the case of a payment of tax falling within any of items 6A, [6BA, 6BB,][1] 6C and 11A to 11M in the Table which relates to a period of less than 6 months but more than 2 months.

(2) But those paragraphs do not apply in the case of a payment mentioned in paragraph 3(1)(*d*).

(3) Paragraph 8K sets out how payments on account of VAT (item 6A) are to be treated for the purposes of paragraphs 8B to 8E.

8B

(1) A penalty period begins to run on the penalty date for the payment of tax.

(2) The penalty period ends with the day 12 months after the date specified in or for the purposes of column 4 for the payment, unless it is extended under paragraph 8C(2)(*c*) or 8H(2)(*c*).

8C

(1) This paragraph applies if—

(*a*) a penalty period has begun under paragraph 8B or 8G because P has failed to make a payment ("payment A"), and

(*b*) before the end of the period, P fails to make another payment ("payment B") falling within the same item in the Table as payment A.

(2) In such a case—

(*a*) paragraph 8B(1) does not apply to the failure to make payment B,

(*b*) P is liable to a penalty under this paragraph for that failure, And (*c*) the penalty period that has begun is extended so that it ends with the day 12 months after the date specified in or for the purposes of column 4 for payment B.

(3) The amount of the penalty under this paragraph is determined by reference to the number of defaults that P has made during the penalty period.

(4) If the default is P's first default during the penalty period, P is liable, at the time of the default, to a penalty of 2% of the amount of the default.

(5) If the default is P's second default during the penalty period, P is liable, at the time of the default, to a penalty of 3% of the amount of the default.

(6) If the default is P's third or a subsequent default during the penalty period, P is liable, at the time of the default, to a penalty of 4% of the amount of the default.

(7) For the purposes of this paragraph—

(*a*) P makes a default when P fails to pay an amount of tax in full on or before the date on which it becomes due and payable;

(*b*) in accordance with sub-paragraph (1)(*b*), the references in sub-paragraphs (3) to (6) to a default are references to a default in relation to the tax to which payments A and B relate;

(*c*) a default counts for the purposes of those sub-paragraphs if (but only if) the period to which the payment relates is less than 6 months;

(*d*) the amount of a default is the amount which P fails to pay.

(8) A penalty period may be extended more than once under subparagraph (2)(*c*).

8D

If any amount of the tax is unpaid after the end of the period of 6 months beginning with the penalty date, P is liable to a penalty of 5% of that amount.

8E

If any amount of the tax is unpaid after the end of the period of 12 months beginning with the penalty date, P is liable to a penalty of 5% of that amount.

Amount of penalty: amounts in respect of periods of 2 months or less

8F

(1) Paragraphs 8G to 8J apply in the case of a payment of tax falling within any of items 6A, 6C and 11A to 11M in the Table which relates to a period of 2 months or less.

(2) But those paragraphs do not apply in the case of a payment mentioned in paragraph 3(1)(*d*).

8G

(1) A penalty period begins to run on the penalty date for the payment of tax.

(2) The penalty period ends with the day 12 months after the date specified in or for the purposes of column 4 for the payment, unless it is extended under paragraph 8C(2)(*c*) or 8H(2)(*c*).

8H

(1) This paragraph applies if—

(*a*) a penalty period has begun under paragraph 8B or 8G because P has failed to make a payment ("payment A"), and

(*b*) before the end of the period, P fails to make another payment ("payment B") falling within the same item in the Table as payment A.

(2) In such a case—

(*a*) paragraph 8G(1) does not apply to the failure to make payment B,

(*b*) P is liable to a penalty under this paragraph for that failure, and

(*c*) the penalty period that has begun is extended so that it ends with the day 12 months after the date specified in or for the purposes of column 4 for payment B.

(3) The amount of the penalty under this paragraph is determined by reference to the number of defaults that P has made during the penalty period.

(4) If the default is P's first, second or third default during the penalty period, P is liable, at the time of the default, to a penalty of 1% of the amount of the default.

(5) If the default is P's fourth, fifth or sixth default during the penalty period, P is liable, at the time of the default, to a penalty of 2% of the amount of the default.

(6) If the default is P's seventh, eighth or ninth default during the penalty period, P is liable, at the time of the default, to a penalty of 3% of the amount of the default.

(7) If the default is P's tenth or a subsequent default during the penalty period, P is liable, at the time of the default, to a penalty of 4% of the amount of the default.

(8) For the purposes of this paragraph—

(*a*) P makes a default when P fails to pay an amount of tax in full on or before the date on which it becomes due and payable;

(*b*) in accordance with sub-paragraph (1)(*b*), the references in sub-paragraphs (3) to (7) to a default are references to a default in relation to the tax to which payments A and B relate;

(*c*) a default counts for the purposes of those sub-paragraphs if (but only if) the period to which the payment relates is less than 6 months;

(*d*) the amount of a default is the amount which P fails to pay.

(9) A penalty period may be extended more than once under subparagraph (2)(*c*).

8I

If any amount of the tax is unpaid after the end of the period of 6 months beginning with the penalty date, P is liable to a penalty of 5% of that amount.

8J

If any amount of the tax is unpaid after the end of the period of 12 months beginning with the penalty date, P is liable to a penalty of 5% of that amount."

Amendments—[1] In the inserted para 8A(1), words inserted by FA 2014 s 103, Sch 22 para 22(1), (6) with effect from 17 July 2014.

8 After paragraph 8J insert—

"Calculation of unpaid VAT: treatment of payments on account

8K

(1) Where P is required, by virtue of an order under section 28 of VATA 1994, to make any payment on account of VAT—

(*a*) each payment is to be treated for the purposes of this Schedule as relating to the prescribed accounting period in respect of which it is to be paid (and not as relating to the interval between the dates on which payments on account are required to be made), and

(*b*) the amount of tax unpaid in respect of the prescribed accounting period is the total of the amounts produced by paragraphs (*a*) and (*b*) of sub-paragraph (3).

(2) In determining that total—

(*a*) if there is more than one amount of POAD or POAT, those amounts are to be added together, and

(*b*) if the amount produced by sub-paragraph (3)(*b*) is less than zero, that amount is to be disregarded.

(3) The amounts are—

(*a*) POAD – POAT, and

(*b*) BPD – BPT.

(4) In this paragraph—

POAD is the amount of any payment on account due in respect of the prescribed accounting period,

POAT is the amount of any payment on account paid on time (that is, on or before the date on which it was required to be made),

BPD (which is the balancing payment due in respect of the prescribed accounting period) is equal to PAPD – POAD, and

BPT (which is the amount paid on time in satisfaction of any liability to pay BPD) is equal to PAPP – POAP.

(5) In sub-paragraph (4)—

PAPD is the amount of VAT due in respect of the prescribed accounting period,

PAPP is the total amount paid, on or before the last day on which P is required to make payments in respect of that period, in satisfaction of any liability to pay PAPD, and

POAP is the total amount paid, on or before that day (but whether or not paid on time), in satisfaction of any liability to pay POAD."

9 (1) Paragraph 11 (assessment) is amended as follows.

(2) In sub-paragraph (4), for "unpaid tax" substitute "tax which was due or payable".

(3) After sub-paragraph (4) insert—

"(4A) A replacement assessment may be made in respect of a penalty if an earlier assessment operated by reference to an overestimate of an amount of tax which was due or payable."

Commencement—Finance (No 3) Act 2010, Schedules 10 and 11 (Income Tax Self Assessment and Pension Schemes) (Appointed Days) Order, SI 2011/703 art 3 (the day appointed for the coming into force of Sch 11 paras 1 and 9 is 6 April 2011 in relation to an amount of tax which is payable in relation to the tax year 2010–11 or any subsequent tax year, and falls within item 1, 12, 18 or 19 of the Table in FA 2009 Sch 56 para 1, or insofar as the tax falls within item 1 of that Table, item 17, 23 or 24 of that Table).

10 For paragraph 16(1) (no liability where there is reasonable excuse for failure) substitute—

"(1) If P satisfies HMRC or (on appeal) the First-tier Tribunal or Upper Tribunal that there is a reasonable excuse for a failure to make a payment—

(*a*) liability to a penalty under any paragraph of this Schedule does not arise in relation to that failure, and

(*b*) the failure does not count as a default for the purposes of paragraphs 6, 8B, 8C, 8G and 8H."

Commencement—Finance (No 3) Act 2010, Schedule 11 (Appointed Day) Order, SI 2011/132 (25 January 2011 appointed for the coming into force of—

- F(No 3)A 2010 Sch 11 paras 2(3), (5), (6), (12), 4, 6;
- F(No 3)A 2010 Sch 11 para 10 for the purposes of the following amounts of tax specified in column 3 of the Table in FA 2009 Sch 56 para 1—
  - item 2 (PAYE Regulations);
  - item 3 (returns under FA 2004 s 254(1));
  - item 4 (FA 2004 s 62); and
  - items 17, 23 and 24 but only insofar as the tax falls within any of items 2, 3 or 4.).

BUDGET RESPONSIBILITY AND NATIONAL AUDIT ACT 2011

(2011 Chapter 4)

An Act to make provision for a Charter for Budget Responsibility and for the publication of Financial Statements and Budget Reports; to establish the Office for Budget Responsibility; to make provision about the Comptroller and Auditor General and to establish a body corporate called the National Audit Office; to amend Schedules 5 and 7 to the Government of Wales Act 2006 in relation to the Auditor General for Wales; and for connected purposes.

[22 March 2011]

BE IT ENACTED by the Queen's most Excellent Majesty, by and with the advice and consent of the Lords Spiritual and Temporal, and Commons, in this present Parliament assembled, and by the authority of the same, as follows:—

PART 1
BUDGET RESPONSIBILITY

1 Charter for Budget Responsibility

(1) The Treasury must prepare a document, to be known as the Charter for Budget Responsibility, relating to the formulation and implementation of fiscal policy and policy for the management of the National Debt.

(2) The Charter must in particular set out—

(*a*) the Treasury's objectives in relation to fiscal policy and policy for the management of the National Debt,

(*b*) the means by which the Treasury's objectives in relation to fiscal policy will be attained ("the fiscal mandate"), and

(*c*) matters to be included in a Financial Statement and Budget Report prepared under section 2.

(3) The Charter may contain such other material as the Treasury considers appropriate (and see also section 6).

(4) The Treasury must lay the Charter before Parliament.

(5) The Treasury may from time to time modify the Charter.

(6) When the Charter is modified the Treasury must lay the modified Charter before Parliament.

(7) The Charter (or the modified Charter) does not come into force until it has been approved by a resolution of the House of Commons.

(8) The Treasury must publish the Charter and any modified Charter once approved by the House of Commons.

Commencement—Budget Responsibility and National Audit Act 2011 (Commencement No 1) Order, SI 2011/892 art 2, Sch 1 (sections 1, 2, 10 come into force on 23 March 2011).

2 Annual Budget documents

(1) The Treasury must prepare a Financial Statement and Budget Report for each financial year.

(2) The contents of a Financial Statement and Budget Report must conform to any provision set out in the Charter.

(3) The Treasury must lay each Financial Statement and Budget Report before Parliament.

(4) The Treasury must publish each Financial Statement and Budget Report.

Commencement—Budget Responsibility and National Audit Act 2011 (Commencement No 1) Order, SI 2011/892 art 2, Sch 1 (sections 1, 2, 10 come into force on 23 March 2011).

3 Office for Budget Responsibility

(1) There is to be a body corporate called the Office for Budget Responsibility.

(2) Schedule 1 contains provision about the Office.

Commencement—Budget Responsibility and National Audit Act 2011 (Commencement No 1) Order, SI 2011/892 art 3, Sch 2 (sections 3–9, Sch 1 come into force on 4 April 2011).

4 Main duty of Office

(1) It is the duty of the Office to examine and report on the sustainability of the public finances.

(2) The duty imposed by this section includes, in particular, the duties imposed by subsections (3) and (4).

(3) The Office must, on at least two occasions for each financial year, prepare—

(*a*) fiscal and economic forecasts, and

(*b*) an assessment of the extent to which the fiscal mandate has been, or is likely to be, achieved.

(4) It must also, on at least one occasion for each financial year, prepare—

(*a*) an assessment of the accuracy of fiscaland economic forecasts previously prepared by it, and

(*b*) an analysis of the sustainability of the public finances.

(5) Any forecast, assessment or analysis prepared by the Office under subsection (3) or (4) must be included in a report.

(6) Any report which the Office makes in pursuance of its duty under this section must include an explanation of the factors which the Office took into account when preparing the report, including (in particular)—

(*a*) the main assumptions made by the Office, and

(*b*) the main risks which the Office considered to be relevant.

Commencement—Budget Responsibility and National Audit Act 2011 (Commencement No 1) Order, SI 2011/892 art 3, Sch 2 (sections 3–9, Sch 1 come into force on 4 April 2011).

5 How main duty is to be performed

(1) The Office has complete discretion in the performance of its duty under section 4 (but subject to subsections (2) and (3) of this section and sections 6 and 7).

(2) The Office must perform that duty objectively, transparently and impartially.

(3) Where any Government policies are relevant to the performance of that duty, the Office—

(*a*) must have regard to those policies, but

(*b*) may not consider what the effect of any alternative policies would be.

Commencement—Budget Responsibility and National Audit Act 2011 (Commencement No 1) Order, SI 2011/892 art 3, Sch 2 (sections 3–9, Sch 1 come into force on 4 April 2011).

6 Guidance as to how main duty is to be performed

(1) The Charter for Budget Responsibility may include guidance to the Office about how it should perform its duty under section 4, including (in particular) guidance about the time at which it is to prepare any forecast, assessment or analysis required to be prepared under subsection (3) or (4) of that section.

(2) But the Charter must not make provision about the methods by which the Office is to make any such forecast, assessment or analysis.

(3) The Office must, in the performance of its duty under section 4, act consistently with any guidance included in the Charter by virtue of this section.

(4) If the Treasury proposes to modify the guidance included in the Charter by virtue of this section, a draft of the modified guidance must be published at least 28 days before the modified Charter is laid before Parliament under section 1(6).

Commencement—Budget Responsibility and National Audit Act 2011 (Commencement No 1) Order, SI 2011/892 art 3, Sch 2 (sections 3–9, Sch 1 come into force on 4 April 2011).

7 Efficiency etc

The Office must aim to carry out its functions efficiently and cost-effectively.

Commencement—Budget Responsibility and National Audit Act 2011 (Commencement No 1) Order, SI 2011/892 art 3, Sch 2 (sections 3–9, Sch 1 come into force on 4 April 2011).

8 Reports

(1) This section applies to any report which the Office makes in pursuance of its duty under section 4.

(2) The Office must—

(*a*) publish the report,

(*b*) lay it before Parliament, and

(*c*) send a copy of it to the Treasury.

Commencement—Budget Responsibility and National Audit Act 2011 (Commencement No 1) Order, SI 2011/892 art 3, Sch 2 (sections 3–9, Sch 1 come into force on 4 April 2011).

9 Right to information

(1) The Office has a right of access (at any reasonable time) to all Government information which it may reasonably require for the purpose of the performance of its duty under section 4.

(2) The Office is entitled to require from any person holding or accountable for any Government information any assistance or explanation which the Office reasonably thinks necessary for that purpose.

(3) "Government information" means information held by any Minister of the Crown or Government department.

(4) This section is subject to any enactment or rule of law which operates to prohibit or restrict the disclosure of information or the giving of any assistance or explanation.

Commencement—Budget Responsibility and National Audit Act 2011 (Commencement No 1) Order, SI 2011/892 art 3, Sch 2 (sections 3–9, Sch 1 come into force on 4 April 2011).

10 Superseded statutory provisions

The following are repealed in consequence of the preceding provisions of this Part—

(*a*) section 27 of, and Schedule 5 to, the Industry Act 1975 (economic model and forecasting);

(*b*) sections 155 to 157 of the Finance Act 1998 (fiscal stability);

(*c*) the Fiscal Responsibility Act 2010.

Commencement—Budget Responsibility and National Audit Act 2011 (Commencement No 1) Order, SI 2011/892 art 2, Sch 1 (sections 1, 2, 10 come into force on 23 March 2011).

PART 2

NATIONAL AUDIT

Miscellaneous and supplementary

26 Transitional provision and consequential amendments

(1) Schedule 4 contains transitional provision.

(2) Schedule 5 contains consequential amendments.

PART 3

FINAL PROVISIONS

28 Power to make consequential provision

(1) The Treasury may by order make such provision as it considers appropriate in consequence of any provision of this Act.

(2) An order under this section may—

(*a*) amend or revoke any provision of subordinate legislation made on or before the last day of the Session in which this Act is passed;

(*b*) include supplementary, incidental, transitional, transitory or saving provision.

(3) An order under this section is to be made by statutory instrument.

(4) A statutory instrument containing an order under this section is subject to annulment in pursuance of a resolution of either House of Parliament.

(5) In this section "subordinate legislation" has the meaning given by section 21(1) of the Interpretation Act 1978.

29 Commencement

(1) This Part comes into force on the day on which this Act is passed.

(2) Section 27 and Schedule 6 come into force at the end of the period of 2 months beginning with the day on which this Act is passed.

(3) The other provisions of this Act come into force in accordance with provision made by order made by statutory instrument by the Treasury.

(4) An order under subsection (3) may—

(*a*) make different provision for different purposes;

(*b*) include supplementary, incidental, consequential, transitional, transitory or saving provision.

Order—Budget Responsibility and National Audit Act 2011 (Commencement No 1) Order, SI 2011/892 art 2, Sch 1 (sections 1, 2, 10 come into force on 23 March 2011; sections 3–9, Sch 1 come into force on 4 April 2011).

30 Extent

(1) Subject to subsection (2), this Act extends to England and Wales, Scotland and Northern Ireland.

(2) The amendment or repeal of any enactment has the same extent as the enactment amended or repealed.

31 Short title

This Act may be cited as the Budget Responsibility and National Audit Act 2011.

SCHEDULE 1

OFFICE FOR BUDGET RESPONSIBILITY

Section 3

Commencement—Budget Responsibility and National Audit Act 2011 (Commencement No 1) Order, SI 2011/892 art 3, Sch 2 (sections 3–9, Sch 1 come into force on 4 April 2011).

Membership

1 (1) The Office is to consist of—

(*a*) a member to chair it, appointed by the Chancellor of the Exchequer with the consent of the Treasury Committee of the House of Commons,

(*b*) 2 other members appointed by the Chancellor of the Exchequer after consultation with the member appointed under paragraph (a) and with the consent of that Committee, and

(*c*) not fewer than 2 members nominated by the Office and appointed by the Chancellor of the Exchequer.

(But see paragraph 3, which makes special provision about the appointment of the initial members of the Office.)

(2) A person may be appointed under sub-paragraph (1)(*a*) or (*b*) only if the person has knowledge or experience likely to be relevant to the performance of the Office's duty under section 4.

Commencement—Budget Responsibility and National Audit Act 2011 (Commencement No 1) Order, SI 2011/892 art 3, Sch 2 (sections 3–9, Sch 1 come into force on 4 April 2011).

Period of appointment and re-appointment

2 (1) An appointment under paragraph 1(1)(a) or (b) is to be for a period of 5 years (but see paragraph 3(5)).

(2) An appointment under paragraph 1(1)(c) is to be for a period of no more than 5 years.

(3) A person may not be appointed under paragraph 1 more than twice.

Commencement—Budget Responsibility and National Audit Act 2011 (Commencement No 1) Order, SI 2011/892 art 3, Sch 2 (sections 3–9, Sch 1 come into force on 4 April 2011).

Appointment of initial members

3 (1) The consent of the Treasury Committee of the House of Commons is not required for the appointment under paragraph 1(1)(*a*) of a person who—

(*a*) immediately before the person's appointment, was chairing the non-statutory Office for Budget Responsibility, and

(*b*) was appointed to do so by the Chancellor of the Exchequer with the consent of that Committee.

(2) The period of the person's appointment under paragraph 1(1)(*a*) is to be taken to have begun with the appointment of that person to chair the non-statutory Office for Budget Responsibility.

(3) The consent of the Treasury Committee of the House of Commons is not required for the appointment under paragraph 1(1)(*b*) of a person who—

(*a*) immediately before the person's appointment, was a member of the non-statutory Office for Budget Responsibility but not chairing it, and

(*b*) was appointed as such a member by the Chancellor of the Exchequer with the consent of that Committee.

(4) The period of appointment under paragraph 1(1)(*b*) of each such person is to be taken to have begun with the appointment of that person as a member of the non-statutory Office for Budget Responsibility.

(5) The first 2 appointments under paragraph 1(1)(*b*) may be for less than 5 years to secure that those appointments and the first appointment under paragraph 1(1)(*a*) each expire at different times.

(6) The first 2 appointments under paragraph 1(1)(*c*) are to be made by the Chancellor of the Exchequer after consultation with the member appointed under paragraph 1(1)(*a*).

Commencement—Budget Responsibility and National Audit Act 2011 (Commencement No 1) Order, SI 2011/892 art 3, Sch 2 (sections 3–9, Sch 1 come into force on 4 April 2011).

Remuneration

4 (1) The Office may, with the approval of the Treasury—

(*a*) pay, or make provision for paying, to a member of the Office such remuneration as the Treasury may determine, and

(*b*) pay, or make provision for paying, to or in respect of a person who is or has been a member of the Office any such pension, allowances or gratuities as the Treasury may determine.

(2) Where—

(*a*) a person ceases to be a member of the Office otherwise than at the end of the period for which the person was appointed, and

(*b*) it appears to the Office and the Treasury that there are circumstances which make it right for the person to receive compensation,

the Office may make a payment to the person of such amount as the Treasury may determine.

Commencement—Budget Responsibility and National Audit Act 2011 (Commencement No 1) Order, SI 2011/892 art 3, Sch 2 (sections 3–9, Sch 1 come into force on 4 April 2011).

Other terms of appointment

5 The Chancellor of the Exchequer may determine other terms of an appointment under paragraph 1.

Commencement—Budget Responsibility and National Audit Act 2011 (Commencement No 1) Order, SI 2011/892 art 3, Sch 2 (sections 3–9, Sch 1 come into force on 4 April 2011).

Termination of appointments

6 (1) A member of the Office may resign by giving written notice to the Chancellor of the Exchequer.

(2) The Chancellor of the Exchequer may terminate the appointment of a member of the Office by giving the member written notice if—

(*a*) the member has been absent from meetings of the Office without the Office's permission for a period of more than 3 months,

(*b*) the member has become bankrupt or has made an arrangement with creditors,

(*c*) the member's estate has been sequestrated in Scotland or the member has entered into a debt arrangement programme under Part 1 of the Debt Arrangement and Attachment (Scotland) Act 2002 (asp 17) as the debtor or has, under Scots law, made a composition or arrangement with, or granted a trust deed for, the member's creditors,

(*d*) the member is unfit to continue the appointment because of misconduct,

(*e*) the member has failed to comply with the terms of the appointment, or

(*f*) the member is otherwise unable, unfit or unwilling to carry out the member's functions.

(3) But the appointment of a member appointed under paragraph 1(1)(a) or (b) is not to be terminated without the consent of the Treasury Committee of the House of Commons.

Commencement—Budget Responsibility and National Audit Act 2011 (Commencement No 1) Order, SI 2011/892 art 3, Sch 2 (sections 3–9, Sch 1 come into force on 4 April 2011).

Status of Office

7 (1) The functions of the Office are to be exercised on behalf of the Crown.

(2) For the purposes of any civil proceedings arising out of those functions—

(*a*) the Crown Proceedings Act 1947 applies to the Office as if it were a government department, and

(*b*) the Crown Suits (Scotland) Act 1857 applies to it as if it were a public department.

(3) The Office's property is to be regarded as held on behalf of the Crown.

Commencement—Budget Responsibility and National Audit Act 2011 (Commencement No 1) Order, SI 2011/892 art 3, Sch 2 (sections 3–9, Sch 1 come into force on 4 April 2011).

Employees

8 (1) The Office may employ staff.

(2) Staff are to be employed on such terms as to remuneration and other matters as the Office may, with the approval of the Minister for the Civil Service, determine.

(3) Service as a member of staff of the Office is employment in the civil service of the State.

(4) The Office must pay to the Minister for the Civil Service, at such times as the Minister may direct, such sums as the Minister may determine in respect of the increase in the sums payable out of money provided by Parliament that is attributable to the provision of pensions, allowances or gratuities under section 1 of the Superannuation Act 1972 payable to or in respect of persons who are or have been members of staff of the Office.

Commencement—Budget Responsibility and National Audit Act 2011 (Commencement No 1) Order, SI 2011/892 art 3, Sch 2 (sections 3–9, Sch 1 come into force on 4 April 2011).

Committees

9 (1) The members appointed under paragraph 1(1)(a) and (b) constitute a committee of the Office to be known as the Budget Responsibility Committee.

(2) The members appointed under paragraph 1(1)(c) constitute a committee of the Office to be known as the Non-executive Committee.

Commencement—Budget Responsibility and National Audit Act 2011 (Commencement No 1) Order, SI 2011/892 art 3, Sch 2 (sections 3–9, Sch 1 come into force on 4 April 2011).

10 (1) The Office may establish other committees.

(2) A committee established by the Office may establish sub-committees.

(3) A committee or sub-committee established under this paragraph may consist of or include persons who are neither members of the Office nor members of its staff.

(4) Appointment as a member of such a committee or sub-committee of a person who is neither a member of the Office nor a member of its staff is to be on such terms as to remuneration and other matters as the Office may, with the approval of the Treasury, determine.

Commencement—Budget Responsibility and National Audit Act 2011 (Commencement No 1) Order, SI 2011/892 art 3, Sch 2 (sections 3–9, Sch 1 come into force on 4 April 2011).

Procedure

11 (1) The Office may determine—

(*a*) its own procedure, and

(*b*) the procedure of any committee or sub-committee established under paragraph 10.

(2) A committee established by paragraph 9 may determine its own procedure.

Commencement—Budget Responsibility and National Audit Act 2011 (Commencement No 1) Order, SI 2011/892 art 3, Sch 2 (sections 3–9, Sch 1 come into force on 4 April 2011).

Delegation of functions

12 (1) The Office may delegate functions to—

(*a*) any of its members,

(*b*) any member of its staff, or

(*c*) any of its committees.

(2) A committee established under paragraph 10 may delegate functions (including functions delegated to it) to a sub-committee.

(3) The Budget Responsibility Committee is to perform the duties imposed by section 4(3) and (4).

(4) Sub-paragraph (1) does not apply to those duties.

(5) The delegation of a function under sub-paragraph (1) or (2) does not prevent the Office or the committee (as the case may be) from carrying out the function itself.

Commencement—Budget Responsibility and National Audit Act 2011 (Commencement No 1) Order, SI 2011/892 art 3, Sch 2 (sections 3–9, Sch 1 come into force on 4 April 2011).

Review by Non-executive Committee

13 The Non-executive Committee must keep under review the way in which the Office's duty under section 4 is performed.

Commencement—Budget Responsibility and National Audit Act 2011 (Commencement No 1) Order, SI 2011/892 art 3, Sch 2 (sections 3–9, Sch 1 come into force on 4 April 2011).

Documentary evidence

14 (1) The application of the Office's seal is to be authenticated by the signature of—

(*a*) a member of the Office, or

(*b*) any person authorised (whether generally or specifically) for the purpose by a member of the Office.

(2) A document purporting to be duly executed under the Office's seal or signed on its behalf—

(*a*) is to be received in evidence, and

(*b*) is to be taken to be executed or signed in that way, unless the contrary is proved.

(3) This paragraph does not extend to Scotland.

Commencement—Budget Responsibility and National Audit Act 2011 (Commencement No 1) Order, SI 2011/892 art 3, Sch 2 (sections 3–9, Sch 1 come into force on 4 April 2011).

Annual report

15 (1) The Office must prepare a report of the performance of its functions in each financial year.

(2) The report must include, in particular, an assessment by the Non-executive Committee of the extent to which the Office's duty under section 4 has been performed in accordance with section 5(1) and (2).

(3) The report relating to a financial year must be prepared as soon as possible after the end of the financial year.

(4) The report must be sent to the Treasury.

(5) The Treasury must lay the report before Parliament.

(6) The Office must publish the report.

(7) "Financial year" means—

(*a*) the period which begins with the day on which this Schedule comes into force and ends with the following 31 March;

(*b*) each successive period of 12 months.

Commencement—Budget Responsibility and National Audit Act 2011 (Commencement No 1) Order, SI 2011/892 art 3, Sch 2 (sections 3–9, Sch 1 come into force on 4 April 2011).

External review

16 (1) The Non-executive Committee must, at least once in every relevant 5-year period, appoint a person or body to review and report on such of the Office's reports as the Committee determines.
(2) In sub-paragraph (1) "the Office's reports" means the reports which—
(*a*) have been made in pursuance of the Office's duty under section 4, and
(*b*) have been published since the relevant date.
(3) The "relevant date" is—
(*a*) in the case of the first review carried out under this paragraph, 1 October 2010;
(*b*) in the case of subsequent reviews, the date of the last review carried out under this paragraph.
(4) A person or body may be appointed under this paragraph only if the person or body has knowledge or experience likely to be relevant to the performance of the Office's duty under section 4.
(5) The Office may, with the approval of the Treasury, make payments to the person or body in respect of the performance of the person's or body's functions under this paragraph.
(6) The Office must—
(*a*) publish each report prepared under this paragraph,
(*b*) lay it before Parliament, and
(*c*) send a copy of it to the Treasury.
(7) In this paragraph "relevant 5-year period" means—
(*a*) the period of 5 years beginning with 1 October 2010;
(*b*) each successive period of 5 years.

Commencement—Budget Responsibility and National Audit Act 2011 (Commencement No 1) Order, SI 2011/892 art 3, Sch 2 (sections 3–9, Sch 1 come into force on 4 April 2011).

Finance

17 (1) The Treasury may make to the Office such payments out of money provided by Parliament as the Treasury considers appropriate for the purpose of enabling the Office to meet its expenses.
(2) Payments are to be made at such times, and subject to any such conditions, as the Treasury considers appropriate.

Commencement—Budget Responsibility and National Audit Act 2011 (Commencement No 1) Order, SI 2011/892 art 3, Sch 2 (sections 3–9, Sch 1 come into force on 4 April 2011).

Accounts and audit

18 (1) The Office must—
(*a*) keep proper accounts and proper records in relation to its accounts, and
(*b*) prepare in respect of each financial year a statement of accounts.
(2) Each statement of accounts must comply with any directions given by the Treasury as to—
(*a*) the information to be contained in it and the manner in which it is to be presented,
(*b*) the methods and principles according to which the statement is to be prepared, and
(*c*) the additional information (if any) which is to be provided for the information of Parliament.
(3) The Office must send a copy of each statement of accounts to—
(*a*) the Treasury, and
(*b*) the Comptroller and Auditor General,
before the end of the month of June next following the financial year to which the statement relates.
(4) The Comptroller and Auditor General must—
(*a*) examine, certify and report on each statement of accounts, and
(*b*) send a copy of each report and certified statement to the Treasury.
(5) The Treasury must lay before Parliament a copy of each such report and certified statement.
(6) "Financial year" has the same meaning as in paragraph 15.

Commencement—Budget Responsibility and National Audit Act 2011 (Commencement No 1) Order, SI 2011/892 art 3, Sch 2 (sections 3–9, Sch 1 come into force on 4 April 2011).

19 The Office must keep under review whether its internal financial controls secure the proper conduct of its financial affairs.

Commencement—Budget Responsibility and National Audit Act 2011 (Commencement No 1) Order, SI 2011/892 art 3, Sch 2 (sections 3–9, Sch 1 come into force on 4 April 2011).

Powers

20 The Office may do anything calculated to facilitate, or conducive or incidental to, the carrying out of any of its functions.

Commencement—Budget Responsibility and National Audit Act 2011 (Commencement No 1) Order, SI 2011/892 art 3, Sch 2 (sections 3–9, Sch 1 come into force on 4 April 2011).

Validity

21 The validity of anything done by the Office (or a committee or sub-committee of the Office) is not affected by—

(*a*) a vacancy, or

(*b*) a defective appointment.

Commencement—Budget Responsibility and National Audit Act 2011 (Commencement No 1) Order, SI 2011/892 art 3, Sch 2 (sections 3–9, Sch 1 come into force on 4 April 2011).

Public records

22 In Schedule 1 to the Public Records Act 1958 (definition of public records), in Part 2 of the Table at the end of paragraph 3, insert at the appropriate place—

"Office for Budget Responsibility."

Commencement—Budget Responsibility and National Audit Act 2011 (Commencement No 1) Order, SI 2011/892 art 3, Sch 2 (sections 3–9, Sch 1 come into force on 4 April 2011).

Parliamentary Commissioner

23 In Schedule 2 to the Parliamentary Commissioner Act 1967 (departments and authorities subject to investigation), insert at the appropriate place—

"Office for Budget Responsibility."

Commencement—Budget Responsibility and National Audit Act 2011 (Commencement No 1) Order, SI 2011/892 art 3, Sch 2 (sections 3–9, Sch 1 come into force on 4 April 2011).

Disqualification

24 In Part 2 of Schedule 1 to the House of Commons Disqualification Act 1975 (bodies of which all members are disqualified), insert at the appropriate place—

"The Office for Budget Responsibility."

Commencement—Budget Responsibility and National Audit Act 2011 (Commencement No 1) Order, SI 2011/892 art 3, Sch 2 (sections 3–9, Sch 1 come into force on 4 April 2011).

25 In Part 2 of Schedule 1 to the Northern Ireland Assembly Disqualification Act 1975 (bodies of which all members are disqualified), insert at the appropriate place—

"The Office for Budget Responsibility."

Commencement—Budget Responsibility and National Audit Act 2011 (Commencement No 1) Order, SI 2011/892 art 3, Sch 2 (sections 3–9, Sch 1 come into force on 4 April 2011).

Race relations

26 (1) In Part 2 of Schedule 1A to the Race Relations Act 1976 (bodies and persons subject to general statutory duty), under the heading "*Regulatory, audit and inspection*" insert at the appropriate place—

"The Office for Budget Responsibility."

(2) The amendment made by sub-paragraph (1) ceases to have effect when the repeal of that Act by Schedule 27 to the Equality Act 2010 has effect for all purposes.

Commencement—Budget Responsibility and National Audit Act 2011 (Commencement No 1) Order, SI 2011/892 art 3, Sch 2 (sections 3–9, Sch 1 come into force on 4 April 2011).

Freedom of information

27 In Part 6 of Schedule 1 to the Freedom of Information Act 2000 (public authorities to which Act applies), insert at the appropriate place—

"The Office for Budget Responsibility."

Commencement—Budget Responsibility and National Audit Act 2011 (Commencement No 1) Order, SI 2011/892 art 3, Sch 2 (sections 3–9, Sch 1 come into force on 4 April 2011).

Equality

28 In Part 1 of Schedule 19 to the Equality Act 2010 (public authorities: general), under the heading "*Industry, business, finance etc*" insert at the appropriate place—

"The Office for Budget Responsibility."

Commencement—Budget Responsibility and National Audit Act 2011 (Commencement No 1) Order, SI 2011/892 art 3, Sch 2 (sections 3–9, Sch 1 come into force on 4 April 2011).

References to Treasury Committee

29 (1) Any reference in this Schedule to the Treasury Committee of the House of Commons—

(*a*) if the name of that Committee is changed, is to be treated as a reference to that Committee by its new name, and

(*b*) if the functions of that Committee (or substantially corresponding functions) become functions of a different Committee of the House of Commons, is to be treated as a reference to the Committee by which those functions are exercisable.

(2) Any question arising under sub-paragraph (1) is to be determined by the Speaker of the House of Commons.

Commencement—Budget Responsibility and National Audit Act 2011 (Commencement No 1) Order, SI 2011/892 art 3, Sch 2 (sections 3–9, Sch 1 come into force on 4 April 2011).

SCHEDULE 4
TRANSITIONAL PROVISION RELATING TO PART 2

Section 26

Transfer of property etc

1 (1) Before the appointed day the Comptroller and Auditor General must—

(*a*) determine the property, rights and liabilities of the Comptroller and Auditor General that are to be transferred to NAO in consequence of the provision made by this Part, and

(*b*) prepare a scheme describing, in the way the Comptroller and Auditor General considers appropriate, that property and those rights and liabilities.

(2) The scheme must be approved by the Public Accounts Commission.

(3) On the appointed day the property, rights and liabilities described in the scheme are transferred to NAO.

(4) Sub-paragraph (3) operates in relation to property, rights and liabilities—

(*a*) whether or not they would otherwise be capable of being transferred,

(*b*) without any instrument or other formality being required, and

(*c*) irrespective of any kind of requirement for consent that would otherwise apply.

(5) In sub-paragraph (1) the references to rights and liabilities include references to rights and liabilities under or in connection with contracts of employment with staff that were appointed under section 3(2) of the National Audit Act 1983.

(6) For any purpose relating to a person who becomes an employee of NAO by virtue of sub-paragraph (3)—

(*a*) a period of employment under section 3(2) of the National Audit Act 1983 (including a period that was counted as such a period by virtue of paragraph 2(3) of Schedule 2 to that Act) is to be treated as a period of employment with NAO, and

(*b*) the transfer to NAO is not to be treated as a break in service.

(7) Anything done by, on behalf of or in relation to the Comptroller and Auditor General in relation to anything transferred by sub-paragraph (3) has effect as if done by, on behalf of or in relation to NAO, so far as necessary or appropriate for continuing its effect on and after the appointed day.

(8) Anything (including legal proceedings) which, immediately before the appointed day, is in the process of being done by, on behalf of or in relation to the Comptroller and Auditor General in relation to anything transferred by sub-paragraph (3) may be continued by, on behalf of or in relation to NAO.

(9) So far as necessary or appropriate in consequence of sub-paragraphs (3) to (8), a reference to the Comptroller and Auditor General in any agreement (whether written or not) or instrument or other document is to be treated as a reference to, or as including a reference to, NAO.

(10) Before the appointed day a person's employment under section 3(2) of the National Audit Act 1983 is to be treated for the purposes of paragraph 1(2)(*c*) and Part 4 of Schedule 2 as if it were employment with NAO.

(11) In this paragraph "the appointed day" means the day appointed for the purposes of this paragraph by an order made by the Treasury by statutory instrument.

Tax consequences of transfers by virtue of paragraph 1(3)

2 (1) For the purposes of the application of Part 5 of the Corporation Tax Act 2009 (loan relationships) in relation to a transfer by virtue of paragraph 1(3), the Comptroller and Auditor General and NAO are to be treated as if, at the time of the transfer, they were members of the same group.

(2) In sub-paragraph (1) the reference to being members of the same group is to be read in accordance with section 335(6) of that Act.

3 (1) For the purposes of Part 8 of the Corporation Tax Act 2009 (intangible fixed assets) a transfer by virtue of paragraph 1(3) of a chargeable intangible asset of the Comptroller and Auditor General is to be treated as a tax-neutral transfer.

(2) Part 4 of the Taxation (International and Other Provisions) Act 2010 (transfer pricing) does not apply in relation to a transfer to which sub-paragraph (1) applies.
(3) For the purposes of section 882 of the Corporation Tax Act 2009 (application of Part 8 to assets created or acquired on or after 1 April 2002) assets acquired by NAO on a transfer by virtue of paragraph 1(3) are to be treated as if they were acquired from a person who at the time of the acquisition was a related party in relation to NAO.
(4) Expressions used in this paragraph and in Part 8 of the Corporation Tax Act 2009 have the same meaning in this paragraph as they have in that Part.

4 For the purposes of the Taxation of Chargeable Gains Act 1992 a disposal constituted by virtue of a transfer by paragraph 1(3) is to be taken (in relation to both the Comptroller and Auditor General and NAO) to be for a consideration such that no gain or loss accrues to the Comptroller and Auditor General.

Old Comptroller and Auditor General to continue to be Comptroller and Auditor General

5 (1) This paragraph applies to the person who is the Comptroller and Auditor General immediately before the appointed day.
(2) On and after the appointed day the person—
(*a*) continues to be the Comptroller and Auditor General and is treated as having been appointed to that office under this Part, and
(*b*) holds the office for 10 years less a period equal to that during which the person was the Comptroller and Auditor General before the appointed day.
(3) The person's remuneration arrangements under section 13 are to be determined jointly by the Prime Minister and the person who chairs the Committee of Public Accounts before the appointed day (but are not to cover any period before the appointed day).
(4) In this paragraph "the appointed day" means the day appointed for the purposes of this paragraph by an order made by the Treasury by statutory instrument.

Provision of services

6 (1) This paragraph applies in relation to anything done by or on behalf of the Comptroller and Auditor General under a power that ceases to be exercisable upon the coming into force of section 16 of this Act.
(2) So far as necessary or appropriate for continuing its effect after the coming into force of section 16, the thing is treated as having been done by or on behalf of the Comptroller and Auditor General under that section.

7 (1) Paragraph 3 of Schedule 3 does not apply in relation to the provision of any services which, at the time that paragraph comes into force, the Comptroller and Auditor General has a contractual duty to provide.
(2) But paragraph 8 of that Schedule applies in relation to any such services as if they were NAO-approved services.

Indemnification

8 (1) The liabilities covered by section 24 of this Act include liabilities that—
(*a*) arise before the coming into force of that section, or
(*b*) arise in relation to any act or omission occurring before the coming into force of that section.
(2) For this purpose section 24(3)(d) covers former members of the staff of the National Audit Office established by section 3 of the National Audit Act 1983.

NAO's procedural rules before rules made under paragraph 18 of Schedule 2

9 (1) This paragraph applies until the first rules under paragraph 18 of Schedule 2 are made.
(2) It applies in relation to any matter to be decided by NAO for the purpose of preparing or making those rules or for the purposes of paragraph 10 of Schedule 3.
(3) The matter is to be decided—
(*a*) at a meeting of NAO at which the person who chairs NAO and at least six other members are present, and
(*b*) by the majority of votes of the members present and voting on the matter.
(4) But the matter may not be decided unless a majority of the members voting on the matter are non-executive members.
(5) If the votes are tied, the person who chairs NAO is to have the casting vote, whether or not that person has already voted on the matter.
(6) It is for the person who chairs NAO to call a meeting of NAO by giving written notice to the other members of the date, time and venue of the meeting.

SCHEDULE 5

CONSEQUENTIAL AMENDMENTS RELATING TO PART 2

Section 26

PART 2

AMENDMENTS

Interpretation Act 1978

12 In Schedule 1 to the Interpretation Act 1978, in the definition of "Comptroller and Auditor General", omit "appointed in pursuance of the Exchequer and Audit Departments Act 1866".

Finance Act 1989

14 (1) Section 182 of the Finance Act 1989 (disclosure of information) is amended as follows.

(2) In subsection (4)(*a*)—

(*a*) in sub-paragraph (i), for "and any member of the staff of the National Audit Office" substitute ", of the National Audit Office and any member or employee of that Office or of any member of the staff of the National Audit Office that was established by section 3 of the National Audit Act 1983", and

(*b*) after that sub-paragraph insert—

"(i *a*) of the Comptroller and Auditor General for Northern Ireland and any member of the staff of the Northern Ireland Audit Office,".

(3) In subsection (6), after "Comptroller" insert "and Auditor General, the Comptroller and Auditor General for Northern Ireland".

(4) In subsection (11), omit paragraphs (*a*) and (*b*).

POSTAL SERVICES ACT 2011

2011 Chapter 5

An Act to make provision for the restructuring of the Royal Mail group and about the Royal Mail Pension Plan; to make new provision about the regulation of postal services, including provision for a special administration regime; and for connected purposes.

[13th June 2011]

BE IT ENACTED by the Queen's most Excellent Majesty, by and with the advice and consent of the Lords Spiritual and Temporal, and Commons, in this present Parliament assembled, and by the authority of the same, as follows:—

PART 1

RESTRUCTURING OF ROYAL MAIL GROUP

Transfer of property etc

10 Taxation provisions relating to re-structuring

Schedule 2 contains taxation provisions.

PART 2

ROYAL MAIL PENSION PLAN

Supplementary provisions

23 Taxation

(1) The Treasury may by regulations make provision for varying the way in which any relevant tax would, apart from the regulations, have effect in relation to—

(a) a new public scheme,

(b) members of a new public scheme, or

(c) a fund within section 21(1)(c).

(2) Regulations under subsection (1) may include provision for treating a new public scheme as a registered pension scheme.

(3) The Treasury may by regulations make provision for varying the way in which any relevant tax would, apart from the regulations, have effect in relation to, or in connection with, anything done in relation to—

(a) the RMPP, or

(b) any members of the RMPP,

by or under, or in consequence of, an order made under this Part.

(4) Regulations under subsection (1) or (3) may include provision for any of the following—

(a) a tax provision not to apply or to apply with modifications,
(b) anything done to have or not to have a specified consequence for the purposes of a tax provision, and
(c) the withdrawal of relief and the charging of a relevant tax.

(5) Provision made by regulations under subsection (1) or (3), other than provision withdrawing a relief or charging a relevant tax, may have retrospective effect.

(6) The Treasury may by regulations make provision, in relation to qualifying accounting periods, for extinguishing such losses made in a trade as they consider are attributable to deductions made for, or in connection with, contributions in respect of qualifying members of the RMPP.

(7) A "qualifying" accounting period is one beginning on or after the date ("the trigger date") on which an order under section 17 is made establishing a new public scheme or transferring qualifying accrued rights to a new public scheme.

(8) Regulations under subsection (6) have effect only if the company whose losses are extinguished is wholly owned by the Crown (within the meaning of Part 1) on the day before the trigger date.

(9) In this section—

"relevant tax" means—

(a) income tax,
(b) capital gains tax,
(c) corporation tax,
(d) inheritance tax,
(e) stamp duty and stamp duty reserve tax, and
(f) stamp duty land tax,

"registered pension scheme" has the same meaning as in Part 4 of the Finance Act 2004,

"tax provision" means any provision made by or under an enactment relating to a relevant tax.

SCHEDULE 2

TAXATION PROVISIONS RELATING TO RE-STRUCTURING ETC

Section 10

Transfer of securities of subsidiaries of original holding company to Crown etc

1 (1) This paragraph applies where—

(a) there is a disposal of securities of a subsidiary of the original holding company to the Secretary of State or the Treasury (or a nominee of either of them) or to a company wholly owned by the Crown, and
(b) immediately before the disposal, the subsidiary was wholly owned by the original holding company.

(2) For the purposes of the Taxation of Chargeable Gains Act 1992 the disposal is to be treated in relation to—

(a) the person making the disposal, and
(b) the person to whom the disposal is made,

as made for a consideration such that no gain or loss accrues to the person making the disposal.

(3) The degrouping provisions are not to apply by reason of the disposal or any agreement to make the disposal (if they otherwise would).

(4) In this Schedule a "degrouping provision" means—

(a) section 179 of the Taxation of Chargeable Gains Act 1992 (company ceasing to be member of group), or
(b) paragraph 3 of Schedule 7 to the Finance Act 2003 (withdrawal of SDLT group relief).

(5) Stamp duty is not chargeable on the instrument effecting the disposal.

(6) This paragraph applies whether or not the disposal is made by or under a transfer scheme under section 8.

2 (1) This paragraph applies where—

(a) paragraph 1(3) has applied at any time in relation to a disposal or an agreement to make a disposal,
(b) there is a subsequent disposal of securities of the subsidiary in relation to which paragraph 1(3) does not apply, and
(c) immediately before the subsequent disposal or the making of an agreement to make it, the subsidiary was a member of a new group.

(2) For the purposes of the application of a degrouping provision in the case of that disposal or agreement—

(a) the company from which the subsidiary acquired relevant assets or chargeable interests is to be treated as if it had been a member of the new group at the time the relevant assets or chargeable interests were acquired, and

(b) that company is to be treated as if it were a member of the new group immediately before the disposal or the making of the agreement mentioned in sub-paragraph (1)(c).

(3) "Relevant assets or chargeable interests" means assets or chargeable interests in relation to which, but for paragraph 1(3), the degrouping provision in question would have applied by reason of the disposal or agreement mentioned in sub-paragraph (1)(a).

(4) In this paragraph—

(a) references to a group have the same meaning as in the degrouping provision in question, and

(b) references to a new group are to a group other than a group of which the subsidiary was a member immediately before the making of a disposal or an agreement in relation to which paragraph 1(3) applied.

Transfers of property, rights and liabilities by transfer schemes

3 In paragraphs 4 to 6—

a "relevant transfer" means a transfer of any property, rights or liabilities by or under a transfer scheme under section 8, and

"transferor" and "transferee" have the same meaning as in Schedule 1.

4 For the purposes of the Taxation of Chargeable Gains Act 1992 a disposal constituted by a relevant transfer is to be treated in relation to the transferor and transferee as made for a consideration such that no gain or loss accrues to the transferor.

5 For the purposes of Chapter 4 of Part 5 of the Corporation Tax Act 2009 (loan relationships: continuity of treatment on transfers within groups or on reorganisations) the transferor and transferee are to be treated in relation to a relevant transfer as if, for the purposes of the transfer, they were members of the same group.

6 (1) For the purposes of Part 8 of the Corporation Tax Act 2009 (intangible fixed assets) a relevant transfer of a chargeable intangible asset is to be treated as tax-neutral.

(2) Part 4 of the Taxation (International and Other Provisions) Act 2010 (transfer pricing) does not apply in relation to a transfer to which sub-paragraph (1) applies.

(3) For the purposes of section 882 of the Corporation Tax Act 2009 (application of Part 8 to assets created or acquired on or after 1 April 2002) assets acquired by a transferee on a relevant transfer are to be treated as if they were acquired from a person who at the time of the acquisition was a related party.

Transfers of securities of original holding company or its subsidiaries

7 (1) This paragraph applies where—

(a) there is a disposal of securities of the original holding company or any of its subsidiaries, and

(b) immediately before the disposal, the original holding company or (as the case may be) the subsidiary was a 51% subsidiary of the Crown.

(2) The degrouping provisions are not to apply by reason of the disposal or any agreement to make the disposal (if they otherwise would).

(3) For the purposes of this paragraph "51% subsidiary" has the same meaning as it has for the purposes of the Corporation Tax Acts (see Chapter 3 of Part 24 of the Corporation Tax Act 2010), but—

(a) the Crown is to be treated as a body corporate, and

(b) for the purpose of determining beneficial ownership the making of an agreement to make the disposal is to be ignored.

8 (1) This paragraph applies where—

(a) paragraph 7 has applied at any time in relation to a disposal or an agreement to make a disposal,

(b) there is a subsequent disposal of securities of the original holding company or any of its subsidiaries in relation to which paragraph 7 does not apply, and

(c) immediately before the subsequent disposal or the making of an agreement to make it, the original holding company or (as the case may be) the subsidiary was a member of a new group.

(2) For the purposes of the application of a degrouping provision in the case of that disposal or agreement—

(a) the company from which the original holding company or (as the case may be) the subsidiary acquired relevant assets or chargeable interests is to be treated as if it had been a member of the new group at the time the relevant assets or chargeable interests were acquired, and

(b) that company is to be treated as if it were a member of the new group immediately before the disposal or the making of the agreement mentioned in sub-paragraph (1)(c).

(3) "Relevant assets or chargeable interests" means assets or chargeable interests in relation to which, but for paragraph 7, the degrouping provision in question would have applied by reason of the disposal or agreement mentioned in sub-paragraph (1)(a).

(4) In this paragraph—

(a) references to a group have the same meaning as in the degrouping provision in question, and

(b) references to a new group are to a group other than a group of which the original holding company or (as the case may be) the subsidiary was a member immediately before the making of a disposal or an agreement in relation to which paragraph 7 applied.

FINANCE ACT 2011

(2011 Chapter 11)

[19 July 2011]

PART 4
PENSIONS

71 Tax provision consequential on Part 1 of Pensions Act 2008 etc

(1) The Treasury may by regulations make provision in relation to any of the relevant taxes in consequence of Part 1 of the Pensions Act 2008 or Part 1 of the Pensions (No 2) Act (Northern Ireland) 2008.

(2) The provision that may be made by regulations under this section includes provision imposing any of the relevant taxes (as well as provisions for exemptions or reliefs).

(3) The relevant taxes are—

(*a*) income tax,
(*b*) capital gains tax,
(*c*) corporation tax,
(*d*) inheritance tax,
(*e*) value added tax,
(*f*) stamp duty land tax,
(*g*) stamp duty, and
(*h*) stamp duty reserve tax.

(4) Regulations under this section may include provision having effect in relation to any time before they are made if the provision does not increase any person's liability to tax.

(5) Regulations under this section may make different provision for different cases.

(6) Regulations under this section may include—

(*a*) provision amending any enactment or instrument, and
(*b*) consequential, supplementary and transitional provision.

(7) Regulations under this section are to be made by statutory instrument.

(8) A statutory instrument containing regulations under this section is subject to annulment in pursuance of a resolution of the House of Commons.

PART 6
OTHER TAXES

Value added tax

74 Business samples

(1) In Schedule 4 to VATA 1994 (matters to be treated as supply of goods or services), paragraph 5 (transfer or disposal of goods forming part of the assets of a business) is amended as follows.

(2) For sub-paragraph (2)(*b*) substitute—

"(*b*) the provision to a person, otherwise than for a consideration, of a sample of goods."

(3) Omit sub-paragraph (3).

75 Zero-rating: splitting of supplies

(1) In Part 2 of Schedule 8 to VATA 1994 (zero-rating: groups), Group 3 (books, etc) is amended as follows.

(2) For "*Note*: Items 1 to 6—" substitute—

"*Notes*:

(1) Items 1 to 6—".

(3) At the end insert—

"(2) Items 1 to 6 do not include goods in circumstances where—

(*a*) the supply of the goods is connected with a supply of services, and
(*b*) those connected supplies are made by different suppliers.

(3) For the purposes of Note (2) a supply of goods is connected with a supply of services if, had those two supplies been made by a single supplier—

(*a*) they would have been treated as a single supply of services, and (*b*) that single supply would have been a taxable supply (other than a zero-rated supply) or an exempt supply."

(4) The amendments made by this section have effect in relation to supplies made on or after the day on which this Act is passed.

76 Academies

(1) In Part 2 of VATA 1994 (reliefs, exemptions and repayments), after section 33A insert—

"33B Refunds of VAT to Academies

(1) This section applies where—

(*a*) VAT is chargeable on—

(i) the supply of goods or services to the proprietor of an Academy,

(ii) the acquisition of any goods from another member State by the proprietor of an Academy, or

(iii) the importation of any goods from a place outside the member States by the proprietor of an Academy, and

(*b*) the supply, acquisition or importation is not for the purposes of any business carried on by the proprietor of the Academy.

(2) The Commissioners shall, on a claim made by the proprietor of the Academy at such time and in such form and manner as the Commissioners may determine, refund to that proprietor the amount of VAT so chargeable.

(3) Subject to subsection (4), the claim must be made before the end of the period of 4 years beginning with the day on which the supply is made or the acquisition or importation takes place.

(4) If the Commissioners so determine, the claim period is such shorter period beginning with that day as the Commissioners may determine.

(5) Subsection (6) applies where goods or services supplied to, or acquired or imported by, the proprietor of the Academy cannot be conveniently distinguished from goods or services supplied to, or acquired or imported by, it for the purpose of a business carried on by that proprietor.

(6) The amount to be refunded under this section is such amount as remains after deducting from the whole of the VAT chargeable on any supply to, or acquisition or importation by, the proprietor of the Academy such proportion of that VAT as appears to the Commissioners to be attributable to the carrying on of the business.

(7) References in this section to VAT do not include any VAT which, by virtue of an order under section 25(7), is excluded from credit under section 25.

(8) In this section—

(*a*) references to the proprietor of an Academy are to the proprietor of the Academy acting in that capacity, and

(*b*) "Academy" and "proprietor" have the same meaning as in the Education Act 1996 (see section 579 of that Act)."

(2) In section 79 of that Act (repayment supplement in respect of certain delayed payments or refunds)—

(*a*) in subsection (1), after paragraph (*c*) insert ", or

(*d*) the proprietor of an Academy who is registered is entitled to a refund under section 33B,",

(*b*) in subsection (5), after paragraph (*c*) insert ", and

(*d*) a supplement paid to the proprietor of an Academy under subsection (1)(d) shall be treated as an amount due to that proprietor by way of refund under section 33B.", and

(*c*) in subsection (6)(*b*) after "33A" insert "or 33B".

(3) In section 90 of that Act (failure of resolution under the Provisional Collection of Taxes Act 1968), in subsection (3) after "33A," insert "33B,".

(4) In Part 2 of Schedule 9 to that Act (exemptions: groups), in Group 14 (supplies of goods where input tax cannot be recovered), in Note (9) after "33A," insert "33B,".

(5) The amendments made by this section have effect in relation to supplies made, and acquisitions and importations taking place, on or after 1 April 2011.

77 Relief from VAT on imported goods of low value

(1) In Schedule 2 to the Value Added Tax (Imported Goods) Relief Order 1984 (SI 1984/746) (reliefs for goods of certain descriptions), in item 8 of Group 8 (consignments of goods not exceeding a certain value), for "£18" substitute "£15".

(2) The amendment of that Schedule by this section is without prejudice to any power to amend that Schedule by subordinate legislation.

(3) The amendment made by this section has effect in relation to goods imported on or after 1 November 2011.

PART 7
ADMINISTRATION ETC

86 Data-gathering powers

(1) Schedule 23 contains provision for officers of Revenue and Customs to obtain data from data-holders.

(2) Schedule 24 contains amendments of Schedule 36 to FA 2008 (information and inspection powers).

87 Mutual assistance for recovery of taxes etc

(1) Schedule 25 contains provision for the purpose of giving effect to Council Directive 2010/24/EU (which concerns mutual assistance for the recovery of claims relating to taxes, duties and other measures).

(2) The Treasury may by regulations make provision for the purpose of giving effect to—

(*a*) any amendments or extensions of Council Directive 2010/24/EU,

(*b*) any EU instrument that—

(i) wholly or partly replaces that Directive or a replacement of it, or

(ii) otherwise makes provision for or in connection with mutual assistance between member States in the recovery of claims relating to taxes, duties and other measures, and

(*c*) any amendments or extensions of any such EU instrument.

(3) Regulations under subsection (2) may amend, replace or repeal Schedule 25 and any other enactment (whenever passed).

(4) Regulations under subsection (2) are to be made by statutory instrument.

(5) An instrument containing regulations under subsection (2) is subject to annulment in pursuance of a resolution of the House of Commons.

PART 8
MISCELLANEOUS PROVISIONS

88 Amendments of section 1 of the Provisional Collection of Taxes Act 1968

(1) Section 1 of the Provisional Collection of Taxes Act 1968 (temporary statutory effect of House of Commons resolutions relating to certain taxes) is amended in accordance with subsections (2) to (7).

(2) In subsection (2) for "(8)" substitute "(9)".

(3) For subsection (3) substitute—

"(3) The period is one expiring at the end of seven months after the date on which the resolution is expressed to take effect or, if no such date is expressed, after the date on which the resolution is passed."

(4) In subsection (5)—

(*a*) in paragraph (*c*) omit "or prorogued", and

(*b*) after paragraph (*c*) insert ", or

(*d*) Parliament is prorogued."

(5) After subsection (5) insert—

"(5A) Subsection (5B) applies in relation to a resolution instead of subsection (5) (*d*) where Parliament is prorogued at the end of a session if—

(*a*) one of the following happens during the session—

(i) a Bill renewing, varying or, as the case may be, abolishing the tax is read a first time by the House, or

(ii) a Bill is amended by the House in Committee or on Report or by any Public Bill Committee of the House so as to include provision for the renewal, variation or, as the case may be, abolition of the tax,

(*b*) the Standing Orders or Sessional Orders of the House provide, or during the session the House orders, that proceedings on the Bill not completed before the end of the session shall be resumed in the next session, and

(*c*) proceedings on the Bill are not completed during the session.

(5B) The resolution shall cease to have statutory effect under this section if, during the period of thirty sitting days beginning with the first sitting day of the next session, no Bill renewing, varying or, as the case may be, abolishing the tax is presented to the House.

(5C) In subsection (5B) "sitting day" means a day on which the House sits.

(5D) Where a Bill is amended as mentioned in subsection (5A)(*a*)(ii), it does not matter for the purposes of subsection (5A)(*b*) if the House orders as mentioned in subsection (5A)(*b*) before the amendment to the Bill is made."

(6) In subsection (6) for "(4) or (5)" substitute "(4), (5) or (5B)".

(7) After subsection (8) insert—

"(9) Subsection (8) does not apply where the later resolution is passed in a different calendar year from that in which the earlier resolution is passed."

(8) Accordingly, the following provisions are repealed—

(*a*) section 205(4) of FA 1993;

(*b*) section 50(1) and (3) of F(No 2)A 1997.

(9) The amendments made by this section come into force on such day as the Treasury may by order made by statutory instrument appoint.

(10) Subject to subsection (11), the amendments do not apply in relation to any resolution passed before the day appointed under subsection (9).

(11) The cases covered by section 1(9) of the Provisional Collection of Taxes Act 1968 (as inserted by subsection (7)) include cases where the earlier resolution (but not the later resolution) is passed before the day appointed under subsection (9).

Commencement—The Finance Act 2011, Section 88 (Appointed Day) Order, SI 2011/2934 (30 December 2011 appointed as the date on which s 88 comes into force).

SCHEDULE 23

DATA-GATHERING POWERS

Section 86(1)

Commentary—*Simon's Taxes* **A4.150**.

HMRC Manuals—Compliance Handbook, CH271400 (amount of penalty).

PART 1
POWER TO OBTAIN DATA

Power to give notice

1 (1) An officer of Revenue and Customs may by notice in writing require a relevant data-holder to provide relevant data.

(2) Part 2 of this Schedule sets out who is a relevant data-holder.

(3) In relation to a relevant data-holder, "relevant data" means data of a kind specified for that type of data-holder in regulations made by the Treasury.

(4) The data that a relevant data-holder may be required to provide—

(*a*) may be general data or data relating to particular persons or matters, and

(*b*) may include personal data (such as names and addresses of individuals).

(5) A notice under this paragraph is referred to as a data-holder notice.

Regulations—Data-gathering Powers (Relevant Data) Regulations, SI 2012/847.
Data-gathering Powers (Relevant Data) (Amendment) Regulations, SI 2015/672.

Purpose of power

2 (1) The power in paragraph 1(1) is exercisable to assist with the efficient and effective discharge of HMRC's tax functions—

(*a*) whether a particular function or more generally, and

(*b*) whether involving a particular taxpayer or taxpayers generally.

(2) It is additional to and is not limited by other powers that HMRC may have to obtain data (for example, in Schedule 36 to FA 2008).

(3) But it may not be used (in place of the power in paragraph 1 of that Schedule) to obtain data required for the purpose of checking the relevant data-holder's own tax position.

(4) Sub-paragraph (3) does not prevent use of the power in paragraph 1(1) of this Schedule to obtain data about a matter mentioned in paragraph 14(3)(*a*) (beneficial ownership of certain payments etc).

(5) Nothing in this paragraph limits the use that may be made of data that have been obtained under this Schedule (see section 17(1) of CRCA 2005).

Specifying relevant data

3 (1) A data-holder notice must specify the relevant data to be provided.

(2) Relevant data may not be specified in a data-holder notice unless an officer of Revenue and Customs has reason to believe that the data could have a bearing on chargeable or other periods ending on or after the applicable day.

(3) The applicable day is the first day of the period of 4 years ending with the day on which the notice is given.

Compliance

4 (1) Relevant data specified in a data-holder notice must be provided by such means and in such form as is reasonably specified in the notice.

(2) If the notice specifies that the data are to be provided by sending them somewhere, the data must be sent to such address and within such period as is reasonably specified in the notice.
(3) If the notice specifies that the data are to be provided by making documents available for inspection somewhere, the documents must be made available for inspection at such place and time as is—

(*a*) reasonably specified in the notice, or
(*b*) agreed between an officer of Revenue and Customs and the data-holder.

(4) A place used solely as a dwelling may not be specified under sub-paragraph (3)(a).
(5) A data-holder notice requiring the provision of specified documents requires the documents to be provided only if they are in the data-holder's possession or power.
(6) A power in this paragraph to specify something in a notice includes power to specify it in a document referred to in the notice.

Approval by tribunal

5 (1) An officer of Revenue and Customs may ask for the approval of the tribunal before giving a data-holder notice.
(2) This does not require an officer to do so (but see paragraph 28(3) for the effect of obtaining approval).
(3) An application for approval under this paragraph may be made without notice (except as required under sub-paragraph (4)).
(4) The tribunal may not approve the giving of a data-holder notice unless—

(*a*) the application for approval is made by, or with the agreement of, an authorised officer,
(*b*) the tribunal is satisfied that, in the circumstances, the officer giving the notice is justified in doing so,
(*c*) the data-holder has been told that the data are to be required and given a reasonable opportunity to make representations to an officer of Revenue and Customs, and
(*d*) the tribunal has been given a summary of any representations made by the data-holder.

(5) Paragraphs (*c*) and (*d*) of sub-paragraph (4) do not apply to the extent that the tribunal is satisfied that taking the action specified in those paragraphs might prejudice any purpose for which the data are required.
(6) A decision by the tribunal under this paragraph is final (despite the provisions of sections 11 and 13 of the Tribunals, Courts and Enforcement Act 2007).
(7) "Authorised officer" means an officer of Revenue and Customs who is, or is a member of a class of officers who are, authorised by the Commissioners for the purposes of this paragraph.

Power to copy documents

6 An officer of Revenue and Customs may take copies of or make extracts from any document provided pursuant to a data-holder notice.

Power to retain documents

7 (1) If an officer of Revenue and Customs thinks it reasonable to do so, HMRC may retain documents provided pursuant to a data-holder notice for a reasonable period.
(2) While a document is being retained, the data-holder may, if the document is reasonably required for any purpose, request a copy of it.
(3) The retention of a document under this paragraph is not to be regarded as breaking any lien claimed on the document.
(4) If a document retained under this paragraph is lost or damaged, the Commissioners are liable to compensate the owner of the document for any expenses reasonably incurred in replacing or repairing the document.

PART 2
RELEVANT DATA-HOLDERS

Introduction

8 (1) This Part of this Schedule sets out who is a relevant data-holder for the purposes of this Schedule.
(2) Descriptions of the various types of data-holder are to be read as including anyone who was previously of such a description.

Salaries, fees, commission etc

9 (1) Each of the following is a relevant data-holder—

(*a*) an employer,

(*b*) a person who is concerned in making payments to or in respect of another person's employees with respect to their employment with that other person,

(*c*) an approved agent within the meaning of section 714 of ITEPA 2003 (which relates to payroll giving), and

(*d*) a person who carries on a business in connection with which relevant payments are or are likely to be made.

(2) Relevant payments are—

(*a*) payments for or in connection with services provided by persons who are not employed in the business, or

(*b*) periodical or lump sum payments in respect of any copyright, public lending right, right in a registered design or design right.

(3) Payments are taken to be made in connection with a business if they are made—

(*a*) in the course of carrying on the business or a part of it, or

(*b*) in connection with the formation, acquisition, development or disposal of the business or a part of it.

(4) Sub-paragraph (1)(*d*) applies to the carrying on of any other kind of activity as it applies to the carrying on of a business, but only if the activity is being carried on by a body of persons (and references in sub-paragraphs (2) and (3) to the business are to be read accordingly).

(5) A reference in this paragraph to the making of payments includes—

(*a*) the provision of benefits, and

(*b*) the giving of any other valuable consideration.

Cross-references—See Data-gathering Powers (Relevant Data) Regulations, SI 2012/847 reg 3 (relevant data for data-holders under this para).

10 (1) This paragraph applies if—

(*a*) services that an individual provides or is obliged to provide under an agency contract are treated under section 44(2) of ITEPA 2003 as the duties of an employment held by the individual with the agency, or

(*b*) remuneration receivable under or in consequence of arrangements falling within section 45 of that Act is treated as earnings from an employment held by an individual with the agency.

(2) For the purposes of paragraph 9—

(*a*) the individual is treated as being employed by the agency, and

(*b*) payments made to the individual under or in consequence of the agency contract, or treated as earnings under section 45 of ITEPA 2003, do not count as "relevant payments".

(3) "Agency contract" and "remuneration" have the same meaning as in Chapter 7 of Part 2 of ITEPA 2003.

11 (1) This paragraph applies if—

(*a*) a person ("A") performs in the United Kingdom duties of an employment,

(*b*) the employment is under or with a person resident outside and not resident in the United Kingdom,

(*c*) the duties performed in the United Kingdom are performed for a continuous period of not less than 30 days, and

(*d*) those duties are performed for the benefit of a person ("B") resident or carrying on a trade, profession or vocation in the United Kingdom.

(2) For the purposes of paragraph 9—

(*a*) B is treated as if B were an employer, but

(*b*) only the name and place of residence of A may be specified for a relevant data-holder of B's type in regulations made under paragraph 1(3).

Cross-references—See Data-gathering Powers (Relevant Data) Regulations, SI 2012/847 reg 4 (relevant data for data-holders under this para).

Interest etc

12 (1) A person by or through whom interest is paid or credited is a relevant data-holder.

(2) For the purposes of this paragraph, the following are to be treated as interest—

(*a*) a dividend in respect of a share in a building society,

(*b*) an amount to which a person holding a deeply discounted security is entitled on the redemption of that security,

(*c*) a foreign dividend, and

(*d*) an alternative finance return.

(3) In sub-paragraph (2)—

"alternative finance return" means—

(*a*) an alternative finance return within the meaning of Part 10A of ITA 2007, and

(*b*) an alternative finance return within the meaning of Part 6 of CTA 2009;

"building society" means a building society within the meaning of the Building Societies Act 1986;

"deeply discounted security" has the same meaning as in Chapter 8 of Part 4 of ITTOIA 2005;

"foreign dividend" means any annual payment, interest or dividend payable out of, or in respect of the funds or securities of—

(*a*) a body of persons that is not resident in the United Kingdom, or

(*b*) a government or public or local authority in a country outside the United Kingdom.

Cross-references—See Data-gathering Powers (Relevant Data) Regulations, SI 2012/847 regs 5–7 (relevant data for data-holders under this para).

Income, assets etc belonging to others

13 A person who (in whatever capacity) is in receipt of money or value of or belonging to another is a relevant data-holder.

Cross-references—See Data-gathering Powers (Relevant Data) Regulations, SI 2012/847 reg 11 (relevant data for data-holders under this para).

[Merchant acquirers etc

13A—(1) A person who has a contractual obligation to make payments to retailers in settlement of payment card transactions is a relevant data-holder.

(2) In this paragraph—

"payment card" includes a credit card, a charge card and a debit card;

"payment card transaction" means any transaction in which a payment card is accepted as payment;

"retailer" means a person who accepts a payment card as payment for any transaction.

(3) In this paragraph any reference to a payment card being accepted as payment includes a reference to any account number or other indicators associated with a payment card being accepted as payment.][1]

Amendments—[1] Para 13A inserted by FA 2013 s 228 with effect in relation to relevant data with a bearing on any period (whether before, on or after 17 July 2013).

Payments derived from securities

14 (1) Each of the following is a relevant data-holder—

(*a*) a person who is the registered or inscribed holder of securities,

(*b*) a person who receives a payment derived from securities or would be entitled to do so if a payment were made,

(*c*) a person who receives a payment treated by the company that makes it as a payment to which section 1033 of CTA 2010 applies (purchase by unquoted trading company of own shares), and

(*d*) a person who receives a chargeable payment within the meaning of Chapter 5 of Part 23 of CTA 2010 (company distributions: demergers).

(2) But, for a relevant data-holder of a type described in this paragraph, data may only be specified in regulations under paragraph 1(3) if the data concern a matter mentioned in sub-paragraph (3).

(3) The matters are—

(*a*) whether the relevant data-holder is the beneficial owner (or sole beneficial owner) of the securities or payment in question,

(*b*) if not—

(i) details of the beneficial owner (or other beneficial owners), and

(ii) if those details are not known or if different, details of the person for whom the securities are held or to whom the payment is or may be paid on, and

(*c*) if there is more than one beneficial owner or more than one person of the kind mentioned in paragraph (*b*)(ii), their respective interests in the securities or payment.

(4) "Payment derived from securities" includes in particular—

(*a*) an amount (whether of income or capital) that is payable out of or in respect of securities or rights attaching to securities, and

(*b*) a payment that is representative of any such amount.

Cross-references—See Data-gathering Powers (Relevant Data) Regulations, SI 2012/847 reg 12 (relevant data for data-holders under this para).

15 (1) A person who makes a payment derived from securities that has been received from or is paid on behalf of another is a relevant data-holder.

(2) "Payment derived from securities" has the same meaning as in paragraph 14.

Cross-references—See Data-gathering Powers (Relevant Data) Regulations, SI 2012/847 reg 13 (relevant data for data-holders under this para).

Grants and subsidies out of public funds

16 (1) A person by whom a payment out of public funds is made by way of grant or subsidy is a relevant data-holder.

(2) For these purposes, a payment is a payment out of public funds if it is provided directly or indirectly by—

(*a*) the Crown,

(*b*) any government, public or local authority whether in the United Kingdom or elsewhere, or

(*c*) any EU institution.

Cross-references—See Data-gathering Powers (Relevant Data) Regulations, SI 2012/847 reg 14 (relevant data for data-holders under this para).

Licences, approvals etc

17 (1) A person by whom licences or approvals are issued or a register is maintained is a relevant data-holder.

(2) "Register" includes—

(*a*) any record or list that a local authority maintains, and

(*b*) any record or list that any other person is required or permitted to maintain by or under an enactment.

Cross-references—See Data-gathering Powers (Relevant Data) Regulations, SI 2012/847 reg 15 (relevant data for data-holders under this para).

Rent and other payments arising from land

18 (1) Each of the following is a relevant data-holder—

(*a*) a lessee (or successor in title of a lessee),

(*b*) an occupier of land,

(*c*) a person having the use of land, and

(*d*) a person who, as agent, manages land or is in receipt of rent or other payments arising from land.

(2) The reference to a person who manages land includes a person who markets property to potential tenants, searches for tenants or provides similar services.

Cross-references—See Data-gathering Powers (Relevant Data) Regulations, SI 2012/847 reg 16 (relevant data for data-holders under this para).

Dealing etc in securities

19 (1) Each of the following is a relevant data-holder—

(*a*) a person who effects or is a party to securities transactions wholly or partly on behalf of others (whether as agent or principal),

(*b*) a person who, in the course of business, acts as registrar or administrator in respect of securities transactions (including a person who manages a clearing house for any terminal market in securities),

(*c*) a person who makes a payment derived from securities to anyone other than the registered or inscribed holder of the securities,

(*d*) a person who makes a payment derived from bearer securities, and

(*e*) an accountable person within the meaning of the Stamp Duty Reserve Tax Regulations 1986 (S.I. 1986/1711).

(2) "Payment derived from securities" has the same meaning as in paragraph 14 (and "payment derived from bearer securities" is to be read accordingly).

(3) "Securities transactions" means—

(*a*) transactions in securities,

(*b*) transactions under which a representative payment has been, is to be or may be made, or

(*c*) the making or receipt of a representative payment.

(4) In sub-paragraph (3)—

"representative payment" means a payment that is representative of an amount payable out of or in respect of securities or rights attaching to securities;

"transactions in securities" means transactions, of whatever description, relating to securities, and includes in particular—

(*a*) the purchase, sale or exchange of securities,

(*b*) issuing or securing the issue of new securities,

(*c*) applying or subscribing for new securities, and

(*d*) altering or securing the alteration of rights attached to securities.

Cross–references—See Data-gathering Powers (Relevant Data) Regulations, SI 2012/847 reg 17 (relevant data for data-holders under this para).

Dealing in other property

20 Each of the following is a relevant data-holder—

(*a*) the committee or other person or body of persons responsible for managing a clearing house for any terminal market in commodities,

(*b*) an auctioneer,

(*c*) a person carrying on a business of dealing in any description of tangible movable property, and

(*d*) a person carrying on a business of acting as an agent or intermediary in dealings in any description of tangible movable property.

Cross–references—See Data-gathering Powers (Relevant Data) Regulations, SI 2012/847 reg 18 (relevant data for data-holders under this para).

Lloyd's

21 A person who is registered as managing agent at Lloyd's in relation to a syndicate of underwriting members of Lloyd's is a relevant data-holder.

Cross–references—See Data-gathering Powers (Relevant Data) Regulations, SI 2012/847 reg 19 (relevant data for data-holders under this para).

Investment plans etc

22 Each of the following is a relevant data-holder—

(*a*) a plan manager (see section 696 of ITTOIA 2005), and

(*b*) an account provider in relation to a child trust fund (as defined in section 3 of the Child Trust Funds Act 2004).

Cross–references—See Data-gathering Powers (Relevant Data) Regulations, SI 2012/847 reg 20 (relevant data for data-holders under this para).

Petroleum activities

23 Each of the following is a relevant data-holder—

(*a*) the holder of a licence granted under Part 1 of the Petroleum Act 1998, and

(*b*) the responsible person in relation to an oil field (within the meaning of Part 1 of OTA 1975).

Cross–references—See Data-gathering Powers (Relevant Data) Regulations, SI 2012/847 reg 21 (relevant data for data-holders under this para).

Insurance activities

24 Each of the following is a relevant data-holder—

(*a*) a person who is involved (in any capacity) in an insurance business (as defined for the purposes of Part 3 of FA 1994),

(*b*) a person who makes arrangements for persons to enter into contracts of insurance, and

(*c*) a person who is concerned in a business that is not an insurance business and who has been involved in the entering into of a contract of insurance that provides cover for any matter associated with the business.

Cross–references—See Data-gathering Powers (Relevant Data) Regulations, SI 2012/847 reg 22 (relevant data for data-holders under this para).

Environmental activities

25 A person who is involved (in any capacity) in any of the following activities is a relevant data-holder—

(*a*) subjecting aggregate to exploitation in the United Kingdom (as defined for the purposes of Part 2 of FA 2001) or connected activities,

(*b*) making or receiving supplies of taxable commodities (as defined for the purposes of Schedule 6 to FA 2000) or connected activities, and

(*c*) landfill disposal (as defined for the purposes of Part 3 of FA 1996).

Cross–references—See Data-gathering Powers (Relevant Data) Regulations, SI 2012/847 reg 23 (relevant data for data-holders under this para).

Settlements

26 (1) Each of the following is a relevant data-holder—

(*a*) a person who makes a settlement,
(*b*) the trustees of a settlement,
(*c*) a beneficiary under a settlement, and
(*d*) any other person to whom income is payable under a settlement.

(2) Section 620 of ITTOIA 2005 (meaning of "settlement" etc) applies for the purposes of this paragraph.

Cross-references—See Data-gathering Powers (Relevant Data) Regulations, SI 2012/847 reg 24 (relevant data for data-holders under this para).

Charities

27 A charity is a relevant data-holder.

Cross-references—See Data-gathering Powers (Relevant Data) Regulations, SI 2012/847 reg 25 (relevant data for data-holders under this para).

PART 3
APPEALS AGAINST DATA-HOLDER NOTICES

Right of appeal

28 (1) The data-holder may appeal against a data-holder notice, or any requirement in such a notice, on any of the following grounds—
(*a*) it is unduly onerous to comply with the notice or requirement,
(*b*) the data-holder is not a relevant data-holder, or
(*c*) data specified in the notice are not relevant data.

(2) Sub-paragraph (1)(*a*) does not apply to a requirement to provide data that form part of the data-holder's statutory records.

(3) Sub-paragraph (1) does not apply if the tribunal approved the giving of the notice in accordance with paragraph 5.

Procedure for appeal

29 (1) Notice of an appeal under paragraph 28 must be given—
(*a*) in writing,
(*b*) before the end of the period of 30 days beginning with the date on which the data-holder notice was given, and
(*c*) to the officer of Revenue and Customs by whom the data-holder notice was given.

(2) It must state the grounds of appeal.

(3) On an appeal that is notified to the tribunal, the tribunal may confirm, vary or set aside the data-holder notice or a requirement in it.

(4) If the tribunal confirms or varies the notice or a requirement in it, the data-holder must comply with the notice or requirement—
(*a*) within such period as is specified by the tribunal, or
(*b*) if the tribunal does not specify a period, within such period as is reasonably specified in writing by an officer of Revenue and Customs following the tribunal's decision.

(5) A decision by the tribunal under this Part is final (despite the provisions of sections 11 and 13 of the Tribunals, Courts and Enforcement Act 2007).

(6) Subject to this paragraph, the provisions of Part 5 of TMA 1970 relating to appeals have effect in relation to appeals under paragraph 28 as they have effect in relation to an appeal against an assessment to income tax.

PART 4
PENALTIES

Penalties for failure to comply

30 (1) If the data-holder fails to comply with a data-holder notice, the data-holder is liable to a penalty of £300.

(2) A reference in this Schedule to failing to comply with a data-holder notice includes—
(*a*) concealing, destroying or otherwise disposing of a material document, or
(*b*) arranging for any such concealment, destruction or disposal.

(3) A document is a material document if, at the time when the data-holder acts—
(*a*) the data-holder has received a data-holder notice requiring the data-holder to provide the document or data contained in the document, or
(*b*) the data-holder has not received such a notice but has been informed by an officer of Revenue and Customs that the data-holder will do so or is likely to do so.

(4) A document is not a material document by virtue of sub-paragraph (3)(*a*) if the data-holder notice has already been complied with, unless—

(*a*) the data-holder has been notified in writing by an officer of Revenue and Customs that the data-holder must continue to preserve the document, and

(*b*) the notification has not been withdrawn.

(5) A document is not a material document by virtue of sub-paragraph (3)(b) if more than 6 months have elapsed since the data-holder was (or was last) informed.

Daily default penalties for failure to comply

31 If—

(*a*) a penalty under paragraph 30 is assessed, and

(*b*) the failure in question continues after the data-holder has been notified of the assessment,

the data-holder is liable to a further penalty, for each subsequent day on which the failure continues, of an amount not exceeding £60 for each such day.

Penalties for inaccurate information or documents

32 (1) This paragraph applies if—

(*a*) in complying with a data-holder notice, the data-holder provides inaccurate data, and

(*b*) condition A, B or C is met.

(2) Condition A is that the inaccuracy is—

(*a*) due to a failure by the data-holder to take reasonable care, or

(*b*) deliberate on the data-holder's part.

(3) Condition B is that the data-holder knows of the inaccuracy at the time the data are provided but does not inform HMRC at that time.

(4) Condition C is that the data-holder—

(*a*) discovers the inaccuracy some time later, and

(*b*) fails to take reasonable steps to inform HMRC.

(5) If this paragraph applies, the data-holder is liable to a penalty not exceeding £3,000.

Failure to comply with time limit

33 A failure to do anything required to be done within a limited period of time does not give rise to liability under paragraph 30 or 31 if the thing was done within such further time (if any) as an officer of Revenue and Customs may have allowed.

Reasonable excuse

34 (1) Liability to a penalty under paragraph 30 or 31 does not arise if the data-holder satisfies HMRC or (on an appeal notified to the tribunal) the tribunal that there is a reasonable excuse for the failure.

(2) For the purposes of this paragraph—

(*a*) an insufficiency of funds is not a reasonable excuse unless attributable to events outside the data-holder's control,

(*b*) if the data-holder relies on another person to do anything, that is not a reasonable excuse unless the data-holder took reasonable care to avoid the failure,

(*c*) if the data-holder had a reasonable excuse for the failure but the excuse has ceased, the data-holder is to be treated as having continued to have the excuse if the failure is remedied without unreasonable delay after the excuse ceased.

Assessment of penalties

35 (1) If the data-holder becomes liable to a penalty under paragraph 30, 31 or 32, HMRC may assess the penalty.

(2) If they do so, they must notify the data-holder.

(3) An assessment of a penalty under paragraph 30 or 31 must be made within the period of 12 months beginning with the latest of the following—

(*a*) the date on which the data-holder became liable to the penalty,

(*b*) the end of the period in which notice of an appeal against the data-holder notice (or a requirement in it) could have been given, and

(*c*) if notice of such an appeal is given, the date on which the appeal is determined or withdrawn.

(4) An assessment of a penalty under paragraph 32 must be made—

(*a*) within the period of 12 months beginning with the date on which the inaccuracy first came to the attention of an officer of Revenue and Customs, and

(*b*) within the period of 6 years beginning with the date on which the data-holder became liable to the penalty.

Right to appeal against penalty

36 The data-holder may appeal against a decision by an officer of Revenue and Customs—

(*a*) that a penalty is payable under paragraph 30, 31 or 32, or

(*b*) as to the amount of such a penalty.

Procedure on appeal against penalty

37 (1) Notice of an appeal under paragraph 36 must be given—

(*a*) in writing,

(*b*) before the end of the period of 30 days beginning with the date on which notification under paragraph 35 was given, and

(*c*) to HMRC.

(2) It must state the grounds of appeal.

(3) On an appeal under paragraph 36(*a*) that is notified to the tribunal, the tribunal may confirm or cancel the decision.

(4) On an appeal under paragraph 36(*b*) that is notified to the tribunal, the tribunal may—

(*a*) confirm the decision, or

(*b*) substitute for the decision another decision that the officer of Revenue and Customs had power to make.

(5) Subject to this paragraph and paragraph 40, the provisions of Part 5 of TMA 1970 relating to appeals have effect in relation to appeals under paragraph 36 as they have effect in relation to an appeal against an assessment to income tax.

Increased daily default penalty

38 (1) This paragraph applies if—

(*a*) a penalty under paragraph 31 is assessed under paragraph 35,

(*b*) the failure in respect of which that assessment is made continues for more than 30 days beginning with the date on which notification of that assessment is given, and

(*c*) the data-holder has been told that an application may be made under this paragraph for an increased daily penalty to be imposed.

(2) If this paragraph applies, an officer of Revenue and Customs may make an application to the tribunal for an increased daily penalty to be imposed on the data-holder.

(3) If the tribunal decides that an increased daily penalty should be imposed, then for each applicable day (see paragraph 39) on which the failure continues—

(*a*) the data-holder is not liable to a penalty under paragraph 31 in respect of the failure, and

(*b*) the data-holder is liable instead to a penalty under this paragraph of an amount determined by the tribunal.

(4) The tribunal may not determine an amount exceeding £1,000 for each applicable day.

(5) But subject to that, in determining the amount the tribunal must have regard to—

(*a*) the likely cost to the data-holder of complying with the data-holder notice,

(*b*) any benefits to the data-holder of not complying with it, and

(*c*) any benefits to anyone else resulting from the data-holder's non-compliance.

39 (1) If a data-holder becomes liable to a penalty under paragraph 38, HMRC must notify the data-holder.

(2) The notification must specify the day from which the increased penalty is to apply.

(3) That day and any subsequent day is an "applicable day" for the purposes of paragraph 38(3).

Enforcement of penalties

40 (1) A penalty under this Schedule must be paid before the end of the period of 30 days beginning with the date mentioned in sub-paragraph (2).

(2) That date is—

(*a*) the date on which notification under paragraph 35 or 39 is given in respect of the penalty, or

(*b*) if (in the case of a penalty under paragraph 30, 31 or 32) a notice of appeal under paragraph 36 is given, the date on which the appeal is finally determined or withdrawn.

(3) A penalty under this Schedule may be enforced as if it were income tax charged in an assessment and due and payable.

Power to change amount of penalties

41 (1) If it appears to the Treasury that there has been a change in the value of money since the last relevant date, they may by regulations substitute for the sums for the time being specified in paragraphs 30(1), 31, 32(5) and 38(4) such other sums as appear to them to be justified by the change.

(2) "Relevant date", in relation to a specified sum, means—

(*a*) the day on which this Act is passed, and

(*b*) each date on which the power conferred by sub-paragraph (1) has been exercised in relation to that sum.

(3) Regulations under this paragraph do not apply to—

(*a*) a failure which began before the date on which they come into force, or

(*b*) an inaccuracy in any data or document provided to HMRC before that date.

Double jeopardy

42 The data-holder is not liable to a penalty under this Schedule in respect of anything in respect of which the data-holder has been convicted of an offence.

PART 5
MISCELLANEOUS PROVISION AND INTERPRETATION

Application of provisions of TMA 1970

43 Subject to the provisions of this Schedule, the following provisions of TMA 1970 apply for the purposes of this Schedule as they apply for the purposes of the Taxes Acts—

(*a*) section 108 (responsibility of company officers),

(*b*) section 114 (want of form), and

(*c*) section 115 (delivery and service of documents).

Regulations

44 (1) Regulations under this Schedule are to be made by statutory instrument.

(2) The first regulations to be made under paragraph 1(3) may not be made unless the instrument containing them has been laid in draft before, and approved by a resolution of, the House of Commons.

(3) Subject to sub-paragraph (2), a statutory instrument containing regulations under this Schedule is subject to annulment in pursuance of a resolution of the House of Commons.

Tax

45 (1) In this Schedule "tax" means any or all of the following—

(*a*) income tax,

(*b*) capital gains tax,

(*c*) corporation tax,

[(*ca*) diverted profits tax,][2]

(*d*) VAT,

(*e*) insurance premium tax,

(*f*) inheritance tax,

(*g*) stamp duty land tax,

(*h*) stamp duty reserve tax,

(*i*) petroleum revenue tax,

(*j*) aggregates levy,

(*k*) climate change levy,

(*l*) landfill tax, and

(*m*) relevant foreign tax.

(2) "Corporation tax" includes any amount assessable or chargeable as if it were corporation tax.

(3) "VAT" means—

(*a*) value added tax charged in accordance with VATA 1994, and

(*b*) value added tax charged in accordance with the law of another member State,

and includes any amount that is recoverable under paragraph 5(2) of Schedule 11 to VATA 1994 (amounts shown on invoices as VAT).

(4) "Relevant foreign tax" means—

(*a*) a tax of a member State, other than the United Kingdom, which is covered by the provisions for the exchange of information under the [Council Directive 2011/16/EU of 15 February 2011 on administrative cooperation in the field of taxation][1] (as amended from time to time), and

(*b*) any tax or duty which is imposed under the law of a territory in relation to which arrangements having effect by virtue of section 173 of FA 2006 (international tax enforcement arrangements) have been made and which is covered by the arrangements.

Amendments—[1] In sub-para (4), words substituted by the European Administrative Co-operation (Taxation) Regulations, SI 2012/3062 reg 6(2) with effect from 1 January 2013.

2 Sub-para (1)(*ca*) inserted by FA 2015 s 105(1) with effect in relation to accounting periods beginning on or after 1 April 2015. For accounting periods that straddle that date, see FA 2015 s 116(2).

Statutory records

46 (1) For the purposes of this Schedule data form part of a data-holder's statutory records if they are data that the data-holder is required to keep and preserve under or by virtue of any enactment relating to tax.
(2) Data cease to form part of a data-holder's statutory records when the period for which the data are required to be preserved under or by virtue of that enactment has expired.

General interpretation

47 In this Schedule—
"address" includes an electronic address;
"body of persons" has the same meaning as in TMA 1970;
"chargeable period" means a tax year, accounting period or other period for which a tax is charged;
"charity" has the meaning given by paragraph 1(1) of Schedule 6 to FA 2010;
"the Commissioners" means the Commissioners for Her Majesty's Revenue and Customs;
"company" has the meaning given by section 288(1) of TCGA 1992;
"data" includes information held in any form;
"the data-holder", in relation to a data-holder notice, means the person to whom the notice is addressed;
"data-holder notice" is defined in paragraph 1;
"dividend" includes any kind of distribution;
"document" includes a copy of a document (see also section 114 of FA 2008);
"employment", "employee" and "employer" have the same meaning as in Parts 2 to 7 of ITEPA 2003 (see, in particular, sections 4 and 5 of that Act);
"HMRC" means Her Majesty's Revenue and Customs;
"local authority" has the meaning given in section 999 of ITA 2007;
"provide" includes make available for inspection;
"specify" includes describe;
"securities" includes—
(*a*) shares and stock,
(*b*) debentures, including debenture stock, loan stock, bonds, certificates of deposit and other instruments creating or acknowledging indebtedness, and
(*c*) warrants or other instruments entitling the holder to subscribe for or otherwise acquire anything within paragraph (*a*) or (*b*),

issued by or on behalf of a person resident in, or a government or public or local authority of, any country (including a country outside the United Kingdom);
"shares" is to be construed in accordance with sections 99 and 103A of TCGA 1992;
"tax functions" means functions relating to tax;
"the tribunal" means the First-tier Tribunal or, where determined by or under the Tribunal Procedure Rules, the Upper Tribunal.

48 A reference in this Schedule to providing data includes—
(*a*) preparing and delivering a return, statement or declaration, and
(*b*) providing documents.

49 (1) A reference in this Schedule to the carrying on of a business also includes—
(*a*) the letting of property,
(*b*) the activities of a charity, and
(*c*) the activities of a government department, a local authority, a local authority association or any other public authority.
(2) "Local authority association" has the meaning given in section 1000 of ITA 2007.

Crown application

50 This Schedule applies to the Crown but not to Her Majesty in Her private capacity (within the meaning of the Crown Proceedings Act 1947).

PART 6
CONSEQUENTIAL PROVISIONS

TMA 1970

51 (1) TMA 1970 is amended as follows.
(2) (*repeals* TMA 1970 ss 13–19, 21, 23–27, 76, 77I)
(3), (4) (*amend* TMA 1970 s 98, Table)
(5) (*inserts* TMA 1970 s 103ZA(*f*))

FA 1973

52 (*repeals* FA 1973 Sch 15 para 2)

FA 1974

53 (1) (*amends* FA 1974 s 24)
(2) Sub-paragraph (1) applies so far as section 24 of FA 1974 continues to have effect (see section 381 of TIOPA 2010).

FA 1986

54 (*repeals* FA 1986 Sch 18 para 8(4), (5))

ICTA

55 (*repeals* TA 1988 ss 42(7), 217(1), 226(4), 768(9), 816(3))

FA 1989

56 (*repeals* FA 1989 Sch 12 para 3)

ITTOIA 2005

57 (*repeals* ITTOIA 2005 ss 302B(3), (4), 647)

FA 2005

58 (*repeals* FA 2005 Sch 2 para 2)

CRCA 2005

59 (*repeals* CRCA 2005 Sch 2 para 2)

FA 2008

60 FA 2008 is amended as follows.

61 (*repeals* FA 2008 s 39(1)(*a*))

62 (1) Schedule 36 (information and inspection powers) is amended as follows.
(2) (*repeals* FA 2008 Sch 36 para 34A)
(3) (*amends* FA 2008 Sch 36 para 61A)

CTA 2009

63 (*repeals* CTA 2009 s 241(3), (4))

CTA 2010

64 (*repeals* CTA 2010 ss 31(1), 465(1), 728, 1046(5)–(7), 1097, 1102(2))

PART 7
APPLICATION OF THIS SCHEDULE

65 (1) This Schedule—
(*a*) comes into force on 1 April 2012, and
(*b*) applies from then on to relevant data with a bearing on any period (whether before, on or after that date), subject to paragraph 3(2).
(2) The provisions repealed or otherwise amended by Part 6 of this Schedule continue to have effect in relation to notices given, or requests made, pursuant to any of the repealed provisions before 1 April 2012 as if the repeals and other amendments had not been made.

SCHEDULE 24

AMENDMENTS OF SCHEDULE 36 FA 2008

Section 86(2)

1 Schedule 36 to FA 2008 (information and inspection powers) is amended as follows.

2 (1) Paragraph 5 (power to obtain information and documents about persons whose identity is not known) is amended as follows.

(2) In sub-paragraph (2), omit "UK".

(3) In sub-paragraph (4)—

(*a*) in paragraph (*b*), for the words from "the Taxes Acts" to the end substitute "the law (including the law of a territory outside the United Kingdom) relating to tax,", and

(*b*) in paragraph (*c*), omit "UK".

(4) Omit sub-paragraph (5).

(5) The amendments made by this paragraph—

(*a*) come into force on 1 April 2012, and

(*b*) apply from then on in relation to tax regardless of when the tax became due (whether before, on or after that date).

3 (1) Paragraph 40A (penalties for inaccurate information and documents) is amended as follows.

(2) In sub-paragraph (1)(*b*), for "A or B" substitute "A, B or C".

(3) After sub-paragraph (3) insert—

"(3A) Condition B is that the person knows of the inaccuracy at the time the information is provided or the document produced but does not inform HMRC at that time."

(4) In sub-paragraph (4), for "B" substitute "C".

(5) The amendments made by this paragraph have effect in relation to any inaccuracy in information provided, or in documents produced, on or after 1 April 2012.

4 (1) After paragraph 49 insert—

"Increased daily default penalty

49A

(1) This paragraph applies if—

(*a*) a penalty under paragraph 40 is assessed under paragraph 46 in respect of a person's failure to comply with a notice under paragraph 5,

(*b*) the failure continues for more than 30 days beginning with the date on which notification of that assessment was issued, and

(*c*) the person has been told that an application may be made under this paragraph for an increased daily penalty to be imposed.

(2) If this paragraph applies, an officer of Revenue and Customs may make an application to the tribunal for an increased daily penalty to be imposed on the person.

(3) If the tribunal decides that an increased daily penalty should be imposed, then for each applicable day (see paragraph 49B) on which the failure continues—

(*a*) the person is not liable to a penalty under paragraph 40 in respect of the failure, and

(*b*) the person is liable instead to a penalty under this paragraph of an amount determined by the tribunal.

(4) The tribunal may not determine an amount exceeding £1,000 for each applicable day.

(5) But subject to that, in determining the amount the tribunal must have regard to—

(*a*) the likely cost to the person of complying with the notice,

(*b*) any benefits to the person of not complying with it, and

(*c*) any benefits to anyone else resulting from the person's non-compliance.

(6) Paragraph 41 applies in relation to the sum specified in sub-paragraph (4) as it applies in relation to the sums mentioned in paragraph 41(1).

49B

(1) If a person becomes liable to a penalty under paragraph 49A, HMRC must notify the person.

(2) The notification must specify the day from which the increased penalty is to apply.

(3) That day and any subsequent day is an "applicable day" for the purposes of paragraph 49A(3).

49C

(1) A penalty under paragraph 49A must be paid before the end of the period of 30 days beginning with the date on which the notification under paragraph 49B is issued.

(2) A penalty under paragraph 49A may be enforced as if it were income tax charged in an assessment and due and payable."

(2) The amendment made by this paragraph has effect in relation to failures to comply with a notice under paragraph 5 that begin on or after 1 April 2012.

5 (1) Paragraph 50 (tax-related penalty) is amended as follows.

(2) In sub-paragraph (1)(*d*), omit "(within the meaning of paragraph 46)".

(3) After sub-paragraph (6) insert—

"(7) In sub-paragraph (1)(*d*) "the relevant date" means—

(*a*) in a case involving an information notice against which a person may appeal, the latest of—

(i) the date on which the person became liable to the penalty under paragraph 39,

(ii) the end of the period in which notice of an appeal against the information notice could have been given, and

(iii) if notice of such an appeal is given, the date on which the appeal is determined or withdrawn, and

(*b*) in any other case, the date on which the person became liable to the penalty under paragraph 39."

(4) The amendments made by this paragraph have effect where a person becomes liable to a penalty under paragraph 39 of Schedule 36 to FA 2008 on or after the day on which this Act is passed.

6 In paragraph 61A (involved third parties), in the first column of item 11 of the Table, after "receiving" insert "supplies of".

SCHEDULE 25
MUTUAL ASSISTANCE FOR RECOVERY OF TAXES ETC

Section 87

MARD

1 In this Schedule "MARD" means Council Directive 2010/24/EU.

HMRC functions

2 (1) The Commissioners are a competent authority in the United Kingdom for the purposes of all matters under MARD.

(2) HMRC is designated as the central liaison office in the United Kingdom for the purposes of all matters under MARD.

Exchange of information

3 (1) No obligation of secrecy imposed by statute or otherwise precludes a public authority (or anyone acting on behalf of a public authority) from disclosing information if the disclosure is made for the purpose of giving effect, or enabling effect to be given, to MARD or a MARD-related instrument.

(2) Sub-paragraph (1) applies, in particular, to any disclosure (to persons in the United Kingdom or elsewhere) in connection with a request or proposed request by or on behalf of an applicant authority of any member State for assistance in accordance with MARD.

(3) Sub-paragraph (2) is not to be taken to limit sub-paragraph (1).

Onward disclosure of information received from HMRC

4 (1) A public authority commits an offence if—

(*a*) it discloses relevant information, and

(*b*) the disclosure is not permitted by sub-paragraph (3).

(2) "Relevant information" is information that—

(*a*) the public authority has received from HMRC by virtue of paragraph 3, and

(*b*) relates to a person whose identity is specified in the disclosure or can be deduced from it.

(3) A disclosure is permitted by this sub-paragraph if it is made—

(*a*) in accordance with paragraph 3,

(*b*) in accordance with another enactment (or an instrument made under an enactment) permitting the disclosure,

(*c*) in pursuance of an order of a court,

(*d*) for the purposes of civil proceedings (whether or not within the United Kingdom),

(*e*) for the purposes of a criminal investigation or criminal proceedings (whether or not within the United Kingdom), (*f*) with the consent of each person to whom the information relates, or

(*g*) with the consent of the Commissioners.

(4) Sub-paragraph (1) applies to each of the following as it applies to a public authority—

(*a*) an employee or agent of the public authority;

(*b*) anyone providing services or exercising functions on behalf of the public authority;

(*c*) anyone authorised by the public authority to receive information on its behalf.

5 (1) It is a defence for a person charged with an offence under paragraph 4 to prove that the person reasonably believed—

(*a*) that the disclosure was lawful, or

(*b*) that the information had already and lawfully been made available to the public.

(2) A person guilty of an offence under paragraph 4 is liable—

(*a*) on conviction on indictment, to imprisonment for a term not exceeding 2 years or a fine, or both;

(*b*) on summary conviction, to imprisonment for a term not exceeding 12 months or a fine not exceeding the statutory maximum, or both.

(3) A prosecution for an offence under paragraph 4 may be instituted in England and Wales [only by or with the consent of the Director of Public Prosecutions.][1]

(4) A prosecution for an offence under paragraph 4 may be instituted in Northern Ireland only—

(*a*) by the Commissioners, or

(*b*) with the consent of the Director of Public Prosecutions for Northern Ireland.

(5) In the application of this paragraph—

(*a*) in England and Wales, in relation to an offence committed before the commencement of section 154(1) of the Criminal Justice Act 2003, or

(*b*) in Northern Ireland,

the reference in sub-paragraph (2)(*b*) to 12 months is to be read as a reference to 6 months.

Amendments—[1] Words in sub-para (3) substituted by the Public Bodies (Merger of the Director of Public Prosecutions and the Director of Revenue and Customs Prosecutions) Order, SI 2014/834 art 3(3), Sch 2 para 75 with effect from 27 March 2014.

Enforcement of foreign claims in the UK

6 (1) This paragraph applies if an applicant authority of another member State makes a request in accordance with MARD for the recovery in the United Kingdom of a claim.

(2) The claim in relation to which such a request is made is referred to as "the foreign claim".

(3) Such steps may be taken by or on behalf of the relevant UK authority to enforce the foreign claim as might be taken (whether or not by the relevant UK authority) to enforce a corresponding UK claim.

(4) "Steps" includes any legal or administrative steps, whether by way of legal proceedings, distress, diligence or otherwise.

(5) See paragraphs 7 and 8 for the meaning of "the relevant UK authority" and "corresponding UK claim".

(6) The steps mentioned in sub-paragraph (3) include exercising any powers of set-off that the relevant UK authority would have been entitled to exercise if the foreign claim had been payable to it under an enactment.

(7) Any enactment or rule of law relating to a corresponding UK claim is to apply, with any necessary adaptations, in relation to the foreign claim.

(8) The enactments applied by sub-paragraph (7) include in particular those relating to the recovery of penalties and to the charging and recovery of interest on unpaid amounts.

The relevant UK authority

7 (1) "The relevant UK authority" is—

(*a*) if the foreign claim relates to anything other than an agricultural levy, the Commissioners;

(*b*) if the foreign claim relates to an agricultural levy and the steps are ones to be taken in or in relation to England, the Commissioners concurrently with the Secretary of State;

(*c*) if the foreign claim relates to an agricultural levy and the steps are ones to be taken in or in relation to Wales, the Commissioners concurrently with the Welsh Ministers;

(*d*) if the foreign claim relates to an agricultural levy and the steps are ones to be taken in or in relation to Scotland, the Commissioners concurrently with the Scottish Ministers;

(*e*) if the foreign claim relates to an agricultural levy and the steps are ones to be taken in or in relation to Northern Ireland, the Commissioners concurrently with the Department of Agriculture and Rural Development.

(2) A reference in this paragraph to claims relating to an agricultural levy includes claims for penalties, fees, surcharges, interest or costs arising in connection with an agricultural levy.

Corresponding UK claim

8 (1) In relation to a foreign claim, "corresponding UK claim" means a claim in the United Kingdom of a kind that appears to the relevant UK authority to correspond most closely to the kind of foreign claim to which the foreign claim belongs.
(2) But if the relevant UK authority concludes that there is nothing in the United Kingdom of a kind that is similar to that kind of foreign claim, "corresponding UK claim" is taken to mean a claim for income tax charged in an assessment and due and payable.

Application of relevant enactments

9 (1) In relation to any kind of foreign claim, the relevant UK authority may by regulations make provision as to the application, non-application or adaptation of any enactment or rule of law relating to corresponding UK claims.
(2) Paragraph 6(7) is subject to any provision so made.

Power to make further provision

10 The Treasury may by regulations make provision about procedural or other supplementary matters for the purpose of giving effect to MARD and any MARD-related instrument.

Contested claims

11 (1) The taking or continuation of steps against a person under paragraph 6(3) must be suspended if the person shows that relevant proceedings are pending, or about to be instituted, before a court, tribunal or other competent body in the member State in question.
(2) "Relevant proceedings" are proceedings relevant to the person's liability on the foreign claim.
(3) Relevant proceedings are "pending" so long as an appeal may be brought against any decision in the proceedings.
(4) Sub-paragraph (1) does not apply to steps that may be taken or continued against the person by the application (by virtue of paragraphs 6(7) and 9) of an enactment or rule of law that permits such steps to be taken or continued in similar circumstances in the case of a corresponding UK claim.
(5) Sub-paragraph (1) ceases to apply if the relevant proceedings are not prosecuted or instituted with reasonable speed.

Claims determined in taxpayer's favour

12 (1) Steps under paragraph 6(3) must not be taken or continued against a person if a final decision on the foreign claim has been given in the person's favour by a court, tribunal or other competent body in the member State in question.
(2) For this purpose, a final decision is one against which no appeal lies or against which an appeal lies within a period that has expired without an appeal having been brought.
(3) If the person shows that such a decision has been given in respect of part of the foreign claim, steps under paragraph 6(3) must not be taken or continued in relation to that part.

Liability to pay

13 In relation to any steps against a person under paragraph 6(3), no question may be raised as to the person's liability on the foreign claim except as mentioned in paragraph 12.

Presumption of validity

14 For the purposes of any steps under paragraph 6(3), a request made by an applicant authority in another member State is taken to be duly made in accordance with MARD unless the contrary is proved.

Regulations

15 (1) Regulations under this Schedule are to be made by statutory instrument.
(2) A statutory instrument containing regulations under this Schedule is subject to annulment in pursuance of a resolution of the House of Commons.

Interpretation

16 In this Schedule—

"agricultural levy" has the meaning given by section 6 of the European Communities Act 1972;

"applicant authority" has the same meaning as in MARD;

"the Commissioners" means the Commissioners for Her Majesty's Revenue and Customs;

"enactment" includes—

(*a*) an Act of the Scottish Parliament,

(*b*) a Measure or Act of the National Assembly for Wales, and

(*c*) any Northern Ireland legislation as defined by section 24(5) of the Interpretation Act 1978;

"HMRC" means Her Majesty's Revenue and Customs;

"MARD-related instrument" means any EU instrument (including one made after the passing of this Act) that lays down detailed rules for implementing MARD;

"public authority" means a person with functions of a public nature;

"requested authority" has the same meaning as in MARD.

Consequential amendments etc

17 (1) Section 134 of and Schedule 39 to FA 2002 (which concern Council Directive 2008/55/EC) are repealed with effect from 1 January 2012.

(2) Any outstanding request for assistance made in accordance with Council Directive 2008/55/EC before that date is to be treated on and after that date for the purposes of this Schedule as if it had been made in accordance with MARD.

18 (1) Section 322 of FA 2004 (mutual assistance: customs union with the Principality of Andorra) is amended as follows.

(2) In subsection (2), in the definition of "the Mutual Assistance Recovery Directive", after "as" insert "MARD has".

(3) In that subsection, for the definition of "the UK mutual assistance provisions" substitute—

""the UK mutual assistance provisions" means the provisions of section 87 of the Finance Act 2011 (mutual assistance for recovery of taxes etc) and Schedule 25 to that Act."

(4) For subsection (3) substitute—

"(3) In the UK mutual assistance provisions as they have effect in accordance with subsection (1)—

(a) references (except for the one in paragraph 1 of Schedule 25) to MARD are to be read as references to the EC-Andorra Mutual Assistance Recovery Decision,

(b) references to another member State are to be read as references to the Principality of Andorra,

(c) references to an applicant authority of another member State are to be read as references to the competent authority of the Principality of Andorra,

(d) references to a MARD-related instrument are to be disregarded, and

(e) paragraph 10 of Schedule 25 (power to make further provision) is to be treated as omitted."

(5) In subsection (4), for "section 134(6) of the Finance Act 2002 and paragraph 3 of Schedule 39" substitute "section 87(2) of the Finance Act 2011 and paragraph 9 of Schedule 25".

(6) The amendments made by this paragraph have effect from 1 January 2012.

(7) Any regulations made by virtue of subsection (4) of section 322 of FA 2004 and in force immediately before 1 January 2012 are to have effect on and after that date as if made by virtue of that subsection as amended by sub-paragraph (5).

Application

19 This Schedule has effect in relation to the recovery of sums becoming due at any time, whether before or after this Act is passed.

FINANCE ACT 2012

(2012 Chapter 14)

CONTENTS

PART 6

EXCISE DUTIES

An Act to grant certain duties, to alter other duties, and to amend the law relating to the National Debt and the Public Revenue, and to make further provision in connection with finance.

[17 July 2012]

PART 6

EXCISE DUTIES

Gambling duties

191 Machine games duty

Schedule 24 contains provision replacing amusement machine licence duty with a new excise duty and making related changes to VATA 1994.

194 Remote gambling: double taxation relief

Schedule 25 contains provision for double taxation relief in respect of remote gambling.

PART 7

VALUE ADDED TAX

196 Changes to the categorisation of supplies

(1) Schedule 26 contains provision about the categorisation of supplies for the purposes of value added tax.

(2) Schedule 27 contains provision for an anti-forestalling charge to value added tax related to changes in the descriptions of exempt or zero-rated supplies.

197 Exempt supplies

(1) In Part 1 of Schedule 9 to VATA 1994 (index to exempt supplies of goods and services), at the appropriate place in the table insert—

"Supplies of services by groups involving cost sharing	Group 16".

(2) In Part 2 of that Schedule (the groups), at the end insert—

"GROUP 16—SUPPLIES OF SERVICES BY GROUPS INVOLVING COST SHARING

Item No

1

The supply of services by an independent group of persons where each of the following conditions is satisfied—

(a) each of those persons is a person who is carrying on an activity ("the relevant activity") which is exempt from VAT or in relation to which the person is not a taxable person within the meaning of Article 9 of Council Directive 2006/ 112/EC,

(b) the supply of services is made for the purpose of rendering the members of the group the services directly necessary for the exercise of the relevant activity,

(c) the group merely claims from its members exact reimbursement of their share of the joint expenses, and

(d) the exemption of the supply is not likely to cause distortion of competition."

(3) In section 31 of that Act (exempt supplies and acquisitions), after subsection (2) insert—

"(3) The Treasury may by regulations make an exemption of a group 16 supply of a description specified in the regulations subject to conditions.

(4) Regulations under subsection (3) may—

(a) make different provision for different cases, and

(b) make consequential or transitional provision (including provision amending this Act).

(5) In subsection (3) "group 16 supply" means a supply falling within Group 16 of Schedule 9."

198 Supply of goods or services by public bodies

(1) VATA 1994 is amended as follows.

(2) In section 41 (application to the Crown)—

(a) omit subsection (2), and

(b) in subsection (3)(b) for "a direction under subsection (2) above," substitute "section 41A,".

(3) After that section insert—

"41A Supply of goods or services by public bodies

(1) This section applies where goods or services are supplied by a body mentioned in Article 13(1) of the VAT Directive (status of public bodies as taxable persons) in the course of activities or transactions in which it is engaged as a public authority.

(2) If the supply is in respect of an activity listed in Annex I to the VAT Directive (activities in respect of which public bodies are to be taxable persons), it is to be treated for the purposes of this Act as a supply in the course or furtherance of a business unless it is on such a small scale as to be negligible.

(3) If the supply is not in respect of such an activity, it is to be treated for the purposes of this Act as a supply in the course or furtherance of a business if (and only if) not charging VAT on the supply would lead to a significant distortion of competition.

(4) In this section "the VAT Directive" means Council Directive 2006/112/ EC on the common system of value added tax."

199 Relief from VAT on low value goods: restriction relating to Channel Islands

(1) In Schedule 2 to the Value Added Tax (Imported Goods) Relief Order 1984 (SI 1984/746) (reliefs for goods of certain descriptions), Group 8 (articles sent for miscellaneous purposes) is amended as follows.

(2) The existing Note becomes Note (1) (and accordingly "*Note*" in Group 8 becomes "*Notes*").

(3) After that Note insert—

"(2) Item 8 does not apply in relation to any goods sent from the Channel Islands under a distance selling arrangement.

(3) For the purposes of Note (2)—

"distance selling arrangement", in relation to any goods, means any transaction, or series of transactions, under which the person to whom the goods are sent receives them from a supplier without the simultaneous physical presence of the person and the supplier at any time during the transaction or series of transactions, and

"supplier" means any person who is acting in a commercial or professional capacity."

(4) The amendment of that Schedule by this section is without prejudice to any power to amend that Schedule by subordinate legislation.

(5) The amendments made by this section have effect in relation to goods imported on or after 1 April 2012.

200 Group supplies using an overseas member

(1) VATA 1994 is amended as follows.

(2) In section 43 (groups of companies), in subsection (2C)(c), after "above" insert "and paragraph 8A of Schedule 6".

(3) In section 83 (appeals), in subsection (1)(v) for "or 2" substitute ", 2 or 8A".

(4) In section 97(4) (orders requiring Parliamentary approval within 28 days of being made), in paragraph (f), after "1A(7)" insert "or 8A(7)".

(5) Schedule 6 (valuation: special cases) is amended as follows.

(6) In paragraph 1 (cases where Commissioners may direct value is open market value), in sub-paragraph (5), after "paragraph", in the second place it occurs, insert "8A or".

(7) After paragraph 8 insert—

"8A (1) This paragraph applies where—

(a) a supply ("the intra-group supply") made by a member of a group ("the supplier") to another member of the group is, by virtue of section 43(2A), excluded from the supplies disregarded under section 43(1)(a), and

(b) the representative member of the group satisfies the Commissioners as to the value of each bought-in supply.

(2) "Bought-in supply", in relation to the intra-group supply, means a supply of services to the supplier to which section 43(2A)(c) to (e) refers, so far as that supply is used by the supplier for making the intra-group supply.

(3) The value of the intra-group supply shall be taken to be the total of the relevant amounts in relation to the bought-in supplies.

(4) The relevant amount in relation to a bought-in supply is the value of the bought-in supply, unless a direction is made under subparagraph (5).

(5) If the value of a bought-in supply is less than its open market value, the Commissioners may direct that the relevant amount in relation to that supply is its open market value.

(6) A direction under this paragraph must be given by notice in writing to the representative member, but no direction may be given more than 3 years after the time of the intra-group supply.

(7) The Treasury may by order vary the provision made by this Schedule about the value of supplies of the kind mentioned in subparagraph (1)(a).

(8) An order under sub-paragraph (7) may include incidental, supplemental, consequential or transitional provision (including provision amending section 43 or 83)."

(8) The amendments made by this section have effect in relation to supplies made on or after the day on which this Act is passed.

201 Face-value vouchers

(1) In Schedule 10A to VATA 1994 (face-value vouchers), after paragraph 7 insert—

"Exclusion of single purpose vouchers

7A

Paragraphs 2 to 4, 6 and 7 do not apply in relation to the issue, or any subsequent supply, of a face-value voucher that represents a right to receive goods or services of one type which are subject to a single rate of VAT."

(2) The amendment made by subsection (1) has effect in relation to supplies of face-value vouchers issued on or after 10 May 2012.

(3) Subsection (4) applies where—

(a) a face-value voucher issued before 10 May 2012 is used on or after that date to obtain goods or services,

(b) paragraphs 2 to 4, 6 and 7 of Schedule 10A to VATA 1994 would not have applied in relation to the issue, or any subsequent supply, of the voucher because of paragraph 7A of that Schedule if the voucher had been issued on or after 10 May 2012, and

(c) VAT is not payable under the law of another member State on the supply of the voucher to the user.

(4) The use of the voucher is to be treated for the purposes of VATA 1994 as a supply of the goods or services by the person from whom they are obtained to the user of the voucher.

202 Power to require notification of arrival of means of transport in UK

In Schedule 11 to VATA 1994 (administration, collection and enforcement), in paragraph 2 (accounting for VAT and payment of VAT), after sub-paragraph (5) insert—

"(5A) Regulations under this paragraph may make provision—

(a) for requiring the relevant person to give to the Commissioners such notification of the arrival in the United Kingdom of goods consisting of a means of transport, at such time and in such form and manner, as may be specified in the regulations or by the Commissioners in accordance with the regulations, and

(b) where notification of the arrival of a means of transport acquired from another member State, or imported from a place outside the member States, is required by virtue of paragraph (a), for requiring any VAT on the acquisition or importation to be paid at such time and in such manner as may be specified in the regulations.

(5B) The provision that may be made by regulations made by virtue of sub-paragraph (5A) includes—

(a) provision for a notification required by virtue of that subparagraph to contain such particulars relating to the notified arrival of the means of transport and any VAT chargeable on its acquisition or importation as may be specified in the regulations or by the Commissioners in accordance with the regulations,

(b) provision for such a notification to be given by a person who is not the relevant person and is so specified, or is of a description so specified,

(c) provision for such a notification to contain a declaration, given in such form and by such person as may be so specified, as to the information contained in the notification, and

(d) supplementary, incidental, consequential or transitional provision (including provision amending any provision made by or under this Act or any other enactment).

(5C) Subsection (3) of section 97 (orders subject to Commons approval) applies to a statutory instrument containing any regulations made by virtue of sub-paragraph (5A) which amend an enactment as it applies to an order within subsection (4) of that section.

(5D) For the purposes of sub-paragraph (5A)—

"means of transport" has the same meaning as it has in this Act in the expression "new means of transport" (see section 95);

"relevant person", in relation to the arrival of a means of transport in the United Kingdom, means—

(a) where the means of transport has been acquired in the United Kingdom from another member State, the person who so acquires it,

(b) where it has been imported from a place outside the member States, the person liable to pay VAT on the importation, and

(c) in any other case—

(i) the owner of the means of transport at the time of its arrival in the United Kingdom, or

(ii) where it is subject to a lease or hire agreement, the lessee or hirer of the means of transport at that time."

203 Non-established taxable persons

Schedule 28 contains provision about non-established taxable persons.

204 Administration of VAT

Schedule 29 contains provision about the administration of VAT.

PART 9

MISCELLANEOUS MATTERS

International matters

218 Agreement between UK and Switzerland

(1) Schedule 36 contains provision giving effect to—

(a) an agreement signed on 6 October 2011 between the United Kingdom and the Swiss Confederation on co-operation in the area of taxation, as amended by a protocol signed by them on 20 March 2012 and by a mutual agreement signed by them on 18 April 2012 implementing article XVIII of that protocol, and

(b) the joint declaration (concerning a tax finality payment) forming an integral part of that protocol.

(2) Schedule 36 comes into force on the day on which the agreement of 6 October 2011 enters into force.

(3) In section 23 of the Constitutional Reform and Governance Act 2010, after subsection (2A) insert—

"(2B) Section 20 does not apply to any treaty referred to in section 218(1) of the Finance Act 2012."

219 Penalties: offshore income etc

In paragraph 21A of Schedule 24 to FA 2007 (classification of territories), in sub-paragraph (4)—

(a) omit "and" at the end of paragraph (b), and

(b) at the end of paragraph (c) insert—

"(d) the existence of any other arrangements between the UK and that territory for co-operation in the area of taxation, and

(e) the quality of any such other arrangements (in particular, the extent to which the co-operation provided for in them assists or is likely to assist in the protection of revenue raised from taxation in the UK)."

Commentary—*Simon's Taxes* **A4.562**.

Financial sector regulation

221 Tax consequences of financial sector regulation

(1) The Treasury may by regulations make provision about the tax consequences in relation to securities of any regulatory requirement imposed by any EU legislation (whenever adopted) or enactment on—

(a) persons who are authorised persons for the purposes of the Financial Services and Markets Act 2000 (see section 31 of that Act), or

(b) parent undertakings (as defined in section 420 of that Act) of such persons.

(2) Regulations under this section may, in particular, make provision—

(a) charging any tax or granting, withdrawing or restricting an exemption or other relief from any tax, and

(b) about the treatment of arrangements the purpose, or one of the main purposes, of which is to secure a tax advantage.

(3) Regulations under this section may provide that a reference in the regulations—

(a) to any EU legislation or enactment,

(b) to any document, or

(c) to any provision of any EU legislation, enactment or document is to be construed as a reference to that legislation, enactment, document or provision as amended from time to time.

(4) Regulations under this section—

(a) may apply (with or without modifications) or disapply any enactment,

(b) may modify, amend, repeal or revoke any enactment,

(c) may make different provision for different cases or different purposes, and

(d) may include incidental, consequential, supplementary or transitional provision.

(5) Regulations under this section are to be made by statutory instrument.

(6) No regulations may be made under this section unless a draft of the statutory instrument containing them has been laid before and approved by a resolution of the House of Commons.

(7) In this section—

"arrangements" includes any arrangements, scheme or understanding of any kind, whether or not legally enforceable and whether involving a single transaction or two or more transactions;

"enactment" includes an enactment contained in subordinate legislation (within the meaning of the Interpretation Act 1978), and includes an enactment whenever passed or made;
"tax" includes stamp duty;
"tax advantage" means—
(a) a relief from tax (including a tax credit) or increased relief from tax,
(b) a repayment of tax or increased repayment of tax,
(c) the avoidance, reduction or delay of a charge to tax or an assessment to tax, or
(d) the avoidance of a possible assessment to tax.

Administration

223 Tax agents: dishonest conduct

(1) Schedule 38 contains provision about tax agents who engage in dishonest conduct.
(2) That Schedule comes into force on such day as the Treasury may by order appoint.
(3) An order under subsection (2)—
(a) may make different provision for different purposes, and
(b) may include transitional provision and savings.
(4) The Treasury may by order make any incidental, supplemental, consequential, transitional or saving provision in consequence of Schedule 38.
(5) An order under subsection (4) may—
(a) make different provision for different purposes, and
(b) make provision amending, repealing or revoking any provision made by or under an Act (whenever passed or made).
(6) An order under this section is to be made by statutory instrument.
(7) A statutory instrument containing an order under subsection (4) is subject to annulment in pursuance of a resolution of the House of Commons.

224 Information powers

(1) Schedule 36 to FA 2008 (information and inspection powers) is amended as follows.
(2) After paragraph 5 insert—

"Power to obtain information about persons whose identity can be ascertained

5A

(1) An authorised officer of Revenue and Customs may by notice in writing require a person to provide relevant information about another person ("the taxpayer") if conditions A to D are met.
(2) Condition A is that the information is reasonably required by the officer for the purpose of checking the tax position of the taxpayer.
(3) Condition B is that—
(a) the taxpayer's identity is not known to the officer, but
(b) the officer holds information from which the taxpayer's identity can be ascertained.
(4) Condition C is that the officer has reason to believe that—
(a) the person will be able to ascertain the taxpayer's identity from the information held by the officer, and
(b) the person obtained relevant information about the taxpayer in the course of carrying on a business.
(5) Condition D is that the taxpayer's identity cannot readily be ascertained by other means from the information held by the officer.
(6) "Relevant information" means all or any of the following—
(a) name,
(b) last known address, and
(c) date of birth (in the case of an individual).
(7) This paragraph applies for the purpose of checking the tax position of a class of persons as for the purpose of checking the tax position of a single person (and references to "the taxpayer" are to be read accordingly)."

(3) In paragraph 6 (notices), in sub-paragraph (1), for "or 5" substitute ", 5 or 5A".
(4) In paragraph 31 (right to appeal against notice given under paragraph 5), after "paragraph 5" insert "or 5A".
(5) Accordingly, in the heading immediately before paragraph 31, at the end insert "*or 5A*".
(6) In section 18D of TMA 1970 (savings income: content of regulations under section 18B), in subsection (1), for "sections 17 and 18" substitute "paragraph 1 of Schedule 23 to the Finance Act 2011 (data-gathering powers)".
(7) The amendments made by subsections (1) to (5) apply for the purpose of checking the tax position of a taxpayer as regards periods or tax liabilities whenever arising (whether before, on or after the day on which this Act is passed).

(8) The amendment made by subsection (6) is treated as having come into force on 1 April 2012.

Commentary—*Simon's Taxes* **A6.317, D1305**.

PART 10

FINAL PROVISIONS

228 Interpretation

(1) In this Act—

"ALDA 1979" means the Alcoholic Liquor Duties Act 1979,
"BGDA 1981" means the Betting and Gaming Duties Act 1981,
"CAA 2001" means the Capital Allowances Act 2001,
"CEMA 1979" means the Customs and Excise Management Act 1979,
"CRCA 2005" means the Commissioners for Revenue and Customs Act 2005,
"CTA 2009" means the Corporation Tax Act 2009,
"CTA 2010" means the Corporation Tax Act 2010,
"F(No 3)A 2010" means the Finance (No 3) Act 2010,
"HODA 1979" means the Hydrocarbon Oil Duties Act 1979,
"ICTA" means the Income and Corporation Taxes Act 1988,
"IHTA 1984" means the Inheritance Tax Act 1984,
"ITA 2007" means the Income Tax Act 2007,
"ITEPA 2003" means the Income Tax (Earnings and Pensions) Act 2003,
"ITTOIA 2005" means the Income Tax (Trading and Other Income) Act 2005,
"OTA 1975" means the Oil Taxation Act 1975,
"PRTA 1980" means the Petroleum Revenue Tax Act 1980,
"TCGA 1992" means the Taxation of Chargeable Gains Act 1992,
"TIOPA 2010" means the Taxation (International and Other Provisions) Act 2010,
"TMA 1970" means the Taxes Management Act 1970,
"TPDA 1979" means the Tobacco Products Duty Act 1979,
"VATA 1994" means the Value Added Tax Act 1994, and
"VERA 1994" means the Vehicle Excise and Registration Act 1994.

(2) In this Act—

"FA", followed by a year, means the Finance Act of that year;
"F(No 2)A", followed by a year, means the Finance (No 2) Act of that year.

229 Short title

This Act may be cited as the Finance Act 2012.

SCHEDULE 24

MACHINE GAMES DUTY

Section 191

PART 1

IMPOSITION OF DUTY

The duty

1 A duty of excise, to be known as machine games duty, is to be charged on the playing of dutiable machine games in the United Kingdom.

Dutiable machine games

2 (1) A "machine game" is a game (whether of skill or chance or both) played on a machine for a prize.

(2) A machine game is "dutiable" if—

(a) the prize or at least one of the prizes that can be won from playing the game on the machine is or includes cash, and
(b) the maximum amount of cash that a player can win from playing the game on the machine exceeds the lowest charge payable for playing the game on the machine.

(3) "Cash" means money or anything that may reasonably be considered to equate to money, including—

(a) anything that can be used in the same way as if it were money, and
(b) anything that allows a person to obtain money on demand or otherwise represents a promise to pay a person money on demand.

(4) The things mentioned in sub-paragraph (3) include—

(a) anything of an intangible nature (such as points), and
(b) anything that a person has as a result of the taking of any step by someone else (such as the crediting of an account).

(5) If an adult would reasonably assume that a machine game satisfies the tests in sub-paragraph (2)(a) and (b) (taking into account the way in which the game is presented and all the other circumstances of the case), the game is taken to be a dutiable machine game, whether or not it does in fact satisfy those tests.

(6) In identifying for the purposes of this paragraph the lowest charge payable for playing a game, any offer that waives or permits a player to pay less than the charge that the player would be required to pay without the offer is disregarded.

(7) Paragraph 3 makes further provision about what counts as a dutiable machine game for the purposes of this Schedule.

3 (1) A game that would otherwise be a dutiable machine game does not count as one if—

(a) it involves betting on future real events,

(b) bingo duty is charged on the playing of it,

(c) lottery duty is charged on the taking of a ticket or chance in it, or

(d) it is a real game of chance and playing it—

(i) amounts to dutiable gaming for the purposes of section 10 of FA 1997, or

(ii) would do so but for subsection (3), (3B) or (4) of that section.

(2) A "real game of chance" is a game of chance (within the meaning of [Part 3 of FA 2014][1]) that is non-virtual.

(3) A game consisting of several stages counts as a dutiable machine game if—

(a) at least one stage would (if played on its own) be a dutiable machine game, or

(b) the stages (taken together) amount to a dutiable machine game.

(4) If more than one game can be played on a given machine, each game is to be considered separately in deciding whether it is a dutiable machine game.

Amendments—

[1] Words in sub-para (2) substituted for words "BGDA 1981" by FA 2014 s 196, Sch 28 para 31(1), (2) with effect from 1 December 2014 (FA 2014 s 198(2)).

4 The Treasury may by order specify criteria to be taken into account in deciding—

(a) whether a particular game (or class of game) falls within the definitions in paragraph 2(1) and (2), and

(b) what counts as a single go at playing a particular game (or class of game).

[Types of machine

5 (1) Machines are divided into three types for the purposes of machine games duty.

(2) A machine is a "type 1 machine" if it can be demonstrated that—

(a) the highest charge payable for playing a dutiable machine game on the machine does not exceed 20p, and

(b) the maximum amount of cash that can be won from playing a dutiable machine game on the machine does not exceed £10.

(3) A machine is a "type 2 machine" if—

(a) it is not a type 1 machine, and

(b) it can be demonstrated that the highest charge payable for playing a dutiable machine game on the machine does not exceed £5.

(4) Any other machine is a "type 3 machine".

(5) The Treasury may by order substitute for a sum for the time being specified in sub-paragraph (2)(a) or (b) or (3)(b) such higher sum as may be specified in the order.][1]

Amendments—[1] Para 5 substituted by FA 2014 s 124(1), (2) with effect in relation to the playing of machine games on or after 1 March 2015.

How the duty is charged

6 (1) Machine games duty is charged on a taxable person's total net takings in an accounting period for each type of machine.

[(2) The amount of the duty is found by—

(a) applying the lower rate to the person's total net takings in the accounting period for type 1 machines,

(b) applying the standard rate to the person's total net takings in the accounting period for type 2 machines,

(c) applying the higher rate to the person's total net takings in the accounting period for type 3 machines, and

(d) aggregating the results.][1]

(3) This is subject to paragraph 10 (negative amounts of duty).

(4) The person's "total net takings" in the accounting period for a type of machine are the sum of the person's net takings in the period for all the relevant machines of that type.

(5) The person's "net takings" in the period for each relevant machine are determined in accordance with paragraphs 7 and 8.

(6) If any of the relevant machines changes type during the accounting period—

(a) the net takings in the part of the period before the change and the net takings in the part after the change are to be allocated separately in calculating the person's total net takings in the period for each type of machine, and

(b) if it is not possible to identify the part of a period to which an amount relates, the amount is to be apportioned on a just and reasonable basis.

(7) For the meaning of "relevant machine" in relation to a taxable person and an accounting period, see paragraph 50.

Amendments—[1] Sub-para (2) substituted by FA 2014 s 124(1), (3) with effect in relation to the playing of machine games on or after 1 March 2015.

Net takings per machine

7 (1) A taxable person's net takings in an accounting period for a relevant machine are—

(a) the takings, less

(b) the payouts.

(2) The takings are the charges that become due at any material time from players for playing dutiable machine games on that machine (irrespective of when the games are played or the prizes are paid out).

(3) The payouts are the prizes (whether cash or non-cash) that are paid out at any material time to players as a result of playing dutiable machine games on that machine (irrespective of when the games are played or the charges become due).

(4) Sub-paragraph (3) does not include prizes paid out to—

(a) a person who is a registrable person in respect of the premises where the machine is located,

(b) a representative or employee of such a person at those premises, or

(c) a person acting for or at the direction of a person within paragraph (a).

(5) Sub-paragraph (3) does not include prizes paid out unlawfully (for example, a prize paid out to a child or young person in breach of a condition attached to an operating licence by virtue of section 83(1)(b) of the Gambling Act 2005).

(6) If it is not reasonably practicable to attribute charges and prizes to dutiable machine games or to apportion them between dutiable machine games and other games or other activities, any attribution or apportionment is to be done on a just and reasonable basis.

(7) "Material time" means any time in the accounting period when the person is liable for machine games duty in respect of the machine.

(8) The Commissioners may by regulations make provision about the point in time at which a charge is taken to become due, or a prize is taken to be paid out, for the purposes of this paragraph.

(9) If a machine game is played in pursuance of an offer that permits the player to pay nothing or less than the charge that the player would be required to pay without the offer, the charge (if any) is treated as becoming due when the player plays the game.

(10) A prize that is paid out using a system involving redemption tickets, points or anything similar is taken to be paid out when the prize is redeemed (rather than when the means of redemption is issued or communicated to the winner).

(11) Sub-paragraphs (9) and (10) do not limit the power in sub-paragraph (8).

8 (1) In calculating the takings and the payouts under paragraph 7, the following amounts are to be left out of account—

(a) amounts arising from playing dutiable machine games on a domestic occasion, and

(b) amounts arising in any other circumstances specified by the Treasury by order.

(2) The power in sub-paragraph (1)(b)—

(a) may be exercised generally or in relation to particular cases or kinds of case, and

(b) may include provision requiring specified conditions to be met before amounts are left out of account.

[The rates

9 (1) The lower rate is 5%.

(2) The standard rate is 20%.

(3) The higher rate is 25%.

(4) If a rate changes during an accounting period—

(a) the old rate is to be applied to the person's total net takings in the part of the period before the change, and

(b) the new rate is to be applied to the person's total net takings in the part of the period after the change.

(5) If it is not possible to identify for the purposes of sub-paragraph (4) the part of the period to which an amount relates, it is to be apportioned on a just and reasonable basis.][1]

Amendments—[1] Para 9 substituted by FA 2014 s 124(1), (4) with effect in relation to the playing of machine games on or after 1 March 2015.

Negative amounts of duty

10 (1) If the calculation of the amount of machine games duty for which a taxable person is liable for an accounting period results in a negative amount ("amount X")—

(a) the amount of machine games duty for which that person is liable for that period is treated as nil, and

(b) the amount of duty for which that person is liable for the next accounting period is to be reduced by amount X.

(2) Sub-paragraph (1) applies to an accounting period whether or not amount X results wholly or partly from the previous application of that subparagraph.

(3) Subject to any reduction required by sub-paragraph (1)(b), the person is not entitled to any repayment or refund of machine games duty in respect of amount X.

Who is liable

11 (1) A person is liable for machine games duty in respect of a machine at any time if at the time—

(a) the person is responsible for the premises where the machine is located (see paragraph 12),

(b) the machine is available there for use by others for playing dutiable machine games on it, and

(c) the machine is not an excluded dual-use machine (see paragraph 13).

(2) If, at any time, there is more than one person who satisfies sub-paragraph (1)(a) to (c) in respect of a machine, each of them is jointly and severally liable for the duty.

(3) A person who is liable for machine games duty in accordance with this paragraph is referred to as a "taxable person".

Responsible for premises

12 (1) This paragraph sets out who is "responsible" for premises for the purposes of paragraph 11.

(2) If a person is registered in respect of premises, that person is responsible for the premises.

(3) A person is "registered" at any time in respect of premises if at the time there is an entry in force for that person in the MGD register in respect of those premises.

(4) If no-one is registered in respect of premises, any person who is a registrable person in respect of the premises or a representative of such a person is responsible for the premises.

(5) Paragraphs 20 to 24 make further provision about registration and registrable persons.

Excluded dual-use machines

13 (1) A machine is an "excluded dual-use machine" if—

(a) it is capable of being used both for playing machine games and for some other purpose that is not related to playing machine games, and

(b) condition A or B is met.

(2) Condition A is that the machine is not designed, adapted or presented in such a way as to—

(a) facilitate its use for playing dutiable machine games, or

(b) draw attention to the possibility of its use for playing such games.

(3) Condition B is that the machine is so designed, adapted or presented but the person mentioned in paragraph 11(1) does not know, and could not reasonably be expected to know, that it is.

(4) References to a machine being "adapted" include a machine to which anything has been done, including the installation of computer software on it.

(5) The Commissioners may by order specify criteria to be taken into account in deciding whether a machine falls within the definition in sub-paragraph (1).

(6) The Treasury may by order amend this paragraph.

Accounting periods

14 (1) An accounting period for machine games duty is a period of 3 consecutive months.

(2) The first day of an accounting period is such day as HMRC may direct.

(3) A direction under sub-paragraph (2) may apply generally or only to a particular case or class of case.

(4) HMRC may agree with a registered person to make either or both of the following changes for the purposes of that person's liability to machine games duty—

(a) to treat specified periods (whether longer or shorter than 3 months) as accounting periods,

(b) to begin accounting periods on days other than those applying by virtue of sub-paragraph (2).

(5) HMRC may by direction make transitional arrangements for periods (whether of 3 months or otherwise) to be treated as accounting periods where—
(a) a person becomes or ceases to be registered, or
(b) an agreement under sub-paragraph (4) begins or ends.
(6) If there is reason to believe that a person who is liable for machine games duty may not discharge that liability as it falls due from time to time—
(a) HMRC may by direction specify shorter periods to be treated as accounting periods for the purposes of that person's liability to machine games duty,
(b) any such direction continues to have effect until it is withdrawn by HMRC (unless otherwise specified in the direction), and
(c) withdrawal of a direction does not prevent the giving of further directions in respect of the same person.

Valuing prizes

15 (1) This paragraph applies in valuing prizes for the purposes of this Schedule (including in determining the maximum amount of cash that can be won from playing a machine game).
(2) The value of a prize includes any portion that—
(a) represents a refund of the charge payable for playing the game, or
(b) is calculated by reference to the amount of any such charge.
(3) The value of a prize in the form of something that is reasonably considered to equate to money is equal to the amount of money to which the thing is reasonably considered to equate.
(4) For a prize in the form of a currency other than sterling or in the form of something that is reasonably considered to equate to such a currency—
(a) the value of the prize is, in relation to any day, the sterling equivalent of that currency determined by reference to the London closing rate for that currency for the previous day, and
(b) for the purposes of paragraph 7(3), the day in relation to which the value is assessed is the last day of the relevant accounting period.
(5) The value of a prize other than cash depends on the person ("A") from whom the person paying out the prize ("B") obtained it—
(a) if A was not connected with B when B obtained the prize from A, the value is the cost to B of obtaining the prize from A,
(b) if A was connected with B when B obtained the prize from A, the value is the smaller of—
(i) the cost to B of obtaining the prize from A, and
(ii) the amount that it would have cost B, at the time B obtained the prize, to obtain it from a person not connected with B.
(6) Whether A is connected with B is to be determined in accordance with section 1122 of CTA 2010.
(7) If the value of a prize other than cash cannot reasonably be determined in accordance with sub-paragraph (5), the value of the prize is such amount as is just and reasonable.
(8) For the purposes of sub-paragraph (5), an amount paid by way of value added tax on the acquisition of a thing is to be treated as part of its cost (whether or not the amount is taken into account for the purpose of a credit or refund).
(9) The Commissioners may by regulations make further provision about the way in which prizes are to be valued for the purposes of this Schedule.
(10) This paragraph applies to a part of a prize as it applies to a whole prize, and references to a prize are to be read accordingly.

Valuing charges

16 (1) This paragraph applies in determining for the purposes of this Schedule the amount of a charge (or the highest or lowest charge) payable or due for playing a machine game.
(2) If the amount of a charge in money's worth cannot be determined, it is assumed to be such amount as is just and reasonable.
(3) If a composite charge is payable or due for the opportunity to play a machine game more than once, the amount of the charge payable or due for each individual go is to be determined on a just and reasonable basis.
(4) If a composite charge is payable or due for the opportunity to play a machine game and for something else, the amount of the charge payable or due for playing the game is to be determined on a just and reasonable basis.
(5) The Commissioners may by regulations make further provision about the way in which the amount of charges is to be determined for the purposes of this Schedule.
(6) Sub-paragraph (7) applies if—
(a) a dutiable machine game is played in pursuance of an offer that permits the player to pay nothing or less than the charge that the player would have been required to pay without the offer,

(b) the offer was made available to the player by way of winnings from an activity in respect of which another duty of excise or value added tax is charged, and

(c) the value of the offer is deductible in calculating the amount of that other duty or value added tax payable in respect of that activity.

(7) The amount of the charge due from the player for playing the dutiable machine game is taken for the purposes of paragraph 7 to be the amount that the player would have been required to pay without the offer.

(8) Regulations under sub-paragraph (5) may include provision extending or modifying the circumstances in which sub-paragraph (7) applies.

Collection and management

17 The Commissioners are responsible for the collection and management of machine games duty.

Returns

18 (1) The Commissioners may make regulations requiring registrable persons to make returns to HMRC in respect of relevant machines.

(2) Regulations under this paragraph may in particular make provision about—

(a) liability to make a return,

(b) timing,

(c) form,

(d) content,

(e) method of making (including provision requiring returns to be made electronically),

(f) declarations,

(g) authentication, and

(h) when a return is to be treated as made.

Regulations—Machine Games Duty Regulations, SI 2012/2500.

Assessment and payment

19 (1) The Commissioners may make regulations about payment of machine games duty.

(2) The regulations may in particular make provision about—

(a) timing,

(b) instalments,

(c) methods of payment (including provision requiring payments to be made electronically),

(d) when payment is to be treated as made, and

(e) the process and effect of assessments by HMRC of amounts due.

(3) Subject to regulations under this paragraph, section 12 of FA 1994 (assessment) applies in relation to liability to pay machine games duty.

Regulations—Machine Games Duty Regulations, SI 2012/2500.

Registration

20 (1) The Commissioners must maintain a register of those responsible for premises where relevant machines are located.

(2) The register is to be known as the MGD register.

(3) A person must not make a relevant machine available for use by others for playing dutiable machine games on it unless a registrable person (whether that person or someone else) is registered in respect of the premises where the machine is located.

(4) Paragraph 21 identifies who is a registrable person in respect of premises.

(5) This paragraph does not apply in relation to a relevant machine if it is reasonable to expect that the only takings and the only payouts in respect of the machine would be amounts that would be left out of account by virtue of paragraph 8.

Registrable persons

21 (1) If a person holds a relevant licence or permit in respect of premises, that person is a registrable person in respect of those premises.

(2) But if the premises are leased to a person ("T") for the purposes of an activity for which an alcohol licence is required and the alcohol licence in respect of the premises is held by someone else, T (and not the licence-holder) is a registrable person in respect of those premises.

(3) If the premises are a stall at a travelling fair, each of the following is a registrable person in respect of the premises—

(a) the holder of the stall, and

(b) the person in charge of the fair.

(4) For premises not falling within any of the preceding sub-paragraphs, each person listed in sub-paragraph (5) is a registrable person in respect of the premises.
(5) The persons are—
(a) a person required to hold a relevant licence or permit in respect of the premises,
(b) an owner, lessee or occupier of the premises,
(c) a person who is responsible to the owner, lessee or occupier for the management of the premises,
(d) a person who is responsible for controlling the use of machines that are made available on the premises for use by others for playing dutiable machine games on them, and
(e) a person who is responsible for controlling the admission of persons to the premises or for providing persons resorting to the premises with goods or services.
(6) "Relevant licence or permit" is defined in paragraph 22.
(7) "Alcohol licence" means—
(a) a premises licence issued under Part 3 of the Licensing Act 2003 that authorises the supply of alcohol for consumption on the licensed premises,
(b) a premises licence issued under Part 3 of the Licensing (Scotland) Act 2005, except where such a licence only applies to the sale of alcohol for consumption off the premises, and
(c) a licence issued under the Licensing (Northern Ireland) Order 1996 (SI 1996/3158 (NI 22)), except where such a licence only applies to the sale of intoxicating liquor by retail for consumption off the premises.
(8) "Travelling fair" means a fair—
(a) consisting wholly or principally of the provision of amusements,
(b) provided wholly or principally by persons who travel from place to place for the purpose of providing such fairs, and
(c) held at a place no part of which has been used for the provision of such a fair on more than 27 days in the same calendar year.

22 (1) A "relevant licence or permit" is—
(a) a licence issued under Part 8 of the Gambling Act 2005,
(b) a family entertainment centre gaming machine permit as defined in section 247 of that Act,
(c) a club gaming permit as defined in section 271 of that Act,
(d) a club machine permit as defined in section 273 of that Act,
(e) a prize gaming permit as defined in section 289 of that Act,
(f) an on-premises alcohol licence or a relevant Scottish licence as defined, in each case, in section 277 of that Act but only if a licence or permit listed above is not held in respect of the same premises,
(g) a club premises certificate granted under Part 4 of the Licensing Act 2003 but only if a licence or permit listed above is not held in respect of the same premises,
(h) a certificate of registration within the meaning of the Betting, Gaming Lotteries and Amusements (Northern Ireland) Order 1985 (SI 1985/1204 (NI 11)),
(i) a bookmaking office licence within the meaning of that Order,
(j) a bingo club licence within the meaning of that Order,
(k) an amusement permit within the meaning of that Order,
(l) a certificate of registration within the meaning of the Registration of Clubs (Northern Ireland) Order 1996 (SI 1996/3159 (NI 23)), or
(m) a licence issued under the Licensing (Northern Ireland) Order 1996 (SI 1996/3158 (NI 22)) but only if a licence, permit or certificate listed above is not held in respect of the same premises.
(2) In sub-paragraph (1), "listed above" means listed in any of the preceding provisions of that sub-paragraph.
(3) The Treasury may by order amend this paragraph to add to, vary or restrict the list in sub-paragraph (1).

Compulsory registration

23 (1) Sub-paragraph (2) applies if—
(a) it appears to HMRC that a relevant machine is being made available by anyone at premises for use by others for playing dutiable machine games on it, and
(b) no-one is registered in respect of the premises.
(2) HMRC may give a notice under this paragraph to any person they believe to be a registrable person in respect of the premises.
(3) The notice is referred to as a "registration notice".
(4) A person to whom a registration notice is given may appeal to an appeal tribunal against the notice.

(5) The appeal may be made on either or both of the following grounds—

(a) that the person is not a registrable person in respect of the premises,

(b) that relevant machines are not being made available at the premises for use by others for playing dutiable machine games on them.

(6) The appeal must be made within the period of 30 days beginning with the date of the registration notice.

(7) If—

(a) no appeal is made within that period, or

(b) an appeal made within that period is dismissed or withdrawn,

HMRC may proceed to register the person in respect of the premises (unless another person has since become registered in respect of them).

(8) Registration under this paragraph is treated as made with effect from the date of the registration notice.

Procedure for registration, de-registration etc

24 (1) The Commissioners may make regulations about registration.

(2) Regulations under this paragraph may in particular make provision about—

(a) the procedure for applying for registration (including provision requiring applications to be made electronically),

(b) the timing of applications,

(c) the information to be provided,

(d) the giving of registration notices and the making of appeals against them,

(e) the procedure for compulsory registration under paragraph 23,

(f) notification of changes to the register,

(g) de-registration, and

(h) re-registration after a person ceases to be registered.

(3) The regulations may permit HMRC to make registration, or continued registration, subject to conditions.

(4) Those conditions may in particular require—

(a) the provision of security for the payment of machine games duty, and

(b) (in the case of a foreign person) the appointment of a United Kingdom representative with responsibility for discharging liability to machine games duty.

(5) In sub-paragraph (4) "foreign person" means a person who—

(a) in the case of an individual, is not usually resident in the United Kingdom,

(b) in the case of a body corporate, does not have an established place of business in the United Kingdom, and

(c) in any other case, does not include an individual who is usually resident in the United Kingdom.

(6) The regulations may include provision for the registration of groups of persons; and may provide for the modification of the provisions of this Part of this Schedule in their application to groups.

(7) The modifications may, for example, include a modification ensuring that, where a representative member of a group is registered in place of the members, each member will be jointly and severally liable for the duty payable by the representative member on behalf of the group.

Regulations—Machine Games Duty Regulations, SI 2012/2500.

Publication of register

25 (1) The MGD register is to contain such details of those who are entered on the register and of the premises in respect of which they are registered as the Commissioners think fit.

(2) The Commissioners may publish the register (or a part of it).

(3) If they choose not to publish it or they choose to publish only a part of it, the Commissioners must nonetheless make arrangements for the provision of a copy of an entry in the register (or the unpublished part of it) to a member of the public on request.

(4) But the Commissioners may refuse a request under sub-paragraph (3) if the person making the request does not pay a fee specified by the Commissioners.

(5) The fee must not exceed the reasonable cost (including any indirect cost) of meeting the request.

Profit-sharers

26 (1) Sub-paragraph (2) applies if—

(a) it appears to HMRC that machine games duty may be chargeable in respect of a machine,

(b) no-one is registered in respect of the premises where the machine is located, and

(c) either—

(i) HMRC do not know the identity of any of those responsible for the premises (see paragraph 12), or

(ii) HMRC do know the identity of one or more such persons but none of them is in the United Kingdom.

(2) HMRC may give a notice under this paragraph to any person they believe to be beneficially entitled to a share of the machine's takings.

(3) The notice must inform the person to whom it is given ("P") that P will become liable to pay a share of the duty in accordance with this paragraph unless, within the specified period—

(a) P provides HMRC with sufficient information to identify a person in the United Kingdom who is responsible for the premises, or

(b) P satisfies HMRC that, when P became beneficially entitled to a share of the machine's takings, P took all reasonable steps to ascertain that a registrable person was registered in respect of the premises.

(4) The specified period is—

(a) such period of 30 days or more as is specified in the notice, or

(b) such other period as may be agreed between HMRC and P.

(5) If P fails to satisfy sub-paragraph (3)(a) or (b) within the specified period, HMRC may assess to the best of their judgement an amount equal to P's share of the machine games duty that would have been due in respect of the machine for an accounting period on the assumptions set out in subparagraph (6).

(6) The assumptions are—

(a) that P had been liable for machine games duty in respect of the machine in the accounting period in accordance with paragraph 11,

(b) that the machine had been the only machine in respect of which P was so liable, and

(c) that the dutiable machine games in respect of which P is beneficially entitled to a share of the takings had been the only dutiable machine games played on the machine.

(7) P's share is a percentage equal to the share of the machine's takings to which P is beneficially entitled.

(8) An assessment under this paragraph may relate to more than one machine, more than one set of premises and more than one accounting period.

(9) But it may not relate to a period that began more than 4 years before the date of the assessment.

(10) An amount assessed under this paragraph is deemed to be an amount of machine games duty assessed under section 12 of FA 1994 and due from P in accordance with regulations under paragraph 19 of this Schedule.

(11) P is not entitled to any repayment from HMRC of an amount assessed under this paragraph if HMRC subsequently identify a person responsible for the premises.

(12) But if, after P has paid such an amount, HMRC make an assessment under section 12 of FA 1994 of an amount of machine games duty due from another person in respect of the same takings from the same machine for the same accounting period, account must be taken in that assessment of the amount paid by P.

Reviews and appeals

27 (1) The decisions mentioned in sub-paragraph (2) are to be treated as if they were listed in subsection (2) of section 13A of FA 1994 (customs and excise reviews and appeals: meaning of "relevant decision") and, accordingly, as if they were relevant decisions for the purposes mentioned in subsection (1) of that section.

(2) The decisions are—

(a) a decision of HMRC to refuse a request for an agreement under paragraph 14,

(b) a decision to give a direction under that paragraph,

(c) a decision not to give such a direction,

(d) a decision of HMRC under regulations by virtue of paragraph 24(2),

(e) a decision of HMRC about security by virtue of paragraph 24(4)(a), and

(f) a decision of HMRC about the appointment of a United Kingdom representative by virtue of paragraph 24(4)(b).

Interest

28 (1) This paragraph applies if an order is made under section 104(3) of FA 2009 appointing a day on which sections 101 to 103 of that Act are to come into force for the purposes of machine games duty.

(2) Interest charged under section 101 of that Act on an amount of machine games duty (or an amount enforceable as if it were machine games duty) may be enforced as if it were an amount of machine games duty payable by the person liable for the amount on which the interest is charged.

Penalties and enforcement

29 In Schedule 24 to FA 2007 (penalties for errors), in the Table in paragraph 1, after the entry relating to remote gaming duty insert—

"Machine games duty	Return under regulations under paragraph 18 of Schedule 24 to FA 2012."

30 In Schedule 41 to FA 2008 (penalties: failure to notify and certain VAT and excise wrongdoing), in the Table in paragraph 1, after the entry relating to remote gaming duty insert—

"Machine games duty	Obligation under paragraph 20(3) of Schedule 24 to FA 2012 (obligation to register in respect of premises)."

31 In Schedule 55 to FA 2009 (penalty for failure to make returns etc), in the Table in paragraph 1, after item 28 insert—

"29	Machine games duty	Return under regulations under paragraph 18 of Schedule 24 to FA 2012".

32 In that Schedule, in each of the following provisions, for "28" substitute "29"—
(a) paragraph 2(1)(b),
(b) paragraph 13A(1), and
(c) paragraph 13F(1).

33 In Schedule 56 to FA 2009 (penalty for failure to make payments on time), in the Table in paragraph 1, after item 11M insert—

"11N	Machine games duty	Amount payable under paragraph 6 of Schedule 24 to FA 2012 (except an amount falling within item 17A, 23 or 24)	The date determined by or under regulations under paragraph 19 of Schedule 24 to FA 2012 as the date by which the amount must be paid".

34 In that Schedule, in each of the following provisions, for "11M" substitute "11N"—
(a) items 17A, 23 and 24 of the Table in paragraph 1,
(b) paragraph 2(c),
(c) paragraph 3(1)(b),
(d) paragraph 8A(1), and
(e) paragraph 8F(1).

35 (1) Contravention of a provision mentioned in sub-paragraph (2) attracts a penalty under section 9 of FA 1994 (penalties) and also attracts daily penalties under that section.
(2) The provisions are—
(a) any provision of regulations made under paragraph 18,
(b) any provision of regulations made under paragraph 19,
(c) paragraph 20(3), and
(d) any provision of regulations made under paragraph 24.

Forfeiture

36 (1) A machine is liable to forfeiture if—
(a) an officer of Revenue and Customs finds it on any premises,
(b) the officer is satisfied that it is being, has been or is about to be made available on the premises for use by others for playing dutiable machine games on it, and
(c) condition A or B is met.
(2) Condition A is that—
(a) no-one is registered in respect of the premises, and

(b) there is a serious risk that any machine games duty chargeable in respect of the machine would not be paid.

(3) Condition B is that the officer is satisfied that an amount of machine games duty has become due and payable in respect of the machine, but has not been paid.

Offences

37 (1) A person commits an offence if the person is knowingly concerned in, or in the taking of steps with a view to, the fraudulent evasion (by that person or any other person) of any machine games duty.

(2) A person guilty of an offence under this paragraph is liable—

(a) on conviction on indictment, to imprisonment for a term not exceeding 7 years or a fine, or both;

(b) on summary conviction, to imprisonment for a term not exceeding 12 months or a fine not exceeding the maximum amount, or both,

(3) The maximum amount is the greater of—

(a) [£20,000][2], and

(b) three times the duty or other amount that is unpaid or the payment of which is sought to be avoided.

(4) In the application of this paragraph—

(a) in England and Wales, in relation to an offence committed before the commencement of section 154(1) of the Criminal Justice Act 2003, or

(b) in Northern Ireland,

the reference in sub-paragraph (2)(b) to 12 months is to be read as a reference to 6 months.

(5) Section 27 of BGDA 1981 (offences by bodies corporate) has effect for the purposes of any offence under this paragraph as it has effect for the purposes of [the offence][1] mentioned in that section.

Cross references See Legal Aid, Sentencing and Punishment of Offenders Act 2012 (Fines on Summary Conviction) Regulations, SI 2015/664 reg 2(1), Sch 1 para 85 (offences under sub-s (1) do not apply for the purposes of the Legal Aid, Sentencing and Punishment of Offenders Act 2012 s 85(1))

Amendments—

1 Words in sub-para (5) substituted for words "the offences" by FA 2014 s 196, Sch 28 para 31(1), (3) with effect from 1 December 2014 (FA 2014 s 198(2)).

2 In sub-para (3)(*a*), figure substituted by the Legal Aid, Sentencing and Punishment of Offenders Act 2012 (Fines on Summary Conviction) Regulations, SI 2015/664 reg 2(2), Sch 2 paras 1, 13 with effect from 12 March 2015 in relation to England and Wales only.

Protection of officers

38 Section 31 of BGDA 1981 applies in relation to machine games duty as it applies in relation to [bingo duty][1].

Amendments—1 Words substituted for words "remote gaming duty" by FA 2014 s 196, Sch 28 para 31(1), (4) with effect from 1 December 2014 (FA 2014 s 198(2)).

Orders and regulations

39 (1) This paragraph applies to orders and regulations under this Part of this Schedule.

(2) Orders and regulations—

(a) may make provision that applies generally or only for specified purposes,

(b) may make different provision for different purposes, and

(c) may include transitional provision and savings.

(3) Regulations may confer a discretion on HMRC.

(4) Orders and regulations are to be made by statutory instrument.

(5) For the purposes of making an order under paragraph 8(1)(b)—

(a) the statutory instrument containing the order must be laid before the House of Commons, and

(b) the order ceases to have effect at the end of the period of 28 days beginning with the day on which it was made unless, during that period, it is approved by a resolution of the House of Commons.

(6) In reckoning the 28-day period, no account is to be taken of any time during which—

(a) Parliament is dissolved or prorogued, or

(b) the House of Commons is adjourned for more than 4 days.

(7) An order ceasing to have effect by virtue of sub-paragraph (5)(b) does not affect—

(a) anything previously done under the order, or

(b) the making of a new order.

(8) A statutory instrument containing an order under paragraph 13(6) or 22(3) may not be made unless a draft of the instrument has been laid before and approved by a resolution of the House of Commons.

(9) Subject to sub-paragraphs (5) and (8), a statutory instrument containing an order or regulations is subject to annulment in pursuance of a resolution of the House of Commons.

Regulations—Machine Games Duty Regulations, SI 2012/2500.

Transitional provision

40 (1) The Commissioners may by notice direct that regulations under paragraph 24 (procedure for registration, de-registration etc) are to apply in relation to the period before the go-live date with the modifications specified in the notice.

(2) A notice under sub-paragraph (1) must be published by the Commissioners.

(3) For a person who, on the go-live date, is responsible for premises where a relevant machine is located, the first accounting period is to be the period beginning with that day and ending with—

(a) the day before the day on which the next accounting period is to begin by virtue of a direction given under paragraph 14(2), or

(b) such other day as is necessary to give effect to an agreement made under paragraph 14(4).

Consequential amendments

41 (1) Section 1(1) of CEMA 1979 (interpretation) is amended as follows.

(2) In the definition of "the revenue trade provisions of the customs and excise Acts", at the end insert—

"(f) the provisions of Part 1 of Schedule 24 to the Finance Act 2012;".

(3) In the definition of "revenue trader", in paragraph (a)—

(a) omit "or" at the end of sub-paragraph (ic),

(b) after that sub-paragraph insert—

"(id) being responsible for premises where relevant machines are located (within the meaning of Part 1 of Schedule 24 to the Finance Act 2012); or", and

(c) in sub-paragraph (ii), for "or (ic)" substitute ", (ic) or (id)".

42 (1) For section 118BC of that Act (inspection powers: gaming duty) substitute—

"118BC Inspection powers: gaming duty and machine games duty

(1) Subsection (2) applies to premises if an officer has reasonable cause to believe that—

(a) section 10 gaming is taking place, has taken place or is about to take place on the premises, or

(b) machines are located on the premises in respect of which a person is, has been or is about to become liable for machine games duty.

(2) The officer may at any reasonable time enter and inspect the premises and inspect—

(a) accounts, records and other documents in the custody or control of any relevant person, and

(b) any relevant equipment.

(3) Subsection (1) does not permit an officer to enter or inspect a particular part of premises if—

(a) the officer has no reasonable cause to believe that paragraph (a) or, as the case may be, (b) of that subsection is satisfied with respect to that particular part, and

(b) the part is used solely as a dwelling.

(4) An officer may at any reasonable time (whether or not as part of an inspection under subsection (2)) require a relevant person or anyone acting on such a person's behalf—

(a) to open relevant equipment, and

(b) to carry out any other operation that may be necessary to enable the officer to ascertain whether any gaming duty or machine games duty is payable in respect of it and, if so, how much.

(5) A "relevant person" is—

(a) in relation to gaming duty, a person who is engaging, or whom the officer reasonably suspects of engaging, in section 10 gaming or in any activity by reason of which the person is or may become liable to gaming duty, and

(b) in relation to machine games duty, a person who is, has been or is about to become liable to machine games duty or whom the officer reasonably suspects of being, having been or being about to become so liable.

(6) "Relevant equipment" is—

(a) in relation to gaming duty, equipment that is being, or the officer reasonably suspects of having been or of being intended to be, used on the premises for or in connection with section 10 gaming, and

(b) in relation to machine games duty, any equipment that is, or the officer reasonably suspects of being, a machine in respect of which a person is, has been or may become liable to machine games duty and any other equipment used in connection with such a machine.

(7) In this section—

(a) "section 10 gaming" means gaming to which section 10 of the Finance Act 1997 applies, and

(b) a reference to premises where a machine is located is to be read in accordance with Part 1 of Schedule 24 to the Finance Act 2012."

(2) In section 118G of that Act (offences under Part 9A), in subsection (1), for "or section 118B" substitute ", 118B or 118BC(4)".

43 In section 2 of BGDA 1981 (bookmakers: general bets), in subsection (2), omit paragraph (d).

44 (1) Section 26H of BGDA 1981 (exemptions from remote gaming duty) is amended as follows.

(2) After subsection (2A) insert—

"(2B) Subsection (2) does not apply in cases where the other gambling tax is machine games duty."

(3) In subsection (3), before paragraph (b) insert—

"(aa) machine games duty,".

45 In Schedule A1 to BGDA 1981 (betting duties: double taxation relief), in paragraph 7, after paragraph (c) insert—

"(ca) machine games duty,".

46 In Schedule 4B to BGDA 1981 (remote gaming duty: double taxation relief), in paragraph 7, after paragraph (c) insert—

"(ca) machine games duty,".

47 In section 12 of FA 1994 (assessment to excise duty), in subsection (2)(c), after "1997" insert "or Part 1 of Schedule 24 to the Finance Act 2012".

48 In section 10 of FA 1997 (gaming duty), for subsection (3AA) substitute—

"(3AA) This section does not apply to the playing of a game in respect of which—

(a) bingo duty or lottery duty is chargeable, or would be chargeable but for an express exception, or

(b) machine games duty is chargeable."

49 In section 7 of the Borders, Citizenship and Immigration Act 2009 (Customs revenue functions of the director), in subsection (2)(e)—

(a) omit "and" at the end of sub-paragraph (vi), and

(b) at the end of sub-paragraph (vii) insert "and

(viii) machine games duty;".

Interpretation

50 In this Part of this Schedule—

"appeal tribunal" means the First-tier Tribunal or, where determined by or under Tribunal Procedure Rules, the Upper Tribunal;

"cash" has the meaning given in paragraph 2 (and "non-cash" is to be read accordingly);

"charge", in relation to a game, means a charge or deduction in money or money's worth, however it is described or levied and whether it becomes due before or after the game is played;

"the Commissioners" means the Commissioners for Her Majesty's Revenue and Customs;

"dutiable machine game" has the meaning given in paragraph 2, subject to paragraphs 3 and 4;

"game" does not include a sport;

"the go-live date" is defined in paragraph 66(5);

"HMRC" means Her Majesty's Revenue and Customs;

"machine" means any apparatus that uses or applies mechanical power, electrical power or both;

"machine game" has the meaning given in paragraph 2;

"MGD register" has the meaning given in paragraph 20;

"money" means money in sterling or any other currency;

"payouts" means prizes paid out to players as a result of playing dutiable machine games on a machine;

"the payouts", in relation to a particular taxable person and accounting period, has the meaning given in paragraph 7;

"premises" includes any place, any means of transport and any stall or other moveable structure;

"prize", in relation to a game—

(a) means a prize in the form of cash or non-cash (or both), however it is described or paid out and whether it is a prize provided by a person making the game available or is winnings of money staked, but

(b) a benefit consisting of nothing more than the opportunity to play the game again does not count as a prize;

"registered" has the meaning given in paragraph 12 (and "registration" is to be read accordingly);

"registrable person" has the meaning given in paragraph 21;

"relevant machine" means—

(a) a machine in respect of which machine games duty is or will be chargeable, or

(b) in relation to a particular taxable person and accounting period, a machine in respect of which that person is liable for machine games duty in that period;

"representative" means a personal representative, trustee in bankruptcy, receiver or liquidator or any other person acting in a representative capacity;

"specified" includes described;

"takings" means charges due from players for playing dutiable machine games on a machine;

"the takings", in relation to a particular taxable person and accounting period, has the meaning given in paragraph 7;

"taxable person" has the meaning given in paragraph 11;

"total net takings" has the meaning given in paragraph 6;

"United Kingdom" includes the territorial sea of the United Kingdom.

51 (1) This Part of this Schedule is to be read in accordance with this paragraph.

(2) A person "plays" a game if the person participates in the game—

(a) whether or not there are other participants in the game, and

(b) whether or not a computer generates images or data taken to represent the actions of other participants in the game.

(3) A reference to the charge (or the lowest or highest charge) payable for playing a machine game—

(a) is a reference to the charge (or the lowest or highest charge) payable for a single go at playing the game, and

(b) includes any charge that entitles the person paying it to play a machine game or to play it at a reduced rate (even if the charge is ostensibly a charge for something else).

(4) A reference to "paying" a charge is to be read, in the case of a charge in money's worth, as a reference to the provision of the thing, or performance of the service, in money's worth.

(5) A reference to a prize (or the maximum amount of cash) that can be won from playing a machine game is a reference to a prize (or the maximum amount of cash) that can be won from a single go at playing the game.

(6) A reference to "paying out" a prize is to be read, in the case of a prize in money's worth, as a reference to the provision of the thing, or performance of the service, in money's worth.

(7) A reference to the premises where a machine is located or made available includes, in the case of a portable machine, the premises where the machine is issued to those wanting to play dutiable machines games on it.

52 The imposition or payment of machine games duty does not make lawful anything that is otherwise unlawful.

PART 2
REMOVAL OF AMUSEMENT MACHINE LICENCE DUTY

Amendment of BGDA 1981

53 The following provisions of BGDA 1981 are omitted—

(a) sections 21 to 26,

(b) section 26H(3)(a),

(c) section 26N(3) and (4), and

(d) Schedules 4 and 4A.

54 (1) Part 3 of that Act (general) is amended as follows.

(2) In section 27 (offences by bodies corporate), for the words from "section 24" to "Schedule 4" substitute "paragraph 13(1) or (3) or 14(1) of Schedule 1 or paragraph 16 of Schedule 3".
(3) In section 31 (protection of officers), for "remote gaming duty or the duty on amusement machine licences" substitute "or remote gaming duty".
(4) In section 33 (interpretation), in subsection (2), for "remote gaming duty or the duty on amusement machine licences" substitute "or remote gaming duty".

Amendment of other enactments

55 In section 102 of CEMA 1979, in subsection (3)(a), omit "or an amusement machine licence".

56 In section 10 of FA 1997 (gaming duty), omit subsection (3A).

57 In Schedule 41 to FA 2008 (penalties: failure to notify and certain VAT and excise wrongdoing), in the Table in paragraph 1, omit the entry relating to amusement machine licence duty.

58 In section 7 of the Borders, Citizenship and Immigration Act 2009 (Customs revenue functions of the director), in subsection (2)(e), omit sub-paragraph (i).

Transitional provision and savings

59 (1) If a licence granted under section 21 of BGDA 1981 is to expire on or after the go-live date, the holder of the licence is entitled to repayment of an amount of duty.
(2) That amount is the difference between—
- (a) the amount of duty actually paid on the licence before the go-live date in accordance with section 23 of that Act, and
- (b) the amount (if less) determined in accordance with sub-paragraph (3).

(3) The amount is to be determined as follows—
Step 1
Calculate the amount of duty that would have been paid if the period for which the licence was granted had been the number of complete months beginning with the date on which the licence was granted and ending immediately before the go-live date. The day immediately following the end of that period of complete months is referred to as "day X".
Step 2
Add to the amount calculated under Step 1 an amount representing the duty payable for the period of days beginning with day X and ending with the day before the go-live date. The duty payable for each such day in that period is to be calculated as 1/365th of the amount of duty payable for a licence of 12 months for a machine of the relevant category.
(4) If—
- (a) duty is being paid on the licence in accordance with arrangements made under paragraph 7A of Schedule 4 to BGDA 1981 (payment of duty by instalments), and
- (b) the amount of duty actually paid on the licence before the go-live date in accordance with section 23 of that Act is less than the amount determined in accordance with sub-paragraph (3),

the difference between those amounts is to be treated under that Act as unpaid duty.
(5) If a person entitled to a repayment of more than £10 under this paragraph has not received the repayment within the period of 90 days beginning with the go-live date—
- (a) the person may give notice to HMRC of that fact,
- (b) the Commissioners must pay interest to the person on the amount of the repayment for the period from the end of that 90-day period until the day on which the repayment is made, and
- (c) any such interest accrues at the rate under section 197 of FA 1996 (rates of interest) that is applicable for Parts 2 and 3 of Schedule 3 to FA 2001 (excise duty payment by Commissioners in case of error or delay).

60 (1) If a licence granted or to be granted under section 21 of BGDA 1981 would expire within the period of 30 days ending with the go-live date, a person may apply—
- (a) for the licence to be treated as extended for the necessary period, or
- (b) for a new amusement machine licence to be treated as granted in its place under Schedule 4 to that Act for the necessary period.

(2) The necessary period is the period from expiry of the licence until immediately before the go-live date.
(3) An application under this paragraph may be made before or after the licence is granted but, if made after the licence is granted, it must be made before the day on which the licence is to expire.
(4) The application must be made to HMRC in such form and manner as HMRC may require.
(5) HMRC must grant the application once it has received payment of an amount of duty payable on the licence (or new licence) in respect of the necessary period.

(6) The amount of duty payable in respect of the necessary period is to be the sum of the amounts payable for each day in that period, each such amount being 1/365th of the duty payable for a licence of 12 months for a machine of the relevant category.
(7) Schedule 4 to BGDA 1981 and any regulations made under that Schedule apply (subject to any modifications specified by the Commissioners in a notice published for the purposes of this paragraph) to an amount of duty payable in accordance with this paragraph as to an amount of duty payable in accordance with section 23 of that Act.
(8) Nothing in this paragraph affects the operation of that Act with respect to the provision of amusement machines in the necessary period in a case where no application is made under this paragraph or an application is not granted.
(9) But if a default licence is granted under Schedule 4A to BGDA 1981 for the necessary period, the amount of duty that may be assessed under paragraph 4 of that Schedule is limited to the amount that would have been payable if an application had been made for a licence under this paragraph.

61 (1) This paragraph applies to licences to be granted under section 21 of BGDA 1981 on or after 2 January 2013 (a "final month licence").
(2) Section 21(3) of that Act has effect as if—
- (a) the requirement to grant amusement machine licences for a period of one or more whole months were omitted, and
- (b) the power to grant amusement machine licences for a period not exceeding 12 months were a power to grant such licences for a period ending with a day that is no later than the day before the go-live date.

(3) The requirement in section 21(4) of that Act to grant special amusement machine licences for a period of 12 months has effect in relation to a final month licence as if it were a requirement to grant a licence for the period beginning with the date of grant and ending with the day before the go-live date.
(4) The amount of duty payable on a final month licence is to be calculated in the manner described in paragraph 60(6).
(5) The Commissioners may by notice direct that Schedules 4 and 4A to BGDA 1981 and any regulations made under those Schedules are to apply to a final month licence with such modifications as may be specified in the notice.
(6) A notice under sub-paragraph (5) must be published by the Commissioners.

62 (1) The enactments repealed by this Part of this Schedule continue to have effect on and after the go-live date in relation to the provision of amusement machines before that date.
(2) Enactments continuing to have effect by virtue of sub-paragraph (1) are to be read with any necessary modifications.
(3) Without prejudice to the generality of sub-paragraph (2), paragraph 4 of Schedule 4A to BGDA 1981 (assessment of amount equivalent to duty) is to be read as if the reference in sub-paragraph (3) to the due date were a reference to the day before the go-live date.

PART 3
VAT EXEMPTION

Amendment of VATA 1994

63 For section 23 of VATA 1994 substitute—

"23 Value of supplies involving relevant machine games
(1) If a person plays a relevant machine game, then for the purposes of VAT the amount paid by the person is to be treated as consideration for a supply of services to that person.
(2) "Relevant machine game" is defined in section 23A.
(3) The value to be taken as the value of supplies made by a person ("the supplier") in the circumstances mentioned in subsection (1) in any period is to be determined as if the consideration for the supplies were reduced by an amount equal to X.
(4) X is the amount (if any) paid out in that period by way of winnings in respect of relevant machine games made available by the supplier (whether the games were played in the same period or an earlier one).
(5) X does not include any winnings paid out to the supplier or a person acting on the supplier's behalf.
(6) Inserting a token into a machine on which a relevant machine game is played is to be treated for the purposes of subsection (1) as the payment of an amount equal to that for which the token can be obtained.
(7) Providing a specified kind of token by way of winnings is to be treated for the purposes of subsection (4) as the payment out of an amount by way of winnings equal to the value of the token.

(8) A specified kind of token is—

(a) a token that can be inserted into the same machine to enable games to be played on the machine, or

(b) a token that is not of such a kind but can be exchanged for money.

(9) The value of a specified kind of token is—

(a) for a token within subsection (8)(a), an amount equal to that for which the token can be obtained, and

(b) for a token within subsection (8)(b), an amount equal to that for which the token can be exchanged.

(10) If it is not reasonably practicable to attribute payments and winnings to relevant machine games or to apportion them between relevant machine games and other games or other activities, any attribution or apportionment is to be done on a just and reasonable basis.

(11) For the purposes of this section, a person plays a game if the person participates in the game—

(a) whether or not there are other participants in the game, and

(b) whether or not a computer generates images or data taken to represent the actions of other participants in the game.

23A Meaning of "relevant machine game"

(1) A "relevant machine game" is a game (whether of skill or chance or both) that—

(a) is played on a machine for a prize, and

(b) is not excluded by subsection (2).

(2) A game is excluded by this subsection if—

(a) takings and payouts in respect of it are taken into account in determining any charge to machine games duty,

(b) it involves betting on future real events,

(c) bingo duty is charged on the playing of it or would be so charged but for paragraphs 1 to 5 of Schedule 3 to the Betting and Gaming Duties Act 1981 (exemptions from bingo duty),

(d) lottery duty is charged on the taking of a ticket or chance in it or would be so charged but for an express exception,

(e) it is a real game of chance and playing it amounts to dutiable gaming for the purposes of section 10 of the Finance Act 1997 or would do so but for subsection (3), (3B) or (4) of that section, or

(f) playing it amounts to remote gaming within the meaning of section 26A of the Betting and Gaming Duties Act 1981 (remote gaming duty: interpretation).

(3) In this section—

"game" does not include a sport;

"machine" means any apparatus that uses or applies mechanical power, electrical power or both;

"prize", in relation to a game, does not include the opportunity to play the game again;

"real game of chance" means a game of chance (within the meaning of the Betting and Gaming Duties Act 1981) that is non-virtual.

(4) The Treasury may by order amend this section."

64 (1) In Part 2 of Schedule 9 to that Act (exemptions: the groups), the provisions of Group 4 are amended as follows.

(2) After Item 1 insert—

"1A The provision of any facilities for the playing of dutiable machine games (as defined in Part 1 of Schedule 24 to the Finance Act 2012) but only to the extent that—

(a) the facilities are used to play such games, and

(b) the takings and payouts in respect of those games are taken into account in determining the charge to machine games duty."

(3) In Note (1)—

(a) for "Item 1 does" substitute "Items 1 and 1A do", and

(b) omit paragraph (d) and the word "or" immediately preceding that paragraph.

(4) After Note (1) insert—

"(1A) Item 1 does not apply to the provision of facilities to the extent that the facilities are used to play a relevant machine game (as defined in section 23A)."

(5) Accordingly—

(a) in Part 2 of Schedule 9, in the heading of Group 4, after "GAMING" insert ", DUTIABLE MACHINE GAMES", and

(b) in Part 1 of that Schedule, in the Index, for "Betting, gaming and lotteries" substitute "Betting, gaming, dutiable machine games and lotteries".

65 (1) Paragraph 9 of Schedule 11 to that Act (administration, collection and enforcement) is amended as follows.
(2) For paragraph (a) substitute—

"(a) to open any machine on which relevant machine games (as defined in section 23A) are capable of being played; and".

(3) In paragraph (b), for "subsection (2) of that section" substitute "section 23(3)".
(4) Accordingly, in the heading immediately before paragraph 9, for "*gaming machines*" substitute "*machines on which relevant machine games are played*".

PART 4
MISCELLANEOUS

Application

66 (1) The provisions of this Schedule have effect as follows.
(2) Part 1 has effect in relation to the playing of machine games on or after 1 February 2013 (and Schedules 55 and 56 to FA 2009, as amended by Part 1 of this Schedule, are taken to have come into force for the purposes of machine games duty on that date).
(3) Part 2 has effect in relation to the provision of amusement machines on or after 1 February 2013.
(4) Part 3 has effect in relation to supplies made on or after that date.
(5) A reference in this Schedule to the "go-live date" is to 1 February 2013.

67 (1) The Treasury may by regulations make transitional or saving provision in connection with the removal of amusement machine licence duty and the introduction of machine games duty.
(2) The power in sub-paragraph (1) is without prejudice to—

(a) the provision made by Part 2 of this Schedule, and
(b) any power in this Schedule apart from this paragraph to make transitional or saving provision in connection with the matters mentioned in sub-paragraph (1).

(3) Regulations under this paragraph are to be made by statutory instrument.
(4) A statutory instrument containing regulations under this paragraph is subject to annulment in pursuance of a resolution of the House of Commons.

SCHEDULE 25

REMOTE GAMBLING: DOUBLE TAXATION RELIEF

Section 193

Consequential amendments

11 (1) The Table in paragraph 1 of Schedule 41 to FA 2008 (penalties: failure to notify and certain VAT and excise wrongdoing) is amended as follows.
(2) In the second column of the entry for general betting duty, for "paragraph 4(1) to (3) of Schedule 1 to BGDA 1981" substitute "paragraph 8(2) of Schedule A1 to BGDA 1981 (obligation to notify reduction etc in qualifying foreign tax) or paragraph 4(1) to (3) of Schedule 1 to that Act".
(3) In the second column of the entry for pool betting duty, for "paragraphs 4(2) and 5(1) of Schedule 1 to BGDA 1981" substitute "paragraph 8(2) of Schedule A1 to BGDA 1981 (obligation to notify reduction etc in qualifying foreign tax) or paragraphs 4(2) and 5(1) of Schedule 1 to that Act".
(4) In the second column of the entry for remote gaming duty, for "to register under regulations under section 26J of BGDA 1981" substitute "to notify under paragraph 8(2) of Schedule 4B to BGDA 1981 (reduction etc in qualifying foreign tax) and obligation to register under regulations under section 26J of that Act".

Commencement

12 The amendments made by this Schedule have effect in relation to accounting periods ending on or after 1 April 2012 (and, accordingly, the first reconciliation period begins with the first accounting period in relation to which the amendments have effect).

SCHEDULE 26

CATEGORISATION OF SUPPLIES

Section 196

Press releases etc—HMRC Brief, 27 September 2012: VAT—addressing borderline anomalies—detailed information sheets published.

PART 1
ZERO-RATED SUPPLIES

Introductory

1 Part 2 of Schedule 8 of VATA 1994 (zero-rating) is amended as follows.

Food

2 (1) Group 1 (food) is amended as follows.
(2) After excepted item 4 insert—
"4A Sports drinks that are advertised or marketed as products designed to enhance physical performance, accelerate recovery after exercise or build bulk, and other similar drinks, including (in either case) syrups, concentrates, essences, powders, crystals or other products for the preparation of such drinks."
(3) In Note (3), omit the words from "and for the purposes of paragraph (b) above" to the end.
(4) After that Note insert—
"(3A) For the purposes of Note (3), in the case of any supplier, the premises on which food is supplied include any area set aside for the consumption of food by that supplier's customers, whether or not the area may also be used by the customers of other suppliers.
(3B) "Hot food" means food which (or any part of which) is hot at the time it is provided to the customer and—
(a) has been heated for the purposes of enabling it to be consumed hot,
(b) has been heated to order,
(c) has been kept hot after being heated,
(d) is provided to a customer in packaging that retains heat (whether or not the packaging was primarily designed for that purpose) or in any other packaging that is specifically designed for hot food, or
(e) is advertised or marketed in a way that indicates that it is supplied hot.
(3C) For the purposes of Note (3B)—
(a) something is "hot" if it is at a temperature above the ambient air temperature, and
(b) something is "kept hot" after being heated if the supplier stores it in an environment which provides, applies or retains heat, or takes other steps to ensure it remains hot or to slow down the natural cooling process.
(3D) In Notes (3B) and (3C), references to food being heated include references to it being cooked or reheated."

Protected buildings

3 (1) Group 6 (protected buildings) is amended as follows.
(2) Omit items 2 and 3 (approved alterations and building materials).
(3) In Note (3), for "(12) to (14) and (22) to (24)" substitute "and (12) to (14)".
(4) For Note (4) substitute—
"(4) For the purposes of item 1, a protected building is not to be regarded as substantially reconstructed unless, when the reconstruction is completed, the reconstructed building incorporates no more of the original building (that is to say, the building as it was before the reconstruction began) than the external walls, together with other external features of architectural or historic interest."
(5) In Note (5), in paragraphs (a), (b) and (c) omit "or other supply".
(6) Omit Notes (6) to (11).

Caravans

4 (1) Group 9 (caravans and houseboats) is amended as follows.
(2) For item 1 substitute—
"1 Caravans which exceed the limits of size of a trailer for the time being permitted to be towed on roads by a motor vehicle having a maximum gross weight of 3,500 kilogrammes and which—
(a) were manufactured to standard BS 3632:2005 approved by the British Standards Institution, or
(b) are second hand, were manufactured to a previous version of standard BS 3632 approved by that Institution and were occupied before 6 April 2013."
(3) In item 3 for "5(3)" substitute "5(4)".
(4) In the Note for "item 3" substitute "item 4".

PART 2
EXEMPT SUPPLIES

Land: self storage and facilities to supply hairdressing services

5 (1) In Part 2 of Schedule 9 to VATA 1994 (exemptions), Group 1 (land) is amended as follows.

(2) In item 1, after paragraph (k) insert—

"(ka) the grant of facilities for the self storage of goods;".

(3) In that item, omit "and" at the end of paragraph (m) and after that paragraph insert—

"(ma) the grant of facilities to a person who uses the facilities wholly or mainly to supply hairdressing services; and".

(4) In that item, in paragraph (n), for "(m)" substitute "(ma)".

(5) After Note (15) insert—

"(15A) In paragraph (ka)—

"facilities for the self storage of goods" means the use of a relevant structure for the storage of goods by the person (or persons) to whom the grant of facilities is made, and "goods" does not include live animals.

(15B) For the purposes of Note (15A), use by a person with the permission of the person (or any of the persons) to whom the grant of facilities is made counts as use by the person (or persons) to whom that grant is made.

(15C) A grant of facilities for the self storage of goods does not fall within paragraph (ka) if—

(a) the person making the grant ("P")—

(i) is doing so in circumstances where the relevant structure used is, or forms part of, a relevant capital item, and

(ii) is connected with any person who uses that relevant structure for the self storage of goods,

(b) the grant is made to a charity which uses the relevant structure solely otherwise than in the course of a business, or

(c) in a case where the relevant structure is part of a building, its use for the storage of goods by the person (or persons) to whom the grant is made is ancillary to other use of the building by that person (or those persons).

(15D) In Notes (15A) and (15C) "relevant structure" means the whole or part of—

(a) a container or other structure that is fully enclosed, or

(b) a unit or building.

(15E) In Note (15C)(a)(i) "relevant capital item" means a capital item which—

(a) is subject to adjustments of input tax deduction by P under regulations made under section 26(3), and

(b) has not yet reached the end of its prescribed period of adjustment."

(6) After Note (16) insert—

"(17) Paragraph (ma) does not apply to a grant of facilities which provides for the exclusive use, by the person to whom the grant is made, of a whole building, a whole floor, a separate room or a clearly defined area, unless the person making the grant or a person connected with that person provides or makes available (directly or indirectly) services related to hairdressing for use by the person to whom the grant is made.

(18) For the purposes of Note (17)—

(a) "services related to hairdressing" means the services of a hairdresser's assistant or cashier, the booking of appointments, the laundering of towels, the cleaning of the facilities subject to the grant, the making of refreshments and other similar services typically used in connection with hairdressing, but does not include the provision of utilities or the cleaning of shared areas in a building, and

(b) it does not matter if the services related to hairdressing are shared with other persons.

(19) For the purposes of Notes (15C) and (17) any question whether a person is connected with any other person is to be determined in accordance with section 1122 of the Corporation Tax Act 2010 (connected person)."

PART 3
SUPPLIES CHARGEABLE AT REDUCED RATE

6 (1) Schedule 7A to VATA 1994 (charged at reduced rate) is amended as follows.

(2) In Part 1 (index to reduced-rate supplies of goods and service), at the appropriate place insert—

"Caravans Group 12"

(3) In Part 2 (the groups), at the end insert—

GROUP 12

CARAVANS

Item No

1

Supplies of caravans which exceed the limits of size of a trailer for the time being permitted to be towed on roads by a motor vehicle having a maximum gross weight of 3,500 kilogrammes.

2

The supply of such services as are described in paragraph 1(1) or 5(4) of Schedule 4 in respect of a caravan within item 1.

NOTE:

This Group does not include—

(a) removable contents other than goods of a kind mentioned in item 4 of Group 5 of Schedule 8, or

(b) the supply of accommodation in a caravan."

PART 4

COMMENCEMENT AND TRANSITIONAL PROVISION

7 (1) Subject to sub-paragraphs (2) and (3), the amendments made by this Schedule come into force on 1 October 2012.

(2) Paragraphs 4 and 6 come into force on 6 April 2013.

(3) Paragraph 3(2) to (6) comes into force, in relation to relevant supplies, on 1 October 2015.

(4) A supply is "relevant" if it is—

(a) a supply of any services, other than excluded services, which is made—

(i) in the course of an approved alteration of a protected building, and

(ii) pursuant to a written contract entered into, or a relevant consent applied for, before 21 March 2012, or

(b) a supply of building materials which is made—

(i) to a person to whom the supplier is supplying services within paragraph (a) which include the incorporation of the materials into the building (or its site) in question, and

(ii) pursuant to a written contract entered into, or a relevant consent applied for, before 21 March 2012.

(5) In relation to supplies made on or after 1 October 2012 but before 1 October 2015, Group 6 has effect as if, for the purposes of item 1 of that Group, a protected building were also regarded as substantially reconstructed if subparagraph (6) or (7) applies.

(6) This sub-paragraph applies if at least three-fifths of the works carried out to effect the reconstruction (measured by reference to cost) are of such a nature that the supply of services (other than excluded services), materials and other items to carry out the works would, if supplied by a taxable person, be relevant supplies.

(7) This sub-paragraph applies if—

(a) at least 10% (measured by reference to cost) of the reconstruction of the protected building was completed before 21 March 2012, and

(b) at least three-fifths of the works carried out to effect the reconstruction (measured by reference to cost) are of such a nature that the supply of services (other than excluded services), materials and other items to carry out the works would, if supplied by a taxable person, be relevant supplies but for the requirement for a written contract to have been entered into or relevant consent to have been applied for before that date.

(8) For the purposes of sub-paragraph (4), works carried out that are not within the scope of the written contract entered into, or the relevant consent applied for, as it stood immediately before 21 March 2012, are not a supply made pursuant to that contract or relevant consent.

(9) In this paragraph—

"excluded services" means the services of an architect, surveyor or other person acting as consultant or in a supervisory capacity;

"Group 6" means Group 6 of Part 2 of Schedule 8 to VATA 1994 (protected buildings);

"relevant consent" means—

(a) in the case of an ecclesiastical building to which section 60 of the Planning (Listed Buildings and Conservation Areas) Act 1990 applies, consent for the approved alterations by a competent body with the authority to approve alterations to such buildings, or

(b) in any other case, consent under any provision of—

(i) Part 1 of the Planning (Listed Buildings and Conservation Areas) Act 1990,

(ii) Part 1 of the Planning (Listed Buildings and Conservation Areas) (Scotland) Act 1997,

(iii) Part 5 of the Planning (Northern Ireland) Order 1991,

(iv) Part 1 of the Ancient Monuments and Archaeological Areas Act 1979, or

(v) Part 2 of the Historic Monuments and Archaeological Objects (Northern Ireland) Order 1995.

(10) The Notes of Group 6 apply in relation to this paragraph as they apply in relation to that Group, except that in applying Notes (9), (10) and (11), references to item 2 are to be read as references to sub-paragraph (4) of this paragraph.

SCHEDULE 27
ANTI-FORESTALLING CHARGE TO VAT

Section 196

Press releases etc—HMRC Brief, 27 September 2012: VAT—addressing borderline anomalies—detailed information sheets published.

PART 1
ANTI-FORESTALLING CHARGE TO VAT

Introductory

1 In this Schedule—

"date of the VAT change" means 1 October 2012;

"pre-change supply" means a supply of a description specified in paragraph 3 which—

(a) is treated as taking place before the date of the VAT change, and

(b) if it had been treated as taking place on that date, would have been charged to VAT at the standard rate as a result of the amendments made by Schedule 26.

The charge

2 (1) There is an anti-forestalling charge to value added tax on any pre-change supply which—

(a) is treated as taking place on or after 21 March 2012, and

(b) is a supply linked to the post-change period (see paragraph 4).

(2) "Chargeable pre-change supply" means a supply to which sub-paragraph (1) applies.

(3) An anti-forestalling charge to value added tax under this Schedule is to be treated for all purposes as if it were value added tax charged in accordance with VATA 1994.

The supplies

3 (1) The descriptions of supplies are—

(a) the supply, in the course of an approved alteration of a protected building, of any services, other than the services of an architect, surveyor or any person acting as consultant or in a supervisory capacity,

(b) the supply of building materials to a person to whom the supplier is supplying services within paragraph (a) which include the incorporation of the materials into the building (or its site),

(c) the grant of facilities for the self storage of goods, or

(d) the grant of a right to receive a supply within paragraph (c).

(2) The Notes to Group 6 in Schedule 8 to VATA 1994 have effect for the purposes of sub-paragraph (1)(a) and (b) as they had effect for the purposes of items 1 to 3 of that Group on 21 March 2012.

(3) For the purposes of this Schedule a right to receive a supply includes—

(a) any option to receive that supply, and

(b) any interest deriving from such an option.

Supplies linked to the post-change period

4 (1) A supply of services within paragraph 3(1)(a) or (c) is linked to the post-change period if, and to the extent that, the services are carried out or provided on or after the date of the VAT change.

(2) A supply of goods within paragraph 3(1)(b) is linked to the post-change period if, and to the extent that, the goods are incorporated into the building concerned (or its site) on or after that date.

(3) A supply within paragraph 3(1)(d) is linked to the post-change period if, and to the extent that, the services to which the grant relates are carried out or provided on or after that date.

Power to modify this Schedule

5 (1) The Treasury may by order modify this Schedule for the purposes of preventing an anti-forestalling charge from arising, in the circumstances specified in the order, in relation to any description of supplies specified in the order.
(2) An order under this paragraph may contain provision having retrospective effect.
(3) An order under this paragraph is to be made by statutory instrument.
(4) A statutory instrument containing an order under this paragraph is subject to annulment in pursuance of a resolution of the House of Commons.

PART 2
LIABILITY AND AMOUNT

Liability

6 (1) An anti-forestalling charge under this Schedule on a chargeable pre-change supply—
(a) is a liability of the supplier (subject to sub-paragraph (2)), and
(b) becomes due on the date of the VAT change (rather than at the time of supply).
(2) If, on the date on which the anti-forestalling charge becomes due, the person who would be liable to pay the charge under sub-paragraph (1)—
(a) is not a taxable person, but
(b) is treated as a member of a group under sections 43A to 43D of VATA 1994,
the anti-forestalling charge is a liability of the representative member of the group.

Amount

7 (1) The amount of the anti-forestalling charge on a chargeable pre-change supply is the amount of VAT that would be chargeable on the supply if it were subject to VAT at 20%.
This is subject to any reduction under sub-paragraph (2).
(2) If the chargeable pre-change supply is not wholly linked to the post-change period, the anti-forestalling charge is the relevant proportion of that amount.
(3) The relevant proportion is—
P / W
where—
P is so much of the consideration for the chargeable supply as is attributable, on a just and reasonable basis, to that part of the supply (or, in the case of a grant of a right, that part of the supply to which the right relates) which is linked to the post-change period;
W is the whole of the consideration for the chargeable pre-change supply.

PART 3
ADMINISTRATION AND INTERPRETATION

Person ceasing to be taxable person before anti-forestalling charge due

8 (1) This paragraph applies if, on the date on which an anti-forestalling charge under this Schedule becomes due ("the due date"), the person who is liable to pay the charge under paragraph 6 is not a taxable person.
(2) The anti-forestalling charge must be accounted for by that person in accordance with VATA 1994 (and regulations made under that Act) as if it were VAT due in the last period for which the person was required to make a return by or under VATA 1994.
(3) If an amount assessed as due by way of an anti-forestalling charge under this Schedule would (in the absence of this sub-paragraph) carry interest from a date earlier than the due date, it is to be treated as only carrying interest from the due date.

Adjustment of contracts following the VAT change

9 (1) This paragraph applies where—
(a) a contract for the supply of goods or services is made before the date of the VAT change, and
(b) there is an anti-forestalling charge under this Schedule on the supply.
(2) The consideration for the supply is to be increased by an amount equal to the anti-forestalling charge, unless the contract provides otherwise.

Invoices

10 Regulations under paragraph 2A of Schedule 11 to VATA 1994 (VAT invoices) may make provision about the provision, replacement or correction of invoices in connection with an anti-forestalling charge under this Schedule.

Regulations—Value Added Tax (Amendment) (No 2) Regulations 2012, SI 2012/1899.

Interpretation: general

11 (1) Expressions used in this Schedule and in VATA 1994 have the same meaning in this Schedule as in that Act.

(2) In this Schedule "treated as taking place" means treated as taking place for the purposes of the charge to VAT.

SCHEDULE 28

NON-ESTABLISHED TAXABLE PERSONS

Section 203

New Schedule 1A

1 In VATA 1994, after Schedule 1 insert—

SCHEDULE 1A

REGISTRATION IN RESPECT OF TAXABLE SUPPLIES: NON-UK ESTABLISHMENT

Liability to be registered

1

(1) A person becomes liable to be registered under this Schedule at any time if conditions A to D are met.

(2) Condition A is that—

(a) the person makes taxable supplies, or

(b) there are reasonable grounds for believing that the person will make taxable supplies in the period of 30 days then beginning.

(3) Condition B is that those supplies (or any of them) are or will be made in the course or furtherance of a business carried on by the person.

(4) Condition C is that the person has no business establishment, or other fixed establishment, in the United Kingdom in relation to any business carried on by the person.

(5) Condition D is that the person is not registered under this Act.

2

(1) A person does not become liable to be registered by virtue of paragraph 1(2)(b) if the reason for believing that taxable supplies will be made in the 30-day period mentioned there is that a business, or part of a business, carried on by a taxable person is to be transferred to the person as a going concern in that period.

(2) But if the transfer takes place, the transferee becomes liable to be registered under this Schedule at the time of the transfer if conditions A to D in paragraph 1 are met in relation to the transferee at that time.

(3) In determining for the purposes of sub-paragraph (2) whether condition B is met, the reference in paragraph 1(3) to a business is to be read as a reference to the business, or part of the business, that is transferred to the transferee.

3

A person is treated as having become liable to be registered under this Schedule at any time when the person would have become so liable under paragraph 1 or 2 but for any registration that is subsequently cancelled under—

(a) paragraph 11,

(b) paragraph 13(3) of Schedule 1,

(c) paragraph 6(2) of Schedule 2,

(d) paragraph 6(3) of Schedule 3, or

(e) paragraph 6(2) of Schedule 3A.

4

(1) A person does not cease to be liable to be registered under this Schedule except in accordance with sub-paragraph (2).

(2) A person who has become liable to be registered under this Schedule ceases to be so liable at any time if the Commissioners are satisfied that—

(a) the person has ceased to make taxable supplies in the course or furtherance of a business carried on by the person, or

(b) the person is no longer a person in relation to whom condition C in paragraph 1 is met.

Notification of liability and registration

5

(1) A person who becomes liable to be registered by virtue of paragraph 1(2)(a) or 2(2) must notify the Commissioners of the liability before the end of the period of 30 days beginning with the day on which the liability arises.
(2) The Commissioners must register any such person (whether or not the person so notifies them) with effect from the beginning of the day on which the liability arises.

6

(1) A person who becomes liable to be registered by virtue of paragraph 1(2)(b) must notify the Commissioners of the liability before the end of the period by reference to which the liability arises.
(2) The Commissioners must register any such person (whether or not the person so notifies them) with effect from the beginning of the period by reference to which the liability arises.

Notification of end of liability

7

(1) A person registered under paragraph 5 or 6 who, on any day, ceases to make or have the intention of making taxable supplies in the course or furtherance of a business carried on by that person must notify the Commissioners of that fact within 30 days beginning with that day.
(2) But the person need not notify the Commissioners if on that day the person would otherwise be liable or entitled to be registered under this Act (disregarding for this purpose the person's registration under this Schedule and any enactment that prevents a person from being liable to be registered under different provisions at the same time).

Cancellation of registration

8

(1) The Commissioners must cancel a person's registration under this Schedule if—
(a) the person satisfies them that the person is not liable to be registered under this Schedule, and
(b) the person requests the cancellation.
(2) The cancellation is to be made with effect from—
(a) the day on which the request is made, or
(b) such later day as may be agreed between the Commissioners and the person.
(3) But the Commissioners must not cancel the registration with effect from any time unless they are satisfied that it is not a time when the person would be subject to a requirement to be registered under this Act.

9

(1) The Commissioners may cancel a person's registration under this Schedule if they are satisfied that the person has ceased to be liable to be registered under this Schedule.
(2) The cancellation is to be made with effect from—
(a) the day on which the person ceased to be so liable, or
(b) such later day as may be agreed between the Commissioners and the person.
(3) But the Commissioners must not cancel the registration with effect from any time unless they are satisfied that it is not a time when the person would be subject to a requirement, or entitled, to be registered under this Act.

10

In determining for the purposes of paragraphs 8 and 9 whether a time is a time when a person would be subject to a requirement, or entitled, to be registered under this Act, so much of any provision of this Act as prevents a person from becoming liable or entitled to be registered when the person is already registered or when the person is so liable under any other provision must be disregarded.

11

(1) The Commissioners may cancel a person's registration under this Schedule if they are satisfied that the person was not liable to be registered under this Schedule on the day on which the person was registered.

(2) The cancellation is to be made with effect from the day on which the person was registered.

12

Paragraphs 8 to 11 are subject to paragraph 18 of Schedule 3B (cancellation of registration under this Schedule of persons seeking to be registered under that Schedule etc).

Exemption from registration

13

(1) The Commissioners may exempt a person from registration under this Schedule if the person satisfies them that the taxable supplies that the person makes or intends to make—

(a) are all zero-rated, or

(b) would all be zero-rated if the person were a taxable person.

(2) The power in sub-paragraph (1) is exercisable only if the person so requests and the Commissioners think fit.

(3) If there is a material change in the nature of the supplies made by a person exempted under this paragraph, the person must notify the Commissioners of the change—

(a) within 30 days beginning with the day on which the change occurred, or

(b) if no particular day is identifiable as that day, within 30 days of the end of the quarter in which the change occurred.

(4) If it appears to the Commissioners that a request under this paragraph should no longer be acted upon on or after any day or has been withdrawn on any day, they must register the person who made the request with effect from that day.

(5) A reference in this paragraph to supplies is to supplies made in the course or furtherance of a business carried on by the person.

Supplementary

14

Any notification required under this Schedule must be made in such form and manner and must contain such particulars as may be specified in regulations or by the Commissioners in accordance with regulations."

Other amendments of VATA 1994

2 VATA 1994 is amended as follows.

3 In section 7 (place of supply of goods), in subsection (4)(c)(ii), after "Schedule 1" insert "or 1A".

4 In section 54 (farmers etc), in subsection (2), after "Schedule 1" insert "or is, has become or has ceased to be liable to be registered under Schedule 1A".

5 In section 55 (customers to account for tax on supplies of gold etc), in subsection (1)—

(a) for "Schedule 1" substitute "Schedules 1 and 1A", and

(b) for "that Schedule" substitute "Schedule 1".

6 In section 55A (customers to account for tax on supplies of goods or services of a kind used in missing trader intra-community fraud), in subsection (3), for "Schedule 1" substitute "Schedules 1 and 1A".

7 In section 69 (breaches of regulatory provisions), in subsection (1)(a), after "Schedule 1," insert "paragraph 7 of Schedule 1A,".

8 In section 73 (failure to make returns etc), in subsection (3)(b), after "Schedule 1," insert "paragraph 9 or 11 of Schedule 1A,".

9 In section 74 (interest on VAT recovered or recoverable by assessment), in subsection (1)(c), after "Schedule 1," insert "under paragraph 13 of Schedule 1A,".

10 In section 77 (assessments: time limits and supplementary assessments), in subsection (4C), after paragraph (a) insert—

"(aa) paragraph 5, 6 or 13(3) of Schedule 1A,".

11 (1) Paragraph 1 of Schedule 1 (registration in respect of taxable supplies) is amended as follows.
(2) In sub-paragraph (1)—
(a) in paragraph (a), after "if" insert "the person is UK-established and", and
(b) in paragraph (b), after "if" insert "the person is UK-established and".
(3) In sub-paragraph (2), for "and the transferee is not registered under this Act at the time of the transfer" substitute ", the transferee is UK-established at the time of the transfer and the transferee is not registered under this Act at that time".
(4) After sub-paragraph (2) insert—
"(2A) In determining the value of a person's supplies for the purposes of sub-paragraph (1)(a) or (2)(a), supplies are to be taken into account (subject to sub-paragraphs (3) to (7)) whether or not the person was UK-established when they were made."
(5) In sub-paragraph (4)(a), after "below," insert "paragraph 11 of Schedule 1A,".
(6) In sub-paragraph (5), after "below," insert "paragraph 11 of Schedule 1A,".
(7) At the end insert—
"(10) A person is "UK-established" if the person has a business establishment, or some other fixed establishment, in the United Kingdom in relation to a business carried on by the person."

12 In paragraph 3 of that Schedule, at the end of paragraph (b) insert "; or (c) is not at that time UK-established (see paragraph 1(10))."

13 Accordingly, in the heading of that Schedule, at the end insert ": UK ESTABLISHMENT".

14 In paragraph 1 of Schedule 2 (registration in respect of supplies from other member States)—
(a) in sub-paragraph (1)(b), after "Schedule 1" insert "or 1A", and
(b) in sub-paragraph (4), after "Schedule 1," insert "paragraph 11 of Schedule 1A,".

15 In paragraph 1 of Schedule 3 (registration in respect of acquisitions from other member States)—
(a) in sub-paragraph (1)(b), after "Schedule 1" insert ", 1A", and
(b) in sub-paragraph (3), after "Schedule 1," insert "paragraph 11 of Schedule 1A,".

16 In paragraph 1 of Schedule 3A (registration in respect of disposals of assets for which a VAT repayment is claimed)—
(a) in sub-paragraph (1), after "Schedule 1," insert "1A,", and
(b) in sub-paragraph (2), after "Schedule 1," insert "paragraph 11 of Schedule 1A,".

17 In paragraph 18 of Schedule 3B (supply of electronic services in member States: special accounting scheme)—
(a) after "Schedule 1", in the first place it occurs, insert "or 1A", and
(b) after "Schedule 1", in the second place it occurs, insert "or, as the case may be, 1A".

Amendments of other Acts

18 In Schedule 41 to FA 2008 (penalties: failure to notify and certain VAT and excise wrongdoing), in the Table in paragraph 1, after the entry for the obligations under Schedule 1 to VATA 1994 insert the following entry—

"Value added tax	Obligations under paragraphs 5, 6 and 13(3) of Schedule 1A to VATA 1994 (obligations to notify liability to register and notify material change in nature of supplies made by person exempted from registration)."

Application

19 The amendments made by this Schedule have effect in relation to supplies made or to be made on or after 1 December 2012.

SCHEDULE 29

ADMINISTRATION OF VAT

Section 204

1 VATA 1994 is amended as follows.

2 (1) Section 18B (fiscally warehoused goods: relief) is amended as follows.
(2) In subsection (1)(d) omit "be in such form and".

(3) In subsection (2)(d) omit "in such form as the Commissioners may by regulations specify".
(4) After subsection (2) insert—

"(2A) A certificate under subsection (1)(d) or (2)(d) must be in such form as may be specified by regulations or by the Commissioners in accordance with regulations."

3 (1) Section 18C (warehouses and fiscal warehouses: services) is amended as follows.
(2) In subsection (1)(c) omit ", in such a form as the Commissioners may by regulations specify,".
(3) After subsection (1) insert—

"(1A) A certificate under subsection (1)(c) must be in such form as may be specified by regulations or by the Commissioners in accordance with regulations."

4 In section 35(2) (refund of VAT to persons constructing certain buildings), for the words following paragraph (c) substitute—

"as may be specified by regulations or by the Commissioners in accordance with regulations."

5 (1) Section 39(3) (repayment of VAT to those in business overseas) is amended as follows.
(2) Before paragraph (a) insert—

"(za) for claims to be made in such form and manner as may be specified in the scheme or by the Commissioners in accordance with the scheme;".

(3) For paragraph (c) substitute—

"(c) for generally regulating—
(i) the time by which claims must be made, and
(ii) the methods by which the amount of any repayment is to be determined and the repayment is to be made."

6 (1) Section 48 (VAT representatives) is amended as follows.
(2) For subsection (1B)(c) substitute—

"(c) Council Regulation (EC) No 904/2010 of 7 October 2010 on administrative cooperation and combating fraud in the field of value added tax."

(3) After subsection (4) insert—

"(4A) Regulations under subsection (4) may require a notification under that subsection to be made in such form and manner, and to contain such particulars, as may be specified in the regulations or by the Commissioners in accordance with the regulations."

7 In section 54(6)(a) (farmers etc)—
(a) omit "the form and manner in which", and
(b) for "is to be made" substitute "to be made in the form and manner specified in the regulations or by the Commissioners in accordance with the regulations".

8 In Schedule 1 (registration in respect of taxable supplies), in paragraph 17 (notifications)—
(a) after "form" insert "and manner", and
(b) for "as the Commissioners may by regulations prescribe" substitute "as may be specified in regulations or by the Commissioners in accordance with regulations."

9 In Schedule 2 (registration in respect of supplies from other member States), in paragraph 9 (notifications)—
(a) after "form" insert "and manner", and
(b) for "as the Commissioners may by regulations prescribe" substitute "as may be specified in regulations or by the Commissioners in accordance with regulations."

10 In Schedule 3 (registration in respect of acquisitions from other member States), in paragraph 10 (notifications)—
(a) after "form" insert "and manner", and
(b) for "as the Commissioners may by regulations prescribe" substitute "as may be specified in regulations or by the Commissioners in accordance with regulations."

11 In Schedule 3A (registration in respect of disposals of assets for which a VAT repayment is claimed), in paragraph 8 (notifications)—
(a) after "form" insert "and manner", and
(b) for "as the Commissioners may by regulations prescribe" substitute "as may be specified in regulations or by the Commissioners in accordance with regulations."

12 (1) Paragraph 2 of Schedule 11 (accounting for VAT and payment of VAT) is amended as follows.
(2) In sub-paragraph (1) (keeping accounts and making returns), insert at the end "or by the Commissioners in accordance with the regulations."
(3) In sub-paragraph (3) (statements containing particulars of certain transactions)—

(a) for paragraph (b) substitute—

"(b) specified by the Commissioners in accordance with the regulations,", and

(b) for "prescribed" substitute "so specified".

(4) In sub-paragraph (3A) (statements containing particulars of certain supplies)—

(a) for paragraph (b) substitute—

"(b) specified by the Commissioners in accordance with the regulations,", and

(b) for "prescribed" substitute "so specified".

(5) In sub-paragraph (3B) (notification of certain events), for "determined by the Commissioners in accordance with powers conferred by the regulations" substitute "by the Commissioners in accordance with the regulations".

(6) In sub-paragraph (4) (notification of acquisition of certain goods), insert at the end "or (in the case of the notification requirement) by the Commissioners in accordance with the regulations".

(7) In sub-paragraph (5)(a) (further provision about notifications), after "regulations" insert "or by the Commissioners in accordance with the regulations".

13 In consequence of the amendments made by this Schedule—

(a) in FA 1996, omit section 30(2), and

(b) in FA 2009, omit section 77(2)(d).

SCHEDULE 36

AGREEMENT BETWEEN UK AND SWITZERLAND

Section 218

Commentary—*Simon's Taxes* **A6.1216**.

PART 1

INTRODUCTION

The Agreement and the Joint Declaration

1 In this Schedule—

(a) "the Agreement" means the agreement signed on 6 October 2011 between the United Kingdom and the Swiss Confederation on co-operation in the area of taxation, as amended by a protocol signed by them on 20 March 2012 and by a mutual agreement signed by them on 18 April 2012 implementing article XVIII of that protocol,

(b) "the Joint Declaration" means the joint declaration (concerning a tax finality payment) forming an integral part of that protocol,

(c) "the start date" is the date on which the Agreement enters into force in accordance with its terms (see Article 44), and

(d) references to a numbered Article are to the Article of that number in the Agreement.

Commentary—*Simon's Taxes* **A6.1216**.

PART 2

THE PAST

Taxes affected

2 (1) The taxes affected by this Part are—

(a) income tax,

(b) capital gains tax,

(c) inheritance tax, and

(d) VAT.

(2) Accordingly, this Part affects—

(a) amounts of income on which income tax is charged,

(b) chargeable gains,

(c) the value of property forming part of the value transferred by a chargeable transfer, and

(d) the value of supplies on which VAT is charged.

(3) An amount falling within one (or more) of those descriptions is referred to as a "taxable amount" and, in relation to such an amount, "tax" means whichever of the taxes mentioned in sub-paragraph (1) is (or are) charged on it.

Commentary—*Simon's Taxes* **A6.1216**.

Application of this Part

3 (1) This Part applies if—

(a) a one-off payment is levied in accordance with Part 2 of the Agreement,

(b) a certificate is issued under Article 9(4) to a person ("P") in respect of that payment, and

(c) the certificate is approved by P or considered approved by virtue of that Article.

(2) The certificate is referred to in this Part as "the Part 2 certificate".

Commentary—*Simon's Taxes* **A6.1216**.

Qualifying amounts

4 (1) The Part 2 certificate applies to taxable amounts in respect of which the conditions in sub-paragraph (2) are met.

(2) The conditions are—

(a) P is liable to tax on the amount,

(b) the amount is untaxed,

(c) the taxable event took place before the start date, and

(d) the necessary link with the certificate can be demonstrated.

(3) The necessary link is—

(a) in a case falling within Article 9(3) (non-UK domiciled individuals opting for self-assessment method), that the amount is included in the omitted taxable base by reference to which the one-off payment was calculated, and

(b) in any other case, that the amount forms part of or is represented by the assets comprised in the relevant capital by reference to which the one-off payment was calculated (referred to in the Agreement as C_r).

(4) For the purposes of sub-paragraph (3)(b), amounts are assumed to be attributed to assets in the way that produces the most beneficial outcome for P.

(5) Paragraph 11 makes further provision about the interpretation of subparagraph (2).

(6) Amounts to which the Part 2 certificate applies in accordance with this paragraph are referred to in this Part as "qualifying amounts".

Commentary—*Simon's Taxes* **A6.1216**.

Eligibility for clearance

5 (1) The effect of the Part 2 certificate depends on whether P is eligible for clearance.

(2) P is "eligible for clearance" if—

(a) none of the circumstances listed in Article 9(13)(a) to (e) apply (tax investigations etc), and

(b) Article 12(1) does not apply (wrongful behaviour in relation to non-UK domiciled status).

(3) Otherwise, P is "not eligible for clearance".

Commentary—*Simon's Taxes* **A6.1216**.

Effect if P eligible for clearance

6 (1) This paragraph sets out the effect of the Part 2 certificate if P is eligible for clearance.

(2) P ceases to be liable to tax on qualifying amounts.

(3) Sub-paragraph (2) does not apply to a qualifying amount if—

(a) the amount was held in the United Kingdom,

(b) at some point during the period beginning with 6 October 2011 and ending immediately before the start date, it ceased to be held in the United Kingdom, and

(c) after that point (but before the start date) it began to be held in Switzerland.

(4) Instead, such part of the one-off payment as is attributable (on a just and reasonable basis) to the qualifying amount is to be treated as if it were a credit allowable against the tax due from P taking account of that amount.

(5) The meaning of tax due "taking account of" an amount is explained in Part 5 of this Schedule.

(6) The form in which a qualifying amount was held in the United Kingdom is irrelevant (so references in sub-paragraph (3) to the amount include an asset representing the amount).

(7) The total qualifying amounts to which sub-paragraphs (2) and (4) can apply as a result of the Part 2 certificate is limited to X.

(8) If the total exceeds X, the particular qualifying amounts to which those subparagraphs apply are assumed to be those that would produce the most beneficial outcome for P.

(9) X is—

(a) in a case falling within Article 9(3), the value of the omitted taxable base by reference to which the one-off payment was calculated, and

(b) in any other case, the value shown in the Part 2 certificate as the value of the relevant capital (C_r).

Commentary—*Simon's Taxes* **A6.1216**.

Ceasing to be liable to tax

7 (1) The result of "ceasing to be liable" to tax on a qualifying amount depends on the tax (or taxes) in respect of which the amount is untaxed.

(2) For income tax or capital gains tax, the result is that the amount is no longer liable to be brought into account in assessing the income tax or capital gains tax due from P for the tax year in which the amount would otherwise be liable to be brought into account.
(3) For inheritance tax, the result is that any inheritance tax due from P in respect of the chargeable transfer and attributable to the property whose value is included in the amount is no longer due from P.
(4) For VAT, the result is that P is no longer required to account for output tax on the amount in determining the VAT payable by P for the prescribed accounting period in which P would otherwise be required to account for output tax on the amount.
(5) But—

(a) ceasing to be liable to tax on a qualifying amount does not affect P's liability to tax on any other amount, and
(b) P's liability to tax on any other amount remains what it would have been, had the qualifying amount been brought into account in calculating that liability.

(6) Accordingly, if the qualifying amount were ever to be brought into account and it were found that the tax assessed on any other amount should have been higher as a result, P would remain liable for the extra tax due on that other amount and for any associated ancillary charge.
(7) For the purposes of sub-paragraphs (5) and (6), the qualifying amount is assumed to form the top slice of the total sum on which P is liable to tax.

Commentary—*Simon's Taxes* **A6.1216**.

Effect if P not eligible for clearance

8 (1) This paragraph sets out the effect of the Part 2 certificate if P is not eligible for clearance.
(2) The one-off payment is to be treated as if it were a credit allowable against the tax due from P taking account of qualifying amounts.
(3) The one-off payment is to be applied for the purposes of sub-paragraph (2)—

(a) in the order specified in sub-paragraph (4), and
(b) subject to that, in the way that produces the most beneficial outcome for P.

(4) The order is—

(a) first, for VAT,
(b) then, for income tax,
(c) then, for capital gains tax, and
(d) finally, for inheritance tax.

Commentary—*Simon's Taxes* **A6.1216**.

Interest, penalties etc

9 (1) Where, by virtue of this Part, P ceases to be liable to tax on a qualifying amount, P also ceases to be liable to any ancillary charge directly connected with that amount.
(2) Where, by virtue of this Part, all or part of a one-off payment is treated as if it were a credit allowable against the tax due from P taking account of a qualifying amount, the credit may also be used to offset any ancillary charge directly connected with that amount.
(3) Sub-paragraph (4) applies in the case of a qualifying amount that is part only of—

(a) an amount of income on which income tax is charged,
(b) a chargeable gain,
(c) the value of property forming part of the value transferred by a chargeable transfer, or
(d) the value of a supply on which VAT is charged.

(4) The amount of any ancillary charge directly connected with that qualifying amount is determined by apportioning the ancillary charge directly connected with the income, gain or value on a just and reasonable basis.

Commentary—*Simon's Taxes* **A6.1216**.

Repayments

10 Nothing in this Part entitles any person to a repayment or refund of tax, save for any repayment or refund to which P may be entitled by virtue of paragraph 6(4) or 8(2) if the credit allowable under that paragraph exceeds the total amount of tax against which the credit is allowable.

Commentary—*Simon's Taxes* **A6.1216**.

Paragraph 4: supplementary provision

11 (1) This paragraph explains how paragraph 4(2) is to be read for each description of taxable amount.
(2) For income and chargeable gains—

(a) the reference to P being "liable to tax" includes a case where P would be so liable if the income or gain were to be remitted to the United Kingdom,

(b) "the taxable event" takes place when the income arises or the gain accrues (whether or not, in a remittance basis case, it is remitted to the United Kingdom), and
(c) the income or gain is "untaxed" if it has not been brought into account in an assessment to income tax or, as the case may be, capital gains tax for the tax year in which it is required to be brought into account.

(3) For the value of property forming part of the value transferred by a chargeable transfer—
(a) "the taxable event" takes place when the chargeable transfer is made (or, in the case of a potentially exempt transfer, when death occurs), and
(b) the value of the property is "untaxed" if it has not been brought into account in determining the value transferred by the chargeable transfer.

(4) For the value of supplies on which VAT is charged—
(a) "the taxable event" takes place when P makes the supply, and
(b) the value of the supply is "untaxed" if output tax on the supply has not been accounted for in determining the VAT payable by P for the prescribed accounting period in which P is required to account for output tax on the supply.

(5) Paragraph 4(2)(a) is not satisfied in a case where P is liable to tax only because the liability has been transferred to P as a result of action taken by HMRC (for example, as a result of a notice given under section 77A of VATA 1994 or a direction given under regulation 81 of the Income Tax (PAYE) Regulations 2003 (SI 2003/2682)).

Commentary—*Simon's Taxes* **A6.1216**.

Refund of one-off payment

12 If a one-off payment is refunded by HMRC in accordance with Article 15(3), this Part ceases to apply with respect to that payment.

Commentary—*Simon's Taxes* **A6.1216**.

PART 3
THE FUTURE: INCOME TAX AND CAPITAL GAINS TAX

Taxes affected

13 The taxes affected by this Part are—
(a) income tax, and
(b) capital gains tax.

Commentary—*Simon's Taxes* **A6.1216**.

Application of this Part

14 (1) This Part applies if—
(a) a sum is levied under Article 19 on an amount of income or a gain of a person, and
(b) a certificate is issued to the person under Article 30(1) in respect of the levying of that sum (or sums that include that sum).

(2) This Part also applies if—
(a) a retention is made under EUSA from an amount of income or a gain of a person,
(b) a tax finality payment, as contemplated by the Joint Declaration, is made on the same income or gain, and
(c) a certificate is issued to the person under the Joint Declaration in respect of the making of that payment (or payments that include that payment).

(3) In this Part—
(a) the person is referred to as "P",
(b) the certificate is referred to as "the relevant certificate",
(c) the amount of income, or the gain, is referred to as "the cleared amount",
(d) the account or deposit (within the meaning of the Agreement) to which the certificate relates (or to which certificates relate that include the certificate) is referred to as "the underlying account", and
(e) the sum levied under Article 19 on the cleared amount or, as the case may be, the tax finality payment made on it is referred to as "the transferred sum".

Commentary—*Simon's Taxes* **A6.1216**.

Effect of relevant certificate

15 (1) The effect of the relevant certificate depends on whether P makes an election under paragraph 16 in respect of the underlying account for the applicable year.

(2) "The applicable year" is the tax year for which P is liable to income tax or, as the case may be, capital gains tax on the cleared amount.

(3) If P makes an election, the transferred sum is to be treated as if it were a credit allowable against the income tax or, as the case may be, capital gains tax due from P for the applicable year.
(4) If P does not make an election, P ceases to be liable to income tax or, as the case may be, capital gains tax on the cleared amount.
(5) Sub-paragraph (4) is to be read in accordance with paragraph 7.
(6) Where P ceases to be liable to tax on the cleared amount, P also ceases to be liable to any ancillary charge directly connected with that amount.
Commentary—*Simon's Taxes* A6.1216.

Election

16 (1) P may make an election under this paragraph in respect of the underlying account for a tax year if all the affected amounts are included in full in a return (or amended return) made by P under Part 2 of TMA 1970 for that tax year.
(2) In relation to a tax year, an amount is an "affected amount" if—
- (a) a certificate is issued to P under Article 30(1) or the Joint Declaration in respect of the levying of a sum, or the making of a tax finality payment, on that amount,
- (b) the account or deposit to which the certificate relates is the underlying account, and
- (c) the amount is required to be brought into account in assessing the income tax or capital gains tax due from P for that tax year.

(3) An election under this paragraph must be made in the return or amended return in which the affected amounts are included.
(4) An election may only be made under this paragraph if it is accompanied by all the relevant certificates relating to the underlying account.
(5) For the purposes of paragraph 15, P is treated as making an election under this paragraph in respect of the underlying account for a tax year if a claim is made under Part 3 of TIOPA 2010 (double taxation relief for special withholding tax) in relation to any of the affected amounts.
(6) Section 143 of TIOPA 2010 (taking account of special withholding tax in calculating income or gains) applies with any necessary modifications in relation to a tax finality payment as it applies in relation to special withholding tax.
Commentary—*Simon's Taxes* A6.1216.

Other credits to be allowed first

17 Other than a credit allowed under Part 3 of TIOPA 2010, any credit for foreign tax allowed under that Act against the income tax or, as the case may be, capital gains tax due from P for the applicable year is to be allowed before effect is given to paragraph 15(3).
Commentary—*Simon's Taxes* A6.1216.

Repayments

18 (1) Sub-paragraph (2) applies if the amount of a credit allowable under paragraph 15(3) exceeds the amount of income tax or, as the case may be, capital gains tax due from P for the applicable year (before set-off).
(2) The excess is to be set against any amount of the other tax (income tax or capital gains tax) due from P for that year.
(3) Nothing in this Part entitles any person to a repayment or refund of tax, save for any repayment to which P may be entitled as a result of paragraph 15(3) if, in relation to a credit allowable under that paragraph, there is any remaining balance after applying—
- (a) sub-paragraph (2), and
- (b) section 138(4)(a) or 140(5)(a) of TIOPA 2010, if applicable to the cleared amount.

Commentary—*Simon's Taxes* A6.1216.

Relationship with special withholding tax rules

19 The Joint Declaration does not count for the purposes of section 136(6)(b) of TIOPA 2010 (definition of "special withholding tax") as a corresponding provision of international arrangements.
Commentary—*Simon's Taxes* A6.1216.

PART 4
THE FUTURE: INHERITANCE TAX

Taxes affected

20 This Part affects inheritance tax.

Application of this Part

21 (1) This Part applies if—

(a) an amount is withheld under Article 32(2) in respect of relevant assets of a deceased person ("P"), and

(b) a certificate is issued under Article 32(6) in respect of the withholding of that amount.

(2) The certificate is referred to in this Part as "the Article 32 certificate".

(3) The relevant assets in relation to which the Article 32 certificate is issued are referred to as "the cleared assets".

(4) Any reference in this Part to "the chargeable transfer" is to the transfer made (under section 4 of IHTA 1984) on P's death.

Commentary—*Simon's Taxes* **A6.1216**.

Effect of Article 32 certificate

22 (1) The cleared assets are to be treated as if they were excluded property in determining the value of P's estate immediately before P's death.

(2) As a result, any ancillary charge directly connected with those assets is also extinguished.

(3) But—

(a) treating the cleared assets as if they were excluded property does not affect any liability to inheritance tax on the rest of P's estate, and

(b) that liability remains what it would have been, had the cleared assets not been treated as excluded property.

(4) Accordingly, if the cleared assets were ever to be included in an account or further account under section 216 or 217 of IHTA 1984 in respect of the chargeable transfer and it were found that the inheritance tax charged on the value of the property in P's estate other than the cleared assets should have been higher, the extra tax charged on the value of that other property remains due, together with any associated ancillary charge.

(5) For the purposes of sub-paragraphs (3) and (4), the value of the cleared assets is assumed to form the highest part of the value transferred by the chargeable transfer.

Commentary—*Simon's Taxes* **A6.1216**.

Election in respect of Article 32 certificates

23 (1) This paragraph applies if the cleared assets for each of the Article 32 certificates issued in respect of P's death are included in full in an account or further account delivered in respect of P's death under section 216 or 217 of IHTA 1984 within the time permitted for delivering such an account or further account.

(2) The person who delivers the account or further account may elect to disapply paragraph 22.

(3) An election under this paragraph must be made in writing at the same time as the account or further account in which all the cleared assets are included, and signed by each person delivering the account or further account.

(4) An election may only be made under this paragraph if it is accompanied by each of the Article 32 certificates.

(5) If an election is made under this paragraph—

(a) paragraph 22 does not apply to the cleared assets for any of the Article 32 certificates issued in respect of P's death, and

(b) the amounts withheld under Article 32(2) are instead to be treated as if they were credits allowable against the inheritance tax due on the value transferred by the chargeable transfer (calculated with the value of all those cleared assets brought into account).

Commentary—*Simon's Taxes* **A6.1216**.

Repayments

24 Nothing in this Part entitles any person to a repayment or refund of tax, save for any repayment to which a person may be entitled as a result of paragraph 23 if the credit allowable under that paragraph exceeds the inheritance tax due from the person on the value transferred by the chargeable transfer.

Commentary—*Simon's Taxes* **A6.1216**.

PART 5
GENERAL PROVISIONS

Information exchange

25 No obligation of secrecy (whether imposed by statute or otherwise) prevents HMRC from disclosing information pursuant to a request made by virtue of Article 36 (reciprocity measures of the United Kingdom).

Commentary—*Simon's Taxes* **A6.1216**.

Amounts recoverable as if they were VAT

26 (1) Part 2 of this Schedule applies to amounts otherwise recoverable under paragraph 5(3) of Schedule 11 to VATA 1994 as a debt due to the Crown (amounts shown on invoices as VAT etc) in the same way as it applies to VAT.

(2) But in the application of Part 2 to such amounts—

(a) a reference to the value of a supply on which VAT is charged is a reference to the value of the supply shown in the invoice mentioned in paragraph 5(2) of that Schedule,

(b) "the taxable event" takes place when the invoice is issued,

(c) the value of the supply shown in the invoice is "untaxed" if the amount otherwise recoverable under paragraph 5(3) of that Schedule has not been recovered, and

(d) "ceasing to be liable" to tax on the value of that supply means that the amount otherwise recoverable is no longer recoverable.

Commentary—*Simon's Taxes* **A6.1216**.

[Transfers to HMRC under Agreement

26A—(1) Income or chargeable gains of a person are to be treated as not remitted to the United Kingdom if conditions A to D are met.

(2) Condition A is that (but for sub-paragraph (1)) the income or gains would be regarded as remitted to the United Kingdom by virtue of the bringing of money to the United Kingdom.

(3) Condition B is that the money is brought to the United Kingdom pursuant to a transfer made to HMRC in accordance with the Agreement.

(4) Condition C (which applies only if the money brought to the United Kingdom is a sum levied under Article 19(2)(*b*)) is that the sum was levied within the period of 45 days beginning with the day on which the amount derived from the income or gain in question was remitted as mentioned in Article 19(2)(*b*).

(5) Condition D is that the transfer is made in relation to a tax year in which section 809B, 809D or 809E of ITA 2007 (application of remittance basis) applies to the person.

(6) Sub-paragraph (1) does not apply in relation to money brought to the United Kingdom if or to the extent that—

(*a*) paragraph 18(2), or section 138(4)(*a*) or 140(5)(*a*) of TIOPA 2010, is applied in relation to it (set-off against other tax liabilities), or

(*b*) it is repaid or refunded by HMRC.][1]

Amendments—

[1] Paras 26A, 26B and preceding heading inserted by FA 2013 s 221. This amendment is treated as having come into force on 1 January 2013.

[26B—(1) This paragraph applies if—

(*a*) but for paragraph 26A(1), income or chargeable gains would have been regarded as remitted to the United Kingdom by virtue of the bringing of money to the United Kingdom, and

(*b*) section 809Q of ITA 2007 (transfers from mixed funds) would have applied in determining the amount that would have been so remitted.

(2) The bringing of the money to the United Kingdom counts as an offshore transfer for the purposes of section 809R(4) of ITA 2007 (composition of mixed fund).][1]

Amendments—[1] Paras 26A, 26B preceding heading inserted by FA 2013 s 221. This amendment is treated as having come into force on 1 January 2013.

General interpretation

27 (1) In this Schedule—

"ancillary charge" means any interest, penalty, surcharge or other ancillary charge;

"assessment", in relation to a tax, includes a determination and also includes an amended assessment or determination (and "assess" is to be read accordingly);

"chargeable gain" means a gain that is a chargeable gain for the purposes of TCGA 1992;

"chargeable transfer" has the meaning given in section 2 of IHTA 1984;

"EUSA" means the agreement dated 26 October 2004 between the European Community and the Swiss Confederation providing for measures equivalent to those laid down in Council Directive 2003/ 48/EC on taxation on savings income in the form of interest payments;

"HMRC" means Her Majesty's Revenue and Customs;

"qualifying amount" is defined in paragraph 4;

"remitted to the United Kingdom" means remitted to the United Kingdom within the meaning of Chapter A1 of Part 14 of ITA 2007;

"the value transferred", in relation to a chargeable transfer, has the meaning given in section 3 of IHTA 1984;

"taxable amount" is defined in paragraph 2;

"VAT" means value added tax charged in accordance with VATA 1994.

(2) An expression used in relation to a tax has the same meaning as in enactments relating to that tax.

(3) A reference to a person being "liable" includes being liable jointly with others.

(4) A reference to the most beneficial outcome for P is a reference to the most beneficial outcome for P with respect to P's liability to tax.

(5) A reference to the tax due "taking account of" a qualifying amount is—

(a) if the amount is an amount of income or a chargeable gain, a reference to the income tax or capital gains tax due for the tax year in which the amount is required to be brought into account (calculated with that amount brought into account),

(b) if the amount is the value of property forming part of the value transferred by a chargeable transfer, a reference to the inheritance tax due on the value transferred by the chargeable transfer (calculated with that amount brought into account),

(c) if the amount is the value of a supply on which VAT is charged, a reference to the VAT payable for the prescribed accounting period in which output tax on the supply is required to be brought into account (calculated with that output tax brought into account), and

(d) if the amount is the value of a supply to which Part 2 applies by virtue of paragraph 26, a reference to the amount otherwise recoverable under paragraph 5(3) of Schedule 11 to VATA 1994 in respect of that supply.

Commentary—*Simon's Taxes* **A6.1216**.

SCHEDULE 38

TAX AGENTS: DISHONEST CONDUCT

Section 223

Commentary—*Simon's Taxes* **A6.321**.

Commencement—Finance Act 2012, Schedule 38 (Tax agents: Dishonest Conduct) (Appointed Day and Savings) Order, SI 2013/279 art 2 (appointed day for the coming into force of Sch 38 is 1 April 2013).

PART 1
INTRODUCTION

Overview

1 This Schedule is arranged as follows—

(a) this Part explains who is a tax agent and what it means to engage in dishonest conduct,

(b) Part 2 sets out the process for establishing whether someone is engaging in or has engaged in dishonest conduct,

(c) Part 3 confers power on HMRC to obtain relevant documents,

(d) Part 4 sets out sanctions for engaging in dishonest conduct,

(e) Part 5 provides for assessment of and appeals against penalties, and

(f) Parts 6 and 7 contain miscellaneous provisions and consequential amendments.

Commentary—*Simon's Taxes* **A6.321**.

Commencement—Finance Act 2012, Schedule 38 (Tax agents: Dishonest Conduct) (Appointed Day and Savings) Order, SI 2013/279 art 2 (appointed day for the coming into force of Sch 38 is 1 April 2013).

Tax agent

2 (1) A "tax agent" is an individual who, in the course of business, assists other persons ("clients") with their tax affairs.

(2) Individuals can be tax agents even if they (or the organisations for which they work) are appointed—

(a) indirectly, or

(b) at the request of someone other than the client.

(3) Assistance with a client's tax affairs includes—

(a) advising a client in relation to tax, and

(b) acting or purporting to act as agent on behalf of a client in relation to tax.

(4) Assistance with a client's tax affairs also includes assistance with any document that is likely to be relied on by HMRC to determine a client's tax position.

(5) Assistance given for non-tax purposes counts as assistance with a client's tax affairs if it is given in the knowledge that it will be, or is likely to be, used by a client in connection with the client's tax affairs.

Commentary—*Simon's Taxes* **A6.321**.

Commencement—Finance Act 2012, Schedule 38 (Tax agents: Dishonest Conduct) (Appointed Day and Savings) Order, SI 2013/279 art 2 (appointed day for the coming into force of Sch 38 is 1 April 2013).

Dishonest conduct

3 (1) An individual "engages in dishonest conduct" if, in the course of acting as a tax agent, the individual does something dishonest with a view to bringing about a loss of tax revenue.
(2) It does not matter whether a loss is actually brought about.
(3) Nor does it matter whether the individual is acting on the instruction of clients.
(4) A loss of tax revenue would be brought about for these purposes if clients were to—
  (a) account for less tax than they are required to account for by law,
  (b) obtain more tax relief than they are entitled to obtain by law,
  (c) account for tax later than they are required to account for it by law, or
  (d) obtain tax relief earlier than they are entitled to obtain it by law.
(5) "Tax" is defined in Part 6 of this Schedule.
(6) "Tax relief" includes—
  (a) any exemption from or deduction or credit against or in respect of tax, and
  (b) any repayment of tax.
(7) A reference in this paragraph to doing something dishonest includes—
  (a) dishonestly omitting to do something, and
  (b) advising or assisting a client to do something that the individual knows to be dishonest.

Commentary—*Simon's Taxes* **A6.322**.
Commencement—Finance Act 2012, Schedule 38 (Tax agents: Dishonest Conduct) (Appointed Day and Savings) Order, SI 2013/279 art 2 (appointed day for the coming into force of Sch 38 is 1 April 2013).

PART 2
ESTABLISHING DISHONEST CONDUCT

Conduct notice

4 (1) This paragraph applies if HMRC determine that an individual is engaging in or has engaged in dishonest conduct.
(2) An authorised officer (or an officer of Revenue and Customs with the approval of an authorised officer) may notify the individual of that determination.
(3) The notice must state the grounds on which the determination was made.
(4) For the effect of notifying the individual, see paragraphs 7(2) and 29(2).
(5) A notice under this paragraph is referred to as a "conduct notice".
(6) In relation to a conduct notice, a reference to "the determination" is to the determination forming the subject of the notice.

Commentary—*Simon's Taxes* **A6.322**.
Commencement—Finance Act 2012, Schedule 38 (Tax agents: Dishonest Conduct) (Appointed Day and Savings) Order, SI 2013/279 art 2 (appointed day for the coming into force of Sch 38 is 1 April 2013).
Cross references—See FA 2014 Sch 34 para 4 (application of this para in relation to the issue of conduct notices to promoters of tax avoidance schemes).

Appeal against determination

5 (1) An individual to whom a conduct notice is given may appeal against the determination.
(2) Notice of appeal must be given—
  (a) in writing to the officer who gave the conduct notice, and
  (b) within the period of 30 days beginning with the day on which the conduct notice was given.
(3) It must state the grounds of appeal.
(4) On an appeal that is notified to the tribunal, the tribunal may confirm or set aside the determination.
(5) Subject to this paragraph, the provisions of Part 5 of TMA 1970 relating to appeals have effect in relation to an appeal under this paragraph as they have effect in relation to an appeal against an assessment to income tax.
(6) Setting aside a determination does not prevent a further conduct notice being given in respect of the same conduct if further evidence emerges.

Commentary—*Simon's Taxes* **A6.322**.
Commencement—Finance Act 2012, Schedule 38 (Tax agents: Dishonest Conduct) (Appointed Day and Savings) Order, SI 2013/279 art 2 (appointed day for the coming into force of Sch 38 is 1 April 2013).

Offence of concealment etc in connection with conduct notice

6 (1) A person ("P") commits an offence if, after a relevant event has occurred, P—
  (a) conceals, destroys or otherwise disposes of a material document, or
  (b) arranges for the concealment, destruction or disposal of a material document.
(2) A "relevant event" occurs if—
  (a) a conduct notice is given to an individual, or

(b) an individual is informed by an officer of Revenue and Customs that a conduct notice will be or is likely to be given to the individual.

(3) A "material document" is any document that could be sought under paragraph 8 as a result of the giving of the conduct notice.

(4) If P acts after the event described in sub-paragraph (2)(a), no offence is committed if P acts—

(a) after the determination has been set aside,

(b) more than 4 years after the conduct notice was given, or

(c) without knowledge of that event.

(5) If P acts before that event but after the event described in sub-paragraph (2)(b), no offence is committed if P acts—

(a) more than 2 years after the individual was, or was last, so informed, or

(b) without knowledge of the event described in sub-paragraph (2)(b).

(6) P acts without knowledge of an event if P—

(a) is not the individual with respect to whom the event has occurred, and

(b) does not know, and could not reasonably be expected to know, that the event has occurred.

(7) A person guilty of an offence under this paragraph is liable—

(a) on summary conviction, to a fine not exceeding the statutory maximum, and

(b) on conviction on indictment, to imprisonment for a term not exceeding 2 years or to a fine, or both.

Commentary—*Simon's Taxes* **A6.322**.

Commencement—Finance Act 2012, Schedule 38 (Tax agents: Dishonest Conduct) (Appointed Day and Savings) Order, SI 2013/279 art 2 (appointed day for the coming into force of Sch 38 is 1 April 2013).

PART 3
POWER TO OBTAIN TAX AGENT'S FILES ETC

Circumstances in which power is exercisable

7 (1) The power in paragraph 8 is exercisable only in case A or case B and only with the approval of the tribunal.

(2) Case A is where a conduct notice has been given to an individual and either—

(a) the time allowed for giving notice of appeal against the determination has expired without any such notice being given, or

(b) notice of appeal against the determination was given within that time, but the appeal has been withdrawn or the determination confirmed.

(3) Case B is where—

(a) an individual has been convicted of an offence relating to tax that involves fraud or dishonesty,

(b) the offence was committed after the individual became a tax agent (whether or not the individual was still a tax agent when it was committed and regardless of the capacity in which it was committed),

(c) either—

(i) the time allowed for appealing against the conviction has expired without any such appeal being brought, or

(ii) an appeal against the conviction was brought within that time, but the appeal has been withdrawn or the conviction upheld, and

(d) no more than 12 months have elapsed since the date on which paragraph (c) was satisfied.

(4) For the purposes of this paragraph, a determination or conviction that is appealed is not considered to have been confirmed or upheld until—

(a) the time allowed for bringing any further appeal has expired, or

(b) if a further appeal is brought within that time, that further appeal has been withdrawn or determined.

(5) In this Schedule, a reference to "the tax agent" is—

(a) in a case falling within case A, a reference to the individual mentioned in sub-paragraph (2), and

(b) in a case falling within case B, a reference to the individual mentioned in sub-paragraph (3).

(6) It does not matter whether the individual is still a tax agent when the power in paragraph 8 is to be exercised.

Commentary—*Simon's Taxes* **A6.323**.

Commencement—Finance Act 2012, Schedule 38 (Tax agents: Dishonest Conduct) (Appointed Day and Savings) Order, SI 2013/279 art 2 (appointed day for the coming into force of Sch 38 is 1 April 2013).

File access notice

8 (1) Subject to paragraph 7, an officer of Revenue and Customs may by notice in writing require any person mentioned in sub-paragraph (2) to provide relevant documents.
(2) The persons are—
(a) the tax agent, and
(b) any other person the officer believes may hold relevant documents.
(3) "Relevant documents" is defined in paragraph 9.
(4) A notice under this paragraph is referred to as a "file access notice".
(5) The person to whom a file access notice is given is referred to as "the document-holder".

Commentary—*Simon's Taxes* **A6.323**.

Commencement—Finance Act 2012, Schedule 38 (Tax agents: Dishonest Conduct) (Appointed Day and Savings) Order, SI 2013/279 art 2 (appointed day for the coming into force of Sch 38 is 1 April 2013).

Relevant documents

9 (1) "Relevant documents" means the tax agent's working papers (whenever acting as a tax agent) and any other documents received, created, prepared or used by the tax agent for the purposes of or in the course of assisting clients with their tax affairs.
(2) It does not matter who owns the papers or other documents.
(3) The reference in sub-paragraph (1) to clients—
(a) includes former clients, and
(b) is not limited to the clients with respect to whom the tax agent is engaging in or has engaged in dishonest conduct.

Commentary—*Simon's Taxes* **A6.323**.

Commencement—Finance Act 2012, Schedule 38 (Tax agents: Dishonest Conduct) (Appointed Day and Savings) Order, SI 2013/279 art 2 (appointed day for the coming into force of Sch 38 is 1 April 2013).

Content of notice

10 (1) A file access notice may require the provision of—
(a) particular relevant documents specified in the notice, or
(b) all relevant documents in the document-holder's possession or power.
(2) A file access notice does not need to identify the clients of the tax agent.
(3) A file access notice addressed to anyone other than the tax agent must name the tax agent.

Commentary—*Simon's Taxes* **A6.323**.

Commencement—Finance Act 2012, Schedule 38 (Tax agents: Dishonest Conduct) (Appointed Day and Savings) Order, SI 2013/279 art 2 (appointed day for the coming into force of Sch 38 is 1 April 2013).

Compliance

11 A file access notice may require documents to be provided—
(a) within such period,
(b) by such means and in such form, and
(c) to such person and at such place,
as is reasonably specified in the notice or in a document referred to in the notice.

Commentary—*Simon's Taxes* **A6.323**.

Commencement—Finance Act 2012, Schedule 38 (Tax agents: Dishonest Conduct) (Appointed Day and Savings) Order, SI 2013/279 art 2 (appointed day for the coming into force of Sch 38 is 1 April 2013).

12 Unless otherwise specified in the notice, a file access notice may be complied with by providing copies of the relevant documents.

Commentary—*Simon's Taxes* **A6.323**.

Commencement—Finance Act 2012, Schedule 38 (Tax agents: Dishonest Conduct) (Appointed Day and Savings) Order, SI 2013/279 art 2 (appointed day for the coming into force of Sch 38 is 1 April 2013).

Approval by tribunal

13 (1) The tribunal may not approve the giving of a file access notice unless—
(a) the application for approval is made by or with the agreement of an authorised officer,
(b) the tribunal is satisfied that the case falls within case A or case B (see paragraph 7),
(c) the tribunal is satisfied that, in the circumstances, the officer giving the notice is justified in doing so,
(d) the document-holder and (where different) the tax agent have been told that relevant documents are to be required and given a reasonable opportunity to make representations to an officer of Revenue and Customs, and
(e) the tribunal has been given a summary of any representations so made.

(2) Nothing in sub-paragraph (1) requires the tribunal to determine whether an individual is engaging in or has engaged in dishonest conduct.
(3) A decision by the tribunal under this paragraph is final (despite the provisions of sections 11 and 13 of the Tribunals, Courts and Enforcement Act 2007).

Commentary—*Simon's Taxes* **A6.323**.
Commencement—Finance Act 2012, Schedule 38 (Tax agents: Dishonest Conduct) (Appointed Day and Savings) Order, SI 2013/279 art 2 (appointed day for the coming into force of Sch 38 is 1 April 2013).

Documents not in person's possession or power

14 A file access notice only requires the document-holder to provide a document if it is in the document-holder's possession or power.

Commentary—*Simon's Taxes* **A6.323**.
Commencement—Finance Act 2012, Schedule 38 (Tax agents: Dishonest Conduct) (Appointed Day and Savings) Order, SI 2013/279 art 2 (appointed day for the coming into force of Sch 38 is 1 April 2013).

Types of information

15 (1) A file access notice does not require the document-holder to provide—
(a) parts of a document that contain information relating to the conduct of a pending appeal relating to tax, or
(b) journalistic material (as defined in section 13 of the Police and Criminal Evidence Act 1984).
(2) A file access notice does not require the document-holder to provide personal records (as defined in section 12 of the Police and Criminal Evidence Act 1984).
(3) But a file access notice may require the document-holder to provide documents that are personal records, omitting any information whose inclusion (whether alone or with other information) makes the original documents personal records.

Commentary—*Simon's Taxes* **A6.323**.
Commencement—Finance Act 2012, Schedule 38 (Tax agents: Dishonest Conduct) (Appointed Day and Savings) Order, SI 2013/279 art 2 (appointed day for the coming into force of Sch 38 is 1 April 2013).

Old documents

16 (1) A file access notice does not require the document-holder to provide a relevant document if—
(a) the whole of the document originated before the back-stop day, and
(b) no part of it has a bearing on tax periods ending on or after that day.
(2) "The back-stop day" is the first day of the period of 20 years ending with the day on which the file access notice is given.

Commentary—*Simon's Taxes* **A6.323**.
Commencement—Finance Act 2012, Schedule 38 (Tax agents: Dishonest Conduct) (Appointed Day and Savings) Order, SI 2013/279 art 2 (appointed day for the coming into force of Sch 38 is 1 April 2013).

Privileged communications between professional legal advisers and clients

17 (1) A file access notice does not require the document-holder to provide any part of a document that is privileged.
(2) For the purposes of this paragraph a document is privileged if it is a document in respect of which a claim to legal professional privilege, or (in Scotland) to confidentiality of communications between client and professional legal adviser, could be maintained in legal proceedings.
(3) Regulations under paragraph 23 of Schedule 36 to FA 2008 (information powers: privileged communications) apply (with any necessary modifications) to disputes under this paragraph as to whether a document is privileged.

Commentary—*Simon's Taxes* **A6.323**.
Commencement—Finance Act 2012, Schedule 38 (Tax agents: Dishonest Conduct) (Appointed Day and Savings) Order, SI 2013/279 art 2 (appointed day for the coming into force of Sch 38 is 1 April 2013).

Power to copy documents

18 If a document is provided pursuant to a file access notice, an officer of Revenue and Customs may take copies of or make extracts from the document.

Commentary—*Simon's Taxes* **A6.323**.
Commencement—Finance Act 2012, Schedule 38 (Tax agents: Dishonest Conduct) (Appointed Day and Savings) Order, SI 2013/279 art 2 (appointed day for the coming into force of Sch 38 is 1 April 2013).

Power to retain documents

19 (1) If a document is provided pursuant to a file access notice, HMRC may retain the document for a reasonable period if an officer of Revenue and Customs thinks it necessary to do so.

(2) While a document is retained—

(a) the document-holder may, if the document is reasonably required for any purpose, request a copy of it, and

(b) an officer of Revenue and Customs must comply with such a request without charge.

(3) The retention of a document under this paragraph is not to be regarded as breaking any lien claimed on the document.

(4) If a document retained under this paragraph is lost or damaged, the Commissioners are liable to compensate the owner of the document for any expenses reasonably incurred in replacing or repairing the document.

Commentary—*Simon's Taxes* **A6.323**.

Commencement—Finance Act 2012, Schedule 38 (Tax agents: Dishonest Conduct) (Appointed Day and Savings) Order, SI 2013/279 art 2 (appointed day for the coming into force of Sch 38 is 1 April 2013).

Appeal against file access notice

20 (1) If the document-holder is a person other than the tax agent, the document-holder may appeal against the file access notice, or any requirement in it, on the ground that it would be unduly onerous to comply with the notice or requirement.

(2) Notice of appeal must be given—

(a) in writing to the officer by whom the file access notice was given, and

(b) within the period of 30 days beginning with the day on which the file access notice was given.

(3) It must state the grounds of appeal.

(4) On an appeal that is notified to the tribunal, the tribunal may confirm, vary or set aside the file access notice or a requirement in it.

(5) If the tribunal confirms or varies the notice or a requirement in it, the document-holder must comply with the notice or requirement—

(a) within such period as is specified by the tribunal, or

(b) if the tribunal does not specify a period, within such period as is reasonably specified in writing by an officer of Revenue and Customs following the tribunal's decision.

(6) A decision by the tribunal under this paragraph is final (despite the provisions of sections 11 and 13 of the Tribunals, Courts and Enforcement Act 2007).

(7) Subject to this paragraph, the provisions of Part 5 of TMA 1970 relating to appeals have effect in relation to an appeal under this paragraph as they have effect in relation to an appeal against an assessment to income tax.

Commentary—*Simon's Taxes* **A6.323**.

Commencement—Finance Act 2012, Schedule 38 (Tax agents: Dishonest Conduct) (Appointed Day and Savings) Order, SI 2013/279 art 2 (appointed day for the coming into force of Sch 38 is 1 April 2013).

Offence of concealment etc in connection with file access notice

21 (1) A person ("P") commits an offence if P—

(a) conceals, destroys or otherwise disposes of a required document, or

(b) arranges for the concealment, destruction or disposal of a required document.

(2) A "required document" is a document within sub-paragraph (3) or subparagraph (4).

(3) A document is within this sub-paragraph if at the time when P acts—

(a) P is required to provide the document by a file access notice, and

(b) either—

(i) the notice has not been complied with, or

(ii) it has been complied with, but P has been notified in writing by an officer of Revenue and Customs that P must continue to preserve the document (and the notification has not been withdrawn).

(4) A document is within this sub-paragraph if at the time when P acts—

(a) P is not required to provide the document by a file access notice,

(b) P has been informed by an officer of Revenue and Customs that P will be or is likely to be so required, and

(c) no more than 6 months have elapsed since P was, or was last, so informed.

(5) A person guilty of an offence under this paragraph is liable—

(a) on summary conviction, to a fine not exceeding the statutory maximum, and

(b) on conviction on indictment, to imprisonment for a term not exceeding 2 years or to a fine, or both.

Commentary—*Simon's Taxes* **A6.323**.

Commencement—Finance Act 2012, Schedule 38 (Tax agents: Dishonest Conduct) (Appointed Day and Savings) Order, SI 2013/279 art 2 (appointed day for the coming into force of Sch 38 is 1 April 2013).

Penalty for failure to comply

22 (1) A person who fails to comply with a file access notice is liable to a penalty of £300.

(2) Failing to comply with a file access notice also includes—

(a) concealing, destroying or otherwise disposing of a required document, or

(b) arranging for any such concealment, destruction or disposal.

(3) "Required document" has the same meaning as in paragraph 21.

Commentary—*Simon's Taxes* **A4.595**.

Commencement—Finance Act 2012, Schedule 38 (Tax agents: Dishonest Conduct) (Appointed Day and Savings) Order, SI 2013/279 art 2 (appointed day for the coming into force of Sch 38 is 1 April 2013).

Daily penalty for failure to comply

23 If the failure continues after notification of a penalty under paragraph 22 has been issued, the person is liable to a further penalty, for each subsequent day on which the failure continues, of an amount not exceeding £60 for each such day.

Commentary—*Simon's Taxes* **A4.595**.

Commencement—Finance Act 2012, Schedule 38 (Tax agents: Dishonest Conduct) (Appointed Day and Savings) Order, SI 2013/279 art 2 (appointed day for the coming into force of Sch 38 is 1 April 2013).

Failure to comply with time limit

24 A failure to do anything required to be done within a limited period of time does not give rise to liability to a penalty under paragraph 22 or 23 if the thing was done within such further time (if any) as an officer of Revenue and Customs may have allowed.

Commentary—*Simon's Taxes* **A4.595**.

Commencement—Finance Act 2012, Schedule 38 (Tax agents: Dishonest Conduct) (Appointed Day and Savings) Order, SI 2013/279 art 2 (appointed day for the coming into force of Sch 38 is 1 April 2013).

Reasonable excuse

25 (1) Liability to a penalty under paragraph 22 or 23 does not arise if the person satisfies HMRC or (on an appeal notified to the tribunal) the tribunal that there is a reasonable excuse for the failure.

(2) For the purposes of this paragraph—

(a) an insufficiency of funds is not a reasonable excuse unless attributable to events outside the person's control,

(b) if the person relies on another person to do anything, that is not a reasonable excuse unless the first person took reasonable care to avoid the failure,

(c) if the person had a reasonable excuse for the failure but the excuse has ceased, the person is to be treated as having continued to have the excuse if the failure is remedied without unreasonable delay after the excuse ceased.

Commentary—*Simon's Taxes* **A4.595**.

Commencement—Finance Act 2012, Schedule 38 (Tax agents: Dishonest Conduct) (Appointed Day and Savings) Order, SI 2013/279 art 2 (appointed day for the coming into force of Sch 38 is 1 April 2013).

PART 4
SANCTIONS FOR DISHONEST CONDUCT

Penalty for dishonest conduct

26 (1) An individual who engages in dishonest conduct is liable to a penalty.

(2) Subject to paragraph 27, the penalty to which the individual is liable is to be—

(a) no less than £5,000, and

(b) no more than £50,000.

(3) In assessing the amount of the penalty, regard must be had to—

(a) whether the individual disclosed the dishonest conduct,

(b) whether that disclosure was prompted or unprompted,

(c) the quality of that disclosure, and

(d) the quality of the individual's compliance with any file access notice in connection with the dishonest conduct.

(4) An individual "discloses" dishonest conduct by—

(a) telling HMRC about it,

(b) giving HMRC reasonable help in identifying the client or clients concerned and in quantifying the loss of tax revenue (if any) brought about by it, and

(c) allowing HMRC access to records for the purpose of ensuring that any such loss is recovered or otherwise properly accounted for.

(5) A disclosure is "unprompted" if it is made at a time when the individual has no reason to believe that HMRC have discovered or are about to discover the dishonest conduct.
(6) Otherwise, a disclosure is "prompted".
(7) In relation to disclosure or compliance, "quality" includes timing, nature and extent.

Commentary—*Simon's Taxes* **A4.595**.
Commencement—Finance Act 2012, Schedule 38 (Tax agents: Dishonest Conduct) (Appointed Day and Savings) Order, SI 2013/279 art 2 (appointed day for the coming into force of Sch 38 is 1 April 2013).

Special reduction

27 (1) This paragraph applies if HMRC propose to assess an individual to a penalty under paragraph 26 of £5,000.
(2) If they think it right because of special circumstances, HMRC may take one or more of the following steps—
(a) reduce the penalty to an amount below £5,000 (which may be nil),
(b) stay the penalty, or
(c) agree a compromise in relation to proceedings for the penalty.
(3) "Special circumstances" does not include—
(a) ability to pay, or
(b) the fact that a loss of tax revenue from a client is balanced by an overpayment by another person (whether or not a client).

Commentary—*Simon's Taxes* **A4.595**.
Commencement—Finance Act 2012, Schedule 38 (Tax agents: Dishonest Conduct) (Appointed Day and Savings) Order, SI 2013/279 art 2 (appointed day for the coming into force of Sch 38 is 1 April 2013).

Power to publish details

28 (1) The Commissioners may publish information about an individual if the individual incurs a penalty under paragraph 26.
(2) The information that may be published is—
(a) the individual's name (including any trading name, previous name or pseudonym),
(b) the individual's address,
(c) the nature of any business carried on by the individual,
(d) the amount of the penalty,
(e) the periods or times to which the dishonest conduct relates,
(f) any other information the Commissioners consider it appropriate to publish in order to make clear the individual's identity, and
(g) the link (if there is one) between the dishonest conduct and any inaccuracy, failure or action as a result of which information is published under section 94 of FA 2009 (which relates to deliberate tax defaulters).
(3) No information may be published under this paragraph if the penalty incurred by the individual is £5,000 or less.
(4) Subsections (5) to (9) and (11) of section 94 of FA 2009 apply to publishing information about an individual under this paragraph as they apply to publishing information about a person under that section.
(5) If, in acting as a tax agent, the individual works or worked for an organisation, sub-paragraph (2)(f) includes power to publish such information about that organisation as the Commissioners consider appropriate in order to make clear the individual's identity.
(6) Before publishing information about the organisation, the Commissioners must—
(a) inform the organisation that they are considering doing so, and
(b) afford the organisation reasonable opportunity to make representations about whether it should be published.

Commentary—*Simon's Taxes* **A4.587**.
Commencement—Finance Act 2012, Schedule 38 (Tax agents: Dishonest Conduct) (Appointed Day and Savings) Order, SI 2013/279 art 2 (appointed day for the coming into force of Sch 38 is 1 April 2013).

PART 5
PENALTIES: ASSESSMENT ETC

Assessment of penalties

29 (1) If a person becomes liable to a penalty under Part 3 or 4 of this Schedule, HMRC may assess the penalty.
(2) But, in the case of a penalty under Part 4, they may only do so if a conduct notice has been given to the person and either—
(a) the time allowed for giving notice of appeal against the determination has expired without notice of appeal being given, or

(b) notice of appeal against the determination was given within the time allowed, but the appeal has been withdrawn or the determination confirmed.

(3) Paragraph 7(4) applies for the purposes of sub-paragraph (2)(b).

(4) If HMRC assess a penalty, they must notify the person.

Commentary—*Simon's Taxes* **A4.595**.

Commencement—Finance Act 2012, Schedule 38 (Tax agents: Dishonest Conduct) (Appointed Day and Savings) Order, SI 2013/279 art 2 (appointed day for the coming into force of Sch 38 is 1 April 2013).

30 (1) HMRC may not assess a penalty under this Schedule after the applicable deadline.

(2) For a penalty under Part 3, the applicable deadline is the end of the period of 12 months beginning with the day on which the person became liable to the penalty.

(3) For a penalty under Part 4, the applicable deadline is the end of the period of 12 months beginning with the later of—

(a) the first day on which HMRC may assess the penalty (see paragraph 29(2)), and

(b) day X.

(4) If a loss of tax revenue is brought about by the dishonest conduct, day X is—

(a) the day immediately following the end of the appeal period for the assessment or determination of the tax revenue lost (or, if more than one client is involved, the end of the last such period), or

(b) if there is no such assessment or determination, the day on which the amount of tax revenue lost is ascertained.

(5) Otherwise, day X is the day on which HMRC ascertain that no loss of tax revenue has been brought about by the dishonest conduct.

(6) In sub-paragraph (4), "appeal period" means the period during which—

(a) an appeal could be brought, or

(b) an appeal that has been brought has not been withdrawn or determined.

Commentary—*Simon's Taxes* **A4.595**.

Commencement—Finance Act 2012, Schedule 38 (Tax agents: Dishonest Conduct) (Appointed Day and Savings) Order, SI 2013/279 art 2 (appointed day for the coming into force of Sch 38 is 1 April 2013).

Appeal against penalty

31 (1) A person may appeal against a decision of HMRC—

(a) that a penalty is payable under Part 3 of this Schedule, or

(b) as to the amount of a penalty payable under Part 3 or 4 of this Schedule.

(2) Notice of appeal must be given—

(a) in writing to HMRC, and

(b) before the end of the period of 30 days beginning with the day on which notification of the penalty was issued.

(3) It must state the grounds of appeal.

(4) On an appeal under sub-paragraph (1)(a) that is notified to the tribunal, the tribunal may confirm or cancel the decision.

(5) On an appeal under sub-paragraph (1)(b) that is notified to the tribunal, the tribunal may—

(a) confirm the decision, or

(b) substitute for the decision another decision that HMRC had power to make.

(6) If, in the case of an appeal against a penalty under Part 4, the tribunal substitutes its decision for HMRC's, the tribunal may rely on paragraph 27 (special reduction)—

(a) to the same extent as HMRC (which may mean applying the same reduction as HMRC to a different starting point), or

(b) to a different extent, but only if the tribunal thinks that HMRC's decision in respect of the application of that paragraph was flawed (when considered in the light of the principles applicable in proceedings for judicial review).

(7) Subject to this paragraph and paragraph 32, the provisions of Part 5 of TMA 1970 relating to appeals have effect in relation to an appeal under this paragraph as they have effect in relation to an appeal against an assessment to income tax.

Commentary—*Simon's Taxes* **A4.595**.

Commencement—Finance Act 2012, Schedule 38 (Tax agents: Dishonest Conduct) (Appointed Day and Savings) Order, SI 2013/279 art 2 (appointed day for the coming into force of Sch 38 is 1 April 2013).

Enforcement of penalty

32 (1) A penalty under this Schedule must be paid—

(a) before the end of the period of 30 days beginning with the day on which notification of the penalty was issued, or

(b) if a notice of appeal under paragraph 31 is given, before the end of the period of 30 days beginning with the day on which the appeal is withdrawn or determined.

(2) A penalty under this Schedule may be enforced as if it were income tax charged in an assessment and due and payable.

Commentary—*Simon's Taxes* **A4.595**.

Commencement—Finance Act 2012, Schedule 38 (Tax agents: Dishonest Conduct) (Appointed Day and Savings) Order, SI 2013/279 art 2 (appointed day for the coming into force of Sch 38 is 1 April 2013).

Double jeopardy

33 A person is not liable to a penalty under this Schedule in respect of anything in respect of which the person has been convicted of an offence.

Commentary—*Simon's Taxes* **A4.595**.

Commencement—Finance Act 2012, Schedule 38 (Tax agents: Dishonest Conduct) (Appointed Day and Savings) Order, SI 2013/279 art 2 (appointed day for the coming into force of Sch 38 is 1 April 2013).

34 (1) A person is not liable to a penalty under this Schedule in respect of anything in respect of which the person is personally liable to a penalty under—

(a) Schedule 24 to FA 2007 (penalties for errors),

(b) Schedule 41 to FA 2008 (penalties for failure to notify etc), or

(c) Schedule 55 to FA 2009 (penalties for failure to make a return etc).

(2) Sub-paragraph (1) applies where, for example, the person is personally liable by virtue of section 48(3) of VATA 1994 (VAT representatives).

Commentary—*Simon's Taxes* **A4.595**.

Commencement—Finance Act 2012, Schedule 38 (Tax agents: Dishonest Conduct) (Appointed Day and Savings) Order, SI 2013/279 art 2 (appointed day for the coming into force of Sch 38 is 1 April 2013).

Power to change amount of penalties

35 (1) If it appears to the Treasury that there has been a change in the value of money since the last relevant day, they may by regulations substitute for the sums for the time being specified in paragraphs 22(1), 23, 26(2), 27(1) and (2)(a) and 28(3) such other sums as appear to them to be justified by the change.

(2) "Relevant day", in relation to a specified sum, means—

(a) the day on which this Act is passed, and

(b) each day on which the power conferred by sub-paragraph (1) has been exercised in relation to that sum.

(3) Regulations under this paragraph do not apply to a failure or conduct that began before the day on which they come into force.

(4) The power to make regulations under this paragraph is exercisable by statutory instrument.

(5) A statutory instrument containing regulations under this paragraph is subject to annulment in pursuance of a resolution of the House of Commons.

Commencement—Finance Act 2012, Schedule 38 (Tax agents: Dishonest Conduct) (Appointed Day and Savings) Order, SI 2013/279 art 2 (appointed day for the coming into force of Sch 38 is 1 April 2013).

PART 6
MISCELLANEOUS PROVISION AND INTERPRETATION

Application of provisions of TMA 1970

36 Subject to the provisions of this Schedule, the following provisions of TMA 1970 apply for the purposes of this Schedule as they apply for the purposes of the Taxes Acts—

(a) section 108 (responsibility of company officers),

(b) section 114 (want of form), and

(c) section 115 (delivery and service of documents).

Commencement—Finance Act 2012, Schedule 38 (Tax agents: Dishonest Conduct) (Appointed Day and Savings) Order, SI 2013/279 art 2 (appointed day for the coming into force of Sch 38 is 1 April 2013).

Tax

37 (1) "Tax" means—

(a) income tax,

(b) capital gains tax,

(c) corporation tax,

(d) construction industry deductions,

(e) VAT,

(f) insurance premium tax,

(g) inheritance tax,

(h) stamp duty land tax,

(i) stamp duty reserve tax,
(j) petroleum revenue tax,
(k) aggregates levy,
(l) climate change levy,
(m) landfill tax, and
(n) any duty of excise other than vehicle excise duty.

(2) "Construction industry deductions" means construction industry deductions under Chapter 3 of Part 3 of FA 2004.

(3) "Corporation tax" includes an amount assessable or chargeable as if it were corporation tax.

(4) "VAT" means—
(a) value added tax charged in accordance with VATA 1994,
(b) amounts recoverable under paragraph 5(2) of Schedule 11 to that Act (amounts shown on invoices as VAT), and
(c) amounts treated as VAT by virtue of regulations under section 54 of that Act (farmers etc).

Commencement—Finance Act 2012, Schedule 38 (Tax agents: Dishonest Conduct) (Appointed Day and Savings) Order, SI 2013/279 art 2 (appointed day for the coming into force of Sch 38 is 1 April 2013).

General interpretation

38 In this Schedule—
"appointed" includes engaged;
"client" (except in paragraph 17)—
(a) has the meaning given in paragraph 2(1), and
(b) in relation to a particular tax agent, means a client of that tax agent;
"the Commissioners" means the Commissioners for Her Majesty's Revenue and Customs;
"conduct notice" has the meaning given in paragraph 4;
"the document-holder" has the meaning given in paragraph 8;
"document" includes a copy of a document (see also section 114 of FA 2008);
"file access notice" has the meaning given in paragraph 8;
"HMRC" means Her Majesty's Revenue and Customs;
"organisation" includes any person or firm carrying on a business;
"specify" includes describe;
"tax period" means a tax year, accounting period or other period in respect of which tax is charged;
"the tribunal" means the First-tier Tribunal or, where determined by or under the Tribunal Procedure Rules, the Upper Tribunal.

Commencement—Finance Act 2012, Schedule 38 (Tax agents: Dishonest Conduct) (Appointed Day and Savings) Order, SI 2013/279 art 2 (appointed day for the coming into force of Sch 38 is 1 April 2013).

39 (1) A reference in this Schedule to clients of a tax agent (or to a tax agent's clients) is a reference to the persons whom the agent assists with their tax affairs.

(2) Sub-paragraph (1) applies even if—
(a) the agent works for an organisation, and
(b) it is the organisation that is appointed to give the assistance.

Commencement—Finance Act 2012, Schedule 38 (Tax agents: Dishonest Conduct) (Appointed Day and Savings) Order, SI 2013/279 art 2 (appointed day for the coming into force of Sch 38 is 1 April 2013).

40 A loss of tax revenue is taken for the purposes of this Schedule to be (or to be capable of being) brought about by dishonest conduct despite the fact that the loss can be recovered or properly accounted for (following discovery of the conduct or otherwise).

Commencement—Finance Act 2012, Schedule 38 (Tax agents: Dishonest Conduct) (Appointed Day and Savings) Order, SI 2013/279 art 2 (appointed day for the coming into force of Sch 38 is 1 April 2013).

41 A reference in this Schedule to working for an organisation includes being a partner or member of an organisation.

Commencement—Finance Act 2012, Schedule 38 (Tax agents: Dishonest Conduct) (Appointed Day and Savings) Order, SI 2013/279 art 2 (appointed day for the coming into force of Sch 38 is 1 April 2013).

42 A reference in a provision of this Schedule to an authorised officer is to an officer of Revenue and Customs who is, or is a member of a class of officers who are, authorised by the Commissioners for the purposes of that provision.

Commencement—Finance Act 2012, Schedule 38 (Tax agents: Dishonest Conduct) (Appointed Day and Savings) Order, SI 2013/279 art 2 (appointed day for the coming into force of Sch 38 is 1 April 2013).

Relationship with other enactments

43 Nothing in this Schedule limits—

(a) any liability a person may have under any other enactment in respect of conduct in respect of which a person is liable to a penalty under this Schedule, or

(b) any power a person may have under any other enactment to obtain relevant documents.

Commencement—Finance Act 2012, Schedule 38 (Tax agents: Dishonest Conduct) (Appointed Day and Savings) Order, SI 2013/279 art 2 (appointed day for the coming into force of Sch 38 is 1 April 2013).

PART 7

CONSEQUENTIAL PROVISIONS

TMA 1970

44 (TMA 1970 is amended as follows.

Commencement—Finance Act 2012, Schedule 38 (Tax agents: Dishonest Conduct) (Appointed Day and Savings) Order, SI 2013/279 art 2 (appointed day for the coming into force of Sch 38 is 1 April 2013).

45 (*repeals* TMA 1970 ss 20A, 20B, 99)

Commencement—Finance Act 2012, Schedule 38 (Tax agents: Dishonest Conduct) (Appointed Day and Savings) Order, SI 2013/279 art 2 (appointed day for the coming into force of Sch 38 is 1 April 2013).

46 (*amends* TMA 1970 s 20BB)

Commencement—Finance Act 2012, Schedule 38 (Tax agents: Dishonest Conduct) (Appointed Day and Savings) Order, SI 2013/279 art 2 (appointed day for the coming into force of Sch 38 is 1 April 2013).

47 (*amends* TMA 1970 s 20D)

Commencement—Finance Act 2012, Schedule 38 (Tax agents: Dishonest Conduct) (Appointed Day and Savings) Order, SI 2013/279 art 2 (appointed day for the coming into force of Sch 38 is 1 April 2013).

48 (*amends* TMA 1970 s 103)

Commencement—Finance Act 2012, Schedule 38 (Tax agents: Dishonest Conduct) (Appointed Day and Savings) Order, SI 2013/279 art 2 (appointed day for the coming into force of Sch 38 is 1 April 2013).

49 (*amends* TMA 1970 s 103ZA)

Commencement—Finance Act 2012, Schedule 38 (Tax agents: Dishonest Conduct) (Appointed Day and Savings) Order, SI 2013/279 art 2 (appointed day for the coming into force of Sch 38 is 1 April 2013).

50 (*amends* TMA 1970 s 118)

Commencement—Finance Act 2012, Schedule 38 (Tax agents: Dishonest Conduct) (Appointed Day and Savings) Order, SI 2013/279 art 2 (appointed day for the coming into force of Sch 38 is 1 April 2013).

OTA 1975

51 (*amends* OTA 1975 Sch 2 para 1(1)).

Commencement—Finance Act 2012, Schedule 38 (Tax agents: Dishonest Conduct) (Appointed Day and Savings) Order, SI 2013/279 art 2 (appointed day for the coming into force of Sch 38 is 1 April 2013).

IHTA 1984

52 (*repeals* IHTA 1984 s 247(4)).

Commencement—Finance Act 2012, Schedule 38 (Tax agents: Dishonest Conduct) (Appointed Day and Savings) Order, SI 2013/279 art 2 (appointed day for the coming into force of Sch 38 is 1 April 2013).

Social Security Contributions and Benefits Act 1992

53 (*amends* SSCBA 1992 s 16).

Commencement—Finance Act 2012, Schedule 38 (Tax agents: Dishonest Conduct) (Appointed Day and Savings) Order, SI 2013/279 art 2 (appointed day for the coming into force of Sch 38 is 1 April 2013).

54 (*amends* SSCBA 1992 Sch 1 para 7B).

Commencement—Finance Act 2012, Schedule 38 (Tax agents: Dishonest Conduct) (Appointed Day and Savings) Order, SI 2013/279 art 2 (appointed day for the coming into force of Sch 38 is 1 April 2013).

Social Security Contributions and Benefits (Northern Ireland) Act 1992

55 (*amends* SSCB(NI)A 1992 Sch 1 para 7B).

Commencement—Finance Act 2012, Schedule 38 (Tax agents: Dishonest Conduct) (Appointed Day and Savings) Order, SI 2013/279 art 2 (appointed day for the coming into force of Sch 38 is 1 April 2013).

Social Security Administration Act 1992

56 (*inserts* SSAA 1992 s 110ZA(2A)).

Commencement—Finance Act 2012, Schedule 38 (Tax agents: Dishonest Conduct) (Appointed Day and Savings) Order, SI 2013/279 art 2 (appointed day for the coming into force of Sch 38 is 1 April 2013).

Social Security Administration (Northern Ireland) Act 1992

57 (*inserts* SSA(NI)A 1992 s 104ZA(2A)).

Commencement—Finance Act 2012, Schedule 38 (Tax agents: Dishonest Conduct) (Appointed Day and Savings) Order, SI 2013/279 art 2 (appointed day for the coming into force of Sch 38 is 1 April 2013).

FA 2003

58 (1) FA 2003 is amended as follows.
(2) (*amends* FA 2003 s 93).
(3) (*repeals* FA 2003 s 96).
(4) (*amends* FA 2003 Sch 13).

Commencement—Finance Act 2012, Schedule 38 (Tax agents: Dishonest Conduct) (Appointed Day and Savings) Order, SI 2013/279 art 2 (appointed day for the coming into force of Sch 38 is 1 April 2013).

FINANCE ACT 2013

AN ACT TO Grant certain duties, to alter other duties, and to amend the law relating to the National Debt and the Public Revenue, and to make further provision in connection with finance.

[17 July 2013]

CONTENTS

PART 4
EXCISE DUTIES AND OTHER TAXES

Value added tax

191 Repayments of value added tax to health service bodies

(1) In section 41 of VATA 1994 (application to the Crown), in subsection (7), after "Board" insert "and a clinical commissioning group, the Health and Social Care Information Centre, the National Health Service Commissioning Board and the National Institute for Health and Care Excellence".

(2) The amendment made by this section is treated as having come into force on 1 April 2013.

192 Valuation of certain supplies of fuel

Schedule 38 contains provision about the valuation of certain supplies of fuel for the purposes of value added tax.

193 Reduced rate for energy-saving materials

(1) Group 2 (installation of energy-saving materials) of Part 2 of Schedule 7A to VATA 1994 (reduced rate supplies of goods and services) is amended as follows.

(2) For items 1 and 2 substitute—

"1 Supplies of services of installing energy-saving materials in residential accommodation.

2 Supplies of energy-saving materials by a person who installs those materials in residential accommodation."

(3) Omit Note 3 (meaning of "use for a relevant charitable purpose").

(4) The amendments made by this section have effect in relation to supplies made on or after 1 August 2013.

PART 6
OTHER PROVISIONS

International matters

221 Agreement between UK and Switzerland

(1) In Schedule 36 to FA 2012 (agreement between UK and Switzerland), after paragraph 26 insert—

"Transfers to HMRC under Agreement

26A

(1) Income or chargeable gains of a person are to be treated as not remitted to the United Kingdom if conditions A to D are met.

(2) Condition A is that (but for sub-paragraph (1)) the income or gains would be regarded as remitted to the United Kingdom by virtue of the bringing of money to the United Kingdom.

(3) Condition B is that the money is brought to the United Kingdom pursuant to a transfer made to HMRC in accordance with the Agreement.

(4) Condition C (which applies only if the money brought to the United Kingdom is a sum levied under Article 19(2)(*b*)) is that the sum was levied within the period of 45 days beginning with the day on which the amount derived from the income or gain in question was remitted as mentioned in Article 19(2)(*b*).

(5) Condition D is that the transfer is made in relation to a tax year in which section 809B, 809D or 809E of ITA 2007 (application of remittance basis) applies to the person.

(6) Sub-paragraph (1) does not apply in relation to money brought to the United Kingdom if or to the extent that—

(*a*) paragraph 18(2), or section 138(4)(*a*) or 140(5)(*a*) of TIOPA 2010, is applied in relation to it (set-off against other tax liabilities), or

(*b*) it is repaid or refunded by HMRC.

26B

(1) This paragraph applies if—

(*a*) but for paragraph 26A(1), income or chargeable gains would have been regarded as remitted to the United Kingdom by virtue of the bringing of money to the United Kingdom, and

(*b*) section 809Q of ITA 2007 (transfers from mixed funds) would have applied in determining the amount that would have been so remitted.

(2) The bringing of the money to the United Kingdom counts as an offshore transfer for the purposes of section 809R(4) of ITA 2007 (composition of mixed fund)."

(2) The amendment made by this section is to be treated as having come into force on 1 January 2013.

222 International agreements to improve tax compliance

(1) The Treasury may make regulations for, or in connection with, giving effect to or enabling effect to be given to—

(*a*) the agreement reached between the Government of the United Kingdom and the Government of the United States of America to improve international tax compliance and to implement FATCA, signed on 12 September 2012;

(*b*) any agreement modifying or supplementing that agreement;

(*c*) any other agreement between the Government of the United Kingdom and the government of another territory which makes provision corresponding, or substantially similar, to that made by an agreement within paragraph (*a*) or (*b*);

(*d*) any arrangements for the exchange of tax information in relation to the United Kingdom and any other territory which make provision corresponding, or substantially similar, to that made by an agreement within paragraph (*a*) or (*b*).

(2) Regulations under this section may in particular—

(*a*) authorise HMRC to require persons specified for the purposes of this paragraph ("relevant financial entities") to provide HMRC with information of specified descriptions;

(*b*) require that information to be provided at such times and in such form and manner as may be specified;

(*c*) impose obligations on relevant financial entities (including obligations to obtain from specified persons details of their place of residence for tax purposes);

(*d*) make provision (including provision imposing penalties) about contravention of, or non-compliance with, the regulations;

(*e*) make provision about appeals in relation to the imposition of any penalty.

(3) Regulations under this section may—

(*a*) provide that a reference in the regulations to an agreement or arrangements to which subsection (1) refers, or a provision of such an agreement or arrangements, is to be construed as a reference to the agreement or arrangements, or provision, as amended from time to time;

(*b*) make different provision in relation to different periods of time;

(*c*) make different provision for different cases or circumstances;

(*d*) contain incidental, supplemental, transitional, transitory or saving provision (including provision amending any enactment).

(4) In this section—

"FATCA" means the provisions commonly known as the Foreign Account Tax Compliance Act in the enactment of the United States of America called the Hiring Incentives to Restore Employment Act;

"HMRC" means Her Majesty's Revenue and Customs;

"specified" means specified in regulations under this section.

(5) The power conferred by this section is without prejudice to any other powers conferred by or under any enactment.

(6) The power of the Treasury to make regulations under this section is exercisable by statutory instrument.

(7) Any statutory instrument containing regulations under this section is subject to annulment in pursuance of a resolution of the House of Commons.

Summer Finance Bill 2015—Summer Finance Bill 2015, as published on 15 July 2015, affects the above provision. Please check the latest version of the Bill and subsequent Finance Act for details.

Regulations—International Tax Compliance (United States of America) Regulations, SI 2013/1962.
International Tax Compliance (United States of America) Regulations, SI 2014/1506.
International Tax Compliance (Crown Dependencies and Gibraltar) (Amendment) Regulations, SI 2015/873.
International Tax Compliance Regulations, SI 2015/878.

Powers

225 Definition of "goods" for certain customs purposes

In section 1(1) of CEMA 1979 (interpretation), in the definition of "goods", for "baggage" substitute "containers".

226 Power to detain goods

(1) Section 139 of CEMA 1979 (provisions as to detention, seizure and condemnation of goods etc) is amended as follows.

(2) After subsection (1) insert—

"(1A) A person mentioned in subsection (1) who reasonably suspects that any thing may be liable to forfeiture under the customs and excise Acts may detain that thing.

(1B) References in this section and Schedule 2A to a thing detained as liable to forfeiture under the customs and excise Acts include a thing detained under subsection (1A)."

(3) In subsection (2), for the words from "either" to the end substitute "deliver that thing to an officer".

(4) In subsection (4), for "the Commissioners at the nearest office of customs and excise" substitute "an officer".

(5) In subsection (5), for "Schedule 3" substitute "Schedules 2A and 3".

(6) After that subsection insert—

"(5A) Schedule 2A contains supplementary provisions relating to the detention of things as liable to forfeiture under the customs and excise Acts."

(7) After Schedule 2 to that Act (composite goods: supplementary provisions as to excise duties and drawbacks) insert—

"SCHEDULE 2A

SUPPLEMENTARY PROVISIONS RELATING TO THE DETENTION OF THINGS AS LIABLE TO FORFEITURE

Section 139(5A)

Interpretation

1

In this Schedule, references (however expressed) to a thing being detained are references to a thing being detained as liable to forfeiture under the customs and excise Acts.

Period of detention

2 (1) This paragraph applies where a thing is detained.

(2) The thing may be detained for 30 days beginning with the day on which the thing is first detained.

(3) The thing is deemed to be seized as liable to forfeiture under the customs and excise Acts if its detention ceases to be authorised under this paragraph.

Notice of detention

3 (1) The Commissioners must take reasonable steps to give written notice of the detention of any thing, and of the grounds for the detention, to any person who to their knowledge was, at the time of the detention, the owner or one of the owners of the thing.

(2) But notice need not be given under sub-paragraph (1) if the detention occurred in the presence of—

- (*a*) the person whose offence or suspected offence occasioned the detention,
- (*b*) the owner or any of the owners of the thing detained or any servant or agent of such an owner, or
- (*c*) in the case of any thing detained on a ship or aircraft, the master or commander.

Unauthorised removal or disposal: penalties etc

4 (1) This paragraph applies where a thing is detained and, with the agreement of a person within sub-paragraph (2) ("the responsible person"), the thing remains at the place where it is first detained (rather than being removed and detained elsewhere).

(2) A person is within this sub-paragraph if the person is—

- (*a*) the owner or any of the owners of the thing at the time it was detained or any servant or agent of such an owner, or
- (*b*) a person whom the person who detains the thing reasonably believes to be a person within paragraph (*a*).

(3) If the responsible person fails to prevent the unauthorised removal or disposal of the thing from the place where it is detained, that failure attracts a penalty under section 9 of the Finance Act 1994 (civil penalties).

(4) The removal or disposal of the thing is unauthorised unless it is done with the permission of a proper officer of Revenue and Customs.

(5) Where any duty of excise is payable in respect of the thing—

- (*a*) the penalty is to be calculated by reference to the amount of that duty (whether it has been paid or not), and
- (*b*) section 9 of the Finance Act 1994 has effect as if in subsection (2)(*a*) the words "5 per cent of" were omitted.

(6) If no duty of excise is payable in respect of the thing, that section has effect as if the penalty provided for by subsection (2)(*b*) of that section were whichever is the greater of—

(*a*) the value of the thing at the time it was first detained, or

(*b*) £250.

5 (1) This paragraph applies where—

(*a*) a thing is detained at a revenue trader's premises,

(*b*) the thing is liable to forfeiture under the customs and excise Acts, and

(*c*) without the permission of a proper officer of Revenue and Customs, the thing is removed from the trader's premises, or otherwise disposed of, by any person.

(2) The Commissioners may seize, as liable to forfeiture under the customs and excise Acts, goods of equivalent value to the thing, from the revenue trader's stock.

(3) For the purposes of this paragraph, a revenue trader's premises include any premises used to hold or store anything for the purposes of the revenue trader's trade, regardless of who owns or occupies the premises."

(8) The amendments made by this section have effect in relation to things detained on or after the day on which this Act is passed.

227 Penalty instead of forfeiture of larger ships

(1) Section 143 of CEMA 1979 (penalty in lieu of forfeiture of larger ship where responsible officer is implicated in offence) is amended as follows.

(2) For subsection (1) (Commissioners' power to impose fine up to £50) substitute—

"(1) This section applies where—

(*a*) any ship of 250 or more tons register would, but for section 142, be liable to forfeiture for, or in connection with, any offence under the customs and excise Acts, and

(*b*) in the opinion of the Commissioners, a responsible officer of the ship is implicated either by the officer's own act, or by neglect, in that offence."

(3) In subsection (3) (Commissioners' power to bring condemnation proceedings)—

(*a*) for the words from the beginning to the first "they" substitute "The Commissioners", and

(*b*) for "£500" substitute "£10,000".

(4) In subsection (4) (power to detain ship pending payment of deposit against fine or condemnation proceedings)—

(*a*) for the words from the beginning to "section, the" substitute "The",

(*b*) for "£50 or, as the case may be, £500" substitute "£10,000", and

(*c*) omit "their final decision or, as the case may be,".

(5) In paragraph (*a*) of subsection (6) (definition of "responsible officer)—

(*a*) after "means" insert "a person who is, or is acting as,",

(*b*) for "or an engineer" substitute ", an engineer or the bosun", and

(*c*) omit the words from "and, in the case of a ship manned" to the end.

(6) After that subsection insert—

"(7) If the Treasury consider that there has been a change in the value of money since the Finance Act 2013 was passed or, as the case may be, since the last occasion when the power conferred by this subsection was exercised, they may by order substitute for the sum for the time being specified in subsections (3) and (4) such other sum as appears to them to be justified by the change.

(8) An order under subsection (7) may not vary the penalty for any conduct occurring before the coming into force of the order.

(9) An order under subsection (7) must be made by statutory instrument.

(10) A statutory instrument containing an order under subsection (7) is subject to annulment in pursuance of a resolution of either House of Parliament."

228 Data-gathering from merchant acquirers etc

(1) In Part 2 of Schedule 23 to FA 2011 (data-gathering powers: relevant data-holders), after paragraph 13 insert—

"*Merchant acquirers etc*

13A

(1) A person who has a contractual obligation to make payments to retailers in settlement of payment card transactions is a relevant data-holder.

(2) In this paragraph—

"payment card" includes a credit card, a charge card and a debit card;

"payment card transaction" means any transaction in which a payment card is accepted as payment;

"retailer" means a person who accepts a payment card as payment for any transaction.

(3) In this paragraph any reference to a payment card being accepted as payment includes a reference to any account number or other indicators associated with a payment card being accepted as payment."

(2) This section applies in relation to relevant data with a bearing on any period (whether before, on or after the day on which this Act is passed).

Payment

230 Penalties: late filing, late payment and errors

Schedule 50 contains provision for, and in connection with, penalties for late filing, late payment and errors.

Administration

233 Self assessment: withdrawal of notice to file etc

Schedule 51 contains provision for, and in connection with, withdrawing a notice under section 8, 8A or 12AA of TMA 1970 and cancelling liability to a penalty under Schedule 55 to FA 2009.

Interim remedies

234 Restrictions on interim payments in proceedings relating to taxation matters

(1) This section applies to an application for an interim remedy (however described), made in any court proceedings relating to a taxation matter, if the application is founded (wholly or in part) on a point of law which has yet to be finally determined in the proceedings.

(2) Any power of a court to grant an interim remedy (however described) requiring the Commissioners for Her Majesty's Revenue and Customs, or an officer of Revenue and Customs, to pay any sum to any claimant (however described) in the proceedings is restricted as follows.

(3) The court may grant the interim remedy only if it is shown to the satisfaction of the court—

(*a*) that, taking account of all sources of funding (including borrowing) reasonably likely to be available to fund the proceedings, the payment of the sum is necessary to enable the proceedings to continue, or

(*b*) that the circumstances of the claimant are exceptional and such that the granting of the remedy is necessary in the interests of justice.

(4) The powers restricted by this section include (for example)—

(*a*) powers under rule 25 of the Civil Procedure Rules 1998 (S.I. 1998/3132);

(*b*) powers under Part II of Rule 29 of the Rules of the Court of Judicature (Northern Ireland) (Revision) 1980 (S.R. 1980 No.346).

(5) This section applies in relation to proceedings whenever commenced, but only in relation to applications made in those proceedings on or after 26 June 2013.

(6) This section applies on and after 26 June 2013.

(7) Subsection (8) applies where, on or after 26 June 2013 but before the passing of this Act, an interim remedy was granted by a court using a power which, because of subsection (6), is to be taken to have been restricted by this section.

(8) Unless it is shown to the satisfaction of the court that paragraph (*a*) or (*b*) of subsection (3) applied at the time the interim remedy was granted, the court must, on an application made to it under this subsection—

(*a*) revoke or modify the interim remedy so as to secure compliance with this section, and

(*b*) if the Commissioners have, or an officer of Revenue and Customs has, paid any sum as originally required by the interim remedy, order the repayment of the sum or any part of the sum as appropriate (with interest from the date of payment).

(9) For the purposes of this section, proceedings on appeal are to be treated as part of the original proceedings from which the appeal lies.

(10) In this section "taxation matter" means anything, other than national insurance contributions, the collection and management of which is the responsibility of the Commissioners for Her Majesty's Revenue and Customs (or was the responsibility of the Commissioners of Inland Revenue or Commissioners of Customs and Excise).

PART 7

FINAL PROVISIONS

235 Interpretation

(1) In this Act—

"ALDA 1979" means the Alcoholic Liquor Duties Act 1979,

"BGDA 1981" means the Betting and Gaming Duties Act 1981,

"CAA 2001" means the Capital Allowances Act 2001,

"CEMA 1979" means the Customs and Excise Management Act 1979,

"CRCA 2005" means the Commissioners for Revenue and Customs Act 2005,

"CTA 2009" means the Corporation Tax Act 2009,
"CTA 2010" means the Corporation Tax Act 2010,
"F(No.3)A 2010" means the Finance (No. 3) Act 2010,
"HODA 1979" means the Hydrocarbon Oil Duties Act 1979,
"ICTA" means the Income and Corporation Taxes Act 1988,
"IHTA 1984" means the Inheritance Tax Act 1984,
"ITA 2007" means the Income Tax Act 2007,
"ITEPA 2003" means the Income Tax (Earnings and Pensions) Act 2003,
"ITTOIA 2005" means the Income Tax (Trading and Other Income) Act 2005,
"OTA 1975" means the Oil Taxation Act 1975,
"TCGA 1992" means the Taxation of Chargeable Gains Act 1992,
"TIOPA 2010" means the Taxation (International and Other Provisions) Act 2010,
"TMA 1970" means the Taxes Management Act 1970,
"TPDA 1979" means the Tobacco Products Duty Act 1979,
"VATA 1994" means the Value Added Tax Act 1994, and
"VERA 1994" means the Vehicle Excise and Registration Act 1994.

(2) In this Act—
"FA", followed by a year, means the Finance Act of that year;
"F(No.2)A", followed by a year, means the Finance (No. 2) Act of that year.

236 Short title

This Act may be cited as the Finance Act 2013.

SCHEDULE 38

VALUATION OF CERTAIN SUPPLIES OF FUEL

Section 192

Introductory

1 VATA 1994 is amended as follows.

Valuation of supplies for private use

2 In Schedule 6 (valuation: special cases), before paragraph 1 insert—

"PART 1

VALUATION OF SUPPLIES OF FUEL FOR PRIVATE USE

Option for valuation on flat-rate basis

A1

(1) This paragraph applies if, in a prescribed accounting period, supplies of goods by a taxable person ("P") arise by virtue of paragraph 5(1) of Schedule 4 (but otherwise than for a consideration) where road fuel which is or has previously been supplied to or imported or manufactured by P in the course of P's business is provided for, or appropriated to, private use.

(2) For this purpose "road fuel is provided for, or appropriated to, private use" if—

(*a*) it is provided or to be provided by P—

(i) to an individual for private use in the individual's own car or a car allocated to the individual, and

(ii) by reason of the individual's employment,

(*b*) where P is an individual, it is appropriated or to be appropriated by P for private use in P's own car, or

(*c*) where P is a partnership, it is provided or to be provided to any of the individual partners for private use in that partner's own car.

(3) P may opt for all supplies of goods within sub-paragraph (1) made by P in the prescribed accounting period to be valued on the flat-rate basis.

(4) On the flat-rate basis, the value of all supplies made to any one individual in respect of any one car is that determined in accordance with an order under paragraph B1.

B1

(1) The Treasury must, by order, make provision about the valuation of supplies on the flat-rate basis.

(2) In particular, an order under this paragraph must—

(*a*) set out a table ("the base valuation table") by reference to which the value of supplies is to be determined until such time as the base valuation table is replaced under paragraph (*b*),

(*b*) provide that at regular intervals—

(i) the amounts specified in the base valuation table are to be revalorised by the Commissioners in accordance with the order, and

(ii) a table (an "updated valuation table") containing the revalorised amounts is to take effect (and replace any existing table) in accordance with the order, and

(*c*) require the Commissioners to publish any updated valuation table before it takes effect, together with a statement specifying the date from which it has effect.

(3) An order under this paragraph may provide for the base valuation table and any updated valuation table to be implemented or supplemented by either or both of the following—

(*a*) rules set out in the order which explain how the value is to be determined by reference to any table;

(*b*) notes set out in the order with respect to the interpretation or application of any table or any rules or notes.

(4) Rules or notes may make different provision for different circumstances or cases.

Interpretation

C1

(1) For the purposes of this Part of this Schedule—

(*a*) any reference to an individual's own car is to be construed as including any car of which for the time being the individual has the use, other than a car allocated to the individual,

(*b*) subject to sub-paragraph (2), a car is at any time to be taken to be allocated to an individual if at that time it is made available (without any transfer of the property in it) either to the individual or to any other person, and is so made available by reason of the individual's employment and for private use, and

(*c*) fuel provided by an employer to an employee and fuel provided to any person for private use in a car which, by virtue of paragraph (*b*), is for the time being taken to be allocated to the employee is to be taken to be provided to the employee by reason of the employee's employment.

(2) For the purposes of this Part of this Schedule, in any prescribed accounting period a car is not regarded as allocated to an individual by reason of the individual's employment if—

(*a*) in that period it was made available to, and actually used by, more than one of the employees of one or more employers and, in the case of each of them, it—

(i) was made available to that employee by reason of the employment, but

(ii) was not in that period ordinarily used by any one of them to the exclusion of the others,

(*b*) in the case of each of the employees, any private use of the car made by the employee in that period was merely incidental to the employee's other use of it in that period, and

(*c*) in that period it was not normally kept overnight on or in the vicinity of any residential premises where any of the employees was residing, except while being kept overnight on premises occupied by the person making the car available to them.

(3) In this Part of this Schedule—

"employment" includes any office, and related expressions are to be construed accordingly;

"car" means a motor car as defined by paragraph 1A(4) and (5);

"road fuel" means hydrocarbon oil as defined by the Hydrocarbon Oil Duties Act 1979 (see section 1(2) of that Act) on which duty has been or is required to be paid in accordance with that Act.

(4) The Treasury may, by order, amend the definition of "road fuel" in sub-paragraph (3).

PART 2
OTHER PROVISIONS".

3 In paragraph 6 of that Schedule (valuation of supplies of goods by virtue of paragraph 5(1) of Schedule 4 etc), in sub-paragraph (1), after "except where" insert "the person making the supply opts under paragraph A1(3) above for valuation on the flat-rate basis or".

4 Omit sections 56 and 57 (fuel for private use).

5 In section 97(4) (orders subject to affirmative procedure), in paragraph (*f*)—

(*a*) after "paragraph" insert "B1, C1(4),", and

(*b*) after "1A(7)" insert ", 2A(4)".

Supplies to employees etc at less than open market value

6 After paragraph 2 of Schedule 6 insert—

"2A

(1) This paragraph applies if—

(*a*) a taxable person ("P") makes a supply of road fuel for a consideration,

(*b*) the recipient of the supply is—

(i) connected with P, or

(ii) an employee or partner of P or a person who is connected with such an employee or partner,

(*c*) the value of the supply would (in the absence of this paragraph) be less than its open market value, and

(*d*) the recipient of the supply is not entitled to credit for the whole of the input tax arising on the supply.

(2) The value of the supply is to be taken to be an amount equal to its open market value.

(3) For the purposes of this paragraph—

(*a*) "road fuel" means hydrocarbon oil as defined by the Hydrocarbon Oil Duties Act 1979 (see section 1(2) of that Act) on which duty has been or is required to be paid in accordance with that Act, and

(*b*) any question whether a person is connected with another is to be determined in accordance with section 1122 of the Corporation Tax Act 2010.

(4) The Treasury may, by order, amend the definition of "road fuel" in sub-paragraph (3)(*a*)."

Commencement and transitional provision

7 (1) The amendments made by paragraphs 2 to 4 come into force in relation to prescribed accounting periods beginning on or after 1 February 2014.

(2) Subject to that, section 56 of VATA 1994 has effect on and after 11 December 2012 as if in subsection (2) of that section for the words after "it is supplied" there were substituted "for consideration."

8 (1) The amendment made by paragraph 6 is to be treated as coming into force on 11 December 2012 and has effect in relation to—

(*a*) supplies of goods on or after the commencement day, and

(*b*) supplies of goods in the period beginning with 11 December 2012 and ending immediately before the commencement day, if and to the extent that the goods are not made available before the end of that period to the person to whom they are supplied.

(2) "The commencement day" means the day on which this Act is passed.

SCHEDULE 50

PENALTIES: LATE FILING, LATE PAYMENT AND ERRORS

Section 230

Amendments to Schedule 24 to FA 2007: penalties for errors

1 (1) In Schedule 24 to FA 2007 (penalties for errors), paragraph 13 (procedure: assessment) is amended as follows.

(2) In sub-paragraph (1)(*c*), after "assessed" insert "(subject to sub-paragraph (1ZB))".

(3) After sub-paragraph (1) insert—

"(1ZA) Sub-paragraph (1ZB) applies where—

(*a*) a person is at any time liable for two or more penalties relating to PAYE returns, or for two or more penalties relating to CIS returns, and (*b*) the penalties ("the relevant penalties") are assessed in respect of more than one tax period ("the relevant tax periods").

(1ZB) A notice under sub-paragraph (1) in respect of any of the relevant penalties may, instead of stating the tax period in respect of which the penalty is assessed, state the tax year or the part of a tax year to which the penalty relates.

(1ZC) For that purpose, a relevant penalty relates to the tax year or the part of a tax year in which the relevant tax periods fall.

(1ZD) For the purposes of sub-paragraph (1ZA)—

"a PAYE return" means a return for the purposes of PAYE regulations;

"a CIS return" means a return for the purposes of regulations under section 70(1)(*a*) of FA 2004 in connection with deductions on account of tax under the Construction Industry Scheme."

Amendments to Schedule 55 to FA 2009: penalty for failure to make returns

2 Schedule 55 (penalty for failure to make returns etc) to FA 2009 is amended in accordance with paragraphs 3 to 9.

3 In paragraph 1 (returns etc in respect of which penalties are to be paid under that Schedule)—

(*a*) in the definition of "penalty date" in sub-paragraph (4), after "document" insert "falling within any of items 1 to 3 and 5 to 13 in the Table";

(*b*) after sub-paragraph (4) insert—

"(4A) The Treasury may by order make such amendments to item 4 in the Table as they think fit in consequence of any amendment, revocation or re-enactment of the regulations mentioned in that item."

4 In the Table at the end of paragraph 1, in item 4 (annual return of payments for purposes of PAYE regulations etc), for the words in the third column substitute—

"Return under any of the following provisions of the Income Tax (PAYE) Regulations 2003 (S.I. 2003/2682)—

(*a*) regulation 67B (real time returns)

(*b*) regulation 67D (exceptions to regulation 67B)".

5 In paragraph 2 (amount of penalty: occasional returns and returns for periods of 6 months or more), for "1 to 5" substitute "1 to 3, 5".

6 After paragraph 6A insert—

"Amount of penalty: real time information for PAYE

6B

Paragraphs 6C and 6D apply in the case of a return falling within item 4 in the Table.

6C

(1) If P fails during a tax month to make a return on or before the filing date, P is liable to a penalty under this paragraph in respect of that month.

(2) But this is subject to sub-paragraphs (3) and (4).

(3) P is not liable to a penalty under this paragraph in respect of a tax month as a result of any failure to make a return on or before the filing date which occurs during the initial period.

(4) P is not liable to a penalty under this paragraph in respect of a tax month falling in a tax year if the month is the first tax month in that tax year during which P fails to make a return on or before the filing date (disregarding for this purpose any failure which occurs during the initial period).

(5) In sub-paragraphs (3) and (4) "the initial period" means the period which—

(*a*) begins with the day in the first tax year on which P is first required to make a return, and

(*b*) is of such duration as is specified in regulations made by the Commissioners,

and for this purpose "the first tax year" means the first tax year in which P is required to make returns.

(6) P may be liable under this paragraph to no more than one penalty in respect of each tax month.

(7) The penalty under this paragraph is to be calculated in accordance with regulations made by the Commissioners.

(8) Regulations under sub-paragraph (7) may provide for a penalty under this paragraph in respect of a tax month to be calculated by reference to either or both of the following matters—

(*a*) the number of persons employed by P, or treated as employed by P for the purposes of PAYE regulations;

(*b*) the number of previous penalties incurred by P under this paragraph in the same tax year.

(9) The Commissioners may by regulations disapply sub-paragraph (3) or (4) in such circumstances as are specified in the regulations.

(10) If P has elected under PAYE regulations to be treated as different employers in relation to different groups of employees, this paragraph applies to P as if—

(*a*) in respect of each group P were a different person, and

(*b*) each group constituted all of P's employees.

(11) Regulations made by the Commissioners under this paragraph may—

(*a*) make different provision for different cases, and

(*b*) include incidental, consequential and supplementary provision.

6D

(1) P may be liable to one or more penalties under this paragraph in respect of extended failures.

(2) In this paragraph an "extended failure" means a failure to make a return on or before the filing date which continues after the end of the period of 3 months beginning with the day after the filing date.

(3) P is liable to a penalty or penalties under this paragraph if (and only if)—

(*a*) HMRC decide at any time that such a penalty or penalties should be payable in accordance with sub-paragraph (4) or (6), and

(*b*) HMRC give notice to P specifying the date from which the penalty, or each penalty, is payable.

(4) HMRC may decide under sub-paragraph (3)(*a*) that a separate penalty should be payable in respect of each unpenalised extended failure in the tax year to date.

(5) In that case the amount of the penalty in respect of each failure is 5% of any liability to make payments which would have been shown in the return in question.

(6) HMRC may decide under sub-paragraph (3)(*a*) that a single penalty should be payable in respect of all the unpenalised extended failures in the tax year to date.

(7) In that case the amount of the penalty in respect of those failures is 5% of the sum of the liabilities to make payments which would have been shown in each of the returns in question.

(8) For the purposes of this paragraph, an extended failure is unpenalised if a penalty has not already been imposed in respect of it under this paragraph (whether in accordance with subparagraph (4) or (6)).

(9) The date specified in the notice under sub-paragraph (3)(*b*) in relation to a penalty—

(*a*) may be earlier than the date on which the notice is given, but

(*b*) may not be earlier than the end of the period mentioned in sub-paragraph (2) in relation to the relevant extended failure.

(10) In sub-paragraph (9)(*b*) "the relevant extended failure" means—

(*a*) the extended failure in respect of which the penalty is payable, or

(*b*) if the penalty is payable in respect of more than one extended failure (in accordance with sub-paragraph (6)), the extended failure with the latest filing date."

7 In paragraph 18 (assessment), for sub-paragraph (5) substitute—

"(5) Sub-paragraph (6) applies if—

(*a*) an assessment in respect of a penalty is based on a liability to tax that would have been shown in a return, and

(*b*) that liability is found by HMRC to be excessive.

(6) HMRC may by notice to P amend the assessment so that it is based upon the correct amount.

(7) An amendment under sub-paragraph (6)—

(*a*) does not affect when the penalty must be paid;

(*b*) may be made after the last day on which the assessment in question could have been made under paragraph 19."

8 (1) Paragraph 19 (assessment) is amended as follows.

(2) In sub-paragraph (2) after "Date A is" insert "—

(*a*) in the case of an assessment of a penalty under paragraph 6C, the last day of the period of 2 years beginning with the end of the tax month in respect of which the penalty is payable, (*b*) in the case of an assessment of a penalty under paragraph 6D, the last day of the period of 2 years beginning with the filing date for the relevant extended failure (as defined in paragraph 6D(10)), and

(*c*) in any other case,".

(3) In sub-paragraph (3)(*a*), after "return" insert "or returns (as the case may be in relation to penalties under section 6C or 6D)".

9 (1) Paragraph 27 (interpretation) is amended as follows.

(2) After sub-paragraph (2) insert—

"(2A) "The Commissioners" means the Commissioners for Her Majesty's Revenue and Customs."

(3) After sub-paragraph (3) insert—

"(3A) "Tax month" means the period beginning with the 6th day of a month and ending with the 5th day of the following month."

Amendments to Schedule 56 to FA 2009: penalty for failure to make payments on time

10 Schedule 56 (penalty for failure to make payments on time) to FA 2009 is amended in accordance with paragraphs 11 to 14.

11 In paragraph 1 (penalty for failure to pay tax), in sub-paragraph (4), for the words from "the date on which" to the end substitute "the day after the date specified in or for the purposes of column 4 of the Table in relation to that amount."

12 (1) Paragraph 6 (amount of penalty: PAYE and CIS amounts) is amended as follows.

(2) For sub-paragraph (1) substitute—

"(1) P is liable to a penalty under this paragraph, in relation to each tax, each time that P makes a default in relation to a tax year."

(3) In sub-paragraph (2)—

(*a*) in the opening words, after "default" insert "in relation to a tax year";

(*b*) in paragraph (*a*), at the end insert "of tax payable in relation to the tax year";

(*c*) in paragraph (*b*), at the end insert "payable in relation to the tax year";

(*d*) in paragraph (*c*), at the end insert "payable in relation to the tax year";

(*e*) in paragraph (*d*), at the end insert "and due for the tax year".

(4) For sub-paragraphs (3) to (7) substitute—

"(3) But where a failure to make one of those payments (or to pay an amount comprising two or more of those payments) would, apart from this sub-paragraph, constitute the first default in relation to a tax year, that failure does not count as a default in relation to that year for the purposes of a penalty under this paragraph.

(4) The amount of the penalty for a default made in relation to a tax year is determined by reference to—

(*a*) the amount of the tax comprised in the default, and

(*b*) the number of previous defaults that P has made in relation to the same tax year.

(5) If the default is P's 1st, 2nd or 3rd default in relation to the tax year, P is liable, at the time of the default, to a penalty of 1% of the amount of tax comprised in the default.

(6) If the default is P's 4th, 5th or 6th default in relation to the tax year, P is liable, at the time of the default, to a penalty of 2% of the amount of tax comprised in the default.

(7) If the default is P's 7th, 8th or 9th default in relation to the tax year, P is liable, at the time of the default, to a penalty of 3% of the amount of tax comprised in the default.

(7A) If the default is P's 10th or subsequent default in relation to the tax year, P is liable, at the time of the default, to a penalty of 4% of the amount of tax comprised in the default."

(5) In sub-paragraph (8), for paragraph (*b*) substitute—

"(*b*) a previous default counts for the purposes of subparagraphs (5) to (7A) even if it is remedied before the time of the default giving rise to the penalty."

(6) After sub-paragraph (8) insert—

"(8A) Regulations made by the Commissioners for Her Majesty's Revenue and Customs may specify—

(*a*) circumstances in which, for the purposes of sub-paragraph (2), a payment of less than the full amount may be treated as a payment in full;

(*b*) circumstances in which sub-paragraph (3) is not to apply.

(8B) Regulations under sub-paragraph (8A) may—

(*a*) make different provision for different cases, and

(*b*) include incidental, consequential and supplementary provision."

13 After paragraph 9 insert—

"*Interaction with other penalties and late payment surcharges*

9A

In the application of the following provisions, no account shall be taken of a penalty under this Schedule—

(*a*) section 97A of TMA 1970 (multiple penalties),

(*b*) paragraph 12(2) of Schedule 24 to FA 2007 (interaction with other penalties), and

(*c*) paragraph 15(1) of Schedule 41 to FA 2008 (interaction with other penalties)."

14 (1) Paragraph 11 (assessment of penalty) is amended as follows.

(2) For sub-paragraph (4A) substitute—

"(4A) If an assessment in respect of a penalty is based on an amount of tax due or payable that is found by HMRC to be excessive, HMRC may by notice to P amend the assessment so that it is based upon the correct amount.

(4B) An amendment made under sub-paragraph (4A)—

(*a*) does not affect when the penalty must be paid;

(*b*) may be made after the last day on which the assessment in question could have been made under paragraph 12."

(3) Omit sub-paragraph (5).

Consequential amendment

15 In consequence of paragraph 7, paragraph 10 of Schedule 10 to the Finance (No. 3) Act 2010 is repealed.

Commencement

16 (1) The amendments made by paragraph 1 have effect in relation to any assessment of a penalty under Schedule 24 to FA 2007 made on or after the day on which this Act is passed.

(2) The amendments made by paragraphs 2 to 9 and 15 have effect for the tax year 2014–15 and subsequent tax years in relation to failures to make returns with a filing date (as defined in paragraph 1(4) of Schedule 55 to FA 2009) on or after 6 April 2014.

(3) The amendments made by paragraphs 10 to 14 have effect for defaults made in relation to the tax year 2014–15 and subsequent tax years (see paragraph 6(2) of Sch.56 to FA 2009 (as amended by paragraph 12(3) of this Schedule) as to when a default is made in relation to a tax year).

SCHEDULE 51

WITHDRAWAL OF NOTICE TO FILE ETC

Section 233

Commentary—*Simon's Taxes* **A4.104**.

TMA 1970

1 TMA 1970 is amended in accordance with paragraphs 2 to 5.

2 (1) Section 7 (notice of liability to income tax and capital gains tax) is amended as follows.

(2) In subsection (1)—

(*a*) for paragraph (*b*) substitute—

"(*b*) falls within subsection (1A) or (1B),", and

(*b*) for "six months from the end of that year" substitute "the notification period".

(3) After subsection (1) insert—

"(1A) A person falls within this subsection if the person has not received a notice under section 8 requiring a return for the year of assessment of the person's total income and chargeable gains.

(1B) A person falls within this subsection if the person—

(*a*) has received a notice under section 8 requiring a return for the year of assessment of the person's total income and chargeable gains, and

(*b*) has received a notice under section 8B withdrawing the notice under section 8.

(1C) In subsection (1) "the notification period" means—

(*a*) in the case of a person who falls within subsection (1A), the period of 6 months from the end of the year of assessment, or

(*b*) in the case of a person who falls within subsection (1B)—

(i) the period of 6 months from the end of the year of assessment, or

(ii) the period of 30 days beginning with the day after the day on which the notice under section 8 was withdrawn,

whichever ends later."

(4) In subsection (2), for the words from "shall have effect" to the end substitute "and subsections (1A) to (1C) have effect as if references to a notice under section 8 were references to a notice under section 8A."

3 After section 8A insert—

"8B Withdrawal by HMRC of notice under section 8 or 8A

(1) This section applies to a person who is given a notice under section 8 or 8A.

(2) Before the end of the withdrawal period, the person may request HMRC to withdraw the notice.

(3) But no request may be made if—

(*a*) the person has made a return under section 8 or 8A in pursuance of the notice under that section, or

(*b*) the person has been served with notice of a determination under section 28C by virtue of the notice under section 8 or 8A having been given to the person.

(4) If, on receiving a request, HMRC decide to withdraw the notice under section 8 or 8A they must do so by giving the person a notice under this section.

(5) A notice under this section must specify the date on which the notice under section 8 or 8A is withdrawn.

(6) For the purposes of subsection (2) "the withdrawal period" means—

(*a*) the period of 2 years beginning with the end of the year of assessment to which the notice under section 8 or 8A relates, or

(*b*) in exceptional circumstances, such extended period as HMRC may agree with the person.

(7) Withdrawal of a notice given to a person under section 8 or 8A in relation to a year of assessment does not prevent HMRC from giving the person a further notice under that section in relation to that year.

(8) See paragraph 17A of Schedule 55 to FA 2009 as to the cancellation of liability to a penalty under any paragraph of that Schedule by including provision in a notice under this section."

4 After section 12AA insert—

"12AAA Withdrawal by HMRC of notice under section 12AA

(1) This section applies to a partner who is required by a notice under section 12AA to deliver a return.

(2) Before the end of the withdrawal period, the partner may request HMRC to withdraw the notice.

(3) But no request may be made if the partner has delivered a return under section 12AA in pursuance of the notice.

(4) If, on receiving a request, HMRC decide to withdraw the notice under section 12AA they must do so by giving the partner a notice under this section.

(5) A notice under this section must specify the date on which the notice under section 12AA is withdrawn.

(6) For the purposes of subsection (2) "the withdrawal period" means—

(*a*) in the case of a partnership which includes one or more companies, the period of 2 years beginning with the end of the period in respect of which the return under section 12AA was required by the notice under that section,

(*b*) in the case of any other partnership, the period of 2 years beginning with the end of the year of assessment to which the notice under section 12AA relates, or

(*c*) in the case of any partnership, such extended period as HMRC may agree with the partner in exceptional circumstances.

(7) Withdrawal of a notice under section 12AA in relation to the period in respect of which the return under that section was required or year of assessment (as the case may be) does not prevent HMRC from serving a further notice under section 12AA requiring a partner to deliver a return in relation to that period or year.

(8) References in subsections (2) to (6) to the partner include references to a successor of the partner (see section 12AA(11)).

(9) See paragraph 17B of Schedule 55 to FA 2009 as to the cancellation of liability to a penalty under any paragraph of that Schedule by including provision in a notice under this section."

5 In section 59B (payment of income and capital gains tax), after subsection (4) insert—

"(4ZA) In a case in which the notice required by section 7 was given following the receipt of a notice under section 8B, subsections (3) and (4) apply as if—

(*a*) the reference to the notice required by section 7 were a reference to the original notice required by that section, and

(*b*) the references to notice under section 8 or 8A were references to the original notice under that section.

(4ZB) In subsection (4ZA) the references to original notices are to notices given before the notice under section 8B."

FA 2008

6 (1) Paragraph 7 of Schedule 41 to FA 2008 (potential lost revenue in respect of failure to comply with relevant obligation) is amended as follows.

(2) After sub-paragraph (1) insert—

"(1A) In the case of an obligation under section 7 of TMA 1970 which arises by virtue of subsection (1B) of that section, the potential lost revenue is so much of any income tax or capital gains tax to which P is liable in respect of the tax year in question as is, by reason of the failure to comply with the obligation—

(*a*) where the period specified in subsection (1C)(*b*)(ii) of that section applies and ends after the relevant date, unpaid at the end of that period, or

(*b*) in any other case, unpaid on the relevant date.

(1B) For the purposes of sub-paragraph (1A) the relevant date is—

(*a*) 31 January following the tax year, or

(*b*) if, after that date, HMRC refund a payment on account in respect of the tax year to P, the day after the refund is issued."

(3) In sub-paragraph (2), after "and a tax year" insert "(not falling within subparagraph (1A))".

FA 2009

7 (1) Paragraph 3 of Schedule 53 to FA 2009 (late payment interest start date: amendments and discovery assessments etc) is amended as follows.

(2) In sub-paragraph (3)—

(*a*) for "as required" substitute "in accordance with a requirement", and

(*b*) after "tax)" insert "that arose by virtue of subsection (1A) of that section".

(3) After that sub-paragraph insert—

"(3A) In the case of a person ("P") who failed to give notice in accordance with a requirement under section 7 of TMA 1970 that arose by virtue of subsection (1B) of that section, the reference in subparagraph (1)(*c*) to an assessment which ought to have been made by P is a reference to the assessment which P would have been required to make if no notice relating to the year of assessment concerned had been withdrawn under section 8B of that Act."

8 In Schedule 55 to that Act (penalty for failure to make returns etc), after paragraph 17 insert—

"Cancellation of penalty

17A

(1) This paragraph applies where—

(*a*) P is liable for a penalty under any paragraph of this Schedule in relation to a failure to make a return falling within item 1 or 2 in the Table, and

(*b*) P makes a request under section 8B of TMA 1970 for HMRC to withdraw a notice under section 8 or 8A of that Act.

(2) The notice under section 8B of TMA 1970 may include provision under this paragraph cancelling liability to the penalty from the date specified in the notice.

17B

(1) This paragraph applies where—

(*a*) P is liable for a penalty under any paragraph of this Schedule in relation to a failure to make a return falling within item 3 in the Table, and

(*b*) a request is made under section 12AAA of TMA 1970 for HMRC to withdraw a notice under section 12AA of that Act.

(2) The notice under section 12AAA of TMA 1970 may include provision under this paragraph cancelling liability to the penalty from the date specified in the notice."

Commencement

9 (1) The amendments made by this Schedule have effect—

(*a*) in relation to a return under section 12AA of TMA 1970 for a partnership which includes one or more companies, in respect of a return for a relevant period beginning on or after 6 April 2012, and

(*b*) in relation to a return under that section for any other partnership, or a return under section 8 or 8A of that Act, in respect of a return for a year of assessment beginning on or after 6 April 2012.

(2) In sub-paragraph (1)(*a*), "relevant period" means a period in respect of which a return is required.

FINANCE ACT 2014

(2014 Chapter 26)

AN ACT TO Grant certain duties, to alter other duties, and to amend the law relating to the National Debt and the Public Revenue, and to make further provision in connection with finance.

[17 July 2014]

CONTENTS

PART 2

EXCISE DUTIES AND OTHER TAXES

Excise and customs duties: general

102 Penalties under section 26 of FA 2003: extension to excise duty

(1) In this section—

"dutiable excise goods" means goods of a class or description subject to any duty of excise, whether or not those goods are in fact chargeable with that duty, and whether or not that duty has been paid on the goods;

"relevant excise rule" means any duty, obligation, requirement or condition imposed by section 78 of CEMA 1979 (customs and excise control of persons entering or leaving the United Kingdom), so far as that section relates to—

(a) dutiable excise goods a person has obtained outside the United Kingdom, or

(b) dutiable excise goods a person has obtained in the United Kingdom without payment of excise duty,

and in respect of which the person is not entitled to exemption from excise duty by virtue of any order under section 13 of the Customs and Excise Duties (General Reliefs) Act 1979 (personal reliefs).

(2) Sections 26 and 27 and 29 to 41 of FA 2003 (taxes and duties on importation and exportation: penalties) apply in relation to excise duty as they apply in relation to a relevant tax or duty (as defined by section 24(2) of that Act) except that, for this purpose, "relevant rule" in sections 26 and 33 means a relevant excise rule.

Regulations—Customs (Contravention of a Relevant Rule) (Amendment) Regulations, SI 2015/636.

Value added tax

103 VAT: special schemes

Schedule 22 contains provision about the supply of electronic services, broadcasting services and telecommunication services.

104 VAT: place of belonging

(1) Section 9 of VATA 1994 (place where supplier or recipient of services belongs) is amended as follows.

(2) In subsection (3)(c), after "usual place of residence" insert "or permanent address".

(3) In subsection (5), for the words from "belonging" to the end substitute "belonging—

(a) in the country in which the person's usual place of residence or permanent address is (except in the case of a body corporate or other legal person);

(b) in the case of a body corporate or other legal person, in the country in which the place where it is established is."

(4) For subsection (6) substitute—

"(6) The reference in subsection (5)(b) to the place where a body corporate or other legal person "is established" is to be read in accordance with Article 13a of Implementing Regulation (EU) No 282/2011 (which is inserted by Council Implementing Regulation (EU) No 1042/2013)."

(5) The amendments made by this section have effect in relation to supplies made on or after 1 January 2015.

105 VAT: place of supply orders: disapplication of transitional provision

(1) Section 97A of VATA 1994 (place of supply orders: transitional provision) is to be ignored for the purpose of giving effect to any new order under section 7A(6) of that Act which—

(a) is expressed as having effect in relation to supplies made on or after 1 January 2015, and

(b) makes provision about the place of supply of electronically supplied services, telecommunication services and radio and television broadcasting services.

(2) In subsection (1) "new order" means an order made on or after the day on which this Act is passed.

(3) Subsection (1) applies only so far as the order makes provision about supplies to which Article 2 of Council Implementing Regulation (EU) No 1042/2013 (transitional provision for changes in the law affecting electronically supplied, telecommunication and radio and television broadcasting services) applies.

106 VAT: supply of services through agents

(1) Section 47 of VATA 1994 (agents) is amended as follows.

(2) In subsection (3), after "services" insert ", other than electronically supplied services and telecommunication services,".

(3) After subsection (3) insert—

"(4) Where electronically supplied services or telecommunication services are supplied through an agent, the supply is to be treated both as a supply to the agent and as a supply by the agent.

(5) For the purposes of subsection (4) "agent" means a person ("A") who acts in A's own name but on behalf of another person within the meaning of Article 28 of Council Directive 2006/112/EC on the common system of value added tax.

(6) In this section "electronically supplied services" and "telecommunication services" have the same meaning as in Schedule 4A (see paragraph 9(3) and (4) and paragraph 8(2) of that Schedule)."

(4) The amendments made by this section have effect in relation to supplies made on or after 1 January 2015.

107 VAT: refunds to health service bodies

(1) In section 41(7) of VATA 1994 (application to the Crown: list of bodies regarded as Government departments) after "Excellence" insert ", Health Education England (established by the Care Act 2014), and the Health Research Authority (also established by that Act),".

(2) In section 41(7) of VATA 1994 as amended by subsection (1)—

(a) for "above," substitute "—
 (a) ",
(b) for the "and" after "1990," substitute—
 "(b) ",
(c) after "1978" insert ",
 (c) ",
(d) for the "and" after "foundation trust" substitute ",
 (d) ",
(e) for the "and" after "Care Trust" substitute ",
 (e) ",
(f) for the "and" after "Health Board" substitute ",
 (f) ",
(g) after "group," insert—
 "(g) ",
(h) after "Centre," insert—
 (h) ",
(i) for the "and" after "Commissioning Board" substitute ",
 (i) ",
(j) before "Health Education England" insert—
 "(j) ",
(k) before "the Health Research Authority" insert—
 "(k) ",
(l) the words from "shall be regarded" to the end are to follow, rather than form part of, the paragraph (k) so formed, and
(m) in those words, for "shall" substitute "are each to".

108 VAT: prompt payment discounts

(1) In Part 2 of Schedule 6 to VATA 1994 (valuation: special cases), for paragraph 4 (prompt payment discounts), substitute—

"4

(1) Sub-paragraph (2) applies where—
 (a) goods or services are supplied for a consideration which is a price in money,
 (b) the terms on which those goods or services are so supplied allow a discount for prompt payment of that price,
 (c) payment of that price is not made by instalments, and
 (d) payment of that price is made in accordance with those terms so that the discount is realised in relation to that payment.

(2) For the purposes of section 19 (value of supply of goods or services) the consideration is the discounted price paid."

(2) The amendment made by this section has effect in relation to relevant supplies made on or after 1 May 2014.

(3) The Treasury may by order made by statutory instrument provide that the amendment has effect in relation to supplies of a description specified in the order made on or after a date so specified (being a date before 1 April 2015).

(4) Subject to that, the amendment has effect in relation to supplies made on or after 1 April 2015.

(5) In this section—

"relevant supply" means a supply of radio or television broadcasting services or telecommunication services made by a taxable person who is not required by or under any enactment to provide a VAT invoice to the person supplied;

"telecommunication services" has the same meaning as in paragraph 8(2) of Schedule 4A to VATA 1994.

PART 6

OTHER PROVISIONS

Financial sector regulation

295 Tax consequences of financial sector regulation

(1) Section 221 of FA 2012 (tax consequences of financial sector regulation) is amended as follows.

(2) In subsection (1) after "imposed" insert ", or which appears to the Treasury likely to be imposed,".

(3) After subsection (4) insert—

"(4A) Where regulations under this section make provision about the tax consequences of any regulatory requirement which appears to the Treasury likely to be imposed by any EU legislation or enactment—

(a) the regulations may be made (and, accordingly, may have effect) before the proposed legislation or enactment is adopted, passed or made, and

(b) failure after the regulations are made to adopt, pass or make the proposed legislation or enactment does not affect the validity of the regulations."

Commentary—*Simon's Taxes* **D7.803**.

PART 7

FINAL PROVISIONS

301 Power to update indexes of defined terms

(1) The Treasury may by order amend any index of defined expressions contained in an Act relating to taxation, so as to make amendments consequential on any enactment.

(2) In this section—

"enactment" means any provision made by or under an Act (whether before or after the passing of this Act);

"index of defined expressions" means a provision contained in an Act relating to taxation which lists where expressions used in the Act, or in a particular part of the Act, are defined or otherwise explained.

(3) The power to make an order under this section is exercisable by statutory instrument.

Commentary—*Simon's Taxes* **A1.150**.

(4) An order under this section is subject to annulment in pursuance of a resolution of the House of Commons.

302 Interpretation

(1) In this Act—

"ALDA 1979" means the Alcoholic Liquor Duties Act 1979,

"BGDA 1981" means the Betting and Gaming Duties Act 1981,

"CAA 2001" means the Capital Allowances Act 2001,

"CEMA 1979" means the Customs and Excise Management Act 1979,

"CRCA 2005" means the Commissioners for Revenue and Customs Act 2005,

"CTA 2009" means the Corporation Tax Act 2009,

"CTA 2010" means the Corporation Tax Act 2010,

"F(No 3)A 2010" means the Finance (No 3) Act 2010,

"IHTA 1984" means the Inheritance Tax Act 1984,

"ITA 2007" means the Income Tax Act 2007,

"ITEPA 2003" means the Income Tax (Earnings and Pensions) Act 2003,

"ITTOIA 2005" means the Income Tax (Trading and Other Income) Act 2005,

"OTA 1975" means the Oil Taxation Act 1975,

"TCGA 1992" means the Taxation of Chargeable Gains Act 1992,

"TIOPA 2010" means the Taxation (International and Other Provisions) Act 2010,

"TMA 1970" means the Taxes Management Act 1970,

"TPDA 1979" means the Tobacco Products Duty Act 1979,

"VATA 1994" means the Value Added Tax Act 1994, and

"VERA 1994" means the Vehicle Excise and Registration Act 1994.

(2) In this Act—

"FA", followed by a year, means the Finance Act of that year, and

"F(No 2)A", followed by a year, means the Finance (No 2) Act of that year.

303 Short title

This Act may be cited as the Finance Act 2014.

SCHEDULE 21

GOODS SHIPPED OR CARRIED AS STORES ON SHIPS OR AIRCRAFT

Section 101

Meaning of "stores"

1 (1) Section 1 of CEMA 1979 (interpretation) is amended as follows.

(2) In subsection (4)(a)(i), for "relevant journey" substitute "journey made by the ship or aircraft".

(3) Omit subsection (4A).

Commencement—Finance Act 2014, Schedule 21 (Commencement) Order, SI 2015/812 (paras 1, 2, 4–9 come into force on 1 April 2015).

Penalties and enforcement

7 In Schedule 55 to FA 2009 (penalty for failure to make returns etc), in the Table in paragraph 1, after item 20 insert—

"20A	Excise duties	Return under regulations under section 60A of the Customs and Excise Management Act 1979".

Commencement—Finance Act 2014, Schedule 21 (Commencement) Order, SI 2015/812 (paras 1, 2, 4–9 come into force on 1 April 2015).

8 In Schedule 56 to FA 2009 (penalty for failure to make payments on time), in the Table in paragraph 1, after item 11G insert—

"11GA	Excise duties	Amount payable under regulations under section 60A of the Customs and Excise Management Act 1979 (except an amount falling within item 17A, 23 or 24).	The date determined by or under regulations under section 60A of the Customs and Excise Management Act 1979 as the date by which the amount must be paid".

Commencement—Finance Act 2014, Schedule 21 (Commencement) Order, SI 2015/812 (paras 1, 2, 4–9 come into force on 1 April 2015).

Commencement

10 (1) Any power to make regulations conferred by virtue of this Schedule comes into force on the day on which this Act is passed.
(2) So far as not already brought into force by virtue of sub-paragraph (1), the amendments made by this Schedule come into force in accordance with provision contained in an order made by statutory instrument by the Commissioners for Her Majesty's Revenue and Customs.

Orders—Finance Act 2014, Schedule 21 (Commencement) Order, SI 2015/812.

11 (1) Schedule 55 to FA 2009 (including the amendments of that Schedule made by Schedule 10 to F(No3)A 2010) is taken to have come into force for the purposes of section 60A of CEMA 1979 on the date on which paragraph 7 of this Schedule comes into force.
(2) Schedule 56 to FA 2009 (including the amendments of that Schedule made by Schedule 11 to F(No3)A 2010) is taken to have come into force for the purposes of section 60A of CEMA 1979 on the date on which paragraph 8 of this Schedule comes into force.

SCHEDULE 22

SUPPLIES OF ELECTRONIC, BROADCASTING AND TELECOMMUNICATION SERVICES: SPECIAL ACCOUNTING SCHEMES

Section 103

PART 1

UNION SCHEME

New Union scheme for accounting for VAT on certain supplies

1 After Schedule 3B to VATA 1994 insert—

"SCHEDULE 3BA

ELECTRONIC, TELECOMMUNICATION AND BROADCASTING SERVICES: UNION SCHEME

PART 1
INTRODUCTION

Overview

1

In this Schedule—

(a) Parts 2 and 3 establish a special accounting scheme (called the "Union scheme") which may be used by certain persons established in the United Kingdom who make supplies of electronically supplied, telecommunication or broadcasting services that are treated as made in other member States;

(b) Part 4 is about persons participating in schemes in other member States that correspond to the Union scheme;

(c) Part 5 is about appeals;

(d) Part 6 contains definitions for the Schedule.

Meaning of "scheme services"

2

(1) In this Schedule "scheme services" means electronically supplied services, broadcasting services or telecommunication services.

(2) In sub-paragraph (1)—

"broadcasting services" means radio and television broadcasting services;

"electronically supplied services" has the same meaning as in Schedule 4A (see paragraph 9(3) and (4) of that Schedule);

"telecommunication services" has the same meaning as in Schedule 4A (see paragraph 8(2) of that Schedule).

PART 2
UNION SCHEME: REGISTRATION

The register

3

Persons registered under the scheme provided for by this Schedule ("the Union scheme") are to be registered in a single register kept by the Commissioners for the purposes of the scheme.

Persons who may be registered

4

(1) A person may register under the Union scheme if all the following conditions are met—

(a) the person makes or intends to make one or more qualifying supplies of scheme services in the course of a business that the person carries on;

(b) either the person's business is established in the United Kingdom or (if the person's business is not established in any member State) the person has a fixed establishment in the United Kingdom;

(c) the person is not barred from registering by sub-paragraph (3), by the second paragraph of Article 369a(2) of Directive 2006/112/EC or by any provision of the Implementing Regulation;

(d) the person is registered under Schedule 1.

(2) A supply of scheme services is a "qualifying supply of scheme services" if the following conditions are met.

1. The recipient of the services must belong in a member State other than the United Kingdom and must not be a relevant business person.

2. The person making the supply must not have a fixed establishment in the

member State in which the recipient belongs.

(3) A person may not be registered under the Union scheme if the person is a participant in a non-UK special scheme (see paragraph 38(1)).

Becoming registered

5

(1) The Commissioners must register under the Union scheme any person who—

(a) satisfies them that the requirements for registration are met, and

(b) makes a request in accordance with this paragraph (a "registration request").

(2) A registration request made by a person must state the person's—

(a) name and postal address, and

(b) electronic addresses (including any websites).

(3) A registration request made by a person must also state—

(a) whether or not the person has begun to make qualifying supplies of scheme services, and

(b) (if applicable) the date on which the person began to do so.

(4) A registration request made by a person must also state—

(a) whether or not the person has previously been identified under a non-UK special scheme, and

(b) (if applicable) the date on which the person was first identified under the scheme concerned.

(5) A registration request—

(a) must contain any further information, and any declaration about its contents, that the Commissioners may by regulations require;

(b) must be made by such electronic means, and in such manner, as the Commissioners may direct or may by regulations require.

Notification of changes etc

6

(1) A person registered under the Union scheme must inform the Commissioners of the date when the person first makes qualifying supplies of scheme services (unless the person has already given the Commissioners the information mentioned in paragraph 5(3)(b)).

(2) That information, and any information a person is required to give under Article 57h of the Implementing Regulation (notification of certain changes), must be communicated by such electronic means, and in such manner, as the Commissioners may direct or may by regulations require.

Cancellation of registration

7

The Commissioners must cancel the registration under the Union scheme of a person if—

(a) the person has ceased to make, or no longer intends to make, supplies of scheme services and has notified them of that fact;

(b) they otherwise determine that the person has ceased to make, or no longer intends to make, supplies of scheme services;

(c) the person has ceased to satisfy any of the other conditions for registration in paragraph 4(1) and has notified them of that fact,

(d) they otherwise determine that the person has ceased to satisfy any of those conditions, or

(e) they determine that the person has persistently failed to comply with the person's obligations under this Schedule or the Implementing Regulation.

PART 3
UNION SCHEME : LIABILITY, RETURNS, PAYMENT ETC

Liability to pay non-UK VAT to Commissioners

8

(1) This paragraph applies where a person—

(a) makes a qualifying supply of scheme services, and

(b) is registered under the Union scheme when the supply is made.

(2) The person is liable to pay to the Commissioners the gross amount of VAT on the supply.

(3) The reference in sub-paragraph (2) to the gross amount of VAT on the supply is to the amount of VAT charged on the supply in accordance with the law of the member State in which the supply is treated as made, without any deduction of VAT pursuant to Article 168 of Directive 2006/112/EC.

Union scheme returns

9

(1) A person who is or has been registered under the Union scheme must submit a return (a "Union scheme return") to the Commissioners for each reporting period.

(2) Each quarter for the whole or part of which a person is registered under the Union scheme is a "reporting period" for that person.

Union scheme returns: further requirements

10

(1) A Union scheme return is to be made out in sterling.

(2) Any conversion from one currency into another for the purposes of sub-paragraph (1) is to be made using the exchange rates published by the European Central Bank—

(a) for the last day of the reporting period to which the Union scheme return relates, or

(b) if no such rate is published for that day, for the next day for which such a rate is published.

(3) A Union scheme return—

(a) must be submitted to the Commissioners within the 20 days after the last day of the reporting period to which it relates;

(b) must be submitted by such electronic means, and in such manner, as the Commissioners may direct or may by regulations require.

Payment

11

(1) A person who is required to submit a Union scheme return must pay, by the deadline for submitting the return, the amounts required in accordance with paragraph 8 in respect of qualifying supplies of scheme services made in the reporting period to which the return relates.

(2) A payment under this paragraph must be made in such manner as the Commissioners may direct or may by regulations require.

Availability of records

12

(1) A person who is registered under the Union scheme must make available to the Commissioners, on request, any obligatory records the person is keeping of transactions entered into by the person while registered under the scheme.

(2) The records must be made available by electronic means.

(3) In sub-paragraph (1) "obligatory records" means records kept in accordance with an obligation imposed in accordance with Article 369k of Directive 2006/112/EC.

Amounts required to be paid to other member States

13

Section 44 of the Commissioners for Revenue and Customs Act 2005 (requirement to pay receipts into the Consolidated Fund) does not apply to any money received for or on account of VAT that is required to be paid to another member State under Article 46 of Council Regulation (EU) No 904/2010.

PART 4
PERSONS REGISTERED UNDER NON-UK SPECIAL SCHEMES

Meaning of "non-UK special scheme"

14

(1) In this Schedule "non-UK special scheme" means any provision of the law of a member State other than the United Kingdom which implements Section 3 of Chapter 6 of Title XII of Directive 2006/ 112/EC.

(2) In relation to a non-UK special scheme, references to the "administering member State" are to the member State under whose law the scheme is established.

Exemption from requirement to register under this Act

15

(1) A participant in a non-UK special scheme is not required to be registered under this Act by virtue of making supplies of scheme services in respect of which the participant is required to make returns under that scheme.

(2) Sub-paragraph (1) overrides any contrary provision in this Act.

(3) Where a participant in a non-UK special scheme who is not registered under this Act ("the unregistered person") makes relevant supplies, it is to be assumed for all purposes of this Act relating to the determination of—

- (a) whether or not VAT is chargeable under this Act on those supplies,
- (b) how much VAT is chargeable under this Act on those supplies,
- (c) the time at which those supplies are treated as taking place, and
- (d) any other matter that the Commissioners may specify by regulations,

that the unregistered person is registered under this Act.

(4) Supplies of scheme services made by the unregistered person are "relevant supplies" if—

- (a) the value of the supplies must be accounted for in a return required to be made by the unregistered person under the non-UK special scheme, and
- (b) the supplies are treated as made in the United Kingdom.

De-registration

16

(1) Sub-paragraph (2) applies where a person who is registered under Schedule 1A—

- (a) satisfies the Commissioners that the person intends to apply for identification under a non-UK special scheme, and
- (b) asks the Commissioners to cancel the person's registration under Schedule 1A.

(2) The Commissioners may cancel the person's registration under Schedule 1A with effect from—

- (a) the day on which the request is made, or
- (b) a later date agreed between the person and the Commissioners.

Scheme participants who are also registered under this Act

17

(1) A person who—

- (a) is a participant in a non-UK special scheme, and
- (b) is also registered, or required to be registered, under this Act,

is not required to discharge any obligation placed on the person as a taxable person, so far as the obligation relates to relevant supplies.

(2) The reference in sub-paragraph (1) to an obligation placed on the person as a taxable person is to an obligation—

(a) to which the person is subject under or by virtue of this Act, and

(b) to which the person would not be subject if the person were neither registered nor required to be registered under this Act.

(3) A supply made by a participant in a non-UK special scheme is a "relevant supply" if—

(a) the value of the supply must be accounted for in a return required to be made by the participant under the non-UK special scheme, and

(b) the supply is treated as made in the United Kingdom.

(4) The Commissioners may by regulations specify cases in relation to which sub-paragraph (1) is not to apply.

(5) In section 25(2) (deduction of input tax from output tax by taxable person) the reference to output tax that is due from the taxable person does not include any VAT that the taxable person is liable under a non-UK special scheme to pay to the tax authorities for the administering member State.

Value of supplies to connected persons

18

In paragraph 1 of Schedule 6 (valuation: supply to connected person at less than market value) the reference to a supply made by a taxable person is to be read as including a supply of scheme services that is made by a participant in a non-UK special scheme (and is treated as made in the United Kingdom).

Refund of VAT on supplies of goods and services supplied to scheme participant

19

The power of the Commissioners to make regulations under section 39 (repayment of VAT to those in business overseas) includes power to make provision for giving effect to the second sentence of Article 369j of Directive 2006/112/EC (which provides for VAT on certain supplies to participants in special accounting schemes to be refunded in accordance with Directive 2008/9/EC).

Assessments: general modifications of section 73

20

(1) For the purposes of this Schedule, section 73 (assessments: incorrect returns etc) is to be read as if—

(a) the reference in subsection (1) of that section to returns required under this Act included relevant non-UK returns, and

(b) references in that section to a prescribed accounting period included a tax period.

(2) See also the modifications in paragraph 21.

(3) In this Schedule "relevant non-UK return" means a non-UK return (see paragraph 38(1)) that is required to be made (wholly or partly) in respect of supplies of scheme services that are treated as made in the United Kingdom.

Assessment in connection with increase in consideration

21

(1) Sub-paragraphs (2) to (4) make modifications of sections 73 and 76 which—

(a) have effect for the purposes of this Schedule, and

(b) are in addition to any other modifications of those sections made by this Schedule.

(2) Section 73 has effect as if the following were inserted after subsection (3) of that section—

"(3A) Where a person has failed to make an amendment or notification that the person is required to make under paragraph 31 of Schedule 3BA in respect of an increase in the consideration for a UK supply (as defined in paragraph 31(7)), the Commissioners may assess the amount of VAT due from the person as a result of the increase to the best of their judgement and notify it to the person.

(3B) An assessment under subsection (3A)—

(a) is of VAT due for the tax period mentioned in paragraph 31(1)(a) of Schedule 3BA;

(b) must be made within the time limits provided for in section 77, and must not be made after the later of—

(i) 2 years after the end of the tax period referred to in paragraph 31(1)(a);

(ii) one year after evidence of facts sufficient in the opinion of the Commissioners to justify making the assessment comes to their knowledge.

(3C) Subject to section 77, where further evidence such as is mentioned in subsection (3B)(b)(ii) comes to the Commissioners' knowledge after they have made an assessment under subsection (3A), another assessment may be made under that subsection, in addition to any earlier assessment."

(3) The reference in section 73(9) to subsection (1) of that section is taken to include a reference to section 73(3A) (as inserted by sub-paragraph (2)).

(4) Section 76 (assessment of amounts due by way of interest etc) is to be read as if the reference in subsection (5) of that section to section 73(1) included a reference to section 73(3A) (as inserted by sub-paragraph (2)).

Assessments: consequential modifications

22

References to prescribed accounting periods in the following provisions are to be read in accordance with the modifications made by paragraphs 20 and 21—

(a) section 74 (interest on VAT recovered or recoverable by assessment);

(b) section 76 (assessment of amounts due by way of penalty, interest or surcharge);

(c) section 77 (assessment: time limits).

Deemed amendments of relevant non-UK returns

23

(1) Where a person who has made a relevant non-UK return makes a claim under paragraph 29(7)(b) (overpayments) in relation to an error in the return, the relevant non-UK return is taken for the purposes of this Act to have been amended by the information in the claim.

(2) Where a person who has made a relevant non-UK return gives the Commissioners a notice relating to the return under paragraph 31(2)(b) (increase or decrease in consideration), the relevant non- UK return is taken for the purposes of this Act to have been amended by that information.

(3) Where (in a case not falling within sub-paragraph (1) or (2)) a person who has made a relevant non-UK return notifies the Commissioners (after the expiry of the period during which the non-UK return may be amended under Article 61 of the Implementing Regulation) of a change that needs to be made to the return to correct an error, or rectify an omission, in it, the relevant non-UK return is taken for the purposes of this Act to have been amended by that information.

(4) The Commissioners may by regulations—

(a) specify within what period and in what form and manner notice is to be given under sub-paragraph (3);

(b) require notices to be supported by documentary evidence described in the regulations.

Interest on VAT: "reckonable date"

24

(1) Sub-paragraph (2) states the "reckonable date" for the purposes of section 74(1) and (2) for any case where an amount carrying interest under that section—

(a) is an amount assessed under section 73(2) (refunds etc) in reliance on paragraph 20, or that could have been so assessed, and

(b) was correctly paid or credited to the person, but would not have been paid or credited to the person had the facts been as they later turn out to be.

(2) The "reckonable date" is the first day after the end of the tax period in which the events occurred as a result of which the Commissioners were authorised to make the assessment (that was or could have been made) under section 73(2).

(3) Sub-paragraph (4) states the "reckonable date" for any other case where an amount carrying interest under section 74 is assessed under section 74(1) or (2) in reliance on paragraph 20, or could have been so assessed.

(4) The "reckonable date" is taken to be the latest date by which a non- UK return was required to be made for the tax period to which the amount assessed relates.

(5) Where section 74(1) or (2) (interest on VAT recovered or recoverable by assessment) applies in relation to an amount assessed under section 73(3A) (as inserted by paragraph 21(2)), the "reckonable date" for the purposes of section 74(1) or (2) is taken to be the day after the end of the tax period referred to in paragraph 31(2).

Default surcharge: notice of special surcharge period

25

(1) A person who is required to make a relevant non-UK return for a tax period is regarded for the purposes of this paragraph and paragraph 26 as being in default in respect of that period if either—

(a) conditions 1A and 2A are met, or

(b) conditions 1B and 2B are met;

(but see also paragraph 27).

(2) For the purposes of sub-paragraph (1)(a)—

(a) condition 1A is that the tax authorities for the administering member State have not received the return by the deadline for submitting it;

(b) condition 2A is that those tax authorities have, in accordance with Article 60a of the Implementing Regulation, issued a reminder of the obligation to submit the return.

(3) For the purposes of sub-paragraph (1)(b)—

(a) condition 1B is that, by the deadline for submitting the return, the tax authorities for the administering member State have received the return but have not received the amount of VAT shown on the return as payable by the person in respect of the tax period;

(b) condition 2B is that those tax authorities have, in accordance with Article 60a of the Implementing Regulation, issued a reminder of the VAT outstanding.

(4) The Commissioners may serve on a person who is in default in respect of a tax period a notice (a "special surcharge liability notice") specifying a period—

(a) ending on the first anniversary of the last day of that tax period, and

(b) beginning on the date of the notice.

(5) A period specified under sub-paragraph (4) is a "special surcharge period".

(6) If a special surcharge liability notice is served in respect of a tax period which ends at or before the end of an existing special surcharge period, the special surcharge period specified in that notice must be expressed as a continuation of the existing special surcharge period (so that the existing period and its extension are regarded as a single special surcharge period).

Further default after service of notice

26

(1) If a person on whom a special surcharge liability notice has been served—

(a) is in default in respect of a tax period ending within the special surcharge period specified in (or extended by) that notice, and

(b) has outstanding special scheme VAT for that tax period,

the person is to be liable to a surcharge of the amount given by sub-paragraph (2).

(2) The surcharge is equal to whichever is the greater of—

(a) £30, and

(b) the specified percentage of the person's outstanding special scheme VAT for the tax period.

(3) The specified percentage depends on whether the tax period is the first, second or third etc in the default period in respect of which the person is in default and has outstanding special scheme VAT, and is—

(a) for the first such tax period, 2%;

(b) for the second such tax period, 5%;

(c) for the third such tax period, 10%;

(d) for each such tax period after the third, 15%.

(4) "Special scheme VAT", in relation to a person, means VAT that the person is liable to pay to the tax authorities for the administering member State under a non-UK special scheme in respect of supplies of scheme services treated as made in the United Kingdom.

(5) A person has "outstanding special scheme VAT" for a tax period if some or all of the special scheme VAT for which the person is liable in respect of that period has not been paid by the deadline for the person to submit a non-UK return for that period (and the amount unpaid is referred to in sub-paragraph (2)(b) as "the person's outstanding special scheme VAT" for the tax period).

Default surcharge: exceptions for reasonable excuse etc

27

(1) A person who would otherwise have been liable to a surcharge under paragraph 26(1) is not to be liable to the surcharge if the person satisfies the Commissioners or, on appeal, the tribunal that, in the case of a default which is material to the surcharge—

(a) the non-UK return or, as the case may be, the VAT shown on that return, was despatched at such a time and in such manner that it was reasonable to expect that it would be received by the tax authorities for the administering member State within the appropriate time limit, or

(b) there is a reasonable excuse for the return or the VAT not having been so despatched.

(2) Where sub-paragraph (1) applies to a person—

(a) the person is treated as not having been in default in respect of the tax period in question, and

(b) accordingly, any special surcharge liability notice the service of which depended on that default is regarded as not having been served.

(3) A default is "material" to a surcharge if—

(a) it is the default which gives rise to the surcharge, under paragraph 26(1), or

(b) it is a default which was taken into account in the service of the special surcharge liability notice on which the surcharge depends and the person concerned has not previously been liable to a surcharge in respect of a tax period ending within the special surcharge period specified in or extended by that notice.

(4) A default is left out of account for the purposes of paragraphs 25(4) and 26(1) if—

(a) the conduct by virtue of which the person is in default is also conduct falling within section 69(1) (breaches of regulatory provisions), and

(b) by reason of that conduct the person concerned is assessed to a penalty under that section.

(5) If the Commissioners, after consultation with the Treasury, so direct, a default in respect of a tax period specified in the direction is to be left out of account for the purposes of paragraphs 25(4) and 26(1).

(6) Section 71(1) (meaning of "reasonable excuse") applies for the purposes of this paragraph as it applies for the purposes of sections 59 to 70.

Interest in certain cases of official error

28

(1) Section 78 (interest in certain cases of official error) applies as follows in relation to a case where, due to an error on the part of the Commissioners—

(a) a person has accounted under a non-UK special scheme for an amount by way of UK VAT that was not UK VAT due from the person, and as a result the Commissioners are liable under paragraph 29 to pay (or repay) an amount to the person, or

(b) (in a case not falling within paragraph (a)), a person has paid, in accordance with an obligation under a non-UK special scheme, an amount by way of UK VAT that was not UK VAT due from the person and which the Commissioners are in consequence liable to repay to the person.

(2) Section 78 has effect as if the condition in section 78(1)(a) were met in relation to that person.

(3) In the application of section 78 as a result of this paragraph, section 78(12)(b) is read as providing that any reference in that section to a return is to a return required to be made under a non-UK special scheme.

(4) In section 78, as it applies as a result of this section, "output tax" has the meaning that that expression would have if the reference in section 24(2) to a "taxable person" were to a "person".

Overpayments

29

(1) A person may make a claim if the person—

(a) has made a non-UK return for a tax period relating wholly or partly to supplies of scheme services treated as made in the United Kingdom,

(b) has accounted to the tax authorities for the administering member State for VAT in respect of those supplies, and

(c) in doing so has brought into account as UK VAT due to those authorities an amount ("the overpaid amount") that was not UK VAT due to them.

(2) A person may make a claim if the person has, as a participant in a non-UK special scheme, paid (to the tax authorities for the administering member State or to the Commissioners) an amount by way of UK VAT that was not UK VAT due ("the overpaid amount"), otherwise than in the circumstances mentioned in sub-paragraph (1)(c).

(3) A person who is or has been a participant in a non-UK special scheme may make a claim if the Commissioners—

(a) have assessed the person to VAT for a tax period, and

(b) in doing so, have brought into account as VAT an amount ("the amount not due") that was not VAT due.

(4) Where a person makes a claim under sub-paragraph (1) or (2), the Commissioners must repay the overpaid amount to the person.

(5) Where a person makes a claim under sub-paragraph (3), the Commissioners must credit the person with the amount not due.

(6) Where—

(a) as a result of a claim under sub-paragraph (3) an amount is to be credited to a person, and

(b) after setting any sums against that amount under or by virtue of this Act, some or all of the amount remains to the person's credit,

the Commissioners must pay (or repay) to the person so much of the amount as remains to the person's credit.

(7) The reference in sub-paragraph (1) to a claim is to a claim made—

(a) by correcting, in accordance with Article 61 of the Implementing Regulation, the error in the non-UK return mentioned in sub-paragraph (1)(a), or

(b) (after the expiry of the period during which the non-UK return may be amended under Article 61) to the Commissioners.

(8) Sub-paragraphs (1) and (2) do not require any amount to be repaid except so far as that is required by Article 63 of the Implementing Regulation.

Overpayments: supplementary

30

(1) In section 80—

(a) subsections (3) to (3C) (unjust enrichment), and

(b) subsections (4A), (4C) and (6) (recovery by assessment of amounts wrongly credited),

have effect as if a claim under paragraph 29(1) were a claim under section 80(1), a claim under paragraph 29(2) were a claim under section 80(1B) and a claim under paragraph 29(3) were a claim under section 80(1A).

(2) In section 80(3) to (3C), (4A), (4C) and (6), as applied by sub-paragraph (1)—

(a) references to the crediting of amounts are to be read as including the payment of amounts;

(b) references to a prescribed accounting period include a tax period.

(3) The Commissioners are not liable to repay the overpaid amount on a claim made—

(a) under paragraph 29(2),or

(b) as mentioned in paragraph 29(7)(b),

if the claim is made more than 4 years after the relevant date.

(4) On a claim made under paragraph 29(3), the Commissioners are not liable to credit the amount not due if the claim is made more than 4 years after the relevant date.

(5) The "relevant date" is—

(a) in the case of a claim under paragraph 29(1), the end of the tax period mentioned in paragraph 29(1)(a), except in the case of a claim resulting from an incorrect disclosure;

(b) in the case of a claim under paragraph 29(1) resulting from an incorrect disclosure, the end of the tax period in which the disclosure was made;

(c) in the case of a claim under paragraph 29(2), the date on which the payment was made;

(d) in the case of a claim under paragraph 29(3), the end of the quarter in which the assessment was made.

(6) A person makes an "incorrect disclosure" where—

(a) the person discloses to the tax authorities in question (whether the Commissioners or the tax authorities for the administering member State) that the person has not brought into account for a tax period an amount of UK VAT due for the period ("the disclosed amount"),

(b) the disclosure is made in a later tax period, and

(c) some or all of the disclosed amount is not in fact VAT due.

Increase or decrease in consideration for a supply

31

(1) This paragraph applies where—

(a) a person makes a non-UK return for a tax period ("the affected tax period") relating (wholly or partly) to a UK supply, and

(b) after the return has been made the amount of the consideration for the UK supply increases or decreases.

(2) The person must, in the tax period in which the increase or decrease is accounted for in the person's business accounts—

(a) amend the non-UK return to take account of the increase or decrease, or

(b) (if the period during which the person is entitled under Article 61 of the Implementing Regulation to amend the non-UK return has expired) notify the Commissioners of the adjustment needed to the figures in the non-UK return because of the increase or decrease.

(3) Where the change to which an amendment or notice under sub-paragraph (2) relates is an increase in the consideration for a UK supply, the person must pay to the tax authorities for the administering member State (in accordance with Article 62 of the Implementing Regulation) or, in a case falling within sub-paragraph (2)(b), the Commissioners, the difference between—

(a) the amount of VAT that was chargeable on the supply before the increase in consideration, and

(b) the amount of VAT that is chargeable in respect of the whole of the increased consideration for the supply.

(4) Where the change to which an amendment or notice under sub-paragraph (2) relates is a decrease in the consideration for a UK supply, the amendment or notice has effect as a claim; and where a claim is made the Commissioners must repay any VAT paid by the person that would not have been VAT due from the person had the consideration for the supply always been the decreased amount.

(5) The Commissioners may by regulations specify—

(a) the latest time by which, and the form and manner in which, a claim or other notice under sub-paragraph (2)(b) must be given;

(b) the latest time by which, and the form in which, a payment under sub-paragraph (3) must be made in a case within sub-paragraph (2)(b).

(6) A payment made under sub-paragraph (3) in a case within sub-paragraph (2)(a) must be made before the end of the tax period referred to in sub-paragraph (2).

(7) In this paragraph "UK supply" means a supply of scheme services that is treated as made in the United Kingdom.

Bad debts

32

Where a participant in a non-UK special scheme—

(a) has submitted a non-UK return to the tax authorities for the administering member State, and

(b) amends the return to take account of the writing-off as a bad debt of the whole or part of the consideration for a supply of scheme services that is treated as made in the United Kingdom,

the amending of the return may be treated as the making of a claim to the Commissioners for the purposes of section 36(2) (bad debts: claim for refund of VAT).

Records relating to supplies in UK

33

(1) A person who is a participant in a non-UK special scheme must keep records of the transactions which the person enters into for the purposes of, or in connection with, relevant supplies.

(2) A supply made by a participant in a non-UK special scheme is a "relevant supply" if—

(a) the value of the supply must be accounted for in a return required to be made by the participant under the non-UK special scheme, and

(b) the supply is treated as made in the United Kingdom.

(3) The records must be sufficiently detailed to enable the Commissioners to determine whether any special scheme return submitted in respect of the supplies is correct.

(4) The records must be made available on request to the Commissioners by electronic means.

(5) Records must be kept for 10 years beginning with the 1 January following the date on which the transaction was entered into.

Penalties for errors: disclosure

34

Where a person corrects a non-UK return in a way that constitutes telling the tax authorities for the administering member State about—

(a) an inaccuracy in the return,

(b) a supply of false information, or

(c) a withholding of information,

the person is regarded as telling HMRC about that for the purposes of paragraph 9 of Schedule 24 to the Finance Act 2007.

Set-offs

35

Where a participant in a non-UK special scheme is liable to pay UK VAT to the tax authorities for the administering member State in accordance with the scheme, the UK VAT is regarded for the purposes of section 130(6) of the Finance Act 2008 (set-off: England, Wales and Northern Ireland) as payable to the Commissioners.

PART 5
APPEALS

36

(1) An appeal lies to the tribunal with respect to any of the following—

(a) a refusal to register a person under the Union scheme;

(b) the cancellation of the registration of any person under the Union scheme;

(c) a refusal to make a repayment under paragraph 29 (overpayments), or a decision by the Commissioners as to the amount of the repayment due under that provision;

(d) a refusal to make a repayment under paragraph 31(4) (decrease in consideration);

(e) any liability to a surcharge under paragraph 26 (default surcharge).

(2) Part 5 of this Act (appeals), and any order or regulations under that Part, have effect as if an appeal under this paragraph were an appeal which lies to the tribunal under section 83(1) (but not under any particular paragraph of that subsection).

37

Where the Commissioners have made an assessment under section 73 in reliance on paragraph 20 or 21—

(a) section 83(1)(p)(i): (appeals against assessments under section 73(1) etc) applies as if the relevant non-UK return were a return under this Act, and

(b) the references in section 84(3) and (5) to the matters mentioned in section 83(1)(p) are to be read accordingly.

PART 6
INTERPRETATION OF SCHEDULE

38

(1) In this Schedule—

"administering member State", in relation to a non-UK special scheme, has the meaning given by paragraph 14(2);

"the Implementing Regulation" means Council Implementing Regulation (EU) No 282/2011;

"non-UK return" means a return required to be made, for a tax period, under a non-UK special scheme;

"non-UK special scheme" has the meaning given by paragraph 14(1);

"participant", in relation to a non-UK special scheme, means a person who is identified under that scheme;

"qualifying supply of scheme services" has the meaning given by paragraph 4(2);

"relevant non-UK return" has the meaning given by paragraph 20(3);

"reporting period" is to be read in accordance with paragraph 9(2);

"scheme services" has the meaning given by paragraph 2;

"tax period" means a period for which a person is required to make a return under a non-UK special scheme;

"UK VAT" means VAT in respect of supplies of scheme services treated as made in the United Kingdom;

"Union scheme" has the meaning given by paragraph 3;

"Union scheme return" has the meaning given by paragraph 9(1).

(2) In relation to a non-UK special scheme (or a non-UK return), references in this Schedule to "the tax authorities" are to the tax authorities for the member State under whose law the non-UK special scheme is established.

(3) References in this Schedule to a supply of scheme services being "treated as made" in the United Kingdom are to its being treated as made in the United Kingdom by paragraph 15 of Schedule 4A."

Power to amend provisions about the Union scheme

2 In section 3A of VATA 1994 (supply of electronic services in member States: special accounting scheme)—

(a) in subsection (2), after "3B" insert "or 3BA";

(b) in subsection (3), for "Schedule 3B" substitute "Schedules 3B and 3BA".

PART 2

NON-UNION SCHEME: AMENDMENTS OF SCHEDULE 3B TO VATA 1994

Introduction

3 Schedule 3B to VATA 1994 (supply of electronic services in member States: special accounting scheme) is amended in accordance with paragraphs 4 to 10.

Extension of non-Union scheme to broadcasting and telecommunication services

4 For paragraph 3 (qualifying supplies) substitute—

"3

(1) In this Schedule "qualifying supply" means a supply of electronically supplied services, telecommunication services or broadcasting services to a person who—

(a) belongs in the United Kingdom or another member State, and

(b) is not a relevant business person.

(2) In sub-paragraph (1)—

"broadcasting services" means radio and television broadcasting services;

"electronically supplied services" has the same meaning as in Schedule 4A (see paragraph 9(3) and (4) of that Schedule);

"telecommunication services" has the same meaning as in Schedule 4A (see paragraph 8(2) of that Schedule)."

5 For the title of the Schedule substitute—

"Electronic, telecommunication and broadcasting services: non-Union scheme".

Consequential and other amendments

6 (1) Part 1 of the Schedule (registration) is amended as follows.

(2) In paragraph 2 (persons who may be registered)—

(a) in sub-paragraph (6) for "Article 26c" substitute "Section 2 of Chapter 6 of Title XII of the VAT Directive";

(b) for sub-paragraph (7) substitute—

"(7) In this Schedule "the VAT Directive" means Directive 2006/112/EC (Title XII of which is amended by Council Directive 2008/8/EC)."

(3) In paragraph 4 (registration request)—

(a) in sub-paragraph (2) for "paragraph 9 below" substitute "Article 58b of Implementing Regulation (EU) No 282/2011";

(b) for sub-paragraph (5) substitute—

"(5) A registration request—

(a) must contain any further information, and any declaration about its contents, that the Commissioners may by regulations require;

(b) must be made by such electronic means, and in such manner, as the Commissioners may direct or may by regulations require."

(4) Omit paragraph 5 (date on which registration takes effect) and the heading before it.

(5) In paragraph 7 (obligation to notify changes)—

(a) omit sub-paragraphs (1) and (2);

(b) in sub-paragraph (3), for "this paragraph" substitute "Article 57h of Implementing Regulation (EU) No 282/2011".

(6) In paragraph 8 (cancellation of registration)—

(a) in sub-paragraph (1)(e), after "this Schedule" insert "or Implementing Regulation (EU) No 282/2011";

(b) omit sub-paragraphs (2) and (3).

(7) Omit paragraph 9 (registration after cancellation for persistent default) and the heading before it.

(8) For the title substitute—

"Non-Union scheme: registration".

7 (1) Part 2 of the Schedule (obligations following registration, etc) is amended as follows.

(2) In paragraph 10 (liability for VAT)—

(a) in sub-paragraph (2), at the end insert "(and the VAT is to be paid without any deduction of VAT pursuant to Article 168 of Directive 2006/112/EC)";

(b) in sub-paragraph (3), omit "that would have been" and for the words from "if the person" to the end substitute "(see paragraph 17(2))";

(c) in sub-paragraph (4), omit "that would have been" and the words from "if the person" to the end;

(d) in sub-paragraph (5) omit paragraph (b) and the "and" before it.

(3) In paragraph 11 (obligation to submit special accounting returns)—

(a) in sub-paragraph (1), for "Controller" substitute "Commissioners";

(b) omit sub-paragraphs (3) to (7).

(4) In paragraph 12 (further obligations with respect to special accounting returns)—

(a) in sub-paragraph (1), for the words from "must" to the end substitute "is to be made out in sterling";

(b) in sub-paragraph (3), for "Controller" substitute "Commissioners".

(5) In paragraph 13 (payment of VAT), in sub-paragraph (1), for the words from "at" to "respect of" substitute "by the deadline for submitting the return, pay to the Commissioners the amount of VAT that the person is liable, in accordance with paragraph 10, to pay on qualifying supplies treated as made by the person in".

(6) In paragraph 15 (Commissioners' power to request production of records), in sub-paragraph (2)(b), for "Article 26c" substitute "Section 2 of Chapter 6 of Title XII of the VAT Directive".

(7) After paragraph 15 insert—

"15A Section 44 of the Commissioners for Revenue and Customs Act 2005 (requirement to pay receipts into the Consolidated Fund) does not apply to any money received for or on account of VAT that is required to be paid to another member State under Article 46 of Council Regulation (EU) No 904/2010."

(8) For the title substitute—

"Non-Union scheme: liability, returns, payment etc".

8 For Part 3 of the Schedule (understatements and overstatements of UK VAT) substitute—

"PART 3

SPECIAL SCHEMES: COLLECTION ETC OF UK VAT

Assessments: general modifications of section 73

16

(1) For the purposes of this Schedule, section 73 (assessments: incorrect returns etc) is to be read as if—

(a) the reference in subsection (1) of that section to returns required under this Act included relevant special scheme returns, and

(b) references in that section to a prescribed accounting period included a tax period.

(2) See also the modifications in paragraph 16A.

(3) In this Schedule "relevant special scheme return" means a special scheme return that is required to be made (wholly or partly) in respect of supplies of scheme services that are treated as made in the United Kingdom.

Assessment in connection with increase in consideration

16A

(1) Sub-paragraphs (2) to (4) make modifications of sections 73 and 76 which—

(a) have effect for the purposes of this Schedule, and

(b) are in addition to any other modifications of those sections made by this Schedule.

(2) Section 73 has effect as if the following were inserted after subsection (3) of that section—

"(3A) Where a person has failed to make an amendment or notification that the person is required to make under paragraph 16K of Schedule 3B in respect of an increase in the consideration for a UK supply (as defined in paragraph 16K(7)), the Commissioners may assess the amount of VAT due from the person as a result of the increase to the best of their judgement and notify it to the person.

(3B) An assessment under subsection (3A)—

(a) is of VAT due for the tax period mentioned in paragraph 16K(1)(a) of Schedule 3B;

(b) must be made within the time limits provided for in section 77, and must not be made after the later of—

(i) 2 years after the end of the tax period referred to in paragraph 16K(1)(a);

(ii) one year after evidence of facts sufficient in the opinion of the Commissioners to justify making the assessment comes to their knowledge.

(3C) Subject to section 77, where further evidence such as is mentioned in subsection (3B)(b)(ii) comes to the Commissioners' knowledge after they have made an assessment under subsection (3A), another assessment may be made under that subsection, in addition to any earlier assessment."

(3) The reference in section 73(9) to subsection (1) of that section is taken to include a reference to section 73(3A) (as inserted by sub-paragraph (2)).

(4) Section 76 (assessment of amounts due by way of interest etc) is to be read as if the reference in subsection (5) of that section to section 73(1) included a reference to section 73(3A) (as inserted by sub-paragraph (2)).

Assessments: consequential modifications

16B

References to prescribed accounting periods in the following provisions are to be read in accordance with the modifications made by paragraphs 16 and 16A—

(a) section 74 (interest on VAT recovered or recoverable by assessment);

(b) section 76 (assessment of amounts due by way of penalty, interest or surcharge);

(c) section 77 (assessment: time limits).

Deemed amendments of relevant special scheme returns

16C

(1) Where a person who has made a relevant special scheme return makes a claim under paragraph 16I(7)(b) (overpayments) in relation to an error in the return, the relevant special scheme return is taken for the purposes of this Act to have been amended by the information in the claim.

(2) Where a person who has made a relevant special scheme return gives the Commissioners a notice relating to the return under paragraph 16K(2)(b) (increase or decrease in consideration), the relevant special scheme return is taken for the purposes of this Act to have been amended by that information.

(3) Where (in a case not falling within sub-paragraph (1) or (2)) a person who has made a relevant special scheme return notifies the Commissioners (after the expiry of the period during which the non-UK return may be amended under Article 61 of the Implementing Regulation) of a change that needs to be made to the return to correct an error, or rectify an omission, in it, the relevant special scheme return is taken for the purposes of this Act to have been amended by that information.

(4) The Commissioners may by regulations—

(a) specify within what period and in what form and manner notice may be given under sub-paragraph (3);

(b) require notices to be supported by documentary evidence described in the regulations.

Interest on VAT: "reckonable date"

16D

(1) Sub-paragraph (2) states the "reckonable date" for the purposes of section 74(1) and (2) for any case where an amount carrying interest under that section—

(a) is an amount assessed under section 73(2) (refunds etc) in reliance on paragraph 16, or that could have been so assessed, and

(b) was correctly paid or credited to the person, but would not have been paid or credited to the person had the facts been as they later turn out to be.

(2) The "reckonable date" is the first day after the end of the tax period in which the events occurred as a result of which the Commissioners were authorised to make the assessment (that was or could have been made) under section 73(2).
(3) Sub-paragraph (4) states the "reckonable date", for any other case where an amount carrying interest under section 74 is assessed under section 74(1) or (2) in reliance on paragraph 16, or could have been so assessed.
(4) The "reckonable date" is taken to be the latest date by which a non-UK return was required to be made for the tax period to which the amount assessed relates.
(5) Where section 74(1) or (2) (interest on VAT recovered or recoverable by assessment) applies in relation to an amount assessed under section 73(3A) (as inserted by paragraph 16A(2)), the "reckonable date" for the purposes of section 74(1) or (2) is taken to be the day after the end of the tax period referred to in paragraph 16K(2).

Default surcharge: notice of special surcharge period

16E

(1) A person who is required to make a relevant special scheme return for a tax period is regarded for the purposes of this paragraph and paragraph 16F as being in default in respect of that period if either—

(a) conditions 1A and 2A are met, or

(b) conditions 1B and 2B are met;

(but see also paragraph 16G).
(2) For the purposes of sub-paragraph (1)(a)—

(a) condition 1A is that the tax authorities for the administering member State have not received the return by the deadline for submitting it;

(b) condition 2A is that those tax authorities have, in accordance with Article 60a of the Implementing Regulation, issued a reminder of the obligation to submit the return.

(3) For the purposes of sub-paragraph (1)(b)—

(a) condition 1B is that, by the deadline for submitting the return, the tax authorities for the administering member State have received the return but have not received the amount of VAT shown on the return as payable by the person in respect of the tax period;

(b) condition 2B is that those tax authorities have, in accordance with Article 60a of the Implementing Regulation, issued a reminder of the VAT outstanding.

(4) The Commissioners may serve on a person who is in default in respect of a tax period a notice (a "special surcharge liability notice") specifying a period—

(a) ending on the first anniversary of the last day of that tax period, and

(b) beginning on the date of the notice.

(5) A period specified under sub-paragraph (4) is a "special surcharge period".
(6) If a special surcharge liability notice is served in respect of a tax period which ends at or before the end of an existing special surcharge period, the special surcharge period specified in that notice must be expressed as a continuation of the existing special surcharge period (so that the existing period and its extension are regarded as a single special surcharge period).

Further default after service of notice

16F

(1) If a person on whom a special surcharge liability notice has been served—

(a) is in default in respect of a tax period ending within the special surcharge period specified in (or extended by) that notice, and

(b) has outstanding special scheme VAT for that tax period,

the person is to be liable to a surcharge of the amount given by sub-paragraph (2).
(2) The surcharge is equal to whichever is the greater of—

(a) £30, and

(b) the specified percentage of the person's outstanding special scheme VAT for the tax period.

(3) The specified percentage depends on whether the tax period is the first, second or third etc in the default period in respect of which the person is in default and has outstanding special scheme VAT, and is—

(a) for the first such tax period, 2%;

(b) for the second such tax period, 5%;
(c) for the third such tax period, 10%;
(d) for each such tax period after the third, 15%.

(4) "Special scheme VAT", in relation to a person, means VAT that the person is liable to pay to the tax authorities for the administering member State under a special scheme in respect of supplies of scheme services treated as made in the United Kingdom.

(5) A person has "outstanding special scheme VAT" for a tax period if some or all of the special scheme VAT for which the person is liable in respect of that period has not been paid by the deadline for the person to submit a special scheme return for that period (and the amount unpaid is referred to in sub-paragraph (2)(b) as "the person's outstanding special scheme VAT" for the tax period).

Default surcharge: exceptions for reasonable excuse etc

16G

(1) A person who would otherwise have been liable to a surcharge under paragraph 16F(1) is not to be liable to the surcharge if the person satisfies the Commissioners or, on appeal, the tribunal that, in the case of a default which is material to the surcharge—

(a) the special scheme return or, as the case may be, the VAT shown on that return, was despatched at such a time and in such manner that it was reasonable to expect that it would be received by the tax authorities for the administering member State within the appropriate time limit, or
(b) there is a reasonable excuse for the return or the VAT not having been so despatched.

(2) Where sub-paragraph (1) applies to a person—

(a) the person is treated as not having been in default in respect of the tax period in question, and
(b) accordingly, any special surcharge liability notice the service of which depended on that default is regarded as not having been served.

(3) A default is "material" to a surcharge if—

(a) it is the default which gives rise to the surcharge, under paragraph 16F(1), or
(b) it is a default which was taken into account in the service of the special surcharge liability notice on which the surcharge depends and the person concerned has not previously been liable to a surcharge in respect of a tax period ending within the special surcharge period specified in or extended by that notice.

(4) A default is left out of account for the purposes of paragraphs 16E(4) and 16F(1) if—

(a) the conduct by virtue of which the person is in default is also conduct falling within section 69(1) (breaches of regulatory provisions), and
(b) by reason of that conduct the person concerned is assessed to a penalty under that section.

(5) If the Commissioners, after consultation with the Treasury, so direct, a default in respect of a tax period specified in the direction is to be left out of account for the purposes of paragraphs 16E(4) and 16F(1).

(6) Section 71(1) (meaning of "reasonable excuse") applies for the purposes of this paragraph as it applies for the purposes of sections 59 to 70.

Interest in certain cases of official error

16H

(1) Section 78 (interest in certain cases of official error) applies as follows in relation to a case where, due to an error on the part of the Commissioners—

(a) a person has accounted, under a special scheme, for an amount by way of UK VAT that was not UK VAT due from the person, and as a result the Commissioners are liable under paragraph 16I to pay (or repay) an amount to the person, or
(b) (in a case not falling within paragraph (a)), a person has paid, in accordance with an obligation under a special scheme, an amount by way of UK VAT that was not UK VAT due from the person and which the Commissioners are in consequence liable to repay to the person.

(2) Section 78 has effect as if the condition in section 78(1)(a) were met in relation to that person.

(3) In the application of section 78 as a result of this paragraph, section 78(12)(b) is read as providing that any reference in that section to a return is to a return required to be made under a special scheme.

(4) In section 78 in its application as a result of this section, "output tax" has the meaning that that expression would have if the reference in section 24(2) to a "taxable person" were to a "person".

Overpayments

16I

(1) A person may make a claim if the person—

(a) has made a special scheme return for a tax period relating wholly or partly to supplies of scheme services treated as made in the United Kingdom,

(b) has accounted to the tax authorities for the administering member State (whether that is the United Kingdom or another member State) for VAT in respect of those supplies, and

(c) in doing so has brought into account as UK VAT due to those authorities an amount ("the overpaid amount") that was not UK VAT due to them.

(2) A person may make a claim if the person has, as a participant in a special scheme, paid (to the tax authorities for the administering member State or to the Commissioners) an amount by way of UK VAT that was not UK VAT due ("the overpaid amount"), otherwise than in the circumstances mentioned in sub-paragraph (1)(c).

(3) A person who is or has been a participant in a special scheme may make a claim if the Commissioners—

(a) have assessed the person to VAT for a tax period, and

(b) in doing so, have brought into account as VAT an amount ("the amount not due") that was not VAT due.

(4) Where a person makes a claim under sub-paragraph (1) or (2), the Commissioners must repay the overpaid amount to the person.

(5) Where a person makes a claim under sub-paragraph (3), the Commissioners must credit the person with the amount not due.

(6) Where—

(a) as a result of a claim under sub-paragraph (3) an amount is to be credited to a person, and

(b) after setting any sums against that amount under or by virtue of this Act, some or all of the amount remains to the person's credit,

the Commissioners must pay (or repay) to the person so much of the amount as remains to the person's credit.

(7) The reference in sub-paragraph (1) to a claim is to a claim made—

(a) by correcting, in accordance with Article 61 of the Implementing Regulation, the error in the non-UK return mentioned in sub-paragraph (1)(a), or

(b) (after the expiry of the period during which the non-UK return may be amended under Article 61) to the Commissioners.

(8) Sub-paragraphs (1) and (2) do not require any amount to be repaid except so far as that is required by Article 63 of the Implementing Regulation.

Overpayments: supplementary

16J

(1) In section 80—

(a) subsections (3) to (3C) (unjust enrichment), and

(b) subsections (4A), (4C) and (6) (recovery by assessment of amounts wrongly credited),

have effect as if a claim under paragraph 16I(1) were a claim under section 80(1), a claim under paragraph 16I(2) were a claim under section 80(1B) and a claim under paragraph 16I(3) were a claim under section 80(1A).

(2) In section 80(3) to (3C), (4A), (4C) and (6), as applied by sub-paragraph (1)—

(a) references to the crediting of amounts are to be read as including the payment of amounts;

(b) references to a prescribed accounting period include a tax period.

(3) The Commissioners are not liable to repay the overpaid amount on a claim made—

(a) under paragraph 16I(2),or

(b) as mentioned in paragraph 16I(7)(b),

if the claim is made more than 4 years after the relevant date.

(4) On a claim made under paragraph 16I(3), the Commissioners are not liable to credit the amount not due if the claim is made more than 4 years after the relevant date.

(5) The "relevant date" is—

(a) in the case of a claim under paragraph 16I(1), the end of the tax period mentioned in paragraph 16I(1)(a), except in the case of a claim resulting from an incorrect disclosure;

(b) in the case of a claim under paragraph 16I(1) resulting from an incorrect disclosure, the end of the tax period in which the disclosure was made;

(c) in the case of a claim under paragraph 16I(2), the date on which the payment was made;

(d) in the case of a claim under paragraph 16I(3), the end of the quarter in which the assessment was made.

(6) A person makes an "incorrect disclosure" where—

(a) the person discloses to the tax authorities in question (whether the Commissioners or the tax authorities for the administering member State) that the person has not brought into account for a tax period an amount of UK VAT due for the period ("the disclosed amount"),

(b) the disclosure is made in a later tax period, and

(c) some or all of the disclosed amount is not in fact VAT due.

Increase or decrease in consideration for a supply

16K

(1) This paragraph applies where—

(a) a person makes a special scheme return for a tax period ("the affected tax period") relating (wholly or partly) to a UK supply, and

(b) after the return has been made the amount of the consideration for the UK supply increases or decreases.

(2) The person must, in the tax period in which the increase or decrease is accounted for in the person's business accounts—

(a) amend the special scheme return to take account of the increase or decrease, or

(b) (if the period during which the person is entitled under Article 61 of the Implementing Regulation to amend the special scheme return has expired) notify the Commissioners of the adjustment needed to the figures in the special scheme return because of the increase or decrease.

(3) Where the change to which an amendment or notice under sub-paragraph (2) relates is an increase in the consideration for a UK supply, the person must pay to the tax authorities for the administering member State (in accordance with Article 62 of the Implementing Regulation) or, in a case falling within sub-paragraph (2)(b), the Commissioners, the difference between—

(a) the amount of VAT that was chargeable on the supply before the increase in consideration, and

(b) the amount of VAT that is chargeable in respect of the whole of the increased consideration for the supply.

(4) Where the change to which an amendment or notice under sub-paragraph (2) relates is a decrease in the consideration for a UK supply, the amendment or notice has effect as a claim; and where a claim is made the Commissioners must repay any VAT paid by the person that would not have been VAT due from the person had the consideration for the supply always been the decreased amount.

(5) The Commissioners may by regulations specify—

(a) the latest time by which, and the form and manner in which, a claim or other notice under sub-paragraph (2)(b) must be given;

(b) the latest time by which, and the form in which, a payment under sub-paragraph (3) must be made in a case within sub-paragraph (2)(b).

(6) A payment made under sub-paragraph (3) in a case within sub-paragraph (2)(a) must be made before the end of the tax period referred to in sub-paragraph (2).

(7) In this paragraph "UK supply" means a supply of scheme services that is treated as made in the United Kingdom.

Bad debts

16L

Where a participant in a special scheme—

(a) has submitted a special scheme return to the tax authorities for the administering member State, and

(b) amends the return to take account of the writing-off as a bad debt of the whole or part of the consideration for a supply of scheme services that is treated as made in the United Kingdom,

the amending of the return may be treated as the making of a claim to the Commissioners for the purposes of section 36(2) (bad debts: claim for refund of VAT).

Penalties for errors: disclosure

16M

Where a person corrects a special scheme return in a way that constitutes telling the tax authorities for the administering member State about—

(a) an inaccuracy in the return,

(b) a supply of false information, or

(c) a withholding of information,

the person is regarded as telling HMRC about that for the purposes of paragraph 9 of Schedule 24 to the Finance Act 2007.

Set-offs

16N

Where a participant in a special scheme is liable to pay UK VAT to the tax authorities for the administering member State in accordance with the scheme, the UK VAT is regarded for the purposes of section 130(6) of the Finance Act 2008 (set-off: England, Wales and Northern Ireland) as payable to the Commissioners."

9

(1) Part 4 of the Schedule (application of provisions relating to VAT) is amended as follows.

(2) Paragraph 17 (registration under VATA 1994) is renumbered as sub-paragraph (1) of that paragraph.

(3) In that paragraph, after sub-paragraph (1) (as renumbered), insert—

"(2) Where a participant in the special scheme ("the scheme participant") makes relevant supplies, it is to be assumed for all purposes of this Act relating to the determination of—

(a) whether or not VAT is chargeable under this Act on those supplies,

(b) how much VAT is chargeable under this Act on those supplies,

(c) the time at which those supplies are treated as taking place, and

(d) any other matter that the Commissioners may specify by regulations,

that the scheme participant is registered under this Act.

(3) Supplies of scheme services made by the scheme participant are "relevant supplies" if—

(a) the value of the supplies must be accounted for in a special scheme return, and

(b) the supplies are treated as made in the United Kingdom."

(4) In paragraph 18 (de-registration), in paragraph (b), for "Article 26c," substitute "Section 2 of Chapter 6 of Title XII of the VAT Directive,".

(5) After paragraph 18 insert—

"Value of supplies to connected persons

18A

In paragraph 1 of Schedule 6 (valuation: supply to connected person at less than market value) the reference to a supply made by a taxable person is to be read as including a supply of scheme services that is made by a participant in the special scheme (and is treated as made in the United Kingdom)."

(6) In paragraph 20 (appeals)—

(a) in sub-paragraph (1), for paragraphs (b) and (c) substitute—

"(b) a refusal to make a repayment under paragraph 16I (overpayments), or a decision by the Commissioners as to the amount of the repayment due under that provision;

(c) a refusal to make a repayment under paragraph 16K(4) (decrease in consideration);

(d) any liability to a surcharge under paragraph 16F (default surcharge)."

(b) after sub-paragraph (2) insert—

"(3) Where the Commissioners have made an assessment under section 73 in reliance on paragraph 16 or 16A—

(a) section 83(1)(p)(i): (appeals against assessments under section 73(1) etc) applies as if the relevant special scheme return were a return under this Act, and

(b) the references in section 84(3) and (5) to the matters mentioned in section 83(1)(p) are to be read accordingly."

(7) Omit paragraph 21 (payments on account of non-UK VAT to other member States) and the heading before it (but see paragraph 7(7) of this Schedule).

(8) For the title substitute—

"Other provisions about special schemes "

10

(1) In Part 5 of the Schedule (supplementary), paragraph 23 (interpretation) is amended as follows.

(2) In sub-paragraph (1)—

(a) for the words from ""Article 26c" to the end of the definition of "the Controller" substitute—

""administering member State", in relation to a special scheme, means the member State under whose law the scheme is established (whether that is the United Kingdom or another member State);

"the Implementing Regulation" means Implementing Regulation (EU) No 282/2011;"

(b) for the definition of "participant in the special scheme", substitute—

""participant in the special scheme" means a person who—

(a) is registered under this Schedule, or

(b) is identified under any provision of the law of another member State which implements Section 2 of Chapter 6 of Title XII of the VAT Directive;"

(c) after the definition of "registration request" insert—

""relevant special scheme return" has the meaning given by paragraph 16(3);"

(d) after the definition of "reporting period" insert—

""scheme services" means electronically supplied services, broadcasting services or telecommunication services (and in this definition "electronically supplied services", "broadcasting services" and

"telecommunication services" have the meaning given by paragraph 3(2));"

(e) after the definition of "special accounting return" insert—

""special scheme" means—

(a) the accounting scheme under this Schedule, or

(b) any other scheme, under the law of another member State, implementing Section 2 of Title XII of Directive 2006/112/EC;

"special scheme return" means—

(a) a special accounting return, or

(b) a value added tax return submitted to the tax authorities of another member State;

"tax period" means—

(a) a reporting period (under the accounting scheme under this Schedule), or

(b) any other period for which a person is required to make a return under a special scheme;

"UK VAT" means VAT which a person is liable to pay (whether in the United Kingdom or another member State) in respect of qualifying supplies treated as made in the United Kingdom at a time when the person is or was a participant in the special scheme;

"value added tax return", in relation to another member State, means any value added tax return required to be submitted under any provision of the law of that member State which implements Article 364 of the VAT Directive (as substituted by Article 5(11) of Council Directive 2008/8/EC);

"the VAT Directive" has the meaning given by paragraph 2(7);".

(3) In sub-paragraph (2)(a), for the words from "virtue" to "2002 VAT Directive)," substitute "paragraph 15 of Schedule 4A (place of supply of electronic, telecommunication and broadcasting services),".

(4) Omit sub-paragraph (3).

PART 3

OTHER AMENDMENTS: UNION AND NON-UNION SCHEMES

11 VATA 1994 is amended in accordance with paragraphs 12 to 16.

12 (1) Section 3A (supply of electronic services in member States: special accounting scheme) is amended as follows.

(2) In subsection (1), after "services" insert ", telecommunication services or broadcasting services".

(3) After subsection (1) insert—

"(1A) Schedule 3BA—

(a) establishes a special accounting scheme for use by persons established in the UK and supplying electronically supplied services, telecommunication services or broadcasting services in other member States, and

(b) makes provision about corresponding schemes in other member States."

(4) For the heading substitute "**Supplies of electronic, telecommunication and broadcasting services: special accounting schemes**."

13 In section 76 (assessment of amounts due by way of penalty, interest or surcharge)—

(a) in subsection (1)(a), for "or 59A," substitute ", section 59A, paragraph 16F of Schedule 3B or paragraph 26 of Schedule 3BA,";

(b) after subsection (3) insert—

"(3A) In the case of a surcharge under paragraph 16F of Schedule 3B or paragraph 26 of Schedule 3BA, the assessment under this section is of an amount due in respect of "the relevant period", that is to say, the tax period (see section 76A) in respect of which the person is in default and in respect of which the surcharge arises.";

(c) in subsection (5), after each "(3)" insert "or (3A)". 14 After section 76 insert—

76A Section 76: cases involving special accounting schemes

(1) References in section 76 to a prescribed accounting period are to be read as including a tax period so far as that is necessary for the purposes of the references in section 76(1)(a) to paragraph 16F of Schedule 3B and paragraph 26 of Schedule 3BA (assessment of surcharge in certain cases involving special accounting schemes).

(2) References in section 77 to a prescribed accounting period are to be read accordingly.

(3) In this section and section 76 "tax period" means a tax period as defined in paragraph 23(1) of Schedule 3B or paragraph 38(1) of Schedule 3BA, as the case requires."

15 In section 77 (assessment: time limits and supplementary assessments)—

(a) in subsection (2), after "subsection (3)" insert "or (3A)";

(b) in subsection (3) after "subsection (3)" insert "or (3A)".

16 In section 80 (repayment of overpaid VAT etc), in subsection (7), after "this section" insert "(and paragraph 16I of Schedule 3B and paragraph 29 of Schedule 3BA)".

17 In section 84(6) (appeals: variation of amounts assessed by way of surcharge etc), after "70," insert "or (as the case requires) paragraph 26 of Schedule 3BA or paragraph 16F of Schedule 3B".

18 In paragraph 12 of Schedule 1A to VATA 1994 (cancellation of registration under that Schedule)—

(a) after "Schedule 3B" insert "and paragraph 16 of Schedule 3BA";

(b) for "that Schedule etc" substitute "the Schedule concerned".

19 (1) Paragraph 1 of Schedule 24 to FA 2007 (penalties for errors) is amended as follows.

(2) In the Table, after the second entry relating to VAT insert—

"VAT	Return under a special scheme."

(3) Before sub-paragraph (5) insert—

"(4A) In this paragraph "return under a special scheme" means any of the following, so far as relating to supplies of services treated as made in the United Kingdom—

(a) a special accounting return under paragraph 11 of Schedule 3B;

(b) a value added tax return submitted under any provision of the law of a member State other than the United Kingdom which implements Article 364 of the VAT Directive (as substituted by Article 5(11) of the Amending Directive);

(c) a value added tax return submitted under any provision of the law of a member State other than the United Kingdom which implements Article 369f of the VAT Directive (as inserted by Article 5(15) of the Amending Directive).

(4B) A value added tax return mentioned in paragraph (b) or (c) of sub-paragraph (4A) is regarded for the purposes of sub-paragraph (1) as given to HMRC when it is submitted to the authority to whom it is required to be submitted.

(4C) In sub-paragraph (4A)—

"the VAT Directive" means Directive 2006/112/EC;

"the Amending Directive" means Council Directive 2008/8/ EC."

20 (1) FA 2009 is amended as follows.

(2) In section 101 (late payment interest on sums due to HMRC), after subsection (9) insert—

"(10) The reference in subsection (1) to amounts payable to HMRC includes—

(a) amounts of UK VAT payable under a non-UK special scheme;

(b) amounts of UK VAT payable under a special scheme;

and references in Schedule 53 to amounts due or payable to HMRC are to be read accordingly.

(11) In subsection (10)—

(a) expressions used in paragraph (a) have the meaning given by paragraph 23(1) of Schedule 3B to VATA 1994 (non-Union scheme);

(b) expressions used in paragraph (b) have the meaning given by paragraph 38(1) of Schedule 3BA to VATA 1994 (Union scheme)."

(3) In section 108 (suspension of penalties during currency of agreement for deferred payment), in the Table in subsection (5), in the entry relating to value added tax, in the second column, after "1994" insert, "or under paragraph 16F of Schedule 3B, or paragraph 26 of Schedule 3BA, to that Act".

21 (1) Schedule 10 to F(No3)A 2010 (which prospectively amends Schedule 55 to FA 2009, which provides for penalties for failure to make returns) is amended as follows.

(2) In paragraph 2—

(a) after sub-paragraph (2) insert—

"(2A) In sub-paragraph (4), in the definition of "filing date", at the end insert "(or, in the case of a return mentioned in item 7AA or 7AB of the Table, to the tax authorities to whom the return is required to be delivered)".";

(b) in the words inserted by sub-paragraph (4), after item 7A, insert—

"7AA	Value added tax	Relevant non-UK return (as defined in paragraph 20(3) of Schedule 3BA to VATA 1994)
7AB	Value added tax	Relevant special scheme return (as defined in paragraph 16(3) of Schedule 3B to VATA 1994)".

(3) In paragraph 7, in the inserted paragraph 13A(1), for "7A, 7B" substitute "7A to 7B".

22 (1) Schedule 11 to F(No3)A 2010 (which prospectively amends Schedule 56 to FA 2009, which provides for penalties for failure to make payments) is amended as follows.

(2) In paragraph 2(7), in the inserted words, after item 6B insert—

"6BA	Value added tax	Amount payable under relevant special scheme return (as defined in paragraph 16(3) of Schedule 3B to VATA 1994) (except an amount falling within item 13A, 13AA, 13AB, 23 or 24)	The date by which the amount must be paid under the law of the member State which has established the special scheme
6BB	Value added tax	Amount payable under relevant non-UK return (as defined in paragraph 20(3) of Schedule 3BA to VATA 1994) (except an amount falling within item 13A, 13AA, 13AB, 23 or 24)	The date by which the amount must be paid under the law of the member State which has established the non-UK special scheme"

(3) In paragraph 2(9), in the inserted words, after item 13A insert—

"13AA	Value added tax	Amount assessed under section 73(1) of VATA 1994, by virtue of paragraph 16 of Schedule 3B to that Act, in the absence of a value added tax return (as defined in paragraph 23(1) of that Schedule)	The date by which the amount would have been required to be paid under the law of the member State under whose law the return was required
13AB	Value added tax	Amount assessed under section 73(1) of VATA 1994, by virtue of paragraph 20 of Schedule 3BA to that Act, in the absence of a relevant non- UK return (as defined in paragraph 38(1) of that Schedule)	The date by which the amount would have been required to be paid under the law of the member State under whose law the return was required"

(4) In paragraph 2(13)(a), in the substituted words, after "6A," insert "6BA, 6BB,".
(5) In paragraph 2(14)(a), in the substituted words, after "6A," insert "6BA, 6BB,".
(6) In paragraph 7, in the inserted paragraph 8A(1), after "6A," insert "6BA, 6BB,".

PART 4
COMMENCEMENT

23 (1) The amendments made by this Schedule (except the amendments made by paragraphs 20(2), 21 and 22) have effect in relation to supplies made on or after 1 January 2015 (but see also paragraphs 24 and 25).
(2) Sub-paragraph (1) does not apply in relation to—
(a) the amendment made by paragraph 6(3)(b);
(b) any amendment so far as it confers power to make regulations.

24 (1) No registration under Schedule 3BA (inserted by paragraph 1) may take effect before 1 January 2015.
(2) A request for registration under Schedule 3BA that is made before 1 October 2014 is to be treated for the purposes of Article 57d of Implementing Regulation (EU) No 282/2011 (as amended by Council Regulation (EU) No 967/2012) (registration to have effect from first day of subsequent quarter) as if it were made on that date.

25 (1) No registration under Schedule 3B that is to be made in reliance on the amendments made by paragraph 4 may take effect before 1 January 2015.
(2) A request for registration under Schedule 3B that is made before 1 October 2014 in reliance on the amendments made by paragraph 4 is to be treated for the purposes of Article 57d of Implementing Regulation (EU) No 282/2011 (as amended by Council Regulation (EU) No 967/2012) as if it were made on that date.

SCHEDULE 28

PART 3: CONSEQUENTIAL AMENDMENTS AND REPEALS

Section 196

PART 2

OTHER AMENDMENTS AND REPEALS

Customs and Excise Management Act 1979

10 CEMA 1979 is amended as follows

11 (1) Section 1(1) (interpretation) is amended as follows.
(2) In the definition of "the revenue trade provisions of the customs and excise Acts", after paragraph (f) insert—

"(g) the provisions of Part 3 of the Finance Act 2014;".

(3) In the definition of "revenue trader"—

(a) in paragraph (a)(ic), for "gaming within the meaning of the Betting and Gaming Duties Act 1981 (see section 33(1))" substitute "any activity that constitutes betting or gaming for the purposes of Part 3 of the Finance Act 2014 (see sections 150, 183 and 188)",

(b) after paragraph (a)(id) insert—

"(ie) the management or administration of any Chapter 1 stake fund, Chapter 2 stake fund or gaming prize fund within the meaning of Part 3 of the Finance Act 2014 (see sections 134, 143 and 154);", and

(c) in paragraph (a)(ii) for "or (id)" substitute ", (id) or (ie)".

Value Added Tax Act 1994

19 (1) Section 23A (meaning of "relevant machine game") of VATA 1994 is amended as follows.
(2) In subsection (2)(f), for "section 26A of the Betting and Gaming Duties Act 1981 (remote gaming duty: interpretation)" substitute "section 154(1) of the Finance Act 2014 (meaning of remote gaming)".
(3) In subsection (3), in the definition of "real game of chance", for "the Betting and Gaming Duties Act 1981" substitute "Part 3 of the Finance Act 2014 (see section 188(1)(b))".

Finance Act 2008

27 (1) The Table in paragraph 1 of Schedule 41 to FA 2008 (penalties: failure to notify and certain VAT and excise wrongdoing) is amended as follows.
(2) For the entries relating to general betting duty and pool betting duty substitute—

"General betting duty	Obligation to register under section 164(2) of FA 2014 (registration of persons liable etc for general betting duty).
Pool betting duty	Obligation to register under section 164(2) of FA 2014 (registration of persons liable etc for pool betting duty)."

(3) For the entry relating to remote gaming duty substitute—

"Remote gaming duty	Obligation to register under section 164(2) of FA 2014 (registration of persons liable etc for remote gaming duty)."

Finance Act 2009

28 FA 2009 is amended as follows.

29 The Table in paragraph 1 of Schedule 55 (penalty for failure to make returns etc) is amended as follows—

(a) in item 23 (general betting duty), for "paragraph 2 of Schedule 1 to BGDA 1981" substitute "section 166 of FA 2014",
(b) in item 24 (pool betting duty), for "paragraph 2A of Schedule 1 to BGDA 1981" substitute "section 166 of FA 2014", and
(c) in item 28 (remote gaming duty), for "26K of BGDA 1981" substitute "166 of FA 2014".

30 (1) The Table in paragraph 1 of Schedule 56 (penalty for failure to make payments on time) is amended as follows.
(2) For items 11H and 11I substitute—

"11H	General betting duty	Amount payable under section 142 of FA 2014	The date determined— (a) under section 142 of FA 2014, or (b) by or under regulations under section 163 or 167 of that Act, as the date by which the amount must be paid
11I	Pool betting duty	Amount payable under section 151 of FA 2014	The date determined— (a) under section 151 of FA 2014, or (b) by or under regulations under section 163 or 167 of that Act, as the date by which the amount must be paid"

(3) For item 11M substitute—

"11M	Remote gaming duty	Amount payable under section 162 of FA 2014	The date determined by or under regulations under section 163 or 167 of FA 2014 as the date by which the amount must be paid"

Finance Act 2012

31 (1) Schedule 24 to FA 2012 (machine games duty) is amended as follows.
(2) In paragraph 3(2), for "BGDA 1981" substitute "Part 3 of FA 2014".
(3) In paragraph 37(5), for "the offences" substitute "the offence".
(4) In paragraph 38, for "remote gaming duty" substitute "bingo duty".

FINANCE ACT 2015

2015 Chapter 11

An Act to grant certain duties, to alter other duties, and to amend the law relating to the National Debt and the Public Revenue, and to make further provision in connection with finance.

26 March 2015

CONTENTS

PART 2

EXCISE DUTIES AND OTHER TAXES

Value Added Tax

66 VAT: refunds to certain charities

(1) In Part 2 of VATA 1994 (reliefs, exemptions and repayments), after section 33B insert—

"33C Refunds of VAT to charities within section 33D

(1) This section applies to a charity that falls within any of the descriptions in section 33D. A charity to which this section applies is referred to in this section as a "qualifying charity".

(2) This section applies where—

(*a*) VAT is chargeable on—

(i) the supply of goods or services to a qualifying charity,

(ii) the acquisition of any goods from another member State by a qualifying charity, or

(iii) the importation of any goods from a place outside the member States by a qualifying charity, and

(*b*) the supply, acquisition or importation is not for the purpose of any business carried on by the qualifying charity.

(3) The Commissioners shall, on a claim made by the qualifying charity at such time and in such form and manner as the Commissioners may determine, refund to the qualifying charity the amount of the VAT so chargeable.

(4) A claim under subsection (3) above in respect of a supply, acquisition or importation must be made before the end of the period of 4 years beginning with the day on which the supply is made or the acquisition or importation takes place.

(5) Subsection (6) applies where goods or services supplied to, or acquired or imported by, a qualifying charity otherwise than for the purpose of any business carried on by the qualifying charity cannot be conveniently distinguished from goods or services supplied to, or acquired or imported by, the qualifying charity for the purpose of such a business.

(6) The amount to be refunded under this section is such amount as remains after deducting from the whole of the VAT chargeable on any supply to, or acquisition or importation by, the qualifying charity such proportion of that VAT as appears to the Commissioners to be attributable to the carrying on of the business.

(7) References in this section to VAT do not include any VAT which, by virtue of an order under section 25(7), is excluded from credit under section 25.

33D Charities to which section 33C applies

Palliative care charities

(1) "Palliative care charity" means a charity the main purpose of which is the provision of palliative care at the direction of, or under the supervision of, a medical professional to persons who are in need of such care as a result of having a terminal illness.

(2) In subsection (1) "medical professional" means—

(*a*) a registered medical practitioner, or

(*b*) a registered nurse.

Air ambulance charities

(3) "Air ambulance charity" means a charity the main purpose of which is to provide an air ambulance service in pursuance of arrangements made by, or at the request of, a relevant NHS body.

(4) In subsection (3) "relevant NHS body" means a body the main purpose of which is to provide ambulance services and which is—

(*a*) an NHS foundation trust in England,

(*b*) an NHS trust in Wales,

(*c*) a Special Health Board constituted under section 2 of the National Health Service (Scotland) Act 1978, or

(*d*) a Health and Social Care trust established under the Health and Personal Social Services (Northern Ireland) Order 1991.

Search and rescue charities

(5) "Search and rescue charity" means a charity that meets condition A or B.

(6) Condition A is that—

(*a*) the main purpose of the charity is to carry out search and rescue activities in the United Kingdom or the UK marine area, and

(*b*) the search and rescue activities carried out by the charity are co-ordinated by a relevant authority.

(7) Condition B is that the main purpose of the charity is to support, develop and promote the activities of a charity which meets condition A.

(8) For the purposes of subsection (6)—

"search and rescue activities" means searching for, and rescuing, persons who are, or may be, at risk of death or serious injury;

"relevant authority" means—

(*a*) the Secretary of State;

(*b*) a police force;

(*c*) the Scottish Fire and Rescue Service;

(*d*) any other person or body specified for the purposes of subsection (6) by an order made by the Treasury;

"police force" means—

(*a*) a police force within the meaning of the Police Act 1996;

(*b*) the Police Service of Scotland;

(*c*) the Police Service of Northern Ireland;

(*d*) the Police Service of Northern Ireland Reserve;

(*e*) the British Transport Police Force;

(*f*) the Civil Nuclear Constabulary;

(*g*) the Ministry of Defence Police;

"UK marine area" has the meaning given by section 42(1) of the Marine and Coastal Access Act 2009.

Medical courier charities

(9) "Medical courier charity" means a charity that meets condition A or B.

(10) Condition A is that the main purpose of the charity is to provide services for the transportation of items intended for use for medical purposes, including in particular—

(*a*) blood;

(*b*) medicines and other medical supplies;

(*c*) items relating to people who are undergoing medical treatment.

(11) Condition B is that the main purpose of the charity is to support, develop and promote the activities of a charity which meets condition A.

(12) In subsection (10) "item" includes any substance."

(2) In section 79 of VATA 1994 (repayment supplement in respect of certain delayed payments or refunds)—

(*a*) in subsection (1), after paragraph (*d*) insert "or

(*e*) a charity which is registered is entitled to a refund under section 33C,";

(*b*) in subsection (5), after paragraph (*d*) insert ", and

(*e*) a supplement paid to a charity under subsection (1)(*e*) shall be treated as an amount due to the charity by way of refund under section 33C.";

(*c*) in subsection (6)(*b*), for "or 33B" substitute ", 33B or 33C".

(3) In section 90 of VATA 1994 (failure of resolution under Provisional Collection of Taxes Act 1968), in subsection (3), after "33B," insert "33C,".

(4) In Schedule 9 to VATA 1994 (exemptions), in Group 14 (supplies of goods where input tax cannot be recovered), in Note (9), after "33B," insert "33C,".

(5) The amendments made by this section have effect in relation to supplies made, and acquisitions and importations taking place, on or after 1 April 2015.

(6) Until section 179 of the Health and Social Care Act 2012 (which abolishes NHS trusts in England) is fully brought into force, references in section 33D of VATA 1994 to an NHS foundation trust in England include an NHS trust in England.

67 VAT: refunds to strategic highways companies

(1) In section 41 of VATA 1994 (application of Act to the Crown), in subsection (7)—

(*a*) after "subsection (6)" insert "each of the following is to be regarded as a body of persons exercising functions on behalf of a Minister of the Crown",

(*b*) omit the "and" after paragraph (*j*), and

(*c*) for the words after paragraph (*k*) substitute—

"(*l*) a strategic highways company appointed under section 1 of the Infrastructure Act 2015."

(2) The amendments made by this section come into force on 1 April 2015.

PART 4
OTHER PROVISIONS

Anti-Avoidance

120 Penalties in connection with offshore matters and offshore transfers

(1) Schedule 20 contains provisions amending—

(*a*) Schedule 24 to FA 2007 (penalties for errors),

(*b*) Schedule 41 to FA 2008 (penalties for failure to notify), and

(*c*) Schedule 55 to FA 2009 (penalties for failure to make returns etc).

(2) That Schedule comes into force on such day as the Treasury may by order appoint.

(3) An order under subsection (2)—

(*a*) may commence a provision generally or only for specified purposes, and

(*b*) may appoint different days for different provisions or for different purposes.

(4) The power to make an order under this section is exercisable by statutory instrument.

PART 5
FINAL PROVISIONS

126 Interpretation

(1) In this Act—

"ALDA 1979" means the Alcoholic Liquor Duties Act 1979,
"CAA 2001" means the Capital Allowances Act 2001,
"CTA 2009" means the Corporation Tax Act 2009,
"CTA 2010" means the Corporation Tax Act 2010,
"IHTA 1984" means the Inheritance Tax Act 1984,
"ITA 2007" means the Income Tax Act 2007,
"ITEPA 2003" means the Income Tax (Earnings and Pensions) Act 2003,
"ITTOIA 2005" means the Income Tax (Trading and Other Income) Act 2005,
"OTA 1975" means the Oil Taxation Act 1975,
"TCGA 1992" means the Taxation of Chargeable Gains Act 1992,
"TIOPA 2010" means the Taxation (International and Other Provisions) Act 2010,
"TMA 1970" means the Taxes Management Act 1970,
"TPDA 1979" means the Tobacco Products Duty Act 1979,
"VATA 1994" means the Value Added Tax Act 1994, and
"VERA 1994" means the Vehicle Excise and Registration Act 1994.

(2) In this Act "FA", followed by a year, means the Finance Act of that year.

127 Short title

This Act may be cited as the Finance Act 2015.

SCHEDULE 20

PENALTIES IN CONNECTION WITH OFFSHORE MATTERS AND OFFSHORE TRANSFERS

Section 120

Penalties for errors

1 Schedule 24 to FA 2007 is amended as follows.

2 (1) Paragraph 4 (penalties payable under paragraph 1) is amended as follows.

(2) After sub-paragraph (1) insert—

"(1A) If the inaccuracy is in category 0, the penalty is—

(*a*) for careless action, 30% of the potential lost revenue,

(*b*) for deliberate but not concealed action, 70% of the potential lost revenue, and

(*c*) for deliberate and concealed action, 100% of the potential lost revenue."

(3) In sub-paragraph (2)—

(*a*) in paragraph (*a*), for "30%" substitute "37.5%",

(*b*) in paragraph (*b*), for "70%" substitute "87.5%", and

(*c*) in paragraph (*c*), for "100%" substitute "125%".

(4) In sub-paragraph (5), for "3" substitute "4".

3 (1) Paragraph 4A (categorisation of inaccuracies) is amended as follows.

(2) For sub-paragraph (1) substitute—

"(A1) An inaccuracy is in category 0 if—

(*a*) it involves a domestic matter,

(*b*) it involves an offshore matter or an offshore transfer, the territory in question is a category 0 territory and the tax at stake is income tax, capital gains tax or inheritance tax, or

(*c*) it involves an offshore matter and the tax at stake is a tax other than income tax, capital gains tax or inheritance tax.

(1) An inaccuracy is in category 1 if—

(*a*) it involves an offshore matter or an offshore transfer,

(*b*) the territory in question is a category 1 territory, and

(*c*) the tax at stake is income tax, capital gains tax or inheritance tax."

(3) In sub-paragraph (2)—

(*a*) in paragraph (*a*), after "matter" insert "or an offshore transfer", and

(*b*) in paragraph (*c*), for "or capital gains tax" substitute ", capital gains tax or inheritance tax".

(4) In sub-paragraph (3)—

(*a*) in paragraph (*a*), after "matter" insert "or an offshore transfer", and

(*b*) in paragraph (*c*), for "or capital gains tax" substitute ", capital gains tax or inheritance tax".

(5) After sub-paragraph (4) insert—

"(4A) Where the tax at stake is inheritance tax, assets are treated for the purposes of sub-paragraph (4) as situated or held in a territory outside the UK if they are so situated or held immediately after the transfer of value by reason of which inheritance tax becomes chargeable.

(4B) An inaccuracy "involves an offshore transfer" if—

(*a*) it does not involve an offshore matter,

(*b*) it is deliberate (whether or not concealed) and results in a potential loss of revenue,

(*c*) the tax at stake is income tax, capital gains tax or inheritance tax, and

(*d*) the applicable condition in paragraph 4AA is satisfied."

(6) In sub-paragraph (5), for the words following "revenue" substitute "and does not involve either an offshore matter or an offshore transfer".

(7) In sub-paragraph (6)(*a*), after "matters" insert "or transfers".

(8) In sub-paragraph (7), for ""Category 1" substitute ""Category 0 territory", "category 1".

4 After paragraph 4A insert—

"4AA

(1) This paragraph makes provision in relation to offshore transfers.

(2) Where the tax at stake is income tax, the applicable condition is satisfied if the income on or by reference to which the tax is charged, or any part of the income—

(*a*) is received in a territory outside the UK, or

(*b*) is transferred before the filing date to a territory outside the UK.

(3) Where the tax at stake is capital gains tax, the applicable condition is satisfied if the proceeds of the disposal on or by reference to which the tax is charged, or any part of the proceeds—

(*a*) are received in a territory outside the UK, or

(*b*) are transferred before the filing date to a territory outside the UK.

(4) Where the tax at stake is inheritance tax, the applicable condition is satisfied if—

(*a*) the disposition that gives rise to the transfer of value by reason of which the tax becomes chargeable involves a transfer of assets, and

(*b*) after that disposition but before the filing date the assets, or any part of the assets, are transferred to a territory outside the UK.

(5) In the case of a transfer falling within sub-paragraph (2)(*b*), (3)(*b*) or (4)(*b*), references to the income, proceeds or assets transferred are to be read as including references to any assets derived from or representing the income, proceeds or assets.

(6) In relation to an offshore transfer, the territory in question for the purposes of paragraph 4A is the highest category of territory by virtue of which the inaccuracy involves an offshore transfer.

(7) "Filing date" means the date when the document containing the inaccuracy is given to HMRC.

(8) "Assets" has the same meaning as in paragraph 4A."

5 In paragraph 10 (standard percentage reductions for disclosure), in the Table in sub-paragraph (2), at the appropriate places insert—

"37.5%	18.75%	0%"
"87.5%	43.75%	25%"
""125%	62.5%	40%"

6 In paragraph 12(5) (interaction with other penalties and late payment surcharges: the relevant percentage)—

(*a*) before paragraph (*a*) insert—

"(za) if the penalty imposed under paragraph 1 is for an inaccuracy in category 0, 100%,", and

(*b*) in paragraph (*a*), for "100%" substitute "125%".

7 (1) Paragraph 21A (classification of territories) is amended as follows.

(2) Before sub-paragraph (1) insert—

"(A1) A category 0 territory is a territory designated as a category 0 territory by order made by the Treasury."

(3) For sub-paragraph (2) substitute—

"(2) A category 2 territory is a territory that is not any of the following—

(*a*) a category 0 territory;

(*b*) a category 1 territory;

(*c*) a category 3 territory."

(4) For sub-paragraph (7) substitute—

"(7) An instrument containing (whether alone or with other provisions) the first order to be made under sub-paragraph (A1) may not be made unless a draft of the instrument has been laid before, and approved by a resolution of, the House of Commons."

8 (1) Paragraph 21B (location of assets etc) is amended as follows.

(2) After sub-paragraph (1) insert—

"(1A) The Treasury may by regulations make provision for determining for the purposes of paragraph 4AA where—

(*a*) income is received or transferred,

(*b*) the proceeds of a disposal are received or transferred, or

(*c*) assets are transferred."

(3) In sub-paragraph (2), for "and capital gains tax" substitute ", capital gains tax and inheritance tax".

Penalties for failure to notify

9 Schedule 41 to FA 2008 is amended as follows.

10 (1) Paragraph 6 (amount of penalty: standard amount) is amended as follows.

(2) After sub-paragraph (1) insert—

"(1A) If the failure is in category 0, the penalty is—

(*a*) for a deliberate and concealed failure, 100% of the potential lost revenue,

(*b*) for a deliberate but not concealed failure, 70% of the potential lost revenue, and

(*c*) for any other case, 30% of the potential lost revenue."

(3) In sub-paragraph (2)—

(*a*) in paragraph (*a*), for "100%" substitute "125%",

(*b*) in paragraph (*b*), for "70%" substitute "87.5%", and

(*c*) in paragraph (*c*), for "30%" substitute "37.5%".

(4) In sub-paragraph (5), for "3" substitute "4".

11 (1) Paragraph 6A (categorisation of failures) is amended as follows.

(2) For sub-paragraph (1) substitute—

"(A1) A failure is in category 0 if—

(*a*) it involves a domestic matter,

(*b*) it involves an offshore matter or an offshore transfer, the territory in question is a category 0 territory and the tax at stake is income tax or capital gains tax, or

(*c*) it involves an offshore matter and the tax at stake is a tax other than income tax or capital gains tax.

(1) A failure is in category 1 if—

(*a*) it involves an offshore matter or an offshore transfer,

(*b*) the territory in question is a category 1 territory, and

(*c*) the tax at stake is income tax or capital gains tax."

(3) In sub-paragraph (2)(*a*), after "matter" insert "or an offshore transfer".

(4) In sub-paragraph (3)(*a*), after "matter" insert "or an offshore transfer".

(5) After sub-paragraph (4) insert—

"(4A) A failure "involves an offshore transfer" if—

(*a*) it does not involve an offshore matter,

(*b*) it is deliberate (whether or not concealed) and results in a potential loss of revenue,

(*c*) the tax at stake is income tax or capital gains tax, and

(*d*) the applicable condition in paragraph 6AA is satisfied."

(6) In sub-paragraph (5), for the words following "revenue" substitute "and does not involve either an offshore matter or an offshore transfer".

(7) In sub-paragraph (6)(*a*), after "matters" insert "or transfers".

(8) Omit sub-paragraph (8).

(9) In sub-paragraph (9), after "paragraph" insert "and paragraph 6AA".

12 After paragraph 6A insert—

"6AA

(1) This paragraph makes provision in relation to offshore transfers.

(2) Where the tax at stake is income tax, the applicable condition is satisfied if the income on or by reference to which the tax is charged, or any part of the income—

(*a*) is received in a territory outside the UK, or

(*b*) is transferred before the calculation date to a territory outside the UK.

(3) Where the tax at stake is capital gains tax, the applicable condition is satisfied if the proceeds of the disposal on or by reference to which the tax is charged, or any part of the proceeds—

(*a*) are received in a territory outside the UK, or

(*b*) are transferred before the calculation date to a territory outside the UK.

(4) In the case of a transfer falling within sub-paragraph (2)(*b*) or (3)(*b*), references to the income or proceeds transferred are to be read as including references to any assets derived from or representing the income or proceeds.

(5) In relation to an offshore transfer, the territory in question for the purposes of paragraph 6A is the highest category of territory by virtue of which the failure involves an offshore transfer.

(6) In this paragraph "calculation date" means the date by reference to which the potential lost revenue is to be calculated (see paragraph 7).

6AB

Regulations under paragraph 21B of Schedule 24 to FA 2007 (location of assets etc) apply for the purposes of paragraphs 6A and 6AA of this Schedule as they apply for the purposes of paragraphs 4A and 4AA of that Schedule."

13 In paragraph 13 (standard percentage reductions for disclosure), in the Table in sub-paragraph (3), at the appropriate places insert—

"37.5%	case A: 12.5% case B: 25%	case A: 0% case B: 12.5%"
"87.5%	43.75%	25%"
"125%	62.5%	40%"

Penalties for failure to make returns etc

14 Schedule 55 to FA 2009 is amended as follows.

15 (1) Paragraph 6 (penalty for failure continuing 12 months after penalty date) is amended as follows.

(2) In sub-paragraph (3A)—

(*a*) before paragraph (*a*) insert—

"(za) for the withholding of category 0 information, 100%,", and

(*b*) in paragraph (*a*), for "100%" substitute "125%".

(3) In sub-paragraph (4A)—

(*a*) before paragraph (*a*) insert—

"(za) for the withholding of category 0 information, 70%,", and

(*b*) in paragraph (*a*), for "70%" substitute "87.5%".

(4) In sub-paragraph (6), for "3" substitute "4".

16 (1) Paragraph 6A (categorisation of information) is amended as follows.

(2) For sub-paragraph (1) substitute—

"(A1) Information is category 0 information if—

(*a*) it involves a domestic matter,

(*b*) it involves an offshore matter or an offshore transfer, the territory in question is a category 0 territory and it is information which would enable or assist HMRC to assess P's liability to income tax, capital gains tax or inheritance tax, or

(*c*) it involves an offshore matter and it is information which would enable or assist HMRC to assess P's liability to a tax other than income tax, capital gains tax or inheritance tax.

(1) Information is category 1 information if—

(*a*) it involves an offshore matter or an offshore transfer,

(*b*) the territory in question is a category 1 territory, and

(*c*) it is information which would enable or assist HMRC to assess P's liability to income tax, capital gains tax or inheritance tax."

(3) In sub-paragraph (2)—

(*a*) in paragraph (*a*), after "matter" insert "or an offshore transfer", and

(*b*) in paragraph (*c*), for "or capital gains tax" substitute ", capital gains tax or inheritance tax".

(4) In sub-paragraph (3)—

(*a*) in paragraph (*a*), after "matter" insert "or an offshore transfer", and

(*b*) in paragraph (*c*), for "or capital gains tax" substitute ", capital gains tax or inheritance tax".

(5) After sub-paragraph (4) insert—

"(4A) If the liability to tax which would have been shown in the return is a liability to inheritance tax, assets are treated for the purposes of sub-paragraph (4) as situated or held in a territory outside the UK if they are so situated or held immediately after the transfer of value by reason of which inheritance tax becomes chargeable.

(4B) Information "involves an offshore transfer" if—

(*a*) it does not involve an offshore matter,

(*b*) it is information which would enable or assist HMRC to assess P's liability to income tax, capital gains tax or inheritance tax,

(*c*) by failing to make the return, P deliberately withholds the information (whether or not the withholding of the information is also concealed), and

(*d*) the applicable condition in paragraph 6AA is satisfied."

(6) In sub-paragraph (5), for the words following "if" substitute "it does not involve an offshore matter or an offshore transfer".

(7) In sub-paragraph (6)(*a*), after "matters" insert "or transfers".

(8) Omit sub-paragraph (8).

(9) In sub-paragraph (9), after "paragraph" insert "and paragraph 6AA".

17 After paragraph 6A insert—

"6AA

(1) This paragraph makes provision in relation to offshore transfers.

(2) Where the liability to tax which would have been shown in the return is a liability to income tax, the applicable condition is satisfied if the income on or by reference to which the tax is charged, or any part of the income—

(*a*) is received in a territory outside the UK, or

(*b*) is transferred before the relevant date to a territory outside the UK.

(3) Where the liability to tax which would have been shown in the return is a liability to capital gains tax, the applicable condition is satisfied if the proceeds of the disposal on or by reference to which the tax is charged, or any part of the proceeds—

(*a*) are received in a territory outside the UK, or

(*b*) are transferred before the relevant date to a territory outside the UK.

(4) Where the liability to tax which would have been shown in the return is a liability to inheritance tax, the applicable condition is satisfied if—

(*a*) the disposition that gives rise to the transfer of value by reason of which the tax becomes chargeable involves a transfer of assets, and

(*b*) after that disposition but before the relevant date the assets, or any part of the assets, are transferred to a territory outside the UK.

(5) In the case of a transfer falling within sub-paragraph (2)(*b*), (3)(*b*) or (4)(*b*), references to the income, proceeds or assets transferred are to be read as including references to any assets derived from or representing the income, proceeds or assets.

(6) In relation to an offshore transfer, the territory in question for the purposes of paragraph 6A is the highest category of territory by virtue of which the information involves an offshore transfer.

(7) "Relevant date" means the date on which P becomes liable to a penalty under paragraph 6.

6AB

Regulations under paragraph 21B of Schedule 24 to FA 2007 (location of assets etc) apply for the purposes of paragraphs 6A and 6AA of this Schedule as they apply for the purposes of paragraphs 4A and 4AA of that Schedule."

18 In paragraph 15 (standard percentage reductions for disclosure), in the Table in sub-paragraph (2), at the appropriate places insert—

"87.5%	43.75%	25%"
"125%	62.5%	40%"

19 In paragraph 17(4) (interaction with other penalties and late payment surcharges), omit the "and" at the end of paragraph (*b*) and after that paragraph insert—

"(*ba*) if one of the penalties is a penalty under paragraph 6(3) or (4) and the information withheld is category 1 information, 125%, and".

SMALL BUSINESS, ENTERPRISE AND EMPLOYMENT ACT 2015

2015 Chapter 26

26 March 2015

PART 1
ACCESS TO FINANCE

Financial information about businesses

8 Disclosure of VAT registration information

(1) The Commissioners for Her Majesty's Revenue and Customs may disclose to a person ("P") any of the information included in the VAT registration of another person ("V") if the disclosure is for the purpose of enabling or assisting P to assess—

(a) V's creditworthiness,
(b) V's compliance with regulatory requirements relating to financial matters, or
(c) the risk of fraud by V.

(2) But subsection (1) does not authorise the Commissioners to disclose any information which is, in the Commissioners' view, financial information relating to any business carried on by V.

(3) If VAT registration information is disclosed to a person in accordance with subsection (1), that person must not further disclose any of the information unless the Commissioners consent to the disclosure.

(4) If VAT registration information is disclosed to a person in accordance with subsection (3) or this subsection, that person must not further disclose any of the information unless the Commissioners consent to the disclosure.

(5) A person does not contravene subsection (3) or (4) by disclosing a financial assessment made wholly or partly in reliance on the VAT registration information, if the financial assessment itself does not include any VAT registration information.

(6) If VAT registration information is disclosed to a person in accordance with subsection (1), (3) or (4), that person must not use that information except for the purposes of making a financial assessment.

(7) A person does not contravene subsection (6) by using, for any purpose, a financial assessment made wholly or partly in reliance on the VAT registration information.

(8) The Commissioners for Her Majesty's Revenue and Customs may make arrangements with any person about disclosures of information to that person (the "recipient") under subsection (1).

(9) The arrangements may (in particular) provide for—

(a) a fee to be payable by the recipient for the disclosure of information;
(b) conditions to apply to the recipient in relation to information disclosed (including conditions relating to the transfer, holding and processing of the information);
(c) financial penalties to be payable by the recipient for a failure to meet conditions which apply to the recipient under the arrangements.

(10) The Treasury may, by regulations, amend this section so that it authorises the Commissioners to disclose VAT registration information included in a person's VAT registration for additional purposes.

(11) In this section—

"financial assessment" means an assessment of a kind mentioned in subsection (1)(a), (b) or (c);

"VAT registration" means registration under the Value Added Tax Act 1994;

"VAT registration information" means information of the kind that the Commissioners are authorised to disclose under subsection (1) (as read with subsection (2)).

(12) Regulations under this section are subject to affirmative resolution procedure.

9 Offences for the purposes of section 8

(1) A person commits an offence if the person discloses information in contravention of section 8(3) or (4).

(2) It is a defence for a person charged with an offence under subsection (1) to prove that the person reasonably believed that the disclosure of the information was lawful.

(3) A person commits an offence if the person uses information in contravention of section 8(6).

(4) It is a defence for a person charged with an offence under subsection (3) to prove that the person reasonably believed that the use of the information was lawful.

(5) Section 19(4) to (7) of the Commissioners for Revenue and Customs Act 2005 apply to an offence under this section as they apply to an offence under section 19 of that Act.

(6) This section is without prejudice to the pursuit of any remedy or the taking of any action in relation to a contravention of section 8(1), (3), (4) or (6) (whether or not this section applies to the contravention).

FINANCE BILL

Note—This is the Summer Finance Bill 2015, as published on 15 July 2015.

At the time of publication, the Bill was expected to be considered by a Public Bill Committee in Autumn 2015, with Committee proceedings due end on Tuesday 20 October 2015 at the latest (Finance Bill programme motion, 21 July 2015).

CONTENTS

A BILL TO Grant certain duties, to alter other duties, and to amend the law relating to the National Debt and the Public Revenue, and to make further provision in connection with finance.

PART 1

PRINCIPAL RATES ETC

Tax lock

2 VAT lock

(1) The rate of value added tax for the time being in force under section 2 of VATA 1994 (standard rate) shall not exceed 20% during the VAT lock period.

(2) The rate of value added tax for the time being in force under section 29A of VATA 1994 (reduced rate) shall not exceed 5% during the VAT lock period.

(3) No supply specified in Schedule 7A to VATA 1994 (charge at reduced rate) at the beginning of the VAT lock period may be removed from it under section 29A(3) of that Act during that period.

(4) No goods, services or supply specified in Schedule 8 to VATA 1994 (zero-rating) at the beginning of the VAT lock period may be removed from it under section 30(4) of that Act during that period.

(5) In this section the "VAT lock period" means the period beginning with the day on which this Act is passed and ending immediately before the date of the first parliamentary general election after that day.

PART 5

EXCISE DUTIES AND OTHER TAXES

Insurance premium tax

43 Insurance premium tax: standard rate

(1) In section 51(2)(b) of FA 1994 (standard rate of insurance premium tax), for "6 per cent" substitute "9.5 per cent".

(2) The amendment made by subsection (1) has effect in relation to a premium falling to be regarded for the purposes of Part 3 of FA 1994 as received under a taxable insurance contract by an insurer on or after 1 November 2015.

(3) The amendment made by subsection (1) does not have effect in relation to a premium which—

- (a) is in respect of a contract made before 1 November 2015, and
- (b) falls to be regarded for the purposes of Part 3 of FA 1994 as received under the contract by the insurer before 1 March 2016 by virtue of regulations under section 68 of that Act (special accounting schemes).

(4) Subsection (3) does not apply in relation to a premium which—

- (a) is an additional premium under a contract,
- (b) falls to be regarded for the purposes of Part 3 of FA 1994 as received under the contract by the insurer on or after 1 November 2015 by virtue of regulations under section 68 of that Act, and
- (c) is in respect of a risk which was not covered by the contract before that date.

(5) In the application of sections 67A to 67C of FA 1994 (announced increase in rate) in relation to the increase made by this section—

- (a) the announcement for the purposes of sections 67A(1) and 67B(1) is to be taken to have been made on 8 July 2015,
- (b) the date of the change is 1 November 2015, and
- (c) the concessionary date is 1 March 2016.

Aggregates levy

44 Aggregates levy: restoration of exemptions

(1) The provisions of Part 2 of FA 2001 (aggregates levy) that were amended or repealed by section 94 of FA 2014 (removal of certain exemptions with effect from 1 April 2014) have effect, and are to be treated as having had effect at all times on or after 1 April 2014, as if the amendments and repeals made by that section had not been made.

(2) Accordingly, sections 94 and 95 of FA 2014 are repealed.

(3) Part 2 of FA 2001, as amended by subsection (1), is further amended in accordance with subsections (4) and (5).

(4) In section 17 (meaning of "aggregate" and "taxable aggregate"), in each of subsections (3)(f) and (4)(a)—

- (a) after "lignite," insert "or", and
- (b) omit "or shale".

(5) In section 18(2) (meaning of "exempt process"), after paragraph (c) insert—

"(ca) in the case of aggregate consisting of shale, any process consisting of a use of the shale that—

(i) is not a use of it as material or support in the construction or improvement of any structure, and

(ii) is not mixing it with anything as part of the process of producing mortar, concrete, tarmacadam, coated roadstone or any similar construction material."

(6) The repeal of section 94 of FA 2014 is to be treated as having come into force on 1 August 2015, and the amendments made by subsections (3) to (5) are to be treated as having come into force on 1 April 2014.

Climate change levy

45 CCL: removal of exemption for electricity from renewable sources

In paragraph 19 of Schedule 6 to FA 2000 (climate change levy: exemption for electricity from renewable sources), in sub-paragraph (3), before paragraph (a) insert—

"(za) it is generated before 1 August 2015,".

PART 6
ADMINISTRATION AND ENFORCEMENT

46 International agreements to improve compliance: client notification

(1) Section 222 of FA 2013 (international agreements to improve tax compliance) is amended as follows.

(2) In subsection (2), in paragraph (c), after "purposes" (but before the closing bracket) insert "and client notification obligations".

(3) In subsection (2), after paragraph (c) insert—

"(ca) impose client notification obligations on specified relevant persons;".

(4) After subsection (2) insert—

"(2A) For the purposes of subsection (2)(c) and (ca) a "client notification obligation" is an obligation to give specified information to—

(a) clients, or
(b) specified clients.

(2B) In subsection (2A) the reference to an obligation to give specified information includes—
(a) any obligation to give the information—
(i) in a specified form or manner;
(ii) at a specified time or specified times;
(b) in the case of a relevant financial entity or relevant person which is a body corporate, an obligation to require a person of which it has control to give the information."

(5) In subsection (4), at the appropriate places insert—
""client" includes—
(a) any client or customer, and
(b) any former client or customer;";
""control" is to be construed in accordance with section 1124 of CTA 2010;";
""relevant person" means—
(a) a tax adviser (as defined by section 272(5) of FA 2014), and
(b) any other person who in the course of business—
(i) gives advice to another person about that person's financial or legal affairs, or
(ii) provides other financial or legal services to another person."

47 Enforcement by deduction from accounts

(1) Schedule 8 contains provision about the enforcement of debts owed to the Commissioners for Her Majesty's Revenue and Customs by making deductions from accounts held with deposit-takers.
(2) The Treasury may, by regulations made by statutory instrument, make consequential, incidental or supplementary provision in connection with any provision made by that Schedule.
(3) Regulations under subsection (2) may amend, repeal or revoke any enactment (whenever passed or made).
(4) "Enactment" includes an enactment contained in subordinate legislation within the meaning of the Interpretation Act 1978.
(5) A statutory instrument containing (whether alone or with other provision) provision amending or repealing an Act may not be made unless a draft of the instrument has been laid before and approved by a resolution of the House of Commons.
(6) Any other statutory instrument containing regulations under subsection (2) is subject to annulment in pursuance of a resolution of the House of Commons.

48 Rate of interest applicable to judgment debts etc in taxation matters

(1) This section applies if a sum payable to or by the Commissioners under a judgment or order given or made in any court proceedings relating to a taxation matter (a "tax-related judgment debt") carries interest as a result of a relevant enactment.
(2) The "relevant enactments" are—
(a) section 17 of the Judgments Act 1838 (judgment debts to carry interest), and
(b) any order under section 74 of the County Courts Act 1984 (interest on judgment debts etc).
(3) The relevant enactment is to have effect in relation to the tax-related judgment debt as if for the rate specified in section 17(1) of the Judgments Act 1838 and any other rate specified in an order under section 74 of the County Courts Act 1984 there were substituted—
(a) in the case of a sum payable to the Commissioners, the late payment interest rate provided for in regulations made by the Treasury under section 103(1) of FA 2009, and
(b) in the case of a sum payable by the Commissioners, the special repayment rate.
(4) Subsection (3) does not affect any power of the court under the relevant enactment to prevent any sum from carrying interest or to provide for a rate of interest which is lower than (and incapable of exceeding) that for which the subsection provides.
(5) If section 44A of the Administration of Justice Act 1970 (interest on judgment debts expressed otherwise than in sterling), or any corresponding provision made under section 74 of the County Courts Act 1984 in relation to the county court, applies to a tax-related judgment debt—
(a) subsection (3) does not apply, but
(b) the court may not specify in an order under section 44A of the Administration of Justice Act 1970, or under any provision corresponding to that section which has effect under section 74 of the County Courts Act 1984, an interest rate which exceeds (or is capable of exceeding)—
(i) in the case of a sum payable to the Commissioners, the rate mentioned in subsection (3)(a), or
(ii) in the case of a sum payable by the Commissioners, the special repayment rate.
(6) The "special repayment rate" is the percentage per annum given by the formula—
$BR + 2$
where BR is the official Bank rate determined by the Bank of England Monetary Policy Committee at the operative meeting.

(7) "The operative meeting", in relation to the special repayment rate applicable in respect of any day, means the most recent meeting of the Bank of England Monetary Policy Committee apart from any meeting later than the 13th working day before that day.

(8) The Treasury may by regulations made by statutory instrument—

(a) repeal subsections (6) and (7), and

(b) provide that the "special repayment rate" for the purposes of this section is the rate provided for in the regulations.

(9) Regulations under subsection (8)—

(a) may make different provision for different purposes,

(b) may either themselves specify a rate of interest or make provision for such a rate to be determined (and to change from time to time) by reference to such rate, or the average of such rates, as may be referred to in the regulations,

(c) may provide for rates to be reduced below, or increased above, what they would otherwise be by specified amounts or by reference to specified formulae,

(d) may provide for rates arrived at by reference to averages to be rounded up or down,

(e) may provide for circumstances in which the alteration of a rate of interest is or is not to take place, and

(f) may provide that alterations of rates are to have effect for periods beginning on or after a day determined in accordance with the regulations ("the effective date") regardless of—

(i) the date of the judgment or order in question, and

(ii) whether interest begins to run on or after the effective date, or began to run before that date.

(10) A statutory instrument containing regulations under subsection (8) is subject to annulment in pursuance of a resolution of the House of Commons.

(11) To the extent that a tax-related judgment debt consists of an award of costs to or against the Commissioners, the reference in section 24(2) of the Crown Proceedings Act 1947 (which relates to interest on costs awarded to or against the Crown) to the rate at which interest is payable upon judgment debts due from or to the Crown is to be read as a reference to the rate at which interest is payable upon tax-related judgment debts.

(12) This section has effect in relation to interest for periods beginning on or after 8 July 2015, regardless of—

(a) the date of the judgment or order in question, and

(b) whether interest begins to run on or after 8 July 2015, or began to run before that date.

(13) Subsection (14) applies where, at any time during the period beginning with 8 July 2015 and ending immediately before the day on which this Act is passed ("the relevant period")—

(a) a payment is made in satisfaction of a tax-related judgment debt, and

(b) the payment includes interest under a relevant enactment in respect of any part of the relevant period.

(14) The court by which the judgment or order in question was given or made must, on an application made to it under this subsection by the person who made the payment, order the repayment of the amount by which the interest paid under the relevant enactment in respect of days falling within the relevant period exceeds the interest payable under the relevant enactment in respect of those days in accordance with the provisions of this section.

(15) In this section—

"the Commissioners" means the Commissioners for Her Majesty's Revenue and Customs;

"taxation matter" means anything, other than national insurance contributions, the collection and management of which is the responsibility of the Commissioners (or was the responsibility of the Commissioners of Inland Revenue or Commissioners of Customs and Excise);

"working day" means any day other than a non-business day as defined in section 92 of the Bills of Exchange Act 1882.

(16) This section extends to England and Wales only.

PART 7

FINAL

49 Interpretation

In this Act—

"CAA 2001" means the Capital Allowances Act 2001,

"CTA 2009" means the Corporation Tax Act 2009,

"CTA 2010" means the Corporation Tax Act 2010,

"FA", followed by a year, means the Finance Act of that year,

"IHTA 1984" means the Inheritance Tax Act 1984,

"ITA 2007" means the Income Tax Act 2007,

"ITEPA 2003" means the Income Tax (Earnings and Pensions) Act 2003,

"ITTOIA 2005" means the Income Tax (Trading and Other Income) Act 2005,

"TCGA 1992" means the Taxation of Chargeable Gains Act 1992,

"TIOPA 2010" means the Taxation (International and Other Provisions) Act 2010,
"TMA 1970" means the Taxes Management Act 1970,
"VATA 1994" means the Value Added Tax Act 1994, and
"VERA 1994" means the Vehicle Excise and Registration Act 1994.

50 Short title
This Act may be cited as the Finance (No. 2) Act 2015.

SCHEDULE 8

ENFORCEMENT BY DEDUCTION FROM ACCOUNTS

Section 47

PART 1

SCHEME FOR ENFORCEMENT BY DEDUCTION FROM ACCOUNTS

Introduction

1 This Part of this Schedule contains provision about the collection of amounts due and payable to the Commissioners by the making of deductions from accounts held with deposit-takers.

"Relevant sum"

2 (1) In this Part of this Schedule "relevant sum", in relation to a person, means a sum that is due and payable by the person to the Commissioners—

(a) under or by virtue of an enactment, or
(b) under a contract settlement,

and in relation to which Conditions A to C are met.
(2) Condition A is that the sum is at least £1,000.
(3) Condition B is that the sum is—

(a) an established debt (see sub-paragraph (5)),
(b) due under section 223 of, or paragraph 6 of Schedule 32 to, FA 2014 (accelerated payment notice or partner payment notice), or
(c) the disputed tax specified in a notice under section 221(2)(b) of FA 2014 (accelerated payment of tax: notice given pending appeal).

(4) Condition C is that HMRC is satisfied that the person is aware that the sum is due and payable by the person to the Commissioners.
(5) A sum that is due and payable to the Commissioners is an "established debt" if there is no possibility that the sum, or any part of it, will cease to be due and payable to the Commissioners on appeal.
(6) For the purposes of sub-paragraph (5) it does not matter whether the reason that there is no such possibility is—

(a) that there is no right of appeal in relation to the sum,
(b) that a period for bringing an appeal has expired without an appeal having been brought, or
(c) that an appeal which was brought has been finally determined or withdrawn;

and any power to grant permission to appeal out of time is to be disregarded.

Information notice

3 (1) This paragraph applies if it appears to HMRC that—

(a) a person has failed to pay a relevant sum, and
(b) that person holds one or more accounts with a deposit-taker.

(2) HMRC may give the deposit-taker a notice under this paragraph (an "information notice") requiring the deposit-taker to provide HMRC with—

(a) prescribed information about accounts held by the person with the deposit-taker,
(b) in relation to any joint account held by the person with the deposit-taker, prescribed information about the other holder or holders of the account, and
(c) any other prescribed information.

(3) HMRC may exercise the power under sub-paragraph (2) only for the purposes of determining whether to give a hold notice to the deposit-taker in respect of the person concerned (see paragraph 4).
(4) Where a deposit-taker is given an information notice, it must comply with the notice as soon as reasonably practicable and, in any event, within the period of 10 working days beginning with the day on which the notice is given to it.
(5) An information notice must explain the effect of—

(a) sub-paragraph (4), and

(b) paragraph 13 (penalties).

Hold notice

4 (1) If it appears to HMRC that—

(a) a person ("P") has failed to pay a relevant sum, and

(b) P holds one or more accounts with a deposit-taker,

HMRC may give the deposit-taker a notice under this paragraph (a "hold notice").

(2) The hold notice must—

(a) specify P's name and last known address,

(b) specify as the "specified amount" an amount that meets the conditions in sub-paragraph (4),

(c) specify as the "safeguarded amount" an amount that meets the requirements set out in sub-paragraphs (6) to (8),

(d) set out any rules which are to apply for the purposes of paragraph 6(5)(b) (priority of accounts subject to a hold notice), and

(e) explain the effect of—

(i) paragraphs 5 to 12 (effect of hold notice, duty to notify account holders etc),

(ii) paragraph 13 (penalties), and

(iii) any regulations under paragraph 19(2)(c) or (d) (powers to restrict the accounts or amounts in relation to which a hold notice may have effect, in addition to the powers to make provision in the hold notice under sub-paragraph (3)(b) and (c)).

For provision about the particular relevant sums to which a hold notice relates see paragraph 7(6)(a)(ii) and (7) (notice to be given by HMRC to P).

(3) The hold notice may—

(a) specify any other information which HMRC considers might assist the deposit-taker in identifying accounts which P holds with it;

(b) specify an account, or description of account, which is to be treated for the purposes of the hold notice and this Part of this Schedule as not being an account held by P with the deposit-taker;

(c) require that an amount specified in the notice is to be treated for the purposes of the hold notice and this Part of this Schedule as if it were not an amount standing to the credit of a specified account held by P.

(4) The amount specified as the specified amount in the hold notice ("the current hold notice") must not exceed so much of the notified sum (see paragraph 7(6) to (8)) as remains after deducting—

(a) the amount specified as the "specified amount" in any hold notice which relates to the same debts as the current hold notice (see subparagraph (5)) and is given to another deposit-taker on the same day as that notice, and

(b) the amount specified as the "specified amount" in any hold notice which relates to the same debts as the current hold notice and is given to a deposit-taker on an earlier day, (unless HMRC has received a notification under paragraph 7(4) in relation to that earlier hold notice).

(5) For the purposes of this paragraph, any two hold notices given in respect of the same person "relate to the same debts" if at least one relevant sum specified in relation to one of those notices by virtue of paragraph 7(7)(a) is the same debt as a relevant sum so specified in relation to the other notice.

(6) The amount specified in the hold notice as the safeguarded amount must be at least £5,000; but this is qualified by sub-paragraphs (7) and (8).

(7) The safeguarded amount must be nil if—

(a) HMRC has previously given a deposit-taker a hold notice ("the earlier hold notice") relating to the same debts as the hold notice mentioned in sub-paragraph (2) ("the new hold notice"), and

(b) within the period of 30 days ending with the day on which the new hold notice is given to the deposit-taker, HMRC has received a notice under paragraph 7 which states that there is a held amount as a result of the earlier hold notice.

(8) HMRC may (in a case not falling within sub-paragraph (7)) determine that an amount less than £5,000 (which may be nil) is to be the safeguarded amount if HMRC considers it appropriate to do so having regard to the value (or aggregate value) in sterling at the relevant time of any amounts which at that time stand to the credit of a qualifying non-sterling account or accounts.

(9) In sub-paragraph (8) "qualifying non-sterling account" means an account which, but for paragraph 5(6)(b) (account not denominated in sterling), would be a relevant account in relation to the hold notice.

(10) For the purposes of sub-paragraph (8), the value in sterling of any amount is to be determined in the prescribed manner; and regulations for the purposes of this sub-paragraph may specify circumstances in which the exchange rate is to be determined in accordance with a notice published by the Commissioners.

(11) In sub-paragraph (8) "the relevant time" means the time when the Commissioners determine the amount to be specified as the "safeguarded amount" under sub-paragraph (2)(c).

(12) HMRC must not on any one day give to a single deposit-taker more than one hold notice relating to the same debts.

Effect of hold notice

5 (1) A deposit-taker to whom a hold notice is given under paragraph 4 must, for each relevant account (see sub-paragraph (6))—

(a) determine whether or not there is a held amount (greater than nil) in relation to that account, and

(b) if there is such a held amount in relation to that account, take the first or second type of action (see sub-paragraph (3)) in respect of that account.

See paragraph 6 for how to determine the held amount in relation to any relevant account.

(2) The deposit-taker must comply with sub-paragraph (1) as soon as is reasonably practicable and, in any event, within the period of 5 working days beginning with the day on which the hold notice is given.

(3) In relation to each affected account (see sub-paragraph (7))—

(a) the first type of action is to put in place such arrangements as are necessary to ensure that the deposit-taker does not do anything, or permit anything to be done, that would reduce the amount standing to the credit of that account below the held amount in relation to that account;

(b) the second type of action is to—

(i) transfer an amount equal to the held amount from the affected account into an account created by the deposit-taker for the sole purpose of containing that transferred amount (a "suspense account"), and

(ii) put in place such arrangements as are necessary to ensure that the deposit-taker does not do anything, or permit anything to be done, that would reduce the amount standing to the credit of that suspense account below the amount that is the held amount in relation to the affected account.

(4) The deposit-taker must maintain any arrangements made under subparagraph (3) until the hold notice ceases to be in force.

(5) A hold notice ceases to be in force when—

(a) the deposit-taker is given a notice cancelling it under paragraph 8(1) or 10 or the hold notice is cancelled under paragraph 11, or

(b) the deposit-taker is given a deduction notice in relation to the hold notice (see paragraph 12).

(6) In this Part of this Schedule "relevant account", in relation to a hold notice, means an account held with the deposit-taker by P, but not including—

(a) an account excluded under paragraph 4(3)(b) or by regulations under paragraph 19(2)(c),

(b) an account not denominated in sterling, or

(c) any suspense account.

(7) For the purposes of this Part of this Schedule, a relevant account is an "affected account" if, as a result of the hold notice, an amount is the held amount in relation to that account (see paragraph 6(1) and (2)).

Determination of held amounts

6 (1) If there is only one relevant account (see paragraph 5(6)) in existence at the time the deposit-taker complies with paragraph 5(1), "the held amount" in relation to that account is—

(a) if the available amount in respect of the account (see sub-paragraph (3)) exceeds the safeguarded amount, so much of the amount of the excess as does not exceed the specified amount, and

(b) if the available amount does not exceed the safeguarded amount, nil.

For the meaning of "the safeguarded amount" and "the specified amount" see paragraph 22(1).

(2) If there is more than one relevant account in existence at the time the deposit-taker complies with paragraph 5(1), "the held amount" in relation to each relevant account is determined as follows—

Step 1

Determine the available amount in respect of each relevant account.

Step 2

Determine the total of the available amounts in respect of all of the relevant accounts.

If that total does not exceed the safeguarded amount, the held amount in relation to each relevant account is nil (and no further steps are to be taken).

In any other case, go to Step 3.

Step 3
Match the safeguarded amount against the available amounts in respect of the relevant accounts, taking those accounts in reverse priority order (see sub-paragraph (6)).
Step 4
Match the specified amount against what remains of the available amounts in respect of the relevant accounts by taking each relevant account in priority order (see sub-paragraph (5)) and matching the specified amount (or, as the case may be, what remains of the specified amount) against the available amount for each account until either—

(a) the specified amount has been fully matched, or
(b) what remains of the available amounts is exhausted.

Where this sub-paragraph applies, "the held amount", in relation to a relevant account—

(i) is so much of the amount standing to the credit of the account as is matched against the specified amount under Step 4, and
(ii) accordingly, is nil if no amount standing to the credit of the account is so matched against the specified amount.

(3) In this paragraph "the available amount" means—

(a) in the case of an account other than a joint account, the amount standing to the credit of that account at the time the deposit-taker complies with paragraph 5(1), or
(b) in the case of a joint account, the appropriate fraction of the amount standing to the credit of that account at that time;

so, if no amount stands to the credit of an account at that time, "the available amount" is nil.
(4) In this paragraph "the appropriate fraction", in relation to a joint account, means—

$1 / N$

where N is the number of persons who together hold the joint account.
(5) In this paragraph "priority order" means such order as the deposit-taker considers appropriate, but the deposit-taker must ensure—

(a) that accounts other than joint accounts always have a higher priority than joint accounts, and
(b) subject to paragraph (a), that any rule set out in the hold notice under paragraph 4(2)(d) is adhered to.

(6) In this paragraph "reverse priority order" means the reverse of the order determined under sub-paragraph (5).
(7) In this paragraph references to an amount standing to the credit of an account are to be read subject to any regulations under paragraph 19(2)(d).

Duty to notify HMRC and account holders etc

7 (1) This paragraph applies where a deposit-taker receives a hold notice.
(2) If the deposit-taker determines that there are one or more affected accounts (see paragraph 5(7)) as a result of the hold notice, the deposit-taker must give HMRC a notice which sets out—

(a) prescribed information about each of the affected accounts held by P,
(b) the amount of the held amount in relation to each such account,
(c) if any of the affected accounts is a joint account held by P and one or more other persons, prescribed information about the other person or persons, and
(d) any other prescribed information.

(3) The notice under sub-paragraph (2) must be given within the period of 5 working days beginning with the day on which the deposit-taker complies with paragraph 5(1).
(4) If the deposit-taker determines that there are no affected accounts as a result of the hold notice, it must give HMRC a notice which—

(a) states that this is the case, and
(b) sets out any other prescribed information.

(5) The notice under sub-paragraph (4) must be given within the period of 5 working days beginning with the day on which the deposit-taker makes that determination.
(6) If HMRC receives a notice under sub-paragraph (2) it must as soon as reasonably practicable—

(a) give P—
 (i) a copy of the hold notice, and
 (ii) a notice under sub-paragraph (7), and
(b) in relation to each affected account, give a notice to each person within sub-paragraph (9) explaining that a hold notice has been given in respect of the account, the effect of the hold notice so far as it relates to the account and the effect of paragraphs 9 to 11.

(7) A notice under this sub-paragraph must comply with the following requirements—

(a) the notice must specify the particular relevant sums (see paragraph 2) to which the hold notice relates;

(b) the details given for that purpose must include a statement, to the best of HMRC's knowledge, of the amount of each of those sums (that is, the unpaid amount) at the date of the notice;

(c) the notice must state the total of the amounts stated under paragraph (b) (if more than one), and

(d) the notice must state that the notified sum for the purposes of the hold notice (see paragraph 4(4)) is equal to—

(i) the total amount specified under paragraph (c) or,

(ii) if paragraph (c) is not applicable, the amount specified under paragraph (b) as the amount of the relevant sum to which the hold notice relates.

(8) In this Part of this Schedule "the notified sum", in relation to a hold notice, means the amount identified as such (or that is to be identified as such) in the notice under sub-paragraph (7).

(9) The persons mentioned in sub-paragraph (6)(b) are—

(a) in the case of a joint account, any holder of the account other than P, and

(b) any person (not falling within paragraph (a)) who is an interested third party in relation to the affected account,

in respect of whom prescribed information has been provided under subparagraph (2)(c) or sufficient information has otherwise been given in the notice under sub-paragraph (2) to enable HMRC to give a notice.

(10) After the deposit-taker has complied with paragraph 5(1), the deposit-taker may, in relation to any affected account, give a notice to—

(a) P,

(b) if the account is a joint account, any other holder of the account, and

(c) any person (not falling within paragraph (b)) who is an interested third party in relation to the account,

which states that a hold notice has been received by the deposit-taker in respect of the account and the effect of that notice so far as it relates to that account.

(11) In this Part of this Schedule "interested third party", in relation to a relevant account, means a person other than P who has a beneficial interest in—

(a) an amount standing to the credit of the account, or

(b) an amount which has been transferred from that account to a suspense account.

(12) But, in relation to a hold notice, an interest which comes into existence after any arrangements under paragraph 5(3) have been put into place is treated as not being a beneficial interest for the purposes of sub-paragraph (11).

Cancellation or variation of effects of hold notice

8 (1) Where a hold notice has been given to a deposit-taker HMRC may, by a notice given to the deposit-taker (a "notice of cancellation or variation")—

(a) cancel the hold notice,

(b) cancel the effect of the hold notice in relation to one or more accounts, or

(c) cancel the effect of the hold notice in relation to any part of the held amount standing to the credit of a particular account or accounts.

In this sub-paragraph references to the effect of a hold notice are to its effect by virtue of paragraph 5(4).

(2) Where HMRC gives a notice under sub-paragraph (1) it must give a copy of that notice to—

(a) P, and

(b) any other person who HMRC considers is affected by the giving of the notice of cancellation or variation and is—

(i) a person who holds a relevant account of which P is also a holder and in respect of whom prescribed information is provided under paragraph 7(2)(c), or

(ii) an interested third party in relation to a relevant account in respect of whom sufficient information has been given in the notice under paragraph 7(2) to enable HMRC to give a notice.

(3) Where the deposit-taker is given a notice under sub-paragraph (1), it must as soon as reasonably practicable and, in any event, within the period of 5 working days beginning with the day the notice is given—

(a) if the notice is given under sub-paragraph (1)(a), cancel the arrangements made under paragraph 5(3) as a result of the notice, and

(b) if the notice is given under sub-paragraph (1)(b) or (c), make such adjustments to those arrangements as are necessary to give effect to the notice.

Making objections to hold notice

9 (1) Where a hold notice is given to a deposit-taker, a person within subparagraph (2) may by a notice given to HMRC (a "notice of objection") object against the hold notice.
(2) The persons who may object are—
(a) P,
(b) any interested third party in relation to an affected account, and
(c) any person (not falling within paragraph (a) or (b)) who is a holder of an affected account which is a joint account,
but only P may object on the ground in sub-paragraph (3)(a).
(3) An objection may only be made on one or more of the following grounds—
(a) that the debts to which the hold notice relates (see paragraph 7(7)(a)) have been wholly or partly paid,
(b) that at the time when the hold notice was given, either there was no sum that was a relevant sum in relation to P or P did not hold any account with the deposit-taker,
(c) that the hold notice is causing or will cause exceptional hardship to the person making the objection or another person, or
(d) that there is an interested third party in relation to one or more of the affected accounts.
(4) A notice of objection must state the grounds of the objection.
(5) Objections under this paragraph may only be made within the period of 30 days beginning with—
(a) in the case of—
(i) P, or
(ii) a person within sub-paragraph (2)(b) or (c) who has not been given a notice under paragraph 7(6)(b),
the day on which a copy of the hold notice is given to P under paragraph 7(6)(a), and
(b) in the case of a person given a notice under paragraph 7(6)(b), the day on which that notice is given.
(6) Sub-paragraph (5) does not apply if HMRC agree to the notice of objection being given after the end of the period mentioned in that sub-paragraph.
(7) HMRC must agree to a notice of objection being given after the end of that period if the following conditions are met—
(a) the person seeking to make the objection has made a request in writing to HMRC to agree to the notice of objection being given;
(b) HMRC is satisfied that there was reasonable excuse for not giving the notice before the relevant time limit, and
(c) HMRC is satisfied that the person complied with paragraph (a) without unreasonable delay after the reasonable excuse ceased.
(8) If a request of the kind referred to in sub-paragraph (7)(a) is made, HMRC must by a notice inform the person making the request whether or not HMRC agrees to the request.
(9) Nothing in Part 5 of TMA 1970 (appeals and other proceedings) applies to an objection under this paragraph.

Consideration of objections

10 (1) HMRC must consider any objections made under paragraph 9 within 30 working days of being given the notice of objection.
(2) Having considered the objections, HMRC must decide whether—
(a) to cancel the hold notice,
(b) to cancel the effect of the hold notice in relation to the held amount, or any part of the held amount, in respect of a particular account or accounts, or
(c) to dismiss the objection.
(3) HMRC must give a notice stating its decision to—
(a) P,
(b) each person other than P who objected, and
(c) any other person who HMRC considers is affected by the decision and is—
(i) a person who holds a relevant account of which P is also a holder and in respect of whom prescribed information is provided under paragraph 7(2)(c), or
(ii) an interested third party in relation to a relevant account in respect of whom sufficient information has been given in the notice under paragraph 7(2) to enable HMRC to give a notice.
(4) HMRC must, by a notice to the deposit-taker—
(a) if it makes a decision under sub-paragraph (2)(a), cancel the hold notice;

(b) if it makes a decision under sub-paragraph (2)(b), cancel the effect of the hold notice in relation to the accounts or amounts in question.

(5) HMRC must give each person to whom HMRC is required to give a notice under sub-paragraph (3) a copy of any notice given to the deposit-taker under sub-paragraph (4).

(6) Where the deposit-taker is given a notice under sub-paragraph (4), it must as soon as reasonably practicable and, in any event, within the period of 5 working days beginning with the day the notice is given—

(a) if the notice is given under sub-paragraph (4)(a), cancel the arrangements mentioned in paragraph 5(3), or

(b) if the notice is given under sub-paragraph (4)(b), make such adjustments to those arrangements as are necessary to give effect to the notice.

(7) In this paragraph references to the effect of a hold notice are to its effect by virtue of paragraph 5(4).

Appeals

11 (1) Where HMRC makes a decision under paragraph (b) or (c) of paragraph 10(2), a person within sub-paragraph (2) may appeal against the hold notice.

(2) The persons who may appeal are—

(a) P,

(b) any interested third party in relation to an affected account, and

(c) any person not falling within paragraph (a) or (b) who is a holder of an affected account which is a joint account.

(3) An appeal may only be made on one or more of the grounds set out in paragraph 9(3) (and for this purpose the reference in paragraph 9(3)(c) to "the objection" is to be read as a reference to the appeal).

(4) An appeal under sub-paragraph (1) must be made—

(a) in England and Wales, to the county court, and

(b) in Northern Ireland, to a county court.

(5) An appeal under this paragraph may only be made within the period of 30 days beginning—

(a) in the case of a person given a notice of HMRC's decision under paragraph 10(3), with the day on which that notice is given to that person, and

(b) in the case of any person within sub-paragraph (2)(b) or (c) to whom such a notice has not been given, the day on which P is given such a notice.

(6) A notice of appeal must state the grounds of appeal.

(7) On an appeal under this paragraph, the court may—

(a) cancel the hold notice,

(b) cancel the effect of the hold notice in relation to the held amount, or any part of the held amount, in respect of a particular account or accounts, or

(c) dismiss the appeal.

(8) Where the deposit-taker is served with an order made by the court under sub-paragraph (7)(a) or (b), the deposit-taker must as soon as reasonably practicable and, in any event, within the period of 5 working days beginning with the day the notice is given take such steps as are necessary to give effect to the order.

(9) Where an appeal on the ground that the hold notice is causing or will cause the person making the appeal or another person exceptional hardship (or a further appeal following such an appeal) is pending, the court to which the appeal is made may, on an application made by the person who made the appeal—

(a) suspend the effect of the hold notice if adequate security is provided in respect of so much of the notified sum as remains unpaid,

(b) suspend the effect of the hold notice in relation to a particular account if adequate security is provided in respect of the held amount in relation to that account, or

(c) suspend the effect of the hold notice in relation to any part of the held amount standing to the credit of a particular account, if adequate security is provided in respect of that part.

(10) In this paragraph references to the effect of a hold notice are to its effect by virtue of paragraph 5(4).

(11) Nothing in Part 5 of TMA 1970 (appeals and other proceedings) applies to an appeal under this paragraph.

Deduction notice

12 (1) If it appears to HMRC that a person in respect of whom a hold notice given to a deposit-taker is in force—

(a) has failed to pay a relevant sum, and

(b) holds an account (or more than one account) with the deposit-taker in respect of which there is a held amount in relation to that sum,

HMRC may give the deposit-taker a deduction notice in respect of that person.

(2) A "deduction notice" is a notice which—

(a) specifies the name of the person concerned,

(b) specifies one or more affected accounts held by that person with the deposit-taker, and

(c) in relation to each such specified account requires the deposit-taker to deduct and pay a qualifying amount (see sub-paragraph (6)) to the Commissioners by a day specified in the notice.

(3) Where a deduction notice specifies a particular affected account—

(a) the deduction required to be made in relation to that account by virtue of sub-paragraph (2)(c) must be made from the appropriate account, that is to say—

(i) if the deposit-taker has by virtue of the hold notice transferred an amount from the specified account into a suspense account, that suspense account, or

(ii) otherwise, the specified account, and

(b) the deposit-taker must not during the period in which the deduction notice is in force do anything, or permit anything to be done (except in accordance with paragraph (a)) that would reduce the amount standing to the credit of the appropriate account below the balance required for the purpose of making that deduction.

(4) A deduction notice must explain the effect of sub-paragraph (4)(b) and paragraph 13 (penalties).

(5) A deduction notice may not be given in respect of an account unless—

(a) the period for making an objection under paragraph 9 has expired and either no objections were made or any objection made has been decided or withdrawn, and

(b) if objections were made and decided, the period for appealing under paragraph 11 has expired and any appeal or further appeal has been finally determined.

(6) In this paragraph "qualifying amount", in relation to an affected account, means an amount not exceeding the held amount in relation to that account (as modified, where applicable, under paragraph 8(3)(b), 10(6)(b) or 11(7)(b)).

(7) The total of the qualifying amounts specified in the deduction notice must not exceed the unpaid amount of the notified sum (see paragraph 7(8)).

(8) HMRC must—

(a) give a copy of the deduction notice to the person in respect of whom it is given, and

(b) in the case of each account in respect of which the notice is given, give a notice to each person within sub-paragraph (9) explaining that a deduction notice has been given in respect of that account and the effect of the deduction notice so far as it relates to that account.

(9) The persons mentioned in sub-paragraph (8)(b) are—

(a) if the account is a joint account, each person other than P who is a holder of the account, and

(b) any person (not falling within paragraph (a))—

(i) who is an interested third party in relation to the account whom HMRC knows will be affected by the deduction notice, and

(ii) about whom HMRC has sufficient information to enable it to give the notice under sub-paragraph (8)(b).

(10) HMRC may, by a notice given to the deposit-taker, amend or cancel the deduction notice, and where it does so it must—

(a) give a copy of the notice under this sub-paragraph to the person in respect of whom the deduction notice was given, and

(b) in the case of each account affected by the amendment or cancellation, give a notice to each person within sub-paragraph (9) explaining the effect of the amendment or cancellation so far as it relates to that account.

(11) The deduction notice—

(a) comes into force at the time it is given to the deposit-taker, and

(b) ceases to be in force at the time—

(i) the deposit-taker is given a notice cancelling it under subparagraph (10), or

(ii) the deposit-taker makes the final payment required by virtue of sub-paragraph (2)(c).

Penalties

13 (1) This paragraph applies to a deposit-taker who—

(a) fails to comply with an information notice,

(b) fails to comply with a hold notice or a deduction notice,

(c) fails to comply with an obligation under paragraph 7(2) in accordance with paragraph 7(3) (obligation to notify HMRC of effects of hold notice),

(d) fails to comply with an obligation under paragraph 7(4) in accordance with paragraph 7(5) (obligation to notify HMRC if no affected accounts),

(e) fails to comply with an obligation under paragraph 8(3) (obligation to cancel or modify effects of hold notice),

(f) fails to comply with an obligation under paragraph 10(6) (obligation to cancel or adjust arrangements to give effect to HMRC's decision of objection), or

(g) following receipt of an information notice or hold notice in relation to an account or accounts held with the deposit-taker by a person ("the affected person"), makes a disclosure of information to the affected person or any other person in circumstances where that disclosure is likely to prejudice HMRC's ability to use the provisions of this Part of this Schedule to recover a relevant sum owed by the affected person.

(2) In sub-paragraph (1)(g), the reference to a disclosure of information does not include the giving of a notice in accordance with paragraph 7(10) to the affected person in respect of a hold notice.

(3) The deposit-taker is liable to a penalty of £300.

(4) If a failure within sub-paragraph (1)(a) to (f) continues after the day on which notice is given under paragraph 14(1) of a penalty in respect of the failure, the deposit-taker is liable to a further penalty or penalties not exceeding £60 for each subsequent day on which the failure continues.

(5) A failure by a deposit-taker to do anything required to be done within a limited period of time does not give rise to liability to a penalty under this paragraph if the deposit-taker did it within such further time, if any, as HMRC may have allowed.

(6) Liability to a penalty under this paragraph does not arise if the person satisfies HMRC or (on an appeal notified to the tribunal) the tribunal that there is a reasonable excuse for the failure or (as the case may be) disclosure.

(7) For the purposes of this paragraph—

(a) where the deposit-taker relies on any other person to do anything, that is not a reasonable excuse unless the deposit-taker took reasonable care to avoid the failure or disclosure, and

(b) where the deposit-taker had a reasonable excuse for the failure but the excuse has ceased, the deposit-taker is to be treated as having continued to have the excuse if the failure is remedied without unreasonable delay after the excuse ceased.

Assessment of penalty

14 (1) Where a deposit-taker becomes liable to a penalty under paragraph 13—

(a) HMRC must assess the penalty, and

(b) if HMRC does so, it must notify the deposit-taker in writing.

(2) An assessment of a penalty by virtue of paragraph (a) of paragraph 13(1) must be made within the period of 12 months beginning with the day on which the deposit-taker becomes liable to the penalty.

(3) An assessment of a penalty under any of paragraphs (b) to (g) of paragraph 13(1) must be made within the period of 12 months beginning with the latest of the following—

(a) the day on which the deposit-taker became liable to the penalty,

(b) the end of the period in which notice of an appeal in respect of the hold notice could have been given, and

(c) if notice of such an appeal is given, the day on which the appeal is finally determined or withdrawn.

Appeal against penalty

15 (1) A deposit-taker may appeal against—

(a) a decision that a penalty is payable by the deposit-taker under paragraph 13, or

(b) a decision as to the amount of such a penalty.

(2) Notice of an appeal must be given to HMRC before the end of the period of 30 days beginning with the day on which the notification under paragraph 14 was given.

(3) Notice of an appeal must state the grounds of appeal.

(4) On an appeal under sub-paragraph (1)(a) that is notified to the tribunal (in accordance with Part 5 of TMA 1970: see below) the tribunal may confirm or cancel the decision.

(5) On an appeal under sub-paragraph (1)(b) that is notified to the tribunal, the tribunal may—

(a) confirm the decision, or

(b) substitute for the decision another decision that HMRC had power to make.

(6) Subject to this paragraph and paragraph 16, the provisions of Part 5 of TMA 1970 relating to appeals have effect in relation to appeals under this paragraph as they have effect in relation to an appeal against an assessment to income tax.

Enforcement of penalty

16 (1) A penalty under paragraph 13 must be paid—

(a) before the end of the period of 30 days beginning with the day on which the notification under paragraph 14 was given, or

(b) if notice of an appeal against the penalty is given, before the end of the period of 30 days beginning with the day on which the appeal is finally determined or withdrawn.

(2) A penalty under paragraph 13 may be enforced as if it were income tax charged in an assessment and due and payable.

Protection of deposit-takers acting in good faith

17 A deposit-taker is not liable for damages in respect of anything done in good faith for the purposes of complying with a hold notice or a deduction notice.

Power to modify amounts and time limits

18 (1) The Commissioners may by regulations amend any of the following provisions by substituting a different amount for the amount for the time being specified there—

(a) paragraph 2(2) (requirement that relevant sum is a minimum amount);

(b) paragraph 4(6) and (8) (threshold for safeguarded amount);

(c) paragraph 13(3) or (4) (level of penalties).

(2) The Commissioners may by regulations amend any of the following provisions by substituting a different period for the period for the time being specified there—

(a) paragraph 3(4) (time limit for complying with information notices);

(b) paragraph 5(2) (time limit for complying with hold notices);

(c) paragraph 7(3) or (5) (time limit for notifying HMRC of effects of hold notice);

(d) paragraph 8(3) (cancellation etc of hold notice: time limit for cancelling or adjusting arrangements);

(e) paragraph 9(5) (time limit for making objections);

(f) paragraph 10(1) (time limit for consideration of objections);

(g) paragraph 10(6) (consideration of objections: time limit for cancelling or adjusting arrangements);

(h) paragraph 11(8) (appeals: time limit for compliance with court order).

Power to make further provision

19 (1) The Commissioners may by regulations make provision supplementing this Part of this Schedule.

(2) The regulations may, in particular, make provision—

(a) about the manner in which a notice or a copy of a notice is to be given under this Part of this Schedule, or the circumstances in which a notice or a copy of a notice is to be treated as given, for the purposes of this Part of this Schedule;

(b) specifying circumstances in which a notice under this Part of this Schedule may not be given;

(c) specifying descriptions of account in respect of which a hold notice or deduction notice has no effect;

(d) specifying circumstances in which amounts standing to the credit of an account are to be treated as not standing to the credit of the account for the purposes of a hold notice or deduction notice;

(e) about fees a deposit-taker may charge a person in respect of whom a notice is given under this Part of this Schedule towards administrative costs in complying with that notice;

(f) with respect to priority as between a notice under this Part of this Schedule and—

(i) any other such notice, or

(ii) any notice or order under any other enactment.

Regulations

20 (1) Regulations under this Part of this Schedule may—

(a) make different provision for different purposes,

(b) include supplementary, incidental and consequential provision, or

(c) make transitional provision and savings.

(2) Regulations under this Part of this Schedule are to be made by statutory instrument.

(3) A statutory instrument containing only regulations within sub-paragraph (4) is subject to annulment in pursuance of a resolution of the House of Commons.

(4) The regulations within this sub-paragraph are—

(a) regulations which prescribe information for the purposes of paragraph 3(2) or any provision of paragraph 7,

(b) regulations under paragraph 4(10),

(c) regulations under paragraph (a), (b), (c), (d), (g) or (h) of paragraph 18(2), or

(d) regulations under paragraph 19(2).

(5) Any other statutory instrument containing regulations under this Part of this Schedule may not be made unless a draft of the instrument has been laid before, and approved by a resolution of, the House of Commons.

Joint accounts

21 In this Part of this Schedule a reference to an account held by a person includes a reference to a joint account held by that person and one or more other persons.

Defined terms

22 (1) In this Part of this Schedule—

"affected account" has the meaning given by paragraph 5(7);

"the Commissioners" means the Commissioners for Her Majesty's Revenue and Customs;

"contract settlement" means an agreement made in connection with any person's liability to make a payment to the Commissioners under or by virtue of an enactment;

"deduction notice" has the meaning given by paragraph 12;

"deposit-taker" means a person who may lawfully accept deposits in the United Kingdom in the course of a business (see sub-paragraph (2));

"HMRC" means Her Majesty's Revenue and Customs;

"hold notice" has the meaning given by paragraph 4;

"information notice" has the meaning given by paragraph 3;

"interested third party", in relation to a relevant account, has the meaning given by paragraph 7(11);

"joint account", in relation to a person, means an account held by the person and one or more other persons;

"notice" means notice in writing;

"notified sum", in relation to a hold notice, has the meaning given by paragraph 7(8);

"prescribed" means prescribed by regulations made by the Commissioners;

"relevant account" (in relation to a hold notice) has the meaning given by paragraph 5(6);

"relevant sum", in relation to a person, has the meaning given by paragraph 2(1);

"the safeguarded amount" (in relation to a hold notice) means the amount specified as the safeguarded amount in the notice (see paragraph 4(2)(c));

"the specified amount" (in relation to a hold notice) means the amount specified as such in the notice (see paragraph 4(2)(b));

"suspense account" has the meaning given by paragraph 5(3)(b)(i);

"the tribunal" means the First-tier Tribunal;

"working day" means a day other than—

(a) Saturday or Sunday,

(b) Christmas Eve, Christmas Day or Good Friday, or

(c) a day which is a bank holiday under the Banking and Financial Dealings Act 1971 in England and Wales or Northern Ireland.

(2) The definition of "deposit-taker" in sub-paragraph (1) is to be read with—

(a) section 22 of the Financial Services and Markets Act 2000 (regulated activities),

(b) any relevant order under that section, and

(c) Schedule 2 to that Act.

Extent

23 This Part of this Schedule extends to England and Wales and Northern Ireland.

PART 2

MISCELLANEOUS AMENDMENTS

FA 2003

40 In Schedule 10 to FA 2003 (stamp duty land tax: returns etc), in paragraph 27, after sub-paragraph (3) insert—

"(4) Where—

(a) action is being taken under Part 1 of Schedule 8 to the Finance (No. 2) Act 2015 (enforcement of deduction from accounts) for the recovery of an amount ("the original amount") of tax charged by a Revenue determination, and

(b) before that action is concluded, the determination is superseded by a self-assessment, that action may be continued as if it were action for the purposes of the recovery of so much of the tax charged by the self-assessment as is due and payable, has not yet been paid and does not exceed the original amount."

FA 2013

41 In Schedule 33 to FA 2013 (annual tax on enveloped dwellings: returns etc), in paragraph 20, after sub-paragraph (3) insert—

"(4) Where—

(a) action is being taken under Part 1 of Schedule 8 to the Finance (No. 2) Act 2015 (enforcement of deduction from accounts) for the recovery of an amount ("the original amount") of tax charged by an HMRC determination, and

(b) before that action is concluded, the determination is superseded by a self-assessment,

that action may be continued as if it were action for the purposes of the recovery of so much of the tax charged by the self-assessment as is due and payable, has not yet been paid and does not exceed the original amount."

Value Added Tax Statutory Instruments

Contents

Chronological list of printed Statutory Instruments

Note—

For list of current, revoked, amending, etc statutory instruments, *see post*.

VAT SIs

SI 2009/3127 Value Added Tax (Supplementary Charge) Order 2009
SI 2010/466 Finance Act 2009, Schedule 56 (Appointed Day and Consequential Provisions) Order 2010
SI 2010/1813 Revenue and Customs (Complaints and Misconduct) Regulations 2010
SI 2010/1878 Finance Act 2009, Sections 101 to 103 (Appointed Day and Supplemental Provision) Order 2010
SI 2010/1879 Taxes and Duties (Interest Rate) Regulations 2010
SI 2010/2239 VAT (Section 55A) (Specified Goods and Services and Excepted Supplies) Order 2010
SI 2010/2655 First-tier Tribunal and Upper Tribunal (Chambers) Order 2010
SI 2010/2880 Single Use Carrier Bags Charge (Wales) Regulations 2010
SI 2010/2924 VAT (Imported Gas, Electricity, Heat and Cooling) Relief Order 2010
SI 2010/2925 VAT (Removal of Gas, Electricity, Heat and Cooling) Order 2010
SI 2011/711 Taxes, etc (Fees for Payment by Internet) Regulations 2011
SI 2011/976 Penalties, Offshore Income etc. (Designation of Territories) Order 2011 SI 2011/1727
SI 2011/1079 International Mutual Administrative Assistance in Tax Matters Order 2011
SI 2011/1727 Charities Act 2006 (Principal Regulators of Exempt Charities) (No. 2) Regulations 2011
SI 2011/2878 Statistics and Registration Service Act 2007 (Disclosure of Value Added Tax Information) Regulations 2011
SI 2011/2931 MARD Regulations 2011
SI 2011/3036 Postal Packets (Revenue and Customs) Regulations 2011
SI 2012/689 Taxes, etc (Fees for Payment by Telephone) Regulations 2012
SI 2012/735 Finance Act 2010, Schedule 6, Part 1 (Further Consequential and Incidental Provision etc) Order 2012
SI 2012/847 Data-gathering Powers (Relevant Data) Regulations 2012
SI 2012/2393 VAT (Refund of VAT to Chief Constables and the Commissioner of Police of the Metropolis) Order 2012
SI 2012/2907 VAT (Relief for European Research Infrastructure Consortia) Order 2012
SI 2013/412 VAT (Refund of Tax to the Natural Resources Body for Wales) Order 2013
SI 2013/2911 VAT (Flat-rate Valuation of Supplies of Fuel for Private Use) Order 2013
SI 2014/1112 VAT (Refund of Tax) Order 2014
SI 2014/1458 VAT (Section 55A) (Specified Goods and Excepted Supplies) Order 2014
SI 2015/449 VAT (Refund of Tax to the London Legacy Development Corporation) Order 2015
SI 2015/776 Single Use Carrier Bags Charges (England) Order 2015

Chronological List of Statutory Instruments

Note—

For list of printed statutory instruments, see above.
SI 1961/1523 Temporary Importation (Commercial Vehicles and Aircraft) Regulations 1961
SI 1965/1776 Rules of the Supreme Court (Revision) 1965 (superseded by SI 1998/3132)
SI 1973/173 VAT (Terminal Markets) Order 1973
SI 1976/1223 Customs Duties (Deferred Payment) Regulations 1976
SI 1976/2028 VAT (Refund of Tax) Order 1976
SI 1977/1017 VAT Tribunals (Amendment) Rules 1977 (revoked)
SI 1977/1760 VAT Tribunals (Amendment) (No 2) Rules 1977 (revoked)
SI 1977/1790 VAT (Imported Goods) Relief Order 1977 (revoked)
SI 1977/1796 VAT (Special Provisions) Order 1977 (revoked)
SI 1978/1064 VAT (Consolidation) Order 1978 (spent)
SI 1978/1129 VAT (Bad Debt Relief) Regulations 1978 (revoked)
SI 1978/1725 Customs Duties (Deferred Payment) (Amendment) Regulations 1978
SI 1978/1883 Customs Duties (Personal Reliefs) (No 1) Order 1968 (Amendment) Order 1978 (revoked)
SI 1979/224 VAT (Supplies by Retailers) (Amendment) Regulations 1979 (revoked)
SI 1979/243 VAT (Finance) Order 1979 (spent)
SI 1979/244 VAT (International Services) Order 1979 (spent)
SI 1979/246 VAT (Medical Goods and Services) Order 1979 (spent)
SI 1979/657 VAT (General) Order 1979 (spent)
SI 1979/1551 Customs Duty (Personal Reliefs) (No 1) Order 1968 (Amendment) Order 1979 (revoked)
SI 1979/1554 VAT (International Services) (No 2) Order 1979 (spent)
SI 1979/1646 VAT (Fuel and Power) (Metrication) Order 1979 (spent)

SI 1980/303 VAT (Gold) Order 1980 (spent)
SI 1980/304 VAT (Terminal Markets) (Amendment) Order 1980
SI 1980/305 VAT (Transport) Order 1980 (spent)
SI 1980/440 VAT (Fuel and Power) Order 1980 (revoked)
SI 1980/442 VAT (Cars) Order 1980 (revoked)
SI 1980/1009 VAT (Imported Goods) Relief Order 1980 (revoked)
SI 1980/1536 VAT (General) Regulations 1980 (revoked)
SI 1980/1537 VAT (Repayment to Community Traders) Regulations 1980 (revoked)
SI 1980/1602 VAT (Health) Order 1980 (spent)
SI 1980/1603 VAT (Special Provisions) (Amending) Order 1980 (revoked)
SI 1980/1604 VAT (Education) Order 1980 (spent)
SI 1980/1909 VAT (Competitions) Order 1980 (spent)
SI 1981/338 VAT (Terminal Markets) (Amendment) Order 1981
SI 1981/365 VAT (Handicapped Persons and Charities) Order 1981 (spent)
SI 1981/663 VAT (General) (Amendment) Regulations 1981 (revoked)
SI 1981/955 VAT (Terminal Markets) (Amendment) (No 2) Order 1981 (revoked)
SI 1981/1080 VAT (General and Bad Debt Relief) (Amendment) Regulations 1981 (revoked)
SI 1981/1530 VAT (General) (Amendment) (No 2) Regulations 1981 (revoked)
SI 1981/1740 VAT (Insurance) Order 1981 (spent)
SI 1981/1741 VAT (Special Provisions) Order 1981 (revoked)
SI 1982/321 VAT (Handicapped Persons and Charities) Order 1982 (spent)
SI 1982/476 VAT (Finance) Order 1982 (spent)
SI 1982/1007 VAT (Double-Glazing) Order 1982 (spent)
SI 1982/1067 VAT (Isle of Man) Order 1982
SI 1982/1068 VAT (Isle of Man) (No 2) Order 1982
SI 1982/1088 VAT (General) (Amendment) Regulations 1982 (revoked)
SI 1982/1471 VAT (General) (Amendment) (No 2) Regulations 1982 (revoked)
SI 1982/1591 Customs Duty (Personal Reliefs) (No 1) Order 1968 (Amendment) Order 1982 (revoked)
SI 1983/295 VAT (General) (Amendment) Regulations 1983 (revoked)
SI 1983/401 VAT (Increase of Registration Limits) Order 1983 (spent)
SI 1983/475 VAT (General) (Amendment) (No 2) Regulations 1983 (revoked)
SI 1983/499 VAT (Health) Order 1983 (spent)
SI 1983/809 VAT (Works of Art, etc) Order 1983 (spent)
SI 1983/1099 VAT (Horses and Ponies) Order 1983 (revoked)
SI 1983/1717 VAT (Charities, Etc) 1983 (revoked)
SI 1983/1828 Customs and Excise Duties (Personal Reliefs for Goods Permanently Imported) Order 1983 (revoked)
SI 1983/1829 Customs and Excise Duties (Personal Reliefs for Goods Temporarily Imported) Order 1983 (revoked)
SI 1984/33 VAT (Cars) (Amendment) Order 1984 (revoked)
SI 1984/155 VAT (General) (Amendment) Regulations 1984 (revoked)
SI 1984/202 VAT (Terminal Markets) (Amendment) Order 1984
SI 1984/342 VAT (Increase of Registration Limits) Order 1984 (spent)
SI 1984/489 VAT (Handicapped Persons) Order 1984 (revoked)
SI 1984/631 VAT (Lifeboats) Order 1984 (revoked)
SI 1984/718 Customs Duty (Personal Reliefs) (No 1) Order 1968 (Amendment) Order 1984 (revoked)
SI 1984/736 VAT (Special Provisions) (Amendment) (No 2) Order 1984 (revoked)
SI 1984/746 VAT (Imported Goods) Relief Order 1984
SI 1984/766 VAT (Charities, etc) Order 1984 (revoked)
SI 1984/767 VAT (Marine etc Insurance) Order 1984 (revoked)
SI 1984/895 C&E Duties (Relief for Imported Legacies) Order 1984 (revoked)
SI 1984/929 VAT (General) (Amendment) (No 2) Regulations 1984 (revoked)
SI 1984/959 VAT (Handicapped Persons) (No 2) Order 1984 (revoked)
SI 1984/1176 Control of Movement of Goods Regulations 1984
SI 1984/1177 Free Zone Regulations 1984
SI 1984/1206 Free Zone (Belfast Airport) Designation Order 1984 (spent)
SI 1984/1207 Free Zone (Birmingham Airport) Designation Order 1984 (revoked)
SI 1984/1208 Free Zone (Cardiff) Designation Order 1984 (spent)
SI 1984/1209 Free Zone (Liverpool) Designation Order 1984 (revoked)
SI 1984/1210 Free Zone (Prestwick Airport) Designation Order 1984 (revoked)

SI 1984/1211 Free Zone (Southampton) Designation Order 1984 (revoked)
SI 1984/1376 VAT (General Amendment) (No 2) Regulations 1984 (revoked)
SI 1984/1685 VAT (Place of Supply) Order 1984 (revoked)
SI 1984/1784 VAT (Optical Appliances) Order 1984 (revoked)
SI 1985/18 VAT (Protected Buildings) Order 1985 (revoked)
SI 1985/105 VAT (General) (Amendment) Regulations 1985 (revoked)
SI 1985/431 VAT (Charities) Order 1985 (revoked)
SI 1985/432 VAT (Finance) Order 1985 (revoked)
SI 1985/433 VAT (Increase of Registration Limits) Order 1985 (spent)
SI 1985/693 VAT (General) (Amendment) (No 2) Regulations 1985 (revoked)
SI 1985/799 VAT (Hiring of Goods) Order 1985 (revoked)
SI 1985/886 VAT (General) Regulations 1985 (revoked)
SI 1985/919 VAT (Handicapped Persons) Order 1985 (revoked)
SI 1985/1046 VAT (Terminal Markets) (Amendment) Order 1985
SI 1985/1101 VAT (Refund of Tax) Order 1985
SI 1985/1375 Customs Duty (Personal Reliefs) (No 1) Order 1968 (Amendment) Order 1985 (revoked)
SI 1985/1376 C&E Duties (Personal Reliefs for Goods Permanently Imported) Order 1983 (Amendment) Order 1985 (spent)
SI 1985/1378 C&E Duties (Relief for Imported Legacies) Order 1984 (Amendment) Order 1985 (revoked)
SI 1985/1384 VAT (Imported Goods) Relief (Amendment) Order 1985 (revoked)
SI 1985/1646 VAT (Temporarily Imported Goods) Relief Order 1985 (revoked)
SI 1985/1650 VAT (General) Regulations 1985 (Amendment) Regulations 1985 (revoked)
SI 1985/1784 The Companies (Department of Trade and Industry) Fees Order 1985 (lapsed)
SI 1985/1900 VAT (Welfare) Order 1985 (revoked)
SI 1986/71 VAT (General) (Amendment) Regulations 1986 (revoked)
SI 1986/260 Postal Packets (Customs and Excise) Regulations 1986 (revoked)
SI 1986/305 VAT (General) (Amendment) (No 2) Regulations 1986 (revoked)
SI 1986/335 VAT (Bad Debt Relief) Regulations 1986 (revoked)
SI 1986/336 VAT (Refund of Tax) Order 1986
SI 1986/337 Finance Act 1985 (Bad Debt Relief) (Commencement) Order 1986 (lapsed)
SI 1986/385 Administrative Receivers (VAT Certificates) Rules 1986 (spent)
SI 1986/530 VAT (Handicapped Persons and Charities) Order 1986 (revoked)
SI 1986/531 VAT (Increase of Registration Limits) Order 1986 (spent)
SI 1986/532 VAT (Refund of Tax) (No 2) Order 1986
SI 1986/590 VAT Tribunals Rules 1986
SI 1986/704 VAT (Land) Order 1986 (revoked)
SI 1986/716 VAT (Land) (No 2) Order 1986 (revoked)
SI 1986/896 VAT (Treatment of Transactions) Order 1986
SI 1986/909 VAT (Repayment Supplement) Regulations 1986 (revoked)
SI 1986/934 Finance Act 1985 (VAT Tribunals Rules) (Appointed Day) Order 1986 (lapsed)
SI 1986/939 VAT (Small Non-Commercial Consignments) Relief Order 1986
SI 1986/968 Finance Act 1985 (Default Surcharge) (Commencement) Order 1986 (lapsed)
SI 1986/969 Finance Act 1985 (Breaches of Regulations) (Appointed Day) Order 1986 (lapsed)
SI 1986/970 Finance Act 1985 (Repayment Supplement) (Appointed Day) Order 1986 (spent)
SI 1986/1019 Postal Packets (Customs and Excise) (Amendment) Regulations 1986
SI 1986/1279 VAT (Repayment Supplement) (No 2) Regulations 1986 (revoked)
SI 1986/1989 VAT (Temporarily Imported Goods) Relief Order 1986 (revoked)
SI 1986/2105 Customs Duty (Personal Reliefs) (No 1) Order 1968 (Amendment) Order 1986 (revoked)
SI 1986/2288 VAT Tribunals Appeals Order 1986
SI 1986/2290 VAT Tribunals (Amendment) Rules 1986
SI 1987/150 VAT (General) (Amendment) Regulations 1987 (revoked)
SI 1987/154 VAT (Small Non-Commercial Consignments) Relief (Amendment) Order 1987 (superseded)
SI 1987/155 VAT (Imported Goods) Relief (Amendment) Order 1987 (superseded)
SI 1987/437 VAT (Charities) Order 1987 (revoked)
SI 1987/438 VAT (Increase of Registration Limits) Order 1987 (spent)
SI 1987/510 VAT (General) (Amendment) (No 2) Regulations 1987 (revoked)
SI 1987/517 VAT (Betting, Gaming and Lotteries) Order 1987 (revoked)

SI 1987/518 VAT (International Services) Order 1987 (revoked)
SI 1987/781 VAT (Construction of Buildings) Order 1987 (spent)
SI 1987/806 VAT (Terminal Markets) (Amendment) Order 1987
SI 1987/860 VAT (Finance) Order 1987 (revoked)
SI 1987/1072 VAT (Construction of Buildings) (No 2) Order 1987 (revoked)
SI 1987/1259 VAT (Education) Order 1987 (revoked)
SI 1987/1427 VAT (Cash Accounting) Regulations 1987 (revoked)
SI 1987/1712 VAT (Supplies by Retailers) (Amendment) Regulations 1987 (revoked)
SI 1987/1806 VAT (Tour Operators) Order 1987
SI 1987/1916 VAT (General) (Amendment) (No 3) Regulations 1987 (revoked)
SI 1987/1919 Insolvency (Amendment) Rules 1987
SI 1987/2015 VAT (Repayments to Third Country Traders) Regulations 1987 (revoked)
SI 1987/2108 VAT (Imported Goods) Relief (Amendment) (No 2) Order 1987
SI 1988/507 VAT (Confectionery) Order 1988 (revoked)
SI 1988/508 VAT (Increase of Registration Limits) Order 1988 (spent)
SI 1988/533 Free Zone (Liverpool) Designation (Variation) Order 1988 (spent)
SI 1988/710 Free Zone (Amendment) Regulations 1988
SI 1988/809 Excise Warehousing (Etc) Regulations 1988
SI 1988/886 VAT (Annual Accounting) Regulations 1988 (revoked)
SI 1988/1124 VAT (Special Provisions) (Amendment) Order 1988 (revoked)
SI 1988/1174 VAT (Goods Imported for Private Purposes) Relief Order 1988 (revoked)
SI 1988/1193 VAT (Imported Goods) Relief (Amendment) Order 1988
SI 1988/1282 VAT (Training) Order 1988 (revoked)
SI 1988/1343 VAT (Repayment Supplement) Regulations 1988 (revoked)
SI 1988/2083 VAT (General) (Amendment) Regulations 1988 (revoked)
SI 1988/2108 VAT (General) (Amendment) (No 2) Regulations 1988 (revoked)
SI 1988/2212 VAT (Imported Goods Relief) (Amendment) (No 2) Order (amending)
SI 1988/2217 VAT (Repayment to Community Traders) (Amendment) Regulations 1988 (revoked)
SI 1989/267 VAT (Educational) Order (revoked)
SI 1989/470 VAT (Fund-Raising Events and Charities Order) 1989 (revoked)
SI 1989/471 VAT (Increase of Registration Limits) Order 1989 (superseded)
SI 1989/472 VAT (Self-supply of Construction Services) Order 1989
SI 1989/959 VAT (Cars) (Amendment) Order 1989 (revoked)
SI 1989/1114 VAT (Water) Order 1989
SI 1989/1132 VAT (General) (Amendment) Regulations 1989 (revoked)
SI 1989/1217 VAT (Refund of Tax) Order 1989 (spent)
SI 1989/1302 VAT (General) (Amendment) (No 2) Regulations 1989 (revoked)
SI 1989/2248 VAT (Accounting and Records) Regulations 1989 (revoked)
SI 1989/2252 Customs Duty (Personal Reliefs) (No 1) Order 1968 (Amendment) Order 1989 (revoked)
SI 1989/2255 VAT (Bad Debt Relief) (Amendment) Regulations 1989 (revoked)
SI 1989/2256 VAT (General) (Amendment) (No 3) Regulations 1989 (revoked)
SI 1989/2259 VAT (Do-It-Yourself Builders) (Refund of Tax) Regulations 1989 (revoked)
SI 1989/2270 Finance Act 1985 (Serious Misdeclaration and Interest on Tax) (Appointed Days) Order 1989 (lapsed)
SI 1989/2271 Finance Act 1989 (Recovery of Overpaid Tax and Administration) (Appointed Days) Order 1989 (lapsed)
SI 1989/2272 VAT (Finance, Health and Welfare) Order 1989 (revoked)
SI 1989/2273 VAT (Small Non-Commercial Consignments Relief) (Amendment) Order 1989 (superseded)
SI 1989/2355 VAT (General) (Amendment) (No 4) Regulations 1989 (revoked)
SI 1990/139 Free Zone (Liverpool) Designation (Variation) Order 1990 (spent)
SI 1990/315 VAT (Cars) (Amendment) Order 1990 (revoked)
SI 1990/420 VAT (Cash Accounting) (Amendment) Regulations 1990 (revoked)
SI 1990/682 VAT (Increase of Registration Limits) Order 1990 (revoked)
SI 1990/750 VAT (Charities) Order 1990 (revoked)
SI 1990/751 VAT (Tour Operators) (Amendment) Order 1990 (revoked in part; otherwise spent)
SI 1990/752 VAT (Transport) Order 1990 (revoked)
SI 1990/1188 VAT (Refund of Tax) (Revocation) Order 1990 (spent)
SI 1990/1943 VAT (Cash Accounting) (Amendment) (No 2) Regulations 1990 (revoked)

SI 1990/2037 VAT (Insurance) Order 1990 (revoked)
SI 1990/2129 VAT (Charities) (No 2) Order 1990 (revoked)
SI 1990/2167 Channel Tunnel (Customs and Excise) Order 1990
SI 1990/2548 VAT (Imported Goods) Relief (Amendment) Order 1990 (superseded)
SI 1990/2553 VAT (Construction of Dwellings and Land) Order 1990 (revoked)
SI 1991/186 VAT Tribunals (Amendment) Rules 1991 (amending)
SI 1991/195 Health and Personal Social Services (Northern Ireland Consequential Amendments) Order 1991
SI 1991/371 VAT (Refunds for Bad Debts) Regulations 1991 (revoked)
SI 1991/532 VAT (Annual Accounting) (Amendment) Regulations 1991 (spent)
SI 1991/691 VAT (General) (Amendment) Regulations 1991 (revoked)
SI 1991/737 VAT (Charities) Order 1991 (revoked)
SI 1991/738 VAT (Increase of Registration Limits) Order 1991 (revoked)
SI 1991/1286 Customs Duty (Personal Reliefs) (Amendment) Order 1991 (revoked)
SI 1991/1287 C&E Duties (Personal Reliefs for Goods Permanently Imported) (Amendment) Order 1991 (revoked)
SI 1991/1293 C&E Duties (Personal Reliefs for Goods Temporarily Imported) (Amendment) Order 1991 (revoked)
SI 1991/1332 VAT (General) (Amendment) (No 2) Regulations 1991 (revoked)
SI 1991/1737 Free Zone (Birmingham Airport) Designation Order 1991 (spent)
SI 1991/1738 Free Zone (Liverpool) Designation Order 1991 (superseded)
SI 1991/1739 Free Zone (Prestwick Airport) Designation Order 1991 (superseded)
SI 1991/1740 Free Zone (Southampton) Designation Order 1991 (superseded)
SI 1991/1754 VAT (Interest on Overpayments etc) (Prescribed Rate) Order 1991 (superseded)
SI 1991/2282 VAT Act 1983 (Interest on Overpayments etc) (Prescribed Rate) (No 2) Order 1991 (superseded)
SI 1991/2306 VAT (Input Tax) (Person Supplied) Order 1991 (revoked)
SI 1991/2312 VAT (General) (Amendment) (No 3) Regulations 1991 (superseded)
SI 1991/2503 VAT (Special Provisions) (Amendment) Order 1991 (revoked)
SI 1991/2534 VAT (Piped Gas) (Metrication) Order 1991 (revoked)
SI 1991/2535 VAT (Small Non-Commercial Consignments) Relief (Amendment) Order 1991
SI 1991/2569 VAT (Buildings and Land) Order 1991 (revoked)
SI 1991/2724 Customs Controls on Importation of Goods Regulations 1991
SI 1991/2727 Free Zone Regulations 1991
SI 1992/627 VAT (Cars) (Amendment) Order 1992 (revoked)
SI 1992/628 VAT (Charities and Aids for Handicapped Persons) Order 1992 (revoked)
SI 1992/629 VAT (Increase of Registration Limits) Order 1992 (revoked)
SI 1992/630 VAT (Treatment of Transactions) Order 1992
SI 1992/644 VAT (Cash Accounting) (Amendment) Regulations 1992 (revoked)
SI 1992/645 VAT (General) (Amendment) Regulations 1992 (revoked)
SI 1992/733 VAT (Increase of Consideration for Fuel) Order 1992 (revoked)
SI 1992/1510 VAT (Payments on Account) Order 1992 (revoked)
SI 1992/1536 VAT (Payments on Account) Regulations 1992 (revoked)
SI 1992/1617 VAT (General) (Amendment) (No 2) Regulations 1992 (superseded)
SI 1992/1654 VAT (Cars) (Amendment) (No 2) Order 1992 (revoked)
SI 1992/1668 VAT (Payments on Account) (No 2) Order 1992 (revoked)
SI 1992/1844 VAT (Payments on Account) (No 2) Regulations 1992 (revoked)
SI 1992/1867 Finance (No 2) Act 1992 (Commencement) Order 1992
SI 1992/2790 Statistics of Trade (Customs and Excise) Regulations 1992
SI 1992/2868 VAT (General) (Amendment) (No 3) Regulations 1992 (superseded)
SI 1992/2979 Finance (No 2) Act 1992 (Commencement No 2 and Transitional Provisions) Order 1992
SI 1992/3065 VAT (Motor Vehicles for the Handicapped) Order 1992 (revoked)
SI 1992/3095 Customs and Excise (Single Market etc) Regulations 1992 (amending)
SI 1992/3096 VAT (EC Sales Statements) Regulations 1992 (revoked)
SI 1992/3097 VAT (Accounting and Records) (Amendment) Regulations 1992 (revoked)
SI 1992/3098 VAT (Repayment to Community Traders) (Amendment) Regulations 1992 (spent)
SI 1992/3099 VAT (Valuation of Acquisitions) Regulations 1992 (revoked)
SI 1992/3100 VAT (Refunds in relation to New Means of Transport) Regulations 1992 (revoked)
SI 1992/3101 VAT (Removal of Goods) (Accounting) Regulations 1992 (revoked)

SI 1992/3102 VAT (General) (Amendment No 4) Regulations 1992 (revoked)
SI 1992/3103 VAT (Flat-rate Scheme for Farmers) Regulations 1992 (revoked)
SI 1992/3111 VAT (Removal of Goods) Order 1992
SI 1992/3118 VAT (Small Non-Commercial Consignments) Relief (Amendment) Order 1992
SI 1992/3119 VAT (Temporarily Imported Goods and Goods Imported for Private Purposes) Reliefs (Revocation) Order 1992 (spent)
SI 1992/3120 VAT (Imported Goods) Relief (Amendment) Order 1992
SI 1992/3121 VAT (Place of Supply of Services) Order 1992
SI 1992/3122 VAT (Cars) Order 1992
SI 1992/3123 VAT (Input Tax) (Specified Supplies) Order 1992 (revoked)
SI 1992/3124 VAT (Imported Gold) Relief Order 1992
SI 1992/3125 VAT (Tour Operators) (Amendment) Order 1992
SI 1992/3126 VAT (Transport) Order 1992 (revoked)
SI 1992/3127 VAT (Means of Transport) Order 1992 (revoked)
SI 1992/3128 VAT (Reverse Charge) Order 1992 (revoked)
SI 1992/3129 VAT (Special Provisions) Order 1992 (revoked)
SI 1992/3130 VAT (Supply of Temporarily Imported Goods) Order 1992
SI 1992/3131 VAT (Tax Free Shops) Order 1992 (revoked)
SI 1992/3132 VAT (Treatment of Transactions) (No 2) Order 1992
SI 1992/3135 Excise Goods (Holding, Movement, Warehousing and REDS) Regulations 1992
SI 1992/3152 Excise Duties (Deferred Payment) Regulations 1992
SI 1992/3153 VAT (Repayments to Third Country Traders) (Amendment) Regulations 1992 (revoked)
SI 1992/3156 Customs and Excise (Personal Reliefs for Special Visitors) Order 1992
SI 1992/3192 Customs Duty (Personal Reliefs) (Amendment) Order 1992 (revoked)
SI 1992/3193 Customs and Excise Duties (Personal Reliefs for Goods Permanently Imported) Order 1992
SI 1992/3220 VAT (Flat-rate Scheme for Farmers) (Designated Activities) Order 1992
SI 1992/3221 VAT (Flat-rate Scheme for Farmers) (Percentage Addition) Order 1992
SI 1992/3222 VAT (Input Tax) Order 1992
SI 1992/3223 VAT (International Services and Transport) Order 1992 (revoked)
SI 1992/3224 Postal Packets (Customs and Excise) (Amendment) Regulations 1992
SI 1992/3283 VAT (Place of Supply of Goods) Order 1992 (revoked)
SI 1993/119 VAT (General) (Amendment) Regulations 1993 (revoked)
SI 1993/192 VAT Act 1983 (Interest on Overpayments etc) (Prescribed Rate) Order 1993 (lapsed)
SI 1993/541 Statistics of Trade (Customs and Excise) (Amendment) Regulations 1993 (revoked)
SI 1993/761 VAT (Accounting and Records) (Amendment) Regulations 1993 (revoked)
SI 1993/762 VAT (Cash Accounting) (Amendment) Regulations 1993 (revoked)
SI 1993/763 VAT (Education) Order 1993 (revoked)
SI 1993/764 VAT (General) (Amendment) (No 2) Regulations 1993 (revoked)
SI 1993/765 VAT (Increase of Consideration for Fuel) Order 1993 (revoked)
SI 1993/766 VAT (Increase of Registration Limits) Order 1993 (revoked)
SI 1993/767 VAT (Protective Boots and Helmets) Order 1993 (revoked)
SI 1993/856 VAT (General) (Amendment) (No 3) Regulations 1993 (revoked)
SI 1993/1124 VAT (Education) (No 2) Order 1993 (revoked)
SI 1993/1222 VAT (Repayments to Third Country Traders) (Amendment) Regulations 1993 (revoked)
SI 1993/1223 VAT (Repayments to Community Traders) (Amendment) Regulations 1993 (revoked)
SI 1993/1224 VAT (General) (Amendment) (No 4) Regulations 1993 (revoked)
SI 1993/1228 Beer Regulations 1993 (amending)
SI 1993/1507 VAT (Supply of Services) Order 1993
SI 1993/1639 VAT (General) (Amendment) (No 5) Regulations 1993 (revoked)
SI 1993/1813 Channel Tunnel (International Agreements) Order 1993 (amending)
SI 1993/1941 VAT (General) (Amendment) (No 6) Regulations 1993 (revoked)
SI 1993/2001 VAT (Payments on Account) Order 1993
SI 1993/2214 Finance Act 1993 (Appointed Day) Order 1993 (revoked)
SI 1993/2328 VAT (Reverse Charge) Order 1993 (revoked)
SI 1993/2498 VAT (Beverages) Order 1993 (revoked)
SI 1993/2951 VAT (Cars) (Amendment) Order 1993 (revoked)

SI 1993/2952 VAT (Increase of Consideration for Fuel) (No 2) Order 1993 (revoked)
SI 1993/2953 VAT (Increase of Registration Limits) (No 2) Order 1993 (revoked)
SI 1993/2954 VAT (Input Tax) (Amendment) Order 1993 (revoked)
SI 1993/3014 Community Customs Code (Consequential Amendment of References) Regulations 1993
SI 1993/3015 Statistics of Trade (Customs and Excise) (Amendment No 2) Regulations 1993
SI 1993/3027 VAT (General) (Amendment) (No 7) Regulations 1993 (revoked)
SI 1993/3028 VAT (Cash Accounting) (Amendment) (No 2) Regulations 1993 (revoked)
SI 1994/143 Free Zone (Prestwick Airport) Designation (Variation) Order 1994 (superseded)
SI 1994/144 Free Zone (Humberside) Designation Order 1994
SI 1994/686 VAT (Tax Free Shops) Order 1994 (revoked)
SI 1994/687 VAT (Sport, Physical Education and Fund-Raising Events) Order 1994 (revoked)
SI 1994/803 VAT (Accounting and Records) (Amendment) Regulations 1994 (revoked)
SI 1994/955 Travellers' Allowances Order 1994
SI 1994/1188 VAT (Education) Order 1994 (revoked)
SI 1994/1234 Finance Act 1994 Section 47, (Appointed Day) Order 1994 (revoked)
SI 1994/1253 Finance Act 1994 Section 47, (Appointed Day) (No 2) Order 1994 (lapsed)
SI 1994/1257 Finance Act 1994 section 45, (Appointed Day) Order 1994 (lapsed)
SI 1994/1405 Channel Tunnel (Miscellaneous Provisions) Order 1994 (amending)
SI 1994/1410 Free Zone (Southampton) Designation (Variation) Order 1994 (amending)
SI 1994/1978 VAT Tribunals Appeals (Northern Ireland) Order 1994
SI 1994/2509 Free Zone (Birmingham Airport) (Substitution of Responsible Authority) Order 1994 (spent)
SI 1994/2542 VAT Act 1994 (Interest on Tax) (Prescribed Rate) Order 1994 (superseded)
SI 1994/2617 VAT Tribunals (Amendment) Rules 1994
SI 1994/2898 Free Zone (Port of Sheerness) Designation Order 1994 (spent)
SI 1994/2905 VAT (Increase of Registration Limits) Order 1994 (superseded)
SI 1994/2914 Statistics of Trade (Customs and Excise) (Amendment) Regulations 1994 (revoked)
SI 1994/2969 VAT (Education) (No 2) Order 1994 (amending)
SI 1994/3013 VAT (Buildings and Land) Order 1994 (revoked)
SI 1994/3014 VAT (Transport) Order 1994 (amending)
SI 1994/3015 VAT (General) (Amendment) Regulations 1994 (revoked)
SI 1994/3128 VAT (Means of Transport) Order 1994 (revoked)
SI 1995/152 VAT (General) (Amendment) Regulations 1995 (revoked)
SI 1995/195 VAT (General) (Amendment) Regulations 1995 (revoked)
SI 1995/279 VAT (Buildings and Land) Order 1995 (revoked)
SI 1995/280 VAT (Construction of Buildings) Order 1995 (amending)
SI 1995/281 VAT (Input Tax) (Amendment) Order 1995
SI 1995/282 VAT (Land) Order 1995 (amending)
SI 1995/283 VAT (Protected Buildings) Order 1995 (amending)
SI 1995/291 VAT (Payments on Account) (Amendment) Order 1995
SI 1995/521 VAT Act 1994 (Interest on Tax) (Prescribed Rate) Order 1995 (superseded)
SI 1995/652 VAT (Supply of Pharmaceutical Goods) Order 1995 (amending)
SI 1995/653 VAT (Transport) Order 1995 (amending)
SI 1995/913 VAT (General) (Amendment) (No 2) Regulations 1995 (revoked)
SI 1995/957 VAT (Special Provisions) (Amendment) Order 1995 (revoked)
SI 1995/958 VAT (Treatment of Transactions) Order 1995
SI 1995/1046 Excise Goods (Drawback) Regulations 1995 (amending)
SI 1995/1067 Free Zone (Humberside) Designation (Variation) Order 1995
SI 1995/1069 VAT (General) (Amendment) (No 3) Regulations 1995 (revoked)
SI 1995/1267 VAT (Input Tax) (Amendment) (No 2) Order 1995
SI 1995/1268 VAT (Special Provisions) Order 1995
SI 1995/1269 VAT (Cars) (Amendment) Order 1995
SI 1995/1280 VAT (General) (Amendment) (No 4) Regulations 1995 (revoked)
SI 1995/1374 Finance Act 1995 section 24 (Appointed Day) Order 1995 (see VATA 1994 s 32)
SI 1995/1385 VAT (Special Provisions) Order 1995 (Amendment) Order 1995
SI 1995/1495 VAT (Tour Operators) (Amendment) Order 1995
SI 1995/1666 VAT (Input Tax) (Amendment) (No 3) Order 1995
SI 1995/1667 VAT (Cars) (Amendment) (No 2) Order 1995
SI 1995/1668 VAT (Supply of Services) (Amendment) Order 1995

SI 1995/1978 VAT (Refund of Tax) Order 1995
SI 1995/2518 VAT Regulations 1995
SI 1995/2946 Statistics of Trade (Customs and Excise) (Amendment) Regulations 1995 (revoked)
SI 1995/2999 VAT (Refund of Tax) (No 2) Order 1995
SI 1995/3037 VAT (Increase of Registration Limits) Order 1995 (superseded)
SI 1995/3038 VAT (Place of Supply of Services) (Amendment) Order 1995
SI 1995/3039 VAT (Ships and Aircraft) Order 1995 (amending)
SI 1995/3040 VAT (Increase of Consideration for Fuel) Order 1995 (amending)
SI 1995/3041 VAT (Tax Free Shops) Order 1995 (revoked)
SI 1995/3042 VAT (Treatment of Transactions) (Trading Stamps) Order 1995 (amending)
SI 1995/3043 VAT (Trading Stamps) Regulations 1995 (amending)
SI 1995/3044 Travellers' Allowances Amendment Order 1995
SI 1995/3147 VAT (Amendment) Regulations 1995
SI 1995/3222 VAT (Imported Goods) Relief (Amendment) Order 1995
SI 1996/165 VAT Act 1994 (Interest on Tax) (Prescribed Rate) Order 1996 (lapsed)
SI 1996/210 VAT (Amendment) Regulations 1996
SI 1996/542 VAT (Annual Accounting) Regulations 1996 (amending)
SI 1996/1196 VAT (Payments on Account) (Amendments) Order 1996
SI 1996/1198 VAT (Amendment) (No 2) Regulations 1996
SI 1996/1249 Finance Act 1996 section 26 (Appointed Day) Order 1996
SI 1996/1250 VAT (Amendment) (No 3) Regulations 1996
SI 1996/1255 VAT (Fiscal Warehousing) (Treatment of Transactions) Order 1996
SI 1996/1256 VAT (Cultural Services) Order 1996 (amending)
SI 1996/1661 VAT (Anti-avoidance (Heating)) Order 1996 (amending)
SI 1996/2098 VAT (Amendment) (No 4) Regulations 1996 (lapsed)
SI 1996/2615 Free Zone (Southampton) Designation (Variation of Area) Order 1996 (superseded)
SI 1996/2948 VAT (Increase of Consideration for Fuel) Order 1996 (superseded)
SI 1996/2949 VAT (Pharmaceutical Chemists) Order 1996 (amending)
SI 1996/2950 VAT (Increase in Registration Limits) Order 1996 (superseded)
SI 1996/2960 VAT (Amendment) (No 5) Regulations 1996
SI 1996/2968 Statistics of Trade (Customs & Excise) (Amendment) Regulations 1996 (revoked)
SI 1996/2992 VAT (Place of Supply of Services) (Amendment) Order 1996
SI 1997/50 VAT (Registered Social Landlords) (No 1) Order 1997 (amending)
SI 1997/51 VAT (Registered Social Landlords) (No 2) Order 1997 (revoked)
SI 1997/255 VAT Tribunals (Amendment) Rules 1997
SI 1997/510 VAT (Finance) Order 1997 (amending)
SI 1997/534 Customs Reviews and Appeals (Tariff and Origin) Regulations 1997 (amending)
SI 1997/994 Free Zone (Port of Sheerness) (Substitution of Responsible Authority) Order 1997
SI 1997/1015 Finance Act 1996 s 197 (Appointed Day) Order 1997 (see FA 1996 s 197)
SI 1997/1016 Air Passenger Duty and Other Indirect Taxes (Interest Rate) Regulations 1997 (revoked)
SI 1997/1086 VAT (Amendment) Regulations 1997
SI 1997/1431 Distress for Customs And Excise Duties and Other Indirect Taxes Regulations 1997
SI 1997/1432 Finance Act 1997, sections 52 and 53, (Appointed Day) Order 1997 (see FA 1997 ss 52 and 53)
SI 1997/1433 Finance Act 1997 (Repeal of Distress and Diligence enactments) (Appointed Day) Order 1997 (see VATA 1994 Sch 11 para 5(4)–(10))
SI 1997/1523 VAT (Reverse Charge) (Anti-avoidance) Order 1997
SI 1997/1524 VAT (Place of Supply of Services) (Amendment) Order 1997
SI 1997/1525 VAT (Amendment) (No 2) Regulations 1997
SI 1997/1603 The Finance Act 1997, section 110 (Appointed Day) Order 1997 (see FA 1997 s 110)
SI 1997/1614 VAT (Amendment) (No 3) Regulations 1997
SI 1997/1615 VAT (Cars) (Amendment) Order 1997
SI 1997/1616 VAT (Special Provisions) (Amendment) Order 1997
SI 1997/1628 VAT (Increase of Registration Limits) Order 1997 (superseded)
SI 1997/1836 VAT (Terminal Markets) (Amendment) Order 1997

SI 1997/2437 VAT (Amendment) (No 4) Regulations 1997
SI 1997/2542 VAT (Payments on Account) (Appeals) Order 1997 (amending)
SI 1997/2558 VAT (Refund of Tax) Order 1997
SI 1997/2744 VAT (Drugs, Medicines and Aids for the Handicapped) Order 1997 (amending)
SI 1997/2864 Statistics of Trade (Customs and Excise) (Amendment) Order 1997
SI 1997/2887 VAT (Amendment) (No 5) Regulations 1997
SI 1998/59 VAT (Amendment) Regulations 1998
SI 1998/759 VAT (Cars) (Amendment) Order 1998
SI 1998/760 VAT (Special Provisions) (Amendment) Order 1998
SI 1998/761 VAT (Increase of Registration Limits) Order 1998 (superseded)
SI 1998/762 VAT (Supply of Services) (Amendment) Order 1998
SI 1998/763 VAT (Place of Supply of Services) (Amendment) Order
SI 1998/765 VAT (Amendment) (No 2) Regulations 1998
SI 1998/1294 VAT (Osteopaths) Order 1998 (amending)
SI 1998/1375 VAT (Reduced Rate) Order 1998 (revoked)
SI 1998/1461 Air Passenger Duty and Other Indirect Taxes (Interest Rate) Regulations 1998
SI 1998/1898 Rules of the Supreme Court (Amendment) 1998
SI 1998/2767 The VAT (Input Tax) (Amendment) Order 1998
SI 1998/2973 The Statistics of Trade (Customs and Excise) (Amendment) Regulations 1998 (revoked)
SI 1998/3086 The Reserve Forces Act 1996 (Consequential Provisions etc) Regulations 1998 (amending)
SI 1999/438 VAT (Amendment) Regulations 1999
SI 1999/593 VAT (Buildings and Land) Order 1999 (revoked)
SI 1999/594 VAT (Finance) Order 1999 (amending)
SI 1999/595 VAT (Increase of Registration Limits) Order 1999 (superseded)
SI 1999/599 VAT (Amendment) (No 2) Regulations 1999
SI 1999/1374 VAT (Amendment) (No 3) Regulations 1999
SI 1999/1575 VAT (Chiropractors) Order 1999 (amending)
SI 1999/1642 VAT (Abolition of Zero-Rating for Tax-Free Shops) Order 1999 (amending)
SI 1999/1994 VAT (Sport, Sports Competitions and Physical Education) Order 1999 (amending)
SI 1999/2076 VAT (Refund of Tax) Order 1999
SI 1999/2831 VAT (Special Provisions) (Amendment) Order 1999
SI 1999/2832 VAT (Cars) (Amendment) Order 1999
SI 1999/2833 VAT (Supplies of Goods where Input Tax cannot be recovered) Order 1999 (amending)
SI 1999/2834 VAT (Subscriptions to Trade Unions, Professional and Other Public Interest Bodies) Order 1999 (amending)
SI 1999/2930 VAT (Input Tax) (Amendment) Order 1999
SI 1999/3029 VAT Regulations 1999 (amending)
SI 1999/3114 VAT (Amendment) (No 4) Regulations 1999
SI 1999/3115 VAT (Importation of Investment Gold) Relief Order 1999
SI 1999/3116 VAT (Investment Gold) Order 1999
SI 1999/3117 VAT (Terminal Markets) Order 1999 (amending)
SI 1999/3118 VAT (Input Tax) (Amendment) (No 2) Order 1999
SI 1999/3119 VAT (Treatment of Transactions) (Amendment) Order 1999
SI 1999/3120 VAT (Special Provisions) (Amendment) (No 2) Order 1999
SI 1999/3121 VAT (Input Tax) (Specified Supplies) Order 1999
SI 1999/3122 Free Zone (Liverpool) Designation (Variation) Order 1999 (superseded)
SI 1999/3269 Statistics of Trade (Customs and Excise) (Amendment) Regulations 1999 (revoked)
SI 2000/221 Civil Procedure (Amendment) Rules 2000
SI 2000/258 VAT (Amendment) Regulations 2000
SI 2000/266 VAT (Deemed Supply of Goods) Order 2000 (amending)
SI 2000/503 VAT (Drugs, Medicines, Aids for the Handicapped and Charities Etc) Order 2000 (amending)
SI 2000/631 Air Passenger Duty and Other Indirect Taxes (Interest Rate) (Amendment) Regulations 2000
SI 2000/634 VAT (Amendment) (No 2) Regulations 2000
SI 2000/794 VAT (Amendment) (No 3) Regulations 2000

SI 2000/802 VAT (Fund-Raising Events by Charities and Other Qualifying Bodies) Order 2000 (amending)
SI 2000/804 VAT (Increase of Registration Limits) Order 2000 (spent)
SI 2000/805 VAT (Charities and Aids for the Handicapped) Order 2000 (amending)
SI 2000/811 VAT (Increase of Consideration for Fuel) Order 2000 (amending)
SI 2000/1046 VAT (Refund of Tax) Order 2000
SI 2000/1515 VAT (Refund of Tax) (No 2) Order 2000
SI 2000/1517 VAT (Protective Helmets) Order 2000 (amending)
SI 2000/1672 VAT (Refund of Tax) (No 3) Order 2000
SI 2000/2954 VAT (Reduced Rate) Order 2000 (revoked)
SI 2000/3227 Statistics of Trade (Customs and Excise) (Amendment) Regulations 2000
SI 2001/630 VAT (Amendment) Regulations 2001
SI 2001/640 VAT (Increase of Registration Limits) Order 2001 (spent)
SI 2001/677 VAT (Amendment) (No 2) Regulations 2001
SI 2001/732 VAT (Protective Helmets) Order 2001 (amending)
SI 2001/735 VAT (Business Gifts of Small Value) Order 2001 (amending)
SI 2001/736 VAT (Consideration for Fuel Provided for Private Use) Order 2001 (amending)
SI 2001/753 VAT (Passenger Vehicles) Order 2001 (amending)
SI 2001/754 VAT (Vehicles Designed or Adapted for Handicapped Persons) Order 2001 (amending)
SI 2001/1149 Postal Services Act 2000 (Consequential Modifications No 1) Order 2001 (amending)
SI 2001/2305 VAT (Conversion of Buildings) Order 2001 (amending)
SI 2001/759 VAT (Electronic Communications) (Incentives) Regulations 2001
SI 2001/2879 VAT (Refund of Tax to Museums and Galleries) Order 2001
SI 2001/2880 Free Zone (Southampton) Designation Order 2001
SI 2001/2881 Free Zone (Liverpool) Designation Order 2001
SI 2001/2882 Free Zone (Prestwick Airport) Designation Order 2001
SI 2001/3073 VAT Tribunals (Amendment) Rules 2001
SI 2001/3337 Air Passenger Duty and Other Indirect Taxes (Interest Rate) (Amendment) Regulations 2001
SI 2001/3453 VAT (Refund of Tax) Order 2001
SI 2001/3500 Transfer of Functions (Miscellaneous) Order 2001 (amending)
SI 2001/3753 VAT (Special Provisions) (Amendment) Order 2001
SI 2001/3754 VAT (Cars) (Amendment) Order 2001
SI 2001/3828 VAT (Amendment)(No 3) Regulations 2001
SI 2001/3887 Statistics of Trade (Customs and Excise) (Amendment) Regulations 2001 (revoked)
SI 2002/1074 VAT (Amendment) Regulations 2002
SI 2002/1098 VAT (Increase of Registration Limits) Order 2002 (spent)
SI 2002/1099 VAT (Consideration for Fuel Provided for Private Use) Order 2002 (amending)
*SI 2002/1100 VAT (Reduced Rate) Order 2002 (amending)*S
SI 2002/1101 VAT (Construction of Buildings) Order 2002 (amending)
SI 2002/1102 VAT (Buildings and Land) Order 2002 (revoked)
SI 2002/1142 VAT (Amendment) (No 2) Regulations 2002
SI 2002/1173 VAT (Transport) Order 2002 (amending)
SI 2002/1280 VAT (Special Provisions) (Amendment) Order 2002
SI 2002/1418 Free Zone (Port of Tilbury) Order 2002
SI 2002/1502 VAT (Cars) (Amendment) Order 2002
SI 2002/1503 VAT (Special Provisions) (Amendment No 2) Order 2002
SI 2002/1935 VAT (Acquisitions) Relief Order 2002
SI 2002/2498 Statistics of Trade (Customs and Excise) (Amendment) Regulations 2002 (revoked)
SI 2002/2813 VAT (Drugs, Medicines, Aids for the Handicapped and Charities Etc) Order 2002 (amends VATA 1994)
SI 2002/2851 VAT Tribunals (Amendment) Rules 2002
SI 2002/2918 VAT (Amendment) (No 3) Regulations 2002
SI 2002/3027 VAT (Amendment) (No 4) Regulations 2002
SI 2003/230 Air Passenger Duty and Other Indirect Taxes (Interest Rate) (Amendment) Regulations 2003
SI 2003/532 VAT (Amendment) Regulations 2003
SI 2003/862 VAT (Place of Supply of Services) (Amendment) Order 2003

SI 2003/863 VAT (Reverse Charge) (Amendment) Order 2003
SI 2003/1055 VAT (Supply of Services) (Amendment) Order 2003
SI 2003/1057 VAT (Consideration for Fuel Provided for Private Use) Order 2003 (amending)
SI 2003/1058 VAT (Increase of Registration Limits) Order 2003 (amending)
SI 2003/1069 VAT (Amendment) (No 2) Regulations 2003
SI 2003/1114 VAT (Amendment) (No 3) Regulations 2003
SI 2003/1485 VAT (Amendment) (No 4) Regulations 2003
SI 2003/2318 VAT (Amendment) (No 5) Regulations 2003
SI 2003/2757 VAT Tribunals (Amendment) Rules 2003
SI 2003/3092 Mutual Assistance Provisions Order 2003 (amending)
SI 2003/3220 VAT (Amendment) (No 6) Regulations 2003
SI 2003/3113 Customs (Contravention of a Relevant Rule) Regulations 2003
SI 2004/674 Recovery of Duties and Taxes etc Due in Other Member States (Corresponding UK Claims, Procedure and Supplementary) Regulations 2004
SI 2004/776 VAT (Consideration for Fuel Provided for Private Use) Order 2004 (amending)
SI 2004/1032 VAT Tribunals (Amendment) Rules 2004
SI 2004/1082 VAT (Amendment) (No 2) Regulations 2004
SI 2004/1501 Criminal Justice (Evidence) (Northern Ireland) Order (amending)
SI 2004/1929 VAT (Disclosure of Avoidance Schemes) Regulations 2004
SI 2004/1931 VAT (Groups: eligibility) Order 2004
SI 2004/1933 VAT (Disclosure of Avoidance Schemes) (Designations) Order 2004
SI 2004/3083 VAT (Insurance) Order 2004 (amending)
SI 2004/3084 VAT (Cars) (Amendment) Order 2004
SI 2004/3085 VAT (Special Provisions) (Amendment) (No 2) Order 2004
SI 2004/3140 VAT (Amendment) (No 4) Regulations 2004
SI 2004/3147 VAT (Imported Gas and Electricity) Relief Order 2004 (revoked)
SI 2004/3150 VAT (Removal of Gas and Electricity) Order 2004 (revoked)
SI 2004/3148 VAT (Place of Supply of Goods) Order 2004
SI 2004/3284 Statistics of Trade (Customs and Excise) (Amendment) Regulations 2004
SI 2004/3343 VAT (Food) Order 2004 (amending)
SI 2005/722 VAT (Fuel Provided for Private Use) Order 2005 (amending)
SI 2005/726 VAT (Reduced Rate) Order 2005 (amending)
SI 2005/727 VAT (Increase of Registration Limits) Order 2005 (amending)
SI 2005/762 VAT (Amendment) Regulations 2005
SI 2005/1133 Revenue and Customs (Inspections) Regulations 2005
SI 2005/1479 Recovery of Taxes etc Due in Other Member States (Amendment of Section 134 of the Finance Act 2002) Regulations 2005
SI 2005/1709 Recovery of Duties and Taxes Etc Due in Other Member States (Corresponding UK Claims, Procedure and Supplementary) (Amendment) Regulations 2005 (amend SI 2004/674)
SI 2005/1724 VAT (Disclosure of Avoidance Schemes) (Designations) (Amendment) Order 2005 (amends SI 2004/1933)
SI 2005/1993 VAT (Refund of Tax to Museums and Galleries) (Amendment) Order 2005 (amends SI 2001/2879)
SI 2005/2231 VAT (Amendment) (No 2) Regulations 2005 (amend SI 1995/2518)
SI 2005/3290 VAT (Input Tax) (Reimbursement by Employers of Employees' Business Use of Road Fuel) Regulations 2005
SI 2005/3291 VAT (Input Tax) (Person Supplied) Order 2005 (revokes SI 1991/2306)
SI 2005/3311 Revenue and Customs (Complaints and Misconduct) Regulations 2005
SI 2005/3328 VAT (Betting, Gaming and Lotteries) Order 2005 (amends VATA 1994)
SI 2005/3329 VAT (Reduced Rate) (No 2) Order 2005 (amends VATA 1994)
SI 2006/587 VAT (Amendment) Regulations 2006 (amend SI 1995/2518)
SI 2006/868 VAT (Consideration for Fuel Provided for Private Use) Order 2006 (amends VATA 1994)
SI 2006/869 VAT (Special Provisions) (Amendment) (No 2) Order 2006 (amends SI 1995/1268)
SI 2006/874 VAT (Cars) (Amendment) Order 2006 (amends SI 1992/3122)
SI 2006/876 VAT (Increase of Registration Limits) Order 2006 (amends VATA 1994)
SI 2006/2685 VAT (Betting, Gaming and Lotteries) Order 2006
SI 2006/2686 VAT (Gaming Machines) Order (amends VATA 1994)
SI 2006/2902 VAT (Amendment) (No 2) Regulations 2006

SI 2006/3216 Statistics of Trade (Customs and Excise) (Amendment) Regulations (amend SI 1992/2790)
SI 2006/3283 *Mutual Assistance Provisions Order 2006* (amends FA 2003)
SI 2006/3292 *VAT (Amendment) (No 3) Regulations 2006*
SI 2007/5 C&E (Personal Reliefs for Special Visitors) (Amendment) Order
SI 2007/206 *VAT (Health and Welfare) Order* (amending)
SI 2007/313 *VAT (Amendment) Regulations 2007*
SI 2007/768 *VAT (Amendment) (No 2) Regulations 2007*
SI 2007/939 *VAT (Amendment of section 77A of the VATA 1994) Order 2007*
SI 2007/941 *VAT (Increase of Registration Limits) Order 2007*
SI 2007/946 *Finance (No 2) Act 2005, Section 2(7), (Appointed Day) Order 2007*
SI 2007/966 *Value Added Tax (Consideration for Fuel Provided for Private Use) Order 2007*
SI 2007/1417 Value Added Tax (Section 55A) (Specified Goods and Excepted Supplies) Order 2007
SI 2007/1418 VAT (Amendment) (No 3) Regulations 2007
SI 2007/1419 Finance Act 2006, Section 19, (Appointed Day) Order 2007
SI 2007/1420 VAT (Payments on Account) (Amendment) Order 2007
SI 2007/1421 VAT (Administration, Collection and Enforcement) Order 2007
SI 2007/1509 Control of Cash (Penalties) Regulations 2007
SI 2007/1599 VAT (Amendment) (No 4) Regulations 2007
SI 2007/1601 Value Added Tax (Reduced Rate) Order 2007
SI 2007/2085 Value Added Tax (Amendment) (No 5) Regulations 2007
SI 2007/2163 VAT (Betting, Gaming and Lotteries) Order 2007 (revoked)
SI 2007/2173 VAT (Supply of Services) (Amendment) Order 2007
SI 2007/2351 VAT Tribunals (Amendment) Rules 2007
SI 2007/2709 Tribunals, Courts and Enforcement Act 2007 (Commencement No 1) Order 2007
SI 2007/2923 *VAT (Special Provisions) (Amendment) Order 2007*
SI 2007/3099 *VAT (Amendment) (No 7) Regulations 2007*
SI 2007/3166 *Finance Act 2007 (Sections 82 to 84 and Schedule 23) (Commencement) Order 2007*
SI 2007/3448 VAT (Reduced Rate) (No 2) Order 2007
SI 2007/3508 Recovery of Duties and Taxes etc Due in Other Member States (Corresponding UK Claims, Procedure and Supplementary) (Amendment) Regulations 2007
SI 2008/556 VAT (Amendment) Regulations 2008
SI 2008/557 Statistics of Trade (Customs and Excise) (Amendment) Regulations 2008
SI 2008/568 Finance Act 2007, Schedule 24 (Commencement and Transitional Provisions) Order 2008
SI 2008/722 *Value Added Tax (Consideration for Fuel Provided for Private Use) Order 2008*
SI 2008/954 *Companies Act 2006 (Consequential Amendments) (Taxes and National Insurance) Order 2008*
SI 2008/1146 Value Added Tax (Buildings and Land) Order 2008
SI 2008/1339 *VAT (Refund of Tax to Museums and Galleries) (Amendment) Order 2008*
SI 2008/1892 *Value Added Tax (Finance) Order 2008 (revoked)*
SI 2008/1948 Taxes (Fees for Payment by Telephone) Regulations 2008
SI 2008/2547 Value Added Tax (Finance) (No 2) Order 2008
SI 2008/2676 Value Added Tax (Reduced Rate) (Supplies of Domestic Fuel or Power) Order
SI 2008/2684 First-tier Tribunal and Upper Tribunal (Chambers) Order 2008
SI 2008/2698 Tribunal Procedure (Upper Tribunal) Rules 2008
SI 2008/2832 Excise Warehousing (Etc) (Amendment) Regulations 2008
SI 2008/2834 Appeals from the Upper Tribunal to the Court of Appeal Order 2008
SI 2008/2835 First-tier Tribunal and Upper Tribunal (Composition of Tribunal) Order 2008
SI 2008/2847 Statistics of Trade (Customs and Excise) (Amendment) (No 2) Regulations 2008
SI 2008/2991 The Taxes (Fees for Payment by Internet) Regulations 2008
SI 2008/3234 Taxes and Duties (Interest Rate) (Amendment) Regulations 2008
SI 2009/56 Transfer of Tribunal Functions and Revenue and Customs Appeals Order 2009
SI 2009/215 VAT (Place of Supply of Goods) Order 2009
SI 2009/217 VAT (Input Tax) (Amendment) Order 2009
SI 2009/404 Finance Act 2008, Schedule 36 (Appointed Day and Savings) Order 2009
SI 2009/273 Tribunal Procedure (First-tier Tribunal) (Tax Chamber) Rules 2009
SI 2009/275 Appeals (Excluded Decisions) Order 2009

SI 2009/403 Finance Act 2008, Schedule 39 (Appointed Day, Transitional Provision and Savings) Order 2009
SI 2009/571 Finance Act 2008, Schedule 40 (Appointed Day, Transitional Provisions and Consequential Amendments) Order 2009
SI 2009/1916 Information Notice: Resolution of Disputes as to Privileged Communications Regulations 2009
SI 2009/1966 Value Added Tax (Buildings and Land) Order 2009
SI 2009/2972 Value Added Tax (Drugs and Medicines) Order 2009
SI 2009/2978 Value Added Tax (Amendment) (No 4) Regulations 2009
SI 2009/3024 Finance Act 2008, Section 128 and Part 2 of Schedule 43 (Appointed Day, Transitional Provisions and Savings) Order 2009
SI 2009/3073 Taxes, etc (Fees for Payment by Telephone) Regulations 2009 (revoked)
SI 2009/3127 Value Added Tax (Supplementary Charge) Order 2009
SI 2010/466 Finance Act 2009, Schedule 56 (Appointed Day and Consequential Provisions) Order 2010
SI 2010/608 Value Added Tax (Refund of Tax to Museums and Galleries) (Amendment) Order 2010
SI 2010/920 Value Added Tax (Increase of Registration Limits) Order 2010
SI 2010/1185 Value Added Tax (Small Non-Commercial Consignments) Relief (Amendment) Order 2010
SI 2010/1813 Revenue and Customs (Complaints and Misconduct) Regulations 2010
SI 2010/1878 Finance Act 2009, Sections 101 to 103 (Appointed Day and Supplemental Provision) Order 2010
SI 2010/1879 Taxes and Duties (Interest Rate) Regulations 2010
SI 2010/2239 VAT (Section 55A) (Specified Goods and Services and Excepted Supplies) Order 2010
SI 2010/2240 VAT (Amendment) (No 2) Regulations 2010
SI 2010/2655 First-tier Tribunal and Upper Tribunal (Chambers) Order 2010
SI 2010/2880 Single Use Carrier Bags Charge (Wales) Regulations 2010
SI 2010/2923 VAT (Place of Supply of Goods) (Amendment) Order 2010
SI 2010/2924 VAT (Imported Gas, Electricity, Heat and Cooling) Relief Order 2010
SI 2010/2925 VAT (Removal of Gas, Electricity, Heat and Cooling) Order 2010
SI 2010/3017 VAT (Exceptions Relating to Supplies not Made to Relevant Business Person) Order 2010
SI 2010/3022 VAT (Amendment) (No. 4) Regulations 2010
SI 2011/21 VAT (Payment on Account) (Amendment) Order 2011
SI 2011/86 VAT (Buildings and Land) Order 2011
SI 2011/254 The Value Added Tax (Amendment) Regulations 2011
SI 2011/711 Taxes, etc (Fees for Payment by Internet) Regulations 2011
SI 2011/976 Penalties, Offshore Income etc. (Designation of Territories) Order 2011
SI 2011/1079 International Mutual Administrative Assistance in Tax Matters Order 2011
SI 2011/1727 Charities Act 2006 (Principal Regulators of Exempt Charities) (No. 2) Regulations 2011
SI 2011/2085 Postal Services Act 2011 (Consequential Modifications and Amendments) Order 2011
SI 2011/2878 Statistics and Registration Service Act 2007 (Disclosure of Value Added Tax Information) Regulations 2011
SI 2011/2931 MARD Regulations 2011
SI 2011/3036 Postal Packets (Revenue and Customs) Regulations 2011
SI 2012/33 Value Added Tax (Amendment) Regulations 2012
SI 2012/58 Value Added Tax (Land Exemption) Order 2012
SI 2012/689 Taxes, etc (Fees for Payment by Telephone) Regulations 2012
SI 2012/735 Finance Act 2010, Schedule 6, Part 1 (Further Consequential and Incidental Provision etc) Order 2012
SI 2012/847 Data-gathering Powers (Relevant Data) Regulations 2012
SI 2012/882 Value Added Tax (Consideration for Fuel Provided for Private Use) Order 2012
SI 2012/883 Value Added Tax (Increase of Registration Limits) Order 2012
SI 2012/1899 Value Added Tax (Amendment) (No 2) Regulations 2012
SI 2012/2393 VAT (Refund of VAT to Chief Constables and the Commissioner of Police of the Metropolis) Order 2012
SI 2012/2787 VAT (Place of Supply of Services) (Transport of Goods) Order 2012
SI 2012/2907 VAT (Relief for European Research Infrastructure Consortia) Order 2012

SI 2012/2951 Value Added Tax (Amendment) (No 3) Regulations 2012
SI 2012/2953 VAT (Removal of Goods) (Amendment) Order 2012
SI 2012/3060 Value Added Tax (Small Non-Commercial Consignments) Relief (Amendment) Order 2012
SI 2013/67 Finance Act 2009, Sections 101 and 102 (Machine Games Duty) (Appointed Day) Order 2013
SI 2013/279 Finance Act 2012, Schedule 38 (Tax Agents: Dishonest Conduct) (Appointed Day and Savings) Order 2013
SI 2013/280 Finance Act 2009, Section 101 (Tax Agents: Dishonest Conduct) (Appointed Day) Order 2013
SI 2013/412 VAT (Refund of Tax to the Natural Resources Body for Wales) Order 2013
SI 2013/430 Value Added Tax (Reduced Rate) (Cable-Suspended Passenger Transport Systems) Order 2013
SI 2013/601 Value Added Tax (Independence Payment) Order 2013
SI 2013/659 Value Added Tax (Consideration for Fuel Provided for Private Use) Order 2013
SI 2013/660 Value Added Tax (Increase of Registration Limits) Order 2013
SI 2013/701 Value Added Tax (Amendment) Regulations 2013
SI 2013/1402 Value Added Tax (Finance) Order 2013
SI 2013/1811 Data-gathering Powers (Relevant Data) (Amendment) Regulations 2013
SI 2013/1897 Value Added Tax (Education) Order 2013
SI 2013/2043 Tribunals, Courts and Enforcement Act 2007 (Commencement No 10) Order 2013
SI 2013/2067 Tribunal Procedure (Amendment No 4) Rules 2013
SI 2013/2241 Value Added Tax (Amendment) (No 2) Regulations 2013
SI 2013/2911 VAT (Flat-rate Valuation of Supplies of Fuel for Private Use) Order 2013
SI 2013/3211 Value Added Tax (Amendment) (No 3) Regulations 2013
SI 2014/514 Tribunal Procedure (Amendment) Rules 2014
SI 2014/548 Value Added Tax (Amendment) Regulations 2014
SI 2014/600 Tribunals, Courts and Enforcement Act 2007 (Consequential, Transitional and Saving Provision) Order 2014
SI 2014/703 Value Added Tax (Increase of Registration Limits) Order 2014
SI 2014/906 Finance Act 2008, Section 127 and Part 1 of Schedule 43 (Appointed Day) Order 2014
SI 2014/1111 VAT (Drugs and Medicines) Order 2014
SI 2014/1112 VAT (Refund of Tax) Order 2014
SI 2014/1264 Revenue and Customs (Amendment of Appeal Provisions for Out of Time Reviews) Order 2014
SI 2014/1458 VAT (Section 55A) (Specified Goods and Excepted Supplies) Order 2014
SI 2014/1497 Value Added Tax (Amendment) (No 2) Regulations 2014
SI 2014/2364 Value Added Tax (Imported Goods) Relief (Amendment) Order 2014
SI 2015/449 VAT (Refund of Tax to the London Legacy Development Corporation) Order 2015
SI 2015/636 Customs (Contravention of a Relevant Rule) (Amendment) Regulations 2015
SI 2015/750 Value Added Tax (Increase of Registration Limits) Order 2015
SI 2015/776 Single Use Carrier Bags Charges (England) Order 2015

Statutory Instruments

1961/1523

TEMPORARY IMPORTATION (COMMERCIAL VEHICLES AND AIRCRAFT) REGULATIONS 1961

Made by the Commissioners of Customs and Excise under the Customs and Excise Act 1952 s 40

Made . . . .*3 August 1961*
Laid before Parliament . . . .*10 August 1961*
Coming into Operation . . . .*14 August 1961*

PART I

1 If any vehicle or aircraft is imported into any part of the United Kingdom other than the Isle of Man and the importer satisfies the Commissioners that—

(*a*) his principal place of business is outside the United Kingdom,
(*b*) the vehicle or aircraft is registered outside the United Kingdom,
(*c*) the vehicle or aircraft is owned and operated by a person whose principal place of business is outside the United Kingdom,
(*d*) the importation is taking place in the course of a journey which has begun and will end outside the United Kingdom,
(*e*) the purpose of the journey is to use the vehicle or aircraft either—
  (i) for the transport of passengers for remuneration or for the industrial or commercial transport of goods from or to a place outside the United Kingdom, or
  (ii) for such other purpose as the Commissioners may in special circumstances allow, and
(*f*) the following provisions of this Part of these Regulations, and such other conditions as may be imposed by the Commissioners, are and will be complied with,

such vehicle or aircraft may be delivered without payment of duty, and duty shall not be payable so long as the Commissioners continue to be so satisfied:

Provided that no vehicle or aircraft may be so delivered without payment of duty if the vehicle or aircraft is principally kept in the United Kingdom or if the importer principally keeps in the United Kingdom any vehicle or aircraft so delivered.

2 The importer shall at the time of importation—

(*a*) produce the vehicle or aircraft to the officer for examination,
(*b*) produce to the officer all documents in his possession which relate to the ownership or foreign registration of the vehicle or aircraft or which in the opinion of the officer might affect the entitlement to delivery of the vehicle or aircraft without payment of duty,
(*c*) if, and as, the Commissioners require, give security for payment of the duty and for compliance with these regulations either—
  (i) by producing a carnet for the vehicle or aircraft issued either to the importer by name, or to another person whose principal place of business is outside the United Kingdom, or
  (ii) by entering into a bond with sureties acceptable to the officer, or
  (iii) by depositing such sum of money or giving such other security as the officer may require,
(*d*) furnish to the officer such documents in such form and containing such particulars as the officer may require.

3 Save as the Commissioners may allow, the vehicle or aircraft while in the United Kingdom—

(*a*) shall not be (or be offered to be) lent, sold, pledged, hired, given away, exchanged or otherwise disposed of, and shall not be used for the purpose of picking up passengers or goods at any place within the United Kingdom for conveyance to another place within the United Kingdom,
(*b*) shall be operated and used only by or on behalf of the owner or operator of the vehicle or aircraft or other person in charge thereof at the time of its importation or by other persons whose principal place of business is outside the United Kingdom who are expressly authorised in writing by the owner or operator of the vehicle or aircraft to operate and use the vehicle or aircraft,

(*c*) shall not be operated or used by, or in the service of, any other person and in particular any person whose principal place of business is in the United Kingdom.

4 The vehicle or aircraft shall be re-exported from the United Kingdom either—

(*a*) in the case of a vehicle or aircraft delivered on importation on production of a carnet, before the expiration of the period of validity of the carnet, or

(*b*) before the expiration of three months from the date of importation, or

(*c*) as soon as the purpose referred to in paragraph (*e*) of Regulation 1 of these Regulations has been served,

whichever is the earliest date, or, in any case,

(*d*) within such period as the Commissioners may allow.

5 The importer shall at the time of re-exportation—

(*a*) produce the vehicle or aircraft and any relevant import documents to the officer, and

(*b*) give such additional information and make such declaration relating to the vehicle or aircraft and the circumstances of its use in the United Kingdom as the officer may require.

PART II

6 If any spare parts or accessories of a vehicle are imported into any part of the United Kingdom other than the Isle of Man by or on behalf of a person whose principal place of business is outside the United Kingdom, and the importer satisfies the Commissioners that

(*a*) the spare parts or accessories—

(i) are imported solely for the purpose of being incorporated in, or used with, a vehicle which has been delivered without payment of duty under the provisions of Part I of these Regulations or under Part I of the Commercial Vehicles (Temporary Importation) Regulations 1952, and

(ii) will be re-exported in, or with, the vehicle before the expiration of the period specified in Regulation 4 of these Regulations which is applicable to that vehicle, and

(*b*) the following provisions of this Part of these Regulations and such other conditions as may be imposed by the Commissioners are and will be complied with,

such spare parts or accessories may be delivered without payment of duty, and duty shall not be payable so long as the Commissioners continue to be so satisfied.

7 The importer shall—

(*a*) at the time of importation of such parts or accessories, if the Commissioners so require, deposit in accordance with the officer's directions such sum of money for securing the duty and compliance with these Regulations, and produce such documents and give such information, as the officer may require,

(*b*) use the spare parts or accessories solely for incorporation in, or with, the vehicle,

(*c*) re-export the spare parts or accessories in, or with, the vehicle before the expiration of the period specified in Regulation 4 of these Regulations which is applicable to that vehicle, and

(*d*) at the time of re-exportation, unless the Commissioners otherwise permit, produce to the officer all used or defective parts or accessories as have been displaced during the incorporation in, or use with, the vehicle by the imported spare parts or accessories, and—

(i) re-export such displaced parts or accessories, or

(ii) destroy them under such conditions as the Commissioners may specify, or

(iii) if the Commissioners so permit, abandon them to the Crown.

PART III

8 If any goods of the following descriptions are imported into any part of the United Kingdom other than the Isle of Man for the purposes hereinafter mentioned—

(*a*) spare parts or equipment imported solely for the purpose of being incorporated in, or used with, any aircraft which is—

(i) registered outside the United Kingdom,

(ii) owned and operated by a person whose principal place of business is outside the United Kingdom, and

(iii) used in international air transport services and in compliance with the provisions of Regulation 3 of these Regulations;

(*b*) aircraft, special tools, spare parts and equipment imported solely for the purpose of being used in the search for, or in the rescue, examination, repair or salvage of, an aircraft which is of the kind referred to in paragraph (*a*) of this Regulation and which has been accidentally lost or damaged;

and if the importer satisfies the Commissioners that the goods will be re-exported as soon as the purpose for which they were imported has been served or before the expiration of such period as may be allowed by the Commissioners, whichever is the earlier, and that the provisions of this Part of these Regulations and such other conditions as may be imposed by the Commissioners are and will be complied with, the goods may be delivered without payment of duty, and duty shall not be payable so long as the Commissioners continue to be so satisfied.

PART IV

9 For the purposes of these Regulations—

(*a*) the principal place of business of a person shall be deemed to be the place from which in the opinion of the Commissioners the control of the business is exercised;

(*b*) a vehicle or aircraft shall be deemed to be not principally kept in the United Kingdom if during the two years immediately preceding the date of importation of the vehicle or aircraft it has been present in the United Kingdom for less than either—

(i) a total of 365 days, or

(ii) such greater number of days as the Commissioners may in special circumstances allow;

(*c*) an importer shall be deemed not to keep a vehicle or aircraft principally in the United Kingdom if he has kept in the United Kingdom during the two years immediately preceding the date of importation of the vehicle or aircraft in question any other vehicle or aircraft which has been delivered without payment of duty under these Regulations or under the Commercial Vehicles (Temporary Importation) Regulations 1952, for an aggregate period of less than either—

(i) a total of 365 days, or

(ii) such greater number of days as the Commissioners may in special circumstances allow.

10 In these Regulations unless the context otherwise requires—

"aircraft" means any aeroplane, airship, balloon, flying machine or glider which is designed for the transport of persons for remuneration or the industrial or commercial transport of goods and also includes any accessories or component parts of any aircraft required for and imported in, or forming part of, such aircraft but does not include any accessories or component parts imported separately;

"carnet" means a carnet de passages en douane or a triptyque which is issued by an association belonging to the Federation Internationale de l'Automobile, the Alliance Internationale de Tourisme or the Federation Aeronautique Internationale, and which is covered by a guarantee given to the Commissioners by an approved association established in the United Kingdom;

"officer" means the proper officer of Customs and Excise;

"United Kingdom" means the United Kingdom including the Isle of Man;

"vehicle" means any motor road vehicle (including a trailer) which is designed for the transport of persons for remuneration or for the industrial or commercial transport of goods and also includes any accessories or component parts of such vehicle required for and imported in, or forming part of, such vehicle, but does not include any accessories or component parts imported separately.

11 The Interpretation Act 1889 shall apply for the interpretation of these Regulations as it applies for the interpretation of an Act of Parliament.

12 The Commercial Vehicles (Temporary Importation) Regulations 1952, are hereby revoked.

13 These Regulations may be cited as the Temporary Importation (Commercial Vehicles and Aircraft) Regulations 1961, and shall come into operation on the 14th day of August 1961.

1973/173

VALUE ADDED TAX (TERMINAL MARKETS) ORDER 1973

Made by the Treasury under FA 1972 s 26, see now VATA 1994, s 50

Made . . . . *6 February 1973*
Laid before the House of Commons . . . . *13 February 1973*
Coming into Operation . . . . *1 April 1973*

Customs and Excise Notices—Notice 701/21: Gold; Notice 701/21A Investment Gold Coins, para 3 (list of investment gold coins).

1 This Order may be cited as the Value Added Tax (Terminal Markets) Order 1973 and shall come into operation on 1st April 1973.

VAT SIs

2—(1) The Interpretation Act 1889[a] shall apply for the interpretation of this Order as it applies for the interpretation of an Act of Parliament.

(2) This Order applies to the following terminal markets—

the London Metal Exchange,
the London Rubber Market,
the London Cocoa Terminal Market,
the London Coffee Terminal Market,
the London Sugar Terminal Market,
the London Vegetable Oil Terminal Market,
the London Wool Terminal Market,
[[the London Bullion Market][8],][2]
[*the London Gold Futures Market,*][4]
. . .[8]
[the London Meat Futures Market,][5]
the London Grain Futures Market, *and*
[the London Soya Bean Meal Futures Market,][1]
the Liverpool Barley Futures Market,
[the International Petroleum Exchange of London,][3]
[the London Potato Futures Market][3] . . .[7]
[the London Platinum and Palladium Market][6] [and the London Securities and Derivatives Exchange Limited (OMLX).][7]

(3) References in this Order to a member of a market include any person ordinarily engaged in dealings on the market.

[(4) Notwithstanding paragraph 3 above, for the purposes of this Order a person is to be regarded as being a member of the London Bullion Market only if that person is a member of the London Bullion Market Association.] [8]

[(5) In this Order—

"investment gold" has the same meaning as that expression has for the purposes of Group 15 of Schedule 9 to the Value Added Tax Act 1994;
"the Act" means the Value Added Tax Act 1994.] [8]

Amendments—[a] IA 1978.

[1] Words in para (2) inserted and the word "and" preceding them deleted, with effect from 8 April 1975, by the VAT (Terminal Markets) (Amendment) Order, SI 1975/385 arts 1, 3.

[2] Words in para (2) inserted by the VAT (Terminal Markets) (Amendment) Order, SI 1980/304 art 2, with effect from 1 April 1980.

[3] Words in para (2) inserted by the VAT (Terminal Markets) (Amendment) Order, SI 1981/338 art 2, with effect from 6 April 1981.

[4] Words in para (2) inserted by the VAT (Terminal Markets) (Amendment) (No 2) Order, SI 1981/955 art 2, with effect from 7 September 1981, and revoked by the VAT (Terminal Markets) (Amendment) Order, SI 1985/1046 with effect from 1 August 1985 following the closure of the London Gold Futures Market on 26 June 1985.

[5] Words in para (2) inserted by the VAT (Terminal Markets) (Amendment) Order, SI 1984/202 art 2, with effect from 16 March 1984.

[6] Words in para (2) inserted by the VAT (Terminal Markets) (Amendment) Order, SI 1987/806 art 2 with effect from 1 June 1987.

[7] Words in para (2) inserted and the word "and" preceding them deleted by the VAT (Terminal Markets) (Amendment) Order, SI 1997/1836 art 2 with effect from 1 September 1997.

[8] Words in para (2) substituted and revoked, and paras (4), (5) added by the VAT (Terminal Markets) Order, SI 1999/3117, arts 2–5 with effect from 1 January 2000.

3—(1) The following supplies of goods or services in the course of dealings on a terminal market to which this Order applies are hereby zero-rated, subject to the conditions specified in this Article—

(*a*) the sale by or to a member of the market of any goods[, other than investment gold,][5] ordinarily dealt with on the market,

(*b*) the grant by or to a member of the market of a right to acquire such goods,

(*c*) where a sale of goods or the grant of a right zero-rated under sub-paragraph (*a*) or (*b*) above is made[,or where a supply of a description falling within article 4 or 5 below is made,][5] in dealings between members of the market acting as agents, the supply by those members to their principals of their services in so acting.

(2) The zero-rating of a sale by virtue of paragraph (1)(*a*) above is subject to the condition that the sale is either—

(*a*) a sale which, as a result of other dealings on the market, does not lead to a delivery of the goods by the seller to the buyer, or

(*b*) a sale by and to a member of the market which—

(i) if the market is the London Metal Exchange, is a sale between members entitled to deal in the ring,

(ii) if the market is the London Cocoa Terminal Market, the London Coffee Terminal Market, [the London Meat Futures Market,][4] [the International Petroleum Exchange of London, the London Potato Futures Market,][3] [the London Soya Bean Meal Futures

Market,][1] the London Sugar Terminal Market, the London Vegetable Oil Terminal Market or the London Wool Terminal Market, is a sale registered with [the International Commodities Clearing House Limited,][2]

(iii) if the market is the London Grain Futures Market, is a sale registered in the Clearing House of the Grain and Feed Trade Association Limited, and

(iv) if the market is the Liverpool Barley Futures Market, is a sale registered at the Clearing House of the Liverpool Corn Trade Association Limited.

(3) The zero-rating of the grant of a right by virtue of paragraph (1)(*b*) above is subject to the condition that either—

(*a*) the right is exercisable at a date later than that on which it is granted, or

(*b*) any sale resulting from the exercise of the right would be a sale with respect to which the condition specified in paragraph (2) above is satisfied.

Amendments—[1] Words in para (2)(*b*)(ii) inserted by the VAT (Terminal Markets) (Amendment) Order, SI 1975/385 arts 1, 4, with effect from 8 April 1975.

[2] Words in para (2)(*b*)(ii) substituted by the VAT (Terminal Markets) (Amendment) Order, SI 1975/385 arts 1, 4, with effect from 8 April 1975.

[3] Words in para (2)(*b*)(ii) inserted by the VAT (Terminal Markets) (Amendment) Order, SI 1981/338, art 3, with effect from 6 April 1981.

[4] Words in para (2)(*b*)(ii) inserted by the VAT (Terminal Markets) (Amendment) Order, SI 1984/202, art 3, with effect from 16 March 1984.

[5] Words in para (1)(*a*), (*c*) inserted by the VAT (Terminal Markets) Order, SI 1999/3117, arts 2, 6, 7, with effect from 1 January 2000.

[**4** Supplies between taxable persons which but for Note 4(*a*) to Group 15 of Schedule 9 to the Act (exemption for investment gold) would have fallen within that Group are hereby zero-rated.][1]

Amendments—[1] This article inserted by the VAT (Terminal Markets) Order, SI 1999/3117, arts 2, 8, with effect from 1 January 2000.

[**5** Subject to articles 6 and 7 below, section 55(1) to (4) of the Act (customers to account for tax on supplies of gold) shall apply to any supply between taxable persons which but for Note 4(*b*) to Group 15 of Schedule 9 to the Act would have fallen within that Group.][1]

Amendments—[1] This article inserted by the VAT (Terminal Markets) Order, SI 1999/3117, arts 2, 8, with effect from 1 January 2000.

[**6** Subject to article 7 below, where a taxable person who is not a member of the London Bullion Market Association makes or receives a supply falling within the description in article 5 is liable to be registered under Schedule 1 or under Schedule 3 to the Act solely by virtue of that supply or acquisition, paragraphs 5 to 8 of Schedule 1 or paragraph 3 of Schedule 3 to the Act (notification of liability and registration) shall not apply.][1]

Amendments—[1] This article inserted by the VAT (Terminal Markets) Order, SI 1999/3117, arts 2, 8, with effect from 1 January 2000.

[**7** Notwithstanding section 55(2) of the Act, where articles 5 and 6 above apply, it shall be for the London Bullion Market Association member, on the non-member's behalf, to keep a record of the supplies and to pay to the Commissioners of Customs and Excise the net amount of VAT, and not for the person who is not a member.][1]

Amendments—[1] This article inserted by the VAT (Terminal Markets) Order, SI 1999/3117, arts 2, 8, with effect from 1 January 2000.

1976/1223

CUSTOMS DUTIES (DEFERRED PAYMENT) REGULATIONS 1976

Made by the Commissioners of Customs and Excise under F(No 2)A 1975 s 16(2) and FA 1976 s 15

Made . . . . *2 August 1976*

Laid before Parliament . . . . *10 August 1976*

Coming into Operation . . . . *1 September 1976*

1 Citation and commencement

These Regulations may be cited as the Customs Duties (Deferred Payment) Regulations 1976 and shall come into operation on 1st September 1976.

2 Interpretation

(1) In these Regulations—

"approved" means approved by the Commissioners [to apply for deferment of payment of duty on behalf of himself or another and "approve" and "approval" shall be construed accordingly][1];

"deferment" means deferment of payment of customs duty granted under these Regulations and "deferred" shall be construed accordingly;

["payment day" means the 15th day of the month next following that in which the amount of duty deferred is entered into the Commissioners' accounts, or in the case of import entries scheduled periodically, the 15th day of the period following that in which deferment is granted (save that where that day in either case falls on a non-working day it shall be the next working day thereafter);][1]

["period" means a period commencing on the 16th day of any month and ending on the 15th day of the month next following.][1]

(2) The Interpretation Act 1889[a] shall apply for the interpretation of these Regulations as it applies for the interpretation of an Act of Parliament.

(3) Where any document used or required for the purpose of deferment refers to a provision of the Customs Duties (Deferred Payment) Regulations 1972 such reference shall, unless the contrary intention appears, be construed as referring to the corresponding provision of these Regulations.

(4) Any approval granted by a Collector under the Customs Duties (Deferred Payments) Regulations 1972 and in force immediately before the commencement of these Regulations shall have effect as if granted under these Regulations.

Notes—[a] IA 1978.

[1] Words in para (1) added and definition of "payment day" in that para substituted by Customs Duties (Deferred Payment) (Amendment) Regulations, SI 1978/1725 reg 4.

3 Application

These Regulations apply in the case of customs duty . . .[1] payable, apart from these Regulations, on the making of entry of goods chargeable therewith.

Amendments—[1] Words revoked by Customs Duties (Deferred Payment) (Amendment) Regulations, SI 1978/1725 reg 5.

4 Approval

(1) A person who wishes to be approved for the purposes of these Regulations shall apply to the Commissioners [in such form and manner as they shall determine][1], furnish security for payment on payment day of the amount of customs duty in respect of which he seeks deferment, and make arrangements with the Commissioners for the payment of that duty on payment day.

(2) If satisfied with the security and arrangements as aforesaid, the Commissioners shall in writing approve the applicant with respect to an amount of customs duty not exceeding that for which he has furnished security;

Provided that such approval may be limited to the deferment of customs duty payable, apart from these Regulations, on the making of entry within any named Collection.

(3) The Commissioners may, for reasonable cause, at any time vary or revoke any approval granted under this Regulation.

(4) A person to whom approval has been granted under this Regulation shall forthwith notify the Commissioners of any change in the particulars furnished, the security given, or the arrangements for payment provided for in paragraph (1) above.

Modifications—VAT Regulations, SI 1995/2518 reg 121A(1)–(4) (modification of this regulation in relation to any VAT chargeable on the importation of goods from places outside the member states).

Amendments—[1] Words in para (1) substituted by Customs Duties (Deferred Payment) (Amendment) Regulations, SI 1978/1725 reg 6.

5 Grant of deferment

Subject to Regulations 3, 4, 6 and 7, the Commissioners shall, upon application by an approved person [in such form and manner as they shall determine][1], grant deferment of customs duty until payment day.

Amendments—[1] Words substituted by Customs Duties (Deferred Payment) (Amendment) Regulations, SI 1978/1725 reg 7.

6 Payment

On each payment day an approved person shall pay to the Commissioners in accordance with the arrangements referred to in Regulation 4(1) the total amount of customs duty of which he has been granted deferment until that payment day.

7 If at any time after entry has been made the Commissioners are satisfied that—

(*a*) the full amount of customs duty payable has not been shown on the entry [or periodic schedule][1] then, save as the Commissioners otherwise allow, the balance shall forthwith be paid by the person making entry of the goods and no deferment in respect thereof shall be permitted;

(*b*) customs duty in excess of the amount payable has been shown on the entry [or periodic schedule][1], the Commissioners shall repay the excess, but the total amount shown shall nevertheless be paid on payment day.

Amendments—[1] Words in paras (*a*), (*b*) added by Customs Duties (Deferred Payment) (Amendment) Regulations, SI 1978/1725 reg 8.

[8 Without prejudice to Regulation 6, for the purposes of—

(*a*) sections 34(1) and 260(1) of the Customs and Excise Act 1952 and the Warehousing Regulations 1975; and

(*b*) any relief by way of repayment or suspension of customs duty, or agricultural levy falling to be treated as such, under—

(i) the Inward Processing Relief Regulations 1977,

(ii) the Customs Duties and Agricultural Levies (Goods for Free Circulation) Regulations 1977,

(iii) Regulation 4 of the Import Duties (Outward Processing Relief) Regulations 1976, and

(iv) Article 4 of the Agricultural Levies (Outward Processing Relief) Order 1976

duty shall be deemed to have been paid at the time when deferment thereof was granted.][1]

Modifications—VAT Regulations, SI 1995/2518 reg 121A(3) (modification of this regulation in relation to any VAT chargeable on the importation of goods from places outside the member states).

Amendments—[1] This regulation substituted by Customs Duties (Deferred Payment) (Amendment) Regulations, SI 1978/1725 reg 9.

1976/2028

VALUE ADDED TAX (REFUND OF TAX) ORDER 1976

Made by the Treasury under FA 1972 s 15(3); see now VATA 1994 s 33(3)

Made . . . .*29 November 1976*
Laid before the House of Commons . . . .*6 December 1976*
Coming into Operation . . . .*1 April 1977*

1 This Order may be cited as the Value Added Tax (Refund of Tax) Order 1976 and shall come into operation on 1st April 1977.

2 The Interpretation Act 1889[1] shall apply for the interpretation of this Order as it applies for the interpretation of an Act of Parliament.

[1] IA 1978.

3 The following bodies are hereby specified for the purposes of section 15 of the Finance Act 1972[1]—

the Commission for Local Administration in England
the Commission for Local Administration in Wales
the Commissioner for Local Administration in Scotland
the Commission for Local Authority Accounts in Scotland.

[1] VATA 1994 s 33.

1982/1067

VALUE ADDED TAX (ISLE OF MAN) ORDER 1982

Made under the Isle of Man Act 1979 s 6

Made . . . .*30 July 1982*
Coming into Operation . . . .*1 October 1982*

1—(1) This Order may be cited as the Value Added Tax (Isle of Man) Order 1982 and shall come into operation on 1st October 1982.

(2) In this Order—

"the United Kingdom Act" means the Finance Act 1972[1];
"the Manx Act" means the Value Added Tax and Other Taxes Act 1973; and
"the Finance Board" means the Finance Board of the Isle of Man,

and any other word or expression used in this Order to which meaning is given in or under Part I of the United Kingdom Act shall have, except where the context otherwise requires, the same meaning in this Order as in or under that Part of that Act.

(3) For the purposes of this Order, the Interpretation Act 1978 shall apply to the Manx Act and to any instrument of a legislative character made thereunder as if the Manx Act were an Act of Parliament.

(4) For the purposes of this Order—

(*a*) a supply shall be treated as made in the United Kingdom if it would be so treated under section 8 or 8A of the United Kingdom Act[2] if Article 2 below were disregarded; and

(*b*) a supply shall be treated as made in the Isle of Man if it would be so treated under one or other of those sections if they were amended by substituting for the words "United Kingdom" wherever they occur the words "Isle of Man".

VAT SIs

Notes—[1] VATA 1994.
[2] VATA 1994 s 7.

2 Subject to the provisions of this Order Part I of the United Kingdom Act shall have effect as if the Isle of Man were part of the United Kingdom.

3—(1) Notwithstanding Article 2 above, the removal of goods to the United Kingdom from the Isle of Man shall be treated for the purposes of Part I of the United Kingdom Act as the importation of those goods into the United Kingdom if they are goods which have previously been imported into or supplied in the United Kingdom or the Isle of Man and either—

(*a*) value added tax was chargeable on that previous importation or supply under Part I of the Manx Act but was not accounted for or paid at the rate which would have applied under Part I of the United Kingdom Act if the importation had been made into, or the supply had been made in, the United Kingdom; or

(*b*) that previous importation or supply was wholly or partly relieved from tax chargeable under Part I of the United Kingdom Act or value added tax chargeable under Part I of the Manx Act subject to a condition and that condition has not been complied with.

(2) The amount of tax chargeable under Part I of the United Kingdom Act on the removal into the United Kingdom from the Isle of Man of such goods as are mentioned in paragraph (1) above shall be reduced by an amount equal to any value added tax chargeable under Part I of the Manx Act which has been accounted for or paid on any earlier importation of those goods into, or supply of those goods in, the United Kingdom or the Isle of Man.

4 Tax shall not be charged under the United Kingdom Act—

(*a*) on the importation of goods into the Isle of Man except where the importation is by a taxable person otherwise than in the course or furtherance of a business carried on by him; or

(*b*) on the importation of goods into the United Kingdom by a person who is a taxable person for the purposes of the Manx Act where the importation is in the course or furtherance of a business carried on by him.

5 Any requirement imposed by or under the Manx Act shall be treated as a requirement imposed by or under the United Kingdom Act.

6 Any permission, direction, notice, determination or other thing given, made or done under the Manx Act by the Finance Board shall be treated as given, made or done by the Commissioners under the United Kingdom Act.

7 Sections 3(3)(*a*), (4), (8) and (9), 5, 14(3), 15, 15A, 17(1), 32(1), 33, 36(1), 43(4)(*b*) and 51 of the United Kingdom Act,[1] section 16 of the Finance Act 1977[2] and section 12(1) of the Finance Act 1978[3] shall have effect as if the references to tax in those sections included references to value added tax chargeable under Part I of the Manx Act.

Notes—[1] VATA 1994 ss 16(1), 24, 32, 33, 35, 39, 97(4)(*b*), 99 and Sch 11 paras 4, 5 and 8.
[2] VATA 1994 s 27.
[3] VATA 1994 s 36.

8 A person who is a taxable person for the purposes of the Manx Act shall be treated as a taxable person for the purposes of sections 18, 27(3), 30(2), 34(1) and 40(1)(*k*) of, and Note (6) to Item 4 of Group 15 of Schedule 4 to, the United Kingdom Act[1] and of section 16 of the Finance Act 1977[2].

Notes—[1] VATA 1994 ss 38, 18(3), 83(*f*), Sch 8, Group 13, item 3 and Note 5 and Sch 11 paras 2(2) and 6.
[2] VATA 1994 s 27.

9 Section 15A of the United Kingdom Act[1] shall not apply to the construction of dwellings within the Isle of Man.

Note—[1] VATA 1994 s 35.

10—(1) This Article shall have effect for enabling the Commissioners to determine for the purposes of section 21 of the United Kingdom Act[1] which member of a group is to be the representative member in cases where supplies are made both in the United Kingdom and in the Isle of Man.

(2) Where bodies corporate, which are treated as members of a group under the said section 21 have establishments both in the United Kingdom and in the Isle of Man, or do not have an establishment in either country, the Commissioners may at any time determine that another member of the group shall be substituted as the representative member from such date as they may determine.

Notes—[1] VATA 1994 s 43.

11—(1) This Article shall have effect, where a person would, apart from this Article, be liable to be registered both under Part I of the United Kingdom Act and under Part I of the Manx Act, for determining, or enabling the Commissioners to determine whether that person is to be registered under the United Kingdom Act or the Manx Act and for transferring a person registered under one Act to the register kept under the other.

(2) A person, who by virtue of paragraph 1(*a*) or (*b*) of Schedule 1 to the United Kingdom Act[1] is liable to be registered shall, if he has an establishment both in the United Kingdom and in the Isle of Man or does not have an establishment in either country, be registered either under Part I of the United Kingdom Act or under Part I of the Manx Act, as the Commissioners shall determine, but unless or until the Commissioners determine that such a person shall be registered under Part I of the Manx Act, he shall be required to be registered under Part I of the United Kingdom Act.
(3) Paragraphs 3, 5 and 6 of Schedule 1 to the United Kingdom Act[2] shall not apply to a person registered or required to be registered under Part I of the Manx Act.
(4) The Commissioners may determine that any person to whom paragraph 3, 5 or 6 of Schedule 1 to the United Kingdom Act[2] applies shall be registered under Part I of the Manx Act.
(5) Where a person, who is or was required to notify the Commissioners under paragraph 3, 5 or 6 of Schedule 1 to the United Kingdom Act,[2] has an establishment in the Isle of Man, he may notify the Isle of Man Finance Board and such notification shall be deemed for the purposes of that paragraph to be notification to the Commissioners.
(6) Any person, registered under Part I of the United Kingdom Act on or after 1st April 1980, who—
(*a*) has no establishment in the Isle of Man, or
(*b*) is the representative member of a group of bodies corporate, within the meaning of section 21 of the United Kingdom Act,[3] no member of which has an establishment in the Isle of Man,
shall notify the Commissioners if, at any later time, he or any member of the group has such an establishment and such notification shall be treated for the purposes of Schedule 1 to the United Kingdom Act and any regulations made thereunder as an event which could necessitate the cancellation of that person's, or that group of bodies corporate's, registration.
(7) Where a person, who is registered under Part I of the United Kingdom Act, has establishments both in the United Kingdom and in the Isle of Man, or does not have an establishment in either country, the Commissioners may, at any time, determine that he shall be registered under Part I of the Manx Act.
(8) Where the Commissioners determine that a person, who is registered under Part I of the United Kingdom Act, shall be registered under Part I of the Manx Act, he shall cease to be, or required to be, registered under Part I of the United Kingdom Act from such date as they may determine, but, for the purposes of paragraph 7 of Schedule 2 to the United Kingdom Act,[4] he shall not cease to be a taxable person.
(9) Where a person, who is registered under Part I of the Manx Act, has establishments both in the United Kingdom and in the Isle of Man or does not have an establishment in either country, the Commissioners may, at any time, determine that he shall be registered under Part I of the United Kingdom Act and, if they so determine, they shall register him with effect from such date as they may determine.
(10) Where a person who was registered under Part I of the Manx Act is, pursuant to a determination of the Commissioners to that effect, registered under Part I of the United Kingdom Act, any amount of value added tax required to be paid under Part I of the Manx Act shall be deemed to have been an amount of tax due under Part I of the United Kingdom Act.
(11) Section 18(1) of the Finance (No 2) Act 1975[5] shall not apply where the person to whom the supply is made is registered under Part I of the Manx Act.

Notes—[1] VATA 1994 Sch 1 para 1.
[2] VATA 1994 Sch 1 paras 5–8.
[3] VATA 1994 s 43.
[4] VATA 1994 Sch 4 para 8.
[5] VATA s 22.

12—(1) For the purposes of Articles 10 and 11 above a person shall be deemed to have an establishment in a country if—
(*a*) there is a place in that country from which he carries on a business; or
(*b*) he carries on business through a branch or agent in that country.
(2) For the purposes of paragraph (1) above an agent is a person who has the authority or capacity to create legal relations between his principal and a third party.

13 In section 8(8)(*bb*) of the United Kingdom Act the words "under either of those Parts" are hereby repealed.

14 This Order revokes—
(*a*) the Value Added Tax (Isle of Man) Order 1980, except so much of it as relates to the Rules, Regulations and Orders specified in Schedule 2 to that Order; and
(*b*) so much of the Value Added Tax (Isle of Man) (No 2) Order 1980 as relates to the amendment of the Finance Act 1972
and accordingly the Finance Acts amended by those Orders shall have effect as if the Orders had not been made.

1982/1068

VALUE ADDED TAX (ISLE OF MAN) (NO 2) ORDER 1982

Made under the Isle of Man Act 1979 s 6

Made ....*30 July 1982*
Coming into Operation ....*1 October 1982*

1—(1) This Order may be cited as the Value Added Tax (Isle of Man) (No 2) Order 1982 and shall come into operation on 1st October 1982.

(2) In this Order—

"the United Kingdom Act" means the Finance Act 1972[a] and "the Manx Act" means the Value Added Tax and Other Taxes Act 1973

and any other word or expression used in this Order to which meaning is given in or under Part I of the United Kingdom Act shall have, except where the context otherwise requires, the same meaning in this Order as in or under that Part of that Act.

(3) For the purposes of this Order, the Interpretation Act 1978 shall apply to the Manx Act and to any instrument of a legislative character made thereunder as if the Manx Act were an Act of Parliament.

Notes—[a] VATA 1994.

2 In statutory instruments made under Part I of the United Kingdom Act references to the United Kingdom shall be construed as including references to the Isle of Man.

3 In the statutory instruments referred to in column 1 of the Schedule to this Order, the word or expression appearing in column 2 thereof shall, to the extent prescribed therein, be construed as including references to their equivalents specified in column 3, whether or not the same word or expression is used in their equivalents in the Manx Act or regulations made thereunder.

4 Regulation 51(4) of the Value Added Tax (General) Regulations 1980 shall not apply to a person determined by the Commissioners under paragraph (7) or (8) of Article 11 of the Value Added Tax (Isle of Man) Order 1982 to be required to be registered under Part I of the Manx Act.

5 Article 2(*a*) of the Tribunals and Inquiries (Value Added Tax Tribunals) Order 1972 and Rule 30(2) of the Value Added Tax Tribunals Rules 1972 shall have effect as if the words "England and Wales" included the Isle of Man.

6 This Order revokes—

(*a*) so much of the Value Added Tax (Isle of Man) Order 1980 as relates to the Rules, Regulations and Orders specified in Schedule 2 to that Order;

(*b*) so much of the Value Added Tax (Isle of Man) (No 2) Order 1980 as relates to the Order specified in the Schedule to that Order; and

(*c*) the Value Added Tax (Isle of Man) (No 3) Order 1980,

and accordingly the instruments amended by those Orders shall have effect as if the Orders had not been made.

SCHEDULE

Article 3

Column 1	Column 2	Column 3
STATUTORY INSTRUMENT	WORDS	MANX EQUIVALENT
The Value Added Tax (Treatment of Transactions) (No 1) Order 1973		
In Article 3(*a*)	"taxable person"	a person defined as such in section 2(2) of the Manx Act
The Value Added Tax (Do-it-yourself Builders) (Relief) Regulations 1975		
In Regulation 1(2)	"value added tax"	value added tax chargeable under Part I of the Manx Act
The Value Added Tax (Bad Debt Relief) Regulations 1978		
In Regulation 4(*b*)(i)	"invoice"	a document defined as such in section 30(2) of the Manx Act

	"Regulations"	the corresponding provisions made under the Manx Act
The Value Added Tax (Cars) Order 1980		
In Article 4(1)	"Tax"	value added tax chargeable under Part I of the Manx Act
	"taxable person", where secondly occurring	a person defined as such in section 2(2) of the Manx Act
In Article 5(2)(*b*)	"tax",	value added tax chargeable under Part I of the Manx Act
In Article 6(1)(*b*)	"tax", where secondly occurring	value added tax chargeable under Part I of the Manx Act
In Article 6(1)(*c*)	"tax", where first occurring	
In Article 6(2)(*c*)	"tax", wherever occurring	
The Value Added Tax (General) Regulations 1980		
In Regulation 8(1)	"taxable person", where secondly occurring	a person defined as such in section 2(2) of the Manx Act
In Regulation 8(3)	"taxable person", where secondly occurring	a person defined as such in section 2(2) of the Manx Act
	"regulation"	the corresponding provision made under the Manx Act
In Regulation 10(1)	"taxable person", where secondly occurring	a person defined as such in section 2(2) of the Manx Act
In Regulations 14 and 15	"the Act"	the corresponding provision of the Manx Act
	"invoice"	a document defined as such in section 30(2) of the Manx Act
In Regulations 16(1)(*b*) and 17	"invoice"	a document defined as such in section 30(2) of the Manx Act
In Regulation 18(1)	"invoice"	a document defined as such in section 30(2) of the Manx Act
In Regulation 18(2)	"invoice", wherever occurring	a document defined as such in section 30(2) of the Manx Act
In Regulation 18(2)(*b*)	"tax"	value added tax chargeable under Part I of the Manx Act
In Regulation 18(2)(*c*)	"tax", where first occurring	
In Regulations 19, 20, 21 and 22	"invoice"	a document defined as such in section 30(2) of the Manx Act
In Regulation 29(1)	"tax", where secondly occurring	value added tax chargeable under Part I of the Manx Act
In Regulation 29(2)	"tax", where first occurring	
In Regulation 29(4)	"tax"	
In Regulation 30(5)	"registered person"	a person defined as such in regulations made under the Manx Act

VAT SIs

In Regulation 33	"taxable person", wherever occurring	a person defined as such in section 2(2) of the Manx Act
	"tax"	value added tax chargeable under Part I of the Manx Act
In Regulation 33(*a*)	"the Act"	the corresponding provisions of the Manx Act
In Regulation 33(*b*)	"registration number", wherever occurring	a number defined as such in regulations made under the Manx Act
In Regulation 33(*a*) and 33(*b*)	"Commissioners"	the Isle of Man Finance Board
In Regulation 34	"tax"	value added tax chargeable under Part I of the Manx Act
	"taxable person"	a person defined as such in section 2(2) of the Manx Act
	"registration number"	a number defined as such in regulations made under the Manx Act
In Regulation 39(*a*)	"taxable person"	a person defined as such in section 2(2) of the Manx Act
In Regulation 39(*c*)(i)	"tax", where secondly occurring	value added tax chargeable under Part I of the Manx Act
	"tax", where first occurring	
	"the Act"	the Manx Act
In Regulation 40(1)(*a*)	"tax", where secondly occurring	value added tax chargeable under Part I of the Manx Act
In Regulation 42	"port", "airport" or "depot", wherever occurring	a place in the Isle of Man corresponding to such a port, airport or depot
In Regulation 55(1)	"proper officer", wherever occurring	a person defined as such in regulations made under the Manx Act
	"tax", where secondly occurring	value added tax chargeable under Part I of the Manx Act
In Regulation 55(1)(*a*)	"registered person"	a person defined as such in regulations made under the Manx Act
	"regulation 8"	the corresponding provision made under the Manx Act
In Regulation 55(1)(*c*) and 55(1)(*d*)	"tax", wherever occurring	value added tax chargeable under Part I of the Manx Act
In Regulation 58(1)	"tax", wherever occurring	value added tax chargeable under Part I of the Manx Act
	"the Act", where first occurring	the Manx Act
	"the Act", where secondly occurring	the corresponding provision of the Manx Act
In Regulation 59(*a*)	"tax", wherever occurring	value added tax chargeable under Part I of the Manx Act
	"Act"	the Manx Act

In Regulation 59(*c*), 59(*e*), 59(*f*) and 59(*g*)	"tax", wherever occurring	value added tax chargeable under Part I of the Manx Act
The Value Added Tax (Repayment to Community Traders) Regulations 1980		
In Regulation 3	"tax", where firstly and secondly occurring	value added tax chargeable under Part I of the Manx Act
In Regulation 4(*b*)(ii)	"tax"	
	"section 8B of the Act"	Section 8B of the Manx Act
In Regulation 6(1)	"tax", wherever occurring	value added tax chargeable under Part I of the Manx Act
In Regulation 7(1)	"tax", where firstly and secondly occurring	value added tax chargeable under Part I of the Manx Act
In Regulation 7(1)(*b*)(ii)	"section 3 of the Act"	Section 3 of the Manx Act
In Regulations 8 and 12	"tax", wherever occurring	value added tax chargeable under Part I of the Manx Act

1984/746

VALUE ADDED TAX (IMPORTED GOODS) RELIEF ORDER 1984

Made by the Treasury under VATA 1983 ss 19(1) and 45(1) and (2) (see now VATA 1994 ss 37(1), 97(1), (5))

Made . . . . *23 May 1984*
Laid before the House of Commons . . . . *5 June 1984*
Coming into Operation . . . . *1 July 1984*

1 Citation and commencement

This Order may be cited as the Value Added Tax (Imported Goods) Relief Order 1984 and shall come into operation on 1st July 1984.

2 Interpretation

(1) In this Order—

["abroad" means a place outside the member States;][3]

"alcoholic beverages" means beverages falling within headings 22.03 to [22.08][2];

"approved" means approved by the Secretary of State;

["exported" means exported to a place outside the member States and "exportation" shall be construed accordingly;][3]

["sent" means sent from a place outside the member States;][3]

["third country" means a place outside the member States;][3]

"tobacco products" has the same meaning as in section 1 of the Tobacco Products Duty Act 1979.

(2) In this Order, references to a heading or sub-heading are references to a heading or sub-heading of the [Combined Nomenclature][1] of the European Economic Community.

(3) Section 48(4) of the Value Added Tax Act 1983[a] (definition of "document" etc) shall not apply for the purposes of this Order.

[(4) Except where it appears in Article 3(2) "import" means import from a place outside the member States and "importation" and "imported" shall be construed accordingly.

(5) Except where it appears in Note (3) to Group 7 of Schedule 2, for "United Kingdom" there shall be substituted "member States".][3]

Notes—

[a] VATA 1994 s 96(6), (7).

[1] Words in para (2) substituted by the VAT (Imported Goods) Relief (Amendment) (No 2) Order, SI 1987/2108 art 3 with effect from 1 January 1988.

[2] Figure substituted for the figure "22.09" by the VAT (Imported Goods) Relief (Amendment) Order, SI 1988/1193 with effect from 1 August 1988.

[3] Definition of "abroad" in para (1) substituted and definitions of "exported", "exportation", "sent" and "third country" and paras (4), (5) inserted by the VAT (Imported Goods) Relief (Amendment) Order, SI 1992/3120 arts 1–3 with effect from 1 January 1993.

3 Application

(1) This Order shall apply without prejudice to relief from tax on the importation of goods afforded under or by virtue of any other enactment.

[(2) Nothing in this Order shall be construed as authorising a person to import anything from a place outside or within the member States in contravention of any prohibition or restriction for the time being in force with respect thereto under or by virtue of any enactment.][1]

Amendments—[1] Para (2) substituted by the VAT (Imported Goods) Relief (Amendment) Order, SI 1992/3120 arts 1, 2, 4 with effect from 1 January 1993.

4 Relief for United Nations goods

No tax shall be payable on the importation, for whatever purpose, of goods produced by the United Nations or by a United Nations organisation, being goods—

(*a*) of a description specified in Part I of Schedule 1 to this Order, or

(*b*) classified under any heading or sub-heading specified in column 1 of Part II of Schedule 1 to this Order and within the limits of relief specified in column 2 thereof in relation to such heading or sub-heading.

5 Relief for goods of other descriptions

(1) Subject to the provisions of this Order, no tax shall be payable on the importation of goods of a description specified in any item in Schedule 2 to this Order.

(2) Schedule 2 shall be interpreted in accordance with the notes therein contained, except that the descriptions of Groups in that Schedule are for ease of reference only and shall not affect the interpretation of the descriptions of items in those Groups.

6 Condition as to use or purpose of goods in Schedule 2

(1) Where relief has been afforded in respect of any goods by virtue of an item comprised in Schedule 2 which describes the goods by reference to a use or purpose, it shall be a condition of the relief that the goods are put to such use or the purpose fulfilled in the United Kingdom.

(2) Without prejudice to paragraph (1) above, where relief has been afforded by virtue of item 5, 6 or 7 of Group 3 of Schedule 2 in respect of goods for demonstration or use, it shall be a condition of the relief that, in the course of, or as a result of, such demonstration or use, the goods are consumed or destroyed or rendered incapable of being used again for the same purpose.

(3) Without prejudice to paragraph (1) above, where relief has been afforded by virtue of item 1 of Group 4 of Schedule 2 in respect of goods for examination, analysis or testing, the relief shall be subject to the following conditions:

(*a*) the examination, analysis or testing shall be completed within such time as the Commissioners may require; and

(*b*) any goods not completely used up or destroyed in the course of, or as a result of, such examination, analysis or testing, and any products resulting therefrom, shall forthwith be destroyed or rendered commercially worthless, or exported.

Note—The words "member States" substituted by the words "United Kingdom" with effect from 1 January 1993 by art 2(5) above.

7 Restriction on disposal of goods in Schedule 2, Group 6

(1) Without prejudice to article 6(1) above and subject to paragraph (2) below, where relief is afforded in respect of any goods by virtue of Group 6 of Schedule 2, it shall be a condition of the relief that the goods are not lent, hired-out or transferred, except in accordance with the provisions of that Group relating to those goods.

(2) Paragraph (1) above shall not apply and relief shall continue to be afforded where goods are lent, hired-out or transferred to an organisation which would be entitled to relief by virtue of Group 6 of Schedule 2, if importing the goods on that date, on condition that—

(*a*) prior notification in writing is received by the Commissioners; and

(*b*) the goods are used solely in accordance with the provisions of Group 6 relating thereto.

8 Supplementary provisions as to goods in Schedule 2, Group 6

Where any goods in respect of which relief has been afforded by virtue of Group 6 of Schedule 2—

(*a*) are to be lent, hired-out, transferred or used except in accordance with the provisions of this Order relating to those goods; or

(*b*) remain in the possession of an organisation which has ceased to fulfil any condition subject to which it is approved,

and written notification thereof is given to the Commissioners, the tax payable on the goods shall be determined as if the goods had been imported on the date when the tax becomes due, provided that where the amount of the tax first relieved is less, such lesser amount shall become payable.

9 Revocation

The Value Added Tax (Imported Goods) Relief (No 1) Order 1973 and the Value Added Tax (Health) Order 1983 are hereby revoked.

SCHEDULE 1

RELIEF FOR GOODS PRODUCED BY THE UNITED NATIONS OR A UNITED NATIONS ORGANISATION

Article 4

PART I

1 Holograms for laser projection.

2 Multi-media kits.

3 Materials for programmed instruction, including materials in kit form, with the corresponding printed materials.

[PART II

Column 1 Heading or sub-heading	Column 2 Limits of Relief
370400 10	Limited to films of an educational, scientific or cultural character.
37 05	Limited to films of an educational, scientific or cultural character.
370690 51	Limited to newsreels (with or without soundtrack) depicting events of current news value at the time of importation and, in the case of each importer, not exceeding two copies of each subject for copying.
370610 99	
370690 91	Limited to—
370690 99	(i) archival film material (with our without soundtrack) intended for use in connection with newsreel films; (ii) recreational film particularly suited for children and young people, and (iii) other films of an educational, scientific or cultural character.
49 11	Limited to— (i) microcards or other information storage media required in computerised information and documentation services of an educational, scientific or cultural character; and (ii) wall charts designed solely for demonstration and education.
85 24	Limited to those of an educational, scientific or cultural character.
90 23	Limited to— (i) patterns, models and wall charts of an educational, scientific or cultural character, designed solely for demonstration and education; and (ii) mock-ups or visualisations of abstract concepts such as molecular structures or mathematical formulae.][1]

Amendments—

[1] Pt II substituted by the VAT (Imported Goods) Relief (Amendment) (No 2) Order, SI 1987/2108 art 4 with effect from 1 January 1988.

SCHEDULE 2

RELIEF FOR GOODS OF OTHER DESCRIPTIONS

Article 5

GROUP 1

CAPITAL GOODS AND EQUIPMENT ON TRANSFER OF ACTIVITIES

Item No

1 Capital goods and equipment imported by a person for the purposes of a business he has ceased to carry on abroad and which he has notified the Commissions is to be carried on by him in the United Kingdom and concerned exclusively with making taxable supplies.

2 . . . [1]

Notes:

(1) "Capital goods and equipment" includes livestock other than livestock in the possession of dealers, but does not include—

(*a*) food of a kind used for human consumption or animal feeding stuffs;

(*b*) fuel;

(*c*) stocks of raw materials and finished or semi-finished products; or

(*d*) any motor vehicle in respect of which deduction of input tax is disallowed by article 4 of the Value Added Tax (Cars) Order 1980.

(2) For the purposes of item 1, a person is not to be treated as intending to carry on a business in the United Kingdom if such business is to be merged with, or absorbed by, another business already carried on there.

(3) Item 1 applies only where the goods—

(*a*) have been used in the course of the business for at least twelve months before it ceased to be carried on abroad;

(*b*) are imported within twelve months of the date on which such business ceased to be carried on abroad, or within such longer period as the Commissioners allow; and

(*c*) are appropriate both to the nature and size of the business to be carried on in the United Kingdom.

(4) . . . [1]

Note—The words "member states" substituted by the words "United Kingdom" with effect from 1 January 1993 by art 2(5) above.

Amendments—[1] Item 2 and Note (4) revoked by the VAT (Imported Goods) Relief (Amendment) Order, SI 1992/3120 arts 1, 2, 5(*a*) with effect from 1 January 1993.

GROUP 2
AGRICULTURE AND ANIMALS

Amendments—Group 2 revoked by the VAT (Imported Goods) Relief (Amendment) Order, SI 1992/3120 arts 1, 2, 5(*a*) with effect from 1 January 1993.

GROUP 3
PROMOTION OF TRADE

Item No

1 Articles of no intrinsic commercial value sent free of charge by suppliers of goods and services for the sole purpose of advertising.

2 Samples of negligible value of a kind and in quantities capable of being used solely for soliciting orders for goods of the same kind.

[3 Printed advertising matter, including catalogues, price lists, directions for use or brochures, which relates to goods for sale or hire by a person established outside the United Kingdom, . . . [2], or to transport, commercial insurance or banking services offered by a person established in a third country, and which clearly displays the name of the person by whom such goods or services are offered.][1]

4 Goods to be distributed free of charge at an event, as small representative samples, for use or consumption by the public.

5 Goods imported solely for the purpose of being demonstrated at an event.

6 Goods imported solely for the purpose of being used in the demonstration of any machine or apparatus displayed at an event.

7 Paints, varnishes, wallpaper and other materials of low value to be used in the building, fitting-out and decoration of a temporary stand at an event.

8 Catalogues, prospectuses, price lists, advertising posters, calendars (whether or not illustrated) unframed photographs and other printed matter or articles advertising goods displayed at an event, supplied without charge for the purpose of distribution free of charge to the public at such event.

Notes:

(1) Where the Commissioners so require, item 2 applies only to goods which are rendered permanently unusable, except as samples, by being torn, perforated, clearly and indelibly marked, or by any other process.

(2) [Save in the case of imported printed matter intended for distribution free of charge and relating to either goods for sale or hire . . . [2], item 3 does not apply to—][1]

(*a*) any consignment containing two or more copies of different documents;

(*b*) any consignment containing two or more copies of the same document, unless the total gross weight of such consignment does not exceed one kilogram; or

(*c*) any goods which are the subject of grouped consignments from the same consignor to the same consignee.

(3) "Event" means any of the following—

(*a*) any trade, industrial, agricultural or craft exhibition, fair or similar show or display, not being an exhibition, fair, show or display organised for private purposes in a shop or on business premises with a view to the sale of the goods displayed;

(*b*) any exhibition or meeting which is primarily organised—

(i) for a charitable purpose, or

(ii) to promote any branch of learning, art, craft, sport or scientific, technical, educational, cultural or trade union activity, or tourism, or

(iii) to promote friendship between peoples, or

(iv) to promote religious knowledge or worship;

(*c*) any meeting of representatives of any international organisation or international group of organisations; and

(*d*) any representative meeting or ceremony of an official or commemorative character.

(4) In item 4, "representative samples" means goods which are—

(*a*) imported free of charge or obtained at such event from goods imported in bulk;

(*b*) identifiable as advertising samples of low value;

(*c*) not easily marketable and, where appropriate, packaged in quantities which are less than the lowest quantity of the same goods as marketed; and

(*d*) intended to be consumed at such event, where the goods comprise foodstuffs or beverages not packaged as described in paragraph (*c*) above.

(5) Items 4, 5 and 6 do not apply to fuels, alcoholic beverages or tobacco products.

(6) Items 4 to 8 apply only where the aggregate value and quantity thereof is appropriate to the nature of the event, the number of visitors and the extent of the exhibitor's participation in it.

Note—The words "member States" substituted by the words "United Kingdom" with effect from 1 January 1993 by art 2(5) above.

Amendments—[1] Item 3 and words at the beginning of Note (2) substituted by the VAT (Imported Goods) Relief (Amendment) (No 2) Order, SI 1988/2212 art 4 with effect from 1 January 1989.

[2] Words in item 3 and Note (2) deleted by the VAT (Imported Goods) Relief (Amendment) Order, SI 1992/3120 arts, 1, 2, 5 with effect from 1 January 1993.

GROUP 4
GOODS FOR TESTING, ETC

Item No

1 Goods imported for the purpose of examination, analysis or testing to determine their composition, quality or other technical characteristics, to provide information or for industrial or commercial research.

Note:

Item 1 does not apply to goods exceeding the quantities necessary for such purposes or where the examination, analysis or testing, itself constitutes a sales promotion.

GROUP 5
HEALTH

Item No

1 Animals specially prepared for laboratory use and sent free of charge to a relevant establishment.

2 . . .[2]

3 Biological or chemical substances sent to a relevant establishment from [a place outside the member States][2].

4 Human blood.

5 Products for therapeutic purposes, derived from human blood.

6 Human (including foetal) organs or tissue for diagnostic or therapeutic purposes or medical research.

7 Reagents for use in blood type grouping or for the detection of blood grouping incompatibilities, by approved institutions or laboratories, exclusively for non-commercial medical or scientific purposes.

8 Reagents for use in the determination of human tissue types by approved institutions or laboratories, exclusively for non-commercial medical or scientific purposes.

9 Pharmaceutical products imported by or on behalf of persons or animals for their use while visiting the United Kingdom to participate in an international sporting event.

[10 Samples of reference substances approved by the World Health Organisation for the quality control of materials used in the manufacture of medicinal products.][1]

Notes:

(1) In items 1, . . .[2] and 3, "relevant establishment" means—

(*a*) a public establishment, or a department of such establishment, principally engaged in education or scientific research; or

(*b*) a private establishment so engaged, which is approved.

(2) Item 3 applies only where the goods fulfil the conditions laid down under or by virtue of [Article 60][1] of Council Regulation (EEC) No 918/83.

(3) Items 4, 5, 6, 7 and 8 include special packaging essential for transport of the goods and any solvents or accessories necessary for their use.

(4) In items 7 and 8, "reagents" means all reagents, whether of human, animal, plant, or other, origin.

[(5) Item 10 applies only to samples addressed to consignees authorised to receive them free of tax.][2]

Note—The words "member States" substituted by the words "United Kingdom" with effect from 1 January 1993 by art 2(5) above.

Amendments—[1] Item 10 and Note (5) added and words in Note (2) substituted by the VAT (Imported Goods) Relief (Amendment) (No 2) Order, SI 1988/2212 art 5 with effect from 1 January 1989.

[2] Words in item 3 substituted and Item 2 and figure in Note (1) revoked by the VAT (Imported Goods) Relief (Amendment) Order SI 1992/3120 arts 1, 2, 5 with effect from 1 January 1993.

GROUP 6
CHARITIES, ETC

Item No

1 Basic necessities obtained without charge for distribution free of charge to the needy by a relevant organisation.

2 Goods donated by a person established abroad to a relevant organisation for use to raise funds at occasional charity events for the benefit of the needy.

3 Equipment and office materials donated by a person established abroad to a relevant organisation for meeting its operating needs or carrying out its charitable aims.

4 Goods imported by a relevant organisation for distribution or loan, free of charge, to victims of a disaster affecting the territory of one or more member States.

5 Goods imported by a relevant organisation for meeting its operating needs in the relief of a disaster affecting the territory of one or more member States.

6 Articles donated to and imported by a relevant organisation for supply to blind or other physically or mentally handicapped persons and which are specially designed for the education, employment or social advancement of such persons.

7 Spare parts, components or accessories for any article of a kind mentioned in item 6, including tools for its maintenance, checking, calibration or repair.

Notes:

(1) In items 1 to 5, "relevant organisation" means a State organisation or other approved charitable or philanthropic organisation.

(2) In item 1, "basic necessities" means food, medicines, clothing, blankets, orthopaedic equipment and crutches, required to meet a person's immediate needs.

(3) Items 1, 2 and 3 do not include alcoholic beverages, tobacco products, coffee, tea or motor vehicles other than ambulances.

(4) Items 2, 3 and 6 do not apply where there is any commercial intent on the part of the donor.

(5) Items 4 and 5 apply only where the Commission of the European Communities has made a Decision authorising importation of the goods.

(6) In item 6, "relevant organisation" means an approved organisation principally engaged in the education of, or the provision of assistance to, blind or other physically or mentally handicapped persons.

(7) In item 6, "supply" means any loan, hiring-out or transfer, for consideration or free of charge, other than on a profit-making basis.

(8) Item 7 applies only where the goods are imported with an article of a kind mentioned in item 6 to which they relate, or, if imported subsequently, are identifiable as being intended for that article, where relief from tax on that article has been afforded by virtue of item 6, or would have been so afforded if such article were imported with the goods which relate to it.

GROUP 7
PRINTED MATTER, ETC

Item No

1 Documents sent free of charge to public services in the United Kingdom.

2 Foreign government publications and publications of official international bodies intended for free distribution.

3 Ballot papers for elections organised by bodies abroad.

4 Specimen signatures and printed circulars concerning signatures, forming part of exchanges of information between bankers or public services.

5 Official printed matter sent to a Central Bank in the United Kingdom.

6 Documents sent by companies incorporated abroad to bearers of, or subscribers to, securities issued by such companies.

7 Files, archives and other documents for use at international meetings, conferences or congresses and reports of such gatherings.

8 Plans, technical drawings, traced designs and other documents sent by any person for the purpose of participating in a competition in the United Kingdom or to obtain or fulfil an order executed abroad.

9 Documents to be used in examinations held in the United Kingdom on behalf of institutions established abroad.

10 Printed forms to be used as official documents in the international movement of vehicles or goods pursuant to international conventions.

11 Printed forms, labels, tickets and similar documents sent to travel agents in the United Kingdom by transport and tourist undertakings abroad.

12 Used commercial documents.

13 Official printed forms from national or international authorities.

14 Printed matter conforming to international standards, for distribution by an association in the United Kingdom and sent by a corresponding association abroad.

15 Documents sent for the purpose of free distribution to encourage persons to visit foreign countries, in particular to attend cultural, tourist, sporting, religious, trade or professional meetings or events.

16 Foreign hotel lists and yearbooks published by or on behalf of official tourist agencies and timetables for foreign transport services, for free distribution.

17 Yearbooks, lists of telephone and telex numbers, hotel lists, catalogues for fairs, specimens of craft goods of negligible value and literature on museums, universities, spas or other similar establishments, supplied as reference material to accredited representatives or correspondents appointed by official national tourist agencies and not intended for distribution.

[18 Official publications issued under the authority of the country of exportation, international institutions, regional or local authorities and bodies governed by public law established in the country of exportation.][1]

[19 Printed matter distributed by foreign political organisations on the occasion of elections to the European Parliament or national elections in the country in which the printed matter originates.][1]

Notes:

[(1) Items 15 and 16 do not apply where the goods contain more than 25 per cent of private commercial advertising.][1]

[(2) Items 18 and 19 apply only to publications or printed matter on which value added tax or any other tax has been paid in the third country from which they have been exported and which have not benefited, by virtue of their exportation, from any relief from payment thereof.][2]

[(3) In Item 19, "foreign political organisations" means those which are officially recognised as such in the United Kingdom.][1]

[(4) In Item 11 "travel agent" includes airlines, national railway undertakings, ferry operators and similar organisations.

(5) In Items 2, 15, 16 and 19 "foreign" means from a country other than the United Kingdom.][2]

Note—Except where it appears in Note (3) above, the words "member States" substituted by the words "United Kingdom" with effect from 1 January 1993 by art 2(5) above.

Amendments—[1] Items 18 and 19 added and Notes (1)–(3) substituted for the original Note by the VAT (Imported Goods) Relief (Amendment) (No 2) Order, SI 1988/2212 art 6 with effect from 1 January 1989.

[2] Note (2) substituted and Notes (4), (5) inserted by the VAT (Imported Goods) Relief (Amendment) Order, SI 1992/3120 arts 1, 2, 5 with effect from 1 January 1993.

GROUP 8

ARTICLES SENT FOR MISCELLANEOUS PURPOSES

Item No

1 Material relating to trademarks, patterns or designs and supporting documents and applications for patents, imported for the purpose of being submitted to bodies competent to deal with protection of copyright or industrial or commercial patent rights.

2 Objects imported for the purpose of being submitted as evidence, or for a like purpose, to a court or other official body in the United Kingdom.

3 Photographs, slides and stereotype mats for photographs, whether or not captioned, sent to press agencies and publishers of newspapers or magazines.

4 Recorded media, including punched cards, sound recordings and microfilm, sent free of charge for the transmission of information.

5 Any honorary decoration conferred by a government or Head of State abroad on a person resident in the United Kingdom and imported on his behalf.

6 Any cup, medal or similar article of an essentially symbolic nature, intended as a tribute to activities in the arts, sciences, sport, or the public service, or in recognition of merit at a particular event, which is either—

(*a*) donated by an authority or person established abroad for the purpose of being presented in the United Kingdom, or

(*b*) awarded abroad to a person resident in the United Kingdom and imported on his behalf.

7 Goods (other than alcoholic beverages or tobacco products) sent on an occasional basis as gifts in token of friendship or goodwill between bodies, public authorities or groups carrying on an activity in the public interest.

8 Any consignment of goods (other than alcoholic beverages, tobacco products, perfumes or toilet waters) not exceeding [£15][2] in value, . . . [1]

[9 Awards, trophies and souvenirs of a symbolic nature and of limited value intended for distribution free of charge at business conferences or similar events to persons normally resident in a country other than the United Kingdom.][1]

Notes:

[(1)] [3] Items 5, 6, 7 and 9 do not apply to any importation of a commercial character.][1]

[(2) Item 8 does not apply in relation to any goods imported on mail order from the Channel Islands.

(3) For the purposes of note (2)—

"mail order" in relation to any goods means any transaction or series of transactions under which a seller (S) sends goods in fulfilment of an order placed remotely,

"remotely" means by any means that do not involve the simultaneous physical presence of S and the person placing the order, and

"seller" does not include any person acting otherwise than in a commercial or professional capacity.][3]

Note—The words "member States" substituted by the words "United Kingdom" with effect from 1 January 1993 by art 2(5) above.

Simon's Tax Cases item 8, *R (on the application of the Minsitry for Economic Development of the States of Jersey) v R&C Comrs; R (on the application of the States of Guernsey) v HM Treasury and anor* [2012] EWHC 7128 (Admin), [2012] STC 1113.

Amendments—[1] Words in item 8 repealed, item 9 added and Note substituted by the VAT (Imported Goods) Relief (Amendment) (No 2) Order, SI 1988/2212 art 7 with effect from 1 January 1989.

[2] In item 8, "£15" substituted for previous value "£18" by FA 2011 s 77(1) with effect in relation to goods imported on or after 1 November 2011. This amendment is without prejudice to any power to amend this Schedule by subordinate legislation (FA 2011 s 77(2)).

[3] Note (1) numbered as such by FA 2012 s 199 with effect in relation to goods imported on or after 1 April 2012. This amendment is made without prejudice to any power to amend this Schedule by subordinate legislation (FA 2012 s 199(4)).

[4] Notes (2), (3) substituted by the VAT (Imported Goods) Relief (Amendment) Order, SI 2014/2364 art 2 with effect in relation to goods imported on or after 26 September 2014.

GROUP 9
WORKS OF ART AND COLLECTORS' PIECES

Item No

1 Works of art and collectors' pieces imported by approved museums, galleries or other institutions for a purpose other than sale.

Note: Item 1 applies only where the goods are—

(*a*) of an educational, scientific or cultural character; and

(*b*) imported free of charge or, if for a consideration, are not supplied to the importer in the course or furtherance of any business.

[GROUP 10
TRANSPORT][1]

[Item No

1 Fuel contained in the standard tanks of a vehicle or of a special container, for use exclusively by such vehicle or such special container.

2 Fuel, not exceeding 10 litres for each vehicle, contained in portable tanks carried by a vehicle, for use exclusively by such vehicle.

3 Lubricants contained in a vehicle, for use exclusively by such vehicle.

4 Litter, fodder and feeding stuffs contained in any means of transport carrying animals, for the use of such animals during their journey.

5 Disposable packings for the stowage and protection of goods during their transportation to the United Kingdom.

Notes:

(1) "Standard tanks" means any of the following—

(*a*) tanks permanently fitted to a vehicle and which are fitted to all vehicles of that type by the manufacturer, to supply directly fuel for the purpose of propulsion and, where appropriate, for the operation, during transport, of refrigeration systems and other systems;

(*b*) gas tanks fitted to vehicles designed for the direct use of gas as a fuel;

(*c*) tanks fitted to ancillary systems with which a vehicle is equipped; and

(*d*) tanks permanently fitted to a special container and which are fitted to all special containers of that type by the manufacturer, to supply directly fuel for the operation, during transport, of refrigeration systems and other systems with which special containers are equipped.

(2) "Vehicle" means any motor road vehicle.

(3) "Special container" means any container fitted with specially designed apparatus for refrigeration systems, oxygenation systems, thermal insulation systems and other systems.

(4) Item 2 does not apply in the case of any special purpose vehicle or a vehicle which, by its type of construction and equipment, is designed for and capable of transporting goods or more than nine persons including the driver.

(5) Item 3 applies only to lubricants necessary for the normal operation of the vehicle during its journey.

(6) Item 5 applies only where the cost of the packings is included in the consideration for the goods transported.][1]

Note—The words "member States" substituted by the words "United Kingdom" with effect from 1 January 1993 by art 2(5) above.

Amendments—[1] This group substituted by the VAT (Imported Goods) Relief (Amendment) (No 2) Order, SI 1988/2212 art 8 with effect from 1 January 1989.

GROUP 11

WAR GRAVES, FUNERALS, ETC

Item No

1 Goods imported by an approved organisation for use in the construction, upkeep or ornamentation of cemeteries, tombs and memorials in the United Kingdom which commemorate war victims of other countries.

2 Coffins containing human remains.

3 Urns containing human ashes.

4 Flowers, wreaths and other ornamental objects accompanying goods described in items 2 or 3.

5 Flowers, wreaths and other ornamental objects, imported without any commercial intent by a person resident abroad, for use at a funeral or to decorate a grave.

Note—The words "member States" substituted by the words "United Kingdom" with effect from 1 January 1993 by art 2(5).

Concession ESC 2.6—American war graves.

1984/1176

CONTROL OF MOVEMENT OF GOODS REGULATIONS 1984

Made by the Commissioners of Customs and Excise under the Customs and Excise Management Act 1979 s 31 and all other enabling powers

Made . . . . *1 August 1984*

Laid before Parliament . . . . *3 August 1984*

Coming into Operation . . . . *6 August 1984*

1 Citation and commencement

These Regulations may be cited as the Control of Movement of Goods Regulations 1984 and shall come into operation on 6th August 1984.

2 Revocation

The Control of Movement of Goods Regulations 1981 are hereby revoked.

3 Interpretation

In these Regulations—

"the Act" means the Customs and Excise Management Act 1979;

"approved place"—

(*a*) in relation to imported goods means a place approved by the Commissioners under section 20 or 25 of the Act for the clearance out of charge of such goods, and

(*b*) in relation to goods intended for export means a place appointed under section 159 of the Act for the examination of goods which is approved by the Commissioners under section 31 of the Act for the examination of such goods before their movement to a place of exportation;

"the loader" shall have the same meaning as in section 57 of the Act; that is to say the owner of the ship or aircraft in which the goods are to be exported or a person appointed by him;

"place of importation" and "place of exportation" shall, where appropriate, include a free zone;

"removal" means a movement of goods which is authorised under these Regulations and "remove" and "removed" shall be construed accordingly;

"removal document" means a document to be obtained from or approved by the Commissioners made in such form and containing such particulars as the Commissioners may direct under section 31(2A) of the Act and for the purpose of regulation 16 shall include a copy of the application referred to in regulations 5, 6 and 7 stamped by the proper officer.

4—(1) These Regulations shall not apply where any goods are moved under the internal or external Community transit procedure.

(2) The application of regulations 11 and 13 of these Regulations to goods carried under the provisions of an international convention having effect in the United Kingdom shall be without prejudice to any such provisions.

5 Restrictions on the movement of goods

Subject to regulation 10, no imported goods not yet cleared from customs and excise charge shall be moved between their place of importation and either an approved place or a free zone and, in the case of transit goods, between their place of importation and a place of exportation unless the movement is authorised by the proper officer upon application made to him.

6 Subject to regulation 10, no goods shall be moved between—

(*a*) a free zone and a place approved for the clearance out of charge of such goods,

(*b*) such a place and a free zone, and

(*c*) a free zone and another free zone,

unless the movement is authorised by the proper officer upon application made to him.

7 Subject to regulations 9 and 10, no goods intended for export and made available at an approved place or a place designated by the proper officer under sections 53(4) or 58(3) of the Act for the purposes of examination shall be moved between any such place and a place of exportation unless the movement is authorised by the proper officer upon application made to him.

8 Save as the Commissioners may otherwise allow, the applications referred to in regulations 5, 6 and 7 above shall be made in writing on a document obtained from or approved by the Commissioners for that purpose and shall be made—

(*a*) in the case of imported goods, by the importer or the person in charge of the goods,

(*b*) in the case of goods intended for export, by the exporter or the person in charge of the goods, and

(*c*) in any other case, by the proprietor of the goods or the person in charge of the goods.

9 Local export control

(1) Where a notice under section 58A(3)(*a*)(i) of the Act is delivered by the exporter such notice shall replace the application required under regulation 7.

(2) Where the notice is for a single movement of goods, if the authority of the proper officer, required under regulation 7, is neither given nor refused by the date and time for the movement specified in that notice, it shall be deemed to be given on the date and immediately before the time so specified.

(3) Where the notice is for more than one movement of goods, if the authority of the proper officer, required under regulation 7, is neither given nor refused, it shall be deemed to be given immediately before each movement commences.

10 Standing permission to remove

Where the Commissioners so permit, during a period specified by them, goods may be moved as contemplated in regulations 5, 6 and 7 without an application to the proper officer; and, unless the proper officer previously gives or refuses his authority, it shall be deemed to be given immediately before the movement commences.

11 Requirement for removal document

Before any removal commences the person by whom, or on whose behalf, the goods are being moved shall be in possession of a removal document.

12 Specification of vehicles etc

(1) The Commissioners may, in respect of any class or description of goods, require that vehicles or containers in which goods of a particular class or description are removed shall be of a type specified by them for the removal of such goods.

(2) Save as provided by paragraph (3) below, no person shall remove any goods in respect of which a requirement under paragraph (1) above has been imposed unless the vehicle or container in which they are carried conforms to such requirement.

(3) The proper officer, upon application made to him by the person in charge of goods to be removed, may for the purposes of the removal in question relax any requirement imposed under paragraph (1) above.

13 Specification of routes
Vehicles and containers proceeding under a removal shall be moved by such routes as the Commissioners may specify.

14 Security of goods, vehicles and containers
(1) Before any goods are removed they or the vehicle or container carrying them shall be secured or identified by any such seals, locks or marks as the Commissioners may specify.
(2) Where in the United Kingdom, seals, locks or marks are affixed for any customs or excise purpose in order to secure or identify the goods to be removed or the vehicles or containers carrying the goods, they shall be so affixed by the proper officer or by such other person as the Commissioners may authorise.

15—(1) Save in the circumstances hereunder mentioned, no person shall at any time during a removal—
(*a*) wilfully break, open or remove any seal, lock or mark affixed for any customs or excise purpose on any goods or to a vehicle or container; or
(*b*) load or unload or assist in the loading or unloading of a vehicle or container.
(2) The circumstances referred to in paragraph (1) above are—
(*a*) where authorisation has been given by the proper officer; or
(*b*) in accordance with any general or special permission given by the Commissioners; or
(*c*) in an emergency in order to safeguard the goods or to protect life or property.

16 Completion of removals, time limits and accidents
(1) Save as the Commissioners otherwise allow, the person in charge of goods proceeding under a removal shall complete the removal by producing the goods, together with the vehicle or container in which they are carried if such vehicle or container has been secured or identified, and delivering a removal document to the proper officer at the approved place or, in the case of goods intended for export, at the place of exportation.
(2) The Commissioners may allow the removal of goods intended for export to be completed by the person in charge of the goods placing them, together with any container in which they are carried if such container has been secured or identified, under the control of the loader and delivering the removal document to him.

17 The person in charge of goods proceeding under a removal shall complete the removal within such period as the Commissioners may specify.

18 Where as a result of an accident or other occurrence arising during a removal a vehicle or container is delayed or diverted from a specified route the person in charge of the goods shall as soon as practicable give sufficient notification of the accident or occurrence as required by the Commissioners to the local office of customs and excise.

1984/1177

FREE ZONE REGULATIONS 1984

Made by the Commissioners of Customs and Excise under CEMA 1979 ss 100B(1), 100C(3) and (4), 100D(1), (2), 125(3) and VATA 1983 s 24 (see now VATA 1994 s 16)

Made . . . . *1 August 1984*
Laid before Parliament . . . . *3 August 1984*
Coming into Operation . . . . *6 August 1984*

PART I
PRELIMINARY

1 Citation and commencement
These Regulations may be cited as the Free Zone Regulations 1984 and shall come into operation on 6th August 1984.

2 Interpretation
In these Regulations—
"chargeable operation" means any operation carried out on Community goods which are free zone goods where, because of Commission Regulation (EEC) 1371/81 and the nature of the operation, agricultural levy becomes chargeable or a negative monetary compensatory amount payable;
["Community goods" means goods which fulfil the conditions of Article 28 of the Treaty on the Functioning of the European Union;][1]
"tax" means value added tax;

VAT SIs

"transfer to another customs procedure providing for suspension of, or relief from, customs duty or agricultural levy" in regulation 11 (requirement for entry) shall not be taken to include the removal of free zone goods from one free zone to another or from a free zone to a place for the clearance out of charge of imported goods.

Amendments—[1] Definition of "Community goods" substituted by the Treaty of Lisbon (Changes in Terminology) Order, SI 2011/1043 art 7, Sch 1 para 3 with effect from 22 April 2011.

PART II
SECURITY OF FREE ZONES

3 Security and recovery of expenditure by Commissioners

The Commissioners may by direction impose obligations on the responsible authority for a free zone to ensure the security of that free zone; and where the responsible authority fails to comply with such direction and the Commissioners thereby incur any expenditure, such expenditure shall be recoverable on demand by the Commissioners as a civil debt from that responsible authority.

4 Residence in free zones not permitted

The responsible authority shall not permit any person to take up residence within a free zone.

PART III
GOODS CHARGEABLE WITH EXCISE DUTY

5 Excise goods which may become free zone goods without payment of excise duty

Goods chargeable with excise duty may be moved into a free zone in accordance with these Regulations without payment of that duty and remain as free zone goods; provided that they are goods which, by or under the customs and excise Acts, the Commissioners may allow to be removed or delivered without payment of excise duty and which have been allowed to be so removed or delivered.

PART IV
MOVEMENT OF GOODS INTO FREE ZONE

6 Goods to become free zone goods

(1) Goods moved into a free zone shall not be free zone goods unless, within [such time as the Commissioners may direct][1], such particulars the Commissioners may direct have been entered in a record to be kept by the occupier of the premises at which the goods are received or, if the Commissioners so direct, by the responsible authority.

(2) . . . [1]

Amendments—[1] Words in para (1) substituted and para (2) revoked by the Free Zone (Amendment) Regulations, SI 1988/710 reg 3 with effect from 10 May 1988.

7 Acknowledgment of Community status of free zone goods

(1) Where the proprietor of free zone goods wishes to obtain an acknowledgment that the goods are Community goods he shall deliver to the proper officer, within the relevant period, a document in such form and containing such particulars as the Commissioners may direct together with such supporting evidence as will enable the officer to establish to his satisfaction that they are Community goods, and, if so satisfied, the proper officer shall provide a written acknowledgment of such Community status.

(2) The written acknowledgment referred to in paragraph (1) above shall consist of a copy of the document containing particulars of the goods, endorsed by the proper officer.

(3) In this regulation "relevant period" shall mean a period not exceeding 7 days from the time the goods become free zone goods or from the time an entry for free circulation under regulation 17(2) is accepted.

8 Goods from another customs procedure

Goods moved into a free zone which are subject to another customs procedure shall not be free zone goods until the proprietor of the goods has presented them to the proper officer and that procedure has been discharged.

PART V
OPERATIONS

9 Operations on free zone goods

(1) Operations on free zone goods shall only be permitted in accordance with this regulation and subject to any prohibition or restriction imposed by or under any enactment for the time being in force.

(2) Any operation is prohibited in which goods that are not free zone goods are mixed with or incorporated into free zone goods.

(3) The Commissioners shall allow, subject to such conditions as they may impose, operations to be carried out on free zone goods as follows—

(*a*) where only Community goods are involved, any operation;

(*b*) where any other goods are involved—

(i) the usual forms of handling listed in Article 1.1 of Council Directive 71/235/EEC,

(ii) processing under customs control for free circulation in accordance with Council Regulation (EEC) 2763/83, or

(iii) any operation carried out in accordance with the Inward Processing Relief Regulations 1977.

(4) A person intending to carry out any operation shall—

(*a*) before commencing an operation referred to in paragraph (3)(*a*) above, inform the proper officer of his intention and, in addition, where the operation is a chargeable operation enter such particulars as the Commissioners may require in a record to be kept by him,

(*b*) before commencing an operation referred to in paragraph (3)(*b*)(i) above, notify the proper officer of his intention, and

(*c*) before commencing any other operation, make a declaration by entering such particulars as the Commissioners may require in a record to be kept by him.

(5) A person intending to carry out an operation referred to in paragraph (3)(*b*)(i) above may, at the time he notifies the proper officer of his intention to carry out the operation, apply for a written acknowledgment that the operation is to commence and the application shall be in such form as the Commissioners may direct and contain such particulars as the Commissioners may require to enable them to apply regulation 25(4).

(6) The written acknowledgment referred to in paragraph (5) above, shall consist of a copy of the application endorsed by the proper officer.

(7) Save as provided by this regulation, free zone goods shall not be used or consumed in a free zone unless they are entered in accordance with regulation 17(1).

(8) Notwithstanding paragraph (3) above, free zone goods chargeable with excise duty which have been removed or delivered without payment of that duty by or under the customs and excise Acts before becoming free zone goods may only be used or consumed in the free zone without payment of that duty where such use or consumption does not affect the relief from excise duty under the requirements of those Acts applicable to the relief; and paragraph (7) above shall only apply to such goods if they are also chargeable with a duty of customs or agricultural levy which has not been paid.

(9) Where an operation is carried out on free zone goods otherwise than in accordance with this regulation, they shall cease to be free zone goods, and shall be liable to forfeiture.

PART VI
ENTRY, REMOVAL AND PAYMENT OF DUTY ETC

10 Procedure for entering free zone goods

(1) Free zone goods, required by these Regulations to be entered, shall be entered by the proprietor of the goods delivering to the proper officer an entry thereof in such form and manner, containing such particulars and accompanied by such documents as the Commissioners may direct.

(2) Acceptance of an entry by the proper officer shall be signified in such manner as the Commissioners may direct.

(3) Where free zone goods are required to be entered under regulation 17, the Commissioners may direct that if the proprietor of the goods—

(*a*) enters such particulars as the Commissioners may direct in a record to be kept by him, and

(*b*) furnishes a schedule to the proper officer at such place and at such intervals as the Commissioners may direct,

an entry of the goods shall be taken to have been delivered and accepted when the particulars are entered in the record.

11 Entry required before removal for home use etc

Subject to regulation 12, before any free zone goods are removed from a free zone for—

(*a*) home use, or

(*b*) transfer to another customs procedure providing for suspension of, or relief from, customs duty or agricultural levy,

the goods shall be entered for such purpose.

12 Removal without entry

(1) Upon application by the proprietor of free zone goods, the Commissioners may allow the goods to be removed from the free zone for the purposes set out in regulation 11 without the goods being entered, if such particulars as the Commissioners may direct are entered in a record to be kept by the proprietor of the goods.

(2) Where goods are allowed to be removed from the free zone in accordance with para-graph (1) above, the proprietor of the goods shall comply with such conditions as the Commissioners may impose.

VAT SIs

13 Goods to be removed after entry etc

Subject to regulations 15 and 16, free zone goods which have been entered under regulation 11 or in respect of which the particulars required under regulation 12 have been entered in the record, shall be removed, forthwith, from the free zone.

14 Removal of goods for export etc

Part V of the Customs and Excise Management Act 1979 (procedures for the export of goods) and any prohibition or restriction on the export of goods or their shipment as stores, imposed by or under any enactment for the time being in force, shall apply to goods removed from a free zone for export or shipment as stores.

15 Restriction on removal of goods

No goods shall be removed from a free zone except with the authority of and in accordance with any requirement made by the proper officer.

16 Payment of duty before removal of goods

Save as the Commissioners may otherwise allow and subject to such conditions as they may impose, no goods shall be removed from a free zone until any customs duty and agricultural levy chargeable thereon has been paid; and where the goods have been entered under regulation 11(*a*), such duty and levy shall be paid at the time the entry is delivered.

17 Entry of goods which are to remain in free zone

(1) Free zone goods to be used or consumed in a free zone, as provided in regulation 9(7), shall be entered for home use.

(2) Where the proprietor of free zone goods wishes to pay any customs duty or agricultural levy chargeable on the goods and for the goods to remain as free zone goods, the goods shall be entered for free circulation.

18 Payment of duty etc on goods to remain in free zone after entry

(1) Where goods are entered under regulation 17, any customs duty and agricultural levy chargeable thereon shall be paid at the time the entry is delivered.

(2) As an exception of paragraph (1) above, where the goods are entered for free circulation, tax on importation shall not be paid at the time customs duty is paid.

19 Agricultural levy chargeable because of chargeable operation

Where agricultural levy becomes chargeable or a negative monetary compensatory amount payable, because of a chargeable operation, a schedule in such form and containing such particulars of the goods and the operation as the Commissioners may direct shall be furnished by the proprietor of the goods to the proper officer at such place and at such intervals as the Commissioners may direct, and any agricultural levy so chargeable shall be paid at the time the schedule is furnished.

20 Customs duty etc deemed to have been paid

For the purposes of these Regulations, customs duty and agricultural levy shall be deemed to have been paid if payment thereof has been deferred under the Customs Duties (Deferred Payment) Regulations 1976, secured to the satisfaction of the Commissioners or otherwise accounted for.

21 Destruction of free zone goods

Subject to such conditions as the Commissioners may impose, free zone goods may be destroyed and no customs duty or agricultural levy shall be payable on them: Provided that where any scrap or waste resulting from their destruction is entered for removal for home use, duty and levy shall be chargeable thereon in accordance with regulation 25.

PART VII
CONTROLS

22 Production of goods

Goods in a free zone shall be produced to the proper officer for examination on request.

23 Segregation etc of goods

The proper officer may require any goods in a free zone to be segregated and marked or otherwise identified.

24 Keeping of records and provision of information

(1) In addition to any requirement in that regard imposed by or under these Regulations, the Value Added Tax Act 1983[a] or the Inward Processing Relief Regulations 1977, the occupier of any premises upon which free zone goods are kept or, where the Commissioners so direct, the responsible authority on his behalf, shall keep such records relating to the goods as the Commissioners may direct.

(2) Any records required to be kept under these Regulations shall be kept in the free zone or such other place as the Commissioners may allow and be kept in such form and be preserved for such time, not exceeding three years from the date the goods are removed from the free zone, as the Commissioners may direct.

(3) The person keeping the record shall—

(*a*) furnish to the Commissioners, within such time and in such form as they may require, such information relating to the goods as the Commissioners may direct, and

(*b*) upon demand made by the proper officer produce to him any records and any document relating to the goods for inspection by the proper officer and permit him to take copies of or to make extracts from them or remove them at a reasonable time and for a reasonable purpose: Provided that if the information that would otherwise be contained in any record or document is not made or preserved in a form which is easily readable or which is not readable without the aid of equipment, the person keeping the record or document, shall, at the request of the proper officer produce the information contained in the record or document in the form of a transcript or other permanent legible reproduction.

Note—[a] VATA 1994.

PART VIII
CUSTOMS DUTY ETC CHARGEABLE ON FREE ZONE GOODS

25 Customs duty chargeable on free zone goods

(1) Except as provided in paragraph (5) of this regulation (compensating products from inward processing), the customs duty and agricultural levy and the rate thereof chargeable, or the negative monetary compensatory amount and the rate thereof payable, on free zone goods—

(*a*) removed from a free zone for home use, or

(*b*) remaining in a free zone after being entered for home use or free circulation;

shall be those in force for goods of that class or description at the time of acceptance of the entry or, where the goods are allowed to be removed without entry, those in force at the time the particulars required under regulation 12 are entered in the record.

(2) The agricultural levy and the rate thereof chargeable or the negative monetary compensatory amount and the rate thereof payable on free zone goods because of a chargeable operation thereon shall be those in force for goods of that class or description at the time the operation commenced.

(3) Except as provided in paragraph (4) below, the value for customs purposes of free zone goods of any class or description shall be that ascertained or accepted by the Commissioners at the time of the acceptance of the entry for home use or free circulation.

(4) Where goods which are removed from a free zone have undergone any of the usual forms of handling referred to in regulation 9(3)(*b*)(i), provided that the proprietor of the goods—

(*a*) if the goods are entered, produces with the entry, or

(*b*) in any other case, produces to the proper officer at such time as the Commissioners may direct,

the written acknowledgment referred to in regulation 9(5), the quantity of goods, their class or description and value shall, at his option, be those accepted or ascertained at the date of the acknowledgment.

(5) Notwithstanding any other provision of this regulation, where any goods imported into the United Kingdom are granted an authorisation, or have been granted in another Member State an authorisation, for inward processing relief and the Commissioners have allowed compensating products, derived from such goods which have become free zone goods, to be entered for home use or free circulation, the customs duty and agricultural levy chargeable shall be either—

(*a*) the amount calculated in accordance with the Inward Processing Relief Regulations 1977, or

(*b*) at the option of the proprietor of the goods and provided that the Commissioners are satisfied that the amount is at least equal to the amount ascertainable under sub-paragraph (*a*) above, the amount calculated in accordance with paragraph (1) above.

(6) In this regulation, "compensating products" shall have the same meaning as in the Inwards Processing Relief Regulations 1977.

PART IX
VALUE ADDED TAX

26 Tax charge on removal from free zone of manufactured goods

. . .

Amendments—This regulation revoked by the Free Zone (Amendment) Regulations, SI 1988/710 reg 4 with effect from 10 May 1988.

27 Relief from import tax following supply to non-registered person

Where free zone goods have been supplied whilst in the free zone to a person who is neither registered or liable to be registered for tax and he enters the goods for home use, the amount of tax payable shall be reduced by the amount of tax paid on the supply.

1985/1101

VALUE ADDED TAX (REFUND OF TAX) ORDER 1985

Made by the Treasury under VATA 1983 s 20(3) (see now VATA 1994 s 33(3))

Made . . . . *17 July 1985*
Laid before the House of Commons . . . . *18 July 1985*
Coming into Operation . . . . *1 August 1985*

1 This Order may be cited as the Value Added Tax (Refund of Tax) Order 1985 and shall come into operation on 1st August 1985.

2 The following bodies established under the Local Government Act 1985 are hereby specified for the purposes of section 20 of the Value Added Tax Act 1983[a]—

The Inner London Education Authority
The Inner London Interim Education Authority
The Northumbria Interim Police Authority
The London Fire and Civil Defence Authority
The London Residuary Body
A metropolitan county Police Authority
A metropolitan county Fire and Civil Defence Authority
A metropolitan county Passenger Transport Authority
A metropolitan county Residuary Body.

Note—[a] VATA 1994 s 33(3).

1986/260

POSTAL PACKETS (CUSTOMS AND EXCISE) REGULATIONS 1986

Amendment—These Regulations revoked by the Postal Packets (Revenue and Customs) Regulations, SI 2011/3036 with effect from 1 January 2012.

1986/336

VALUE ADDED TAX (REFUND OF TAX) ORDER 1986

Made by the Treasury under VATA 1983 s 20(3) (see now VATA 1994 s 33(3))

Made . . . . *25 February 1986*
Laid before the House of Commons . . . . *27 February 1986*
Coming into Operation . . . . *1 April 1986*

1 This Order may be cited as the Value Added Tax (Refund of Tax) Order 1986 and shall come into operation on 1st April 1986.

2 The following bodies are hereby specified for the purposes of section 20 of the Value Added Tax Act 1983[a]:

A probation committee constituted by section 47(*a*) of, and paragraph 2 of Schedule 3 to, the Powers of Criminal Courts Act 1973
A magistrates' courts committee established under section 19 of the Justices of the Peace Act 1979
The charter trustees constituted by section 246(4) or (5) of the Local Government Act 1972.

Note—[a] VATA 1994 s 33.

1986/532

VALUE ADDED TAX (REFUND OF TAX) (NO 2) ORDER 1986

Made by the Treasury under VATA 1983 s 20(3) (see now VATA 1994 s 33(3))

Made . . . . *18 March 1986*
Laid before the House of Commons . . . . *18 March 1986*
Coming into Operation . . . . *1 April 1986*

1 This Order may be cited as the Value Added Tax (Refund of Tax) (No 2) Order 1986 and shall come into operation on 1st April 1986.

2 The following bodies are hereby specified for the purposes of section 20 of the Value Added Tax Act 1983[1]—

Authorities established under section 10 of the Local Government Act 1985.

Note—[1] VATA 1994 s 33.

1986/590

VALUE ADDED TAX TRIBUNALS RULES 1986

Made by the Commissioners of Customs and Excise, under VATA 1983 Sch 8 para 9 (see now VATA 1994 Sch 12 para 9)

Made . . . . *26 March 1986*
Laid before the House of Commons . . . . . . *9 April 1986*
Coming into Operation . . . . *1 May 1986*

Revocation—These Regulations revoked by the Transfer of Tribunal Functions and Revenue and Customs Appeals Order, SI 2009/56 art 3, Sch 2 para 187(*c*) with effect from 1 April 2009.

1986/896

VALUE ADDED TAX (TREATMENT OF TRANSACTIONS) ORDER 1986

Made by the Treasury under VATA 1983 s 3(3) (see now VATA 1994 s 5(3)(c))

Made . . . . *22 May 1986*
Laid before the House of Commons . . . . . . *3 June 1986*
Coming into Operation . . . . *1 July 1986*

1 Citation and commencement

This Order may be cited as the Value Added Tax (Treatment of Transactions) Order 1986 and shall come into operation on 1st July 1986.

2 Interpretation

In this Order—

"articles in pawn" means articles subject to a pledge;
"pawnee", "pawnor" and "pledge" have the same meaning as in section 189 of the Consumer Credit Act 1974.

3 Treatment of Transaction

The following description of a transaction shall be treated as neither a supply of goods nor a supply of services:

the supply by a taxable person of goods the property in which passed to him as a pawnee by virtue of section 120(1)(a) of the Consumer Credit Act 1974–

(*a*) where the supply is to a person who was pawnor of those goods, and
(*b*) where the supply is made not later than three months from the date when the taxable person acquired the property in the goods.

1986/939

VALUE ADDED TAX (SMALL NON-COMMERCIAL CONSIGNMENTS) RELIEF ORDER 1986

Made by the Treasury under VATA 1983 s 19(1) (see now VATA 1994 s 37(1))

Made . . . . *3 June 1986*
Laid before the House of Commons . . . . . . *9 June 1986*
Coming into Operation . . . . *1 July 1986*

1 Citation and commencement

This Order may be cited as the Value Added Tax (Small Non-Commercial Consignments) Relief Order 1986 and shall come into operation on 1st July 1986.

2 Revocation

The Value Added Tax (Imported Goods) Relief Order 1980 and the Value Added Tax (Imported Goods) Relief (Amendment) Order 1985 are hereby revoked.

3 Relief from value added tax

(1) Subject to the provisions of this Order, no tax is payable on the importation [from a place outside the member States][1] of goods forming part of a small consignment of a non-commercial character.

(2) In this Order "small consignment" means a consignment (not forming part of a larger consignment) containing goods with a value for customs purposes not exceeding [£36][2].

(3) For the purposes of this Order a consignment is of a non-commercial character only if the following requirements are met, namely—

(*a*) it is consigned by one private individual to another;

(*b*) it is not imported for any consideration in money or money's worth;

(*c*) it is intended solely for the personal use of the consignee or that of his family and not for any commercial purpose.

Amendments—[1] Words in para (1) inserted by the VAT (Small Non-Commercial Consignments) Relief (Amendment) Order, SI 1992/3118 with effect from 1 January 1993.

[2] Figure in para (2) substituted by the VAT (Small Non-Commercial Consignments) Relief (Amendment) Order, SI 2012/3060 art 2 with effect from 1 January 2013. Figure was previously £40 (with effect from 28 April 2010).

[4 Conditions of relief

No relief shall be given under this Order unless the consignment is of an occasional nature.][1]

Amendments—[1] This article substituted by the VAT (Small Non-Commercial Consignments) Relief (Amendment) Order, SI 1992/3118 with effect from 1 January 1993.

5 Quantitative restriction on relief for certain goods

Where a small consignment of a non-commercial character contains goods of any of the following descriptions, namely—

(*a*) tobacco products (being cigarettes, cigars or smoking tobacco);

(*b*) alcohol and alcoholic beverages (being spirits or wine), tafia and saké; or

(*c*) perfumes or toilet waters,

in excess of the quantity shown in relation to goods of that description in the Schedule to this Order, no relief under this Order shall be given in respect of any goods of that description contained in that consignment.

6 Relief not applicable to travellers' baggage

This Order does not apply to goods contained in the baggage of a person entering the United Kingdom or carried with such a person.

SCHEDULE

Article 5

(1) Tobacco products—	
Cigarettes	50
Or	
cigarillos (cigars with a maximum weight each of 3 grammes)	25
Or	
Cigars	10
Or	
smoking tobacco	50 grammes
(2) Alcohol and alcoholic beverages—	
distilled beverages and spirits of an alcoholic strength exceeding 22% by volume; undenatured ethyl alcohol of 80% by volume and over	1 litre
Or	
distilled beverages and spirits, and aperitifs with a wine or alcohol base, tafia, saké or similar beverages of an alcoholic strength of 22% by volume or less; sparkling wines and fortified wines	1 litre
Or	
still wines	2 litres
(3) Perfumes	50 grammes
Or	
toilet waters	[250 millilitres][1]

Amendments—

[1] Words in para (3) substituted by the VAT (Small Non-Commercial Consignments) Relief (Amendment) Order, SI 1991/2535 arts 1, 2 with effect from 30 November 1991.

1986/2288

VALUE ADDED TAX TRIBUNALS APPEALS ORDER 1986

Made by the Lord Chancellor under FA 1985 s 26 (see now VATA 1994 s 86)

Made . . . .*18 December 1986*
Laid before Parliament . . . .*22 December 1986*
Coming into Operation . . . .*12 January 1987*

Revocation—These Regulations revoked by the Transfer of Tribunal Functions and Revenue and Customs Appeals Order, SI 2009/56 art 3, Sch 2 para 187(*d*) with effect from 1 April 2009.

1987/1806

VALUE ADDED TAX (TOUR OPERATORS) ORDER 1987

Made by the Treasury under VATA 1983 ss 3(3), 6(6), 16(4), 37A(1)–(2), 48(6) (see now VATA 1994 ss 5(3), 7(11), 30(4), 53(1), (2), 96(9))

Made . . . .*14 October 1987*
Laid before the House of Commons . . . .*21 October 1987*
Coming into force . . . .*1 April 1988*

1 Citation and Commencement

This Order may be cited as the Value Added Tax (Tour Operators) Order 1987 and shall come into force on 1st April 1988.

2 Supplies to which this Order applies

This Order shall apply to any supply of goods or services by a tour operator where the supply is for the benefit of travellers.

3 Meaning of "designated travel service"

(1) Subject to paragraphs (2) . . . [1] and (4) of this article, a "designated travel service" is a supply of goods or services—

(*a*) acquired for the purposes of his business; and

(*b*) supplied for the benefit of a traveller without material alteration or further processing;

by a tour operator in a member State of the European Community in which he has established his business or has a fixed establishment.

(2) The supply of one or more designated travel services, as part of a single transaction, shall be treated as a single supply of services.

(3) . . . [1]

(4) The supply of goods and services of such description as the Commissioners of Customs and Excise may specify shall be deemed not to be a designated travel service.

Press releases etc—C&E News Release 50/95 24-10-95 (guidance for tour operators on in-house supplies of transport, supplies as agent and supplies to businesses).

Business Brief 2/96 9-2-96 (guidance on the VAT treatment of commission for transport only sales by travel agents).

Simon's Tax Cases—*Secret Hotels2 Ltd (formerly Med Hotels Ltd) v R&C Comrs* [2012] EWCA Civ 1571, [2013] STC 452; *Secret Hotels2 Ltd (formerly Med Hotels Ltd) v R&C Comrs* [2014] UKSC 16, [2014] STC 937.

Amendments—[1] Reference in sub-para (1) and whole of sub-para (3) revoked by the Value Added Tax (Tour Operators) (Amendment) Order, SI 2009/3166 arts 2, 3 with effect in relation to supplies made on or after 1 January 2010.

4 Time of supply

(1) Sections 4 and 5 of the Value Added Tax Act 1983[a] shall not apply to any supply comprising in whole or in part a designated travel service.

(2) Subject to paragraphs (3) and (4) of this article, all supplies comprising in whole or in part a designated travel service shall, at the election of the tour operator making the supplies, be treated as taking place either—

(*a*) when the traveller commences a journey or occupies any accommodation supplied, whichever is the earlier; or

(*b*) when any payment is received by the tour operator in respect of that supply which, when aggregated with any earlier such payment, exceeds 20 per cent of the total consideration, to the extent covered by that and any earlier such payment, save in so far as any earlier such payment has already been treated as determining the time of part of that supply.

(3) Save as the Commissioners of Customs and Excise may otherwise allow, all supplies comprising in whole or in part a designated travel service made by the same tour operator shall, subject to paragraph (4) of this article, be treated as taking place at the time determined under one only of the methods specified in paragraph (2) of this article.

VAT SIs

(4) Where—

(*a*) a tour operator uses the method specified in paragraph (2)(*b*) to determine the time of a supply; and

(*b*) payment is not received in respect of all or part of the supply;

notwithstanding paragraph (3), the time of any part of that supply, which has not already been determined under paragraph (2)(b), shall be determined in accordance with paragraph (2)(a).

Note—[a] VATA 1994 s 6.

[5 Place of supply

(1) . . . [2]

(2) A designated travel service shall be treated [for the purposes of this Act][2] as supplied in the member State in which the tour operator has established his business or, if the supply was made from a fixed establishment, in the member State in which the fixed establishment is situated.][1]

Amendments—[1] This article substituted by the VAT (Tour Operators) (Amendment) Order, SI 1992/3125 with effect from 1 January 1993.

[2] In para (2) words inserted, para (1) repealed and article treated as made under VATA 1994 s 7A(6)(*c*), by FA 2009 s 76, Sch 36 para 13 with effect in relation to supplies made on or after 1 January 2010.

6

. . .

Note—This article amended VAT (Place of Supply) Order, SI 1984/1685 arts 4, 5 (revoked).

7 Value of a designated travel service

Subject to articles [8, 9 and 9A][1] of this Order, the value of a designated travel service shall be determined by reference to the difference between sums paid or payable to and sums paid or payable by the tour operator in respect of that service, calculated in such manner as the Commissioners of Customs and Excise shall specify.

Simon's Tax Cases—*C&E Comrs v First Choice Holidays* [2000] STC 609, [2004] STC 1407.

Amendments—[1] Words substituted by the Value Added Tax (Tour Operators) (Amendment) Order, SI 2009/3166 arts 2, 4 with effect in relation to supplies made on or after 1 January 2010.

8—(1) Where—

(*a*) a supply of goods or services is acquired for a consideration in money by a tour operator, for the purpose of supplying a designated travel service, and

(*b*) the value of the supply is (apart from this article) greater than its open market value, and

(*c*) the person making the supply and the tour operator to whom it is made are connected,

the Commissioners of Customs and Excise may direct that the value of the supply shall be deemed to be its open market value for the purpose of calculating the value of the designated travel service.

(2) A direction under this article shall be given by notice in writing to the tour operator acquiring the supply, but no direction may be given more than three years after the time of the supply.

(3) A direction given to a tour operator under this paragraph, in respect of a supply acquired by him, may include a direction that the value of any supply—

(*a*) which is acquired by him after the giving of the notice, or after such later date as may be specified in the notice, and

(*b*) as to which the conditions in sub-paragraph (*a*) to (*c*) of paragraph (1) above are satisfied,

shall be deemed to be its open market value for the purpose of calculating the value of the designated travel service.

(4) For the purposes of this article any question whether a person is connected with another shall be determined in accordance with section 533 of the Income and Corporation Taxes Act 1970[1].

Note—[1] TA 1988 s 839.

9—(1) Where—

(*a*) goods and services have been acquired prior to the commencement of this Order; and

(*b*) input tax credit has been claimed in respect of those goods and services; and

(*c*) the goods and services are supplied as a designated travel service or as part of a designated travel service after the commencement of this Order;

article 7 of this Order shall not apply in determining the value of that part of a designated travel service referable to goods and services on which input tax has been claimed.

(2) The value of that part of the designated travel service to which, by virtue of paragraph (1) of this article, article 7 of this Order does not apply shall be calculated in accordance with section 10 of the Value Added Tax Act 1983[1].

Note—[1] VATA 1994 s 19.

[9A—(1) Where—

(*a*) goods or services have been supplied to a tour operator by a taxable person before 1st January 2010,

(*b*) the tour operator claims input tax in respect of those goods or services, and (*c*) the tour operator supplies those goods or services on or after 1st January 2010 as a designated travel service, or as part of a designated travel service, without material alteration or further processing, to a taxable person who ordered the supply for use in the United Kingdom by that person for the purpose of that person's business other than by way of re-supply,

article 7 of this Order shall not apply in determining the value of that part of the designated travel service which is referable to the goods or services in respect of which input tax is claimed.

(2) The value of that part of a designated travel service to which, by virtue of paragraph (1), article 7 of this Order does not apply, shall be calculated in accordance with section 19 of the Value Added Tax Act 1994.][1]

Amendments—[1] This article inserted by the Value Added Tax (Tour Operators) (Amendment) Order, SI 2009/3166 arts 2, 5 with effect in relation to supplies made on or after 1 January 2010.

10 . . .

Amendments—This article revoked by the VAT (Tour Operators) (Amendment) Order, SI 1995/1495 art 2 with effect from 1 January 1996.

11 . . .

Amendments—This article revoked by the VATA 1994 s 100(2), Sch 15.

12 Disallowance of input tax

[Subject to article 9A of this Order,][2] input tax on goods or services acquired by a tour operator for re-supply as a designated travel service shall be excluded from credit under sections 14 and 15 of the Value Added Tax Act 1983[1].

Note—[1] VATA 1994 ss 24–26.

Amendments—[2] Words inserted by the Value Added Tax (Tour Operators) (Amendment) Order, SI 2009/3166 arts 2, 6 with effect in relation to supplies made on or after 1 January 2010.

13 Disqualification from membership of group of companies

A tour operator shall not be eligible to be treated as a member of a group for the purposes of section 29 of the Value Added Tax Act 1983[1] if any other member of the proposed or existing group—

(*a*) has an overseas establishment;

(*b*) makes supplies outside the United Kingdom which would be taxable supplies if made within the United Kingdom; and

(*c*) supplies goods or services which will become, or are intended to become, a designated travel service.

Note—[1] VATA 1994 s 43.

14 Option not to treat supply as designated travel service

(1) Where a tour operator supplies a designated travel service he may treat that supply as not being a designated travel service if:

(*a*) there are reasonable grounds for believing that the value of all such supplies in the period of one year then beginning will not exceed one per cent of all supplies made by him during that period; and

(*b*) he makes no supplies of designated travel services consisting of accommodation or transport.

(2) For the purposes of this article the value of any supplies shall be calculated in accordance with section 10 of the Value Added Tax Act 1983[1].

Note—[1] VATA 1994 s 19.

1988/809

EXCISE WAREHOUSING (ETC) REGULATIONS 1988

Made by the Commissioners of Customs and Excise under CEMA 1979 s 93 and ALDA 1979 ss 2(3A), 15 and 56(1)

Made . . . . *29 April 1988*
Laid before Parliament . . . . *9 May 1988*
Coming into force . . . . *1 June 1988*

ARRANGEMENT OF REGULATIONS

VAT SIs

PART I
PRELIMINARY

1 Citation and commencement

These Regulations may be cited as the Excise Warehousing (Etc) Regulations 1988 and shall come into force on 1st June 1988, but the Commissioners may give consent and agree conditions, restrictions or requirements under regulation 5 (variation of provisions at request of occupier or proprietor) before that date.

2 Interpretation

In these Regulations, unless the context otherwise requires—

"duty" means excise duty;

"occupier" means the occupier of an excise warehouse, and in the case of a distiller's warehouse means the distiller;

"package" includes any bundle, case, carton, cask, or other container whatsoever;

"proprietor" means the proprietor of goods in an excise warehouse or of goods which have been in, or are to be deposited in, or are treated as being in, an excise warehouse, and "proprietorship" shall be construed accordingly;

"warehoused" means warehoused or rewarehoused in an excise warehouse, and "warehousing" and "rewarehousing" shall be construed accordingly.

3 Application

(1) Except as provided by or under the Hydrocarbon Oil Duties Act 1979 Parts I to IV of these Regulations apply to all goods chargeable with a duty of excise.

(2) Part V of these Regulations applies for all purposes of the Alcoholic Liquor Duties Act 1979.

4 Designated file

(1) For the purposes of these Regulations delivery to the proper officer of anything in writing—

(*a*) shall be effected by placing it in the relevant designated file; and

(*b*) the time of such delivery shall be when it is placed in that designated file,

but the proper officer may direct that delivery shall be effected in another manner.

(2) Nothing in a designated file shall be removed without the permission of the proper officer.

(3) Nothing in a designated file shall be altered in any way, and an amendment to anything in it shall be made by depositing a notice of amendment in the designated file.

(4) The designated file shall be kept at such place as the Commissioners direct and, if kept at the excise warehouse, shall be provided by the occupier.

(5) The designated file shall be a receptacle approved by the Commissioners for the secure keeping of written material, and different files may be approved for different purposes.

(6) For the purposes of these Regulations delivery to the proper officer of anything not in writing shall be effected in such manner, and be subject to such conditions, as the Commissioners direct.

5 Variation of provisions at request of occupier or proprietor

(1) The Commissioners may, if they see fit, consent in writing to an application by an occupier or proprietor for variation of any condition, restriction or requirement contained in or arising under regulations 11 to 24 below, and may make that consent subject to compliance with such other condition, restriction or requirement (as the case may be) as may be agreed by them and the applicant in writing.

(2) Where under paragraph (1) above any condition or restriction is varied or another is substituted for it, then, if the varied or substituted condition or restriction is one—

(*a*) subject to which goods may be deposited in, secured in, kept in or removed from an excise warehouse or made available there to their owner for any prescribed purpose; or

(*b*) subject to which an operation may be carried out on goods in an excise warehouse,

breach of the varied or substituted condition or restriction shall give rise to forfeiture of those goods, provided that breach of the original condition or restriction would have given rise to forfeiture.

6 . . .

Amendments—This regulation revoked by Excise Goods (Drawback) Regulations, SI 1995/1046, Pt V, reg 15(*a*) with effect from 1 June 1995.

7 Manner of Commissioners' directions etc

(1) Where, by or under these Regulations, it is provided that the Commissioners may—

(*a*) make a direction or requirement;

(*b*) give their permission or consent;

(*c*) grant approval; or

(*d*) impose a condition or restriction,

then they may do so only in writing; and they may make a direction or requirement or impose a condition or restriction by means of a public notice.

(2) Any request for the proper officer to give his permission or grant approval under these Regulations shall, if he or the Commissioners direct, be made in writing.

(3) Any right granted to the Commissioners or the proper officer by these Regulations to—

(*a*) make a direction or requirement;

(*b*) give permission or consent;

(*c*) grant approval; or

(*d*) impose a condition or restriction,

shall include a right to revoke, vary or replace any such direction, requirement, permission, consent, approval, condition or restriction.

8 Form of entries etc

(1) Except as the Commissioners otherwise allow, and subject to paragraph (2) below, any entry, account, notice, specification, record or return required by or under these Regulations shall be in writing.

(2) This regulation does not apply to the records referred to in regulation 22(3) and (4) below (records kept for the purposes of any relevant business or activity).

9 Revocation

The Excise Warehousing (Etc) Regulations 1982 and the Excise Warehousing (Etc) (Amendment) Regulations 1986 are hereby revoked.

PART II
PROCEDURES FOR EXCISE WAREHOUSES AND WAREHOUSED GOODS

10 Time of warehousing

Goods brought to an excise warehouse for warehousing shall be deemed to be warehoused when they are put in the excise warehouse.

10A Goods to which section 46 of the Customs and Excise Management Act 1979 applies

Amendments—Regulation revoked by the Excise Goods (Holding, Movement and Duty Point) Regulations, SI 2010/593 reg 91, Sch 3 with effect in relation to goods imported on or after 1 January 2011.

11 Receipt of goods into warehouse

(1) Subject to paragraph (6) below, when goods are warehoused the occupier shall immediately deliver to the proper officer an entry of the goods in such form and containing such particulars as the Commissioners direct.

(2) When goods are warehoused the occupier shall take account of the goods and deliver a copy of that account to the proper officer by the start of business on the next day after warehousing that the warehouse is open.

(3) The occupier shall, if there is any indication that the goods may have been subject to loss or tampering in the course of removal to the excise warehouse, immediately inform the proper officer and retain the goods intact for his examination.

(4) [Except in any case to which the Excise Goods (Holding, Movement and Duty Point) Regulations 2010 apply], the occupier shall, within 5 days of goods being warehoused, send a certificate of receipt for the goods to the person from whom they were received identifying the goods and stating the quantity which has been warehoused.][2]

[(4A) Where goods are warehoused in circumstances where duty may be drawn back the certificate of receipt mentioned in paragraph (4) above shall—

(*a*) be in such form and contain such particulars as the Commissioners may require, and

(*b*) be endorsed on one of the copies of the warehousing advice note that accompanied the goods,

and in this paragraph "warehousing advice note" means a document (in such form and containing such particulars as the Commissioners may require) drawn up by the person to whom the certificate of receipt will be sent.][1]

(5) Except as the proper officer otherwise allows the occupier shall give only one receipt required by paragraph (4) above for each lot or parcel of goods warehoused.

(6) In the case of spirits warehoused at the distillery where they were produced satisfaction of the requirements of regulation 21 of the Spirits Regulations 1982 shall be deemed to be compliance with the requirements of entry and account in paragraphs (1) and (2) above.

(7) Should the occupier fail to comply with any condition or restriction imposed by or under paragraphs (1), (2), (3) or (6) above any goods in respect of which the failure occurred shall be liable to forfeiture.

Amendments—[1] Para (4A) inserted by Excise Goods (Drawback) Regulations, SI 1995/1046, Pt V, reg 15(*b*) with effect from 1 June 1995.

[2] In para (4), words substituted for words "Except as the proper officer may otherwise allow," by the Excise Goods (Holding, Movement and Duty Point) Regulations, SI 2010/593 reg 90, Sch 2 paras 1, 2 with effect from 1 April 2010.

12 Securing, marking and taking stock of warehoused goods

(1) The occupier shall take all necessary steps to ensure that no access is had to warehoused goods other than as allowed by or under these Regulations.

(2) Goods shall be warehoused in the packages and lots in which they were first entered for warehousing.

(3) The occupier shall—

(*a*) legibly and uniquely mark and keep marked warehoused goods so that at any time they can be identified in the stock records; and

(*b*) stow warehoused goods so that safe and easy access may be had to each package or lot.

(4) The occupier shall, when required by the proper officer to do so, promptly produce to him any warehoused goods which have not lawfully been removed from the warehouse.

(5) The occupier shall take stock of all goods in the warehouse—

(*a*) monthly in the case of bulk goods in vats or in storage tanks; and

(*b*) annually in the case of all other goods,

and shall take stock at such other times and to such extent as the Commissioners may for reasonable cause require.

(6) In accordance with the Commissioners' directions the occupier shall—

(*a*) balance his stock accounts and reconcile the quantities of those balances with his Excise Warehouse Returns; and

(*b*) balance his stock accounts so that they can be compared with the result of any stock-taking.

(7) The occupier shall notify the proper officer immediately in writing of any deficiency, surplus or other discrepancy concerning stocks or records of stocks whenever or however discovered.

(8) Any goods—

(*a*) found not to be marked in accordance with paragraph (3) above; or
(*b*) found to be in excess of the relevant stock account and not immediately notified to the proper officer,

shall be liable to forfeiture.

13 Proprietor's examination of goods

The proprietor of warehoused goods may, provided that the occupier has first given his consent and has given at least 6 hours' notice to the proper officer—
(*a*) examine the goods and their packaging;
(*b*) take any steps necessary to prevent any loss therefrom; or
(*c*) display them for sale.

14 Operations

(1) Except as provided by or under this regulation or by or under sections 57 and 58 of the Alcoholic Liquor Duties Act 1979 (mixing of spirits with made-wine or wine), no operation shall be carried out on warehoused goods.
(2) The Commissioners may allow the operations described in Schedule 1 to these Regulations to be carried out on warehoused goods, and may allow other operations if they are satisfied that the control of the goods and the security and collection of the revenue will not be prejudiced.
(3) Save as the proper officer may allow in cases of emergency for the preservation of the goods, no operation shall be commenced unless the occupier has delivered to the proper officer a notice of the proposed operation with a specification of the goods involved, and 24 hours have elapsed following the delivery of that notice.
(4) Before commencing any operation on goods the occupier shall ensure that an account is taken of those goods and that immediately after completion of the operation an account is taken of the out-turn quantities.
(5) The occupier shall deliver to the proper officer a notice containing such detail of the accounts required by paragraph (4) above as the proper officer requires.
(6) The occupier shall ensure that—
(*a*) any operation is carried out in part of the warehouse approved by the Commissioners for that purpose, or in such other part as the proper officer allows; and
(*b*) such other requirements as the proper officer may impose in any particular circumstances are observed.
(7) Any goods in respect of which this regulation is not observed shall be liable to forfeiture.
(8) Nothing in paragraph (2) above shall permit the mixing of spirits with wine or made-wine while that operation is excluded from the provisions of section 93(2)(*c*) of the Customs and Excise Management Act 1979.

15 Removal from warehouse—occupier's responsibilities

The occupier shall ensure that—
(*a*) notice of intention to remove the goods is given to the proper officer in accordance with any directions made by the Commissioners;
(*b*) an entry of the goods is delivered to the proper officer in such form and containing such particulars as the Commissioners may direct;
(*c*) no goods are removed until any duty chargeable has been paid, secured, or otherwise accounted for;
(*d*) no goods are removed contrary to any condition or restriction imposed by the proper officer;
(*e*) an account of the goods is taken in such manner and to such extent as the proper officer requires and a copy of the account is delivered to the proper officer; . . .[2]
(*f*) [except in any case to which the Excise Goods (Holding, Movement and Duty Point) Regulations 2010 apply,][1] when goods are removed other than for home use, a certificate of receipt is obtained showing that all the goods arrived at the place to which they were entered on removal and, if no such receipt is obtained within 21 days of the removal, notice of that fact is given to the proper officer for the excise warehouse from which the goods were removed[; and
(*g*) in any case where, in accordance with regulations made under section 60A of the Customs and Excise Management Act 1979, authorisation is required to ship goods as stores without payment of duty, a copy of the authorisation is obtained before the goods are removed.][2]

Amendments—[1] In para (*f*), words inserted by the Excise Goods (Holding, Movement and Duty Point) Regulations, SI 2010/593 reg 90, Sch 2 paras 1, 2 with effect from 1 April 2010.
[2] In para (*e*), word revoked, in para (*f*), word substituted for full stop, and para (*g*) inserted by the Excise Goods (Aircraft and Ship's Stores) Regulations, SI 2015/368 regs 13, 14 with effect in relation to excise goods—
– supplied to be shipped as stores on or after 1 April 2015;
– shipped as stores on or after 1 April 2015; or
– carried as stores on or after 1 April 2015, where they were shipped on or after that date.

VAT SIs

16 Removal from warehouse—entry

(1) Goods may be entered for removal from warehouse for—

(*a*) home use, if so eligible;

(*b*) exportation;

(*c*) shipment as stores; or

(*d*) removal to the Isle of Man [;

provided that, where goods are warehoused in circumstances where duty may be drawn back they may not, under this paragraph, be entered for removal from warehouse for any purpose that may result in their being consumed in the United Kingdom or the Isle of Man][2].

(2) The Commissioners may allow goods to be entered for removal from warehouse for—

(*a*) rewarehousing in another excise warehouse;

(*b*) temporary removal for such purposes and such periods as they may allow;

(*c*) scientific research and testing;

(*d*) removal to premises where goods of the same class or description may, by or under the customs and excise Acts, be kept without payment of excise duty;

(*e*) denaturing or destruction; or

(*f*) such other purpose as they permit,

and may by direction impose conditions and restrictions on the entry of goods or classes of goods for any of the above purposes.

(3) Save as the Commissioners direct no goods may be removed from warehouse unless they have been entered in accordance with this regulation.

(4), (5) . . .

[(6) In any case where, in accordance with regulations made under section 60A of the Customs and Excise Management Act 1979, authorisation is required to ship goods as stores without payment of duty, goods entered for shipment as stores may be removed from warehouse without payment of duty only if a copy of the authorisation has been given to the occupier.][2]

Note—Paras (4), (5) excepted from subordinate legislation (applied by the VATA 1994 s 16(1)) by the VAT Regulations, SI 1995/2518 reg 119.

Amendments—[1] Words in para (1) inserted by Excise Goods (Drawback) Regulations, SI 1995/1046, Pt V, reg 15(*c*) with effect from 1 June 1995.

[2] Para 6 inserted by the Excise Goods (Aircraft and Ship's Stores) Regulations, SI 2015/368 regs 13, 15 with effect in relation to excise goods—

– supplied to be shipped as stores on or after 1 April 2015;

– shipped as stores on or after 1 April 2015; or

– carried as stores on or after 1 April 2015, where they were shipped on or after that date.

17 Removal from warehouse—general

(1) Any goods removed from an excise warehouse without payment of duty as samples or for scientific research and testing and which are no longer required for the purpose for which they were removed shall be—

(*a*) destroyed to the satisfaction of the proper officer;

(*b*) rewarehoused in an excise warehouse; or

(*c*) diverted to home use on payment of the duty chargeable thereon.

(2) The proper officer may require any goods entered for removal from an excise warehouse for any purpose, other than home use, to be secured or identified by the use of a seal, lock or mark, and any such requirement may continue after the goods have been removed.

(3) In such cases as the Commissioners may direct the proper officer may impose conditions and restrictions on the removal of goods from an excise warehouse in addition to those imposed elsewhere in these Regulations.

(4) Any goods in respect of which any of the provisions of these Regulations relating to removal of goods from an excise warehouse (other than regulation 15(*f*)) is contravened shall be liable to forfeiture.

(5) The Commissioners may direct that any provision of these Regulations relating to removal of goods from an excise warehouse shall not apply in the case of hydrocarbon oils.

[(6) Subject to paragraph (7) below, goods entered for removal from an excise warehouse for any of the purposes set out in regulation 16 above shall be accompanied by an accompanying document that has been completed and is used in accordance with the instructions for completion and use set out on the reverse of copy 1 of that document.

(7) Paragraph (6) above does not apply to—

(*a*) goods entered for removal for home use, shipment as stores or denaturing;

(*b*) goods entered for removal for use by a person to whom section 13A of the Customs and Excise Duties (General Reliefs) Act 1979 (reliefs from duties and taxes for persons enjoying certain immunities and privileges) applies;

(*c*) goods entered for removal that are, in accordance with regulations made under section 12(1) of the Customs and Excise Duties (General Reliefs) Act 1979 (supply of duty-free goods to Her Majesty's ships), to be treated as exported;

(*d*) spirits entered for removal for use by a person authorised to receive them in accordance with section 8 of the Alcoholic Liquor Duties Act 1979 (remission of duty in respect of spirits used for medical or scientific purposes);

(*e*) goods entered for removal for exportation in circumstances to which Part II of the Excise Goods (Accompanying Documents) Regulations 2002 apply;

[(*ea*) goods entered for removal for exportation in circumstances to which Part 6 of the Excise Goods (Holding, Movement and Duty Point) Regulations 2010 apply;

(*eb*) goods entered for removal in circumstances to which Part 8 of the Excise Goods (Holding, Movement and Duty Point) Regulations 2010 apply;][2]

(*f*) goods that are being lawfully moved under the cover of a single administrative document; or

(*g*) any goods that are entered for removal from an excise warehouse for any of the purposes set out in regulation 16 above before 1st October 2002 if those goods are accompanied by a document that has been approved by the Commissioners for that purpose.

(8) If there is a contravention of, or failure to comply with, paragraph (6) above, the excise duty point for excise goods that are required by this regulation to be accompanied by an accompanying document is the time those goods were removed from the excise warehouse.

(9) The person liable to pay the excise duty at the excise duty point is—

(*a*) the person who arranged for the security required by regulation 16(5) above, or

(*b*) if regulation 16(5) above was not complied with, the authorized warehousekeeper.

(10) Any person whose conduct caused a contravention of, or failure to comply with, paragraph (6) above is jointly and severally liable to pay the excise duty with the person specified in paragraph (9) above.

(11) Any excise duty that any person is liable to pay by virtue of this regulation must be paid immediately.

(12) In this regulation—

"single administrative document" has the same meaning as in Commission Regulation (EEC) No 2454/93;

"accompanying document" means the document set out in Schedule 4 below.][1]

Amendments—[1] Paras (6)–(12) added by the Excise Goods (Accompanying Documents) Regulations, SI 2002/501 reg 27(1), (3) with effect from 1 April 2002.

[2] Sub-paras (7)(*ea*), (*eb*) inserted by the Excise Goods (Holding, Movement and Duty Point) Regulations, SI 2010/593 reg 90, Sch 2 paras 1, 2 with effect from 1 April 2010.

18 Entry of goods not in warehouse

Except in such cases as the Commissioners direct, goods which are to be warehoused and goods which have been lawfully removed from an excise warehouse without payment of duty may, with the permission of the proper officer, be entered or further entered by their proprietor for any of the purposes referred to in paragraphs (1) and (2) of regulation 16 above as if they were to be removed from the excise warehouse:

Provided that where any such goods are packaged and part only is to be further entered, that part shall consist of one or more complete packages.

19 Samples

(1) The Commissioners may make directions—

(*a*) allowing the proprietor of warehoused goods to draw samples thereof for such purposes and subject to such conditions as they specify; and

(*b*) . . .

and no sample shall be drawn or removed except as allowed by, and in accordance with directions and conditions under, this regulation.

(2) Any samples drawn or removed in breach of this regulation shall be liable to forfeiture.

Note—Para (1)(*b*) excepted from subordinate legislation (applied by the VATA 1994 s 16(1)) by the VAT Regulations, SI 1995/2518 reg 119.

PART III
RETURNS AND RECORDS

20 Returns

(1) The occupier shall complete and sign an Excise Warehouse Return and shall deliver such return to the proper officer within 14 days of the end of the stock period to which it relates.

(2) A return shall be in such form and contain such particulars of goods received into, stored in and delivered from an excise warehouse as the Commissioners direct, and different provisions may be made for goods of different classes or descriptions.

(3) The Commissioners may direct that separate returns be made in respect of goods of different classes or descriptions.

(4) The occupier shall support each return with such schedules and further information relating to the goods as the Commissioners may require.

(5) "Stock period" means one calendar month or such other period, not exceeding 5 weeks, as the proper officer, at the request of the occupier, allows.

21 Records to be kept

(1) The occupier shall, in relation to goods in an excise warehouse, keep the records prescribed by Schedule 2 to these Regulations.

(2) The proprietor of goods in an excise warehouse, or of goods which have been removed from an excise warehouse without payment of duty, or which are to be warehoused, may be required by the proper officer to keep the records prescribed by Schedule 3 to these Regulations in so far as they relate to his proprietorship of the goods.

(3) In addition to the other records required by this regulation the occupier shall, in relation to his occupation of the warehouse, keep such records of the receipt and use of goods received into the excise warehouse other than for warehousing therein as the proper officer requires.

(4) Records required by or under this regulation shall—

(*a*) be entered up promptly;

(*b*) identify the goods to which they relate;

(*c*) in the case of an occupier be kept at the warehouse;

(*d*) in the case of a proprietor be kept at his principal place of business in the United Kingdom, or at such other place as the proper officer allows; and

(*e*) be kept in such form and manner and contain such information as the Commissioners direct.

22 Preservation of records

(1) The occupier shall preserve, for not less than 3 years from the lawful removal of the goods or such shorter period as the Commissioners direct, all records which he is required to keep by virtue of regulation 21(1) above, but no record shall be destroyed until the relevant stock accounts have been balanced and any discrepancy reconciled.

(2) The proprietor shall preserve, for not less than 3 years from when he ceased to be the proprietor of the goods, or for such shorter period as the Commissioners direct, all records which he is required to keep by virtue of regulation 21(2) above.

(3) Each occupier and proprietor shall preserve all records (other than those referred to in paragraphs (1) and (2) above) kept by him for the purposes of any relevant business or activity for not less than 3 years from the events recorded in them, except that such records need not be preserved if they are records which (or records of a class which) the Commissioners have directed as not needing preservation.

(4) The requirements to preserve records imposed by paragraph (3) above may be discharged by the preservation in a form approved by the Commissioners of the information contained in those records.

23 Production of records

(1) The occupier or the proprietor shall, when required by the Commissioners, produce or cause to be produced to the proper officer any records, copy records or information which he was required by these Regulations to preserve.

(2) Production under paragraph (1) above shall—

(*a*) take place at such reasonable time as the proper officer requires; and

(*b*) take place at the excise warehouse or at such other place as the proper officer may reasonably require.

(3) The proper officer may inspect, copy or take extracts from and may remove at a reasonable time and for a reasonable period any record produced or required to be produced to him under this regulation, and the occupier and proprietor shall permit such inspection, copying, extraction and removal.

(4) Where the records required to be produced by this regulation are preserved in a form which is not readily legible, or which is legible only with the aid of equipment, the occupier or proprietor shall, if the proper officer so requires, produce a transcript or other permanently legible reproduction of the records and shall permit the proper officer to retain that reproduction.

24 Information for the protection of the revenue

(1) The occupier or the proprietor shall furnish the Commissioners with any information relating to any relevant business or activity of his which they specify as information which they think it is necessary or expedient for them to be given for the protection of the revenue.

(2) Such information shall be furnished to the Commissioners within such time, and at such place and in such form as they may reasonably require.

25 Further provision as to records

For the purposes of regulations 21 to 24 above, in relation to a proprietor—

(*a*) goods which are to be warehoused shall be treated as if they were warehoused in the warehouse to which they are being removed; and

(*b*) goods which have been removed from warehouse without payment of duty shall be treated as if they were warehoused in the warehouse from which they have been removed.

PART IV
DUTY CHARGEABLE ON WAREHOUSED GOODS

26 Duty chargeable on goods removed for home use

The duty and the rate thereof chargeable on any warehoused goods removed from an excise warehouse for home use shall be those in force for goods of that class or description at the time of their removal.

27 Duty chargeable on goods diverted to home use after removal without payment of duty

(1) The duty and the rate thereof chargeable on any goods removed from an excise warehouse without payment of duty and in respect of which duty is payable under regulation 17(1)(*c*) above shall be those in force for goods of that class or description at the time of payment of the duty.

(2) The duty and the rate thereof chargeable on any goods which have been entered for home use under regulation 18 above shall be those in force for goods of that class or description—

(*a*) where removal for home use is allowed under section 119 of the Customs and Excise Management Act 1979 on the giving of security for the duty chargeable thereon, at the time of giving of the security, or

(*b*) in any other case, at the time of payment.

28 Duty chargeable on missing or deficient goods

The duty and the rate thereof chargeable on any goods found to be missing or deficient and upon which duty is payable under section 94 of the Customs and Excise Management Act 1979 shall be those in force for goods of that class or description at the time the loss or deficiency occurred:

Provided that where that time cannot be ascertained to the proper officer's satisfaction, the rate of duty chargeable on such goods shall be the highest rate applicable thereto from the time of their deposit in the excise warehouse, or, where appropriate, from the time that the last account of them was taken, until the loss or deficiency came to the notice of the proper officer.

29 Calculation of duty

(1) Where duty is charged on any such goods as are referred to in regulation 26 above, the quantity of those goods shall be ascertained by reference to any account taken in accordance with these Regulations at the time of their removal from the excise warehouse or, if no account is taken, the quantity declared to and accepted by the proper officer as the quantity of goods being removed or, if greater, the actual quantity of goods being removed.

(2) Where duty is charged on any such goods as are referred to in regulations 27 or 28 above the quantity of such goods shall be ascertained by reference to the last account taken in accordance with these Regulations, or, if no account has been taken, the quantity declared to and accepted by the proper officer as the quantity of goods on which duty is to be charged, or, if greater, the actual quantity of goods.

30 Ascertainment of quantity by taking an account

(1) Where the quantity of warehoused goods is to be ascertained by taking an account thereof, it shall be ascertained for the purposes of these Regulations by reference to weight, measure, strength, original gravity or number as the case may require.

(2) Where under these Regulations an occupier is required to deliver a copy of an account of goods he shall deliver to the proper officer a notice giving such details of the account as the proper officer requires, and the taking of the account shall not be complete until that notice has been delivered.

PART V
ASCERTAINMENT OF DUTY BY REFERENCE TO LABELS ETC

31 Ascertainment of duty by reference to labels etc

(1) Subject to paragraph (2) of this regulation, for the purpose of charging duty on any spirits, wine or made-wine contained in any bottle or other container the strength, weight and volume of the spirits, wine or made-wine shall be ascertained conclusively by reference to any information given on the bottle or other container by means of a label, or otherwise, or by reference to any documents relating to the bottle or other container, notwithstanding any other legal provision.

(2) The method of ascertaining the strength, weight or volume, or any of them, referred to in paragraph (1) above shall not be used if another method would produce a result upon which a greater amount of duty would be charged than would be the case if the method in paragraph (1) above were used.

SCHEDULE 1
OPERATIONS WHICH MAY BE PERMITTED ON WAREHOUSED GOODS

(Regulation 14(2))

1 Sorting, separating, packing or repacking and such other operations as are necessary for the preservation, sale, shipment or disposal of the goods.

VAT SIs

2 The rectifying and compounding of spirits.
3 The rendering sparkling of wine and made-wine.
4 The mixing of a fermented liquor or a liquor derived from a fermented liquor with any other liquor or substance so as to produce made-wine.
5 The mixing of lime or lemon juice with spirits for shipment as stores or for exportation.
6 Denaturing.
7 Reducing.
8 Marrying.
9 Blending.

SCHEDULE 2

RECORDS TO BE KEPT BY THE OCCUPIER

(Regulation 21(1))

Records of—

(*a*) goods deposited in the excise warehouse, from where and from whom received, and date of warehousing;

[(*aa*) any certificate or other document that accompanied beer that contained a statement of the amount of beer produced in the brewery where the beer was produced;][1]

(*b*) goods removed from the excise warehouse, the purpose of the removal, date of removal and (if the purpose of the removal is other than for home use) the place to which the goods are removed;

(*c*) stock of warehoused goods;

(*d*) deficiencies and increases in stock;

(*e*) operations performed;

(*f*) deficiencies and increases in operation;

(*g*) accounts taken of goods deposited in the excise warehouse, removed from the excise warehouse, put into operation, received from operation, and of stocks in the excise warehouse;

(*h*) samples drawn from warehoused goods, samples removed from warehouse, and the person to whom samples are delivered;

(*i*) the manner in which duty is paid or accounted for when goods chargeable with duty are removed for home use;

(*j*) the manner in which security is given when goods chargeable with duty are removed for purposes other than home use, and the dates when certificates of receipt or shipment are received;

[(*jj*) a copy of any authorisation which is required, in accordance with regulations made under section 60A of the Customs and Excise Management Act 1979, to ship goods as stores without payment of duty;][2]

(*k*) notices delivered to the proper officer and of the manner and time of delivery;

(*l*) times when the excise warehouse is opened and closed;

(*m*) names and titles of keyholders to the excise warehouse;

(*n*) the name and address of the proprietor of each lot or parcel of goods, and of changes of proprietorship.

Amendments—[1] Paragraph (*aa*) inserted by the Beer and Excise Warehousing (Amendment) Regulations, SI 2002/1265 reg 3(1), (2) with effect from 1 June 2002.

[2] Paragraph (*jj*) inserted by the Excise Goods (Aircraft and Ship's Stores) Regulations, SI 2015/368 regs 13, 16 with effect in relation to excise goods—

- supplied to be shipped as stores on or after 1 April 2015;
- shipped as stores on or after 1 April 2015; or
- carried as stores on or after 1 April 2015, where they were shipped on or after that date.

SCHEDULE 3

RECORDS WHICH THE PROPRIETOR MAY BE REQUIRED TO KEEP

(Regulation 21(2))

Records of

(*a*) goods which are to be warehoused in an excise warehouse;

(*b*) goods which have been warehoused in an excise warehouse;

(*c*) goods which have been removed from an excise warehouse otherwise than for home use on payment of the duty chargeable, and all movements of such goods;

(*d*) his stock of goods in each excise warehouse;

(*e*) operations performed;

(*f*) samples drawn, removed from warehouse and, where that removal is other than on payment of the duty chargeable, their use, location and disposal;

(*g*) the time and manner in which the duty chargeable on goods to which regulation 21(2) relates is paid, secured or accounted for.

Note—Sch 4, as inserted by SI 2002/501 reg 27(1), (4), has not been reproduced.

[SCHEDULE 5

PARTICULARS WHICH MUST BE CONTAINED IN A DOCUMENT

Regulation 10A

1 Date of entry of the goods and their entry number.

2 Importer's name and address.

3 The name, address and approval number of the excise warehouse to which the goods are to be moved.

4 A description of the goods and their quantity.]

Amendments—This Schedule inserted by the Excise Warehousing (Etc) (Amendment) Regulations, SI 2008/2832 regs 2, 3(2) with effect from 1 December 2008.

Schedule revoked by the Excise Goods (Holding, Movement and Duty Point) Regulations, SI 2010/593 reg 91, Sch 3 with effect from 1 January 2011.

1989/472

VALUE ADDED TAX (SELF-SUPPLY OF CONSTRUCTION SERVICES) ORDER 1989

Made by the Treasury under VATA 1983 ss 3(6), (8) and 29(2) (see now VATA 1994 ss 5(6), (8) and 43(2))

Made .... *14 March 1989*

Laid before the House of Commons .... *14 March 1989*

Coming into force .... *1 April 1989*

1 This Order may be cited as the Value Added Tax (Self-supply of Construction Services) Order 1989 and shall come into force on 1st April 1989.

2 In this Order "the Act" means the Value Added Tax Act 1983 [VATA 1994].

3—(1) Where a person, in the course or furtherance of a business carried on by him, for the purpose of that business and otherwise than for a consideration, performs any of the following services, that is to say—

(*a*) the construction of a building; or

(*b*) the extension or other alteration of, or the construction of an annexe to, any building such that additional floor area of not less than 10 per cent of the floor area of the original building is created; or

(*c*) the construction of any civil engineering work; or

(*d*) in connection with any such services as are described in sub-paragraph (*a*), (*b*) or (*c*) above, the carrying out of any demolition work contemporaneously with or preparatory thereto,

then, subject to each of the conditions specified in paragraph (2) below being satisfied, those services shall be treated for the purposes of the Act as both supplied to him for the purpose of that business and supplied by him in the course or furtherance of it.

(2) The conditions mentioned in paragraph (1) above are that—

(*a*) the value of such services is not less than £100,000; and

(*b*) such services would, if supplied for a consideration in the course or furtherance of a business carried on by a taxable person, be chargeable to tax at a rate other than nil.

(3) The preceding provisions of this article shall apply in relation to any bodies corporate which are treated for the purposes of section 29 of the Act[a] as members of a group as if those bodies were one person, but anything done which would fall to be treated by virtue of this Order as services supplied to and by that person shall be treated as supplied to and by the representative member.

Note—[a] VATA 1994 s 43.

4—(1) The value of any supply of services which is to be treated as taking place by virtue of this Order is the open market value of such services.

(2) Where any services of a description specified in article 3(1) above are in the process of being performed on the day this Order comes into force, the value of such services for the purposes of this Order shall be the value of such part of those services as are performed on or after that day.

VAT SIs

1989/1114

VALUE ADDED TAX (WATER) ORDER 1989

Made by the Treasury under VATA 1983 s 3(3) (see now VATA 1994 s 5(3)) and all other enabling powers

Made ....*3 July 1989*
Laid before the House of Commons ....*11 July 1989*
Coming into force ....*1 August 1989*

1 This Order may be cited as the Value Added Tax (Water) Order 1989 and shall come into force on 1st August 1989.

2 The supply of water insofar as it is not otherwise a supply of goods shall be treated as a supply of goods and not as a supply of services.

1990/2167

CHANNEL TUNNEL (CUSTOMS AND EXCISE) ORDER 1990

Made by the Commissioners of Customs and Excise under the Channel Tunnel Act 1987 ss 11(1)(a), (c), (d), (g), (h), 11(2), 11(3)(a), (d), 13(1) and (2) and all other enabling powers

Made ....*1 November 1990*
Laid before Parliament ....*9 November 1990*
Coming into force ....*1 December 1990*

1 Citation and commencement

This Order may be cited as the Channel Tunnel (Customs and Excise) Order 1990 and shall come into force on 1st December 1990.

2 Interpretation

(1) In this Order—

"the Act of 1979" means the Customs and Excise Management Act 1979;
"the Act of 1987" means the Channel Tunnel Act 1987;
"customs approved area" has the meaning given by article 3(1) below;
"the tunnel" except in the expression "tunnel system" means that part of the tunnel system comprising the tunnels specified in section 1(7)(*a*) of the Act 1987 or any of those tunnels.

(2) In this Order the following expressions have the meanings assigned to them by section 1 of the Act of 1979:

"approved wharf";
"the boundary";
"commander";
"the Commissioners";
"the customs and excise Acts";
"customs and excise airport";
"goods";
"officer";
"owner";
"port";
["proper";][1]
"ship";
"shipped" and cognate expressions.

(3)–(5) . . .

Amendments—[1] Words in para (2) inserted by Channel Tunnel (International Arrangements) Order, SI 1993/1813 art 8 Sch 5 Pt II paras 7, 8(*a*) with effect from 2 August 1993.

Note—Paras (3)–(5) outside the scope of the coverage of legislation in this handbook.

3 Channel tunnel customs approved areas

. . .

Note—This article is outside the scope of the coverage of legislation in this handbook.

4 Modification of the Act of 1979

The Act of 1979 shall be modified in accordance with the provisions of the Schedule to this Order.

5 Time of importation, exportation etc

. . .

Note—This article is outside the scope of the coverage of legislation in this handbook.

SCHEDULE
MODIFICATIONS OF THE ACT OF 1979
Article 4

[Part II of the Act of 1979: Administration

A1 In section 17(1) (disposal of duties, etc) the reference to Great Britain shall be construed as including a reference to a control zone in France [or Belgium][2].][1]

Amendments—[1] Paras A1, A2 inserted by Channel Tunnel (International Agreements) Order, SI 1993/1813 art 8 Sch 5 Pt II para 11 with effect from 2 August 1993.

[2] Words in para A1 inserted by Channel Tunnel (Miscellaneous Provisions) Order, SI 1994/1405 art 8 Sch 4 para 7 as from a day to be appointed.

Part III of the Act of 1979: Customs and Excise Control Areas

[A2—(1) For the purposes of section 21 (control of movement of aircraft, etc, into and out of the United Kingdom) references to an aircraft shall be treated as including references to a through train, and in relation to such trains section 21 shall be construed in accordance with sub-paragraphs (2) to (5).

(2) References to a customs and excise airport shall be construed as references to a terminal control point or a place which is a customs approved area.

(3) References to a flight shall be construed as references to a journey, and the reference in section 21(4) to flying shall be construed accordingly.

(4) References to landing shall be construed as references to stopping for the purpose of enabling passengers or crew to board or leave the train or goods to be loaded onto or unloaded from it.

(5) References to the commander of an aircraft shall be construed as references to the train manager of a train.][1]

Amendments—[1] Paras A1, A2 inserted by Channel Tunnel (International Agreements) Order, SI 1993/1813 art 8 Sch 5 Pt II para 11 with effect from 2 August 1993.

Part IV of the Act of 1979: Control of Importation

6 In section 42(1)(*a*) (power to regulate the unloading, removal, etc of imported goods) the reference to a ship arriving at a port shall be construed as including a reference to a vehicle arriving [at a place which is a customs approved area either in France or through the tunnel from France][1] at a customs approved area through the tunnel from France.

Amendments—[1] Words in para 6 inserted by Channel Tunnel (International Arrangements) Order, SI 1993/1813 arts 1, 8 Sch 5 Pt II paras 19–21, 32, 33, with effect from 2 August 1993.

[7 In section 49(1) (forfeiture of goods improperly imported)—

(*a*) the reference in paragraph (*a*)(ii) to goods unloaded from any aircraft in the United Kingdom shall be construed as including a reference to goods unloaded from a through train or shuttle train which has brought them into the United Kingdom and a reference to goods otherwise brought through the tunnel into the United Kingdom; and

(*b*) the reference in paragraph (*c*) to goods found to have been concealed on board any aircraft shall be construed as including references to goods found concealed—

(i) on a through train or shuttle train has brought them into the United Kingdom,

(ii) on a through train while it constitutes a control zone in France [or Belgium][2], or

(iii) in a road vehicle in a control zone in France within the tunnel system.][1]

Amendments—[1] Para 7 substituted by Channel Tunnel (International Arrangements) Order, SI 1993/1813 arts 1, 8 Sch 5 Pt II paras 19–21, 32, 33, with effect from 2 August 1993.

[2] Words in paras 7(*b*)(ii) inserted by Channel Tunnel (Miscellaneous Provisions) Order, SI 1994/1405 arts 1, 8 Sch 4 para 7 as from a day to be appointed.

8 Section 50(2) (penalty for improper importation of goods) shall have effect as if—

(*a*) any person who unloads or assists or is otherwise concerned in the unloading of those goods mentioned in section 50(1) from any vehicle which has arrived from France through the tunnel [or Belgium][2][, or who brings or assists or is otherwise concerned in the bringing of such goods into a control zone in France [or Belgium][2],][1] were a person who unships such goods in a port; and

(*b*) any person who removes or assists or is otherwise concerned in the removal of such goods from any customs approved area were a person who removes such goods from an approved wharf.

Amendments—[1] Words in para 8(*a*) inserted by Channel Tunnel (International Arrangements) Order, SI 1993/1813 arts 1, 8 Sch 5 Pt II paras 19–21, 32, 33, with effect from 2 August 1993.

[2] Words in para 8(*a*) inserted by Channel Tunnel (Miscellaneous Provisions) Order, SI 1994/1405 arts 1, 8 Sch 4 para 7 as from a day to be appointed.

Part XI of the Act of 1979: Detention of Persons, Forfeiture and Legal Proceedings

22 In section 146(1) (service of process) the reference in paragraph (*c*) to an aircraft shall be construed as including a reference to a vehicle which has arrived from or is departing to France through the tunnel[, and in relation to such a vehicle the second reference to the United Kingdom shall be construed as including a reference to a control zone in France within the tunnel system][1].

Amendments—[1] Words in para 22 inserted by Channel Tunnel (International Arrangements) Order, SI 1993/1813 arts 1, 8 Sch 5 Pt II paras 19–21, 32, 33, with effect from 2 August 1993.

23 In section 154(2) (proof of certain other matters) any reference to goods loaded or to be loaded into or unloaded from an aircraft shall be construed respectively as including references to goods loaded or to be loaded onto or unloaded from a vehicle which is departing to or has arrived from France through the tunnel.

24 In section 159(1) (power to examine and take account of goods) the reference in paragraph (*c*) to goods which have been loaded into a ship shall be construed as including a reference to goods which have been loaded onto a vehicle for exportation through the tunnel.

[25 The persons to whom section 164 (search of persons) applies shall be taken to include any person who is—

(*a*) in the tunnel system in the United Kingdom;

(*b*) in a through train in the United Kingdom;

(*c*) in, entering or leaving a customs approved area in the United Kingdom; or

(*d*) in a control zone in France [or Belgium][2].][1]

Amendments—[1] Para 25 substituted by Channel Tunnel (International Arrangements) Order, SI 1993/1813 arts 1, 8 Sch 5 Pt II paras 19–21, 32, 33, with effect from 2 August 1993.

[2] Words in para 25(*d*) inserted by Channel Tunnel (Miscellaneous Provisions) Order, SI 1994/1405 arts 1, 8 Sch 4 para 7 as from a day to be appointed.

1991/2306

VALUE ADDED TAX (INPUT TAX) (PERSON SUPPLIED) ORDER 1991

Amendment—This Order revoked by the VAT (Input Tax) (Person Supplied) Order, SI 2005/3291 with effect from 1 January 2006.

1991/2724

CUSTOMS CONTROLS ON IMPORTATION OF GOODS REGULATIONS 1991

Made by the Commissioners of Customs and Excise under the European Communities Act 1972 s 2(2) and all other enabling powers

Made . . . . *4 December 1991*

Laid before the House of Commons . . . . *11 December 1991*

Coming into force . . . . *1 January 1992*

Note—Amending provisions and provisions outside the scope of this Handbook have not been reproduced.

1 Citation and commencement

These Regulations may be cited as the Customs Controls on Importation of Goods Regulations 1991 and shall come into force on 1st January 1992.

2 Interpretation

In these Regulations—

"the Act" means the Customs and Excise Management Act 1979;

"the Commissioners" means the Commissioners of Customs and Excise;

"the Council Regulation" means [Council Regulation (EEC) No 2913/92][1];

["the Commission Regulation" means the Commission Regulation (EEC) No 2454/93][1]

"the customs and excise Acts" has the same meaning as in section 1(1) of the Act.

Amendments—[1] Words substituted and definition "the Commission Regulation" inserted by Community Customs Code (Consequential Amendment of References) Regulations, SI 1993/3014 reg 4(1), (2) with effect from 1 January 1994.

3 Presentation

(1) Notification to the Commissioners of the arrival of goods as required by [Article 40][1], of the Council Regulation shall be made in the form prescribed in Schedule 1 or a form to the like effect approved by the Commissioners.

(2) Where a computerised inventory system has been approved by the Commissioners presentation may consist in a computerised record capable of being printed out.

(3) Within three hours of its arrival at the wharf or airport at which a ship or aircraft carrying the goods is to unload them, notification of such arrival, as required by [Article 40][1], of the Council Regulation shall be made at the customs office for the wharf or airport; should such notification be impossible due to the office being closed during that period, the period shall end at the expiration of one hour following the re-opening of the office.

Amendments—[1] Words in paras (1), (3) substituted by Community Customs Code (Consequential Amendment of References) Regulations, SI 1993/3014 reg 4(1), (3), (4) with effect from 1 January 1994.

4 Summary declaration

The summary declaration required under [Article 43][1] of the Council Regulation shall be in the form prescribed in Schedule 2 or a form to the like effect approved by the Commissioners.

Amendments—[1] Words substituted by Community Customs Code (Consequential Amendment of References) Regulations, SI 1993/3014 reg 4(1), (5) with effect from 1 January 1994.

5 Entry

(1) For the purposes of [Article 49][2] of the Council Regulation the goods shall be entered not later than—

(*a*) [forty-five][1] days from the date on which the summary declaration is lodged in the case of goods carried by sea; or

(*b*) [twenty][1] days from the date on which the summary declaration is lodged in the case of goods carried otherwise than by sea.

(2) The entry shall be delivered by the importer to the proper officer . . . [1]

(3) Except with the permission of the Commissioners no entry shall be delivered before the goods have been presented at the proper office of customs and excise.

(4) Where the Commissioners permit an entry to be delivered before presentation of the goods, the goods must be presented to the proper office of customs and excise within such time as the Commissioners may allow; and if the goods are not so presented the entry shall be treated as not having been delivered.

(5) Acceptance of an entry by the proper officer shall be signified in such manner as the Commissioners may direct.

Amendments—[1] Word in paras (1)(*a*), (*b*) substituted and words in para (2) revoked by Customs and Excise (Single Market etc) Regulations, SI 1992/3095 reg 7(*a*) with effect from 1 January 1993.

[2] Words in para (1) substituted by Community Customs Code (Consequential Amendment of References) Regulations, SI 1993/3014 reg 4(1), (6) with effect from 1 January 1994.

1991/2727

FREE ZONE REGULATIONS 1991

Made by the Commissioners of Customs and Excise under the European Communities Act 1972 s 2(2) and all other enabling powers

Made . . . . *4 December 1991*
Laid before Parliament . . . . *11 December 1991*
Coming into force . . . . *1 January 1992*

1 Citation and commencement

These Regulations may be cited as the Free Zone Regulations 1991 and shall come into force on 1st January 1992.

2 Interpretation

In these Regulations—

"the Act" means the Customs and Excise Management Act 1979;

"the customs and excise Acts" has the same meaning as in section 1(1) of the Act;

"relevant Community provision" means any provision of a Community Regulation specified in the first and second columns of the Schedule.

3 Repeals

(1) Subject to paragraph (2) below, the following sections of the Act are hereby repealed—

section 100B (free zone regulations),

section 100C (free zone goods: customs duties, etc), except for subsection (4),

section 100D (free zone regulations: supplemental), and

section 100E (control of trading in free zones).

(2) This regulation shall not have effect in relation to the application of the following provisions of the Act by virtue of section 24(1) of the Value Added Tax Act 1983—

section 100B (free zone regulations),

section 100C(1) (free zone goods) insofar as the subsection purports to apply to goods chargeable with customs duty, and section 100C(3) (scope of free zone regulations).

4, 5 Amendments
(*amend* CEMA 1979 ss 1(1), 100C(4)).

6 Offences, penalty and forfeiture
In the event of any contravention or failure to comply with—

(*a*) any relevant Community provision; or
(*b*) any requirement or condition imposed by or under any such provision; or
(*c*) any undertaking given pursuant to any such provision or requirement; or
(*d*) any regulation made under section 100B of the Act in its continued application by virtue of regulation 3(2) above; or
(*e*) any regulation made under section 100C(4) of the Act,

the person responsible for the contravention or failure shall be liable on summary conviction to a penalty of level 3 on the standard scale together with a penalty of £40 for each day on which the contravention or failure continues and any goods in respect of which the offence was committed shall be liable to forfeiture.

7 Supplementary
(1) Section 139 of and Schedule 3 to the Act (detention, seizure and condemnation of goods) shall apply to any goods where liable to forfeiture under regulation 6 above as if the goods were liable to forfeiture under the customs and excise Acts.
(2) Sections 144 to 148 and 150 to 155 of the Act (proceedings for offences, mitigation of penalties, proof and other matters) shall apply in relation to offences and penalties under regulation 6 above and proceedings for such offences or for condemnation of any thing as being forfeited under that regulation as they apply in relation to offences and penalties and proceedings for offences or for condemnation under the customs and excise Acts.

[SCHEDULE
RELEVANT COMMUNITY PROVISIONS
Regulation 2

(1) *Community Regulation*	(2) *Relevant Provision*	(3) *Subject Matter of Provision*
Council Regulation (EEC) No 2913/92	Article 59	All goods intended to be placed under a customs procedure shall be covered by a declaration for that customs procedure
	Article 101(*a*)	Warehousekeeper to ensure that goods in warehouse are not removed from customs supervision
	Article 101(*b*)	Warehousekeeper to fulfil obligations arising from storage of goods
	Article 101(*c*)	Warehousekeeper to comply with conditions of authorisation
	Article 105	Designated person to keep stock records in approved form
	Article 110	Temporary removal requires authorisation
	Article 111	Transfer requires authorisation
Commission Regulation (EEC) No 2454/93	Article 513	Failure to make presentation of goods and lodge declaration
	Article 269	Authorised use of simplified procedures
	Article 517	Stock records to be made available to the supervising office
	Articles 522, 523 and 532	Authorisation for usual forms of handling
	Article 527	Inventory to be furnished when required
	Articles 223, 528 and 864	Treatment without customs approved formalities
	Articles 529–534	Requirement for export declaration

Article 536	Customs status and identification of Community goods.][1]

Amendments—

[1] This Schedule substituted by Community Customs Code (Consequential Amendment of References) Regulations, SI 1993/3014 Sch 1 with effect from 1 January 1994.

1992/630

VALUE ADDED TAX (TREATMENT OF TRANSACTIONS) ORDER 1992

Made by the Treasury, under VATA 1983 s 3(3) (see now VATA 1994 s 5(3)) and all other enabling powers

Made . . . .*10 March 1992*
Laid before the House of Commons . . . .*10 March 1992*
Coming into force . . . .*1 April 1992*

1 This Order may be cited as the Value Added Tax (Treatment of Transactions) Order 1992 and shall come into force on 1st April 1992.

2 Where an employer gives an employee a choice between—
(*a*) a particular rate of wages, salary or emoluments, or
(*b*) in the alternative a lower rate of wages, salary or emoluments and, in addition, the right to the private use of a motor car provided by the employer,
and the employee chooses the alternative described in paragraph (*b*) above, then the provision to the employee of the right to use the motor car privately shall be treated as neither a supply of goods nor a supply of services (if it otherwise would be) to the extent only that the consideration for the provision of the motor car for the employee's private use is the difference between the wages, salary or emoluments available to him under paragraphs (*a*) and (*b*) of this article.

1992/2790

STATISTICS OF TRADE (CUSTOMS AND EXCISE) REGULATIONS 1992

Made by the Commissioners of Customs and Excise under the European Communities Act 1972 s 2(2) and all other enabling powers

Made . . . .*6 November 1992*
Laid before parliament . . . .*10 November 1992*
Coming into force . . . .*1 December 1992*

Commentary—*De Voil Indirect Tax Service* **V5.276.**
Cross references—See Commission Regulation 3046/92/EEC of 22 October 1992.

1 Citation, commencement and interpretation

(1) These Regulations may be cited as the Statistics of Trade (Customs and Excise) Regulations 1992 and shall come into force on 1st December 1992.
(2) In these Regulations—
"the Act" means the Customs and Excise Management Act 1979;
. . .[1]
. . .[3]
"authorised person" means any person acting under the authority of the Commissioners;
. . .[1]
. . .[3]
"document" includes in addition to a document in writing—
(*a*) any photograph;
(*b*) any disc, tape, sound track or other device in which sounds or other data (not being visual images) are recorded so as to be capable (with or without the aid of some other equipment) of being reproduced therefrom; and
(*c*) any film, negative, tape or other device in which one or more visual images are recorded so as to be capable (as aforesaid) of being reproduced therefrom;
"film" includes a microfilm;
. . .[3]
["Intrastat" refers to the data collection system established and implemented by—
(*a*) Council and European Parliament Regulation (EC) No 638/2004 ("establishing Regulation"); and

VAT SIs

(*b*) Commission Regulation (EC) No 1982/2004 ("implementing Regulation");][2]

. . .

["periodic declaration" refers to the means of providing the simplified information in regulations 3(1) and 3(2) (VAT return) or to a supplementary declaration in regulation 4;][2]

. . .[3]

. . .[1]

. . .[3]

(3) In these Regulations, unless defined above, words and expressions shall have the meanings assigned to them by section 1 of the Act [or have the same meaning as in the establishing or implementing Regulation][2].

Amendments—[1] Definitions in para (2) revoked by Statistics of Trade (Customs and Excise) (Amendment) Regulations, SI 1997/2864 with effect from 1 January 1998 (previously inserted by Statistics of Trade (Customs and Excise) (Amendment) Regulations, SI 1993/541 reg 3).

[2] In para (2), definition of "Intrastat" substituted for that of "Intrastat system", and definition of "periodic declaration" substituted; and words in para (3) inserted; by the Statistics of Trade (Customs and Excise) (Amendment) Regulations, SI 2004/3284 regs 1(3), 2 with effect from 1 January 2005.

[3] Definitions revoked by SI 2004/3284 regs 1(3), 5, Schedule with effect from 1 January 2005. The revoked definitions are those of "arrival stage", "assimilation threshold", "dispatch stage", "goods", "Member State", "Principal Regulation", "reference period", "register of intra-Community operators", "supplementary declaration" and "Threshold Regulation".

2 [Application of Intrastat

(1) For the purposes of the United Kingdom's statistical territory (see Article 4(1) of the establishing Regulation), Intrastat is under the care and management of the Commissioners of Customs and Excise (the "Commissioners").

(2) For the purposes mentioned in paragraph (1), the Commissioners are—

(*a*) "customs" within Article 5(2) of the establishing Regulation (provision to national authority of statistical information on other goods at least once a month);

(*b*) the "national authority" within—

(i) Articles 5(2), 8(1), 8(2), 9(1) and 11 of the establishing Regulation (other goods, etc; register of intra-Community operators; identification of parties responsible for providing information; information that must be collected; statistical confidentiality); and

(ii) Articles 5, 13(4), 17(4), 21(4), 22(4) and 23(2) of the implementing Regulation (identification of persons who have declared goods for fiscal purposes; simplification for certain individual transactions; access to additional data sources in the case of vessels and aircraft, sea products, spacecraft and electricity);

(*c*) the "tax administration" within—

(i) Articles 8(2) and 8(3) of the establishing Regulation (duty to furnish lists of persons who have declared that they have supplied goods to or acquired goods from other Member States; duty to furnish information provided for fiscal purposes which could improve quality of statistics; duty to bring the Intrastat obligations to the attention of VAT-registered traders); and

(ii) Article 5 of the implementing Regulation (duty to provide specified information to identify persons who have declared goods for fiscal purposes).

(3) Also, for the purposes mentioned in paragraph (1), the duties or discretions expressed in the following Articles as those of the "Member States" must be performed or exercised by the Commissioners—

(*a*) Articles 10(6), 12 and 13 of the establishing Regulation (sending information on thresholds to Commission; transmission of that data; quality of that data and yearly quality report to Commission); and

(*b*) Articles 10, 16(2), 18, 19(3), 20(3), 23(3), 24(2), 25(2), 25(4) to 25(7) and 26(1) of the implementing Regulation (reporting nature of transaction; application of specific rules for staggered consignments, motor vehicle and aircraft parts, goods delivered to vessels and aircraft, offshore installations, electricity, military goods; transmission of data to Commission; yearly quality report to Commission).

(4) The Commissioners may do anything necessary for and reasonably incidental to any Article mentioned in paragraphs (2) and (3).

This paragraph is additional to any other basis for their doing so.

(5) For the purposes of Article 9 of the establishing Regulation (information that must or may be collected), the Commissioners must only collect information in accordance with Regulations 3, 4 and 4A (simplified information and supplementary declaration).][1]

Amendments—[1] Regulations 2–4A substituted for regulations 2–4 by the Statistics of Trade (Customs and Excise) (Amendment) Regulations, SI 2004/3284 regs 1(3), 3 with effect from 1 January 2005.

[3 [Information collected on the value added tax return]

[(1) The Commissioners may treat the following information collected in accordance with regulations made under section 58 of, and Schedule 11 paragraphs 2(1) and 2(11) to, the Value Added Tax Act 1994 (information collected on the VAT return) for Intrastat purposes (see Article 10(1) of the establishing Regulation)—

(*a*) information about the value of supplies of goods and related costs to other Member States;

(*b*) information about the value of acquisitions of goods and related costs from other Member States.][2]

[(2) If the annual value of [intra-EU][3] 'dispatches' (see Articles 3, 7, and 10(2) of the establishing Regulation) of a party is at or below £250,000, that party may be treated as exempt from providing Intrastat information concerning dispatches, and therefore that party is not subject to regulation 4 (supplementary declarations) in respect of such information.

(3) If the annual value of [intra-EU][3] 'arrivals' (see Articles 3, 7, and 10(2) of the establishing Regulation) of a party is at or below [£1,500,000][4], that party may be treated as exempt from providing Intrastat information concerning arrivals, and therefore that party is not subject to regulation 4 (supplementary declarations) in respect of such information.][3]][1]

Amendments—[1] Regulations 2–4A substituted for regulations 2–4 by the Statistics of Trade (Customs and Excise) (Amendment) Regulations, SI 2004/3284 regs 1(3), 3 with effect from 1 January 2005.

[2] Heading, and para (1) substituted by the Statistics of Trade (Customs and Excise) (Amendment) Regulations, SI 2006/3216 regs 2, 3 with effect from 1 January 2007.

[3] Paras (2), (3) substituted by the Statistics of Trade (Customs and Excise) (Amendment) Regulations, SI 2009/2974, reg 2(1) with effect from 1 January 2010.

[4] In para (3), figure substituted by the Statistics of Trade (Customs and Excise) (Amendment) Regulations, SI 2014/3135, reg 2 with effect from 1 January 2015.

[4 [Supplementary declarations

(1) A party that in relation to the United Kingdom is responsible for providing the information (see Article 7 of the establishing Regulation) must provide it to the Commissioners by means of electronic communication in the appropriate form specified in a current Commissioners' direction.

(2) That party must provide all the information sought by the appropriate form, in accordance with the establishing and implementing Regulations.

(3) But that party need provide the "delivery terms" information sought by the appropriate form only if that party's annual value of intra-EU trade relevant to that form (namely, value of "arrivals" or value of "dispatches") exceeds £16,000,000.

(4) That party must use the coding mentioned in Article 11 of the implementing Regulation in providing any "delivery terms" information pursuant to paragraph (1) and this paragraph (and see also Article 9(2)(d) of the establishing Regulation).

(5) That party must deliver the completed supplementary declaration to the Commissioners no later than the 21st day of the month following the end of the reference period to which it relates.

Only the reference period in Article 6(1) of the establishing Regulation applies in relation to the supplementary declaration ("calendar month of dispatch or arrival of the goods".)

But the reference periods in Article 3 of the Implementing Regulation may be used instead if a current Commissioners' direction so permits in the interests of better administration ("calendar month" of "chargeable event" or in which "declaration is accepted").

(6) direction under paragraph (1) or (5) is not current for the purposes of the relevant paragraph to the extent that it is varied, replaced or revoked by another Commissioners' direction.][1], [2]

Amendments—[1] Regulations 2–4A substituted for regulations 2–4 by the Statistics of Trade (Customs and Excise) (Amendment) Regulations, SI 2004/3284 regs 1(3), 3 with effect from 1 January 2005.

[2] Regulation 4 substituted by the Statistics of Trade (Customs and Excise) (Amendment) Regulations, SI 2012/532 reg 3 with effect from 1 April 2012.

4A [Administration of rules concerning specific goods and movements

(1) The Commissioners must give directions as to matters of administration for the proper application of these Regulations in the case of the rules set out in Articles 16, 17, 19, 20, 21, 22, 23 and 24 of the implementing Regulation (rules concerning specific goods and movements – staggered consignments, vessels and aircraft, goods delivered to vessels and aircraft, offshore installations, sea products, spacecraft, electricity, military goods).

(2) The Commissioners may give such a direction in the case of the rules set out in Articles 15 and 18 of that Regulation (industrial plant, motor vehicle and aircraft parts).

(3) Regulation 4 (supplementary declarations) is subject to every current direction under this regulation.

(4) A direction is not current for the purposes of paragraph (3) to the extent that it is varied, replaced or revoked by another such direction.][1]

Amendments—[1] Regulations 2–4A substituted for regulations 2–4 by the Statistics of Trade (Customs and Excise) (Amendment) Regulations, SI 2004/3284 regs 1(3), 3 with effect from 1 January 2005.

5 Duty to keep and retain records

(1) Every person who is mentioned in the register of intra-Community operators, shall—

(*a*) keep a copy of every periodic declaration . . . [1] he makes [or delivers or which is made or delivered][2] on his behalf;

(*b*) keep copies of all documents which he or anyone acting on his behalf used for the purpose of compiling [his periodic declarations][1];

(*c*) produce or cause to be produced [periodic declarations and documents][1] mentioned in paragraphs (*a*) and (*b*) above when required to do so by an authorised person;

(*d*) permit an authorised person exercising the powers mentioned in paragraph (*c*) above to make [copies or extracts of those periodic declarations and documents][1] or to remove them for a reasonable period.

(2) The Commissioners may require [periodic declarations and documents][1] mentioned in paragraph (1) above to be preserved for such period not exceeding six years as they may require.

(3) For the purpose of exercising any powers granted by this regulation an authorised person may at any reasonable time enter premises used in connection with the carrying on of a business by a person mentioned in the register of intra-Community operators or another person compiling periodic declarations on his behalf.

Amendments—[1] Words in para (1)(*a*) revoked and words in paras (1)(*b*), (*c*), (*d*), (2) substituted by Statistics of Trade (Customs and Excise) (Amendment) Regulations, SI 1997/2864 reg 6 with effect from 1 January 1998.

[2] Words in para (1)(*a*) substituted by the Statistics of Trade (Customs and Excise) (Amendment) Regulations, SI 2004/3284 regs 1(3), 4(1) with effect from 1 January 2005.

6 Offences and evidence

(1) If any person required to [deliver][2] a supplementary declaration in accordance with [these Regulations][2] fails to do so he shall be liable on summary conviction to a penalty not exceeding level 4 on the standard scale.

(2) Any failure to [deliver][2] a supplementary declaration includes a failure to [provide][2] such supplementary declaration in the form and manner required by these Regulations . . . [3].

(3) Subject to paragraph (4) below, for the purpose of the rules against charging more than one offence in the same information—

(*a*) failure to [deliver][2] one or more supplementary declarations of trade in goods dispatched to other Member States for any given reference period shall constitute one offence; and

(*b*) failure to [deliver][2] one or more supplementary declarations of trade in goods [arriving][2] from other Member States for any given reference period shall constitute one offence.

(4) If the failure in respect of which a person is convicted under paragraph (1) above is continued after the conviction he shall be guilty of a further offence and may on summary conviction thereof be punished accordingly.

(5) . . . [3]

(5A) . . . [1]

(6) . . . [3]

(7) In any proceedings for an offence mentioned in this regulation it shall be a defence for the accused to prove that he took all reasonable precautions and exercised all due diligence to avoid the commission of such an offence by himself, any person under his control or any person to whom he transferred the task of providing information in accordance with [and subject to Article 7(2) of the establishing Regulation][2].

[(8) Liability to a penalty under paragraphs (1) and (2) does not arise in relation to a failure under paragraph (1) of regulation 4 if a party satisfies the Commissioners that there is a reasonable excuse for the failure.

(9) For the purposes of paragraph (8), where a party relies on any other person to do anything, that is not a reasonable excuse unless that party took reasonable care to avoid the relevant act or failure.][4]

Amendments—[1] Para (5A) and words in para (6) revoked by Statistics of Trade (Customs and Excise) (Amendment) Regulations, SI 1997/2864 reg 7 with effect from 1 January 1998.

[2] Words in paras (1), (2), (3), (7) substituted by the Statistics of Trade (Customs and Excise) (Amendment) Regulations, SI 2004/3284 regs 1(3), 4(2)–(6) with effect in relation to acts, or omissions, occurring after 31 December 2004.

[3] Words in para (2) revoked, and paras (5), (6) revoked, by SI 2004/3284 regs 1(3), 5, Schedule with effect from 1 January 2005.

[4] Paras (8), (9) inserted by the Statistics of Trade (Customs and Excise) (Amendment) Regulations, SI 2012/532 reg 4 with effect from 1 April 2012.

7—(1) In any legal proceedings, whether civil or criminal, where any question arises concerning a document furnished[, provided, delivered][2] or created for the purposes of the Intrastat system this regulation shall apply.

(2) Where any document does not consist of legible visual images its . . . [1] content may be proved in any proceedings by production of a copy of the information in the form of legible visual images.

Amendments—[1] Words in para (2) revoked by Statistics of Trade (Customs and Excise) (Amendment) Regulations, SI 1993/541 reg 7 with effect from 1 April 1993.

[2] Words in para (1) inserted by the Statistics of Trade (Customs and Excise) (Amendment) Regulations, SI 2004/3284 regs 1(3), 4(7) with effect in relation to acts, or omissions, occurring after 31 December 2004.

8—(1) A certificate of the Commissioners—

(*a*) that a person was or was not a party responsible for providing information in accordance with the Intrastat system;
(*b*) that a person was or was not mentioned in the register of intra-Community operators;
(*c*) that any information required for purposes connected with the Intrastat system has not been given or had not been given at any date;
(*d*) that a copy produced in accordance with paragraph (2) of regulation 7 above is, both as to form and content, identical to that received by electronic means in accordance with [regulation 4(1)][2] above

shall be sufficient evidence of that fact until the contrary is proved.

(2) A photograph of any document furnished[, provided or delivered][1] to the Commissioners for the purposes of these Regulations and certified by them to be such a photograph shall be admissible in any proceedings, whether civil or criminal, to the same extent as the document itself.

(3) Any document purporting to be a certificate under paragraph (1) or (2) above shall be deemed to be such a certificate until the contrary is proved.

Amendments—[1] Words in para (2) inserted, by the Statistics of Trade (Customs and Excise) (Amendment) Regulations, SI 2004/3284 regs 1(3), 4(8), (9) with effect in relation to acts, or omissions, occurring after 31 December 2004.
[2] Words in para (1)(*d*) substituted by the Statistics of Trade (Customs and Excise) (Amendment) Regulations, SI 2012/532 reg 5 with effect from 1 April 2012.

9 Access to recorded information

(1) Where, on an application by an authorised person, a justice of the peace or, in Scotland, a justice (within the meaning of section 462 of the Criminal Procedure (Scotland) Act 1975) is satisfied that there are reasonable grounds for believing—

(*a*) that an offence in connection with the Intrastat system is being, has been or is about to be committed, and
(*b*) that any recorded information (including any document of any nature whatsoever) which may be required as evidence for the purpose of any proceedings in respect of such an offence is in the possession of any person,

he may make an order in accordance with this regulation.

(2) An order made in accordance with this regulation is an order that the person who appears to the justice to be in possession of the recorded information to which the application relates shall—

(*a*) give an authorised person access to it, and
(*b*) permit an authorised person to remove and take away any of it which he reasonably considers necessary,

not later than the end of the period of seven days beginning on the date of the order or the end of such longer period as the order may specify.

(3) The reference in sub-paragraph (2)(*a*) above to giving an authorised person access to the recorded information to which the application relates includes a reference to permitting the authorised person to take copies of it or to make extracts from it.

(4) Where the recorded information consists of information contained in a computer, an order made in accordance with this regulation shall have effect as an order to produce the information in a form in which it is visible and legible and, if the authorised person wishes to remove it, in a form in which it can be removed.

10—(1) An authorised person who removes anything in the exercise of a power conferred by or under regulation 9 above shall, if so requested by a person showing himself—

(*a*) to be the occupier of premises from which it was removed, or
(*b*) to have had custody or control of it immediately before the removal,

provide that person with a record of what he removed.

(2) The authorised person shall provide the record within a reasonable time from the making of the request for it.

(3) Subject to paragraph (7) below, if a request for permission to be granted access to anything which—

(*a*) has been removed by an authorised person, and
(*b*) is retained by the Commissioners for the purpose of investigating an offence,

is made to the officer in overall charge of the investigation by a person who had custody or control of the thing immediately before it was so removed or by someone acting on behalf of such a person, the officer shall allow the person who made the request access to it under the supervision of an authorised person.

(4) Subject to paragraph (7) below, if a request for a photograph or copy of any such thing is made to the officer in overall charge of the investigation by a person who had custody or control of the thing immediately before it was so removed, or by someone acting on behalf of such a person, the officer shall—

(*a*) allow the person who made the request access to it under the supervision of an authorised person for the purpose of photographing it or copying it; or
(*b*) photograph or copy it, or cause it to be photographed or copied.

(5) Where anything is photographed or copied under sub-paragraph (4)(*b*) above the photograph or copy shall be supplied to the person who made the request.

(6) The photograph or copy shall be supplied within a reasonable time from the making of the request.

(7) There is no duty under this regulation to grant access to, or to supply a photograph or copy of, anything if the officer in overall charge of the investigation for the purposes of which it was removed has reasonable grounds for believing that to do so would prejudice—

(*a*) that investigation;

(*b*) the investigation of an offence other than the offence for the purposes of the investigation of which the thing was removed; or

(*c*) any criminal proceedings which may be brought as a result of—

(i) the investigation of which he is in charge, or

(ii) any such investigation as is mentioned in sub-paragraph (*b*) above.

(8) Any reference in this regulation to the officer in overall charge of the investigation is a reference to the person whose name and address are endorsed on the order concerned as being the officer so in charge.

11—(1) Where, on an application made as mentioned in paragraph (2) below, the appropriate judicial authority is satisfied that a person has failed to comply with a requirement imposed by regulation 10 above, the authority may order that person to comply with the requirement within such time and in such manner as may be specified in the order.

(2) An application under paragraph (1) above shall be made—

(*a*) in the case of a failure to comply with any of the requirements imposed by paragraphs (1) and (2) of regulation 10 above, by the occupier of the premises from which the thing in question was removed or by the person who had custody or control of it immediately before it was so removed, and

(*b*) in any other case, by the person who has such custody or control.

(3) In this regulation "the appropriate judicial authority" means—

(*a*) in England and Wales, a magistrates' court;

(*b*) in Scotland, the sheriff; and

(*c*) in Northern Ireland, a court of summary jurisdiction, as defined in Article 2 (2) (*a*) of the Magistrates' Court (Northern Ireland) Order 1981.

(4) In England and Wales and Northern Ireland, an application for an order under this regulation shall be made by way of complaint; and sections 21 and 42(2) of the Interpretation Act (Northern Ireland) 1954 shall apply as if any reference in those provisions to any enactment included a reference to this regulation.

12 Supplementary

Where in connection with the operation of the Intrastat system a person is convicted of an offence contrary to section 167(1) or section 168(1) of the Act, section 167(2)(*a*) and section 168(2)(*a*) of the Act shall have effect as if, in each case, for the words "6 months" there were substituted the words "3 months".

[**13** The following provisions of the Act shall apply to these Regulations as they apply to the customs and excise Acts—

Sections 145 to 148 (proceedings for offences, etc);

Sections 150 to 154 (incidental provisions as to legal proceedings, mitigation of penalties, proof and other matters).][1]

Amendments—[1] This regulation added by Statistics of Trade (Customs and Excise) (Amendment No 2) Regulations, SI 1993/3015 regs 2, 4 with effect from 1 January 1994.

SCHEDULE

Regulation 4

Amendments—Schedule repealed by the Statistics of Trade (Customs and Excise) (Amendment) Regulations, SI 2012/532 reg 6 with effect from 1 April 2012.

1992/3111

VALUE ADDED TAX (REMOVAL OF GOODS) ORDER 1992

Made by the Treasury under VATA 1983 s 3(3) (see now VATA 1994 s 5(3)) and all other enabling powers

Made . . . . *9 December 1992*

Laid before the House of Commons . . . . *11 December 1992*

Coming into force . . . . *1 January 1993*

1 This Order may be cited as the Value Added Tax (Removal of Goods) Order 1992 and shall come into force on 1st January 1993.

2 In this Order—

"the Act" means the Value Added Tax Act 1983[a];

"the member State of arrival" means the member State to which the goods are removed;

"the member State of dispatch" means the member State from which the goods are removed;

"the owner" means the person who is carrying on the business of which the goods form part of the assets;

"registered" means either registered under the Act or registered under the provisions of the law of another member State corresponding thereto;

"temporary importation relief" means relief, other than partial relief, from payment of any duty incurred on the entry of goods into the territory of the Community which is afforded by virtue of any of the Community Regulations specified in the Schedule to this Order.

Note—[a] VATA 1994.

3 For the purposes of this Order, a person is treated as being established in a member State if he has there a business establishment or some other fixed establishment or carries on a business there through a branch or agency.

4 Subject to article 5 below, paragraph 5A of Schedule 2 to the Act[a] shall not apply to the following removals of goods from a member State to a place in any other member State—

(*a*) where the supply of the goods would be treated as having been made in a Member State other than the member State of dispatch by virtue of section 6(2A), (2B) or (2C) of the Act;[b]

(*b*) where the supply of the goods would be treated as having been made in the member State of dispatch by virtue of the Value Added Tax (Place of Supply of Goods) Order 1992;

(*c*) where the goods have been removed by or under the directions of the owner for the purpose of—

(i) his delivering them to a person to whom he is supplying those goods; or

(ii) his taking possession of them from a person who is supplying those goods to him,

and that supply is or will be zero-rated by virtue of section 16(6) or (7) of the Act;[c]

(*d*) . . . [1]

[(*e*) where—

(i) the goods have been removed to another member State for the purpose of delivering them to a person (other than the owner) who is to value or carry out any work on them in that member State; and

(ii) the owner intends that the goods will be returned to him by their removal to the member State of dispatch upon completion of the valuation or work;][1]

(*f*) where—

(i) the owner is established in the member State of dispatch and is not established in the member State of arrival;

(ii) they are removed for the sole purpose of their being used by the owner in the course of a supply of services to be made by him;

(iii) at the time of their removal there exists a legally binding obligation to make that supply of services; and

(iv) the owner intends to remove them to the member State of dispatch upon his ceasing to use them in the course of making the supply;

(*g*) where—

(i) temporary importation relief would have been afforded had the goods been imported from a place outside the member States; and

(ii) the owner intends to export the goods to a place outside the member States or remove them to a member State other than the member State of arrival, in either case, not later than 2 years after the day upon which the goods were removed;

(*h*) where the goods are removed in accordance with an intention described in paragraph [(*e*)][1], (*f*)(iv) or (*g*)(ii) above;

(*i*) . . . [1]

Notes—[a] VATA 1994 Sch 4 para 6.

[b] VATA 1994 s 7(3)–(5).

[c] VATA 1994 s 30(6), (8).

Cross references—See VAT (Removal of Goods) (Accounting) Regulations, SI 1992/3101 reg 3 (goods removed from a member State to a place in any other member State; removal falling within paras (*d*)–(*g*) above).

Amendments—[1] Paras (*d*), (*i*) revoked, para (*e*) substituted, and in para (*h*) reference substituted for reference "(d)(iii)", by the VAT (Removal of Goods) (Amendment) Order, SI 2012/2953 art 2(1), (2) with effect from 1 January 2013.

5 In the case of a removal falling within paragraph [(*e*)][1], (*f*) or (*g*) above, it shall be a condition of paragraph 5A of Schedule 2 to the Act[a] not applying that the relevant intention of the owner is fulfilled.

Note—[a] VATA 1994 Sch 4 para 6.

Cross references—See VAT (Removal of Goods) (Accounting) Regulations, SI 1992/3101 reg 3 (owner's obligation to make entry on VAT account where condition in this article is not complied with and tax has become payable).

Amendments—[1] Reference substituted for reference "(*d*)" by the VAT (Removal of Goods) (Amendment) Order, SI 2012/2953 art 2(1), (3) with effect from 1 January 2013.

SCHEDULE

COMMUNITY LEGISLATION RELATING TO TEMPORARY IMPORTATION RELIEF

Article 2

Council Regulation (EEC) No 3599/82
Council Regulation (EEC) No 1855/89
Council Regulation (EEC) No 3312/89
Commission Regulation (EEC) No 2249/91.

1992/3121

VALUE ADDED TAX (PLACE OF SUPPLY OF SERVICES) ORDER 1992

Made by the Treasury under VATA 1983 s 6(6) (see now VATA 1994 s 7(11)) and all other enabling powers

Made . . . . *9 December 1992*
Laid before the House of Commons . . . . *11 December 1992*
Coming into force . . . . *1 January 1993*

PART I

PRELIMINARY

1 Citation and commencement

This Order may be cited as the Value Added Tax (Place of Supply of Services) Order 1992 and shall come into force on 1st January 1993.

2 Interpretation

In this Order—

"the Act" means the [Value Added Tax Act 1994][1];

"ancillary transport services" means loading, unloading, handling and similar activities;

"intra-Community transport of goods" means the transportation of goods which begins in one member State and ends in a different member State;

"pleasure cruise" includes a cruise wholly or partly for the purposes of education or training;

"registration number" means an identifying number assigned to a person by a member State for the purposes of value added tax in that member State.

Amendments—[1] Words substituted by the VAT (Place of Supply of Services) (Amendment) Order, SI 1995/3038 art 3, with effect from 1 January 1996.

3 Revocation

The Value Added Tax (Place of Supply) Order 1984 is hereby revoked.

PART II

4 Rules For Determining Place Of Supply Of Services

The rules for determining where a supply of goods or of services is made shall be varied in accordance with the following provisions of this Order.

5 Services relating to land

Where a supply of services consists of—

(*a*) the grant, assignment or surrender of—

(i) any interest in or right over land;

(ii) a personal right to call for or be granted any interest in or right over land; or

(iii) a licence to occupy land or any other contractual right exercisable over or in relation to land;

(*b*) any works of construction, demolition, conversion, reconstruction, alteration, enlargement, repair or maintenance of a building or civil engineering work;

(*c*) services such as are supplied by estate agents, auctioneers, architects, surveyors, engineers and others involved in matters relating to land,

it shall be treated as made where the land in connection with which the supply is made is situated.

6 Transport

Subject to articles 7 and 10 below, services consisting of the transportation of passengers or goods shall be treated as supplied in the country in which the transportation takes place, and only to the extent that it takes place in that country.

7 For the purposes of article 6 above, there shall be treated as taking place wholly in a country any transportation which takes place partly outside the territorial jurisdiction of that country where—

(*a*) it takes place in the course of a journey between two points in that country, whether or not as part of a longer journey involving travel to or from another country; and

(*b*) the means of transport used does not put in or land in another country in the course of the journey between those two points.

8 Any—

(*a*) goods or services provided as part of a pleasure cruise; or

(*b*) services consisting of the transportation of any luggage or motor vehicle accompanying (in either case) a passenger,

shall be treated as supplied in the same place as the transportation of the passenger is treated as supplied (whether or not they would otherwise be treated as supplied separately); and, for the purpose of this article, a pleasure cruise shall be treated as the transportation of passengers.

Simon's Tax Cases—*C&E Comrs v Peninsular and Oriental Steam Navigation Co Ltd* [1996] STC 698; *Pendragon plc and ors v R&C Comrs* [2012] UKUT 90 (TCC), [2012] STC 1638.

9 Subject to article 14 below, where a supply consists of ancillary transport services, it shall be treated as made where those services are physically performed.

10 Subject to article 14 below, where a supply of services consists of the intra-Community transport of goods, it shall be treated as made in the member State in which the transportation of the goods begins.

11 Services of intermediaries

Subject to article 14 below, where services consist of the making of arrangements for the intra-Community transport of goods or of any other activity intended to facilitate the making of such a supply, they shall be treated as supplied in the member State where the transportation of the goods begins.

12 Subject to article 14 below, where services consist of the making of arrangements for the supply by or to another person of ancillary transport services in connection with the intra-Community transport of goods or of any other activity intended to facilitate the making of such a supply, they shall be treated as supplied in the member State where the ancillary transport services are physically performed.

13 Subject to article 14 below, where services consist of the making of arrangements for a supply by or to another person or of any other activity intended to facilitate the making of such a supply, being a supply which is not of a description within articles 9 or 10 above or 16 below, those services shall be treated as supplied in the same place as the supply by or to that other person is treated as made.

14 Use of customer's registration number

Where a supply of services—

(*a*) falls within articles 10 to 13 above; . . .[1]

[(*aa*) consists of the valuation of, or work carried out on, any goods [which are then dispatched or transported out of the member state where those services were physically carried out][2]; or][1]

(*b*) consists of ancillary transport services provided in connection with the intra-Community transport of goods,

and the recipient of those services makes use, for the purpose of the supply, of a registration number, then, notwithstanding any provision of this Order to the contrary, the supply shall be treated as made in the member State which issued the registration number if, and only if, the supply would otherwise be treated as taking place in a different member State.

Amendments—[1] Words revoked, and sub-para (*aa*) inserted, by the VAT (Place of Supply of Services) (Amendment) Order, SI 1995/3038 art 4, with effect from 1 January 1996.

[2] Words in sub-para (*aa*) substituted by the VAT (Place of Supply of Services)(Amendment) Order, SI 1996/2992 with effect from 1 January 1997.

15 Services supplied where performed

Where a supply of services consists of—

(*a*) cultural, artistic, sporting, scientific, educational or entertainment services;

(*b*) services relating to exhibitions, conferences or meetings;
(*c*) services ancillary to, including those of organising, any supply of a description within paragraph (*a*) or (*b*) above; [or][2]
(*d*) the valuation of, or work carried out on, any goods, [save as provided by Article 14 above,][1]

it shall be treated as made where the services are physically carried out.

Amendments—[1] Words in sub-para (*d*) added by the VAT (Place of Supply of Services) (Amendment) Order, SI 1995/3038 art 5, with effect from 1 January 1996.
[2] Word "or" at end of sub-para (*c*) inserted by the VAT (Place of Supply of Services) (Amendment) Order, SI 1996/2992 with effect from 1 January 1997.

16 Services supplied where received

Where a supply consists of any services of a description specified in any of [paragraphs 1 to 8 of Schedule 5][1] to the Act, and the recipient of that supply—
(*a*) belongs in a country, other than the Isle of Man, which is not a member State; or
[(*b*) is a person who belongs in a member State, but in a country other than that in which the supplier belongs, and who—
(i) receives the supply for the purpose of a business carried on by him; and
(ii) is not treated as having himself supplied the services by virtue of section 8 of the Act,
it shall be treated as made where the recipient belongs.][1]

Simon's Tax Cases—*Diversified Agency Services Ltd v C&E Comrs* [1996] STC 398.

Amendments—[1] Words in square brackets substituted by the VAT (Place of Supply of Services) (Amendment) Order, SI 1995/3038 art 6, with effect from 1 January 1996.

[**16A** Where a supply consists of any services of a description specified in paragraph 7C of Schedule 5 to the Act and—
(*a*) the recipient of the supply is a person who belongs in a member State;
(*b*) he does not receive it for the purposes of a business carried on by him;
(*c*) it is received from a person who belongs in a country, other than the Isle of Man, which is not a member State,

it shall be treated as made where the recipient belongs.][1]

Amendments—[1] Article 16A inserted by the VAT (Place of Supply of Services) (Amendment) Order, SI 2003/862 arts 2, 3 with effect for any services supplied after 30 June 2003.

[17 [Services supplied where enjoyed]

Amendments—Heading substituted by the VAT (Place of Supply of Services) (Amendment) Order, SI 2003/862 arts 2, 4 with effect for any services supplied after 30 June 2003.

Where a supply of services consists of—
(*a*) the letting on hire of any means of transport; or
[(*b*) services described in paragraph 7, 7A or 7B of Schedule 5 to the Act; or][2]
[(*c*) services described in paragraph 7C of that Schedule, when received by a person for the purposes of a business carried on by him,][2]

and those services would be treated, apart from this article, as supplied in the United Kingdom, they shall not be treated as supplied in the United Kingdom to the extent that the effective use and enjoyment of the services takes place outside the member States.][1]

Amendments—[1] Substituted by the VAT (Place of Supply of Services) (Amendment) Order, SI 1998/763 in relation to any services supplied on or after 18 March 1998.
[2] Paras (*b*), (*c*) substituted for para (*b*), by SI 2003/862 arts 2, 5 with effect for any services supplied after 30 June 2003.

[**18** Where a supply of services consists of—
(*a*) the letting on hire of any means of transport; or
[(*b*) services described in paragraph 7, 7A or 7B of Schedule 5 to the Act; or][2]
[(*c*) services described in paragraph 7C of that Schedule, when received by a person for the purposes of a business carried on by him,][2]

and those services would be treated, apart from this article, as supplied in a place outside the member States, they shall be treated as supplied in the United Kingdom to the extent that the effective use and enjoyment of the services takes place in the United Kingdom.][1]

Amendments—[1] Substituted by the VAT (Place of Supply of Services) (Amendment) Order, SI 1998/763 in relation to any services supplied on or after 18 March 1998.
[2] Paras (*b*), (*c*) substituted for para (*b*), by SI 2003/862 arts 2, 5 with effect for any services supplied after 30 June 2003.

19 . . .

Amendments—This paragraph revoked by the VAT (Place of Supply of Services) (Amendment) Order, SI 1998/763 in relation to any services supplied on or after 18 March 1998.

20 . . .

Amendments—This paragraph revoked by the VAT (Place of Supply of Services) (Amendment) Order, SI 1998/763 in relation to any services supplied on or after 18 March 1998.

[21—(1) The place of supply of a right to services shall be the same as [the place in which the supply of the services to which the right relates would be treated as made if made by the supplier of the right to the recipient of the right][2] (whether or not the right is exercised).
(2) The reference to a right to services in paragraph (1) above shall include a reference to any right, option or priority with respect to the supply of services and to the supply of an interest deriving from any right to services.][1]

Simon's Tax Cases—art 21(1) *R&C Comrs v Arachchige* [2011] STC 33.

Amendments—[1] This paragraph inserted by the VAT (Place of Supply of Services) (Amendment) Order, SI 1997/1524 in relation to any services performed on or after 1 July 1997.

[2] Words in para (1) substituted by the Value Added Tax (Place of Supply of Services) (Amendment) Order, SI 2006/1683 arts 2, 3 with effect from 1 August 2006.

1992/3122

VALUE ADDED TAX (CARS) ORDER 1992

Made by the Treasury under VATA 1983 ss 3(3), 3(5), 18(1), 18(2), 18(3), 18(4), 18(5), 18(6) and 29(2) (see now VATA 1994 ss 5(3), (5), 32(1)–(6), 43(2)) and all other enabling powers

Made . . . . *9 December 1992*
Laid before the House of Commons . . . . *11 December 1992*
Coming into force . . . . *1 January 1993*

1 Citation and commencement

This Order may be cited as the Value Added Tax (Cars) Order 1992 and shall come into force on 1st January 1993.

2[Interpretation

(1)] [4] In this Order—

"the Act" means the Value Added Tax Act [1994][1];

["the Manx Act" means [the Value Added Tax Act 1996][2]][1]

. . . [3]

"finance agreement" means an agreement for the sale of goods whereby the property in those goods is not to be transferred until the whole of the price has been paid and the seller retains the right to repossess the goods;

. . . [5]

["Motor car" means any motor vehicle of a kind normally used on public roads which has three or more wheels and either—

(*a*) is constructed or adapted solely or mainly for the carriage of passengers; or

(*b*) has to the rear of the driver's seat roofed accommodation which is fitted with side windows or which is constructed or adapted for the fitting of side windows;

but does not include—

(i) vehicles capable of accommodating only one person;

(ii) vehicles which meet the requirements of Schedule 6 to the Road Vehicles (Construction and Use) Regulations 1986 and are capable of carrying twelve or more seated persons;

(iii) vehicles of not less than three tonnes unladen weight (as defined in the Table to regulation 3(2) of the Road Vehicles (Construction and Use) Regulations 1986);

(iv) vehicles constructed to carry a payload (the difference between a vehicle's kerb weight (as defined in the Table to regulation 3(2) of the Road Vehicles (Construction and Use) Regulations 1986) and its maximum gross weight (as defined in that Table)) of one tonne or more;

(v) caravans, ambulances and prison vans;

(vi) vehicles constructed for a special purpose other than the carriage of persons and having no other accommodation for carrying persons than such as is incidental to that purpose;][3]

["auctioneer" means a person who sells or offers for sale goods at any public sale where persons become purchasers by competition, being the highest bidders.][1]

(2) . . . [5]

Press releases etc—Business Brief 16/04, 9-6-2004, clarifying HMRC's interpretation of the definition of a motor car; see also notice posted on HMRC website on 27 October 2006 concerning car derived vans and combi vans.

Simon's Tax Cases—*C&E Comrs v Jeynes (T/A Midland International (Hire) Caterers)* [1984] STC 30*; *Withers of Winsford Ltd v C&E Comrs* [1988] STC 431*.

Amendments—[1] Figure in the definition of "the Act" substituted for the figure "1983", and definitions "the Manx Act" and "auctioneer" inserted by the VAT (Cars) (Amendment) Order, SI 1995/1269 arts 2, 3 with effect from 1 June 1995.

[2] Words in the definition of "the Manx Act" substituted by the VAT (Cars) (Amendment) Order, SI 1998/759 with effect from 17 March 1998.

[3] Definition of "car dealer" revoked, and definition of "Motor car" substituted, by the VAT (Cars) (Amendment) Order, SI 1999/2832, arts 2, 3, with effect from 1 December 1999.

4 Para (1) numbered as such, definition of "insurer" substituted, and para (2) inserted, by the Financial Services and Markets Act 2000 (Consequential Amendments and Repeals) Order, SI 2001/3649 art 432 with effect from 1 December 2001.

5 In para (1), definition of "insurer" repealed, and para (2) repealed, by the VAT (Cars) (Amendment) Order, SI 2004/3084 with effect from 1 January 2005.

3 Revocations

The provisions specified in the first column of the Schedule to this Order are hereby revoked to the extent specified in the second column of that Schedule.

4 Treatment of transactions

(1) [Subject to paragraphs (1A) to (2) below,][2] each of the following descriptions of transactions shall be treated as neither a supply of goods nor a supply of services—

(*a*) the disposal of a used motor car by a person who repossessed it under the terms of a finance agreement, where the motor car is in the same condition as it was in when it was repossessed;

(*b*) the disposal of a used motor car by an insurer who has taken it in the settlement of a claim under a policy of insurance, where the motor car is disposed of in the same condition as it was in when it was so taken;

(*c*) the disposal of a motor car for no consideration . . .[2]

[(*d*) services in connection with a supply of a used motor car provided by an agent acting in his own name to the purchaser of the motor car the consideration for which is taken into account by virtue of article 8(8) below in calculating the price at which the agent sold the motor car.][1]

[(*e*) services in connection with the sale of a used motor car provided by an auctioneer acting in his own name to the vendor or the purchaser of the motor car the consideration for which is taken into account by virtue of article 8(9) below in calculating the price at which the auctioneer obtained (or as the case may be) sold the motor car.][1]

[(*f*) a relevant supply of services by a taxable person to whom a motor car has been let on hire or supplied or by whom a motor car has been acquired from another member State or imported.][2]

[(1A) Paragraph (1) above shall not apply in relation to a case falling within paragraph (1)(*a*) to (*c*) above unless the tax on any previous supply, acquisition or importation was wholly excluded from credit under section 25 of the Act.][2]

[(1AA) Paragraph (1)(*a*) above shall not apply where adjustment, whether or not made under regulation 38 of the Value Added Regulations 1995, has taken account, or may later take account, of VAT on the initial supply under the finance agreement as a result of repossession and the motor car delivered under that agreement was delivered on or after 1st September 2006.][3]

[(1B) Paragraph (1) above shall not apply in relation to a case falling within paragraph (1)(*f*) above unless the tax on any previous letting on hire, supply, acquisition or importation was wholly or partly excluded from credit under section 25 of the Act.][2]

[(1C) For the purposes of paragraph (1)(*f*) above a relevant supply of service is—

(*a*) the letting on hire of a motor car to any person for no consideration or for a consideration which is less than that which would be payable in money if it were a commercial transaction conducted at arms length; or

(*b*) the making available of a motor car (otherwise than by letting it on hire) to any person (including, where the taxable person is an individual, himself, and where the taxable person is a partnership, a partner) for private use, whether or not for a consideration.][2]

(2) Nothing in paragraph (1)(*a*) or (*b*) above shall be construed as meaning that a transaction is not a supply for the purposes of section [11(1)(*a*)][1] of the Act.

Simon's Tax Cases—*C & E Comrs v General Motors Acceptance Corporation (UK) plc* [2004] STC 577.

Amendments—1 Figures in para (2) substituted, and paras (1)(*d*), (*e*) added, by the VAT (Cars) (Amendment) Order, SI 1995/1269 art 4 with effect from 1 June 1995.

2 Words in para (1) sub-para (*f*) and paras (1A)–(1C) inserted, and words in para (1)(*c*) revoked by the VAT (Cars) (Amendment) (No 2) Order, SI 1995/1667 art 3 with effect from 1 August 1995.

3 Para (1AA) inserted by the VAT (Cars) (Amendment) Order, SI 2006/874 with effect from 13 April 2006 in relation to finance agreements entered into on or after that date. For these purposes, "finance agreement" has the meaning given in SI 1992/3122 art 2(1).

[4A Paragraph 5(4) of Schedule 4 to the Act shall not apply in relation to a motor car to which [article 5][2] below applies which is used or made available in circumstances where, but for the operation of that paragraph, it would be treated by virtue of [that article][2] as supplied to and by a taxable person.][1]

Amendments—1 This article inserted by the VAT (Cars) (Amendment) (No 2) Order, SI 1995/1667 art 4 with effect from 1 August 1995.

2 Words substituted by the VAT (Cars) (Amendment) Order, SI 1999/2832, arts 2, 4, with effect from 1 December 1999.

[5 Self-supplies

(1) This article applies to any motor car—

(*a*) which has been produced by a taxable person otherwise than by the conversion of a vehicle obtained by him;

(*b*) which has been produced by the taxable person by the conversion of another vehicle (whether a motor car or not) and in relation to which the condition in paragraph (2) below is satisfied; . . . [2]

(*c*) which was supplied to, or acquired from another member State or imported by, a taxable person and in relation to which the condition in paragraph (2) below is satisfied[;

(*d*) which was transferred to a taxable person as an asset of a business or part of a business in the course of the transfer of that business or part of a business as a going concern—

(i) in circumstances where the transfer was treated as neither a supply of goods nor a supply of services by virtue of an Order made or having effect as if made under section 5(3) of the Act;

(ii) in the hands of the transferor or any predecessor of his the motor car was one to which this article applied by virtue of sub-paragraph (*a*), (*b*) or (*c*) above; and

(iii) the motor car has not been treated as supplied by virtue of this article to and by the transferor or any of his predecessors.][2].

(2) The condition referred to in paragraph (1)(*b*) and (*c*) above is that the tax on the supply to, or acquisition or importation by, the taxable person of the motor car or the vehicle from which it was converted, as the case may be, was not wholly excluded from credit under section 25 of the Act.

[(2A) For the purposes of paragraph (1)(*d*) above a person is a predecessor of a transferor if—

(*a*) he transferred the motor car as an asset of a business or part of a business which he transferred as a going concern—

(i) to the transferor, or

(ii) where the motor car has been the subject of more than one such transfer, to a person who made one of those transfers; and

(*b*) the transfer of the motor car was treated as neither a supply of goods nor a supply of services by virtue of any Order made or having effect as if made under section 5(3) of the Act.][2]

[(3) Where a motor car to which this article applies—

(*a*) has not been supplied by the taxable person in the course or furtherance of a business carried on by him; and

(*b*) is used by him such that had it been supplied to, or imported or acquired from another member State by him at that time, his entitlement to credit under section 25 of the Act in respect of the VAT chargeable on such a supply, importation or acquisition from another member State would have been wholly excluded by virtue of article 7 of the Value Added Tax (Input Tax) Order 1992,

it shall be treated for the purposes of the Act as both supplied to him for the purposes of a business carried on by him and supplied by him for the purposes of that business.][2]][1]

Press releases etc—C&E Business Briefs 10/95 23-5-95 and 15/95 31-7-95 and VAT Information Sheet 12/95 1-6-95 (detailed guidance on rules governing supplies of business cars).

Note—It is believed that the comma after the word "time" in para (3)(*b*) should actually appear after the word "him".

Amendments—[1] This article substituted by the VAT (Cars) (Amendment) (No 2) Order, SI 1995/1667 arts 2, 5 with effect from 1 August 1995.

[2] Word "or" at end of para (1)(*b*) revoked, words at end of para (1), and para (3), substituted, and para (2A) inserted, by the VAT (Cars) (Amendment) Order, SI 1999/2832, arts 2, 5, 6, 7, with effect from 1 December 1999.

6, 6A . . .

Amendments—These articles revoked by the VAT (Cars) (Amendment) Order, SI 1999/2832, arts 2, 8, with effect from 1 December 1999.

7 [Article 5][2] above shall apply in relation to any bodies corporate which are treated for the purposes of section [43][1] of the Act as members of a group as if those bodies were one person, but any motor car which would fall to be treated as supplied to and by that person shall be treated as supplied to and by the representative member.

Amendments—[1] Figure substituted for the figure "29" by the VAT (Cars) (Amendment) Order, SI 1995/1269 art 6 with effect from 1 June 1995.

[2] Words substituted by the VAT (Cars) (Amendment) Order, SI 1999/2832, arts 2, 9, with effect from 1 December 1999.

[8 Relief for second-hand motor cars

(1) Subject to complying with such conditions (including the keeping of such records and accounts) as the Commissioners may direct in a notice published by them for the purposes of this Order or may otherwise direct, and subject to paragraph (3) below, where a person supplies a used motor car which he took possession of in any of the circumstances set out in paragraph (2) below, he may opt to account for the VAT chargeable on the supply on the profit margin on the supply instead of by reference to its value.

(2) The circumstances referred to in paragraph (1) above are that the taxable person took possession of the motor car pursuant to—

(*a*) a supply in respect of which no VAT was chargeable under the Act or under Part I of the Manx Act;

VAT SIs

(*b*) a supply on which VAT was chargeable on the profit margin in accordance with paragraph (1) above, or a corresponding provision made under the Manx Act or a corresponding provision of the law of another member State;

[(*bb*) a supply [received before 1 March 2000][3] to which the provisions of article 7(4) of the Value Added Tax (Input Tax) Order 1992 applied;][2]

[(*c*) a de-supplied transaction, other than an article 5 transaction;

(*d*) subject to paragraph (2A) below, an article 5 transaction.][5]

[(2A) An article 5 transaction does not fall within sub-paragraph (*d*) of paragraph (2) above unless the taxable person has a relevant predecessor in title.][5]

(3) This article does not apply to—

(*a*) a supply which is a letting on hire;

(*b*) the supply by any person of a motor car which was produced by him, if it was neither previously supplied by him in the course or furtherance of any business carried on by him nor treated as so supplied by virtue of article 5 above;

(*c*) any supply if an invoice or similar document showing an amount as being VAT or as being attributable to VAT is issued in respect of the supply;

(*d*) . . .[2]

(4) . . .[2]

(5) Subject to paragraph (6) below, for the purposes of determining the profit margin—

(*a*) the price at which the motor car was obtained shall be calculated as follows—

(i) (where the taxable person took possession of the used motor car pursuant to a supply) in the same way as the consideration for the supply would be calculated for the purposes of the Act;

(ii) (where the taxable person is a sole proprietor and the used motor car was supplied to him in his private capacity) in the same way as the consideration for the supply to him as a private individual would be calculated for the purposes of the Act;

[(iii) (where the taxable person took possession of the motor car pursuant to a de-supplied transaction, other than an article 5 transaction) by taking the price he paid pursuant to the transaction;

(iv) (where the taxable person took possession of the motor car pursuant to an article 5 transaction) by taking the price at which his relevant predecessor in title obtained the motor car;][5]

(*b*) the price at which the motor car is sold shall be calculated in the same way as the consideration for the supply would be calculated for the purposes of the Act;

(*c*) . . .[5]

(6) Subject to paragraph (7) below, where the taxable person is an agent acting in his own name the price at which the motor car was obtained shall be calculated in accordance with paragraph 5(*a*) above but the selling price calculated in accordance with paragraph 5(*b*) above shall be increased by the amount of any consideration payable to the taxable person in respect of services supplied by him to the purchaser in connection with the supply of the motor car.

(7) Instead of calculating the price at which the motor car was obtained or supplied in accordance with paragraph (6) above, an auctioneer acting in his own name may—

[(*a*) calculate the price at which the motor car was obtained by deducting from the successful bid the amount of the commission payable to him under his contract with the vendor for the sale of the motor car;][4]

(*b*) calculate the price at which the motor car was supplied by adding to the successful bid the consideration for any supply of services by him to the purchaser in connection with the sale of the motor car,

in either (or both) cases excluding the consideration for supplies of services that are not chargeable to VAT.][1].

[(8) For the purposes of this article—

"article 5 transaction" means a transaction which is a de-supplied transaction by virtue of a provision of article 5 of the Value Added Tax (Special Provisions) Order 1995 or a corresponding provision made under the Manx Act;

"de-supplied transaction" means a transaction which was treated by virtue of any Order made or having effect as if made under section 5(3) of the Act or under the corresponding provisions of the Manx Act as being neither a supply or goods nor a supply of services.][5]

[(9) For the purposes of this article a person is a relevant predecessor in title of a taxable person if—

(*a*) he is the person from whom the taxable person took possession of the motor car and himself took possession of it pursuant to a transaction within any of sub-paragraphs (*a*) to (*c*) of sub-paragraph (2) above; or

(*b*) where the motor car has been the subject of a succession of two or more article 5 transactions (culminating in the article 5 transaction to which the taxable person was a party), he was a party to one of those transactions and himself took possession of the motor car pursuant to a transaction within any of sub-paragraphs (*a*) to (*c*) of sub-paragraph (2) above.][5]

Press releases etc—C&E Press Notice 25-6-82 ("Premium and Nearly New" cars with value higher than list price sold by non-franchised dealers are unused for VAT purposes; "Personal import" cars acquired by the VAT registered dealers are also unused for VAT purposes when sold).
C&E Business Briefs 10/95 23-5-95 and 15/95 31-7-95 and VAT Information Sheet 12/95 1-6-95 (detailed guidance on rules governing supplies of business cars).

Amendments—[1] This article substituted by the VAT (Cars) (Amendment) Order, SI 1995/1269 art 7 with effect from 1 June 1995.

[2] Para (2)(*bb*) inserted and paras (3)(*d*), (4) revoked by the VAT (Cars) (Amendment) (No 2) Order, SI 1995/1667 art 8 with effect from 1 August 1995.

[3] In para 8(2)(*bb*) words inserted by the VAT (Cars) (Amendment) Order, SI 1999/2832, arts 2, 10, with effect from 1 March 2000.

[4] Para (7)(*a*) substituted by the VAT (Cars) (Amendment) Order, SI 2001/3754 art 3 with effect from 2 January 2002.

[5] Sub-paras (2)(*c*), (*d*) substituted, sub-paras (5)(*a*)(iii), (iv) substituted for sub-para (5)(*a*)(iii), sub-para (5)(*c*) revoked, and paras (8), (9) added, by the VAT (Cars) (Amendment) Order, SI 2002/1502 with effect from 1 July 2002. For further provisions as to the effect of that Order see SI 2002/1502 art 1(2).

Note—The Commissioners have confirmed that the cross reference in art 8(6) should refer to paras (5)(*a*) and (5)(*b*) above and not paras 5(*a*) and 5(*b*), as stated in the amending order SI 1995/1269 art 7.

1992/3124

VALUE ADDED TAX (IMPORTED GOLD) RELIEF ORDER 1992

Made by the Treasury under VATA 1983 s 19(1) (see now VATA 1994 s 37(1)) and all other enabling powers

Made . . . . *9 December 1992*
Laid before the House of Commons . . . . *11 December 1992*
Coming into force . . . . *1 January 1993*

1 This Order may be cited as the Value Added Tax (Imported Gold) Relief Order 1992 and shall come into force on 1st January 1993.

2 The tax chargeable upon the importation of gold (including gold coins) from a place outside the Member States shall not be payable where the importation is by a Central Bank.

3 The Value Added Tax (Imported Goods) Relief Order 1977 is hereby revoked.

1992/3130

VALUE ADDED TAX (SUPPLY OF TEMPORARILY IMPORTED GOODS) ORDER 1992

Made by the Treasury under VATA 1983 s 3(3) (see now VATA 1994 s 5(3)) and all other enabling powers

Made . . . . *9 December 1992*
Laid before the House of Commons . . . . *11 December 1992*
Coming into force . . . . *1 January 1993*

1 This Order may be cited as the Value Added Tax (Supply of Temporarily Imported Goods) Order 1992 and shall come into force on 1st January 1993.

2—(1) Where goods held under temporary importation arrangements are supplied, that supply shall be treated as neither a supply of goods nor a supply of services provided that—
(*a*) the goods remain eligible for temporary importation arrangements; and
(*b*) the supply is to a person established outside the member States.

(2) "Goods held under temporary importation arrangements" means goods placed under customs arrangements with total relief from customs duty within the meaning of Council Regulation (EEC) No 3599/82, whether or not the goods are subject to customs duty.

1992/3132

VALUE ADDED TAX (TREATMENT OF TRANSACTIONS) (NO 2) ORDER 1992

Made by the Treasury under VATA 1983 s 8A(4) (see now VATA 1994 s 11(4)) and all other enabling powers

Made . . . . *9 December 1992*
Laid before the House of Commons . . . . *11 December 1992*

VAT SIs

Coming into force . . . . *1 January 1993*

1 This Order may be cited as the Value Added Tax (Treatment of Transactions) (No 2) Order 1992, and shall come into force on 1st January 1993.

2—(1) Where gold is supplied to a Central Bank by a supplier in another member State, and the transaction involves the removal of the gold from that or some other member State to the United Kingdom, the taking possession of the gold by the Central Bank concerned is not to be treated for the purposes of the Value Added Tax Act 1983[1] as the acquisition of goods from another member State.
(2) For the purposes of this article, gold includes gold coins.

Note—[1] VATA 1994.

1992/3135

EXCISE GOODS (HOLDING, MOVEMENT, WAREHOUSING AND REDS) REGULATIONS 1992

Made by the Commissioners of Customs and Excise under CEMA 1979 ss 93, 100G, 100H and 127A and F(No 2)A 1992 ss 1, 2

Made . . . . *10 December 1992*
Laid before Parliament . . . . *14 December 1992*
Coming into force . . . . *1 January 1993*

Revocation—These Regulations revoked by Excise Goods (Holding, Movement and Duty Point) Regulations, SI 2010/593 reg 91, Sch 3 with effect from 1 April 2010.

1992/3152

EXCISE DUTIES (DEFERRED PAYMENT) REGULATIONS 1992

Made by the Commissioners of Customs and Excise under CEMA 1979 ss 93, 127A; ALDA 1979 ss 13, 15, 56, 62(5); HODA 1979 ss 21, 24 and the ECA 1972 s 2(2)

Made . . . . *10 December 1992*
Laid before Parliament . . . . *11 December 1992*
Coming into force . . . . *1 January 1993*

PART I
PRELIMINARY

1 Citation, commencement and revocation

(1) These Regulations may be cited as the Excise Duties (Deferred Payment) Regulations 1992 and shall come into force on 1st January 1993.
(2) The Excise Duties (Deferred Payment) Regulations 1983, the Excise Duties (Hydrocarbon Oils) (Deferred Payment) Regulations 1985; the Excise Duties (Deferred Payment) (Amendment) Regulations 1986 and the Excise Duties (Deferred Payment) (Amendment) Regulations 1989 are hereby revoked.

2 Interpretation

In these Regulations—

"approved person" means a person approved by the Commissioners under regulation 4 below;
"business day" means a day which is a business day within the meaning of section 92 of the Bills of Exchange Act 1882;
"hydrocarbon oils" means goods (except petrol substitutes, power methylated spirits and road fuel gas) chargeable with excise duty by virtue of the Hydrocarbon Oil Duties Act 1979 and includes composite goods containing hydrocarbon oils on which goods excise duty is chargeable;
"imported by a registered excise dealer and shipper" includes any importation where goods are moved under the instructions of a registered excise dealer and shipper or are, in accordance with registered excise dealers and shippers regulations, deemed to be so moved;
"made-wine" includes composite goods containing made-wine on which goods excise duty is chargeable;
"spirits" includes composite goods containing spirits on which good excise duty is chargeable;
"payment day" has the meaning given by regulation 5 below;
"wine" includes composite goods containing wine on which goods excise duty is chargeable.

3 Application

These Regulations shall apply to goods on which excise duty would, but for deferment granted by these Regulations, be payable on or after 1st January 1993; being goods of any of the following descriptions—

(*a*) wine, made-wine, cider, spirits, hydrocarbon oils; and

(*b*) beer imported by a registered excise dealer and shipper.

PART II

DEFERMENT OF EXCISE DUTY

4 Approved persons

(1) A person who wishes to be granted excise duty deferment under these Regulations shall apply to be approved for excise duty deferment purposes.

(2) When approving a person under this regulation the Commissioners may specify the maximum amount of excise duty which may be deferred by that person at any time under that approval.

(3) When approving a person under this regulation the Commissioners may limit the approval to deferment in respect of goods which are at specified places.

(4) A person may be approved separately under this regulation in respect of different places.

(5) The Commissioners may, for reasonable cause, at any time vary or revoke any approval granted under this regulation.

5 Deferment

(1) Deferment shall be granted upon the giving of notice by an approved person that he wishes excise duty in respect of any goods to be deferred until a day, to be known as "payment day", provided that the notice is given in such form and manner and contains such particulars as the Commissioners may require and provided that the provisions of these Regulations are complied with.

(2) Subject to regulation 6 below, on each payment day an approved person shall pay to the Commissioners the total amount of excise duty of which he has been granted deferment until that payment day.

(3) Payment day shall be—

(*a*) in the case of beer imported by a registered excise dealer and shipper, the 25th day of the month following the month in which the duty would, but for deferment granted by these Regulations, be payable;

(*b*) in the case of any goods other than beer imported by a registered excise dealer and shipper, the 15th day of the month following the month in which the duty on those goods would, but for deferment granted by these Regulations, be payable;

(*c*) in the case of hydrocarbon oils delivered for home use from a refinery or other premises used for the production of hydrocarbon oil or from an excise warehouse on or after the 15th day of one month and not later than the 14th day of the next month, the last business day of that next month; and

(*d*) in any other case, where the duty on those goods would, but for deferment granted by these Regulations, be payable on or after the 15th day of one month and not later than the 14th day of the next month, either—

(i) the 29th day of that next month; or

(ii) where that next month has only 28 days, the 28th day of that month;

provided that where the payment day would, if determined in accordance with the foregoing provisions of this paragraph, fall on a day upon which the Bank of England is closed, the payment day shall be, in the case mentioned in sub-paragraph (b) above the next business day following that day and, in any other case, the last business day preceding that day.

6 Set-offs

(1) Subject to paragraph (2) below an approved person shall set-off all sums to which he is entitled as rebate under section 11 of the Hydrocarbon Oil Duties Act 1979 all sums to which he is entitled to repayment under section 15 of that Act[, regulation 3(1)(*b*) of the Hydrocarbon Oil Duties (Marine Voyages Reliefs) Regulations 1996][1] and such other sums as the Commissioners may allow against excise duty required to be paid by him on payment day under regulation 5 above.

(2) An approved person shall not set-off those sums referred to in paragraph (1) above unless on or before the said payment day he submits to the Commissioners a claim for set-off in such form and manner and containing such particulars as they may require.

(3) Rebate shall not be set-off under paragraph (1) above at a payment day earlier than that on which duty deferred under these Regulations, in respect of which the rebate exists, would have been due.

Amendments—[1] Words in para (1) inserted by Hydrocarbon Oil Duties (Marine Voyages Reliefs) Regulations, SI 1996/2537 reg 15 with effect from 1 November 1996.

7 Adjustments

(1) If a notice has been given under regulation 5 above or any other document has been submitted to the Commissioners in respect of excise duty deferment and the Commissioners are satisfied that the full amount of excise duty payable has not been shown then, save as the Commissioners may otherwise allow, the balance of excise duty shall be paid forthwith.

(2) If a notice has been given under regulation 5 above or any other document has been submitted to the Commissioners in respect of excise duty deferment and the Commissioners are satisfied that excise duty in excess of the amount payable has been shown other than by reason of a set-off under regulation 6 above, the Commissioners shall repay or give credit for that excess, but the total amount shown shall nonetheless be paid on payment day.

PART III

REQUIREMENTS TO BE OBSERVED

8 Security

A person who is approved for the purpose of applying for deferment of excise duty shall provide such security for that duty in such form and manner and in such amount as the Commissioners may require.

9 Conditions

The Commissioners may make any approval of a person or any grant of deferment of duty subject to any condition or requirement and conditions or requirements may be added to or varied at any time by the Commissioners.

10 Change of Circumstances

Any person who has applied to be approved or has been approved under regulation 4 above shall notify the Commissioners immediately of any change in circumstances which materially affects any application for approval or for deferment of duty or any security given by him under these Regulations.

PART IV

RELATIONSHIP TO OTHER ENACTMENTS

11 Purposes for which excise duty is treated as paid

Without prejudice to regulation 5 above for the purposes of the following enactments excise duty shall be deemed to have been paid at the time when deferment was granted—

(*a*) sections 24(2)(*b*), [43(1), 49(1)(*a*)][1], 51, 67(1)(*b*), 96(1)(*a*), 127 and 162 of the Customs and Excise Management Act 1979;

(*b*) sections 10(2)(*a*) and 11(1)(*a*) of the Customs and Excise Duties (General Reliefs) Act 1979;

(*c*) sections 16, 21, 22(1), 22(3A), 22(5), 42 and 43 of the Alcoholic Liquor Duties Act 1979;

(*d*) sections 9(4), 15(1), 17(1), . . .[1], 19(3), 19A(1) and 20(1) of the Hydrocarbon Oils Duties Act 1979.

[(*e*) regulation 3(1)(*b*) of the Hydrocarbon Oil Duties (Marine Voyages Reliefs) Regulations 1996][1]

Amendments—[1] Words in (*a*) substituted by, words in (*d*) deleted by, and (*e*) above inserted by Hydrocarbon Oil Duties (Marine Voyages Reliefs) Regulations, SI 1996/2537 reg 15 with effect from 1 November 1996.

12 Savings for requirements of other Regulations

Nothing in these Regulations shall be taken to remove any obligation placed upon any person to comply with the requirements or conditions imposed by or under any other Regulations relating to the goods in respect of which payment of duty is deferred under these Regulations, except in so far as those other Regulations relate to the date for payment of duty and deferment of that payment is granted under these Regulations.

1992/3156

CUSTOMS AND EXCISE (PERSONAL RELIEFS FOR SPECIAL VISITORS) ORDER 1992

Made by the Commissioners of Customs and Excise under the Customs and Excise Duties (General Reliefs) Act 1979 s 13A and all other enabling powers

Made . . . . *10 December 1992*
Laid before the House of Commons . . . . *11 December 1992*
Coming into force . . . . *1 January 1993*

PART I

PRELIMINARY

1 This Order may be cited as the Customs and Excise (Personal Reliefs for Special Visitors) Order 1992 and shall come into force on 1st January 1993.

PART II

INTERPRETATION

2 In this Order—

"acquisition" means an acquisition of goods from another member State within the meaning of section 2A of the Value Added Tax Act 1983[a] and "acquired" shall be construed accordingly;

"duty" means any duty of customs or duty of excise;

"importation" means an importation from a place outside the member States, and "imported" shall be construed accordingly;

"relief" means the remission of any duty or tax which is chargeable and which a person, whether the person upon whom the relief is conferred or some other person, would be liable to pay were it not for the relief conferred;

"supply" means a supply within the meaning of section 3 of the Value Added Tax Act 1983[b] and "supplied" shall be construed accordingly;

"tax" means value added tax;

"United Kingdom national" means a British citizen, a British Dependent Territories citizen, a British National (Overseas) or a British Overseas citizen;

"used", in relation to a person's use of consumable property, includes having the property at his disposal;

"warehouse" means a warehouse within the meaning of section 1(1) of the Customs and Excise Management Act 1979 [the premises in respect of which a person is registered under section 41A, 47, or 62(2) of the Alcoholic Liquor Duties Act 1979, the premises in respect of which a person holds an excise licence under section 54(2) or 55(2) of that Act, or premises registered for the safe storage of tobacco products in accordance with regulations made under section 7(1)(b) of the Tobacco Products Duty Act 1979;][1] and "removal from warehouse" shall be construed accordingly.

Notes—[a] VATA 1994 s 10.

[b] VATA 1994 s 5.

[1] Words in definition of "warehouse" inserted by the Customs and Excise (Personal Reliefs for Special Visitors) (Amendment) Order, SI 2007/5 arts 1, 2 with effect from 1 February 2007.

PART III

CONDITIONS ATTACHING TO PART VI RELIEFS

3 In this Part—

"entitled person" means an entitled person for the purposes of Part VI.

4 It shall be a condition of the relief conferred under article 16 below that the entitled person deliver or cause to be delivered to the supplier of the motor vehicle a certificate in the form numbered 1 in the Schedule to this Order—

(*a*) containing full information in respect of the matters specified therein; and

(*b*) signed—

(i) as to Part A, by the entitled person upon whom the relief is conferred;

(ii) as to Part B, by the head of the mission or other body or organisation of which the entitled person is a member;

(iii) as to Part C, by the Secretary of State or a person authorised to sign on his behalf; and

(iv) as to Part D, by the supplier,

before the supply is made.

PART IV

CONDITIONS ATTACHING TO PART VII RELIEFS

5—(1) In this Part—

"entitled person" means an entitled person for the purposes of Part VII.

(2) For the purposes of articles 6 and 7 below, any reference to a certificate shall be construed as including a reference to a copy of such a certificate.

6—(1) It shall be a condition of relief conferred under article 19 below that the entitled person deliver or cause to be delivered in accordance with paragraph (2) below five certificates in the form numbered 2 in the Schedule to this Order—

(*a*) containing full information in respect of the matters specified therein; and (*b*) signed—

(i) as to Part A, by the entitled person upon whom the relief is conferred; and

(ii) as to Part B, by the officer commanding the visiting force or other body or organisation of which the entitled person is a member or by a person authorised to sign on his behalf.

(2) The certificates referred to in paragraph (1) above shall be delivered before the supply is made as follows:

(*a*) two certificates shall be delivered to the visiting force or other body or organisation of which the entitled person is a member;

(*b*) two certificates shall be delivered to the proper officer; and

(*c*) one certificate shall be delivered to the supplier of the motor vehicle.

7—(1) It shall be a condition of relief conferred under article 20 below in respect of a motor vehicle that the entitled person deliver or cause to be delivered in accordance with paragraph (2) below four certificates in the form numbered 3 in the Schedule to this Order—

(*a*) containing full information in respect of the matters specified therein; and

(*b*) signed—

(i) as to Part A, by the entitled person upon whom the relief is conferred; and

(ii) as to Part B, by the officer commanding the visiting force or other body or organisation of which the entitled person is a member or by a person authorised to sign on his behalf.

(2) The certificates referred to in paragraph (1) above shall be delivered before the goods are removed by or on behalf of the entitled person as follows:

(*a*) one certificate shall be delivered to the visiting force or other body or organisation of which the entitled person is a member; and

(*b*) three certificates shall be delivered to the proper officer.

PART V
CONDITIONS ATTACHING TO ALL RELIEFS

8 In this Part—

"entitled person" means an entitled person for the purposes of either Part VI or Part VII of this Order.

9 An entitled person upon whom any relief is conferred under any Part of this Order shall be bound by the conditions described in the following provisions of this Part and in Part III or IV above, as the case may be.

10—(1) It shall be a condition of the relief that the goods shall not be lent, hired-out, given as security or transferred by the entitled person or any other person without the prior authorisation in writing of the Commissioners.

(2) Where the Commissioners authorise such disposal as is mentioned in paragraph (1) above, they may discharge the relief and the entitled person to whom the relief was afforded shall forthwith pay the duty or tax at the rate then in force, provided that where a lower rate was in force when relief was afforded the amount payable shall be determined by reference to the lower rate.

11 It shall be a condition of the relief that the goods are used exclusively by the entitled person or members of his family forming part of his household.

12 Where relief has been afforded and subsequently the Commissioners are not satisfied that any condition attaching to such relief, whether by virtue of a provision of this Order or otherwise, has been complied with, then, unless the Commissioners sanction the non-compliance in writing, the duty or tax shall become payable forthwith and the goods shall be liable to forfeiture.

13 Where relief has been afforded, but any duty or tax subsequently becomes payable by virtue of article 12 above, the following persons shall be jointly and severally liable to pay it—

(*a*) the entitled person upon whom the relief was conferred;

(*b*) any person who, at or after the time of the non-compliance with the condition which has caused the duty or tax to become payable, has been in possession of the goods.

PART VI
DIPLOMATS ETC

14 In this Part—

"entitled person" means:

(*a*) any person enjoying any privilege or immunity by virtue of his being—

(i) a diplomatic agent for the purposes of the Diplomatic Privileges Act 1964
(ii) a senior officer of the Commonwealth Secretariat for the purposes of the Commonwealth Secretariat Act 1966
(iii) a consular officer for the purposes of the Consular Relations Act 1968
(iv) a representative or a person recognised as holding a rank equivalent to a diplomatic agent for the purposes of the International Organisations Act 1968 or

(*b*) any person enjoying, under or by virtue of section 2 of the European Communities Act 1972 any privilege or immunity similar to those enjoyed under or by virtue of the enactments referred to in paragraph (*a*) above by the persons therein specified,

who is neither a United Kingdom national nor a permanent resident of the United Kingdom.

15 Where any tobacco product or beverage containing alcohol is removed from warehouse in the course of its being supplied to an entitled person, payment of any duty or tax chargeable in respect of the removal from warehouse or supply shall not be required.

16—(1) Subject to the following provisions of this article, where an entitled person purchases a motor vehicle which has been manufactured in a country, other than the United Kingdom, which is—
(*a*) a member State; or
(*b*) a member of the European Free Trade Association,
payment of any tax chargeable in respect of the supply shall not be required.
(2) No relief shall be afforded under paragraph (1) above if the entitled person has previously been afforded relief in respect of any other motor vehicle, whether under paragraph (1) above or otherwise, unless he has disposed of all previous motor vehicles in respect of which relief has been so afforded and paid any duty or tax which was required to be paid under article 10(2) above.
(3) Where the spouse [or civil partner][1] of the entitled person is present in the United Kingdom, paragraph (2) above shall apply as if the words "(or all but one)" were inserted after the words "motor vehicles".

Amendment—[1] Words in para (3) inserted by the Civil Partnership Act 2004 (Amendments to Subordinate Legislation) Order, SI 2005/2114 art 2(1), Sch 1 para 5 with effect from 5 December 2005.

17 Nothing in this Part of this Order shall be taken as conferring relief in respect of any duty or tax which is subject to remission or refund by or under any of the enactments referred to in article 14 above.

PART VII
VISITING FORCES AND HEADQUARTERS

18 In this Part—
"entitled person" means a person who is—
(*a*) for the purposes of any provision of the Visiting Forces Act 1952 a serving member of a visiting force of a country, other than the United Kingdom, which is a party to the North Atlantic Treaty, or a person recognised by the Secretary of State as a member of a civilian component of such a force, or
(*b*) a person who is a military or civilian member of a headquarters or organisation designated for the purposes of any provision of the International Headquarters and Defence Organisations Act 1964

who is neither a United Kingdom national nor a permanent resident of the United Kingdom.

19 Subject to article 22 below, where an entitled person purchases a motor vehicle which has been manufactured in a country which is—
(*a*) a member State; or
(*b*) a member of the European Free Trade Association,
payment of any tax in respect of the supply shall not be required.

20 Subject to article 22 below, where an entitled person imports, acquires or removes from warehouse any goods, payment of any duty or tax chargeable in respect of the importation, acquisition or removal from warehouse shall not be required.

21 Subject to article 22 below, where a gift of goods, other than tobacco products or beverages containing alcohol, is made to an entitled person by dispatching them to him from a place outside the United Kingdom, payment of any duty or tax chargeable in respect of their acquisition or importation shall not be required.

22—(1) No relief shall be afforded under this Part of this Order in respect of a motor vehicle if the entitled person has previously been afforded relief under this Order in respect of any other motor vehicle, unless he has disposed of all previous motor vehicles in respect of which relief has been so afforded and paid any duty or tax which was required to be paid under article 10(2) above.

(2) Where the spouse [or civil partner][1] of the entitled person is present in the United Kingdom, paragraph (1) above shall apply as if the words "(or all but one)" were inserted after the words "motor vehicles".

Amendment—[1] Words in para (2) inserted by the Civil Partnership Act 2004 (Amendments to Subordinate Legislation) Order, SI 2005/2114 art 2(1), Sch 1 para 5 with effect from 5 December 2005.

SCHEDULE

FORM NO 1—CERTIFICATE FOR USE IN CONNECTION WITH THE PURCHASE OF AN EC (NOT UK) OR EFTA ORIGIN VEHICLE FREE OF VALUE ADDED TAX (C 428) (ARTICLE 4).

FORM NO 2—VISITING FORCES' CERTIFICATE OF ENTITLEMENT TO RELIEF FROM DUTY AND VAT ON THE PURCHASE OF A MOTOR VEHICLE (C&E 941A) (ARTICLE 6(1)).

FORM NO 3—VISITING FORCES' CERTIFICATE OF ENTITLEMENT TO RELIEF FROM DUTY AND VAT ON THE IMPORT/WITHDRAWAL FROM WAREHOUSE OF A MOTOR VEHICLE (C 941) (ARTICLE 7(1)).

Note—See Forms C428, C&E 941A, C941 set out on the following pages.

Article 4

FORM 1

Certificate for use in Connection with the Purchase of an EC (not UK) or EFTA Origin Vehicle free of Value Added Tax

Part A: To be completed by entitled person

Surname	Forenames	Rank or status

Embassy/High Commission/International Organisation

Signature of entitled person. .... Date ....

Part B: Certificate by Head of Mission

Official Stamp

Signature ....

Name ....
(BLOCK LETTERS)

Part C: Certificate by Foreign & Commonwealth Office

This is to certify that the above named is entitled to purchase an EC or EFTA origin vehicle at a VAT exclusive price.

Signature .... Department .... Date ....

Part D: Particular of Vehicle (to be completed by supplier)

Make and model	Engine number	Chassis number
Vehicle registration mark	Year of manufacture	

Name of supplier ....

Signature of supplier .... Date ....

C 428 CD3433/N3(12/92) F 3690( )

Article 6(1)

HM Customs and Excise

Visiting Forces' Certificate of Entitlement to Relief from Duty and Value Added Tax on the Import/Withdrawal from Warehouse of a Motor Vehicle or on the Acquisition of a New Means of Transport

Please complete four copies.

Part A: To be completed by entitled person

Surname	Forenames	Rank and Service No.

Base in the UK to which assigned

Private address in the UK

***Particulars of vehicle/new means of transport**

Make and model	Engine number	Chassis/Hull/Airframe number
Registration mark		Year of manufacture

Declaration

I declare that:-

I am a member of *the civilian component of/the .... visiting forces and that the details given above are true and complete.

Signature of entitled person. .... Date ....

Part B Certificate by Visiting Force

I certify that .... is a member of *the civilian component of/the visiting forces serving in the United Kingdom.

Signature .... Date ....

Name and rank (in BLOCK LETTERS) ....

For official use	Date stamp

* *delete as necessary*

C&E 941 PCU (October 1997)

HM Customs and Excise

Visiting Forces' Certificate of Entitlement to Relief from Duty and Value Added Tax on the Import/Withdrawal from Warehouse of a Motor Vehicle or on the Acquisition of a New Means of Transport

Please complete four copies.

Part A: To be completed by entitled person

Surname	Forenames	Rank and Service No.

Base in the UK to which assigned

Private address in the UK

***Particulars of vehicle/new means of transport**

Make and model	Engine number	Chassis/Hull/Airframe number
Registration mark		Year of manufacture

Declaration

I declare that:-

I am a member of *the civilian component of/the .... visiting forces and that the details given above are true and complete.

Signature of entitled person. .... Date ....

Part B Certificate by Visiting Force

I certify that .... is a member of *the civilian component of/the visiting forces serving in the United Kingdom.

Signature .... Date ....

Name and rank (in BLOCK LETTERS) ....

For official use	Date stamp

* *delete as necessary*

C&E 941

PCU (October 1997)

1992/3193

CUSTOMS AND EXCISE DUTIES (PERSONAL RELIEFS FOR GOODS PERMANENTLY IMPORTED) ORDER 1992

Made by the Commissioners of Customs and Excise under CED(GR)A 1979 ss 7, 13.

Made .... *16 December 1992*
Laid before the House of Commons .... *17 December 1992*
Coming into force .... *1 January 1993*

PART I

PRELIMINARY

1 Citation and commencement

This order may be cited as the Customs and Excise Duties (Personal Reliefs for Goods Permanently Imported) Order 1992 and shall come into force on 1st January 1993.

2 Interpretation

In this Order—

"declared for relief" has the meaning assigned to it by article 8 below;

"household effects" means furnishing and equipment for personal household use;

"motor vehicle" shall include a trailer;

"normal residence" means a person's principal place of abode situated in the country where he is normally resident;

"normally resident" has the meaning assigned to it by article 3 below;

"occupational ties" shall not include attendance by a pupil or student at a school, college or university;

"personal ties" shall mean family or social ties to which a person devotes most of his time not devoted to occupational ties;

"property" means any personal property intended for personal use or for meeting household needs and shall include household effects, household provisions, household pets and riding animals, cycles, motor vehicles, caravans, pleasure boats and private aircraft, provided that there shall be excluded any goods which, by their nature or quantity, indicate that they are being imported for a commercial purpose;

"third country", shall have the meaning given by Article 3.1 of Council Directive 77/388/EEC;

"used", in relation to a person's use of consumable property, shall include having the property at his disposal.

3 Rules for determining where a person is normally resident

(1) This article shall apply for the purpose of determining, in relation to this Order, where a person is normally resident.

(2) A person shall be treated as being normally resident in the country where he usually lives—

(*a*) for a period of, or periods together amounting to, at least 185 days in a period of twelve months;

(*b*) because of his occupational ties; and

(*c*) because of his personal ties.

(3) In the case of a person with no occupational ties, paragraph (2) above shall apply with the omission of sub-paragraph (*b*), provided his personal ties show close links with that country.

(4) Where a person has his occupational ties in one country and his personal ties in another country, he shall be treated as being normally resident in the latter country provided that either—

(*a*) his stay in the former country is in order to carry out a task of a definite duration, or

(*b*) he returns regularly to the country where he has his personal ties.

(5) Notwithstanding paragraph (4) above, a United Kingdom citizen whose personal ties are in the United Kingdom but whose occupational ties are in a third country may for the purposes of relief under this Order be treated as normally resident in the country of his occupational ties, provided he has lived there for a period of, or periods together amounting to, at least 185 days in a period of twelve months.

4 Supplementary

For the purposes of this Order—

(*a*) any reference to a person who has been normally resident in a third country and who intends to become normally resident in the United Kingdom shall be taken as a reference to a person who intends to comply with the requirements of paragraphs (2), (3) or (4) of article 3 above, as the case may be, for being treated as normally resident in the United Kingdom;

(*b*) the date on which a person becomes normally resident in the United Kingdom shall be the date when having given up his normal residence in a third country he is in the United Kingdom for the purpose of fulfilling such intention as is mentioned in paragraph (*a*) above.

PART II

PROVISIONS COMMON TO CERTAIN RELIEFS

5 Property may be in separate consignments

Except as otherwise provided by this Order, where property in respect of which relief is afforded is permitted to be imported over a period it may be imported in more than one consignment during such period.

6 Condition as to security for certain importations

Where any goods are declared for relief under this Order—

(*a*) before the date on which a person becomes normally resident in the United Kingdom, or

(*b*) if he intends to become so resident on the occasion of his marriage before such marriage has taken place,

the relief shall be subject to the condition that there is furnished to the Commissioners such security as they may require.

7 Restriction on disposal without authorisation

(1) Except as provided by or under this Order, where relief is afforded under any Part of this Order, it shall be a condition of the relief that the goods are not lent, hired-out, given as security or transferred in the United Kingdom within a period of twelve months from the date on which relief was afforded, unless such disposal is authorised by the Commissioners.

(2) Where the Commissioners authorise any such disposal as is mentioned in paragraph (1) above, they may discharge the relief and the person to whom the relief was afforded shall forthwith pay tax at the rate then in force, provided that where a lower rate was in force when relief was afforded the amount payable shall be determined by reference to the lower rate.

PART III

PROVISIONS COMMON TO ALL RELIEFS

8 Goods to be declared for relief

(1) A person shall not be entitled to relief from payment of duty or tax in respect of any goods under any Part of this Order unless the goods are declared for relief to the proper officer.

(2) For the purposes of this Order, the expression "declared for relief" shall refer to the act by which a person applies for relief on importation of the goods or on their removal from another customs procedure and includes, as the case may be, any declaration under section 78 of the Customs and Excise Management Act 1979 or any entry under the Postal Packets (Customs and Excise) Regulations 1986, the Excise Warehousing (Etc) Regulations 1988, or regulation 5 of the Customs Controls on Importation of Goods Regulations 1991, or any entry required by Article 40 of Commission Regulation (EEC) No 2561/90.

9 Fulfilment of intention to be a condition

Where relief from payment of duty or tax is afforded under any Part of this Order subject to a specified intention on the part of a person in relation to his becoming normally resident in the United Kingdom, or the use of the goods in respect of which relief is afforded, it shall be a condition of the relief that such intention be fulfilled.

10 Enforcement

Where relief from payment of duty or tax has been afforded under any Part of this Order and subsequently the Commissioners are not satisfied that any condition subject to which such relief was afforded has been complied with, then, unless the Commissioners sanction the non-compliance, the duty or tax shall become payable forthwith by the person to whom relief was afforded (except to the extent that the Commissioners may see fit to waive payment of the whole or any part thereof) and the goods shall be liable to forfeiture.

PART IV

11 Persons Transferring Their Normal Residence From A Third Country

(1) Subject to the provisions of this Part, a person entering the United Kingdom shall not be required to pay any duty or tax chargeable in respect of property imported into the United Kingdom on condition that—

(*a*) he has been normally resident in a third country for a continuous period of at least twelve months;

(*b*) he intends to become normally resident in the United Kingdom;

(*c*) the property has been in his possession and used by him in the country where he has been normally resident, for a period of at least six months before its importation;

(*d*) the property is intended for his personal or household use in the United Kingdom; and

(*e*) the property is declared for relief—

(i) not earlier than six months before the date on which he becomes normally resident in the United Kingdom, and

(ii) not later than twelve months following that date.

(2) A person shall not be afforded relief under this Part unless the Commissioners are satisfied that the goods have borne, in their country of origin or exportation, the customs or other duties and taxes to which goods of that class or description are normally liable and that such goods have not, by reason of their exportation, been subject to any exemption from, or refund of, such duties and taxes as aforesaid, or any turnover tax, excise duty or other consumption tax.

(3) For the purposes of this Part, "property" shall not include—

(*a*) beverages containing alcohol;
(*b*) tobacco products;
(*c*) any motor road vehicle which by its type of construction and equipment is designed for and capable of transporting more than nine persons including the driver, or goods, or any special purpose vehicle or mobile workshop; and
(*d*) articles for use in the exercise of a trade or profession, other than portable instruments of the applied or liberal arts.

12 Supplementary
Where the Commissioners are satisfied that a person has given up his normal residence in a third country but is prevented by occupational ties from becoming normally resident in the United Kingdom immediately, they may allow property to be declared for relief earlier than as prescribed in article 11(1)(*e*)(i) above, subject to such conditions and restrictions as they think fit.

PART V
ADDITIONAL RELIEF FOR PROPERTY IMPORTED ON MARRIAGE FROM A THIRD COUNTRY

13 Relief
(1) Subject to the provisions of this article, in addition to the relief afforded by Part IV, a person entering the United Kingdom shall not be required to pay any duty or tax chargeable in respect of property imported into the United Kingdom on condition that—
(*a*) he has been normally resident in a third country for a continuous period of at least twelve months;
(*b*) he intends to become normally resident in the United Kingdom on the occasion of his marriage; and
(*c*) the property is declared for relief within the period provided by article 15 below.
(2) In this article "property" shall be limited to household effects and trousseaux, other than tobacco products and beverages containing alcohol.

14 Wedding gifts
(1) Subject to the provisions of this article, a person to whom article 13(1) above applies shall not be required to pay any duty or tax chargeable in respect of any wedding gift imported into the United Kingdom by him or on his behalf on condition that such wedding gift is—
(*a*) given or intended to be given to him on the occasion of his marriage by a person who is normally resident in a third country;
(*b*) declared for relief within the period provided by article 15 below.
(2) Relief shall not be afforded under this article in respect of any wedding gift the value of which exceeds £800.
(3) For the purpose of affording relief from any duty or tax under this article, a wedding gift shall be treated as if it were liable to Community customs duty and, valued in accordance with the rules applicable to such duty.
(4) In this article "wedding gift" means any property customarily given on the occasion of a marriage, other than tobacco products or beverages containing alcohol.

15 Time limit for relief
The property to which this Part applies shall be declared for relief—
(*a*) not earlier than two months before the date fixed for the solemnisation of the marriage; and
(*b*) not later than four months following the date of the marriage.

PART VI
PUPILS AND STUDENTS

16 Relief for scholastic equipment
(1) Without prejudice to relief afforded under any other Part of this Order and subject to the provisions of this article, a person entering the United Kingdom shall not be required to pay any duty or tax chargeable in respect of scholastic equipment imported into the United Kingdom on condition that—
(*a*) he is a pupil or student normally resident in a third country who has been accepted to attend a full-time course at a school, college or university in the United Kingdom; and
(*b*) such equipment belongs to him and is intended for his personal use during the period of his studies.
(2) For the purposes of this article, "scholastic equipment" shall mean household effects which represent the normal furnishings for the room of a pupil or student, clothing, uniforms, and articles or instruments normally used by pupils or students for the purpose of their studies, including calculators or typewriters.
(3) The provisions of article 7 above shall not apply to relief afforded under this Part.

PART VII

HONORARY DECORATIONS, AWARDS AND GOODWILL GIFTS

17 Relief for honorary decorations and awards

Subject to article 20 below, a person entering the United Kingdom shall not be required to pay any duty or tax chargeable on the importation into the United Kingdom of any goods on condition that—

(*a*) he is normally resident in the United Kingdom; and

(*b*) such goods comprise—

(i) any honorary decoration which has been conferred on him by a government in a third country or

(ii) any cup, medal or similar article of an essentially symbolic nature which has been awarded to him in a third country as a tribute to his activities in the arts, sciences, sport, or the public service, or in recognition of merit at a particular event.

18 Relief for gifts received by official visitors in a third country

Subject to article 20 below, a person entering the United Kingdom shall not be required to pay any duty or tax chargeable on the importation into the United Kingdom of any goods on condition that—

(*a*) he is normally resident in the United Kingdom;

(*b*) he is returning from an official visit to a third country;

(*c*) the goods were given to him by the host authorities of such country on the occasion of his visit; and

(*d*) the goods are not intended for a commercial purpose.

19 Relief for gifts brought by official visitors

Subject to article 20 below, a person entering the United Kingdom shall not be required to pay any duty or tax chargeable on the importation into the United Kingdom of any goods on condition that—

(*a*) he is normally resident in a third country;

(*b*) he is paying an official visit to the United Kingdom;

(*c*) the goods are in the nature of an occasional gift which he intends to offer to the host authorities during his visit; and

(*d*) the goods are not intended for a commercial purpose.

20 Supplementary

(1) Part II shall not apply to relief afforded under this Part.

(2) No relief shall be afforded under this Part in respect of beverages containing alcohol, tobacco products or importations having a commercial character.

PART VIII

PERSONAL PROPERTY ACQUIRED BY INHERITANCE

21 Relief for legacies imported from a third country

(1) Without prejudice to relief afforded under any other Part of this Order and subject to the provisions of this article, a person who has become entitled as a legatee to property situated in a third country shall not be required to pay any duty or tax chargeable on the importation thereof into the United Kingdom, on condition that—

(*a*) he is either—

(i) normally resident in the United Kingdom or the Isle of Man; or

(ii) a secondary resident who is not normally resident in a third country; or

(iii) an eligible body;

(*b*) he furnishes proof to the officer of his entitlement as legatee to the property; and

(*c*) save as the Commissioners otherwise allow, the property is imported by or for such person not later than two years from the date on which his entitlement as legatee is finally determined.

(2) No relief shall be afforded under paragraph (1) above in respect of goods specified in the Schedule to this Order.

(3) For the purposes of this Part—

"eligible body" means a body solely concerned with carrying on a non-profit making activity and which is incorporated in the United Kingdom or the Isle of Man;

"secondary resident" means a person who, without being normally resident in the United Kingdom or the Isle of Man has a home situated in the United Kingdom which he owns or is renting for at least twelve months.

PART IX

22 Revocation

. . .

Note—Effect has been given for the revocations made by this article.

SCHEDULE

Article 21(2)

1 Beverages contain alcohol.

2 Tobacco products.

3 Any motor road vehicle which, by its type of construction and equipment, is designed for and capable of transporting more than nine persons including the driver, or goods, or any special purpose vehicle or mobile workshop.

4 Articles, other than portable instruments of the applied or liberal arts, used in the exercise of a trade or profession before his death by the person from whom the legatee has acquired them.

5 Stocks of new materials and finished or semi-finished products.

6 Livestock and stocks of agricultural products exceeding the quantities appropriate to normal family requirements.

1992/3220

VALUE ADDED TAX (FLAT-RATE SCHEME FOR FARMERS) (DESIGNATED ACTIVITIES) ORDER 1992

Made by the Treasury under VATA 1983 s 37B(8) (see now VATA 1994 s 54(8)) and all other enabling powers

Made . . . .*16 December 1992*

Laid before the House of Commons . . . .*17 December 1992*

Coming into force . . . .*1 January 1993*

1 This Order may be cited as the Value Added Tax (Flat-rate Scheme for Farmers) (Designated Activities) Order 1992, and shall come into force on 1st January 1993.

2—(1) Subject to paragraph (2) below, the activities described in any part of the Schedule to this order are designated activities for the purposes of section 37B of the Value Added Tax Act 1983[a].

(2) The activities described in Part VI of the Schedule are not designated activities for the purposes of section 37B of the Act, unless:

(*a*) the person performing them also carries out designated activities falling within one or more of Parts I to V of the Schedule (other designated activities), and

(*b*) in carrying out the activities described in Part VI—

(i) he performs them himself, or they are performed by his employees (or both), and

(ii) any equipment he uses in carrying them out, or hires to another, for agricultural purposes is equipment which he also uses for carrying out his other designated activities.

Note—[a] VATA 1994 s 54.

SCHEDULE

Article 2

PART I

CROP PRODUCTION

1 General agriculture, including viticulture.

2 Growing of fruit and of vegetables, flowers and ornamental plants, whether in the open or under glass.

3 Production of mushrooms, spices, seeds and propagating materials; nurseries.

PART II

STOCK FARMING

1 General stock farming.

2 Poultry farming.

3 Rabbit farming.

4 Beekeeping.

5 Silkworm farming.

6 Snail farming.

PART III

FORESTRY

1 Growing, felling and general husbandry of trees in a forest, wood or copse.

PART IV
FISHERIES

1 Fresh-water fishing.
2 Fish farming.
3 Breeding of mussels, oysters and other molluscs and crustaceans.
4 Frog farming.

PART V
PROCESSING

1 The processing by a person of products deriving from his activities falling within Parts I to IV above, using only such means as are normally employed in the course of such activities.

PART VI
SERVICES

1 Field work, reaping and mowing, threshing, bailing, collecting, harvesting, sowing and planting.
2 Packing and preparing for market (including drying, cleaning, grinding, disinfecting and ensilaging) of agricultural products for market.
3 Storage of agricultural products.
4 Stock minding, rearing and fattening.
5 Hiring out of equipment for use in any of the activities described in this Schedule.
6 Technical assistance in relation to any of the activities described in this Schedule.
7 Destruction of weeds and pests, dusting and spraying of crops and land.
8 Operation of irrigation and drainage equipment.
9 Lopping, tree felling and other forestry services.

1992/3221

VALUE ADDED TAX (FLAT-RATE SCHEME FOR FARMERS) (PERCENTAGE ADDITION) ORDER 1992

Made by the Treasury under VATA 1983 s 37B(4) (see now VATA 1994 s 54(4)) and all other enabling powers

Made . . . . *16 December 1992*
Laid before the House of Commons . . . . *17 December 1992*
Coming into force . . . . *1 January 1993*

1 This Order may be cited as the Value Added Tax (Flat-rate Scheme for Farmers) (Percentage Addition) Order 1992, and shall come into force on 1st January 1993.

2 The percentage referred to in section 37B(4) of the Value Added Tax Act 1983[1] shall be 4 per cent.

Note—[1] VATA 1994 s 54(5).

1992/3222

VALUE ADDED TAX (INPUT TAX) ORDER 1992

Made by the Treasury under VATA 1983 s 14(10) (see now VATA 1994 s 25(7)) and all other enabling powers

Made . . . . *16 December 1992*
Laid before the House of Commons . . . . *17 December 1992*
Coming into force . . . . *1 January 1993*

1 Citation and commencement
This Order may be cited as the Value Added Tax (Input Tax) Order 1992, and shall come into force on 1st January 1993.

2 Interpretation
In this Order—

"the Act" means the Value Added Tax Act [1994][1];
"the Manx Act" means the Value Added Tax and Other Taxes Act 1973;
["antiques" means objects other than works of art or collectors' items, which are more than 100 years old;][2]

["collectors' items" means any collection or collector's piece falling within section 21(5) of the Act but excluding investment gold coins within the meaning of Note 1(*b*) and (*c*) to Group 15 of Schedule 9 to the Act;][4]

["building materials" means any goods the supply of which would be zero-rated if supplied by a taxable person to a person to whom he is also making a supply of a description within either item 2 or item 3 of Group 5, or item 2 of Group 6, of Schedule 8 to the Act][1]

. . . [2]

["Motor car" means any motor vehicle of a kind normally used on public roads which has three or more wheels and either—

(*a*) is constructed or adapted solely or mainly for the carriage of passengers; or

(*b*) has to the rear of the driver's seat roofed accommodation which is fitted with side windows or which is constructed or adapted for the fitting of side windows;

but does not include—

(i) vehicles capable of accommodating only one person;

(ii) vehicles which meet the requirements of Schedule 6 to the Road Vehicles (Construction and Use) Regulations 1986 and are capable of carrying [12][5] or more seated persons;

[(ii *a*) vehicles which would otherwise meet the requirements of sub-paragraph (ii) but which can carry fewer than 12 seated persons solely because they have been adapted for wheelchair users;][5]

(iii) vehicles of not less than three tonnes unladen weight (as defined in the Table to regulation 3(2) of the Road Vehicles (Construction and Use) Regulations 1986);

(iv) vehicles constructed to carry a payload (the difference between a vehicle's kerb weight (as defined in the Table to regulation 3(2) of the Road Vehicles (Construction and Use) Regulations 1986) and its maximum gross weight (as defined in that Table) of one tonne or more;

(v) caravans, ambulances and prison vans;

(vi) vehicles constructed for a special purpose other than the carriage of persons and having no other accommodation for carrying persons than such as is incidental to that purpose;][3]

["motor dealer" means a person whose business consists in whole or in part of obtaining supplies of, or acquiring from another member State or importing, new or second-hand motor cars for resale with a view to making an overall profit on the sale of them (whether or not a profit is made on each sale);

"motor manufacturer" means a person whose business consists in whole or part of producing motor cars including producing motors cars by conversion of a vehicle (whether a motor car or not);][3]

. . . [2]

. . . [3]

. . . [2]

["Second-hand goods" means tangible moveable property (including motor cars) that is suitable for further use as it is or after repair other than works of art, collectors' items or antiques and other than precious metals and precious stones;][2]

["stock in trade" means new or second-hand motor cars (other than second-hand motor cars which are not qualifying motor cars within the meaning of article 7(2A) below) which are—

(*a*) produced by a motor manufacturer or, as the case may require, supplied to or acquired from another member State or imported by a motor dealer, for the purpose of resale, and

(*b*) are intended to be sold by—

(i) a motor manufacturer within 12 months of their production, or

(ii) by a motor dealer within 12 months of their supply, acquisition from another member State or importation, as the case may require,

and such motor cars shall not cease to be stock in trade where they are temporarily put to a use in the motor manufacturer's or, as the case may be, the motor dealer's business which involves making them available for private use;][3]

["work of art" has the same meaning as in section 21 of the Act.][4]

Amendments—[1] Word in the definition "the Act" substituted, and the definition "building materials" inserted, by the VAT (Input Tax) (Amendment) Order, SI 1995/281 art 3 with effect from 1 March 1995.

[2] Definitions of "caravan", "firearms", "motorcycle", "works of art", "antiques" and "collectors' pieces" revoked and the definitions of "antiques", and "Second-hand goods" inserted by the VAT (Input Tax) (Amendment) (No 2) Order, SI 1995/1267 art 3 with effect from 1 June 1995.

[3] Definition of "motor car" substituted, definitions of "motor dealer", "motor manufacturer" and "stock in trade" inserted, and definition of "printed matter" revoked, by the VAT (Input Tax) (Amendment) Order, SI 1999/2930, arts 2, 3 with effect from 1 December 1999.

[4] Definitions of "collectors' items" and "work of art" substituted (both definitions originally inserted by SI 1995/1267) by the VAT (Input Tax) (Amendment) (No 2) Order, SI 1999/3118, arts 2, 3, with effect from 1 January 2000.

VAT SIs

[5] In definition of "motor car", figure "12" substituted for word "twelve" and sub-para (*b*)(ii *a*) inserted, by the VAT (Input Tax) (Amendment) Order, SI 2009/217 art 2 with effect from 6 April 2009.

3 Revocations

The provisions specified in the first column of the Schedule to this Order are hereby revoked to the extent specified in the second column of that Schedule.

[4 Disallowance of input tax

(1) Subject to paragraph (4) below, tax charged on the—

(*a*) supply;

(*b*) acquisition from another member State; or

(*c*) importation,

of any goods such as are described in paragraph (2) below which are supplied to, or acquired from another member State or imported by, a taxable person in the circumstances described in paragraph (3) below shall be excluded from any credit under section 25 of the Act.

(2) The goods referred to in paragraph (1) above are—

(*a*) works of art, antiques and collectors' items;

(*b*) second-hand goods.

(3) The circumstances of the supply, acquisition from another member State or importation referred to in paragraph (1) above are—

(*a*) a supply on which, by virtue of an Order made under Section 50A of the Act or a corresponding provision of the Manx Act or by virtue of a corresponding provision of the law of another member State, VAT was chargeable on the profit margin;

[(*aa*) . . .][2]

(*b*) (if the goods are a work of art, an antique or a collectors' item) the taxable person imported it himself;

(*c*) (if the goods are a work of art) it was supplied to the taxable person by, or acquired from another member State by him from its creator or his successor in title;

(4) Paragraph (1) above shall only apply to exclude from credit, tax chargeable on a supply of goods to or an acquisition or importation of goods by a taxable person in the circumstances set out in paragraph (3)(*b*) and (*c*) above if the taxable person—

(*a*) has opted to account for VAT chargeable on his supplies of such goods on the profit margin and

(*b*) has not elected to account for VAT chargeable on his supply of the goods by reference to its value, in accordance with the provisions of an Order made under section 50A of the Act.][1]

Amendments—[1] This article substituted by the VAT (Input Tax) (Amendment) (No 2) Order, SI 1995/1267 art 4 with effect from 1 June 1995.

[2] Para (3)(*aa*) revoked by the VAT (Input Tax) (Amendment) Order, SI 1999/2930, arts 2, 4, with effect from 1 March 2000 (previously inserted by the VAT (Input Tax) (Amendment) (No 3) Order, SI 1995/1666 art 3).

5—(1) Tax charged on any goods or services supplied to a taxable person, or on any goods acquired by a taxable person, or on any goods imported by a taxable person, is to be excluded from any credit under section [25][1] of the Act, where the goods or services in question are used or to be used by the taxable person for the purposes of business entertainment [unless the entertainment is provided for an overseas customer of the taxable person and is of a kind and on a scale which is reasonable, having regard to all the circumstances][3].

(2) Where, by reason of the operation of paragraph (1) above, a taxable person has claimed no input tax on . . . [2]a supply of any services, tax shall be charged on a supply by him of the goods in question not being a letting on hire or on a supply by him of the services in question, as if that supply were for a consideration equal to the excess of—

[(*a*) the consideration for which the services are supplied by him, over

(*b*) the consideration for which the services were supplied to him,][2]

and accordingly shall not be charged unless there is such an excess.

(3) For the purposes of this article, "business entertainment" means entertainment including hospitality of any kind provided by a taxable person in connection with a business carried on by him, but does not include the provision of any such entertainment for either or both—

(*a*) employees of the taxable person;

(*b*) if the taxable person is a body corporate, its directors or persons otherwise engaged in its management,

unless the provision of entertainment for persons such as are mentioned in sub-paragraph (a) and (b) above is incidental to its provisions for others.

[(4) For the purposes of this article "overseas customer", in relation to a taxable person, means—

(*a*) any person who is not ordinarily resident nor carrying on a business in the United Kingdom or the Isle of Man and avails himself or herself, or may be expected to avail himself or herself, in the course of a business carried on by that person outside the United Kingdom and the Isle of Man, of any goods or services the supply of which forms part of the taxable person's business; and (*b*) any person who is not ordinarily resident in the United Kingdom or the Isle of Man and is acting, in relation to such goods or services, on behalf of an overseas customer as defined in paragraph (a) above or on behalf of any government or public authority outside the United Kingdom and the Isle of Man.][3]

Press releases etc—C&E Business Brief 21/95 8-10-95 (entertaining of guests at staff parties constitutes "business entertainment").

Simon's Tax Cases—Art 5(1), *C&E Comrs v Plant* [1994] STC 232*; *Thorn EMI plc v C&E Comrs* [1995] STC 674*; *BMW (GB) Ltd v Comrs of Customs and Excise* [1997] STC 824; *C&E Comrs v Kilroy Television Co Ltd* [1997] STC 901.

Art 5(3), [1997] STC 824, *C&E Comrs v Kilroy Television Co Ltd* [1997] STC 901.

Amendments—[1] Figure in para (1) substituted by the VAT (Input Tax) (Amendment) Order, SI 1995/281 art 5 with effect from 1 March 1995.

[2] Words in para (2) revoked, and paras (2)(*a*), (*b*) substituted, by the VAT (Input Tax) (Amendment) Order, SI 1999/2930, arts 2, 5, with effect from 1 March 2000.

[3] Words in para (1), and whole of para (4), inserted, by the VAT (Input Tax) (Amendment) Order, SI 2011/1071 art 2 with effect from 1 May 2011.

[6 Where a taxable person constructing, or effecting any works to a building, in either case for the purpose of making a grant of a major interest in it or any part of it or its site which is of a description in Schedule 8 to the Act, incorporates goods other than building materials in any part of the building or its site, input tax on the supply, acquisition or importation of the goods shall be excluded from credit under section 25 of the Act.][1]

Simon's Tax Cases—*C&E Comrs v Westbury Developments (Worthing) Lt* d [1981] STC 72*; *C&E Comrs v McLean Homes Midland Ltd* [1993] STC 335*.

Amendments—[1] Substituted by the VAT (Input Tax) (Amendment) Order, SI 1995/281 art 6 with effect from 1 March 1995.

7—(1) Subject to paragraph (2) [to (2H)][2] below tax charged on—

(*a*) the supply [(including a letting on hire)][2] to a taxable person;

(*b*) the acquisition by a taxable person from another member State; or

(*c*) the importation by a taxable person,

of a motor car shall be excluded from any credit under section [25][1] of the Act.

[(2) Paragraph (1) above does not apply where—

(*a*) the motor car is—

(i) a qualifying motor car;

(ii) [supplied (including on a letting on hire) to][3], or acquired from another member State or imported by, a taxable person; and

(iii) the relevant condition is satisfied;

[(*aa*) the motor car forms part of the stock in trade of a motor manufacturer or a motor dealer;][4]

(*b*) the supply is a letting on hire of a motor car which is not a qualifying motor car [(other than a supply on a letting on hire of a motor car which is not a qualifying motor car by virtue only of the application of paragraph (2C) below, to a person whose supply on a letting on hire prior to 1st August 1995 resulted in the application of that paragraph)][3];

(*c*) the motor car is unused and is supplied to a taxable person whose only taxable supplies are concerned with the letting of motor cars on hire to another taxable person whose business consists predominantly of making supplies of a description falling within item 14 of Group 12 of Schedule 8 to the Act; or

(*d*) the motor car is unused and is supplied on a letting on hire to a taxable person whose business consists predominantly of making supplies of a description falling within item 14 of Group 12 of Schedule 8 to the Act, by a taxable person whose only taxable supplies are concerned with the letting on hire of motor cars to such a taxable person.][2]

[(2A) Subject to paragraph (2B) and (2C) below, for the purposes of paragraph (2)(*a*) [and (*b*)][4] above a motor car is a qualifying motor car if—

(*a*) it has never been supplied, acquired from another member State, or imported in circumstances in which the VAT on that supply, acquisition or importation was wholly excluded from credit as input tax by virtue of paragraph (1) above; or

(*b*) a taxable person has elected for it to be treated as such.

(2B) A taxable person may only elect for a motor car to be treated as a qualifying motor car if it—

(*a*) is first registered on or after 1st August 1995;

(*b*) was supplied to, or acquired from another member State or imported by, him prior to that date in circumstances in which the VAT on that supply, acquisition or importation was wholly excluded from credit as input tax by virtue of paragraph (1) above; and

(*c*) had not been supplied on a letting on hire by him prior to 1st August 1995.

VAT SIs

(2C) A motor car that is supplied, acquired from another member State or imported on or after 1st August 1995 and which would, apart from this paragraph, be a qualifying motor car by virtue of sub-paragraph (*a*) of paragraph (2A) above shall not be such a car if it was supplied on a letting on hire prior to that date by the person to whom it is supplied or by whom it is acquired or imported (as the case may be).

(2D) References in this article to registration of a motor car mean registration in accordance with section 21 of the Vehicle Excise and Registration Act 1994.

(2E) For the purposes of paragraph (2)(*a*) above the relevant condition is that the letting on hire, supply, acquisition or importation (as the case may be) is to a taxable person who intends to use the motor car either—

(*a*) exclusively for the purposes of a business carried on by him, but this is subject to paragraph (2G) below; or

(*b*) primarily for a relevant purpose.

(2F) For the purposes of paragraph (2E) above a relevant purpose, in relation to a motor car which is let on hire or supplied to, or acquired or imported by, a taxable person (as the case may be), is any of the following purposes—

(*a*) to provide it on hire with the services of a driver for the purpose of carrying passengers;

(*b*) to provide it for self-drive hire; or

(*c*) to use it as a vehicle in which instruction in the driving of a motor car is to be given by him.

(2G) A taxable person shall not be taken to intend to use a motor car exclusively for the purposes of a business carried on by him if he intends to—

(*a*) let it on hire to any person either for no consideration or for a consideration which is less than that which would be payable in money if it were a commercial transaction conducted at arms length; or

(*b*) make it available (otherwise than by letting it on hire) to any person (including, where the taxable person is an individual, himself, or where the taxable person is a partnership, a partner) for private use, whether or not for a consideration.

(2H) Where paragraph (1) above applies to a supply of a motor car on a letting on hire it shall apply to the tax charged on that supply as if for the word "tax" there were substituted "one half of the tax".][2]

(3) In this article—

(*a*) . . . [2]

(*b*) "self-drive hire" means hire where the hirer is the person normally expected to drive the motor car and the period of hire to each hirer, together with the period of hire of any other motor car expected to be hired to him by the taxable person—

(i) will normally be less than 30 consecutive days; and

(ii) will normally be less than 90 days in any period of 12 months.

(4), (5) . . . [5]

Commentary—*De Voil Indirect Tax Service* **V3.449**.

Press releases etc—C&E Business Brief 15/95 31-7-95 (Further developments or treatment of business cars).

Simon's Tax Cases—*C&E Comrs v Jeynes (T/A Midland International (Hire) Caterers)* [1984] STC 30*.

Art 7(1), *Group Ltd v C&E Comrs* [1996] STC 898.

Art 7(2), *C&E Comrs v Elm Milk Ltd* [2005] STC 776.

Art 7(2C), *C&E Comrs v BRS Automotive Ltd* [1998] STC 1210.

Art 7(2E), *C&E Comrs v Skellett (t/a Vidcom Computer Services)* [2004] STC 201; *C&E Comrs v Robbins* [2005] STC 1103; *Thompson (trading as Thompson (HAS) & Co) v C&E Comrs* [2005] STC 1777; *R&C Comrs v Shaw* [2007] STC 1525.

Art 7(2G), *C&E Comrs v Skellett (t/a Vidcom Computer Services)* [2004] STC 201; *C&E Comrs v Elm Milk Ltd* [2005] STC 776; *C&E Comrs v Robbins* [2005] STC 1103; *Thompson (trading as Thompson (HAS) & Co) v C&E Comrs* [2005] STC 1777; *R&C Comrs v Shaw* [2007] STC 1525.

Cross reference—See VAT Regulations, SI 1995/2518 (requirement to state on VAT invoice for a supply of a letting of a car, other than for self-drive hire, whether it is a qualifying vehicle under para (2A) above).

See EC Council Decision 98/198/EC of 9 March 1998 (authorisation for UK to restrict to 50% the input tax recoverable by hirers or lessees of cars used partly for private purposes).

Amendments—[1] Words in paras (1), (2)(*d*), (*f*), (4), (5)(*b*) substituted by the VAT (Input Tax) (Amendment) Order, SI 1995/281 art 7 with effect from 1 March 1995.

[2] Words in para (1), and paras (2A)–(2H) inserted, words in para (1), para (2) and the words in para (4) substituted, and para (3)(*a*) revoked by the VAT (Input Tax) (Amendment) (No 3) Order, SI 1995/1666 arts 4–8 with effect from 1 August 1995.

[3] Words in paras (2)(*a*)(ii) substituted and (2)(*b*) inserted by the VAT (Input Tax) (Amendment) Order, SI 1998/2767 with effect from 13 November 1998.

[4] Para (2)(*aa*), and words in para (2A), inserted by the VAT (Input Tax) (Amendment) Order, SI 1999/2930, arts 2, 6(*a*), (*b*), with effect from 1 December 1999.

[5] Paras (4), (5) revoked by the VAT (Input Tax) (Amendment) Order, SI 1999/2930, arts 2, 6(*c*), with effect from 1 March 2000.

SCHEDULE

REVOCATIONS

Article 3

Note—Effect has been given to the revocations made by this Schedule.

1992/3283

VALUE ADDED TAX (PLACE OF SUPPLY OF GOODS) ORDER 1992

Amendment—This Order revoked by the VAT (Place of Supply of Goods) Order, SI 2004/3148 reg 3 with effect from 1 January 2005.

1993/1507

VALUE ADDED TAX (SUPPLY OF SERVICES) ORDER 1993

Made by the Treasury under VATA 1983 s 3(4), (8) (see now VATA 1994 s 5(4), (8)) and all other enabling powers

Made . . . . *15 June 1993*
Laid before the House of Commons . . . . *16 June 1993*
Coming into force . . . . *1 August 1993*

1 This Order may be cited as the Value Added Tax (Supply of Services) Order 1993 and shall come into force on 1st August 1993.

HMRC Manuals—VAT Guidance V1-3: Supply and consideration, para 6.1 (private or non-business use of services).

2 In this Order—

"the Act" means the Value Added Tax Act [1994][1].

Amendments—[1] Year substituted by the VAT (Supply of Services) (Amendment) Order, SI 1995/1668 art 3 with effect from 1 August 1995.

3 Subject to articles [6, 6A and 7][1] below, where a person carrying on a business puts services which have been supplied to him to any private use or uses them, or makes them available to any person for use, for a purpose other than a purpose of the business he shall be treated for the purposes of the Act as supplying those services in the course or furtherance of the business [except for the purposes of determining whether tax on the supply of the services to him is input tax of his under section 24 of the Act][2].

Press releases etc—C&E Business Brief 17/94 12-9-94 (minor and occasional changes of use to private or non-business use should be ignored).

Amendments—[1] Words substituted by the VAT (Supply of Services) (Amendment) Order, SI 1995/1668 art 4 with effect from 1 August 1995.

[2] Words inserted by the VAT (Supply of Services) (Amendment) Order, SI 2003/1055 art 3. SI 2003/1055 comes into force on 10 April 2003, with effect for supplies made to a taxable person after 9 April 2003.

3A, 3B

Note—Articles 3A, 3B revoked following the ECJ decision in *P Charles and T S Charles-Tijmens v Staatssecretaris van Financiën* (Case C-434/03).

Amendments—Articles 3A, 3B revoked by the VAT (Supply of Services) (Amendment) Order, SI 2007/2173 art 2 with effect from 1 September 2007.

4 In the case of a business carried on by an individual, this Order shall apply to services used, or made available for use, by himself personally.

5 The value of a supply which a person is treated as making by virtue of this Order shall be taken to be that part of the value of the supply of the services to him as fairly and reasonably represents the cost to him of providing the services.

Press releases etc—C&E Business Brief 17/94 12-9-94 (in calculating the cost of private or non-business use, a taxpayer can use his normal accounting convention for depreciating comparable business assets or any other fair and reasonable basis).

6 This Order shall not apply in respect of any services—

(*a*) which are used, or made available for use, for a consideration;

(*b*) except those in respect of which the person carrying on the business [has or will become][2] entitled under sections [25 and 26][1] of the Act to credit for the whole or any part of the tax on their supply to him;

VAT SIs

(*c*) in respect of which any part of the tax on their supply to the person carrying on the business was not counted as being input tax of his by virtue of an apportionment made under section [24(5)][1] of the Act; or

(*d*) of a description within paragraph 10(1) of Schedule [6][1] to the Act.

Amendments—[1] Words substituted by the VAT (Supply of Services) (Amendment) Order, SI 1995/1668 art 5 with effect from 1 August 1995.

[2] Words substituted by the VAT (Supply of Services) (Amendment) Order, SI 1998/762 with effect from 18 March 1998.

[6A—(1) This Order shall not apply to any supply of services consisting of the letting on hire of a motor car where one half of the tax on that letting on hire was excluded from credit under section 25 of the Act by virtue of article 7 of the Value Added Tax (Input Tax) Order 1992.

(2) In paragraph (1) above, "motor car" has the same meaning as in article 2 of the Value Added Tax (Input Tax) Order 1992.][1]

Amendments—[1] This article inserted by the VAT (Supply of Services) (Amendment) Order, SI 1995/1668 art 6 with effect from 1 August 1995.

7 Nothing in this Order shall be construed as making any person liable for any tax which, taken together with any tax for which he was liable as a result of a previous supply of the same services which he was treated as making by virtue of this Order, would exceed the amount of input tax for which he [has or will become entitled][1] to [credit under sections 25 and 26 of the Act][1] in respect of the services used, or made available for use, by him; and, where the tax chargeable would otherwise exceed the amount of that credit—

(*a*) he shall not be treated as making a supply of the services where the amount of that credit has already been equalled or exceeded; and

(*b*) in any other case, the value of the supply shall be reduced accordingly.

Amendments—[1] Words substituted by the VAT (Supply of Services) (Amendment) Order, SI 1998/762 with effect from 18 March 1998.

[8 Where—

(*a*) there is a supply of any of the assets of a business of a person ('the transferor') to a person to whom the whole or any part of that business is transferred as a going concern ('the transferee'), and

(*b*) that supply is treated in accordance with an Order made under section 5(3) of the Act (or under an enactment re-enacted in section 5(3) of the Act) as being neither a supply of goods nor a supply of services,

the liability of the transferee to tax in accordance with articles 5, 6(b) and 7 above, shall be determined as if the transferor and the transferee were the same person.][1]

Amendments—[1] Inserted by the VAT (Supply of Services) (Amendment) Order, SI 1998/762 with effect from 18 March 1998.

[9 Where a transferor has himself acquired any assets by way of a supply falling within paragraphs (*a*) and (*b*) of article 8 above, that article shall have the effect of requiring the person from whom those assets were acquired to be treated for the purposes of determining the liability of the transferee to tax in accordance with articles 5, 6(*b*) and 7 above as the same person as the transferor and the transferee, and so on in the case of any number of successive supplies falling within those paragraphs.][1]

Amendments—[1] Inserted by the VAT (Supply of Services) (Amendment) Order, SI 1998/762 with effect from 18 March 1998.

1993/2001

VALUE ADDED TAX (PAYMENTS ON ACCOUNT) ORDER 1993

Made by the Treasury under VATA 1983 s 38C(1)–(2), (4), (5) (see now VATA 1994 s 28(1), (2), (4), (5)) and all other enabling powers

Made . . . .*9 August 1993*

Laid before the House of Commons . . . .*9 August 1993*

Coming into force . . . .*2 September 1993*

1 Citation and commencement

This Order may be cited as the Value Added Tax (Payments on Account) Order 1993 and shall come into force on 2nd September 1993.

2 Interpretation

(1) In this Order—

"the Act" means the Value Added Tax Act [1994][1];

"the basic period" means, in relation to a taxable person falling within article 5 or 6 below, the period of one year in which there ended the prescribed accounting periods in respect of which his liability to pay a total amount of tax exceeding [the figure specified in article 5(1) or 6(1)][3] caused him to become such a taxable person;

"Controller" means the Controller, Customs and Excise, Value Added Tax Central Unit;

. . .[2]

"reference period" has the meaning ascribed to it in article 11(1) below.

(2) Any reference in articles 13 to 15 below to the total amount of tax by reference to which a taxable person's payments on account fall to be calculated being "reduced accordingly" or "increased accordingly" is in each case a reference to a reduction or increase of the same proportion as the difference between the total amount of tax by reference to which his payments on account are currently calculated and the total amount of tax, excluding the tax on goods imported from countries other than member States, which he was, or (as the case may be) which the Commissioners are satisfied that he will be, liable to pay in respect of the prescribed accounting periods the ends of which fall within the year referred to in the relevant provision of the article in question.

Amendments—[1] Substituted by SI 1996/1196 art 3 with effect from 1 June 1996.

[2] Definition of "credit transfer" repealed by SI 1996/1196 with effect from 1 June 1996.

[3] In para (1), in definition of "the basic period", words substituted for figure "£2,000,000" by the VAT (Payments on Account) (Amendment) Order, SI 2011/21 art 2(*a*) with effect from 1 June 2011.

2A [Supplies to which section 55A(6) of the Act applies (customers to account for tax on supplies of a kind used in missing trader intra-community fraud)

Where, on application, a taxable person satisfies the Commissioners that, by reason solely of any amount that he is liable to pay by virtue of section 55A(6) of the Act—

(*a*) he falls within article 5 or 6 below, or

(*b*) the amount of each of his payments on account is increased,

then, with effect from the date of the approval by the Commissioners of the application, any amount that he is so liable to pay by virtue of that section shall be disregarded for the purposes of those articles or, as the case may be, the calculation of the amount of each of his payments on account.][1]

Amendments—[1] Article 2A inserted by the VAT (Payments on Account) (Amendment) Order, SI 2007/1420 art 2 with effect from 1 June 2007.

3 Revocation

(1) Subject to paragraph (2) below, the Value Added Tax (Payments on Account) (No 2) Order 1992 is hereby revoked.

(2) The duty under the Value Added Tax (Payments on Account) (No 2) Order 1992 of any taxable person to make a payment on account in respect of a prescribed accounting period beginning before 2nd September 1993 shall not be affected by the revocation of that Order which shall continue to have effect in relation to any such payment on account.

4 Payments on account

(1) A taxable person falling within article 5 or 6 below shall be under a duty to pay, on account of any tax he may become liable to pay in respect of each prescribed accounting period exceeding one month beginning on or after [1st April each year][1] amounts (in this Order referred to as "payments on account") determined in accordance with this Order at times so determined, provided that in the case of a taxable person falling within article 6 below there shall be no duty to pay such amounts in respect of a prescribed accounting period other than one beginning after the basic period.

[(2) Where such a taxable person has a prescribed accounting period exceeding one month which begins on or after 2nd March each year and ends on or before 30th June each year, he shall be under a like duty to make payments on account also in respect of that prescribed accounting period.][1]

Amendments—[1] Words in para (1) and whole of para (2) substituted by the VAT (Payments on Account) (Amendment) Order, SI 1995/291 arts 3, 4 with effect from 2 March 1995.

[5 Persons to whom this Order applies

(1) Subject to paragraph (2) below and article 16 below, a taxable person falls within this article in any year if the total amount of tax which he was liable to pay in respect of the prescribed accounting periods the ends of which fell within the period of one year ending on the last day of his last prescribed accounting period ending before the previous 1st December exceeded [£2,300,000][2].

(2) Where in any year ending 30th November a prescribed accounting period of the taxable person did not begin on the first day or did not end on the last day of a month, the period of one year shall, for the purpose of this article, be regarded as having comprised those prescribed account periods which related to the tax periods ending within the year ending 30th November of that year to which references are shown in the certificate of registration issued to him][1].

Amendments—[1] Substituted by the VAT (Payments on Account) (Amendment) Order, SI 1995/291 art 5 with effect from 2 March 1995.

[2] In para (1), figure "£2,300,000" substituted for figure "£2,000,000" by the VAT (Payments on Account) (Amendment) Order, SI 2011/21 art 2(*b*) with effect from 1 December 2011.

6—(1) Subject to paragraph (2) below and article 16 below, a taxable person who does not fall within article 5 above shall fall within this article if the total amount of tax which he was liable to pay in respect of the prescribed accounting periods the ends of which fell within any one period of one year ending on the last day of a prescribed accounting period of his ending after [30th November of the previous year][1] exceeded [£2,300,000][2].

(2) Where in the period of the year referred to in paragraph (1) above a prescribed accounting period of the taxable person did not begin on the first day or did not end on the last day of a month, that period of one year shall, for the purpose of this article, be regarded as having comprised those prescribed accounting periods which related to the tax periods ending within that period of one year to which references are shown in the certificate of registration issued to him.

Amendments—[1] Words in para (1) substituted by the VAT (Payments on Account) (Amendment) Order, SI 1995/291 art 6 with effect from 2 March 1995.

[2] In para (1), figure substituted for figure "£2,000,000" by the VAT (Payments on Account) (Amendment) Order, SI 2011/21 art 2(*c*) with effect from 1 June 2011.

7 Cessation of duty to make payments on account

If the total amount of tax which a taxable person who is under a duty to make payments on account was liable to pay in respect of the prescribed accounting periods the ends of which fell within any one period of one year ending after the end of the basic period was less than [£1,800,000][1], then, with effect from the date of the written approval by the Commissioners of a written application by the taxable person to that effect, he shall not be under a duty to make payments on account.

Amendments—[1] Figure substituted for figure "£1,600,000" by the VAT (Payments on Account) (Amendment) Order, SI 2011/21 art 2(*d*) with effect from 1 June 2011.

8 Time for payment

[Subject to article 9 below][1], in respect of each prescribed accounting period a payment on account shall be made to the Controller not later than—

(*a*) the last day of the month next following the end of the first complete month included therein, and

(*b*) the last day of the month next following the end of the second complete month included therein.

Amendments—[1] Words substituted by the VAT (Payments on Account) (Amendment) Order, SI 1996/1196 art 4 with effect from 1 June 1996.

9 . . . [1] where a prescribed accounting period does not begin on the first day or does not end on the last day of a month—

(*a*) the first payment on account shall be made not later than the last day of the month next following the end of the first complete month included therein, and

(*b*) the second payment on account shall be made not later than the last day of the month next following the end of the second complete month included therein,

except that where—

(i) a prescribed accounting period does not comprise more complete months than one, the first payment on account shall be made not later than the last day of that month and the second payment on account shall be made not later than the end of the prescribed accounting period, or

(ii) a prescribed accounting period comprises an incomplete month followed by two complete months, the first payment on account shall be made not later than the end of the first complete month and the second payment on account shall be made not later than the end of the second complete month, or

(iii) a prescribed accounting period comprises an incomplete month followed by two complete months and an incomplete month, the first payment on account shall be made not later than the end of the first complete month and the second payment on account shall be made not later than the end of the second complete month.

Amendments—[1] Words deleted by the VAT (Payments on Account) (Amendment) Order, SI 1996/1196 art 5 with effect from 1 June 1996.

10 . . .

Amendments—This article deleted by the VAT (Payments on Account) (Amendment) Order, SI 1996/1196 art 6 with effect from 1 June 1996.

11 Calculation of the payments on account

(1) Subject to paragraph (2) below and articles [12A,][2], 13, 14 and 15 below, the amount of each payment on account to be made by a taxable person who falls within article 5 above shall equal [one twenty-fourth][3] of the total amount of tax, excluding the tax on goods imported from countries other than member States, which he was liable to pay in respect of the prescribed accounting periods the ends of which fell within the period (in this Order referred to as "the reference period")—

[(*a*) 1st October to 30th September in the basic period where he has a prescribed accounting period beginning in April in any year in which he is under a duty to make payments on account,][1]

[(*b*) 1st November to 31st October in the basic period where he has a prescribed accounting period beginning in May in any year in which he is under a duty to make payments on account, and][1]

[(*c*) 1st December to 30th November in the basic period where he has a prescribed accounting period beginning in June in any year in which he is under a duty to make payments on account.][1]

(2) Where in the period of the year mentioned in sub-paragraph (*a*), (*b*) or (*c*) of paragraph (1) above a prescribed accounting period of the taxable person did not begin on the first day or did not end on the last day of a month, the reference period shall, for the purpose of paragraph (1), be regarded as having comprised those prescribed accounting periods which related to the tax periods ending within the period of the year mentioned in sub-paragraph (*a*), (*b*) or (*c*) of paragraph (1) as appropriate to which references are shown in the certificate of registration issued to him.

Amendments—[1] Para (1) (*a*)–(*c*) substituted by the VAT (Payments on Account) (Amendment) Order, SI 1995/291 arts 7–9 with effect from 2 March 1995.

[2] Words inserted by the VAT (Payments on Account) (Amendment) Order, SI 1996/1196 art 7 with effect from 1 June 1996.

[3] Words substituted by the VAT (Payments on Account) (Amendment) Order, SI 1996/1196 art 7 with effect from 1 June 1996.

12 Subject to articles [12A][1], 13, 14 and 15 below, the amount of each payment on account to be made by a taxable person who falls within article 6 above shall equal [one twenty-fourth][2] of the total amount of tax, excluding the tax on goods imported from countries other than member States, which he was liable to pay in respect of the prescribed accounting periods the ends of which fell within the basic period.

Amendments—[1] Words inserted by the VAT (Payments on Account) (Amendment) Order, SI 1996/1196 art 8 with effect from 1 June 1996.

[2] Words substituted by the VAT (Payments on Account) (Amendment) Order, SI 1996/1196 art 8 with effect from 1 June 1996.

[12A—(1) Subject to paragraph (5) below a taxable person who is under a duty to make payments on account may instead of paying the amount calculated in accordance with paragraphs 11 or 12 above elect to pay an amount equal to his liability to VAT (excluding the tax on goods imported from countries other than member States) for the preceding month.

(2) A person making an election under paragraph (1) above shall notify the Commissioners in writing of—

(*a*) the election, and

(*b*) the date (being a date not less than 30 days after the date of the notification) on which it is to take effect.

(3) Subject to paragraph (4) below, an election under paragraph (1) above shall continue to have effect until a date notified by the taxable person in writing to the Commissioners, which date shall not be earlier than the first anniversary of the date on which the election took effect.

(4) Where the Commissioners are satisfied that an amount paid by a person who has elected in accordance with paragraph (1) above is less than the amount required to be paid by virtue of that paragraph the Commissioners may notify the taxable person in writing that his election shall cease to have effect from a date specified in the notification.

(5) A person may not make an election under paragraph (1) above within 12 months of the date on which any previous election made by him ceased to have effect by virtue of paragraph (4) above.][1]

Amendments—[1] This article inserted by the VAT (Payments on Account) (Amendment) Order, SI 1996/1196 art 10 with effect from 1 June 1996.

13 If—

(*a*) the total amount of tax, excluding the tax on goods imported from countries other than member States, which the taxable person was liable to pay in respect of the prescribed accounting periods the ends of which fell within any one period of one year—

(i) in the case of a taxable person who falls within article 5 above, ending after the end of his reference period was less than 80 per cent of the total amount of tax relevant in his case under article 11 above, or

(ii) in the case of a taxable person who falls within article 6 above, ending after the end of the basic period was less than 80 per cent of the total amount of tax referred to in article 12, or

(*b*) where such a period of one year has not ended, the Commissioners are satisfied that the total amount of tax, excluding the tax on goods imported from countries other than member States, which the taxable person will be liable to pay in respect of the prescribed accounting periods the ends of which fall within that year will be less than 80 per cent of the total amount of tax referred to in sub-paragraph (i) or (ii) (as the case may be) of paragraph (*a*) above,

then, with effect from the date of the written approval by the Commissioners of a written application by the taxable person to that effect, but subject to article 14 below, the total amount of tax by

VAT SIs

reference to which his payments on account fall to be calculated shall be reduced accordingly and the amount of each payment on account beginning with the first payment on account which falls to be made after the date of that approval shall equal [one twenty-fourth][1] of the reduced amount.

Amendments—[1] Words substituted by the VAT (Payments on Account) (Amendment) Order, SI 1996/1196 art 9 with effect from 1 June 1996.

14 If the total amount of tax, excluding the tax on goods imported from countries other than member States, which the taxable person was liable to pay in respect of the prescribed accounting periods the ends of which fell within any one period of one year—

(*a*) in the case of a taxable person who falls within article 5 above, ending after the end of his reference period exceeded by 20 per cent. or more the total amount of tax by reference to which his payments on account are currently calculated, or

(*b*) in the case of a taxable person who falls within article 6 above, ending after the end of the basic period exceeded by 20 per cent. or more the total amount of tax by reference to which his payments on account are currently calculated,

then, with effect from the end of the period of one year first mentioned, but subject to article 15 below, the total amount of tax by reference to which his payments on account fall to be calculated shall be increased accordingly and the amount of each payment on account beginning with the first payment on account which falls to be made after the end of that period of one year shall equal [one twenty-fourth][1] of the increased amount.

Amendments—[1] Words substituted by the VAT (Payments on Account) (Amendment) Order, SI 1996/1196 art 9 with effect from 1 June 1996.

15 Where the payments on account payable by a taxable person have been increased by virtue of article 14 above and—

(*a*) the total amount of tax, excluding the tax on goods imported from countries other than member States, which he was liable to pay in respect of the prescribed accounting periods the ends of which fell within any one period of one year ending after such increase has taken effect was less than 80 per cent of the total amount of tax by reference to which his payments on account are currently calculated, or

(*b*) where such a period of one year has not ended, the Commissioners are satisfied that the total amount of tax, excluding the tax on goods imported from countries other than member States, which he will be liable to pay in respect of the prescribed accounting periods the ends of which fall within that year will be less than 80 per cent of the total amount of tax by reference to which his payments on account are currently calculated.

then, with effect from the date of the written approval by the Commissioners of a written application by the taxable person to that effect, the total amount of tax by reference to which his payments on account fall to be calculated shall be reduced accordingly and the amount of each payment on account beginning with the first payment on account which falls to be made after the date of that approval shall equal [one twenty-fourth][1] of the reduced amount.

Amendments—[1] Words substituted by the VAT (Payments on Account) (Amendment) Order, SI 1996/1196 art 9 with effect from 1 June 1996.

16 Business carried on in divisions

(1) Subject to paragraph (3) below, where the registration under the Act of a body corporate is and was throughout the prescribed accounting periods mentioned in article 5(1) or 6(1) above in the names of divisions under section 31(1) of the Act[a] and those divisions are the same divisions, that body corporate shall not be under a duty to make payments on account by virtue of falling within article 5 or 6 above but shall be under a duty to make payments on account by reference to the business of any division if the total amount of tax which it was liable to pay in respect of the prescribed accounting periods of that division the ends of which fell within the period of one year ending on the last day of—

(*a*) that division's last prescribed accounting period ending before [1st December of the previous year][1], or

(*b*) a prescribed accounting period of that division ending after [30th November of the previous year][1],

and which was referable to the business of that division exceeded [the figure specified in article 5(1) or 6(1) respectively][2].

[(2) Where a relevant division has a prescribed accounting period exceeding one month which begins on or after 2nd March each year and ends on or before 30th June each year, the body corporate shall be under a like duty to make payments on account also in respect of that prescribed accounting period.][1]

(3) Articles 5(2) and 6(2) above shall apply for the purposes of this article as if for the references therein to the taxable person there were substituted references to a relevant division.

(4) Where payments on account fall to be made under this article, they shall be calculated and made separately in the case of each relevant division as if it were a taxable person and shall be remitted to the Controller through that division.

(5) In relation to a body corporate to which this article applies, references in articles 7, 13, 14 and 15 above to—

(*a*) the total amount of tax which a taxable person was or will be liable to pay shall be construed as references to the total amount of such tax referable to the business of a relevant division; and

(*b*) an application by the taxable person shall be construed as references to an application by the division in respect of which the application is made.

(6) In this article "relevant division" means a division by reference to the business of which a body corporate is under a duty to make payments on account by virtue of paragraph (1) above.

Notes—[a] VATA 1994 s 46(1).

[1] Words in para (1) and whole of para (2) substituted by the VAT (Payments on Account) (Amendment) Order, SI 1995/291 arts 11, 12 with effect from 2 March 1995.

[2] In para (1), words substituted for figure "£2,000,000" by the VAT (Payments on Account) (Amendment) Order, SI 2011/21 art 2(*e*) with effect from 1 June 2011.

17 Groups of companies

This Order shall apply in relation to any bodies corporate which are treated as members of a group under [section 43][1] of the Act as if those bodies were one taxable person; and where there is a duty to make a payment on account it shall be the responsibility of the representative member, except that in default of payment by the representative member it shall be the joint and several responsibility of each member of the group.

Amendments—[1] Words substituted by the VAT (Payments on Account) (Amendment) Order, SI 1996/1196 art 11 with effect from 1 June 1996.

1994/144

FREE ZONE (HUMBERSIDE) DESIGNATION ORDER 1994

Made by the Treasury under CEMA 1979 s 100A

Made . . . .*26 January 1994*

Coming into force . . . .*1 February 1994*

1 Citation and commencement

This Order may be cited as the Free Zone (Humberside) Designation Order 1994 and shall come into force on 1st February 1994.

2 Designation of area as free zone

(1) An area of 10.322 acres, in the parish of Stoneferry in the County of Humberside, shown enclosed by a red line on a map (in this article referred to as "the map"), being of a scale of 1:500, and signed by a Collector of Customs and Excise, shall be a free zone.

(2) The map shall be kept by the Commissioners at their Headquarters, New King's Beam House, 22 Upper Ground, London SE1 9PJ and a copy thereof at the offices of the responsible authority.

(3) The map or a copy thereof may, on application, be inspected by members of the public at reasonable hours without charge.

Cross reference—See Free Zone (Humberside) Designation (Variation) Order, SI 1995/1067.

3 Appointment of responsible authority

The responsible authority for the free zone shall be Transport Development Group Limited whose Registered Office is at Windsor House, 50 Victoria Street, London SW1H 0NR.

4 Period of validity of Order

This Order shall have effect for a period of 10 years from the date of coming into force.

5 Conditions imposed on responsible authority

The responsible authority shall—

(*a*) maintain an office in the free zone or such other place as the Commissioners may allow at which shall be kept any records, for which the responsible authority is responsible, relating to the free zone and the business carried on therein;

(*b*) keep separate accounts in connection with the free zone;

(*c*) provide such information in connection with the free zone and the operation thereof to any person authorised by the Treasury, as that person may reasonably require;

(*d*) provide, free of expense to the Crown, such accommodation and facilities including furniture, fittings and equipment as the Commissioners may reasonably require and such accommodation and facilities shall be properly maintained, heated, lighted, ventilated and kept clean by the responsible authority;

(*e*) provide, free of expense to the Crown, such area of land within the free zone as the Commissioners may reasonably require for the examination of goods and vehicles and shall provide and maintain such appliances and afford such other facilities which are reasonably necessary to enable an account to be taken of any goods or make any examination or search.

6 Health and safety

Without prejudice to the responsibilities of persons occupying premises within the free zone, the responsible authority shall ensure that the working conditions within the free zone are safe and without risk to the health and safety of persons employed by the Commissioners and shall comply with any requirements concerning health and safety imposed by any competent authority.

1994/955

TRAVELLERS' ALLOWANCES ORDER 1994

Made by the Commissioners of Customs and Excise under CED(GR)A 1979 s 13(1) and (3)

Made . . . . *28 March 1994*
Laid before the House of Commons . . . . *29 March 1994*
Coming into force . . . . *1 April 1994*

1 This Order may be cited as the Travellers' Allowances Order 1994 and shall come into force on 1st April 1994.

2—(1) Subject to the following provisions of this Order a person who has travelled from a third country shall on entering the United Kingdom be relieved from payment of value added tax and excise duty on goods of the descriptions and in the quantities shown in the Schedule to this Order . . . [1] contained in his personal luggage.

(2) For the purposes of this article—

(*a*) goods shall be treated as contained in a person's personal luggage where they are carried with or accompanied by the person or, if intended to accompany him, were at the time of his departure for the United Kingdom consigned by him as personal luggage to the transport operator with whom he travelled;

(*b*) a person shall not be treated as having travelled from a third country by reason only of his having arrived from its territorial waters or air space;

[(*c*) "third country"—

(i) shares the definition that applies to that expression for the purposes of Council Directive 2007/74/EC (this is termed "outside country" below) (see both indents of Article 3(1) of the Directive) (value added tax and excise duty exemptions for travellers from outside the Member States of the European Union, etc); but

(ii) it incorporates the definition that applies for the purposes of that Directive to "territory where the Community provisions on VAT or excise duty, or both do not apply" (this is termed "outside territory" below) (see both indents of Article 3(2) of that Directive); but

(iii) any outside territory where those "Community provisions on VAT" do apply (or where that Directive regards them as applying) is not a third country for value added tax purposes; and

(iv) any outside territory where those "Community provisions on . . . excise duty" do apply (or where that Directive regards them as applying) is not a third country for excise duty purposes.][1]

[(3) Where the person's journey involved transit through an outside country, or began in outside territory, this Order applies if that person is unable to establish to an officer of Revenue and Customs that the goods contained in that person's personal luggage were acquired subject to the general conditions governing taxation on the domestic market of a member State and do not qualify for any refunding of value added tax or excise duty.
(See Article 2 of Council Directive 2007/74/EC (transit, etc).)][1]

Amendments—[1] Words in para (1) revoked, para (2)(*c*) substituted, and para (3) inserted, by the Travellers' Allowances (Amendment) Order, SI 2008/3058 art 2, Sch paras 1–3 with effect from 1 December 2008.

3 The reliefs afforded under this Order are subject to the condition that the goods in question, as indicated by their nature or quantity or otherwise, are not imported for a commercial purpose nor are used for such purpose; and if that condition is not complied with in relation to any goods, those goods shall, unless the non-compliance was sanctioned by the Commissioners, be liable to forfeiture. [That condition is complied with, for example, where an occasional importation consists exclusively of goods intended as presents, or of goods for the personal or family use of the person in question. (See Article 6 of Council Directive 2007/74/EC (non-commercial imports).)][1]

Amendments—[1] Words inserted, by the Travellers' Allowances (Amendment) Order, SI 2008/3058 art 2, Sch para 4 with effect from 1 December 2008.

4 No relief shall be afforded under this Order to any person under the age of 17 in respect of tobacco products[, alcoholic beverages and alcohol][1].

Amendments—[1] Words substituted, by the Travellers' Allowances (Amendment) Order, SI 2008/3058 art 2, Sch para 5 with effect from 1 December 2008.

5 . . .

Note—Effect has been given to the revocations made by this article.

SCHEDULE . . . [1]

Article 2

[Description	*Quantity*
Goods other than fuel and those described below	Total value [£390][2] or less, if the person travelled by air or sea. Total value [£270][2] or less, if the person did not travel by air or sea. Notes: (a) . . . [2] (b) Private pleasure-flying or private pleasure-sea-navigation does not constitute travel by air or sea for these purposes. This refers to the use of an aircraft or a sea-going vessel by its owner or the person who enjoys its use either through hire or through any other means, for purposes other than commercial and in particular other than for the carriage of passengers or goods or for the supply of services for consideration or for the purposes of public authorities. (c) The value of an individual item must not be split up. (d) The value of the person's personal luggage if imported temporarily or re-imported following its temporary export, and of medicinal products required to meet the person's personal needs, is excluded from consideration. (e) This relief corresponds to Articles 3(3), 3(4), 5 (the exclusion of fuel), 7(1), 7(3), 7(4) and 15 of Council Directive 2007/74/EC.
Alcoholic beverages and alcohol, other than beer and still wine	1 litre of alcohol and alcoholic beverages of an alcoholic strength exceeding 22% by volume, or undenatured ethyl alcohol of 80% by volume and over; or 2 litres of alcohol and alcoholic beverages of an alcoholic strength not exceeding 22% by volume. Notes: (f) Each respective amount represents 100% of the total relief afforded for alcohol and alcoholic beverages. (g) For any one person, the relief applies to any combination of the types of alcohol and alcoholic beverage described, provided that the aggregate of the percentages used up from the relief the person is afforded for such alcohol and alcoholic beverage does not exceed 100%. (h) This relief corresponds to Articles 9(1) and 9(2) of that Directive.
Beer	16 litres or less Notes: (i) This relief corresponds to Article 9(3) of that Directive (beer).
Still wine	4 litres or less Notes: (j) This relief corresponds to Article 9(3) of that Directive (still wine).

[Description	*Quantity*
Tobacco products	200 cigarettes, or 100 cigarillos, or 50 cigars, or 250 grams of smoking tobacco. Notes: (k) Each respective amount represents 100% of the total relief afforded for tobacco products. (l) For any one person, the relief applies to any combination of tobacco products provided that the aggregate of the percentages used up from the relief the person is afforded for such products does not exceed 100%. (m) A cigarillo is a cigar of maximum weight 3 grams. (n) This relief corresponds to Articles 8(1) and 8(4) of that Directive.][1]

Amendments—

1 Table substituted, and words in previous table heading revoked, by the Travellers' Allowances (Amendment) Order, SI 2008/3058 art 2, Sch para 6 with effect from 1 December 2008.

2 In column 2, figures substituted and Note (a) revoked, by the Travellers' Allowances (Amendment) Order, SI 2009/3172 arts 2, 3 with effect where the person in question enters the UK on or after 1 January 2010.

1994/1978

VALUE ADDED TAX TRIBUNALS APPEALS (NORTHERN IRELAND) ORDER 1994

Revocation—These Regulations revoked by the Transfer of Tribunal Functions and Revenue and Customs Appeals Order, SI 2009/56 art 3, Sch 2 para 187(*g*) with effect from 1 April 2009.

1995/958

VALUE ADDED TAX (TREATMENT OF TRANSACTIONS) ORDER 1995

Made by the Treasury under VATA 1994 s 5(3)

Made . . . . *30 March 1995*
Laid before the House of Commons . . . . *31 March 1995*
Coming into force in accordance with article 1 . . . . *1 May 1995*

1 This Order may be cited as the Value Added Tax (Treatment of Transactions) Order 1995 and shall come into force on the day that the Finance Bill 1995 is passed.

[2 In this Order "work of art" has the same meaning as in section 21 of the Value Added Tax Act 1994.][1]

Amendments—[1] This article substituted by the VAT (Treatment of Transactions) (Amendment) Order, SI 1999/3119, arts 2, 3, with effect from 1 January 2000.

3—(1) Subject to paragraph (3) below, the transfer of ownership in—

(*a*) second-hand goods imported from a place outside the member States with a view to their sale by auction;

(*b*) works of art imported from a place outside the member States for the purposes of exhibition, with a view to possible sale,

at a time when the second-hand goods or works of art, as the case may be, are still subject to arrangements for temporary importation with total exemption from import duty in accordance with Articles 137 to 141 and paragraph 1 of Article 144 of Council Regulation (EEC) No 2913/92 . . . [1], shall be treated as neither a supply of goods nor a supply of services.

(2) Subject to paragraph (3) [and article 4][1] below, the provision of any services relating to a transfer of ownership falling within paragraph (1)(*a*) or (*b*) above shall be treated as neither a supply of goods nor a supply of services.

(3) Paragraphs (1) and (2) above shall not apply in relation to any transfer of ownership in second-hand goods which is effected otherwise than by sale by auction.

Amendments—[1] Words in art 3(1) revoked, words in 3(2), and whole of new art 4 inserted, by the Value Added Tax (Treatment of Transactions and Special Provisions) (Amendment) Order, SI 2006/2187, art 2(1)–(3), with effect from 1 September 2006.

[4—(1) Article 3(1) does not apply where—

(*a*) any goods falling within paragraph (2) are sold by auction at a time when they are subject to the procedure specified in paragraph (3), and (*b*) arrangements made by or on behalf of the purchaser of the goods following the sale by auction result in the importation of the goods from a place outside the member States.

(See section 21(2A) of the Value Added Tax Act 1994.)

(2) The goods that fall within this paragraph are—

(*a*) any work of art;

(*b*) any antique, not falling within sub-paragraph (a) or (c), that is more than one hundred years old;

(*c*) any collection or collector's piece that is of zoological, botanical, mineralogical, anatomical, historical, archaeological, palaeontological, ethnographic, numismatic or philatelic interest.

(See sections 21(5) to 21(6C) of the Value Added Tax Act 1994.)

(3) That procedure is the customs procedure for temporary importation with total relief from import duties provided for in Articles 137 to 141 of Council Regulation (EEC) No 2913/92 establishing the Community Customs Code.

(See section 21(2B) of the Value Added Tax Act 1994.)][1]

Amendments—[1] Words in art 3(1) revoked, words in 3(2), and whole of new art 4 inserted, by the Value Added Tax (Treatment of Transactions and Special Provisions) (Amendment) Order, SI 2006/2187, art 2(1)–(3), with effect from 1 September 2006.

1995/1067

FREE ZONE (HUMBERSIDE) DESIGNATION (VARIATION) ORDER 1995

Made by the Treasury under CEMA 1979 s 100A(4)(a)(ii)

Made . . . .*11 April 1995*
Coming into force . . . .*12 April 1995*

1 This Order may be cited as the Free Zone (Humberside) Designation (Variation) Order 1995 and shall come into force on 12th April 1995.

2 The area designated a free zone by the Free Zone (Humberside) Designation Order 1994 shall be varied so as to consist of the area of 4.479 hectares in the parish of Stoneferry in the County of Humberside, shown enclosed by a red line on a map (being of a scale of 1:500), marked "Map referred to in article 2 of the Free Zone (Humberside) Designation (Variation) Order 1995", signed by a Collector of Customs and Excise and dated 2nd February 1995.

3 The map referred to in article 2 above shall be kept by the Commissioners at their Headquarters, New King's Beam House, 22 Upper Ground, London SE1 9PJ (and a copy thereof at the offices of Transport Development Group Limited) in substitution for the map referred to in article 2 of the Free Zone (Humberside) Designation Order 1994.

Cross references—See Free Zone (Humberside) Designation Order, SI 1994/144.

1995/1268

VALUE ADDED TAX (SPECIAL PROVISIONS) ORDER 1995

Made by the Treasury under VATA 1994 ss 5(3), (5), 11(4), 43(2), 50A

Made . . . .*10 May 1995*
Laid before the House of Commons . . . .*10 May 1995*
Coming into force . . . .*1 June 1995*

1 Citation and commencement

This Order may be cited as the Value Added Tax (Special provisions) Order 1995, and shall come into force on 1st June 1995.

2[Interpretation

(1)] [4] In this Order—

"finance agreement" means an agreement for the sale of goods whereby the property in those goods is not to be transferred until the whole of the price has been paid and the seller retains the right to repossess the goods;

. . .[6]

"marine mortgage" means a mortgage which is registered in accordance with the [Merchant Shipping Act 1995][7] and by virtue of which a boat (but not any share thereof) is made a security for a loan;

"aircraft mortgage" means a mortgage which is registered in accordance with the Mortgaging of Aircraft Order 1972 and by virtue of which an aircraft is made security for a loan;

"the Act" means the Value Added Tax Act 1994;

"the Manx Act" means [the Value Added Tax Act 1996][1];

["work of art" has the same meaning as in section 21 of the Act.][3]

"antiques" means objects other than works of art or collectors' items, which are more than 100 years old;

["collectors' items" means any collection or collector's piece falling within section 21(5) of the Act but excluding investment gold coins within the meaning of Note 1(*b*) and (*c*) to Group 15 of Schedule 9 to the Act;][3]

["Motor car" means any motor vehicle of a kind normally used on public roads which has three or more wheels and either—

(*a*) is constructed or adapted solely or mainly for the carriage of passengers; or

(*b*) has to the rear of the driver's seat roofed accommodation which is fitted with side windows or which is constructed or adapted for the fitting of side windows;

but does not include—

(i) vehicles capable of accommodating only one person;

(ii) vehicles which meet the requirements of Schedule 6 to the Road Vehicles (Construction and Use) Regulations 1986 and are capable of carrying twelve or more seated persons;

(iii) vehicles of not less than three tonnes unladen weight (as defined in the Table to regulation 3(2) of the Road Vehicles (Construction and Use) Regulations 1986);

(iv) vehicles constructed to carry a payload (the difference between a vehicle's kerb weight (as defined in the Table to regulation 3(2) of the Road Vehicles (Construction and Use) Regulations 1986) and its maximum gross weight (as defined in that Table)) of one tonne or more;

(v) caravans, ambulances and prison vans;

(vi) vehicles constructed for a special purpose other than the carriage of persons and having no other accommodation for carrying persons than such as is incidental to that purpose;][2]

"second-hand goods" means tangible movable property that is suitable for further use as it is or after repair, other than motor cars, works of art, collectors' items or antiques and other than precious metals and precious stones;

"printed matter" includes printed stationery but does not include anything produced by typing, duplicating or photo-copying;[5]

"auctioneer" means a person who sells or offers for sale goods at any public sale where persons become purchasers by competition, being the highest bidders.

(2) . . .[6]

Amendments—[1] Words substituted by the VAT (Special Provisions) (Amendment) Order, SI 1998/760 with effect from 18 March 1998.

[2] Definition of "Motor car" substituted by the VAT (Special Provisions) (Amendment) Order, SI 1999/2831, art 2, with effect from 1 December 1999.

[3] Definitions of "collectors' items" and "work of art" substituted by the VAT (Special Provisions) (Amendment) (No 2) Order, SI 1999/3120, arts 2, 3, with effect from 1 January 2000.

[4] Para (1) numbered as such, definition of "insurer" substituted, and para (2) inserted, by the Financial Services and Markets Act 2000 (Consequential Amendments and Repeals) Order, SI 2001/3649 art 500 with effect from 1 December 2001.

[5] Definition of "printed matter" revoked by the VAT (Special Provisions) (Amendment) Order, SI 2002/1280 arts 2, 3 with effect from 1 June 2002. See SI 2002/1280 art 1(2) for circumstances in which this amendment shall not have effect.

[6] In para (1), definition of "insurer" repealed, and para (2) repealed, by the VAT (Special Provisions) (Amendment) (No 2) Order, SI 2004/3085 with effect from 1 January 2005.

[7] In definition of "marine mortgage", words substituted by the Value Added Tax (Treatment of Transactions and Special Provisions) (Amendment) Order, SI 2006/2187, art 3(1), with effect from 1 September 2006.

3 . . .

Note—Effect has been given to the revocations made by this article.

4 Treatment of transactions

(1) Each of the following descriptions of transactions shall be treated as neither a supply of goods nor a supply of services—

(*a*) the disposal of any of the goods described in paragraph (3) below by a person who repossessed them under the terms of a finance agreement;

(*b*) the disposal of any of the goods described in paragraph (3) below by an insurer who has taken possession of them in settlement of a claim under a policy of insurance;

(*c*) the disposal of a boat by a mortgagee after he has taken possession thereof under the terms of a marine mortgage;

(*d*) the disposal of an aircraft by a mortgagee after he has taken possession thereof under the terms of an aircraft mortgage;

if, in each case, the goods so disposed of are in the same condition at the time of disposal as they were when they were repossessed or taken into possession, as the case may be, and if a supply of them in the United Kingdom by the person from whom in each case they were obtained would not have been chargeable with VAT, or would have been chargeable with VAT on less than the full value of such supply.

[(1A) Paragraph (1)(*a*) above shall not apply where adjustment, whether or not made under regulation 38 of the Value Added Tax Regulations 1995, has taken account, or may later take account, of VAT on the initial supply under the finance agreement as a result of repossession and the goods delivered under that agreement were delivered on or after 1st September 2006.][2]

(2) Paragraph (1) of this article shall not apply to reimported goods which were previously exported from the United Kingdom or the Isle of Man free of VAT chargeable under the Act or VAT chargeable under Part I of the Manx Act by reason of the zero-rating provisions of either [Act, or][1] regulations made under either Act, or to imported goods which have not borne VAT chargeable under either of those Acts in the United Kingdom or the Isle of Man.

(3) The goods referred to in subparagraphs (*a*) and (*b*) of paragraph (1) above are as follows:

(*a*) works of art, antiques and collectors' items;

(*b*) second-hand goods.

Amendments—[1] Words in para (2) inserted by the VAT (Special Provisions) Order 1995 (Amendment) Order, SI 1995/1385 art 2 with effect from 1 June 1995.

[2] Para (1A) inserted by the VAT (Special Provisions) (Amendment) (No 2) Order, SI 2006/869 with effect from 13 April 2006 in relation to finance agreements entered into on or after that date. For these purposes, "finance agreement" has the meaning given in SI 1995/1268 art 2(1).

5—(1) Subject to paragraph (2) below, there shall be treated as neither a supply of goods nor a supply of services the following supplies by a person of assets of his business—

(*a*) their supply to a person to whom he transfers his business as a going concern where—

(i) the assets are to be used by the transferee in carrying on the same kind of business, whether or not as part of any existing business, as that carried on by the transferor, and

(ii) in a case where the transferor is a taxable person, the transferee is already, or immediately becomes as a result of the transfer, a taxable person or a person defined as such in [section 3(1)][1] of the Manx Act;

(*b*) their supply to a person to whom he transfers part of his business as a going concern where—

(i) that part is capable of separate operation,

(ii) the assets are to be used by the transferee in carrying on the same kind of business, whether or not as part of any existing business, as that carried on by the transferor in relation to that part, and

(iii) in a case where the transferor is a taxable person, the transferee is already, or immediately becomes as a result of the transfer, a taxable person or a person defined as such in [section 3(1)][1] of the Manx Act.

(2) A supply of assets shall not be treated as neither a supply of goods nor a supply of services by virtue of paragraph (1) above to the extent that it consists of—

(*a*) a grant which would, but for an [option which the transferor has exercised][3], fall within item 1 of Group 1 of Schedule 9 to the Act; or

(*b*) a grant of a fee simple which falls within paragraph (*a*) of item 1 of Group 1 of Schedule 9 to the Act,

unless [the conditions contained in paragraph (2A) below are satisfied][2].

[(2A) The conditions referred to in paragraph (2) above are that the transferee has, no later than the relevant date—

(*a*) [exercised an option][3] in relation to the land which has effect on the relevant date and has given any written notification of the [option required by paragraph 20 of Schedule 10][3] to the Act; and

(*b*) notified the transferor that paragraph (2B) below does not apply to him.][2]

[(2B) This paragraph applies to a transferee where—

(*a*) the supply of the asset that is to be transferred to him would become, in relation to him, a capital item as described in regulation 113 of the Value Added Tax Regulations 1995 if the supply of that asset to him—

(i) were to be treated as neither a supply of goods nor a supply of services; or

(ii) were not so treated; and

(*b*) his supplies of that asset will, or would fall, to be exempt supplies by virtue of [paragraph 12 of Schedule 10][3] to the Act.][2]

(3) In paragraph (2) of this article—

. . . [3]

["option" means an option to tax any land having effect under Part 1 of Schedule 10 to the Act;][3]

"relevant date" means the date upon which the grant would have been treated as having been made or, if there is more than one such date, the earliest of them;

"transferor" and "transferee" include a relevant associate of either respectively as defined in [paragraph 3 of Schedule 10][3] to the Act.

(4) There shall be treated as neither a supply of goods nor a supply of services the assignment by an owner of goods comprised in a hire-purchase or conditional sale agreement of his rights and interest thereunder, and the goods comprised therein, to a bank or other financial institution.

Press releases etc—C&E Business Brief 16/99 20-7-99 (timing of an election to tax on property forming part of the assets of a TOGC).

Simon's Tax Cases—*Higher Education Statistics Agency v C&E Comrs* [2000] STC 332; *Royal Bank of Scotland v R&C Comrs* [2012] EWHC 9 (Ch), [2012] STC 797.

Art 5(1), *Abbey National plc v C&E Comrs* [2001] STC 297.

Amendments—[1] Words substituted by the VAT (Special Provisions) (Amendment) Order, SI 1998/760 with effect from 18 March 1998.

[2] Words in para (2) substituted, and paras (2A), (2B) inserted, by the VAT (Special Provisions) (Amendment) Order, SI 2004/779 with effect from 18 March 2004.

[3] Words in paras (2)(*a*), (2A)(*a*), (2B)(*b*), (3) substituted, in para (3) definition of "election" revoked, and definition of "option" inserted, by the Value Added Tax (Buildings and Land) Order, SI 2008/1146, art 6, Sch 1 para 15 with effect in relation to supplies made on or after 1 June 2008, subject to savings in Sch 2 of the Order.

6 The following description of transaction shall be treated as a supply of services and not as a supply of goods—

the exchange of a reconditioned article for an unserviceable article of a similar kind by a person who regularly offers in the course of his business to provide a reconditioning facility by that means.

7 The following description of transaction shall not be treated as the acquisition of goods from another member State—

the removal of goods to the United Kingdom in pursuance of a supply to a taxable person, made by a person in another member State, where VAT on that supply is to be accounted for and paid in another member State by reference to the profit margin on the supply by virtue of the law of that member State corresponding to section 50A of the Act and any Orders made thereunder.

8 The following description of transaction shall be treated as neither a supply of goods nor a supply of services—

the removal of goods to the United Kingdom in pursuance of a supply to a person, made by a person in another member State where VAT on that supply is to be accounted for and paid in another member State by reference to the profit margin on the supply by virtue of the law of that member State corresponding to section 50A of the Act and any Orders made thereunder.

9 The following description of transaction shall be treated as neither a supply of goods nor a supply of services—

services in connection with a supply of goods provided by an agent acting in his own name to the purchaser of the goods the consideration for which is taken into account by virtue of article 12(6) below in calculating the price at which the agent obtained the goods.

10 The following description of transaction shall be treated as neither a supply of goods nor a supply of services—

services in connection with the sale of goods provided by an auctioneer acting in his own name to the vendor or the purchaser of the goods the consideration for which is taken into account by virtue of article 12(7) below in calculating the price at which the auctioneer obtained (or as the case may be) sold the goods.

10A [Goods put to private use or used, or made available for use, for non-business purposes
Paragraph 5(4) of Schedule 4 to the Act shall not apply to goods (including land treated as goods for the purposes of that paragraph by virtue of paragraph 9 of that Schedule) which have no economic life for the purposes of Part 15A of the Value Added Tax Regulations 1995 at the time when they are used or made available for use.][1]

Amendments—[1] Para 10A inserted by the VAT (Special Provisions) (Amendment) Order, SI 2007/2923 arts 2, 3 with effect from 1 November 2007 in relation to the use, on or after that date, of goods or land held or used for the purposes of a business: SI 2007/2923 art 1.

11 Self-supply

(1) Where a person in the course or furtherance of any business carried on by him produces printed matter and the printed matter—

(a) is not supplied to another person or incorporated in other goods produced in the course or furtherance of that business; but

(b) is used by him for the purpose of a business carried on by him,

then, subject to paragraph (2) below, the printed matter shall be treated for the purposes of the Act as both supplied to him for the purpose of that business and supplied by him in the course or furtherance of that business.

(2) Paragraph (1) of this article does not apply if—

(a) the person is a fully taxable person;

(b) the value of the supplies falling to be treated as made by and to that person would not, if those were the only supplies made or to be made by that person, make him liable to be registered for VAT pursuant to the provisions of Schedule 1 to the Act; or

(c) the Commissioners, being satisfied that the VAT (if any) which would be attributable to the supplies after allowing for any credit under sections 25 and 26 of the Act would be negligible, have given, and have not withdrawn, a direction that the paragraph is not to apply.

(3) For the purposes of paragraph (2)(a) above, a person is a fully taxable person if the only input tax of his to which he is not entitled to credit at the end of any prescribed accounting period or longer period is input tax which is excluded from any credit under section 25 of the Act by virtue of any Order made under sub-section (7) of that section.

(4) The preceding provisions of this article shall apply in relation to any bodies corporate which are treated for the purposes of section 43 of the Act as members of a group as if those bodies were one person, but any printed matter which would fall to be treated as supplied to and by that person shall be treated as supplied to and by the representative member.

Amendment—Revoked by the VAT (Special Provisions) (Amendment) Order, SI 2002/1280 arts 2, 3 with effect from 1 June 2002. See SI 2002/1280 art 1(2) for circumstances in which this amendment shall not have effect.

12 Relief for certain goods

(1) Without prejudice to article 13 below and subject to complying with such conditions as the Commissioners may direct in a notice published by them for the purposes of this Order or may otherwise direct and subject to paragraph (4) below, where a person supplies goods of a description in paragraph (2) below, of which he took possession in any of the circumstances set out in paragraph (3) below, he may opt to account for the VAT chargeable on the supply on the profit margin on the supply instead of by reference to its value.

(2) The supplies referred to in paragraph (1) above are supplies of—

(*a*) works of art, antiques and collectors' items;

(*b*) second-hand goods.

(3) The circumstances mentioned in paragraph (1) above are—

[(*a*) that the taxable person took possession of the goods pursuant to—

(i) a supply in respect of which no VAT was chargeable under the Act or under Part I of the Manx Act;

(ii) a supply on which VAT was chargeable on the profit margin in accordance with paragraph (1) above or a corresponding provision made under the Manx Act or a corresponding provision of the law of another member State;

[(iii) a de-supplied transaction, other than an article 5 transaction;

(iv) subject to paragraph (3A) below, an article 5 transaction;][4]

(v) (if the goods are a work of art) a supply to the taxable person by, or an acquisition from another member State by him from its creator or his successor in title;][1]

(*b*) (if the goods are a work of art, an antique or a collectors' item) that they were imported by the taxable person himself[, which includes – if the taxable person is an auctioneer – the auctioneer having placed them in the customs procedure for temporary importation with total relief from import duties provided for in Articles 137 to 141 of Council Regulation (EEC) No 2913/92 establishing the Community Customs Code][5].

[(3A) An article 5 transaction does not fall within paragraph (iv) of paragraph (3)(*a*) above unless the taxable person has a relevant predecessor in title.][4]

(4) A taxable person—

(*a*) may not opt under paragraph (1) above where—

(i) the supply is a letting on hire;

(ii) an invoice or similar document showing an amount as being VAT or as being attributable to VAT is issued in respect of the supply;

(iii) the supply is of an air gun unless the taxable person is registered for the purposes of the Firearms Act 1968; or

(iv) the supply is of goods which are being disposed of in the circumstances mentioned in article 4(1)(*a*)(*b*)(*c*) or (*d*) above but which is not disregarded by virtue of that article;

(*b*) may only exercise the option under paragraph (1) above in relation to supplies of—

(i) works of art of which he took possession in the circumstances mentioned in paragraph [(3)(*a*)(v)][2] above, or

(ii) works of art, antiques or collectors' items of which he took possession in circumstances set out in paragraph (3)(*b*) above,

if at the same time he exercises the option in relation to the other.

(5) Subject to paragraph (6) below, for the purposes of determining the profit margin—

(*a*) the price at which goods were obtained shall be calculated as follows—

(i) (where the taxable person took possession of the goods pursuant to a supply) in the same way as the consideration for the supply would be calculated for the purposes of the Act;

(ii) (where the taxable person is a sole proprietor and the goods were supplied to him in his private capacity) in the same way as the consideration for the supply to him as a private individual would be calculated for the purposes of the Act;

(iii) (where the goods are a work of art which was acquired from another member State by the taxable person pursuant to a supply to him by the creator of the item or his successor in title) in the same way as the value of the acquisition would be calculated for the purposes of the Act plus the VAT chargeable on the acquisition;

(iv) (where the goods are a work of art, an antique or a collectors' item which the taxable person has imported himself[, which includes – if the taxable person is an auctioneer – the auctioneer having placed them in the customs procedure for temporary importation with total relief from import duties mentioned in article 12(3)(*b*)][5]) in the same way as the value of the goods for the purpose of charging VAT on their importation would be calculated for the purposes of the Act plus any VAT chargeable on their importation;

[(v) (where the taxable person took possession of the goods pursuant to a de-supplied transaction, other than an article 5 transaction) by taking the price he paid pursuant to the transaction;

(vi) (where the taxable person took possession of the goods pursuant to an article 5 transaction) by taking the price at which his relevant predecessor in title obtained the goods;][4]

(*b*) the price at which goods are sold shall be calculated in the same way as the consideration for the supply would be calculated for the purposes of the Act[;

(*c*) . . .[4]

(6) Subject to paragraph (7) below, where the taxable person is an agent acting in his own name the price at which the goods were obtained shall be calculated in accordance with paragraph (5)(*a*) above, but the selling price calculated in accordance with paragraph (5)(*b*) above shall be increased by the amount of any consideration payable to the taxable person in respect of services supplied by him to the purchaser in connection with the supply of the goods.

(7) Instead of calculating the price at which goods were obtained or supplied in accordance with paragraph (6) above an auctioneer acting in his own name may—

[(*a*) calculate the price at which they were obtained by deducting from the successful bid the amount of the commission payable to him under his contract with the vendor for the sale of the goods;][3]

(*b*) calculate the price at which they were supplied by adding to the successful bid the consideration for any supply of services by him to the purchaser in connection with the sale of the goods,

in either (or both) cases excluding the consideration for supplies of services that are not chargeable to VAT.

(8) Where a taxable person opts under paragraph (1) above in respect of goods of which he took possession in the circumstances set out in paragraph [(3)(*a*)(v)][2] and (*b*) above, the exercise of the option shall—

(*a*) be notified by him to the Commissioners in writing;

(*b*) have effect from the date of that notification or such later date as may be specified therein;

(*c*) subject to paragraph (9) below, apply to all supplies of such goods made by the taxable person in the period ending 2 years after the date on which it first had effect or the date on which written notification of its revocation is given to the Commissioners, whichever is the later.

(9) Notwithstanding paragraph (8)(*c*) above a taxable person may elect to account for VAT chargeable on any particular supply of such goods by reference to the value of that supply.

[(10) For the purposes of this article—

"article 5 transaction" means a transaction which is a de-supplied transaction by virtue of a provision of article 5 above or a corresponding provision made under the Manx Act;

"de-supplied transaction" means a transaction which was treated by virtue of any Order made or having effect as if made under section 5(3) of the Act or under the corresponding provisions of the Manx Act as being neither a supply of goods nor a supply of services.

(11) For the purposes of this article a person is a relevant predecessor in title of a taxable person if—

(*a*) he is the person from whom the taxable person took possession of the goods and himself took possession of them in any of the circumstances described in paragraph (3) above, but not pursuant to an article 5 transaction; or (*b*) where the goods have been the subject of a succession of two or more article 5 transactions (culminating in the article 5 transaction to which the taxable person was a party), he was a party to one of those transactions and himself took possession of the goods in any of the circumstances described in paragraph (3) above, but not pursuant to an article 5 transaction.][4]

Amendments—[1] Para (3)(*a*) substituted by the VAT (Special Provisions) (Amendment) Order SI 1997/1616 with effect from 3 July 1997.

[2] Words in paras (4)(*b*)(i), (8) substituted, by the VAT (Special Provisions) (Amendment) Order, SI 1998/760 with effect from 18 March 1998.

[3] Para (7)(*a*) substituted by the VAT (Special Provisions) (Amendment) Order, SI 2001/3753 art 3 with effect from 2 January 2002.

[4] Sub-paras (3)(*a*)(iii), (iv) substituted, para (3A) inserted, sub-paras (5)(*a*)(v), (vi) substituted for sub-para (5)(*a*)(v), sub-para (5)(*c*) revoked, and paras (10), (11) added, by the VAT (Special Provisions) (Amendment) (No 2) Order, SI 2002/1503 with effect from 1 July 2002. For further provisions as to the effect of that Order see SI 2002/1503 art 1(2).

[5] Words in paras (3)(*b*) and (5)(*a*)(iv) inserted by the Value Added Tax (Tax Treatment of Transactions and Special Provisions) (Amendment) Order, SI 2006/2187, art 3(2), (3), with effect from 1 September 2006.

13 Global Accounting

(1) Subject to complying with such conditions as the Commissioners may direct in a notice published by them for the purposes of this Order or may otherwise direct, and subject to paragraph (2) below, a taxable person who has opted under article 12(1) above may account for VAT on the total profit margin on goods supplied by him during a prescribed accounting period, calculated in accordance with paragraph (3) below, instead of the profit margin on each supply.

(2) Paragraph (1) above does not apply to supplies of—

(*a*) motor vehicles;
(*b*) aircraft;
(*c*) boats and outboard motors;
(*d*) caravans and motor caravans;
(*e*) horses and ponies;
(*f*) any other individual items whose value calculated in accordance with article 12(5)(*a*) above, exceeds £500.

[(3) The total profit margin for a prescribed accounting period shall be the amount (if any) by which the total selling price calculated in accordance with paragraph (4) below, exceeds the total purchase price calculated in accordance with paragraph (5) below.][1]

(4) For the purposes of paragraph (3) above the total selling price shall be calculated by aggregating for all goods sold during the period the prices (calculated in accordance with article 12(5) or (6) above as appropriate) for which they were sold.

(5) For the purposes of paragraph (3) above the total purchase price shall be calculated by aggregating for all goods obtained during the period the prices (calculated in accordance with article 12(5) above) at which they were obtained and adding to that total the amount (if any) carried forward from the previous period in accordance with paragraph (6) below.

(6) If in any prescribed accounting period the total purchase price calculated in accordance with paragraph (5) above exceeds the total selling price, the excess amount shall be carried forward to the following prescribed accounting period for inclusion in the calculation of the total purchase price for that period.

Amendments—[1] Para (3) substituted by the VAT (Special Provisions) (Amendment) (No 2) Order, SI 1999/3120, arts 2, 4, with effect from 1 January 2000.

1995/1978

VALUE ADDED TAX (REFUND OF TAX) ORDER 1995

Made by the Treasury under VATA 1994 s 33(3)

Made .... *26 July 1995*
Laid before the House of Commons .... *26 July 1995*
Coming into force .... *18 August 1995*

1 This Order may be cited as the Value Added Tax (Refund of Tax) Order 1995 and shall come into force on 18th August 1995.

2 The Environment Agency (a body corporate established by section 1 of the Environment Act 1995) is hereby specified for the purposes of section 33 of the Value Added Tax Act 1994.

Amendments—Para (3) substituted by the VAT (Special Provisions) (Amendment) (No 2) Order SI 1999/3120 arts 2, 4 with effect from 1 January 2000.

1995/2518

VALUE ADDED TAX REGULATIONS 1995

Made by the Commissioners of Customs and Excise under VATA 1994 ss 3(4), 6(14), 7(9), 8(4), 12(3), 14(3), 16(1) and (2), 18(5), (5A), 24(3), (4), (6), 25(1), (4), (6), 26(1), (3), (4), 28(3), (4) and (5), 30(8), 35(2), 36(5), 37(3) and (4), 38, 39(1), 40(3), 46(2), (4), 48(3)(b), (4), (6), 49(2), (3), 52, 54(1), (2), (3), (6), 58, 79(3), 80(6), 88(3), (5), 92(4), 93(1), (2), 95(5), 97(1) and Sch 1 para 17, Sch 2 para 9, Sch 3 para 10, Sch 7 paras 2(1)–(2), and Sch 11 paras 2(1)–(12), 5(4), (9), 6(1)–(2) and 7(1)

Made . . . .*27 September 1995*

Laid before the House of Commons . . . .*28 September 1995*

Coming into force . . . .*20 October 1995*

ARRANGEMENT OF REGULATIONS

VAT SIs

VAT SIs

VAT SIs

Cross reference—See VAT (Isle of Man) (No 2) Order, SI 1982/1068 reg 3, Sch; VATA 1994, Sch 13 para 23 (modifications consequential on treatment of UK and Isle of Man as a single area for VAT purposes).

PART I
PRELIMINARY

1 Citation and commencement

These Regulations may be cited as the Value Added Tax Regulations 1995 and shall come into force on 20th October 1995.

Former regulation—VAT (General) Regulations, SI 1985/886 reg 1.

2 Interpretation—general

(1) In these Regulations unless the context otherwise requires—

"the Act" means the Value Added Tax Act 1994 and any reference to a Schedule to the Act includes a reference to a Schedule as amended from time to time by Order of the Treasury;

["alphabetical code" means the alphabetical prefix as set out below which shall be used to identify the member State—

Austria—AT
Belgium—BE
[Bulgaria—BG][4]
Cyprus—CY
Czech Republic—CZ
Denmark—DK
Estonia—EE
Finland—FI
France—FR
Germany—DE
Greece—EL
Hungary—HU
Ireland—IE
Italy—IT
Latvia—LV
Lithuania—LT
Luxembourg—LU
Malta—MT
Netherlands—NL
Poland—PL
Portugal—PT
[Romania—RO][4]
Slovakia—SK
Slovenia—SI
Spain—ES
Sweden—SE
United Kingdom—GB][3]

"Collector" includes Deputy Collector and Assistant Collector;

"the Community" means the European Community;

"continental shelf" means a designated area within the meaning of the Continental Shelf Act 1964;

"Controller" means the Controller, Customs and Excise Value Added Tax Central Unit;

"datapost packet" means a postal packet containing goods which is posted in the United Kingdom as a datapost packet for transmission to a place outside the United Kingdom in accordance with the terms of a contract entered into between [a universal service provider][6] and the sender of the packet; or which is received at a post office [a universal service provider][6] in the United Kingdom from a place outside the United Kingdom for transmission and delivery in the United Kingdom [by that universal service provider][6] as if it were a datapost packet;

["fiscal or other warehousing regime" means "fiscal warehousing regime or warehousing regime";][1]

. . . [6]

["post office" has the same meaning as in section 125(1) of the Postal Services Act 2000][6]

["postal packet" has the same meaning as in Part 3 of the Postal Services Act 2011][6]

"prescribed accounting period", subject to regulation 99(I), means a period such as is referred to in regulation 25;

"proper officer" means the person appointed or authorised by the Commissioners to act in respect of any matter in the course of his duties;

"registered person" means a person registered by the Commissioners under [Schedule 1, [1A,][5] 2, 3 or 3A][2] to the Act;

"registration number" means the number allocated by the Commissioners to a taxable person in the certificate of registration issued to him;

"return" means a return which is required to be made in accordance with regulation 25;

"specified date" means the date specified in a person's application for registration for the purpose of VAT as that on which he expects to make his first taxable supply.

["universal service provider" means a person who provides a universal postal service (within the meaning of Part 3 of the Postal Services Act 2011) or part of such a service, in the United Kingdom][6]

(2) A reference in these Regulations to "this Part" is a reference to the Part of these Regulations in which that reference is made.

(3) In these Regulations any reference to a form [specified in a notice published by the Commissioners][7] shall include a reference to a form which the Commissioners are satisfied is a form to the like effect.

Former regulations—Para (1): VAT (General) Regulations, SI 1985/886 reg 2(1); VAT (General) (Amendment) Regulations, SI 1992/3102 regs 1, 3, SI 1993/1941 regs 2, 3, SI 1995/152 reg 3.

Para (2): None.

Para (3): VAT (General) Regulations, SI 1985/886 reg 2(2).

Amendments—[1] Definition of "fiscal or other warehousing regime" inserted by the VAT (Amendment) (No 3) Regulations, SI 1996/1250 reg 4 with effect from 1 June 1996.

[2] Words in definition of "registered person" substituted by the VAT (Amendment) (No 3) Regulations, SI 2000/794 regs 2, 3 with effect from 22 March 2000.

[3] Definition of "alphabetical code" substituted by the VAT (Amendment) (No 2) Regulations, SI 2004/1082 regs 2, 3 with effect from 1 May 2004.

[4] In para (1) entries inserted by the VAT (Amendment) (No 3) Regulations, SI 2006/3292 regs 2, 3 with effect from 1 January 2007.

[5] In para (1), in definition of "registered person", reference inserted, and in para (3), words substituted for words "prescribed in Schedule 1 to these Regulations", by the VAT (Amendment) (No 2) Regulations, SI 2012/1899 regs 3, 4 with effect from 15 October 2012.

[6] In para (1) words in the definition of "datapost packet" substituted, definitions inserted, and definition of "the Post office Company" revoked by the Postal Services Act 2011 (Consequential Modifications and Amendments) Order, SI 2011/2085 art 5(1), Sch 16 para 31 with effect from 1 October 2011.

3 Revocations and savings

(1) The Regulations described in Schedule 2 to these Regulations are hereby revoked.

(2) Anything begun under or for the purpose of any Regulations revoked by these Regulations shall be continued under or, as the case may be, for the purpose of the corresponding provision of these Regulations.

(3) Where any document used or required for the purpose of VAT refers to a provision of a regulation revoked by these Regulations, such reference shall, unless the context otherwise requires, be construed as a reference to the corresponding provision of these Regulations.

Former regulation—VAT (General) Regulations, SI 1985/886 reg 3.

4 Requirement, direction, demand or permission

Any requirement, direction, demand or permission by the Commissioners, under or for the purposes of these Regulations, may be made or given by a notice in writing, or otherwise.

Former regulation—VAT (General) Regulations, SI 1985/886 reg 67.

4A [Electronic communication

(1) A specified communication may be made to the Commissioners using an electronic communications system.

(2) Where an electronic communications system is used it must take a form approved by the Commissioners in a specific or general direction.

(3) A direction under paragraph (2) may in particular—

(*a*) modify or dispense with any requirement of a form mentioned in regulation 2(3) used to make a specified communication;

(*b*) specify different forms of electronic communications system for different cases; and

(*c*) specify different circumstances in which the electronic communications system may be used, or not used, by or on behalf of the person required to make the communication and specify different circumstances for different cases.

(4) An electronic communications system shall incorporate an electronic validation process.

(5) Subject to paragraph (6) below and unless the contrary is proved—

(*a*) the use of an electronic communications system shall be presumed to have resulted in the making of a communication to the Commissioners only if this has been successfully recorded as such by the relevant electronic validation process;

(*b*) the time of making a communication to the Commissioners using an electronic communications system shall be presumed to be the time recorded as such by the relevant electronic validation process; and

(*c*) the person delivering a communication to the Commissioners shall be presumed to be the person identified as such by any relevant feature of the electronic communications system.

(6) No communication shall be treated as having been made using an electronic communications system unless it is in the form required by paragraph (2).

(7) A communication made using an electronic communications system carries the same consequences as a communication made in paper form.

(8) In paragraph (2) "direction" refers only to a current direction, and a direction is not current to the extent that it is varied, replaced or revoked by another Commissioners' direction.][1]

Amendments—[1] Regs 4A, 4B inserted by the VAT (Amendment) (No 2) Regulations, SI 2012/1899 regs 3, 5 with effect from 15 October 2012.

[4B—

(1) A specified communication is—

(*a*) an application under section 43B(1), (2)(d) or (3) of the Act (Groups: applications);

(*b*) a notification under regulation 5(1), (2) or (3) (registration and notification);

(*c*) an application under regulation 6(1)(d) (transfer of a going concern);

(*d*) a notification under regulation 10(1) or (4) (VAT representatives);

(*e*) an application under regulation 52(1) (annual accounting scheme: eligibility);

(*f*) a notification under regulation 54(2) (annual accounting scheme: termination);

(*g*) a notification under regulation 55(1)(d) (annual accounting scheme: termination);

(*h*) a notification under regulation 55B(1)(a) (flat-rate scheme for small businesses: notification of desire to join the scheme); . . .[2]

(*i*) a notification under regulation 55Q(1)(e) (flat-rate scheme for small businesses: notification of decision to withdraw from the scheme); [and

(*j*) a notification under paragraph (3)[, (3A) or (4)][3] of regulation 148A (notification of the arrival in the United Kingdom of motorised land vehicles and payment of VAT).][2]][1]

Amendments—[1] Regs 4A, 4B inserted by the VAT (Amendment) (No 2) Regulations, SI 2012/1899 regs 3, 5 with effect from 15 October 2012.

[2] In para (*h*), word "and" revoked, and para (*j*) and preceding word "and" inserted, by the VAT (Amendment) Regulations, SI 2013/701 regs 3, 4 with effect from 15 April 2013.

[3] Words in para (*j*) inserted by the Value Added Tax (Amendment) Regulations, SI 2014/548 regs 2, 3 with effect from 1 April 2014.

PART II
REGISTRATION AND PROVISIONS FOR SPECIAL CASES

[5 Registration and notification

(1) Where any person is required under paragraph 5(1)[, 6(1) or 7(1)][2] of Schedule 1, [paragraph 5(1), 6(1) or (13)(3) of Schedule 1A][3] paragraph 3(1) of Schedule 2, paragraph 3(1) of Schedule 3 or paragraph 3(1) or 4(1) of Schedule 3A to the Act to notify the Commissioners of his liability to be registered, the notification shall contain the particulars (including the declaration) set out [in the relevant form specified in a notice published by the Commissioners and shall be made in that form][3]; provided that, where the notification is made by a partnership, the notification shall also contain the particulars set out in [the relevant form specified in a notice published by the Commissioners][3].

(2) Every registered person except one to whom paragraph 11, 12, 13(1), (2) or (3) of Schedule 1, [paragraph 7, 8 or 9(1) of Schedule 1A,][3] paragraph 5 of Schedule 2, paragraph 5 of Schedule 3 or paragraph 5 of Schedule 3A of the Act applies, shall, within 30 days of any changes being made in the name, constitution or ownership of his business, or of any other event occurring which may necessitate the variation of the register or cancellation of his registration, notify the Commissioners . . . [3] of such change or event and furnish them with full particulars thereof.

(3) Every notification by a registered person under paragraph 11 or 12 of Schedule 1, paragraph 5 of Schedule 2, paragraph 5 of Schedule 3 or paragraph 5 of Schedule 3A to the Act . . . [3] shall state—

(*a*) the date on which he ceased to make, or have the intention of making, taxable supplies; or

(*b*) where paragraph 12(*a*) of Schedule 1 to the Act applies, the date on which he ceased to make, or have the intention of making, supplies within paragraph 10(2) of that Schedule; or

(*c*) where paragraph 12(*b*) of Schedule 1 to the Act applies, the date on which he made, or formed the intention of making, taxable supplies; or

(*d*) where paragraph 5(1) of Schedule 2 to the Act applies, the date on which he ceased to be registrable by virtue of paragraph 5(4) of that Schedule; or

(*e*) where paragraph 5(1) of Schedule 3 to the Act applies, the date on which he ceased to be registrable by virtue of paragraph 5(3) of that Schedule; or

(*f*) where paragraph 5(1) of Schedule 3A to the Act applies, the date on which he ceased to make, or have the intention of making, relevant supplies within the meaning of paragraph 9 of that Schedule.][1]

(4)–(14) . . . [3]

Former regulations—VAT (General) Regulations, SI 1985/886 reg 4(1)–(3); VAT (General) (Amendment) Regulations, SI 1992/3102 regs 2, 4.

Amendments—[1] This regulation substituted by the VAT (Amendment) (No 3) Regulations, SI 2000/794 regs 2, 4 with effect from 22 March 2000.

[2] Words in para (1) substituted for the words "or 6(1)", and paras (4)–(14) inserted, by the VAT (Amendment) (No 3) Regulations, SI 2004/1675 regs 1, 2 with effect from 22 July 2004.

[3] In para (1), words inserted, and words substituted for words "in forms numbered 1, 6, 7 and 7A respectively in Schedule 1 to these Regulations and shall be made in those forms" and words "the form numbered 2 in that Schedule", in para (2), words inserted and words "in writing" revoked, in para (3), words "shall be made in writing to the Commissioners and" revoked, and paras (4)–(14) revoked, by the VAT (Amendment) (No 2) Regulations, SI 2012/1899 regs 3, 6 with effect from 15 October 2012.

6 Transfer of a going concern

(1) Where—

(*a*) a business [or part of a business][3] is transferred as a going concern,

(*b*) the registration under Schedule 1 [or 1A][4] to the Act of the transferor has not already been cancelled,

(*c*) on the transfer of the business [or part of it][3] the registration of the transferor [under either Schedule][4] is to be cancelled and either the transferee becomes liable to be registered [under either Schedule][4] or the Commissioners agree to register him [under paragraph 9 of Schedule 1 to the Act][4], and

(*d*) an application is made in [the form specified in a notice published by the Commissioners][4] by or on behalf of both the transferor and the transferee of that business [or the part transferred][3],

the Commissioners may as from the date of the said transfer [cancel the registration under Schedule 1 or 1A to the Act of the transferor and register the transferee under Schedule 1 or 1A to the Act as appropriate with the registration number previously allocated to the transferor][4]

(2) An application under paragraph (1) above shall constitute notification for the purposes of paragraph 11 of Schedule 1 [or paragraph 7 of Schedule 1A][4] to the Act.

(3) Where the transferee of a business [or part of a business][3] has under paragraph (1) above been registered under Schedule 1 [or 1A][4] to the Act in substitution for the [transferor of it][3], and with the transferor's registration number—

(*a*) any liability of the transferor existing at the date of the transfer to make a return or to account for or pay VAT under regulation 25 or [40][2] shall become the liability of the transferee,

(*b*) any right of the transferor, whether or not existing at the date of the transfer, to credit for, or to repayment of, input tax shall become the right of the transferee, . . . [1]

(*c*) any right of either the transferor, whether or not existing at the date of the transfer, or the transferee to payment by the Commissioners under section 25(3) of the Act shall be satisfied by payment to either of them.

[(*d*) any right of the transferor, whether or not existing at the date of the transfer, to claim a refund under section 36 of the Act shall become the right of the transferee, . . . [3]

(*e*) any liability of the transferor, whether or not existing at the date of the transfer, to account for an amount under Part XIXA of these Regulations, shall become that of the transferee][1][, and

(*f*) any records relating to the business which, by virtue of these Regulations or a direction made by the Commissioners, are required to be preserved for any period after the transfer shall be preserved by the transferee unless the Commissioners, at the request of the transferor, otherwise direct.][3]

(4) In addition to the provisions set out in paragraph (3) above, where the transferee of a business [or part of a business][3] has been registered in substitution for, and with the registration number of, the transferor during a prescribed accounting period [subsequent to that in which the transfer took place][3] but with effect from [the date of the transfer][3], and any—

(*a*) return has been made,

(*b*) VAT has been accounted for and paid, or

(*c*) right to credit for input tax has been claimed,

either by or in the name of the transferee or the transferor, it shall be treated as having been done by the transferee.

Former regulations—VAT (General) Regulations, SI 1985/886 reg 4(4), (5), (7), (8); VAT (General) (Amendment) Regulations, SI 1992/3102 regs 2, 4.

Amendments—[1] Word "and" in para (3)(*b*) deleted and paras (3)(*d*), (*e*) inserted by the VAT (Amendment) Regulations, SI 1997/1086 reg 3 with effect from 1 May 1997.

[2] In para (3)(*a*), figure substituted for "41" by the VAT (Amendment) (No 3) Regulations, SI 2004/1675 regs 1(1), (3), 3 with effect from 22 July 2004.

[3] Words in sub-s (1) inserted, words in sub-ss (3), (4) inserted and substituted, and sub-s (3)(*f*) and preceding word "and" inserted, by the Value Added Tax (Amendment) (No 5) Regulations, SI 2007/2085 regs 2–5 with effect from 1 September 2007, in relation to transfers of going concerns pursuant to contracts entered into on or after that date.

[4] In para (1), in sub-para (b) words inserted, in sub-para (c), words substituted for words "under that Schedule" and "under paragraph 9 of that Schedule", in sub-para (d) words substituted for words "the form numbered 3 in Schedule 1 to these Regulations", and words "cancel the registration under Schedule 1 to the Act of the transferor and register the transferee under that Schedule with the registration number previously allocated to the transferor." revoked, and words in paras (2), (3) inserted, by the VAT (Amendment) (No 2) Regulations, SI 2012/1899 regs 3, 7 with effect from 15 October 2012.

7 Notice by partnership

(1) Where any notice is required to be given for the purposes of the Act or these Regulations by a partnership, it shall be the joint and several liability of all the partners to give such notice, provided that a notice given by one partner shall be a sufficient compliance with any such requirement.

(2) Where, in Scotland, a body of persons carrying on a business which includes the making of taxable supplies is a partnership required to be registered, any notice shall be given and signed in the manner indicated in section 6 of the Partnership Act 1890.

Former regulation—VAT (General) Regulations, SI 1985/886 reg 9.

8 Representation of club, association or organisation

Anything required to be done by or under the Act, these regulations or otherwise by or on behalf of a club, association or organisation, the affairs of which are managed by its members or a committee or committees of its members, shall be the joint and several responsibility of—

(*a*) every member holding office as president, chairman, treasurer, secretary or any similar office; or in default of any thereof,

(*b*) every member holding office as a member of a committee; or in default of any thereof,

(*c*) every member,

provided that if it is done by any official, committee member or member referred to above, that shall be sufficient compliance with any such requirement.

Former regulation—VAT (General) Regulations, SI 1985/886 reg 10.

9 Death, bankruptcy or incapacity of taxable person

(1) If a taxable person dies or becomes bankrupt or incapacitated, the Commissioners may, from the date on which he died or became bankrupt or incapacitated treat as a taxable person any person carrying on that business until some other person is registered in respect of the taxable supplies made or intended to be made by that taxable person in the course or furtherance of his business or the incapacity ceases, as the case may be; and the provisions of the Act and of any Regulations made thereunder shall apply to any person so treated as though he were a registered person.

(2) Any person carrying on such business shall, within 21 days of commencing to do so, inform the Commissioners in writing of that fact and of the date of the death, [the date of the bankruptcy order][1] or of the nature of the incapacity and the date on which it began.

(3) In relation to a company which is a taxable person, the references in paragraph (1) above to the taxable person becoming bankrupt or incapacitated shall be construed as references to the company going into liquidation or receivership or [entering administration][2].

Former regulations—VAT (General) Regulations, SI 1985/886 reg 11; VAT (General) (Amendment) Regulations, SI 1985/1650 reg 7.

Simon's Tax Cases—*Sargent v C&E Comrs* [1995] STC 398*.

Amendments—[1] Words in square brackets inserted by the VAT (Amendment) (No 3) Regulations, SI 1996/1250 reg 5 with effect from 1 June 1996.

[2] Words in para (3) substituted by the Enterprise Act 2002 (Insolvency) Order, SI 2003/2096 art 5, Schedule paras 55, 56 with effect from 15 September 2003. However, this amendment does not apply in any case where a petition for an administration order was presented before that date: SI 2003/2096 arts 1, 6.

10 VAT representatives

(1) Where any person is appointed by virtue of section 48 of the Act to be the VAT representative of another (in this regulation referred to as "his principal"), the VAT representative shall notify the Commissioners of his appointment [in the form specified in a notice published by the Commissioners][2] within 30 days of the date on which his appointment became effective and the notification shall contain the particulars (including the declaration) set out [in that notice][2].

(2) The notification referred to in this regulation shall be accompanied by evidence of the VAT representative's appointment.

(3) Where a person is appointed by virtue of section 48 of the Act to be a VAT representative, the Commissioners shall register the name of that VAT representative against the name of his principal in the register kept for the purposes of the Act.

(4) Every VAT representative who is registered in accordance with this regulation shall, within 30 days of any changes being made in the name, constitution or ownership of his business or of his ceasing to be a person's VAT representative, or of any other event occurring which may necessitate the variation of the register, notify the Commissioners in writing of such change, cessation or event and furnish them with full particulars thereof.

(5) For the purposes of this regulation the date upon which the appointment of a VAT representative ("the first VAT representative") shall be regarded as having ceased shall be treated as being whichever is the earliest of the following times—

(*a*) when the Commissioners receive any notification in accordance with regulation 5(2), or

(*b*) when the Commissioners receive a notification of appointment in accordance with paragraph (1) above of a person other than the first VAT representative, or

(*c*) when the Commissioners receive a notification of cessation in accordance with regulation 5(2), or

(*d*) when the Commissioners receive a notification of cessation in accordance with paragraph (4) above, or

(*e*) when a VAT representative dies, becomes insolvent or becomes incapacitated,

provided that if the Commissioners have not received a notification such as is mentioned in all or any of sub-paragraphs (a), (c) or (d) above and another person has been appointed as a VAT representative by virtue of section 48 of the Act, the Commissioners may treat the date of cessation as the date of appointment of that other person.

(6) In relation to a company which is a VAT representative, the references in paragraph (5)(*e*) above to the VAT representative becoming insolvent or incapacitated shall be construed as references to its going into liquidation or receivership or [entering administration][1].

Former regulations—VAT (General) Regulations, SI 1985/886 reg 10A; VAT (General) (Amendment) Regulations, SI 1992/3102.

Amendments—[1] Words in para (6) substituted by the Enterprise Act 2002 (Insolvency) Order, SI 2003/2096 art 5, Schedule paras 55, 57 with effect from 15 September 2003. However, this amendment does not apply in any case where a petition for an administration order was presented before that date: SI 2003/2096 arts 1, 6.

[2] In para (1), words substituted for words "on the form numbered 8 in Schedule 1 to these Regulations" and words "in that form", by the VAT (Amendment) (No 2) Regulations, SI 2012/1899 regs 3, 8 with effect from 15 October 2012.

11 Notification of intended section 14(1) supplies by intermediate suppliers

(1) An intermediate supplier who has made or intends to make a supply to which he wishes section 14(1) of the Act to apply shall notify the Commissioners and the customer in writing of his intention to do so.

(2) A notification under this regulation shall contain the following particulars—

(*a*) the name and address of the intermediate supplier,

(*b*) the number including the alphabetical code, by which the intermediate supplier is identified for VAT purposes, which was used or is to be used for the purpose of the supply to him by the original supplier,

(*c*) the date upon which the goods were first delivered or are intended to be first delivered, and

(*d*) the name, address and registration number of the customer to whom the goods have been supplied or are to be supplied.

(3) A notification under this regulation shall be made no later than the provision, in accordance with regulation 18, of the first invoice in relation to the supply to which it relates, and sent to—

(*a*) the office designated by the Commissioners for the receipt of such notifications, and

(*b*) the customer.

(4) Notifications under this regulation shall be made separately in relation to each customer to whom it is intended to make supplies to which the intermediate supplier wishes section 14(1) of the Act to apply.

(5) Where an intermediate supplier has complied with the requirements of this regulation in relation to the first supply to a customer to which section 14(1) of the Act applies, those requirements shall be deemed to have been satisfied in relation to all subsequent supplies to that customer while the intermediate supplier continues to belong in another member State.

Former regulations—VAT (General) Regulations, SI 1985/886 reg 10B; VAT (General) (Amendment) Regulations, SI 1993/1941 regs 2, 4.

12 Notification of intended section 14(2) supplies by persons belonging in other member States

(1) A person belonging in another member State who has made or who intends to make a supply to which he wishes section 14(2) of the Act to apply shall notify the Commissioners and the registered person in writing of his intention to do so.

(2) A notification under this regulation shall contain the following particulars—

(*a*) the name and address of the person belonging in another member State,

(*b*) the number including the alphabetical code by which the person belonging in another member State is identified for VAT purposes in the member State in which he belongs,

(*c*) the date upon which the installation or assembly of the goods was commenced or is intended to commence, and

(*d*) the name, address and registration number of the registered person to whom the goods have been supplied or are to be supplied.

(3) A notification under this regulation shall be made no later than the provision, in accordance with regulation 19, of the first invoice in relation to the supply to which it relates, and sent to—

(*a*) the office designated by the Commissioners for the receipt of such notifications, and

(*b*) the registered person to whom the goods are to be supplied.

(4) Notifications under this regulation shall be made separately in relation to each registered person to whom it is intended to make supplies to which the person belonging in another member State wishes section 14(2) of the Act to apply.

(5) Where a person belonging in another member State has complied with the requirements of this regulation in relation to the first supply to a registered person to which section 14(2) of the Act applies, those requirements shall be deemed to have been satisfied in relation to all subsequent supplies to that registered person while the person making the supply continues to belong in another member State.

Former regulations—VAT (General) Regulations, SI 1985/886 reg 10C; VAT (General) (Amendment) Regulations, SI 1993/1941 regs 2, 5.

PART III
VAT INVOICES AND OTHER INVOICING REQUIREMENTS

A13 [Interpretation of Part 3

Amendments—This regulation revoked by the VAT (Amendment) (No 3) Regulations, SI 2012/2951 reg 2(1), (2) with effect from 1 January 2013.

13 Obligation to provide a VAT invoice

(1) Save as otherwise provided in these Regulations, where a registered person—

(*a*) makes a taxable supply in the United Kingdom to a taxable person, or

(*b*) makes a supply of goods or services . . .[3] to a person in another member State [for the purpose of any business activity carried out by that person][3], or

(*c*) receives a payment on account in respect of a supply he has made or intends to make from a person in another member State,

he shall provide such persons as are mentioned above with a VAT invoice [(unless, in the case of that supply, he is entitled to issue and issues a VAT invoice pursuant to section 18C(1)(e) of the Act and regulation 145D(1) below in relation to the supply by him of specified services performed on or in relation to goods while those goods are subject to a fiscal or other warehousing regime)][1].

[(1A) Paragraph (1)(*b*) above shall not apply where the supply is an exempt supply which is made to a person in a member State which does not require an invoice to be issued for the supply.][3]

[(1B) Paragraph (1)(*b*) shall not apply in the case of a supply which falls within Group 2 or Group 5 of Schedule 9 to the Act.][4]

(2) The particulars of the VAT chargeable on a supply of goods described in paragraph 7 of Schedule 4 to the Act shall be provided, on a sale by auction, by the auctioneer, and, where the sale is otherwise than by auction, by the person selling the goods, on a document containing the particulars prescribed in regulation 14(1); and such a document issued to the buyer shall be treated for the purposes of paragraph (1)(*a*) above as a VAT invoice provided by the person by whom the goods are deemed to be supplied in accordance with the said paragraph 7.

[(3) Where a registered person provides a document to himself ("a self-billed invoice") that purports to be a VAT invoice in respect of a supply of goods or services to him by another registered person, that document shall be treated as the VAT invoice required to be provided by the supplier under paragraph (1)(*a*) if it complies with the conditions set out in paragraph (3A) and with any further conditions that may be contained in a notice published by the Commissioners or may be imposed in a particular case.][2]

[(3A) The following conditions must be complied with if a self-billed invoice is to be treated as a VAT invoice—

(*a*) it must have been provided pursuant to a prior agreement ("a self-billing agreement") entered into between the supplier of the goods or services to which it relates and the recipient of the goods or services ("the customer") and which satisfies the requirements in paragraph (3B);

(*b*) it must contain the particulars required under regulation 14(1) or (2);

(*c*) it must relate to a supply or supplies made by a supplier who is a taxable person.][1]

[(3B) A self-billing agreement must—

(*a*) authorise the customer to produce self-billed invoices in respect of supplies made by the supplier for a specified period . . .[4];

(*b*) specify that the supplier will not issue VAT invoices in respect of supplies covered by the agreement;

(*c*) specify that the supplier will accept each self-billed invoice created by the customer in respect of supplies made to him by the supplier;

(*d*) specify that the supplier will notify the customer if he ceases to be a taxable person or if he changes his registration number.][1]

[(3C) Without prejudice to any term of a self-billing agreement, it shall be treated as having expired when—

(*a*) the business of the supplier is transferred as a going concern;

(*b*) the business of the customer is transferred as a going concern;

(*c*) the supplier ceases to be registered for VAT.][1]

[(3D) In addition to the matters set out in paragraph (3B)—

(*a*) conditions that must be complied with may be set out in a notice published by the Commissioners;

(*b*) the Commissioners may impose further conditions in particular cases.][1]

[(3E) Where a customer in another member State provides a document to himself in respect of a supply of goods or services to him by a registered person, that document shall be treated as the VAT invoice required to be provided by the supplier under paragraph 1(*b*) or (*c*) if it complies with the conditions set out in paragraph (3A).][1]

[(3F) For the purposes of the following, a self-billed invoice will not be treated as issued by the supplier (however the supplier may be described in the provision concerned)—

(*a*) regulation 84(2)(*b*)(ii);

(*b*) regulation 85(1)(*b*);

(*c*) regulation 85(2);

(*d*) regulation 86(1);

(*e*) regulation 86(2)(*b*);

(*f*) regulation 86(3);

(*g*) regulation 88(1)(*b*);

(*h*) regulation 89(*b*)(ii);

(*i*) regulation 90(1)(*b*);

(*j*) regulation 90(2);

(*k*) regulation 91;

(*l*) regulation 92(*b*);

(*m*) regulation 93(1)(*b*);

(*n*) regulation 94B(6)(*a*).][2]

(4) Where the person who makes a supply to which regulation 93 relates gives an authenticated receipt containing the particulars required under regulation 14(1) to be specified in a VAT invoice in respect of that supply, that document shall be treated as the VAT invoice required to be provided under paragraph (1)(*a*) above on condition that no VAT invoice or similar document which was intended to be or could be construed as being a VAT invoice for the supply to which the receipt relates is issued.

(5) [With the exception of the supplies referred to in paragraph (6),][4] the documents specified in paragraphs (1), (2), (3) and (4) above shall be provided within 30 days of the time when the supply is treated as taking place under section 6 of the Act, or within such longer period as the Commissioners may allow in general or special directions.

[(6) The documents specified in paragraphs (1), (2), (3) and (4) shall—

(*a*) in the case of a supply of goods falling within section 6(7) of the Act, be provided by the 15th day of the month following that in which the removal in question takes place; and

(*b*) in the case of a supply of services falling within regulation 82, be provided by the 15th day of—

(i) the month following the month in which the services are treated as being performed under regulation 82(2),

(ii) the month following the month during which the services are treated as separately and successively made as a result of payments being made under regulation 82(4), or

(iii) the January following the 31st December on which the services are treated as being supplied under regulation 82(6).

(7) Both the supplier and the customer shall ensure the authenticity of the origin, the integrity of the content and the legibility of an invoice for such time as the invoice is required to be preserved.

(8) In this regulation—

(*a*) "authenticity of the origin" of an invoice means the assurance of either the identity of the supplier of the underlying goods or services or the issuer of that invoice;

(*b*) "integrity of the content" of an invoice means that the content required by regulation 14 has not been altered.][4]

Former regulations—VAT (General) Regulations, SI 1985/886 reg 12; VAT (General) (Amendment) Regulations, SI 1992/3102 reg 8.

Cross reference—See VAT Regulations, SI 1995/2518 reg 20 (disapplication of this regulation to certain supplies made in UK).

Customs and Excise Notices—Notice 701/48 Corporate purchasing cards, para 3.3 (the line item detail VAT invoice).

Amendments—[1] Words in para (1) inserted by the VAT (Amendment) (No 3) Regulations, SI 1996/1250 reg 6 with effect from 1 June 1996.

[2] Para (3) substituted, paras (3A)–(3F) inserted, by the VAT (Amendment) (No 6) Regulations, SI 2003/3220 regs 1(1)(*b*), 2, 4 with effect from 1 January 2004.

[3] Words in para (1) revoked and inserted, and para (1A) inserted, by the Value Added Tax (Amendment) (No 5) Regulations, SI 2007/2085 regs 2, 6 with effect from 1 October 2007.

[4] Paras (1B), (6)–(8) inserted, in para (3B)(*a*) words revoked, and words in para (5) inserted, by the VAT (Amendment) (No 3) Regulations, SI 2012/2951 reg 2(1), (3) with effect from 1 January 2013.

[13A Electronic invoicing

(1) This regulation applies where a document is provided by a registered person [in any electronic format][2] that purports to be a VAT invoice in respect of a supply of goods or services.

[(2) The document is not to be treated as the VAT invoice required to be provided by the supplier under regulation 13(1) unless the use of the electronic invoice is accepted by the customer.

(3) When the document is a self-billed invoice that purports to be a VAT invoice, paragraph (2) applies as if the reference to the supplier is to the customer and the reference to the customer is to the supplier.

(4) In this regulation "electronic invoice" means an invoice that contains the particulars required by regulation 14 and which has been issued and received in any electronic format.][2]][1]

Amendments—[1] Inserted by the VAT (Amendment No 6) Regulations, SI 2003/3220 regs 1(1)(*b*), 2, 5 with effect from 1 January 2004.

[2] In para (1), words substituted for words "by electronic transmission", and paras (2)–(4) substituted, by the VAT (Amendment) (No 3) Regulations, SI 2012/2951 reg 2(1), (4) with effect from 1 January 2013.

[13B Where a VAT invoice or part of a VAT invoice is in a language other than English the Commissioners may, by notice in writing, require that an English translation of the invoice is provided to them by a person who has received such an invoice in the United Kingdom within 30 days of the date of the notice.][1]

Amendments—[1] Inserted by the VAT (Amendment) (No 6) Regulations, SI 2003/3220 regs 1(1)(*b*), 2, 6 with effect from 1 January 2004.

14 Contents of VAT invoice

(1) Subject to paragraph (2) below and regulation 16 [and save as the Commissioners may otherwise allow][2], a registered person providing a VAT invoice in accordance with regulation 13 shall state thereon the following particulars—

(*a*) [a sequential number based on one or more series which uniquely identifies the document][6],

(*b*) the time of the supply,

(*c*) the date of the issue of the document,

(*d*) the name, address and registration number of the supplier,

(*e*) the name and address of the person to whom the goods or services are supplied,

(*f*) . . .[3]

(*g*) a description sufficient to identify the goods or services supplied,

(*h*) for each description, the quantity of the goods or the extent of the services, and the rate of VAT and the amount payable, excluding VAT, expressed in [any currency][3],

(*i*) the gross total amount payable, excluding VAT, expressed in [any currency][3],

(*j*) the rate of any cash discount offered,

(*k*) . . .[3]

(*l*) the total amount of VAT chargeable, expressed in sterling,

[(*m*) the unit price.][3]

[(*n*) where a margin scheme is applied under section 50A or section 53 of the Act, [the reference "margin scheme: works of art", "margin scheme: antiques or collectors' items", "margin scheme: second-hand goods", or "margin scheme: tour operators" as appropriate][7]

(*o*) where a VAT invoice relates in whole or part to a supply where the person supplied is liable to pay the tax, [the reference "reverse charge"]][7]][6]

(2) [Save as the Commissioners may otherwise allow, where a registered person provides a person in another member State with a VAT invoice or any document that refers to a VAT invoice and is intended to amend it, he must ensure that it states thereon the following particulars—][4]

(*a*) the information specified in sub-paragraphs [(*a*) to (*e*), (*g*), [(*j*), (*m*), (*n*) and (*o*)][6]][4] of paragraph (1) above,
(*b*) the letters "GB" as a prefix to his registration number,
(*c*) the registration number, if any, of the recipient of the supply of goods or services and which registration number, if any, shall contain the alphabetical code of the member State in which that recipient is registered,
(*d*) the gross amount payable, excluding VAT,
(*e*) where the supply is of a new means of transport (as defined in section 95 of the Act) a description sufficient to identify it as such,
(*f*) for each description, the quantity of the goods or the extent of the services, and where a positive rate of VAT is chargeable, the rate of VAT and the amount payable, excluding VAT, expressed in sterling, . . .[6]
(*g*) where the supply of goods is a taxable supply, the information as specified in [sub-paragraph (*l*)][4] of paragraph (1) above[, and
(*h*) where the supply is an exempt or zero-rated supply, a relevant reference or any indication that the supply is exempt or zero-rated as appropriate][6].

(3) Where a taxable supply takes place as described in section 6(2)(*c*) or section 6(5) of the Act, any consignment or delivery note or similar document or any copy thereof issued by the supplier before the time of supply shall not, notwithstanding that it may contain all the particulars set out in paragraph (1) above, be treated as a VAT invoice provided it is endorsed "This is not a VAT invoice".
(4) Where a registered person provides an invoice containing the particulars specified in paragraphs (1) and (3) above, and specifies thereon any goods or services which are the subject of an exempt or zero-rated supply, he shall distinguish on the invoice between the goods or services which are the subject of an exempt, zero-rated or other supply and state separately the gross total amount payable in respect of each supply and rate.
(5) . . .[6]
[(6) Where a registered person provides a VAT invoice relating in whole or in part to a supply of the letting on hire of a motor car other than for self-drive hire, he shall state on the invoice whether that motor car is a qualifying vehicle under article 7(2A) of the Value Added Tax (Input Tax) Order 1992.][1]
[(7) Where a registered person provides documents in batches to the same recipient [in any electronic format][7] that purport to be VAT invoices in respect of supplies of goods or services made to, or received by, him, as an exception to the requirements in regulation 14(1) and 14(2), details common to each such document need only be stated once for each batch file.][5]
[(8) In this regulation, a "relevant reference" is—
(*a*) a reference to the appropriate provision of Council Directive 2006/112/EC, or
(*b*) a reference to the corresponding provision of the Act.][6]

Former regulations—VAT (General) Regulations, SI 1985/886 reg 13; VAT (General) (Amendment) Regulations, SI 1992/3102 reg 9, SI 1993/856 reg 3.
VAT Notices—Notice 701/48 Corporate purchasing cards, para 3.3 (the line item detail VAT invoice).
Press releases etc—VAT Information Sheet 13/95 1-9-95 (contents of a VAT invoice from supplier to card company in respect of purchases using a corporate purchasing card).
HMRC Brief 36/07, 10-4-07 (Input tax deduction without a valid VAT invoice: revised Statement of Practice).
HMRC Brief 51/07, 24-7-07 (modifications made to the format of invoices with effect from 1 October 2007).
Cross reference—See VAT Regulations, SI 1995/2518 reg 20 (disapplication of this regulation to certain supplies made in UK).
Amendments—[1] Para (6) inserted by the VAT (Amendment) Regulations, SI 1995/3147 reg 3, with effect from 1 January 1996.
[2] Words in paras (1) and (2) inserted by the VAT (Amendment) (No 3) Regulations, SI 1996/1250 reg 7 with effect from 1 June 1996.
[3] In para (1), sub-paras (*f*) and (*k*) revoked, words in sub-paras (*h*) and (*i*) substituted, and sub-para (*m*) inserted, by the VAT (Amendment) (No 6) Regulations, SI 2003/3220 regs 1(1)(*b*), 2, 7 with effect from 1 January 2004.
[4] Words at beginning of sub-para (2), and in sub-paras (2)(*a*), (*g*) substituted by SI 2003/3220 regs 1(1)(*b*), 2, 8 with effect from 1 January 2004.
[5] Sub-para (7) inserted by SI 2003/3220 regs 1(1)(*b*), 2, 9 with effect from 1 January 2004.
[6] Words in paras (1), (2) substituted and inserted, para (5) revoked, and para (8) inserted, by the Value Added Tax (Amendment) (No 5) Regulations, SI 2007/2085 regs 2, 7 with effect from 1 October 2007.
[7] In para (1)(*n*), words substituted for words "a relevant reference or any indication that a margin scheme has been applied,", in para (1)(*o*), words substituted for words "a relevant reference or any indication that the supply is one where the customer is liable to pay the tax.", and in para (7), words substituted for words "by electronic transmission", by the VAT (Amendment) (No 3) Regulations, SI 2012/2951 reg 2(1), (5) with effect from 1 January 2013.

15 Change of rate, credit notes

Where there is a change in the rate of VAT in force under section 2 [or 29A][1] of the Act or in the descriptions of exempt[, zero-rated or reduced-rate][1] supplies, and a VAT invoice which relates to a supply in respect of which an election is made under section 88 of the Act was issued before the election was made, the person making the supply shall, within [45 days][2] after any such change, [or within such longer period as the Commissioners may allow in general or special directions,][2] provide the person to whom the supply was made with a credit note headed "Credit note-change of VAT rate" and containing the following particulars—

(*a*) the identifying number and date of issue of the credit note,
(*b*) the name, address and registration number of the supplier,
(*c*) the name and address of the person to whom the supply is made,
(*d*) the identifying number and date of issue of the VAT invoice,
(*e*) a description sufficient to identify the goods or services supplied, and
(*f*) the amount being credited in respect of VAT.

Former regulation—VAT (General) Regulations, SI 1985/886 reg 14.

Cross reference—See VAT Regulations, SI 1995/2518 reg 20 (disapplication of this regulation to certain supplies made in UK).

Amendments—[1] Words inserted, and words substituted for the words "or zero-rated", by the VAT (Amendment) (No 4) Regulations, SI 2003/1485 regs 2, 3 with effect from 1 July 2003.

[2] Figure substituted and words inserted, by the VAT (Amendment) (No 2) Regulations, SI 2008/3021 regs 2, 3 with effect from 1 December 2008.

15A [Change of rate, supplementary charge invoices

Where a supplementary charge is due under Schedule 3 to the Finance Act 2009 [or Schedule 2 to the Finance (No 2) Act 2010][2] in respect of a supply and a VAT invoice has been issued in relation to that supply which invoice does not include the supplementary charge, the person making the supply shall, within 45 days after the date when the supplementary charge becomes due, provide the person to whom the supply is made with an invoice headed "Supplementary charge invoice" and containing the following particulars—

(*a*) the identifying number and date of issue of the supplementary charge invoice,
(*b*) the amount of the supplementary charge to VAT,
(*c*) the name, address and registration number of the supplier,
(*d*) the name and address of the person to whom the supply is made, and
(*e*) the identifying number and date of issue of the VAT invoice.][1]

Amendments—[1] Reg 15A inserted by the VAT (Amendment) (No 5) Regs, SI 2009/3241, regs 2, 3 with effect from 1 January 2010.

[2] Words inserted by the VAT (Amendment) (No 3) Regulations, SI 2010/2940 regs 2, 3 with effect from 4 January 2011.

15B [Change of liability: anti-forestalling invoices

(1) Where—

(*a*) an anti-forestalling charge is due under Schedule 27 to the Finance Act 2012 in relation to any supply,
(*b*) the person making the supply ("the supplier") would have been required to provide the person to whom the supply is made ("the recipient") with a VAT invoice under regulation 13 in respect of the supply at the time it was made had the supply been subject to the standard rate of VAT at that time, and
(*c*) where the supply has been included in a VAT invoice, the supplier has not included the anti-forestalling charge in that VAT invoice,

the supplier shall, within 45 days after the date when the anti-forestalling charge becomes due, provide the recipient with an invoice headed "Anti-forestalling charge invoice" and containing the particulars specified in paragraph (2) or (3) as appropriate.

(2) Where the supply has not been included in a VAT invoice, the particulars are the particulars required in regulation 14.

(3) Where the supply has been included in a VAT invoice which does not include the anti-forestalling charge, the particulars are—

(*a*) the identifying number and date of issue of the anti-forestalling charge invoice,
(*b*) the amount of the anti-forestalling charge to VAT,
(*c*) the name, address and registration number of the supplier,
(*d*) the name and address of the recipient, and
(*e*) the identifying number and date of issue of the VAT invoice in which the supply was previously included.][1]

Amendments—[1] Reg 15B inserted by the VAT (Amendment) (No 2) Regulations, SI 2012/1899 regs 3, 9 with effect from 1 October 2012.

16 Retailers' invoices

(1) Subject to paragraph (2) below, a registered person who is a retailer shall not be required to provide a VAT invoice, except that he shall provide such an invoice at the request of a customer who is a taxable person in respect of any supply to him; but, in that event, if, but only if, the consideration for the supply does not exceed [£250][1] and the supply is other than to a person in another member State, the VAT invoice need contain only the following particulars—

(*a*) the name, address and registration number of the retailer,
(*b*) the time of the supply,
(*c*) a description sufficient to identify the goods or services supplied,
(*d*) the total amount payable including VAT, and
(*e*) for each rate of VAT chargeable, the gross amount payable including VAT, and the VAT rate applicable.

VAT SIs

(2) Where a registered person provides an invoice in accordance with this regulation, the invoice shall not contain any reference to any exempt supply.

Former regulations—VAT (General) Regulations, SI 1985/886 reg 15; VAT (General) (Amendment) Regulations, SI 1992/3102 reg 10.

Cross reference—See VAT Regulations, SI 1995/2518 reg 20 (disapplication of this regulation to certain supplies made in UK).

Amendments—[1] Figure substituted by the VAT (Amendment) (No 6) Regulations, SI 2003/3220 regs 1(1)(*b*), 2, 10 with effect from 1 January 2004.

[16A Simplified invoices

In any case where the consideration for a supply does not exceed £250 and the supply is other than to a person in another member State, the VAT invoice that a registered person is required to provide need contain only the following particulars—

(*a*) the name, address and registration number of the supplier;

(*b*) the time of the supply;

(*c*) a description sufficient to identify the goods or services supplied;

(*d*) the total amount payable including VAT; and

(*e*) for each rate of VAT chargeable, the gross amount payable including VAT, and the VAT rate applicable.][1]

Amendments—[1] Regulation 16A inserted by the VAT (Amendment) (No 3) Regulations, SI 2012/2951 reg 2(1), (6) with effect from 1 January 2013.

17 Section 14(6) supplies to persons belonging in other member States

(1) Where a registered person makes a supply such as is mentioned in section 14(6) of the Act he shall provide the person supplied with an invoice in respect of that supply.

[(2) An invoice provided under this regulation shall comply with the requirements of regulations 13 and 14.][1]

Former regulations—VAT (General) Regulations, SI 1985/886 reg 15A; VAT (General) (Amendment) Regulations, SI 1993/1941 regs 2, 8.

Cross reference—See VAT Regulations, SI 1995/2518 reg 20 (disapplication of this regulation to certain supplies made in UK).

Amendments—[1] Para (2) substituted by the Value Added Tax (Amendment) (No 5) Regulations, SI 2007/2085 regs 2, 8 with effect from 1 October 2007.

18 Section 14(1) supplies by intermediate suppliers

(1) On each occasion that an intermediate supplier makes or intends to make a supply to which he wishes section 14(1) of the Act to apply he shall, subject to paragraph (3) below, provide the customer with an invoice.

(2) An invoice provided under this regulation by an intermediate supplier shall—

(*a*) comply with the provisions of the law corresponding, in relation to the member State which provided the intermediate supplier with the identification number for VAT purposes used or to be used by him for the purpose of the supply to him by the original supplier of the goods which were subsequently removed to the United Kingdom, to regulation 17,

(*b*) be provided no later than 15 days after the time that the supply of the goods would, but for section 14(1) of the Act, have been treated as having taken place by or under section 6 of the Act,

(*c*) cover no less than the extent of the supply which would, but for section 14(1) of the Act, have been treated as having taken place by or under section 6 of the Act at the time that such an invoice is provided, . . . [1]

(*d*) . . . [1]

(3) Where an intermediate supplier makes a supply such as is mentioned in paragraph (1) above, and he has already provided the customer with an invoice that complies with the requirements of sub-paragraphs (*a*), (*c*) and (*d*) of paragraph (2) above, he shall not be required to provide the customer with a further invoice in relation to that supply.

(4) Where an intermediate supplier makes a supply such as is mentioned in paragraph (1) above and he provides the customer with an invoice such as is described in paragraphs (2) and (3) above, that invoice shall be treated as if it were an invoice for the purpose of regulation 83.

(5) Where an intermediate supplier makes a supply such as is mentioned in paragraph (1) above and he provides the customer with an invoice that complies only with the requirements of paragraph (2)(*a*) above, that invoice shall, for the purposes of this regulation only, be treated as if it were a VAT invoice.

Former regulations—VAT (General) Regulations, SI 1985/886 reg 15B; VAT (General) (Amendment) Regulations, SI 1993/1941 regs 2, 8.

Cross reference—See VAT Regulations, SI 1995/2518 reg 20 (disapplication of this regulation to certain supplies made in UK).

Amendments—[1] Para (2)(*d*) and preceding word "and" revoked by the Value Added Tax (Amendment) (No 5) Regulations, SI 2007/2085 regs 2, 9 with effect from 1 October 2007.

19 Section 14(2) supplies by persons belonging in other member States

(1) On each occasion that a person belonging in another member State makes or intends to make a supply to which he wishes section 14(2) of the Act to apply he shall, subject to paragraph (3) below, provide the registered person with an invoice.

(2) An invoice provided under this regulation by a person belonging in another member State shall—

(*a*) comply with the provisions of the law of the member State in which he belongs corresponding in relation to that member State to the provisions of regulation 14,

(*b*) be provided no later than 15 days after the time that the supply of the goods would, but for section 14(2) of the Act, have been treated as having taken place by or under section 6 of the Act,

(*c*) cover no less than the extent of the supply which would, but for section 14(2) of the Act, have been treated as having taken place by or under section 6 of the Act at the time that such an invoice is provided, . . . [1]

(*d*) . . . [1]

(3) Where a person belonging in another member State makes a supply such as is mentioned in paragraph (1) above, and he has already provided the registered person with an invoice that complies with the requirements of sub-paragraphs (*a*), (*c*) and (*d*) of paragraph (2) above, he shall not be required to provide the registered person with a further invoice in relation to that supply.

(4) Where a person belonging in another member State makes a supply such as is mentioned in paragraph (1) above and he provides the registered person with an invoice such as is described in paragraphs (2) and (3) above, that invoice shall be treated as if it were an invoice for the purpose of regulation 83.

(5) Where a person belonging in another member State makes a supply such as is mentioned in paragraph (1) above, and he provides the registered person with an invoice that complies only with the requirements of paragraph (2)(*a*) above, that invoice shall, for the purposes of this regulation only, be treated as if it were a VAT invoice.

Former regulations—VAT (General) Regulations, SI 1985/886 reg 15C; VAT (General) (Amendment) Regulations, SI 1993/1941 regs 2, 8.

Cross reference—See VAT Regulations, SI 1995/2518 reg 20 (disapplication of this regulation to certain supplies made in UK).

Amendments—[1] Para (2)(*d*) and preceding word "and" revoked by the Value Added Tax (Amendment) (No 5) Regulations, SI 2007/2085 regs 2, 10 with effect from 1 October 2007.

20 General

Regulations 13, 14, 15, 16, 17, 18 and 19 shall not apply to the following supplies made in the United Kingdom—

(*a*) any zero-rated supply other than a supply for the purposes of an acquisition in another member State,

(*b*) any supply to which an order made under section 25(7) of the Act applies,

(*c*) any supply on which VAT is charged although it is not made for consideration, or

(*d*) any supply to which an order made under section 32 of the Act applies.

Former regulations—VAT (General) Regulations, SI 1985/886 reg 16; VAT (General) (Amendment) Regulations, SI 1992/3102 reg 11, SI 1993/1941 regs 2, 9.

PART IV
EC SALES STATEMENTS

[21 Interpretation of Part IV

In this Part—

"EU supply of goods" means a supply falling within paragraph 22(1) and "EU supplies of goods" shall be construed accordingly;

"EU supply of services" means a supply falling within paragraph 22A(1) and "EU supplies of services" shall be construed accordingly;

"first relevant figure" means, up to and including 31st December 2011, £70,000 excluding VAT and thereafter £35,000 excluding VAT;

"NMT supply of goods" means a supply falling within paragraph 22C(1) and "NMT supplies of goods" shall be construed accordingly;

"registered in another member State" means registered in accordance with the measures adopted by the competent authority in another member State for the purposes of the common system of VAT and "registered in that member State" and "registered in other member States" shall be construed accordingly;

"second relevant figure" means the sum of the amount mentioned in paragraph 1(1)(*a*) of Schedule 1 to the Act as that paragraph has effect from time to time and £25,500;

"supply of goods" does not include either a supply of gas supplied through the natural gas distribution network or a supply of electricity;

"value" in the phrases "value of EU supplies", "value of the taxable person's taxable supplies" and "value of the taxable person's supplies" means the consideration for the supplies and includes, if the supply is a supply of goods, the costs of any freight transport services and services ancillary to the transport of the goods charged by the supplier to the customer.][1]

Amendments—[1] Reg 21 substituted by the VAT (Amendment) (No 5) Regs, SI 2009/3241, regs 2, 4 with effect from 1 January 2010.

VAT SIs

[22 Submission of statements

(1) Every taxable person who makes a supply of goods—

(*a*) to a person who, at the time of the supply, was registered in another member State and those goods were dispatched or transported to that or another member State, or

(*b*) to which section 14(6) of the Act applies, or

(*c*) which falls within paragraph 6 of Schedule 4 to the Act to a person who, at the time of the supply, was registered in another member State,

shall submit a statement to the Commissioners.

(2) The statement shall—

[(*a*) be made in the form specified in a notice published by the Commissioners,][2]

(*b*) contain, in respect of the EU supplies of goods which have been made within the period in respect of which the statement is made, such information as the Commissioners shall from time to time prescribe, and

(*c*) contain a declaration that the information provided in the statement is true and complete.

(3)

(*a*) Subject to paragraphs (4) to (6) below, the statement shall be submitted in respect of the month in which the EU supply of goods is made.

(*b*) Where during the period specified in sub-paragraph (*a*) above the taxable person (*a*)—

(i) ceases to be registered under Schedule 1 to the Act, and

(ii) no other person has been registered with the registration number of and in substitution for A,

the last day of that period is to be treated as being the same date as the effective date of A's deregistration.

(4)

(*a*) This sub-paragraph applies where, in each of the four quarters preceding the quarter in which the supply is made ("the relevant quarter"), the total value of EU supplies of goods made by the taxable person (*a*) did not exceed the first relevant figure.

(*b*) This sub-paragraph applies where, in the relevant quarter, the total value of EU supplies of goods made by A did not exceed the first relevant figure.

(*c*) Where sub-paragraphs (*a*) and (*b*) above apply, A may submit the statement in respect of the relevant quarter.

(*d*) Where—

(i) sub-paragraph (*a*) above applies, and

(ii) sub-paragraph (*b*) above does not apply,

A may submit a statement in respect of the period beginning with the first day of the relevant quarter and ending on the last day of the month in which the total value of EU supplies of goods made by A in that quarter first exceeded the relevant figure.

(*e*) Where during the relevant quarter specified in sub-paragraph (*c*) above A—

(i) ceases to be registered under Schedule 1 to the Act, and

(ii) no other person has been registered with the registration number of and in substitution for A,

the last day of that period is to be treated as being the same date as the effective date of A's deregistration.

(5)

(*a*) A statement may be submitted in respect of the year mentioned in sub-paragraphs (i) to (iv) below provided that the taxable person making the statement (*a*) has not, during that year, made a supply of a new means of transport and the Commissioners are satisfied either that—

(i) at the end of any month, the value of A's taxable supplies in the period of one year then ending is less than the second relevant figure, or

(ii) at any time there are reasonable grounds for believing that the value of A's taxable supplies in the period of one year beginning at that or any later time will not exceed the second relevant figure,

and either that—

(iii) at the end of any month, the value of A's supplies to persons registered in other member States in the period of one year then ending is less than £11,000, or

(iv) at any time, there are reasonable grounds for believing that the value of A's supplies to persons registered in other member States in the period of one year beginning at that or any later time will not exceed £11,000.

(*b*) Where during a period specified in sub-paragraph (*a*) above A—

(i) ceases to be registered under Schedule 1 to the Act, and

(ii) no other person has been registered with the registration number of and in substitution for A, the last day of that period is to be treated as being the same date as the effective date of A's deregistration.

(6) A taxable person (*a*) who is permitted under regulation 25 to make a return in respect of a period longer than 3 months may submit a statement under paragraph (1) above in respect of a period identical to the period permitted for the making of the return provided that A has not, during that period, made a supply of a new means of transport and the Commissioners are satisfied either that—

(*a*) at the end of any month, the value of A's taxable supplies in the period of one year then ending is less than £145,000, or

(*b*) at any time, there are reasonable grounds for believing that the value of A's taxable supplies in the period of one year beginning at that or any later time will not exceed £145,000,

and either that—

(*c*) at the end of any month, the value of A's supplies to persons registered in other member States in the period of one year then ending is less than £11,000, or

(*d*) at any time, there are reasonable grounds for believing that the value of A's supplies to persons registered in other member States in the period of one year beginning at that or any later time will not exceed £11,000.][1]

Amendments—[1] Reg 22 substituted by the VAT (Amendment) (No 5) Regs, SI 2009/3241, regs 2, 5 with effect from 1 January 2010.

[2] Para (2)(a) substituted by the VAT (Amendment) (No 2) Regulations, SI 2012/1899 regs 3, 10 with effect from 15 October 2012.

[22A—(1) Every taxable person who has made a supply of services to a person in a member State other than the United Kingdom in circumstances where the recipient is required to pay VAT on the supply in accordance with the provisions of the law of that other member State giving effect to Article 196 of Council Directive 2006/112/EC shall submit a statement to the Commissioners.

(2) The statement shall be—

[(*a*) made in the form specified in a notice published by the Commissioners,][2]

(*b*) contain, in respect of the EU supplies of services which have been made within the period to which the statement relates, such information as the Commissioners shall from time to time prescribe, and

(*c*) contain a declaration that the information provided in the statement is true and complete.

(3)

(*a*) Subject to paragraph (4) below the statement may be submitted in respect of the period of the month or the quarter in which the EU supply of services has been made.

(*b*) Where during a period mentioned in sub-paragraph (*a*) above the taxable person (*a*)—

(i) ceases to be registered under Schedule 1 to the Act, and

(ii) no other person has been registered with the registration number of and in substitution for A,

the last day of that period is to be treated as being the same date as the effective date of A's deregistration.

(4) A taxable person (*a*) who is permitted under regulation 25 to make a return in respect of a period longer than 3 months may make a statement under paragraph (1) above in respect of a period identical to the period permitted for the making of the return provided that A has not, during that period, made a supply of a new means of transport and the Commissioners are satisfied either that—

(*a*) at the end of any month, the value of A's taxable supplies in the period of one year then ending is less than £145,000, or

(*b*) at any time, there are reasonable grounds for believing that the value of A's taxable supplies in the period of one year beginning at that or any later time will not exceed £145,000,

and either that—

(*c*) at the end of any month, the value of A's supplies to persons registered in other member States in the period of one year then ending is less than £11,000, or

(*d*) at any time, there are reasonable grounds for believing that the value of A's supplies to persons registered in other member States in the period of one year beginning at that or any later time will not exceed £11,000.][1]

Amendments—[1] Regs 22A–22C inserted by the VAT (Amendment) (No 5) Regs, SI 2009/3241, regs 2, 6 with effect from 1 January 2010.

[2] Para (2)(a) substituted by the VAT (Amendment) (No 2) Regulations, SI 2012/1899 regs 3, 11 with effect from 15 October 2012.

[22B—(1) Where statements are to be submitted under regulation 22 and 22A in respect of periods ending on the same day, the statements may be submitted on a single form.

(2) A taxable person may submit a statement under regulation 22 or 22A on paper or on-line using an electronic portal provided by the Commissioners for that purpose.

(3) A taxable person who is required to submit a statement under regulation 22 or 22A must do so—

(*a*) where the statement is submitted on-line, not later than 21 days from the end of the period to which the statement relates,

VAT SIs

(*b*) in every other case, not later than 14 days from the end of the period to which the statement relates.][1]

Amendments—[1] Regs 22A–22C inserted by the VAT (Amendment) (No 5) Regs, SI 2009/3241, regs 2, 6 with effect from 1 January 2010.

[22C—(1) Every taxable person who in any quarter makes a supply of a new means of transport to a person ("the acquirer")—

(*a*) for the purposes of acquisition by that acquirer in another member State, and

(*b*) where the acquirer is not, at the time of the acquisition, registered in that member State,

shall submit a statement to the Commissioners.

(2)

(*a*) The statement shall be submitted in respect of the quarter in which the NMT supply of goods is made.

(*b*) Where during the period mentioned in sub-paragraph (*a*) above the taxable person (*a*)—

(i) ceases to be registered under Schedule 1 to the Act, and

(ii) no other person has been registered with the registration number of and in substitution for A,

the last day of that period is to be treated as being the same date as the effective date of A's deregistration.

(3) The statement shall—

[(*a*) be made in the form specified in a notice published by the Commissioners,][2]

(*b*) contain, in respect of the NMT supplies of goods which have been made within the period in respect of which the statement is made, such information as the Commissioners shall from time to time prescribe,

(*c*) contain a declaration that the information provided in the statement is true and complete, and

(*d*) be submitted within 42 days of the end of the period to which it relates.][1]

Amendments—[1] Regs 22A–22C inserted by the VAT (Amendment) (No 5) Regs, SI 2009/3241, regs 2, 6 with effect from 1 January 2010.

[2] Para (3)(a) substituted by the VAT (Amendment) (No 2) Regulations, SI 2012/1899 regs 3, 12 with effect from 15 October 2012.

23 Final statements

Amendments—Reg 23 repealed by the VAT (Amendment) (No 5) Regs, SI 2009/3241, regs 2, 7 with effect from 1 January 2010.

[PART 4A

REVERSE CHARGE SALES STATEMENTS

23A Interpretation of Part 4A

In this Part—

"relevant supply" means a supply of goods to which section 55A(6) of the Act applies (customers to account for tax on supplies of goods of a kind used in missing trader intra-community fraud) [other than a supply of gas or electricity][2];

"statement" means the statement which a taxable person is required to submit in accordance with this Part of these Regulations.][1]

Amendments—[1] Regs 23A–23C inserted by the VAT (Amendment) (No 3) Regulations, SI 2007/1418 regs 2, 3 with effect from 1 June 2007.

[2] In definition of "relevant supply" words inserted by the VAT (Amendment) (No 2) Regulations, SI 2014/1497 reg 3 with effect in relation to supplies made on or after 1 July 2014 and returns required by reg 25 below made for any prescribed accounting period which commences on or after that date.

[23B Notification of first relevant supply

(1) On the first occasion on which a person makes a relevant supply, he must notify the Commissioners of that fact within 30 days of the day on which the supply is made.

(2) The notification referred to in paragraph (1) must be made on-line by using a portal provided by the Commissioners.

(3) If the portal referred to in paragraph (2) is unavailable for any reason, the Commissioners may allow the notification to be made by email.][1]

Amendments—[1] Regs 23A–23C inserted by the VAT (Amendment) (No 3) Regulations, SI 2007/1418 regs 2, 3 with effect from 1 June 2007.

[23C Submission of Statements

(1) Every taxable person who, in any prescribed accounting period, has made a relevant supply must, in relation to that period, submit to the Commissioners, no later than the day by which he is required to make a return for that period and in such a form and manner as may be determined by the Commissioners in a notice published by them (or otherwise), a statement containing the following prescribed particulars—

(*a*) his registration number;

(*b*) the registration number of each person to whom he has made a relevant supply; and (*c*) for each month falling within the prescribed accounting period, the total value of the relevant supplies made to each person mentioned in sub-paragraph (*b*).

(2) If, in any prescribed accounting period, no relevant supplies are made, a statement to that effect must be submitted to the Commissioners in such form and manner as may be determined by them in a notice published by them (or otherwise).

(3) Sub-paragraph (2) does not apply where a taxable person has notified the Commissioners that he has ceased making relevant supplies without intending subsequently to make such supplies.

(4) A statement must contain a declaration made by the taxable person that it is true and complete.][1]

Amendments—[1] Regs 23A–23C inserted by the VAT (Amendment) (No 3) Regulations, SI 2007/1418 regs 2, 3 with effect from 1 June 2007.

23D [Notification of cessation and recommencement of relevant supplies

Where a person—

(*a*) ceases making relevant supplies without intending subsequently to make such supplies, or

(*b*) has fallen within paragraph (*a*) above but nonetheless starts to make relevant supplies again,

he shall, within 30 days of so ceasing or, as the case may be, of so recommencing, notify the Commissioners of that fact in such form and manner as may be determined in a notice published by them (or otherwise).][1]

Amendments—[1] Regulation inserted by the VAT (Amendment) (No 4) Regulations, SI 2007/1599 regs 2, 3 with effect from 1 July 2007.

[PART 4B

PROVISION OF INFORMATION RELATING TO ARRIVALS AND DISPATCHES

23E Interpretation of Part 4B

(1) In this Part—

"establishing Regulation" means the Council and European Parliament Regulation (EC) No 638/2004;

"implementing Regulation" means the Commission Regulation (EC) N. 1982/2004;

"statistics Regulations" means the Statistics of Trade (Customs and Excise) Regulations 1992;

(2) In this Part—

"arrivals and dispatches" means those arrivals and dispatches for which a responsible party is required to provide information under the establishing Regulation, implementing Regulation and the statistics Regulations;

"for Intrastat purposes" means for any purpose under the establishing Regulation, implementing Regulation or the statistics Regulations;

"reference period" means the period applicable under Article 6(1) of the establishing Regulation or such other period directed by the Commissioners pursuant to regulation 4(3) of the statistics Regulations;

"responsible party" means a taxable person who is required by Article 7 of the establishing Regulation and regulation 3 of the statistics Regulations to provide information in relation to arrivals and dispatches;

"supplementary declaration" means the relevant form set out in the Schedule to the statistics Regulations;

"delivery terms", "nature of the transaction", "partner Member State", "quantity of the goods" and "value of the goods" shall have the same meaning as in the establishing Regulation and implementing Regulation.][1]

Amendments—[1] This regulation inserted by the VAT (Amendment) Regulations 2008, SI 2008/556 reg 2 with effect from 1 April 2008; SI 2008/556 reg 1.

23F—(1) A responsible party shall provide the information in paragraph (2) relating to arrivals and dispatches to the Commissioners.

(2) The information is—

(*a*) the registration number of the responsible party,

(*b*) the reference period,

(*c*) whether the information relates to arrival or dispatch,

(*d*) the commodity, identified by the eight digit code of the Combined Nomenclature as defined in Council Regulation (EEC) No 2658/87 of 23 July 1987 as amended on the tariff and statistical nomenclature and the Common Customs Tariff,

(*e*) the partner Member State,

(*f*) the value of the goods,

(*g*) the quantity of the goods,

(*h*) the nature of the transaction.

(3) A responsible party to whom regulation 4(2) of the statistics Regulations applies shall also provide the delivery terms relating to arrivals and dispatches to the Commissioners.

VAT SIs

(4) The information required by paragraphs (2) and (3) shall be provided in the supplementary declaration in which, and for the same reference period as, information is provided relating to those arrivals and dispatches for Intrastat purposes.][1]

Amendments—[1] This regulation inserted by the VAT (Amendment) Regulations, SI 2008/556 reg 2 with effect from 1 April 2008: SI 2008/556 reg 1.

PART V
ACCOUNTING, PAYMENT AND RECORDS

24 Interpretation of Part V

In this Part—

"increase in consideration" means an increase in the consideration due on a supply made by a taxable person which is evidenced by a credit or debit note or any other document having the same effect and "decrease in consideration" is to be interpreted accordingly;

"insolvent person" means—

(*a*) an individual who has been adjudged bankrupt;

(*b*) a company in relation to which—

(i) a voluntary arrangement under Part I of the Insolvency Act 1986 has been approved,

(ii) [an administrator has been appointed][3],

(iii) an administrative receiver has been appointed,

(iv) a resolution for voluntary winding up has been passed, or

(v) an order for its winding-up has been made by the court at a time when it had not already gone into liquidation by passing a resolution for voluntary winding-up;

["investment gold" has the same meaning as that expression has for the purposes of Group 15 of Schedule 9 to the Act;][1]

"negative entry" means an amount entered into the VAT account as a negative amount;

"positive entry" means an amount entered into the VAT account as a positive amount;

"VAT allowable portion", "VAT payable portion" and "VAT account" have the meanings given in regulation [32][2];

"the Removal Order" means the Value Added Tax (Removal of Goods) Order 1992;

"the owner" has the same meaning as in article 2 of the Removal Order.

Former regulations—VAT (Accounting and Records) Regulations, SI 1989/2248 reg 1(2); VAT (Removal of Goods) (Accounting) Regulations, SI 1992/3101 reg 2.

Simon's Tax Cases—*C&E Comrs v General Motors Acceptance Corp (UK) plc* [2004] STC 577.

Amendments—[1] Definition of "investment gold" inserted by the VAT (Amendment) (No 4) Regulations, SI 1999/3114, regs 2, 3, with effect from 1 January 2000.

[2] In the definition of "VAT allowable portion", "VAT payable portion" and "VAT account", figure "32" substituted for "33" by the VAT (Amendment) (No 4) Regulations, SI 2003/1485 regs 2,4 with effect from 1 July 2003.

[3] Words in definition of "insolvent person" substituted by the Enterprise Act 2002 (Insolvency) Order, SI 2003/2096 art 5, Schedule paras 55, 58 with effect from 15 September 2003. However, this amendment does not apply in any case where a petition for an administration order was presented before that date: SI 2003/2096 arts 1, 6.

25 Making of returns

(1) Every person who is registered or was or is required to be registered shall, in respect of every period of a quarter or in the case of a person who is registered, every period of 3 months ending on the dates notified either in the certificate of registration issued to him or otherwise, not later than the last day of the month next following the end of the period to which it relates, make to the Controller a return [in the manner prescribed in regulation 25A][4] showing the amount of VAT payable by or to him and containing full information in respect of the other matters specified in the form and a declaration, [signed by that person or by a person authorised to sign on that person's behalf][4], that the return is [correct][4] and complete;

provided that—

(*a*) the Commissioners may allow or direct a person to make returns in respect of periods of one month and to make those returns within one month of the periods to which they relate;

(*b*) the first return shall be for the period which includes the effective date determined in accordance with [Schedules 1, [1A,][5] 2, 3 and 3A][2] to the Act upon which the person was or should have been registered, and the said period shall begin on that date;

(*c*) where the Commissioners consider it necessary in any particular case to vary the length of any period or the date on which any period begins or ends or by which any return shall be made, they may allow or direct any person to make returns accordingly, whether or not the period so varied has ended;

(*d*) where the Commissioners consider it necessary in any particular case, they may allow or direct a person to make returns to a specified address.

(2) Any person to whom the Commissioners give any direction in pursuance of the proviso to paragraph (1) above shall comply therewith.

(3) Where for the purposes of this Part the Commissioners have made a requirement of any person pursuant to regulation 30—

(*a*) the period in respect of which taxable supplies were being made by the person who died or became incapacitated shall end on the day previous to the date when death or incapacity took place; and

(*b*) subject to sub-paragraph (1)(*c*) above, a return made on his behalf shall be made in respect of that period no later than the last day of the month next following the end of that period; and

(*c*) the next period shall start on the day following the aforesaid period and it shall end, and all subsequent periods shall begin and end, on the dates previously determined under paragraph (1) above.

(4) Any person who—

(*a*) ceases to be liable to be registered, or

(*b*) ceases to be entitled to be registered under either or both of paragraphs 9 and 10 of Schedule 1[, paragraph 4 of Schedule 2 or paragraph 4 of Schedule 3][5] to the Act,

shall, unless another person has been registered with his registration number in substitution for him under regulation 6, make to the Controller a final return [in the manner prescribed in regulation 25A][4] and any such return shall contain full information in respect of the matters specified in the form and a declaration, [signed by that person or by a person authorised to sign on that person's behalf][4], that the return is [correct][4] and complete and shall be made, in the case of a person who was or is registered, within one month of the effective date for cancellation of his registration, and in the case of any other person, within one month of the date upon which he ceases to be liable to be registered, and in either case shall be in respect of the final period ending on the date aforementioned and be in substitution for the return for the period in which such date occurs.

(4A)–(4M) . . . [4]

(5) The Commissioners may allow VAT chargeable in any period to be treated as being chargeable in such later period as they may specify.

Former regulations—VAT (General) Regulations, SI 1985/886 reg 58; VAT (General) (Amendment) Regulations, SI 1986/1900 reg 3, SI 1987/1916 reg 9, SI 1988/2108 reg 7.

Cross reference—See VAT Regulations, SI 1995/2518 reg 6(3) (transfer of a going concern: transferee assuming liabilities of transferor).

Press releases etc—Business Brief 27/97, 21-11-97 (VAT treatment of compensation payments).

Simon's Tax Cases—*Hindle and another (trading as D J Baker Bar) v C&E Comrs* [2004] STC 412; *R&C Comrs v Raj Restaurant (a firm) and others* [2009] STC 729; *R (oao BMW AG and anor) v R&C Comrs* [2009] STC 963.

Amendments—[1] Paras (4A)–(4L) inserted by the VAT (Amendment) Regulations, SI 2000/258 regs 2, 3 with effect from 1 March 2000 (but see notes 3, 4 below).

[2] Words in para (1)(*b*) substituted by the VAT (Amendment) (No 3) Regulations, SI 2000/794 regs 2, 5 with effect from 22 March 2000.

[3] In para (4A), words revoked, para (4D) substituted, in para (4F), words substituted, and paras (4J)–(4M) substituted for previous paras (4J)–(4L), by the VAT (Amendment) (No 3) Regulations, SI 2004/1675 regs 1(1), (3), 4 with effect from 22 July 2004.

[4] In para (1), words substituted for words "on the form numbered 4 in Schedule 1 to these Regulations ("Form 4")", "signed by him" and "true", in para (4), words substituted for words "on the form numbered 5 in Schedule 1 to these Regulations ("Form 5")", "signed by him" and "true", and paras (4A)–(4M) revoked, by the Value Added Tax (Amendment) (No 4) Regulations, SI 2009/2978 regs 2, 3 with effect from 1 December 2009.

[5] In paras (1)(*b*), (4)(*b*) words inserted, by the VAT (Amendment) (No 2) Regulations, SI 2012/1899 regs 3, 13 with effect from 15 October 2012.

[25A—(1) Where a person makes a return required by regulation 25 using electronic communications, such a method of making a return shall be referred to in this Part as an "electronic return system".

(2) Where a person makes a return [or a final return on the relevant form specified in a notice published by the Commissioners][4], such a method of making a return shall be referred to in this Part as a "paper return system".

[(3) Subject to paragraph (6) below, a person who is registered for VAT must make a return required by regulation 25 using an electronic return system [that that person is required or authorised to use][5] whether or not such a person is registered in substitution for another person under regulation 6 (transfer of a going concern).][3]

(4) In any case where an electronic return system is not used, a return must be made using a paper return system.

(5) . . . [3]

(6) . . . [3] A person—

(*a*) who the Commissioners are satisfied is a practising member of a religious society or order whose beliefs are incompatible with the use of electronic communications, or

(*b*) to whom an insolvency procedure as described in any of paragraphs (*a*) to (*f*) of section 81(4B) of the Act is applied . . . [3][, or

VAT SIs

(*c*) for whom the Commissioners are satisfied that it is not reasonably practicable to make a return using an electronic return system (including any electronic return system that that person is authorised to use) for reasons of disability, age, remoteness of location or any other reason][5],

[is not required to make a return required by regulation 25 using an electronic return system][3].

(7) . . . [3]

(8) Where an electronic return system is used, it must take a form approved by the Commissioners in a specific or general direction.

(9) Where a paper return system is used, a return required by regulation 25(1) [or 25(4) must be made on the relevant form specified in a notice published by the Commissioners][4].

(10) A direction under paragraph (8) above may in particular—

(*a*) modify or dispense with any requirement of [the relevant form specified in a notice published by the Commissioners][4],

(*b*) specify circumstances in which the electronic return system may be used, or not used, by or on behalf of the person required to make the return,

[(*c*) approve telephone filing as a form of electronic return system for use by specified categories of persons.][5]

For the purposes of sub-paragraph (*b*), the direction may specify different circumstances for different cases.

(11) An electronic return system shall incorporate an electronic validation process.

(12) Subject to paragraph (13) below and unless the contrary is proved—

(*a*) the use of an electronic return system shall be [presumed][2] to have resulted in the making of the return to the Controller only if this has been successfully recorded as such by the relevant electronic validation process,

(*b*) the time of making the return to the Controller using an electronic return system shall be . . . [2] presumed to be the time recorded as such by the relevant electronic validation process, and

(*c*) the person delivering the return to the Controller shall be presumed to be the person identified as such by any relevant feature of the electronic return system.

(13) No return shall be treated as having been made using an electronic return system unless it is in the form required by paragraph (8) above.

The requirement in paragraph (8) above incorporates the matters mentioned in paragraph (10) above.

(14) A return made using an electronic return system carries the same consequences as a return made using a paper return system, except in relation to any matter for which alternative or additional provision is made by or under this regulation.

(15) [Subject to paragraph (15A)][3] in relation to returns made for prescribed accounting periods which end on or after 31 March 2011, a . . . [3] person who fails to comply with paragraph (3) above is liable to a penalty.

[(15A) A person who—

(*a*) on 31 March 2012 was registered for VAT with an effective date of registration before that date,

(*b*) was not as at 31 March 2012 required to make a return required by regulation 25 using an electronic return system, and

(*c*) fails to comply with paragraph (3),

is only liable to a penalty in relation to returns made for prescribed accounting periods which end on or after 31 March 2013.][3]

(16) But a . . . [3] person who has a reasonable excuse for so failing to comply is not liable to a penalty.

(17) The table below sets out the penalties depending on the level of turnover.

Annual VAT exclusive turnover	*Penalty*
£22,800,001 and above	*£400*
£5,600,001 to £22,800,000	*£300*
£100,001 to £5,600,000	*£200*
£100,000 and under	*£100*

(18) A person may appeal against the Commissioners' decision to impose a penalty only on the ground that—

(*a*) that person is not [a person required to make a return required by regulation 25 using an electronic return system][3],

(*b*) the amount of the penalty is incorrect,

(*c*) paragraph (3) above was complied with, or

(*d*) paragraph (16) above applies.

(19) In calculating a person's annual VAT exclusive turnover for the purposes of . . .[3] the table in paragraph (17) above, the Commissioners shall use any available figures which they determine to be fair and reasonable in the circumstances and such figures shall be taken to be the correct figures for the purposes of the calculation.

(20) Additional time is allowed to make—

(*a*) a return using an electronic return system or a paper return system for which any related payment is made solely by means of electronic communications (see regulation 25(1)—time for making return, and regulations 40(2) to 40(4)—payment of VAT), or

(*b*) a return using an electronic return system for which no payment is required to be made.

That additional time is only as the Commissioners may allow in a specific or general direction, and such a direction may allow different times for different means of payment.

The Commissioners need not give a direction pursuant to this paragraph.

(21) Where a corporate body is registered in the names of its divisions pursuant to section 46(1) of the Act, each such separately registered division is "a person" for the purposes of paragraphs . . .[3] (12) and (19) above.

(22) In this regulation—

(*a*) . . .[3]

(*b*) a reference to an appeal is a reference to an appeal made under section 83(1)(*zc*) of the Act,

(*c*) "reasonable excuse" shall have the same limitation as it does in section 71(1)(*b*) of the Act.

(23) In paragraphs (8) and (20) above "direction" and "direct" refer only to a current direction, and a direction is not current to the extent that it is varied, replaced or revoked by another Commissioners' direction.][1]

Amendments—

[1] Reg 25A inserted by the Value Added Tax (Amendment) (No 4) Regulations, SI 2009/2978 regs 2, 4 with effect from 1 December 2009.

[2] Word in para (12)(*a*), substituted, and word in para (12)(*b*) revoked, by the Value Added Tax (Amendment) Regulations, SI 2010/559 reg 2, 3 with effect from 1 April 2010.

[3] Para (3) substituted, paras (5), (7) revoked, in para (6) words revoked and substituted, in para (15) words inserted and word revoked, para (15A) inserted, in para (16) word revoked, in para (18)(*a*) words substituted, in paras (19), (21) words revoked, and para (22)(*a*) revoked, by the VAT (Amendment) Regulations, SI 2012/33 regs 3–14 with effect in relation to returns required by reg 25 of these regulations made for any prescribed accounting period which commences on or after 1 April 2012.

[4] In para (2), words substituted for words "on the form numbered 4 in Schedule 1 to these Regulations ("Form 4") or, in the case of a final return, on the form numbered 5 in Schedule 1 to these Regulations ("Form 5")", in para (9), words substituted for words "must be made on Form 4 and a return required by regulation 25(4) must be made on Form 5.", and in para (10)(*a*), words substituted for words "Form 4 or Form 5 (as appropriate)", by the VAT (Amendment) (No 2) Regulations, SI 2012/1899 regs 3, 14 with effect from 15 October 2012.

[5] Words in para (3) inserted, para (6)(*c*) and preceding word "or" inserted, and para (10)(*c*) inserted, VAT (Amendment) (No 2) Regulations, SI 2014/1497 reg 4 with effect in relation to supplies made on or after 1 July 2014 and returns required by reg 25 below made for any prescribed accounting period which commences on or after that date.

26 Accounting for VAT on an acquisition by reference to the value shown on an invoice

Where the time of the acquisition of any goods from another member State is determined by reference to the issue of an invoice such as is described in regulation 83, VAT shall be accounted for and paid in respect of the acquisition only on so much of its value as is shown on that invoice.

Former regulations—VAT (General) Regulations, SI 1985/886 reg 58A; VAT (General) (Amendment) Regulations, SI 1992/3102 reg 45.

Simon's Tax Cases—reg 26(1)(*c*), *Bjellica (T/A Eddy's Domestic Appliances) v C&E Comrs* [1995] STC 329*.

27 Supplies under Schedule 4, paragraph 7

Where goods are deemed to be supplied by a taxable person by virtue of paragraph 7 of Schedule 4 to the Act, the auctioneer on a sale by auction or, where the sale is otherwise than by auction, the person selling the goods, shall, whether or not registered under the Act, within 21 days of the sale—

(*a*) furnish to the Controller a statement showing—

(i) his name and address and, if registered, his registration number,

(ii) the name, address and registration number of the person whose goods were sold,

(iii) the date of the sale,

(iv) the description and quantity of goods sold at each rate of VAT, and

(v) the amount for which they were sold and the amount of VAT charged at each rate,

(*b*) pay the amount of VAT due, and

(*c*) send to the person whose goods were sold a copy of the statement referred to in sub-paragraph (*a*) above, and the auctioneer or person selling the goods, as the case may be, and the person whose goods were sold shall exclude the VAT chargeable on that supply of those goods from any return made under these Regulations.

Former regulation—VAT (General) Regulations, SI 1985/886 reg 59.

VAT SIs

28 Estimation of output tax

Where the Commissioners are satisfied that a person is not able to account for the exact amount of output tax chargeable in any period, he may estimate a part of his output tax for that period, provided that any such estimated amount shall be adjusted and exactly accounted for as VAT chargeable in the next prescribed accounting period or, if the exact amount is still not known and the Commissioners are satisfied that it could not with due diligence be ascertained, in the next but one prescribed accounting period.

Former regulation—VAT (General) Regulations, SI 1985/886 reg 61.

29 Claims for input tax

(1) [Subject to paragraph (1A) below][2], and save as the Commissioners may otherwise allow or direct either generally or specially, a person claiming deduction of input tax under section 25(2) of the Act shall do so on a return made by him for the prescribed accounting period in which the VAT became chargeable [save that, where he does not at that time hold the document or invoice required by paragraph (2) below, he shall make his claim on the return for the first prescribed accounting period in which he holds that document or invoice][2].

[(1A) [Subject to paragraph (1B)][2] the Commissioners shall not allow or direct a person to make any claim for deduction of input tax in terms such that the deduction would fall to be claimed more than [4 years][2] after the date by which the return for [the first prescribed accounting period in which he was entitled to claim that input tax in accordance with paragraph (1) above][2] is required to be made.][1]

[(1B) The Commissioners shall not allow or direct a person to make any claim for deduction of input tax where the return for the first prescribed accounting period in which the person was entitled to claim that input tax in accordance with paragraph (1) above was required to be made on or before 31st March 2006.][2]

(2) At the time of claiming deduction of input tax in accordance with paragraph (1) above, a person shall, if the claim is in respect of—

(*a*) a supply from another taxable person, hold the document which is required to be provided under regulation 13;

(*b*) a supply under section 8(1) of the Act, hold the relative invoice from the supplier;

(*c*) an importation of goods, hold a document authenticated or issued by the proper officer, showing the claimant as importer, consignee or owner and showing the amount of VAT charged on the goods;

(*d*) goods which have been removed from warehouse, hold a document authenticated or issued by the proper officer showing the claimant's particulars and the amount of VAT charged on the goods;

(*e*) an acquisition by him from another member State of any goods other than a new means of transport, hold a document required by the authority in that other member State to be issued showing his registration number including the prefix "GB", the registration number of the supplier including the alphabetical code of the member State in which the supplier is registered, the consideration for the supply exclusive of VAT, the date of issue of the document and description sufficient to identify the goods supplied; or

(*f*) an acquisition by him from another member State of a new means of transport, hold a document required by the authority in that other member State to be issued showing his registration number including the prefix "GB", the registration number of the supplier including the alphabetical code of the member State in which the supplier is registered, the consideration for the supply exclusive of VAT, the date of issue of the document and description sufficient to identify the acquisition as a new means of transport as specified in section 95 of the Act;

provided that where the Commissioners so direct, either generally or in relation to particular cases or classes of cases, a claimant shall hold [or provide][1] such other . . . [1] evidence of the charge to VAT as the Commissioners may direct.

(3) Where the Commissioners are satisfied that a person is not able to claim the exact amount of input tax to be deducted by him in any period, he may estimate a part of his input tax for that period, provided that any such estimated amount shall be adjusted and exactly accounted for as VAT deductible in the next prescribed accounting period or, if the exact amount is still not known and the Commissioners are satisfied that it could not with due diligence be ascertained, in the next but one prescribed accounting period.

[(4) Nothing in this regulation shall entitle a taxable person to deduct more than once input tax incurred on goods imported or acquired by him or on goods or services supplied to him.][2]

Commentary—*De Voil Indirect Tax Service* **V3.415, V5.415**.

Former regulations—Para (1): VAT (General) Regulations, SI 1985/886 reg 62(1); VAT (General) (Amendment) Regulations, SI 1987/1916 reg 10.

Para (2): VAT (General) Regulations, SI 1985/886 reg 62(1A); VAT (General) (Amendment) Regulations, SI 1992/3102 reg 47.

Para (3): VAT (General) Regulations, SI 1985/886 reg 62(2).

Press releases etc—Business Brief 4/02 22-2-02 (Late claims to input tax submitted before 1 May 1997).
Business Brief 13/06 24-8-06 (Court of Appeal Judgment in Michael Fleming t/a Bodycraft).
Simon's Tax Cases—Para (1A), *Local Authorities Mutual Investment Trust v C&E Comrs* [2004] STC 246; *Fleming (t/a Bodycraft) v R&C Comrs, Condé Nast Publications Ltd v R&C Comrs* [2008] STC 324.
Para (2), *Best Buys Ltd v R&C Comrs* [2012] UKUT 44 (TCC), [2012] STC 885.
Amendments—[1] Words in para (2) substituted, and word revoked, by the VAT (Amendment) (No 3) Regulations, SI 2003/1114 with effect from 16 April 2003.
[2] In paras (1), words substituted for words "Subject to paragraphs (1A) and (2) below", and words inserted, in para (1A), words inserted and words substituted for words "3 years" and "the prescribed accounting period in which the VAT became chargeable" respectively, and paras (1B), (4) inserted, by the VAT (Amendment) Regulations, SI 2009/586 regs 2, 3 with effect from 1 April 2009.

30 Persons acting in a representative capacity

Where any person subject to any requirements under this Part dies or becomes incapacitated and control of his assets passes to another person, being a personal representative, trustee in bankruptcy, receiver, liquidator or person otherwise acting in a representative capacity, that other person shall, if the Commissioners so require and so long as he has such control, comply with these requirements, provided that any requirement to pay VAT shall only apply to that other person to the extent of the assets of the deceased or incapacitated person over which he has control; and save to the extent aforesaid this Part shall apply to such a person, so acting, in the same way as it would have applied to the deceased or incapacitated person had that person not been deceased or incapacitated.

Former regulation—VAT (General) Regulations, SI 1985/886 reg 63.

31 Records

(1) Every taxable person shall, for the purpose of accounting for VAT, keep the following records—

(*a*) his business and accounting records,

(*b*) his VAT account,

(*c*) copies of all VAT invoices issued by him,

(*d*) all VAT invoices received by him,

[(*da*) all certificates—

(i) prepared by him relating to acquisitions by him of goods from other member States, or

(ii) given to him relating to supplies by him of goods or services,][1]

provided that, owing to provisions in force which concern fiscal or other warehousing regimes, those acquisitions or supplies are either zero-rated or treated for the purposes of the Act as taking place outside the United Kingdom,

(*e*) documentation received by him relating to acquisitions by him of any goods from other member States,

(*f*) copy documentation issued by him relating to the transfer, dispatch or transportation of goods by him to other member States,

(*g*) documentation received by him relating to the transfer, dispatch or transportation of goods by him to other member States,

(*h*) documentation relating to importations and exportations by him, and

(*i*) all credit notes, debit notes, or other documents which evidence an increase or decrease in consideration that are received, and copies of all such documents that are issued by him.

[(*j*) a copy of any self-billing agreement within regulation 13(3A) to which he is a party;][2]

[(*k*) where he is a customer, party to a self-billing agreement within regulation 13(3A), the name, address and VAT registration number of each supplier with whom he has entered into a self-billing agreement.][2]

(2) The Commissioners may—

(*a*) in relation to a trade or business of a description specified by them, or

(*b*) for the purposes of any scheme established by, or under, Regulations made under the Act,

supplement the list of records required in paragraph (1) above by a notice published by them for that purpose.

(3) Every person who, at a time when he is not a taxable person, acquires in the United Kingdom from another member State any goods which are subject to a duty of excise or consist of a new means of transport shall, for the purposes of accounting for VAT, keep such records with respect to the acquisition as may be specified in any notice published by the Commissioners in pursuance of this regulation.

Former regulations—Paras (1), (2): VAT (Accounting and Records) Regulations, SI 1989/2248 reg 2(1), (2); VAT (Accounting and Records) (Amendment) Regulations, SI 1992/3097 reg 3.
Para (3): VAT (Accounting and Records) Regulations, SI 1989/2248 reg 2A; VAT (Accounting and Records) (Amendment) Regulations, SI 1992/3097 reg 4.
Amendments—[1] Para (1)(*da*) inserted by the VAT (Amendment) (No 3) Regulations, SI 1996/1250 reg 8 with effect from 1 June 1996.
[2] Para (1)(*j*), (*k*) inserted by the VAT (Amendment) (No 6) Regulations, SI 2003/3220 regs 1(1)(*b*), 2, 11 with effect from 1 January 2004.

[31A—(1) This regulation applies where a person—

VAT SIs

(*a*) makes a supply of investment gold of a description falling within item 1 of Group 15 of Schedule 9 to the Act, or

(*b*) makes a supply of a description falling within item 2 of Group 15 of Schedule 9 to the Act, which subsequently results in the transfer of the possession of the investment gold.

(2) Subject to paragraph (6) below (and save as the Commissioners may otherwise allow in relation to supplies where the value is less than an amount equivalent to 15,000 euro at a rate specified in any notice published by the Commissioners for the purposes of this regulation) in addition to the requirements upon every taxable person under this Part, a person making a supply of a description falling within paragraph (1) above shall—

(*a*) without prejudice to regulations 13 and 14, issue an invoice in respect of the supply containing such details as may be specified in a notice published by the Commissioners for the purposes of this regulation;

(*b*) keep and maintain a record of the supply containing such details as may be specified in a notice published by the Commissioners for the purposes of this regulation;

(*c*) retain such documents in relation to the supply as may be specified in a notice published by the Commissioners for the purposes of this regulation;

(*d*) keep and maintain a record of the recipient of the supply containing such particulars pertaining to the recipient as may be specified in a notice published by the Commissioners for the purposes of this regulation;

(*e*) keep and maintain such other records and documents as may be specified in a notice published by the Commissioners for the purposes of this regulation to allow the proper identification of each recipient of the supply;

(*f*) notify the Commissioners in writing that he is making such supplies within 28 days of the first supply,

(*g*) furnish to the Commissioners such information in relation to his making of the supply as may be specified in a notice published by them.

(3) A taxable person shall keep and maintain, together with the account he is required to keep and maintain under regulation 32 below, a record of exempt supplies of a description falling within item 1 or 2 of Group 15 of Schedule 9 to the Act, that he makes to another taxable person.

(4) Where there is a sale of investment gold, which would if that person were supplying investment gold in the course or furtherance of any business, fall within item 1 or 2 of Group 15 of Schedule 9 to the Act, by a person who is not trading in investment gold, to a person who is so trading, the purchaser shall issue on behalf of the seller an invoice containing such particulars as may be set out in a notice published by the Commissioners for the purposes of this regulation and the seller shall sign such form of declaration as may be set out in a notice published by the Commissioners for the purposes of this regulation.

(5) The records required to be kept and the documents required to be retained under paragraphs (1) to (4) above shall be preserved for a minimum period of 6 years.

(6) Paragraphs (2) to (5) above shall not apply to any person in respect of a supply by him of a description falling within item 1 or 2 of Group 15 of Schedule 9 to the Act the value of which does not exceed £5,000, unless the total value of those supplies to any person over the last 12 months exceeds £10,000.][1]

Amendments—[1] This Regulation inserted by the VAT (Amendment) (No 4) Regulations, SI 1999/3114, regs 2, 4, with effect from 1 January 2000.

[31B Where a person receives a supply of a description falling within article 31A(1) above that person shall retain the purchase invoice in relation to that supply for a minimum period of 6 years.][1]

Amendments—[1] This Regulation inserted by the VAT (Amendment) (No 4) Regulations, SI 1999/3114, regs 2, 4, with effect from 1 January 2000.

[31C Paragraph 10(2) of Schedule 11 to the Act shall apply in relation to supplies of a description falling within items 1 and 2 of Group 15 of Schedule 9 to the Act as it applies in relation to the supply of goods under taxable supplies.][1]

Amendments—[1] This Regulation inserted by the VAT (Amendment) (No 4) Regulations, SI 1999/3114, regs 2, 4, with effect from 1 January 2000.

32 The VAT account

(1) Every taxable person shall keep and maintain, in accordance with this regulation, an account to be known as the VAT account.

(2) The VAT account shall be divided into separate parts relating to the prescribed accounting periods of the taxable person and each such part shall be further divided into 2 portions to be known as "the VAT payable portion" and "the VAT allowable portion".

(3) The VAT payable portion for each prescribed accounting period shall comprise—

(*a*) a total of the output tax due from the taxable person for that period,

(*b*) a total of the output tax due on acquisitions from other member States by the taxable person for that period, [(*ba*) a total of the tax which the taxable person is required to account for and pay on behalf of the supplier,][1]

(*c*) every correction or adjustment to the VAT payable portion which is required or allowed by regulation 34, 35[, 38, or 38A][1], and

(*d*) every adjustment to the amount of VAT payable by the taxable person for that period which is required, or allowed, by or under any Regulations made under the Act.

(4) The VAT allowable portion for each prescribed period shall comprise—

(*a*) a total of the input tax allowable to the taxable person for that period by virtue of section 26 of the Act,

(*b*) a total of the input tax allowable in respect of acquisitions from other member States by the taxable person for that period by virtue of section 26 of the Act,

(*c*) every correction or adjustment to the VAT allowable portion which is required or allowed by regulation 34, 35 or 38, and

(*d*) every adjustment to the amount of input tax allowable to the taxable person for that period which is required, or allowed, by or under any Regulations made under the Act.

Former regulations—VAT (Accounting and Records) Regulations, SI 1989/2248 reg 4; VAT (Accounting and Records) (Amendment) Regulations, SI 1992/3097 reg 6.

Amendments—[1] Words in para (3)(*b*) inserted, and words in para (3)(*c*) substituted, by the VAT (Amendment) (No 3) Regulations, SI 2007/1418 regs 2, 4 with effect from 1 June 2007.

33 The register of temporary movement of goods to and from other member States

(1) Every taxable person shall keep and maintain, in accordance with this regulation, a register to be known as the register of temporary movement of goods to and from other member States.

(2) Where goods have been moved to or received from another member State and they are to be returned within a period of 2 years of the date of their first removal or receipt, as the case may be, the register shall contain the following information—

(*a*) the date of removal of goods to another member State,

(*b*) the date of receipt of the goods mentioned in sub-paragraph (*a*) above when they are returned from the member State mentioned in that sub-paragraph or another member State,

(*c*) the date of receipt of goods from another member State,

(*d*) the date of removal of the goods mentioned in sub-paragraph (*c*) above when they are returned to the member State mentioned in that sub-paragraph or another member State,

(*e*) a description of the goods sufficient to identify them

(*f*) a description of any process, work or other operation carried out on the goods either in the United Kingdom or in another member State,

(*g*) the consideration for the supply of the goods, and

(*h*) the consideration for the supply of any processing, work or other operation carried out on the goods either in the United Kingdom or another member State.

(3) The Commissioners may in relation to a trade or business of a description specified by them supplement the list of information required in paragraph (2) above by a notice published by them for that purpose.

Former regulations—VAT (Accounting and Records) Regulations, SI 1989/2248 reg 4A; VAT (Accounting and Records) (Amendment) Regulations, SI 1992/3097 reg 7.

[**33A** A person making supplies of a description falling within article 4 of the Value Added Tax (Terminal Markets) Order 1973 shall not be required to keep in relation to those supplies the records specified in regulations 31 (save for paragraph (1)(*a*) of that regulation), 31A, 32 and 33 of these Regulations.][1]

Amendments—[1] This Regulation inserted by the VAT (Amendment) (No 4) Regulations, SI 1999/3114, regs 2, 5, with effect from 1 January 2000.

[**33B** Where a person of a description in article 6 of the Value Added Tax (Terminal Markets) Order 1973 who makes or receives supplies of a description falling within that article, the following Parts of these Regulations shall not apply in relation to those supplies, that is to say—]

(*a*) Part IV;

(*b*) Part V.][1]

Amendments—[1] This Regulation inserted by the VAT (Amendment) (No 4) Regulations, SI 1999/3114, regs 2, 5, with effect from 1 January 2000.

34 Correction of errors

(1) [Subject to paragraph (1A) below][1] this regulation applies where a taxable person has made a return, or returns, to the Controller which overstated or understated his liability to VAT or his entitlement to a payment under section 25(3) of the Act.

[(1A) Subject to paragraph (1B) [and (1C)][3] below, any overstatement or understatement in a return where—

(*a*) a period of [4 years][3] has elapsed since the end of the prescribed accounting period for which the return was made; and (*b*) the taxable person has not (in relation to that overstatement or understatement) corrected his VAT account in accordance with this regulation before the end of the prescribed accounting period during which that period of [4 years][3] has elapsed,

shall be disregarded for the purposes of this regulation; and in paragraphs (2) to (6) of this regulation "overstatement", "understatement" and related expressions shall be construed accordingly.][1]

[(1B) Paragraph (1A) above does not apply where—

(*a*) the overstatement or understatement is discovered in a prescribed accounting period which begins before 1st May 1997; and

(*b*) the return for that prescribed accounting period has not been made, and was not required to have been made, before that date.][1]

[(1C) Where paragraph (1B) above does not apply, any overstatement or understatement in a return shall be disregarded for the purposes of this regulation where the prescribed accounting period for which the return was made or required to be made ended on or before 31st March 2006.][3]

(2) In this regulation—

(*a*) "under-declarations of liability" means the aggregate of—

(i) the amount (if any) by which credit for input tax was overstated in any return, and

(ii) the amount (if any) by which output tax was understated in any return;

(*b*) "over-declarations of liability" means the aggregate of—

(i) the amount (if any) by which credit for input tax was understated in any return, and

(ii) the amount (if any) by which output tax was overstated in any return.

(3) Where, in relation to all such overstatements or understatements discovered by the taxable person during a prescribed accounting period, the difference between—

(*a*) under-declarations of liability, and

(*b*) over-declarations of liability,

does not exceed [£50,000][2], the taxable person may correct his VAT account in accordance with this regulation.

[But if Box 6 of the taxable person's return for the prescribed accounting period must contain a total less than £5,000,000, the difference must not for these purposes exceed 1% of that total [unless the difference is £10,000 or less][3].

(Box 6 must contain the total value of sales and all other outputs excluding any VAT – [see regulations 25 and 25A and the relevant forms specified in a notice published by the Commissioners][4].)][2]

(4) In the VAT payable portion—

(*a*) where the amount of any overstatements of output tax is greater than the amount of any understatements of output tax a negative entry shall be made for the amount of the excess; or

(*b*) where the amount of any understatements of output tax is greater than the amount of any overstatements of output tax a positive entry shall be made for the amount of the excess.

(5) In the VAT allowable portion—

(*a*) where the amount of any overstatements of credit for input tax is greater than the amount of any understatements of credit for input tax a negative entry shall be made for the amount of the excess; or

(*b*) where the amount of any understatements of credit for input tax is greater than the amount of any overstatements of credit for input tax a positive entry shall be made for the amount of the excess.

(6) Every entry required by this regulation shall—

(*a*) be made in that part of the VAT account which relates to the prescribed accounting period in which the overstatements or understatements in any earlier returns were discovered,

(*b*) make reference to the returns to which it applies, and

(*c*) make reference to any documentation relating to the overstatements or understatements.

(7) Where the conditions referred to in paragraph (3) above do not apply, the VAT account may not be corrected by virtue of this regulation.

Former regulations—VAT (Accounting and Records) Regulations, SI 1989/2248 reg 5; VAT (Accounting and Records) (Amendment) Regulations, SI 1993/761, SI 1994/803.

Simon's Tax Cases—*R (on the application of Capital Accommodation (London) Ltd v R&C Comrs* [2012] UKUT 276 (TCC), [2013] STC 303.

Cross reference—See VAT Regulations, SI 1995/2518 reg 39(4) (returns correcting earlier returns to which this regulation applies).

Press releases etc—Business Brief 2/98 27-1-98 (VAT: three year time limit for refunds).

Business Brief 13/06 24-8-06 (Court of Appeal Judgment in Michael Fleming t/a Bodycraft).

Amendments—[1] Words in para (1), and paras (1A) and (1B), inserted by the VAT (Amendment) Regulations, SI 1997/1086 reg 5 with effect from 1 May 1997.

[2] In para (3) figure substituted for figure "£2,000", and final two sentences inserted, by the Value Added Tax, etc (Correction of Errors, etc) Regulations, SI 2008/1482 reg 2(1) with effect from 1 July 2008. These amendments only have effect in relation to the overstatements or understatements of liability to VAT in reg 34(3) which taxable persons first discover during their prescribed accounting periods that begin on 1 July 2008 or later: SI 2008/1482 reg 2(2).

3 In para (1A), words inserted and words substituted for words "3 years", para (1C) inserted, and words in para (3) substituted for words "unless the difference is less than £10,000", by the VAT (Amendment) Regulations, SI 2009/586 regs 2, 4 with effect from 1 April 2009.

4 In para (3), words substituted for words "see regulation 25 and Schedule 1 Forms 4 and 5", by the VAT (Amendment) (No 2) Regulations, SI 2012/1899 regs 3, 15 with effect from 15 October 2012.

35 Where a taxable person has made an error—

(*a*) in accounting for VAT, or

(*b*) in any return made by him,

then, unless he corrects that error in accordance with regulation 34, he shall correct it in such manner and within such time as the Commissioners may require.

Former regulation—VAT (General) Regulations, SI 1985/886 reg 64.

Simon's Tax Cases—*Victoria and Albert Museum Trustees v C&E Comrs* [1996] STC 1016*; *R (on the application of Cardiff County Council) v C&E Comrs* [2002] STC 1318; *R (on the application of Capital Accommodation (London) Ltd v R&C Comrs* [2012] UKUT 276 (TCC), [2013] STC 303.

Cross reference—See VAT Regulations, SI 1995/2518 reg 39(4) (returns correcting earlier returns to which this regulation applies).

Press releases etc—Business Brief 2/98 27-1-98 (VAT: three year time limit for refunds).

Business Brief 13/06 24-8-06 (Court of Appeal Judgment in Michael Fleming t/a Bodycraft).

36 Notification of acquisition of goods subject to excise duty by non-taxable persons and payment of VAT

(1) Where—

(*a*) a taxable acquisition of goods subject to excise duty takes place in the United Kingdom,

(*b*) the acquisition is not in pursuance of a taxable supply, and

(*c*) the person acquiring the goods is not a taxable person at the time of the acquisition,

the person acquiring the goods shall notify the Commissioners of the acquisition at the time of the acquisition or the arrival of the goods in the United Kingdom, whichever is the later.

(2) The notification shall be in writing in the English language and shall contain the following particulars—

(*a*) the name and current address of the person acquiring the goods,

(*b*) the time of the acquisition,

(*c*) the date when the goods arrived in the United Kingdom,

(*d*) the value of the goods including any excise duty payable, and

(*e*) the VAT due upon the acquisition.

(3) The notification shall include a declaration, signed by the person who is required to make the notification, that all the information entered in it is true and complete.

(4) Any person required to notify the Commissioners of an acquisition of goods subject to excise duty shall pay the VAT due upon the acquisition at the time of notification and, in any event, no later than the last day on which he is required by this regulation to make such notification.

(5) Where a person required to make notification dies or becomes incapacitated and control of his assets passes to another person, being a personal representative, trustee in bankruptcy, receiver, liquidator or person otherwise acting in a representative capacity, that other person shall, so long as he has such control, be required to make the notification referred to in this regulation, provided that the requirement to pay the VAT due upon the acquisition shall apply to that other person only to the extent of the assets of the deceased or incapacitated person over which he has control and, save to the extent aforesaid, this regulation shall apply to such person so acting in the same way as it would have applied to the deceased or incapacitated person had that person not been deceased or incapacitated.

Former regulations—VAT (General) Regulations, SI 1985/886 reg 64C; VAT (General) (Amendment) Regulations, SI 1992/3102 reg 44.

37 [Claims for credit for, or repayment of, overstated or overpaid VAT][1]

Any claim under section 80 of the Act shall be made in writing to the Commissioners and shall, by reference to such documentary evidence as is in the possession of the claimant, state the amount of the claim and the method by which that amount was calculated.

Former regulation—VAT (Accounting and Records) Regulations, SI 1989/2248 reg 6.

Amendments—1 Heading substituted by the VAT (Amendment) (No 2) Regulations, SI 2005/2231 reg 2 with effect from 1 September 2005 in relation to claims made under VATA 1994 s 80 on or after that date.

38 Adjustments in the course of business

(1) . . . [3] This regulation applies where—

(*a*) there is an increase in consideration for a supply, or

(*b*) there is a decrease in consideration for a supply,

which includes an amount of VAT and the increase or decrease occurs after the end of the prescribed accounting period in which the original supply took place.

[(1A) Subject to paragraph (1B) below, this regulation does not apply to any increase or decrease in consideration which occurs more than 3 years after the end of the prescribed accounting period in which the original supply took place.][1, 3]

VAT SIs

[(1B) Paragraph (1A) above does not apply where—

(a) the increase or decrease takes place during a prescribed accounting period beginning before 1st May 1997; and

(b) the return for the prescribed accounting period in which effect is given to the increase or decrease in the business records of the taxable person has not been made, and was not required to have been made, before that date.][1, 3]

[(1C) Where an increase or decrease in consideration relates to a supply in respect of which it is for the recipient, on the supplier's behalf, to account for and pay the tax, the prescribed accounting period referred to in paragraph (1) is that of the recipient, and not the maker, of the supply. But this paragraph does not apply to the circumstances referred to in regulation 38A.][2]

[Where this regulation applies, both the taxable person who makes the supply and a taxable person who receives the supply shall adjust their respective VAT accounts in accordance with the provisions of this regulation.][3]

(3) [Subject to paragraph (3A) below,][2] the maker of the supply shall—

(*a*) in the case of an increase in consideration, make a positive entry; or

(*b*) in the case of a decrease in consideration, make a negative entry,

for the relevant amount of VAT in the VAT payable portion of his VAT account.

[(3A) Where an increase or decrease in consideration relates to a supply on which the VAT has been accounted for and paid by the recipient of the supply, any entry required to be made under paragraph (3) shall be made in the recipient's VAT account and not that of the supplier.][2]

(4) The recipient of the supply, if he is a taxable person, shall—

(*a*) in the case of an increase in consideration, make a positive entry; or

(*b*) in the case of a decrease in consideration, make a negative entry,

for the relevant amount of VAT in the VAT allowable portion of his VAT account.

(5) Every entry required by this regulation shall, except where paragraph (6) below applies, be made in that part of the VAT account which relates to the prescribed accounting period in which the increase or decrease is given effect in the business accounts of the [relevant][3] taxable person.

(6) Any entry required by this regulation to be made in the VAT account of an insolvent person shall be made in that part of the VAT account which relates to the prescribed accounting period in which the supply was made or received.

(7) None of the circumstances to which this regulation applies is to be regarded as giving rise to any application of regulations 34 and 35.

Former regulation—VAT (Accounting and Records) Regulations, SI 1989/2248 reg 7.

Simon's Tax Cases—*C&E Comrs v McMaster Stores (Scotland) Ltd (in receivership)* [1995] STC 846*.

C&E Comrs v General Motors Acceptance Corp (UK) plc [2004] STC 577; *GMAC UK plc v R&C Comrs*; *BT plc v R&C Comrs* [2012] UKUT 279 (TCC), [2012] STC 2349.

Amendments—[1] Words in paras (1A) and (1B), inserted by the VAT (Amendment) Regulations, SI 1997/1086 reg 6 with effect from 1 May 1997.

[2] Paras (1C), (3A), and words in para (3) inserted, by the VAT (Amendment) (No 3) Regulations, SI 2007/1418 regs 2, 4(*b*) with effect from 1 June 2007.

[3] In para (1), words "Subject to paragraph (1A) below," repealed, paras (1A), (1B) repealed, para (2) substituted, and in para (5) word inserted, by the VAT (Amendment) Regulations, SI 2009/586 regs 2, 5 with effect from 1 April 2009.

[38ZA—(1) Where—

(*a*) there is a decrease in consideration for a supply of goods which includes an amount of VAT and the decrease occurs after the end of the prescribed accounting period in which the original supply took place,

(*b*) the supply is the final supply in a chain of supplies made by taxable persons which relates to the same goods,

(*c*) the decrease in consideration is as a result of a relevant payment (which may form part of a larger payment that includes an element of compensation) that reduces the taxable amount which serves as a basis for determination of the VAT payable by the first supplier, and

(*d*) the amount of the relevant payment equates to the whole, or a proportion, of the price paid for the goods by the final consumer to the final supplier and does not exceed the amount so paid,

then, in regulation 38(2), the reference to "the taxable person who makes the supply" shall include a reference to the first supplier and the reference to "a taxable person who receives the supply" shall include a reference to a final consumer who is a taxable person.

(2) In this regulation—

"cash refund" includes a payment made by cheque or equivalent but does not include the provision of a face-value voucher falling within Schedule 10A to the Act;

"final consumer" means the recipient of the supply referred to in paragraph (1)(b);

"final supplier" means the person who makes the supply referred to in paragraph (1)(b);

"first supplier" means the first person in the chain of supplies that ends with the final consumer;

"relevant payment" means—

(*a*) a cash refund made by the first supplier direct to the final consumer—

(i) to reflect the reduced value (including a reduction to nil) of goods which are faulty, damaged or otherwise do not fully meet expectations of the final consumer,

(ii) as a result of a product recall, or

(iii) in accordance with the terms of a sales promotion scheme operated by the first supplier under the terms of which the final consumer is required to provide proof of purchase of specified goods to the first supplier; or

(*b*) a reimbursement made by the first supplier direct to the final supplier—

(i) which equates to the redemption value of a money-off coupon issued by the first supplier and used by the final consumer in part payment for goods purchased from the final supplier, or

(ii) to redeem a money-off coupon issued by the first supplier in any of the circumstances specified in sub-paragraph (*a*)(i) or (ii) and used by the final consumer in full or part payment for goods purchased from the final supplier.

(3) Where the rate of VAT applicable to the supply made by the first supplier differs from the rate of VAT applicable to the supply made by the final supplier, the adjustment made by the first supplier shall be at the rate of VAT applied by the final supplier.][1]

Amendments—[1] Reg 38ZA inserted by the Value Added Tax (Amendment) Regulations, SI 2014/548 regs 2, 4 with effect from 1 April 2014.

[38A Adjustments where a supply becomes, or ceases to be, a supply to which section 55A(6) of the Act applies (customers to account for tax on supplies of goods [or services] of a kind used in missing trader intra-community fraud)

(1) Where regulation 38 applies and—

(*a*) as a result of an increase in consideration for a supply it becomes one to which section 55A(6) of the Act applies; or

(*b*) as a result of a decrease in consideration for a supply it ceases to be one to which that section applies,

both the maker, and the recipient, of the supply shall make such entries in the VAT payable portion of their VAT accounts as are necessary to account for that fact.

(2) Paragraphs (5) and (6) of regulation 38 shall apply to any entry required by this regulation as they apply to any entry required by that regulation.

(3) None of the circumstances to which this regulation applies is to be regarded as giving rise to any application of regulations 34 and 35.]

Amendments—Reg inserted by the VAT (Amendment) (No 3) Regulations, SI 2007/1418 regs 2, 4(c) with effect from 1 June 2007.

Words in heading inserted by the VAT (Amendment) (No 2) Regulations, SI 2010/2240 regs 2, 3(1) with effect from 1 November 2010.

39 Calculation of returns

(1) Where a person is required by regulations made under the Act to make a return to the Controller, the amounts to be entered on that return shall be determined in accordance with this regulation.

(2) In the box opposite the legend "VAT due in this period on sales and other outputs" shall be entered the aggregate of all the entries in the VAT payable portion of that part of the VAT account which relates to the prescribed accounting period for which the return is made, except that the total of the output tax due in that period on acquisitions from other member States shall be entered instead in the box opposite the legend "VAT due in this period on acquisitions from other EC member States".

(3) In the box opposite the legend "VAT reclaimed in this period on purchases and other inputs" (including acquisitions from other member States) shall be entered the aggregate of all the entries in the VAT allowable portion of that part of the VAT account which relates to the prescribed accounting period for which the return is made.

(4) Where any correction has been made and a return calculated in accordance with these Regulations then any such return shall be regarded as correcting any earlier returns to which regulations 34 and 35 apply.

Former regulations—VAT (Accounting and Records) Regulations, SI 1989/2248 reg 8; VAT (Accounting and Records) (Amendment) Regulations, SI 1992/3097 reg 8.

40 VAT to be accounted for on returns and payment of VAT

[(1) Any person making a return shall in respect of the period to which the return relates account in that return for—

(*a*) all his output tax,

[(*aa*) all VAT which he is required to pay on behalf of the supplier.][4]

(*b*) all VAT for which he is accountable by virtue of Part XVI of these Regulations,

(*c*) all VAT which he is required to pay as a result of the removal of goods from a fiscal warehousing regime, and (*d*) all VAT which he is required to pay as a result of a supply of specified services (performed on or in relation to goods at a time when they are subject to a warehousing regime) being zero-rated under section 18C(1) of the Act where—

(i) that warehousing regime is one where goods are stored without payment of any duty of excise,

(ii) those goods are subject to a duty of excise,

(iii) those goods have been the subject of an acquisition from another member State and the material time for that acquisition was while those goods were subject to that warehousing regime, and,

(iv) there was no supply of those goods while they were subject to that warehousing regime.

The amounts to be entered on that return shall be determined in accordance with these Regulations.

(2) Any person required to make a return shall pay to the Controller such amount of VAT as is payable by him in respect of the period to which the return relates not later than the last day on which he is required to make that return.

[(2A) Where a return is made [or is required to be made][5] in accordance with [regulations 25 and 25A][5] above using an electronic return system, the relevant payment to the Controller required by paragraph (2) above shall be made solely by means of electronic communications that are acceptable to the Commissioners for this purpose.][2]

[(2B) With effect from 1st April 2010, where a person makes any payment to the Controller required by paragraph (2) above by cheque (whether or not in contravention of paragraph (2A) above)—

(*a*) the payment shall be treated as made on the day when the cheque clears to the account of the Controller, and

(*b*) that shall be the day when payment of any VAT shown as due on the return is to be treated as received by the Commissioners for the purposes of section 59 of the Act.

(2C) For the purposes of this regulation, the day on which a cheque clears to the account of the Controller is the second business day following but not including the date of its receipt.

(2D) In this regulation a "business day" is any day except—

(*a*) Saturday, Sunday, Good Friday or Christmas Day;

(*b*) a bank holiday under the Banking and Financial Dealings Act 1971;

(*c*) a day appointed by Royal proclamation as a public fast or thanksgiving day;

(*d*) a day declared by an order under section 2(1) of the Banking and Financial Dealings Act 1971 to be a non-business day.][5]

(3) The requirements of paragraphs (1) or (2) above shall not apply where the Commissioners allow or direct otherwise.][1]

[(4) A direction under paragraph (3) may in particular allow additional time for a payment mentioned in paragraph (2) that is made by means of electronic communications.

The direction may allow different times for different means of payment.][3]

[(5) Later payment so allowed does not of itself constitute a default for the purposes of section 59 of the Act (default surcharge).][3]

Former regulation—VAT (General) Regulations, SI 1985/886 reg 60.

Simon's Tax Cases—*Hindle and another (trading as DJ Baker Bar) v C&E Comrs* [2004] STC 412.

Amendments—[1] This Regulation substituted by the VAT (Amendment) (No 3) Regulations, SI 1996/1250 reg 9 with effect from 1 June 1996.

[2] Para (2A) inserted by the VAT (Amendment) Regulations, SI 2000/258 regs 2, 4 with effect from 1 March 2000.

[3] Paras (4), (5) inserted by the VAT (Amendment) (No 3) Regulations, SI 2004/1675 regs 1(1), (3), 5 with effect from 22 July 2004.

[4] Para (1)(*aa*) inserted by the VAT (Amendment) (No 3) Regulations, SI 2007/1418 regs 2, 4(*d*) with effect from 1 June 2007.

[5] In para (2A), words inserted and words substituted for words "regulation 25", and paras (2B)–(2D) inserted, by the Value Added Tax (Amendment) (No 4) Regulations, SI 2009/2978 regs 2, 5 with effect from 1 December 2009.

[40A—Where the Commissioners in exercise of their power under section 28(2A) of the Act have directed the manner in which payments on account under section 28 of the Act are to be made, a person who is liable to make such payments shall also pay any amount of VAT payable in respect of a return for any prescribed accounting period in the like manner.][1]

Amendments—[1] This Regulation inserted by the VAT (Amendment) (No 2) Regulations, SI 1996/1198 reg 3 with effect from 1 June 1996.

41 Accounting etc by reference to the duty point, and prescribed accounting period in which VAT on certain supplies is to be treated as being chargeable

(1) Where in respect of—

(*a*) any supply by a taxable person of dutiable goods, or

(*b*) an acquisition by any person from another member State of dutiable goods,

the time of supply or acquisition, as the case may be, precedes the duty point in relation to those goods, the VAT in respect of that supply or acquisition shall be accounted for and paid, and any question as to the inclusion of any duty in the value of the supply or acquisition shall be determined, by reference to the duty point or by reference to such later time as the Commissioners may allow.

(2) . . . [1]

Former regulations—Para (1): VAT (General) Regulations, SI 1985/886 reg 60A; VAT (General) (Amendment) Regulations, SI 1992/3102 reg 46.

Paras (2), (3): VAT (General) Regulations, SI 1985/886 reg 58ZA; VAT (General) (Amendment) Regulations, SI 1995/1069 reg 4.

Cross reference—See VAT Regulations, SI 1995/2518 reg 6(3) (transfer of a going concern: transferee assuming liabilities of transferor).

Amendments—[1] Paras (2) and (3) deleted by the VAT (Amendment) (No 3) Regulations, SI 1996/1250 reg 10 with effect from 1 June 1996 except that where 28 April 1996 fell within a taxable person's prescribed accounting period which ended on or after 1 June 1996, the amendment had effect in relation to that taxable person from the day after the end of that prescribed accounting period.

42 Accounting for VAT on the removal of goods

(1) This regulation applies where goods have been removed from a member State to a place in any other member State, and that removal falls within any of paragraphs (*d*), (*f*) or (*g*) of article 4 of the Removal Order.

(2) Except where paragraph (3) below applies in respect of the same prescribed accounting period, the owner shall not make any entry in the VAT payable portion of that part of his VAT account which relates to the prescribed accounting period in which he would be liable to account for any VAT chargeable in respect of the removal.

(3) Where—

(*a*) the condition described in article 5 of the Removal Order has not been complied with, and

(*b*) an amount of VAT has become payable,

the owner shall make a positive entry for the relevant amount of VAT in the VAT payable portion of that part of his VAT account which relates to the prescribed accounting period in which the condition was not complied with.

Former regulation—VAT (Removal of Goods) (Accounting) Regulations, SI 1992/3101 reg 3.

43 Goods removed from warehousing regime

(1) This regulation applies to a registered person who is an approved person within the meaning of the Excise Duties (Deferred Payment) Regulations 1992 in respect of goods which are at a specified warehouse.

(2) [Where a person to whom this regulation applies is—

(*a*) the person who is liable under section 18(4)(*b*) of the Act to pay VAT on a supply of goods while the goods are subject to a warehousing regime, or

(*b*) liable under section 18D(2) of the Act to pay VAT on a supply of services to which section 18C(3) of the Act applies (specified services performed on or in relation to goods which are subject to a warehousing regime),

he may pay that VAT at or before the relevant time determined in accordance with paragraph (3) below instead of at the time provided for by sections 18(4)(b) or 18D(2)(a) of the Act.][1]

(3) For the purposes of paragraph (2) above the relevant time means—

(*a*) in relation to hydrocarbon oils, the 15th day of the month immediately following the month in which the hydrocarbon oils were removed from the warehousing regime;

(*b*) in relation to any other goods subject to a duty of excise, the day (payment day) on which the registered person is required to pay the excise duty on the goods in accordance with regulation 5 of the Excise Duties (Deferred Payment) Regulations 1992.

(4) Where any goods of a kind chargeable to a duty of excise qualify for any relief of that duty, that relief shall be disregarded for the purposes of determining the relevant time under paragraph (3) above.

Amendments—[1] Para (2) substituted by the VAT (Amendment) (No 3) Regulations, SI 1996/1250 reg 11 with effect from 1 June 1996.

[PART VA
REIMBURSEMENT ARRANGEMENTS]

Commentary—*De Voil Indirect Tax Service* **V5.159**.

Note—Part VA inserted after Part V by the VAT (Amendment) (No 5) Regulations, SI 1998/59 with effect from 11 February 1998. Regulations 37A to 37H within Part VA were incorrectly numbered. An amending statutory instrument, SI 1999/438, has now been issued. Regulations 37A to 37H have been renumbered in sequence, from 43A to 43H, with effect from 1 April 1999.

[43A Interpretation of Part VA

In this Part—

["claim" means—

(*a*) a claim made under section 80 of the Act for credit of an amount accounted for to the Commissioners or assessed by them as output tax which was not output tax due to them; or

(*b*) a claim made under paragraph 16I of Schedule 3B, or paragraph 29 of Schedule 3BA, to the Act (claims which have effect for the purpose of section 80(3) of the Act as if they were section 80 claims), and "claimed" and "claimant" are to be construed accordingly;][3]

"reimbursement arrangements" means any arrangements (whether made before, on or after 30th January 1998) for the purposes of a claim which—

(*a*) are made by a claimant for the purpose of securing that he is not unjustly enriched by the [crediting][2] of any amount in pursuance of the claim; and

(*b*) provide for the reimbursement of persons (consumers) who have, for practical purposes, borne the whole or any part of the [original amount brought into account as output tax that was not output tax due][2];

"relevant amount" means that part (which may be the whole) of the amount of a claim which the claimant has reimbursed or intends to reimburse to consumers.][1]

Amendments—[1] This regulation inserted by the VAT (Amendment) (No 5) Regulations, SI 1998/59 with effect from 11 February 1998.

[2] In the definition of "reimbursement arrangements", words substituted, by the VAT (Amendment) (No 2) Regulations, SI 2005/2231 reg 3 with effect from 1 September 2005 in relation to claims made under VATA 1994 s 80 on or after that date.

[3] Definition of "claim" substituted by the VAT (Amendment) (No 3) Regulations, SI 2014/2430 regs 2, 3 with effect from 1 January 2015.

[43B Reimbursement arrangements—general

Without prejudice to regulation 43H below, for the purposes of section 80(3) of the Act (defence by the Commissioners that [crediting][2] by them of an amount claimed would unjustly enrich the claimant) reimbursement arrangements made by a claimant shall be disregarded except where they—

(*a*) include the provisions described in regulation 43C below; and

(*b*) are supported by the undertakings described in regulation 43G below.][1]

Amendments—[1] This regulation inserted by the VAT (Amendment) (No 5) Regulations, SI 1998/59 with effect from 11 February 1998.

[2] Word substituted by the VAT (Amendment) (No 2) Regulations, SI 2005/2231 reg 4 with effect from 1 September 2005 in relation to claims made under VATA 1994 s 80 on or after that date.

[43C Reimbursement arrangements—provisions to be included

The provisions referred to in regulation 43B(*a*) above are that—

(*a*) reimbursement for which the arrangements provide will be completed by no later than 90 days after the [crediting of the amount][2] to which it relates;

(*b*) no deduction will be made from the relevant amount by way of fee or charge (howsoever expressed or effected);

(*c*) reimbursement will be made only in cash or by cheque;

[(*d*) any part of the relevant amount credited to the claimant that is not reimbursed by the time mentioned in paragraph (*a*) above will be notified by the claimant to the Commissioners;][2]

[(*da*) any part of the relevant amount paid (or repaid) to the claimant that is not reimbursed by the time mentioned in paragraph (*a*) above will be repaid by the claimant to the Commissioners;][2]

(*e*) any interest paid by the Commissioners on any relevant amount [paid (or repaid)][2] by them will also be treated by the claimant in the same way as the relevant amount falls to be treated under paragraphs (*a*) and (*b*) above; and

(*f*) the records described in regulation 43E below will be kept by the claimant and produced by him to the Commissioners, or to an officer of theirs in accordance with regulation 43F below.][1]

Amendments—[1] This regulation inserted by the VAT (Amendment) (No 5) Regulations, SI 1998/59 with effect from 11 February 1998.

[2] Words substituted, and paras (*d*), (*da*) substituted for para (*d*) by the VAT (Amendment) (No 2) Regulations, SI 2005/2231 reg 5 with effect from 1 September 2005 in relation to claims made under VATA 1994 s 80 on or after that date.

43D [Notifications and repayments to the Commissioners

The claimant shall give any notification to the Commissioners that he is required to give by virtue of regulation 43C(*d*) above and, without any prior demand, make any repayment to the Commissioners that he is required to make by virtue of regulation 43C(*da*) and (*e*) above within 14 days of the expiration of the 90 days referred to in regulation 43C(*a*) above.][1]

Amendments—[1] This regulation substituted by the VAT (Amendment) (No 2) Regulations, SI 2005/2231 reg 6 with effect from 1 September 2005 in relation to claims made under VATA 1994 s 80 on or after that date.

[43E Records

The claimant shall keep records of the following matters—

(*a*) the names and addresses of those consumers whom he has reimbursed or whom he intends to reimburse;

(*b*) the total amount reimbursed to each such consumer;

(*c*) the amount of interest included in each total amount reimbursed to each consumer;

(*d*) the date that each reimbursement is made.][1]

Amendments—[1] This regulation inserted by the VAT (Amendment) (No 5) Regulations, SI 1998/59 with effect from 11 February 1998.

[43F Production of records

(1) Where a claimant is given notice in accordance with paragraph (2) below, he shall, in accordance with such notice produce to the Commissioners, or to an officer of theirs, the records that he is required to keep pursuant to regulation 43E above.

(2) A notice given for the purposes of paragraph (1) above shall—

(*a*) be in writing;

(*b*) state the place and time at which, and the date on which the records are to be produced; and

(*c*) be signed and dated by the Commissioners, or by an officer of theirs,

and may be given before or after, or both before and after the Commissioners have [credited][2] the relevant amount to the claimant.][1]

Amendments—[1] This regulation inserted by the VAT (Amendment) (No 5) Regulations, SI 1998/59 with effect from 11 February 1998.

[2] Word in para (2) substituted by the VAT (Amendment) (No 2) Regulations, SI 2005/2231 reg 7 with effect from 1 September 2005 in relation to claims made under VATA 1994 s 80 on or after that date.

[43G Undertakings

(1) Without prejudice to regulation 43H(*b*) below, the undertakings referred to in regulation 43B(*b*) above shall be given to the Commissioners by the claimant no later than the time at which he makes the claim for which the reimbursement arrangements have been made.

(2) The undertakings shall be in writing, shall be signed and dated by the claimant, and shall be to the effect that—

(*a*) at the date of the undertakings he is able to identify the names and addresses of those consumers whom he has reimbursed or whom he intends to reimburse;

(*b*) he will apply the whole of the relevant amount [credited][2] to him, without any deduction by way of fee or charge or otherwise, to the reimbursement in cash or by cheque, of such consumers by no later than 90 days after his receipt of that amount (except insofar as he has already so reimbursed them);

(*c*) he will apply any interest paid to him on the relevant amount [paid (or repaid)][2] to him wholly to the reimbursement of such consumers by no later than 90 days after his receipt of that interest;

[(*d*) he will notify the Commissioners of the whole or such part of the relevant amount credited to him as he fails to apply in accordance with the undertakings mentioned in sub-paragraphs (*b*) and (*c*) above;][2]

[(*da*) he will repay to the Commissioners without demand the whole or such part of the relevant amount paid (or repaid) to him or of any interest paid to him as he fails to apply in accordance with the undertakings mentioned in sub-paragraphs (*b*) and (*c*) above;][2]

(*e*) he will keep the records described in regulation 43E above; and

(*f*) he will comply with any notice given to him in accordance with regulation 43F above concerning the production of such records.][1]

Amendments—[1] This regulation inserted by the VAT (Amendment) (No 5) Regulations, SI 1998/59 with effect from 11 February 1998.

[2] In para (2), words substituted, and sub-paras (*d*), (*da*) substituted for sub-para (*d*), by the VAT (Amendment) (No 2) Regulations, SI 2005/2231 reg 8 with effect from 1 September 2005 in relation to claims made under VATA 1994 s 80 on or after that date.

43H Reimbursement arrangements made before 11th February 1998

Amendment—This regulation revoked by the VAT (Amendment) (No 2) Regulations, SI 2005/2231 reg 9 with effect from 1 September 2005 in relation to claims made under VATA 1994 s 80 on or after that date.

PART VI
PAYMENTS ON ACCOUNT

44 Interpretation of Part VI

In this Part—

"body corporate" means a body corporate which is under a duty to make payments on account by virtue of the Value Added Tax (Payments on Account) Order 1993 and "relevant division" means a division of a body corporate by reference to the business of which that body corporate is under such a duty;

"payments on account" has the same meaning as in the Value Added Tax (Payments on Account) Order 1993.

Former regulation—VAT (Payments on Account) (No 2) Regulations, SI 1992/1844 regs 2, 7(1).

45 Payments on Account

Save in a case to which regulation 48 applies, the Commissioners shall give to a taxable person who is under a duty to make payments on account notification in writing of—

(*a*) the amounts that he is under a duty to pay,

(*b*) how those amounts have been calculated, and

(*c*) the times for payment of those amounts.

VAT SIs

Former regulation—VAT (Payments on Account) (No 2) Regulations, SI 1992/1844 reg 4.

46 Save in a case to which regulation 48 applies, if in respect of a prescribed accounting period the total amount of the payment on account made by the taxable person exceeds the amount of VAT due from him in respect of that period, the amount of excess shall be paid to him by the Commissioners if and to the extent that it is not required by section 81 of the Act to be set against any sum which he is liable to pay to them.

Former regulation—VAT (Payments on Account) (No 2) Regulations, SI 1992/1844 reg 5.

[46A—(1) A payment on account and a payment in respect of a return to which regulation 40A above applies shall not be treated as having been made by the last day on which it is required to be made unless it is made in such a manner as secures that all the transactions can be completed that need to be completed before the whole of the amount becomes available to the Commissioners.

(2) For the purposes of this regulation and regulation 47 below, references to a payment being made by any day include references to its being made on that day.][1]

Amendments—[1] This regulation inserted by the VAT (Amendment) (No 2) Regulations, SI 1996/1198 reg 4 with effect from 1 June 1996.

47 Where a taxable person fails to make a payment on account by the last day by which he is required to make it, that payment on account shall be recoverable as if it were VAT due from him.

Former regulation—VAT (Payments on Account) (No 2) Regulations, SI 1992/1844 reg 6.

48—(1) The Commissioners shall notify a relevant division in writing of—

(*a*) the amounts of the payments on account that the body corporate is under a duty to make by reference to the business of that division,

(*b*) how those amounts have been calculated, and

(*c*) the times for payment of those amounts.

(2) If in respect of a prescribed accounting period the total amount of the payments on account made by a body corporate by reference to the business of a particular relevant division exceeds the amount of VAT due from the body corporate in respect of that period by reference to that business, the amount of the excess shall be paid to the body corporate through that division by the Commissioners if and to the extent that it is not required by section 81 of the Act to be set against any sum which the body corporate is liable to pay to them.

(3) Section 81 of the Act shall not require any amount which is due to be paid by the Commissioners to a body corporate under paragraph (2) above by reference to the business of a particular relevant division to be set against any sum due from the body corporate otherwise than by reference to that business or to the liabilities of the body corporate arising in connection with that division.

Former regulation—VAT (Payments on Account) (No 2) Regulations, SI 1992/1844 reg 7(2)–(4).

[PART VII

ANNUAL ACCOUNTING][1]

Amendments—[1] This Part (regs 49–55) substituted by the VAT (Annual Accounting) Regulations, SI 1996/542 with effect, in the case of a taxable person who was on 31 March 1996 authorised to use the annual accounting scheme under the VAT Regulations, SI 1995/2518 reg 50, from the first day of his next current accounting year, and in respect of any other taxable person, from 1 April 1996.

[49 Interpretation of Part VII

In this Part—

"authorised person" means a person who has been authorised by the Commissioners in accordance with regulation 50(1), and "authorised" and "authorisation" shall be construed accordingly;

"transitional accounting period" means the period commencing on the first day of a person's prescribed accounting period in which the Commissioners authorise him to use the scheme, and ending on the day immediately preceding the first day of that person's first current accounting year, and is a prescribed accounting period within the meaning of section 25(1) of the Act;

"current accounting year" means the period of 12 months commencing on a date indicated by the Commissioners in their notification of authorisation of a person, or while a person remains authorised the most recent anniversary thereof, and is a prescribed accounting period within the meaning of section 25(1) of the Act;

"the scheme" means the annual accounting scheme established by regulations 50 and 51;

"credit transfer" means the transfer of funds from one bank account to another under a mandate given by the payer to the bank making the transfer;

["the quarterly sum" means—

(*a*) in the case of a taxable person who has been registered for at least 12 months—

(i) immediately preceding the first day of his current accounting year, or

(ii) for the purposes of regulation 51, immediately preceding the first day of his transitional accounting period,

a sum equal to 25 per cent. of the total amount of VAT that he was liable to pay to the Commissioners in respect of those 12 months; or

(*b*) in any other case, a sum equal to 25 per cent of the total amount of VAT that the Commissioners are satisfied he will be liable to pay to the Commissioners in respect of the next 12 months;][2]

"the agreed quarterly sum" means a sum agreed with the Commissioners, not being less than [25 per cent][2] of a taxable person's estimated liability for VAT in his current accounting year;

["the monthly sum" means—

(*a*) in the case of a taxable person who has been registered for at least 12 months—

(i) immediately preceding the first day of his current accounting year, or

(ii) for the purposes of regulation 51, immediately preceding the first day of his transitional accounting period,

a sum equal to 10 per cent of the total amount of VAT that he was liable to pay to the Commissioners in respect of those 12 months; or

(*b*) in any other case, a sum equal to 10 per cent. of the total amount of VAT that the Commissioners are satisfied he will be liable to pay to the Commissioners in respect of the next 12 months;][2]

"the agreed monthly sum" means a sum agreed with the Commissioners, not being less than 10 per cent of a taxable person's estimated liability for VAT, in his current accounting year;

"working day" means any day of the week other than Saturday, Sunday, a bank holiday or a public holiday;

"relevant quarterly date" means the last working day of the fourth and, where a period has such months, the seventh and the tenth months of a transitional accounting period;

"relevant monthly date" means the last working day of the fourth and each successive month of a transitional accounting period.][1]

Amendments—[1] This regulation substituted by the VAT (Annual Accounting) Regulations, SI 1996/542 with effect, in the case of a taxable person who was on 31 March 1996 authorised to use the annual accounting scheme under the VAT Regulations, SI 1995/2518 reg 50, from the first day of his next current accounting year, and in respect of any other taxable person, from 1 April 1996.

[2] Definitions of "the quarterly sum" and "the monthly sum" substituted, and definition of "the agreed monthly sum" amended, by the VAT (Amendment) (No 2) Regulations, SI 2002/1142 regs 1–3 with effect—

(a) in the case of a taxable person who is on 24 April 2002 authorised under the Value Added Tax Regulations, SI 1995/2518 reg 50, from the first day of his next prescribed accounting period beginning after that date; and

(b) in the case of any other taxable person, from 25 April 2002.

[50 Annual accounting scheme

(1) The Commissioners may, subject to the requirements of this Part, authorise a taxable person to pay and account for VAT by reference to any transitional accounting period, and any subsequent current accounting year at such times, and for such amounts, as may be determined in accordance with the scheme.

(2) A taxable person authorised to pay and account for VAT in accordance with the scheme shall—

(*a*) pay to the Commissioners by credit transfer—

[(i) where the taxable person and Commissioners agree to such payment pattern, the quarterly sum, or as the case may be the agreed quarterly sum, no later than the last working day of each of the fourth, seventh and tenth months of his current accounting year;][2]

(ii) in all other cases, the monthly sum, or as the case may be, the agreed monthly sum, in nine equal monthly instalments, commencing on the last working day of the fourth month of his current accounting year; and

(*b*) make by the last working day of the second month following the end of that current accounting year a return in respect of that year, together with any outstanding payment due to the Commissioners in respect of his liability for VAT for the current accounting year declared on that return.

(3) . . . [2]][1]

Amendments—[1] This regulation substituted by the VAT (Annual Accounting) Regulations, SI 1996/542 with effect, in the case of a taxable person who was on 31 March 1996 authorised to use the annual accounting scheme under the VAT Regulations, SI 1995/2518 reg 50, from the first day of his next current accounting year, and in respect of any other taxable person, from 1 April 1996.

[2] Para (2)(*a*)(i) substituted, and para (3) revoked, by the VAT (Amendment) (No 2) Regulations, SI 2002/1142 regs 1, 2, 4 with effect—

(a) in the case of a taxable person who is on 24 April 2002 authorised under the Value Added Tax Regulations, SI 1995/2518 reg 50, from the first day of his next prescribed accounting period beginning after that date; and

(b) in the case of any other taxable person, from 25 April 2002.

[51 An authorised person shall, where in any given case the transitional accounting period is—

(*a*) 4 months or more—

[(i) where the taxable person and Commissioners agree to such payment pattern, pay to the Commissioners by credit transfer on each relevant quarterly date the quarterly sum;][2] or

(ii) in all other cases, pay to the Commissioners by credit transfer on each relevant monthly date the monthly sum; and

(iii) make by the last working day of the second month following the end of his transitional accounting period a return in respect of that period, together with any outstanding payment due to the Commissioners in respect of his liability for VAT declared on that return; or

(*b*) less than 4 months, make by the last working day of the first month following the end of his transitional accounting period a return in respect of that period, together with any outstanding payment due to the Commissioners in respect of his liability for VAT declared on that return.][1]

Amendments—[1] This regulation substituted by the VAT (Annual Accounting) Regulations, SI 1996/542 with effect, in the case of a taxable person who was on 31 March 1996 authorised to use the annual accounting scheme under the VAT Regulations, SI 1995/2518 reg 50, from the first day of his next current accounting year, and in respect of any other taxable person, from 1 April 1996.

[2] Para (*a*)(i) substituted by the VAT (Amendment) (No 2) Regulations, SI 2002/1142 regs 1, 2, 5 with effect—

(a) in the case of a taxable person who is on 24 April 2002 authorised under the Value Added Tax Regulations, SI 1995/2518 reg 50, from the first day of his next prescribed accounting period beginning after that date; and

(b) in the case of any other taxable person, from 25 April 2002.

[52 Admission to the scheme

(1) A taxable person shall be eligible to apply for authorisation under regulation 50(1) if—

(*a*) . . . [2]

(*b*) he has reasonable grounds for believing that the value of taxable supplies made or to be made by him in the period of 12 months beginning on the date of his application for authorisation will not exceed [£1,350,000][2];

(*c*) his registration is not in the name of a group under section 43(1) of the Act;

(*d*) his registration is not in the name of a division under section 46(1) of the Act; and

(*e*) he has not in the 12 months preceding the date of his application for authorisation ceased to operate the scheme.

(1A) . . . [2]

(2) The Commissioners may refuse to authorise a person under regulation 50(1) where they consider it necessary to do so for the protection of the revenue.][1]

Amendments—[1] This regulation substituted by the VAT (Annual Accounting) Regulations, SI 1996/542 with effect, in the case of a taxable person who was on 31 March 1996 authorised to use the annual accounting scheme under the VAT Regulations, SI 1995/2518 reg 50, from the first day of his next current accounting year, and in respect of any other taxable person, from 1 April 1996.

[2] Paras (1)(*a*), (1A) revoked, and figure in para (1)(*b*) substituted, by the VAT (Amendment) Regulations, SI 2006/587 regs 1(2), (5), 2 with effect from 1 April 2006.

[53—(1) An authorised person shall continue to account for VAT in accordance with the scheme until he ceases to be authorised.

(2) An authorised person ceases to be authorised when—

(*a*) at the end of any [transitional accounting period][3] or current accounting year the value of taxable supplies made by him in that period or, as the case may be, year has exceeded [£1,600,000][2]; or

(*b*) his authorisation is terminated in accordance with regulation 54 below;

(*c*) he—

(i) becomes insolvent and ceases to trade, other than for the purpose of disposing of stocks and assets; or

(ii) ceases business or ceases to be registered; or

(iii) dies, becomes bankrupt or incapacitated;

(*d*) he ceases to operate the scheme of his own volition.][1]

Amendments—[1] This regulation substituted by the VAT (Annual Accounting) Regulations, SI 1996/542 with effect, in the case of a taxable person who was on 31 March 1996 authorised to use the annual accounting scheme under the VAT Regulations, SI 1995/2518 reg 50, from the first day of his next current accounting year, and in respect of any other taxable person, from 1 April 1996.

[2] Figure in sub-para (2)(*a*) substituted by the VAT (Amendment) Regulations, SI 2006/587 regs 1(2), (5), 3 with effect from 1 April 2006.

[3] In sub-para (2)(*a*), words substituted by the VAT (Amendment) (No 2) Regulations, SI 2003/1069 regs 1(1), 2, 4 with effect from 10 April 2003.

[54—(1) The Commissioners may terminate an authorisation in any case where—

(*a*) a false statement has been made by or on behalf of an authorised person in relation to his application for authorisation; or

(*b*) an authorised person fails to make by the due date a return in accordance with regulation 50(2)(*b*) or regulation 51(*a*)(iii) or (*b*); or
(*c*) an authorised person fails to make any payment prescribed in regulation 50 or 51; or
(*d*) where they receive a notification in accordance with paragraph (2) below; or
(*e*) at any time during an authorised person's transitional accounting period or current accounting year they have reason to believe, that the value of taxable supplies he will make during the period or as the case may be year, will exceed [£1,600,000][2]; or
(*f*) it is necessary to do so for the protection of the revenue; or
(*g*) an authorised person has not, in relation to a return made by him prior to authorisation, paid to the Commissioners all such sums shown as due thereon; or
(*h*) an authorised person has not, in relation to any assessment made under either section 73 or section 76 of the Act, paid to the Commissioners all such sums shown as due thereon.

(2) Where an authorised person has reason to believe that the value of taxable supplies made by him during a transitional accounting period or current accounting year will exceed [£1,600,000][2], he shall within 30 days notify the Commissioners in writing.][1]

Amendments—[1] This regulation substituted by the VAT (Annual Accounting) Regulations, SI 1996/542 with effect, in the case of a taxable person who was on 31 March 1996 authorised to use the annual accounting scheme under the VAT Regulations, SI 1995/2518 reg 50, from the first day of his next current accounting year, and in respect of any other taxable person, from 1 April 1996.
[2] Figures in paras (1)(*e*), (2) substituted by the VAT (Amendment) Regulations, SI 2006/587 regs 1(2), (5), 3 with effect from 1 April 2006.

[55—(1) The date from which an authorised person ceases to be authorised in accordance with Regulation 53(2) shall be—
(*a*) where regulation 53(2)(*a*) applies, the day following the last day of the relevant transitional accounting period or current accounting year;
(*b*) where regulation 53(2)(*b*) applies, the day on which the Commissioners terminate his authorisation;
(*c*) where regulation 53(2)(*c*) applies, the day on which any one of the events mentioned in that paragraph occurs; and
(*d*) where regulation 53(2)(*d*) applies, the date on which the Commissioners are notified in writing of the authorised persons decision to cease using the scheme.

(2) Where an authorised person ceases to be authorised, he or as the case may be, his representative, shall—
(*a*) if his authorisation ceases before the end of his transitional accounting period or current accounting year, make a return within 2 months of the date specified in paragraph (1)(*b*), (1)(*c*) or (1)(*d*) above, together with any outstanding payment due to the Commissioners in respect of his liability for VAT for that part of the period or year arising before the date he ceased to be authorised; or
(*b*) if his authorisation ceases at the end of his transitional accounting period or current accounting year, make a return together with any outstanding payment due to the Commissioners in respect of his liability for VAT in accordance with regulation 51 or 50 above; and

in either case, from the day following the day on which he ceases to be authorised, account for and pay VAT as provided for otherwise than under this Part.][1]

Amendments—[1] This regulation substituted by the VAT (Annual Accounting) Regulations, SI 1996/542 with effect, in the case of a taxable person who was on 31 March 1996 authorised to use the annual accounting scheme under the VAT Regulations, SI 1995/2518 reg 50, from the first day of his next current accounting year, and in respect of any other taxable person, from 1 April 1996.

[PART VIIA
FLAT-RATE SCHEME FOR SMALL BUSINESSES

55A Interpretation of Part VIIA

(1) In this Part—

. . . [2]

"capital expenditure goods" means any goods of a capital nature but does not include any goods acquired by a flat-rate trader (whether before he is a flat-rate trader or not)—
(*a*) for the purpose of resale or incorporation into goods supplied by him,
(*b*) for consumption by him within one year, or
(*c*) to generate income by being leased, let or hired;

. . . [2]

["EDR" means the day with effect from which a person is registered under the Act;][2]
"end date" has the meaning given in regulation 55Q(2);
"flat-rate trader" means a person who is, for the time being, authorised by the Commissioners in accordance with regulation 55B(1);
"relevant purchase" has the meaning given in regulation 55C;

VAT SIs

"start date" has the meaning given in regulation 55B(2);
"the scheme" means the flat-rate scheme for small businesses established by this Part;
"the Table" means the table set out in regulation 55K.

(2) For the purposes of this Part, a person is associated with another person at any time if that other person makes supplies in the course or furtherance of a business carried on by him, and—

(*a*) the business of one is under the dominant influence of the other, or
(*b*) the persons are closely bound to one another by financial, economic and organisational links.][1]

[(3) For the purposes of this Part, "relevant date", in relation to a flat-rate trader, means any of the following—

(*a*) his start date;
(*b*) the first day of the prescribed accounting period current at any anniversary of his start date;
(*c*) any day on which he first carries on a new business activity;
(*d*) any day on which he no longer carries on an existing business activity;
(*e*) any day with effect from which the Table is amended in relation to him;
(*f*) where regulation 55JB (reduced rate for newly registered period) applies—
(i) the day that his newly registered period begins, and
(ii) the first anniversary of his EDR.][2]

Amendments—[1] This Part inserted by the VAT (Amendment) (No 2) Regulations, SI 2002/1142 regs 1, 7 with effect from 25 April 2002.

[2] Definition of "amendment date" and "change date" revoked, definition of "EDR" inserted, and para (3) inserted, by the VAT (Amendment) (No 6) Regulations, SI 2003/3220 regs 1(1)(*b*), 2, 18(1) with effect from 1 January 2004.

55B [Flat-rate scheme for small businesses

(1) The Commissioners may, subject to the requirements of this Part, authorise a taxable person to account for and pay VAT in respect of his relevant supplies in accordance with the scheme with effect from—

(*a*) the beginning of his next prescribed accounting period after the date on which the Commissioners are notified . . .[2] of his desire to be so authorised, or
(*b*) such earlier or later date as may be agreed between him and the Commissioners.

(2) The date with effect from which a person is so authorised shall be known as his start date.

(3) The Commissioners may refuse to so authorise a person if they consider it is necessary for the protection of the revenue that he is not so authorised.

(4) A flat-rate trader shall continue to account for VAT in accordance with the scheme until his end date.][1]

Amendments—[1] This Part inserted by the VAT (Amendment) (No 2) Regulations, SI 2002/1142 regs 1, 7 with effect from 25 April 2002.

[2] Words revoked by the VAT (Amendment) (No 6) Regulations, SI 2003/3220 regs 1(1)(*b*), 2, 17 with effect from 1 January 2004.

55C [Relevant supplies and purchases

(1) Subject to paragraphs (3)[, (5) and (6)][2], any—

(*a*) supply of any goods or services to,
(*b*) acquisition of any goods from another member State by, or
(*c*) importation of any goods from a place outside the member States by,

a flat-rate trader is a relevant purchase of his.

(2) Subject to the following provisions of this regulation, any supply made by a person when he is not a flat-rate trader is not a relevant supply of his.

(3) Subject to [paragraphs (4) and (6)][2] below, where—

(*a*) a supply is made to, or made by, a person at a time when he is not a flat-rate trader, and
(*b*) the operative date for VAT accounting purposes is, by virtue of regulation 57 (cash accounting scheme), a date when he is a flat-rate trader,

that supply is a relevant supply or a relevant purchase of his, as the case may be, if otherwise it would not be by virtue of paragraph (2) above.

(4) Where a person—

(*a*) is entitled to any credit for input tax in respect of the supply to, or acquisition or importation by, him of capital expenditure goods,
(*b*) claims any such credit, and
(*c*) makes a supply of those capital expenditure goods,

the supply made by him is not a relevant supply of his, if otherwise it would be.

(5) Where by virtue of any provision of, or made under, the Act a supply is treated as made by a flat-rate trader, whether to himself or otherwise, that supply is neither a relevant supply nor a relevant purchase of his.][1]

[(6) Where a supply of goods [or services][3] to which section 55A(6) of the Act applies (customers to account for tax on supplies of goods [or services][3] of a kind used in missing trader intra-community fraud) is made to, or made by, a flat rate trader, that supply is neither a relevant purchase nor a relevant supply of his.][2]

Amendments—[1] This Part inserted by the VAT (Amendment) (No 2) Regulations, SI 2002/1142 regs 1, 7 with effect from 25 April 2002.

[2] Words in paras (1), (3) substituted, and para (6) inserted, by the VAT (Amendment) (No 3) Regulations, SI 2007/1418 regs 2, 5 with effect from 1 June 2007.

[3] Words in para (6) inserted by the VAT (Amendment) (No 2) Regulations, SI 2010/2240 regs 2, 3(2) with effect from 1 November 2010.

55D [Method of accounting

Subject to [regulations 55H and 55JB][2] below, for any prescribed accounting period of a flat-rate trader, the output tax due from him in respect of his relevant supplies shall be deemed to be the appropriate percentage of his relevant turnover for that period][1]

Amendments—[1] This regulation inserted by the VAT (Amendment) (No 2) Regulations, SI 2002/1142 regs 1, 7 with effect from 25 April 2002.

[2] Words substituted by the VAT (Amendment) (No 6) Regulations, SI 2003/3220 regs 1(1)(*b*), 2, 18(2) with effect from 1 January 2004.

55E [Input tax

(1) For any prescribed accounting period of a flat-rate trader, he is entitled to credit for input tax in respect of any relevant purchase of his of capital expenditure goods with a value, together with the VAT chargeable, of more than £2,000.

(2) Where paragraph (1) above applies, the whole of the input tax on the goods concerned shall be regarded as used or to be used by the flat-rate trader exclusively in making taxable supplies.

(3) Section 26B(5) of the Act shall not apply to prevent a taxable person from being entitled to credit for input tax in respect of any supply, acquisition or importation by him that is not a relevant purchase of his.

(4) Nothing in this regulation gives an entitlement to credit for input tax where such entitlement is excluded by virtue of any order made under section 25(7) of the Act.][1]

Amendments—[1] This Part inserted by the VAT (Amendment) (No 2) Regulations, SI 2002/1142 regs 1, 7 with effect from 25 April 2002.

55F [Exceptional claims for VAT relief

(1) This regulation applies where—

(*a*) the first prescribed accounting period for which a taxable person is authorised to account for and pay VAT in accordance with the scheme is the first prescribed accounting period for which he is, or is required to be, registered under the Act, and

(*b*) the taxable person makes a claim in accordance with regulation 111 (exceptional claims for VAT relief).

(2) Where this regulation applies, section 26B(5) of the Act shall not apply to prevent the taxable person from being entitled to credit for input tax in relation to the matters for which he makes the claim described in paragraph (1)(b) above.

(3) Where—

(*a*) this regulation applies, and

(*b*) the Commissioners authorise the claim described in paragraph (1)(b) above,

the whole of the input tax on the goods or services concerned shall be regarded as used or to be used by the taxable person exclusively in making taxable supplies.][1]

Amendments—[1] This Part inserted by the VAT (Amendment) (No 2) Regulations, SI 2002/1142 regs 1, 7 with effect from 25 April 2002.

55G [Determining relevant turnover

(1) The Commissioners shall prescribe, in a notice published by them, three methods to determine when supplies are to be treated as taking place for the purpose of ascertaining the relevant turnover of a flat-rate trader for a particular period, as follows—

(*a*) "the basic turnover method", which shall be a method based on consideration for supplies taking place in a period;

(*b*) "the cash turnover method", which shall be a method based on the actual consideration received in a period;

(*c*) "the retailer's turnover method", which shall be a method based on the daily gross takings of a retailer.

(2) When exercising their power to prescribe these methods, the Commissioners shall prescribe what rules are to apply when a flat-rate trader ceases to use one of the methods and begins to use a different method.

(3) In any prescribed accounting period, a flat-rate trader must use one of the methods to determine the value of his relevant turnover.][1]

Amendments—[1] This Part inserted by the VAT (Amendment) (No 2) Regulations, SI 2002/1142 regs 1, 7 with effect from 25 April 2002.

[55H—(1) The appropriate percentage to be applied by a flat-rate trader for any prescribed accounting period, or part of a prescribed accounting period (as the case may be), shall be determined in accordance with this regulation and regulations 55JB and 55K.

(2) For any prescribed accounting period—

(*a*) beginning with a relevant date, the appropriate percentage shall be that specified in the Table for the category of business that he is expected, at the relevant date, on reasonable grounds, to carry on in that period;

(*b*) current at his start date but not beginning with his start date, the appropriate percentage shall be that specified in the Table for the category of business that he is expected, at his start date, on reasonable grounds, to carry on in the remainder of the period;

(*c*) not falling within (*a*) or (*b*), the appropriate percentage shall be that applicable to his relevant turnover at the end of the previous prescribed accounting period.

(3) Except that, where a relevant date other than his start date occurs on a day other than the first day of a prescribed accounting period, the following rules shall apply for the remainder of that prescribed accounting period—

(*a*) for the remaining portion, the appropriate percentage shall be that specified in the Table for the category of business that he is expected, at the relevant date, on reasonable grounds, to carry on in that period;

(*b*) "remaining portion" means that part of the prescribed accounting period in which the relevant date occurs—

(i) starting with the relevant date, and

(ii) ending on the last day of that prescribed accounting period;

(*c*) the appropriate percentage specified in sub-paragraph (*a*) shall be applied to his relevant turnover in the remaining portion described;

(*d*) if the rules set out in paragraphs (*a*) to (*c*) apply and then another relevant date occurs in the same prescribed accounting period, then—

(i) the existing remaining portion ends on the day before the latest relevant date,

(ii) another remaining portion begins on the latest relevant date, and

(iii) the rules in paragraph (*a*) to (*c*) shall be applied again in respect of the latest remaining portion.][1]

Amendments—[1] Substituted for regulations 55H–55JA by the VAT (Amendment) (No 6) Regulations, SI 2003/3220 regs 1(1)(*b*), 2, 19(1) with effect from 1 January 2004.

55JB [Reduced appropriate percentage for newly registered period

(1) This regulation applies where a flat-rate trader's start date falls within one year of his EDR.

(2) Except that this regulation does not apply where—

(*a*) the Commissioners received notification of, or otherwise became fully aware of, his liability to be registered more than one year after his EDR, or

(*b*) his end date or the first anniversary of his EDR falls before 1st January 2004.

(3) At any relevant date on or after 1st January 2004 falling within his newly registered period, the Table shall be read as if each percentage specified in the right-hand column were reduced by one.

(4) A flat-rate trader's "newly registered period" is the period—

(*a*) beginning with the later of—

(i) his start date; and

(ii) the day the Commissioners received notification of, or otherwise became fully aware of, his liability to be registered under the Act, and

(*b*) ending on the day before the first anniversary of his EDR.][1]

Amendments—[1] Inserted by the VAT (Amendment) (No 6) Regulations, SI 2003/3220 regs 1(1)(*b*), 2, 19(2) with effect from 1 January 2004.

55K [Category of business

(1) Where, at a relevant date, a flat-rate trader is expected, on reasonable grounds, to carry on business in more than one category in the period concerned, paragraph (3) below shall apply.

(2) . . .[2]

(3) He shall be regarded as being expected, on reasonable grounds, to carry on that category of business which is expected, on reasonable grounds, to be his main business activity in that period.

(4) In paragraph (3) above, his main business activity in a period is to be determined by reference to the respective proportions of his relevant turnover expected, on reasonable grounds, to be generated by each business activity expected, on reasonable grounds, to be carried on in the period.][1]

[Table

Category of business	*Appropriate percentage*
Accountancy or book-keeping	14.5
Advertising	11
Agricultural services	11
Any other activity not listed elsewhere	12

Category of business	*Appropriate percentage*
Architect, civil and structural engineer or surveyor	14.5
Boarding or care of animals	12
Business services that are not listed elsewhere	12
Catering services including restaurants and takeaways	12.5
Computer and IT consultancy or data processing	14.5
Computer repair services	10.5
Dealing in waste or scrap	10.5
Entertainment or journalism	12.5
Estate agency or property management services	12
Farming or agriculture that is not listed elsewhere	6.5
Film, radio, television or video production	13
Financial services	13.5
Forestry or fishing	10.5
General building or construction services*	9.5
Hairdressing or other beauty treatment services	13
Hiring or renting goods	9.5
Hotel or accommodation	10.5
Investigation or security	12
Labour-only building or construction services*	14.5
Laundry or dry-cleaning services	12
Lawyer or legal services	14.5
Library, archive, museum or other cultural activity	9.5
Management consultancy	14
Manufacturing fabricated metal products	10.5
Manufacturing food	9
Manufacturing that is not listed elsewhere	9.5
Manufacturing yarn, textiles or clothing	9
Membership organisation	8
Mining or quarrying	10
Packaging	9
Photography	11
Post offices	5
Printing	8.5
Publishing	11
Pubs	6.5
Real estate activity not listed elsewhere	14
Repairing personal or household goods	10
Repairing vehicles	8.5
Retailing food, confectionary, tobacco, newspapers or children's clothing	4
Retailing pharmaceuticals, medical goods, cosmetics or toiletries	8
Retailing that is not listed elsewhere	7.5
Retailing vehicles or fuel	6.5
Secretarial services	13
Social work	11

Category of business	*Appropriate percentage*
Sport or recreation	8.5
Transport or storage, including couriers, freight, removals and taxis	10
Travel agency	10.5
Veterinary medicine	11
Wholesaling agricultural products	8
Wholesaling food	7.5
Wholesaling that is not listed elsewhere	8.5
(1) * "Labour-only building or construction services" means building or construction services where the value of materials supplied is less than 10 per cent of relevant turnover from such services; any other building or construction services are "general building or construction services"][3]	

Cross reference—VAT (Amendment) Regulations, SI 2004/767 reg 2(3) ("his main business activity" in a period (as mentioned in Note 4 below) is to be determined by reference to reg 55K(4) above).

Amendments—

[1] This Part inserted by the VAT (Amendment) (No 2) Regulations, SI 2002/1142 regs 1, 7 with effect from 25 April 2002.

[2] Para (2) revoked by the VAT (Amendment) (No 6) Regulations, SI 2003/3220 regs 1(1)(*b*), 2, 18(3) with effect from 1 January 2004.

[3] Table substituted by the VAT (Amendment) (No 3) Regulations, SI 2010/2940 regs 2, 4 with effect from 4 January 2011.

55L [Admission to Scheme

(1) A taxable person shall be eligible to be authorised to account for VAT in accordance with the scheme at any time if—

(*a*) there are reasonable grounds for believing that—

(i) the value of taxable supplies to be made by him in the period of one year then beginning will not exceed [£150,000][2], and

(ii) . . . [3]

(*b*) he—

(i) is not a tour operator,

(ii) is not required to carry out adjustments in relation to a capital item under Part XV, or

(iii) does not intend to opt to account for the VAT chargeable on a supply made by him by reference to the profit margin on the supply, in accordance with the provisions of any Order made under section 50A of the Act,

(*c*) he has not, in the period of one year preceding that time—

(i) been convicted of any offence in connection with VAT,

(ii) made any payment to compound proceedings in respect of VAT under section 152 of the Customs and Excise Management Act 1979,

(iii) been assessed to a penalty under section 60 of the Act, or

(iv) ceased to operate the scheme, and

(*d*) he is not, and has not been within the past 24 months—

(i) eligible to be registered for VAT in the name of a group under section 43A of the Act,

(ii) registered for VAT in the name of a division under section 46(1) of the Act, or

(iii) associated with another person.

(2) In determining the value of a person's taxable supplies . . . [3] for the purposes of paragraph (1)(*a*)—

(*a*) any supply of goods or services that are capital assets of the business in the course or furtherance of which they are supplied, and

(*b*) any supply of services treated as made by the recipient by virtue of section 8 of the Act (reverse charge on supplies from abroad),

shall be disregarded.

(3) Notwithstanding the above, where a person has been—

(*a*) eligible to be registered for VAT in the name of a group under section 43A of the Act,

(*b*) registered for VAT in the name of a division under section 46(1) of the Act, or

(*c*) associated with another person,

in the period of 24 months before the date of his application, he shall not be authorised, unless the Commissioners are satisfied that such authorisation poses no risk to the revenue.][1]

Amendments—[1] This Part inserted by the VAT (Amendment) (No 2) Regulations, SI 2002/1142 regs 1, 7 with effect from 25 April 2002.

[2] In sub-para (1)(*a*)(i), "£150,000" substituted for "£100,000", by the VAT (Amendment) (No 2) Regulations, SI 2003/1069 regs 1(1), 2, 7(1) with effect from 10 April 2003.

[3] Para (1)(*a*)(ii) revoked, and in para (2) words "or income" revoked, by the VAT (Amendment) Regulations, SI 2009/586 regs 2, 6 with effect from 1 April 2009.

55M [Withdrawal from the scheme

(1) Subject to paragraph (2) below, a flat-rate trader ceases to be eligible to be authorised to account for VAT in accordance with the scheme where—

(*a*) at any anniversary of his start date, the total value of his income in the period of one year then ending is more than [£230,000][3],

(*b*) there are reasonable grounds to believe that the total value of his income in the period of 30 days then beginning will exceed [£230,000][3],

(*c*) he becomes a tour operator,

(*d*) he intends to acquire, construct or otherwise obtain a capital item within the meaning of regulation 112(2),

(*e*) he opts to account for the VAT chargeable on a supply made by him by reference to the profit margin on the supply, in accordance with the provisions of any Order made under section 50A of the Act,

(*f*) he becomes—

(i) eligible to be registered for VAT in the name of a group under section 43A of the Act,

(ii) registered for VAT in the name of a division under section 46(1) of the Act, or

(iii) associated with another person,

(*g*) he opts to withdraw from the scheme, or

(*h*) his authorisation is terminated in accordance with regulation 55P below.

(2) A flat-rate trader does not cease to be eligible to be authorised by virtue of paragraph (1)(*a*) above if the Commissioners are satisfied that the total value of his income in the period of one year then beginning will not exceed [£191,500][3].

(3) In determining the value of a flat-rate trader's income for the purposes of paragraphs (1)(*a*) and (*b*) and (2) above, any supply of goods or services that are capital assets of the business in the course or furtherance of which they are supplied, shall be disregarded.

[(4) For the purposes of this regulation, "income" shall be calculated in accordance with the method specified in regulation 55G(1) (determining relevant turnover) used by the business to determine the value of its turnover whilst accounting for VAT under the scheme.

(5) Where a business has used more than one method to determine the value of its turnover whilst accounting for VAT under the scheme, the method referred to in paragraph (4) above shall be the most recent method used.][2]][1]

Amendments—[1] This Part inserted by the VAT (Amendment) (No 2) Regulations, SI 2002/1142 regs 1, 7 with effect from 25 April 2002.

[2] Paras (4), (5) inserted by the VAT (Amendment) Regulations, SI 2009/586 regs 2, 7 with effect from 1 April 2009.

[3] In para (1)(*a*), (*b*) "£230,000" substituted for "£225,000", in para (2) "£191,500" substituted for "£187,500" by the VAT (Amendment) (No 3) Regulations, SI 2010/2940 regs 2, 5 with effect from 4 January 2011.

55N [Notification

[(1) Where—

(*a*) at the first day of the prescribed accounting period current at any anniversary of his start date,

(*b*) the appropriate percentage to be applied by a flat-rate trader in accordance with regulation 55H(2)(*a*) for the prescribed accounting period just beginning differs from that applicable to his relevant turnover at the end of the previous prescribed accounting period,

he must notify the Commissioners of that fact within 30 days of the first day of the prescribed accounting period current at the anniversary of his start date.][2]

[(2) Where a flat-rate trader begins to carry on a new business activity or ceases to carry on an existing business activity, he must notify the Commissioners of—

(*a*) that fact,

(*b*) the date that is the relevant date described by regulation 55A(3)(*c*) or (*d*) (as the case may be), and

(*c*) the appropriate percentage to be applied to the period immediately before that relevant date and immediately after it,

within 30 days of that relevant date.][2]

(3) Where any of sub-paragraphs (*a*) to (*g*) of regulation 55M(1) apply, the flat-rate trader shall notify the Commissioners of that fact within 30 days.

(4) Any notification required by this regulation shall be given in writing.][1]

Amendments—[1] This Part inserted by the VAT (Amendment) (No 2) Regulations, SI 2002/1142 regs 1, 7 with effect from 25 April 2002.

[2] Paras (1), (2) substituted by the VAT (Amendment) (No 6) Regulations, SI 2003/3220 regs 1(1)(*b*), 2, 18(4) with effect from 1 January 2004.

55P [Termination by the Commissioners

The Commissioners may terminate the authorisation of a flat-rate trader at any time if—

(*a*) they consider it necessary to do so for the protection of the revenue, or

VAT SIs

(*b*) a false statement was made by, or on behalf of, him in relation to his application for authorisation.][1]

Amendments—[1] This Part inserted by the VAT (Amendment) (No 2) Regulations, SI 2002/1142 regs 1, 7 with effect from 25 April 2002.

55Q [Date of withdrawal from the scheme

(1) The date on which a flat-rate trader ceases to be authorised to account for VAT in accordance with the scheme shall be—

(*a*) where regulation 55M(1)(*a*) applies—

(i) in the case of a person who is authorised in accordance with regulation 50(1) (annual accounting scheme), the end of the prescribed accounting period in which the relevant anniversary occurred, or the end of the month next following, whichever is the earlier, or

(ii) in all other cases, the end of the prescribed accounting period in which the relevant anniversary occurred,

(*b*) where regulation 55M(1)(*b*) applies, the beginning of the period of 30 days in question,

(*c*) where regulation 55M(1)(*c*), (*d*), or (*f*) applies, the date the event occurred,

(*d*) where regulation 55M(1)(*e*) applies, the beginning of the prescribed accounting period for which he makes the election described by that provision,

(*e*) where regulation 55M(1)(*g*) applies, the date on which the Commissioners are notified in writing of his decision to cease using the scheme, or such earlier or later date as may be agreed between them and him, and

(*f*) where regulation 55M(1)(*h*) applies, the date of issue of a notice of termination by the Commissioners or such earlier or later date as may be directed in the notification.

(2) The date with effect from which a person ceases to be so authorised shall be known as his end date.][1]

Amendments—[1] This Part inserted by the VAT (Amendment) (No 2) Regulations, SI 2002/1142 regs 1, 7 with effect from 25 April 2002.

55R [Self-supply on withdrawal from scheme

(1) This regulation applies where—

(*a*) a person continues to be a taxable person after his end date,

(*b*) for any prescribed accounting period for which he was a flat-rate trader, he was entitled to, and claimed, credit for input tax in respect of any capital expenditure goods, and

(*c*) he did not, whilst he was a flat-rate trader, make a supply of those goods.

(2) Where this regulation applies, those goods shall be treated for the purposes of the Act as being, on the day after his end date, both supplied to him for the purpose of his business and supplied by him in the course or furtherance of his business.

(3) The value of a supply of goods treated under paragraph (2) above as made to or by a person shall be determined as though it were a supply falling within paragraph 6(1) of Schedule 6 to the Act.][1]

Amendments—[1] This Part inserted by the VAT (Amendment) (No 2) Regulations, SI 2002/1142 regs 1, 7 with effect from 25 April 2002.

55S [Adjustments in respect of stock on hand at withdrawal from scheme

(1) This regulation applies where—

(*a*) a person continues to be a taxable person after his end date,

(*b*) at his end date, he has stock on hand in respect of which he is not entitled to credit for input tax, and

(*c*) the value of the stock on hand referred to in sub-paragraph (*b*) above exceeds the value of his stock on hand in respect of which he was entitled to credit for input tax, at his start date.

(2) Where this regulation applies, the taxable person, for the prescribed accounting period following that in which his end date falls, is entitled to credit for input tax in respect of his stock on hand in such amount as may be determined in accordance with a notice published by the Commissioners.][1]

Amendments—[1] This Part inserted by the VAT (Amendment) (No 2) Regulations, SI 2002/1142 regs 1, 7 with effect from 25 April 2002.

55T [Amendment by Notice

The Commissioners may vary the terms of any method prescribed by them for the purposes of regulations 55G or 55S by publishing a fresh notice or publishing a notice that amends an existing notice.][1]

Amendments—[1] This Part inserted by the VAT (Amendment) (No 2) Regulations, SI 2002/1142 regs 1, 7 with effect from 25 April 2002.

55U [Reverse charges

Section 8 of the Act (reverse charge on supplies from abroad) shall not apply to any relevant supply or relevant purchase of a flat-rate trader.][1]

Amendments—[1] This Part inserted by the VAT (Amendment) (No 2) Regulations, SI 2002/1142 regs 1, 7 with effect from 25 April 2002.

55V [Bad Debt Relief

(1) This regulation applies where—

(*a*) a person has made a relevant supply,

(*b*) he has used the cash turnover method to determine the value of his relevant turnover for the prescribed accounting period in which the relevant supply was made,

(*c*) he has not accounted for and paid VAT on the supply,

(*d*) the whole or any part of the consideration for the supply has been written off in his accounts as a bad debt, and

(*e*) a period of 6 months (beginning with the date of the supply) has elapsed.

(2) Where this regulation applies—

(*a*) section 36 of the Act (bad debts) and any regulations made thereunder shall apply as if the conditions set out in subsection (1) of that section are satisfied, and

(*b*) the amount of refund of VAT to which the person is entitled under that section shall be the VAT chargeable on the relevant supply described in paragraph (1) above less the flat-rate amount.

(3) In paragraph (2)(*b*) above, the flat-rate amount is—

$$A \times B$$

where—

A is the appropriate percentage applicable for the prescribed accounting period, or part thereof, in which the relevant supply was made, and

B is the value of the relevant supply together with the VAT chargeable thereon.][1]

Amendments—[1] This Part inserted by the VAT (Amendment) (No 2) Regulations, SI 2002/1142 regs 1, 7 with effect from 25 April 2002.

PART VIII

CASH ACCOUNTING

56 Interpretation of Part VIII

In this Part—

"money" means banknotes or coins;

"notice" means any notice published pursuant to this Part.

Former regulations—VAT (Cash Accounting) Regulations, SI 1987/1427 reg 2; VAT (Cash Accounting) (Amendment) Regulations, SI 1993/762 reg 3.

57 Cash accounting scheme

A taxable person may, subject to this Part and to such conditions as are described in a notice published by the Commissioners, account for VAT in accordance with a scheme (hereinafter referred to in this Part as "the scheme") by which the operative dates for VAT accounting purposes shall be—

(*a*) for output tax, the day on which payment or other consideration is received or the date of any cheque, if later; and

(*b*) for input tax, the date on which payment is made or other consideration is given, or the date of any cheque, if later.

Former regulations—VAT (Cash Accounting) Regulations, SI 1987/1427 reg 3; VAT (Cash Accounting) (Amendment) Regulations, SI 1993/762 reg 4.

[57A—(1) A person shall not account for VAT in accordance with the scheme in respect of any relevant supplies or relevant purchases of his.

(2) In this regulation, "relevant supplies" and "relevant purchases" have the same meanings as in Part VIIA (flat-rate scheme for small businesses).][1]

Amendments—[1] Regulation inserted by the VAT (Amendment) (No 2) Regulations, SI 2002/1142 regs 1, 8 with effect from 25 April 2002.

[58 Admission to the scheme

(1) Without prejudice to paragraph (4) below, a taxable person shall be eligible to begin to operate the scheme from the beginning of any prescribed accounting period if—

(*a*) he has reasonable grounds for believing that the value of taxable supplies to be made by him in the period of one year then beginning will not exceed [£1,350,000][2],

(*b*) he has made all returns which he is required to make, and has—

(i) paid to the Commissioners all such sums shown as due on those returns and on any assessments made either under section 76 of, or Schedule 11 to, the Act, or

(ii) agreed an arrangement with the Commissioners for any outstanding amount of such sums as are referred to in sub-paragraph (i) above to be paid in instalments over a specific period, and

(*c*) he has not in the period of one year preceding that time—

(i) been convicted of any offence in connection with VAT,

(ii) made any payment to compound proceedings in respect of VAT under section 152 of the Customs and Excise Management Act 1979(*c*),

(iii) been assessed to a penalty under section 60 of the Act, or

(iv) by virtue of regulation 64(1), ceased to be entitled to continue to operate the scheme.

(2) The scheme shall not apply to—

(*a*) lease purchase agreements;

(*b*) hire purchase agreements;

(*c*) conditional sale agreements;

(*d*) credit sale agreements;

(*e*) supplies where a VAT invoice is issued and full payment of the amount shown on the invoice is not due for a period in excess of 6 months from the date of the issue of the invoice; . . .[3]

(*f*) supplies of goods or services in respect of which a VAT invoice is issued in advance of the delivery or making available of the goods or the performance of the services as the case may be[; or

(*g*) supplies of goods [or services][4] in respect of which it is for the recipient, on the supplier's behalf, to account for and pay the VAT.][3].

(3) Sub-paragraph (2)(*f*) above shall not apply where goods have been delivered or made available in part or where services have been performed in part and the VAT invoice in question relates solely to that part of the goods which have been delivered or made available or that part of the services which have been performed.

(4) A person shall not be entitled to begin to operate the scheme if the Commissioners consider it is necessary for the protection of the revenue that he shall not be so entitled.][1]

Amendments—[1] This regulation substituted by the VAT (Amendment) (No 3) Regulations, SI 1997/1614 reg 3 with effect from 3 July 1997.

[2] Figure in sub-para (1)(*a*) substituted by the VAT (Amendment) (No 2) Regulations, SI 2007/768 regs 2, 3 with effect from 1 April 2007.

[3] Words in sub-para (2)(*f*) revoked, and sub-para (2)(*g*) and preceding word "or" inserted, by the VAT (Amendment) (No 3) Regulations, SI 2007/1418 regs 2, 6 with effect from 1 June 2007.

[4] Words in para (2)(*g*) inserted by the VAT (Amendment) (No 2) Regulations, SI 2010/2240 regs 2, 3(3) with effect from 1 November 2010.

59 Without prejudice to the right of a person to withdraw from the scheme, the Commissioners may vary the terms of the scheme by publishing a fresh notice [or publishing a notice which amends an existing notice][1].

Former regulation—VAT (Cash Accounting) Regulations, SI 1987/1427 reg 5.
Amendments—[1] Words inserted by the VAT (Amendment) (No 3) Regulations, SI 1997/1614 reg 3 with effect from 3 July 1997.

[60—(1) Without prejudice to regulation 64 below, a person shall withdraw from the scheme immediately at the end of a prescribed accounting period of his if the value of taxable supplies made by him in the period of one year ending at the end of the prescribed accounting period in question has exceeded [£1,600,000][2].

(2) Subject to regulations 61 to 63 below a person may withdraw from the scheme at the end of any prescribed accounting period.

(3) The requirements in paragraph (1) above shall not apply where the Commissioners allow or direct otherwise.][1]

Amendments—[1] This regulation substituted by the VAT (Amendment) (No 3) Regulations, SI 1997/1614 reg 5 with effect from 3 July 1997.

[2] Figure in sub-s (1) substituted by the VAT (Amendment) (No 2) Regulations, SI 2007/768 regs 2, 4 with effect from 1 April 2007.

[61—(1) Subject to paragraph (2), a person who ceases to operate the scheme, either of his own volition or because the value of taxable supplies made by him exceeds the level provided for in regulation 60(1), must—

(*a*) settle up, or

(*b*) apply transitional arrangements.

(2) Where the value of taxable supplies made by a person in the period of three months ending at the end of the prescribed accounting period in which he ceased to operate the scheme has exceeded [£1,350,000][2], he may not apply transitional arrangements.

(3) In paragraph (1)(*a*), "settle up" means account for and pay on a return made for the prescribed accounting period in which he ceased to operate the scheme—

(*a*) all VAT that he would have been required to pay to the Commissioners during the time when he operated the scheme, if he had not then been operating the scheme, minus

(*b*) all VAT accounted for and paid to the Commissioners in accordance with the scheme, subject to any adjustment for credit for input tax.

(4) In paragraph (1)(*b*), "apply transitional arrangements" means continue to operate the scheme in respect of his scheme supplies for 6 months after the end of the prescribed accounting period in which he ceased to operate the scheme.

(5) In paragraph (4), "scheme supplies" means supplies made and received while he operated the scheme that are not excluded from the scheme by virtue of regulation 57A or 58 or conditions described in a notice.

(6) Where a person chooses to apply transitional arrangements, he shall account for and pay on a return made for the first prescribed accounting period that ends 6 months or more after the end of the prescribed accounting period in which he ceased to operate the scheme—

(*a*) all VAT that he would have been required to pay to the Commissioners during the time when he operated the scheme, if he had not then been operating the scheme, minus

(*b*) all VAT accounted for and paid to the Commissioners in accordance with the scheme (including any VAT accounted for and paid because he applied transitional arrangements), subject to any adjustment for credit for input tax.][1]

Amendments—[1] This regulation substituted by the VAT (Amendment) Regulations, SI 2004/767 regs 3, 9 with effect from 1 April 2004.

[2] Figure in sub-s (2) substituted by the VAT (Amendment) (No 2) Regulations, SI 2007/768 regs 2, 5 with effect from 1 April 2007.

[62 Where a person operating the scheme becomes insolvent he shall within 2 months of the date of insolvency account for VAT due on all supplies made and received up to the date of insolvency which has not otherwise been accounted for, subject to any credit for input tax.][1]

Amendments—[1] This regulation substituted by the VAT (Amendment) (No 3) Regulations, SI 1997/1614 reg 7 with effect from 3 July 1997.

63—[(1) Where a person operating the scheme ceases business or ceases to be registered he shall within 2 months or such longer period as the Commissioners may allow, make a return accounting for, and pay, VAT due on all supplies made and received up to the date of cessation which has not otherwise been accounted for, subject to any adjustment for credit for input tax.

(2) Where a business or part of a business carried on by a person operating the scheme is transferred as a going concern and regulation 6(1) does not apply, the transferor shall within 2 months or such longer period as the Commissioners may allow, make a return accounting for, and pay, VAT due on all supplies made and received which has not otherwise been accounted for, subject to credit for input tax.][1]

(3) Where a business carried on by a person operating the scheme is transferred in circumstances where regulation [6(1)][2] applies, the transferee shall continue to account for and pay VAT as if he were a person operating the scheme on supplies made and received by the transferor prior to the date of transfer.

Amendments—[1] Paras (1) and (2) substituted by the VAT (Amendment) (No 3) Regulations, SI 1997/1614 reg 8 with effect from 3 July 1997.

[2] Number substituted for "6(2)" by the VAT (Amendment) (No 3) Regulations, SI 1997/1614 reg 8 with effect from 3 July 1997.

[64 Withdrawal from the scheme

(1) A person shall not be entitled to continue to operate the scheme where—

(*a*) he has, while operating the scheme, been convicted of an offence in connection with VAT or has made a payment to compound such proceedings under section 152 of the Customs and Excise Management Act 1979,

(*b*) he has while operating the scheme been assessed to a penalty under section 60 of the Act,

(*c*) he has failed to leave the scheme as required by regulation 60(1) above, or

(*d*) the Commissioners consider it necessary for the protection of the revenue that he shall not be so entitled.

(2) A person who, by virtue of paragraph (1) above, ceases to be entitled to continue to operate the scheme shall account for and pay on a return made for the prescribed accounting period in which he ceased to be so entitled—

(*a*) all VAT which he would have been required to pay to the Commissioners during the time when he operated the scheme, if he had not then been operating the scheme, less

(*b*) all VAT accounted for and paid to the Commissioners in accordance with the scheme, subject to any adjustment for credit for input tax.][1]

Amendments—[1] This regulation substituted by the VAT (Amendment) (No 3) Regulations, SI 1997/1614 reg 9 with effect from 3 July 1997.

64A [Bad debt relief

Where a person accounts for and pays VAT in relation to a supply in accordance with regulation 61(3) or (6) or 64(2), he shall be treated for the purposes of section 36(1)(*a*) of the Act as having accounted for and paid VAT on the supply in the prescribed accounting period in which he ceased to operate the scheme.][1]

Amendments—[1] This regulation inserted by the VAT (Amendment) Regulations, SI 2004/767 regs 3, 10 with effect from 1 April 2004.

VAT SIs

65 Accounting

(1) Except in the circumstances set out in regulations 61 to 63, VAT shall be accounted for and paid to the Commissioners by the due date prescribed for the accounting period in which payment or other consideration for the supply is received.

(2) Input tax may be credited either in the prescribed accounting period in which payment or consideration for a supply is given, or in such later period as may be agreed with the Commissioners.

(3) A person operating the scheme shall obtain and keep for a period of 6 years, or such lesser period as the Commissioners may allow, a receipted and dated VAT invoice from any taxable person to whom he has made a payment in money in respect of a taxable supply, and in such circumstances a taxable person must on request provide such a receipted and dated VAT invoice.

(4) A person operating the scheme shall keep for a period of 6 years, or such lesser period as the Commissioners may allow, a copy of any receipt which he gives under paragraph (3) above.

Former regulations—VAT (Cash Accounting) Regulations, SI 1987/1427 reg 12; VAT (Cash Accounting) (Amendment) Regulations, SI 1993/762 reg 8.

PART IX
SUPPLIES BY RETAILERS

66 Interpretation of Part IX

In this Part—

["flat-rate trader" has the meaning given in regulation 55A;][1]

"notice" means any notice or leaflet published by the Commissioners pursuant to this Part;

"scheme" means a method as referred to in regulation 67.

Former regulations—VAT (Supplies by Retailers) Regulations, SI 1972/1148 reg 1(2), VAT (Supplies by Retailers) (Amendment) Regulations, SI 1979/224.

Amendments—[1] Definition of "flat-rate trader" inserted by the VAT (Amendment) (No 2) Regulations, SI 2002/1142 regs 1, 9(*a*) with effect from 25 April 2002.

67 Retail schemes

(1) The Commissioners may permit the value which is to be taken as the value, in any prescribed accounting period or part thereof, of supplies by a retailer which are taxable at other than the zero rate to be determined by a method agreed with that retailer or by any method described in a notice published by the Commissioners for that purpose; and they may publish any notice accordingly.

(2) The Commissioners may vary the terms of any method by—

(*a*) publishing a fresh notice,

(*b*) publishing a notice which amends an existing notice, or

(*c*) adapting any method by agreement with any retailer.

Former regulations—VAT (Supplies by Retailers) Regulations, SI 1972/1148 reg 2; VAT (Supplies by Retailers) (Amendment) Regulations, SI 1979/224.

Simon's Tax Cases—*C&E Comrs v Kingfisher plc* [1994] STC 63*; *C&E Comrs v Co-operative Wholesale Society Ltd* [1995] STC 983*.

68 The Commissioners may refuse to permit the value of taxable supplies to be determined in accordance with a scheme if it appears to them—

(*a*) that the use of any particular scheme does not produce a fair and reasonable valuation during any period,

(*b*) that it is necessary to do so for the protection of the revenue, or

(*c*) that the retailer could reasonably be expected to account for VAT in accordance with regulations made under paragraph 2(1) of Schedule 11 to the Act.

Former regulations—VAT (Supplies by Retailers) Regulations, SI 1972/1148 reg 3; VAT (Supplies by Retailers) (Amendment) Regulations, SI 1987/1712 reg 2.

69 No retailer may at any time use more than one scheme except as provided for in any notice or as the Commissioners may otherwise allow.

Former regulation—VAT (Supplies by Retailers) Regulations, SI 1972/1148 reg 4.

[69A No retailer may use a scheme at any time for which he is a flat-rate trader.][1]

Amendments—[1] Regulation inserted by the VAT (Amendment) (No 2) Regulations, SI 2002/1142 regs 1, 9(*b*) with effect from 25 April 2002.

70 Notification of use of a scheme

. . .

Amendments—This regulation revoked by the VAT (Amendment) (No 4) Regulations, SI 1997/2437 with effect from 1 November 1997.

71[Changing schemes

(1)] [1] Save as the Commissioners may otherwise allow, a retailer who accounts for VAT on the basis of taxable supplies valued in accordance with any scheme shall, so long as he remains a taxable person, continue to do so for a period of not less than one year from the adoption of that scheme by him, and any change by a retailer from one scheme to another shall be made at the end of any complete year reckoned from the beginning of the prescribed accounting period in which he first adopted the scheme.

[(2) Paragraph (1) shall not apply where a retailer ceases to operate a scheme solely because he becomes a flat-rate trader.][1]

Former regulation—VAT (Supplies by Retailers) Regulations, SI 1972/1148 reg 6.

Amendments—[1] Para (1) numbered as such, and para (2) added, by the VAT (Amendment) (No 2) Regulations, SI 2002/1142 regs 1, 9(*c*) with effect from 25 April 2002.

72 Ceasing to use a scheme

(1) A retailer shall notify the Commissioners before ceasing to account for VAT on the basis of taxable supplies valued in accordance with these regulations.

(2) A retailer may be required to pay VAT on such proportion as the Commissioners may consider fair and reasonable of any sums due to him at the end of the prescribed accounting period in which he last used a scheme.

Former regulation—VAT (Supplies by Retailers) Regulations, SI 1972/1148 reg 7.

73 Supplies under Schedule 8, Group 1

. . .

Amendments—This regulation revoked by the VAT (Amendment) (No 4) Regulations, SI 1997/2437 with effect from 1 November 1997.

74 Supplies under Schedule 8, Group 12

. . .

Amendments—This regulation revoked by the VAT (Amendment) (No 4) Regulations, SI 1997/2437 with effect from 1 November 1997.

75 Change in VAT

Where pursuant to any enactment there is a change in the VAT charged on any supply, including a change to or from no VAT being charged on such supply, a retailer using any scheme shall take such steps relating to that scheme as are directed in any notice applicable to him or as may be agreed between him and the Commissioners.

Former regulations—VAT (Supplies by Retailers) Regulations, SI 1972/1148 reg 9; VAT (Supplies by Retailers) (Amendment) Regulations, SI 1975/274.

PART X
TRADING STAMPS

76 Interpretation of Part X

. . .

Amendments—This Part (regs 76–80) revoked by the VAT (Trading Stamps) Regulations, SI 1995/3043 reg 2, with effect from 1 June 1996.

77–80 Trading stamp scheme

. . .

Amendments—This Part (regs 76–80) revoked by the VAT (Trading Stamps) Regulations, SI 1995/3043 reg 2, with effect from 1 June 1996.

PART XI
TIME OF SUPPLY AND TIME OF ACQUISITION

81 Goods for private use and free supplies of services

(1) Where the services referred to in paragraph 5(4) of Schedule 4 to the Act are supplied for any period, they shall be treated as being supplied on the last day of the supplier's prescribed accounting period, or of each such accounting period, in which the goods are made available or used.

(2) Where services specified in an order made by the Treasury under section 5(4) of the Act are supplied for any period, they shall be treated as being supplied on the last day of the supplier's prescribed accounting period, or of each such accounting period, in which the services are performed.

Former regulation—VAT (General) Regulations, SI 1985/886 reg 17.

[82 Services from outside the United Kingdom

(1) This paragraph applies to services which are treated as being made by a person under section 8(1) of the Act which are not services to which paragraph (3) below applies.

(2) Subject to paragraphs (5) and (7) below, the services to which paragraph (1) above applies shall be treated as being made when they are performed.

(3) This paragraph applies to services which are treated as being made by a person under section 8(1) of the Act and which are supplied for a period for a consideration the whole or part of which is determined or payable periodically or from time to time.

(4) Subject to paragraphs (5), (6) and (7) below, services to which paragraph (3) above applies shall be treated as separately and successively made at the end of the periods in respect of which payments are made or invoices issued and to the extent covered by the relevant payment or invoice.

(5) Where—

(*a*) in the case of a supply of services to which paragraph (1) above applies, a payment is made in respect of the supply before the time applicable under paragraph (2) above, or

(*b*) in the case of services to which paragraph (3) above applies, either—

(i) a payment is made at a time that is earlier than the end of the period to which it relates, or

(ii) a payment is made which is not made in respect of any identified period, or

(*c*) a payment is made in respect of services—

(i) which are performed on or before 31stDecember 2009, or

(ii) in respect of which a period as described in paragraph (4) above has ended on or before that date, or

(iii) which the recipient has received the benefit of on or before that date,

the services shall be treated as being made at the time the payment is made.

(6) Where the supply of services to which paragraph (3) above applies—

(*a*) commences before 1st January and continues after 31st December of any year, and

(*b*) during that year no invoice is issued that has effect for the purposes of paragraph (4) above, and

(*c*) no payment is made in respect of that supply,

the services supplied during that year shall be treated as being supplied on the 31st December of that year to the extent that the recipient has received the benefit of them.

(7) Services for which the consideration is not in money and which have been supplied during a period which—

(*a*) commences on the day following the last day of the last complete prescribed accounting period in 2009 which is applicable to the recipient of the services, and

(*b*) ends on 31st December 2009,

shall be treated as being supplied on 31st December 2009.][1]

Amendments—[1] Reg 82 substituted by the VAT (Amendment) (No 5) Regs, SI 2009/3241, regs 2, 10 with effect from 1 January 2010.

82A [Goods supplied by persons outside the United Kingdom

Goods which are treated as supplied by a person under section 9A of the Act shall be treated as being supplied when the goods are paid for or, if the consideration is not in money, on the last day of the prescribed accounting period in which the goods are removed or made available.][1]

Amendments—[1] Regulation 82A inserted by the VAT (Amendment) (No 4) Regulations, SI 2004/3140 reg 4 with effect from 1 January 2005 in relation to supplies made on or after that date: SI 2004/3140 reg 2(1).

83 Time of acquisition

Where the time that goods are acquired from another member State falls to be determined in accordance with section 12(1)(*b*) of the Act by reference to the day of the issue, in respect of the transaction in pursuance of which the goods are acquired, of an invoice of such description as the Commissioners may by regulations prescribe, the invoice shall be one which is issued by the supplier [or the customer and which, in either case, is issued under the provisions of the law of the member State where the goods were supplied, corresponding in relation to that member State to the provisions of regulations 13, 13A and 14.][1]

Former regulations—VAT (General) Regulations, SI 1985/886 reg 18A; VAT (General) (Amendment) Regulations, SI 1992/3102 reg 12.

Cross references—See VAT Regulations, SI 1995/2518 reg 18(4) (invoices for certain supplies by intermediate suppliers: treatment as invoices for the purposes of this regulation);

VAT Regulations, SI 1995/2518 reg 19(4) (invoices for certain supplies by persons belonging in other member states: treatment as invoices for the purposes of this regulation).

Amendments—[1] Words substituted by the VAT (Amendment) (No 6) Regulations, SI 2003/3220 regs 1(1)(*b*), 2, 12 with effect from 1 January 2004.

84 Supplies of land—special cases

(1) Where by or under any enactment an interest in, or right over, land is compulsorily purchased and, at the time determined in accordance with section 6(2) or (3) of the Act, the person (the grantor) from whom it is purchased does not know the amount of payment that he is to receive in respect of the purchase then goods or, as the case may require, services shall be treated as supplied each time the grantor receives any payment for the purchase.

(2) [[Subject to paragraphs (3) to (5)][2] below,][1] where a person (the grantor) grants or assigns the fee simple in any land, and at the time of the grant or assignment, the total consideration for it is not determinable, then goods shall be treated as separately and successively supplied at the following times—

(*a*) the time determined in accordance with section 6(2), (4), (5), (6) . . .[4] or (10) of the Act, as the case may require, and

(*b*) the earlier of the following times—

(i) each time that any part of the consideration which was not determinable at the time mentioned in sub-paragraph (*a*) above is received by the grantor, or

(ii) each time that the grantor issues a VAT invoice in respect of such a part.

[(3) Paragraph (2) above shall not apply in relation to a grant or assignment falling within item 1(*a*) of Group 1 of Schedule 9 to the Act where any of the persons specified in paragraph (4) below intend or expect to occupy the land on a date before a date ten years after completion of the building or civil engineering work on the land, without being in occupation of it [wholly, or substantially wholly,][5] for eligible purposes.][3]

[(4) The persons referred to in paragraph (3) above are—

(*a*) the grantor;

(*b*) any person who, with the intention or in the expectation that occupation of the land on a date before a date ten years after completion of the building or civil engineering work would not be [wholly, or substantially wholly,][5] for eligible purposes—

(i) provides finance for the grantor's development of the land, or

(ii) has entered into any agreement arrangement or understanding (whether or not legally enforceable) to provide finance for the grantor's development of the land;

(*c*) any person who is connected with any person of a description within sub-paragraph (*a*) or (*b*) above.][3]

[(5) For the purposes of this regulation—

(*a*) Note (2) to Group 1 of Schedule 9 to the Act shall apply in determining when a building or civil engineering work is completed;

[(*b*) paragraph 16 of Schedule 10 to the Act shall have effect for determining the meaning of "eligible purposes" and "occupation";

(*ba*) whether a person's occupation is "wholly, or substantially wholly," for eligible purposes shall be determined in the same way as it is for the purposes of paragraph 15 of that Schedule;][5]

(*c*) "the grantor's development of the land" means any acquisition by the grantor of an interest in the land, building or civil engineering work and includes the construction of the building or civil engineering work;

(*d*) "providing finance" has the same meaning as in [paragraph 14(3) of Schedule 10][5] to the Act, subject to any appropriate modifications, but does not include paying the consideration for the grantor's grant or assignment within paragraph (3) above;

(*e*) any question whether one person is connected with another shall be determined in accordance with section 839 [of the Taxes Act; but this is subject to sub-paragraph (*f*);

(*f*) a company is not connected with another company only because both are under the control of—

(i) the Crown,

(ii) a Minister of the Crown,

(iii) a government department, or

(iv) a Northern Ireland department;

(*g*) "company" and "control" have the same meaning as in section 839 of the Taxes Act.][6]][3]

Former regulations—VAT (General) Regulations, SI 1985/886 reg 18B; VAT (General) (Amendment) Regulations, SI 1992/3102 reg 12.

Amendments—[1] Words in para (2) inserted, and paras (3)–(9) inserted, by the VAT (Amendment) (No 3) Regulations, SI 2002/2918 with effect from 28 November 2002 in relation to grants or assignments made after 27 November 2002.

[2] Words in para (2) substituted by the VAT (Amendment) (No 2) Regulations, SI 2003/1069 regs 1(3), 2, 8 in relation to grants or assignments made after 9 April 2003.

[3] Paras (3)–(5) substituted for paras (3)–(9) by the VAT (Amendment) (No 2) Regulations, SI 2003/1069 regs 1(3), 2, 9 in relation to grants or assignments made after 9 April 2003.

[4] Reference revoked by the VAT (Amendment) (No 6) Regulations, SI 2003/3220 regs 1(1)(*b*), 2, 13 with effect from 1 January 2004.

[5] Words in paras (3), (4)(*b*) substituted, in para (5) sub-paras (*b*), (*ba*) substituted for previous sub-para (*b*), and words in para (5)(*d*) substituted, by the Value Added Tax (Buildings and Land) Order, SI 2008/1146, art 6, Sch 1 paras 16, 17 with effect in relation to supplies made on or after 1 June 2008, subject to savings in Sch 2 of the Order.

[6] Words in para (5)(*e*) substituted for words "of the Income and Corporation Taxes Act 1988." by the Value Added Tax (Amendment) (No 3) Regulations, SI 2009/1967 regs 2, 3 with effect from 15 August 2009.

85 Leases treated as supplies of goods

(1) Subject to paragraph (2) below, where the grant of a tenancy or lease is a supply of goods by virtue of paragraph 4 of Schedule 4 to the Act, and the whole or part of the consideration for that grant is payable periodically or from time to time, goods shall be treated as separately and successively supplied at the earlier of the following times—

(*a*) each time that a part of the consideration is received by the supplier, or

(*b*) each time that the supplier issues a VAT invoice relating to the grant.

(2) Where in respect of the grant of a tenancy or lease such as is mentioned in paragraph (1) above the supplier, at or about the beginning of any period not exceeding one year, issues a VAT invoice containing, in addition to the particulars specified in regulation 14, the following particulars—

(*a*) the dates on which any parts of the consideration are to become due for payment in the period,

(*b*) the amount payable (excluding VAT) on each such date, and

(*c*) the rate of VAT in force at the time of the issue of the VAT invoice and the amount of VAT chargeable in accordance with that rate on each of such payments,

goods shall be treated as separately and successively supplied each time that a payment in respect of the tenancy or lease becomes due or is received by the supplier, whichever is the earlier.

(3) Where, on or before any of the dates that a payment is due as stated on an invoice issued as described in paragraph (2) above, there is a change in the VAT chargeable on supplies of the description to which the invoice relates, that invoice shall cease to be treated as a VAT invoice in respect of any such supplies for which payments are due after the change (and not received before the change).

Former regulations—VAT (General) Regulations, SI 1985/886 reg 19; VAT (General) (Amendment) Regulations, SI 1989/1132 reg 3.

Simon's Tax Cases—reg 85(1), *Royal & Sun Alliance Insurance Group plc v C&E Comrs* [2000] STC 933, [2003] STC 832.

86 Supplies of water, gas or any form of power, heat, refrigeration [or other cooling,]or ventilation

(1) Except in relation to a supply to which subsections (7) and (8) of section 6 of the Act apply, and subject to paragraphs (2) and (3) below, a supply of—

(*a*) water other than

(i) distilled water, deionised water and water of similar purity, and

(ii) water comprised in any of the excepted items set out in Group 1 of Schedule 8 to the Act, or

(*b*) coal gas, water gas, producer gases or similar gases, or

(*c*) petroleum gases, or other gaseous hydrocarbons, in a gaseous state, or

(*d*) any form of power, heat, refrigeration [or other cooling,][1] or ventilation,

shall be treated as taking place each time that a payment in respect of the supply is received by the supplier, or a VAT invoice relating to the supply is issued by the supplier, whichever is the earlier.

(2) Subject to paragraph (3) below, where the whole or part of the consideration for a supply such as is described in paragraph (1)(*a*), (*b*) or (*c*) above or of power in the form of electricity is determined or payable periodically or from time to time, goods shall be treated as separately and successively supplied at the earlier of the following times—

(*a*) each time that a part of the consideration is received by the supplier, or

(*b*) each time that the supplier issues a VAT invoice relating to the supply.

(3) Where separate and successive supplies as described in paragraph (2) above are made under an agreement which provides for successive payments, and the supplier at or about the beginning of any period not exceeding one year, issues a VAT invoice containing, in addition to the particulars specified in regulation 14, the following particulars—

(*a*) the dates on which payments under the agreement are to become due in the period,

(*b*) the amount payable (excluding VAT) on each such date, and

(*c*) the rate of VAT in force at the time of issue of the VAT invoice and the amount of VAT chargeable in accordance with that rate on each of such payments,

goods shall be treated as separately and successively supplied each time that payment in respect of the supply becomes due or is received by the supplier, whichever is the earlier.

(4) Where, on or before any of the dates that a payment is due as stated on an invoice issued as described in paragraph (3) above, there is a change in the VAT chargeable on supplies of the description to which the invoice relates, that invoice shall cease to be treated as a VAT invoice in respect of any such supplies for which payments are due after the change (and not received before the change).

(5) A supply mentioned in paragraph (1)(a), (*b*), (*c*) or (*d*) above to which subsections (7) and (8) of section 6 of the Act apply shall be treated as taking place on the day of the issue of a VAT invoice in respect of the supply.[2]

Former regulations—VAT (General) Regulations, SI 1985/886 reg 20; VAT (General) (Amendment) Regulations, SI 1989/1132 reg 4, SI 1992/3102 reg 13.

Amendments—[1] Words in heading and in para (1)(*d*) inserted by the VAT (Amendment) (No 4) Regulations, SI 2010/3022 regs 2, 3 with effect in relation to supplies made on or after 1 January 2011.

[2] Para (5) revoked by the VAT (Amendment) (No 3) Regulations, SI 2012/2951 reg 2(1), (7) with effect from 1 January 2013.

87 Acquisitions of water, gas or any form of power, heat, refrigeration [or other cooling] or ventilation

Where goods described in regulation 86(1)(*a*), (*b*), (*c*) or (*d*) are acquired from another member State and the whole or part of any consideration comprised in the transaction in pursuance of which the goods are acquired is payable periodically, or from time to time, goods shall be treated as separately and successively acquired on each occasion that [an invoice such as is described in regulation 83 is issued.][1], [2]

Former regulations—VAT (General) Regulations, SI 1985/886 reg 20A; VAT (General) (Amendment) Regulations, SI 1992/3102 reg 14.

Amendments—[1] Words substituted by the VAT (Amendment) (No 6) Regulations, SI 2003/3220 regs 1(1)(*b*), 2, 14 with effect from 1 January 2004.

[2] Regulation 87 revoked by the VAT (Amendment) (No 3) Regulations, SI 2012/2951 reg 2(1), (8) with effect from 1 January 2013.

Words in heading inserted by the VAT (Amendment) (No 4) Regulations, SI 2010/3022 regs 2, 4 with effect in relation to supplies made on or after 1 January 2011.

88 Supplier's goods in possession of buyer

(1) Except in relation to a supply mentioned in section 6(2)(*c*) of the Act, or to a supply to which subsections (7) and (8) of section 6 of the Act apply, where goods are supplied under an agreement whereby the supplier retains the property therein until the goods or part of them are appropriated under the agreement by the buyer and in circumstances where the whole or part of the consideration is determined at that time, a supply of any of the goods shall be treated as taking place at the earliest of the following dates—

(*a*) the date of appropriation by the buyer,

(*b*) the date when a VAT invoice is issued by the supplier, or

(*c*) the date when a payment is received by the supplier.

(2) If, within 14 days after appropriation of the goods or part of them by the buyer as mentioned in paragraph (1) above, the supplier issues a VAT invoice in respect of goods appropriated [or a self-billed invoice fulfilling the conditions in regulation 13(3A) is issued by the customer][1], the provisions of section 6(5) of the Act shall apply to that supply.

Former regulations—VAT (General) Regulations, SI 1985/886 reg 21(1), (2); VAT (General) (Amendment) Regulations, SI 1992/3102 reg 15.

Amendments—[1] Words inserted by the VAT (Amendment) (No 6) Regulations, SI 2003/3220 regs 1(1)(*b*), 2, 15 with effect from 1 January 2004.

89 Retention payments

Where any contract [other than one of a description falling within regulation 93 below][1] for the supply of goods (other than for a supply to which subsections (7) and (8) of section 6 of the Act apply) or for the supply of services provides for the retention of any part of the consideration by a person pending full and satisfactory performance of the contract, or any part of it, by the supplier, goods or services (as the case may require) shall be treated as separately and successively supplied at the following times—

(*a*) the time determined in accordance with section 6(2), (3), (4), (5), (6), . . . [2] (10) or (13) of the Act, as the case may require, and

(*b*) the earlier of the following times—

(i) the time that a payment in respect of any part of the consideration which has been retained, pursuant to the terms of the contract, is received by the supplier, or

(ii) the time that the supplier issues a VAT invoice relating to any such part.

Former regulations—VAT (General) Regulations, SI 1985/886 reg 22; VAT (General) (Amendment) Regulations, SI 1992/3102 reg 16.

Amendments—[1] Words inserted by the VAT (Amendment) (No 5) Regulations, SI 1997/2887 with effect from 1 January 1998.

[2] Reference revoked by the VAT (Amendment) (No 6) Regulations, SI 2003/3220 regs 1(1)(*b*), 2, 16 with effect from 1 January 2004.

90 Continuous supplies of services

(1) Subject to paragraph (2) below, where services[, except those to which regulation 93 applies,][2] are supplied for a period for a consideration the whole or part of which is determined or payable periodically or from time to time, they shall be treated as separately and successively supplied at the earlier of the following times—

(*a*) each time that a payment in respect of the supplies is received by the supplier, or

(*b*) each time that the supplier issues a VAT invoice relating to the supplies.

(2) Where separate and successive supplies of services as described in paragraph (1) above are made under an agreement which provides for successive payments, and the supplier at or about the beginning of any period not exceeding one year, issues a VAT invoice containing, in addition to the particulars specified in regulation 14, the following particulars—

(*a*) the dates on which payments under the agreement are to become due in the period,

(*b*) the amount payable (excluding VAT) on each such date, and (*c*) the rate of VAT in force at the time of issue of the VAT invoice and the amount of VAT chargeable in accordance with that rate on each of such payments,

services shall be treated as separately and successively supplied each time that a payment in respect of them becomes due or is received by the supplier, whichever is the earlier.

(3) Where, on or before any of the dates that a payment is due as stated on an invoice issued as described in paragraph (2) above, there is a change in the VAT chargeable on supplies of the description to which the invoice relates, that invoice shall cease to be treated as a VAT invoice in respect of any such supplies for which payments are due after the change (and not received before the change).

[(4) This regulation shall not apply to any relevant services—

(*a*) where the period to which a payment falling within paragraph (1), (2) or (3) above relates, ends before 1st July 1997; or

(*b*) which are treated as supplied on 1st July 1997 by virtue of regulation 90A below.][1]

[(5) In this regulation and in regulations 90A and 90B below, "relevant services" means services within the description contained in paragraph 7A of Schedule 5 to the Act (*c*) which are treated as supplied in the United Kingdom by virtue of [article 18][3] of the Value Added Tax (Place of Supply of Services) Order 1992.][1]

Former regulations—VAT (General) Regulations, SI 1985/886 reg 23; VAT (General) (Amendment) Regulations, SI 1989/1132 reg 5.

Simon's Tax Cases—*C&E Comrs v British Telecom plc* [1996] STC 818*.

Reg 90(1), *B J Rice & Associates v C&E Comrs* [1996] STC 581*; *Royal & Sun Alliance Insurance Group plc v C&E Comrs* [2000] STC 933, [2003] STC 832.

Reg 90(1)(*a*), *C&E Comrs v British Telecom plc* [1995] STC 239*.

Amendments—[1] Paras (4) and (5) inserted by the VAT (Amendment) (No 2) Regulations, SI 1997/1525 with effect from 1 July 1997.

[2] Words inserted by the VAT (Amendment) (No 5) Regulations, SI 1997/2887 with effect from 1 January 1998.

[3] Words amended by the VAT (Amendment) (No 2) Regulations, SI 1998/765 with effect from 18 March 1998.

[90A Where—

(*a*) relevant services are supplied for a period for a consideration the whole or part of which is determined or payable periodically or from time to time;

(*b*) the period covered by the payment referred to in sub-paragraph (*c*) below ends on or after 1st July 1997; and

(*c*) a payment in respect of the services was made before 1st July 1997,

the services shall be treated as supplied on 1st July 1997.][1]

Amendments—[1] This regulation inserted by the VAT (Amendment) (No 2) Regulations, SI 1997/1525 with effect from 1 July 1997.

[90B Where relevant services are treated as supplied on or after 1st July 1997 by virtue of regulation 90 or 90A above, the supply shall be treated as taking place only to the extent covered by the lower of—

(*a*) the payment; and

(*b*) so much of the payment as is properly attributable to such part of the period covered by the payment as falls after 30th June 1997.][1]

Amendments—[1] This regulation inserted by the VAT (Amendment) (No 2) Regulations, SI 1997/1525 with effect from 1 July 1997.

91 Royalties and similar payments

Where the whole amount of the consideration for a supply of services was not ascertainable at the time when the services were performed and subsequently the use of the benefit of those services by a person other than the supplier gives rise to any payment of consideration for that supply which is—

(*a*) in whole or in part determined or payable periodically or from time to time or at the end of any period,

(*b*) additional to the amount, if any, already payable for the supply, and

(*c*) not a payment to which regulation 90 applies,

a further supply shall be treated as taking place each time that a payment in respect of the use of the benefit of those services is received by the supplier or a VAT invoice is issued by the supplier, whichever is the earlier.

Former regulation—VAT (General) Regulations, SI 1985/886 reg 24.

92 Supplies of services by barristers and advocates

Services supplied by a barrister, or in Scotland, by an advocate, acting in that capacity, shall be treated as taking place at whichever is the earliest of the following times—

(*a*) when the fee in respect of those services is received by the barrister or advocate,

(*b*) when the barrister or advocate issues a VAT invoice in respect of them, or

(*c*) the day when the barrister or advocate ceases to practise as such.

Former regulation—VAT (General) Regulations, SI 1985/886 reg 25.

[93 Supplies in the construction industry

(1) Where services, or services together with goods, are supplied in the course of the construction, alteration, demolition, repair or maintenance of a building or any civil engineering work under a contract which provides for payment for such supplies to be made periodically or from time to time, those services or goods and services shall be treated as separately and successively supplied at the earliest of the following times—

(*a*) each time that a payment is received by the supplier,

(*b*) each time that the supplier issues a VAT invoice, or

(*c*) where the services are services to which paragraph (2) below applies, to the extent that they have not already been treated as supplied by virtue of sub-paragraphs (*a*) and (*b*) above—

(i) if the services were performed on or after 9th December 1997 and before 9th June 1999, the day which falls eighteen months after the date on which those services were performed, or

(ii) if the services are performed on or after 9th June 1999, the day on which the services are performed.

(2) This paragraph applies if, at the time the services were, or as the case may require, are performed—

(*a*) it was, or as the case may require, is the intention or expectation of—

(i) the supplier, or

(ii) a person responsible for financing the supplier's cost of supplying the services or services together with goods,

that relevant land would, or as the case may require, will become (whether immediately or eventually) exempt land or, as the case may be, continue (for a period at least) to be such land, or

(*b*) the supplier had, or as the case may require, has received (and used in making his supply) any supply of services or of services together with goods the time of supply of which—

(i) was, or

(ii) but for the issue by the supplier of those services or services together with goods of a VAT invoice (other than one which has been paid in full), would have been,

determined by virtue of paragraph (1)(c) above.

(3) For the purposes of this regulation "relevant land" is land on which the building or civil engineering work to which the construction services relate is, or as the case may be, was situated.

(4) In this regulation references to a person's being responsible for financing the supplier's cost of supplying the services or goods and services are references to his being a person who, with the intention or in the expectation that relevant land will become, or continue (for a period at least) to be, exempt land—

(*a*) has provided finance for the supplier's cost of supplying the services or services together with goods, or

(*b*) has entered into any agreement, arrangement or understanding (whether or not legally enforceable) to provide finance for the supplier's cost of supplying the services or services together with goods.

(5) In this regulation references to providing finance for the supplier's cost of supplying services or services together with goods are references to doing any one or more of the following, that is to say—

(*a*) directly or indirectly providing funds for meeting the whole or any part of the supplier's cost of supplying the services or services together with goods,

(*b*) directly or indirectly procuring the provision of such funds by another,

(*c*) directly or indirectly providing funds for discharging, in whole or in part any liability that has been or may be incurred by any person for or in connection with the raising of funds to meet the supplier's cost of supplying the services or services together with goods,

(*d*) directly or indirectly procuring that any such liability is or will be discharged, in whole or in part, by another.

(6) The references in paragraph (5) above to the provision of funds for a purpose referred to in that paragraph include references to—

(*a*) the making of a loan of funds that are or are to be used for that purpose,

(*b*) the provision of any guarantee or other security in relation to such a loan,

(*c*) the provision of any of the consideration for the issue of any shares or other securities issued wholly or partly for raising those funds, or

(*d*) any other transfer of assets or value as a consequence of which any of those funds are made available for that purpose,

but do not include references to funds made available to the supplier by paying to him the whole or any part of the consideration payable for the supply of the services or services together with goods.

(7) In this regulation references to the supplier's cost of supplying the services or services together with goods are to—

(*a*) amounts payable by the supplier for supplies to him of services or of goods used or to be used by him in making the supply of services or of services together with goods, and

(*b*) the supplier's staff and other internal costs of making the supply of services or of services together with goods.

(8) For the purposes of this regulation relevant land is exempt land if—

(*a*) the supplier,

(*b*) a person responsible for financing the supplier's cost of supplying the services or goods and services, or

(*c*) a person connected with the supplier or with a person responsible for financing the supplier's cost of supplying the services or goods and services,

is in occupation of the land without being in occupation of it wholly or mainly for eligible purposes.

(9) For the purposes of this regulation, but subject to paragraphs (11) and (13) below, a person's occupation at any time of any land is not capable of being occupation for eligible purposes unless he is a taxable person at that time.

(10) Subject to paragraphs (11) and (13) below, a taxable person in occupation of any land shall be taken for the purposes of this regulation to be in occupation of that land for eligible purposes to the extent only that his occupation of that land is for the purpose of making supplies which—

(*a*) are or are to be made in the course or furtherance of a business carried on by him, and

(*b*) are supplies of such a description that any input tax of his which was wholly attributable to those supplies would be input tax for which he would be entitled to credit.

(11) For the purposes of this regulation—

(*a*) occupation of land by a body to which section 33 of the Act applies is occupation of the land for eligible purposes to the extent that the body occupies the land for purposes other than those of a business carried on by that body, and

(*b*) any occupation of land by a government department (within the meaning of section 41 of the Act) is occupation of the land for eligible purposes.

(12) For the purposes of this regulation, where land of which a person is in occupation—

(*a*) is being held by that person in order to be put to use by him for particular purposes, and

(*b*) is not land of which he is in occupation for any other purpose,

that person shall be deemed, for so long as the conditions in sub-paragraphs (a) and (b) above are satisfied, to be in occupation of the land for the purposes for which he proposes to use it.

(13) Paragraphs (9) to (12) above shall have effect where land is in the occupation of a person who—

(*a*) is not a taxable person, but

(*b*) is a person whose supplies are treated for the purposes of the Act as supplies made by another person who is a taxable person,

as if the person in occupation of the land and that other person were a single taxable person.

(14) For the purposes of this regulation a person shall be taken to be in occupation of any land whether he occupies it alone or together with one or more other persons and whether he occupies all of that land or only part of it.

(15) For the purposes of this regulation, any question as to whether one person is connected with another shall be determined in accordance with section 839 of the Taxes Act[; but this is subject to paragraph (16)][2].

[(16) For the purposes of this regulation—

(*a*) a company is not connected with another company only because both are under the control of—

(i) the Crown,

(ii) a Minister of the Crown,

(iii) a government department, or

(iv) a Northern Ireland department; and

(*b*) "company" and "control" have the same meaning as in section 839 of the Taxes Act][2].][1]

Commentary—*De Voil Indirect Tax Service* **V3.140**.

Former regulation—VAT (General) Regulations, SI 1985/886 reg 26.

Press releases etc—VAT information Sheet 7/99 22-6-99 (new anti-avoidance rules).

Simon's Tax Cases—*Metropolitan Borough of Wirral v C&E Comrs* [1995] STC 597*.

Cross reference—See VAT Regulations, SI 1995/2518 reg 13(4) (authenticated receipts for supplies within this regulation: treatment as VAT invoices).

Amendments—[1] Para substituted by the VAT (Amendment) (No 3) Regulations, SI 1999/1374 with effect from 9 June 1999.

[2] Words in para (15), and whole of para (16), inserted, by the Value Added Tax (Amendment) (No 3) Regulations, SI 2009/1967 regs 2, 4, 5 with effect from 15 August 2009.

94 General

[Subject to regulation 90B above, where under this Part][1] of these Regulations a supply is treated as taking place each time that a payment (however expressed) is received or an invoice is issued, the supply is to be treated as taking place only to the extent covered by the payment or invoice.

Former regulations—VAT (General) Regulations, SI 1985/886 reg 27; VAT (General) (Amendment) Regulations, SI 1992/3102 reg 17.

Amendments—[1] Words substituted for the words "Where under this Part" by the VAT (Amendment) (No 2) Regulations, SI 1997/1525 with effect from 1 July 1997.

[94A In this Part a reference to receipt of payment (however expressed) includes a reference to receipt by a person to whom a right to receive it has been assigned.][1]

Amendments—[1] This regulation inserted by the VAT (Amendment) (No 2) Regulations, SI 1999/599 reg 3, and shall have effect in respect of payments received on or after 10 March 1999.

[94B—(1) This regulation applies in relation to the following supplies where they are provided in the circumstances referred to in paragraph (2) below—

(*a*) supplies falling within regulation 85 above (leases treated as supplies of goods) other than any supply which is exempt by virtue of Group 1 of Schedule 9 to the Act or would be exempt but for the operation of [Part 1 of Schedule 10][2] to the Act;

(*b*) supplies falling within regulation 86(1) to (4) above (supplies of water, gas or any form of power, heat, refrigeration or ventilation);

(*c*) supplies falling within regulation 90 above (continuous supplies of services) other than any supply which is exempt by virtue of Group 1 of Schedule 9 to the Act or would be exempt but for the operation of [Part 1 of Schedule 10][2] to the Act.

(2) The circumstances referred to in paragraph (1) above are—

(*a*) that the person making the supply and the person to whom it is made are connected with each other, or

(*b*) one of those persons is an undertaking in relation to which the other is a group undertaking (except where both undertakings are treated under sections 43A to 43C of the Act as members of the same group), and

(*c*) the supply is subject to the rates of VAT prescribed in section 2 or section 29A of the Act.

(3) But this regulation does not apply where a person can show that a person to whom he has made a supply of a description falling within paragraph (1) above is entitled under sections 25 and 26 of the Act to credit for all of the VAT on that supply.

[(4) For the purposes of paragraph (2)—

(*a*) any question whether one person is connected with another shall be determined in accordance with section 839 of the Taxes Act;

(*b*) a company is not connected with another company only because both are under the control of—

(i) the Crown,

(ii) a Minister of the Crown,

(iii) a government department, or

(iv) a Northern Ireland department;

(*c*) "company" and "control" have the same meaning as in section 839 of the Taxes Act; and

(*d*) "undertaking" and "group undertaking" have the same meaning as in section 1161 of the Companies Act 2006.][3]

(5) Where this regulation applies, goods or services shall, to the extent that they have not already been treated as supplied by virtue of the regulations specified in paragraph (1) above (or any provision of the Act or other regulations made under the Act), and to the extent that they have been provided, be treated as separately and successively supplied—

(*a*) in the case of supplies the provision of which commenced on or before 1st October 2003, at the end of the period of twelve months after that date;

(*b*) in the case of supplies the provision of which commenced after 1st October 2003, at the end of the period of twelve months after the supplies commenced; or

(*c*) where the Commissioners are satisfied that each category of supply has been adequately identified, on such other period end date nominated for each category and falling within the period specified in sub-paragraph (5)(*a*) or (*b*) above as may be notified by the taxable person to the Commissioners in writing,

and thereafter at the end of each subsequent period of twelve months.

(6) But where the person making the supply, within the period of six months after the time applicable under paragraph (5) above either—

(*a*) issues a VAT invoice in respect of it, or

(*b*) receives a payment in respect of it,

the supply shall, to the extent that it has not been treated as taking place at some other time by virtue of the regulations specified in paragraph (1) above (or any provision of the Act or other regulations made under the Act), be treated as taking place at the time the invoice is issued or the payment is

VAT SIs

received, unless the person making the supply has notified the Commissioners in writing that he elects not to avail himself of this paragraph.

(7) The Commissioners may, at the request of a taxable person, allow paragraph (6) above to apply in relation to supplies made by him (or such supplies as may be specified) as if for the period of six months there were substituted such other period as may be prescribed by them.

(8) A taxable person may after the start of any period to be established under paragraph (5) above—

(*a*) in relation to some or all of his supplies, and

(*b*) where the Commissioners give their approval,

select an alternative period end date falling before the end of that period (which end date but for this paragraph would be established under paragraph (5) above), from which date subsequent periods of twelve months will end.

(9) A date selected and approved under paragraph (8) above shall be the date which establishes the end of the taxable person's current period.

(10) For the purposes of paragraph (8) above, a reference to a period end established under paragraph (5) above includes a reference to a period end established by an earlier application of paragraph (8) above.

(11) Where the supply is one of the leasing of assets, and that leasing depends on one or more other leases of those assets (the superior lease or leases), then the reference in paragraph (2) above to the person making the supply includes a reference to any lessor of a superior lease.

(12) For the purposes of paragraph (11) above, a reference to the leasing of assets includes a reference to any letting, hiring or rental of assets however described, and "lessor" shall be construed accordingly.

(13) For the purposes of this regulation, goods or services are provided at the time when and to the extent that, the recipient receives the benefit of them.

(14) Where this regulation applies, the regulations specified in paragraph (1) above shall not apply to the extent that supplies have been treated as having taken place under this regulation.][1]

Amendments—[1] Regulation 94B inserted by the VAT (Amendment) (No 5) Regulations, SI 2003/2318 regs 2, 3 with effect from 1 October 2003. This insertion has effect for supplies of goods or services the benefit of which was received after the coming into force of SI 2003/2318.

[2] Words in para (1)(*a*), (*c*) substituted by the Value Added Tax (Buildings and Land) Order, SI 2008/1146, art 6, Sch 1 paras 16, 18 with effect in relation to supplies made on or after 1 June 2008, subject to savings in Sch 2 of the Order.

[3] Para (4) substituted by the Value Added Tax (Amendment) (No 3) Regulations, SI 2009/1967 regs 2, 6 with effect from 15 August 2009.

95 Supplies spanning change of rate etc

Section 88 of the Act shall apply as if the references in subsection (2) of that section to section 6(4), (5), (6) and (10) of the Act included references to regulations 81, 82, [82A,][2] 84, 85, 86(1) to (4) . . . [,][1] 88 to 93 [and 94B][1] of these Regulations.

Former regulations—VAT (General) Regulations, SI 1985/886 reg 28; VAT (General) (Amendment) Regulations, SI 1992/3102 reg 18.

Amendments—[1] This regulation amended by the VAT (Amendment) (No 5) Regulations, SI 2003/2318 regs 2, 4 with effect from 1 October 2003. The amendments have effect for supplies of goods or services the benefit of which was received after the coming into force of SI 2003/2318.

[2] Reference inserted by the VAT (Amendment) (No 4) Regulations, SI 2004/3140 reg 5 with effect from 1 January 2005 in relation to supplies made on or after that date: SI 2004/3140 reg 2(1).

PART XII

VALUATION OF ACQUISITIONS

96 Interpretation of Part XII

In this Part—

"relevant transaction", in relation to any acquisition of goods from another member State, and "relevant time" in relation to any such acquisition, have the meanings given in paragraph 5 of Schedule 7 to the Act.

Former regulation—VAT (Valuation of Acquisitions) Regulations, SI 1992/3099 reg 2(3).

97 Valuation of acquisitions

(1) Subject to paragraph (2) below, the value of the relevant transaction in relation to any goods acquired in the United Kingdom from another member State where—

(*a*) the goods are charged in connection with their removal to the United Kingdom with a duty of excise; or

(*b*) on that removal are subject, in accordance with any provision for the time being having effect for transitional purposes in connection with the accession of any State to the European Communities, to any Community customs duty or agricultural levy of the Economic Community,

shall be taken, for the purposes of the Act, to be the sum of its value apart from paragraph 2 of Schedule 7 to the Act and the amount, so far as not already included in that value, of the excise duty,

Community customs duty or, as the case may be, agricultural levy which has been or is to be paid in respect of those goods.

(2) Paragraph (1) above does not apply to a transaction in pursuance of which there is an acquisition of goods which, under subsection (4) of section 18 of the Act, is treated as taking place before the duty point within the meaning of that section.

Former regulation—VAT (Valuation of Acquisitions) Regulations, SI 1992/3099 reg 2(1), (2).

PART XIII
PLACE OF SUPPLY

98 Distance sales from the United Kingdom

(1) Where a person has exercised an option in the United Kingdom corresponding to an option mentioned in paragraph 1(2) of Schedule 2 to the Act, in respect of supplies involving the removal of goods to another member State, he shall notify the Commissioners in writing of the exercise of that option not less than 30 days before the date on which the first supply to which the option relates is made,

(2) The notification referred to in paragraph (1) above shall contain the name of the member State to which the goods have been, or are to be, removed under the direction or control of the person making the supply.

(3) Any person who has notified the Commissioners in accordance with paragraph (1) above shall within 30 days of the date of the first supply as is mentioned in that paragraph furnish to the Commissioners documentary evidence that he has notified the member State of the exercise of his option,

(4) Where a person has notified the Commissioners in accordance with paragraph (1) above he may withdraw his notification by giving a further written notification but that further notification must specify the date upon which the first notification is to be withdrawn, which date must not be earlier than—

(*a*) the 1st January which is, or next follows, the second anniversary of the date of the making of the first supply mentioned above to which the option relates, and

(*b*) the day 30 days after the receipt by the Commissioners of the further notification, and not later than 30 days before the date of the first supply which he intends to make after the withdrawal.

Former regulations—VAT (General) Regulations, SI 1985/886 reg 9A; VAT (General) (Amendment) Regulations, SI 1993/1224.

PART XIV
INPUT TAX AND PARTIAL EXEMPTION

99 Interpretation of Part XIV and longer periods

(1) In this Part—

[(*a*) "exempt input tax" means input tax incurred by a taxable person on goods imported or acquired by, or goods or services supplied to, him in so far as they are used by him or are to be used by him, or a successor of his, in making exempt supplies, or supplies outside the United Kingdom which would be exempt if made in the United Kingdom, other than any input tax which is allowable under regulation [101][5] [[102,][4] 103, 103A or 103B][3];

and "successor" in this paragraph has the same meaning as in regulation 107D;][2]

(*b*) "prescribed accounting period" means—

(i) a prescribed accounting period such as is referred to in regulation 25, or

(ii) a special accounting period, where the first prescribed accounting period would otherwise be 6 months or longer, save that this paragraph shall not apply where the reference to the prescribed accounting period is used solely in order to identify a particular return;

(*c*) "special accounting period" means each of a succession of periods of the same length as the next prescribed accounting period which does not exceed 3 months, and—

(i) the last such period shall end on the day before the commencement of that next prescribed accounting period, and

(ii) the first such period shall commence on the effective date of registration determined in accordance with Schedule 1[, [1A,][7] 2, 3 or 3A][1] to the Act and end on the day before the commencement of the second such period;

(*d*) the "tax year" of a taxable person means—

(i) the first period of 12 calendar months commencing on the first day of April, May or June, according to the prescribed accounting periods allocated to him, next following his effective date of registration determined in accordance with Schedule 1[, [1A,][7] 2, 3 or 3A][1] to the Act, or

(ii) any subsequent period of 12 calendar months commencing on the day following the end of his first, or any subsequent, tax year,

VAT SIs

save that the Commissioners may approve or direct that a tax year shall be a period of other than 12 calendar months or that it shall commence on a date other than that determined in accordance with paragraph (i) or (ii) above;

(*e*) the "registration period" of a taxable person means the period commencing on his effective date of registration determined in accordance with Schedule 1[, [1A,][7] 2, 3 or 3A][1] to the Act and ending on the day before the commencement of his first tax year.

[(1A) In this Part "non-business VAT" has the meaning given in section 24(5)(b) of the Act.][6]

(2) In this Part, any reference to goods or services shall be construed as including a reference to anything which is supplied by way of a supply of goods or a supply of services respectively.

(3) The provisions of paragraphs (4), (5), (6) and (7) below shall be used for determining the longer period applicable to taxable persons under this Part.

(4) A taxable person who incurs exempt input tax during any tax year shall have applied to him a longer period which shall correspond with that tax year unless he did not incur exempt input tax during his immediately preceding tax year or registration period, in which case his longer period shall—

(*a*) begin on the first day of the first prescribed accounting period in which he incurs exempt input tax, and

(*b*) end on the last day of that tax year,

except where he incurs exempt input tax only in the last prescribed accounting period of his tax year, in which case no longer period shall be applied to him in respect of that tax year.

(5) A taxable person who incurs exempt input tax during his registration period shall have applied to him a longer period which shall begin on the first day on which he incurs exempt input tax and end on the day before the commencement of his first tax year.

(6) In the case of a taxable person ceasing to be taxable during a longer period applicable to him, that longer period shall end on the day when he ceases to be taxable.

(7) The Commissioners may approve in the case of a taxable person who incurs exempt input tax, or a class of such persons, that a longer period shall apply which need not correspond with a tax year.

Former regulations—Para (1): VAT (General) Regulations, SI 1985/886 reg 29(1); VAT (General) (Amendment) Regulations, SI 1992/645, regs 1–3, SI 1992/3102 reg 19, SI 1993/1639 reg 3.

Para (2): VAT (General) Regulations, SI 1985/886 reg 29(1A); VAT (General) (Amendment) Regulations, SI 1992/3102 reg 19.

Paras (3)–(7): VAT (General) Regulations, SI 1985/886 reg 29(2)–(6); VAT (General) (Amendment) Regulations, SI 1992/645, regs 1–3.

Amendments—[1] Words in para (1)(*c*), (*d*), (*e*) inserted by the VAT (Amendment) (No 3) Regulations, SI 2000/794 regs 2, 6 with effect from 22 March 2000.

[2] Para (1)(*a*) substituted by the VAT (Amendment) Regulations, SI 2002/1074 regs 2, 3, with effect for input tax incurred by a taxable person on goods imported or acquired by, or goods or services supplied to, him after 17 April 2002.

[3] In sub-para (1)(*a*), references substituted by the VAT (Amendment) (No 4) Regulations, SI 2004/3140 reg 9 with effect from 3 December 2004: SI 2004/3140 reg 2(3).

[4] Reference in para (1)(*a*) inserted by the VAT (Amendment) (No 2) Regulations, SI 2007/768 regs 2, 6 with effect from 1 April 2007.

[5] Reference in para (1)(*a*) inserted by the VAT (Amendment) (No 2) Regulations, SI 2009/820 regs 2, 3 with effect in relation to input tax incurred by a taxable person on goods imported or acquired by, or goods or services supplied to, him on or after 1 April 2009. Where 31 March 2009 falls within the prescribed accounting period of a taxable person, the amendments made by SI 2009/820 shall not, in relation to that taxable person, have effect until the day after the end of that prescribed accounting period (SI 2009/820reg 1(2)).

[6] Para (1A) inserted by the VAT (Amendment) (No 4) Regulations, SI 2010/3022 regs 2, 5 with effect from 1 January 2011.

[7] In para (1), words inserted by the VAT (Amendment) (No 2) Regulations, SI 2012/1899 regs 3, 16 with effect from 15 October 2012.

100 Nothing in this Part shall be construed as allowing a taxable person to deduct the whole or any part of VAT on the importation or acquisition by him of goods or the supply to him of goods or services where those goods or services are not used or to be used by him in making supplies in the course or furtherance of a business carried on by him.

Former regulations—VAT (General) Regulations, SI 1985/886 reg 29A; VAT (General) (Amendment) Regulations, SI 1993/1639 reg 4.

101 Attribution of input tax to taxable supplies

(1) Subject to regulation regulations [102, 103A, 105A and 106ZA][2], the amount of input tax which a taxable person shall be entitled to deduct provisionally shall be that amount which is attributable to taxable supplies in accordance with this regulation.

(2) [Subject to paragraph (8) below and regulation 107(1)(*g*)(ii),][5] in respect of each prescribed accounting period—

(*a*) goods imported or acquired by and . . . [1] goods or services supplied to, the taxable person in the period shall be identified,

(*b*) there shall be attributed to taxable supplies the whole of the input tax on such of those goods or services as are used or to be used by him exclusively in making taxable supplies, (*c*) no part of the input tax on such of those goods or services as are used or to be used by him exclusively in making exempt supplies, or in carrying on any activity other than the making of taxable supplies, shall be attributed to taxable supplies, . . .[5]

(*d*) [where a taxable person does not have an immediately preceding longer period and subject to subparagraph (*e*) below,][5] there shall be attributed to taxable supplies such proportion of the [residual input tax][5] as bears the same ratio to the total of such input tax as the value of taxable supplies made by him bears to the value of all supplies made by him in the period,

[(*e*) the attribution required by subparagraph (*d*) above may be made on the basis of the extent to which the goods or services are used or to be used by him in making taxable supplies,

(*f*) where a taxable person has an immediately preceding longer period and subject to subparagraph (*g*) below, his residual input tax shall be attributed to taxable supplies by reference to the percentage recovery rate for that immediately preceding longer period, and

(*g*) the attribution required by subparagraph (*f*) above may be made using the calculation specified in subparagraph (*d*) above provided that that calculation is used for all the prescribed accounting periods which fall within any longer period applicable to a taxable person.][5]

(3) In calculating the proportion under paragraph (2)(*d*) [or (g)][5] above, there shall be excluded—

(*a*) any sum receivable by the taxable person in respect of any supply of capital goods used by him for the purposes of his business,

(*b*) any sum receivable by the taxable person in respect of any of the following descriptions of supplies made by him, where such supplies are incidental to one or more of his business activities—

[(i) any supply of a description falling within Group 5 of Schedule 9 to the Act,

(ii) any other financial transaction, and

(iii) any real estate transaction,][4]

(*c*) that part of the value of any supply of goods on which output tax is not chargeable by virtue of any order made by the Treasury under section 25(7) of the Act unless the taxable person has imported, acquired or been supplied with the goods for the purpose of selling them, [5]

(*d*) the value of any supply which, under or by virtue of any provision of the Act, the taxable person makes to himself, [and][5]

"(*e*) supplies of a description falling within paragraph (8) below.][5]

(4) The ratio calculated for the purpose of paragraph (2)(*d*)[, (*e*) or (*g*)][5] above shall be expressed as a percentage and, if that percentage is not a whole number, it shall be rounded up [as specified in paragraph (5) below][3].

[(5) The percentage shall be rounded up—

(*a*) where in any prescribed accounting period or longer period which is applied the amount of input tax which is available for attribution under paragraph 2(*d*)[, (*e*) or (*g*)][5] above prior to any such attribution being made does not amount to more than £400,000 per month on average, to the next whole number, and

(*b*) in any other case, to two decimal places.][3]

[(6) For the purposes of this regulation, a "real estate transaction" includes any grant, assignment (including any transfer, disposition or sale), surrender or reverse surrender of any interest in, right over or licence to occupy land.][4]

[(7) In this regulation "taxable supplies" include supplies of a description falling within regulation 103.

(8) Input tax incurred on goods or services acquired by or supplied to a taxable person which are used or to be used by him in whole or in part in making—

(*a*) supplies falling within either item 1 or item 6 of Group 5 of Schedule 9 to the Act; or

(*b*) supplies made from an establishment situated outside the United Kingdom,

shall, whether the supply in question is made within or outside the United Kingdom, be attributed to taxable supplies on the basis of the extent to which the goods or services are used or to be used by him in making taxable supplies.

(9) For the purposes of this regulation in relation to a taxable person—

(*a*) "immediately preceding longer period" means the longer period applicable to him which ends immediately before the longer period in which the prescribed accounting period in respect of which he is making the attribution required by paragraph (2)(*d*) to (*g*) above falls;

(*b*) "percentage recovery rate" means the amount of relevant residual input tax which he was entitled to attribute to taxable supplies under regulation 107(1)(*a*) to (*d*), expressed as a percentage of the total amount of the residual input tax which fell to be so attributed and rounded up in accordance with paragraphs (4) and (5) above;

(*c*) "relevant residual input tax" means all residual input tax other than that which falls to be attributed under paragraph (8) above.

(10) In this regulation "residual input tax" means input tax incurred by a taxable person on goods or services which are used or to be used by him in making both taxable and exempt supplies.][5]

VAT SIs

Commentary—*De Voil Indirect Tax Service* **V3.460–V3.467**.

Former regulations—Paras (1), (2): VAT (General) Regulations, SI 1985/886 reg 30(1), (2); VAT (General) (Amendment) Regulations, SI 1992/645 regs 1–3, SI 1992/3102 reg 20.

Paras (3), (4): VAT (General) Regulations, SI 1985/886 reg 30(3), (4); VAT (General) (Amendment) Regulations, SI 1992/645 regs 1–3, SI 1992/3102 reg 20.

Para (5): VAT (General) Regulations, SI 1985/886 reg 30(2A); VAT (General) (Amendment) Regulations, SI 1995/1069 reg 3.

Simon's Tax Cases—*C&E Comrs v Harpcombe Ltd* [1996] STC 726*; *C&E Comrs v Southern Primary Housing Association Ltd* [2003] STC 525; *Banbury Visionplus Ltd v R&C Comrs and other appeals* [2006] STC 1568; *MBNA Europe Bank Ltd v R&C Comrs* [2006] STC 2089; *Royal Bank of Scotland Group plc v R&C Comrs* [2008] STC 1485.

Reg 101(1), *C&E Comrs v Dennis Rye Ltd* [1996] STC 27*.

Reg 101(2), *Dial-a-Phone Ltd v C&E Comrs* [2003] STC 192; [2004] STC 987.

Reg 101(2)(*c*), (*d*), *RAP Group plc v C&E Comrs* [2000] STC 980; *Mayflower Theatre Trust Ltd v R&C Comrs* [2007] STC 880.

Reg 101(2)(*d*), *C&E Comrs v Liverpool Institute for Performing Arts* [2001] STC 891*.

Reg 101(3), *C&E Comrs v JDL Ltd* [2001] STC 1.

Amendments—[1] Words in para (2)(*a*) deleted by the VAT (Amendment) (No 3) Regulations, SI 1996/1250 reg 14, with effect from 1 June 1996 except that where 28 April 1996 fell within a taxable person's prescribed accounting period which ended on or after 1 June 1996, the Amendment has effect in relation to that taxable person from the day after the end of that prescribed accounting period.

[2] In para (1), reference substituted for "regulation 102 and 103A" by the VAT (Amendment) Regulations, SI 2010/559 regs 2, 4 with effect from 1 April 2010.

[3] Words in para (4) substituted for words "to the whole next number", and para (5) inserted, by the VAT (Amendment) Regulations, SI 2005/762 reg 3 with effect from 1 April 2005. Where 31 March 2005 falls within the prescribed accounting period of a taxable person, the amendments shall not, in relation to that taxable person, have effect until the day after the end of that prescribed accounting period: SI 2005/762 reg 1.

[4] In para (3) sub-paras (i)–(iii) substituted for original sub-paras (i)–(v), and para (6) inserted, by the VAT (Amendment) (No 2) Regulations, SI 2007/768 regs 2, 7 with effect from 1 April 2007.

[5] In para (2), words inserted at beginning, at end of sub-para (*c*) word "and" repealed, in sub-para (*d*) words inserted at beginning and words substituted for words "input tax on such of those goods or services as are used or to be used by him in making both taxable and exempt supplies", and sub-paras (*e*)–(*g*) inserted, in para (3), words inserted, in sub-para (*c*) word "and" repealed, sub-para (*e*) and preceding word "and" inserted, in paras (4), (5), words inserted, and paras (7)–(10) inserted, by the VAT (Amendment) (No 2) Regulations, SI 2009/820 regs 2, 4 with effect in relation to input tax incurred by a taxable person on goods imported or acquired by, or goods or services supplied to, him on or after 1 April 2009. Where 31 March 2009 falls within the prescribed accounting period of a taxable person, the amendments made by SI 2009/820 shall not, in relation to that taxable person, have effect until the day after the end of that prescribed accounting period (SI 2009/820reg 1(2)).

102 Use of other methods

(1) Subject to [paragraphs (2) and (9)][3] below and [regulations 103, 103A[, 103B, 105A and 106ZA][5]][1], the Commissioners may approve or direct the use by a taxable person of a method other than that specified in regulation 101[1] . . . .

[(1A) A method approved or directed under paragraph (1) above—

(*a*) shall be in writing,

(*b*) may attribute input tax which would otherwise fall to be attributed under regulation 103 provided that, where it attributes any such input tax, it shall attribute it all, and

(*c*) shall identify the supplies in respect of which it attributes input tax by reference to the relevant paragraph or paragraphs of section 26(2) of the Act.][3]

(2) Notwithstanding any provision of any method approved or directed to be used under this regulation which purports to have the contrary effect, in calculating the proportion of any input tax on goods or services used or to be used by the taxable person in making both taxable and exempt supplies which is to be treated as attributable to taxable supplies, the value of any supply [of a description falling within regulation [101(3)(*a*) to (*d*)][4] whether made within or outside the United Kingdom][3] shall be excluded.

(3) A taxable person using a method as approved or directed to be used by the Commissioners under paragraph (1) above shall continue to use that method unless the Commissioners approve or direct the termination of its use.

(4) Any direction under paragraph (1) or (3) above shall take effect from the date upon which the Commissioners give such direction or from such later date as they may specify.

[(5) Any approval given or direction made under this regulation shall only have effect if it is in writing in the form of a document which identifies itself as being such an approval or direction.][2]

[(6) Where a taxable person who is using a method which has been approved or directed under this regulation incurs input tax of the description in paragraph (7) below, that input tax shall be attributed to taxable supplies to the extent that the goods or services are used or to be used in making taxable supplies expressed as a proportion of the whole use or intended use.][2]

[(7) The input tax referred to in paragraph (6) above is input tax—

(*a*) the attribution of which to taxable supplies is not prescribed in whole or in part by the method referred to in paragraph (6) above, and

(*b*) which does not fall to be attributed to taxable or other supplies as specified under regulations 103, 103A or 103B.][2]

[(8) Where the input tax specified in paragraph (7)(*a*) above is input tax the attribution of which to taxable supplies is only in part not prescribed by the method, only that part the attribution of which is not so prescribed shall fall within that paragraph.][2]

[(9) With effect from 1st April 2007 the Commissioners shall not approve the use of a method under this regulation unless the taxable person has made a declaration to the effect that to the best of his knowledge and belief the method fairly and reasonably represents the extent to which goods or services are used by or are to be used by him in making taxable supplies.

(10) The declaration referred to in paragraph (9) above shall—

(*a*) be in writing,

(*b*) be signed by the taxable person or by a person authorised to sign it on his behalf, and

(*c*) include a statement that the person signing it has taken reasonable steps to ensure that he is in possession of all relevant information.

(11) Where it appears to the Commissioners that a declaration made under this regulation is incorrect in that—

(*a*) the method does not fairly and reasonably represent the extent to which goods or services are used by or are to be used by the taxable person in making taxable supplies, and

(*b*) the person who signed the declaration knew or ought reasonably to have known this at the time when the declaration was made by the taxable person,

they may subject to paragraph (12) below serve on the taxable person a notice to that effect setting out their reasons in support of that notification and stating the effect of the notice.

(12) The Commissioners shall not serve a notice under this regulation unless they are satisfied that the overall result of the application of the method is an over-deduction of input tax by the taxable person.

(13) Subject to paragraph (14) below, the effect of a notice served under this regulation is that regulation 102B(1) shall apply to the person served with the notice in relation to—

(*a*) prescribed accounting periods commencing on or after the effective date of the method, and

(*b*) longer periods to the extent of that part of the longer period falling on or after the effective date of the method, save that no adjustment shall be required in relation to any part of any prescribed accounting period,

unless or until the method is terminated under regulation 102(3).

(14) In relation to any past prescribed accounting periods, the Commissioners may assess the amount of VAT due to the best of their judgement and notify it to the taxable person unless they allow him to account for the difference in such manner and within such time as they may require.

(15) The service of a notice on a taxable person under this regulation shall be without prejudice to the Commissioners' powers to serve a notice on him under regulation 102A and any notice served under regulation 102A shall take priority in relation to the periods which it covers.

(16) In this regulation "the effective date of the method" is the date when the method to which the declaration relates first takes effect and may predate the date when the declaration was made.

(17) In this regulation and in regulations 102A, 102B, 102C and 107, where paragraph (1A)(*b*) above applies, "taxable supplies" includes supplies of a description falling within regulation 103.][3]

Commentary—*De Voil Indirect Tax Service* **V3.460–V3.467**.

Former regulations—Para (1): VAT (General) Regulations, SI 1985/886 reg 31(1); VAT (General) (Amendment) Regulations, SI 1992/645 regs 1–3, SI 1994/3015 reg 3.

Para (2): VAT (General) Regulations, SI 1985/886 reg 31(1A); VAT (General) (Amendment) Regulations, SI 1994/3015 reg 3.

Paras (3), (4): VAT (General) Regulations, SI 1985/886 reg 31(2), (3); VAT (General) (Amendment) Regulations, SI 1992/645 regs 1–3.

Simon's Tax Cases—*Kwik-Fit (GB) Ltd v C&E Comrs* [1998] STC 159; *Banbury Visionplus Ltd v R&C Comrs and other appeals* [2006] STC 1568; *MBNA Europe Bank Ltd v R&C Comrs* [2006] STC 2089; *DCM (Optical Holdings) Ltd v R&C Comrs* [2008] STC 1294.

Press releases etc—HMRC Brief 23/07, 14-3-07 (guidance on preparing and submitting the new Declaration required for all partial exemption special method applications approved on or after 1 April 2007, including a template for the Declaration).

Amendments—[1] In para (1), references substituted by the VAT (Amendment) (No 4) Regulations, SI 2004/3140 reg 11 with effect from 3 December 2004: SI 2004/3140 reg 2(3).

[2] Paras (5)–(8) inserted by the VAT (Amendment) Regulations, SI 2005/762 reg 4 with effect from 1 April 2005.

[3] Words in para (1) substituted and omitted, paras (1A) and (9)–(17) inserted, and words in para (2) substituted, by the VAT (Amendment) (No 2) Regulations, SI 2007/768 regs 2, 8 with effect from 1 April 2007.

[4] In para (2), words substituted for words "101(3)" by the VAT (Amendment) (No 2) Regulations, SI 2009/820 regs 2, 5 with effect in relation to input tax incurred by a taxable person on goods imported or acquired by, or goods or services supplied to, him on or after 1 April 2009. Where 31 March 2009 falls within the prescribed accounting period of a taxable person, the amendments made by SI 2009/820 shall not, in relation to that taxable person, have effect until the day after the end of that prescribed accounting period (SI 2009/820 reg 1(2)).

[5] In para (1), reference substituted for "and 103B" by the VAT (Amendment) Regulations, SI 2010/559 regs 2, 5 with effect from 1 April 2010.

[102ZA

(1) A taxable person who is required to make an apportionment under section 24(5) of the Act in relation to goods or services which are used or are to be used partly for business purposes and partly for other purposes may effect that apportionment using a method provided for in regulation 102(1).

(2) Where the taxable person referred to in paragraph (1) is not a fully taxable person, the method used shall be the only method used to calculate that person's deductible input tax.

(3) Where a person who was a fully taxable person at the time when the method was approved subsequently incurs exempt input tax, regulation 102B shall apply from the date on which that person first incurs such exempt input tax.

(4) Where a person effects the apportionment referred to in paragraph (1) using a method provided for in regulation 102(1)—

(*a*) regulations 102(1A) to (17) and 102A to 102C shall apply;

(*b*) regulations 105A, 106 and 106ZA shall not apply; and

(*c*) for the purposes of defining a longer period and determining an adjustment of attribution under regulation 107, "exempt input tax" shall include non-business VAT.

(5) In this regulation, a fully taxable person is a person who, disregarding paragraph (4)(*c*), has not incurred any exempt input tax in that person's current or immediately preceding (if any) tax year or registration period.][1]

Amendments—[1] Reg 102ZA inserted by the VAT (Amendment) (No 4) Regulations, SI 2010/3022 regs 2, 6with effect from 1 January 2011.

[102A—(1) [Notwithstanding the Commissioners' powers to serve a notice under regulation 102,][2] where a taxable person—

(*a*) is for the time being using a method approved or directed under regulation 102, and

(*b*) that method does not fairly and reasonably represent the extent to which goods or services are used by him or are to be used by him in making taxable supplies,

the Commissioners may serve on him a notice to that effect, setting out their reasons in support of that notification and stating the effect of the notice.

(2) The effect of a notice served under this regulation is that regulation 102B shall apply to the person served with the notice in relation to—

(*a*) prescribed accounting periods commencing on or after the date of the notice or such later date as may be specified in the notice, and

(*b*) longer periods to the extent of that part of the longer period falling on or after the date of the notice or such later date as may be specified in the notice.][1]

Simon's Tax Cases—*Vision Express (UK) Ltd v R&C Comrs* [2010] STC 742.

Amendments—[1] Regulations 102A–102C inserted by the VAT (Amendment) (No 6) Regulations, SI 2003/3220 regs 1(1)(*b*), (2), 2, 21 with effect for input tax incurred by a taxable person on goods imported or acquired by, or goods or services supplied to, him after 31 December 2003.

[2] Words in para (1) inserted by the VAT (Amendment) (No 2) Regulations, SI 2007/768 regs 2, 9 with effect from 1 April 2007.

[102B—(1) Where this regulation applies, a taxable person shall calculate the difference between—

(*a*) the attribution made by him in any prescribed accounting period or longer period, and

(*b*) an attribution which represents the extent to which the goods or services are used by him or are to be used by him in making taxable supplies,

and account for the difference on the return for that prescribed accounting period or on the return on which that longer period adjustment is required to be made, except where the Commissioners allow another return to be used for this purpose.

(2) This regulation shall apply from the date prescribed under regulation 102A(2) or 102C(2), unless or until the method referred to in regulation 102A(1)(*a*) or 102C(1)(*a*) is terminated under regulation 102(3).][1]

Amendments—[1] Regulations 102A–102C inserted by the VAT (Amendment) (No 6) Regulations, SI 2003/3220 regs 1(1)(*b*), (2), 2, 21 with effect for input tax incurred by a taxable person on goods imported or acquired by, or goods or services supplied to, him after 31 December 2003.

[102C—(1) Subject to regulation 102A, where a taxable person—

(*a*) is for the time being using a method approved or directed under regulation 102, and

(*b*) that method does not fairly and reasonably represent the extent to which goods or services are used by him or are to be used by him in making taxable supplies,

the taxable person may serve on the Commissioners a notice to that effect, setting out his reasons in support of that notification.

(2) Where the Commissioners approve a notice served under this regulation, the effect is that regulation 102B shall apply to the person serving the notice in relation to—

(*a*) prescribed accounting periods commencing on or after the date of the notice or such later date as may be specified in the notice, and

(*b*) longer periods to the extent of that part of the longer period falling on or after the date of the notice or such later date as may be specified in the notice.][1]

Amendments—[1] Regulations 102A–102C inserted by the VAT (Amendment) (No 6) Regulations, SI 2003/3220 regs 1(1)(*b*), (2), 2, 21 with effect for input tax incurred by a taxable person on goods imported or acquired by, or goods or services supplied to, him after 31 December 2003.

103 Attribution of input tax to foreign and specified supplies

Other than where it falls to be attributed under [regulation 101 or][4] a method approved or directed by the Commissioners under regulation 102,][3] . . . [2] Input tax incurred by a taxable person in any prescribed accounting period on goods imported or acquired by, or goods or services supplied to, him which are used or to be used by him in whole or in part in making—

(*a*) supplies outside the United Kingdom which would be taxable supplies if made in the United Kingdom, or

(*b*) supplies specified in an Order under section 26(2)(*c*) of the Act, [other than supplies of a description falling within regulation 103A below,][1]

shall be attributed to taxable supplies to the extent that the goods or services are so used or to be used expressed as a proportion of the whole use or intended use.

(2), (3) . . . [2]

Former regulations—VAT (General) Regulations, SI 1985/886 reg 32; VAT (General) (Amendment) Regulations, SI 1994/3015 reg 4.

Simon's Tax Cases—*C&E Comrs v Liverpool Institute for Performing Arts* [2001] STC 891*; *MBNA Europe Bank Ltd v R&C Comrs* [2006] STC 2089.

Amendments—[1] Words inserted by the VAT (Amendment) (No 4) Regulations, SI 1999/3114, regs 2, 7, with effect from 1 January 2000.

[2] Paragraph numbering and paras (2), (3) revoked by the VAT (Amendment) (No 4) Regulations, SI 2004/3140 reg 7 with effect from 3 December 2004: SI 2004/3140 reg 2(3).

[3] Words inserted by the VAT (Amendment) (No 2) Regulations, SI 2007/768 regs 2, 10 with effect from 1 April 2007.

[4] Words inserted by the VAT (Amendment) (No 2) Regulations, SI 2009/820 regs 2, 6 with effect in relation to input tax incurred by a taxable person on goods imported or acquired by, or goods or services supplied to, him on or after 1 April 2009. Where 31 March 2009 falls within the prescribed accounting period of a taxable person, the amendments made by SI 2009/820 shall not, in relation to that taxable person, have effect until the day after the end of that prescribed accounting period (SI 2009/820reg 1(2)).

[103A [Attribution of input tax to investment gold]

(1) This regulation applies to a taxable person who makes supplies of a description falling within item 1 or 2 of Group 15 of Schedule 9 to the Act.]

(2) Input tax incurred by him in any prescribed accounting period in respect of supplies by him of a description falling within paragraph (1) above shall be allowable as being attributable to those supplies only to the following extent, that is to say where it is incurred—

(*a*) on investment gold supplied to him which but for an election made under the Value Added Tax (Investment Gold) Order 1999, or but for Note 4(*b*) to Group 15 of Schedule 9 to the Act would have fallen within item 1 or 2 of that Group, or on investment gold acquired by him;

(*b*) on a supply to him, an acquisition by him, or on an importation by him of gold other than investment gold which is to be transformed by him or on his behalf into investment gold;

(*c*) on services supplied to him comprising a change of form, weight or purity of gold.

(3) Where a taxable person produces investment gold or transforms any gold into investment gold he shall also be entitled to credit for input tax incurred by him on any goods or services supplied to him, any acquisitions of goods by him or any importations of goods by him, but only to the extent that they are linked to the production or transformation of that gold into investment gold.

(4) Where input tax has been incurred on goods or services which are used or to be used in making supplies of a description falling within item 1 or 2 of Group 15 of Schedule 9 to the Act and any other supply, that input tax shall be attributed to the supplies falling within item 1 or 2 to the extent that the goods or services are so used or to be used, expressed as a proportion of the whole use or intended use.

(5) Where input tax is attributed to supplies of a description falling within item 1 or 2 of Group 15 to Schedule 9 to the Act under paragraph (4) above, the taxable person shall be entitled to credit for only so much input tax as is reasonably allowable under paragraph (2) or (3) above.

(6) For the purpose of attributing input tax to supplies of a description falling within item 1 or 2 of Group 15 of Schedule 9 to the Act under paragraph (4) above, any input tax of the description in that paragraph shall be deemed to be the only input tax incurred by the taxable person in the prescribed accounting period concerned.]

Amendments—This Regulation inserted by the VAT (Amendment) (No 4) Regulations, SI 1999/3114, regs 2, 8, with effect from 1 January 2000.

Heading inserted by the VAT (Amendment) (No 2) Regulations, SI 2007/768 regs 2, 11 with effect from 1 April 2007.

103B [Attribution of input tax incurred on services and related goods used to make financial supplies

(1) This regulation applies to a taxable person who incurs input tax in the circumstances specified in paragraph (2) below.

(2) [Other than where it falls to be attributed under regulation 101,][2] where—

(*a*) input tax has been incurred by a taxable person in any prescribed accounting period on supplies to him of any of the services specified in paragraph (4) below and of any related goods, and (*b*) those services and related goods are used or to be used by the taxable person in making both a relevant supply and any other supply, and

(*c*) the relevant supply is incidental to one or more of the taxable person's business activities,

that input tax shall be attributed to taxable supplies to the extent that the services or related goods are so used or to be used expressed as a proportion of the whole use or intended use, notwithstanding any provision of any input tax attribution method that the taxable person is required or allowed to use which purports to have the contrary effect.

(3) In this regulation—

(*a*) "relevant supply" means a supply of a description falling within item 1 or 6 of Group 5 of Schedule 9 to the Act and any supply of the same description which is made in another member State; and

(*b*) "taxable supplies" includes supplies of a description falling within regulation 103.

(4) The services referred to in paragraph (2)(*a*) above are services supplied by—

(*a*) accountants;

(*b*) advertising agencies;

(*c*) bodies which provide listing and registration services;

(*d*) financial advisers;

(*e*) lawyers;

(*f*) marketing consultants;

(*g*) persons who prepare and design documentation; and

(*h*) any person or body which provides similar services to those specified in sub-paragraphs (*a*) to (*g*) above.][1]

Amendments—[1] Regulation 103B inserted by the VAT (Amendment) (No 4) Regulations, SI 2004/3140 reg 8 with effect from 3 December 2004 in relation to input tax incurred by a taxable person on goods imported or acquired by, or goods and services supplied to, him on or after that date: SI 2004/3140 reg 2(2).

[2] Words inserted in para (2) by the VAT (Amendment) (No 2) Regulations, SI 2009/820 regs 2, 7 with effect in relation to input tax incurred by a taxable person on goods imported or acquired by, or goods or services supplied to, him on or after 1 April 2009. Where 31 March 2009 falls within the prescribed accounting period of a taxable person, the amendments made by SI 2009/820 shall not, in relation to that taxable person, have effect until the day after the end of that prescribed accounting period (SI 2009/820reg 1(2)).

104 Attribution of input tax on self-supplies

Where under or by virtue of any provision of the Act a person makes a supply to himself, the input tax on that supply shall not be allowable as attributable to that supply.

Former regulation—VAT (General) Regulations, SI 1985/886 reg 32A; VAT (General) (Amendment) Regulations, SI 1992/645 regs 1–3.

105 Treatment of input tax attributable to exempt supplies as being attributable to taxable supplies

. . .

Amendments—This regulation revoked by the VAT (Amendment) (No 2) Regulations, SI 1999/599 reg 4, with effect from 10 March 1999, unless the taxable person was registered prior to that date when it shall have effect from the commencement of the first tax year commencing on or after 10 March 1999.

[105A—(1) Subject to regulation 106ZA(1), where, in relation to a taxable person, total input tax incurred less any input tax incurred on goods or services used or to be used exclusively in making taxable supplies—

(*a*) in any prescribed accounting period, or

(*b*) in any applicable longer period,

does not amount to more than £625 per month on average, all input tax incurred in that period shall be treated as attributable to taxable supplies provided that the value of exempt supplies does not exceed one half of the value of all supplies.

(2) In the application of paragraph (1) above to a longer period—

(*a*) any treatment of input tax as attributable to taxable supplies in any prescribed accounting period shall be disregarded, and

(*b*) the amount of input tax incurred on goods or services used or to be used exclusively in making taxable supplies must reflect any changes in use or intention during that period.

(3) In this regulation—

(*a*) "taxable supplies" includes supplies of a description falling within regulation 103, and

(*b*) "exempt supplies" means any supplies that are not taxable supplies.][1]

Amendments—[1] Reg 105A inserted by the VAT (Amendment) Regulations, SI 2010/559, regs 2, 6 with effect from 1 April 2010.

[106—(1) [Where regulation 105A does not apply then, subject to regulations 106A and 106ZA(1)][3], where relevant input tax—

(*a*) in any prescribed accounting period, or

(*b*) in the case of a longer period, taken together with the amount of any adjustment in respect of that period under regulation 107B—

(i) does not amount to more than £625 per month on average, and

(ii) does not exceed one half of all his input tax for the period concerned,

all such input tax in that period shall be treated as attributable to taxable supplies.

(2) In the application of paragraph (1) above to a longer period—

(*a*) any treatment of relevant input tax as attributable to taxable supplies in any prescribed accounting period shall be disregarded, and

(*b*) no account shall be taken of any amount or amounts which may be deductible or payable under regulation 115.

(3) For the purposes of this regulation, relevant input tax is input tax attributed under regulations 101, 102, 103, 103A[, 103B][2] and, where the case arises, regulation 107, to exempt supplies or to supplies outside the United Kingdom which would be exempt if made in the United Kingdom (not being supplies specified in an Order made under section 26(2)(*c*) of the Act).][1]

Former regulations—VAT (General) Regulations, SI 1985/886 reg 33A; VAT (General) (Amendment) Regulations, SI 1992/645 regs 1–3, SI 1994/3015 reg 5.

Amendments—[1] Regulation substituted by the VAT (Amendment) Regulations, SI 2002/1074 regs 2, 4 with effect for input tax incurred by a taxable person on goods imported or acquired by, or goods or services supplied to, him after 17 April 2002.

[2] In para (3), reference inserted by the VAT (Amendment) (No 4) Regulations, SI 2004/3140 reg 12 with effect from 3 December 2004: SI 2004/3140 reg 2(3).

[3] Words in para (1) substituted for "Subject to regulation 106A" by the VAT (Amendment) Regulations, SI 2010/559, regs 2, 7 with effect from 1 April 2010.

[106ZA (1) A taxable person who—

(*a*) was entitled to attribute his input tax to taxable supplies under regulation 105A(1)(*b*) or regulation 106(1)(*b*) in his immediately preceding longer period, and

(*b*) does not expect to incur more than £1,000,000 input tax in his current longer period,

may treat input tax incurred in each prescribed accounting period within his current longer period as attributable to taxable supplies, provided that he does so for all of the prescribed accounting periods that fall within that longer period.

(2) For the purposes of this regulation in relation to a taxable person, "immediately preceding longer period" means the longer period applicable to that person which ends immediately before the longer period in which the prescribed accounting period in respect of which he is making the attribution under paragraph (1) above falls.][1]

Amendments—[1] Reg 106ZA inserted by the VAT (Amendment) Regulations, SI 2010/559, regs 2, 8 with effect from 1 April 2010.

[106A—(1) This regulation applies where regulation 107A applies.

(2) Where, taken together with the amount of any adjustment under regulation 107A, input tax attributed under regulations 101, 103[, 103A and 103B][2] to exempt supplies, or to supplies outside the United Kingdom which would be exempt if made in the United Kingdom (in each case not being supplies specified in an Order made under section 26(2)(*c*) of the Act)—

(*a*) does not amount to more than £625 per month on average, and

(*b*) does not exceed one half of all his input tax for the period concerned,

all such input tax in that period shall be treated as attributable to taxable supplies.

(3) Where, in accordance with regulations 101, 103[, 103A and 103B][2], a taxable person has attributed an amount of input tax to exempt supplies, or to supplies outside the United Kingdom which would be exempt if made in the United Kingdom (in each case not being supplies specified in an Order made under section 26(2)(c) of the Act) and, after applying regulation 107A, he is entitled to treat all his input tax as attributable to taxable supplies under paragraph (2) above, he shall—

(*a*) calculate the difference between—

(i) the total amount of input tax for that prescribed accounting period, and

(ii) the amount of input tax deducted in that prescribed accounting period, taken together with the amount of any adjustment under regulation 107A, and

(*b*) include this difference as an under-deduction in a return for the first prescribed accounting period next following the prescribed accounting period referred to in regulation 107A(1), except where the Commissioners allow another return to be used for this purpose.

(4) Where in a prescribed accounting period a taxable person has treated input tax as attributable to taxable supplies under regulation 106(1) but is not entitled to do so because of the operation of paragraph (2) above, he shall include the amount so treated as an over-deduction in a return for the first prescribed accounting period next following the prescribed accounting period referred to in regulation 107A(1), except where the Commissioners allow another return to be used for this purpose.

(5) But where a registered person has his registration cancelled at or before the end of the prescribed accounting period referred to in regulation 107A(1), he shall account for any adjustment under this regulation on his final return.][1]

Amendments—[1] Regulation inserted by the VAT (Amendment) Regulations, SI 2002/1074 regs 2, 5 with effect for input tax incurred by a taxable person on goods imported or acquired by, or goods or services supplied to, him after 17 April 2002.

VAT SIs

2 In paras (2), (3), reference substituted by the VAT (Amendment) (No 4) Regulations, SI 2004/3140 reg 13 with effect from 3 December 2004: SI 2004/3140 reg 2(3).

107 Adjustment of attribution

(1) [Subject to regulation 105A(1)(*b*),][3] Where a taxable person to whom a longer period is applicable has provisionally attributed an amount of input tax to taxable supplies in accordance with a method [or treated an amount of input tax as attributable to taxable supplies under regulation 105A(1)(*a*) or regulation 106ZA(1)][3] . . . [2] and save as the Commissioners may dispense with the following requirement to adjust, he . . . [2]—

[(*a*) shall, subject to [subparagraphs (*b*), (*c*), (*d*) and (*da*) below][3], determine for the longer period the amount of input tax which is attributable to taxable supplies according to the method used in the prescribed accounting periods,

(*b*) shall, where he has provisionally attributed input tax in accordance with regulation 101(2)(*e*) in any prescribed accounting period, determine for the longer period the amount of residual input tax which is attributable to taxable supplies on the basis of the extent to which the goods or services are used or to be used by him in making taxable supplies,

(*c*) may, where he has not provisionally attributed input tax in accordance with regulation 101(2)(*e*) but was nevertheless entitled to do so, determine for the longer period the amount of residual input tax which is attributable to taxable supplies on the basis of the extent to which the goods or services are used or to be used by him in making taxable supplies,

(*d*) shall, where he has provisionally attributed residual input tax under regulation 101(2)(*f*), determine for the longer period the amount of residual input tax which is attributable to taxable supplies using the calculation specified in regulation 101(2)(*d*) subject to the provisions of regulation 101(3) to (5),

[(*da*) shall, where he has treated an amount of input tax as attributable to taxable supplies under regulation 105A(1)(*a*) or regulation 106ZA(1), determine for the longer period the amount of input tax that is attributable to taxable supplies in accordance with sub-paragraphs (*a*) to (*d*) above as appropriate,][3]

(*e*) shall[, except where a taxable person is using a method provided for in regulation 102(1) to make the apportionment referred to in regulation 102ZA(1),][4] apply the tests set out in regulation 106 to determine whether all input tax in the longer period in question shall be treated as attributable to taxable supplies,

(*f*) shall calculate the difference between the amount of input tax determined to be attributable to taxable supplies under subparagraphs (*a*) to (*e*) above and the amounts of input tax, if any, which were deducted in the returns for the prescribed accounting periods, and

(*g*) shall include any such amount of over-deduction or under-deduction in a return for—

(i) the first prescribed accounting period next following the longer period, or

(ii) the last prescribed accounting period in the longer period,

except where the Commissioners allow another return to be used.][2]

[(2) Where a taxable person makes no adjustment as required by paragraph (1) above, the requirement shall be that the adjustment is made in the return for the first prescribed accounting period next following the longer period.][2]

[(3) But where a registered person has his registration cancelled at or before the end of a longer period, he shall account for any adjustment under this regulation on his final return.][1]

[(4) In this regulation "residual input tax" has the same meaning as in regulation 101(10).][2]

Former regulation—VAT (General) Regulations, SI 1985/886 reg 34; VAT (General) (Amendment) Regulations, SI 1992/645 regs 1–3.

Amendments—1 Para (3) added by the VAT (Amendment) Regulations, SI 2002/1074 regs 2, 6 with effect for input tax incurred by a taxable person on goods imported or acquired by, or goods or services supplied to, him after 17 April 2002.

2 In para (1), words ", and where all his exempt input tax in that longer period cannot be treated as attributable to taxable supplies under regulation 106," and "shall" revoked, and sub-paras (*a*)–(*g*) substituted for previous sub-paras (*a*)–(*c*), para (2) substituted, and para (4) inserted, by the VAT (Amendment) (No 2) Regulations, SI 2009/820 regs 2, 8 with effect in relation to input tax incurred by a taxable person on goods imported or acquired by, or goods or services supplied to, him on or after 1 April 2009. Where 31 March 2009 falls within the prescribed accounting period of a taxable person, the amendments made by SI 2009/820 shall not, in relation to that taxable person, have effect until the day after the end of that prescribed accounting period (SI 2009/820 reg 1(2)).

3 Words in para (1) inserted, words in para (1)(*a*) substituted and para (*da*) inserted, by the VAT (Amendment) Regulations, SI 2010/559, regs 2, 9 with effect from 1 April 2010.

4 Words in para (1)(*e*) inserted by the VAT (Amendment) (No 4) Regulations, SI 2010/3022 regs 2, 7 with effect from 1 January 2011.

[107A—(1) This regulation applies where a taxable person has made an attribution under regulation 101(2)(*b*) and (*d*) and the prescribed accounting period does not form part of a longer period, and the attribution differs substantially from one which represents the extent to which the goods or services are used by him or are to be used by him, or a successor of his, in making taxable supplies.

(2) Where this regulation applies, the taxable person shall calculate the difference and account for it on the return for the first prescribed accounting period next following the prescribed accounting period referred to in paragraph (1) above, except where the Commissioners allow another return to be used for this purpose.

(3) But where a registered person has his registration cancelled at or before the end of the prescribed accounting period referred to in paragraph (1) above, he shall account for any adjustment under this regulation on his final return.][1]

Amendments—[1] Regulations 107A–107E inserted by the VAT (Amendment) Regulations, SI 2002/1074 regs 2, 7 with effect for input tax incurred by a taxable person on goods imported or acquired by, or goods or services supplied to, him after 17 April 2002.

[107B—(1) [Other than where input tax falls to be attributed under regulation 101(8) or regulation 107(1)(*b*) or (*c*),][2] this regulation applies where a taxable person has made an attribution under [regulation 107(1)(*a*) or (*d*)][2] according to the method specified in regulation 101 and that attribution differs substantially from one which represents the extent to which the goods or services are used by him or are to be used by him, or a successor of his, in making taxable supplies.

(2) Where this regulation applies the taxable person shall—

(*a*) calculate the difference, and

(*b*) in addition to any amount required to be included under [regulation 107(1)(*g*)][2], account for the amount so calculated on the return for the first prescribed accounting period next following the longer period [or the return for the last prescribed accounting period in the longer period if applicable][2], except where the Commissioners allow another return to be used for this purpose.

(3) But where a registered person has his registration cancelled at or before the end of a longer period, he shall account for any adjustment under this regulation on his final return.][1]

Amendments—[1] Regulations 107A–107E inserted by the VAT (Amendment) Regulations, SI 2002/1074 regs 2, 7 with effect for input tax incurred by a taxable person on goods imported or acquired by, or goods or services supplied to, him after 17 April 2002.

[2] In para (1), words inserted and words substituted for words "regulation 107(1)(*a*)", in para (2)(*b*), words substituted for words "regulation 107(1)(*c*)" and words inserted, by the VAT (Amendment) (No 2) Regulations, SI 2009/820 regs 2, 9 with effect in relation to input tax incurred by a taxable person on goods imported or acquired by, or goods or services supplied to, him on or after 1 April 2009. Where 31 March 2009 falls within the prescribed accounting period of a taxable person, the amendments made by SI 2009/820 shall not, in relation to that taxable person, have effect until the day after the end of that prescribed accounting period (SI 2009/820reg 1(2)).

[107C For the purposes of regulations 107A and 107B, a difference is substantial if it exceeds—

(*a*) £50,000; or

(*b*) 50% of the amount of input tax falling to be apportioned under regulation 101(2)(*d*) within the prescribed accounting period referred to in regulation 107A(1), or longer period, as the case may be, but is not less than £25,000.][1]

Amendments—[1] Regulations 107A–107E inserted by the VAT (Amendment) Regulations, SI 2002/1074 regs 2, 7 with effect for input tax incurred by a taxable person on goods imported or acquired by, or goods or services supplied to, him after 17 April 2002.

[107D For the purposes of regulations 107A and 107B a person is the successor of another if he is a person to whom that other person has—

(*a*) transferred assets of his business by a transfer of that business, or part of it, as a going concern; and

(*b*) the transfer of the assets is one falling by virtue of an Order under section 5(3) of the Act to be treated as neither a supply of goods nor a supply of services;

and the reference in this regulation to a person's successor includes references to the successors of his successors through any number of transfers.][1]

Amendments—[1] Regulations 107A–107E inserted by the VAT (Amendment) Regulations, SI 2002/1074 regs 2, 7 with effect for input tax incurred by a taxable person on goods imported or acquired by, or goods or services supplied to, him after 17 April 2002.

[107E—(1) Regulations 107A and 107B shall not apply where the amount of input tax falling to be apportioned under regulation 101(2)(*d*) within the prescribed accounting period referred to in regulation 107A(1), or longer period, as the case may be, does not exceed—

(*a*) in the case of a person who is a group undertaking in relation to one or more other undertakings (other than undertakings which are treated under sections 43A to 43C of the Act as members of the same group as the person), £25,000 per annum, adjusted in proportion for a period that is not 12 months; or

(*b*) in the case of any other person, £50,000 per annum, adjusted in proportion for a period that is not 12 months.

(2) For the purposes of paragraph (1) above, "undertaking" and "group undertaking" have the same meaning as in [section 1161 of the Companies Act 2006][2].][1]

Amendments—[1] Regulations 107A–107E inserted by the VAT (Amendment) Regulations, SI 2002/1074 regs 2, 7 with effect for input tax incurred by a taxable person on goods imported or acquired by, or goods or services supplied to, him after 17 April 2002.

[2] Words in sub-para (2) substituted by the Companies Act 2006 (Consequential Amendments) (Taxes and National Insurance) Order, SI 2008/954 arts 43, 45 with effect from 6 April 2008.

[107F The references in regulations 107C and 107E to an apportionment under regulation 101(2)(*d*) in relation to a longer period include cases where the apportionment is made under regulation 107(1)(*a*) or (*d*) using the calculation specified in regulation 101(2)(*d*).][1]

Amendments—[1] This para inserted by the VAT (Amendment) (No 2) Regulations, SI 2009/820 regs 2, 10 with effect in relation to input tax incurred by a taxable person on goods imported or acquired by, or goods or services supplied to, him on or after 1 April 2009. Where 31 March 2009 falls within the prescribed accounting period of a taxable person, the amendments made by SI 2009/820 shall not, in relation to that taxable person, have effect until the day after the end of that prescribed accounting period (SI 2009/820reg 1(2)).

108—(1) This regulation applies where a taxable person has deducted an amount of input tax which has been attributed to taxable supplies because he intended to use the goods or services in making either—

(*a*) taxable supplies, or

(*b*) both taxable and exempt supplies,

and during a period of 6 years commencing on the first day of the prescribed accounting period in which the attribution was determined and before that intention is fulfilled, he uses or forms an intention to use the goods or services concerned in making exempt supplies or, in the case of an attribution within sub-paragraph (a) above, in making both taxable and exempt supplies.

(2) Subject to regulation 110 and save as the Commissioners otherwise allow where this regulation applies the taxable person shall on the return for the prescribed accounting period in which the use occurs or the intention is formed, as the case may be, account for an amount equal to the input tax which has ceased to be attributable to taxable supplies in accordance with the method which he was required to use when the input tax was first attributed and he shall repay the said amount to the Commissioners.

(3) For the purposes of this regulation any question as to the nature of any supply shall be determined in accordance with the provisions of the Act and any Regulations or Orders made thereunder in force at the time when the input tax was first attributed.

Former regulations—VAT (General) Regulations, SI 1985/886 reg 35; VAT (General) (Amendment) Regulations, SI 1992/645 regs 1–3, SI 1993/1639 reg 6.

Simon's Tax Cases—*C&E Comrs v Svenska International plc* [1999] STC 406*, *C&E Comrs v Wiggett Construction Ltd* [2001] STC 933.

reg 108(1), *Tremerton Ltd v C&E Comrs* [1999] STC 1039.

109—(1) This regulation applies where a taxable person has incurred an amount of input tax which has not been attributed to taxable supplies because he intended to use the goods or services in making either—

(*a*) exempt supplies, or

(*b*) both taxable and exempt supplies,

and during a period of 6 years commencing on the first day of the prescribed accounting period in which the attribution was determined and before that intention is fulfilled, he uses or forms an intention to use the goods or services concerned in making taxable supplies or, in the case of an attribution within sub-paragraph (a) above, in making both taxable and exempt supplies.

(2) Subject to regulation 110 and where this regulation applies, the Commissioners shall, on receipt of an application made by the taxable person in such form and manner and containing such particulars as they may direct, pay to him an amount equal to the input tax which has become attributable to taxable supplies in accordance with the method which he was required to use when the input tax was first attributed.

(3) For the purposes of this regulation any question as to the nature of any supply shall be determined in accordance with the provisions of the Act and any Regulations or Orders made thereunder in force at the time when the input tax was first attributed.

Former regulations—VAT (General) Regulations, SI 1985/886 reg 36; VAT (General) (Amendment) Regulations, SI 1992/645 regs 1–3, SI 1993/1639 reg 7.

Simon's Tax Cases—*Royal & Sun Alliance Insurance Group plc v C&E Comrs* [2000] STC 933, [2003] STC 832; *Community Housing Association Ltd v R&C Comrs* [2009] STC 1324.

[110—(1) Subject to paragraph (2) below, in this regulation, in regulations [103B,][2] 108 and 109 above and in Part XV of these Regulations—

(*a*) "exempt supplies" includes supplies outside the United Kingdom which would be exempt if made in the United Kingdom, other than supplies of a description falling within subparagraph (*b*) below; and

(*b*) "taxable supplies" includes supplies of a description falling within regulation [103][2] above.

(2) Subject to paragraph (3) below, for the purposes of identifying the use, or intended use, of goods and services in regulations 108 and 109 above and in Part XV of these Regulations—

(*a*) "exempt supplies" shall be construed as including supplies of a description falling within regulation 103A(1) above, but only to the extent that there is, or would be, no credit for input tax on goods and services under that regulation; and

(*b*) "taxable supplies" shall be construed as including supplies of a description falling within regulation 103A(1) above, but only to the extent that there is, or would be, credit for input tax on goods and services under that regulation.

(3) Any adjustment under regulations 108 and 109 above shall not cause any more or any less input tax to be credited, as the case may be, in respect of supplies of a description falling within regulation 103A(1) above than would be allowed or required under that regulation.

(4) Subject to [regulations 103 and 103B][2], where—

(*a*) regulation 108 or 109 applies,

(*b*) the use to which the goods or services concerned are put, or to which they are intended to be put, includes the making of any supplies outside the United Kingdom, and

(*c*) at the time when the taxable person was first required to attribute the input tax he was not required to use a method approved or directed under regulation 102 or that method did not provide expressly for the attribution of input tax attributable to supplies outside the United Kingdom,

the amount for which the taxable person shall be liable to account under regulation 108 or the amount which he is entitled to be paid under regulation 109, as the case may be, shall be calculated by reference to the extent to which the goods or services concerned are used or intended to be used in making taxable supplies, expressed as a proportion of the whole use or intended use.

[(5) In regulations 108 and 109 a reference to—

(*a*) "exempt supplies" includes a reference to non-business activities that give rise to an amount of non-business VAT;

(*b*) a method which a taxable person is required to use includes a reference to an apportionment which a taxable person is required to make under section 24(5) of the Act.][3]][1]

Former regulations—VAT (General) Regulations, SI 1985/886 reg 36A; VAT (General) (Amendment) Regulations, SI 1993/1639 reg 8, SI 1994/3015 reg 6.

Amendments—[1] This Regulation substituted by the VAT (Amendment) (No 4) Regulations, SI 1999/3114, regs 2, 9, with effect from 1 January 2000.

[2] Reference inserted in para (1), and references substituted in paras (1)(*b*), (4), by the VAT (Amendment) (No 4) Regulations, SI 2004/3140 reg 14 with effect from 3 December 2004: SI 2004/3140 reg 2(3).

[3] Para (5) inserted by the VAT (Amendment) (No 4) Regulations, SI 2010/3022 regs 2, 8 with effect in relation to input tax incurred by a taxable person on goods imported or acquired by, or goods or services supplied to, that taxable person on or after 1 January 2011.

111 Exceptional claims for VAT relief

(1) Subject to paragraphs (2) and (4) below, on a claim made in accordance with paragraph (3) below, the Commissioners may authorise a taxable person to treat as if it were input tax—

(*a*) VAT on the supply of goods or services to the taxable person before the date with effect from which he was, or was required to be, registered, or paid by him on the importation or acquisition of goods before that date, for the purpose of a business which either was carried on or was to be carried on by him at the time of such supply or payment, and

(*b*) in the case of a body corporate, VAT on goods obtained for it before its incorporation, or on the supply of services before that time for its benefit or in connection with its incorporation, provided that the person to whom the supply was made or who paid VAT on the importation or acquisition—

(i) became a member, officer or employee of the body and was reimbursed, or has received an undertaking to be reimbursed, by the body for the whole amount of the price paid for the goods or services,

(ii) was not at the time of the importation, acquisition or supply a taxable person, and

(iii) imported, acquired or was supplied with the goods, or received the services, for the purpose of a business to be carried on by the body and has not used them for any purpose other than such a business,

[(2) No VAT may be treated as if it were input tax under paragraph (1) above—

(*a*) in respect of—

(i) goods or services which had been supplied, or

(ii) save as the Commissioners may otherwise allow, goods which had been consumed,

by the relevant person before the date with effect from which the taxable person was, or was required to be, registered;

(*b*) subject to paragraph (2A)[, (2C) and (2D)][3] below, in respect of goods which had been supplied to, or imported or acquired by, the relevant person more than [4 years][3] before the date with effect from which the taxable person was, or was required to be, registered;

VAT SIs

(c) in respect of services performed upon goods to which sub-paragraph (a) or (b) above applies; . . .[4]

(d) in respect of services which had been supplied to the relevant person more than 6 months before the date with effect from which the taxable person was, or was required to be, registered; [or

(e) in respect of capital items of a description falling within regulation 113.][4]][1]

[(2A) Paragraph (2)(b) above does not apply where—

(a) the taxable person was registered before 1st May 1997; and

(b) he did not make any returns before that date.

(2B) In paragraph (2) above references to the relevant person are references to—

(a) the taxable person; or

(b) in the case of paragraph (1)(b) above, the person to whom the supply had been made, or who had imported or acquired the goods, as the case may be.][1]

[(2C) Where the relevant person was, or was required to be, registered on or before 1st April 2009, no VAT may be treated as if it were input tax under paragraph (1) above in respect of goods which were supplied to, or imported or acquired by the relevant person more than 3 years before the date with effect from which that person was, or was required to be, registered.

(2D) Where the relevant person was or was required to be registered on or before 31st March 2010 and paragraph (2C) above does not apply, no VAT may be treated as if it were input tax under paragraph (1) above in respect of goods which were supplied to, or imported or acquired by, the relevant person on or before 31st March 2006.][3]

(3) [Subject to paragraph (3A) and (3B) below, a][1] claim under paragraph (1) above shall, save as the Commissioners may otherwise allow, be made on [the first return the taxable person is required to make][2] and, as the Commissioners may require, be supported by invoices and other evidence.

[(3A) Where the taxable person was registered before 1st May 1997 and has not made any returns before that date paragraph (3) above shall have effect as if for the words "the first return the taxable person is required to make" there were substituted the words "the first return the taxable person makes".

(3B) [Subject to paragraph (3C)][3] the Commissioners shall not allow a person to make any claim under paragraph (3) above in terms such that the VAT concerned would fall to be claimed as if it were input tax more than [4 years][3] after the date by which the first return he is required to make is required to be made.][1]

[(3C) The Commissioners shall not allow a person to make any claim under paragraph (3) above in the circumstances where the first return the taxable person was required to make was required to be made on or before 31st March 2006.][3]

(4) A taxable person making a claim under paragraph (1) above shall compile and preserve for such period as the Commissioners may require—

(a) in respect of goods, a stock account showing separately quantities purchased, quantities used in the making of other goods, date of purchase and date and manner of subsequent disposals of both such quantities, and

(b) in respect of services, a list showing their description, date of purchase and date of disposal, if any.

(5) [Subject to paragraph (6) below][1] if a person who has been, but is no longer, a taxable person makes a claim in such manner and supported by such evidence as the Commissioners may require, they may pay to him the amount of any VAT on the supply of services to him after the date with effect from which he ceased to be, or to be required to be, registered and which was attributable to any taxable supply made by him in the course or furtherance of any business carried on by him when he was, or was required to be, registered.

[(6) Subject to paragraph (7) [and (8)][3] below, no claim under paragraph (5) above may be made more than [4 years][3] after the date on which the supply of services was made.

(7) Paragraph (6) above does not apply where—

(a) the person ceased to be, or ceased to be required to be, registered before 1st May 1997; and

(b) the supply was made before that date.][1]

[(8) No claim may be made under paragraph (5) above in relation to a supply of services which was made on or before 31st March 2006.][3]

Former regulations—VAT (General) Regulations, SI 1985/886 reg 37; VAT (General) (Amendment) Regulations, SI 1992/645 regs 1–3, SI 1992/3102 reg 22.

Amendments—[1] Para (2) substituted and paras (2A), (2B), (3A), (3B), (6), (7) and words in paras (3), (5) inserted by the VAT (Amendment) Regulations, SI 1997/1086 reg 7 with effect from 1 May 1997.

[2] Words in para (3) substituted by SI 1997/1086 reg 7 with effect from 1 May 1997.

[3] In paras (2)(b), (3B), (6), words inserted and words substituted for words "3 years", paras (2C), (2D), (3C), (8) inserted, by the VAT (Amendment) Regulations, SI 2009/586 regs 2, 8 with effect from 1 April 2009.

[4] In para (2)(c), word "or" revoked, and para (2)(e) and preceding word "or" inserted, by the VAT (Amendment) (No 4) Regulations, SI 2010/3022 regs 2, 9 with effect in relation to any person registering for VAT on or after 1 January 2011.

PART XV
ADJUSTMENTS TO THE DEDUCTION OF INPUT TAX ON CAPITAL ITEMS

112 Interpretation of Part XV

(1) Any expression used in this Part to which a meaning is given in Part XIV of these Regulations shall, unless the contrary intention appears, have the same meaning in this Part as it has in that Part [and in particular, exempt supplies and taxable supplies shall be accorded the same meanings as defined in regulation 110 above][1].

(2) Any reference in this Part to a capital item shall be construed as a reference to a capital item to which this Part applies by virtue of regulation 113, being an item which a person [who has or acquires an interest in the item in question][2] (hereinafter referred to as "the owner") uses in the course or furtherance of a business carried on by him, and for the purpose of that business, otherwise than solely for the purpose of selling the item.

[(3) In this regulation and in regulation 114, an interest includes an interest which is treated as being supplied to a person under [paragraph 37(1)][3] of Schedule 10 to the Act provided that the numerator of the fraction in [paragraph 37(3)][3] of that Schedule is [36][3] or more.

(4) The reference to "owner" in paragraph (2) shall be taken to refer to—

(*a*) subject to sub-paragraph (*b*), the transferee where the whole or part of a capital item is transferred from one person to another and that transfer is not treated as a supply for the purposes of VAT; and

(*b*) the representative member of a group under section 43 of the Act if the capital item is owned by a member of the group.

(5) Where the owner is a transferee or representative member, that person shall be treated as having done everything that the transferor or group member (as may be the case) has done in respect of the capital item.][2]

Former regulations—VAT (General) Regulations, SI 1985/886 reg 37A; VAT (General) (Amendment) Regulations, SI 1989/2355 reg 4, SI 1992/645 regs 2, 4.

Press releases etc—Business Brief 30/97 19-12-97 (Statement of practice on a budget change to the capital goods scheme).

Amendments—[1] Words in para (1) inserted by the VAT (Amendment) (No 4) Regulations, SI 1999/3114, regs 2, 10, with effect from 1 January 2000.

[2] Words in para (2), and whole of paras (3)–(5), inserted, by the VAT (Amendment) (No 4) Regulations, SI 2010/3022 regs 2, 10 with effect from 1 January 2011.

[3] In para (3), words substituted for words "paragraph 37(3)", "paragraph 37(5)" and "3", by the VAT (Amendment) Regulations, SI 2011/254 regs 2, 3 with effect in relation to supplies treated as made under VATA 1994 Sch 10 where the building that is supplied was completed on or after 1 March 2011.

[113 Capital items to which this Part applies

(1) The capital items to which this Part applies are any of the items specified in paragraph (2) on or in relation to which the owner incurs VAT bearing capital expenditure of a type specified in paragraph (3), the value of which is not less than that specified in paragraph (4).

(2) The items are—

(*a*) land;

(*b*) a building or part of a building;

(*c*) a civil engineering work or part of a civil engineering work;

(*d*) a computer or an item of computer equipment;

(*e*) an aircraft;

(*f*) a ship, boat or other vessel.

(3) The expenditure—

(*a*) in the case of an item falling within paragraph (2)(*a*) or (*d*), is the expenditure relating to its acquisition;

(*b*) in the case of an item falling within paragraph (2)(*b*), (*c*), (*e*) or (*f*), is the expenditure relating to its—

(i) acquisition,

(ii) construction (including where appropriate manufacture),

(iii) refurbishment,

(iv) fitting out,

(v) alteration, or

(vi) extension (including the construction of an annex).

(4) The value for the purposes of paragraph (3) is—

(*a*) not less than £250,000 where the item falls within paragraph (2)(*a*), (*b*) or (*c*);

(*b*) not less than £50,000 where the item falls within paragraph (2)(*d*), (*e*) or (*f*).][1]

Amendments—[1] Reg 113 substituted by the VAT (Amendment) (No 4) Regulations, SI 2010/3022 regs 2, 11 with effect in relation to input tax incurred by a taxable person on goods imported or acquired by, or goods or services supplied to, that taxable person on or after 1 January 2011.

[113A—(1) This regulation applies where—

(*a*) the owner of an item described by regulation 113(2)(a) to (c) ("O") (or a person to whom O has granted an interest in that item) uses that item to make a grant that falls within item 1(ka) of Group 1 of Schedule 9 to the Act,

(*b*) apart from this regulation, the item would not be a capital item to which this Part applies,

(*c*) O has, no later than 31st March 2013, decided to treat the item as a capital item for the purposes of this Part, and

(*d*) O has made a written record of that decision specifying the date that it was made.

(2) Where this regulation applies, for the item in question—

(*a*) for "£250,000" in regulation 113(4)(a) substitute "£1", but

(*b*) no adjustment of deductions of input tax shall be made under this Part for any intervals ending before 1st October 2012 that fall within the period of adjustment for the capital item as prescribed in regulation 114.][1]

Amendments—[1] Reg 113A inserted by the VAT (Amendment) (No 2) Regulations, SI 2012/1899 regs 3, 17 with effect from 1 October 2012.

114 Period of adjustment

(1) The proportion (if any) of the total input tax on a capital item which may be deducted under Part XIV shall be subject to adjustments in accordance with the provisions of this Part.

(2) Adjustments shall be made over a period determined in accordance with the following paragraphs of this regulation.

[(3) Subject to paragraphs (3A) and (3B), the period of adjustment is—

(*a*) 10 successive intervals in the case of a capital item of a description falling within regulation 113(2)(*a*) to (*c*);

(*b*) 5 successive intervals in the case of a capital item of a description falling within regulation 113(2)(*d*) to (*f*),

determined in accordance with paragraphs (4) to (5B) and (7).

(3A) If, at the time of the owner's first use, the number of intervals specified in paragraph (3)(*a*) or (*b*) (as may be the case) exceeds the number of complete years that the owner's interest in the capital item has to run by more than one, the number of intervals shall be reduced to one more than the number of complete years that the owner's interest has to run calculated from the date of the owner's first use of the item (but not to less than three intervals).

(3B) Where the owner's interest falls within regulation 112(3), the number of intervals shall be the same as the numerator of the fraction in [paragraph 37(5)][4] of Schedule 10 to the Act [divided by 12 and rounded up to the next whole number][4].

(3C) Where paragraph (3A) or (3B) applies, the relevant denominator in regulation 115(1) shall be adjusted accordingly.

(3D) Where a person who registers for VAT already owns an item of a description falling within regulation 113, for the purposes of calculating the period of adjustment—

(*a*) one complete interval shall be deducted for each complete year which has elapsed since the date of that person's first use of the capital item prior to the date of VAT registration, and

(*b*) the first interval applicable to the capital item which ends after the date of VAT registration shall be treated as a subsequent interval for the purposes of regulation 115(1).

(4) Subject to paragraphs (5A), (5B) and (7), the first interval applicable to a capital item shall commence on the day on which the owner first uses the capital item and shall end on the day before the start of his next tax year whether or not this is his first tax year.][3]

(5) Subject to [paragraphs (5A), (5B) and (7)][2] below, each subsequent interval applicable to a capital item shall correspond with a longer period applicable to the owner, or if no longer period applies to him, a tax year of his.

[(5A) On the first occasion during the period of adjustment applicable to a capital item that the owner of the item—

(*a*) being a registered person subsequently becomes a member of a group under section 43 of the Act;

(*b*) being a member of a group under section 43 ceases to be a member of that group (whether or not he becomes a member of another such group immediately thereafter); or

(*c*) transfers the item in the course of the transfer of his business or part of his business as a going concern (the item therefore not being treated as supplied) in circumstances where the new owner is not, under regulation 6(1) above, registered with the registration number of and in substitution for the transferor,

the interval then applying shall end on the day before he becomes a member of a group or the day that he ceases to be a member of the group or transfers the business or part of the business (as the case may require) and thereafter each subsequent interval (if any) applicable to the capital item shall end on the successive anniversaries of that day..][1]

[(5B) Where the extent to which a capital item is used in making taxable supplies does not change between what would, but for this paragraph, have been the first interval and the first subsequent interval applicable to it and the length of the two intervals taken together does not exceed 12 months the first interval applicable to the capital item shall end on what would have been the day that the first subsequent interval expired.][1]

(6) . . .[2]

[(7) Where the owner of a capital item transfers it during the period of adjustment applicable to it in the course of the transfer of his business or a part of his business as a going concern (the item therefore not being treated as supplied) and the new owner is, under regulation 6(1) above, registered with the registration number of, and in substitution for the transferor, the interval applying to the capital item at the time of the transfer shall end on the last day of the longer period applying to the new owner immediately after the transfer or, if no longer period then applies to him, shall end on the last day of his tax year following the day of transfer.][2]

Former regulations—VAT (General) Regulations, SI 1985/886 reg 37C; VAT (General) (Amendment) Regulations, SI 1989/2355 reg 4, SI 1992/3102 reg 24.

Press releases etc—Business Brief 30/97 19-12-97 (Statement of practice on a budget change to the capital goods scheme).

Amendments—[1] Paras (5A) and (5B), inserted by the VAT (Amendment) (No 3) Regulations, SI 1997/1614 reg 11 with effect from 3 July 1997.

[2] Words in para (5) substituted, para (6) deleted and para (7) substituted by SI 1997/1614 reg 11 with effect from 3 July 1997.

[3] Paras (3)–(4) substituted for previous paras (3), (4) by the VAT (Amendment) (No 4) Regulations, SI 2010/3022 regs 2, 12 with effect in relation to any capital item where the first interval of its adjustment period (as determined under the law prior to SI 2010/3022 regs 5 to 15 coming into force) has not started before 1 January 2011.

[4] In para (3B), words substituted for words "paragraph 37(5)", and words inserted, by the VAT (Amendment) Regulations, SI 2011/254 regs 2, 4 with effect in relation to supplies treated as made under VATA 1994 Sch 10 where the building that is supplied was completed on or after 1 March 2011.

115 Method of adjustment

(1) Where in a subsequent interval applicable to a capital item, the extent to which it is used in making taxable supplies increases from the extent to which it was so used [or to be used at the time that the original entitlement to deduction of the input tax was determined][3], the owner may deduct for that subsequent interval an amount calculated as follows—

(*a*) where the capital item falls within [regulation 114(3)(b)][5]—

$$\frac{\text{the total input tax on the capital sum}}{5} \times \text{the adjustment percentage;}$$

(*b*) where the capital item falls within [regulation 114(3)(*a*)][5]—

$$\frac{\text{the total input tax on the capital sum}}{10} \times \text{the adjustment percentage;}$$

(2) Where in a subsequent interval applicable to a capital item, the extent to which it is used in making taxable supplies decreases from the extent to which it was so used [or to be used at the time that the original entitlement to deduction of the input tax was determined][3], the owner shall pay to the Commissioners for that subsequent interval an amount calculated in the manner described in paragraph (1) above.

[(3) Paragraph (3ZA) applies where, during an interval other than the last interval applicable to a capital item, the owner—

(*a*) supplies the whole or part of his interest in the capital item, or

(*b*) is deemed to supply the whole or part of his interest in the capital item, or

(*c*) would have been deemed to supply the whole of his interest in the capital item but for the fact that the VAT on the deemed supply (whether by virtue of its value or because it is zero-rated or exempt) would not have exceeded the sum specified in paragraph 8(1)(*c*) of Schedule 4 to the Act.

(3ZA) If the supply (or deemed supply) of the capital item referred to in paragraph (3) is—

(*a*) a taxable supply, the owner shall be treated as using the whole or part (as may be the case) of the capital item for each of the remaining complete intervals applicable to it wholly in making taxable supplies, or

(*b*) an exempt supply, the owner shall be treated as not using the whole or part (as may be the case) of the capital item for any of the remaining complete intervals applicable to it in making any taxable supplies,

and, in each case, the owner shall, except where paragraph (3A) applies, calculate for each of the remaining complete intervals applicable to the capital item, in accordance with paragraph (1) or (2) as the case may require, such amount as the owner may deduct or be liable to pay to the Commissioners.][5]

VAT SIs

[(3A) This paragraph applies if the total amount of input tax deducted or deductible by the owner of a capital item as a result of the initial deduction, any adjustments made under paragraph (1) or (2) above and the adjustment which would apart from this paragraph fall to be made under [paragraph (3ZA)][5] above would exceed the output tax chargeable by him [on the supply of the whole or part of that capital item][5].][2]

[(3B) Save as the Commissioners may otherwise allow, where paragraph (3A) above applies the owner may deduct, or as the case may require, shall pay to the Commissioners such amount as results in the total amount of input tax deducted or deductible being equal to the output tax chargeable by him [on the supply of the whole or part of the capital item][5].][2]

[(4) If a capital item is irretrievably lost or stolen or is totally destroyed, no further adjustment shall be made in respect of any remaining complete intervals applicable to it.][5]

[(5) Subject to paragraph (5A), for the purposes of this Part—

"the adjustment percentage" means the difference (if any) between the extent, expressed as a percentage, to which the whole or part as appropriate of the capital item was used or to be used for the making of taxable supplies at the time the original entitlement to deduction of the input tax was determined and the extent to which the whole or part of it as appropriate is so used, or is treated under paragraph (3ZA) as being so used, in the subsequent interval in question;

"the original entitlement to deduction" means the entitlement to deduction under sections 24 to 26 of the Act and regulations made under those sections;

"the total input tax on the capital item" means—

in relation to any capital item, all VAT incurred by the owner on the capital expenditure on that item (whether or not the person incurring it is VAT registered at the time that it is incurred) including any non-business VAT; and

where a person is treated as making a supply to himself under [paragraph 37(1)][7] of Schedule 10 to the Act, the VAT charged on that supply;

"VAT bearing capital expenditure" means capital expenditure on which VAT is charged at the standard rate or at a reduced rate.][6]

[(5A) Where paragraph (3ZA) applies in respect of part of a capital item, for the remaining complete intervals the total VAT incurred on the capital item as defined in paragraph (5) shall be reduced accordingly.

(5B) The person responsible for making an adjustment under paragraph (1), (2) or (3ZA) shall be the person who is treated as the owner of the capital item under regulation 112 at the point immediately prior to the end of the interval in question or, in the case of an adjustment under paragraph (3ZA), the event specified in paragraph (3).][5]

(6) [Subject to [paragraphs (9) and (11)][5] below][1] a taxable person claiming any amount pursuant to paragraph (1) above, or liable to pay any amount pursuant to paragraph (2) above, shall include such amount in a return for the second prescribed accounting period next following the interval to which that amount relates, except where the Commissioners allow another return to be used for this purpose . . . [5]

(7) [Subject to [paragraphs (9) and (11)][5] below][1] a taxable person claiming any amount or amounts, or liable to pay any amount or amounts, pursuant to paragraph [(3ZA)][5] above, shall include such amount or amounts in a return for the second prescribed accounting period next following the interval in which the supply (or deemed supply) in question takes place except where the Commissioners allow another return to be used for this purpose.

[(8) For the purposes of paragraph (9), a "specified return" means a return specified in paragraph (6) or (7).][5]

(9) . . . [5] The Commissioners shall not allow the taxable person to use a return other than a specified return unless it is the return for a prescribed accounting period commencing within 4 years of the end of the prescribed accounting period to which the specified return relates.

(10) . . . [5]][4]

[(11) Where a person is required to make an adjustment under paragraph (1), (2) or (3ZA) at a time when he is no longer registered for VAT, he shall make the required adjustment in his final VAT return.][5]

Commentary—*De Voil Indirect Tax Service* **V3.470**.

Former regulations—VAT (General) Regulations, SI 1985/886 reg 37D; VAT (General) (Amendment) Regulations, SI 1989/2355 reg 4.

Press releases etc—Business Brief 30/97 19-12-97 (Statement of practice on a budget change to the capital goods scheme).

Simon's Tax Cases—*Centralan Property Ltd v C&E Comrs* [2006] STC 1542.

–reg 115(2), *Gateshead Talmudical College v R&C Comrs* [2011] UKUT 131 (TCC), [2011] STC 1593.

Amendments—[1] Words in paras (6) and (7) inserted by the VAT (Amendment) Regulations, SI 1997/1086 reg 8 with effect from 1 May 1997.

[2] Paras (3A), (3B), inserted by the VAT (Amendment) (No 3) Regulations, SI 1997/1614 reg 12 with effect from 3 July 1997.

[4] Words in paras (1), (2) substituted by the VAT (Amendment) (No 2) Regulations, SI 1999/599 reg 6 with effect from subsequent adjustment intervals commencing on or after 10 March 1999.

[7] Paras (8)–(10) substituted for previous para (8), by the VAT (Amendment) Regulations, SI 2009/586 regs 2, 9 with effect from 1 April 2009.

[8] In paras (1)(*a*), (*b*), (3A), (3B), (7) words substituted, paras (3), (3ZA) substituted for previous para (3), paras (4), (8) substituted, paras (5A), (5B) inserted, in para (6) words substituted and revoked, in para (9) words revoked, para (10) revoked, and para (11) inserted, by the VAT (Amendment) (No 4) Regulations, SI 2010/3022 regs 2, 13(*a*)–(*f*), (*h*)–(*n*) with effect from 1 January 2011.

[9] Para (5) substituted by the VAT (Amendment) (No 4) Regulations, SI 2010/3022 regs 2, 13(*g*) with effect in relation to input tax incurred by a taxable person on goods imported or acquired by, or goods or services supplied to, that taxable person on or after 1 January 2011.

[10] In para (5), words substituted for words "paragraph 37(3)" by the VAT (Amendment) Regulations, SI 2011/254 regs 2, 5 with effect in relation to supplies treated as made under VATA 1994 Sch 10 where the building that is supplied was completed on or after 1 March 2011.

116 Ascertainment of taxable use of a capital item

(1) Subject to regulation 115(3) [and (3B)][2] and paragraphs (2)[, (A2)][2] and (3) below, for the purposes of this Part, an attribution of the total input tax on the capital item shall be determined for each subsequent interval applicable to it [in accordance with the provisions of sections 24 to 26 of the Act and regulations made under those sections as they apply to that interval][3] and the proportion of the input tax thereby determined to be attributable to taxable supplies shall be treated as being the extent to which the capital item is used in making taxable supplies in that subsequent interval.

[(A2) Subject to paragraph (2) below, the attribution of the total input tax on a capital item for subsequent intervals determined in accordance with regulation 114(5A) above shall be determined by such method as is agreed with the Commissioners.][2]

(2) In any particular case the Commissioners may allow another method by which, or may direct the manner in which, the extent to which a capital item is used in making taxable supplies in any subsequent interval applicable to it is to be ascertained.

(3) Where the owner of a building which is a capital item of his grants or assigns a tenancy or lease in the whole or any part of that building and that grant or assignment is a zero-rated supply to the extent only as provided by—

(*a*) note [(14)][1] to Group 5 of Schedule 8 to the Act, or

(*b*) that note as applied to Group 6 of that Schedule by note [(3)][1] to Group 6, or

(*c*) paragraph 8 of Schedule 13 to the Act,

any subsequent exempt supply of his arising directly from that grant or assignment shall be disregarded in determining the extent to which the capital item is used in making taxable supplies in any interval applicable to it.

Former regulations—VAT (General) Regulations, SI 1985/886 reg 37E; VAT (General) (Amendment) Regulations, SI 1989/2355 reg 4, SI 1992/645 regs 2, 5.

Press releases etc—Business Brief 30/97 19-12-97 (Statement of practice on a budget change to the capital goods scheme).

Simon's Tax Cases—*C&E Comrs v R & R Pension Fund Trustees* [1996] STC 889*.

Amendments—[1] Figures in para (3) substituted by the VAT (Amendment) Regulations, SI 1995/3147 reg 5, with effect from 1 January 1996.

[2] Words in para (1) above, and para (A2) above, inserted by the VAT (Amendment) (No 3) Regulations, SI 1997/1614 reg 13 with effect from 3 July 1997.

[3] In para (1), words substituted by the VAT (Amendment) (No 4) Regulations, SI 2010/3022 regs 2, 14 with effect from 1 January 2011.

[PART 15A

GOODS USED FOR NON-BUSINESS PURPOSES DURING THEIR ECONOMIC LIFE][1]

Note—The VAT (Amendment) (No 7) Regulations, SI 2007/3099 revoke and replace the VAT (Amendment) (No 6) Regulations, SI 2007/2922. This revocation was necessary owing to a typographical error in the recital powers pursuant to which the No 6 Regulations were made. The No 7 Regulations make the amendments to the VAT Regulations, SI 2003/2518, which were intended to be made by the No 6 Regulations.

Amendments—[1] Part 15A (regs 116A–116N) inserted by the VAT (Amendment) (No 7) Regulations, SI 2007/3099 regs 3, 4 with effect from 1 November 2007: SI 2007/3099 reg 1(2)(*b*).

116A [Application

This Part makes provision for calculating the full cost to a person of providing the supply of services ("relevant supply") that is treated as made pursuant to paragraph 5(4) of Schedule 4 to the Act where goods that are held or used for the purposes of a business are used for private or non-business purposes. Where goods that are held or used for the purposes of a business have an economic life (see regulations 116C, 116D, 116G and 116L) at the time when they are used for private or non-business purposes, the value or part of the value of the relevant supply which is referable to that use on or after 1st November 2007 shall be calculated in accordance with the regulations in this Part.][1]

Amendments—[1] Part 15A (regs 116A–116N) inserted by the VAT (Amendment) (No 7) Regulations, SI 2007/3099 regs 3, 4 with effect from 1 November 2007: SI 2007/3099 reg 1(2)(*b*).

116B Interpretation of this Part

(1) In this Part—

"full cost of the goods" means the full cost of the goods to the person (being the person making the relevant supply or any of his predecessors) who, in relation to the VAT on the goods mentioned in paragraph 5(5) of Schedule 4 to the Act, is described in that paragraph as being entitled to—

(*a*) credit under sections 25 and 26 of the Act; or

(*b*) a repayment under the scheme made under section 39 of the Act;

[but, in relation to any goods which are relevant assets, the full cost shall exclude any costs on which VAT was incurred on or after 1 January 2011;][2]

"goods" includes land forming part of the assets of, or held or used for the purposes of, a business which is treated as goods for the purposes of paragraph 5 of Schedule 4 to the Act by virtue of paragraph 9 of that Schedule and references to goods being held or used for the purposes of a business shall be construed accordingly;

"predecessor" has the same meaning as it does in paragraph 5 of Schedule 4 to the Act.

["relevant asset" has the same meaning as it has in section 24(5B) of the Act.][2]

(2) In this Part, references to a period of time comprising a number of months shall be computed to two decimal places where that period does not comprise a whole number of months.][1]

Amendments—[1] Part 15A (regs 116A–116N) inserted by the VAT (Amendment) (No 7) Regulations, SI 2007/3099 regs 3, 4 with effect from 1 November 2007: SI 2007/3099 reg 1(2)(*b*).

[2] In para (1), in definition of "the full cost of the goods", words inserted, and definition of "relevant asset" inserted, by the VAT (Amendment) (No 4) Regulations, SI 2010/3022 regs 2, 15 with effect from 1 January 2011.

116C [Economic life of goods

Goods held or used for the purposes of a business have an economic life being (subject to regulations 116G and 116L) the period of time commencing on the day when they are first used for any purpose after they have been supplied to, or acquired or imported by, a person or any of his predecessors and lasting for a period of—

(*a*) 120 months in the case of land, a building or part of a building (but this is subject to regulation 116D);

(*b*) 60 months for all other goods.][1]

Amendments—[1] Part 15A (regs 116A–116N) inserted by the VAT (Amendment) (No 7) Regulations, SI 2007/3099 regs 3, 4 with effect from 1 November 2007: SI 2007/3099 reg 1(2)(*b*).

[116D Where the economic life of the interest of a person, or any of his predecessors, in land, a building or part of a building commences at a time when that interest has less than 120 months to run at that time, it shall be limited to the number of months remaining before expiry of that interest and element B of the formula in regulation 116E and element D of the formula in regulation 116L shall be construed accordingly.][1]

Amendments—[1] Part 15A (regs 116A–116N) inserted by the VAT (Amendment) (No 7) Regulations, SI 2007/3099 regs 3, 4 with effect from 1 November 2007: SI 2007/3099 reg 1(2)(*b*).

116E [Value of a relevant supply

Subject to regulations 116F, 116H and 116I, the value of a relevant supply is the amount determined using the formula—

$$\frac{A}{B} \times (C \times U\%)$$

where—

A is the number of months in the prescribed accounting period during which the relevant supply occurs which fall within the economic life of the goods concerned;

B is the number of months of the economic life of the goods concerned or, in the case of an economic life commencing on 1st November 2007 by virtue of regulation 116L, what would have been its duration if it had been determined according to regulation 116C or 116G as appropriate;

C is the full cost of the goods excluding any increase resulting from a supply of goods or services giving rise to a new economic life; and

U% is the extent, expressed as a percentage, to which the goods are put to any private use or used, or made available for use, for non-business purposes as compared with the total use made of the goods during the part of the prescribed accounting period occurring within the economic life of the goods.][1]

Amendments—[1] Part 15A (regs 116A–116N) inserted by the VAT (Amendment) (No 7) Regulations, SI 2007/3099 regs 3, 4 with effect from 1 November 2007: SI 2007/3099 reg 1(2)(*b*).

[116F Where a prescribed accounting period in which a relevant supply occurs immediately follows a prescribed accounting period during which the goods whose use gives rise to that supply were not used or made available for use for any purpose, element "A" of the formula in regulation 116E shall (without prejudice to any other element of the formula) comprise the total number of months falling within the economic life concerned covered by—

(*a*) the prescribed accounting period in which the relevant supply occurs; and

(*b*) all preceding prescribed accounting periods which commence after the end of the prescribed accounting period during which the goods were last used or made available for use for any purpose before the prescribed accounting period in which the relevant supply occurs.][1]

Amendments—[1] Part 15A (regs 116A–116N) inserted by the VAT (Amendment) (No 7) Regulations, SI 2007/3099 regs 3, 4 with effect from 1 November 2007: SI 2007/3099 reg 1(2)(*b*).

116G [Later increase in the full cost of goods

Where—

(*a*) a supply of goods or services is made to a person or any of his predecessors in respect of any goods held or used for the purposes of a business (whether or not the goods have an economic life in relation to that person at that time);

(*b*) VAT is chargeable on that supply which is eligible (in whole or part) for credit under sections 25 and 26 of the Act or repayment under section 39 of the Act; and

(c) by virtue of that supply, the full cost of the goods is greater than their full cost immediately before that supply,

a new economic life shall, without prejudice to any other economic life having effect in relation to those goods, be treated as commencing in respect of them in accordance with regulation 116C as if they had been supplied, acquired or imported at the time when the supply of goods or services is made.][1]

Amendments—[1] Part 15A (regs 116A–116N) inserted by the VAT (Amendment) (No 7) Regulations, SI 2007/3099 regs 3, 4 with effect from 1 November 2007: SI 2007/3099 reg 1(2)(*b*).

116H [Value of relevant supplies made during a new economic life

Subject to regulation 116I, the calculation of the value of a relevant supply made during a new economic life in accordance with the formula in regulation 116E is varied so that—

C is the increase in the full cost of the goods resulting from the supply of the goods or services giving rise to the new economic life; and

U% is the extent, expressed as a percentage, to which the goods are put to any private use or used, or made available for use, for non-business purposes as compared with the total use made of the goods during the part of the prescribed accounting period occurring during the new economic life of the goods.][1]

Amendments—[1] Part 15A (regs 116A–116N) inserted by the VAT (Amendment) (No 7) Regulations, SI 2007/3099 regs 3, 4 with effect from 1 November 2007: SI 2007/3099 reg 1(2)(*b*).

116I [Value of relevant supplies of goods which have two or more economic lives

Where a relevant supply occurs in relation to goods that have two or more economic lives at the time when they are put to private use or used, or made available for use, for non-business purposes, the value of that supply shall be such amount as represents the total of the amounts calculated in accordance with regulation 116E (as varied by regulation 116H as appropriate) in respect of those economic lives.][1]

Amendments—[1] Part 15A (regs 116A–116N) inserted by the VAT (Amendment) (No 7) Regulations, SI 2007/3099 regs 3, 4 with effect from 1 November 2007: SI 2007/3099 reg 1(2)(*b*).

116J [Transitional provisions

Regulation 116L applies to an economic life that—

(*a*) would be treated as commencing before 1st November 2007 if that regulation did not apply; and

(*b*) relates to goods that, before that day, have been put to any private use or used, or made available for use, for non-business purposes by the person described in regulation 116K or any of his predecessors (whether or not a relevant supply arising from that use has been treated as made before that day).][1]

Amendments—[1] Part 15A (regs 116A–116N) inserted by the VAT (Amendment) (No 7) Regulations, SI 2007/3099 regs 3, 4 with effect from 1 November 2007: SI 2007/3099 reg 1(2)(*b*).

[116K The person referred to in regulation 116J(b) is the person who holds or uses the goods concerned for the purposes of his business on 1st November 2007.][1]

Amendments—[1] Part 15A (regs 116A–116N) inserted by the VAT (Amendment) (No 7) Regulations, SI 2007/3099 regs 3, 4 with effect from 1 November 2007: SI 2007/3099 reg 1(2)(*b*).

[116L An economic life of goods to which this regulation applies shall be treated as commencing on 1st November 2007 and lasting for the period of time determined using the formula—

VAT SIs

$$D \times \frac{(E-F)}{E}$$

where—

D is the number of months which would have been the duration of the economic life concerned if it had commenced in accordance with regulation 116C or had been treated as having commenced in accordance with that regulation by virtue of regulation 116G;

E is the value of element "C" of the formula contained in regulation 116E (as varied where appropriate in relation to that economic life by regulation 116H) for the purpose of determining the whole or, where the use occurs at a time when the goods have two or more economic lives at that time, part of the value of a relevant supply arising from the use of the goods during the economic life concerned;

F is the value determined using the formula—

$$\frac{(G \times 100)}{(X\% \times 100)}$$

where—

G is the total value of relevant supplies of the goods on which VAT has been or will be accounted for in respect of such relevant supplies arising from the goods being put to any private use or used, or made available for use, for non-business purposes before 1st November 2007 (whether or not such supplies are treated as made before or after that day) to the extent that the value of the relevant supplies comprised in the total value was determined by reference to the value of element "E" of the formula used in this regulation in respect of the economic life concerned; and

X% is the extent, expressed as a percentage, to which the goods have been put to any private use or used, or made available for use, for non-business purposes during the period described in regulation 116M as compared with the total use made of the goods in that period.][1]

Amendments—[1] Part 15A (regs 116A–116N) inserted by the VAT (Amendment) (No 7) Regulations, SI 2007/3099 regs 3, 4 with effect from 1 November 2007: SI 2007/3099 reg 1(2)(*b*).

[116M The period referred to in regulation 116L is the period of time commencing at the time when the economic life concerned would have commenced if it had commenced in accordance with regulation 116C or had been treated as having commenced in accordance with that regulation by virtue of regulation 116G and ending immediately before 1st November 2007.][1]

Amendments—[1] Part 15A (regs 116A–116N) inserted by the VAT (Amendment) (No 7) Regulations, SI 2007/3099 regs 3, 4 with effect from 1 November 2007: SI 2007/3099 reg 1(2)(*b*).

[116N Where a person has claimed deduction of input tax on goods which was incurred within the period of two years ending on 21st March 2007, he may withdraw that claim in whole or part as if it were made in error (but not so as to render him liable to any penalty or payment of interest in respect of that claim) provided that

(*a*) the goods have not been used for any purpose before the claim is withdrawn;

(*b*) he intends or expects that the goods will be put to private or non-business purposes during their economic life;

(*c*) the withdrawal is in respect of-

(i) all of the input tax claimed on the goods; or

(ii) the part of the input tax claimed on the goods which is referable to his intended use of those goods for purposes other than those of his business; and

(*d*) the withdrawal is made in accordance with regulation 35 (whatever the amount of the claim that is withdrawn) before 1st February 2008.][1]

Amendments—[1] Part 15A (regs 116A–116N) inserted by the VAT (Amendment) (No 7) Regulations, SI 2007/3099 regs 3, 4 with effect from 1 November 2007: SI 2007/3099 reg 1(2)(*b*).

PART XVI
IMPORTATIONS, EXPORTATIONS AND REMOVALS

117 Interpretation of Part XVI

(1) In regulation 127 "approved inland clearance depot" means any inland premises approved by the Commissioners for the clearance of goods for customs and excise purposes.

(2) For the purposes of regulation 128 "container" means an article of transport equipment (lift-van, moveable tank or other similar structure)—

(*a*) fully or partially enclosed to constitute a compartment intended for containing goods,

(*b*) of a permanent character and accordingly strong enough to be suitable for repeated use,

(*c*) specially designed to facilitate the carriage of goods, by one or more modes of transport, without intermediate reloading,
(*d*) designed for ready handling, particularly when being transferred from one mode of transport to another,
(*e*) designed to be easy to fill and to empty, and
(*f*) having an internal volume of one cubic metre or more,

and the term "container" shall include the accessories and equipment of the container, appropriate for the type concerned, provided that such accessories and equipment are carried with the container, but shall not include vehicles, accessories or spare parts of vehicles, or packaging.

(3) [. . .][2]

[(4) In [regulation][3] 131 "goods" does not include—
(*a*) a motor-vehicle, or
(*b*) a boat intended to be exported under its own power.][1]

(5), (6) . . . [1]

(7) For the purposes of regulation 129 "overseas authority" means any country other than the United Kingdom or any part of or place in such a country or the government of any such country, part or place.

[(7A) In [regulation][3] 131 the words "overseas visitor" refer to a traveller who is not established within the member States.

(7B) For the purposes of paragraph (7A) above, a traveller is not established within the member States only if that traveller's domicile or habitual residence is situated outside the member States.

(7C) Solely for the purposes of paragraph (7B) above, the traveller's domicile or habitual residence is the place entered as such in a valid—
(*a*) identity document,
(*b*) identity card, or
(*c*) passport.

(7D) A document referred to in subparagraph (*a*), (*b*) or (*c*) of paragraph (7C) above is valid for the purposes of that paragraph only if—
(*a*) it is so recognised by the Commissioners; and
(*b*) it is not misleading as to the traveller's true place of domicile or habitual residence.][2]

(8) In [regulation 132][2] "overseas visitor" means a person who, during the 2 years immediately preceding . . . [2] the date of the application mentioned in regulation 132, has not been in the member States for more than 365 days, or who, . . . [2] during the 6 years immediately preceding the date of the application has not been in the member States for more than 1,095 days.

(9) . . . [3]

(10) In regulations 140 and 144 "customs territory of the Community" has the same meaning as it has for the purposes of Council Regulation (EEC) No 2913 No 92.

[(11) In this Part references to Council Regulation (EEC) No 2913/92 (the Community Customs Code) and Commission Regulation (EEC) No 2454/93 (which contains provisions implementing the Community Customs Code) shall be read as references to those instruments as—
(*a*) amended by the Act concerning the accession of the Czech Republic, the Republic of Estonia, the Republic of Cyprus, the Republic of Latvia, the Republic of Lithuania, the Republic of Hungary, the Republic of Malta, the Republic of Poland, the Republic of Slovenia and the Slovak Republic, signed at Athens on 16th April 2003,
(*b*) amended, modified or otherwise affected by the Act concerning the conditions of Accession of the Republic of Bulgaria and Romania and the adjustments to the Treaties on which the European Union is founded, signed at Luxembourg on 25th April 2005 and Council Regulation (EC) No 1791/2006 (which contains consequential amendments to the Customs Code).][4]

Former regulations—Para (1): VAT (General) Regulations, SI 1985/886 reg 38(1).
Para (2): VAT (General) Regulations, SI 1985/886 reg 38(3).
Paras (3), (4) (as originally enacted): VAT (General) Regulations, SI 1985/886 reg 38(5), (6); VAT (General) (Amendment) Regulations, SI 1992/3102 reg 25.
Paras (5)–(9) (as originally enacted): VAT (General) Regulations, SI 1985/886 reg 38(8)–(12); VAT (General) (Amendment) Regulations, SI 1992/3102 reg 25, SI 1995/913 reg 3.
Para (10): VAT (General) Regulations, SI 1985/886 reg 38(14); VAT (General) (Amendment) Regulations, SI 1995/152 reg 4.

Amendments—[1] Para (4) substituted and paras (5), (6) revoked by the VAT (Amendment) Regulations, SI 1996/210 regs 8, 9, with effect from 1 March 1996.
[2] Para (3) revoked, paras (7A) to (7D) inserted and words in para (8) substituted and revoked by the VAT (Amendment) Regulations, SI 1999/438 reg 10, with effect from 1 April 1999.
[3] Word in paras (4), (7A) substituted for the words "regulations 130 and" and "regulations 130(*a*)(i) and" respectively, and para (9) revoked, by the VAT (Amendment) (No 4) Regulations, SI 2003/1485 regs 2, 5 with effect for supplies made after 30 June 2003.
[4] Para (11) substituted by the VAT (Amendment) (No 3) Regulations, SI 2006/3292 regs 2, 4 with effect from 1 January 2007.

VAT SIs

118 Enactments excepted

There shall be excepted from the enactments which are to apply as mentioned in section 16(1) of the Act—

(*a*) the Alcoholic Liquor Duties Act 1979—

(i) section 7 (exemption from duty on spirits in articles used for medical purposes),

(ii) section 8 (repayment of duty on spirits for medical or scientific purposes),

(iii) section 9 (remission of duty on spirits for methylation),

(iv) section 10 (remission of duty on spirits for use in art or manufacture),

(v) section 22(4) (drawback on exportation of tinctures or spirits of wine), and

(vi) sections 42 and 43 (drawback on exportation and warehousing of beer),

(*b*) the Hydrocarbon Oil Duties Act 1979—

(i) section 9 (relief for certain industrial uses),

(ii) section 15 (drawback of duty on exportation etc of certain goods),

(iii) section 16 (drawback of duty on exportation etc of power methylated spirits),

(iv) section 17 (repayment of duty on heavy oil used by horticultural producers),

(v) section 18 (repayment of duty on fuel for ships in home waters),

(vi) section 19 (repayment of duty on fuel used in fishing boats etc),

(vii) section 20 (relief from duty on oil contaminated or accidentally mixed in warehouse), and

(viii) section 20AA (power to allow reliefs),

(*c*) the Customs and Excise Management Act 1979—

(i) section 43(5) (provisions as to duty on re-imported goods),

(ii) section 125(1) and (2) (valuation of goods for the purpose of ad valorem duties),

(iii) section 126 (charge of excise duty on manufactured or composite imported articles), and

(iv) section 127(1)(*b*) (determination of disputes as to duties on imported goods),

(*d*) the Customs and Excise Duties (General Reliefs) Act 1979 other than sections 8 and 9(*b*),

(*e*) the Isle of Man Act 1979, sections 8 and 9 (removal of goods from Isle of Man to United Kingdom), . . . [1]

(*f*) the Tobacco Products Duty Act 1979, section 2(2) (remission or repayment of duty on tobacco products)[, and

(*g*) the Finance Act 1999, sections 126 and 127 (interest on unpaid customs debts and on certain repayments relating to customs duty)][1].

Former regulations—VAT (General) Regulations, SI 1985/886 reg 39; VAT (General) (Amendment) Regulations, SI 1992/3102 reg 26.

Amendments—[1] Word "and" at end of para (*e*) revoked, and para (*g*) and the word "and" immediately preceding it added by the VAT (Amendment) (No 2) Regulations, SI 2000/634 regs 2, 3 with effect from 1 April 2000.

[119 Regulations excepted

The provision made by or under the following subordinate legislation shall be excepted from applying as mentioned in section 16(1) of the Act—

(*a*) regulations 16(4) and (5) and 19(1)(*b*) of the Excise Warehousing (Etc) Regulations 1988 (certain removals from warehouse);

(*b*) any regulations made under section 197(2)(*f*) of the Finance Act 1996 (rate of interest on overdue customs duty and on repayments of amounts paid by way of customs duty).][1]

Former regulations—VAT (General) Regulations, SI 1985/886 reg 39B; VAT (General) (Amendment) Regulations, SI 1992/3102 reg 27.

Amendments—[1] This regulation substituted by the VAT (Amendment) (No 2) Regulations, SI 2000/634 regs 2, 4 with effect from 1 April 2000.

120 Community legislation excepted

(1) Council Regulation (EEC) No 918/83 on conditional reliefs from duty on the final importation of goods, and any implementing Regulations made thereunder shall be excepted from the Community legislation which is to apply as mentioned in section 16(1) of the Act.

(2) The following Articles shall be excepted from the Community legislation which is to apply as mentioned in section 16(1) of the Act—

(*a*) in Council Regulation (EEC) No 2913/92 establishing the Community Customs Code—

(i) Articles 126 to 128 (drawback system of inward processing relief),

(ii) . . . [2]

(iii) Article 137 so far as it relates to partial relief on temporary importation, and Article 142,

(iv) Articles 145 to 160 (outward processing),

(v) . . . [4] . . . [1]

(vi) Article 229(*b*) (interest payable on a customs debt),

[(vii) Articles 232(1)(*b*), (2) and (3) (interest on arrears of duty), and

(viii) Article 241, second and third sentences only (interest on certain repayments by the authorities),][1]

[(*b*) in Commission Regulation (EEC) No 2454/93 which contains provisions implementing the Community Customs Code—

(i) Articles 496 to 523, Articles 536 to 544 and Article 550 (but only to the extent that these Articles apply to the drawback system of inward processing relief),

(ii) Article 519 (compensatory interest),

(iii) Articles 585 to 592 (outward processing) (and Articles 496 to 523 to the extent that they are relevant to outward processing),

(iv) . . . [4]][3]

(3) Council Regulation (EEC) No 2658/87 on the tariff and statistical nomenclature and on the Common Customs Tariff and implementing Regulations made thereunder (end use relief), save and in so far as the said Regulations apply to goods admitted into territorial waters—

(*a*) in order to be incorporated into drilling or production platforms, for purposes of the construction, repair, maintenance, alteration or fitting-out of such platforms, or to link such drilling or production platforms to the mainland of the United Kingdom, or

(*b*) for the fuelling and provisioning of drilling or production platforms,

shall be excepted from the Community legislation which is to apply as mentioned in section 16(1) of the Act.

Former regulations—VAT (General) Regulations, SI 1985/886 reg 40(1)–(3); VAT (General) (Amendment) Regulations, SI 1992/3102 reg 28, SI 1993/3027 regs 2, 3.

Amendments—[1] Words in para (2)(*a*)(v) revoked and para (2)(*a*)(vii), (viii) added by the VAT (Amendment) (No 2) Regulations, SI 2000/634 regs 2, 5 with effect from 1 April 2000.

[2] In para (2), sub-paras (*a*)(ii), (*b*)(ii) revoked by the VAT (Amendment) Regulations, SI 2001/630 reg 3 with effect for goods imported after 31 March 2001.

[3] Sub-para (2)(*b*) substituted by the VAT (Amendment)(No 5) Regulations, SI 2003/2318 regs 2, 5 with effect from 1 October 2003. This substitution has effect for supplies of goods or services the benefit of which was received after the coming into force of SI 2003/2318.

[4] Paras (2)(*a*)(v), (2)(*b*)(iv) revoked by the VAT (Amendment) Regulations, SI 2006/587 regs 1(3), (5), 5 with effect from 6 April 2006.

[121 Adaptations

(1) The provision made by the following enactments shall apply, as mentioned in section 16(1) of the Act, subject to the adaptations prescribed by this regulation.

(2) Section 125(3) of the Customs and Excise Management Act 1979 (valuation of goods) shall have effect as if the reference to the preceding subsections of that section included a reference to section 21 of the Act.

(3) Section 129 of the Finance Act 1999 (recovery of certain amounts by the Commissioners) shall be regarded as providing for the recovery of a repayment of any relevant VAT (import VAT).][1]

Former regulations—VAT (General) Regulations, SI 1985/886 reg 39A; VAT (General) (Amendment) Regulations, SI 1992/3102 reg 27.

Amendments—[1] This regulation substituted by the VAT (Amendment) (No 2) Regulations, SI 2000/634 regs 2, 6 with effect from 1 April 2000.

[121A—(1) The application of the Customs Duties (Deferred Payment) Regulations 1976 in relation to any VAT chargeable on the importation of goods from places outside the member States is subject to the following prescribed adaptations.

(2) In regulation 4(1) (application for approval), regard "security" as being "appropriate security (which may be nil if there is no risk to the payment)".

(3) In regulation 4(2) (security and payment arrangements), regard there being a second sub-paragraph as follows—

"Provided that the amount in question may exceed that of the security in the case of nil security.".

(4) For regulation 4(3) (variations and revocations of approval), regard any Commissioners' variation consequent on the adaptations prescribed by this regulation as only being able to have effect after 30th November 2003.

(5) Before "and" at the end of regulation 8(*a*) (deemed payment for certain purposes at time deferment granted), regard there being—

"(*aa*) Article 74(1) of Council Regulation (EEC) No 2913/92 (Community Customs Code) (no release of goods unless customs debt paid or secured);".][1]

Amendments—[1] This regulation inserted by the VAT (Amendment) (No 5) Regulations, SI 2003/2318 regs 2, 6 with effect from 1 October 2003. This insertion has effect for supplies of goods or services the benefit of which was received after the coming into force of SI 2003/2318.

[121B—(1) The application of Council Regulation (EEC) No 2913/92 (Community Customs Code) in relation to any VAT chargeable on the importation of goods from places outside the member States is subject to the following prescribed adaptations.

VAT SIs

(2) But the adaptation in paragraph (5) only applies to the extent that the Commissioners grant deferment of payment of the relevant VAT with nil security.

(3) In Article 218(1) second sub-paragraph (single entry in the accounts), after "secured" regard there being "if required".

(4) In Article 225 first sub-paragraph (deferment of payment conditional on security), after "applicant" regard there being "(but the customs authorities may waive this condition if there is no risk to the payment)".

(5) Regard Article 225 as not being subject to Article 192 (fixing amount of security).][1]

Amendments—[1] This regulation inserted by the VAT (Amendment) (No 5) Regulations, SI 2003/2318 regs 2, 6 with effect from 1 October 2003. This insertion has effect for supplies of goods or services the benefit of which was received after the coming into force of SI 2003/2318.

[121C—(1) The application of Commission Regulation (EEC) No 2454/93 (implementation of Community Customs Code) in relation to any VAT chargeable on the importation of goods from places outside the member States is subject to the following prescribed adaptations.

(2) But the adaptations in paragraphs (3) and (4) only apply to the extent that the Commissioners grant deferment of payment of the relevant VAT with nil security.

(3) Regard Articles 244, 248(1), 257(3), 257(4), 258, 262(1) and 876a(1) (circumstances in which duties have to be or are taken as having to be secured) as providing that the provision of security is at the discretion of the customs authorities.

(4) Regard Articles 244, 248(1), 257(3), 257(4) and 876a(1) (circumstances in which duties have to be secured) as not being subject to Article 192 of Council Regulation (EEC) No 2913/92 (Community Customs Code) (fixing amount of security).][1]

Amendments—[1] This regulation substituted by the VAT (Amendment) (No 5) Regulations, SI 2003/2318 regs 2, 6 with effect from 1 October 2003.

121D [Adaptations and exceptions for the application of returned goods relief

(1) The application of Council Regulation (EEC) No 2913/92 (Community Customs Code) and Commission Regulation (EEC) No 2454/93 (implementation Regulation) in relation to any VAT chargeable on the importation of goods from places outside the member States is subject to the following prescribed adaptations.

(2) Regard—

(*a*) Articles 185 to 187 of the Community Customs Code (returned Community goods and returned compensating products), and

(*b*) Articles 844 to 856 and Article 882 of the implementation Regulation (returned Community goods and returned compensating products),

as only applying in the case and to the extent of a reimportation to the United Kingdom by the person who originally exported or re-exported the relevant Community goods or compensating products from the VAT territory of the Community.

That VAT territory is the territorial application of Council Directive 77/388/EEC in accordance with Title III of that Directive (territorial application).

(3) Regard the amount of the relief mentioned in Article 186 of the Community Customs Code (returned Community goods) as reduced by the amount of any unpaid VAT.

(4) Regard the amount legally owed in Article 187 of the Community Customs Code (returned compensating products) as reduced by the amount of any paid VAT.

(5) For the purposes of paragraphs (3) and (4)—

(*a*) "VAT" includes value added tax charged in accordance with the law of another member State (see sections 92(1), 92(2) and 96(1) of the Act);

(*b*) "unpaid" refers to any part of the VAT charged and due on—

(i) a supply or acquisition of the goods in a member State before the reimportation, or

(ii) an importation of the goods from outside the member States before the reimportation,

but repaid, remitted or otherwise not paid;

(*c*) "paid" refers to any part of the VAT charged, due and paid on—

(i) a supply or acquisition of the goods in a member State before the reimportation, or

(ii) an importation of the goods from outside the member States before the reimportation,

and without any actual, or prospect of, repayment or remission;

(*d*) a sum for which there is or was under the law of a member State an entitlement or right to a deduction or refund within Article 17 of Council Directive 77/388/EEC (origin and scope of the right to deduct) is neither "unpaid" nor "paid".

(6) In the circumstances described by paragraph (7) or (8)—

(*a*) Articles 185 to 187 of the Community Customs Code (returned goods), and

(*b*) Articles 844 to 856 and Article 882 of the implementation Regulation (returned goods),

are excepted from the Community legislation which is to apply as mentioned in section 16(1) of the Act (application of customs legislation in relation to import VAT).

(7) These circumstances are that—

(*a*) the reimporter contemplated by those Articles makes a supply of, or concerning, the goods whilst under the inward processing procedure or in the course of, or after, the relevant exportation, re-exportation or reimportation,

(*b*) the place of that supply for the purposes of VAT is determined by or under section 7 of the Act (place of supply) as being outside the United Kingdom, and

(*c*) the goods nevertheless are or may be stored or physically used in the United Kingdom by or under the direction of that reimporter or the person to whom that supply is made ("recipient").

For these purposes, "reimporter" and "recipient" include someone connected with either person or both persons as determined in accordance with section 839 of the Taxes Act.

(8) These circumstances are that the goods in question were supplied at any time to any person pursuant to regulations 131 to 133 (supplies to persons departing from the member States) or pursuant to any corresponding provision of the Isle of Man.

(9) For the purposes of the Articles of the Community Customs Code and implementation Regulation mentioned in paragraph (2)—

(*a*) regard the description of the customs territory of the Community in Article 3 of the Community Customs Code as being substituted with a description of the VAT territory (see paragraph (2));

(*b*) regard the following references as including a reference to the completion of the formalities referred to in Article 33a(1)(*a*) of Council Directive 77/388/EEC (formalities relating to entry of goods into VAT territory from territory considered a third territory)—

(i) "released for free circulation" in the definition of "Community goods" in Article 4(7), second indent and Article 185(1) of the Community Customs Code;

(ii) "entered" and "declared" for "release for free circulation" in, or for the purposes of, Articles 844(4), 848(1), 848(2), 849(1) and 849(5) of the implementation Regulation;

(*c*) regard the following references as including a reference to the completion of the formalities referred to in Article 33a(2)(*a*) of Council Directive 77/388/EEC (or to a declaration under those formalities) (formalities relating to dispatch or transport of goods from Member State to territory considered a third territory)—

(i) "customs export formalities" in Articles 844(1), 849(1), 849(2) and 849(3) of the implementation Regulation;

(ii) "export declaration" in Article 848(1) of that Regulation;

(iii) "customs formalities relating to their exportation" in Articles 844(4) and 849(1) of that Regulation;

(*d*) regard—

(i) the definition of "import duties" in Article 4(10) of the Community Customs Code as defining instead VAT charged on the importation of goods from places outside the member States in accordance with the Act; and

(ii) the references to "import duty" and "duty" in Article 185(1), second sub-paragraph, second indent and Article 187 of the Community Customs Code as references to such VAT.

(10) The references to Council Directive 77/388/EEC in paragraphs (2), (5)(*d*), (9)(*b*) and (9)(*c*) embrace relevant amendments up to and including 6th April 2006 only.][1]

Amendments—[1] Regulation 121D inserted by the VAT (Amendment) Regulations, SI 2006/587 regs 1(3)–(5), 4 with effect from 6 April 2006. This amendment applies to any reimportation of goods occurring once it is in force.

122 Postal importations by registered persons in the course of business

Goods imported by post from places outside the member States, other than by datapost packet, not exceeding £2,000 in value, or such greater sum as is determined for the time being by the Commissioners, by a registered person in the course of a business carried on by him may, with the authority of the proper officer, be delivered without payment of VAT if—

(*a*) the registered person has given such security as the Commissioners may require, and

(*b*) his registration number is shown on the customs declaration attached to or accompanying the package,

and save as the Commissioners may otherwise allow he shall account for VAT chargeable on the goods on their importation together with any VAT chargeable on the supply of goods or services by him or on the acquisition of goods by him from another member State in a return furnished by him in accordance with these Regulations for the prescribed accounting period during which the goods were imported.

Former regulations—VAT (General) Regulations, SI 1985/886 reg 41; VAT (General) (Amendment) Regulations, SI 1992/3102 reg 29.

123 Temporary importations

(1) Subject to such conditions as the Commissioners may impose, the VAT chargeable on the importation of goods from a place outside the member States shall not be payable where—

(*a*) a taxable person makes a supply of goods which is to be zero-rated in accordance with sub-paragraphs (*a*)(i) and (ii), and (*b*) of section 30(8) of the Act,

(*b*) the goods so imported are the subject of that supply, and

(*c*) the Commissioners are satisfied that—

(i) the importer intends to remove the goods to another member State, and

(ii) the importer is importing the goods in the course of a supply by him of those goods in accordance with the provisions of sub-paragraphs (*a*)(i) and (ii), and (*b*) of section 30(8) of the Act and any Regulations made thereunder.

(2) As a condition of granting the relief afforded by paragraph (1) above the Commissioners may require the deposit of security, the amount of which shall not exceed the amount of VAT chargeable on the importation.

(3) The relief afforded by paragraph (1) above shall continue to apply provided that the importer—

(*a*) removes the goods to another member State within one month of the date of importation or within such longer period as the Commissioners may allow, and

(*b*) supplies the goods in accordance with sub-paragraphs (*a*)(i) and (ii), and (*b*) of section 30(8) of the Act and any Regulations made thereunder.

Former regulations—VAT (General) Regulations, SI 1985/886 reg 42; VAT (General) (Amendment) Regulations, SI 1992/3102 reg 30.

124 Reimportation of certain goods by non-taxable persons

Amendment—Regulation 124 revoked by the VAT (Amendment) Regulations, SI 2006/587 regs 1(3), (5), 5 with effect from 6 April 2006.

125 Reimportation of certain goods by taxable persons

Amendment—Regulation 125 revoked by the VAT (Amendment) Regulations, SI 2006/587 regs 1(3), (5), 5 with effect from 6 April 2006.

126 Reimportation of goods exported for treatment or process

Subject to such conditions as the Commissioners may impose, VAT chargeable on the importation of goods from a place outside the member States which have been temporarily exported from the member States and are reimported after having undergone repair, process or adaptation outside the member States, or after having been made up or reworked outside the member States, shall be payable as if such treatment or process had been carried out in the United Kingdom, if the Commissioners are satisfied that—

(*a*) at the time of exportation the goods were intended to be reimported after completion of the treatment or process outside the member States, and

(*b*) the ownership in the goods was not transferred to any other person at exportation or during the time they were abroad.

Former regulations—VAT (General) Regulations, SI 1985/886 reg 48; VAT (General) (Amendment) Regulations, SI 1992/3102 reg 35.

127 Supplies to export houses

. . .

Former regulations—VAT (General) Regulations, SI 1985/886 reg 49; VAT (General) (Amendment) Regulations, SI 1992/3102 reg 36.

Amendments—This regulation revoked by the VAT (Amendment) Regulations, SI 1999/438 reg 11, with effect from 1 April 1999.

128 Export of freight containers

Where the Commissioners are satisfied that a container is to be exported to a place outside the member States, its supply, subject to such conditions as they may impose, shall be zero-rated.

Former regulations—VAT (General) Regulations, SI 1985/886 reg 50; VAT (General) (Amendment) Regulations, SI 1992/3102 reg 37.

129 Supplies to overseas persons

(1) Where the Commissioners are satisfied that—

(*a*) goods intended for export to a place outside the member States have been supplied . . . [2] to—

(i) a person not resident in the United Kingdom,

(ii) a trader who has no business establishment in the United Kingdom from which taxable supplies are made, or

(iii) an overseas authority, and

(*b*) the goods were exported to a place outside the member States,

the supply, subject to such conditions as they may impose, shall be zero-rated.

(2) . . . [1]

Former regulations—VAT (General) Regulations, SI 1985/886 reg 51; VAT (General) (Amendment) Regulations, SI 1992/3102 reg 38.

Amendments—[1] Para (2) revoked by the VAT (Amendment) (No 4) Regulations, SI 2003/1485 regs 2, 6 with effect for supplies made after 30 June 2003.

[2] In para (1)(*a*), words ", otherwise than to a taxable person," revoked by the VAT (Amendment) (No 2) Regulations, SI 2013/2241 regs 2, 3 with effect in relation to supplies made on or after 1 October 2013.

130 . . . Supplies to persons departing from the member States

Amendment—This regulation revoked by the VAT (Amendment) (No 4) Regulations, SI 2003/1485 regs 2, 6 with effect for supplies made after 30 June 2003.

131—(1) Where the Commissioners are satisfied that—

(*a*) goods have been supplied to a person who is an overseas visitor and who, at the time of the supply, intended to depart from the member States [before the end of the third month following that in which the supply is effected][1] and that the goods should accompany him,

(*b*) save as they may allow, the goods were produced to the competent authorities for the purposes of the common system of VAT in the member State from which the goods were finally exported to a place outside the member States, and

(*c*) the goods were exported to a place outside the member States,

the supply, subject to such conditions as they may impose, shall be zero-rated.

(2) . . . [2]

Former regulations—VAT (General) Regulations, SI 1985/886 reg 54; VAT (General) (Amendment) Regulations, SI 1992/3102 reg 41.

Amendments—[1] Words in para (1)(*a*) substituted by the VAT (Amendment) Regulations, SI 1995/3147 reg 6, with effect from 1 January 1996.

[2] Para (2) revoked by the VAT (Amendment) (No 4) Regulations, SI 2003/1485 regs 2, 6 with effect for supplies made after 30 June 2003.

132 The Commissioners may, on application by an overseas visitor who intends to depart from the member States within 15 months and remain outside the member States for a period of at least 6 months, permit him within 12 months of his intended departure to purchase, from a registered person, a . . . [1] motor vehicle without payment of VAT, for subsequent export, and its supply, subject to such conditions as they may impose, shall be zero-rated.

Former regulations—VAT (General) Regulations, SI 1985/886 reg 56; VAT (General) (Amendment) Regulations, SI 1992/3102 reg 43.

Amendments—[1] Word revoked by the VAT (Amendment) Regulations, SI 2000/258 regs 2, 6 with effect from 1 April 2000.

133 The Commissioners may, on application by any person who intends to depart from the member States within 9 months and remain outside the member States for a period of at least 6 months, permit him within 6 months of his intended departure to purchase, from a registered person, a . . . [1] motor vehicle without payment of VAT, for subsequent export, and its supply, subject to such conditions as they may impose, shall be zero-rated.

Former regulations—VAT (General) Regulations, SI 1985/886 reg 57; VAT (General) (Amendment) Regulations, SI 1992/3102 reg 43.

Amendments—[1] Word revoked by the VAT (Amendment) Regulations, SI 2000/258 regs 2, 6 with effect from 1 April 2000.

134 Supplies to persons taxable in another member State

Where the Commissioners are satisfied that—

(*a*) a supply of goods by a taxable person involves their removal from the United Kingdom,

(*b*) the supply is to a person taxable in another member State,

(*c*) the goods have been removed to another member State, and

(*d*) the goods are not goods in relation to whose supply the taxable person has opted, pursuant to section 50A of the Act, for VAT to be charged by reference to the profit margin on the supply,

the supply, subject to such conditions as they may impose, shall be zero-rated.

Former regulations—VAT (General) Regulations, SI 1985/886 reg 57A; VAT (General) (Amendment) Regulations, SI 1992/3102 reg 44, SI 1995/1280 reg 3.

Simon's Tax Cases—*McMahon (trading as Irish Cottage Trading Co) v R&C Comrs* [2012] UKUT 106 (TCC), [2012] STC 1859 .

135 Supplies of goods subject to excise duty to persons who are not taxable in another member State

Where the Commissioners are satisfied that—

(*a*) a supply by a taxable person of goods subject to excise duty involves their removal from the United Kingdom to another member State,

(*b*) that supply is other than to a person taxable in another member State and the place of supply is not, by virtue of section 7(5) of the Act, treated as outside the United Kingdom,

(*c*) the goods have been removed to another member State in accordance with the provisions of the [Excise Goods (Holding, Movement and Duty Point) Regulations 2010][1], and

(*d*) the goods are not goods in relation to whose supply the taxable person has opted, pursuant to section 50A of the Act, for VAT to be charged by reference to the profit margin on the supply,

the supply, subject to such conditions as they may impose, shall be zero-rated.

Former regulations—VAT (General) Regulations, SI 1985/886 reg 57B; VAT (General) (Amendment) Regulations, SI 1992/3102 reg 44, SI 1995/1280 reg 4.

AMENDMENTS—

1 In para (*c*), words substituted for words "Excise Goods (Holding, Movement, Warehousing and REDS) Regulations 1992" by the VAT (Amendment) (No 2) Regulations, SI 2013/2241 regs 2, 5 with effect in relation to supplies made on or after 1 October 2013.

136 Territories to be treated as excluded from or included in the territory of the Community and of the member States

For the purposes of the Act the following territories shall be treated as excluded from the territory of the Community—

(*a*) the Channel Islands,

(*b*) Andorra,

(*c*) San Marino, and

(*d*) the Aland Islands.

Former regulations—VAT (General) Regulations, SI 1985/886 reg 57D(1); VAT (General) (Amendment) Regulations, SI 1992/3102 reg 44, SI 1995/152 reg 5.

137 For the purposes of the Act the following territories shall be treated as excluded from the territory of the member States and the territory of the Community—

(*a*) the Canary Islands (Kingdom of Spain),

[(*b*) Guadeloupe, French Guiana, Martinique, Mayotte, Réunion and Saint-Martin (French Republic), and][1]

(*c*) Mount Athos (Hellenic Republic).

Former regulations—VAT (General) Regulations, SI 1985/886 reg 57D(2); VAT (General) (Amendment) Regulations, SI 1992/3102 reg 44.

Amendments—[1] Para (*b*) substituted by the Value Added Tax (Amendment) (No 3) Regulations 2013/3211 regs 2, 3 with effect from 1 January 2014.

138—[(1) For the purposes of the Act the territory of the Community shall be treated as excluding—

(*a*) Austria, Finland and Sweden ("the 1995 acceding States"),

(*b*) the Czech Republic, Estonia, Cyprus, Latvia, Lithuania, Hungary, Malta, Poland, Slovakia and Slovenia ("the 2004 acceding States"), and

(*c*) Bulgaria and Romania ("the 2007 acceding states")

in relation to goods to which this regulation applies.][1]

(2) Subject to [paragraph 4][1] below, the goods to which this regulation applies are—

(*a*) goods which are the subject of a supply made in an acceding State before [the date specified in paragraph (5)][1] and which in pursuance of that supply are removed to the United Kingdom on or after [the date specified in paragraph (6)][1] being goods in the case of which provisions of the law of the acceding State in question having effect for purposes corresponding to those of subsection (6)(*a*) or (so far as it applies to exportations) subsection (8) of section 30 of the Act have prevented VAT from being charged on that supply, and

(*b*) goods which were subject to a suspension regime before 1st January 1995, which by virtue of any Community legislation were to remain, for VAT purposes only, subject to that regime for a period beginning with that date and which cease to be subject to that regime on or after 20th October 1995.

(3) For the purposes of paragraph (2)(*b*) above, goods shall be treated as having become subject to a suspension regime if—

(*a*) on their entry into the territory of the Community—

(i) they were placed under a temporary admission procedure with full exemption from import duties, in temporary storage, in a free zone, or under customs warehousing arrangements or inward processing arrangements, or

(ii) they were admitted into the territorial waters of the United Kingdom for the purpose of being incorporated into drilling or production platforms, for the purposes of the construction, repair, maintenance, alteration or fitting-out of such platforms, for the purpose of linking such platforms to the mainland of the United Kingdom, or for the purpose of fuelling or provisioning such platforms, or

(*b*) they were placed under any customs transit procedure in pursuance of a supply made in the course of a business,

and (in the case in question) the time that any Community customs debt in relation to the goods would be incurred in the United Kingdom if the accession to the European Union of the acceding States were disregarded would fall to be determined by reference to the matters mentioned in sub-paragraph (a) or (b) above.

(4) This regulation does not apply to the following goods—

(*a*) goods which are exported on or after [the date specified in paragraph (6)][1] to a place outside the member States, (*b*) goods which are not means of transport and are removed on or after [the date specified in paragraph (6)][1] from a temporary admission procedure such as is referred to in paragraph (3)(*a*)(i) above, in order to be returned to the person in an acceding State who had exported them from that State,

(*c*) means of transport which are removed on or after [the date specified in paragraph (6)][1] from a temporary admission procedure such as is referred to in paragraph (3)(*a*)(i) above and which—

(i) were first brought into service before [the date specified in paragraph (7)][1], or

(ii) have a value not exceeding £4,000, or

(iii) have been charged in an acceding State with VAT which has not been remitted or refunded by reason of their exportation and to such other tax (if any) to which means of transport of that class or description are normally chargeable.

[(5) For the purposes of paragraphs (2) and (4) the specified date—

(*a*) in relation to the 1995 acceding states is 1st January 1995;

(*b*) in relation to the 2004 acceding states is 1st May 2004; and

(*c*) in relation to the 2007 acceding states is 1st January 2007.

(6) For the purposes of paragraphs (2) and (4) the specified date—

(*a*) in relation to the 1995 acceding states is 20th October 1995;

(*b*) in relation to the 2004 acceding states 1st May 2004; and

(*c*) in relation to the 2007 acceding states 1st January 2007.

(7) For the purposes of paragraph (4)(*c*)(i) the specified date—

(*a*) in relation to the 1995 acceding states is 1st January 1987;

(*b*) in relation to the 2004 acceding states is 1st May 2006; and

(*c*) in relation to the 2007 acceding states is 1st January 1999.][1]

Former regulations—VAT (General) Regulations, SI 1985/886 reg 57DA; VAT (General) (Amendment) Regulations, SI 1995/152 reg 6.

Amendments—[1] Paras (1), (5) and words in paras (2), (4) substituted, by the VAT (Amendment) (No 3) regulations, SI 2006/3292 regs 2, 5 with effect from 1 January 2007.

139 For the purposes of the Act the following territories shall be treated as included in the territory of the member States and the territory of the Community—

(i) the Principality of Monaco (French Republic), . . . [1]

(ii) the Isle of Man (United Kingdom)[, and

(iii) the United Kingdom Sovereign Base Areas of Akrotiri and Dhekelia (Cyprus).][1]

Former regulations—VAT (General) Regulations, SI 1985/886 reg 57E; VAT (General) (Amendment) Regulations, SI 1992/3102 reg 44.

Amendments—[1] Word in para (i) revoked, and para (iii) and word preceding it inserted, by the VAT (Amendment) (No 2) Regulations, SI 2004/1082 regs 2, 6 with effect from 1 May 2004.

140 Entry and exit formalities

(1) Where goods enter the United Kingdom from the territories prescribed in regulation 136 or 137 the formalities relating to the entry of goods into the customs territory of the Community contained in Council Regulation (EEC) No 2913/92, Commission Regulation (EEC) No 2454/93 and the Customs Controls on Importation of Goods Regulations 1991, shall be completed.

(2) Where goods are exported from the United Kingdom to the territories prescribed in regulation 136 or 137 the formalities relating to the export of goods to a place outside the customs territory of the Community contained in Council Regulation (EEC) No 2913/92 and Commission Regulation (EEC) No 2454/93 shall be completed.

Former regulations—VAT (General) Regulations, SI 1985/886 reg 57F; VAT (General) (Amendment) Regulations, SI 1992/3102 reg 44, SI 1993/3027 regs 2, 4.

141 Use of the internal Community transit procedure

Where goods enter the United Kingdom from the territories prescribed in regulation 136 or 137 and the said goods are intended for another member State, or other destination outside the United Kingdom transport of the goods to which destination involves their passage through another member State, the internal Community transit procedure described in Council Regulation (EEC) No 2913/92 and Commission Regulation (EEC) No 2454/93 shall apply.

Former regulations—VAT (General) Regulations, SI 1985/886 reg 57G; VAT (General) (Amendment) Regulations, SI 1992/3102 reg 44.

142 Customs and excise legislation to be applied

Subject to regulation 143, where goods are imported into the United Kingdom from the territories prescribed in regulation 136 or 137 customs and excise legislation shall apply (so far as relevant) in relation to any VAT chargeable upon such importation with the same exception and adaptations as are prescribed in regulations 118, 119, 120 and 121 in relation to the application of section 16(1) of the Act.

Former regulations—VAT (General) Regulations, SI 1985/886 reg 57H; VAT (General) (Amendment) Regulations, SI 1992/3102 reg 44.

143 Where goods are imported into the United Kingdom from the territories prescribed in regulation 137, section 4 of the Finance (No 2) Act 1992 (enforcement powers) shall apply in relation to any VAT chargeable upon such importation as if references in that section to "member States" excluded the territories prescribed in regulation 137.

Former regulations—VAT (General) Regulations, SI 1985/886 reg 57I; VAT (General) (Amendment) Regulations, SI 1992/3102 reg 44.

144 Where goods are exported from the United Kingdom to the territories prescribed in regulation 136 or 137 the provisions relating to the export of goods to a place outside the customs territory of the Community contained in Council Regulation (EEC) No 2913/92 and Commission Regulation (EEC) No 2454/93 shall apply for the purpose of ensuring the correct application of the zero rate of VAT to such goods.

Former regulations—VAT (General) Regulations, SI 1985 No 886 reg 57J; VAT (General) (Amendment) Regulations, SI 1992/3102 reg 44.

145—(1) Subject to paragraph (2) below, where goods are exported from the United Kingdom to the territories prescribed in regulation 136 or 137 the provisions made by or under the Customs and Excise Management Act 1979 in relation to the exportation of goods to places outside the member States shall apply (so far as relevant) for the purpose of ensuring the correct application of the zero rate of VAT to such goods.

(2) Where goods are being exported from the United Kingdom to the territories prescribed in regulation 137, section 4 of the Finance (No 2) Act 1992 (enforcement powers) shall apply to such goods as if references in that section to "member States" excluded the territories prescribed in regulation 137.

[PART XVI(A)][1]

FISCAL AND OTHER WAREHOUSING REGIMES

Amendments—[1] This Part inserted by the VAT (Amendment) (No 3) Regulations, SI 1996/1250 reg 13 with effect from 1 June 1996.

145A Interpretation of Part XVI(A)

(1) In this Part unless the context otherwise requires—

"eligible goods" has the meaning given by section 18B(6);

"fiscal warehouse" includes all fiscal warehouses kept by the same fiscal warehousekeeper;

"material time" has the meaning given by section 18F(1) in the case of a fiscal warehousing regime and section 18(6) in the case of a warehousing regime;

"regulation" or "regulations" refers to the relevant regulation or regulations of these Regulations; and

"section" or "sections" refers to the relevant section or sections of the Act.

(2) For the purposes of this Part, where a fiscal warehousekeeper keeps one or more fiscal warehouses there shall be associated with him a single fiscal warehousing regime; and "relevant fiscal warehousekeeper", "relevant fiscal warehouse", "relevant fiscal warehousing regime", "his fiscal warehouse", "his fiscal warehousing regime" and similar expressions shall be construed in this light.

145B Fiscal warehousing certificates

(1) The certificate referred to in section 18B(1)(*d*) (certificate relating to acquisitions in or intended for fiscal warehousing) and the certificate referred to in section 18B(2)(*d*) (supplies of goods intended for fiscal warehousing) shall contain the information indicated [in the form specified in a notice published by the Commissioners][1].

(2) A certificate prepared under section 18B(1)(*d*) by an acquirer who is not a taxable person shall be kept by him for a period of six years commencing on the day the certificate is prepared; and he shall produce it to a proper officer when that officer requests him to do so.

Amendments—[1] In para (1), words substituted for words "in the form numbered 17 in Schedule 1 to these Regulations", by the VAT (Amendment) (No 2) Regulations, SI 2012/1899 regs 3, 18 with effect from 15 October 2012.

145C Certificates connected with services in fiscal or other warehousing regimes

The certificate referred to in section 18C(1)(*c*) (certificate required for the zero-rating of certain services performed on or in relation to goods while those goods are subject to a fiscal or other warehousing regime) shall contain the information indicated [in the form specified in a notice published by the Commissioners][1].

Amendments—[1] Words substituted for words "in the form numbered 18 in Schedule 1 to these Regulations", by the VAT (Amendment) (No 2) Regulations, SI 2012/1899 regs 3, 19 with effect from 15 October 2012.

145D VAT invoices relating to services performed in fiscal or other warehousing regimes

(1) This regulation applies to the invoice referred to in section 18C(1)(*e*) (invoice required for the zero-rating of the supply of certain services performed on or in relation to goods while those goods are subject to a fiscal or other warehousing regime).

(2) The invoice shall be known as a VAT invoice and shall state the following particulars (unless the Commissioners allow any requirement of this paragraph to be relaxed or dispensed with)—

(*a*) an identifying number,

(*b*) the material time of the supply of the services in question,

(*c*) the date of the issue of the invoice,

(*d*) the name, an address and the registration number of the supplier,

(*e*) the name and an address of the person to whom the services are supplied,

(*f*) a description sufficient to identify the nature of the services supplied,

(*g*) the extent of the services and the amount payable, excluding VAT, expressed in sterling,

(*h*) the rate of any cash discount offered,

(*i*) the rate of VAT as zero per cent, and

(*j*) a declaration that in respect of the supply of services in question, the requirements of section 18C(1) will be or have been satisfied.

(3) The supplier of the services in question shall issue the invoice to the person to whom the supply is made within thirty days of the material time of that supply of services (or within such longer period as the Commissioners may allow in general or special directions).

145E Fiscal warehousing regimes

(1) Upon any eligible goods entering a fiscal warehouse the relevant fiscal warehousekeeper shall record their entry in his relevant fiscal warehousing record.

(2) Eligible goods shall only be subject to or in a fiscal warehousing regime at any time—

(*a*) while they are allocated to that regime in the relevant fiscal warehousing record;

(*b*) while they are not identified in that record as having been transferred; or,

(*c*) prior to their removal from that regime.

145F The fiscal warehousing record and stock control

(1) In addition to the records referred to in regulation 31, a fiscal warehousekeeper shall maintain a fiscal warehousing record for any fiscal warehouse in respect of which he is the relevant fiscal warehousekeeper.

(2) The fiscal warehousing record may be maintained in any manner acceptable to the Commissioners. In particular, it shall be capable of—

(*a*) ready use by any proper officer in the course of his duties; and

(*b*) reproduction into a form suitable for any proper officer to readily use at a place other than the relevant fiscal warehouse.

(3) Subject to paragraph (4) below, the fiscal warehousing record shall have the features and shall comply with the requirements set out in Schedule 1A to these Regulations.

(4) In respect of any goods the relevant fiscal warehousing record shall not be required to record events more than six years following—

(*a*) the transfer or removal of those goods from the relevant fiscal warehousing regime; or,

(*b*) the exit of those goods from the relevant fiscal warehouse (in the case of goods which were not allocated to the relevant fiscal warehousing regime).

(5) A fiscal warehousekeeper, upon receiving a request to do so from any proper officer, shall—

(*a*) produce his fiscal warehousing record to that officer and permit him to inspect or take copies of it or of any part of it (as that officer shall require); or,

(*b*) facilitate and permit that officer to inspect any goods which are stored or deposited in his fiscal warehouse (whether or not those goods are allocated to the relevant fiscal warehousing regime).

145G Fiscal warehousing transfers in the United Kingdom

(1) Subject to paragraphs (2) and (3) below, a fiscal warehousekeeper ("the original fiscal warehousekeeper") may permit eligible goods which are subject to his fiscal warehousing regime ("the original regime") to be transferred to another fiscal warehousing regime ("the other regime") without those goods being treated as removed from the original regime.

(2) The original fiscal warehousekeeper shall not allow eligible goods to exit from his fiscal warehouse in pursuance of this regulation before he receives a written undertaking from the fiscal warehousekeeper in relation to that other fiscal warehousing regime ("the other fiscal warehousekeeper") that, in respect of those eligible goods, the other fiscal warehousekeeper will comply with the requirements of paragraph (3) below.

(3) The other fiscal warehousekeeper, upon the entry of the goods to his fiscal warehouse, shall—

(*a*) record that entry in his fiscal warehousing record; and,

(*b*) allocate those goods to his fiscal warehousing regime.

VAT SIs

Furthermore, within 30 days commencing with the day on which those goods left the original fiscal warehouse, he shall—

(*c*) deliver or cause to be delivered to the original fiscal warehousekeeper a certificate in a form acceptable to the Commissioners confirming that he has recorded the entry of those goods to his fiscal warehouse and allocated them to his fiscal warehousing regime; and,

(*d*) retain a copy of that certificate as part of his fiscal warehousing record.

145H Removal of goods from a fiscal warehousing regime and transfers overseas

(1) Without prejudice to sections 18F(5), 18F(6) and the following paragraphs of this regulation, eligible goods which are allocated to a fiscal warehousing regime shall only be removed from that regime at the time and in any of the following circumstances—

(*a*) when an entry in respect of those eligible goods is made in the relevant fiscal warehousing record which indicates the time and date of their removal from that regime;

(*b*) when the eligible goods are moved outside the fiscal warehouse in respect of which they are allocated to a fiscal warehousing regime (except in the case of movements between fiscal warehouses kept by the same fiscal warehousekeeper); or,

(*c*) at the time immediately preceding a retail sale of those eligible goods.

The person who shall be treated as the person who removes or causes the removal of the relevant goods from the relevant fiscal warehousing regime in any of the circumstances described above shall be, as the case requires, either the person who causes any of those circumstances to occur or, in the case of sub-paragraph (*c*), the person who makes the retail sale referred to there.

(2) Subject to paragraph (3) below, eligible goods which are subject to a fiscal warehousing regime shall not be treated as removed from that regime but shall be treated as transferred or as being in the process of transfer, as the case requires, in any of the following circumstances—

(*a*) where the goods in question are transferred or are in the process of transfer to another fiscal warehousing regime in pursuance of regulation 145G(1) above;

(*b*) where the goods in question are transferred or are in the process of transfer to arrangements which correspond in effect, under the law of another member State, to section 18B(3) (fiscal warehousing) whether or not those arrangements also correspond in effect to section 18C(1) (zero-rating of certain specified services performed in a fiscal or other warehousing regime);

(*c*) where the goods in question are exported or are in the process of being exported to a place outside the member States; or,

(*d*) where the goods in question are moved temporarily to a place other than the relevant fiscal warehouse for repair, processing, treatment or other operations (subject to the prior agreement of and to conditions to be imposed by the Commissioners).

(3) Where any relevant document referred to in paragraph (4) below is not received by the relevant fiscal warehousekeeper within the time period indicated there (commencing on the day on which the relevant eligible goods leave his fiscal warehouse), he shall—

(*a*) make an entry by way of adjustment to his fiscal warehousing record to show the relevant goods as having been removed from his fiscal warehousing regime at the time and on the day when they left;

(*b*) identify in his fiscal warehousing record the person on whose instructions he allowed the goods to leave his fiscal warehouse as the person removing those goods and that person's address and registration number (if any); and,

(*c*) notify the person on whose instructions he allowed the goods to leave his fiscal warehouse that the relevant document has not been received by him in time.

(4) The document and time period referred to in paragraph (3) above is, as the case requires, either—

(*a*) the certificate referred to in regulation 145G(3)(*c*) confirming the completion of a transfer of eligible goods from the relevant fiscal warehousing regime to another fiscal warehousing regime (30 days);

(*b*) a document evidencing the completion of the transfer of the eligible goods from the relevant fiscal warehousing regime directly to arrangements which correspond, in another member State, to fiscal warehousing (60 days); or,

(*c*) a document evidencing the export of the eligible goods from the relevant fiscal warehousing regime to a place outside the member States (60 days).

145I—(1) A fiscal warehousekeeper shall not remove or allow the removal of any eligible goods from his fiscal warehousing regime at any time before—

(*a*) he has inspected and placed on his fiscal warehousing record a copy of the relevant document issued by the Commissioners under regulation 145J(1) (removal document); or,

(*b*) he is provided with the registration number of a person registered under the Act and a written undertaking from that person that any VAT payable by that person as the result of any removal of eligible goods from that fiscal warehousing regime will be accounted for on that person's return in accordance with regulation 40(1)(*c*).

(2) Without prejudice to section 18E, where a fiscal warehousekeeper allows the removal of any eligible goods to take place from his fiscal warehousing regime otherwise than in accordance with this regulation, he shall be jointly and severally liable with the person who removes the goods for the payment of the VAT payable under section 18D(2) to the Commissioners.

(3) Paragraphs (1) and (2) above shall not apply to a removal which is the result of an entry in the relevant fiscal warehousing record made by the relevant fiscal warehousekeeper in compliance with regulation 145H(3)(*a*) (non-receipt of a document following transfer or export).

145J—

(1) The Commissioners may, in respect of a person who is seeking to remove or cause the removal of eligible goods from a fiscal warehousing regime,—

(*a*) accept from or on behalf of that person payment of the VAT payable (if any) as a result of that removal, and

(*b*) issue to that person a document bearing a reference or identification number.

(2) The Commissioners need not act in accordance with paragraph (1) above unless, as the case requires, they are satisfied as to—

(*a*) the value and material time of any supply of the relevant goods in the fiscal warehousing regime which is treated as taking place in the United Kingdom under section 18B(4) and the status of the person who made that supply;

(*b*) the nature and quantity of the relevant eligible goods;

(*c*) the value of any relevant self-supplies of specified services treated as made under section 18C(3) in the course or furtherance of his business by the person who is to remove the relevant goods, or by the person on whose behalf the goods are to be removed, at the time they are removed from the fiscal warehousing regime; and

(*d*) the nature and material time of any relevant supplies of specified services in respect of which the self-supplies referred to in sub-paragraph (*c*) above are treated as being identical (certain supplies of services on or in relation to goods while those goods are subject to the fiscal warehousing regime).

(3) In paragraph (2)(*a*) above 'status' is a reference to whether the person in question—

(*a*) is or is required to be registered under the Act, or

(*b*) would be required to be registered under the Act were it not for paragraph 1(9) of Schedule 1 to the Act, paragraph 1(7) of Schedule 2 to the Act, paragraph 1(6) of Schedule 3 to the Act, or any of those provisions.

[145K Place of supply of goods subject to warehousing regime

(1) Section 18(1) (supply of goods subject to warehousing regime and before duty point treated as taking place outside the United Kingdom) shall not apply in the following prescribed circumstances.

(2) The circumstances are—

(*a*) that there is a supply of goods that would but for this regulation be treated for the purposes of the Act as taking place outside the United Kingdom by virtue of section 18(1);

(*b*) the whole or part of the business carried on by the supplier of those goods consists in supplying to a number of persons goods to be sold, by them or others, by retail;

(*c*) that supplier is a taxable person (or would be a taxable person but for section 18(1)); and

(*d*) that supply is to a person who is not a taxable person, and

(i) consists in a supply of goods to that person to be sold, by that person, by retail, or

(ii) consists in a supply of goods to that person by retail.][1]

Amendments—[1] This regulation inserted by the VAT (Amendment) (No 2) Regulations, SI 2005/2231 reg 10 with effect from 1 September 2005.

PART XVII

[MEANS OF TRANSPORT]

146 Interpretation of Part XVII

In this Part—

"claim" means a claim for a refund of VAT made pursuant to section 40 of the Act and "claimant" shall be construed accordingly;

"competent authority" means an authority having powers under the laws in force in any member State to register a vehicle for road use in that member State;

"first entry into service" in relation to a new means of transport means the time determined in relation to that means of transport under regulation 147;

"registration" means registration for road use in a member State corresponding in relation to that member State to registration in accordance with the Vehicles Excise and Registration Act 1994.

Former regulations—VAT (General) Regulations, SI 1985/886 reg 64B(3); VAT (General) (Amendment) Regulations, SI 1992/3102 reg 44; VAT (Refunds in relation to New Means of Transport) Regulations, SI 1992/3100 reg 1(2).

Amendments—Heading to Part 17 substituted by the VAT (Amendment) Regulations, SI 2013/701 regs 3, 5 with effect from 15 April 2013. Heading previously read "New Means of Transport".

VAT SIs

147 First entry into service of a means of transport

(1) For the purposes of section 95 of the Act a means of transport is to be treated as having first entered into service—

(*a*) in the case of a ship or aircraft—

(i) when it is delivered from its manufacturer to its first purchaser or owner, or on its first being made available to its first purchaser or owner, whichever is the earlier, or

(ii) if its manufacturer takes it into use for demonstration purposes, on its being first taken into such use, and

(*b*) in the case of a motorised land vehicle—

(i) on its first registration for road use by the competent authority in the member State of its manufacture or when a liability to register for road use is first incurred in the member State of its manufacture, whichever is the earlier,

(ii) if it is not liable to be registered for road use in the member State of its manufacture, on its removal by its first purchaser or owner, or on its first delivery or on its being made available to its first purchaser, whichever is the earliest, or

(iii) if its manufacturer takes it into use for demonstration purposes, on its first being taken into such use.

(2) Where the times specified in paragraph (1) above cannot be established to the Commissioners' satisfaction, a means of transport is to be treated as having first entered into service on the issue of an invoice relating to the first supply of the means of transport.

Former regulations—VAT (General) Regulations, SI 1985/886 reg 64B(1), (2); VAT (General) (Amendment) Regulations, SI 1992/3102 reg 44.

148 Notification of acquisition of new [ships or new aircraft] by non-taxable persons and payment of VAT

(1) Where—

(*a*) a taxable acquisition of a new [ship or new aircraft][1] takes place in the United Kingdom,

(*b*) the acquisition is not in pursuance of a taxable supply, and

(*c*) the person acquiring the goods is not a taxable person at the time of the acquisition,

the person acquiring the goods shall notify the Commissioners of the acquisition within [14][1] days of the time of the acquisition or the arrival of the goods in the United Kingdom, whichever is the later.

(2) The notification shall be in writing in the English language and shall contain the following particulars—

(*a*) the name and current address of the person acquiring the new [ship or new aircraft][1],

(*b*) the time of the acquisition,

(*c*) the date when the new [ship or new aircraft][1] arrived in the United Kingdom,

(*d*) a full description of the new [ship or new aircraft][1] which shall include any . . . [1] hull or airframe identification number and engine number,

(*e*) the consideration for the transaction in pursuance of which the new [ship or new aircraft][1] was acquired,

(*f*) the name and address of the supplier in the member State from which the new [ship or new aircraft][1] was acquired,

(*g*) the place where the new [ship or new aircraft][1] can be inspected, and

(*h*) the date of notification.

(3) The notification shall include a declaration, signed by the person who is required to make the notification or a person authorised in that behalf in writing, that all the information entered in it is true and complete.

(4) The notification shall be made at, or sent to, any office designated by the Commissioners for the receipt of such notifications.

(5) Any person required to notify the Commissioners of an acquisition of a new [ship or new aircraft][1] shall pay the VAT due upon the acquisition at the time of notification or within 30 days of the Commissioners issuing a written demand to him detailing the VAT due and requesting payment.

Former regulations—VAT (General) Regulations, SI 1985/886 reg 64A; VAT (General) (Amendment) Regulations, SI 1992/3102 reg 44.

Amendments—[1] In heading to s 148 and throughout s 148 itself, words substituted for words "means of transport', in para (1), figure substituted for figure "7", and in para (2)(*d*) words "registration mark allocated to it by any competent authority in another member State prior to its arrival in the United Kingdom and any chassis," revoked, by the VAT (Amendment) Regulations, SI 2013/701 regs 3, 6 with effect from 15 April 2013. Note that these amendments do not have effect in relation to the arrival in the UK on or before 14 April 2013 of a new means of transport that is a motorised land vehicle (SI 2013/701 reg 6(3)).

[148A Notification of the arrival in the United Kingdom of motorised land vehicles and payment of VAT

(1) This regulation applies to a means of transport that is a motorised land vehicle (see section 95 of, and paragraph 2(5D) of Schedule 11 to, the Act) (a "land vehicle").

(2) In this regulation an "excepted relevant person" means a relevant person (see paragraph 2(5D) of Schedule 11 to the Act) who is—

(*a*) bringing a land vehicle into the United Kingdom which that person has the approval of the Secretary of State to register and license in the United Kingdom in accordance with Parts 1 and 2 of the Vehicle Excise and Registration Act 1994 using a secure registration and licensing system (whether automated or paper based);

(*b*) importing a land vehicle into the United Kingdom and who is not a taxable person acting as such in relation to the arrival of the land vehicle in the United Kingdom;

(*c*) bringing a land vehicle into the United Kingdom which—

(i) is not required to be registered for road use in the United Kingdom, and

(ii) is to remain in the United Kingdom for a period (continuous or otherwise) of not more than 6 months in any 12 months; or

(*d*) bringing a land vehicle into the United Kingdom which has remained registered for road use in the United Kingdom during the period when it has been outside the United Kingdom.

(3) A relevant person other than an excepted relevant person must notify the Commissioners of the arrival in the United Kingdom of a land vehicle within 14 days of the date of the arrival.

[(3A) Where a person falling within paragraph (2)(*a*) makes a decision that the land vehicle in question will not be registered using the secure registration and licensing system (whether because it is not required to be registered for road use in the United Kingdom or for any other reason), that person must notify the Commissioners of the arrival of that land vehicle in the United Kingdom within 14 days of the date of that decision.][2]

[(4) Where a person falling within paragraph (2)(*c*) makes a decision—

(*a*) to register the land vehicle in question for road use in the United Kingdom, or

(*b*) to keep the land vehicle in the United Kingdom for a period longer than that specified in sub-paragraph (*c*)(ii) in circumstances where that land vehicle is not required to be registered for road use in the United Kingdom,

that person must notify the Commissioners of the arrival in the United Kingdom of that land vehicle within 14 days of the date of that decision.][2]

(5) In this regulation "registered for road use in the United Kingdom" means registered for such use in accordance with the Vehicle Excise and Registration Act 1994 and "register for road use in the United Kingdom" is to be construed accordingly.

(6) A person required to notify under paragraph (3) or (4) may authorise a third party to notify on that person's behalf.

(7) The notification shall be made in the English language.

(8) A notification under paragraph (3) or (4) must—

(*a*) contain the particulars listed in paragraph (9);

(*b*) include a declaration by the person required to notify the arrival in the United Kingdom of a land vehicle or a person authorised on that person's behalf that all the information entered in it is true and complete; and

(*c*) when made in paper form, be made at or sent to any office designated by the Commissioners for the receipt of such notifications.

(9) The particulars referred to in paragraph (8)(*a*) are—

(*a*) the name and current address of the person bringing the land vehicle into the United Kingdom;

(*b*) the date when the land vehicle arrived in the United Kingdom;

(*c*) . . . [2]

(*d*) a full description of the land vehicle which shall include any vehicle registration mark allocated to it by any competent authority in another member State prior to its arrival and any chassis identification number;

(*e*) where applicable, the registration number of the person bringing the land vehicle into the United Kingdom;

(*f*) the date of the notification;

(*g*) in the case of an acquisition arising from a deemed supply under paragraph 6 of Schedule 4 to the Act—

(i) the value of the transaction determined in accordance with paragraph 3 of Schedule 7 to the Act, and

(ii) details of any relief claimed or to be claimed in relation to the acquisition under Item 2(*f*) of Group 12 of Schedule 8 to the Act (zero rating: drugs, medicines, aids for the handicapped etc);

(*h*) in the case of any other acquisition—

(i) the consideration for the transaction in pursuance of which the land vehicle was acquired,

(ii) the name and address of the supplier in the member State from which the land vehicle was acquired, and

(iii) details of any relief claimed or to be claimed in relation to the acquisition under Item 2(*f*) of Group 12 of Schedule 8 to the Act;

(*i*) in the case of an import—

VAT SIs

(i) the price actually paid or payable for the land vehicle including any deposit, commission and fees,

(ii) the entry number of the Customs declaration as defined in paragraph 17 of Article 4 of Council Regulation (EEC) No 2913/92 of 12 October 1992 establishing the Community Customs Code, and

(iii) the relevant commodity code entered on the Customs declaration; and

(*j*) any other particulars specified in a notice published by the Commissioners (which includes such a notice as revised or replaced from time to time).

[(9A) In any case falling within paragraph (3A) or (4), the date of the relevant decision is to be treated as the date of the arrival in the United Kingdom of the land vehicle in question for the purposes of paragraph (9)(b).][2]

(10) Any person required under paragraph (3) or (4) to notify the Commissioners of an arrival which is an acquisition must pay any VAT due on the acquisition at the time and in the manner prescribed in paragraphs (12) to (16) as appropriate.

(11) In the case of an import of a land vehicle, any requirements to notify the importation and pay any tax, duty of customs or duty of excise due as may be prescribed in any of the enactments referred to in section 16(1)(*a*) and (*b*) of the Act shall apply in addition to any requirements imposed by or under this regulation.

(12) Where—

(*a*) the arrival is a taxable acquisition which takes place in the United Kingdom, and

(*b*) the person acquiring the land vehicle is not a taxable person acting as such in relation to the acquisition of the land vehicle,

payment shall be made at the time of notification

(13) Where—

(*a*) the arrival is a taxable acquisition which takes place in the United Kingdom, and

(*b*) the person acquiring the land vehicle is a taxable person acting as such in relation to the acquisition of the land vehicle,

payment shall be made in accordance with paragraph (15).

(14) Where the arrival is an acquisition arising from a deemed supply under paragraph 6 of Schedule 4 to the Act, payment shall be made in accordance with paragraph (15).

(15) Where this paragraph applies, payment shall be made in accordance with regulation 40 having been accounted for in the appropriate return required by regulation 25.

(16) In any case where—

(*a*) VAT due is required to be paid at the time of notification under paragraph (12), and

(*b*) notification is made under regulation 4A,

the relevant payment shall be made solely by means of electronic communications that are acceptable to the Commissioners for this purpose.][1]

Amendments—[1] Reg 148A inserted by the VAT (Amendment) Regulations, SI 2013/701 regs 3, 7 with effect from 15 April 2013. Note that this amendment does not have effect in relation to the arrival in the UK on or before 14 April 2013 of a new means of transport that is a motorised land vehicle (SI 2013/701 reg 6(3)).

[2] Paras (3A), (9A) inserted, para (4) substituted, and para (9)(*c*) revoked, by the Value Added Tax (Amendment) Regulations, SI 2014/548 regs 2, 5 with effect from 1 April 2014.

149 Refunds in relation to new means of transport

A claimant shall make his claim in writing no earlier than one month and no later than 14 days prior to making the supply of the new means of transport by virtue of which the claim arises.

Former regulation—VAT (Refunds in relation to New Means of Transport) Regulations, SI 1992/3100 reg 2.

150 The claim shall be made at, or sent to, any office designated by the Commissioners for the receipt of such claims.

Former regulation—VAT (Refunds in relation to New Means of Transport) Regulations, SI 1992/3100 reg 3.

151 The claim shall contain the following information—

(*a*) the name, current address and telephone number of the claimant,

(*b*) the place where the new means of transport is kept and the times when it may be inspected,

(*c*) the name and address of the person who supplied the new means of transport to the claimant,

(*d*) the price paid by the claimant for the supply to him of the new means of transport excluding any VAT,

(*e*) the amount of any VAT paid by the claimant on the supply to him of the new means of transport,

(*f*) the amount of any VAT paid by the claimant on the acquisition of the new means of transport from another member State or on its importation from a place outside the member States,

(*g*) the name and address of the proposed purchaser, the member State to which the new means of transport is to be removed, and the date of the proposed purchase,

(*h*) the price to be paid by the proposed purchaser,

(*i*) a full description of the new means of transport including, in the case of motorised land vehicles, its mileage since its first entry into service and, in the case of ships and aircraft, its hours of use since its first entry into service,

(*j*) in the case of a ship, its length in metres,

(*k*) in the case of an aircraft, its take-off weight in kilograms,

(*l*) in the case of a motorised land vehicle powered by a combustion engine, its displacement or cylinder capacity in cubic centimetres, and in the case of an electrically propelled motorised land vehicle, its maximum power output in kilowatts, described to the nearest tenth of a kilowatt, and

(*m*) the amount of the refund being claimed.

Former regulation—VAT (Refunds in relation to New Means of Transport) Regulations, SI 1992/3100 reg 4.

152 The claim shall be accompanied by the following documents—

(*a*) the invoice issued by the person who supplied the new means of transport to the claimant or such other documentary evidence of purchase as is satisfactory to the Commissioners,

(*b*) in respect of a new means of transport imported from a place outside the member States by the claimant, documentary evidence of its importation and of the VAT paid thereon, and

(*c*) in respect of a new means of transport acquired by the claimant from another member State, documentary evidence of the VAT paid thereon.

Former regulation—VAT (Refunds in relation to New Means of Transport) Regulations, SI 1992/3100 reg 5.

153 The claim shall include a declaration, signed by the claimant or a person authorised by him in that behalf in writing, that all the information entered in or accompanying it is true and complete.

Former regulation—VAT (Refunds in relation to New Means of Transport) Regulations, SI 1992/3100 reg 6.

154 The claim shall be completed by the submission to the Commissioners of—

(*a*) the sales invoice or similar document identifying the new means of transport and showing the price paid by the claimant's customer, and

(*b*) documentary evidence that the new means of transport has been removed to another member State.

Former regulation—VAT (Refunds in relation to New Means of Transport) Regulations, SI 1992/3100 reg 7.

155 Supplies of new means of transport to persons departing to another member State

The Commissioners may, on application by a person who is not taxable in another member State and who intends—

(*a*) to purchase a new means of transport in the United Kingdom, and

(*b*) to remove that new means of transport to another member State,

permit that person to purchase a new means of transport without payment of VAT, for subsequent removal to another member State within 2 months of the date of supply and its supply, subject to such conditions as they may impose, shall be zero-rated.

Former regulations—VAT (General) Regulations, SI 1985/886 reg 57C; VAT (General) (Amendment) Regulations, SI 1992/3102 reg 44.

PART XVIII

BAD DEBT RELIEF (THE OLD SCHEME)

156–164 Interpretation of Part XVIII

. . .

Amendments—This part revoked by the VAT (Amendment) Regulations, SI 1997/1086 reg 9 with effect from 1 May 1997.

PART XIX

BAD DEBT RELIEF (THE NEW SCHEME)

Note—With effect for the purposes of the making of any refund or repayment after 9 March 1999, but not anything received on or before that day, Part XIX, other than reg 171, of these regulations shall, subject to provisions made under VATA 1994 s 36, be read as if a reference to a payment being received by the claimant includes a payment received by a person to whom a right to receive it has been assigned by virtue of FA 1999 s 12(4).

165 Interpretation of Part XIX

In this Part—

"claim" means a claim in accordance with regulations 166 [or 166AA,][2] and 167 for a refund of VAT to which a person is entitled by virtue of section 36 of the Act and "claimant" shall be construed accordingly;

"payment" means any payment or part-payment which is made by any person . . . [1] by way of consideration for a supply regardless of whether such payment extinguishes the purchaser's debt to the claimant or not;

"purchaser" means a person to whom the claimant made a relevant supply;

"refunds for bad debts account" has the meaning given in regulation 168;

"relevant supply" means any taxable supply upon which a claim is based;

"return" means the return which the claimant is required to make in accordance with regulation 25 [but "relevant non-UK return" has the meaning given by paragraph 20(3) of Schedule 3BA to the Act and "relevant special scheme return" has the meaning given by paragraph 16(3) of Schedule 3B to the Act][2];

"security" means—

(*a*) in relation to England, Wales and Northern Ireland, any mortgage, charge, lien or other security, and

(*b*) in relation to Scotland, any security (whether heritable or moveable), any floating charge and any right of lien or preference and right of retention (other than a right of compensation or set-off).

["tax period" has the meaning given by paragraph 23(1) of Schedule 3B or paragraph 38(1) of Schedule 3BA (as the case may require) to the Act.][2]

Former regulation—VAT (Refunds for Bad Debts) Regulations, SI 1991/371 reg 2.

Amendments—[1] In definition of "payment" words revoked by the VAT Regulations, SI 1999/3029, regs 2, 3 with effect from 1 December 1999.

[2] In definitions of "claim" and "return" words inserted, and definition of "tax period' inserted, by the VAT (Amendment) (No 3) Regulations, SI 2014/2430 regs 2, 4 with effect from 1 January 2015.

165A [Time within which a claim must be made

(1) Subject to paragraph (3) [and (4)][2] below, a claim shall be made within the period of [4 years and 6 months][2] following the later of—

(*a*) the date on which the consideration (or part) which has been written off as a bad debt becomes due and payable to or to the order of the person who made the relevant supply; and

(*b*) the date of the supply.

(2) A person who is entitled to a refund by virtue of section 36 of the Act, but has not made a claim within the period specified in paragraph (1) shall be regarded for the purposes of this Part as having ceased to be entitled to a refund accordingly.

(3) This regulation does not apply insofar as the date mentioned at sub-paragraph (*a*) or (*b*) of paragraph (1) above, whichever is the later, falls before 1st May 1997.

[(4) A person shall be regarded for the purposes of this Part as having ceased to be entitled to a refund where the date mentioned at subparagraph (*a*) or (*b*) of paragraph (1) above, whichever is the later, is on or before 30th September 2005.][2]][1]

Amendments—[1] This regulation inserted by the VAT (Amendment) Regulations, SI 1997/1086 reg 10 with effect from 1 May 1997.

[2] In para (1), words inserted and words substituted for words "3 years and 6 months", and para (4) inserted, by the VAT (Amendment) Regulations, SI 2009/586 regs 2, 10 with effect from 1 April 2009.

166 The making of a claim to the Commissioners

(1) [Subject to regulation 166AA, and][2] save as the Commissioners may otherwise allow or direct, the claimant shall make a claim to the Commissioners by including the correct amount of the refund in the box opposite the legend "VAT reclaimed in this period on purchases and other inputs" on his return [for the prescribed accounting period in which he becomes entitled to make the claim or, subject to regulation 165A, any later return][1].

(2) If at a time the claimant becomes entitled to a refund he is no longer required to make returns to the Commissioners he shall make a claim to the Commissioners in such form and manner as they may direct.

Former regulation—VAT (Refunds for Bad Debts) Regulations, SI 1991/371 reg 3.

Amendments—[1] Words in para (1) inserted by the VAT (Amendment) Regulations, SI 1997/1086 reg 11 with effect from 1 May 1997.

[2] Words in para (1) inserted by the VAT (Amendment) (No 3) Regulations, SI 2014/2430 regs 2, 5(1) with effect from 1 January 2015.

[166AA The making of a claim to the Commissioners: special accounting schemes

(1) This regulation applies where the VAT on the relevant supply was accounted for on a relevant non-UK return or a relevant special scheme return.

(2) Where this regulation applies, the claimant must make the claim by—

(*a*) amending, in accordance with Article 61 of the Implementing Regulation, that relevant non-UK return or relevant special scheme return; or

(*b*) (where the period during which a person is entitled to make such an amendment has expired) notifying the Commissioners of the claim in writing in the English language.][1]

Amendments—[1] Reg 166AA inserted by the VAT (Amendment) (No 3) Regulations, SI 2014/2430 regs 2, 5(2) with effect from 1 January 2015.

166A [Notice to purchaser of claim

Where the purchaser is a taxable person[, and the relevant supply was made before 1st January 2003][2] the claimant shall not before, but within 7 days from, the day he makes a claim give to the purchaser a notice in writing containing the following information—

(*a*) the date of issue of the notice;

(*b*) the date of the claim;

(*c*) the date and number of any VAT invoice issued in relation to each relevant supply;
(*d*) the amount of the consideration for each relevant supply which the claimant has written off as a bad debt;
(*e*) the amount of the claim.][1]

Press releases etc—Business Brief 5/98 10-2-98 (VAT bad debt relief—insolvency practitioners).
Amendments—[1] This regulation inserted by the VAT (Amendment) Regulations, SI 1997/1086 reg 12 with effect from 1 May 1997.
[2] Words inserted by the VAT (Amendment) (No 4) Regulations, SI 2002/3027 regs 2, 3 with effect from 1 January 2003.

167 Evidence required of the claimant in support of the claim

Save as the Commissioners may otherwise allow, the claimant, before he makes a claim, shall hold in respect of each relevant supply—
(*a*) either—
(i) a copy of any VAT invoice which was provided in accordance with Part III of these Regulations, or
(ii) where there was no obligation to provide a VAT invoice, a document which shows the time, nature and purchaser of the relevant goods and services, and the consideration therefore,
(*b*) records or any other documents showing that he has accounted for and paid the VAT thereon, and
(*c*) records or any other documents showing that the consideration has been written off in his accounts as a bad debt.

Former regulation—VAT (Refunds for Bad Debts) Regulations, SI 1991/371 reg 4.

168 Records required to be kept by the claimant

(1) Any person who makes a claim to the Commissioners shall keep a record of that claim.
(2) Save as the Commissioners may otherwise allow, the record referred to in paragraph (1) above shall consist of the following information in respect of each claim made—
(*a*) in respect of each relevant supply for that claim—
(i) the amount of VAT chargeable,
(ii) the prescribed accounting period in which the VAT chargeable was accounted for and paid to the Commissioners,
(iii) the date and number of any invoice issued in relation thereto or, where there is no such invoice, such information as is necessary to identify the time, nature and purchaser thereof, and
(iv) any payment received therefor,
(*b*) the outstanding amount to which the claim relates,
(*c*) the amount of the claim, . . . [1]
(*d*) the prescribed accounting period in which the claim was made[, and
(*e*) a copy of the notice required to be given in accordance with regulations 166A.][1]
(3) Any records created in pursuance of this regulation shall be kept in a single account to be known as the "refunds for bad debts account".
[(4) Where regulation 166AA applies, "prescribed accounting period" in this regulation is to be read as "tax period".][2]

Former regulation—VAT (Refunds for Bad Debts) Regulations, SI 1991/371 reg 5.
Amendments—[1] Word "and" in para 2(*c*) deleted and para (2)(*e*) and word "and" at end of para (2)(*d*) inserted by the VAT (Amendment) Regulations, SI 1997/1086 reg 13 with effect from 1 May 1997.
[2] Para (4) inserted by the VAT (Amendment) (No 3) Regulations, SI 2014/2430 regs 2, 6 with effect from 1 January 2015.

169 Preservation of documents and records and duty to produce

(1) Save as the Commissioners may otherwise allow, the claimant shall preserve the documents, invoices and records which he holds in accordance with regulations 167 and 168 for a period of 4 years from the date of the making of the claim.
(2) Upon demand made by an authorised person the claimant shall produce or cause to be produced any such documents, invoices and records for inspection by the authorised person and permit him to remove them at a reasonable time and for a reasonable period.

Former regulation—VAT (Refunds for Bad Debts) Regulations, SI 1991/371 reg 6.

170 Attribution of payments

(1) [Subject to regulation 170A below, where][1]—
(*a*) the claimant made more than one supply (whether taxable or otherwise) to the purchaser, and
(*b*) a payment is received in relation to those supplies,
the payment shall be attributed to each such supply in accordance with the rules set out in paragraphs (2) and (3) below.

VAT SIs

(2) The payment shall be attributed to the supply which is the earliest in time and, if not wholly attributed to that supply, thereafter to supplies in the order of the dates on which they were made, except that attribution under this paragraph shall not be made to any supply if the payment was allocated to that supply by the purchaser at the time of payment and the consideration for that supply was paid in full.

(3) Where—

(*a*) the earliest supply and other supplies to which the whole of the payment could be attributed under this regulation occur on one day, or

(*b*) the supplies to which the balance of the payment could be attributed under this regulation occur on one day,

the payment shall be attributed to those supplies by multiplying, for each such supply, the payment received by a fraction of which the numerator is the outstanding consideration for that supply and the denominator is the total outstanding consideration for those supplies.

Former regulation—VAT (Refunds for Bad Debts) Regulations, SI 1991/371 reg 7.

Simon's Tax Cases—*Abbey National plc v C&E Comrs* [2006] STC 1.

Amendments—[1] Words substituted by the VAT (Amendment) (No 4) Regulations, SI 2002/3027 regs 2, 4 with effect from 1 January 2003.

[170A [Attribution of payments received under certain credit agreements

(1) This regulation applies where—

(*a*) the claimant made a supply of goods and, in connection with that supply, a supply of credit;

(*b*) those supplies were made under a hire purchase, conditional sale or credit sale agreement; and

(*c*) a payment is received in relation to those supplies (other than a payment of an amount upon which interest is not charged).

(2) Where the supply of goods was made before 1st September 2006 the payment shall be attributed in accordance with the rule set out in paragraph (5).

(3) Where the supply of goods was made on or after 1st September 2006 and before 1st September 2007 the payment may be attributed in accordance with the rule set out in paragraph (5) or (6).

(4) Where the supply of goods was made on or after 1st September 2007 the payment shall be attributed in accordance with the rule set out in paragraph (6).

(5) Where this paragraph applies, the payment shall be attributed—

(*a*) as to the amount obtained by multiplying it by the fraction A/B, to the supply of credit; and

(*b*) as to the balance, to the supply of goods,

where—

A is the total of the interest on the credit provided under the agreement under which the supplies are made (determined as at the date of the making of the agreement); and

B is the total amount payable under the agreement, less any amount upon which interest is not charged.

(6) Where this paragraph applies, the payment shall be attributed—

(*a*) in respect of payments made on or before termination of the agreement,

(i) as to the amount obtained by multiplying it by the fraction A/B, to the supply of credit; and

(ii) as to the balance, to the supply of goods,

where—

A is the total of the interest on the credit provided under the agreement, less any rebate of interest granted, less any interest attributable to any unpaid instalments prior to the termination; and

B is the total amount payable under the agreement being the total of *A* plus the total for the goods.

"Total for the goods" means the amount due for the goods under the agreement, less any reduction as a consequence of termination, less any amount upon which interest is not charged, less any part of the total due for the goods which is unpaid at the time of termination.

(*b*) in respect of payments made after termination of the agreement, between the supply of goods and the supply of credit according to the proportion of the balances due at the time the payment is made.

(7) Where an agreement provides for a variation of the rate of interest after the date of the making of the agreement then, for the purposes of the calculation in paragraph (5), it shall be assumed that the rate is not varied.][1]

Press releases etc—HMRC Brief 14/07 (Changes to the rules on bad debt relief for goods supplied on credit terms).

Amendments—[1] This regulation substituted by the VAT (Amendment) Regulations, SI 2007/313 regs 2, 3 with effect from 1 March 2007.

[171 Repayment of a refund

(1) [Subject to regulation 171A,][5] where a claimant—

(*a*) has received a refund upon a claim, and

(*b*) either—

(i) a payment for the relevant supply is subsequently received, or

(ii) a payment is, by virtue of regulation 170 or 170A, treated as attributed to the relevant supply, or

(iii) the consideration for any relevant supply upon which the claim to refund is based is reduced after the claim is made,

he shall repay to the Commissioners such an amount as equals the amount of the refund, or the balance thereof, multiplied by a fraction of which the numerator is the amount so received or attributed, and the denominator is the amount of the outstanding consideration, or such an amount as is equal to the negative entry made in the VAT allowable portion of his VAT account as provided for in regulation 38.][4]

(2) [Subject to regulation 171B,][5] the claimant shall repay to the Commissioners the amount referred to in paragraph (1) above by including that amount in the box opposite the legend "VAT due in this period on sales and other outputs" on his return for the prescribed accounting period in which the payment is received.

(3) [Subject to regulation 171B and,][5] save as the Commissioners may otherwise allow, where the claimant fails to comply with the requirements of regulation 167, 168, 169[, 170 or 170A][2] he shall repay to the Commissioners the amount of the refund obtained by the claim to which the failure to comply relates; and he shall repay the amount by including that amount in the box opposite the legend "VAT due in this period on sales and other outputs" on his return for the prescribed accounting period which the Commissioners shall designate for that purpose.

(4) If at the time the claimant is required to repay any amount, he is no longer required to make returns to the Commissioners, he shall repay such amount to the Commissioners at such time and in such form and manner as they may direct.

[(5) For the purposes of this regulation[, but subject to paragraph (6) below,][3] a reference to payment shall not include a reference to a payment received by a person to whom a right to receive it has been assigned.][1]

[(6) Paragraph (5) above does not apply where any person to whom the right to receive a payment has been assigned (whether by the claimant or any other person) is connected to the claimant.][3]

[(7) Any question for the purposes of paragraph (6) above whether any person is connected to the claimant shall be determined in accordance with section 839 of the Taxes Act.][3]

[(8) Paragraphs (6) and (7) above apply where the right to receive a payment is assigned on or after 11th December 2003.][3]

Former regulation—VAT (Refunds for Bad Debts) Regulations, SI 1991/371 reg 8.

Amendments—[1] Para (5) added by the VAT Regulations, SI 1999/3029, regs 2, 4 with effect from 1 December 1999.

[2] Words substituted by the VAT (Amendment) (No 4) Regulations, SI 2002/3027 regs 2, 6 with effect from 1 January 2003.

[3] 3 Words in para (5) inserted, and paras (6)–(8), inserted by the VAT (Amendment) (No 6) Regulations, SI 2003/3220 regs 1(1)(*a*), 2, 22, 23 with effect from 11 December 2003.

[4] Para (1) substituted by the VAT (Amendment) Regulations, SI 2007/313 regs 2, 4 with effect from 1 March 2007.

[5] In paras (1), (2), (3) words inserted by the VAT (Amendment) (No 3) Regulations, SI 2014/2430 regs 2, 7(1)–(3) with effect from 1 January 2015.

[171A Calculation of repayment where reduction in consideration: special accounting schemes

In a case falling within sub-paragraph (*b*)(iii) of regulation 171(1) where the VAT on the relevant supply was accounted for on a relevant non-UK return or a relevant special scheme return, the amount to be repaid is such an amount as is equal to the amount by which the VAT chargeable on the relevant supply is reduced.][1]

Amendments—[1] Regs 171A, 171B inserted by the VAT (Amendment) (No 3) Regulations, SI 2014/2430 regs 2, 7(4) with effect from 1 January 2015.

[171B Timing and method of repayments: special accounting schemes

(1) Where—

(*a*) the VAT on the relevant supply was accounted for on a relevant non-UK return or a relevant special scheme return, and

(*b*) a repayment is required by regulation 171(1),

that repayment must be made no later than twenty days after the end of the tax period in which the payment for the relevant supply is received or the reduction in consideration is accounted for in the claimant's business accounts.

(2) Where—

(*a*) the VAT on the relevant supply was accounted for on a relevant non-UK return or a relevant special scheme return, and

(*b*) a repayment is required by regulation 171(3),

that repayment must be made no later than twenty days after the end of the tax period in which the failure to comply first occurred.

(3) In either case the repayment must be made by—

(*a*) amending (in accordance with Article 61 of the Implementing Regulation) the relevant non-UK return or the relevant special scheme return for the tax period in which the VAT on the relevant supply was brought into account, or

(*b*) (where the period during which a person is entitled to make such an amendment has expired) sending the sum due to the Commissioners.][1]

Amendments—[1] Regs 171A, 171B inserted by the VAT (Amendment) (No 3) Regulations, SI 2014/2430 regs 2, 7(4) with effect from 1 January 2015.

172 Writing off debts

(1) This regulation shall apply for the purpose of ascertaining whether, and to what extent, the consideration is to be taken to have been written off as a bad debt.

[(1A) Neither the whole nor any part of the consideration for a supply shall be taken to have been written off in accounts as a bad debt until a period of not less than six months has elapsed from the time when such whole or part first became due and payable to or to the order of the person who made the [relevant supply][2].][1]

[(2) Subject to paragraph (1A) the whole or any part of the consideration for a [relevant supply][2] shall be taken to have been written off as a bad debt when an entry is made in relation to that supply in the refunds for bad debt account in accordance with regulation 168.][1]

(3) Where the claimant owes an amount of money to the purchaser which can be set off, the consideration written off in the accounts shall be reduced by the amount so owed.

(4) Where the claimant holds in relation to the purchaser an enforceable security, the consideration written off in the accounts of the claimant shall be reduced by the value of that security.

Former regulation—VAT (Refunds for Bad Debts) Regulations, SI 1991/371 reg 9.

Amendments—[1] Para (1A) inserted by, and para (2) substituted by, VAT (Amendment) (No 5) Regulations, SI 1996/2960 with effect from 17 December 1996.

[2] Words in paras (1A) and (2) substituted by the VAT (Amendment) Regulations, SI 1997/1086 reg 14 with effect from 1 May 1997.

172A [Writing off debts—margin schemes

(1) This regulation applies where, by virtue of the claimant's having exercised an option under an order made under section 50A of the Act, the VAT chargeable on the relevant supply is charged by reference to the profit margin.

(2) Where this regulation applies the consideration for the relevant supply which is to be taken to have been written off as a bad debt shall not exceed the relevant amount.

(3) For the purposes of paragraph (2) above the relevant amount is—

(*a*) where either—

(i) no payment has been received in relation to the relevant supply, or

(ii) the total of such payments as have been received does not exceed the non-profit element,

the profit margin; or

(*b*) where the total of such payments as have been received exceeds the non-profit element, the amount (if any) by which the consideration for the relevant supply exceeds that total.

(4) In paragraph (3) above—

"non-profit element" means the consideration for the relevant supply less the profit margin.][1]

Amendments—[1] This regulation inserted by the VAT (Amendment) Regulations, SI 1997/1086 reg 15 with effect from 1 May 1997.

172B [Writing off debts—tour operators margin scheme

(1) This regulation applies where, by virtue of an order under section 53 of the Act, the value of the relevant supply falls to be determined otherwise than in accordance with section 19 of the Act.

(2) Where this regulation applies the consideration for the relevant supply which is to be taken to have been written off as a bad debt shall not exceed the relevant amount.

(3) For the purposes of paragraph (2) above the relevant amount is—

(*a*) where either—

(i) no payment has been received in relation to the relevant supply, or

(ii) the total of any such payments as have been received does not exceed the non-profit element,

the profit element; or

(*b*) where the total of such payments as have been received exceeds the non-profit element, the amount (if any) by which the consideration for the relevant supply exceeds that total.

(4) In this regulation—

"non-profit element" means the consideration for the relevant supply less the profit element;

"profit element" means the sum of—

(*a*) the value of the relevant supply; and

(*b*) the VAT chargeable on the relevant supply.][1]

Amendments—[1] This regulation inserted by the VAT (Amendment) Regulations, SI 1997/1086 reg 15 with effect from 1 May 1997.

[PART XIXA
REPAYMENT OF INPUT TAX WHERE CLAIM MADE UNDER PART XIX][1]

Cross References—See Reg 6(3) above (liability under this Part on transfer of going concern).

Amendments—[1] This part inserted by the VAT (Amendment) Regulations, SI 1997/1086 reg 16 with effect from 1 May 1997.

172ZC [Application

This Part applies where the relevant supply was made before 1st January 2003.][1]

Amendments—[1] This regulation inserted by the VAT (Amendment) (No 4) Regulations, SI 2002/3027 regs 2, 7 with effect from 1 January 2003.

172C [Interpretation of Part XIXA

Any expression used in this Part to which a meaning is given in Part XIX of these Regulations shall, unless the contrary intention appears, have the same meaning in this Part as it has in that Part.][1]

Amendments—[1] This regulation inserted by the VAT (Amendment) Regulations, SI 1997/1086 reg 16 with effect from 1 May 1997.

172D [Repayment of input tax

(1) Where—

(*a*) a claim has been made; and

(*b*) the purchaser has claimed deduction of the whole or part of the VAT on the relevant supply as input tax ('the deduction'),

the purchaser shall make an entry in his VAT account in accordance with paragraphs (2) and (3) below.

(2) The purchaser shall make a negative entry in the VAT allowable portion of that part of his VAT account which relates to the prescribed accounting period of his in which the claim has been made.

(3) The amount of the negative entry referred to in paragraph (2) above shall be such amount as is found by multiplying the amount of the deduction by a fraction of which the numerator is the amount of the claim and the denominator is the total VAT chargeable on the relevant supply.

(4) None of the circumstances to which this regulation applies is to be regarded as giving rise to any application of regulations 34 and 35.] [1]

Amendments—[1] This regulation inserted by the VAT (Amendment) Regulations, SI 1997/1086 reg 15 with effect from 1 May 1997.

172E [Restoration of an entitlement to credit for input tax

(1) Where—

(*a*) the purchaser has made an entry in his VAT account in accordance with regulation 172D ("the input tax repayment");

(*b*) he has made the return for the prescribed accounting period concerned, and has paid any VAT payable by him in respect of that period; and

(*c*) the claimant has made a repayment in accordance with regulation 171 in relation to the claim concerned,

the purchaser shall make an entry in his VAT account in accordance with paragraphs (2) and (3) below.

(2) The purchaser shall make a positive entry in the VAT allowable portion of that part of his VAT account which relates to the prescribed accounting period of his in which the repayment has been made.

(3) The amount of the positive entry referred to in paragraph (2) above shall be such amount as is found by multiplying the amount of the input tax repayment by a fraction of which the numerator is the amount repaid by the claimant and the denominator is the total amount of the claim.

(4) None of the circumstances to which this regulation applies is to be regarded as giving rise to any application of regulations 34 and 35.][1]

Amendments—[1] This regulation inserted by the VAT (Amendment) Regulations, SI 1997/1086 reg 16 with effect from 1 May 1997.

[PART XIXB
REPAYMENT OF INPUT TAX WHERE CONSIDERATION NOT PAID][1]

Amendments—[1] This Part inserted by the VAT (Amendment) (No 4) Regulations, SI 2002/3027 regs 2, 8 with effect from 1 January 2003.

172F [Application

This Part applies where the supply in relation to which a person has claimed credit for input tax was made on or after 1st January 2003.][1]

Amendments—[1] This regulation inserted by the VAT (Amendment) (No 4) Regulations, SI 2002/3027 regs 2, 8 with effect from 1 January 2003.

VAT SIs

172G [Interpretation

In this Part—

"relevant period" means 6 months following—

(i) the date of the supply, or

(ii) if later, the date on which the consideration for the supply, or (as the case may be) the unpaid part of it, became payable.][1]

Amendments—[1] This regulation inserted by the VAT (Amendment) (No 4) Regulations, SI 2002/3027 regs 2, 8 with effect from 1 January 2003.

172H [Repayment of input tax

(1) Subject to paragraph (5) below, where a person—

(*a*) has not paid the whole or any part of the consideration for a supply by the end of the relevant period; and

(*b*) has claimed deduction of the whole or part of the VAT on the supply as input tax ("the deduction"),

he shall make an entry in his VAT account in accordance with paragraphs (2) and (3) below.

(2) The person shall make a negative entry in the VAT allowable portion of that part of his VAT account which relates to the prescribed accounting period of his in which the end of the relevant period falls.

(3) The amount of the negative entry referred to in paragraph (2) above shall be such amount as is found by multiplying the amount of the deduction by a fraction of which the numerator is the amount of the consideration for the supply which has not been paid before the end of the relevant period and the denominator is the total consideration for the supply.

(4) None of the circumstances to which this regulation applies is to be regarded as giving rise to any application of regulations 34 and 35.

(5) This regulation does not apply where, for input tax, the operative date for VAT accounting purposes is the date mentioned in regulation 57(*b*) above.][1]

Amendments—[1] This regulation inserted by the VAT (Amendment) (No 4) Regulations, SI 2002/3027 regs 2, 8 with effect from 1 January 2003.

172I [Restoration of an entitlement to credit for input tax

(1) Where a person—

(*a*) has made an entry in his VAT account in accordance with regulation 172H ("the input tax repayment");

(*b*) has made the return for the prescribed accounting period concerned, and has paid any VAT payable by him in respect of that period; and

(*c*) after the end of the relevant period, has paid the whole or part of the consideration for the supply in relation to which the input tax repayment was made,

he shall make an entry in his VAT account in accordance with paragraphs (2) and (3) below in respect of each such payment made.

(2) The person shall make a positive entry in the VAT allowable portion of that part of his VAT account which relates to the prescribed accounting period of his in which payment of the whole or part of the consideration was made.

(3) The amount of the positive entry referred to in paragraph (2) above shall be such amount as is found by multiplying the amount of the input tax repayment by a fraction of which the numerator is the amount of the payment referred to in paragraph (1) (*c*) above and the denominator is [that consideration for the supply which was not paid before the end of the relevant period][2].

(4) None of the circumstances to which this regulation applies is to be regarded as giving rise to any application of regulations 34 and 35.

(5) . . .[2]][1]

Amendments—[1] This regulation inserted by the VAT (Amendment) (No 4) Regulations, SI 2002/3027 regs 2, 8 with effect from 1 January 2003.

[2] Words in para (3) substituted, and para (5) revoked, by the VAT (Amendment) Regulations, SI 2003/532 with effect from 1 April 2003.

172J [Attribution of payments

The rules on the attribution of payments in regulation 170 and, as the case may be, [170A(5)][2] above shall apply for determining whether anything paid is to be taken as paid by way of consideration for a particular supply.][1]

Amendments—[1] This regulation inserted by the VAT (Amendment) (No 4) Regulations, SI 2002/3027 regs 2, 8 with effect from 1 January 2003.

[2] Figure substituted by the VAT (Amendment) Regulations, SI 2007/313 regs 2, 5 with effect from 1 March 2007.

[PART 19C

ADJUSTMENT OF OUTPUT TAX IN RESPECT OF SUPPLIES TO WHICH SECTION 55A (6) OF THE ACT APPLIES

172K This Part applies where a person is entitled, by virtue of section 26AB(2) of the Act, to make an adjustment to the amount of VAT which he is required to account for and pay under section 55A(6) of the Act ("the adjustment").][1]

Amendments—[1] Regs 172K–172N inserted by the VAT (Amendment) (No 3) Regulations, SI 2007/1418 regs 2, 7 with effect from 1 June 2007.

[172L Adjustment of output tax

(1) The person must make the adjustment by making a negative entry in the VAT payable portion of that part of his VAT account which relates to the same prescribed accounting period of his as that in which he is required to make an entry in accordance with regulation 172H(2).

(2) The amount of the negative entry referred to in paragraph (1) above must be equal to the amount of the entry that is required to be made in accordance with regulation 172H(2).][1]

Amendments—[1] Regs 172K–172N inserted by the VAT (Amendment) (No 3) Regulations, SI 2007/1418 regs 2, 7 with effect from 1 June 2007.

[172M Readjustment of output tax

(1) Where a person—

(*a*) has made an entry in his VAT account in accordance with regulation 172L; and

(*b*) in relation to the same supply, he subsequently makes an entry in his VAT account in accordance with regulation 172I,

he must make an entry in his VAT account in accordance with paragraphs (2) and (3) below.

(2) The person must make a positive entry in the VAT payable portion of that part of his VAT account which relates to the same prescribed accounting period of his as that in which he makes an entry in accordance with regulation 172I.

(3) The amount of the positive entry referred to in paragraph (2) above must be equal to the amount of the entry he makes in accordance with regulation 172I.][1]

Amendments—[1] Regs 172K–172N inserted by the VAT (Amendment) (No 3) Regulations, SI 2007/1418 regs 2, 7 with effect from 1 June 2007.

[172N None of the circumstances to which this Part applies is to be regarded as giving rise to any application of regulations 34 and 35.][1]

Amendments—[1] Regs 172K–172N inserted by the VAT (Amendment) (No 3) Regulations, SI 2007/1418 regs 2, 7 with effect from 1 June 2007.

PART XX

REPAYMENTS TO COMMUNITY TRADERS

173 Interpretation of Part XX

(1) In this Part—

. . .[1]

"claimant" means a person making a claim under this Part or a person on whose behalf such a claim is made;

["claimant's member State" means the member State in which the claimant is established;][1]

. . .[1]

["principal VAT Directive" means Council Directive 2006/112/EC;

"refund Directive" means Council Directive 2008/9/EC;

"repayment period" means a period of time falling within one of the periods described in regulation 173G;

"repayment year" means the period of 12 calendar months commencing on 1st January.][1]

[(2) For the purposes of this Part, a person (P) is treated as being established in a country if—

(*a*) P has there a business establishment or some other fixed establishment from which business transactions are effected; or

(*b*) P's usual place of residence is there where P has no such establishment as is described in sub-paragraph (*a*) above in that country or elsewhere.][1]

(3) For the purposes of this Part—

(*a*) a person carrying on business through a branch or agency in any country is treated as having there an establishment from which business transactions are effected, . . .[1]

(*b*) "usual place of residence", in relation to a body corporate, means the place where it is legally constituted.

[(*c*) a reference to Article 170 of the principal VAT Directive is a reference to that Article—

(i) as amended by Article 2(3) of the Council Directive 2008/8/EC, and

(ii) as applied in the claimant's member State;

(*d*) a reference to Article 214 of the principal VAT Directive is a reference to that Article—

VAT SIs

(i) as amended by Article 2(8) of Council Directive 2008/8/EC, and

(ii) as applied in the claimant's member State;

(*e*) a reference to any other Article in the principal VAT Directive or to any Article in the refund Directive is a reference to such Article as applied in the claimant's member State; and

(*f*) a reference to Council Regulation (EC) No 1798/2003 is a reference to that Regulation as amended by Council Regulations (EC) No 885/2004, (EC) No 1791/2006, (EC) No 143/2008 and (EC) No 37/2009.][1]

Former regulation—VAT (Repayment to Community Traders) Regulations, SI 1980/1537 reg 2.

1 Definitions "calendar year" and "official authority" substituted, definitions inserted, para (2) substituted, word "and" deleted and paras 3(*c*)–(*f*) inserted, by the VAT (Amendment) (No 5) Regs, SI 2009/3241, regs 2, 11 with effect from 1 January 2010. Note that a claim for repayment of VAT in accordance with Part 20 made before 1 January 2010 shall be determined and, if appropriate, repayment made in accordance with this Part as it stood before the amendments made by SI 2009/3241 (see reg 18).

[173A Repayments of VAT

(1) The Commissioners shall make a repayment of VAT described in regulation 173B in accordance with this Part if—

(*a*) the VAT is incurred in the repayment period covered by a repayment application;

(*b*) the claimant is a person to whom this Part applies;

(*c*) the claimant makes a claim for repayment of the VAT in accordance with this Part; and

(*d*) the Commissioners are satisfied that the claimant is entitled to the repayment.

(2) Where—

(*a*) a repayment application covering a repayment period has been submitted in accordance with this Part; and

(*b*) a claim for repayment of VAT incurred in the repayment period covered by that repayment application is omitted from the repayment application,

the claim for repayment of that VAT may be made by means of a repayment application covering a later repayment period falling within the repayment year in which the VAT was incurred.][1]

Amendments—[1] Regs 173A–173X inserted by the VAT (Amendment) (No 5) Regs, SI 2009/3241, regs 2, 12 with effect from 1 January 2010. Note that a claim for repayment of VAT in accordance with Part 20 made before 1 January 2010 shall be determined and, if appropriate, repayment made in accordance with this Part as it stood before the amendments made by SI 2009/3241 (see reg 18).

[173B—(1) The VAT referred to in regulation 173A is VAT charged on—

(*a*) an importation of goods by the claimant from a place outside the member States; and

(*b*) supplies of goods or services made to the claimant in the United Kingdom if that VAT would be input tax of the claimant if the claimant were a taxable person.

(2) A claim for repayment may not be made in respect of VAT charged on—

(*a*) an importation of goods in respect of which the VAT charged is eligible for other relief;

(*b*) a supply or importation of goods which the claimant has removed or intends to remove to another member State, or which the claimant has exported or intends to export to a place outside the member States;

(*c*) a supply or importation of goods or a supply of services which the claimant has used or intends to use for the purpose of any supply by the claimant in the United Kingdom other than a supply described in regulation 173E(*b*)(i), (ii)[, (iii) or (iv)][2];

(*d*) a supply or importation of goods or a supply of services which if made to a taxable person would be excluded from credit under section 25 of the Act (payment of VAT by reference to accounting periods and credit for input tax against output tax); or

(*e*) a supply or importation of goods or a supply of services to a travel agent which is for the direct benefit of a traveller other than the travel agent or the travel agent's employee.

(3) In this regulation "travel agent" includes a tour operator and any person who purchases and re-supplies services of a kind enjoyed by travellers.][1]

Amendments—[1] Regs 173A–173X inserted by the VAT (Amendment) (No 5) Regs, SI 2009/3241, regs 2, 12 with effect from 1 January 2010. Note that a claim for repayment of VAT in accordance with Part 20 made before 1 January 2010 shall be determined and, if appropriate, repayment made in accordance with this Part as it stood before the amendments made by SI 2009/3241 (see reg 18).

2 In para (2)(*c*), words substituted for words "or (iii)" by the VAT (Amendment) (No 3) Regulations, SI 2014/2430 regs 2, 8(1)(*a*) with effect from 1 January 2015.

[173C—(1) This regulation applies to VAT charged on the goods or services described in regulation 173B(1) which—

(*a*) are not goods or services described in regulation 173B(2); and

(*b*) are used by the claimant both for transactions—

(i) giving rise to a right of deduction as required by Articles 168, 169 and 170 of the principal VAT Directive, and

(ii) transactions that do not give rise to a right of deduction.

(2) The VAT to which this regulation applies is repayable only to the extent of the deductible proportion of that VAT.

(3) The deductible proportion of any VAT is the proportion of that VAT that the claimant would be entitled to deduct in accordance with Articles 173, 174 and 175 of the principal VAT Directive if the VAT were chargeable in the claimant's member State.][1]

Amendments—[1] Regs 173A–173X inserted by the VAT (Amendment) (No 5) Regs, SI 2009/3241, regs 2, 12 with effect from 1 January 2010. Note that a claim for repayment of VAT in accordance with Part 20 made before 1 January 2010 shall be determined and, if appropriate, repayment made in accordance with this Part as it stood before the amendments made by SI 2009/3241 (see reg 18).

[173D—(1) This regulation applies where—

(*a*) a claim ("the original claim") for repayment of VAT to the extent of the deductible proportion of that VAT described in regulation 173C has been made; and

(*b*) the deductible proportion used in making the claim was determined on a provisional basis as described in Article 175(2) of the principal VAT Directive.

(2) Where the amount of VAT claimed in the original claim is less than the VAT that would have been repayable if the deductible proportion had been determined by reference to the final proportion described in Article 175(3) of the principal VAT Directive, the VAT representing the difference between the two amounts may be claimed by means of a repayment application submitted during the adjustment year as if that VAT had been incurred during the repayment period covered by that repayment application.

(3) Where the amount of VAT claimed in the original claim is more than the VAT that would have been repayable if the deductible proportion had been determined by reference to the final proportion described in Article 175(3) of the principal VAT Directive, the VAT representing the difference between the two amounts must be repaid to the Commissioners—

(*a*) by way of adjustment of a repayment claim made by means of a repayment application submitted in the adjustment year, or

(*b*) if no repayment claim is made as described in sub-paragraph (*a*) above, the payment back to the Commissioners must be made pursuant to a declaration submitted using the electronic portal set up by the claimant's member State for the purpose of facilitating repayments of VAT in accordance with the refund Directive before the expiry of the adjustment year.

(4) In this regulation "adjustment year" means the repayment year beginning immediately after the repayment year in which the repayment period of the original claim occurred or would have occurred if the original claim had been made in respect of the repayment period when the VAT was incurred.][1]

Amendments—[1] Regs 173A–173X inserted by the VAT (Amendment) (No 5) Regs, SI 2009/3241, regs 2, 12 with effect from 1 January 2010. Note that a claim for repayment of VAT in accordance with Part 20 made before 1 January 2010 shall be determined and, if appropriate, repayment made in accordance with this Part as it stood before the amendments made by SI 2009/3241 (see reg 18).

[173E Persons to whom this Part applies

This Part applies to a person who is established in and who carries on business in a member State other than the United Kingdom for the whole of a repayment period other than a person who—

(*a*) is established in the United Kingdom during any part of the repayment period;

(*b*) makes supplies in the United Kingdom of goods or services during any part of the repayment period other than—

(i) transport of freight outside the United Kingdom or to or from a place outside the United Kingdom or services ancillary thereto,

(ii) services where the VAT on the supply is payable solely by the person to whom the services are supplied in accordance with the provisions of section 8 of the Act (reverse charge on supplies received from abroad), and

(iii) goods where the VAT on the supply is payable solely by the person to whom they are supplied as provided for in section 9A (reverse charge on gas and electricity supplied by persons outside the United Kingdom) or 14 (acquisitions from persons belonging in other member States) of the Act;

[(iv) scheme services within paragraph 2 of Schedule 3BA to the Act supplied by a person who—

(*a*) is required to account for the VAT on those supplies on a non-UK return; and

(*b*) is not a registered person.][2]

(*c*) during any part of the repayment period, does not undertake or intend to undertake transactions in the member State where that person is established which afford that person a right of deduction in accordance with Articles 168 and 169 of the principal VAT Directive as applied in the member State where that person is established;

(*d*) makes or intends to make supplies in the repayment period upon which VAT was not or would not be charged by virtue of their being within the exemption afforded to small enterprises under Articles 284, 285, 286 and 287 of the principal VAT Directive as applied in the member State in which that person is established; or

VAT SIs

(*e*) makes or intends to make supplies in the repayment period which are covered by the flat-rate scheme for farmers provided for in Articles 295 to 305 of the principal VAT Directive as applied in the member State in which that person is established.][1]

Amendments—[1] Regs 173A–173X inserted by the VAT (Amendment) (No 5) Regs, SI 2009/3241, regs 2, 12 with effect from 1 January 2010. Note that a claim for repayment of VAT in accordance with Part 20 made before 1 January 2010 shall be determined and, if appropriate, repayment made in accordance with this Part as it stood before the amendments made by SI 2009/3241 (see reg 18).

[2] Para (*b*)(iv) inserted by the VAT (Amendment) (No 3) Regulations, SI 2014/2430 regs 2, 8(2) with effect from 1 January 2015.

[173F Time when VAT is incurred

(1) Paragraphs (2) to (4) below apply for determining the time when VAT is incurred for the purposes of a claim under this Part.

(2) VAT charged on the importation of goods is treated as incurred at the time when the VAT becomes chargeable.

(3) Where a supply of goods or services is treated as made at or before the time when the VAT invoice relating to it is issued, the VAT on that supply will be treated as incurred at the time when the VAT invoice is issued.

(4) Where a supply of goods or services is treated as made after the time when the VAT invoice relating to it is issued, the VAT will be treated as incurred at the time when the supply is treated as made.][1]

Amendments—[1] Regs 173A–173X inserted by the VAT (Amendment) (No 5) Regs, SI 2009/3241, regs 2, 12 with effect from 1 January 2010. Note that a claim for repayment of VAT in accordance with Part 20 made before 1 January 2010 shall be determined and, if appropriate, repayment made in accordance with this Part as it stood before the amendments made by SI 2009/3241 (see reg 18).

[173G Repayment period

A repayment period may be for a period of time covering—

(*a*) a repayment year;

(*b*) three or more consecutive months occurring wholly within a repayment year; or

(*c*) the remainder of a repayment year where the period commences after 30th September in that year.][1]

Amendments—[1] Regs 173A–173X inserted by the VAT (Amendment) (No 5) Regs, SI 2009/3241, regs 2, 12 with effect from 1 January 2010. Note that a claim for repayment of VAT in accordance with Part 20 made before 1 January 2010 shall be determined and, if appropriate, repayment made in accordance with this Part as it stood before the amendments made by SI 2009/3241 (see reg 18).

[173H Minimum total claim for a repayment period

(1) A claim for a repayment period must not be made unless the total amount claimed for the period is equal to or exceeds the minimum amount specified in paragraph (2) below.

(2) The minimum amount specified for a repayment period is—

(*a*) £35 in respect of the repayment period described in regulation 173G(*a*);

(*b*) £295 in respect of the repayment period described in regulation 173G(*b*); and

(*c*) £35 in respect of the repayment period described in regulation 173G(*c*).][1]

Amendments—[1] Regs 173A–173X inserted by the VAT (Amendment) (No 5) Regs, SI 2009/3241, regs 2, 12 with effect from 1 January 2010. Note that a claim for repayment of VAT in accordance with Part 20 made before 1 January 2010 shall be determined and, if appropriate, repayment made in accordance with this Part as it stood before the amendments made by SI 2009/3241 (see reg 18).

[173I Requirements for a claim for repayment of VAT

A claim for repayment of VAT under this Part must be made by means of a repayment application that—

(*a*) is addressed to the United Kingdom;

(*b*) contains the information required in regulations 173L and 173M completed in the English language;

(*c*) is submitted at any time before the day specified in regulation 173P using the electronic portal set up by the claimant's member State for the purpose of facilitating repayments of VAT in accordance with the refund Directive.][1]

Amendments—[1] Regs 173A–173X inserted by the VAT (Amendment) (No 5) Regs, SI 2009/3241, regs 2, 12 with effect from 1 January 2010. Note that a claim for repayment of VAT in accordance with Part 20 made before 1 January 2010 shall be determined and, if appropriate, repayment made in accordance with this Part as it stood before the amendments made by SI 2009/3241 (see reg 18).

[173J Where a claim for repayment of VAT under this Part comprises or includes a claim made in respect of a supply or importation described in regulation 173K, copies of such documentary evidence of an entitlement to deduct VAT as could be required of a taxable person claiming deduction of input tax in accordance with regulation 29 (requirements in connection with making claims for deduction of input tax) must be submitted using the electronic portal described in regulation 173I(*c*) at the same time as the repayment application in respect of that VAT.][1]

Amendments—[1] Regs 173A–173X inserted by the VAT (Amendment) (No 5) Regs, SI 2009/3241, regs 2, 12 with effect from 1 January 2010. Note that a claim for repayment of VAT in accordance with Part 20 made before 1 January 2010 shall be determined and, if appropriate, repayment made in accordance with this Part as it stood before the amendments made by SI 2009/3241 (see reg 18).

[173K The supplies or importations referred to in regulation 173J are—

(*a*) a supply of goods or services of a value equal to or exceeding £750;

(*b*) an importation of goods of a value equal to or exceeding £750; and

(*c*) a supply or importation of fuel of a value equal to or exceeding £200.][1]

Amendments—[1] Regs 173A–173X inserted by the VAT (Amendment) (No 5) Regs, SI 2009/3241, regs 2, 12 with effect from 1 January 2010. Note that a claim for repayment of VAT in accordance with Part 20 made before 1 January 2010 shall be determined and, if appropriate, repayment made in accordance with this Part as it stood before the amendments made by SI 2009/3241 (see reg 18).

[173L Contents of a repayment application

(1) A repayment application must contain the following information—

(*a*) the claimant's name and full address;

(*b*) an address for contact by electronic means;

(*c*) a description of the claimant's business activity for which the goods or services were acquired by reference to the appropriate harmonised code contained in revision 2 of the common statistical classification of economic activities referred to as "NACE Rev. 2" established by the European Parliament and Council Regulation (EC) No 1983/2006;

(*d*) the repayment period covered by the application;

(*e*) a declaration that the claimant has made no supply falling within paragraph (2) below during any part of the repayment period;

(*f*) the VAT identification number or tax reference number by which the claimant is identified for VAT purposes in the claimant's member State in accordance with Articles 214, 239 or 240 of the principal VAT Directive;

(*g*) the details of the bank account to which the claimant requests the Commissioners to repay the VAT claimed; and

(*h*) the information described in regulation 173M in relation to every importation of goods or supply in respect of which repayment of VAT charged thereon is claimed in the repayment application.

(2) A supply is within this paragraph if it is a supply of goods or services made in the United Kingdom other than a supply mentioned in regulation 173E(*b*)(i), (ii)[, (iii) or (iv)][2].][1]

Amendments—[1] Regs 173A–173X inserted by the VAT (Amendment) (No 5) Regs, SI 2009/3241, regs 2, 12 with effect from 1 January 2010. Note that a claim for repayment of VAT in accordance with Part 20 made before 1 January 2010 shall be determined and, if appropriate, repayment made in accordance with this Part as it stood before the amendments made by SI 2009/3241 (see reg 18).

[2] In para (2), words substituted for words "or (iii)" by the VAT (Amendment) (No 3) Regulations, SI 2014/2430 regs 2, 8(1)(*b*) with effect from 1 January 2015.

[173M In respect of every importation of goods or supply in respect of which repayment of VAT charged thereon is claimed, a repayment application must contain the following information—

(*a*) the full name and address of the supplier;

(*b*) except in the case of an importation of goods, the registration number of the supplier and the prefix "GB" or such other prefix by which the United Kingdom is identified in accordance with the requirements of Article 215 of the principal VAT Directive;

(*c*) the date of issue of, and the unique sequential number identifying, the document authenticated or issued by a proper officer in respect of the importation of goods or the VAT invoice issued in respect of the supply;

(*d*) the value of the supply or of the imported goods (expressed in sterling) as determined under the Act but excluding the VAT chargeable on the supply or importation;

(*e*) the amount (expressed in sterling) of VAT chargeable on the supply or importation;

(*f*) the amount of VAT on the supply or importation eligible for repayment under this Part expressed in sterling;

(*g*) where applicable, the fraction described in regulation 173N, expressed as a percentage; and

(*h*) the nature of goods and services acquired, described in accordance with regulation 173O.][1]

Amendments—[1] Regs 173A–173X inserted by the VAT (Amendment) (No 5) Regs, SI 2009/3241, regs 2, 12 with effect from 1 January 2010. Note that a claim for repayment of VAT in accordance with Part 20 made before 1 January 2010 shall be determined and, if appropriate, repayment made in accordance with this Part as it stood before the amendments made by SI 2009/3241 (see reg 18).

[173N The fraction referred to in regulation 173M(*g*) is the fraction described in Article 174(1) of the principal VAT Directive that would determine the deductible proportion of the VAT that the claimant would be entitled to deduct in accordance with Articles 173, 174 and 175 of that Directive if the VAT were chargeable in the claimant's member State.][1]

Amendments—[1] Regs 173A–173X inserted by the VAT (Amendment) (No 5) Regs, SI 2009/3241, regs 2, 12 with effect from 1 January 2010. Note that a claim for repayment of VAT in accordance with Part 20 made before 1 January 2010 shall be determined and, if appropriate, repayment made in accordance with this Part as it stood before the amendments made by SI 2009/3241 (see reg 18).

[173O—(1) The nature of the goods or services in respect of which repayment of VAT under this Part is claimed must be described by reference to—

(*a*) the harmonised numerical codes in paragraph (2) below; and

(*b*) where paragraph (3) below applies, the harmonised numerical codes for the goods and services concerned referred to in paragraph (4) below.

(2) The harmonised numerical codes referred to in paragraph (1) above are—

(*a*) code 1 in respect of fuel;

(*b*) code 2 in respect of hiring of means of transport;

(*c*) code 3 in respect of expenditure relating to means of transport (other than the goods and services referred to by codes 1 and 2);

(*d*) code 4 in respect of road tolls and road user charges;

(*e*) code 5 in respect of travel expenses, such as taxi fares and public transport fares;

(*f*) code 6 in respect of accommodation;

(*g*) code 7 in respect of food, drink and restaurant services;

(*h*) code 8 in respect of admissions to fairs and exhibitions;

(*i*) code 9 in respect of expenditures on luxuries, amusements and entertainment;

(*j*) code 10 in respect of other goods and services.

(3) This paragraph applies where the goods or services in respect of which repayment of VAT under this Part is claimed fall within any of the descriptions of goods or services represented by such of the harmonised numerical codes contained in the annex to Commission Regulation (EC) No 1174/2009 as listed in paragraph (4) below.

(4) The harmonised numerical codes referred to in paragraph (3) above are codes 1.6, 2.2, 2.4, 2.5.1, 2.5.2, 2.6.1, 2.6.2, 2.7, 2.9.1, 2.9.2, 3.2.1, 3.2.2, 3.2.3, 3.4.1, 3.4.2, 3.5.1, 3.5.2, 3.6.1, 3.6.2, 3.7.1, 3.7.2, 3.8.1, 3.8.2, 3.9, 3.10, 3.12, 5.1, 5.2, 5.3.1, 5.3.2, 6.1, 6.2, 6.4.1, 6.4.2, 6.6, 7.1.1, 7.1.2, 7.2.1, 7.2.2, 7.4, 8.1, 8.2, 9.1, 9.2, 9.3.1, 9.3.2, 9.4, 9.5, 9.6, 9.7, 10,1, 10.2, 10.3, 10.4.1, 10.4.2, 10.4.3, 10.5.1, 10.5.2, 10.5.3, 10.6, 10.7, 10.8, 10.9.1, 10.9.2, 10.9.3, 10.9.4, 10.10, 10.11, 10.12, 10.13, 10.14, 10.15, 10.16.1, 10.16.2, 10.16.3, 10.16.4, 10.17.1 and 10.17.2.

(5) Goods or services which fall within harmonised numerical code 10 in paragraph (2)(j) above but which do not fall within any of the harmonised numerical codes specified in paragraph (4) above must be expressly described in addition to their description by reference to harmonised code 10.][1]

Amendments—[1] Regs 173A–173X inserted by the VAT (Amendment) (No 5) Regs, SI 2009/3241, regs 2, 12 with effect from 1 January 2010. Note that a claim for repayment of VAT in accordance with Part 20 made before 1 January 2010 shall be determined and, if appropriate, repayment made in accordance with this Part as it stood before the amendments made by SI 2009/3241 (see reg 18).

[173P Day by which a claim under this Part must be made

(1) [Subject to paragraph (1A),][2] the day before which a repayment application in respect of a repayment period must be submitted in accordance with regulation 173I(*c*) is 1st October of the repayment year immediately following the repayment year in which the repayment period covered by the repayment application falls.

[(1A) A repayment application in respect of a repayment period falling within the repayment year commencing on 1st January 2009 must be submitted in accordance with regulation 173I(c) before 1st April 2011.][2]

(2) A repayment application will be treated as having been submitted in accordance with regulation 173I(*c*) only if its submission is successfully recorded by the validation process of the electronic portal described in that regulation.

(3) The time of submission of a repayment application will be conclusively presumed to be the time recorded as such by the electronic portal.

(4) The Commissioners must, by electronic means, notify a claimant of the day on which the claimant's repayment application is received by the Commissioners.][1]

Amendments—[1] Regs 173A–173X inserted by the VAT (Amendment) (No 5) Regs, SI 2009/3241, regs 2, 12 with effect from 1 January 2010. Note that a claim for repayment of VAT in accordance with Part 20 made before 1 January 2010 shall be determined and, if appropriate, repayment made in accordance with this Part as it stood before the amendments made by SI 2009/3241 (see reg 18).

[2] Words in para (1), and whole of para (1A), inserted, by the VAT (Amendment) (No 3) Regulations, SI 2010/2940 regs 2, 6 with effect from 4 January 2011.

[173Q Notification of entitlement to repayment

(1) The Commissioners must notify a claimant whether they are satisfied that the claimant is entitled to repayment of VAT claimed under this Part before the expiry of the relevant period applicable to the VAT in question.

(2) If the Commissioners are not satisfied that the claimant is entitled to repayment of any VAT claimed, they must state their reasons in the notification.

(3) If the Commissioners do not, in relation to any VAT claimed for repayment under this Part, notify a claimant in accordance with paragraph (1) above, they shall be deemed to have refused to make payment of the VAT in question for the purposes of section 83(1)(ha) of the Act (appeals against refusal by the Commissioners to make repayment).][1]

Amendments—[1] Regs 173A–173X inserted by the VAT (Amendment) (No 5) Regs, SI 2009/3241, regs 2, 12 with effect from 1 January 2010. Note that a claim for repayment of VAT in accordance with Part 20 made before 1 January 2010 shall be determined and, if appropriate, repayment made in accordance with this Part as it stood before the amendments made by SI 2009/3241 (see reg 18).

[173R Requests for further information or a document

(1) This regulation applies where, in order for the Commissioners to satisfy themselves whether a claimant is entitled to a repayment of VAT under this Part, information or the production of a document is requested by means of—

(*a*) a notice pursuant to Schedule 36 of the Finance Act 2008 (information and inspection powers); or

(*b*) a request to the competent authority of another member State in accordance with Council Regulation (EC) No 1798/2003 and Commission Regulation (EC) No 1925/2004.

(2) A request for information or the production of a document made to a claimant or competent authority of a member State must be made by electronic means.

(3) In any other case, a request for information or a document must be made by—

(*a*) electronic means if such means are available to the recipient of the request; or

(*b*) such other means as are expedient.

(4) A request for information or a document must be made before the expiry of the relevant period applicable to the VAT in question.

(5) There is no limit on the number of requests for information or documents that may be made before the expiry of relevant period applicable to the VAT in question.

(6) The question whether a request for information or the production of a document has been made before the expiry of a relevant period applicable to any VAT shall take account of any extension of the 4-month period mentioned in regulation 173S by virtue of regulations 173T and 173U resulting from a request that has already been made but no account shall be taken of any further extension to the relevant period that would arise if the request in question were to be made.

(7) In this regulation, references to the competent authority of a member State are references to the authorities listed as competent authorities in relation to the member States in Article 2 of Council Regulation (EC) No 1798/2003.][1]

Amendments—[1] Regs 173A–173X inserted by the VAT (Amendment) (No 5) Regs, SI 2009/3241, regs 2, 12 with effect from 1 January 2010. Note that a claim for repayment of VAT in accordance with Part 20 made before 1 January 2010 shall be determined and, if appropriate, repayment made in accordance with this Part as it stood before the amendments made by SI 2009/3241 (see reg 18).

[173S Relevant period applicable to any VAT for which repayment is claimed

The relevant period applicable to any VAT for which repayment is claimed in this Part is the period which—

(*a*) commences on the day when the Commissioners receive the repayment application in respect of the VAT claimed, and

(*b*) ends 4 months after that day unless the end of that period is determined in accordance with regulations 173T or 173U.][1]

Amendments—[1] Regs 173A–173X inserted by the VAT (Amendment) (No 5) Regs, SI 2009/3241, regs 2, 12 with effect from 1 January 2010. Note that a claim for repayment of VAT in accordance with Part 20 made before 1 January 2010 shall be determined and, if appropriate, repayment made in accordance with this Part as it stood before the amendments made by SI 2009/3241 (see reg 18).

[173T Extension of the relevant period by virtue of the making of a request for information or a document

(1) Where a request for information or the production of a document as described in regulation 173R is made, then, subject to paragraphs (2), (3) and (4) below and regulation 173U, the relevant period applicable to the VAT in question shall end on the expiry of 2 months from the day on which the Commissioners receive the information or document requested.

(2) Where, by virtue of paragraph (1) above, the relevant period applicable to any VAT would end before the expiry of 6 months from the date on which the Commissioners received the repayment application for the VAT in question, the relevant period shall end on the expiry of that 6-month period.

(3) Where, by virtue of paragraph (1) above, the relevant period applicable to any VAT would end after the expiry of 8 months from the day on which the Commissioners received the repayment application for the VAT in question, the relevant period shall end on the expiry of that 8 month period.

VAT SIs

(4) Where the Commissioners do not receive the information or a document requested before the expiry of 1 month from the date on which the request reaches the intended recipient of it, the end of the relevant period shall be determined in accordance with this regulation as if the Commissioners had received the requested information or document upon the expiry of that 1-month period.][1]

Amendments—[1] Regs 173A–173X inserted by the VAT (Amendment) (No 5) Regs, SI 2009/3241, regs 2, 12 with effect from 1 January 2010. Note that a claim for repayment of VAT in accordance with Part 20 made before 1 January 2010 shall be determined and, if appropriate, repayment made in accordance with this Part as it stood before the amendments made by SI 2009/3241 (see reg 18).

[173U Extension of the relevant period where more than one request for information or a document is made in relation to the same VAT

(1) This regulation applies to determine the end of the relevant period applicable to any VAT where more than one request for information or the production of a document as described in regulation 173R is made in relation to that VAT.

(2) Where the requests are—

(*a*) made on different days; or

(*b*) received by the recipients of the requests on different days,

the end of the relevant period shall be determined in accordance with regulation 173T as if all of the requests were comprised in a single request ("composite request") made on the latest day when a request forming part of the composite request was made.

(3) The question whether information or a document requested by a composite request has been provided to the Commissioners within the 1-month period mentioned in regulation 173T(4) shall be determined as if the composite request had been received on the latest day on which any of the requests forming part of the composite request is received.][1]

Amendments—[1] Regs 173A–173X inserted by the VAT (Amendment) (No 5) Regs, SI 2009/3241, regs 2, 12 with effect from 1 January 2010. Note that a claim for repayment of VAT in accordance with Part 20 made before 1 January 2010 shall be determined and, if appropriate, repayment made in accordance with this Part as it stood before the amendments made by SI 2009/3241 (see reg 18).

[173V Time when a repayment of VAT must be made

(1) VAT to which a claimant is entitled to repayment under this Part must be paid by the Commissioners within 10 business days of the expiry of the relevant period in relation to that VAT.

(2) For these purposes, a "business day" is any day except—

(*a*) Saturday, Sunday, Good Friday or Christmas Day;

(*b*) a bank holiday under the Banking and Financial Dealings Act 1971;

(*c*) a day appointed by Royal proclamation as a public fast or thanksgiving day; or

(*d*) a day declared by an order under section 2(1) of the Banking and Financial Dealings Act 1971 to be a non-business day.][1]

Amendments—[1] Regs 173A–173X inserted by the VAT (Amendment) (No 5) Regs, SI 2009/3241, regs 2, 12 with effect from 1 January 2010. Note that a claim for repayment of VAT in accordance with Part 20 made before 1 January 2010 shall be determined and, if appropriate, repayment made in accordance with this Part as it stood before the amendments made by SI 2009/3241 (see reg 18).

[173W Interest on late payments

(1) Where the Commissioners fail to repay VAT to which a claimant is entitled to repayment under this Part before the expiry of the period described in regulation 173V, they must pay interest on that amount to the claimant for the applicable period.

(2) The "applicable period" is the period—

(*a*) beginning upon the expiry of the period described in regulation 173V, and

(*b*) ending on the day on which the Commissioners authorise the repayment to the claimant.

(3) Interest under this regulation shall be payable at the same rate as would have been payable if the Commissioners had been required to pay interest to the claimant pursuant to section 78 of the Act during the applicable period.

(4) Where—

(*a*) a claimant is requested to provide information or produce a document by a notice described in regulation 173R, and

(*b*) the claimant fails to provide the information or to produce the document within 1 month of receiving the notice,

the Commissioners shall not be liable to pay any interest under this regulation in respect of the VAT in relation to which the request was made even if the claimant provides the information or produces the document requested at a later time.

(5) The Commissioners shall not be liable to pay interest under this regulation during any period where a claimant has not provided to the Commissioners the documents described in regulation 173J that are required to be submitted at the same time as a repayment application in respect of supplies or importations described in regulation 173K.][1]

Amendments—[1] Regs 173A–173X inserted by the VAT (Amendment) (No 5) Regs, SI 2009/3241, regs 2, 12 with effect from 1 January 2010. Note that a claim for repayment of VAT in accordance with Part 20 made before 1 January 2010 shall be determined and, if appropriate, repayment made in accordance with this Part as it stood before the amendments made by SI 2009/3241 (see reg 18).

[173X Where—

(*a*) any amount has been paid to any person by way of interest under regulation 173W, but

(*b*) that person was not entitled to that amount under that regulation,

the amount paid shall be treated for the purposes of the Act as if it had been an amount paid to that person by way of interest under section 78 of the Act (interest in certain cases of official error) in circumstances where that person was not entitled to that amount under that section.][1]

Amendments—[1] Regs 173A–173X inserted by the VAT (Amendment) (No 5) Regs, SI 2009/3241, regs 2, 12 with effect from 1 January 2010. Note that a claim for repayment of VAT in accordance with Part 20 made before 1 January 2010 shall be determined and, if appropriate, repayment made in accordance with this Part as it stood before the amendments made by SI 2009/3241 (see reg 18).

174–179

Revocation—Regs 174–179, and preceding headings, revoked by the VAT (Amendment) (No 5) Regs, SI 2009/3241, regs 2, 13 with effect from 1 January 2010. Note that a claim for repayment of VAT in accordance with Part 20 made before 1 January 2010 shall be determined and, if appropriate, repayment made in accordance with this Part as it stood before the amendments made by SI 2009/3241 (see reg 18).

180 Deduction of bank charges

Where any repayment is to be made to a claimant in the country in which he is established, the Commissioners may reduce the amount of the repayment by the amount of any bank charges or costs incurred as a result thereof.

Former regulation—VAT (Repayment to Community Traders) Regulations, SI 1980/1537 reg 9.

181 Treatment of claim . . .

For the purposes of section 73 of the Act any claim made under this Part shall be treated as a return required under paragraph 2 of Schedule 11 [made in respect of a prescribed accounting period comprising the repayment period of the claim] to the Act.

Former regulation—VAT (Repayment to Community Traders) Regulations, SI 1980/1537 reg 10.

Amendment—Words "and repayment claimed" omitted from cross-heading, and words in reg 181 inserted, by the VAT (Amendment) (No 5) Regs, SI 2009/3241, regs 2, 14, 15 with effect from 1 January 2010. Note that a claim for repayment of VAT in accordance with Part 20 made before 1 January 2010 shall be determined and, if appropriate, repayment made in accordance with this Part as it stood before the amendments made by SI 2009/3241 (see reg 18).

182 For the purpose of section 83(c) of the Act repayments claimed under this Part shall be treated as the amount of any input tax which may be credited to a person.

Former regulation—VAT (Repayment to Community Traders) Regulations, SI 1980/1537 reg 11.

Amendment—Reg 182 repealed by the VAT (Amendment) (No 5) Regs, SI 2009/3241, regs 2, 15 with effect from 1 January 2010. Note that a claim for repayment of VAT in accordance with Part 20 made before 1 January 2010 shall be determined and, if appropriate, repayment made in accordance with this Part as it stood before the amendments made by SI 2009/3241 (see reg 18).

183 . . . incorrect claims

If any claimant furnishes or sends to the Commissioners for the purposes of this Part any document which is false or which has been altered after issue to that person, the Commissioners may refuse to repay any VAT claimed by that claimant for the period of 2 years from the date when the claim, in respect of which the false or altered document was furnished or sent, was made.

Former regulation—VAT (Repayment to Community Traders) Regulations, SI 1980/1537 reg 12.

Amendment—Words "False, altered or" in cross heading, and Reg 183, repealed by the VAT (Amendment) (No 5) Regs, SI 2009/3241, regs 2, 15 with effect from 1 January 2010. Note that a claim for repayment of VAT in accordance with Part 20 made before 1 January 2010 shall be determined and, if appropriate, repayment made in accordance with this Part as it stood before the amendments made by SI 2009/3241 (see reg 18).

184 Where any sum has been repaid to a claimant as a result of an incorrect claim, the amount of any subsequent repayment to that claimant may be reduced by the said sum.

Former regulation—VAT (Repayment to Community Traders) Regulations, SI 1980/1537 reg 13.

PART XXI

REPAYMENTS TO THIRD COUNTRY TRADERS

185 Interpretation of Part XXI

(1) In this Part—

"claimant" means a person making a claim under this Part or a person on whose behalf a claim is made and any agent acting on his behalf as his VAT representative;

"official authority" means any-government body or agency in any country which is recognised by the Commissioners as having authority to act for the purposes of this Part;

"prescribed year" means the period of 12 months beginning on the first day of July in any year;

VAT SIs

"VAT representative" means any person established in the United Kingdom and registered for VAT purposes in accordance with the provisions of Schedule 1 to the Act who acts as agent on behalf of a claimant;

"third country" means a country other than those comprising the member States of the European Community;

"trader" means a person carrying on a business who is established in a third country and who is not a taxable person in the United Kingdom.

(2) For the purposes of this Part, a person is treated as being established in a country if—

(*a*) he has there a business establishment, or

(*b*) he has no such establishment (there or elsewhere) but his permanent address or usual place of residence is there.

(3) For the purposes of this Part—

(*a*) a person carrying on business through a branch or agency in any country is treated as being established there, and

(*b*) where the person is a body corporate its usual place of residence shall be the place where it is legally constituted.

Former regulation—VAT (Repayments to Third Country Traders) Regulations, SI 1987/2015 reg 2.

186 Repayments of VAT

Subject to the other provisions of this Part a trader shall be entitled to be repaid VAT charged on goods imported by him into the United Kingdom in respect of which no other relief is available or on supplies made to him in the United Kingdom if that VAT would be input tax of his were he a taxable person in the United Kingdom.

Former regulation—VAT (Repayments to Third Country Traders) Regulations, SI 1987/2015 reg 3.
Simon's Tax Cases—*SRI International v R&C Comrs* [2011] UKUT 240 (TCC), [2011] STC 1614.

187 VAT representatives

The Commissioners may, as a condition of allowing a repayment under this Part, require a trader to appoint a VAT representative to act on his behalf.

Former regulation—VAT (Repayments to Third Country Traders) Regulations, SI 1987/2015 reg 4.

188 Persons to whom this Part applies

(1) Save as the Commissioners may otherwise allow, a trader to whom this Part applies who is established in a third country having a comparable system of turnover taxes will not be entitled to any refunds under this Part unless that country provides reciprocal arrangements for refunds to be made to taxable persons who are established in the United Kingdom.

(2) This Part shall apply to any trader but not if during any period determined under regulation 192—

(*a*) he was established in any of the member States of the European Community, or

(*b*) he made supplies in the United Kingdom of goods or services other than—

(i) transport of freight outside the United Kingdom to or from a place outside the United Kingdom or services ancillary thereto,

(ii) services where the VAT on the supply is payable solely by the person to whom they are supplied in accordance with the provisions of section 8 of the Act, and

(iii) goods where the VAT on the supply is payable solely by the person to whom they are supplied.

Former regulations—VAT (Repayments to Third Country Traders) Regulations, SI 1987/2015 reg 5; VAT (Repayments to Third Country Traders) (Amendment) Regulations, SI 1993/1222 reg 3.

189 Supplies and importations to which this Part applies

This Part applies to any supply of goods or services made in the United Kingdom or to any importation of goods into the United Kingdom on or after 1st July 1994 but does not apply to any supply or importation which—

(*a*) the trader has used or intends to use for the purpose of any supply by him in the United Kingdom, or

(*b*) has been exported or is intended for exportation from the United Kingdom by or on behalf of the trader.

Former regulation—VAT (Repayments to Third Country Traders) Regulations, SI 1987/2015 reg 6.

190 VAT which will not be repaid

(1) The following VAT shall not be repaid—

(*a*) VAT charged on a supply which if made to a taxable person would be excluded from any credit under section 25 of the Act,

(*b*) VAT charged on a supply to a travel agent which is for the direct benefit of a traveller other than the travel agent or his employee,

[(*c*) VAT charged on a supply used or to be used in making supplies of a description falling within article 3 of the Value Added Tax (Input Tax) (Specified Supplies) Order 1999.][1]

(2) In this regulation a travel agent includes a tour operator or any person who purchases and resupplies services of a kind enjoyed by travellers.

Former regulation—VAT (Repayments to Third Country Traders) Regulations, SI 1987/2015 reg 7.

Amendments—[1] Sub-para (1)(*c*) inserted by the VAT (Amendment) (No 4) Regulations, SI 2004/3140 reg 15 with effect from 3 December 2004 in relation to VAT charged on or after that date: SI 2004/3140 reg 2(4).

191 Method of claiming

(1) A person claiming a repayment of VAT under this Part shall—

(*a*) complete in the English language and send to the Commissioners either [the form specified in a notice published by the Commissioners][1], or a like form produced by any official authority, containing full information in respect of all the matters specified in the said form and a declaration as therein set out, and

(*b*) at the same time furnish—

(i) a certificate of status issued by the official authority of the third country in which the trader is established either on [the form specified in a notice published by the Commissioners][1] or on a like form produced by the official authority, and

(ii) such documentary evidence of an entitlement to deduct input tax as may be required of a taxable person claiming a deduction of input tax in accordance with the provisions of regulation 29.

(2) Where the Commissioners are in possession of a certificate of status issued not more than 12 months before the date of the claim, the claimant shall not be required to furnish a further such certificate.

(3) The Commissioners shall refuse to accept any document referred to in paragraph (1)(*b*)(ii) above if it bears an official stamp indicating that it had been furnished in support of an earlier claim.

Amendments—[1] In para (1)(*a*), words substituted for words "the form numbered 9 in Schedule 1 to these Regulations", and in para (1)(b), words substituted for words "the form numbered 10 in Schedule 1 to these Regulations", by the VAT (Amendment) (No 2) Regulations, SI 2012/1899 regs 3, 20 with effect from 15 October 2012.

192 Time within which a claim must be made

(1) A claim shall be made not later than 6 months after the end of the prescribed year in which the VAT claimed was charged and shall be in respect of VAT charged on supplies or on importations made during a period of not less than 3 months and not more than 12 months, provided that a claim may be made in respect of VAT charged on supplies or on importations made during a period of less than 3 months where that period represents the final part of the prescribed year.

(2) No claim shall be made for less than £16.

(3) No claim shall be made for less than £130 in respect of VAT charged on supplies or on importations made during a period of less than the prescribed year except where that period represents the final part of the prescribed year.

Former regulation—VAT (Repayments to Third Country Traders) Regulations, SI 1987/2015 reg 9.

193 Deduction of bank charges

Where any repayment is to be made to a claimant in the country in which he is established, the Commissioners may reduce the amount of the repayment by the amount of any bank charges or costs incurred as a result thereof.

194 Treatment of claim

For the purposes of section 73 of the Act any claim made under this Part shall be treated as a return required under paragraph 2 of Schedule 11 to the Act [made in respect of a prescribed accounting period].

Former regulation—VAT (Repayments to Third Country Traders) Regulations, SI 1987/2015 reg 10.

Amendment—Words "and repayment claimed" omitted from cross heading, and words inserted in reg 194, by the VAT (Amendment) (No 5) Regs, SI 2009/3241, regs 2, 17 with effect from 1 January 2010.

195 For the purpose of section 83(c) of the Act repayments claimed under this Part shall be treated as the amount of any input tax which may be credited to a person.

Former regulation—VAT (Repayments to Third Country Traders) Regulations, SI 1987/2015 reg 11.

Amendment—Reg 195 repealed by the VAT (Amendment) (No 5) Regs, SI 2009/3241, regs 2, 17 with effect from 1 January 2010.

196 False, altered or incorrect claims

If any claimant furnishes or sends to the Commissioners for the purposes of this Part any document which is false or which has been altered after issue to that person the Commissioners may refuse to repay any VAT claimed by that claimant for the period of 2 years from the date when the claim in respect of which the false or altered documents were furnished or sent, was made.

197 Where any sum has been repaid to a claimant as a result of an incorrect claim, the amount of any subsequent repayment to that claimant may be reduced by the said sum.

VAT SIs

PART XXII
REPAYMENT SUPPLEMENT

198 Computation of period

In computing the period of 30 days referred to in section 79(2)(*b*) of the Act, periods referable to the following matters shall be left out of account—

(*a*) the raising and answering of any reasonable inquiry relating to the requisite return or claim,

(*b*) the correction by the Commissioners of any errors or omissions in that requisite return or claim, and

(*c*) in any case to which section 79(1)(*a*) of the Act applies, the following matters, namely—

(i) any such continuing failure to submit returns as is referred to in section 25(5) of the Act, and

(ii) compliance with any such condition as is referred to in paragraph 4(1) of Schedule 11 to the Act.

Former regulation—VAT (Repayment Supplement) Regulation, SI 1988/1343 reg 4.
Simon's Tax Cases—*C&E Comrs v L Rowland & Co (Retail) Ltd* [1992] STC 647*.

199 Duration of period

For the purpose of determining the duration of the periods referred to in regulation 198, the following rules shall apply—

(*a*) in the case of the period mentioned in regulation 198(*a*), it shall be taken to have begun on the date when the Commissioners first raised the inquiry and it shall be taken to have ended on the date when they received a complete answer to their inquiry;

(*b*) in the case of the period mentioned in regulation 198(*b*), it shall be taken to have begun on the date when the error or omission first came to the notice of the Commissioners and it shall be taken to have ended on the date when the error or omission was corrected by them;

(*c*) in the case of the period mentioned in regulation 198(*c*)(i), it shall be determined in accordance with a certificate of the Commissioners under paragraph 14(1)(*b*) of Schedule 11 to the Act;

(*d*) in the case of the period mentioned in regulation 198(*c*)(ii), it shall be taken to have begun on the date of the service of the written notice of the Commissioners which required the production of documents or the giving of security, and it shall be taken to have ended on the date when they received the required documents or the required security.

Former regulation—VAT (Repayment Supplement) Regulations, SI 1988/1343 reg 5.
Simon's Tax Cases—*C&E Comrs v L Rowland & Co (Retail) Ltd* [1992] STC 647*.

PART XXIII
REFUNDS TO "DO-IT-YOURSELF" BUILDERS

200 Interpretation of Part XXIII

In this Part—

"claim" means a claim for refund of VAT made pursuant to section 35 of the Act, and "claimant" shall be construed accordingly;

"relevant building" means a building in respect of which a claimant makes a claim.

Former regulation—VAT ("Do-It-Yourself" Builders) (Refund of Tax) Regulations, SI 1989/2259 reg 2.

201 Method and time for making claim

A claimant shall make his claim in respect of a relevant building by—

(*a*) furnishing to the Commissioners no later than 3 months after the completion of the building [the relevant form for the purposes of the claim][1] containing the full particulars required therein, and

(*b*) at the same time furnishing to them—

(i) a certificate of completion obtained from a local authority or such other documentary evidence of completion of the building as is satisfactory to the Commissioners,

(ii) an invoice showing the registration number of the person supplying the goods, whether or not such an invoice is a VAT invoice, in respect of each supply of goods on which VAT has been paid which have been incorporated into the building or its site,

(iii) in respect of imported goods which have been incorporated into the building or its site, documentary evidence of their importation and of the VAT paid thereon,

(iv) documentary evidence that planning permission for the building had been granted, and

(v) a certificate signed by a quantity surveyor or architect that the goods shown in the claim were or, in his judgement, were likely to have been, incorporated into the building or its site.

Former regulation—VAT ("Do-It-Yourself" Builders) (Refund of Tax) Regulations, SI 1989/2259 reg 3.
Simon's Tax Cases—*R&C Comrs v Patel* [2014] UKUT 361 (TCC), [2015] STC 148.
Amendments—[1] In para (*a*), words substituted for words "the form numbered 11 in Schedule 1 to these Regulations", by the Value Added Tax (Amendment) (No 3) Regulations, SI 2009/1967 regs 2, 7 with effect from 15 August 2009.

[**201A**—The relevant form for the purposes of a claim is—

(*a*) form VAT 431NB where the claim relates to works described in section 35(1A)(*a*) or (*b*) of the Act; and

(*b*) form VAT 431C where the claim relates to works described in section 35(1A)(*c*) of the Act.][1]

Amendments—[1] Section 201A substituted by the VAT (Amendment) (No 2) Regulations, SI 2012/1899 regs 3, 21 with effect from 15 October 2012.

PART XXIV

FLAT-RATE SCHEME FOR FARMERS

202 Interpretation of Part XXIV

In this Part—

"certified person" means a person certified as a flat-rate farmer for the purposes of the flat- rate scheme under regulation 203 and "certified" and "certification" shall be construed accordingly.

Former regulation—VAT (Flat-rate Scheme for Farmers) Regulations, SI 1992/3103 reg 1(2).

203 Flat-rate scheme

(1) The Commissioners shall, if the conditions mentioned in regulation 204 are satisfied, certify that a person is a flat-rate farmer for the purposes of the flat-rate scheme (hereinafter in this Part referred to as "the scheme").

(2) Where a person is for the time being certified in accordance with this regulation, then (whether or not that person is a taxable person) any supply of goods or services made by him in the course or furtherance of the relevant part of his business shall be disregarded for the purpose of determining whether he is, has become or has ceased to be liable or entitled to be registered under Schedule 1 [or 1A][1] to the Act.

Former regulation—VAT (Flat-rate Scheme for Farmers) Regulations, SI 1992/3103 reg 2.

Amendments—[1] In para (2), words inserted by the VAT (Amendment) (No 2) Regulations, SI 2012/1899 regs 3, 22 with effect from 15 October 2012.

204 Admission to the scheme

The conditions mentioned in regulation 203 are that—

(*a*) the person satisfies the Commissioners that he is carrying on a business involving one or more designated activities,

(*b*) he has not in the 3 years preceding the date of his application for certification—

(i) been convicted of any offence in connection with VAT,

(ii) made any payment to compound proceedings in respect of VAT under section 152 of the Customs and Excise Management Act 1979 as applied by section 72(12) of the Act,

(iii) been assessed to a penalty under section 60 of the Act,

(*c*) he makes an application for certification on the form [specified in a notice published by the Commissioners][1], and

(*d*) he satisfies the Commissioners that he is a person in respect of whom the total of the amounts as are mentioned in regulation 209 relating to supplies made in the year following the date of his certification will not exceed by £3,000 or more the amount of input tax to which he would otherwise be entitled to credit in that year.

Former regulation—VAT (Flat-rate Scheme for Farmers) Regulations, SI 1992/3103 reg 3.

Amendments—[1] In para (*c*), words substituted for words "numbered 14 in Schedule 1 to these Regulations", by the VAT (Amendment) (No 2) Regulations, SI 2012/1899 regs 3, 23 with effect from 15 October 2012.

205 Certification

Where the Commissioners certify that a person is a flat-rate farmer for the purposes of the scheme, the certificate issued by the Commissioners shall be effective from—

(*a*) the date on which the application for certification is received by the Commissioners,

(*b*) with the agreement of the Commissioners, an earlier date to that mentioned in sub-paragraph (*a*) above, or

(*c*) if the person so requests, a later date which is no more than 30 days after the date mentioned in sub-paragraph (*a*) above,

provided that any certificate shall not be effective from a date before the date when the person's registration under Schedule 1[, 1A][1] or 3 to the Act is cancelled and a certificate shall not be effective from a date earlier than 1st January 1993.

Former regulation—VAT (Flat-rate Scheme for Farmers) Regulations, SI 1992/3103 reg 4.

Amendments—[1] Words inserted by the VAT (Amendment) (No 2) Regulations, SI 2012/1899 regs 3, 24 with effect from 15 October 2012.

206 Cancellation of certificates

(1) The Commissioners may cancel a person's certificate in any case where—

(*a*) a statement false in a material particular was made by him or on his behalf in relation to his application for certification,

(*b*) he has been convicted of an offence in connection with VAT or has made a payment to compound such proceedings under section 152 of the Customs and Excise Management Act 1979 as applied by section 72(12) of the Act,
(*c*) he has been assessed to a penalty under section 60 of the Act,
(*d*) he ceases to be involved in designated activities,
(*e*) he dies, becomes bankrupt or incapacitated,
(*f*) he is liable to be registered under Schedule 1[, 1A][1] or 3 to the Act,
(*g*) he makes an application in writing for cancellation,
(*h*) he makes an application in writing for registration under Schedule 1 or 3 to the Act, and such application shall be deemed to be an application for cancellation of his certificate,
(*i*) they consider it is necessary to do so for the protection of the revenue, or
(*j*) they are not satisfied that any of the grounds for cancellation of a certificate mentioned in sub-paragraphs (*a*) to (*h*) above do not apply.

(2) Where the Commissioners cancel a person's certificate in accordance with paragraph (1) above, the effective date of the cancellation shall be for each of the cases mentioned respectively in that paragraph as follows—
(*a*) the date when the Commissioners discover that such a statement has been made,
(*b*) the date of his conviction or the date on which a sum is paid to compound proceedings,
(*c*) 30 days after the date when the assessment is notified,
(*d*) the date of the cessation of designated activities,
(*e*) the date on which he died, became bankrupt or incapacitated,
(*f*) the effective date of registration,
(*g*) not less than one year after the effective date of his certificate or such earlier date as the Commissioners may agree,
(*h*) not less than one year after the effective date of his certificate or such earlier date as the Commissioners may agree,
(*i*) the date on which the Commissioners consider a risk to the revenue arises, or
(*j*) the date mentioned in sub-paragraphs (*a*) to (*h*) above as appropriate.

Former regulation—VAT (Flat-rate Scheme for Farmers) Regulations, SI 1992/3103 reg 5.
Amendments—[1] Words inserted in para (1)(*f*) by the VAT (Amendment) (No 2) Regulations, SI 2012/1899 regs 3, 25 with effect from 15 October 2012.

207 Death, bankruptcy or incapacity of certified person

(1) If a certified person dies or becomes bankrupt or incapacitated, the Commissioners may, from the date on which he died or became bankrupt or incapacitated treat as a certified person any person carrying on those designated activities until some other person is certified in respect of the designated activities or the incapacity ceases, as the case may be; and the provisions of the Act and of any Regulations made thereunder shall apply to any person so treated as though he were a certified person.

(2) Any person carrying on such designated activities shall, within 30 days of commencing to do so, inform the Commissioners in writing of that fact and of the date of the death, or of the nature of the incapacity and the date on which it began.

(3) In relation to a company which is a certified person, the references in regulation 206(1)(*e*) and (2)(*e*) and in paragraph (1) above to the certified person becoming bankrupt or incapacitated shall be construed as references to its going into liquidation or receivership or [entering administration][1].

Former regulation—VAT (Flat-rate Scheme for Farmers) Regulations, SI 1992/3103 reg 6.
Amendments—[1] Words in para (3) substituted by the Enterprise Act 2002 (Insolvency) Order, SI 2003/2096 art 5, Schedule paras 55, 59 with effect from 15 September 2003. However, this amendment does not apply in any case where a petition for an administration order was presented before that date: SI 2003/2096 arts 1, 6.

208 Further certification

Where a person who has been certified and is no longer so certified makes a further application under regulation 204, that person shall not be certified for a period of 3 years from the date of the cancellation of his previous certificate except—
(*a*) the Commissioners may certify from the date of his further application a person who has not been registered under Schedule 1[, 1A][1] or 3 to the Act at any time since the cancellation of his previous certificate; and
(*b*) where the circumstances as are mentioned in paragraph 8(1)(*c*) of Schedule 4 to the Act apply, the Commissioners may certify the person mentioned in that paragraph on a date after the expiry of one year from the date of the cancellation of his previous certificate.

Former regulation—VAT (Flat-rate Scheme for Farmers) Regulations, SI 1992/3103 reg 7.
Amendments—[1] Words inserted in para (*a*) by the VAT (Amendment) (No 2) Regulations, SI 2012/1899 regs 3, 25 with effect from 15 October 2012.

209 Claims by taxable persons for amounts to be treated as credits for input tax

(1) The amount referred to in section 54(4) of the Act and included in the consideration for any taxable supply which is made—

(*a*) in the course or furtherance of the relevant part of his business by a person who is for the time being certified under this part,

(*b*) at a time when that person is not a taxable person, and

(*c*) to a taxable person,

shall be treated, for the purpose of determining the entitlement of the person supplied to credit under sections 25 and 26 of the Act, as VAT on a supply to that person.

(2) Subject to paragraph (3) below and save as the Commissioners may otherwise allow or direct generally or specially, a taxable person claiming entitlement to a credit of an amount as is mentioned in paragraph (1) above shall do so on the return made by him for the prescribed accounting period in which the invoice specified in paragraph (3) below is issued by a certified person.

(3) A taxable person shall not be entitled to credit as is mentioned in paragraph (1) above unless there has been issued an invoice containing the following particulars—

(*a*) an identifying number,

(*b*) the name, address and certificate number of the certified person by whom the invoice is issued,

(*c*) the name and address of the person to whom the goods or services are supplied,

(*d*) the time of the supply,

(*e*) a description of the goods or services supplied,

(*f*) the consideration for the supply or, in the case of any increase or decrease in the consideration, the amount of that increase or decrease excluding the amount as is mentioned in paragraph (1) above, and

(*g*) the amount as is mentioned in paragraph (1) above which amount shall be entitled "Flat-rate Addition" or "FRA".

Former regulation—VAT (Flat-rate Scheme for Farmers) Regulations, SI 1992/3103 reg 8.

210 Duty to keep records

(1) Every certified person shall, for the purposes of the scheme, keep and preserve the following records—

(*a*) his business and accounting records, and

(*b*) copies of all invoices specified in regulation 209(3) issued by him or on his behalf.

(2) Every certified person shall comply with such requirements with respect to the keeping, preservation and production of records as the Commissioners may notify to him.

(3) Every certified person shall keep and preserve such records as are required by paragraph (1) above or by notification for a period of 6 years or such lesser period as the Commissioners may allow.

Former regulation—VAT (Flat-rate Scheme for Farmers) Regulations, SI 1992/3103 reg 9.

211 Production of records

(1) Every certified person shall—

(*a*) upon demand made by an authorised person, produce or cause to be produced for inspection by that person—

(i) at the principal place of business of the person upon whom the demand is made or at such other place as the authorised person may reasonably require, and

(ii) at such time as the authorised person may reasonably require,

any documents specified in regulation 210(1), and

(*b*) permit an authorised person to take copies of, or make extracts from, or remove at a reasonable time and for a reasonable period, any document produced under paragraph (1)(*a*) above.(2) Where a document removed by an authorised person under paragraph (1)(*b*) above is reasonably required for the proper conduct of a business, he shall, as soon as practicable, provide a copy of that document, free of charge, to the person by whom it was produced or caused to be produced.

(3) Where any documents removed under paragraph (1)(*b*) above are lost or damaged, the Commissioners shall be liable to compensate their owner for any expenses reasonably incurred by him in replacing or repairing the documents.

Former regulation—VAT (Flat-rate Scheme for Farmers) Regulations, SI 1992/3103 reg 10.

PART XXV
DISTRESS AND DILIGENCE

[A212 In this Part—

"Job Band" followed by a number between "1" and "12" means the band for the purposes of pay and grading in which the job an officer performs is ranked in the system applicable to Customs and Excise.][1]

Amendments—[1] This Regulation inserted by the VAT (Amendment) (No 4) Regulations, SI 1996/2098 with effect from 2 September 1996.

VAT SIs

212 Distress

. . .

Amendments—This regulation revoked by the Customs and Excise Duties and Other Indirect Taxes Regulations, SI 1997/1431 with effect from 1 July 1997. See SI 1997/1431 for the replacement provisions.

213 Diligence

In Scotland, the following provisions shall have effect—

(*a*) where the Commissioners are empowered to apply to the Sheriff for a warrant to authorise a Sheriff Officer to recover any amount of VAT or any sum recoverable as if it were VAT remaining due and unpaid, any application, and any certificate required to accompany that application, may be made on their behalf by a Collector of Customs and Excise or an officer of rank not below that of [Job Band 7][1];

(*b*) where, during the course of a poinding and sale in accordance with Schedule 5 to the Debtors (Scotland) Act 1987 the Commissioners are entitled as a creditor to do any acts, then any such acts, with the exception of the exercise of the power contained in paragraph 18(3) of that Schedule, may be done on their behalf by a Collector of Customs and Excise or an officer of rank not below that of [Job Band 7][1].

Former regulations—VAT (General) Regulations, SI 1985/886 reg 66; VAT (General) (Amendment) Regulations, SI 1988/2083 reg 2, SI 1993/3027 regs 2, 8.

Amendments—[1] Words in (*a*) and (*b*) above substituted by the VAT (Amendment) (No 4) Regulations, SI 1996/2098 with effect from 2 September 1996.

[PART 26
[UK UNION AND NON-UNION SPECIAL ACCOUNTING SCHEMES: REGISTRATION, NOTIFICATION OF CHANGES, AND RETURNS]]

AmendmentsPart 26 (regs 214–218) inserted by the VAT (Amendment) (No 3) Regulations, SI 2014/2430 regs 2, 9 with effect from 1 October 2014.

Heading to Part 26 substituted by the VAT (Amendment) (No 3) Regulations, SI 2014/2430 regs 2, 10(2) with effect from 1 January 2015. Heading previously read as follows "UK Union and Non-Union Special Accounting Schemes: Registration".

[214 Interpretation

(1) In this Part—

'applicant' means a person making a registration request under paragraph 4 of Schedule 3B or paragraph 5 of Schedule 3BA to the Act;

'principal VAT Directive' means Council Directive 2006/112/EC.

(2) In regulations 215 and 216, references to a number allocated under Article 362 of the principal VAT Directive mean a number allocated at any time under that Article.][1]

Amendments[1] Part 26 (regs 214–218) inserted by the VAT (Amendment) (No 3) Regulations, SI 2014/2430 regs 2, 9 with effect from 1 October 2014.

[215 Registration requests: Non-Union scheme

A registration request under paragraph 4 of Schedule 3B to the Act must contain details of—

(*a*) any VAT identification number or tax reference number by which the applicant is identified for VAT purposes by any member State in accordance with Article 214, Article 239 or Article 240 of the principal VAT Directive, and the name of that member State;

(*b*) any number previously allocated to the applicant by any member State under Article 362 of the principal VAT Directive, or otherwise for the purposes of Article 369d of the principal VAT Directive, and the name of that member State.][1]

Amendments[1] Part 26 (regs 214–218) inserted by the VAT (Amendment) (No 3) Regulations, SI 2014/2430 regs 2, 9 with effect from 1 October 2014.

[216 Registration requests: Union scheme

A registration request under paragraph 5 of Schedule 3BA to the Act must contain the following information—

(*a*) any VAT identification number or tax reference number by which the applicant is identified for VAT purposes by any member State in accordance with Article 214, Article 239 or Article 240 of the principal VAT Directive, and the name of that member State;

(*b*) any number previously allocated to the applicant by any member State under Article 362 of the principal VAT Directive, or otherwise for the purposes of Article 369d of the principal VAT Directive, and the name of that member State;

(*c*) where the applicant has previously been identified under a non-UK special scheme, the date the applicant ceased to be so identified;

(*d*) whether the applicant is treated as a member of a group under any of sections 43A to 43D of the Act; and

(*e*) the name of any member States in which the applicant has a fixed establishment, and the address of each such fixed establishment.][1]

Amendments[1] Part 26 (regs 214–218) inserted by the VAT (Amendment) (No 3) Regulations, SI 2014/2430 regs 2, 9 with effect from 1 October 2014.

[217 Registration requests: declaration

A registration request under paragraph 4 of Schedule 3B or paragraph 5 of Schedule 3BA to the Act must also contain a declaration by the applicant that the information the applicant has provided in the registration request is accurate and complete to the best of the applicant's knowledge.][1]

Amendments[1] Part 26 (regs 214–218) inserted by the VAT (Amendment) (No 3) Regulations, SI 2014/2430 regs 2, 9 with effect from 1 October 2014.

[[**218** The following communications must be made by using the electronic portal set up by the Commissioners for the purpose of implementing Sections 2 and 3 of Chapter 6 of Title XII to the principal VAT Directive—

(*a*) a registration request under paragraph 4 of Schedule 3B or paragraph 5 of Schedule 3BA to the Act;

(*b*) the information required by paragraph 7 of Schedule 3B or paragraph 6 of Schedule 3BA to the Act;

(*c*) a return required under paragraph 11 of Schedule 3B or paragraph 9 of Schedule 3BA to the Act.][2]][1]

Amendments[1] Part 26 (regs 214–218) inserted by the VAT (Amendment) (No 3) Regulations, SI 2014/2430 regs 2, 9 with effect from 1 October 2014.

[2] Reg 218 substituted by the VAT (Amendment) (No 3) Regulations, SI 2014/2430 regs 2, 10(1) with effect from 1 January 2015.

[PART 27

NON-UK UNION AND NON-UNION SPECIAL ACCOUNTING SCHEMES: ADJUSTMENTS, CLAIMS AND ERROR CORRECTION

219 In this Part, 'tax period' has the meaning given by paragraph 23(1) of Schedule 3B or paragraph 38(1) of Schedule 3BA (as the case may require) to the Act.][1]

Amendments—[1] Part 27 (regs 219–223) inserted by the VAT (Amendment) (No 3) Regulations, SI 2014/2430 regs 2, 11 with effect from 1 January 2015.

[220 Correction of errors on non-UK and special scheme returns more than 3 years after the date the original return was required to be made

(1) In this regulation 'notice' means a notice given under paragraph 16C(3) of Schedule 3B or paragraph 23(3) of Schedule 3BA to the Act.

(2) A person giving a notice (P) must do so—

(*a*) no later than 4 years after the end of the tax period in respect of which the return identified in the notice was required to be made; and

(*b*) in writing in the English language.

(3) P must also provide such documentary evidence in support of the notice as P possesses.][1]

Amendments—[1] Part 27 (regs 219–223) inserted by the VAT (Amendment) (No 3) Regulations, SI 2014/2430 regs 2, 11 with effect from 1 January 2015.

[221 Claims in respect of overpaid VAT

(1) A person making a claim under paragraph 16I(1) of Schedule 3B, or paragraph 29(1) of Schedule 3BA, to the Act must provide to the Commissioners at the time of making the claim a statement in writing in the English language explaining how the claim is calculated.

(2) A person making a claim under any other provision of paragraph 16I of Schedule 3B, or paragraph 29 of Schedule 3BA, to the Act must—

(i) make that claim to the Commissioners; and

(ii) provide to the Commissioners at the time of making the claim a statement in writing in the English language explaining how the claim is calculated.][1]

Amendments—[1] Part 27 (regs 219–223) inserted by the VAT (Amendment) (No 3) Regulations, SI 2014/2430 regs 2, 11 with effect from 1 January 2015.

[222 Increases or decreases in consideration occurring more than 3 years after the end of the affected tax period

(1) A claim or other notice made under paragraph 16K(2)(*b*) of Schedule 3B or paragraph 31(2)(*b*) of Schedule 3BA to the Act must be made in writing in the English language.

(2) A person making a payment—

(*a*) under paragraph 16K(3) of Schedule 3B to the Act in a case falling within paragraph 16K(2)(*b*) of that Schedule; or

(*b*) under paragraph 31(3) of Schedule 3BA to the Act in a case falling within paragraph 31(2)(*b*) of that Schedule,

must do so no later than twenty days after the end of the tax period in which the increase in consideration is accounted for in the person's business accounts.][1]

Amendments—[1] Part 27 (regs 219–223) inserted by the VAT (Amendment) (No 3) Regulations, SI 2014/2430 regs 2, 11 with effect from 1 January 2015.

[223 Scheme participants who are also taxable persons: disapplication of paragraph 17(1)

(1) Paragraph 17(1) of Schedule 3BA to the Act is not to apply in the case of an input tax obligation.

(2) In this regulation 'input tax obligation' means an obligation imposed on a taxable person relating to a claim to deduction under section 25(2) of the Act or to payment of a VAT credit.][1]

Amendments—[1] Part 27 (regs 219–223) inserted by the VAT (Amendment) (No 3) Regulations, SI 2014/2430 regs 2, 11 with effect from 1 January 2015.

SCHEDULE 1

Regulation 5(1)

Amendments—Schedule 1 revoked by the VAT (Amendment) (No 2) Regulations, SI 2012/1899 regs 3, 27 with effect from 15 October 2012.

Form No 1: Application for VAT Registration

HM Revenue & Customs

Value Added Tax (VAT) Application for registration

You can apply online

Go to **www.hmrc.gov.uk** and follow the links for 'Do it online'.

How to fill in this form

- Please write clearly in **black ink** and use **capital letters**.
- If you need more space for any answers, continue on a separate sheet of paper.
- If you need help, look at the VAT1 (Notes) or phone our VAT Helpline on **0845 010 9000**.

You may have to send us other forms and supporting information as well as this form; you will be told what is needed as you work through the form.

You can download any forms you need from **www.hmrc.gov.uk** or phone our VAT Helpline.

About the business

1 **Status of the business**

Sole proprietors: please enter your full name – first name(s) followed by surname

Partnerships: please enter your trading name. Or, if you do not have one, enter the full names of all the partners. *Partnerships must also complete form VAT2 and enclose it with this form.*

If you need more space, use a separate sheet of paper. ***Partnerships now go to Question 5.***

Corporate or unincorporated bodies: please enter the name of the company, club, association, trust, charity, etc.

2 **If the business has a trading name, enter it here**

3 **If the business is a corporate body registered in the UK, enter the following details from the Certificate of Incorporation**

Certificate number

Date of incorporation *DD MM YYYY*

Country of incorporation

If the business is an unincorporated body, enter the type (for example, club, association, trust, charity, etc.)

4 **Are you registering as the Representative Member or nominated corporate body of a VAT group?**

Read the glossary in the Notes for a definition of 'VAT group'.

Yes ☐ No ☐

If Yes, complete and enclose forms VAT50 and VAT51.

5 **Business contact details**

Business address, that is, the principal place where most of the day to day running of the business is carried out.

Postcode

Contact phone number

Business fax number

Business mobile phone number

Business email address

Business website address

VAT SIs

About the business continued

6 Business activities

Read the note for Question 6.

If the business activities are land or property-related, you will need to provide further information in form VAT5L *VAT registration - land and property.*

Main activities

Other activities

If you need more space, use a separate sheet of paper.

7 Are you (or any of the partners or directors in this business) **currently involved, or in the last two years have been involved, in any other business in the UK or Isle of Man** (VAT registered or not) **either as a sole proprietor, partner or director?**

Read the note for Question 7.

Yes No

If Yes, complete the boxes below.

Business 1: name

Business 1: VAT number (if applicable)

Tick if still trading

Business 2: name

Business 2: VAT number (if applicable)

Tick if still trading

If you need to show details of more than two businesses, use a separate sheet of paper.

About the business continued

8 UK bank or building society account

Read the note for Question 8.

Name of bank or building society

Account name

Sort code

Account number

About your VAT registration

Taking over a going concern

9 Are you registering for VAT because you have:

- **taken over** (or are about to take over) **a business** (or part of a business) **as a going concern,**

OR

- **changed** (or are about to change) **the legal status of a VAT registered business?**

Important: *read the note for Question 9 before you answer.*

Yes No

If No, go to Question 13 - ignore Questions 10 to 12.

If Yes , enter the date the transfer or change took place or is intended to take place. DD MM YYYY

This will be your effective date of registration.

10 What is the previous owner's name?

11 Enter the previous owner's VAT number (if applicable)

12 Do you want to keep the previous owner's VAT number?

Important: *read the note for Question 12 before you answer.*

Yes No

If Yes, you and the previous owner will need to complete form VAT68 and enclose it with this form.

Now go to Question 19 - ignore Questions 13 to 18.

About your VAT registration *continued*

Voluntary registration

13 Are you applying for voluntary registration because your turnover is below the registration threshold?

Important: *read the note for Question 13 before you answer.*

Yes ☐ No ☐

If No, go to Question 14.

If Yes, tick one of the boxes below.

My turnover is below the current registration threshold but I want to register now. ☐

I intend to make taxable supplies in the future. ☐

I am established, or have a fixed establishment, in the UK and make, or intend to make, supplies only outside the UK. ☐

What date do you wish to be registered from? *DD MM YYYY*

☐☐ ☐☐ ☐☐☐☐

Go to Question 19 - ignore Questions 14 to 18.

Compulsory registration

Important: *read the notes for Questions 14 to16 before you answer.* Enter dates as *DD MM YYYY or MM YYYY*

14 Are you registering because your taxable turnover has gone over the registration threshold in any past period of 12 months or less?

Yes ☐ No ☐

If Yes, enter the month and year when this occurred.

☐☐ ☐☐☐☐

15 Are you registering because you had an expectation on any date that your taxable turnover would go over the registration threshold in the next 30 DAYS ALONE?

Yes ☐ No ☐

If Yes, enter the date you first expected this to happen.

☐☐ ☐☐ ☐☐☐☐

16 Are you registering because you are a non established taxable person making or intending to make taxable supplies in the UK?

Yes ☐ No ☐

If Yes, at any time on or after 1 December 2012, what was the earliest date that the business either made or had an intention to make taxable supplies in the next 30 days?

☐☐ ☐☐ ☐☐☐☐

Exemption from registration

17 Do you want to apply for exemption from registration?

Read the note for Question 17.

You can apply for exemption from registration if most of your supplies are zero-rated.

Yes ☐ No ☐

If Yes, estimate the value of your zero-rated supplies over the next 12 months.

£ ☐☐,☐☐☐,☐☐☐,☐☐☐ . 0 0

If you answered Yes to any of Questions 14 to 16, and are not requesting exemption from registration, go to Question 18.

Earlier registration

18 Application for earlier registration

Enter the month and year you want to be registered from. *DD MM YYYY*

☐☐ ☐☐ ☐☐☐☐

Go to Question 19.

VAT repayment

19 Do you expect the VAT on your purchases to regularly exceed the VAT on your taxable supplies?

Read the note for Question 19.

Yes ☐ No ☐

If Yes, say why.

If you need more space, use a separate sheet of paper.

About your VAT registration continued

Your turnover

20 **Enter your estimate of your taxable supplies in the next 12 months**

£ . 0 0

21 **Do you expect to make any exempt supplies?**
Look at the list of VAT terms in the Notes if you need more information about exempt supplies.

Yes No

22 **Do you expect to buy goods from other EU member states in the next 12 months?**
Read the note for Question 22.

Yes No

If Yes, enter the total estimated value.

£ . 0 0

Do you expect to sell goods to other EU member states in the next 12 months?

Yes No

If Yes, enter the total estimated value.

£ . 0 0

Applicant details and declaration

This section must be completed by:

- the sole owner of the business, or a partner, or
- a director or the company secretary or an authorised signatory of a corporate body, or
- an officer or official applying on behalf of an unincorporated body, for example, secretary, trustee, or
- an authorised agent.

If this form is being signed by an authorised signatory, or an authorised agent, the details of the person authorising you must be shown at Question 23.

23 **Applicant details**
First name(s) followed by surname

Home address

Postcode

If you have lived at this address for less than three years, enter details of your previous address.

Applicant details and declaration continued

Previous home address (if applicable)

Postcode

Home phone number

Date of birth *DD MM YYYY*

National Insurance number

If you are a non-UK national and do not have a National Insurance number, enter your tax identification number in your country of origin and the name of that country.

24 **I declare that the information given in this form and accompanying documents is true and complete**
Signature

Date *DD MM YYYY*

Capacity in which you signed this application
(for example, proprietor, trustee, company secretary)

Please use the Checklist on page 8 of the Notes to make sure you send everything we have asked for.

Where to send your completed form

For all standard registration applications send to:

Wolverhampton Registration Unit
Deansgate
62 - 70 Tettenhall Road
WOLVERHAMPTON
WV1 4TZ

For applications to register a VAT group or if you wish to keep the previous owner's VAT Registration Number send to:

Grimsby Registration Unit
Imperial House
77 Victoria Street
GRIMSBY
DN31 1DB

5013734

Amendments—Form 1 substituted by the Value Added Tax (Amendment) (No 2) Regulations, SI 2006/2902, reg 3, Sch 1, with effect from 1 December 2006.

Schedule 1 revoked by the VAT (Amendment) (No 2) Regulations, SI 2012/1899 regs 3, 27 with effect from 15 October 2012.

Form No: 2: Partnership Details

VALUE ADDED TAX
Partnership Details

HM Customs and Excise

For official use only

Date of receipt

Each partner should complete one of the sections below.

Please start at the beginning of each line and leave a space between words.

Please use BLOCK CAPITALS and write clearly in ink.

Registration No. (where known)

1

Full name

Home address

Postcode

Home telephone

Mobile telephone

National Insurance Number or Tax Identifier in country of origin

Signature

Date

Partner details

2

Full name

Home address

Postcode

Home telephone

Mobile telephone

National Insurance Number or Tax Identifier in country of origin

Signature

Date

SPECIMEN

Partner details

3

Full name

Home address

Postcode

Home telephone

Mobile telephone

National Insurance Number or Tax Identifier in country of origin

Signature

Date

Partner details

4

Full name

Home address

Postcode

Home telephone

Mobile telephone

National Insurance Number or Tax Identifier in country of origin

Signature

Date

VAT 2 PT (December 2001) *Please continue overleaf*

5 Partner details

Full name

Home address

Postcode

Home telephone　Mobile telephone

National Insurance Number or Tax Identifier in country of origin

Signature　Date

6 Partner details

Full name

Home address

Postcode

Home telephone　Mobile telephone

National Insurance Number or Tax Identifier in country of origin

Signature　Date

7 Partner details

Full name

Home address

Postcode

Home telephone　Mobile telephone

National Insurance Number or Tax Identifier in country of origin

Signature　Date

8 Partner details

Full name

Home address

Postcode

Home telephone　Mobile telephone

National Insurance Number or Tax Identifier in country of origin

Signature　Date

9 Partner details

Full name

Home address

Postcode

Home telephone　Mobile telephone

National Insurance Number or Tax Identifier in country of origin

Signature　Date

VAT 2 reverse (1201)

Amendments—Schedule 1 revoked by the VAT (Amendment) (No 2) Regulations, SI 2012/1899 regs 3, 27 with effect from 15 October 2012.

Form No 3: Application to use previous owner's VAT registration number following the transfer of a business as a going concern

Regulation 6

HM Customs and Excise

Value Added Tax

Transfer of a business as a going concern

SPECIMEN

Request for Transfer of a Registration number

When you have filled in this form and signed it please send it to:

Important : You must complete this form if you want to keep the registration number of the previous owner. **You must also complete form VAT 1.** Once the transfer of the number has been allowed, it cannot be revoked.

VAT 68 IB (September 2000)

The following notes will help you to fill in this form. Remember both parts of the form must be completed - the first part by the new owner and the second part by the previous owner.

Who can ask for a number to be transferred?

If you are taking over a business as a going concern, or changing the status of your business (for example, from sole proprietor to a limited company, or partnership) you can, if you wish, apply for the previous owner's VAT registration number to be transferred to you.

When can I ask for a registration number to be transferred?

You can ask for a number to be transferred if:

- you are not already registered for VAT; **but**
- you become either liable or entitled to registration from the date the business is transferred to you; **and**
- the previous owner's registration will be cancelled from that date. (If the previous owner is still liable to be registered he cannot pass his number on to you); **and**
- the previous owner agrees to the transfer of the number.

Transfer of the number will **not** normally be allowed if the previous owner:

- has a Surcharge Assessment which remains unpaid or is the subject of an appeal;
- was a member of a group registration;
- was registered but had made no taxable supplies.

How do I apply and when?

Both you and the previous owner must agree to the transfer of the number. You must **both** fill in and sign this form as soon as the business is transferred and **before** the previous owner asks for his registration to be cancelled. We will treat this form as the previous owner's request for cancellation of his registration.

Who has to sign the form?

You must fill in and sign Part 1 and the previous owner must fill in and sign Part 2 of this form.

If you are simply changing the status of your business, (for example, from a sole proprietor to a limited company) you may have to sign both parts of the form if you are, or represent, both the new and previous owner.

If a partnership is involved, **all** the partners must sign the form.

If the previous owner was a sole proprietor and has died, or a partnership and one of the partners has died, the executor must sign the form.

What to do when you have filled in the form.

You must send this request to the address shown on the front of this form. If you have not already done so, you must also send a fresh form VAT 1 (and form VAT 2 if you are a partnership) to cover this change of ownership. We will write to tell you whether your application has been allowed.

If you have any difficulty completing this form, or require further advice, please contact the office shown on the front of this form.

IMPORTANT: The conditions that you and the previous owner must agree to are set out on the application form and are legally binding. This means that not only will you be liable for any outstanding VAT from the previous owners registration but the previous owner will no longer be entitled to any repayments of VAT or unclaimed input tax, whether these amounts refer to periods before or after the transfer.

Both parts of this Application Form must be filled in

Part 1 To be completed by the new owner

If you are the new legal entity or owner of the business, please read this form carefully and answer all the questions in Part 1.

1. Please give your full name, or your trading name if you have one;

2. Please give your legal status, eg sole proprietor, partnership, limited company

3. I took over the business as a going concern on

4. Please give the name of the previous owner;

5. I apply to use the previous owner's VAT registration number from the above date. The number is;

6. If this application is allowed, I agree to the following conditions:

- I will send in my first VAT return to Customs and Excise, with all the VAT due for the whole of the period shown on the form;
- I will send in any outstanding returns which are due from the previous owner;
- I will pay Customs and Excise any VAT due on supplies made by the previous owner before the business was transferred - including any VAT on stocks and assets kept by the previous owner.
- I agree that any VAT return made by the previous owner for a period after the transfer date will be treated as made by me; and
- I will have no right to claim any money paid by Customs and Excise to the previous owner, before the VAT registration number was transferred.

Signature(s)

(Proprietor, partners, director, company secretary, executor)

Date

Part 2 To be completed by the previous owner

If you are the former legal entity or the previous owner of the business, please read this form carefully and answer all the questions in Part 2.

1. Please give your full name, or your trading name if you have one;

2. Please give your legal status, eg sole proprietor, partnership, limited company

3. I transferred my business / changed my legal status on

4. Please give the name of the new owner;

5. I wish to cancel my VAT registration number from the above date because I am no longer liable or eligible to be registered. I agree to transfer my number to the new owner. The number is

6. If this application is allowed, I agree to the following conditions:

- I will have no right to claim any money paid by Customs and Excise to the new owner.
- I agree that the new owner will be entitled to reclaim any input tax which Customs and Excise would normally have paid to me if the number had not been transferred; and

7. I have retained stocks and assets valued at

£

8. Please give an address where we can contact you after the business has been taken over by the new owner.

Signature(s)

(Proprietor, partners, director, company secretary, executor)

Date

SPECIMEN

VAT 68 page 2 (09/00)

VAT SIs

Checklist:

- Have you and the previous owner signed the form?
- Have you already filled in and returned a form VAT 1 to cover this change of ownership? If not, send it in with this form. Your application for the number to be transferred to you cannot be processed without an accompanying VAT 1.
- Have all the partners signed the form?
- Have you completed a VAT 2 if you are a partnership.
- Have you included a copy of the certificate of incorporation if you are a limited company.

Remember:

- That your registration will cover all your business activities.
- You are now liable for any VAT due on supplies made by the previous owner, even if they come to light after the transfer.
- The previous owner no longer has any right to repayments of tax, even if they refer to the period prior to the transfer.

Please return the completed form to the address shown on the front of this form.

Data Protection Act 1998

HM Customs and Excise collects information in order to administer the taxes for which it is responsible (such as VAT, insurance premium tax, excise duties, air passenger duty, landfill tax), and for detecting and preventing crime.

Where the law permits we may also get information about you from third parties, or give information to them, for example in order to check its accuracy, prevent or detect crime or protect public funds in other ways. These third parties may include the police, other government departments and agencies.

VAT 68 page 2R (09/00)

Amendments—Form 3 substituted by the Value Added Tax (Amendment) (No 3) Regulations, SI 2001/3828 with effect from 1 January 2002.

Schedule 1 revoked by the VAT (Amendment) (No 2) Regulations, SI 2012/1899 regs 3, 27 with effect from 15 October 2012.

Form No 4: VAT Return

Regulations 23, 25(4)

HM Revenue & Customs

Value Added Tax Return

For official use

Registration Number | Period

If your completed return and all the VAT payable are not received by the due date you will be in default and may be liable to a financial penalty

Due Date:

For official use D O R only

Please read the notes on the back before you fill in this form or if you use a special VAT accounting scheme. Fill in all boxes clearly in black ink, and write 'none' where necessary. **Don't put a dash or leave a box blank. If there are no pence write '00' in the pence column. Do not** enter more than one amount in any box. If there is a minus amount in boxes 1 to 4, enclose the figure in brackets.

For official use

	Box	£	p
VAT due in this period on sales and other outputs	1		
VAT due in this period on acquisitions from other EC Member States	2		
Total VAT due (the sum of boxes 1 and 2)	3		
VAT reclaimed in this period on purchases and other inputs (including acquisitions from the EC)	4		
NET VAT to be paid to HMRC or reclaimed by you (Difference between boxes 3 and 4)	5		
Total value of sales and all other outputs excluding any VAT, include your box 8 figure	6		00
Total value of purchases and all other inputs excluding any VAT, include your box 9 figure	7		00
Total value of all supplies of goods and related costs, excluding any VAT, to other EC Member States	8		00
Total value of all acquisitions of goods and related costs, excluding any VAT, from other EC Member States	9		00

DECLARATION You, or someone on your behalf, must sign below. **A false declaration can result in prosecution.**

Full name of signatory (in capital letters) I, ______ declare that the information given above is correct and complete to the best of my knowledge and belief.

Signature ______ Date *DD MM YYYY*

VAT 100 v05C PAGE 1 HMRC 08/09

Online VAT returns

If you would prefer not to continue completing this paper version of the VAT return, you can apply to file an electronic version online. You can find out more about online VAT returns at **www.hmrc.gov.uk**

How do I fill in my VAT return?

A summary of how to fill in each box is shown below. Detailed information on how to fill in this form is in Notice 700/12 ***Filling in your VAT return.*** **This is available online at www.hmrc.gov.uk**

If you need any further advice on filling in your return, please phone our Helpline on **0845 010 9000**.

There is also an online guide on completing your VAT return at **www.hmrc.gov.uk** by selecting 'VAT' followed by 'VAT Returns and accounts' and 'VAT Returns: how to complete and submit a return box by box'.

Box 1

Enter the VAT due on all goods and services you supplied.

Box 2

Enter the VAT due from you on purchases of goods (and related costs) from VAT registered customers in other Member States of the European Community.

Box 3

Enter the total of boxes 1 and 2 added together. This is your 'output VAT' for the period.

Box 4

Enter the total amount of VAT charged on your business purchases. This is your 'input VAT' for the period.

Box 5

Take the figures in boxes 3 and 4 and deduct the smaller amount from the larger amount. Enter the difference in box 5. If this amount is under £1, you need not send any payment, nor will any repayment be made to you. However, you must still fill in this form and send it to the VAT Central Unit.

Box 6

Enter the total value of all your business sales but leave out any VAT. You must include the value of your EC supplies shown in box 8.

Box 7

Enter the total value of all your business purchases but leave out any VAT. You must include the value of your EC purchases shown in box 9.

Box 8

Enter the total value of supplies of goods (and related costs) supplied to other EC Member States. Leave out any VAT. If you enter an amount in box 8 you must also include that amount in your box 6 entry.

Box 9

Enter the total value of goods (and related costs) purchased from other EC Member States. Leave out any VAT. If you enter an amount in box 9 you must also include that amount in your box 7 entry.

What if I use a special VAT accounting scheme?

If you use a VAT accounting scheme there are different rules for completing some of the boxes on the VAT return. For further information, please see section 4 of Notice 700/12 ***Filling in your VAT return*** if you use any of the following schemes:

- **Flat Rate Scheme.**
- Cash Accounting Scheme.
- Annual Accounting Scheme.
- Margin Scheme for second-hand goods.

or you:

- supply or receive goods under reverse charge accounting arrangements
- are in the Payments on Account (POA) regime.

How do I correct errors made on previous returns?

You may be able to correct errors in VAT returns for the preceding three years by using boxes 1 and 4 on the return for the period of discovery. Net errors of £10,000 or less can be included in your return. Net errors between £10,000 and £50,000 can be included provided they do not exceed 1% of the total value of your sales (before correction) shown in box 6. Net errors exceeding £50,000 and those above £10,000 that exceed 1% of the box 6 amount must be separately notified. For further information see Notice 700/45 ***How to correct VAT errors and make adjustments or claims.***

How do I pay?

Information on how to pay is also available on our website at **www.hmrc.gov.uk** by selecting 'Paying HMRC' followed by 'VAT' or by phoning our Helpline on **0845 010 9000**. Please allow enough time for payment to reach us by the due date. We suggest you allow at least three working days for this. If the due date falls on a weekend or bank holiday please ensure payment is received by the previous bank working day.

1. Direct payment

Using the internet, telephone banking, BACS Direct Credit or CHAPS, provide your bank or building society with the following information to make a direct payment:

- payment amount
- account name: HMRC VAT
- sort code: 08-32-00
- account number: 11963155
- your VAT registration number

2. At your bank

If your bank or building society offers this service we can send you a book of payslips to use. Phone us on **01702 366376** or **01702 366314** or email **electronicpaymentteam@hmrc.gsi.gov.uk**. Take the payslip and payment to any branch of your bank. Other banks may not accept payment. Any cheque must be drawn on your bank, and made payable to 'HM REVENUE & CUSTOMS ONLY'.

3. Credit card or debit card

If you have a credit or debit card (except American Express or Diners Club cards) issued by a UK bank you can pay over the internet using the BillPay service. To make your payment you will need your:

- Credit or debit card details
- VAT registration number

If you pay by any of the above methods you may receive up to seven extra calendar days for the return and payment to reach us.

4. Post

If you use this method, make your cheque payable to 'HM REVENUE & CUSTOMS ONLY' followed by your VAT registration number and send your return and payment to us in the envelope provided. The envelope provided is for VAT payments only. You must not include any other payments.

Further information on deadlines for filing your return and making payment is available online at **www.hmrc.gov.uk** by selecting 'VAT' followed by 'VAT Returns and accounts' and 'Deadlines for your VAT Return and payment'.

Where do I send my return?

Return should be posted using the reply envelope provided. If you have mislaid this envelope, the address to send your return to is:

VAT Controller
VAT Central Unit
BX5 5AT

How do I notify business changes?

You must tell the National Registration Service about any changes in your business circumstances, including a change of address.
You can write to:

HM Revenue & Customs
Imperial House
77 Victoria Street
Grimsby
Lincolnshire
DN31 1DB

Or go online at **www.hmrc.gov.uk** and select 'VAT' followed by 'Changing or cancelling your VAT registration'.

VAT 100 Page 2 HMRC 08/09

Amendments—Forms 4 and 5 substituted by the Value Added Tax (Amendment) (No 4) Regulations, SI 2009/2978 regs 2, 6 with effect from 1 December 2009.

Schedule 1 revoked by the VAT (Amendment) (No 2) Regulations, SI 2012/1899 regs 3, 27 with effect from 15 October 2012.

Form No 5: Final VAT Return

Regulation 5(1)

HM Revenue & Customs

Final Value Added Tax Return

For official use

Registration Number

Period

9999

If your completed return and all the VAT payable are not received by the due date you will be in default and may be liable to a financial penalty

Due Date:

For official use D O R only

Please read the notes on the back before you fill in this form or if you use a special VAT accounting scheme. Fill in all boxes clearly in black ink, and write 'none' where necessary. **Don't put a dash or leave a box blank. If there are no pence write '00' in the pence column.** Do not enter more than one amount in any box. If there is a minus amount in boxes 1 to 4, enclose the figure in brackets.

For official use

	Box	£	p
VAT due in this period on sales and other outputs	1		
VAT due in this period on acquisitions from other EC Member States	2		
Total VAT due (the sum of boxes 1 and 2)	3		
VAT reclaimed in this period on purchases and other inputs (including acquisitions from the EC)	4		
NET VAT to be paid to HMRC or reclaimed by you (Difference between boxes 3 and 4)	5		
Total value of sales and all other outputs excluding any VAT. Include your box 8 figure	6		00
Total value of purchases and all other inputs excluding any VAT. Include your box 9 figure.	7		00
Total value of all supplies of goods and related costs, excluding any VAT, to other EC Member States	8		00
Total value of all acquisitions of goods and related costs, excluding any VAT, from other EC Member States.	9		00

DECLARATION You, or someone on your behalf, must sign below. **A false declaration can result in prosecution.**

Full name of signatory (in capital letters) I, ____________ declare that the information given above is correct and complete to the best of my knowledge and belief.

Signature ____________ Date *DD MM YYYY*

VAT 193 v05C PAGE 1 HMRC 08/09

How do I fill in my VAT return?

A summary of how to fill in each box is shown below. Detailed information on how to fill in this form is in Notice 700/12 ***Filling in your VAT return.* This is available online at www.hmrc.gov.uk**

If you need any further advice on filling in your return, please phone our Helpline on **0845 010 9000.**

There is also an online guide on completing your VAT return at **www.hmrc.gov.uk** by selecting 'VAT' followed by 'VAT Returns and accounts' and 'VAT Returns: how to complete and submit a return box by box'.

Box 1

Enter the VAT due on all goods and services you supplied. You must also include VAT due on stocks and assets you hold at the close of business on the day your registration is cancelled unless the VAT on their value is under £1,000

Box 2

Enter the VAT due from you on purchases of goods (and related costs) from VAT registered customers in other Member States of the European Community

Box 3

Enter the total of boxes 1 and 2 added together. This is your 'output VAT' for the period.

Box 4

Enter the total amount of VAT charged on your business purchases. This is your 'input VAT' for the period.

Box 5

Take the figures in boxes 3 and 4 and deduct the smaller amount from the larger amount. Enter the difference in box 5. If this amount is under £1, you need not send any payment, nor will any repayment be made to you. However, you must still fill in this form and send it to the VAT Central Unit.

Box 6

Enter the total value of all your business sales but leave out any VAT. You must include the value of your EC supplies shown in box 8.

Box 7

Enter the total value of all your business purchases but leave out any VAT. You must include the value of your EC purchases shown in box 9.

Box 8

Enter the total value of supplies of goods (and related costs) supplied to other EC Member States. Leave out any VAT. If you enter an amount in box 8 you must also include that amount in your box 6 entry

Box 9

Enter the total value of goods (and related costs) purchased from other EC Member States. Leave out any VAT. If you enter an amount in box 9 you must also include that amount in your box 7 entry

What if I use a special VAT accounting scheme?

If you use a VAT accounting scheme there are different rules for completing some of the boxes on the VAT return. For further information, please see section 4 of Notice 700/12 ***Filling in your VAT return*** if you use any of the following schemes:

- **Flat Rate Scheme.**
- Cash Accounting Scheme
- Annual Accounting Scheme
- Margin Scheme for second-hand goods

or you

- supply or receive goods under reverse charge accounting arrangements
- are in the Payments on Account (POA) regime

How do I correct errors made on previous returns?

You may be able to correct errors in VAT returns for the preceding three years by using boxes 1 and 4 on the return for the period of discovery. Net errors of £10,000 or less can be included in your return. Net errors between £10,000 and £50,000 can be included provided they do not exceed 1% of the total value of your sales (before correction) shown in box 6. Net errors exceeding £50,000 and those above £10,000 that exceed 1% of the box 6 amount must be separately notified. For further information see Notice 700/45 ***How to correct VAT errors and make adjustments or claims.***

How do I pay?

Information on how to pay is also available on our website at **www.hmrc.gov.uk** by selecting 'Paying HMRC' followed by 'VAT' or by phoning our Helpline on **0845 010 9000**. Please allow enough time for payment to reach us by the due date. We suggest you allow at least three working days for this. If the due date falls on a weekend or bank holiday please ensure payment is received by the previous bank working day.

1. Direct payment

Using the internet, telephone banking, BACS Direct Credit or CHAPS, provide your bank or building society with the following information to make a direct payment:

- payment amount
- account name: HMRC VAT
- sort code: 08-32-00
- account number: 11963155
- your VAT registration number

2. At your bank

If your bank or building society offers this service we can send you a book of payslips to use. Phone us on **01702 366376** or **01702 366314** or email **electronicpaymentteam@hmrc.gsi.gov.uk** Take the payslip and payment to any branch of your bank. Other banks may not accept payment. Any cheque must be drawn on your bank, and made payable to 'HM REVENUE & CUSTOMS ONLY'.

3. Credit card or debit card

If you have a credit or debit card (except American Express or Diners Club cards) issued by a UK bank you can pay over the internet using the BillPay service. To make your payment you will need your:

- Credit or debit card details
- VAT registration number

If you pay by any of the above methods you may receive up to seven extra calendar days for the return and payment to reach us.

4. Post

If you use this method, make your cheque payable to 'HM REVENUE & CUSTOMS ONLY' followed by your VAT registration number and send your return and payment to us in the envelope provided. The envelope provided is for VAT payments only. You must not include any other payments.

Further information on deadlines for filing your return and making payment is available online at **www.hmrc.gov.uk** by selecting 'VAT' followed by 'VAT Returns and accounts' and Deadlines for your VAT Return and payment'.

Selling your business?

If you are selling all or part of your business as a going concern, the transfer of assets is not normally treated as a taxable supply and you must not charge VAT. For further information please see section 1.4 of Notice 700/11 Cancelling your registration.

Where do I send my return?

Return should be posted using the reply envelope provided. If you have mislaid this envelope, the address to send your return to is:

VAT Controller
VAT Central Unit
BX5 5AT

VAT 193 Page 2 HMRC 08/09

Amendments—Forms 4 and 5 substituted by the Value Added Tax (Amendment) (No 4) Regulations, SI 2009/2978 regs 2, 6 with effect from 1 December 2009.

Schedule 1 revoked by the VAT (Amendment) (No 2) Regulations, SI 2012/1899 regs 3, 27 with effect from 15 October 2012.

Form No 6: Application for VAT Registration—Distance Selling

Regulation 5(1)

1. Enter the NAME of the PERSON MAKING DISTANCE SALES to the UK. Write in BLOCK LETTERS and leave a space between words

2. Enter the NAME of the UK TAX REPRESENTATIVE (see note 2)

3. Please give the ADDRESS of the TAX REPRESENTATIVE or the ADDRESS of the PERSON NAMED at box 1 if a tax representative has not been appointed

Phone No.

Postcode

4. Describe your main BUSINESS ACTIVITY IN FULL please (See note 4)

5. Who is the BUSINESS OWNED by? (See Note 5 and tick ONE BOX only)

Sole Proprietor

or Partnership Please ensure you ALSO complete form VAT 2.

or Limited Company

or Other Please give details

6. Enter your UK BANK DETAILS or YOUR TAX REPRESENTATIVE'S BANK DETAILS: (See Note 6)

Bank Sort Code Account Number or Giro Bank Account Number

7. Do you use a COMPUTER FOR ACCOUNTING? (See Note 7 and tick one box only) YES NO

8. Has the value of your DISTANCE SALES to customers in the UK exceeded the UK distance selling threshold at any time in the calendar year commencing 1st January 1993 or any subsequent calendar year?

YES and I exceeded the threshold on Go to 11

NO Go to 9

VAT 1A CD 3429/1/N3 (11/92)

9. Have you exercised the OPTION TO MAKE THE PLACE OF SUPPLY THE UK, although you have NOT exceeded the UK threshold? (see note 9)

Tick one box

NO ☐ Go to 10

YES ☐ and the option was exercised in EC Country ☐ on ☐☐☐

Please enter the date of your first taxable supply in the UK ☐☐☐

10. Do you intend to make distance sales of GOODS LIABLE TO EXCISE DUTY to the UK?

NO ☐ Go to 12

YES ☐ Please enter the estimated date of your first taxable supply in the UK. ☐☐☐

11. (See note 11 - this is VERY IMPORTANT)

I am REQUIRED TO BE REGISTERED from ☐☐☐

But I would LIKE TO BE REGISTERED from this earlier date ☐☐☐ Go to 13

12. Do you intend to exercise the OPTION TO MAKE THE PLACE OF SUPPLY of your distance sales the UK?

NO ☐

YES ☐ Please enter the estimated date of your first taxable supply in the UK ☐☐☐

The date from which I wish to be registered is ☐☐☐

13. Please enter the ESTIMATED VALUE OF DISTANCE SALES you expect to make to the UK in the next 12 months

£ ☐

14. **Declaration**

I ....

(Full name in BLOCK LETTERS)

declare that all the entered details and information in any accompanying documents are correct and complete

Signature ....

Tick one box

Proprietor ☐ Partner ☐ Director ☐

Company Secretary ☐ Authorised Official (including tax representative) ☐ Trustee ☐

CD 3429/2/N3(11/92)

HM Customs and Excise

VALUE ADDED TAX

Application for Registration: Distance Selling

Return Form to:

For Official use

Issue code

Date of receipt

VAT 1A CD 3429/N3(11/92) F 8658

SPECIMEN

For official use

Local office code and registration number

Name

Trade name

E D R — D M Y

Stagger Status

Trade classification

Taxable Turnover

Rept. Vol. 2 Oversize name address Comp. user Group Div Intg Overseas

Intg. EC

Value of Sales to EC

Value of purchases from EC

Registration	Obligatory/Voluntary	Exemption	Intending	Transfer of Regn No.
Approved - Initial/date				
Refused - Initial/date				
Letter issued - initial/date	Letter	Letter	Letter	Approval letter

Application For VAT Registration

You should read the notes in the registration booklet "Should I be Registered for VAT?- Distance Selling" which will help you to answer these questions.

Please write clearly in black ink.

CD 3429(11/92)

Do not detach

Amendments—Schedule 1 revoked by the VAT (Amendment) (No 2) Regulations, SI 2012/1899 regs 3, 27 with effect from 15 October 2012.

Form No 7: Application for VAT Registration Acquisitions

Regulation 5(1)

Value Added Tax

Application for Registration: Acquisitions

SPECIMEN

For office use	Issuing office
Issue code: ______ Date of receipt: ______	

VAT 1B Page 1 PCU(February 1997)

Value Added Tax

Application for Registration: Acquisitions

Before you start, please read the Notice "Should I be registered for VAT? - Acquisitions". The notes in part 2 will help you to answer the questions on this form. If you do not answer the questions correctly it may take longer to register you and give you a registration number. Write clearly in ***black*** *ink and use CAPITAL LETTERS.*

1 Please give your full name

- *if you are a limited company give your company name*
- *if you are a partnership give your trading name. If you do not have a trading name give the names of all the partners*

Name:

2 Please give your trading name (if different from the name given at 1)

Trading name:

3 Please give the address of your principal place of business

- *this should be where the day-to-day running of your business takes place*

Business address:

Post code:

Phone no:

Fax no:

4 Describe your main business activity (see note 4)

5 Who owns the business?

- *If you are a partnership please remember to fill in form VAT 2 as well as this form*

Please tick ☑

Limited company ☐ Give details from your certificate of incorporation:

Certificate number | Date of certificate

Sole proprietor ☐ Partnership ☐

Other ☐ If other, give details below:

6 Please give your bank details

- *this question must be completed in all cases*

Bank sort code | Account number

or Girobank account number

Please tick box if you do not have a bank account: ☐

7 Do you use a computer for accounting?

- *If you use a computer let us know the type of computer and software you use, in a separate letter*

Please tick ☑

Yes ☐ No ☐

8 Have you made any acquisitions yet?

- *If you are not sure what **'acquisitions'** means paragraph 1 of the Notice will help you*
- *If you have not yet made any acquisitions **you must enclose evidence** to show that you are going to in the future*

Please tick ☑

Yes ☐ I made my first acquisition on [| |]

No ☐ but I intend to start on [| |]

9 Have the value of your acquisitions from persons in other EC countries exceeded the registration limit at any time in the calendar year commencing 1 January 1993 or any subsequent calendar year?

Please tick ☑

Yes ☐ I went over the limit on [| |]

because the value of my acquisitions from 1 January amounted to £ [ ]

No ☐ The value of my acquisitions from 1 January amounted to £ [ ]

10 Do you expect the value of the acquisitions you will make in the next 30 days alone will go over the registration limit?

Please tick ☑

Yes ☐ Go to 11

No ☐ Go to 12

11 From what date must you be registered for VAT?

- *If you have answered Yes to either question 9 or 10 then give the date from which you **have** to be registered (note 11 in part 2 of the Notice will help you)*
- *If you want to be registered from an earlier date fill in the date in the box provided*

I have to be registered from [| |]

I would like to be registered from this earlier date [| |]

12 I do not need to be registered but I want to be registered

- *only answer this question if you have not yet reached the registration limit but want to be registered on a voluntary basis*

I want to be registered from [| |]

13 Do you make taxable supplies in the UK?

Please tick ☑

Yes ☐ Please give the estimated value of taxable supplies you have made in the last 12 months £ [ ]

No ☐

14 Do you want exemption from registration because all your acquisitions are zero-rated?

- *if you are asking for exemption from registration enter the expected value of your zero-rated acquisitions in the next 12 months, in the box provided*

Please tick ☑

Yes ☐ Value of zero-rated acquisitions £ ☐

No ☐

15 Please complete and sign the declaration

Declaration

I, ☐

(enter your full name in CAPITAL LETTERS) declare that the information given on this form and contained in any accompanying document is true and complete.

Signature ☐ *Mr, Mrs, Miss, Ms*

Date ☐

Please tick ☑

Proprietor ☐ Director ☐
Trustee ☐ Partner ☐
Company Secretary ☐ Authorised official ☐

SPECIMEN

For office use

Local office code and registration number ☐

EDR D M Y ☐ Stagger ☐ Status ☐

Name ☐

Trade name ☐

Trade classification ☐ Taxable Turnover ☐

Rept.	Vol.	Oversize name address	Comp. user	Group Div	Intg	Overseas	Intg. EC	Value of Sales to EC	Value of Purchases from EC
	3								

Registration	Obligatory/Voluntary	Exemption	Intending	Transfer of Regn No.
Approved - Initial/date				
Refused - Initial/date				
Letter issued - Initial/date	Letter	Letter	Letter	Approval letter

VAT 1B Page 2R(02/97)

Amendments—Schedule 1 revoked by the VAT (Amendment) (No 2) Regulations, SI 2012/1899 regs 3, 27 with effect from 15 October 2012.

Form No 7A: VAT Registration Notification

Regulation 5(1)

Value Added Tax

VAT Registration Notification

This notification form must only be filled in if you have to register because you are making relevant supplies in the UK and you have no place of business here. Section 7 of VAT Notice 700/4 *Registration for VAT: Non-established taxable persons* gives more information about this and will help you to answer the questions on the form.

Please answer all questions. Write clearly in black ink and use CAPITAL LETTERS

Name

1. Sole proprietors - please give your full name.
   Partnerships - please give your trading name. If you do not have one, give the names of all partners (*partnerships must also complete form VAT 2*).
   Corporate or unincorporated bodies - please give the name of the company, club, association etc.

2. Do you have a trading name? Yes ☐ No ☐

   Please give the trading name of the business.

SPECIMEN

Business address

3. Please give the address of your principal place of business.

   Postcode

   Phone number

   Fax number

Tax representative

4. If you have appointed a tax representative to deal with your VAT matters in the UK please give details below.

   Name

   Address

   Phone number

   Postcode

   Fax number

VAT1C IB(March 2000)

VAT SIs

Status

5. What is the structure/legal status of the business? (*Please tick*)

Sole proprietor ☐ Partnership ☐

Corporate body ☐ (*Please give your company incorporation details*)

Certificate number ☐ Date ☐

Unincorporated body ☐ Please give details ☐

Business activities

6. What does your business do or intend to do? Tell us about your current or intended business activities.

Bank details

7. Please give your UK bank details or your tax representative's bank details.

Sort code ☐ Account number ☐

or

Girobank account number ☐

No bank account (*please tick*) ☐

SPECIMEN

Computer accounts

8. Is your accounting system computerised?

Yes (*Give details below*) ☐ No ☐

Computer type ☐

Software ☐ Version ☐

Relevant supplies

9. Have you made any relevant supplies yet? (*Please tick one box*)

☐ Yes, I made my first relevant supply on ☐

☐ No, but I expect to make my first relevant supply on ☐

VAT1C IB(March 2000)

10. When did you first have reasonable grounds to believe that you were going to make relevant supplies?

Date [ ]

11. What value of relevant supplies do you expect to make in the next 12 months?

£ [ ]

12. Do you make any other taxable supplies in the UK?

Yes [ ] No [ ]

If, **"*Yes*"**, enter the estimated value of all taxable supplies, other than your relevant supplies, that you expect to make in the UK in the next 12 months.

£ [ ]

Transfer of assets

13. Are you registering because VAT has been recovered by a predecessor in connection with the relevant supplies you have made, or intend to make?

Yes [ ] No [ ]

If **"*Yes*"**, give the name(s) and address(es) of the person(s) who recovered VAT under either the Eighth or Thirteeneth Directive refund schemes.

Exemption

14. Do you want exemption from registration because your relevant supplies are wholly zero-rated?

Yes [ ] No [ ]

If **"*Yes*"**, give the expected value of your zero-rated supplies in the next 12 months.

Zero-rated relevant supplies [ ]

Other VAT registrations

15. Are you involved in, or have you (or any other partners or directors in your business) been involved in any other businesses in the past 5 years?

Yes [ ] No [ ]

If **"*Yes*"**, give the names and VAT registration numbers of these businesses.

(Continue on a separate sheet, if necessary)

Declaration

16. I declare that the information given on this form and contained in any accompanying document is true and complete.

Signature		Date	
Full name			

What is your position in the business? *(Please tick)*

Proprietor	☐	Partner	☐	Director	☐
Company Secretary	☐	Trustee	☐	Other	☐

If "Other", give details

Checklist

- Have you answered every question?
- Have you signed the form?
- Partnership? Remember to complete Form VAT 2
- Appointing a tax representative? Remember to complete Form VAT1TR

SPECIMEN

What to do next

When you have completed and signed the form, please send it to the VAT Registration Unit specified in VAT Notice 700/4 *Registration for VAT: Non-established taxable persons.* If you have any problems completing the form please contact the Registration Unit.

Usually we will register you and give you a VAT registration number within 15 working days of receiving your form, provided you have given all the necessary information.

For office use

Local office code and registration number | D | M | Y | Stagger | Status

Name

Trade name | Trade classification | Taxable turnover

Rept. | Vol. | Oversize name address | Comp. user | Group Div | Intg. | Overseas | Intg. EC | Value of Sales to EC | Value of Purchases from EC

Registration	Obligatory/Voluntary	Exemption	Intending	Transfer of Regn No
Approved - Initial/date				
Refused - Initial/date				
Form issued - Initial/date	VAT9/ other	VAT8	Letter	Approval letter

VAT1C IB(March 2000)

Amendments—Form 7A inserted by the VAT (Amendment) (No 3) Regulations, SI 2000/794 regs 2, 7 with effect from 22 March 2000.

Schedule 1 revoked by the VAT (Amendment) (No 2) Regulations, SI 2012/1899 regs 3, 27 with effect from 15 October 2012.

Form No 8: Appointment of Tax Representative

Appointment of Tax Representative

You should read the notes in the registration booklet *"Should I be registered VAT? - Distance Selling"* which will help you to answer these questions.

Please write clearly in black ink.

1. Who is the business owned by? Please give the persons full **name** and **address** of the principal place of business.

Phone No. ____________ Postcode ____________

Please give the VAT Registration number in EC country of origin

Please give the UK VAT Registration number (if any)

2. Enter the full name and address of the UK Tax Representative

Phone No. ____________ Postcode ____________

3. Please give the date of appointment of Tax Representative and VAT registration number (if any)

Date of appointment

VAT Registration number

4. Declaration

We, ...and

Full name of PRINCIPAL in BLOCK LETTERS)

....

(Full name of TAX REPRESENTATIVE in BLOCK LETTERS)

declare that all the entered details and information in any accompanying documents are correct and complete

Signature of Principal .... Date ....

Tick one box

Proprietor ☐ Partner ☐ Director ☐

Company Secretary ☐ Authorised Official ☐ Trustee ☐

Signature of Tax Representative .... Date ....

Tick one box

Proprietor ☐ Partner ☐ Director ☐

Company Secretary ☐ Authorised Official ☐ Trustee ☐

CD 3428/N3(11/92)

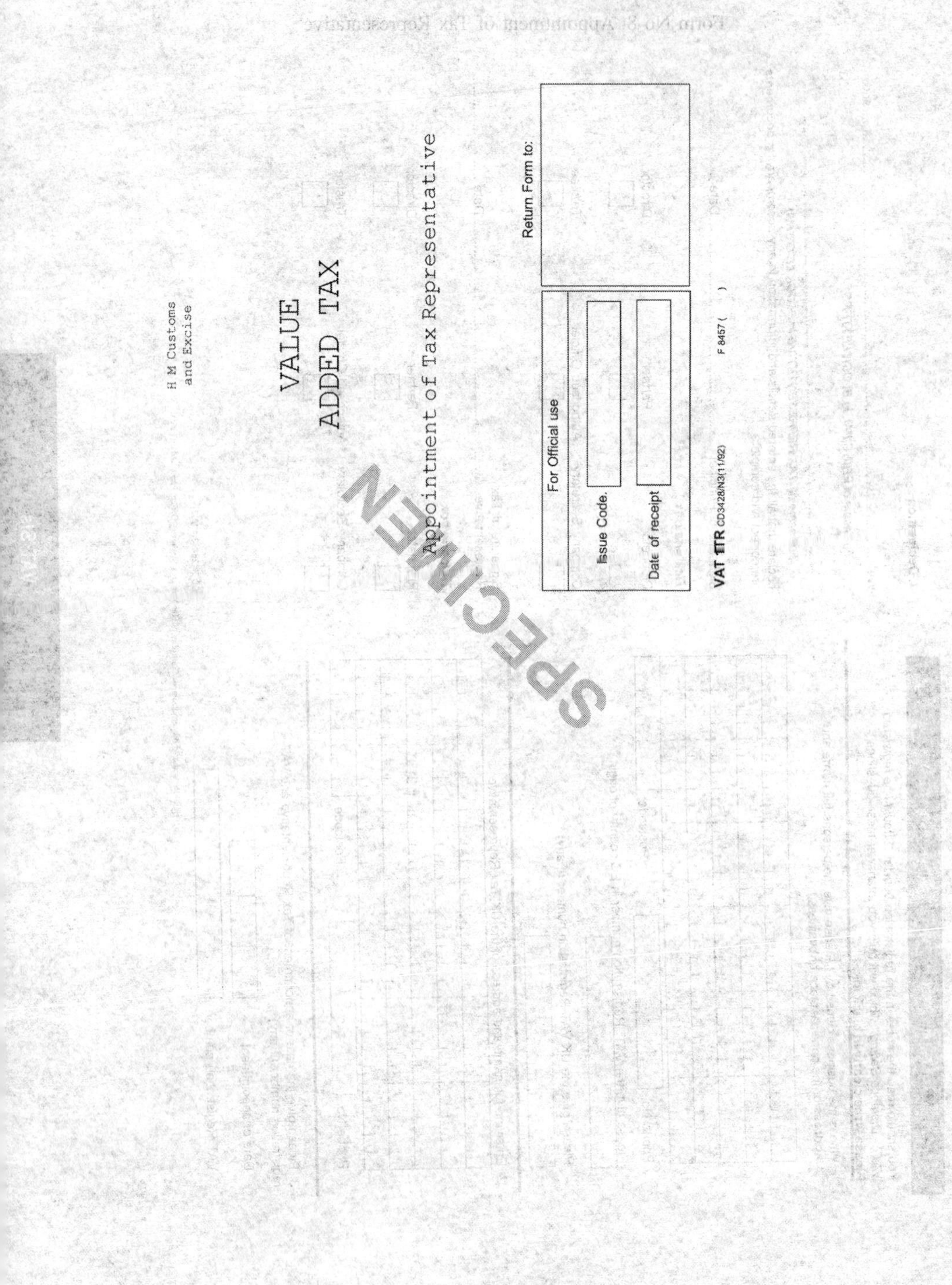
H M Customs and Excise

VALUE ADDED TAX

Appointment of Tax Representative

Return Form to:

For Official use

Issue Code.

Date of receipt

VAT 1TR CD3428/N3(11/92)

F 8457 ( )

Amendments—Schedule 1 revoked by the VAT (Amendment) (No 2) Regulations, SI 2012/1899 regs 3, 27 with effect from 15 October 2012.

Form No 9: Application by a business person not established in the Community for Refund of VAT

Regulation 191(1)(*b*)

HM Revenue & Customs

Application for refund of VAT

By a business person who **is not** established in the community

Read the VAT65A (Notes) before completing this form.

HM Revenue & Customs
VAT Overseas Repayments
8th/13th Directive
PO Box 34
Foyle House
Duncreggan Road
Londonderry
BT48 7AE
Northern Ireland

Enter your Unique Reference Number (URN), only if this is **not** your first application

Is this form being completed by an agent on behalf of a trader? *Enter 'X' if it is.*

1 Your forename(s) and surname or name of business

House name/number and street name

Place, *for the UK this will be your town and county*

Country

Postal reference, *for the UK this will be your postcode*

2 Nature of applicant's business

3 **For the country in which you are established, or have your domicile, or have your normal place of residence, give the following**

Tax/Business registration number

Name of the official authority

Address of the official authority

4 Period covered by this application *MM YY*

From to

5 Total amount of refund requested. *See itemised schedules*

£

6 **Enter details of the account where you would like to receive the payment of your requested refund**

Non-UK bank account UK bank account

Postal account

IBAN

Currency of account

Bank SWIFT code

Bank identifier code

Account in the name of

Name of bank

Address of bank

7 **Number of items enclosed** *excluding itemised schedules*

Documents

Invoices

Import documents

Declaration

8 **I hereby declare that:**

a) the goods or services specified on the itemised schedule(s) were used for the following business activities in the UK.

b) in the UK during the period covered by this application, I engaged in (*put 'X' in appropriate box*)

no supply of goods or services

only the provision of services in respect of which tax is payable solely by the person to whom they are supplied

only the provision of certain supporting exempted transport services.

c) the details given in this application are true.

I agree to pay back any monies wrongfully obtained

Signature

Date *DD MM YYYY, for example 21 10 2008*

Place application signed

Contact phone number

Fax number

Email address

SPECIMEN

You must complete the itemised schedule at question 9 on page 3. If you need more space, use as many copies of the VAT65/65A (CS) continuation sheet as you need. You must send us two copies of each schedule.

Unique Reference Number (URN), if you have one

Schedule number 0 1

9 **Itemised schedule of VAT amounts relating to the period covered by this application**

1) Each document submitted should be consecutively numbered starting with 1. The number should be inserted in the top right-hand corner. Enter details across the columns in respect of each invoice submitted. If you do not have enough space use the VAT65/65A (CS) continuation sheet or acceptable alternative version (see under *General* in the Notes). Attach this firmly to the application form.

2) You are reminded that when tax is incurred by taxable persons who receive VAT group treatment, the group representative member must apply on behalf of all the members. As the supporting invoices produced will not necessarily be addressed to the representative member, the status certificate must also contain the names of those group members who incurred the tax.

3) Refunds of tax incurred may only be claimed subject to the rules of each state. Brief details of supplies in each Member State on which tax cannot be reclaimed are given in HMRC Notice 723.
Tax incurred on the following supplies will not be refunded by any Member State:
(a) supplies of goods which have been or are about to be exported, and
(b) supplies to travel agents which are for the direct benefit of travellers. Under this scheme the term 'travel agent' includes tour operators or any person who purchases or re-supplies services to travellers.

SPECIMEN

Number	Nature of goods or services	Name of supplier	Address of supplier	VAT registration number	Date of invoice *dd/mm/yyyy*	Invoice number	Amount of tax £

Unique Reference Number, if you have one

Page total £

Page 3

VAT SIs

Amendments—Schedule 1 revoked by the VAT (Amendment) (No 2) Regulations, SI 2012/1899 regs 3, 27 with effect from 15 October 2012.

Form No 10: Certificate of Status of Business Person

Regulation 201(*a*)

HM Customs and Excise

Certificate of Status of Business Person

The undersigned ....
(Name and address of official authority)

certifies that ....
(Name of business person)

....
(Nature of activity)

....

....
(Address of the Establishment)

is a registered business person in ....
(Name of county)

*his registration number being | | | |

Date ....

Signature ....

Office date stamp

....
(Name and grade)

*If the applicant does not have a registration number, the official authority should state the reason for this.

SPECIMEN

VAT 66A CD 3298/N6(07/92) F 8609( )

Amendments—Schedule 1 revoked by the VAT (Amendment) (No 2) Regulations, SI 2012/1899 regs 3, 27 with effect from 15 October 2012.

Form 11A: VAT refunds for DIY housebuilders—Claim form for new houses

Regulations 21, 22, 23

HM Revenue & Customs

VAT refunds for DIY housebuilders Claim form for new houses

Official use only
Claim reference number

To claim back the VAT you have paid on building materials used to construct your new house, answer the questions on this claim form. The information you give at part B will show us whether you are eligible to claim back the VAT. Refer to the notes that came with this claim form. If you are not sure how to answer a question, phone the Helpline on **0300 200 3700**.

A Personal details

Answer all the questions in this part. If you leave any answer blank we may reject your claim

1 Your full name, including your title *Mr, Mrs, Miss, etc.*
If a charity, name of charity for whom the building has been constructed

2 If more than one claimant, title and full name of other claimant(s)

3 Your daytime contact phone numbers

4 Your address

Postcode

Is this the building you are claiming for?

No Yes

5 Your National Insurance number

6 Certified date of completion for the building
If you do not have a completion certificate leave blank

DD MM YYYY

7 Date you occupied the building

DD MM YYYY

8 If you or anyone connected with this claim have an interest or association with a VAT registered business, enter the VAT registration number(s) below:

B Are you eligible to claim?

Refer to the guidance notes

9 Is the property that you have built a new build?
By new build we mean a building that has been constructed from scratch which does not incorporate any part of an existing building

No Yes

10 Is your claim for the fit out and finish of a building shell?

No Yes

If you have answered No to questions 9 and 10 you will not be eligible to claim

11 Has the work been done on a completed dwelling purchased from a developer, builder or private vendor?

No Yes

If Yes, you are not eligible to claim

12 Has Planning Permission been granted for your new build?
To obtain a VAT refund you must provide evidence that the works are lawful and send to us a copy of the Planning Permission

No Yes

13 Do the terms of your Planning Permission (or similar permission) prevent the separate disposal, or separate use, of the new building from any other pre-existing building?

No Yes

14 Has a Building Regulation Completion Certificate been granted by the local authority or by an approved inspector registered with the local authority building control?

No Yes

If No, give details about what you will be providing instead

VAT SIs

Claimant: enter your full name here

15 Have you got your approved plans from your Local Authority?

No ☐ Yes ☐

16 Are you intending to live in the property you are claiming for?

No ☐ Yes ☐

If No, provide the address of the new build and explain why you have carried out the work

17 Are you claiming for any other building(s)?

No ☐ Yes ☐

If Yes, give details about the other building(s) and explain why

Continue to complete the rest of this claim form only if you have answered questions 9 to 17, have checked the notes and are sure that you qualify for a VAT refund using this scheme.

C Details of the property that has been constructed

18 Type of building
For example, a house, bungalow, apartment/flat, etc.

Is the building detached, semi-detached, terraced?

Number of storeys

Number of reception rooms

Number of bedrooms

Number of bathrooms/en-suites

Number of kitchen/utility rooms

If there are other rooms not described above, tell us how many there are and describe their purpose below

19 How many garages do you have (or intend to have)?

Number of integral

Number of detached

20 Will you be occupying it/them with the property you are constructing?

No ☐ Yes ☐

If No, explain what you will be doing with them

Claimant: enter your full name here

D Details of the goods supplied to you for which you will be claiming back VAT where the VAT amounts are shown separately on the invoice

Remember, you can only claim for building materials **and** you must send in the original invoices.
The invoices should be in your name. If they are not in your name, you must explain why.
For further advice about how to complete this part, refer to the notes.

Reference/ invoice number	Date of invoice	Description of invoice item	Supplier's name	VAT paid

D Total

VAT SIs

Claimant: enter your full name here

D Details of the goods supplied to you for which you will be claiming back VAT where the VAT amounts are shown separately on the invoice *Continued*

Reference/ invoice number	Date of invoice	Description of invoice item	Supplier's name	VAT paid	
			Balance brought forward		

D **Total**

Claimant: enter your full name here

E Details of the goods supplied to you for which you will be claiming back VAT at the standard rate where VAT amounts are not shown separately on the invoice

Remember, you can only claim for building materials **and** you must send in the original invoices.

The invoices should be in your name. If they are not in your name, you must explain why.

For further advice about how to complete this part, refer to the notes.

Reference/ invoice number	Date of invoice	Description of invoice item	Supplier's name	Total paid

Total paid

E **Total VAT calculated** *see notes*

Claimant: enter your full name here

E Details of the goods supplied to you for which you will be claiming back VAT at the standard rate where VAT amounts are not shown separately on the invoice *Continued*

Reference/ invoice number	Date of invoice	Description of invoice item	Supplier's name	Total paid	
			Balance brought forward		

Total paid

E Total VAT calculated *see notes*

Claimant: enter your full name here

F Sending in your claim

Summary, checklist and declaration

21 Summary

To check what is needed here, refer to the notes

Total amount of VAT claimed from part D

£ .

Total amount of VAT claimed from part E

£ .

Total amount of VAT to claim back from parts D + E

£ .

22 Bank account details

Give us details of the account into which you would prefer us to send your VAT refund

Full name(s) of account holder(s)

Sort code

Account number

Must be at least 8 digits. Lead with zeros if less

23 Checklist

Make sure you send all documents as requested to help us deal with your claim quickly. If you do not provide us with the correct documents we may reject your claim.

Have you enclosed the following documents?

Full Planning Permission No Yes

Or

Outline Planning Permission and Approval of Reserved Matters No Yes

*Note: **both** documents are needed*

And

Completion Certificate or other acceptable evidence No Yes

A full set of building plans No Yes

Original invoices *filed in the same order as listed on the schedules* No Yes

If any of the invoices have not been made out in your name, explain why in the box provided below

24 Do you give your authority for us to discuss your claim with your agent or accountant?

No Yes

If Yes, give details of your agent or accountant here

25 Declaration

If you give incomplete or inaccurate information in this claim, we may charge you a financial penalty or prosecute you.

I declare that:

- I am only reclaiming VAT which was correctly charged to me and which I paid on goods I bought or imported from a VAT registered supplier
- all the details and information on this form and any accompanying documents are correct
- I have read the attached guidance notes.

VAT registered persons

I confirm no other claim has been or will be made for these supplies and where the purchase of goods has been invoiced to my VAT registered business, I have not and will not claim this VAT through my VAT return.

Charity builders

The building being claimed for is to be used solely for the purpose of the charity named in question 1 of this claim form.

Signature(s)

Date *DD MM YYYY*

VAT431NB Page 7

Amendments—Forms 11A and 11B substituted for previous Form 11, by the Value Added Tax (Amendment) (No 3) Regulations, SI 2009/1967 regs 2, 9 with effect from 15 August 2009.

Schedule 1 revoked by the VAT (Amendment) (No 2) Regulations, SI 2012/1899 regs 3, 27 with effect from 15 October 2012.

VAT SIs

Form 11B: VAT refunds for DIY housebuilders—Claim form for conversions

Regulations 21, 22, 23

HM Revenue & Customs

VAT refunds for DIY housebuilders
Claim form for conversions

Official use only
Claim reference number

To claim back the VAT you have paid on building materials and services used for your conversion, answer the questions on this claim form. The information you give at part B will show us whether you are eligible to claim back the VAT. Refer to the notes that came with this claim form. If you are not sure how to answer a question, phone the Helpline on **0300 200 3700**.

A Personal details

Answer all the questions in this part. If you leave any answer blank we may reject your claim

1 Your full name, including your title *Mr, Mrs, Miss, etc.*

2 If more than one claimant, title and full name of other claimant(s)

3 Your daytime contact phone numbers

4 Your address

Postcode

Is this the building you are claiming for?

No Yes

5 Your National Insurance number

6 Certified date of completion for the building
If you do not have a completion certificate leave blank

DD MM YYYY

7 Date you occupied the building

DD MM YYYY

8 If you or anyone connected with this claim have an interest or association with a VAT registered business, enter the VAT registration number(s) below:

B Are you eligible to claim?

Refer to the guidance notes

9 Have you converted a non-residential building?
By conversion we mean converting a non-residential building into a dwelling

No Yes

10 Have you carried out works to a building that has previously been lived in?

No Yes

11 Have you got evidence that the building has been empty for 10 years or more before works started?

No Yes

If No, you are not eligible to claim

12 Are you 'fitting out or finishing' a converted non-residential building?

No Yes

13 Has work been done on a completed dwelling purchased from a developer, builder or private vendor?

No Yes

If Yes, you are not eligible to claim

14 Has Planning Permission been granted for your conversion/renovation/alteration works?
To obtain a VAT refund you must provide evidence that the works are lawful and send to us a copy of the Planning Permission

No Yes

If No, explain the reason why below

Claimant: enter your full name here

15 Do the terms of your Planning Permission (or similar permission) prevent the separate disposal, or separate use, of the converted property from any other pre-existing building?

No ☐ Yes ☐

16 Has a Building Regulation Completion Certificate been granted by the local authority or an approved inspector registered with the local authority building control?

No ☐ Yes ☐

If No, refer to notes and give details about what you will be providing instead

17 Have you got your approved plans from your Local Authority?

No ☐ Yes ☐

18 Are you intending to live in the property you are claiming for?

No ☐ Yes ☐

If No, provide the address of the conversion and explain why you have carried out the works

19 Are you claiming for any other building(s)?

No ☐ Yes ☐

If Yes, give details about the other building(s) and explain why

Continue to complete the rest of this claim form only if you have answered questions 9 to 19, have checked the notes and are sure that you qualify for a VAT refund using this scheme.

C Details of the property that has been converted

20 What was the building before you started your works?

Type of building

For example, barn conversion, house, apartment/flat, etc.

Is the building detached, semi-detached, terraced?

Number of storeys

Number of reception rooms

Number of bedrooms

Number of bathrooms/en-suites

Number of kitchen/utility rooms

If there are other rooms not described above, tell us how many there are and describe their purpose below

21 How many garages do you have (or intend to have)?

Number of integral

Number of detached

22 Will you be occupying it/them with the property you are converting?

No ☐ Yes ☐

If No, explain what you will be doing with them

VAT SIs

Claimant: enter your full name here

D Details of the goods and services for which you will be claiming back VAT where the VAT amounts are shown separately on the invoice

Remember, you must send in the original invoices. The invoices should be in your name.
If they are not in your name, you must explain why.
For further advice about how to complete this part, refer to the notes.

Reference/ invoice number	Date of invoice	Description of invoice item	Supplier's name	VAT paid
			D Total	

Claimant: enter your full name here

D Details of the goods and services supplied to you for which you will be claiming back VAT where the VAT amounts are shown separately on the invoice *Continued*

Reference/ invoice number	Date of invoice	Description of invoice item	Supplier's name	VAT paid
			Balance brought forward	

D **Total**

VAT SIs

Claimant: enter your full name here

E Details of the goods and services for which you will be claiming back VAT at the standard rate where VAT amounts are not shown separately on the invoice

Remember, you must send in the original invoices. The invoices should be in your name.
If they are not in your name, you must explain why.
For further advice about how to complete this part, refer to the notes.

Reference/ invoice number	Date of invoice	Description of invoice item	Supplier's name	Total paid

Total paid

E **Total VAT calculated** *see notes*

Claimant: enter your full name here

E Details of the goods and services supplied to you for which you will be claiming back VAT at the standard rate where VAT amounts are not shown separately on the invoice ***Continued***

Reference/ invoice number	Date of invoice	Description of invoice item	Supplier's name	Total paid
			Balance brought forward	

Total paid

E **Total VAT calculated** *see notes*

Claimant: enter your full name here

F Details of the goods and services for which you will be claiming back VAT at the reduced rate where VAT amounts are not shown separately on the invoice

Remember, you must send in the original invoices. The invoices should be in your name.
If they are not in your name, you must explain why.
For further advice about how to complete this part, refer to the notes.

Reference/ invoice number	Date of invoice	Description of invoice item	Supplier's name	Total paid

Total paid

F **Total VAT calculated** *see notes*

Claimant: enter your full name here

F Details of the goods and services for which you will be claiming back VAT at the reduced rate where VAT amounts are not shown separately on the invoice ***Continued***

Reference/ invoice number	Date of invoice	Description of invoice item	Supplier's name	Total paid
			Balance brought forward	

Total paid 0.00

F **Total VAT calculated** *see notes*

VAT SIs

Claimant: enter your full name here

G Sending in your claim

Summary, checklist and declaration

23 Summary

To check what is needed here, refer to the notes

Total amount of VAT claimed from part D

£ ☐☐☐☐☐☐ · ☐☐

Total amount of VAT claimed from part E

£ ☐☐☐☐☐☐ · ☐☐

Total amount of VAT claimed from part F

£ ☐☐☐☐☐☐ · ☐☐

Total amount of VAT to claim back from parts D + E + F

£ ☐☐☐☐☐☐ · ☐☐

24 Bank account details

Give us details of the account into which you would prefer us to send your VAT refund

Full name(s) of account holder(s)

Sort code

☐☐ – ☐☐ – ☐☐

Account number

Must be at least 8 digits. Lead with zeros if less

☐☐☐☐☐☐☐☐

25 Checklist

Make sure you send all documents as requested to help us deal with your claim quickly. If you do not provide us with the correct documents we may reject your claim.

Have you enclosed the following documents?

Evidence that the building has been empty for 10 years or more before you started your works No ☐ Yes ☐

Full Planning Permission No ☐ Yes ☐

Or

Outline Planning Permission **and** Approval of Reserved Matters No ☐ Yes ☐

Note: ***both*** *documents are needed*

And

Completion Certificate or other acceptable evidence No ☐ Yes ☐

A full set of building plans No ☐ Yes ☐

Original invoices *filed in the same order as listed on the schedules* No ☐ Yes ☐

If any of the invoices have not been made out in your name, explain why in the box below

26 Do you give your authority for us to discuss your claim with your agent or accountant?

No ☐ Yes ☐

If Yes, give details of your agent or accountant here

27 Declaration

If you give incomplete or inaccurate information in this claim, we may charge you a financial penalty or prosecute you.

I declare that:

- I am only reclaiming VAT which was correctly charged to me and which I paid on goods/services I bought or imported from a VAT registered supplier
- all the details and information on this form and any accompanying documents are correct
- I have read the attached guidance notes.

VAT registered persons

I confirm no other claim has been or will be made for these supplies and where the purchase of goods has been invoiced to my VAT registered business, I have not and will not claim this VAT through my VAT return.

Signature(s)

Date *DD MM YYYY*

☐☐ ☐☐ ☐☐☐☐

VAT431C Page 9

Amendments—Forms 11A and 11B substituted for previous Form 11, by the Value Added Tax (Amendment) (No 3) Regulations, SI 2009/1967 regs 2, 9 with effect from 15 August 2009.

Schedule 1 revoked by the VAT (Amendment) (No 2) Regulations, SI 2012/1899 regs 3, 27 with effect from 15 October 2012.

Form No 12: VAT EC Sales List

Regulation 22(6), 23

HM Revenue & Customs

Value Added Tax EC Sales List

If blank, please enter your name and address here

Please enter the following details. If you don't, we won't be able to use the information you give on the rest of this form.

VAT Registration Number

Branch/subsidiary identifier **Period reference** ***MM YY***

To avoid a penalty, please make sure this form reaches HMRC **within 14 days** of the period end date.

Enter the dates in the format DD MM YYYY

to

Period for services from to

If you move, transfer, supply or sell goods or supply services to other EU countries you have to complete an EC sales list. If you have not been involved in any such transactions during this period, you **do not** need to complete this form.

If you file your EC Sales List online, you will get an extra seven days to do so. To find out more go to **www.hmrc.gov.uk** and under *do it online* select *VAT online*.

Before you start, please enter your details at the top of this page. When we receive this form we will scan it, so please write clearly in black ink and leave blank any boxes that don't apply to you. The notes on page 2 will help you complete the rest of this form. If you have more than eight transactions to record, please use a VAT101A *Continuation sheet*. See page 2 for details.

For further advice go to **www.hmrc.gov.uk** or phone our Helpline on **0845 010 9000** (Monday to Friday, 8am to 8pm)

	Country code	Customer VAT Registration Number	Total value of supplies In pound sterling	Indicator
1			£ . 00	
2			£ . 00	
3			£ . 00	
4			£ . 00	
5			£ . 00	
6			£ . 00	
7			£ . 00	
8			£ . 00	

Declaration You, or someone on your behalf, must sign below.

I declare that the information given on this form and any continuation sheets is correct and complete to the best of my knowledge.

Signature

Contact number *in case we need to speak to you*

Full name of signatory in capital letters

Date DD MM YYYY

Number of pages to this list

VAT101MAN **PAGE 1** **HMRC 10/09**

VAT SIs

Before you start

Monthly Sales Lists

If you supply goods and services and are required to file your EC Sales List for goods monthly:

- you may report **goods only** in months 1 and 2 and report **goods** for the month and **services** for the whole quarter in month 3, or
- you can report goods and services each month.

Simplified annual EC Sales List (ESL) for supplies of goods

If HM Revenue & Customs has given you approval to submit a simplified annual ESL because you have low levels of supplies of goods to other EC countries, you are not required to enter the actual value of supplies.

Instead, enter a nominal total value of £1. Then follow the rest of the guidance about the VAT Registration Number and the indicator box.

How to fill in this form

- Write inside the boxes. Use black ink and capital letters.
- If you make a mistake, please cross it out and write the correct information below it.
- Leave blank any boxes that don't apply to you – please don't strike through them. Do not write 'none'.
- Only include your sales for the period(s) shown on page 1.
- Enter each type of sale on a separate line.

Country code

Enter your customer's country code. This is made up of two letters. It can only be one of the codes shown below.

EC country codes

Austria	AT	Germany	DE	Netherlands	NL
Belgium	BE	Greece	EL	Poland	PL
Bulgaria	BG	Hungary	HU	Portugal	PT
Cyprus	CY	Ireland	IE	Romania	RO
Czech Republic	CZ	Italy	IT	Slovak Republic	SK
Denmark	DK	Latvia	LV	Slovenia	SI
Estonia	EE	Lithuania	LT	Spain	ES
Finland	FI	Luxembourg	LU	Sweden	SE
France	FR	Malta	MT		

Customer's VAT Registration Number

Enter your customer's VAT Registration Number starting from the left hand side.

Please do not include the country code in this column, or any spaces, dashes or comma. If you need to, refer to Notice 725 *The Single Market* to check how VAT numbers for each of the EC countries are formatted.

One of the conditions for zero-rating supplies of goods and services to other EC countries is that you must provide a **valid** VAT Registration Number for each of your customers.

You can check that a number is valid on the Europa website.

Go to www.ec.europa.eu/taxation_customs/vies

Total values of supplies and the indicator box

In all cases, enter the total, rounded down to the nearest pound sterling. Enter each amount starting from the right hand side. We have already added the zero pence and decimal point for you. Please **do not** add commas.

If you have a minus figure to enter because the value of credit notes is greater than the total value of supplies, enter a minus sign in a white box **before** each value.

Please note that you may need up to three lines for each customer. This is because the total value of **each type of sale** needs to be entered. For example, if you have supplied goods direct **and** as a triangulated sale **and** have supplied a service, you must complete three lines for that customer. Further guidance is given below.

- If you supplied goods, enter the value (including related costs) of all the goods supplied to that customer (deducting credit notes where appropriate). Leave the indicator column **blank**.

  Related costs include services which form part of the **goods**, such as freight and insurance charges.
- If you were an intermediate supplier in a triangulated sale, enter the total value of the supplies to each customer on a separate line from any other supplies made to that customer. Enter 2 in the indicator column.
- If you have supplied services which were subject to the reverse charge in the customer's member state, enter the total value of these supplies on a separate line. Enter 3 in the indicator column.

Other forms you may need

If you need more space please do not add lines to this form. Please use the form VAT101A *Continuation sheet*.

If you need to correct any data supplied in a previous period or supply previously omitted data, please do so on form VAT101B *Correction to EC Sales List*.

To obtain any of these forms, please go to www.hmrc.gov.uk select Find a Form and enter the form number (for example, *VAT101A* or *VAT101B*). Or phone the Helpline on **0845 010 9000** and ask for copies.

What to do next

When you have completed and signed this form please send it in the addressed envelope to:

HM Revenue & Customs
Comben House
Farriers Way
Liverpool
L75 1AY

To avoid penalty, please make sure this form reaches us on time.

Need help?

If you need further guidance on EC Sales Lists please refer to Notice 725 *The Single Market* which is available online.

Go to **www.hrmc.gov.uk** or phone the Helpline on **0845 010 9000** Monday to Friday, 8am to 8pm.

VAT101MAN **PAGE 2**

Amendments—Form 12 substituted by SI 2009/3241, regs 2, 8, Schedule, with effect from 1 January 2010.

Schedule 1 revoked by the VAT (Amendment) (No 2) Regulations, SI 2012/1899 regs 3, 27 with effect from 15 October 2012.

Form No 13: New means of transport for removal from the UK to another Member State of the European Community

Regulation 204(c)

HM Revenue & Customs

New means of transport

Removal from the UK to another member state of the European Community

See notes overleaf before completing.

For the supplier to complete

Title and full name

Full UK address

Phone

VAT Registration number

GB

Details of the new means of transport *(tick one box)*

Motorised land vehicle ☐ Ship ☐ Aircraft ☐

Make	
Model	
Colour	
Registration number	
Date of issue of the plates	
Engine number	
Chassis/Hull/Airframe number	
Name of vessel	
Number of kilometers/hours of navigation/hours of flight (if different from nil)	
Invoice number and date	
Date of supply	
Purchase price	
VAT not paid at time of supply	

I declare that:

- the information given above is correct
- the New Means of Transport described above complies with the definition given in Notice 728 about VAT and the Single Market.

Signature

Date

For the purchaser to complete

Title and full name

Full UK address *(if applicable)*

Phone

Full address in Member State of destination

Phone

Member State of destination of the new means of transport in which VAT will be paid

Are you a UK Resident? *(Tick one box)*

No ☐ Yes ☐

Are you a serving member of HM Forces or a dependant of a Serving Member of HM Forces? *(Tick one box)*

No ☐ Yes ☐

I declare that:

- the information I have given is correct
- I have read Notice 728 and the notes overleaf
- I intend to remove the New Means of Transport described on this form from the UK to the Member State of Destination within two months of the date of supply
- I intend to notify the fiscal authority in that Member State and pay any tax due
- I understand that if I fail to remove the New Means of Transport described on this form within two months of the date of supply it will become liable to forfeiture and UK taxes will become due.

Signature

Date

Notes

This form should only be used for removals of new means of transport to other member states of the European Community, by persons not registered for VAT.

Notice 728 (for unregistered purchasers) define what a new means of transport is. They explain the circumstances in which a new means of transport may be obtained free of taxes.

Before completing this form please read the relevant notice and the following information carefully.

You can download the VAT Notices from our website at **www.hmrc.gov.uk** or you can phone our National Advice Service on **0845 01 09 000** for advice.

The following are member states of the EC:

Austria
Belgium
Bulgaria
*Cyprus
Czech Republic
Denmark
Estonia
Finland
France (including Monaco)
Germany
Greece
Hungary
Ireland
Italy
Latvia
Lithuania
Luxembourg
Malta
Netherlands
Poland
Portugal (including the Azores and Maderia)
Romania
Slovakia
Slovenia
Spain (including the Balearic Islands)
Sweden and the UK (including the Isle of Man).

**The European Commission has advised that, as the situation stands at present, the application of the 6th Directive shall be suspended in those area of Cyprus in which the Government of the Republic of Cyprus does not exercise effective control. Transactions with those areas will continue from 1 May 2004 to be treated as non-EU transactions.*

To the supplier

- When this form has been completed send the original to:
  HM Revenue & Customs
  Personal Transport Unit
  Freight Clearance Centre
  Lord Warden Square
  Western Docks
  Dover
  Kent
  CT17 9DN.
- Give the first copy to the purchaser.
- Retain the second copy for your records.
- Attach the third copy to the application for a registration number (this only applies when the new means of transport is a motor vehicle).

To the purchaser

You must remove the new means of transport from the UK to the member state of destination within two months of the date of the supply. The date of supply is the earlier of either:

- the date of the invoice for the purchase of the new means of transport, or
- the 15th day of the month after that in which you received the new means of transport or it was despatched to you.

You must notify HM Revenue & Customs immediately if for any reason you change your intention to remove the new means of transport to the member of state of destination within two months of the date of supply.

The supplier will provide you with a copy of this form. You should retain this for production to the tax authority in the member state of destination.

The law relating to this scheme is in section 30(8) of the Value Added Tax Act 1994.

HM Revenue & Customs

New means of transport

Removal from the UK to another member state of the European Community

See notes overleaf before completing.

For the supplier to complete

Title and full name

Full UK address

Phone

VAT Registration number

GB

Details of the new means of transport *(tick one box)*

Motorised land vehicle ☐ Ship ☐ Aircraft ☐

Make	
Model	
Colour	
Registration number	
Date of issue of the plates	
Engine number	
Chassis/Hull/Airframe number	
Name of vessel	
Number of kilometers/hours of navigation/hours of flight (if different from nil)	
Invoice number and date	
Date of supply	
Purchase price	
VAT not paid at time of supply	

I declare that:

- the information given above is correct
- the New Means of Transport described above complies with the definition given in Notice 728 about VAT and the Single Market.

Signature

Date

For the purchaser to complete

Title and full name

Full UK address *(if applicable)*

Phone

Full address in Member State of destination

Phone

Member State of destination of the new means of transport in which VAT will be paid

Are you a UK Resident? *(Tick one box)*

No ☐ Yes ☐

Are you a serving member of HM Forces or a dependant of a Serving Member of HM Forces? *(Tick one box)*

No ☐ Yes ☐

I declare that:

- the information I have given is correct
- I have read Notice 728 and the notes overleaf
- I intend to remove the New Means of Transport described on this form from the UK to the Member State of Destination within two months of the date of supply
- I intend to notify the fiscal authority in that Member State and pay any tax due
- I understand that if I fail to remove the New Means of Transport described on this form within two months of the date of supply it will become liable to forfeiture and UK taxes will become due.

Signature

Date

Notes

This form should only be used for removals of new means of transport to other member states of the European Community, by persons not registered for VAT.

Notice 728 (for unregistered purchasers) define what a new means of transport is. They explain the circumstances in which a new means of transport may be obtained free of taxes.

Before completing this form please read the relevant notice and the following information carefully.

You can download the VAT Notices from our website at **www.hmrc.gov.uk** or you can phone our National Advice Service on **0845 01 09 000** for advice.

The following are member states of the EC:

Austria
Belgium
Bulgaria
*Cyprus
Czech Republic
Denmark
Estonia
Finland
France (including Monaco)
Germany
Greece
Hungary
Ireland
Italy
Latvia
Lithuania
Luxembourg
Malta
Netherlands
Poland
Portugal (including the Azores and Maderia)
Romania
Slovakia
Slovenia
Spain (including the Balearic Islands)
Sweden and the UK (including the Isle of Man).

**The European Commission has advised that, as the situation stands at present, the application of the 6th Directive shall be suspended in those area of Cyprus in which the Government of the Republic of Cyprus does not exercise effective control. Transactions with those areas will continue from 1 May 2004 to be treated as non-EU transactions.*

To the supplier

- When this form has been completed send the original to:
  HM Revenue & Customs
  Personal Transport Unit
  Freight Clearance Centre
  Lord Warden Square
  Western Docks
  Dover
  Kent
  CT17 9DN.
- Give the first copy to the purchaser.
- Retain the second copy for your records.
- Attach the third copy to the application for a registration number (this only applies when the new means of transport is a motor vehicle).

To the purchaser

You must remove the new means of transport from the UK to the member state of destination within two months of the date of the supply. The date of supply is the earlier of either:

- the date of the invoice for the purchase of the new means of transport, or
- the 15th day of the month after that in which you received the new means of transport or it was despatched to you.

You must notify HM Revenue & Customs immediately if for any reason you change your intention to remove the new means of transport to the member of state of destination within two months of the date of supply.

The supplier will provide you with a copy of this form. You should retain this for production to the tax authority in the member state of destination.

The law relating to this scheme is in section 30(8) of the Value Added Tax Act 1994.

HM Revenue & Customs

New means of transport

Removal from the UK to another member state of the European Community

See notes overleaf before completing.

For the supplier to complete

Title and full name

Full UK address

Phone

VAT Registration number

GB

Details of the new means of transport *(tick one box)*

Motorised land vehicle ☐ Ship ☐ Aircraft ☐

Make	
Model	
Colour	
Registration number	
Date of issue of the plates	
Engine number	
Chassis/Hull/Airframe number	
Name of vessel	
Number of kilometers/hours of navigation/hours of flight (if different from nil)	
Invoice number and date	
Date of supply	
Purchase price	
VAT not paid at time of supply	

I declare that:

- the information given above is correct
- the New Means of Transport described above complies with the definition given in Notice 728 about VAT and the Single Market.

Signature

Date

For the purchaser to complete

Title and full name

Full UK address *(if applicable)*

Phone

Full address in Member State of destination

Phone

Member State of destination of the new means of transport in which VAT will be paid

Are you a UK Resident? *(Tick one box)*

No ☐ Yes ☐

Are you a serving member of HM Forces or a dependant of a Serving Member of HM Forces? *(Tick one box)*

No ☐ Yes ☐

I declare that:

- the information I have given is correct
- I have read Notice 728 and the notes overleaf
- I intend to remove the New Means of Transport described on this form from the UK to the Member State of Destination within two months of the date of supply
- I intend to notify the fiscal authority in that Member State and pay any tax due
- I understand that if I fail to remove the New Means of Transport described on this form within two months of the date of supply it will become liable to forfeiture and UK taxes will become due.

Signature

Date

Notes

This form should only be used for removals of new means of transport to other member states of the European Community, by persons not registered for VAT.

Notice 728 (for unregistered purchasers) define what a new means of transport is. They explain the circumstances in which a new means of transport may be obtained free of taxes.

Before completing this form please read the relevant notice and the following information carefully.

You can download the VAT Notices from our website at **www.hmrc.gov.uk** or you can phone our National Advice Service on **0845 01 09 000** for advice.

The following are member states of the EC:

Austria
Belgium
Bulgaria
*Cyprus
Czech Republic
Denmark
Estonia
Finland
France (including Monaco)
Germany
Greece
Hungary
Ireland
Italy
Latvia
Lithuania
Luxembourg
Malta
Netherlands
Poland
Portugal (including the Azores and Maderia)
Romania
Slovakia
Slovenia
Spain (including the Balearic Islands)
Sweden and the UK (including the Isle of Man).

**The European Commission has advised that, as the situation stands at present, the application of the 6th Directive shall be suspended in those area of Cyprus in which the Government of the Republic of Cyprus does not exercise effective control. Transactions with those areas will continue from 1 May 2004 to be treated as non-EU transactions.*

To the supplier

- When this form has been completed send the original to:
  HM Revenue & Customs
  Personal Transport Unit
  Freight Clearance Centre
  Lord Warden Square
  Western Docks
  Dover
  Kent
  CT17 9DN.
- Give the first copy to the purchaser.
- Retain the second copy for your records.
- Attach the third copy to the application for a registration number (this only applies when the new means of transport is a motor vehicle).

To the purchaser

You must remove the new means of transport from the UK to the member state of destination within two months of the date of the supply. The date of supply is the earlier of either:

- the date of the invoice for the purchase of the new means of transport, **or**
- the 15th day of the month after that in which you received the new means of transport or it was despatched to you.

You must notify HM Revenue & Customs immediately if for any reason you change your intention to remove the new means of transport to the member of state of destination within two months of the date of supply.

The supplier will provide you with a copy of this form. You should retain this for production to the tax authority in the member state of destination.

The law relating to this scheme is in section 30(8) of the Value Added Tax Act 1994.

HM Revenue & Customs

New means of transport

Removal from the UK to another member state of the European Community

See notes overleaf before completing.

For the supplier to complete

Title and full name

Full UK address

Phone

VAT Registration number

GB

Details of the new means of transport *(tick one box)*

Motorised land vehicle ☐ Ship ☐ Aircraft ☐

Make	
Model	
Colour	
Registration number	
Date of issue of the plates	
Engine number	
Chassis/Hull/Airframe number	
Name of vessel	
Number of kilometers/hours of navigation/hours of flight (if different from nil)	
Invoice number and date	
Date of supply	
Purchase price	
VAT not paid at time of supply	

I declare that:

- the information given above is correct
- the New Means of Transport described above complies with the definition given in Notice 728 about VAT and the Single Market.

Signature

Date

For the purchaser to complete

Title and full name

Full UK address *(if applicable)*

Phone

Full address in Member State of destination

Phone

Member State of destination of the new means of transport in which VAT will be paid

Are you a UK Resident? *(Tick one box)*

No ☐ Yes ☐

Are you a serving member of HM Forces or a dependant of a Serving Member of HM Forces? *(Tick one box)*

No ☐ Yes ☐

I declare that:

- the information I have given is correct
- I have read Notice 728 and the notes overleaf
- I intend to remove the New Means of Transport described on this form from the UK to the Member State of Destination within two months of the date of supply
- I intend to notify the fiscal authority in that Member State and pay any tax due
- I understand that if I fail to remove the New Means of Transport described on this form within two months of the date of supply it will become liable to forfeiture and UK taxes will become due.

Signature

Date

Notes

This form should only be used for removals of new means of transport to other member states of the European Community, by persons not registered for VAT.

Notice 728 (for unregistered purchasers) define what a new means of transport is. They explain the circumstances in which a new means of transport may be obtained free of taxes.

Before completing this form please read the relevant notice and the following information carefully.

You can download the VAT Notices from our website at **www.hmrc.gov.uk** or you can phone our National Advice Service on **0845 01 09 000** for advice.

The following are member states of the EC:

Austria
Belgium
Bulgaria
*Cyprus
Czech Republic
Denmark
Estonia
Finland
France (including Monaco)
Germany
Greece
Hungary
Ireland
Italy
Latvia
Lithuania
Luxembourg
Malta
Netherlands
Poland
Portugal (including the Azores and Maderia)
Romania
Slovakia
Slovenia
Spain (including the Balearic Islands)
Sweden and the UK (including the Isle of Man).

**The European Commission has advised that, as the situation stands at present, the application of the 6th Directive shall be suspended in those area of Cyprus in which the Government of the Republic of Cyprus does not exercise effective control. Transactions with those areas will continue from 1 May 2004 to be treated as non-EU transactions.*

To the supplier

- When this form has been completed send the original to:
  HM Revenue & Customs
  Personal Transport Unit
  Freight Clearance Centre
  Lord Warden Square
  Western Docks
  Dover
  Kent
  CT17 9DN.
- Give the first copy to the purchaser.
- Retain the second copy for your records.
- Attach the third copy to the application for a registration number (this only applies when the new means of transport is a motor vehicle).

To the purchaser

You must remove the new means of transport from the UK to the member state of destination within two months of the date of the supply. The date of supply is the earlier of either:

- the date of the invoice for the purchase of the new means of transport, **or**
- the 15th day of the month after that in which you received the new means of transport or it was despatched to you.

You must notify HM Revenue & Customs immediately if for any reason you change your intention to remove the new means of transport to the member of state of destination within two months of the date of supply.

The supplier will provide you with a copy of this form. You should retain this for production to the tax authority in the member state of destination.

The law relating to this scheme is in section 30(8) of the Value Added Tax Act 1994.

Amendments—Schedule 1 revoked by the VAT (Amendment) (No 2) Regulations, SI 2012/1899 regs 3, 27 with effect from 15 October 2012.

Form No 14: Flat Rate Scheme for Agriculture—Application for Certification

Regulation 178(1)(a)

HM Customs and Excise

Value Added Tax

Flat Rate Scheme for Agriculture

Application for Certification

Notes to help you complete this form are on the reverse. Please read them carefully

1. Please enter your FULL NAME in BLOCK LETTERS. (See note 1)

2. Please enter the ADDRESS of your BUSINESS. (See note 2)

Postcode Tel No.

3. Please describe your BUSINESS INCLUDING NON-FARMING ACTIVITIES. (See note 3)

4. Please enter the ESTIMATED VALUE of AGRICULTURAL SUPPLIES you expect to make in the next 12 months. (see note 4)

5. Please enter the ESTIMATED VALUE of SUPPLIES OF OTHER GOODS and SERVICES which you expect to make in the next 12 months. (See note 5)

6. Please enter the DATE from which you wish your CERTIFICATE TO BE EFFECTIVE. (See note 6)

7. Please enter your VAT REGISTRATION NUMBER. Write "NONE" if you are not registered for VAT. (See note 7)

8. **You must complete the following declaration** :

I ....
(enter your full name in BLOCK LETTERS)

declare that the information entered on this form is true and complete.

I apply for cancellation of the VAT registration shown at box 7 abov e.

Signature .... Date ....

Tick one box Proprietor ☐ Director ☐ Trustee ☐ Partner ☐ Company Secretary ☐ Authorised Official ☐

SPECIMEN

For Official Use

Initials and Date

All'd LVO TC Abbreviated name

Ref'd EDC

VAT 98 PT (March 2001)

Notes

VAT Notice 700/46 - "Agricultural Flat Rate Scheme" will help you to decide whether to apply to become a flat rate farmer and will help you in completing this form.

1. Enter the name of the owner of the business as follows:

   Sole Proprietor: enter your full name, leave a space between words.

   Partnership: enter the trading name of the partnership if you have one, and the full names of all partners. If there is not enough room on the form continue on a sheet of paper and attach it to the form.

   Limited company: enter the name of the company.

   Other: enter the name of the association etc (the trading name if it has one).

2. Enter the full business address, telephone number and post code of the person or persons named at box 1. This must be an address where farming activities are carried on.

3. Give a brief description eg "sheep farmer" and include any non-farming activities. Enclose a separate note if there is not enough room, but there is no need to provide more than basic details especially if you are presently registered for VAT.

4. Enter here your best estimate of the value of your farming supplies for the next 12 months. **Exclude** subsidies paid directly to you and any income from non-farming activities eg bed & breakfast. A full list of farming activities is in the notice.

5. This figure is your best estimate of the value of your **non-farming** taxable supplies in the next 12 months. If this value is greater than the VAT registration limit you **do not** qualify as a flat rate farmer.

6. You can apply for a certificate up to 30 days in advance of when you want it to start. But a certificate can not be dated before the day on which we receive your application.

7. If you are registered for VAT you **must** enter your VAT registration number here so that we can cancel your registration. **Do not** enter the VAT number of any associated business eg if you are applying for a certificate as a sole proprietor and you are also a partner in another business **do not** enter the partnership number.

The declaration at the foot of the form **must** be completed. ***If any of the information given in the form is false your certificate will be cancelled and you will be liable to a financial penalty if you have charged flat rate additions.***

When you have completed this form send it to the local VAT office which is nearest to the farm address you have entered at Box 2. The VAT office address can be found in the telephone directory under "Customs and Excise".

Data Protection Act 1998

HM Customs and Excise collects information in order to administer the taxes for which it is responsible (such as VAT, insurance premium tax, excise duties, air passenger duty, landfill tax), and for detecting and preventing crime.
Where the law permits we may also get information about you from third parties, or give information to them, for example in order to check its accuracy, prevent or detect crime or protect public funds in other ways. These third parties may include the police, other government departments and agencies.

VAT 98 Reverse (03/01)

Amendments—Schedule 1 revoked by the VAT (Amendment) (No 2) Regulations, SI 2012/1899 regs 3, 27 with effect from 15 October 2012.

Form No 15: Application by a business person established in the Community for Refund of VAT

Regulation 178(1)(b)(i)

HM Revenue & Customs

Application for refund of VAT

By a business person who **is** established in the community

Read the VAT65 (Notes) before completing this form.

HM Revenue & Customs
VAT Overseas Repayments
8th/13th Directive
PO Box 34
Foyle House
Duncreggan Road
Londonderry
BT48 7AE
Northern Ireland

Enter your Unique Reference Number (URN), only if this is **not** your first application

Is this form being completed by an agent on behalf of a trader? *Enter 'X' if it is.*

1 Your forename(s) and surname or name of business

House name/number and street name

Place, *for the UK this will be your town and county*

Country

Postal reference, *for the UK this will be your postcode*

2 Nature of applicant's business

3 **For the country in which you are established, or have your domicile, or have your normal place of residence, give the following**

Tax/Business registration number

Name of the official authority

Address of the official authority

4 Period covered by this application *MM YY*

From to

5 Total amount of refund requested. *See itemised schedules*

£

6 **Enter details of the account where you would like to receive the payment of your requested refund**

Non-UK bank account UK bank account

Postal account

IBAN

Currency of account

Bank SWIFT code

Bank identifier code

SPECIMEN

VAT SIs

Account in the name of

Name of bank

Address of bank

7 **Number of items enclosed** *excluding itemised schedules*

Documents

Invoices

Import documents

Declaration

8 **I hereby declare that:**

a) the goods or services specified on the itemised schedule(s) were used for the following business activities in the UK.

b) in the UK during the period covered by this application, I engaged in (*put 'X' in appropriate box*)

no supply of goods or services

only the provision of services in respect of which tax is payable solely by the person to whom they are supplied

only the provision of certain supporting exempted transport services.

c) the details given in this application are true.

I agree to pay back any monies wrongfully obtained

Signature

Date *DD MM YYYY, for example 21 10 2008*

Place application signed

Contact phone number

Fax number

Email address

You must complete the itemised schedule at question 9 on page 3. If you need more space, use as many copies of the VAT65/65A (CS) continuation sheet as you need. You must send us two copies of each schedule.

Unique Reference Number (URN), if you have one

Schedule number 0 1

9 Itemised schedule of VAT amounts relating to the period covered by this application

1) Each document submitted should be consecutively numbered starting with 1. The number should be inserted in the top right-hand corner. Enter details across the columns in respect of each invoice submitted. If you do not have enough space use the VAT65/65A (CS) continuation sheet or acceptable alternative version (see under *General* in the Notes). Attach this firmly to the application form.

2) You are reminded that when tax is incurred by taxable persons who receive VAT group treatment, the group representative member must apply on behalf of all the members. As the supporting invoices produced will not necessarily be addressed to the representative member, the status certificate must also contain the names of those group members who incurred the tax.

3) Refunds of tax incurred may only be claimed subject to the rules of each state. Brief details of supplies in each Member State on which tax cannot be reclaimed are given in HMRC Notice 723.
Tax incurred on the following supplies will not be refunded by any Member State:
(a) supplies of goods which have been or are about to be exported, and
(b) supplies to travel agents which are for the direct benefit of travellers. Under this scheme the term 'travel agent' includes tour operators or any person who purchases or re-supplies services to travellers.

SPECIMEN

Number	Nature of goods or services	Name of supplier	Address of supplier	VAT registration number	Date of invoice *dd/mm/yyyy*	Invoice number	Amount of tax £

Unique Reference Number, if you have one

Page total £

Page 3

Amendments—Schedule 1 revoked by the VAT (Amendment) (No 2) Regulations, SI 2012/1899 regs 3, 27 with effect from 15 October 2012.

VAT SIs

Form No 16: Certificate of Status of Taxable Person

Regulation 145B

HM Customs and Excise

Certificate of Status of Taxable Person

The undersigned

....

(Name of local VAT office)

certifies that

Name of taxable person
Address
Nature of activity

is a taxable person for the purposes of Value Added Tax, whose Registration number is

Date ....

Office stamp

Signature ....

....

(Name and grade)

VAT 66 CD 1017/N6(07/91) F 5037 (NOV 90) NKBH 9646 50M (11/92)

Amendments—Schedule 1 revoked by the VAT (Amendment) (No 2) Regulations, SI 2012/1899 regs 3, 27 with effect from 15 October 2012.

Form No 17[1]

CERTIFICATE REQUIRED TO SECURE RELIEF FROM VAT ON PURCHASED OR ACQUIRED GOODS INTENDED TO BE PLACED IN A FISCAL WAREHOUSING REGIME

Information to be indicated:

I (full name)

(status in company)

Of (name and address of company)

declare that (name of company) intends to enter to the fiscal warehousing regime at the fiscal warehouse shown below on (date), or within . . . days commencing today, the goods indicated below:

- name and address of fiscal warehouse
- authorisation number of the fiscal warehousekeeper
- description of goods
- quantity of goods

I certify that the supply of goods/acquisition is eligible to be relieved from VAT under the following provisions of the Value Added Tax Act 1994 [*delete as appropriate*]:

sections 18B(2)(d)/18B(3) (purchases) or sections 18B(1)(d)/18B(3) (acquisitions).

(signature)

(date)

NOTE: You should be aware that there are severe penalties for making a false declaration. If there is any doubt about the eligibility of the goods or about the fiscal warehouse to which they are being sent you should consult the local Customs and Excise office before preparing the certificate. *A copy of the certificate should be filed with the supplier's invoice and a copy of the delivery note.*

Regulation 145C

Form No 18

CERTIFICATE REQUIRED TO SECURE ZERO-RATING OF SERVICES (OTHER THAN THE SUPPLY OF WAREHOUSING) PERFORMED IN A FISCAL OR OTHER WAREHOUSE

Information to be indicated:

I (full name)

(status in company)

of (name and address of company)

declare that the goods shown below are subject to a fiscal or other warehousing regime at the place indicated below:

- description of goods
- quantity of goods
- warehouse stock number
- name and address of fiscal or other warehouse
- authorisation number of the relevant warehousekeeper/warehouse

and that the following services are to be performed on the goods in the fiscal or other warehouse:

I certify that the supply of services is eligible to be zero-rated for VAT purposes under section 18C(1) of the Value Added Tax Act 1994.

(signature)

(date)

NOTE: You should be aware that there are severe penalties for making a false declaration. If there is any doubt about a supply being entitled to zero-rating you should consult the local Customs and Excise office before signing and giving the certificate. *A copy of the certificate should be filed with the supplier's invoice which should refer to section 18C(1) of the Value Added Tax Act 1994 to be eligible for zero-rating.*

Amendments—Forms 17, 18 added by the VAT (Amendment) (No 3) Regulations, SI 1996/1250 reg 15, Sch 1, with effect from 1 June 1996.

Schedule 1 revoked by the VAT (Amendment) (No 2) Regulations, SI 2012/1899 regs 3, 27 with effect from 15 October 2012.

[SCHEDULE 1A

Regulation 145F

Amendments—This Schedule inserted by the VAT (Amendment) (No 3) Regulations, SI 1996/1250 reg 16, with effect from 1 June 1996.

The fiscal warehousing record which is referred to in paragraph (3) of regulation 145F shall have the features and comply with the requirements set out below.

1

Goods in and out of a fiscal warehouse and its regime

(*a*) It shall accurately identify any eligible goods which enter or exit the fiscal warehouse, their nature and quantity, and the time and date when they so enter or exit.

(*b*) It shall accurately identify any goods which are not eligible goods and which enter or exit the fiscal warehouse for storage (other than goods which enter for purposes wholly incidental to such storage), their nature and quantity, and time and date when they so enter or exit.

(*c*) It shall accurately identify all eligible goods which are allocated to or removed from the fiscal warehousing regime associated with the relevant fiscal warehousekeeper, the time and date when the allocation or removal takes place, and the location of the eligible goods while they are allocated to the relevant regime.

(*d*) It shall accurately identify as "transferred goods" all eligible goods which are transferred directly from the fiscal warehousing regime to another fiscal warehousing regime, the time and date when the transfer starts, and the address of the fiscal warehouse to which the goods in question are transferred.

(*e*) It shall accurately identify as "transferred goods" all eligible goods which are transferred directly from the fiscal warehousing regime to corresponding arrangements in another member State under regulation 145H(2)(*b*), the date and time when the transfer starts, and the address of the place in the other member State to which the goods in question are transferred.

(*f*) It shall accurately identify as "transferred goods (by reason of export)" all eligible goods which are directly exported from the fiscal warehousing regime to a place outside the member States under regulation 145H(2)(*c*), the date and time when the movement of the goods which is directly associated with the export starts, and the address of the place outside the member States to which the goods in question are consigned.

2

Specified services performed in a fiscal warehouse

It shall accurately identify the nature of any services which are performed on or in relation to eligible goods while those goods are allocated to the relevant fiscal warehousing regime, the date when the services are performed, the particular eligible goods on or in relation to which they are performed, and the name, address and registration number (if any) of the supplier of those services.

3

Documents relating to transfers and specified services

(*a*) It shall include the written undertaking from the other fiscal warehousekeeper relating to a transfer made within the United Kingdom referred to in regulation 145G(2), the certificate from the other fiscal warehousekeeper confirming a transfer made within the United Kingdom referred to in regulation 145G(3)(*c*), and it shall relate them to the relevant transfer.

(*b*) It shall include the copy of the certificate relating to a transfer received by the relevant fiscal warehousekeeper from another fiscal warehousing regime within the United Kingdom referred to in regulation 145G(3)(*d*) and it shall relate that copy to the relevant allocation to his relevant fiscal warehousing regime.

(*c*) It shall include the document relating to the completion of a transfer to corresponding arrangements in another member State referred to in regulation 145H(4)(*b*) and it shall relate that document to the relevant transfer.

(*d*) It shall include the document relating to the completion of an export to a place outside the member States referred to in regulation 145H(4)(*c*) and it shall relate that document to the export in question.

4

Procedures where transfers are not completed

(*a*) It shall be adjusted to show a removal (and not a transfer) where the certificate of transfer within the United Kingdom referred to in regulation 145G(3)(*c*) is not received in time from the other fiscal warehousekeeper.

(*b*) It shall be adjusted to show a removal (and not a transfer) where the document referred to in articles 145H(4)(*b*) or 145H(4)(*c*) concerning goods which have been transferred to corresponding arrangements in another member State, or which have been exported to a place outside the member States, is not received in time.

(*c*) It shall evidence any notification made under regulation 145H(3)(*c*) to the person on whose instructions the goods were allowed to leave the fiscal warehouse.

5

Removals from a fiscal warehousing regime

(*a*) It shall identify the name and address of any person who at any time removes or causes the removal of any goods from the fiscal warehousing regime and that person's registration number if he is registered under the Act.

(*b*) It shall include a copy of the removal document issued by the Commissioners under regulation 145J(1) and shall relate it to the relevant removal.

6

Miscellaneous

(*a*) It shall incorporate any modifications to the features or requirements set out in paragraphs 1 to 5 above which the Commissioners may require in respect of the relevant fiscal warehousekeeper.

(*b*) A fiscal warehousekeeper may, with the prior agreement of the Commissioners, maintain a fiscal warehousing record in which any of the features or requirements set out in paragraphs 1 to 5 above are relaxed or dispensed with.

SCHEDULE 2

REVOCATIONS

Regulation 3(1)

Note—The revocations listed in this Schedule have been taken into effect.

1995/2999

VALUE ADDED TAX (REFUND OF TAX) (NO 2) ORDER 1995

Made by the Treasury under VATA 1994 s 33(3)

Made . . . . *22 November 1995*
Laid before the House of Commons . . . . *22 November 1995*
Coming into force . . . . *15 December 1995*

1 This Order may be cited as the Value Added Tax (Refund of Tax) (No 2) Order 1995 and shall come into force on 15th December 1995.

2 The following bodies are hereby specified for the purposes of section 33 of the Value Added Tax Act 1994:

A National Park authority (within the meaning of section 63 of the Environmental Act 1995)
A fire authority constituted by a combination scheme made under section 6 of the Fire Services Act 1947.

1996/1255

VALUE ADDED TAX (FISCAL WAREHOUSING) (TREATMENT OF TRANSACTIONS) ORDER 1996

Made by the Treasury under VATA 1994 s 5(3)

Made . . . . *8 May 1996*
Laid before the House of Commons . . . . *9 May 1996*
Coming into force . . . . *1 June 1996*

1 This Order may be cited as the Value Added Tax (Fiscal Warehousing) (Treatment of Transactions) Order 1996 and shall come into force on 1st June 1996.

2—(1) In this Order—
"eligible goods" has the meaning given by section 18B(6) of the Act;
"material time" has the meaning given by section 18F(1) of the Act;

VAT SIs

"supply" means a supply for the purposes of section 5(2)(*a*) of the Act; and,
"the Act" means the Value Added Tax Act 1994.

(2) In construing article 3(2) below any supply referred to in that article must be treated as taking place at the material time for that supply.

3—(1) A transaction fulfilling the description set out in paragraph (2) below shall be treated as a supply of goods and not as a supply of services.

(2) The description referred to in paragraph (1) above is that there is a supply (which is not a retail transaction) involving the transfer of any undivided share of property in eligible goods and either—

(*a*) that supply takes place while the goods in question are subject to a fiscal warehousing regime, or

(*b*) the transferee causes the goods in question to be placed in a fiscal warehousing regime after receiving that supply but before the supply, if any, which next occurs involving the transfer of any property in those goods.

1997/994

FREE ZONE (PORT OF SHEERNESS) (SUBSTITUTION OF RESPONSIBLE AUTHORITY) ORDER 1997

Made by the Treasury under CEMA 1979 s 100A(4)(b)

Made . . . . *19 March 1997*
Coming into force . . . . *1 April 1997*

1 This Order may be cited as the Free Zone (Port of Sheerness) (Substitution of Responsible Authority) Order 1997 and shall come into force on 1st April 1997.

2 The responsible authority for the area designated a free zone by article 2(1) of the Free Zone (Port of Sheerness) Designation Order 1994 shall, in substitution for the Medway Ports Limited who were appointed by article 3 of that Order, be Port of Sheerness Limited, whose Registered Office is at Maritime Centre, Port of Liverpool, Liverpool L21 1LA.

1997/1431

DISTRESS FOR CUSTOMS AND EXCISE DUTIES AND OTHER INDIRECT TAXES REGULATIONS 1997

Made by the Commissioners of Customs and Excise under FA 1997 ss 51(1)–(3)

Made . . . . *9 June 1997*
Laid before House of Commons . . . . *9 June 1997*
Coming into force . . . . *1 July 1997*

Revocation—These regulations revoked by the Tribunals, Courts and Enforcement Act 2007 (Consequential, Transitional and Saving Provision) Order 2014, SI 2014/600 art 7, Schedule Pt 2 to the extent that they apply to England and Wales only.

1 Citation and Commencement

These Regulations may be cited as The Distress for Customs and Excise Duties and Other Indirect Taxes Regulations 1997 and shall come into force on 1st July 1997.

2 Interpretation

(1) In these Regulations—

"authorised person" means a person acting under the authority of the Commissioners;
"costs" means any costs, charges, expenses and fees;
"officer" means, subject to section 8(2) of the Customs and Excise Management Act 1979, a person commissioned by the Commissioners pursuant to section 6(3) of that Act;
"person in default" means a person who has refused or neglected to pay any relevant tax due from him;
"relevant tax" means any of the following—

. . .

(*b*) value added tax;

. . .

"VAT Act" means the Value Added Tax Act 1994;
"walking possession agreement" means an agreement under which, in consideration of any goods and chattels distrained upon being allowed to remain in the custody of the person in default and of the delaying of their sale, that person—

(*a*) acknowledges that the goods and chattels specified in the agreement are under distraint and held in walking possession; and

(*b*) undertakes that, except with the consent of the Commissioners and subject to such conditions as they may impose, he will not remove or allow the removal of any of the specified goods and chattels from the place named in the agreement;

"1994 Act" means Part III of the Finance Act 1994;

"1996 Act" means Part III of the Finance Act 1996;

(2) Any reference in these Regulations to an amount of relevant tax includes a reference to any amount recoverable as if it were an amount of that relevant tax.

Note—Words omitted are not relevant for the purposes of VAT.

3 Revocations and transitional provisions

(1) The Regulations specified in Schedule 3 are hereby revoked to the extent set out there.

(2) Where a warrant is signed before the coming into force of these Regulations, these Regulations shall apply to anything done, after these Regulations come into force, in relation to that warrant or as a consequence of distress being levied.

4 Levying distress

(1) Subject to regulation 5 below, if upon written demand a person neglects or refuses to pay any relevant tax due from him an officer may levy distress on the goods and chattels of that person and by warrant signed by him direct any authorised person to levy such distress.

(2) Where a warrant has been signed, distress shall be levied by or under the direction of, and in the presence of, the authorised person.

(3) Subject to regulation 6 below, distress may be levied on any goods and chattels located at any place whatever including on a public highway.

5 Restrictions on levying distress

(1) . . .

(2) Where an amount of VAT is due under section 73(9) of the VAT Act no distress shall be levied before expiry of the last day on which the person who is liable to pay the amount concerned is required, by rules made under paragraph 9 of Schedule 12 to the VAT Act, to serve a notice of appeal with respect to that amount.

Note—Words omitted are not relevant for the purposes of VAT.

6 Goods and chattels not subject to levy

No distress shall be levied on any goods and chattels mentioned in Schedule 1 which at the time of levy are located in a place and used for a purpose mentioned in that Schedule.

7 Times for levying distress

(1) Subject to paragraph (2) below, a levy of distress shall commence only during the period between eight o'clock in the morning and eight o'clock at night on any day of the week but it may be continued thereafter outside that period until the levy is completed.

(2) Where a person holds himself out as conducting any profession, trade or business during hours which are partly within and partly outside, or wholly outside the period mentioned in paragraph (1) above, a levy of distress may be commenced at any time during that period or during the hours of any day in which he holds himself out as conducting that profession, trade or business and it may be continued thereafter outside that period or those hours until the levy is completed.

8 Costs

(1) A person in respect of whose goods and chattels a warrant has been signed shall be liable to pay to an officer or authorised person all costs, in connection with anything done under these Regulations described in column 1 of Schedule 2, as determined in accordance with column 2 of that Schedule.

(2) An authorised person may, after deducting and accounting for the amount of relevant tax to the Commissioners, retain costs from any amount received.

9 Sale

If any person upon whose goods and chattels distress has been levied does not pay the amount of relevant tax due together with costs within 5 days of a levy, an officer or authorised person may sell the distress for payment of the amount of relevant tax and costs; and the officer or authorised person, after deducting and retaining the amount of relevant tax and costs shall restore any surplus to the owner of the goods upon which distress was levied.

10 Disputes as to costs

(1) In the case of any dispute as to costs, the amount of those costs shall be taxed by a district judge of the county court of the district where the distress was levied, and he may make such order as he thinks fit as to the costs of the taxation.

(2) In the application of this regulation to Northern Ireland, in the case of any dispute as to costs, the amount of those costs shall be taxed in the same manner as costs in equity suits or proceedings in the county court in Northern Ireland.

SCHEDULE 1

GOODS AND CHATTELS NOT SUBJECT TO LEVY

Regulation 6

1 Any of the following goods and chattels which are located in a dwelling house at which distress is being levied and are reasonably required for the domestic needs of any person residing in that dwelling house—

(*a*) beds and bedding;
(*b*) household linen;
(*c*) chairs and settees;
(*d*) tables;
(*e*) food;
(*f*) lights and light fittings;
(*g*) heating appliances;
(*h*) curtains;
(*i*) floor coverings;
(*j*) furniture, equipment and utensils used for cooking, storing or eating food;
(*k*) refrigerators;
(*l*) articles used for cleaning, mending, or pressing clothes;
(*m*) articles used for cleaning the home;
(*n*) furniture used for storing—
 (i) clothing, bedding or household linen;
 (ii) articles used for cleaning the home;
 (iii) utensils used for cooking or eating food;
(*o*) articles used for safety in the home;
(*p*) toys for the use of any child within the household;
(*q*) medical aids and medical equipment.

2 Any of the following items which are located in premises used for the purposes of any profession, trade or business—

(*a*) fire fighting equipment for use on the premises;
(*b*) medical aids and medical equipment for use on the premises.

SCHEDULE 2

SCALE OF COSTS

Regulation 8(1)

Matter	*Costs*
(1)	*(2)*
1 For attending to levy distress where payment is made of an amount of relevant tax due and distress is not levied:	£12·50.
2 For levying distress—	
(*a*) where an amount of relevant tax demanded and due does not exceed £100:	£12·50.
(*b*) where an amount of relevant tax demanded and due exceeds £100:	12½% on the first £100,
	4% on the next £400,
	2½% on the next £1,500,
	1% on the next £8,000,
	¼% on any additional sum.
3 For taking possession of distrained goods—	
(*a*) where a person remains in physical possession of goods at the place where distress was levied (the person to provide his own food and lodgings):	£4·50 per day.
(*b*) where possession is taken under a walking possession agreement:	£7·00.
4 For appraising goods upon which distress has been levied:	Reasonable costs of appraisement.

5 For arranging removal and storage of goods upon which distress has been levied:	Reasonable costs of arrangement.
6 For removing and storing goods upon which distress has been levied:	Reasonable costs of removal and storage.
7 For advertising the sale of goods upon which distress has been levied:	Reasonable costs of advertising.
8 For selling the distress—	
(*a*) where a sale by auction is held at the auctioneer's premises:	15% of the sum realised.
(*b*) where a sale by auction is held elsewhere:	$7^1/_2$% of the sum realised and auctioneer's reasonable costs.
(*c*) where a sale by other means is undertaken:	$7^1/_2$% of the sum realised and reasonable costs.

9 In addition to any amount specified in this scale in respect of the supply of goods or services on which value added tax is chargeable there may be added a sum equivalent to value added tax at the appropriate rate on that amount.

1997/1523

VALUE ADDED TAX (REVERSE CHARGE) (ANTI-AVOIDANCE) ORDER 1997

Made by the Treasury under VATA 1994 s 8(5), (7)–(8)

Made . . . . *30 June 1997*
Laid before the House of Commons . . . . *30 June 1997*
Coming into force in accordance with . . . . *article 1*

1 Citation and commencement

This Order may be cited as the Value Added Tax (Reverse Charge) (Anti-avoidance) Order 1997 and shall apply in relation to any services performed on or after 1st July 1997.

2 Interpretation

In this Order—

"the Act" means the Value Added Tax Act 1994;

"the Regulations" means the Value Added Tax Regulations 1995;

"relevant telecommunications services" means services within the description which by virtue of this Order is inserted as paragraph 7A of Schedule 5 to the Act;

"relevant period" means such part of a period over which relevant telecommunications services are performed as falls after 30th June 1997;

"a supply of relevant telecommunications services by virtue of a right" means a supply of relevant telecommunications services performed on or after 1st July 1997 which is made by virtue of the exercise of a right which had been granted before 1st July 1997.

3 Insertion of telecommunications services into Schedule 5 to the Act

[*Amends VATA 1994 Sch 5*]

4 Modification of the effect of regulation 82 of the Regulations

(1) Where a supply of relevant telecommunications services is treated as if it were a taxable supply by virtue of section 8(1) or 43(2B) of the Act, the effect of regulation 82 of the Regulations shall be modified as follows—

(*a*) it shall have no effect in relation to relevant telecommunications services which are performed or which, by virtue of article 10 below, are treated as performed before 1st July 1997;

(*b*) it shall have no effect in relation to relevant telecommunications services which are wholly chargeable to VAT in another member State;

(*c*) where—

(i) relevant telecommunications services are performed on or after 1st July 1997; and

(ii) a payment in respect of those services has been made before that date,

it shall have effect in relation to those services as if the payment was made on 1st July 1997.

(2) Where the circumstances mentioned in paragraph (3) below apply—

(*a*) relevant telecommunications services which are paid for on or after 1st July 1997 shall be treated as being supplied only to the extent covered by the lower of—

(i) so much of the payment as exceeds the part of the payment for the supply by reference to which VAT is chargeable in another member State; and

(ii) so much of the payment as is properly attributable to the relevant period; and

(*b*) relevant telecommunications services which are supplied for a consideration which is not in money shall be treated as being supplied only to the extent covered by the lower of—

(i) so much of the consideration as exceeds the part of the consideration for the supply by reference to which VAT is chargeable in another member State; and

(ii) so much of the consideration as is properly attributable to the relevant period.

(3) The circumstances referred to in paragraph (2) above and article 7 below are that—

(*a*) relevant telecommunications services are performed on or after 1st July 1997; and

(*b*) either—

(i) the services are chargeable to VAT in part in another member State; or

(ii) the period over which the services are performed commenced before 1st July 1997.

5 Treatment of a right to relevant telecommunications services

(1) Subject to article 6 below, where the circumstances mentioned in article 8(3) below apply the time at which and extent to which a supply of relevant telecommunications services by virtue of a right is to be treated as made shall be determined as if the supply of relevant telecommunications services and the right were a single supply of which the supply of the right and each of those supplies constituted different parts.

(2) Without prejudice to the generality of paragraph (1) above, the payment for a right to relevant telecommunications services or the consideration for that right, as the case may be, shall, for the purposes of article 4 above, be treated as if it were the payment or the consideration for the relevant telecommunications services supplied by virtue of the right.

6 Rights not exercised before 1st July 1997

Where—

(*a*) the circumstances mentioned in article 8(3) below apply;

(*b*) a right to relevant telecommunications services is exercised on or after 1st July 1997,

(*c*) the consideration for the right was in money; and

(*d*) a payment in respect of the right was made before 1st July 1997,

the payment shall be deemed to have been made at the time of the exercise of the right.

7 Value of supply of relevant telecommunications services

Where the circumstances mentioned in article 4(3) above apply, the effect of paragraph 8 of Schedule 6 to the Act shall be modified so that the value of the supply treated as made shall be taken—

(*a*) in a case where the consideration for which the relevant telecommunications services were in fact supplied was a consideration in money, to be such amount as is equal to the lower of—

(i) so much of the consideration as exceeds the part of the consideration for the supply by reference to which VAT is chargeable in another member State; and

(ii) so much of the consideration as is properly attributable to the relevant period; and

(*b*) in a case where that consideration did not consist or not wholly consist of money, to be such amount in money as is equivalent to the lower of—

(i) so much of the consideration as exceeds the part of the consideration for the supply by reference to which VAT is chargeable in another member State; and

(ii) so much of the consideration as is properly attributable to the relevant period.

8 Value of relevant telecommunications services supplied by virtue of a right

(1) For the purposes of paragraph 8 of Schedule 6 to the Act and article 7 above, where the circumstances mentioned in paragraph (3) below apply, the consideration for which the relevant telecommunications services were in fact supplied shall be deemed to be the higher of—

(*a*) the consideration for which the services were in fact received; and

(*b*) the lower of—

(i) the open market value of the relevant telecommunications services which were in fact supplied which shall be valued as if they had not been supplied by virtue of the right; and

(ii) the amount determined in accordance with paragraph (2) below.

(2) The amount referred to in paragraph (1)(*b*)(ii) above is the sum of—

(*a*) the consideration for which the relevant telecommunications services were in fact supplied; and

(*b*) the consideration for the right to those services,

reduced by the open market value of the right to the relevant telecommunications services which shall be valued as if the right was a right to those services to be supplied at the open market value for those services determined in accordance with paragraph (1)(b)(i) above.

(3) The circumstances referred to in paragraph (1) above are that—

(*a*) there is a supply of relevant telecommunications services by virtue of a right; and (*b*) the consideration for the relevant telecommunications services which were in fact supplied is less than the open market value of those services which shall be valued as if they had not been supplied by virtue of the right.

9 Meaning of a right to relevant telecommunications services

References in this Order to a right to relevant telecommunications services include references to any right, option or priority with respect to a supply of relevant telecommunications services, and to any interest deriving from any right to relevant telecommunications services.

10 Time when relevant telecommunications services are treated as performed

(1) For the purposes of this Order relevant telecommunications services which are supplied for a consideration the whole or part of which is determined or payable periodically or from time to time or in respect of which statements or invoices are issued periodically or from time to time, shall be treated as performed on the expiration of the period to which a payment, statement or invoice (as the case may be) relates.

(2) Where paragraph (1) above applies the services shall be treated as performed to the extent covered by the payment, statement or invoice.

1997/2558

VALUE ADDED TAX (REFUND OF TAX) ORDER 1997

Made by the Treasury under VATA 1994 s 33(3)

Made . . . . *27 October 1997*
Laid before the House of Commons . . . . *28 October 1997*
Coming into force . . . . *1 December 1997*

1 This Order may be cited as the Value Added Tax (Refund of Tax) Order 1997 and shall come into force on 1 December 1997.

2 The following bodies are hereby specified for the purposes of section 33 of the Value Added Tax Act 1994—

charter trustees established by an Order made under section 17 of the Local Government Act 1992 or by any other statutory instrument made under Part II of that Act.

1998/1461

AIR PASSENGER DUTY AND OTHER INDIRECT TAXES (INTEREST RATE) REGULATIONS 1998

Made by the Treasury under FA 1996 s 197

Made . . . . *15 June 1998*
Laid before the House of Commons . . . . *15 June 1998*
Coming into force . . . . *6 July 1998*

1 Citation and commencement

These Regulations may be cited as the Air Passenger Duty and Other Indirect Taxes (Interest Rate) Regulations 1998 and shall come into force on 6th July 1998.

2 Interpretation

(1) In these Regulations unless the context otherwise requires—

"established rate" means—

(*a*) on the coming into force of these Regulations, [6 per cent][1] per annum; and

(*b*) in relation to any day after the first reference day after the coming into force of these Regulations, the reference rate found on the immediately preceding reference day;

"operative day" means the [[twelfth][3] working day after the reference day][2];

"reference day" means the [. . .[3] working day following the day on which the most recent meeting of the Monetary Policy Committee of the Bank of England took place][2];

"section 197" means section 197 of the Finance Act 1996;

the "relevant enactments" are those referred to in regulations 4(1) and 5(1) below;

"working day" means any day other than a non-business day within the meaning of section 92 of the Bills of Exchange Act 1882.

[(2) In these Regulations the reference rate found on a reference date is the official bank rate determined by the most recent meeting of the Monetary Policy Committee of the Bank of England.][3]

Amendments—[1] Words substituted by the Air Passenger Duty and Other Indirect Taxes (Interest Rate) (Amendment) Regulations, SI 2000/631 regs 2, 3 with effect from 1 April 2000.

[2] In para (1), in definition of "operative day" words substituted for words "sixth day of each month", and in definition of "reference day" words substituted for words "twelfth working day before the next operative day" by the Taxes and Duties (Interest Rate) (Amendment) Regulations, SI 2008/3234 reg 3(1), (2) with effect from 7 January 2009.

[3] In para (1), in definition of "operative day" word substituted for word "eleventh" and in definition of "reference day", word "second" revoked, and para (2) substituted, by the Taxes and Duties (Interest Rate) (Amendment) Regulations, SI 2009/2032 regs 15, 16 with effect from 12 August 2009.

2A [Applicable rate of interest equal to zero

In determining the rate of interest applicable under section 197 for the purposes of any enactments referred to in these Regulations, if the result is less than zero the rate shall be treated as zero for those purposes.[2]][1]

Amendments—[1] Regulation 2A inserted by the Taxes and Duties (Interest Rate) (Amendment) Regulations, SI 2008/3234 reg 3(1), (3) with effect from 7 January 2009.

[2] This regulation revoked by the Taxes and Duties (Interest Rate) (Amendment) Regulations, SI 2009/2032 regs 15, 17 with effect from 12 August 2009.

3 The Air Passenger Duty and Other Indirect Taxes (Interest Rate) Regulations 1997 are hereby revoked.

4 [Applicable rate of interest payable to the Commissioners of Customs and Excise in connection with excise duties, insurance premium tax, VAT, landfill tax, and customs duty

(1) For the purposes of—

(*a*) [section 60(8) of, and paragraphs 7 and 8(1) of Schedule 6 to,][4] the Finance Act 1994,

(*b*) paragraph 21 of Schedule 7 to that Act,

(*c*) [sections 74 and 85A(3)][4] of the Value Added Tax Act 1994,

(*d*) [section 56(5) of and][4] paragraph 26 of Schedule 5 to the Finance Act 1996,

(*e*) paragraph 17 of Schedule 5 to the Finance Act 1997, . . . [2]

(*f*) section 126 of the Finance Act 1999, [. . .[3]

(*g*) paragraphs 41(2)(*f*), 70(1)(*b*)[, 81(3) and 123(6)][3] of Schedule 6 to the Finance Act 2000 (climate change levy),][2] [and

(*h*) sections 25(2)(*f*)[, 30(3)(f) and 42(6)][4] of, and paragraphs 6 and 8(3)(*a*) of Schedule 5 to, the Finance Act 2001 (aggregates levy),][3]

the rate applicable under section 197 shall, subject to paragraph (2) below, be 8.5 per cent per annum.

(2) Where, on any reference day after the coming into force of these Regulations, the reference rate found on that day differs from the established rate, the rate applicable under section 197 of the Finance Act 1996 for the purposes of the enactments referred to in paragraph (1) above shall, from the next operative day, be the percentage per annum determined in accordance with the formula specified in paragraph (3) below.

(3) The formula specified in this paragraph is—

$$RR + 2.5,$$

where RR is the reference rate referred to in paragraph (2) above.][1]

[(4) With effect from 1st November 2001 the rate of interest prescribed in paragraph (1) above for the purposes of paragraph 17 of Schedule 5 to the Finance Act 1997 also applies in the application of that paragraph to assessments under paragraph 14 or 15 of that Schedule as amended by paragraph 19 of Schedule 3 to the Finance Act 2001.][2]

Amendments—[1] This regulation substituted by the Air Passenger Duty and Other Indirect Taxes (Interest Rate) (Amendment) Regulations, SI 2000/631 regs 2, 4 with effect from 1 April 2000.

[2] Word "and" in para (1)(*e*) revoked, and paras (1)(*g*) and (4) added by the Air Passenger Duty and Other Indirect Taxes (Interest Rate) (Amendment) Regulations, SI 2001/3337 regs 1, 2 with effect from 1 November 2001.

[3] The word "and" in para (1)(*f*) revoked, and para (1)(*h*) inserted, by the Air Passenger Duty and Other Indirect Taxes (Interest Rate) (Amendment) Regulations, SI 2003/230 regs 2, 3 with effect from 1 April 2003.

[4] In para (1), in sub-para (a) words substituted for words "paragraph 7 of Schedule 6 to", in sub-para (c) words substituted for words "section 74", in sub-para (d) words inserted, in sub-para (g) words substituted for words "and 81(3)", and in sub-para (h) words substituted for words "and 30(3)(f)", by the Transfer of Tribunal Functions and Revenue and Customs Appeals Order, SI 2009/56 art 3, Sch 2 paras 38, 39 with effect from 1 April 2009.

5 [Applicable rate of interest payable by the Commissioners of Customs and Excise in connection with air passenger duty, insurance premium tax, VAT, landfill tax, and customs duty

(1) For the purposes of—

(*a*) [Parts 2 and 3 of Schedule 3 to the Finance Act 2001 (interest payable on repayments etc)][2],

(*b*) paragraph 22 of Schedule 7 to that Act,

[(*ba*) section 60(6) of the Finance Act 1994,][4]

(*c*) [sections 78 and 85A(2)][4] of the Value Added Tax Act 1994,

(*d*) [section 56(3) and (4) of and][4] paragraph 29 of Schedule 5 to the Finance Act 1996, . . . [2]

(*e*) section 127 of the Finance Act 1999, [. . .[3]

(*f*) paragraphs 62(3)(*f*)[, 66, 123(4) and 123(5)][4] of Schedule 6 to the Finance Act 2000 (climate change levy)][2][, and

(*g*) [section 42(4) and (5) of and][4] paragraphs 2 and 6(1)(*b*) of Schedule 8 to the Finance Act 2001 (aggregates levy),][3]

the rate applicable under section 197 of the Finance Act 1996 shall be 5 per cent per annum.

(2) Where, on a reference day after the coming into force of these Regulations, the reference rate found on that date differs from the established rate, the rate applicable under section 197 for the purposes of the enactments referred to in paragraph (1) above shall, from the next operative day, be the [higher of—

(*a*) 0.5% per annum, and

(*b*) the percentage per annum found by applying the formula specified in paragraph (3).][5]

[(3) The formula specified in this paragraph is—

$$RR - 1,$$

where RR is the reference rate referred to in paragraph (2).][5]][1]

Amendments—[1] This regulation substituted by the Air Passenger Duty and Other Indirect Taxes (Interest Rate) (Amendment) Regulations, SI 2000/631 regs 2, 5 with effect from 1 April 2000.

[2] In para (1), words in sub-para (*a*) substituted, word "and" in sub-para (*d*) revoked, and sub-para (*f*) added by the Air Passenger Duty and Other Indirect Taxes (Interest Rate) (Amendment) Regulations, SI 2001/3337 regs 1, 3 with effect from 1 November 2001.

[3] Word "and" in para (1)(*e*) revoked, and para (1)(*g*) inserted, by the Air Passenger Duty and Other Indirect Taxes (Interest Rate) (Amendment) Regulations, SI 2003/230 regs 2, 4 with effect from 1 April 2003.

[4] In para (1), sub-para (*ba*) inserted, in sub-para (*c*) words substituted for words "section 78", in sub-paras (*d*), (*g*) words inserted, and in sub-para (*f*) words substituted for words "and 66", by the Transfer of Tribunal Functions and Revenue and Customs Appeals Order, SI 2009/56 art 3, Sch 2 paras 38, 40 with effect from 1 April 2009.

[5] In para (2), words substituted, and para (3) substituted, by the Taxes and Duties (Interest Rate) (Amendment) Regulations, SI 2009/2032 regs 15, 17 with effect from 12 August 2009.

6 Effect of change in applicable rate

Where the rate applicable under section 197 for the purposes of any of the relevant enactments changes on an operative day by virtue of these Regulations, that change shall have effect for periods beginning on or after the operative day in relation to interest running from before that day as well as in relation to interest running from, or from after that day.

7 Where the rate applicable under section 197 for the purposes of any of the relevant enactments changes on an operative day by virtue of these Regulations, the rate in force immediately prior to any change shall continue to have effect for periods immediately prior to the change and so on in the case of any number of successive changes.

8 Applicable rate of interest prior to the coming into force of these Regulations

The rate applicable under section 197 for interest running from before the date these Regulations come into force in relation to periods prior to that date shall be specified for the relevant enactments in the following Tables—

Table 1
Paragraph 7 of Schedule 6 to the Finance Act 1994

Interest for any period	*Rate*
From 1st November 1994 and before 6th February 1996	5·5 per cent
After 5th February 1996 and before 6th July 1998	6·25 per cent

Table 2
Paragraph 21 of Schedule 7 to the Finance Act 1994

Interest for any period	*Rate*
From 1st October 1994 and before 6th February 1996	5·5 per cent
After 5th February 1996 and before 6th July 1998	6·25 per cent

Table 3
Section 74 of the Value Added Tax Act 1994

Interest for any period	*Rate*
from 1st April 1990 and before 6th November 1990	13 per cent

VAT SIs

after 5th November 1990 and before 6th March 1991	12·25 per cent
after 5th March 1991 and before 6th May 1991	11·5 per cent
after 5th May 1991 and before 6th July 1991	10·75 per cent
after 5th July 1991 and before 6th October 1991	10 per cent
after 5th October 1991 and before 6th November 1992	9·25 per cent
after 5th November 1992 and before 6th December 1992	7·75 per cent
after 5th December 1992 and before 6th March 1993	7 per cent
after 5th March 1993 and before 6th January 1994	6·25 per cent
after 5th January 1994 and before 6th October 1994	5·5 per cent
after 5th October 1994 and before 6th March 1995	6·25 per cent
after 5th March 1995 and before 6th February 1996	7 per cent
after 5th February 1996 and before 6th July 1998	6·25 per cent

Table 4
Paragraph 26 of Schedule 5 to the Finance Act 1996

Interest for any period	*Rate*
from 1st April 1997 and before 6th July 1998	6·25 per cent

Table 5
Paragraph 9 of Schedule 6 to the Finance Act 1994

Interest for any period	*Rate*
from 1st November 1994 and before 1st April 1997	8 per cent
after 31st March 1997 and before 6th July 1998	6 per cent

Table 6
Paragraph 22 of Schedule 7 to the Finance Act 1994

Interest for any period	*Rate*
after 1st October 1994 and before 1st April 1997	8 per cent
after 31st March 1997 and before 6th July 1998	6 per cent

Table 7
Section 78 of the Value Added Tax Act 1994

Interest for any period	*Rate*
from 1st April 1973 and before 1st March 1974	8 per cent
after 28th February 1974 and before 1st February 1977	9 per cent
after 31st January 1977 and before 1st March 1979	10 per cent
after 28th February 1979 and before 1st January 1980	12·5 per cent
after 31st December 1979 and before 1st January 1981	15 per cent
after 31st December 1980 and before 1st December 1981	12·5 per cent
after 30th November 1981 and before 1st March 1982	15 per cent
after 28th February 1982 and before 1st July 1982	14 per cent
after 30th June 1982 and before 1st April 1983	13 per cent
after 31st March 1983 and before 1st April 1984	12·5 per cent
after 31st March 1984 and before 1st August 1986	12 per cent
after 31st July 1986 and before 1st January 1987	11·5 per cent
after 31st December 1986 and before 1st April 1987	12·25 per cent
after 31st March 1987 and before 1st November 1987	11·75 per cent
after 31st October 1987 and before 1st December 1987	11·25 per cent

after 30th November 1987 and before 1st May 1988	11 per cent
after 30th April 1988 and before 1st August 1988	9·5 per cent
after 31st July 1988 and before 1st November 1988	11 per cent
after 31st October 1988 and before 1st January 1989	12·25 per cent
after 31st December 1988 and before 1st November 1989	13 per cent
after 31st October 1989 and before 1st April 1991	14·25 per cent
after 31st March 1991 and before [16th October 1991][1]	12 per cent
after 15th October 1991 and before 6th February 1993	10·25 per cent
aftcr 5th February 1993 and before 1st April 1997	8 per cent
after 31st March 1997 and before 6th July 1998	6 per cent

Table 8
Paragraph 29 of Schedule 5 to the Finance Act 1996

Interest for any period	*Rate*
from 1st April 1997 and before 6th July 1998	6 per cent

Amendments—

[1] Words in square brackets in Table 7 substituted by the Air Passenger Duty and Other Indirect Taxes (Interest Rate) (Amendment) Regulations, SI 2000/631 regs 2, 6 with effect from 1 April 2000.

1999/2076

VALUE ADDED TAX (REFUND OF TAX) ORDER 1999

Made by the Treasury under VATA 1994 s 33(3)

Made . . . . *21 July 1999*
Laid before the House of Commons . . . . *22 July 1999*
Coming into force . . . . *1 September 1999*

Commentary—*De Voil Indirect Tax Service* **V6.154, V6.155.**

1 This Order may be cited as the Value Added Tax (Refund of Tax) Order 1999 and shall come into force on 1st September 1999.

2 The Broads Authority (a body corporate established by section 1 of the Norfolk and Suffolk Broads Act 1988) is hereby specified for the purposes of section 33 of the Value Added Tax Act 1994.

1999/3115

VALUE ADDED TAX (IMPORTATION OF INVESTMENT GOLD) RELIEF ORDER 1999

Made by the Treasury under VATA 1994 s 37(1) and FA 1999 s 13(3) and (4)

Made . . . . *19 November 1999*
Laid before the House of Commons . . . . *22 November 1999*
Coming into force . . . . *1 January 2000*

1 This Order may be cited as the Value Added Tax (Importation of Investment Gold) Relief Order 1999 and shall come into force on 1st January 2000.

2 In this Order—

"Investment gold" has the same meaning as in Group 15 of Schedule 9 to the Value Added Tax Act 1994.

3 VAT shall not be chargeable on the importation of investment gold from places outside the member States.

1999/3116

VALUE ADDED TAX (INVESTMENT GOLD) ORDER 1999

Made by the Treasury under VATA 1994 ss 31(2), 55(6) and 96(9) and FA 1999 s 13(2) and (4)

Made . . . .*19 November 1999*
Laid before the House of Commons . . . .*22 November 1999*
Coming into force . . . .*1 January 2000*

Customs and Excise Notices—Notice 701/21: Gold.

1 Citation, commencement and interpretation

(1) This Order may be cited as the Value Added Tax (Investment Gold) Order 1999 and shall come into force on 1st January 2000 and shall have effect in relation to supplies made on or after that date.

(2) In this Order—

"the Commissioners" means the Commissioners of Customs and Excise;

"the Act" means the Value Added Tax Act 1994.

"relevant supply" means a supply of investment gold within the meaning of item 1 or 2 of Group 15 of Schedule 9 to the Act made by a taxable person, to another taxable person and "relevant supplies" shall be construed accordingly.

2 Exemption for investment gold

(*Amends the Value Added Tax Act 1994, Sch 9.*)

3 Election to waive exemption

(1) Subject to paragraphs (2), (6), (7) and (8) below, where an election under this paragraph has effect in relation to a relevant supply by a taxable person who produces or transforms investment gold, which supply would (apart from this paragraph) fall within item 1 or 2 of Group 15 of Schedule 9 to the Act, the supply shall not fall within that Group.

(2) An election under paragraph (1) above (or an election having the like effect) or an election under paragraph (5) below shall apply in respect of an individual relevant supply made and shall have effect on or after the day from which the election is made.

(3) Subject to complying with such conditions as the Commissioners may direct in notices published by them for the purposes of this Order, the Commissioners may permit a taxable person to make elections in respect of relevant supplies by him of a description falling within paragraph (4) below having the like effect to an election under paragraph (1) above.

(4) The supplies referred to in paragraph (3) above are those relevant supplies where the investment gold supplied falls within the description in Note (1)(*a*) contained in Group 15 of Schedule 9 to the Act, made by a taxable person who in the normal course of his business makes supplies of gold for industrial purposes.

(5) Subject to paragraphs (6) to (8) below, where a taxable person has made a relevant supply in respect of which an election under paragraph (1) above (or an election having the like effect) has been made, the supply of services by his agent directly linked to the relevant supply and which supply of services would (apart from this paragraph) fall within item 3 of Group 15 of Schedule 9 to the Act shall, if the agent so elects, not fall within that Group.

(6) A person making a relevant supply in respect of which an election to waive exemption under this article has been made shall comply with such conditions as the Commissioners may specify in notices published by them for the purposes of this Order including conditions relating to the notification of an election.

(7) An election made under paragraph (1) above (or an election having the like effect) and an election made under paragraph (5) above shall be irrevocable.

(8) Where the Commissioners have permitted a person to make elections under paragraph (3) above, they may withdraw that permission where it appears to them to be necessary to do so for the protection of the revenue and accordingly the permission shall cease to have effect from such date as may be specified in a notification from the Commissioners.

4 Customers to account for tax on supplies of investment gold

Section 55(1) to (4) of the Act shall apply to all supplies of a description which but for an election made under article 3 above would fall within item 1 or 2 of Group 15 of Schedule 9 to the Act.

1999/3121

VALUE ADDED TAX (INPUT TAX) (SPECIFIED SUPPLIES) ORDER 1999

Made by the Treasury under VATA 1994 s 26(2)(c)

Made . . . .*19 November 1999*

Laid before the House of Commons ....22 November 1999
Coming into force ....1 January 2000

1 This Order may be cited as the Value Added Tax (Input Tax) (Specified Supplies) Order 1999 and shall come into force on 1st January 2000 and shall have effect in relation to supplies made on or after that date.

2 The supplies described in articles 3 and 4 below are hereby specified for the purposes of section 26(2)(*c*) of the Value Added Tax Act 1994.

3 Services—

(*a*) which are supplied to a person who belongs outside the member States;
(*b*) which are directly linked to the export of goods to a place outside the member States; or
(*c*) which consist of the provision of intermediary services within the meaning of item 4 of Group 2, or item 5 of Group 5, of Schedule 9 to the Value Added Tax Act 1994 in relation to any transaction specified in paragraph (*a*) or (*b*) above,

provided the supply is exempt, or would have been exempt if made in the United Kingdom, by virtue of any item of Group 2, or any of items 1 to 6 and item 8 of Group 5, of Schedule 9 to the Value Added Tax Act 1994.

4 Supplies made either in or outside the United Kingdom which fall, or would fall, within item 1 or 2 of Group 15 of Schedule 9 to the Value Added Tax Act 1994 (investment gold).

5 (Revokes the Value Added Tax (Input Tax) (Specified Supplies) Order 1992, SI 1992/3123.)

VAT SIs

2000/1046

VALUE ADDED TAX (REFUND OF TAX) ORDER 2000

Made by the Treasury under VATA 1994 s 33(3)

Made ....12 April 2000
Laid before the House of Commons ....13 April 2000
Coming into force ....8 May 2000

Commentary—*De Voil Indirect Tax Service* **V6.154, V6.155**.

1 This Order may be cited as the Value Added Tax (Refund of Tax) Order 2000 and shall come into force on 8th May 2000.

2 The Greater London Authority (a body corporate established by section 1 of the Greater London Authority Act 1999) is specified for the purposes of section 33 of the Value Added Tax Act 1994.

2000/1515

VALUE ADDED TAX (REFUND OF TAX) (NO 2) ORDER 2000

Made by the Treasury under VATA 1994 s 33(3)

Made ....7 June 2000
Laid before the House of Commons ....8 June 2000
Coming into force ....3 July 2000

Commentary—*De Voil Indirect Tax Service* **V6.162**.

1 This Order may be cited as the Value Added Tax (Refund of Tax) (No 2) Order 2000 and shall come into force on 3rd July 2000.

2 The London Fire and Emergency Planning Authority (the body corporate reconstituted by section 328 of, and Schedule 28 to, the Greater London Authority Act 1999) is specified for the purposes of section 33 of the Value Added Tax Act 1994.

2000/1672

VALUE ADDED TAX (REFUND OF TAX) (NO 3) ORDER 2000

Made by the Treasury under VATA 1994 s 33(3)

Made ....26 June 2000
Laid before the House of Commons ....26 June 2000

Coming into force . . . .*17 July 2000*

Commentary—*De Voil Indirect Tax Service* **V6.162**.

1 This Order may be cited as the Value Added Tax (Refund of Tax) (No 3) Order 2000 and shall come into force on 17th July 2000.

2 Transport for London (the body corporate established by section 154 of the Greater London Authority Act 1999) is specified for the purposes of section 33 of the Value Added Tax Act 1994.

2001/759

VALUE ADDED TAX (ELECTRONIC COMMUNICATIONS) (INCENTIVES) REGULATIONS 2001

Made by the Commissioners of Customs and Excise under FA 2000 Sch 38

Made . . . .*7 March 2001*
Laid before the House of Commons . . . .*8 March 2001*
Coming into force . . . .*1 April 2001*

Amendment—These regulations revoked by the VAT (Amendment) (No 3) Regulations, SI 2004/1675 reg 1(1), (2) with effect from 22 July 2004.

2001/2879

VALUE ADDED TAX (REFUND OF TAX TO MUSEUMS AND GALLERIES) ORDER 2001

Made by the Treasury under VATA 1994 s 33A(9)

Made . . . .*9 August 2001*
Laid before the House of Commons . . . .*9 August 2001*
Coming into force . . . .*1 September 2001*

Commentary—*De Voil Indirect Tax Service* **V5.162**.

1 This Order may be cited as the Value Added Tax (Refund of Tax to Museums and Galleries) Order 2001 and comes into force on 1st September 2001.

2 Section 33A of the Value Added Tax Act 1994 applies to the bodies listed in column 1 of the Schedule to this Order.

3 The museums and galleries listed in column 2 of the Schedule are, for the purposes of section 33A of the Value Added Tax Act 1994, relevant museums and galleries in relation to the bodies listed opposite them in the Schedule.

4 Where column 3 of the Schedule indicates a particular date, in the case of the museum or gallery to be found opposite that date, section 33A of the Value Added Tax Act 1994 shall apply as if, in subsection (1)(*c*) of that section, that date were substituted for 1st April 2001.

SCHEDULE

Articles 2, 3 and 4

Column 1	*Column 2*	*Column 3*
Body	*Relevant museums and galleries*	*Later date to be substituted for 1st April 2001*
British Museum	British Museum Great Russell Street London WC1B 3DG	
Imperial War Museum	Imperial War Museum Lambeth Road London SE1 6HZ	1st December 2001
	IWM North Trafford Wharf Road Trafford Park	1st April 2002

	Manchester M17 1TZ	
The National Gallery	The National Gallery Trafalgar Square London WC2N 5ND	
National Maritime Museum	National Maritime Museum	1st December 2001
	[The Royal Observatory Astronomy Centre Blackheath Avenue London SE10 8JX	3 March 2008][5]
	[The Queen's House Romney Road London SE10 9NF	3 March 2008][5]
National Museums and Galleries on Merseyside	Walker Art Gallery William Brown Street Liverpool L3 8EL	1st December 2001
	[World Museum Liverpool][3] William Brown Street Liverpool L3 8EN	1st December 2001
	Merseyside Maritime Museum Albert Dock Liverpool L3 4AQ	1st December 2001
	[Museum of Liverpool][3] Pier Head Liverpool L3 1PZ	1st December 2001
	The Lady Lever Art Gallery Port Sunlight Village Bebington Wirral Merseyside [CH62 5EQ][3]	1st December 2001
	Sudley House Mossley Hill Road Liverpool L18 8BX	1st December 2001
	[Collections Management Division/Development Office National Museums Liverpool Midland Railway Building 1 Peter Street Liverpool L1 6BL][5]	1st December 2001
	. . . [5]	. . . [5]
	[International Slavery Museum [Dr Martin Luther King Jr Building][6] Albert Dock Liverpool L3 4AX][3]	[1st April 2006][3]
National Portrait Gallery	National Portrait Gallery St Martin's Place London WC2H 0HE	
Natural History Museum	Natural History Museum Cromwell Road London SW7 5BD	1st December 2001
	Natural History Museum Zoological Museum	1st December 2001

	Akeman Street Tring Herts HP23 6AD	
Royal Armouries	The Royal Armouries Armouries Drive Leeds West Yorkshire LS10 1LT	1st December 2001
	Royal Armouries at Fort Nelson Fort Nelson Down End Road Fareham Hants PO17 6AD	1st December 2001
[Science Museum Group][6]	Science Museum South Kensington London SW7 2DD	1st December 2001
	[National Media Museum][5] Bradford West Yorkshire BD1 1LQ	
	National Railway Museum Leeman Road York YO26 4XJ	1st December 2001
	Science Museum Wroughton Airfield Swindon Wilts SN4 9NS	1st April 2002
	. . . [6]	. . . [6]
	[Locomotion, The National Railway Museum at Shildon Shildon County Durham DL4 1PQ.][1]	[10th February 2003][1]
	[Museum of Science and Industry in Manchester Liverpool Road Castlefield Manchester M3 4FP][6]	[1st December 2001][6]
Tate Gallery	Tate Britain Millbank London SW1P 4RG Tate Modern Bankside London SE1 9TG Tate Liverpool Albert Dock Liverpool L3 4BB	
Victoria and Albert Museum	Victoria and Albert Museum Cromwell Road London SW7 2RL	22nd November 2001
	Bethnal Green Museum of Childhood Cambridge Heath Road London E2 9PA	*22nd November 2001*[4]
	[Victoria and Albert Museum	[1st December 2014][6]

	Blythe House 23 Blythe Road Hammersmith London W14 0QX][6]	
	. . .[4]	. . .[4]
The Wallace Collection	The Wallace Collection Hertford House Manchester Square London W1U 3BN	
. . .[6]		
Sir John Soane's Museum	Sir John Soane's Museum 13 Lincoln's Inn Fields London WC2A 3BP	
Museum of London	Museum of London London Wall London EC2Y 5NH	1st December 2001
	Museum of London Archaeological Service	1st March 2002
	[Museum of London West India Quay Canary Wharf London E14 4AL][4]	[1st April 2010][4]
	Mortimer Wheeler House 46 Eagle Wharf Road London N1	
Geffrye Museum	Geffrye Museum Kingsland Road London E2 8EA	
Horniman Museum	Horniman Museum 100 London Road Forest Hill London SE23 3PQ	
British Library	British Library 96 Euston Road London NW1 2DB (in respect of the historical collections in its galleries, temporary exhibitions and other related public programmes and events)	
The National Army Museum	The National Army Museum Royal Hospital Road Chelsea London SW3 4HT	
The Royal Air Force Museum	The Royal Air Force Museum Hendon London NW9 5LL	1st December 2001
	[The Royal Air Force Museum Cosford Shifnal Shropshire TF11 8UP][3]	[24th August 2005][1]
[The National Museum of Wales][4]	[National Museum Cardiff][4] Cathays Park	

VAT SIs

	Cardiff CF10 3NP National Museums of Welsh History: [National Roman Legion Museum][4] High Street Caerleon [NP18 1AE][4] Segontium Roman Fort Museum Beddgelert Road Caernarfon Gwynedd LL55 2LN [St Fagans: National History Museum][4] St Fagans Cardiff CF5 6XB National Museums of Welsh Industry: [National Slate Museum][4] Llanberis Gwynedd LL55 4TY [Big Pit: National Coal Museum][4] Blaenafon Torfaen NP4 9XP [National Wool Museum][4] Drefach Felindre Llandysul SA44 5UP [Collections Centre Heol Crochendy Parc Nantgarw Pontypridd CF15 7QT][6]	
	[National Waterfront Museum Swansea Maritime Quarter Victoria Road Swansea SA1 1SN][1]	18th October 2001][1]
	. . . [6]	
The National Library of Wales	The National Library of Wales Aberystwyth Ceredigion SY23 3BU (in respect of the historical collections in its galleries, temporary exhibitions and other related public programmes and events)	
National Museums and Galleries of Northern Ireland	Ulster Museum Botanic Gardens Belfast BT9 5AB Armagh County Museum The Mall East Armagh	
National Museums of Scotland	Royal Scottish Museum Chambers Street Edinburgh EH1 1JF Museum of Scotland Chambers Street Edinburgh EH1 1JF	

	. . . [5]	
National Galleries of Scotland	National Gallery of Scotland The Mound Edinburgh EH2 2EL Scottish National Portrait Gallery Queen Street Edinburgh EH2 1JD Scottish National Gallery of Modern Art Belford Road Edinburgh EH4 3DR Dean Gallery Belford Road Edinburgh EH4 3DR	
National Library of Scotland	National Library of Scotland George IV Bridge Edinburgh EH1 1EW National Library of Scotland 33 Salisbury Place Edinburgh (in respect of the historical collections in its galleries, temporary exhibitions and other related public programmes and events)	
[Keele University	Keele University Art Gallery Keele Arts Keele University, Staffordshire ST5 5BG	1 August 2004
Lancaster University	Peter Scott Gallery Lancaster University Lancaster LA1 4YW	1 August 2004
	Ruskin Library Lancaster University Lancaster LA1 4YH	1 August 2004
London Metropolitan University	The Women's Library London Metropolitan University Old Castle Street London E1 7NT	1 August 2004
Manchester Metropolitan University	Manchester Metropolitan University Special Collections Sir Kenneth Green Library All Saints Manchester M15 6BH	1 August 2004
. . . [5]	. . . [5]	. . . [5]
Queen's University, Belfast	The Naughton Gallery at Queen's and Queen's University Art Collection Lanyon Building Queen's University Belfast BT7 1NN	1 August 2004
. . . [5]	. . . [5]	. . . [5]
The Royal Academy of Music	York Gate Collections	1 August 2004

VAT SIs

	Royal Academy of Music Marylebone Road London NW1 5HT	
The Royal College of Surgeons of England	Hunterian Museum at the Royal College of Surgeons 35–43 Lincoln's Inn Fields London WC2A 3PE	1 August 2004
University of Aberdeen	[King's Museum 90 High Street Aberdeen AB24 3HE][6]	1 August 2004
	[Natural Philosophy Collection of Scientific Instruments][6] University of Aberdeen Department of Physics Fraser Noble Building King's College Aberdeen Scotland AB24 3UE	1 August 2004
	Zoology Museum University of Aberdeen Zoology Building Tillydrone Avenue Aberdeen Scotland AB24 2TZ	1 August 2004
	[Special Collections Centre The Sir Duncan Rice Library Bedford Road Aberdeen AB23 3AA][6]	[5th December 2011][6]
University of Birmingham	Barber Institute of Fine Arts University of Birmingham Edgbaston Birmingham B15 2TS	1 August 2004
	Lapworth Museum of Geology University of Birmingham Edgbaston Birmingham B15 2TT	1 August 2004
University of Bristol	[University of Bristol Cartoon Archive][5] Cantocks Close Bristol BS8 1UP	1 August 2004
University of Cambridge	Sedgwick Museum of Earth Sciences 3 Downing Street Cambridge CB2 3EQ	1 August 2004
	University Museum of Zoology Cambridge Downing Street Cambridge CB2 3EJ	1 August 2004
	The Fitzwilliam Museum Cambridge Trumpington Street Cambridge CB2 1RB	1 August 2004
	[Museum of Archaeology and Anthropology Downing Street Cambridge CB2 3DZ][4]	[15th May 2007][4]

	[Kettle's Yard Castle Street Cambridge CB3 0AQ][6]	[1st December 2014][6]
University College Chichester	Otter Gallery University College Chichester Bishop Otter Campus College Lane Chichester W Sussex PO19 6PE	1 August 2004
University of East Anglia	The Sainsbury Centre for Visual Arts University of East Anglia Norwich NR4 7TJ	28 October 2004
University of Edinburgh	Talbot Rice Gallery The University of Edinburgh Old College South Bridge Edinburgh EH8 9YL	1 August 2004
University of Exeter	The Bill Douglas Centre for the History of Cinema and Popular Culture The Old Library Prince of Wales Road Exeter EX4 4SB	1 August 2004
University of Glamorgan	University of Glamorgan Artworks Collection Oriel y Bont The University of Glamorgan Treforest Pontypridd CF37 1DL	1 August 2004
University of Glasgow	Hunterian Museum Gilbert Scott Building University of Glasgow University Avenue Glasgow G12 8QQ	1 August 2004
	Hunterian Art Gallery 82 Hillhead Street University of Glasgow Glasgow G12 8QQ	1 August 2004
	Zoology Museum Graham Kerr Building University of Glasgow University Avenue Glasgow G12 8QQ	1 August 2004
University of Hull	University of Hull Art Collection University of Hull Hull HU6 7RX	1 August 2004
University of Kent	Centre for the Study of Cartoons and Caricature Templeman Library University of Kent Canterbury CT2 7NU	1 August 2004
University of Manchester	. . . [5]	. . . [5]

VAT SIs

	The John Rylands Library 150 Deansgate Manchester M3 3EH	1 August 2004
	The Manchester Museum Oxford Road Manchester M13 9PL	1 August 2004
	Whitworth Art Gallery The University of Manchester Oxford Road Manchester M15 6ER	1 August 2004
University of Newcastle upon Tyne	[GNM Hancock][5] Barras Bridge Newcastle upon Tyne NE2 4PT	28 February 2005
	Hatton Gallery University of Newcastle upon Tyne Newcastle upon Tyne [NE1 4JA][5]	1 August 2004
	. . . [5]	. . . [5]
	. . . [5]	. . . [5]
University of Northumbria at Newcastle	University Gallery and Baring Wing Northumbria University Sandyford Road Newcastle-upon-Tyne NE1 8ST	1 August 2004
University of Oxford	Ashmolean Museum of Art and Archaeology Beaumont Street Oxford OX1 2PH	1 August 2004
	Oxford University Museum of Natural History Parks Road Oxford OX1 3PW	
	Pitt Rivers Museum South Parks Road Oxford OX1 3PP	1 August 2004
	[Museum of the History of Science	[1st April 2007][3]
	[The Weston Library (New Bodleian) Bodleian Libraries (in respect of the historical collections in its galleries, temporary exhibitions and other related public programmes and events) Broad Street Oxford OX1 3EG][5]	14 September 2010][5]
University of Reading	Cole Museum of Zoology School of Animal and Microbial Sciences University of Reading Whiteknights Reading RG6 6AJ	1 August 2004
	Museum of English Rural Life University of Reading Redlands Road Reading RG15EX	1 August 2004
	Ure Museum of Greek Archaeology University of Reading	1 August 2004

	Room 38 HUMUSS Building Whiteknights Reading RG6 6AH	
. . . [6]		
[Aberystwyth University][5]	Ceramics Gallery [Aberystwyth University][5] Buarth Mawr Aberystwyth Ceredigion SY23 1NG	1 August 2004
	School of Art Gallery and Museum [Aberystwyth University][5] Buarth Mawr Aberystwyth Ceredigion SY23 1NG	1 August 2004
University of Wales Swansea	Egypt Centre University of Wales Swansea Singleton Park Swansea SA2 8PP	1 August 2004][2]
[People's History Museum	People's History Museum [Left Bank Spinningfields][5] Manchester M3 3ER	9th August 2005
National Football Museum	National Football Museum [National Football Museum Urbis Building Cathedral Gardens Manchester M4 3BG Sir Tom Finney Way Deepdale Preston PR1 6PA	1st July 2005 1 December 2012][5]
University of Liverpool	The Victoria Gallery and Museum The Foundation Building 765 Brownlow Hill Liverpool L69 7ZX	24th October 2005]National Football Museum Urbis Building Cathedral Gardens Manchester M4 3BG[3]
[University of Bath	Holburne Museum of Art Great Pulteney Street Bath BA2 4DB	19 December 2008
University of St Andrews	Museum of the University of St Andrews 7a The Scores St Andrews KY16 9AR	1st August 2006
	Gateway Galleries North Haugh St Andrews KY16 9ST	1st April 2006
University of the Arts London	[Museum and Study Collection Central Saint Martins Granary Building 1 Granary Square	[1st September 2008][4]

	London N1C 4AA][6]	
[University of Leeds	The Stanley and Audrey Burton Gallery University of Leeds Parkinson Building Woodhouse Lane Leeds LS2 9JT	3 March 2008][5]
[UK Border Agency National Museum	Seized! The Borders and Customs Uncovered Basement of Merseyside Maritime Museum Albert Dock Liverpool L1 4AQ	1 December 2012][5]
[Design Museum	Design Museum 224 Kensington High Street London W8 6NQ	1st November 2010
University of Leicester	Embrace Arts Centre Fielding Johnson Building University Road Leicester LE1 7RH	1st December 2014
Design Dundee Ltd	V & A Dundee University of Dundee Nethergate Dundee DD1 4HN	1st December 2014
	V & A Dundee University of Abertay Dundee Kydd Building Bell Street Dundee DD1 1HG	1st December 2014
	V & A Dundee Earl Grey Place Dundee DD1 4DF	1st December 2014
National Coal Mining Museum for England	National Coal Mining Museum for England Caphouse Colliery New Road Overton Wakefield West Yorkshire WF4 4RH	1st April 2002][6]

Amendments—

1 Entries inserted by the VAT (Refund of Tax to Museums and Galleries) Order, SI 2004/1709 with effect from 1 August 2004.

2 Entries inserted by the VAT (Refund of Tax to Museums and Galleries) (Amendment) Order, SI 2005/1993 with effect from 10 August 2005.

3 Entries substituted and inserted by the VAT (Refund of Tax to Museums and Galleries) (Amendment) Order, SI 2008/1339 with effect from 1 July 2008.

4 Entries inserted, substituted and revoked, by the Value Added Tax (Refund of Tax to Museums and Galleries) (Amendment) Order, SI 2010/608, with effect from 26 March 2010.

5 Entries inserted, substituted and revoked by the Value Added Tax (Refund of Tax to Museums and Galleries) (Amendment) Order, SI 2012/2731 with effect from 1 December 2012.

6 Entries inserted, substituted and revoked by the Value Added Tax (Refund of Tax to Museums and Galleries) (Amendment) Order, SI 2014/2858 with effect from 1 December 2014.

2001/2880

FREE ZONE (SOUTHAMPTON) DESIGNATION ORDER 2001

Made by the Treasury under the Customs and Excise Management Act 1979 s 100A

Made . . . . *9 August 2001*
Coming into force . . . . *10 August 2001*

1 Citation and commencement

This Order may be cited as The Free Zone (Southampton) Designation Order 2001 and shall come into force on 10th August 2001.

2 Designation of area as free zone

(1) An area of 3.2436 hectares, in the City of Southampton, Hampshire, shown enclosed by a red line on a map (in this article referred to as "the map"), being of a scale of 1:2500, and signed by a Collector of Customs and Excise, shall be a free zone.

[(2) The map shall be kept by the Commissioners and a copy of the map shall be kept at the offices of the responsible authority.][1]

(3) The map or the copy thereof may, on application, be inspected by members of the public at reasonable hours without charge.

Amendments—[1] Paragraph (2) substituted by the Free Zone Designations (Amendments) Order, SI 2006/1834 art 2 with effect from 1 August 2006.

3 Appointment of responsible authority

The responsible authority for the free zone shall be Southampton Free Trade Zone Limited whose Registered Office is 150 Holborn, London EC1N 2LR.

4 Period of validity of Order

This Order shall have effect for a period of 10 years from the date of coming into force.

5 Conditions imposed on responsible authority

The responsible authority shall—

(*a*) maintain an office in the free zone or at such other place as the Commissioners may allow at which shall be kept any records, for which the responsible authority is responsible, relating to the free zone and the business carried on therein;

(*b*) keep separate accounts in connection with the free zone;

(*c*) provide such information in connection with the free zone and the operation thereof to any person authorised by the Treasury, as that person may reasonably require;

(*d*) provide, free of expense to the Crown, such accommodation and facilities including furniture, fittings and equipment as the Commissioners may reasonably require and such accommodation and facilities shall be properly maintained, heated, lighted, ventilated and kept clean by the responsible authority;

(*e*) provide, free of expense to the Crown, such area of land within the free zone as the Commissioners may reasonably require for the examination of goods and vehicles and shall provide and maintain such appliances and afford such other facilities which are reasonably necessary to enable an account to be taken of any goods or make any examination or search;

(*f*) not permit a person to establish or carry on any trade or business in the free zone unless that person is authorised by the Commissioners to carry on such a trade or business in the free zone.

6 Health and safety

Without prejudice to the responsibilities of persons occupying premises within the free zone, the responsible authority shall ensure that the working conditions within the free zone are safe and without risk to the health and safety of persons employed by the Commissioners and shall comply with any requirements concerning health and safety imposed by any competent authority.

2001/2881

FREE ZONE (LIVERPOOL) DESIGNATION ORDER 2001

Made by the Treasury under the Customs and Excise Management Act 1979 s 100A

Made . . . . *9 August 2001*
Coming into force . . . . *10 August 2001*

1 Citation and commencement

This Order may be cited as The Free Zone (Liverpool) Designation Order 2001 and shall come into force on 10th August 2001.

VAT SIs

2 Designation of area as free zone

(1) An area of 383.28 hectares, in the County of Merseyside, comprising 269.56 hectares in the Metropolitan Borough of Sefton, 77.87 hectares in the Metropolitan Borough of Wirral and 35.85 hectares within the City of Liverpool, shown enclosed by a red line on a map (in this article referred to as "the map"), being of a scale of 1:2500, and signed by a Collector of Customs and Excise, shall be a free zone.

[(2) The map shall be kept by the Commissioners and a copy of the map shall be kept at the offices of the responsible authority.][1]

(3) The map or the copy thereof may, on application, be inspected by members of the public at reasonable hours without charge.

Amendments—[1] Paragraph (2) substituted by the Free Zone Designations (Amendments) Order, SI 2006/1834 art 2 with effect from 1 August 2006.

[3 Appointment of responsible authority

The responsible authority for the free zone shall be the Mersey Docks and Harbour Company, whose Head Office is at Maritime Centre, Port of Liverpool, L21 1LA.][1]

Amendments—[1] Article substituted by the Free Zone Designations (Amendments) Order, SI 2006/1834 art 3 with effect from 1 August 2006.

4 Period of validity of Order

This Order shall have effect for a period of 10 years from the date of coming into force.

5 Conditions imposed on responsible authority

The responsible authority shall—

(*a*) maintain an office in the free zone or at such other place as the Commissioners may allow at which shall be kept any records, for which the responsible authority is responsible, relating to the free zone and the business carried on therein;

(*b*) keep separate accounts in connection with the free zone;

(*c*) provide such information in connection with the free zone and the operation thereof to any person authorised by the Treasury, as that person may reasonably require;

(*d*) provide, free of expense to the Crown, such accommodation and facilities including furniture, fittings and equipment as the Commissioners may reasonably require and such accommodation and facilities shall be properly maintained, heated, lighted, ventilated and kept clean by the responsible authority;

(*e*) provide, free of expense to the Crown, such area of land within the free zone as the Commissioners may reasonably require for the examination of goods and vehicles and shall provide and maintain such appliances and afford such other facilities which are reasonably necessary to enable an account to be taken of any goods or make any examination or search;

(*f*) not permit a person to establish or carry on any trade or business in the free zone unless that person is authorised by the Commissioners to carry on such a trade or business in the free zone.

6 Health and safety

Without prejudice to the responsibilities of persons occupying premises within the free zone, the responsible authority shall ensure that the working conditions within the free zone are safe and without risk to the health and safety of persons employed by the Commissioners and shall comply with any requirements concerning health and safety imposed by any competent authority.

2001/2882

FREE ZONE (PRESTWICK AIRPORT) DESIGNATION ORDER 2001

Made by the Treasury under the Customs and Excise Management Act 1979 s 100A

Made . . . . *9 August 2001*
Coming into force . . . . *10 August 2001*

1 Citation and commencement

This Order may be cited as The Free Zone (Prestwick Airport) Designation Order 2001 and shall come into force on 10th August 2001.

2 Designation of area as free zone

(1) An area of 7.0359 acres (2.8475 hectares), in the parish of Ayr in the County of Ayr, shown enclosed by a red line on a map (in this article referred to as "the map"), being of a scale of 1:500, and signed by the Head of Business Services, HM Customs and Excise, Scotland, shall be a free zone.

[(2) The map shall be kept by the Commissioners and a copy of the map shall be kept at the offices of the responsible authority.][1]

(3) The map or the copy thereof may, on application, be inspected by members of the public at reasonable hours without charge.

Amendments—[1] Paragraph (2) substituted by the Free Zone Designations (Amendments) Order, SI 2006/1834 art 2 with effect from 1 August 2006.

3 Appointment of responsible authority

The responsible authority for the free zone shall be Freeport Scotland Ltd whose Registered Office is at County Buildings (Financial Services), Wellington Square, Ayr KA7 2PL.

4 Period of validity of Order

This Order shall have effect for a period of 10 years from the date of coming into force.

5 Conditions imposed on responsible authority

The responsible authority shall—

(*a*) maintain an office in the free zone or at such other place as the Commissioners may allow at which shall be kept any records, for which the responsible authority is responsible, relating to the free zone and the business carried on therein;

(*b*) keep separate accounts in connection with the free zone;

(*c*) provide such information in connection with the free zone and the operation thereof to any person authorised by the Treasury, as that person may reasonably require;

(*d*) provide, free of expense to the Crown, such accommodation and facilities including furniture, fittings and equipment as the Commissioners may reasonably require and such accommodation and facilities shall be properly maintained, heated, lighted, ventilated and kept clean by the responsible authority;

(*e*) provide, free of expense to the Crown, such area of land within the free zone as the Commissioners may reasonably require for the examination of goods and vehicles and shall provide and maintain such appliances and afford such other facilities which are reasonably necessary to enable an account to be taken of any goods or make any examination or search;

(*f*) not permit a person to establish or carry on any trade or business in the free zone unless that person is authorised by the Commissioners to carry on such a trade or business in the free zone.

6 Health and safety

Without prejudice to the responsibility of persons occupying premises within the free zone, the responsible authority shall ensure that the working conditions within the free zone are safe and without risk to the health and safety of persons employed by the Commissioners and shall comply with any requirements concerning health and safety imposed by any competent authority.

2001/3453

VALUE ADDED TAX (REFUND OF TAX) ORDER 2001

Made by the Treasury under the Value Added Tax Act 1994 s 33(3)

Made . . . . *22 October 2001*
Laid . . . . *23 October 2001*
Coming into force . . . . *1 December 2001*

1 This Order may be cited as the Value Added Tax (Refund of Tax) Order 2001 and shall come into force on 1st December 2001.

2 The Greater London Magistrates' Courts Authority (the body corporate established by section 30A of the Justice of the Peace Act 1997) is specified for the purposes of section 33 of the Value Added Tax Act 1994.

2002/1280

VALUE ADDED TAX (SPECIAL PROVISIONS) (AMENDMENT) ORDER 2002

Made by the Treasury under VATA 1994 ss 5(5), 43(2)

Made . . . . *8 May 2002*
Laid before the House of Commons . . . . *9 May 2002*
Coming into force . . . . *1 June 2002*

1—(1) This Order may be cited as the Value Added Tax (Special Provisions) (Amendment) Order 2002 and comes into force on 1st June 2002.

VAT SIs

(2) This Order shall not have effect where a person produces printed matter (other than printed matter of a description specified in Group 3 of Schedule 8 to the Value Added Tax Act 1994) from goods—

(*a*) the supply of which to him is treated by virtue of section 6(4) of the Value Added Tax Act 1994 as taking place before 1st June 2002; and

(*b*) which he neither collects nor takes delivery of before that date.

2–4 (*Amend the Value Added Tax (Special Provisions) Order, SI 1995/1268*)

2002/1418

FREE ZONE (PORT OF TILBURY) DESIGNATION ORDER 2002

Made by the Treasury under CEMA 1979 s 100A

Made . . . . *24 May 2002*

Coming into force . . . . *2 June 2002*

1 Citation and commencement

This Order may be cited as The Free Zone (Port of Tilbury) Designation Order 2002 and shall come into force on 2nd June 2002.

2 Designation of area as free zone

(1) An area of 766.9 acres in the Borough of Thurrock in the County of Essex, shown enclosed by a red line on a map (being of a scale of 1:5000), marked "Map referred to in article 2 of the Free Zone (Port of Tilbury) Designation Order 2002" signed by a Deputy Collector of Customs and Excise and dated 19th May 2002, shall be a Free Zone.

[(2) The map shall be kept by the Commissioners and a copy of the map shall be kept at the offices of the responsible authority.][1]

(3) The map or the copy thereof may, on application, be inspected by members of the public at reasonable hours without charge.

Amendments—[1] Paragraph (2) substituted by the Free Zone Designations (Amendments) Order, SI 2006/1834 art 2 with effect from 1 August 2006.

3 Appointment of responsible authority

The responsible authority for the free zone shall be Port of Tilbury London Limited whose Registered Office is at Leslie Ford House, Tilbury Dock, Essex RM18 7EH.

4 Period of validity of Order

This Order shall have effect for a period of 10 years from the date of coming into force.

5 Conditions imposed on responsible authority

The responsible authority shall—

(*a*) maintain an office in the free zone or at such other place as the Commissioners may allow at which shall be kept any records, for which the responsible authority is responsible, relating to the free zone and the business carried on therein;

(*b*) keep separate accounts in connection with the free zone;

(*c*) provide such information in connection with the free zone and the operation thereof to any person authorised by the Treasury, as that person may reasonably require;

(*d*) provide, free of expense to the Crown, such accommodation and facilities including furniture, fittings and equipment as the Commissioners may reasonably require and such accommodation and facilities shall be properly maintained, heated, lighted, ventilated and kept clean by the responsible authority;

(*e*) provide, free of expense to the Crown, such area of land within the free zone as the Commissioners may reasonably require for the examination of goods and vehicles and shall provide and maintain such appliances and afford such other facilities which are reasonably necessary to enable an account to be taken of any goods or make any examination or search;

(*f*) not permit a person to establish or carry on any trade or business in the free zone unless that person is authorised by the Commissioners to carry on such a trade or business in the free zone.

6 Health and safety

Without prejudice to the responsibilities of persons occupying premises within the free zone, the responsible authority shall ensure that the working conditions within the free zone are safe and without risk to the health and safety of persons employed by the Commissioners and shall comply with any requirements concerning health and safety imposed by any competent authority.

2002/1502

VALUE ADDED TAX (CARS) (AMENDMENT) ORDER 2002

Made by the Treasury under VATA 1994 s 50A(1), (5), (8)

Made . . . . *10 June 2002*
Laid before the House of Commons . . . . *10 June 2002*
Coming into force . . . . *1 July 2002*

1—(1) This Order may be cited as the Value Added Tax (Cars) (Amendment) Order 2002 and comes into force on 1st July 2002.

(2) This Order shall not have effect where the taxable person took possession of the motor car pursuant to—

(*a*) an assignment which is an article 5 transaction solely by virtue of article 5(4) of the Value Added Tax (Special Provisions) Order 1995 or a corresponding provision made under the Manx Act; or

(*b*) a transaction forming part of a succession of two or more article 5 transactions, at least one of which was such an assignment,

if the assignment or, where there is a succession of transactions comprising two or more assignments, any of the assignments takes effect before 1st July 2002.

(3) In this article—

"article 5 transaction" means a transaction which is treated as being neither a supply of goods nor a supply of services by virtue of a provision of article 5 of the Value Added Tax (Special Provisions) Order 1995 or a corresponding provision made under the Manx Act;

"the Manx Act" means the Value Added Tax Act 1996.

2 (*amends the Value Added Tax (Cars) Order, SI 1992/3122 art 8*)

2002/1503

VALUE ADDED TAX (SPECIAL PROVISIONS) (AMENDMENT) (NO 2) ORDER 2002

Made by the Treasury under VATA 1994 s 50A(1), (5), (8)

Made . . . . *10 June 2002*
Laid before the House of Commons . . . . *10 June 2002*
Coming into force . . . . *1 July 2002*

1—(1) This Order may be cited as the Value Added Tax (Special Provisions) (Amendment) (No 2) Order 2002 and comes into force on 1st July 2002.

(2) This Order shall not have effect where the taxable person took possession of the goods pursuant to—

(*a*) an assignment which is an article 5 transaction solely by virtue of article 5(4) of the Value Added Tax (Special Provisions) Order 1995 or a corresponding provision made under the Manx Act; or

(*b*) a transaction forming part of a succession of two or more article 5 transactions, at least one of which was such an assignment,

if the assignment or, where there is a succession of transactions comprising two or more assignments, any of the assignments takes effect before 1st July 2002.

(3) In this article—

"article 5 transaction" means a transaction which is treated as being neither a supply of goods nor a supply of services by virtue of a provision of article 5 of the Value Added Tax (Special Provisions) Order 1995 or a corresponding provision made under the Manx Act;

"the Manx Act" means the Value Added Tax Act 1996.

2 (*amends the Value Added Tax (Special Provisions) Order, SI 1995/1268 art 12*)

2002/1935

VALUE ADDED TAX (ACQUISITIONS) RELIEF ORDER 2002

Made by the Treasury under VATA 1994 s 36A

Made . . . . *25 July 2002*

VAT SIs

Laid before the House of Commons . . . .*25 July 2002*
Coming into force . . . .*15 August 2002*

1 This Order may be cited as the Value Added Tax (Acquisitions) Relief Order 2002 and comes into force on 15th August 2002.

2 Subject to article 3 below, no VAT shall be payable on any acquisition from another member State of any goods where, if they were imported from a place outside the member States, relief from payment of VAT would be given by the Value Added Tax (Imported Goods) Relief Order 1984 (as amended from time to time).

3 The relief given by this Order in respect of the acquisition of any goods shall be subject to the same conditions as those to which, by virtue of the Value Added Tax (Imported Goods) Relief Order 1984 (as amended from time to time), relief under that Order would be subject in the case of an importation of those goods.

2003/3113

CUSTOMS (CONTRAVENTION OF A RELEVANT RULE) REGULATIONS 2003

Made by the Treasury under FA 2003 s 26(1), (2), (3), (4), (41)

Made . . . .*2 December 2003*
Laid before the House of Commons . . . .*2 December 2003*
Coming into force . . . .*23 December 2003*

1 Citation and Commencement
These Regulations may be cited as the Customs (Contravention of a Relevant Rule) Regulations 2003 and shall come into force on 23rd December 2003.

2 Interpretation
In these Regulations—

"the Act" means the Customs and Excise Management Act 1979;

. . .[3]

. . .[3]

"the 1994 Act" means the Finance Act 1994;

"the Code" means Council Regulation 2913/92/EEC;

["Customs" means Her Majesty's Revenue and Customs, the Secretary of State by whom customs functions are exercisable or the Director of Border Revenue;][1]

[functions exercised under these Regulations by the Secretary of State by whom customs functions are exercisable are general customs functions in accordance with the Borders, Citizenship and Immigration Act 2009 and those exercised by the Director of Border Revenue are customs revenue functions in accordance with the same Act;][1]

. . .[1]

. . .[3]

. . .[3]

. . .[3]

. . .[3]

["customs territory" has the meaning given by Article 3 of the Code to "customs territory of the Community";][2]

. . .[3]

"the Implementing Regulation" means Commission Regulation 2454/93/EEC as it implements the Code;

"the Importation Regulations" means the Customs Controls on Importation of Goods Regulations 1991;

. . .[3]

. . .[3]

. . .[3]

. . .[3]

. . .[3]

. . .[3]

. . .[3]

. . .[3]

. . .[3]

. . .[1]

Amendments—[1] Definition of "Customs" substituted and following words inserted, definition of "Customs authority of the United Kingdom" and following words, and definition of "the Transit Regulations", revoked, by the Customs (Contravention of a Relevant Rule) (Amendment) Regulations, SI 2009/3164 regs 2, 3 with effect from 24 December 2009.

[2] Definition of "customs territory" inserted by the Customs (Contravention of a Relevant Rule) (Amendment) Regulations, SI 2011/2534, regs 2, 3 with effect from 15 November 2011.

[3] Definitions revoked by the Customs (Contravention of a Relevant Rule) (Amendment) Regulations, SI 2015/636 regs 2, 3 with effect from 2 April 2015.

3 Relevant Rule and Amount of Penalty

(1) The Schedule to these regulations shall have effect.

(2) An entry in Column 1 of the Schedule specifies the relevant rule or the description of a relevant rule in the case of any relevant tax or duty to which it applies for the purposes of section 26(1) of the Finance Act 2003 (Penalty for contravention of relevant rule).

(3) An entry in Column 2 of the Schedule adjacent to an entry in Column 1 specifies a person, of the description there laid out, who shall be liable to a penalty under section 26 of the Finance Act 2003 (where his conduct contravenes the relevant rule or a relevant rule of the description specified for the purposes of that section).

(4) An entry in Column 3 of the Schedule adjacent to an entry in Columns 1 and 2 specifies for the purposes of section 26(1) of the Finance Act 2003 the maximum amount of the penalty which may be imposed upon a person specified for the purposes of that section as liable for that contravention of that specified relevant rule.

(5) Any description of a relevant rule specified in Column 1 and any description of a person prescribed in Column 2 of the Schedule is without prejudice to the effect of any directly applicable Community provision so described or description of a person responsible contained in that provision so described.

(6) A specified relevant rule or description of a person shall be construed in accordance with the effect and scope of that directly applicable Community provision referred to in Column 1.

[(7) [Where as a consequence of these Regulations, a person is liable to a penalty under section 26 of the Finance Act 2003][2] and the conduct giving rise to the liability continues after the date specified in a notice in writing given to that person by the Commissioners, that continuation of the conduct—

(*a*) shall constitute a further contravention of the same rule; and

(*b*) shall make that person liable to a separate penalty accordingly.][1]

Amendments—[1] Para (7) inserted by the Customs (Contravention of a Relevant Rule) (Amendment) Regulations, SI 2011/2534, regs 2, 4 with effect from 15 November 2011.

[2] In para (7), words substituted by the Customs (Contravention of a Relevant Rule) (Amendment) Regulations, SI 2015/636 regs 2, 4 with effect from 2 April 2015.

SCHEDULE

Regulation 3

Column 1	*Column 2*	*Column 3*
Description of relevant Rule/Relevant Rule of a description	*Person of a description*	*Penalty for contravention*
Report		
[Sections 20, 22 and 25 of the Act		
Any condition or restriction attaching to any approval given under section 20, 22 or 25 of the Act.	The approved person.	£1,000.
Section 21(1) and (3)(b) of the Act		
Except where permitted, not to cause, or permit, to land an aircraft other than at a customs and excise airport (which, in the case of flights departing the UK, must be as specified in the clearance application), except with Customs' permission or for unavoidable cause.	The commander of the aircraft.	£2,500.
Section 21(2) of the Act		
Except as permitted by Customs, not to bring into the United Kingdom, in an aircraft, at any place other than a customs and excise airport, goods being imported from within the customs territory.	The person bringing in the goods.	£2,500.
Section 21(3)(a) of the Act		

Except where permitted, not to depart on a flight to a place or area outside the United Kingdom from any place in the United Kingdom other than a customs and excise airport.	The person departing.	£2,500.
Section 21(4)(a) of the Act		
In the case of landing other than as permitted under sections 21(1) or (3), (a) to make immediate report (b) not to permit goods to be unloaded from the aircraft (c) not to permit any crew or passengers to leave its vicinity (d) to comply with any directions given by an officer.	The commander of the aircraft.	£2,500.
Section 21(4)(b) of the Act		
In the case of landing other than as permitted under sections 21(1) or (3), no passenger or crew member to leave the immediate vicinity of the aircraft without the consent of an officer or constable.	The passenger or crew member in question.	£2,500.
Section 33(1) of the Act		
To allow an officer to board and inspect an aircraft and all goods and documents carried in and relating to it.	The commander of the aircraft.	£2,500.
Section 33(2) of the Act		
To permit an officer to enter and inspect an aerodrome.	The person in control of the aerodrome.	£2,500.
Section 33(3) of the Act		
To keep the prescribed records of flights to and from that aerodrome; to permit an officer to make copies and take extracts from such records.	The person in control of the aerodrome.	£2,500.
Section 34(1) of the Act		
Any instructions given under section 34(1) of the Act.	The commander of the aircraft.	£2,500.
	The owner of the aircraft.	£2,500.][4]
Section 35(1) of the Act		
To report in such form and manner containing such particulars as Customs direct.	The master.	£1,000
	Person authorised by the master.	£1,000
	Commander of the aircraft.	
[Ship's Report, Importation and Exportation by Sea Regulations 1981][4]:		
Regulation 3		
Completion of the forms directed by Customs under s 35(1) by the master, or a person authorised by him (as Customs permit).	The master	£1,000
	Person authorised by the master.	£1,000
Regulation 4		
Delivery of a duly completed report:	The master.	£1,000
(a) to a boarding officer immediately on request;	Person authorised by the master.	£1,000
(b) to the place designated within three hours of the ship having reached its place of loading or unloading; or		
(c) on the expiration of twenty four hours following arrival within the limits of the port when a ship has not arrived at its place of loading or unloading.		
Regulation 5		

To retain on board as long as the ship remains within the limits of the port a copy of the form of report for inspection by an officer.	The master.	£1,000
[Aircraft (Customs and Excise) Regulations 1981][4]**:**		
Regulation 4(1)		
Delivery to the proper officer of:	Commander of the aircraft.	£1,000
(a) a General Declaration;		
(b) particulars of the goods on the aircraft; and		
(c) a list in duplicate of the stores on board the aircraft.		
Section 35(6) of the Act		
To answer all such question relating to:	The master.	£1,000
(a) the ship or aircraft;	Person authorised by the master.	£1,000
(b) the goods carried therein;		
(c) the crew; and	Commander of the aircraft.	£1,000
(d) the voyage or flight		
as put to him by the proper officer.		
Section 35(7) of the Act		
Where prior to report:	The master.	£1,000
(a) bulk is broken;	Person authorised by the master.	£1,000
(b) stowage of any goods is altered to facilitate unloading of any part thereof before making report;	Commander of the aircraft.	£1,000
(c) any part of the goods are staved, destroyed, thrown overboard; or		
(d) a container opened		
and no proper explanation is given to the satisfaction of Customs.		
[Section 64(1) of the Act		
Except as permitted by Customs, no ship or aircraft requiring clearance under this section should depart from a port or customs and excise airport to a destination outside the member States and the Isle of Man, without a valid clearance.	The master of the ship.	£1,000.
	The commander of the aircraft.	£1,000.
Section 71(1) of the Act		
To deliver a report to the proper officer as directed.	The master of the ship.	£500.
Section 72(2) and (3)(b) of the Act		
Any requirement made under section 72(2) or (3)(b) of the Act.	The master of the ship.	£500.
Section 77(1) of the Act		
Any requirement made under section 77(1) of the Act.	The person of whom the requirement is made.	£1,000.
Section 78(1) of the Act		

(a) A person (P) entering the United Kingdom must, at such place and in such manner as Customs may direct, declare any thing contained in P's baggage or carried with P which P has obtained outside the United Kingdom and in respect of which P is not entitled to exemption from duty and tax by virtue of any order under section 13 of the Customs and Excise Duties (General Reliefs) Act 1979 (personal reliefs).	Any person.	£1,000.
(b) A person (P) entering the United Kingdom must, at such place and in such manner as Customs may direct, declare any thing contained in P's baggage or carried with P which, being dutiable goods or chargeable goods, P has obtained in the United Kingdom without payment of duty or tax and in respect of which P is not entitled to exemption from duty and tax by virtue of any order under section 13 of the Customs and Excise Duties (General Reliefs) Act 1979.	Any person.	£1,000.
Section 158(1) and (3) of the Act		
Provision and maintenance of appliances, facilities and fittings; keeping the appliances in an approved place; allowing use of the same at any time to a proper officer; all necessary assistance to be given.	The person on whom the obligation falls.	£1,000.
The Control of Movement of Goods Regulations 1984		
Not to move or interfere with goods to which the Regulations apply other than in accordance with the Regulations.	The person moving or interfering with the goods.	£2,500.][4]
Goods brought into the [customs territory][3] (United Kingdom)		
[[Articles 36a and 36b of the Code and Articles 183, 184a and 184c of the Implementing Regulation		
Goods brought into the customs territory to be covered by a summary declaration, lodged within the applicable time-limits, by the prescribed means, to the prescribed office of entry and containing the requisite particulars.	Where a declaration has not been lodged, the person upon whom the obligation to lodge the declaration falls.	£1,000.
	Where a declaration has been lodged, the person who lodges the declaration.	£1,000.][4]
Article 183d(1) of the Implementing Regulation—first sentence		
The operator of an active means of transport entering the customs territory must (except in the circumstances identified in article 183a) submit a 'diversion request' message if that means of transport arrives first at a customs office in a member state not declared on the Entry Summary Declaration.	The operator of the active means of transport.	£2,500
Article 183d(1) of the Implementing Regulation—second sentence		
The diversion request message must contain the particulars set out in Annex 30 of the Implementing Regulation.	The operator of the active means of transport.	£1,000
Article 184 of the Implementing Regulation		

Goods covered by a summary declaration which have not been unloaded and have not yet been assigned a customs-approved treatment or use must be re-presented intact whenever the Customs so require.	The person who has made the summary declaration.	£1,000
	Any person who holds the goods after they have been unloaded in order to move or store them.	£1,000
Article 184g of the Implementing Regulation—first sentence		
The operator of an active means of transport entering the customs territory or his agent must notify Customs of its arrival at the office of entry.	The operator of the active means of transport.	£2,500
Article 184g of the Implementing Regulation—second sentence		
The notification must contain all the particulars necessary for the identification of the entry summary declarations lodged in respect of all goods carried on that means of transport.	The operator of the active means of transport.	£1,000
Article 186 of the Implementing Regulation		
Non-Community goods presented to Customs shall be covered by a summary declaration for temporary storage in the form prescribed by Customs. The declaration must be lodged no later than at presentation.	The person who presents the goods.	£1,000][3]
Article 38 of the Code		
To convey the goods to the customs office designated or free zone by the route specified, without delay and in accordance with the instructions of Customs.	Person bringing the goods into the [customs territory][3].	£1,000
	Any person who assumes responsibility for the carriage of the goods after they have been brought into the [customs territory][3].	£1,000
Article 39 of the Code		
Pursuant to Article 39, to inform without delay the Customs of:	In respect of Article 39(1) the person bringing the goods into the [customs territory][3]; or	£1,000
(a) the inability to comply with Article 38(1) due to unforeseen circumstances or force majeure; and	Any person who assumes responsibility for the carriage of the goods after they have been brought into the customs territory.	£1,000
(b) the precise location of the goods where the unforeseen circumstances or force majeure does not result in the total loss of the goods.	In respect of Article 39(2), the person bringing the vessel or aircraft into the customs territory, or in respect of either provision any other person acting in his place.	£1,000
Presentation of Goods to Customs		
. . .[3]	. . .[3]	. . .[3]

VAT SIs

Regulation 3 of the Importation Regulations		
To notify Customs:		
(a) of the arrival of goods in the prescribed form or where approved, by computerised record capable of being printed out; and	The person who brought the goods into the customs territory.	£1,000
(b) to make such notification within three hours of the arrival of the ship at the wharf or aircraft at the airport, or if the customs office is closed within one hour following the re-opening of the office.	The person who assumes responsibility for carriage of the goods following entry.	£1,000
Article 42 of the Code		
To seek permission of the Customs before examination or sampling of goods in order that they may be assigned a customs approved treatment or use.	The person authorised to assign the goods a customs approved treatment or use.	£1,000
	Any person able to present the goods or to have them presented. A person subject to a specific obligation in relation to goods being assigned to a customs approved treatment or use.	£1,000
	Any person doing so on his behalf.	£1,000
. . . [3]	. . . [3]	. . . [3]
Article 46 of the Code		
Goods shall:		
(a) except in the event of imminent danger, only be unloaded or transhipped from the means of transport with the permission of Customs and in places designated or approved or;	The person who brought the goods into the customs territory.	£1,000
	The person who assumes responsibility for the carriage of the goods following entry into the Customs territory.	£1,000
(b) be unloaded and unpacked as required by Customs for the purposes of inspecting the goods and means of transport.	The person responsible for the contravention of the Importation Regulations.	£1,000
Where permission is not required, Customs shall be informed forthwith of the unloading or transhipment of the goods.		
Article 47 of the Code		
Goods shall not be removed from their original position without permission of Customs.	The person who brought the goods into the [customs territory][3].	£1,000
	The person who assumes responsibility for the carriage of goods following entry into the customs territory.	£1,000
[Directions made on 2 August 2011 under section 30 of the Act		

No goods to which section 30 applies to be moved except:	The declarant.	£1,000
(a) on the instructions of a proper officer;		
(b) in the manner and under the conditions specified by a proper officer.	The person who moves the goods.	£1,000][3]
Articles 48 and 49 and 59 of the Code and Regulation 5 of the Importation Regulation		
Goods shall be assigned to a customs approved treatment or use within the period prescribed in Article 49.	The person who brought the goods into the [customs territory][3].	
Entry to a customs approved treatment or use shall be effected by the delivery of an appropriate declaration presented to the proper officer pursuant to regulation 5.	The person who is able to present the goods to customs.	
	The importer within the meaning of the Act	£1,000
Article 51 of the Code		
Goods in temporary storage shall be stored only at places approved and under the conditions laid down by Customs.	The person bringing the goods into the [customs territory][3]	£1,000
The provision of security where required by Customs.	The person who removed the goods from customs supervision.	£1,000
	The person who participated in such removal.	£1,000
	The person required to fulfil the obligations arising from temporary storage.	£1,000
Customs Declarations		
Article 59 of the Code		
Goods intended to be placed under a customs procedure shall be covered by a declaration.	Any person who is able to present the goods in question together with the documents required for the application of the rules governing the procedure.	£2,500
	A specific person (where acceptance of a declaration imposes particular obligations on that specific person).	£2,500
	An agent acting on his behalf.	£2,500
	By a direct agent in the case of a specific person.	£2,500
Articles 62 and 77 of the Code and Article 199 of the Implementing Regulation		
Section 167(3) of the Act		
Declarations shall be:		

(a) made on a form corresponding to the official specimen prescribed for the purpose;	Any person who is able to present the goods in question together with the documents required for the application of the rules governing the customs procedure.	£2,500
(b) signed and contain all the particulars necessary for implementation of the provisions of the customs procedure; and		£2,500
(c) accompanied by all the documents required for implementation of the provisions of the customs procedure.	A specific person (where acceptance of a declaration imposes particular obligations on that specific person).	
	By an agent on his behalf.	£2,500
	By a direct agent in the case of a specific person.	£2,500
[Article 201 of the Implementing Regulation		
The customs declaration must be lodged at one of the following customs offices: (a) the customs office responsible for the place of presentation; (b) the customs office responsible in the place where the exporter is established or from which the goods are exported.	The declarant.	£1,000][3]
Authorised economic operators		
[. . .[4] Article 14w of the Implementing Regulation		
To inform Customs of all factors arising after an authorised economic operator certificate has been granted which may influence its continuation or content.	The authorised economic operator.	£2,500.][1]
[Simplified and Local Procedures][4]		
[Articles 253(6) and 253(7) of the Implementing Regulation		
A person authorised for the simplified or local clearance procedure must: (a) comply with the relevant conditions, meet the relevant criteria and comply with the relevant obligations; (b) inform Customs of all factors arising after authorisation has been granted which may influence its continuation or content.	The authorised person.	£2,500][3]
[Articles 76 of the Code and Article 260 of the Implementing Regulation		
The simplified declaration or the document or documents permitted in lieu of it must: (a) contain at least the particulars for a simplified declaration set out in Annex 30A; (b) be accompanied by all documents which may be required to secure the release of the goods to free circulation; (c) bear a reference to any general release authorisation; (d) where the goods are entered for the relevant procedure by means of an entry in the records, bear the date of such entry. A supplementary declaration must be furnished.	The declarant	£2,500][3]
. . .[3]	. . .[3]	. . .[3]

. . . [4]		
. . . [4]		
. . . [4]	. . . [4]	. . . [4]
	. . . [4]	. . . [4]
Customs Procedure with Economic Impact		
[Articles 85 and 87 of the Code][4]	The person to whom the authorisation for use of any customs procedure with economic impact is issued.	£2,500
To comply with a condition (including special conditions governing the procedure in question) of an immediately enforceable binding decision of Customs, in respect of an authorisation or transferred obligations for use of any customs procedure with economic impact referred to in Articles 85 to 87a	Any person to whom the conditions or obligations of a customs procedure with economic impact are transferred.	£2,500
To notify Customs of all factors arising after the authorisation is granted and which may influence its continuation or content.	Any authorised person.	£2,500
Articles 105 of the Code . . . [4]		
. . . [4] the designated person shall keep stock records of all the goods placed under the customs warehousing procedure in the form approved by Customs.	The designated person.	£1,000
End Use		
Articles 6, 7, 21, 82, 85 to 87 and 90 of the Code and Article 292 and 293 of the Implementing Regulation		
To comply with a condition of an immediately enforceable binding decision of Customs in respect of an authorisation or a transferred obligation under end-use referred to in Article 21 or 82.	The person to whom the authorisation for End Use is issued.	£2,500
Free Zones		
Articles 6, 7, 167 and 172 of the Code and Articles 800 and 801 of the Implementing Regulation		
To comply with a condition of an immediately enforceable binding decision of Customs in respect of an approval for a free zone.	The person to whom the approval for a free zone has been granted.	£2,500
[Article 176 of the Code		
To keep stock records in the form approved by Customs.	The designated person.	£1,000.][4]
Transit		
[Customs status of goods and Community transit		
Article 94(1) of the Code		
To provide a guarantee.	The principal to the transit operation.	£2,500.
Article 96(1) and (2) of the Code		
Obligation to:		
(a) produce the goods intact at the customs office of destination by the prescribed time limit and duly observe the measures adopted by Customs to ensure identification of the goods;	The principal to the transit operation.	£2,500.

VAT SIs

	A carrier or recipient of goods who accepts the goods knowing they are moving under Community transit.	£2,500.
(b) observe the provisions relating to the Community transit procedure.	The principal to the transit operation.	£2,500.
. . . [4]		
. . . [4]	. . . [4]	. . . [4]
. . . [4]		
. . . [4]	. . . [4]	. . . [4]
Article 324d of the Implementing Regulation		
Obligation for T2L or other commercial documents to contain the endorsement "signature waived" in place of the authorised consignor's signature.	The authorised consignor.	£2,500.
Article 448(5) as it applies to Article 324e(5) of the Implementing Regulation		
Obligation to notify all offences and irregularities to the customs authorities.	The shipping company.	£2,500.
Article 359(1) of the Implementing Regulation		
To present the consignment and the transit accompanying document at each office of transit.	The carrier.	£2,500.
Article 360(1) of the Implementing Regulation		
In the circumstances described in Article 360(1)(a) to (e) (prescribed itinerary changed, seals broken, goods transferred to another means of transport, goods unloaded, or in the event of some other incident or accident capable of affecting the ability of the principal or carrier to comply with his obligations), to make the necessary entries in the transit accompanying document and present it with the consignment to the customs authorities of the Member State in whose territory the means of transport is located.	The carrier.	£2,500.
Article 361(1) of the Implementing Regulation		
To present the goods and the required documents at the office of destination during the days and hours appointed for opening; or, where allowed by the office of destination and at the request and expense of the party concerned, outside the appointed days and hours or at any other place.	The principal.	£2,500.
	The carrier.	£2,500.
Articles 6 and 7 of the Code and Articles 372 to 376 of the Implementing Regulation		
To comply with a condition of authorisation (including the conditions for use of simplifications and operating and control methods) of an immediately enforceable binding decision of Customs to authorise simplifications of Community transit.	The principal.	£2,500.
	The consignee.	
Article 377(1) of the Implementing Regulation		

To inform the customs authorities of any factor arising after the authorisation was granted which may influence its continuation or content.	The authorisation holder.	£2,500.
Article 408(1) of the Implementing Regulation		
Obligation to:		
(a) immediately inform the office of destination responsible of the arrival of the goods by the "arrival notification" message including all incidents during transport;	The authorised consignee.	£2,500.
(b) wait for the "unloading message" before starting the unloading;	The authorised consignee.	£2,500.
(c) send the "unloading remarks" message in accordance with the time limit and procedure stipulated;	The authorised consignee.	£2,500.
(d) make available or send to the office of destination a copy of the transit accompanying document which accompanied the goods according to the arrangement provided in the authorisation.	The authorised consignee.	£2,500.
Article 353(3) of the Implementing Regulation		
To obtain the approval of the customs authorities to use a written transit declaration in the fallback procedure under paragraph 2(b) when the principal's computer system and/ or network is/ are not functioning.	The principal.	£2,500.
Point 5 of Annex 37d to the Implementing Regulation		
To inform the customs authorities when the principal's computer system and/ or network is/ are available again.	The principal.	£2,500.
Point 15 of Annex 37d to the Implementing Regulation		
Under the fallback procedure, to present a transit advice note in the required form to each office of transit.	The carrier.	£2,500.
Point 30.1 of Annex 37d to the Implementing Regulation		
Under the fallback procedure, to send to the office of destination without delay the Transit Accompanying Document or Copies No 4 and No 5 of the transit declaration which accompanied the goods, indicating the date of arrival, the condition of any seals affixed and any irregularity.	The authorised consignee.	£2,500.][1]
[Provisions concerning bananas		
. . .[4]		
. . .[4]	. . .[4]	. . .[4]
Article 290c and Annexes 38b and 38c of the Implementing Regulation		
To draw up a banana weighing certificate in accordance with the required procedure and in the required form.	Authorised weigher.	£2,500.][1]
Information and Records		
Article 14 of the Code and section 23 of the 1994 Act		

VAT SIs

Any obligation to provide, furnish, or produce information or documents to Customs (whether subject to time limit or reasonable demand) in such form as may reasonably be required for examination, copying or making extracts or removal for such purposes and whether for a reasonable or specified period.	The person directly or indirectly involved in the customs operation concerned for the purposes of trade in goods.	£1,000
	Any person carrying on a trade or business within the meaning of section 20 of the 1994 Act.	£1,000
[Article 16 of the Code, the Customs Traders (Accounts and Records) Regulations 1995		
To keep and preserve records as required by Article 16 of the Code and by the Regulations.	The person upon whom the obligation falls.	£1,000.][4]
Assistance in Examination of goods		
Articles 241 and 243 of the Implementing Regulation		
To render Customs:	The declarant.	£1,000
(a) satisfactory assistance to facilitate examination or sampling of goods; and	The person designated by the declarant to be present at the examination of the goods.	£1,000
(b) where necessary, by a deadline set by that authority.		
[The Postal Packets (Revenue and Customs) Regulations 2011 Regulations 17, 18(1) and 19		
All foreign postal packets	The sender.	£1,000.
(a) to be accompanied by a customs declaration in the appropriate form, completed in one of the permitted languages, legibly, accurately and in full, and	The postal operator.	£2,500.
(b) in the cases to which regulation 18(1) applies, to be labelled or distinguished as required by that regulation.		
Regulation 18(2)		
On accepting a packet satisfying the requirements of regulation 18(1) to give the sender a duly endorsed certificate of sending.	The postal operator.	£2,500.
Regulation 21		
When so requested by a customs officer, to produce any packet to that officer or open it for that officer's examination.	The postal operator.	£2,500.
Regulation 22(3)		
To return, destroy or deliver up to Customs goods for which no proper account is given within the requisite period.	The postal operator.	£2,500.
Regulation 23		
To pay over to Customs any sums due to them recovered under section 105(3) of the Postal Services Act 2000.	The postal operator.	£2,500.][4]
Preference		
Section 80 of the Act		

(a) To furnish information in such form and within such time as may be specified; (b) To produce for inspection, copying or the taking of extracts, invoices, bills of lading, books or documents specified; as Customs or an officer may require for the purpose of verifying or investigating any certificate or other evidence under any Community requirement;	Any person appearing to the Customs or an officer to have been concerned in any way with the goods, or with any goods from which directly or indirectly they have been produced or manufactured, or to have been concerned with the obtaining or furnishing of the certificate or evidence.	£1,000
	The exporter	£1,000
(i) as to the origin of goods; or		
(ii) as to payments made or relief from duty allowed in any country or territory.		
[Articles 27 and 20(3)(d) of the Code and the agreements therein referred to, which the Community has concluded with certain countries or groups of countries and which provide for the granting of preferential tariff treatment and which require that penalties shall be imposed on any person who draws up or causes to be drawn up a document which contains incorrect information for the purpose of obtaining preferential treatment for products		
Not to draw up, or cause to be drawn up, a document which contains incorrect information for the purpose of obtaining a preferential treatment for products.	Any person drawing up or causing to be drawn up such a document.	£2,500.
Articles 5 and 62 of the Code and Articles 84 and 199 of the Implementing Regulation		
Submission of an accurate, authentic proof of origin or equivalent declaration with attached documents in compliance with any obligation under a particular international agreement entered into by the Community applying as part of the law of the United Kingdom in relation to a relevant tax or duty by virtue of directly applicable Community legislation.	The declarant or representative lodging the proof of origin or equivalent declaration with Customs.	£2,500.][1]
[Reliefs from customs duty and import VAT		
Articles 8, 16, 33, 48, 52, 64, 71, 72, 78, 79 of Council Regulation 1186/2009		
Not to lend, hire out, transfer or (in the case of Articles 8, 16 and 33) give as security goods admitted duty-free under the Regulation without (a) prior notification to Customs; and (b) payment of any import duties arising.	In respect of non-notification: the person lending, hiring, transferring the goods or giving them as security.	£1,000.
	In respect of non-payment of duties: the person to whom the relief has been given.	£1,000.
Articles 52, 65 and 80 of Council Regulation 1186/2009		
To inform Customs where the conditions for entitlement cease to be fulfilled or where the goods are to be used other than for the permitted purposes.	The institution or organisation in question.	£1,000.

The Customs and Excise (Personal Reliefs for Special Visitors) Order 1992		
The conditions for relief set out in the Order.	The entitled person.	£1,000.][4]

Amendments—

[1] After the last entry under the heading "Customs Declarations", entries inserted, entries under heading "Transit" substituted, entries under heading "Provisions concerning bananas" inserted, and entry relating to "Preference" beginning "Article 199" substituted, by the Customs (Contravention of a Relevant Rule) (Amendment) Regulations, SI 2009/3164 regs 2, 4–7 with effect from 24 December 2009.

[2] In entry under the heading "Regulation 9 of the Postal packets Regulations", words substituted by the Postal Services Act 2011 (Consequential Modifications and Amendments) Order, SI 2011/2085 art 5(1), Sch 1 para 57 with effect from 1 October 2011.

[3] In entries in columns 1 and 2, words substituted; under the heading "Goods brought into the customs territory of the Community (United Kingdom)" entries inserted; under the heading "Presentation of Goods to Customs" entry revoked and entries inserted; under heading "Customs Declarations" entry inserted; and under the heading "Simplified Procedures" entries substituted and entry revoked, by the Customs (Contravention of a Relevant Rule) (Amendment) Regulations, SI 2011/2534 regs 2, 5–12 with effect from 15 November 2011.

[4] Entries revoked, substituted and inserted, and in column 1, words substituted and revoked by the Customs (Contravention of a Relevant Rule) (Amendment) Regulations, SI 2015/636 regs 2, 5 with effect from 2 April 2015.

2004/674

RECOVERY OF DUTIES AND TAXES ETC DUE IN OTHER MEMBER STATES (CORRESPONDING UK CLAIMS, PROCEDURE AND SUPPLEMENTARY) REGULATIONS 2004

Made by the Treasury under FA 2002 Sch 39 para 3(1),(2),(3) and the Commissioners of Customs and Excise and the Commissioners of Inland Revenue, under FA 2002 Sch 39 paras 2(2) and 3(4)

Made . . . . 9 March 2004
Laid before the House of Commons . . . . 10 March 2004
Coming into force . . . . 1 April 2004

Amendments—These regulations revoked by the MARD Regulations, SI 2011/2931 reg 18, Schedule with effect from 1 January 2012.

2004/1929

VALUE ADDED TAX (DISCLOSURE OF AVOIDANCE SCHEMES) REGULATIONS 2004

Made by the Treasury under VATA 1994 Sch 11A paras 6(2), (3), 9(1) and 13

Made . . . . 22 July 2004
Laid before the House of Commons . . . . 22 July 2004
Coming into force . . . . 1 August 2004

1 Citation, commencement and interpretation

(1) These Regulations may be cited as the Value Added Tax (Disclosure of Avoidance Schemes) Regulations 2004 and come into force on 1st August 2004.

(2) In these Regulations "Schedule 11A" means Schedule 11A to the Value Added Tax Act 1994.

2 Time of notification

(1) Where paragraph 6(1)(*a*) of Schedule 11A applies (VAT return affected by a notifiable scheme), the time prescribed for the purposes of paragraph 6(2) and (3) of that Schedule (duty to notify Commissioners) is the 30th day from the end of the last day specified by or under regulation 25 of the Value Added Tax Regulations 1995 for making the return.

(2) Where paragraph 6(1)(*b*) of Schedule 11A applies (claim for repayment of output tax or an increase in credit for input tax based on a scheme), the time prescribed for the purposes of paragraph 6(2) and (3) of that Schedule is the 30th day from the end of the date the claim is made.

[(3) Where paragraph 6(1)(*c*) of Schedule 11A applies (non-deductible tax less than it would be but for a scheme), the time prescribed for the purposes of paragraph 6(2) and (3) of that Schedule is the 30th day from the end of the last day specified by or under regulation 25 of the Value Added Tax Regulations 1995 for making a return in respect of the relevant prescribed accounting period.

(4) For the purposes of paragraph (3) relevant prescribed accounting period means the period in which the taxable person's non-deductible tax is less than it would be but for any notifiable scheme to which he is party.

(5) Paragraph (1) shall not have effect in relation to any scheme listed in Column 1 of the Schedule where the beginning of the prescribed accounting period for which the VAT return is made is earlier than the date shown opposite that scheme in Column 2 of the Schedule.

(6) Paragraph (2) shall not have effect in relation to any scheme listed in Column 1 of the Schedule where the beginning of the prescribed accounting period in relation to which the claim is made is earlier than the date shown opposite that scheme in Column 2 of the Schedule.][1]

Amendments—[1] Paras (3)–(6) substituted for former paras (3), (4) by the Value Added Tax (Disclosure of Avoidance Schemes) (Amendment) Regulations, SI 2005/2009 arts 2, 3 with effect from 1 August 2005.

3 Form and manner of notification

Notification of a scheme pursuant to paragraph 6(2) or 6(3) of Schedule 11A shall be made in such form and manner as may be specified in a notice published by the Commissioners and not withdrawn by a further notice.

4 Information to be notified

(1) For the purposes of paragraph 6(3) of Schedule 11A (duty to notify the Commissioners of a scheme other than a designated scheme) and paragraph 9(1) of that Schedule (voluntary notification of scheme) the following information is prescribed—

(*a*) any provision designated in accordance with paragraph 4 of Schedule 11A (designation of provisions included in or associated with avoidance schemes) which is included in or associated with the scheme;

(*b*) how the scheme gives rise to a tax advantage, including, insofar as material to the tax advantage—

(i) a description of each arrangement, transaction or series of transactions;

(ii) their sequence;

(iii) their timing, or the intervals between them; and

(iv) the goods or services involved;

(*c*) how the involvement of any party to the scheme contributes to the obtaining of the tax advantage; and

(*d*) any provision having the force of law in the United Kingdom or elsewhere relied upon as giving rise to the tax advantage.

(2) A tax advantage is considered to have been obtained or to be obtained and any arrangement, transaction or series of transactions is considered to have taken place or to take place provided a taxable person has treated or intends to treat it as having been obtained or taken place for the purposes of—

(*a*) a return required under the Value Added Tax Act 1994; . . .[1]

(*b*) a claim for repayment of output tax or an increase in credit for input tax[; or

(*c*) reducing the amount of his non-deductible tax.][1]

Amendments—[1] In para (2), word "or" at end of sub-para (*a*) revoked, and sub-para (*c*) and preceding word "or" inserted by the Value Added Tax (Disclosure of Avoidance Schemes) (Amendment) Regulations, SI 2005/2009 arts 2, 4 with effect from 1 August 2005.

SCHEDULE

Regulations 2(5) and 2(6)

Row	*Column 1*	*Column 2*
	Scheme	*Date*
(a)	Any scheme allocated a reference number from 1 to 8 by the Value Added Tax (Disclosure of Avoidance Schemes) (Designations) Order 2004.	1st August 2004
(b)	Any scheme that includes, or is associated with, a provision of a description falling within paragraphs 1 to 7 of Schedule 2 to the Value Added Tax (Disclosure of Avoidance Schemes) (Designations) Order 2004.	1st August 2004
(c)	Any scheme allocated the reference number 9 or 10 by the Value Added Tax (Disclosure of Avoidance Schemes) (Designations) Order 2004 and which does not fall within row (b) above.	1st August 2005
(d)	Any scheme that includes, or is associated with, a provision of a description falling within paragraph 8 of Schedule 2 to the Value Added Tax (Disclosure of Avoidance Schemes) (Designations) Order 2004 and which does not fall within rows (a) or (b) above.	1st August 2005][1]

Amendments—

[1] Schedule inserted by the Value Added Tax (Disclosure of Avoidance Schemes) (Amendment) Regulations, SI 2005/2009 arts 2, 5 with effect from 1 August 2005.

2004/1931

VALUE ADDED TAX (GROUPS: ELIGIBILITY) ORDER 2004

Made by the Treasury under VATA 1994 s 43AA(1)–(4)

Made . . . .*22 July 2004*
Laid before the House of Commons . . . .*22 July 2004*
Coming into force . . . .*1 August 2004*

1 Citation and commencement

This Order may be cited as the Value Added Tax (Groups: eligibility) Order 2004 and comes into force on 1st August 2004.

2 Modification regarding section 43A of the Value Added Tax Act 1994

A body corporate that is a specified body is eligible to be treated as a member of a group if, in addition to satisfying the conditions set out in section 43A(1) of the Value Added Tax Act 1994 ("the Act"), it satisfies both the benefits condition and the consolidated accounts condition.

3 Specified bodies

(1) A body corporate to which this article applies is a specified body for the purposes of this Order if it carries on a relevant business activity and—

(*a*) the value of the group's supplies in the year then ending has exceeded £10 million; or

(*b*) there are reasonable grounds for believing that the value of the group's supplies in the year then beginning will exceed that amount.

(2) For the purposes of determining the value mentioned in sub-paragraph (*b*) of paragraph (1), a body that is not a member of the group shall be deemed to be a member.

(3) Subject to paragraph (4), this article applies to a body corporate which, at any time when the relevant business activity is being carried on—

(*a*) is not a wholly-owned subsidiary of a person who controls all of the other members of the group (or, where the person is or will be a member of the group, all of the other members apart from himself);

(*b*) is managed, directly or indirectly, in respect of the business activity concerned, by a third party in the course or furtherance of a business carried on by him; or

(*c*) is the sole general partner of a limited partnership.

(4) This article does not apply to—

(*a*) a body corporate that controls all of the members of the group (or, where it is a member of the group, all of the members apart from itself);

(*b*) a body corporate whose activities another body corporate is empowered by statute to control;

(*c*) a body corporate whose only activity is acting as the trustee of a pension scheme; or

(*d*) a charity.

(5) In this article—

(*a*) a body corporate is a wholly-owned subsidiary of a person if it is a wholly-owned subsidiary of his within the meaning given by section [1159 of and Schedule 6 to][1] the Companies Act [2006][1], or would be if the person were a company;

(*b*) in determining whether a body corporate is a wholly-owned subsidiary of a person, the membership of any excepted individual who is not acting on behalf of another person shall be disregarded;

(*c*) "pension scheme" means an occupational pension scheme established under a trust and "occupational pension scheme" has the meaning given by section 1 of the Pension Schemes Act 1993.

Amendments—[1] In para (5)(*a*), words substituted for words "736 of" and "1985", by the Companies Act 2006 (Consequential Amendments) (Taxes and National Insurance) Order, SI 2009/1890 art 4(1)(*k*) with effect from 1 October 2009.

4 Relevant business activities

(1) A business activity is a relevant business activity if it involves making one or more supplies of goods or services to one or more members of the group and—

(*a*) those supplies are not incidental to that business activity;

(*b*) at least one of those supplies is or would be chargeable to VAT at a rate other than zero; and

(*c*) the representative member is not or would not be entitled to credit for the whole of the VAT on such supplies as fall within sub-paragraph (*b*) as input tax.

(2) In determining for the purposes of paragraph (1) whether—

(*a*) a body corporate makes any supplies to any members of the group;

(*b*) a supply would be chargeable to VAT at a rate other than zero;

(*c*) the representative member would not be entitled to credit for the whole of the VAT on the supply as input tax, a body corporate that is a member of the group shall be deemed not to be a member.

5 The benefits condition

(1) The benefits condition is satisfied unless more than 50% of the benefits of the relevant business activity accrue, directly or indirectly, to one or more third parties.

(2) For the purposes of paragraph (1), benefits that accrue to a person in his capacity as a member of a body corporate which controls all of the other members of the group (or, where the body is or will be a member of the group, all of the other members apart from itself) shall not be regarded as accruing to a third party.

(3) The following are benefits of a business activity for the purposes of paragraph (1)—

(*a*) profits (whether or not distributed);

(*b*) charges for managing the business activity (including charges for providing staff to manage it);

(*c*) the amounts, if any, by which any other charges made to the body exceed the open market value of the goods or services concerned.

(4) For the purposes of paragraph (1), if there are no such benefits, the business activity shall be deemed to generate profits of £100.

6 The consolidated accounts condition

(1) The consolidated accounts condition is satisfied if—

(*a*) consolidated accounts prepared for a person who controls all of the other members of the group (or, where the person is or will be a member of the group, all of the other members apart from himself) would be required by generally accepted accounting practice to include accounts for the specified body as his subsidiary; and

(*b*) consolidated accounts prepared for a third party would not be required by generally accepted accounting practice to include accounts for the specified body as his subsidiary.

(2) For the purpose of the application of paragraph (1) at a particular time—

(*a*) the reference to consolidated accounts is a reference to consolidated accounts—

(i) for a period including that time, and

(ii) insofar as they relate to that time,

(*b*) any principle of generally accepted accounting practice that permits accounts of a subsidiary undertaking to be excluded from a consolidation as being immaterial shall be disregarded;

(*c*) the reference to consolidated accounts prepared for a person is a reference to consolidated accounts of a kind that could be prepared for him in accordance with generally accepted accounting practice, for which purpose it does not matter—

(i) whether accounts are actually prepared for him (whether for a particular period or at all), or

(ii) in particular, whether he is required to prepare accounts.

(3) In this article "generally accepted accounting practice"—

(*a*) has the meaning given by section 50(1) of the Finance Act 2004;

(*b*) in relation to any time when that section does not have effect, has the meaning given by section 836A of the Income and Corporation Taxes Act 1988.

7 Interpretation etc

(1) In determining—

(*a*) the value of the supplies made by a body corporate that is the sole general partner of a limited partnership (a "general partner");

(*b*) whether a general partner is carrying on a relevant business activity;

(*c*) whether the benefits condition is satisfied in relation to a general partner;

(*d*) whether the consolidated accounts condition is satisfied in relation to a general partner,

articles 3(1) and (2), 4(1), 5 and 6 shall apply as if references to the body or specified body, as the case requires, are references to the limited partnership.

(2) A person is a third party for the purposes of this Order if—

(*a*) he does not control the body corporate and all of the other members of the group;

(*b*) a person who controls the body corporate and all of the other members of the group does not control him; and

(*c*) he is not an excepted individual.

(3) An individual is an excepted individual if he is—

(*a*) an employee or director of the body; or

(*b*) where the body is a limited liability partnership, a member of the body.

(4) Any reference in this Order to "the group" is to the group of which the body corporate is a member or to which an application under section 43B(1) or (2)(*a*) of the Act relates, as the case may require.

(5) Any reference in this Order to a person controlling a body corporate includes a reference to his controlling the body together with one or more other individuals with whom he is carrying on a business in partnership.

2004/1933

VALUE ADDED TAX (DISCLOSURE OF AVOIDANCE SCHEMES) (DESIGNATIONS) ORDER 2004

Made by the Treasury under VATA 1994 s 97(3)

Made ....*22 July 2004*
Laid before the House of Commons ....*22 July 2004*
Coming into force ....*1 August 2004*

1 Citation and commencement

This Order may be cited as the Value Added Tax (Disclosure of Avoidance Schemes) (Designations) Order 2004 and comes into force on 1st August 2004.

2 Interpretation

(1) In this Order "the Act" means the Value Added Tax Act 1994.

(2) Any reference in this Order to "Schedule 8" or "Schedule 9" is a reference to that Schedule to the Act.

(3) For the purposes of this Order a person is connected with another where—

(*a*) one of them is an undertaking in relation to which the other is a group undertaking; or

(*b*) both of them are connected to the same trust.

(4) For the purposes of this Order a person is connected to a trust where—

(*a*) he is the settlor of the trust, a trustee or beneficiary of it, or

(*b*) he holds any shares in a company in accordance with the terms of the trust, or is a person on whose behalf such shares are held.

(5) For the purposes of this Order "undertaking" and "group undertaking" have the meaning given by [section 1161 of the Companies Act 2006][1].

(6) A scheme is treated as fitting a description contained in the first column of Schedule 1 to this Order even if any feature of that scheme is not actually present (whether as a matter of law or for any other reason), provided a taxable person has treated that feature as being present for the purpose of making—

(*a*) a return required under the Act; or

(*b*) a claim for the repayment of output tax or an increase in credit for input tax.

(7) A provision is treated as fitting a description contained in Schedule 2 to this Order even if it, or any feature of it, is not actually present (whether as a matter of law or for any other reason), provided a taxable person has treated that feature as being present for the purpose of making—

(*a*) a return required under the Act; or

(*b*) a claim for the repayment of output tax or an increase in credit for input tax.

Amendments—[1] Words in para (5) substituted by the Companies Act 2006 (Consequential Amendments) (Taxes and National Insurance) Order, SI 2008/954 arts 53 with effect from 6 April 2008.

3 Designation of avoidance schemes and provisions included in or associated with avoidance schemes

(1) The schemes described in the first column of Schedule 1 to this Order are designated schemes for the purposes of paragraph 3 of Schedule 11A to the Act and are allocated the reference numbers shown in the second column of Schedule 1.

(2) The provisions described in Schedule 2 to this Order are provisions designated for the purposes of paragraph 4 of Schedule 11A to the Act.

SCHEDULES

SCHEDULE 1

Article 3(1)

Description of Scheme	**Reference Number**
First grant of a major interest in a building	**1**

Any scheme comprising or including the first grant of a major interest in any building of a description falling within item 1(*a*) of Group 5 of Schedule 8 (construction of buildings etc.) where—

(*a*) the grant is made to a person connected with the grantor; and

(*b*) the grantor, or any body corporate treated as a member of a VAT group under section 43 of the Act of which the grantor is a member, attributes to that grant input tax incurred by him—

(i) in respect of a service charge relating to the building; or

Description of Scheme **Reference Number**

(ii) in connection with any extension, enlargement, repair, maintenance or refurbishment of the building, other than for remedying defects in the original construction.

Payment handling service 2

Any scheme comprising or including a retail supply of goods or services together with a linked supply to the same customer, where the total consideration for the retail supply and the linked supply is no different, or not significantly different, from what it would be for the retail sale alone.

NOTE

"Linked supply" means a supply by the retailer or any other person that—

(*a*) relates to the means of payment used for the retail supply; and

(*b*) is a supply of a description falling within Group 5 of Schedule 9 (finance).

Value shifting 3

Any scheme comprising or including a retail supply of goods or services together with a linked supply to the same customer where—

(*a*) the linked supply is a separate supply under the terms of any agreement made by the customer;

(*b*) part of the total consideration for the retail supply and the linked supply is attributed to the linked supply by the terms of any such agreement; and

(*c*) the total consideration for the retail supply and the linked supply is no different, or not significantly different, from what it would be for the retail supply alone.

NOTES

(1) "Retail supply" means a supply by retail upon which VAT is charged at the rate in force under section 2(1) of the Act (rate of VAT)

(2) "Linked supply" means a supply of goods or services made by the retailer or any other person which is zero-rated or exempt.

Leaseback agreement 4

Any scheme comprising or including the supply of goods, or the leasing or letting on hire of goods, ("the relevant supply") by a taxable person to a connected relevant person where—

(*a*) the taxable person or another taxable person connected with him, including the relevant person, is entitled to credit for all the input tax arising on the purchase of the goods;

(*b*) the relevant person uses the goods in the course or furtherance of a business carried on by him, and for the purpose of that business, otherwise than for the purpose of selling, or leasing or letting on hire, the goods; and

(*c*) the relevant person or a person connected with him has directly or indirectly provided funds for meeting more than 90% of the cost of the goods.

NOTES

(1) "Relevant person" means any person who, in respect of the relevant supply, is not entitled to credit for all the input tax wholly attributable to the supplies he makes.

(2) The provision of funds includes—

(*a*) the making of a loan of funds; and

(*b*) the provision of any consideration for the issue of any shares or other securities issued wholly or partly for raising the funds.

(3) The grant, assignment or surrender of a major interest in land is not a supply of goods for the purposes of this scheme.

Extended approval period 5

Any scheme comprising or including a retail supply of goods where—

(*a*) the goods are sent or taken on approval or sale or return or similar terms;

(*b*) payment for the supply is required in full by the retailer before the expiry of any approval, return or similar period; and

(*c*) for the purposes of accounting for VAT, the retailer treats the goods as supplied on a date after the date on which payment is received in full.

Groups: third party suppliers 6

Description of Scheme	**Reference Number**

Any scheme comprising or including supplies made to one or more group members by a specified body in relation to which the benefits condition is not satisfied.

NOTE

The Value Added Tax (Groups: eligibility) Order 2004 shall apply for the purposes of determining whether—

(*a*) a body corporate is a specified body; and

(*b*) the benefits condition is satisfied in relation to it.

Exempt education or vocational training by a non-profit making body **7**

Any scheme comprising or including the conduct of a relevant business by a non-profit making body where—

(*a*) it receives a relevant supply from a connected taxable person who is not an eligible body; and

(*b*) in any one prescribed accounting period the value of all such relevant supplies is equal to or more than 20% of the cost of making the supplies comprising the relevant business.

NOTES

(1) "Relevant business" means a business whose activities consist wholly or mainly of the supply of education or vocational training to persons who are not taxable persons.

(2) "Non-profit making body" means a body within Note (1)(*e*) of Group 6 of Schedule 9 (Education) which is not otherwise within Note 1.

(3) "Relevant supply" means the supply, including the leasing or letting on hire, for use in a relevant business of—

(*a*) a capital item used in the course or furtherance of the relevant business, and for the purpose of that business, otherwise than solely for the purpose of selling, or leasing or letting on hire, the item;

(*b*) staff;

(*c*) management services;

(*d*) administration services; or

(*e*) accountancy services.

(4) "Eligible body" has the meaning given by Note (1) of Group 6 of Schedule 9.

(5) "Vocational training" has the meaning given by Note (3) of Group 6 of Schedule 9, but does not include vocational training of a description falling within item 5 or 5A of that Group.

Taxable education or vocational training by a non-eligible body **8**

Any scheme comprising or including the conduct of a relevant business by a non-eligible body connected to an eligible body where—

(*a*) the non-eligible body benefits or intends to benefit the eligible body by way of gift, dividend or otherwise; or

(*b*) the eligible body makes any supply to the non-eligible body which is a relevant supply and, in any one prescribed accounting period, the value of all such relevant supplies is equal to or more than 20% of the cost of making the supplies comprising the relevant business.

NOTES

(1) "Eligible body" has the meaning given by Note (1) of Group 6 of Schedule 9.

(2) "Relevant business" means a business whose activities consist wholly or mainly of the taxable supply of education or vocational training.

(3) "Vocational training" has the meaning given by Note (3) of Group 6 of Schedule 9.

(4) "Relevant supply" means the supply, or leasing or letting on hire, for use in a relevant business of—

(*a*) a capital item used in the course or furtherance of the relevant business, and for the purpose of that business, otherwise than solely for the purpose of selling, or leasing or letting on hire, the item;

(*b*) staff;

(*c*) management services;

Description of Scheme	Reference Number
(*d*) administration services; or	
(*e*) accounting services.	
[Cross-border face-value vouchers	
Any scheme comprising or including the supply of a relevant service by a person belonging in the United Kingdom (the UK supplier) to a person belonging in a member State other than the United Kingdom (the non-UK recipient) where—	9
(a) the service is used, or intended to be used, in whole or in part, by the non-UK recipient or any other person belonging in another member State for the purposes of supplying a relevant service to a person belonging in the United Kingdom (the retail supply);	
(b) the recipient of the retail supply uses a face-value voucher issued by a person belonging in a country other than the United Kingdom to obtain that supply;	
(c) the person making the retail supply does not account for VAT on that supply in the United Kingdom or any other member State; and	
(d) the UK supplier and the person making the retail supply are connected persons.	
NOTES	
(1) "Face-value voucher" means tokens, stamps or vouchers of a description falling within paragraph 1(1) of Schedule 10A to the Act (face-value vouchers).	
(2) "Relevant service" means a supply of a description specified in any of paragraphs 7A to 7C of Schedule 5 to the Act (services supplied where received).	
(3) References in this scheme to the retail supply shall not include any supply of a relevant service made to a taxable person.	
Surrender of relevant lease	
Any scheme comprising or including the surrender by an occupier of a building of a relevant lease, tenancy or licence to occupy where—	10
(a) the occupier or any person connected to him is a relevant person;	
(b) the building is a capital item for the purposes of regulation 113 of the Value Added Tax Regulations 1995;	
(c) before the surrender the occupier paid relevant VAT and was not entitled to full credit for, or refund of, that VAT under any provision of the Act or regulations;	
(d) following the surrender the occupier continues to occupy at least 80% of the area previously occupied; and	
(e) following the surrender the occupier pays no relevant VAT or pays less than 50% of the relevant VAT paid before the surrender.	
NOTES	
(1) Relevant lease, tenancy or licence to occupy means any lease of, tenancy of or licence to occupy the building granted or assigned to the occupier where—	
(a) an election under paragraph 2 of Schedule 10 (election to waive exemption) has been made in relation to the building; and	
(b) that election has not been revoked in accordance with paragraph 3(5) of Schedule 10.	
(2) Relevant person means any person who—	
(a) is a lessor of the building;	
(b) is an owner of the building for the purposes of regulation 113 of the VAT Regulations 1995; and	
(c) has made an election under paragraph 2 of Schedule 10 in relation to the building.	
(3) Relevant VAT means VAT on rent paid or payable by the occupier in relation to the building.	
(4) Surrender includes any termination by the occupier of the relevant lease, tenancy or licence to occupy where he has entered into any agreement, arrangement or understanding (whether legally binding or not) with the lessor regarding that termination.	
(5) Building includes any part of that building.][1]	

VAT SIs

Amendments—[1] Entry inserted by the VAT (Disclosure of Avoidance Schemes) (Designations) (Amendment) Order, SI 2005/1724 arts 2, 3 with effect from 1 August 2005.

SCHEDULE 2

Article 3(2)

PART 1
PROVISIONS ASSOCIATED WITH SCHEMES

Confidentiality condition

1 An agreement preventing or limiting the disclosure of how a scheme gives rise to a tax advantage.

The sharing of the tax advantage with another party to the scheme or with the promoter

2—(1) An agreement that the tax advantage to a person accruing from the operation of the scheme be shared to any extent with another party to it or another person promoting it.

(2) A person is a promoter of a scheme if, in the course of a trade, profession or business which involves the provision to other persons of services relating to taxation—

(*a*) he is to any extent responsible for the design of the proposed arrangements; or

(*b*) he invites persons to enter into contracts for the implementation of the proposed arrangements.

Fee payable to a promoter which is in whole or in part contingent on tax savings from the scheme

3—(1) An agreement that payment to a promoter of the scheme be contingent in whole or in part on the tax advantage accruing from the operation of the scheme.

(2) A person is a promoter of a scheme if, in the course of a trade, profession or business which involves the provision to other persons of services relating to taxation—

(*a*) he is to any extent responsible for the design of the proposed arrangements; or

(*b*) he invites persons to enter into contracts for the implementation of the proposed arrangements.

PART 2
PROVISIONS INCLUDED IN SCHEMES

Prepayment between connected parties

4—(1) A payment for a supply of goods or services between connected persons—

(*a*) before the time applicable under section 6(2) or (3) of the Act; or

(*b*) where the supply is a continuous supply and the payment is before the goods or services are provided.

(2) A supply is a continuous supply if it is a supply to which regulation 85 (leases treated as supplies of goods), 86 (supplies of water, gas or any form of power, heat, refrigeration or ventilation), 90 (continuous supply of services), 91 (royalties and similar payments) or 93 (supplies in the construction industry) of the Value Added Tax Regulations 1995 applies.

(3) For the purposes of paragraph (1)(*b*) goods or services are provided at the time when, and to the extent that, the recipient receives the benefit of them.

Funding by loan, share subscription or subscription in securities

5 The funding in whole or in part of a supply of goods or services between connected persons by means of a loan between connected persons or the subscription for shares in, or securities issued by, a connected person.

Off-shore loops

6—(1) A supply of a relevant service which is used or intended to be used, in whole or in part, directly or indirectly, in making to a person belonging in the United Kingdom, a supply which is zero-rated, exempt or treated as made in another country (and not in the United Kingdom) by virtue of section 7(10) of the Act (place of supply of services).

(2) A "relevant service" is a service of a description falling within—

(*a*) article 3(*a*) of the Value Added Tax (Input Tax) (Specified Supplies) Order 1999 (services supplied to a person who belongs outside the member States);

(*b*) article 3(*b*) of that Order (services directly linked to the export of goods to a place outside the member States), insofar as they are supplies of a description falling within item 2 of Group 5 of Schedule 9 (the making of any advance or any credit); or (*c*) article 3(*c*) of that Order (the provision of intermediary insurance or financial services); or is a supply of a description specified in any of paragraphs 1 to 8 of Schedule 5 to the Act (services supplied where received), and the recipient of that supply belongs in a country, other than the Isle of Man, which is not a member State.

Property transactions between connected persons

7—(1) A relevant grant where—

(*a*) the grantor or grantee of the interest or right is a person who is not entitled to credit for all the input tax wholly attributable to the supplies he makes;

(*b*) any work of construction, alteration, demolition, repair, maintenance or civil engineering has been or is to be carried out on the land; and

(*c*) the grant is made to a person connected with the grantor.

(2) "Relevant grant" means the grant of any interest in or right over land or of any licence to occupy land or, in relation to land in Scotland, any personal right to call for or be granted any such interest or right, other than a grant of a description falling within item 1 of Group 5 (first grant of a major interest by a person constructing a building designed for dwelling, or intended for use solely for residential or charitable purposes; or by a person converting a non-residential building to residential use) or item 1 of Group 6 (first grant of a major interest in a protected building by a person reconstructing it) of Schedule 8.

(3) "Grant" includes an assignment or surrender and the supply made by the person to whom an interest is surrendered when there is a reverse surrender.

[Issue of face-value vouchers

8—(1) The issue of face-value vouchers for consideration.

(2) Paragraph 1 does not apply where—

(*a*) the issuer expects, on reasonable grounds, that at least 75% of the face-value of the vouchers will be redeemed within three years of the date on which the vouchers were issued; and

(*b*) the vouchers were issued to relevant persons.

(3) A relevant person is

(*a*) any person who is not connected with the issuer; or

(*b*) any body corporate—

(i) which is a member of the same VAT group as the issuer for the purposes of section 43 of the Act; and

(ii) which does not intend to supply the vouchers, directly or indirectly, to any person connected with the issuer outside that VAT group.

(4) "Face-value vouchers" means tokens, stamps or vouchers of a description falling within paragraph 1(1) of Schedule 10A to the Act (face-value vouchers) and "face-value" has the meaning given by paragraph 1(2) of that Schedule.][1]

Amendments—[1] This paragraph inserted by the VAT (Disclosure of Avoidance Schemes) (Designations) (Amendment) Order, SI 2005/1724 arts 2, 4 with effect from 1 August 2005.

2004/3147

VAT (IMPORTED GAS AND ELECTRICITY) RELIEF ORDER 2004

Made . . . . .30 *November 2004*

Laid before the House of Commons . . . . .2 *December 2004*

Coming into force . . . . .1 *January 2005*

Whereas it appears necessary to the Treasury that the relief from value added tax provided by this Order should be allowed with a view to conforming with Article 14.1(k) of Council Directive No. 77/388 EEC and Article 249 of the Treaty establishing the European Community:

Now, therefore, the Treasury, in exercise of the powers conferred on them by section 37(1) of the Value Added Tax Act 1994, hereby make the following Order:

1 This Order may be cited as the Value Added Tax (Imported Gas and Electricity) Relief Order 2004 and shall come into force on 1 January 2005 in relation to goods imported on or after that date.[1]

Amendments—[1] This Order revoked by the VAT (Imported Gas, Electricity, Heat and Cooling) Relief Order, SI 2010/2924 art 2 with effect in relation to goods imported on or after 1 January 2011.

2 The VAT chargeable on the importation from a place outside the member States of-

(*a*) *gas through the natural gas distribution network or*

(*b*) *electricity*

shall not be payable.[1]

Amendments—[1] This Order revoked by the VAT (Imported Gas, Electricity, Heat and Cooling) Relief Order, SI 2010/2924 art 2 with effect in relation to goods imported on or after 1 January 2011.

2004/3148

VALUE ADDED TAX (PLACE OF SUPPLY OF GOODS) ORDER 2004

Made . . . . *30 November 2004*
Laid before the House of Commons . . . . *2 December 2004*
Coming into force . . . . *1 January 2005*

The Treasury, in exercise of the powers conferred on them by sections 7(11) and 9A of the Value Added Tax Act 1994, hereby make the following Order:

PART 1
PRELIMINARY

1 Citation and commencement

(1) This Order may be cited as the Value Added Tax (place of supply of goods) Order 2004 and shall come into force on 1 January 2005.

(2) Part 3 (supplies of gas and electricity) has effect in relation to supplies made on or after 1 January 2005.

2 Rules for determining place of supply

The rules for determining where a supply of goods is made shall be varied in accordance with the following provisions of this Order.

3 Revocation

The Value Added Tax (Place of Supply of Goods) Order 1992 is hereby revoked.

PART 2
GOODS SUPPLIED ON BOARD SHIPS, AIRCRAFT AND TRAINS

4 Interpretation of Part 2

In this Part—

"Community transport" means the transportation of passengers between the point of departure and the point of arrival in the course of which-

(*a*) there is a stop in a Member State other than that in which lies the point of departure and

(*b*) there is no stop in a country which is not a Member State

"homeward stage" means that part of the return trip which ends at the first stop in the country in which the return trip commenced and which involves only such other stops, if any, as are in Member States where there have previously been stops (in the course of that return trip)

"pleasure cruise" includes a cruise wholly or partly for the purposes of education or training

"point of arrival" means the last place in the Member States where it is expected that passengers who have commenced their journey at a place in a Member State will terminate their journey or, where there is to follow a leg which will involve a stop in a place outside the Member States, the last such place before such leg is undertaken

"point of departure" means the first place in the Member States where it is expected that passengers will commence their journey or, where there has been a leg which involved a stop in a place outside the Member States, the first such place after such leg has been completed

"return trip" means any journey involving two or more countries where it is expected that the means of transport will stop in the country from which it originally departed.

5 Subject to articles 6 to 8, where goods are supplied on board a ship, aircraft or train in the course of a Community transport, those goods shall be treated as supplied at the point of departure.

6 Subject to articles 7 and 8, any goods supplied on board a [ship, aircraft or train][1] in the course of a Community transport for consumption on board shall be treated as supplied outside the Member States.

Amendments—[1] Words substituted for words "ship or aircraft" by the VAT (Place of Supply of Goods) Order, SI 2009/215 arts 2, 3 with effect from 6 April 2009.

7 For the purposes of this Part—

(*a*) part of transportation where it is expected that a different means of transport will be used shall be treated as separate transportation and

(*b*) the homeward stage of a return trip shall be treated as separate transportation.

8 This Part shall not apply to any goods supplied as part of a pleasure cruise.

PART 3

SUPPLIES OF GAS[,, ELECTRICITY, HEAT OR COOLING]

Amendments—Words in heading substituted for words "and Electricity" by the VAT (Place of Supply of Goods) (Amendment) Order, SI 2010/2923 art 2(1), (2) with effect in relation to supplies made on or after 1 January 2011.

9 Interpretation of Part 3

In this Part—

(*a*) "the Act" means the Value Added Tax Act 1994

(*b*) "dealer" means a person whose principal activity in respect of receiving supplies of relevant goods is the re-selling of those goods and whose own consumption of those goods is negligible

[(*c*) "relevant goods" means—

(i) gas supplied through a natural gas system situated within the territory of a member State or any network connected to such a system,

(ii) electricity, and

(iii) heat or cooling supplied through a network;][1]

(*d*) "re-selling" for the purposes of article 9(*b*) does not include—

(i) re-sale as part of a single composite supply of other goods or services or

(ii) re-sale as a supply that falls to be disregarded under section 43(1)(*a*) of the Act where relevant goods are to be effectively used and consumed by a member of a VAT group

(*e*) "VAT group" means any bodies corporate treated under sections 43A to 43C of the Act as members of a group.

Amendments—[1] Para (*c*) substituted by the VAT (Place of Supply of Goods) (Amendment) Order, SI 2010/2923 art 2(1), (3) with effect in relation to supplies made on or after 1 January 2011.

10 Relevant goods supplied to a dealer shall be treated as supplied at the place where that dealer has established his business or has a fixed establishment to which the relevant goods are supplied or, in the absence of such a place of business or fixed establishment, the place where he has his permanent address or usually resides.

11 Subject to articles 12 and 13, supplies of relevant goods not falling within article 10 above shall be treated as supplied at-

(*a*) the place where the recipient of the supply has effective use and consumption of the goods or

(*b*) in relation to any part of the goods not consumed, the place where the recipient of the supply has established his business or has a fixed establishment to which the goods are supplied, or in the absence of such place of business or fixed establishment, the place where he has his permanent address or usually resides.

12 Where the recipient of supplies of relevant goods supplies those goods as part of a single composite supply of other goods or services, that constitutes effective use and consumption by him of the goods for the purposes of article 11(*a*).

13 The supply of relevant goods to a member of a VAT group, where the goods are effectively used and consumed by a member of that group, shall constitute effective use and consumption of the goods for the purposes of article 11(*a*).

14 For the purposes of section 9A of the Act (reverse charge on [certain goods][1] supplied by persons outside the United Kingdom) a person is outside the United Kingdom if he has established his business or has a fixed establishment outside the United Kingdom or, in the absence of such a place of business or fixed establishment, the place where he has his permanent address or usually resides is outside the United Kingdom.

Amendments—[1] Words substituted for words "gas and electricity" by the VAT (Place of Supply of Goods) (Amendment) Order, SI 2010/2923 art 2(1), (4) with effect in relation to supplies made on or after 1 January 2011.

2005/1133

REVENUE AND CUSTOMS (INSPECTIONS) REGULATIONS 2005

Made by the Treasury under the Commissioners for Revenue and Customs Act 2005 ss 27(1) and (2)

Made . . . . *7 April 2005*
Laid before Parliament . . . . *8 April 2005*
Coming into force . . . . *29 April 2005*

1 Citation and commencement

These Regulations may be cited as the Revenue and Customs (Inspections) Regulations 2005 and shall come into force on 29th April 2005.

2 Interpretation

(1) In these Regulations—

"the Act" means the Commissioners for Revenue and Customs Act 2005;

"appropriate inspectors" means in relation to—

(*a*) an inspection in England and Wales, the inspectors of constabulary,

(*b*) an inspection in Scotland, the inspectors of constabulary and the Scottish inspectors acting jointly,

(*c*) an inspection in Northern Ireland, the Northern Ireland inspectors;

"Chairman" means the Commissioner for the time being designated as chairman of Her Majesty's Revenue and Customs in Letters Patent under section 1(1) of the Act;

"civil penalty" means any penalty for which the Commissioners have power under any enactment to make an assessment or a demand;

"Commissioners" means the Commissioners for Revenue and Customs;

"criminal investigation" means any investigation for the purpose of considering whether an offence has been committed or discovering by whom an offence has been committed;

"Director" means the Director of Revenue and Customs Prosecutions;

"inspectors of constabulary" means Her Majesty's Inspectors of Constabulary;

"officer" means an officer of Revenue and Customs;

"revenue" has the meaning given by section 5(4) of the Act;

"risk" means the likelihood of an officer or the Commissioners doing or omitting to do something which affects—

(*a*) the prevention, detection or investigation of an offence by an officer or the Commissioners,

(*b*) any criminal proceedings in England and Wales conducted by the Director,

(*c*) any criminal proceedings conducted in Scotland under the direction of the Lord Advocate or a procurator fiscal, or

(*d*) any criminal proceedings conducted in Northern Ireland by the Commissioners or the Director of Public Prosecutions for Northern Ireland,

and the possible effect of such an act or omission on the prevention, detection or investigation of that offence or those proceedings.

(2) A reference to the Scottish inspectors or to the Northern Ireland inspectors has the same meaning as in section 27(6) of the Act.

3 Inspection Functions: England and Wales

(1) The inspectors of constabulary may carry out inspections in England and Wales for the purpose of assessing the effectiveness of the following conduct—

(*a*) any acts or omissions of an officer or the Commissioners in connection with the prevention, detection or investigation of an offence by him or them, or

(*b*) any acts or omissions of an officer or the Commissioners in connection with criminal proceedings conducted by the Director.

(2) The inspectors of constabulary may carry out inspections in England and Wales to assess the effectiveness of any matter described in regulation 6.

(3) The inspectors of constabulary may exercise the powers under this regulation on their own initiative or at the request of the Chancellor of the Exchequer or the Commissioners but the Chancellor of the Exchequer may not make a request to carry out an inspection in relation to a particular person.

(4) The chief inspector of constabulary may include in his report under section 54(4) of the Police Act 1996 (annual reports) a report on the Commissioners and officers.

4 Inspection Functions: Scotland

(1) The inspectors of constabulary and the Scottish inspectors may jointly carry out inspections in Scotland for the purpose of assessing the effectiveness of the following conduct—

(*a*) any acts or omissions of an officer or the Commissioners in connection with the prevention, detection or investigation of an offence by him or them, or

(*b*) any acts or omissions of an officer or the Commissioners in connection with criminal proceedings conducted under the direction of the Lord Advocate or a procurator fiscal.

(2) The inspectors of constabulary and the Scottish inspectors may jointly carry out inspections in Scotland to assess the effectiveness of any matter described in regulation 6.

(3) The inspectors of constabulary and the Scottish inspectors may jointly exercise the powers under this regulation on their own initiative or at the request of the Chancellor of the Exchequer or the Commissioners but the Chancellor of the Exchequer may not make a request to carry out an inspection in relation to a particular person.

5 Inspection Functions: Northern Ireland

(1) The Northern Ireland inspectors may carry out inspections in Northern Ireland for the purpose of assessing the effectiveness of the following conduct—

(*a*) any acts or omissions of an officer or the Commissioners in connection with the prevention, detection or investigation of an offence by him or them, or

(*b*) any acts or omissions of an officer or the Commissioners in connection with criminal proceedings conducted in Northern Ireland by the Commissioners or the Director of Public Prosecutions for Northern Ireland.

(2) The Northern Ireland inspectors may carry out inspections in Northern Ireland to assess the effectiveness of any of the matters described in regulation 6.

(3) The Northern Ireland inspectors may exercise the powers under this regulation on their own initiative or at the request of the Chancellor of the Exchequer or the Commissioners but the Chancellor of the Exchequer may not make a request to carry out an inspection in relation to a particular person.

6 Inspection of means of dealing with risks

The matters to which regulations 3(2), 4(2) and 5(2) apply are—

(*a*) any method devised by or for Her Majesty's Revenue and Customs for identifying and dealing with a risk;

(*b*) any measures devised by or for Her Majesty's Revenue and Customs for assuring that an officer or the Commissioners are properly applying that method, and

(*c*) the operation of any such method or measures by an officer or the Commissioners.

7 Access

(1) This regulation applies to an inspection carried out under regulation 3, 4 or 5.

(2) For the purposes of an inspection the Commissioners shall provide to the appropriate inspectors such of the following as are reasonably required by the appropriate inspectors—

(*a*) access to any premises belonging to the Commissioners;

(*b*) access to any system operated by or on behalf of the Commissioners for storing and retrieving information electronically;

(*c*) any information or documents held by the Commissioners.

(3) For the purposes of an inspection an officer shall provide to the appropriate inspectors such information or documents held by him as are reasonably required by the inspectors.

8 Inspections of guidance

The appropriate inspectors may, if the Chancellor of the Exchequer or the Commissioners request them to do so, carry out an inspection of—

(*a*) the operation of any guidance issued by the Commissioners to officers for assessing or demanding a civil penalty instead of carrying out a criminal investigation into any matter or vice versa, or

(*b*) the operation of any guidance issued by the Commissioners for using other powers to secure any revenue, for the collection and management of which the Commissioners are responsible, instead of assessing or demanding a civil penalty or carrying out a criminal investigation.

9 Reports

(1) Where—

(*a*) the inspectors of constabulary carry out an inspection under regulation 3 or 8,

(*b*) the inspectors of constabulary and the Scottish inspectors jointly carry out an inspection under regulation 4 or 8, or

(*c*) the Northern Ireland inspectors carry out an inspection under regulation 5 or 8,

they shall provide a report of the inspection to the Chancellor of the Exchequer.

(2) Subject to paragraph (3), the Chancellor of the Exchequer shall arrange for any report received by him to be published.

(3) The Chancellor of the Exchequer may exclude from publication under paragraph (2) any part of a report if, in his opinion, the publication of that part—

(*a*) would be against the interests of national security;

(*b*) might jeopardise the safety of any person;

(*c*) would contravene section 29(2) of the Act, or

(*d*) might prejudice the prevention or detection of crime or the apprehension or prosecution of offenders.

(4) The Chancellor of the Exchequer shall send a copy of the published report to the Chairman.

(5) The Commissioners shall—

(*a*) prepare comments on the published report;

(*b*) send a copy of the comments to the Chancellor of the Exchequer before such date as may be specified by him;

(*c*) publish the comments in such manner as appears to the Commissioners to be appropriate.

(6) Where the inspectors of constabulary and the Scottish inspectors provide a report of an inspection to the Chancellor of the Exchequer he shall send a copy of the published report to the Scottish Ministers.

10 Appointment of assistant inspectors and staff officers

(1) Section 56 of the Police Act 1996 (appointment of assistant inspectors and staff officers) shall have effect subject to the following modifications—

(*a*) in section 56(1) after "constabulary" insert "for the purpose of carrying out functions under the Revenue and Customs (Inspections) Regulations 2005", and

(*b*) in section 56(2) for "Members of a police force" substitute "Officers of Revenue and Customs".

(2) Section 34 of the Police (Scotland) Act 1967 (appointment of assistant inspectors and staff officers)shall have effect subject to the following modifications—

(*a*) in section 34(1) after "constabulary" insert "for the purpose of carrying out functions under the Revenue and Customs (Inspections) Regulations 2005", and

(*b*) in section 34(1A) for "Constables" substitute "Officers of Revenue and Customs".

11 Payment

(1) The Commissioners shall pay to the inspectors of constabulary, for functions carried out by those inspectors under these Regulations, such amount as may be agreed between the Commissioners and those inspectors or, in the absence of an agreement, such amount as the Treasury, after consultation with the Secretary of State, may determine.

(2) The Commissioners shall pay to the inspectors of constabulary and the Scottish inspectors, for functions carried out jointly by those inspectors under these Regulations, such amount as may be agreed between the Commissioners and those inspectors or, in the absence of an agreement, such amount as the Treasury, after consultation with the Secretary of State and Scottish Ministers, may determine.

(3) The Commissioners shall pay to the Northern Ireland inspectors for functions carried out by those inspectors under these Regulations such amount as may be agreed between the Commissioners and those inspectors or, in the absence of an agreement, such amount as the Treasury, after consultation with the Secretary of State, may determine.

2005/3290

VALUE ADDED TAX (INPUT TAX) (REIMBURSEMENT BY EMPLOYERS OF EMPLOYEES' BUSINESS USE OF ROAD FUEL) REGULATIONS 2005

Made by HMRC Commissioners under VATA 1994 s 24(6)(a)

Made . . . . *30 November 2005*

Laid before the House of Commons . . . . *30 November 2005*

Coming into force . . . . *1 January 2006*

Commentary—*De Voil Indirect Tax Service* **V3.436**.

1 These Regulations may be cited as the Value Added Tax (Input Tax) (Reimbursement by Employers of Employees' Business Use of Road Fuel) Regulations 2005 and come into force on 1st January 2006.

2 Regulation 5 shall apply where—

(*a*) road fuel is supplied to a taxable person (employer) in circumstances where it is delivered to and paid for by his employee acting in his name and on his behalf for use by him (the employee) either in whole or in part for the purposes of the taxable person's business; and

(*b*) the taxable person has agreed to reimburse and does so reimburse his employee for the cost of the road fuel so used in one of the ways specified in regulations 3 and 4.

3 Where all the road fuel is used for the purposes of the taxable person's business, by payment of the actual cost of the road fuel.

4 Where only part of the road fuel is used for the purposes of the taxable person's business, by payment of either—

(*a*) an amount which represents the actual cost of the road fuel so used determined by—

(i) the total distances travelled by the vehicle in which the road fuel is used for the purposes of the taxable person's business; and

(ii) the cylinder capacity of that vehicle; or

(*b*) the actual cost of the road fuel in circumstances where the taxable person will account for output tax on any private use under section 57 of the Value Added Tax Act 1994.

5 Where this regulation applies, subject to regulation 6, the amount of input tax to be deducted by the taxable person under section 24(1) of the Value Added Tax Act 1994 in relation to the supply of road fuel referred to in regulation 2 shall be quantified by reference to the amount paid by him to his employee as reimbursement under regulation 3 or 4, as the case may be.

6 These regulations only apply where the taxable person holds a VAT invoice which contains the details prescribed by regulation 14(1), regulation 14(2) or regulation 16(1) of the Value Added Tax Regulations 1995 as may be applicable and, where so required, is made out to him as the recipient of the supply.

7 In these regulations, "use for the purposes of the taxable person's business" means use for those purposes by the taxable person (employer) in making onward taxable supplies.

2005/3311

REVENUE AND CUSTOMS (COMPLAINTS AND MISCONDUCT) REGULATIONS 2005

Revocation—These Regs revoked by the Revenue and Customs (Complaints and Misconduct) Regulations, SI 2010/1813 reg 2 with effect from 5 August 2010. However, where an allegation in respect of the conduct by an officer came to the attention of the appropriate authority before 5 August 2010, nothing in SI 2010/1813 shall apply and these Regs shall continue to have effect.

Made by the Treasury under CRCA 2005 ss 28(1) and (2), and 29(3)

Made . . . . *1 December 2005*
Laid before Parliament . . . . *2 December 2005*
Coming into force . . . . *28 December 2005*

1 ***Citation, commencement and extent***

(1) These Regulations may be cited as the Revenue and Customs (Complaints and Misconduct) Regulations 2005 and shall come into force on 28th December 2005.

(2) These Regulations extend to England and Wales.

Revocation—These Regs revoked by the Revenue and Customs (Complaints and Misconduct) Regulations, SI 2010/1813 reg 2 with effect from 5 August 2010. However, where an allegation in respect of the conduct by an officer came to the attention of the appropriate authority before 5 August 2010, nothing in SI 2010/1813 shall apply and these Regs shall continue to have effect.

2 ***Interpretation***

In these Regulations—

"2002 Act" means the Police Reform Act 2002;

"Commission" means the Independent Police Complaints Commission;

"Commissioners" means the Commissioners for Her Majesty's Revenue and Customs;

"Complaints Regulations" means the Police (Complaints and Misconduct) Regulations 2004;

"conduct matter" has the meaning given by section 12 of the 2002 Act;

"functions" has the meaning given by section 51(2)(a) of the Commissioners for Revenue and Customs Act 2005;

"Investigatory Powers Order" means the Independent Police Complaints Commission (Investigatory Powers) Order 2004;

"officers" means officers of Revenue and Customs;

"Staff Conduct Regulations" means the Independent Police Complaints Commission (Staff Conduct) Regulations 2004.

Revocation—These Regs revoked by the Revenue and Customs (Complaints and Misconduct) Regulations, SI 2010/1813 reg 2 with effect from 5 August 2010. However, where an allegation in respect of the conduct by an officer came to the attention of the appropriate authority before 5 August 2010, nothing in SI 2010/1813 shall apply and these Regs shall continue to have effect.

3 ***Application of provisions of Part 2 of the 2002 Act with modifications***

(1) The provisions specified in paragraphs (2), (3) and (4) shall apply for the purpose of conferring functions on the Commission in relation to the Commissioners and officers.

(2) Sections 9 to 29 of the 2002 Act shall have effect with the modifications made by Schedule 1 to these Regulations.

(3) Schedule 2 to the 2002 Act shall have effect with the modifications made by Schedule 2 to these Regulations.

(4) Paragraphs 10 to 24, 27 and 29 of Schedule 3 to the 2002 Act shall have effect with the modifications made by Schedule 3 to these Regulations.

(5) Paragraphs 1 to 9, 25, 26 and 28 of Schedule 3 to the 2002 Act shall have effect with the modifications made by Schedule 3 to these Regulations.
(6) The provisions specified in—
(*a*) *paragraphs (2), (3) and (4) shall have effect from the date these Regulations come into force;*
(*b*) *paragraph (5) shall have effect from 1st April 2006.*
(7) The references in regulations 5, 8 and 9(1) to Part 2 of the 2002 Act are references to Part 2 of the 2002 Act as modified by Schedules 1, 2 and 3 to these Regulations.

Revocation—These Regs revoked by the Revenue and Customs (Complaints and Misconduct) Regulations, SI 2010/1813 reg 2 with effect from 5 August 2010. However, where an allegation in respect of the conduct by an officer came to the attention of the appropriate authority before 5 August 2010, nothing in SI 2010/1813 shall apply and these Regs shall continue to have effect.

4 *Application of the Investigatory Powers Order, the Complaints Regulations and the Staff Conduct Regulations with modifications*
(1) The provisions specified in paragraph (2) shall apply for the purpose of conferring functions on the Commission in relation to the Commissioners and officers.
(2) From the date these Regulations come into force—
(*a*) *the Investigatory Powers Order shall have effect,*
(*b*) *the Complaints Regulations shall have effect with the modifications made by Part 1 of Schedule 4 to these Regulations, and*
(*c*) *the Staff Conduct Regulations shall have effect with the modifications made by Part 2 of Schedule 4 to these Regulations.*
(3) The references in regulations 5, 8 and 9(1) to—
(*a*) *the Complaints Regulations,*
(*b*) *the Staff Conduct Regulations,*
are references to those Regulations as modified by Parts 1 and 2 of Schedule 4 to these Regulations.

Revocation—These Regs revoked by the Revenue and Customs (Complaints and Misconduct) Regulations, SI 2010/1813 reg 2 with effect from 5 August 2010. However, where an allegation in respect of the conduct by an officer came to the attention of the appropriate authority before 5 August 2010, nothing in SI 2010/1813 shall apply and these Regs shall continue to have effect.

[4A—(1) For the purpose of the application of the Complaints Regulations under regulation 4, the amendments made to those Regulations by the provisions specified in paragraph (2) shall apply.
(2) The provisions specified are—
(*a*) *regulation 26 of the Serious Organised Crime and Police Act 2005 (Powers of Arrest) (Consequential Amendments) Order 2005, and*
(*b*) *regulation 2 of the Police (Complaints and Misconduct) (Amendment) Regulations 2006.*
(3) This regulation has effect from 27th July 2006.][1]

Revocation—These Regs revoked by the Revenue and Customs (Complaints and Misconduct) Regulations, SI 2010/1813 reg 2 with effect from 5 August 2010. However, where an allegation in respect of the conduct by an officer came to the attention of the appropriate authority before 5 August 2010, nothing in SI 2010/1813 shall apply and these Regs shall continue to have effect.
Amendments—[1] This regulation inserted by the Revenue and Customs (Complaints and Misconduct) (Amendment) Regulations, SI 2006/1748 reg 3 with effect from 27 July 2006.

5 *Disclosure of information*
Where the Commission, or any person acting on its behalf, obtains information in the course of performing a function under these Regulations it or he may not disclose it except as permitted by Part 2 of the 2002 Act or the Complaints Regulations.

Revocation—These Regs revoked by the Revenue and Customs (Complaints and Misconduct) Regulations, SI 2010/1813 reg 2 with effect from 5 August 2010. However, where an allegation in respect of the conduct by an officer came to the attention of the appropriate authority before 5 August 2010, nothing in SI 2010/1813 shall apply and these Regs shall continue to have effect.

6 *Use of information*
Where the Commission, or any person acting on its behalf, obtains information in the course of performing a function under these Regulations it or he may not use it for any purpose other than the performance of a function under these Regulations.

Revocation—These Regs revoked by the Revenue and Customs (Complaints and Misconduct) Regulations, SI 2010/1813 reg 2 with effect from 5 August 2010. However, where an allegation in respect of the conduct by an officer came to the attention of the appropriate authority before 5 August 2010, nothing in SI 2010/1813 shall apply and these Regs shall continue to have effect.

7 *Payments*
(1) The Commissioners shall pay such amount to the Secretary of State in respect of functions performed by the Commission under these Regulations as may be agreed between the Commissioners and the Commission.
(2) In the absence of an agreement, the Commissioners shall pay such amount in respect of those functions as the Treasury, after consultation with the Secretary of State, shall determine.

Revocation—These Regs revoked by the Revenue and Customs (Complaints and Misconduct) Regulations, SI 2010/1813 reg 2 with effect from 5 August 2010. However, where an allegation in respect of the conduct by an officer came to the attention of the appropriate authority before 5 August 2010, nothing in SI 2010/1813 shall apply and these Regs shall continue to have effect.

8 Complaints about conduct occurring before 1st April 2006

Nothing in Part 2 of the 2002 Act, the Investigatory Powers Order, the Complaints Regulations or the Staff Conduct Regulations shall have effect in relation to a complaint made about the conduct of a Commissioner or an officer occurring before 1st April 2006.

Revocation—These Regs revoked by the Revenue and Customs (Complaints and Misconduct) Regulations, SI 2010/1813 reg 2 with effect from 5 August 2010. However, where an allegation in respect of the conduct by an officer came to the attention of the appropriate authority before 5 August 2010, nothing in SI 2010/1813 shall apply and these Regs shall continue to have effect.

9 Conduct matter occurring before 1st April 2006

(1) Subject to paragraph (2), nothing in Part 2 of the 2002 Act, the Investigatory Powers Order, the Complaints Regulations or the Staff Conduct Regulations shall have effect in relation to a conduct matter relating to the conduct of a Commissioner or an officer occurring before 1st April 2006.

(2) Paragraph (1) does not apply to any conduct matter which the appropriate authority may refer to the Commission under paragraph 13(2) of Schedule 3 to the 2002 Act.

Revocation—These Regs revoked by the Revenue and Customs (Complaints and Misconduct) Regulations, SI 2010/1813 reg 2 with effect from 5 August 2010. However, where an allegation in respect of the conduct by an officer came to the attention of the appropriate authority before 5 August 2010, nothing in SI 2010/1813 shall apply and these Regs shall continue to have effect.

SCHEDULE 1

MODIFICATION OF SECTIONS 9 TO 29 OF THE 2002 ACT

Regulation 3(2)

1 At the end of section 9(3) insert—

"(g) *any person who holds or has held office or employment as a Commissioner or officer.*".

Revocation—These Regs revoked by the Revenue and Customs (Complaints and Misconduct) Regulations, SI 2010/1813 reg 2 with effect from 5 August 2010. However, where an allegation in respect of the conduct by an officer came to the attention of the appropriate authority before 5 August 2010, nothing in SI 2010/1813 shall apply and these Regs shall continue to have effect.

2—(1) Section 10 shall be modified as follows.

(2) In subsection (1) after "the Commission" insert ", in relation to the Commissioners and officers,".

(3) In subsection (1)(a) for "police authorities and chief officers" substitute "the Commissioners".

(4) In subsection (1)(e) omit "and also of police practice in relation to other matters,".

(5) Omit subsection (1)(f).

(6) In subsection (2)(a) for "persons serving with the police" substitute—

"Commissioners or officers which the appropriate authority—

(i) *has a duty to refer to the Commission under paragraph 4(1) of Schedule 3 or,*

(ii) *may refer to the Commission under paragraph 4(2) or (3) of Schedule 3;".*

(7) In subsection (2)(b) for the words from "appears that" to the end substitute—

"appears that—

(i) *there may have been conduct by such persons which constitutes or involves the commission of a criminal offence or behaviour justifying disciplinary proceedings, and*

(ii) *that conduct or behaviour is conduct or behaviour which the appropriate authority has a duty to refer to the Commission under paragraph 13(1) of Schedule 3 or may refer to the Commission under paragraph 13(2) or (3) of that Schedule.".*

(8) In subsection (2)(ba) for "a person serving with the police" insert "an officer".

(9) Omit subsection (3).

(10) In subsection (4)(a) for "subsections (1) and (3)" insert "subsection (1)".

(11) In subsection (5)(a) after "functions" insert "in relation to the Commissioners and officers".

(12) Omit subsections (7)(b) and *(c).*

(13) In subsection (8) for the words from "control of a police force" to the end substitute "control of Her Majesty's Revenue and Customs by the Commissioners".

VAT SIs

Revocation—These Regs revoked by the Revenue and Customs (Complaints and Misconduct) Regulations, SI 2010/1813 reg 2 with effect from 5 August 2010. However, where an allegation in respect of the conduct by an officer came to the attention of the appropriate authority before 5 August 2010, nothing in SI 2010/1813 shall apply and these Regs shall continue to have effect.

3—(1) Section 11 shall be modified as follows.
(2) In subsections (1), (2), (3), and (5) for "Secretary of State" insert "Chancellor of the Exchequer".
(3) Omit subsection (4)(b).
(4) In subsection (6) for the words from "under subsection (1)" to the end substitute "under subsection (1) to the Commissioners".
(5) In subsection (7) for the words from "under subsection (3)" to the end substitute "under subsection (3) to the Commissioners".
(6) Omit subsections (8) and (9).
(7) In subsection (10) for paragraphs (a) to *(g)* substitute—
"*(a) the Chancellor of the Exchequer, and*
(b) the Commissioners.".
(8) In the heading for "Reports to the Secretary of State" substitute "Reports to the Chancellor of the Exchequer".

Revocation—These Regs revoked by the Revenue and Customs (Complaints and Misconduct) Regulations, SI 2010/1813 reg 2 with effect from 5 August 2010. However, where an allegation in respect of the conduct by an officer came to the attention of the appropriate authority before 5 August 2010, nothing in SI 2010/1813 shall apply and these Regs shall continue to have effect.

4—(1) Section 12 shall be modified as follows.
(2) In subsections (1) and (2) for "a person serving with the police" substitute "a Commissioner or an officer".
(3) In subsections (2B)(a), [*(2B)(b)*,][1] (2C)*(a)* and (2D) for "a person serving with the police" (on each occasion the words occur) substitute "an officer".

Revocation—These Regs revoked by the Revenue and Customs (Complaints and Misconduct) Regulations, SI 2010/1813 reg 2 with effect from 5 August 2010. However, where an allegation in respect of the conduct by an officer came to the attention of the appropriate authority before 5 August 2010, nothing in SI 2010/1813 shall apply and these Regs shall continue to have effect.

Amendments—[1] Reference inserted by the Revenue and Customs (Complaints and Misconduct) (Amendment) Regulations, SI 2006/1748 reg 4 with effect from 27 July 2006.

5—(1) Section 14 shall be modified as follows.
(2) In subsection (1) for the words from "control of a police force" to the end substitute "control of Her Majesty's Revenue and Customs by the Commissioners".
(3) Omit subsections (2) and (3).

Revocation—These Regs revoked by the Revenue and Customs (Complaints and Misconduct) Regulations, SI 2010/1813 reg 2 with effect from 5 August 2010. However, where an allegation in respect of the conduct by an officer came to the attention of the appropriate authority before 5 August 2010, nothing in SI 2010/1813 shall apply and these Regs shall continue to have effect.

6—(1) Section 15 shall be modified as follows.
(2) In subsection (1)—
(a) *for the words in paragraph (a)* substitute "the Commissioners and ";
(b) *omit paragraph (b);*
(c) *for "it or he is" substitute "they are or he is" and for "that force" substitute "Her Majesty's Revenue and Customs".*
(3) In subsection (3)—
(a) *for paragraph (a)* substitute—
"*(a) the Commission requires the chief officer of a police force to provide a member of his force for appointment under paragraph 17A or 18A of Schedule 3,*";
(b) *omit paragraphs (b)* and *(c);*
(c) *omit "or Director General".*
(4) In subsection (4)—
(a) *omit paragraphs (c)* and *(d)*, and
(b) *after paragraph (d)* insert—
"*(e) the Commissioners,*".
(5) In subsection (5)—
(a) *omit paragraphs (c)* and *(d);*
(b) *for "16, 17 or 18" substitute "17A or 18A".*
(6) After subsection (5) insert—

"(5A) It shall be the duty of the [designated permanent secretary][1], the Chairman and Commissioners to ensure that a person appointed under paragraph 16,17, 17A, 18 or 18A of Schedule 3 to carry out an investigation is given all such assistance and co-operation in the carrying out of that investigation as that person may reasonably require.".

(7) Omit subsections (6) and (7).

Revocation—These Regs revoked by the Revenue and Customs (Complaints and Misconduct) Regulations, SI 2010/1813 reg 2 with effect from 5 August 2010. However, where an allegation in respect of the conduct by an officer came to the attention of the appropriate authority before 5 August 2010, nothing in SI 2010/1813 shall apply and these Regs shall continue to have effect.

Amendments—[1] In sub-para (6), in sub-s (5A) (as set out), words substituted for words "Head of the Home Civil Service" by the Constitutional Reform and Governance Act 2010 s 19, Sch 2 para 22(1), (2) with effect from 11 November 2010 (by virtue os SI 2010/2703 art 2(*a*)).

7—(1) Section 16 shall be modified as follows.

(2) In subsection (1)—

(*a*) *in paragraph (a)—*

(i) *for "one" substitute "a";*

(ii) *omit "to another";*

(iii) *delete "or";*

(*b*) *at the end of paragraph (b)* insert "; or";

(*c*) *after paragraph (b)* insert—

"(*c*) *a police force provides assistance by agreement under paragraph 17A(2) or 18A(2) of Schedule 3.".*

(3) In subsection (2)—

(*a*) *in paragraph (a)* for—

(i) *"one police force to another" substitute "a police force",*

(ii) *"the first force ("the assisting force")" substitute "that force";*

(iii) *in sub-paragraph (i) for "a member of the other force" substitute "a Commissioner or an officer";*

(iv) *in sub-paragraph (ii) for "a member of the other force" substitute "an officer";*

(*b*) *in paragraph (b)—*

(i) *omit "(the assisting force)";*

(ii) *in sub-paragraph (i) for "not a member of that force" substitute "a Commissioner or an officer";*

(iii) *in sub-paragraph (ii) for "not a member of that force" substitute "an officer".*

(4) In subsection (3)—

(*a*) *for "one police force to another" substitute "a police force";*

(*b*) *for "police authority maintaining that other police force" substitute "appropriate authority";*

(*c*) *for "the assisting force" substitute "that force";*

(*d*) *omit "(if any)";*

(*e*) *in paragraph (b)*(i) after "generally" insert "and the Commissioners", and

(*f*) *in paragraph (b)*(ii) omit "by one police force to another".

(5) After subsection (3) there shall be inserted—

"(3A) Subsection (3) shall have effect in relation to assistance which a police force provides by agreement under paragraph 17A (2) or 18A (2) of Schedule 3 as if the reference in that subsection to required to be provided were a reference to provided by agreement under paragraph 17A(2) or 18A(2) of Schedule 3.".

(6) Omit subsections (5), (6) and (7).

Revocation—These Regs revoked by the Revenue and Customs (Complaints and Misconduct) Regulations, SI 2010/1813 reg 2 with effect from 5 August 2010. However, where an allegation in respect of the conduct by an officer came to the attention of the appropriate authority before 5 August 2010, nothing in SI 2010/1813 shall apply and these Regs shall continue to have effect.

8—(1) Section 17 shall be modified as follows.

(2) From the beginning of subsection (1) to the end of paragraph (b) of that subsection substitute "It shall be the duty of the Commissioners".

(3) In subsection (2)—

(*a*) *for the words "every police authority and of every chief officer" substitute "the Commissioners", and*

(*b*) *in paragraph (a)* for the words "that authority and or chief officer" substitute "the Commissioners".

(4) In subsection (4)—

(*a*) *for the words "a police authority or chief officer" substitute "the Commissioners", and*

VAT SIs

(*b*) *in paragraph* (*a*) for the words "that authority and or chief officer" substitute "the Commissioners".

Revocation—These Regs revoked by the Revenue and Customs (Complaints and Misconduct) Regulations, SI 2010/1813 reg 2 with effect from 5 August 2010. However, where an allegation in respect of the conduct by an officer came to the attention of the appropriate authority before 5 August 2010, nothing in SI 2010/1813 shall apply and these Regs shall continue to have effect.

9—(1) Section 18 shall be modified as follows.

(2) In subsection (1)(a)—

(*a*) *for paragraphs (i) and (ii) substitute "the Commissioners"; and*

(*b*) *for "that force" substitute "Her Majesty's Revenue and Customs".*

(3) In subsection (1) for "the authority or, as the case may be, of the chief officer" substitute "the Commissioners".

(4) In subsection (2)(a) for "the force in question" substitute "the Commissioners".

(5) In subsection (3) for "the authority or chief officer" substitute "the Commissioners".

(6) In subsection (5)(b) for "police authorities and chief officers" substitute "the Commissioners".

(7) In the heading to the section for "police premises" substitute "Her Majesty's Revenue and Customs premises".

Revocation—These Regs revoked by the Revenue and Customs (Complaints and Misconduct) Regulations, SI 2010/1813 reg 2 with effect from 5 August 2010. However, where an allegation in respect of the conduct by an officer came to the attention of the appropriate authority before 5 August 2010, nothing in SI 2010/1813 shall apply and these Regs shall continue to have effect.

10—(1) Section 22 shall be modified as follows.

(2) In subsection (1) for the words from "guidance" to the end of paragraph (c) substitute "guidance to the Commissioners and officers".

(3) In subsection (3)—

(*a*) *for paragraph (a)* substitute—

"(*a*) *the Commissioners and";*

(*b*) *omit paragraph (b).*

(4) In subsection (4) for "the Secretary of State" substitute "the Chancellor of the Exchequer".

(5) Omit subsection (5)(c).

Revocation—These Regs revoked by the Revenue and Customs (Complaints and Misconduct) Regulations, SI 2010/1813 reg 2 with effect from 5 August 2010. However, where an allegation in respect of the conduct by an officer came to the attention of the appropriate authority before 5 August 2010, nothing in SI 2010/1813 shall apply and these Regs shall continue to have effect.

11 Omit sections 25 and 26.

Revocation—These Regs revoked by the Revenue and Customs (Complaints and Misconduct) Regulations, SI 2010/1813 reg 2 with effect from 5 August 2010. However, where an allegation in respect of the conduct by an officer came to the attention of the appropriate authority before 5 August 2010, nothing in SI 2010/1813 shall apply and these Regs shall continue to have effect.

12—(1) Section 29 shall be modified as follows.

(2) In subsection (1)—

(*a*) *for the definition of "the appropriate authority" substitute the following definition—*

""the appropriate authority"—

(*a*) *in relation to the Chairman, the Deputy Chairman, a Commissioner or an officer or in relation to any complaint, matter or*

investigation relating to the conduct of such a person, means—

(i) if that person is the Chairman or Deputy Chairman, the [designated permanent secretary],

(ii) if that person is a Commissioner, the Chairman, or

(iii) if that person is an officer, the Commissioners" and

(*b*) *in relation to a death or serious injury matter and the relevant officer, means the Commissioners.";*

(*b*) *after the definition of "the appropriate authority" insert—*

""the Chairman" means the chairman of the Commissioners";

(*c*) *after the definition of "the Commission" insert—*

""the Commissioners" means the Commissioners for Her Majesty's Revenue and Customs;";

(*d*) *after the definition of "conduct matter" insert—*

""the Deputy Chairman" means the Deputy Chairman of the Commissioners";

[(*da*) *after the definition of "the Deputy Chairman" insert—*

""the designated permanent secretary" means the permanent secretary in the civil service of the State designated by the Minister for the Civil Service for the purposes of this Part;"][1]

(*e*) *for the definition of "disciplinary proceedings" substitute—*

""disciplinary proceedings" means any proceedings or management process during which the conduct of the Chairman, Deputy Chairman, a Commissioner or an officer is considered in order to determine whether a sanction or punitive measure should be imposed against him in relation to that conduct;";

(*f*) *after the definition of "local resolution" insert the following definition—*

""officers" means officers of Revenue and Customs;", and

(*g*) *omit the definitions of "local resolution", "relevant force", and "senior officer".*

(3) In subsection (1A) for "person serving with the police (within the meaning of section 12(7))" substitute "officer" and for "such person" substitute "such officer".

(4) In subsection (1B) for "persons serving with the police" substitute "officers".

(5) Omit subsection (7).

(6) In subsection (3) for the words from "falling within" to the end of that subsection substitute "who is a Commissioner or an officer (whether at the time of the conduct or any subsequent time)".

(7) In subsection (4)—

(*a*) *for paragraph (a)* substitute—

"(*a*) *a person who, at the time when the conduct was supposed to have taken place in relation to him, was a Commissioner or an officer (whether or not he was on duty in his capacity as a Commissioner or officer at that time).";*

(*b*) *omit paragraph (b)*(i);

(*c*) *for "person falling within subsection (3)(a)* to (*d*)" substitute "Commissioner or officer".

Revocation—These Regs revoked by the Revenue and Customs (Complaints and Misconduct) Regulations, SI 2010/1813 reg 2 with effect from 5 August 2010. However, where an allegation in respect of the conduct by an officer came to the attention of the appropriate authority before 5 August 2010, nothing in SI 2010/1813 shall apply and these Regs shall continue to have effect.

Amendments—[1] In sub-para (2)(*a*), in definition "the appropriate authority" (as set out), in para (*a*)(i) words substituted for words "Head of the Home Civil Service", and sub-para (2)(*da*) inserted, by the Constitutional Reform and Governance Act 2010 s 19, Sch 2 para 22(1)–(3) with effect from 11 November 2010 (by virtue of SI 2010/2703, art 2(*a*)).

SCHEDULE 2

MODIFICATION OF SCHEDULE 2 TO THE 2002 ACT

Regulation 3(3)

1 After paragraph 6(2) insert—

"(2A) The Commission may make arrangements with the Commissioners under which officers of Revenue and Customs are engaged on temporary service with the Commission.".

Revocation—These Regs revoked by the Revenue and Customs (Complaints and Misconduct) Regulations, SI 2010/1813 reg 2 with effect from 5 August 2010. However, where an allegation in respect of the conduct by an officer came to the attention of the appropriate authority before 5 August 2010, nothing in SI 2010/1813 shall apply and these Regs shall continue to have effect.

2 In paragraph 17(1)(c) after "Secretary of State" insert ", the Treasury".

Revocation—These Regs revoked by the Revenue and Customs (Complaints and Misconduct) Regulations, SI 2010/1813 reg 2 with effect from 5 August 2010. However, where an allegation in respect of the conduct by an officer came to the attention of the appropriate authority before 5 August 2010, nothing in SI 2010/1813 shall apply and these Regs shall continue to have effect.

SCHEDULE 3

MODIFICATION OF SCHEDULE 3 TO THE 2002 ACT

Regulations 3(4) and (5)

1—(1) Paragraph 1 shall be modified as follows.

(2) For sub-paragraph (1) substitute—

"(1) Where—

(*a*) *complaint is made to the [designated permanent secretary] about the conduct of the Chairman or Deputy Chairman, or*

(*b*) *the [designated permanent secretary] becomes aware that a complaint about the conduct of the Chairman or Deputy Chairman has been made to the Commission,*

the [designated permanent secretary] shall take all such steps as appear to him to be appropriate for the purposes of Part 2 of this Act for obtaining and preserving evidence relating to the conduct complained of.".

(3) After sub-paragraph (1) insert—

"(1A) Where—

(*a*) *a complaint is made to the Chairman about the conduct of a Commissioner, or* (*b*) *the Chairman becomes aware that a complaint about the conduct of a Commissioner has been made to the Commission,*

the Chairman shall take all such steps as appear to him to be appropriate for the purposes of Part 2 of this Act for obtaining and preserving evidence relating to the conduct complained of.".

(4) For sub-paragraph (2) substitute—

"(2) Where—

(*a*) *a complaint is made to the Commissioners about the conduct of an officer, or*

(*b*) *the Commissioners become aware that a complaint about the conduct of an officer has been made to the Commission,*

the Commissioners shall take all such steps as appear to them to be appropriate for the purposes of Part 2 of this Act for obtaining and preserving evidence relating to the conduct complained of.".

(5) For sub-paragraph (3) substitute—

"(3) The duty of the—

(*a*) *[designated permanent secretary] under sub-paragraph (1);*

(*b*) *Chairman under sub-paragraph (1A);*

(*c*) *Commissioners under sub-paragraph (2),*

must be performed as soon as practicable after the complaint is made or, as the case may be, he or they become aware of it.".

(6) In sub-paragraph (4) for—

(*a*) *"he shall" substitute "he or they shall";*

(*b*) *"he is satisfied" substitute "he is or they are satisfied"; and*

(*c*) *"appearing to him" substitute "appearing to him or them".*

(7) Omit sub-paragraph (5).

(8) In sub-paragraph (6)—

(*a*) *for "a chief officer" substitute—*

"the—

(*a*) *[designated permanent secretary];*

(*b*) *Chairman;*

(*c*) *Commissioners,";*

(*b*) *the words after "a chief officer" become full out words;*

(*c*) *for "he may" substitute "he or they may", and*

(*d*) *omit "by the police authority maintaining his force or".*

Revocation—These Regs revoked by the Revenue and Customs (Complaints and Misconduct) Regulations, SI 2010/1813 reg 2 with effect from 5 August 2010. However, where an allegation in respect of the conduct by an officer came to the attention of the appropriate authority before 5 August 2010, nothing in SI 2010/1813 shall apply and these Regs shall continue to have effect.

Amendments—Words "designated permanent secretary" substituted for words "Head of the Home Civil Service" by the Constitutional Reform and Governance Act 2010 s 19, Sch 2 para 23 with effect from 11 November 2010 (by virtue os SI 2010/2703 art 2(*a*)).

2—*(1) Paragraph 2 shall be modified as follows.*

(2) In sub-paragraph (1)(a) for "police authority or chief officer who is" substitute "[designated permanent secretary], Chairman or Commissioners who is or are".

(3) In sub-paragraph (2)—

(*a*) *for "a police authority, it" substitute "[designated permanent secretary] or Chairman, he";*

(*b*) *in paragraph (a)* for "it is itself" substitute "he is himself"; and

(*c*) *in paragraph (b)* for "it determines that it" substitute "he determines that he".

(4) In sub-paragraph (3) for—

(*a*) *"a chief officer, he shall" substitute "the Commissioners, they shall";*

(*b*) *"he is himself" substitute "they are themselves"; and*

(*c*) *"he determines that he is not" substitute "they determine that they are not".*

(5) In sub-paragraph (5) for "a police authority or a chief officer gives" substitute "[designated permanent secretary], Chairman or Commissioners gives or give".

(6) For sub-paragraph (6) substitute—

"(6) Where—

(*a*) *the [designated permanent secretary] or Chairman determines, in the case of any complaint made to him, that he is himself the appropriate authority,*

(*b*) *the Commissioners determine, in the case of any complaint made to them, that they are themselves the appropriate authority, or*

(*c*) *a complaint is notified to the[designated permanent secretary], Chairman or Commissioners under this paragraph,* the [designated permanent secretary], Chairman or Commissioners shall record the complaint.".

Revocation—These Regs revoked by the Revenue and Customs (Complaints and Misconduct) Regulations, SI 2010/1813 reg 2 with effect from 5 August 2010. However, where an allegation in respect of the conduct by an officer came to the attention of the appropriate authority before 5 August 2010, nothing in SI 2010/1813 shall apply and these Regs shall continue to have effect.

Amendments—Words "designated permanent secretary" substituted for words "Head of the Home Civil Service" by the Constitutional Reform and Governance Act 2010 s 19, Sch 2 para 23 with effect from 11 November 2010 (by virtue os SI 2010/2703 art 2(*a*)).

3—(1) Paragraph 3 shall be modified as follows.

(2) In sub-paragraph (1) for "a police authority or chief officer" substitute "[designated permanent secretary], Chairman or Commissioners".

(3) In sub-paragraph (2)—

(*a*) *for "police authority or chief officer" and "authority or chief officer" substitute (on each occasion) "[designated permanent secretary], Chairman or Commissioners"*

(*b*) *for "decides" substitute "decides or decide" and*

(*c*) *in paragraph* (*c*) for "that complainant's right to appeal" substitute "whether the complainant has a right to appeal".

(4) In sub-paragraph (3)—

(*a*) *for "police authority or chief officer" substitute "[designated permanent secretary], Chairman or Commissioners"; and*

(*b*) *after "paragraph" insert "if, but only if, the failure is in respect of conduct which the [designated permanent secretary], Chairman or Commissioners is or are required to refer to the Commission under paragraph 4(1)(a)* or (*b*).".

(5) In sub-paragraph (4)—

(*a*) *in paragraph (b)* for "police authority or chief officer" substitute "[designated permanent secretary], Chairman or Commissioners"; and

(*b*) *for "a police authority or chief officer" substitute "the [designated permanent secretary], Chairman or Commissioners".*

(6) In sub-paragraph (6) for—

(*a*) *"police authority or, as the case may be, the chief officer" substitute "[designated permanent secretary], Chairman or, as the case may be, the Commissioners"; and*

(*b*) *"police authority or chief officer" substitute "[designated permanent secretary], Chairman or Commissioners".*

Revocation—These Regs revoked by the Revenue and Customs (Complaints and Misconduct) Regulations, SI 2010/1813 reg 2 with effect from 5 August 2010. However, where an allegation in respect of the conduct by an officer came to the attention of the appropriate authority before 5 August 2010, nothing in SI 2010/1813 shall apply and these Regs shall continue to have effect.

Amendments—Words "designated permanent secretary" substituted for words "Head of the Home Civil Service" by the Constitutional Reform and Governance Act 2010 s 19, Sch 2 para 23 with effect from 11 November 2010 (by virtue os SI 2010/2703 art 2(*a*)).

4—(1) Paragraph 4 shall be modified as follows.

[(1A) After sub-paragraph (1) insert—

"(1A) The obligation on the [designated permanent secretary][2] under sub-paragraph (1)(*a*) or (*b*) to refer a complaint about the conduct of a person in respect of whom he is the appropriate authority arises only if the [designated permanent secretary][2] is satisfied that the complaint contains an indication that a criminal offence may have been committed by that person.

(1B) The obligation on the Chairman or the Commissioners under sub-paragraph (1)(*a*) or (1)(*b*) to refer a complaint about the conduct of a person in respect of whom he is or they are the appropriate authority arises only if he is or they are satisfied that the complaint contains an indication that the person may have—

(*a*) *committed a criminal offence; or*

(*b*) *behaved in a manner which would justify the bringing of disciplinary proceedings and that such behaviour (if it had taken place) would be likely to lead to the termination of that person's office or employment.".]*[1]

(2) In sub-paragraph (3)—

(*a*) *for "a police authority" substitute "the [designated permanent secretary]*[2]*";*

(*b*) *in paragraph (a)* for "chief officer of police of the police force maintained by that authority" substitute "Chairman"; and

(*c*) *in paragraph (b)* for "the police authority" substitute "the [designated permanent secretary][2]".

(3) In sub-paragraph (5)(b) for "a police authority or chief officer" substitute "the [designated permanent secretary][2], Chairman or Commissioners".

(4) In sub-paragraph (6)—

VAT SIs

(*a*) *for "A police authority or chief officer which refers" substitute "Where the [designated permanent secretary]*[2]*, Chairman or Commissioners refers or refer";*

(*b*) *after "paragraph" insert "he or they"; and*

(*c*) *in paragraph (b)* for "that authority or chief officer" substitute "the [designated permanent secretary][2], Chairman or Commissioners".

Revocation—These Regs revoked by the Revenue and Customs (Complaints and Misconduct) Regulations, SI 2010/1813 reg 2 with effect from 5 August 2010. However, where an allegation in respect of the conduct by an officer came to the attention of the appropriate authority before 5 August 2010, nothing in SI 2010/1813 shall apply and these Regs shall continue to have effect.

Amendments—[1] Sub-para (1A) inserted by the Revenue and Customs (Complaints and Misconduct) (Amendment) Regulations, SI 2006/1748 reg 5(1), (2) with effect from 27 July 2006.

[2] Words "designated permanent secretary" substituted for words "Head of the Home Civil Service" by the Constitutional Reform and Governance Act 2010 s 19, Sch 2 para 23 with effect from 11 November 2010 (by virtue os SI 2010/2703 art 2(*a*)).

5—(1) Paragraph 5 shall be modified as follows.

(2) In sub-paragraph (1) for "a police authority or chief officer" substitute "the [designated permanent secretary], Chairman or Commissioners".

(3) In sub-paragraph (2) for "paragraph 6" substitute "sub-paragraph (2A)".

(4) After sub-paragraph (2) insert—

"(2A) In a case to which sub-paragraph (2) applies the appropriate authority shall not be required by virtue of any of the provisions of this Schedule to take any action in relation to the complaint but may handle the complaint in whatever manner it thinks fit, or take no action in relation to the complaint.".

(5) For sub-paragraph 3(b) substitute—

"(*b*) *to the person complained against.".*

Revocation—These Regs revoked by the Revenue and Customs (Complaints and Misconduct) Regulations, SI 2010/1813 reg 2 with effect from 5 August 2010. However, where an allegation in respect of the conduct by an officer came to the attention of the appropriate authority before 5 August 2010, nothing in SI 2010/1813 shall apply and these Regs shall continue to have effect.

Amendments—Words "designated permanent secretary" substituted for words "Head of the Home Civil Service" by the Constitutional Reform and Governance Act 2010 s 19, Sch 2 para 23 with effect from 11 November 2010 (by virtue os SI 2010/2703 art 2(*a*)).

6—(1) Paragraph 6 shall be modified as follows.

(2) For sub-paragraph (2) substitute—

"(2) The appropriate authority shall not be required by virtue of any provisions of this Schedule to take any action in relation to the complaint but may handle the complaint in whatever manner it thinks fit or take no action in relation to the complaint.".

(3) Omit sub-paragraphs (3) to (7).

Revocation—These Regs revoked by the Revenue and Customs (Complaints and Misconduct) Regulations, SI 2010/1813 reg 2 with effect from 5 August 2010. However, where an allegation in respect of the conduct by an officer came to the attention of the appropriate authority before 5 August 2010, nothing in SI 2010/1813 shall apply and these Regs shall continue to have effect.

7 Omit paragraphs 7, 8 and 9.

Revocation—These Regs revoked by the Revenue and Customs (Complaints and Misconduct) Regulations, SI 2010/1813 reg 2 with effect from 5 August 2010. However, where an allegation in respect of the conduct by an officer came to the attention of the appropriate authority before 5 August 2010, nothing in SI 2010/1813 shall apply and these Regs shall continue to have effect.

8—(1) Paragraph 10 shall be modified as follows.

(2) In sub-paragraph (1)—

(*a*) *in paragraph (a)* for—

(i) *"a police authority or chief officer" (on both occasions where it occurs) substitute "the [designated permanent secretary]*[2]*, Chairman or Commissioners";*

(ii) *for "has received" substitute "has or have received"; and*

(iii) *for "that authority or chief officer" substitute "the [designated permanent secretary]*[2]*, Chairman or Commissioners";*

(*b*) *in paragraph (b)* for "that authority or chief officer" substitute "the [designated permanent secretary][2], Chairman or Commissioners".

(3) In sub-paragraph (2)—

(*a*) *for "The authority or chief officer" substitute "The [designated permanent secretary]*[2]*, Chairman or Commissioners";*

(*b*) *in paragraph (a)* for "it or, as the case may be, he is" substitute "he is or, as the case may be, they are"; and

(*c*) *in paragraph (b)* for "if it or he is not" substitute "if he is or they are not".

(4) In sub-paragraph (3)—

(a) at the beginning insert "Subject to sub-paragraphs (3A) and (3B),";[1]

(b) for "a police authority or chief officer determines" substitute "the [designated permanent secretary][2]*, Chairman or Commissioners determines or determine";*

(c) for "it or, as the case may be, he is" substitute "he is, or as the case may be, they are", and

(d) for "it or he" substitute "he or they".

(5) After sub-paragraph (3) insert—

"(3A) Nothing in sub-paragraph (3) shall require the Head of the Home Civil Service, as the appropriate authority, to record a conduct matter if he is satisfied that matter falls within subsection 12(1)(b) of this Act.

(3B) Nothing in sub-paragraph (3) shall require the Chairman or the Commissioners, as the appropriate authority, to record a conduct matter if he is or they are satisfied that—

(a) the matter falls within subsection 12(1)(b) of this Act; and

(b) any disciplinary proceedings which were brought would be unlikely to result in the termination of an office or employment.".[1]

Revocation—These Regs revoked by the Revenue and Customs (Complaints and Misconduct) Regulations, SI 2010/1813 reg 2 with effect from 5 August 2010. However, where an allegation in respect of the conduct by an officer came to the attention of the appropriate authority before 5 August 2010, nothing in SI 2010/1813 shall apply and these Regs shall continue to have effect.

Amendments—[1] Sub-paras (4)(*a*), (5) revoked by the Revenue and Customs (Complaints and Misconduct) (Amendment) Regulations, SI 2006/1748 reg 5(1), (3) with effect from 27 July 2006.

[2] Words "designated permanent secretary" substituted for words "Head of the Home Civil Service" by the Constitutional Reform and Governance Act 2010 s 19, Sch 2 para 23 with effect from 11 November 2010 (by virtue os SI 2010/2703 art 2(*a*)).

9—(1) Paragraph 11 shall be modified as follows.

(2) In sub-paragraph (1)—

(a) at the beginning insert "Subject to paragraphs (2A) and (2B),";[1]

(b) in paragraph (a) for "police authority or chief officer who is" substitute "[designated permanent secretary][2], Chairman or Commissioners who is or are".

(3) After sub-paragraph (2) insert—

"(2A) Nothing in sub-paragraph (1) shall require the Head of the Home Civil Service, as the appropriate authority, to record a conduct matter if he is satisfied that the matter falls within section 12(1)(b) of this Act.

(2B) Nothing in sub-paragraph (1) shall require the Chairman or the Commissioners, as the appropriate authority, to record a conduct matter if he is or they are satisfied that—

(a) the matter falls within section 12(1)(b) of this Act; and

(b) any disciplinary proceedings which were brought would be unlikely to result in the termination of an office or employment.".[1]

Revocation—These Regs revoked by the Revenue and Customs (Complaints and Misconduct) Regulations, SI 2010/1813 reg 2 with effect from 5 August 2010. However, where an allegation in respect of the conduct by an officer came to the attention of the appropriate authority before 5 August 2010, nothing in SI 2010/1813 shall apply and these Regs shall continue to have effect.

Amendments—[1] Sub-paras (2)(*a*), (3) revoked by the Revenue and Customs (Complaints and Misconduct) (Amendment) Regulations, SI 2006/1748 reg 5(1), (3) with effect from 27 July 2006.

[2] Words "designated permanent secretary" substituted for words "Head of the Home Civil Service" by the Constitutional Reform and Governance Act 2010 s 19, Sch 2 para 23 with effect from 11 November 2010 (by virtue os SI 2010/2703 art 2(*a*)).

10—(1) Paragraph 12 shall be modified as follows.

(2) Omit sub-paragraph (1).

(3) For sub-paragraph (2) substitute—

"(2) Where—

(a) the [designated permanent secretary] becomes aware of any recordable matter relating to the conduct of the Chairman or Deputy Chairman;

(b) the Chairman becomes aware of any recordable matter relating to the conduct of a Commissioner; or

(c) the Commissioners become aware of any recordable matter relating to the conduct of an officer,

it shall be his or their duty to take all such steps as appear to him or them to be appropriate for the purposes of Part 2 of this Act for obtaining and preserving the evidence relating to that matter.".

(4) For sub-paragraph (3) substitute—

"(3) The duty under sub-paragraph (2) of—

(a) the [designated permanent secretary];

(b) the Chairman;

(c) the Commissioners,

VAT SIs

must be performed as soon as practicable after he becomes or they become aware of the matter in question.".

(5) In sub-paragraph (4) for—

(a) "he shall be under a duty, until he is" substitute "he or they shall be under a duty until he is or they are"; and

(b) "appearing to him" substitute "appearing to him or them".

(6) Omit sub-paragraph (5).

(7) In sub-paragraph (6)—

(a) for "the chief officer" substitute "the Chairman or Commissioners";

(b) for "he may be directed" substitute "he or they may be directed"; and

(c) omit "by the police authority maintaining his force or".

Revocation—These Regs revoked by the Revenue and Customs (Complaints and Misconduct) Regulations, SI 2010/1813 reg 2 with effect from 5 August 2010. However, where an allegation in respect of the conduct by an officer came to the attention of the appropriate authority before 5 August 2010, nothing in SI 2010/1813 shall apply and these Regs shall continue to have effect.

Amendments—Words "designated permanent secretary" substituted for words "Head of the Home Civil Service" by the Constitutional Reform and Governance Act 2010 s 19, Sch 2 para 23 with effect from 11 November 2010 (by virtue os SI 2010/2703 art 2(*a*)).

11—(1) Paragraph 13 shall be modified as follows.

(2) In sub-paragraph (1) for—

(a) "a police authority or a chief officer" substitute "the [designated permanent secretary][2]*, Chairman or Commissioners", and*

(b) "the authority or chief officer is" substitute "any of those persons is or are".

[(2A) After sub-paragraph (1) insert—

"(1A) Sub-paragraph (1) is subject to sub-paragraphs (1B) and (1C).

(1B) The obligation on the [designated permanent secretary][2] under sub-paragraph (1)(a) or (1)(b) to refer a recordable conduct matter in respect of a person for whom he is the appropriate authority arises only if the [designated permanent secretary][2] is satisfied that the matter is one in respect of which there is an indication that a criminal offence may have been committed by that person.

(1C) The obligation on the Chairman or the Commissioners under sub-paragraph (1)(*a*) or (1)(*b*) to refer a recordable conduct matter in respect of a person for whom he is or they are the appropriate authority arises only if he is or they are satisfied that the matter is one in respect of which there is an indication that the person may have—

(*a*) *committed a criminal offence; or*

(*b*) *behaved in a manner which would justify the bringing of disciplinary proceedings and that such behaviour (if it had taken place) would be likely to lead to the termination of that person's office or employment."]*[1]

(3) In sub-paragraph (3)—

(a) for "a police authority maintaining any police force" substitute "the [designated permanent secretary][2]*";*

(b) in paragraph (a) for "chief officer of police of that force" substitute "Chairman"; and

(c) in paragraph (b) for "police authority" substitute "[designated permanent secretary][2]".

(4) In sub-paragraph (5)(b) for "a police authority or chief officer" substitute "the [designated permanent secretary][2], Chairman or Commissioners".

(5) In sub-paragraph (6)—

(a) in paragraph (a) for "a police authority or chief officer refers" substitute "the [designated permanent secretary][2], Chairman or Commissioners refers or refer";

(b) in paragraph (b) for "that authority or chief officer does not" substitute "the [designated permanent secretary][2], Chairman or Commissioners does or do not"; and

(c) for "that authority or chief officer" substitute "the [designated permanent secretary][2]*, Chairman or Commissioners".*

Revocation—These Regs revoked by the Revenue and Customs (Complaints and Misconduct) Regulations, SI 2010/1813 reg 2 with effect from 5 August 2010. However, where an allegation in respect of the conduct by an officer came to the attention of the appropriate authority before 5 August 2010, nothing in SI 2010/1813 shall apply and these Regs shall continue to have effect.

Amendments—[1] Sub-para(2A) inserted by the Revenue and Customs (Complaints and Misconduct) (Amendment) Regulations, SI 2006/1748 reg 5(1), (4) with effect from 27 July 2006.

[2] Words "designated permanent secretary" substituted for words "Head of the Home Civil Service" by the Constitutional Reform and Governance Act 2010 s 19, Sch 2 para 23 with effect from 11 November 2010 (by virtue os SI 2010/2703 art 2(*a*)).

12—(1) Paragraph 14 shall be modified as follows.

(2) In sub-paragraph (1) for "a police authority or chief officer" substitute "the [designated permanent secretary], Chairman or Commissioners".

(3) In sub-paragraph (2)—

(a) after "recordable conduct matter" insert "referred by the [designated permanent secretary], Chairman or Commissioners";

(b) for "appropriate authority" substitute "[designated permanent secretary], Chairman or Commissioners";

(c) for "that authority" (on the first occasion those words appear) substitute "by him or them"; and

(d) for "that authority" (on the second occasion those words appear) substitute "he or they".

Revocation—These Regs revoked by the Revenue and Customs (Complaints and Misconduct) Regulations, SI 2010/1813 reg 2 with effect from 5 August 2010. However, where an allegation in respect of the conduct by an officer came to the attention of the appropriate authority before 5 August 2010, nothing in SI 2010/1813 shall apply and these Regs shall continue to have effect.

Amendments—Words "designated permanent secretary" substituted for words "Head of the Home Civil Service" by the Constitutional Reform and Governance Act 2010 s 19, Sch 2 para 23 with effect from 11 November 2010 (by virtue os SI 2010/2703 art 2(*a*)).

13—(1) Paragraph 14A shall be modified as follows.

(2) For sub-paragraph (1) substitute—

"(1) Where a DSI matter comes to the attention of the Commissioners, being the appropriate authority, it shall be their duty to record that matter.".

Revocation—These Regs revoked by the Revenue and Customs (Complaints and Misconduct) Regulations, SI 2010/1813 reg 2 with effect from 5 August 2010. However, where an allegation in respect of the conduct by an officer came to the attention of the appropriate authority before 5 August 2010, nothing in SI 2010/1813 shall apply and these Regs shall continue to have effect.

14—(1) Paragraph 14B shall be modified as follows.

(2) Omit sub-paragraph (1).

(3) In sub-paragraph (2)—

(a) for the words from "Where" to the end of paragraph (b) substitute "Where a DSI matter comes to the attention of the Commissioners";

(b) for "his duty" substitute "their duty"; and

(c) for "to him" substitute "to them".

(4) In sub-paragraph (3) for "chief officer's" substitute "Commissioners'" and for "he becomes" substitute "they become".

(5) In sub-paragraph (4) for "he shall" substitute "they shall", "he is" substitute "they are" and "to him" substitute "to them".

(6) Omit sub-paragraph (5).

(7) In sub-paragraph (6) for "chief officer" substitute "Commissioners", for "he" substitute "they" and omit "by the police authority maintaining his force or".

Revocation—These Regs revoked by the Revenue and Customs (Complaints and Misconduct) Regulations, SI 2010/1813 reg 2 with effect from 5 August 2010. However, where an allegation in respect of the conduct by an officer came to the attention of the appropriate authority before 5 August 2010, nothing in SI 2010/1813 shall apply and these Regs shall continue to have effect.

15—(1) Paragraph 14D shall be modified as follows.

(2) In sub-paragraph (1) for "a police authority or a chief officer" substitute "the Commissioners".

Revocation—These Regs revoked by the Revenue and Customs (Complaints and Misconduct) Regulations, SI 2010/1813 reg 2 with effect from 5 August 2010. However, where an allegation in respect of the conduct by an officer came to the attention of the appropriate authority before 5 August 2010, nothing in SI 2010/1813 shall apply and these Regs shall continue to have effect.

16—(1) Paragraph 15 shall be modified as follows.

(2) After sub-paragraph (4)(b) insert—

"*(bb) an investigation by a police force under the supervision of the Commission;*".

(3) In sub-paragraph (4)(c) substitute "the appropriate authority" for "that authority".

(4) After sub-paragraph (4)(c) insert—

"*(cc) an investigation by a police force under the management of the Commission;*".

(5) After sub-paragraph (4) insert—

"(4A) An investigation relating to any conduct of the Chairman, Deputy Chairman or other Commissioners under this paragraph may only be carried out in the form specified in sub-paragraph (4)(*bb*), (4)(*cc*) or (4)(*d*).".

Revocation—These Regs revoked by the Revenue and Customs (Complaints and Misconduct) Regulations, SI 2010/1813 reg 2 with effect from 5 August 2010. However, where an allegation in respect of the conduct by an officer came to the attention of the appropriate authority before 5 August 2010, nothing in SI 2010/1813 shall apply and these Regs shall continue to have effect.

17—(1) Paragraph 16 shall be modified as follows.

(2) In sub-paragraph (1) omit paragraph (a).

(3) Omit sub-paragraph (2).

(4) For sub-paragraph (3) substitute—

"(3) It shall be the duty of the appropriate authority to appoint an officer to investigate the complaint or matter."

(5) Omit [sub-paragraphs (4) and (5)][1].

Revocation—These Regs revoked by the Revenue and Customs (Complaints and Misconduct) Regulations, SI 2010/1813 reg 2 with effect from 5 August 2010. However, where an allegation in respect of the conduct by an officer came to the attention of the appropriate authority before 5 August 2010, nothing in SI 2010/1813 shall apply and these Regs shall continue to have effect.

Amendments—[1] Sub-para (4) substituted, and in sub-para (5), words substituted for the words "sub-paragraph (5)" by the Revenue and Customs (Complaints and Misconduct) (Amendment) Regulations, SI 2006/1748 reg 5(1), (5), (6) with effect from 27 July 2006.

18—(1) Paragraph 17 shall be modified as follows.

(2) In sub-paragraph (2) for the words from "appoint" to the end of the sub-paragraph substitute "appoint an officer to investigate the complaint or matter.".

(3) In sub-paragraph (4)(a) for "sub-paragraph 2(*a*) or (*b*)" substitute "sub-paragraph (2)".

(4) Omit sub-paragraphs (6) and (6A).

Revocation—These Regs revoked by the Revenue and Customs (Complaints and Misconduct) Regulations, SI 2010/1813 reg 2 with effect from 5 August 2010. However, where an allegation in respect of the conduct by an officer came to the attention of the appropriate authority before 5 August 2010, nothing in SI 2010/1813 shall apply and these Regs shall continue to have effect.

19 After paragraph 17 insert—

"17A—

(1) This paragraph applies where the Commission determines that there should be an investigation by a police force under the supervision of the Commission.

(2) The Commission shall—

(*a*) *identify the police force whose force area includes the geographical area to which the subject matter of the complaint, recordable conduct matter or DSI matter most closely relates, and*

(*b*) *take steps to obtain the agreement of—*

(i) *the chief officer of police of that force, and*

(ii) *the appropriate authority,*

to the appointment by the Commission of that force to carry out the investigation.

(3) In the event that no agreement is reached under sub-paragraph (2) the Commission may require the chief officer of police of any police force it considers appropriate to carry out the investigation.

(4) A chief officer of police of a police force who agrees to or is required to carry out an investigation shall, if he has not already done so, appoint a person serving with the police who is a member of that force to investigate that complaint.

(5) Sub-paragraphs (3) to (5) and (7) of paragraph 17 shall apply as they apply to an investigation by the appropriate authority which the Commission has determined is one that it should supervise and the references to the appropriate authority in those sub-paragraphs shall be treated as references to the chief officer of police concerned.

(6) An appointment of a person under sub-paragraph (4) or (5) shall be notified by the chief officer of police concerned to the appropriate authority.".

Revocation—These Regs revoked by the Revenue and Customs (Complaints and Misconduct) Regulations, SI 2010/1813 reg 2 with effect from 5 August 2010. However, where an allegation in respect of the conduct by an officer came to the attention of the appropriate authority before 5 August 2010, nothing in SI 2010/1813 shall apply and these Regs shall continue to have effect.

20 After paragraph 18 insert—

"18A—

(1) This paragraph applies where the Commission determines that there should be an investigation by a police force under the management of the Commission.

(2) The Commission shall—

(*a*) *identify the police force whose force area includes the geographical area to which the subject matter of the complaint, recordable conduct matter or DSI matter most closely relates, and*

(*b*) *take steps to obtain the agreement of—*

(i) *the chief officer of police of that force, and*

(ii) *the appropriate authority,*

to the appointment by the Commission of that force to carry out the investigation.

(3) In the event that no agreement is reached under sub-paragraph (2) the Commission may require the chief officer of police of any police force it considers appropriate to carry out the investigation.

(4) A chief officer of police of a police force who agrees to or is required to carry out an investigation shall, if he has not already done so, appoint a person serving with the police who is a member of that force to investigate that complaint or matter.

(5) Sub-paragraphs (3) to (5) of paragraph 17 shall apply as they apply to an investigation by the appropriate authority which the Commission has determined is one that it should supervise and the references to the appropriate authority in those sub-paragraphs shall be treated as references to the chief officer of police concerned.

(6) An appointment of a person under sub-paragraph (4) or (5) shall be notified by the chief officer of police concerned to the appropriate authority.

(7) The person appointed to investigate the complaint or matter shall, in relation to that investigation, be under the direction and control of the Commission.".

Revocation—These Regs revoked by the Revenue and Customs (Complaints and Misconduct) Regulations, SI 2010/1813 reg 2 with effect from 5 August 2010. However, where an allegation in respect of the conduct by an officer came to the attention of the appropriate authority before 5 August 2010, nothing in SI 2010/1813 shall apply and these Regs shall continue to have effect.

21 Omit paragraphs 19(3) and (3A).

Revocation—These Regs revoked by the Revenue and Customs (Complaints and Misconduct) Regulations, SI 2010/1813 reg 2 with effect from 5 August 2010. However, where an allegation in respect of the conduct by an officer came to the attention of the appropriate authority before 5 August 2010, nothing in SI 2010/1813 shall apply and these Regs shall continue to have effect.

22—(1) Paragraph 20 shall be modified as follows.

(2) Omit sub-paragraph (1)(a).

(3) In paragraph 20(3) after "Director of Public Prosecutions" insert "or, as the case may be, the Director of Revenue and Customs Prosecutions".

Revocation—These Regs revoked by the Revenue and Customs (Complaints and Misconduct) Regulations, SI 2010/1813 reg 2 with effect from 5 August 2010. However, where an allegation in respect of the conduct by an officer came to the attention of the appropriate authority before 5 August 2010, nothing in SI 2010/1813 shall apply and these Regs shall continue to have effect.

23 Omit paragraphs 20A to 20I.

Revocation—These Regs revoked by the Revenue and Customs (Complaints and Misconduct) Regulations, SI 2010/1813 reg 2 with effect from 5 August 2010. However, where an allegation in respect of the conduct by an officer came to the attention of the appropriate authority before 5 August 2010, nothing in SI 2010/1813 shall apply and these Regs shall continue to have effect.

24—(1) Paragraph 21A shall be modified as follows.

(2) In sub-paragraphs (1) and (3) for "a person serving with the police" substitute "an officer".

(3) In sub-paragraph (1) after "18" insert "or 18A".

(4) In sub-paragraph (3) for "16 or 17" substitute "16, 17 or 17A".

Revocation—These Regs revoked by the Revenue and Customs (Complaints and Misconduct) Regulations, SI 2010/1813 reg 2 with effect from 5 August 2010. However, where an allegation in respect of the conduct by an officer came to the attention of the appropriate authority before 5 August 2010, nothing in SI 2010/1813 shall apply and these Regs shall continue to have effect.

25 In paragraph 22(2) for "17 or 18" substitute "17, 17A, 18 or 18A".

Revocation—These Regs revoked by the Revenue and Customs (Complaints and Misconduct) Regulations, SI 2010/1813 reg 2 with effect from 5 August 2010. However, where an allegation in respect of the conduct by an officer came to the attention of the appropriate authority before 5 August 2010, nothing in SI 2010/1813 shall apply and these Regs shall continue to have effect.

26—(1) In paragraph 23(2)(c) after "Director of Public Prosecutions" insert "or the Director of Revenue and Customs Prosecutions".

(2) In paragraphs 23(3), (4) and (6)(b) after "Director of Public Prosecutions" insert "or, as the case may be, the Director of Revenue and Customs Prosecutions".

Revocation—These Regs revoked by the Revenue and Customs (Complaints and Misconduct) Regulations, SI 2010/1813 reg 2 with effect from 5 August 2010. However, where an allegation in respect of the conduct by an officer came to the attention of the appropriate authority before 5 August 2010, nothing in SI 2010/1813 shall apply and these Regs shall continue to have effect.

27 In paragraphs 24(2)(b), (3), (4) and (6)(*b*) after "Director of Public Prosecutions" insert "or, as the case may be, the Director of Revenue and Customs Prosecutions".

Revocation—These Regs revoked by the Revenue and Customs (Complaints and Misconduct) Regulations, SI 2010/1813 reg 2 with effect from 5 August 2010. However, where an allegation in respect of the conduct by an officer came to the attention of the appropriate authority before 5 August 2010, nothing in SI 2010/1813 shall apply and these Regs shall continue to have effect.

28 In paragraphs 24A(4), 24B(1) and 24C(1) for "a person serving with the police" substitute (on each occasion where the words occur) "an officer".

Revocation—These Regs revoked by the Revenue and Customs (Complaints and Misconduct) Regulations, SI 2010/1813 reg 2 with effect from 5 August 2010. However, where an allegation in respect of the conduct by an officer came to the attention of the appropriate authority before 5 August 2010, nothing in SI 2010/1813 shall apply and these Regs shall continue to have effect.

29 Omit paragraph 25(2A).

Revocation—These Regs revoked by the Revenue and Customs (Complaints and Misconduct) Regulations, SI 2010/1813 reg 2 with effect from 5 August 2010. However, where an allegation in respect of the conduct by an officer came to the attention of the appropriate authority before 5 August 2010, nothing in SI 2010/1813 shall apply and these Regs shall continue to have effect.

30 In paragraph 27(3) for "any person serving with the police" substitute "any officer".

Revocation—These Regs revoked by the Revenue and Customs (Complaints and Misconduct) Regulations, SI 2010/1813 reg 2 with effect from 5 August 2010. However, where an allegation in respect of the conduct by an officer came to the attention of the appropriate authority before 5 August 2010, nothing in SI 2010/1813 shall apply and these Regs shall continue to have effect.

SCHEDULE 4

Regulation 4(2)

PART 1
MODIFICATION OF THE COMPLAINTS REGULATIONS

1 Omit regulation 4.

Revocation—These Regs revoked by the Revenue and Customs (Complaints and Misconduct) Regulations, SI 2010/1813 reg 2 with effect from 5 August 2010. However, where an allegation in respect of the conduct by an officer came to the attention of the appropriate authority before 5 August 2010, nothing in SI 2010/1813 shall apply and these Regs shall continue to have effect.

2—(1) In regulation 6(2) for the words from "consent" to the end of the paragraph substitute—
"consent—

(i) *in the case of an investigation carried out by an appointed person who is an officer, of the Director of Revenue and Customs Prosecutions, or*

(ii) *in any other case, of the Director of Public Prosecutions,*

to the imposition thereof."

(2) In regulation 6(3) for—

(a) "a chief officer" substitute "the [designated permanent secretary], Chairman or Commissioners";

(b) "consulting him" substitute "consulting him or them";

(c) "he may make" substitute "he or they may make".

Revocation—These Regs revoked by the Revenue and Customs (Complaints and Misconduct) Regulations, SI 2010/1813 reg 2 with effect from 5 August 2010. However, where an allegation in respect of the conduct by an officer came to the attention of the appropriate authority before 5 August 2010, nothing in SI 2010/1813 shall apply and these Regs shall continue to have effect.

Amendments—Words "designated permanent secretary" substituted for words "Head of the Home Civil Service" by the Constitutional Reform and Governance Act 2010 s 19, Sch 2 para 23 with effect from 11 November 2010 (by virtue os SI 2010/2703 art 2(*a*)).

3 Omit regulations 7(2)(b) and *7(7)(c).*

Revocation—These Regs revoked by the Revenue and Customs (Complaints and Misconduct) Regulations, SI 2010/1813 reg 2 with effect from 5 August 2010. However, where an allegation in respect of the conduct by an officer came to the attention of the appropriate authority before 5 August 2010, nothing in SI 2010/1813 shall apply and these Regs shall continue to have effect.

4—(1) In regulation 8(1) for "a police authority or chief officer" substitute "the [designated permanent secretary], Chairman or Commissioners".

(2) In regulation 8(2)(c) for "the police force or police authority which" substitute "the [designated permanent secretary], Chairman or Commissioners who".

(3) In regulations 8(3)(a) and (7) for "police authority or chief officer" substitute "[designated permanent secretary], Chairman or Commissioners".

(4) In regulation 8(5) for "A police authority or chief officer" substitute "The [designated permanent secretary], Chairman or Commissioners".

Revocation—These Regs revoked by the Revenue and Customs (Complaints and Misconduct) Regulations, SI 2010/1813 reg 2 with effect from 5 August 2010. However, where an allegation in respect of the conduct by an officer came to the attention of the appropriate authority before 5 August 2010, nothing in SI 2010/1813 shall apply and these Regs shall continue to have effect.

Amendments—Words "designated permanent secretary" substituted for words "Head of the Home Civil Service" by the Constitutional Reform and Governance Act 2010 s 19, Sch 2 para 23 with effect from 11 November 2010 (by virtue os SI 2010/2703 art 2(*a*)).

5 Omit regulation 9.

Revocation—These Regs revoked by the Revenue and Customs (Complaints and Misconduct) Regulations, SI 2010/1813 reg 2 with effect from 5 August 2010. However, where an allegation in respect of the conduct by an officer came to the attention of the appropriate authority before 5 August 2010, nothing in SI 2010/1813 shall apply and these Regs shall continue to have effect.

6—(1) Regulation 12 shall be modified as follows.

(2) After paragraph (1)(b) insert—

"(*c*) *preventing the disclosure of any information held by the Revenue and Customs in connection with a function of the Revenue and Customs which—*

(i) *is obtained from the [designated permanent secretary], Chairman, Commissioners or an officer, and*

(ii) *relates to a person whose identity is specified in the disclosure or can be deduced from it.".*

(3) After paragraph (1) insert—

"(1A) Paragraph (1)(*c*) does not apply to any information about internal administrative arrangements of Her Majesty's Revenue and Customs (whether relating to Commissioners, officers or others).".

(4) After paragraph (2) insert—

"(2A) The Commission shall consult the appropriate authority in any case under paragraph (1)(*c*) before deciding whether or not it is satisfied under paragraph (2).".

(5) After paragraph (3) insert—

"(4) In this regulation "the Revenue and Customs" means—

(*a*) *the Commissioners;*

(*b*) *an officer;*

(*c*) *a person acting on behalf of the Commissioners or an officer;*

(*d*) *a committee established by the Commissioners;*

(*e*) *a member of a committee established by the Commissioners;*

(*f*) *the Commissioners of Inland Revenue (or any committee or staff of theirs or anyone acting on their behalf);*

(*g*) *the Commissioners of Customs and Excise (or any committee or staff of theirs or anyone acting on their behalf), and*

(*h*) *a person specified in section 6(2) or 7(3) of the Commissioners for Revenue and Customs Act 2005.".*

Revocation—These Regs revoked by the Revenue and Customs (Complaints and Misconduct) Regulations, SI 2010/1813 reg 2 with effect from 5 August 2010. However, where an allegation in respect of the conduct by an officer came to the attention of the appropriate authority before 5 August 2010, nothing in SI 2010/1813 shall apply and these Regs shall continue to have effect.

Amendments—Words "designated permanent secretary" substituted for words "Head of the Home Civil Service" by the Constitutional Reform and Governance Act 2010 s 19, Sch 2 para 23 with effect from 11 November 2010 (by virtue os SI 2010/2703 art 2(*a*)).

7—(1) In regulation 18(1) for "17 or 18" substitute "17, 17A, 18 or 18A".

(2) Omit regulations 18(1)(d), (2) and (3).

Revocation—These Regs revoked by the Revenue and Customs (Complaints and Misconduct) Regulations, SI 2010/1813 reg 2 with effect from 5 August 2010. However, where an allegation in respect of the conduct by an officer came to the attention of the appropriate authority before 5 August 2010, nothing in SI 2010/1813 shall apply and these Regs shall continue to have effect.

8 In regulation 21 for "person serving with the police" substitute "Commissioner or an officer".

Revocation—These Regs revoked by the Revenue and Customs (Complaints and Misconduct) Regulations, SI 2010/1813 reg 2 with effect from 5 August 2010. However, where an allegation in respect of the conduct by an officer came to the attention of the appropriate authority before 5 August 2010, nothing in SI 2010/1813 shall apply and these Regs shall continue to have effect.

9 In regulation 24—

(*a*) *for "Every police authority and chief officer" substitute "The [designated permanent secretary][2], Chairman and Commissioners", and*

(*b*) *in paragraphs (a)*[, (*b*) and (*ab*)][1] *for* "it or him" substitute "him or them".

Revocation—These Regs revoked by the Revenue and Customs (Complaints and Misconduct) Regulations, SI 2010/1813 reg 2 with effect from 5 August 2010. However, where an allegation in respect of the conduct by an officer came to the attention of the appropriate authority before 5 August 2010, nothing in SI 2010/1813 shall apply and these Regs shall continue to have effect.

Amendments—[1] In sub-para (*b*), words substituted for the words "and (*b*)" by the Revenue and Customs (Complaints and Misconduct) (Amendment) Regulations, SI 2006/1748 reg 6(1), (2) with effect from 27 July 2006.

[2] Words "designated permanent secretary" substituted for words "Head of the Home Civil Service" by the Constitutional Reform and Governance Act 2010 s 19, Sch 2 para 23 with effect from 11 November 2010 (by virtue os SI 2010/2703 art 2(*a*)).

10—*(1) In regulation 25(1) for "a police authority or chief officer" substitute "the [designated permanent secretary], Chairman or Commissioners".*

(2) In regulation 25(3) for "(a) and *(b)"* substitute "(*a*), (*b*) and (*c*)".

Revocation—These Regs revoked by the Revenue and Customs (Complaints and Misconduct) Regulations, SI 2010/1813 reg 2 with effect from 5 August 2010. However, where an allegation in respect of the conduct by an officer came to the attention of the appropriate authority before 5 August 2010, nothing in SI 2010/1813 shall apply and these Regs shall continue to have effect.

Amendments—Words "designated permanent secretary" substituted for words "Head of the Home Civil Service" by the Constitutional Reform and Governance Act 2010 s 19, Sch 2 para 23 with effect from 11 November 2010 (by virtue os SI 2010/2703 art 2(*a*)).

11—*(1) Regulation 26 shall be modified as follows.*

(2) In paragraph (1) for—

(a) "chief officer" substitute "the [designated permanent secretary][2]*, Chairman or Commissioners";*

(b) "on him" substitute "on him or them"; and

(c) "an officer" substitute "a person".

(3) In paragraph (2) for sub-paragraphs (a) to *(c)* substitute—

"*(a) in the case of the [designated permanent secretary]*[2]*, to a member of the Senior Civil Service;*

(b) in the case of the Chairman, to a member of the Senior Civil Service employed in the service of the Commissioners;

(c) in the case of the Commissioners, to an officer.".

(4) Omit paragraph (3).

(5) For paragraph (4) substitute—

"(4) The [designated permanent secretary][2], Chairman or Commissioners shall not, in any particular case, delegate any power or duty under paragraph (1) to a person who has acted as investigating officer in that case.".

(6) In paragraph (5) for "a chief constable" substitute "the Head of the Home Civil Service, Chairman or Commissioners".[1]

Revocation—These Regs revoked by the Revenue and Customs (Complaints and Misconduct) Regulations, SI 2010/1813 reg 2 with effect from 5 August 2010. However, where an allegation in respect of the conduct by an officer came to the attention of the appropriate authority before 5 August 2010, nothing in SI 2010/1813 shall apply and these Regs shall continue to have effect.

Amendments—[1] Sub-para (6) revoked by the Revenue and Customs (Complaints and Misconduct) (Amendment) Regulations, SI 2006/1748 reg 6(1), (3) with effect from 27 July 2006.

[2] Words "designated permanent secretary" substituted for words "Head of the Home Civil Service" by the Constitutional Reform and Governance Act 2010 s 19, Sch 2 para 23 with effect from 11 November 2010 (by virtue os SI 2010/2703 art 2(*a*)).

12 *Omit regulations 28, 29 and 30.*

Revocation—These Regs revoked by the Revenue and Customs (Complaints and Misconduct) Regulations, SI 2010/1813 reg 2 with effect from 5 August 2010. However, where an allegation in respect of the conduct by an officer came to the attention of the appropriate authority before 5 August 2010, nothing in SI 2010/1813 shall apply and these Regs shall continue to have effect.

PART 2
MODIFICATION OF THE STAFF CONDUCT REGULATIONS

1 In regulation 2(3)(*a*)(i) for "person serving with the police" substitute "Commissioner or officer".

Revocation—These Regs revoked by the Revenue and Customs (Complaints and Misconduct) Regulations, SI 2010/1813 reg 2 with effect from 5 August 2010. However, where an allegation in respect of the conduct by an officer came to the attention of the appropriate authority before 5 August 2010, nothing in SI 2010/1813 shall apply and these Regs shall continue to have effect.

2007/1417

VALUE ADDED TAX (SECTION 55A) (SPECIFIED GOODS AND EXCEPTED SUPPLIES) ORDER 2007

Made by the Treasury under VATA 1994 s 55A(9), (10), (11) and (14)

Made . . . . *10 May 2007*
Laid before the House of Commons . . . . *10 May 2007*
Coming into force . . . . *1 June 2007*

Revocation—This Order revoked by the Value Added Tax (Section 55A) (Specified Goods and Services and Excepted Supplies) Order, SI 2010/2239 art 2 with effect in relation to supplies made on or after 1 November 2010.

1 ***Citation and commencement***

This Order may be cited as the Value Added Tax (Section 55A) (Specified Goods and Excepted Supplies) Order 2007 and comes into force on 1st June 2007.

2 ***Interpretation***

In this Order—

"public electronic communications service" has the same meaning as in section 151 of the Communications Act 2003;

"specified goods" means goods of a description specified in article 3;

"the Act" means the Value Added Tax Act 1994.

3 ***Specified Goods***

For the purposes of section 55A of the Act (customers to account for tax on supplies of goods of a kind used in missing trader intra-community fraud) the goods of a description specified below are goods to which that section applies—

(*a*) *mobile telephones, whether or not they have any function in addition to the transmitting and receiving of spoken messages;*

(*b*) *integrated circuit devices, such as central processing units and microprocessor units, in a state prior to integration into end user products.*

4 ***Excepted supplies***

For the purposes of section 55A of the Act, a supply of a description specified below is an excepted supply—

(*a*) *a supply of specified goods where the value of the supply is less than £5000;*

(*b*) *a supply of specified goods where the supply is of a description specified in an order made under section 50A of the Act (margin schemes) and, in accordance with such an order, the supplier opts to account for the VAT chargeable on the supply on the profit margin on the supply instead of by reference to its value;*

(*c*) *a supply of a mobile telephone where, at the time a person enters into the agreement to purchase the telephone—*

(i) *he enters into an agreement (including the renewal or extension of an existing agreement) with a provider of a public electronic communications service for the supply, in relation to that telephone, of such a service, and*

(ii) *that agreement is not one that requires periodical pre-payments in order to use the service ("Pay as You Go");*

(*d*) *a transfer or disposal of specified goods for no consideration that is treated as a supply of goods by virtue of paragraph 5(1) of Schedule 4 to the Act.*

5 Article 4(*a*) does not apply to a supply of specified goods where—

(*a*) *the supply is particularised on the same VAT invoice as a supply, or supplies, of other specified goods, and*

(*b*) *the total value of the supplies equals or exceeds £5000.*

2007/1509

CONTROL OF CASH (PENALTIES) REGULATIONS 2007

Made by the Treasury under ECA 1972 s 2(2), being designated for the purposes of that subsection in relation to measures relating to preventing the use of the financial system for the purpose of money laundering and measures relating to the movement of capital and to payments between Member States and between Member States and countries which are not Member States:

Made .... *22 May 2007*
Laid before Parliament .... *23 May 2007*
Coming into force .... *15 June 2007*

1 Citation and commencement

These Regulations may be cited as the Control of Cash (Penalties) Regulations 2007 and come into force on 15th June 2007.

2 Interpretation

In these Regulations—

VAT SIs

"Community Regulation" means European Parliament and Council Regulation (EC) No 1889/2005 on controls of cash entering or leaving the Community

"The Commissioners" means the Commissioners for Her Majesty's Revenue and Customs.

["tribunal" means the First-tier Tribunal or, where determined by or under Tribunal Procedure Rules, the Upper Tribunal.][1]

Amendments—[1] Definition of "tribunal" inserted by the Transfer of Tribunal Functions and Revenue and Customs Appeals Order, SI 2009/56 art 3, Sch 2 paras 160, 161 with effect from 1 April 2009.

3 Power to impose penalties

(1) The Commissioners may impose a penalty of such amount as they consider appropriate, not exceeding £5000, on a person failing to comply with article 3 of the Community Regulation (obligation to declare cash of a value of 10,000 euros or more).

[(2) Where the Commissioners decide to impose a penalty under this regulation, they must forthwith—

(*a*) Where the Commissioners decide to impose a penalty under this regulation, they must forthwith—

(*b*) offer the person a review under regulation 4A.][1]

(3) Where a person is liable to a penalty under this regulation, the Commissioners may reduce the penalty to such amount (including nil) as they think proper.

Amendments—[1] Para (2) substituted by the Transfer of Tribunal Functions and Revenue and Customs Appeals Order, SI 2009/56 art 3, Sch 2 paras 160, 162 with effect from 1 April 2009.

4 [Appeals]

(1) Any person who is the subject of a decision to impose a penalty under regulation 3 may by notice in writing to the Commissioners require them to review that decision.

(2)–(5) . . . [1]

Amendments—[1] Heading and words in para (1) substituted, and paras (2)–(5) revoked by the Transfer of Tribunal Functions and Revenue and Customs Appeals Order, SI 2009/56 art 3, Sch 2 paras 160, 163 with effect from 1 April 2009.

[4A Offer of review

(1) The Commissioners must offer a person (P) a review of a decision that has been notified to P if an appeal lies under regulation 4 in respect of the decision.

(2) The offer of the review must be made by notice given to P at the same time as the decision is notified to P.

(3) This regulation does not apply to the notification of the conclusions of a review.][1]

Amendments—[1] Regulations 4A–4F inserted by the Transfer of Tribunal Functions and Revenue and Customs Appeals Order, SI 2009/56 art 3, Sch 2 paras 160, 164 with effect from 1 April 2009.

[4B Review by the Commissioners

(1) The Commissioners must review a decision if—

(*a*) they have offered a review of the decision under regulation 4A, and

(*b*) P notifies the Commissioners accepting the offer within 30 days from the date of the document containing the notification of the offer.

(2) But P may not notify acceptance of the offer if P has already appealed to the tribunal under regulation 4F.

(3) The Commissioners shall not review a decision if P has appealed to the tribunal under regulation 4F in respect of the decision.][1]

Amendments—[1] Regulations 4A–4F inserted by the Transfer of Tribunal Functions and Revenue and Customs Appeals Order, SI 2009/56 art 3, Sch 2 paras 160, 164 with effect from 1 April 2009.

[4C Extensions of time

(1) If under regulation 4A, the Commissioners have offered P a review of a decision, the Commissioners may within the relevant period notify P that the relevant period is extended.

(2) If notice is given the relevant period is extended to the end of 30 days from—

(*a*) the date of the notice, or

(*b*) any other date set out in the notice or a further notice.

(3) In this regulation "relevant period" means—

(*a*) the period of 30 days referred to in regulation 4B(1)(*b*), or

(*b*) if notice has been given under paragraph (1) that period as extended (or as most recently extended) in accordance with paragraph (2).][1]

Amendments—[1] Regulations 4A–4F inserted by the Transfer of Tribunal Functions and Revenue and Customs Appeals Order, SI 2009/56 art 3, Sch 2 paras 160, 164 with effect from 1 April 2009.

[4D Review out of time

(1) This regulation applies if—

(*a*) the Commissioners have offered a review of a decision under regulation 4A, and

(*b*) P does not accept the offer within the time allowed under regulation 4B(1)(*b*) or 4C(2).

(2) The Commissioners must review the decision under regulation 4C if—

(*a*) after the time allowed, P notifies the Commissioners in writing requesting a review out of time,
(*b*) the Commissioners are satisfied that P had a reasonable excuse for not accepting the offer or requiring review within the time allowed, and
(*c*) the Commissioners are satisfied that P made the request without unreasonable delay after the excuse had ceased to apply.

(3) The Commissioners shall not review a decision if P has appealed to the tribunal under regulation 4F in respect of the decision.][1]

Amendments—[1] Regulations 4A–4F inserted by the Transfer of Tribunal Functions and Revenue and Customs Appeals Order, SI 2009/56 art 3, Sch 2 paras 160, 164 with effect from 1 April 2009.

[4E Nature of review etc

(1) This regulation applies if the Commissioners are required to undertake a review under regulation 4B or 4D.

(2) The nature and extent of the review are to be such as appear appropriate to the Commissioners in the circumstances.

(3) For the purpose of paragraph (2), the Commissioners must, in particular, have regard to steps taken before the beginning of the review—
(*a*) by the Commissioners in reaching the decision, and
(*b*) by any person in seeking to resolve disagreement about the decision.

(4) The review must take account of any representations made by P at a stage which gives the Commissioners a reasonable opportunity to consider them.

(5) The review may conclude that the decision is to be—
(*a*) upheld,
(*b*) varied, or
(*c*) cancelled.

(6) The Commissioners must give P notice of the conclusions of the review and their reasoning within—
(*a*) a period of 45 days beginning with the relevant date, or
(*b*) such other period as the Commissioners and P may agree.

(7) In paragraph (6) "relevant date" means—
(*a*) the date the Commissioners received P's notification accepting the offer of a review (in a case falling within regulation 4A), or
(*b*) the date on which the Commissioners decided to undertake the review (in a case falling within regulation 4D).

(8) Where the Commissioners are required to undertake a review but do not give notice of the conclusions within the time period specified in paragraph (6), the review is to be treated as having concluded that the decision is upheld.

(9) If paragraph (8) applies, the Commissioners must notify P of the conclusion which the review is treated as having reached.][1]

Amendments—[1] Regulations 4A–4F inserted by the Transfer of Tribunal Functions and Revenue and Customs Appeals Order, SI 2009/56 art 3, Sch 2 paras 160, 164 with effect from 1 April 2009.

[4F Bringing of appeals

(1) An appeal under regulation 4 is to be made to the tribunal before—
(*a*) the end of the period of 30 days beginning with the date of the document notifying the decision to which the appeal relates, or
(*b*) if later, the end of the relevant period (within the meaning of regulation 4C).

(2) But that is subject to paragraphs (3) to (5).

(3) In a case where the Commissioners are required to undertake a review under regulation 4B—
(*a*) an appeal may not be made until the conclusion date, and
(*b*) any appeal is to be made within the period of 30 days beginning with the conclusion date.

[(4) In a case where HMRC are requested to undertake a review in accordance with regulation 9D—
(*a*) an appeal may not be made to an appeal tribunal—
(i) unless HMRC have notified P as to whether or not a review will be undertaken, and
(ii) if HMRC have notified P that a review will be undertaken, until the conclusion date;
(*b*) any appeal where sub-paragraph (*a*)(ii) applies is to be made within the period of 30 days beginning with the conclusion date;
(*c*) if HMRC have notified P that a review will not be undertaken, an appeal may be made only if the appeal tribunal gives permission to do so.][2]

(5) In a case where regulation 4E(8) applies, an appeal may be made at any time from the end of the period specified in regulation 4E(6) to the date 30 days after the conclusion date.

(6) An appeal may be made after the end of the period specified in paragraph (1), (3)(*b*), (4)(*b*) or (5) if the tribunal gives permission to do so.

(7) In this regulation "conclusion date" means the date of the document notifying the conclusions of the review.][1]

Amendments—[1] Regulations 4A–4F inserted by the Transfer of Tribunal Functions and Revenue and Customs Appeals Order, SI 2009/56 art 3, Sch 2 paras 160, 164 with effect from 1 April 2009.

[2] Para 4 substituted by the Revenue and Customs (Amendment of Appeal Provisions for Out of Time Reviews) Order, SI 2014/1264 art 10 with effect in relation to requests for a review out of time notified to HMRC on or after 1 June 2014.

[5 Settling of appeals by agreement

Section 85 of the Value Added Tax Act 1994 (settling of appeals by agreement) shall have effect as if the reference to section 83 of that Act included a reference to regulation 4 above.][1]

Amendments—[1] Regulation 5 substituted by the Transfer of Tribunal Functions and Revenue and Customs Appeals Order, SI 2009/56 art 3, Sch 2 paras 160, 165 with effect from 1 April 2009.

6 On an appeal under regulation [4][1], the tribunal has the power to—

(*a*) quash or vary any decision of the Commissioners, including the power to reduce any penalty to such amount (including nil) as it thinks proper; and

(*b*) substitute its own decision for any decision quashed on appeal.

Amendments—[1] Reference substituted by the Transfer of Tribunal Functions and Revenue and Customs Appeals Order, SI 2009/56 art 3, Sch 2 paras 160, 166 with effect from 1 April 2009.

[7 (1) An appeal shall not be entertained unless—

(*a*) the amount which the Commissioners have imposed by way of a penalty has been paid to them; or

(i) the Commissioners are satisfied (on the application of the appellant), or

(ii) the tribunal decides (the Commissioners not being so satisfied and on the application of the appellant),

that the requirement would cause the appellant to suffer hardship.

(2) Notwithstanding the provisions of sections 11 and 13 of the Tribunals, Courts and Enforcement Act 2007, the decision of the tribunal as to the issue of hardship is final.

Amendments—[1] Regulation 7 substituted by the Transfer of Tribunal Functions and Revenue and Customs Appeals Order, SI 2009/56 art 3, Sch 2 paras 160, 167 with effect from 1 April 2009.

8 Retention of cash detained

Where the Commissioners have imposed a penalty under regulation 3 they may deduct from any cash detained pursuant to article 4(2) of the Community Regulation the amount of the penalty, and upon expiry of the period for appealing, or where an appeal has been made upon determination of the appeal, the amount payable shall be forfeit to them.

2007/2126

INTERNATIONAL MUTUAL ADMINISTRATIVE ASSISTANCE IN TAX MATTERS ORDER 2007

A draft of this Order was laid before the House of Commons in accordance with FA 2006 s 173(7) and approved by a resolution of that House. Accordingly, Her Majesty, in exercise of the powers conferred upon Her by FA 2006 s 173(1)–(3), by and with the advice of Her Privy Council, orders as follows—

Made . . . . *25 July 2007*

Commentary—*Simon's Taxes* **A2.304, E6.455.**

1 Citation

This Order may be cited as the International Mutual Administrative Assistance in Tax Matters Order 2007.

2 Mutual administrative assistance arrangements to have effect

It is declared that—

(*a*) arrangements relating to international tax enforcement that fall within the joint Council of Europe/Organisation for Economic Co-operation and Development Convention on Mutual Administrative Assistance in Tax Matters, signed on behalf of the United Kingdom on 24 May 2007, have been made in relation to the other signatory territories, and

(*b*) it is expedient that those arrangements have effect.

2007/2709

TRIBUNALS, COURTS AND ENFORCEMENT ACT 2007 (COMMENCEMENT NO 1) ORDER 2007

Made by the Lord Chancellor under TCEA 2007 s 148(5)

Made . . . .*13 September 2007*

1 Citation and interpretation

(1) This Order may be cited as the Tribunals, Courts and Enforcement Act 2007 (Commencement No 1) Order 2007.

(2) In this Order, "the Act" means the Tribunals, Courts and Enforcement Act 2007.

2 Provisions coming into force on 19th September 2007

The following provisions of the Act come into force on 19th September 2007—

(*a*) sections 1, 2, 7(1) and (9), 9(3), 10(3), 11(5)(*f*) and (6) to (8), 13(6), (8)(*f*), (9), (10), (14) and (15), 18(10) and (11), 20(3), (6) and (7), 21(6), 22, 27(5) and (6), 30 to 42, 45(3), 49, 54, 58, 59, 61 and 144(1), (5) and (7);

(*b*) section 46 to the extent that it relates to Schedule 5;

(*c*) section 48(1) to the extent that it relates to the following paragraphs of Schedule 8—

(i) paragraphs 31(1) to (3), 62, 63 and 65(1) and (2); and

(ii) paragraph 65(3) to the extent that it relates to the Senior President of Tribunals;

(*d*) section 48(2) to the extent that it relates to paragraphs 1, 2 and 12(2) of Schedule 9;

(*e*) sections 50(1) to (5) and (7), 51 and 52 for the purposes of paragraph 3 of Schedule 1;

(*f*) section 144(11) to the extent that it relates to Part 1 and section 51;

(*g*) in Schedule 1, paragraphs 1 to 11;

(*h*) in Schedule 4, paragraph 15;

(*i*) Schedule 5;

(*j*) Schedule 6; and

(*k*) in Schedule 7, paragraphs 25(2) to (7) and 26 to 28.

VAT SIs

3 Provisions coming into force on 1st November 2007

The following provisions of the Act come into force on 1st November 2007—

(*a*) sections 44, 45(1) and (2) and 146;

(*b*) section 48(1) to the extent that it relates to the following paragraphs of Schedule 8—

(i) paragraphs 2, 3, 8 to 12, 14, 15, 17, 19 to 23, 30(*a*) to (*c*), 32, 33(1) and (2), 49 to 52 and 56 to 61;

(ii) paragraphs 4, 5, 7 and 53 to the extent that they relate to the Administrative Justice and Tribunals Council and to the Scottish Committee of the Administrative Justice and Tribunals Council; and

(iii) paragraph 18 to the extent that it relates to the Administrative Justice and Tribunals Council;

(*c*) in Schedule 7—

(i) paragraphs 1 to 6, 10(1)(*a*) and (*b*), (2)(*a*) and (*b*), (3)(*a*) and (*b*) and (4), 12, 13, 14(1), (2), (3)(*a*) and (4), 15 to 18, 20, 21(1), (2), (4) and (5), 22(1)(*a*) and (*b*) and (2), 23 and 25(1);

(ii) paragraphs 11 and 22(3) to the extent that they relate to the Administrative Justice and Tribunals Council and to the Scottish Committee of the Administrative Justice and Tribunals Council; and

(iii) paragraph 21(6) to the extent that it relates to reports made by the Administrative Justice and Tribunals Council; and

(*d*) in Part 1 of Schedule 23, the entries relating to—

(i) the House of Commons Disqualification Act 1975;

(ii) the Northern Ireland Assembly Disqualification Act 1975;

(iii) the Race Relations Act 1976;

(iv) the Estate Agents Act 1979;

(v) sections 1, 2, 3, 4 and 13(5)(*c*) of the Tribunals and Inquiries Act 1992;

(vi) the Scotland Act 1998 (Cross-Border Public Authorities) (Adaptation of Functions etc) Order 1999 to the extent that Schedule 9 applies to sections 2 and 4 of the Tribunals and Inquiries Act 1992;

(vii) the Freedom of Information Act 2000; and

(viii) the Scottish Public Services Ombudsman Act 2002 (Consequential Provisions and Modifications) Order 2004.

4 Provisions coming into force on 1st December 2007

Section 48(1) of the Act comes into force on 1st December 2007 to the extent that it relates to paragraphs 35 to 39 of Schedule 8.

5 Provisions coming into force on 1st April 2008

The following provisions of the Act come into force on 1st April 2008—

(*a*) sections 139 and 140; and

(*b*) Schedule 22.

6 Provisions coming into force on 1st June 2008

The following provisions of the Act come into force on 1st June 2008—

(*a*) all paragraphs of Schedule 7, except paragraph 24, to the extent that they are not already in force; and

(*b*) section 48(1) to the extent that it relates to the following paragraphs of Schedule 8—

(i) paragraphs 4 and 5 to the extent that they relate to the Welsh Committee of the Administrative Justice and Tribunals Council;

(ii) paragraphs 7, 18 and 53, to the extent that they are not already in force; and

(iii) paragraph 30(*d*).

2007/3298

TRANSFER OF FUNDS (INFORMATION ON THE PAYER) REGULATIONS 2007

Made .... *22 November 2007*

Laid before Parliament .... *23 November 2007*

Coming into force .... *15 December 2007*

The Treasury are a government department designated for the purposes of section 2(2) of the European Communities Act 1972 in relation to the prevention of money laundering and terrorist financing;

The Treasury, in exercise of the powers conferred on them by section 2(2) of the European Communities Act 1972 and by sections 168(4)(*b*), 402(1)(*b*), 417(1) and 428(3) of the Financial Services and Markets Act 2000, make the following Regulations:

PART 1
GENERAL

1 Citation, commencement etc

(1) These Regulations may be cited as the Transfer of Funds (Information on the Payer) Regulations 2007 and come into force on 15th December 2007.

(2) These Regulations are prescribed for the purposes of sections 168(4)(*b*) (appointment of persons to carry out investigations in particular cases) and 402(1)(*b*) (power of the Authority to institute proceedings for certain other offences) of the 2000 Act.

2 Interpretation

(1) In these Regulations—

"the 2000 Act" means the Financial Services and Markets Act 2000;

"authorised person" means a person who is authorised for the purposes of the 2000 Act;

"the Authority" means the Financial Services Authority;

"the Commissioners" means the Commissioners for Her Majesty's Revenue and Customs;

"money laundering" means an act which falls within section 340(11) of the Proceeds of Crime Act 2002;

"notice" means a notice in writing;

"the payments regulation" means Regulation 1781/2006/EC of the European Parliament and of the Council of 15th November 2006 on information on the payer accompanying transfers of funds;

"supervisory authority" in relation to any payment service provider means the supervisory authority specified for such a payment service provider by regulation 3;

"terrorist financing" means an offence under—

(*a*) section 15 (fund-raising), 16 (use and possession), 17 (funding arrangements), 18 (money laundering) or 63 (terrorist finance: jurisdiction) of the Terrorism Act 2000;

(*b*) paragraph 7(2) or (3) of Schedule 3 to the Anti-Terrorism, Crime and Security Act 2001 (freezing orders);

(*c*) article 7, 8 or 10 of the Terrorism (United Nations Measures) Order 2006; or

(*d*) article 7, 8 or 10 of the Al-Qaida and Taliban (United Nations Measures) Order 2006;

(2) Unless otherwise defined, expressions used in these Regulations and the payments regulation have the same meaning as in the payments regulation.
(3) References in these Regulations to numbered Articles are references to Articles of the payments regulation.

PART 2
SUPERVISION

3 Supervisory authorities

(1) The Authority is the supervisory authority for payment service providers who are authorised persons.
(2) The Commissioners are the supervisory authority for payment service providers who are not authorised persons.

4 Duties of supervisory authorities

(1) A supervisory authority must effectively monitor the payment service providers for whom it is the supervisory authority and take necessary measures for the purpose of securing compliance by such payment service providers with the requirements of the payments regulation.
(2) A supervisory authority which, in the course of carrying out any of its functions under these Regulations, knows or suspects that a payment service provider is or has engaged in money laundering or terrorist financing must promptly inform the Serious Organised Crime Agency.
(3) A disclosure made under paragraph (2) is not to be taken to breach any restriction, however imposed, on the disclosure of information.
(4) The functions of the Authority under these Regulations shall be treated for the purposes of Parts 1, 2 and 4 of Schedule 1 to the 2000 Act (the Financial Services Authority) as functions conferred on the Authority under that Act.

5 Costs of supervision

(1) The Authority and the Commissioners may impose charges on payment service providers supervised by them.
(2) Charges levied under paragraph (1) must not exceed such amount as the Authority or the Commissioners (as the case may be) consider will enable them to meet any expenses reasonably incurred by them in carrying out their functions under these Regulations or for any incidental purpose.
(3) Without prejudice to the generality of paragraph (2), a charge may be levied in respect of each of the premises at which a payment service provider carries on (or proposes to carry on) business.
(4) The Authority must apply amounts paid to it by way of penalties imposed under regulation 11 towards expenses incurred in carrying out its functions under these Regulations or for any incidental purpose.

PART 3
ENFORCEMENT

Powers of Supervisory Authorities

6 Interpretation

In this Part—

"officer", except in regulations 10(3) and 16, means—

(*a*) an officer of the Authority, including a member of the Authority's staff or an agent of the Authority; or

(*b*) an officer of Revenue and Customs;

"recorded information" includes information recorded in any form and any document of any nature.

7 Power to require information from, and attendance of, relevant and connected persons

(1) An officer may, by notice to a payment service provider or to a person connected with a payment service provider, require the payment service provider or the connected person, as the case may be—

(*a*) to provide such information as may be specified in the notice;

(*b*) to produce such recorded information as may be so specified; or

(*c*) to attend before an officer at a time and place specified in the notice and answer questions.

(2) For the purposes of paragraph (1), a person is connected with a payment service provider if he is, or has at any time been, in relation to the payment service provider, a person listed in Schedule 1 to these Regulations.
(3) An officer may exercise powers under this regulation only if the information sought to be obtained as a result is reasonably required in connection with the exercise by the supervisory authority for which he acts of its functions under these Regulations.
(4) Where an officer requires information to be provided or produced pursuant to paragraph (1)(*a*) or (*b*)—

VAT SIs

(*a*) the notice must set out the reasons why the officer requires the information to be provided or produced; and

(*b*) such information must be provided or produced—

(i) before the end of such reasonable period as may be specified in the notice; and

(ii) at such place as may be so specified.

(5) In relation to information recorded otherwise than in legible form, the power to require production of it includes a power to require the production of a copy of it in legible form or in a form from which it can readily be produced in visible and legible form.

(6) The production of a document does not affect any lien which a person has on the document.

(7) A person may not be required under this regulation to provide or produce information or to answer questions which that person would be entitled to refuse to provide, produce or answer on grounds of legal professional privilege in proceedings in the High Court, except that a lawyer may be required to provide the name and address of his client.

(8) Subject to paragraphs (9) and (10), a statement made by a person in compliance with a requirement imposed on that person under paragraph (1)(*c*) is admissible in evidence in any proceedings, so long as it also complies with any requirements governing the admissibility of evidence in the circumstances in question.

(9) In criminal proceedings in which a person is charged with an offence to which this paragraph applies—

(*a*) no evidence relating to the statement may be adduced; and

(*b*) no question relating to it may be asked,

by or on behalf of the prosecution unless evidence relating to it is adduced, or a question relating to it is asked, in the proceedings by or on behalf of that person.

(10) Paragraph (9) applies to any offence other than one under—

(*a*) section 5 of the Perjury Act 1911 (false statements without oath);

(*b*) section 44(2) of the Criminal Law (Consolidation) (Scotland) Act 1995 (false statements and declarations); or

(*c*) Article 10 of the Perjury (Northern Ireland) Order 1979 (false unsworn statements).

(11) In the application of this regulation to Scotland, the reference in paragraph (7) to—

(*a*) proceedings in the High Court is to be read as a reference to proceedings in the Court of Session; and

(*b*) an entitlement on grounds of legal professional privilege is to be read as a reference to an entitlement on the grounds of confidentiality of communications—

(i) between a professional legal adviser and his client; or

(ii) made in connection with or in contemplation of legal proceedings and for the purposes of those proceedings.

8 Entry, inspection without a warrant etc

(1) Where an officer has reasonable cause to believe that any premises are being used by a payment service provider in connection with the payment service provider's business or professional activities, he may on producing evidence of his authority at any reasonable time—

(*a*) enter the premises;

(*b*) inspect the premises;

(*c*) observe the carrying on of business or professional activities by the payment service provider;

(*d*) inspect any recorded information found on the premises;

(*e*) require any person on the premises to provide an explanation of any recorded information or to state where it may be found;

(*f*) inspect any cash found on the premises.

(2) An officer may take copies of, or make extracts from, any recorded information found under paragraph (1).

(3) Paragraphs (1)(*d*) and (*e*) and (2) do not apply to recorded information which the payment service provider would be entitled to refuse to disclose on grounds of legal professional privilege in proceedings in the High Court, except that a lawyer may be required to provide the name and address of his client and, for this purpose, regulation 7(11) applies to this paragraph as it applies to regulation 7(7).

(4) An officer may exercise powers under this regulation only if the information sought to be obtained as a result is reasonably required in connection with the exercise by the supervisory authority for which he acts of its functions under these Regulations.

(5) In this regulation, "premises" means any premises other than premises used only as a dwelling.

9 Entry to premises under warrant

(1) A justice may issue a warrant under this paragraph if satisfied on information on oath given by an officer that there are reasonable grounds for believing that the first, second or third set of conditions is satisfied.

(2) The first set of conditions is—

(*a*) that there is on the premises specified in the warrant recorded information in relation to which a requirement could be imposed under regulation 7(1)(*b*); and

(*b*) that if such a requirement were to be imposed—

(i) it would not be complied with; or

(ii) the recorded information to which it relates would be removed, tampered with or destroyed.

(3) The second set of conditions is—

(*a*) that a person on whom a requirement has been imposed under regulation 7(1)(*b*) has failed (wholly or in part) to comply with it; and

(*b*) that there is on the premises specified in the warrant recorded information which has been required to be produced.

(4) The third set of conditions is—

(*a*) that an officer has been obstructed in the exercise of a power under regulation 8; and

(*b*) that there is on the premises specified in the warrant recorded information or cash which could be inspected under regulation 8(1)(*d*) or (*f*).

(5) A justice may issue a warrant under this paragraph if satisfied on information on oath given by an officer that there are reasonable grounds for suspecting that—

(*a*) an offence under these Regulations has been, is being or is about to be committed by a payment service provider; and

(*b*) there is on the premises specified in the warrant recorded information relevant to whether that offence has been, or is being or is about to be committed.

(6) A warrant issued under this regulation shall authorise an officer—

(*a*) to enter the premises specified in the warrant;

(*b*) to search the premises and take possession of any recorded information or anything appearing to be recorded information specified in the warrant or to take, in relation to any such recorded information, any other steps which may appear to be necessary for preserving it or preventing interference with it;

(*c*) to take copies of, or extracts from, any recorded information specified in the warrant;

(*d*) to require any person on the premises to provide an explanation of any recorded information appearing to be of the kind specified in the warrant or to state where it may be found;

(*e*) to use such force as may reasonably be necessary.

(7) Where a warrant is issued by a justice under paragraph (1) or (5) on the basis of information on oath given by an officer of the Authority, for "an officer" in paragraph (6) substitute "a constable".

(8) In paragraphs (1), (5) and (7), "justice" means—

(*a*) in relation to England and Wales, a justice of the peace;

(*b*) in relation to Scotland, a justice within the meaning of section 307 of the Criminal Procedure (Scotland) Act 1995 (interpretation);

(*c*) in relation to Northern Ireland, a lay magistrate.

(9) In the application of this regulation to Scotland, the references in paragraphs (1), (5) and (7) to information on oath are to be read as references to evidence on oath.

10 Failure to comply with information requirement

(1) If, on an application made by a supervisory authority it appears to the court that a person (the "information defaulter") has failed to do something that he was required to do under regulation 7(1), the court may make an order under this regulation.

(2) An order under this regulation may require the information defaulter—

(*a*) to do the thing that he failed to do within such period as may be specified in the order;

(*b*) otherwise to take such steps to remedy the consequences of the failure as may be so specified.

(3) If the information defaulter is a body corporate, a partnership or an unincorporated body of persons which is not a partnership, the order may require any officer of the body corporate, partnership or body, who is (wholly or partly) responsible for the failure to meet such costs of the application as are specified in the order.

(4) In this regulation, "court" means—

(*a*) in England and Wales and Northern Ireland, the High Court or the county court;

(*b*) in Scotland, the Court of Session or the sheriff court.

Civil Penalties, Review and Appeals

11 Power to impose civil penalties

(1) A supervisory authority may impose a penalty of such amount as it considers appropriate on a payment service provider in respect of any transfer of funds to which the payments regulation applies—

(*a*) in the case of the payment service provider of the payer, if he fails to comply with any requirement in—

(i) Article 5(1) read with Article 6(1) (information accompanying transfers of funds within the EEA);

VAT SIs

(ii) Article 5(2) read with Article 5(3) or (4) (whichever is relevant) (verification of information);
(iii) Article 5(5) (record keeping);
(iv) Article 6(2) (information to be provided following request);
(v) Article 7(1) read with Article 7(2) (information accompanying transfers of funds from the EEA to outside the EEA);

(*b*) in the case of the payment service provider of the payee, if he fails to comply with any requirement in Article 8 (detection of missing information), 9(1) (transfers of funds with missing or incomplete information), 9(2) sub-paragraph 2 (reporting) or 11 (record keeping);

(*c*) in the case of the intermediary payment service provider, if he fails to comply with any requirement in Article 12 (keeping information on the payer with the transfer) or 13(3), (4) or (5) (use of a payment system with technical limitations);

and, for this purpose, "appropriate" means effective, proportionate and dissuasive.

(2) The supervisory authority must not impose a penalty on a person under paragraph (1) where there are reasonable grounds for it to be satisfied that the person took all reasonable steps and exercised all due diligence to ensure that the requirement would be complied with.

(3) In deciding whether a person has failed to comply with any requirement of the payments regulation, the supervisory authority must consider whether the person followed any relevant guidance which was at the time—

(*a*) issued by a supervisory authority or any other appropriate body;
(*b*) approved by the Treasury; and
(*c*) published in a manner approved by the Treasury as suitable in their opinion to bring the guidance to the attention of persons likely to be affected by it.

(4) In paragraph (3), an "appropriate body" means any body which regulates or is representative of any trade, profession, business or employment carried on by the payment service provider.

(5) Where the Commissioners decide to impose a penalty under this regulation, they must give the payment service provider notice of—

(*a*) their decision to impose the penalty and its amount;
(*b*) the reasons for imposing the penalty;
(*c*) the right to a review under regulation 12; and
(*d*) the right to appeal under regulation 13(1)(*b*).

(6) Where the Authority proposes to impose a penalty under this regulation, it must give the payment service provider notice of—

(*a*) its proposal to impose the penalty and the proposed amount;
(*b*) the reasons for imposing the penalty; and
(*c*) the right to make representations to it within a specified period (which may not be less than 28 days).

(7) The Authority must then decide, within a reasonable period, whether to impose a penalty under this regulation and it must give the payment service provider notice of—

(*a*) its decision not to impose a penalty; or
(*b*) the following matters—
(i) its decision to impose a penalty and the amount;
(ii) the reasons for its decision; and
(iii) the right to appeal under regulation 13(1)(*a*).

(8) A penalty imposed under this regulation is payable to the supervisory authority which imposes it.

12 Review procedure

(1) Any payment service provider who is the subject of a decision by the Commissioners to impose a penalty under regulation 11 may by notice to the Commissioners require them to review that decision.

(2) The Commissioners need not review any decision unless the notice requiring the review is given within 45 days beginning with the date on which they first gave notice of the decision to the payment service provider requiring the review.

(3) Where the Commissioners are required under this regulation to review any decision they must either—

(*a*) confirm the decision; or
(*b*) withdraw or vary the decision and take such further steps (if any) in consequence of the withdrawal or variation as they consider appropriate.

(4) Where the Commissioners do not, within 45 days beginning with the date on which the review was required by a payment service provider, give notice to that person of their determination of the review, they are to be taken for the purposes of these Regulations to have confirmed the decision.

13 Appeals

(1) A payment service provider may appeal from a decision by—

(*a*) the Authority under regulation 11(7); and
(*b*) the Commissioners on a review under regulation 12.

(2) An appeal from a decision by—

(*a*) the Authority is to the Financial Services and Markets Tribunal; and

(*b*) the Commissioners is to a VAT and duties tribunal.

(3) The provisions of Part 9 of the 2000 Act (hearings and appeals), subject to the modifications set out in paragraph 1 of Schedule 2, apply in respect of appeals to the Financial Services and Markets Tribunal made under this regulation as they apply in respect of references made to that Tribunal under that Act.

(4) The provisions of Part 5 of the Value Added Tax Act 1994 (appeals), subject to the modifications set out in paragraph 2 of Schedule 2, apply in respect of appeals to a VAT and duties tribunal made under this regulation as they apply in respect of appeals made to such a tribunal under section 83 (appeals) of that Act.

(5) A VAT and duties tribunal hearing an appeal under paragraph (2) has the power to—

(*a*) quash or vary any decision of the supervisory authority, including the power to reduce any penalty to such amount (including nil) as they think proper; and

(*b*) substitute their own decision for any decision quashed on appeal.

Criminal Offences

14 Offences

(1) A payment service provider is guilty of an offence in respect of any transfer of funds to which the payments regulation applies—

(*a*) in the case of the payment service provider of the payer, if he fails to comply with any requirement in—

(i) Article 5(1) read with Article 6(1) (information accompanying transfers of funds within the EEA);

(ii) Article 5(2) read with Article 5(3) or (4) (whichever is relevant) (verification of information);

(iii) Article 5(5) (record keeping);

(iv) Article 6(2) (information to be provided following request);

(v) Article 7(1) read with Article 7(2) (information accompanying transfers of funds from the EEA to outside the EEA);

(*b*) in the case of the payment service provider of the payee, if he fails to comply with any requirement in Article 8 (detection of missing information), 9(1) or the third paragraph of Article 9 (transfers of funds with missing or incomplete information) or Article 11 (record keeping);

(*c*) in the case of the intermediary payment service provider, if he fails to comply with any requirement in Article 12 (keeping information on the payer with the transfer) or 13(3), (4) or (5) (use of a payment system with technical limitations).

(2) A payment service provider who is guilty of an offence under paragraph (1) is liable—

(*a*) on summary conviction, to a fine not exceeding the statutory maximum;

(*b*) on conviction on indictment, to imprisonment for a term not exceeding two years, to a fine or to both.

(3) In deciding whether a person has committed an offence under paragraph (1), the court must consider whether the person followed any relevant guidance which was at the time—

(*a*) issued by a supervisory authority or any other appropriate body;

(*b*) approved by the Treasury; and

(*c*) published in a manner approved by the Treasury as suitable in their opinion to bring the guidance to the attention of persons likely to be affected by it.

(4) In paragraph (3), an "appropriate body" means any body which regulates or is representative of any trade, profession, business or employment carried on by the alleged offender.

(5) A person is not guilty of an offence under this regulation if he took all reasonable steps and exercised all due diligence to avoid committing the offence.

(6) Where a person is convicted of an offence under this regulation, he shall not also be liable to a penalty under regulation 11.

15 Prosecution of offences

(1) Proceedings for an offence under regulation 14 may be instituted by—

(*a*) the Director of Revenue and Customs Prosecutions or by order of the Commissioners;

(*b*) the Director of Public Prosecutions; or

(*c*) the Director of Public Prosecutions for Northern Ireland.

(2) Proceedings for an offence under regulation 14 may be instituted only against a payment service provider or, where the payment service provider is a body corporate, a partnership or an unincorporated association, against any person who is liable to be proceeded against under regulation 16.

(3) Where proceedings under paragraph (1) are instituted by order of the Commissioners, the proceedings must be brought in the name of an officer of Revenue and Customs.

(4) Where the Commissioners investigate, or propose to investigate, any matter with a view to determining—

(*a*) whether there are grounds for believing that an offence under regulation 14 has been committed by any person; or

(*b*) whether a person should be prosecuted for such an offence,

that matter is to be treated as an assigned matter within the meaning of section 1(1) of the Customs and Excise Management Act 1979.

(5) Paragraphs (1) and (3) do not extend to Scotland and, in its application to the Commissioners acting in Scotland, paragraph (4)(*b*) shall be read as referring to the Commissioners determining whether to refer the matter to the Crown Office and Procurator Fiscal Service with a view to the Procurator Fiscal determining whether a person should be prosecuted for such an offence.

16 Offences by bodies corporate etc

(1) If an offence under regulation 14 committed by a body corporate is shown—

(*a*) to have been committed with the consent or the connivance of an officer of the body corporate; or

(*b*) to be attributable to any neglect on his part,

the officer as well as the body corporate is guilty of an offence and liable to be proceeded against and punished accordingly.

(2) If an offence under regulation 14 committed by a partnership is shown—

(*a*) to have been committed with the consent or the connivance of a partner; or

(*b*) to be attributable to any neglect on his part,

the partner as well as the partnership is guilty of an offence and liable to be proceeded against and punished accordingly.

(3) If an offence under regulation 14 committed by an unincorporated association (other than a partnership) is shown—

(*a*) to have been committed with the consent or the connivance of an officer of the association; or

(*b*) to be attributable to any neglect on his part,

the officer as well as the association is guilty of an offence and liable to be proceeded against and punished accordingly.

(4) If the affairs of a body corporate are managed by its members, paragraph (1) applies in relation to the acts and defaults of a member in connection with his functions of management as if he were a director of the body.

(5) Proceedings for an offence alleged to have been committed by a partnership or an unincorporated association must be brought in the name of the partnership or association (and not in that of its members).

(6) A fine imposed on the partnership or association on its conviction of an offence is to be paid out of the funds of the partnership or association.

(7) Rules of court relating to the service of documents are to have effect as if the partnership or association were a body corporate.

(8) In proceedings for an offence brought against the partnership or association—

(*a*) section 33 of the Criminal Justice Act 1925 (procedure on charge of offence against corporation) and Schedule 3 to the Magistrates' Courts Act 1980 (corporations) apply as they do in relation to a body corporate;

(*b*) section 70 of the Criminal Procedure (Scotland) Act 1995 (proceedings against bodies corporate) applies as it does in relation to a body corporate;

(*c*) section 18 of the Criminal Justice (Northern Ireland) Act 1945 (procedure on charge) and Schedule 4 to the Magistrates' Courts (Northern Ireland) Order 1981 (corporations) apply as they do in relation to a body corporate.

(9) In this regulation—

"officer"—

(*a*) in relation to a body corporate, means a director, manager, secretary, chief executive, member of the committee of management, or a person purporting to act in such a capacity; and

(*b*) in relation to an unincorporated association, means any officer of the association or any member of its governing body, or a person purporting to act in such capacity; and

"partner" includes a person purporting to act as a partner.

PART 4
MISCELLANEOUS

17 Recovery of charges and penalties through the court

Any charge or penalty imposed on a payment service provider by a supervisory authority under regulation 5(1) or 11(1) is a debt due from that person to the authority, and is recoverable accordingly.

18 Transfers between the United Kingdom and the Channel Islands and the Isle of Man

In determining whether a person has failed to comply with any requirement in the payments regulation, any transfer of funds between the United Kingdom and—

(*a*) the Channel Islands; or

(*b*) the Isle of Man,

shall be treated as a transfer of funds within the United Kingdom.

SCHEDULE 1

CONNECTED PERSONS

Regulation 7(2)

Corporate Bodies

1 If the payment service provider is a body corporate ("BC"), a person who is or has been—

(*a*) an officer or manager of BC or of a parent undertaking of BC;

(*b*) an employee of BC;

(*c*) an agent of BC or of a parent undertaking of BC

Partnerships

2 If the payment service provider is a partnership, a person who is or has been a member, manager, employee or agent of the partnership.

Unincorporated Associations

3 If the payment service provider is an unincorporated association of persons which is not a partnership, a person who is or has been an officer, manager, employee or agent of the association.

Individuals

4 If the payment service provider is an individual, a person who is or has been an employee or agent of that individual.

SCHEDULE 2

MODIFICATIONS IN RELATION TO APPEALS

Regulation 13(3) and (4)

THE VALUE ADDED TAX ACT 1994

2 Part 5 of the Value Added Tax Act 1994 (appeals) is modified as follows—

(*a*) omit section 84; and

(*b*) in section 87, in paragraph (*a*) of each of subsections (1), (2) and (3), omit ", or is recoverable as, VAT".

Note—Provisions beyond the scope of this publication have not been reproduced.

2008/568

FINANCE ACT 2007, SCHEDULE 24 (COMMENCEMENT AND TRANSITIONAL PROVISIONS) ORDER 2008

Made by the Treasury under FA 2007 s 97

Made . . . . *3 March 2008*

1 Citation and interpretation

(1) This Order may be cited as the Finance Act 2007, Schedule 24 (Commencement and Transitional Provisions) Order 2008.

(2) In this Order "Schedule 24" means Schedule 24 to the Finance Act 2007 and a reference to a paragraph (without more) is a reference to that paragraph of Schedule 24.

(3) In this Order—

"HMRC" means Her Majesty's Revenue and Customs;

"relevant documents" means documents given to HMRC of a kind listed in the Table in paragraph 1;

"relevant tax" means any tax mentioned in the Table in paragraph 1; and

"tax period" has the meaning given in paragraph 28(g).

2 Appointed days

The days appointed for the coming into force of Schedule 24 are—

(*a*) 1st April 2008 in relation to relevant documents relating to tax periods commencing on or after that date;

(*b*) 1st April 2008 in relation to assessments falling within paragraph 2 for tax periods commencing on or after that date;

(*c*) 1st July 2008 in relation to relevant documents relating to claims under the Thirteenth Council Directive (arrangements for the refund of value added tax to persons not established in Community territory) for years commencing on or after that date;

(*d*) 1st January 2009 in relation to relevant documents relating to claims under the Eighth Council Directive (arrangements for the refund of value added tax to taxable persons not established in the territory of the country) for years commencing on or after that date;

(*e*) 1st April 2009 in relation to documents relating to all other claims for repayments of relevant tax made on or after 1st April 2009 which are not related to a tax period; and

(*f*) in any other case, 1st April 2009 in relation to documents given where a person's liability to pay relevant tax arises on or after that date.

3 Transitional provision

Notwithstanding article 2, no person shall be liable to a penalty under Schedule 24 in respect of any tax period for which a return is required to be made before 1st April 2009.

4 Saving

Notwithstanding paragraph 29(*d*) (consequential amendments), sections 60 and 61 of the Value Added Tax Act 1994 (VAT evasion) shall continue to have effect with respect to conduct involving dishonesty which does not relate to an inaccuracy in a document or a failure to notify HMRC of an under-assessment by HMRC.

2008/1146

VALUE ADDED TAX (BUILDINGS AND LAND) ORDER 2008

Made by the Treasury under FA 2006 s 17(1)–(5)

Made . . . . *21 April 2008*

Laid before the House of Commons . . . . *22 April 2008*

Coming into force . . . . *1 June 2008*

1 Citation, commencement and effect

(1) This Order may be cited as the Value Added Tax (Buildings and Land) Order 2008 and comes into force on 1st June 2008.

(2) This Order, apart from article 4, has effect in relation to supplies made on or after 1st June 2008.

(3) Article 4 has effect in relation to supplies made on or after 1st June 2020.

(4) Paragraphs (2) and (3) are subject to Schedule 2 (transitional provisions and savings).

2 Rewrite of Schedule 10 to VATA 1994

(*inserts* new VATA 1994 Sch 10).

3–5 (*These amendments are already in force and are therefore not reproduced*)

6 Consequential amendments, repeals and revocations

Schedule 1 contains consequential amendments, repeals and revocations.

7 Transitional provisions and savings

Schedule 2 contains transitional provisions and savings.

SCHEDULE 1

CONSEQUENTIAL AMENDMENTS, REPEALS AND REVOCATIONS

Article 6

Note—The amendments effected by Sch 1 are already in force and are therefore not reproduced here.

SCHEDULE 2

TRANSITIONAL PROVISIONS AND SAVINGS

Article 7

PART 1

GENERAL PROVISIONS

1 The re-enactment by article 2 of this Order of any provision of Schedule 10 to VATA 1994 in a rewritten form does not affect the continuity of the law.

2 Paragraph 1 does not apply to any change in the law relating to that provision effected by that article.

3 Any thing which—

(*a*) has been done, or has effect as if done, under or for the purposes of a provision (a "superseded provision") of Schedule 10 to VATA 1994 as it stood before being rewritten, and

(*b*) is in force or effective immediately before the commencement of the corresponding rewritten provision,

has effect after that commencement as if done under or for the purposes of the rewritten provision.

4 Any reference (express or implied) in any enactment, instrument or document to—

(*a*) a rewritten provision, or

(*b*) things done or falling to be done under or for the purposes of a rewritten provision,

is to be read as including, in relation to times, circumstances or purposes in relation to which any corresponding superseded provision had effect, a reference to the superseded provision or (as the case may be) things done or falling to be done under or for the purposes of the superseded provision.

5 Any reference (express or implied) in any enactment, instrument or document to—

(*a*) a superseded provision, or

(*b*) things done or falling to be done under or for the purposes of a superseded provision,

is to be read as including, in relation to times, circumstances or purposes in relation to which any corresponding rewritten provision has effect, a reference to the rewritten provision or (as the case may be) things done or falling to be done under or for the purposes of the rewritten provision.

6 Paragraphs 1 to 5 have effect instead of section 17(2) of the Interpretation Act 1978 (but do not affect the operation of any other provision of that Act).

7 Paragraphs 4 and 5 have effect only in so far as the context permits.

PART 2

OTHER PROVISION

Elections made before 1st November 1989

8—(1) An election under paragraph 2 of Schedule 10 to VATA 1994 which was made before 1st November 1989 continues to have effect in accordance with paragraph 3(1)(b) of that Schedule.

(2) In this paragraph any reference to Schedule 10 to VATA 1994 is to that Schedule as it stood before being rewritten by article 2 of this Order.

Elections made before 1st March 1995

9—(1) An election under paragraph 2 of Schedule 10 to VATA 1994 which was made before 1st March 1995 continues to have effect in accordance with paragraph 3(6)(a) of that Schedule.

(2) In this paragraph any reference to Schedule 10 to VATA 1994 is to that Schedule as it stood before being rewritten by article 2 of this Order.

Developers of certain non-residential buildings etc

10 The fact that paragraphs 5 to 7 of Schedule 10 to VATA 1994 (as it stood before being rewritten by article 2 of this Order) are not rewritten by that article is not to affect—

(*a*) the continued operation of Part 15 of the Value Added Tax Regulations 1995 (adjustments to the deduction of input tax on capital items) in relation to supplies treated as made on or before 1st March 1997, or

(*b*) the continued operation of paragraph (*b*) of item 1 in Group 1 of Schedule 9 to VATA 1994, as read with Note (7), in relation to supplies made before 1st June 2020.

Option made before 1st June 2008 specifying a description of land

11 The fact that the words ", or of a description specified," in paragraph 3(2) of Schedule 10 to VATA 1994 (as it stood before being rewritten by article 2 of this Order) are not rewritten by that article is not to affect the continued operation of an option to tax any land—

(*a*) which was made before 1st June 2008, and

(*b*) which specified a description of land.

2008/1948

TAXES (FEES FOR PAYMENT BY TELEPHONE) REGULATIONS 2008

Made by the Commissioners for Her Majesty's Revenue and Customs under FA 2008 s 136(1) and (3)

Made .... *22 July 2008*
Laid before the House of Commons .... *22 July 2008*
Coming into force .... *13 August 2008*

Revocation—These regulations revoked by the Taxes, etc (Fees for Payment by Telephone) Regulations 2009, SI 2009/3073.

2008/2684

FIRST-TIER TRIBUNAL AND UPPER TRIBUNAL (CHAMBERS) ORDER 2008

Made .... *13 October 2008*
Laid before Parliament .... *15 October 2008*
Coming into force .... *3 November 2008*

The Lord Chancellor, with the concurrence of the Senior President of Tribunals, makes the following Order in exercise of the power conferred by section 7(1) and (9) of the Tribunals, Courts and Enforcement Act 2007.

1 Citation and commencement

This Order may be cited as the First-tier Tribunal and Upper Tribunal (Chambers) Order 2008 and shall come into force on 3rd November 2008.

2 First-tier Tribunal Chambers

The First-tier Tribunal shall be organised into the following chambers—

(*a*) the Social Entitlement Chamber;
(*b*) the War Pensions and Armed Forces Compensation Chamber; . . . [1]
(*c*) the Health, Education and Social Care Chamber;
[(*d*) the Tax Chamber.][1]
[(*e*) the General Regulatory Chamber.][2]
[(*f*) the Immigration and Asylum Chamber.][3]

Amendments—[1] In para (*b*), word "and" repealed, and para (*d*) inserted, by the First-tier Tribunal and Upper Tribunal (Chambers) (Amendment) Order, SI 2009/196 arts 2, 3 with effect from 1 April 2009.

[2] Para (*e*) inserted by the First-tier Tribunal and Upper Tribunal (Chambers) (Amendment No 3) Order, SI 2009/1590 arts 2, 3 with effect from 1 September 2009.

[3] Para (*f*) inserted by the First-tier Tribunal and Upper Tribunal (Chambers) (Amendment) Order, SI 2010/40, arts 6, 7 with effect from 15 February 2010.

3 Functions of the Social Entitlement Chamber

To the Social Entitlement Chamber are assigned all functions relating to appeals—

[(*a*) in cases regarding support for asylum seekers, failed asylum seekers, persons designated under section 130 of the Criminal Justice and Immigration Act 2008, or the dependants of any such persons;][1]
(*b*) in criminal injuries compensation cases;
(*c*) regarding entitlement to, payments of, or recovery or recoupment of payments of, social security benefits, child support, vaccine damage payment, [health in pregnancy grant,][2] [and][4] tax credits . . . [4][, with the exception of—
  [(*a* i) appeals under section 11 of the Social Security Contributions (Transfer of Functions, etc) Act 1999 (appeals against decisions of Her Majesty's Revenue and Customs);][3]
  (i) appeals in respect of employer penalties or employer information penalties (as defined in section 63(11) and (12) of the Tax Credits Act 2002);
  (ii) appeals under regulation 28(3) of the Child Trust Funds Regulations 2004;][1]
[(*ca*) regarding saving gateway accounts with the exception of appeals against requirements to account for an amount under regulations made under section 14 of the Saving Gateway Accounts Act 2009;
(*cb*) regarding child trust funds with the exception of appeals against requirements to account for an amount under regulations made under section 22(4) Child Trust Funds Act 2004 in relation to section 13 of that Act;][4]
(*d*) regarding payments in consequence of diffuse mesothelioma;
(*e*) regarding a certificate or waiver decision in relation to NHS charges;
(*f*) regarding entitlement to be credited with earnings or contributions;
(*g*) against a decision as to whether an accident was an industrial accident.

Amendments—[1] Para (*a*) substituted and words in para (*c*) inserted, by the First-tier Tribunal and Upper Tribunal (Chambers) (Amendment) Order, SI 2009/196 arts 2, 4 with effect from 1 April 2009.

[2] Words in para (*c*) inserted by the First-tier Tribunal and Upper Tribunal (Chambers) (Amendment No 2) Order, SI 2009/1021 arts 2, 3 with effect from 1 June 2009.

[3] Para (*c*)(*a* i) inserted by the First-tier Tribunal and Upper Tribunal (Chambers) (Amendment No 3) Order, SI 2009/1590 arts 2, 4 with effect from 1 September 2009.

[4] Word in para (*c*), and paras (*ca*), (*cb*) inserted, and words "and child trust funds" in para (*c*) omitted, by the First-tier Tribunal and Upper Tribunal (Chambers) (Amendment) Order, SI 2010/40, arts 6, 8, with effect from 18 January 2010.

4 Functions of the War Pensions and Armed Forces Compensation Chamber

To the War Pensions and Armed Forces Compensation Chamber are assigned all functions relating to appeals under the War Pensions (Administrative Provisions) Act 1919 and the Pensions Appeal Tribunals Act 1943.

5 Functions of the Health, Education and Social Care Chamber

To the Health Education and Social Care Chamber are assigned all functions relating to—

(*a*) an appeal against a decision related to children with special educational needs;

(*b*) a claim of disability discrimination in the education of a child;

(*c*) an application or an appeal against a decision or determination related to work with children or vulnerable adults;

(*d*) an appeal against a decision related to registration in respect of [the][1] provision of health or social care;

[(*dd*) an application in respect of, or an appeal against a decision related to, the provision of health care or health services;][1]

(*e*) an appeal against a decision related to registration in respect of social workers and social care workers;

(*f*) an appeal against a decision related to the provision of childcare;

(*g*) an appeal against a decision related to an independent school or other independent educational institution;

(*h*) applications and references by and in respect of patients under the provisions of the Mental Health Act 1983 or paragraph 5(2) of the Schedule to the Repatriation of Prisoners Act 1984.

Amendments—[1] Word in para (*d*), and whole of para (*dd*), inserted, by First-tier Tribunal and Upper Tribunal (Chambers) (Amendment) Order, SI 2010/40, arts 6, 9, with effect from 18 January 2010.

[5A Functions of the Tax Chamber

To the Tax Chamber are assigned all functions, except those functions assigned to the Social Entitlement Chamber by article 3 or to the [Tax and Chancery][2] Chamber by article 8, relating to—

(*a*) an appeal, application, reference or other proceeding in respect of a function of the Commissioners for Her Majesty's Revenue and Customs or an officer of Revenue and Customs;

(*b*) an appeal in respect of the exercise by the Serious Organised Crime Agency of general Revenue functions or Revenue inheritance tax functions (as defined in section 323 of the Proceeds of Crime Act 2002).][1]

Amendments—[1] Article 5A inserted by the First-tier Tribunal and Upper Tribunal (Chambers) (Amendment) Order, SI 2009/196 arts 2, 5 with effect from 1 April 2009.

[2] Words substituted for words "Finance and Tax" by the First-tier Tribunal and Upper Tribunal (Chambers) (Amendment) Order, SI 2010/40, regs 6, 10 with effect from 6 April 2010.

[5B Functions of the General Regulatory Chamber

To the General Regulatory Chamber are assigned all functions relating to—

(*a*) proceedings in respect of the decisions and actions of regulatory bodies which are not assigned to the Health, Education and Social Care Chamber by article 5;

(*b*) matters referred to the First-tier Tribunal under Schedule 1D to the Charities Act 1993; and

(*c*) the determination of remuneration for carrying mail-bags in a ship or aircraft.][1]

Amendments—[1] Article inserted by the First-tier Tribunal and Upper Tribunal (Chambers) (Amendment No 3) Order, SI 2009/1590 arts 2, 5 with effect from 1 September 2009.

[5C Functions of the Immigration and Asylum Chamber of the First-tier Tribunal

To the Immigration and Asylum Chamber of the First-tier Tribunal are assigned all functions relating to immigration and asylum matters, except for matters assigned to—

(*a*) the Social Entitlement Chamber by article 3(*a*); and

(*b*) the General Regulatory Chamber by article 5B(*a*).][1]

Amendments—[1] Article 5C inserted by the First-tier Tribunal and Upper Tribunal (Chambers) (Amendment) Order, SI 2010/40, arts 6, 11 with effect from 15 February 2010.

[6 Upper Tribunal Chambers

The Upper Tribunal shall be organised into the following chambers—

(*a*) the Administrative Appeals Chamber;

[(*b*) the Tax and Chancery Chamber;][3]

[(*c*) the Lands Chamber.][2]][1]

[(*d*) the Immigration and Asylum Chamber of the Upper Tribunal.][4]

Amendments—[1] Article 6 substituted by the First-tier Tribunal and Upper Tribunal (Chambers) (Amendment) Order, SI 2009/196 arts 2, 6 with effect from 1 April 2009.

[2] Para (*c*) inserted by the First-tier Tribunal and Upper Tribunal (Chambers) (Amendment No 2) Order, SI 2009/1021 arts 2, 4 with effect from 1 June 2009.

[3] Para (*b*) substituted by the First-tier Tribunal and Upper Tribunal (Chambers) (Amendment No 3) Order, SI 2009/1590 arts 2, 6 with effect from 1 September 2009.

[4] Para (*d*) inserted by the First-tier Tribunal and Upper Tribunal (Chambers) (Amendment) Order, SI 2010/40 arts 6, 12 with effect from 15 February 2010.

7 Functions of the Administrative Appeals Chamber

To the Administrative Appeals Chamber are assigned all functions relating to—

(*a*) an appeal—

(i) against a decision made by [the First-tier Tribunal, except [an appeal assigned to the Tax and Chancery Chamber by article 8(1)(*a*)][2] [or the Immigration and Asylum Chamber of the Upper Tribunal by article 9A(*a*)][3]][1];

(ii) under section 5 of the Pensions Appeal Tribunals Act 1943 (assessment decision) against a decision of the Pensions Appeal Tribunal in Northern Ireland established under paragraph 1(2) of Schedule 1 to the Pensions Appeal Tribunals Act 1943;

(iii) against a decision of the Pensions Appeal Tribunal in Scotland established under paragraph 1(2) of Schedule 1 to the Pensions Appeal Tribunals Act 1943;

(iv) against a decision of the Mental Health Review Tribunal for Wales established under section 65 of the Mental Health Act 1983c;

(v) against a decision of the Special Educational Needs Tribunal for Wales;

(vi) under section 4 of the Safeguarding Vulnerable Groups Act 2006 (appeals);

[(vii) against a decision of the Information Commissioner transferred to the Upper Tribunal from the First-tier Tribunal under Tribunal Procedure Rules;

(viii) against a decision of a traffic commissioner.][2]

(*b*) an application[, except an application assigned to the Tax and Chancery Chamber by article 8(*e*), for the Upper Tribunal][2]—

(i) to grant the relief mentioned in section 15(1) of the Tribunal, Courts and Enforcement Act 2007 (Upper Tribunal's "judicial review" jurisdiction);

(ii) to exercise the powers of review under section 21(2) of that Act (Upper Tribunal's "judicial review" jurisdiction: Scotland);

[(*c*) a matter referred to the Upper Tribunal by the First-tier Tribunal under section 9(5)(*b*) of the Tribunals, Courts and Enforcement Act 2007, [except where the reference is assigned to the Tax and Chancery Chamber by article 8(1)(*d*)][2] [or the Immigration and Asylum Chamber of the Upper Tribunal by article 9A(*b*)][3].][1]

[(*d*) a determination or decision under section 4 of the Forfeiture Act 1982.][2]

Amendments—[1] In para (*a*)(i) words substituted, and para (*c*) inserted, by the First-tier Tribunal and Upper Tribunal (Chambers) (Amendment) Order, SI 2009/196 arts 2, 7 with effect from 1 April 2009.

[2] In para (*a*)(i) words substituted for words "decisions made in the Tax Chamber", para (*a*)(vii), (viii) inserted, in para (*b*), words inserted, in para (*c*), words substituted for words "unless the reference is made by the Tax Chamber", and para (*d*) inserted, by the First-tier Tribunal and Upper Tribunal (Chambers) (Amendment No 3) Order, SI 2009/1590 arts 2, 7 with effect from 1 September 2009.

[3] Words in paras (*a*)(i), (*c*) inserted by the First-tier Tribunal and Upper Tribunal (Chambers) (Amendment) Order, SI 2010/40, arts 6, 13 with effect from 15 February 2010.

8 Functions of the Tax and Chancery Chamber

(1) To the Tax and Chancery Chamber are assigned all functions relating to—

(*a*) an appeal against a decision of the First-tier Tribunal made—

(i) in the Tax Chamber; or

(ii) in a charities case;

[(*aa*) a reference or appeal in respect of—

(i) a decision of the Financial Services Authority;

(ii) a decision of the Bank of England; or

(iii) a decision of a person relating to the assessment of any compensation or consideration under the Banking (Special Provisions) Act 2008;

(*ab*) a reference in respect of a decision of the Pensions Regulator;][2]

(*b*) an application under paragraph 50(1)(*d*) of Schedule 36 to the Finance Act 2008;

(*c*) proceedings transferred to the Upper Tribunal under Tribunal Procedure Rules—

(i) from the Tax Chamber of the First-tier Tribunal; or

(ii) from the First-tier Tribunal in a charities case;

(*d*) a matter referred to the Upper Tribunal under section 9(5)(*b*) of the Tribunals, Courts and Enforcement Act 2007—

(i) by the Tax Chamber of the First-tier Tribunal; or

(ii) by the First-tier Tribunal in a charities case;

(*e*) an application for the Upper Tribunal to grant the relief mentioned in section 15(1) of the Tribunals, Courts and Enforcement Act 2007 (Upper Tribunal's "judicial review" jurisdiction), or to exercise the powers of review under section 21(2) of that Act (Upper Tribunal's "judicial review" jurisdiction: Scotland), which relates to—

(i) a decision of the First-tier Tribunal mentioned in paragraph (*a*)(i) or (ii);

(ii) a function of the Commissioners for Her Majesty's Revenue and Customs or an officer of Revenue and Customs, with the exception of any function in respect of which an appeal would be allocated to the Social Entitlement Chamber by article 3;

(iii) the exercise by the Serious Organised Crime Agency of general Revenue functions or Revenue inheritance tax functions (as defined in section 323 of the Proceeds of Crime Act 2002), with the exception of any function in relation to which an appeal would be allocated to the Social Entitlement Chamber by article 3;

(iv) a function of the Charity Commission[, or one of the bodies mentioned in paragraph (*aa*) or (*ab*)][2].

(2) In this article "a charities case" means an appeal or application in respect of a decision, order or direction of the Charity Commission, or a reference under Schedule 1D of the Charities Act 1993.][1]

Amendments—[1] Article 8 substituted by the First-tier Tribunal and Upper Tribunal (Chambers) (Amendment No 3) Order, SI 2009/1590 arts 2, 8 with effect from 1 September 2009.

[2] Paras (*aa*), (*ab*), and words in para (*e*)(iv), inserted, by the First-tier Tribunal and Upper Tribunal (Chambers) (Amendment) Order, SI 2010/40, arts 6, 14 with effect from 6 April 2010.

[9 Functions of the Lands Chamber

To the Lands Chamber are assigned—

(*a*) all functions relating to—

(i) compensation and other remedies for measures taken which affect the ownership, value, enjoyment or use of land or water, or of rights over or property on land or water;

(ii) appeals from decisions of leasehold valuation tribunals, residential property tribunals and valuation tribunals;

(iii) appeals on questions of the value of land or interests in land arising in tax proceedings; and

(iv) proceedings in respect of restrictive covenants, blight notices or the obstruction of light;

(*b*) the Upper Tribunal's function as arbitrator under section 1(5) of the Lands Tribunal Act 1949; and

(*c*) any other functions transferred to the Upper Tribunal by the Transfer of Tribunal Functions (Lands Tribunal and Miscellaneous Amendments) Order 2009.][1]

Amendments—[1] Articles 9, 10 inserted by the First-tier Tribunal and Upper Tribunal (Chambers) (Amendment No 2) Order, SI 2009/1021 arts 2, 5 with effect from 1 June 2009.

[9A Functions of the Immigration and Asylum Chamber of the Upper Tribunal

To the Immigration and Asylum Chamber of the Upper Tribunal are assigned all functions relating to—

(*a*) an appeal against a decision of the First-tier Tribunal made in the Immigration and Asylum Chamber of the First-tier Tribunal; and

(*b*) a matter referred to the Upper Tribunal under section 9(5)(*b*) of the Tribunals, Courts and Enforcement Act 2007 by the Immigration and Asylum Chamber of the First-tier Tribunal.][1]

Amendments—[1] Article 9A inserted by the First-tier Tribunal and Upper Tribunal (Chambers) (Amendment) Order, SI 2010/40, arts 6, 15 with effect from 15 February 2010.

[10 Resolution of doubt or dispute as to chamber

If there is any doubt or dispute as to the chamber in which a particular matter is to be dealt with, the Senior President of Tribunals may allocate that matter to the chamber which appears to the Senior President of Tribunals to be most appropriate.][1]

Amendments—[1] Articles 9, 10 inserted by the First-tier Tribunal and Upper Tribunal (Chambers) (Amendment No 2) Order, SI 2009/1021 arts 2, 5 with effect from 1 June 2009.

[11 Re-allocation of a case to another chamber

(1) Subject to paragraph (2), the Chamber President of the chamber to which a case has been assigned or allocated by or under this Order may allocate that case to another chamber within the same tribunal, by giving a direction to that effect.

(2) A Chamber President may give a direction under paragraph (1) only if the Chamber President of the chamber to which the case is to be allocated has first consented to the giving of the direction.

(3) A direction under paragraph (1) may be given at any point in the proceedings.][1]

Amendments—[1] Article 11 inserted by the First-tier Tribunal and Upper Tribunal (Chambers) (Amendment) Order, SI 2010/40, arts 6, 16 with effect from 18 January 2010.

2008/2692

QUALIFICATIONS FOR APPOINTMENT OF MEMBERS TO THE FIRST-TIER TRIBUNAL AND UPPER TRIBUNAL ORDER 2008

Made . . . . *15 October 2008*

Laid before Parliament . . . . *15 October 2008*

Coming into force . . . . *3 November 2008*

The Lord Chancellor, with the concurrence of the Senior President of Tribunals, makes the following Order in exercise of the powers conferred by paragraph 2(2) of Schedule 2 and paragraph 2(2) of Schedule 3 to the Tribunals, Courts and Enforcement Act 2007.

1 [(1)] This Order may be cited as the Qualifications for Appointment of Members to the First-tier Tribunal and Upper Tribunal Order 2008 and shall come into force on 3rd November 2008.

[(2) In this Order "registered medical practitioner" means a fully registered person within the meaning of the Medical Act 1983 whether or not they hold a licence to practise under that Act.]

2 (1) A person is eligible for appointment as a member of the First-tier Tribunal or the Upper Tribunal who is not a judge of those tribunals if paragraph (2), (3) or (4) applies.

(2) This paragraph applies to a person who is—

(*a*) a registered medical practitioner;

(*b*) a registered nurse;

(*c*) a registered dentist;

[(*ca*) a registered optometrist;]

(*d*) a clinical psychologist;

(*e*) an educational psychologist;

(*f*) a pharmacologist;

(*g*) a veterinary surgeon or a veterinary practitioner registered under the Veterinary Surgeons Act 1966;

(*h*) a Member or Fellow of the Royal Institution of Chartered Surveyors; or

(*i*) an accountant who is a member of—

(i) the Institute of Chartered Accountants in England and Wales;

(ii) the Institute of Chartered Accountants in Scotland;

(iii) the Institute of Chartered Accountants in Ireland;

(iv) the Institute of Certified Public Accountants in Ireland;

(v) the Association of Chartered Certified Accountants;

(vi) the Chartered Institute of Management Accountants; or

(vii) the Chartered Institute of Public Finance and Accountancy.

(3) This paragraph applies to a person. . . who is experienced in dealing with the physical or mental needs of disabled persons because they—

(*a*) work with disabled persons in a professional or voluntary capacity; or

(*b*) are themselves disabled.

[(3A) A person is not eligible for appointment under paragraph (3) if they are a registered medical practitioner.]

(4) This paragraph applies to a person who has substantial experience—

(*a*) of service in Her Majesty's naval, military, or air forces;

(*b*) of educational, child care, health, or social care matters;

(*c*) of dealing with victims of violent crime;

(*d*) in transport operations and its law and practice;

(*e*) in the regulatory field;

(*f*) in consumer affairs;

(*g*) in an industry, trade or business sector and the matters that are likely to arise as issues in the course of disputes with regulators of such industries, trades or businesses;

(*h*) in tax matters and related tax procedures;

(*i*) in a business, trade[, charity] or not-for-profit organisation;

[(*j*) in immigration services or the law and procedure relating to immigration;

(*k*) of data protection;

(*l*) of freedom of information (including environmental information) rights;

(*m*) of service as a Member or Senior Officer of a local authority in England].

2008/2698

TRIBUNAL PROCEDURE (UPPER TRIBUNAL) RULES 2008

Made by the Tribunal Procedure Committee, after consulting in accordance with TCEA 2007 Sch 5 para 28(1), under TCEA 2007 ss 10(3), 16(9), 22, 29(3), (4), Sch 5.

The Lord Chancellor has allowed the Rules in accordance with TCEA 2007 Sch 5 para 28(3).

Made .... *9 October 2008*
Laid before Parliament .... *15 October 2008*
Coming into force .... *3 November 2008*

PART 1
INTRODUCTION

1 Citation, commencement, application and interpretation

(1) These Rules may be cited as the Tribunal Procedure (Upper Tribunal) Rules 2008 and come into force on 3rd November 2008.

(2) These Rules apply to proceedings before the Upper Tribunal [except proceedings in the Lands Chamber][2].

(3) In these Rules—

"the 2007 Act" means the Tribunals, Courts and Enforcement Act 2007;

["appellant" means—

(a) a person who makes an appeal, or applies for permission to appeal, to the Upper Tribunal;

(b) in proceedings transferred or referred to the Upper Tribunal from the First-tier Tribunal, a person who started the proceedings in the First-tier Tribunal; or

(c) a person substituted as an appellant under rule 9(1) (substitution and addition of parties);][1]

["applicant" means—

(*a*) a person who applies for permission to bring, or does bring, judicial review proceedings before the Upper Tribunal and, in judicial review proceedings transferred to the Upper Tribunal from a court, includes a person who was a claimant or petitioner in the proceedings immediately before they were transferred; or

(*b*) a person who refers a financial services case [or a wholesale energy case][11] to the Upper Tribunal;][5]

["appropriate national authority" means, in relation to an appeal, the Secretary of State, the Scottish Ministers[, the Department of the Environment in Northern Ireland][8] or the Welsh Ministers, as the case may be;

["asylum case" means proceedings before the Upper Tribunal on appeal against a decision in proceedings under section 82, 83 or 83A of the Nationality, Immigration and Asylum Act 2002 in which a person claims that removal from, or a requirement to leave, the United Kingdom would breach the United Kingdom's obligations under the Convention relating to the Status of Refugees done at Geneva on 28 July 1951 and the Protocol to the Convention;][4]

["authorised person" means—

(*a*) an examiner appointed by the Secretary of State under section 66A of the Road Traffic Act 1988;

(*b*) an examiner appointed by the Department of the Environment in Northern Ireland under Article 74 of the Road Traffic (Northern Ireland) Order 1995; or

(*c*) any person authorised in writing by the Department of the Environment in Northern Ireland for the purposes of the Goods Vehicles (Licensing of Operators) Act (Northern Ireland) 2010;

and includes a person acting under the direction of such an examiner or other authorised person, who has detained the vehicle to which an appeal relates;][8]

["disability discrimination in schools case" means proceedings concerning discrimination in the education of a child or young person or related matters;][12]

. . .[1]

"dispose of proceedings" includes, unless indicated otherwise, disposing of a part of the proceedings;

"document" means anything in which information is recorded in any form, and an obligation under these Rules or any practice direction or direction to provide or allow access to a document or a copy of a document for any purpose means, unless the Upper Tribunal directs otherwise, an obligation to provide or allow access to such document or copy in a legible form or in a form which can be readily made into a legible form;

["fast-track case" means an asylum case or an immigration case where the person who appealed to the First-tier Tribunal—

VAT SIs

(*a*) was detained under the Immigration Acts at a place specified in [rule 2(3) of the Schedule to the Tribunal Procedure (First-tier Tribunal) (Immigration and Asylum Chamber) Rules 2014][13] when the notice of decision that was the subject of the appeal to the First-tier Tribunal was served on the appellant;

(*b*) remains so detained; and

(*c*) the First-tier Tribunal or the Upper Tribunal has not directed that the case cease to be treated as a fast-track case;][4]

["financial services case" means a reference to the Upper Tribunal in respect of—

[(*a*) a decision of the Financial Conduct Authority;

(*aa*) a decision of the Prudential Regulation Authority;][9]

(*b*) a decision of the Bank of England;

(*c*) a decision of the Pensions Regulator; . . . [11]

(*d*) a decision of a person relating to the assessment of any compensation or consideration under the Banking (Special Provisions) Act 2008 or the Banking Act 2009;] [or[5]

(*e*) any determination, calculation or dispute which may be referred to the Upper Tribunal under the Financial Services and Markets Act 2000 (Contribution to Costs of Special Resolution Regime) Regulations 2010(2) (and in these Rules a decision in respect of which a reference has been made to the Upper Tribunal in a financial services case includes any such determination, calculation or, except for the purposes of rule 5(5), dispute relating to the making of payments under the Regulations).][6]

. . . [10]

"hearing" means an oral hearing and includes a hearing conducted in whole or in part by video link, telephone or other means of instantaneous two-way electronic communication;

["immigration case" means proceedings before the Upper Tribunal on appeal against a decision in proceedings under section 40A of the British Nationality Act 1981, section 82 of the Nationality, Immigration and Asylum Act 2002, or regulation 26 of the Immigration (European Economic Area) Regulations 2006 that are not an asylum case;][4]

["immigration judicial review proceedings" means judicial review proceedings which are designated as an immigration matter—

(*a*) in a direction made in accordance with Part 1 of Schedule 2 to the Constitutional Reform Act 2005 specifying a class of case for the purposes of section 18(6) of the 2007 Act; or

(*b*) in an order of the High Court in England and Wales made under section 31A(3) of the Senior Courts Act 1981, transferring to the Upper Tribunal an application of a kind described in section 31A(1) of that Act;][10]

"interested party" means—

(*a*) a person who is directly affected by the outcome sought in judicial review proceedings, and has been named as an interested party under rule 28 or 29 (judicial review), or has been substituted or added as an interested party under rule 9 [(addition, substitution and removal of parties)][5] . . . [5];

(*b*) in judicial review proceedings transferred to the Upper Tribunal under section 25A(2) or (3) of the Judicature (Northern Ireland) Act 1978 or section 31A(2) or (3) of the Supreme Court Act 1981, a person who was an interested party in the proceedings immediately before they were transferred to the Upper Tribunal; [and

(*c*) in a financial services case [or a wholesale energy case][11], any person other than the applicant who could have referred the case to the Upper Tribunal and who has been added or substituted as an interested party under rule 9 (addition, substitution and removal of parties);][5]

"judicial review proceedings" means proceedings within the jurisdiction of the Upper Tribunal pursuant to section 15 or 21 of the 2007 Act, whether such proceedings are started in the Upper Tribunal or transferred to the Upper Tribunal;

. . . [1]

"mental health case" means proceedings before the Upper Tribunal on appeal against a decision in proceedings under the Mental Health Act 1983 or paragraph 5(2) of the Schedule to the Repatriation of Prisoners Act 1984;

["national security certificate appeal" means an appeal under section 28 of the Data Protection Act 1998 or section 60 of the Freedom of Information Act 2000 (including that section as applied and modified by regulation 18 of the Environmental Information Regulations 2004);][3]

"party" means a person who is an appellant, an applicant, a respondent or an interested party in proceedings before the Upper Tribunal, a person who has referred a question [or matter][5] to the Upper Tribunal or, if the proceedings have been concluded, a person who was an appellant, an applicant, a respondent or an interested party when the [Upper][10] Tribunal finally disposed of all issues in the proceedings;

"permission" includes leave in cases arising under the law of Northern Ireland;

"practice direction" means a direction given under section 23 of the 2007 Act;

["QCS Board" means a Board constituted under Part 2 of the Transport Act 2000;
"quality contracts scheme" has the meaning provided for in section 124(3) (quality contracts scheme) of the Transport Act 2000;
"quality contracts scheme case" means proceedings in the Upper Tribunal under Part 2 of the Transport Act 2000;][14]
["relevant minister" means the Minister or designated person responsible for the signing of the certificate to which a national security certificate appeal relates;][3]
["reference", in a financial services case, includes an appeal;][5]
"respondent" means—

(*a*) in an appeal, or application for permission to appeal, against a decision of another tribunal, any person other than the appellant who—
  (i) was a party before that other tribunal;
  (ii) . . . [1]
  (iii) otherwise has a right of appeal against the decision of the other tribunal and has given notice to the Upper Tribunal that they wish to be a party to the appeal;

(*b*) in an appeal [other than a road transport case][8], the person who made the decision;

(*c*) in judicial review proceedings—
  (i) in proceedings started in the Upper Tribunal, the person named by the applicant as the respondent;
  (ii) in proceedings transferred to the Upper Tribunal under section 25A(2) or (3) of the Judicature (Northern Ireland) Act 1978 or section 31A(2) or (3) of the Supreme Court Act 1981, a person who was a defendant in the proceedings immediately before they were transferred;
  (iii) in proceedings transferred to the Upper Tribunal under section 20(1) of the 2007 Act, a person to whom intimation of the petition was made before the proceedings were transferred, or to whom the Upper Tribunal has required intimation to be made;

[(*ca*) in proceedings transferred or referred to the Upper Tribunal from the First-tier Tribunal, a person who was a respondent in the proceedings in the First-tier Tribunal;][1]

(*d*) in a reference under the Forfeiture Act 1982, the person whose eligibility for a benefit or advantage is in issue; . . . [5]

[(*da*) in a financial services case—
  (i) where the case is a multiple regulator case, both the primary and secondary regulator as defined in Schedule 3 to these rules (but subject to the operation of paragraph 4A(3) of that Schedule);
  (ii) where the case is a single regulator case, the maker of the decision in respect of which a reference has been made; or][9]

[(*db*) in a wholesale energy case, in relation to Great Britain, the Gas and Electricity Markets Authority or, in relation to Northern Ireland, the Northern Ireland Authority for Utility Regulation; or][11]

(*e*) a person substituted or added as a respondent under rule 9 (substitution and addition of parties);

["road transport case" means an appeal against a decision of a traffic commissioner or the Department of the Environment in Northern Ireland;][8]
["special educational needs case" means proceedings concerning the education of a child or young person who has or may have special educational needs, including proceedings relating to—

(*a*) an EHC needs assessment within the meaning of section 36(2) of the Children and Families Act 2014(b); . . . [14]

[(*aa*) a detained person's EHC needs assessment within the meaning of section 70(5) of the Children and Families Act 2014(; or][14]

(*b*) an EHC plan within the meaning of section 37(2) of that Act,

of such a child or young person;][12]
["tribunal" does not include a traffic commissioner;][2]
["wholesale energy case" means a reference to the Upper Tribunal in respect of a decision of—

(*a*) in relation to Great Britain, the Gas and Electricity Markets Authority under the Electricity and Gas (Market Integrity and Transparency) (Enforcement etc.) Regulations 2013; or

(*b*) in relation to Northern Ireland, the Northern Ireland Authority for Utility Regulation under the Electricity and Gas (Market Integrity and Transparency) (Enforcement etc.) Regulations (Northern Ireland) 2013;][11]

VAT SIs

. . . [1]
"working day" means any day except a Saturday or Sunday, Christmas Day, Good Friday or a bank holiday under section 1 of the Banking and Financial Dealings Act 1971.
["young person" means, in relation to a special educational needs case or a disability discrimination in schools case, a person over compulsory school age but under 25;][12]

Amendments—[1] In para (3), definition of "appellant" substituted, definitions of "disability discrimination in schools case", "legal representative" and "special educational needs case" repealed, in definition of "respondent", sub-para (*a*)(ii) repealed and sub-para (*ca*) inserted, by the Tribunal Procedure (Amendment) Rules, SI 2009/274 rules 3, 5 with effect from 1 April 2009.

2 In paras (2), (3) words inserted by the Tribunal Procedure (Amendment No 2) Rules, SI 2009/1975 rules 7, 8 with effect from 1 September 2009.

3 Definitions inserted by the Tribunal Procedure (Amendment) Rules, SI 2010/43, rules 5, 6, with effect from 18 January 2010.

4 Definitions inserted by the Tribunal Procedure (Amendment No 2) Rules, SI 2010/44, rules 2, 3, with effect from 15 February 2010.

5 Definition of "applicant" substituted, definitions of "financial services case" and "reference" inserted, in definition of "interested party" words in sub-para (*a*) substituted and word "and" revoked, and sub-para (*c*) and preceding word "and" inserted, in definition of "party" words inserted, in definition of "respondent" in sub-para (*d*) word "or" revoked, by the Tribunal Procedure (Upper Tribunal) (Amendment) Rules, SI 2010/747 rules 2, 4 with effect from 6 April 2010.

6 In definition of "financial services case" sub-para (*e*) and preceding word "or" inserted by the Tribunal Procedure (Amendment) Rules SI 2011/651 rule 8(1), (2) with effect from 1 April 2011.

8 In definition of "appropriate national authority", words inserted, definition of "authorised person" substituted, in definition of "respondent", words substituted for words "against any other decision except a decision of a traffic commissioner", and definition of "road transport case" inserted, by the Tribunal Procedure (Amendment No 2) Rules, SI 2012/1363 rules 4, 5 with effect from 1 July 2012.

9 In definition of "financial services case" paras (*a*), (*aa*) substituted for previous para (*a*), and in definition of "respondent" para (*da*) substituted, by the Tribunal Procedure (Amendment No 2) Rules, SI 2013/606 rule 2(1), (2) with effect from 1 April 2013.

10 In para (3), definition of "fresh claim proceedings" revoked, definition of "immigration judicial review proceedings" inserted, and in the definition of "party" word inserted, by the Tribunal Procedure (Amendment No 4) Rules, SI 2013/2067 rules 2, 4 with effect from 1 November 2013.

11 In definition of "applicant", words in para (*b*) inserted, in definition of "financial services case", word in para (*c*) revoked, in definition of "interested party", words in para (*c*) inserted, in definition of "respondent", para (*db*) inserted, and definition of "wholesale energy case" inserted by the Tribunal Procedure (Amendment) Rules, SI 2014/514 rules 2, 4 with effect from 6 April 2014.

12 Definitions of "disability discrimination in schools case", "special educational needs case" and "young person" inserted by the Tribunal Procedure (Amendment No 3) Rules, SI 2014/2128 rules 2, 4(*a*), (*c*), (*d*) with effect from 1 September 2014.

13 In definition of "fast-track case" words substituted for words "Schedule 2 to the Asylum and Immigration Tribunal (Fast Track Procedure) Rules 2005" by the Tribunal Procedure (Amendment No 3) Rules, SI 2014/2128 rules 2, 4(*b*) with effect from 20 October 2014.

14 Definitions of ""QCS Board", "quality contracts scheme", and "quality contracts scheme case" inserted, and in definition of "special educational needs case", in sub-para (*a*), word "or" revoked and sub-para (*aa*) inserted, by the Tribunal Procedure (Amendment) Rules, SI 2015/1510 arts 2, 3 with effect from 21 August 2015.

2 Overriding objective and parties' obligation to co-operate with the Upper Tribunal

(1) The overriding objective of these Rules is to enable the Upper Tribunal to deal with cases fairly and justly.

(2) Dealing with a case fairly and justly includes—

(*a*) dealing with the case in ways which are proportionate to the importance of the case, the complexity of the issues, the anticipated costs and the resources of the parties;

(*b*) avoiding unnecessary formality and seeking flexibility in the proceedings;

(*c*) ensuring, so far as practicable, that the parties are able to participate fully in the proceedings;

(*d*) using any special expertise of the Upper Tribunal effectively; and

(*e*) avoiding delay, so far as compatible with proper consideration of the issues.

(3) The Upper Tribunal must seek to give effect to the overriding objective when it—

(*a*) exercises any power under these Rules; or

(*b*) interprets any rule or practice direction.

(4) Parties must—

(*a*) help the Upper Tribunal to further the overriding objective; and

(*b*) co-operate with the Upper Tribunal generally.

3 Alternative dispute resolution and arbitration

(1) The Upper Tribunal should seek, where appropriate—

(*a*) to bring to the attention of the parties the availability of any appropriate alternative procedure for the resolution of the dispute; and

(*b*) if the parties wish and provided that it is compatible with the overriding objective, to facilitate the use of the procedure.

(2) Part 1 of the Arbitration Act 1996 does not apply to proceedings before the Upper Tribunal.

PART 2
GENERAL POWERS AND PROVISIONS

4 Delegation to staff

(1) Staff appointed under section 40(1) of the 2007 Act (tribunal staff and services) may, with the approval of the Senior President of Tribunals, carry out functions of a judicial nature permitted or required to be done by the Upper Tribunal.

(2) The approval referred to at paragraph (1) may apply generally to the carrying out of specified functions by members of staff of a specified description in specified circumstances.

(3) Within 14 days after the date on which the Upper Tribunal sends notice of a decision made by a member of staff under paragraph (1) to a party, that party may apply in writing to the Upper Tribunal for that decision to be considered afresh by a judge.

5 Case management powers

(1) Subject to the provisions of the 2007 Act and any other enactment, the Upper Tribunal may regulate its own procedure.

(2) The Upper Tribunal may give a direction in relation to the conduct or disposal of proceedings at any time, including a direction amending, suspending or setting aside an earlier direction.

(3) In particular, and without restricting the general powers in paragraphs (1) and (2), the Upper Tribunal may—

(*a*) extend or shorten the time for complying with any rule, practice direction or direction;

(*b*) consolidate or hear together two or more sets of proceedings or parts of proceedings raising common issues, or treat a case as a lead case;

(*c*) permit or require a party to amend a document;

(*d*) permit or require a party or another person to provide documents, information, evidence or submissions to the Upper Tribunal or a party;

(*e*) deal with an issue in the proceedings as a preliminary issue;

(*f*) hold a hearing to consider any matter, including a case management issue;

(*g*) decide the form of any hearing;

(*h*) adjourn or postpone a hearing;

(*i*) require a party to produce a bundle for a hearing;

(*j*) stay (or, in Scotland, sist) proceedings;

(*k*) transfer proceedings to another court or tribunal if that other court or tribunal has jurisdiction in relation to the proceedings and—

(i) because of a change of circumstances since the proceedings were started, the Upper Tribunal no longer has jurisdiction in relation to the proceedings; or

(ii) the Upper Tribunal considers that the other court or tribunal is a more appropriate forum for the determination of the case;

(*l*) suspend the effect of its own decision pending an appeal or review of that decision;

(*m*) in an appeal, or an application for permission to appeal, against the decision of another tribunal, suspend the effect of that decision pending the determination of the application for permission to appeal, and any appeal;

[(*n*) require any person, body or other tribunal whose decision is the subject of proceedings before the Upper Tribunal to provide reasons for the decision, or other information or documents in relation to the decision or any proceedings before that person, body or tribunal.][1]

[(4) The Upper Tribunal may direct that a fast-track case cease to be treated as a fast-track case if—

(*a*) all the parties consent; [or][6]

(*b*) the Upper Tribunal is satisfied that . . . [6] the appeal or application could not be justly determined if it were treated as a fast-track case. . . . [6]

(*c*) . . . [6]][2]

[(5) In a financial services case, the Upper Tribunal may direct that the effect of the decision in respect of which the reference has been made is to be suspended pending the determination of the reference, if it is satisfied that to do so would not prejudice—

(*a*) the interests of any persons (whether consumers, investors or otherwise) intended to be protected by that notice; . . . [4]

(*b*) the smooth operation or integrity of any market intended to be protected by that notice[; or][4]

[(*c*) the stability of the financial system of the United Kingdom.][4]

(6) Paragraph (5) does not apply in the case of a reference in respect of a decision of the Pensions Regulator.][3]

[(7) In a wholesale energy case, the Upper Tribunal may direct that the effect of the decision in respect of which the reference has been made is to be suspended pending the determination of the reference.][5]

Amendments—[1] Para (3)(*n*) substituted by the Tribunal Procedure (Amendment No 2) Rules, SI 2009/1975 rules 7, 9 with effect from 1 September 2009.

[2] Para (4) inserted by the Tribunal Procedure (Amendment No 2) Rules, SI 2010/44 rules 2, 4, with effect from 15 February 2010.

VAT SIs

3 Paras (5), (6) inserted, by the Tribunal Procedure (Upper Tribunal) (Amendment) Rules, SI 2010/747 rules 2, 5 with effect from 6 April 2010.

4 In para (5), word "or" at end of sub-para (*a*) revoked, and sub-para (*c*) and preceding word "or" inserted, by the Tribunal Procedure (Amendment No 2) Rules, SI 2013/606 rule 2(1), (3) with effect from 1 April 2013.

5 Para (7) inserted by the Tribunal Procedure (Amendment) Rules, SI 2014/514 rules 2, 5 with effect from 6 April 2014.

6 In para (4), in sub-para (*a*) word inserted, in sub-para (*b*) words "there are exceptional circumstances which suggest that" revoked, and sub-para (*c*) revoked, by the Tribunal Procedure (Amendment No 3) Rules, SI 2014/2128 rules 2, 5 with effect from 20 October 2014.

6 Procedure for applying for and giving directions

(1) The Upper Tribunal may give a direction on the application of one or more of the parties or on its own initiative.

(2) An application for a direction may be made—

(*a*) by sending or delivering a written application to the Upper Tribunal; or

(*b*) orally during the course of a hearing.

(3) An application for a direction must include the reason for making that application.

(4) Unless the Upper Tribunal considers that there is good reason not to do so, the Upper Tribunal must send written notice of any direction to every party and to any other person affected by the direction.

(5) If a party or any other person sent notice of the direction under paragraph (4) wishes to challenge a direction which the Upper Tribunal has given, they may do so by applying for another direction which amends, suspends or sets aside the first direction.

7 Failure to comply with rules etc

(1) An irregularity resulting from a failure to comply with any requirement in these Rules, a practice direction or a direction, does not of itself render void the proceedings or any step taken in the proceedings.

(2) If a party has failed to comply with a requirement in these Rules, a practice direction or a direction, the Upper Tribunal may take such action as it considers just, which may include—

(*a*) waiving the requirement;

(*b*) requiring the failure to be remedied;

(*c*) exercising its power under rule 8 (striking out a party's case); or

(*d*) except in [a mental health case, an asylum case or an immigration case][1], restricting a party's participation in the proceedings.

(3) Paragraph (4) applies where the First-tier Tribunal has referred to the Upper Tribunal a failure by a person to comply with a requirement imposed by the First-tier Tribunal—

(*a*) to attend at any place for the purpose of giving evidence;

(*b*) otherwise to make themselves available to give evidence;

(*c*) to swear an oath in connection with the giving of evidence;

(*d*) to give evidence as a witness;

(*e*) to produce a document; or

(*f*) to facilitate the inspection of a document or any other thing (including any premises).

(4) The Upper Tribunal may exercise its power under section 25 of the 2007 Act (supplementary powers of the Upper Tribunal) in relation to such non-compliance as if the requirement had been imposed by the Upper Tribunal.

Amendments—1 In para (2)(*d*), words substituted for words "mental health cases" by the Tribunal Procedure (Amendment No 2) Rules, SI 2010/44 rules 2, 5, with effect from 15 February 2010.

8 Striking out a party's case

[(1A) Except for paragraph (2), this rule does not apply to an asylum case or an immigration case.][2]

[(1) The proceedings, or the appropriate part of them, will automatically be struck out—

(*a*) if the appellant or applicant has failed to comply with a direction that stated that failure by the appellant or applicant to comply with the direction would lead to the striking out of the proceedings or part of them; or

[(*b*) in immigration judicial review proceedings, when a fee has not been paid, as required, in respect of an application under rule 30(4) or upon the grant of permission.][4]][3]

(2) The Upper Tribunal must strike out the whole or a part of the proceedings if the Upper Tribunal—

(*a*) does not have jurisdiction in relation to the proceedings or that part of them; and

(*b*) does not exercise its power under rule 5(3)(k)(i) (transfer to another court or tribunal) in relation to the proceedings or that part of them.

(3) The Upper Tribunal may strike out the whole or a part of the proceedings if—

(*a*) the appellant or applicant has failed to comply with a direction which stated that failure by the appellant or applicant to comply with the direction could lead to the striking out of the proceedings or part of them;

(*b*) the appellant or applicant has failed to co-operate with the Upper Tribunal to such an extent that the Upper Tribunal cannot deal with the proceedings fairly and justly; or (*c*) in proceedings which are not an appeal from the decision of another tribunal or judicial review proceedings, the Upper Tribunal considers there is no reasonable prospect of the appellant's or the applicant's case, or part of it, succeeding.

(4) The Upper Tribunal may not strike out the whole or a part of the proceedings under paragraph (2) or (3)(*b*) or (*c*) without first giving the appellant or applicant an opportunity to make representations in relation to the proposed striking out.

(5) If the proceedings have been struck out under paragraph (1) or (3)(*a*), the appellant or applicant may apply for the proceedings, or part of them, to be reinstated.

(6) An application under paragraph (5) must be made in writing and received by the Upper Tribunal within 1 month after the date on which the Upper Tribunal sent notification of the striking out to the appellant or applicant.

(7) This rule applies to a respondent [or an interested party][1] as it applies to an appellant or applicant except that—

(*a*) a reference to the striking out of the proceedings is to be read as a reference to the barring of the respondent [or interested party][1] from taking further part in the proceedings; and

(*b*) a reference to an application for the reinstatement of proceedings which have been struck out is to be read as a reference to an application for the lifting of the bar on the respondent [or interested party][1] . . . [1] taking further part in the proceedings.

(8) If a respondent [or an interested party][1] has been barred from taking further part in proceedings under this rule and that bar has not been lifted, the Upper Tribunal need not consider any response or other submission made by that respondent [or interested party, and may summarily determine any or all issues against that respondent or interested party][1].

Amendments—[1] In para (7), words inserted and word repealed, and in sub-s (8), words inserted, by the Tribunal Procedure (Amendment) Rules, SI 2009/274 rules 3, 6 with effect from 1 April 2009.

[2] Para (1A) inserted by the Tribunal Procedure (Amendment No 2) Rules, SI 2010/44 rules 2, 6, with effect from 15 February 2010.

[3] Para (1) substituted by the Tribunal Procedure (Upper Tribunal) (Amendment) Rules, SI 2011/2343 rules 2, 5 with effect from 17 October 2011.

[4] Para (1)(*b*) substituted by the Tribunal Procedure (Amendment No 4) Rules, SI 2013/2067 rules 2, 5 with effect from 1 November 2013. Para (1)(*b*) previously read as follows—

"(*b*) when a fee has not been paid upon the grant of permission in fresh claim proceedings as required.".

[Addition, substitution and removal of parties

9—(1) The Upper Tribunal may give a direction adding, substituting or removing a party as an appellant, a respondent or an interested party.

(2) If the Upper Tribunal gives a direction under paragraph (1) it may give such consequential directions as it considers appropriate.

(3) A person who is not a party may apply to the Upper Tribunal to be added or substituted as a party.

(4) If a person who is entitled to be a party to proceedings by virtue of another enactment applies to be added as a party, and any conditions applicable to that entitlement have been satisfied, the Upper Tribunal must give a direction adding that person as a respondent or, if appropriate, as an appellant.][1]

[(5) In an asylum case, the United Kingdom Representative of the United Nations High Commissioner for Refugees ("the United Kingdom Representative") may give notice to the Upper Tribunal that the United Kingdom Representative wishes to participate in the proceedings.

(6) If the United Kingdom Representative gives notice under paragraph (5)—

(i) the United Kingdom Representative is entitled to participate in any hearing; and

(ii) all documents which are required to be sent or delivered to parties must be sent or delivered to the United Kingdom Representative.][2]

Amendments—[1] Rule 9 substituted by the Tribunal Procedure (Amendment No 2) Rules, SI 2009/1975 rules 7, 10 with effect from 1 September 2009.

[2] Paras (5), (6) inserted by the Tribunal Procedure (Amendment No 2) Rules, SI 2010/44 rules 2, 7, with effect from 15 February 2010.

[10 Orders for costs

(1) The Upper Tribunal may not make an order in respect of costs (or, in Scotland, expenses) in proceedings [transferred or referred by, or on appeal from,][2] another tribunal except—

[(*aa*) in a national security certificate appeal, to the extent permitted by paragraph (1A);][3]

(*a*) in proceedings [transferred by, or on appeal from,][2] the Tax Chamber of the First-tier Tribunal; or

(*b*) to the extent and in the circumstances that the other tribunal had the power to make an order in respect of costs (or, in Scotland, expenses).

[(1A) In a national security certificate appeal—

(*a*) the Upper Tribunal may make an order in respect of costs or expenses in the circumstances described at paragraph (3)(*c*) and (*d*);

(*b*) if the appeal is against a certificate, the Upper Tribunal may make an order in respect of costs or expenses against the relevant Minister and in favour of the appellant if the Upper Tribunal allows the appeal and quashes the certificate to any extent or the Minister withdraws the certificate;

(*c*) if the appeal is against the application of a certificate, the Upper Tribunal may make an order in respect of costs or expenses—

(i) against the appellant and in favour of any other party if the Upper Tribunal dismisses the appeal to any extent; or

(ii) in favour of the appellant and against any other party if the Upper Tribunal allows the appeal to any extent.][3]

(2) The Upper Tribunal may not make an order in respect of costs or expenses under section 4 of the Forfeiture Act 1982.

(3) In other proceedings, the Upper Tribunal may not make an order in respect of costs or expenses except—

(*a*) in judicial review proceedings;

(*b*) *in proceedings transferred from the Tax Chamber of the First-tier Tribunal;*[2]

(*c*) under section 29(4) of the 2007 Act (wasted costs) [and costs incurred in applying for such costs][5]; . . . [4]

(*d*) if the Upper Tribunal considers that a party or its representative has acted unreasonably in bringing, defending or conducting the proceedings [or

(*e*) if, in a financial services case [or a wholesale energy case][7], the Upper Tribunal considers that the decision in respect of which the reference was made was unreasonable.][4]

(4) The Upper Tribunal may make an order for costs (or, in Scotland, expenses) on an application or on its own initiative.

(5) A person making an application for an order for costs or expenses must—

(*a*) send or deliver a written application to the Upper Tribunal and to the person against whom it is proposed that the order be made; and

(*b*) send or deliver with the application a schedule of the costs or expenses claimed sufficient to allow summary assessment of such costs or expenses by the Upper Tribunal.

(6) An application for an order for costs or expenses may be made at any time during the proceedings but may not be made later than 1 month after the date on which the Upper Tribunal sends—

(*a*) a decision notice recording the decision which finally disposes of all issues in the proceedings; or

[(*b*) notice under rule 17(5) that a withdrawal which ends the proceedings has taken effect.][5]

(7) The Upper Tribunal may not make an order for costs or expenses against a person (the "paying person") without first—

(*a*) giving that person an opportunity to make representations; and

(*b*) if the paying person is an individual and the order is to be made under paragraph (3)(*a*), (*b*) or (*d*), considering that person's financial means.

(8) The amount of costs or expenses to be paid under an order under this rule may be ascertained by—

(*a*) summary assessment by the Upper Tribunal;

(*b*) agreement of a specified sum by the paying person and the person entitled to receive the costs or expenses ("the receiving person"); or

(*c*) assessment of the whole or a specified part of the costs or expenses[, including the costs or expenses of the assessment,][5] incurred by the receiving person, if not agreed.

(9) Following an order for assessment under paragraph (8)(*c*), the paying person or the receiving person may apply—

(*a*) in England and Wales, to the High Court or the Costs Office of the Supreme Court (as specified in the order) for a detailed assessment of the costs on the standard basis or, if specified in the order, on the indemnity basis; and the Civil Procedure Rules 1998 shall apply, with necessary modifications, to that application and assessment as if the proceedings in the tribunal had been proceedings in a court to which the Civil Procedure Rules 1998 apply;

(*b*) in Scotland, to the Auditor of the Court of Session for the taxation of the expenses according to the fees payable in that court; or

(*c*) in Northern Ireland, to the Taxing Office of the High Court of Northern Ireland for taxation on the standard basis or, if specified in the order, on the indemnity basis.

[(10) Upon making an order for the assessment of costs, the [Upper][6] Tribunal may order an amount to be paid on account before the costs or expenses are assessed.][5]][1]

Simon's Tax Cases—10, *Capital Air Services Ltd v R&C Comrs* [2011] STC 617; *Leeds City Council v R&C Comrs* [2014] UKUT 350 (TCC), [2015] STC 168.

Amendments—[1] Rule 10 substituted, by the Tribunal Procedure (Amendment) Rules, SI 2009/274 rules 3, 7 with effect from 1 April 2009.

[2] In para (1), (1)(*a*), words substituted, and para (3)(*b*) revoked, by the Tribunal Procedure (Amendment No 2) Rules, SI 2009/1975 rules 7, 11 with effect from 1 September 2009.

[3] Paras (1)(*aa*), (1A) inserted by the Tribunal Procedure (Amendment) Rules, SI 2010/43, rules 5, 7, with effect from 18 January 2010.

[4] In para (3)(*c*), word "or" revoked, and para (3)(*e*) and preceding word "or" inserted, by the Tribunal Procedure (Upper Tribunal) (Amendment) Rules, SI 2010/747 rules 2, 6 with effect from 6 April 2010.

[5] In paras (3), (8)(*c*) words inserted, para (6)(*b*) substituted, and para (10) inserted, by the Tribunal Procedure (Amendment) Rules, SI 2013/477 rules 49–53 with effect from 1 April 2013.

[6] Word in para (10) inserted by the Tribunal Procedure (Amendment No 4) Rules, SI 2013/2067 rules 2, 6 with effect from 1 November 2013.

[7] In para (3)(*e*), words inserted by the Tribunal Procedure (Amendment) Rules, SI 2014/514 rules 2, 6 with effect from 6 April 2014.

11 Representatives

(1) [Subject to paragraph (5A),][5] a party may appoint a representative (whether a legal representative or not) to represent that party in the proceedings [save that a party in an asylum or immigration case may not be represented by any person prohibited from representing by section 84 of the Immigration and Asylum Act 1999][4].

(2) If a party appoints a representative, that party (or the representative if the representative is a legal representative) must send or deliver to the Upper Tribunal . . . [1] written notice of the representative's name and address.

[(2A) If the Upper Tribunal receives notice that a party has appointed a representative under paragraph (2), it must send a copy of that notice to each other party.][1]

(3) Anything permitted or required to be done by a party under these Rules, a practice direction or a direction may be done by the representative of that party, except signing a witness statement.

(4) A person who receives due notice of the appointment of a representative—

(*a*) must provide to the representative any document which is required to be provided to the represented party, and need not provide that document to the represented party; and

(*b*) may assume that the representative is and remains authorised as such until they receive written notification that this is not so from the representative or the represented party.

(5) [Subject to paragraph (5B),][5] at a hearing a party may be accompanied by another person whose name and address has not been notified under paragraph (2) but who, subject to paragraph (8) and with the permission of the Upper Tribunal, may act as a representative or otherwise assist in presenting the party's case at the hearing.

[(5A) In [immigration judicial review][6] proceedings, a party may appoint as a representative only a person authorised under the Legal Services Act 2007 to undertake the conduct of litigation in the High Court.

(5B) At a hearing of [immigration judicial review][6] proceedings, rights of audience before the Upper Tribunal are restricted to persons authorised to exercise those rights in the High Court under the Legal Services Act 2007.][5]

(6) Paragraphs (2) to (4) do not apply to a person who accompanies a party under paragraph (5).

(7) In a mental health case if the patient has not appointed a representative the Upper Tribunal may appoint a legal representative for the patient where—

(*a*) the patient has stated that they do not wish to conduct their own case or that they wish to be represented; or

(*b*) the patient lacks the capacity to appoint a representative but the Upper Tribunal believes that it is in the patient's best interests for the patient to be represented.

(8) In a mental health case a party may not appoint as a representative, or be represented or assisted at a hearing by—

(*a*) a person liable to be detained or subject to guardianship or after-care under supervision, or who is a community patient, under the Mental Health Act 1983; or

(*b*) a person receiving treatment for mental disorder at the same hospital [or][2] home as the patient.

[(9) In this rule "legal representative" means [a person who, for the purposes of the Legal Services Act 2007, is an authorised person in relation to an activity which constitutes the exercise of a right of audience or the conduct of litigation within the meaning of that Act][3], [a qualified person as defined in section 84(2) of the Immigration and Asylum Act 1999,][4] an advocate or solicitor in Scotland or a barrister or solicitor in Northern Ireland.][1]

[(10) In an asylum case or an immigration case, an appellant's representative before the First-tier Tribunal will be treated as that party's representative before the Upper Tribunal, unless the Upper Tribunal receives notice—

(*a*) of a new representative under paragraph (2) of this rule; or

(*b*) from the appellant stating that they are no longer represented.][4]

Amendments—[1] In para (2), words repealed, and paras (2A), (9) inserted, by the Tribunal Procedure (Amendment) Rules, SI 2009/274 rules 3, 8 with effect from 1 April 2009.

[2] In para (8)(*b*) word inserted by the Tribunal Procedure (Amendment No 2) Rules, SI 2009/1975 rules 7, 12 with effect from 1 September 2009.

[3] In para (9), words substituted for by the Tribunal Procedure (Amendment) Rules, SI 2010/43, rules 5, 8, with effect from 18 January 2010.

VAT SIs

4 Words in paras (1), (9), and whole of para (10), inserted, by the Tribunal Procedure (Amendment No 2) Rules, SI 2010/44 rules 2, 8, with effect from 15 February 2010.

5 In paras (1), (5), words inserted, and paras (5A), (5B) inserted, by the Tribunal Procedure (Upper Tribunal) (Amendment) Rules, SI 2011/2343 rules 2, 6 with effect from 17 October 2011.

6 In paras (5A), (5B) words substituted for words "fresh claim" by the Tribunal Procedure (Amendment No 4) Rules, SI 2013/2067 rules 2, 7 with effect from 1 November 2013.

12 Calculating time

(1) An act required by these Rules, a practice direction or a direction to be done on or by a particular day must be done by 5pm on that day.

(2) If the time specified by these Rules, a practice direction or a direction for doing any act ends on a day other than a working day, the act is done in time if it is done on the next working day.

(3) In a special educational needs case or a disability discrimination in schools case, the following days must not be counted when calculating the time by which an act must be done—

(*a*) 25th December to 1st January inclusive; and

(*b*) any day in August.

[(3A) In an asylum case or an immigration case, when calculating the time by which an act must be done, in addition to the days specified in the definition of "working days" in rule 1 (interpretation), the following days must also not be counted as working days—

(*a*) 27th to 31st December inclusive. . . . [2]

(*b*) . . . [2]][1]

(4) Paragraph (3) [or (3A)][1] does not apply where the Upper Tribunal directs that an act must be done by or on a specified date.

(5) . . . [2]

Amendments—[1] Para (3A) and words in para (4) inserted by the Tribunal Procedure (Amendment No 2) Rules, SI 2010/44 rules 2, 9, with effect from 15 February 2010.

2 Para (5) revoked by the Tribunal Procedure (Amendment No 3) Rules, SI 2014/2128 rules 2, 6(b) with effect from 1 September 2014.

Para (5) previously read as follows—

"(5) In this rule—

"disability discrimination in schools case" means proceedings concerning disability discrimination in the education of a child or related matters; and

"special educational needs case" means proceedings concerning the education of a child who has or may have special educational needs.".[1]

3 Para (3A)(*b*) and preceding word "and" revoked, by the Tribunal Procedure (Amendment No 3) Rules, SI 2014/2128 rules 2, 6 with effect from 20 October 2014. Para (3A)(*b*) previously read as follows—

"(*b*) in a fast-track case, 24th December, Maundy Thursday, or the Tuesday after the last Monday in May.".

13 Sending and delivery of documents

(1) Any document to be provided to the Upper Tribunal under these Rules, a practice direction or a direction must be—

(*a*) sent by pre-paid post or [by document exchange, or delivered by hand,][1] to the address specified for the proceedings;

(*b*) sent by fax to the number specified for the proceedings; or

(*c*) sent or delivered by such other method as the Upper Tribunal may permit or direct.

(2) Subject to paragraph (3), if a party provides a fax number, email address or other details for the electronic transmission of documents to them, that party must accept delivery of documents by that method.

(3) If a party informs the Upper Tribunal and all other parties that a particular form of communication, other than pre-paid post or delivery by hand, should not be used to provide documents to that party, that form of communication must not be so used.

(4) If the Upper Tribunal or a party sends a document to a party or the Upper Tribunal by email or any other electronic means of communication, the recipient may request that the sender provide a hard copy of the document to the recipient. The recipient must make such a request as soon as reasonably practicable after receiving the document electronically.

(5) The Upper Tribunal and each party may assume that the address provided by a party or its representative is and remains the address to which documents should be sent or delivered until receiving written notification to the contrary.

[(6) Subject to paragraph (7), if a document submitted to the Upper Tribunal is not written in English, it must be accompanied by an English translation.

(7) In proceedings that are in Wales or have a connection with Wales, a document or translation may be submitted to the [Upper][3] Tribunal in Welsh.][2]

Amendments—[1] Words in para (1)(*a*) substituted by the Tribunal Procedure (Amendment) Rules, SI 2009/274 rules 3, 10 with effect from 1 April 2009.

2 Paras (6), (7) inserted by the Tribunal Procedure (Amendment No 2) Rules, SI 2010/44 rules 2, 10, with effect from 15 February 2010.

[3] Word in para (7) inserted by the Tribunal Procedure (Amendment No 4) Rules, SI 2013/2067 rules 2, 8 with effect from 1 November 2013.

14 Use of documents and information

(1) The Upper Tribunal may make an order prohibiting the disclosure or publication of—

(*a*) specified documents or information relating to the proceedings; or

(*b*) any matter likely to lead members of the public to identify any person whom the Upper Tribunal considers should not be identified.

(2) The Upper Tribunal may give a direction prohibiting the disclosure of a document or information to a person if—

(*a*) the Upper Tribunal is satisfied that such disclosure would be likely to cause that person or some other person serious harm; and

(*b*) the Upper Tribunal is satisfied, having regard to the interests of justice, that it is proportionate to give such a direction.

(3) If a party ("the first party") considers that the Upper Tribunal should give a direction under paragraph (2) prohibiting the disclosure of a document or information to another party ("the second party"), the first party must—

(*a*) exclude the relevant document or information from any documents that will be provided to the second party; and

(*b*) provide to the Upper Tribunal the excluded document or information, and the reason for its exclusion, so that the Upper Tribunal may decide whether the document or information should be disclosed to the second party or should be the subject of a direction under paragraph (2).

(4) The Upper Tribunal must conduct proceedings as appropriate in order to give effect to a direction given under paragraph (2).[1]

(5) If the Upper Tribunal gives a direction under paragraph (2) which prevents disclosure to a party who has appointed a representative, the Upper Tribunal may give a direction that the documents or information be disclosed to that representative if the Upper Tribunal is satisfied that—

(*a*) disclosure to the representative would be in the interests of the party; and

(*b*) the representative will act in accordance with paragraph (6).

(6) Documents or information disclosed to a representative in accordance with a direction under paragraph (5) must not be disclosed either directly or indirectly to any other person without the Upper Tribunal's consent.

(7) Unless the Upper Tribunal gives a direction to the contrary, information about mental health cases and the names of any persons concerned in such cases must not be made public.

[(8) The Upper Tribunal may, on its own initiative or on the application of a party, give a direction that certain documents or information must or may be disclosed to the Upper Tribunal on the basis that the Upper Tribunal will not disclose such documents or information to other persons, or specified other persons.

(9) A party making an application for a direction under paragraph (8) may withhold the relevant documents or information from other parties until the Upper Tribunal has granted or refused the application.

(10) In a case involving matters relating to national security, the Upper Tribunal must ensure that information is not disclosed contrary to the interests of national security.

(11) The Upper Tribunal must conduct proceedings and record its decision and reasons appropriately so as not to undermine the effect of an order made under paragraph (1), a direction given under paragraph (2) or (8) or the duty imposed by paragraph (10).][1]

Amendments—[1] Para (4) revoked, and paras (8)–(11) inserted, by the Tribunal Procedure (Amendment No 2) Rules, SI 2009/1975 rules 7, 13 with effect from 1 September 2009.

15 Evidence and submissions

(1) Without restriction on the general powers in rule 5(1) and (2) (case management powers), the Upper Tribunal may give directions as to—

(*a*) issues on which it requires evidence or submissions;

(*b*) the nature of the evidence or submissions it requires;

(*c*) whether the parties are permitted or required to provide expert evidence, and if so whether the parties must jointly appoint a single expert to provide such evidence;

(*d*) any limit on the number of witnesses whose evidence a party may put forward, whether in relation to a particular issue or generally;

(*e*) the manner in which any evidence or submissions are to be provided, which may include a direction for them to be given—

(i) orally at a hearing; or

(ii) by written submissions or witness statement; and

(*f*) the time at which any evidence or submissions are to be provided.

(2) The Upper Tribunal may—

(*a*) admit evidence whether or not—

(i) the evidence would be admissible in a civil trial in the United Kingdom; or

(ii) the evidence was available to a previous decision maker; or

(*b*) exclude evidence that would otherwise be admissible where—

(i) the evidence was not provided within the time allowed by a direction or a practice direction;

(ii) the evidence was otherwise provided in a manner that did not comply with a direction or a practice direction; or

(iii) it would otherwise be unfair to admit the evidence.

[(2A) In an asylum case or an immigration case—

(*a*) if a party wishes the Upper Tribunal to consider evidence that was not before the First-tier Tribunal, that party must send or deliver a notice to the Upper Tribunal and any other party—

(i) indicating the nature of the evidence; and

(ii) explaining why it was not submitted to the First-tier Tribunal; and

(*b*) when considering whether to admit evidence that was not before the First-tier Tribunal, the Upper Tribunal must have regard to whether there has been unreasonable delay in producing that evidence.][1]

(3) The Upper Tribunal may consent to a witness giving, or require any witness to give, evidence on oath, and may administer an oath for that purpose.

Amendments—[1] Para (2A) inserted by the Tribunal Procedure (Amendment No 2) Rules, SI 2010/44 rules 2, 11, with effect from 15 February 2010.

16 Summoning or citation of witnesses and orders to answer questions or produce documents

(1) On the application of a party or on its own initiative, the Upper Tribunal may—

(*a*) by summons (or, in Scotland, citation) require any person to attend as a witness at a hearing at the time and place specified in the summons or citation; or

(*b*) order any person to answer any questions or produce any documents in that person's possession or control which relate to any issue in the proceedings.

(2) A summons or citation under paragraph (1)(*a*) must—

(*a*) give the person required to attend 14 days' notice of the hearing or such shorter period as the Upper Tribunal may direct; and

(*b*) where the person is not a party, make provision for the person's necessary expenses of attendance to be paid, and state who is to pay them.

(3) No person may be compelled to give any evidence or produce any document that the person could not be compelled to give or produce on a trial of an action in a court of law in the part of the United Kingdom where the proceedings are due to be determined.

[(4) A person who receives a summons, citation or order may apply to the Upper Tribunal for it to be varied or set aside if they did not have an opportunity to object to it before it was made or issued.

(5) A person making an application under paragraph (4) must do so as soon as reasonably practicable after receiving notice of the summons, citation or order.

(6) A summons, citation or order under this rule must—

(*a*) state that the person on whom the requirement is imposed may apply to the Upper Tribunal to vary or set aside the summons, citation or order, if they did not have an opportunity to object to it before it was made or issued; and

(*b*) state the consequences of failure to comply with the summons, citation or order.][1]

Amendments—[1] Paras (4)–(6) substituted for previous para (4) by the Tribunal Procedure (Amendment) Rules, SI 2009/274 rules 3, 11 with effect from 1 April 2009.

17 Withdrawal

(1) Subject to paragraph (2), a party may give notice of the withdrawal of its case, or any part of it—

(*a*) . . . [2] by sending or delivering to the Upper Tribunal a written notice of withdrawal; or

(*b*) orally at a hearing.

(2) Notice of withdrawal will not take effect unless the Upper Tribunal consents to the withdrawal except in relation to an application for permission to appeal.

(3) A party which has withdrawn its case may apply to the Upper Tribunal for the case to be reinstated.

(4) An application under paragraph (3) must be made in writing and be received by the Upper Tribunal within 1 month after—

(*a*) the date on which the Upper Tribunal received the notice under paragraph (1)(*a*); or

(*b*) the date of the hearing at which the case was withdrawn orally under paragraph (1)(*b*).

(5) The Upper Tribunal must notify each party in writing [that a withdrawal has taken effect][2] under this rule.

[(6) Paragraph (3) does not apply to a financial services case other than a reference against a penalty.][1]

Amendments—[1] Para (6) inserted, by the Tribunal Procedure (Upper Tribunal) (Amendment) Rules, SI 2010/747 rules 2, 7 with effect from 6 April 2010.

[2] In para (1)(*a*), words "at any time before a hearing to consider the disposal of the proceedings (or, if the Tribunal disposes of the proceedings without a hearing, before that disposal)," repealed, and in para (5), words substituted for words "of a withdrawal", by the Tribunal Procedure (Amendment) Rules, SI 2013/477 rules 49, 54 with effect from 1 April 2013.

[17A Appeal treated as abandoned or finally determined in an asylum case or an immigration case

(1) A party to an asylum case or an immigration case before the Upper Tribunal must notify the [Upper][2] Tribunal if they are aware that—

(*a*) the appellant has left the United Kingdom;

(*b*) the appellant has been granted leave to enter or remain in the United Kingdom;

(*c*) a deportation order has been made against the appellant; or

(*d*) a document listed in paragraph 4(2) of Schedule 2 to the Immigration (European Economic Area) Regulations 2006 has been issued to the appellant.

(2) Where an appeal is treated as abandoned pursuant to section 104(4) or (4A) of the Nationality, Immigration and Asylum Act 2002 or paragraph 4(2) of Schedule 2 to the Immigration (European Economic Area) Regulations 2006, or as finally determined pursuant to section 104(5) of the Nationality, Immigration and Asylum Act 2002, the Upper Tribunal must send the parties a notice informing them that the appeal is being treated as abandoned or finally determined.

(3) Where an appeal would otherwise fall to be treated as abandoned pursuant to section 104(4A) of the Nationality, Immigration and Asylum Act 2002, but the appellant wishes to pursue their appeal, the appellant must send or deliver a notice, which must comply with any relevant practice directions, to the Upper Tribunal and the respondent so that it is received within thirty days of the date on which the notice of the grant of leave to enter or remain in the United Kingdom was sent to the appellant.

(4) Where a notice of grant of leave to enter or remain is sent electronically or delivered personally, the time limit in paragraph (3) is twenty eight days.

(5) Notwithstanding rule 5(3)(*a*) (case management powers) and rule 7(2) (failure to comply with rules etc), the Upper Tribunal must not extend the time limits in paragraph (3) and (4).][1]

Amendments—[1] Rule 17A inserted by the Tribunal Procedure (Amendment No 2) Rules, SI 2010/44 rules 2, 12, with effect from 15 February 2010.

[2] Word in para (1) inserted by the Tribunal Procedure (Amendment No 4) Rules, SI 2013/2067 rules 2, 9 with effect from 1 November 2013.

18 Notice of funding of legal services

If a party is granted funding of legal services at any time, that party must as soon as practicable—

(*a*)

(i) if [civil legal services (within the meaning of section 8 of the Legal Aid, Sentencing and Punishment of Offenders Act 2012) are provided under arrangements made for the purposes of Part 1 of that Act or by][1] the Northern Ireland Legal Services Commission, send a copy of the [certificate or][1] funding notice to the Upper Tribunal; or

(ii) if funding is granted by the Scottish Legal Aid Board, send a copy of the legal aid certificate to the Upper Tribunal; and

(*b*) notify every other party in writing that funding has been granted.

Amendments—[1] In para (*a*)(i), words substituted for words "funding is granted by the Legal Services Commission or", and words inserted, by the Tribunal Procedure (Amendment) Rules, SI 2013/477 rules 49, 55 with effect from 1 April 2013.

[19 Confidentiality in social security and child support cases

(1) Paragraph (4) applies to an appeal against a decision of the First-tier Tribunal—

(*a*) in proceedings under the Child Support Act 1991 in the circumstances described in paragraph (2), other than an appeal against a reduced benefit decision (as defined in section 46(10)(*b*) of the Child Support Act 1991, as that section had effect prior to the commencement of section 15(*b*) of the Child Maintenance and Other Payments Act 2008); or

(*b*) in proceedings where the parties to the appeal include former joint claimants who are no longer living together in the circumstances described in paragraph (3).

(2) The circumstances referred to in paragraph (1)(*a*) are that—

(*a*) in the proceedings in the First-tier Tribunal in respect of which the appeal has been brought, there was an obligation to keep a person's address confidential; or

(*b*) an absent parent, non-resident parent or person with care would like their address or the address of the child to be kept confidential and has given notice to that effect to the Upper Tribunal—

(i) in an application for permission to appeal or notice of appeal;

(ii) within 1 month after an enquiry by the Upper Tribunal; or

(iii) when notifying any subsequent change of address after proceedings have been started.

(3) The circumstances referred to in paragraph (1)(*b*) are that—

(*a*) in the proceedings in the First-tier Tribunal in respect of which the appeal has been brought, there was an obligation to keep a person's address confidential; or

(*b*) one of the former joint claimants would like their address to be kept confidential and has given notice to that effect to the Upper Tribunal—

(i) in an application for permission to appeal or notice of appeal;

(ii) within 1 month after an enquiry by the Upper Tribunal; or

(iii) when notifying any subsequent change of address after proceedings have been started.

VAT SIs

(4) Where this paragraph applies, the Secretary of State or other decision maker and the Upper Tribunal must take appropriate steps to secure the confidentiality of the address and of any information which could reasonably be expected to enable a person to identify the address, to the extent that the address or that information is not already known to each other party.

(5) In this rule—

"absent parent", "non-resident parent" and "person with care" have the meanings set out in section 3 of the Child Support Act 1991;

"joint claimants" means the persons who made a joint claim for a jobseeker's allowance under the Jobseekers Act 1995, a tax credit under the Tax Credits Act 2002 or in relation to whom an award of universal credit is made under Part 1 of the Welfare Reform Act 2012.][1]

Amendments—[1] Rule 19 substituted by the Tribunal Procedure (Amendment No 3) Rules, SI 2014/2128 rules 2, 7 with effect from 20 October 2014.

20 Power to pay expenses and allowances

(1) In proceedings brought under section 4 of the Safeguarding Vulnerable Groups Act 2006 . . . [1], the Secretary of State may pay such allowances for the purpose of or in connection with the attendance of persons at hearings as the Secretary of State may, with the consent of the Treasury, determine.

(2) Paragraph (3) applies to proceedings on appeal from a decision of—

(*a*) the First-tier Tribunal in proceedings under the Child Support Act 1991, section 12 of the Social Security Act 1998 or paragraph 6 of Schedule 7 to the Child Support, Pensions and Social Security Act 2000;

(*b*) the First-tier Tribunal in a war pensions and armed forces case (as defined in the Tribunal Procedure (First-tier Tribunal) (War Pensions and Armed Forces Compensation Chamber) Rules 2008); or

(*c*) a Pensions Appeal Tribunal for Scotland or Northern Ireland.

(3) The Lord Chancellor (or, in Scotland, the Secretary of State) may pay to any person who attends any hearing such travelling and other allowances, including compensation for loss of remunerative time, as the Lord Chancellor (or, in Scotland, the Secretary of State) may determine.

Amendments—[1] Words in para (1) repealed by the Tribunal Procedure (Amendment) Rules, SI 2009/274 rules 3, 12 with effect from 1 April 2009.

[Procedure for applying for a stay of a decision pending an appeal

20A—(1) This rule applies where another enactment provides in any terms for the Upper Tribunal to stay or suspend, or to lift a stay or suspension of, a decision which is or may be the subject of an appeal to the Upper Tribunal ("the substantive decision") pending such appeal.

(2) A person who wishes the Upper Tribunal to decide whether the substantive decision should be stayed or suspended must make a written application to the Upper Tribunal which must include—

(*a*) the name and address of the person making the application;

(*b*) the name and address of any representative of that person;

(*c*) the address to which documents for that person should be sent or delivered;

(*d*) the name and address of any person who will be a respondent to the appeal;

(*e*) details of the substantive decision and any decision as to when that decision is to take effect, and copies of any written record of, or reasons for, those decisions; and

(*f*) the grounds on which the person making the application relies.

(3) In the case of an application under paragraph (2) [in a road transport case][2]—

(*a*) the person making the application must notify the [decision maker][2] when making the application;

(*b*) within 7 days of receiving notification of the application the [decision maker][2] must send or deliver written reasons for refusing or withdrawing the stay—

(i) to the Upper Tribunal; and

(ii) to the person making the application, if the [decision maker][2] has not already done so.

(4) If the Upper Tribunal grants a stay or suspension following an application under this rule—

(*a*) the Upper Tribunal may give directions as to the conduct of the appeal of the substantive decision; and

(*b*) the Upper Tribunal may, where appropriate, grant the stay or suspension subject to conditions.

(5) Unless the Upper Tribunal considers that there is good reason not to do so, the Upper Tribunal must send written notice of any decision made under this rule to each party.][1]

Amendments—[1] Rule inserted by the Tribunal Procedure (Amendment No 2) Rules, SI 2009/1975 rules 7, 14 with effect from 1 September 2009.

[2] In para (3), words substituted for words "for a stay of a decision of a traffic commissioner" and "traffic commissioner" (in each place), by the Tribunal Procedure (Amendment No 2) Rules, SI 2012/1363 rules 4, 6 with effect from 1 July 2012.

PART 3

[PROCEDURE FOR CASES IN][1] THE UPPER TRIBUNAL

Amendments—[1] Words substituted by the Tribunal Procedure (Amendment) Rules, SI 2009/274 rules 3, 13 with effect from 1 April 2009.

21 Application to the Upper Tribunal for permission to appeal

(1) This rule applies to an application for permission to appeal to the Upper Tribunal against any decision.[1]

(2) A person may apply to the Upper Tribunal for permission to appeal to the Upper Tribunal against a decision of another tribunal only if—

(*a*) they have made an application for permission to appeal to the tribunal which made the decision challenged; and

(*b*) that application has been refused or has not been admitted [or has been granted only on limited grounds][3].

(3) An application for permission to appeal must be made in writing and received by the Upper Tribunal no later than—

(*a*) in the case of an application under section 4 of the Safeguarding Vulnerable Groups Act 2006, 3 months after the date on which written notice of the decision being challenged was sent to the appellant; . . . [2]

[(*aa*) . . . [4], in an asylum case or an immigration case where the appellant is in the United Kingdom at the time that the application is made—

(i) [14][4] days after the date on which notice of the First-tier Tribunal's refusal of permission was sent to the appellant; or

(ii) if the case is a fast-track case, four working days after the date on which notice of the First-tier Tribunal's refusal of permission was sent to the appellant;][2]

(*ab*) . . . [4]

(*b*) otherwise, a month after the date on which the tribunal that made the decision under challenge sent notice of its refusal of permission to appeal, or refusal to admit the application for permission to appeal, to the appellant.

(3A) . . . [4]

(4) The application must state—

(*a*) the name and address of the appellant;

(*b*) the name and address of the representative (if any) of the appellant;

(*c*) an address where documents for the appellant may be sent or delivered;

(*d*) details (including the full reference) of the decision challenged;

(*e*) the grounds on which the appellant relies; and

(*f*) whether the appellant wants the application to be dealt with at a hearing.

(5) The appellant must provide with the application a copy of—

(*a*) any written record of the decision being challenged;

(*b*) any separate written statement of reasons for that decision; and

(*c*) if the application is for permission to appeal against a decision of another tribunal, the notice of refusal of permission to appeal, or notice of refusal to admit the application for permission to appeal, from that other tribunal.

(6) If the appellant provides the application to the Upper Tribunal later than the time required by paragraph (3) or by an extension of time allowed under rule 5(3)(*a*) (power to extend time)—

(*a*) the application must include a request for an extension of time and the reason why the application was not provided in time; and

(*b*) unless the Upper Tribunal extends time for the application under rule 5(3)(*a*) (power to extend time) the Upper Tribunal must not admit the application.

(7) If the appellant makes an application to the Upper Tribunal for permission to appeal against the decision of another tribunal, and that other tribunal refused to admit the appellant's application for permission to appeal because the application for permission or for a written statement of reasons was not made in time—

(*a*) the application to the Upper Tribunal for permission to appeal must include the reason why the application to the other tribunal for permission to appeal or for a written statement of reasons, as the case may be, was not made in time; and

(*b*) the Upper Tribunal must only admit the application if the Upper Tribunal considers that it is in the interests of justice for it to do so.

[(8) In this rule, a reference to notice of a refusal of permission to appeal is to be taken to include a reference to notice of a grant of permission to appeal on limited grounds.][3]

Note—In rule 21(2)(*a*), the reference to the tribunal which made the decision challenged is to be read as a reference to the First-tier Tribunal (SI 2009/196 art 9).

Amendments—[1] Para (1) revoked by the Tribunal Procedure (Amendment No 2) Rules, SI 2009/1975 rules 7, 15 with effect from 1 September 2009.

[2] Word "and" in para (3)(*a*) repealed, and para (3)(*aa*) inserted, by the Tribunal Procedure (Amendment No 2) Rules, SI 2010/44 rules 2, 13, with effect from 15 February 2010.

3 Words in para (2)(*b*) inserted, and para (8) inserted by the Tribunal Procedure (Amendment) Rules, SI 2014/514 rules 2, 7 with effect from 6 April 2014.

4 In para (3)(*aa*), words "subject to paragraph (3A)" revoked, in para (3)(*aa*)(i), words substituted for words "seven working", and paras (3)(*ab*), (3A) revoked, by the Tribunal Procedure (Amendment No 3) Rules, SI 2014/2128 rules 2, 8 with effect from 20 October 2014.

22 Decision in relation to permission to appeal

(1) [Except where rule 22A (special procedure for providing notice of a refusal of permission to appeal in an asylum case) applies][4] if the Upper Tribunal refuses permission to appeal [or refuses to admit a late application for permission][3], it must send written notice of the refusal and of the reasons for the refusal to the appellant.

(2) If the Upper Tribunal gives permission to appeal—

(*a*) the Upper Tribunal must send written notice of the permission, and of the reasons for any limitations or conditions on such permission, to each party;

(*b*) subject to any direction by the Upper Tribunal, the application for permission to appeal stands as the notice of appeal and the Upper Tribunal must send to each respondent a copy of the application for permission to appeal and any documents provided with it by the appellant; and

(*c*) the Upper Tribunal may, with the consent of the appellant and each respondent, determine the appeal without obtaining any further response.

[(3) Paragraph (4) applies where the Upper Tribunal, without a hearing, determines an application for permission to appeal—

(*a*) against a decision of—

(i) the Tax Chamber of the First-tier Tribunal;

(ii) the Health, Education and Social Care Chamber of the First-tier Tribunal;

[(iia) the General Regulatory Chamber of the First-tier Tribunal;][2]

[(iib) the Property Chamber of the First-tier Tribunal;][3]

(iii) the Mental Health Review Tribunal for Wales; or

(iv) the Special Educational Needs Tribunal for Wales; or

(*b*) under section 4 of the Safeguarding Vulnerable Groups Act 2006.][1]

(4) In the circumstances set out at paragraph (3) the appellant may apply for the decision to be reconsidered at a hearing if the Upper Tribunal—

(*a*) refuses permission to appeal [or refuses to admit a late application for permission][3]; or

(*b*) gives permission to appeal on limited grounds or subject to conditions.

(5) An application under paragraph (4) must be made in writing and received by the Upper Tribunal within 14 days after the date on which the Upper Tribunal sent written notice of its decision regarding the application to the appellant.

Amendments—[1] Para (3) substituted by the Tribunal Procedure (Amendment) Rules, SI 2009/274 rules 3, 14 with effect from 1 April 2009.

2 Para (3)(*a*)(iia) inserted by the Tribunal Procedure (Amendment No 2) Rules, SI 2009/1975 rules 7, 16 with effect from 1 September 2009.

3 In paras (1), (4)(*a*), words inserted, and para (3)(*a*)(iib) inserted, by the Tribunal Procedure (Amendment) Rules, SI 2014/514 rules 2, 8 with effect from 6 April 2014.

4 In para (1) words substituted for words "Subject to rule 40A" by the Tribunal Procedure (Amendment No 3) Rules, SI 2014/2128 rules 2, 9 with effect from 20 October 2014.

[22A Special procedure for providing notice of a refusal of permission to appeal in an asylum case

(1) This rule applies to a decision in an asylum case to refuse permission to appeal or to refuse to admit a late application for permission to appeal, where—

(*a*) the appellant is not the Secretary of State;

(*b*) at the time the application is made the appellant is in the United Kingdom; and

(*c*) the decision is not made in a fast-track case.

(2) The Upper Tribunal must provide written notice of the refusal and of the reasons for the refusal ("the notice") to the Secretary of State as soon as reasonably practicable.

(3) The Secretary of State must—

(*a*) send the notice to the appellant not later than 30 days after the Upper Tribunal provided it to the Secretary of State; and

(*b*) as soon as practicable after doing so, inform the Upper Tribunal of the date on which, and the means by which, it was sent.

(4) If the Secretary of State does not give the Upper Tribunal the information required by paragraph (3)(*b*) within 31 days after the notice was provided to the Secretary of State, the Upper Tribunal must send the notice to the appellant as soon as reasonably practicable.][1]

Amendments—[1] Rule 22A inserted by the Tribunal Procedure (Amendment No 3) Rules, SI 2014/2128 rules 2, 10 with effect from 20 October 2014.

23 Notice of appeal

[(1) This rule applies—

(*a*) to proceedings on appeal to the Upper Tribunal for which permission to appeal is not required, except proceedings to which rule 26A [or 26B][3] applies;

(*b*) if another tribunal has given permission for a party to appeal to the Upper Tribunal; or

(*c*) subject to any other direction by the Upper Tribunal, if the Upper Tribunal has given permission to appeal and has given a direction that the application for permission to appeal does not stand as the notice of appeal.

[(1A) In an asylum case or an immigration case in which the First-tier Tribunal has given permission to appeal, subject to any direction of the First-tier Tribunal or the Upper Tribunal, the application for permission to appeal sent or delivered to the First-tier Tribunal stands as the notice of appeal and accordingly paragraphs (2) to (6) of this rule do not apply.][2]

(2) The appellant must provide a notice of appeal to the Upper Tribunal so that it is received within 1 month after—

(*a*) the date that the tribunal that gave permission to appeal sent notice of such permission to the appellant; or

[(*b*) if permission to appeal is not required, the date on which notice of decision to which the appeal relates—

(i) was sent to the appellant; or

(ii) in a quality contracts scheme case, if the notice was not sent to the appellant, the date on which the notice was published in a newspaper in accordance with the requirement of section 125 (notice and consultation requirements) of the Transport Act 2000.][5][1]

(3) The notice of appeal must include the information listed in rule 21(4)(*a*) to (*e*) (content of the application for permission to appeal) and, where the Upper Tribunal has given permission to appeal, the Upper Tribunal's case reference.

(4) If another tribunal has granted permission to appeal, the appellant must provide with the notice of appeal a copy of—

(*a*) any written record of the decision being challenged;

(*b*) any separate written statement of reasons for that decision; and

(*c*) the notice of permission to appeal.

(5) If the appellant provides the notice of appeal to the Upper Tribunal later than the time required by paragraph (2) or by an extension of time allowed under rule 5(3)(*a*) (power to extend time)—

(*a*) the notice of appeal must include a request for an extension of time and the reason why the notice was not provided in time; and

(*b*) unless the Upper Tribunal extends time for the notice of appeal under rule 5(3)(*a*) (power to extend time) the Upper Tribunal must not admit the notice of appeal.

[(6) When the Upper Tribunal receives the notice of appeal it must send a copy of the notice and any accompanying documents—

(*a*) to each respondent; or

(*b*) in a road transport case, to—

(i) the decision maker;

(ii) the appropriate national authority; and

(iii) in a case relating to the detention of a vehicle, the authorised person.][4]][1]

[(7) Paragraph (6)(*a*) does not apply in a quality contracts scheme case, in respect of which Schedule A1 makes alternative and further provision.][5]

Amendments—[1] Paras (1), (2), (6) substituted by the Tribunal Procedure (Amendment No 2) Rules, SI 2009/1975 rules 7, 17 with effect from 1 September 2009.

[2] Para (1A) inserted by the Tribunal Procedure (Amendment No 2) Rules, SI 2010/44 rules 2, 14, with effect from 15 February 2010.

[3] In para (1)(*a*), figure inserted, by the Tribunal Procedure (Upper Tribunal) (Amendment) Rules, SI 2010/747 rules 2, 8 with effect from 6 April 2010.

[4] Para (6)(*b*) substituted by the Tribunal Procedure (Amendment No 2) Rules, SI 2012/1363 rules 4, 7 with effect from 1 July 2012.

[5] Para (2)(*b*) substituted and para (7) inserted by the Tribunal Procedure (Amendment) Rules, SI 2015/1510 arts 2, 4 with effect from 21 August 2015. Para (2)(*b*) previously read as follows—

"(*b*) if permission to appeal is not required, the date on which notice of decision to which the appeal relates was sent to the appellant.".

24 Response to the notice of appeal

[(1) This rule and rule 25 do not apply to [a road transport case][5], in respect of which Schedule 1 makes alternative provision.

(1A) Subject to any direction given by the Upper Tribunal, a respondent may provide a response to a notice of appeal.][2]

(2) Any response provided under paragraph [(1A)][3] must be in writing and must be sent or delivered to the Upper Tribunal so that it is received—

[(*a*) if an application for permission to appeal stands as the notice of appeal, no later than one month after the date on which the respondent was sent notice that permission to appeal had been granted;][4]

VAT SIs

[(*aa*) in a fast-track case, [two days][6] before the hearing of the appeal; or][4]
[(*ab*) in a quality contracts scheme case, no later than 1 month after the date on which a copy of the notice of appeal is sent to the respondent;][7]
(*b*) in any other case, no later than 1 month after the date on which the Upper Tribunal sent a copy of the notice of appeal to the respondent.

(3) The response must state—
(*a*) the name and address of the respondent;
(*b*) the name and address of the representative (if any) of the respondent;
(*c*) an address where documents for the respondent may be sent or delivered;
(*d*) whether the respondent opposes the appeal;
(*e*) the grounds on which the respondent relies, including [(in the case of an appeal against the decision of another tribunal)][2] any grounds on which the respondent was unsuccessful in the proceedings which are the subject of the appeal, but intends to rely in the appeal; and
(*f*) whether the respondent wants the case to be dealt with at a hearing.

(4) If the respondent provides the response to the Upper Tribunal later than the time required by paragraph (2) or by an extension of time allowed under rule 5(3)(*a*) (power to extend time), the response must include a request for an extension of time and the reason why the [response][1] was not provided in time.

(5) When the Upper Tribunal receives the response it must send a copy of the response and any accompanying documents to the appellant and each other party.

[(6) Paragraph (5) does not apply in a quality contracts scheme case, in respect of which Schedule A1 makes alternative and further provision.][7]

Note—Publisher's note: SI 2015/1510 art 5(1) inserts para (1)(*ab*). It is the publisher's belief that the intention was to insert para (2)(*ab*), and the amendment has been made on that basis.

Amendments—[1] Word in para (4) substituted by the Tribunal Procedure (Amendment) Rules, SI 2009/274 rules 3, 15 with effect from 1 April 2009.

[2] Paras (1), (1A) substituted for previous para (1), in para (2)(*a*), words substituted for words "if the application for permission", and in para (3)(*e*), words inserted, by the Tribunal Procedure (Amendment No 2) Rules, SI 2009/1975 rules 7, 18 with effect from 1 September 2009.

[3] In para (2), reference substituted for reference "(1)" by the Tribunal Procedure (Amendment) Rules, SI 2010/43, rules 5, 9, with effect from 18 January 2010.

[4] Para (2)(*a*) substituted, and para (2)(*aa*) inserted, by the Tribunal Procedure (Amendment No 2) Rules, SI 2010/44 rules 2, 15, with effect from 15 February 2010.

[5] In para (1), words substituted for words "an appeal against a decision of a traffic commissioner" by the Tribunal Procedure (Amendment No 2) Rules, SI 2012/1363 rules 4, 8 with effect from 1 July 2012.

[6] In para (2)(*aa*), words substituted for words "one day" by the Tribunal Procedure (Amendment No 3) Rules, SI 2014/2128 rules 2, 11 with effect from 20 October 2014.

[7] Paras (2)(*ab*), (6) inserted by the Tribunal Procedure (Amendment) Rules, SI 2015/1510 arts 2, 5 with effect from 21 August 2015.

25 Appellant's reply

(1) Subject to any direction given by the Upper Tribunal, the appellant may provide a reply to any response provided under rule 24 (response to the notice of appeal).

(2) [Subject to paragraph (2A), any][1] reply provided under paragraph (1) must be in writing and must be sent or delivered to the Upper Tribunal so that it is received within one month after the date on which the Upper Tribunal sent a copy of the response to the appellant.

[(2A) In an asylum case or an immigration case, the time limit in paragraph (2) is—
(*a*) one month after the date on which the Upper Tribunal sent a copy of the response to the appellant, or five days before the hearing of the appeal, whichever is the earlier; and
(*b*) in a fast-track case, the day of the hearing.][1]

[(2B) In a quality contracts scheme case, the time limit in paragraph (2) is 1 month from the date on which the respondent sent a copy of the response to the appellant.][2]

(3) When the Upper Tribunal receives the reply it must send a copy of the reply and any accompanying documents to each respondent.

[(4) Paragraph (3) does not apply in a quality contracts scheme case, in respect of which Schedule A1 makes alternative and further provision.][2]

Amendments—[1] In para (2), words substituted, and para (2A) inserted, by the Tribunal Procedure (Amendment No 2) Rules, SI 2010/44 rules 2, 16, with effect from 15 February 2010.

[2] Paras (2B), (4) inserted by the Tribunal Procedure (Amendment) Rules, SI 2015/1510 arts 2, 6 with effect from 21 August 2015.

26 References under the Forfeiture Act 1982

(1) If a question arises which is required to be determined by the Upper Tribunal under section 4 of the Forfeiture Act 1982, the person to whom the application for the relevant benefit or advantage has been made must refer the question to the Upper Tribunal.

(2) The reference must be in writing and must include—
(*a*) a statement of the question for determination;
(*b*) a statement of the relevant facts;
(*c*) the grounds upon which the reference is made; and

(*d*) an address for sending documents to the person making the reference and each respondent.

(3) When the Upper Tribunal receives the reference it must send a copy of the reference and any accompanying documents to each respondent.

(4) Rules 24 (response to the notice of appeal) and 25 (appellant's reply) apply to a reference made under this rule as if it were a notice of appeal.

[26A Cases transferred or referred to the Upper Tribunal, applications made directly to the Upper Tribunal and proceedings without notice to a respondent]

[(1) Paragraphs (2) and (3) apply to—

(*a*) a case transferred or referred to the Upper Tribunal from the First-tier Tribunal; or

(*b*) a case, other than an appeal or a case to which rule 26 (references under the Forfeiture Act 1982) applies, which is started by an application made directly to the Upper Tribunal.][2]

(2) In a case to which this paragraph applies—

(*a*) the Upper Tribunal must give directions as to the procedure to be followed in the consideration and disposal of the proceedings; ...[4]

[(*aa*) in a reference under Schedule 1D of the Charities Act 1993, the Upper Tribunal may give directions providing for an application to join the proceedings as a party and the time within which it may be made; and][4]

(*b*) the preceding rules in this Part will only apply to the proceedings to the extent provided for by such directions.

(3) If a case or matter to which this paragraph applies is to be determined without notice to or the involvement of a respondent—

(*a*) any provision in these Rules requiring a document to be provided by or to a respondent; and

(*b*) any other provision in these Rules permitting a respondent to participate in the proceedings

does not apply to that case or matter.][1]

[(4) Schedule 2 makes further provision for national security certificate appeals transferred to the Upper Tribunal.][3]

Amendments—[1] Rule 26 inserted by the Tribunal Procedure (Amendment) Rules, SI 2009/274 rules 3, 16 with effect from 1 April 2009.

[2] Para (1) substituted by the Tribunal Procedure (Amendment No 2) Rules, SI 2009/1975 rules 7, 19 with effect from 1 September 2009.

[3] Para (4) inserted by the Tribunal Procedure (Amendment) Rules, SI 2010/43, rules 5, 10 with effect from 18 January 2010.

[4] In para (2), in sub-para (*a*), word "and" revoked, and sub-para (*aa*) inserted, by the Tribunal Procedure (Amendment) Rules, SI 2012/500, rule 5 with effect from 6 April 2012.

[26B Financial services cases [and wholesale energy cases][2]

Schedule 3 makes provision for financial services cases [and wholesale energy cases][2].][1]

Amendments—[1] Para inserted by the Tribunal Procedure (Upper Tribunal) (Amendment) Rules, SI 2010/747 rules 2, 9 with effect from 6 April 2010.

[2] Words in heading and text inserted by the Tribunal Procedure (Amendment) Rules, SI 2014/514 rules 2, 9, 10 with effect from 6 April 2014.

PART 4
JUDICIAL REVIEW PROCEEDINGS IN THE UPPER TRIBUNAL

27 Application of this Part to judicial review proceedings transferred to the Upper Tribunal

(1) When a court transfers judicial review proceedings to the Upper Tribunal, the Upper Tribunal—

(*a*) must notify each party in writing that the proceedings have been transferred to the Upper Tribunal; and

(*b*) must give directions as to the future conduct of the proceedings.

(2) The directions given under paragraph (1)(*b*) may modify or disapply for the purposes of the proceedings any of the provisions of the following rules in this Part.

(3) In proceedings transferred from the Court of Session under section 20(1) of the 2007 Act, the directions given under paragraph (1)(*b*) must—

(*a*) if the Court of Session did not make a first order specifying the required intimation, service and advertisement of the petition, state the Upper Tribunal's requirements in relation to those matters;

(*b*) state whether the Upper Tribunal will consider summary dismissal of the proceedings; and

(*c*) where necessary, modify or disapply provisions relating to permission in the following rules in this Part.

28 Applications for permission to bring judicial review proceedings

(1) A person seeking permission to bring judicial review proceedings before the Upper Tribunal under section 16 of the 2007 Act must make a written application to the Upper Tribunal for such permission.

(2) Subject to paragraph (3), an application under paragraph (1) must be made promptly and, unless any other enactment specifies a shorter time limit, must be sent or delivered to the Upper Tribunal so that it is received no later than 3 months after the date of the decision[, action or omission][1] to which the application relates.

(3) An application for permission to bring judicial review proceedings challenging a decision of the First-tier Tribunal may be made later than the time required by paragraph (2) if it is made within 1 month after the date on which the First-tier Tribunal sent—

(*a*) written reasons for the decision; or

(*b*) notification that an application for the decision to be set aside has been unsuccessful, provided that that application was made in time.

(4) The application must state—

(*a*) the name and address of the applicant, the respondent and any other person whom the applicant considers to be an interested party;

(*b*) the name and address of the applicant's representative (if any);

(*c*) an address where documents for the applicant may be sent or delivered;

(*d*) details of the decision challenged (including the date, the full reference and the identity of the decision maker);

(*e*) that the application is for permission to bring judicial review proceedings;

(*f*) the outcome that the applicant is seeking; and

(*g*) the facts and grounds on which the applicant relies.

(5) If the application relates to proceedings in a court or tribunal, the application must name as an interested party each party to those proceedings who is not the applicant or a respondent.

(6) The applicant must send with the application—

(*a*) a copy of any written record of the decision in the applicant's possession or control; and

(*b*) copies of any other documents in the applicant's possession or control on which the applicant intends to rely.

(7) If the applicant provides the application to the Upper Tribunal later than the time required by paragraph (2) or (3) or by an extension of time allowed under rule 5(3)(*a*) (power to extend time)—

(*a*) the application must include a request for an extension of time and the reason why the application was not provided in time; and

(*b*) unless the Upper Tribunal extends time for the application under rule 5(3)(*a*) (power to extend time) the Upper Tribunal must not admit the application.

(8) [Except where rule 28A(2)(*a*) (special provisions for [immigration judicial review][3] proceedings) applies,][2] when the Upper Tribunal receives the application it must send a copy of the application and any accompanying documents to each person named in the application as a respondent or interested party.

Amendments—[1] In para (2), words inserted by the Tribunal Procedure (Amendment) Rules, SI 2009/274 rules 3, 17 with effect from 1 April 2009.

[2] In para (8), words inserted by the Tribunal Procedure (Upper Tribunal) (Amendment) Rules, SI 2011/2343 rules 2, 7 with effect from 17 October 2011.

[3] In para (8), words substituted for words "fresh claim", by the Tribunal Procedure (Amendment No 4) Rules, SI 2013/2067 rules 2, 10 with effect from 1 November 2013.

[28A Special provisions for [immigration judicial review] proceedings

(1) The Upper Tribunal must not accept an application for permission to bring [immigration judicial review][2] proceedings unless it is either accompanied by any required fee or the Upper Tribunal accepts an undertaking that the fee will be paid.

(2) Within 9 days of making an application referred to in paragraph (1), an applicant must provide—

(*a*) a copy of the application and any accompanying documents to each person named in the application as a respondent or an interested party; and

(*b*) the Upper Tribunal with a written statement of when and how this was done.][1]

Amendments—[1] Rule 28A inserted by the Tribunal Procedure (Upper Tribunal) (Amendment) Rules, SI 2011/2343 rules 2, 8 with effect from 17 October 2011.

[2] In heading and in para (1), words substituted for words "fresh claim", by the Tribunal Procedure (Amendment No 4) Rules, SI 2013/2067 rules 2, 11 with effect from 1 November 2013.

29 Acknowledgment of service

(1) A person who is sent [or provided with][3] a copy of an application for permission under rule 28(8) (application for permission to bring judicial review proceedings) [or rule 28A(2)(a) (special provisions for [immigration judicial review][4] proceedings)][3] and wishes to take part in the proceedings must [provide][3] to the Upper Tribunal an acknowledgment of service so that it is received no later than 21 days after the date on which the Upper Tribunal sent[, or in [immigration judicial review][4] proceedings the applicant provided,][3] a copy of the application to that person.

(2) An acknowledgment of service under paragraph (1) must be in writing and state—

(*a*) whether the person intends to [support or][1] oppose the application for permission;

(*b*) their grounds for any [support or][1] opposition under sub-paragraph (*a*), or any other submission or information which it considers may assist the Upper Tribunal; and (*c*) the name and address of any other person not named in the application as a respondent or interested party whom the person providing the acknowledgment considers to be an interested party.

(2A) In [immigration judicial review][4] proceedings, a person who provides an acknowledgement of service under paragraph (1) must also provide a copy to—

(a) the applicant; and

(b) any other person named in the application under rule 28(4)(a) or acknowledgement of service under paragraph (2)(c)

no later than the time specified in paragraph (1).][3]

(3) A person who is [provided with][3] a copy of an application for permission under rule 28(8) [or 28A(2)(*a*)][3] but does not provide an acknowledgment of service [to the Upper Tribunal][3] may not take part in the application for permission [unless allowed to do so by the Upper Tribunal][2], but may take part in the subsequent proceedings if the application is successful.

Amendments—[1] In para (2), words inserted by the Tribunal Procedure (Amendment) Rules, SI 2009/274 rules 3, 17 with effect from 1 April 2009.

[2] In para (3) words inserted by the Tribunal Procedure (Amendment) Rules SI 2011/651 rule 8(1), (3) with effect from 1 April 2011.

[3] In para (1) words inserted and word substituted; para (2A) inserted; and in para (3), words substituted and words inserted; by the Tribunal Procedure (Upper Tribunal) (Amendment) Rules, SI 2011/2343 rules 2, 9 with effect from 17 October 2011.

[4] In para (1) in both places, and in para (2A), words substituted for words "fresh claim", by the Tribunal Procedure (Amendment No 4) Rules, SI 2013/2067 rules 2, 12 with effect from 1 November 2013.

30 Decision on permission or summary dismissal, and reconsideration of permission or summary dismissal at a hearing

(1) The Upper Tribunal must send to the applicant, each respondent and any other person who provided an acknowledgment of service to the Upper Tribunal, and may send to any other person who may have an interest in the proceedings, written notice of—

(*a*) its decision in relation to the application for permission; and

[(*b*) the reasons for any—

(i) refusal of the application or refusal to admit the late application, or

(ii) limitations or conditions on permission.][3]

(2) In proceedings transferred from the Court of Session under section 20(1) of the 2007 Act, where the Upper Tribunal has considered whether summarily to dismiss of the proceedings, the Upper Tribunal must send to the applicant and each respondent, and may send to any other person who may have an interest in the proceedings, written notice of—

(*a*) its decision in relation to the summary dismissal of proceedings; and

(*b*) the reasons for any decision summarily to dismiss part or all of the proceedings, or any limitations or conditions on the continuation of such proceedings.

(3) Paragraph (4) applies where the Upper Tribunal, without a hearing—

(*a*) determines an application for permission to bring judicial review proceedings by—

(i) refusing permission or refusing to admit the late application, or

(ii) giving permission on limited grounds or subject to conditions.][3]

(*b*) in proceedings transferred from the Court of Session, summarily dismisses part or all of the proceedings, or imposes any limitations or conditions on the continuation of such proceedings.

(4) [Subject to paragraph (4A), in][2] the circumstances specified in paragraph (3) the applicant may apply for the decision to be reconsidered at a hearing.

[(4A) Where the Upper Tribunal refuses permission to bring immigration judicial review proceedings [or refuses to admit a late application for permission to bring such proceedings][3] and considers the application to be totally without merit, it shall record that fact in its decision notice and, in those circumstances, the applicant may not request the decision to be reconsidered at a hearing.][2]

(5) An application under paragraph (4) must be made in writing and must be sent or delivered to the Upper Tribunal so that it is received within 14 days[, or in [immigration judicial review][2] proceedings 9 days,][1] after the date on which the Upper Tribunal sent written notice of its decision regarding the application to the applicant.

Amendments—[1] In para (5), words inserted by the Tribunal Procedure (Upper Tribunal) (Amendment) Rules, SI 2011/2343 rules 2, 10 with effect from 17 October 2011.

[2] In para (4) words substituted for word "In", para (4A) inserted, and in para (5) words substituted for words "fresh claim", by the Tribunal Procedure (Amendment No 4) Rules, SI 2013/2067 rules 2, 13 with effect from 1 November 2013. Note that the amendments relating to paras (4) and (4A) do not apply to fresh claim proceedings where an application for permission to bring judicial review proceedings was issued in the Upper Tribunal before 1 November 2013, or an application for permission to apply for judicial review was transferred to the Upper Tribunal by the High Court under the Senior Courts Act 1981 s 31A before 1 November 2013. "Fresh claim proceedings" has the meaning in rule 1(3) of these Rules as it was in force immediately before 1 November 2013 (SI 2013/2067 rule 29).

[3] Paras (1)(*b*), (3)(*a*) substituted, and in para (4A), words inserted by the Tribunal Procedure (Amendment) Rules, SI 2014/514 rules 2, 11 with effect from 6 April 2014.

31 Responses

(1) Any person to whom the Upper Tribunal has sent notice of the grant of permission under rule 30(1) (notification of decision on permission), and who wishes to contest the application or support it on additional grounds, must provide detailed grounds for contesting or supporting the application to the Upper Tribunal.

(2) Any detailed grounds must be provided in writing and must be sent or delivered to the Upper Tribunal so that they are received not more than 35 days after the Upper Tribunal sent notice of the grant of permission under rule 30(1).

32 Applicant seeking to rely on additional grounds

The applicant may not rely on any grounds, other than those grounds on which the applicant obtained permission for the judicial review proceedings, without the consent of the Upper Tribunal.

33 Right to make representations

Each party and, with the permission of the Upper Tribunal, any other person, may—

(*a*) submit evidence, except at the hearing of an application for permission;

(*b*) make representations at any hearing which they are entitled to attend; and

(*c*) make written representations in relation to a decision to be made without a hearing.

[33A Amendments and additional grounds resulting in transfer of proceedings to the High Court in England and Wales

(1) This rule applies only to judicial review proceedings arising under the law of England and Wales.

(2) In relation to such proceedings—

(*a*) the powers of the Upper Tribunal to permit or require amendments under rule 5(3)(*c*) extend to amendments which would, once in place, give rise to an obligation or power to transfer the proceedings to the High Court in England and Wales under section 18(3) of the 2007 Act or paragraph (3);

(*b*) except with the permission of the Upper Tribunal, additional grounds may not be advanced, whether by an applicant or otherwise, if they would give rise to an obligation or power to transfer the proceedings to the High Court in England and Wales under section 18(3) of the 2007 Act or paragraph (3).

(3) Where the High Court in England and Wales has transferred judicial review proceedings to the Upper Tribunal under any power or duty and subsequently the proceedings are amended or any party advances additional grounds—

(*a*) if the proceedings in their present form could not have been transferred to the Upper Tribunal under the relevant power or duty had they been in that form at the time of the transfer, the Upper Tribunal must transfer the proceedings back to the High Court in England and Wales;

(*b*) subject to sub-paragraph (*a*), where the proceedings were transferred to the Upper Tribunal under section 31A(3) of the Senior Courts Act 1981(power to transfer judicial review proceedings to the Upper Tribunal), the Upper Tribunal may transfer proceedings back to the High Court in England and Wales if it appears just and convenient to do so.][1]

Amendments—[1] Rule 33A inserted by the Tribunal Procedure (Upper Tribunal) (Amendment) Rules, SI 2011/2343 rules 2, 11 with effect from 17 October 2011.

PART 5
HEARINGS

34 Decision with or without a hearing

(1) Subject to [paragraphs (2) and (3)][1], the Upper Tribunal may make any decision without a hearing.

(2) The Upper Tribunal must have regard to any view expressed by a party when deciding whether to hold a hearing to consider any matter, and the form of any such hearing.

[(3) In immigration judicial review proceedings, the Upper Tribunal must hold a hearing before making a decision which disposes of proceedings.

(4) Paragraph (3) does not affect the power of the Upper Tribunal to—

(*a*) strike out a party's case, pursuant to rule 8(1)(*b*) or 8(2);

(*b*) consent to withdrawal, pursuant to rule 17;

(*c*) determine an application for permission to bring judicial review proceedings, pursuant to rule 30; or

(*d*) make a consent order disposing of proceedings, pursuant to rule 39,

without a hearing.][1]

Amendments—[1] In para (1) words substituted for words "paragraph (2)", and paras (3), (4) inserted, by the Tribunal Procedure (Amendment No 4) Rules, SI 2013/2067 rules 2, 14 with effect from 1 November 2013.

35 Entitlement to attend a hearing

[(1)] [1]Subject to rule 37(4) (exclusion of a person from a hearing), each party is entitled to attend a hearing.

[(2) In a national security certificate appeal the relevant Minister is entitled to attend any hearing.][1]

Amendments—[1] Para (1) numbered as such, and para (2) inserted, by the Tribunal Procedure (Amendment) Rules, SI 2010/43, rules 5, 11, with effect from 18 January 2010.

36 Notice of hearings

(1) The Upper Tribunal must give each party entitled to attend a hearing reasonable notice of the time and place of the hearing (including any adjourned or postponed hearing) and any change to the time and place of the hearing.

(2) The period of notice under paragraph (1) must be at least 14 days except that—

(*a*) in applications for permission to bring judicial review proceedings, the period of notice must be at least 2 working days; . . . [1]

[(*aa*) in a fast-track case the period of notice must be at least one working day; and][1]

(*b*) [in any case other than a fast-track case][1] the Upper Tribunal may give shorter notice—

(i) with the parties' consent; or

(ii) in urgent or exceptional cases.

Amendments—[1] Word "and" at end of para (2)(*a*) repealed, and para (2)(*aa*) and words in para (2)(*b*) inserted, by the Tribunal Procedure (Amendment No 2) Rules, SI 2010/44 rules 2, 17, with effect from 15 February 2010.

[36A Special time limits for hearing an appeal in a fast-track case

(1) Subject to rule 36(2)(*aa*) (notice of hearings) and paragraph (2) of this rule, where permission to appeal to the Upper Tribunal has been given in a fast-track case, the Upper Tribunal must start the hearing of the appeal not later than—

(*a*) [five][2] working days after the date on which the First-tier Tribunal or the Upper Tribunal sent notice of its grant of permission to appeal to the appellant; or

(*b*) where the notice of its grant of permission to appeal is sent electronically or delivered personally, two working days after the date on which the First-tier Tribunal or the Upper Tribunal sent notice of its grant of permission to appeal to the appellant.

(2) If the Upper Tribunal is unable to arrange for the hearing to start within the time specified in paragraph (1), it must set a date for the hearing as soon as is reasonably practicable.][1]

Amendments—[1] Rule 36A inserted by the Tribunal Procedure (Amendment No 2) Rules, SI 2010/44 rules 2, 18, with effect from 15 February 2010.

[2] In para (1)(*a*), word substituted for word "four" by the Tribunal Procedure (Amendment No 3) Rules, SI 2014/2128 rules 2, 13 with effect from 20 October 2014.

37 Public and private hearings

(1) Subject to the following paragraphs, all hearings must be held in public.

(2) The Upper Tribunal may give a direction that a hearing, or part of it, is to be held in private.

[(2A) In a national security certificate appeal, the Upper Tribunal must have regard to its duty under rule 14(10) (no disclosure of information contrary to the interests of national security) when considering whether to give a direction that a hearing, or part of it, is to be held in private.][3]

(3) Where a hearing, or part of it, is to be held in private, the Upper Tribunal may determine who is entitled to attend the hearing or part of it.

(4) The Upper Tribunal may give a direction excluding from any hearing, or part of it—

(*a*) any person whose conduct the Upper Tribunal considers is disrupting or is likely to disrupt the hearing;

(*b*) any person whose presence the Upper Tribunal considers is likely to prevent another person from giving evidence or making submissions freely;

(*c*) any person who the Upper Tribunal considers should be excluded in order to give effect to [the requirement at rule 14(11) (prevention of disclosure or publication of documents and information)][2]; . . . [1]

(*d*) any person where the purpose of the hearing would be defeated by the attendance of that person[; or

(*e*) a person under [18, other than a young person who is a party in a special educational needs case or a disability discrimination in schools case][4]][1].

(5) The Upper Tribunal may give a direction excluding a witness from a hearing until that witness gives evidence.

Amendments—[1] In para (4), word "or" in sub-para (*c*) repealed, and sub-para (*e*) and preceding word "or" inserted, by the Tribunal Procedure (Amendment) Rules, SI 2009/274 rules 3, 19 with effect from 1 April 2009.

[2] In para (4)(*c*), words substituted by the Tribunal Procedure (Amendment No 2) Rules, SI 2009/1975 rules 7, 20 with effect from 1 September 2009.

[3] Para (2A) inserted by the Tribunal Procedure (Amendment) Rules, SI 2010/43, rules 5, 12, with effect from 18 January 2010.

[4] In para (4)(*e*), words substituted for words "the age of eighteen years" by the Tribunal Procedure (Amendment No 3) Rules, SI 2014/2128 rules 2, 13 with effect from 1 September 2014.

38 Hearings in a party's absence

If a party fails to attend a hearing, the Upper Tribunal may proceed with the hearing if the Upper Tribunal—

(*a*) is satisfied that the party has been notified of the hearing or that reasonable steps have been taken to notify the party of the hearing; and

VAT SIs

(*b*) considers that it is in the interests of justice to proceed with the hearing.

PART 6
DECISIONS

39 Consent orders

(1) The Upper Tribunal may, at the request of the parties but only if it considers it appropriate, make a consent order disposing of the proceedings and making such other appropriate provision as the parties have agreed.

(2) Notwithstanding any other provision of these Rules, the [Upper][2] Tribunal need not hold a hearing before making an order under paragraph (1) . . . [1].

Amendments—[1] In para (2), words repealed by the Tribunal Procedure (Amendment) Rules, SI 2009/274 rules 3, 20 with effect from 1 April 2009.

[2] Word in para (2) inserted by the Tribunal Procedure (Amendment No 4) Rules, SI 2013/2067 rules 2, 15 with effect from 1 November 2013.

40 Decisions

(1) The Upper Tribunal may give a decision orally at a hearing.

[(1A) Subject to paragraph (1B), in immigration judicial review proceedings, a decision which disposes of proceedings shall be given at a hearing.

(1B) Paragraph (1A) does not affect the power of the Upper Tribunal to—

(*a*) strike out a party's case, pursuant to rule 8(1)(*b*) or 8(2);

(*b*) consent to withdrawal, pursuant to rule 17;

(*c*) determine an application for permission to bring judicial review proceedings, pursuant to rule 30; or

(*d*) make a consent order disposing of proceedings, pursuant to rule 39,

without a hearing.][6]

(2) . . . [1] [Except where [rule 22 (decision in relation to permission to appeal) or rule 22A (special procedure for providing notice of a refusal of permission to appeal in an asylum case)][7] applies,][4] The Upper Tribunal must provide to each party as soon as reasonably practicable after making [a decision (other than a decision under Part 7) which finally disposes of all issues in the proceedings or of a preliminary issue dealt with following a direction under rule 5(3)(*e*)[5]]—

(*a*) a decision notice stating the [Upper][5] Tribunal's decision; and

(*b*) notification of any rights of review or appeal against the decision and the time and manner in which such rights of review or appeal may be exercised.

(3) [Subject to rule [14(11) (prevention of disclosure or publication of documents and information)][2],][1] the Upper Tribunal must provide written reasons for its decision with a decision notice provided under paragraph (2)(*a*) unless—

(*a*) the decision was made with the consent of the parties; or

(*b*) the parties have consented to the Upper Tribunal not giving written reasons.

(4) The [Upper][2] Tribunal may provide written reasons for any decision to which paragraph (2) does not apply.

[(5) In a national security certificate appeal, when the Upper Tribunal provides a notice or reasons to the parties under this rule, it must also provide the notice or reasons to the relevant Minister and the Information Commissioner, if they are not parties.][3]

Amendments—[1] In para (2), words repealed, and in para (3), words inserted, by the Tribunal Procedure (Amendment) Rules, SI 2009/274 rules 3, 21 with effect from 1 April 2009.

[2] In para (3), words substituted, and in para (4), word inserted, by the Tribunal Procedure (Amendment No 2) Rules, SI 2009/1975 rules 7, 21 with effect from 1 September 2009.

[3] Para (5) inserted by the Tribunal Procedure (Amendment) Rules, SI 2010/43, rules 5, 13, with effect from 18 January 2010.

[4] Words in para (2) inserted by the Tribunal Procedure (Amendment No 2) Rules, SI 2010/44 rules 2, 19, with effect from 15 February 2010.

[5] In para (2), words substituted for words ", a decision which finally disposes of all issues in the proceedings (except a decision under Part 7)", and in sub-para (*a*) word inserted, by the Tribunal Procedure (Amendment) Rules, SI 2013/477 rules 49, 56 with effect from 1 April 2013.

[6] Paras (1A), (1B) inserted by the Tribunal Procedure (Amendment No 4) Rules, SI 2013/2067 rules 2, 16 with effect from 1 November 2013.

[7] In para (2), words substituted for words "rule 40A (special procedure for providing notice of a decision relating to an asylum case)" by the Tribunal Procedure (Amendment No 3) Rules, SI 2014/2128 rules 2, 14 with effect from 20 October 2014.

[40A Special procedure for providing notice of a decision relating to an asylum case

[(1) This rule applies to a decision of the Upper Tribunal in an asylum case—

(*a*) *to refuse (or not to admit) an application for permission to appeal to the Upper Tribunal made by the person who appealed to the First-tier Tribunal; or*

(*b*) *on an appeal under section 11 of the 2007 Act,*

where—

(i) *at the time the application or appeal (as the case may be) is made the person who appealed to the First-tier Tribunal is in the United Kingdom; and*

(ii) *the decision is not made in a fast track case.]*[2]

(2) The Upper Tribunal must provide to the Secretary of State for the Home Department as soon as reasonably practicable—

(*a*) *a decision notice stating the Upper Tribunal's decision; and*

(*b*) *a statement of any right of appeal against the decision and the time and manner in which such a right of appeal may be exercised.*

(3) The Secretary of State must, subject to paragraph (5)—

(*a*) *send the documents listed in paragraph (2) to the other party not later than 30 days after the Upper Tribunal sent them to the Secretary of State for the Home Department; and*

(*b*) *as soon as practicable after sending the documents listed in paragraph (2), notify the Upper Tribunal on what date and by what means they were sent*

(4) If the Secretary of State does not notify the Upper Tribunal under paragraph (3)(*b*) within 31 days after the documents listed in paragraph (2) were sent, the Upper Tribunal must send the notice of decision to the other party as soon as reasonably practicable.

(5) If the Secretary of State applies for permission to appeal under section 13 of the 2007 Act, the Secretary of State must send the documents listed in paragraph (2) to the other party no later than the date on which the application for permission is sent to the Upper Tribunal.][1], [3]

Amendments—[1] Rule 40A inserted by the Tribunal Procedure (Amendment No 2) Rules, SI 2010/44 rules 2, 20, with effect from 15 February 2010.

[2] Para (1) substituted by the Tribunal Procedure (Amendment No 2) Rules, SI 2014/1505 rules 2, 4 with effect from 30 June 2014.

[3] Rule 40A revoked by the Tribunal Procedure (Amendment No 3) Rules, SI 2014/2128 rules 2, 15 with effect from 20 October 2014.

PART 7
CORRECTING, SETTING ASIDE, REVIEWING AND APPEALING DECISIONS OF THE UPPER TRIBUNAL

41 Interpretation

In this Part—

"appeal"[, except in rule 44(2) (application for permission to appeal),][1] means the exercise of a right of appeal under section 13 of the 2007 Act; and

"review" means the review of a decision by the Upper Tribunal under section 10 of the 2007 Act.

Amendments—[1] Words in definition of "appeal" inserted by the Tribunal Procedure (Amendment) Rules, SI 2009/274 rules 3, 22 with effect from 1 April 2009.

42 Clerical mistakes and accidental slips or omissions

The Upper Tribunal may at any time correct any clerical mistake or other accidental slip or omission in a decision or record of a decision by—

(*a*) sending notification of the amended decision, or a copy of the amended record, to all parties; and

(*b*) making any necessary amendment to any information published in relation to the decision or record.

43 Setting aside a decision which disposes of proceedings

(1) The Upper Tribunal may set aside a decision which disposes of proceedings, or part of such a decision, and re-make the decision or the relevant part of it, if—

(*a*) the Upper Tribunal considers that it is in the interests of justice to do so; and

(*b*) one or more of the conditions in paragraph (2) are satisfied.

(2) The conditions are—

(*a*) a document relating to the proceedings was not sent to, or was not received at an appropriate time by, a party or a party's representative;

(*b*) a document relating to the proceedings was not sent to the Upper Tribunal at an appropriate time;

(*c*) a party, or a party's representative, was not present at a hearing related to the proceedings; or

(*d*) there has been some other procedural irregularity in the proceedings.

(3) [Except where paragraph (4) applies,][1] a party applying for a decision, or part of a decision, to be set aside under paragraph (1) must make a written application to the Upper Tribunal so that it is received no later than 1 month after the date on which the [Upper][2] Tribunal sent notice of the decision to the party.

[(4) In an asylum case or an immigration case, the written application referred to in paragraph (3) must be sent or delivered so that it is received by the Upper Tribunal—

(*a*) where the person who appealed to the First-tier Tribunal is in the United Kingdom at the time that the application is made, no later than twelve days after the date on which the Upper Tribunal or, as the case may be in an asylum case, the Secretary of State for the Home Department, sent notice of the decision to the party making the application; or

VAT SIs

(*b*) where the person who appealed to the First-tier Tribunal is outside the United Kingdom at the time that the application is made, no later than thirty eight days after the date on which the Upper Tribunal sent notice of the decision to the party making the application.

(5) Where a notice of decision is sent electronically or delivered personally, the time limits in paragraph (4) are ten working days.][1]

Amendments—[1] Words at start of para (3), and whole of paras (4), (5), inserted, by the Tribunal Procedure (Amendment No 2) Rules, SI 2010/44 rules 2, 21, with effect from 15 February 2010.

[2] Word in para (3) inserted by the Tribunal Procedure (Amendment No 4) Rules, SI 2013/2067 rules 2, 17 with effect from 1 November 2013.

44 Application for permission to appeal

(1) [Subject to [paragraphs (4A) and (4B)][6],][5] a person seeking permission to appeal must make a written application to the Upper Tribunal for permission to appeal.

(2) Paragraph (3) applies to an application under paragraph (1) in respect of a decision—

(*a*) on an appeal against a decision in a social security and child support case (as defined in the Tribunal Procedure (First-tier Tribunal) (Social Entitlement Chamber) Rules 2008);

(*b*) on an appeal against a decision in proceedings in the War Pensions and Armed Forces Compensation Chamber of the First-tier Tribunal; . . . [1]

[(*ba*) on an appeal against a decision of a Pensions Appeal Tribunal for Scotland or Northern Ireland; or][1]

(*c*) in proceedings under the Forfeiture Act 1982.

(3) Where this paragraph applies, the application must be sent or delivered to the Upper Tribunal so that it is received within 3 months after the date on which the Upper Tribunal sent to the person making the application—

(*a*) written notice of the decision;

(*b*) notification of amended reasons for, or correction of, the decision following a review; or

(*c*) notification that an application for the decision to be set aside has been unsuccessful.

[(3A) An application under paragraph (1) in respect of a decision in an asylum case or an immigration case must be sent or delivered to the Upper Tribunal so that it is received within the appropriate period after the Upper Tribunal or, as the case may be in an asylum case, the Secretary of State for the Home Department, sent any of the documents in paragraph (3) to the party making the application.

(3B) The appropriate period referred to in paragraph (3A) is as follows—

(*a*) where the person who appealed to the First-tier Tribunal is in the United Kingdom at the time that the application is made—

(i) [twelve working days][4]; or

(ii) if the party making the application is in detention under the Immigration Acts, seven working days; and

(*b*) where the person who appealed to the First-tier Tribunal is outside the United Kingdom at the time that the application is made, thirty eight days.

(3C) Where a notice of decision is sent electronically or delivered personally, the time limits in paragraph (3B) are—

(*a*) in sub-paragraph (*a*)(i), ten working days;

(*b*) in sub-paragraph (*a*)(ii), five working days; and

(*c*) in sub-paragraph (*b*), ten working days.][2]

[(3D) An application under paragraph (1) in respect of a decision in a financial services case must be sent or delivered to the Upper Tribunal so that it is received within 14 days after the date on which the Upper Tribunal sent to the person making the application—

(*a*) written notice of the decision;

(*b*) notification of amended reasons for, or correction of, the decision following a review; or

(*c*) notification that an application for the decision to be set aside has been unsuccessful.][3]

(4) Where paragraph (3)[, (3A)[, (3D) or (4C);][6]][3] does not apply, an application under paragraph (1) must be sent or delivered to the Upper Tribunal so that it is received within 1 month after the latest of the dates on which the Upper Tribunal sent to the person making the application—

(*a*) written reasons for the decision;

(*b*) notification of amended reasons for, or correction of, the decision following a review; or

(*c*) notification that an application for the decision to be set aside has been unsuccessful.

[(4A) Where a decision that disposes of immigration judicial review proceedings is given at a hearing, a party may apply at that hearing for permission to appeal, and the Upper Tribunal must consider at the hearing whether to give or refuse permission to appeal.

(4B) Where a decision that disposes of immigration judicial review proceedings is given at a hearing and no application for permission to appeal is made at that hearing—

(*a*) the Upper Tribunal must nonetheless consider at the hearing whether to give or refuse permission to appeal; and

(*b*) if permission to appeal is given to a party, it shall be deemed for the purposes of section 13(4) of the 2007 Act to be given on application by that party.

(4C) Where a decision that disposes of immigration judicial review proceedings is given pursuant to rule 30 and the Upper Tribunal records under rule 30(4A) that the application is totally without merit, an application under paragraph (1) must be sent or delivered to the Upper Tribunal so that it is received within 7 days after the later of the dates on which the Upper Tribunal sent to the applicant—

(*a*) written reasons for the decision; or

(*b*) notification of amended reasons for, or correction of, the decision following a review.][6]

(5) The date in paragraph (3)(*c*) or (4)(*c*) applies only if the application for the decision to be set aside was made within the time stipulated in rule 43 (setting aside a decision which disposes of proceedings) or any extension of that time granted by the Upper Tribunal.

(6) If the person seeking permission to appeal provides the application to the Upper Tribunal later than the time required by paragraph (3)[, (3A)][2][, (3D)][3] or (4), or by any extension of time under rule 5(3)(a) (power to extend time)—

(*a*) the application must include a request for an extension of time and the reason why the application notice was not provided in time; and

(*b*) unless the Upper Tribunal extends time for the application under rule 5(3)(*a*) (power to extend time) the Upper Tribunal must refuse the application.

(7) An application under paragraph (1) [or (4A)(*a*)][5] must—

(*a*) identify the decision of the [Upper][6] Tribunal to which it relates;

(*b*) identify the alleged error or errors of law in the decision; and

(*c*) state the result the party making the application is seeking.

Amendments—[1] In para (2), in sub-para (*b*), word "or" repealed, and sub-para (*ba*) inserted, by the Tribunal Procedure (Amendment) Rules, SI 2009/274 rules 3, 23 with effect from 1 April 2009.

[2] Paras (3A)–(3C), and references in para (6), inserted, by the Tribunal Procedure (Amendment No 2) Rules, SI 2010/44 rules 2, 22, with effect from 15 February 2010.

[3] Para (3D) inserted, reference in para (4) substituted and reference in para (6) inserted, by the Tribunal Procedure (Upper Tribunal) (Amendment) Rules, SI 2010/747 rules 2, 10 with effect from 6 April 2010.

[4] In para (3B)(*a*)(i) words substituted by the Tribunal Procedure (Amendment) Rules, SI 2011/651 rule 8(1), (4) with effect from 1 April 2011.

[5] Words in paras (1), (7) inserted, by the Tribunal Procedure (Upper Tribunal) (Amendment) Rules, SI 2012/2890 rules 2, 3 with effect from 11 December 2012.

[6] In para (1), words substituted for words "paragraph (4A)", in para (4), words substituted for words "or (3D)", paras (4A)–(4C) substituted for previous para (4A), and in para (7)(*a*) word inserted, by the Tribunal Procedure (Amendment No 4) Rules, SI 2013/2067 rules 2, 18 with effect from 1 November 2013.

45 Upper Tribunal's consideration of application for permission to appeal

(1) On receiving an application for permission to appeal the Upper Tribunal may review the decision in accordance with rule 46 (review of a decision), but may only do so if—

(*a*) when making the decision the Upper Tribunal overlooked a legislative provision or binding authority which could have had a material effect on the decision; or

(*b*) since the Upper Tribunal's decision, a court has made a decision which is binding on the Upper Tribunal and which, had it been made before the Upper Tribunal's decision, could have had a material effect on the decision.

(2) If the Upper Tribunal decides not to review the decision, or reviews the decision and decides to take no action in relation to the decision or part of it, the Upper Tribunal must consider whether to give permission to appeal in relation to the decision or that part of it.

(3) The Upper Tribunal must [provide][1] a record of its decision to the parties as soon as practicable.

(4) If the Upper Tribunal refuses permission to appeal it must [provide][1] with the record of its decision—

(*a*) a statement of its reasons for such refusal; and

(*b*) notification of the right to make an application to the relevant appellate court for permission to appeal and the time within which, and the method by which, such application must be made.

(5) The Upper Tribunal may give permission to appeal on limited grounds, but must comply with paragraph (4) in relation to any grounds on which it has refused permission.

Amendments—[1] In paras (3), (4) word substituted for word "send" by the Tribunal Procedure (Amendment No 4) Rules, SI 2013/2067 rules 2, 19 with effect from 1 November 2013.

46 Review of a decision

[(1) The Upper Tribunal may only undertake a review of a decision pursuant to rule 45(1) (review on an application for permission to appeal).][1]

(2) The Upper Tribunal must notify the parties in writing of the outcome of any review and of any rights of review or appeal in relation to the outcome.

(3) If the Upper Tribunal decides to take any action in relation to a decision following a review without first giving every party an opportunity to make representations, the notice under paragraph (2) must state that any party that did not have an opportunity to make representations may apply for such action to be set aside and for the decision to be reviewed again.

Amendments—[1] Para (1) substituted by the Tribunal Procedure (Upper Tribunal) (Amendment) Rules, SI 2011/2343 rules 2, 12 with effect from 17 October 2011.

47 [Setting aside] a decision in proceedings under the Forfeiture Act 1982

(1) A person who referred a question to the Upper Tribunal under rule 26 (references under the Forfeiture Act 1982) must refer the Upper Tribunal's previous decision in relation to the question to the Upper Tribunal if they—

(*a*) consider that the decision should be [set aside and re-made under this rule][1]; or

(*b*) have received a written application for the decision to be [set aside and re-made under this rule][1] from the person to whom the decision related.

(2) The Upper Tribunal may [set aside the decision, either in whole or in part, and re-make it][1] if—

(*a*) ...[1]

(*b*) the decision was made in ignorance of, or was based on a mistake as to, some material fact; or

(*c*) there has been a relevant change in circumstances since the decision was made.

[(3) Rule 26(2) to (4), Parts 5 and 6 and this Part apply to a reference under this rule as they apply to a reference under rule 26(1).][1]

Amendments—[1] In heading, paras (1) (*a*), (*b*), (2), words substituted; para 2(*a*) revoked; and para (3) substituted for previous paras (3)–(5); by the Tribunal Procedure (Upper Tribunal) (Amendment) Rules, SI 2011/2343 rules 2, 13 with effect from 17 October 2011.

[48 Power to treat an application as a different type of application

The [Upper][2] Tribunal may treat an application for a decision to be corrected, set aside or reviewed, or for permission to appeal against a decision, as an application for any other one of those things.][1]

Amendments—[1] Rule 48 inserted by the Tribunal Procedure (Amendment No 3) Rules, SI 2010/2653 rule 8 with effect from 29 November 2010.

[2] Word inserted by the Tribunal Procedure (Amendment No 4) Rules, SI 2013/2067 rules 2, 20 with effect from 1 November 2013.

[SCHEDULE A1

PROCEDURE IN QUALITY CONTRACTS SCHEME CASES]

Rule 23

Amendments—[1] Schedule A1inserted by the Tribunal Procedure (Amendment) Rules, SI 2015/1510 arts 2, 7 with effect from 21 August 2015.

[1 This Schedule applies to quality contracts scheme cases.][1]

Amendments—[1] Schedule A1inserted by the Tribunal Procedure (Amendment) Rules, SI 2015/1510 arts 2, 7 with effect from 21 August 2015.

[Notice of appeal

2 The appellant must send or deliver to the Upper Tribunal the notice of appeal together with the following materials —

(*a*) a copy of the notice of the decision being challenged;

(*b*) a copy of any separate written statement of reasons;

(*c*) copies of the most significant documents (or relevant extracts) on which the appellant relies in support of the grounds stated in its notice of appeal, including—

(i) the quality contracts scheme (or relevant extracts); and

(ii) any report of the QCS Board (or relevant extracts); and

(*d*) a list of the materials referred to in sub-paragraphs (*a*) to (*c*) and where such materials may be accessed (e.g. link to internet webpage).][1]

Amendments—[1] Schedule A1inserted by the Tribunal Procedure (Amendment) Rules, SI 2015/1510 arts 2, 7 with effect from 21 August 2015.

[3 The appellant must, at the same time as sending its notice of appeal to the Upper Tribunal in accordance with paragraph 2, send a copy of the notice of appeal and of the additional materials to the respondent.][1]

Amendments—[1] Schedule A1inserted by the Tribunal Procedure (Amendment) Rules, SI 2015/1510 arts 2, 7 with effect from 21 August 2015.

[4 The Upper Tribunal must send a copy of the notice of appeal and a copy of the list referred to in paragraph 2(*d*) to the appropriate national authority.][1]

Amendments—[1] Schedule A1inserted by the Tribunal Procedure (Amendment) Rules, SI 2015/1510 arts 2, 7 with effect from 21 August 2015.

[5 The Upper Tribunal may, upon receipt of the notice of appeal, direct the respondent to—

(*a*) give notice in at least one newspaper circulating in the area to which the scheme relates that a notice of appeal has been received;

(*b*) give written notice to the persons consulted under section 125(3) (notice and consultation requirements) of the Transport Act 2000 and (if the case may be) those not consulted under section 125(3) but who in the opinion of the QCS Board, under section 126D(1)(*b*) (consideration of proposed schemes by boards) of that Act, ought to have been so consulted, that a notice of appeal has been received;

(*c*) make arrangements for a place or website where copies of the notice of appeal and any response or reply and in each case their accompanying documents may be inspected;

(*d*) ensure that each notice provided for in sub-paragraphs (*a*) and (*b*) states—

(i) where copies of the notice of appeal and other documents relating to the proceedings may be inspected; and

(ii) where information about the procedure for applying to be added as a party may be found.][1]

Amendments—[1] Schedule A1inserted by the Tribunal Procedure (Amendment) Rules, SI 2015/1510 arts 2, 7 with effect from 21 August 2015.

[Response to the notice of appeal

6 A respondent must send or deliver to the Upper Tribunal its response to the notice of appeal together with the following materials —

(*a*) a copy of the most significant documents (or relevant extracts) on which the respondent relies in support of the response;

(*b*) a list of those documents.][1]

Amendments—[1] Schedule A1inserted by the Tribunal Procedure (Amendment) Rules, SI 2015/1510 arts 2, 7 with effect from 21 August 2015.

[**7** The respondent must, at the same time as providing its response to the Upper Tribunal in accordance with paragraph 6, provide copies of that response and of those materials to—

(*a*) the appellant; and

(*b*) the appropriate national authority.][1]

Amendments—[1] Schedule A1inserted by the Tribunal Procedure (Amendment) Rules, SI 2015/1510 arts 2, 7 with effect from 21 August 2015.

[8 Any directions given by the Upper Tribunal to the respondent under paragraph 5 are also to be regarded as directions to the respondent to make available for inspection copies of its response and accompanying materials.][1]

Amendments—[1] Schedule A1inserted by the Tribunal Procedure (Amendment) Rules, SI 2015/1510 arts 2, 7 with effect from 21 August 2015.

[Appellant's reply

9 The appellant must send or deliver to the Upper Tribunal its reply (if any) to a response under paragraph 6 together with the following materials—

(*a*) a copy of any additional documents (or relevant extracts) relied on in support of the reply;

(*b*) a list of those documents.][1]

Amendments—[1] Schedule A inserted by the Tribunal Procedure (Amendment) Rules, SI 2015/1510 arts 2, 7 with effect from 21 August 2015.

[10 The appellant must, at the same time as providing its reply to the Upper Tribunal in accordance with paragraph 9, provide a copy of that reply and of those materials to the respondent.][1]

Amendments—[1] Schedule A1inserted by the Tribunal Procedure (Amendment) Rules, SI 2015/1510 arts 2, 7 with effect from 21 August 2015.

[11 The Upper Tribunal must send a copy of the appellant's reply and a copy of the list of documents referred to in paragraph 9(b) to the appropriate national authority.][1]

Amendments—[1] Schedule A1inserted by the Tribunal Procedure (Amendment) Rules, SI 2015/1510 arts 2, 7 with effect from 21 August 2015.

[12 Any directions given by the Upper Tribunal to the respondent under paragraph 5 are also to be regarded as directions to the respondent to make available for inspection copies of the appellant's reply and accompanying materials.][1]

Amendments—[1] Schedule A1inserted by the Tribunal Procedure (Amendment) Rules, SI 2015/1510 arts 2, 7 with effect from 21 August 2015.

[Adding further parties

13 Any person who wishes to be added as a party to the proceedings, and has given notice to the respondent that they received the notice of the appeal in consequence of a direction made under paragraph 5, must apply to the Upper Tribunal in accordance with rule 9 within 1 month of the date on which they received notice of the appeal.][1]

Amendments—[1] Schedule A inserted by the Tribunal Procedure (Amendment) Rules, SI 2015/1510 arts 2, 7 with effect from 21 August 2015.

[14 Any application to be added as a party must state—

(*a*) *the name and address of the person making the application;*

(*b*) *the name and address of the representative (if any) of that person;*

(*c*) *an address where documents for that person may be sent or delivered;*

(*d*) *whether or not copies of the notice of appeal, any response and any reply has been inspected, along with their accompanying documents;*

(*e*) *whether the person making the application supports or opposes the appeal; and*

(*f*) *the grounds relied upon for adding the person as a party.]*[1]

Amendments—[1] Schedule A1inserted by the Tribunal Procedure (Amendment) Rules, SI 2015/1510 arts 2, 7 with effect from 21 August 2015.

[15 The person making the application must provide the following materials with the application—

(*a*) *a copy of the most significant documents (or relevant extracts) on which the person relies in support of the application, if not already listed by a party; and*

(*b*) *a list of the documents referred to in sub-paragraph (a).]*[1]

Amendments—[1] Schedule A1inserted by the Tribunal Procedure (Amendment) Rules, SI 2015/1510 arts 2, 7 with effect from 21 August 2015.

[16 The Upper Tribunal must notify the parties of any application to be joined as a party and send a copy of the list of documents with the notification.][1]

Amendments—[1] Schedule A1inserted by the Tribunal Procedure (Amendment) Rules, SI 2015/1510 arts 2, 7 with effect from 21 August 2015.

[17 The Upper Tribunal may give further directions relating to any application to be added as a party and generally as to the conduct of the case.][1]

Amendments—[1] Schedule A1inserted by the Tribunal Procedure (Amendment) Rules, SI 2015/1510 arts 2, 7 with effect from 21 August 2015.

[SCHEDULE 1

Rule 24(1)

Procedure after the notice of appeal in [road transport cases]

1 This Schedule applies to [road transport cases][1].

Amendments—[1] In Schedule heading, words substituted for words "appeals against decisions of traffic commissioners", and in para 1, words substituted for words "an appeal against the decision of a traffic commissioner", by the Tribunal Procedure (Amendment No 2) Rules, SI 2012/1363 rules 4, 9 with effect from 1 July 2012.

2 The only parties to the appeal are the appellant and any person added as a party under rule 9 [(addition, substitution and removal of parties)][1].

Amendments—[1] Words substituted by the Tribunal Procedure (Upper Tribunal) (Amendment) Rules, SI 2010/747 rules 2, 11 with effect from 6 April 2010.

3 On receipt of a copy of a notice of appeal under rule 23(6)(*b*), the [decision maker][1] must send to the Upper Tribunal a copy (and, on request, further copies) of—

(*a*) a written record of the decision appealed against and reasons for the decision;

(*b*) all documents produced to the [decision maker][1] in connection with the decision;

(*c*) if a public inquiry was held, the transcript of the inquiry or, if no such transcript was produced, the [decision maker's][1] note of the inquiry; and

[(*d*) in an appeal under—

(i) section 50 of the Public Passenger Vehicles Act 1981(a) or section 37 of the Goods Vehicles (Licensing of Operators) Act 1995(b), or

(ii) section 35 of the Goods Vehicles (Licensing of Operators) Act (Northern Ireland) 2010,

a list of the names and addresses of objectors and representors.][1]

Amendments—[1] Words substituted for words "traffic commissioner" and "traffic commissioner's", and para (*d*) substituted, by the Tribunal Procedure (Amendment No 2) Rules, SI 2012/1363 rules 4, 9 with effect from 1 July 2012.

4 On receipt of a list under paragraph 3(*d*) the Upper Tribunal must send a copy of the notice of appeal—

(*a*) where the appellant had applied for, or for the variation of, an operator's licence, to each person who made an objection to the application;

(*b*) where the appellant had made an objection to an application for, or (in the case of a goods vehicle operator's licence) for the variation of, an operator's licence, to the person who made the application and to every other person who made an objection to the application; . . . [1]

(*c*) in an appeal under section 37(5) of the Goods Vehicles (Licensing of Operators) Act 1995, [to][2] each person who made representations under section 12(4) or 19(2) of that Act against the application for, or for the variation of, the operator's licence in question.

[(*d*) in an appeal under section 35(5) of the Goods Vehicles (Licensing of Operators) Act (Northern Ireland) 2010, to each person who made representations under section 11(4) or 18(2) of that Act.][1]

Amendments—[1] In para (*b*) word "and" revoked, and para (*d*) inserted, by the Tribunal Procedure (Amendment No 2) Rules, SI 2012/1363 rules 4, 9 with effect from 1 July 2012.

[2] Word in para (*c*) inserted by the Tribunal Procedure (Amendment) Rules, SI 2013/477 rules 49, 57(*a*) with effect from 1 April 2013. Note that this amendment is repeated in SI 2014/2128 rule 16.

5 The appropriate national authority and any person to whom the Upper Tribunal has sent a copy of the notice of appeal under paragraph 4 may apply for a direction under rule 9(2) adding them as a respondent.

6 An application under paragraph 5 must be sent or delivered to the Upper Tribunal so that it is received within 14 days of the date that the Upper Tribunal sent a copy of the notice of appeal to the person making the application.

7 If a person . . . [1] makes an application in accordance with paragraphs 5 and 6, the Upper Tribunal must give a direction under rule 9(2) adding that person as a respondent.

Amendments—[1] Words "specified in paragraph 8" repealed by the Tribunal Procedure (Amendment) Rules, SI 2013/477 rules 49, 57(*b*) with effect from 1 April 2013.

8 The persons specified for the purposes of paragraph 7 are—

(*a*) *the appropriate national authority;*

(*b*) *an objector who was sent a copy of the notice of appeal under paragraph 4(*a*) or (*b*); and*

(*c*) *a person who made an application and was sent a copy of the notice of appeal under paragraph 4(*b*).*[1]

Amendments—[1] Para 8 repealed by the Tribunal Procedure (Amendment) Rules, SI 2013/477 rules 49, 57(*c*) with effect from 1 April 2013.

9 The Upper Tribunal must notify each other party of any application under paragraph 3 and the Upper Tribunal's decision in respect of each such application.

10 Any party may make a request to the Upper Tribunal for copies of specified documents provided by the [decision maker][1] under paragraph 3.

Amendments—[1] Words substituted for words "traffic commissioner", by the Tribunal Procedure (Amendment No 2) Rules, SI 2012/1363 rules 4, 9 with effect from 1 July 2012.

11 On receiving a request under paragraph 9 the Upper Tribunal—

(*a*) must provide the requested copies unless it considers the request unreasonable; and

(*b*) if it considers the request unreasonable, give details of why it considers the request unreasonable.][1]

Amendments—[1] Schedule inserted by the Tribunal Procedure (Amendment No 2) Rules, SI 2009/1975 rules 7, 22 with effect from 1 September 2009.

[SCHEDULE 2

ADDITIONAL PROCEDURE IN NATIONAL SECURITY CERTIFICATE CASES

Rule 26A(4)

1 This Schedule applies only to national security certificate appeals.

2 Following the transfer of the appeal from the First-tier Tribunal, the Upper Tribunal must provide a copy of the notice of appeal to the respondent, the relevant Minister and the Information Commissioner.

3 The relevant Minister must send or deliver to the Upper Tribunal a copy of the certificate to which the appeal relates, and a response to the notice of appeal, not later than 42 days after the date on which the relevant Minister received a copy of the notice of appeal.

VAT SIs

4 In an appeal under section 28(4) of the Data Protection Act 1998 or section 60(1) of the Freedom of Information Act 2000 (including that subsection as applied and modified by regulation 18 of the Environmental Information Regulations 2004), the relevant Minister's response must state whether the relevant Minister intends to oppose the appeal and, if so set out—

(*a*) a summary of the circumstances relating to the issue of the certificate;

(*b*) the reason for the issue of the certificate;

(*c*) the grounds on which the relevant Minister relies in opposing the appeal; and

(*d*) a statement of the evidence on which the relevant Minister relies in support of those grounds.

5 In an appeal under section 28(6) of the Data Protection Act 1998 or section 60(4) of the Freedom of Information Act 2000 (including that subsection as applied and modified by regulation 18 of the Environmental Information Regulations 2004), the relevant Minister's response must state whether the relevant Minister intends to make representations in relation to the appeal and, if so set out—

(*a*) the extent to which the relevant Minister intends to support or oppose the appeal;

(*b*) the grounds on which the relevant Minister relies in supporting or opposing the appeal; and

(*c*) a statement of the evidence on which the relevant Minister relies in support of those grounds.

6 The Upper Tribunal must—

(*a*) subject to paragraph 11, provide the relevant Minister's response and any other response to the appellant, the Information Commissioner and any respondent; and

(*b*) send a copy of any other response to the relevant Minister.

7 On grounds of the need to ensure that information is not disclosed contrary to the interests of national security, the relevant Minster may—

(*a*) object to the disclosure of the relevant Minister's response to the appellant, the Information Commissioner or any respondent, by sending a notice to the Upper Tribunal with the response; or

(*b*) object to the disclosure of any other response to the Information Commissioner or any respondent, by sending a notice to the Upper Tribunal within 42 days of the date on which the relevant Minister received a copy of the response.

8 A notice under paragraph 7 must—

(*a*) state the reason for the objection; and

(*b*) in the case of a notice under paragraph 7(*a*) and to the extent that it is possible to do so, be accompanied by a version of the relevant Minister's response in a form that can be shown to the appellant, the Commissioner or, as the case may be, a respondent.

9 Before the Upper Tribunal gives a direction, issues a summons or citation, or produces or publishes a written record of, or reasons for, a decision—

(*a*) the Upper Tribunal must notify the relevant Minister of the proposed action; and

(*b*) if the relevant Minister considers that the proposal would cause information that is or would be exempt by virtue of a provision in Part 2 of the Freedom of Information Act 2000 to be disclosed, the relevant Minister may object to the proposal by sending a notice to the Upper Tribunal [so that the Upper Tribunal receives the notice within 14 days of the date that the Minister received notice of the proposal][1].

Amendments—[1] Words substituted by the Tribunal Procedure (Upper Tribunal) (Amendment) Rules, SI 2010/747 rules 2, 12 with effect from 6 April 2010.

10 When deciding whether to uphold an objection made by the relevant Minister—

(*a*) any hearing must take place in the absence of the parties;

(*b*) if the Upper Tribunal is minded to overrule the relevant Minister's objection, or to require the relevant Minister to provide a version of the relevant Minister's response in a form other than one provided under paragraph 8(*b*) above, the Upper Tribunal must invite the relevant Minister to make representations; and

(*c*) if the Upper Tribunal overrules an objection in relation to the disclosure of a response, the [Upper][1] Tribunal must not disclose, or require the relevant Minister to disclose, any material the subject of the objection unless the relevant Minister relies upon that material in opposing the appeal.

Amendments—[1] Word in para (*c*) inserted by the Tribunal Procedure (Amendment No 4) Rules, SI 2013/2067 rules 2, 21(*a*) with effect from 1 November 2013.

11 Where the relevant Minister may object to the disclosure of a response or proposed action by the Upper Tribunal, the Upper Tribunal may not proceed with that disclosure or that proposed action unless—

(*a*) the time for the relevant Minister to object has expired; and (*b*) the relevant Minister has not objected, or the [Upper][2] Tribunal has overruled the relevant Minister's objection and, in the case of the disclosure of a response, may proceed with the disclosure under paragraph 10(*c*).][1]

Amendments—[1] Schedule 2 inserted by the Tribunal Procedure (Amendment) Rules, SI 2010/43, rules 5, 14, with effect from 18 January 2010.

[2] Word in para (*b*) inserted by the Tribunal Procedure (Amendment No 4) Rules, SI 2013/2067 rules 2, 21(*b*) with effect from 1 November 2013.

[SCHEDULE 3

PROCEDURE IN FINANCIAL SERVICES CASES [AND WHOLESALE ENERGY CASES]

Rule 26B

Amendments—Words in heading inserted by the Tribunal Procedure (Amendment) Rules, SI 2014/514 rules 2, 12 with effect from 6 April 2014.

Interpretation

1 In this Schedule—

["further material" means—

(*a*) in a single regulator case, documents which—

(i) were considered by the respondent in reaching or maintaining the decision to give the notice in respect of which the reference has been made; or

(ii) were obtained by the respondent in connection with the matter to which that notice relates (whether they were obtained before or after giving the notice) but which were not considered by it in reaching or maintaining that decision;

but does not include documents on which the respondent relies in support of the referred action;

(*b*) in a multiple regulator case—

(i) in relation to a respondent who is the primary regulator, documents which—

(*aa*) were considered by that regulator in reaching or maintaining its decision to give the notice in respect of which the reference has been made; or

(*bb*) were obtained by that regulator in connection with the matter to which that notice relates (whether they were obtained before or after the notice was given) but which were not considered by that regulator in reaching or maintaining its decision;

(ii) in relation to a respondent who is the secondary regulator, documents which—

(*aa*) were considered by that regulator in reaching or maintaining its decision to take the secondary regulator action in relation to the notice in respect of which the reference has been made; or

(*bb*) were obtained by that regulator in connection with the matter to which that notice relates (whether they were obtained before or after the notice was given) but which were not considered by that regulator in reaching or maintaining its decision;

but does not include documents on which either the primary regulator or the secondary regulator relies;][2]

["multiple regulator case" means a case where—

(*a*) any of the Financial Conduct Authority, the Prudential Regulation Authority or the Bank of England has given the notice in respect of which the reference has been made; and

(*b*) such notice stated that another of those regulators had decided to take one of the following actions—

(i) to refuse a consent where such consent is required under the 2000 Act;

(ii) to give a conditional consent under the 2000 Act; or

(iii) to direct another regulator to take an action or not to take an action under the 2000 Act;][2]

["primary regulator" means, in a multiple regulator case, the regulator giving the notice;][2]

"reference notice" means the written notice required in making a reference in a financial services case [or a wholesale energy case][3];

["referred action" means—

(*a*) in a single regulator case, the act (or proposed act) on the part of the respondent that gave rise to the reference; and

(*b*) in a multiple regulator case, the act (or proposed act) on the part of the primary regulator that gave rise to the reference;][2]

["secondary regulator action" means an action taken by a secondary regulator, as stated in the notice given by the primary regulator;][2]

["secondary regulator" means, in a multiple regulator case, a regulator specified in the notice other than the primary regulator;][2]

["single regulator case" means a case that is not a multiple regulator case;][2]

"the 2000 Act" means the Financial Services and Markets Act 2000[;][1]

"the 2013 Regulations" means the Electricity and Gas (Market Integrity and Transparency) (Enforcement etc.) Regulations 2013;

"the 2013 (NI) Regulations" means the Electricity and Gas (Market Integrity and Transparency) (Enforcement etc.) Regulations (Northern Ireland) 2013.][13]

Amendments—[1] Schedule 3 inserted by the Tribunal Procedure (Upper Tribunal) (Amendment) Rules, SI 2010/747 rules 2, 13 with effect from 6 April 2010.

[2] Definitions inserted, and definitions of "further material" and "referred action" substituted, by the Tribunal Procedure (Amendment No 2) Rules, SI 2013/606 rule 2(1), (4) with effect from 1 April 2013.

[3] Words inserted in definition of "reference notice", and definitions of "the 2013 Regulations" and "the 2013 (NI) Regulations" inserted by the Tribunal Procedure (Amendment) Rules, SI 2014/514 rules 2, 13(*a*), (*b*) with effect from 6 April 2014.

Reference notice

[2 (1) A reference notice must be signed by or on behalf of the applicant and sent or delivered by the applicant to the Upper Tribunal.

(2) A reference notice must be received by the Upper Tribunal no later than 28 days after notice was given of the decision in respect of which the reference is made.

(3) The reference notice must state—

(*a*) the name and address of the applicant;

(*b*) the name and address of the applicant's representative (if any);

(*c*) if no representative is named under sub-paragraph (*b*), an address where documents for the applicant may be sent or delivered; and

(*d*) the issues that the applicant wishes the Upper Tribunal to consider.

(4) The applicant must send or deliver to the Upper Tribunal with the reference notice a copy of the notice of the decision in respect of which the reference has been made.

[(5) At the same time the applicant must send a copy of the reference notice—

(*a*) in a single regulator case, to the respondent; and

(*b*) in a multiple regulator case, to each of the primary and secondary regulators.][2]][1]

Amendments—[1] Schedule 3 inserted by the Tribunal Procedure (Upper Tribunal) (Amendment) Rules, SI 2010/747 rules 2, 13 with effect from 6 April 2010.

[2] Sub-para (5) substituted by the Tribunal Procedure (Amendment No 2) Rules, SI 2013/606 rule 2(1), (5) with effect from 1 April 2013.

Register of references and decisions

[3 (1) The Upper Tribunal must keep a register of references and decisions in financial services cases [and wholesale energy cases][3].

(2) The register must be open to inspection by any person without charge and at all reasonable hours.

[(3) The Upper Tribunal may direct that the register is not to include particulars of a reference if it is satisfied that it is necessary to do so having regard [in particular to—

(*a*) any unfairness to the applicant or, except as regards a reference in respect of a decision of the Prudential Regulation Authority, any prejudice to the interests of consumers that might otherwise result;

(*b*) as regards a reference in respect of a decision of the Financial Conduct Authority, any detriment to the stability of the UK financial system;

(*c*) as regards a reference in respect of a decision of the Prudential Regulation Authority, any prejudice to the safety and soundness of persons authorised by it, or where section 2C of the 2000 Act applies, any prejudice to securing the appropriate degree of protection for policy holders; or

(*d*) as regards a reference under the 2013 Regulations or the 2013 (NI) Regulations any detriment to the stability of the wholesale energy market as defined in those Regulations.][3]

(4) Upon receiving a reference notice, the Upper Tribunal must—

(*a*) subject to any direction given under sub-paragraph (3), enter particulars of the reference in the register; and

(*b*) notify the parties either that it has done so or that it will not include particulars in the register, as the case may be.

[(5) In a multiple regulator case, notification under sub-paragraph (4)(*b*) must be given to each of the primary and secondary regulators.][2]][1]

Amendments—[1] Schedule 3 inserted by the Tribunal Procedure (Upper Tribunal) (Amendment) Rules, SI 2010/747 rules 2, 13 with effect from 6 April 2010.

[2] Sub-para (5) inserted by the Tribunal Procedure (Amendment No 2) Rules, SI 2013/606 rule 2(1), (6) with effect from 1 April 2013.

[3] Words in sub-para (1) inserted, and in sub-para (3), words substituted by the Tribunal Procedure (Amendment) Rules, SI 2014/514 rules 2, 13(*c*) with effect from 6 April 2014.

[Respondent's statement of case in a single regulator case]

[4 (1) The respondent [in a single regulator case][2] must send or deliver a written statement ("a statement of case") in support of the referred action so that it is received by the Upper Tribunal no later than 28 days after the day on which the respondent received from the Upper Tribunal the notification required by paragraph 3(4)(*b*).

(2) The statement of case must—

(*a*) identify the statutory provisions providing for the referred action;

(*b*) state the reasons for the referred action; and

(*c*) set out all the matters and facts upon which the respondent relies to support the referred action.

(3) The respondent must provide with the statement of case a list of—

(*a*) any documents on which the respondent relies in support of the referred action; and

(*b*) any further material which in the opinion of the respondent might undermine the decision to take that action.

(4) At the same time as it sends or delivers the statement of case, the respondent must send to the applicant a copy of the statement of case and of the list referred to in sub-paragraph (3).][1]

Amendments—[1] Schedule 3 inserted by the Tribunal Procedure (Upper Tribunal) (Amendment) Rules, SI 2010/747 rules 2, 13 with effect from 6 April 2010.

[2] Heading substituted and words in sub-para (1) inserted, by the Tribunal Procedure (Amendment No 2) Rules, SI 2013/606 rule 2(1), (7) with effect from 1 April 2013.

Respondents' statements of case in a multiple regulator case

[4A (1) This paragraph applies in a multiple regulator case.

(2) The primary regulator must send or deliver either—

(*a*) a written statement (a "statement of case") in support of the referred action; or

(*b*) a written notification that it does not itself advance a case in support of the referred action,

so that it is received by the Upper Tribunal no later than 28 days after the day on which the primary regulator received from the Upper Tribunal the notification required by paragraph 3(4)(*b*).

(3) A primary regulator providing a written notification under sub-paragraph (2)(*b*) must send or deliver a copy to the secondary regulator and the applicant and upon so doing—

(*a*) the primary regulator shall not be required to take further steps in the proceedings unless the Upper Tribunal gives a direction to the contrary under rule 6; and

(*b*) the respondent shall be the secondary regulator unless the Upper Tribunal orders otherwise.

(4) The secondary regulator must send or deliver a written statement ("a statement of case") in support of its decision to take the secondary regulator action so that it is received by the Upper Tribunal no later than 28 days after the day on which the secondary regulator received from the Upper Tribunal the notification required by paragraph 3(4)(*b*).

(5) A statement of case must—

(*a*) identify the statutory provisions providing for the referred action;

(*b*) state the reasons in support for the referred action; and

(*c*) set out all the matters and facts upon which the regulator relies to support the referred action.

(6) A regulator must provide with the statement of case a list of—

(*a*) all documents on which it relies in support of the referred action;

(*b*) any further material which, in the opinion of the regulator, might undermine its decision to—

(i) in the case of a primary regulator; take the referred action; and

(ii) in the case of a secondary regulator; take the secondary regulator action.

(7) The primary regulator and the secondary regulator must send to the applicant and the other regulator a copy of any statement of case required by sub-paragraphs (2) and (4) above and of the list referred to in sub-paragraph (6).][1]

Amendments—[1] Para 4A inserted by the Tribunal Procedure (Amendment No 2) Rules, SI 2013/606 rule 2(1), (8) with effect from 1 April 2013.

Applicant's reply

[5—(1) The applicant must send or deliver a written reply so that it is received by the Upper Tribunal no later than 28 days after—

[(*a*) in a single regulator case, on the date on which the applicant received a copy of the statement of case;

(*aa*) in a multiple regulator case, on the first date on which the applicant was in receipt of all the statements and, where relevant, notifications required under paragraphs 4A(2) and 4A(4); or][2]

(*b*) if [a respondent][2] amends its statement of case, the date on which the applicant received a copy of the amended statement of case.

(2) The reply must—

(*a*) state the grounds on which the applicant relies in the reference;

(*b*) identify all matters contained in [the respondent's statement of case (or, where applicable, respondents' statements of case)][2] which are disputed by the applicant; . . . [2]

(*c*) state the applicant's reasons for disputing them.

(3) The applicant must send with the reply a list of all the documents on which the applicant relies in support of his case.

(4) At the same time the applicant must send to [all other parties][2] a copy of the reply and of the list referred to in sub-paragraph (3).

[(5) Where the primary regulator has provided a written notification under paragraph 4A(2)(*b*), if the applicant wishes the Tribunal to direct that further steps in the proceedings be taken by the primary regulator, an application must be made at the time of sending the reply.][2]

Amendments—[1] Schedule 3 inserted by the Tribunal Procedure (Upper Tribunal) (Amendment) Rules, SI 2010/747 rules 2, 13 with effect from 6 April 2010.

[2] In sub-para (1), paras (*a*), (*aa*) substituted for previous para (*a*), and words in para (*b*) substituted; in sub-para (2)(*b*) words substituted and word "and" revoked; in sub-para (4) words substituted; and sub-para (5) inserted; by the Tribunal Procedure (Amendment No 2) Rules, SI 2013/606 rule 2(1), (9) with effect from 1 April 2013.

Secondary disclosure by [a respondent]

[6—(1) After the applicant's reply has been sent or delivered, if there is any further material which might reasonably be expected to assist the applicant's case as disclosed by the applicant's reply and which is not listed in the list [(or lists)][2] provided in accordance with paragraph 4(3) [(or paragraph 4A(6) where applicable)][2], the respondent [(or the respondents)][2] must send or deliver to the Upper Tribunal a list [(or lists)][2] of such further material.

(2) Any list required to be sent or delivered by sub-paragraph (1) must be sent or delivered so that it is received no later than 14 days after the day on which the respondent [in question][2] received the applicant's reply.

(3) At the same time as it sends or delivers any list required by sub-paragraph (1) [a respondent must send a copy to the applicant (and where applicable the other parties)][2].][1]

Amendments—[1] Schedule 3 inserted by the Tribunal Procedure (Upper Tribunal) (Amendment) Rules, SI 2010/747 rules 2, 13 with effect from 6 April 2010.

[2] Words in heading substituted, words in sub-paras (1), (2) inserted, and words in sub-para (3) substituted, by the Tribunal Procedure (Amendment No 2) Rules, SI 2013/606 rule 2(1), (10) with effect from 1 April 2013.

Exceptions to disclosure

[7—(1) A list provided in accordance with paragraph 4(3)[, 4A(6)][2] or 6(1) need not include any document that relates to a case involving a person other than the applicant which was taken into account by the respondent [providing the list][2] in the applicant's case only for the purposes of comparison with other cases.

(2) A list provided in accordance with paragraph 4(3)[, 4A(6)][2], 5(3) or 6(1) need not include any document that is material the disclosure of which for the purposes of or in connection with any legal proceedings is prohibited by section 17 of the Regulation of Investigatory Powers Act 2000.

(3) A list provided in accordance with paragraph 4(3)[, 4A(6)][2], 5(3) or 6(1) need not include any document in respect of which an application has been or is being made under sub-paragraph (4).

(4) A party may apply to the Upper Tribunal (without giving notice to any other party) for a direction authorising the party making the application not to include in the list required by paragraph 4(3)[, 4A(6)][2], 5(3) or 6(1) a document on the ground that disclosure of the document—

(*a*) would not be in the public interest; or

(*b*) would not be fair, having regard to—

(i) the likely significance of the document to the applicant in relation to the matter referred to the Upper Tribunal; and

(ii) the potential prejudice to the commercial interests of a person other than the applicant which would be caused by disclosure of the document.

(5) For the purpose of deciding an application by a party under sub-paragraph (4), the Upper Tribunal may—

(*a*) require the document to be produced to the Upper Tribunal together with a statement of the reasons why its inclusion in the list would—

(i) in the case of an application under sub-paragraph (4)(*a*), not be in the public interest; or

(ii) in the case of an application under sub-paragraph (4)(*b*), not be fair; and

(*b*) invite any other party to make representations.

(6) If the Upper Tribunal refuses an application under sub-paragraph (4), it must direct the party—

(*a*) to revise its list so as to include the document; and

(*b*) to send or deliver a copy of the revised list to the Upper Tribunal and to any other party.

[(7) A party ("P") who has sent or delivered a list under paragraph 4(3), 4A(6), 5(3) or 6(1) must, upon the request of another party, provide that other party with a copy of any document which P has which is specified in the list, or make it available for inspection or copying, and if P does not have it, tell the other party where to the best of P's knowledge and belief it may be found.][2]

(8) Sub-paragraph (7) does not apply to any document that is a protected item.

(9) In this paragraph "protected item" has the meaning provided by section 413 of the 2000 Act, section 311(2) of the Pensions Act 2004 or article 283(2) of the Pensions (Northern Ireland) Order 2005 [or regulation 52(2) of the 2013 Regulations or regulation 51(2) of the 2013 (NI) Regulations][3].][1]

Amendments—[1] Schedule 3 inserted by the Tribunal Procedure (Upper Tribunal) (Amendment) Rules, SI 2010/747 rules 2, 13 with effect from 6 April 2010.

[2] Words in sub-paras (1)–(4) inserted, and sub-para (7) substituted, by the Tribunal Procedure (Amendment No 2) Rules, SI 2013/606 rule 2(1), (11) with effect from 1 April 2013.

[3] Words in sub-para (9) inserted by the Tribunal Procedure (Amendment) Rules, SI 2014/514 rules 2, 13(*d*) with effect from 6 April 2014.

Subsequent notices in relation to the referred action

[8—Where, after a reference notice has been sent or delivered, [a respondent][2] gives the applicant any further, amended or supplementary notice in relation to the referred action, [that respondent][2] must without delay send or deliver a copy of that notice to the Upper Tribunal.][1]

Amendments—[1] Schedule 3 inserted by the Tribunal Procedure (Upper Tribunal) (Amendment) Rules, SI 2010/747 rules 2, 13 with effect from 6 April 2010.

[2] Words substituted by the Tribunal Procedure (Amendment No 2) Rules, SI 2013/606 rule 2(1), (12) with effect from 1 April 2013.

References by third parties

[9—(1) In the case of any reference made by an applicant under section 393 of the 2000 Act[, regulation 40 of the 2013 Regulations or regulation 40 of the 2013 (NI) Regulations][3] (third party rights) these rules apply subject to the modifications set out in this paragraph.

(2) In this paragraph—

(*a*) if the reference was made under section 393(9) of the 2000 Act[, regulation 40(9) of the 2013 Regulations or regulation 40(9) of the 2013 (NI) Regulations][3] (reference to the Upper Tribunal by a third party to whom a decision notice was copied), the notice of the decision in respect of which the reference has been made is the decision notice which was copied to the applicant by the respondent [that gave the notice][2]; and

(*b*) if the reference was made under section 393(11) of the 2000 Act[, regulation 40(11) of the 2013 Regulations or regulation 40(11) of the 2013 (NI) Regulations][3] (reference to the Upper Tribunal by a third party who alleges that they were not given a copy of a decision notice), the notice of the decision in respect of which the reference has been made is the decision notice which the applicant alleges was not copied to them.

(3) If the reference was made under section 393(11) of the 2000 Act[, regulation 40(11) of the 2013 Regulations or regulation 40(11) of the 2013 (NI) Regulations][3], paragraph 2(4) does not apply.

[(4) The duties of a respondent to—

(*a*) set out information under paragraphs 4(2), 4A(2), 4A(4) or 4A(5); or

(*b*) list material under paragraphs 4(3), 4A(6) or 6(1);

apply only to information or material which relate to the matters referred to the Upper Tribunal in accordance with section 393(9) or (as the case may be) section 393(11) of the 2000 Act[, regulation 40(9) or, as the case may be, regulation 40(11) of the 2013 Regulations, or regulation 40(9) or, as the case may be, regulation 40(11) of the 2013 (NI) Regulations][3].][2]][1]

Amendments—[1] Schedule 3 inserted by the Tribunal Procedure (Upper Tribunal) (Amendment) Rules, SI 2010/747 rules 2, 13 with effect from 6 April 2010.

[2] Words in sub-para (2)(*a*) inserted, and sub-para (4) substituted, by the Tribunal Procedure (Amendment No 2) Rules, SI 2013/606 rule 2(1), (13) with effect from 1 April 2013.

[3] Words inserted by the Tribunal Procedure (Amendment) Rules, SI 2014/514 rules 2, 13(*e*) with effect from 6 April 2014.

2008/2834

APPEALS FROM THE UPPER TRIBUNAL TO THE COURT OF APPEAL ORDER 2008

Made . . . . *29 October 2008*

Coming into force in accordance with . . . . *article 1*

The Lord Chancellor makes the following Order in exercise of the power conferred by section 13(6) of the Tribunals, Courts and Enforcement Act 2007.

A draft of this Order was laid before Parliament and approved by a resolution of each House of Parliament in accordance with section 49(5) of that Act.

1 This Order may be cited as the Appeals from the Upper Tribunal to the Court of Appeal Order 2008 and shall come into force on 3rd November 2008.

2 Permission to appeal to the Court of Appeal in England and Wales or leave to appeal to the Court of Appeal in Northern Ireland shall not be granted unless the Upper Tribunal or, where the Upper Tribunal refuses permission, the relevant appellate court, considers that—

(*a*) the proposed appeal would raise some important point of principle or practice; or

(*b*) there is some other compelling reason for the relevant appellate court to hear the appeal.

2008/2835

FIRST-TIER TRIBUNAL AND UPPER TRIBUNAL (COMPOSITION OF TRIBUNAL) ORDER 2008

Made . . . . *29 October 2008*

Coming into force . . . . *3 November 2008*

The Lord Chancellor makes the following Order in exercise of the powers conferred by section 145(1) of, and paragraph 15 of Schedule 4 to, the Tribunals, Courts and Enforcement Act 2007.

In accordance with paragraph 15(8) of that Act the Lord Chancellor has consulted the Senior President of Tribunals.

In accordance with section 49(5) of that Act a draft of this instrument was laid before Parliament and approved by a resolution of each House of Parliament.

1 Citation and commencement

This Order may be cited as the First-tier Tribunal and Upper Tribunal (Composition of Tribunal) Order 2008 and comes into force on 3rd November 2008.

2 Number of members of the First-tier Tribunal

(1) The number of members of the tribunal who are to decide any matter that falls to be decided by the First-tier Tribunal must be determined by the Senior President of Tribunals in accordance with paragraph (2).

(2) The Senior President of Tribunals must have regard to—

(*a*) where the matter which falls to be decided by the tribunal fell to a tribunal in a list in Schedule 6 to the Tribunals, Courts and Enforcement Act 2007 before its functions were transferred by order under section 30(1) of that Act, any provision made by or under any enactment for determining the number of members of that tribunal; and

(*b*) the need for members of tribunals to have particular expertise, skills or knowledge.

3 Number of members of the Upper Tribunal

(1) The number of members of the tribunal who are to decide any matter that falls to be decided by the Upper Tribunal is one unless determined otherwise under paragraph (2).

(2) The tribunal may consist of two or three members if the Senior President of Tribunals so determines.

4 Tribunal consisting of single member

(1) Where a matter is to be decided by a single member of a tribunal, it must be decided by a judge of the tribunal unless paragraph (2) applies.

(2) The matter may be decided by one of the other members of the tribunal if the Senior President of Tribunals so determines.

5 Tribunal consisting of two or more members

The following articles apply where a matter is to be decided by two or more members of a tribunal.

6 The number of members who are to be judges of the tribunal and the number of members who are to be other members of the tribunal must be determined by the Senior President of Tribunals.

7 The Senior President of Tribunals must select one of the members (the "presiding member") to chair the tribunal.

8 If the decision of the tribunal is not unanimous, the decision of the majority is the decision of the tribunal; and the presiding member has a casting vote if the votes are equally divided.

2009/56

TRANSFER OF TRIBUNAL FUNCTIONS AND REVENUE AND CUSTOMS APPEALS ORDER 2009

Made . . . . *18th January 2009*
Coming into force . . . . *1st April 2009*

The Lord Chancellor and the Treasury make the following Order in exercise of the powers conferred by sections 30(1) and (4), 31(1), (2) and (9) and 38 of, and paragraph 30 of Schedule 5 to, the Tribunals, Courts and Enforcement Act 2007 and section 124(1) to (7) of the Finance Act 2008.

A draft of this Order was laid before Parliament and approved by resolution of each House of Parliament in accordance with section 49(5) of the Tribunals, Courts and Enforcement Act 2007 and section 124(9) of the Finance Act 2008.

1 Citation and commencement

(1) This Order may be cited as the Transfer of Tribunal Functions and Revenue and Customs Appeals Order 2009.
(2) This Order comes into force on 1st April 2009.

2 The existing tribunals

In this Order "existing tribunals" means—

(*a*) the Commissioners for the general purposes of the income tax established under section 2 of the Taxes Management Act 1970;
(*b*) the Commissioners for the special purposes of the Income Tax Acts established under section 4 of the Taxes Management Act 1970;
(*c*) the VAT and duties tribunals established under Schedule 12 to the Value Added Tax Act 1994;
(*d*) the tribunal established under section 706 of the Income and Corporation Taxes Act 1988; and
(*e*) the tribunal established under section 704 of the Income Tax Act 2007.

3 Transfer of functions, consequential and other amendments

(1) Schedule 1 contains amendments to primary legislation which—
(*a*) transfer functions of existing tribunals, and
(*b*) make consequential and other provision (including provision about reviews of decisions by Her Majesty's Revenue and Customs).
(2) Schedule 2 contains amendments to secondary legislation which—
(*a*) transfer functions of existing tribunals, and
(*b*) make consequential and other provision (including provision about reviews of decisions by Her Majesty's Revenue and Customs).

4 Abolition of existing tribunals

The existing tribunals (apart from the Commissioners for the general purposes of the income tax) are abolished.

5 Transfer of members of existing tribunals

A person who, immediately before this Order comes into force, holds an office listed in column 1 of any of the following tables is to hold the office or offices listed in the corresponding entry in column 2 of that table—

The Special Commissioners	
1 Office held	2 Office or offices to be held
Commissioner for the special purposes of the Income Tax Acts appointed under section 4 of the Taxes Management Act 1970	Transferred-in judge of the Upper Tribunal

VAT SIs

Deputy Commissioner for the special purposes of the Income Tax Acts appointed under section 4A of the Taxes Management Act 1970	Transferred-in judge of the First-tier Tribunal and deputy judge of the Upper Tribunal

VAT and duties tribunals	
1 Office held	*2 Office or offices to be held*
President of VAT and duties tribunals appointed under paragraph 2 of Schedule 12 to the Value Added Tax Act 1994	Transferred-in judge of the Upper Tribunal
Person appointed to a panel of chairmen of a VAT and duties tribunal under paragraph 7 of Schedule 12 to the Value Added Tax Act 1994	Transferred-in judge of the First-tier Tribunal and deputy judge of the Upper Tribunal
Person appointed to a panel of other members of a VAT and duties tribunal under paragraph 7 of Schedule 12 to the Value Added Tax Act 1994	Transferred-in other member of the First-tier Tribunal

Tribunal established under section 706 ICTA 1988	
1 Office held	*2 Office or offices to be held*
Chairman of the tribunal appointed under section 706(1)(*a*) of the Income and Corporation Taxes Act 1988	Transferred-in judge of the Upper Tribunal
Other member of the tribunal appointed under section 706(1)(*b*) of the Income and Corporation Taxes Act 1988	Transferred-in other member of the First-tier Tribunal

Tribunal established under section 704 ITA 2007	
1 Office held	*2 Office or offices to be held*
Chairman of the tribunal appointed under section 704(1)(*a*) of the Income Taxes Act 2007	Transferred-in judge of the Upper Tribunal
Other member of the tribunal appointed under section 704(1)(*b*) of the Income Taxes Act 2007	Transferred-in other member of the First-tier Tribunal

6 Transitionals and savings

Schedule 3 contains—

(*a*) transitional provision, and

(*b*) saving provision.

SCHEDULE 1

CONSEQUENTIAL AMENDMENTS AND SUPPLEMENTAL PROVISIONS—PRIMARY LEGISLATION

Article 3

Note—The amendments made by this Schedule are already in force and are therefore not reproduced.

SCHEDULE 2

CONSEQUENTIAL AMENDMENTS AND SUPPLEMENTAL PROVISIONS—SECONDARY LEGISLATION

Article 3

Note—The amendments made by this Schedule are already in force and are therefore not reproduced.

SCHEDULE 3

TRANSITIONAL AND SAVING PROVISIONS

Article 6

General

1—(1) In this Schedule—

"commencement date" means the date on which this Order comes into force;

"enactment" includes subordinate legislation (within the meaning of the Interpretation Act 1978);

"HMRC" means Her Majesty's Revenue and Customs;

"tribunal" means the First-tier Tribunal or, where determined by or under Tribunal Procedure Rules, the Upper Tribunal.

(2) For the purposes of this Schedule there are "current proceedings" if, before the commencement date—

(*a*) any party has served notice on an existing tribunal for the purpose of beginning proceedings before the existing tribunal, and

(*b*) the existing tribunal has not concluded proceedings arising by virtue of that notice.

Simon's Tax Cases—*ATEC Associates Ltd v R&C Comrs* [2010] STC 1882.

Former VAT and duties tribunals matters (except VAT)

2—(1) This paragraph applies in relation to the following decisions—

(*a*) any relevant decision which HMRC notify before the commencement date, unless—

(i) the period to require a review of the decision has expired before that date, or

(ii) a review of the decision has been required before that date;

(*b*) any relevant review decision which HMRC notify before the commencement date unless—

(i) the period to serve notice of appeal against the decision on an existing tribunal has expired before that date, or

(ii) notice of appeal against the decision has been served on an existing tribunal before that date.

(2) On and after the commencement date, the following enactments continue to apply (subject to sub-paragraphs (3) and (4)) as they applied immediately before that date—

(*a*) the review and appeal provisions,

(*b*) rule 4(2) of the Value Added Tax Tribunals Rules 1986, and

(*c*) any other enactments that apply in relation to relevant decisions or relevant review decisions.

(3) Those enactments apply subject to Tribunal Procedure Rules.

(4) Any reference to an existing tribunal is to be substituted with a reference to the tribunal.

(5) Any time period which has started to run before the commencement date and has not expired will continue to apply.

(6) In this paragraph—

"relevant decision" means a decision to which a review and appeal provision applies (apart from a relevant review decision);

"relevant review decision" means a decision—

(*a*) that is made on a review of a relevant decision, and

(*b*) to which a review and appeal provision applies,

and includes a relevant decision that is treated as having been confirmed under a review and appeal provision.

"review and appeal provisions" means—

(*a*) sections 14 to 16 of the Finance Act 1994,

(*b*) sections 59 and 60 of the Finance Act 1994,

(*c*) sections 54 to 56 of the Finance Act 1996,

(*d*) paragraphs 121 to 123 of Schedule 6 to the Finance Act 2000,

(*e*) sections 40 to 42 of the Finance Act 2001,

(*f*) sections 33 to 37 of the Finance Act 2003,

(*g*) regulations 9 to 13 of the Export (Penalty) Regulations 2003,

(*h*) regulations 4 to 7 of the Control of Cash (Penalties) Regulations 2007,

(*i*) regulations 43 and 44 of the Money Laundering Regulations 2007, and

(*j*) regulations 12 and 13 of the Transfer of Funds (Information on the Payer) Regulations 2007.

3—(1) This paragraph applies in relation to a relevant decision if, before the commencement date—

VAT SIs

(*a*) HMRC have notified the relevant decision, and

(*b*) a review of the decision has begun under a review and appeal provision (whether or not a relevant review decision has been notified).

(2) On and after the commencement date the following enactments continue to apply (subject to sub-paragraphs (3) and (4)), as they applied immediately before that date—

(*a*) the review and appeal provisions,

(*b*) rule 4(2) of the VAT Tribunals Rules 1986, and

(*c*) any other enactments that apply in relation to relevant decisions or relevant review decisions.

(3) Those enactments apply subject to Tribunal Procedure Rules.

(4) Any reference to an existing tribunal is to be substituted with a reference to the tribunal.

(5) Any time period which has started to run before the commencement date and has not expired will continue to apply.

(6) On and after the commencement date, no notification offering or requiring a review may be given under any review and appeal provision or any other enactments that are applicable to the decision as they apply after that date.

(7) In this paragraph "review and appeal provision", "relevant decision" and "relevant review decision" have the same meaning as in paragraph 2.

Former VAT and duties tribunals matters: VAT

4—(1) This paragraph applies if, before the commencement date—

(*a*) HMRC have notified a decision relating to a matter to which section 83 of the Value Added Tax Act 1994 applies, and

(*b*) no party has served notice on a VAT and duties tribunal for the purpose of beginning proceedings before such a tribunal in relation to that decision.

(2) On and after the commencement date, the following enactments continue to apply (subject to sub-paragraphs (3) and (4)) as they applied immediately before that date—

(*a*) the Value Added Tax Act 1994,

(*b*) rule 4(2) of the VAT Tribunals Rules 1986, and

(*c*) any other enactments that are applicable to the decision.

(3) Those enactments apply subject to Tribunal Procedure Rules.

(4) Any reference to an existing tribunal is to be substituted with a reference to the tribunal.

(5) Any time period which has started to run before the commencement date and has not expired will continue to apply.

Matters formerly heard by existing tribunals (except VAT and duties tribunals)

5—(1) This paragraph applies if, before the commencement date—

(*a*) a notice of appeal has been given to HMRC; but

(*b*) no party has served notice on an existing tribunal for the purpose of beginning proceedings before the existing tribunal in relation to that appeal.

(2) Where the date on which a review is required or offered falls on or before 31 March 2010, the period for HMRC to give notice of their conclusions for the purposes of the relevant provision is to be 90 days (but without prejudice to any power to agree to a different period).

(3) In this paragraph—

"review" means a review under—

(*a*) section 49B or 49C of the Taxes Management Act 1970, or

(*b*) any other enactment which, as amended by this Order, contains provisions corresponding to section 49B or 49C for review to be required or offered;

"relevant provision" means—

(*a*) in the case of a review under section 49B or 49C of the Taxes Management Act 1970, section 49E(6) of that Act, or

(*b*) in the case of a review under any other enactment amended by this Order, the provision that corresponds to section 49E(6) of the Taxes Management Act 1970 in relation to that review.

Current proceedings

6 Any current proceedings are to continue on and after the commencement date as proceedings before the tribunal.

7—(1) This paragraph applies to current proceedings that are continued before the tribunal by virtue of paragraph 6.

(2) Where a hearing before an existing tribunal (except for the Commissioners for the general purposes of the income tax) began before the commencement date but was not completed by that date, the tribunal must be comprised for the continuation of that hearing of the person or persons who began it.

(3) The tribunal may give any direction to ensure that proceedings are dealt with fairly and justly and, in particular, may—

(*a*) apply any provision in procedural rules which applied to the proceedings before the commencement date; or

(*b*) disapply any provision of Tribunal Procedure Rules.

(4) In sub-paragraph (3) "procedural rules" means any provision (whether called rules or not) regulating practice or procedure before an existing tribunal.

(5) Any direction or order made or given in proceedings which is in force immediately before the commencement date remains in force on and after that date as if it were a direction or order of the tribunal relating to proceedings before that tribunal.

(6) A time period which has started to run before the commencement date and which has not expired will continue to apply.

(7) An order for costs may only be made if, and to the extent that, an order could have been made before the commencement date (on the assumption, in the case of costs actually incurred after that date, that they had been incurred before that date).

Cases to be remitted by courts

8 Any case to be remitted by a court on or after the commencement date in relation to an existing tribunal shall be remitted to the tribunal.

Decisions of VAT and duties tribunals and courts: interest and payment

9—(1) This paragraph applies in relation to any decision of a VAT and duties tribunal made before the commencement date.

(2) On and after that date, the following provisions continue to apply as they applied immediately before that date—

(*a*) section 84(8) of the Value Added Tax Act 1994 (VAT),

(*b*) section 60(6) to (8) of the Finance Act 1994 (insurance premium tax),

(*c*) paragraphs 8 and 10 of Schedule 6 to the Finance Act 1994 (air passenger duty),

(*d*) section 56(3) to (5) of the Finance Act 1996 (landfill tax),

(*e*) paragraph 123(4) to (6) of Schedule 6 to the Finance Act 2000 (climate change levy),

(*f*) section 42(4) to (6) of the Finance Act 2001 (aggregates levy),

(*g*) paragraph 14(4) of Schedule 3 to the Finance Act 2001 (excise and customs).

10—(1) This paragraph applies if an appeal from a decision of a VAT and duties tribunal, or from a court, is made before the commencement date.

(2) Section 85B of the Value Added Tax Act 1994 does not apply in relation to that decision.

Decisions of existing tribunals: rights of appeal, reviews and irregularities

11—(1) This paragraph applies to a decision of an existing tribunal if, immediately before the commencement date—

(*a*) an appeal lies to a court from that decision,

(*b*) an application may be or has been made to an existing tribunal seeking a review of that decision, or

(*c*) the existing tribunal wishes to correct an irregularity.

(2) Except as provided for in sub-paragraph (3), on and after the commencement date such rights of appeal shall lie from the decision as would lie from a decision of the First-tier Tribunal made on or after that date.

(3) Subject to the modifications specified in sub-paragraphs (4) and (5) the following enactments continue to apply for the purposes of a case to be stated, a review, or for correcting an irregularity in respect of any decision of the Commissioners for the general purposes of the income tax made before the commencement date, as if the amendments in this Order had not been made—

(*a*) sections 56 and 58 of the Taxes Management Act 1970,

(*b*) regulations 17 and 20 to 24 of the General Commissioners (Jurisdiction and Procedure) Regulations 1994, and

(*c*) the General Commissioners of Income Tax (Costs) Regulations 2001.

(4) Section 56(6) of the Taxes Management Act 1970 is modified so that for "the Commissioners" there is substituted "the tribunal".

(5) Section 58 of the Taxes Management Act 1970 is modified as follows—

(*a*) omit subsection (2B); and

(*b*) in subsection (2C) omit "or on an appeal under section 56A of this Act".

(6) In article 4 of the Tribunals, Courts and Enforcement Act 2007 (Commencement No 6 and Transitional Provisions) Order 2008—

(*a*) for "section 56 of the 1970 Act (statement of case for opinion of the High Court)" substitute "sections 56(3) and (11) and 58 of the 1970 Act (statement of case for opinion of the High Court) and regulations 17 and 20 to 24 of the General Commissioners (Jurisdiction and Procedure) Regulations 1994 (review of tribunal's final determination, stated case procedures and correction of irregularities)"; and

(*b*) after "commenced" insert ", and the amendments to the 1970 Act and the revocation of the General Commissioners (Jurisdiction and Procedure) Regulations 1994, the General Commissioners (Jurisdiction and Procedure) (Amendment) Regulations 1999, the General Commissioners (Jurisdiction and Procedure) (Amendment) Regulations 2005 and the General Commissioners and Special Commissioners (Jurisdiction and Procedure) (Amendment) Regulations 2007 (as they relate to the General Commissioners) in the Transfer of Tribunal Functions and Revenue and Customs Appeals Order 2009 had not been made".

Existing tribunals—staff

12 Staff appointed to the existing tribunals (except to the Commissioners for the general purposes of the income tax) before the commencement date are, on and after that date, to be treated, for the purpose of any enactment, as if they had been appointed by the Lord Chancellor under section 40(1) of the Tribunals, Courts and Enforcement Act 2007 (tribunal staff and services).

Transitional: general

13—(1) In so far as appropriate in consequence of this Order, a reference in an enactment, instrument or other document to an existing tribunal, or a member or official of an existing tribunal (however expressed) is to be taken to be a reference to the tribunal.

(2) Sub-paragraph (1) does not apply to any reference that is amended by Schedule 1 or 2.

2009/196

FIRST-TIER TRIBUNAL AND UPPER TRIBUNAL (CHAMBERS) (AMENDMENT) ORDER 2009

Made. . . . .*9 February 2009*
Laid before Parliament. . . . .*13 February 2009*
Coming into force. . . . .*1 April 2009*

The Lord Chancellor, with the concurrence of the Senior President of Tribunals, makes the following Order in exercise of the power conferred by sections 7(1) and (9) and 145 of the Tribunals, Courts and Enforcement Act 2007.

Note—This Order revoked, except for the purposes of article 9, by the First-tier Tribunal and Upper Tribunal (Chambers) Order, SI 2010/2655 art 1(2), Schedule with effect from 29 November 2010.

9 Transitional provision

(1) This article applies to an appeal which lies to the to the Upper Tribunal by virtue of paragraph 11(2) of Schedule 3 to the Transfer of Tribunal Functions and Revenue and Customs Appeals Order 2009 (transitional provisions) against a decision of—

(*a*) the Commissioners for the general purposes of the income tax established under section 2 of the Taxes Management Act 1970;

(*b*) the Commissioners for the special purposes of the Income Tax Acts established under section 4 of the Taxes Management Act 1970;

(*c*) the VAT and duties tribunals established under Schedule 12 to the Value Added Tax Act 1994;

(*d*) the tribunal established under section 706 of the Income and Corporation Taxes Act 1988; or

(*e*) the tribunal established under section 704 of the Income Tax Act 2007.

(2) In rule 21(2)(*a*) of the Tribunal Procedure (Upper Tribunal) Rules 2008 (application to the Upper Tribunal for permission to appeal) the reference to the tribunal which made the decision challenged is to be read as a reference to the First-tier Tribunal.

2009/273

TRIBUNAL PROCEDURE (FIRST-TIER TRIBUNAL) (TAX CHAMBER) RULES 2009

Made . . . .*5 February 2009*

Laid before Parliament . . . .*13 February 2009*
Coming into force . . . .*1 April 2009*

After consulting in accordance with paragraph 28(1) of Schedule 5 to the Tribunals, Courts and Enforcement Act 2007, the Tribunal Procedure Committee has made the following Rules in exercise of the power conferred by sections 9(3), 22 and 29(3) of, and Schedule 5 to, that Act.

The Lord Chancellor has allowed the Rules in accordance with paragraph 28(3) of Schedule 5 to the Tribunals, Courts and Enforcement Act 2007.

PART 1

INTRODUCTION

1 Citation, commencement, application and interpretation

(1) These Rules may be cited as the Tribunal Procedure (First-tier Tribunal) (Tax Chamber) Rules 2009 and come into force on 1st April 2009.

[(2) These Rules apply to proceedings before the Tax Chamber of the First-tier Tribunal.][1]

(3) In these Rules—

"the 2007 Act" means the Tribunals, Courts and Enforcement Act 2007;

"appellant" means—

(*a*) the person who starts proceedings (whether by bringing or notifying an appeal, by making an originating application, by a reference, or otherwise);

(*b*) in proceedings started jointly by more than one person, such persons acting jointly or each such person, as the context requires;

(*c*) a person substituted as an appellant under rule 9 (substitution and addition of parties);

"Basic case" means a case allocated to the Basic category under rule 23 (allocation of cases to categories);

["CAA case" means an application under section 563 of the Capital Allowances Act 2001;][3]

"Complex case" means a case allocated to the Complex category under rule 23 (allocation of cases to categories);

["Compliance Officer" means the Compliance Officer for IPSA;][1]

"Default Paper case" means a case allocated to the Default Paper category under rule 23 (allocation of cases to categories);

"document" means anything in which information is recorded in any form, and an obligation under these Rules to provide or allow access to a document or a copy of a document for any purpose means, unless the Tribunal directs otherwise, an obligation to provide or allow access to such document or copy in a legible form or in a form which can be readily made into a legible form;

["financial restrictions civil penalty case" means an appeal under paragraph 26(3) or 28(1) of Schedule 7 to the Counter-Terrorism Act 2008;][3]

"hearing" means an oral hearing and includes a hearing conducted in whole or in part by video link, telephone or other means of instantaneous two-way electronic communication;

["HMRC" means Her Majesty's Revenue and Customs but also includes—

(*a*) the Serious Organised Crime Agency when carrying out functions under section 317 of the Proceeds of Crime Act 2002; and

(*b*) the Director of Border Revenue when carrying out functions under section 7 of the Borders, Citizenship and Immigration Act 2009;][1]

["IPSA" means the Independent Parliamentary Standards Authority;

"MP expenses case" means an appeal under the Parliamentary Standards Act 2009;][1]

"party" means a person who is (or was at the time that the Tribunal disposed of the proceedings) an appellant or respondent in proceedings before the Tribunal;

"practice direction" means a direction given under section 23 of the 2007 Act;

["respondent" means—

(*a*) in a case other than an MP expenses case—

(i) HMRC, where HMRC is not an appellant;

(ii) in proceedings brought by HMRC alone, a person against whom the proceedings are brought or to whom the proceedings relate;

(*b*) in a MP expenses case, the Compliance Officer; and

(*c*) in any case, a person substituted or added as a respondent under rule 9 (substitution and addition of parties);][1]

"Standard case" means a case allocated to the Standard category under rule 23 (allocation of cases to categories);

. . . [2]

"Tribunal" means the First-tier Tribunal.

Amendments—[1] Para (2) substituted, in para (3) definitions of "Compliance Officer", "IPSA", and "MP expense case" inserted, and definitions of "HMRC" and "respondent" substituted, by the Tribunal Procedure (Amendment No 3) Rules, SI 2010/2653 rule 6(1)–(3) with effect from 29 November 2010.

[2] In para (3) definition of "Tax Chamber" repealed by the Tribunal Procedure (Amendment) Rules, SI 2011/651 rule 5(1), (2) with effect from 1 April 2011.

[3] Definitions of "CAA case" and "financial restrictions civil penalty case" inserted by the Tribunal Procedure (Amendment) Rules, SI 2013/477 rules 33, 34 with effect from 1 April 2013.

2 Overriding objective and parties' obligation to co-operate with the Tribunal

(1) The overriding objective of these Rules is to enable the Tribunal to deal with cases fairly and justly.

(2) Dealing with a case fairly and justly includes—

(*a*) dealing with the case in ways which are proportionate to the importance of the case, the complexity of the issues, the anticipated costs and the resources of the parties;

(*b*) avoiding unnecessary formality and seeking flexibility in the proceedings;

(*c*) ensuring, so far as practicable, that the parties are able to participate fully in the proceedings;

(*d*) using any special expertise of the Tribunal effectively; and

(*e*) avoiding delay, so far as compatible with proper consideration of the issues.

(3) The Tribunal must seek to give effect to the overriding objective when it—

(*a*) exercises any power under these Rules; or

(*b*) interprets any rule or practice direction.

(4) Parties must—

(*a*) help the Tribunal to further the overriding objective; and

(*b*) co-operate with the Tribunal generally.

Simon's Tax Cases—*R&C Comrs v Ingenious Games LLP and others* [2014] UKUT 62 (TCC), [2014] STC 1416.

3 Alternative dispute resolution and arbitration

(1) The Tribunal should seek, where appropriate—

(*a*) to bring to the attention of the parties the availability of any appropriate alternative procedure for the resolution of the dispute; and

(*b*) if the parties wish and provided that it is compatible with the overriding objective, to facilitate the use of the procedure.

(2) Part 1 of the Arbitration Act 1996 does not apply to proceedings before the Tribunal.

PART 2

GENERAL POWERS AND PROVISIONS

4 Delegation to staff

(1) Staff appointed under section 40(1) of the 2007 Act (tribunal staff and services) may, with the approval of the Senior President of Tribunals, carry out functions of a judicial nature permitted or required to be done by the Tribunal.

(2) The approval referred to at paragraph (1) may apply generally to the carrying out of specified functions by members of staff of a specified description in specified circumstances.

(3) Within 14 days after the date that the Tribunal sends notice of a decision made by a member of staff pursuant to an approval under paragraph (1) to a party, that party may make a written application to the Tribunal requiring that decision to be considered afresh by a judge.

5 Case management powers

(1) Subject to the provisions of the 2007 Act and any other enactment, the Tribunal may regulate its own procedure.

(2) The Tribunal may give a direction in relation to the conduct or disposal of proceedings at any time, including a direction amending, suspending or setting aside an earlier direction.

(3) In particular, and without restricting the general powers in paragraphs (1) and (2), the Tribunal may by direction—

(*a*) extend or shorten the time for complying with any rule, practice direction or direction, unless such extension or shortening would conflict with a provision of another enactment setting down a time limit;

(*b*) consolidate or hear together two or more sets of proceedings or parts of proceedings raising common issues, or treat a case as a lead case (whether in accordance with rule 18 (lead cases) or otherwise);

(*c*) permit or require a party to amend a document;

(*d*) permit or require a party or another person to provide documents, information or submissions to the Tribunal or a party;

(*e*) deal with an issue in the proceedings as a preliminary issue;

(*f*) hold a hearing to consider any matter, including a case management hearing;

(*g*) decide the form of any hearing;

(*h*) adjourn or postpone a hearing;

(*i*) require a party to produce a bundle for a hearing;

(*j*) stay (or, in Scotland, sist) proceedings;

(*k*) transfer proceedings to another tribunal if that other tribunal has jurisdiction in relation to the proceedings and, because of a change of circumstances since the proceedings were started—
  (i) the Tribunal no longer has jurisdiction in relation to the proceedings; or
  (ii) the Tribunal considers that the other tribunal is a more appropriate forum for the determination of the case;

(*l*) suspend the effect of its own decision pending the determination by the Tribunal or the Upper Tribunal, as the case may be, of an application for permission to appeal, a review or an appeal.

Simon's Tax Cases—*R&C Comrs v Ingenious Games LLP and others* [2014] UKUT 62 (TCC), [2014] STC 1416.

6 Procedure for applying for and giving directions

(1) The Tribunal may give a direction on the application of one or more of the parties or on its own initiative.

(2) An application for a direction may be made—
  (*a*) by sending or delivering a written application to the Tribunal; or
  (*b*) orally during the course of a hearing.

(3) An application for a direction must include the reasons for making that application.

(4) Unless the Tribunal considers that there is good reason not to do so, the Tribunal must send written notice of any direction to every party and to any other person affected by the direction.

(5) If a party or other person sent notice of the direction under paragraph (4) wishes to challenge a direction which the Tribunal has given, they may do so by applying for another direction which amends, suspends or sets aside the first direction.

7 Failure to comply with rules etc

(1) An irregularity resulting from a failure to comply with any requirement in these Rules, a practice direction or a direction does not of itself render void the proceedings or any step taken in the proceedings.

(2) If a party has failed to comply with a requirement in these Rules, a practice direction or a direction, the Tribunal may take such action as it considers just, which may include—
  (*a*) waiving the requirement;
  (*b*) requiring the failure to be remedied;
  (*c*) exercising its power under rule 8 (striking out a party's case);
  (*d*) restricting a party's participation in proceedings; or
  (*e*) exercising its power under paragraph (3).

(3) The Tribunal may refer to the Upper Tribunal, and ask the Upper Tribunal to exercise its power under section 25 of the 2007 Act (Upper Tribunal to have powers of High Court or Court of Session) in relation to, any failure by a person to comply with a requirement imposed by the Tribunal—
  (*a*) to attend at any place for the purpose of giving evidence;
  (*b*) otherwise to make themselves available to give evidence;
  (*c*) to swear an oath in connection with the giving of evidence;
  (*d*) to give evidence as a witness;
  (*e*) to produce a document; or
  (*f*) to facilitate the inspection of a document or any other thing (including any premises).

8 Striking out a party's case

(1) The proceedings, or the appropriate part of them, will automatically be struck out if the appellant has failed to comply with a direction that stated that failure by a party to comply with the direction would lead to the striking out of the proceedings or that part of them.

(2) The Tribunal must strike out the whole or a part of the proceedings if the Tribunal—
  (*a*) does not have jurisdiction in relation to the proceedings or that part of them; and
  (*b*) does not exercise its power under rule 5(3)(k)(i) (transfer to another court or tribunal) in relation to the proceedings or that part of them.

(3) The Tribunal may strike out the whole or a part of the proceedings if—
  (*a*) the appellant has failed to comply with a direction which stated that failure by the appellant to comply with the direction could lead to the striking out of the proceedings or part of them;
  (*b*) the appellant has failed to co-operate with the Tribunal to such an extent that the Tribunal cannot deal with the proceedings fairly and justly; or
  (*c*) the Tribunal considers there is no reasonable prospect of the appellant's case, or part of it, succeeding.

(4) The Tribunal may not strike out the whole or a part of the proceedings under paragraphs (2) or (3)(*b*) or (*c*) without first giving the appellant an opportunity to make representations in relation to the proposed striking out.

(5) If the proceedings, or part of them, have been struck out under paragraphs (1) or (3)(*a*), the appellant may apply for the proceedings, or part of them, to be reinstated.

(6) An application under paragraph (5) must be made in writing and received by the Tribunal within 28 days after the date that the Tribunal sent notification of the striking out to the appellant.

(7) This rule applies to a respondent as it applies to an appellant except that—

(*a*) a reference to the striking out of the proceedings must be read as a reference to the barring of the respondent from taking further part in the proceedings; and

(*b*) a reference to an application for the reinstatement of proceedings which have been struck out must be read as a reference to an application for the lifting of the bar on the respondent taking further part in the proceedings.

(8) If a respondent has been barred from taking further part in proceedings under this rule and that bar has not been lifted, the Tribunal need not consider any response or other submissions made by that respondent, and may summarily determine any or all issues against that respondent.

Simon's Tax Cases—*R&C Comrs v Fairford Group plc and another* [2014] UKUT 329 (TCC), [2015] STC 156.

9 Substitution and addition of parties

(1) The Tribunal may give a direction substituting a party if—

(*a*) the wrong person has been named as a party; or

(*b*) the substitution has become necessary because of a change in circumstances since the start of proceedings.

(2) The Tribunal may give a direction adding a person to the proceedings as a respondent.

(3) A person who is not a party to proceedings may make an application to be added as a party under this rule.

(4) If the Tribunal refuses an application under paragraph (3) it must consider whether to permit the person who made the application to provide submissions or evidence to the Tribunal.

(5) If the Tribunal gives a direction under paragraph (1) or (2) it may give such consequential directions as it considers appropriate.

10 Orders for costs

(1) The Tribunal may only make an order in respect of costs (or, in Scotland, expenses)—

(*a*) under section 29(4) of the 2007 Act (wasted costs) [and costs incurred in applying for such costs][2];

(*b*) if the Tribunal considers that a party or their representative has acted unreasonably in bringing, defending or conducting the proceedings; . . . [1]

(*c*) if—

(i) the proceedings have been allocated as a Complex case under rule 23 (allocation of cases to categories); and

(ii) the taxpayer (or, where more than one party is a taxpayer, one of them) has not sent or delivered a written request to the Tribunal, within 28 days of receiving notice that the case had been allocated as a Complex case, that the proceedings be excluded from potential liability for costs or expenses under this sub-paragraph; [or

(*d*) in a MP expenses case, if—

(i) the case has been allocated as a Complex case under rule 23 (allocation of cases to categories); and

(ii) the appellant has not sent or delivered a written request to the Tribunal, within 28 days of receiving notice that the case had been allocated as a Complex case, that the proceedings be excluded from potential liability for costs or expenses under this sub-paragraph.][1]

(2) The Tribunal may make an order under paragraph (1) on an application or of its own initiative.

(3) A person making an application for an order under paragraph (1) must—

(*a*) send or deliver a written application to the Tribunal and to the person against whom it is proposed that the order be made; and

(*b*) send or deliver with the application a schedule of the costs or expenses claimed in sufficient detail to allow the Tribunal to undertake a summary assessment of such costs or expenses if it decides to do so.

(4) An application for an order under paragraph (1) may be made at any time during the proceedings but may not be made later than 28 days after the date on which the Tribunal sends—

(*a*) a decision notice recording the decision which finally disposes of all issues in the proceedings; or

(*b*) notice [under rule 17(2) of its receipt of a withdrawal][2] which ends the proceedings.

(5) The Tribunal may not make an order under paragraph (1) against a person (the "paying person") without first—

(*a*) giving that person an opportunity to make representations; and

(*b*) if the paying person is an individual, considering that person's financial means.

(6) The amount of costs (or, in Scotland, expenses) to be paid under an order under paragraph (1) may be ascertained by—

(*a*) summary assessment by the Tribunal;

(*b*) agreement of a specified sum by the paying person and the person entitled to receive the costs or expenses (the "receiving person"); or (*c*) assessment of the whole or a specified part of the costs or expenses[, including the costs or expenses of the assessment,][2] incurred by the receiving person, if not agreed.

(7) Following an order for assessment under paragraph (6)(*c*) the paying person or the receiving person may apply—

(*a*) in England and Wales, to a county court, the High Court or the Costs Office of the Supreme Court (as specified in the order) for a detailed assessment of the costs on the standard basis or, if specified in the order, on the indemnity basis; and the Civil Procedure Rules 1998 shall apply, with necessary modifications, to that application and assessment as if the proceedings in the tribunal had been proceedings in a court to which the Civil Procedure Rules 1998 apply;

(*b*) in Scotland, to the Auditor of the Sheriff Court or the Court of Session (as specified in the order) for the taxation of the expenses according to the fees payable in that court; or

(*c*) in Northern Ireland, to the Taxing Office of the High Court of Northern Ireland for taxation on the standard basis or, if specified in the order, on the indemnity basis.

[(7A) Upon making an order for the assessment of costs, the Tribunal may order an amount to be paid on account before the costs or expenses are assessed.][2]

(8) In this rule "taxpayer" means a party who is liable to pay, or has paid, the tax, duty, levy or penalty to which the proceedings relate or part of such tax, duty, levy or penalty, or whose liability to do so is in issue in the proceedings;

Amendments—[1] In para (1), word "or" in sub-para (*b*) revoked and sub-para (*d*) and preceding word "or" inserted, by the Tribunal Procedure (Amendment No 3) Rules, SI 2010/2653 rule 6(1), (4) with effect from 29 November 2010.

[2] In paras (1)(*a*), (6)(*c*) words inserted, in para (4) words substituted for words "of a withdrawal under rule 17 (withdrawal)", and para (7A) inserted, by the Tribunal Procedure (Amendment) Rules, SI 2013/477 rules 33, 35–38 with effect from 1 April 2013.

11 Representatives

(1) A party may appoint a representative (whether a legal representative or not) to represent that party in the proceedings.

(2) If a party appoints a representative, that party (or the representative if the representative is a legal representative) must send or deliver to the Tribunal and to each other party to the proceedings written notice of the representative's name and address.

(3) Anything permitted or required to be done by a party under these Rules, a practice direction or a direction may be done by the representative of that party, except signing a witness statement.

(4) A person who receives due notice of the appointment of a representative—

(*a*) must provide to the representative any document which is required to be provided to the represented party, and need not provide that document to the represented party; and

(*b*) may assume that the representative is and remains authorised as such until they receive written notification that this is not so from the representative or the represented party.

(5) At a hearing a party may be accompanied by another person who, with the permission of the Tribunal, may act as a representative or otherwise assist in presenting the party's case at the hearing.

(6) Paragraphs (2) to (4) do not apply to a person (other than an appointed representative) who accompanies a party in accordance with paragraph (5).

(7) In this rule "legal representative" means [a person who, for the purposes of the Legal Services Act 2007, is an authorised person in relation to an activity which constitutes the exercise of a right of audience or the conduct of litigation within the meaning of that Act][1], an advocate or solicitor in Scotland, or a barrister or solicitor in Northern Ireland.

Amendments—[1] In para (7), words substituted by the Tribunal Procedure (Amendment) Rules, SI 2010/43, rule 16, with effect from 18 January 2010.

12 Calculating time

(1) An act required by these Rules, a practice direction or a direction to be done on or by a particular day must be done before 5pm on that day.

(2) If the time specified by these Rules, a practice direction or a direction for doing any act ends on a day other than a working day, the act is done in time if it is done on the next working day.

(3) In this rule "working day" means any day except a Saturday or Sunday, Christmas Day, Good Friday or a bank holiday under section 1 of the Banking and Financial Dealings Act 1971.

13 Sending and delivery of documents

(1) Any document to be provided to the Tribunal under these Rules, a practice direction or a direction must be—

(*a*) sent by pre-paid post or document exchange, or delivered by hand, to the address specified for the proceedings; or

(*b*) sent or delivered by such other method as the Tribunal may permit or direct.

(2) Subject to paragraph (3), if a party or representative provides a fax number, email address or other details for the electronic transmission of documents to them, that party or representative must accept delivery of documents by that method.

(3) If a party informs the Tribunal and all other parties that a particular form of communication (other than pre-paid post or delivery by hand) should not be used to provide documents to that party, that form of communication must not be so used.
(4) If the Tribunal or a party sends a document to a party or the Tribunal by email or any other electronic means of communication, the recipient may request that the sender provide a hard copy of the document to the recipient. The recipient must make such a request as soon as reasonably practicable after receiving the document electronically.
(5) The Tribunal and each party may assume that the address provided by a party or its representative is and remains the address to which documents should be sent or delivered until receiving written notification to the contrary.

14 Use of documents and information

The Tribunal may make an order prohibiting the disclosure or publication of—

(*a*) specified documents or information relating to the proceedings; or
(*b*) any matter likely to lead members of the public to identify any person whom the Tribunal considers should not be identified.

15 Evidence and submissions

(1) Without restriction on the general powers in rule 5(1) and (2) (case management powers), the Tribunal may give directions as to—

(*a*) issues on which it requires evidence or submissions;
(*b*) the nature of the evidence or submissions it requires;
(*c*) whether the parties are permitted or required to provide expert evidence, and if so whether the parties must jointly appoint a single expert to provide such evidence;
(*d*) any limit on the number of witnesses whose evidence a party may put forward, whether in relation to a particular issue or generally;
(*e*) the manner in which any evidence or submissions are to be provided, which may include a direction for them to be given—
  (i) orally at a hearing; or
  (ii) by written submissions or witness statement; and
(*f*) the time at which any evidence or submissions are to be provided.

(2) The Tribunal may—

(*a*) admit evidence whether or not the evidence would be admissible in a civil trial in the United Kingdom; or
(*b*) exclude evidence that would otherwise be admissible where—
  (i) the evidence was not provided within the time allowed by a direction or a practice direction;
  (ii) the evidence was otherwise provided in a manner that did not comply with a direction or a practice direction; or
  (iii) it would otherwise be unfair to admit the evidence.

(3) The Tribunal may consent to a witness giving, or require any witness to give, evidence on oath, and may administer an oath for that purpose.

16 Summoning or citation of witnesses and orders to answer questions or produce documents

(1) On the application of a party or on its own initiative, the Tribunal may—

(*a*) by summons (or, in Scotland, citation) require any person to attend as a witness at a hearing at the time and place specified in the summons or citation;
(*b*) order any person to answer any questions or produce any documents in that person's possession or control which relate to any issue in the proceedings.

(2) A summons or citation under paragraph (1)(*a*) must—

(*a*) give the person required to attend at least 14 days' notice of the hearing, or such shorter period as the Tribunal may direct; and
(*b*) where the person is not a party, make provision for the person's necessary expenses of attendance to be paid, and state who is to pay them.

(3) No person may be compelled to give any evidence or produce any document that the person could not be compelled to give or produce on a trial of an action in a court of law in the part of the United Kingdom where the proceedings are due to be determined.
(4) A person who receives a summons, citation or order may apply to the Tribunal for it to be varied or set aside if they did not have an opportunity to object to it before it was made or issued.
(5) A person making an application under paragraph (4) must do so as soon as reasonably practicable after receiving notice of the summons, citation or order.
(6) A summons, citation or order under this rule must—

(*a*) state that the person on whom the requirement is imposed may apply to the Tribunal to vary or set aside the summons, citation or order, if they did not have an opportunity to object to it before it was made or issued; and (*b*) state the consequences of failure to comply with the summons, citation or order.

17 Withdrawal

(1) Subject to any provision in an enactment relating to withdrawal or settlement of particular proceedings, a party may give notice to the Tribunal of the withdrawal of the case made by it in the Tribunal proceedings, or any part of that case—

(*a*) . . . [1] by sending or delivering to the Tribunal a written notice of withdrawal; or

(*b*) orally at a hearing.

(2) The Tribunal must notify each . . . [1] party in writing of [its receipt of][1] a withdrawal under this rule.

(3) A party who has withdrawn their case may apply to the Tribunal for the case to be reinstated.

(4) An application under paragraph (3) must be made in writing and be received by the Tribunal within 28 days after—

(*a*) the date that the Tribunal received the notice under paragraph (1)(*a*); or

(*b*) the date of the hearing at which the case was withdrawn orally under paragraph (1)(*b*).

Amendments—[1] In para (1)(*a*), words "at any time before a hearing to consider the disposal of the proceedings (or, if the Tribunal disposes of the proceedings without a hearing, before that disposal)," repealed, in para (2), word "other" repealed and words inserted, by the Tribunal Procedure (Amendment) Rules, SI 2013/477 rules 33, 39 with effect from 1 April 2013.

18 Lead cases

(1) This rule applies if—

(*a*) two or more cases have been started before the Tribunal;

(*b*) in each such case the Tribunal has not made a decision disposing of the proceedings; and

(*c*) the cases give rise to common or related issues of fact or law.

(2) The Tribunal may give a direction—

(*a*) specifying one or more cases falling under paragraph (1) as a lead case or lead cases; and

(*b*) staying (or, in Scotland, sisting) the other cases falling under paragraph (1) ("the related cases").

(3) When the Tribunal makes a decision in respect of the common or related issues—

(*a*) the Tribunal must send a copy of that decision to each party in each of the related cases; and

(*b*) subject to paragraph (4), that decision shall be binding on each of those parties.

(4) Within 28 days after the date that the Tribunal sent a copy of the decision to a party under paragraph (3)(*a*), that party may apply in writing for a direction that the decision does not apply to, and is not binding on the parties to, that case.

(5) The Tribunal must give directions in respect of cases which are stayed or sisted under paragraph (2)(*b*), providing for the disposal of or further steps in those cases.

(6) If the lead case or cases are withdrawn or disposed of before the Tribunal makes a decision in respect of the common or related issues, the Tribunal must give directions as to—

(*a*) whether another case or other cases are to be heard as a lead case or lead cases; and

(*b*) whether any direction affecting the related cases should be set aside or amended.

PART 3
PROCEDURE BEFORE THE TRIBUNAL

CHAPTER 1
STARTING PROCEEDINGS AND ALLOCATION OF CASES TO CATEGORIES

19 Proceedings without notice to a respondent

If a case or matter is to be determined without notice to or the involvement of a respondent—

(*a*) any provision in these Rules requiring a document to be provided by or to a respondent; and

(*b*) any other provision in these Rules permitting a respondent to participate in the proceedings

does not apply to that case or matter.

20 Starting appeal proceedings

[(1) A person making or notifying an appeal to the Tribunal under any enactment must start proceedings by sending or delivering a notice of appeal to the Tribunal.][1]

(2) The notice of appeal must include—

(*a*) the name and address of the appellant;

(*b*) the name and address of the appellant's representative (if any);

(*c*) an address where documents for the appellant may be sent or delivered;

(*d*) details of the decision appealed against;

(*e*) the result the appellant is seeking; and

(*f*) the grounds for making the appeal.

(3) The appellant must provide with the notice of appeal a copy of any written record of any decision appealed against, and any statement of reasons for that decision, that the appellant has or can reasonably obtain.

[(4) If the notice of appeal is provided after the end of any period specified in an enactment referred to in paragraph (1) but the enactment provides that an appeal may be made or notified after that period with the permission of the Tribunal—

(*a*) the notice of appeal must include a request for such permission and the reason why the notice of appeal was not provided in time; and

(*b*) unless the Tribunal gives such permission, the Tribunal must not admit the appeal.][1]

(5) When the Tribunal receives the notice of appeal it must give notice of the proceedings to the respondent.

Amendments—[1] Paras (1), (4) substituted by the Tribunal Procedure (Amendment No 3) Rules, SI 2010/2653 rule 6(1), (5) with effect from 29 November 2010.

21 Starting proceedings by originating application or reference

(1) Where an enactment provides for a person or persons to make an originating application or reference to the Tribunal, the appellant must start proceedings by providing an application notice or notice of reference to the Tribunal within any time limit imposed by that enactment.

(2) The application notice or notice of reference must state—

(*a*) the name and address of the appellant;

(*b*) the name and address of the appellant's representative (if any);

(*c*) an address where documents for the appellant may be sent or delivered;

(*d*) the name and address of each respondent (if any);

(*e*) the facts relevant to the originating application or reference;

(*f*) the result the appellant is seeking (if any); and

(*g*) the grounds for making the originating application or reference.

(3) If the appellant provides the application notice or notice of reference to the Tribunal later than the time required by paragraph (1) or by any extension of time under rule 5(3)(*a*) (power to extend time)—

(*a*) the application notice or notice of reference must include a request for an extension of time and the reason why the application notice or notice of reference was not provided in time; and

(*b*) unless the Tribunal extends time for the application notice or notice of reference under rule 5(3)(*a*) (power to extend time) the Tribunal must not admit the application notice or notice of reference.

[(3A) The power of the Tribunal under these Rules to extend time for starting proceedings shall not apply in a CAA case.][1]

(4) When the Tribunal receives an application notice or a notice of reference it must send a copy of the notice and any accompanying document to any respondent.

Amendments—[1] Para (3A) inserted by the Tribunal Procedure (Amendment) Rules, SI 2013/477 rules 33, 40 with effect from 1 April 2013.

22 Hardship applications

(1) This rule applies where an enactment provides, in any terms, that an appeal may not proceed if the liability to pay the amount in dispute is outstanding unless HMRC or the Tribunal consent to the appeal proceeding.

(2) When starting proceedings, the appellant must include or provide the following in or with the notice of appeal—

(*a*) a statement as to whether the appellant has paid the amount in dispute;

(*b*) if the appellant has not paid the amount in dispute, a statement as to the status or outcome of any application to HMRC for consent to the appeal proceeding; and

(*c*) if HMRC have refused such an application, an application to the Tribunal for consent to the appeal proceeding.

(3) An application under paragraph (2)(*c*) must include the reasons for the application and a list of any documents the appellant intends to produce or rely upon in support of that application.

(4) If the appellant requires the consent of HMRC or the Tribunal before the appeal may proceed, the Tribunal must stay the proceedings until any applications to HMRC or the Tribunal in that respect have been determined.

23 Allocation of cases to categories

[(1) When the Tribunal receives a notice of appeal, application notice or notice of reference, the Tribunal must give a direction—

(*a*) in an MP expenses case[, a financial restrictions civil penalty case or a CAA case][2], allocating the case to one of the categories set out in paragraph (2)(*c*) or (*d*); and

(*b*) in any other case, allocating the case to one of the categories set out in paragraph (2).][1]

(2) The categories referred to in paragraph (1) are—

(*a*) Default Paper cases, which will usually be disposed of without a hearing;

(*b*) Basic cases, which will usually be disposed of after a hearing, with minimal exchange of documents before the hearing;
(*c*) Standard cases, which will usually be subject to more detailed case management and be disposed of after a hearing; and
(*d*) Complex cases, in respect of which see paragraphs (4) and (5) below.

(3) The Tribunal may give a further direction re-allocating a case to a different category at any time, either on the application of a party or on its own initiative.

(4) The Tribunal may allocate a case as a Complex case under paragraph (1) or (3) only if the Tribunal considers that the case—
(*a*) will require lengthy or complex evidence or a lengthy hearing;
(*b*) involves a complex or important principle or issue; or
(*c*) involves a large financial sum.

(5) If a case is allocated as a Complex case—
(*a*) rule 10(1)(*c*) (costs in Complex cases) applies to the case; and
(*b*) rule 28 (transfer of Complex cases to the Upper Tribunal) applies to the case.

Simon's Tax Cases—*Capital Air Services Ltd v R&C Comrs* [2010] STC 2726.

Amendments—[1] Para (1) substituted by the Tribunal Procedure (Amendment No 3) Rules, SI 2010/2653 rule 6(1), (6) with effect from 29 November 2010.
[2] Words in para (1)(*a*) inserted by the Tribunal Procedure (Amendment) Rules, SI 2013/477 rules 33, 41 with effect from 1 April 2013.

CHAPTER 2

PROCEDURE AFTER ALLOCATION OF CASES TO CATEGORIES

24 Basic cases

(1) This rule applies to Basic cases.

(2) Rule 25 (respondent's statement of case) does not apply and, subject to paragraph (3) and any direction given by the Tribunal, the case will proceed directly to a hearing.

(3) If the respondent intends to raise grounds for contesting the proceedings at the hearing which have not previously been communicated to the appellant, the respondent must notify the appellant of such grounds.

(4) If the respondent is required to notify the appellant of any grounds under paragraph (3), the respondent must do so—
(*a*) as soon as reasonably practicable after becoming aware that such is the case; and
(*b*) in sufficient detail to enable the appellant to respond to such grounds at the hearing.

25 Respondent's statement of case

[(1) A respondent must send or deliver a statement of case to the Tribunal, the appellant and any other respondent so that it is received—
(*a*) in a Default Paper case, within 42 days after the Tribunal sent the notice of appeal or a copy of the application notice or notice of reference;
(*b*) in an MP expenses case, within 28 days after the Tribunal sent the notice of appeal; or
(*c*) in a Standard or Complex case other than an MP expenses case, within 60 days after the Tribunal sent the notice of appeal or a copy of the application notice or notice of reference.][1]

(2) A statement of case must—
(*a*) in an appeal, state the legislative provision under which the decision under appeal was made; and
(*b*) set out the respondent's position in relation to the case.

(3) A statement of case may also contain a request that the case be dealt with at a hearing or without a hearing.

(4) If a respondent provides a statement of case to the Tribunal later than the time required by paragraph (1) or by any extension allowed under rule 5(3)(*a*) (power to extend time), the statement of case must include a request for an extension of time and the reason why the statement of case was not provided in time.

Amendments—[1] Para (1) substituted by the Tribunal Procedure (Amendment No 3) Rules, SI 2010/2653 rule 6(1), (7) with effect from 29 November 2010.

26 Further steps in a Default Paper case

(1) This rule applies to Default Paper cases.

(2) The appellant may send or deliver a written reply to the Tribunal so that it is received within 30 days after the date on which the respondent sent to the appellant the statement of case to which the reply relates.

(3) The appellant's reply may—
(*a*) set out the appellant's response to the respondent's statement of case;

(*b*) provide any further information (including, where appropriate, copies of the documents containing such information) which has not yet been provided to the Tribunal and is relevant to the case; and

(*c*) contain a request that the case be dealt with at a hearing.

(4) The appellant must send or deliver a copy of any reply provided under paragraph (2) to each respondent at the same time as it is provided to the Tribunal.

(5) If the appellant provides a reply to the Tribunal later than the time required by paragraph (2) or by any extension allowed under rule 5(3)(*a*) (power to extend time), the reply must include a request for an extension of time and the reason why the reply was not provided in time.

(6) Following receipt of the appellant's reply, or the expiry of the time for the receipt of the appellant's reply then, unless it directs otherwise and subject in any event to paragraph (7), the Tribunal must proceed to determine the case without a hearing.

(7) If any party has made a written request to the Tribunal for a hearing, the Tribunal must hold a hearing before determining the case.

27 Further steps in a Standard or Complex case

(1) This rule applies to Standard and Complex cases.

(2) Subject to any direction to the contrary, within 42 days after the date the respondent sent the statement of case (or, where there is more than one respondent, the date of the final statement of case) each party must send or deliver to the Tribunal and to each other party a list of documents—

(*a*) of which the party providing the list has possession, the right to possession, or the right to take copies; and

(*b*) which the party providing the list intends to rely upon or produce in the proceedings.

(3) A party which has provided a list of documents under paragraph (2) must allow each other party to inspect or take copies of the documents on the list (except any documents which are privileged).

28 Transfer of Complex cases to the Upper Tribunal

(1) If a case has been allocated as a Complex case the Tribunal may, with the consent of the parties, refer a case [or a preliminary issue][1] to the President of the Tax Chamber [of the First-tier Tribunal][2] with a request that the case [or issue][1] be considered for transfer to the Upper Tribunal.

[(2) If a case or issue has been referred by the Tribunal under paragraph (1), the President of the Tax Chamber may, with the concurrence of the President of the Tax and Chancery Chamber of the Upper Tribunal, direct that the case or issue be transferred to and determined by the Upper Tribunal.][1]

Amendments—[1] In para (1) words inserted, and para (2) substituted, by the Tribunal Procedure (Amendment No 3) Rules, SI 2010/2653 rule 6(1), (8) with effect from 29 November 2010.

[2] In para (1) words inserted by the Tribunal Procedure (Amendment) Rules, SI 2011/651 rule 5(1), (3) with effect from 1 April 2011.

CHAPTER 3

HEARINGS

29 Determination with or without a hearing

(1) Subject to rule 26(6) (determination of a Default Paper case without a hearing) and the following paragraphs in this rule, the Tribunal must hold a hearing before making a decision which disposes of proceedings, or a part of proceedings, unless—

(*a*) each party has consented to the matter being decided without a hearing; and

(*b*) the Tribunal considers that it is able to decide the matter without a hearing.

(2) This rule does not apply to decisions under Part 4 (correcting, setting aside, reviewing and appealing Tribunal decisions).

(3) The Tribunal may dispose of proceedings, or a part of proceedings, without a hearing under rule 8 (striking out a party's case).

30 Entitlement to attend a hearing

Subject to rules 19 (proceedings without notice to a respondent) and 32(4) (exclusion from a hearing), each party to proceedings is entitled to attend a hearing.

31 Notice of hearings

(1) The Tribunal must give each party entitled to attend a hearing reasonable notice of the time and place of any hearing (including any adjourned or postponed hearing) and any changes to the time and place of any hearing.

(2) In relation to a hearing to consider the disposal of proceedings, the period of notice under paragraph (1) must be at least 14 days except that the Tribunal may give less than 14 days' notice—

(*a*) with the parties' consent; or

(*b*) in urgent or exceptional circumstances.

32 Public and private hearings

(1) Subject to the following paragraphs, all hearings must be held in public.

(2) The Tribunal may give a direction that a hearing, or part of it, is to be held in private if the Tribunal considers that restricting access to the hearing is justified—

(*a*) in the interests of public order or national security;

(*b*) in order to protect a person's right to respect for their private and family life;

(*c*) in order to maintain the confidentiality of sensitive information;

(*d*) in order to avoid serious harm to the public interest; or

(*e*) because not to do so would prejudice the interests of justice.

(3) Where a hearing, or part of it, is to be held in private, the Tribunal may determine who is permitted to attend the hearing or part of it.

(4) The Tribunal may give a direction excluding from any hearing, or part of it—

(*a*) any person whose conduct the Tribunal considers is disrupting or is likely to disrupt the hearing;

(*b*) any person whose presence the Tribunal considers is likely to prevent another person from giving evidence or making submissions freely;

(*c*) any person where the purpose of the hearing would be defeated by the attendance of that person; or

(*d*) a person under the age of eighteen years.

(5) The Tribunal may give a direction excluding a witness from a hearing until that witness gives evidence.

(6) If the Tribunal publishes a report of a decision resulting from a hearing which was held wholly or partly in private, the Tribunal must, so far as practicable, ensure that the report does not disclose information which was referred to only in a part of the hearing that was held in private (including such information which enables the identification of any person whose affairs were dealt with in the part of the hearing that was held in private) if to do so would undermine the purpose of holding the hearing in private.

33 Hearings in a party's absence

If a party fails to attend a hearing the Tribunal may proceed with the hearing if the Tribunal—

(*a*) is satisfied that the party has been notified of the hearing or that reasonable steps have been taken to notify the party of the hearing; and

(*b*) considers that it is in the interests of justice to proceed with the hearing.

CHAPTER 4
DECISIONS

34 Consent orders

(1) The Tribunal may, at the request of the parties but only if it considers it appropriate, make a consent order disposing of the proceedings and making such other appropriate provision as the parties have agreed.

(2) Notwithstanding any other provision of these Rules, the Tribunal need not hold a hearing before making an order under paragraph (1), or provide reasons for the order.

35 Notice of decisions and reasons

(1) The Tribunal may give a decision orally at a hearing.

(2) The Tribunal must provide to each party within 28 days after making [a decision (other than a decision under Part 4) which finally disposes of all issues in proceedings or of a preliminary issue dealt with following a direction under rule 5(3)(*e*)][1], or as soon as practicable thereafter, a decision notice which—

(*a*) states the Tribunal's decision; and

(*b*) notifies the party of any right of appeal against the decision and the time within which, and the manner in which, the right of appeal may be exercised.

(3) Unless each party agrees that it is unnecessary, the decision notice must—

(*a*) include a summary of the findings of fact and reasons for the decision; or

(*b*) be accompanied by full written findings of fact and reasons for the decision.

(4) If the Tribunal provides no findings and reasons, or summary findings and reasons only, in or with the decision notice, a party to the proceedings may apply for full written findings and reasons, and must do so before making an application for permission to appeal under rule 39 (application for permission to appeal).

(5) An application under paragraph (4) must be made in writing and be sent or delivered to the Tribunal so that it is received within 28 days after the date that the Tribunal sent or otherwise provided the decision notice under paragraph (2) to the party making the application.

(6) The Tribunal must send a full written statement of findings and reasons to each party within 28 days after receiving an application for full written reasons made in accordance with paragraphs (4) and (5), or as soon as practicable thereafter.

Amendments—[1] In para (2), words substituted for words "a decision which finally disposes of all issues in proceedings (except a decision under Part 4)" by the Tribunal Procedure (Amendment) Rules, SI 2013/477 rules 33, 42 with effect from 1 April 2013.

PART 4
CORRECTING, SETTING ASIDE, REVIEWING AND APPEALING TRIBUNAL DECISIONS

36 Interpretation

In this Part—

"appeal" means the exercise of a right of appeal against a decision of the Tribunal; and

"review" means the review of a decision by the Tribunal under section 9 of the 2007 Act.

37 Clerical mistakes and accidental slips or omissions

The Tribunal may at any time correct any clerical mistake or other accidental slip or omission in a decision, direction or any document produced by it, by—

(*a*) sending notification of the amended decision or direction, or a copy of the amended document, to all parties; and

(*b*) making any necessary amendment to any information published in relation to the decision, direction or document.

38 Setting aside a decision which disposes of proceedings

(1) The Tribunal may set aside a decision which disposes of proceedings, or part of such a decision, and re-make the decision, or the relevant part of it, if—

(*a*) the Tribunal considers that it is in the interests of justice to do so; and

(*b*) one or more of the conditions in paragraph (2) is satisfied.

(2) The conditions are—

(*a*) a document relating to the proceedings was not sent to, or was not received at an appropriate time by, a party or a party's representative;

(*b*) a document relating to the proceedings was not sent to the Tribunal at an appropriate time;

(*c*) there has been some other procedural irregularity in the proceedings; or

(*d*) a party, or a party's representative, was not present at a hearing related to the proceedings.

(3) A party applying for a decision, or part of a decision, to be set aside under paragraph (1) must make a written application to the Tribunal so that it is received no later than 28 days after the date on which the Tribunal sent notice of the decision to the party.

(4) If the Tribunal sets aside a decision or part of a decision under this rule, the Tribunal must notify the parties in writing as soon as practicable.

39 Application for permission to appeal

(1) A person seeking permission to appeal must make a written application to the Tribunal for permission to appeal.

(2) An application under paragraph (1) must be sent or delivered to the Tribunal so that it is received no later than 56 days after the latest of the dates that the Tribunal sends to the person making the application—

[(*za*) the relevant decision notice;][1]

[(*a*) where—

(i) the decision disposes of all issues in the proceedings; or

(iii) subject to paragraph (2A), the decision disposes of a preliminary issue dealt with following a direction under rule 5(3)(e),

full written reasons for the decision;][1]

(*b*) notification of amended reasons for, or correction of, the decision following a review; or

(*c*) notification that an application for the decision to be set aside has been unsuccessful.

[(2A) The Tribunal may direct that the 56 days within which a party may send or deliver an application for permission to appeal against a decision that disposes of a preliminary issue shall run from the date of the decision that disposes of all issues in the proceedings.][1]

(3) The date in paragraph (2)(*c*) applies only if the application for the decision to be set aside was made within the time stipulated in rule 38 (setting aside a decision which disposes of proceedings), or any extension of that time granted by the Tribunal.

(4) If the person seeking permission to appeal sends or delivers the application to the Tribunal later than the time required by paragraph (2) or by any extension of time under rule 5(3)(*a*) (power to extend time)—

(*a*) the application must include a request for an extension of time and the reason why the application notice was not provided in time; and

(*b*) unless the Tribunal extends time for the application under rule 5(3)(*a*) (power to extend time) the Tribunal must not admit the application.

(5) An application under paragraph (1) must—

(*a*) identify the decision of the Tribunal to which it relates;

(*b*) identify the alleged error or errors in the decision; and

(*c*) state the result the party making the application is seeking.

Amendments—[1] Para (2)(*za*) inserted, para (2)(*a*) substituted, and para (2A) inserted, by the Tribunal Procedure (Amendment) Rules, SI 2013/477 rules 33, 43 with effect from 1 April 2013.

40 Tribunal's consideration of application for permission to appeal

(1) On receiving an application for permission to appeal the Tribunal must first consider, taking into account the overriding objective in rule 2, whether to review the decision in accordance with rule 41 (review of a decision).

(2) If the Tribunal decides not to review the decision, or reviews the decision and decides to take no action in relation to the decision, or a part of it, the Tribunal must consider whether to give permission to appeal in relation to the decision or that part of it.

(3) The Tribunal must send a record of its decision to the parties as soon as practicable.

(4) If the Tribunal refuses permission to appeal it must send with the record of its decision—

(*a*) a statement of its reasons for such refusal; and

(*b*) notification of the right to make an application to the Upper Tribunal for permission to appeal and the time within which, and the method by which, such application must be made.

(5) The Tribunal may give permission to appeal against part only of the decision or on limited grounds, but must comply with paragraph (4) in relation to any part of the decision or grounds on which it has refused permission.

41 Review of a decision

(1) The Tribunal may only undertake a review of a decision—

(*a*) pursuant to rule 40(1) (review on an application for permission to appeal); and

(*b*) if it is satisfied that there was an error of law in the decision.

(2) The Tribunal must notify the parties in writing of the outcome of any review, unless the Tribunal decides to take no action following the review.

(3) The Tribunal may not take any action in relation to a decision following a review without first giving every party an opportunity to make representations in relation to the proposed action.

42 Power to treat an application as a different type of application

The Tribunal may treat an application for a decision to be corrected, set aside or reviewed, or for permission to appeal against a decision, as an application for any other one of those things.

2009/275

APPEALS (EXCLUDED DECISIONS) ORDER 2009

Made by the Lord Chancellor under the Tribunals, Courts and Enforcement Act 2007 ss 11(5)(f) and 13(8)(f).

Made . . . .*5 February 2009*

Laid before Parliament . . . .*13 February 2009*

Coming into force . . . .*1 April 2009*

1 Citation and commencement

This Order may be cited as the Appeals (Excluded Decisions) Order 2009 and comes into force on 1st April 2009.

2 [Excluded decisions

For the purposes of section 11(1) of the Tribunals, Courts and Enforcement Act 2007, the following decisions of the First-tier Tribunal are excluded decisions—

(*a*) a decision under section 103 of the Immigration and Asylum Act 1999 (appeals); and

(*b*) a decision under paragraphs 22, 23, 24, 29, 30, 31, 32 and 33 of Schedule 2 to the Immigration Act 1971.][1]

Amendments—[1] Art 2 substituted by the Tribunals, Courts and Enforcement Act 2007 (Miscellaneous Provisions) Order, SI 2010/41 arts 2, 3 with effect from 15 February 2010.

3 For the purposes of sections 11(1) and 13(1) of the Tribunals, Courts and Enforcement Act 2007, the following decisions of the First-tier Tribunal or the Upper Tribunal are excluded decisions—

(*a*) any decision under section 20(7), (8B) or (8G)(*b*) (power to call for documents of taxpayer and others), 20B(1B) or (6) (restrictions on powers under sections 20 and 20A) or 20BB(2)(*a*) (falsification etc of documents) of the Taxes Management Act 1970;

(*b*) any decision under section 35A(2) (variation of undertakings), 79A(2) (variation of undertakings) or 219(1A) (power to require information) of the Inheritance Tax Act 1984;

(*c*) any decision under section 152(5) (notification of taxable amount of certain benefits) or 215(7) (advance clearance by Board of distributions and payments) of the Income and Corporation Taxes Act 1988;

(*d*) any decision under section 138(4) of the Taxation of Chargeable Gains Act 1992 (procedure for clearance in advance);

(*e*) any decision under section 187(5) or (6) (returns and information) of, or paragraph 3(2) or 6(2) of Schedule 21 (restrictions on powers under section 187) to, the Finance Act 1993;

(*f*) any decision under paragraph 91(5) of Schedule 15 to the Finance Act 2000 (corporate venturing scheme: advance clearance);

(*g*) any decision under paragraph 88(5) of Schedule 29 to the Finance Act 2002 (gains and losses from intangible fixed assets: transfer of business or trade);

(*h*) any decision under paragraph 2, 4, 7, 9, 10, 11 or 24 of Schedule 13 to the Finance Act 2003 (stamp duty land tax: information powers);

(*i*) any decision under section 306A (doubt as to notifiability), 308A (supplemental information), 313B (reasons for non-disclosure: supporting information) or 314A (order to disclose) of the Finance Act 2004;

(*j*) any decision under section 697(4) of the Income Tax Act 2007 (opposed notifications: determinations by tribunal);

(*k*) any decision under regulation 10(3) of the Venture Capital Trust (Winding up and Mergers) (Tax) Regulations 2004 (procedure for Board's approval);

(*l*) any decision under regulation 5A (doubt as to notifiability), 7A (supplemental information), 12B (reasons for non-disclosure: supporting information) or 12C (order to disclose) of the National Insurance Contributions (Application of Part 7 of the Finance Act 2004) Regulations 2007;

(*m*) any procedural, ancillary or preliminary decision made in relation to an appeal against a decision under section 40A of the British Nationality Act 1981, section 82, 83 or 83A of the Nationality, Immigration and Asylum Act 2002, or regulation 26 of the Immigration (European Economic Area) Regulations 2006.][1]

Amendments—[1] Art 3 substituted by the Tribunals, Courts and Enforcement Act 2007 (Miscellaneous Provisions) Order, SI 2010/41 arts 2, 3 with effect from 15 February 2010.

4 Revocations

The Appeals (Excluded Decisions) Order 2008 and the Appeals (Excluded Decisions) (Amendment) Order 2008 are revoked.

2009/403

FINANCE ACT 2008, SCHEDULE 39 (APPOINTED DAY, TRANSITIONAL PROVISION AND SAVINGS) ORDER 2009

Made by the Treasury under FA 2008 s 118(2) and (3)

Made . . . .*26 February 2009*

1 Citation and interpretation

(1) This Order may be cited as the Finance Act 2008, Schedule 39 (Appointed Day, Transitional Provision and Savings) Order 2009.

(2) In this Order a reference to a paragraph (without more) is a reference to that paragraph of Schedule 39 to the Finance Act 2008.

(3) In this Order—

"the Taxes Acts" has the meaning given in section 118(1) of the Taxes Management Act 1970;
"TMA 1970" means the Taxes Management Act 1970;
"VATA 1994" means the Value Added Tax Act 1994.

2 Appointed days

(1) The day appointed for the coming into force of paragraphs 32 to 36 is 1st April 2009.

(2) Subject to article 10(2), the day appointed for the coming into force of paragraphs 1 to 31 and 37 to 66 is 1st April 2010.

3 Transitional provisions and savings

Paragraph 33 is disregarded where, for the purposes of section 33A of VATA 1994 (refunds of VAT to museums and galleries), the day on which the supply was made or the acquisition or importation took place was on or before 31st March 2006.

4 Paragraph 34 is disregarded—

(*a*) where, for the purposes of section 77 of VATA 1994 (assessments: time limits and supplementary assessments), the end of the prescribed accounting period or the importation, acquisition or event giving rise to the penalty, as appropriate, occurred on or before 31st March 2006, and (*b*) where, after a person's death, a sum is assessed as due by reason of some conduct (however described) of the deceased, including a sum due by way of penalty, interest or surcharge, and the date of the death is on or before 31st March 2006.

5 Paragraph 35 is disregarded where, for the purposes of a claim under section 78 of VATA 1994 (interest in certain cases of official error), the end of the applicable period to which the claim relates was on or before 31st March 2006.

6 Paragraph 36 is disregarded where, for the purposes of section 80 of VATA 1994 (credit for, or repayment of, overstated or overpaid VAT), the relevant date is on or before 31st March 2006.

7 Section 36(1A)(*b*) and (*c*) of TMA 1970 (fraudulent and negligent conduct) shall not apply where the year of assessment is 2008-09 or earlier, except where the assessment on the person ("P") is for the purposes of making good to the Crown a loss of tax attributable to P's negligent conduct or the negligent conduct of a person acting on P's behalf.

8 Paragraph 46(2A)(*b*) and (*c*) of Schedule 18 to the Finance Act 1998 (general time limits for assessments) shall not apply where the end of the accounting period to which the assessment relates is on or before 31st March 2010, except in a case involving negligence on the part of—

(*a*) the company, or
(*b*) a person acting on behalf of the company, or
(*c*) a person who was a partner of the company at the relevant time.

9 Section 77(4A)(*c*) and (*d*) of VATA 1994 (value added tax: assessments: time limits and supplementary assessments) shall not apply where the end of the prescribed accounting period or the importation, acquisition or event giving rise to the penalty, as appropriate, occurred on or before 31 March 2010, except where VAT has been lost in circumstances giving rise to a penalty under section 67 of VATA 1994 (failure to notify and unauthorised issue of invoices).

10—(1) This article applies where an event specified in paragraph 4 below relates to a year of assessment in respect of which a person ("P") has not been given notice under—

(*a*) section 8 of TMA 1970 (personal return),
(*b*) section 8A of TMA 1970 (trustee's return), or
(*c*) section 12AA of TMA 1970 (partnership return),

within one year of the end of the year of assessment.

(2) Where this article applies, the day appointed for the coming into force of paragraphs 1 to 31 and 37 to 65 is 1st April 2012.

(3) But this article does not apply if, as regards P and a year of assessment, any income which ought to have been assessed to income tax or chargeable gains which ought to have been assessed to capital gains tax, have not been assessed, or an assessment to tax has become insufficient, or any relief which has been given has become excessive.

(4) The events referred to in paragraph (1) above are—

(*a*) an assessment on P to income tax or capital gains tax,
(*b*) a claim by or on behalf of P, provided for by any provision of the Taxes Acts, and
(*c*) a notice given by P under section 711 of the Income Tax (Earnings and Pensions Act) 2003 (right to make a return).

(5) Nothing in this article has any application where P is a company.

2009/404

FINANCE ACT 2008, SCHEDULE 36 (APPOINTED DAY AND SAVINGS) ORDER 2009

Made by the Treasury under FA 2008 s 113(2) and (3)

Made . . . . *26 February 2009*

1 Citation and interpretation

(1) This Order may be cited as the Finance Act 2008, Schedule 36 (Appointed Day and Savings) Order 2009.

(2) In this Order a reference to a paragraph (without more) is a reference to that paragraph of Schedule 36 to the Finance Act 2008.

2 Appointed day

The day appointed for the coming into force of Schedule 36 to the Finance Act 2008 is 1st April 2009.

3 Savings

Where a notice is given under section 19A of the Taxes Management Act 1970 ("TMA 1970") (power to call for documents for purposes of enquiries) on or before 31st March 2009, for the purposes of that notice—

(*a*) the provisions contained in that section and in section 97AA of TMA 1970 (penalties for failure to produce documents under section 19A) shall continue to have effect on and after 1st April 2009;

(*b*) the amendments made by paragraphs 71 and 75 (consequential amendments) shall be disregarded.

4 Where a notice is given under section 20 of TMA 1970 (power to call for documents of taxpayer and others) on or before 31st March 2009, for the purposes of that notice—

(*a*) the provisions contained in that section and in section 20BB of TMA 1970 (offence of falsification etc of documents) shall continue to have effect on and after 1st April 2009;

(*b*) the amendments made by paragraphs 68, 70 and 76 (consequential amendments) shall be disregarded.

5 Where a notice is given under paragraph 6 of Schedule 1A to TMA 1970 (power to call for documents for the purposes of enquiries) on or before 31st March 2009, for the purposes of that notice—

(*a*) the provisions contained in paragraphs 6 and 6A (power to appeal against notice to produce documents) of that Schedule shall continue to have effect on and after 1st April 2009;

(*b*) the amendments made by paragraphs 72 and 75 (consequential amendments) shall be disregarded.

6 Where a notice is given under section 767C of the Income and Corporation Taxes Act (change in company ownership: information) on or before 31st March 2009, for the purposes of that notice—

(*a*) the provisions contained in that section shall continue to have effect on and after 1st April 2009;

(*b*) the amendments made by paragraph 73(*a*), 80, 81 and 82 (consequential amendments) shall be disregarded.

7 Where a notice is given under paragraph 27 of Schedule 18 to the Finance Act 1998 (company tax returns) on or before 31st March 2009, the provisions contained in paragraphs 27, 28 and 29 of that Schedule (notice to produce documents etc for purposes of enquiry into company tax return, power to appeal against such notices and penalty for failure to produce such documents etc) shall continue to have effect on and after 1st April 2009 for the purposes of that notice.

8 Where a notice is given for the purposes of regulation 5 (amendment of syndicate determinations and HMRC enquiries) of the Lloyd's Underwriters (Tax) Regulations 2005 on or before 31st March 2009, the provisions of paragraphs 27 to 29 of Schedule 18 to the Finance Act 1998 shall continue to have effect on and after 1st April 2009, with appropriate modification, for the purposes of that regulation.

9 In relation to a notice given on or before 31st March 2009, for the purposes of the application of section 20 of TMA 1970 (with sections 20B and 20BB of that Act) to—

(*a*) section 110ZA of the Social Security Administration Act 1992 (Class 1, 1A, 1B or 2 contributions: powers to call for documents etc),

(*b*) section 104ZA of the Social Security Administration (Northern Ireland) Act 1992 (Class 1, 1A, 1B or 2 contributions: powers to call for documents etc), and

(*c*) section 25 of the Tax Credits Act 2002 (payments of working tax credit by employers),

the amendments made respectively by paragraphs 84, 85 and 90 shall be disregarded.

10 In relation to a notice given on or before 31st March 2009, for the purposes of the application of—

(*a*) subsections (1) to (8) and 8(*c*) to 9 of section 20 of TMA 1970 (powers to call for information relevant to liability to income tax, corporation tax or capital gains tax), and

(*b*) sections 20B, 20BB and 20D of that Act so far as relating to those subsections,

to section 174 of the Finance Act 2006 (international tax enforcement arrangements: information powers), the amendments made by paragraph 91 shall be disregarded.

11 Where a notice is given on or before 31st March 2009, the amendments made by paragraph 78 (amendment to section 12(3) (secrecy) of the National Savings Bank Act 1971) shall be disregarded so far as they affect the notice.

12 In consequence of the preceding provisions of this Order, the amendments made by paragraph 92 shall be disregarded so far as they affect any notice referred to in those provisions, given on or before 31st March 2009.

2009/511

FINANCE ACT 2008, SCHEDULE 41 (APPOINTED DAY AND TRANSITIONAL PROVISIONS) ORDER 2009

Made . . . . *5 March 2009*

The Treasury make the following Order in exercise of the powers conferred by sections 122 and 123 of the Finance Act 2008:

1 Citation and interpretation

(1) This Order may be cited as the Finance Act 2008, Schedule 41 (Appointed Day and Transitional Provisions) Order 2009.

(2) In this Order a reference to a paragraph (without more) is a reference to that paragraph of Schedule 41 to the Finance Act 2008.

(3) In this Order—

"relevant excise provision" has the meaning given in paragraph 3(1);

"relevant obligation" means an obligation specified in the Table in paragraph 1;

"unauthorised issue of an invoice" has the meaning given in paragraph 2(2).

2 Appointed day

The day appointed for the coming into force of Schedule 41 to the Finance Act 2008 is 1st April 2010.

3 That Schedule has effect—

(*a*) in relation to any relevant obligation arising on or after that date;

(*b*) in relation to any unauthorised issue of an invoice taking place on or after that date;

(*c*) in relation to any act which enables HMRC to assess an amount as duty under a relevant excise provision and which is done on or after that date; and

(*d*) in relation to any act giving rise to a penalty under paragraph 4 (handling goods subject to unpaid excise duty) which is done on or after that date.

4 Transitional provisions

Paragraph 25 (consequential repeals), paragraph 29 of Schedule 24 to the Finance Act 2007 and paragraph 21 of Schedule 40 to the Finance Act 2008 repeal the following provisions only in so far as those provisions relate to conduct involving dishonesty which gives rise to a penalty under Schedule 41 to the Finance Act 2008—

(*a*) in the Value Added Tax Act 1994—

(i) sections 60 and 61 (VAT evasion), and

(ii) section 67(1)(*b*) (failure to notify);

(*b*) in the Finance Act 1994—

(i) section 8 (penalty for evasion of excise duty), and

(ii) paragraphs 12 and 13 of Schedule 7 (insurance premium tax: civil penalties);

(*c*) paragraphs 18 and 19 of Schedule 5 to the Finance Act 1996 (landfill tax: civil penalties: evasion and misdeclaration or neglect);

(*d*) paragraphs 98 and 99 of Schedule 6 to the Finance Act 2000 (climate change levy: civil penalties: evasion, liability of directors and misdeclaration or neglect);

(*e*) in Schedule 6 to the Finance Act 2001—

(i) paragraphs 7 and 8 (aggregates levy: civil penalties: evasion, liability of directors and misdeclaration or neglect); and

(ii) paragraph 9A(5)(*b*) (penalty under paragraph 7 above); and

(*f*) section 133(2) to (4) of the Finance Act 2002 (aggregates levy: amendments to provisions about civil penalties).

VAT SIs

2009/571

FINANCE ACT 2008, SCHEDULE 40 (APPOINTED DAY, TRANSITIONAL PROVISIONS AND CONSEQUENTIAL AMENDMENTS) ORDER 2009

Made by the Treasury under FA 2008 s 122

Made . . . .*9 March 2009*

Laid before the House of Commons . . . .*10 March 2009*

Coming into force . . . .*1 April 2009*

1 Citation and interpretation

(1) This Order may be cited as the Finance Act 2008, Schedule 40 (Appointed Day, Transitional Provisions and Consequential Amendments) Order 2009 and comes into force on 1st April 2009.

(2) In this Order a reference to a paragraph (without more) is a reference to that paragraph of Schedule 40 to the Finance Act 2008.

(3) In this Order—

"filing date", in relation to a relevant document, means—

(i) where the document is required to be given to HMRC, the date by which it is required to be given, and

(ii) where the document is not required to be given to HMRC, the date on which it is given;

"HMRC" means Her Majesty's Revenue and Customs;

"relevant documents" means documents given to HMRC of a kind inserted in the Table in paragraph 1 of Schedule 24 by paragraph 2(4) or (5);

"relevant tax" means any tax inserted in the Table in paragraph 1 of Schedule 24 by paragraph 2(4) or (5);

"Schedule 24" means Schedule 24 to the Finance Act 2007; and

"tax period" has the meaning given in paragraph 28(*g*) of Schedule 24.

2 Appointed day

The day appointed for the coming into force of Schedule 40 to the Finance Act 2008 is 1st April 2009.

3 In their application in relation to penalties payable under paragraph 1 of Schedule 24 (error in taxpayer's document), the entries inserted by paragraph 2(4) and (5) shall have effect in relation to—

(*a*) relevant documents—

(i) which relate to tax periods commencing on or after 1st April 2009, and

(ii) for which the filing date is on or after 1st April 2010;

(*b*) relevant documents relating to all claims for repayments of relevant tax made on or after 1st April 2010 which are not related to a tax period;

(*c*) relevant documents produced under regulations under section 256 of the Inheritance Tax Act 1984 ("IHTA 1984") (regulations about accounts, etc), where the date of death is on or after 1st April 2009; and

(*d*) in any other case, relevant documents given where a person's liability to pay relevant tax arises on or after 1st April 2010.

4 In their application in relation to penalties payable under paragraph 1A of Schedule 24 (error in taxpayer's document attributable to another person), the entries inserted by paragraph 2(4) and (5) shall have effect in relation to—

(*a*) relevant documents—

(i) which relate to tax periods commencing on or after 1st April 2009, and

(ii) for which the filing date is on or after 1st April 2010;

(*b*) relevant documents relating to all claims for repayments of relevant tax made on or after 1st April 2010 which are not related to a tax period;

(*c*) relevant documents produced under regulations under section 256 of IHTA 1984 (regulations about accounts, etc) where the date of death is on or after 1st April 2009; and

(*d*) in any other case, relevant documents given where a person's liability to pay relevant tax arises on or after 1st April 2010.

5 In their application in relation to assessments falling within paragraph 2 of Schedule 24 (under-assessment by HMRC), the entries inserted by paragraph 2(4) and (5) shall have effect in relation to tax periods commencing on or after 1st April 2009, where the filing date for the relevant document is on or after 1st April 2010.

6 Transitional provisions

(1) Paragraph 21 (consequential repeals) repeals the provisions listed in paragraph (2) only in so far as those provisions relate to conduct involving dishonesty which relates to—

(*a*) an inaccuracy in a document, or

(*b*) a failure to notify HMRC of an under-assessment by HMRC.

(2) The provisions referred to in paragraph (1) are—

(*a*) in the Finance Act 1994—

(i) section 8 (penalty for evasion of excise duty), and

(ii) paragraphs 12 and 13 of Schedule 7 (insurance premium tax: civil penalties),

(*b*) paragraphs 18 and 19 of Schedule 5 to the Finance Act 1996 (landfill tax: civil penalties: evasion and misdeclaration or neglect),

(*c*) paragraphs 98 and 99 of Schedule 6 to the Finance Act 2000 (climate change levy: civil penalties: evasion, liability of directors and misdeclaration or neglect),

(*d*) in Schedule 6 to the Finance Act 2001—

(i) paragraphs 7 and 8 (aggregates levy: civil penalties: evasion, liability of directors and misdeclaration or neglect), and

(ii) paragraph 9A(5)(*b*) (penalty under paragraph 7 above),

(*e*) section 133(2) to (4) of the Finance Act 2002 (aggregates levy: amendments to provisions about civil penalties).

7 Notwithstanding paragraph 29(*d*) of Schedule 24 (consequential amendments), sections 60 and 61 of the Value Added Tax Act 1994 (VAT evasion) shall continue to have effect with respect to conduct involving dishonesty which does not relate to an inaccuracy in a document or a failure to notify HMRC of an under-assessment by HMRC.

8 Consequential amendments to enactments

Schedule 1 contains amendments of enactments in consequence of the provisions omitted by paragraph 21 and by paragraph 29 of Schedule 24.

9 Schedule 2 contains consequential amendments to secondary legislation.

SCHEDULE 1

CONSEQUENTIAL AMENDMENTS—PRIMARY LEGISLATION

Article 8

Value Added Tax Act 1994

22 The Value Added Tax Act 1994 is amended as follows.

23 In section 66(7) (failure to submit EC sales statement or statement relating to section 55A)—

(*a*) after "76" insert "and Schedule 24 to the Finance Act 2007", and

(*b*) after "any penalty under this section" insert "or that Schedule".

24 In section 69(9)(*c*) (breaches of regulatory provisions) after "section 60 or 63" insert " or a penalty under Schedule 24 to the Finance Act 2007".

25 In section 69A(7)(*a*) (breach of record-keeping requirements etc in relation to transactions in gold) after "section 60" insert "or a penalty for a deliberate inaccuracy under Schedule 24 to the Finance Act 2007".

26 In section 69B(7)(*a*) (breach of record keeping requirements imposed by directions) after "section 60" insert "or a penalty for a deliberate inaccuracy under Schedule 24 to the Finance Act 2007".

27 In paragraph 10(3)(*b*) of Schedule 11A(*a*) (disclosure of avoidance schemes) after "section 60" insert "or a penalty for a deliberate inaccuracy under Schedule 24 to the Finance Act 2007".

SCHEDULE 2

CONSEQUENTIAL AMENDMENTS—SECONDARY LEGISLATION

Article 9

Duty Stamps Regulations 2006

42 The Duty Stamps Regulations 2006 are amended as follows.

43 For regulation 10(8) substitute—

"(8) A relevant penalty is a penalty that has been assessed and notified under Schedule 24 to the Finance Act 2007 (penalties for errors) and that has not been withdrawn or quashed."

VAT SIs

2009/1177

VALUE ADDED TAX (REFUND OF TAX TO CHARTER TRUSTEES AND CONSERVATORS) ORDER 2009

Made by the Treasury under VATA 1994 s 33(3)(*k*)

Made . . . . *7 May 2009*
Laid before the House of Commons . . . . *8 May 2009*
Coming into force:
Articles 1 and 2 . . . . *1 June 2009*
Remainder . . . . *1 April 2010*

1 Citation and commencement

This Order may be cited as the Value Added Tax (Refund of Tax to Charter Trustees and Conservators) Order 2009 and shall come into force—

(*a*) for the purposes of articles 1 and 2 on 1st June 2009, and
(*b*) for all other purposes on 1st April 2010.

2 Charter Trustees

The following bodies are specified for the purposes of section 33 of the Value Added Tax Act 1994—

(*a*) the Charter Trustees for the City of Chester,
(*b*) the Charter Trustees for Crewe,
(*c*) the Charter Trustees for the City of Durham,
(*d*) the Charter Trustees for Ellesmere Port, and
(*e*) the Charter Trustees for Macclesfield.

3 Wimbledon and Putney Commons Conservators

The Wimbledon and Putney Commons Conservators are specified for the purposes of section 33 of the Value Added Tax Act 1994.

2009/1916

INFORMATION NOTICE: RESOLUTION OF DISPUTES AS TO PRIVILEGED COMMUNICATIONS REGULATIONS 2009

Made by the Commissioners for HMRC under FA 2008 Sch 36 para 23(3) and (4)

Made . . . . *16 July 2009*
Laid before the House of Commons . . . . *17 July 2009*
Coming into force . . . . *7 August 2009*

1 Citation and commencement

These Regulations may be cited as the Information Notice: Resolution of Disputes as to Privileged Communications Regulations 2009 and come into force on 7th August 2009.

2 Interpretation

In these Regulations—

"document" means information, a document or part of a document;

a "document in dispute" is a document over which there is a dispute between HMRC and a person who has been given an information notice as to whether the document is privileged;

"officer" means an officer of Revenue and Customs;

a "person acting on behalf of" a taxpayer or a third party means any person who is acting on behalf of a taxpayer or third party in relation to an information notice;

"Schedule 36" means Schedule 36 to the Finance Act 2008;

"taxpayer" means a person who is given a notice under paragraph 1 of Schedule 36;

"third party" means a person who is given a notice under paragraph 2 or paragraph 5 of Schedule 36;

"working day" means any day except a Saturday, Sunday, Christmas Day, Good Friday or a bank holiday under section 1 of the Banking and Financial Dealings Act 1971.

3 Application of these Regulations

These Regulations apply where there is a dispute between HMRC and a person to whom an information notice has been given either—

(*a*) during the course of correspondence, or

(*b*) during the course of an inspection of premises under Schedule 36,

as to whether a document is privileged.

4 Requirement to provide information and produce documents not in dispute

Nothing in these Regulations shall affect—

(*a*) the requirement under an information notice to provide information or produce a document, which is not in dispute; or

(*b*) the power under Schedule 36 to inspect premises.

5 Procedure where information notice given in correspondence is in dispute

(1) The following procedure applies where there is a dispute falling within regulation 3(*a*).

(2) On receipt of the information notice, the taxpayer, third party or person acting on their behalf shall—

(*a*) by the date given in the notice for providing information or producing documents, specify in a list each document, required under the information notice, which is in dispute, with a description of the nature and contents of that document;

(*b*) serve that list on HMRC.

(3) But no description of a document or type of document is required where such description would itself give rise to a dispute over privilege.

(4) Within twenty working days of receiving the list referred to in sub-paragraph (2), HMRC must notify the person who served the list of any documents on the list that it requires to be produced and which it considers are not privileged.

(5) On receipt of notification under paragraph (4), the taxpayer, third party or person acting on their behalf must make an application to the First-tier Tribunal to consider and resolve the dispute and must include copies of the documents which remain in dispute with that application.

(6) The taxpayer, third party or person acting on their behalf shall provide HMRC with proof of service under paragraph (2)(*b*).

(7) Service for the purposes of paragraph (2)(*b*) must take place within a reasonable time to be agreed between the taxpayer, third party or person acting on their behalf and HMRC but in any event no later than twenty working days after the date given in the notice for providing information or producing documents.

(8) An application under paragraph (5) must be made within a reasonable time to be agreed between the taxpayer, third party or person acting on their behalf and HMRC but in any event no later than twenty working days of the date of the notification required under paragraph (4).

6 Procedure where information notice given during inspection of premises is in dispute

(1) The following procedure applies where there is a dispute falling within regulation 3(*b*).

(2) On receipt of the information notice, the taxpayer, third party or person acting on their behalf shall indicate to the officer carrying out the inspection each document, required under the information notice, which is in dispute.

(3) The taxpayer, third party or person acting on their behalf must place the document or documents in dispute, or a copy of such document or documents, in an appropriate container which prevents the contents being visible.

(4) The container shall be—

(*a*) sealed, labelled and signed by that person;

(*b*) countersigned by the officer; and

(*c*) given into the custody of the officer.

(5) The officer shall deliver the container to the First-tier Tribunal with the seal intact within forty-two working days of having taken custody of it together with an application to that Tribunal to consider and resolve the dispute.

7 Compliance with information notice

Where a taxpayer or third party who has received an information notice, or a person acting on their behalf, complies with the procedure set out in regulation 5 or, as the case may be, regulation 6, those persons shall be treated as having complied with the information notice in relation to the documents in dispute until the First-tier Tribunal decides the status of the document or until an agreement has been reached under regulation 10.

8 Finding of the First-tier Tribunal

When an application is made under regulation 5(5) or 6(5), the First-tier Tribunal shall—

(*a*) resolve the dispute by confirming whether and to what extent the document, is or is not privileged;

(*b*) direct which part or parts of a document (if any) shall be disclosed.

9 The First-tier Tribunal must ensure that any document in dispute, or any copy of such document, is not inappropriately disclosed to any person pending the Tribunal's consideration of the status of the document.

10 Resolution of disputes by agreement

A dispute falling within regulation 3 may be resolved at any time by HMRC and the person to whom an information notice has been given reaching an agreement, whether in writing or otherwise.

2009/2972

VALUE ADDED TAX (DRUGS AND MEDICINES) ORDER 2009

Made . . . . *9 November 2009*

Laid before the House of Commons . . . . *10 November 2009*

Coming into force . . . . *2 December 2009*

The Treasury, in exercise of the powers conferred by sections 30(4) and 96(9) of the Value Added Tax Act 1994, make the following Order:

1 This Order may be cited as the Value Added Tax (Drugs and Medicines) Order 2009, and comes into force on 2nd December 2009 and has effect in relation to supplies made on or after that date.

2 (1) Group 12 of Schedule 8 to the Value Added Tax Act 1994 (zero-rating: drugs, medicines, aids for the handicapped, etc) is varied as follows.

3 For items 1 and 1A substitute—

"**1** The supply of any qualifying goods dispensed to an individual for that individual's personal use on the prescription of an appropriate practitioner where the dispensing is—

(*a*) by a registered pharmacist, or

(*b*) in accordance with a requirement or authorisation under a relevant provision."

4 In Note (1) omit "or item 1A".

5 In Note (2A) for "items 1 and 1A" substitute "item 1".

6 Insert after Note (2A)—

"(2B) In item 1 "appropriate practitioner" means—

(*a*) a registered medical practitioner;

(*b*) a person registered in the dentists' register under the Dentists Act 1984;

(*c*) a community practitioner nurse prescriber;

(*d*) a nurse independent prescriber;

(*e*) an optometrist independent prescriber;

(*f*) a pharmacist independent prescriber;

(*g*) a supplementary prescriber.

For the purposes of this Note "community practitioner nurse prescriber", "nurse independent prescriber", "optometrist independent prescriber", "pharmacist independent prescriber" and "supplementary prescriber" have the meanings given in article 1(2) of the Prescription Only Medicines (Human Use) Order 1997.

(2C) In item 1 "registered pharmacist" means a person who is—

(*a*) registered in the Register of Pharmacists maintained under the Pharmacists and Pharmacy Technicians Order 2007, or

(*b*) registered in the register of pharmaceutical chemists kept under the Pharmacy (Northern Ireland) Order 1976.

(2D) In item 1 "relevant provision" means—

(*a*) article 57 of the Health and Personal Social Services (Northern Ireland) Order 1972;

(*b*) regulation 20 of the National Health Service (Pharmaceutical Services) Regulations 1992;

(*c*) regulation 12 of the Pharmaceutical Services Regulations (Northern Ireland) 1997;

(*d*) paragraph 44 of Schedule 5 to the National Health Service (General Medical Services Contracts) (Scotland) Regulations 2004;

(*e*) paragraph 15 of Schedule 1 to the National Health Service (Primary Medical Services Section 17C Agreements) (Scotland) Regulations 2004;

(*f*) paragraphs 47 and 49 of Schedule 6 to the National Health Service (General Medical Services Contracts) Regulations 2004;

(*g*) paragraph 44 of Schedule 5 to the Health and Personal Social Services (General Medical Services Contracts) Regulations (Northern Ireland) 2004;

(*h*) paragraphs 46, 48 and 49 of Schedule 5 to the National Health Service (Personal Medical Services Agreements) Regulations 2004;

(*i*) paragraph 47 of Schedule 6 to the National Health Service (General Medical Services Contracts) (Wales) Regulations 2004;

(*j*) regulation 60 of the National Health Service (Pharmaceutical Services) Regulations 2005.".

7 In Note (5) omit "1A,".

2009/3024

FINANCE ACT 2008, SECTION 128 AND PART 2 OF SCHEDULE 43 (APPOINTED DAY, TRANSITIONAL PROVISION AND SAVINGS) ORDER 2009

Made . . . . 9 November 2009

The Commissioners for Her Majesty's Revenue and Customs, in exercise of the powers conferred by section 129(4) and (5) of the Finance Act 2008 make the following Order:

1 Citation and interpretation

(1) This Order may be cited as The Finance Act 2008, Section 128 and Part 2 of Schedule 43 (Appointed Day, Transitional Provision and Savings) Order 2009.

2 In this Order "FA 2008" means the Finance Act 2008.

3 Appointed day

The day appointed for the coming into force of Section 128 of, and Part 2 of Schedule 43 to, FA 2008 is 23rd November 2009.

4 Transitional Provision and Savings

(1) If, before the commencement date, a warrant has been granted under—

(*a*) section 63 of the Taxes Management Act 1970 (recovery of tax in Scotland);

(*b*) section 121B of the Social Security Administration Act 1992 (recovery of contributions etc in Scotland);

(*c*) section 52 of the Finance Act 1997 (recovery of relevant tax in Scotland); or

(*d*) paragraph 3 of Schedule 12 to the Finance Act 2003 (recovery of stamp duty land tax by diligence in Scotland).

that warrant shall continue to have effect according to the provisions under which it was granted.

5 (1) The amendments made by paragraph 13(1) and (2) of Schedule 43 to FA 2008 to the Debtors (Scotland) Act 1987 shall not have effect in relation to—

(*a*) actions commenced under section 1 (time to pay directions); or

(*b*) applications made under section 5 (time to pay orders);

before the commencement date.

(2) The amendment made by paragraph 13(3) of Schedule 43 to FA 2008 to the definition of "summary warrant" in section 106 (interpretation) of the Debtors (Scotland) Act 1987 shall not apply to summary warrants granted before the commencement date.

2009/3073

TAXES, ETC (FEES FOR PAYMENT BY TELEPHONE) REGULATIONS 2009

Made by the Treasury under FA 2008 s 136

Made . . . . 20 November 2009

Laid before the House of Commons . . . . 23 November 2009

Coming into force . . . . 14 December 2009

Revocation—These Regulations revoked by the Taxes, etc. (Fees for Payment by Telephone) Regulations, SI 2012/689 with effect from 2 April 2012.

2009/3127

VALUE ADDED TAX (SUPPLEMENTARY CHARGE) ORDER 2009

Made . . . . 30 November 2009

Laid before the House of Commons . . . . 1 December 2009

Coming into force . . . . 31 December 2009

The Treasury, in exercise of the powers conferred by paragraph 15 of Schedule 3 (VAT: supplementary charge and orders changing rate) to the Finance Act 2009, make the following Order:

VAT SIs

1 This Order may be cited as the Value Added Tax (Supplementary Charge) Order 2009 and comes into force on 31st December 2009.

2 There is no supplementary charge on a supply of goods within paragraph 2 of Schedule 3 to the Finance Act 2009 if—

(*a*) the only relevant condition met is condition D,

(*b*) the VAT invoice—

(i) relates to a supply of goods made under a hire-purchase, conditional sale or credit sale agreement,

(ii) forms part of that agreement, and

(iii) is issued in accordance with normal commercial practice in relation to a supply made under such an agreement, and

(*c*) the basic time of supply of the goods is intended and expected to be within six months of the date of the VAT invoice which relates to the supply.

3 In this Order—

(*a*) "normal commercial practice" means the normal commercial practice of the supplier at a time when an increase in the rate of VAT in force under section 2 of the Value Added Tax Act 1994 is not expected, and

(*b*) "basic time of supply" has the meaning given in paragraph 4(1) of Schedule 3 to the Finance Act 2009.

2010/22

TRANSFER OF TRIBUNAL FUNCTIONS ORDER 2010

Made . . . . 6th January 2010

Coming into force in accordance with article 1

The Lord Chancellor makes the following Order in exercise of the powers conferred by sections 30(1) and (4), 31(1), (2) and (9) and 38 of, and paragraph 30 of Schedule 5 to, the Tribunals, Courts and Enforcement Act 2007.

The Welsh Ministers have consented to the making of this Order in so far as their consent is required by section 30(8) of that Act.

A draft of this Order was laid before Parliament and approved by a resolution of each House of Parliament in accordance with section 49(5) of that Act.

1 Citation, commencement and extent

(1) This Order may be cited as the Transfer of Tribunal Functions Order 2010 and, subject to paragraph (2), comes into force on 18th January 2010.

(2) The following provisions of this Order come into force on 6th April 2010—

(a) paragraph (5);

(b) article 2(2), (3)(b) and (4);

(c) article 3 in respect of the Financial Services and Markets Tribunal;

(d) Schedule 1 in respect of the Financial Services and Markets Tribunal and the Pensions Regulator Tribunal;

(e) in Schedule 2, paragraphs 3(c)(i), 4(c), 5 to 9, 12 to 14, 15(c), 17(b), 18(b), 20 to 23, 43 to 49, 74 to 89, 92(h) to (k) and 141 to 151;

(f) in Schedule 3, paragraphs 16 to 38, 90 to 94, 140 to 142, 143(d), 144 to 146, 148 to 158, 176 to 189 and 191 to 200; and

(g) Part 2 of Schedule 4.

(3) Subject as follows, this Order extends to England and Wales, Scotland and Northern Ireland.

(4) Except as provided by paragraph (5), an amendment, repeal or revocation of any enactment by any provision of Schedule 2, 3 or 4 extends to the part or parts of the United Kingdom to which the enactment extends.

(5) The amendments, repeals and revocations made by the following provisions do not extend to Northern Ireland—

(a) in Schedule 2, paragraphs 5(b), 9(b), 77 to 79, 83 to 85, 88, 142(b) and 143(b);

(b) in Schedule 3, paragraphs 90 to 94;

(c) in Part 2 of Schedule 4, the entries relating to—

(i) the Tribunals, Courts and Enforcement Act 2007 in so far as it relates to paragraph 40 of Schedule 10;

(ii) the Pensions Act 2008;

(iii) the Pensions Regulator Tribunal Rules 2005; and

(iv) the Lord Chancellor (Transfer of Functions and Supplementary Provisions) (No 2) Order 2006.

2 Transfer of functions of certain tribunals

(1) The functions of the following tribunals are transferred to the First-tier Tribunal—

(a) tribunals drawn from the Adjudication Panel for England;
(b) the Claims Management Services Tribunal;
(c) the Gambling Appeals Tribunal;
(d) the Immigration Services Tribunal; and
(e) the Family Health Services Appeal Authority.

(2) The functions of the Financial Services and Markets Tribunal are transferred to the Upper Tribunal.

(3) The functions of the following tribunals are transferred to the First-tier Tribunal and the Upper Tribunal with the question as to which one of them is to exercise the functions in a particular case being determined by, or under, Tribunal Procedure Rules—

(a) the Information Tribunal; and
(b) subject to paragraph (4), the Pensions Regulator Tribunal.

(4) The functions of the Pensions Regulator Tribunal exercisable in relation to Northern Ireland are not transferred.

3 Abolition of tribunals

The tribunals mentioned in article 2(1), (2) and (3)(a) are abolished.

4 Persons becoming judges and other members of the First-tier Tribunal and the Upper Tribunal

A person who, immediately before this Order comes into force, holds an office listed in a part of Schedule 1, is to hold the office or offices set out in the corresponding entry in the table below.

Part of Schedule 1	*Office or offices*
Part 1	Transferred-in judge of the Upper Tribunal
Part 2	Transferred-in other member of the Upper Tribunal
Part 3	Deputy judge of the Upper Tribunal and transferred in judge of the First-tier Tribunal
Part 4	Transferred-in judge of the First-tier Tribunal
Part 5	Transferred-in other member of the First-tier Tribunal

5 Consequential, transitional and saving provisions

(1) Schedule 2 contains amendments to primary legislation as a consequence of the transfers effected by this Order.

(2) Schedule 3 contains amendments to secondary legislation as a consequence of the transfers effected by this Order.

(3) Schedule 4 contains repeals and revocations as a consequence of the amendments in Schedules 2 and 3.

(4) Schedule 5 contains transitional and saving provisions.

SCHEDULE 5

TRANSITIONAL AND SAVING PROVISIONS

Article 5(4)

Interpretation of Schedule 5

1 In this Schedule—

"old tribunal" means a tribunal, the functions of which are transferred by article 2, but does not include the Pensions Regulator Tribunal in respect of its functions exercisable in Northern Ireland;

"new tribunal" means—

(a) the Upper Tribunal, in respect of—

(i) the functions of the Financial Services and Markets Tribunal and the Pensions Regulator Tribunal;

(ii) the functions of the Information Tribunal of deciding appeals under section 28 of the Data Protection Act 1998 or section 60 of the Freedom of Information Act 2000 (including that section as applied and modified by regulation 18 of the Environmental Information Regulations 2004) (appeals in relation to national security certificates);

(b) the First-tier Tribunal, in respect of—

(i) the tribunal functions mentioned in article 2(1);

(ii) the functions of the Information Tribunal other than those mentioned in paragraph (a)(ii);

"transfer date" means the date on which the functions of an old tribunal are transferred to a new tribunal by article 2.

Transitional and saving provisions

2 Any proceedings before an old tribunal which are pending immediately before the transfer date shall continue on and after the transfer date as proceedings before the new tribunal.

3 (1) The following sub-paragraphs apply where proceedings are continued in a new tribunal by virtue of paragraph 2.

(2) Where a hearing began before the transfer date but was not completed by that date, the new tribunal must be comprised for the continuation of that hearing of the person or persons who began it.

(3) The new tribunal may give any direction to ensure that proceedings are dealt with fairly and, in particular, may—

(a) apply any provision in procedural rules which applied to the proceedings before the transfer date; or

(b) disapply provisions of Tribunal Procedure Rules.

(4) In sub-paragraph (3) "procedural rules" means provision (whether called rules or not) regulating practice or procedure before a tribunal.

(5) Any direction or order given or made in proceedings which is in force immediately before the transfer date remains in force on and after that date as if it were a direction or order of the new tribunal.

(6) A time period which has started to run before the transfer date and which has not expired shall continue to apply.

(7) An order for costs may only be made if, and to the extent that, an order for costs could have been made by the old tribunal before the transfer date.

4 Paragraph 5 applies where—

(a) an appeal lies to a court from any decision made by an old tribunal before the transfer date;

(b) that right of appeal has not been exercised; and

(c) the time to exercise that right of appeal has not expired prior to the transfer date.

5 In the circumstances set out at paragraph 4, such of the following provisions as is appropriate shall apply as if the decision were a decision made on or after the transfer date by the new tribunal—

(a) section 11 of the Tribunals, Courts and Enforcement Act 2007 (right to appeal to Upper Tribunal);

(b) section 13 of the Tribunals, Courts and Enforcement Act 2007 (right to appeal to Court of Appeal);

(c) section 78(9A) to (9D) or section 78B(4) to (7) of the Local Government Act 2000 (as inserted or amended by Schedule 2 to this Order).

6 Any case to be remitted by a court on or after the transfer date and which, if it had been remitted before the transfer date, would have been remitted to an old tribunal, shall be remitted to the new tribunal.

7 Staff appointed to an old tribunal before the transfer date are to be treated on and after that date, for the purpose of any enactment, as if they had been appointed by the Lord Chancellor under section 40(1) of the Tribunals, Courts and Enforcement Act 2007 (tribunal staff and services).

8 A decision made by an old tribunal before the transfer date is to be treated on or after the transfer date as a decision of the new tribunal.

2010/466

FINANCE ACT 2009, SCHEDULE 56 (APPOINTED DAY AND CONSEQUENTIAL PROVISIONS) ORDER 2010

Made . . . . *25 February 2010*

Laid before the House of Commons. . . . . *26 February 2010*

Coming into force. . . . . .6 *April 2010*

The Treasury make the following Order in exercise of the powers conferred by section 107 of the Finance Act 2009.

1 Citation, commencement and interpretation

This Order may be cited as the Finance Act 2009, Schedule 56 (Appointed Day and Consequential Provisions) Order 2010 and shall come into force on 6th April 2010.

2 In this Order—

"Schedule 56" means Schedule 56 to the Finance Act 2009;

"tax quarter" means any of the following (inclusive) periods—

6th April to 5th July, 6th July to 5th October, 6th October to 5th January and 6th January to 5th April;

"tax month" means the period beginning on the 6th day of a calendar month and ending on the 5th day of the following calendar month;

"tax period" means a tax quarter or tax month;

"section 254 period" means each period of three months ending with 31st March, 30th June, 30th September or 31st December as provided for in section 254(2) of the Finance Act 2004.

3 Appointed day

(1) In relation to those amounts of tax which are specified in paragraph (2), and are—

(*a*) chargeable in respect of a tax period starting on or after 6th April 2010, or

(*b*) chargeable in respect of a section 254 period ending on or after 30th September 2010

the day appointed for the coming into force of Schedule 56 is 6th April 2010.

(2) The amounts of tax referred to in paragraph (1) are the following amounts specified in column 3 of the Table in paragraph 1 of Schedule 56—

(*a*) items 2, 3 and 4, and

(*b*) items 17, 23 and 24 but only insofar as the tax falls within any of items 2,3 or 4.

4 Consequential provisions and savings

(1) Regulations 203 (default surcharge) and 204 (surcharge notice and appeal) of the Income Tax (Pay As You Earn) Regulations 2003 are omitted subject to the savings set out in paragraph (3).

(2) Regulations 48 (default surcharge) and 49 (surcharge notice and appeal) of the Income Tax (Construction Industry Scheme) Regulations 2005 are omitted subject to the savings set out in paragraph (3).

(3) The regulations referred to in paragraphs (1) and (2) shall continue to have effect in relation to surcharges arising in respect of late payments of tax where the tax was chargeable in respect of a tax period ending on or before 5th April 2010.

(4) Paragraph 110 of Schedule 2 (consequential amendments and supplemental provisions—secondary legislation) to the Transfer of Tribunal Functions and Revenue and Customs Appeals Order 2009 is omitted.

2010/1813

REVENUE AND CUSTOMS (COMPLAINTS AND MISCONDUCT) REGULATIONS 2010

Made . . . . .14 *July 2010*

Laid before Parliament . . . . .15 *July 2010*

Coming into force . . . . .5 *August 2010*

The Treasury make the following Regulations in exercise of the powers conferred by sections 28(1), (2) and (6) and 29(3) of the Commissioners for Revenue and Customs Act 2005.

Commentary—*Simon's Taxes* **A5.403**.

PART 1
GENERAL

1 Citation and commencement

These Regulations may be cited as the Revenue and Customs (Complaints and Misconduct) Regulations 2010 and shall come into force on 5th August 2010.

2 Revocation and transitional provision

(1) Subject to paragraph (2), the Revenue and Customs (Complaints and Misconduct) Regulations 2005 and the Revenue and Customs (Complaints and Misconduct) (Amendment) Regulations 2006 are revoked.

VAT SIs

(2) Where an allegation in respect of the conduct by an officer came to the attention of the appropriate authority before the 5th August 2010, nothing in these Regulations shall apply and the Revenue and Customs (Complaints and Misconduct) Regulations 2005 shall continue to have effect.

3 Interpretation

(1) In these Regulations—

"2002 Act" means the Police Reform Act 2002;

"appropriate authority"—

(*a*) in relation to the Commissioners or an officer or in relation to any complaint, matter or investigation relating to the conduct of such a person, means—

(i) if that person is the Chairman, the Chief Executive or the Permanent Secretary for Tax, the Head of the Home Civil Service,

(ii) if that person is a Commissioner, the Chief Executive unless that Commissioner is the Chairman, the Permanent Secretary for Tax or the Chief Executive, or

(iii) if that person is an officer, the Commissioners (other than the Chairman, the Chief Executive and the Permanent Secretary for Tax), and

(*b*) in relation to a death or serious injury matter and the relevant officer, means the Commissioners (other than the Chairman, the Chief Executive and the Permanent Secretary for Tax);

"the Chairman" means the Chairman of the Board of HMRC;

"the Chief Executive" means the Chief Executive of HMRC;

"chief officer" means the chief officer of police of any police force;

"the Commissioners" unless a contrary intention appears, means the Commissioners for Her Majesty's Revenue and Customs and for the purposes of these Regulations includes the Chairman (and unless a contrary intention appears, "Commissioner" is to be construed accordingly);

"complainant" shall be construed in accordance with paragraph (4);

"complaint" has the meaning given by regulation 9 (complaints, matters and persons to which these Regulations apply);

"conduct" includes acts, omissions and statements (whether actual, alleged or inferred);

"conduct matter" has the meaning given by regulation 9;

"death or serious injury matter" and "DSI matter" have the meaning given by regulation 9;

"disciplinary proceedings" means any proceedings or management process during which the conduct of the Commissioners or an officer is considered in order to determine whether a sanction or punitive measure should be imposed against that person in relation to that conduct;

"document" means anything in which information of any description is recorded;

"function" in relation to the Commissioners or officers has the meaning given by section 51(2) of the Commissioners for Revenue and Customs Act 2005;

"HMRC" means Her Majesty's Revenue and Customs;

"information" includes estimates and projections, and statistical analyses;

"IPCC" means the Independent Police Complaints Commission and has the meaning given by section 9(1) of the 2002 Act;

"officer" means, unless the context otherwise requires, an officer of Revenue and Customs;

"the Permanent Secretary for Tax" means HMRC's Permanent Secretary for Tax;

"the person complained against", in relation to a complaint, means the person whose conduct is the subject-matter of the complaint;

"the person investigating", in relation to a complaint, recordable conduct matter or DSI matter, means the person appointed or designated to investigate that complaint or matter;

"recordable conduct matter" means—

(*a*) a conduct matter that is required to be recorded by the appropriate authority under regulation 23 (conduct matters arising in civil proceedings) or 24 (recording etc of conduct matters in other cases), or has been so recorded; or

(*b*) except in paragraph (3) of regulation 19 (initial handling and recording of complaints), any matter brought to the attention of the appropriate authority under that paragraph;

"relevant offence" means—

(*a*) an offence for which the sentence is fixed by law,

(*b*) an offence for which a person of 18 years or over (not previously convicted) may be sentenced to imprisonment for a term of seven years or more (or might be so sentenced but for the restrictions imposed by section 33 of the Magistrates' Courts Act 1980);

"serious injury" means a fracture, a deep cut, a deep laceration or an injury causing damage to an internal organ or the impairment of any bodily function.

(2) In these Regulations "the relevant officer", in relation to a DSI matter, means the officer—

(*a*) who arrested the person who has died or suffered serious injury,

(*b*) in whose custody that person was at the time of the death or serious injury, or

(*c*) with whom that person had the contact in question;

and where there is more than one such officer it means, subject to paragraph (3), the one who so dealt with that person last before the death or serious injury occurred.

(3) Where it cannot be determined which of two or more officers dealt with a person last before a death or serious injury occurred, the "relevant officer" is the most senior of them.

(4) References in these Regulations to the complainant, in relation to anything which is or purports to be a complaint, are references—

(*a*) except in the case of anything which is or purports to be a complaint falling within regulation 9(1)(*d*) (complaints, matters and persons to which these Regulations apply), to the person by whom the complaint or purported complaint was made; and

(*b*) in that case, to the person on whose behalf the complaint or purported complaint was made;

but where any person is acting on another's behalf for the purposes of any complaint or purported complaint, anything that is to be or may be done under these Regulations by or in relation to the complainant may be done, instead, by or in relation to the person acting on the complainant's behalf.

(5) Subject to paragraph (6), references in these Regulations, in relation to any conduct or anything purporting to be a complaint about any conduct, to a member of the public include references to any person who is a Commissioner or an officer (whether at the time of the conduct or any subsequent time).

(6) In these Regulations references, in relation to any conduct or to anything purporting to be a complaint about any conduct, to a member of the public do not include references to—

(*a*) a person who, at the time when the conduct was supposed to have taken place in relation to that person, was a Commissioner or an officer (whether or not that person was on duty in that person's capacity as a Commissioner or officer at that time), or

(*b*) a person who at the time when that person is supposed to have been adversely affected by it, or to have witnessed it, was on duty in that person's capacity as a Commissioner or officer.

(7) For the purposes of these Regulations, a person is adversely affected if that person suffers any form of loss or damage, distress or inconvenience, if that person is put in danger or if that person is otherwise unduly put at risk of being adversely affected.

(8) References in these Regulations to the investigation of any complaint or matter by the appropriate authority on its own behalf, under the supervision of the IPCC, under the management of the IPCC or by the IPCC itself shall be construed as references to its investigation in accordance with—

(*a*) regulation 44 (investigations by the appropriate authority on its own behalf),

(*b*) regulation 45 (investigations supervised by the IPCC),

(*c*) regulation 46 (investigations by a police force under the management or under the supervision of the IPCC),

(*d*) regulation 47 (investigations managed by the IPCC), or

(*e*) regulation 48 (investigations by the IPCC itself).

4 Application: general

These Regulations shall apply for the purpose of conferring functions on the IPCC in relation to the Commissioners and officers, in the exercise of their functions in or in relation to England and Wales.

5 Application of the 2002 Act

(1) Sections 9 (the Independent Police Complaints Commission), 19 (use of investigatory powers by or on behalf of the IPCC), 22 (power of the IPCC to issue guidance), 23 (regulations), 24 (consultation on regulations) and 27 (conduct of the IPCC's staff) of the 2002 Act shall apply to the Commissioners and officers with the following modifications.

(2) In section 22 of the 2002 Act—

(*a*) for subsection (1) substitute—

"(1) The Commission may issue guidance to Her Majesty's Revenue and Customs and any person it sees fit concerning the exercise or performance by the persons to whom the guidance is issued, of any powers or duties specified in subsection (2).";

(*b*) in subsection (2) for "persons serving with the police" substitute "persons serving with Her Majesty's Revenue and Customs";

(*c*) for subsection (3) substitute—

"(3) Before issuing any guidance under this section, the Commission shall consult Her Majesty's Revenue and Customs and any person it sees fit.";

(*d*) in subsection (4) for "the Secretary of State" substitute "the Chancellor of the Exchequer";

(*e*) omit subsection (5)(*c*).

(3) In section 23 of the 2002 Act—

(*a*) in subsection (2)(k), for "a person serving with the police" substitute "a person serving with Her Majesty's Revenue and Customs";

(*b*) in subsection (2)(p), for "chief officers" substitute "the Commissioners for Her Majesty's Revenue and Customs".

(4) In section 24 of the 2002 Act—

(*a*) at the end of paragraph (*a*) insert "and Her Majesty's Revenue and Customs";

(*b*) omit paragraphs (*b*) and (*c*).

6 Temporary service and copies of accounts

(1) The IPCC may make arrangements with the Commissioners under which officers are engaged on temporary service with the IPCC.

(2) Copies of the statement referred to in paragraph 17(1)(*c*) of Schedule 2 to the 2002 Act (accounts) shall also be sent to the Treasury.

7 General functions of the IPCC in relation to the Commissioners and officers

(1) The functions of the IPCC in relation to the Commissioners and officers shall be—

(*a*) to secure the maintenance by the IPCC itself, and by the Commissioners, of suitable arrangements with respect to the matters mentioned in paragraph (2);

(*b*) to keep under review all arrangements maintained with respect to those matters;

(*c*) to secure that arrangements maintained with respect to those matters comply with the requirements of the following provisions of this Part, are efficient and effective and contain and manifest an appropriate degree of independence;

(*d*) to secure that public confidence is established and maintained in the existence of suitable arrangements with respect to those matters and with the operation of the arrangements that are in fact maintained with respect to those matters;

(*e*) to make such recommendations, and to give such advice, for the modification of the arrangements maintained with respect to those matters, as appear, from the carrying out by the IPCC of its other functions, to be necessary or desirable.

(2) Those matters are—

(*a*) the handling of complaints made about the conduct of the Commissioners or officers which the appropriate authority—

(i) has a duty to refer to the IPCC under regulation 28(1) (reference of complaints to the IPCC), or

(ii) may refer to the IPCC under regulation 28(4) or (5);

(*b*) the recording of matters from which it appears that—

(i) there may have been conduct by such persons which constitutes or involves the commission of a criminal offence or behaviour justifying disciplinary proceedings, and

(ii) that conduct or behaviour is conduct or behaviour which the appropriate authority has a duty to refer to the IPCC under regulation 30(1) (reference of conduct matters to the IPCC) or may refer to the IPCC under regulation 30(5) or (6) of these Regulations;

(*c*) the recording of matters from which it appears that a person has died or suffered serious injury during, or following, contact with an officer;

(*d*) the manner in which any such complaints or any such matters as are mentioned in sub-paragraph (*b*) or (*c*) are investigated or otherwise handled and dealt with.

(3) It shall be the duty of the IPCC—

(*a*) to exercise the powers and perform the duties conferred on it by the following provisions of these Regulations in the manner that it considers best calculated for the purpose of securing the proper carrying out of its functions under paragraph (1), and

(*b*) to secure that arrangements exist which are conducive to, and facilitate, the reporting of misconduct by persons in relation to whose conduct the IPCC has functions.

(4) It shall also be the duty of the IPCC—

(*a*) to enter into arrangements with the chief inspector of constabulary for the purpose of securing co-operation, in the carrying out of their respective functions in relation to the Commissioners and officers, between the IPCC and the inspectors of constabulary, and

(*b*) to provide those inspectors with all such assistance and co-operation as may be required by those arrangements, or as otherwise appears to the IPCC to be appropriate, for facilitating the carrying out by those inspectors of their functions.

(5) Subject to the other provisions of these Regulations, the IPCC may do anything which appears to it to be calculated to facilitate, or is incidental or conducive to, the carrying out of its functions.

(6) The IPCC may, in connection with the making of any recommendation or the giving of any advice to any person for the purpose of carrying out its function under paragraph (1)(*e*), impose any such charge on that person for anything done by the IPCC for the purposes of, or in connection with, the carrying out of that function as it thinks fit.

(7) Nothing in these Regulations shall confer any function on the IPCC in relation to so much of any complaint or conduct matter as relates to the direction and control of HMRC by the Commissioners.

8 Reports to the Chancellor of the Exchequer

(1) As soon as practicable after the end of each of its financial years, the IPCC shall also make a report to the Chancellor of the Exchequer ("the Chancellor") on the carrying out of its functions during that year.

(2) The IPCC shall also make such reports to the Chancellor about matters relating generally to the carrying out of its functions as the Chancellor may, from time to time, require.

(3) The IPCC may, from time to time, make such other reports to the Chancellor as it considers appropriate for drawing the Chancellor's attention to matters which—

(*a*) have come to the IPCC's notice, and

(*b*) are matters that it considers should be drawn to the Chancellor's attention by reason of their gravity or of other exceptional circumstances.

(4) The IPCC shall prepare such reports containing advice and recommendations as it thinks appropriate for the purpose of carrying out its function under regulation 7(1)(*e*) (general functions of the IPCC in relation to Commissioners and officers).

(5) Where the Chancellor receives any report under this regulation, the Chancellor shall—

(*a*) in the case of every annual report under paragraph (1), and

(*b*) in the case of any other report, if and to the extent that the Chancellor considers it appropriate to do so,

lay a copy of the report before Parliament and cause the report to be published.

(6) The IPCC shall send a copy of every annual report under paragraph (1) to the Commissioners.

(7) The IPCC shall send a copy of every report under paragraph (3) to the Commissioners.

(8) The IPCC shall send a copy of every report under paragraph (4) to—

(*a*) the Chancellor of the Exchequer, and

(*b*) the Commissioners.

(9) The IPCC shall send a copy of every report made or prepared by it under paragraphs (3) or (4) to such of the persons (in addition to those specified in the preceding paragraphs) who—

(*a*) are referred to in the report, or

(*b*) appear to the IPCC otherwise to have a particular interest in its contents,

as the IPCC thinks fit.

9 Complaints, matters and persons to which these Regulations apply

(1) In these Regulations references to a complaint are references (subject to the following provisions of this regulation) to any complaint about the conduct of a Commissioner or an officer which is made (whether in writing or otherwise) by—

(*a*) a member of the public who claims to be the person in relation to whom the conduct took place;

(*b*) a member of the public not falling within sub-paragraph (*a*) who claims to have been adversely affected by the conduct;

(*c*) a member of the public who claims to have witnessed the conduct;

(*d*) a person acting on behalf of a person falling within any of sub-paragraphs (*a*) to (*c*).

(2) In these Regulations "conduct matter" means (subject to the following provisions of this regulation, and regulation 19(3)) any matter which is not and has not been the subject of a complaint but in the case of which there is an indication (whether from the circumstances or otherwise) that a Commissioner or an officer may have—

(*a*) committed a criminal offence, or

(*b*) behaved in a manner which would justify the bringing of disciplinary proceedings.

(3) In these Regulations "death or serious injury matter" ("DSI matter") means any circumstance (other than those which are or have been the subject of a complaint or which amount to a conduct matter)—

(*a*) in or in consequence of which a person has died or has sustained serious injury, and

(*b*) in relation to which the requirements of either paragraph (4) or (5) are satisfied.

(4) The requirements of this paragraph are that at the time of the death or serious injury the person—

(*a*) had been arrested by an officer and had not been released from that arrest, or

(*b*) was otherwise detained in the custody of an officer.

(5) The requirements of this paragraph are that—

(*a*) at or before the time of the death or serious injury the person had contact (of whatever kind, and whether direct or indirect) with an officer who was acting in the execution of duties, and

(*b*) there is an indication that the contact may have caused (whether directly or indirectly) or contributed to the death or serious injury.

(6) In paragraph (3) the reference to a person includes an officer, but in relation to such a person "contact" in paragraph (5) does not include contact that the officer has whilst acting in the execution of duties.

(7) The complaints that are complaints for the purposes of these Regulations by virtue of paragraph (1)(*b*) do not, except in a case falling within paragraph (8), include any made by or on behalf of a person who claims to have been adversely affected as a consequence only of having seen or heard the conduct, or any of the alleged effects of the conduct.

(8) A case falls within this paragraph if—

(*a*) it was only because the person in question was physically present, or sufficiently nearby, when the conduct took place or the effects occurred that the person was able to see or hear the conduct or its effects, or (*b*) the adverse effect is attributable to, or was aggravated by, the fact that the person in relation to whom the conduct took place was already known to the person claiming to have suffered the adverse effect.

(9) For the purposes of this regulation a person shall be taken to have witnessed conduct if, and only if—

(*a*) that person acquired knowledge of that conduct in a manner which would make that person a competent witness capable of giving admissible evidence of that conduct in criminal proceedings, or

(*b*) that person possesses or controls anything which would in any such proceedings constitute admissible evidence of that conduct.

(10) For the purposes of these Regulations a person falling within paragraph (1)(*a*) to (*c*) shall not be taken to have authorised another person to act on that person's behalf unless—

(*a*) that other person is for the time being designated for the purposes of these Regulations by the IPCC as a person through whom complaints may be made, or is of a description of persons so designated, or

(*b*) the other person has been given, and is able to produce, the written consent to such action, of the person on whose behalf that action is taken.

10 Handling of complaints, conduct matters and DSI matters etc

These Regulations shall have effect subject to regulation 11 (direction and control matters).

11 Direction and control matters

Nothing in these Regulations shall have effect with respect to so much of any complaint as relates to the direction and control of HMRC by the Commissioners.

PART 2

COMPLAINTS AND MISCONDUCT

12 Co-operation, assistance and information

(1) It shall be the duty of the Commissioners to ensure that they are kept informed, in relation to HMRC, about all matters falling within paragraph (2).

(2) Those matters are—

(*a*) matters with respect to which any provision of these Regulations has effect;

(*b*) anything which is done under or for the purposes of any such provision; and

(*c*) any obligations to act or refrain from acting that have arisen by or under these Regulations, but have not yet been complied with or have been contravened.

(3) Where the IPCC requires the chief officer of a police force to provide a member of that person's force for appointment under regulation 46 or 47, it shall be the duty of the chief officer to whom the requirement is addressed to comply with it.

(4) It shall be the duty of the Commissioners to provide the IPCC and every member of the IPCC's staff with all such assistance as the IPCC or that member of staff may reasonably require for the purposes of, or in connection with, the carrying out of any investigation by the IPCC under these Regulations.

(5) It shall be the duty of the Commissioners to ensure that a person appointed under regulation 42 to carry out an investigation is given all such assistance and co-operation in the carrying out of that investigation as that person may reasonably require.

(6) It shall be the duty of the Head of the Home Civil Service and the Commissioners to ensure that a person appointed under regulation 44, 45, 46 or 47 to carry out an investigation is given all such assistance and co-operation in the carrying out of that investigation as that person may reasonably require.

13 Disclosure of information

Where the IPCC, or any person acting on its behalf, obtains information in the course of performing a function under these Regulations, that information may not be disclosed except as permitted under these Regulations or as otherwise prescribed by law.

14 Use of information

Where the IPCC or any person acting on its behalf, obtains information in the course of performing a function under these Regulations, that information may not be used for any purpose other than in the performance of a function under these Regulations or as otherwise prescribed by law.

15 Payments

(1) The Commissioners shall pay such amount to the Secretary of State in respect of functions performed by the IPCC under these Regulations as may be agreed between the Commissioners and the IPCC.

(2) In the absence of an agreement, the Commissioners shall pay such amount in respect of those functions as the Treasury, after consultation with the Secretary of State, shall determine.

16 Payment for assistance with investigations

(1) This regulation applies where—

(*a*) a police force is required to provide assistance in connection with an investigation under Part 6 of these Regulations (investigations);

(*b*) a police force is required to provide assistance in such a connection to the IPCC; or

(*c*) a police force provides assistance by agreement under regulation 46(2).

(2) For the purposes of this regulation—

(*a*) assistance is required to be provided by a police force in connection with an investigation under Part 6 of these Regulations if the chief officer of that force complies with a requirement under regulation 12(3) (co-operation, assistance and information) that is made in connection with—

(i) an investigation relating to the conduct of a person who, at the time of the conduct, was a Commissioner or an officer, or

(ii) an investigation of a DSI matter in relation to which the relevant officer was, at the time of the death or serious injury, an officer; and

(*b*) assistance is required to be provided in such a connection by a police force to the IPCC if the chief officer of that force complies with a requirement under regulation 12(6) that is made in connection with—

(i) an investigation relating to the conduct of a person who, at the time of the conduct, was a Commissioner or an officer, or

(ii) an investigation of a DSI matter in relation to which the relevant officer was, at the time of the death or serious injury, an officer.

(3) Where the assistance is required to be provided by a police force, the appropriate authority shall pay to the [local policing body][1] maintaining that force such contribution towards the costs of the assistance—

(*a*) as may be agreed between them; or

(*b*) in the absence of an agreement, as may be determined in accordance with any arrangements which—

(i) have been agreed to by [local policing bodies][1] generally and the Commissioners, and

(ii) are for the time being in force with respect to the making of contributions towards the costs of assistance provided, in connection with investigations under Part 6 of these Regulations; or

(*c*) in the absence of any such arrangements, as may be determined by the Secretary of State.

(4) Paragraph (3) shall have effect in relation to assistance which a police force provides by agreement under regulation 46(2) as if the reference in that paragraph to required to be provided were a reference to provided by agreement under regulation 46(2).

(5) Where the assistance is required to be provided by a police force to the IPCC, the IPCC shall pay to the [local policing body][1] maintaining the assisting force such contribution (if any) towards the costs of the assistance—

(*a*) as may be agreed between the IPCC and that authority; or

(*b*) in the absence of an agreement, as may be determined in accordance with any arrangements which—

(i) have been agreed to by [local policing bodies][1] generally and by the IPCC, and

(ii) are for the time being in force with respect to the making of contributions towards the costs of assistance provided, in connection with investigations under this Part, to the IPCC; or

(*c*) in the absence of any such arrangements, as may be determined by the Secretary of State.

Amendments—

[1] In paras (3) and (5), words substituted, and in paras 3(*b*)(*I*) and 5(*b*)(*I*), words substituted, by the Revenue and Customs (Complaints and Misconduct) (Amendment) Regulations, SI 2011/3061 reg 2 with effect from 16 January 2012.

PART 3

HANDLING OF COMPLAINTS AND CONDUCT MATTERS ETC

17 Duties to preserve evidence relating to complaints

(1) This regulation applies where condition A or B is met.

(2) Condition A is that—

(*a*) a complaint is made to an appropriate authority about the conduct of an individual, and

(*b*) that authority is the appropriate authority in relation to that individual.

(3) Condition B is that—

(*a*) an appropriate authority becomes aware that a complaint has been made to the IPCC, and

(*b*) that authority is the appropriate authority in relation to that individual.

(4) The appropriate authority shall take all such steps as appear to that authority to be appropriate for the purposes of these Regulations for obtaining and preserving evidence relating to the conduct complained of.

VAT SIs

(5) The duty of the appropriate authority under paragraph (4) must be performed as soon as practicable after the complaint is made or after it becomes aware of the complaint.

(6) After that, the appropriate authority shall be under a duty, until it is satisfied that it is no longer necessary to do so, to continue to take the steps from time to time appearing to that authority to be appropriate for the purposes of these Regulations for obtaining and preserving evidence relating to the conduct complained of.

(7) It shall be the duty of the appropriate authority to take all such specific steps for obtaining or preserving evidence relating to any conduct that is the subject-matter of a complaint as it may be directed by the IPCC to take for the purposes of this regulation.

18 Delegation of powers and duties

(1) Subject to paragraph (3), the appropriate authority may delegate all or any of the powers or duties conferred or imposed on it by or under these Regulations to a person mentioned in paragraph (2).

(2) Those powers or duties may be delegated—

(*a*) in the case of the Head of the Home Civil Service, to a member of the Senior Civil Service;

(*b*) in the case of the Chief Executive, to a member of the Senior Civil Service employed in the service of the Commissioners;

(*c*) in the case of a Commissioner (other than the Chief Executive), to an officer.

(3) The appropriate authority shall not, in any particular case, delegate any power or duty under paragraph (1) to a person who has acted as investigating officer in that case.

19 Initial handling and recording of complaints

(1) Where a complaint is made to the IPCC—

(*a*) it shall ascertain whether the complainant is content for the appropriate authority to be notified of the complaint, and

(*b*) it shall give notification of the complaint to the appropriate authority if, and only if, the complainant is so content.

(2) Where a complaint is made to an appropriate authority, the authority shall—

(*a*) determine whether or not it is the appropriate authority in relation to the complaint, and

(*b*) if it determines that it is not, give notification of the complaint to the appropriate authority for the individual complained against.

(3) Where the IPCC—

(*a*) is prevented by paragraph (1)(*b*) from notifying any complaint to the appropriate authority, and

(*b*) considers that it is in the public interest for the subject-matter of the complaint to be brought to the attention of the appropriate authority and recorded under regulation 24,

the IPCC may bring that matter to the appropriate authority's attention under that regulation as if it were a recordable conduct matter, and (if it does so) the following provisions of these Regulations shall have effect accordingly as if it were such a matter.

(4) Where the IPCC or the appropriate authority gives notification of a complaint under paragraph (1) or (2) or the IPCC brings any matter to the appropriate authority's attention under paragraph (3), the person who gave the notification or, as the case may be, the IPCC shall notify the complainant—

(*a*) that the notification has been given and of what it contained, or

(*b*) that the matter has been brought to the appropriate authority's attention to be dealt with otherwise than as a complaint.

(5) Where—

(*a*) an appropriate authority, in the case of any complaint made to it, decides that it is the appropriate authority, or

(*b*) a complaint is notified to the appropriate authority under this regulation,

the appropriate authority shall record the complaint.

(6) Nothing in this regulation shall require the notification or recording by any person of any complaint about any conduct if—

(*a*) that person is satisfied that the subject-matter of the complaint has been, or is already being, dealt with by means of criminal or disciplinary proceedings against the person whose conduct it was, or

(*b*) the complaint has been withdrawn.

20 Keeping of records

The appropriate authority shall keep records, in such form as the IPCC shall determine, of—

(*a*) every complaint and purported complaint that is made to it;

(*b*) every conduct matter recorded by it under regulation 23(3) (conduct matters arising in civil proceedings);

(*c*) every DSI matter recorded by it under regulation 32 (duty to record DSI matters);

(*d*) every exercise of a power or performance of a duty under these Regulations.

21 Failures to notify or record a complaint

(1) This regulation applies where anything which is or purports to be a complaint in relation to which regulation 19 (initial handling and recording of complaints) has effect is received by the Head of the Home Civil Service, the Chief Executive or the Commissioners (other than the Chairman, the Chief Executive and the Permanent Secretary) (whether in consequence of having been made directly or of a notification under that regulation).

(2) Where the Head of the Home Civil Service, the Chief Executive or the Commissioners (other than the Chairman, the Chief Executive and the Permanent Secretary) decides or decide not to take action under regulation 19 for notifying or recording the whole or any part of what has been received, the Head of the Home Civil Service, the Chief Executive or the Commissioners (other than the Chairman, the Chief Executive and the Permanent Secretary) shall notify the complainant of the following matters—

(*a*) the decision to take no action, and, if that decision relates to only part of what was received, the part in question;

(*b*) the grounds on which the decision was made; and

(*c*) whether the complainant has a right to appeal against that decision under this regulation.

(3) The complainant shall have a right of appeal to the IPCC against any failure by the Head of the Home Civil Service, the Chief Executive or the Commissioners (other than the Chairman, the Chief Executive and the Permanent Secretary) to make a determination under regulation 19 or to notify or record anything under that regulation if, but only if, the failure is in respect of conduct which the Head of the Home Civil Service, the Chief Executive or the Commissioners (other than the Chairman, the Chief Executive and the Permanent Secretary) is required to refer to the IPCC under regulation 28(1)(*a*) or (*b*) (reference of complaints to the IPCC).

(4) On an appeal under this regulation, the IPCC shall—

(*a*) determine whether any action under regulation 19 should have been taken in the case in question, and

(*b*) if the IPCC finds in the complainant's favour, give to the Head of the Home Civil Service, the Chief Executive or the Commissioners (other than the Chairman, the Chief Executive and the Permanent Secretary) such directions as the IPCC considers appropriate, as to the action to be taken for making a determination, or for notifying or recording what was received,

and it shall be the duty of the Head of the Home Civil Service, the Chief Executive or the Commissioners (other than the Chairman, the Chief Executive and the Permanent Secretary) to comply with any directions given under sub-paragraph (*b*).

(5) Directions under paragraph (4)(*b*) may require action taken in pursuance of the directions to be treated as taken in accordance with any such provision of regulation 19 as may be specified in the direction.

(6) The IPCC—

(*a*) shall give notification both to the Head of the Home Civil Service, the Chief Executive or the Commissioners (other than the Chairman, the Chief Executive and the Permanent Secretary), as the case may be, and to the complainant, of any determination made by it under this regulation, and

(*b*) shall give notification to the complainant of any direction given by it to the Head of the Home Civil Service, the Chief Executive or the Commissioners (other than the Chairman, the Chief Executive and the Permanent Secretary) under this regulation.

22 Handling of complaints by the appropriate authority

(1) This regulation applies where a complaint has been recorded by the appropriate authority unless the complaint—

(*a*) is one which has been, or must be, referred to the IPCC under regulation 28 (reference of complaints to the IPCC), and

(*b*) is not for the time being either referred back to the authority under regulation 29 (duties of the IPCC on references under regulation 28) or the subject of a determination under regulation 38 (power of the IPCC to determine the form of an investigation).

(2) The appropriate authority shall not be required by virtue of any provisions of these Regulations to take any action in relation to the complaint but may handle the complaint in whatever manner it thinks fit, or take no action in relation to the complaint.

23 Conduct matters arising in civil proceedings

(1) This regulation applies where—

(*a*) the appropriate authority has received notification (whether or not under this regulation) that civil proceedings relating to any matter have been brought by a member of the public against it, or it otherwise appears to the appropriate authority that such proceedings are likely to be so brought, and

(*b*) it appears to the appropriate authority (whether at the time of the notification or at any time subsequently) that those proceedings involve or would involve a conduct matter.

(2) The appropriate authority—

(*a*) shall consider whether it is the appropriate authority in relation to the conduct matter in question, and

(*b*) if it is not, shall notify the person who is the appropriate authority about the proceedings, or the proposal to bring them, and about the circumstances that make it appear as mentioned in paragraph (1)(*b*).

(3) Where the appropriate authority determines for the purposes of this regulation that it is the appropriate authority in relation to any conduct matter, it shall record that matter.

(4) Where the appropriate authority records any matter under this regulation it—

(*a*) shall first determine whether the matter is one which it is required to refer to the IPCC under regulation 30 (reference of conduct matters to the IPCC) or is one which it would be appropriate so to refer, and

(*b*) if it is not required so to refer the matter and does not do so, may deal with the matter in such other manner (if any) as it may determine.

(5) Nothing in paragraph (3) shall require the appropriate authority to record any conduct matter if it is satisfied that the matter has been, or is already being, dealt with by means of criminal or disciplinary proceedings against the person to whose conduct the matter relates.

(6) For the purposes of this regulation civil proceedings involve a conduct matter if—

(*a*) they relate to such a matter, or

(*b*) they are proceedings that relate to a matter in relation to which a conduct matter, or evidence of a conduct matter, is or may be relevant.

24 Recording etc of conduct matters in other cases

(1) Where—

(*a*) a conduct matter comes (otherwise than as mentioned in regulation 23 (conduct matters arising in civil proceedings)) to the attention of the appropriate authority in relation to that matter, and

(*b*) it appears to the appropriate authority that the conduct involved in that matter falls within paragraph (2),

it shall be the duty of the appropriate authority to record that matter.

(2) Conduct falls within this paragraph if (assuming it to have taken place)—

(*a*) it appears to have resulted in the death of any person or in serious injury to any person;

(*b*) a member of the public has been adversely affected by it; or

(*c*) it is of a description specified in paragraph (3).

(3) The following descriptions of conduct are specified for the purposes of paragraph (2)—

(*a*) a serious assault, as defined in guidance issued by the IPCC;

(*b*) a serious sexual offence, as defined in guidance issued by the IPCC;

(*c*) serious corruption, as defined in guidance issued by the IPCC;

(*d*) a criminal offence or behaviour liable to result in disciplinary proceedings which was aggravated by discriminatory behaviour on the grounds of a person's race, sex, religion, or other status identified in guidance by the IPCC;

(*e*) a relevant offence;

(*f*) conduct whose gravity or other exceptional circumstances make it appropriate to record the matter in which the conduct is involved; or

(*g*) conduct which is alleged to have taken place in the same incident as one in which conduct within sub-paragraphs (*a*) to (*e*) is alleged.

(4) Where the appropriate authority records any matter under this regulation it—

(*a*) shall first determine whether the matter is one which it is required to refer to the IPCC under regulation 30 (reference of conduct matters to the IPCC) or is one which it would be appropriate to so refer, and

(*b*) if it is not required so to refer the matter and does not do so, may deal with the matter in such other manner (if any) as it may determine.

(5) Nothing in paragraph (1) shall require the appropriate authority to record any conduct matter if it is satisfied that the matter has been, or is already being, dealt with by means of criminal or disciplinary proceedings against the person to whose conduct the matter relates.

(6) If it appears to the IPCC—

(*a*) that any matter that has come to its attention is a recordable conduct matter, but

(*b*) that that matter has not been recorded by the appropriate authority,

the IPCC may direct the appropriate authority to record that matter; and it shall be the duty of that authority to comply with the direction.

25 Duties to preserve evidence relating to conduct matters

(1) Where the appropriate authority becomes aware of any recordable matter relating to the conduct of an individual, it shall be the duty of that authority to take all such steps as appear to it to be appropriate for the purposes of these Regulations for obtaining and preserving the evidence relating to that matter.

(2) The duty of the appropriate authority under paragraph (1) must be performed as soon as practicable after it becomes aware of the matter in question.
(3) After that, the appropriate authority shall be under a duty until it is satisfied that it is no longer necessary to do so, to continue to take the steps from time to time appearing to it to be appropriate for the purposes of these Regulations for obtaining and preserving evidence relating to the matter.
(4) It shall be the duty of the appropriate authority to take all such specific steps for obtaining or preserving evidence relating to any recordable conduct matter, as it may be directed by the IPCC to take for the purposes of these Regulations.

26 Complaints against a person who has subsequently ceased to serve with HMRC

Where a complaint or conduct matter relates to the conduct of a person who has ceased to be a Commissioner or an officer since the time of the conduct, these Regulations shall apply in relation to such person as if they did not include any requirement for an appropriate authority to determine whether disciplinary proceedings should be brought against a person whose conduct is reported to the appropriate authority.

PART 4
REFERRAL OF MATTERS TO THE IPCC

27 Recording and reference of conduct and DSI matters

(1) Any conduct matter which is required to be referred to the IPCC shall be referred in such manner as the IPCC specifies and—
- (*a*) if the matter falls within paragraph (1)(*a*) or (*b*) of regulation 30, not later than the end of the day following the day on which it first becomes clear to the appropriate authority that the conduct matter is one to which that paragraph applies, and
- (*b*) if the matter falls within paragraph (1)(*c*) of that regulation, not later than the end of the day following the day on which the IPCC notifies the appropriate authority that the conduct matter is to be referred.

(2) Any DSI matter which is required to be referred to the IPCC shall be referred in such manner as the IPCC specifies and—
- (*a*) in a case where the IPCC directs that the matter be referred to it, within time limits defined in guidance issued by the IPCC, but no later than the end of the day following the day on which the IPCC so directs;
- (*b*) in any other case, within time limits defined in guidance issued by the IPCC, but no later than the end of the day following the day on which the matter first comes to the attention of the appropriate authority.

28 Reference of complaints to the IPCC

(1) It shall be the duty of the appropriate authority to refer a complaint to the IPCC where the complaint is—
- (*a*) one alleging that the conduct complained of has resulted in death or serious injury;
- (*b*) any complaint not falling within paragraph (*a*) but alleging conduct which constitutes—
  - (i) a serious assault, as defined in guidance issued by the IPCC;
  - (ii) a serious sexual offence, as defined in guidance issued by the IPCC;
  - (iii) serious corruption, as defined in guidance issued by the IPCC;
  - (iv) a criminal offence or behaviour which is liable to lead to a disciplinary sanction and which in either case was aggravated by discriminatory behaviour on the grounds of a person's race, sex, religion, or other status identified in guidance by the IPCC;
  - (v) a relevant offence;
- (*c*) a complaint which arises from the same incident as one in which any conduct falling within paragraph (*a*) or (*b*) is alleged; or
- (*d*) one in respect of which the IPCC notifies the appropriate authority that it requires the complaint in question to be referred to the IPCC for its consideration.

(2) The obligation on the Head of the Home Civil Service under paragraph (1)(*a*) or (*b*) to refer a complaint about the conduct of a person in respect of whom the Head of the Home Civil Service is the appropriate authority arises only if the Head of the Home Civil Service is satisfied that the complaint contains an indication that a criminal offence may have been committed by that person.
(3) The obligation on the Chief Executive or the Commissioners (other than the Chairman, the Chief Executive and the Permanent Secretary for Tax) under paragraph (1)(*a*) or (*b*) to refer a complaint about the conduct of a person in respect of whom the Chief Executive is or the Commissioners are the appropriate authority arises only if the Chief Executive is or the Commissioners are satisfied that the complaint contains an indication that the person may have—
- (*a*) committed a criminal offence, or
- (*b*) behaved in a manner which would justify the bringing of disciplinary proceedings and that such behaviour (if it had taken place) would be likely to lead to the termination of that person's office or employment.

VAT SIs

(4) In a case where there is no obligation under paragraph (1) to make a reference, the appropriate authority may refer a complaint to the IPCC if that authority considers that it would be appropriate to do so by reason of—

(*a*) the gravity of the subject-matter of the complaint; or

(*b*) any exceptional circumstances.

(5) In a case in which a reference under paragraph (1) or (4) is neither made nor required to be made, the Head of the Home Civil Service may refer a complaint to the IPCC if—

(*a*) it is one in relation to which the Chief Executive is the appropriate authority; and

(*b*) the Head of the Home Civil Service considers that it would be appropriate to do so by reason of—

(i) the gravity of the subject-matter of the complaint, or

(ii) any exceptional circumstances.

(6) Where a complaint is required to be referred to the IPCC under paragraph (1)(*a*), (*b*) or (*c*), notification of the complaint shall be given to the IPCC—

(*a*) not later than the end of the day following the day on which it first becomes clear to the appropriate authority that the complaint is one to which that sub-paragraph applies, and

(*b*) in such manner as the IPCC specifies.

(7) Where a complaint is required to be referred to the IPCC under paragraph (1)(*d*), notification of the complaint shall be given to the IPCC—

(*a*) not later than the end of the day following the day on which the IPCC notifies the appropriate authority that the complaint is to be referred, and

(*b*) in such manner as the IPCC specifies.

(8) Subject to paragraph (10), the power—

(*a*) of the IPCC by virtue of paragraph (1)(*d*) to require a complaint to be referred to it, and

(*b*) of the appropriate authority to refer a complaint to the IPCC under paragraph (2) or (3),

shall each be exercisable at any time irrespective of whether the complaint is already being investigated by any person or has already been considered by the IPCC.

(9) Where the appropriate authority refers a complaint to the IPCC under this regulation it shall give a notification of the making of the reference—

(*a*) to the complainant, and

(*b*) except in a case where it appears to the appropriate authority that to do so might prejudice a possible future investigation of the complaint, to the person complained against.

(10) A complaint that has already been referred to the IPCC under this regulation on a previous occasion—

(*a*) shall not be required to be referred again under this regulation unless the IPCC so directs, and

(*b*) shall not be referred in exercise of any power conferred by this regulation unless the IPCC consents.

29 Duties of the IPCC on references under regulation 28

(1) It shall be the duty of the IPCC, in the case of every complaint referred to it by the appropriate authority, to determine whether or not it is necessary for the complaint to be investigated.

(2) Where the IPCC determines under this regulation that it is not necessary for a complaint to be investigated, it may, if it thinks fit, refer the complaint back to the appropriate authority in accordance with paragraph (3).

(3) In a case to which paragraph (2) applies, the appropriate authority shall not be required by virtue of any provisions of these Regulations to take any action in relation to the complaint but may handle the complaint in whatever manner it thinks fit, or take no action in relation to the complaint.

(4) Where the IPCC refers a complaint back under paragraph (2), it shall give a notification of the making of the reference back—

(*a*) to the complainant, and

(*b*) to the person complained against.

30 Reference of conduct matters to the IPCC

(1) It shall be the duty of the appropriate authority to refer a recordable conduct matter to the IPCC (whether or not the case falls within regulation 23), if—

(*a*) that matter relates to any incident or circumstances in or in consequence of which any person has died or suffered serious injury;

(*b*) that matter is of a description specified in paragraph (2); or

(*c*) the IPCC notifies the appropriate authority that it requires that matter to be referred to the IPCC for its consideration.

(2) Any matter which relates to conduct falling within the following descriptions is specified for the purposes of paragraph (1)(*b*)—

(*a*) a serious assault, as defined in guidance issued by the IPCC;

(*b*) a serious sexual offence, as defined in guidance issued by the IPCC;

(*c*) serious corruption, as defined in guidance issued by the IPCC;

(*d*) a criminal offence or behaviour which is liable to lead to a disciplinary sanction and which in either case was aggravated by discriminatory behaviour on the grounds of a person's race, sex, religion, or other status identified in guidance issued by the IPCC;

(*e*) a relevant offence; or

(*f*) conduct which is alleged to have taken place in the same incident as one in which conduct within sub-paragraphs (*a*) to (*e*) is alleged.

(3) The obligation on the Head of the Home Civil Service under paragraph (1)(*a*) or (*b*) to refer a recordable conduct matter in respect of a person for whom the Head of the Home Civil Service is the appropriate authority arises only if the Head of the Home Civil Service is satisfied that the matter is one in respect of which there is an indication that a criminal offence may have been committed by that person.

(4) The obligation on the appropriate authority under paragraph (1)(*a*) or (*b*) to refer a recordable conduct matter in respect of a person for whom it is the appropriate authority arises only if it is satisfied that the matter is one in respect of which there is an indication that the person may have—

(*a*) committed a criminal offence, or

(*b*) behaved in a manner which would justify the bringing of disciplinary proceedings and that such behaviour (if it had taken place) would be likely to lead to the termination of that person's office or employment.

(5) In any case where there is no obligation under paragraph (1) to make a reference, the appropriate authority may refer a recordable conduct matter to the IPCC if that authority considers that it would be appropriate to do so by reason of—

(*a*) the gravity of the matter, or

(*b*) any exceptional circumstances.

(6) In a case in which a reference under paragraph (1) or (5) is neither made nor required to be made, the Head of the Home Civil Service may refer any recordable conduct matter to the IPCC if—

(*a*) it is one in relation to which the Chief Executive is the appropriate authority, and

(*b*) the Head of the Home Civil Service considers that it would be appropriate to do so by reason of—

(i) the gravity of the matter, or

(ii) any exceptional circumstances.

(7) Where there is an obligation under this regulation to refer any matter to the IPCC, it must be so referred within such period as may be provided for by regulation 27.

(8) Subject to paragraph (10), the power—

(*a*) of the IPCC by virtue of paragraph (1)(*c*) to require a matter to be referred to it, and

(*b*) of the appropriate authority to refer any matter to the IPCC under paragraph (5) or (6),

shall each be exercisable at any time irrespective of whether the matter is already being investigated by any person or has already been considered by the IPCC.

(9) Where—

(*a*) the appropriate authority refers a matter to the IPCC under this regulation, and

(*b*) it does not consider that to do so might prejudice a possible future investigation of that matter,

it shall give a notification of the making of the reference to the person to whose conduct that matter relates.

(10) A matter that has already been referred to the IPCC under this regulation on a previous occasion—

(*a*) shall not be required to be referred again under this regulation unless the IPCC so directs, and

(*b*) shall not be referred in exercise of any power conferred by this regulation unless the IPCC consents.

31 Duties of the IPCC on references under regulation 30

(1) It shall be the duty of the IPCC, in the case of every recordable conduct matter referred to it by the appropriate authority under regulation 30, to determine whether or not it is necessary for the matter to be investigated.

(2) Where the IPCC determines under this regulation that it is not necessary for a recordable conduct matter referred by the appropriate authority to be investigated, it may if it thinks fit refer the matter back to the appropriate authority to be dealt with by it in such manner (if any) as the appropriate authority may determine.

(3) Where—

(*a*) the IPCC refers a matter back to the appropriate authority under this regulation, and

(*b*) the IPCC does not consider that to do so might prejudice a possible future investigation of that matter,

the IPCC shall give a notification of the making of the reference to the person to whose conduct that matter relates.

PART 5
HANDLING DEATH AND SERIOUS INJURY (DSI)

32 Duty to record DSI matters

(1) Where a DSI matter comes to the attention of the appropriate authority, it shall be the duty of the appropriate authority to record that matter.

(2) If it appears to the IPCC—

(*a*) that any matter that has come to its attention is a DSI matter, but

(*b*) that that matter has not been recorded by the appropriate authority,

the IPCC may direct the appropriate authority to record that matter; and it shall be the duty of that authority to comply with the direction.

33 Duty to preserve evidence relating to DSI matters

(1) Where a DSI matter comes to the attention of the appropriate authority it shall be the duty of that authority to take all such steps as appear to it to be appropriate for the purposes of these Regulations for obtaining and preserving evidence relating to that matter.

(2) The duty of the appropriate authority under paragraph (1) must be performed as soon as practicable after it becomes aware of the matter in question.

(3) After that, the appropriate authority shall be under a duty to continue to take the steps from time to time appearing to it to be appropriate for the purposes of these Regulations for obtaining and preserving evidence relating to the matter, until it is satisfied that it is no longer necessary to do so.

(4) It shall be the duty of the appropriate authority to take all such specific steps for obtaining or preserving evidence relating to any DSI matter as it may be directed to take for the purposes of this regulation by the IPCC.

34 Reference of DSI matters to the IPCC

(1) It shall be the duty of the appropriate authority to refer a DSI matter to the IPCC.

(2) The appropriate authority must do so within the period specified in regulation 27(2) (recording and reference of conduct matters).

(3) A matter that has already been referred to the IPCC under this regulation on a previous occasion shall not be required to be referred again under this regulation unless the IPCC so directs.

35 Duties of IPCC on references under regulation 34

(1) It shall be the duty of the IPCC, in the case of every DSI matter referred to it by the appropriate authority, to determine whether or not it is necessary for the matter to be investigated.

(2) Where the IPCC determines under this regulation that it is not necessary for a DSI matter to be investigated, it may if it thinks fit refer the matter back to the appropriate authority to be dealt with by it in such manner (if any) as the appropriate authority may determine.

36 Procedure where conduct matter is revealed during investigation of DSI matter

(1) If during the course of an investigation of a DSI matter it appears to a person designated under regulation 47 or 48 or appointed to undertake an investigation under the management of the IPCC under regulation 46, that there is an indication that the person whose conduct is in question may have—

(*a*) committed a criminal offence, or

(*b*) behaved in a manner which would justify the bringing of disciplinary proceedings,

the person so appointed shall make a submission to that effect to the IPCC.

(2) If, after considering a submission under paragraph (1), the IPCC determines that there is such an indication, it shall—

(*a*) notify the appropriate authority in relation to the DSI matter and (if different) the appropriate authority in relation to the person whose conduct is in question of its determination, and

(*b*) send to it (or each of them) a copy of the submission under paragraph (1).

(3) If during the course of an investigation of a DSI matter it appears to a person appointed under regulation 44 or 45 or appointed to undertake an investigation under the supervision of the IPCC under regulation 46, that there is an indication that the person whose conduct is in question may have—

(*a*) committed a criminal offence, or

(*b*) behaved in a manner which would justify the bringing of disciplinary proceedings,

the person so appointed shall make a submission to that effect to the appropriate authority in relation to the DSI matter.

(4) If, after considering a submission under paragraph (3), the appropriate authority determines that there is such an indication, it shall—

(*a*) if it is not the appropriate authority in relation to the person whose conduct is in question, notify that other authority of its determination and send to that authority a copy of the submission under paragraph (3), and

(*b*) notify the IPCC of its determination and send to it a copy of the submission under paragraph (3).

(5) Where the appropriate authority in relation to the person whose conduct is in question—

(*a*) is notified of a determination by the IPCC under paragraph (2),

(*b*) (in a case where it is also the appropriate authority in relation to the DSI matter) makes a determination under paragraph (4), or

(*c*) (in a case where it is not the appropriate authority in relation to the DSI matter) is notified by that other authority of a determination by it under paragraph (4),

it shall record the matter under regulation 24 (recording etc of conduct matters in other cases) as a conduct matter (and the other provisions of these Regulations shall apply in relation to that matter accordingly).

(6) Where a DSI matter is recorded under regulation 24 as a conduct matter by virtue of paragraph (5)—

(*a*) the person investigating the DSI matter shall (subject to any determination made by the IPCC under regulation 38(6)) continue the investigation as if appointed or designated to investigate the conduct matter, and

(*b*) the other provisions of these Regulations shall apply in relation to that matter accordingly.

PART 6
INVESTIGATIONS

37 Inspections of HMRC premises on behalf of the IPCC

(1) Where—

(*a*) the IPCC requires the Commissioners to allow a person nominated for the purpose by the IPCC to have access to any premises occupied for the purposes of HMRC and to documents and other things on those premises, and

(*b*) the requirement is imposed for any of the purposes mentioned in paragraph (2),

it shall be the duty of the Commissioners to secure that the required access is allowed to the nominated person.

(2) Those purposes are—

(*a*) the purposes of any examination by the IPCC of the efficiency and effectiveness of the arrangements made by the Commissioners for handling complaints or dealing with recordable conduct matters or DSI matters;

(*b*) the purposes of any investigation by the IPCC under this Part or of any investigation carried out under its supervision or management.

(3) A requirement imposed under this regulation for the purposes mentioned in paragraph (2)(*a*) must be notified to the Commissioners at least 48 hours before the time at which access is required.

(4) Where—

(*a*) a requirement imposed under this regulation for the purposes mentioned in paragraph (2)(*a*) requires access to any premises, document or thing to be allowed to any person, but

(*b*) there are reasonable grounds for not allowing that person to have the required access at the time at which that person seeks to have it,

the obligation to secure that the required access is allowed shall have effect as an obligation to secure that the access is allowed to that person at the earliest practicable time after there cease to be any such grounds as that person may specify.

(5) The provisions of this regulation are in addition to, and without prejudice to—

(*a*) the rights of entry, search and seizure that are or may be conferred on—

(i) a person designated for the purposes of regulation 48 (investigations by the IPCC itself), or

(ii) any person who otherwise acts on behalf of the IPCC,

in that person's capacity as a constable or as a person with the powers and privileges of a constable; or

(*b*) the obligations of the Commissioners under regulations 12 (co-operation, assistance and information) and 53 (provision of information to the IPCC).

38 Power of the IPCC to determine the form of an investigation

(1) This regulation applies where—

(*a*) a complaint or recordable conduct matter or DSI matter is referred to the IPCC; and

(*b*) the IPCC determines that it is necessary for the complaint or matter to be investigated.

(2) It shall be the duty of the IPCC to determine the form which the investigation shall take.

(3) In making a determination under paragraph (2) the IPCC shall have regard to the seriousness of the case and the public interest.

(4) The only forms which the investigation may take in accordance with a determination made under this regulation are—

(*a*) an investigation by the appropriate authority on its own behalf;

(*b*) an investigation by the appropriate authority under the supervision of the IPCC;

VAT SIs

(*c*) an investigation by a police force under the supervision of the IPCC;
(*d*) an investigation by the appropriate authority under the management of the IPCC;
(*e*) an investigation by a police force under the management of the IPCC;
(*f*) an investigation by the IPCC.

(5) An investigation under this regulation relating to any conduct of the Commissioners may only be carried out in the form specified in paragraph (4)(*c*), (4)(*e*) or (4)(*f*).

(6) The IPCC may at any time make a further determination under this regulation to replace an earlier one.

(7) Where a determination under this regulation replaces an earlier determination under this regulation, or relates to a complaint or matter in relation to which the appropriate authority has already begun an investigation on its own behalf, the IPCC may give—

(*a*) the appropriate authority, and
(*b*) any person previously appointed to carry out the investigation,

such directions as it considers appropriate for the purpose of giving effect to the new determination.

(8) It shall be the duty of a person to whom a direction is given under paragraph (7) to comply with it.

(9) The IPCC shall notify the appropriate authority of any determination that it makes under this regulation in relation to a particular complaint or recordable conduct matter or DSI matter.

39 Appointment of persons to carry out investigations

No person shall be appointed to carry out an investigation under regulation 44, 45, 46 or 47—

(*a*) unless that person has an appropriate level of knowledge, skills and experience to plan and manage the investigation;
(*b*) if that person's involvement could reasonably give rise to a concern as to whether that person could act impartially under these Regulations; or
(*c*) if that person works, directly or indirectly, under the management of the person whose conduct is being investigated.

40 Power of the IPCC to impose requirements in relation to an investigation which it is supervising

(1) For the purposes of regulation 45(6) the requirements which may be imposed by the IPCC on a person appointed to investigate a complaint, recordable conduct matter or DSI matter are, subject to paragraphs (2) and (3), any reasonable requirements as to the conduct of the investigation as appear to the IPCC to be necessary.

(2) Where at any stage of an investigation of a complaint, recordable conduct matter or DSI matter the possibility of criminal proceedings arises, the IPCC shall not, under paragraph (1), impose any requirement relating to the obtaining or preservation of evidence of a criminal offence without first obtaining the consent—

(*a*) in the case of an investigation carried out by an appointed person who is an officer, of the Director of Revenue and Customs Prosecutions, or
(*b*) in any other case, of the Director of Public Prosecutions,

to the imposition of any such requirement.

(3) The IPCC shall not, under paragraph (1), impose any requirement relating to the resources to be made available by the appropriate authority, for the purposes of an investigation, without first consulting it and having regard to any representations it may make.

41 Combining and splitting investigations

(1) An appropriate authority which is carrying out an investigation on its own behalf may—

(*a*) combine that investigation with another such investigation, or
(*b*) split that investigation into two or more such separate investigations,

if it considers that it is more efficient and effective, or is otherwise in the public interest, to do so.

(2) Subject to paragraph (3), where the IPCC is supervising, managing or carrying out an investigation, it may—

(*a*) combine that investigation with another investigation, or
(*b*) split that investigation into two or more separate investigations,

if it considers that it is more efficient and effective, or is otherwise in the public interest, to do so.

(3) The IPCC shall not take any action under paragraph (2) in relation to a supervised or managed investigation except after consultation with the appropriate authority.

(4) Nothing in this regulation shall prevent the IPCC from determining—

(*a*) that where an investigation is split into two or more separate investigations, those investigations may take different forms, or
(*b*) that two or more separate investigations which take different forms (including an investigation being carried out by the appropriate authority on its own behalf) may be combined into a single investigation.

42 Power of the IPCC to discontinue an investigation

(1) If, following a determination under regulation 29 (duties of the IPCC on reference under regulation 28), 31 (duties of the IPCC on reference under regulation 30) or 35 (duties of the IPCC on reference under regulation 34), it appears at any time to the IPCC (whether on an application by the appropriate authority or otherwise) that a complaint or matter that is being investigated—

(*a*) by the appropriate authority on its own behalf, or

(*b*) under the supervision or management of the IPCC,

is of a description of complaint or matter specified in paragraph (5), the IPCC may by order require the discontinuance of the investigation.

(2) Where the IPCC makes an order under this regulation or discontinues an investigation being carried out in accordance with regulation 48 (investigations by the IPCC itself), it shall give notification of the discontinuance—

(*a*) to the appropriate authority;

(*b*) to every person entitled to be kept properly informed in relation to the subject matter of the investigation under regulation 55 (duty to provide information for other persons); and

(*c*) in a case where the investigation that is discontinued is an investigation of a complaint, to the complainant.

(3) Where an investigation of a complaint or recordable conduct matter or DSI matter is discontinued in accordance with this regulation—

(*a*) the IPCC may give the appropriate authority directions to do any such things as it is authorised to direct under paragraphs (11) and (12);

(*b*) the IPCC may itself take any such steps of a description specified in regulations so made as it considers appropriate for purposes connected with the discontinuance of the investigation; and

(*c*) subject to the preceding paragraphs, neither the appropriate authority nor the IPCC shall take any further action in accordance with the provisions of these Regulations in relation to that complaint or matter.

(4) The appropriate authority shall comply with any directions given to it under paragraph (3).

(5) The descriptions of complaint or matter are—

(*a*) one in which the complainant refuses to co-operate to the extent that the IPCC considers that it is not reasonably practicable to continue the investigation;

(*b*) one which the IPCC considers is vexatious, oppressive or otherwise an abuse of the procedures for dealing with complaints, conduct matters or DSI matters;

(*c*) one which is repetitious, as defined in paragraph (6); and

(*d*) one which the IPCC otherwise considers is such as to make it not reasonably practicable to proceed with the investigation.

(6) A complaint is repetitious only if—

(*a*) it is substantially the same as a previous complaint (whether made by or on behalf of the same or a different complainant), or it concerns substantially the same conduct as a previous conduct matter;

(*b*) it contains no fresh allegations which significantly affect the account of the conduct complained of;

(*c*) no fresh evidence, being evidence which was not reasonably available at the time the previous complaint was made, is tendered in support of it; and

(*d*) as respects the previous complaint or conduct matter, either—

(i) the requirements of regulation 67(9) or 68(11) (determination by the appropriate authority of what action to take) were complied with;

(ii) the IPCC gave the appropriate authority a direction under paragraph (11)(*b*) (requirement to dispense with the requirements of these Regulations); or

(iii) the complainant gave such notification of the withdrawal of the complaint as is mentioned in regulation 43(1)(*a*) (complainant withdraws the complaint).

(7) The cases in which the IPCC is authorised to discontinue an investigation that is being carried out in accordance with regulation 48 are any cases where the complaint, conduct matter or DSI matter under investigation falls within paragraph (5) of this regulation.

(8) Any application by an appropriate authority to the IPCC for an order that it discontinue an investigation shall be in writing and shall be accompanied by—

(*a*) a copy of the complaint, and

(*b*) a memorandum from the appropriate authority containing a summary of the investigation undertaken so far and explaining the reasons for the application to discontinue the investigation.

(9) The appropriate authority shall—

(*a*) send the complainant a copy of any such application on the same day as the day on which the application is sent to the IPCC, and

(*b*) supply any further information requested by the IPCC for the purpose of considering that application.

VAT SIs

(10) The IPCC shall not require the discontinuance of an investigation in a case where there has been no application to do so by the appropriate authority unless it has consulted with that authority.

(11) A direction given to an appropriate authority by the IPCC under paragraph (3) may—

(*a*) require the appropriate authority to produce an investigation report on the discontinued investigation under regulation 66 and to take any subsequent steps under these Regulations;

(*b*) where the investigation concerned a complaint, require the appropriate authority to dispense with the requirements of these Regulations as respects that complaint;

(*c*) direct the appropriate authority to handle the matter in whatever manner (if any) that authority thinks fit.

(12) For the purposes of this regulation the steps that may be taken by the IPCC where an investigation is discontinued are—

(*a*) to produce an investigation report on the discontinued investigation and take any subsequent steps required under these Regulations;

(*b*) where the investigation concerned a complaint, to dispense with the requirements of these Regulations as respects that complaint;

(*c*) to handle the matter in whatever manner it thinks fit.

43 Withdrawn and discontinued complaints

(1) If an appropriate authority receives from a complainant notification in writing signed by the complainant or by a solicitor or other authorised agent on the complainant's behalf to the effect either—

(*a*) that the complainant withdraws the complaint, or

(*b*) that the complainant does not wish any further steps to be taken in consequence of the complaint,

the appropriate authority shall forthwith record the withdrawal or the fact that the complainant does not wish any further steps to be taken, as the case may be, and subject to the following provisions of this regulation, the provisions of these Regulations shall cease to apply in respect of that complaint.

(2) Where a complainant gives such notification as is mentioned in paragraph (1) to the IPCC but, so far as is apparent to the IPCC, has not sent that notification to the appropriate authority, then—

(*a*) the IPCC shall send a copy of the notification to the appropriate authority;

(*b*) that appropriate authority shall record the withdrawal or the fact that the complainant does not wish any further steps to be taken, as the case may be; and

(*c*) subject to the following provisions of this regulation, the provisions of these Regulations shall cease to apply in respect of that complaint.

(3) Where a complainant gives such notification as is mentioned in paragraph (1) to an appropriate authority, or where the appropriate authority receives a copy of a notification under paragraph (2), and it relates to a complaint—

(*a*) which was referred to the IPCC under regulation 28(1) (reference of complaints to the IPCC) and which has not been referred back to the appropriate authority under regulation 29(2);

(*b*) which the appropriate authority knows is currently the subject of an appeal to the IPCC under regulation 21 (failures to notify or record a complaint), or 74 (appeals to the IPCC with respect to an investigation; or

(*c*) which was notified to the appropriate authority by the IPCC under regulation 19(1) (initial handling and recording of complaints),

the appropriate authority shall notify the IPCC that it has recorded the withdrawal of the complaint or the fact that the complainant does not wish any further steps to be taken, as the case may be.

(4) In a case falling within paragraph (3)(*a*), the IPCC shall determine whether it is in the public interest for the complaint to be treated as a recordable conduct matter, and shall notify the appropriate authority of its decision.

(5) In a case falling within sub-paragraphs (*b*) or (*c*) of paragraph (3), the appropriate authority shall also—

(*a*) determine whether it is in the public interest for the complaint to be treated as a recordable conduct matter, and

(*b*) notify the IPCC of its determination and the reasons for the determination.

(6) Where a determination is made that a complaint is to be treated as a recordable conduct matter, the provisions of these Regulations shall apply to that matter.

(7) Where a complainant gives such notification as is mentioned in paragraph (1) to an appropriate authority, or where an appropriate authority receives a copy of a notification under paragraph (2), and that notification relates to a complaint which does not fall within any of sub-paragraphs (*a*) to (*c*) of paragraph (3)—

(*a*) the appropriate authority shall determine whether it is in the public interest for the complaint to be treated as a recordable conduct matter;

(*b*) if the complaint is to be treated as a recordable conduct matter, the provisions of these Regulations shall apply to that matter;

(*c*) if the complaint is not to be treated as a recordable conduct matter, the provisions of these Regulations shall cease to apply in respect of that complaint.

(8) In a case where—

(*a*) a complaint has been subjected to an investigation by the appropriate authority on its own behalf;

(*b*) the complaint is currently subject to an appeal to the IPCC under regulation 74; and

(*c*) the appropriate authority has notified the IPCC under paragraph (5)(*b*) that it has determined that the complaint is not to be treated as a recordable conduct matter,

the IPCC shall consider whether it is in the public interest for that determination to be reversed, and if so it shall instruct the appropriate authority to reverse the decision.

(9) Where a complainant indicates the wish to withdraw the complaint or the wish that no further steps are to be taken in consequence of the complaint, but the complainant fails to provide a notification to that effect in writing signed by or on behalf of the complainant—

(*a*) in the case of an indication received by the appropriate authority, the authority shall take the steps set out in paragraph (10);

(*b*) in the case of an indication received by the IPCC, the IPCC shall refer the matter to the appropriate authority which shall take the steps set out in paragraph (10).

(10) Those steps are—

(*a*) the appropriate authority shall write to the complainant to ascertain whether the complainant wishes to withdraw the complaint or does not wish any further steps to be taken in consequence of the complaint;

(*b*) if the complainant indicates the wish to withdraw the complaint or does not wish any further steps to be taken in consequence of the complaint, or if the complainant fails to reply within 21 days from the date of the communication under sub-paragraph (*a*), the appropriate authority shall treat the indication as though it had been received in writing signed by the complainant;

(*c*) if the complainant indicates the wish not to withdraw the complaint, or the wish that further steps be taken in consequence of the complaint, the appropriate authority shall start or resume the investigation as the case may be.

(11) The appropriate authority shall notify the person complained against if—

(*a*) it records the withdrawal of a complaint or the fact that the complainant does not wish any further steps to be taken;

(*b*) it determines that a complaint shall be treated as a recordable conduct matter;

(*c*) the IPCC determines that a complaint shall be treated as a recordable conduct matter;

(*d*) the IPCC instructs it to reverse a decision not to treat a complaint as a recordable conduct matter; or

(*e*) the provisions of these Regulations cease to apply in respect of a complaint.

(12) But nothing in paragraph (11) shall require the appropriate authority to make a notification if it has previously decided under regulation 61(3) (copies of complaints etc) not to notify the person complained against of the complaint because it is of the opinion that that—

(*a*) might prejudice any criminal investigation or pending proceedings, or

(*b*) would be contrary to the public interest.

44 Investigations by the appropriate authority on its own behalf

(1) This regulation applies where the appropriate authority is required by virtue of any determination made by the IPCC under regulation 38 (power of the IPCC to determine the form of an investigation) to make arrangements for a complaint or recordable conduct matter or DSI matter to be investigated by the appropriate authority on its own behalf.

(2) It shall be the duty of the appropriate authority to appoint an officer to investigate the complaint or matter.

(3) The person to be appointed under this regulation to investigate any DSI matter in relation to which the relevant officer is the Chairman, the Chief Executive or the Permanent Secretary for Tax is the Head of the Home Civil Service.

45 Investigations supervised by the IPCC

(1) This regulation applies where the IPCC has determined that it should supervise the investigation by the appropriate authority of any complaint or recordable conduct matter or DSI matter.

(2) On being given notice of that determination, the appropriate authority shall, if it has not already done so, appoint an officer to investigate the complaint or matter.

(3) The IPCC may require that no appointment is made under paragraph (2) unless it has given notice to the appropriate authority that it approves the person whom that authority proposes to appoint.

(4) Where a person has already been appointed to investigate the complaint or matter, or is selected under this regulation for appointment, and the IPCC is not satisfied with that person, the IPCC may require the appropriate authority, as soon as reasonably practicable after being required to do so—

(*a*) to select another person falling within paragraph (2) to investigate the complaint or matter, and

(*b*) to notify the IPCC of the person selected.

(5) Where a selection made in pursuance of a requirement under paragraph (4) has been notified to the IPCC, the appropriate authority shall appoint that person to investigate the complaint or matter if, but only if, the IPCC notifies the authority that it approves the appointment of that person.

(6) The person appointed to investigate the complaint or matter shall comply with all the requirements of regulation 40.

46 Investigation by a police force under the management or under the supervision of the IPCC

(1) This regulation applies where the IPCC determines that there should be an investigation by a police force under the management or supervision of the IPCC.

(2) The IPCC shall—

(*a*) identify the police force whose force area includes the geographical area to which the subject matter of the complaint, recordable conduct matter or DSI matter most closely relates, and

(*b*) take steps to obtain the agreement of—

(i) the chief officer of police of that force, and

(ii) the appropriate authority,

to the appointment by the IPCC of that force to carry out the investigation.

(3) In the event that no agreement is reached under paragraph (2) the IPCC may require the chief officer of police of any police force it considers appropriate to carry out the investigation.

(4) A chief officer of police of a police force who agrees to or is required to carry out an investigation shall, if that person has not already done so, appoint a person serving with the police who is a member of that force to investigate that complaint or matter.

(5) Paragraphs (3) to (6) of regulation 45 (investigations supervised by the IPCC) shall apply as they apply to an investigation by the appropriate authority which the IPCC has determined is one that it should supervise; and the references to the appropriate authority in those paragraphs shall be treated as references to the chief officer of police concerned.

(6) An appointment of a person under paragraph (4) or (5) shall be notified by the chief of police concerned to the appropriate authority.

(7) The person appointed to investigate the complaint or matter shall, in relation to an investigation under the management of the IPCC, be under the direction and control of the IPCC.

(8) The person appointed to investigate the complaint or matter shall comply with all such requirements in relation to the carrying out of that investigation as may be imposed by these Regulations.

47 Investigations managed by the IPCC

(1) This regulation applies where the IPCC has determined that it should manage the investigation by the appropriate authority of any complaint or recordable conduct matter or DSI matter.

(2) Paragraphs (2) to (5) of regulation 45 shall apply as they apply in the case of an investigation which the IPCC has determined is one that it should supervise.

(3) The person appointed to investigate the complaint or matter shall, in relation to that investigation, be under the direction and control of the IPCC.

48 Investigations by the IPCC itself

(1) This regulation applies where the IPCC has determined that it should itself carry out the investigation of a complaint or recordable conduct matter or DSI matter.

(2) The IPCC shall designate both—

(*a*) a member of the IPCC's staff to take charge of the investigation on behalf of the IPCC, and

(*b*) all such other members of the IPCC's staff as are required by the IPCC to assist that member.

(3) A member of the IPCC's staff who—

(*a*) is designated under paragraph (2) in relation to any investigation, but

(*b*) does not already, by virtue of section 97(8) of the Police Act 1996, have all the powers and privileges of a constable throughout England and Wales and the adjacent United Kingdom waters,

shall, for the purposes of the carrying out of the investigation and all purposes connected with it, have all those powers and privileges throughout England and Wales and those waters.

(4) A member of the IPCC's staff who is not a constable shall not, as a result of paragraph (3), be treated as being in police service for the purposes of—

(*a*) section 280 of the Trade Union and Labour Relations (Consolidation) Act 1992 (person in police service excluded from definitions of "worker" and "employee"); or

(*b*) section 200 of the Employment Rights Act 1996 (certain provisions of that Act not to apply to persons in police service).

(5) References in this regulation to the powers and privileges of a constable—

(*a*) are references to any power or privilege conferred by or under any enactment (including one passed after the making of these Regulations) on a constable; and

(b) shall have effect as if every such power were exercisable, and every such privilege existed, throughout England and Wales and the adjacent United Kingdom waters (whether or not that is the case apart from this paragraph).

(6) In this regulation "United Kingdom waters" means the sea and other waters within the seaward limits of the United Kingdom's territorial sea.

49 Relinquishing the IPCC's supervision or management of an investigation

(1) This regulation applies where the IPCC—

(a) relinquishes the management of an investigation in favour of a supervised investigation or an investigation by the appropriate authority on its own behalf, or

(b) relinquishes the supervision of an investigation in favour of an investigation by the appropriate authority on its own behalf.

(2) The IPCC—

(a) shall notify the appropriate authority, the complainant, any interested person within the meaning of regulation 55 (duty to provide information for other persons) and the person complained against of its decision, and the reasons for that decision; and

(b) shall send to the appropriate authority any documentation and evidence gathered during its investigations as will assist the appropriate authority to carry out its functions under these Regulations.

(3) But nothing in paragraph (2)(a) shall require the IPCC to make a notification to the person complained against if it is of the opinion that that might prejudice any criminal investigation or pending proceedings or would be contrary to the public interest.

50 Circumstances in which an investigation or other procedure may be suspended

(1) Subject to the provisions of this regulation, proceedings under these Regulations shall proceed without delay.

(2) In a case investigated by the IPCC or under the management of the IPCC, the IPCC may suspend any investigation or other procedure under these Regulations which would, if it were to continue, prejudice any criminal proceedings. Before referring a case to misconduct proceedings, the IPCC shall decide whether misconduct proceedings may prejudice any criminal proceedings.

(3) For any period during which the IPCC considers misconduct proceedings would prejudice any criminal proceedings, no such misconduct proceedings shall take place.

(4) Where a witness who is or may be a witness in any criminal proceedings is to be or may be asked to provide evidence in misconduct proceedings, the IPCC shall consult the relevant prosecutor (and when doing so must inform the prosecutor of the names and addresses of all such witnesses) before making a decision under paragraph (2).

(5) For the purposes of this regulation, "relevant prosecutor" means the Director of Public Prosecutions or any other person who has or is likely to have responsibility for criminal proceedings.

(6) In a case under the supervision of the IPCC or undertaken by the appropriate authority on its own behalf, the appropriate authority may, subject to paragraph (7), suspend any investigation or other procedure under these Regulations which would, if it were to continue, prejudice any criminal investigation or proceedings.

(7) The IPCC may direct that any investigation or other procedure under these Regulations which is liable to be suspended under paragraph (6) shall continue if it is of the view that it is in the public interest to make such a direction.

(8) The IPCC shall consult the appropriate authority before making such a direction.

51 Resumption of investigation after criminal proceedings

(1) Where the whole or part of the investigation of a complaint has been suspended until the conclusion of criminal proceedings, and after the conclusion of those proceedings the complainant has failed to express the wish for the investigation to start or to be resumed, the IPCC or, as the case may be, the appropriate authority, shall take the steps set out in paragraph (2).

(2) The IPCC or the appropriate authority shall take all reasonable steps to contact the complainant to ascertain whether the complainant wants the investigation to start or to be resumed as the case may be.

(3) If the complainant expresses the wish for the investigation to start or be resumed, the IPCC or the appropriate authority shall start or resume the investigation as the case may be.

(4) If the complainant indicates that the complainant does not want the investigation to start or to be resumed, or if the complainant fails to reply within 21 days of the date of the letter to the complainant by the IPCC or the appropriate authority, the IPCC or the appropriate authority, as the case may be, shall determine whether it is in the public interest for the complaint to be treated as a recordable conduct matter.

(5) If the IPCC or the appropriate authority determines that it is not in the public interest for the complaint to be treated as a recordable conduct matter, the provisions of these Regulations shall cease to apply to the complaint.

VAT SIs

(6) If the IPCC or the appropriate authority determines that it is in the public interest for the complaint to be treated as a recordable conduct matter, it shall be treated as such under these Regulations.

(7) The IPCC or the appropriate authority shall notify the person complained against if paragraph (5) or (6) applies.

(8) But nothing in paragraph (7) shall require the IPCC or the appropriate authority to make a notification if it is of the opinion that that might prejudice any criminal investigation or pending proceedings or would be contrary to the public interest.

52 Restrictions on proceedings pending the conclusion of an investigation

(1) No criminal or disciplinary proceedings shall be brought in relation to any matter which falls to be determined under these Regulations until a report on that investigation has been submitted to the IPCC or to the appropriate authority under regulation 66 (final reports on investigations: complaints, conduct matters and certain DSI matters) or 69 (final reports on investigations: other DSI matters).

(2) Nothing in this regulation shall prevent the bringing of criminal or disciplinary proceedings in respect of any conduct at any time after the discontinuance of the investigation in accordance with the provisions of these Regulations which relate to that conduct.

(3) The restrictions imposed by this regulation in relation to the bringing of criminal proceedings shall not apply to the bringing of criminal proceedings by the Director of Public Prosecutions or, as the case may be, the Director of Revenue and Customs Prosecutions in any case in which it appears to that person that there are exceptional circumstances which make it undesirable to delay the bringing of such proceedings.

PART 7
PROVISION OF INFORMATION

53 Provision of information to the IPCC

(1) It shall be the duty of the Commissioners at such times, in such circumstances and in accordance with such other requirements as may be set out in these Regulations, to provide the IPCC with all such information and documents as may be specified or described in these Regulations.

(2) It shall also be the duty of the Commissioners—

(*a*) to provide the IPCC with all such other information and documents specified or described in a notification given by the IPCC to the Commissioners, and

(*b*) to produce or deliver up to the IPCC all such evidence and other things so specified or described,

as appear to the IPCC to be required by it for the purposes of the carrying out of any of its functions.

(3) Anything falling to be provided, produced or delivered up by any person in pursuance of a requirement imposed under paragraph (2) must be provided, produced or delivered up in such form, in such manner and within such period as may be specified in—

(*a*) the notification imposing the requirement; or

(*b*) in any subsequent notification given by the IPCC to that person for the purposes of this paragraph.

(4) Nothing in this regulation shall require the Commissioners—

(*a*) to provide the IPCC with any information or document, or to produce or deliver up any other thing, before the earliest time at which it is practicable for the Commissioners to do so; or

(*b*) to provide, produce or deliver up anything at all in a case in which it never becomes practicable for the Commissioners to do so.

(5) A requirement imposed under this regulation may authorise or require information or documents to which it relates to be provided to the IPCC electronically.

54 Duty to keep the complainant informed

(1) Subject to regulation 60, in any case in which there is an investigation of a complaint in accordance with the provisions of these Regulations—

(*a*) by the IPCC, or

(*b*) under its management,

it shall be the duty of the IPCC to provide the complainant with all such information as will keep the complainant properly informed of all the matters specified in paragraph (4) while the investigation is being carried out and subsequently.

(2) Subject to regulation 60, in any case in which there is an investigation of a complaint in accordance with the provisions of these Regulations—

(*a*) by the appropriate authority on its own behalf, or

(*b*) under the supervision of the IPCC,

it shall be the duty of the appropriate authority to provide the complainant with all such information as will keep the complainant properly informed, while the investigation is being carried out and subsequently, of all the matters specified in paragraph (4).

(3) Where paragraph (2) applies, it shall be the duty of the IPCC to give the appropriate authority all such directions as it considers appropriate for securing that that authority complies with its duty under that paragraph; and it shall be the duty of the appropriate authority to comply with any direction so given.

(4) The matters of which the complainant must be kept properly informed are—

(*a*) the progress of the investigation;

(*b*) any provisional findings of the person carrying out the investigation;

(*c*) whether any report has been submitted under regulation 69 (final reports on investigations: other DSI matters);

(*d*) the action (if any) that is taken in respect of the matters dealt with in any such report; and

(*e*) the outcome of any such action.

(5) It shall be the duty of a person appointed to carry out an investigation under these Regulations to provide the IPCC or, as the case may be, the appropriate authority, with all such information as the IPCC or that authority may reasonably require for the purpose of performing its duty under this regulation.

55 Duty to provide information for other persons

(1) A person has an interest in being kept properly informed about the handling of a complaint or recordable conduct matter or DSI matter which is the subject of an investigation in accordance with the provisions of these Regulations if—

(*a*) it appears to the IPCC or to an appropriate authority that that person is a person falling within paragraph (2) or (3); and

(*b*) that person has indicated consent to the provision of information in accordance with this regulation and that consent has not been withdrawn.

(2) A person falls within this paragraph if, in the case of a complaint or recordable conduct matter, that person—

(*a*) is a relative of a person whose death is the alleged result from the conduct complained of or to which the recordable conduct matter relates;

(*b*) is a relative of a person whose serious injury is the alleged result from that conduct and that person is incapable of making a complaint;

(*c*) has suffered serious injury as the alleged result of that conduct.

(3) A person falls within this paragraph if, in the case of a DSI matter, that person—

(*a*) is a relative of the person who has died;

(*b*) is a relative of the person who has suffered serious injury and that person is incapable of making a complaint;

(*c*) is the person who has suffered serious injury.

(4) A person who does not fall within paragraph (2) or (3) has an interest in being kept properly informed about the handling of a complaint, recordable conduct matter or DSI matter if—

(*a*) the IPCC or an appropriate authority considers that that person has an interest in the handling of the complaint, conduct matter or DSI matter which is sufficient to make it appropriate for information to be provided to that person in accordance with this regulation; and

(*b*) that person has indicated consent to the provision of information in accordance with this regulation.

(5) In relation to a complaint, this section confers no rights on the complainant.

(6) A person who has an interest in being kept properly informed about the handling of a complaint, conduct matter or DSI matter is referred to in this regulation as an "interested person".

(7) In any case in which there is an investigation of the complaint, recordable conduct matter or DSI matter in accordance with the provisions of these Regulations—

(*a*) by the IPCC, or

(*b*) under its management,

it shall be the duty of the IPCC to provide the interested person with all such information as will keep the interested person properly informed of all the matters specified in paragraph (10) while the investigation is being carried out and subsequently.

(8) In any case in which there is an investigation of the complaint, recordable conduct matter or DSI matter in accordance with the provisions of these Regulations—

(*a*) by the appropriate authority on its own behalf, or

(*b*) under the supervision of the IPCC,

it shall be the duty of the appropriate authority to provide the interested person with all such information as will keep the interested person properly informed of all the matters specified in paragraph (10) while the investigation is being carried out and subsequently.

(9) Where paragraph (8) applies, it shall be the duty of the IPCC to give the appropriate authority all such directions as it considers appropriate for securing that that authority complies with its duty under that paragraph; and it shall be the duty of the appropriate authority to comply with any direction given to it under this paragraph.

(10) The matters of which the interested person must be kept properly informed are—

(*a*) the progress of the investigation;

(*b*) any provisional findings of the person carrying out the investigation;
(*c*) whether the IPCC or the appropriate authority has made a determination under regulation 36 (procedure where conduct matter is revealed during investigation of a DSI matter);
(*d*) whether any report has been submitted under regulation 66 or 69;
(*e*) the action (if any) that is taken in respect of the matters dealt with in any such report; and
(*f*) the outcome of any such action.

(11) The duties imposed by this regulation on the IPCC and the appropriate authority in relation to any complaint, recordable conduct matter or DSI matter shall be performed in such manner, and shall have effect subject to such exceptions, as may be provided for by regulation 60.

(12) Paragraph (5) of regulation 54 (duty to keep the complainant informed) applies for the purposes of this regulation as it applies for the purposes of that regulation.

(13) In this regulation "relative" means any spouse, partner, parent or adult child.

56 Written notices

(1) If during the course of an investigation of a complaint or matter which falls to be determined under these Regulations it appears to the person investigating that there is an indication that the person whose conduct is in question may have—
(*a*) committed a criminal offence, or
(*b*) behaved in a manner which would justify the bringing of disciplinary proceedings,
the person investigating the complaint or matter must give a notification to the person whose conduct is in question that complies with paragraph (2).

(2) The notification must—
(*a*) provide sufficient details of the complaint or matter in question so that the person whose conduct is in question may make representations to the person investigating the complaint or matter;
(*b*) give the information about the effect of regulation 57 (duty to consider submissions from the person whose conduct is in question);
(*c*) set out the time limits for providing the person investigating the complaint or matter with relevant statements and relevant documents for the purposes of regulation 57(2);
(*d*) give such information that may be set out in guidance.

(3) Paragraphs (1) and (2) do not apply for so long as the person investigating the complaint or the matter considers that giving the notification might prejudice—
(*a*) the investigation, or
(*b*) any other investigation (including, in particular, a criminal investigation).

(4) In this regulation and regulations 57 and 58, the person whose conduct is in question—
(*a*) in relation to an investigation of a complaint, means the person in respect of whom it appears to the person investigating that there is the indication mentioned in paragraph (1);
(*b*) in relation to an investigation of a recordable conduct matter, means the person to whose conduct the investigation relates.

(5) In this regulation—
(*a*) "relevant document" means—
(i) a document relating to any complaint or matter under investigation, and
(ii) includes such a document containing suggestions as to lines of inquiry to be pursued or witness to be interviewed;
(*b*) "relevant statement" means an oral or written statement relating to any complaint or matter under investigation.

57 Duty to consider submissions from the person whose conduct is in question

(1) This regulation applies where a notification under regulation 56 (written notices) has been issued to the person whose conduct is in question.

(2) If before the expiry of the appropriate time limit notified in pursuance of regulation 56(2)—
(*a*) the person whose conduct is in question provides the person investigating the complaint or matter with a relevant statement or a relevant document, or
(*b*) any person provides the person investigating the complaint or matter with a relevant document,
the person investigating must consider the statement or document.

58 Duty to provide certain information to the appropriate authority

(1) This regulation applies during the course of an investigation under these Regulations.

(2) The person investigating the complaint or matter must supply the appropriate authority with such information in that person's possession as the appropriate authority may reasonably request for the purpose mentioned in paragraph (3).

(3) That purpose is determining whether the person whose conduct is in question should be, or should remain, suspended from duty.

59 Manner in which duties to provide information to the complainant are to be performed

(1) For the purposes of regulations 54(4) (duty to keep the complainant informed) and 55(10) (duty to provide information for other persons), the manner in which the IPCC or, as the case may be, an appropriate authority, shall perform the duties imposed by those regulations is as follows.

(2) The IPCC, in a case falling within regulation 54(1) or 55(7) (investigation of a complaint, conduct matter or DSI matter by or under the management of the IPCC), shall inform the complainant or, as the case may be, the interested person—

(*a*) of the progress of the investigation promptly, and in any event—

(i) if there has been no previous notification, within four weeks of the start of the investigation; and

(ii) in any other case, within four weeks of the previous notification; and

(*b*) of any provisional findings of the person carrying out the investigation as frequently as the IPCC determines to be appropriate in order for the complainant to be kept properly informed.

(3) An appropriate authority, in a case falling within regulation 54(2) (duty to keep the complainant informed or 55(8) (duty to provide information for other persons), shall inform the complainant or the interested person (as the case may be)—

(*a*) of the progress of the investigation promptly and in any event—

(i) if there has been no previous notification, within four weeks of the start of the investigation; and

(ii) in any other case, within four weeks of the previous notification; and

(*b*) of any provisional findings of the person carrying out the investigation as frequently as the appropriate authority determines to be appropriate in order for the complainant to be kept properly informed.

(4) When an investigation has been completed, each complainant and interested person shall be notified—

(*a*) of the date on which the final report under regulation 66 (final reports on investigations: complaints, conduct matters and certain DSI matters) is likely to be submitted; and

(*b*) of the date on which the notification under regulation 67(11) (action by the IPCC in response to an investigation report under regulation 66) or 68(12) (action by the appropriate authority in response to an investigation report under regulation 66) is likely to be given.

(5) In performing the duties imposed by regulations 54(1) and (2), 55(7) and (8), 67(11) and 68(12), the IPCC or, as the case may be, the appropriate authority, shall determine whether it is appropriate to offer, or to accede to a request for, a meeting with a complainant or, as the case may be, an interested person.

(6) As soon as practicable after any such meeting, the IPCC or, as the case may be, the appropriate authority, shall send to the complainant or interested person a written record of the meeting and an account of how any concerns of that person will be addressed.

(7) As soon as practicable after any misconduct hearing or other action that is taken in respect of the matters dealt with in any report submitted under regulation 66, the IPCC or, as the case may be, the appropriate authority, shall notify any complainant and interested person of the outcome of that hearing or action, including the fact and outcome of any appeal against the findings of or sanctions imposed by such a hearing.

(8) If the IPCC or, as the case may be, the appropriate authority, considers that an investigation has made minimal or no progress since the previous notification, then the next notification may be made by any means that in the opinion of the IPCC or, as the case may be, the appropriate authority, is suitable.

60 Exceptions to the duty to keep the complainant informed and to provide information for other persons

(1) Subject to paragraph (2), the duties mentioned in regulation 54(1) and (2) (duty to keep the complainant informed), regulation 55(7) and (8) (duty to provide information for other persons) and in regulations 67(11) and 68(12) shall not apply in circumstances where in the opinion of the IPCC, or, as the case may be, of the appropriate authority, the non-disclosure of information is necessary for the purpose of—

(*a*) preventing the premature or inappropriate disclosure of information that is relevant to, or may be used in, any actual or prospective criminal proceedings;

(*b*) preventing the disclosure of information in any circumstances in which its non-disclosure—

(i) is in the interests of national security;

(ii) is for the purposes of the prevention or detection of crime, or the apprehension or prosecution of offenders;

(iii) is required on proportionality grounds; or

(iv) is otherwise necessary in the public interest; or

(*c*) preventing the disclosure of any information held by HMRC in connection with its functions which—

(i) is obtained from the Head of the Home Civil Service, the Chief Executive, the Commissioners or an officer, and

(ii) relates to a person whose identity is specified in the disclosure or can be deduced from it.

(2) Paragraph (1)(*c*) does not apply to any information relating to internal administrative arrangements of HMRC (whether relating to the Commissioners, officers or others).

(3) The IPCC or, as the case may be, the appropriate authority, shall not conclude that the non-disclosure of information is necessary under paragraph (1) unless it is satisfied that—

(*a*) there is a real risk of the disclosure of that information causing an adverse effect; and

(*b*) that adverse effect would be significant.

(4) The IPCC shall consult the appropriate authority in any case under paragraph (1)(*c*) before deciding whether or not it is satisfied under paragraph (3).

(5) Without prejudice to the generality of paragraph (1), the IPCC, or, as the case may be, the appropriate authority, shall consider whether the non-disclosure of information is justified under that paragraph in circumstances where—

(*a*) that information is relevant to, or may be used in, any actual or prospective disciplinary proceedings;

(*b*) the disclosure of that information may lead to the contamination of the evidence of witnesses during such proceedings;

(*c*) the disclosure of that information may prejudice the welfare or safety of any third party;

(*d*) that information constitutes criminal intelligence.

61 Copies of complaints etc

(1) Where a complaint is recorded under regulation 19(6) (initial handling and recording of complaints), the appropriate authority shall—

(*a*) supply to the complainant a copy of the record made of that complaint; and

(*b*) subject to paragraphs (2) to (4), supply to the person complained against a copy of the complaint.

(2) A copy of a complaint supplied under this regulation may be in a form which keeps anonymous the identity of the complainant or of any other person.

(3) The appropriate authority may decide not to supply such a copy of a complaint if it is of the opinion that to do so—

(*a*) might prejudice any criminal investigation or pending proceedings, or

(*b*) would otherwise be contrary to the public interest.

(4) Where the appropriate authority decides not to supply such a copy, it shall keep that decision under regular review.

62 Notification of actions and decisions

(1) So far as not covered by regulation 67(11) and (12) and regulation 74(11) and (12) (appeals to the IPCC with respect to an investigation), where the IPCC takes any action or decisions in consequence of it having received a memorandum under regulation 67(9) or regulation 74(3), it shall notify such action or decisions, together with an explanation of its reasons for having taken them, to—

(*a*) the appropriate authority;

(*b*) the complainant and any other interested person within the meaning of regulation 55(2) and (3); and

(*c*) subject to paragraph (2), the person complained against.

(2) The IPCC may decide not to give such a notification and explanation to the person complained against if it is of the opinion that that notification might prejudice any criminal investigation, pending proceedings, or review of the complaint.

63 Information for complainant about disciplinary recommendations

(1) Where—

(*a*) the IPCC makes recommendations under regulation 71 (duties with respect to disciplinary proceedings) in the case of an investigation of a complaint, and

(*b*) the appropriate authority notifies the IPCC that the recommendations have been accepted,

the IPCC shall notify the complainant and every person entitled to be kept properly informed in relation to the complaint under regulation 55 of that fact and of the steps that have been, or are to be taken, by the appropriate authority to give effect to it.

(2) Where in the case of an investigation of a complaint the appropriate authority—

(*a*) notifies the IPCC that it does not (either in whole or in part) accept recommendations made by the IPCC under regulation 71, or

(*b*) fails to take steps to give full effect to any such recommendations,

it shall be the duty of the IPCC to determine what further steps (if any) to take under that regulation.

(3) It shall be the duty of the IPCC to notify the complainant and every person entitled to be kept properly informed in relation to the complaint under regulation 55—

(*a*) of any determination under paragraph (2) not to take further steps under regulation 71; and (*b*) where it determines under that paragraph to take further steps under that regulation, of the outcome of the taking of those steps.

64 Register to be kept by the IPCC

(1) The IPCC shall establish and maintain a register of all information supplied to it by the appropriate authority under these Regulations.

(2) Subject to paragraph (3), the IPCC may publish or otherwise disclose to any person any information held on the register provided that the publication or disclosure is necessary for or conducive to the purpose of—

(*a*) learning lessons from the handling of, or demonstrating the thoroughness and effectiveness of, investigations by the IPCC or of managed or supervised investigations;

(*b*) raising public awareness of the complaints system; or

(*c*) improving the complaints system.

(3) Information may not be published or disclosed in circumstances where in the opinion of the IPCC the non-disclosure of information is necessary for the purposes mentioned in regulation 60(1)(*a*) and (*b*) (exceptions to the duty to keep the complainant informed and to provide information for other persons).

65 Manner and time limits of notifications

(1) Any notification to be given under these Regulations shall—

(*a*) unless otherwise specified in these Regulations or determined in guidance issued by the IPCC, be given in writing; and

(*b*) unless otherwise specified in these Regulations, be made within such period as the IPCC may determine in guidance.

(2) No time limit mentioned in these Regulations or determined by the IPCC shall apply in any case where exceptional circumstances prevent that time limit being complied with.

PART 8

REPORTS AND RECOMMENDATIONS

66 Final reports on investigations: complaints, conduct matters and certain DSI matters

(1) This regulation applies on the completion of an investigation of—

(*a*) a complaint, or

(*b*) a conduct matter.

(2) A person appointed under regulation 44 (investigation by the appropriate authority on its own behalf) shall submit a report on that person's investigation to the appropriate authority.

(3) A person appointed under regulation 45 (investigations supervised by the IPCC), 46 (investigations by a police force under the management or under the supervision of the IPCC), or 47 (investigations managed by the IPCC) shall—

(*a*) submit a report on that person's investigation to the IPCC; and

(*b*) send a copy of that report to the appropriate authority.

(4) In relation to a matter that was formerly a DSI matter but has been recorded as a conduct matter in pursuance of regulation 36(5) (procedure where conduct matter is revealed during investigation of a DSI matter), the references in paragraphs (2) and (3) of this regulation to the appropriate authority are references to—

(*a*) the appropriate authority in relation to the DSI matter; and

(*b*) (where different) the appropriate authority in relation to the person whose conduct is in question.

(5) A person designated under regulation 48 (investigations by the IPCC itself) as the person in charge of an investigation by the IPCC itself shall submit a report on the investigation to the IPCC.

(6) A person submitting a report under this regulation shall not be prevented by any obligation of secrecy imposed by any rule of law or otherwise from including all such matters in the report as that person thinks fit.

(7) A person who has submitted a report on an investigation under this regulation on an investigation within regulation 57(1) (duty to consider submissions from the person whose conduct is in question) must supply the appropriate authority with such copies of further documents or other items in that person's possession as the authority may request.

(8) The appropriate authority may only make a request under paragraph (7) in respect of a copy of a document or other item if the authority—

(*a*) considers that the document or item is of relevance to the investigation, and

(*b*) requires a copy of the document or the item for either or both of the purposes mentioned in paragraph (9).

(9) Those purposes are—

(*a*) complying with any obligation which the authority has under the disciplinary proceedings in relation to any person whose conduct is the subject-matter of the investigation;

VAT SIs

(*b*) ensuring that any such officer (a person whose conduct is in question) receives a fair hearing at any disciplinary proceedings in respect of any such conduct of that officer.

67 Action by the IPCC in response to an investigation report under regulation 66

(1) This regulation applies where—

(*a*) a report on an investigation carried out under the management of the IPCC is submitted to it under paragraph (3) of regulation 66 (final report on investigations: complaints, conduct matters and certain DSI matters); or

(*b*) a report on an investigation carried out by a person designated by the IPCC is submitted to it under paragraph (5) of that regulation.

(2) On receipt of the report, the IPCC—

(*a*) if it appears that the appropriate authority has not already been sent a copy of the report, shall send a copy of the report to that authority;

(*b*) shall determine whether the conditions set out in paragraphs (3) and (4) are satisfied in respect of the report;

(*c*) if it determines that those conditions are so satisfied, shall notify the Director of Public Prosecutions or the Director of Revenue and Customs Prosecutions of the determination and send the Director a copy of the report; and

(*d*) shall notify the appropriate authority and the persons mentioned in paragraph (7) of its determination under sub-paragraph (*b*) and of any action taken by it under sub-paragraph (*c*).

(3) The first condition is that the report indicates that a criminal offence may have been committed by a person to whose conduct the investigation related.

(4) The second condition is that the circumstances are such that, in the opinion of the IPCC, it is appropriate for the matters dealt with in the report to be considered by the Director of Public Prosecutions or, as the case may be, the Director of Revenue and Customs Prosecutions.

(5) The Director of Public Prosecutions or, as the case may be, the Director of Revenue and Customs Prosecutions shall notify the IPCC of any decision of the Director to take, or not to take, action in respect of the matters dealt with in any report a copy of which has been sent to the Director under paragraph (2)(*c*).

(6) It shall be the duty of the IPCC to notify the persons mentioned in paragraph (7) if criminal proceedings are brought against any person by the Director of Public Prosecutions or, as the case may be, the Director of Revenue and Customs Prosecutions in respect of any matters dealt with in a report copied to the Director under paragraph (2)(*c*).

(7) Those persons are—

(*a*) in the case of a complaint, the complainant and every person entitled to be kept properly informed in relation to the complaint under regulation 55 (duty to provide information for other persons); and

(*b*) in the case of a recordable conduct matter, every person entitled to be kept properly informed in relation to that matter under that regulation.

(8) On receipt of the report, the IPCC shall also notify the appropriate authority that it must—

(*a*) determine—

(i) whether any officer (person whose conduct is in question) has a case to answer in respect of their conduct or has no case to answer, and

(ii) what action (if any) the authority is required to, or will in its discretion, take in respect of the matters dealt with in the report; and

(*b*) determine what other action (if any) the authority will in its discretion take in respect of those matters.

(9) On receipt of a notification under paragraph (8) the appropriate authority shall make those determinations and submit a memorandum to the IPCC which—

(*a*) sets out the determinations the authority has made; and

(*b*) if the appropriate authority has decided in relation to any person whose conduct is the subject-matter of the report that disciplinary proceedings should not be brought against that person, sets out its reasons for so deciding.

(10) On receipt of a memorandum under paragraph (9), the IPCC shall—

(*a*) consider the memorandum and whether the appropriate authority has made the determinations under paragraph (8)(*a*) that the IPCC considers appropriate in respect of the matters dealt with in the report;

(*b*) determine, in the light of its consideration of those matters, whether or not to make recommendations under regulation 71 (duties with respect to disciplinary proceedings); and

(*c*) make such recommendations (if any) under that regulation as it thinks fit.

(11) On the making of a determination under paragraph (10)(*b*) the IPCC shall give a notification—

(*a*) in the case of a complaint, to the complainant and to every person entitled to be kept properly informed in relation to the complaint under regulation 55; and

(*b*) in the case of a recordable conduct matter, to every person entitled to be kept properly informed in relation to that matter under that regulation.

(12) The notification required by paragraph (11) is one setting out—

(*a*) the findings of the report;

(*b*) the IPCC's determination under paragraph (10)(*b*); and

(*c*) the action which the appropriate authority is to be recommended to take as a consequence of the determination.

(13) Regulation 60 shall have effect in relation to the duties imposed on the IPCC by paragraph (11) of this regulation.

(14) Except so far as may be otherwise provided by these Regulations, the IPCC shall be entitled (notwithstanding any obligation of secrecy imposed by any rule of law or otherwise) to discharge the duty to give a person mentioned in paragraph (11) notification of the findings of the report by sending that person a copy of the report.

(15) In relation to a DSI matter in respect of which a determination has been made under regulation 36(2) or (4) (procedure where conduct matter is revealed during the investigation of a DSI matter), the references in this regulation to the appropriate authority are references to the appropriate authority in relation to the person whose conduct is in question.

68 Action by the appropriate authority in response to an investigation report under regulation 66

(1) This regulation applies where—

(*a*) a report of an investigation is submitted to the appropriate authority in accordance with regulation 66(2); or

(*b*) a copy of a report on an investigation carried out under the supervision of the IPCC is sent to the appropriate authority in accordance with regulation 66(3).

(2) On receipt of the report or (as the case may be) of the copy, the appropriate authority—

(*a*) shall determine whether the conditions set out in paragraphs (3) and (4) are satisfied in respect of the report;

(*b*) if it determines that those conditions are so satisfied, shall notify the Director of Public Prosecutions or, as the case may be, the Director of Revenue and Customs Prosecutions of the determination and send the Director a copy of the report; and

(*c*) shall notify the persons mentioned in paragraph (7) of its determination under sub-paragraph (*a*) and of any action taken by it under sub-paragraph (*b*).

(3) The first condition is that the report indicates that a criminal offence may have been committed by a person to whose conduct the investigation related.

(4) The second condition is that the circumstances are such that, in the opinion of the appropriate authority, it is appropriate for the matters dealt with in the report to be considered by the Director of Public Prosecutions or, as the case may be, the Director of Revenue and Customs Prosecutions.

(5) The Director of Public Prosecutions or, as the case may be, the Director of Revenue and Customs Prosecutions shall notify the appropriate authority of any decision of the Director to take, or not to take, action in respect of the matters dealt with in any report a copy of which has been sent to the Director under paragraph (2).

(6) It shall be the duty of the appropriate authority to notify the persons mentioned in paragraph (7) if criminal proceedings are brought against any person by the Director of Public Prosecutions or, as the case may be, the Director of Revenue and Customs Prosecutions in respect of any matters dealt with in a report copied to the Director under paragraph (2)(*b*).

(7) Those persons are—

(*a*) in the case of a complaint, the complainant and every person entitled to be kept properly informed in relation to the complaint under regulation 55 (duty to provide information for other persons); and

(*b*) in the case of a recordable conduct matter, every person entitled to be kept properly informed in relation to that matter under that regulation.

(8) In the case of a report falling within paragraph (1)(*b*) which relates to a recordable conduct matter, the appropriate authority shall also notify the IPCC of its determination under paragraph (2)(*a*).

(9) On receipt of such a notification that the appropriate authority has determined that the conditions in paragraphs (3) and (4) are not satisfied in respect of the report, the IPCC—

(*a*) shall make its own determination as to whether those conditions are so satisfied; and

(*b*) if it determines that they are so satisfied, shall direct the appropriate authority to notify the Director of Public Prosecutions or, as the case may be, the Director of Revenue and Customs Prosecutions of the IPCC's determination and send the Director a copy of the report.

(10) It shall be the duty of the appropriate authority to comply with any direction given to it under paragraph (9)(*b*).

(11) On receipt of the report or (as the case may be) copy, the appropriate authority shall also—

(*a*) determine—

(i) whether any person to whose conduct the investigation related has a case to answer in respect of their conduct or has no case to answer, and

(ii) what action (if any) the authority is required to, or will in its discretion, take in respect of the matters dealt with in the report; and

(*b*) determine what other action (if any) the authority will in its discretion take in respect of those matters.

(12) On the making of the determinations under paragraph (11) the appropriate authority shall give a notification—

(*a*) in the case of a complaint, to the complainant and to every person entitled to be kept properly informed in relation to the complaint under regulation 55; and

(*b*) in the case of a recordable conduct matter, to every person entitled to be kept properly informed in relation to that matter under that regulation.

(13) The notification required by paragraph (12) is one setting out—

(*a*) the findings of the report;

(*b*) the determinations the authority has made under paragraph (11); and

(*c*) the complainant's right of appeal under regulation 74 (appeals to the IPCC with respect to an investigation).

(14) Regulation 60 shall have effect in relation to the duties imposed on the appropriate authority by paragraph (12) of this regulation.

(15) Except so far as may be otherwise provided by these Regulations, the appropriate authority shall be entitled (notwithstanding any obligation of secrecy imposed by any rule of law or otherwise) to discharge the duty to give a person mentioned in paragraph (12) notification of the findings of the report by sending that person a copy of the report.

(16) In relation to a DSI matter in respect of which a determination has been made under regulation 36(2) or (4), the references in this regulation to the appropriate authority are references to the appropriate authority in relation to the person whose conduct is in question.

69 Final reports on investigations: other DSI matters

(1) This regulation applies on the completion of an investigation of a DSI matter in respect of which neither the IPCC nor the appropriate authority has made a determination under regulation 36(2) or (4) (procedure where conduct matter is revealed during investigation of DSI matter).

(2) The person investigating shall—

(*a*) submit a report on the investigation to the IPCC; and

(*b*) send a copy of that report to the appropriate authority.

(3) A person submitting a report under this regulation shall not be prevented by any obligation of secrecy imposed by any rule of law or otherwise from including all such matters in that report as that person thinks fit.

70 Action by the IPCC in response to an investigation report under regulation 69

(1) On receipt of the report referred to in regulation 69, the IPCC shall determine whether the report indicates that an officer may have—

(*a*) committed a criminal offence; or

(*b*) behaved in a manner which would justify the bringing of disciplinary proceedings.

(2) If the IPCC determines under paragraph (1) that there is no indication in the report that an officer may have—

(*a*) committed a criminal offence; or

(*b*) behaved in a manner which would justify the bringing of disciplinary proceedings,

it shall make such recommendations or give such advice (if any) under regulation 7 as it considers necessary or desirable.

(3) Paragraph (2) does not affect any power of the IPCC to make recommendations or give advice under regulation 7 in other cases (whether arising under these Regulations or otherwise).

(4) If the IPCC determines under paragraph (1) that the report indicates that an officer may have—

(*a*) committed a criminal offence; or

(*b*) behaved in a manner which would justify the bringing of disciplinary proceedings,

it shall notify the appropriate authority in relation to the person whose conduct is in question of its determination, and, if it appears that the appropriate authority has not already been sent a copy of the report, send a copy of the report to that authority.

(5) Where the appropriate authority in relation to the person whose conduct is in question is notified of a determination by the IPCC under paragraph (4), it shall record the matter under regulation 24 (recording etc of conduct matters in other cases) as a conduct matter (and the other provisions of these Regulations shall apply in relation to that matter accordingly).

(6) Where a DSI matter is recorded under regulation 24 as a conduct matter by virtue of paragraph (5)—

(*a*) the person investigating the DSI matter shall (subject to any determination made by the IPCC under regulation 38(6) (power of the IPCC to determine the form of an investigation—further determination)) investigate the conduct matter as if appointed or designated to do so, and

(*b*) the other provisions of these Regulations shall apply in relation to that matter accordingly.

71 Duties with respect to disciplinary proceedings

(1) This regulation applies where, in the case of any investigation, the appropriate authority—

(*a*) has given, or is required to give, a notification under regulation 68(12) (action by the appropriate authority in response to an investigation report under regulation 66) of the action it is proposing to take in relation to the matters dealt with in any report of the investigation; or

(*b*) has submitted, or is required to submit, a memorandum to the IPCC under regulation 67 (action by the IPCC in response to an investigation report under regulation 66) or 74 (appeals to the IPCC with respect to an investigation) setting out the action that it is proposing to take in relation to those matters.

(2) Subject to regulation 52 (restrictions on proceedings pending the conclusion of an investigation) and to any recommendations or directions under this regulation, it shall be the duty of the appropriate authority—

(*a*) to take the action which has been or is required to be notified or, as the case may be, which is or is required to be set out in the memorandum; and

(*b*) in a case where that action consists of or includes the bringing of disciplinary proceedings, to secure that those proceedings, once brought, are proceeded with to a proper conclusion.

(3) Where this regulation applies by virtue of paragraph (1)(*b*), the IPCC may make a recommendation to the appropriate authority in respect of any person whose conduct is in question—

(*a*) that the person has a case to answer in respect of their conduct or has no case to answer in relation to their conduct to which the investigation related;

(*b*) that disciplinary proceedings of the form specified in the recommendation are brought against that person in respect of the conduct to which the investigation related; or

(*c*) that any disciplinary proceedings brought against that person are modified so as to deal with such aspects of that conduct as may be so specified;

and it shall be the duty of the appropriate authority to notify the IPCC whether it accepts the recommendation and (if it does) to set out in the notification the steps that it is proposing to take to give effect to it.

(4) If, after the IPCC has made a recommendation under this regulation, the appropriate authority does not take steps to secure that full effect is given to the recommendation—

(*a*) the IPCC may direct the appropriate authority to take steps for that purpose; and

(*b*) it shall be the duty of the appropriate authority to comply with the direction.

(5) A direction under paragraph (4) may, to such extent as the IPCC thinks fit, set out the steps to be taken by the appropriate authority in order to give effect to the recommendation.

(6) Where the IPCC gives the appropriate authority a direction under this regulation, it shall supply the appropriate authority with a statement of its reasons for doing so.

(7) Where disciplinary proceedings have been brought in accordance with a recommendation or direction under this regulation, it shall be the duty of the authority to ensure that they are proceeded with to a proper conclusion.

(8) The IPCC may at any time withdraw a direction given under this regulation; and paragraph (7) shall not impose any obligation in relation to any time after the withdrawal of the direction.

(9) The appropriate authority shall keep the IPCC informed—

(*a*) in a case in which this regulation applies by virtue of paragraph (1)(*b*), of whatever action it takes in pursuance of its duty under paragraph (2); and

(*b*) in every case of a recommendation or direction under this regulation, of whatever action it takes in response to that recommendation or direction.

72 Complaints against a person whose identity is unascertained

(1) Where a complaint or conduct matter relates to the conduct of a person whose identity is unascertained at the time at which the complaint is made or the conduct matter is recorded, or whose identity is not ascertained during or subsequent to, the investigation of the complaint or recordable conduct matter, these Regulations shall apply in relation to such a person as if it did not include—

(*a*) any requirement for the person complained against to be given a notification or an opportunity to make representations;

(*b*) any requirement for the IPCC or the appropriate authority to determine whether a criminal offence may have been committed by the person whose conduct has been the subject-matter of an investigation, or to take any action in relation to such a determination;

(*c*) any requirement for an appropriate authority to determine whether disciplinary proceedings should be brought against a person whose conduct is the subject-matter of a report.

(2) Where the identity of such a person is subsequently ascertained, the IPCC and the appropriate authority shall take such action in accordance with these Regulations as they see fit, regardless of any previous action taken.

VAT SIs

PART 9
APPEALS

73 Appeals to the IPCC: failures to notify or record a complaint

(1) An appeal under regulation 21 (failures to notify or record a complaint) against any failure referred to in regulation 21(3) shall be made within 28 days of the date on which notification of that failure is made or sent to the complainant under regulation 21(2).

(2) Any such appeal shall be made in writing and shall state—

(*a*) details of the complaint;

(*b*) the date on which the complaint was made;

(*c*) the name of the Head of the Home Civil Service, the Chief Executive or the Commissioner (other than the Chairman, the Chief Executive and the Permanent Secretary) who gave notification of the failure;

(*d*) the grounds for the appeal; and

(*e*) the date on which the complainant was notified of the determination or of the failure to record the complaint.

(3) Where the IPCC receives such an appeal it shall—

(*a*) notify the Head of the Home Civil Service, the Chief Executive or the Commissioners (other than the Chairman, the Chief Executive and the Permanent Secretary) concerned of the appeal, and

(*b*) request any information from any person which it considers necessary to dispose of the appeal.

(4) Where the IPCC receives an appeal which fails to comply with one or more of the requirements mentioned in paragraph (2), it may decide to proceed as if those requirements had been complied with.

(5) The Head of the Home Civil Service, the Chief Executive or the Commissioners (other than the Chairman, the Chief Executive and the Permanent Secretary) shall supply to the IPCC any information requested under paragraph (3)(*b*).

(6) The IPCC shall determine the outcome of the appeal as soon as practicable.

(7) The IPCC shall notify the complainant and the Head of the Home Civil Service, the Chief Executive or the Commissioners (other than the Chairman, the Chief Executive and the Permanent Secretary) concerned of the reasons for its determination.

(8) The IPCC may extend the time period mentioned in paragraph (1) in any case where it is satisfied that by reason of the special circumstances of the case it is just to do so.

74 Appeals to the IPCC with respect to an investigation

(1) This regulation applies where a complaint has been subjected to—

(*a*) an investigation by the appropriate authority on its own behalf; or

(*b*) an investigation under the supervision of the IPCC.

(2) The complainant shall have the following rights of appeal to the IPCC—

(*a*) a right of appeal on the grounds that the complainant has not been provided with adequate information—

(i) about the findings of the investigation; or

(ii) about any determination of the appropriate authority relating to the taking (or not taking) of action in respect of any matters dealt with in the report on the investigation;

(*b*) a right of appeal against the findings of the investigation;

(*c*) a right of appeal against any determination by the appropriate authority that a person to whose conduct the investigation related has a case to answer in respect of that person's conduct or has no case to answer;

(*d*) a right of appeal against any determination by the appropriate authority relating to the taking (or not taking) of action in respect of any matters dealt with in the report; and

(*e*) a right of appeal against any determination by the appropriate authority under regulation 68(2)(*a*) (action by the appropriate authority in response to an investigation report under regulation 66), as a result of which it is not required to send the Director of Public Prosecutions or, as the case may be, the Director of Revenue and Customs Prosecutions a copy of the report.

(3) On the bringing of an appeal under this regulation, the IPCC may require the appropriate authority to submit a memorandum to the IPCC which—

(*a*) sets out whether the appropriate authority has determined that a person to whose conduct the investigation related has a case to answer in respect of that person's conduct or has no case to answer;

(*b*) if the appropriate authority is proposing to take any action, sets out what action it is proposing to take;

(*c*) if the appropriate authority has decided in relation to a person to whose conduct the investigation related, that disciplinary proceedings should not be brought against that person, sets out its reasons for so deciding; and (*d*) if the appropriate authority made a determination under regulation 68(2)(*a*) as a result of which it is not required to send the Director of Public Prosecutions or, as the case may be, the Director of Revenue and Customs Prosecutions, a copy of the report relating to the investigation, sets out the reasons for that determination;

and it shall be the duty of the appropriate authority to comply with any requirement under this paragraph.

(4) Where the IPCC so requires on the bringing of any appeal under this regulation in the case of an investigation by the appropriate authority on its own behalf, the appropriate authority shall provide the IPCC with a copy of the report of the investigation.

(5) On an appeal under this regulation, the IPCC shall determine such of the following as it considers appropriate in the circumstances—

(*a*) whether the complainant has been provided with adequate information about the matters mentioned in paragraph (2)(*a*);

(*b*) whether the findings of the investigation need to be reconsidered; and

(*c*) whether the appropriate authority—

(i) has made such a determination as is mentioned in paragraph (3)(*a*) that the IPCC considers to be appropriate in respect of matters dealt with in the report, and

(ii) has determined that it is required to or will, in its discretion, take the action (if any) that the IPCC considers to be so appropriate; and

(*d*) whether the conditions set out in regulation 68(3) and (4) are satisfied in respect of the report on the investigation.

(6) Where, on an appeal under this regulation, the IPCC determines that the complainant has not been provided with adequate information about any matter, the IPCC shall give the appropriate authority all such directions as the IPCC considers appropriate for securing that the complainant is properly informed.

(7) Nothing in paragraph (6) shall authorise the IPCC to require the disclosure of any information the disclosure of which to the appellant has been or is capable of being withheld by virtue of regulation 60.

(8) Where, on an appeal under this regulation, the IPCC determines that the findings of the investigation need to be reconsidered, it shall either—

(*a*) review those findings without an immediate further investigation; or

(*b*) direct that the complaint be re-investigated.

(9) Where, on an appeal under this regulation, the IPCC determines that the appropriate authority has not made a determination as to whether there is a case for a person to whose conduct the investigation related to answer that the IPCC considers appropriate or has not determined that it is required to or will, in its discretion, take the action in respect of the matters dealt with in the report that the IPCC considers appropriate, the IPCC shall—

(*a*) determine, in the light of that determination, whether or not to make recommendations under regulation 71 (duties with respect to disciplinary proceedings); and

(*b*) make such recommendations (if any) under that regulation as it thinks fit.

(10) Where, on an appeal under this regulation, the IPCC determines that the conditions set out in regulation 68(3) and (4) are satisfied in respect of the report, it shall direct the appropriate authority—

(*a*) to notify the Director of Public Prosecutions or, as the case may be, the Director of Revenue and Customs Prosecutions, of the IPCC's determination; and

(*b*) to send the Director a copy of the report.

(11) The IPCC shall give notification of any determination under this regulation—

(*a*) to the appropriate authority;

(*b*) to the complainant;

(*c*) to every person entitled to be kept properly informed in relation to the complaint under regulation 55 (duty to provide information for other persons); and

(*d*) except in a case where it appears to the IPCC that to do so might prejudice any proposed review or re-investigation of the complaint, to the person complained against.

(12) The IPCC shall also give notification of any directions given to the appropriate authority under this regulation—

(*a*) to the complainant;

(*b*) to every person entitled to be kept properly informed in relation to the complaint under regulation 55; and

(*c*) except in a case where it appears to the IPCC that to do so might prejudice any proposed review or re-investigation of the complaint, to the person complained against.

(13) It shall be the duty of the appropriate authority to comply with any directions given to it under this regulation.

(14) Any appeal made by a complainant under this regulation shall be made within 28 days of the date on which the appropriate authority sends a notification to the complainant of its determination under regulation 68(12) as to what action (if any) it will take in respect of the matters dealt with in the investigation report.

(15) Any such appeal shall be in writing and shall state—

(*a*) details of the complaint;

(*b*) the date on which the complaint was made;

(*c*) the grounds for the appeal; and

(*d*) the date on which the complainant received notification under regulation 68(12).

(16) Where the IPCC receives such an appeal, it shall request any information from any person which it considers necessary to dispose of the appeal.

(17) Where the IPCC receives an appeal which fails to comply with one or more of the requirements mentioned in paragraph (15), it may decide to proceed as if those requirements had been complied with.

(18) The appropriate authority shall supply to the IPCC any further information requested of it under paragraph (16).

(19) The IPCC shall determine the outcome of the appeal as soon as practicable.

(20) The IPCC shall notify the complainant and the appropriate authority of the reasons for its determination.

(21) The IPCC may extend the time period mentioned in paragraph (14) in any case where it is satisfied that by reason of the special circumstances of the case it is just to do so.

75 Reviews and re-investigations following an appeal

(1) On a review under regulation 74(8)(*a*) (appeals to the IPCC with respect to an investigation) of the findings of an investigation, the powers of the IPCC shall be, according to its determination on that review, to do one or more of the following—

(*a*) to uphold the findings in whole or in part;

(*b*) to give the appropriate authority such directions as the IPCC thinks fit—

(i) as to the carrying out by the appropriate authority of its own review of the findings,

(ii) as to the information to be provided to the complainant, and

(iii) generally as to the handling of the matter in future;

(*c*) to direct that the complaint be re-investigated.

(2) Where the IPCC directs under regulation 74 or paragraph (1) that a complaint be re-investigated, it shall make a determination of the form that the re-investigation should take.

(3) Paragraphs (3) to (8) of regulation 38 (power of the IPCC to determine the form of an investigation) shall apply in relation to a determination under paragraph (2) as they apply in the case of a determination under that regulation.

(4) The provisions of these Regulations shall apply in relation to any re-investigation in pursuance of a direction under regulation 74(9) or paragraph (1) as they apply in relation to any investigation in pursuance of a determination under regulation 38.

(5) The IPCC shall give notification of any determination made by it under this regulation—

(*a*) to the appropriate authority;

(*b*) to the complainant;

(*c*) to every person entitled to be kept properly informed in relation to the complaint under regulation 55 (duty to provide information for other persons); and

(*d*) except in a case where it appears to the IPCC that to do so might prejudice any proposed re-investigation of the complaint, to the person complained against.

(6) The IPCC shall also give notification of any directions given to the appropriate authority under this regulation—

(*a*) to the complainant;

(*b*) to every person entitled to be kept properly informed in relation to the complaint under regulation 55; and

(*c*) except in a case where it appears to the IPCC that to do so might prejudice any proposed review or re-investigation of the complaint, to the person complained against.

2010/1878

FINANCE ACT 2009, SECTIONS 101 TO 103 (APPOINTED DAY AND SUPPLEMENTAL PROVISION) ORDER 2010

Made . . . . *21 July 2010*

The Treasury make the following Order in exercise of the powers conferred by section 104(3) to (5) of the Finance Act 2009.

1 Citation

This Order may be cited as the Finance Act 2009, Sections 101 to 103 (Appointed Day and Supplemental Provision) Order 2010.

2 Appointed day

The day appointed as the day on which sections 101 to 103 of the Finance Act 2009 come into force for the purposes of bank payroll tax (including any penalties assessed in relation to that tax) is 31st August 2010.

3 Supplemental provision

Interest charged under section 101 of the Finance Act 2009 (late payment interest on sums due to HMRC) on an amount enforceable as if it were bank payroll tax may be enforced as if it were an amount of bank payroll tax.

2010/1879

TAXES AND DUTIES (INTEREST RATE) REGULATIONS 2010

Made .... *21 July 2010*

Laid .... *22 July 2010*

Coming into force .... *31 August 2010*

The Treasury make the following Order in exercise of the powers conferred by section 103 of the Finance Act 2009.

Revocation—

These regulations revoked by the Taxes and Duties, etc (Interest Rate) Regulations, SI 2011/2446 reg 7 with effect from 31 October 2011.

2010/2239

VALUE ADDED TAX (SECTION 55A) (SPECIFIED GOODS AND SERVICES AND EXCEPTED SUPPLIES) ORDER 2010

Made .... *13 September 2010*

Laid before the House of Commons .... *14 September 2010*

Coming into force .... *1 November 2010*

The Treasury, in exercise of the powers conferred by sections 55A(9), (10), (11) and (14) of the Value Added Tax Act 1994, make the following Order:

1 Citation, commencement and effect

(1) This Order may be cited as the Value Added Tax (Section 55A) (Specified Goods and Services and Excepted Supplies) Order 2010.

(2) This Order shall come into force on 1st November 2010 and has effect in relation to supplies made on or after that date.

2 Revocation

The Value Added Tax (Section 55A) (Specified Goods and Excepted Supplies) Order 2007 is revoked.

3 Interpretation

In this Order—

"the Act" means the Value Added Tax Act 1994;

"allowance" has the meaning given in Article 3 of the Directive;

"certified emission reduction" has the meaning given in Article 3 of the Directive;

"the Directive" means Directive 2003/87/EC of the European Parliament and of the Council establishing a scheme for greenhouse gas emission allowance trading within the Community and amending Council Directive 96/61/EC;

"emission reduction unit" has the meaning given in Article 3 of the Directive;

"operator" has the meaning given in Article 3 of the Directive;

"public electronic communications service" has the meaning given in section 151 of the Communications Act 2003.

4 The application of section 55A of the Act to specified goods and services

The goods and services specified in articles 5 and 6 are goods and services to which section 55A of the Act (customers to account for tax on supplies of goods or services of a kind used in missing trader intra-community fraud) applies.

5 Specified goods

The goods referred to in article 4 are—

(*a*) a mobile telephone, whether or not it has any function in addition to the transmitting and receiving of spoken messages;

(*b*) an integrated circuit device, such as a central processing unit and microprocessor unit, in a state prior to integration into an end user product.

6 Specified services

The services referred to in article 4 are—

(*a*) a transfer of an allowance;

(*b*) a transfer of an emission reduction unit which can be used by an operator for compliance with the scheme established by the Directive;

(*c*) a transfer of a certified emission reduction which can be used by an operator for compliance with the scheme established by the Directive.

7 Excepted supplies

For the purposes of section 55A of the Act a supply of a description specified below is an excepted supply—

(*a*) a supply of specified goods where the value of the supply is less than £5000;

(*b*) a supply of specified goods where the supply is of a description specified in an order made under section 50A of the Act (margin schemes) and, in accordance with such an order, the supplier opts to account for the VAT chargeable on the supply on the profit margin on the supply instead of by reference to its value;

(*c*) a supply of a mobile telephone where, at the time a person enters into the agreement to purchase the telephone—

(i) he enters into an agreement (including the renewal or extension of an existing agreement) with a provider of a public electronic communications service for the supply, in relation to that telephone, of such a service, and

(ii) that agreement is not one that requires periodical pre-payments in order to use the service ("Pay as You Go");

(*d*) a transfer or disposal of specified goods for no consideration that is treated as a supply of goods by virtue of paragraph 5(1) of Schedule 4 to the Act.

8 Article 7(*a*) does not apply to a supply of specified goods where—

(*a*) the supply is particularised on the same VAT invoice as a supply, or supplies, of other specified goods, and

(*b*) the total value of the supplies equals or exceeds £5000.

2010/2655

FIRST-TIER TRIBUNAL AND UPPER TRIBUNAL (CHAMBERS) ORDER 2010

Made . . . . *28 October 2010*

Laid before Parliament . . . . *2 November 2010*

Coming into force . . . . *29 November 2010*

The Lord Chancellor, with the concurrence of the Senior President of Tribunals, makes the following Order in exercise of the power conferred by section 7(1) and (9) of the Tribunals, Courts and Enforcement Act 2007.

1 Citation, commencement and revocations

(1) This Order may be cited as the First-tier Tribunal and Upper Tribunal (Chambers) Order 2010 and comes into force on 29th November 2010.

(2) The Orders listed in the first column of the Schedule to this Order are revoked to the extent specified in the second column.

2 First-tier Tribunal Chambers

The First-tier Tribunal shall be organised into the following chambers—

(*a*) the General Regulatory Chamber;

(*b*) the Health, Education and Social Care Chamber;

(*c*) the Immigration and Asylum Chamber;

[(*cc*) the Property Chamber;][1]

(*d*) the Social Entitlement Chamber;

(*e*) the Tax Chamber;

(*f*) the War Pensions and Armed Forces Compensation Chamber.

Amendments—[1] Para (*cc*) inserted by First-tier Tribunal and Upper Tribunal (Chambers) (Amendment) Order, SI 2013/1187 arts 2, 3 with effect from 1 July 2013.

3 Functions of the General Regulatory Chamber

To the General Regulatory Chamber are allocated all functions related to—

(*a*) proceedings in respect of the decisions and actions of regulatory bodies which are not allocated to the Health, Education and Social Care Chamber by article 4 or to the Tax Chamber by article 7;

(*b*) matters referred to the First-tier Tribunal under Schedule 1D to the Charities Act 1993 (references to Tribunal);

(*c*) the determination of remuneration for carrying mail-bags in a ship or aircraft.

4 Functions of the Health, Education and Social Care Chamber

To the Health, Education and Social Care Chamber are allocated all functions related to—

(*a*) an appeal against a decision related to children with special educational needs;

(*b*) a claim of disability discrimination in the education of a child;

(*c*) an application or an appeal against a decision or determination related to work with children or vulnerable adults;

(*d*) an appeal against a decision related to registration in respect of the provision of health or social care;

(*e*) an application in respect of, or an appeal against a decision related to, the provision of health care or health services;

(*f*) an appeal against a decision related to registration in respect of social workers and social care workers;

(*g*) an appeal against a decision related to the provision of childcare;

(*h*) an appeal against a decision related to an independent school or other independent educational institution;

(*i*) applications and references by and in respect of patients under the provisions of the Mental Health Act 1983 or paragraph 5(2) of the Schedule to the Repatriation of Prisoners Act 1984.

5 Functions of the Immigration and Asylum Chamber of the First-tier Tribunal

To the Immigration and Asylum Chamber of the First-tier Tribunal are allocated all functions related to immigration and asylum matters, with the exception of matters allocated to—

(*a*) the Social Entitlement Chamber by article 6(*a*);

(*b*) the General Regulatory Chamber by article 3(*a*).

[5A Functions of the Property Chamber

To the Property Chamber are allocated all functions conferred on the First-tier Tribunal relating to—

(*a*) a reference by the Chief Land Registrar and any other application, matter or appeal under the Land Registration Act 2002;

(*b*) proceedings under any of the enactments referred to in section 6A(2) of the Agriculture (Miscellaneous Provisions) Act 1954 or the Hill Farming Act 1946;

(*c*) housing etc, under the Housing Act 2004;

(*d*) leasehold property;

(*e*) residential property;

(*f*) rents;

(*g*) the right to buy;

[(*h*) proceedings relating to mobile homes and caravan sites.][2]]

[(*I*) proceedings for approval by the First-tier Tribunal of the exercise of a power of entry, made under paragraph 6B of Schedule 9 to the Local Government Finance Act 1988 or under section 25A of the Local Government Finance Act 1992.][3]][1]

Amendments—[1] Article 5A inserted by First-tier Tribunal and Upper Tribunal (Chambers) (Amendment) Order, SI 2013/1187 arts 2, 4 with effect from 1 July 2013.

[2] Para (*h*) substituted by the First-tier Tribunal and Upper Tribunal (Chambers) (Amendment) Order, SI 2014/1901 art 2(1), (2) with effect from 8 August 2014.

[3] Para (*I*) inserted by the First-tier Tribunal and Upper Tribunal (Chambers) (Amendment) Order, SI 2015/1563 art 2(1), (2) with effect from 1 October 2015.

6 Functions of the Social Entitlement Chamber

To the Social Entitlement Chamber are allocated all functions related to appeals—

(*a*) in cases regarding support for asylum seekers, failed asylum seekers, persons designated under section 130 of the Criminal Justice and Immigration Act 2008, or the dependants of any such persons;

(*b*) in criminal injuries compensation cases;

VAT SIs

(*c*) regarding entitlement to, payments of, or recovery or recoupment of payments of, social security benefits, child support, vaccine damage payments, health in pregnancy grant and tax credits, with the exception of—

(i) appeals under section 11 of the Social Security Contributions (Transfer of Functions, etc) Act 1999 (appeals against decisions of Her Majesty's Revenue and Customs);

(ii) appeals in respect of employer penalties or employer information penalties (as defined in section 63(11) and (12) of the Tax Credits Act 2002);

(iii) appeals under regulation 28(3) of the Child Trust Funds Regulations 2004;

(*d*) regarding saving gateway accounts with the exception of appeals against requirements to account for an amount under regulations made under section 14 of the Saving Gateway Accounts Act 2009;

(*e*) regarding child trust funds with the exception of appeals against requirements to account for an amount under regulations made under section 22(4) of the Child Trust Funds Act 2004 in relation to section 13 of that Act;

[(*ea*) appealable decisions within the meaning of section 56(3) of the Childcare Payments Act 2014;][1]

(*f*) regarding payments in consequence of diffuse mesothelioma;

(*g*) regarding a certificate or waiver decision in relation to NHS charges;

(*h*) regarding entitlement to be credited with earnings or contributions;

(*i*) against a decision as to whether an accident was an industrial accident.

Amendments—[1] Para (*ea*) inserted by the First-tier Tribunal and Upper Tribunal (Chambers) (Amendment) Order, SI 2015/1563 art 2(1), (3) with effect from 1 October 2015..

7 Functions of the Tax Chamber

To the Tax Chamber are allocated all functions, except those functions allocated to the Social Entitlement Chamber by article 6 or to the Tax and Chancery Chamber of the Upper Tribunal by article 13, related to an appeal, application, reference or other proceeding in respect of—

(*a*) a function of the Commissioners for Her Majesty's Revenue and Customs or an officer of Revenue and Customs;

(*b*) the exercise by the Serious Organised Crime Agency of general Revenue functions or Revenue inheritance tax functions (as defined in section 323 of the Proceeds of Crime Act 2002);

(*c*) the exercise by the Director of Border Revenue of functions under section 7 of the Borders, Citizenship and Revenue Act 2009;

(*d*) a function of the Compliance Officer for the Independent Parliamentary Standards Authority.

8 Functions of the War Pensions and Armed Forces Compensation Chamber

To the War Pensions and Armed Forces Compensation Chamber are allocated all functions related to appeals under the War Pensions (Administrative Provisions) Act 1919 and the Pensions Appeal Tribunals Act 1943.

9 Upper Tribunal Chambers

The Upper Tribunal shall be organised into the following chambers—

(*a*) the Administrative Appeals Chamber;

(*b*) the Immigration and Asylum Chamber of the Upper Tribunal;

(*c*) the Lands Chamber;

(*d*) the Tax and Chancery Chamber.

10 Functions of the Administrative Appeals Chamber

To the Administrative Appeals Chamber are allocated all functions related to—

(*a*) an appeal—

(i) against a decision made by the First-tier Tribunal, except an appeal allocated to the Tax and Chancery Chamber by article 13(*a*) or the Immigration and Asylum Chamber of the Upper Tribunal by article 11(*a*);

(ii) under section 5 of the Pensions Appeal Tribunals Act 1943 (appeals against assessment of extent of disablement) against a decision of the Pensions Appeal Tribunal in Northern Ireland established under paragraph 1(3) of the Schedule to the Pensions Appeal Tribunals Act 1943 (constitution, jurisdiction and procedure of Pensions Appeal Tribunals);

(iii) against a decision of the Pensions Appeal Tribunal in Scotland established under paragraph 1(2) of the Schedule to the Pensions Appeal Tribunals Act 1943;

(iv) against a decision of the Mental Health Review Tribunal for Wales established under section 65 of the Mental Health Act 1983 (Mental Health Review Tribunals);

(v) against a decision of the Special Educational Needs Tribunal for Wales;

(vi) under section 4 of the Safeguarding Vulnerable Groups Act 2006 (appeals);

(vii) transferred to the Upper Tribunal from the First-tier Tribunal under Tribunal Procedure Rules, except an appeal allocated to the Tax and Chancery Chamber by article 13(1)(*e*);

[(viii) against a decision in a road transport case;][1]

(*b*) an application, except an application allocated to another chamber by article 11(*c*)[, (*d*) or (*e*)][3], 12(*c*) or 13(*g*), for the Upper Tribunal—

(i) to grant the relief mentioned in section 15(1) of the Tribunals, Courts and Enforcement Act 2007 (Upper Tribunal's "judicial review" jurisdiction);

(ii) to exercise the powers of review under section 21(2) of that Act (Upper Tribunal's "judicial review" jurisdiction: Scotland);

(*c*) a matter referred to the Upper Tribunal by the First-tier Tribunal—

(i) under section 9(5)(*b*) of the Tribunals, Courts and Enforcement Act 2007 (review of decision of First-tier Tribunal), or

(ii) under Tribunal Procedure Rules relating to non-compliance with a requirement of the First-tier Tribunal,

except where the reference is allocated to another chamber by article 11(*b*) or 13(*f*);

(*d*) a determination or decision under section 4 of the Forfeiture Act 1982;

(*e*) proceedings, or a preliminary issue, transferred under Tribunal Procedure Rules to the Upper Tribunal from the First-tier Tribunal, except those allocated to [the Lands Chamber by article 12(*cc*) or to][2] the Tax and Chancery Chamber by article 13(1)(*e*).

Amendments—[1] Para (*a*)(viii) substituted by the First-tier Tribunal and Upper Tribunal (Chambers) (Amendment) Order, SI 2012/1673 arts 2, 3 with effect from 20 July 2012.

[2] Words in para (*e*) inserted by the First-tier Tribunal and Upper Tribunal (Chambers) (Amendment) Order, SI 2013/1187 arts 2, 5 with effect from 1 July 2013.

[3] Words in para (*b*) substituted for words "or (*d*)" by the First-tier Tribunal and Upper Tribunal (Chambers) (Amendment No 2) Order, SI 2013/2068 arts 2, 3 with effect from 1 November 2013.

11 Functions of the Immigration and Asylum Chamber of the Upper Tribunal

To the Immigration and Asylum Chamber of the Upper Tribunal are allocated all functions related to—

(*a*) an appeal against a decision of the First-tier Tribunal made in the Immigration and Asylum Chamber of the First-tier Tribunal;

(*b*) a matter referred to the Upper Tribunal under section 9(5)(*b*) of the Tribunals, Courts and Enforcement Act 2007 or under Tribunal Procedure Rules by the Immigration and Asylum Chamber of the First-tier Tribunal;

[(*c*) an application for the Upper Tribunal to grant relief mentioned in section 15(1) of the Tribunals, Courts and Enforcement Act 2007 (Upper Tribunal's "judicial review" jurisdiction), or to exercise the power of review under section 21(2) of that Act (Upper Tribunal's "judicial review" jurisdiction: Scotland), which is made by a person who claims to be a minor from outside the United Kingdom challenging a defendant's assessment of that person's age;

(*d*) an application for the Upper Tribunal to exercise the powers of review under section 21(2) of the Tribunals, Court and Enforcement Act (Upper Tribunal's "judicial review" jurisdiction: Scotland), which relates to a decision of the First-tier Tribunal mentioned in paragraph (a);

(*e*) an application for the Upper Tribunal to grant relief mentioned in section 15(1) of the Tribunals, Courts and Enforcement Act 2007 (Upper Tribunal's "judicial review" jurisdiction), which is designated as an immigration matter—

(i) in a direction made in accordance with Part 1 of Schedule 2 to the Constitutional Reform Act 2005 specifying a class of case for the purposes of section 18(6) of the Tribunals, Courts and Enforcement Act 2007; or

(ii) in an order of the High Court in England and Wales made under section 31A(3) of the Senior Courts Act 1981, transferring to the Upper Tribunal an application of a kind described in section 31A(1) of that Act.][1]

Amendments—[1] Paras (*c*)–(*e*) substituted for previous paras (*c*), (*d*), by the First-tier Tribunal and Upper Tribunal (Chambers) (Amendment No 2) Order, SI 2013/2068 arts 2, 4 with effect from 1 November 2013. Paras (*c*), (*d*) previously read as follows—

"(*c*) an application for the Upper Tribunal to grant the relief mentioned in section 15(1) of the Tribunals, Courts and Enforcement Act 2007 (Upper Tribunal's "judicial review" jurisdiction), or to exercise the powers of review under section 21(2) of that Act (Upper Tribunal's "judicial review" jurisdiction: Scotland), which—

(i) relates to a decision of the First-tier Tribunal mentioned in paragraph (*a*); or

(ii) is made by a person who claims to be a minor from outside the United Kingdom challenging a defendant's assessment of that person's age.

an application meeting the condition specified in section 31A(8) of the Senior Courts Act 1981 made to the Upper Tribunal or transferred to it by the High Court in England and Wales, to grant the relief mentioned in section 15(1) (Upper Tribunal's "judicial review" jurisdiction) of the Tribunals, Courts and Enforcement Act 2007.".

12 Functions of the Lands Chamber

To the Lands Chamber are allocated—

(*a*) all functions related to—

(i) compensation and other remedies for measures taken which affect the ownership, value, enjoyment or use of land or water, or of rights over or property in land or water;

[(ii) appeals from decisions of—

(*aa*) the First-tier Tribunal made in the Property Chamber other than appeals allocated to the Tax and Chancery Chamber by article 13(*h*);

(*ab*) leasehold valuation tribunals in Wales, residential property tribunals in Wales, rent assessment committees in Wales, the Agricultural Land Tribunal in Wales or the Valuation Tribunal for Wales;

(*ac*) the Valuation Tribunal for England;][1]

(iii) the determination of questions of the value of land or an interest in land arising in tax proceedings;

(iv) proceedings in respect of restrictive covenants, blight notices or the obstruction of light;

(*b*) the Upper Tribunal's function as arbitrator under section 1(5) of the Lands Tribunal Act 1949;

(*c*) an application for the Upper Tribunal to grant the relief mentioned in section 15(1) of the Tribunals, Courts and Enforcement Act 2007 (Upper Tribunal's "judicial review" jurisdiction) which relates to a decision of a tribunal mentioned in sub-paragraph (*a*)(ii);

[(*cc*) any case which may be transferred under Tribunal Procedure Rules to the Upper Tribunal from the Property Chamber of the First-tier Tribunal in relation to functions listed in article 5A(*c*) to (*h*);][1]

(*d*) any other functions transferred to the Upper Tribunal by the Transfer of Tribunal Functions (Lands Tribunal and Miscellaneous Amendments) Order 2009.

Amendments—[1] Para (*a*)(ii) substituted, and para (*cc*) inserted, by the First-tier Tribunal and Upper Tribunal (Chambers) (Amendment) Order, SI 2013/1187 arts 2, 6 with effect from 1 July 2013. Para (*a*)(ii) previously read as follows—

"(ii) appeals from decisions of leasehold valuation tribunals, residential property tribunals, the Valuation Tribunal for England or the Valuation Tribunal for Wales;".

13 Functions of the Tax and Chancery Chamber

(1) To the Tax and Chancery Chamber are allocated all functions related to—

(*a*) an appeal against a decision of the First-tier Tribunal made—

(i) in the Tax Chamber;

(ii) in the General Regulatory Chamber in a charities case;

(*b*) a reference or appeal in respect of—

(i) a decision of the [Financial Conduct Authority or the Prudential Regulation Authority][2];

(ii) a decision of the Bank of England;

(iii) a decision of a person related to the assessment of any compensation or consideration under the Banking (Special Provisions) Act 2008;

(iv) a determination or dispute within the meaning of regulation 14(5) or 15 of the Financial Services and Management Act 2000 (Contribution to Costs of Special Resolution Regime) Regulations 2010;

(*c*) a reference in respect of a decision of the Pensions Regulator;

(*d*) an application under paragraph 50(1)(*d*) of Schedule 36 to the Finance Act 2008;

(*e*) proceedings, or a preliminary issue, transferred to the Upper Tribunal under Tribunal Procedure Rules—

(i) from the Tax Chamber of the First-tier Tribunal;

(ii) from the General Regulatory Chamber of the First-tier Tribunal in a charities case;

(*f*) a matter referred to the Upper Tribunal under section 9(5)(*b*) of the Tribunals, Courts and Enforcement Act 2007 or under Tribunal Procedure Rules relating to non-compliance with a requirement of the First-tier Tribunal—

(i) by the Tax Chamber of the First-tier Tribunal;

(ii) by the General Regulatory Chamber of the First-tier Tribunal in a charities case;

(*g*) an application for the Upper Tribunal to grant the relief mentioned in section 15(1) of the Tribunals, Courts and Enforcement Act 2007 (Upper Tribunal's "judicial review" jurisdiction), or to exercise the powers of review under section 21(2) of that Act (Upper Tribunal's "judicial review" jurisdiction: Scotland), which relates to—

(i) a decision of the First-tier Tribunal mentioned in paragraph (1)(*a*)(i) or (ii);

(ii) a function of the Commissioners for Her Majesty's Revenue and Customs or an officer of Revenue and Customs, with the exception of any function in respect of which an appeal would be allocated to the Social Entitlement Chamber by article 6;

(iii) the exercise by the Serious Organised Crime Agency of general Revenue functions or Revenue inheritance tax functions (as defined in section 323 of the Proceeds of Crime Act 2002), with the exception of any function in relation to which an appeal would be allocated to the Social Entitlement Chamber by article 6;

(iv) a function of the Charity Commission, or one of the bodies mentioned in sub-paragraph (*b*) or (*c*);

[(*h*) an appeal against a decision of the First-tier Tribunal made in the Property Chamber in a case mentioned in article 5A(*a*).][1]

(2) In this article "a charities case" means an appeal or application in respect of a decision, order or direction of the Charity Commission, or a reference under Schedule 1D to the Charities Act 1993.

Amendments—[1] Para (1)(*h*) inserted by the First-tier Tribunal and Upper Tribunal (Chambers) (Amendment) Order, SI 2013/1187 arts 2, 7 with effect from 1 July 2013.

[2] In para)1)(*b*)(i), words substituted for words "Financial Services Authority" by the First-tier Tribunal and Upper Tribunal (Chambers) (Amendment) Order, SI 2014/1901 art 2(1), (3) with effect from 8 August 2014.

14 Resolution of doubt or dispute as to chamber

If there is any doubt or dispute as to the chamber in which a particular matter is to be dealt with, the Senior President of Tribunals may allocate that matter to the chamber which appears to the Senior President of Tribunals to be most appropriate.

15 Re-allocation of a case to another chamber

At any point in the proceedings, the Chamber President of the chamber to which a case or any issue in that case has been allocated by or under this Order may, with the consent of the corresponding Chamber President, allocate that case or that issue to another chamber within the same tribunal, by giving a direction to that effect.

SCHEDULE

REVOCATIONS

article 1(2)

Orders revoked	*Extent to which revoked*
The First-tier Tribunal and Upper Tribunal (Chambers) Order 2008, SI 2008/2684.	The whole Order.
The First-tier Tribunal and Upper Tribunal (Chambers) (Amendment) Order 2009, SI 2009/196.	The whole Order, except for the purposes of article 9 (transitional provision).
The First-tier Tribunal and Upper Tribunal (Chambers) (Amendment No 2) Order 2009, SI 2009/1021.	The whole Order.
The First-tier Tribunal and Upper Tribunal (Chambers) (Amendment No 3) Order 2009, SI 2009/1590.	The whole Order.
The First-tier Tribunal and Upper Tribunal (Chambers) (Amendment) Order 2010 SI 2010/40.	The whole Order.

2010/2880 (W 238)

SINGLE USE CARRIER BAGS CHARGE (WALES) REGULATIONS 2010

Made . . . . *30 November 2010*

Coming into force . . . . *1 October 2011*

The Welsh Ministers make these Regulations in exercise of the powers conferred by sections 77(2) and 90(3)(a) and (b) of, and paragraphs 1, 2, 3(1)(a) and (2)(a), 4 to 8, 9(1) and (2), 10, 12, 16 to 19 and 21 of Schedule 6 to, the Climate Change Act 2008.

The Welsh Ministers are satisfied in accordance with paragraph 23 of Schedule 6 to that Act that every county council and county borough council in Wales will act in accordance with the principles referred to in that paragraph when exercising a power conferred by these Regulations to impose a civil sanction.

A draft of these Regulations has been laid before, and approved by resolution of, the National Assembly for Wales pursuant to section 77(4)(a) and (b) of, and paragraph 27(3) of Schedule 6 to, the Climate Change Act 2008.

VAT SIs

PART 1

INTRODUCTION

1 Title, commencement and application

(1) The title of these Regulations is the Single Use Carrier Bags Charge (Wales) Regulations 2010.

(2) These Regulations apply in relation to Wales and come into force on 1 October 2011.

2 Interpretation

(1) In these Regulations—

["the charge" ("*y tâl*") means the minimum consideration that must be paid by a customer by virtue of regulation 6(2);][1]

["consideration" ("cydnabyddiaeth") includes any chargeable VAT;]

"enforcement costs recovery notice" ("*hysbysiad adennill costau gorfodi*") has the meaning given in regulation 16(1);

"functions" ("*swyddogaethau*") includes powers and duties;

"late payment penalty" ("*cosb am dalu'n hwyr*") means any increase in an amount payable—

(a) as a fixed monetary penalty, by virtue of paragraph 10 of Schedule 2;

(b) as a variable monetary penalty, by virtue of paragraph 9 of Schedule 3;

(c) as a non-compliance penalty, by virtue of paragraph 8 of Schedule 4;

"non-compliance penalty notice" ("*hysbysiad o gosb am beidio â chydymffurfio*") has the meaning given in paragraph 5(4) of Schedule 4;

"record" ("*cofnod*") means the information specified in regulation 8(3);

"reporting year" ("*blwyddyn adrodd*") means—

(a) the period starting on the date on which these Regulations come into force and ending on 6 April 2012;

(b) thereafter, the period commencing 7 April in one year and ending on 6 April the following year; the first such period to commence 7 April 2012;

"specified sum" ("*swm penodedig*") has the meaning given in paragraph 4(2) of Schedule 2;

["VAT" ("TAW") has the meaning given in section 96 of the Value Added Tax Act 1994.]

(2) References to—

(a) a notice of intent in relation to a fixed monetary penalty, are references to a notice of intent served under paragraph 3(1) of Schedule 2;

(b) a final notice in relation to a fixed monetary penalty, are references to a final notice served under paragraph 6(5) of Schedule 2;

(c) to a notice of intent in relation to a discretionary requirement, are references to a notice of intent served under paragraph 3(1) of Schedule 3;

(d) to a final notice in relation to a discretionary requirement, are references to a final notice served under paragraph 5(6) of Schedule 3;

(e) to a notice of intent in relation to a non-compliance penalty, are references to a notice of intent served under paragraph 3(1) of Schedule 4.

(3) References to single use carrier bags attracting the charge are references to those single use carrier bags to which regulation 6 applies.

Amendments—

1 In para (1), definition of "the charge" substituted, and definitions of "consideration" and "VAT" inserted, by the Single Use Carrier Bags Charge (Wales) (Amendment) Regulations, SI 2011/2184 regs 2, 3 with effect from 1 October 2011.

3 Meaning of "single use carrier bag"

(1) In these Regulations "single use carrier bag" ("*bag siopa untro*") means a bag fitting the description in paragraph (2) or (3)—

(2) A bag fits the description in this paragraph if—

(a) it is made wholly or mainly of paper, plant-based material or natural starch; and

(b) it is not specifically manufactured for multiple reuse.

(3) A bag fits the description in this paragraph if it is a plastic bag—

(a) which does not meet all of the specifications in paragraph (4); or

(b) which meets all of the specifications in paragraph (4) but is not intended for multiple reuse (*see* paragraph (5)).

(4) The specifications are—

(a) both of the bag's dimensions are greater than 404 millimetres ("mm");

(b) at least one of the bag's dimensions is greater than 439 mm;

(c) the bag is manufactured from material which is greater than 49 microns in thickness.

(5) A plastic bag is intended for multiple reuse if—

(a) it is purchased by the customer; and

(b) when worn out, it is returnable to the seller from whom it was purchased to be replaced free of charge.

(6) In this regulation—

"dimensions" ("*dimensiynau*") means width or height;

"plastic bag" ("*bag plastig*") means a bag which is made wholly or mainly of plastic.

4 Meaning of "seller"

(1) In these Regulations "seller" ("*gwerthwr*") means a person who in the course of trade or business—

(a) sells goods from a place in Wales;

(b) sells goods which are delivered to persons in Wales.

But this is subject to paragraph (2).

(2) Where a person (A) sells goods in A's capacity as an officer or employee of another person (B), then for the purposes of these Regulations B is the seller in those circumstances, and not A.

5 Administrator

(1) A local authority is to administer the provision made by these Regulations and accordingly, is the administrator for its area.

(2) In paragraph (1) the reference to a local authority is a reference to a county or county borough council.

PART 2
THE CHARGE

[6 Requirement to charge

(1) A seller must charge for every single use carrier bag supplied new—

(a) at the place in Wales where the goods are sold, for the purpose of enabling the goods to be taken away;

(b) for the purpose of enabling the goods to be delivered to persons in Wales.

This is subject to regulation 7.

(2) The amount that a seller must charge is such amount as ensures that the consideration paid by a customer for each single use carrier bag is not less than 5 pence.][1]

Amendments—[1] Reg 6 substituted by the Single Use Carrier Bags Charge (Wales) (Amendment) Regulations, SI 2011/2184 regs 2, 4 with effect from 1 October 2011.

7 Exemption from the requirement to charge

Regulation 6 does not apply in relation to the supply of single use carrier bags of the kinds described in Schedule 1 and that Schedule has effect accordingly.

PART 3
RECORDS AND PUBLICATION

[7A Application of this Part

(1) This Part applies to a seller in relation to any reporting year in which the seller meets the condition in paragraph (2).

(2) The condition is that on the first day of the reporting year the seller employs ten or more full time equivalent members of staff.][1]

Amendments—[1] Reg 7A inserted by the Single Use Carrier Bags Charge (Wales) (Amendment) Regulations, SI 2011/2184 regs 2, 5 with effect from 1 October 2011.

[8 Record-keeping

(1) A seller must keep a record of the information specified in paragraph (3) for every reporting year.

(2) Records must be retained by a seller for a period of three years beginning on 31 May in the reporting year following that to which a record relates.

(3) The information is—

(*a*) the number of single use carrier bags supplied which attract the charge;

(*b*) the amount received by way of consideration for single use carrier bags which attract the charge;

(*c*) the amount received by way of the charge;

(*d*) the net proceeds of the charge;

(*e*) a breakdown of how the amount which represents the difference between the amount received by way of the charge and the net proceeds of the charge has been arrived at, including—

(i) the apportionment between any chargeable VAT and reasonable costs;

(ii) the apportionment between different heads of reasonable costs;

(*f*) the uses to which the net proceeds of the charge have been put.

(4) The following are the amounts specified for the purposes of the definition of "net proceeds of the charge" in paragraph 7(4) of Schedule 6 to the Climate Change Act 2008—

(*a*) any amount in excess of the charge received by way of consideration for single use carrier bags which attract the charge;

(*b*) any amount of chargeable VAT received by way of the charge;

(*c*) the amount of any reasonable costs.

(5) In this regulation "reasonable costs" ("*costau rhesymol*") means—

(*a*) costs reasonably incurred by a seller to enable the seller to comply with these Regulations;

(*b*) costs reasonably incurred by a seller to enable the seller to communicate information about the charge to customers.

This is subject to paragraph (6).

(6) In relation to the first reporting year, "reasonable costs" includes costs reasonably incurred by a seller before the date on which these Regulations come into force—

(*a*) to enable the seller to comply with these Regulations;

(*b*) to enable the seller to communicate information about the charge to customers.][1]

Amendments—[1] Reg 8 substituted by the Single Use Carrier Bags Charge (Wales) (Amendment) Regulations, SI 2011/2184 regs 2, 6 with effect from 1 October 2011.

9 Availability of records

(1) This regulation applies where a person mentioned in paragraph (4) requests a seller in writing to supply a record for a reporting year.

(2) If the request is received during the retention period for the record in question, the seller must provide a copy of that record to the person who requested it within 28 days of receiving the written request.

(3) The retention period is the three year period for which any particular record must be retained under regulation 8(2).

(4) The persons are—

(a) the Welsh Ministers;

(b) a member of the public.

10 Publication of records

(1) A seller must publish the record for a reporting year if the conditions in paragraph (2) are met by the seller in relation to the reporting year in question.

(2) The conditions are—

(a) that the seller is a taxable person for the purposes of the Value Added Tax Act 1994;

(b) that the seller supplies 1000 or more single use carrier bags which attract the charge.

(3) A seller must publish the record on or before 31 May in the reporting year following that to which the record relates.

(4) The record must remain published until 31 May in the following reporting year.

(5) Publication must be by way of—

(a) the seller's internet site; or

(b) the display of a notice containing the record in all of the seller's premises in Wales to which customers have access.

(6) If a seller publishes the record by way of its internet site—

(a) the record must be displayed prominently on the seller's home page; or

(b) if the record is to be displayed elsewhere on the seller's internet site, a link to the record must be displayed prominently on the seller's home page.

(7) If a seller publishes the record in the way described in paragraph (5)(b), the notice must be displayed in a prominent position so that it is clearly visible to, and readable by, customers.

PART 4
BREACHES

11 Breaches

(1) A seller breaches these Regulations if, as a result of having failed to take all reasonable steps necessary to enable it to do so, a seller fails to comply with a requirement mentioned in paragraph (2).

(2) The requirements are—

(a) the requirement to charge in accordance with regulation 6;

(b) the requirement to keep records in accordance with regulation 8;

(c) the requirement to retain records in accordance with regulation 8;

(d) the requirement to supply records in accordance with regulation 9;

(e) the requirement to publish records in accordance with regulation 10.

(3) A seller breaches these Regulations if, without reasonable cause, a seller—

(a) gives false or misleading information to an administrator;

(b) otherwise obstructs or fails to assist an administrator in the conduct of its functions under these Regulations.

PART 5
CIVIL SANCTIONS

12 Civil sanctions

The following Schedules have effect—

(a) Schedule 2, which makes provision for fixed monetary penalties;
(b) Schedule 3, which makes provision for discretionary requirements.

13 Combination of penalties

[(1) An administrator may not serve a notice of intent in relation to a fixed monetary penalty on a seller in any of the following circumstances—

(*a*) where a discretionary requirement has been imposed on that seller in relation to the same breach;
(*b*) where the seller has discharged liability to a fixed monetary penalty in respect of the same breach by payment of a specified sum;
(*c*) where a fixed monetary penalty has previously been imposed in respect of the same act or omission.][1]

(2) An administrator may not serve a notice of intent in relation to a discretionary requirement on a seller in any of the following circumstances—

(a) where a fixed monetary penalty has been imposed on that seller in relation to the same breach;
(b) where the seller has discharged liability to a fixed monetary penalty in respect of the same breach by payment of a specified sum;
(c) where a discretionary requirement has previously been imposed in respect of the same act or omission.

Amendments—[1] Para (1) substituted by the Single Use Carrier Bags Charge (Wales) (Amendment) Regulations, SI 2011/2184 regs 2, 7 with effect from 1 October 2011.

PART 6
ENFORCEMENT AND NON-COMPLIANCE

14 Enforcement powers

(1) An administrator has the powers of enforcement in this regulation.

(2) The powers are—

(a) to make test purchases of goods for the purposes of ascertaining whether these Regulations are being complied with;
(b) to inspect any goods and to enter any premises at any reasonable time (other than domestic premises) for the purposes of ascertaining whether these Regulations are being complied with;
(c) if an administrator reasonably believes that there has been a failure to comply with a requirement of these Regulations—
 (i) to question a seller or officers or employees of a seller;
 (ii) to require the production of documents or the provision of information.

(3) In this regulation "domestic premises" ("*mangre ddomestig*") means premises used wholly or mainly as a private dwelling.

(4) An administrator seeking to exercise a power under paragraph (2)(b) or (c) must produce evidence of identity and authority if requested by a person who is, or appears to be—

(a) the seller, or an officer or employee of the seller;
(b) an owner or occupier of any premises in which the administrator seeks to exercise the power concerned.

(5) Nothing in paragraph (2) compels the production of any document of which—

(a) in England and Wales or Northern Ireland, that person would on grounds of legal professional privilege be entitled to withhold production on an order for discovery in an action in the County Court or High Court; or
(b) in Scotland, that person would on grounds of confidentiality of communications be entitled to withhold production on an order for the production of documents in an action in the Court of Session.

15 Non-monetary discretionary requirements: enforcement

Schedule 4 makes provision for the imposition of monetary penalties in cases where a seller fails to comply with a non-monetary discretionary requirement and that Schedule has effect accordingly.

16 Enforcement costs recovery

(1) An administrator may serve a notice ("an enforcement costs recovery notice") on a seller on whom a discretionary requirement is imposed requiring that seller to pay the costs incurred by the administrator in relation to the imposition of the discretionary requirement up to the time of its imposition ("enforcement costs").

(2) Enforcement costs include, in particular—

(a) investigation costs;
(b) administration costs;
(c) costs of obtaining expert advice (including legal advice).

(3) An enforcement costs recovery notice must specify the amount required to be paid and must include information as to—
(a) how payment may be made;
(b) the date by which payment must be made;
(c) the right of appeal; and
(d) the consequences of failure to make payment by the date it is due.
(4) The date referred to in paragraph (3)(b) must be at least 28 days later than the date on which the enforcement costs recovery notice is served on the seller.
(5) Enforcement costs must be paid by the seller by the date specified in the enforcement costs recovery notice.
(6) But paragraph (5) is subject to the remaining provisions of this regulation and to regulation 21(4) (suspension of requirements and notices pending appeal).
(7) If a decision of an administrator under this regulation is the subject of an appeal, then to the extent that that decision is upheld, the seller must pay the enforcement costs within 28 days of the day on which the appeal is determined.
(8) An administrator must provide a detailed breakdown of the costs specified in an enforcement costs recovery notice if requested to do so by the seller on whom the notice is served.
(9) A seller is not liable to pay any costs shown by that seller to have been unnecessarily incurred.
(10) A seller may appeal—
(a) against a decision of an administrator to impose a requirement to pay costs;
(b) against a decision of an administrator as to the amount of those costs.

17 Recovery of payments
An administrator may recover any fixed monetary penalty, variable monetary penalty, non-compliance penalty, enforcement costs or late payment penalty—
(a) as a civil debt;
(b) on the order of a court, as if payable under a court order.

18 Publicity for imposition of civil sanctions
(1) An administrator may give a publicity notice to a seller on whom a civil sanction has been imposed.
(2) The following is the information specified for the purposes of paragraph 19(2)(b) of Schedule 6 to the Climate Change Act 2008—
(a) the type of civil sanction concerned;
(b) the grounds on which the sanction was imposed;
(c) if the sanction was a fixed or variable monetary penalty, the amount of that penalty;
(d) if the sanction was a non-monetary discretionary requirement, the nature of the requirement in question.
(3) A publicity notice must—
(a) specify the manner of publication required;
(b) specify the time for compliance with the notice;
(c) require the seller to provide evidence of compliance with the notice within a time specified in the notice.
(4) If a seller fails to comply with a publicity notice within the time specified under paragraph (3)(b), the administrator may—
(a) publicise the information required to be publicised by the notice; and
(b) recover the costs of doing so from the seller in question.
(5) Where an administrator publicises information under paragraph (4)(a) it must do so in a way it considers most likely to bring the information to the attention of members of the public in its area.

PART 7
ADMINISTRATION

19 Scope of administrators' powers
The functions conferred on an administrator by these Regulations are exercisable by an administrator in, and in relation to, its area.

20 Withdrawing or amending a notice
(1) An administrator may at any time in writing—
(a) withdraw a notice of intent or a final notice in relation to a fixed monetary penalty;
(b) withdraw a notice of intent or final notice in relation to a variable monetary penalty or reduce the amount specified in the notice;
(c) withdraw a notice of intent or a final notice in relation to a non-monetary discretionary requirement or amend the steps specified in the notice so as to reduce the amount of work necessary to comply with the notice;

(d) withdraw a notice of intent in relation to a non-compliance penalty or reduce the amount specified in the notice;
(e) withdraw a non-compliance penalty notice or reduce the amount specified in the notice;
(f) withdraw an enforcement costs recovery notice or reduce the amount specified in the notice.

(2) An administrator must consult the seller in question before withdrawing or amending a notice under paragraph (1).

(3) But paragraph (2) does not apply in any case where it is impracticable to consult the seller concerned.

21 Appeals

(1) An appeal under these Regulations is to the First-tier Tribunal ("the Tribunal").

(2) In any appeal where the commission of a breach is an issue requiring determination, the administrator must prove that breach on the balance of probabilities.

(3) In any other case the Tribunal must determine the standard of proof.

(4) A requirement or notice which is the subject of an appeal is suspended pending the determination of the appeal.

(5) The Tribunal may, in relation to the imposition of a requirement or service of a notice—
(a) withdraw the requirement or notice;
(b) confirm the requirement or notice;
(c) take such steps as the administrator could take in relation to the act or omission giving rise to the requirement or notice;
(d) remit the decision whether to confirm the requirement or notice, or any matter relating to that decision, to the administrator.

22 Guidance as to use of civil sanctions

(1) An administrator must publish guidance about its use of civil sanctions under these Regulations.

(2) The guidance must contain the relevant information (see paragraphs (5) and (6)).

(3) An administrator must revise the guidance where appropriate.

(4) An administrator must have regard to the guidance or revised guidance in exercising its functions.

(5) In the case of guidance relating to a fixed monetary penalty, the relevant information referred to in paragraph (2) is information as to—
(a) the circumstances in which the penalty is likely to be imposed;
(b) the circumstances in which the penalty may not be imposed;
(c) the amount of the penalty;
(d) how liability for the penalty may be discharged and the effect of discharge;
(e) rights to make representations and objections; and
(f) rights of appeal.

(6) In the case of guidance relating to a discretionary requirement, the relevant information referred to in paragraph (2) is information as to—
(a) the circumstances in which the requirement is likely to be imposed;
(b) the circumstances in which the requirement may not be imposed;
(c) in the case of a variable monetary penalty, the matters likely to be taken into account by the administrator in determining the amount of the penalty (including, where relevant, any discounts for voluntary reporting of non-compliance);
(d) rights to make representations and objections; and
(e) rights of appeal.

23 Additional guidance

(1) An administrator must publish guidance about how it will exercise the powers conferred by regulation 15 and Schedule 4 (non-compliance penalties) and regulation 16 (enforcement costs recovery).

(2) The guidance must include, in particular, information as to—
(a) the circumstances in which the powers are likely to be exercised;
(b) matters to be taken into account in determining the amounts involved;
(c) rights of appeal.

(3) An administrator must revise the guidance where appropriate.

(4) An administrator must have regard to the guidance or revised guidance in exercising its functions.

24 Consultation on guidance

Before publishing any guidance or revised guidance under these Regulations an administrator must consult—
(a) the Welsh Ministers;
(b) the Local Better Regulation Office;
(c) the Confederation of British Industry;

(d) the Federation of Small Businesses;
(e) the British Retail Consortium.

25 Publication of enforcement action

(1) An administrator must from time to time publish reports specifying—

(a) the cases in which a civil sanction for a breach of these Regulations has been imposed;
(b) where the civil sanction is a fixed monetary penalty, the cases in which liability to the penalty has been discharged in accordance with paragraph 4 of Schedule 2 (discharge of liability following notice of intent).

(2) In paragraph (1)(a) the reference to cases in which the civil sanction has been imposed does not include cases where the sanction has been imposed but overturned on appeal.

(3) An administrator must not publish a report in any case where the Welsh Ministers notify the administrator in writing that it would be inappropriate to do so.

Jane Davidson

Minister for Environment, Sustainability and Housing, one of the Welsh Ministers

30 November 2010

SCHEDULE 1

Regulation 7

Exemptions

1 (1) The kinds of single use carrier bags to which regulation 6 does not apply are—

[(*za*) bags used solely to contain one or more items of the following kinds—
(i) unpackaged food for human or animal consumption;
(ii) unpackaged loose seeds, bulbs, corms or rhizomes;
(iii) any unpackaged axe, knife, knife blade or razor blade;
(iv) unpackaged goods contaminated by soil;
(v) items from the categories specified in sub-paragraph (2);][1]

(a)–(d) . . .[1]

(e) bags used solely to contain packaged—
(i) uncooked fish or fish products;
(ii) uncooked meat or meat products;
(iii) uncooked poultry or poultry products,

and in respect of which the maximum dimensions are 205 millimetres ("mm") (width) x 125 mm (gusset width) x 458 mm (height inclusive of handles);

(f) . . .[1]

(g) bags used to contain purchases made on board ships, trains, aircraft, coaches or buses;
(h) bags used to contain purchases made in an area designated by the Secretary of State as a security restricted area under section 11A of the Aviation Security Act 1982;
[(i) mail order dispatch and courier bags;][1]
(j) bags which—
(i) are made wholly from paper;
(ii) have maximum dimensions of 175 mm (width) x 260 mm (height);
(iii) do not have a gusset; and
(iv) do not have a handle;
(k) bags which—
(i) are made wholly or mainly from plastic;
(ii) have maximum dimensions of 125 mm (width) x 125 mm (height);
(iii) do not have a gusset; and
(iv) do not have a handle;
(l) bags which—
(i) are made wholly from paper;
(ii) have maximum dimensions of 80 mm (width) x 50 mm (gusset width) x 155 mm (height); and
(iii) do not have a handle;
(m) gusseted liners used to line or cover boxes, crates or other containers of a similar nature;
(n) bags used solely to contain live aquatic creatures in water;
(o) . . .[1]

(2) The specified categories are—

[(a) medicinal products or listed appliances sold in accordance with a prescription issued by a registered medical practitioner, a dentist, a supplementary prescriber, a nurse independent prescriber, an independent nurse prescriber, an optometrist independent prescriber, a pharmacist independent prescriber, a physiotherapist independent prescriber, a podiatrist or a chiropodist independent prescriber or an EEA health professional;][4]

(b) where sold . . . [1] otherwise than in accordance with paragraph (a), pharmacy medicine.

(3) In this paragraph—

"dentist" ("*deintydd*") means a person registered in the dentists register kept under section 14 of the Dentists Act 1984;

"EEA health professional" ("*proffesiynolyn iechyd yr AEE*") has the meaning given in regulation [213(1) of the Human Medicines Regulations 2012][2];

"independent nurse prescriber" ("*nyrs sy'n rhagnodi'n annibynnol*") has the meaning given in regulation 2(1) of the [National Health Service (Pharmaceutical Services) (Wales) Regulations 2013][3];

"listed appliances" ("*cyfarpar rhestredig*") means listed appliances within the meaning of any of the following—

(a) section 80 of the National Health Service (Wales) Act 2006;

(b) article 63 of the Health and Personal Social Services (Northern Ireland) Order 1972;

(c) section 27 of the National Health Service (Scotland) Act 1978;

(d) section 126 of the National Health Service Act 2006;

"medicinal product" ("*cynnyrch meddyginiaethol*") has the meaning given in section 130 of the Medicines Act 1968;

"pharmacy medicine" ("*meddyginiaeth fferyllol*") [has the meaning given in regulation 5(5) of the Human Medicines Regulations 2012][2];][2];

["physiotherapist independent prescriber" ("ffisiotherapydd-ragnodydd annibynnol") has the meaning given in regulation 2(1) of the National Health Service (Pharmaceutical Services) (Wales) Regulations 2013;][4]

["podiatrist or chiropodist independent prescriber" ("podiatrydd-ragnodydd neu giropodydd-ragnodydd annibynnol") has the meaning given in regulation 2(1) of the National Health Service (Pharmaceutical Services) (Wales) Regulations 2013;][4]

"prescription only medicine" ("*meddyginiaeth drwy bresgripsiwn yn unig*") means [has the meaning given in regulation 5(3) of the Human Medicines Regulations

"supplementary prescriber" ("*rhagnodydd atodol*"), "nurse independent prescriber" ("*nyrs-ragnodydd annibynnol*"), "optometrist independent prescriber" ("*optometrydd-ragnodydd annibynnol*") and "pharmacist independent prescriber" ("*fferyllydd-ragnodydd annibynnol*") each have the meanings respectively ascribed to them in [regulation 8(1) of the Human Medicines Regulations 2012][2];

"unpackaged" ("*heb ei becynnu*") means wholly or partly unwrapped.

Amendments—[1] In sub-para (1), para (*za*) inserted, paras (*a*)–(*d*), (*f*), (*o*) revoked, para (*i*) substituted, and in sub-para (2) words "or supplied" revoked, by the Single Use Carrier Bags Charge (Wales) (Amendment) Regulations, SI 2011/2184 regs 2, 8 with effect from 1 October 2011.

[2] In sub-para (3), in definitions of "EEA health professional", "pharmacy medicine", "prescription only medicine" and "supplementary prescriber", words substituted by the Human Medicines Regulations, SI 2012/1916 reg 348, Sch 34 para 101 with effect from 14 August 2012.

[3] In sub-para (1), in definition of "independent nurse prescriber", words substituted for words "National Health Service (Pharmaceutical Services) Regulations 1992" by the National Health Service (Pharmaceutical Services) (Wales) Regulations, SI 2013/898 reg 50(1), Sch 7 para 6 with effect from 10 May 2013.

[4] Sub-para (2)(*a*) substituted, in sub-para (3) definitions of "physiotherapist independent prescriber" and "podiatrist or chiropodist independent prescriber" inserted by the National Health Service (Physiotherapist, Podiatrist or Chiropodist Independent Prescribers) (Miscellaneous Amendments) (Wales) Regulations, SI 2014/2292 reg 5 with effect from 24 September 2014.

SCHEDULE 2

FIXED MONETARY PENALTIES

Regulation 12

PART 1

IMPOSITION OF FIXED MONETARY PENALTIES AND PROCEDURE

Power to impose fixed monetary penalty

1 (1) An administrator may by notice impose a fixed monetary penalty on a seller who breaches these Regulations in the circumstances specified in regulation 11(1).

(2) An administrator may exercise the power conferred by sub-paragraph (1) in relation to a case if it is satisfied on the balance of probabilities that the breach has occurred.

Fixed monetary penalties

2 The amount of penalty which can be imposed by an administrator as a fixed monetary penalty in any case is the amount specified in the second column of the table in Part 2 by reference to the kind of breach concerned.

Notice of Intent

3 (1) Where an administrator proposes to impose a fixed monetary penalty on a seller, the administrator must serve a notice of intent on that seller.

(2) A notice of intent must—

(a) state the amount of the penalty;

(b) offer the seller the opportunity to discharge its liability to the penalty by paying the specified sum within 28 days beginning with the day on which the notice is received;

(c) include information as to—

(i) the grounds for the proposal to impose the fixed monetary penalty;

(ii) the effect of payment of the specified sum;

(iii) the right to make representations and objections conferred by paragraph 5;

(iv) the circumstances in which the administrator may not impose the fixed monetary penalty;

(v) the 28 day period within which liability to the fixed monetary penalty may be discharged by virtue of paragraph 4;

(vi) the 28 day period within which representations and objections may be made;

(vii) how payment may be made.

Discharge of liability following notice of intent

4 (1) A seller's liability to a fixed monetary penalty is discharged if the seller pays the specified sum within 28 days beginning with the day on which the notice of intent to which it relates was received.

(2) The specified sum is the amount specified in the third column of the table in Part 2 by reference to the kind of breach concerned.

Making representations and objections

5 (1) This paragraph applies if a seller does not discharge its liability to a fixed monetary penalty by payment of the specified sum.

(2) Within 28 days of the day on which the notice of intent was received by the seller, the seller may make written representations and objections to the administrator in relation to the proposed imposition of the fixed monetary penalty.

Decision whether to impose a fixed monetary penalty

6 (1) At the end of the 28 day period for making representations and objections under paragraph 5, the administrator must decide whether to impose the fixed monetary penalty.

(2) In making a decision under this paragraph an administrator must take into consideration any representations or objections made by the seller in accordance with that paragraph.

(3) An administrator may not decide to impose a fixed monetary penalty in any of the following circumstances—

(a) if liability to a fixed monetary penalty in respect of the same breach has been discharged by payment of the specified sum;

(b) if a fixed monetary penalty has previously been imposed in respect of the same breach;

(c) if a discretionary requirement has been imposed in respect of the same act or omission;

(4) Without restricting the power under sub-paragraph (1), an administrator may decide not to impose a fixed penalty if the administrator considers that in all the circumstances of the case it would be inexpedient to do so.

(5) Where the administrator decides to impose the fixed monetary penalty it must do so by serving the final notice on the seller.

(6) The final notice must comply with paragraph 7.

Contents of final notice

7 The final notice must include information as to—

(a) the grounds for imposing the fixed monetary penalty;

(b) the administrator's response to any representation and objections made by the seller;

(c) the amount of the penalty;

(d) how payment may be made;

(e) the period of 56 days within which payment must be made;

(f) the effect of paragraph 9 (early payment discount);

(g) the effect of paragraph 10 (late payment penalty);

(h) rights of appeal; and

(i) the consequences of non-payment.

Payment

8 (1) A fixed monetary penalty must be paid by a seller within 56 days beginning with the day on which the final notice imposing it was received.

But this is subject to regulation 21(4) (suspension of requirements and notices pending appeal).

(2) If a decision to impose a fixed monetary penalty is the subject of an appeal then if that decision is upheld, the penalty must be paid by the seller within 28 days beginning with the day on which the appeal is determined.

Early payment discount

9 A seller may discharge its liability to a fixed monetary penalty by paying 50% of the amount of the penalty within 28 days beginning with the day on which the final notice imposing it was received.

Late payment penalty

10 If a fixed monetary penalty is not paid within the period allowed in accordance with paragraph 8 the amount of the penalty is increased by 50%.

Grounds of appeal

11 (1) A seller may appeal against an administrator's decision to impose a fixed monetary penalty.

(2) The grounds of appeal are—

(a) that the decision was based on an error of fact;

(b) that the decision was wrong in law;

(c) that the decision was unreasonable for any other reason;

(d) any other reason.

PART 2

FIXED MONETARY PENALTY AMOUNTS AND SPECIFIED SUMS

Breach	*Amount of penalty which can be imposed as a fixed monetary penalty*	*Specified sums*
Failure to comply with the requirement to charge in accordance with regulation 6 (regulation 11(1) and (2))	£200	£100
Failure to keep records in accordance with regulation 8 (regulation 11(1) and (2))	£100	£50
Failure to retain records in accordance with regulation 8 (regulation 11(1) and (2))	£100	£50
Failure to supply records in accordance with regulation 9 (regulation 11(1) and (2))	£100	£50
Failure to publish records in accordance with regulation 10 (regulation 11(1) and (2))	£100	£50

SCHEDULE 3

DISCRETIONARY REQUIREMENTS

Regulation 12

PART 1

IMPOSITION OF DISCRETIONARY REQUIREMENTS AND PROCEDURE

Power to impose discretionary requirements

1 (1) An administrator may by notice impose one or more discretionary requirements on a seller who breaches these Regulations.

(2) An administrator may exercise the power conferred by sub-paragraph (1) in relation to a case if it is satisfied on the balance of probabilities that the breach has occurred.

Variable monetary penalties: maximum amounts

2 The maximum penalty which may be imposed by an administrator as a variable monetary penalty in respect of any particular kind of breach is the amount specified in the second column of the table in Part 2 by reference to the kind of breach concerned.

Notice of intent

3 (1) Where an administrator proposes to impose one or more discretionary requirements on a seller, the administrator must serve a notice of intent on that seller.

(2) The notice of intent must—

(a) if the administrator proposes to impose a non-monetary discretionary requirement—

(i) specify the steps that the administrator proposes the seller be required to take;

(ii) specify the time period within which the administrator proposes that those steps are to be completed;

(b) if the administrator proposes to impose a variable monetary penalty, specify the amount of penalty proposed;

(c) include information as to—

(i) the grounds for the proposal to impose the one or more discretionary requirements;

(ii) the right to make representations and objections conferred by paragraph 4;

(iii) the circumstances in which the administrator may not impose the one or more discretionary requirements;

(iv) the 28 day period within which representations and objections may be made;

(v) in the case of a variable monetary penalty, how payment may be made.

Making representations and objections

4 Within 28 days beginning with the day on which the notice of intent is received by the seller, the seller may make written representations and objections to the administrator in relation to the proposed imposition of the one or more discretionary requirements.

Decision whether to impose discretionary requirements

5 (1) After the end of the 28 day period for making representations and objections under paragraph 4, the administrator must decide whether to—

(a) impose the one or more discretionary requirements with or without modifications; or

(b) impose any other discretionary requirement that the administrator has the power to impose under this Schedule.

(2) In making a decision under this paragraph an administrator must take into consideration any representations or objections made by the seller in accordance with paragraph 4.

(3) An administrator may not decide to impose a discretionary requirement in any of the following circumstances—

(a) if a discretionary requirement has previously been imposed in relation to the same act or omission;

(b) if liability to a fixed monetary penalty in respect of the same breach has been discharged by payment of a specified sum;

(c) if a fixed monetary penalty has been imposed in respect of the same breach.

(4) An administrator may not decide under this paragraph to impose a fixed monetary penalty in place of a discretionary requirement.

(5) Without restricting the power under sub-paragraph (1), an administrator may decide not to impose a discretionary requirement if the administrator considers that in all the circumstances of the case it would be inexpedient to do so.

(6) Where an administrator decides to impose a discretionary requirement it must do so by serving the final notice on the seller.

(7) The final notice must comply with paragraph 6.

Contents of a final notice

6 The final notice must include information as to—

(a) the grounds for imposing the one or more discretionary requirements;

(b) the administrator's response to any representation and objections made by the seller, including the effect (if any) on the amount of any variable monetary penalty imposed;

(c) where the discretionary requirement is a non-monetary discretionary requirement—

(i) the steps the seller is required to take;

(ii) the period within which those steps must be completed;

(d) where the discretionary requirement is a variable monetary penalty—

(i) the amount of the penalty;

(ii) how payment may be made;

(iii) the period within which payment must be made;

(iv) the effect of paragraph 8 (early payment discount)

(v) the effect of paragraph 9 (late payment penalty);

(e) rights of appeal; and

(f) the consequences of failing to comply with the notice.

Payment

7 (1) A variable monetary penalty must be paid by a seller within 56 days beginning with the day on which the final notice imposing it was received.

But this is subject to regulation 21(4) (suspension of requirements and notices pending appeal).

(2) If the decision to impose a variable monetary penalty is the subject of an appeal then to the extent that that decision is upheld, the penalty must be paid by the seller within 28 days beginning with the day on which the appeal is determined.

Early payment discount

8 A seller may discharge its liability to a variable monetary penalty by paying 50% of the amount of the penalty within 28 days beginning with the day on which the final notice imposing it is received.

Late payment penalty

9 If a variable monetary penalty is not paid within the period allowed in accordance with paragraph 7 the amount payable is increased by 50%.

Grounds of appeal

10 (1) A seller may appeal against an administrator's decision to impose a discretionary requirement.

(2) The grounds of appeal are—

(a) that the decision was based on an error of fact;

(b) that the decision was wrong in law;

(c) in case of a variable monetary penalty, that the amount of the penalty is unreasonable;

(d) in the case of a non-monetary discretionary requirement, that the nature of the requirement is unreasonable;

(e) that the decision was unreasonable for any other reason;

(f) any other reason.

PART 2
VARIABLE MONETARY PENALTIES: MAXIMUM AMOUNTS

Breach	*Maximum amount which may be imposed as a variable monetary penalty*
Failure to comply with the requirement to charge in accordance with regulation 6 (regulation 11(1) and (2))	£5,000
Failure to keep records in accordance with regulation 8 (regulation 11(1) and (2))	£5,000
Failure to retain records in accordance with regulation 8 (regulation 11(1) and (2))	£5,000
Failure to supply records in accordance with regulation 9 (regulation 11(1) and (2))	£5,000
Failure to publish records in accordance with regulation 10 (regulation 11(1) and (2))	£5,000
Without reasonable cause, giving false or misleading information to an administrator (regulation 11(3))	£20,000
Without reasonable cause, otherwise obstructing or failing to assist an administrator in the conduct of its functions under these Regulations (regulation 11(3))	£20,000

SCHEDULE 4
NON-MONETARY DISCRETIONARY REQUIREMENTS: ENFORCEMENT

Regulation 15

1 (1) In this Schedule—

"specified steps" ("*camau penodedig*") means the steps specified in a final notice under paragraph 6(c)(i) of Schedule 3;

"specified period" ("*cyfnod penodedig*") means the period specified in a final notice under paragraph 6(c)(ii) of Schedule 3.

(2) A reference in this Schedule to a complete failure is a reference to a seller having taken none of the specified steps within the specified period.

(3) A reference in this Schedule to a partial failure is a reference to a seller having taken at least one, but not all, of the specified steps within the specified period.

Power to impose non-compliance penalties

2 (1) If a seller fails to comply with a non-monetary discretionary requirement an administrator may by notice impose a non-compliance penalty on the seller.

(2) A non-compliance penalty may be imposed in respect of a complete or partial failure to comply with a non-monetary discretionary requirement.

(3) A non-compliance penalty may be imposed irrespective of whether a variable monetary penalty was imposed in addition to the non-discretionary requirement to which the non-compliance penalty relates.

(4) The amount of a non-compliance penalty is to be determined by the administrator.

(5) But the maximum penalty which may be imposed by an administrator as a non-compliance penalty is the amount specified in sub-paragraph (6) by reference to the kind of failure concerned.

(6) The maximum penalties are—

(a) £5,000 in relation to a partial failure;

(b) £5,000 in relation to a complete failure.

Notice of intent

3 (1) Where an administrator proposes to impose a non-compliance penalty on a seller, the administrator must serve on that seller a notice of what is proposed (a "notice of intent").

(2) A notice of intent must include information as to—

(a) the kind of failure in relation to which the administrator proposes to impose the non-compliance penalty;

(b) the specified steps which remain to be taken by the seller concerned;

(c) the amount of the penalty proposed;

(d) how payment may be made;

(e) the date by which payment would be due;

(f) the consequences of failure to make payment by the date it is due;

(g) the right to make representations and objections conferred by paragraph 4;

(h) the 28 day period within which representations and objections may be made;

(i) the circumstances (if any) in which the administrator may be inclined to reduce the amount of the penalty proposed.

Making representations and objections

4 Within 28 days beginning with the date on which the notice of intent is received by the seller, the seller may make written representations and objections to the administrator in relation to the proposed imposition of a non-compliance penalty.

Decision whether to impose a non-compliance penalty

5 (1) After the end of the 28 day period for making representations and objections under paragraph 4, the administrator must decide whether to impose the non-compliance penalty with or without modifications.

(2) Without restricting the power under sub-paragraph (1), an administrator may decide not to impose a non-compliance penalty if the administrator considers that in all the circumstances of the case it would be inexpedient to do so.

(3) In making a decision under this paragraph an administrator must take into consideration any representations or objections made by the seller in accordance with paragraph 4.

(4) Where an administrator decides to impose a non-compliance penalty it must do so by serving a notice ("a non-compliance penalty notice") on the seller.

(5) A non-compliance penalty notice must comply with paragraph 6.

Contents of a non-compliance penalty notice

6 (1) A non-compliance penalty notice must include information as to—

(a) the grounds for imposing the non-compliance penalty;

(b) the administrator's response to any representations and objections made by the seller, including the effect (if any) on the amount of the penalty imposed;

(c) the amount of the penalty;

(d) how payment may be made;

(e) the date by which payment must be made;

(f) the right of appeal; and

(g) the consequences of failure to make payment by the date it is due.

(2) A non-compliance penalty must be paid by a seller within 56 days beginning with the date on which the notice imposing it was received.

(3) But this is subject to sub-paragraph (4) and regulation 21(4) (suspension of requirements and notices pending determination of an appeal).

(4) If the requirements of the non-monetary discretionary requirement are complied with before the 56 days expire, the non-compliance penalty is not payable.

(5) A seller on whom a non-compliance penalty notice is served may appeal against it.

(6) The grounds of appeal are—

(a) that the decision to serve the notice was based on an error of fact;

(b) that the decision was wrong in law;

(c) that the amount of the penalty was unreasonable;

(d) that the decision was unfair or unreasonable for any other reason;

(e) any other reason.

Payment of non-compliance penalties following appeal

7 If a non-compliance penalty notice is the subject of an appeal, then to the extent that the notice is upheld, the penalty must be paid by the seller within 28 days beginning with the day on which the appeal is determined.

Non-compliance penalties: late payment penalty

8 If a non-compliance penalty is not paid within the period allowed by paragraph 6(2) or (as the case may be) by paragraph 7, the amount payable is increased by 50%.

2010/2924

VALUE ADDED TAX (IMPORTED GAS, ELECTRICITY, HEAT AND COOLING) RELIEF ORDER 2010

Made . . . . *8 December 2010*
Laid before the House of Commons . . . . *9 December 2010*
Coming into force . . . . *1 January 2011*

The Treasury make the following Order in exercise of the powers conferred by section 37(1) of the Value Added Tax Act 1994.

It appears to the Treasury that it is expedient to make this Order having regard to the need to conform with Article 143(1)(l) of Council Directive 2006/112/EC.

1 Citation, commencement and effect

(1) This Order may be cited as the Value Added Tax (Imported Gas, Electricity, Heat and Cooling) Relief Order 2010.

(2) This Order comes into force on 1st January 2011 and has effect in relation to goods imported on or after that date.

2 Revocation of the Value Added Tax (Imported Gas and Electricity) Relief Order 2004

(revokes the VAT (Imported Gas and Electricity) Relief Order, SI 2004/3147).

3 Relief from value added tax

The VAT chargeable on the importation from a place outside the member States of—

(*a*) gas—

(i) through a natural gas system or any network connected to such a system, or

(ii) fed in from a vessel transporting gas into a natural gas system or any upstream pipeline network,

(*b*) electricity, or

(*c*) heat or cooling supplied through a network,

shall not be payable.

2010/2925

VALUE ADDED TAX (REMOVAL OF GAS, ELECTRICITY, HEAT AND COOLING) ORDER 2010

Made . . . . *8 December 2010*
Laid before the House of Commons . . . . *9 December 2010*
Coming into force . . . . *1 January 2011*

The Treasury, in exercise of the powers conferred by section 5(3) of the Value Added Tax Act 1994, make the following Order:

1 Citation, commencement and effect

(1) This Order may be cited as the Value Added Tax (Removal of Gas, Electricity, Heat and Cooling) Order 2010.

(2) This Order comes into force on 1st January 2011 and has effect in relation to supplies made on or after that date.

VAT SIs

2 Revocation of the Value Added Tax (Removal of Gas and Electricity) Order 2004

(revokes the VAT (Removal of Gas and Electricity) Order, SI 2004/3150)

3 The application of paragraph 6(1) of Schedule 4 to the Value Added Tax Act 1994

Paragraph 6(1) of Schedule 4 (matters to be treated as supply of goods or services) to the Value Added Tax Act 1994 shall not apply to the removal of—

(*a*) gas through a natural gas system situated within the territory of a member State or any network connected to such a system,

(*b*) electricity, or

(*c*) heat or cooling supplied through a network.

2011/711

TAXES, ETC (FEES FOR PAYMENT BY INTERNET) REGULATIONS 2011

Made . . . . *9th March 2011*

Laid before the House of Commons . . . . *10th March 2011*

Coming into force . . . . *1st April 2011*

The Commissioners for Her Majesty's Revenue and Customs make the following Regulations in exercise of the powers conferred by section 136(1) to (3) of the Finance Act 2008.

In accordance with section 136(2) of that Act, the Commissioners expect that they, or the person authorised by them, will be required to pay a fee in connection with amounts paid where internet authorisation is given for the payment to be made by credit card.

1 Citation, commencement, effect and interpretation

(1) These Regulations may be cited as the Taxes, etc (Fees for Payment by Internet) Regulations 2011.

(2) These Regulations come into force on 1st April 2011 and have effect in relation to any payment made by credit card on or after that date where internet authorisation is given to make that payment.

(3) In these Regulations "internet authorisation" means authorisation given by a credit card issuer via the internet.

2 Fee payable where internet authorisation is given to make a payment by credit card

(1) Where—

(*a*) internet authorisation is given for a person to make a payment by credit card, and

(*b*) that person makes the payment to the Commissioners or a person authorised by the Commissioners,

the person must also pay a fee of 1.4 % of the amount of that payment.

(2) The fee must be paid by being added to the payment (so that, accordingly, the person must make a single overall payment, consisting of the payment and the fee).

(3) In these Regulations "credit card" means a card which—

(*a*) is a credit-token within section 14(1)(*b*) of the Consumer Credit Act 1974, or

(*b*) would be a credit-token falling within that enactment were the card to be given to an individual.

3 Revocation

The Taxes (Fees for Payment by Internet) Regulations 2008 are revoked.

2011/976

PENALTIES, OFFSHORE INCOME ETC (DESIGNATION OF TERRITORIES) ORDER 2011

Made . . . . *28 March 2011*

Coming into force . . . . *6 April 2011*

The Treasury make the following Order in exercise of the powers conferred by paragraph 21A(1) to (4) of Schedule 24 to the Finance Act 2007.

In accordance with paragraph 21A(7) of Schedule 24 to that Act, a draft of this instrument was laid before the House of Commons and approved by a resolution of that House.

1 Citation and commencement

This Order may be cited as the Penalties, Offshore Income etc (Designation of Territories) Order 2011 and comes into force on 6th April 2011.

2 Designation of territories

The territories specified in the left hand column of the Table in the Schedule to this Order are designated as category 1 territories for the purposes of Schedule 24 to the Finance Act 2007 (penalties for errors).

3 The territories specified in the right hand column of the Table in the Schedule to this Order are designated as category 3 territories for the purposes of Schedule 24 to the Finance Act 2007.

SCHEDULE

Articles 2 and 3

Designated Territories

Category 1 territories	*Category 3 territories*
Anguilla	Albania
Aruba	Algeria
Australia	Andorra
Belgium	. . .[1]
Bulgaria	. . .[1]
Canada	. . .[1]
Cayman Islands	. . .[1]
Cyprus	. . .[1]
Czech Republic	Bonaire, Sint Eustatius and Saba
Denmark (not including Faroe Islands and Greenland)	Brazil
Estonia	Cameroon
Finland	Cape Verde
France	Colombia
Germany	Congo, Republic of the
Greece	Cook Islands
Guernsey	Costa Rica
Hungary	Curaçao
Ireland	Cuba
Isle of Man	Democratic People's Republic of Korea
Italy	. . .[1]
Japan	Dominican Republic
Korea, South	Ecuador
Latvia	El Salvador
[Liechtenstein][1]	Gabon
Lithuania	. . .[1]
Malta	Guatemala
Montserrat	Honduras
Netherlands (not including Bonaire, Sint Eustatius and Saba)	Iran
New Zealand (not including Tokelau)	Iraq
Norway	Jamaica
Poland	Kyrgyzstan
Portugal	Lebanon
Romania	Macau
Slovakia	Marshall Islands
Slovenia	. . .[1]
Spain	Micronesia, Federated States of
Sweden	Monaco
[Switzerland][1]	Nauru
United States of America (not including overseas territories and possessions)	Nicaragua

	Niue
	Palau
	Panama
	Paraguay
	Peru
	. . . [1]
	. . . [1]
	. . . [1]
	. . . [1]
	Seychelles
	Sint Maarten
	Suriname
	Syria
	Tokelau
	Tonga
	Trinidad and Tobago
	United Arab Emirates
	Uruguay

Amendments—

[1] In Table, entries in left-hand column inserted and entries in right-hand column revoked by the Penalties, Offshore Income etc. (Designation of Territories) (Amendment) Order, SI 2013/1618 with effect from 24 July 2013. Revoked entries read as follows—

"Antigua and Barbuda"
"Armenia"
"Bahrain"
"Barbados"
"Belize"
"Dominica"
"Grenada"
"Mauritius"
"Saint Kitts and Nevis"
"San Marino"
"Saint Lucia"
"Saint Vincent and the Grenadines"

2011/1079

INTERNATIONAL MUTUAL ADMINISTRATIVE ASSISTANCE IN TAX MATTERS ORDER 2011

Made . . . . *7th April 2011*

At the Court at Windsor Castle, the 7th day of April 201

Present,

The Queen's Most Excellent Majesty in Council

A draft of this Order was laid before the House of Commons in accordance with section 173(7) of the Finance Act 2006 and approved by a resolution of that House.

Accordingly, Her Majesty, in exercise of the power conferred upon Her by sections 173(1) to (3) of the Finance Act 2006, by and with the advice of Her Privy Council, orders as follows—

1 Citation

This Order may be cited as the International Mutual Administrative Assistance in Tax Matters Order 2011.

2 Mutual administrative assistance arrangements to have effect

It is declared that—

(a) the arrangements relating to international tax enforcement set out in the joint Council of Europe/Organisation for Economic Co-operation and Development Convention on Mutual Administrative Assistance in Tax Matters, as varied by the arrangements specified in the Protocol set out in the Schedule to this Order, have been made with the other signatories, and

(b) it is expedient that the arrangements should have effect.

SCHEDULE

Article 2

PROTOCOL AMENDING THE CONVENTION ON MUTUAL ADMINISTRATIVE ASSISTANCE IN TAX MATTERS

Preamble

The member States of the Council of Europe and the member countries of the Organisation for Economic Co-operation and Development (OECD), signatories of this Protocol,

Considering that the Convention on Mutual Administrative Assistance in Tax Matters, done at Strasbourg on 25 January 1988 (hereinafter "the Convention"), was concluded before agreement was reached on the internationally agreed standard to exchange information in tax matters;

Considering that a new cooperative environment has emerged since the Convention was concluded;

Considering that it is desirable that a multilateral instrument is made available to allow the widest number of States to obtain the benefit of the new co-operative environment and at the same time to implement the highest international standards of co-operation in the tax field;

Have agreed as follows:

ARTICLE I

1 The seventh recital of the Preamble to the Convention shall be deleted and replaced by the following:

"Convinced therefore that States should carry out measures or supply information, having regard to the necessity of protecting the confidentiality of information, and taking account of international instruments for the protection of privacy and flows of personal data;"

2 The following shall be added after the seventh recital of the Preamble to the Convention:

"Considering that a new co-operative environment has emerged and that it is desirable that a multilateral instrument is made available to allow the widest number of States to obtain the benefits of the new co-operative environment and at the same time implement the highest international standards of co-operation in the tax field;"

ARTICLE II

Article 4 of the Convention shall be deleted and replaced by the following:

"Article 4—General provision

1

The Parties shall exchange any information, in particular as provided in this section, that is foreseeably relevant for the administration or enforcement of their domestic laws concerning the taxes covered by this Convention.

2

Deleted.

3

Any Party may, by a declaration addressed to one of the Depositaries, indicate that, according to its internal legislation, its authorities may inform its resident or national before transmitting information concerning him, in conformity with Articles 5 and 7."

ARTICLE III

1 The term "and" in paragraph 1.b of Article 18 of the Convention shall be replaced by the term ", or".

2 The reference to "Article 19" in paragraph 1.f of Article 18 of the Convention shall be replaced by a reference to "Article 21.2.g".

VAT SIs

ARTICLE IV

Article 19 of the Convention shall be deleted.

ARTICLE V

Article 21 of the Convention shall be deleted and replaced by the following:

"Article 21—Protection of persons and limits to the obligation to provide assistance

1

Nothing in this Convention shall affect the rights and safeguards secured to persons by the laws or administrative practice of the requested State.

2

Except in the case of Article 14, the provisions of this Convention shall not be construed so as to impose on the requested State the obligation:

(a) to carry out measures at variance with its own laws or administrative practice or the laws or administrative practice of the applicant State;

(b) to carry out measures which would be contrary to public policy (ordre public);

(c) to supply information which is not obtainable under its own laws or its administrative practice or under the laws of the applicant State or its administrative practice;

(d) to supply information which would disclose any trade, business, industrial, commercial or professional secret, or trade process, or information, the disclosure of which would be contrary to public policy (ordre public);

(e) to provide administrative assistance if and insofar as it considers the taxation in the applicant State to be contrary to generally accepted taxation principles or to the provisions of a convention for the avoidance of double taxation, or of any other convention which the requested State has concluded with the applicant State;

(f) to provide administrative assistance for the purpose of administering or enforcing a provision of the tax law of the applicant State, or any requirement connected therewith, which discriminates against a national of the requested State as compared with a national of the applicant State in the same circumstances;

(g) to provide administrative assistance if the applicant State has not pursued all reasonable measures available under its laws or administrative practice, except where recourse to such measures would give rise to disproportionate difficulty;

(h) to provide assistance in recovery in those cases where the administrative burden for that State is clearly disproportionate to the benefit to be derived by the applicant State.

3

If information is requested by the applicant State in accordance with this Convention, the requested State shall use its information gathering measures to obtain the requested information, even though the requested State may not need such information for its own tax purposes. The obligation contained in the preceding sentence is subject to the limitations contained in this Convention, but in no case shall such limitations, including in particular those of paragraphs 1 and 2, be construed to permit a requested State to decline to supply information solely because it has no domestic interest in such information.

4

In no case shall the provisions of this Convention, including in particular those of paragraphs 1 and 2, be construed to permit a requested State to decline to supply information solely because the information is held by a bank, other financial institution, nominee or person acting in an agency or a fiduciary capacity or because it relates to ownership interests in a person."

ARTICLE VI

Paragraphs 1 and 2 of Article 22 shall be deleted and replaced with the following:

"1

Any information obtained by a Party under this Convention shall be treated as secret and protected in the same manner as information obtained under the domestic law of that Party and, to the extent needed to ensure the necessary level of protection of personal data, in accordance with the safeguards which may be specified by the supplying Party as required under its domestic law.

2

Such information shall in any case be disclosed only to persons or authorities (including courts and administrative or supervisory bodies) concerned with the assessment, collection or recovery of, the enforcement or prosecution in respect of, or the determination of appeals in relation to, taxes of that Party, or the oversight of the above. Only the persons or authorities mentioned above may use the information and then only for such purposes. They may, notwithstanding the provisions of paragraph 1, disclose it in public court proceedings or in judicial decisions relating to such taxes."

ARTICLE VII

Paragraph 2 of Article 27 of the Convention shall be deleted and replaced by the following:

"2

Notwithstanding paragraph 1, those Parties which are member States of the European Union can apply, in their mutual relations, the possibilities of assistance provided for by the Convention in so far as they allow a wider co-operation than the possibilities offered by the applicable European Union rules."

ARTICLE VIII

1 The following paragraphs shall be added at the end of Article 28 of the Convention:

"4

Any member State of the Council of Europe or any member country of OECD which becomes a Party to the Convention after the entry into force of the Protocol amending this Convention, opened for signature on 27th May 2010 (the "2010 Protocol"), shall be a Party to the Convention as amended by that Protocol, unless they express a different intention in a written communication to one of the Depositaries.

5

After the entry into force of the 2010 Protocol, any State which is not a member of the Council of Europe or of the OECD may request to be invited to sign and ratify this Convention as amended by the 2010 Protocol. Any request to this effect shall be addressed to one of the Depositaries, who shall transmit it to the Parties. The Depositary shall also inform the Committee of Ministers of the Council of Europe and the OECD Council. The decision to invite States which so request to become Party to this Convention shall be taken by consensus by the Parties to the Convention through the co-ordinating body. In respect of any State ratifying the Convention as amended by the 2010 Protocol in accordance with this paragraph, this Convention shall enter into force on the first day of the month following the expiration of a period of three months after the date of deposit of the instrument of ratification with one of the Depositaries.

6

The provisions of this Convention, as amended by the 2010 Protocol, shall have effect for administrative assistance related to taxable periods beginning on or after 1 January of the year following the one in which the Convention, as amended by the 2010 Protocol, entered into force in respect of a Party, or where there is no taxable period, for administrative assistance related to charges to tax arising on or after 1 January of the year following the one in which the Convention, as amended by the 2010 Protocol, entered into force in respect of a Party. Any two or more Parties may mutually agree that the Convention, as amended by the 2010 Protocol, shall have effect for administrative assistance related to earlier taxable periods or charges to tax.

7

Notwithstanding paragraph 6, for tax matters involving intentional conduct which is liable to prosecution under the criminal laws of the applicant Party, the provisions of this Convention, as amended by the 2010 Protocol, shall have effect from the date of entry into force in respect of a Party in relation to earlier taxable periods or charges to tax."

2 The following subparagraph shall be added after subparagraph e of paragraph 1 of Article 30 of the Convention:

"(f) to apply paragraph 7 of Article 28 exclusively for administrative assistance related to taxable periods beginning on or after 1 January of the third year preceding the one in which the Convention, as amended by the 2010 Protocol, entered into force in respect of a Party, or where there is no taxable period, for administrative assistance related to charges to tax arising on or after 1 January of the third year preceding the one in which the Convention, as amended by the 2010 Protocol, entered into force in respect of a Party."

3 The words "and any Party to this Convention" shall be added after the words "member countries of the OECD" in paragraph 1 of Article 32 of the Convention.

ARTICLE IX

1 This Protocol shall be open for signature by the Signatories to the Convention. It is subject to ratification, acceptance or approval. A signatory may not ratify, accept or approve this Protocol unless it has previously or simultaneously ratified, accepted or approved the Convention. Instruments of ratification, acceptance or approval shall be deposited with one of the Depositaries.

2 This Protocol shall enter into force on the first day of the month following the expiration of a period of three months after the date on which five Parties to the Convention have expressed their consent to be bound by the Protocol in accordance with the provisions of paragraph 1.

3 In respect of any Party to the Convention which subsequently expresses its consent to be bound by it, the Protocol shall enter into force on the first day of the month following the expiration of a period of three months after the date of the deposit of the instrument of ratification, acceptance or approval.

ARTICLE X

1 The Depositary with whom an act, notification or communication has been accomplished, shall notify the member States of the Council of Europe, the member countries of OECD and any Party to the Convention as amended by this Protocol of:

(a) any signature;

(b) the deposit of any instrument of ratification, acceptance or approval;

(c) any date of entry into force of this Protocol in accordance with the provisions of Article IX;

(d) any other act, notification or communication relating to this Protocol.

2 The Depositary receiving a communication or making a notification in pursuance of the provisions of paragraph 1 shall inform the other Depositary thereof.

3 The Depositaries shall transmit to the member States of the Council of Europe and the member countries of the OECD a certified copy of this Protocol.

4 When this Protocol enters into force in accordance with Article IX, one of the Depositaries shall establish the text of the Convention as amended by this Protocol and shall send a certified copy to all the Parties to the Convention as amended by this Protocol.

In witness whereof the undersigned, being duly authorised thereto, have signed the Protocol.

Done at Paris, this 27th day of May 2010, in English and French, both texts being equally authentic, in two copies, one of which shall be deposited in the archives of the Council of Europe and the other in the archives of the OECD.

2011/2878

STATISTICS AND REGISTRATION SERVICE ACT 2007 (DISCLOSURE OF VALUE ADDED TAX INFORMATION) REGULATIONS 2011

Made .... *28th November 2011*

Coming into force .... *29th November 2011*

The Minister for the Cabinet Office makes these Regulations in exercise of the powers conferred by sections 47(1)(a), (6) and (7)(a) of the Statistics and Registration Service Act 2007.

In accordance with section 47(8)(b) of that Act these Regulations are made with the consent of the Treasury.

In accordance with section 47(9) of that Act the Minister for the Cabinet Office and the Treasury are satisfied that the disclosure authorised by these Regulations is required by the Statistics Board to enable it to carry out the functions in relation to which the disclosure is authorised, and the disclosure is in the public interest.

In accordance with section 65(5)(b) of that Act a draft of these Regulations has been approved by resolution of each House of Parliament.

1 Citation and commencement

These Regulations may be cited as the Statistics and Registration Service Act 2007 (Disclosure of Value Added Tax Information) Regulations 2011 and come into force on the day after the day on which they are made.

2 Interpretation

In these Regulations—

"the Act" means the Statistics and Registration Service Act 2007;

"Commissioners" means the Commissioners for Her Majesty's Revenue and Customs appointed under section 1 of the Commissioners for Revenue and Customs Act 2005; and "return" means a return made in accordance with the Value Added Tax (General) Regulations 1985 or the Value Added Tax Regulations 1995.

3 Disclosure of Value Added Tax Information

The Commissioners may disclose to the Statistics Board—

(a) information which relates to the estimated or actual value of business purchases, excluding value added tax, contained in a return made to the Commissioners on or after 1st October 1985; and

(b) the date which is recorded by the Commissioners as the date on which such a return was received.

4 Purposes for which disclosure is authorised

Information disclosed under regulation 3 may only be used by the Statistics Board for the production of business or economic statistics under section 20 (production of statistics) of the Act.

5 Restrictions on disclosure of personal information by the Statistics Board

In the application of section 39(4) of the Act to personal information which is disclosed to the Statistics Board under regulation 3—

(a) paragraph (a) applies only to the extent that—

(i) a disclosure is required by any enactment; or

(ii) a disclosure is permitted by section 41 (disclosure of information to service providers) of the Act but only in connection with the purposes specified in regulation 4; and

(b) paragraphs (d), (f) and (h) do not apply.

VAT SIs

2011/2931

MARD REGULATIONS 2011

Made . . . . *8th December 2011*

Laid before the House of Commons . . . . *9th December 2011*

Coming into force . . . . *1st January 2012*

The Treasury make regulations 1 to 7 and 9 to 18 of these Regulations exercising their powers in paragraph 10 of Schedule 25 to the Finance Act 2011.

The Commissioners for Her Majesty's Revenue and Customs make regulations 1(1) and 8 of these Regulations exercising the powers in paragraph 9 of that Schedule.

1 Citation, commencement and interpretation

(1) These Regulations may be cited as the MARD Regulations 2011 and come into force on 1 January 2012.

(2) The Articles mentioned in these Regulations are those of MARD.

(3) Regulations 2(1), 4(1), 5(1), 6, 7(2), 7(4) and 13(2) each applies to any Article it mentions only where the relevant UK authority is the requested authority in that Article.

(4) Regulations 9, 10(1), 11, 12 and 13(3) each applies to any Article it mentions only where an applicant authority of the United Kingdom is the applicant authority in that Article.

Claims, etc to the United Kingdom (ie relevant UK authority is the requested authority in MARD)

2 Exchange of information

(1) The relevant UK authority must comply with the provision made by Article 5 in relation to the requested authority.

(2) This is subject to Articles 5(2) and 5(3).

3 A United Kingdom public authority that is to make a refund in Article 6 may follow that Article.

4 (1) The relevant UK authority must make and carry out the agreement and arrangements for which Article 7(1) makes provision in relation to the requested authority, to the extent that this will promote the mutual assistance provided for in MARD.

(2) This is subject to Articles 7(3) and 21(2).

5 Enforcement of foreign claims in the UK

(1) The relevant UK authority must comply with the provision made by Articles 8, 9(1), 13(2), 13(3), 13(5), 14(1), 16, 18(4) and 19(3) in relation to the requested authority.

(2) For Article 8: this is subject to Article 8(2).

(3) For Article 16: paragraph (1) and regulation 7 apply in a way that gives effect to Article 17.

6 (1) The relevant UK authority may follow Article 13(4), first sentence.

(2) Where it does so, that authority must follow Article 13(4), second sentence.

7 (1) Articles 12, 14(1), 14(2), 15(2) second and third sub-paragraphs, and 18 apply to a foreign claim.
(2) The relevant UK authority must follow Article 15(2), first sub-paragraph, second sentence.
(3) The provision in paragraph (1) for Articles 12 and 14 also apply where the foreign claim is based on a revised instrument in Article 15(2), third sub-paragraph.
(4) The relevant UK authority may follow Articles 18(1) and 18(2).
(5) The relevant UK authority may follow Article 18(3) where the United Kingdom is the Member State in that Article.

8 In the application of the Finance Act 2009, Schedule 49 to any kind of foreign claim for which the relevant UK authority is the Commissioners, the sum payable in paragraph 1(1) of that Schedule includes a foreign claim.

Claims, etc from the United Kingdom (ie a UK authority is the applicant authority in MARD)

9 Request for notification of certain documents relating to claims
Any applicant authority of the United Kingdom must ensure compliance or comply with the provision made by Articles 8(1) and 8(2) in relation to the applicant authority.

10 Requests for recovery, and conditions governing them
(1) Any applicant authority of the United Kingdom must comply with the provision made by Articles 10(2) and 11 in relation to the applicant authority.
(2) A request in either Article by an applicant authority of the United Kingdom must comply with Article 12(1) (except for the obligations that Article places on the requested Member State).
The request may be accompanied by the other documents as mentioned in Article 12(2).

11 Disputes
Any applicant authority of the United Kingdom must comply with the provision made by Articles 14(3) and 14(4), third sub-paragraph, third sentence in relation to the applicant authority.

12 Amendment or withdrawal of UK request for recovery assistance
Any applicant authority of the United Kingdom must comply with the provision made by Article 15 in relation to the applicant authority.

Claims within MARD: general

13 Questions on limitation
(1) Article 19 applies to a foreign claim and to a claim for which the applicant Member State is the United Kingdom, as appropriate.
(2) The relevant UK authority must comply with the provision made by Article 19(3) in relation to the requested authority.
(3) Any applicant authority of the United Kingdom must comply with the provision made by Article 19(3) in relation to the applicant authority.

14 Costs
(1) The relevant UK authority and an applicant authority of the United Kingdom may follow respectively Article 20(2), second sub-paragraph in relation to the requested and applicant authorities, as appropriate to the circumstances.
(2) United Kingdom public authorities must seek to ensure compliance with Article 20(2), first sub-paragraph and with Article 20(3).

15 Standard forms and means of communication
(1) Article 21(1) applies where the United Kingdom is the requested Member State or the applicant Member State in that Article, as appropriate.
(2) This is subject to Article 21(3).

16 Use of languages
(1) The documents mentioned in Article 22(1) sent from the United Kingdom must comply with that Article.
(2) Where those documents are sent to the United Kingdom, the second sentence of that Article applies provided that the United Kingdom public authority concerned has agreed with the sending Member State as mentioned in that sentence.
(3) This paragraph applies in relation to documents covered by Article 22(3) where the relevant UK authority is the requested authority or an applicant authority of the United Kingdom is the applicant authority in that Article.
The former authority may impose, and the latter authority must obey, the requirement in that Article. Either authority may enter the bilateral agreement in that Article.
(4) English is the only official language in cases where the United Kingdom is the requested Member State in Articles 22(1) and 22(3), or is the applicant Member State in Article 22(2).

17 Disclosure of information and documents
(1) Articles 23(1) and 23(6) apply where the United Kingdom is the Member State receiving the information within those Articles.

(2) Any United Kingdom public authority in question must seek to ensure that the United Kingdom complies with Articles 23(3) and 23(5) where the United Kingdom is the Member State providing the information, or is the Member State from which it originates, within those Articles.
(3) The relevant UK authority may follow Article 23(4), first sentence where it is the requested authority in that Article.
(4) An applicant authority of the United Kingdom may follow Article 23(4), first sentence where it is the applicant authority in that Article.
(5) Paragraphs (3) and (4) are subject to the second and third sentences of Article 23(4), and to Article 23(5), being satisfied.

Statutory instruments revoked

18 Statutory instruments revoked

The Regulations in the table in the Schedule are revoked.

SCHEDULE

TABLE OF STATUTORY INSTRUMENTS REVOKED

Regulation 18

(1)	(2)
Regulations revoked	References
The Recovery of Duties and Taxes Etc Due in Other Member States (Corresponding UK Claims, Procedure and Supplementary) Regulations 2004	SI 2004/674
The Recovery of Agricultural Levies Due in Other Member States Regulations 2004	SI 2004/800
The Recovery of Duties and Taxes Etc Due in Other Member States (Corresponding UK Claims, Procedure and Supplementary) (Amendment) Regulations 2005	SI 2005/1709
The Recovery of Duties and Taxes Etc Due in Other Member States (Corresponding UK Claims, Procedure and Supplementary) (Amendment) Regulations 2007	SI 2007/3508
The Schedule 39 to the Finance Act 2002 and Recovery of Taxes etc Due in Other Member States (Amendment) Regulations 2010	SI 2010/792

2011/3036

POSTAL PACKETS (REVENUE AND CUSTOMS) REGULATIONS 2011

Made . . . .*19th December 2011*

Laid before the House of Commons . . . .*20th December 2011*

Coming into force . . . .*10th January 2012*

The Treasury, in exercise of the powers conferred by sections 105(2) and 122 of the Postal Services Act 2000, and on the recommendation of the Commissioners for Her Majesty's Revenue and Customs and the Secretary of State, make the following Regulations.

1 Citation and commencement

These Regulations may be cited as the Postal Packets (Revenue and Customs) Regulations 2011 and come into force on 10th January 2012.

2 Definitions

In these Regulations—

"the Act of 1979" means the Customs and Excise Management Act 1979;

"CN22" and "CN23" mean the customs declaration forms for postal items described under those names in the provisions of the Universal Postal Convention and detailed regulations made thereunder which are for the time being in force;

"the Commissioners" means the Commissioners for Her Majesty's Revenue and Customs;

"the customs and excise Acts" has the meaning given by section 1(1) of the Act of 1979;

"the Customs and Excise Acts 1979" has the meaning given by section 1(1) of the Act of 1979;

"customs officer" means an officer of Revenue and Customs;

VAT SIs

"the customs territory" means the territories which, in accordance with Article 3 of Council Regulation 2913/92/EEC (as amended from time to time), comprise the customs territory of the Community;

"duty" includes value added tax and any other charge on imported goods; and

"exporter" and "importer" have the meanings given by section 1(1) of the Act of 1979.

3 Revocations

The Postal Packets (Customs and Excise) Regulations 1986 are revoked.

4 The Postal Packets (Revenue and Customs) Regulations 2007 are revoked.

5 Application of Section 105 of the Postal Services Act 2000

Section 105 of the Postal Services Act 2000 applies to all foreign postal packets.

6 Modifications and Exceptions

In its application to foreign postal packets, the Act of 1979 is subject to the modifications and exceptions made by regulations 7 and 8.

7 Section 159 (power to examine and take account of goods) has effect as if—

(a) in subsection (2), for "at such place as the Commissioners appoint for the purpose" there were substituted "at the place of importation, the place of exportation or any premises where loading, unloading, sorting, distribution, handling or storage of foreign postal packets (within the meaning of section 105 of the Postal Services Act 2000) takes place", and

(b) in subsection (8), for the words after "the Commissioners may" there were substituted "accept as the account of those goods for that purpose an account taken by the postal operator concerned or by a person authorised for that purpose by that postal operator.".

8 Paragraph 1(1) of Schedule 3 (notice of seizure) does not apply where the seizure was made in the presence of an officer of the postal operator concerned, authorised for the purpose by that postal operator.

9 In its application to foreign postal packets carried by a universal service provider acting in that capacity, the Act of 1979 is subject to the modifications and exceptions made by regulations 10 to 16.

10 Section 5 (time of importation, exportation, etc) has effect as if—

(a) subsections (3) and (5) were omitted, and

(b) for subsection (4) there were substituted—

"(4) The time of exportation of goods is the time when they are posted (or redirected) in the United Kingdom for transmission to a place outside the customs territory.".

11 Subsection (3) of section 40 (sale of uncleared goods deposited in Queen's warehouse) applies to goods deposited under regulation 22(4) as it applies to goods deposited by a proper officer under that section.

12 Section 43 (duty on imported goods) has effect as if—

(a) subsection (1) were omitted, and

(b) in subsection (2)(c), for sub-paragraphs (i) and (ii) there were substituted "those in force at the time when the officer assesses the amount of duty".

13 Section 49 (forfeiture of goods improperly imported) has effect as if subsection (1)(a) were omitted.

14 Section 53 (entry outwards of goods) has effect as if in subsection (8)—

(a) for "shipped for exportation or as stores or are waterborne for such shipment" there were substituted "exported"; and

(b) for "shipping or making waterborne" there were substituted "exportation".

15 Section 77 (information in relation to goods imported or exported) applies in relation to any foreign postal packet and its contents as it applies in relation to goods.

16 Section 99 (provisions as to deposit in Queen's warehouse) applies to any goods deposited in a Queen's Warehouse under regulation 22(4) as it applies to goods so deposited under or by virtue of the Customs and Excise Acts 1979.

17 Customs declarations for foreign postal packets carried by a universal service provider

All foreign postal packets carried by a universal service provider—

(a) posted to the United Kingdom from a place outside the customs territory, or

(b) posted in the United Kingdom to a place outside the customs territory, must be accompanied by a customs declaration in form CN22 or CN23 as appropriate, completed accurately and in full.

18 Declarations and labelling of packets for exportation

(1) Except where regulation 17 applies, every postal packet containing goods to be exported by post without payment of any duty to which they are subject, or on drawback or repayment of such duty, must—

(a) be accompanied by a customs declaration fully stating the nature, quantity and value of the goods which it contains or of which it consists and such other particulars as the Commissioners or the postal operator concerned may require,

(b) have affixed to its outer cover in the form and manner required by the Commissioners a label printed with the words "Exported by Post under Revenue and Customs control" or be distinguished in such other manner as the Commissioners may require.

(2) Where the requirements of paragraph (b) have been fulfilled, the postal operator concerned must endorse a certificate of posting on the appropriate document and give it to the sender.

19 Language of declarations

The declarations referred to in regulations 17 and 18 shall be completed legibly in English, French or the language of the destination country.

20 Liability to forfeiture of non-compliant foreign postal packets

(1) Where—

(a) the contents of a foreign postal packet are not in accordance with the accompanying customs declaration, or

(b) a foreign postal packet is not accompanied by the prescribed declaration, completed in accordance with these Regulations, or

(c) a foreign postal packet is not labelled in accordance with these Regulations,

the packet and all its contents shall be liable to forfeiture.

(2) Subject to regulation 8, section 139 (provisions as to detention, seizure and condemnation of goods, etc) of and Schedule 3 to the Act of 1979 shall apply to anything liable to forfeiture under paragraph (1) above as they apply to goods liable to forfeiture under that Act.

21 Production and examination of postal packets

Where a customs officer so requires, in relation to any foreign postal packet, the proper officer of the postal operator concerned must—

(a) produce the packet to that customs officer; or

(b) open the packet for examination by that customs officer.

22 Power to require an entry or account and disposal of goods for which no entry or no proper account is given

(1) This regulation applies to goods contained in postal packets which are brought into the United Kingdom from outside the customs territory.

(2) A customs officer may send to the addressee of the postal packet in which the goods are contained, or to any other person who is for the time being the importer of the goods, a notice requiring entry to be made of them or requiring a full and accurate account of them to be delivered to the officer.

(3) Where such entry is not made or such account is not delivered within 28 days of the date of the notice or within such longer period as the Commissioners may allow, then the postal operator concerned shall either—

(a) return the goods to the sender of the packet in which they were contained or otherwise export them from the customs territory in accordance with any request or indication appearing on the packet, or

(b) in accordance with arrangements agreed with the Commissioners, destroy the goods, or

(c) if required by the Commissioners, deliver them to any customs officer.

(4) Where the goods have been delivered to a customs officer under paragraph (3)(c) of this regulation, that officer may deposit the goods in a Queen's warehouse.

(5) This regulation is without prejudice to the Commissioners' powers of seizure if the goods are liable to forfeiture under these Regulations or any other provisions of the customs and excise Acts.

(6) This regulation is without prejudice to the Commissioners' power to refuse customs clearance for the goods.

23 Payment of duty and other sums

(1) A postal operator must pay over to the Commissioners any sums due to them which are recovered by that postal operator pursuant to section 105(3) of the Postal Services Act 2000.

(2) Where any sums due to the Commissioners and demanded by a postal operator pursuant to section 105(3) of the Postal Services Act 2000 are not paid to that postal operator, that postal operator may, with the agreement of the Commissioners, dispose of the goods contained in the postal packet concerned as that postal operator sees fit.

24 Authorisation of postal operator to perform duties of importer or exporter
The postal operator concerned is authorised to perform, in relation to any postal packet or its contents, such of the duties which the customs and excise Acts require the importer or exporter to perform as the Commissioners may require.

25 The Postal Services Act 2000
Nothing in these Regulations authorises any article to be brought into or sent out of the United Kingdom by post contrary to any provision of the Postal Services Act 2000.

26 UK Border Agency
References in these Regulations to the Commissioners shall include a reference to the Secretary of State by whom general customs functions are exercisable and the Director of Border Revenue.

2012/689

TAXES, ETC (FEES FOR PAYMENT BY TELEPHONE) REGULATIONS 2012

Made . . . . 5th March 2012
Laid before the House of Commons . . . . 6th March 2012
Coming into force . . . . 2nd April 2012

The Commissioners for Her Majesty's Revenue and Customs make the following Regulations in exercise of the powers conferred by section 136 of the Finance Act 2008.

In accordance with section 136(2) of that Act, the Commissioners expect that they, or the person authorised by them, will be required to pay a fee in connection with amounts paid where telephone authorisation is given to make a payment by credit card.

1 Citation and commencement
These Regulations may be cited as the Taxes, etc (Fees for Payment by Telephone) Regulations 2012 and come into force on 2nd April 2012.

2 Fee payable for telephone payments made by credit card
(1) A person who—
(a) gives telephone authorisation to make a payment by credit card, and
(b) makes a payment to the Commissioners or the person authorised by the Commissioners,
must also pay a fee of 1.5% of the amount of that payment.
(2) The fee must be paid by being added to the payment (so that, accordingly, the person must make a single overall payment, consisting of the payment and the fee).
(3) In these Regulations "credit card" means a card which—
(a) is a credit-token within section 14(1)(b) of the Consumer Credit Act 1974, or
(b) would be a credit-token falling within that enactment were the card to be given to an individual.

3 Revocation
The Taxes, etc (Fees for Payment by Telephone) Regulations 2009 are revoked.

2012/735

FINANCE ACT 2010, SCHEDULE 6, PART 1 (FURTHER CONSEQUENTIAL AND INCIDENTAL PROVISION ETC) ORDER 2012

Made . . . . 8th March 2012
Laid before the House of Commons . . . . 9th March 2012
Coming into force . . . . 1st April 2012

The Commissioners for Her Majesty's Revenue and Customs make the following Order in exercise of the powers conferred by paragraph 29(1) and (2) of Schedule 6 to the Finance Act 2010.

The provision made by this Order appears appropriate in consequence of, or otherwise in connection with, Part 1 of that Schedule.

1 Citation, commencement and effect
This Order may be cited as the Finance Act 2010, Schedule 6, Part 1 (Further Consequential and Incidental Provision etc) Order 2012 and comes into force on 1st April 2012.

2 (1) Article 5 has effect in relation to—
(a) a supply of goods or services (including anything treated as such a supply) made on or after 1st April 2012,
(b) an acquisition of goods from another member State on or after 1st April 2012, and

(c) an importation of goods from a place outside the member States on or after 1st April 2012.

(2) In paragraph 1—

"acquisition of goods from another member State" shall be construed in accordance with section 11 of VATA 1994;

"another member State" has the meaning given by section 96(1) of VATA 1994;

"importation of goods from a place outside the member States" shall be construed in accordance with section 15 of VATA 1994;

"supply" shall be construed in accordance with section 5 of VATA 1994.

3 Article 6 has effect—

(a) for corporation tax purposes, for accounting periods beginning on or after 1st April 2012, and

(b) for capital gains tax purposes, for the tax year 2012-13 and subsequent tax years.

4 Article 7 has effect—

(a) for corporation tax purposes, for accounting periods beginning on or after 1st April 2012, and

(b) for income tax purposes, for the tax year 2012-13 and subsequent tax years.

5 Definition of "charity" for the purposes of value added tax

(1) The definition of "charity" in section 1(1) of the Charities Act 2011 ceases to apply for the purposes of enactments relating to value added tax to which it would otherwise apply.

(2) Accordingly, by virtue of paragraph 33(2) of Schedule 6 to the Finance Act 2010, the definition of "charity" in Part 1 of that Schedule applies for the purposes of those enactments.

6 Definition of "charity" for the purposes of capital gains tax

. . .

7 Amendment of CTA 2009

2012/847

DATA-GATHERING POWERS (RELEVANT DATA) REGULATIONS 2012

Made . . . . *14th March 2012*

Coming into force . . . . *1st April 2012*

A draft of these Regulations was laid before, and approved by a resolution of, the House of Commons under paragraph 44(2) of Schedule 23 to the Finance Act 2011.

Accordingly the Treasury make the following Regulations in exercise of the power conferred by paragraph 1(3) of Schedule 23 to the Finance Act 2011.

1 Citation, commencement and interpretation

These Regulations may be cited as the Data-gathering Powers (Relevant Data) Regulations 2012 and come into force on 1st April 2012.

2 In these Regulations "Schedule 23" means Schedule 23 to the Finance Act 2011.

3 Salaries, fees, commission etc

(1) The relevant data for a data-holder of the type described in paragraph 9(1)(a) of Schedule 23 are information relating to all payments made by the employer that relate to the employment (referred to in this regulation as "employment related payments").

(2) The relevant data for a data-holder of the type described in paragraph 9(1)(b) are information relating to payments by any other person who has made employment related payments to the employer's employees or to the employees of another person.

(3) Information relating to apportioned expenses incurred partly in respect of employment related payments and partly in, or in connection with, other matters are relevant data for the purposes of paragraph 9(1)(a) and 9(1)(b).

(4) The relevant data for a data-holder of the type described in paragraph 9(1)(c) are information and documents relating to the donations made under Part 12 of the Income Tax (Earnings and Pensions) Act 2003 (payroll giving).

(5) For the purposes of paragraph 9(1)(d) and, where relevant, paragraph 9(4)—

(a) the relevant data are information relating to relevant payments made in connection with a business, or a part of a business;

(b) particulars of the following payments are not relevant data—

(i) payments from which income tax is deductible; and

(ii) payments made to any one person where the total of those payments, particulars of which would otherwise fall to be provided, does not exceed £500.

VAT SIs

4 The relevant data for a data-holder of the type described in paragraph 11 of Schedule 23 are the data described in paragraph 11(2)(b).

5 Interest etc

(1) The relevant data for a data-holder of the type described in paragraph 12 of Schedule 23 are information and documents relating to accounts or sums on which relevant interest is payable, including but not limited to the data in regulations 8, 9 and 10.

(2) "Relevant interest" means interest paid or credited—

(a) on money received or retained in the United Kingdom; and

(b) either without deduction of income tax or after deduction of income tax.

6 Information relating to the following payments is not relevant data for the purposes of a data-holder of the type described in paragraph 12—

(a) a payment in respect of a certificate of deposit within the meaning given by section 1019 of the Income Tax Act 2007;

(b) a payment in respect of an investment or a deposit held by a branch of a person to whom a data-holder notice is issued, where the branch is situated in a territory other than the United Kingdom;

(c) a payment falling within regulation 9(c) or 10(d) if the name and address of the person to whom the interest was paid or credited is not the person beneficially entitled to the interest;[1]

(d) a payment in respect of an investment under a plan provided for by regulations made under Chapter 3 of Part 6 of the Income Tax (Trading and Other Income) Act 2005;

(e) a payment to or a receipt for a person other than an individual (in whatever capacity the individual is acting), except where the case falls within regulation 9(c) or 10(d) [or where the relevant data-holder is carrying on a trade or business and, in the ordinary course of the operations thereof, receives or retains money in such circumstances that interest becomes payable thereon][1];

(f) any other payment not falling within any of paragraphs (a) to (e) which is specified in the data-holder notice as being a payment in respect of which information is not required.

Amendments—

[1] Para (c) revoked, and words in para (e) inserted, by the Data-gathering Powers (Relevant Data) (Amendment) Regulations, SI 2013/1811 regs 2, 3 with effect from 1 September 2013.

7 (1) Information is not relevant data for the purposes of a data-holder of the type described in paragraph 12 if it is in respect of a relevant dormant account before the balance of the account is paid out to the account-holder following a repayment claim (such payment being referred to in this regulation as the repayment claim being "settled").

(2) Where a repayment claim to the balance of a dormant account is settled, all interest paid, credited or included in the balance of the account, during and at the end of the relevant dormant period, is relevant data for the purposes of paragraph 12 and shall be treated—

(a) as paid at the time the repayment claim is settled; and

(b) as if the bank or building society in question had retained the balance of the account, in the ordinary course of the operations of its trade or business.

(3) If the data-holder notice specifies the year of assessment in which the relevant dormant period for any account ends, the notice shall (unless it states otherwise) be deemed to require as relevant data the inclusion of information for all relevant dormant accounts, in respect of which repayment claims were settled in that year.

(4) Information in respect of a relevant dormant account which, at the time it first became a relevant dormant account, was a plan provided for by regulations made under Chapter 3 of Part 6 of the Income Tax (Trading and Other Income) Act 2005 (individual investment plans) is not relevant data for the purpose of paragraph 12.

(5) In this regulation—

"relevant dormant account" has the meaning in section 39(2) of the Finance Act 2008;

"relevant dormant period" means the period between the time when a dormant account becomes a relevant dormant account and the time at which a repayment claim is settled; and

"repayment claim" means a repayment claim mentioned in section 5(6) of the Dormant Bank and Building Society Accounts Act 2008 ("the Dormant Accounts Act").

Other terms used have the same meaning as in the Dormant Accounts Act.

8 If a payment is made in circumstances in which a certificate has been supplied under regulation 4 of the Income Tax (Deposit-takers and Building Societies) (Interest Payments) Regulations 2008

. . . [1]

(a) the name and address of the person or persons by or on behalf of whom a certificate has been given in connection with the payment ("the beneficiary") if other than the person or persons to whom the payment was made;

(b) the date of birth of the beneficiary;

(c) the national insurance number or tax identification number of the beneficiary (or confirmation that a national insurance number or tax identification number is not held) for any account in respect of which the payment was made opened on or after 6th April 2013, and for any account opened earlier if such number is provided to the deposit-taker or building society;
(d) notification of the fact that the account in respect of which the payment was made is or was one in connection with which a certificate or certificates had been given which had not ceased to be valid at the 5th April in the year in which the payment was made or at the date of closure of the account, if earlier in that year;
(e) the reference number of the account referred to in paragraph (d) and, where necessary for identifying the account, the branch of the payer where the account is held;
(f) where the payment was made to two or more account-holders each of whom was beneficially entitled to the payment, notification of that fact and, if known, the number of such persons;
(g) the national insurance numbers or tax identification numbers of persons referred to in paragraph (f) other than the beneficiary referred to in paragraphs (b) and (c) (or confirmation that a national insurance number or tax identification number is not held) for any account opened on or after 6th April 2013, and for any account opened earlier if such number is provided to the deposit-taker or building society;
(h) where a certificate was given by or on behalf of one, or more, but not all, of the persons referred to in paragraph (f) and had not ceased to be valid at the 5th April in the year in which the payment was made or at the date of closure of the account, if earlier in that year, notification of those facts;
(i) where the payment was the first payment made in respect of an account, notification of that fact;
(j) where the payment was in a currency other than sterling and the amount of the payment is recorded in that currency in the data provided under a data-holder notice notification of the fact that the amount is so recorded and the specification of the currency concerned.

Amendments—[1] Words revoked by the Data-gathering Powers (Relevant Data) (Amendment) Regulations, SI 2015/672 reg 2 with effect from 6 April 2015.

9 In cases to which regulation 8 does not apply, the relevant data relating to payments in respect of deposits are—
(a) the reference number of the account in respect of which a payment was made and, where necessary for identifying the account, the branch of the payer where the account is held;
(b) where a payment was made to two or more account holders, notification of that fact and, if known, the number of such persons;
(c) where the payment was made without deduction of tax by virtue of a declaration made after 5th April 2001 under section 858, 859, 860 or 861 of the Income Tax Act 2007—
(i) the name and principal residential address of the individual beneficially entitled to the payment or, if more than one, of each individual entitled to the payment; or
(ii) where the person beneficially entitled to the payment is a Scottish partnership, all the partners in which are individuals, the name and principal residential address of each of the partners;
(d) in a case falling within paragraph (c) notification of the fact that the account in respect of which the payment was made was one in respect of which a declaration had been made as mentioned in that paragraph;
(e) the national insurance number or tax identification number (or confirmation that a national insurance number or tax identification number is not held) of the person or, where paragraph (b) applies, each person to whom a payment was made for any account opened on or after 6th April 2013, and for any account opened earlier if such number is provided to the deposit-taker or building society;
(f) where a payment made in the course of the year was the first payment in respect of an account, notification of that fact;
(g) where a payment was in a currency other than sterling and the amount of the payment is recorded in that currency in the data provided under a data-holder notice notification of the fact that the amount is so recorded and the specification of the currency concerned.

10 In cases to which regulation 8 does not apply, the relevant data relating to payments and receipts of interest other than payments in respect of deposits are—
(a) identification of the security or investment in respect of which the payment was made or received;
(b) where a payment or receipt was in a currency other than sterling and the amount of the payment is recorded in that currency in the data provided under a data-holder notice notification of the fact that the amount is so recorded and the specification of the currency concerned;

(c) where a payment was made to, or the receipt was for, two or more persons, notification of that fact and, if known, the number of such persons;

(d) where a payment was made without deduction of tax by virtue of a declaration made under regulation 31 of the Authorised Investment Funds (Tax) Regulations 2006, the name and principal residential address of the person beneficially entitled to the payment, or if more than one, of each person beneficially entitled to the payment;

(e) in a case falling within paragraph (d), notification of the fact that the account in respect of which the payment was made was one in respect of which the declaration had been made.

11 Income, assets etc belonging to others

The relevant data for a data-holder of the type described in paragraph 13 of Schedule 23 are—

(a) information relating to the money or value received; and

(b) the name and address of the beneficial owner of the money or value.

[11A Merchant acquirers etc

(1) The relevant data for a data-holder of the type described in paragraph 13A of Schedule 23 are—

(a) in relation to a retailer, information relating to payment card transactions recorded against a merchant account, including the currency these payment card transactions were made in;

(b) the reference number of the account into which payments are made by the relevant data-holder to the retailer and, where necessary for identifying the account, the branch where the account is held;

(c) any unique identifier which has been allocated to a retailer, for the purposes of identifying the retailer, as part of the business arrangement between the relevant data-holder and the retailer;

(d) any identifier which has been allocated to a retailer, for the purposes of classifying the trade of the retailer, as part of the business arrangement between the relevant data-holder and the retailer;

(e) any unique identifier which has been allocated to a retailer's merchant account, for the purposes of identifying this merchant account, as part of the business arrangement between the relevant data-holder and the retailer;

(f) the name, address, telephone number, e-mail address, website address and VAT number ("relevant details") of a retailer and, if different, the relevant details associated with a merchant account.

(2) In this regulation—

"merchant account" means an account held by a retailer with the relevant data-holder, by reference to which the amount due to be paid by the relevant data-holder to the retailer in settlement of payment card transactions is calculated; and

"VAT number" means "registration number" for the purposes of paragraph (1) of regulation 2 of the Value Added Tax Regulations 1995.][1]

Amendments—[1] Reg 11A inserted by the Data-gathering Powers (Relevant Data) (Amendment) Regulations, SI 2013/1811 regs 2, 5 with effect from 1 September 2013.

12 Payments derived from securities

The relevant data for a data-holder of the type described in paragraph 14 of Schedule 23 are—

(a) whether the relevant data-holder is the beneficial owner (or sole beneficial owner) of the securities or payment in question;

(b) if not—

(i) details of the beneficial owner (or other beneficial owners); and

(ii) if those details are not known or if different, details of the person for whom the securities are held or to whom the payment is or may be paid on; and

(c) if there is more than one beneficial owner or more than one person of the kind mentioned in paragraph (b)(ii), their respective interests in the securities or payment.

13 The relevant data for a data-holder of the type described in paragraph 15 of Schedule 23 are details of the amounts paid that were received from or paid on behalf of another person including the name and address of each such person.

14 Grants and subsidies out of public funds

The relevant data for a data-holder of the type described in paragraph 16 of Schedule 23 are—

(a) the name and address of the person to whom the payment has been made or on whose behalf the payment has been received;

(b) the amount of the payment so made or received; and

(c) the address of any property in respect of which the payment has been made.

15 Licences, approvals etc

The relevant data for a data-holder of the type described in paragraph 17 of Schedule 23 are—

(a) the name and address of anyone who is or has been the holder of a licence or approval or to whom an entry in the register relates or related;
(b) particulars of the licence, approval or entry;
(c) information relating to any application for such a licence or approval or for entry on that register.

16 Rent and other payments arising from land

(1) The relevant data for a data-holder of the type described in paragraph 18 of Schedule 23 are—
(a) information relating to the terms applying to the lease, occupation or use of land;
(b) information relating to any consideration given for the grant or assignment of the tenancy;
(c) information relating to any person on whose behalf the land is managed or the payments received, including particulars of payments arising from the land.
(2) In this regulation—
(a) "lease" includes an agreement for a lease, and any tenancy, but does not include a mortgage or heritable security;
(b) "lessee" includes a successor in title of a lease; and
(c) in relation to Scotland, "assignment" means an assignation.

17 Dealing etc in securities

(1) The relevant data for a data-holder of the type described in paragraph 19 of Schedule 23 are—
(a) information and documents relating to securities transactions in respect of which that person is a relevant data-holder; and
(b) in relation to a person who carries on a business of effecting public issues or placings or otherwise effects public issues or placings, information relating to the issue, allotment or placing of the public issues or placings.
(2) In this regulation—
(a) "placing" means a placing of shares or securities in a company; and
(b) "public issue" means a public issue of shares or securities in a company.

18 Dealing in other property

The relevant data for a data-holder of the type described in paragraph 20 of Schedule 23 are—
(a) particulars of any transactions effected through a clearing house;
(b) particulars of any transaction which meets the following conditions—
(i) the transaction is effected by or through that person;
(ii) in the transaction, an asset which is tangible moveable property is disposed of; and
(iii) the amount or value of the consideration for the disposal exceeds, in the hands of the recipient, £6,000.

19 Lloyd's

The relevant data for a data-holder of the type described in paragraph 21 of Schedule 23 are information and documents relating to, and to the activities of, the syndicate of underwriting members of Lloyd's.

20 Investment plans etc

The relevant data for a data-holder of the type described in paragraph 22 of Schedule 23 are—
(a) information and documents relating to the plan, including investments which are or have been held under the plan;
(b) information and documents relating to the child trust fund including investments which are or have been held under the fund.

21 Petroleum activities

The relevant data for a data-holder of the type described in paragraph 23 of Schedule 23 are—
(a) particulars of transactions in connection with any activities authorised by a petroleum licence as a result of which any person is or might be liable to tax by virtue of section 276 of the Taxation of Chargeable Gains Act 1992, section 1313 of the Corporation Tax Act 2009 or section 874 of the Income Tax (Trading and Other Income) Act 2005;
(b) particulars of earnings or money treated as earnings, which constitute employment income (see section 7(2)(a) or (b) of the Income Tax (Earnings and Pensions) Act 2003) or other payments paid or payable in respect of duties or services performed in an area in which those activities may be carried on under the petroleum licence;
(c) particulars of the persons to whom such earnings, money or other payments were paid and are payable;
(d) information and documents relating to the oil field.

VAT SIs

22 Insurance activities

The relevant data for a data-holder of the type described in paragraph 24 of Schedule 23 are—

(a) information and documents relating to contracts of insurance entered into in the course of an insurance business;

(b) if paragraph 24(b) or (c) applies, information and documents relating to the contracts of insurance.

23 Environmental activities

The relevant data for a data-holder of the type described in paragraph 25 of Schedule 23 are—

(a) information and documents relating to aggregates levy matters in which the person is or has been involved;

(b) information and documents relating to climate change levy matters in which the person is or has been involved;

(c) information and documents relating to any landfill disposal.

24 Settlements

The relevant data for a data-holder of the type described in paragraph 26 of Schedule 23 are information and documents relating to the settlement in question and to income or gains arising to the settlement.

25 Charities

The relevant data for a data-holder of the type described in paragraph 27 of Schedule 23 are information relating to donations to the charity that are eligible for tax relief under any of the following provisions

(a) section 257 of the Taxation of Chargeable Gains Act 1992 (gifts to charities etc);

(b) section 63(2)(a) or (aa) of the Capital Allowances Act 2001(cases in which disposal value is nil);

(c) Part 12 of the Income Tax (Earnings and Pensions) Act 2003 (payroll giving);

(d) section 108 of the Income Tax (Trading and Other Income) Act 2005 (gifts of trading stock to charities etc);

(e) Chapter 2 or 3 of Part 8 of the Income Tax Act 2007 (gift aid, gifts of shares, securities and real property to charities etc);

(f) section 105 of the Corporation Tax Act 2009 (gifts of trading stock to charities etc); and

(g) Part 6 of the Corporation Tax Act 2010 (charitable donations relief).

2012/2393

VALUE ADDED TAX (REFUND OF VAT TO CHIEF CONSTABLES AND THE COMMISSIONER OF POLICE OF THE METROPOLIS) ORDER 2012

Made . . . . *17th September 2012*
Laid before the House of Commons . . . . *18th September 2012*
Coming into force . . . . *15th November 2012*

The Treasury make the following Order in exercise of the power conferred by section 33(3)(k) of the Value Added Tax Act 1994.

1 This Order may be cited as the Value Added Tax (Refund of Tax to Chief Constables and the Commissioner of Police of the Metropolis) Order 2012 and comes into force on 15 November 2012:

2 The following bodies are specified for the purposes of section 33 of the Value Added Tax Act 1994—

(*a*) a chief constable established under section 2 of the Police Reform and Social Responsibility Act 2011,

(*b*) the Commissioner of Police of the Metropolis established under section 4 of that Act.

2012/2907

VALUE ADDED TAX (RELIEF FOR EUROPEAN RESEARCH INFRASTRUCTURE CONSORTIA) ORDER 2012

Made . . . . *20th November 2012*
Laid before the House of Commons . . . . *21st November 2012*

Coming into force . . . . *1st January 2013*

The Treasury make the following Order in exercise of the powers conferred by sections 30(4), 36A, 37(1) and 96(9) of the Value Added Tax Act 1994.

It appears to the Treasury that it is expedient to make this Order having regard to the need to conform with Articles 3(1)(a), 143(1)(g) and 151(1)(b) of Council Directive 2006/112/EC on the common system of value added tax.

1 Citation, commencement and effect

(1) This Order may be cited as the Value Added Tax (Relief for European Research Infrastructure Consortia) Order 2012 and comes into force on 1st January 2013.

(2) This Order has effect in relation to importations, acquisitions or supplies made on or after 1st January 2013.

2 Relief from value added tax on importation or acquisition of goods

(1) No VAT shall be chargeable on the importation of goods from a place outside the member States, or on the acquisition of goods from another member State, by an ERIC.

(2) Paragraph (1) applies only where the following requirements are met—

- (a) the statutory seat of the ERIC referred to in Article 8(1) of Council Regulation (EC) No 723/2009 on the Community legal framework for a European Research Infrastructure Consortium is located in a member State,
- (b) the goods are for the official use of the ERIC,
- (c) relief is not precluded by the limitations and conditions laid down in the agreement between the members of the ERIC referred to in Article 5(1)(d) of Council Regulation (EC) No 723/2009, and
- (d) a certificate in writing has been given to the Commissioners on behalf of the ERIC that the requirements in paragraphs (a), (b) and (c) are met in relation to the importation or acquisition.

(3) In this article "ERIC" means a body set up as a European Research Infrastructure Consortium by a decision under Article 6(1)(a) of Council Regulation (EC) No 723/2009.

3 Amendment of Schedule 8 to the Value Added Tax Act 1994

(inserts Group 18 into VATA 1994 Sch 8)

2013/412

VALUE ADDED TAX (REFUND OF TAX TO THE NATURAL RESOURCES BODY FOR WALES) ORDER 2013

Made . . . . *25 February 2013*

Laid before the House of Commons . . . . *26 February 2013*

Coming into force . . . . *19 March 2013*

The Treasury make the following Order in exercise of the power conferred by section 33(3)(k) of the Value Added Tax Act 1994:

1 Citation and Commencement

This Order may be cited as the Value Added Tax (Refund of Tax to the Natural Resources Body for Wales) Order 2013 and comes into force on 19th March 2013.

2 The Natural Resources Body for Wales (also known as Corff Adnoddau Naturiol Cymru)

The Natural Resources Body for Wales (also known as Corff Adnoddau Naturiol Cymru) is specified for the purposes of section 33 of the Value Added Tax Act 1994.

2013/2911

VALUE ADDED TAX (FLAT-RATE VALUATION OF SUPPLIES OF FUEL FOR PRIVATE USE) ORDER 2013

Made . . . . *18 November 2013*

Laid before the House of Commons . . . . *18 November 2013*

Coming into force . . . . *1 February 2014*

The Treasury make the following Order in exercise of the powers conferred by paragraph B1 of Schedule 6 to the Value Added Tax Act 1994.

1 Citation and commencement

This Order may be cited as the Value Added Tax (Flat-rate Valuation of Supplies of Fuel for Private Use) Order 2013 and comes into force on 1st February 2014.

VAT SIs

2 Flat-rate basis of valuation of supplies of fuel for private use

The value of all supplies of road fuel made to any one individual in respect of any one car for a prescribed accounting period is to be determined in accordance with—

(a) the valuation table, and

(b) the notes to the valuation table.

3 The "valuation table" is—

(a) the updated valuation table having effect during the period, or

(b) if no table has been published under article 7, the table set out in Schedule 1 to this Order ("the base valuation table").

4 The "notes to the valuation table" are the notes set out in Schedule 2 to this Order.

5 Revalorisation of the flat-rate valuation of supplies

The Commissioners must revalorise the amounts specified in the base valuation table in accordance with the method set out in Schedule 3 to this Order in such time that the first revalorisation takes place prior to 1st May 2014 and thereafter each revalorisation must be no more than twelve months after the previous revalorisation.

6 On each occasion that the Commissioners revalorise, a table (an "updated valuation table") containing the revalorised amounts is to take effect (and replace the existing valuation table) from the date the Commissioners specify ("the revalorisation start date").

7 The Commissioners must publish the updated valuation table before the revalorisation start date together with a statement specifying the revalorisation start date.

SCHEDULE 1

BASE VALUATION TABLE

Article 3

Description of vehicle: vehicle's CO_2 emissions figure	VAT inclusive consideration for a 12 month prescribed accounting period £	VAT inclusive consideration for a 3 month prescribed accounting period £	VAT inclusive consideration for a 1 month prescribed accounting period £
120 or less	675.00	168.00	56.00
125	1,010.00	253.00	84.00
130	1,080.00	269.00	89.00
135	1,145.00	286.00	95.00
140	1,215.00	303.00	101.00
145	1,280.00	320.00	106.00
150	1,350.00	337.00	112.00
155	1,415.00	354.00	118.00
160	1,485.00	371.00	123.00
165	1,550.00	388.00	129.00
170	1,620.00	404.00	134.00
175	1,685.00	421.00	140.00
180	1,755.00	438.00	146.00
185	1,820.00	455.00	151.00
190	1,890.00	472.00	157.00
195	1,955.00	489.00	163.00
200	2,025.00	506.00	168.00
205	2,090.00	523.00	174.00
210	2,160.00	539.00	179.00
215	2,225.00	556.00	185.00
220	2,295.00	573.00	191.00
225 or more	2,360.00	590.00	196.00

Note—The following valuation table, published under art 7 of this Order, provides the flat-rate amounts, as revalorised, for prescribed accounting periods beginning on or after **1 May 2015**—

Description of vehicle: vehicle's CO_2 emissions figure	VAT inclusive consideration for a 12 month prescribed accounting period £	VAT inclusive consideration for a 3 month prescribed accounting period £	VAT inclusive consideration for a 1 month prescribed accounting period £
120 or less	536.00	133.00	44.00
125	802.00	200.00	66.00
130	857.00	213.00	70.00
135	909.00	227.00	75.00
140	965.00	240.00	80.00
145	1,016.00	254.00	84.00
150	1,072.00	267.00	88.00
155	1,123.00	281.00	93.00
160	1,179.00	294.00	97.00
165	1,231.00	308.00	102.00
170	1,286.00	320.00	106.00
175	1,338.00	334.00	111.00
180	1,393.00	347.00	115.00
185	1,445.00	361.00	119.00
190	1,501.00	374.00	124.00
195	1,552.00	388.00	129.00
200	1,608.00	401.00	133.00
205	1,660.00	415.00	138.00
210	1,715.00	428.00	142.00
215	1,767.00	441.00	146.00
220	1,822.00	455.00	151.00
225 or more	1,874.00	468.00	155.00

HMRC's VAT fuel scale charge pages are available at: www.gov.uk/fuel-scale-charge.

SCHEDULE 2
NOTES TO THE VALUATION TABLE
Article 4

1 For a car of a description in the first column of the valuation table, the value on the flat-rate basis of all supplies of road fuel made to any one individual in respect of that car for a prescribed accounting period is the amount specified under whichever of the second, third or fourth columns corresponds with the length of the prescribed accounting period.

2 Where a CO22 emissions figure is specified in relation to a car in a UK approval certificate or in a certificate of conformity issued by a manufacturer in another member state corresponding to a UK approval certificate ("corresponding certificate of conformity"), the car's CO22 emissions figure for the purposes of the valuation table is determined as follows—

(a) if only one figure is specified in the certificate, that figure is the car's CO22 emissions figure for those purposes;

(b) if more than one figure is specified in the certificate, the figure specified as the CO22 (combined) emissions figure is the car's CO22 emissions figure for those purposes;

(c) if separate CO22 emissions figures are specified for different fuels, the lowest figure specified, or, in a case within sub-paragraph (b), the lowest CO22 (combined) emissions figure specified is the car's CO22 emissions figure for those purposes.

3 For the purpose of paragraph 2, if the car's CO22 emissions figure is not a multiple of 5 it is rounded down to the nearest multiple of 5 for those purposes.

4 Where no UK approval certificate or corresponding certificate of conformity is issued in relation to a car, or where a certificate is issued but no emissions figure is specified in it, the car's CO22 emissions figure for the purposes of the valuation table is—

(a) 140 if its cylinder capacity is 1,400 cubic centimetres or less,

(b) 175 if its cylinder capacity exceeds 1,400 cubic centimetres but does not exceed 2,000 cubic centimetres, and

(c) 220 or more if its cylinder capacity exceeds 2,000 cubic centimetres.

5 For the purpose of paragraph 4, the car's cylinder capacity is the capacity of its engine as calculated for the purposes of the Vehicle Excise and Registration Act 1994.

6 In any case where—

(a) in a prescribed accounting period, there are supplies of fuel for private use to an individual in respect of one car for a part of the period and in respect of another car for another part of the period, and

(b) at the end of that period one of those cars neither belongs to, nor is allocated to, the individual,

the flat-rate value of the supplies is determined as if the supplies made to the individual during those parts of the period were in respect of only one car.

7 (1) Where paragraph 6 applies, the value of the supplies is to be determined as follows—

(a) if each of the 2 or more cars falls within the same description of car specified in the valuation table, the value specified in the valuation table for that description of car applies for the whole of the prescribed accounting period, and

(b) if one of those cars falls within a description of car specified in that table which is different from the others, the value of the supplies is the aggregate of the relevant fractions of the consideration appropriate for each description of car in the valuation table.

(2) "The relevant fraction" in relation to any car is that which the part of the prescribed accounting period in which fuel was supplied for private use in respect of the car bears to the whole of that period.

8 "CO22 emissions figure" means a CO22 emissions figure expressed in grams per kilometre driven.

9 "UK approval certificate" means a certificate issued under—

(a) Section 58(1) or (4) of the Road Traffic Act 1988, or

(b) Article 31A(4) or (5) of the Road Traffic (Northern Ireland) Order 1981.

10 "Company car" means a car that is made available for private use (without any transfer of the property in it) by an employer to an employee, or member of an employee's family or household, by reason of the employee's employment for which fuel is provided for private use.

SCHEDULE 3

METHOD FOR REVALORISATION OF AMOUNTS SPECIFIED IN THE BASE VALUATION TABLE

Article 5

1 The amounts in the base valuation table are to be revalorised in accordance with the following steps—

2 *Step 1—establishing the current fuel price*

In respect of each fuel (unleaded petrol and diesel) the current average retail price of a litre of fuel in the UK is to be ascertained from reliable data. The resulting figures ("the current fuel prices") are to be rounded down to the nearest whole penny.

3 *Step 2—calculating the prospective excise duty differences*

If a change in the rate of excise duty liable to be charged on road fuel is due in the period beginning on the date that the Commissioners revalorise the amounts in the base valuation table and ending a calendar year after the next revalorisation start date the prospective increase or decrease in the amount of excise duty chargeable per litre of each of the fuels is to be calculated by—

(a) adding the amount of VAT that is applicable to the increased or decreased amount of excise duty chargeable and rounding down the resultant figures to the nearest whole penny,

(b) dividing the number of days of the calendar year beginning on the revalorisation start date in which the increase or decrease in excise duty is likely to apply by 365 (or 366 in a leap year) and expressing the result of that calculation as a percentage rounded down to two decimal places, and

(c) multiplying the increased or decreased amount calculated in accordance with sub-paragraph (a) in respect of each of the fuels by the percentage calculated in accordance with sub-paragraph (b), each resultant figure is to be rounded down to the nearest whole penny.

If the valuation table is intended to have effect for less than a full calendar year the periods specified in sub-paragraph (b) above must be amended accordingly.

4 *Step 3—calculating the duty inclusive fuel price*
For each fuel, the prospective excise duty difference calculated in accordance with step 2 is to be added to, or deducted from, the current fuel price. The resultant figure is the "duty inclusive fuel price".

5 *Step 4—calculating the percentage price difference*
The percentage price difference for each of the fuels is to be calculated using the following formula—

$A/B \times 100/1$

where "*A*" represents the duty inclusive fuel price for each fuel and "*B*" represents the average retail price per litre as at 11th March 2013 of that fuel. The average retail price of diesel and unleaded petrol (rounded down to the nearest whole penny) as at 11th March 2013 was £1.47 and £1.40 per litre respectively. The resulting percentages are to be rounded down to two decimal places.

6 *Step 5—calculating the weighted percentage price difference*
If the percentage price difference for each fuel is not the same, the average is to be calculated by weighting according to the relative number of petrol and diesel company cars in the UK (ascertained from reliable data) by using the following formula—

$(C \times E/E + F) + (D \times F/E + F)$

where "*C*" and "*D*" represent the percentage price differences for petrol and diesel respectively and "*E*" and "*F*" are the numbers of petrol and diesel company cars respectively. The resulting percentage is to be rounded down to two decimal places.

7 *Step 6—calculating the increase or decrease in the amounts in the table*
Each amount specified in the base valuation table is to be amended by multiplying that amount by the weighted percentage price difference rounded down to the nearest whole pound.

2014/1112

VALUE ADDED TAX (REFUND OF TAX) ORDER 2014

Made . . . . *28 April 2014*
Laid before the House of Commons . . . . . . *29 April 2014*
Coming into force . . . . *20 May 2014*

The Treasury make the following Order in exercise of the power conferred by section 33(3)(*k*) of the Value Added Tax Act 1994:

1 Citation and commencement

This Order may be cited as the Value Added Tax (Refund of Tax) Order 2014 and comes into force on 20th May 2014.

2 Bodies specified for the purposes of section 33 of the Value Added Tax Act 1994

The following bodies are specified for the purposes of section 33 of the Value Added Tax Act 1994—

(*a*) the Barnsley, Doncaster, Rotherham and Sheffield Combined Authority established by article 3 of the Barnsley, Doncaster, Rotherham and Sheffield Combined Authority Order 2014;

(*b*) the Durham, Gateshead, Newcastle Upon Tyne, North Tyneside, Northumberland, South Tyneside and Sunderland Combined Authority established by article 3 of the Durham, Gateshead, Newcastle Upon Tyne, North Tyneside, Northumberland, South Tyneside and Sunderland Combined Authority Order 2014;

(*c*) the Greater Manchester Combined Authority established by article 3 of the Greater Manchester Combined Authority Order 2011;

(*d*) the Halton, Knowsley, Liverpool, St Helens, Sefton and Wirral Combined Authority established by article 3 of the Halton, Knowsley, Liverpool, St Helens, Sefton and Wirral Combined Authority Order 2014; and

(*e*) the West Yorkshire Combined Authority established by article 3 of the West Yorkshire Combined Authority Order 2014.

2014/1458

VALUE ADDED TAX (SECTION 55A) (SPECIFIED GOODS AND EXCEPTED SUPPLIES) ORDER 2014

Made .... *9 June 2014*
Laid before the House of Commons .... *9 June 2014*
Coming into force .... *1 July 2014*

The Treasury, in exercise of the power conferred on them by section 55A(9), (10), (11) and (14) of the Value Added Tax Act 1994, make the following Order.

1 Citation and commencement

(1) This Order may be cited as the Value Added Tax (Section 55A) (Specified Goods and Excepted Supplies) Order 2014.

(2) This Order comes into force on 1st July 2014 and has effect in relation to supplies made on or after that date.

2 Interpretation

In this Order—

"accredited FIT installation" has the meaning specified in article 2(1) of the Feed-in Tariffs Order 2012;

"the Act" means the Value Added Tax Act 1994;

"directed utility" means a person who is treated as a gas or electricity utility pursuant to a direction made under sub-paragraph 1, or regulations made under sub-paragraph 2, of paragraph 151 of Part 14 of Schedule 6 to the Finance Act 2000;

"specified goods" means the goods specified in article 4;

"supply licence" means —

(*a*) a licence granted under section 7A(1) of the Gas Act 1986 (licensing of gas suppliers and gas shippers);

(*b*) a licence granted under section 6(1)(*d*) of the Electricity Act 1989 (licences authorising supply, etc.);

(*c*) a licence granted under article 8(1)(*c*) of the Gas (Northern Ireland) Order 1996 (licences authorising supply, etc.); or

(*d*) a licence granted under article 10(1)(*c*) of the Electricity (Northern Ireland) Order 1992 (licences authorising supply, etc.);

"third party intermediary" means a person who purchases specified goods from a utility in order to make an onward supply of those goods to an end user for consumption, in circumstances where the goods are delivered directly to the end user by the utility;

"utility" has the meaning given by paragraph 150(1) of Part 14 of Schedule 6 to the Finance Act 2000.

3 Application of section 55A of the Act

(1) Section 55A of the Act (customers to account for tax on supplies of goods or services of a kind used in missing trader intra-Community fraud) applies to goods of a description specified in article 4.

(2) The supplies specified in article 5 are excepted supplies for the purposes of section 55A of the Act.

4 Specified goods

The goods referred to in article 3(1) are—

(*a*) gas supplied through a natural gas system situated within the territory of a member State or any network connected to such a system; and

(*b*) electricity.

5 Excepted supplies

The supplies referred to in article 3(2) are—

(*a*) a supply of specified goods made by a person who holds a supply licence in relation to that supply;

(*b*) a supply of specified goods by a directed utility to an end user for consumption;

(*c*) a supply of specified goods deemed to have been made pursuant to a contract under—

(i) paragraph 3(1) or (2) of Schedule 6 to the Electricity Act 1989 (the electricity code: deemed contracts in certain cases);

(ii) paragraph 8(1) or (2) of Schedule 2B to the Gas Act 1986 (the gas code: deemed contracts in certain cases);

(iii) paragraph 3(1) or (2) of Schedule 6 to the Electricity (Northern Ireland) Order 1992 (the electricity supply code: deemed contracts); or

(iv) section 12(1) or (2) of the Energy Act (Northern Ireland) 2011 (gas: deemed contracts for supply in certain cases);

(*d*) a supply of specified goods made to a directed utility for the purpose of —

(i) consumption by the directed utility, or

(ii) onward supply by the directed utility to an end user for consumption;

(*e*) a supply of specified goods made by a person who, in relation to that supply, is exempted from the requirement to hold a supply licence under —

(i) article 5 of the Gas Exemptions Order 2011 (supplier exemptions);

(ii) paragraph 1, 2, 4 or 5 of Schedule 2A to the Gas Act 1986 (exceptions to prohibition on unlicensed activities);

(iii) article 7(1) of the Gas (Northern Ireland) Order 1996 (exemptions);

(iv) article 3(1)(*c*) of, and Schedule 4 to, the Electricity (Class Exemptions from the Requirements for a Licence) Order 2001;

(v) article 9(1) of the Electricity (Northern Ireland) Order 1992 (exemptions); or

(vi) article 3(1)(*c*) of, and Schedule 3 to, the Electricity (Class Exemptions from the Requirement for a Licence) Order (Northern Ireland) 2013;

(*f*) a supply to which section 9A of the Act (reverse charge on gas, electricity, heat or cooling supplied by persons outside the United Kingdom) applies;

(*g*) a supply of electricity made by an accredited FIT installation;

(*h*) a supply of specified goods—

(i) to a third party intermediary; or

(ii) by a third party intermediary;

(*i*) any other supply of specified goods which is not a wholesale supply.

VAT SIs

2015/449

VALUE ADDED TAX (REFUND OF TAX TO THE LONDON LEGACY DEVELOPMENT CORPORATION) ORDER 2015

The Treasury make the following Order in exercise of the power conferred by section 33(3)(k) of the Value Added Tax Act 1994:

Made . . . . *3 March 2015*
Laid before the House of Commons . . . . *4 March 2015*
Coming into force . . . . *1 April 2015*

1 Citation and commencement

This Order may be cited as the Value Added Tax (Refund of Tax to the London Legacy Development Corporation) Order 2015 and comes into force on 1st April 2015.

2 The London Legacy Development Corporation

The London Legacy Development Corporation, established by article 3 of the London Legacy Development Corporation (Establishment) Order 2012, is specified for the purposes of section 33 of the Value Added Tax Act 1994.

2015/776

SINGLE USE CARRIER BAGS CHARGES (ENGLAND) ORDER 2015

Made . . . . *19 March 2015*
Coming into force in accordance with . . . . *article 1(c)*

The Secretary of State is satisfied in accordance with paragraph 23 of Schedule 6 to the Climate Change Act 2008 ("the CCA 2008") that each administrator appointed by article 5(1) will act in accordance with the principles that:

(*a*) regulatory activities should be carried out in a way that is transparent, accountable, proportionate and consistent;

(*b*) regulatory activities should be targeted only at cases in which action is needed.

A draft of this Order has been laid before and approved by a resolution of each House of Parliament in accordance with:

(*c*) section 77(4) of, and paragraph 27(2) of Schedule 6 to, the CCA 2008;

(*d*) section 20(3) of the Regulatory Enforcement and Sanctions Act 2008 Act ("the RESA 2008").

The Secretary of State makes this Order in exercise of the powers conferred by section 90(3) and (5) of, and Schedule 6 to, the CCA 2008 and section 4(4)(a) of the RESA 2008.

PART 1
INTRODUCTION

1 Citation, application, commencement and expiry

This Order—

(*a*) may be cited as the Single Use Carrier Bags Charges (England) Order 2015;
(*b*) applies in relation to England;
(*c*) comes into force—
  (i) for the purposes of article 18(1), one month after the day on which it is made;
  (ii) for all other purposes, on 5th October 2015;
(*d*) ceases to have effect on 5th October 2022.

2 Interpretation

In this Order—

"breach" has the meaning given in article 6;
"enforcement costs recovery notice" has the meaning given in article 12(1);
"lightweight plastic material" means synthetic or semi-synthetic material made from polyamide, polyethylene, polylactic acid, polyvinyl chloride or other polymer, or any combination of polymers, the thickness of which is not greater than 70 microns;
"non-compliance penalty notice" has the meaning given in paragraph 3(4) of Schedule 7;
"record" means a record required to be kept in accordance with paragraph 1 of Schedule 3;
"reporting year" has the meaning given in paragraph 3 of Schedule 3;
"seller" has the meaning given in Schedule 1;
"single use carrier bag" has the meaning given in Schedule 2;
"SUCB" means a single use carrier bag;
"VAT" has the meaning given in section 96 of the Value Added Tax Act 1994.

PART 2
SELLERS' OBLIGATIONS

3 Obligation to charge

A seller must charge a minimum of 5 pence (including any VAT) for each SUCB supplied in a reporting year—

(*a*) at the place in England where the goods are sold, for the purpose of enabling the goods to be taken away; or
(*b*) for the purpose of enabling the goods to be delivered to persons in England.

4 Obligations in relation to records

Schedule 3 (records) has effect.

PART 3
ADMINISTRATORS AND ENFORCEMENT

5 Administrators

(1) The relevant local authority is appointed as the administrator.
(2) In paragraph (1), "the relevant local authority" is—
  (*a*) in the case of a SUCB supplied at a place in England where goods are sold, for the purpose of enabling the goods to be taken away, the local authority with responsibility for the area in which the goods are sold;
  (*b*) in the case of a SUCB dispatched from a place in England, in the course of the delivery of goods to a person in England, the local authority with responsibility for the area from which the goods are dispatched;
  (*c*) in the case of a SUCB dispatched from a place outside England, in the course of the delivery of goods to a person in England, the local authority with responsibility for the area for which the goods are destined.
(3) In this article, "local authority" means, in relation to—
  (*a*) the City of London, the Common Council for the City of London;
  (*b*) an area in the rest of London, the London borough council for that area;
  (*c*) the Isles of Scilly, the Council of the Isles of Scilly;
  (*d*) an area in the rest of England, the county council for that area or where there is no county council for that area, the district council for that area.

6 Breach

A seller breaches this Order if, without reasonable cause, the seller—

(*a*) fails to—

(i) charge in accordance with article 3;

(ii) keep records in accordance with paragraph 1 of Schedule 3; or

(iii) supply records in accordance with paragraph 2 of Schedule 3; or

(*b*) gives false or misleading information to, or otherwise obstructs or fails to assist, an administrator exercising its functions under this Order.

7 Powers of enforcement

(1) An administrator may, for the purpose of enforcing this Order—

(*a*) enter a seller's premises at any reasonable time;

(*b*) inspect a seller's goods;

(*c*) make test purchases of a seller's goods;

(*d*) require a seller to produce documents or to provide information;

(*e*) question a seller or officers or employees of a seller.

(2) An administrator may only exercise the powers in paragraph (1)(*d*) or (*e*) if it reasonably believes that a breach has occurred.

(3) An administrator seeking to exercise a power under paragraph (1) must produce evidence of identity and authority if requested by a person who is, or appears to be—

(*a*) the seller, or an officer or employee of the seller;

(*b*) the owner or occupier of any premises in which the administrator seeks to exercise the power concerned.

(4) Nothing in paragraph (1) compels the production of any document of which—

(*a*) in England and Wales or Northern Ireland, that person would on grounds of legal professional privilege be entitled to withhold production on an order for discovery in an action in the County Court or High Court;

(*b*) in Scotland, that person would on grounds of confidentiality of communications be entitled to withhold production on an order for the production of documents in an action in the Court of Session.

(5) In this article, "premises" means premises other than those used wholly or mainly as a private dwelling.

8 Duties to report and publish guidance

Schedule 4 (reporting and guidance) has effect.

PART 4

SANCTIONS, APPEALS ETC

9 Power to impose fixed monetary penalty

(1) An administrator may by notice impose a fixed monetary penalty on a seller if satisfied on the balance of probabilities that a breach has occurred.

(2) Schedule 5 (fixed monetary penalties: amounts and procedure) has effect.

10 Power to impose one or more discretionary requirements

(1) An administrator may by notice impose one or more discretionary requirements on a seller if satisfied on the balance of probabilities that a breach has occurred.

(2) An administrator may only exercise the power conferred by paragraph (1) in relation to a case if a discretionary requirement has not been imposed on the seller on a previous occasion in relation to the same act or omission.

(3) Schedule 6 (discretionary requirements: amounts and procedure) has effect.

11 Power to impose non-compliance penalty

(1) If a seller fails to comply with a non-monetary discretionary requirement, an administrator may by notice impose a non-compliance penalty on the seller.

(2) A non-compliance penalty may be imposed irrespective of whether a variable monetary penalty has also been imposed.

(3) The maximum amount which may be imposed in any case is £5,000.

(4) Schedule 7 (non-compliance penalties: procedure) has effect.

12 Power to recover costs

(1) An administrator may serve a notice (an "enforcement costs recovery notice") on a seller on whom a discretionary requirement is imposed requiring the seller to pay the costs incurred by the administrator in relation to the imposition of the discretionary requirement up to the time of its imposition ("enforcement costs").

(2) In paragraph (1), the reference to "costs" includes—

(*a*) investigation costs;

(*b*) administration costs;

(*c*) costs of obtaining expert advice (including legal advice).

(3) An enforcement costs recovery notice must specify the amount required to be paid and must include information as to—

VAT SIs

(*a*) methods of payment;
(*b*) the date by which payment must be made;
(*c*) the right of appeal;
(*d*) the consequences of failure to make payment by the due date.

(4) The date referred to in paragraph (3)(*b*) must be at least 28 days later than the date on which the enforcement costs recovery notice is served on the seller.

(5) Enforcement costs must be paid by the seller by the date specified in the enforcement costs recovery notice.

(6) To the extent that a decision of an administrator is upheld on appeal, the seller must pay the enforcement costs within the period of 28 days beginning with the day on which the appeal is determined.

(7) An administrator must provide a detailed breakdown of the costs specified in an enforcement costs recovery notice if requested to do so by the seller on whom the notice is served.

(8) A seller is not liable to pay any costs shown by the seller to have been unnecessarily incurred.

13 Power to require publicity

(1) An administrator may give a publicity notice to a seller on whom a civil sanction has been imposed.

(2) A publicity notice means a notice requiring the seller to publicise—
(*a*) the fact that a civil sanction has been imposed;
(*b*) the type of civil sanction;
(*c*) the grounds on which the sanction was imposed;
(*d*) if the sanction was a fixed or variable monetary penalty, the amount of that penalty;
(*e*) if the sanction was a non-monetary discretionary requirement, the nature of the requirement in question.

(3) A publicity notice must—
(*a*) specify the manner of publication required;
(*b*) specify the time for compliance with the notice;
(*c*) require the seller to provide evidence of compliance with the notice within a time specified in the notice.

(4) If a seller fails to comply with a publicity notice within the time specified under paragraph (3)(*b*), the administrator may—
(*a*) publicise the information;
(*b*) recover the costs of doing so from the seller.

(5) Where an administrator publicises information under paragraph (4)(*a*), it must do so in a way it considers most likely to bring the information to the attention of members of the public in its area.

14 Power to withdraw or amend notice

(1) An administrator may at any time in writing—
(*a*) withdraw a notice of intent or final notice served under Schedule 5;
(*b*) withdraw, or reduce an amount specified in, a notice of intent or final notice relating to a variable monetary penalty served under Schedule 6;
(*c*) amend the steps specified in a notice of intent or final notice relating to a non-monetary discretionary requirement served under Schedule 6 so as to reduce the amount of work necessary to comply with the notice;
(*d*) withdraw, or reduce the amount specified in, a notice of intent or non-compliance penalty notice served under Schedule 7;
(*e*) withdraw, or reduce the amount specified in, an enforcement costs recovery notice served under article 12(1).

(2) An administrator must consult the seller before withdrawing or amending a notice under paragraph (1) save where it is impracticable to do so.

15 Power to recover payments

An administrator may recover the amount of any fixed monetary penalty, variable monetary penalty, non-compliance penalty or enforcement costs as if payable under a court order.

16 Appeals

(1) A seller may appeal on any ground to the First-tier Tribunal against an administrator's decision to—
(*a*) impose a fixed monetary penalty under article 9(1);
(*b*) impose a discretionary requirement under article 10(1);
(*c*) impose a non-compliance penalty under article 11(1);
(*d*) require payment of costs under article 12(1).

(2) A requirement or notice which is the subject of an appeal is suspended pending the determination or withdrawal of the appeal.

(3) The First-tier Tribunal may, in relation to the imposition of a requirement or service of a notice under this Order—
(*a*) withdraw the requirement or notice;

(*b*) confirm the requirement or notice;
(*c*) take such steps as the administrator could have taken in relation to the act or omission giving rise to the requirement or notice;
(*d*) remit the decision whether to confirm the requirement or notice, or any matter relating to that decision, to the administrator.

17 Amendment of Schedule 3 to the Regulatory Enforcement and Sanctions Act 2008

In Schedule 3 to the Regulatory Enforcement and Sanctions Act 2008 (enactments specified for purposes of section 4(1): definition of "relevant function"), at the appropriate place insert—

"Single Use Carrier Bags Charges (England) Order 2015 (SI 2015/776)".

18 Review

(1) Before 5th October 2015, the Secretary of State must—
(*a*) complete a review of industry standards for the biodegradability of lightweight plastic material; and
(*b*) lay a copy of a report before Parliament setting out the conclusions of the review, in particular—
(i) whether it appears to the Secretary of State that there exists an industry standard appropriate for the purposes of an exclusion from the obligations specified in Part 2 on grounds of biodegradability; and
(ii) if so, how that exclusion would be implemented.

(2) Before 5th October 2020, the Secretary of State must—
(*a*) carry out a review of this Order;
(*b*) set out the conclusions of the review in a report; and
(*c*) publish the report.

(3) The report in paragraph (2) must in particular—
(*a*) set out the objectives intended to be achieved by the regulatory system established by this Order;
(*b*) assess the extent to which those objectives are achieved;
(*c*) assess whether those objectives remain appropriate and, if so, the extent to which they could be achieved with a system that imposes less regulation.

19 Transitional and saving provision

Article 1(d) does not have effect in relation to the requirement to—
(*a*) keep a record in accordance with paragraph 1(3) of Schedule 3, in so far as the record relates to the reporting year beginning with 7th April 2022 ("the final year");
(*b*) supply a record in accordance with paragraph 2 of Schedule 3, in so far as the record relates to the final year;
(*c*) publish a record in accordance with paragraph 1 of Schedule 4, in so far as the record relates to the final year;
(*d*) publish a report in accordance with paragraph 2 of Schedule 4, in so far as the report relates to the period beginning with 5th October 2020 and ending with 4th October 2022.

SCHEDULE 1
SELLERS

Article 2

Meaning

1 A seller means a person who sells goods and employs 250 or more employees on the first day of a reporting year.

Number of employees of a person

2 (1) For the purposes of this Schedule, the number of employees of a person is taken to be the number of that person's full-time equivalent employees.

(2) The number of full-time equivalent employees of a person is calculated as follows—

TH/37.5

where TH is the total number of hours per week for which all the employees of the person are contracted to work.

Employees

3 (1) In this Schedule, "employee" means an individual who has entered into or works under a contract of employment.

(2) In sub-paragraph (1), "contract of employment" means a contract of service, whether express or implied, and (if it is express) whether oral or in writing.

SCHEDULE 2
SINGLE USE CARRIER BAGS

Article 2

Meaning

1 A SUCB means an unused bag made of lightweight plastic material with handles, other than an excluded bag.

Excluded bags

2 (1) The following are excluded bags—

Name	Description
(*a*) Unwrapped food bag	A bag intended to be used solely to contain wholly or partly unwrapped food for human or animal consumption.
(*b*) Unwrapped loose seeds bag	A bag intended to be used solely to contain wholly or partly unwrapped loose seeds, bulbs, corns, rhizomes, flowers or goods contaminated by soil.
(*c*) Unwrapped blades bag	A bag intended to be used solely to contain wholly or partly unwrapped axes, knives, knife blades or razor blades.
(*d*) Prescription-only medicine bag	A bag intended to be used solely to contain a prescription-only medicine, a pharmacy medicine or a listed appliance sold in accordance with a prescription issued by a doctor, dentist, supplementary prescriber, nurse independent prescriber, independent nurse prescriber, optometrist independent prescriber, pharmacist independent prescriber or EEA health professional.
(*e*) Uncooked meat food bag	A bag intended to be used solely to contain uncooked fish or fish products, meat or meat products or poultry or poultry products.
(*f*) Live aquatic creatures bag	A bag intended to be used solely to contain live aquatic creatures in water.
(*g*) Returnable multiple reuse bag	A bag which is sold for an amount not less than the minimum amount specified in article 3 and which— (i) is intended to be returnable to the seller from whom it was purchased to be replaced free of charge; (ii) is made from material the thickness of which is not less than 50 microns but not greater than 70 microns; and (iii) disregarding the width of any gussets, or the height of any handles extending above the main body of the bag— (*aa*) has a width and height greater (in each case) than 404 mm; and (*bb*) has a width or height greater (in either case) than 439 mm.
(*h*) Woven plastic bag	A bag the material of which is made by interlacing long threads passing in one direction with others at a right angle to them.
(*I*) Transit goods bag	A bag which is intended to be used to carry goods in a transit place.

(2) For the purposes of determining whether a bag falls within the description in paragraph 2(1)(*a*), (*b*), (*c*), (*d*) or (*e*), the fact that the bag may be intended to be used to contain items referred to in the description relating to any other of those bags is to be disregarded.

(3) In sub-paragraph (1)—

"dentist" means a person registered in the dentists register kept under section 14 of the Dentists Act 1984;

"doctor", "nurse independent prescriber", "optometrist independent prescriber", "pharmacist independent prescriber" and "supplementary prescriber" have the meaning given in regulation 8(1) of the Human Medicines Regulations 2012;

"EEA health professional" has the meaning given in regulation 213(1) of the Human Medicines Regulations 2012;

"independent nurse prescriber" has the meaning given in regulation 2(1) of the National Health Service (Pharmaceutical and Local Pharmaceutical Services) Regulations 2013;

"listed appliance" means a listed appliance within the meaning of—

(*a*) section 80 of the National Health Service (Wales) Act 2006;

(*b*) Article 63 of the Health and Personal Social Services (Northern Ireland) Order 1972;

(*c*) section 27 of the National Health Service (Scotland) Act 1978; or

(*d*) section 126 of the National Health Service Act 2006;

"pharmacy medicine" and "prescription-only medicine" have the meaning given in regulation 5(3) and (5) of the Human Medicines Regulations 2012;

"transit place" means on board a ship, train, aircraft, coach or bus, or in an area designated by the Secretary of State as a security restricted area under section 11A of the Aviation Security Act 1982.

VAT SIs

SCHEDULE 3
RECORDS

Article 4

Record-keeping

1 (1) A seller must keep a record in relation to a reporting year if required to charge in that year in accordance with article 3.

(2) The record must include the following information—

(*a*) the number of SUCBs supplied by the seller during the reporting year;

(*b*) in relation to those bags—

(i) the gross proceeds of the charge;

(ii) the amount of any VAT received by way of the gross proceeds of the charge;

(iii) the amount of any reasonable costs;

(iv) the apportionment between any different kinds of reasonable costs;

(v) the net proceeds of the charge;

(vi) the uses to which the net proceeds of the charge have been put.

(3) The seller must keep the record for a period of three years beginning with 31st May in the reporting year following that to which the record relates.

(4) The amounts specified for the purposes of the definition of "net proceeds of the charge" in paragraph 7(4) of Schedule 6 to the Climate Change Act 2008 are—

(*a*) the amount of any VAT received by way of the gross proceeds of the charge; and

(*b*) the amount of any reasonable costs.

(5) For the purposes of sub-paragraph (3), in relation to the reporting year beginning with 7th April 2022, the period of three years begins with 31st May 2023.

(6) In this paragraph, "reasonable costs" means costs reasonably incurred completing transactions, communicating information, obtaining expert advice or carrying on similar activities to enable the seller to comply with this Order.

Supply of records

2 (1) The seller must supply a copy of the record to the Secretary of State.

(2) The record must be supplied—

(*a*) on or before 31st May in the reporting year following that to which the record relates;

(*b*) in an electronic or other format reasonably required by the Secretary of State for the purposes of publishing the records or producing statistics.

(3) If a person writes to the seller asking them to supply the record during the retention period, the seller must provide a copy of that record to the person who requested it within the period of 28 days beginning with the day on which the written request is received.

(4) For the purposes of sub-paragraph (2)(*a*), in relation to the reporting year beginning with 7th April 2022, the date on or before which the record must be supplied is 31st May 2023.
(5) In sub-paragraph (3), "the retention period" means the three-year period for which the record must be retained in accordance with paragraph 1(3) and (if applicable) (5).

Meaning of reporting year

3 For the purposes of this Schedule, each of the following is a "reporting year"—
(*a*) the period beginning with 5th October 2015 and ending with 6th April 2016;
(*b*) each period of 12 months beginning with 7th April in the period of 6 years beginning with 7th April 2016;
(*c*) the period beginning with 7th April 2022 and ending with 4th October 2022.

SCHEDULE 4
REPORTING AND GUIDANCE

Article 8

Publication of records

1 (1) The Secretary of State must publish every record supplied to the Secretary of State in accordance with paragraph 2 of Schedule 3 on or before 31st July in the reporting year following that to which the record relates.
(2) The record must be published by way of a notice displayed in a prominent position on a website.
(3) The record must remain published for a period of one year beginning with the day after the date of its publication in accordance with sub-paragraph (1).
(4) For the purposes of sub-paragraph (1), in relation to the reporting year beginning with 7th April 2022, the date on or before which the report must be published is 31st July 2023.

Publication of report about enforcement action

2 (1) An administrator must publish a report for the period—
(*a*) beginning with 5th October 2015 and ending with 4th October 2017;
(*b*) beginning with 5th October 2017 and ending with 4th October 2020; and
(*c*) beginning with 5th October 2020 and ending with 4th October 2022.
(2) The report must be published, in relation to the period beginning with—
(*a*) 5th October 2015, on or before 31st May 2018;
(*b*) 5th October 2017, on or before 31st May 2021;
(*c*) 5th October 2020, on or before 31st May 2023.
(3) The report must be—
(*a*) published in a prominent position on the administrator's website; and
(*b*) available for inspection at the administrator's office.
(4) The report must specify—
(*a*) the cases in which a civil sanction has been imposed;
(*b*) where the civil sanction is a fixed monetary penalty, the cases in which liability to the penalty has been discharged pursuant to paragraph 3 of Schedule 5.
(5) The report must remain published, and be available for inspection at the administrator's office, for a period of three years beginning with the day after the date of its publication in accordance with sub-paragraph (2).
(6) In sub-paragraph (4)(*a*), the reference to the imposition of a civil sanction does not include cases where a civil sanction was imposed but overturned on appeal.
(7) An administrator must not publish a report where the Secretary of State notifies the administrator in writing not to do so.

Guidance as to use of civil sanctions

3 (1) An administrator must publish guidance about its use of civil sanctions under this Order.
(2) The guidance must contain—
(*a*) in relation to a fixed monetary penalty, information as to—
(i) the circumstances in which the penalty is likely to be imposed;
(ii) the circumstances in which the penalty may not be imposed;
(iii) the amount of the penalty;
(iv) how liability for the penalty may be discharged and the effect of discharge;
(v) the right to make representations and objections;
(vi) the right of appeal;
(*b*) in relation to a discretionary requirement, information as to—

(i) the circumstances in which the requirement is likely to be imposed;
(ii) the circumstances in which the requirement may not be imposed;
(iii) in the case of a variable monetary penalty, the matters likely to be taken into account by the administrator in determining the amount of the penalty (including, where relevant, any discounts for voluntary reporting of non-compliance);
(iv) the right to make representations and objections;
(v) the right of appeal.

(3) An administrator must revise the guidance where appropriate.
(4) An administrator must publish revised guidance within the period of 28 days beginning with the day on which the guidance is revised.
(5) Before publishing any guidance or revised guidance, an administrator must consult the Secretary of State and the British Retail Consortium.
(6) An administrator must have regard to the guidance or revised guidance in exercising its functions under this Order.

SCHEDULE 5

FIXED MONETARY PENALTIES: AMOUNTS AND PROCEDURE

Article 9(2)

PART 1

FIXED MONETARY PENALTIES: AMOUNTS

1 The amount of penalty which may be imposed as a fixed monetary penalty in any case is as follows—

Breach	*Amount*
Fails to comply with the requirement to charge in accordance with article 3	£200
Fails to keep records in accordance with paragraph 1 of Schedule 3	£100
Fails to supply records in accordance with paragraph 2 of Schedule 3	£100

PART 2

FIXED MONETARY PENALTIES: PROCEDURE

Notice of intent

2 (1) An administrator who proposes to impose a fixed monetary penalty on a seller must serve a notice of intent on that seller.
(2) But an administrator may not serve a notice of intent on a seller in relation to a breach where a discretionary requirement has been imposed on the seller in relation to the same breach.
(3) A notice of intent must—

(*a*) state the amount of the penalty;
(*b*) offer the seller the opportunity to discharge its liability by paying the amount specified in paragraph 3 within the period of 28 days beginning with the day on which the notice was received;
(*c*) include information as to—
(i) the grounds for the proposal to impose the penalty;
(ii) the right to make representations and objections;
(iii) the 28-day period within which representations and objections may be made;
(iv) the circumstances in which the administrator may not impose the penalty;
(v) methods of payment.

Discharge of liability following notice of intent

3 (1) A seller's liability to a fixed monetary penalty is discharged by paying the specified sum within the period of 28 days beginning with the day on which the notice of intent to which it relates is received.
(2) The specified sum is—

Breach	*Sum*

Fails to comply with the requirement to charge in accordance with article 3	£100
Otherwise	£50

Making representations and objections

4 (1) This paragraph applies if a seller does not discharge its liability to a fixed monetary penalty by payment of the amount specified in paragraph 3(1).
(2) Within the period of 28 days beginning with the day on which the notice of intent is received, the seller may make written representations and objections to the administrator in relation to the proposed imposition of the penalty.

Decision whether to impose a fixed monetary penalty

5 (1) After the end of the 28-day period for making representations and objections under paragraph 4(2), the administrator must decide whether to impose the fixed monetary penalty.
(2) The administrator must take into consideration any representations or objections made by the seller under paragraph 4(2).
(3) An administrator may not impose the penalty if the administrator discovers that its proposal to impose the penalty was based on an error of fact, wrong in law or unreasonable.
(4) Where an administrator decides to impose the penalty it must do so by serving the final notice on the seller.

Contents of final notice

6 The final notice must include information as to—
(a) the grounds for imposing the fixed monetary penalty;
(b) the administrator's response to any representation and objections made by the seller;
(c) the amount of the penalty;
(d) methods of payment;
(e) the period of 56 days within which payment must be made;
(f) the right to, and effect of, early payment under paragraph 8;
(g) the right of appeal;
(h) the consequences of non-payment, including the imposition of a late payment penalty in accordance with paragraph 9.

Payment

7 (1) A fixed monetary penalty must be paid by a seller within the period of 56 days beginning with the day on which the final notice imposing it is received.
(2) If a decision to impose a penalty is upheld on appeal, the seller must pay the penalty within the period of 28 days beginning with the day on which the appeal is determined.

Early payment discount

8 A seller may discharge its liability to a fixed monetary penalty by paying 50% of the amount of the penalty within the period of 28 days beginning with the day on which the final notice imposing it is received.

Late payment penalty

9 If a fixed monetary penalty is not paid within the period specified in paragraph 7(1) or (if applicable) (2), the amount of the penalty is increased by 50%.

SCHEDULE 6
DISCRETIONARY REQUIREMENTS: AMOUNTS AND PROCEDURE

Article 10(3)

PART 1
VARIABLE MONETARY PENALTIES: MAXIMUM AMOUNTS

1 The maximum amount of variable monetary penalty which may be imposed in any case is as follows—

Breach	*Maximum amount*
Fails to comply with the requirement to charge in accordance with article 3	£5,000
Fails to keep records in accordance with paragraph 1 of Schedule 3	£5,000
Fails to supply records in accordance with paragraph 2 of Schedule 3	£5,000
Gives false or misleading information to, or otherwise obstructs or fails to assist, an administrator	£20,000

PART 2

DISCRETIONARY REQUIREMENTS: PROCEDURE

Notice of intent

2 (1) Where an administrator proposes to impose a discretionary requirement on a seller, the administrator must serve a notice of intent on that seller.

(2) But an administrator may not serve a notice of intent on a seller in relation to a breach where—

(*a*) a fixed monetary penalty has been imposed on the seller in relation to the same breach; or

(*b*) the seller has discharged liability to a fixed monetary penalty in relation that breach pursuant to paragraph 3(1) of Schedule 5.

(3) The notice of intent must—

(*a*) if the administrator proposes to impose a non-monetary discretionary requirement—

(i) specify the steps that the administrator proposes the seller be required to take;

(ii) specify the time period within which the administrator proposes that those steps are to be taken;

(*b*) if the administrator proposes to impose a variable monetary penalty, specify the amount of penalty proposed;

(*c*) include information as to—

(i) the grounds for the proposal to impose the discretionary requirement;

(ii) the right to make representations and objections;

(iii) the 28-day period within which representations and objections may be made;

(iv) the circumstances in which the administrator may not impose the discretionary requirements;

(v) in the case of a variable monetary penalty, methods of payment.

Making representations and objections

3 Within the period of 28 days beginning with the day on which the notice of intent is received, the seller may make written representations and objections to the administrator in relation to the proposed imposition of the discretionary requirement.

Decision whether to impose discretionary requirements

4 (1) After the end of the 28-day period for making representations and objections under paragraph 3, the administrator must decide whether to impose—

(*a*) the discretionary requirement with or without modifications; or

(*b*) any other discretionary requirement that the administrator has power to impose under this Schedule.

(2) The administrator must take into consideration any representations or objections made by the seller under paragraph 3.

(3) An administrator may not impose a discretionary requirement if the administrator discovers that its proposal to impose the requirement was—

(*a*) based on an error of fact;

(*b*) wrong in law;

(*c*) in relation to the amount of any variable monetary penalty, unreasonable;

(*d*) in relation to the nature of any non-monetary discretionary requirement, unreasonable;

(*e*) unreasonable for any other reason.

(4) An administrator may not impose a fixed monetary penalty in place of a discretionary requirement.

(5) Where an administrator decides to impose a discretionary requirement it must do so by serving the final notice on the seller.

Contents of a final notice

5 The final notice must include information as to—

(*a*) the grounds for imposing the discretionary requirement;

(*b*) the administrator's response to any representation and objections made by the seller, including any effect on the amount of any variable monetary penalty imposed;

(*c*) where the discretionary requirement is a non-monetary discretionary requirement—

(i) the steps the seller is required to take;

(ii) the period within which those steps must be taken;

(*d*) where the discretionary requirement is a variable monetary penalty—

(i) the amount of the penalty;

(ii) methods of payment;

(iii) the period within which payment must be made;

(iv) the right to, and effect of, early payment under paragraph 7;

(*e*) the right of appeal;

(*f*) the consequences of failing to comply with the notice, including the imposition of a late payment penalty in accordance with paragraph 8.

Payment

6 (1) A variable monetary penalty must be paid by a seller within the period of 56 days beginning with the day on which the final notice imposing it is received.

(2) To the extent that a decision to impose a penalty is upheld on appeal, the seller must pay the penalty within the period of 28 days beginning with the day on which the appeal is determined.

Early payment discount

7 A seller may discharge its liability to a variable monetary penalty by paying 50% of the amount of the penalty within the period of 28 days beginning with the day on which the final notice imposing it is received.

Late payment penalty

8 If a variable monetary penalty is not paid within the period specified in paragraph 6(1) or (if applicable) (2), the amount of the penalty is increased by 50%.

SCHEDULE 7

NON-COMPLIANCE PENALTIES: PROCEDURE

Article 11(4)

Notice of intent

1 (1) Where an administrator proposes to impose a non-compliance penalty on a seller, the administrator must serve a notice of intent on that seller.

(2) The notice of intent must include information as to—

(*a*) the grounds for the proposal to impose the penalty;

(*b*) the amount of the penalty proposed;

(*c*) methods of payment;

(*d*) the date by which payment would be due;

(*e*) the consequences of failure to make payment by the due date;

(*f*) the right to make representations and objections;

(*g*) the 28-day period within which representations and objections may be made;

(*h*) the circumstances (if any) in which the administrator may reduce the amount of the penalty proposed.

Making representations and objections

2 Within the period of 28 days beginning with the day on which the notice of intent is received, the seller may make written representations and objections to the administrator in relation to the proposed imposition of a non-compliance penalty.

Decision whether to impose a non-compliance penalty

3 (1) After the end of the 28-day period for making representations and objections under paragraph 2, the administrator must decide whether to impose the non-compliance penalty with or without modifications.

(2) An administrator may decide not to impose a non-compliance penalty if the administrator considers that in all the circumstances of the case it would be inexpedient to do so.

(3) The administrator must take into consideration any representations or objections made by the seller under paragraph 2.

(4) Where an administrator decides to impose a non-compliance penalty it must do so by serving a notice (a "non-compliance penalty notice") on the seller.

Contents of a non-compliance penalty notice

4 (1) A non-compliance penalty notice must include information as to—

(*a*) the grounds for imposing the non-compliance penalty;

(*b*) the administrator's response to any representations and objections made by the seller, including any effect on the amount of the penalty imposed;

(*c*) the amount of the penalty;

(*d*) methods of payment;

(*e*) the date by which payment must be made;

(*f*) the right of appeal;

(*g*) the consequences of failure to make payment by the due date.

(2) A non-compliance penalty must be paid by a seller within the period of 56 days beginning with the date on which the notice imposing it was received.

(3) If the requirements of the non-monetary discretionary requirement are complied with before the 56-day period expires, the liability to pay the non-compliance penalty is discharged.

(4) If a non-compliance penalty notice is the subject of an appeal, then to the extent that the notice is upheld, the penalty must be paid by the seller within the period of 28 days beginning with the day on which the appeal is determined.

Late payment penalty

5 If a fixed monetary penalty is not paid within the period specified in paragraph 4(2) or (if applicable) (4) the amount of the penalty is increased by 50%.

Value Added Tax EU legislation

VAT EU

Contents

Note—The following list comprises EU legislation currently in force and reproduced on the following pages. See below for the full list in chronological order showing legislation which is currently in force, repealed or amending.

2013 establishing an action programme to improve the operation of taxation systems in the European Union for the period 2014-2020 (Fiscalis 2020) and repealing Decision No 1482/2007/EC.

17/2014: Commission Implementing Regulation of 10 January 2014 laying down the standardised form for the notification for a special measure under the Quick Reaction Mechanism against VAT fraud.

EU Decisions

89/466: Council Decision of 18 July 1989 authorising derogation from Council Directive 77/388/EEC art 11(A)(1)(*b*).

89/534: Council Decision authorising derogation from Council Directive 77/388/EEC art 11A(1)(*a*).

92/621: Council Decision of 21 December 1992 authorising application of a particular measure in accordance with Council Directive 77/388/EEC art 22(12)(*b*).

93/609: Council Decision of 22 November 1993 authorising derogation from Council Directive 77/388/EEC art 22(12)(*a*).

95/252: Council Decision of 29 June 1995 authorising derogation from Council Directive 77/388/EEC arts 6 and 17.

2006/659: Council Decision of 25 September 2006 authorising the United Kingdom to introduce a special measure derogating from Articles 5(6) and 11(A)(1)(*b*) of Directive 77/388/EEC on the harmonisation of the laws of the Member States relating to turnover taxes.

2009/439: Council Decision of 5 May 2009 amending Decision 2007/250/EC authorising the United Kingdom to introduce a special measure derogating from Article 193 of Directive 2006/112/EC on the common system of value added tax.

2012/C 198/05: Commission Decision of 3 July 2012 setting up the EU VAT Forum.

2013/52/EU: Council Decision of 22 January 2013 authorising enhanced cooperation in the area of financial transaction tax.

Commission Recommendation

2012/771/EU: Commission Recommendation of 6 December 2012 regarding measures intended to encourage third countries to apply minimum standards of good governance in tax matters.

Chronological list of EU legislation

Note—

This list comprises amending or repealed legislation and legislation currently in force. Amending and repealed titles are printed in italics.

See above for the shorter list comprising legislation currently in force and reproduced on the following pages.

1957

Treaty on the Functioning of the EU (previously the Treaty Establishing the European Community).

1967

EC 1967/67/227: *First Council Directive of 11 April 1967* (repealed by Council Directive 2006/112/EC).

EC 1967/ 67/228: *Second Council Directive of 11 2April 1967 on the harmonisation of legislation of Member States concerning turnover taxes Structure and procedures for application of the common system of value added tax* (repealed by Council Directive 77/388)

1969

EC 1969/69/169: *Council Directive of 28 May 1969 on the harmonisation of provisions laid down by law, regulation or administrative action relating to exemption from turnover tax on imports in international travel.* (repealed by Council Directive 2007/74/EC)

EC 1969/69/463: *Third Council Directive of 9 December 1969* (amends Directive 67/227)

1976

EC 1976/76/308: *Council Directive of 15 March 1976 on mutual assistance for the recovery of claims resulting from operations forming part of the system of financing the European Agricultural Guidance and Guarantee Fund, and of agricultural levies and customs duties [and in respect of value added tax].* (repealed by Council Directive 2008/55/EC).

1977

EC 1977/77/388: *Sixth Council Directive of 17 May 1977* (repealed by Council Directive 2006/112/EC).

EC 1977/77/799: *Council Directive of 19 December 1977 concerning mutual assistance by the competent authorities of the Member States in the fields of direct taxation and value added tax* (repealed).

1978

EC 1978/ 78/1035: *Council Directive of 19 December 1978 on the exemption from taxes of imports of small consignments of goods of a non-commercial character from third countries* (repealed).

1979

EC 1979/79/1070: *Council Directive of 6 December 1979* (amends Directive 77/799).

EC 1979/79/1072: *Eighth Council Directive of 6 December 1979* (repealed by Council Directive 2008/9/EC)

1980

EC 1980/1224/80: *Council Regulation of 28 May 1980 on the valuation of goods for customs purposes* (repealed by Council Regulation 2913/92 art 251).

EC 1980/1494/80: *Commission Regulation of 11 June 1980 on interpretative notes and generally accepted accounting principles for the purposes of customs value* (repealed by Commission Regulation 2454/93 art 913).

EC 1980/1495/80: *Commission Regulation of 11 June 1980 implementing certain provisions of Articles 1, 3 and 8 of Council Regulations (EEC) No 1224/80 on the valuation of goods for customs purposes* (repealed by Commission Regulation 2454/93 art 913).

EC 1980/1496/80: *Commission Regulation of 11 June 1980 on the declaration of particulars relating to customs value and on documents to be furnished* (repealed by Commission Regulation 2454/93 art 913).

EC 1980/3177/80: *Commission Regulation of 5 December 1980 on the place of introduction to be taken into consideration in applying article 14(2) of Council Regulation (EEC) No 1224/80 on the valuation of goods for customs purposes* (repealed by Commission Regulation 2454/93 art 913).

EC 1980/3179/80: *Commission Regulation of 5 December 1980 on postal charges to be taken into consideration when determining the customs value of goods sent by post* (repealed by Commission Regulation 2454/93 art 913).

1981

EC 1981/1577/81: *Commission Regulation of 12 June 1981 establishing a system of simplified procedures for the determination of the customs value of certain perishable goods* (repealed by Commission Regulation 2454/93 art 913).

1983

EC 1983/83/181: *Council Directive of 28 March 1983 determining the scope of Article 14 (1) (d) of Directive 77/388/EEC as regards exemption from value added tax on the final importation of certain goods.* (repealed by Council Directive 2009/132/EC)

EC 1983/3158/83: *Commission Regulation of 9 November 1983 on the incidence of royalties and licence fees in customs value* (repealed by Commission Regulation 2454/93 art 913).

1984

EC 1984/84/386: *Tenth Council Directive of 31 July 1984* (amends Directive 77/388) (repealed by Council Directive 2006/112/EC)

EC 1984/2151/84: *Council Regulation of 23 July 1984 on the customs territory of the Community* (repealed by Council Regulation 2913/92 art 251).

1985

EC 1985/1766/85: *Commission Regulation of 27 June 1985 on the rates of exchange to be used in the determination of customs value* (repealed by Commission Regulation 2454/93 art 913).

1986

EC 1986/86/356: *Council Decision of 21 July 1986 authorising the UK to apply flat-rate measures in respect of the non-deductible VAT charged on fuel expenditure in company cars* (Repealed by Council Decision 2006/659/EC art 4, with effect from 30 April 2007)

EC 1986/86/560: Thirteenth Council Directive of 17 November 1986.

1989

EC 1989/ 89/465: *Eighteenth Council Directive of 18 July 1989* (repealed).

EC 1989/89/466: Council Decision of 18 July 1989 authorising derogation from Council Directive 77/388/EEC art 11(A)(1)(*b*).

EC 1989/89/534: Council Decision authorising derogation from Council Directive 77/388/EEC art 11A(1)(*a*).

1991

EC 1991/91/680: Council Directive of 16 December 1991 supplementing the common

VAT EU

system of VAT and amending Directive 77/388/EEC with a view to the abolition of fiscal frontiers.

EC 1991/3330/91: *Council Regulation of 7 November 1991 on the statistics relating to the trading of goods between member States* (repealed by European Parliament and Council Regulation 638/2004 art 15).

1992

EC 1992/92/77: *Council Directive of 19 October 1992* (amends Directive 77/388) (repealed by Council Directive 2006/112/EC).

EC 1992/ 92/111: *Council Directive of 14 December 1992 amending Directive 77/388/EEC and introducing simplification measures with regard to value added tax* (repealed).

EC 1992/92/546: *Council Decision of 23 November 1992 authorising derogation from Council Directive 77/388/EEC art 28e(1).* (spent)

EC 1992/92/621: Council Decision of 21 December 1992 authorising application of a particular measure in accordance with Council Directive 77/388/EEC art 22(12)(*b*).

EC 1992/2256/92: *Commission Regulation of 31 July 1992 on statistical thresholds for the statistics on trade between member States* (repealed by Commission Regulation (EC) 1901/2000 art 49).

EC 1992/2913/92: *Council Regulation of 12 October 1992 establishing the Community Customs Code* (repealed 23 June 2013 by Regulation 450/2008/EC).

EC 1992/3046/92: Commission Regulation of 22 October 1992 laying down provisions implementing and amending Council Regulation (EEC) No 3330/91 on the statistics relating to the trading of goods between Member States.

EC 1992/ 3590/92: *Commission Regulation of 11 December 1992 concerning the statistical information media for statistics on trade between Member States* (repealed).

EC 1992/3903/92: *Commission Regulation of 21 December 1992 on air transport costs to be included in customs value* (repealed by Commission Regulation 2454/93 art 913).

1993

EC 1993/93/111: *Council Decision of 15 February 1993 authorising derogation from Council Directive 77/388/EEC art 17.* (spent)

EC 1993/93/204: *Council Decision of 5 April 1993 authorising derogation from Council Directive 77/388/EEC arts 5(8) and 21(1)(a).* (spent)

EC 1993/93/563: Council Decision of 25 October 1993 authorising derogation from Council Directive 77/388/EEC arts 2(1) and 17 (spent).

EC 1993/93/609: Council Decision of 22 November 1993 authorising derogation from Council Directive 77/388/EEC art 22(12)(*a*).

EC 1993/2454/93: Commission Regulation of 2 July 1993 laying down provisions for the implementation of Council Regulation No 2913/92/EEC establishing the Community Customs Code.

1994

EC 1994/94/4: Council Directive of 14 February 1994 amending Directives 69/169/EEC and 77/388/EEC—allowances for travellers from third countries and limits on tax-free purchases in intra-Community travel.

EC 1994/94/5: *Council Directive of 14 February 1994 supplementing the common system of VAT and amending Directive 77/388/EEC with regard to special arrangements applicable to second-hand goods, works of art, collectors' items and antiques* (repealed).

1995

EC 1995/95/7: *Council Directive of 10 April 1995 amending Directive 77/388/EEC and introducing new simplification measures with regard to VAT—scope of certain exemptions and practical arrangements for implementing them* (amends Directive 77/388/EEC) (repealed by Council Directive 2006/112/EC).

EC 1995/95/252: Council Decision of 29 June 1995 authorising derogation from Council Directive 77/388/EEC arts 6 and 17.

1997

ECDEC97/214: *Council Decision of 17 March 1997 authorising derogation from Council Directive 77/388/EEC art 9* (spent).

ECDEC97/375: *Council Decision of 9 June 1997 authorising derogation from Council Directive 77/388/EEC art 17* (repealed).

EC 1997/97/860: *Commission Regulation of 14 May 1997 amending Regulation (EEC) No 3046/92 with regard to the reporting of the value of goods* (repealed).

EC 1997/97/1427: Commission Regulation of 23 July 1997 amending Regulation (EEC) No 2454/93 laying down provisions for the implementation of Council Regulation (EEC) No

2913/92 establishing the Community Customs Code.

1998

EC 1998/98/23: *Council Decision of 19 December 1997 authorising the United Kingdom to extend application of a measure derogating from Article 28e(1) of the Sixth Council Directive 77/388/EEC on the harmonisation of the laws of the Member States relating to turnover taxes.* (repealed by Council Directive 2006/69/EC)

EC 1998/75/98: Commission Regulation of 12 January 1998 amending Regulation (EEC) No 2454/93 laying down provisions for the implementation of Council Regulation (EEC) No 2913/92 establishing the Community Customs Code.

EC 1998/98/94/EC: Council Directive of 14 December 1998 amending Directive 94/4/EC and extending the temporary derogation applicable to Germany and Austria.

EC 1998/98/80: *Council Directive of 12 October 1998 supplementing the common system of value added tax and amending Directive 77/388/EEC—special scheme for investment gold* (repealed by Council Directive 2006/112/EC).

EC 1998/98/198: *Council Decision of 9 March 1998 authorising the United Kingdom to extend application of a measure derogating from Articles 6 and 17 of the Sixth Council Directive (77/388/EEC) on the harmonisation of the laws of the Member States relating to turnover taxes.* (spent)

EC 1998/1677/98: Commission Regulation of 29 July 1998 amending Regulation (EEC) No 2454/93 laying down provisions for the implementation of Council Regulation (EEC) No 2913/92 establishing the Community Customs Code.

EC 1998/98/2535: *Commission Regulation of 26 November 1998 amending Regulation (EEC) No 3046/92 with regard to information provided by the tax authorities* (repealed).

1999

EC 1999/99/49/EC: *Council Directive of 25 May 1999 amending, with regard to the level of standard rate, Directive 77/388/EEC on the common system of VAT* (repealed by Council Directive 2006/112/EC).

EC 1999/99/59/EC: *Council Directive of 17 June 1999 amending with regard to the VAT arrangements applicable to telecommunication services, Directive 77/388/EEC* (repealed by Council Directive 2006/112/EC).

EC 1999/99/79: Council Decision of 18 January 1999 amending Article 3 of Decision 98/198/EC.

2000

EC 2000/ 17/EC: *Council Directive of 30 March 2000 amending Directive 77/388/EEC on the common system of VAT: transitional provisions granted to the Republic of Austria and the Portuguese Republic* (repealed by Council Directive 2006/112/EC).

EC 2000/ 65/EC: *Council Directive of 17 October 2000 amending Directive 77/388/EEC as regards the determination of the person liable for payment of VAT* (repealed by Council Directive 2006/112/EC).

EC 2000/ 185/EC: *Council Decision of 28 February 2000 authorising Member States to apply a reduced rate of VAT to certain labour-intensive services in accordance with the procedure provided for in Article 28(6) of Directive 77/388/EEC.* (spent)

EC 2000/ 435/EC: Council Decision of 29 June 2000 amending Decisions 97/375/EC, 97/510/EC, 98/20/EC, 98/23/EC and 98/161/EC.

EC 2000/ 1602/EC: Commission Regulation of 24 July 2000 amending Regulation 2454/93/EEC laying down provisions for the implementation of Council Regulation 2913/92/EEC establishing the Community Customs Code.

EC 2000/ 2700/EC: *Parliament and Council Regulation amending Council Regulation 2913/92/EEC establishing the Community Customs Code* (implicitly repealed by Regulation 2008/450/EC).

EC 2000/ 2787: Commission Regulation amending Regulation (EEC) No 2454/93 laying down provisions for the implementation of Council Regulation 2913/92/EEC establishing the Community Customs Code.

2001

4/EC: *Council Direction amending the sixth Directive (77/388/EEC) on the common system of value added tax, with regard to the length of time during which the minimum standard rate is to be applied* (repealed by Council Directive 2006/112/EC).

44/EC: *Council Direction amending Directive 76/308/EEC on mutual assistance for the recovery of claims resulting from operations forming part of the system of financing the European Agricultural Guidance and Guarantee Fund, and of agricultural levies and customs duties and in respect of value added tax and certain excise duties* (spent).

115/EC: *Council Directive amending Directive 77/388/EEC with a view to simplifying, modernising and harmonising the conditions laid down for invoicing in respect of value added tax* (repealed by Council Directive 2006/112/EC).

2002

38/EC: *amending and temporarily amending Council Directive 77/388 EEC as regards the value added tax arrangements applicable to radio and television broadcasting services and certain electronically supplied services* (repealed).

92/EC: *amending Directive 77/388/EEC to extend the facility allowing Member States to apply reduced rates of VAT to certain labour-intensive services* (repealed by Council Directive 2006/112/EC).

94/EC: *laying down detailed rules for implementing certain provisions of Council Directive 76/308/EEC on mutual assistance for the recovery of claims relating to certain levies, duties, taxes and other measures* (repealed).

954/EC: *Council Decision of 3 December 2002 extending the period of application of Decision 2000/185/EC authorising Member States to apply a reduced rate of VAT to certain labour-intensive services in accordance with the procedure provided for in Article 28(6) of Directive 77/388/EEC* (spent).

2003

881/EC: Commission Regulation amending Regulation (EEC) No 2454/93 laying down provisions for the implementation of Council Regulation (EEC) No 2913/92 establishing the Community Customs Code.

1798/03: Council Regulation of 7 October 2003 on administrative cooperation in the field of value added tax and repealing Regulation (EEC) No 218/92.

2004

638/04: Regulation of the European Parliament and of the Council of 31 March 2004 on Community statistics relating to the trading of goods between Member States and repealing Council Regulation (EEC) No 3330/91.

1925/04: *Commission Regulation of 29 October 2004 laying down detailed rules for implementing certain provisions of Council Regulation No 1798/2003 concerning administrative cooperation in the field of VAT* (repealed).

1982/04: Commission Regulation of 18 November 2004 implementing Regulation (EC) No 638/2004 of the European Parliament and of the Council on Community statistics relating to the trading of goods between Member States and repealing Commission Regulations (EC) No 1901/2000 and (EEC) No 3590/92.

2005

1777/05: *Council Regulation of 17 October 2005 laying down implementing measures for Directive 77/388/EEC on the common system of value added tax* (spent).

2006

2006/79 Council Directive of 5 October 2006 on the exemption from taxes of imports of small consignments of goods of a non-commercial character from third countries (codified version).

2006/112: Council Directive of 28 November 2006 on the common system of value added tax.

2006/659: Council Decision of 25 September 2006 authorising the United Kingdom to introduce a special measure derogating from Articles 5(6) and 11(A)(1)(*b*) of Directive 77/388/EEC on the harmonisation of the laws of the Member States relating to turnover taxes.

2006/774: *Council Decision of 7 November 2006 authorising certain Member States to apply a reduced rate of VAT to certain labour-intensive services in accordance with the procedure provided for in Article 28(6) of Directive 77/388/EEC* (spent).

2007

2007/133: *Council Decision of 30 January 2007 authorising Estonia, Slovenia, Sweden and the United Kingdom to apply a special measure derogating from Article 167 of Directive 2006/112/EC on the common system of value added tax* (spent).

2007/250 *Council Decision of 16 April 2007 authorising the United Kingdom to introduce a special measure derogating from Article 193 of Directive 2006/112/EC on the common system of value added tax* (spent).

2007/884: *Council Decision of 20 December 2007 authorising the United Kingdom to continue to apply a measure derogating from Articles 26(1)(a), 168 and 169 of Directive 2006/112/EC on the common system of value added tax* (spent on 31 December 2013).

2008

2008/8: Council Directive of 12 February 2008 amending Directive 2006/112/EC as regards the place of supply of services.

2008/9: Council Directive of 12 February 2008 laying down detailed rules for the refund of value added tax, provided for in Directive 2006/112/EC, to taxable persons not established in the Member State of refund but established in another Member State.

2008/55: *Council Directive of 26 May 2008 on mutual assistance for the recovery of claims relating to certain levies, duties, taxes and other measures* (repealed).

67/2008: Commission Regulation of 25 January 2008 amending Regulation (EC) No 3199/93 on the mutual recognition of procedures for the complete denaturing of alcohol for the purposes of exemption from excise duty.

117/2008: Council Directive of 16 December 2008 amending Directive 2006/112/EC on the common system of value added tax to combat tax evasion connected with intra-Community transactions.

143/2008: Council Regulation of 12 February 2008 amending Regulation (EC) No 1798/2003 as regards the introduction of administrative cooperation and the exchange of information concerning the rules relating to the place of supply of services, the special schemes and the refund procedure for value added tax.

450/2008: *Regulation of the European Parliament and of the Council of 23 April 2008 laying down the Community Customs Code (Modernised Customs Code)* (repealed by Regulation 952/2013 of the European Parliament and of the Council of 9 October 2013).

1179/2008: *Commission Regulation of 28 November 2008 laying down detailed rules for implementing certain provisions of Council Directive 2008/55/EC on mutual assistance for the recovery of claims relating to certain levies, duties, taxes and other measures* (repealed by Council Implementing Regulation 2011/1189/EC)

2009

37/2009: Council Regulation of 16 December 2008 amending Regulation (EC) No 1798/2003 on administrative cooperation in the field of value added tax, in order to combat tax evasion connected with intra-Community transactions.

47/2009: Council Directive of 5 May 2009 amending Directive 2006/112/EC as regards reduced rates of value added tax.

69/2009: Council Directive of 25 June 2009 amending Directive 2006/112/EC on the common system of value added tax as regards tax evasion linked to imports.

2009/132: Council Directive of 19 October 2009 determining the scope of Article 143(b) and (c) of Directive 2006/112/EC as regards exemption from value added tax on the final importation of certain goods.

2009/162: Council Directive of 22 December 2009 amending various provisions of Directive 2006/112/EC on the common system of value added tax.

222/2009: Regulation of the European Parliament and of the Council of 11 March 2009 amending Regulation (EC) No 638/2004 on Community statistics relating to the trading of goods between Member States.

2009/439: Council Decision of 5 May 2009 amending Decision 2007/250/EC authorising the United Kingdom to introduce a special measure derogating from Article 193 of Directive 2006/112/EC on the common system of value added tax.

2010

2010/23 Council Directive of 16 March 2010 amending Directive 2006/112/EC on the common system of value added tax, as regards an optional and temporary application of the reverse charge mechanism in relation to supplies of certain services susceptible to fraud (applies until 30 June 2015).

2010/24 Council Directive of 16 March 2010 concerning mutual assistance for the recovery of claims relating to taxes, duties and other measures.

2010/45 Council Directive of 13 July 2010 amending Directive 2006/112/EC on the common system of value added tax as regards the rules on invoicing.

904/2010: Council Regulation of 7 October 2010 on administrative cooperation and combating fraud in the field of value added tax (recast).

2010/66 Council Directive of 14 October 2010 amending Directive 2008/9/EC laying down detailed rules for the refund of value added tax, provided for in Directive 2006/112/EC, to taxable persons not established in the Member State of refund but established in another Member State.

2010/88 Council Directive of 7 December 2010 amending Directive 2006/112/EC on the common system of value added tax, with regard to the duration of the obligation to respect a minimum standard rate.

2011

2011/16 Council Directive of 15 February 2011 on administrative cooperation in the field of taxation and repealing Directive 77/799/EEC.

282/2011: Council Implementing Regulation of 15 March 2011 laying down implementing measures for Directive 2006/112/EC on the common system of value added tax.

1189/2011: Council Implementing Regulation of 18 November 2011 laying down detailed rules in relation to certain provisions of Council Directive 2010/24/EU concerning mutual assistance for the recovery of claims relating to taxes, duties and other measures.

2011/363 *Council Implementing Decision of 20 June 2011 authorising Romania to introduce a special measure derogating from Article 193 of Directive 2006/112/EC on the common system of value added tax (applied until 31 May 2013)* (spent).

2012

79/2012: Commission Implementing Regulation of 31 January 2012 laying down detailed rules for implementing certain provisions of Council Regulation (EU) No 904/2010 concerning administrative cooperation and combating fraud in the field of value added tax.

815/2012: Commission Implementing Regulation of 13 September 2012 laying down detailed rules for the application of Council Regulation (EU) No 904/2010, as regards special schemes for non-established taxable persons supplying telecommunications, broadcasting or electronic services to non-taxable persons.

1156/2012/EU: Commission Implementing Regulation of 6 December 2012 laying down detailed rules for implementing certain provisions of Council Directive 2011/16/EU on administrative cooperation in the field of taxation.

2012/C 198/05: Commission Decision of 3 July 2013 setting up the EU VAT Forum.

2012/771: Commission Recommendation of 6 December 2012 regarding measures intended to encourage third countries to apply minimum standards of good governance in tax matters.

2013

2013/42 Council Directive of 22 July 2013 amending Directive 2006/112/EC on the common system of value added tax, as regards a Quick Reaction Mechanism against VAT fraud.

2013/43 Council Directive of 22 July 2013 amending Directive 2006/112/EC on the common system of value added tax, as regards an optional and temporary application of the reverse charge mechanism in relation to supplies of certain goods and services susceptible to fraud.

2013/52/EU: Council Decision of 22 January 2013 authorising enhanced cooperation in the area of financial transaction tax.

2013/517: Council Regulation of 13 May 2013 adapting certain regulations and decisions in the fields of free movement of goods, freedom of movement for persons, company law, competition policy, agriculture, food safety, veterinary and phytosanitary policy, transport policy, energy, taxation, statistics, trans-European networks, judiciary and fundamental rights, justice, freedom and security, environment, customs union, external relations, foreign, security and defence policy and institutions, by reason of the accession of the Republic of Croatia.

952/2013 Regulation of the European Parliament and of the Council of 9 October 2013 laying down the Union Customs Code.

1042/2013 Council Implementing Regulation of 7 October 2013 amending Implementing Regulation (EU) No 282/2011 as regards the place of supply of services.

1286/2013 Regulation of the European Parliament and of the Council of 11 December 2013 establishing an action programme to improve the operation of taxation systems in the European Union for the period 2014-2020 (Fiscalis 2020) and repealing Decision No 1482/2007/EC.

2014

17/2014 Commission Implementing Regulation of 10 January 2014 laying down the standardised form for the notification for a special measure under the Quick Reaction Mechanism against VAT fraud.

Treaty on the Functioning of the EU

CONSOLIDATED VERSION OF THE TREATY ON THE FUNCTIONING OF THE EUROPEAN UNION

Notes—Date of publication in OJ: OJ C83, 30.03.2010, p 47.
Commencement: 1 December 2009.
This is the Treaty on the Functioning of the European Union as consolidated following the Treaty of Lisbon, which came into force on 1 December 2009. Only those Articles of particular relevance are printed here. Cross-references to the equivalent article in the pre-Lisbon version of the Treaty are given at the beginning of each of the Articles reproduced which have such equivalents; these cross-references are part of the official text.

PART THREE

UNION POLICIES AND INTERNAL ACTIONS

TITLE IV

FREE MOVEMENT OF PERSONS, SERVICES AND CAPITAL

Chapter 1
WORKERS

Article 45 (ex Article 39 TEC)

1. Freedom of movement for workers shall be secured within the Union.
2. Such freedom of movement shall entail the abolition of any discrimination based on nationality between workers of the Member States as regards employment, remuneration and other conditions of work and employment.
3. It shall entail the right, subject to limitations justified on grounds of public policy, public security or public health:
(*a*) to accept offers of employment actually made;
(*b*) to move freely within the territory of Member States for this purpose;
(*c*) to stay in a Member State for the purpose of employment in accordance with the provisions governing the employment of nationals of that State laid down by law, regulation or administrative action;
(*d*) to remain in the territory of a Member State after having been employed in that State, subject to conditions which shall be embodied in regulations to be drawn up by the Commission.
4. The provisions of this Article shall not apply to employment in the public service.

Commentary—*Simon's Taxes* **D2.204.**

Simon's Tax Cases—*Zurstrassen v Administration des Contributions Directes* [2001] STC 1102*; *R (on the application of Professional Contractors Group Ltd and others) v IRC* [2002] STC 165; *Ritter-Coulais and another v Finanzamt Germersheim* [2006] STC 1111; *EC Commission v Kingdom of Denmark (supported by Kingdom of Sweden)* [2007] STC 1392; *Proceedings brought by Turpeinen* [2008] STC 1; *Schwarz and another v Finanzamt Bergisch Gladbach; EC Commission v Germany* [2008] STC 1357; *Luxembourg v Lakebrink and another* [2008] STC 2482; *EC Commission v Sweden* [2008] STC 2546; *Schulz-Delzers and anor v Finanzamt Stuttgart III* (Case C-240/10) [2011] STC 2144.

Article 46 (ex Article 40 TEC)

The European Parliament and the Council shall, acting in accordance with the ordinary legislative procedure and after consulting the Economic and Social Committee, issue directives or make regulations setting out the measures required to bring about freedom of movement for workers, as defined in Article 45, in particular:
(*a*) by ensuring close cooperation between national employment services;
(*b*) by abolishing those administrative procedures and practices and those qualifying periods in respect of eligibility for available employment, whether resulting from national legislation or from agreements previously concluded between Member States, the maintenance of which would form an obstacle to liberalisation of the movement of workers;
(*c*) by abolishing all such qualifying periods and other restrictions provided for either under national legislation or under agreements previously concluded between Member States as imposed on workers of other Member States conditions regarding the free choice of employment other than those imposed on workers of the State concerned;

(*d*) by setting up appropriate machinery to bring offers of employment into touch with applications for employment and to facilitate the achievement of a balance between supply and demand in the employment market in such a way as to avoid serious threats to the standard of living and level of employment in the various regions and industries.

Article 47 (ex Article 41 TEC)

Member States shall, within the framework of a joint programme, encourage the exchange of young workers.

Article 48 (ex Article 42 TEC)

The European Parliament and the Council shall, acting in accordance with the ordinary legislative procedure, adopt such measures in the field of social security as are necessary to provide freedom of movement for workers; to this end, they shall make arrangements to secure for employed and self-employed migrant workers and their dependants:

(*a*) aggregation, for the purpose of acquiring and retaining the right to benefit and of calculating the amount of benefit, of all periods taken into account under the laws of the several countries;

(*b*) payment of benefits to persons resident in the territories of Member States.

Where a member of the Council declares that a draft legislative act referred to in the first subparagraph would affect important aspects of its social security system, including its scope, cost or financial structure, or would affect the financial balance of that system, it may request that the matter be referred to the European Council. In that case, the ordinary legislative procedure shall be suspended. After discussion, the European Council shall, within four months of this suspension, either:

(a) refer the draft back to the Council, which shall terminate the suspension of the ordinary legislative procedure; or

(b) take no action or request the Commission to submit a new proposal; in that case, the act originally proposed shall be deemed not to have been adopted.

Chapter 2

RIGHT OF ESTABLISHMENT

Article 49 (ex Article 43 TEC)

Within the framework of the provisions set out below, restrictions on the freedom of establishment of nationals of a Member State in the territory of another Member State shall be prohibited. Such prohibition shall also apply to restrictions on the setting-up of agencies, branches or subsidiaries by nationals of any Member State established in the territory of any Member State.

Freedom of establishment shall include the right to take up and pursue activities as self-employed persons and to set up and manage undertakings, in particular companies or firms within the meaning of the second paragraph of Article 54, under the conditions laid down for its own nationals by the law of the country where such establishment is effected, subject to the provisions of the Chapter relating to capital.

Simon's Tax Cases—*Cadbury Schweppes plc v IRC* [2006] STC 1908; *Test Claimants in the Thin Cap Group Litigation v IRC* [2007] STC 906; *Finanzamt Dinslaken v Meindl (Meindl-Berger, third party)* [2007] STC 314*; *Finanzamt Offenbach am Main-Land v Keller Holding GmbH* [2007] STC 962*; *Foulser v MacDougall (Insp of Taxes)* [2007] STC 973*; *CLT-UFA SA v Finanzamt Köln-West* [2007] STC 1303*; *EC Commission v Kingdom of Denmark (supported by Kingdom of Sweden)* [2007] STC 1392; *Marks & Spencer plc v Halsey (Insp of Taxes)*[2008] STC 526; *N v Inspecteur van de Belastingdienst Oost/kantoor Almelo* [2008] STC 436; *Proceedings brought by Oy AA* [2008] STC 991; *Schwarz and another v Finanzamt Bergisch Gladbach; EC Commission v Germany* [2008] STC 1357; *Rewe Zentralfinanz eG (as universal legal successor of ITS Reisen GmbH) v Finanzamt Köln-Mitte* [2008] STC 2785; *Deutsche Shell v Finanzamt für Großunternehmen in Hamberg* [2008] STC 1721; *Vodafone 2 v R&C Comrs (No 2)* [2008] STC 2391; *EC Commission v Sweden* [2008] STC 2546; *Columbus Container Services BVBA & Co v Finanzamt Bielefeld-Innenstsadt* [2008] STC 2554; *Finanzamt Hamburg-Am Tierpark v Burda GmbH (formerly Burda Verlagsbeteiligungen GmbH)* [2008] STC 2996; *Lidl Belgium GmbH & Co KG v Finanzamt Heilbronn* [2008] STC 3229; *Talotta v Belgium* [2008] STC 3261; *Société Papillon v Ministère du budget, des comptes publics et de la fonction publique* [2009] STC 542; Vodafone 2 v R&C Comrs (No 2) [2009] STC 1480; *Aberdeen Property Fininvest Alpha Oy* [2009] STC 1945; *X Holding BV v Staatssecretaris van Financien* [2010] STC 941; *Test Claimants in the FII Group Litigation v R&C Comrs* [2010] STC 1251; *Gaz de France—Berliner Investissement SA v Bundeszentralamt für Steuern* [2010] STC 1519; *CIBA v APEH* [2010] STC 1680; *Schmelz v Finanzamt Waldviertel* (Case C-97/09) [2011] STC 88, *Test Claimants in the Thin Cap Group Litigation v R&C Comrs* [2011] EWCA Civ 127, [2011] STC 738; *National Grid Indus BV v Inspecteur van de Belastingdienst Rijnmond/kantoor Rotterdam* (Case C-371/10) [2012] STC 114; *Ministre du Budget, des Comptes piblics et de la Fonction publique v Accor* (Case C-310/09) [2012] STC 438; *Societe d'Investissement pour l'Agriculture Tropicale SA v Belgium* (Case C-318/10) [2012] STC 1988; *R&C Comrs v Philips Electronics UK Ltd* (Case C-18/11) [2013] STC 41; *European Commission v Belgium* (Case C-387/11) [2013] STC 587; *Inspecteur van de Belastingdienst/Noord/kantoor Groningen v SCA Group Holding BV and joined applications* (Joined Cases C-39/13, C-40/13 and C-41/13) [2014] STC 2107; *Felixstowe Dock and Railway Company Ltd and Others v v R&C Comrs* (Case C-80/12) [2014] STC 1489; *Nordea Bank Danmark A/S v Skatteministeriet* (Case C-48/13) [2015] STC 34.

Article 50 (ex Article 44 TEC)

1. In order to attain freedom of establishment as regards a particular activity, the European Parliament and the Council, acting in accordance with the ordinary legislative procedure and after consulting the Economic and Social Committee, shall act by means of directives.

2. The European Parliament, the Council and the Commission shall carry out the duties devolving upon them under the preceding provisions, in particular:

(*a*) by according, as a general rule, priority treatment to activities where freedom of establishment makes a particularly valuable contribution to the development of production and trade;

(*b*) by ensuring close cooperation between the competent authorities in the Member States in order to as-certain the particular situation within the Union of the various activities concerned;

(*c*) by abolishing those administrative procedures and practices, whether resulting from national legislation or from agreements previously concluded between Member States, the maintenance of which would form an obstacle to freedom of establishment;

(*d*) by ensuring that workers of one Member State employed in the territory of another Member State may remain in that territory for the purpose of taking up activities therein as self-employed persons, where they satisfy the conditions which they would be required to satisfy if they were entering that State at the time when they intended to take up such activities;

(*e*) by enabling a national of one Member State to acquire and use land and buildings situated in the territory of another Member State, in so far as this does not conflict with the principles laid down in Article 39(2);

(*f*) by effecting the progressive abolition of restrictions on freedom of establishment in every branch of activity under consideration, both as regards the conditions for setting up agencies, branches or subsidiaries in the territory of a Member State and as regards the subsidiaries in the territory of a Member State and as regards the conditions governing the entry of personnel belonging to the main establishment into manage-rial or supervisory posts in such agencies, branches or subsidiaries;

(*g*) by coordinating to the necessary extent the safeguards which, for the protection of the interests of members and others, are required by Member States of companies or firms within the meaning of the second paragraph of Article 54 with a view to making such safeguards equivalent throughout the Union;

(*h*) by satisfying themselves that the conditions of establishment are not distorted by aids granted by Member States.

Article 51 (ex Article 45 TEC)

The provisions of this Chapter shall not apply, so far as any given Member State is concerned, to activities which in that State are connected, even occasionally, with the exercise of official authority.

The European Parliament and the Council, acting in accordance with the ordinary legislative procedure, may rule that the provisions of this Chapter shall not apply to certain activities.

Article 52 (ex Article 46 TEC)

1. The provisions of this Chapter and measures taken in pursuance thereof shall not prejudice the applicability of provisions laid down by law, regulation or administrative action providing for special treatment for foreign nationals on grounds of public policy, public security or public health.

2. The European Parliament and the Council shall, acting in accordance with the ordinary legislative procedure, issue directives for the coordination of the abovementioned provisions.

Article 53 (ex Article 47 TEC)

1. In order to make it easier for persons to take up and pursue activities as self-employed persons, the European Parliament and the Council shall, acting in accordance with the ordinary legislative procedure, issue directives for the mutual recognition of diplomas, certificates and other evidence of formal qualifications and for the coordination of the provisions laid down by law, regulation or administrative action in Member States concerning the taking-up and pursuit of activities as self-employed persons.

2. In the case of the medical and allied and pharmaceutical professions, the progressive abolition of restrictions shall be dependent upon coordination of the conditions for their exercise in the various Member States.

Article 54 (ex Article 48 TEC)

Companies or firms formed in accordance with the law of a Member State and having their registered office, central administration or principal place of business within the Union shall, for the purposes of this Chapter, be treated in the same way as natural persons who are nationals of Member States.

"Companies or firms" means companies or firms constituted under civil or commercial law, including co-operative societies, and other legal persons governed by public or private law, save for those which are non-profit-making.

Simon's Tax Cases—*Bosal Holding BV v Staatssecretaris van Financiën* [2003] STC 1483; *Schilling and anor v Finanzamt Nürnburg-Süd* [2005] STC 1756; *Cadbury Schweppes plc and another v IRC* [2006] STC 1908; *Marks & Spencer plc v Halsey (Inspector of Taxes)* [2008] STC 526; *Rewe Zentralfinanz eG (as universal legal successor of ITS Reisen GmbH) v Finanzamt Köln-Mitte* [2008] STC 2785; *Deutsche Shell v Finanzamt für Großunternehmen in Hamberg* [2008] STC 1721; *Aberdeen Property Fininvest Alpha Oy* [2009] STC 1945; *X Holding BV v Staatssecretaris van Financien* [2010] STC 941; *Gaz de France—Berliner Investissement SA v Bundeszentralamt für Steuern* [2010] STC 1519; *CIBA v APEH* [2010] STC 1680; *Inspecteur van de Belastingdienst/Noord/kantoor Groningen v SCA Group Holding BV and joined applications* (Joined Cases C-39/13, C-40/13 and C-41/13) [2014] STC 2107; *Felixstowe Dock and Railway Company Ltd and Others v v R&C Comrs* (Case C-80/12) [2014] STC 1489; *Nordea Bank Danmark A/S v Skatteministeriet* (Case C-48/13) [2015] STC 34.

Article 55 (ex Article 294 TEC)

Member States shall accord nationals of the other Member States the same treatment as their own nationals as regards participation in the capital of companies or firms within the meaning of Article 54, without prejudice to the application of the other provisions of the Treaties.

Chapter 3

SERVICES

Article 56 (ex Article 49 TEC)

Within the framework of the provisions set out below, restrictions on freedom to provide services within the Union shall be prohibited in respect of nationals of Member States who are established in a Member State other than that of the person for whom the services are intended.

The European Parliament and the Council, acting in accordance with the ordinary legislative procedure, may extend the provisions of the Chapter to nationals of a third country who provide services and who are established within the Union.

Simon's Tax Cases—*Proceedings brought by Danner* [2002] STC 1283; *Försäkringsaktiebolaget Skandia (publ) and another v Riksskatteverket* [2003] STC 1361; *Laboratoires Fournier SA v Direction des verifications nationales et internationales* [2006] STC 538; *EC Commission v French Republic* [2007] STC 54; *EC Commission v Kingdom of Denmark (supported by Kingdom of Sweden)* [2007] STC 1392; *R (on the application of the Federation of Tour Operators and others) v HM Treasury* [2008] STC 547; *Centro Equestre da Lezíria Grande Lda v Bundesamt für Finanzen* [2008] STC 2250; *X v Staatssecretaris van Financiën* [2009] STC 2441; *Schmelz v Finanzamt Waldviertel* (Case C-97/09) [2011] STC 88, *Test Claimants in the ACT Group Litigation (Classes 2 and 4) and anor v R&C Comrs* [2010] EWCA Civ 1480, [2011] STC 872; *XBV and anor v Staatssecretaris van Financien* (Cases C-24/12 and C-27/12) [2014] STC 2394.

Article 57 (ex Article 50 TEC)

Services shall be considered to be "services" within the meaning of the Treaties where they are normally provided for remuneration, in so far as they are not governed by the provisions relating to freedom of movement for goods, capital and persons.

"Services" shall in particular include:

(*a*) activities of an industrial character;

(*b*) activities of a commercial character;

(*c*) activities of craftsmen;

(*d*) activities of the professions.

Without prejudice to the provisions of the Chapter relating to the right of establishment, the person providing a service may, in order to do so, temporarily pursue his activity in the Member State where the service is provided, under the same conditions as are imposed by that State on its own nationals.

Article 58 (ex Article 51 TEC)

1. Freedom to provide services in the field of transport shall be governed by the provisions of the Title relating to transport.

2. The liberalisation of banking and insurance services connected with movements of capital shall be effected in step with the liberalisation of movement of capital.

Article 59 (ex Article 52 TEC)

1. In order to achieve the liberalisation of a specific service, the European Parliament and the Council, acting in accordance with the ordinary legislative procedure and after consulting the Economic and Social Committee, shall issue directives.

2. As regards the directives referred to in paragraph 1, priority shall as a general rule be given to those services which directly affect production costs or the liberalisation of which helps to promote trade in goods.

Article 60 (ex Article 53 TEC)

The Member States shall endeavour to undertake the liberalisation of services beyond the extent required by the directives issued pursuant to Article 59(1), if their general economic situation and the situation of the economic sector concerned so permit.

To this end, the Commission shall make recommendations to the Member States concerned.

Article 61 (ex Article 54 TEC)

As long as restrictions on freedom to provide services have not been abolished, each Member State shall apply such restrictions without distinction on grounds of nationality or residence to all persons providing services within the meaning of the first paragraph of Article 56.

Article 62 (ex Article 55 TEC)

The provisions of Articles 51 to 54 shall apply to the matters covered by this Chapter.

CHAPTER 4—CAPITAL AND PAYMENTS

Article 63 (ex Article 56)

1. Within the framework of the provisions set out in this Chapter, all restrictions on the movement of capital between Member States and between Member States and third countries shall be prohibited.
2. Within the framework of the provisions set out in this Chapter, all restrictions on payments between Member States and between Member States and third countries shall be prohibited.

Statement of Practice SP 2/92—Movements of capital between residents of EC Member States.

Simon's Tax Cases—*EC Commission v Belgium* [2000] STC 830; *EC Commission v French Republic* [2007] STC 54; *Kerckhaert and Morres v Belgian State* [2007] STC 1349; *EC Commission v Kingdom of Denmark (supported by Kingdom of Sweden)* [2007] STC 1392; *Holböck v Finanzamt Salzburg-Land* [2008] STC 92; *Heirs of van Hilten-van der Heijden v Inspecteur van de Belastingdienst/Particulieren/Ondernemingen buitenland te Heerlen* [2008] STC 1245; *Européene et Luxembourgeoise d'investissements SA v Directeur général des impôts and another* [2008] STC 1762; *Hollmann v Fazenda Publica* [2008] STC 1874; *Bouanich v Skatteverket* [2008] STC 2020; *Meilicke and others v Finanzamt Bonn-Innenstadt* [2008] STC 2267; *Columbus Container Services BVBA & Co v Finanzamt Bielefeld-Innenstsadt* [2008] STC 2554; *Amurta SGPS v Inspecteur van de Belastingdienst/Amsterdam* [2008] STC 2851; *Skatteverket v A* [2009] STC 405; *Persche v Finanzamt Lüdenscheid* [2009] STC 586; *X v Staatssecretaris van Financiën* [2009] STC 2441; *Glaxo Wellcome GmbH & Co KG v Finanzamt München II* [2010] STC 244; *Test Claimants in the FII Group Litigation v R&C Comrs* [2010] STC 1251*, *Haribo Lakritzen Hans Riegel Betriebs gmbhH and anor v Finanzamt Linz* (Joined Cases C-436/08 and C-437/08) [2011] STC 917, *Missionwerk Werner Heukelbach eV v Belgium* (Case C-25/10) [2011] STC 985, *Schroder v Finanzamt Hameln* (Case C-450/09) [2011] STC 1248, *R (on the application of Shiner and another) v R&C Comrs* [2011] EWCA Civ 892, [2011] STC 1878; *European Commission v Germany* (Case C-284/09) [2011] STC 2392; *Ministre du Budget, des Comptes piblics et de la Fonction publique v Accor* (Case C-310/09) [2012] STC 438; *Santander Asset Management SGIIC SA, on behalf of FIM Santander Top 25 Fi v Directeur des residents a l'etranger et des services generaux and other cases* (Joined cases C-338/11 to C-347/11) [2012] STC 1785; *European Commission v Republic of Finland* (Case C-342/10) [2013] STC 280; *European Commission v Belgium* (Case C-387/11) [2013] STC 587; *Test Claimants in the FII Group Litigation v R&C Comrs* (Case C-35/11) [2013] STC 612; *Trustees of the BT Pension Scheme v R&C Comrs* [2013] UKUT 105 (TCC), [2013] STC 1781; *Prudential Assurance Co Ltd and anor v R&C Comrs* [2014] EWHC 3249 (Ch), [2014] STC 1236; *DMC Beteiligungsgesellschaft mbH v Finanzamt Hamburg-Mitte* (Case C-164/12) [2014] STC 1345; *Emerging Markets Series of DFA Investment Trust Company v Dyrektor Izby Skarbowej w Bydgoszczy* (Case C-190/12) [2014] STC 1660; *Kronos International Inc v Finanzamt Leverkusen* (Case C-47/12) [2015] STC 351.

Article 64 (ex Article 57 TEC)

1. The provisions of Article 63 shall be without prejudice to the application to third countries of any restrictions which exist on 31 December 1993 under national or Union law adopted in respect of the movement of capital to or from third countries involving direct investment - including in real estate - establishment, the provision of financial services or the admission of securities to capital markets. In respect of restrictions existing under national law in Bulgaria, Estonia and Hungary, the relevant date shall be 31 December 1999.
2. Whilst endeavouring to achieve the objective of free movement of capital between Member States and third countries to the greatest extent possible and without prejudice to the other Chapters of the Treaties, the European Parliament and the Council, acting in accordance with the ordinary legislative procedure, shall adopt the measures on the movement of capital to or from third countries involving direct investment - including investment in real estate - establishment, the provision of financial services or the admission of securities to capital markets.
3. Notwithstanding paragraph 2, only the Council, acting in accordance with a special legislative procedure, may unanimously, and after consulting the European Parliament, adopt measures which constitute a step backwards in Union law as regards the liberalisation of the movement of capital to or from third countries.

Simon's Tax Cases—*Holböck v Finanzamt Salzburg-Land* [2008] STC 92; *Test Claimants in the FII Group Litigation v R&C Comrs* [2010] STC 1251*.

Article 65 (ex Article 58 TEC)

1. The provisions of Article 63 shall be without prejudice to the right of Member States:
   (*a*) to apply the relevant provisions of their tax law which distinguish between taxpayers who are not in the same situation with regard to their place of residence or with regard to the place where their capital is invested;
   (*b*) to take all requisite measures to prevent infringements of national law and regulations, in particular in the field of taxation and the prudential supervision of financial institutions, or to lay down procedures for the declaration of capital movements for purposes of administrative or statistical information, or to take measures which are justified on grounds of public policy or public security.

2. The provisions of this Chapter shall be without prejudice to the applicability of restrictions on the right of establishment which are compatible with the Treaties.
3. The measures and procedures referred to in paragraphs 1 and 2 shall not constitute a means of arbitrary discrimination or a disguised restriction on the free movement of capital and payments as defined in Article 63.
4. In the absence of measures pursuant to Article 64(3), the Commission or, in the absence of a Commission decision within three months from the request of the Member State concerned, the Council, may adopt a decision stating that restrictive tax measures adopted by a Member State concerning one or more third countries are to be considered compatible with the Treaties in so far as they are justified by one of the objectives of the Union and compatible with the proper functioning of the internal market. The Council shall act unanimously on application by a Member State.

Simon's Tax Cases—*Royal Bank of Scotland v Greek State* [2000] STC 733; *Bouanich v Skatteverket* [2008] STC 2020; *Meilicke and others v Finanzamt Bonn-Innenstadt* [2008] STC 2267; *Amurta SGPS v Inspecteur van de Belastingdienst/Amsterdam* [2008] STC 2851; *Santander Asset Management SGIIC SA, on behalf of FIM Santander Top 25 Fi v Directeur des residents a l'etranger et des services generaux and other cases* (Joined cases C-338/11 to C-347/11) [2012] STC 1785; *Emerging Markets Series of DFA Investment Trust Company v Dyrektor Izby Skarbowej w Bydgoszczy* (Case C-190/12) [20134] STC 1660.

Article 66 (ex Article 59 TEC)

Where, in exceptional circumstances, movements of capital to or from third countries cause, or threaten to cause, serious difficulties for the operation of economic and monetary union, the Council, on a proposal from the Commission and after consulting the European Central Bank, may take safeguard measures with regard to third countries for a period not exceeding six months if such measures are strictly necessary.

[TITLE VII (EX TITLE VI)—COMMON RULES ON COMPETITION, TAXATION AND APPROXIMATION OF LAW

CHAPTER 2—TAX PROVISIONS

Article 110 (ex Article 90)

No Member State shall impose, directly or indirectly, on the products of other Member States any internal taxation of any kind in excess of that imposed directly or indirectly on similar domestic products.
Furthermore, no Member State shall impose on the products of other Member States any internal taxation of such a nature as to afford indirect protection to other products.

Simon's Tax Cases—*EC Commission v Kingdom of Spain* [1993] STC 150*; *EC Commission v Hellenic Republic* [1993] STC 160*; *EC Commission v French Republic (Case C-276/91)* [1997] STC 584*; [1997] *Fazenda Pública v Fricarnes SA* [1997] STC 1348*.

Article 111 (ex Article 91 TEC)

Where products are exported to the territory of any Member State, any repayment of internal taxation shall not exceed the internal taxation imposed on them whether directly or indirectly.

Article 112 (ex Article 92 TEC)

In the case of charges other than turnover taxes, excise duties and other forms of indirect taxation, remissions and repayments in respect of exports to other Member States may not be granted and countervailing charges in respect of imports from Member States may not be imposed unless the measures contemplated have been previously approved for a limited period by the Council on a proposal from the Commission.

Article 113 (ex Article 93 TEC)

The Council shall, acting unanimously in accordance with a special legislative procedure and after consulting the European Parliament and the Economic and Social Committee, adopt provisions for the harmonisation of legislation concerning turnover taxes, excise duties and other forms of indirect taxation to the extent that such harmonisation is necessary to ensure the establishment and the functioning of the internal market and to avoid distortion of competition.

CHAPTER 3—APPROXIMATION OF LAWS

Article 114 (ex Article 95)

1. Save where otherwise provided in the Treaties, the following provisions shall apply for the achievement of the objectives set out in Article 26. The European Parliament and the Council shall, acting in accordance with the ordinary legislative procedure and after consulting the Economic and Social Committee, adopt the measures for the approximation of the provisions laid down by law, regulation or administrative action in Member States which have as their object the establishment and functioning of the internal market.
2. Paragraph 1 shall not apply to fiscal provisions, to those relating to the free movement of persons nor to those relating to the rights and interests of employed persons.

3. The Commission, in its proposals envisaged in paragraph 1 concerning health, safety, environmental protection and consumer protection, will take as a base a high level of protection, taking account in particular of any new development based on scientific facts. Within their respective powers, the European Parliament and the Council will also seek to achieve this objective.
4. If, after the adoption of a harmonisation measure by the European Parliament and the Council, by the Council or by the Commission, a Member State deems it necessary to maintain national provisions on grounds of major needs referred to in Article 36, or relating to the protection of the environment or the working environment, it shall notify the Commission of these provisions as well as the grounds for maintaining them.
5. Moreover, without prejudice to paragraph 4, if, after the adoption of a harmonisation measure by the European Parliament and the Council, by the Council or by the Commission, a Member State deems it necessary to introduce national provisions based on new scientific evidence relating to the protection of the environment or the working environment on grounds of a problem specific to that Member State arising after the adoption of the harmonisation measure, it shall notify the Commission of the envisaged provisions as well as the grounds for introducing them.
6. The Commission shall, within six months of the notifications as referred to in paragraphs 4 and 5, approve or reject the national provisions involved after having verified whether or not they are a means of arbitrary discrimination or a disguised restriction on trade between Member States and whether or not they shall constitute an obstacle to the functioning of the internal market.
In the absence of a decision by the Commission within this period the national provisions referred to in paragraphs 4 and 5 shall be deemed to have been approved.
When justified by the complexity of the matter and in the absence of danger for human health, the Commission may notify the Member State concerned that the period referred to in this paragraph may be extended for a further period of up to six months.
7. When, pursuant to paragraph 6, a Member State is authorised to maintain or introduce national provisions derogating from a harmonisation measure, the Commission shall immediately examine whether to propose an adaptation to that measure.
8. When a Member State raises a specific problem on public health in a field which has been the subject of prior harmonisation measures, it shall bring it to the attention of the Commission which shall immediately examine whether to propose appropriate measures to the Council.
9. By way of derogation from the procedure laid down in Articles 258 and 259, the Commission and any Member State may bring the matter directly before the Court of Justice of the European Union if it considers that another Member State is making improper use of the powers provided for in this Article.
10. The harmonisation measures referred to above shall, in appropriate cases, include a safeguard clause authorising the Member States to take, for one or more of the non-economic reasons referred to in Article 36, provisional measures subject to a Union control procedure.

Article 115 (ex Article 94)

Without prejudice to Article 114, the Council shall, acting unanimously in accordance with a special legislative procedure and after consulting the European Parliament and the Economic and Social Committee, issue directives for the approximation of such laws, regulations or administrative provisions of the Member States as directly affect the establishment or functioning of the internal market.

Article 116 (ex Article 96)

Where the Commission finds that a difference between the provisions laid down by law, regulation or administrative action in Member States is distorting the conditions of competition in the internal market and that the resultant distortion needs to be eliminated, it shall consult the Member States concerned.
If such consultation does not result in an agreement eliminating the distortion in question, the European, Parliament and the Council, acting in accordance with the ordinary legislative procedure, shall issue the necessary directives. Any other appropriate measures provided for in the Treaties may be adopted.

Article 117 (ex Article 97)

1. Where there is a reason to fear that the adoption or amendment of a provision laid down by law, regulation or administrative action may cause distortion within the meaning of Article 116, a Member State desiring to proceed therewith shall consult the Commission. After consulting the Member States, the Commission shall recommend to the States concerned such measures as may be appropriate to avoid the distortion in question.
2. If a State desiring to introducc or amend its own provisions does not comply with the recommendation addressed to it by the Commission, other Member States shall not be required, pursuant to Article 116, to amend their own provisions in order to eliminate such distortion. If the Member State which has ignored the recommendation of the Commission causes distortion detrimental only to itself, the provisions of Article 116 shall not apply.

Article 118

In the context of the establishment and functioning of the internal market, the European Parliament and the Council, acting in accordance with the ordinary legislative procedure, shall establish measures for the creation of European intellectual property rights to provide uniform protection of intellectual property rights throughout the Union and for the setting up of centralised Union-wide authorisation, coordination and supervision arrangements. The Council, acting in accordance with a special legislative procedure, shall by means of regulations establish language arrangements for the European intellectual property rights. The Council shall act unanimously after consulting the European Parliament.

[TITLE VIII (EX TITLE VII)—ECONOMIC AND MONETARY POLICY

Article 119 (ex Article 4 TEC)

1. For the purposes set out in Article 3 of the Treaty on European Union, the activities of the Member States and the Union shall include, as provided in the Treaties, the adoption of an economic policy which is based on the close coordination of Member States' economic policies, on the internal market and on the definition of common objectives, and conducted in accordance with the principle of an open market econ-omy with free competition.

2. Concurrently with the foregoing, and as provided in the Treaties and in accordance with the procedures set out therein, these activities shall include a single currency, the euro, and the definition and conduct of a single monetary policy and exchange-rate policy the primary objective of both of which shall be to maintain price stability and, without prejudice to this objective, to support the general economic policies in the Union, in accordance with the principle of an open market economy with free competition.

3. These activities of the Member States and the Union shall entail compliance with the following guiding principles: stable prices, sound public finances and monetary conditions and a sustainable balance of payments.

[CHAPTER 1—ECONOMIC POLICY

Article 120 (ex Article 98)

Member States shall conduct their economic policies with a view to contributing to the achievement of the objectives of the Union, as defined in Article 3 of the Treaty on European Union, and in the context of the broad guidelines referred to in Article 121(2). The Member States and the Union shall act in accordance with the principle of an open market economy with free competition, favouring an efficient allocation of resources, and in compliance with the principles set out in Article 119.

PART SIX

INSTITUTIONAL AND FINANCIAL PROVISIONS

TITLE I—INSTITUTIONAL PROVISIONS

CHAPTER 1—THE INSTITUTIONS

SECTION 5—THE COURT OF JUSTICE OF THE EUROPEAN UNION

Article 251 (ex Article 221 TEC)

The Court of Justice shall sit in chambers or in a Grand Chamber, in accordance with the rules laid down for that purpose in the Statute of the Court of Justice of the European Union.

When provided for in the Statute, the Court of Justice may also sit as a full Court.

Article 252 (ex Article 222 TEC)

The Court of Justice shall be assisted by eight Advocates-General. Should the Court of Justice so request, the Council, acting unanimously, may increase the number of Advocates-General.

It shall be the duty of the Advocate-General, acting with complete impartiality and independence, to make, in open court, reasoned submissions on cases which, in accordance with the Statute of the Court of Justice of the European Union, require his involvement.

Article 253 (ex Article 223 TEC)

The Judges and Advocates-General of the Court of Justice shall be chosen from persons whose independence is beyond doubt and who possess the qualifications required for appointment to the highest judicial offices in their respective countries or who are jurisconsults of recognised competence; they shall be appointed by common accord of the governments of the Member States for a term of six years, after consultation of the panel provided for in Article 255.

Every three years there shall be a partial replacement of the Judges and Advocates-General, in accordance with the conditions laid down in the Statute of the Court of Justice of the European Union.

The Judges shall elect the President of the Court of Justice from among their number for a term of three years. He may be re-elected.

Retiring Judges and Advocates-General may be reappointed.

The Court of Justice shall appoint its Registrar and lay down the rules governing his service.

The Court of Justice shall establish its Rules of Procedure. Those Rules shall require the approval of the Council.

Article 254 (ex Article 224 TEC)

The number of Judges of the General Court shall be determined by the Statute of the Court of Justice of the European Union. The Statute may provide for the General Court to be assisted by Advocates-General.

The members of the General Court shall be chosen from persons whose independence is beyond doubt and who possess the ability required for appointment to high judicial office. They shall be appointed by common accord of the governments of the Member States for a term of six years, after consultation of the panel provided for in Article 255. The membership shall be partially renewed every three years. Retiring members shall be eligible for reappointment.

The Judges shall elect the President of the General Court from among their number for a term of three years. He may be re-elected.

The General Court shall appoint its Registrar and lay down the rules governing his service.

The General Court shall establish its Rules of Procedure in agreement with the Court of Justice. Those Rules shall require the approval of the Council.

Unless the Statute of the Court of Justice of the European Union provides otherwise, the provisions of the Treaties relating to the Court of Justice shall apply to the General Court.

Article 255

A panel shall be set up in order to give an opinion on candidates' suitability to perform the duties of Judge and Advocate-General of the Court of Justice and the General Court before the governments of the Member States make the appointments referred to in Articles 253 and 254.

The panel shall comprise seven persons chosen from among former members of the Court of Justice and the General Court, members of national supreme courts and lawyers of recognised competence, one of whom shall be proposed by the European Parliament. The Council shall adopt a decision establishing the panel's operating rules and a decision appointing its members. It shall act on the initiative of the President of the Court of Justice.

Article 256 (ex Article 225 TEC)

1. The General Court shall have jurisdiction to hear and determine at first instance actions or proceedings referred to in Articles 263, 265, 268, 270 and 272, with the exception of those assigned to a specialised court set up under Article 257 and those reserved in the Statute for the Court of Justice. The Statute may provide for the General Court to have jurisdiction for other classes of action or proceeding.

Decisions given by the General Court under this paragraph may be subject to a right of appeal to the Court of Justice on points of law only, under the conditions and within the limits laid down by the Statute.

2. The General Court shall have jurisdiction to hear and determine actions or proceedings brought against decisions of the specialised courts.

Decisions given by the General Court under this paragraph may exceptionally be subject to review by the Court of Justice, under the conditions and within the limits laid down by the Statute, where there is a serious risk of the unity or consistency of Union law being affected.

3. The General Court shall have jurisdiction to hear and determine questions referred for a preliminary ruling under Article 267, in specific areas laid down by the Statute.

Where the General Court considers that the case requires a decision of principle likely to affect the unity or consistency of Union law, it may refer the case to the Court of Justice for a ruling.

Decisions given by the General Court on questions referred for a preliminary ruling may exceptionally be subject to review by the Court of Justice, under the conditions and within the limits laid down by the Statute, where there is a serious risk of the unity or consistency of Union law being affected.

Article 257 (ex Article 225A TEC)

The European Parliament and the Council, acting in accordance with the ordinary legislative procedure, may establish specialised courts attached to the General Court to hear and determine at first instance certain classes of action or proceeding brought in specific areas. The European Parliament and the Council shall act by means of regulations either on a proposal from the Commission after consultation of the Court of Justice or at the request of the Court of Justice after consultation of the Commission.

The regulation establishing a specialised court shall lay down the rules on the organisation of the court and the extent of the jurisdiction conferred upon it.

Decisions given by specialised courts may be subject to a right of appeal on points of law only or, when provided for in the regulation establishing the specialised court, a right of appeal also on matters of fact, before the General Court.

The members of the specialised courts shall be chosen from persons whose independence is beyond doubt and who possess the ability required for appointment to judicial office. They shall be appointed by the Council, acting unanimously.
The specialised courts shall establish their Rules of Procedure in agreement with the Court of Justice. Those Rules shall require the approval of the Council.
Unless the regulation establishing the specialised court provides otherwise, the provisions of the Treaties relating to the Court of Justice of the European Union and the provisions of the Statute of the Court of Justice of the European Union shall apply to the specialised courts. Title I of the Statute and Article 64 thereof shall in any case apply to the specialised courts.

Article 258 (ex Article 226 TEC)

If the Commission considers that a Member State has failed to fulfil an obligation under the Treaties, it shall deliver a reasoned opinion on the matter after giving the State concerned the opportunity to submit its observations.

If the State concerned does not comply with the opinion within the period laid down by the Commission, the latter may bring the matter before the Court of Justice of the European Union.

Article 259 (ex Article 227 TEC)

A Member State which considers that another Member State has failed to fulfil an obligation under the Treaties may bring the matter before the Court of Justice of the European Union.

Before a Member State brings an action against another Member State for an alleged infringement of an obligation under the Treaties, it shall bring the matter before the Commission.

The Commission shall deliver a reasoned opinion after each of the States concerned has been given the opportunity to submit its own case and its observations on the other party's case both orally and in writing.

If the Commission has not delivered an opinion within three months of the date on which the matter was brought before it, the absence of such opinion shall not prevent the matter from being brought before the Court.

Article 260 (ex Article 228 TEC)

1. If the Court of Justice of the European Union finds that a Member State has failed to fulfil an obligation under the Treaties, the State shall be required to take the necessary measures to comply with the judgment of the Court.
2. If the Commission considers that the Member State concerned has not taken the necessary measures to comply with the judgment of the Court, it may bring the case before the Court after giving that State the opportunity to submit its observations. It shall specify the amount of the lump sum or penalty payment to be paid by the Member State concerned which it considers appropriate in the circumstances.

If the Court finds that the Member State concerned has not complied with its judgment it may impose a lump sum or penalty payment on it.

This procedure shall be without prejudice to Article 259.

3. When the Commission brings a case before the Court pursuant to Article 258 on the grounds that the Member State concerned has failed to fulfil its obligation to notify measures transposing a directive adopted under a legislative procedure, it may, when it deems appropriate, specify the amount of the lump sum or penalty payment to be paid by the Member State concerned which it considers appropriate in the circumstances.

If the Court finds that there is an infringement it may impose a lump sum or penalty payment on the Member State concerned not exceeding the amount specified by the Commission. The payment obligation shall take effect on the date set by the Court in its judgment.

Article 261 (ex Article 229 TEC)

Regulations adopted jointly by the European Parliament and the Council, and by the Council, pursuant to the provisions of the Treaties, may give the Court of Justice of the European Union unlimited jurisdiction with regard to the penalties provided for in such regulations.

Article 262 (ex Article 229A TEC)

Without prejudice to the other provisions of the Treaties, the Council, acting unanimously in accordance with a special legislative procedure and after consulting the European Parliament, may adopt provisions to confer jurisdiction, to the extent that it shall determine, on the Court of Justice of the European Union in disputes relating to the application of acts adopted on the basis of the Treaties which create European intellectual property rights. These provisions shall enter into force after their approval by the Member States in accordance with their respective constitutional requirements.

Article 263 (ex Article 230 TEC)

The Court of Justice of the European Union shall review the legality of legislative acts, of acts of the Council, of the Commission and of the European Central Bank, other than recommendations and opinions, and of acts of the European Parliament and of the European Council intended to produce legal effects vis-à-vis third parties. It shall also review the legality of acts of bodies, offices or agencies of the Union intended to produce legal effects vis-à-vis third parties.

It shall for this purpose have jurisdiction in actions brought by a Member State, the European Parliament, the Council or the Commission on grounds of lack of competence, infringement of an essential procedural requirement, infringement of the Treaties or of any rule of law relating to their application, or misuse of powers.

The Court shall have jurisdiction under the same conditions in actions brought by the Court of Auditors, by the European Central Bank and by the Committee of the Regions for the purpose of protecting their prerogatives.

Any natural or legal person may, under the conditions laid down in the first and second paragraphs, institute proceedings against an act addressed to that person or which is of direct and individual concern to them, and against a regulatory act which is of direct concern to them and does not entail implementing measures.

Acts setting up bodies, offices and agencies of the Union may lay down specific conditions and arrangements concerning actions brought by natural or legal persons against acts of these bodies, offices or agencies intended to produce legal effects in relation to them.

The proceedings provided for in this Article shall be instituted within two months of the publication of the measure, or of its notification to the plaintiff, or, in the absence thereof, of the day on which it came to the knowledge of the latter, as the case may be.

Article 264 (ex Article 231 TEC)

If the action is well founded, the Court of Justice of the European Union shall declare the act concerned to be void.

However, the Court shall, if it considers this necessary, state which of the effects of the act which it has declared void shall be considered as definitive.

Article 265 (ex Article 232 TEC)

Should the European Parliament, the European Council, the Council, the Commission or the European Central Bank, in infringement of the Treaties, fail to act, the Member States and the other institutions of the Union may bring an action before the Court of Justice of the European Union to have the infringement established. This Article shall apply, under the same conditions, to bodies, offices and agencies of the Union which fail to act.

The action shall be admissible only if the institution, body, office or agency concerned has first been called upon to act. If, within two months of being so called upon, the institution, body, office or agency concerned has not defined its position, the action may be brought within a further period of two months.

Any natural or legal person may, under the conditions laid down in the preceding paragraphs, complain to the Court that an institution, body, office or agency of the Union has failed to address to that person any act other than a recommendation or an opinion.

Article 266 (ex Article 233 TEC)

The institution whose act has been declared void or whose failure to act has been declared contrary to the Treaties shall be required to take the necessary measures to comply with the judgment of the Court of Justice of the European Union.

This obligation shall not affect any obligation which may result from the application of the second paragraph of Article 340.

Article 267 (ex Article 234 TEC)

The Court of Justice of the European Union shall have jurisdiction to give preliminary rulings concerning:

(a) the interpretation of the Treaties;

(b) the validity and interpretation of acts of the institutions, bodies, offices or agencies of the Union;

Where such a question is raised before any court or tribunal of a Member State, that court or tribunal may, if it considers that a decision on the question is necessary to enable it to give judgment, request the Court to give a ruling thereon.

Where any such question is raised in a case pending before a court or tribunal of a Member State against whose decisions there is no judicial remedy under national law, that court or tribunal shall bring the matter before the Court.

Simon's Tax Cases—*Grattan plc v R&C Comrs* [2011] UKUT 399 (TCC), [2011] STC 2342.

If such a question is raised in a case pending before a court or tribunal of a Member State with regard to a person in custody, the Court of Justice of the European Union shall act with the minimum of delay.

Article 268 (ex Article 235 TEC)

The Court of Justice of the European Union shall have jurisdiction in disputes relating to compensation for damage provided for in the second and third paragraphs of Article 340.

Article 269

The Court of Justice shall have jurisdiction to decide on the legality of an act adopted by the European Council or by the Council pursuant to Article 7 of the Treaty on European Union solely at the request of the Member State concerned by a determination of the European Council or of the Council and in respect solely of the procedural stipulations contained in that Article.

Such a request must be made within one month from the date of such determination. The Court shall rule within one month from the date of the request.

Article 270 (ex Article 236 TEC)

The Court of Justice of the European Union shall have jurisdiction in any dispute between the Union and its servants within the limits and under the conditions laid down in the Staff Regulations of Officials and the Conditions of Employment of other servants of the Union.

Article 271 (ex Article 237 TEC)

The Court of Justice of the European Union shall, within the limits hereinafter laid down, have jurisdiction in disputes concerning:

(a) the fulfilment by Member States of obligations under the Statute of the European Investment Bank. In this connection, the Board of Directors of the Bank shall enjoy the powers conferred upon the Commission by Article 258;

(b) measures adopted by the Board of Governors of the European Investment Bank. In this connection, any Member State, the Commission or the Board of Directors of the Bank may institute proceedings under the conditions laid down in Article 263;

(c) measures adopted by the Board of Directors of the European Investment Bank. Proceedings against such measures may be instituted only by Member States or by the Commission, under the conditions laid down in Article 263, and solely on the grounds of non-compliance with the procedure provided for in Article 19(2), (5), (6) and (7) of the Statute of the Bank;

(d) the fulfilment by national central banks of obligations under the Treaties and the Statute of the ESCB and of the ECB. In this connection the powers of the Governing Council of the European Central Bank in respect of national central banks shall be the same as those conferred upon the Commission in respect of Member States by Article 258. If the Court finds that a national central bank has failed to fulfil an obligation under the Treaties, that bank shall be required to take the necessary measures to comply with the judgment of the Court.

Article 272 (ex Article 238 TEC)

The Court of Justice of the European Union shall have jurisdiction to give judgment pursuant to any arbitration clause contained in a contract concluded by or on behalf of the Union, whether that contract be governed by public or private law.

Article 273 (ex Article 239 TEC)

The Court of Justice shall have jurisdiction in any dispute between Member States which relates to the subject matter of the Treaties if the dispute is submitted to it under a special agreement between the parties.

Article 274 (ex Article 240 TEC)

Save where jurisdiction is conferred on the Court of Justice of the European Union by the Treaties, disputes to which the Union is a party shall not on that ground be excluded from the jurisdiction of the courts or tribunals of the Member States.

Article 275

The Court of Justice of the European Union shall not have jurisdiction with respect to the provisions relating to the common foreign and security policy nor with respect to acts adopted on the basis of those provisions.

However, the Court shall have jurisdiction to monitor compliance with Article 40 of the Treaty on European Union and to rule on proceedings, brought in accordance with the conditions laid down in the fourth paragraph of Article 263 of this Treaty, reviewing the legality of decisions providing for restrictive measures against natural or legal persons adopted by the Council on the basis of Chapter 2 of Title V of the Treaty on European Union.

Article 276

In exercising its powers regarding the provisions of Chapters 4 and 5 of Title V of Part Three relating to the area of freedom, security and justice, the Court of Justice of the European Union shall have no jurisdiction to review the validity or proportionality of operations carried out by the police or other law-enforcement services of a Member State or the exercise of the responsibilities incumbent upon Member States with regard to the maintenance of law and order and the safeguarding of internal security.

Article 277 (ex Article 241 TEC)

Notwithstanding the expiry of the period laid down in Article 263, sixth paragraph, any party may, in proceedings in which an act of general application adopted by an institution, body, office or agency of the Un-ion is at issue, plead the grounds specified in Article 263, second paragraph, in order to invoke before the Court of Justice of the European Union the inapplicability of that act.

Article 278 (ex Article 242 TEC)

Actions brought before the Court of Justice of the European Union shall not have suspensory effect. The Court may, however, if it considers that circumstances so require, order that application of the contested act be suspended.

Article 279 (ex Article 243 TEC)

The Court of Justice of the European Union may in any cases before it prescribe any necessary interim measures.

Article 280 (ex Article 244 TEC)

The judgments of the Court of Justice of the European Union shall be enforceable under the conditions laid down in Article 299.

Article 281 (ex Article 245 TEC)

The Statute of the Court of Justice of the European Union shall be laid down in a separate Protocol. The European Parliament and the Council, acting in accordance with the ordinary legislative procedure, may amend the provisions of the Statute, with the exception of Title I and Article 64. The European Parliament and the Council shall act either at the request of the Court of Justice and after consultation of the Commission, or on a proposal from the Commission and after consultation of the Court of Justice.

CHAPTER 2—LEGAL ACTS OF THE UNION, ADOPTION PROCEDURES AND OTHER PROVISIONS

SECTION 1 THE LEGAL ACTS OF THE UNION

Article 288 (ex Article 249)

To exercise the Union's competences, the institutions shall adopt regulations, directives, decisions, recommendations and opinions.

A regulation shall have general application. It shall be binding in its entirety and directly applicable in all Member States.

A directive shall be binding, as to the result to be achieved, upon each Member State to which it is addressed, but shall leave to the national authorities the choice of form and methods.

A decision shall be binding in its entirety. A decision which specifies those to whom it is addressed shall be binding only on them.

Recommendations and opinions shall have no binding force.

Article 288 (ex Article 249 TEC)

EU Council Directives

SIXTH COUNCIL DIRECTIVE (77/388/EEC) OF 17 MAY 1977 ON THE HARMONISATION OF THE LAWS OF THE MEMBER STATES RELATING TO TURNOVER TAXES—COMMON SYSTEM OF VALUE ADDED TAX: UNIFORM BASIS OF ASSESSMENT

(77/388/EEC)

Note—See OJ L145, 13.6.1977, p 1.

Repeal—This Directive repealed by Council Directive of 28 November 2006 on the common system of value added tax (2006/112/EC). For correlation table, see Annex XII of that Directive.

Cross references—See F(No 2)A 1992 s 14(2) (provisions to give effect to the requirements of this Directive as amended by Directive 91/680/EEC in connection with abolition of fiscal frontiers between member States).

THE COUNCIL OF THE EUROPEAN COMMUNITIES

Having regard to the Treaty establishing the European Economic Community, and in particular Articles 99 and 100 thereof,

Having regard to the proposal from the Commission,

Having regard to the opinion of the European Parliament (OJ C40, 8.4.74, p 25),

Having regard to the opinion of the Economic and Social Committee (OJ C139, 12.11.74, p 15),

Whereas all Member States have adopted a system of value added tax in accordance with the first and second Council Directives of 11 April 1967 on the harmonisation of the laws of the Member States relating to turnover taxes (OJ 71, 14.4.67, pp 1301–1367);

Whereas the Decision of 21 April 1970 on the replacement of financial contributions from Member States by the Communities' own resources (OJ L94, 28.4.70, p 19) provides that the budget of the Communities shall, irrespective of other revenue, be financed entirely from the Communities' own resources; whereas these resources are to include those accruing from value added tax and obtained by applying a common rate of tax on a basis of assessment determined in a uniform manner according to Community rules;

Whereas further progress should be made in the effective removal of restrictions on the movement of persons, goods, services and capital and the integration of national economies;

Whereas account should be taken of the objective of abolishing the imposition of tax on the importation and the remission of tax on exportation in trade between Member States; whereas it should be ensured that the common system of turnover taxes is non-discriminatory as regards the origin of goods and services, so that a common market permitting fair competition and resembling a real internal market may ultimately be achieved;

Whereas, to enhance the non-discriminatory nature of the tax, the term "taxable person" must be clarified to enable the Member States to extend it to cover persons who occasionally carry out certain transactions;

Whereas the term "taxable transaction" has led to difficulties, in particular as regards transactions treated as taxable transactions; whereas these concepts must be clarified;

Whereas the determination of the place where taxable transactions are effected has been the subject of conflicts concerning jurisdiction as between Member States, in particular as regards supplies of goods for assembly and the supply of services; whereas although the place where a supply of services is effected should in principle be defined as the place where the person supplying the services has his principal place of business, that place should be defined as being in the country of the person to whom the services are supplied, in particular in the case of certain services supplied between taxable persons where the cost of the services is included in the price of the goods;

Whereas the concepts of chargeable event and of the charge to tax must be harmonised if the introduction and any subsequent alterations of the Community rate are to become operative at the same time in all Member States;

Whereas the taxable base must be harmonised so that the application of the Community rate to taxable transactions leads to comparable results in all the Member States;

Whereas the rates applied by Member States must be such as to allow the normal deduction of the tax applied at the preceding stage;

Whereas a common list of exemptions should be drawn up so that the Communities' own resources may be collected in a uniform manner in all the Member States;

Whereas the rules governing deductions should be harmonised to the extent that they affect the actual amounts collected; whereas the deductible proportion should be calculated in a similar manner in all the Member States;

Whereas it should be specified which persons are liable to pay tax, in particular as regards services supplied by a person established in another country;

Whereas the obligations of taxpayers must be harmonised as far as possible so as to ensure the necessary safeguards for the collection of taxes in a uniform manner in all the Member States; whereas taxpayers should, in particular, make a periodic aggregate return of their transactions, relating to both inputs and outputs where this appears necessary for establishing and monitoring the basis of assessment of own resources;

Whereas Member States should nevertheless be able to retain their special schemes for small undertakings, in accordance with common provisions, and with a view to closer harmonisation; whereas Member States should remain free to apply a special scheme involving flat rate rebates of input value added tax to farmers not covered by normal schemes; whereas the basic principles of this scheme should be established and a common method adopted for calculating the value added of these farmers for the purposes of collecting own resources;

Whereas the uniform application of the provisions of this Directive should be ensured; whereas to this end a Community procedure for consultation should be laid down; whereas the setting up of a Value Added Tax Committee would enable the Member States and the Commission to co-operate closely;

Whereas Member States should be able, within certain limits and subject to certain conditions, to take or retain special measures derogating from this Directive in order to simplify the levying of tax or to avoid fraud or tax avoidance;

Whereas it might appear appropriate to authorise Member States to conclude with non-member countries or international organisations agreements containing derogations from this Directive;

Whereas it is vital to provide for a transitional period to allow national laws in specified fields to be gradually adapted,

HAS ADOPTED THIS DIRECTIVE:

TITLE I: INTRODUCTORY PROVISIONS

Article 1

Member States shall modify their present value added tax systems in accordance with the following Articles.

They shall adopt the necessary laws, regulations and administrative provisions so that the systems as modified enter into force at the earliest opportunity and by 1 January 1978 at the latest.

TITLE II: SCOPE

Article 2

The following shall be subject to value added tax:

1 *the supply of goods or services effected for consideration within the territory of the country by a taxable person acting as such;*

2 *the importation of goods.*

Commentary—*De Voil Indirect Tax Service* **V2.101**.

Note—Council Decision 93/563/EEC, art 1 allows derogation from para 1 above.

Simon's Tax Cases—*C&E Comrs v Church Schools Foundation Ltd;* [2001] STC 1661; *C&E Comrs v Polok* [2002] STC 361; *Kretztechnik AG v Finanzamt Linz* [2005] STC 1118; *Hotel Scandic Gåsabäck AB v Riksskatteverket* [2005] STC 1311; *Lebara Ltd v R&C Comrs* (Case C-520/10) [2012] STC 1536; *Danove riaditel'stvo Slovenskej republiky v Profitube spol sro* (Case C-165/11) [2013] STC 538.

Art 2(1), *Halifax plc and others v C&E Comrs* [2006] STC 919; *University of Huddersfield Higher Education Corporation v C&E Comrs* [2006] STC 980; *Elliniko Dimosio v Karageorgou and others* [2006] STC 1654; *Ministero dell'Economia e delle Finanze and another v FCE Bank plc* [2007] STC 165; *Everything Everywhere Ltd (formerly T-Mobile (UK) Ltd) v R&C Comrs* (Case C-276/09) [2011] STC 316; *Finanzamt Essen-NordOst v GFKL Financial Services AG* (Case C-93/10) [2012] STC 79.

Cross references—See VAT Regulations, SI 1995/2518 reg 10 (implementation of para 1 above).

TITLE III: TERRITORIAL APPLICATION

[Article 3

1. For the purposes of this Directive—

- *"territory of a Member State" shall mean the territory of the country as defined in respect of each Member State in paragraphs 2 and 3,*
- *"Community" and "territory of the Community" shall mean the territory of the Member States as defined in respect of each Member State in paragraphs 2 and 3,*
- *"third territory" and "third country" shall mean any territory other than those defined in paragraphs 2 and 3 as the territory of a Member State.*

2. For the purposes of this Directive, the "territory of the country" shall be the area of application of the Treaty establishing the European Economic Community as defined in respect of each Member State in Article 227.

3. The following territories of individual Member States shall be excluded from the territory of the country:

- *Federal Republic of Germany:*
  the Island of Heligoland,
  the territory of Büsingen,
- *Kingdom of Spain:*
  Ceuta,
  Melilla,
- *Republic of Italy:*
  Livigno,
  Campione d'Italia,
  the Italian waters of Lake Lugano.

The following territories of individual Member States shall also be excluded from the territory of the country:

- *Kingdom of Spain:*
  the Canary Islands,
- *French Republic:*
  the overseas departments,
- *Hellenic Republic:*
  'Αγιο 'Οροζ.

[[4. By way of derogation from paragraph 1, in view of:

- *the conventions and treaties which the Principality of Monaco and the Isle of Man have concluded respectively with the French Republic and the United Kingdom of Great Britain and Northern Ireland,*
- *the Treaty concerning the Establishment of the Republic of Cyprus, the Principality of Monaco, the Isle of Man and the United Kingdom Sovereign Base Areas of Akrotiri and Dhekelia shall not be treated for the purpose of the application of this Directive as third territories.]*[3]

Member States shall take the measures necessary to ensure that transactions originating in or intended for—

- *the Principality of Monaco are treated as transactions originating in or intended for the French Republic,*
- *the Isle of Man are treated as transactions originating in or intended for the United Kingdom of Great Britain and Northern Ireland.]*[2]

[— the United Kingdom Sovereign Base Areas of Akrotiri and Dhekelia are treated as transactions originating in or intended for the Republic of Cyprus.][3]

5. If the Commission considers that the provisions laid down in paragraphs 3 and 4 are no longer justified, particularly in terms of fair competition or own resources, it shall submit appropriate proposals to the Council.][1]

Amendments—[1] Article 3 replaced by EEC Council Directive 91/680; OJ L376, 31.12.1991, p 1 art 1(1).
[2] Para 4 replaced by EEC Council Directive 92/111, art 1.1; OJ L384, 30.12.92.
[3] In para 4, words replaced and words inserted by the 2003 Act of Accession Protocol No 3 Annex Part Two (OJ L236; 23.9.2003 p 940).

Simon's Tax Cases—*Danove riaditel'stvo Slovenskej republiky v Profitube spol sro* (Case C-165/11) [2013] STC 538.

TITLE IV: TAXABLE PERSONS

Article 4

1. "Taxable person" shall mean any person who independently carries out in any place any economic activity specified in paragraph 2, whatever the purpose or results of that activity.

2. The economic activities referred to in paragraph 1 shall comprise all activities of producers, traders and persons supplying services including mining and agricultural activities and activities of the professions. The exploitation of tangible or intangible property for the purpose of obtaining income therefrom on a continuing basis shall also be considered an economic activity.

3. Member States may also treat as a taxable person anyone who carries out, on an occasional basis, a transaction relating to the activities referred to in paragraph 2 and in particular one of the following:

(a) the supply before first occupation of buildings or parts of buildings and the land on which they stand; Member States may determine the conditions of application of this criterion to transformations of buildings and the land on which they stand.

Member States may apply criteria other than that of first occupation, such as the period elapsing between the date of completion of the building and the date of first supply or the period elapsing between the date of first occupation and the date of subsequent supply, provided that these periods do not exceed five years and two years respectively.

"A building" shall be taken to mean any structure fixed to or in the ground;

(b) the supply of building land.

"Building land" shall mean any unimproved or improved land defined as such by the Member States.

4. The use of the word "independently" in paragraph 1 shall exclude employed and other persons from the tax in so far as they are bound to an employer by a contract of employment or by any other legal ties creating the relationship of employer and employee as regards working conditions, remuneration and the employer's liability.

Subject to the consultations provided for in Article 29, each Member State may treat as a single taxable person persons established in the territory of the country who, while legally independent, are closely bound to one another by financial, economic and organisational links.

[A Member State exercising the option provided for in the second subparagraph, may adopt any measures needed to prevent tax evasion or avoidance through the use of this provision.][1]

5. States, regional and local government authorities and other bodies governed by public law shall not be considered taxable persons in respect of the activities or transactions in which they engage as public authorities, even where they collect dues, fees, contributions or payments in connection with these activities or transactions.

However, when they engage in such activities or transactions, they shall be considered taxable persons in respect of these activities or transactions where treatment as non-taxable persons would lead to significant distortions of competition.

In any case, these bodies shall be considered taxable persons in relation to the activities listed in Annex D, provided they are not carried out on such a small scale as to be negligible.

Member States may consider activities of these bodies which are exempt under Article 13 or 28 as activities which they engage in as public authorities.

Commentary—*De Voil Indirect Tax Service* **V2.101, V2.108**.

Simon's Tax Cases—Art 4, *Gabalfrisa SL v Agencia Estatale Administracion Tributaria* [2002] STC 535; *I/S Fini H v Skatteministeriet* [2005] STC 903; *Finanzamt Offenbach am Main-Land v Faxworld Vorgründungsgesellschaft Peter Hünninghausen und Wolfgang Klein GbR* [2005] STC 1192; *Waterschap Zeeuws Vlaanderen v Staatssecretaris van Financiën* [2005] STC 1298; *Elliniko Dimosio v Karageorgou and others* [2006] STC 1654; *Finanzamt Essen-NordOst v GFKL Financial Services AG* (Case C-93/10) [2012] STC 79; *Finanzamt Freistadt Rohrbach Urfahr v Unabhängiger Finanzsenat Außenstelle Linz (in the presence of Fuchs)* (Case C-219/12) [2012] STC 114; *Finanzamt Saarlouis* (Case C-204/13) [2014] STC 1916.

Art 4(1), *Intercommunale voor Zeewaterontzilting (in liquidation) v Belgian State* [1996] STC 569; *ICAEW v C&E Comrs* [1999] STC 398; *Halifax plc and others v C&E Comrs* [2006] STC 919; *University of Huddersfield Higher Education Corporation v C&E Comrs* [2006] STC 980.

Art 4(2), *ICAEW v C&E Comrs* [1999] STC 398; *C&E Comrs v Yarburgh Children's Trust* [2002] STC 207; *Cibo Participations SA v Directeur regional des impots du Nord-Pas-de-Calais* [2002] STC 460; *Empresa de Desenvolvimento Mineiro SGPS SA (EDM) v Fazenda Pública (Ministério Público, intervening)* [2005] STC 65.

Art 4(3)(*b*), *Gemeente Emmen v Belastingdienst Grote Ondernemingen* [1996] STC 496; *JJ Komen en Zonen Beheer Heerhugowaard BV v Sttatssecretaris can Financien* (Case C-326/11) [2012] STC 2415.

Art 4(4), *Osman v C&E Comrs* [1989] STC 596; *Ayuntamiento de Sevilla v Recaudadores de las Zonas Primera y Segunda* [1993] STC 659; *C&E Comrs v Thorn Materials Supply Ltd and Thorn Resources Ltd* [1998] STC 725; *C&E Comrs v Barclays Bank plc, CA* [2001] STC 1558; *Ampliscientifica Srl and anor v Ministero Dell'Economia e delle Finanze and anor* [2011] STC 566.

Art 4(5), *R v C&E Comrs, ex p Greater Manchester Police Authority* [2001] STC 406, *CA; EC Commission v UK* [2000] STC 777; *Fazenda Pública v Câmera Municipal do Porto (Ministério Público, third party)* [2001] STC 560; *Customs and Excise Commissioners v Isle of Wight Council* [2005] STC 257; *Edinburgh Telford College v R'C Comrs* [2006] STC 1291; *Finanzamt Eisleben v Feuerbestattungsverein Halle eV (Lutherstadt Eisleben, joined party)* [2006] STC 2043.

Amendments—[1] Words in sub-para (4) inserted by Council Directive 2006/69/EC art 1(1), with effect from 13 August 2006, (OJ L 221, 12.8.2006, p 9).

TITLE V:
TAXABLE TRANSACTIONS

Article 5 Supply of goods

1. "Supply of goods" shall mean the transfer of the right to dispose of tangible property as owner.

2. Electric current, gas, heat, refrigeration and the like shall be considered tangible property.

3. Member States may consider the following to be tangible property:

(a) certain interest in immovable property;

(b) rights in rem giving the holder thereof a right of user over immovable property;

(c) shares or interests equivalent to shares giving the holder thereof de jure or de facto rights of ownership or possession over immovable property or part thereof.

4. The following shall also be considered supplies within the meaning of paragraph 1:

(a) the transfer, by order made by or in the name of a public authority or in pursuance of the law, of the ownership of property against payment of compensation;

(b) the actual handing over of goods, pursuant to a contract for the hire of goods for a certain period or for the sale of goods on deferred terms, which provides that in the normal course of events ownership shall pass at the latest upon payment of the final instalment;

(c) the transfer of goods pursuant to a contract under which commission is payable on purchase or sale.

[5. Member States may consider the handing over of certain works of construction to be supplies within the meaning of paragraph 1.][1]

6. The application by a taxable person of goods forming part of his business assets for his private use or that of his staff, or the disposal thereof free of charge or more generally their application for purposes other than those of his business, where the value added tax on the goods in question or the component parts thereof was wholly or partly deductible, shall be treated as supplies made for consideration. However, applications for the giving of samples or the making of gifts of small value for the purposes of the taxable person's business shall not be so treated.

7. Member States may treat as supplies made for consideration:

(a) the application by a taxable person for the purposes of his business of goods produced, constructed, extracted, processed, purchased or imported in the course of such business, where the value added tax on such goods, had they been acquired from another taxable person, would not be wholly deductible;

(b) the application of goods by a taxable person for the purposes of a non-taxable transaction, where the value added tax on such goods became wholly or partly deductible upon their acquisition or upon their application in accordance with sub-paragraph (a);

(c) except in those cases mentioned in paragraph 8, the retention of goods by a taxable person or his successors when he ceases to carry out a taxable economic activity where the value added tax on such goods became wholly or partly deductible upon their acquisition or upon their application in accordance with sub-paragraph (a).

8. In the event of a transfer, whether for consideration or not or as a contribution to a company, of a totality of assets or part thereof, Member States may consider that no supply of goods has taken place and in that event the recipient shall be treated as the successor to the transferor. [Where appropriate, Member States may, in cases where the recipient is not wholly liable to tax, take the measures necessary to prevent distortion of competition. They may also adopt any measures needed to prevent tax evasion or avoidance through the use of this provision.][2]

Cross references—See Council Decision EEC 93/204, art 1; OJ L88, 8.4.93 (derogation from para 8 above granted to the UK).

Simon's Tax Cases—art 5, *Finanzamt Uelzen v Armbrecht* [1995] STC 997; *R&C Comrs v Loyalty Management Ltd* (Case C-53/09) [2010] STC 2651; *Baxi Group Ltd v R&C Comrs* (Case C-55/09) [2010] STC 2651; *Finanzampt Burgdorf v Bog and other references* (Joned Cases C-497/09, C-499/09, C-501/09 and C-502/09) [2011] STC 1221; *Grattan plc v R&C Comrs* (C-310/11) [2013] STC 502.

Art 5(1), *van Tiem v Staatssecretaris van Financiën* [1993] STC 91; *British Airways plc v C&E Comrs* [1996] STC 1127; *, *Stewart (t/a GT Shooting) v C&E Comrs* [2002] STC 255; *Halifax plc and others v C&E Comrs* [2006] STC 919; *University of Huddersfield Higher Education Corporation v C&E Comrs* [2006] STC 980; *Finanzamt Ludenscheid v Schriever* (Case C-444/10) [2012] STC 633.

Art 5(3), *DTZ Zadelhoff vif v Sttatssecretaris van Financien* (C-259/11) [2012] STC 2271.

Art 5(3)(*b*), *van Tiem v Staatssecretaris van Financiën* [1993] STC 91; *Stichting 'Goed Wonen' v Staatssecretaris van Financiën* [2003] STC 1137.

Art 5(6), *Kuwait Petroleum (GB) Ltd v C&E Comrs* [2001] STC 62; *Finanzamt Burgdorf v Fischer, Finanzamt Düsseldorf-Mettman v Brandenstein* [2001] STC 1356; *Hotel Scandic Gåsabäck AB v Riksskatteverket* [2005] STC 1311; *Church of England Children's Society v Revenue and Customs Commissioners* [2005] STC 1644.

Art 5(7)(*a*), *C&E Comrs v Robert Gordon's College* [1995] STC 1093; *Staatssecretaris van Financien v Gemeente Vlaardingen* (Case C-299/11) [2013] STC 478.

Art 5(8), *Abbey National plc v C&E Comrs* [2001] STC 297; *Zita Modes Sàrl v Administration de l'Enregistrment et des Domaines* [2005] STC 1059; *Finanzamt Offenbach am Main-Land v Faxworld Vorgründungsgesellschaft Peter Hünninghausen und Wolfgang Klein GbR* [2005] STC 1192; *Finanzamt Ludenscheid v Schriever* (Case C-444/10) [2012] STC 633; *Staatssecretaris van Financiën v X BV* (Case C-651/11) [2013] STC 1893.

Amendments—[1] Para 5 replaced by EC Council Directive 95/7, art 1(1): OJ L102, 5.5.95, p 18 with effect from 25 May 1995.

VAT EC

[2] Words in para (8) inserted by Council Directive 2006/69/EC art 1(2), with effect from 13 August 2006, (OJ L 221, 12.8.2006, p 9).

Article 6 Supply of services

1. "Supply of services" shall mean any transaction which does not constitute a supply of goods within the meaning of Article 5.

Such transactions may include inter alia:

- *assignments of intangible property whether or not it is the subject of a document establishing title,*
- *obligations to refrain from an act or to tolerate an act or situation,*
- *the performances of services in pursuance of an order made by or in the name of a public authority or in pursuance of the law.*

2. The following shall be treated as supplies of services for consideration:

(a) the use of goods forming part of the assets of a business for the private use of the taxable person or of his staff or more generally for purposes other than those of his business where the value added tax on such goods is wholly or partly deductible;

(b) supplies of services carried out free of charge by the taxable person for his own private use or that of his staff or more generally for purposes other than those of his business.

Member States may derogate from the provisions of this paragraph provided that such derogation does not lead to distortion of competition.

3. In order to prevent distortion of competition and subject to the consultations provided for in Article 29, Member States may treat as a supply of services for consideration the supply by a taxable person of a service for the purposes of his undertaking where the value added tax on such a service, had it been supplied by another taxable person, would not be wholly deductible.

4. Where a taxable person acting in his own name but on behalf of another takes part in a supply of services, he shall be considered to have received and supplied those services himself.

5. Article 5(8) shall apply in like manner to the supply of services.

Commentary—*De Voil Indirect Tax Service* **V3.470**.

Simon's Tax Cases—*Mirror Group Newspapers Ltd v Customs and Excise Commissioners* [2000] STC 156; *Swedish State v Stockholm Lindopark AB, Stockholm Lindopark AB v Swedish State* [2001] STC 103; *Trinity Mirror plc (formerly Mirror Group Newspapers Ltd) v C&E Comrs* [2001] STC 192; *R&C Comrs v Loyalty Management Ltd* (Case C-53/09) [2010] STC 2651; *Baxi Group Ltd v R&C Comrs* (Case C-55/09) [2010] STC 2651, *Finanzampt Burgdorf v Bog and other references* (Joned Cases C-497/09, C-499/09, C-501/09 and C-502/09) [2011] STC 1221.

art 6(1), *Faaborg-Gelting Linien A/S v Finanzamt Flensburg* (Case C-231/94) [1996] STC 774; *Landboden-Agrardienste GmbH & Co KG v Finanzamt Calau* (Case C-384/95) [1998] STC 171; *Halifax plc and others v C&E Comrs* [2006] STC 919; *University of Huddersfield Higher Education Corporation v C&E Comrs* [2006] STC 980.

art 6(2), *Enkler v Finanzamt Homburg* (Case C-230/94) [1996] STC 1316; *Julius Fillibeck Söhne Gmbh & Co KG v Finanzamt Neustadt* (Case C-258/95) [1998] STC 513; *Hotel Scandic Gåsabäck AB v Riksskatteverket* [2005] STC 1311; *Charles and another v Staatssecretaris van Financiën* [2006] STC 1429; *van Laarhoven v Staatssecretaris van Financiën* (Case C-594/10) [2012] STC 1023; *Belgium v BLM SA* (Case C-436/10) [2012] STC 1564; *X v Staatssecretaris van Financien* (C-334/10) [2012] STC 2288.

art 6(2)(*a*), *Victoria and Albert Museum Trustees v C&E Comrs* [1996] STC 1016; *Finanzamt München III v Mohsche* (Case C-193/91) [1997] STC 195; *Seeling v Finanzamt Starnberg* [2003] STC 805.

art 6(3), *C&E Comrs v Robert Gordon's College* [1995] STC 1093.

art 6(4), *Belgium v Henfling and others (acting as administrators in the insolvency of Tierce Franco-Belge SA)* (C-464/10) [2011] STC 1851.

art 6(5), *Finanzamt Offenbach am Main-Land v Faxworld Vorgründungsgesellschaft Peter Hünninghausen und Wolfgang Klein GbR* [2005] STC 1192; *Staatssecretaris van Financiën v X BV* (Case C-651/11) [2013] STC 1893.

Article 7 Imports

[1. "Importation of goods" shall mean:

(a) the entry into the Community of goods which do not fulfil the conditions laid down in Articles 9 and 10 of the Treaty establishing the European Economic Community or, where the goods are covered by the Treaty establishing the European Coal and Steel Community, are not in free circulation;

[(b) the entry into the Community of goods from a third territory, other than the goods covered by (a).][2]

2. The place of import of goods shall be the Member State within the territory of which the goods are when they enter the Community.

3. Notwithstanding paragraph 2, where goods referred to in paragraph 1(a) are, on entry into the Community, placed under one of the arrangements referred to in Article 16(1)(B)[(a), (b), (c) and (d)],[3] *under arrangements for temporary importation with total exemption from import duty or under external transit arrangements, the place of import of such goods shall be the Member State within the territory of which they cease to be covered by those arrangements.*

[Similarly, when goods referred to in paragraph 1(b) are placed, on entry into the Community, under one of the procedures referred to in Article 33a(1)(b) or (c), the place of import shall be the Member State within whose territory this procedure ceases to apply.][4]*]*[1]

Amendments—[1] Article 7 replaced by EEC Council Directive 91/680; OJ L376, 31.12.1991, p 1 art 1(2).

[2] Para 1(*b*) replaced by EEC Council Directive 92/111, art 1.2; OJ L384, 30.12.92.

[3] Words in para 3 added by EEC Council Directive 92/111, art 1.3, OJ L384, 30.12.92.
[4] Words in para 3 replaced by EEC Council Directive 92/111, art 1.3, OJ L384, 30.12.92.
Simon's Tax Cases—*Danove riaditel'stvo Slovenskej republiky v Profitube spol sro* (Case C-165/11) [2013] STC 538.

TITLE VI:
PLACE OF TAXABLE TRANSACTIONS

Article 8 Supply of goods

1. The place of supply of goods shall be deemed to be:

(a) in the case of goods dispatched or transported either by the supplier or by the person to whom they are supplied or by a third person: the place where the goods are at the time when dispatch or transport to the person to whom they are supplied begins. Where the goods are installed or assembled, with or without a trial run, by or on behalf of the supplier, the place of supply shall be deemed to be the place where the goods are installed or assembled. In cases where the installation or assembly is carried out [in a Member State other than][1] that of the supplier, [the Member State within the territory of which the installation or assembly is carried out][1] shall take any necessary steps to avoid double taxation in that State;

(b) in the case of goods not dispatched or transported: the place where the goods are when the supply takes place;

[(c) in the case of goods supplied on board ships, aircraft or trains during the part of a transport of passengers effected in the Community: at the point of the departure of the transport of passengers

[(d) in the case of the supply of gas through the natural gas distribution system, or of electricity, to a taxable dealer: the place where that taxable dealer has established his business or has a fixed establishment for which the goods are supplied, or, in the absence of such a place of business or fixed establishment, the place where he has his permanent address or usually resides.

"Taxable dealer" for the purposes of this provision means a taxable person whose principal activity in respect of purchases of gas and electricity is reselling such products and whose own consumption of these products is negligible.][5]

[(e) in the case of the supply of gas through the natural gas distribution system, or of electricity, where such a supply is not covered by point (d): the place where the customer has effective use and consumption of the goods. Where all or part of the goods are not in fact consumed by this customer, these non consumed goods are deemed to have been used and consumed at the place where he has established his business or has a fixed establishment for which the goods are supplied. In the absence of such a place of business or fixed establishment, he is deemed to have used and consumed the goods at the place where he has his permanent address or usually resides.][5]

For the purposes of applying this provision—

— "part of a transport of passengers effected in the Community" shall mean the part of the transport effected, without a stop in a third territory, between the point of departure and the point of arrival of the transport of passengers,

— "the point of departure of the transport of passengers" shall mean the first point of passenger embarkation foreseen within the Community, where relevant after a leg outside the Community,

— "the point of arrival of the transport of passengers" shall mean the last point of disembarkation of passengers foreseen within the Community of passengers who embarked in the Community, where relevant before a leg outside the Community.

In the case of a return trip, the return leg shall be considered to be a separate transport.

The Commission shall, by 30 June 1993 at the latest, submit to the Council a report accompanied, if necessary, by appropriate proposals on the place of taxation of goods supplied for consumption and services, including restaurant services, provided for passengers on board ships, aircraft or trains.

By 31 December 1993, after consulting the European Parliament, the Council shall take a unanimous decision on the Commission proposal.

Until 31 December 1993, Member States may exempt or continue to exempt goods supplied for consumption on board whose place of taxation is determined in accordance with the above provisions, with the right to deduct the value added tax paid at an earlier stage.][3]

[2. By way of derogation from paragraph 1(a), where the place of departure of the consignment or transport of goods is in a third territory, the place of supply by the importer as defined in [Article 21(4)][4] and the place of any subsequent supplies shall be deemed to be within the Member State of import of the goods.][2]

Cross references—See VAT (Place of Supply of Goods) Order, SI 1992/3283 (implementation of para 1(*c*) above).
Simon's Tax Cases—art 8(1)(*a*), *Grattan plc v R&C Comrs* (C-310/11) [2013] STC 502.
art 8(1)(*c*), *Peninsular and Oriental Steam Navigation Co v C&E Comrs* [2000] STC 488; *Köhler v Finanzamt Düsseldorf-Nord* [2006] STC 469.
Amendments—[1] Words in para 1(*a*) substituted by EEC Council Directive 91/680; OJ L376, 31.12.1991, p 1 art 1(3), (4), (5).
[2] Para 2 replaced by EEC Council Directive 91/680; OJ L376, 31.12.1991, p 1 art 1(3), (4), (5).

VAT EC

3 Para 1(*c*) replaced by EEC Council Directive 92/111, art 1.4; OJ L384, 30.12.92.
4 Words "Article 21(4)" substituted for "Article 21(2)" by Council Directive 2000/65/EC art 1(6) with effect from 21 October 2000; OJ L269 p 44, 21.10.00. Member states must bring into force the measures necessary to comply with these provisions not later than 31 December 2001.
5 Para 1(*d*), (*e*) inserted by Council Directive 2003/92/EC art 1(1); OJ L260, 11.10.2003 p 8.

Article 9 Supply of services

1. The place where a service is supplied shall be deemed to be the place where the supplier has established his business or has a fixed establishment from which the service is supplied or, in the absence of such a place of business or fixed establishment, the place where he has his permanent address or usually resides.

2. However:

(a) the place of the supply of services connected with immovable property, including the services of estate agents and experts, and of services for preparing and co-ordinating construction works, such as the services of architects and of firms providing on-site supervision, shall be the place where the property is situated;

(b) the place where transport services are supplied shall be the place where transport takes place, having regard to the distances covered;

(c) the place of the supply of services relating to:

— cultural, artistic, sporting, scientific, educational, entertainment or similar activities, including the activities of the organisers of such activities, and where appropriate, supply of ancillary services,

— ancillary transport activities such as loading, handling and similar activities,

— valuations of movable tangible property,

— work on movable tangible property,

shall be the place where those services are physically carried out;

[(d) . . .][1]

(e) the place where the following services are supplied when performed for customers established outside the Community or for taxable persons established in the Community but not in the same country as the supplier, shall be the place where the customer has established his business or has a fixed establishment to which the service is supplied or, in the absence of such a place, the place where he has his permanent address or usually resides:

— transfers and assignments of copyrights, patents, licences, trade marks and similar rights,

— advertising services,

— services of consultants, engineers, consultancy bureaux, lawyers, accountants and other similar services, as well as data processing and the supplying of information,

— obligations to refrain from pursuing or exercising, in whole or in part, a business activity or a right referred to in this point (e),

— banking, financial and insurance transactions including reinsurance, with the exception of the hire of safes,

— the supply of staff,

— the services of agents who act in the name and for the account of another, when they procure for their principal the services referred to in this point (e).

[— the hiring out of movable tangible property with the exception of all forms of transport;][2]

[— the provision of access to, and of transport or transmission through, natural gas and electricity distribution systems and the provision of other directly linked services.][5]

[— Telecommunications. Telecommunications services shall be deemed to be services relating to the transmission, emission or reception of signals, writing, images and sounds or information of any nature by wire, radio, optical or other electromagnetic systems, including the related transfer or assignment of the right to use capacity for such transmission, emission or reception. Telecommunications services within the meaning of this provision shall also include provision of access to global information networks;][3]

[— radio and television broadcasting services,][4]

[— electronically supplied services, inter alia, those described in Annex L.][4]

[(f) the place where services referred to in the last indent of sub-paragraph (e) are supplied when performed for non-taxable persons who are established, have their permanent address or usually reside in a Member State, by a taxable person who has established his business or has a fixed establishment from which the service is supplied outside the Community or, in the absence of such a place of business or fixed establishment, has his permanent address or usually resides outside the Community, shall be the place where the non-taxable person is established, has his permanent address or usually resides.][4]

[3. In order to avoid double taxation, non-taxation or the distortion of competition, the Member States may, with regard to the supply of services referred to in paragraph 2(e), except for the services referred to in the last indent when supplied to non-taxable persons, and also with regard to the hiring out of forms of transport consider:][4]

(a) the place of supply of services, which under this Article would be situated within the territory of the country, as being situated outside the Community where the effective use and enjoyment of the services take place outside the Community;

(b) the place of supply of services, which under this Article would be situated outside the Community, as being within the territory of the country where the effective use and enjoyment of the services take place within the territory of the country.

[4. In the case of telecommunications services and radio and television broadcasting services referred to in paragraph 2(e) when performed for non-taxable persons who are established, have their permanent address or usually reside in a Member State, by a taxable person who has established his business or has a fixed establishment from which the service is supplied outside the Community, or in the absence of such a place of business or fixed establishment, has his permanent address or usually resides outside the Community, Member States shall make use of paragraph 3(b).][4]

Commentary—*De Voil Indirect Tax Service* **V2.101**, **V3.166**, **V3.192**.

Note—Council decision 97/214 allows derogation from this Article.

Press releases etc—Written Answer. OJ C140, 21.5.94 (treatment of compensation payments for destroyed or stolen property subject to leasing contracts governed by para 2(*e*) above).

Business Brief 12/98 21.5.98 (Overseas businesses established in the UK through agencies).

Simon's Tax Cases—art 9, *Diversified Agency Services Ltd v C&E Comrs* [1996] STC 398; *(Case C-167/95)* [1997] STC 1287; *C&E Comrs v Chinese Channel (Hong Kong) Ltd* [1998] STC 347, *R (on the application of IDT Card Services Ireland Ltd) v Customs and Excise Commissioners* [2005] STC 314; *R&C Comrs v IDT Card Services Ireland Ltd* [2006] STC 1252.

Art 9(1), *ARO Lease BV v Inspecteur der Belastingdienst Grote Ondernemingen, Amsterdam* (Case C-190/95) [1997] STC 1272; *Lease Plan Luxembourg SA v Belgium* (Case C-390/96) [1998] STC 628; *EC Commission v French Republic* [2001] STC 156; *RAL (Channel Islands) and others v C&E Comrs* [2005] STC 1025; *Ministero dell'Economia e delle Finanze and another v FCE Bank plc* [2007] STC 165.

Art 9(2)(*b*), *EC Commission v Hellenic Republic* (Case C-331\94) [1996] STC 1168; *Reisebüro Binder GmbH v Finanzamt Stuttgart-Körperschaften* (Case C-116/96) [1998] STC 604.

Art 9(2)(*c*), *Dudda v Finanzamt Bergisch Gladbach* (Case C-327/94) [1996] STC 1290; *RAL (Channel Islands) and others v C&E Comrs* [2005] STC 1025; *Ministre de l'Économie, des Finances et de l'Industrie v Gillian Beach Ltd* [2006] STC 1080; *Kronospan Mielec sp z oo v Dyrektor Izby Skarbowej w Rzeszowie* (Case C-222/09) [2011] STC 80.

Art 9(2)(*d*), *Hamann v Finanzamt Hamburg-Eimsbüttel* [1991] STC 193.

Art 9(2)(*e*), *EC Commission v Grand Duchy of Luxembourg* (Case C-69/92) [1997] STC 712; *von Hoffmann v Finanzamt Trier* [1997] STC 1321; *Synidcat des Producteurs Independants (SPI) v Ministere de l'Economie, des Finances et de l'Industry* [2001] STC 523; *Design Concept SA v Flanders Expo SA* [2003] STC 912; *R&C Comrs v Zurich Insurance Co* [2006] STC 1694; *Kronospan Mielec sp z oo v Dyrektor Izby Skarbowej w Rzeszowie* (Case C-222/09) [2011] STC 80.

Cross references—See VAT (Place of Supply of Services) Order, SI 1992/3121 (implementation of paras 2, 3 above).

Amendments—[1] Para 2(*d*) deleted by art 1 of the Tenth Council Directive of 31 July 1984: 84/386/EEC; see OJ L208, 3.8.1984, p 58.

[2] Words in para 2(*e*) added by art 1 of the Tenth Council Directive of 31 July 1984: 84/386/EEC; see OJ L208. 3.8.1984, p 58.

[3] Indent added to s 9(2)(*e*) and para 4 inserted by Council Directive of 17 June 1999: 99/59/EC; see OJ L162/64, 26.6.1999.

[4] This article is temporarily amended by Council Directive 2002/38 art 1 para 1 (OJ L 128; 15.05.02). Two more indents added to para 2(*e*), and point (*f*) added; the introductory phrase to para 3 substituted, and para 4 substituted, with effect for a period of three years from 1 July 2003: see Council Directive 2002/38/EC art 4.

[5] Indent added to para 2(*e*) by Council Directive 2003/92/EC, art 1(2); OJ L260, 11.10.2003 p 8.

TITLE VII:
CHARGEABLE EVENT AND CHARGEABILITY OF TAX

Article 10

1

(a) "Chargeable event" shall mean the occurrence by virtue of which the legal conditions necessary for tax to become chargeable are fulfilled.

(b) The tax becomes "chargeable" when the tax authority becomes entitled under the law at a given moment to claim the tax from the person liable to pay, notwithstanding that the time of payment may be deferred.

2. The chargeable event shall occur and the tax shall become chargeable when the goods are delivered or the services are performed. Deliveries of goods other than those referred to in Article 5(4)(b) and supplies of services which give rise to successive statements of account or payments shall be regarded as being completed at the time when the periods to which such statements of account or payments pertain expire. [Member States may in certain cases provide that continuous supplies of goods and services which take place over a period of time shall be regarded as being completed at least at intervals of one year.][2]

However, where a payment is to be made on account before the goods are delivered or the services are performed, the tax shall become chargeable on receipt of the payment and on the amount received.

By way of derogation from the above provisions, Member States may provide that the tax shall become chargeable, for certain transactions or for certain categories of taxable person, either:

— no later than the issue of the invoice . . .[3]*, or*

— no later than receipt of the price, or

VAT EC

— *where an invoice . . .* [3] *is not issued, or is issued late, within a specified period from the date of the chargeable event.*

[3. The chargeable event shall occur and the tax shall become chargeable when the goods are imported. Where goods are placed under one of the arrangements referred to in Article 7(3) on entry into the Community, the chargeable event shall occur and the tax shall become chargeable only when the goods cease to be covered by those arrangements.

However, where imported goods are subject to customs duties, to agricultural levies or to charges having equivalent effect established under a common policy, the chargeable event shall occur and the tax shall become chargeable when the chargeable event for those Community duties occurs and those duties become chargeable.

Where imported goods are not subject to any of those Community duties, Member States shall apply the provisions in force governing customs duties as regards the occurrence of the chargeable event and the moment when the tax becomes chargeable.] [1]

Simon's Tax Cases—art 10, *Ufficio IVA di Trapani v Italittica SpA* (Case C-144/94) [1995] STC 1059; *Balocchi v Ministero delle Finanze* [1997] STC 640; *Société Financière d'Investissements SPRL v Belgium* [2000] STC 164.

Art 10(2), *C&E Comrs v British Telecom plc* [1996] STC 818; *BUPA Hospitals Ltd and another v C&E Comrs* [2006] STC 967.

Art 10(3), *Pezzullo Molini Pastifici Mangimifici SpA v Ministero delle Finanze* (Case C-166/94) [1996] STC 1236.

Amendments—[1] Article 10(3) replaced by EEC Council Directive 91/680; OJ L376, 31.12.1991, p 1 art 1(6).

[2] Words in art 10(2) inserted by Council Directive 2000/65/EC art 1(1) with effect from 21 October 2000; OJ L269 p 44, 21.10.00. Member states must bring into force the measures necessary to comply with these provisions not later than 31 December 2001.

[3] Words in art 10(2) revoked by Council Directive 2001/115/EC art 4(1) (see OJ L 015; 17.01.02).

TITLE VIII:
TAXABLE AMOUNT

Article 11

A. Within the territory of the country

1. The taxable amount shall be:

(a) in respect of supplies of goods and services other than those referred to in (b), (c) and (d) below, everything which constitutes the consideration which has been or is to be obtained by the supplier from the purchaser, the customer or a third party for such supplies including subsidies directly linked to the price of such supplies;

(b) in respect of supplies referred to in Article 5(6) and (7), the purchase price of the goods or of similar goods or, in the absence of a purchase price, the cost price, determined at the time of supply;

(c) in respect of supplies referred to in Article 6(2), the full cost to the taxable person of providing the services;

(d) in respect of supplies referred to in Article 6(3), the open market value of the services supplied.

. . . [6]

2. The taxable amount shall include:

(a) taxes, duties, levies and charges, excluding the value added tax itself;

(b) incidental expenses such as commission, packing, transport and insurance costs charged by the supplier to the purchaser or customer. Expenses covered by a separate agreement may be considered to be incidental expenses by the Member States.

3. The taxable amount shall not include:

(a) price reductions by way of discount for early payment;

(b) price discounts and rebates allowed to the customer and accounted for at the time of the supply;

(c) the amounts received by a taxable person from his purchaser or customer as repayment for expenses paid out in the name and for the account of the latter and which are entered in his books in a suspense account. The taxable person must furnish proof of the actual amount of this expenditure and may not deduct any tax which may have been charged on these transactions.

[4. By way of derogation from paragraphs 1, 2 and 3, Member States which, on 1 January 1993, did not avail themselves of the option provided for in the third sub-paragraph of Article 12(3)(a) may, where they avail themselves of the option provided for in Title B(6), provide that, for the transactions referred to in the second sub-paragraph of Article 12(3)(c), the taxable amount shall be equal to a fraction of the amount determined in accordance with paragraphs 1, 2 and 3.

That fraction shall be determined in such a way that the value added tax thus due is, in any event, equal to at least 5% of the amount determined in accordance with paragraphs 1, 2 and 3.] [3]

[5. Member States shall have the option of including in the taxable amount in respect of the supply of goods and services, the value of exempt investment gold within the meaning of Article 26b, which has been provided by the customer to be used as a basis for working and which as a result, loses its VAT exempt investment gold status when such goods and services are supplied. The value to be used is the open market value of the investment gold at the time that those goods and services are supplied.

6. In order to prevent tax evasion or avoidance, Member States may take measures to ensure that the taxable amount in respect of a supply of goods or services shall be the open market value. The option shall be applied only in respect of supplies of goods and services involving family or other close personal ties, management, ownership, membership, financial or legal ties as defined by the Member State. For these purposes legal ties may include the relationship between an employer and employee or the employee's family, or any other closely connected persons.

The option in the first subparagraph may apply only in any of the following circumstances:

(a) where the consideration is lower than the open market value and the recipient of the supply does not have a full right of deduction under Article 17;

(b) where the consideration is lower than the open market value and the supplier does not have a full right of deduction under Article 17 and the supply is subject to an exemption under Article 13 or Article 28(3)(b);

(c) where the consideration is higher than the open market value and the supplier does not have a full right of deduction under Article 17.

Member States may restrict the categories of suppliers or recipients to whom the measures in the first and the second subparagraph shall apply.

Member States shall inform the Committee established in accordance with Article 29 of any new national measure adopted pursuant to the provisions of this paragraph.

7. For the purposes of this Directive, "open market value" shall mean the full amount that, in order to obtain the goods or services in question at that time, a customer at the same marketing stage at which the supply of goods or services takes place, would have to pay, under conditions of fair competition, to a supplier at arm's length within the territory of the Member State in which the supply is subject to tax.

Where no comparable supply of goods or services can be ascertained, "open market value" shall mean, in respect of goods, an amount that is not less than the purchase price of the goods or of similar goods or, in the absence of a purchase price, the cost price, determined at the time of supply; in respect of services it shall mean not less than the full cost to the taxable person of providing the service.][6]

B. Importation of goods

[1. The taxable amount shall be the value for customs purposes, determined in accordance with the Community provisions in force; this shall also apply for the import of goods referred to in Article 7(1)(b).][2]

2. . . . *(repealed by Directive 91/680)*

[3. The taxable amount shall include, in so far as they are not already included:

(a) taxes, duties, levies and other charges due outside the importing Member State and those due by reason of importation, excluding the value added tax to be levied;

(b) incidental expenses, such as commission, packing, transport and insurance costs, incurred up to the first place of destination within the territory of the importing Member State.
"First place of destination" shall mean the place mentioned on the consignment note or any other document by means of which the goods are imported into the importing Member State. In the absence of such an indication, the first place of destination shall be taken to be the place of the first transfer of cargo in the importing Member State.
[The incidental expenses referred to above shall also be included in the taxable amount where they result from transport to another place of destination within the territory of the Community if that place is known when the chargeable event occurs.][5]

4. The taxable amount shall not include those factors referred to in A(3)(a) and (b).

5. When goods have been temporarily exported [from the Community][1] *and are re-imported after having undergone abroad repair, processing or adaptation, or after having been made up or reworked [outside the Community]*[1], *Member States shall take steps to ensure that the treatment of the goods for value added tax purposes is the same as that which would have applied to the goods in question had the above operations been carried out within the territory of the country.*

[6. By way of derogation from paragraphs 1 to 4, Member States which, on 1 January 1993, did not avail themselves of the option provided for in the third sub-paragraph of Article 12(3)(a) may provide that for imports of the works of art, collectors' items and antiques defined in Article 26a(A)(a), (b) and (c), the taxable amount shall be equal to a fraction of the amount determined in accordance with paragraphs 1 to 4.

That fraction shall be determined in such a way that the value added tax thus due on the import is, in any event, equal to at least 5% of the amount determined in accordance with paragraphs 1 to 4.][4]

C. Miscellaneous provisions

1. In the case of cancellation, refusal or total or partial non-payment, or where the price is reduced after the supply takes place, the taxable amount shall be reduced accordingly under conditions which shall be determined by the Member States.
However, in the case of total or partial non-payment, Member States may derogate from this rule.
[2. Where information for determining the taxable amount on importation is expressed in a currency other than that of the Member State where assessment takes place, the exchange rate shall be determined in accordance with the Community provisions governing the calculation of the value for customs purposes.
Where information for the determination of the taxable amount of a transaction other than an import transaction is expressed in a currency other than that of the Member State where assessment takes place, the exchange rate applicable shall be the latest selling rate recorded, at the time the tax becomes chargeable, on the most representative exchange market or markets of the Member State concerned, or a rate determined by reference to that or those markets, in accordance with the . . . down by that Member State. However, for some of those transactions or for certain categories of taxable person, Member States may continue to apply the exchange rate determined in accordance with the Community provisions in force governing the calculation of the value for customs purposes.][1]
3. As regards returnable packing costs, Member States may:
- *either exclude them from the taxable amount and take the necessary measures to see that this amount is adjusted if the packing is not returned,*
- *or include them in the taxable amount and take the necessary measures to see that this amount is adjusted where the packing is in fact returned.*

Note—Some words are missing in the second paragraph of art 11(C)(2) which is reproduced above as it appears in the EEC Official Journal.

Press releases etc—Business Brief 21/97, 3.10.97 (bad debt relief scheme changes for barter transactions).

Simon's Tax Cases—*Direct Cosmetics Ltd and Laughtons Photographs Ltd v C&E Comrs* [1988] STC 540; *BP Supergas Anonimos Etairia Geniki Emporiki-Viomichaniki kai Antiprossopeion v Greece* (Case C-62/93) [1995] STC 805; *C&E Comrs v Bugeja* [2000] STC 1; *C&E Comrs v Plantiflor Ltd* [2000] STC 137.

Art 11A, *Trafalgar Tours Ltd v C&E Comrs* [1990] STC 127.

Art 11A(1), *Muy's en De Winter's Bouw-en Aannemingsbedrijf BV v Staatssecretaris van Financiën* [1997] STC 665; *Rosgill Group Ltd v C&E Comrs* [1997] STC 811; *Nell Gwynn House Maintenance Fund Trustees v C&E Comrs* [1999] STC 79; *Marks and Spencer plc v C&E Comrs (Case C-62/00)* [2002] STC 1036; *Campsa Estaciones de Servicio SA v Administracion del Estada* (Case C-285/10) [2011] STC 1603.

Art 11A(1)(*a*), *Town and County Factors Ltd v C&E Comrs* (Case C-498/99) [2002] STC 1263; *EC Commission v Federal Republic of Germany (United Kingdom intervening)*, [2003] STC 301; *Yorkshire Co-operatives Ltd v C&E Comrs* [2003] STC 234; *Office des Produits Wallons ASBL v Belgium* [2003] STC 1100; *Lex Services plc v C&E Comrs* [2004] STC 73; *R&C Comrs v Loyalty Management Ltd* (Case C-53/09) [2010] STC 2651; *Baxi Group Ltd v R&C Comrs* (Case C-55/09) [2010] STC 2651; *International Bingo Technology SA v Tribunal Económico-Administrativo Regional de Cataluña (TEARC)* (Case C-377/11) [2013] STC 661; *Le Rayon d'Or SARL v Ministre de l'Economie et des Finances* (Case C-151/13) [2014] STC 1165.

Art 11A(1)(*b*), *Staatssecretaris van Financien v Gemeente Vlaardingen* (Case C-299/11) [2013] STC 478.

Art 11A(1)(*c*), *Köhne v Finanzamt München III* [1990] STC 749; *Enkler v Finanzamt Homburg* (Case C-230/94) [1996] STC 1316; *van Laarhoven v Staatssecretaris van Financiën* (Case C-594/10) [2012] STC 1023.

Art 11A(2)(*b*), *C&E Comrs v British Telecom plc* [1999] STC 758.

Art 11A(3), *Nell Gwynn House Maintenance Fund Trustees v C&E Comrs* [1999] STC 79; *Finanzamt Dusseldorf-Mitte v Ibero Tours GmbH* (Case C-300/12) [2014] STC 991.

Art 11A(3)(*b*), *Boots Co plc v C&E Comrs* [1990] STC 387; *Kuwait Petroleum (GB) Ltd v C&E Comrs* [1999] STC 488, [2001] STC 62, *Freemans v C&E Comrs* [2001] STC 960.

Art 11A(3)(*c*), *C&E Comrs v Plantiflor* [2002] STC 1132.

Art 11C(1), *Elida Gibbs Ltd v C&E Comrs* (Case C-317/94) [1996] STC 1387; *Goldsmiths (Jewellers) Ltd v C&E Comrs* (Case C-330/95) [1997] STC 1073; *Yorkshire Co-operatives Ltd v C&E Comrs* [2003] STC 234; *Simpson & Marwick (a firm) v R&C Comrs* [2011] UKUT 498 (TCC), [2012] STC 611; *GMAC UK plc v R&C Comrs*; *BT plc v R&C Comrs* [2012] UKUT 279 (TCC), [2012] STC 2349; *R&C Comrs v GMAC UK plc* (Case C-589/12) [2014] STC 2603; *British Telecommunications plc v R&C Comrs* [2014] EWCA Civ 433, [2014] STC 1926.

Amendments—[1] Article 11(B), (C) amended by EEC Council Directive 91/680; OJ L376, 31.12.1991, p 1, art 1(8), (9), (10).
[2] Para (B)(1) replaced by EEC Council Directive 92/111, art 1.5; OJ L384, 30.12.92.
[3] Para (A)(4) added by EEC Council Directive 94/5, arts 1(1), 4; OJ L60, 3.3.94. For commencement, see art 4 of the Directive printed *post*; see p 678.
[4] Para (B)(6) added by EEC Council Directive 94/5, arts 1(1), 4; OJ L60, 3.3.94.
[5] Words in para (B)(3)(*b*) replaced by EC Council Directive 95/7, art 1(2): OJ L102, 5.5.95, p 18 with effect from 25 May 1995.
[6] Words in para (A)(1)(*d*) repealed, and para (A)(5)–(7) inserted, by Council Directive 2006/69/EC art 1(3), with effect from 13 August 2006, (OJ L 221, 12.8.2006, p 9).

TITLE IX: RATES

Article 12

1. The rate applicable to taxable transactions shall be that in force at the time of the chargeable event. However:

(a) in the cases provided for in the second and third sub-paragraphs of Article 10(2), the rate to be used shall be that in force when the tax becomes chargeable;

[(b) in the cases provided for in the second and third sub-paragraphs of Article 10(3), the rate applicable shall be that in force at the time when the tax becomes chargeable.]

2. In the event of changes in the rates, Member States may:

— effect adjustments in the cases provided for in paragraph 1(a) in order to take account of the rate applicable at the time when the goods or services were supplied,

— adopt all appropriate transitional measures.

[3.

[(a) [The standard rate of value added tax shall be fixed by each Member State as a percentage of the taxable amount and shall be the same for the supply of goods and for the supply of services. From 1 January 2006 until 31 December 2010, the standard rate may not be less than 15%.][9]

[The Council shall decide, in accordance with Article 93 of the Treaty, on the level of the standard rate to be applied after 31 December 2010.][9]

[Member states may also apply either one or two reduced rates. These rates shall be fixed as a percentage of the taxable amount which may not be less than 5% and shall apply only to supplies of the categories of goods and services specified in Annex H.][7]

[The third subparagraph shall not apply to the services referred to in the last indent of Article 9(2)(e).][8]

[(b) Member States may apply a reduced rate to supplies of natural gas, electricity and district heating provided that no risk of distortion of competition exists. A Member State intending to apply such a rate must inform the Commission before doing so. The Commission shall give a decision on the existence of a risk of distortion of competition. If the Commission has not taken that decision within three months of the receipt of the information a risk of distortion of competition is deemed not to exist.][10]

[(c) Member States may provide that the reduced rate, or one of the reduced rates, which they apply in accordance with the third paragraph of (a) shall also apply to imports of works of art, collectors' items and antiques as referred to in Article 26a(A)(a), (b) and (c).

Where they avail themselves of this option, Member States may also apply the reduced rate to supplies of works of art, within the meaning of Article 26a(A)(a):

— effected by their creator or his successors in title,

— effected on an occasional basis by a taxable person other than a taxable dealer, where these works of art have been imported by the taxable person himself or where they have been supplied to him by their creator or his successors in title or where they have entitled him to full deduction of value added tax.][4]

(d) . . . [5]

(e) . . .][6]

Member States will take all necessary measures to combat fraud in this area from 1 January 1993. These measures may include the introduction of a system of accounting for VAT on supplies of gold between taxable persons in the same Member State which provides for the payment of tax by the buyer on behalf of the seller and a simultaneous right for the buyer to a deduction of the same amount of tax as input tax.][2]

4. . . . [2] *Each reduced rate shall be so fixed that the amount of value added tax resulting from the application thereof shall be such as in the normal way to permit the deduction therefrom of the whole of the value added tax deductible under the provisions of Article 17.*

[On the basis of a report from the Commission, the Council shall, starting in 1994, review the scope of the reduced rates every two years. The Council, acting unanimously on a proposal from the Commission, may decide to alter the list of goods and services in Annex H.][2]

[By 30 June 2007 at the latest the Commission shall present to the European Parliament and the Council an overall assessment report on the impact of reduced rates applying to locally supplied services, including restaurant services, notably in terms of job creation, economic growth and the proper functioning of the internal market, based on a study carried out by an independent economic think-tank.][10]

[5. Subject to paragraph 3(c), the rate applicable on the importation of goods shall be that applied to the supply of like goods within the territory of the country.][7]

[6. The Portuguese Republic may apply to transactions carried out in the autonomous regions of the Azores and Madeira and to direct imports to those regions, reduced rates in comparison to those applying on the mainland.][1]

Commentary—*De Voil Indirect Tax Service* **V4.401**.

VAT EC

Simon's Tax Cases—*Marks and Spencer plc v C&E Comrs* [2000] STC 16.

Art 12(3)(*a*), *EC Commission v French Republic (Republic of Finland intervening)* [2001] STC 919; *EC Commission v Federal Republic of Germany* [2006] STC 1587.

Amendments—[1] Para 6 added by the Act of Accession 1985, art 26 Annex I Part V point 2; see OJ L302, 15.11.85, p 167.

[2] Para 3 substituted and words in para 4 repealed and added by EEC Council Directive 92/77; see OJ L316, 31.10.92.

[4] Para 3(*c*) replaced by EEC Council Directive 94/5, arts 1(2), 4; OJ L60, 3.3.94. For commencement, see art 4 of the Directive printed *post*.

[5] Para 3(*d*) deleted by EC Council Directive 96/42, art 1, with effect from 1 January 1995; see OJ L170, 9.7.96, p 34.

[6] Para 3(*e*) deleted by EC Council Directive 98/80, art 2; with effect from 17 October 1998; see OJ L281, 17.10.98.

[7] Para 3(*a*) replaced by EC Council Directive 96/95, art 1; OJ L338, 28.12.96.

[8] This article is temporarily amended by Council Directive 2002/38 art 1 para 2 (OJ L 128; 15.05.02). A further sub-paragraph is added to para 3(*a*) with effect for a period of three years from 1 July 2003: see Council Directive 2002/38/EC art 4.

[9] Words in para (3)(*a*) substituted by Council Directive 2005/92 art 1; (see OJ L 345; 28.12.2005, p 19).

[10] Para (3)(*b*) substituted, and words in para (4) substituted, by Council Directive 2006/18 art 1(1); see OJ L 051; 22.2.2006, p 12.

TITLE X: EXEMPTIONS

Article 13 Exemptions within the territory of the country

A. Exemptions for certain activities in the public interest

1. Without prejudice to other Community provisions, Member States shall exempt the following under conditions which they shall lay down for the purpose of ensuring the correct and straightforward application of such exemptions and of preventing any possible evasion, avoidance or abuse:

(a) the supply by the public postal services of services other than passenger transport and telecommunications services, and the supply of goods incidental thereto;

(b) hospital and medical care and closely related activities undertaken by bodies governed by public law or, under social conditions comparable to those applicable to bodies governed by public law, by hospitals, centres for medical treatment or diagnosis and other duly recognised establishments of a similar nature;

(c) the provision of medical care in the exercise of the medical and paramedical professions as defined by the Member State concerned;

(d) supplies of human organs, blood and milk;

(e) services supplied by dental technicians in their professional capacity and dental prostheses supplied by dentists and dental technicians;

(f) services supplied by independent groups of persons whose activities are exempt from or are not subject to value added tax, for the purpose of rendering their members the services directly necessary for the exercise of their activity, where these groups merely claim from their members exact reimbursement of their share of the joint expenses, provided that such exemption is not likely to produce distortion of competition;

(g) the supply of services and of goods closely linked to welfare and social security work, including those supplied by old people's homes, by bodies governed by public law or by other organisations recognised as charitable by the Member State concerned;

(h) the supply of services and of goods closely linked to the protection of children and young persons by bodies governed by public law or by other organisations recognised as charitable by the Member State concerned;

(i) children's or young people's education, school or university education, vocational training or retraining, including the supply of services and of goods closely related thereto, provided by bodies governed by public law having such as their aim or by other organisations defined by the Member State concerned as having similar objects;

(j) tuition given privately by teachers and covering school or university education;

(k) certain supplies of staff by religious or philosophical institutions for the purpose of sub-paragraphs (b), (g), (h) and (i) of this Article and with a view to spiritual welfare;

(l) supply of services and goods closely linked thereto for the benefit of their members in return for a subscription fixed in accordance with their rules by non-profit-making organisations with aims of a political, trade-union, religious, patriotic, philosophical, philanthropic or civic nature, provided that this exemption is not likely to cause distortion of competition;

(m) certain services closely linked to sport or physical education supplied by non-profit-making organisations to persons taking part in sport or physical education;

(n) certain cultural services and goods closely linked thereto supplied by bodies governed by public law or by other cultural bodies recognised by the Member State concerned;

(o) the supply of services and goods by organisations whose activities are exempt under the provisions of sub-paragraphs (b), (g), (h), (i), (l), (m) and (n) above in connection with fund-

raising events organised exclusively for their own benefit provided that exemption is not likely to cause distortion of competition. Member States may introduce any necessary restrictions in particular as regards the number of events or the amount of receipts which give entitlement to exemption;

(*p*) *the supply of transport services for sick or injured persons in vehicles specially designed for the purpose by duly authorised bodies;*

(*q*) *activities of public radio and television bodies other than those of a commercial nature.*

Commentary—*De Voil Indirect Tax Service* **V4.146**, **V4.161**.

Note—Art 13A(1)(*c*) implemented by the Value Added Tax (Chiropractors) Order, SI 1999/1575 which inserts VATA 1994 Sch 9 Item 1(*cb*), with effect from 29 June 1999.

Simon's Tax Cases—Art 13A(1), *EC Commission v United Kingdom* [1988] STC 251; *Christoph-Dornier-Stiftung für Klinische Psychologie v Finanzamt Gießen* [2005] STC 228.

Art 13A(1)(*b*), *Gregg v Comrs of Customs and Excise* (Case C-216/97) [1999] STC 934; *C&E Comrs v Kingscrest Associates Ltd (t/a Kingscrest Residential Care Homes)* [2002] STC 490; *Diagnostiko & Therapeftiko Kentro Athinon-Ygeia AE v Ipourgos Ikonomikon* [2006] STC 1349.

Art 13A(1)(*c*), *Barkworth v C&E Comrs* [1988] STC 771; *C&E Comrs v Leightons Ltd* [1995] STC 458; *D v W (Osterreicher Bundesschatz intervening)* [2002] STC 1200; *d'Ambrumenil and another v C&E Comrs Unterpertinger v Pensionsversicherungsanstalt der Arbeiter* [2005] STC 650; *Solleveld and another v Staatssecretaris van Financiën* [2007] STC 71; *Finanzamt Leverkusen v Verigen Transplantation Service International AG* (Case C-156/09) [2011] STC 255; *Finanzamt Dortmund-West v Klinikum Dortmund GmbH* (Case C-366/12) [2014] STC 2197.

Art 13A(1)(*f*), *Assurandør-Societetet, acting on behalf of Taksatorringen v Skatteministeriet* [2006] STC 1842.

Art 13A(1)(*g*), *Yoga for Health Foundation v C&E Comrs* [1984] STC 630; *International Bible Students Association v C&E Comrs* [1988] STC 412; *Bulthuis-Griffioen v Inspector der Omzetbelasting* (Case C-453/93) [1995] STC 954; *Gregg v Comrs of C&E* (Case C-216/97) [1999] STC 934; *Kingscrest Associates Ltd and another v C&E Comrs* [2005] STC 1547.

Art 13A(1)(*i*), [1998] STC 784, *Pilgrims Language Courses Ltd v C&E Comrs* [1999] STC 874; *North of England Zoological Society v C&E Comrs* [1999] STC 1027; *C&E Comrs v University of Leicester Student's Union, CA* [2002] STC 147; *EC Commission v Federal Republic of Germany (Case C-287/00)* [2002] STC 982.

Art 13A(1)(*l*), *Institute of Leisure and Amenity Management v C&E Comrs* [1988] STC 602; *Committee of Directors of Polytechnics v C&E Comrs* [1992] STC 873; *Institute of Motor Industry v C&E Comrs* (Case C-149/97) [1998] STC 1219; *Expert Witness Institute v C&E Comrs, CA* [2002] STC 42.

Art 13A(1)(*m*), *EC Commission v Spain (supported by United Kingdom, intervener)* (Case C-124/96) [1998] STC 1237; *Swedish State v Stockholm Lindopark AB, Stockholm Lindopark AB v Swedish State* [2001] STC 103; *Messenger Leisure Developments Ltd v Revenue and Customs Commissioners* [2005] STC 1078.

Art 13A(1)(*n*), *R&C Comrs v British Film Institute* [2014] UKUT 370 (TCC), [2015] STC 99.

2

(*a*) *Member States may make the granting to bodies other than those governed by public law of each exemption provided for in 1(b), (g), (h), (i), (l), (m) and (n) of this Article subject in each individual case to one or more of the following conditions:*

— *they shall not systematically aim to make a profit, but any profits nevertheless arising shall not be distributed, but shall be assigned to the continuance or improvement of the services supplied,*

— *they shall be managed and administered on an essentially voluntary basis by persons who have no direct or indirect interest, either themselves or through intermediaries, in the results of the activities concerned,*

— *they shall charge prices approved by the public authorities or which do not exceed such approved prices or, in respect of those services not subject to approval, prices lower than those charged for similar services by commercial enterprises subject to value added tax,*

— *exemption of the services concerned shall not be likely to create distortions of competition such as to place at a disadvantage commercial enterprises liable to value added tax.*

(*b*) *The supply of services or goods shall not be granted exemption as provided for in (1)(b), (g), (h), (i), (l), (m) and (n) above if:*

— *it is not essential to the transactions exempted,*

— *its basic purpose is to obtain additional income for the organisation by carrying out transactions which are in direct competition with those of commercial enterprises liable for value added tax.*

Commentary—*De Voil Indirect Tax Service* **V4.146**.

Press releases etc—Business Brief 13/98, 9.6.98 (VAT exemption for osteopaths' service).

Simon's Tax Cases—Art 13A(1)(*b*), *Diagnostiko & Therapeftiko Kentro Athinon-Ygeia AE v Ipourgos Ikonomikon* [2006] STC 1349.

Art 13A(1)(*j*), *Marcus Webb Golf Professional v R&C Comrs* [2012] UKUT 378 (TCC), [2013] STC 574.

Art 13A(1)(*o*), *Loughborough Students Union v R&C Comrs* [2014] STC 357, [2013] UKUT 517 (TCC).

Art 13A(2)(*a*), *C&E Comrs v Bell Concord Educational Trust Ltd* [1989] STC 264; *EC Commission v Spain* (Case C-124/96) [1998] STC 1237.

Art 13A(2)(*b*), *C&E Comrs v Pilgrims Language Courses Ltd* [1998] STC 784.

B. Other exemptions

Without prejudice to other Community provisions, Member States shall exempt the following under conditions which they shall lay down for the purpose of ensuring the correct and straightforward application of the exemptions and of preventing any possible evasion, avoidance or abuse;

(a) insurance and reinsurance transactions, including related services performed by insurance brokers and insurance agents;

(b) the leasing or letting of immovable property excluding:

1 the provisions of accommodation, as defined in the laws of the Member States, in the hotel sector or in sectors with a similar function, including the provision of accommodation in holiday camps or on sites developed for use as camping sites;

2 the letting of premises and sites for parking vehicles;

3 lettings of permanently installed equipment and machinery;

4 hire of safes.

Member States may apply further exclusions to the scope of this exemption;

(c) supplies of goods used wholly for an activity exempted under this Article or under Article 28(3)(b) when these goods have not given rise to the right to deduction, or of goods on the acquisition or production of which, by virtue of Article 17(6), value added tax did not become deductible;

(d) the following transactions:

1 the granting and the negotiation of credit and the management of credit by the person granting it;

2 the negotiation of or any dealings in credit guarantees or any other security for money and the management of credit guarantees by the person who is granting the credit;

3 transaction, including negotiation, concerning deposit and current accounts, payments, transfers, debts, cheques and other negotiable instruments, but excluding debt collection and factoring;

4 transactions, including negotiation, concerning currency, bank notes and coins used as legal tender, with the exception of collectors' items; "collectors' items" shall be taken to mean gold, silver or other metal coins or bank notes which are not normally used as legal tender or coins of numismatic interest;

5 transactions, including negotiation, excluding management and safe-keeping, in shares, interests in companies or associations, debentures and other securities, excluding:

— documents establishing title to goods,

— the rights or securities referred to in Article 5(3);

6 management of special investment funds as defined by Member States;

(e) the supply at fact value of postage stamps valid for use for postal services within the territory of the country, fiscal stamps, and other similar stamps;

(f) betting, lotteries and other forms of gambling, subject to conditions and limitations laid down by each Member State;

(g) the supply of buildings or parts thereof, and of the land on which they stand, other than as described in Article 4(3)(a);

(h) the supply of land which has not been built on other than building land as described in Article 4(3)(b).

Commentary—*De Voil Indirect Tax Service* **V4.111**, **V4.131**, **V4.136**.

Simon's Tax Cases—Art 13B(*a*) *Skandinaviska Enskilda Banken AB Momsgrupp v Skatterverket* (Case C-540/09) [2011] STC 1125; *Royal Bank of Scotland v R&C Comrs* [202] EWHC 9 (Ch), [2012] STC 797.

Art 13B(*a*), Item 4, *Century Life plc v C&E Comrs* [2001] STC 38, CA, *Re Forsakringsaktiebolaget Skandia (publ)* [2001] STC 754; *CR Smith Glaziers (Dunfermline) Ltd v C&E Comrs* [2003] STC 419; *Staatssecretaris van Financiën v Arthur Andersen & Co Accountants cs* [2005] STC 508; *Assurandør-Societetet, acting on behalf of Taksatorringen v Skatteministeriet* [2006] STC 1842.

Art 13B(*b*), *Sinclair Collis Ltd v C&E Comrs* [2003] STC 898; *Stichting 'Goed Wonen' v Staatssecretaris van Financiën* [2003] STC 1137; *Belgian State v Temco Europe SA* [2005] STC 1451; *Fonden Marselisborg Lystbådehavn v Skatteministeriet* [2006] STC 1467; *Abbey National plc v C&E Comrs* [2006] STC 1961; *MacDonal Resorts Ltd v R&C Comrs* (Case C-270/09) [2011] STC 412; *Belgium v BLM SA* (Case C-436/10) [2012] STC 1564; *Leichenich v Ansbert Peffekoven and Ingo Horeis* (Case C-532/11) [2013] STC 846.

Art 13B(*b*)(1), *Lubbock Fine & Co v C&E Comrs* (Case C-63/92) [1994] STC 101; *Blasi v Finanzamt München I* (Case C-346/95) [1998] STC 336.

Art 13B(*b*)(2), *Skatteministeriet v Henriksen* [1990] STC 768; *Fonden Marselisborg Lystbådehavn v Skatteministeriet* [2006] STC 1467.

Art 13B(*c*), *EC Commission v Italian Republic* (Case C-43/95) [1997] STC 1062; *Jyske Finans A/S v Skatteministeriet (Nordania Finans A/S and BG Factoring A/S intervening)* [2006] STC 1744; *R&C Comrs v Axa UK plc* [2011] EWCA Civ 1607, [2012] STC 754.

Art 13B(*d*) *Skandinaviska Enskilda Banken AB Momsgrupp v Skatterverket* (Case C-540/09) [2011] STC 1125.

Art 13B(*d*)(1), *Primback Ltd v C&E Comrs* [1996] STC 757; *Muy's en De Winter's Bouw-en Aannemingsbedrijf BV v Staatssecretaris van Financiën* [1997] STC 665; *C&E Comrs v Civil Service Motoring Association Ltd* [1998] STC 111; *C&E Comrs v Lloyds TSB Group Ltd* [1998] STC 528.

Art 13B(*d*)(3), *C&E Comrs v FDR Ltd* [2000] STC 672; *C&E Comrs v BAA plc; Institute of Directors v C&E Comrs* [2003] STC 35, CA; *Finanzamt Groß-Gerau v MKG-Kraftfahrzeuge-Factory GmbH* [2003] STC 951; *Bookit Ltd v R&C Comrs* [2006] STC 1367; *ATP PensionService A/S v Skatteministeriet* (Case C-461/12) [2014] STC 2145.

Art 13B(*d*)(3), (5) *Sparekassernes Datacenter (SDC) v Skatteministeriet* (Case C-2/95) [1997] STC 932; *F&I Services Ltd v C&E Comrs* [2000] STC 364; *C&E Comrs v Electronic Data Systems Ltd* [2003] STC 688; *Bookit Ltd v R&C Comrs* [2006] STC 1367; *Proceedings brought by Nordea Pankki Suomi Oyj* (C-350/10) [2011] STC 1956; *Granton Advertising BV v Inspecteur van de Belastingdienst Haaglanden/kantoor Den Haag* (C-461/12) [2014] STC 2375.

Art 13B(*d*)(5), *Ivory & Sime Trustlink Ltd v C&E Comrs* [1998] STC 597; *CSC Financial Services Ltd v C&E Comrs (Case C-235/00)* [2002] STC 57; *DTZ Zadelhoff vif v Sttatssecretaris van Financien* (C-259/11) [2012] STC 2271.

Art 13B(*d*)(6), *Abbey National plc and another v C&E Comrs* [2006] STC 1136; *Wheels Common Investment Fund Trustees Ltd and others v R&C Comrs* (Case C-424/11) [2014] STC 49; *ATP PensionService A/S v Skatteministeriet* (Case C-461/12) [2014] STC 2145.

Art 13B(*f*), *R v Ryan* [1994] STC 446; *C&E Comrs v Feehan* [1995] STC 75; *Ivory & Sime Trustlink Ltd v C&E Comrs* [1995] STC 708; *United Utilities plc v C&E Comrs* [2006] STC 1423; *Belgium v Henfling and others (acting as administrators in the insolvency of Tierce Franco-Belge SA)* (C-464/10) [2011] STC 1851.

Art 13B(*g*), *JJ Komen en Zonen Beheer Heerhugowaard BV v Sttatssecretaris can Financien* (Case C-326/11) [2012] STC 2415.

Art 13B(*h*), *C&E Comrs v Parkinson* [1989] STC 51; *Gemeente Emmen v Belastingdienst Grote Ondernemingen* (Case C-468/93) [1996] STC 496; *Rank Group plc v R&C Comrs* (Cases C-259/10 and C-260/10) [2012] STC 22; *Staatssecretaris van Financien v Gemeente Vlaardingen* (Case C-299/11) [2013] STC 478.

C. Options

Member States may allow taxpayers a right of option for taxation in cases of:

(a) letting and leasing of immovable property;

(b) the transactions covered in B(d), (g) and (h) above.

Member States may restrict the scope of this right of option and shall fix the details of its use.

Commentary—*De Voil Indirect Tax Service* **V4.115**.

Simon's Tax Cases—*Belgocodex SA v Belgium* [2000] STC 351; *Stichting 'Goed Wonen' v Staatssecretaris van Financiën* [2003] STC 1137; *Administration de l'enregistrement et des domains, État du grand-duché de Luxembourg v Vermietungsgesellschaft Objekt Kirchberg SARL* [2005] STC 1345; *Marlow Gardner & Cooke Ltd Directors' Pension Scheme v R&C Comrs* [2006] STC 2014.

Article 14 Exemptions on importation

1. Without prejudice to other Community provisions, Member States shall exempt the following under conditions which they shall lay down for the purpose of ensuring the correct and straightforward application of such exemption and of preventing any possible evasion, avoidance or abuse:

(a) final importation of goods of which the supply by a taxable person would in all circumstances be exempted within the country;

(b) . . . (repealed by Directive 91/680)

. . . [3]

(d) final importation of goods qualifying for exemption from customs duties other than as provided for in the Common Customs Tariff . . . [1] *However, Member States shall have the option of not granting exemption where this would be liable to have a serious effect on conditions of competition . . .* [1]*; [This exemption shall also apply to the import of goods, within the meaning of Article 7(1)(b), which would be capable of benefiting from the exemption set out above if they had been imported within the meaning of Article 7(1)(a).]* [2]

(e) reimportation by the person who exported them of goods in the state in which they were exported, where they qualify for exemption from customs duties or would qualify therefor if they were imported from a third country;

(f) . . . [1]

(g) importations of goods:

— under diplomatic and consular arrangements, which qualify for exemption from customs duties . . . [1]*,*

— by international organisations recognised as such by the public authorities of the host country, and by members of such organisations, within the limits and under the conditions laid down by the international conventions establishing the organisations or by headquarters agreements,

— into the territory of Member States which are parties to the North Atlantic Treaty by the armed forces of other States which are parties to that Treaty for the use of such forces or the civilian staff accompanying them or for supplying their messes or canteens where such forces take part in the common defence effort;

[— the exemptions set out in the third indent shall extend to imports by and supplies of goods and services to the forces of the United Kingdom stationed in the island of Cyprus pursuant to the Treaty of Establishment concerning the Republic of Cyprus, dated 16 August 1960, which are for the use of the forces or the civilian staff accompanying them or for supplying their messes or canteens.] [5]

(h) importation into ports by sea fishing undertakings of their catches, unprocessed or after undergoing preservation for marketing but before being supplied;

VAT EC

(i) the supply of services, in connection with the importation of goods where the value of such services is included in the taxable amount in accordance with Article 11B(3)(b);
(j) importation of gold by Central Banks;
[(k) import of gas through the natural gas distribution system, or of electricity.][4]
2. The Commission shall submit to the Council at the earliest opportunity proposals designed to lay down Community tax rules clarifying the scope of the exemptions referred to in paragraph 1 and detailed rules for their implementation.
Until the entry into force of these rules, Member States may:
— *maintain their national provisions in force on matters related to the above provisions,*
— *adapt their national provisions to minimise distortion of competition and in particular the non-imposition or double imposition of value added tax within the Community,*
— *use whatever administrative procedures they consider most appropriate to achieve exemption.*

Member States shall inform the Commission, which shall inform the other Member States, of the measures they have adopted and are adopting pursuant to the preceding provisions.

Simon's Tax Cases—art 14(1), *Ministère Public and Ministre des Finances du Royaume de Belgique v Ledoux* [1991] STC 553.

Cross references—See VAT (Imported Goods) Relief Order, SI 1984/746 (provisions implementing para 1(*a*) above).
VAT (Imported Gold) Relief Order, SI 1992/3124 (provisions to conform with para 1(*j*) above).
Customs and Excise (Personal Reliefs for Special Visitors) Order, SI 1992/3156 (provisions implementing para 1(*g*) above);
Council Directive 83/181/EEC (clarifying the scope of art 1(*d*));
Council Directive 85/362/EEC (clarifying the scope of art 14(1)(*c*)).

Amendments—[1] Article 14(1) amended by EEC Council Directive 91/680; OJ L376, 31.12.91, p 1.
[2] Words in para (1)(*d*) added by EEC Council Directive 92/111, art 1.8; OJ L384, 30.12.92.
[3] Para (1)(*e*) deleted by EEC Council Directive 92/111, art 1.8; OJ L384, 30.12.92.
[4] Para 1(*k*) inserted by Council Directive 2003/92/EC, art 1(3); OJ L260, 11.10.2003 p 8.
[5] Words in para 1(*g*) inserted by the 2003 Act of Accession Protocol No 3 Annex Part Three para 2(*a*); OJ L 236; 23.9.2003 p 940.

Article 15 [Exemption of exports from the Community and like transactions and international transport][1]

Without prejudice to other Community provisions Member States shall exempt the following under conditions which they shall lay down for the purpose of ensuring the correct and straightforward application of such exemptions and of preventing any evasion, avoidance or abuse:
1. the supply of goods dispatched or transported to a destination [outside the Community][1]*; by or on behalf of the vendor;*
2. the supply of goods dispatched or transported to a destination [outside the Community][1]*; by or on behalf of a purchaser not established within the territory of the country, with the exception of goods transported by the purchaser himself for the equipping, fuelling and provisioning of pleasure boats and private aircraft or any other means of transport for private use;*
[In the case of the supply of goods to be carried in the personal luggage of travellers, this exemption shall apply on condition that:
— *the traveller is not established within the Community,*
— *the goods are transported to a destination outside the Community before the end of the third month following that in which the supply is effected,*
— *the total value of the supply, including value added tax, is more than the equivalent in national currency of ECU 175, fixed in accordance with Article 7(2) of Directive 69/169/EEC; however, Member States may exempt a supply with a total value of less than that amount.*

For the purposes of applying the second subparagraph:
— *a traveller not established within the Community shall be taken to mean a traveller whose domicile or habitual residence is not situated within the Community. For the purposes of this provision, "domicile or habitual residence" shall mean the place entered as such in a passport, identity card or other identity documents which the Member State within whose territory the supply takes place recognises as valid,*
— *proof of exportation shall be furnished by means of the invoice or other document in lieu thereof, endorsed by the customs office where the goods left the Community.*

Each Member State shall transmit to the Commission specimens of the stamps it uses for the endorsement referred to in the second indent of the third subparagraph. The Commission shall transit this information to the tax authorities in the other Member States.][5]
[3. the supply of services consisting of work on movable property acquired or imported for the purpose of undergoing such work within the territory of the Community, and dispatched or transported out of the Community by the person providing the services or by the customer if [not established within the territory of the country][4] *or on behalf of either of them;]*[1]
4. the supply of goods for the fuelling and provisioning of vessels:
(a) used for navigation on the high seas and carrying passengers for reward or used for the purpose of commercial, industrial or fishing activities;

(b) used for rescue or assistance at sea, or for inshore fishing, with the exception, for the latter, of ships' provisions;
(c) of war, as defined in subheading 89.01 A of the Common Customs Tariff, leaving the country and bound for foreign ports or anchorages.

[The Commission shall submit to the Council as soon as possible proposals to establish Community fiscal rules specifying the scope of and practical arrangements for implementing this exemption and the exemptions provided for in (5) to (9). Until these rules come into force, Member States may limit the extent of the exemption provided for in this paragraph.][3]

5. the supply, modification, repair, maintenance, chartering and hiring of the sea-going vessels referred to in paragraph 4(a) and (b) and the supply, hiring, repair and maintenance of equipment—including fishing equipment—incorporated or used therein;

6. the supply, modification, repair, maintenance, chartering and hiring of aircraft used by airlines operating for reward chiefly on international routes, and the supply, hiring, repair and maintenance of equipment incorporated or used therein;

7. the supply of goods for the fuelling and provisioning of aircraft referred to in paragraph 6;

8. the supply of services other than those referred to in paragraph 5, to meet the direct needs of the sea-going vessels referred to in that paragraph or of their cargoes;

9. the supply of services other than those referred to in paragraph 6, to meet the direct needs of aircraft referred to in that paragraph or of their cargoes;

10. supplies of goods and services:
- *under diplomatic and consular arrangements,*
- *to another Member State and intended for the forces of any Member State which is a party to the North Atlantic Treaty, other than the Member State of destination itself, for the use of those forces or of the civilian staff accompanying them, or for supplying their messes or canteens when such forces take part in the common defence effort,]*[1]
- *to international organisations recognised as such by the public authorities of the host country, and to members of such organisations, within the limits and under the conditions laid down by the international conventions establishing the organisations or by headquarters agreements,*
- *effected within a Member State which is a party to the North Atlantic Treaty and intended either for the use of the forces of other States which are parties to that Treaty or of the civilian staff accompanying them, or for supplying their messes or canteens when such forces take part in the common defence effort.*

This exemption shall be [subject to [limitations][3] *laid down by the host Member State]*[1] *until Community tax rules are adopted.*

[In cases where the goods are not dispatched or transported out of the country, and in the case of services, the benefit of the exemption may be given by means of a refund of the tax.][3]

11. supplies of gold to Central Banks;

12. goods supplied to approved bodies which export them [from the Community][1] *as part of their humanitarian, charitable or teaching activities [outside the Community]*[1]*. This exemption may be implemented by means of a refund of the tax;*

[13. The supply of services, including transport and ancillary operations, but excluding the supply of services exempted in accordance with Article 13, where these are directly connected with the export of goods or imports of goods covered by the provisions of Article 7(3) or Article 16(1), Title A.][4]

14. services supplied by brokers and other intermediaries, acting in the name and for account of another person, where they form part of transactions specified in this Article, or of transactions carried out [outside the Community][1]*.*

This exemption does not apply to travel agents who supply in the name and for account of the traveller services which are supplied in other Member States.

[15. The Portuguese Republic may treat sea and air transport between the islands making up the autonomous regions of the Azores and Madeira and between those regions and the mainland in the same way as international transport.][2]

Simon's Tax Cases—art 15, *Staatssecretaris van Financiën v Velker International Oil Co Ltd NV* [1991] STC 640; *Lange v Finanzamt Fürstenfeldbruck* (Case C-111/92) [1997] STC 564.

art 15(4)(*a*), (5), *Luxembourg and anor v Feltgen (administrator in the bankruptcy of Bacino Charter Co SA) and Anor* (Case C-116/10) [2011] STC 994

Cross references—See VATA 1994 Sch 8, Groups 7 and 8 (implementation of paras 3 and 4 above).

Customs and Excise (Personal Reliefs for Special Visitors) Order, SI 1992/3156 (implementation of para 10 above).

VAT (Amendment) Regulations, SI 2000/258 (implementation of para 2 above).

Amendments—[1] Paras 3, 14 amended by EEC Council Directive 91/680; OJ L376, 31.12.1991, p 1.

[2] Para 15 added by the Act of Accession 1985, art 26 Annex I Part V point 2; see OJ L302, 15.11.1985, p 167.

[3] Words in paras 3, 4, 10 replaced by EEC Council Directive 92/111, art 1.9; OJ L384, 30.12.92.

[4] Para 13 replaced by EEC Council Directive 92/111, art 1.9; OJ L384, 30.12.92.

[5] Words in para 2 replaced by Council Directive 95/7, art 1.3: OJ L102, 5.5.95, p 18 with effect from 25 May 1995.

VAT EC

Article 16 Special exemptions linked to international goods traffic

1. Without prejudice to other Community tax provisions, Member States may, subject to the consultations provided for in Article 29, take special measures designed to exempt all or some of the following transactions, provided that they are not aimed at final use and/or consumption and that the amount of value added tax due on cessation of the arrangements on situations referred to at A to E corresponds to the amount of tax which would have been due had each of these transactions been taxed within the territory of the country:

A *imports of goods which are intended to be placed under warehousing arrangements other than customs;*

B *supplies of goods which are intended to be:*

(a) produced to customs and, where applicable, placed in temporary storage;

(b) placed in a free zone or in a free warehouse;

(c) placed under customs warehousing arrangements or inward processing arrangements;

(d) admitted into territorial waters:

— *in order to be incorporated into drilling or production platforms, for purposes of the construction, repair, maintenance, alteration or fitting-out of such platforms, or to link such drilling or production platforms to the mainland,*

— *for the fuelling and provisioning of drilling or production platforms;*

(e) placed, within the territory of the country, under warehousing arrangements other than customs warehousing.

For the purposes of this Article, warehouses other than customs warehouses shall be taken to be:

— *for products subject to excise duty, the places defined as tax warehouses for the purposes of Article 4(b) of Directive 92/12/EEC,*

— *for goods other than those subject to excise duty, the places defined as such by the Member States. However, Member States may not provide for warehousing arrangements other than customs warehousing where the goods in question are intended to be supplied at the retail stage.*

Nevertheless, Member States may provide for such arrangements for goods intended for:

— *taxable persons for the purposes of supplies effected under the conditions laid down in Article 28k,*

— *tax-free shops within the meaning of Article 28k, for the purposes of supplies to travellers taking flights or sea crossings to third countries, where those supplies are exempt pursuant to Article 15,*

— *taxable persons for the purposes of supplies to travellers on board aircraft or vessels during a flight or sea crossing where the place of arrival is situated outside the Community,*

— *taxable persons for the purposes of supplies effected free of tax pursuant to Article 15, point 10.*

The places referred to in (a), (b), (c) and (d) shall be as defined by the Community customs provisions in force;

C supplies of services relating to the supplies of goods referred to in B;

D supplies of goods and of services carried out:

(a) in the places listed in B(a), (b), (c) and (d) and still subject to one of the situations specified therein;

(b) in the places listed in B(e) and still subject, within the territory of the country, to the situation specified therein.

Where they exercise the option provided for in (a) for transactions effected in customs warehouses, Member States shall take the measures necessary to ensure that they have defined warehousing arrangements other than customs warehousing which permit the provisions in (b) to be applied to the same transactions concerning goods listed in Annex J which are effected in such warehouses other than customs warehouses;

E supplies:

— *of goods referred to in Article 7(1)(a) still subject to arrangements for temporary importation with total exemption from import duty or to external transit arrangements,*

— *of goods referred to in Article 7(1)(b) still subject to the internal Community transit procedure provided for in Article 33a,*

as well as supplies of services relating to such supplies.

By way of derogation from the first subparagraph of Article 21(1)(a), the person liable to pay the tax due in accordance with the first subparagraph shall be the person who causes the goods to cease to be covered by the arrangements or situations listed in this paragraph.

When the removal of goods from the arrangements or situations referred to in this paragraph gives rise to importation within the meaning of Article 7(3), the Member State of import shall take the measures necessary to avoid double taxation within the country.][1]

[1a. Where they exercise the option provided for in paragraph 1, Member States shall take the measures necessary to ensure that intra-Community acquisitions of goods intended to be placed under one of the arrangements or in one of the situations referred to in paragraph 1(B) benefit from the same provisions as supplies of goods effected within the country under the same conditions.][1]

2. Subject to the consultation provided for in Article 29, Member States may opt to exempt [intra-Community acquisitions of goods made by a taxable person and][1] *imports for and supplies of goods to a taxable person intending to export them [outside the Community]*[1] *as they are or after processing, as well as supplies of services linked with his export business, up to a maximum equal to the value of his exports during the preceding 12 months.*

[When they take up this option the Member States shall, subject to the consultation provided for in Article 29, extend the benefit of this exemption to intra-Community acquisitions of goods by a taxable person, imports for and supplies of goods to a taxable person intending to supply them, as they are or after processing, under the conditions laid down in Article 28c(A), as well as supplies of services relating to such supplies, up to a maximum equal to the value of his supplies of goods effected under the conditions laid down in Article 28c(A) during the preceding twelve months.

Member States may set a common maximum amount for transactions which they exempt under the first and second subparagraphs.][1]

3. The Commission shall submit to the Council at the earliest opportunity proposals concerning common arrangements for applying value added tax to the transactions referred to in paragraphs 1 and 2.

Cross references—See Council Directive 85/362/EEC (common arrangements for goods subject to temporary importation arrangements).

Amendments—[1] Art 16(1) substituted, para (1A) added and para (2) amended by EC Council Directive 95/7, art 1(9): OJ L102, 5.5.95, p 18 with effect from 25 May 1995.

Simon's Tax Cases—*Danove riaditel'stvo Slovenskej republiky v Profitube spol sro* (Case C-165/11) [2013] STC 538; *Equoland Soc coop arl v Agenzia delle Dogane—Ufficio delle Dogane di Livorno* (Case C-272/13) [2014] STC 2487.

TITLE XI:
DEDUCTIONS

Article 17 Origin and scope of the right to deduct

1. The right to deduct shall arise at the time when the deductible tax becomes chargeable.

[2. In so far as the goods and services are used for the purposes of his taxable transactions, the taxable person shall be entitled to deduct from the tax which he is liable to pay:

[(a) value added tax due or paid within the territory of the country in respect of goods or services supplied or to be supplied to him by another taxable person;][3]

(b) value added tax due or paid in respect of imported goods within the territory of the country;

(c) value added tax due pursuant to Articles 5(7)(a), 6(3) and 28a(6);

(d) value added tax due pursuant to Article 28a(1)(a).][1]

[3. Member States shall also grant every taxable person the right to the deduction or refund of the value added tax referred to in paragraph 2 in so far as the goods and services are used for the purposes of:

(a) transactions relating to the economic activities referred to in Article 4(2), carried out in another country, which would be deductible if they had been performed within the territory of the country;

[(b) transactions which are exempt pursuant to Article 14(1)(g) and (i), 15, 16(1)(B),(C), (D) or (E) or (2) or 28c(A) and (C),][4]*;*

(c) any of the transactions exempt pursuant to Article 13(B)(a) and (d)(1) to (5), when the customer is established outside the Community or when those transactions are directly linked with goods to be exported to a country outside the Community.][1]

[4. The refund of value added tax referred to in paragraph 3 shall be effected:

— to taxable persons who are not established within the territory of the country but who are established in another Member State in accordance with the detailed implementing rules laid down in Directive 79/1072/EEC.

— to taxable persons who are not established within the territory of the Community, in accordance with the detailed implementing rules laid down in Directive 86/560/EEC.]

[For the purposes of applying the above:

(a) the taxable persons referred to in Article 1 of Directive 79/1072/EEC shall also be considered for the purposes of applying the said Directive as taxable persons who are not established in the country when, inside the territory of the country, they have only carried out supplies of goods and services to a person who has been designated as the person liable to pay the tax in accordance with [Article 21(1)(a), (1)(c) or (1)(f) or Article 21(2)(c)][5]*;*

(b) the taxable persons referred to in Article 1 of Directive 86/560/EEC shall also be considered for the purposes of applying the said Directive as taxable persons who are not established in the Community when, inside the territory of the country, they have only carried out supplies of goods and services to a person who has been designated as the person liable to pay the tax in accordance with [Article 21(1)(a), or (1)(f) or Article 21(2)(c)][5]*;*

(c) Directives 79/1072/EEC and 86/560/EEC shall not apply to supplies of goods which are, or may be, exempted under Article 28c(A) when the goods supplied are dispatched or transported by the acquirer or for his account.][2]*]*[1]

5. As regards goods and services to be used by a taxable person both for transactions covered by paragraphs 2 and 3, in respect of which value added tax is deductible, and for transactions in respect of which value added tax is not deductible, only such proportion of the value added tax shall be deductible as is attributable to the former transactions.

This proportion shall be determined, in accordance with Article 19, for all the transactions carried out by the taxable person.

However, Member States may:

(a) authorise the taxable person to determine a proportion for each sector of his business, provided that separate accounts are kept for each sector;

(b) compel the taxable person to determine a proportion for each sector of his business and to keep separate accounts for each sector;

(c) authorise or compel the taxable person to make the deduction on the basis of the use of all or part of the goods and services;

(d) authorise or compel the taxable person to make the deduction in accordance with the rule laid down in the first sub-paragraph, in respect of all goods and services used for all transactions referred to therein;

(e) provide that where the value added tax which is not deductible by the taxable person is insignificant it shall be treated as nil.

6. Before a period of four years at the latest has elapsed from the date of entry into force of this Directive, the Council, acting unanimously on a proposal from the Commission, shall decide what expenditure shall not be eligible for a deduction of value added tax. Value added tax shall in no circumstances be deductible on expenditure which is not strictly business expenditure, such as that on luxuries, amusements or entertainment.

Until the above rules come into force, Member States may retain all the exclusions provided for under their national laws when this Directive comes into force.

7. Subject to the consultation provided for in Article 29, each Member State may, for cyclical economic reasons, totally or partly exclude all or some capital goods or other goods from the system of deductions. To maintain identical conditions of competition, Member States may, instead of refusing deduction, tax the goods manufactured by the taxable person himself or which he has purchased in the country or imported, in such a way that the tax does not exceed the value added tax which would have been charged on the acquisition of similar goods.

Commentary—*De Voil Indirect Tax Service* **V2.101**, **V.3.401**, **V3.460**.

Note—Council Decision 93/563/EEC, art 3 allows derogation from this Article.

Simon's Tax Cases—*Kretztechnik AG v Finanzamt Linz* [2005] STC 1118; *Stichting 'Goed Wonen' v Staatssecretaris van Financiën* [2006] STC 833; *Halifax plc and others v C&E Comrs* [2006] STC 919; *University of Huddersfield Higher Education Corporation v C&E Comrs* [2006] STC 980; *Fiscale eenheid PPG Holdings BV cs te Hoogezand v Inspecteur van de Belastingdienst/Noord/kantoor Groningen* (Case C-26/12) [2014] STC 175; *Le Crédit Lyonnais v Ministre du Budget, des Comptes publics et de la Réforme de l'État* (Case C-388/11) [2014] STC 245.

Art 17(2), *EC Commission v French Republic (United Kingdom intervening)* [2003] STC 372, 390; *BUPA Purchasing Ltd and others v C&E Comrs* [2003] STC 1203; *Finanzamt Offenbach am Main-Land v Faxworld Vorgründungsgesellschaft Peter Hünninghausen und Wolfgang Klein GbR* [2005] STC 1192; *Finanzamt Bergisch Gladbach v HE* [2007] STC 128; *R&C Comrs v Loyalty Management Ltd* (Case C-53/09) [2010] STC 2651; *Baxi Group Ltd v R&C Comrs* (Case C-55/09) [2010] STC 2651; *Varzim Sol – Turismo, Jogo e Animacao SA v Fazenda Publica* (Case C-25/11) [2012] STC 971; *Finanzamt Saarlouis* (Case C-204/13) [2014] STC 1916.

Art 17(2)(*a*), *Finanzamt Uelzen v Armbrecht* [1995] STC 997; *C&E Comrs v Southern Primary Housing Association Ltd* [2003] STC 525; *EC Commission v Kingdom of the Netherlands (United Kingdom intervening)* [2003] STC 1506; *C&E Comrs v Southern Primary Housing Association Ltd* [2004] STC 209.

Art 17(2)(*b*), *Veleclair SA v Ministre du budget, des comptes publics et de la reforme de l'Etat* (Case C-414/10) [2012] STC 1281.

Art 17(3)(*a*), *R&C Comrs v RBS Deutschland Holdings GmbH* (Case C-277/09) [2011] STC 345.

Art 17(5), *Cibo Participations SA v Directeur regional des impots du Nord-Pas-de-Calais* [2002] STC 460; *Dial-a-Phone Ltd v C&E Comrs,* [2003] STC 192; *EC Commission v Kingdom of Spain* [2006] STC 1087; *EC Commission v French Republic (Kingdom of Spain, intervening)* [2006] STC 1098; *Varzim Sol – Turismo, Jogo e Animacao SA v Fazenda Publica* (Case C-25/11) [2012] STC 971; *Finanzamt Hildeshein v BLC Baumarkt GmbH & Co KG* (Case C-511/10) [2013] STC 521; *International Bingo Technology SA v Tribunal Económico-Administrativo Regional de Cataluña (TEARC)* (Case C-377/11) [2013] STC 661; *Fazenda Publica v Banco Mais SA* (Case C-183/13) [2014] STC 2325.

Art 17(6), *Group Ltd v C&E Comrs* [1996] STC 898; *Royscot Leasing Ltd v C&E Comrs* [1999] STC 998; *EC Commission v French Republic (United Kingdom intervening)* [2003] STC 372, 390; *Charles and another v Staatssecretaris van Financiën* [2006] STC 1429.

Cross reference—For directives adopted under art 17(4), see the Eighth Council Directive 79/1072/EEC; see OJ L331, 27.12.1979, p 11 and the Thirteenth Council Directive 86/560/EEC; see OJ L326, 21.11.1986, p 40.

VAT (Input Tax) (Specified Supplies) Order, SI 1992/3123 (partial implementation of para 3 above).

VAT Regulations, SI 1995/2518 reg 175 (implementation of para 4 above); reg 188(2)(*b*)(ii) (implementation of para 4 above).

Amendments—[1] Paras 2–4 substituted by Council Directive 91/680/EEC of 16 December 1991 which inserted art 28f(1)with effect from 1 January 1993 for the transitional period specified in art 28l.

[2] Words in para 4 added by Council Directive 92/111/EEC art 1(18); OJ L 384, 30.12.92.

3 Para 2(*a*) substituted by Council Directive 95/7/EEC art 1(10) with effect from 25 May 1995; OJ L 102, 15.5.95.

4 Para 3(*b*) (which was substituted by the 2003 Act of Accession Protocol No 3 Annex Part Three para 2(*b*); OJ L 236; 23.9.2003 p 940) substituted by Council Directive 2004/66 art 1, Annex V para 1(*c*); OJ L 168; 1.5.2004 p 35).

5 Words in para 4 substituted by Council Directive 2006/69/EC art 1(4), with effect from 13 August 2006, (OJ L 221, 12.8.2006, p 9).

Article 18 Rules governing the exercise of the right to deduct

[1. To exercise his right of deduction, a taxable person must:

(a) in respect of deductions pursuant to Article 17(2)(a), hold an invoice drawn up in accordance with Article 22(3);

(b) in respect of deductions pursuant to Article 17(2)(b), hold an import document specifying him as consignee or importer and stating or permitting the calculation of the amount of tax due;

(c) in respect of deductions pursuant to Article 17(2)(c), comply with the formalities established by each Member State;

(d) when he is required to pay the tax as a customer or purchaser where [Article 21(1) or Article 21(2)(c)][2] applies, comply with the formalities laid down by each Member State;

(e) in respect of deductions pursuant to Article 17(2)(d), set out in the declaration provided for in Article 22(4) all the information needed for the amount of the tax due on his intra-Community acquisitions of goods to be calculated and hold an invoice in accordance with Article 22(3).][1]

2. The taxable person shall effect the deduction by subtracting from the total amount of value added tax due for a given tax period the total amount of the tax in respect of which, during the same period, the right to deduct has arisen and can be exercised under the provisions of paragraph 1.

However, Member States may require that as regards taxable persons who carry out occasional transactions as defined in Article 4(3), the right to deduct shall be exercised only at the time of the supply.

3. Member States shall determine the conditions and procedures whereby a taxable person may be authorised to make a deduction which he has not made in accordance with the provisions of paragraphs 1 and 2.

[3a. Member States may authorise a taxable person who does not hold an invoice in accordance with Article 22(3) to make the deduction referred to in Article 17(2)(d); they shall determine the conditions and arrangements for applying this provision.][1]

4. Where for a given tax period the amount of authorised deductions exceeds the amount of tax due, the Member States may either make a refund or carry the excess forward to the following period according to conditions which they shall determine.

However, Member States may refuse to refund or carry forward if the amount of the excess is insignificant.

Commentary—*De Voil Indirect Tax Service* **V3.401**.

Simon's Tax Cases—*Local Authorities Mutual Investment Trust v C&E Comrs* [2004] STC 246 *R (on the application of UK Tradecorp Ltd) v Customs and Excise Commissioners* [2005] STC 138.

art 18(1)(*a*), *Reisdorf v Finanzamt Köln-West* [1997] STC 180; *EC Commission v Kingdom of the Netherlands (United Kingdom intervening)* [2003] STC 1506; *Finanzamt Gummersbach v Bockemühl* [2005] STC 934; *Finanzamt Bergisch Gladbach v HE* [2007] STC 128.

Art 18(4), *Garage Molenheide BVBA, Schepens, Bureau Rik Decan-Business Research & Development NV (BRD) and Sanders BVBA v Belgium* (Joined cases C-286/94, C-340/95, C-401/95 and C-47/96) [1998] STC 126.

Cross references—See Title XVI *a*, arts 28 *f* para 2, 28l, *post* (transitional arrangements for the taxation of trade between member States);

VAT Regulations, SI 1995/2518 reg 29(2) (implementation of this article).

Amendments—1 Para 1 substituted and para 3a inserted by Council Directive 91/680/EEC of 16 December 1991 which inserted art 28f with effect from 1 January 1993 for the transitional period specified in art 28l.

2 Words in para 1(*d*) substituted by Council Directive 2006/69/EC art 1(5), with effect from 13 August 2006, (OJ L 221, 12.8.2006, p 9).

Article 19 Calculation of the deductible proportion

1. The proportion deductible under the first sub-paragraph of Article 17(5) shall be made up of a fraction having:

— *as numerator, the total amount, exclusive of value added tax, of turnover per year attributable to transactions in respect of which value added tax is deductible under Article 17(2) and (3),*

— *as denominator, the total amount, exclusive of value added tax, of turnover per year attributable to transactions included in the numerator and to transactions in respect of which value added tax is not deductible. The Member States may also include in the denominator the amount of subsidies, other than those specified in Article 11A(1)(a).*

The proportion shall be determined on an annual basis, fixed as a percentage and rounded up to a figure not exceeding the next unit.

2. By way of derogation from the provisions of paragraph 1, there shall be excluded from the calculation of the deductible proportion, amounts of turnover attributable to the supplies of capital goods used by the taxable person for the purposes of his business. Amounts of turnover attributable to transactions specified in Article 13B(d), in so far as these are incidental transactions, and to incidental real estate and financial transactions shall also be excluded. Where Member States exercise the option provided under Article 20(5) not to require adjustment in respect of capital goods, they may include disposals of capital goods in the calculation of the deductible proportion.

3. The provisional proportion for a year shall be that calculated on the basis of the preceding year's transactions. In the absence of any such transactions to refer to, or where they were insignificant in amounts, the deductible proportion shall be estimated provisionally, under supervision of the tax authorities, by the taxable person from his own forecasts. However, Member States may retain their current rules.

Deductions made on the basis of such provisional proportion shall be adjusted when the final proportion is fixed during the next year.

Commentary—*De Voil Indirect Tax Service* **V3.460**.

Simon's Tax Cases—art 19, *Dwyer Property Ltd v C&E Comrs* [1995] STC 1035; *C&E Comrs v Liverpool Institute for Performing Arts* [2001] STC 891; *Varzim Sol – Turismo, Jogo e Animacao SA v Fazenda Publica* (Case C-25/11) [2012] STC 971.

Art 19(1), *Sofitam SA (formerly Satam SA) v Ministre chargé du Budget* (Case C-333/91), ECJ [1997] STC 226; *Floridienne SA and anor v Belgian State* [2000] STC 1044; *EC Commission v Kingdom of Spain* [2006] STC 1087; *EC Commission v French Republic (Kingdom of Spain, intervening)* [2006] STC 1098; *Finanzamt Hildeshein v BLC Baumarkt GmbH & Co KG* (Case C-511/10) [2013] STC 521; *International Bingo Technology SA v Tribunal Económico-Administrativo Regional de Cataluña (TEARC)* (Case C-377/11) [2013] STC 661; *Le Crédit Lyonnais v Ministre du Budget, des Comptes publics et de la Réforme de l'État* (Case C-388/11) [2014] STC 245.

Art 19(2), *Régie Dauphinoise—Cabinet A Forest SARL v Ministre du Budget* (Case C-306/94) [1996] STC 1176; *C&E Comrs v JDL Ltd* [2001] STC 1; *Empresa de Desenvolvimento Mineiro SGPS SA (EDM) v Fazenda Pública (Ministério Público, intervening)* [2005] STC 65.

Article 20 Adjustments of deductions

1. The initial deduction shall be adjusted according to the procedures laid down by the Member States, in particular:

- *(a) where that deduction was higher or lower than that to which the taxable person was entitled,*
- *(b) where after the return is made some change occurs in the factors used to determine the amount to be deducted, in particular where purchases are cancelled or price reductions are obtained; however, adjustment shall not be made in case of transactions remaining totally or partially unpaid and of destruction, loss or theft of property duly proved or confirmed, nor in the case of applications for the purpose of making gifts of small value and giving samples specified in Article 5(6). However, Member States may require adjustment in cases of transactions remaining totally or partially unpaid and of theft.*

2. In the case of capital goods, adjustments shall be spread over five years including that in which the goods were acquired or manufactured. The annual adjustment shall be made only in respect of one-fifth of the tax imposed on the goods. The adjustment shall be made on the basis of the variations in the deduction entitlement in subsequent years in relation to that for the year in which the goods were acquired or manufactured.

By way of derogation from the preceding sub-paragraph, Member States may base the adjustment on a period of five full years starting from the time at which the goods are first used.

[In the case of immovable property acquired as capital goods, the adjustment period may be extended up to 20 years.][1]

3. In the case of supply during the period of adjustment capital goods shall be regarded as if they had still been applied for business use by the taxable person until expiry of the period of adjustment. Such business activities are presumed to be fully taxed in cases where the delivery of the said goods is taxed; they are presumed to be fully exempt where the delivery is exempt. The adjustment shall be made only once for the whole period of adjustment still to be covered.

However, in the latter case, Member States may waive the requirement for adjustment in so far as the purchaser is a taxable person using the capital goods in question solely for transactions in respect of which value added tax is deductible.

4. For the purposes of applying the provisions of paragraphs 2 and 3, Member States may:

- *define the concept of capital goods,*
- *indicate the amount of the tax which is to be taken into consideration for adjustment,*
- *adopt any suitable measures with a view to ensuring that adjustment does not involve any unjustified advantage,*
- *permit administrative simplifications.*

[Member States may also apply paragraphs 2 and 3 to services which have characteristics similar to those normally attributed to capital goods.][2]

5. If in any Member State the practical effect of applying paragraphs 2 and 3 would be insignificant, that Member State may subject to the consultation provided for in Article 29 forego application of these paragraphs having regard to the need to avoid distortion of competition, the overall tax effect in the Member State concerned and the need for due economy of administration.

6. Where the taxable person transfers from being taxed in the normal way to a special scheme or vice versa, Member States may take all necessary measures to ensure that the taxable person neither benefits nor is prejudiced unjustifiably.

Commentary—*De Voil Indirect Tax Service* **V3.470**.

Simon's Tax Cases—Art 20, *Lennartz v Finanzamt München III* (Case C-97/90) [1995] STC 514; *C&E Comrs v University of Wales College, Cardiff* [1995] STC 611; *Waterschap Zeeuws Vlaanderen v Staatssecretaris van Financiën* [2005] STC 1298; *Stichting 'Goed Wonen' v Staatssecretaris van Financiën* [2006] STC 833.

Art 20(1)(*b*), *Tremerton Ltd v C&E Comrs* [1999] STC 1039; *Finanzamt Burgdorf v Fischer, Finanzamt Düsseldorf-Mettman v Brandenstein* [2001] STC 1356.

Art 20(2), *Finanzamt Uelzen v Armbrecht* (Case C-291/92) [1995] STC 997.

Art 20(3), *Centralan Property Ltd v C&E Comrs* [2006] STC 1542.

Amendments—[1] Words in para (2) replaced by EC Council Directive 95/7, art 1(4): OJ L102, 5.5.95, p 18 with effect from 25 May 1995.

[2] Words in para 4 inserted by Council Directive 2006/69/EC art 1(6), with effect from 13 August 2006, (OJ L 221, 12.8.2006, p 9).

TITLE XII:
PERSONS LIABLE FOR PAYMENT FOR TAX

[Article 21 Persons liable for payment for tax

1. Under the internal system, the following shall be liable to pay value added tax—

[(a) the taxable person carrying out the taxable supply of goods or of services, except for the cases referred to in (b), (c) and (f). Where the taxable supply of goods or of services is effected by a taxable person who is not established within the territory of the country, Member States may, under the conditions determined by them, lay down that the person liable to pay tax is the person for whom the taxable supply of goods or of services is carried out;][3]

(b) taxable persons to whom services covered by Article 9(2)(e) are supplied or persons who are identified for value added tax purposes within the territory of the country to whom services covered by Article 28b(C), (D), (E) and (F) are supplied, if the services are carried out by a taxable person not established within the territory of the country;

(c) the person to whom the supply of goods is made when the following conditions are met—

— the taxable operation is a supply of goods made under the conditions laid down in Article 28c(E)(3),

— the person to whom the supply of goods is made is another taxable person or a non-taxable legal person identified for the purposes of value added tax within the territory of the country,

— the invoice issued by the taxable person not established within the territory of the country conforms to Article 22(3).

However, Member States may provide a derogation from this obligation, where the taxable person who is not established within the territory of the country has appointed a tax representative in that country;

(d) any person who mentions the value added tax on an invoice . . . [2]*;*

(e) any person effecting a taxable intra-Community acquisition of goods.

[(f) persons who are identified for value added tax purposes within the territory of the country and to whom goods are supplied under the conditions set out in Article 8(1)(d) or (e), if the supplies are carried out by a taxable person not established within the territory of the country.][3]

2. By way of derogation from the provisions of paragraph 1—

(a) where the person liable to pay tax in accordance with the provisions of paragraph 1 is a taxable person who is not established within the territory of the country, Member States may allow him to appoint a tax representative as the person liable to pay tax. This option shall be subject to conditions and procedures laid down by each Member State;

(b) where the taxable transaction is effected by a taxable person who is not established within the territory of the country and no legal instrument exists, with the country in which that taxable person is established or has his seat, relating to mutual assistance similar in scope to that laid down by Directives 76/308/EEC and 77/799/EEC and by Council Regulation (EEC) No 218/ 92 of 27 January 1992 on administrative co-operation in the field of indirect taxation (VAT), Member States may take steps to provide that the person liable for payment of the tax shall be a tax representative appointed by the non-established taxable person.

[(c) where the following supplies are carried out, Member States may lay down that the person liable to pay tax is the taxable person to whom those supplies are made:

(i) the supply of construction work, including repair, cleaning, maintenance, alteration and demolition services in relation to immovable property, as well as the handing over of construction works considered to be a supply of goods by virtue of Article 5(5);

(ii) the supply of staff engaged in activities covered by (i);

(iii) the supply of immovable property, as referred to in Article 13(B)(g) and (h), where the supplier has opted for taxation of the supply pursuant to point (C)(b) of that Article;

(iv) the supply of used material, used material which cannot be re-used in the same state, scrap, industrial and non industrial waste, recyclable waste, part processed waste and certain goods and services, as identified in Annex M;

(v) the supply of goods provided as security by one taxable person to another in execution of that security;

(vi) the supply of goods following the cession of the reservation of ownership to an assignee and the exercising of this right by the assignee;

(vii) the supply of immovable property sold by the judgment debtor in a compulsory sale procedure.

For the purposes of this point, Member States may provide that a taxable person who also carries out activities or transactions that are not considered to be taxable supplies of goods or services in accordance with Article 2 shall be deemed to be a taxable person in respect of supplies received as referred to in the first subparagraph. A non-taxable body governed by public law, may be deemed to be a taxable person in respect of supplies received as referred to in (v), (vi) and (vii).

For the purposes of this point, Member States may specify the supplies of goods and services covered, and the categories of suppliers or recipients to whom these measures may apply. They may also limit the application of this measure to some of the supplies of goods and services listed in Annex M.

Member States shall inform the Committee established in accordance with Article 29 of any new national measure adopted pursuant to the provisions of this point.][4]

3. In the situations referred to in paragraphs 1 and 2, Member States may provide that someone other than the person liable for payment of the tax shall be held jointly and severally liable for payment of the tax.

4. On importation, value added tax shall be payable by the person or persons designated or accepted as being liable by the Member State into which the goods are imported.][1]

Commentary—*De Voil Indirect Tax Service* **V1.285, V5.186**.

Note—The amendments made by note 3 below were expressed in Council Directive 2003/92 to be made to the version of this article "set out in article 28gh". On a strict reading, this would imply that the amendment be made to the version set out in note 1 below. However, this does not work, and the amendment has been made to the current text of art 21.

Simon's Tax Cases—art 21(1)(*b*), *Finanzamt Deggendorf v Stoppelkamp* (Case C–421/10) [2011] STC 2358.

art 21(1)(*c*), *Finanzamt Osnabrück-Land v Langhorst* (Case C-141/96) [1997] STC 1357; *EMI Group Electronics Ltd v Coldicott* [1997] STC 1372; *Schmeink & Cofreth AG & Co KG v Finanzamt Borken*; *Strobel v Fananzamt Esslingen* (Case C-454/98) [2000] STC 810; *Elliniko Dimosio v Karageorgou and others* [2006] STC 1654.

21(3), *C&E Comrs and another v Federation of Technological Industries and others* [2006] STC 1483.

Cross references—See Council Decision EEC 93/204, art 1; OJ L88, 8.4.93 (derogation from para 1(*a*) above granted to the UK);

VATA 1994 Sch 5 para 9.

Amendments—[1] Article 21 substituted by Council Directive 2000/65/EC art 1(4) with effect from 21 October 2000; OJ L269 p 44, 21.10.00. Member states must bring into force the measures necessary to comply with these provisions not later than 31 December 2001.

[2] Words repealed by Council Directive 2001/115/EC art 4(5); see OJ L 015; 17.01.02.

[3] In para (1), point (*a*) substituted, and point (*f*) inserted, by Council Directive 2003/92 art 1(4), (5) (OJ L 260; 11.10.2003 p 8).

[4] Para 2(*c*) inserted by Council Directive 2006/69/EC art 1(7), with effect from 13 August 2006, (OJ L 221, 12.8.2006, p 9).

TITLE XIII:
OBLIGATIONS OF PERSONS LIABLE FOR PAYMENT

[Article 22 Obligations under the internal system:

1

[(a) Every taxable person shall state when his activity as a taxable person commences, changes or ceases. Member States shall, subject to conditions which they lay down, allow the taxable person to make such statements by electronic means, and may also require that electronic means are used.][10]

(b) Without prejudice to (a), every taxable person referred to in Article 28a(1)(a), second subparagraph, shall state that he is effecting intra-Community acquisitions of goods when the conditions for application of the derogation provided for in that Article are not fulfilled.

(c) Member States shall take the measures necessary to identify by means of an individual number:

[— Every taxable person, with the exception of those referred to in Article 28a(4), who, within the territory of the country, effects supplies of goods or of services giving him the right of deduction, other than supplies of goods or of services for which tax is payable solely by the customer or the recipient in accordance with Article 21(1)(a),(b),(c) or (f). However, Member States need not identify certain taxable persons referred to in article 4(3),][12]

— every taxable person referred to in paragraph 1(b) and every taxable person who exercises the option provided for in the third subparagraph of Article 28a(1)(a),

[— every taxable person who, within the territory of the country, effects intra-Community acquisitions of goods for the purposes of his operations relating to the economic activities referred to in Article 4(2) carried out abroad.][2]

(d) Each individual identification number shall have a prefix in accordance with ISO International Standard No 3166—alpha 2—by which the Member State of issue may be identified. [Nevertheless, the Hellenic Republic shall be authorised to use the prefix "EL".][11]

(e) Member States shall take the measures necessary to ensure that their identification systems distinguish the taxable persons referred to in (c) and to ensure the correct application of the transitional arrangements for the taxation of intra-Community transactions as laid down in this Title.

2

(a) Every taxable person shall keep accounts in sufficient detail for value added tax to be applied and inspected by the tax authority.

[(b) Every taxable person shall keep a register of the goods he has dispatched or transported or which have been dispatched or transported on his behalf out of the territory defined in Article 3 but within the Community for the purposes of the transactions referred to in the fifth, sixth and seventh indents of Article 28a(5)(b).

Every taxable person shall keep sufficiently detailed accounts to permit the identification of goods dispatched to him from another Member State by or on behalf of a taxable person identified for purposes of value added tax in that other Member State, in connection with which a service has been provided pursuant to the third or fourth indent of Article 9(2)(c);][9]

[3.

(a) Every taxable person shall ensure that an invoice is issued, either by himself or by his customer or, in his name and on his behalf, by a third party, in respect of goods or services which he has supplied or rendered to another taxable person or to a non-taxable legal person. Every taxable person shall also ensure that an invoice is issued, either by himself or by his customer or, in his name and on his behalf, by a third party, in respect of the supplies of goods referred to in Article 28b(B)(1) and in respect of goods supplied under the conditions laid down in Article 28c(A).

Every taxable person shall likewise ensure that an invoice is issued, either by himself or by his customer or, in his name and on his behalf, by a third party, in respect of any payment on account made to him before any supplies of goods referred to in the first subparagraph and in respect of any payment on account made to him by another taxable person or non-taxable legal person before the provision of services is completed.

Member States may impose on taxable persons an obligation to issue an invoice in respect of goods or services other than those referred to in the preceding subparagraphs which they have supplied or rendered on their territory. When they do so, Member States may impose fewer obligations in respect of these invoices than those listed under points (b), (c) and (d).

The Member States may release taxable persons from the obligation to issue an invoice in respect of goods or services which they have supplied or rendered in their territory and which are exempt, with or without refund of the tax paid at the preceding stage, pursuant to Article 13, Article 28(2)(a) and Article 28(3)(b).

Any document or message that amends and refers specifically and unambiguously to the initial invoice is to be treated as an invoice. Member States in whose territory goods or services are supplied or rendered may allow some of the obligatory details to be left out of such documents or messages.

Member States may impose time limits for the issue of invoices on taxable persons supplying goods and services in their territory.

Under conditions to be laid down by the Member States in whose territory goods or services are supplied or rendered, a summary invoice may be drawn up for several separate supplies of goods or services.

Invoices may be drawn up by the customer of a taxable person in respect of goods or services supplied or rendered to him by that taxable person, on condition that there is at the outset an agreement between the two parties, and on condition that a procedure exists for the acceptance of each invoice by the taxable person supplying the goods or services. The Member States in whose territory the goods or services are supplied or rendered shall determine the terms and conditions of the agreement and of the acceptance procedures between the taxable person and his customer.

Member States may impose further conditions on the issue of invoices by the customers of taxable persons supplying goods or services on their territory. For example, they may require that such invoices be issued in the name and on behalf of the taxable person. Such conditions must always be the same wherever the customer is established.

VAT EC

Member States may also lay down specific conditions for taxable persons supplying goods or services in their territory in cases where the third party, or the customer, who issues invoices is established in a country with which no legal instrument exists relating to mutual assistance similar in scope to that laid down by Council Directive 76/308/EEC of 15 March 1976 on mutual assistance for the recovery of claims relating to certain levies, duties, taxes and other measures(6), Council Directive 77/799/EEC of 19 December 1977 concerning mutual assistance by the competent authorities of the Member States in the field of direct and indirect taxation(7) and by Council Regulation (EEC) No 218/92 of 27 January 1992 on administrative cooperation in the field of indirect taxation (VAT)(8).

(b) *Without prejudice to the specific arrangements laid down by this Directive, only the following details are required for VAT purposes on invoices issued under the first, second and third subparagraphs of point (a):*
- *the date of issue;*
- *a sequential number, based on one or more series, which uniquely identifies the invoice,*
- *the VAT identification number referred to in paragraph 1(c) under which the taxable person supplied the goods or services;*
- *where the customer is liable to pay tax on goods supplied or services rendered or has been supplied with goods as referred to in Article 28c(A), the VAT identification number as referred to in paragraph 1(c) under which the goods were supplied or the services rendered to him;*
- *the full name and address of the taxable person and of his customer;*
- *the quantity and nature of the goods supplied or the extent and nature of the services rendered;*
- *the date on which the supply of goods or of services was made or completed or the date on which the payment on account referred to in the second subparagraph of point (a) was made, insofar as that a date can be determined and differs from the date of issue of the invoice;*
- *the taxable amount per rate or exemption, the unit price exclusive of tax and any discounts or rebates if they are not included in the unit price;*
- *the VAT rate applied;*
- *the VAT amount payable, except where a specific arrangement is applied for which this Directive excludes such a detail;*
- *where an exemption is involved or where the customer is liable to pay the tax, reference to the appropriate provision of this directive, to the corresponding national provision, or to any indication that the supply is exempt or subject to the reverse charge procedure;*
- *where the intra-Community supply of a new means of transport is involved, the particulars specified in Article 28a(2);*
- *where the margin scheme is applied, reference to Article 26 or 26a, to the corresponding national provisions, or to any other indication that the margin scheme has been applied;*
- *where the person liable to pay the tax is a tax representative within the meaning of Article 21(2), the VAT identification number referred to in paragraph 1(c) of that tax representative, together with his full name and address.*

Member States may require taxable persons established on their territory and supplying goods or services on their territory to indicate the VAT identification number referred to in paragraph 1(c) of their customer in cases other than those referred to in the fourth indent of the first subparagraph.

Member States shall not require invoices to be signed.

The amounts which appear on the invoice may be expressed in any currency, provided that the amount of tax to be paid is expressed in the national currency of the Member State where the supply of goods or services takes place, using the conversion mechanism laid down in Article 11 C(2).

Where necessary for control purposes, Member States may require invoices in respect of goods supplied or services rendered in their territory and invoices received by taxable persons in their territory to be translated into their national languages.

(c) *Invoices issued pursuant to point (a) may be sent either on paper or, subject to an acceptance by the customer, by electronic means.*

Invoices sent by electronic means shall be accepted by Member States provided that the authenticity of the origin and integrity of the contents are guaranteed:
- *by means of an advanced electronic signature within the meaning of Article 2(2) of Directive 1999/93/EC of the European Parliament and of the Council of 13 December 1999 on a Community framework for electronic signatures(9); Member States may however ask for the advanced electronic signature to be based on a qualified certificate and created by a secure-signature-creation device, within the meaning of Article 2(6) and (10) of the aforementioned Directive;*
- *or by means of electronic data interchange (EDI) as defined in Article 2 of Commission Recommendation 1994/820/EC of 19 October 1994 relating to the legal aspects of*

electronic data interchange(10) when the agreement relating to the exchange provides for the use of procedures guaranteeing the authenticity of the origin and integrity of the data; however Member States may, subject to conditions which they lay down, require that an additional summary document on paper is necessary.

Invoices may, however, be sent by other electronic means subject to acceptance by the Member State(s) concerned. The Commission will present, at the latest on 31 December 2008, a report, together with a proposal, if appropriate, amending the conditions on electronic invoicing in order to take account of possible future technological developments in this field.

Member States may not impose on taxable persons supplying goods or services in their territory any other obligations or formalities relating to the transmission of invoices by electronic means. However, they may provide, until 31 December 2005, that the use of such a system is to be subject to prior notification.

Member States may lay down specific conditions for invoices issued by electronic means for goods or services supplied in their territory from a country with which no legal instrument exists relating to mutual assistance similar in scope to that laid down by Directives 76/308/EEC and 77/799/EEC and by Regulation (EEC) No 218/92.

When batches containing several invoices are sent to the same recipient by electronic means, the details that are common to the individual invoices may be mentioned only once if, for each invoice, all the information is accessible.

(d) Every taxable person shall ensure that copies of invoices issued by himself, by his customer or, in his name and on his behalf, by a third party, and all the invoices which he has received are stored.

For the purposes of this Directive, the taxable person may decide the place of storage provided that he makes the invoices or information stored there available without undue delay to the competent authorities whenever they so request. Member States may, however, require taxable persons established in their territory to notify them of the place of storage, if it is outside their territory. Member States may, in addition, require taxable persons established in their territory to store within the country invoices issued by themselves or by their customers or, in their name and on their behalf, by a third party, as well as all the invoices which they have received, when the storage is not by electronic means guaranteeing full on-line access to the data concerned.

The authenticity of the origin and integrity of the content of the invoices, as well as their readability, must be guaranteed throughout the storage period. As regards the invoices referred to in the third subparagraph of point (c), the information they contain may not be altered; it must remain legible throughout the aforementioned period.

The Member States shall determine the period for which taxable persons must store invoices relating to goods or services supplied in their territory and invoices received by taxable persons established in their territory.

In order to ensure that the conditions laid down in the third subparagraph are met, Member States referred to in the fourth subparagraph may require that invoices be stored in the original form in which they were sent, whether paper or electronic. They may also require that when invoices are stored by electronic means, the data guaranteeing the authenticity of the origin and integrity of the content also be stored.

Member States referred to in the fourth subparagraph may impose specific conditions prohibiting or restricting the storage of invoices in a country with which no legal instrument exists relating to mutual assistance similar in scope to that laid down by Directives 76/308/EEC, 77/799/EEC and by Regulation (EEC) No 218/92 and to the right of access by electronic means, download and use referred to in Article 22a.

Member States may, subject to conditions which they lay down, require the storage of invoices received by non-taxable persons.

(e) For the purposes of points (c) and (d), transmission and storage of invoices 'by electronic means' shall mean transmission or making available to the recipient and storage using electronic equipment for processing (including digital compression) and storage of data, and employing wires, radio transmission, optical technologies or other electromagnetic means.

For the purposes of this Directive, Member States shall accept documents or messages in paper or electronic form as invoices if they meet the conditions laid down in this paragraph.][11]

4

[(a) Every taxable person shall submit a return by a deadline to be determined by Member States. That deadline may not be more than two months later than the end of each tax period. The tax period shall be fixed by each Member State at one month, two months or a quarter. Member States may, however, set different periods provided that they do not exceed one year. Member States shall, subject to conditions which they lay down, allow the taxable person to make such returns by electronic means, and may also require that electronic means are used.][10]

VAT EC

(b) The return shall set out all the information needed to calculate the tax that has become chargeable and the deductions to be made including, where appropriate, and in so far as it seems necessary for the establishment of the basis of assessment, the total value of the transactions relative to such tax and deductions and the value of any exempt transactions.

(c) The return shall also set out:

— on the one hand, the total value, less value added tax, of the supplies of goods referred to in Article 28c(A) on which tax has become chargeable during the period.

The following shall also be added: the total value, less value added tax, of the supplies of goods referred to in the second sentence of Article 8(1)(a) and in Article 28b(B)(1) effected within the territory of another Member State for which tax has become chargeable during the return period where the place of departure of the dispatch or transport of the goods is situated in the territory of the country,

[— on the other hand, the total amount, less value-added tax of the intra-Community acquisitions of goods referred to in Article 28a(1) and (6) effected within the territory of the country on which tax has become chargeable.

The following shall also be added: the total value, less value-added tax, of the supplies of goods referred to in the second sentence of Article 8(1)(a) and in Article 28(b)(B)(1) effected in the territory of the country on which tax has become chargeable during the return period, where the place of departure of the dispatch or transport of the goods is situated within the territory of another Member State, and the total amount, less value-added tax, of the supplies of goods made within the territory of the country for which the taxable person has been designated as the person liable for the tax in accordance with Article 28c(E)(3) and under which the tax has become payable in the course of the period covered by the declaration.][3]

5. Every taxable person shall pay the net amount of the value added tax when submitting the regular return. Member States may, however, set a different date for the payment of that amount or may demand an interim payment.

6

[(a) Member States may require a taxable person to submit a statement, including all the particulars specified in paragraph 4, concerning all transactions carried out in the preceding year. That statement shall provide all the information necessary for any adjustments. Member States shall, subject to conditions which they lay down, allow the taxable person to make such statements by electronic means, and may also require that electronic means are used.][10]

[(b) [Every taxable person identified for value added tax purposes shall also submit a recapitulative statement of the acquirers identified for value added tax purposes to whom he has supplied goods under the conditions provided for in Article 28c(A)(a) and (d), and of consignees identified for value added tax purposes in the transactions referred to in the fifth subparagraph.][9]][4]

[The recapitulative statement shall be drawn up for each calendar quarter within a period and in accordance with procedures to be determined by the Member States, which shall take the measures necessary to ensure that the provisions concerning administrative cooperation in the field of indirect taxation are in any event complied with. Member States shall, subject to conditions which they lay down, allow the taxable person to make such statements by electronic means, and may also require that electronic means are used.][10]

The recapitulative statement shall set out:

— the number by which the taxable person is identified for purposes of value added tax in the territory of the country and under which he effected supplies of goods in the conditions laid down in [Article 28c(A)(a)][5],

[— the number by which each person acquiring goods is identified for purposes of value added tax in another Member State and under which the goods were supplied to him,][9]

— for each person acquiring goods, the total value of the supplies of goods effected by the taxable person. Those amounts shall be declared for the calendar quarter during which the tax became chargeable.

The recapitulative statement shall also set out:

— for the supplies of goods covered by [Article 28c(A)(d)][6], the number by means of which the taxable person is identified for purposes of value added tax in the territory of the

country, the number by which he is identified in the Member State of arrival of the dispatch or transport [and the total amount of the supplies, determined in accordance with Article 28e(2)][7]*,*

— *the amounts of adjustments made pursuant to Article 11(C)(1). Those amounts shall be declared for the calendar quarter during which the person acquiring the goods is notified of the adjustment.*

. . .[9]

[In the cases set out in the third subparagraph of Article 28b (A) (2), the taxable person identified for value added tax purposes within the territory of the country shall mention in a clear way on the recapitulative statement:

— *the number by which he is identified for value added tax purposes within the territory of the country and under which he carried out the intra-Community acquisition and the subsequent supply of goods,*

— *the number by which, within the territory of the Member State of arrival of the dispatch or transport of the goods, the consignee of the subsequent supply by the taxable person is identified,*

— *and, for each consignee, the total amount, less value added tax, of the supplies made by the taxable person within the territory of the Member State of arrival of the dispatch or transport of the goods. These amounts shall be declared for the calendar quarter during which the tax became chargeable]*[7]

(c) *By way of derogation from (b), Member States may:*

— *require recapitulative statements to be filed on a monthly basis,*

— *require that recapitulative statements give additional particulars.*

(d) *In the case of supplies of new means of transport effected under the conditions laid down in Article 28c(A)(b) by a taxable person identified for purposes of value added tax to a purchaser not identified for purposes of value added tax or by a taxable person as defined in Article 28a(4), Member States shall take the measures necessary to ensure that the vendor communicates all the information necessary for value added tax to be applied and inspected by the tax authority.*

(e) *Member States may require taxable persons who in the territory of the country effect intra-Community acquisitions of goods as defined in Article 28a(1)(a) and (6) to submit statements giving details of such acquisitions provided, however, that such statements may not be required for a period of less than one month.*

Member States may also require persons who effect intra-Community acquisitions of new means of transport as defined in Article 28a(1)(b) to provide, when submitting the return referred to in paragraph 4, all the information necessary for value added tax to be applied and inspected by the tax authority.

7. Member States shall take the measures necessary to ensure that those persons who, in accordance with Article 21(1) and (2), are considered to be liable to pay the tax instead of a taxable person not established within the territory of the country comply with the obligations relating to declaration and payment set out in this Article; they shall also take the measures necessary to ensure that those persons who, in accordance with Article 21(3), are held to be jointly and severally liable for payment of the tax comply with the obligations relating to payment set out in this Article.][10]

8. Member States may impose other obligations which they deem necessary for the correct collection of the tax and for the prevention of evasion, subject to the requirement of equal treatment for domestic transactions and transactions carried out between Member States by taxable persons and provided that such obligations do not, in trade between Member States, give rise to formalities connected with the crossing of frontiers.

[The option provided for in the first subparagraph cannot be used to impose additional obligations over and above those laid down in paragraph 3.][11]

9

(a) *Member States may release from certain or all obligations:*

— *taxable persons carrying out only supplies of goods or of services which are exempt pursuant to Articles 13 and 15,*

— *taxable persons eligible for the exemption from tax provided for in Article 24 and for the derogation provided for in Article 28a(1)(a), second subparagraph,*

— *taxable persons carrying out none of the transactions referred to in paragraph 4(c).*

[Without prejudice to the provisions laid down in point (d), Member States may not, however, release the taxable persons referred to in the third indent from the obligations referred to in Article 22(3).][11]

(b) *Member States may release taxable persons other than those referred to in (a) from certain of the obligations referred to in 2(a).*

(c) *Member States may release taxable persons from payment of the tax due where the amount involved is insignificant.*

VAT EC

[(d) Subject to consultation of the Committee provided for in Article 29 and under the conditions which they may lay down, Member States may provide that invoices in respect of goods supplied or services rendered in their territory do not have to fulfil some of the conditions laid down in paragraph 3(b) in the following cases:
— when the amount of the invoice is minor, or
— when commercial or administrative practice in the business sector concerned or the technical conditions under which the invoices are issued make it difficult to comply with all the requirements referred to in paragraph 3(b).
In any case, these invoices must contain the following:
— the date of issue,
— identification of the taxable person,
— identification of the type of goods supplied or services rendered,
— the tax due or the information needed to calculate it.
The simplified arrangements provided for in this point may not be applied to transactions referred to in paragraph 4(c).][11]

[(e) In cases where Member States make use of the option provided for in the third indent of point (a) to refrain from allocating a number as referred to in paragraph 1(c) to taxable persons who do not carry out any of the transactions referred to in paragraph 4(c), and where the supplier or the customer have not been allocated an identification number of this type, the invoice should feature instead another number called the tax reference number, as defined by the Member States concerned.
When the taxable person has been allocated an identification number as referred to in paragraph 1(c), the Member States referred to in the first subparagraph may also require the invoice to show:
— for services rendered referred to in Article 28b(C), (D), (F) and (F) and for supplies of goods referred to in Article 28c(A) and (E) point 3, the number referred to in paragraph 1(c) and the tax reference number of the supplier;
— for other supplies of goods and services, only the tax reference number of the supplier or only the number referred to in paragraph 1(c).][11]

10. Member States shall take measures to ensure that non-taxable legal persons who are liable for the tax payable in respect of intra-Community acquisitions of goods covered by the first subparagraph of Article 28a(1)(a) comply with the above obligations relating to declaration and payment and that they are identified by an individual number as defined in paragraph 1(c), (d) and (e).

11. [In the case of intra-Community acquisitions of products subject to excise duty referred to in Article 28a(1)(c) as well as][8] *in the case of intra-Community acquisitions of new means of transport covered by Article 28a(1)(b), Member States shall adopt arrangements for declaration and subsequent payment.*

12. Acting unanimously on a proposal from the Commission, the Council may authorise any Member State to introduce particular measures to simplify the statement obligations laid down in paragraph 6(b). Such simplification measures, which shall not jeopardise the proper monitoring of intra-Community transactions, may take the following forms:

(a) Member States may authorise taxable persons who meet the following three conditions to file one-year recapitulative statements indicating the numbers by which the persons to whom those taxable persons have supplied goods under the conditions laid down in Article 28c(A) are identified for purposes of value added tax in other Member States:
— the total annual value, less value added tax, of their supplies of goods or provisions of services, as defined in Articles 5, 6 and 28a(5), does not exceed by more than ECU 35,000 the amount of the annual turnover which is used as a reference for application of the exemption from tax provided for in Article 24,
— the total annual value, less value added tax, of supplies of goods effected by them under the conditions laid down in Article 28c(A) does not exceed the equivalent in national currency of ECU 15,000,
— supplies of goods effected by them under the conditions laid down in Article 28c(A) are other than supplies of new means of transport;

(b) Member States which set at over three months the tax period for which taxable persons must submit the returns provided for in paragraph 4 may authorise such persons to submit recapitulative statements for the same period where those taxable persons meet the following three conditions—
— the overall annual value, less value added tax, of the goods and the services they supply, as defined in Articles 5, 6 and 28a(5), does not exceed the equivalent in national currency of ECU 200,000,
— the total annual value, less value added tax, of supplies of goods effected by them under the conditions laid down in Article 28c(A) does not exceed the equivalent in national currency of ECU 15,000,

— *supplies of goods effected by them under the conditions laid down in Article 28c(A) are other than supplies of new means of transport.]*[1]

Commentary—*De Voil Indirect Tax Service* **V1.285, V2.101, V3.401, V3.415, V5.186**.

Note—The amendment made by note 12 below was expressed in Council Directive 2003/92 to be made to the version of this article "set out in article 28h". On a strict reading, this would imply that the amendment be made to the version set out in note 1 below. However, this does not work, and the amendment has been made to the current text of art 21.

Simon's Tax Cases—art 22, *Bjellica (T/A Eddy's Domestic Appliances) v C&E Comrs* [1995] STC 329; *C&E Comrs and another v Federation of Technological Industries and others* [2006] STC 1483.

Art 22(3), *Reisdorf v Finanzamt Köln-West* (Case C-85/95) [1997] STC 180; *Finanzamt Bergisch Gladbach v HE* [2007] STC 128.

Art 22(3)(*c*), *Finanzamt Osnabrück-Land v Langhorst* (Case C-141/96) [1997] STC 1357; *EMI Group Electronics Ltd v Coldicott* [1997] STC 1372.

Art 22(4), (5), *Balocchi v Ministero delle Finanze* [1997] STC 640.

Art 22(8), *EC Commission v Kingdom of Spain* (Case C-96/91) [1996] STC 672; *Eismann Alto Adige Srl v Ufficio IVA di Bolzano* (Case C-217/94) [1996] STC 1374.

Cross references—See Council Directive 92/111, art 4, para 1; OJ L384, 30.12.92 (member States may provide that information relating to certain transactions referred to in para 6(*b*) of art 22 for which tax becomes payable during January–March 1993 must appear on summary statement for the quarter April–June 1993),

Council Directive 92/111 art 4 para 2 (extension of time limit to 31 December 1993 for adoption of laws, etc under certain provisions of this article);

EEC Council Decision 92/621; OJ L408, 31.12.92 (as provided by para 12 above, the UK is authorised to introduce a particular measure in accordance with para 12(*b*) above to simplify the obligations laid down in para 6(*b*) above regarding recapitulative statements).

Council Decision EC 93/609, *post* (derogation from para 6(*b*) above granted to the UK);

VAT Regulations, SI 1995/2518 regs 5, 6, 13, 14, 16, 20, 36, 148 (implementation of this article);

VAT Regulations, SI 1995/2518 regs 24, 31–34, 37–39 (regulations requiring compliance with para 2 above);

SI 1995/2518 regs 21–23 (regulations requiring compliance with para 6 above).

Amendments—[1] Article 22 substituted by Council Directive 91/680/EEC of 16 December 1991 which inserted art 28h below with effect from 1 January 1993 for the transitional period specified in art 28l.

[2] Words in para 1(*c*) inserted by EEC Council Directive 92/111, art 1(20); OJ L384, 30.12.92.

[3] Words in para 4(*c*) replaced by EEC Council Directive 92/111, art 1(20); OJ L384, 30.12.92.

[4] Para 6(*b*) replaced by EEC Council Directive 92/111, art 1(20); OJ L384, 30.12.92.

[5] Words in para 6(*b*) replaced by EEC Council Directive 92/111, art 1(20); OJ L384, 30.12.92.

[6] Words in para 6(*b*) replaced by EEC Council Directive 92/111, art 1(20); OJ L384, 30.12.92.

[7] Words in para 6(*b*) replaced and words inserted by EEC Council Directive 92/111, art 1(20); OJ L384, 30.12.92.

[8] Words in para 11 inserted by EEC Council Directive 92/111, art 1(20); OJ L384, 30.12.92.

[9] Para (2)(*b*), first indent of second sub-para in para 3(*b*), first sub-para of para 6(*b*) and second indent in third sub-para of para 6(*b*) replaced and the fifth sub-para of para 6(*b*) repealed by EC Council Directive 95/7, art 1(12): OJ L102, 15.5.95, p 18 with effect from 25 May 1995.

[10] Paras 1(*a*), 4(*a*), 6(*a*) and words in para 6(*b*) substituted by Council Directive 2002/38/EC art 2 with effect from 15 May 2002: see OJ L 128; 15.5.02.

[11] Words inserted in para 1(*d*), para 3 substituted, words inserted in paras 8, 9(*a*), and paras 9(*d*), (*e*) inserted, by Council Directive 2001/115/EEC art 2; see OJ L 015, 17.01.02.

[12] In para (1), the first indent in point (*c*) substituted by Council Directive 2003/92 art 1(6); see OJ L 260; 11.10.2003 p 8.

[Article 22a Right of access to invoices stored by electronic means in another Member State

When a taxable person stores invoices which he issues or receives by an electronic means guaranteeing on-line access to the data and when the place of storage is in a Member State other than that in which he is established, the competent authorities in the Member State in which he is established shall have a right, for the purpose of this directive, to access by electronic means, download and use these invoices within the limits set by the regulations of the Member State where the taxable person is established and as far as that State requires for control purposes.][1]

Amendments—[1] This article inserted by Council Directive 2001/115/EEC art 3; see OJ L 015, 17.01.02.

Article 23 Obligations in respect of imports

As regards imported goods, Member States shall lay down the detailed rules for the making of the declarations and payments.

In particular, Member States may provide that the value added tax payable on importation of goods by taxable persons or persons liable to tax or certain categories of these two need not be paid at the time of importation, on condition that the tax is mentioned as such in a return to be submitted under Article 22(4).

TITLE XIV: SPECIAL SCHEMES

Article 24 Special scheme for small undertakings

1. Member States which might encounter difficulties in applying the normal tax scheme to small undertakings by reason of their activities or structure shall have the option, under such conditions and within such limits as they may set but subject to the consultation provided for in Article 29, of applying simplified procedures such as flat-rate schemes for charging and collecting the tax provided they do not lead to a reduction thereof.

2. Until a date to be fixed by the Council acting unanimously on a proposal from the Commission, but which shall not be later than that on which the charging of tax on imports and the remission of tax on exports in trade between the Member States are abolished:

(a) Member States which have made use of the option under Article 14 of the second Council Directive of 11 April 1967 to introduce exemptions or graduated tax relief may retain them and the arrangements for applying them if they conform with the value added tax system.
Those Member States which apply an exemption from tax to taxable persons whose annual turnover is less than the equivalent in national currency of 5,000 European units of account at the conversion rate of the day on which this Directive is adopted, may increase this exemption up to 5,000 European units of account.
Member States which apply graduated tax relief may neither increase the ceiling of the graduated tax reliefs nor render the conditions for the granting of it more favourable;

(b) Member States which have not made use of this option may grant an exemption from the tax to taxable persons whose annual turnover is at the maximum equal to the equivalent in national currency of 5,000 European units of account at the conversion rate of the day on which this Directive is adopted; where appropriate, they may grant graduated tax relief to taxable persons whose annual turnover exceeds the ceiling fixed by the Member States for the application of exemption;

(c) Member States which apply an exemption from tax to taxable persons whose annual turnover is equal to or higher than the equivalent in national currency of 5,000 European units of account at the conversion rate of the day on which this Directive is adopted, may increase it in order to maintain its value in real terms.

3. The concepts of exemption and graduated tax relief shall apply to the supply of goods and services by small undertakings.
Member States may exclude certain transactions from the arrangements provided for in paragraph 2. The provisions of paragraph 2 shall not, in any case, apply to the transactions referred to in Article 4(3).
[In all circumstances supplies of new means of transport effected under the conditions laid down in Article 28c(A) as well as supplies of goods and services effected by a taxable person who is not established in the territory of the country shall be excluded from the exemption from tax under paragraph 2.][1]

4. The turnover which shall serve as a reference for the purposes of applying the provisions of paragraph 2 shall consist of the amount, exclusive of value added tax, of goods and services supplied as defined in Articles 5 and 6, to the extent that they are taxed, including transactions exempted with refund of tax previously paid in accordance with Article 28(2), and the amount of the transactions exempted pursuant to Article 15, the amount of real property transactions, the financial transactions referred to in Article 13B(d), and insurance services, unless these transactions are ancillary transactions.
However, disposals of tangible or intangible capital assets of an undertaking shall not be taken into account for the purposes of calculating turnover.

5. Taxable persons exempt from tax shall not be entitled to deduct tax in accordance with the provisions of Article 17, nor to show the tax on their invoices . . .[2]

6. Taxable persons eligible for exemption from tax may opt either for the normal value added tax scheme or for the simplified procedures referred to in paragraph 1. In this case they shall be entitled to any graduated tax relief which may be laid down by national legislation.

7. Subject to the application of paragraph 1, taxable persons enjoying graduated relief shall be treated as taxable persons subject to the normal value added tax scheme.

8. At four-yearly intervals, and for the first time on 1 January 1982, and after consultation of the Member States, the Commission shall report to the Council on the application of the provisions of this Article. It shall as far as may be necessary, and taking into account the needs to ensure the long-term convergence of national regulations, attach to this report proposals for:

(a) improvements to be made to the special scheme for small undertakings;

(b) the adaptation of national systems as regards exemptions and graduated value added tax relief;

(c) the adaptation of the limit of 5,000 European units of account mentioned in paragraph 2.

9. The Council will decide at the appropriate time whether the realisation of the objective referred to in Article 4 of the First Council Directive of 11 April 1967 requires the introduction of a special scheme for small undertakings and will, if appropriate, decide on the limits and common implementing conditions of this scheme. Until the introduction of such a scheme, Member States may retain their own special schemes which they will apply in accordance with the provisions of this Article and of subsequent acts of the Council.

Simon's Tax Cases—*Direct Cosmetics Ltd and Laughtons Photographs Ltd v C&E Comrs* [1988] STC 540; *C&E Comrs v Eastwood Care Homes (Ilkeston) Ltd and others* [2001] STC 1629; *Schmelz v Finanzamt Waldviertel* (Case C-97/09) [2011] STC 88.

Amendments—[1] Words in para 3 (which were inserted by Council Directive 91/680/EEC of 16 December 1991 which inserted art 28i below from 1 January 1993 for the transitional period specified in art 28l) replaced by Council Directive 92/111/EEC art 1(20); OJ L384, 30.12.92.

[2] Words in para 5 revoked by Council Directive 2001/115/EC art 4(2); see OJ L 015; 17.01.02.

[Article 24a

In implementing Article 24(2) to (6), the following Member States may grant an exemption from value added tax to taxable persons whose annual turnover is less than the equivalent in national currency at the conversion rate on the date of their accession:

— *in the Czech Republic: EUR 35 000;*
— *in Estonia: EUR 16 000;*
— *in Cyprus: EUR 15 600;*
— *in Latvia: EUR 17 200;*
— *in Lithuania: EUR 29 000;*
— *in Hungary: EUR 35 000;*
— *in Malta: EUR 37 000 when the economic activity consists principally in the supply of goods, EUR 24 300 when the economic activity consists principally in the supply of services with a low value added (high inputs), and EUR 14 600 in other cases, namely service providers with a high value added (low inputs);*
— *in Poland: EUR 10 000;*
— *in Slovenia: EUR 25 000;*
— *in Slovakia: EUR 35 000.]*[1]

Amendments—[1] Article 24 bis, which was inserted by the 2003 Act of Accession Annex II Chapter 9 para 3(*a*), is replaced by Article 24a, by virtue of Council Directive 2004/66 art 1, Annex Part V para 1(*a*) (OJ L 168; 1.5.2004 p 35).

Article 25 Common flat-rate scheme for farmers

1. Where the application to farmers of the normal value added tax scheme, or the simplified scheme provided for in Article 24, would give rise to difficulties, Member States may apply to farmers a flat-rate scheme tending to offset the value added tax charged on purchases of goods and services made by the flat-rate farmers pursuant to this Article.

2. For the purposes of this Article, the following definitions shall apply:

"farmer": taxable person who carries on his activity in one of the undertakings defined below,

"agricultural, forestry or fisheries undertakings": an undertaking considered to be such by each Member State within the framework of the production activities listed in Annex A,

"flat-rate farmer": a farmer subject to the flat-rate scheme provided for in paragraphs 3 et seq,

"agricultural products": goods produced by an agricultural, forestry or fisheries undertaking in each Member State as a result of the activities listed in Annex A,

"agricultural service": any service as set out in Annex B supplied by a farmer using his labour force and/or by means of the equipment normally available on the agricultural, forestry or fisheries undertaking operated by him,

"value added tax charge on inputs": the amount of the total value added tax attaching to the goods and services purchased by all agricultural, forestry and fisheries undertakings of each Member State subject to the flat-rate scheme where such tax would be deductible under Article 17 by a farmer subject to the normal value added tax scheme,

"flat-rate compensation percentages": the percentages fixed by Member States in accordance with paragraph 3 and applied by them in the cases specified in paragraph 5 to enable flat-rate farmers to offset at a fixed rate the value added tax charge on inputs,

"flat-rate compensation": the amount arrived at by applying the flat-rate compensation percentage provided for in paragraph 3 to the turnover of the flat-rate farmer in the cases referred to in paragraph 5.

3. Member States shall fix the flat-rate compensation percentages, where necessary, and shall notify the Commission before applying them. Such percentages shall be based on macro-economic statistics for flat-rate farmers alone for the preceding three years. They may not be used to obtain for flat-rate farmers refunds greater than the value added tax charges on imports. Member States shall have the option of reducing such percentages to a nil rate. The percentage may be rounded up or down to the nearest half point.

Member States may fix varying flat-rate compensation percentages for forestry, for the different sub-divisions of agriculture and for fisheries.

4. Member States may release flat-rate farmers from the obligations imposed upon taxable persons by Article 22.

[When they exercise this option, Member States shall take the measures necessary to ensure the correct application of the transitional arrangements for the taxation of intra-Community transactions as laid down in Title XVIa.][1]

[5. The flat-rate percentages provided for in paragraph 3 shall be applied to the prices, exclusive of tax, of:

(a) agricultural products supplied by flat-rate farmers to taxable persons other than those eligible within the territory of the country for the flat-rate scheme provided for in this Article;

VAT EC

(b) agricultural products supplied by flat-rate farmers, under the conditions laid down in Article 28c(A), to non-taxable legal persons not eligible, in the Member State of arrival of the dispatch or transport of the agricultural products thus supplied, for the derogation provided for in Article 28a(1)(a), second sub-paragraph;

(c) agricultural services supplied by flat-rate farmers to taxable persons other than those eligible within the territory of the country for the flat-rate scheme provided for in this Article.

This compensation shall exclude any other form of deduction.][1]

[6. In the case of the supplies of agricultural products and of agricultural services referred to in paragraph 5, Member States shall provide for the flat-rate compensation to be paid either:

(a) by the purchaser or customer. In that event, the taxable purchaser or customer shall be authorised, as provided for in Article 17 and in accordance with the procedures laid down by the Member States, to deduct from the tax for which he is liable within the territory of the country the amount of the flat-rate compensation he has paid to flat-rate farmers.

Member States shall refund to the purchaser or customer the amount of the flat-rate compensation he has paid to flat-rate farmers in respect of any of the following transactions:

- *supplies of agricultural products effected under the conditions laid down in Article 28c(A) to taxable persons, or to non-taxable legal persons acting as such in another Member State within which they are not eligible for the derogation provided for in the second subparagraph of Article 28a(1)(a),*
- *supplies of agricultural products effected under the conditions laid down in Article 15 and in Article 16(1)(B), (D) and (E) to taxable purchasers established outside the Community, provided that the products are used by those purchasers for the purposes of the transactions referred to in Article 17(3)(a) and (b) or for the purposes of services which are deemed to be supplied within the territory of the country and on which tax is payable solely by the customers under Article 21(1)(b),*
- *supplies of agricultural services to taxable customers established within the Community but in other Member States or to taxable customers established outside the Community, provided that the services are used by those customers for the purposes of the transactions referred to in Article 17(3)(a) and (b) and for the purposes of services which are deemed to be supplied within the territory of the country and on which tax is payable solely by the customers under Article 21(1)(b).*

Member States shall determine the method by which the refunds are to be made; in particular, they may apply Article 17(4); or

(b) by the public authorities.][1]

7. Member States shall make all necessary provisions to check properly the payment of the flat-rate compensation to the flat-rate farmers.

8. As regards all supplies of agricultural products and agricultural services other than those covered by paragraph 5, the flat-rate compensation is deemed to be paid by the purchaser or customer.

9. Each Member State may exclude from the flat-rate scheme certain categories of farmers and farmers for whom the application of the normal value added tax scheme, or the simplified scheme provided for in Article 24(1), would not give rise to administrative difficulties.

[Whenever they exercise the option provided for in this Article, Member States shall take all measures necessary to ensure that the same method of taxation is applied to supplies of agricultural products effected under the conditions laid down in Article 28b(B)(1), whether the supply is effected by a flat-rate farmer or by a taxable person other than a flat-rate farmer.][1]

10. Every flat-rate farmer may opt, subject to the rule and conditions to be laid down by each Member State, for application of the normal value added tax scheme or, as the case may be, the simplified scheme provided for in Article 24(1).

11. The Commission shall, before the end of the fifth year following the entry into force of this Directive, present to the Council new proposals concerning the application of the value added tax to transactions in respect of agricultural products and services.

12. . . .

Note—Para 12 is not relevant to this work.

Simon's Tax Cases—*Finanzamt Rendsburg v Harbs* [2006] STC 340.

Cross references—See VATA 1994 s 54(8) (special treatment for certified farmers as regards registration for VAT purposes).

Amendments—[1] Words in paras 4, 9 added and paras 5 and 6 substituted by Council Directive 91/680/EEC of 16 December 1991 which inserts art 28j; below with effect from 1 January 1993 for the transitional period specified in art 28l.

Article 26 Special scheme for travel agents

1. Member States shall apply value added tax to the operations of travel agents in accordance with the provisions of this Article, where the travel agents deal with customers in their own name and use the supplies and services of other taxable persons in the provision of travel facilities. This Article shall not apply to travel agents who are acting only as intermediaries and accounting for tax in accordance with Article 11 A(3)(c). In this Article travel agents include tour operators.

2. All transactions performed by the travel agent in respect of a journey shall be treated as a single service supplied by the travel agent to the traveller. It shall be taxable in the Member State in which the travel agent has established his business or has a fixed establishment from which the travel agent has provided the services. The taxable amount and the price exclusive of tax, within the meaning of Article 22(3)(b), in respect of this service shall be the travel agent's margin, that is to say, the difference between the total amount to be paid by the traveller, exclusive of value added tax, and the actual cost to the travel agent of supplies and services provided by other taxable persons where these transactions are for the direct benefit of the traveller.

3. If transactions entrusted by the travel agent to other taxable persons are performed by such persons outside the Community, the travel agent's service shall be treated as an exempted intermediary activity under Article 15(14). Where these transactions are performed both inside and outside the Community, only that part of the travel agent's service relating to transactions outside the Community may be exempted.

4. Tax charged to the travel agent by other taxable persons on the transactions described in paragraph 2 which are for the direct benefit of the traveller, shall not be eligible for deduction or refund in any Member State.

Simon's Tax Cases—*C&E Comrs v DFDS A/S* [1997] STC 384; *C&E Comrs v Madgett and Baldwin (T/A Howden Court Hotel) v C&E Comrs* (Joined cases C-308/96 and C-94/97) [1998] STC 1189; *C&E Comrs v First Choice Holidays* [2000] STC 609, [2003] STC 934; *MyTravel plc v C&E Comrs* [2005] STC 1617; *Finanzamt Heidelberg v 1st internationale Sprach- und Studienreisen GmbH* [2006] STC 52.

Cross references—See the VAT (Tour Operators) Order 1987, SI 1987/1806.

Press releases etc—Business Brief 12/98 21.5.98 (Overseas businesses established in the UK through agencies).

[Article 26a Special arrangements applicable to second-hand goods, works of art, collectors' items and antiques

A Definitions

For the purposes of this Article, and without prejudice to other Community provisions:

(a) works of art shall mean the objects referred to in (a) of Annex I.
However, Member States shall have the option of not considering as 'works of art' the items mentioned in the final three indents in (a) in Annex I;

(b) collectors items shall mean the objects referred to in (b) of Annex I;

(c) antiques shall mean the objects referred to in (c) of Annex I;

(d) second-hand goods shall mean tangible movable property that is suitable for further use as it is or after repair, other than works of art, collectors' items or antiques and other than precious metals or precious stones as defined by the Member States;

(e) taxable dealer shall mean a taxable person who, in the course of his economic activity, purchases or acquires for the purposes of his undertaking, or imports with a view to resale, second-hand goods and/or works of art, collectors' items or antiques, whether that taxable person is acting for himself or on behalf of another person pursuant to a contract under which commission is payable on purchase or sale;

(f) organiser of a sale by public auction shall mean any taxable person who, in the course of his economic activity, offers goods for sale by public auction with a view to handing them over to the highest bidder;

(g) principal of an organiser of a sale by public auction shall mean any person who transmits goods to an organiser of a sale by public auction under a contract under which commission is payable on a sale subject to the following provisions:
- *the organiser of the sale by public auction offers the goods for sale in his own name but on behalf of his principal,*
- *the organiser of the sale by public auction hands over the goods, in his own name but on behalf of his principal, to the highest bidder at the public auction.*

B Special arrangements for taxable dealers

1. In respect of supplies of second-hand goods, works of act, collectors' items and antiques effected by taxable dealers, Member States shall apply special arrangements for taxing the profit margin made by the taxable dealer, in accordance with the following provisions.

2. The supplies of goods referred to in paragraph 1 shall be supplies, by a taxable dealer, of second-hand goods, works of art, collectors' items or antiques supplied to him within the Community:
- *by a non-taxable person, or*
- *by another taxable person, in so far as the supply of goods by that other taxable person is exempt in accordance with Article 13(B)(c), or*
- *by another taxable person in so far as the supply of goods by that other taxable person qualifies for the exemption provided for in Article 24 and involves capital assets, or*
- *by another taxable dealer, in so far as the supply of goods by that other taxable dealer was subject to value added tax in accordance with these special arrangements.*

VAT EC

3. The taxable amount of the supplies of goods referred to in paragraph 2 shall be the profit margin made by the taxable dealer, less the amount of value added tax relating to the profit margin. That profit margin shall be equal to the difference between the selling price charged by the taxable dealer for the goods and the purchase price.

For the purposes of this paragraph, the following definitions shall apply:

- *selling price shall mean everything which constitutes the consideration, which has been, or is to be, obtained by the taxable dealer from the purchaser or a third party, including subsidies directly linked to that transaction, taxes, duties, levies and charges and incidental expenses such as commission, packaging, transport and insurance costs charged by the taxable dealer to the purchaser but excluding the amounts referred to in Article 11(A)(3),*
- *purchase price shall mean everything which constitutes the consideration defined in the first indent, obtained, or to be obtained, from the taxable dealer by his supplier.*

4. Member States shall entitle taxable dealers to opt for application of the special arrangements to supplies of:

(a) works of art, collectors' items or antiques which they have imported themselves;
(b) works of art supplied to them by their creators or their successors in title;
(c) works of art supplied to them by a taxable person other than a taxable dealer where the supply by that other taxable person was subject to the reduced rate pursuant to Article 12(3)(c).

Member States shall determine the detailed rules for exercising this option which shall in any event cover a period at least equal to two calendar years.

If the option is taken up, the taxable amount shall be determined in accordance with paragraph 3. For supplies of works of art, collectors' items or antiques which the taxable dealer has imported himself, the purchase price to be taken into account in calculating the margin shall be equal to the taxable amount on importation, determined in accordance with Article 11(B), plus the value added tax due or paid on importation.

5. Where they are effected in the conditions laid down in Article 15, the supplies of second-hand goods, works of art, collectors' items or antiques subject to the special arrangements for taxing the margin shall be exempt.

6. Taxable persons shall not be entitled to deduct from the tax for which they are liable the value added tax due or paid in respect of goods which have been, or are to be, supplied to them by a taxable dealer, in so far as the supply of those goods by the taxable dealer is subject to the special arrangements for taxing the margin.

7. In so far as goods are used for the purpose of supplies by him subject to the special arrangements for taxing the margin, the taxable dealer shall not be entitled to deduct from the tax for which he is liable:

(a) the value added tax due or paid in respect of works of art, collectors' items or antiques which he has imported himself;
(b) the value added tax due or paid in respect of works of which have been, or are to be, supplied to him by their creators or their successors in title;
(c) the value added tax due or paid in respect of works of art which have been, or are to be, supplied to him by a taxable person other than a taxable dealer.

8. Where he is led to apply both the normal arrangements for value added tax and the special arrangements for taxing the margin, the taxable dealer must follow separately in his accounts the transactions falling under each of these arrangements, according to rules laid down by the Member States,

9. The taxable dealer may not indicate separately on the invoices which he issues, . . .[2] *tax relating to supplies of goods which he makes subject to the special arrangements for taxing the margin.*

10. In order to simplify the procedure for charging the tax and subject to the consultation provided for in Article 29, Member States may provide that, for certain transactions or for certain categories of taxable dealers, the taxable amount of supplies of goods subject to the special arrangements for taxing the margin shall be determined for each tax period during which the taxable dealer must submit the return referred to in Article 22(4).

In that event, the taxable amount for supplies of goods to which the same rate of value added tax is applied shall be the total margin made by the taxable dealer less the amount of value added tax relating to that margin.

The total margin shall be equal to the difference between:

- *the total amount of supplies of goods subject to the special arrangements for taxing the margin effected by the taxable dealer during the period; that amount shall be equal to the total selling prices determined in accordance with paragraph 3, and*
- *the total amount of purchases of goods as referred to in paragraph 2 effected, during that period, by the taxable dealer; that amount shall be equal to the total purchase prices determined in accordance with paragraph 3.*

Member States shall take the necessary measures to ensure that the taxable persons concerned do not enjoy unjustified advantages or sustain unjustified loss.

11. The taxable dealer may apply the normal value added tax arrangements to any supply covered by the special arrangements pursuant to paragraph 2 or 4.
Where the taxable dealer applies the normal value added tax arrangements to:
- *(a) the supply of a work of art, collectors' item or antique which he has imported himself, he shall be entitled to deduct from his tax liability the value added tax due or paid on the import of those goods;*
- *(b) the supply of a work of art supplied to him by its creator or his successors in title, he shall be entitled to deduct from his tax liability the value added tax due or paid for the work of art supplied to him;*
- *(c) the supply of a work of art supplied to him by a taxable person other than a taxable dealer, he shall be entitled to deduct from his tax liability the value added tax due or paid for the work of art supplied to him.*

This right to deduct shall arise at the time when the tax due for the supply in respect of which the taxable dealer opts for application of the normal value added tax arrangements become chargeable.

C Special arrangements for sales by public auction

1. By way of derogation from B, Member States may determine, in accordance with the following provisions, the taxable amount of supplies of second-hand goods, works of art, collectors' items or antiques effected by an organiser of sales by public auction, acting in his own name, pursuant to a contract under which commission is payable on the sale of those goods by public auction, on behalf of:
- *a non-taxable person, or*
- *another taxable person, in so far as the supply of goods, within the meaning of Article 5(4)(c), by that other taxable person is exempt in accordance with Article 13(B)(c), or*
- *another taxable person, in so far as the supply of goods, within the meaning of Article 5(4)(c), by that other taxable person qualifies for the exemption provided for in Article 24 and involves capital assets, or*
- *a taxable dealer, in so far as the supply of goods, within the meaning of Article 5(4)(c), by that other taxable dealer, is subject to tax in accordance with the special arrangements for taxing the margin provided for in B.*

2. The taxable amount of each supply of goods referred to in paragraph 1 shall be the total amount invoiced in accordance with paragraph 4 to the purchaser by the organiser of the sale by public auction, less:
- *the net amount paid or to be paid by the organiser of the sale by public auction to his principal, determined in accordance with paragraph 3, and*
- *the amount of the tax due by the organiser of the sale by public auction in respect of his supply.*

3. The net amount paid or to be paid by the organiser of the sale by public auction to his principal shall be equal to the difference between:
- *the price of the goods at public auction, and*
- *the amount of the commission obtained or to be obtained by the organiser of the sale by public auction from his principal, under the contract whereby commission is payable on the sale.*

4. The organiser of the sale by public auction must issue to the purchaser an invoice . . . [2] *itemising:*
- *the auction price of the goods,*
- *taxes, dues, levies and charges,*
- *incidental expenses such as commission, packing, transport and insurance costs charged by the organiser to the purchaser of the goods.*

That invoice must not indicate any value added tax separately.

5. The organiser of the sale by public auction to whom the goods were transmitted under a contract whereby commission is payable on a public auction sale must issue a statement to his principal.
That statement must itemise the amount of the transaction, ie the auction price of the goods less the amount of the commission obtained or to be obtained from the principal.
A statement so drawn up shall serve as the invoice which the principal, where he is a taxable person, must issue to the organiser of the sale by public auction in accordance with Article 22(3).

6. Organisers of sales by public auction who supply goods under the conditions laid down in paragraph 1 must indicate in their accounts, in suspense accounts:
- *the amounts obtained or to be obtained from the purchaser of the goods,*
- *the amount reimbursed or to be reimbursed to the vendor of the goods.*

These amounts must be duly substantiated.

7. The supply of goods to a taxable person who is an organiser of sales by public auction shall be regarded as being effected when the sale of those goods by public auction is itself effected.

D Transitional arrangements for the taxation of trade between Member States

During the period referred to in Article 281, Member States shall apply the following provisions:

- *(a) supplies of new means of transport, within the meaning of Article 28a(2), effected within the conditions laid down in Article 28c(A) shall be excluded from the special arrangements provided for in B and C;*
- *(b) by way of derogation from Article 28a(1)(a), intra-Community acquisitions of second-hand goods, works of art, collectors' items or antiques shall not be subject to value added tax where the vendor is a taxable dealer acting as such and the goods acquired have been subject to tax in the Member State of departure of the dispatch or transport, in accordance with the special arrangements for taxing the margin provided for in B, or where the vendor is an organiser of sales by public auction acting as such and the goods acquired have been subject to tax in the Member State of departure of the dispatch or transport, in accordance with the special arrangements provided for in C;*
- *(c) Articles 28b(B) and 28c(A)(a), (c) and (d) shall not apply to supplies of goods subject to value added tax in accordance with either of the special arrangements laid down in B and C.]*[1]

Commentary—*De Voil Indirect Tax Service* **V3.532.**
Simon's Tax Cases—Art 26a, *Pendragon plc and ors v R&C Comrs* [2012] UKUT 90 (TCC), [2012] STC 1638.
Art 26aA(*e*), *Jyske Finans A/S v Skatteministeriet (Nordania Finans A/S and BG Factoring A/S intervening)* [2006] STC 1744.
Amendments—[1] This Article inserted by Council Directive 94/5/EEC, arts 1(3), 4; OJ L60, 3.3.94. For commencement, see art 4 of the Directive.
[2] Words repealed by Council Directive 2001/115/EC art 4(2), (3); see OJ L 015; 17.01.02.

[Article 26b Special scheme for investment gold

A Definition

For the purposes of this Directive, and without prejudice to other Community provisions: 'investment gold' shall mean:

- *(i) gold, in the form of a bar or a wafer of weights accepted by the bullion markets, of a purity equal to or greater than 995 thousandths, whether or not represented by securities. Member States may exclude from the scheme small bars or wafers of a weight of 1g or less;*
- *(ii) gold coins which:*
  - *— are of a purity equal to or greater than 900 thousandths,*
  - *— are minted after 1800,*
  - *— are or have been legal tender in the country of origin, and*
  - *— are normally sold at a price which does not exceed the open market value of the gold contained in the coins by more than 80%.*

Such coins are not, for the purpose of this Directive, considered to be sold for numismatic interest. Each Member State shall inform the Commission before 1 July each year, starting in 1999, of the coins meeting these criteria which are traded in that Member State. The Commission shall publish a comprehensive list of these coins in the 'C' series of the Official Journal of the European Communities before 1 December each year. Coins included in the published list shall be deemed to fulfil these criteria for the whole year for which the list is published.

Note—See VAT Notice 701/21A, para 3 for the list of investment gold coins.

B Special arrangements applicable to investment gold transactions

Member States shall exempt from value added tax the supply, intra-Community acquisition and importation of investment gold, including investment gold represented by certificates for allocated or unallocated gold or traded on gold accounts and including, in particular, gold loans and swaps, involving a right of ownership or claim in respect of investment gold, as well as transactions concerning investment gold involving futures and forward contracts leading to a transfer of right of ownership or claim in respect of investment gold.
Member States shall also exempt services of agents who act in the name and for the account of another when they intervene in the supply of investment gold for their principal.

C Option to tax

Member States shall allow taxable persons who produce investment gold or transform any gold into investment gold as defined in A a right of option for taxation of supplies of investment gold to another taxable person which would otherwise be exempt under B.

Member States may allow taxable persons, who in their trade normally supply gold for industrial purposes, a right of option for taxation of supplies of investment gold as defined in A(i) to another taxable person, which would otherwise be exempt under B. Member States may restrict the scope of this option.
Where the supplier has exercised a right of option for taxation pursuant to the first or second paragraph, Member States shall allow a right of option for taxation for the agent in respect of the services mentioned in the second paragraph of B.
Member States shall specify the details of the use of these options, and shall inform the Commission of the rules of application for the exercise of these options in that Member State.

D Right of deduction

1. Taxable persons shall be entitled to deduct—
- *(a) tax due or paid in respect of investment gold supplied to them by a person who has exercised the right of option under C or supplied to them pursuant to the procedure laid down in G;*
- *(b) tax due or paid in respect of supply to them, or intra-Community acquisition or importation by them, of gold other than investment gold which is subsequently transformed by them or on their behalf into investment gold;*
- *(c) tax due or paid in respect of services supplied to them consisting of change of form, weight or purity of gold including investment gold,*

if their subsequent supply of this gold is exempt under this Article.
2. Taxable persons who produce investment gold or transform any gold into investment gold, shall be entitled to deduct tax due or paid by them in respect of supplies, or intra-Community acquisition or importation of goods or services linked to the production or transformation of that gold as if their subsequent supply of the gold exempted under this Article were taxable.

E Special obligations for traders in investment gold

Member States shall, as a minimum, ensure that traders in investment gold keep account of all substantial transactions in investment gold and keep the documentation to allow identification of the customer in such transactions.
Traders shall keep this information for a period of at least five years.
Member States may accept equivalent obligations under measures adopted pursuant to other Community legislation, such as Council Directive 91/308/EEC of 10 June 1991 on prevention of the use of the financial system for the purpose of money laundering, to meet the requirements of the first paragraph.
Member States may lay down stricter obligations, in particular on special record keeping or special accounting requirements.

VAT EC

F Reverse charge procedure

By way of derogation from Article 21(1)(a), as amended by Article 28g, in the case of supplies of gold material or semi-manufactured products of a purity of 325 thousandths or greater, or supplies of investment gold where an option referred to in C of this Article has been exercised, Member States may designate the purchaser as the person liable to pay the tax, according to the procedures and conditions, which they shall lay down. When they exercise this option, Member States shall take the measures necessary to ensure that the person designated as liable for the tax due fulfils the obligations to submit a statement and to pay the tax in accordance with Article 22.

G Procedure for transactions on a regulated gold bullion market

1. A Member State may, subject to consultation provided for under Article 29, disapply the exemption for investment gold provided for by this special scheme in respect of specific transactions, other than intra-Community supplies or exports, concerning investment gold taking place in that Member State:
- *(a) between taxable persons who are members of a bullion market regulated by the Member State concerned, and*
- *(b) where the transaction is between a member of a bullion market regulated by the Member State concerned and another taxable person who is not a member of that market.*

Under these circumstances, these transactions shall be taxable and the following shall apply.
2

(a) *For transactions under 1(a), for the purpose of simplification, the Member State shall authorise suspension of the tax to be collected as well as dispense with the recording requirements of value added tax.*

(b) *For transactions under 1(b), the reverse charge procedure under F shall be applicable. Where a non-member of the bullion market would not, other than for these transactions, be liable for registration for VAT in the relevant Member State, the member shall fulfil the fiscal obligations on behalf of the non-member, according to the provisions of that Member State.]*[1]

Amendments—[1] This Article inserted by Council Directive 98/80/EC, art 1; OJ L281, 17.10.98. For commencement, see art 4 of the Directive printed *post*.

[Article 26c Special scheme for non-established taxable persons supplying electronic services to non-taxable persons

A Definitions

For the purposes of this Article, the following definitions shall apply without prejudice to other Community provisions:

(a) *'non-established taxable person' means a taxable person who has neither established his business nor has a fixed establishment within the territory of the Community and who is not otherwise required to be identified for tax purposes under Article 22;*

(b) *'electronic services' and 'electronically supplied services' means those services referred to in the last indent of Article 9(2)(e);*

(c) *'Member State of identification' means the Member State which the non-established taxable person chooses to contact to state when his activity as a taxable person within the territory of the Community commences in accordance with the provisions of this Article;*

(d) *'Member State of consumption' means the Member State in which the supply of the electronic services is deemed to take place according to Article 9(2)(f);*

(e) *'value added tax return' means the statement containing the information necessary to establish the amount of tax that has become chargeable in each Member State.*

B Special scheme for electronically supplied services

1. Member States shall permit a non-established taxable person supplying electronic services to a non-taxable person who is established or has his permanent address or usually resides in a Member State to use a special scheme in accordance with the following provisions. The special scheme shall apply to all those supplies within the Community.

2. The non-established taxable person shall state to the Member State of identification when his activity as a taxable person commences, ceases or changes to the extent that he no longer qualifies for the special scheme. Such a statement shall be made electronically.

The information from the non-established taxable person to the Member State of identification when his taxable activities commence shall contain the following details for the identification: name, postal address, electronic addresses, including websites, national tax number, if any, and a statement that the person is not identified for value added tax purposes within the Community. The non-established taxable person shall notify the Member State of identification of any changes in the submitted information.

3. The Member State of identification shall identify the non-established taxable person by means of an individual number. Based on the information used for this identification, Member States of consumption may keep their own identification systems.

The Member State of identification shall notify the non-established taxable person by electronic means of the identification number allocated to him.

4. The Member State of identification shall exclude the non-established taxable person from the identification register if:

(a) *he notifies that he no longer supplies electronic services, or*

(b) *it otherwise can be assumed that his taxable activities have ended, or*

(c) *he no longer fulfils the requirements necessary to be allowed to use the special scheme, or*

(d) *he persistently fails to comply with the rules concerning the special scheme.*

5. The non-established taxable person shall submit by electronic means to the Member State of identification a value added tax return for each calendar quarter whether or not electronic services have been supplied. The return shall be submitted within 20 days following the end of the reporting period to which the return refers.

The value added tax return shall set out the identification number and, for each Member State of consumption where tax has become due, the total value, less value added tax, of supplies of electronic services for the reporting period and total amount of the corresponding tax. The applicable tax rates and the total tax due shall also be indicated.

6. The value added tax return shall be made in euro. Member States which have not adopted the euro may require the tax return to be made in their national currencies. If the supplies have been made in other currencies, the exchange rate valid for the last date of the reporting period shall be used when completing the value added tax return. The exchange shall be done following the exchange rates published by the European Central Bank for that day, or, if there is no publication on that day, on the next day of publication.

7. The non-established taxable person shall pay the value added tax when submitting the return. Payment shall be made to a bank account denominated in euro, designated by the Member State of identification. Member States which have not adopted the euro may require the payment to be made to a bank account denominated in their own currency.

8. Notwithstanding Article 1(1) of Directive 86/560/EEC, the non-established taxable person making use of this special scheme shall, instead of making deductions under Article 17(2) of this Directive, be granted a refund according to Directive 86/560/EEC. Articles 2(2),2(3) and 4(2)of Directive 86/560/EEC shall not apply to the refund related to electronic supplies covered by this special scheme.

9. The non-established taxable person shall keep records of the transactions covered by this special scheme in sufficient detail to enable the tax administration of the Member State of consumption to determine that the value added tax return referred to in paragraph 5 is correct. These records should be made available electronically on request to the Member State of identification and to the Member State of consumption. These records shall be maintained for a period of 10 years from the end of the year when the transaction was carried out.

10. Article 21(2)(b) shall not apply to a non-established taxable person who has opted for this special scheme.][1]

Amendments—[1] Article 26c is temporarily inserted by Council Directive 2002/38 art 1 para 3 (OJ L 128; 15.05.02) with effect for a period of three years from 1 July 2003: see Council Directive 2002/38/EC art 4.

TITLE XV:
SIMPLIFICATION PROCEDURES

Article 27

[1. The Council, acting unanimously on a proposal from the Commission, may authorise any Member State to introduce special measures for derogation from the provisions of this Directive, in order to simplify the procedure for charging the tax or to prevent certain types of tax evasion or avoidance. Measures intended to simplify the procedure for charging the tax, except to a negligible extent, may not affect the overall amount of the tax revenue of the Member State collected at the stage of final consumption.][1]

[2. A Member State wishing to introduce the measure referred to in paragraph 1 shall send an application to the Commission and provide it with all the necessary information. If the Commission considers that it does not have all the necessary information, it shall contact the Member State concerned within two months of receipt of the application and specify what additional information is required. Once the Commission has all the information it considers necessary for appraisal of the request it shall within one month notify the requesting Member State accordingly and it shall transmit the request, in its original language, to the other Member States.][1]

[3. Within three months of giving the notification referred to in the last sentence of paragraph 2, the Commission shall present to the Council either an appropriate proposal or, should it object to the derogation requested, a communication setting out its objections.][1]

[4. In any event, the procedure set out in paragraphs 2 and 3 shall be completed within eight months of receipt of the application by the Commission.][1]

5. Those Member States which apply on 1 January 1977 special measures of the type referred to in paragraph 1 above may retain them providing they notify the Commission of them before 1 January 1978 and providing that where such derogations are designed to simplify the procedure for charging tax they conform with the requirement laid down in paragraph 1 above.

Simon's Tax Cases—art 27, *C&E Comrs v Next plc* [1995] STC 651; *Primback Ltd v C&E Comrs* [1996] STC 757; *Finanzamt Bergisch Gladbach v Skripalle* (Case C-63/96) [1997] STC 1035; *Finanzamt Sulingen v Sudholz* [2005] STC 747; *Campsa Estaciones de Servicio SA v Administracion del Estada* (Case C-285/10) [2011] STC 1603.

Art 27(1), *Genius Holding BV v Staatssecretaris van Financiën* [1991] STC 239; *'K' Line Air Service Europe BV v Eulaerts NV and Belgian State* (Case C-131/91) [1996] STC 597.

Amendments—[1] Paras 1, 2, 3 replaced by Council Directive 2004/7 art 1 (OJ L 027; 30.1.2004 p 44).

VAT EC

TITLE XVI:
TRANSITIONAL PROVISIONS

Article 28

1. Any provisions brought into force by the Member States under the provisions of the first four indents of Article 17 of the second Council Directive of 11 April 1967 shall cease to apply, in each Member State, as from the respective dates on which the provisions referred to in the second paragraph of Article 1 of this Directive come into force.

[1a. Until a date which may not be later than 30 June 1999, the United Kingdom of Great Britain and Northern Ireland may, for imports of works of art, collectors' items or antiques which qualified for an exemption on 1 January 1993, apply Article 11(B)(6) in such a way that the value added tax due on importation is, in any event, equal to 2·5% of the amount determined in accordance with Article 11(B)(1) to (4).][3]

[2. Notwithstanding Article 12(3), the following provisions shall apply during the transitional period referred to in Article 281.

(a) *Exemptions with refund of the tax paid at the preceding stage and reduced rates lower than the minimum rate laid down in Article 12(3) in respect of the reduced rates, which were in force on 1 January 1991 and which are in accordance with Community law, and satisfy the conditions stated in the last indent of Article 17 of the second Council Directive of 11 April 1967, may be maintained.*

Member States shall adopt the measures necessary to ensure the determination of own resources relating to these operations.

In the event that the provisions of this paragraph create for Ireland distortions of competition in the supply of energy products for heating and lighting, Ireland may, on specific request, be authorised by the Commission to apply a reduced rate to such supplies, in accordance with Article 12(3). In that case, Ireland shall submit its request to the Commission together with all necessary information. If the Commission has not taken a decision within three months of receiving the request, Ireland shall be deemed to be authorised to apply the proposed reduced rates.

(b) *Member States which, at 1 January 1991 in accordance with Community law, applied exemptions with refund of tax paid at the preceding stage, or reduced rates lower than the minimum laid down in Article 12(3) in respect of the reduced rates, to goods and services other than those specified in Annex H, may apply the reduced rate or one of the two reduced rates provided for in Article 12(3) to any such supplies.*

(c) *Member States which under the terms of Article 12(3) will be obliged to increase their standard rate as applied at 1 January 1991 by more than 2%, may apply a reduced rate lower than the minimum laid down in Article 12(3) in respect of the reduced rate to supplies of categories of goods and services specified in Annex H. Furthermore, those Member States may apply such a rate to restaurant services, children's clothing, children's footwear and housing. Member States may not introduce exemptions with refund of the tax at the preceding stage on the basis of this paragraph.*

(d) *Member States which at 1 January 1991 applied a reduced rate to restaurant services, children's clothing, children's footwear and housing, may continue to apply such a rate to such supplies.*

(e) *Member States which at 1 January 1991 applied a reduced rate to supplies of goods and services other than those specified in Annex H may apply the reduced rate or one of the two reduced rates provided for in Article 12(3) to such supplies, provided that the rate is not lower than 12%.*

[This provision may not apply to supplies of second-hand goods, works of art, collectors' items or antiques subject to value added tax in accordance with one of the special arrangements provided for in Article 26a(B) and (C).][4]

(f) *The Hellenic Republic may apply VAT rates up to 30% lower than the corresponding rates applied in mainland Greece in the departments of Lesbos, Chios, Samos, the Dodecanese and the Cyclades, and on the following islands in the Aegean: Thasos, Northern Sporades, Samothrace and Skiros.*

(g) *On the basis of a report from the Commission, the Council shall, before 31 December 1994, re-examine the provisions of subparagraphs (a) to (f) above in relation to the proper functioning of the internal market in particular. In the event of significant distortions of competition arising, the Council, acting unanimously on a proposal from the Commission, shall adopt appropriate measures.]*[2]

[(h) *Member States which, on 1 January 1993, were availing themselves of the option provided for in Article 5(5)(a) as in force on that date, may apply to supplies under a contract to make up work the rate applicable to the goods after making up.*

For the purposes of applying this provision, supplies under a contract to make up work shall be deemed to be delivery by a contractor to his customer of movable property made or assembled by the contractor from materials or objects entrusted to him by the customer for this purpose, whether or not the contractor has provided any part of the materials used.][6]

[(i) Member States may apply a reduced rate to supplies of live plants (including bulbs, roots and the like, cut flowers and ornamental foliage) and wood for use as firewood][7]

[(j) the Republic of Austria may apply one of the two reduced rates provided for in the third subparagraph of Article 12(3)(a) to the letting of immovable property for residential use, provided that the rate is not lower than 10%.

(k) the Portuguese Republic may apply one of the two reduced rates provided for in the third subparagraph of Article 12(3)(a) to restaurant services, provided that the rate is not lower than 12%.][9]

3. During the transitional period referred to in paragraph 4, Member States may:

(a) continue to subject to tax the transactions exempt under Article 13 or 15 set out in Annex E to this Directive;

(b) continue to exempt the activities set out in Annex F under conditions existing in the Member State concerned;

(c) grant to taxable persons the option for taxation of exempt transactions under the conditions set out in Annex G;

(d) continue to apply provisions derogating from the principle of immediate deduction laid down in the first paragraph of Article 18(2);

(e) continue to apply measures derogating from the provisions of Articles 5(4)(c)[5]*, 6(4) and 11A(3)(c);*

(f) provide that for supplies of buildings and building land purchased for the purpose of resale by a taxable person for whom tax on the purchase was not deductible, the taxable amount shall be the difference between the selling price and the purchase price;

(g) by way of derogation from Articles 17(3) and 26(3), continue to exempt without repayment of input tax the services of travel agents referred to in Article 26(3). This derogation shall also apply to travel agents acting in the name and on account of the traveller.

[3a. Pending a decision by the Council, which, under Article 3 of Directive 89/465/EEC, is to act on the abolition of the transitional derogations provided for in paragraph 3, Spain shall be authorised to exempt the transactions referred to in point 2 of Annex F in respect of services rendered by authors and the transactions referred to in points 23 and 25 of Annex F.][1]

4. The transitional period shall last initially for five years as from 1 January 1978. At the latest six months before the end of this period, and subsequently as necessary, the Council shall review the situation with regard to the derogations set out in paragraph 3 on the basis of a report from the Commission and shall unanimously determine on a proposal from the Commission, whether any or all of these derogations shall be abolished.

5. At the end of the transitional period passenger transport shall be taxed in the country of departure for that part of the journey taking place within the Community according to the detailed rules of procedure to be laid down by the Council acting unanimously on a proposal from the Commission.

[6. The Council, acting unanimously on a proposal from the Commission, may authorise any Member State to apply until 31 December 2010 at the latest the reduced rates provided for in the third subparagraph of Article 12(3)(a) to services listed in a maximum of two of the categories set out in Annex K. In exceptional cases, a Member State may be authorised to apply the reduced rates to services belonging to three of the aforementioned categories.][10]

The services concerned must satisfy the following requirements—

(a) they must be labour-intensive;

(b) they must be largely provided direct to final consumers;

(c) they must be mainly local and not likely to create distortions of competition;

(d) there must be a close link between the lower prices resulting from the rate reduction and the foreseeable increase in demand and employment.

The application of a reduced rate must not prejudice the smooth functioning of the internal market.

[Any Member State wishing to apply for the first time after 31 December 2005 a reduced rate to one or more of the services mentioned in the first subparagraph pursuant to this provision shall inform the Commission before 31 March 2006. It shall communicate to it before that date all relevant particulars concerning the new measures it wishes to introduce, and in particular the following:

(a) scope of the measure and detailed description of the services concerned;

(b) particulars showing that the conditions laid down in the second and third subparagraphs have been met;

(c) particulars showing the budgetary cost of the measure envisaged.][10]

Those Member States authorised to apply the reduced rate referred to in the first sub-paragraph shall, before 1 October 2002, draw up a detailed report containing an overall assessment of the measure's effectiveness in terms notably of job creation and efficiency.

VAT EC

Before 31 December 2002 the Commission shall forward a global evaluation report to the Council and Parliament accompanied, if necessary, by a proposal for appropriate measures for a final decision on the VAT rate applicable to labour-intensive services.][8]

Commentary—*De Voil Indirect Tax Service* **V4.275**.

Simon's Tax Cases—*EC Commission v Federal Republic of Germany* [1996] STC 843; *Marks and Spencer plc v C&E Comrs* [2000] STC 16.

Art 28(2), *EC Commission v United Kingdom* [1988] STC 456; *Jubilee Hall Recreation Centre Ltd v C&E Comrs* [1997] STC 414; *Talacre Beach Caravan Sales Ltd v C&E Comrs* [2006] STC 1671.

Art 28(2)(*a*), *Marks and Spencer plc v C&E Comrs* [1999] STC 205; *Marks and Spencer plc v C&E Comrs, University of Sussex v C&E Comrs* [2004] STC 1.

Art 28(3), *Jetair NV and anor v FOD Financien* (Case C-599/12) [2014] STC 1088.

Art 28(3)(*b*), *Norbury Developments Ltd v C&E Comrs* [1999] STC 511; *Idéal Tourisme SA v Belgian State* [2001] STC 1386.

Art 28(3)(*b*), (*c*), *Finanzamt Goslar v Breistsohl* [2001] STC 355.

Note—Art 17 of the Second Council Directive reads as follows—

> *Article 17*
>
> With a view to the transition from the present systems of turnover taxes to the common system of value added tax, Member States may:
>
> — adopt transitional measures to levy the tax in advance;
>
> — apply, during a certain transitional period, in respect of capital goods, the method of deduction by annual instalments (deductions *pro rata temporis*);
>
> — exclude, in whole or in part, during a certain transitional period, capital goods from the deduction system provided for in Article 11;
>
> and, subject to the consultations mentioned in Article 16:
>
> — authorise (in order to grant relief, total or partial, but general in scope, from the turnover tax charged up to the time of introducing value added tax) standard deductions in respect of capital goods not yet written off and of stocks in hand at that time. Member States may, however, restrict such deductions to goods exported during a period of one year from the introduction of value added tax. In that event, such deductions shall only be allowed in respect of stocks in hand at the time referred to above and exported in an unaltered state;
>
> — provide for reduced rates or even exemptions with refund, if appropriate, of the tax paid at the preceding stage, where the total incidence of such measures does not exceed that of the reliefs applied under the present system. Such measures may only be taken for clearly defined social reasons and for the benefit of the final consumer, and may not remain in force after the abolition of the imposition of tax on importation and the remission of tax on exportation in trade between Member States.

Amendment—[1] Para 3a added by EEC Council Regulation 91/680; OJ L376, 31.12.1991, p 1.

[2] Para 2 replaced by EEC Council Directive 92/77; OJ L316, 31.10.92.

[3] Para 1a inserted by EEC Council Directive 94/5, arts 1(4), 4; OJ L60, 3.3.94. For commencement, see art 4 of the Directive printed *post*.

[4] Words in para 2(*e*) added by EEC Council Directive 94/5, arts 1(5), 4; OJ L60, 3.3.94.

[5] Derogation in para 3(*e*) relating to art 5(4)(*c*) deleted by EEC Council Directive 94/5, arts 1(8), 4; OJ L60, 3.3.94.

[6] Para (2)(*h*) added by EC Council Directive 95/7, art 1(5): OJ L102, 5.5.95, p 18 with effect from 25 May 1995.

[7] Para 2(*i*) added by EC Council Directive 96/42, art 1, with effect from 1 January 1995; see OJ L 170, 9.7.96, p 34.

[8] Para 6 added by EC Council Directive 99/85, art 1(1), with effect from 28 October 1999; see OJ L 277, 28.10.99, p 34.

[9] Para 2(*j*), (*k*) added by EC Council Directive 2000/17, art 1, with effect from 1 January 1999 until the end of the transitional period referred to in Article 281; see OJ L84, 5.4.00, p 24.

[10] Words in para 6 substituted by Council Directive 2006/18 art 1(2); see OJ L 051; 22.2.2006, p 12.

[TITLE XVIA:
TRANSITIONAL ARRANGEMENTS FOR THE TAXATION OF TRADE BETWEEN MEMBER STATES]

Note—For the period of application of this Title, see art 28 *l post*.

Amendments—This Title (arts 28 *a*–28 *m*) added by EEC Council Directive 91/680; OJ L376, 31.12.1991, p 1.

Article 28a Scope

1. The following shall also be subject to value added tax:

(a) intra-Community acquisitions of goods for consideration within the territory of the country by a taxable person acting as such or by a non-taxable legal person where the vendor is a taxable person acting as such who is not eligible for the tax exemption provided for in Article 24 and who is not covered by the arrangements laid down in the second sentence of Article 8(1)(a) or in Article 28b(B)(1).

[By way of derogation from the first subparagraph, intra-Community acquisitions of goods made under the conditions set out in paragraph 1a by a taxable person or non-taxable legal person shall not be subject to value added tax.][1]

Member States shall grant taxable persons and non-taxable legal persons eligible under the second subparagraph the right to opt for the general scheme laid down in the first subparagraph. Member States shall determine the detailed rules for the exercise of that option, which shall in any case apply for two calendar years;

(b) intra-Community acquisitions of new means of transport effected for consideration within the country by taxable persons or non-taxable legal persons who qualify for the derogation provided for in the second subparagraph of (a) or by any other non-taxable person.

[(c) the intra-Community acquisition of goods which are subject to excise duties effected for consideration within the territory of the country by a taxable person or a non-taxable legal person who qualifies for the derogation referred to in the second subparagraph of point (a), and for which the excise duties become chargeable within the territory of the country pursuant to Directive 92/12/EEC.][2]

[1a. The following shall benefit from the derogation set out in the second subparagraph of paragraph 1(a):

(a) intra-Community acquisitions of goods whose supply within the territory of the country would be exempt pursuant to Article 15(4) to (10);

(b) intra-Community acquisitions of goods other than those at (a), made—

— *by a taxable person for the purpose of his agricultural, forestry or fisheries undertaking, subject to the flat-rate scheme set out in Article 25, by a taxable person who carries out only supplies of goods or services in respect of which value added tax is not deductible, or by a non-taxable legal person,*

— *for a total amount not exceeding, during the current calendar year, a threshold which the Member States shall determine but which may not be less than the equivalent in national currency of ECU 10 000, and*

— *provided that the total amount of intra-Community acquisitions of goods did not, during the previous calendar year, exceed the threshold referred to in the second indent.*

The threshold which serves as the reference for the application of the above shall consist of the total amount, exclusive of value added tax due or paid in the Member State from which the goods are dispatched or transported, of intra-Community acquisitions of goods other than new means of transport and other than goods subject to excise duty.][3]

2. For the purposes of this Title:

(a) the following shall be considered as "means of transport": vessels exceeding 7·5 metres in length, aircraft the take-off weight of which exceeds 1,550 kilograms and motorised land vehicles the capacity of which exceeds 48 cubic centimetres or the power of which exceeds 7·2 kilowatts, intended for the transport of persons or goods, except for the vessels and aircraft referred to in Article 15(5) and (6);

[(b) the means of transport referred to in (a) shall not be considered to be 'new' where both of the following conditions are simultaneously fulfilled:

— *they were supplied more than three months after the date of first entry into service. However, this period shall be increased to six months for the motorised land vehicles defined in (a),*

— *they have travelled more than 6,000 kilometres in the case of land vehicles, sailed for more than 100 hours in the case of vessels, or flown for more than 40 hours in the case of aircraft.*

Member States shall lay down the conditions under which the above facts can be regarded as established.][6]

3. "Intra-Community acquisition of goods" shall mean acquisition of the right to dispose as owner of movable tangible property dispatched or transported to the person acquiring the goods by or on behalf of the vendor or the person acquiring the goods to a Member State other than that from which the goods are dispatched or transported.

Where goods acquired by a non-taxable legal person are dispatched or transported from a third territory and imported by that non-taxable legal person into a Member State other than the Member State of arrival of the goods dispatched or transported, the goods shall be deemed to have been dispatched or transported from the Member State of import. That Member State shall grant the importer as defined in [Article 21(4)][8] *a refund of the value added tax paid in connection with the importation of the goods in so far as the importer establishes that his acquisition was subject to value added tax in the Member State of arrival of the goods dispatched or transported.*

4. Any person who from time to time supplies a new means of transport under the conditions laid down in Article 28c(A) shall also be regarded as a taxable person.

The Member State within the territory of which the supply is effected shall grant the taxable person the right of deduction on the basis of the following provisions:

— *the right of deduction shall arise and may be exercised only at the time of the supply,*

— *the taxable person shall be authorised to deduct the value added tax included in the purchase price or paid on the importation or intra-Community acquisition of the means of transport, up to an amount not exceeding the tax for which he would be liable if the supply were not exempt.*

Member States shall lay down detailed rules for the implementation of these provisions.

5. [The following shall be treated as supplies of goods effected for consideration:][7]

(a) . . .[7]

(b) the transfer by a taxable person of goods from his undertaking to another Member State.

VAT EC

The following shall be regarded as having been transferred to another Member State: any tangible property dispatched or transported by or on behalf of the taxable person out of the territory defined in Article 3 but within the Community for the purposes of his undertaking, other than for the purposes of one of the following transactions:

- *the supply of the goods in question by the taxable person within the territory of the Member State of arrival of the dispatch or transport under the conditions laid down in the second sentence of Article 8(1)(a) and in Article 28b(B)(1),*
- *the supply of the goods in question by the taxable person under the conditions laid down in Article 8(1)(c),*
- *the supply of the goods in question by the taxable person within the territory of the country under the conditions laid down in Article 15 or in Article 28c(A),*

. . . [7]

[— *the supply of a service performed for the taxable person and involving work on the goods in question physically carried out in the Member State in which the dispatch or transport of the goods ends, provided that the goods, after being worked upon, are re-dispatched to that taxable person in the Member State from which they had initially been dispatched or transported.*][7]

- *temporary use of the goods in question within the territory of the Member State of arrival of the dispatch or transport of the goods for the purposes of the supply of services by the taxable person established within the territory of the Member State of departure of the dispatch or transport of the goods,*
- *temporary use of the goods in question, for a period not exceeding 24 months, within the territory of another Member State in which the import of the same goods from a third country with a view to temporary use would be eligible for the arrangements for temporary importation with full exemption from import duties.*

[— *the supply of gas through the natural gas distribution system, or of electricity, under the conditions set out in Article 8(1)(d) or (e).*][9]

[However, when one of the conditions to which the benefit of the above is subordinated is no longer met, the goods shall be considered as having been transferred to a destination in another Member State. In this case, the transfer is carried out at the moment that the condition is no longer met.][4]

6. The intra-Community acquisition of goods for consideration shall include the use by a taxable person for the purposes of his undertaking of goods dispatched or transported by or on behalf of that taxable person from another Member State within the territory of which the goods were produced, extracted, processed, purchased, acquired as defined in paragraph 1 or imported by the taxable person within the framework of his undertaking into that other Member State.

[The following shall also be deemed to be an intra-Community acquisition of goods effected for consideration: the appropriation of goods by the forces of a State party to the North Atlantic Treaty, for their use or for the use of the civilian staff accompanying them, which they have not acquired subject to the general rules governing taxation on the domestic market of one of the Member States, when the importation of these goods could not benefit from the exemption set out in Article 14(1)(g).][5]

7. Member States shall take measures to ensure that transactions which would have been classed as "supplies of goods" as defined in paragraph 5 or Article 5 if they had been carried out within the territory of the country by a taxable person acting as such are classed as "intra-Community acquisitions of goods".

Cross references—See VATA 1994 s 95(2) (implementation of para 2(*a*) above);
VAT Regulations, SI 1995/2518 regs 146, 147 (implementation of this article).
VAT Regulations, SI 1995/2518 regs 149–154 (regulations in implementing para 4 above).

Amendments—[1] Words in para 1(*a*) replaced by EEC Council Directive 92/111, art 1.10; OJ L384, 30.12.92.

[2] Para 1(*c*) added by EEC Council Directive 92/111, art 1.10; OJ L384, 30.12.92.

[3] Para 1a inserted by EEC Council Directive 92/111, art 1.10; OJ L384, 30.12.92.

[4] Sub-para added to para 5(*b*) by EEC Council Directive 92/111, art 1.10; OJ L384, 30.12.92.

[5] Sub-para added to para 6 by EEC Council Directive 92/111, art 1.10; OJ L384, 30.12.92.

[6] Para 2(b) replaced by EEC Council Directive 94/5, arts 1(6), 4; OJ L60, 3.3.94. For commencement, see art 4 of the Directive printed post.

[7] The words in the first pair of square brackets in para 5 and words in sub-para (*b*) replaced, and para 5(*a*) and the words omitted from sub-para (*b*) repealed by EC Council Directive 95/7, art 1(6): OJ L102, 5.5.95, p 18 with effect from 25 May 1995.

[8] Words "Article 21(4)" substituted for "Article 21(2)" by Council Directive 2000/65/EC art 1(6) with effect from 21 October 2000; OJ L269 p 44, 21.10.00. Member states must bring into force the measures necessary to comply with these provisions not later than 31 December 2001.

[9] Words in para 5 inserted by Council Directive 2003/92/EC art 1(7); OJ L260, 11.10.2003 p 8.

Article 28b Place of transactions

A Place of the intra-Community acquisition of goods

1. The place of the intra-Community acquisition of goods shall be deemed to be the place where the goods are at the time when dispatch or transport to the person acquiring them ends.

2. Without prejudice to paragraph 1, the place of the intra-Community acquisition of goods referred to in Article 28a(1)(a) shall, however, be deemed to be within the territory of the Member State which issued the value added tax identification number under which the person acquiring the goods made the acquisition, unless the person acquiring the goods establishes that that acquisition has been subject to tax in accordance with paragraph 1.

If, however, the acquisition is subject to tax in accordance with paragraph 1 in the Member State of arrival of the dispatch or transport of the goods after having been subject to tax in accordance with the first subparagraph, the taxable amount shall be reduced accordingly in the Member State which issued the value added tax identification number under which the person acquiring the goods made the acquisition.

[For the purposes of applying the first subparagraph, the intra-Community acquisition of goods shall be deemed to have been subject to tax in accordance with paragraph 1 when the following conditions have been met—

- *the acquirer establishes that he has effected this intra-Community acquisition for the needs of a subsequent supply effected in the Member State referred to in paragraph 1 and for which the consignee has been designated as the person liable for the tax due in accordance with Article 28c(E)(3),*
- *the obligations for declaration set out in the last subparagraph of Article 22(6)(b) have been satisfied by the acquirer.]*[1]

B Place of the supply of goods

1. By way of derogation from Article 8(1)(a) and (2), the place of the supply of goods dispatched or transported by or on behalf of the supplier from a Member State other than that of arrival of the dispatch or transport shall be deemed to be the place where the goods are when dispatch or transport to the purchaser ends, where the following conditions are fulfilled:

- *the supply of goods is effected for a taxable person eligible for the derogation provided for in the second subparagraph of Article 28a(1)(a), for a non-taxable legal person who is eligible for the same derogation or for any other non-taxable person,*
- *the supply is of goods other than new means of transport and other than goods supplied after assembly or installation, with or without a trial run, by or on behalf of the supplier.*

Where the goods thus supplied are dispatched or transported from a third territory and imported by the supplier into a Member State other than the Member State of arrival of the goods dispatched or transported to the purchaser, they shall be regarded as having been dispatched or transported from the Member State of import.

2. However, where the supply is of goods other than products subject to excise duty, paragraph 1 shall not apply to supplies of goods dispatched or transported to the same Member State of arrival of the dispatch or transport where:

- *the total value of such supplies, less value added tax, does not in one calendar year exceed the equivalent in national currency of ECU 100,000, and*
- *the total value, less value added tax, of the supplies of goods other than products subject to excise duty effected under the conditions laid down in paragraph 1 in the previous calendar year did not exceed the equivalent in national currency of ECU 100,000.*

The Member State within the territory of which the goods are when dispatch or transport to the purchaser ends may limit the thresholds referred to above to the equivalent in national currency of ECU 35,000 where that Member State fears that the threshold of ECU 100,000 referred to above would lead to serious distortions of the conditions of competition. Member States which exercise this option shall take the measures necessary to inform the relevant public authorities in the Member State of dispatch or transport of the goods.

Before 31 December 1994, the Commission shall report to the Council on the operation of the special ECU 35,000 thresholds provided for in the preceding subparagraph. In that report the Commission may inform the Council that the abolition of the special thresholds will not lead to serious distortions of the conditions of competition. Until the Council takes a unanimous decision on a Commission proposal, the preceding subparagraph shall remain in force.

3. The Member State within the territory of which the goods are at the time of departure of the dispatch or transport shall grant those taxable persons who effect supplies of goods eligible under paragraph 2 the right to choose that the place of such supplies shall be determined in accordance with paragraph 1.

The Member States concerned shall determine the detailed rules for the exercise of that option, which shall in any case apply for two calendar years.

VAT EC

C Place of the supply of services in the intra-Community transport of goods

1. By way of derogation from Article 9(2)(b), the place of the supply of services in the intra-Community transport of goods shall be determined in accordance with paragraphs 2, 3 and 4. For the purposes of this Title the following definitions shall apply:

- *"the intra-Community transport of goods" shall mean transport where the place of departure and the place of arrival are situated within the territories of two different Member States[.]*[2]

[The transport of goods where the place of departure and the place of arrival are situated within the territory of the country shall be treated as intra-Community transport of goods where such transport is directly linked to transport of goods where the place of departure and the place of arrival are situated within the territories of two different Member States;][2]

- *"the place of departure" shall mean the place where the transport of goods actually starts, leaving aside distance actually travelled to the place where the goods are,*
- *"the place of arrival" shall mean the place where the transport of goods actually ends.*

2. The place of the supply of services in the intra-Community transport of goods shall be the place of departure.
3. However, by way of derogation from paragraph 2, the place of the supply of services in the intra-Community transport of goods rendered to customers identified for purposes of value added tax in a Member State other than that of the departure of the transport shall be deemed to be within the territory of the Member State which issued the customer with the value added tax identification number under which the service was rendered to him.
4. Member States need not apply the tax to that part of the transport corresponding to journeys made over waters which do not form part of the territory of the Community as defined in Article 3.

D Place of the supply of services ancillary to the intra-Community transport of goods

By way of derogation from Article 9(2)(c), the place of the supply of services involving activities ancillary to the intra-Community transport of goods, rendered to customers identified for purposes of value added tax in a Member State other than that within the territory of which the services are physically performed, shall be deemed to be within the territory of the Member State which issued the customer with the value added tax identification number under which the service was rendered to him.

E Place of the supply of services rendered by intermediaries

1. By way of derogation from Article 9(1), the place of the supply of services rendered by intermediaries, acting in the name and for the account of other persons, where they form part of the supply of services in the intra-Community transport of goods, shall be the place of departure.
However, where the customer for whom the services rendered by the intermediary are performed is identified for purposes of value added tax in a Member State other than that of the departure of the transport, the place of the supply of services rendered by an intermediary shall be deemed to be within the territory of the Member State which issued the customer with the value added tax identification number under which the service was rendered to him.
2. By way of derogation from Article 9(1), the place of the supply of services rendered by intermediaries acting in the name and for the account of other persons, where they form part of the supply of services the purpose of which is activities ancillary to the intra-Community transport of goods, shall be the place where the ancillary services are physically performed.
However, where the customer of the services rendered by the intermediary is identified for purposes of value added tax in a Member State other than that within the territory of which the ancillary service is physically performed, the place of supply of the services rendered by the intermediary shall be deemed to be within the territory of the Member State which issued the customer with the value added tax identification number under which the service was rendered to him by the intermediary.
3. By way of derogation from Article 9(1), the place of the supply of services rendered by intermediaries acting in the name and for the account of other persons, when such services form part of transactions other than those referred to in paragraph 1 or 2 or in Article 9(2)(e), shall be the place where those transactions are carried out.
However, where the customer is identified for purposes of value added tax in a Member State other than that within the territory of which those transactions are carried out, the place of supply of the services rendered by the intermediary shall be deemed to be within the territory of the Member State which issued the customer with the value added tax identification number under which the service was rendered to him by the intermediary.

[F Place of the supply of services in the case of valuations of or work on movable tangible

property

By way of derogation from Article 9(2)(c), the place of the supply of services involving valuations or work on movable tangible property, provided to customers identified for value added tax purposes in a Member State other than the one where those services are physically carried out, shall be deemed to be in the territory of the Member State which issued the customer with the value added tax identification number under which the service was carried out for him.
This derogation shall not apply where the goods are not dispatched or transported out of the Member State where the services were physically carried out.][2]

Cross references—See VAT (Place of Supply of Services) Order, SI 1992/3121 (implementation of paras C, D, E above); VAT Regulations, SI 1995/2518 reg 98 (implementation of para B.3 above);
EEC Council Directive 92/111, art 4, para 2; OJ L384, 30.12.92 (extension of time limit to 31 December 1993 for adoption of laws, etc under certain provisions of this article).

Simon's Tax Cases—Art 28c(A), *Criminal proceedings against R* (Case C-285/09) [2011] STC 138.

Amendments—[1] Words in para A.2 added by EEC Council Directive 92/111, art 1.11; OJ L384, 30.12.92.
[2] Words in para C(1) and para F inserted and full point in para C(1) replaced by EC Council Directive 95/7, art 1(7): OJ L102, 5.5.95, p 18 with effect from 25 May 1995.

Article 28c Exemptions

A Exempt supplies of goods

Without prejudice to other Community provisions and subject to conditions which they shall lay down for the purpose of ensuring the correct and straightforward application of the exemptions provided for below and preventing any evasion, avoidance or abuse, Member States shall exempt:

(a) supplies of goods, [as defined in Article 5][4]*, dispatched or transported by or on behalf of the vendor or the person acquiring the goods out of the territory referred to in Article 3 but within the Community, effected for another taxable person or a non-taxable legal person acting as such in a Member State other than that of the departure of the dispatch or transport of the goods.*
This exemption shall not apply to supplies of goods by taxable persons exempt from tax pursuant to Article 24 or to supplies of goods effected for taxable persons or non-taxable legal persons who qualify for the derogation in the second subparagraph of Article 28a(1)(a);

(b) supplies of new means of transport, dispatched or transported to the purchaser by or on behalf of the vendor or the purchaser out of the territory referred to in Article 3 but within the Community, effected for taxable persons or non-taxable legal persons who qualify for the derogation provided for in the second subparagraph of Article 28a(1)(a) or for any other non-taxable person;

[(c) the supply of goods subject to excise duty dispatched or transported to the purchaser, by the vendor, by the purchaser or on his behalf, outside the territory referred to in Article 3 but inside the Community, effected for taxable persons or non-taxable legal persons who qualify for the derogation set out in the second subparagraph of Article 28a(1)(a), when the dispatch or transport of the goods is carried out in accordance with Article 7(4) and (5), or Article 16 of Directive 92/12/EEC.
This exemption shall not apply to supplies of goods subject to excise duty effected by taxable persons who benefit from the exemption from tax set out in Article 24;][1]

[(d) the supply of goods, within the meaning of Article 28a(5)(b), which benefit from the exemptions set out above if they have been made on behalf of another taxable person.][2]

B Exempt intra-Community acquisitions of goods

Without prejudice to other Community provisions and subject to conditions which they shall lay down for the purpose of ensuring the correct and straightforward application of the exemptions provided for below and preventing any evasion, avoidance or abuse, Member States shall exempt:

(a) the intra-Community acquisition of goods the supply of which by taxable persons would in all circumstances be exempt within the territory of the country;

(b) the intra-Community acquisition of goods the importation of which would in all circumstances be exempt under Article 14(1);

(c) the intra-Community acquisition of goods where, pursuant to Article 17(3) and (4), the person acquiring the goods would in all circumstances be entitled to full reimbursement of the value added tax due under Article 28a(1).

C Exempt transport services

VAT EC

Member States shall exempt the supply of intra-Community transport services involved in the dispatch or transport of goods to and from the islands making up the autonomous regions of the Azores and Madeira as well as the dispatch or transport of goods between those islands.

D Exempt importation of goods

Where goods dispatched or transported from a third territory are imported into a Member State other than that of arrival of the dispatch or transport, Member States shall exempt such imports where the supply of such goods by the importer as defined in [Article 21(4)][6] is exempt in accordance with paragraph A.
Member States shall lay down the conditions governing this exemption with a view to ensuring its correct and straightforward application and preventing any evasion, avoidance or abuse.

[E Other exemptions

1. (substitutes art 16(1) and adds art 16(1A)).
2. (amends Art 16(2)).
3. Member States shall take specific measures to ensure that value added tax is not charged on the intra-Community acquisition of goods effected, within the meaning of Article 28b(A)(1), within its territory when the following conditions are met—

— *the intra-Community acquisition of goods is effected by a taxable person who is not established in the territory of the country but who is identified for value added tax purposes in another Member State,*
— *the intra-Community acquisition of goods is effected for the purpose of a subsequent supply of goods made by a taxable person in the territory of the country,*
— *the goods so acquired by this taxable person are directly dispatched or transported from another Member State than that in which he is identified for value added tax purposes and destined for the person for whom he effects the subsequent supply,*
— *the person to whom the subsequent supply is made is a taxable person or a non-taxable legal person who is identified for value added tax purposes within the territory of the country,*
— *the person to whom the subsequent supply is made has been designated in accordance with [Article 21(1)(c)][5] as the person liable for the tax due on the supplies effected by the taxable person not established within the territory of the country.][3]*

Simon's Tax Cases—art 28cA(a), *McMahon (trading as Irish Cottage Trading Co) v R&C Comrs* [2012] UKUT 106 (TCC), [2012] STC 1859 ; *Marcus Webb Golf Professional v R&C Comrs* [2012] UKUT 378 (TCC), [2013] STC 574.

Cross references—See VATA 1994 Sch 8, Group 8, item 14 (implementation of para C above);
Customs and Excise (Personal Reliefs for Special Visitors) Order, SI 1992/3156 (implementation of para B above);
VAT Regulations, SI 1995/2518 regs 134, 135, 155 (implementation of para A above),
VAT Regulations, SI 1995/2518 reg 123 (implementation of para D above);
EEC Council Directive 92/111, art 4, para 2; OJ L384, 30.12.92 (extension of time limit to 31 December 1993 for adoption of laws, etc under certain provisions of this article).

Amendments—[1] Para A(*c*) replaced by EEC Council Directive 92/111, art 1.12; OJ L384, 30.12.92.
[2] Para A(*d*) added by EEC Council Directive 92/111, art 1.12; OJ L384, 30.12.92.
[3] Para E replaced by EEC Council Directive 92/111, art 1.13; OJ L384, 30.12.92.
[4] Words in para (A)(*a*) replaced by EC Council Direction 95/7, art 7(8): OJ L102, 5.5.95, p 18 with effect from 25 May 1995.
[5] Words in fifth indent of art 28c(E)(3) substituted by Council Directive 2000/65/EC art 1(3) with effect from 21 October 2000; OJ L269 p 44, 21.10.00. Member states must bring into force the measures necessary to comply with these provisions not later than 31 December 2001.
[6] Words "Article 21(4)" substituted for "Article 21(2)" by Council Directive 2000/65/EC art 1(6) with effect from 21 October 2000; OJ L269 p 44, 21.10.00. Member states must bring into force the measures necessary to comply with these provisions not later than 31 December 2001.

Article 28d Chargeable event and chargeability of tax

1. The chargeable event shall occur when the intra-Community acquisition of goods is effected. The intra-Community acquisition of goods shall be regarded as being effected when the supply of similar goods is regarded as being effected within the territory of the country.
2. For the intra-Community acquisition of goods, tax shall become chargeable on the 15th day of the month following that during which the chargeable event occurs.
3. [By way of derogation from paragraph 2, tax shall become chargeable on the issue of the invoice . . . [3]. provided for in the first subparagraph of Article 22(3)(a) where that invoice . . . [3] is issued to the person acquiring the goods before the fifteenth day of the month following that during which the taxable event occurs.][1]
4. By way of derogation from Article 10(2) and (3), tax shall become chargeable for supplies of goods effected under the conditions laid down in Article 28c(A) on the 15th day of the month following that during which the chargeable event occurs.

[However, tax shall become chargeable on the issue of the invoice provided for in the first subparagraph of Article 22(3)(a) . . . where that invoice . . . [3] *is issued before the fifteenth day of the month following that during which the taxable event occurs.]*[2]

Amendments—[1] Para 3 replaced by EEC Council Directive 92/111, art 1.14; OJ L384, 30.12.92.
[2] Words in para 4 replaced by EEC Council Directive 92/111, art 1.15; OJ L384, 30.12.92.
[3] Words in paras 3, 4 repealed by Council Directive 2001/115/EC art 4(4); see OJ L 015; 17.01.02.

Article 28e Taxable amount and rate applicable

1. In the case of the intra-Community acquisition of goods, the taxable amount shall be established on the basis of the same elements as those used in accordance with Article 11(A) to determine the taxable amount for supply of the same goods within the territory of the country. [In particular, in the case of the intra-Community acquisition of goods referred to in Article 28a(6), the taxable amount shall be determined in accordance with Article 11(A)(1)(b) and paragraphs 2 and 3.][1]

Member States shall take the measures necessary to ensure that the excise duty due or paid by the person effecting the intra-Community acquisition of a product subject to excise duty is included in the taxable amount in accordance with Article 11(A)(2)(a). [When, after the moment the intra-Community acquisition of goods was effected, the acquirer obtains the refund of excise duties paid in the Member State from which the goods were dispatched or transported, the taxable amount shall be reduced accordingly in the Member State where the intra-Community acquisition took place.][2]

[2. For the supply of goods referred to in Article 28c(A)(d), the taxable amount shall be determined in accordance with Article 11(A)(1)(b) and paragraphs 2 and 3.][3]

[3.] [3] *The tax rate applicable to the intra-Community acquisition of goods shall be that in force when the tax becomes chargeable.*

[4.] [3] *The tax rate applicable to the intra-Community acquisition of goods shall be that applied to the supply of like goods within the territory of the country.*

Cross references—See VAT Regulations, SI 1995/2518 reg 41(1) (implementation of this article);
EEC Council Directive 92/546, art 1; OJ L351, 2.12.92 (derogation from para 1 above granted to the UK).

Amendments—[1] Words in para 1 replaced by EEC Council Directive 92/111, art 1.16; OJ L384, 30.12.92.
[2] Words in para 1 added by EEC Council Directive 92/111, art 1.16; OJ L384, 30.12.92.
[3] Para 2 inserted by EEC Council Directive 92/111, art 1.17; OJ L384, 30.12.92.

Article 28f Right of deduction

Notes—Para 1 replaces art 17(2), (3), (4).
Para 2 replaces art 18(1).
Para 3 inserts art 18(3a).

Article 28g Persons liable for payment of the tax

Note—This article replaces art 21.

Cross references—See EEC Council Directive 92/111, art 4 para 2; OJ L384, 30.12.92 (extension of time limit to 31 December 1993 for adoption of laws, etc under certain provisions of this article).

Article 28h Obligations of persons liable for payment

Note—This article replaces art 22.

Article 28i Special scheme for small undertakings

Note—This article amends art 24(3).
Simon's Tax Cases—*Schmelz v Finanzamt Waldviertel* (Case C-97/09) [2011] STC 88.

Article 28j Common flat-rate scheme for farmers

Note—Para 1 amends art 25(4).
Para 2 replaces art 25(5), (6).
Para 3 amends art 25(9).

Article 28k Miscellaneous provisions

The following provisions shall apply until 30 June 1999:

1. Member States may exempt supplies by tax-free shops of goods to be carried away in the personal luggage of travellers taking intra-Community flights or sea crossings to other Member States. For the purposes of this Article:

- *(a) "tax-free shop" shall mean any establishment situated within an airport or port which fulfils the conditions laid down by the competent public authorities pursuant, in particular, to paragraph 5;*
- *(b) "traveller to another Member State" shall mean any passenger holding a transport document for air or sea travel stating that the immediate destination is an airport or port situated in another Member State;*
- *(c) "intra-Community flight or sea crossing" shall mean any transport, by air or sea, starting within the territory of the country as defined in Article 3, where the actual place of arrival is situated within another Member State.*

Supplies of goods effected by tax-free shops shall include supplies of goods effected on board aircraft or vessels during intra-Community passenger transport.

VAT EC

This exemption shall also apply to supplies of goods effected by tax-free shops in either of two Channel Tunnel terminals, for passengers holding valid tickets for the journey between those two terminals.

2. Eligibility for the exemption provided for in paragraph 1 shall apply only to supplies of goods:

[(a) the total value of which per person per journey does not exceed ECU 90.

By way of derogation from Article 28m, Member States shall determine the equivalent in national currency of the above amount in accordance with Article 7(2) of Directive 69/169/EEC.][1]

Where the total value of several items or of several supplies of goods per person per journey exceeds those limits, the exemption shall be granted up to those amounts, on the understanding that the value of an item may not be split;

(b) involving quantities per person per journey not exceeding the limits laid down by the Community provisions in force for the movement of travellers between third countries and the Community.

The value of supplies of goods effected within the quantitative limits laid down in the previous sub-paragraph shall not be taken into account for the application of (a).

3. Member States shall grant every taxable person the right to a deduction or refund of the value added tax referred to in Article 17(2) in so far as the goods and services are used for the purposes of his supplies of goods exempt under this Article.

4. Member States which exercise the option provided for in Article 16(2) shall also grant eligibility under that provision to imports, intra-Community acquisitions and supplies of goods to a taxable person for the purposes of his supplies of goods exempt pursuant to this Article.

5. Member States shall take the measures necessary to ensure the correct and straightforward application of the exemptions provided for in this Article and to prevent any evasion, avoidance or abuse.

Cross references—See VATA 1994 Sch 8, Group 14 (implementation of this article).

Amendments—[1] Words in para 2 substituted by Council Directive 94/4/EC of 14 February 1994, arts 2, 4 with effect from 3 March 1994 (date on which the Directive was published in the Official Journal); see OJ L60, 3.3.94, p 14.

Article 28l Period of application

The transitional arrangements provided for in this Title shall enter into force on 1 January 1993. Before 31 December 1994 the Commission shall report to the Council on the operation of the transitional arrangements and submit proposals for a definitive system.

The transitional arrangements shall be replaced by a definitive system for the taxation of trade between Member States based in principle on the taxation in the Member State of origin of the goods or services supplied. To that end, after having made a detailed examination of that report and considering that the conditions for transition to the definitive system have been fulfilled satisfactorily, the Council, acting unanimously on a proposal from the Commission and after consulting the European Parliament, shall decide before 31 December 1995 on the arrangements necessary for the entry into force and the operation of the definitive system.

The transitional arrangements shall enter into force for four years and shall accordingly apply until 31 December 1996. The period of application of the transitional arrangements shall be extended automatically until the date of entry into force of the definitive system and in any event until the Council has decided on the definitive system.

[Article 28m Rate of conversion

To determine the equivalents in their national currencies of amounts expressed in ecus in this Title Member States shall use the rate of exchange applicable on 16 December 1991. However, Bulgaria, the Czech Republic, Estonia, Cyprus, Latvia, Lithuania, Hungary, Malta, Poland, Romania, Slovenia and Slovakia shall use the rate of exchange applicable on the date of their accession.][1]

Amendments—[1] This article substituted by Council Directive 2006/98/EC art 1, Annex Part 2(a) (OJ L 363, 20.12.2006, p 129).

[Article 28n Transitional measures

1. When goods:

— entered the territory of the country within the meaning of Article 3 before 1 January 1993,

and

— were placed, on entry into the territory of that country, under one of the regimes referred to in Article 14(1)(b) or (c), or Article 16(1)(A),

and

— have not left that regime before 1 January 1993, the provisions in force at the moment the goods were placed under that regime shall continue to apply for the period, as determined by those provisions, the goods remain under that regime.

2. The following shall be deemed to be an import of goods within the meaning of Article 7(1):

(a) the removal, including irregular removal, of goods from the regime referred to in Article 14(1)(c) under which the goods were placed before 1 January 1993 under the conditions set out in paragraph 1;

(b) the removal, including irregular removal, of goods from the regime referred to in Article 16(1)(A) under which the goods were placed before 1 January 1993 under the conditions set out in paragraph 1;

(c) the termination of a Community internal transit operation started before 1 January 1993 in the Community for the purpose of supply of goods for consideration made before 1 January 1993 in the Community by a taxable person acting as such;

(d) the termination of an external transit operation started before 1 January 1993;

(e) any irregularity or offence committed during an external transit operation started under the conditions set out in (c) or any Community external transit operation referred to in (d);

(f) the use within the country, by a taxable or non-taxable person, of goods which have been supplied to him, before 1 January 1993, within another Member State, where the following conditions are met—

— the supply of these goods has been exempted, or was likely to be exempted, pursuant to Article 15(1) and (2),

— the goods were not imported within the country before 1 January 1993.

For the purpose of the application of (c), the expression "Community internal transit operation" shall mean the dispatch or transport of goods under the cover of the internal Community transit arrangement or under the cover of a T2 L document or the intra-Community movement carnet, or the sending of goods by post.

3. In the cases referred to in paragraph 2(a) to (e), the place of import, within the meaning of Article 7(2), shall be the Member State within whose territory the goods cease to be covered by the regime under which they were placed before 1 January 1993.

4. By way of derogation from Article 10(3), the import of the goods within the meaning of paragraph 2 of this Article shall terminate without the occurrence of a chargeable event when:

(a) the imported goods are dispatched or transported outside the Community within the meaning of Article 3;

or

(b) the imported goods, within the meaning of paragraph 2(a), are other than a means of transport and are dispatched or transported to the Member State from which they were exported and to the person who exported them;

or

(c) the imported goods, within the meaning of paragraph 2(a), are means of transport which were acquired or imported before 1 January 1993, in accordance with the general conditions of taxation in force on the domestic market of a Member State, within the meaning of Article 3, and/or have not been subject by reason of their exportation to any exemption from or refund of value added tax.

This condition shall be deemed to be fulfilled when the date of the first use of the means of transport was before 1 January 1985 or when the amount of tax due because of the importation is insignificant.][1]

Amendments—[1] This article added by EEC Council Directive 92/111, art 1.22; OJ L384, 30.12.92.

VAT EC

[TITLE XVIB: TRANSITIONAL PROVISIONS APPLICABLE IN THE FIELD OF SECOND-HAND GOODS, WORKS OF ART, COLLECTORS' ITEMS AND ANTIQUES]

Note—For commencement of this Title, see EEC Council Directive 94/5, art 4.

Amendments—This Title (art 28 *o*) inserted by EEC Council Directive 94/5, arts 1 (7), 4; OJ L60, 3.3.94. For commencement, see art 4 of the Directive.

Article 28o

1. Member States which at 31 December 1992 were applying special tax arrangements other than those provided for in Article 26a(B) to supplies of second-hand means of transport effected by taxable dealers may continue to apply those arrangements during the period referred to in Article 281 in so far as they comply with, or are adjusted to comply with, the following conditions:

(a) the special arrangements shall apply only to supplies of the means of transport referred to in Article 28a(2)(a) and regarded as second-hand goods within the meaning of Article 26a(A)(d), effected by taxable dealers within the meaning of Article 26a(A)(e), and subject to the special tax arrangements for taxing the margin pursuant to Article 26a(B)(1) and (2). Supplies of new means of transport within the meaning of Article 28a(2)(b) that are carried out under the conditions specified in Article 28c(A) shall be excluded from these special arrangements;

(b) the tax due in respect of each supply referred to in (a) is equal to the amount of tax that would be due if that supply had been subject to the normal arrangements for value added tax, less the amount of value added tax regarded as being incorporated in the purchase price of the means of transport by the taxable dealer;

(c) the tax regarded as being incorporated in the purchase price of the means of transport by the taxable dealer shall be calculated according to the following method:

— the purchase price to be taken into account shall be the purchase price within the meaning of Article 26a(B)(3),

— that purchase price paid by the taxable dealer shall be deemed to include the tax that would have been due if the taxable dealer's supplier had subjected the supply to the normal value added tax arrangements,

— the rate to be taken into account shall be the rate applicable within the meaning of Article 12(1), in the Member State within which the place of the supply to the taxable dealer, determined in accordance with Article 8, is deemed to be situated;

(d) the tax due in respect of each supply as referred to in (a), determined in accordance with the provisions of (b), may not be less than the amount of tax that would be due if that supply had been subject to the special arrangements for taxing the margin in accordance with Article 26a(B)(3).

For the application of the above provisions, the Member States have the option of providing that if the supply had been subject to the special arrangements for taxation of the margin, that margin would not have been less than 10% of the selling price, within the meaning of B(3);

(e) the taxable dealer shall not be entitled to indicate separately on the invoices he issues, . . . [2] *tax relating to supplies which he is subjecting to the special arrangements;*

(f) taxable persons shall not be entitled to deduct from the tax for which they are liable tax due or paid in respect of second-hand means of transport supplied to them by a taxable dealer, in so far as the supply of those goods by the taxable dealer is subject to the tax arrangements in accordance with (a);

(g) by way of derogation from Article 28a(1)(a), intra-Community acquisitions of means of transport are not subject to value added tax where the vendor is a taxable dealer acting as such and the second-hand means of transport acquired has been subject to the tax, in the Member State of departure of the dispatch or transport, in accordance with (a);

(h) Articles 28b(B) and 28c(A)(a) and (d) shall not apply to supplies of second-hand means of transport subject to tax in accordance with (a).

2. By way of derogation from the first sentence of paragraph 1, the Kingdom of Denmark shall be entitled to apply the special tax arrangements laid down in paragraph 1(a) to (h) during the period referred to in Article 28l.

3. Where they apply the special arrangements for sales by public auction provided for in Article 26a(C), Member States shall also apply these special arrangements to supplies of second-hand means of transport effected by an organiser of sales by public auction acting in his own name, pursuant to a contract under which commission is payable on the sale of those goods by public auction, on behalf of a taxable dealer, in so far as the supply of the second-hand means of transport, within the meaning of Article 5(4)(c), by that other taxable dealer, is subject to tax in accordance with paragraphs 1 and 2.

4. For supplies by a taxable dealer of works of art, collectors' items or antiques that have been supplied to him under the conditions provided for in Article 26a(B)(2), the Federal Republic of Germany shall be entitled, until 30 June 1999, to provide for the possibility for taxable dealers to apply either the special arrangements for taxable dealers, or the normal VAT arrangements according to the following rules:

(a) for the application of the special arrangements for taxable dealers to these supplies of goods, the taxable amount shall be determined in accordance with Article 11(A)(1), (2) and (3);

(b) in so far as the goods are used for the needs of his operations which are taxed in accordance with (a), the taxable dealer shall be authorised to deduct from the tax for which he is liable:

— the value added tax due or paid for works of art, collectors' items or antiques which are or will be supplied to him by another taxable dealer, where the supply by that other taxable dealer has been taxed in accordance with (a),

— the value added tax deemed to be included in the purchase price of the works of art, collectors' items or antiques which are or will be supplied to him by another taxable dealer, where the supply by that other taxable dealer has been subject to value added tax in accordance with the special arrangements for the taxation of the margin provided for in Article 26a(B), in the Member State within whose territory the place of that supply, determined in accordance with Article 8, is deemed to be situated.

This right to deduct shall arise at the time when the tax due for the supply taxed in accordance with (a) becomes chargeable;

(c) for the application of the provisions laid down in the second indent of (b), the purchase price of the works of art, collectors' items or antiques the supply of which by a taxable dealer is taxed in accordance with (a) shall be determined in accordance with Article 26a(B)(3) and the tax deemed to be included in this purchase price shall be calculated according to the following method:

— the purchase price shall be deemed to include the value added tax that would have been due if the taxable margin made by the supplier had been equal to 20% of the purchase price,

— *the rate to be taken into account shall be the rate applicable, within the meaning of Article 12(1), in the Member State within whose territory the place of the supply that is subject to the special arrangements for taxation of the profit margin, determined in accordance with Article 8, is deemed to be situated;*

(d) where he applies the normal arrangements for value added tax to the supply of a work of art, collectors' item or antique which has been supplied to him by another taxable dealer and where the goods have been taxed in accordance with (a), the taxable dealer shall be authorised to deduct from his tax liability the value added tax referred to in (b);

(e) the category of rates applicable to these supplies of goods shall be that which was applicable on 1 January 1993;

(f) for the application of the fourth indent of Article 26a(B)(2), the fourth indent of Article 26a(C)(1) and Article 26a(D)(b) and (c), the supplies of works of art, collectors' items or antiques, taxed in accordance with (a), shall be deemed by Member States to be supplies subject to value added tax in accordance with the special arrangements for taxation of the profit margin provided for in Article 26a(B);

(g) where the supplies of works of art, collectors' items or antiques taxed in accordance with (a) are effected under the conditions provided for in Article 28c(A), the invoice issued in accordance with Article 22(3) shall contain an endorsement indicating that the special taxation arrangements for taxing the margin provided for in Article 28o(4) have been applied.][1]

Amendments—[1] This Title (art 28 *o*) inserted by EEC Council Directive 94/5, arts 1(7), 4; OJ L60, 3.3.94. For commencement, see art 4 of the Directive printed *post*.

[2] Words in para 1(*e*) repealed by Council Directive 2001/115/EC art 4(6); see OJ L 015; 17.01.02.

[TITLE XVIC:
TRANSITIONAL MEASURES APPLICABLE IN THE CONTEXT OF THE ACCESSION TO THE EUROPEAN UNION OF AUSTRIA, FINLAND AND SWEDEN ON 1 JANUARY 1995, OF THE CZECH REPUBLIC, ESTONIA, CYPRUS, LATVIA, LITHUANIA, HUNGARY, MALTA, POLAND, SLOVENIA AND SLOVAKIA ON 1 MAY 2004, AND OF BULGARIA AND ROMANIA ON 1 JANUARY 2007]

Amendments—This Heading replaced by Council Directive 2006/98/EC art 1, Annex Part 2(b) (OJ L 363, 20.12.2006, p 129).

Article 28p

1. For the purpose of applying this Article:

— *"Community" shall mean the territory of the Community as defined in Article 3 before accession,*

[— "new Member States" shall mean the territory of the Member States acceding to the European Union on 1 January 1995, on 1 May 2004 and on 1 January 2007, as defined for each of those Member States in Article 3 of this Directive,][2]

— *"enlarged Community" shall mean the territory of the community as defined in Article 3, after accession.*

2. When goods:

— *entered the territory of the Community or of one of the new Member States before the date of accession, and*

— *were placed, on entry into the territory of the Community or of one of the new Member States, under a temporary admission procedure with full exemption from import duties, under one of the regimes referred to in Article 16(1)(B)(a) to (d) or under a similar regime in one of the new Member States, and*

— *have not left that regime before the date of accession,*

the provisions in force at the moment the goods were placed under that regime shall continue to apply until the goods leave this regime, after the date of accession.

3. When goods:

— *were placed, before the date of accession, under the common transit procedure or under another customs transit procedure, and*

— *have not left that procedure before the date of accession,*

the provisions in force at the moment the goods were placed under that procedure shall continue to apply until the goods leave this procedure, after the date of accession.

For the purposes of the first indent, "common transit procedure" shall mean the measures for the transport of goods in transit between the Community and the countries of the European Free Trade Association (EFTA) and between the EFTA countries themselves, as provided for in the Convention of 20 May 1987 on a common transit procedure.

4. The following shall be deemed to be an importation of goods within the meaning of Article 7(1) where it is shown that the goods were in free circulation in one of the new Member States or in the Community;

VAT EC

(a) the removal, including irregular removal, of goods from a temporary admission procedure under which they were placed before the date of accession under the conditions set out in paragraph 2;

(b) the removal, including irregular removal, of goods either from one of the regimes referred to in Article 16(1)(B)(a) to (d) or from a similar regime under which they were placed before the date of accession under the conditions set out in paragraph 2;

(c) the termination of one of the procedures referred to in paragraph 3 which was started before the date of accession in one of new Member States for the purposes of a supply of goods for consideration effected before that date in that Member State by a taxable person acting as such;

(d) any irregularity or offence committed during one of the procedures referred to in paragraph 3 under the conditions set out at (c).

5. The use after the date of accession within a Member State, by a taxable or non-taxable person, of goods supplied to him before the date of accession within the Community or one of the new Member States shall also be deemed to be an importation of goods within the meaning of Article 7(1) where the following conditions are met:

— the supply of those goods has been exempted, or was likely to be exempted, either under Article 15(1) and (2) or under a similar provision in the new Member States,

— the goods were not imported into one of the new Member States or into the Community before the date of accession.

6. In the cases referred to in paragraph 4, the place of import within the meaning of Article 7(3) shall be the Member State within whose territory the goods cease to be covered by the regime under which they were placed before the date of accession.

7. By way of derogation from Article 10(3), the importation of goods within the meaning of paragraphs 4 and 5 of this Article shall terminate without the occurrence of a chargeable event when:

(a) the imported goods are dispatched or transported outside the enlarged Community; or

(b) the imported goods within the meaning of paragraph 4(a) are other than means of transport and are redispatched or transported to the Member State from which they were exported and to the person who exported them; or

(c) the imported goods within the meaning of paragraph 4(a) are means of transport which were acquired or imported before the date of accession in accordance with the general conditions of taxation in force on the domestic market of one of the new Member States or of one of the Member States of the Community and/or have not been subject, by reason of their exportation, to any exemption from, or refund of, value added tax.

[This condition shall be deemed to be fulfilled in the following cases:

— when, in respect of Austria, Finland and Sweden, the date of the first use of the means of transport was before 1 January 1987;

— when, in respect of the Czech Republic, Estonia, Cyprus, Latvia, Lithuania, Hungary, Malta, Poland, Slovenia and Slovakia, the date of the first use of the means of transport was before 1 May 1996;

— when in respect of Bulgaria and Romania, the date of the first use of the means of transport was before 1 January 1999;

— when the amount of tax due by reason of the importation is insignificant.][3]*]*[1]

Amendments—[1] This title added by EC Council Directive 94/76, art 1; OJ L365, 31.12.94 p 53.

[2] Words in paras (1), (7) replaced by Council Directive 2006/98/EC art 1, Annex Part 2(c), (d) (OJ L 363, 20.12.2006, p 129).

[3] Words in para (7) replaced by the 2003 Act of Accession Annex II Chapter 9 para 3(*d*) (OJ L 236; 23.9.2003 p 555).

TITLE XVII:
VALUE ADDED TAX COMMITTEE

Article 29

1. An Advisory Committee on value added tax, hereinafter called "the Committee", is hereby set up.

2. The Committee shall consist of representatives of the Member States and of the Commission.

The chairman of the Committee shall be a representative of the Commission.

Secretarial services for the Committee shall be provided by the Commission.

3. The Committee shall adopt its own rules of procedure.

4. In addition to points subject to the consultation provided for under this Directive, the Committee shall examine questions raised by its chairman, on his own initiative or at the request of the representative of a Member State, which concern the application of the Community provisions on value added tax.

[Article 29a Implementing measures

The Council, acting unanimously on a proposal from the Commission, shall adopt the measures necessary to implement this Directive.][1]

Amendments—[1] This Article inserted by Council Directive 2004/7 art 2 (OJ L 027; 30.1.2004 p 44).

TITLE XVIII: MISCELLANEOUS

[Article 30 International agreements

1. The Council, acting unanimously on a proposal from the Commission, may authorise any Member State to conclude with a third country or an international organisation an agreement which may contain derogations from this Directive.

2. A Member State wishing to conclude such an agreement shall send an application to the Commission and provide it with all the necessary information. If the Commission considers that it does not have all the necessary information, it shall contact the Member State concerned within two months of receipt of the application and specify what additional information is required. Once the Commission has all the information it considers necessary for appraisal of the request it shall within one month notify the requesting Member State accordingly and it shall transmit the request, in its original language, to the other Member States.

3. Within three months of giving the notification referred to in the last sentence of paragraph 2, the Commission shall present to the Council either an appropriate proposal or, should it object to the derogation requested, a communication setting out its objections.

4. In any event, the procedure set out in paragraphs 2 and 3 shall be completed within eight months of receipt of the application by the Commission.][1]

Amendments—[1] This Article replaced by Council Directive 2004/7 art 3 (OJ L 027; 30.1.2004 p 44).

Article 31 Unit of account

1. The unit of account used in this Directive shall be the European unit of account (EUA) defined by Decision 75/250/EEC (OJ L104, 24.4.75, p 35).

2. When converting this unit of account into national currencies, Member States shall have the option of rounding the amounts resulting from this conversion either upwards or downwards by up to 10 per cent.

Article 32 Second-hand goods

Amendment—This article deleted by EEC Council Directive 94/5, arts 1(9), 4; OJ L60, 3.3.94; with effect as mentioned in art 4 of the Directive printed *post*.

[Article 33][1]

1. Without prejudice to other Community provisions, in particular those laid down in the Community provisions in force relating to the general arrangements for the holding, movement and monitoring of products subject to excise duty, this Directive shall not prevent a Member State from maintaining or introducing taxes on insurance contracts, taxes on betting and gambling, excise duties, stamp duties and, more generally, any taxes, duties or charges which cannot be characterised as turnover taxes, provided however that those taxes, duties or charges do not, in trade between Member States, give rise to formalities connected with the crossing of frontiers.

2. Any reference in this Directive to products subject to excise duty shall apply to the following products as defined by current Community provisions:

- *mineral oils,*
- *alcohol and alcoholic beverages,*
- *manufactured tobacco.*

Simon's Tax Cases—*Fazenda Pública v Solisnor-Estaleiros Navais SA* (Case C-130/96) [1998] STC 191; *R v C&E Comrs, ex p Lunn Poly Ltd* [1998] STC 649; *SPAR österreichische Warenhandels AG v Finanzlandesdirektion für Salzburg* [1998] STC 960.

Amendments—[1] Article 33 replaced by EEC Council Directive 91/680; OJ L376, 31.12.1991, p 1.

[Article 33a][1]

[1. Goods referred to in Article 7(1)(b) entering the Community from a territory which forms part of the customs territory of the Community but which is considered as a third territory for the purposes of applying this Directive shall be subject to the following provisions:

(a) the formalities relating to the entry of such goods into the Community shall be the same as those laid down by the Community customs provisions in force for the import of goods into the customs territory of the Community;

(b) when the place of arrival of the dispatch or transport of these goods is situated outside the Member State where they enter the Community, they shall circulate in the Community under the internal Community transit procedure laid down by the Community customs provisions in force, insofar as they have been the subject of a declaration placing them under this regime when the goods entered the Community;

(c) when at the moment of their entry into the Community the goods are found to be in one of the situations which would qualify them, if they were imported within the meaning of Article 7(1)(a), to benefit from one of the arrangements referred to in Article 16(1)(B)(a), (b), (c) and (d), or under a temporary arrangement in full exemption from import duties, the Member States shall take measures ensuring that the goods may remain in the Community under the same conditions as those laid down for the application of such arrangements.

2. Goods not referred to in Article 7(1)(a) dispatched or transported from a Member State to a destination in a territory that forms parts of the customs territory of the Community but which is considered as a third territory for the purposes of applying this Directive shall be subject to the following provisions:

(a) the formalities relating to the export of those goods outside the territory of the Community shall be the same as the Community customs provisions in force in relation to export of goods outside the customs territory of the Community;

(b) for goods which are temporarily exported outside the Community, in order to be reimported, the Member States shall take the measures necessary to ensure that, on reimportation into the Community, such goods may benefit from the same provisions as if they had been temporarily exported outside the customs territory of the Community.][1]

Cross references—See VAT Regulations, SI 1995/2518 regs 140, 141 (implementation of this article).

Amendments—[1] This art replaced by EEC Council Directive 92/111, art 1.23; OJ L384, 30.12.92 p 47.

TITLE XIX:
FINAL PROVISIONS

Article 34

For the first time on 1 January 1982 and thereafter every two years, the Commission shall, after consulting the Member States, send the Council a report on the application of the common system of value added tax in the Member States. This report shall be transmitted by the Council to the European Parliament.

Article 35

At the appropriate time the Council acting unanimously on a proposal from the Commission, after receiving the opinion of the European Parliament and of the Economic and Social Committee, and in accordance with the interests of the common market, shall adopt further Directives on the common system of value added tax, in particular to restrict progressively or to repeal measures taken by the Member States by way of derogation from the system, in order to achieve complete parallelism of the national value added tax systems and thus permit the attainment of the objective stated in Article 4 of the first Council Directive of 11 April 1967.

Article 36

The fourth paragraph of Article 2 and Article 5 of the first Council Directive of 11 April 1967 are repealed.

Article 37

Second Council Directive 67/228/EEC of 11 April 1967 on value added tax shall cease to have effect in each Member State as from the respective dates on which the provisions of this Directive are brought into application.

Article 38

This Directive is addressed to the Member States.

Done at Brussels, 17 May 1977.

ANNEX A
LIST OF AGRICULTURAL PRODUCTION ACTIVITIES

I CROP PRODUCTION

1. General agriculture, including viticulture

2. Growing of fruit (including olives) and of vegetables, flowers and ornamental plants, both in the open and under glass

3. Production of mushrooms, spices, seeds and propagating materials; nurseries.

II STOCK FARMING TOGETHER WITH CULTIVATION

1. General stock farming

2. Poultry farming

3. Rabbit farming

4. Beekeeping

5. Silkworm farming

6. Snail farming.

III FORESTRY

IV FISHERIES

1. Fresh-water fishing

2. Fish farming

3. Breeding of mussels, oysters and other molluscs and crustaceans

4. Frog farming.

V WHERE A FARMER PROCESSES, USING MEANS NORMALLY EMPLOYED IN AN AGRICULTURAL, FORESTRY OR FISHERIES UNDERTAKING, PRODUCTS DERIVING ESSENTIALLY FROM HIS AGRICULTURAL PRODUCTION, SUCH PROCESSING SHALL ALSO BE REGARDED AS AGRICULTURAL PRODUCTION.

Simon's Tax Cases—*Grattan plc v R&C Comrs* (Case C-310/11) [2013] STC 502.

ANNEX B

LIST OF AGRICULTURAL SERVICES

Supplies of agricultural services which normally play a part in agricultural production shall be considered the supply of agricultural services, and include the following in particular:

- *field work, reaping and mowing, threshing, baling, collecting, harvesting, sowing and planting*
- *packing and preparation for market, for example drying, cleaning, grinding, disinfecting and ensilage of agricultural products*
- *storage of agricultural products*
- *stock minding, rearing and fattening*
- *hiring out, for agricultural purposes, of equipment normally used in agricultural, forestry or fisheries undertakings*
- *technical assistance*
- *destruction of weeds and pests, dusting and spraying of crops and land*
- *operation of irrigation and drainage equipment*
- *lopping, tree felling and other forestry services.*

Simon's Tax Cases—*Finanzamt Rendsburg v Harbs* [2006] STC 340.

ANNEX C

COMMON METHOD OF CALCULATION

(The classification used in this Annex is that used in the Economic Accounts for Agriculture of the Statistical Office of the European Communities (SOEC))

Note—This Annex is not relevant to this work.

ANNEX D

LIST OF THE ACTIVITIES REFERRED TO IN THE THIRD PARAGRAPH OF ARTICLE 4(5)

1. Telecommunications
2. The supply of water, gas, electricity and steam
3. The transport of goods
4. Port and airport services
5. Passenger transport
6. Supply of new goods manufactured for sale
7. The transactions of agricultural intervention agencies in respect of agricultural products carried out pursuant to Regulations on the common organisation of the market in these products
8. The running of trade fairs and exhibitions
9. Warehousing
10. The activities of commercial publicity bodies
11. The activities of travel agencies
12. The running of staff shops, co-operatives and industrial canteens and similar institutions
13. Transactions other than those specified in Article 13 A(1)(q), of radio and television bodies

ANNEX E

TRANSACTIONS REFERRED TO IN ARTICLE 28(3)(A)

1. . . . [1]
2. Transactions referred to in Article 13A(1)(e)
3–6 . . . [1]
7. Transactions referred to in Article 13A(1)(q)
8.–10. . . . [1]
11. Supplies covered by Article 13B(g) in so far as they are made by taxable persons who were entitled to deduction of input tax on the building concerned
12.–14. . . . [1]
15. The services of travel agents referred to in Article 26, and those of travel agents acting in the name and on account of the traveller, for journeys outside the Community

Amendments—[1] The transactions referred to in points 1, 3–6, 8–10, and 12–14 abolished with effect from 1 January 1990 by art 1(1) of the Eighteenth Council Directive 89/465/EEC of 18 July 1989; see OJ L 226, 3.8.1989, p 21.

ANNEX F

TRANSACTIONS REFERRED TO IN ARTICLE 28(3)(B)

1. Admission to sporting events

2. Services supplied by authors, artists, performers, lawyers and other members of the liberal professions, other than the medical and paramedical professions, in so far as they are not services specified in Annex B to the second Council Directive of 11 April 1967

3. . . . [1]

4. . . . [2]

5. Telecommunications services supplied by public postal services and supplies of goods incidental thereto

6. Services supplied by undertakers and cremation services, together with goods related thereto

7. Transactions carried out by blind persons or workshops for the blind provided these exemptions do not give rise to significant distortion of competition

8. The supply of goods and services to official bodies responsible for the construction, setting out and maintenance of cemeteries, graves and monuments commemorating war dead

9. . . . [3]

10. Transactions of hospitals not covered by Article 13A(1)(b)

11. . . . [4]

12. The supply of water by public authorities

13. . . . [2]

14. . . . [1]

15. . . . [2]

16. Supplies of those buildings and land described in Article 4(3)

17. Passenger transport

The transport of goods such as luggage or motor vehicles accompanying passengers and the supply of services related to the transport of passengers, shall only be exempted in so far as the transport of the passengers themselves is exempt

18.–22. . . . [1]

23. The supply, modification, repair, maintenance, chartering and hiring of aircraft, including equipment incorporated or used therein, used by State institutions

24. . . . [2]

25. The supply, modification, repair, maintenance, chartering and hiring of warships

26. . . . [5]

27 The services of travel agents referred to in Article 26, and those of travel agents acting in the name and on account of the traveller, for journeys within the Community

Simon's Tax Cases—Item 6, *Network Insurance Brokers Ltd v C&E Comrs* [1998] STC 742.

Item 16, *Norbury Developments Ltd v C&E Comrs* (Case C-136/97) [1999] STC 511.

Amendments—[1] The transactions referred to in points 3, 14 and 18–22 abolished with effect from 1 January 1990 by art 1(2) of the Eighteenth Council Directive 89/465/EEC of 18 July 1989; see OJ L226, 3.8.1989, p 21.

[2] The transactions referred to in points 4, 13, 15 and 24 abolished with effect from 1 January 1991 by, art 2 of the Eighteenth Council Directive 89/465/EEC of 18 July 1989; see OJ L226, 3.8.1989.

[3] The transaction referred to in point 9 abolished with effect from 1 January 1992 by the Eighteenth Council Directive 89/465/EEC of 18 July 1989, art 2; see OJ L226, 3.8.1989.

[4] The transactions referred to in point 11 abolished with effect from 1 January 1993 by the Eighteenth Council Directive 89/465/EEC of 18 July 1989, art 2; see OJ L226, 3.8.1989.

[5] The transaction referred to in point 26 abolished with effect from 17 October 1998 by EC Council Directive 98/80, art 2; with effect from 17 October 1998; see OJ L281, 17.10.98 printed *post*.

ANNEX G

RIGHT OF OPTION

1. The right of option referred to in Article 28(3)(c) may be granted in the following circumstances:

(a) in the case of transactions specified in Annex E:
Member States which already exempt these supplies but also give the right of option for taxation, may maintain this right of option

(b) in the case of transactions specified in Annex F:
Member States which provisionally maintain the right to exempt such supplies may grant taxable persons the right to opt for taxation

2. Member States already granting a right of option for taxation not covered by the provisions of paragraph 1 above may allow taxpayers exercising it to maintain it until at the latest the end of three years from the date the Directive comes into force.

Simon's Tax Cases—Annex H, category 1, *Finanzampt Burgdorf v Bog and other references* (Joned Cases C-497/09, C-499/09, C-501/09 and C-502/09) [2011] STC 1221

[ANNEX H][1]

LIST OF SUPPLIES OF GOODS AND SERVICES WHICH MAY BE SUBJECT TO REDUCED RATES OF VAT

In transposing the categories below which refer to goods into national legislation, Member States may use the combined nomenclature to establish the precise coverage of the category concerned.

Category	*Description*
1	*Foodstuffs (including beverages but excluding alcoholic beverages) for human and animal consumption; live animals, seeds, plants and ingredients normally intended for use in preparation of foodstuffs; products normally intended to be used to supplement or substitute foodstuffs*
2	*Water supplies*
3	*Pharmaceutical products of a kind normally used for health care, prevention of diseases and treatment for medical and veterinary purposes, including products used for contraception and sanitary protection*
4	*Medical equipment, aids and other appliances normally intended to alleviate or treat disability, for the exclusive personal use of the disabled, including the repair of such goods, and children's car seats*
5	*Transport of passengers and their accompanying luggage*
6	*Supply, including on loan by libraries, of books (including brochures, leaflets and similar printed matter, children's picture, drawing or colouring books, music printed or in manuscript, maps and hydrographic or similar charts), newspapers and periodicals, other than material wholly or substantially devoted to advertising matter*
7	*Admissions to shows, theatres, circuses, fairs, amusement parks, concerts, museums, zoos, cinemas, exhibitions and similar cultural events and facilities*
	Reception of broadcasting services
8	*Services supplied by or royalties due to writers, composers and performing artists*
9	*Supply, construction, renovation and alteration of housing provided as part of a social policy*
10	*Supplies of goods and services of a kind normally intended for use in agricultural production but excluding capital goods such as machinery or buildings*
11	*Accommodation provided by hotels and similar establishments including the provision of holiday accommodation and the letting of camping sites and caravan parks*
12	*Admission to sporting events*
13	*Use of sporting facilities*
14	*Supply of goods and services by organisations recognised as charities by Member States and engaged in welfare or social security work, insofar as these supplies are not exempt under Article 13*
15	*Services supplied by undertakers and cremation services, together with the supply of goods related thereto*
16	*Provision of medical and dental care as well as thermal treatment in so far as these services are not exempt under Article 13*
17	*Services supplied in connection with street cleaning, refuse collection and waste treatment, other than the supply of such services by bodies referred to in Article 4(5)*

Amendments—

[1] Annex H added by EEC Council Directive 92/77, art 1; OJ L316, 31.10.92 p 1.

[ANNEX I][1]

WORKS OF ART, COLLECTORS' ITEMS AND ANTIQUES

For the purposes of this Directive:

(a) "works of art" shall mean:

VAT EC

- *pictures, collages and similar decorative plaques, paintings and drawings, executed entirely by hand by the artist, other than plans and drawings for architectural, engineering, industrial, commercial, topographical or similar purposes, hand-decorated manufactured articles, theatrical scenery, studio back cloths or the like of painted canvas (CN code 9701),*
- *original engravings, prints and lithographs, being impressions produced in limited numbers directly in black and white or in colour of one or of several plates executed entirely by hand by the artist, irrespective of the process or of the material employed by him, but not including any mechanical or photomechanical process (CN code 9702 00 00),*
- *original sculptures and statuary, in any material, provided that they are executed entirely by the artist; sculpture casts the production of which is limited to eight copies and supervised by the artist or his successors in title (CN code 9703 00 00); on an exceptional basis, in cases determined by the Member States, the limit of eight copies may be exceeded for statuary casts produced before 1 January 1989,*
- *tapestries (CN code 5805 00 00) and wall textiles (CN code 6304 00 00) made by hand from original designs provided by artists, provided that there are not more than eight copies of each,*
- *individual pieces of ceramics executed entirely by the artist and signed by him,*
- *enamels on copper, executed entirely by hand, limited to eight numbered copies bearing the signature of the artist or the studio, excluding articles of jewellery and goldsmiths' and silversmiths' wares,*
- *photographs taken by the artist, printed by him or under his supervision, signed and numbered and limited to 30 copies, all sizes and mounts included;*

(b) "collectors' items" shall mean:

- *postage or revenue stamps, postmarks, first-day covers, pre-stamped stationery and the like, franked, or if unfranked not being of legal tender and not being intended for use as legal tender (CN code 9704 00 00),*
- *collections and collectors' pieces of zoological, botanical, mineralogical, anatomical, historical, archaeological, palaeontological, ethnographic or numismatic interest (CN code 9705 00 00);*

(c) "antiques" shall mean objects other than works of art or collectors' items, which are more than 100 years old (CN code 9706 00 00).][1]

Amendments—[1] Annex I added by EEC Council Directive 94/5, arts 1(10), 4; OJ L60, 3.3.94. For commencement, see art 4 of the Directive printed *post*.

[ANNEX J]

Description of goods	*CN code*
Tin	*8001*
Copper	*7402* *7403* *7405* *7408*
Zinc	*7901*
Nickel	*7502*
Aluminium	*7601*
Lead	*7801*
Indium	*ex 8112 91* *ex 8112 99*
Cereals	*1001 to 1005* *1006: unprocessed rice only* *1007 to 1008*
Oil seeds and oleaginous fruit *Coconuts, Brazil nuts and cashew nuts* *Other nuts* *Olives*	*1201 to 1207* *0801* *0802* *0711 20*
Grains and seeds (including soya beans)	*1201 to 1207*
Coffee, not roasted	*0901 11 00*

Description of goods	*CN code*
	0901 12 00
Tea	*0902*
Cocoa beans, whole or broken, raw or roasted	*1801*
Raw sugar	*1701 11* *1701 12*
Rubber, in primary forms or in plates, sheets or strip	*4001* *4002*
Wool	*5101*
Chemicals in bulk	*Chapters 28 and 29*
Mineral oils (including propane and butane; also including crude petroleum oils)	*2709* *2710* *2711 12* *2711 13*
Silver	*7106*
Platinum (palladium, rhodium)	*7110 11 00* *7110 21 00* *7110 31 00*
Potatoes	*0701*
Vegetable oils and fats and their fractions, whether or not refined, but not chemically modified	*1507 to 1515*

Amendments—Annex J added by EC Council Directive 95/7, art 1(13), Annex, with effect from 25 May 1995; OJ L 102, 5.5.95, p 18.

[ANNEX K][1]

LIST OF SUPPLIES OF SERVICES REFERRED TO IN ARTICLE 28(6)

1. Small services of repairing—

— bicycles,

— shoes and leather goods,

— clothing and household linen (including mending and alteration).

2. Renovation and repairing of private dwellings, excluding materials which form a significant part of the value of the supply.

3. Window cleaning and cleaning in private households.

4. Domestic care services (eg home help and care of the young, elderly, sick or disabled).

5. Hairdressing.][1]

Amendments—

[1] Annex K added by EC Council Directive 99/85, art 1(1), Annex, with effect from 28 October 1999; see OJ L 277, 28.10.99, p 34.

[ANNEX L

ILLUSTRATIVE LIST OF ELECTRONICALLY SUPPLIED SERVICES REFERRED TO IN ARTICLE 9(2)(E)

1. Website supply, web-hosting, distance maintenance of programmes and equipment.

2. Supply of software and updating thereof.

3. Supply of images, text and information, and making databases available.

4. Supply of music, films and games, including games of chance and gambling games, and of political, cultural, artistic, sporting, scientific and entertainment broadcasts and events.

5. Supply of distance teaching.

Where the supplier of a service and his customer communicates via electronic mail, this shall not of itself mean that the service performed is an electronic service within the meaning of the last indent of Article 9(2)(e).][1]

Amendments—[1] Annex L added by Council Directive 2002/38 Annex (OJ L 128; 15.05.02).

VAT EC

[ANNEX M

LIST OF SUPPLIES OF GOODS AND SERVICES AS REFERRED TO IN ARTICLE 21(2)(C)(IV)

(a) the supply of ferrous and non ferrous waste, scrap, and used materials including that of semi-finished products resulting from the processing, manufacturing or melting down of ferrous and non-ferrous metals and their alloys;

(b) the supply of ferrous and non-ferrous semi-processed products and certain associated processing services;

(c) the supply of residues and other recyclable materials consisting of ferrous and non-ferrous metals, their alloys, slag, ash, scale and industrial residues containing metals or their alloys and the supply of selection, cutting, fragmenting and pressing services for these products;

(d) the supply of, and certain processing services relating to, ferrous and non-ferrous waste as well as parings, scrap, waste and used and recyclable material consisting of cullet, glass, paper, paperboard and board, rags, bone, leather, imitation leather, parchment, raw hides and skins, tendons and sinews, twine, cordage, rope, cables, rubber and plastic;

(e) the supply of the materials referred to in this annex after processing in the form of cleaning, polishing, selection, cutting, fragmenting, pressing or casting into ingots;

(f) the supply of scrap and waste from the working of base materials.][1]

Amendments—[1] Annex M added by Council Directive 2006/69/EC art 1(8), with effect from 13 August 2006, (OJ L 221, 12.8.2006, p 9).

EIGHTH COUNCIL DIRECTIVE (79/1072/EEC) OF 6 DECEMBER 1979 ON THE HARMONISATION OF THE LAWS OF THE MEMBER STATES RELATING TO TURNOVER TAXES—ARRANGEMENTS FOR THE REFUND OF VALUE ADDED TAX TO TAXABLE PERSONS NOT ESTABLISHED IN THE TERRITORY OF THE COUNTRY

(79/1072/EEC)

Note—See OJ L331, 27.12.1979, p 11.

Repeal—This Directive repealed by Council Directive 2008/9/EC of 12 February 2008, art 28(2) with effect from 1 January 2010. However, provisions of this Directive shall continue to apply to refund applications submitted before 1 January 2010. References to this Directive shall be construed as references to Directive 2008/9/EC except for refund applications submitted before 1 January 2010. See below for the text of Directive 2008/9/EC.

THE COUNCIL OF THE EUROPEAN COMMUNITIES

Having regard to the Treaty establishing the European Economic Community,

Having regard to Sixth Council Directive 77/388/EEC of 17 May 1977 on the harmonisation of the laws of the Member States relating to turnover taxes—Common system of value added tax (uniform basis of assessment) (OJ No L145, 13.6.1977, p 1), and particular Article 17(4) thereof,

Having regard to the proposal from the Commission (OJ No C26, 1.2.1978, p 5),

Having regard to the opinion of the European Parliament (OJ No C39, 12.2.1979, p 14),

Having regard to the opinion of the Economic and Social Committee (OJ No C269, 13.11.1978, p 51),

Whereas, pursuant to Article 17(4) of Directive 77/288/EEC, the Council is to adopt Community rules laying down the arrangements governing refunds of value added tax, referred to in paragraph 3 of the said Article, to taxable persons not established in the territory of the country;

Whereas rules are required to ensure that a taxable person established in the territory of one member country can claim for tax which has been invoiced to him in respect of supplies of goods or services in another Member State or which has been paid in respect of imports into that other Member State, thereby avoiding double taxation;

Whereas discrepancies between the arrangements currently in force in Member States, which give rise in some cases to deflection of trade and distortion of competition, should be eliminated;

Whereas the introduction of Community rules in this field will mark progress towards the effective liberalisation of the movement of persons, goods and services, thereby helping to complete the process of economic integration;

Whereas such rules must not lead to the treatment of taxable persons differing according to the Member State in the territory of which they are established;

Whereas certain forms of tax evasion or avoidance should be prevented;

Whereas, under Article 17(4) of Directive 77/388/EEC, Member States may refuse the refund or impose supplementary conditions in the case of taxable persons not established in the territory of the Community; whereas steps should, however, also be taken to ensure that such taxable persons are not eligible for refunds on more favourable terms than those provided for in respect of Community taxable persons;

Whereas, initially, only the Community arrangements contained in this Directive should be adopted; whereas these arrangements provide, in particular, that decisions in respect of applications for refund should be notified within six months of the date on which such applications were lodged; whereas refunds should be made within the same period; whereas, for a period of one year from the final date laid down for the implementation of these arrangements, the Italian Republic should be authorised to notify the decisions taken by its competent services with regard to applications lodged by taxable persons not established within its territory and to make the relevant refunds within nine months, in order to enable the Italian Republic to reorganise the system at present in operation, with a view to applying the Community system;

Whereas further arrangements will have to be adopted by the Council to supplement the Community system; whereas, until the latter arrangements enter into force, Member States will refund the tax on the services and the purchases of goods which are not covered by this Directive, in accordance with the arrangements which they adopt pursuant to Article 17(4) of Directive 77/388/EEC,

HAS ADOPTED THIS DIRECTIVE:

Article 1

For the purposes of this Directive, 'a taxable person not established in the territory of the country' shall mean a person as referred to in Article 4(1) of Directive 77/388/EEC who, during the period referred to in the first and second sentences of the first sub-paragraph of Article 7(1), has had in that country neither the seat of his economic activity, nor a fixed establishment from which business transactions are effected, nor, if no such seat or fixed establishment exists, his domicile or normal place of residence, and who, during the same period, has supplied no goods or services deemed to have been supplied in that country, with the exception of:

(*a*) *transport services and services ancillary thereto, exempted pursuant to Article 14(1)(i), Article 15 or Article 16(1), B, C and D of Directive 77/388/EEC;*

(*b*) *services provided in cases where tax is payable solely by the person to whom they are supplied, pursuant to Article 21(1)(b)* of Directive 77/388/EEC.

Simon's Tax Cases—*Daimler AG and another v Skatteverket* (Joined cases C-318/11 and C-319/11) [2013] STC 670.

Article 2

Each Member State shall refund to any taxable person who is not established in the territory of the country but who is established in another Member State, subject to the conditions laid down below, any value added tax charged in respect of services or movable property supplied to him by other taxable persons in the territory of the country or charged in respect of the importation of goods into the country, in so far as such goods and services are used for the purposes of the transactions referred to in Article 17(3)(a) and (*b*) of Directive 77/388/EEC and of the provision of services referred to in Article 1(*b*).

Simon's Tax Cases—*Ministre du Budget and Ministre de l'Economie et des Finances v Societe Monte Dei Paschi Di Siena* [2001] STC 1029.

Article 3

To qualify for refund, any taxable person as referred to in Article 2 who supplies no goods or services deemed to be supplied in the territory of the country shall:

(*a*) *submit to the competent authority referred to in the first paragraph of Article 9 an application modelled on the specimen contained in Annex A, attaching originals of invoices or import documents. Member States shall make available to applicants an explanatory notice which shall in any event contain the minimum information set out in Annex C;*

(*b*) *produce evidence, in the form of a certificate issued by the official authority of the State in which he is established, that he is a taxable person for the purposes of value added tax in that State. However, where the competent authority referred to in the first paragraph of Article 9 already has such evidence in its possession, the taxable person shall not be bound to produce new evidence for a period of one year from the date of issue of the first certificate by the official authority of the State in which he is established. Member States shall not issue certificates to any taxable persons who benefit from tax exemption pursuant to Article 24(2) of Directive 77/388/EEC;*

(*c*) *certify by means of a written declaration that he has supplied no goods or services deemed to have been supplied in the territory of the country during the period referred to in the first and second sentences of the first subparagraph of Article 7(1);*

VAT EC

(*d*) *undertake to repay any sum collected in error.*

Press releases etc—Business Brief 6/94 3-3-94 (refunds from Italy: delay: advice on completion of application form: translation of relevant regulations).

Simon's Tax Cases—art 3(*a*), *Société Général des Grandes Sources d'Eaux Minérales Françaises v Bundesamt für Finanzen* [1998] STC 981.

Art 3(*b*), *Debouche v Inspecteur der Invoerrechten en Accijnzen* (Case C-302/93) [1996] STC 1406; *Planzer Luxembourg Sàrl v Bundeszentralamt für Steuern* [2008] STC 1113.

Article 4

To be eligible for the refund, any taxable person as referred to in Article 2 who has supplied in the territory of the country no goods or services deemed to have been supplied in the country other than the services referred to in Article 1(a) and (*b*) *shall:*

(*a*) *satisfy the requirements laid down in Article 3(a),* (*b*) and (*d*);

(*b*) *certify by means of a written declaration that, during the period referred to in the first and second sentences of the first subparagraph of Article 7(1), he has supplied no goods or services deemed to have been supplied in the territory of the country other than services referred to in Article 1(a)* and (*b*).

Article 5

For the purposes of this Directive, goods and services in respect of which tax may be refundable shall satisfy the conditions laid down in Article 17 of Directive 77/388/EEC as applicable in the Member State of refund.

This Directive shall not apply to supplies of goods which are, or may be, exempted under item 2 of Article 15 of Directive 77/388/EEC.

Simon's Tax Cases—*Debouche v Inspecteur der Invoerrechten en Accijnzen* (Case C-302/93) [1996] STC 1406, *Ministre du Budget and Ministre de l'Economie et des Finances v Societe Monte Dei Paschi Di Siena* [2001] STC 1029.

Article 6

Member States may not impose on the taxable persons referred to in Article 2 any obligation, in addition to those referred to in Articles 3 and 4, other than the obligation to provide, in specific cases, the information necessary to determine whether the application for refund is justified.

Article 7

1. The application for refund provided for in Articles 3 and 4 shall relate to invoiced purchases of goods or services or to imports made during a period of not less than three months or not more than one calendar year. Applications may, however, relate to a period of less than three months where the period represents the remainder of a calendar year. Such applications may also relate to invoices or import documents not covered by previous applications and concerning transactions completed during the calendar year in question. Applications shall be submitted to the competent authority referred to in the first paragraph of Article 9 within six months of the end of the calendar year in which the tax became chargeable.

If the application relates to a period of less than one calendar year but not less than three months, the amount for which application is made may not be less than the equivalent in national currency of 200 European units of account; if the application relates to a period of a calendar year or the remainder of a calendar year, the amount may not be less than the equivalent in national currency of 25 European units of account.

2. The European unit of account used shall be that defined in the Finance Regulation of 21 December 1977 (OJ No L 356, 31.12.1977, p 1), as determined on 1 January of the year of the period referred to in the first and second sentences of the first subparagraph of paragraph 1. Member States may round up or down, by up to 10%, the figures resulting from this conversion into national currency.

3. The competent authority referred to in the first paragraph of Article 9 shall stamp each invoice and/or import document to prevent their use for further application and shall return them within one month.

4. Decisions concerning applications for refund shall be announced within six months of the date when the applications, accompanied by all the necessary documents required under this Directive for examination of the application, are submitted to the competent authority referred to in paragraph 3. Refunds shall be made before the end of the above mentioned period, at the applicant's request, in either the Member State of refund or the State in which he is established. In the latter case, the bank charges for the transfer shall be payable by the applicant.

The grounds for refusal of an application shall be stated. Appeals against such refusals may be made to the competent authorities in the Member State concerned, subject to the same conditions as to form and time limits as those governing claims for refunds made by taxable persons established in the same State.

5. Where a refund has been obtained in a fraudulent or in any other irregular manner, the competent authority referred to in paragraph 3 shall proceed directly to recover the amounts wrongly paid and any penalties imposed, in accordance with the procedure applicable in the Member State concerned, without prejudice to the provisions relating to mutual assistance in the recovery of value added tax. In the case of fraudulent applications which cannot be made the subject of an administrative penalty, in accordance with national legislation, the Member State concerned may refuse for a maximum period of two years from the date on which the fraudulent application was submitted any further refund to the taxable person concerned. Where an administrative penalty has been imposed but has not been paid, the Member State concerned may suspend any further refund to the taxable person concerned until it has been paid.

Simon's Tax Cases—*Ministero dell'Economia e delle Finanze and another v Elsacom NV* (Case C-294/11) [2012] STC 2053.

Article 8

Amendments—Article 8 deleted by art 7 of the Thirteenth Council Directive of 17 November 1986: 86/560/EEC; see OJ L326, 21.11.1986, p 40.

Article 9

Member States shall make known, in an appropriate manner, the competent authority to which the application referred to in Article 3(a) and in Article 4(*a*) are to be submitted.

The certificates referred to in Article 3(b) and in Article 4(*a*), establishing that the person concerned is a taxable person, shall be modelled on the specimens contained in Annex B.

Simon's Tax Cases—*Planzer Luxembourg Sàrl v Bundeszentralamt für Steuern* [2008] STC 1113.

Article 10

Member States shall bring into force the provisions necessary to comply with this Directive no later than 1 January 1981. This Directive shall apply only to applications for refunds concerning value added tax charged on invoiced purchases of goods or services or in imports made as from that date. Member States shall communicate to the Commission the texts of the main provisions of national law which they adopt in the field covered by this Directive. The Commission shall inform the other Member States thereof.

Article 11

By a way of derogation from Article 7(4), the Italian Republic may, until 1 January 1982, extend the period referred to in this paragraph from six to nine months.

Article 12

Three years after the date referred to in Article 10, the Commission shall, after consulting the Member States, submit a report to the Council on the application of this Directive, and in particular Articles 3, 4 and 7 thereof.

Article 13

This Directive is addressed to the Member States.

ANNEX A

ANNEX A

SPECIMEN

Is this your first application?
If not, please give tax reference number

Receipt stamp

Competent authority to which the application is addressed ▶

Application for refund of value added tax by a taxable person not established in the country
(Read the explanatory notes before filling in)

SPECIMEN

1	Surname and forenames or name of firm of applicant
	Street and house number
	Postal code, place and country
2	Nature of applicant's business
3	Particulars of the tax office and VAT registration number in the country in which the applicant is established or has his domicile or normal place of residence
4	Period to which the application refers — from: month, year; to: month, year
5	Total amount of refund requested (in figures) (see overleaf for itemized list)
6	The applicant requests the refund of the amount shown in 5 in the manner described in 7.
7	Method of settlement requested (*) Bank account ☐ Postal account ☐
	Account number — Code number of financial body
	Account in the name of
	Name and address of the financial body
8	Number of documents enclosed: .... Invoices: .... Import documents: ....
9	The applicant hereby declares:

(*) Insert X in the appropriate box ▶ (item 7)

(a) that the goods or services specified overleaf were used for his activities as a taxable person during:
....
....

(b) that in the country in which the refund is being requested, and during the period covered by this application, he engaged in:

☐ (*) no supply of goods or services,
☐ (*) only the provision of services in respect of which tax is payable solely by the person to whom they are supplied,
☐ (*) only in the provision of certain exempted transport services and services ancillary thereto;

(*) Insert X in the appropriate box ▶

(c) that the particulars given in this application are true.

The applicant undertakes to pay back any monies wrongfully obtained.

.... (Place) on .... (Date) .... (Signature)

10 Statement itemizing VAT amounts relating to the period covered by this application

No	Nature of the goods or services	Name, VAT registration number, if known, and address of supplier of goods or services	Date and number of invoice or import document	Amount of tax refund applied for	For official use only
			Total		

For official use only

VAT EC

ANNEX B

ANNEX B

SPECIMEN

CERTIFICATE OF STATUS OF TAXABLE PERSON

The undersigned ....
(Name and address of competent authority)

certifies that ....
(Surname and forenames or name of firm)

....
(Nature of activity)

....
(Address of the establishment)

is a taxable person for the purposes of value added tax, his registration number being[1] ....

....

....
(Date)

Official Stamp

....
(Signature, name and grade)

Note.—[1] If the applicant does not have a VAT registration number, the competent authority shall state the reason for this.

ANNEX C

Minimum information to be given in explanatory notes

A. The application shall be drawn up on a form printed in one of the official languages of the European Communities. This form shall, however, be completed in the language of the country of refund.

B. The application shall be completed in block capitals and be submitted, by 30 June of the year following that to which the application relates, to the competent authority of the State to which the application is made (see D below).

C. The VAT registration number in the country of refund shall be given, if it is known to the applicant.

[D. The application shall be submitted to the relevant competent authorities, ie for:

— *Belgium:*
— *Denmark:*
— *Germany:*
— *Greece:*
— *Spain:*
— *France:*
— *Ireland:*
— *Italy:*
— *Luxembourg:*
— *the Netherlands:*
— *Austria:*
— *Portugal:*
— *Finland:*
— *Sweden:*
— *the United Kingdom:]*[1]
[— *the Czech Republic: Financní úrad pro Prahu 1]*[2]
[— *Estonia: Maksuamet]*[2]
[— *Cyprus:* Υπουργειο Οικονομικων, Τμημα Τελωνειων, Υπηρεσια ΦΠΑ*]*[2]
[— *Latvia: Valsts ienemumu dienesta Lielo nodoklu maksataju parvalde]*[2]
[— *Lithuania: Vilniaus apskrities valstybine mokesčiu inspekcija]*[2]
[— *Hungary: Adó-és Pénzügyi Ellenorzési Hivatal]*[2]
[— *Malta: Id-Dipartiment tat-Taxxa fuq il-Valur Mizÿjud fil-Ministeru tal-Finanzi]*[2]
[— *Poland: Drugi Urzad Skarbowy Warszawa Sródmiescie]*[2]
[— *Slovenia: Davčni urad Ljubljana]*[2]
[— *Slovakia: Danovy úrad Bratislava I]*[2]
[— *Bulgaria: . . . . ;*
— *Romania: . . . .]*[4]

E. The application shall refer to purchases of goods or services invoiced or to imports made during a period of not less than three months or more than one calendar year. However, it may relate to a period of less than three months where this period represents the remainder of a calendar year. Such an application may also relate to invoices or import documents not covered by previous applications and concerning transactions made during the calendar year in question.

F. In 9 (a), the applicant shall describe the nature of the activities for which he has acquired the goods or received the services referred to in the application for refund of the tax (eg participation in the International . . . . Fair, held in . . . . from . . . . stand No . . . ., or international carriage of goods as from . . . . to . . . . on . . . .).

G. The application shall be accompanied by a certificate issued by the official authority of the State in which the applicant is established and which provides evidence that he is a taxable person for the purposes of value added tax in that State. However, where the competent authority referred to in D above already has such evidence in its possession, the applicant shall not be bound to produce new evidence for a period of one year from the date of issue of the first certificate.

H. The application shall be accompanied by the originals of the invoices or import documents showing the amount of value added tax borne by the applicant.

[I. The application may be used for more than one invoice or import document but the total amount of VAT claimed for 19 . . . . may not be less than:

BEF/LUF . . .
DKK . . .
DEM . . .
GRD . . .
PTE . . .
FRF . . .
IEP . . .
ITL . . .
NLG . . .
ATS . . .
ESP . . .
FIM . . .
SEK . . .
GBP . . .
[CZK . . . *]*[3]

VAT EC

[EEK . . .][3]
[CYP . . .][3]
[LVL . . .][3]
[LTL . . .][3]
[HUF . . .][3]
[MTL . . .][3]
[PLN . . .][3]
[SIT . . .][3]
[SKK . . .][3]
[BGN . . .
RON . . . [4]*]*

if the period to which it relates is less than one calendar year but not less than three months or less than:

BEF/LUF . . .
DKK . . .
DEM . . .
GRD . . .
PTE . . .
FRF . . .
IEP . . .
ITL . . .
NLG . . .
ATS . . .
ESP . . .
FIM . . .
SEK . . .
GBP . . .
[CZK . . .][3]
[EEK . . .][3]
[CYP . . .][3]
[LVL . . .][3]
[LTL . . .][3]
[HUF . . .][3]
[MTL . . .][3]
[PLN . . .][3]
[SIT . . .][3]
[SKK . . .][3]
[BGN . . .
RON . . .][4]

if the period to which it relates is one calendar year or less than three months,][1]

J. Exempted transport services are those carried out in connection with the international carriage of goods, including—subject to certain conditions—transport associated with the transit, export or import of goods.

K. Any refund obtained improperly may render the offender liable to the fines or penalties laid down by the law of the State which has made the refund.

L. The authority in the country of refund reserves the right to make refunds by cheque or money order addressed to the applicant.

Amendments—[1] Points D and I substituted by the Act of Accession of 1994, art 29, Annex I; see OJ L1, 1.1.95, p 213.

[2] Words added to Point D by the 2003 Act of Accession Annex II Chapter 9 para 5(*a*) (OJ L 236; 23.9.2003 p 555).

[3] Words added to Point I by the 2003 Act of Accession Annex II Chapter 9 para 5(*b*), (*c*) (OJ L 236; 23.9.2003 p 555)

[4] Entries added to points D, I by Council Directive 2006/98/EC art 1, Annex Part 4(a)–(c) (OJ L 363, 20.12.2006, p 129).

THIRTEENTH COUNCIL DIRECTIVE (86/560/EEC) OF 17 NOVEMBER 1986 ON THE HARMONISATION OF THE LAWS OF THE MEMBER STATES RELATING TO TURNOVER TAXES—ARRANGEMENTS FOR THE REFUND OF VALUE ADDED TAX TO TAXABLE PERSONS NOT ESTABLISHED IN COMMUNITY TERRITORY

(86/560/EEC)

Note—See OJ L326, 21.11.86, p 40.

THE COUNCIL OF THE EUROPEAN COMMUNITIES,

Having regard to the Treaty establishing the European Economic Community, and in particular Articles 99 and 100 thereof,

Having regard to the Sixth Council Directive 77/388/EEC of 17 May 1977 on the harmonisation of the laws of the Member States relating to turnover taxes—Common system of value added tax: uniform basis of assessment (OJ L145, 13.6.77, p 1), and in particular Article 17 (4) thereof,

Having regard to the proposal from the Commission (OJ C223, 27.8.82, p 5, OJ C196, 23.7.83, p 6),

Having regard to the opinion of the European Parliament (OJ C161, 20.6.83, p 111),

Having regard to the opinion of the Economic and Social Committee (OJ C176, 4.7.83, p 22),

Whereas Article 8 of Directive 79/1072/EEC (OJ L331, 27.12.79, p 11) on the arrangements for the refund of value added tax to taxable persons not established in the territory of the country provides that in the case of taxable persons not established in the territory of the Community, Member States may refuse refunds or impose special conditions;

Whereas there is a need to ensure the harmonious development of trade relations between the Community and third countries based on the provisions of Directive 79/1072/EEC, while taking account of the varying situations encountered in third countries;

Whereas certain forms of tax evasion or avoidance should be prevented,

HAS ADOPTED THIS DIRECTIVE—

Article 1

For the purposes of this Directive—

1. "A taxable person not established in the territory of the Community" shall mean a taxable person as referred to in Article 4(1) of Directive 77/388/EEC who, during the period referred to in Article 3(1) of this Directive, has had in that territory neither his business nor a fixed establishment from which business transactions are effected, nor, if no such business or fixed establishment exists, his permanent address or usual place of residence, and who, during the same period, has supplied no goods or services deemed to have been supplied in the Member State referred to in Article 2, with the exception of—

(*a*) transport services and services ancillary thereto, exempted pursuant to Article 14(1)(*i*), Article 15 or Article 16(1), B, C and D of Directive 77/388/EEC;

(*b*) services provided in cases where tax is payable solely by the person to whom they are supplied, pursuant to Article 21(1)(*b*) of Directive 77/388/EEC;

2. "Territory of the Community" shall mean the territories of the Member States in which Directive 77/388/EEC is applicable.

Simon's Tax Cases—*Planzer Luxembourg Sàrl v Bundeszentralamt für Steuern* [2008] STC 1113.

Article 2

1. Without prejudice to Articles 3 and 4, each Member State shall refund to any taxable person not established in the territory of the Community, subject to the conditions set out below, any value added tax charged in respect of services rendered or moveable property supplied to him in the territory or the country by other taxable persons or charged in respect of the importation of goods into the country, in so far as such goods and services are used for the purposes of the transactions referred to in Article 17(3)(*a*) and (*b*) of Directive 77/388/EEC or of the provision of services referred to in point 1(*b*) of Article 1 of this Directive.

2. Member States may make the refunds referred to in paragraph 1 conditional upon the granting by third States of comparable advantages regarding turnover taxes.

3. Member States may require the appointment of a tax representative.

Simon's Tax Cases—*Rízení Letového Provozu CR sp v Bundesamt für Finanzen* [2007] STC 1509.

VAT EC

Article 3

1. The refunds referred to in Article 2(1) shall be granted upon application by the taxable person. Member States shall determine the arrangements for submitting applications, including the time limits for doing so, the period which applications should cover, the authority competent to receive them and the minimum amounts in respect of which applications may be submitted. They shall also determine the arrangements for making refunds, including the time limits for doing so. They shall impose on the applicant such obligations as are necessary to determine whether the application is justified and to prevent fraud, in particular the obligation to provide proof that he is engaged in an economic activity in accordance with Article 4(1) of Directive 77/388/EEC. The applicant must certify, in a written declaration, that, during the period prescribed, he has not carried out any transaction which does not fulfil the conditions laid down in point 1 of Article 1 of this Directive.
2. Refunds may not be granted under conditions more favourable than those applied to Community taxable persons.

Article 4

1. For the purposes of this Directive, eligibility for refunds shall be determined in accordance with Article 17 of Directive 77/388/EEC as applied in the Member State where the refund is paid.
2. Member States may, however, provide for the exclusion of certain expenditure or make refunds subject to additional conditions.
3. This Directive shall not apply to supplies of goods which are or may be exempted under point 2 of Article 15 of Directive 77/388/EEC.

Article 5

1. Member States shall bring into force the laws, regulations and administrative provisions necessary to comply with this Directive by 1 January 1988 at the latest. This Directive shall apply only to applications for refunds concerning value added tax charged on purchases of goods or services invoiced or on imports effected on or after that date.
2. Member States shall communicate to the Commission the main provisions of national law which they adopt in the field covered by this Directive and shall inform the Commission of the use they make of the option afforded by Article 2(2). The Commission shall inform the other Member States thereof.

Article 6

Within three years of the date referred to in Article 5, the Commission shall, after consulting the Member States, submit a report to the Council and to the European Parliament on the application of this Directive, particularly as regards the application of Article 2(2).

Article 7

As from the date on which this Directive is implemented, and at all events by the date mentioned in Article 5, the last sentence of Article 17(4) of Directive 77/388/EEC and Article 8 of Directive 79/1072/EEC shall cease to have effect in each Member State.

Article 8

This Directive is addressed to the Member States.

Done at Brussels, 17 November 1986.

COUNCIL DIRECTIVE (91/680/EEC) OF 16 DECEMBER 1991 SUPPLEMENTING THE COMMON SYSTEM OF VALUE ADDED TAX AND AMENDING DIRECTIVE 77/388/EEC WITH A VIEW TO THE ABOLITION OF FISCAL FRONTIERS

(91/680/EEC)

Note—See OJ L376 31.12.1991, p 1.

THE COUNCIL OF THE EUROPEAN COMMUNITIES,

Having regard to the Treaty establishing the European Economic Community, and in particular Article 99 thereof,

Having regard to the proposal from the Commission,

Having regard to the opinion of the European Parliament,

Having regard to the opinion of the Economic and Social Committee,

Whereas Article 8a of the Treaty defines the internal market as an area without internal frontiers in which the free movement of goods, persons, services and capital is ensured in accordance with the provisions of the Treaty;

Whereas the completion of the internal market requires the elimination of fiscal frontiers between Member States and that to that end the imposition of tax on imports and the remission of tax on exports in trade between Member States be definitively abolished;

Whereas fiscal controls at internal frontiers will be definitively abolished as from 1 January 1993 for all transactions between Member States;

Whereas the imposition of tax on imports and the remission of tax on exports must therefore apply only to transactions with territories excluded from the scope of the common system of value added tax;

Whereas, however, in view of the conventions and treaties applicable to them, transactions originating in or intended for the Principality of Monaco and the Isle of Man must be treated as transactions originating in or intended for the French Republic and the United Kingdom of Great Britain and Northern Ireland respectively;

Whereas the abolition of the principle of the imposition of tax on imports in relations between Member States will make provisions on tax exemptions and duty-free allowances superfluous in relations between Member States; whereas, therefore, those provisions should be repealed and the relevant Directives adapted accordingly;

Whereas the achievement of the objective referred to in Article 4 of the First Council Directive of 11 April 1967, as last amended by the Sixth Directive 77/388/EEC, requires that the taxation of trade between Member States be based on the principle of the taxation in the Member State of origin of goods and services supplied without prejudice, as regards Community trade between taxable persons, to the principle that tax revenue from the imposition of tax at the final consumption stage should accrue to the benefit of the Member State in which that final consumption takes place;

Whereas, however, the determination of the definitive system that will bring about the objectives of the common system of value added tax on goods and services supplied between Member States requires conditions that cannot be completely brought about by 31 December 1992;

Whereas, therefore, provision should be made for a transitional phase, beginning on 1 January 1993 and lasting for a limited period, during which provisions intended to facilitate transition to the definitive system for the taxation of trade between Member States, which continues to be the medium-term objective, will be implemented;

Whereas during the transitional period intra-Community transactions carried out by taxable persons other than exempt taxable persons should be taxed in the Member States of destination, at those Member States' rates and under their conditions;

Whereas intra-Community acquisitions of a certain value by exempt persons or by non-taxable legal persons and certain intra-Community distance selling and supplies of new means of transport to individuals or exempt or non-taxable bodies should also be taxed, during the transitional period, in the Member States of destination, at those Member States' rates and under their conditions, in so far as such transactions would, in the absence of special provisions, be likely to cause significant distortions of competition between Member States;

Whereas the necessary pursuit of a reduction of administrative and statistical formalities for undertakings, particularly small and medium-sized undertakings, must be reconciled with the implementation of effective control measures and the need, on both economic and tax grounds, to maintain the quality of Community statistical instruments;

Whereas advantage must be taken of the transitional period of taxation of intra-Community trade to take measures necessary to deal with both the social repercussions in the sectors affected and the regional difficulties, in frontier regions in particular, that might follow the abolition of the imposition of tax on imports and of the remission of tax on exports in trade between Member States; whereas Member States should therefore be authorised, for a period ending on 30 June 1999, to exempt supplies of goods carried out within specified limits by duty-free shops in the context of air and sea travel between Member States;

Whereas the transitional arrangements will enter into force for four years and will accordingly apply until 31 December 1996; whereas they will be replaced by a definitive system for the taxation of trade between Member States based on the principle of the taxation of goods and services supplied in the Member State of origin, so that the objective referred to in Article 4 of the First Council Directive of 11 April 1967 is achieved;

Whereas to that end the Commission will report to the Council before 31 December 1994 on the operation of the transitional arrangements and make proposals for the details of the definitive system for the taxation of trade between Member States; whereas the Council, considering that the conditions for transition to the definitive system have been fulfilled satisfactorily, will decide before 31 December 1995 on the arrangements necessary for the entry into force and the operation of the definitive system, the transitional arrangements being automatically continued until the entry into force of the definitive system and in any event until the Council has decided on the definitive system;

Whereas, accordingly, Directive 77/388/EEC, as last amended by Directive 89/465/EEC should be amended,

HAS ADOPTED THIS DIRECTIVE:

Simon's Tax Cases—*Eismann Alto Adige Srl v Ufficio IVA di Bolzano* [1996] STC 1374.

Article 1

Directive 77/388/EEC is hereby amended as follows:

Note—Amendments made by this article have been incorporated in Directive 77/388/EEC.

Article 2

1. The following Directives shall cease to have effect on 31 December 1992 as regards relations between Member States:

— Directive 83/181/EEC, as last amended by Directive 89/219/EEC,

— Directive 85/362/EEC.

2. The provisions on value added tax laid down in the following Directive shall cease to have effect on 31 December 1992:

— Directive 74/651/EEC, as last amended by Directive 88/663/EEC,

— Directive 83/182/EEC,

— Directive 83/183/EEC, as amended by Directive 89/604/EEC.

3. The provisions of Directive 69/169/EEC as last amended by Directive 91/191/EEC relating to value added tax shall cease to have effect on 31 December 1992 as regards relations between Member States.

Article 3

1. Member States shall adapt their present value added tax systems to this Directive.

They shall bring into force such laws, regulations and administrative provisions as are necessary for their arrangements thus adapted to Article 1(1) to (20) and (22) to (24) and 2 of this Directive to enter into force on 1 January 1993.

2. Member States shall inform the Commission of the provisions which they adopt to apply this Directive.

3. Member States shall communicate to the Commission the texts of the provisions of national law which they adopt in the field governed by this Directive.

4. When Member States adopt such measures they shall include a reference to this Directive or shall accompany them by such a reference on the occasion of their official publication.

The manner in which such references shall be made shall be laid down by the Member States.

Article 4

This Directive is addressed to the Member States.

COUNCIL DIRECTIVE (94/4/EC) OF 14 FEBRUARY 1994 AMENDING DIRECTIVES 69/169/EEC AND 77/388/EEC AND INCREASING THE LEVEL OF ALLOWANCES FOR TRAVELLERS FROM THIRD COUNTRIES AND THE LIMITS ON TAX-FREE PURCHASES IN INTRA-COMMUNITY TRAVEL

(94/4/EC)

Note—See OJ L60 03.03.1994, p 14.

THE COUNCIL OF THE EUROPEAN UNION,

Having regard to the Treaty establishing the European Community, and in particular Article 99 thereof,

Having regard to the proposal from the Commission,

Having regard to the opinion of the European Parliament,

Having regard to the opinion of the Economic and Social Committee,

Whereas Article 1(1) of Council Directive 69/169/EEC of 28 May 1969 on the harmonisation of provisions laid down by law, regulation or administrative action relating to exemption from turnover tax and excise duty on imports in international travel provides for allowances in respect of goods contained in the personal luggage of travellers coming from third countries on condition that such imports have no commercial character;

Whereas the total value of the goods eligible for this exemption may not exceed ECU 45 per person; whereas, in accordance with Article 1(2) of Directive 69/169/EEC, Member States may reduce the allowance to ECU 23 for travellers under 15 years of age;

Whereas account must be taken of measures in favour of travellers recommended by specialised international organisations, in particular the measures contained in Annex F.3 to the International Convention on the Simplification and Harmonisation of Customs Procedures;

Whereas these objectives could be attained by increasing the allowances;

Whereas it is necessary to provide, for a limited period, a derogation for Germany, taking into account the economic difficulties likely to be caused by the amount of the allowances, particularly as regards travellers entering the territory of that Member State by land frontiers linking Germany to countries other than Member States and the EFTA members or by means of coastal navigation coming from the said countries;

Whereas there are special links between continental Spain and the Canary Islands, Ceuta and Melilla;

Whereas it is necessary to ensure, during the period when these sales are authorised pursuant to the provisions of Article 28k of Council Directive 77/388/EEC of 17 May 1977 on the harmonisation of the laws of the Member States relating to turnover taxes—Common system of value added tax: uniform basis of assessment, that the real value of goods likely to be sold in tax-free shops to travellers on intra-Community flights or sea crossings is maintained,

HAS ADOPTED THIS DIRECTIVE:

Article 1

Note—Article 1 amends Directive 69/169/EEC, arts 1, 7 *b*.

Article 2

Note—Article 2 amends Directive 77/388/EEC, art 28 *k*.

Repeal—Article 2 repealed by Council Directive 2006/112/EC Annex XI with effect from 1 January 2007.

Article 3

1. Member States shall bring into force the provisions necessary to comply with this Directive by 1 April 1994 at the latest. They shall forthwith inform the Commission thereof.

When Member States adopt these provisions, they shall contain a reference to this Directive or shall be accompanied by such reference on the occasion of their official publication. The methods of making such a reference shall be laid down by the Member States.

[2. By way of derogation from paragraph 1, the Federal Republic of Germany and the Republic of Austria shall be authorised to bring into force the measures necessary to comply with this Directive by 1 January [2003][2] at the latest for goods imported by travellers entering German or Austrian territory by a land frontier linking Germany or Austria to countries other than Member States and the EFTA members or, where applicable, by means of coastal navigation coming from the said countries.][1]

[However, those Member States shall apply an allowance of not less than ECU 100 from 1 January 1999 to imports by the travellers referred to in the preceding subparagraph. They shall jointly increase that amount gradually, with a view to applying the limit in force in the Community to the said imports by 1 January 2003 at the latest.][3]

3. Member States shall communicate to the Commission the text of the provisions of domestic law which they adopt in the field covered by this Directive.

Amendments—[1] Paragraph 2 replaced by Directive 94/75/EC, art 1; OJ L365, 31.12.1994, p 52.

[2] Words in brackets replaced by Directive 98/94/EC, art 1; OJ L 358, 31.12.1998, p 105, 106 with effect from 31 December 1998.

[3] Replaced by Directive 98/94/EC, art 1; OJ L 358, 31.12.1998, p 105, 106 with effect from 31 December 1998.

Article 4

This Directive shall enter into force on the day of its publication in the *Official Journal of the European Communities*.

Article 5

This Directive is addressed to the Member States.

COUNCIL DIRECTIVE (2006/79/EC) OF 5 OCTOBER 2006 ON THE EXEMPTION FROM TAXES OF IMPORTS OF SMALL CONSIGNMENTS OF GOODS OF A NON-COMMERCIAL CHARACTER FROM THIRD COUNTRIES (CODIFIED VERSION)

(2006/79/EC)

Note—See OJ L 286, 17.10.2006 p 15.

THE COUNCIL OF THE EUROPEAN UNION,

Having regard to the Treaty establishing the European Community, and in particular Article 93 thereof,

Having regard to the proposal from the Commission,

Having regard to the opinion of the European Parliament[1],

Having regard to the opinion of the European Economic and Social Committee[2],

Whereas:

(1) Council Directive 78/1035/EEC of 19 December 1978 on the exemption from taxes of imports of small consignments of goods of a non-commercial character from third countries[3] has been substantially amended several times[4]. In the interests of clarity and rationality, the said Directive should be codified.

(2) Provision should be made for the exemption from turnover taxes and excise duties of imports of small consignments of goods of a non-commercial character from third countries.

(3) To that end the limits within which such exemption is to be applied should, for practical reasons, be as far as possible the same as those laid down for the Community arrangements for exemption from customs duties in Council Regulation (EEC) No 918/83 of 28 March 1983 setting up a Community system of reliefs from customs duty[5].

(4) It is necessary to set special limits for certain products because of the high level of taxation to which they are at present subject in the Member States.

(5) This Directive should be without prejudice to the obligations of the Member States relating to the time-limits for transposition into national law of the Directives set out in Annex I, Part B,

Notes—[1] Not yet published in the Official Journal.

[2] Not yet published in the Official Journal.

[3] OJ L 366, 28.12.1978, p. 34. Directive as last amended by the 1994 Act of Accession.

[4] See Annex I, Part A.

[5] OJ L 105, 23.4.1983, p. 1. Regulation as last amended by the 2003 Act of Accession.

HAS ADOPTED THIS DIRECTIVE:

Article 1

1. Goods in small consignments of a non-commercial character sent from a third country by private persons to other private persons in a Member State shall be exempt on importation from turnover tax and excise duty.

2. For the purposes of paragraph 1, "small consignments of a non-commercial character" shall mean consignments which:

(*a*) are of an occasional nature;

(*b*) contain only goods intended for the personal or family use of the consignees, the nature and quantity of which do not indicate that they are being imported for any commercial purpose;

(*c*) contain goods with a total value not exceeding EUR 45;

(*d*) are sent by the sender to the consignee without payment of any kind.

Article 2

1. Article I shall apply to the goods listed below subject to the following quantitative limits:

(*a*) tobacco products

(i) 50 cigarettes,

or

(ii) 25 cigarillos (cigars of a maximum weight of three grams each),

or

(iii) 10 cigars,

or

(iv) 50 grams of smoking tobacco;

(*b*) alcohol and alcoholic beverages:

(i) distilled beverages and spirits of an alcoholic strength exceeding 22% vol.; undenatured ethyl alcohol of 80% vol. and over: one standard bottle (up to 1 litre),

or

(ii) distilled beverages and spirits, and aperitifs with a wine or alcohol base, tafia, saké or similar beverages of an alcoholic strength of 22% vol. or less; sparkling wines, fortified wines: one standard bottle (up to 1 litre),

or

(iii) still wines: two litres;

(*c*) perfumes: 50 grams,

or

toilet waters: 0,25 litre or eight ounces;

(*d*) coffee: 500 grams,

or

coffee extracts and essences: 200 grams;

(*e*) tea: 100 grams,

or

tea extracts and essences: 40 grams.

2. Member States shall have the right to reduce the quantities of the products referred to in paragraph 1 eligible for exemption from turnover tax and excise duties, or to abolish exemption for such products altogether.

Article 3

Any goods listed in Article 2 which are contained in a small consignment of a non-commercial character in quantities exceeding those laid down in the said Article shall be excluded in their entirety from exemption.

Article 4

1. The euro equivalent in national currency which shall apply for the implementation of this Directive shall be fixed once a year. The rates applicable shall be those obtaining on the first working day of October with effect from 1 January of the following year.
2. Member States may round off the amounts in national currency resulting from the conversion of the amounts in euros provided for in Article 1(2), provided such rounding-off does not exceed EUR 2.
3. Member States may maintain the amount of the exemption in force at the time of the annual adjustment provided for in paragraph 1 if, prior to the rounding-off provided for in paragraph 2, conversion of the amount of the exemption expressed in euros would result in a change of less than 5% in the exemption expressed in national currency.

Article 5

Member States shall communicate to the Commission the text of the main provisions of national law which they adopt in the field covered by this Directive. The Commission shall inform the other Member States thereof.

Article 6

Directive 78/1035/EEC shall be repealed, without prejudice to the obligations of the Member States relating to the time-limits for transposition into national law of the Directives set out in Annex I, Part B.
References to the repealed Directive shall be construed as references to this Directive and shall be read in accordance with the correlation table in Annex II.

Article 7

This Directive shall enter into force on the 20th day following its publication in the Official Journal of the European Union.

Article 8

This Directive is addressed to the Member States.

Done at Luxembourg, ... 5 October 2006.

For the Council
The President
K. Rajamäki

ANNEX I

PART A

REPEALED DIRECTIVE WITH ITS SUCCESSIVE AMENDMENTS

Council Directive 78/1035/EEC[1] (OJ L 366, 28.12.1978, p. 34)	
Council Directive 81/933/EEC (OJ L 338, 25.11.1981, p. 24)	only Article 2
Council Directive 85/576/EEC (OJ L 372, 31.12.1985, p. 30)	

Notes—

[1] Directive 78/1035/EEC was also amended by the 1994 Act of Accession.

PART B

TIME-LIMITS FOR TRANSPOSITION INTO NATIONAL LAW

(referred to in Article 6)

Directive	Time-limit for transposition
78/1035/EEC	1 January 1979
81/933/EEC	31 December 1981
85/576/EEC	30 June 1986

ANNEX II

CORRELATION TABLE

Directive 78/1035/EEC	This Directive
Article 1(1)	Article 1(1)
Article 1(2), first indent	Article 1(2)(*a*)
Article 1(2), second indent	Article 1(2)(*b*)
Article 1(2), third indent	Article 1(2)(*c*)
Article 1(2), fourth indent	Article 1(2)(*d*)
Article 2(1)(*a*), from "50 cigarettes" to "50 grams of smoking tobacco"	Article 2(1)(*a*)(i) to (iv)
Article 2(1)(*b*)	Article 2(1)(*b*)
Article 2(1)(*b*), first indent	Article 2(1)(*b*)(i)
Article 2(1)(*b*), second indent	Article 2(1)(*b*)(ii)
Article 2(1)(*b*), third indent	Article 2(1)(*b*)(iii)
Article 2(1)(*c*), (*d*) and (*e*)	Article 2(1)(*c*), (*d*) and (*e*)
Article 2(2)	Article 2(2)
Article 2(3)	—
Article 3	Article 3
Article 4(1)	—
Article 4(2)	Article 4(1)
Article 4(3)	Article 4(2)
Article 4(4)	Article 4(3)
Article 5(1)	—
Article 5(2)	Article 5
—	Article 6
—	Article 7
Article 6	Article 8
—	Annex I

— Annex II

VAT EC

COUNCIL DIRECTIVE 2006/112/EC OF 28 NOVEMBER 2006 ON THE COMMON SYSTEM OF VALUE ADDED TAX

(2006/112/EC)

Note—This Directive repeals Council Directives 67/227/EEC (First Council Directive of 11 April 1967) and 77/388 (Sixth Council Directive of 17 May 1977). For correlation table, see Annex XII.

ARRANGEMENT OF CONTENTS

SECTION 3:
Particular provisions

CHAPTER 3:
TEMPORARY PROVISIONS FOR PARTICULAR LABOUR-INTENSIVE SERVICES

CHAPTER 4:
SPECIAL PROVISIONS APPLYING UNTIL THE ADOPTION OF DEFINITIVE ARRANGEMENTS

CHAPTER 5:
TEMPORARY PROVISIONS

TITLE IX:
EXEMPTIONS

CHAPTER 1:
GENERAL PROVISIONS

CHAPTER 2:
EXEMPTIONS FOR CERTAIN ACTIVITIES IN THE PUBLIC INTEREST

CHAPTER 3:
EXEMPTIONS FOR OTHER ACTIVITIES

CHAPTER 4:
EXEMPTIONS FOR INTRA-COMMUNITY TRANSACTIONS

SECTION 1:
Exemptions related to the supply of goods

SECTION 2:
Exemptions for intra-Community acquisitions of goods

SECTION 3:
Exemptions for certain transport services

CHAPTER 5:
EXEMPTIONS ON IMPORTATION

CHAPTER 6:
EXEMPTIONS ON EXPORTATION

CHAPTER 7:
EXEMPTIONS RELATED TO INTERNATIONAL TRANSPORT

CHAPTER 8:
EXEMPTIONS RELATING TO CERTAIN TRANSACTIONS TREATED AS EXPORTS

CHAPTER 9:
EXEMPTIONS FOR THE SUPPLY OF SERVICES BY INTERMEDIARIES

CHAPTER 10:
EXEMPTIONS FOR TRANSACTIONS RELATING TO INTERNATIONAL TRADE

SECTION 1:
Customs warehouses, warehouses other than customs warehouses and similar arrangements

SECTION 2:
Transactions exempted with a view to export and in the framework of trade between the Member States

SECTION 3:
Provisions common to Sections 1 and 2

TITLE X:
DEDUCTIONS

CHAPTER 1:

ORIGIN AND SCOPE OF RIGHT OF DEDUCTION

CHAPTER 2:

PROPORTIONAL DEDUCTION

CHAPTER 3:

RESTRICTIONS ON THE RIGHT OF DEDUCTION

CHAPTER 4:

RULES GOVERNING EXERCISE OF THE RIGHT OF DEDUCTION

CHAPTER 5:

ADJUSTMENT OF DEDUCTIONS

TITLE XI:
OBLIGATIONS OF TAXABLE PERSONS AND CERTAIN NON-TAXABLE PERSONS

CHAPTER 1:

OBLIGATION TO PAY

SECTION 1:

Persons liable for payment of VAT to the tax authorities

SECTION 2:

Payment arrangements

CHAPTER 2:

IDENTIFICATION

CHAPTER 3:

INVOICING

SECTION 1:

Definition

SECTION 2:

Concept of invoice

SECTION 3:

Issue of invoices

SECTION 4:

Content of invoices

SECTION 5:

Sending invoices by electronic means

SECTION 6:

Simplification measures

CHAPTER 4:

ACCOUNTING

SECTION 1:

Definition

SECTION 2:

General obligations

SECTION 3:

Specific obligations relating to the storage of all invoices

SECTION 4:

Right of access to invoices stored by electronic means in another Member State

CHAPTER 5:

RETURNS

CHAPTER 6:

RECAPITULATIVE STATEMENTS

CHAPTER 7:

MISCELLANEOUS PROVISIONS

CHAPTER 8:

OBLIGATIONS RELATING TO CERTAIN IMPORTATIONS AND EXPORTATIONS

SECTION 1:

Importation

SECTION 2:

Exportation

TITLE XII:
SPECIAL SCHEMES

CHAPTER 1:

SPECIAL SCHEME FOR SMALL ENTERPRISES

SECTION 1:
Simplified procedures for charging and collection

SECTION 2:

Exemptions or graduated relief

SECTION 3:
Reporting and review

CHAPTER 2:

COMMON FLAT-RATE SCHEME FOR FARMERS

CHAPTER 3:

SPECIAL SCHEME FOR TRAVEL AGENTS

CHAPTER 4:

SPECIAL ARRANGEMENTS FOR SECOND-HAND GOODS, WORKS OF ART, COLLECTORS' ITEMS AND ANTIQUES

SECTION 1:

Definitions

SECTION 2:

Special arrangements for taxable dealers

SUBSECTION 1:
Margin scheme

SUBSECTION 2:

Transitional arrangements for second-hand means of transport

SECTION 3:

Special arrangements for sales by public auction

SECTION 4:

Measures to prevent distortion of competition and tax evasion

CHAPTER 5:

SPECIAL SCHEME FOR INVESTMENT GOLD

SECTION 1:

General provisions

SECTION 2:

Exemption from VAT

SECTION 3:

Taxation option

SECTION 4:

Transactions on a regulated gold bullion market

SECTION 5:

Special rights and obligations for traders in investment gold

CHAPTER 6:

SPECIAL SCHEME FOR NON-ESTABLISHED TAXABLE PERSONS SUPPLYING ELECTRONIC SERVICES TO NON-TAXABLE PERSONS

SECTION 1:

General provisions

SECTION 2:

Special scheme for electronically supplied services

TITLE XIII:
DEROGATIONS

CHAPTER 1:

DEROGATIONS APPLYING UNTIL THE ADOPTION OF DEFINITIVE ARRANGEMENTS

SECTION 1:

Derogations for States which were members of the Community on 1 January 1978

SECTION 2:

Derogations for States which acceded to the Community after 1 January 1978

SECTION 3:

Provisions common to Sections 1 and 2

CHAPTER 2:

DEROGATIONS SUBJECT TO AUTHORISATION

SECTION 1:

Simplification measures and measures to prevent tax evasion or avoidance

SECTION 2:

International agreements

TITLE XIV:
MISCELLANEOUS

CHAPTER 1:

IMPLEMENTING MEASURES

CHAPTER 2:

VAT COMMITTEE

CHAPTER 3:

CONVERSION RATES

CHAPTER 4:

0THER TAXES, DUTIES AND CHARGES

TITLE XV:
FINAL PROVISIONS

CHAPTER 1:

TRANSITIONAL ARRANGEMENTS FOR THE TAXATION OF TRADE BETWEEN MEMBER STATES

CHAPTER 2:

TRANSITIONAL MEASURES APPLICABLE IN THE CONTEXT OF ACCESSION TO THE EUROPEAN UNION

CHAPTER 3:

TRANSPOSITION AND ENTRY INTO FORCE

THE COUNCIL OF THE EUROPEAN UNION,

Having regard to the Treaty establishing the European Community, and in particular Article 93 thereof,

Having regard to the proposal from the Commission,

Having regard to the Opinion of the European Parliament,

Having regard to the Opinion of the European Economic and Social Committee,

Whereas:

(1) Council Directive 77/388/EEC of 17 May 1977 on the harmonisation of the laws of the Member States relating to turnover taxes — Common system of value added tax: uniform basis of assessment[1] has been significantly amended on several occasions. Now that new amendments are being made to the said Directive, it is desirable, for reasons of clarity and rationalisation that the Directive should be recast.

(2) The recast text should incorporate all those provisions of Council Directive 67/227/EEC of 11 April 1967 on the harmonisation of legislation of Member States concerning turnover taxes[2] which are still applicable. That Directive should therefore be repealed.

(3) To ensure that the provisions are presented in a clear and rational manner, consistent with the principle of better regulation, it is appropriate to recast the structure and the wording of the Directive although this will not, in principle, bring about material changes in the existing legislation. A small number of substantive amendments are however inherent to the recasting exercise and should nevertheless be made. Where such changes are made, these are listed exhaustively in the provisions governing transposition and entry into force.

(4) The attainment of the objective of establishing an internal market presupposes the application in Member States of legislation on turnover taxes that does not distort conditions of competition or hinder the free movement of goods and services. It is therefore necessary to achieve such harmonisation of legislation on turnover taxes by means of a system of value added tax (VAT), such as will eliminate, as far as possible, factors which may distort conditions of competition, whether at national or Community level.

(5) A VAT system achieves the highest degree of simplicity and of neutrality when the tax is levied in as general a manner as possible and when its scope covers all stages of production and distribution, as well as the supply of services. It is therefore in the interests of the internal market and of Member States to adopt a common system which also applies to the retail trade.

(6) It is necessary to proceed by stages, since the harmonisation of turnover taxes leads in Member States to alterations in tax structure and appreciable consequences in the budgetary, economic and social fields.

(7) The common system of VAT should, even if rates and exemptions are not fully harmonised, result in neutrality in competition, such that within the territory of each Member State similar goods and services bear the same tax burden, whatever the length of the production and distribution chain.

(8) Pursuant to Council Decision 2000/597/EC, Euratom, of 29 September 2000 on the system of the European Communities' own resources[3], the budget of the European Communities is to be financed, without prejudice to other revenue, wholly from the Communities' own resources. Those resources are to include those accruing from VAT and obtained through the application of a uniform rate of tax to bases of assessment determined in a uniform manner and in accordance with Community rules.

(9) It is vital to provide for a transitional period to allow national laws in specified fields to be gradually adapted.

(10) During this transitional period, intra-Community transactions carried out by taxable persons other than exempt taxable persons should be taxed in the Member State of destination, in accordance with the rates and conditions set by that Member State.

(11) It is also appropriate that, during that transitional period, intra-Community acquisitions of a certain value, made by exempt persons or by non-taxable legal persons, certain intra-Community distance selling and the supply of new means of transport to individuals or to exempt or non-taxable bodies should also be taxed in the Member State of destination, in accordance with the rates and conditions set by that Member State, in so far as such transactions would, in the absence of special provisions, be likely to cause significant distortion of competition between Member States.

(12) For reasons connected with their geographic, economic and social situation, certain territories should be excluded from the scope of this Directive.

(13) In order to enhance the non-discriminatory nature of the tax, the term 'taxable person' should be defined in such a way that the Member States may use it to cover persons who occasionally carry out certain transactions.

(14) The term 'taxable transaction' may lead to difficulties, in particular as regards transactions treated as taxable transactions. Those concepts should therefore be clarified.

(15) With a view to facilitating intra-Community trade in work on movable tangible property, it is appropriate to establish the tax arrangements applicable to such transactions when they are carried out for a customer who is identified for VAT purposes in a Member State other than that in which the transaction is physically carried out.

(16) A transport operation within the territory of a Member State should be treated as the intra-Community transport of goods where it is directly linked to a transport operation carried out between Member States, in order to simplify not only the principles and arrangements for taxing those domestic transport services but also the rules applicable to ancillary services and to services supplied by intermediaries who take part in the supply of the various services.

(17) Determination of the place where taxable transactions are carried out may engender conflicts concerning jurisdiction as between Member States, in particular as regards the supply of goods for assembly or the supply of services. Although the place where a supply of services is carried out should in principle be fixed as the place where the supplier has established his place of business, it should be defined as being in the Member State of the customer, in particular in the case of certain services supplied between taxable persons where the cost of the services is included in the price of the goods.

(18) It is necessary to clarify the definition of the place of taxation of certain transactions carried out on board ships, aircraft or trains in the course of passenger transport within the Community.

(19) Electricity and gas are treated as goods for VAT purposes. It is, however, particularly difficult to determine the place of supply. In order to avoid double taxation or non taxation and to attain a genuine internal market free of barriers linked to the VAT regime, the place of supply of gas through the natural gas distribution system, or of electricity, before the goods reach the final stage of consumption, should therefore be the place where the customer has established his business. The supply of electricity and gas at the final stage, that is to say, from traders and distributors to the final consumer, should be taxed at the place where the customer actually uses and consumes the goods.

(20) In the case of the hiring out of movable tangible property, application of the general rule that supplies of services are taxed in the Member State in which the supplier is established may lead to substantial distortion of competition if the lessor and the lessee are established in different Member States and the rates of taxation in those States differ. It is

therefore necessary to establish that the place of supply of a service is the place where the customer has established his business or has a fixed establishment for which the service has been supplied or, in the absence thereof, the place where he has his permanent address or usually resides.

(21) However, as regards the hiring out of means of transport, it is appropriate, for reasons of control, to apply strictly the general rule, and thus to regard the place where the supplier has established his business as the place of supply.

(22) All telecommunications services consumed within the Community should be taxed to prevent distortion of competition in that field. To that end, telecommunications services supplied to taxable persons established in the Community or to customers established in third countries should, in principle, be taxed at the place where the customer for the services is established. In order to ensure uniform taxation of telecommunications services which are supplied by taxable persons established in third territories or third countries to non-taxable persons established in the Community and which are effectively used and enjoyed in the Community, Member States should, however, provide for the place of supply to be within the Community.

(23) Also to prevent distortions of competition, radio and television broadcasting services and electronically supplied services provided from third territories or third countries to persons established in the Community, or from the Community to customers established in third territories or third countries, should be taxed at the place of establishment of the customer.

(24) The concepts of chargeable event and of the chargeability of VAT should be harmonised if the introduction of the common system of VAT and of any subsequent amendments thereto are to take effect at the same time in all Member States.

(25) The taxable amount should be harmonised so that the application of VAT to taxable transactions leads to comparable results in all the Member States.

(26) To prevent loss of tax revenues through the use of connected parties to derive tax benefits, it should, in specific limited circumstances, be possible for Member States to intervene as regards the taxable amount of supplies of goods or services and intra-Community acquisitions of goods.

(27) In order to combat tax evasion or avoidance, it should be possible for Member States to include within the taxable amount of a transaction which involves the working of investment gold provided by a customer, the value of that investment gold where, by virtue of being worked, the gold loses its status of investment gold. When they apply these measures, Member States should be allowed a certain degree of discretion.

(28) If distortions are to be avoided, the abolition of fiscal controls at frontiers entails, not only a uniform basis of assessment, but also sufficient alignment as between Member States of a number of rates and rate levels.

(29) The standard rate of VAT in force in the various Member States, combined with the mechanism of the transitional system, ensures that this system functions to an acceptable degree. To prevent divergences in the standard rates of VAT applied by the Member States from leading to structural imbalances in the Community and distortions of competition in some sectors of activity, a minimum standard rate of 15 % should be fixed, subject to review.

(30) In order to preserve neutrality of VAT, the rates applied by Member States should be such as to enable, as a general rule, deduction of the VAT applied at the preceding stage.

(31) During the transitional period, certain derogations concerning the number and the level of rates should be possible.

(32) To achieve a better understanding of the impact of reduced rates, it is necessary for the Commission to prepare an assessment report on the impact of reduced rates applied to locally supplied services, notably in terms of job creation, economic growth and the proper functioning of the internal market.

(33) In order to tackle the problem of unemployment, those Member States wishing to do so should be allowed to experiment with the operation and impact, in terms of job creation, of a reduction in the VAT rate applied to labour-intensive services. That reduction is also likely to reduce the incentive for the businesses concerned to join or remain in the black economy.

(34) However, such a reduction in the VAT rate is not without risk for the smooth functioning of the internal market and for tax neutrality. Provision should therefore be made for an authorisation procedure to be introduced for a period that is fixed but sufficiently long, so that it is possible to assess the impact of the reduced rates applied to locally supplied services. In order to make sure that such a measure remains verifiable and limited, its scope should be closely defined.

(35) A common list of exemptions should be drawn up so that the Communities' own resources may be collected in a uniform manner in all the Member States.

(36) For the benefit both of the persons liable for payment of VAT and the competent administrative authorities, the methods of applying VAT to certain supplies and intra-Community acquisitions of products subject to excise duty should be aligned with the

procedures and obligations concerning the duty to declare in the case of shipment of such products to another Member State laid down in Council Directive 92/12/EEC of 25 February 1992 on the general arrangements for products subject to excise duty and on the holding, movement and monitoring of such products[4].

(37) The supply of gas through the natural gas distribution system, and of electricity is taxed at the place of the customer. In order to avoid double taxation, the importation of such products should therefore be exempted from VAT.

(38) In respect of taxable operations in the domestic market linked to intra-Community trade in goods carried out during the transitional period by taxable persons not established within the territory of the Member State in which the intra-Community acquisition of goods takes place, including chain transactions, it is necessary to provide for simplification measures ensuring equal treatment in all the Member States. To that end, the provisions concerning the taxation system and the person liable for payment of the VAT due in respect of such operations should be harmonised. It is however, necessary to exclude in principle from such arrangements goods that are intended to be supplied at the retail stage.

(39) The rules governing deductions should be harmonised to the extent that they affect the actual amounts collected. The deductible proportion should be calculated in a similar manner in all the Member States.

(40) The scheme which allows the adjustment of deductions for capital goods over the lifetime of the asset, according to its actual use, should also be applicable to certain services with the nature of capital goods.

(41) It is appropriate to specify the persons liable for payment of VAT, particularly in the case of services supplied by a person who is not established in the Member State in which the VAT is due.

(42) Member States should be able, in specific cases, to designate the recipient of supplies of goods or services as the person liable for payment of VAT. This should assist Member States in simplifying the rules and countering tax evasion and avoidance in identified sectors and on certain types of transactions.

(43) Member States should be entirely free to designate the person liable for payment of the VAT on importation.

(44) Member States should be able to provide that someone other than the person liable for payment of VAT is to be held jointly and severally liable for its payment.

(45) The obligations of taxable persons should be harmonised as far as possible so as to ensure the necessary safeguards for the collection of VAT in a uniform manner in all the Member States.

(46) The use of electronic invoicing should allow tax authorities to carry out their monitoring activities. It is therefore appropriate, in order to ensure the internal market functions properly, to draw up a list, harmonised at Community level, of the particulars that must appear on invoices and to establish a number of common arrangements governing the use of electronic invoicing and the electronic storage of invoices, as well as for self-billing and the outsourcing of invoicing operations.

(47) Subject to conditions which they lay down, Member States should allow certain statements and returns to be made by electronic means, and may require that electronic means be used.

(48) The necessary pursuit of a reduction in the administrative and statistical formalities to be completed by businesses, particularly small and medium-sized enterprises, should be reconciled with the implementation of effective control measures and the need, on both economic and tax grounds, to maintain the quality of Community statistical instruments.

(49) Member States should be allowed to continue to apply their special schemes for small enterprises, in accordance with common provisions, and with a view to closer harmonisation.

(50) Member States should remain free to apply a special scheme involving flat rate rebates of input VAT to farmers not covered by the normal scheme. The basic principles of that special scheme should be established and a common method adopted, for the purposes of collecting own resources, for calculating the value added by such farmers.

(51) It is appropriate to adopt a Community taxation system to be applied to second-hand goods, works of art, antiques and collectors' items, with a view to preventing double taxation and the distortion of competition as between taxable persons.

(52) The application of the normal VAT rules to gold constitutes a major obstacle to its use for financial investment purposes and therefore justifies the application of a special tax scheme, with a view also to enhancing the international competitiveness of the Community gold market.

(53) The supply of gold for investment purposes is inherently similar to other financial investments which are exempt from VAT. Consequently, exemption appears to be the most appropriate tax treatment for supplies of investment gold.

(54) The definition of investment gold should cover gold coins the value of which primarily reflects the price of the gold contained. For reasons of transparency and legal certainty, a yearly list of coins covered by the investment gold scheme should be drawn up, providing security for the operators trading in such coins. That list should be without prejudice to the exemption of coins which are not included in the list but which meet the criteria laid down in this Directive.

(55) In order to prevent tax evasion while at the same time alleviating the financing burden for the supply of gold of a degree of purity above a certain level, it is justifiable to allow Member States to designate the customer as the person liable for payment of VAT.

(56) In order to facilitate compliance with fiscal obligations by operators providing electronically supplied services, who are neither established nor required to be identified for VAT purposes within the Community, a special scheme should be established. Under that scheme it should be possible for any operator supplying such services by electronic means to non-taxable persons within the Community, if he is not otherwise identified for VAT purposes within the Community, to opt for identification in a single Member State.

(57) It is desirable for the provisions concerning radio and television broadcasting and certain electronically supplied services to be put into place on a temporary basis only and to be reviewed in the light of experience within a short period of time.

(58) It is necessary to promote the uniform application of the provisions of this Directive and to that end an advisory committee on value added tax should be set up to enable the Member States and the Commission to cooperate closely.

(59) Member States should be able, within certain limits and subject to certain conditions, to introduce, or to continue to apply, special measures derogating from this Directive in order to simplify the levying of tax or to prevent certain forms of tax evasion or avoidance.

(60) In order to ensure that a Member State which has submitted a request for derogation is not left in doubt as to what action the Commission plans to take in response, time-limits should be laid down within which the Commission must present to the Council either a proposal for authorisation or a communication setting out its objections.

(61) It is essential to ensure uniform application of the VAT system. Implementing measures are appropriate to realise that aim.

(62) Those measures should, in particular, address the problem of double taxation of cross-border transactions which can occur as the result of divergences between Member States in the application of the rules governing the place where taxable transactions are carried out.

(63) Although the scope of the implementing measures would be limited, those measures would have a budgetary impact which for one or more Member States could be significant. Accordingly, the Council is justified in reserving to itself the right to exercise implementing powers.

(64) In view of their limited scope, the implementing measures should be adopted by the Council acting unanimously on a proposal from the Commission.

(65) Since, for those reasons, the objectives of this Directive cannot be sufficiently achieved by the Member States and can therefore be better achieved by at Community level, the Community may adopt measures, in accordance with the principle of subsidiarity as set out in Article 5 of the Treaty. In accordance with the principle of proportionality, as set out in that Article, this Directive does not go beyond what is necessary in order to achieve those objectives.

(66) The obligation to transpose this Directive into national law should be confined to those provisions which represent a substantive change as compared with the earlier Directives. The obligation to transpose into national law the provisions which are unchanged arises under the earlier Directives.

(67) This Directive should be without prejudice to the obligations of the Member States in relation to the time-limits for transposition into national law of the Directives listed in Annex XI, Part B,

1 OJ L 145, 13.6.1977, p. 1. Directive as last amended by Directive 2006/98/EC (OJ L 221, 12.8.2006, p. 9).
2 OJ 71, 14.4.1967, p. 1301. Directive as last amended by Directive 69/ 463/EEC (OJ L 320 of 20.12.1969, p. 34).
3 OJ L 253, 7.10.2000, p. 42.
4 OJ L 76, 23.3.1992, p. 1. Directive as last amended by Directive 2004/106/EC (OJ L 359, 4.12.2004, p. 30).

HAS ADOPTED THIS DIRECTIVE:

TITLE I

SUBJECT MATTER AND SCOPE

Article 1

1. This Directive establishes the common system of value added tax (VAT).

2. The principle of the common system of VAT entails the application to goods and services of a general tax on consumption exactly proportional to the price of the goods and services, however many transactions take place in the production and distribution process before the stage at which the tax is charged.
On each transaction, VAT, calculated on the price of the goods or services at the rate applicable to such goods or services, shall be chargeable after deduction of the amount of VAT borne directly by the various cost components.
The common system of VAT shall be applied up to and including the retail trade stage.

Simon's Tax Cases—Art 1(2), *Société Financière d'Investissements SPRL v Belgium* [2000] STC 164*; *Belgocodex SA v Belgium* [2000] STC 351*; *Midland Bank Plc v C&E Comrs* [2000] STC 501*; *C&E Comrs v Southern Primary Housing Association Ltd* [2003] STC 525*; *C&E Comrs v Southern Primary Housing Association Ltd* [2004] STC 209*; *JD Wetherspoon plc v R&C Comrs* [2009] STC 1022*; *Metropol Spielstatten Unternehmergesellschaft (haftungsbeschrankt) v Finanzamt Hamburg-Bergedorf* (Case C-440/12) [2014] STC 505.

Article 2

1. The following transactions shall be subject to VAT:
  (*a*) the supply of goods for consideration within the territory of a Member State by a taxable person acting as such;
  (*b*) the intra-Community acquisition of goods for consideration within the territory of a Member State by:
    (i) a taxable person acting as such, or a non-taxable legal person, where the vendor is a taxable person acting as such who is not eligible for the exemption for small enterprises provided for in Articles 282 to 292 and who is not covered by Articles 33 or 36;
    (ii) in the case of new means of transport, a taxable person, or a non-taxable legal person, whose other acquisitions are not subject to VAT pursuant to Article 3(1), or any other non-taxable person;
    (iii) in the case of products subject to excise duty, where the excise duty on the intra-Community acquisition is chargeable, pursuant to Directive 92/12/EEC, within the territory of the Member State, a taxable person, or a non-taxable legal person, whose other acquisitions are not subject to VAT pursuant to Article 3(1);
  (*c*) the supply of services for consideration within the territory of a Member State by a taxable person acting as such;
  (*d*) the importation of goods.

2. (*a*) For the purposes of point (ii) of paragraph 1(*b*), the following shall be regarded as 'means of transport', where they are intended for the transport of persons or goods:
  (i) motorised land vehicles the capacity of which exceeds 48 cubic centimetres or the power of which exceeds 7,2 kilowatts;
  (ii) vessels exceeding 7,5 metres in length, with the exception of vessels used for navigation on the high seas and carrying passengers for reward, and of vessels used for the purposes of commercial, industrial or fishing activities, or for rescue or assistance at sea, or for inshore fishing;
  (iii) aircraft the take-off weight of which exceeds 1 550 kilograms, with the exception of aircraft used by airlines operating for reward chiefly on international routes.

(*b*) These means of transport shall be regarded as 'new' in the cases:
  (i) of motorised land vehicles, where the supply takes place within six months of the date of first entry into service or where the vehicle has travelled for no more than 6 000 kilometres;
  (ii) of vessels, where the supply takes place within three months of the date of first entry into service or where the vessel has sailed for no more than 100 hours;
  (iii) of aircraft, where the supply takes place within three months of the date of first entry into service or where the aircraft has flown for no more than 40 hours.

(*c*) Member States shall lay down the conditions under which the facts referred to in point (*b*) may be regarded as established.

[3. "Products subject to excise duty" shall mean energy products, alcohol and alcoholic beverages and manufactured tobacco, as defined by current Community legislation, but not gas supplied through a natural gas system situated within the territory of the Community or any network connected to such a system.]

Commentary—*De Voil Indirect Tax Service* **V2.101**.

Simon's Tax Cases—*C&E Comrs v Church Schools Foundation Ltd**; [2001] STC 1661*; *C&E Comrs v Polok* [2002] STC 361*; *Kretztechnik AG v Finanzamt Linz* [2005] STC 1118*; *Hotel Scandic Gåsabäck AB v Riksskatteverket* [2005] STC 1311*; *Société thermale d'Eugénie-les-Bains v Ministère de l'Economie, des Finances et de l'Industrie* [2008] STC 2470*; *X v Skatteverket* (Case c-84/09) [2011] STC 189.

Art 2(1), *University of Huddersfield Higher Education Corporation v C&E Comrs* [2006] STC 980*; *Elliniko Dimosio v Karageorgou and others* [2006] STC 1654*; *Ministero dell'Economia e delle Finanze v FCE Bank plc* [2007] STC 165*; *EC Commission v United Kingdom* [2007] STC 1211*; *Aktiebolaget NN v Skatteverket* [2008] STC 3203*; *Skatteverket v AB SKF* [2010] STC 419; *Astra Zeneca UK Ltd v R&C Comrs* [2010] STC 2298*; *Serebryannay vek EOOD v Direktor na Direktsia "Obzhalvane i upravlenie na izpalnenieto" -Varna pri Tsentralno upravlenie na Natsionalna agentsia za prihodite.* (Case C-283/12) [2014] STC 427.

VAT EC

Amendments—Article 2(3) substituted by Council Directive 2009/162/EU art 1 with effect from 15 January 2010 (OJ L 10, 15.1.2010, p 14).

Article 3

1. By way of derogation from Article 2(1)(*b*)(i), the following transactions shall not be subject to VAT:

(*a*) the intra-Community acquisition of goods by a taxable person or a non-taxable legal person, where the supply of such goods within the territory of the Member State of acquisition would be exempt pursuant to Articles 148 and 151;

(*b*) the intra-Community acquisition of goods, other than those referred to in point (*a*) and Article 4, and other than new means of transport or products subject to excise duty, by a taxable person for the purposes of his agricultural, forestry or fisheries business subject to the common flat-rate scheme for farmers, or by a taxable person who carries out only supplies of goods or services in respect of which VAT is not deductible, or by a non-taxable legal person.

2. Point (*b*) of paragraph 1 shall apply only if the following conditions are met:

(*a*) during the current calendar year, the total value of intra-Community acquisitions of goods does not exceed a threshold which the Member States shall determine but which may not be less than EUR 10 000 or the equivalent in national currency;

(*b*) during the previous calendar year, the total value of intra-Community acquisitions of goods did not exceed the threshold provided for in point (*a*).

The threshold which serves as the reference shall consist of the total value, exclusive of VAT due or paid in the Member State in which dispatch or transport of the goods began, of the intra-Community acquisitions of goods as referred to under point (b) of paragraph 1.

3. Member States shall grant taxable persons and non-taxable legal persons eligible under point (*b*) of paragraph 1 the right to opt for the general scheme provided for in Article 2(1)(*b*)(i).

Member States shall lay down the detailed rules for the exercise of the option referred to in the first subparagraph, which shall in any event cover a period of two calendar years.

Article 4

In addition to the transactions referred to in Article 3, the following transactions shall not be subject to VAT:

(*a*) the intra-Community acquisition of second-hand goods, works of art, collectors' items or antiques, as defined in points (1) to (4) of Article 311(1), where the vendor is a taxable dealer acting as such and VAT has been applied to the goods in the Member State in which their dispatch or transport began, in accordance with the margin scheme provided for in Articles 312 to 325;

(*b*) the intra-Community acquisition of second-hand means of transport, as defined in Article 327(3), where the vendor is a taxable dealer acting as such and VAT has been applied to the means of transport in the Member State in which their dispatch or transport began, in accordance with the transitional arrangements for second-hand means of transport;

(*c*) the intra-Community acquisition of second-hand goods, works of art, collectors' items or antiques, as defined in points (1) to (4) of Article 311(1), where the vendor is an organiser of sales by public auction, acting as such, and VAT has been applied to the goods in the Member State in which their dispatch or transport began, in accordance with the special arrangements for sales by public auction.

TITLE II
TERRITORIAL SCOPE

Article 5

For the purposes of applying this Directive, the following definitions shall apply:

(1) 'Community' and 'territory of the Community' mean the territories of the Member States as defined in point (2);

(2) 'Member State' and 'territory of a Member State' mean the territory of each Member State of the Community to which the Treaty establishing the European Community is applicable, in accordance with Article 299 of that Treaty, with the exception of any territory referred to in Article 6 of this Directive;

(3) 'third territories' means those territories referred to in Article 6;

(4) 'third country' means any State or territory to which the Treaty is not applicable.

Article 6

1. This Directive shall not apply to the following territories forming part of the customs territory of the Community:

(*a*) Mount Athos;

(*b*) the Canary Islands;

[(*c*) the French territories referred to in Article 349 and Article 355(1) of the Treaty on the Functioning of the European Union;][1]
(*d*) the Åland Islands;
(*e*) the Channel Islands.

2. This Directive shall not apply to the following territories not forming part of the customs territory of the Community:
(*a*) the Island of Heligoland;
(*b*) the territory of Büsingen;
(*c*) Ceuta;
(*d*) Melilla;
(*e*) Livigno;
(*f*) Campione d'Italia;
(*g*) the Italian waters of Lake Lugano.

Amendments—[1] Para 1(*c*) substituted by Council Directive 2013/61/EU art 1 with effect from 1 January 2014 (OJ L 353, 28.12.2013, p 5). Para 1(*c*) previously read as follows—

"(*c*) the French overseas departments;".

Article 7

1. In view of the conventions and treaties concluded with France, the United Kingdom and Cyprus respectively, the Principality of Monaco, the Isle of Man and the United Kingdom Sovereign Base Areas of Akrotiri and Dhekelia shall not be regarded, for the purposes of the application of this Directive, as third countries.

2. Member States shall take the measures necessary to ensure that transactions originating in or intended for the Principality of Monaco are treated as transactions originating in or intended for France, that transactions originating in or intended for the Isle of Man are treated as transactions originating in or intended for the United Kingdom, and that transactions originating in or intended for the United Kingdom Sovereign Base Areas of Akrotiri and Dhekelia are treated as transactions originating in or intended for Cyprus.

Article 8

If the Commission considers that the provisions laid down in Articles 6 and 7 are no longer justified, particularly in terms of fair competition or own resources, it shall present appropriate proposals to the Council.

TITLE III
TAXABLE PERSONS

Article 9

1. 'Taxable person' shall mean any person who, independently, carries out in any place any economic activity, whatever the purpose or results of that activity.

Any activity of producers, traders or persons supplying services, including mining and agricultural activities and activities of the professions, shall be regarded as 'economic activity'. The exploitation of tangible or intangible property for the purposes of obtaining income therefrom on a continuing basis shall in particular be regarded as an economic activity.

2. In addition to the persons referred to in paragraph 1, any person who, on an occasional basis, supplies a new means of transport, which is dispatched or transported to the customer by the vendor or the customer, or on behalf of the vendor or the customer, to a destination outside the territory of a Member State but within the territory of the Community, shall be regarded as a taxable person.

Commentary—*De Voil Indirect Tax Service* **V2.101, V2.108**.

Simon's Tax Cases—Art 9(1), *ICAEW v C&E Comrs* [1999] STC 398*; *C&E Comrs v Yarburgh Children's Trust* [2002] STC 207*; *Cibo Participations SA v Directeur regional des impots du Nord-Pas-de-Calais* [2002] STC 460*; *Empresa de Desenvolvimento Mineiro SGPS SA (EDM) v Fazenda Pública (Ministério Público, intervening)* [2005] STC 65*; *University of Huddersfield Higher Education Corporation v C&E Comrs* [2006] STC 980*; *T-Mobile Austria GmbH and others v Republic of Austria* [2008] STC 184*; *Hutchison 3G UK Ltd and others v C&E Comrs* [2008] STC 218*; *R v Hashash* [2008] STC 1158*; *van der Steen v Inspecteur van de Belastingdienst* [2008] STC 2379*; *SPÖ Landesorganisation Kärnten v Finanzamt Klagenfurt* [2010] STC 287*; *Skatteverket v AB SKF* [2010] STC 419; *Slaby v Minster Finansow / Kuc and anor v Dyrektor Izby Skarbowej w Warszawie* (Cases C-180/10 and C-181/10) [2011] STC 2230; *Kopalnia Odrykwokowa Polski Trawertyn P Granatowicz, M Wasiewicz, spolka jawna v Dyrektor Izby Skarbowej w Poznaniu* (Case C-280/10) [2012] STC 1085; *Klub OOD v Direktsia 'Obzhalvane I upravlenie na izpalnenieto'—Varna pri Tsentralno upravlenie na Natsionalnata agentsia za prihodite* (Case C-153/11) [2012] STC 1129.

Article 10

The condition in Article 9(1) that the economic activity be conducted 'independently' shall exclude employed and other persons from VAT in so far as they are bound to an employer by a contract of employment or by any other legal ties creating the relationship of employer and employee as regards working conditions, remuneration and the employer's liability.

Simon's Tax Cases—*Osman v C&E Comrs* [1989] STC 596*; *Ayuntamiento de Sevilla v Recaudadores de las Zonas Primera y Segunda* [1993] STC 659*; *C&E Comrs v Thorn Materials Supply Ltd and Thorn Resources Ltd* [1998] STC 725*; *C&E Comrs v Barclays Bank plc, CA* [2001] STC 1558*; *van der Steen v Inspecteur van de Belastingdienst* [2008] STC 2379*.

Article 11

After consulting the advisory committee on value added tax (hereafter, the 'VAT Committee'), each Member State may regard as a single taxable person any persons established in the territory of that Member State who, while legally independent, are closely bound to one another by financial, economic and organisational links.

A Member State exercising the option provided for in the first paragraph, may adopt any measures needed to prevent tax evasion or avoidance through the use of this provision.

Simon's Tax Cases—*Osman v C&E Comrs* [1989] STC 596*; *Ayuntamiento de Sevilla v Recaudadores de las Zonas Primera y Segunda* [1993] STC 659*; *C&E Comrs v Thorn Materials Supply Ltd and Thorn Resources Ltd* [1998] STC 725*; *C&E Comrs v Barclays Bank plc, CA* [2001] STC 1558*; *van der Steen v Inspecteur van de Belastingdienst* [2008] STC 2379*.

Article 12

1. Member States may regard as a taxable person anyone who carries out, on an occasional basis, a transaction relating to the activities referred to in the second subparagraph of Article 9(1) and in particular one of the following transactions:

(*a*) the supply, before first occupation, of a building or parts of a building and of the land on which the building stands;

(*b*) the supply of building land.

2. For the purposes of paragraph 1(*a*), 'building' shall mean any structure fixed to or in the ground.

Member States may lay down the detailed rules for applying the criterion referred to in paragraph 1(a) to conversions of buildings and may determine what is meant by 'the land on which a building stands'.

Member States may apply criteria other than that of first occupation, such as the period elapsing between the date of completion of the building and the date of first supply, or the period elapsing between the date of first occupation and the date of subsequent supply, provided that those periods do not exceed five years and two years respectively.

3. For the purposes of paragraph 1(*b*), 'building land' shall mean any unimproved or improved land defined as such by the Member States.

Simon's Tax Cases—*Gemeente Emmen v Belastingdienst Grote Ondernemingen* [1996] STC 496*; *Don Bosco Onroerend Goed BV v Staatssecretaris van Financiën* [2010] STC 476*; *Slaby v Minster Finansow / Kuc and anor v Dyrektor Izby Skarbowej w Warszawie* (Cases C-180/10 and C-181/10) [2011] STC 2230.

Article 13

1. States, regional and local government authorities and other bodies governed by public law shall not be regarded as taxable persons in respect of the activities or transactions in which they engage as public authorities, even where they collect dues, fees, contributions or payments in connection with those activities or transactions.

However, when they engage in such activities or transactions, they shall be regarded as taxable persons in respect of those activities or transactions where their treatment as non-taxable persons would lead to significant distortions of competition.

In any event, bodies governed by public law shall be regarded as taxable persons in respect of the activities listed in Annex I, provided that those activities are not carried out on such a small scale as to be negligible.

[2. Member States may regard activities, exempt under Articles 132, 135, 136 and 371, Articles 374 to 377, Article 378(2), Article 379(2) or Articles 380 to 390b, engaged in by bodies governed by public law as activities in which those bodies engage as public authorities.]

Commentary—*De Voil Indirect Tax Service* **V2.108**.

Simon's Tax Cases—*Fazenda Pública v Câmera Municipal do Porto (Ministério Público, third party)* [2001] STC 560*; *Edinburgh Telford College v R&C Comrs* [2006] STC 1291*; *Finanzamt Eisleben v Feuerbestattungsverein Halle eV (Lutherstadt Eisleben, joined party)* [2006] STC 2043*; *T-Mobile Austria GmbH and others v Republic of Austria* [2008] STC 184*; *Hutchison 3G UK Ltd and others v C&E Comrs* [2008] STC 218*; *R&C Comrs v Isle of Wight Council and others* [2008] STC 614; *Finanzamt Oschatz v Zweckverband zur Trinkwasserversorgung und Abwasserbeseitigung Torgau-Westelbien* [2009] STC 1*; *R&C Comrs v Isle of Wight Council and others* [2009] STC 1098*; *Cambridge University v R&C Comrs* [2009] STC 1288; *Finanzamt Dusseldorf-Sud v SALIX Grundstucks-Vermietungsgesellschaft mbH & Co Object Offenback KG* [2009] STC 1607*.

Press releases etc—HMRC Brief 27/08 (now reissued as 96/09), (interpretation of "bodies governed by public law" and "special legal regime", reconsidered by HMRC).

Amendments—Article 13(2) substituted by Council Directive 2009/162/EU art 1(2) with effect from 15 January 2010 (OJ L 10, 15.1.2010, p 14).

TITLE IV
TAXABLE TRANSACTIONS

CHAPTER 1
SUPPLY OF GOODS

Article 14

1. 'Supply of goods' shall mean the transfer of the right to dispose of tangible property as owner.
2. In addition to the transaction referred to in paragraph 1, each of the following shall be regarded as a supply of goods:
   (*a*) the transfer, by order made by or in the name of a public authority or in pursuance of the law, of the ownership of property against payment of compensation;
   (*b*) the actual handing over of goods pursuant to a contract for the hire of goods for a certain period, or for the sale of goods on deferred terms, which provides that in the normal course of events ownership is to pass at the latest upon payment of the final instalment;
   (*c*) the transfer of goods pursuant to a contract under which commission is payable on purchase or sale.
3. Member States may regard the handing over of certain works of construction as a supply of goods.

Commentary—*De Voil Indirect Tax Service* **V3.119**.

Simon's Tax Cases—Art 14(1), *van Tiem v Staatssecretaris van Financiën* [1993] STC 91*; *British Airways plc v C&E Comrs* [1996] STC 1127*; *, *Stewart (t/a GT Shooting) v C&E Comrs* [2002] STC 255*; *Halifax plc and others v C&E Comrs* [2006] STC 919*; *University of Huddersfield Higher Education Corporation v C&E Comrs* [2006] STC 980*; *R&C Comrs v Loyalty Management UK Ltd* [2007] STC 536*; *Aktiebolaget NN v Skatteverket* [2008] STC 3203*; *Graphic Procédé v Ministère du Budget, des Comptes publics et de la Fonction publique* [2010] STC 918*; *Dixons Retail plc v R&C Comrs* (Case C-494/12) [2014] STC 375.

Art 14(2)(*c*), *EC Commission v United Kingdom* [2007] STC 1211*.

Article 15

[1. Electricity, gas, heat or cooling energy and the like shall be treated as tangible property.]
2. Member States may regard the following as tangible property:
   (*a*) certain interests in immovable property;
   (*b*) rights in rem giving the holder thereof a right of use over immovable property;
   (*c*) shares or interests equivalent to shares giving the holder thereof de jure or de facto rights of ownership or possession over immovable property or part thereof.

Simon's Tax Cases—Art 15(2), *van Tiem v Staatssecretaris van Financiën* [1993] STC 91*; *Stichting 'Goed Wonen' v Staatssecretaris van Financiën* [2003] STC 1137*.

Amendments—Article 15(1) substituted by Council Directive 2009/162/EU art 1(3) with effect from 15 January 2010 (OJ L 10, 15.1.2010, p 14).

Article 16

The application by a taxable person of goods forming part of his business assets for his private use or for that of his staff, or their disposal free of charge or, more generally, their application for purposes other than those of his business, shall be treated as a supply of goods for consideration, where the VAT on those goods or the component parts thereof was wholly or partly deductible.

However, the application of goods for business use as samples or as gifts of small value shall not be treated as a supply of goods for consideration.

Simon's Tax Cases—*Kuwait Petroleum (GB) Ltd v C&E Comrs* [2001] STC 62*; *Finanzamt Burgdorf v Fischer, Finanzamt Düsseldorf-Mettman v Brandenstein* [2001] STC 1356*; *Hotel Scandic Gåsabäck AB v Riksskatteverket* [2005] STC 1311*; *Church of England Children's Society v Revenue and Customs Commissioners* [2005] STC 1644*; *EMI Group Ltd v R&C Comrs* [2010] STC 2609*.

Article 17

1. The transfer by a taxable person of goods forming part of his business assets to another Member State shall be treated as a supply of goods for consideration.

'Transfer to another Member State' shall mean the dispatch or transport of movable tangible property by or on behalf of the taxable person, for the purposes of his business, to a destination outside the territory of the Member State in which the property is located, but within the Community.
2. The dispatch or transport of goods for the purposes of any of the following transactions shall not be regarded as a transfer to another Member State:
   (*a*) the supply of the goods by the taxable person within the territory of the Member State in which the dispatch or transport ends, in accordance with the conditions laid down in Article 33;
   (*b*) the supply of the goods, for installation or assembly by or on behalf of the supplier, by the taxable person within the territory of the Member State in which dispatch or transport of the goods ends, in accordance with the conditions laid down in Article 36;
   (*c*) the supply of the goods by the taxable person on board a ship, an aircraft or a train in the course of a passenger transport operation, in accordance with the conditions laid down in Article 37;

[(*d*) the supply of gas through a natural gas system situated within the territory of the Community or any network connected to such a system, the supply of electricity or the supply of heat or cooling energy through heating or cooling networks, in accordance with the conditions laid down in Articles 38 and 39;]

(*e*) the supply of the goods by the taxable person within the territory of the Member State, in accordance with the conditions laid down in Articles 138, 146, 147, 148, 151 or 152;

[(*f*) the supply of a service performed for the taxable person and consisting in valuations of, or work on, the goods in question physically carried out within the territory of the Member State in which dispatch or transport of the goods ends, provided that the goods, after being valued or worked upon, are returned to that taxable person in the Member State from which they were initially dispatched or transported;]

(*g*) the temporary use of the goods within the territory of the Member State in which dispatch or transport of the goods ends, for the purposes of the supply of services by the taxable person established within the Member State in which dispatch or transport of the goods began;

(*h*) the temporary use of the goods, for a period not exceeding twenty-four months, within the territory of another Member State, in which the importation of the same goods from a third country with a view to their temporary use would be covered by the arrangements for temporary importation with full exemption from import duties.

3. If one of the conditions governing eligibility under paragraph 2 is no longer met, the goods shall be regarded as having been transferred to another Member State. In such cases, the transfer shall be deemed to take place at the time when that condition ceases to be met.

Amendments—Article 17(2)(*d*) substituted by Council Directive 2009/162/EU art 1(3) with effect from 15 January 2010 (OJ L 10, 15.1.2010, p 14).

Article 17(2)(*f*) substituted by Council Directive 2010/45 art 1(1) with effect from 11 August 2010 (OJ L 189, 22.7.2010, p 1). The deadline for implementation of Directive 2010/45/EU is 31 December 2012.

"(*f*) the supply of a service performed for the taxable person and consisting of work on the goods in question physically carried out within the territory of the Member State in which dispatch or transport of the goods ends, provided that the goods, after being worked upon, are returned to that taxable person in the Member State from which they were initially dispatched or transported;".

Article 18

Member States may treat each of the following transactions as a supply of goods for consideration:

(*a*) the application by a taxable person for the purposes of his business of goods produced, constructed, extracted, processed, purchased or imported in the course of such business, where the VAT on such goods, had they been acquired from another taxable person, would not be wholly deductible;

(*b*) the application of goods by a taxable person for the purposes of a non-taxable area of activity, where the VAT on such goods became wholly or partly deductible upon their acquisition or upon their application in accordance with point (*a*);

(*c*) with the exception of the cases referred to in Article 19, the retention of goods by a taxable person, or by his successors, when he ceases to carry out a taxable economic activity, where the VAT on such goods became wholly or partly deductible upon their acquisition or upon their application in accordance with point (*a*).

Simon's Tax Cases—*C&E Comrs v Robert Gordon's College* [1995] STC 1093*; *Gemeente Leusden and another v Staatssecretaris van Financiën* [2007] STC 776*.

Article 19

In the event of a transfer, whether for consideration or not or as a contribution to a company, of a totality of assets or part thereof, Member States may consider that no supply of goods has taken place and that the person to whom the goods are transferred is to be treated as the successor to the transferor.

Member States may, in cases where the recipient is not wholly liable to tax, take the measures necessary to prevent distortion of competition. They may also adopt any measures needed to prevent tax evasion or avoidance through the use of this Article.

Simon's Tax Cases—*Abbey National plc v C&E Comrs* [2001] STC 297*; *Zita Modes Sàrl v Administration de l'Enregistrment et des Domaines* [2005] STC 1059*; *Finanzamt Offenbach am Main-Land v Faxworld Vorgründungsgesellschaft Peter Hünninghausen und Wolfgang Klein GbR* [2005] STC 1192*; *Skatteverket v AB SKF* [2010] STC 419.

CHAPTER 2

INTRA-COMMUNITY ACQUISITION OF GOODS

Article 20

'Intra-Community acquisition of goods' shall mean the acquisition of the right to dispose as owner of movable tangible property dispatched or transported to the person acquiring the goods, by or on behalf of the vendor or the person acquiring the goods, in a Member State other than that in which dispatch or transport of the goods began.

Where goods acquired by a non-taxable legal person are dispatched or transported from a third territory or a third country and imported by that non-taxable legal person into a Member State other than the Member State in which dispatch or transport of the goods ends, the goods shall be regarded as having been dispatched or transported from the Member State of importation. That Member State shall grant the importer designated or recognised under Article 201 as liable for payment of VAT a refund of the VAT paid in respect of the importation of the goods, provided that the importer establishes that VAT has been applied to his acquisition in the Member State in which dispatch or transport of the goods ends.

Simon's Tax Cases—*X v Skatteverket* (Case C-84/09) [2011] STC 189.

Article 21

The application by a taxable person, for the purposes of his business, of goods dispatched or transported by or on behalf of that taxable person from another Member State, within which the goods were produced, extracted, processed, purchased or acquired within the meaning of Article 2(1)(*b*), or into which they were imported by that taxable person for the purposes of his business, shall be treated as an intra-Community acquisition of goods for consideration.

[Article 22

The application by the armed forces of a State party to the North Atlantic Treaty, for their use or for the use of the civilian staff accompanying them, of goods which they have not purchased subject to the general rules governing taxation on the domestic market of a Member State shall be treated as an intra-Community acquisition of goods for consideration, where the importation of those goods would not be eligible for the exemption provided for in Article 143(1)(*h*).]

Amendments—Article 22 substituted by Council Directive 2009/69/EC art 1 with effect from 24 July 2009. See OJ L 175, 4.7.2009 p 12.

Article 23

Member States shall take the measures necessary to ensure that a transaction which would have been classed as a supply of goods if it had been carried out within their territory by a taxable person acting as such is classed as an intra-Community acquisition of goods.

CHAPTER 3

SUPPLY OF SERVICES

Article 24

1. 'Supply of services' shall mean any transaction which does not constitute a supply of goods.
2. 'Telecommunications services' shall mean services relating to the transmission, emission or reception of signals, words, images and sounds or information of any nature by wire, radio, optical or other electromagnetic systems, including the related transfer or assignment of the right to use capacity for such transmission, emission or reception, with the inclusion of the provision of access to global information networks.

Commentary—*De Voil Indirect Tax Service* **V3.470.**

Simon's Tax Cases—art 24(1), *Faaborg-Gelting Linien A/S v Finanzamt Flensburg* [1996] STC 774*; *Landboden-Agrardienste GmbH & Co KG v Finanzamt Calau* [1998] STC 171*; *Halifax plc and others v C&E Comrs* [2006] STC 919*; *University of Huddersfield Higher Education Corporation v C&E Comrs* [2006] STC 980*; *R&C Comrs v Loyalty Management UK Ltd* [2007] STC 536*; *Graphic Procédé v Ministère du Budget, des Comptes publics et de la Fonction publique* [2010] STC 918*.

Article 25

A supply of services may consist, inter alia, in one of the following transactions:

(*a*) the assignment of intangible property, whether or not the subject of a document establishing title;

(*b*) the obligation to refrain from an act, or to tolerate an act or situation;

(*c*) the performance of services in pursuance of an order made by or in the name of a public authority or in pursuance of the law.

Commentary—*De Voil Indirect Tax Service* **V3.470.**

Simon's Tax Cases—*Faaborg-Gelting Linien A/S v Finanzamt Flensburg* (Case C-231/94) [1996] STC 774*; *Landboden-Agrardienste GmbH & Co KG v Finanzamt Calau* (Case C-384/95) [1998] STC 171*; *Halifax plc and others v C&E Comrs*

VAT EC

[2006] STC 919*; *University of Huddersfield Higher Education Corporation v C&E Comrs* [2006] STC 980*; *R&C Comrs v Loyalty Management UK Ltd* [2007] STC 536*; *Graphic Procédé v Ministère du Budget, des Comptes publics et de la Fonction publique* [2010] STC 918*.

Article 26

1. Each of the following transactions shall be treated as a supply of services for consideration:

(*a*) the use of goods forming part of the assets of a business for the private use of a taxable person or of his staff or, more generally, for purposes other than those of his business, where the VAT on such goods was wholly or partly deductible;

(*b*) the supply of services carried out free of charge by a taxable person for his private use or for that of his staff or, more generally, for purposes other than those of his business.

2. Member States may derogate from paragraph 1, provided that such derogation does not lead to distortion of competition.

Commentary—*De Voil Indirect Tax Service* **V3.470**.

Simon's Tax Cases—*Seeling v Finanzamt Starnberg* [2003] STC 805*; *Finanzamt Offenbach am Main-Land v Faxworld Vorgründungsgesellschaft Peter Hünninghausen und Wolfgang Klein GbR* 2005] STC 1192*; *Hotel Scandic Gåsabäck AB v Riksskatteverket* [2005] STC 1311*; *Charles and another v Staatssecretaris van Financiën* [2006] STC 1429*; *Danfoss A/S and anor v Skatteministeriet* [2009] STC 701*; *Vereniging Noordelijke Land en Tuinbouw Organisatie v Staatssecretaris van Financiën* [2009] STC 935*; *Puffer v Unabhängiger Finanzsenat Außenstella Linz* [2009] STC 1693*; *X Holding BV v Staatssecretaris van Financiën* [2010] STC 1221*.

Article 27

In order to prevent distortion of competition and after consulting the VAT Committee, Member States may treat as a supply of services for consideration the supply by a taxable person of a service for the purposes of his business, where the VAT on such a service, were it supplied by another taxable person, would not be wholly deductible.

Article 28

Where a taxable person acting in his own name but on behalf of another person takes part in a supply of services, he shall be deemed to have received and supplied those services himself.

Article 29

Article 19 shall apply in like manner to the supply of services.

CHAPTER 4

IMPORTATION OF GOODS

Article 30

'Importation of goods' shall mean the entry into the Community of goods which are not in free circulation within the meaning of Article 24 of the Treaty.

In addition to the transaction referred to in the first paragraph, the entry into the Community of goods which are in free circulation, coming from a third territory forming part of the customs territory of the Community, shall be regarded as importation of goods.

TITLE V

PLACE OF TAXABLE TRANSACTIONS

CHAPTER 1

PLACE OF SUPPLY OF GOODS

SECTION 1

Supply of goods without transport

Article 31

Where goods are not dispatched or transported, the place of supply shall be deemed to be the place where the goods are located at the time when the supply takes place.

Commentary—*De Voil Indirect Tax Service* **V3.171–178**.

Simon's Tax Cases—*EMAG Handel Eder OHG v Finanzlandesdirektion für Kärnten* [2007] STC 1461*.

SECTION 2

Supply of goods with transport

Article 32

Where goods are dispatched or transported by the supplier, or by the customer, or by a third person, the place of supply shall be deemed to be the place where the goods are located at the time when dispatch or transport of the goods to the customer begins.

However, if dispatch or transport of the goods begins in a third territory or third country, both the place of supply by the importer designated or recognised under Article 201 as liable for payment of VAT and the place of any subsequent supply shall be deemed to be within the Member State of importation of the goods.

Commentary—*De Voil Indirect Tax Service* **V3.112**.
Simon's Tax Cases—*Aktiebolaget NN v Skatteverket* [2008] STC 3203*.

Article 33

1. By way of derogation from Article 32, the place of supply of goods dispatched or transported by or on behalf of the supplier from a Member State other than that in which dispatch or transport of the goods ends shall be deemed to be the place where the goods are located at the time when dispatch or transport of the goods to the customer ends, where the following conditions are met:
   (*a*) the supply of goods is carried out for a taxable person, or a non-taxable legal person, whose intra-Community acquisitions of goods are not subject to VAT pursuant to Article 3 (1) or for any other non-taxable person;
   (*b*) the goods supplied are neither new means of transport nor goods supplied after assembly or installation, with or without a trial run, by or on behalf of the supplier.

2. Where the goods supplied are dispatched or transported from a third territory or a third country and imported by the supplier into a Member State other than that in which dispatch or transport of the goods to the customer ends, they shall be regarded as having been dispatched or transported from the Member State of importation.

Article 34

1. Provided the following conditions are met, Article 33 shall not apply to supplies of goods all of which are dispatched or transported to the same Member State, where that Member State is the Member State in which dispatch or transport of the goods ends:
   (*a*) the goods supplied are not products subject to excise duty;
   (*b*) the total value, exclusive of VAT, of such supplies effected under the conditions laid down in Article 33 within that Member State does not in any one calendar year exceed EUR 100 000 or the equivalent in national currency;
   (*c*) the total value, exclusive of VAT, of the supplies of goods, other than products subject to excise duty, effected under the conditions laid down in Article 33 within that Member State did not in the previous calendar year exceed EUR 100 000 or the equivalent in national currency.

2. The Member State within the territory of which the goods are located at the time when their dispatch or transport to the customer ends may limit the threshold referred to in paragraph 1 to EUR 35 000 or the equivalent in national currency, where that Member State fears that the threshold of EUR 100 000 might cause serious distortion of competition.

Member States which exercise the option under the first subparagraph shall take the measures necessary to inform accordingly the competent public authorities in the Member State in which dispatch or transport of the goods begins.

3. The Commission shall present to the Council at the earliest opportunity a report on the operation of the special EUR 35 000 threshold referred to in paragraph 2, accompanied, if necessary, by appropriate proposals.

4. The Member State within the territory of which the goods are located at the time when their dispatch or transport begins shall grant those taxable persons who carry out supplies of goods eligible under paragraph 1 the right to opt for the place of supply to be determined in accordance with Article 33.

The Member States concerned shall lay down the detailed rules governing the exercise of the option referred to in the first subparagraph, which shall in any event cover two calendar years.

Article 35

Articles 33 and 34 shall not apply to supplies of second-hand goods, works of art, collectors' items or antiques, as defined in points (1) to (4) of Article 311(1), nor to supplies of second-hand means of transport, as defined in Article 327(3), subject to VAT in accordance with the relevant special arrangements.

Article 36

Where goods dispatched or transported by the supplier, by the customer or by a third person are installed or assembled, with or without a trial run, by or on behalf of the supplier, the place of supply shall be deemed to be the place where the goods are installed or assembled.

Where the installation or assembly is carried out in a Member State other than that of the supplier, the Member State within the territory of which the installation or assembly is carried out shall take the measures necessary to ensure that there is no double taxation in that Member State.

Commentary—*De Voil Indirect Tax Service* **V3.171–178**.
Simon's Tax Cases—*EMAG Handel Eder OHG v Finanzlandesdirektion für Kärnten* [2007] STC 1461*; *Aktiebolaget NN v Skatteverket* [2008] STC 3203*.

SECTION 3

Supply of goods on board ships, aircraft or trains

Article 37

1. Where goods are supplied on board ships, aircraft or trains during the section of a passenger transport operation effected within the Community, the place of supply shall be deemed to be at the point of departure of the passenger transport operation.

2. For the purposes of paragraph 1, 'section of a passenger transport operation effected within the Community' shall mean the section of the operation effected, without a stopover outside the Community, between the point of departure and the point of arrival of the passenger transport operation. 'Point of departure of a passenger transport operation' shall mean the first scheduled point of passenger embarkation within the Community, where applicable after a stopover outside the Community.

'Point of arrival of a passenger transport operation' shall mean the last scheduled point of disembarkation within the Community of passengers who embarked in the Community, where applicable before a stopover outside the Community.

In the case of a return trip, the return leg shall be regarded as a separate transport operation.

3. The Commission shall, at the earliest opportunity, present to the Council a report, accompanied if necessary by appropriate proposals, on the place of taxation of the supply of goods for consumption on board and the supply of services, including restaurant services, for passengers on board ships, aircraft or trains.

Pending adoption of the proposals referred to in the first subparagraph, Member States may exempt or continue to exempt, with deductibility of the VAT paid at the preceding stage, the supply of goods for consumption on board in respect of which the place of taxation is determined in accordance with paragraph 1.

Commentary—*De Voil Indirect Tax Service* **V3.177**.

Simon's Tax Cases—*Peninsular and Oriental Steam Navigation Co v C&E Comrs* [2000] STC 488*; *Köhler v Finanzamt Düsseldorf-Nord* [2006] STC 469*.

[SECTION 4

Supplies of gas through a natural gas system, of electricity and of heat or cooling energy through heating and cooling networks

Article 38

1. In the case of the supply of gas through a natural gas system situated within the territory of the Community or any network connected to such a system, the supply of electricity, or the supply of heat or cooling energy through heating or cooling networks to a taxable dealer, the place of supply shall be deemed to be the place where that taxable dealer has established his business or has a fixed establishment for which the goods are supplied or, in the absence of such a place of business or fixed establishment, the place where he has his permanent address or usually resides.

2. For the purposes of paragraph 1, "taxable dealer" shall mean a taxable person whose principal activity in respect of purchases of gas, electricity, heat or cooling energy is reselling those products and whose own consumption of those products is negligible.

Amendments—Section 4 (Arts 38, 39) substituted by Council Directive 2009/162/EU art 1(5) with effect from 15 January 2010 (OJ L 10, 15.1.2010, p 14).

Article 39

In the case of the supply of gas through a natural gas system situated within the territory of the Community or any network connected to such a system, the supply of electricity or the supply of heat or cooling energy through heating or cooling networks, where such a supply is not covered by Article 38, the place of supply shall be deemed to be the place where the customer effectively uses and consumes the goods.

Where all or part of the gas, electricity or heat or cooling energy is not effectively consumed by the customer, those non-consumed goods shall be deemed to have been used and consumed at the place where the customer has established his business or has a fixed establishment for which the goods are supplied. In the absence of such a place of business or fixed establishment, the customer shall be deemed to have used and consumed the goods at the place where he has his permanent address or usually resides.]

Amendments—Section 4 (Arts 38, 39) substituted by Council Directive 2009/162/EU art 1(5) with effect from 15 January 2010 (OJ L 10, 15.1.2010, p 14).

CHAPTER 2

PLACE OF AN INTRA-COMMUNITY ACQUISITION OF GOODS

Article 40

The place of an intra-Community acquisition of goods shall be deemed to be the place where dispatch or transport of the goods to the person acquiring them ends.

Simon's Tax Cases—*Staatssecretaris van Financiën v X* [2010] STC 1701*.

Article 41

Without prejudice to Article 40, the place of an intra-Community acquisition of goods as referred to in Article 2(1)(*b*)(i) shall be deemed to be within the territory of the Member State which issued the VAT identification number under which the person acquiring the goods made the acquisition, unless the person acquiring the goods establishes that VAT has been applied to that acquisition in accordance with Article 40.

If VAT is applied to the acquisition in accordance with the first paragraph and subsequently applied, pursuant to Article 40, to the acquisition in the Member State in which dispatch or transport of the goods ends, the taxable amount shall be reduced accordingly in the Member State which issued the VAT identification number under which the person acquiring the goods made the acquisition.

Simon's Tax Cases—*Staatssecretaris van Financiën v X* [2010] STC 1701*.

Article 42

The first paragraph of Article 41 shall not apply and VAT shall be deemed to have been applied to the intra-Community acquisition of goods in accordance with Article 40 where the following conditions are met:

(*a*) the person acquiring the goods establishes that he has made the intra-Community acquisition for the purposes of a subsequent supply, within the territory of the Member State identified in accordance with Article 40, for which the person to whom the supply is made has been designated in accordance with Article 197 as liable for payment of VAT;

(*b*) the person acquiring the goods has satisfied the obligations laid down in Article 265 relating to submission of the recapitulative statement.

Simon's Tax Cases—*Staatssecretaris van Financiën v X* [2010] STC 1701*.

[CHAPTER 3

PLACE OF SUPPLY OF SERVICES

SECTION 1

Definitions

Article 43

For the purpose of applying the rules concerning the place of supply of services:

1. a taxable person who also carries out activities or transactions that are not considered to be taxable supplies of goods or services in accordance with Article 2(1) shall be regarded as a taxable person in respect of all services rendered to him;

2. a non-taxable legal person who is identified for VAT purposes shall be regarded as a taxable person.]

Commentary—*De Voil Indirect Tax Service* **V2.101, V3.166, V3.192.**

Simon's Tax Cases—*Lease Plan Luxembourg SA v Belgium* (Case C-390/96) [1998] STC 628*; *EC Commission v French Republic* [2001] STC 156*; *RAL (Channel Islands) and others v C&E Comrs* [2005] STC 1025*; *Ministero dell'Economia e delle Finanze and another v FCE Bank plc* [2007] STC 165*.

Amendments—Chapter 3 substituted by Council Directive 2008/8/EC art 2 with effect from 1 January 2010 (OJ L 44, 20.2.2008 p 11).

[SECTION 2

General rules

Article 44

The place of supply of services to a taxable person acting as such shall be the place where that person has established his business. However, if those services are provided to a fixed establishment of the taxable person located in a place other than the place where he has established his business, the place of supply of those services shall be the place where that fixed establishment is located. In the absence of such place of establishment or fixed establishment, the place of supply of services shall be the place where the taxable person who receives such services has his permanent address or usually resides.]

Amendments—Chapter 3 substituted by Council Directive 2008/8/EC art 2 with effect from 1 January 2010 (OJ L 44, 20.2.2008 p 11).

[Article 45

The place of supply of services to a non-taxable person shall be the place where the supplier has established his business. However, if those services are provided from a fixed establishment of the supplier located in a place other than the place where he has established his business, the place of supply of those services shall be the place where that fixed establishment is located. In the absence of such place of establishment or fixed establishment, the place of supply of services shall be the place where the supplier has his permanent address or usually resides.]

Commentary—*De Voil Indirect Tax Service* **V3.188**.

Simon's Tax Cases—*Heger Rudi GmbH v Finanzamt Graz-Stadt* [2008] STC 2679*; *RCI Europe v R&C Comrs* [2009] STC 2407*.

Amendments—Chapter 3 substituted by Council Directive 2008/8/EC art 2 with effect from 1 January 2010 (OJ L 44, 20.2.2008 p 11).

[SECTION 3

Particular provisions

SUBSECTION 1

Supply of services by intermediaries

Article 46

The place of supply of services rendered to a non-taxable person by an intermediary acting in the name and on behalf of another person shall be the place where the underlying transaction is supplied in accordance with this Directive.]

Commentary—*De Voil Indirect Tax Service* **V2.101, V3.166, V3.192**.

Simon's Tax Cases—*EC Commission v Hellenic Republic* (Case C-331\94) [1996] STC 1168*; *Reisebüro Binder GmbH v Finanzamt Stuttgart-Körperschaften* (Case C-116/96) [1998] STC 604*.

Amendments—Chapter 3 substituted by Council Directive 2008/8/EC art 2 with effect from 1 January 2010 (OJ L 44, 20.2.2008 p 11).

[SUBSECTION 2

Supply of services connected with immovable property

Article 47

The place of supply of services connected with immovable property, including the services of experts and estate agents, the provision of accommodation in the hotel sector or in sectors with a similar function, such as holiday camps or sites developed for use as camping sites, the granting of rights to use immovable property and services for the preparation and coordination of construction work, such as the services of architects and of firms providing on-site supervision, shall be the place where the immovable property is located.]

Simon's Tax Cases—*Minister Finansów v RR Donnelley Global Turnkey Solutions Poland sp. zoo* (Case C-155/12) [2014] STC 131.

Amendments—Chapter 3 substituted by Council Directive 2008/8/EC art 2 with effect from 1 January 2010 (OJ L 44, 20.2.2008 p 11).

[SUBSECTION 3

Supply of transport

Article 48

The place of supply of passenger transport shall be the place where the transport takes place, proportionate to the distances covered.]

Amendments—Chapter 3 substituted by Council Directive 2008/8/EC art 2 with effect from 1 January 2010 (OJ L 44, 20.2.2008 p 11).

[Article 49

The place of supply of the transport of goods, other than the intra-Community transport of goods, to non-taxable persons shall be the place where the transport takes place, proportionate to the distances covered.]

Amendments—Chapter 3 substituted by Council Directive 2008/8/EC art 2 with effect from 1 January 2010 (OJ L 44, 20.2.2008 p 11).

[Article 50

The place of supply of the intra-Community transport of goods to non-taxable persons shall be the place of departure.]

Amendments—Chapter 3 substituted by Council Directive 2008/8/EC art 2 with effect from 1 January 2010 (OJ L 44, 20.2.2008 p 11).

[Article 51

"Intra-Community transport of goods" shall mean any transport of goods in respect of which the place of departure and the place of arrival are situated within the territories of two different Member States.

"Place of departure" shall mean the place where transport of the goods actually begins, irrespective of distances covered in order to reach the place where the goods are located and "place of arrival" shall mean the place where transport of the goods actually ends.]

Amendments—Chapter 3 substituted by Council Directive 2008/8/EC art 2 with effect from 1 January 2010 (OJ L 44, 20.2.2008 p 11).

[Article 52

Member States need not apply VAT to that part of the intra-Community transport of goods to non-taxable persons taking place over waters which do not form part of the territory of the Community.]

Simon's Tax Cases—*Inter-Mark Group sp zoo sp komandytowa w Poznaniu v Minster Finansow* (Case C-530/09) [2012] STC 156.

Amendments—Chapter 3 substituted by Council Directive 2008/8/EC art 2 with effect from 1 January 2010 (OJ L 44, 20.2.2008 p 11).

[SUBSECTION 4

Supply of cultural, artistic, sporting, scientific, educational, entertainment and similar services, ancillary transport services and valuations of and work on movable property.]

Amendments—Chapter 3 substituted by Council Directive 2008/8/EC art 2 with effect from 1 January 2010 (OJ L 44, 20.2.2008 p 11).

[Article 53

The place of supply of services in respect of admission to cultural, artistic, sporting, scientific, educational, entertainment or similar events, such as fairs and exhibitions, and of ancillary services related to the admission, supplied to a taxable person, shall be the place where those events actually take place.]

Amendments—Chapter 3 substituted by Council Directive 2008/8/EC art 2 with effect from 1 January 2010 (OJ L 44, 20.2.2008 p 11).

Articles 53, 54 substituted, by Council Directive 2008/8/EC art 3 with effect from 1 January 2011 (OJ L 44, 20.2.2008 p 11). Articles 53, 54 previously read as follows—

> "**Article 53** The place of supply of services and ancillary services relating to cultural, artistic, sporting, scientific, educational, entertainment or similar activities, such as fairs and exhibitions, including the supply of services of the organisers of such activities, shall be the place where those activities are physically carried out.".
>
> "**Article 54** The place of supply of the following services to non-taxable persons shall be the place where the services are physically carried out:
>
> (a) ancillary transport activities such as loading, unloading, handling and similar activities;
>
> (b) valuations of and work on movable tangible property.

[Article 54

(1) The place of supply of services and ancillary services, relating to cultural, artistic, sporting, scientific, educational, entertainment or similar activities, such as fairs and exhibitions, including the supply of services of the organisers of such activities, supplied to a non-taxable person shall be the place where those activities actually take place.

(2) The place of supply of the following services to a nontaxable person shall be the place where the services are physically carried out:

(*a*) ancillary transport activities such as loading, unloading, handling and similar activities;

(*b*) valuations of and work on movable tangible property.]

Amendments—Chapter 3 substituted by Council Directive 2008/8/EC art 2 with effect from 1 January 2010 (OJ L 44, 20.2.2008 p 11).

Articles 53, 54 substituted by Council Directive 2008/8/EC art 3 with effect from 1 January 2011 (OJ L 44, 20.2.2008 p 11).

[SUBSECTION 5

Supply of restaurant and catering services

Article 55

The place of supply of restaurant and catering services other than those physically carried out on board ships, aircraft or trains during the section of a passenger transport operation effected within the Community, shall be the place where the services are physically carried out.]

Amendments—Chapter 3 substituted by Council Directive 2008/8/EC art 2 with effect from 1 January 2010 (OJ L 44, 20.2.2008 p 11).

[SUBSECTION 6

Hiring of means of transport

Article 56

1. The place of short-term hiring of a means of transport shall be the place where the means of transport is actually put at the disposal of the customer.

[2. The place of hiring, other than short-term hiring, of a means of transport to a non-taxable person shall be the place where the customer is established, has his permanent address or usually resides.

VAT EC

However, the place of hiring a pleasure boat to a non-taxable person, other than short-term hiring, shall be the place where the pleasure boat is actually put at the disposal of the customer, where this service is actually provided by the supplier from his place of business or a fixed establishment situated in that place.

3. For the purposes of paragraphs 1 and 2, "short-term" shall mean the continuous possession or use of the means of transport throughout a period of not more than thirty days and, in the case of vessels, not more than 90 days.]]

Simon's Tax Cases—*Inter-Mark Group sp zoo sp komandytowa w Poznaniu v Minster Finansow* (Case C-530/09) [2012] STC 156.

art 56(1)(*e*), *Finanzamt Frankfurt am Main V-Hochst v Deutsche Bank AG* (Case C-44/11) [2012] STC 1951.

Amendments—Chapter 3 substituted by Council Directive 2008/8/EC art 2 with effect from 1 January 2010 (OJ L 44, 20.2.2008 p 11).

New paras 2, 3 substituted for previous para 2, by Council Directive 2008/8/EC art 4 with effect from 1 January 2013 (OJ L 44, 20.2.2008 p 11). Para 2 previously read as follows—

> "2. For the purposes of paragraph 1, "short-term" shall mean the continuous possession or use of the means of transport throughout a period of not more than thirty days and, in the case of vessels, not more than ninety days.".

[SUBSECTION 7

Supply of restaurant and catering services for consumption on board ships, aircraft or trains

Article 57

1. The place of supply of restaurant and catering services which are physically carried out on board ships, aircraft or trains during the section of a passenger transport operation effected within the Community, shall be at the point of departure of the passenger transport operation.

2. For the purposes of paragraph 1, "section of a passenger transport operation effected within the Community" shall mean the section of the operation effected, without a stopover outside the Community, between the point of departure and the point of arrival of the passenger transport operation.

"Point of departure of a passenger transport operation" shall mean the first scheduled point of passenger embarkation within the Community, where applicable after a stopover outside the Community.

"Point of arrival of a passenger transport operation" shall mean the last scheduled point of disembarkation within the Community of passengers who embarked in the Community, where applicable before a stop-over outside the Community.

In the case of a return trip, the return leg shall be regarded as a separate transport operation.]

Amendments—Chapter 3 substituted by Council Directive 2008/8/EC art 2 with effect from 1 January 2010 (OJ L 44, 20.2.2008 p 11).

[SUBSECTION 8

Supply of telecommunications, broadcasting and electronic services to non-taxable persons

Article 58

The place of supply of the following services to a non-taxable person shall be the place where that person is established, has his permanent address or usually resides:

(a) telecommunications services;
(b) radio and television broadcasting services;
(c) electronically supplied services, in particular those referred to in Annex II.

Where the supplier of a service and the customer communicate via electronic mail, that shall not of itself mean that the service supplied is an electronically supplied service.][1]

Cross-references—See VATA 1994 Sch 3BA (electronic, telecommunication and broadcasting services: Union scheme, from 1 January 2015).

Amendments—[1] Sub-s 8 substituted by Council Directive 2008/8/EC art 5(1) with effect from 1 January 2015 (OJ L 44, 20.2.2008 p 11). Sub-s 8 previously read as follows—

> "*Subsection 8*
>
> *Supply of electronic services to non-taxable persons*
>
> **Article 58**
>
> The place of supply of electronically supplied services, in particular those referred to in Annex II, when supplied to non-taxable persons who are established in a Member State, or who have their permanent address or usually reside in a Member State, by a taxable person who has established his business outside the Community or has a fixed establishment there from which the service is supplied, or who, in the absence of such a place of business or fixed establishment, has his permanent address or usually resides outside the Community, shall be the place where the non-taxable person is established, or where he has his permanent address or usually resides.
>
> Where the supplier of a service and the customer communicate via electronic mail, that shall not of itself mean that the service supplied is an electronically supplied service.".

[SUBSECTION 9

Supply of services to non-taxable persons outside the Community

Article 59

The place of supply of the following services to a non-taxable person who is established or has his permanent address or usually resides outside the Community, shall be the place where that person is established, has his permanent address or usually resides:

(*a*) transfers and assignments of copyrights, patents, licences, trade marks and similar rights;
(*b*) advertising services;
(*c*) the services of consultants, engineers, consultancy firms, lawyers, accountants and other similar services, as well as data processing and the provision of information;
(*d*) obligations to refrain from pursuing or exercising, in whole or in part, a business activity or a right referred to in this Article;
(*e*) banking, financial and insurance transactions including reinsurance, with the exception of the hire of safes;
(*f*) the supply of staff;
(*g*) the hiring out of movable tangible property, with the exception of all means of transport;
[(*h*) the provision of access to a natural gas system situated within the territory of the Community or to any network connected to such a system, to the electricity system or to heating or cooling networks, or the transmission or distribution through these systems or networks, and the provision of other services directly linked thereto;][2]
(*i*) *telecommunications services;*[3]
(*j*) *radio and television broadcasting services;*[3]
(*k*) *electronically supplied services, in particular those referred to in Annex II.*[3]

Where the supplier of a service and the customer communicate via electronic mail, that shall not of itself mean that the service supplied is an electronically supplied service.][1]

Commentary—*De Voil Indirect Tax Service* **V2.101**, **V3.166**, **V3.192**.

Simon's Tax Cases—*EC Commission v Grand Duchy of Luxembourg* (Case C-69/92) [1997] STC 712*; *von Hoffmann v Finanzamt Trier* [1997] STC 1321*; *Synidcat des Producteurs Independants (SPI) v Ministere de l'Economie, des Finances et de l'Industry* [2001] STC 523*; *Design Concept SA v Flanders Expo SA* [2003] STC 912*; *R&C Comrs v Zurich Insurance Co* [2006] STC 1694*; *R&C Comrs v Zurich Insurance Co* [2007] STC 1756*; *EC Commission v Germany* [2008] STC 2906*; *Kollektivavtalsstiftelsen TRR Trygghetsrådet v Skatteverket* [2009] STC 526.

Amendments—[1] Chapter 3 substituted by Council Directive 2008/8/EC art 2 with effect from 1 January 2010 (OJ L 44, 20.2.2008 p 11).

[2] Point (*h*) substituted by Council Directive 2009/162/EU art 1(6) with effect from 15 January 2010 (OJ L 10, 15.1.2010, p 14).

[3] Points (*i*), (*j*), (*k*) repealed by Council Directive 2008/8/EC art 5(2) with effect from 1 January 2015 (OJ L 44, 20.2.2008 p 11).

[SUBSECTION 10

Prevention of double taxation or non-taxation

[Article 59a

In order to prevent double taxation, non-taxation or distortion of competition, Member States may, with regard to services the place of supply of which is governed by Articles 44, 45, 56, 58 and 59:

(a) consider the place of supply of any or all of those services, if situated within their territory, as being situated outside the Community if the effective use and enjoyment of the services takes place outside the Community;
(b) consider the place of supply of any or all of those services, if situated outside the Community, as being situated within their territory if the effective use and enjoyment of the services takes place within their territory.][1]

Amendments—[1] Article 59a substituted by Council Directive 2008/8/EC art 5(3) with effect from 1 January 2015 (OJ L 44, 20.2.2008 p 11). Article 59a previously read as follows—

"In order to prevent double taxation, non-taxation or distortion of competition, Member States may, with regard to services the place of supply of which is governed by Articles 44, 45, 56 and 59:

consider the place of supply of any or all of those services, if situated within their territory, as being situated outside the Community if the effective use and enjoyment of the services takes place outside the Community;

consider the place of supply of any or all of those services, if situated outside the Community, as being situated within their territory if the effective use and enjoyment of the services takes place within their territory.

However, this provision shall not apply to the electronically supplied services where those services are rendered to non-taxable persons not established within the Community.".

Article 59b

Member States shall apply Article 59a(b) to telecommunications services and radio and television broadcasting services, as referred to in point (*j*) of the first paragraph of Article 59, supplied to non-taxable persons who are established in a Member State, or who have their permanent address or usually reside in a Member State, by a taxable person who has established his business outside the Community or has a fixed establishment there from which the services are supplied, or who, in the absence of such a place of business or fixed establishment, has his permanent address or usually resides outside the Community.[1]

Amendments—[1] Article 59b repealed by Council Directive 2008/8/EC art 5(3) with effect from 1 January 2015 (OJ L 44, 20.2.2008 p 11).

CHAPTER 4

PLACE OF IMPORTATION OF GOODS

Article 60

The place of importation of goods shall be the Member State within whose territory the goods are located when they enter the Community.

Article 61

By way of derogation from Article 60, where, on entry into the Community, goods which are not in free circulation are placed under one of the arrangements or situations referred to in Article 156, or under temporary importation arrangements with total exemption from import duty, or under external transit arrangements, the place of importation of such goods shall be the Member State within whose territory the goods cease to be covered by those arrangements or situations.

Similarly, where, on entry into the Community, goods which are in free circulation are placed under one of the arrangements or situations referred to in Articles 276 and 277, the place of importation shall be the Member State within whose territory the goods cease to be covered by those arrangements or situations.

Simon's Tax Cases—*Dansk Transport og Logistik v Skatteministeriet* [2010] STC 1711*.

TITLE VI
CHARGEABLE EVENT AND CHARGEABILITY OF VAT

CHAPTER 1

GENERAL PROVISIONS

Article 62

For the purposes of this Directive:

(1) 'chargeable event' shall mean the occurrence by virtue of which the legal conditions necessary for VAT to become chargeable are fulfilled;

(2) VAT shall become 'chargeable' when the tax authority becomes entitled under the law, at a given moment, to claim the tax from the person liable to pay, even though the time of payment may be deferred.

CHAPTER 2

SUPPLY OF GOODS OR SERVICES

Article 63

The chargeable event shall occur and VAT shall become chargeable when the goods or the services are supplied.

Article 64

1. Where it gives rise to successive statements of account or successive payments, the supply of goods, other than that consisting in the hire of goods for a certain period or the sale of goods on deferred terms, as referred to in point (*b*) of Article 14 (2), or the supply of services shall be regarded as being completed on expiry of the periods to which such statements of account or payments relate.

[2. Continuous supplies of goods over a period of more than one calendar month which are dispatched or transported to a Member State other than that in which the dispatch or transport of those goods begins and which are supplied VAT-exempt or which are transferred VAT-exempt to another Member State by a taxable person for the purposes of his business, in accordance with the conditions laid down in Article 138, shall be regarded as being completed on expiry of each calendar month until such time as the supply comes to an end.

Supplies of services for which VAT is payable by the customer pursuant to Article 196, which are supplied continuously over a period of more than one year and which do not give rise to statements of account or payments during that period, shall be regarded as being completed on expiry of each calendar year until such time as the supply of services comes to an end.

Member States may provide that, in certain cases other than those referred to in the first and second subparagraphs, the continuous supply of goods or services over a period of time is to be regarded as being completed at least at intervals of one year.][1]

Amendments—[1] Para 2 substituted by Council Directive 2010/45 art 1(2) with effect from 11 August 2010 (OJ L 189, 22.7.2010, p 1). The deadline for implementation of Directive 2010/45/EU is 31 December 2012. Para 2 previously read as follows—

"2. Supplies of services for which VAT is payable by the customer pursuant to Article 196, which are supplied continuously over a period of more than one year and which do not give rise to statements of account or payments during that period shall be regarded as being completed on expiry of each calendar year until such time as the supply of services comes to an end.

Member States may provide that, in certain cases other than those referred to in the previous paragraph, the continuous supply of goods or services over a period of time is to be regarded as being completed at least at intervals of one year.".

Article 65

Where a payment is to be made on account before the goods or services are supplied, VAT shall become chargeable on receipt of the payment and on the amount received.

Simon's Tax Cases—*FIRIN OOD v Direktor na Direktsia 'Obzhalvane i danachno-osiguritelna praktika' Veliko Tarnovo pri Tsentralno upravlenie na Natsionalnata agentsia za prihodite* (Case C-107/13) [2014] STC 1581.

Article 66

By way of derogation from Articles 63, 64 and 65, Member States may provide that VAT is to become chargeable, in respect of certain transactions or certain categories of taxable person at one of the following times:

(*a*) no later than the time the invoice is issued;

(*b*) no later than the time the payment is received;

[(*c*) where an invoice is not issued, or is issued late, within a specified time no later than on expiry of the time- limit for issue of invoices imposed by Member States pursuant to the second paragraph of Article 222 or where no such time-limit has been imposed by the Member State, within a specified period from the date of the chargeable event.

The derogation provided for in the first paragraph shall not, however, apply to supplies of services in respect of which VAT is payable by the customer pursuant to Article 196 and to supplies or transfers of goods referred to in Article 67.][1]

Amendments—[1] Words substituted by Council Directive 2010/45 art 1(3) with effect from 11 August 2010 (OJ L 189, 22.7.2010, p 1). The deadline for implementation of Directive 2010/45/EU is 31 December 2012. Words previously read as follows—

"(*c*) where an invoice is not issued, or is issued late, within a specified period from the date of the chargeable event.

The derogation provided for in the first paragraph shall not, however, apply to supplies of services in respect of which VAT is payable by the customer pursuant to Article 196.".

[Article 67

Where, in accordance with the conditions laid down in Article 138, goods dispatched or transported to a Member State other than that in which dispatch or transport of the goods begins are supplied VAT-exempt or where goods are transferred VAT-exempt to another Member State by a taxable person for the purposes of his business, VAT shall become chargeable on issue of the invoice, or on expiry of the time limit referred to in the first paragraph of Article 222 if no invoice has been issued by that time.

Article 64(1), the third subparagraph of Article 64(2) and Article 65 shall not apply with respect to the supplies and transfers of goods referred to in the first paragraph.][1]

Amendments—[1] Article substituted by Council Directive 2010/45 art 1(4) with effect from 11 August 2010 (OJ L 189, 22.7.2010, p 1). The deadline for implementation of Directive 2010/45/EU is 31 December 2012. Article previously read as follows—

"1. Where, in accordance with the conditions laid down in Article 138, goods dispatched or transported to a Member State other than that in which dispatch or transport of the goods begins are supplied VAT-exempt or where goods are transferred VAT-exempt to another Member State by a taxable person for the purposes of his business, VAT shall become chargeable on the 15th day of the month following that in which the chargeable event occurs.

2. By way of derogation from paragraph 1, VAT shall become chargeable on issue of the invoice provided for in Article 220, if that invoice is issued before the 15th day of the month following that in which the chargeable event occurs.".

CHAPTER 3

INTRA-COMMUNITY ACQUISITION OF GOODS

Article 68

The chargeable event shall occur when the intra-Community acquisition of goods is made.

The intra-Community acquisition of goods shall be regarded as being made when the supply of similar goods is regarded as being effected within the territory of the relevant Member State.

[Article 69

In the case of the intra-Community acquisition of goods, VAT shall become chargeable on issue of the invoice, or on expiry of the time limit referred to in the first paragraph of Article 222 if no invoice has been issued by that time.][1]

Amendments—[1] Article substituted by Council Directive 2010/45 art 1(5) with effect from 11 August 2010 (OJ L 189, 22.7.2010, p 1). The deadline for implementation of Directive 2010/45/EU is 31 December 2012. Article previously read as follows—

"1. In the case of the intra-Community acquisition of goods, VAT shall become chargeable on the 15th day of the month following that in which the chargeable event occurs.

2. By way of derogation from paragraph 1, VAT shall become chargeable on issue of the invoice provided for in Article 220, if that invoice is issued before the 15th day of the month following that in which the chargeable event occurs.".

CHAPTER 4

IMPORTATION OF GOODS

Article 70

The chargeable event shall occur and VAT shall become chargeable when the goods are imported.

Simon's Tax Cases—*Dansk Transport og Logistik v Skatteministeriet* [2010] STC 1711*.

Article 71

1. Where, on entry into the Community, goods are placed under one of the arrangements or situations referred to in Articles 156, 276 and 277, or under temporary importation arrangements with total exemption from import duty, or under external transit arrangements, the chargeable event shall occur and VAT shall become chargeable only when the goods cease to be covered by those arrangements or situations.

However, where imported goods are subject to customs duties, to agricultural levies or to charges having equivalent effect established under a common policy, the chargeable event shall occur and VAT shall become chargeable when the chargeable event in respect of those duties occurs and those duties become chargeable.

2. Where imported goods are not subject to any of the duties referred to in the second subparagraph of paragraph 1, Member States shall, as regards the chargeable event and the moment when VAT becomes chargeable, apply the provisions in force governing customs duties.

Simon's Tax Cases—*Pezzullo Molini Pastifici Mangimifici SpA v Ministero delle Finanze* [1996] STC 1236*; *Dansk Transport og Logistik v Skatteministeriet* [2010] STC 1711*.

TITLE VII

TAXABLE AMOUNT

CHAPTER 4

IMPORTATION OF GOODS

Note—This Chapter number and heading appear to be erroneous. In accordance with the Arrangement of Contents the Chapter number and heading should instead read "Chapter 1 Definition".

Article 72

For the purposes of this Directive, 'open market value' shall mean the full amount that, in order to obtain the goods or services in question at that time, a customer at the same marketing stage at which the supply of goods or services takes place, would have to pay, under conditions of fair competition, to a supplier at arm's length within the territory of the Member State in which the supply is subject to tax.

Where no comparable supply of goods or services can be ascertained, 'open market value' shall mean the following:

(1) in respect of goods, an amount that is not less than the purchase price of the goods or of similar goods or, in the absence of a purchase price, the cost price, determined at the time of supply;

(2) in respect of services, an amount that is not less than the full cost to the taxable person of providing the service.

CHAPTER 2

SUPPLY OF GOODS OR SERVICES

Article 73

In respect of the supply of goods or services, other than as referred to in Articles 74 to 77, the taxable amount shall include everything which constitutes consideration obtained or to be obtained by the supplier, in return for the supply, from the customer or a third party, including subsidies directly linked to the price of the supply.

Simon's Tax Cases—*Town and County Factors Ltd v C&E Comrs* (Case C-498/99) [2002] STC 1263*; *EC Commission v Federal Republic of Germany (United Kingdom intervening)*, [2003] STC 301*; *Yorkshire Co-operatives Ltd v C&E Comrs* [2003] STC 234*; *Office des Produits Wallons ASBL v Belgium* [2003] STC 1100*; *Lex Services plc v C&E Comrs* [2004] STC 73*; *Total UK Ltd v R&C Comrs* [2008] STC 19*; *Ministero dell'Economia e delle Finanze v Part Service Srl* [2008] STC 3132*; *Fiscale eenheid Koninklijke Ahold NV v Staatssecretaris van Financiën* [2009] STC 45*; *JD Wetherspoon plc v R&C Comrs* [2009] STC 1022*; *ADSITS Balkan and Sea Properties and another v Direktor na Direktsia 'Obzhalvane l upravlenie na izpalnenieto' — Varna pri Tsentralno upravlenie na Natsionalnata agentsia za prihodite* (Joined cases C-621/10 and C-129/11) [2012] STC 1819; *Dixons Retail plc v R&C Comrs* (Case C-494/12) [2014] STC 375; *Metropol Spielstatten Unternehmergesellschaft (haftungsbeschrankt) v Finanzamt Hamburg-Bergedorf* (Case C-440/12) [2014] STC 505.

Article 74

Where a taxable person applies or disposes of goods forming part of his business assets, or where goods are retained by a taxable person, or by his successors, when his taxable economic activity ceases, as referred to in Articles 16 and 18, the taxable amount shall be the purchase price of the goods or of similar goods or, in the absence of a purchase price, the cost price, determined at the time when the application, disposal or retention takes place.

Article 75

In respect of the supply of services, as referred to in Article 26, where goods forming part of the assets of a business are used for private purposes or services are carried out free of charge, the taxable amount shall be the full cost to the taxable person of providing the services.

Simon's Tax Cases—*Köhne v Finanzamt München III* [1990] STC 749*; *Enkler v Finanzamt Homburg* (Case C-230/94) [1996] STC 1316*; *Hausgemeinschaft Jörg und Stefanie Wollny v Finanzamt Landshut* [2008] STC 1618*.

Article 76

In respect of the supply of goods consisting in transfer to another Member State, the taxable amount shall be the purchase price of the goods or of similar goods or, in the absence of a purchase price, the cost price, determined at the time the transfer takes place.

Article 77

In respect of the supply by a taxable person of a service for the purposes of his business, as referred to in Article 27, the taxable amount shall be the open market value of the service supplied.

Article 78

The taxable amount shall include the following factors:

(*a*) taxes, duties, levies and charges, excluding the VAT itself;

(*b*) incidental expenses, such as commission, packing, transport and insurance costs, charged by the supplier to the customer.

For the purposes of point (b) of the first paragraph, Member States may regard expenses covered by a separate agreement as incidental expenses.

Simon's Tax Cases—*C&E Comrs v British Telecom plc* [1999] STC 758*; *Lidl & Companhia v Fazenda Publica* (C-106/10) [2011] STC 1979.

Article 79

The taxable amount shall not include the following factors:

(*a*) price reductions by way of discount for early payment;

(*b*) price discounts and rebates granted to the customer and obtained by him at the time of the supply;

(*c*) amounts received by a taxable person from the customer, as repayment of expenditure incurred in the name and on

behalf of the customer, and entered in his books in a suspense account.

The taxable person must furnish proof of the actual amount of the expenditure referred to in point (c) of the first paragraph and may not deduct any VAT which may have been charged.

Simon's Tax Cases—*Boots Co plc v C&E Comrs* [1990] STC 387*; *Nell Gwynn House Maintenance Fund Trustees v C&E Comrs* [1999] STC 79*; *Kuwait Petroleum (GB) Ltd v C&E Comrs* [2001] STC 62*; *Freemans v C&E Comrs* [2001] STC 960*; *C&E Comrs v Plantiflor* [2002] STC 1132*; *Lidl & Companhia v Fazenda Publica* (C-106/10) [2011] STC 1979.

Article 80

1. In order to prevent tax evasion or avoidance, Member States may in any of the following cases take measures to ensure that, in respect of the supply of goods or services involving family or other close personal ties, management, ownership, membership, financial or legal ties as defined by the Member State, the taxable amount is to be the open market value:

(*a*) where the consideration is lower than the open market value and the recipient of the supply does not have a full right of deduction under Articles 167 to 171 and Articles 173 to 177;

(*b*) where the consideration is lower than the open market value and the supplier does not have a full right of deduction under Articles 167 to 171 and Articles 173 to 177 and the supply is subject to an exemption under Articles 132, 135, 136, 371, 375, 376, 377, 378(2), 379(2) or [Articles 380 to 390b];

(*c*) where the consideration is higher than the open market value and the supplier does not have a full right of deduction under Articles 167 to 171 and Articles 173 to 177.

For the purposes of the first subparagraph, legal ties may include the relationship between an employer and employee or the employee's family, or any other closely connected persons.

2. Where Member States exercise the option provided for in paragraph 1, they may restrict the categories of suppliers or recipients to whom the measures shall apply.

3. Member States shall inform the VAT Committee of national legislative measures adopted pursuant to paragraph 1 in so far as these are not measures authorised by the Council prior to 13 August 2006 in accordance with Article 27 (1) to (4) of Directive 77/388/EEC, and which are continued under paragraph 1 of this Article.

Amendments—In para (1)(*b*), the words substituted for "Articles 380 to 390" by Council Directive 2009/162/EU art 1(7) with effect from 15 January 2010 (OJ L 10, 15.1.2010, p 14).

Simon's Tax Cases—*ADSITS Balkan and Sea Properties and another v Direktor na Direktsia 'Obzhalvane I upravlenie na izpalnenieto' — Varna pri Tsentralno upravlenie na Natsionalnata agentsia za prihodite* (Joined cases C-621/10 and C-129/11) [2012] STC 1819.

Article 81

Member States which, at 1 January 1993, were not availing themselves of the option under Article 98 of applying a reduced rate may, if they avail themselves of the option under Article 89, provide that in respect of the supply of works of art, as referred to in Article 103(2), the taxable amount is to be equal to a fraction of the amount determined in accordance with Articles 73, 74, 76, 78 and 79.

The fraction referred to in the first paragraph shall be determined in such a way that the VAT thus due is equal to at least 5% of the amount determined in accordance with Articles 73, 74, 76, 78 and 79.

Article 82

Member States may provide that, in respect of the supply of goods and services, the taxable amount is to include the value of exempt investment gold within the meaning of Article 346, which has been provided by the customer to be used as basis for working and which as a result, loses its VAT exempt investment gold status when such goods and services are supplied. The value to be used is the open market value of the investment gold at the time that those goods and services are supplied.

CHAPTER 3
INTRA-COMMUNITY ACQUISITION OF GOODS

Article 83

In respect of the intra-Community acquisition of goods, the taxable amount shall be established on the basis of the same factors as are used in accordance with Chapter 1 to determine the taxable amount for the supply of the same goods within the territory of the Member State concerned. In the case of the transactions, to be treated as intra-Community acquisitions of goods, referred to in Articles 21 and 22, the taxable amount shall be the purchase price of the goods or of similar goods or, in the absence of a purchase price, the cost price, determined at the time of the supply.

Article 84

1. Member States shall take the measures necessary to ensure that the excise duty due from or paid by the person making the intra-Community acquisition of a product subject to excise duty is included in the taxable amount in accordance with point (*a*) of the first paragraph of Article 78.

2. Where, after the intra-Community acquisition of goods has been made, the person acquiring the goods obtains a refund of the excise duty paid in the Member State in which dispatch or transport of the goods began, the taxable amount shall be reduced accordingly in the Member State in the territory of which the acquisition was made.

CHAPTER 4
IMPORTATION OF GOODS

Article 85

In respect of the importation of goods, the taxable amount shall be the value for customs purposes, determined in accordance with the Community provisions in force.

Article 86

1. The taxable amount shall include the following factors, in so far as they are not already included:

(*a*) taxes, duties, levies and other charges due outside the Member State of importation, and those due by reason of importation, excluding the VAT to be levied;

(*b*) incidental expenses, such as commission, packing, transport and insurance costs, incurred up to the first place of destination within the territory of the Member State of importation as well as those resulting from transport to another place of destination within the Community, if that other place is known when the chargeable event occurs.

2. For the purposes of point (*b*) of paragraph 1, 'first place of destination' shall mean the place mentioned on the consignment note or on any other document under which the goods are imported into the Member State of importation. If no such mention is made, the first place of destination shall be deemed to be the place of the first transfer of cargo in the Member State of importation.

Article 87

The taxable amount shall not include the following factors:

(*a*) price reductions by way of discount for early payment;

(*b*) price discounts and rebates granted to the customer and obtained by him at the time of importation.

Article 88

Where goods temporarily exported from the Community are reimported after having undergone, outside the Community, repair, processing, adaptation, making up or re-working, Member States shall take steps to ensure that the tax treatment of the goods for VAT purposes is the same as that which would have been applied had the repair, processing, adaptation, making up or re-working been carried out within their territory.

Article 89

Member States which, at 1 January 1993, were not availing themselves of the option under Article 98 of applying a reduced rate may provide that in respect of the importation of works of art, collectors' items and antiques, as defined in points (2), (3) and (4) of Article 311(1), the taxable amount is to be equal to a fraction of the amount determined in accordance with Articles 85, 86 and 87.

The fraction referred to in the first paragraph shall be determined in such a way that the VAT thus due on the importation is equal to at least 5% of the amount determined in accordance with Articles 85, 86 and 87.

Simon's Tax Cases—*EC Commission v United Kingdom* [2007] STC 1211*.

CHAPTER 5
MISCELLANEOUS PROVISIONS

Article 90

1. In the case of cancellation, refusal or total or partial nonpayment, or where the price is reduced after the supply takes place, the taxable amount shall be reduced accordingly under conditions which shall be determined by the Member States.

2. In the case of total or partial non-payment, Member States may derogate from paragraph 1.

Simon's Tax Cases—*Elida Gibbs Ltd v C&E Comrs* (Case C-317/94) [1996] STC 1387*; *Goldsmiths (Jewellers) Ltd v C&E Comrs* (Case C-330/95) [1997] STC 1073*; *Yorkshire Co-operatives Ltd v C&E Comrs* [2003] STC 234*; *Minister Finansow v Kraft Foods Polska SA* (Case C-588/10) [2012] STC 787; *FIRIN OOD v Direktor na Direktsia 'Obzhalvane i danachno-osiguritelna praktika' Veliko Tarnovo pri Tsentralno upravlenie na Natsionalnata agentsia za prihodite* (Case C-107/13) [2014] STC 1581.

Article 91

1. Where the factors used to determine the taxable amount on importation are expressed in a currency other than that of the Member State in which assessment takes place, the exchange rate shall be determined in accordance with the Community provisions governing the calculation of the value for customs purposes.

2. Where the factors used to determine the taxable amount of a transaction other than the importation of goods are expressed in a currency other than that of the Member State in which assessment takes place, the exchange rate applicable shall be the latest selling rate recorded, at the time VAT becomes

VAT EC

chargeable, on the most representative exchange market or markets of the Member State concerned, or a rate determined by reference to that or those markets, in accordance with the rules laid down by that Member State.

[Member States shall accept instead the use of the latest exchange rate published by the European Central Bank at the time the tax becomes chargeable. Conversion between currencies other than the euro shall be made by using the euro exchange rate of each currency. Member States may require that they be notified of the exercise of this option by the taxable person.

However, for some of the transactions referred to in the first subparagraph or for certain categories of taxable persons, Member States may use the exchange rate determined in accordance with the Community provisions in force governing the calculation of the value for customs purposes.][1]

Amendments—[1] In para 2, second and third sub-paras substituted by Council Directive 2010/45 art 1(6) with effect from 11 August 2010 (OJ L 189, 22.7.2010, p 1). The deadline for implementation of Directive 2010/45/EU is 31 December 2012. Words previously read as follows—

> "However, for some of the transactions referred to in the first subparagraph or for certain categories of taxable persons, Member States may use the exchange rate determined in accordance with the Community provisions in force governing the calculation of the value for customs purposes.".

Article 92

As regards the costs of returnable packing material, Member States may take one of the following measures:

(*a*) exclude them from the taxable amount and take the measures necessary to ensure that this amount is adjusted if the packing material is not returned;

(*b*) include them in the taxable amount and take the measures necessary to ensure that this amount is adjusted if the packing material is in fact returned.

TITLE VIII
RATES

CHAPTER 1
APPLICATION OF RATES

Article 93

The rate applicable to taxable transactions shall be that in force at the time of the chargeable event.

However, in the following situations, the rate applicable shall be that in force when VAT becomes chargeable:

(*a*) in the cases referred to in Articles 65 and 66;

(*b*) in the case of an intra-Community acquisition of goods;

(*c*) in the cases, concerning the importation of goods, referred to in the second subparagraph of Article 71(1) and in Article 71(2).

Article 94

1. The rate applicable to the intra-Community acquisition of goods shall be that applied to the supply of like goods within the territory of the Member State.

2. Subject to the option under Article 103(1) of applying a reduced rate to the importation of works of art, collectors' items or antiques, the rate applicable to the importation of goods shall be that applied to the supply of like goods within the territory of the Member State.

Article 95

Where rates are changed, Member States may, in the cases referred to in Articles 65 and 66, effect adjustments in order to take account of the rate applying at the time when the goods or services were supplied.

Member States may also adopt all appropriate transitional measures.

CHAPTER 2
STRUCTURE AND LEVEL OF RATES

SECTION 1
Standard rate

Article 96

Member States shall apply a standard rate of VAT, which shall be fixed by each Member State as a percentage of the taxable amount and which shall be the same for the supply of goods and for the supply of services.

[Article 97

From 1 January 2011 until 31 December 2015, the standard rate may not be lower than 15 %.][1]

Commentary—*De Voil Indirect Tax Service* **V4.401**.

Simon's Tax Cases—*EC Commission v French Republic (Republic of Finland intervening)* [2001] STC 919*; *EC Commission v Federal Republic of Germany* [2006] STC 1587*; *Finanzamt Oschatz v Zweckverband zur Trinkwasserversorgung und Abwasserbeseitigung Torgau-Westelbien* [2009] STC 1*.

Amendments—[1] Article 97 substituted by Council Directive 2010/88/EU art 1 with effect from 11 December 2010. Article 97 previously read as follows—

"1. From 1 January 2006 until 31 December 2010, the standard rate may not be less than 15%.

2. The Council shall decide, in accordance with Article 93 of the Treaty, on the level of the standard rate to be applied after 31 December 2010.".

SECTION 2
Reduced rates

Article 98

1. Member States may apply either one or two reduced rates.

2. The reduced rates shall apply only to supplies of goods or services in the categories set out in Annex III.

[The reduced rates shall not apply to electronically supplied services.][1]

3. When applying the reduced rates provided for in paragraph 1 to categories of goods, Member States may use the Combined Nomenclature to establish the precise coverage of the category concerned.

Commentary—*De Voil Indirect Tax Service* **V4.401**.

Simon's Tax Cases—*EC Commission v French Republic (Republic of Finland intervening)* [2001] STC 919*; *EC Commission v Federal Republic of Germany* [2006] STC 1587*; *Finanzamt Oschatz v Zweckverband zur Trinkwasserversorgung und Abwasserbeseitigung Torgau-Westelbien* [2009] STC 1*; *European Commission v France* (Case C-94/09) [2012] STC 573; *European Commission v Spain* (Case C-360/11) [2013] STC 2236.

Amendments—[1] Second sub-para substituted by Council Directive 2008/8/EC art 2(2) with effect from 1 January 2010 (OJ L 44, 20.2.2008 p 11). Text previously read as follows—

"The reduced rates shall not apply to the services referred to in point (k) of Article 56(1).".

Article 99

1. The reduced rates shall be fixed as a percentage of the taxable amount, which may not be less than 5%.

2. Each reduced rate shall be so fixed that the amount of VAT resulting from its application is such that the VAT deductible under Articles 167 to 171 and Articles 173 to 177 can normally be deducted in full.

Article 100

On the basis of a report from the Commission, the Council shall, starting in 1994, review the scope of the reduced rates every two years.

The Council may, in accordance with Article 93 of the Treaty, decide to alter the list of goods and services set out in Annex III.

Article 101

By 30 June 2007 at the latest the Commission shall present to the European Parliament and the Council an overall assessment report on the impact of reduced rates applying to locally supplied services, including restaurant services, notably in terms of job creation, economic growth and the proper functioning of the internal market, based on a study carried out by an independent economic think-tank.

SECTION 3
Particular provisions

[Article 102

After consultation of the VAT Committee, each Member State may apply a reduced rate to the supply of natural gas, electricity or district heating.]

Amendments—Article 102 substituted by Council Directive 2009/162/EU art 1(8) with effect from 15 January 2010 (OJ L 10, 15.1.2010, p 14).

Article 103

1. Member States may provide that the reduced rate, or one of the reduced rates, which they apply in accordance with Articles 98 and 99 is also to apply to the importation of works of art, collectors' items and antiques, as defined in points (2), (3) and (4) of Article 311(1).

2. If Member States avail themselves of the option under paragraph 1, they may also apply the reduced rate to the following transactions:

(*a*) the supply of works of art, by their creator or his successors in title;

(*b*) the supply of works of art, on an occasional basis, by a taxable person other than a taxable dealer, where the works of art have been imported by the taxable person himself, or where they have been supplied to him by their creator or his successors in title, or where they have entitled him to full deduction of VAT.

Article 104

Austria may, in the communes of Jungholz and Mittelberg (Kleines Walsertal), apply a second standard rate which is lower than the corresponding rate applied in the rest of Austria but not less than 15%.

[Article 104a

Cyprus may apply one of the two reduced rates provided for in Article 98 to the supply of liquid petroleum gas (LPG) in cylinders.][1]

Amendments—[1] Article 104a inserted by Council Directive 2009/47/EC art 1 with effect from 1 June 2009 (OJ L 116, 9.5.2009 p 18).

[Article 105

1. Portugal may apply one of the two reduced rates provided for in Article 98 to the tolls on bridges in the Lisbon area.

2. Portugal may, in the case of transactions carried out in the autonomous regions of the Azores and Madeira and of direct importation into those regions, apply rates lower than those applying on the mainland.][1]

Amendments—[1] Article 105 substituted by Council Directive 2009/47/EC art 1 with effect from 1 June 2009 (OJ L 116, 9.5.2009 p 18). Text previously read as follows:

"Portugal may, in the case of transactions carried out in the autonomous regions of the Azores and Madeira and of direct importation into those regions, apply rates lower than those applying on the mainland.".

CHAPTER 3

TEMPORARY PROVISIONS FOR PARTICULAR LABOUR-INTENSIVE SERVICES[1]

Amendments—[1] Chapter 3 repealed by Council Directive 2009/47/EC art 1 with effect from 1 June 2009 (OJ L 116, 9.5.2009 p 18).

Article 106

The Council may, acting unanimously on a proposal from the Commission, allow Member States to apply until 31 December 2010 at the latest the reduced rates provided for in Article 98 to services listed in Annex IV.

The reduced rates may be applied to services from no more than two of the categories set out in Annex IV.

In exceptional cases a Member State may be allowed to apply the reduced rates to services from three of those categories.[1]

Amendments—[1] Chapter 3 repealed by Council Directive 2009/47/EC art 1 with effect from 1 June 2009 (OJ L 116, 9.5.2009 p 18).

Article 107

The services referred to in Article 106 must meet the following conditions:

(*a*) *they must be labour-intensive;*

(*b*) *they must largely be provided direct to final consumers;*

(*c*) *they must be mainly local and not likely to cause distortion of competition.*

There must also be a close link between the decrease in prices resulting from the rate reduction and the foreseeable increase in demand and employment. Application of a reduced rate must not prejudice the smooth functioning of the internal market.[1]

Amendments—[1] Chapter 3 repealed by Council Directive 2009/47/EC art 1 with effect from 1 June 2009 (OJ L 116, 9.5.2009 p 18).

Article 108

Any Member State wishing to apply for the first time after 31 December 2005 a reduced rate to one or more of the services referred to in Article 106 pursuant to this Article shall inform the Commission accordingly no later than 31 March 2006. It shall communicate to it before that date all relevant information concerning the new measures it wishes to introduce, in particular the following:

(*a*) *scope of the measure and detailed description of the services concerned;*

(*b*) *particulars showing that the conditions laid down in Article 107 have been met;*

(*c*) *particulars showing the budgetary cost of the measure envisaged.*[1]

Amendments—[1] Chapter 3 repealed by Council Directive 2009/47/EC art 1 with effect from 1 June 2009 (OJ L 116, 9.5.2009 p 18).

CHAPTER 4

SPECIAL PROVISIONS APPLYING UNTIL THE ADOPTION OF DEFINITIVE ARRANGEMENTS

Article 109

Pending introduction of the definitive arrangements referred to in Article 402, the provisions laid down in this Chapter shall apply.

Simon's Tax Cases—*Marks & Spencer plc v R&C Comrs* [2008] STC 1408*.

Article 110

Member States which, at 1 January 1991, were granting exemptions with deductibility of the VAT paid at the preceding stage or applying reduced rates lower than the minimum laid down in Article 99 may continue to grant those exemptions or apply those reduced rates.

The exemptions and reduced rates referred to in the first paragraph must be in accordance with Community law and must have been adopted for clearly defined social reasons and for the benefit of the final consumer.

Article 111

Subject to the conditions laid down in the second paragraph of Article 110, exemptions with deductibility of the VAT paid at the preceding stage may continue to be granted in the following cases:

(*a*) by Finland in respect of the supply of newspapers and periodicals sold by subscription and the printing of publications distributed to the members of corporations for the public good;

(*b*) by Sweden in respect of the supply of newspapers, including radio and cassette newspapers for the visually impaired, pharmaceutical products supplied to hospitals or on prescription, and the production of, or other related services concerning, periodicals of non-profit-making organisations;

[(*c*) by Malta in respect of the supply of foodstuffs for human consumption and pharmaceuticals.][1]

Amendments—[1] Para (*c*) inserted by Council Directive 2009/47/EC art 1 with effect from 1 June 2009 (OJ L 116, 9.5.2009 p 18).

Article 112

If the provisions of Article 110 cause for Ireland distortion of competition in the supply of energy products for heating and lighting, Ireland may, on specific request, be authorised by the Commission to apply a reduced rate to such supplies, in accordance with Articles 98 and 99.

In the case referred to in the first paragraph, Ireland shall submit a request to the Commission, together with all necessary information. If the Commission has not taken a decision within three months of receiving the request, Ireland shall be deemed to be authorised to apply the reduced rates proposed.

Article 113

Member States which, at 1 January 1991, in accordance with Community law, were granting exemptions with deductibility of the VAT paid at the preceding stage or applying reduced rates lower than the minimum laid down in Article 99, in respect of goods and services other than those specified in Annex III, may apply the reduced rate, or one of the two reduced rates, provided for in Article 98 to the supply of such goods or services.

Article 114

1. Member States which, on 1 January 1993, were obliged to increase their standard rate in force at 1 January 1991 by more than 2% may apply a reduced rate lower than the minimum laid down in Article 99 to the supply of goods and services in the categories set out in Annex III.

[The Member States referred to in the first subparagraph may also apply such a rate to children's clothing and children's footwear and housing.][1]

2. Member States may not rely on paragraph 1 to introduce exemptions with deductibility of the VAT paid at the preceding stage.

Amendments—[1] In para 1, second sub-para substituted by Council Directive 2009/47/EC art 1 with effect from 1 June 2009 (OJ L 116, 9.5.2009 p 18). Text previously read as follows—

"The Member States referred to in the first subparagraph may also apply such a rate to restaurant services, children's clothing, children's footwear and housing.".

[Article 115

Member States which, at 1 January 1991, were applying a reduced rate to children's clothing, children's footwear or housing may continue to apply such a rate to the supply of those goods or services.][1]

Amendments—[1] Article 115 substituted by Council Directive 2009/47/EC art 1 with effect from 1 June 2009 (OJ L 116, 9.5.2009 p 18). Text previously read as follows—

"**Article 115**

Member States which, at 1 January 1991, were applying a reduced rate to restaurant services, children's clothing, children's footwear or housing may continue to apply such a rate to the supply of those goods or services.".

Article 116

Portugal may apply one of the two reduced rates provided for in Article 98 to restaurant services, provided that the rate is not lower than 12%.[1]

Amendments—[1] Article 116 repealed by Council Directive 2009/47/EC art 1 with effect from 1 June 2009 (OJ L 116, 9.5.2009 p 18).

Article 117

1. For the purposes of applying Article 115, Austria may continue to apply a reduced rate to restaurant services.[1]

2. Austria may apply one of the two reduced rates provided for in Article 98 to the letting of immovable property for residential use, provided that the rate is not lower than 10%.

Amendments—[1] Para 1 repealed by Council Directive 2009/47/EC art 1 with effect from 1 June 2009 (OJ L 116, 9.5.2009 p 18).

Article 118

Member States which, at 1 January 1991, were applying a reduced rate to the supply of goods or services other than those specified in Annex III may apply the reduced rate, or one of the two reduced rates, provided for in Article 98 to the supply of those goods or services, provided that the rate is not lower than 12%.

The first paragraph shall not apply to the supply of second-hand goods, works of art, collectors' items or antiques, as defined in points (1) to (4) of Article 311(1), subject to VAT in accordance with the margin scheme provided for in Articles 312 to 325 or the arrangements for sales by public auction.

Article 119

For the purposes of applying Article 118, Austria may apply a reduced rate to wines produced on an agricultural holding by the producer-farmer, provided that the rate is not lower than 12%.

Article 120

Greece may apply rates up to 30% lower than the corresponding rates applied in mainland Greece in the departments of Lesbos, Chios, Samos, the Dodecanese and the Cyclades, and on the islands of Thassos, the Northern Sporades, Samothrace and Skiros.

Article 121

Member States which, at 1 January 1993, regarded work under contract as the supply of goods may apply to the delivery of work under contract the rate applicable to the goods obtained after execution of the work under contract.

For the purposes of applying the first paragraph, 'delivery of work under contract' shall mean the handing over by a contractor to his customer of movable property made or assembled by the contractor from materials or objects entrusted to him by the customer for that purpose, whether or not the contractor has provided any part of the materials used.

Article 122

Member States may apply a reduced rate to the supply of live plants and other floricultural products, including bulbs, roots and the like, cut flowers and ornamental foliage, and of wood for use as firewood.

CHAPTER 5

TEMPORARY PROVISIONS

[Article 123

The Czech Republic may, until 31 December 2010, continue to apply a reduced rate of not less than 5% to the supply of construction work for residential housing not provided as part of a social policy, excluding building materials.][1]

Amendments—[1] Article 123 substituted by Council Directive 2007/75/EC of 20 December 2007, art 1(1) with effect from 1 January 2008.

Article 124

. . .[1]

Amendments—[1] Article 124 repealed by Council Directive 2007/75/EC of 20 December 2007, art 1(2) with effect from 1 January 2008.

Article 125

1. Cyprus may, [until 31 December 2010][1], continue to grant an exemption with deductibility of VAT paid at the preceding stage in respect of the supply of pharmaceuticals and foodstuffs for human consumption, with the exception of ice cream, ice lollies, frozen yoghurt, water ice and similar products and savoury food products (potato crisps/sticks, puffs and similar products packaged for human consumption without further preparation).

2. *Cyprus may continue to apply a reduced rate of not less than 5% to the supply of restaurant services, [until 31 December 2010][1] or until the introduction of definitive arrangements, as referred to in Article 402, whichever is the earlier.*[2]

Amendments—[1] Words substituted by Council Directive 2007/75/EC of 20 December 2007, art 1(3) with effect from 1 January 2008.

[2] Para 2 repealed by Council Directive 2009/47/EC art 1 with effect from 1 June 2009 (OJ L 116, 9.5.2009 p 18).

Article 126

. . . [1]

Amendments—[1] Article 126 repealed by Council Directive 2007/75/EC of 20 December 2007, art 1(4) with effect from 1 January 2008.

Article 127

Malta may, until [31 December 2010][1], continue to grant an exemption with deductibility of VAT paid at the preceding stage in respect of the supply of foodstuffs for human consumption and pharmaceuticals.

Amendments—[1] Words substituted by Council Directive 2007/75/EC of 20 December 2007, art 1(5) with effect from 1 January 2008.

Amendments—Article 127 repealed by Council Directive 2009/47/EC art 1 with effect from 1 January 2011 (OJ L 116, 9.5.2009 p 18).

[Article 128

1. Poland may, until 31 December 2010, grant an exemption with deductibility of VAT paid at the preceding stage in respect of the supply of certain books and specialist periodicals.

2. *Poland may, until 31 December 2010 or until the introduction of definitive arrangements, as referred to in Article 402, whichever is the earlier, continue to apply a reduced rate of not less than 7% to the supply of restaurant services.*[2]

3. Poland may, until 31 December 2010, continue to apply a reduced rate of not less than 3% to the supply of foodstuffs as referred to in point (1) of Annex III.

4. Poland may, until 31 December 2010, continue to apply a reduced rate of not less than 7% to the supply of services, not provided as part of a social policy, for construction, renovation and alteration of housing, excluding building materials, and to the supply before first occupation of residential buildings or parts of residential buildings, as referred to in Article 12(1)(*a*).][1]

Amendments—[1] Article 128 substituted by Council Directive 2007/75/EC of 20 December 2007, art 1(6) with effect from 1 January 2008.

[2] Para 2 repealed by Council Directive 2009/47/EC art 1 with effect from 1 June 2009 (OJ L 116, 9.5.2009 p 18).

Article 129

1. *Slovenia may, [until 31 December 2010][1] or until the introduction of definitive arrangements as referred to in Article 402, whichever is the earlier, continue to apply a reduced rate of not less than 8.5% to the preparation of meals.*[2]

2. Slovenia may, [until 31 December 2010][1], continue to apply a reduced rate of not less than 5% to the supply of construction, renovation and maintenance work for residential housing not provided as part of a social policy, excluding building materials.

Amendments—[1] Words substituted by Council Directive 2007/75/EC of 20 December 2007, art 1(7) with effect from 1 January 2008.

[2] Para 1 repealed by Council Directive 2009/47/EC art 1 with effect from 1 June 2009 (OJ L 116, 9.5.2009 p 18).

Article 130

. . . [1]

Amendments—[1] Article 130 repealed by Council Directive 2007/75/EC of 20 December 2007, art 1(8) with effect from 1 January 2008.

TITLE IX
EXEMPTIONS

CHAPTER 1
GENERAL PROVISIONS

Article 131

The exemptions provided for in Chapters 2 to 9 shall apply without prejudice to other Community provisions and in accordance with conditions which the Member States shall lay down for the purposes of ensuring the correct and straightforward application of those exemptions and of preventing any possible evasion, avoidance or abuse.

Simon's Tax Cases—*BDV Hungary Trading Kft, in liquidation, v Nemzeti Adó- és Vámhivatal Közép-magyarországi Regionális Adó Főigazgatósága* (Case C-563/12) [2014] STC 1015.

CHAPTER 2

EXEMPTIONS FOR CERTAIN ACTIVITIES IN THE PUBLIC INTEREST

Article 132

1. Member States shall exempt the following transactions:

(*a*) the supply by the public postal services of services other than passenger transport and telecommunications services, and the supply of goods incidental thereto;

(*b*) hospital and medical care and closely related activities undertaken by bodies governed by public law or, under social conditions comparable with those applicable to bodies governed by public law, by hospitals, centres for medical treatment or diagnosis and other duly recognised establishments of a similar nature;

(*c*) the provision of medical care in the exercise of the medical and paramedical professions as defined by the Member State concerned;

(*d*) the supply of human organs, blood and milk;

(*e*) the supply of services by dental technicians in their professional capacity and the supply of dental prostheses by dentists and dental technicians;

(*f*) the supply of services by independent groups of persons, who are carrying on an activity which is exempt from VAT or in relation to which they are not taxable persons, for the purpose of rendering their members the services directly necessary for the exercise of that activity, where those groups merely claim from their members exact reimbursement of their share of the joint expenses, provided that such exemption is not likely to cause distortion of competition;

(*g*) the supply of services and of goods closely linked to welfare and social security work, including those supplied by old people's homes, by bodies governed by public law or by other bodies recognised by the Member State concerned as being devoted to social wellbeing;

(*h*) the supply of services and of goods closely linked to the protection of children and young persons by bodies governed by public law or by other organisations recognised by the Member State concerned as being devoted to social wellbeing;

(*i*) the provision of children's or young people's education, school or university education, vocational training or retraining, including the supply of services and of goods closely related thereto, by bodies governed by public law having such as their aim or by other organisations recognised by the Member State concerned as having similar objects;

(*j*) tuition given privately by teachers and covering school or university education;

(*k*) the supply of staff by religious or philosophical institutions for the purpose of the activities referred to in points (*b*), (*g*), (*h*) and (*i*) and with a view to spiritual welfare;

(*l*) the supply of services, and the supply of goods closely linked thereto, to their members in their common interest in return for a subscription fixed in accordance with their rules by non-profit-making organisations with aims of a political, trade-union, religious, patriotic, philosophical, philanthropic or civic nature, provided that this exemption is not likely to cause distortion of competition;

(*m*) the supply of certain services closely linked to sport or physical education by non-profit-making organisations to persons taking part in sport or physical education;

(*n*) the supply of certain cultural services, and the supply of goods closely linked thereto, by bodies governed by public law or by other cultural bodies recognised by the Member State concerned;

(*o*) the supply of services and goods, by organisations whose activities are exempt pursuant to points (*b*), (*g*), (*h*), (*i*), (*l*), (*m*) and (*n*), in connection with fund-raising events organised exclusively for their own benefit, provided that exemption is not likely to cause distortion of competition;

(*p*) the supply of transport services for sick or injured persons in vehicles specially designed for the purpose, by duly authorised bodies;

(*q*) the activities, other than those of a commercial nature, carried out by public radio and television bodies.

2. For the purposes of point (*o*) of paragraph 1, Member States may introduce any restrictions necessary, in particular as regards the number of events or the amount of receipts which give entitlement to exemption.

Commentary—*De Voil Indirect Tax Service* **V4.146, V4.161**.

Simon's Tax Cases—*EC Commission v United Kingdom* [1988] STC 251*; *Christoph-Dornier-Stiftung für Klinische Psychologie v Finanzamt Gießen* [2005] STC 228*.

Art 132(1), *Gregg v Comrs of Customs and Excise* (Case C-216/97) [1999] STC 934*; *C&E Comrs v Kingscrest Associates Ltd (t/a Kingscrest Residential Care Homes)* [2002] STC 490*; *Diagnostiko & Therapeftiko Kentro Athinon-Ygeia AE v Ipourgos Ikonomikon* [2006] STC 1349*.

Art 132(1)(a), *R (on the application of TNT Post UK Ltd) v R&C Comrs* [2009] STC 1438*.

Art 132(1)(*b*), *LuP GmbH v Finanzamt Bochum-Mitte* [2008] STC 1742*; *CopyGene A/S v Skatteministeriet* [2010] STC 1799*.

Art 132(1)(*c*), *C&E Comrs v Leightons Ltd* [1995] STC 458*; *D v W (Osterreicher Bundesschatz intervening)* [2002] STC 1200*; *d'Ambrumenil and another v C&E Comrs Unterpertinger v Pensionsversicherungsanstalt der Arbeiter* [2005] STC 650*; *Solleveld and another v Staatssecretaris van Financiën* [2007] STC 71*; *LuP GmbH v Finanzamt Bochum-Mitte* [2008] STC 1742*.

Art 132(1)(*d*), *Belgium v De Fruytier* [2010] STC 1792*.

Art 132(1)(*e*), *Administration de l'enregistrement et des domaines v Eurodental Sàrl* (Case C-240/05) [2007] STC 275*; *VDP Dental Laboratory NV v Staatssecretaris van Financiën* [2007] STC 474*.

Art 132(1)(*f*), *Assurandør-Societetet, acting on behalf of Taksatorringen v Skatteministeriet* [2006] STC 1842*; *Stichting Centraal Begeleidingsorgaan voor de Intercollegiale Toetsing v Staatssecretaris van Financiën* [2009] STC 869*.

Art 132(1)(*g*), *Bulthuis-Griffioen v Inspector der Omzetbelasting* (Case C-453/93) [1995] STC 954*; *Gregg v Comrs of C&E* (Case C-216/97) [1999] STC 934*; *Kingscrest Associates Ltd and another v C&E Comrs* [2005] STC 1547*; *Staatssecretaris van Financiën v Stichting Kinderopvang Enschede* [2007] STC 294*.

Art 132(1)(*h*), *Staatssecretaris van Financiën v Stichting Kinderopvang Enschede* [2007] STC 294*.

Art 132(1)(*i*), *North of England Zoological Society v C&E Comrs* [1999] STC 1027*; *C&E Comrs v University of Leicester Student's Union, CA* [2002] STC 147*; *EC Commission v Federal Republic of Germany (Case C-287/00)* [2002] STC 982*; *Staatssecretaris van Financiën v Stichting Kinderopvang Enschede* [2007] STC 294*; *Stichting Regionaal Opleidingen Centrum Noord-Kennermerland/West-Friesland (Horizon College) v Staatssecretaris van Financiën* [2008] STC 2145*; *R&C Comrs v Brockenhurst College* [2014] UKUT 46 (TCC); [2014] STC 1332.

Art 132(1)(*j*), *R&C Comrs v Empowerment Enterprises Ltd* [2008] STC 1835; *Haderer v Finanzamt Wilmersdorf* [2008] STC 2171*.

Art 132(1)(*l*), *Institute of Leisure and Amenity Management v C&E Comrs* [1988] STC 602*; *Committee of Directors of Polytechnics v C&E Comrs* [1992] STC 873*; *Institute of Motor Industry v C&E Comrs* (Case C-149/97) [1998] STC 1219*; *Expert Witness Institute v C&E Comrs, CA* [2002] STC 42*; *British Association for Shooting and Conservation Ltd v R&C Comrs* [2009] STC 1421*.

Art 132(1)(*m*), *EC Commission v Spain (supported by United Kingdom, intervener)* (Case C-124/96) [1998] STC 1237*; *Swedish State v Stockholm Lindopark AB, Stockholm Lindopark AB v Swedish State* [2001] STC 103*; *Messenger Leisure Developments Ltd v Revenue and Customs Commissioners* [2005] STC 1078*; *Canterbury Hockey Club and another v R&C Comrs* [2008] STC 3351*; *Město Žamberk v Finanční ředitelství v Hradci Králové* (case C-18/12) [2014] STC 1703.

Art 132(1)(*n*), *Bournemouth Symphony Orchestra v C&E Comrs, Loughborough Festival Opera v R&C Comrs* [2007] STC 198*.

Article 133

Member States may make the granting to bodies other than those governed by public law of each exemption provided for in points (*b*), (*g*), (*h*), (*i*), (*l*), (*m*) and (*n*) of Article 132(1) subject in each individual case to one or more of the following conditions:

(*a*) the bodies in question must not systematically aim to make a profit, and any surpluses nevertheless arising must not be distributed, but must be assigned to the continuance or improvement of the services supplied;

(*b*) those bodies must be managed and administered on an essentially voluntary basis by persons who have no direct or indirect interest, either themselves or through intermediaries, in the results of the activities concerned;

(*c*) those bodies must charge prices which are approved by the public authorities or which do not exceed such approved prices or, in respect of those services not subject to approval, prices lower than those charged for similar services by commercial enterprises subject to VAT;

(*d*) the exemptions must not be likely to cause distortion of competition to the disadvantage of commercial enterprises subject to VAT.

Member States which, pursuant to Annex E of Directive 77/388/ EEC, on 1 January 1989 applied VAT to the transactions referred to in Article 132(1)(m) and (n) may also apply the conditions provided for in point (d) of the first paragraph when the said supply of goods or services by bodies governed by public law is granted exemption.

Commentary—*De Voil Indirect Tax Service* **V4.146**.

Simon's Tax Cases—*C&E Comrs v Bell Concord Educational Trust Ltd* [1989] STC 264*; *EC Commission v Spain* (Case C-124/96) [1998] STC 1237*; *LuP GmbH v Finanzamt Bochum-Mitte* [2008] STC 1742*.

Article 134

The supply of goods or services shall not be granted exemption, as provided for in points (*b*), (*g*), (*h*), (*i*), (*l*), (*m*) and (*n*) of Article 132(1), in the following cases:

(*a*) where the supply is not essential to the transactions exempted;

(*b*) where the basic purpose of the supply is to obtain additional income for the body in question through transactions which are in direct competition with those of commercial enterprises subject to VAT.

Commentary—*De Voil Indirect Tax Service* **V4.146**.

Simon's Tax Cases—*C&E Comrs v Pilgrims Language Courses Ltd* [1998] STC 784*; *Canterbury Hockey Club and another v R&C Comrs* [2008] STC 3351*.

CHAPTER 3

EXEMPTIONS FOR OTHER ACTIVITIES

Article 135

1. Member States shall exempt the following transactions:

(*a*) insurance and reinsurance transactions, including related services performed by insurance brokers and insurance agents;

(*b*) the granting and the negotiation of credit and the management of credit by the person granting it;

(*c*) the negotiation of or any dealings in credit guarantees or any other security for money and the management of credit guarantees by the person who is granting the credit;

(*d*) transactions, including negotiation, concerning deposit and current accounts, payments, transfers, debts, cheques and other negotiable instruments, but excluding debt collection;

(*e*) transactions, including negotiation, concerning currency, bank notes and coins used as legal tender, with the exception of collectors' items, that is to say, gold, silver or other metal coins or bank notes which are not normally used as legal tender or coins of numismatic interest;

(*f*) transactions, including negotiation but not management or safekeeping, in shares, interests in companies or associations, debentures and other securities, but excluding documents establishing title to goods, and the rights or securities referred to in Article 15(2);

(*g*) the management of special investment funds as defined by Member States;

(*h*) the supply at face value of postage stamps valid for use for postal services within their respective territory, fiscal stamps and other similar stamps;

(*i*) betting, lotteries and other forms of gambling, subject to the conditions and limitations laid down by each Member State;

(*j*) the supply of a building or parts thereof, and of the land on which it stands, other than the supply referred to in point (*a*) of Article 12(1);

(*k*) the supply of land which has not been built on other than the supply of building land as referred to in point (*b*) of Article 12(1);

(*l*) the leasing or letting of immovable property.

2. The following shall be excluded from the exemption provided for in point (*l*) of paragraph 1:

(*a*) the provision of accommodation, as defined in the laws of the Member States, in the hotel sector or in sectors with a similar function, including the provision of accommodation in holiday camps or on sites developed for use as camping sites;

(*b*) the letting of premises and sites for the parking of vehicles;

(*c*) the letting of permanently installed equipment and machinery;

(*d*) the hire of safes.

Member States may apply further exclusions to the scope of the exemption referred to in point (l) of paragraph 1.

Commentary—*De Voil Indirect Tax Service* **V4.111**, **V4.131**, **V4.136**.

Simon's Tax Cases—Art 135, *Ford Motor Company Ltd v R&C Comrs* [2008] STC 1016*; *RLRE Tellmer Property sro v Finanční ředitelství v Ustí nad Labem* [2009] STC 2006*; *Swiss Re Germany Holding GmbH v Finanzamt München für Körperschaften* [2010] STC 189*.

Art 135(1)(*a*), *CR Smith Glaziers (Dunfermline) Ltd v C&E Comrs* [2003] STC 419*; *Staatssecretaris van Financiën v Arthur Andersen & Co Accountants cs* [2005] STC 508*; *Assurandør-Societetet, acting on behalf of Taksatorringen v Skatteministeriet* [2006] STC 1842*; *EC Commission v Hellenic Republic* [2007] STC 194*; *JCM Beheer BV v Staatssecretaris van Financiën* [2008] STC 3360*; *InsuranceWide.com Services Ltd v R&C Comrs, R&C Comrs v Trader Media Group Ltd* [2010] STC 1572*.

Art 135(1)(*b*), *Primback Ltd v C&E Comrs* [1996] STC 757*; *Muy's en De Winter's Bouw-en Aannemingsbedrijf BV v Staatssecretaris van Financiën* [1997] STC 665*; *C&E Comrs v Civil Service Motoring Association Ltd* [1998] STC 111*; *C&E Comrs v Lloyds TSB Group Ltd* [1998] STC 528*; *Ludwig v Finanzamt Luckenwalde* [2008] STC 1640*.

Art 135(1)(*c*), *Velvet & Steel Immobilien und Handels GmbH v Finanzamt Hamburg-Eimsbüttel* [2008] STC 922*.

Art 135(1)(*d*), *Sinclair Collis Ltd v C&E Comrs* [2003] STC 898*; *Stichting 'Goed Wonen' v Staatssecretaris van Financiën* [2003] STC 1137*; *Belgian State v Temco Europe SA* [2005] STC 1451*; *Fonden Marselisborg Lystbådehavn v Skatteministeriet* [2006] STC 1467*; *Abbey National plc v C&E Comrs* [2006] STC 1961*; *Scottish Exhibition Centre Ltd v R&C Comrs* [2008] STC 967*.

Art 135(1)(*f*) *F&I Services Ltd v C&E Comrs* [2000] STC 364*; *CSC Financial Services Ltd v C&E Comrs (Case C-235/00)* [2002] STC 57*; *C&E Comrs v Electronic Data Systems Ltd* [2003] STC 688*; *Bookit Ltd v R&C Comrs* [2006] STC 1367*; *Skatteverket v AB SKF* [2010] STC 419; *Finanzamt Frankfurt am Main V-Hochst v Deutsche Bank AG* (Case C-44/11) [2012] STC 1951.

Art 135(1)(*g*), *Abbey National plc v C&E Comrs* [2006] STC 1136*; *JP Morgan Fleming Claverhouse Investment Trust plc v R&C Comrs* [2008] STC 1180*; *Finanzamt Frankfurt am Main V-Hochst v Deutsche Bank AG* (Case C-44/11) [2012] STC 1951; *Wheels Common Investment Fund Trustees Ltd and others v R&C Comrs* (Case C-424/11) [2014] STC 49.

Art 135(1)(*i*), *R v Ryan* [1994] STC 446*; *C&E Comrs v Feehan* [1995] STC 75*; *Ivory & Sime Trustlink Ltd v C&E Comrs* [1995] STC 708*; *United Utilities plc v C&E Comrs* [2006] STC 1423*; *Finanzamt Gladbeck v Linneweber, Finanzamt Herne-West v Akritidis* [2008] STC 1069*; *R&C Comrs v Rank Group plc* [2009] STC 2304*; *Leo-Libera GmbH v Finanzamt Buchholz in der Nordheide* [2010] STC 1950; *Metropol Spielstatten Unternehmergesellschaft (haftungsbeschrankt) v Finanzamt Hamburg-Bergedorf* (Case C-440/12) [2014] STC 505.

Art 135(1)(*j*), *Don Bosco Onroerend Goed BV v Staatsecretaris van Financiën* [2010] STC 476*.

Art 135(1)(*k*), *C&E Comrs v Parkinson* [1989] STC 51*; *Gemeente Emmen v Belastingdienst Grote Ondernemingen* (Case C-468/93) [1996] STC 496*.

Art 135(1)(*l*), *Ministero della Finanze—Ufficio IVA di Milano v Co.GE.P. Srl* [2008] STC 2744*; *Walderdorff v Finanzamt Waldviertel* [2008] STC 3079*; *Holland (t/a The Studio Hair Company) v R&C Comrs, Vigdor Ltd v R&C Comrs* [2009] STC 150*; *R&C Comrs v UK Storage Company (SW) Ltd* [2012] UKUT 359 (TCC), [2013] STC 361; *Finnamore (trading as Hanbidge Storage Services) v R&C Comrs* [2014] UKUT 336 (TCC), [2014] STC 2754.

Art 135(2)(*a*), *Lubbock Fine & Co v C&E Comrs* (Case C-63/92) [1994] STC 101*; *Blasi v Finanzamt München I* (Case C-346/95) [1998] STC 336*.

Art 135(2)(*b*), *Skatteministeriet v Henriksen* [1990] STC 768*; *Fonden Marselisborg Lystbådehavn v Skatteministeriet* [2006] STC 1467*.

Article 136

Member States shall exempt the following transactions:

(*a*) the supply of goods used solely for an activity exempted under Articles 132, 135, 371, 375, 376 and 377, Article 378 (2), Article 379(2) and [Articles 380 to 390b], if those goods have not given rise to deductibility;

(*b*) the supply of goods on the acquisition or application of which VAT was not deductible, pursuant to Article 176.

Amendments—In Article 136(*a*), the words substituted for "Articles 380 to 390" by Council Directive 2009/162/EU art 1(9) with effect from 15 January 2010 (OJ L 10, 15.1.2010, p 14).

Simon's Tax Cases—*Bawaria Motors Sp z oo v Minister Finansow* (C-160/11) [2012] STC 2088.

Article 137

1. Member States may allow taxable persons a right of option for taxation in respect of the following transactions:

(*a*) the financial transactions referred to in points (*b*) to (*g*) of Article 135(1);

(*b*) the supply of a building or of parts thereof, and of the land on which the building stands, other than the supply referred to in point (*a*) of Article 12(1);

(*c*) the supply of land which has not been built on other than the supply of building land referred to in point (*b*) of Article 12(1);

(*d*) the leasing or letting of immovable property.

2. Member States shall lay down the detailed rules governing exercise of the option under paragraph 1.

Member States may restrict the scope of that right of option.

Commentary—*De Voil Indirect Tax Service* **V4.115**.

Simon's Tax Cases—*Belgocodex SA v Belgium* [2000] STC 351*; *Stichting 'Goed Wonen' v Staatssecretaris van Financiën* [2003] STC 1137*; *Administration de l'enregistrement et des domains, État du grand-duché de Luxembourg v Vermietungsgesellschaft Objekt Kirchberg SARL* [2005] STC 1345*; *Marlow Gardner & Cooke Ltd Directors' Pension Scheme v R&C Comrs* [2006] STC 2014; *Proceedings brought by Uudenkaupungin kaupunki* [2008] STC 2329*.

CHAPTER 4

EXEMPTIONS FOR INTRA-COMMUNITY TRANSACTIONS

SECTION 1

Exemptions related to the supply of goods

Article 138

1. Member States shall exempt the supply of goods dispatched or transported to a destination outside their respective territory but within the Community, by or on behalf of the vendor or the person acquiring the goods, for another taxable person, or for a non-taxable legal person acting as such in a Member State other than that in which dispatch or transport of the goods began.

2. In addition to the supply of goods referred to in paragraph 1, Member States shall exempt the following transactions:

(*a*) the supply of new means of transport, dispatched or transported to the customer at a destination outside their respective territory but within the Community, by or on behalf of the

VAT EC

vendor or the customer, for taxable persons, or non-taxable legal persons, whose intra-Community acquisitions of goods are not subject to VAT pursuant to Article 3(1), or for any other non-taxable person;

(*b*) the supply of products subject to excise duty, dispatched or transported to a destination outside their respective territory but within the Community, to the customer, by or on behalf of the vendor or the customer, for taxable persons, or non-taxable legal persons, whose intra-Community acquisitions of goods other than products subject to excise duty are not subject to VAT pursuant to Article 3(1), where those products have been dispatched or transported in accordance with Article 7(4) and (5) or Article 16 of Directive 92/12/EEC;

(*c*) the supply of goods, consisting in a transfer to another Member State, which would have been entitled to exemption under paragraph 1 and points (*a*) and (*b*) if it had been made on behalf of another taxable person.

Simon's Tax Cases—*EMAG Handel Eder OHG v Finanzlandesdirektion für Kärnten* [2007] STC 1461*; *X v Skatteverket* (Case C-84/09) [2011] STC 189; *Mecsek-Gabona Kft v Nemzeti Ado-es Vamhivatal Del-dunantuli Regionalis Ado Foigazgatosaga* (Case C-273/11) [2013] STC 171.

Article 139

1. The exemption provided for in Article 138(1) shall not apply to the supply of goods carried out by taxable persons who are covered by the exemption for small enterprises provided for in Articles 282 to 292.

Nor shall that exemption apply to the supply of goods to taxable persons, or non-taxable legal persons, whose intra-Community acquisitions of goods are not subject to VAT pursuant to Article 3(1).

2. The exemption provided for in Article 138(2)(*b*) shall not apply to the supply of products subject to excise duty by taxable persons who are covered by the exemption for small enterprises provided for in Articles 282 to 292.

3. The exemption provided for in Article 138(1) and (2)(*b*) and (*c*) shall not apply to the supply of goods subject to VAT in accordance with the margin scheme provided for in Articles 312 to 325 or the special arrangements for sales by public auction.

The exemption provided for in Article 138(1) and (2)(c) shall not apply to the supply of second-hand means of transport, as defined in Article 327(3), subject to VAT in accordance with the transitional arrangements for second-hand means of transport.

Simon's Tax Cases—*EMAG Handel Eder OHG v Finanzlandesdirektion für Kärnten* [2007] STC 1461*.

SECTION 2

Exemptions for intra-community acquisitions of goods

Article 140

Member States shall exempt the following transactions:

(*a*) the intra-Community acquisition of goods the supply of which by taxable persons would in all circumstances be exempt within their respective territory;

[(*b*) the intra-Community acquisition of goods the importation of which would in all circumstances be exempt under points (*a*), (*b*) and (*c*) and (*e*) to (*l*) of Article 143(1);]

(*c*) the intra-Community acquisition of goods where, pursuant to Articles 170 and 171, the person acquiring the goods would in all circumstances be entitled to full reimbursement of the VAT due under Article 2(1)(*b*).

Amendments—Point (*b*) substituted by Council Directive 2009/69/EC art 1 with effect from 24 July 2009. See OJ L 175, 4.7.2009 p 12).

Article 141

Each Member State shall take specific measures to ensure that VAT is not charged on the intra-Community acquisition of goods within its territory, made in accordance with Article 40, where the following conditions are met:

(*a*) the acquisition of goods is made by a taxable person who is not established in the Member State concerned but is identified for VAT purposes in another Member State;

(*b*) the acquisition of goods is made for the purposes of the subsequent supply of those goods, in the Member State concerned, by the taxable person referred to in point (*a*);

(*c*) the goods thus acquired by the taxable person referred to in point (*a*) are directly dispatched or transported, from a Member State other than that in which he is identified for VAT purposes, to the person for whom he is to carry out the subsequent supply;

(*d*) the person to whom the subsequent supply is to be made is another taxable person, or a non-taxable legal person, who is identified for VAT purposes in the Member State concerned;

(*e*) the person referred to in point (*d*) has been designated in accordance with Article 197 as liable for payment of the VAT due on the supply carried out by the taxable person who is not established in the Member State in which the tax is due.

SECTION 3

Exemptions for certain transport services

Article 142

Member States shall exempt the supply of intra-Community transport of goods to and from the islands making up the autonomous regions of the Azores and Madeira, as well as the supply of transport of goods between those islands.

CHAPTER 5

EXEMPTIONS ON IMPORTATION

Article 143

[1.] Member States shall exempt the following transactions:

(*a*) the final importation of goods of which the supply by a taxable person would in all circumstances be exempt within their respective territory;

(*b*) the final importation of goods governed by Council Directives 69/169/EEC (;1), 83/181/EEC (;2) and 2006/79/ EC (;3);

(*c*) the final importation of goods, in free circulation from a third territory forming part of the Community customs territory, which would be entitled to exemption under point (*b*) if they had been imported within the meaning of the first paragraph of Article 30;

(*d*) the importation of goods dispatched or transported from a third territory or a third country into a Member State other than that in which the dispatch or transport of the goods ends, where the supply of such goods by the importer designated or recognised under Article 201 as liable for payment of VAT is exempt under Article 138;

(*e*) the reimportation, by the person who exported them, of goods in the state in which they were exported, where those goods are exempt from customs duties;

(*f*) the importation, under diplomatic and consular arrangements, of goods which are exempt from customs duties;

[(*fa*) the importation of goods by the European Community, the European Atomic Energy Community, the European Central Bank or the European Investment Bank, or by the bodies set up by the Communities to which the Protocol of 8 April 1965 on the privileges and immunities of the European Communities applies, within the limits and under the conditions of that Protocol and the agreements for its implementation or the headquarters agreements, in so far as it does not lead to distortion of competition;]

[(*g*) the importation of goods by international bodies, other than those referred to in point (fa), recognised as such by the public authorities of the host Member State, or by members of such bodies, within the limits and under the conditions laid down by the international conventions establishing the bodies or by headquarters agreements;]

(*h*) the importation of goods, into Member States party to the North Atlantic Treaty, by the armed forces of other States party to that Treaty for the use of those forces or the civilian staff accompanying them or for supplying their messes or canteens where such forces take part in the common defence effort;

(*i*) the importation of goods by the armed forces of the United Kingdom stationed in the island of Cyprus pursuant to the Treaty of Establishment concerning the Republic of Cyprus, dated 16 August 1960, which are for the use of those forces or the civilian staff accompanying them or for supplying their messes or canteens;

(*j*) the importation into ports, by sea fishing undertakings, of their catches, unprocessed or after undergoing preservation for marketing but before being supplied;

(*k*) the importation of gold by central banks;

[(*l*) the importation of gas through a natural gas system or any network connected to such a system or fed in from a vessel transporting gas into a natural gas system or any upstream pipeline network, of electricity or of heat or cooling energy through heating or cooling networks].

[2. The exemption provided for in paragraph 1(*d*) shall apply in cases when the importation of goods is followed by the supply of goods exempted under Article 138(1) and (2)(*c*) only if at the time of importation the importer has provided to the competent authorities of the Member State of importation at least the following information:

(*a*) his VAT identification number issued in the Member State of importation or the VAT identification number of his tax representative, liable for payment of the VAT, issued in the Member State of importation;

(*b*)the VAT identification number of the customer, to whom the goods are supplied in accordance with Article 138(1), issued in another Member State, or his own VAT identification number issued in the Member State in which the dispatch or transport of the goods ends when the goods are subject to a transfer in accordance with Article 138(2)(*c*);

(*c*) the evidence that the imported goods are intended to be transported or dispatched from the Member State of importation to another Member State.

VAT EC

However, Member States may provide that the evidence referred to in point (*c*) be indicated to the competent authorities only upon request.]

Simon's Tax Cases—*Ministère Public and Ministre des Finances du Royaume de Belgique v Ledoux* [1991] STC 553*.

Notes—(1) Council Directive 69/169/EEC of 28 May 1969 on the harmonisation of provisions laid down by Law, Regulation or Administrative Action relating to exemption from turnover tax and excise duty on imports in international travel (OJ L 133, 4.6.1969, p. 6). Directive as last amended by Directive 2005/93/EC (OJ L 346, 29.12.2005, p. 16).

(2) Council Directive 83/181/EEC of 28 March 1983 determining the scope of Article 14(1)(*d*) of Directive 77/388/EEC as regards exemption from value added tax on the final importation of certain goods (OJ L 105, 23.4.1983, p. 38). Directive as last amended by the 1994 Act of Accession.

(3) Council Directive 2006/79/EC of 5 October 2006 on the exemption from taxes of imports of small consignments of goods of a non-commercial character from third countries (codified version) (OJ L 286, 17.10.2006, p. 15).

Amendments—Introductory words numbered as para 1, and para 2 inserted, by Council Directive 2009/69/EC art 1 with effect from 24 July 2009. See OJ L 175, 4.7.2009 p 12).

In para 1, point (*fa*) inserted and point (*g*) substituted by Council Directive 2009/162/EU art 1(10) with effect from 15 January 2010 (OJ L 10, 15.1.2010, p 14). Points (*g*) and (*l*) previously read as follows:

"(*g*) the importation of goods by international bodies recognised as such by the public authorities of the host Member State, or by members of such bodies, within the limits and under the conditions laid down by the international conventions establishing the bodies or by headquarters agreements;"

"(*l*) the importation of gas through the natural gas distribution system, or of electricity.".

Article 144

Member States shall exempt the supply of services relating to the importation of goods where the value of such services is included in the taxable amount in accordance with Article 86(1)(*b*).

Article 145

1. The Commission shall, where appropriate, as soon as possible, present to the Council proposals designed to delimit the scope of the exemptions provided for in Articles 143 and 144 and to lay down the detailed rules for their implementation.

2. Pending the entry into force of the rules referred to in paragraph 1, Member States may maintain their national provisions in force.

Member States may adapt their national provisions so as to minimise distortion of competition and, in particular, to prevent non-taxation or double taxation within the Community.

Member States may use whatever administrative procedures they consider most appropriate to achieve exemption.

3. Member States shall notify to the Commission, which shall inform the other Member States accordingly, the provisions of national law which are in force, in so far as these have not already been notified, and those which they adopt pursuant to paragraph 2.

CHAPTER 6

EXEMPTIONS ON EXPORTATION

Article 146

1. Member States shall exempt the following transactions:

(*a*) the supply of goods dispatched or transported to a destination outside the Community by or on behalf of the vendor;

(*b*) the supply of goods dispatched or transported to a destination outside the Community by or on behalf of a customer not established within their respective territory, with the exception of goods transported by the customer himself for the equipping, fuelling and provisioning of pleasure boats and private aircraft or any other means of transport for private use;

(*c*) the supply of goods to approved bodies which export them out of the Community as part of their humanitarian, charitable or teaching activities outside the Community;

(*d*) the supply of services consisting in work on movable property acquired or imported for the purpose of undergoing such work within the Community, and dispatched or transported out of the Community by the supplier, by the customer if not established within their respective territory or on behalf of either of them;

(*e*) the supply of services, including transport and ancillary transactions, but excluding the supply of services exempted in accordance with Articles 132 and 135, where these are directly connected with the exportation or importation of goods covered by Article 61 and Article 157(1)(*a*).

2. The exemption provided for in point (*c*) of paragraph 1 may be granted by means of a refund of the VAT.

Simon's Tax Cases—Art 146, *BDV Hungary Trading Kft, in liquidation, v Nemzeti Adó- és Vámhivatal Közép-magyarországi Regionális Adó Főigazgatósága* (Case C-563/12) [2014] STC 1015.

Art 146(1)(*e*), *R&C Comrs v EB Central Services Ltd and another* [2008] STC 2209*; *Navicon SA v Administración del Estrado* [2008] STC 2693*; *Netto Supermarket GmbH & Co OHG v Finanzamt Machin* [2008] STC 3280*.

Article 147

1. Where the supply of goods referred to in point (*b*) of Article 146(1) relates to goods to be carried in the personal luggage of travellers, the exemption shall apply only if the following conditions are met:

(*a*) the traveller is not established within the Community;

(*b*) the goods are transported out of the Community before the end of the third month following that in which the supply takes place;

(*c*) the total value of the supply, including VAT, is more than EUR 175 or the equivalent in national currency, fixed annually by applying the conversion rate obtaining on the first working day of October with effect from 1 January of the following year.

However, Member States may exempt a supply with a total value of less than the amount specified in point (c) of the first subparagraph.

2. For the purposes of paragraph 1, 'a traveller who is not established within the Community' shall mean a traveller whose permanent address or habitual residence is not located within the Community. In that case 'permanent address or habitual residence' means the place entered as such in a passport, identity card or other document recognised as an identity document by the Member State within whose territory the supply takes place.

Proof of exportation shall be furnished by means of the invoice or other document in lieu thereof, endorsed by the customs office of exit from the Community.

Each Member State shall send to the Commission specimens of the stamps it uses for the endorsement referred to in the second subparagraph. The Commission shall forward that information to the tax authorities of the other Member States.

Simon's Tax Cases—*Netto Supermarket GmbH & Co OHG v Finanzamt Machin* [2008] STC 3280*.

CHAPTER 7

EXEMPTIONS RELATED TO INTERNATIONAL TRANSPORT

Article 148

Member States shall exempt the following transactions:

(*a*) the supply of goods for the fuelling and provisioning of vessels used for navigation on the high seas and carrying passengers for reward or used for the purpose of commercial, industrial or fishing activities, or for rescue or assistance at sea, or for inshore fishing, with the exception, in the case of vessels used for inshore fishing, of ships' provisions;

(*b*) the supply of goods for the fuelling and provisioning of fighting ships, falling within the combined nomenclature (CN) code 8906 10 00, leaving their territory and bound for ports or anchorages outside the Member State concerned;

(*c*) the supply, modification, repair, maintenance, chartering and hiring of the vessels referred to in point (*a*), and the supply, hiring, repair and maintenance of equipment, including fishing equipment, incorporated or used therein;

(*d*) the supply of services other than those referred to in point (*c*), to meet the direct needs of the vessels referred to in point (*a*) or of their cargoes;

(*e*) the supply of goods for the fuelling and provisioning of aircraft used by airlines operating for reward chiefly on international routes;

(*f*) the supply, modification, repair, maintenance, chartering and hiring of the aircraft referred to in point (*e*), and the supply, hiring, repair and maintenance of equipment incorporated or used therein;

(*g*) the supply of services, other than those referred to in point (*f*), to meet the direct needs of the aircraft referred to in point (*e*) or of their cargoes.

Simon's Tax Cases—Art 148(*c*), *R&C Comrs v Stone, The Kei* [2008] STC 2501*; *Navicon SA v Administración del Estrado* [2008] STC 2693*.

Art 148(*g*), *R&C Comrs v EB Central Services Ltd* [2008] STC 2209*.

Article 149

Portugal may treat sea and air transport between the islands making up the autonomous regions of the Azores and Madeira and between those regions and the mainland as international transport.

Article 150

1. The Commission shall, where appropriate, as soon as possible, present to the Council proposals designed to delimit the scope of the exemptions provided for in Article 148 and to lay down the detailed rules for their implementation.

2. Pending the entry into force of the provisions referred to in paragraph 1, Member States may limit the scope of the exemptions provided for in points (*a*) and (*b*) of Article 148.

CHAPTER 8

EXEMPTIONS RELATING TO CERTAIN TRANSACTIONS TREATED AS EXPORTS

Article 151

1. Member States shall exempt the following transactions:

(*a*) the supply of goods or services under diplomatic and consular arrangements;

[(*aa*)the supply of goods or services to the European Community, the European Atomic Energy Community, the European Central Bank or the European Investment Bank, or to the bodies set up by the Communities to which the Protocol of 8 April 1965 on the privileges and immunities of the European Communities applies, within the limits and under the conditions of that Protocol and the agreements for its implementation or the headquarters agreements, in so far as it does not lead to distortion of competition;]

[(*b*) the supply of goods or services to international bodies, other than those referred to in point (aa), recognised as such by the public authorities of the host Member States, and to members of such bodies, within the limits and under the conditions laid down by the international conventions establishing the bodies or by headquarters agreements;]

(*c*) the supply of goods or services within a Member State which is a party to the North Atlantic Treaty, intended either for the armed forces of other States party to that Treaty for the use of those forces, or of the civilian staff accompanying them, or for supplying their messes or canteens when such forces take part in the common defence effort;

(*d*) the supply of goods or services to another Member State, intended for the armed forces of any State which is a party to the North Atlantic Treaty, other than the Member State of destination itself, for the use of those forces, or of the civilian staff accompanying them, or for supplying their messes or canteens when such forces take part in the common defence effort;

(*e*) the supply of goods or services to the armed forces of the United Kingdom stationed in the island of Cyprus pursuant to the Treaty of Establishment concerning the Republic of Cyprus, dated 16 August 1960, which are for the use of those forces, or of the civilian staff accompanying them, or for supplying their messes or canteens.

Pending the adoption of common tax rules, the exemptions provided for in the first subparagraph shall be subject to the limitations laid down by the host Member State.

2. In cases where the goods are not dispatched or transported out of the Member State in which the supply takes place, and in the case of services, the exemption may be granted by means of a refund of the VAT.

Amendments—In para (1), point (*aa*) inserted and point (*b*) substituted, by Council Directive 2009/162/EU art 1(11) with effect from 15 January 2010 (OJ L 10, 15.1.2010, p 14).

Simon's Tax Cases—Art 151(1)(c), *Able UK Ltd v R&C Comrs* [2011] UKUT 193 (TCC)[2011] STC 1110

Article 152

Member States shall exempt the supply of gold to central banks.

CHAPTER 9

EXEMPTIONS FOR THE SUPPLY OF SERVICES BY INTERMEDIARIES

Article 153

Member States shall exempt the supply of services by intermediaries, acting in the name and on behalf of another person, where they take part in the transactions referred to in Chapters 6, 7 and 8, or of transactions carried out outside the Community.

The exemption referred to in the first paragraph shall not apply to travel agents who, in the name and on behalf of travellers, supply services which are carried out in other Member States.

CHAPTER 10

EXEMPTIONS FOR TRANSACTIONS RELATING TO INTERNATIONAL TRADE

SECTION 1

Customs warehouses, warehouses other than customs warehouses and similar arrangements

Article 154

For the purposes of this Section, 'warehouses other than customs warehouses' shall, in the case of products subject to excise duty, mean the places defined as tax warehouses by Article 4(*b*) of Directive 92/12/EEC and, in the case of products not subject to excise duty, the places defined as such by the Member States.

Article 155

Without prejudice to other Community tax provisions, Member States may, after consulting the VAT Committee, take special measures designed to exempt all or some of the transactions referred to in this Section, provided that those measures are not aimed at final use or consumption and that the amount of VAT due on cessation of the arrangements or situations referred to in this Section corresponds to the amount of tax which would have been due had each of those transactions been taxed within their territory.

Article 156

1. Member States may exempt the following transactions:
   (*a*) the supply of goods which are intended to be presented to customs and, where applicable, placed in temporary storage;
   (*b*) the supply of goods which are intended to be placed in a free zone or in a free warehouse;
   (*c*) the supply of goods which are intended to be placed under customs warehousing arrangements or inward processing arrangements;
   (*d*) the supply of goods which are intended to be admitted into territorial waters in order to be incorporated into drilling or production platforms, for purposes of the construction, repair, maintenance, alteration or fitting-out of such platforms, or to link such drilling or production platforms to the mainland;
   (*e*) the supply of goods which are intended to be admitted into territorial waters for the fuelling and provisioning of drilling or production platforms.

2. The places referred to in paragraph 1 shall be those defined as such by the Community customs provisions in force.

Article 157

1. Member States may exempt the following transactions:
   (*a*) the importation of goods which are intended to be placed under warehousing arrangements other than customs warehousing;
   (*b*) the supply of goods which are intended to be placed, within their territory, under warehousing arrangements other than customs warehousing.

2. Member States may not provide for warehousing arrangements other than customs warehousing for goods which are not subject to excise duty where those goods are intended to be supplied at the retail stage.

Article 158

1. By way of derogation from Article 157(2), Member States may provide for warehousing arrangements other than customs warehousing in the following cases:
   (*a*) where the goods are intended for tax-free shops, for the purposes of the supply of goods to be carried in the personal luggage of travellers taking flights or sea crossings to third territories or third countries, where that supply is exempt pursuant to point (*b*) of Article 146(1);
   (*b*) where the goods are intended for taxable persons, for the purposes of carrying out supplies to travellers on board an aircraft or a ship in the course of a flight or sea crossing where the place of arrival is situated outside the Community;
   (*c*) where the goods are intended for taxable persons, for the purposes of carrying out supplies which are exempt from VAT pursuant to Article 151.

2. Where Member States exercise the option of exemption provided for in point (*a*) of paragraph 1, they shall take the measures necessary to ensure the correct and straightforward application of this exemption and to prevent any evasion, avoidance or abuse.

3. For the purposes of point (*a*) of paragraph 1, 'tax-free shop' shall mean any establishment which is situated within an airport or port and which fulfils the conditions laid down by the competent public authorities.

Article 159

Member States may exempt the supply of services relating to the supply of goods referred to in Article 156, Article 157(1)(*b*) or Article 158.

Article 160

1. Member States may exempt the following transactions:
   (*a*) the supply of goods or services carried out in the locations referred to in Article 156(1), where one of the situations specified therein still applies within their territory;
   (*b*) the supply of goods or services carried out in the locations referred to in Article 157(1)(*b*) or Article 158, where one of the situations specified in Article 157(1)(*b*) or in Article 158 (1) still applies within their territory.

2. Where Member States exercise the option under point (*a*) of paragraph 1 in respect of transactions effected in customs warehouses, they shall take the measures necessary to provide for warehousing arrangements other than customs warehousing under which point (*b*) of paragraph 1 may be applied to the same transactions when they concern goods listed in Annex V and are carried out in warehouses other than customs warehouses.

Article 161

Member States may exempt supply of the following goods and of services relating thereto:

(*a*) the supply of goods referred to in the first paragraph of Article 30 while they remain covered by arrangements for temporary importation with total exemption from import duty or by external transit arrangements;

(*b*) the supply of goods referred to in the second paragraph of Article 30 while they remain covered by the internal Community transit procedure referred to in Article 276.

Article 162

Where Member States exercise the option provided for in this Section, they shall take the measures necessary to ensure that the intra-Community acquisition of goods intended to be placed under one of the arrangements or in one of the situations referred to in Article 156, Article 157(1)(*b*) or Article 158 is covered by the same provisions as the supply of goods carried out within their territory under the same conditions.

Article 163

If the goods cease to be covered by the arrangements or situations referred to in this Section, thus giving rise to importation for the purposes of Article 61, the Member State of importation shall take the measures necessary to prevent double taxation.

SECTION 2

Transactions exempted with a view to export and in the framework of trade between the Member States

Article 164

1. Member States may, after consulting the VAT Committee, exempt the following transactions carried out by, or intended for, a taxable person up to an amount equal to the value of the exports carried out by that person during the preceding 12 months:

(*a*) intra-Community acquisitions of goods made by the taxable person, and imports for and supplies of goods to the taxable person, with a view to their exportation from the Community as they are or after processing;

(*b*) supplies of services linked with the export business of the taxable person.

2. Where Member States exercise the option of exemption under paragraph 1, they shall, after consulting the VAT Committee, apply that exemption also to transactions relating to supplies carried out by the taxable person, in accordance with the conditions specified in Article 138, up to an amount equal to the value of the supplies carried out by that person, in accordance with the same conditions, during the preceding 12 months.

Article 165

Member States may set a common maximum amount for transactions which they exempt pursuant to Article 164.

SECTION 3

Provisions common to Sections 1 and 2

Article 166

The Commission shall, where appropriate, as soon as possible, present to the Council proposals concerning common arrangements for applying VAT to the transactions referred to in Sections 1 and 2.

TITLE X
DEDUCTIONS

CHAPTER 1
ORIGIN AND SCOPE OF RIGHT OF DEDUCTION

Article 167

A right of deduction shall arise at the time the deductible tax becomes chargeable.

Simon's Tax Cases—*Proceedings brought by Uudenkaupungin kaupunki* [2008] STC 2329*.

[Article 167a

Member States may provide within an optional scheme that the right of deduction of a taxable person whose VAT solely becomes chargeable in accordance with Article 66(b) be postponed until the VAT on the goods or services supplied to him has been paid to his supplier.

Member States which apply the optional scheme referred to in the first paragraph shall set a threshold for taxable persons using the scheme within their territory, based on the annual turnover of the taxable person calculated in accordance with Article 288. That threshold may not be higher than EUR 500 000 or the equivalent in national currency. Member States may increase that threshold up to EUR 2 000 000 or the equivalent in national currency after consulting the VAT Committee. However, such consultation of the VAT Committee shall not be required for Member States which applied a threshold higher than EUR 500 000 or the equivalent in national currency on 31 December 2012.

Member States shall inform the VAT Committee of national legislative measures adopted pursuant to the first paragraph.][1]

Amendments—[1] Article inserted by Council Directive 2010/45 art 1(7) with effect from 11 August 2010 (OJ L 189, 22.7.2010, p 1). The deadline for implementation of Directive 2010/45/EU is 31 December 2012.

Article 168

In so far as the goods and services are used for the purposes of the taxed transactions of a taxable person, the taxable person shall be entitled, in the Member State in which he carries out these transactions, to deduct the following from the VAT which he is liable to pay:

(*a*) the VAT due or paid in that Member State in respect of supplies to him of goods or services, carried out or to be carried out by another taxable person;

(*b*) the VAT due in respect of transactions treated as supplies of goods or services pursuant to Article 18(*a*) and Article 27;

(*c*) the VAT due in respect of intra-Community acquisitions of goods pursuant to Article 2(1)(*b*)(i);

(*d*) the VAT due on transactions treated as intra-Community acquisitions in accordance with Articles 21 and 22;

(*e*) the VAT due or paid in respect of the importation of goods into that Member State.

Simon's Tax Cases—*Skatteverket v AB SKF* [2010] STC 419; *Eon Asset Menidjmunt OOD v Direktor na Direktsia 'Obzhalvane I upravlenie na izpalnenieto' —Varna pr Tsentralno upravlenie na Natsionalnata agentsia za prihodite* (Case C-118/11) [2012] STC 982; *Kopalnia Odrykwokowa Polski Trawertyn P Granatowicz, M Wasiewicz, spolka jawna v Dyrektor Izby Skarbowej w Poznaniu* (Case C-280/10) [2012] STC 1085; *Klub OOD v Direktsia 'Obzhalvane I upravlenie na izpalnenieto'—Varna pri Tsentralno upravlenie na Natsionalnata agentsia za prihodite* (Case C-153/11) [2012] STC 1129; *Bonik EOOD v Direktor na Direktsia "Obzhalvane I upravlenie na izpalnenieto" - Varna pri Tsentralno upravlenie na Natsionalnata agentsia za prihodite* (Case C-285/11) [2013] STC 773; *FIRIN OOD v Direktor na Direktsia 'Obzhalvane i danachno-osiguritelna praktika' Veliko Tarnovo pri Tsentralno upravlenie na Natsionalnata agentsia za prihodite* (Case C-107/13) [2014] STC 1581.

[168a

1. In the case of immovable property forming part of the business assets of a taxable person and used both for purposes of the taxable person's business and for his private use or that of his staff, or, more generally, for purposes other than those of his business, VAT on expenditure related to this property shall be deductible in accordance with the principles set out in Articles 167, 168, 169 and 173 only up to the proportion of the property's use for purposes of the taxable person's business.

By way of derogation from Article 26, changes in the proportion of use of immovable property referred to in the first subparagraph shall be taken into account in accordance with the principles provided for in Articles 184 to 192 as applied in the respective Member State.

2. Member States may also apply paragraph 1 in relation to VAT on expenditure related to other goods forming part of the business assets as they specify.]

Amendments—Article 168a inserted by Council Directive 2009/162/EU art 1(12) with effect from 15 January 2010 (OJ L 10, 15.1.2010, p 14).

Article 169

In addition to the deduction referred to in Article 168, the taxable person shall be entitled to deduct the VAT referred to therein in so far as the goods and services are used for the purposes of the following:

(*a*) transactions relating to the activities referred to in the second subparagraph of Article 9(1), carried out outside the Member State in which that tax is due or paid, in respect of which VAT would be deductible if they had been carried out within that Member State;

(*b*) transactions which are exempt pursuant to Articles 138, 142 or 144, Articles 146 to 149, Articles 151, 152, 153 or 156, Article 157(1)(*b*), Articles 158 to 161 or Article 164;

(*c*) transactions which are exempt pursuant to points (*a*) to (*f*) of Article 135(1), where the customer is established outside the Community or where those transactions relate directly to goods to be exported out of the Community.

Simon's Tax Cases—Art 169(*c*), *European Commission v United Kingdom* [2010] STC 2364..

Article 170

[All taxable persons who, within the meaning of Article 1 of Directive 86/560/EEC, Article 2(1) and Article 3 of Directive 2008/9/EC and Article 171 of this Directive, are not established in the Member State in which they purchase goods and services or import goods subject to VAT shall be entitled to obtain a refund of that VAT insofar as the goods and services are used for the purposes of the following:][1]

(*a*) transactions referred to in Article 169;

(*b*) transactions for which the tax is solely payable by the customer in accordance with Articles 194 to 197 or Article 199.

Amendments—[1] Introductory sentence substituted by Council Directive 2008/8/EC art 2(3) with effect from 1 January 2010 (OJ L 44, 20.2.2008 p 11). Text previously read as follows—

VAT EC

> "All taxable persons who, within the meaning of Article 1 of Directive 79/1072/EEC, Article 1 of Directive 86/560/EEC and Article 171 of this Directive, are not established in the Member State in which they purchase goods and services or import goods subject to VAT shall be entitled to obtain a refund of that VAT in so far as the goods and services are used for the purposes of the following:".

Article 171

[1. VAT shall be refunded to taxable persons who are not established in the Member State in which they purchase goods and services or import goods subject to VAT but who are established in another Member State, in accordance with the detailed rules laid down in Directive 2008/9/EC.[1]

The taxable persons referred to in Article 1 of Directive 79/1072/ EEC shall also, for the purposes of applying that Directive, be regarded as taxable persons who are not established in the Member State concerned where, in the Member State in which they purchase goods and services or import goods subject to VAT, they have only carried out the supply of goods or services to a person designated in accordance with Articles 194 to 197 or Article 199 as liable for payment of VAT.

2. VAT shall be refunded to taxable persons who are not established within the territory of the Community in accordance with the detailed implementing rules laid down in Directive 86/ 560/EEC.

The taxable persons referred to in Article 1 of Directive 86/560/ EEC shall also, for the purposes of applying that Directive, be regarded as taxable persons who are not established in the Community where, in the Member State in which they purchase goods and services or import goods subject to VAT, they have only carried out the supply of goods or services to a person designated in accordance with Articles 194 to 197 or Article 199 as liable for payment of VAT.

[3. Directive 86/560/EEC shall not apply to:

(*a*) amounts of VAT which according to the legislation of the Member State of refund have been incorrectly invoiced;

(*b*) invoiced amounts of VAT in respect of supplies of goods the supply of which is, or may be, exempt pursuant to Article 138 or Article 146(1)(*b*).][1]

Amendments—[1] Paras 1, 3 substituted by Council Directive 2008/8/EC art 2(4) with effect from 1 January 2010 (OJ L 44, 20.2.2008 p 11). Text previously read as follows—

"1. VAT shall be refunded to taxable persons who are not established in the Member State in which they purchase goods and services or import goods subject to VAT but who are established in another Member State, in accordance with the detailed implementing rules laid down in Directive 79/1072/EEC."

"3. Directives 79/1072/EEC[(1)] and 86/560/EEC[(2)] shall not apply to the supply of goods which is, or may be, exempted pursuant to Article 138 where the goods thus supplied are dispatched or transported by or on behalf of the person acquiring the goods."

Notes to former para 3 previously read as follows—

"(1) Eighth Council Directive 79/1072/EEC of 6 December 1979 on the harmonization of the laws of the Member States relating to turnover taxes — Arrangements for the refund of value added tax to taxable persons not established in the territory of the country (OJ L 331, 27.12.1979, p. 11). Directive as last amended by the 2003 Act of Accession.

(2) Thirteenth Council Directive 86/560/EEC of 17 November 1986 on the harmonization of the laws of the Member States relating to turnover taxes – Arrangements for the refund of value added tax to taxable persons not established in Community territory (OJ L 326, 21.11.1986, p. 40).

[Article 171a

Member States may, instead of granting a refund of VAT pursuant to Directives 86/560/EEC or 2008/9/EC on those supplies of goods or services to a taxable person in respect of which the taxable person is liable to pay the tax in accordance with Articles 194 to 197 or Article 199, allow deduction of this tax pursuant to the procedure laid down in Article 168. The existing restrictions pursuant to Article 2(2) and Article 4(2) of Directive 86/560/EEC may be retained.

To that end, Member States may exclude the taxable person who is liable to pay the tax from the refund procedure pursuant to Directives 86/560/EEC or 2008/9/EC.][1]

Amendments—[1] Article 171A inserted by Council Directive 2008/8/EC art 2(4) with effect from 1 January 2010 (OJ L 44, 20.2.2008 p 11).

Article 172

1. Any person who is regarded as a taxable person by reason of the fact that he supplies, on an occasional basis, a new means of transport in accordance with the conditions specified in Article 138(1) and (2)(*a*) shall, in the Member State in which the supply takes place, be entitled to deduct the VAT included in the purchase price or paid in respect of the importation or the intra-Community acquisition of this means of transport, up to an amount not exceeding the amount of VAT for which he would be liable if the supply were not exempt.

A right of deduction shall arise and may be exercised only at the time of supply of the new means of transport.

2. Member States shall lay down detailed rules for the implementation of paragraph 1.

CHAPTER 2
PROPORTIONAL DEDUCTION

Article 173

1. In the case of goods or services used by a taxable person both for transactions in respect of which VAT is deductible pursuant to Articles 168, 169 and 170, and for transactions in respect of which VAT is not deductible, only such proportion of the VAT as is attributable to the former transactions shall be deductible.

The deductible proportion shall be determined, in accordance with Articles 174 and 175, for all the transactions carried out by the taxable person.

2. Member States may take the following measures:

(*a*) authorise the taxable person to determine a proportion for each sector of his business, provided that separate accounts are kept for each sector;

(*b*) require the taxable person to determine a proportion for each sector of his business and to keep separate accounts for each sector;

(*c*) authorise or require the taxable person to make the deduction on the basis of the use made of all or part of the goods and services;

(*d*) authorise or require the taxable person to make the deduction in accordance with the rule laid down in the first subparagraph of paragraph 1, in respect of all goods and services used for all transactions referred to therein;

(*e*) provide that, where the VAT which is not deductible by the taxable person is insignificant, it is to be treated as nil.

Commentary—*De Voil Indirect Tax Service* **V2.101, V.3.401, V3.460.**

Simon's Tax Cases—*Cibo Participations SA v Directeur regional des impots du Nord-Pas-de-Calais* [2002] STC 460*; *Dial-a-Phone Ltd v C&E Comrs,* [2003] STC 192*; *EC Commission v Kingdom of Spain* [2006] STC 1087*; *EC Commission v French Republic (Kingdom of Spain, intervening)* [2006] STC 1098*; *Proceedings brought by Uudenkaupungin kaupunki* [2008] STC 2329*; *Royal Bank of Scotland Group plc v R&C Comrs* [2009] STC 461*.

Article 174

1. The deductible proportion shall be made up of a fraction comprising the following amounts:

(*a*) as numerator, the total amount, exclusive of VAT, of turnover per year attributable to transactions in respect of which VAT is deductible pursuant to Articles 168 and 169;

(*b*) as denominator, the total amount, exclusive of VAT, of turnover per year attributable to transactions included in the numerator and to transactions in respect of which VAT is not deductible.

Member States may include in the denominator the amount of subsidies, other than those directly linked to the price of supplies of goods or services referred to in Article 73.

2. By way of derogation from paragraph 1, the following amounts shall be excluded from the calculation of the deductible proportion:

(*a*) the amount of turnover attributable to supplies of capital goods used by the taxable person for the purposes of his business;

(*b*) the amount of turnover attributable to incidental real estate and financial transactions;

(*c*) the amount of turnover attributable to the transactions specified in points (*b*) to (*g*) of Article 135(1) in so far as those transactions are incidental.

3. Where Member States exercise the option under Article 191 not to require adjustment in respect of capital goods, they may include disposals of capital goods in the calculation of the deductible proportion.

Commentary—*De Voil Indirect Tax Service* **V3.460.**

Simon's Tax Cases—*Dwyer Property Ltd v C&E Comrs* [1995] STC 1035*; *C&E Comrs v Liverpool Institute for Performing Arts* [2001] STC 891*; *António Jorge Lda v Fazenda Pública* [2008] STC 2533*.

Art 174(1), *Sofitam SA (formerly Satam SA) v Ministre chargé du Budget* (Case C-333/91), ECJ [1997] STC 226*; *Floridienne SA and anor v Belgian State* [2000] STC 1044*; *EC Commission v Kingdom of Spain* [2006] STC 1087*; *EC Commission v French Republic (Kingdom of Spain, intervening)* [2006] STC 1098*; *Royal Bank of Scotland Group plc v R&C Comrs* [2009] STC 461*.

Art 174(2), *Régie Dauphinoise—Cabinet A Forest SARL v Ministre du Budget* (Case C-306/94) [1996] STC 1176*; *C&E Comrs v JDL Ltd* [2001] STC 1*; *Empresa de Desenvolvimento Mineiro SGPS SA (EDM) v Fazenda Pública (Ministério Público, intervening)* [2005] STC 65*; *Nordania Finans A/S and another v Skatteministeriet* [2008] STC 3314*; *NCC Construction Danmark A/S v Skattenministeriet* [2010] STC 532*.

Article 175

1. The deductible proportion shall be determined on an annual basis, fixed as a percentage and rounded up to a figure not exceeding the next whole number.

2. The provisional proportion for a year shall be that calculated on the basis of the preceding year's transactions. In the absence of any such transactions to refer to, or where they were insignificant in amount, the deductible proportion shall be estimated provisionally, under the supervision of the tax authorities, by the taxable person on the basis of his own forecasts.

However, Member States may retain the rules in force at 1 January 1979 or, in the case of the Member States which acceded to the Community after that date, on the date of their accession.

3. Deductions made on the basis of such provisional proportions shall be adjusted when the final proportion is fixed during the following year.

Commentary—*De Voil Indirect Tax Service* **V3.460**.

Simon's Tax Cases—*Dwyer Property Ltd v C&E Comrs* [1995] STC 1035*; *C&E Comrs v Liverpool Institute for Performing Arts* [2001] STC 891*; *António Jorge Lda v Fazenda Pública* [2008] STC 2533*.

CHAPTER 3

RESTRICTIONS ON THE RIGHT OF DEDUCTION

Article 176

The Council, acting unanimously on a proposal from the Commission, shall determine the expenditure in respect of which VAT shall not be deductible. VAT shall in no circumstances be deductible in respect of expenditure which is not strictly business expenditure, such as that on luxuries, amusements or entertainment.

Pending the entry into force of the provisions referred to in the first paragraph, Member States may retain all the exclusions provided for under their national laws at 1 January 1979 or, in the case of the Member States which acceded to the Community after that date, on the date of their accession.

Commentary—*De Voil Indirect Tax Service* **V2.101**, **V3.401**, **V3.460**.

Simon's Tax Cases—*Group Ltd v C&E Comrs* [1996] STC 898*; *Royscot Leasing Ltd v C&E Comrs* [1999] STC 998*; *EC Commission v French Republic (United Kingdom intervening)* [2003] STC 372, 390*; *Charles and another v Staatssecretaris van Financiën* [2006] STC 1429*; *Proceedings brought by Uudenkaupungin kaupunki* [2008] STC 2329*; *Danfoss A/S and anor v Skatteministeriet* [2009] STC 701*; *Puffer v Unabhängiger Finanzsenat Außenstella Linz* [2009] STC 1693*; *X Holding BV v Staatssecretaris van Financiën* [2010] STC 1221*; *Eon Asset Menidjmunt OOD v Direktor na Direktsia 'Obzhalvane I upravlenie na izpalnenieto'—Varna pr Tsentralno upravlenie na Natsionalnata agentsia za prihodite* (Case C-118/11) [2012] STC 982.

Article 177

After consulting the VAT Committee, each Member State may, for cyclical economic reasons, totally or partly exclude all or some capital goods or other goods from the system of deductions.

In order to maintain identical conditions of competition, Member States may, instead of refusing deduction, tax goods manufactured by the taxable person himself or goods which he has purchased within the Community, or imported, in such a way that the tax does not exceed the amount of VAT which would be charged on the acquisition of similar goods.

CHAPTER 4

RULES GOVERNING EXERCISE OF THE RIGHT OF DEDUCTION

Article 178

In order to exercise the right of deduction, a taxable person must meet the following conditions:

[(*a*) for the purposes of deductions pursuant to Article 168(a), in respect of the supply of goods or services, he must hold an invoice drawn up in accordance with Sections 3 to 6 of Chapter 3 of Title XI;][1]

(*b*) for the purposes of deductions pursuant to Article 168(*b*), in respect of transactions treated as the supply of goods or services, he must comply with the formalities as laid down by each Member State;

[(*c*) for the purposes of deductions pursuant to Article 168(c), in respect of the intra-Community acquisition of goods, he must set out in the VAT return provided for in Article 250 all the information needed for the amount of VAT due on his intra-Community acquisitions of goods to be calculated and he must hold an invoice drawn up in accordance with Sections 3 to 5 of Chapter 3 of Title XI;][1]

(*d*) for the purposes of deductions pursuant to Article 168(*d*), in respect of transactions treated as intra-Community acquisitions of goods, he must complete the formalities as laid down by each Member State;

(*e*) for the purposes of deductions pursuant to Article 168(*e*), in respect of the importation of goods, he must hold an import document specifying him as consignee or importer, and stating the amount of VAT due or enabling that amount to be calculated;

(*f*) when required to pay VAT as a customer where Articles 194 to 197 or Article 199 apply, he must comply with the formalities as laid down by each Member State.

Amendments—[1] Paras (*a*), (*c*) substituted by Council Directive 2010/45 art 1(8) with effect from 11 August 2010 (OJ L 189, 22.7.2010, p 1). The deadline for implementation of Directive 2010/45/EU is 31 December 2012. Those paras previously read as follows—

"(*a*) for the purposes of deductions pursuant to Article 168(*a*), in respect of the supply of goods or services, he must hold an invoice drawn up in accordance with Articles 220 to 236 and Articles 238, 239 and 240;"

"(c) for the purposes of deductions pursuant to Article 168(*c*), in respect of the intra-Community acquisition of goods, he must set out in the VAT return provided for in Article 250 all the information needed for the amount of the VAT due on his intra-Community acquisitions of goods to be calculated and he must hold an invoice drawn up in accordance with Articles 220 to 236;".

Simon's Tax Cases—*Kopalnia Odrykwokowa Polski Trawertyn P Granatowicz, M Wasiewicz, spolka jawna v Dyrektor Izby Skarbowej w Poznaniu* (Case C-280/10) [2012] STC 1085.

Article 179

The taxable person shall make the deduction by subtracting from the total amount of VAT due for a given tax period the total amount of VAT in respect of which, during the same period, the right of deduction has arisen and is exercised in accordance with Article 178.

However, Member States may require that taxable persons who carry out occasional transactions, as defined in Article 12, exercise their right of deduction only at the time of supply.

Article 180

Member States may authorise a taxable person to make a deduction which he has not made in accordance with Articles 178 and 179.

[Article 181

Member States may authorise a taxable person who does not hold an invoice drawn up in accordance with Sections 3 to 5 of Chapter 3 of Title XI to make the deduction referred to in Article 168(c) in respect of his intra- Community acquisitions of goods.][1]

Amendments—[1] Article substituted by Council Directive 2010/45 art 1(9) with effect from 11 August 2010 (OJ L 189, 22.7.2010, p 1). The deadline for implementation of Directive 2010/45/EU is 31 December 2012. Article previously read as follows—

"Member States may authorise a taxable person who does not hold an invoice drawn up in accordance with Articles 220 to 236 to make the deduction referred to in Article 168(*c*) in respect of his intra-Community acquisitions of goods.".

Article 182

Member States shall determine the conditions and detailed rules for applying Articles 180 and 181.

Article 183

Where, for a given tax period, the amount of deductions exceeds the amount of VAT due, the Member States may, in accordance with conditions which they shall determine, either make a refund or carry the excess forward to the following period.

However, Member States may refuse to refund or carry forward if the amount of the excess is insignificant.

Commentary—*De Voil Indirect Tax Service* **V3.401**.

Simon's Tax Cases—*Garage Molenheide BVBA, Schepens, Bureau Rik Decan-Business Research & Development NV (BRD) and Sanders BVBA v Belgium* (Joined cases C-286/94, C-340/95, C-401/95 and C-47/96) [1998] STC 126*; *Alstom Power Hydro v Valsts ieņēmumu dienests* [2010] STC 777*.

CHAPTER 5

ADJUSTMENT OF DEDUCTIONS

Article 184

The initial deduction shall be adjusted where it is higher or lower than that to which the taxable person was entitled.

Article 185

1. Adjustment shall, in particular, be made where, after the VAT return is made, some change occurs in the factors used to determine the amount to be deducted, for example where purchases are cancelled or price reductions are obtained.

2. By way of derogation from paragraph 1, no adjustment shall be made in the case of transactions remaining totally or partially unpaid or in the case of destruction, loss or theft of property duly proved or confirmed, or in the case of goods reserved for the purpose of making gifts of small value or of giving samples, as referred to in Article 16.

However, in the case of transactions remaining totally or partially unpaid or in the case of theft, Member States may require adjustment to be made.

Commentary—*De Voil Indirect Tax Service* **V3.470**.

Simon's Tax Cases—*Tremerton Ltd v C&E Comrs* [1999] STC 1039*; *Finanzamt Burgdorf v Fischer, Finanzamt Düsseldorf-Mettman v Brandenstein* [2001] STC 1356*; *TETS Haskovo AD v Direktor na Direktsia 'Obzhalvane I upravlenie na izpalnenieto' — Varna pri Tsentralno upravlenie na Natsionalnata agentsia za prihodite* (Case C-234/11) [2013] STC 243; *PIGI — Pavleta Dimova ET v Direktor na Direktsia 'Obzhalvane I upravlenie na izpalnenieto' — Varna pri Tsentralno upravlenie na Natsionalnata agentsia za prihodite* (Case C-550/11) [2013] STC 272; *FIRIN OOD v Direktor na Direktsia 'Obzhalvane i danachno-osiguritelna praktika' Veliko Tarnovo pri Tsentralno upravlenie na Natsionalnata agentsia za prihodite* (Case C-107/13) [2014] STC 1581.

Article 186

Member States shall lay down the detailed rules for applying Articles 184 and 185.

Article 187

1. In the case of capital goods, adjustment shall be spread over five years including that in which the goods were acquired or manufactured.

Member States may, however, base the adjustment on a period of five full years starting from the time at which the goods are first used.

In the case of immovable property acquired as capital goods, the adjustment period may be extended up to 20 years.

2. The annual adjustment shall be made only in respect of one-fifth of the VAT charged on the capital goods, or, if the adjustment period has been extended, in respect of the corresponding fraction thereof.

The adjustment referred to in the first subparagraph shall be made on the basis of the variations in the deduction entitlement in subsequent years in relation to that for the year in which the goods were acquired, manufactured or, where applicable, used for the first time.

Commentary—*De Voil Indirect Tax Service* **V3.470**.

Simon's Tax Cases—*Finanzamt Uelzen v Armbrecht* (Case C-291/92) [1995] STC 997*; *Gemeente Leusden and another v Staatssecretaris van Financiën* [2007] STC 776*.

Article 188

1. If supplied during the adjustment period, capital goods shall be treated as if they had been applied to an economic activity of the taxable person up until expiry of the adjustment period.

The economic activity shall be presumed to be fully taxed in cases where the supply of the capital goods is taxed.

The economic activity shall be presumed to be fully exempt in cases where the supply of the capital goods is exempt.

2. The adjustment provided for in paragraph 1 shall be made only once in respect of all the time covered by the adjustment period that remains to run. However, where the supply of capital goods is exempt, Member States may waive the requirement for adjustment in so far as the purchaser is a taxable person using the capital goods in question solely for transactions in respect of which VAT is deductible.

Commentary—*De Voil Indirect Tax Service* **V3.470**.

Simon's Tax Cases—*Centralan Property Ltd v C&E Comrs* [2006] STC 1542*.

Article 189

For the purposes of applying Articles 187 and 188, Member States may take the following measures:

(*a*) define the concept of capital goods;

(*b*) specify the amount of the VAT which is to be taken into consideration for adjustment;

(*c*) adopt any measures needed to ensure that adjustment does not give rise to any unjustified advantage;

(*d*) permit administrative simplifications.

Article 190

For the purposes of Articles 187, 188, 189 and 191, Member States may regard as capital goods those services which have characteristics similar to those normally attributed to capital goods.

Article 191

If, in any Member State, the practical effect of applying Articles 187 and 188 is negligible, that Member State may, after consulting the VAT Committee, refrain from applying those provisions, having regard to the overall impact of VAT in the Member State concerned and the need for administrative simplification, and provided that no distortion of competition thereby arises.

Article 192

Where a taxable person transfers from being taxed in the normal way to a special scheme or vice versa, Member States may take all measures necessary to ensure that the taxable person does not enjoy unjustified advantage or sustain unjustified harm.

TITLE XI

OBLIGATIONS OF TAXABLE PERSONS AND CERTAIN NON-TAXABLE PERSONS

CHAPTER 1

OBLIGATION TO PAY

SECTION 1

Persons liable for payment of VAT to the tax authorities

[Article 192a

For the purposes of this Section, a taxable person who has a fixed establishment within the territory of the Member State where the tax is due shall be regarded as a taxable person who is not established within that Member State when the following conditions are met:

(*a*) he makes a taxable supply of goods or of services within the territory of that Member State;

(*b*) an establishment which the supplier has within the territory of that Member State does not intervene in that supply.][1]

Amendments—[1] Article 192a inserted by Council Directive 2008/8/EC art 2(5) with effect from 1 January 2010 (OJ L 44, 20.2.2008 p 11).

Article 193

VAT shall be payable by any taxable person carrying out a taxable supply of goods or services, except where it is payable by another person in the cases referred to in [Articles 194 to 199b][1] and Article 202.

Simon's Tax Cases—*FIRIN OOD v Direktor na Direktsia 'Obzhalvane i danachno-osiguritelna praktika' Veliko Tarnovo pri Tsentralno upravlenie na Natsionalnata agentsia za prihodite* (Case C-107/13) [2014] STC 1581.

Amendments—[1] Words substituted for words "Articles 194 to 199" by Council Directive 2013/43/EU art 1(1) with effect from 15 August 2013 until 31 December 2018 (OJ L 201, 26.7.2013, p 4).

Article 194

1. Where the taxable supply of goods or services is carried out by a taxable person who is not established in the Member State in which the VAT is due, Member States may provide that the person liable for payment of VAT is the person to whom the goods or services are supplied.

2. Member States shall lay down the conditions for implementation of paragraph 1.

Article 195

VAT shall be payable by any person who is identified for VAT purposes in the Member State in which the tax is due and to whom goods are supplied in the circumstances specified in Articles 38 or 39, if the supplies are carried out by a taxable person not established within that Member State.

[Article 196

VAT shall be payable by any taxable person, or non-taxable legal person identified for VAT purposes, to whom the services referred to in Article 44 are supplied, if the services are supplied by a taxable person not established within the territory of the Member State.][1]

Amendments—[1] Article 196 substituted, by Council Directive 2008/8/EC art 2(7) with effect from 1 January 2010 (OJ L 44, 20.2.2008 p 11). Text previously read as follows—

"**Article 196**

VAT shall be payable by any taxable person to whom the services referred to in Article 56 are supplied or by any person identified for VAT purposes in the Member State in which the tax is due to whom the services referred to in Articles 44, 47, 50, 53, 54 and 55 are supplied, if the services are supplied by a taxable person not established in that Member State.".

Article 197

1. VAT shall be payable by the person to whom the goods are supplied when the following conditions are met:

(*a*) the taxable transaction is a supply of goods carried out in accordance with the conditions laid down in Article 141;

(*b*) the person to whom the goods are supplied is another taxable person, or a non-taxable legal person, identified for VAT purposes in the Member State in which the supply is carried out;

[(*c*) the invoice issued by the taxable person not established in the Member State of the person to whom the goods are supplied is drawn up in accordance with Sections 3 to 5 of Chapter 3.][1]

2. Where a tax representative is appointed as the person liable for payment of VAT pursuant to Article 204, Member States may provide for a derogation from paragraph 1 of this Article.

Amendments—[1] Para 1(*c*) substituted by Council Directive 2010/45 art 1(10) with effect from 11 August 2010 (OJ L 189, 22.7.2010, p 1). The deadline for implementation of Directive 2010/45/EU is 31 December 2012. That para previously read as follows—

"(*c*) the invoice issued by the taxable person not established in the Member State of the person to whom the goods are supplied is drawn up in accordance with Articles 220 to 236.".

VAT EC

Article 198

1. Where specific transactions relating to investment gold between a taxable person who is a member of a regulated gold bullion market and another taxable person who is not a member of that market are taxed pursuant to Article 352, Member States shall designate the customer as the person liable for payment of VAT.

If the customer who is not a member of the regulated gold bullion market is a taxable person required to be identified for VAT purposes in the Member State in which the tax is due solely in respect of the transactions referred to in Article 352, the vendor shall fulfil the tax obligations on behalf of the customer, in accordance with the law of that Member State.

2. Where gold material or semi-manufactured products of a purity of 325 thousandths or greater, or investment gold as defined in Article 344(1) is supplied by a taxable person exercising one of the options under Articles 348, 349 and 350, Member States may designate the customer as the person liable for payment of VAT.

3. Member States shall lay down the procedures and conditions for implementation of paragraphs 1 and 2.

Article 199

1. Member States may provide that the person liable for payment of VAT is the taxable person to whom any of the following supplies are made:

(*a*) the supply of construction work, including repair, cleaning, maintenance, alteration and demolition services in relation to immovable property, as well as the handing over of construction works regarded as a supply of goods pursuant to Article 14(3);

(*b*) the supply of staff engaged in activities covered by point (*a*);

(*c*) the supply of immovable property, as referred to in Article 135(1)(*j*) and (*k*), where the supplier has opted for taxation of the supply pursuant to Article 137;

(*d*) the supply of used material, used material which cannot be re-used in the same state, scrap, industrial and non industrial waste, recyclable waste, part processed waste and certain goods and services, as listed in Annex VI;

(*e*) the supply of goods provided as security by one taxable person to another in execution of that security;

(*f*) the supply of goods following the cession of a reservation of ownership to an assignee and the exercising of this right by the assignee;

(*g*) the supply of immovable property sold by a judgment debtor in a compulsory sale procedure.

2. When applying the option provided for in paragraph 1, Member States may specify the supplies of goods and services covered, and the categories of suppliers or recipients to whom these measures may apply.

3. For the purposes of paragraph 1, Member States may take the following measures:

(*a*) provide that a taxable person who also carries out activities or transactions that are not considered to be taxable supplies of goods or services in accordance with Article 2 shall be regarded as a taxable person in respect of supplies received as referred to in paragraph 1 of this Article;

(*b*) provide that a non-taxable body governed by public law, shall be regarded as a taxable person in respect of supplies received as referred to in points (*e*), (*f*) and (*g*) of paragraph 1.

4. Member States shall inform the VAT Committee of national legislative measures adopted pursuant to paragraph 1 in so far as these are not measures authorised by the Council prior to 13 August 2006 in accordance with Article 27(1) to (4) of Directive 77/388/EEC, and which are continued under paragraph 1 of this Article.

Simons Tax Cases*Promociones y Construcciones BJ 200 SL* (Case C-125/12) [2014] STC 237

[Article 199a

1. [Member States may, until 31 December 2018 and for a minimum period of two years, provide that the person liable for payment of VAT is the taxable person to whom any of the following supplies are made:]

(*a*) the transfer of allowances to emit greenhouse gases as defined in Article 3 of Directive 2003/87/EC of the European Parliament and of the Council of 13 October 2003 establishing a scheme for greenhouse gas emission allowance trading within the Community [], transferable in accordance with Article 12 of that Directive;

(*b*) the transfer of other units that may be used by operators for compliance with the same Directive.

(*c*) supplies of mobile telephones, being devices made or adapted for use in connection with a licensed network and operated on specified frequencies, whether or not they have any other use;

(*d*) supplies of integrated circuit devices such as microprocessors and central processing units in a state prior to integration into end user products;

(*e*) supplies of gas and electricity to a taxable dealer as defined in Article 38(2);

(*f*) supplies of gas and electricity certificates;

(*g*) supplies of telecommunication services as defined in Article 24(2);
(*h*) supplies of game consoles, tablet PC's and laptops;
(*i*) supplies of cereals and industrial crops including oil seeds and sugar beet, that are not normally used in the unaltered state for final consumption;
(*j*) supplies of raw and semi-finished metals, including precious metals, where they are not otherwise covered by point (*d*) of Article 199(1), the special arrangements for second-hand goods, works of art, collector's items and antiques pursuant to Articles 311 to 343 or the special scheme for investment gold pursuant to Articles 344 to 356.][2]

1a. Member States may lay down the conditions for the application of the mechanism provided for in paragraph 1.

1b. The application of the mechanism provided for in paragraph 1 to the supply of any of the goods or services listed in points (*c*) to (*j*) of that paragraph is subject to the introduction of appropriate and effective reporting obligations on taxable persons who supply the goods or services to which the mechanism provided for in paragraph 1 applies.][2]

[2. Member States shall inform the VAT Committee of the application of the mechanism provided for in paragraph 1 on the introduction of any such mechanism and shall provide the following information to the VAT Committee:

(*a*) the scope of the measure applying the mechanism together with the type and the features of the fraud, and a detailed description of accompanying measures, including any reporting obligations on taxable persons and any control measures;
(*b*) actions taken to inform the relevant taxable persons of the introduction of the application of the mechanism;
(*c*) evaluation criteria to enable comparison between fraudulent activities in relation to the goods and services listed in paragraph 1 before and after the application of the mechanism, fraudulent activities in relation to other goods and services before and after the application of the mechanism, and any increase in other types of fraudulent activities before and after the application of the mechanism;
(*d*) the date of commencement and the period to be covered by the measure applying the mechanism.][2]

3. [Member States applying the mechanism provided for in paragraph 1 shall, on the basis of the evaluation criteria provided for under point (c) of paragraph 2, submit a report to the Commission no later than 30 June 2017.][2]

[(*a*) the impact on fraudulent activities in relation to supplies of goods or services covered by the measure;][2]
(*b*) the possible shift of fraudulent activities to goods or other services;
(*c*) the compliance costs for taxable persons resulting from the measure.

[4. Each Member State that has detected a shift in trends of fraudulent activities in its territory in relation to the goods or services listed in paragraph 1 from the date of entry into force of this Article with respect to such goods or services, shall submit a report to the Commission in that respect no later than 30 June 2017.

5. Before 1 January 2018, the Commission shall present to the European Parliament and to the Council an overall assessment report on the effects of the mechanism provided for in paragraph 1 on combatting fraud.][2]][1]

Amendments—[1] Article 199a inserted by Council Directive 2010/23/EU with effect from 9 April 2010 (OJ L 72, 20.03.2010, p 1).

[2] In para 1, first sentence substituted and sub-paras (*c*)–(*j*) inserted, paras 1a, 1b inserted, para 2 substituted, in para 3, first sentence and sub-para (*a*) substituted, and paras 4, 5 substituted for previous para 4, by Council Directive 2013/43/EU art 1(2) with effect from 15 August 2013 until 31 December 2018 (OJ L 201, 26.7.2013, p 4). Before these amendments, art 199a read as follows—

"Article 199a

1. Member States may, until 30 June 2015 and for a minimum period of two years, provide that the person liable for payment of VAT is the taxable person to whom any of the following supplies are made:

the transfer of allowances to emit greenhouse gases as defined in Article 3 of Directive 2003/87/EC of the European Parliament and of the Council of 13 October 2003 establishing a scheme for greenhouse gas emission allowance trading within the Community [], transferable in accordance with Article 12 of that Directive;

the transfer of other units that may be used by operators for compliance with the same Directive.

2. Member States shall inform the Commission of the application of the mechanism provided for in paragraph 1 on the introduction of any such mechanism and shall provide the following information to the Commission:

a statement on the scope of the measure applying the mechanism and a detailed description of accompanying measures, including any reporting obligations on taxable persons and any control measures;

evaluation criteria to enable comparison between fraudulent activities in relation to the services listed in paragraph 1 before and after the application of the mechanism, fraudulent activities in relation to other services before and after the application of the mechanism, and any increase in other types of fraudulent activities before and after the application of the mechanism;

the date of commencement and the period to be covered by the measure applying the mechanism.

VAT EC

3. Member States applying the mechanism provided for in paragraph 1 shall, on the basis of the evaluation criteria provided for under paragraph 2(b), submit a report to the Commission no later than 30 June 2014. The report shall clearly indicate the information to be treated as confidential and the information which may be published. The report shall provide a detailed assessment of the measure's overall effectiveness and efficiency, in particular as regards:

the impact on fraudulent activities in relation to supplies of services covered by the measure;

the possible shift of fraudulent activities to goods or other services;

the compliance costs for taxable persons resulting from the measure.

4. Each Member State that has detected, as from the entry into force of this Article, a shift in trends of fraudulent activities in its territory in relation to the services listed in paragraph 1, shall submit a report to the Commission in that respect no later than 30 June 2014.".

[Article 199b

1. A Member State may, in cases of imperative urgency and in accordance with paragraphs 2 and 3, designate the recipient as the person liable to pay VAT on specific supplies of goods and services by derogation from Article 193 as a Quick Reaction Mechanism ("QRM") special measure to combat sudden and massive fraud liable to lead to considerable and irreparable financial losses.

The QRM special measure shall be subject to appropriate control measures by the Member State with respect to taxable persons who supply the goods or services to which that measure applies, and shall be for a period not exceeding nine months.

2. A Member State wishing to introduce a QRM special measure as provided for in paragraph 1 shall send a notification to the Commission using the standardised form established in accordance with paragraph 4 and at the same time send it to the other Member States. The Member State shall provide the Commission with the information indicating the sector concerned, the type and the features of the fraud, the existence of imperative grounds of urgency, the sudden and massive character of the fraud and its consequences in terms of considerable and irreparable financial losses. If the Commission considers it does not have all the necessary information, it shall contact the Member State concerned within two weeks of receipt of the notification and specify what additional information is required. Any additional information provided by the Member State concerned to the Commission shall at the same time be sent to the other Member States. If the additional information provided is not sufficient, the Commission shall inform the Member State concerned thereof within one week.

The Member State wishing to introduce a QRM special measure as provided for in paragraph 1 shall at the same time also make an application to the Commission in accordance with the procedure laid down in Article 395(2) and (3).

3. Once the Commission has all the information it considers necessary for appraisal of the notification referred to in the first subparagraph of paragraph 2, it shall notify the Member States thereof. Where it objects to the QRM special measure, it shall produce a negative opinion within one month of that notification, and shall inform the Member State concerned and the VAT Committee thereof. Where the Commission does not object, it shall confirm this in writing to the Member State concerned and to the VAT Committee within the same time period. The Member State may adopt the QRM special measure from the date of receipt of that confirmation. In appraising the notification, the Commission shall take into account the views of any other Member State sent to it in writing.

4. The Commission shall adopt an implementing act establishing a standardised form for the submission of the notification for the QRM special measure referred to in paragraph 2 and of the information referred to in the first subparagraph of paragraph 2. That implementing act shall be adopted in accordance with the examination procedure referred to in paragraph 5.

5. Where reference is made to this paragraph, Article 5 of Regulation (EU) No 182/2011 of the European Parliament and of the Council shall apply and for this purpose the committee shall be the committee established by Article 58 of Council Regulation (EU) No 904/2010.]

Amendments—Article 199b inserted by Council Directive 2013/42/EU art 1 with effect from 15 August 2013 until 31 December 2018 (OJ L 201, 26.7.2013, p 1).

Article 200

VAT shall be payable by any person making a taxable intra-Community acquisition of goods.

Article 201

On importation, VAT shall be payable by any person or persons designated or recognised as liable by the Member State of importation.

Article 202

VAT shall be payable by any person who causes goods to cease to be covered by the arrangements or situations listed in Articles 156, 157, 158, 160 and 161.

Article 203

VAT shall be payable by any person who enters the VAT on an invoice.

Article 204

1. Where, pursuant to Articles 193 to 197 and Articles 199 and 200, the person liable for payment of VAT is a taxable person who is not established in the Member State in which the VAT is due, Member States may allow that person to appoint a tax representative as the person liable for payment of the VAT.

Furthermore, where the taxable transaction is carried out by a taxable person who is not established in the Member State in which the VAT is due and no legal instrument exists, with the country in which that taxable person is established or has his seat, relating to mutual assistance similar in scope to that provided for in Directive 76/308/EEC :[1] and Regulation (EC) No 1798/2003 :[1]), Member States may take measures to provide that the person liable for payment of VAT is to be a tax representative appointed by the non-established taxable person.

[However, Member States may not apply the option referred to in the second subparagraph to a taxable person not established within the Community, within the meaning of point (1) of Article 358a, who has opted for the special scheme for telecommunications, broadcasting or electronic services.][1]

2. The option under the first subparagraph of paragraph 1 shall be subject to the conditions and procedures laid down by each Member State.

(1) Council Directive 76/308/EEC of 15 March 1976 on mutual assistance for the recovery of claims relating to certain levies, duties, taxes and other measures (OJ L 73, 19.3.1976, p. 18.). Directive as last amended by the Act of Accession of 2003.

Cross-references—See VATA 1994 Sch 3BA (electronic, telecommunication and broadcasting services: Union scheme, from 1 January 2015).

Amendments—[1] In para 1, third sub-para substituted by Council Directive 2008/8/EC art 5(4) with effect from 1 January 2015 (OJ L 44, 20.2.2008 p 11). That sub-para previously read as follows—

"However, Member States may not apply the option referred to in the second subparagraph to a non-established taxable person, within the meaning of point (1) of Article 358, who has opted for the special scheme for electronically supplied services.".

Article 205

In the situations referred to in Articles 193 to 200 and Articles 202, 203 and 204, Member States may provide that a person other than the person liable for payment of VAT is to be held jointly and severally liable for payment of VAT.

SECTION 2
Payment arrangements

Article 206

Any taxable person liable for payment of VAT must pay the net amount of the VAT when submitting the VAT return provided for in Article 250. Member States may, however, set a different date for payment of that amount or may require interim payments to be made.

Article 207

Member States shall take the measures necessary to ensure that persons who are regarded as liable for payment of VAT in the stead of a taxable person not established in their respective territory, in accordance with Articles 194 to 197 and Articles 199 and 204, comply with the payment obligations set out in this Section.

Member States shall also take the measures necessary to ensure that those persons who, in accordance with Article 205, are held to be jointly and severally liable for payment of the VAT comply with these payment obligations.

Article 208

Where Member States designate the customer for investment gold as the person liable for payment of VAT pursuant to Article 198(1) or if, in the case of gold material, semi-manufactured products, or investment gold as defined in Article 344(1), they exercise the option provided for in Article 198(2) of designating the customer as the person liable for payment of VAT, they shall take the measures necessary to ensure that he complies with the payment obligations set out in this Section.

Article 209

Member States shall take the measures necessary to ensure that non-taxable legal persons who are liable for payment of VAT due in respect of intra-Community acquisitions of goods, as referred to in Article 2(1)(*b*)(i), comply with the payment obligations set out in this Section.

Article 210

Member States shall adopt arrangements for payment of VAT on intra-Community acquisitions of new means of transport, as referred to in Article 2(1)(*b*)(ii), and on intra-Community acquisitions of products subject to excise duty, as referred to in Article 2(1)(*b*)(iii).

Article 211

Member States shall lay down the detailed rules for payment in respect of the importation of goods.

In particular, Member States may provide that, in the case of the importation of goods by taxable persons or certain categories thereof, or by persons liable for payment of VAT or certain categories thereof, the VAT due by reason of the importation need not be paid at the time of importation, on condition that it is entered as such in the VAT return to be submitted in accordance with Article 250.

Article 212

Member States may release taxable persons from payment of the VAT due where the amount is insignificant.

CHAPTER 2

IDENTIFICATION

Article 213

1. Every taxable person shall state when his activity as a taxable person commences, changes or ceases.

Member States shall allow, and may require, the statement to be made by electronic means, in accordance with conditions which they lay down.

2. Without prejudice to the first subparagraph of paragraph 1, every taxable person or non-taxable legal person who makes intra-Community acquisitions of goods which are not subject to VAT pursuant to Article 3(1) must state that he makes such acquisitions if the conditions, laid down in that provision, for not making such transactions subject to VAT cease to be fulfilled.

Article 214

1. Member States shall take the measures necessary to ensure that the following persons are identified by means of an individual number:

(*a*) every taxable person, with the exception of those referred to in Article 9(2), who within their respective territory carries out supplies of goods or services in respect of which VAT is deductible, other than supplies of goods or services in respect of which VAT is payable solely by the customer or the person for whom the goods or services are intended, in accordance with Articles 194 to 197 and Article 199;

(*b*) every taxable person, or non-taxable legal person, who makes intra-Community acquisitions of goods subject to VAT pursuant to Article 2(1)(*b*) and every taxable person, or non-taxable legal person, who exercises the option under Article 3(3) of making their intra-Community acquisitions subject to VAT;

(*c*) every taxable person who, within their respective territory, makes intra-Community acquisitions of goods for the purposes of transactions which relate to the activities referred to in the second subparagraph of Article 9(1) and which are carried out outside that territory.

[(*d*) every taxable person who within their respective territory receives services for which he is liable to pay VAT pursuant to Article 196;

(*e*) every taxable person, established within their respective territory, who supplies services within the territory of another Member State for which VAT is payable solely by the recipient pursuant to Article 196.][1]

2. Member States need not identify certain taxable persons who carry out transactions on an occasional basis, as referred to in Article 12.

Amendments—[1] Para 1(*d*), (*e*) inserted, by Council Directive 2008/8/EC art 2(8) with effect from 1 January 2010 (OJ L 44, 20.2.2008 p 11).

Article 215

Each individual VAT identification number shall have a prefix in accordance with ISO code 3166 — alpha 2 — by which the Member State of issue may be identified.

Nevertheless, Greece may use the prefix 'EL'.

Article 216

Member States shall take the measures necessary to ensure that their identification systems enable the taxable persons referred to in Article 214 to be identified and to ensure the correct application of the transitional arrangements for the taxation of intra-Community transactions, as referred to in Article 402.

CHAPTER 3

INVOICING

SECTION 1

Definition

[Article 217

For the purposes of this Directive, "electronic invoice" means an invoice that contains the information required in this Directive, and which has been issued and received in any electronic format.][1]

Amendments—[1] Article substituted by Council Directive 2010/45 art 1(11) with effect from 11 August 2010 (OJ L 189, 22.7.2010, p 1). The deadline for implementation of Directive 2010/45/EU is 31 December 2012. Article previously read as follows—

> "For the purposes of this Chapter, 'transmission or provision by electronic means' shall mean transmission or provision to the addressee of data using electronic equipment for processing (including digital compression) and storage, and employing wire, radio, optical or other electromagnetic means.".

SECTION 2

Concept of invoice

Article 218

For the purposes of this Directive, Member States shall accept documents or messages on paper or in electronic form as invoices if they meet the conditions laid down in this Chapter.

Article 219

Any document or message that amends and refers specifically and unambiguously to the initial invoice shall be treated as an invoice.

SECTION 3

Issue of invoices

[219a

Without prejudice to Articles 244 to 248, the following shall apply:

(1) Invoicing shall be subject to the rules applying in the Member State in which the supply of goods or services is deemed to be made, in accordance with the provisions of Title V.

(2) By way of derogation from point (1), invoicing shall be subject to the rules applying in the Member State in which the supplier has established his business or has a fixed establishment from which the supply is made or, in the absence of such place of establishment or fixed establishment, the Member State where the supplier has his permanent address or usually resides, where:

(*a*) the supplier is not established in the Member State in which the supply of goods or services is deemed to be made, in accordance with the provisions of Title V, or his establishment in that Member State does not intervene in the supply within the meaning of Article 192a, and the person liable for the payment of the VAT is the person to whom the goods or services are supplied.

However where the customer issues the invoice (self-billing), point (1) shall apply.

(*b*) the supply of goods or services is deemed not to be made within the Community, in accordance with the provisions of Title V.][1]

Amendments—[1] Article inserted by Council Directive 2010/45 art 1(12) with effect from 11 August 2010 (OJ L 189, 22.7.2010, p 1). The deadline for implementation of Directive 2010/45/EU is 31 December 2012.

[Article 220

1 Every taxable person shall ensure that, in respect of the following, an invoice is issued, either by himself or by his customer or, in his name and on his behalf, by a third party:

(1) supplies of goods or services which he has made to another taxable person or to a non-taxable legal person;

(2) supplies of goods as referred to in Article 33;

(3) supplies of goods carried out in accordance with the conditions specified in Article 138;

(4) any payment on account made to him before one of the supplies of goods referred to in points (1) and (2) was carried out;

(5) any payment on account made to him by another taxable person or non-taxable legal person before the provision of services was completed.

2 By way of derogation from paragraph 1, and without prejudice to Article 221(2), the issue of an invoice shall not be required in respect of supplies of services exempted under points (a) to (g) of Article 135(1).][1]

Amendments—[1] Article substituted by Council Directive 2010/45 art 1(13) with effect from 11 August 2010 (OJ L 189, 22.7.2010, p 1). The deadline for implementation of Directive 2010/45/EU is 31 December 2012. Article previously read as follows—

> "Every taxable person shall ensure that, in respect of the following, an invoice is issued, either by himself or by his customer or, in his name and on his behalf, by a third party:
>
> (1) supplies of goods or services which he has made to another taxable person or to a non-taxable legal person;
>
> (2) supplies of goods as referred to in Article 33;
>
> (3) supplies of goods carried out in accordance with the conditions specified in Article 138;
>
> (4) any payment on account made to him before one of the supplies of goods referred to in points (1), (2) and (3) was carried out;
>
> (5) any payment on account made to him by another taxable person or non-taxable legal person before the provision of services was completed.".

[Article 220a

1 Member States shall allow taxable persons to issue a simplified invoice in any of the following cases:

(*a*) where the amount of the invoice is not higher than EUR 100 or the equivalent in national currency;

(*b*) where the invoice issued is a document or message treated as an invoice pursuant to Article 219.

2 Member States shall not allow taxable persons to issue a simplified invoice where invoices are required to be issued pursuant to points (2) and (3) of Article 220(1) or where the taxable supply of goods or services is carried out by a taxable person who is not established in the Member State in which the VAT is due, or whose establishment in that Member State does not intervene in the supply within the meaning of Article 192a, and the person liable for the payment of VAT is the person to whom the goods or services are supplied.][1]

Amendments—[1] Article inserted by Council Directive 2010/45 art 1(14) with effect from 11 August 2010 (OJ L 189, 22.7.2010, p 1). The deadline for implementation of Directive 2010/45/EU is 31 December 2012.

[Article 221

1 Member States may impose on taxable persons an obligation to issue an invoice in accordance with the details required under Article 226 or 226b in respect of supplies of goods or services other than those referred to in Article 220(1).

2 Member States may impose on taxable persons who have established their business in their territory or who have a fixed establishment in their territory from which the supply is made, an obligation to issue an invoice in accordance with the details required in Article 226 or 226b in respect of supplies of services exempted under points (a) to (g) of Article 135(1) which those taxable persons have made in their territory or outside the Community.

3 Member States may release taxable persons from the obligation laid down in Article 220(1) or in Article 220a to issue an invoice in respect of supplies of goods or services which they have made in their territory and which are exempt, with or without deductibility of the VAT paid in the preceding stage, pursuant to Articles 110 and 111, Article 125(1), Article 127, Article 128(1), Article 132, points (h) to (l) of Article 135(1), Articles 136, 371, 375, 376 and 377, Articles 378(2) and 379(2) and Articles 380 to 390b.][1]

Amendments—[1] Articles 221–225 substituted by Council Directive 2010/45 art 1(15) with effect from 11 August 2010 (OJ L 189, 22.7.2010, p 1). The deadline for implementation of Directive 2010/45/EU is 31 December 2012. Article 221 previously read as follows—

> "1. Member States may impose on taxable persons an obligation to issue an invoice in respect of supplies of goods or services made in their territory, other than those referred to in Article 220.
>
> Member States may, in respect of the invoices referred to in the first subparagraph, impose fewer obligations than those laid down in Articles 226, 230, 233, 244 and 246.
>
> 2. Member States may release taxable persons from the obligation laid down in Article 220 to issue an invoice in respect of supplies of goods or services which they have made in their territory and which are exempt, with or without deductibility of the VAT paid at the preceding stage, pursuant to Articles 110 and 111, Article 125(1), Article 127, Article 128 (1), Articles 132, 135, 136, 371, 375, 376 and 377, Article 378 (2), Article 379(2) and Articles 380 to 390b.".

[Article 222

For supplies of goods carried out in accordance with the conditions specified in Article 138 or for supplies of services for which VAT is payable by the customer pursuant to Article 196, an invoice shall be issued no later than on the fifteenth day of the month following that in which the chargeable event occurs.

For other supplies of goods or services Member States may impose time limits on taxable persons for the issue of invoices.][1]

Amendments—[1] Articles 221–225 substituted by Council Directive 2010/45 art 1(15) with effect from 11 August 2010 (OJ L 189, 22.7.2010, p 1). The deadline for implementation of Directive 2010/45/EU is 31 December 2012. Article 222 previously read as follows—

> "Member States may impose time limits on taxable persons for the issue of invoices when supplying goods or services in their territory.".

[Article 223

Member States shall allow taxable persons to issue summary invoices which detail several separate supplies of goods or services provided that VAT on the supplies mentioned in the summary invoice becomes chargeable during the same calendar month.

Without prejudice to Article 222, Member States may allow summary invoices to include supplies for which VAT has become chargeable during a period of time longer than one calendar month.[1]

Amendments—[1] Articles 221–225 substituted by Council Directive 2010/45 art 1(15) with effect from 11 August 2010 (OJ L 189, 22.7.2010, p 1). The deadline for implementation of Directive 2010/45/EU is 31 December 2012. Article 223 previously read as follows—

"In accordance with conditions to be laid down by the Member States in whose territory goods or services are supplied, a summary invoice may be drawn up for several separate supplies of goods or services.".

[Article 224

Invoices may be drawn up by the customer in respect of the supply to him, by a taxable person, of goods or services, where there is a prior agreement between the two parties and provided that a procedure exists for the acceptance of each invoice by the taxable person supplying the goods or services. Member State may require that such invoices be issued in the name and on behalf of the taxable person.[1]

Amendments—[1] Articles 221–225 substituted by Council Directive 2010/45 art 1(15) with effect from 11 August 2010 (OJ L 189, 22.7.2010, p 1). The deadline for implementation of Directive 2010/45/EU is 31 December 2012. Article 224 previously read as follows—

"1. Invoices may be drawn up by the customer in respect of the supply to him, by a taxable person, of goods or services, if there is a prior agreement between the two parties and provided that a procedure exists for the acceptance of each invoice by the taxable person supplying the goods or services.

2. The Member States in whose territory the goods or services are supplied shall determine the terms and conditions of such prior agreements and of the acceptance procedures between the taxable person and the customer.

3. Member States may impose further conditions on taxable persons supplying goods or services in their territory concerning the issue of invoices by the customer. They may, in particular, require that such invoices be issued in the name and on behalf of the taxable person.

The conditions referred to in the first subparagraph must always be the same wherever the customer is established.".

[Article 225

Member States may impose specific conditions on taxable persons in cases where the third party, or the customer, who issues invoices is established in a country with which no legal instrument exists relating to mutual assistance similar in scope to that provided for in Directive 2010/24/EU (*) and Regulation (EC) No 1798/2003 (**).

Notes—(*) Council Directive 2010/24/EU of 16 March 2010 concerning mutual assistance for the recovery of claims relating to taxes, duties and other measures (OJ L 84, 31.3.2010, p. 1).

(**) Council Regulation (EC) No 1798/2003 of 7 October 2003 on administrative cooperation in the field of value added tax (OJ L 264, 15.10.2003, p. 1).

Amendments—[1] Articles 221–225 substituted by Council Directive 2010/45 art 1(15) with effect from 11 August 2010 (OJ L 189, 22.7.2010, p 1). The deadline for implementation of Directive 2010/45/EU is 31 December 2012. Article 225 previously read as follows—

"Member States may impose specific conditions on taxable persons supplying goods or services in their territory in cases where the third party, or the customer, who issues invoices is established in a country with which no legal instrument exists relating to mutual assistance similar in scope to that provided for in Directive 76/308/EEC and Regulation (EC) No 1798/2003.".

SECTION 4

Content of invoices

Article 226

Without prejudice to the particular provisions laid down in this Directive, only the following details are required for VAT purposes on invoices issued pursuant to Articles 220 and 221:

(1) the date of issue;

(2) a sequential number, based on one or more series, which uniquely identifies the invoice;

(3) the VAT identification number referred to in Article 214 under which the taxable person supplied the goods or services;

(4) the customer's VAT identification number, as referred to in Article 214, under which the customer received a supply of goods or services in respect of which he is liable for payment of VAT, or received a supply of goods as referred to in Article 138;

(5) the full name and address of the taxable person and of the customer;

(6) the quantity and nature of the goods supplied or the extent and nature of the services rendered;

(7) the date on which the supply of goods or services was made or completed or the date on which the payment on account referred to in points (4) and (5) of Article 220 was made, in so far as that date can be determined and differs from the date of issue of the invoice;

[(*7a*) where the VAT becomes chargeable at the time when the payment is received in accordance with Article 66(b) and the right of deduction arises at the time the deductible tax becomes chargeable, the mention "Cash accounting";][1]

(8) the taxable amount per rate or exemption, the unit price exclusive of VAT and any discounts or rebates if they are not included in the unit price;

(9) the VAT rate applied;

(10) the VAT amount payable, except where a special arrangement is applied under which, in accordance with this Directive, such a detail is excluded;

VAT EC

[(10a) where the customer receiving a supply issues the invoice instead of the supplier, the mention "Self-billing";][1]

[(11) in the case of an exemption, reference to the applicable provision of this Directive, or to the corresponding national provision, or any other reference indicating that the supply of goods or services is exempt;][1]

[(11a) where the customer is liable for the payment of the VAT, the mention "Reverse charge";][1]

(12) in the case of the supply of a new means of transport made in accordance with the conditions specified in Article 138 (1) and (2)(*a*), the characteristics as identified in point (*b*) of Article 2(2);

[(13) where the margin scheme for travel agents is applied, the mention "Margin scheme — Travel agents"

(14) where one of the special arrangements applicable to second-hand goods, works of art, collectors' items and antiques is applied, the mention "Margin scheme — Second-hand goods"; "Margin scheme — Works of art" or "Margin scheme — Collector's items and antiques" respectively;][1]

(15) where the person liable for payment of VAT is a tax representative for the purposes of Article 204, the VAT identification number, referred to in Article 214, of that tax representative, together with his full name and address.

Amendments—[1] Paras (7a), (10a), (11a) inserted, paras (11), (13), (14) substituted, by Council Directive 2010/45 art 1(16) with effect from 11 August 2010 (OJ L 189, 22.7.2010, p 1). The deadline for implementation of Directive 2010/45/EU is 31 December 2012. Substituted previously read as follows—

"(11) in the case of an exemption or where the customer is liable for payment of VAT, reference to the applicable provision of this Directive, or to the corresponding national provision, or any other reference indicating that the supply of goods or services is exempt or subject to the reverse charge procedure;".

"(13) where the margin scheme for travel agents is applied, reference to Article 306, or to the corresponding national provisions, or any other reference indicating that the margin scheme has been applied;".

"(14) where one of the special arrangements applicable to second-hand goods, works of art, collectors' items and antiques is applied, reference to Articles 313, 326 or 333, or to the corresponding national provisions, or any other reference indicating that one of those arrangements has been applied;".

[226a

Where the invoice is issued by a taxable person, who is not established in the Member State where the tax is due or whose establishment in that Member State does not intervene in the supply within the meaning of Article 192a, and who is making a supply of goods or services to a customer who is liable for payment of VAT, the taxable person may omit the details referred to in points (8), (9) and (10) of Article 226 and instead indicate, by reference to the quantity or extent of the goods or services supplied and their nature, the taxable amount of those goods or services.][1]

Amendments—[1] Article nserted by Council Directive 2010/45 art 1(17) with effect from 11 August 2010 (OJ L 189, 22.7.2010, p 1). The deadline for implementation of Directive 2010/45/EU is 31 December 2012.

[226b

As regards simplified invoices issued pursuant to Article 220a and Article 221(1) and (2), Member States shall require at least the following details:

(*a*) the date of issue;

(*b*) identification of the taxable person supplying the goods or services;

(*c*) identification of the type of goods or services supplied;

(*d*) the VAT amount payable or the information needed to calculate it;

(*e*) where the invoice issued is a document or message treated as an invoice pursuant to Article 219, specific and unambiguous reference to that initial invoice and the specific details which are being amended.

They may not require details on invoices other than those referred to in Articles 226, 227 and 230.';][1]

Amendments—[1] Article nserted by Council Directive 2010/45 art 1(17) with effect from 11 August 2010 (OJ L 189, 22.7.2010, p 1). The deadline for implementation of Directive 2010/45/EU is 31 December 2012.

Article 227

Member States may require taxable persons established in their territory and supplying goods or services there to indicate the VAT identification number, referred to in Article 214, of the customer in cases other than those referred to in point (4) of Article 226.

Article 228

Member States in whose territory goods or services are supplied may allow some of the compulsory details to be omitted from documents or messages treated as invoices pursuant to Article 219.[1]

Amendments—[1] Article repealed by Council Directive 2010/45 art 1(18) with effect from 11 August 2010 (OJ L 189, 22.7.2010, p 1). The deadline for implementation of Directive 2010/45/EU is 31 December 2012.

Article 229

Member States shall not require invoices to be signed.

[Article 230

The amounts which appear on the invoice may be expressed in any currency, provided that the amount of VAT payable or to be adjusted is expressed in the national currency of the Member State, using the conversion rate mechanism provided for in Article 91.][1]

Amendments—[1] Article substituted by Council Directive 2010/45 art 1(19) with effect from 11 August 2010 (OJ L 189, 22.7.2010, p 1). The deadline for implementation of Directive 2010/45/EU is 31 December 2012. Article previously read as follows—

"The amounts which appear on the invoice may be expressed in any currency, provided that the amount of VAT payable is expressed in the national currency of the Member State in which the supply of goods or services takes place, using the conversion mechanism laid down in Article 91.".

Article 231

For control purposes, Member States may require invoices in respect of supplies of goods or services in their territory and invoices received by taxable persons established in their territory to be translated into their national languages.[1]

Amendments—[1] Article repealed by Council Directive 2010/45 art 1(20) with effect from 11 August 2010 (OJ L 189, 22.7.2010, p 1). The deadline for implementation of Directive 2010/45/EU is 31 December 2012.

SECTION 5

[Paper invoices and electronic invoices]

[Article 232

The use of an electronic invoice shall be subject to acceptance by the recipient.][1]

Amendments—[1] Section 5 heading, and Article 232 substituted, by Council Directive 2010/45 art 1(21) with effect from 11 August 2010 (OJ L 189, 22.7.2010, p 1). The deadline for implementation of Directive 2010/45/EU is 31 December 2012. Article previously read as follows—

"Invoices issued pursuant to Section 2 may be sent on paper or, subject to acceptance by the recipient, they may be sent or made available by electronic means.".

[Article 233

1. The authenticity of the origin, the integrity of the content and the legibility of an invoice, whether on paper or in electronic form, shall be ensured from the point in time of issue until the end of the period for storage of the invoice.

Each taxable person shall determine the way to ensure the authenticity of the origin, the integrity of the content and the legibility of the invoice. This may be achieved by any business controls which create a reliable audit trail between an invoice and a supply of goods or services.

"Authenticity of the origin" means the assurance of the identity of the supplier or the issuer of the invoice.

"Integrity of the content" means that the content required according to this Directive has not been altered.

2. Other than by way of the type of business controls described in paragraph 1, the following are examples of technologies that ensure the authenticity of the origin and the integrity of the content of an electronic invoice:

(*a*) an advanced electronic signature within the meaning of point (2) of Article 2 of Directive 1999/93/EC of the European Parliament and of the Council of 13 December 1999 on a Community framework for electronic signatures (*), based on a qualified certificate and created by a secure signature creation device, within the meaning of points (6) and (10) of Article 2 of Directive 1999/93/EC;

(*b*) electronic data interchange (EDI), as defined in Article 2 of Annex 1 to Commission Recommendation 1994/820/EC of 19 October 1994 relating to the legal aspects of electronic data interchange (**), where the agreement relating to the exchange provides for the use of procedures guaranteeing the authenticity of the origin and integrity of the data.][1]

Notes—(*) OJ L 13, 19.1.2000, p 12.

(**) OJ L 338, 28.12.1994, p 98.

Amendments—[1] Article 233 substituted, by Council Directive 2010/45 art 1(23) with effect from 11 August 2010 (OJ L 189, 22.7.2010, p 1). The deadline for implementation of Directive 2010/45/EU is 31 December 2012. Article previously read as follows—

"1. Invoices sent or made available by electronic means shall be accepted by Member States provided that the authenticity of the origin and the integrity of their content are guaranteed by one of the following methods:

by means of an advanced electronic signature within the meaning of point (2) of Article 2 of Directive 1999/93/EC of the European Parliament and of the Council of 13 December 1999 on a Community framework for electronic signatures :[1]);

by means of electronic data interchange (EDI), as defined in Article 2 of Commission Recommendation 1994/820/EC of 19 October 1994 relating to the legal aspects of electronic data interchange :[2], if the agreement relating to the exchange provides for the use of procedures guaranteeing the authenticity of the origin and integrity of the data.

Invoices may, however, be sent or made available by other electronic means, subject to acceptance by the Member States concerned.

VAT EC

2. For the purposes of point (*a*) of the first subparagraph of paragraph 1, Member States may also ask for the advanced electronic signature to be based on a qualified certificate and created by a secure-signature-creation device, within the meaning of points (6) and (10) of Article 2 of Directive 1999/93/EC.

3. For the purposes of point (*b*) of the first subparagraph of paragraph 1, Member States may also, subject to conditions which they lay down, require that an additional summary document on paper be sent.".

Article 234

Member States may not impose on taxable persons supplying goods or services in their territory any other obligations or formalities relating to the sending or making available of invoices by electronic means.

[Article 235

Member States may lay down specific conditions for electronic invoices issued in respect of goods or services supplied in their territory from a country with which no legal instrument exists relating to mutual assistance similar in scope to that provided for in Directive 2010/24/EU and Regulation (EC) No 1798/2003.][1]

Amendments—[1] Articles 235–237 substituted by Council Directive 2010/45 art 1(24) with effect from 11 August 2010 (OJ L 189, 22.7.2010, p 1). The deadline for implementation of Directive 2010/45/EU is 31 December 2012. Article 235 previously read as follows—

"Member States may lay down specific conditions for invoices issued by electronic means in respect of goods or services supplied in their territory from a country with which no legal instrument exists relating to mutual assistance similar in scope to that provided for in Directive 76/308/EEC and Regulation (EC) No 1798/2003.".

[Article 236

Where batches containing several electronic invoices are sent or made available to the same recipient, the details common to the individual invoices may be mentioned only once where, for each invoice, all the information is accessible.][1]

Amendments—[1] Articles 235–237 substituted by Council Directive 2010/45 art 1(24) with effect from 11 August 2010 (OJ L 189, 22.7.2010, p 1). The deadline for implementation of Directive 2010/45/EU is 31 December 2012. Article 236 previously read as follows—

"Where batches containing several invoices are sent or made available to the same recipient by electronic means, the details common to the individual invoices may be mentioned only once if, for each invoice, all the information is accessible.".

[Article 237

By 31 December 2016 at the latest, the Commission shall present to the European Parliament and the Council an overall assessment report, based on an independent economic study, on the impact of the invoicing rules applicable from 1 January 2013 and notably on the extent to which they have effectively led to a decrease in administrative burdens for businesses, accompanied where necessary by an appropriate proposal to amend the relevant rules.][1]

Amendments—[1] Articles 235–237 substituted by Council Directive 2010/45 art 1(24) with effect from 11 August 2010 (OJ L 189, 22.7.2010, p 1). The deadline for implementation of Directive 2010/45/EU is 31 December 2012. Article 237 previously read as follows—

"The Commission shall present, at the latest on 31 December 2008, a report and, if appropriate, a proposal amending the conditions applicable to electronic invoicing in order to take account of future technological developments in that field.".

SECTION 6

Simplification measures

Article 238

[1. After consulting the VAT Committee, Member States may, in accordance with conditions which they may lay down, provide that in the following cases only the information required pursuant to Article 226b shall be entered on invoices in respect of supplies of goods or services:

(*a*) where the amount of the invoice is higher than EUR 100 but not higher than EUR 400, or the equivalent in national currency;

(*b*) where commercial or administrative practice in the business sector concerned or the technical conditions under which the invoices are issued make it particularly difficult to comply with all the obligations referred to in Article 226 or 230.][1]

2. . . .[1]

[3. The simplified arrangements provided for in paragraph 1 shall not be applied where invoices are required to be issued pursuant to points (2) and (3) of Article 220(1) or where the taxable supply of goods or services is carried out by a taxable person who is not established in the Member State in which the VAT is due or whose establishment in that Member State does not intervene in the supply within the meaning of Article 192a and the person liable for the payment of VAT is the person to whom the goods or services are supplied.][1]

Amendments—[1] Paras 1, 3 substituted, and para 2 repealed, by Council Directive 2010/45 art 1(25) with effect from 11 August 2010 (OJ L 189, 22.7.2010, p 1). The deadline for implementation of Directive 2010/45/EU is 31 December 2012. Article 238 previously read as follows—

"After consulting the VAT Committee, Member States may, in accordance with conditions which they may lay down, provide that in the following cases some of the information required under Article 226 and 230, subject to options taken up by Member States under Articles 227, 228 and 231, need not be entered on invoices in respect of supplies of goods or services in their territory:

where the amount of the invoice is minor;

where commercial or administrative practice in the business sector concerned or the technical conditions under which the invoices are issued make it difficult to comply with all the obligations referred to in Articles 226 and 230.

3. Invoices must, in any event, contain the following information:

the date of issue;

identification of the taxable person;

identification of the type of goods or services supplied;

the VAT amount payable or the information needed to calculate it.

3. The simplified arrangements provided for in paragraph 1 may not be applied to the transactions referred to in Articles 20, 21, 22, 33, 36, 138 and 141.".

Article 239

In cases where Member States make use of the option under point (*b*) of the first subparagraph of Article 272(1) of not allocating a VAT identification number to taxable persons who do not carry out any of the transactions referred to in Articles 20, 21, 22, 33, 36, 138 and 141, and where the supplier or the customer has not been allocated an identification number of that type, another number called the tax reference number, as defined by the Member States concerned, shall be entered on the invoice instead.

Article 240

Where the taxable person has been allocated a VAT identification number, the Member States exercising the option under point (*b*) of the first subparagraph of Article 272(1) may also require the invoice to show the following:

(1) in respect of the supply of services, as referred to in Articles 44, 47, 50, 53, 54 and 55, and the supply of goods, as referred to in Articles 138 and 141, the VAT identification number and the tax reference number of the supplier;

(2) in respect of other supplies of goods or services, only the tax reference number of the supplier or only the VAT identification number.

CHAPTER 4

ACCOUNTING

SECTION 1

Definition

Article 241

For the purposes of this Chapter, 'storage of an invoice by electronic means' shall mean storage of data using electronic equipment for processing (including digital compression) and storage, and employing wire, radio, optical or other electromagnetic means.

SECTION 2

General obligations

Article 242

Every taxable person shall keep accounts in sufficient detail for VAT to be applied and its application checked by the tax authorities.

[Article 243

1. Every taxable person shall keep a register of the goods dispatched or transported by him, or on his behalf, to a destination outside the territory of the Member State of departure but within the Community for the purposes of transactions consisting in valuations of those goods or work on them or their temporary use as referred to in points (f), (g) and (h) of Article 17(2).

2. Every taxable person shall keep accounts in sufficient detail to enable the identification of goods dispatched to him from another Member State, by or on behalf of a taxable person identified for VAT purposes in that other Member State, and used for services consisting in valuations of those goods or work on those goods.][1]

Amendments—[1] Article 243 substituted by Council Directive 2010/45 art 1(26) with effect from 11 August 2010 (OJ L 189, 22.7.2010, p 1). The deadline for implementation of Directive 2010/45/EU is 31 December 2012. Article 243 previously read as follows—

VAT EC

"1. Every taxable person shall keep a register of the goods dispatched or transported, by that person or on his behalf, to a destination outside the territory of the Member State of departure but within the Community for the purposes of transactions consisting in work on those goods or their temporary use as referred to in points (*f*), (*g*) and (*h*) of Article 17 (2).

2. Every taxable person shall keep accounts in sufficient detail to enable the identification of goods dispatched to him from another Member State, by or on behalf of a taxable person identified for VAT purposes in that other Member State, and used for services consisting in valuations of those goods or work on those goods as referred to in point (*c*) of Article 52.".

SECTION 3

Specific obligations relating to the storage of all invoices

Article 244

Every taxable person shall ensure that copies of the invoices issued by himself, or by his customer or, in his name and on his behalf, by a third party, and all the invoices which he has received, are stored.

Article 245

1. For the purposes of this Directive, the taxable person may decide the place of storage of all invoices provided that he makes the invoices or information stored in accordance with Article 244 available to the competent authorities without undue delay whenever they so request.

2. Member States may require taxable persons established in their territory to notify them of the place of storage, if it is outside their territory.

Member States may also require taxable persons established in their territory to store within that territory invoices issued by themselves or by their customers or, in their name and on their behalf, by a third party, as well as all the invoices that they have received, when the storage is not by electronic means guaranteeing full on-line access to the data concerned.

Article 246

The authenticity of the origin and the integrity of the content of the invoices stored, as well as their legibility, must be guaranteed throughout the storage period.

In respect of the invoices referred to in the second subparagraph of Article 233(1), the details they contain may not be altered and must remain legible throughout the storage period.[1]

Amendments—[1] Article 246 repealed by Council Directive 2010/45 art 1(27) with effect from 11 August 2010 (OJ L 189, 22.7.2010, p 1). The deadline for implementation of Directive 2010/45/EU is 31 December 2012.

Article 247

1. Each Member State shall determine the period throughout which taxable persons must ensure the storage of invoices relating to the supply of goods or services in its territory and invoices received by taxable persons established in its territory.

[2. In order to ensure that the requirements laid down in Article 233 are met, the Member State referred to in paragraph 1 may require that invoices be stored in the original form in which they were sent or made available, whether paper or electronic. Additionally, in the case of invoices stored by electronic means, the Member State may require that the data guaranteeing the authenticity of the origin of the invoices and the integrity of their content, as provided for in Article 233, also be stored by electronic means.

3. The Member State referred to in paragraph 1 may lay down specific conditions prohibiting or restricting the storage of invoices in a country with which no legal instrument exists relating to mutual assistance similar in scope to that provided for in Directive 2010/24/EU and Regulation (EC) No 1798/2003 or to the right referred to in Article 249 to access by electronic means, to download and to use.][1]

Amendments—[1] Paras 2, 3 substituted by Council Directive 2010/45 art 1(28) with effect from 11 August 2010 (OJ L 189, 22.7.2010, p 1). The deadline for implementation of Directive 2010/45/EU is 31 December 2012. Those paras previously read as follows—

"2. In order to ensure that the conditions laid down in Article 246 are met, the Member State referred to in paragraph 1 may require that invoices be stored in the original form in which they were sent or made available, whether paper or electronic. Additionally, in the case of invoices stored by electronic means, the Member State may require that the data guaranteeing the authenticity of the origin of the invoices and the integrity of their content, as provided for in the first paragraph of Article 246, also be stored.

3. The Member State referred to in paragraph 1 may lay down specific conditions prohibiting or restricting the storage of invoices in a country with which no legal instrument exists relating to mutual assistance similar in scope to that provided for in Directive 76/308/EEC and Regulation (EC) No 1798/2003 or to the right referred to in Article 249 to access by electronic means, to download and to use.".

Article 248

Member States may, subject to conditions which they lay down, require the storage of invoices received by non-taxable persons.

[Article 248a

For control purposes, and as regards invoices in respect of supplies of goods or services supplied in their territory and invoices received by taxable persons established in their territory, Member States may, for certain taxable persons or certain cases, require translation into their official languages. Member States may, however, not impose a general requirement that invoices be translated.][1]

Amendments—[1] Article 248a inserted by Council Directive 2010/45 art 1(29) with effect from 11 August 2010 (OJ L 189, 22.7.2010, p 1). The deadline for implementation of Directive 2010/45/EU is 31 December 2012.

SECTION 4

Right of access to invoices stored by electronic means in another Member State

[Article 249

For control purposes, where a taxable person stores, by electronic means guaranteeing online access to the data concerned, invoices which he issues or receives, the competent authorities of the Member State in which he is established and, where the VAT is due in another Member State, the competent authorities of that Member State, shall have the right to access, download and use those invoices.][1]

Amendments—[1] Article 249 substituted by Council Directive 2010/45 art 1(30) with effect from 11 August 2010 (OJ L 189, 22.7.2010, p 1). The deadline for implementation of Directive 2010/45/EU is 31 December 2012. Article 249 previously read as follows—

> "Where a taxable person stores invoices which he issues or receives by electronic means guaranteeing on-line access to the data and where the place of storage is in a Member State other than that in which he is established, the competent authorities in the Member State in which he is established shall, for the purposes of this Directive, have the right to access those invoices by electronic means, to download and to use them, within the limits set by the rules of the Member State in which the taxable person is established and in so far as those authorities require for control purposes.".

CHAPTER 5

RETURNS

Article 250

1. Every taxable person shall submit a VAT return setting out all the information needed to calculate the tax that has become chargeable and the deductions to be made including, in so far as is necessary for the establishment of the basis of assessment, the total value of the transactions relating to such tax and deductions and the value of any exempt transactions.

2. Member States shall allow, and may require, the VAT return referred to in paragraph 1 to be submitted by electronic means, in accordance with conditions which they lay down.

Article 251

In addition to the information referred to in Article 250, the VAT return covering a given tax period shall show the following:

(*a*) the total value, exclusive of VAT, of the supplies of goods referred to in Article 138 in respect of which VAT has become chargeable during this tax period;

(*b*) the total value, exclusive of VAT, of the supplies of goods referred to in Articles 33 and 36 carried out within the territory of another Member State, in respect of which VAT has become chargeable during this tax period, where the place where dispatch or transport of the goods began is situated in the Member State in which the return must be submitted;

(*c*) the total value, exclusive of VAT, of the intra-Community acquisitions of goods, or transactions treated as such, pursuant to Articles 21 or 22, made in the Member State in which the return must be submitted and in respect of which VAT has become chargeable during this tax period;

(*d*) the total value, exclusive of VAT, of the supplies of goods referred to in Articles 33 and 36 carried out in the Member State in which the return must be submitted and in respect of which VAT has become chargeable during this tax period, where the place where dispatch or transport of the goods began is situated within the territory of another Member State;

(*e*) the total value, exclusive of VAT, of the supplies of goods carried out in the Member State in which the return must be submitted and in respect of which the taxable person has been designated, in accordance with Article 197, as liable for payment of VAT and in respect of which VAT has become chargeable during this tax period.

Article 252

1. The VAT return shall be submitted by a deadline to be determined by Member States. That deadline may not be more than two months after the end of each tax period.

2. The tax period shall be set by each Member State at one month, two months or three months. Member States may, however, set different tax periods provided that those periods do not exceed one year.

Article 253

Sweden may apply a simplified procedure for small and medium-sized enterprises, whereby taxable persons carrying out only transactions taxable at national level may submit VAT returns three months after the end of the annual direct tax period.

Article 254

In the case of supplies of new means of transport carried out in accordance with the conditions specified in Article 138(2)(*a*) by a taxable person identified for VAT purposes for a customer not identified for VAT purposes, or by a taxable person as defined in Article 9(2), Member States shall take the measures necessary to ensure that the vendor communicates all the information needed for VAT to be applied and its application checked by the tax authorities.

Article 255

Where Member States designate the customer of investment gold as the person liable for payment of VAT pursuant to Article 198 (1) or if, in the case of gold material, semi-manufactured products or investment gold as defined in Article 344(1), they exercise the option provided for in Article 198(2) of designating the customer as the person liable for payment of VAT, they shall take the measures necessary to ensure that he complies with the obligations relating to submission of a VAT return set out in this Chapter.

Article 256

Member States shall take the measures necessary to ensure that persons who are regarded as liable for payment of VAT in the stead of a taxable person not established within their territory, in accordance with Articles 194 to 197 and Article 204, comply with the obligations relating to submission of a VAT return, as laid down in this Chapter.

Article 257

Member States shall take the measures necessary to ensure that non-taxable legal persons who are liable for payment of VAT due in respect of intra-Community acquisitions of goods, as referred to in Article 2(1)(*b*)(i), comply with the obligations relating to submission of a VAT return, as laid down in this Chapter.

Article 258

Member States shall lay down detailed rules for the submission of VAT returns in respect of intra-Community acquisitions of new means of transport, as referred to in Article 2(1)(*b*)(ii), and intra-Community acquisitions of products subject to excise duty, as referred to in Article 2(1)(*b*)(iii).

Article 259

Member States may require persons who make intra-Community acquisitions of new means of transport as referred to in Article 2 (1)(*b*)(ii), to provide, when submitting the VAT return, all the information needed for VAT to be applied and its application checked by the tax authorities.

Article 260

Member States shall lay down detailed rules for the submission of VAT returns in respect of the importation of goods.

Article 261

1. Member States may require the taxable person to submit a return showing all the particulars specified in Articles 250 and 251 in respect of all transactions carried out in the preceding year. That return shall provide all the information necessary for any adjustments.

2. Member States shall allow, and may require, the return referred to in paragraph 1 to be submitted by electronic means, in accordance with conditions which they lay down.

CHAPTER 6
RECAPITULATIVE STATEMENTS

[Article 262

Every taxable person identified for VAT purposes shall submit a recapitulative statement of the following:

(*a*) the acquirers identified for VAT purposes to whom he has supplied goods in accordance with the conditions specified in Article 138(1) and (2)(*c*);

(*b*) the persons identified for VAT purposes to whom he has supplied goods which were supplied to him by way of intra-Community acquisitions referred to in Article 42;

(*c*) the taxable persons, and the non-taxable legal persons identified for VAT purposes, to whom he has supplied services, other than services that are exempted from VAT in the Member State where the transaction is taxable, and for which the recipient is liable to pay the tax pursuant to Article 196.][1]

Amendments—[1] Article 262 substituted by Council Directive 2008/8/EC art 2(9) with effect from 1 January 2010 (OJ L 44, 20.2.2008 p 11). Text previously read as follows—

"**Article 262**

Every taxable person identified for VAT purposes shall submit a recapitulative statement of the acquirers identified for VAT purposes to whom he has supplied goods in accordance with the conditions specified in Article 138(1) and (2)(*c*), and of the persons identified for VAT purposes to whom he has supplied goods which were supplied to him by way of intra-Community acquisitions referred to in Article 42.".

[Article 263

1. The recapitulative statement shall be drawn up for each calendar month within a period not exceeding one month and in accordance with procedures to be determined by the Member States.

1a. However, Member States, in accordance with the conditions and limits which they may lay down, may allow taxable persons to submit the recapitulative statement for each calendar quarter within a time limit not exceeding one month from the end of the quarter, where the total quarterly amount, excluding VAT, of the supplies of goods as referred to in Articles 264(1)(*d*) and 265(1)(*c*) does not exceed either in respect of the quarter concerned or in respect of any of the previous four quarters the sum of EUR 50000 or its equivalent in national currency.

The option provided for in the first subparagraph shall cease to be applicable after the end of the month during which the total value, excluding VAT, of the supplies of goods as referred to in Article 264(1)(*d*) and 265(1)(*c*) exceeds, in respect of the current quarter, the sum of EUR 50000 or its equivalent in national currency. In this case, a recapitulative statement shall be drawn up for the month(s) which has (have) elapsed since the beginning of the quarter, within a time limit not exceeding one month.

1b. Until 31 December 2011, Member States are allowed to set the sum mentioned in paragraph 1a at EUR 100000 or its equivalent in national currency.

1c. In the case of supplies of services as referred to in Article 264(1)(*d*), Member States, in accordance with the conditions and limits which they may lay down, may allow taxable persons to submit the recapitulative statement for each calendar quarter within a time limit not exceeding one month from the end of the quarter.

Member States may, in particular, require the taxable persons who carry out supplies of both goods and services as referred to in Article 264(1)(*d*) to submit the recapitulative statement in accordance with the deadline resulting from paragraphs 1 to 1b.

2. Member States shall allow, and may require, the recapitulative statement referred to in paragraph 1 to be submitted by electronic file transfer, in accordance with conditions which they lay down.][1]

Amendments—[1] Article 263 substituted by Council Directive 2008/117/EC art 1 with effect from 21 January 2009. The deadline for implementation of this Directive is 1 January 2010 (OJ L 14, 20.1.2009 p 7). Text previously read as follows—

"Article 263

1. The recapitulative statement shall be drawn up for each calendar quarter within a period and in accordance with procedures to be determined by the Member States. Member States may, however, provide that recapitulative statements are to be submitted on a monthly basis.
2. Member States shall allow, and may require, the recapitulative statements referred to in paragraph 1 to be submitted by electronic means, in accordance with conditions which they lay down.".

Article 264

1. The recapitulative statement shall set out the following information:

[(*a*) the VAT identification number of the taxable person in the Member State in which the recapitulative statement must be submitted and under which he has carried out the supply of goods in accordance with the conditions specified in Article 138(1) and under which he effected taxable supplies of services in accordance with the conditions laid down in Article 44;

(*b*) the VAT identification number of the person acquiring the goods or receiving the services in a Member State other than that in which the recapitulative statement must be submitted and under which the goods or services were supplied to him;][1]

(*c*) the VAT identification number of the taxable person in the Member State in which the recapitulative statement must be submitted and under which he has carried out a transfer to another Member State, as referred to in Article 138(2)(*c*), and the number by means of which he is identified in the Member State in which the dispatch or transport ended;

[(*d*) for each person who acquired goods or received services, the total value of the supplies of goods and the total value of the supplies of services carried out by the taxable person;][1]

(*e*) in respect of supplies of goods consisting in transfers to another Member State, as referred to in Article 138(2)(*c*), the total value of the supplies, determined in accordance with Article 76;

(*f*) the amounts of adjustments made pursuant to Article 90.

[2. The value referred to in paragraph 1(*d*) shall be declared for the period of submission established in accordance with Article 263(1) to (1 *c*) during which VAT became chargeable.

The amounts referred to in paragraph 1(f) shall be declared for the period of submission established in accordance with Article 263(1) to (1 *c*) during which the person acquiring the goods was notified of the adjustment.][2]

VAT EC

Amendments—[1] Para 1(*a*), (*b*), (*d*) substituted, by Council Directive 2008/8/EC art 2(10) with effect from 1 January 2010 (OJ L 44, 20.2.2008 p 11). Text previously read as follows—

"(*a*) the VAT identification number of the taxable person in the Member State in which the recapitulative statement must be submitted and under which he has carried out the supply of goods in accordance with the conditions specified in Article 138(1);

(*b*) the VAT identification number of the person acquiring the goods in a Member State other than that in which the recapitulative statement must be submitted and under which the goods were supplied to him;".

"(*d*) for each person who acquired goods, the total value of the supplies of goods carried out by the taxable person;".

[2] Para 2 substituted by Council Directive 2008/117/EC art 1 with effect from 21 January 2009. The deadline for implementation of this Directive is 1 January 2010 (OJ L 14, 20.1.2009 p 7). Text previously read as follows—

"2. The value referred to in point (*d*) of paragraph 1 shall be declared for the calendar quarter during which VAT became chargeable.

The amounts referred to in point (f) of paragraph 1 shall be declared for the calendar quarter during which the person acquiring the goods was notified of the adjustment.".

Article 265

1. In the case of intra-Community acquisitions of goods, as referred to in Article 42, the taxable person identified for VAT purposes in the Member State which issued him with the VAT identification number under which he made such acquisitions shall set the following information out clearly on the recapitulative statement:

(*a*) his VAT identification number in that Member State and under which he made the acquisition and subsequent supply of goods;

(*b*) the VAT identification number, in the Member State in which dispatch or transport of the goods ended, of the person to whom the subsequent supply was made by the taxable person;

(*c*) for each person to whom the subsequent supply was made, the total value, exclusive of VAT, of the supplies made by the taxable person in the Member State in which dispatch or transport of the goods ended.

[2. The value referred to in paragraph 1(*c*) shall be declared for the period of submission established in accordance with Article 263(1) to (1 *b*) during which VAT became chargeable.][1]

Amendments—[1] Para 2 substituted by Council Directive 2008/117/EC art 1 with effect from 21 January 2009. The deadline for implementation of this Directive is 1 January 2010 (OJ L 14, 20.1.2009 p 7). Text previously read as follows—

"2. The value referred to in point (*c*) of paragraph 1 shall be declared for the calendar quarter during which VAT became chargeable.".

Article 266

By way of derogation from Articles 264 and 265, Member States may provide that additional information is to be given in recapitulative statements.

Article 267

Member States shall take the measures necessary to ensure that those persons who, in accordance with Articles 194 and 204, are regarded as liable for payment of VAT, in the stead of a taxable person who is not established in their territory, comply with the obligation to submit a recapitulative statement as provided for in this Chapter.

Article 268

Member States may require that taxable persons who, in their territory, make intra-Community acquisitions of goods, or transactions treated as such, pursuant to Articles 21 or 22, submit statements giving details of such acquisitions, provided, however, that such statements are not required in respect of a period of less than one month.

Article 269

Acting unanimously on a proposal from the Commission, the Council may authorise any Member State to introduce the special measures provided for in Articles 270 and 271 to simplify the obligation, laid down in this Chapter, to submit a recapitulative statement. Such measures may not jeopardise the proper monitoring of intra-Community transactions.

Article 270

By virtue of the authorisation referred to in Article 269, Member States may permit taxable persons to submit annual recapitulative statements indicating the VAT identification numbers, in another Member State, of the persons to whom those taxable persons have supplied goods in accordance with the conditions specified in Article 138(1) and (2)(*c*), where the taxable persons meet the following three conditions:

(*a*) the total annual value, exclusive of VAT, of their supplies of goods and services does not exceed by more than EUR 35 000, or the equivalent in national currency, the amount of the annual turnover which is used as a reference for application of the exemption for small enterprises provided for in Articles 282 to 292;

(*b*) the total annual value, exclusive of VAT, of supplies of goods carried out by them in accordance with the conditions specified in Article 138 does not exceed EUR 15 000 or the equivalent in national currency;

(*c*) none of the supplies of goods carried out by them in accordance with the conditions specified in Article 138 is a supply of new means of transport.

Article 271

By virtue of the authorisation referred to in Article 269, Member States which set at over three months the tax period in respect of which taxable persons must submit the VAT return provided for in Article 250 may permit such persons to submit recapitulative statements in respect of the same period where those taxable persons meet the following three conditions:

(*a*) the total annual value, exclusive of VAT, of their supplies of goods and services does not exceed EUR 200 000 or the equivalent in national currency;

(*b*) the total annual value, exclusive of VAT, of supplies of goods carried out by them in accordance with the conditions specified in Article 138 does not exceed EUR 15 000 or the equivalent in national currency;

(*c*) none of the supplies of goods carried out by them in accordance with the conditions specified in Article 138 is a supply of new means of transport.

CHAPTER 7
MISCELLANEOUS PROVISIONS

Article 272

1. Member States may release the following taxable persons from certain or all obligations referred to in Chapters 2 to 6:

(*a*) taxable persons whose intra-Community acquisitions of goods are not subject to VAT pursuant to Article 3(1);

(*b*) taxable persons carrying out none of the transactions referred to in Articles 20, 21, 22, 33, 36, 138 and 141;

(*c*) taxable persons carrying out only supplies of goods or of services which are exempt pursuant to Articles 132, 135 and 136, Articles 146 to 149 and Articles 151, 152 or 153;

(*d*) taxable persons covered by the exemption for small enterprises provided for in Articles 282 to 292;

(*e*) taxable persons covered by the common flat-rate scheme for farmers.

[Member States may not release the taxable persons referred to in point (b) of the first subparagraph from the invoicing obligations laid down in Sections 3 to 6 of Chapter 3 and Section 3 of Chapter 4.][1]

2. If Member States exercise the option under point (*e*) of the first subparagraph of paragraph 1, they shall take the measures necessary to ensure the correct application of the transitional arrangements for the taxation of intra-Community transactions.

3. Member States may release taxable persons other than those referred to in paragraph 1 from certain of the accounting obligations referred to in Article 242.

Amendments—[1] In para 1, second sub-para substituted by Council Directive 2010/45 art 1(31) with effect from 11 August 2010 (OJ L 189, 22.7.2010, p 1). The deadline for implementation of Directive 2010/45/EU is 31 December 2012. That para previously read as follows—

"Member States may not release the taxable persons referred to in point (b) of the first subparagraph from the invoicing obligations laid down in Articles 220 to 236 and Articles 238, 239 and 240.".

Article 273

Member States may impose other obligations which they deem necessary to ensure the correct collection of VAT and to prevent evasion, subject to the requirement of equal treatment as between domestic transactions and transactions carried out between Member States by taxable persons and provided that such obligations do not, in trade between Member States, give rise to formalities connected with the crossing of frontiers.

The option under the first paragraph may not be relied upon in order to impose additional invoicing obligations over and above those laid down in Chapter 3.

Simon's Tax Cases—*Minister Finansow v Kraft Foods Polska SA* (Case C-588/10) [2012] STC 787; *Mahageben kft v Nemzeti Adó- és Vámhivatal Dél-dunántúli Regionális Adó Főigazgatósága; David v Nemzeti Adó- és Vámhivatal Észak-alföldi Regionális Adó Főigazgatósága* (Joined cases C-80/11 and C-142/11) [2012] STC 1934.

VAT EC

CHAPTER 8
OBLIGATIONS RELATING TO CERTAIN IMPORTATIONS AND EXPORTATIONS

SECTION 1
Importation

Article 274

Articles 275, 276 and 277 shall apply to the importation of goods in free circulation which enter the Community from a third territory forming part of the customs territory of the Community.

Article 275

The formalities relating to the importation of the goods referred to in Article 274 shall be the same as those laid down by the Community customs provisions in force for the importation of goods into the customs territory of the Community.

Article 276

Where dispatch or transport of the goods referred to in Article 274 ends at a place situated outside the Member State of their entry into the Community, they shall circulate in the Community under the internal Community transit procedure laid down by the Community customs provisions in force, in so far as they have been the subject of a declaration placing them under that procedure on their entry into the Community.

Article 277

Where, on their entry into the Community, the goods referred to in Article 274 are in one of the situations which would entitle them, if they were imported within the meaning of the first paragraph of Article 30, to be covered by one of the arrangements or situations referred to in Article 156, or by a temporary importation arrangement with full exemption from import duties, Member States shall take the measures necessary to ensure that the goods may remain in the Community under the same conditions as those laid down for the application of those arrangements or situations.

SECTION 2
Exportation

Article 278

Articles 279 and 280 shall apply to the exportation of goods in free circulation which are dispatched or transported from a Member State to a third territory forming part of the customs territory of the Community.

Article 279

The formalities relating to the exportation of the goods referred to in Article 278 from the territory of the Community shall be the same as those laid down by the Community customs provisions in force for the exportation of goods from the customs territory of the Community.

Article 280

In the case of goods which are temporarily exported from the Community, in order to be reimported, Member States shall take the measures necessary to ensure that, on reimportation into the Community, such goods may be covered by the same provisions as would have applied if they had been temporarily exported from the customs territory of the Community.

TITLE XII
SPECIAL SCHEMES

CHAPTER 1
SPECIAL SCHEME FOR SMALL ENTERPRISES

SECTION 1
Simplified procedures for charging and collection

Article 281

Member States which might encounter difficulties in applying the normal VAT arrangements to small enterprises, by reason of the activities or structure of such enterprises, may, subject to such conditions and limits as they may set, and after consulting the VAT Committee, apply simplified procedures, such as flat-rate schemes, for charging and collecting VAT provided that they do not lead to a reduction thereof.

SECTION 2
Exemptions or graduated relief

Article 282

The exemptions and graduated tax relief provided for in this Section shall apply to the supply of goods and services by small enterprises.

Article 283

1. The arrangements provided for in this Section shall not apply to the following transactions:

(*a*) transactions carried out on an occasional basis, as referred to in Article 12;

(*b*) supplies of new means of transport carried out in accordance with the conditions specified in Article 138(1) and (2)(*a*);

(*c*) supplies of goods or services carried out by a taxable person who is not established in the Member State in which the VAT is due.

2. Member States may exclude transactions other than those referred to in paragraph 1 from the arrangements provided for in this Section.

Simon's Tax Cases—*Schmelz v Finanzamt Waldviertel* (Case C-97/09) [2011] STC 88.

Article 284

1. Member States which have exercised the option under Article 14 of Council Directive 67/228/EEC of 11 April 1967 on the harmonisation of legislation of Member States concerning turnover taxes — Structure and procedures for application of the common system of value added tax ;[1] of introducing exemptions or graduated tax relief may retain them, and the arrangements for applying them, if they comply with the VAT rules.

2. Member States which, at 17 May 1977, exempted taxable persons whose annual turnover was less than the equivalent in national currency of 5 000 European units of account at the conversion rate on that date, may raise that ceiling up to EUR 5 000.

Member States which applied graduated tax relief may neither raise the ceiling for graduated tax relief nor render the conditions for the granting of it more favourable.

(1) OJ 71, 14.4.1967, p. 1303/67. Directive repealed by Directive 77/ 388/EEC.

Article 285

Member States which have not exercised the option under Article 14 of Directive 67/228/EEC may exempt taxable persons whose annual turnover is no higher than EUR 5 000 or the equivalent in national currency.

The Member States referred to in the first paragraph may grant graduated tax relief to taxable persons whose annual turnover exceeds the ceiling fixed by them for its application.

Article 286

Member States which, at 17 May 1977, exempted taxable persons whose annual turnover was equal to or higher than the equivalent in national currency of 5 000 European units of account at the conversion rate on that date, may raise that ceiling in order to maintain the value of the exemption in real terms.

Article 287

Member States which acceded after 1 January 1978 may exempt taxable persons whose annual turnover is no higher than the equivalent in national currency of the following amounts at the conversion rate on the day of their accession:

(1) Greece: 10 000 European units of account;
(2) Spain: ECU 10 000;
(3) Portugal: ECU 10 000;
(4) Austria: ECU 35 000;
(5) Finland: ECU 10 000;
(6) Sweden: ECU 10 000;
(7) Czech Republic: EUR 35 000;
(8) Estonia: EUR 16 000;
(9) Cyprus: EUR 15 600;
(10) Latvia: EUR 17 200;
(11) Lithuania: EUR 29 000;
(12) Hungary: EUR 35 000;
(13) Malta: EUR 37 000 if the economic activity consists principally in the supply of goods, EUR 24 300 if the economic activity consists principally in the supply of services with a low value added (high inputs), and EUR 14 600 in other cases, namely supplies of services with a high value added (low inputs);
(14) Poland: EUR 10 000;
(15) Slovenia: EUR 25 000;
(16) Slovakia: EUR 35 000.
[(17) Bulgaria: EUR 25 600;
(18) Romania: EUR 35 000.]

Amendments—Points (17), (18) inserted by Council Directive 2009/162/EU art 1(14) with effect from 15 January 2010 (OJ L 10, 15.1.2010, p 14).

VAT EC

Article 288

The turnover serving as a reference for the purposes of applying the arrangements provided for in this Section shall consist of the following amounts, exclusive of VAT:

(1) the value of supplies of goods and services, in so far as they are taxed;

(2) the value of transactions which are exempt, with deductibility of the VAT paid at the preceding stage, pursuant to Articles 110 or 111, Article 125(1), Article 127 or Article 128(1);

(3) the value of transactions which are exempt pursuant to Articles 146 to 149 and Articles 151, 152 or 153;

(4) the value of real estate transactions, financial transactions as referred to in points (*b*) to (*g*) of Article 135(1), and insurance services, unless those transactions are ancillary transactions.

However, disposals of the tangible or intangible capital assets of an enterprise shall not be taken into account for the purposes of calculating turnover.

Article 289

Taxable persons exempt from VAT shall not be entitled to deduct VAT in accordance with Articles 167 to 171 and Articles 173 to 177, and may not show the VAT on their invoices.

Article 290

Taxable persons who are entitled to exemption from VAT may opt either for the normal VAT arrangements or for the simplified procedures provided for in Article 281. In this case, they shall be entitled to any graduated tax relief provided for under national legislation.

Article 291

Subject to the application of Article 281, taxable persons enjoying graduated relief shall be regarded as taxable persons subject to the normal VAT arrangements.

Article 292

The arrangements provided for in this Section shall apply until a date to be fixed by the Council in accordance with Article 93 of the Treaty, which may not be later than that on which the definitive arrangements referred to in Article 402 enter into force.

SECTION 3

Reporting and review

Article 293

Every four years starting from the adoption of this Directive, the Commission shall present to the Council, on the basis of information obtained from the Member States, a report on the application of this Chapter, together, where appropriate and taking into account the need to ensure the long-term convergence of national regulations, with proposals on the following subjects:

(1) improvements to the special scheme for small enterprises;

(2) the adaptation of national systems as regards exemptions and graduated tax relief;

(3) the adaptation of the ceilings provided for in Section 2.

Article 294

The Council shall decide, in accordance with Article 93 of the Treaty, whether a special scheme for small enterprises is necessary under the definitive arrangements and, if appropriate, shall lay down the common limits and conditions for the implementation of that scheme.

CHAPTER 2

COMMON FLAT-RATE SCHEME FOR FARMERS

Article 295

1. For the purposes of this Chapter, the following definitions shall apply:

(1) 'farmer' means any taxable person whose activity is carried out in an agricultural, forestry or fisheries undertaking;

(2) 'agricultural, forestry or fisheries undertaking' means an undertaking regarded as such by each Member State within the framework of the production activities listed in Annex VII;

(3) 'flat-rate farmer' means any farmer covered by the flat-rate scheme provided for in this Chapter;

(4) 'agricultural products' means goods produced by an agricultural, forestry or fisheries undertaking in each Member State as a result of the activities listed in Annex VII;

(5) 'agricultural services' means services, and in particular those listed in Annex VIII, supplied by a farmer using his labour force or the equipment normally employed in the agricultural, forestry or fisheries undertaking operated by him and normally playing a part in agricultural production;

(6) 'input VAT charged' means the amount of the total VAT attaching to the goods and services purchased by all agricultural, forestry and fisheries undertakings of each Member State

subject to the flat-rate scheme where such tax would be deductible in accordance with Articles 167, 168 and 169 and Articles 173 to 177 by a farmer subject to the normal VAT arrangements;

(7) 'flat-rate compensation percentages' means the percentages fixed by Member States in accordance with Articles 297, 298 and 299 and applied by them in the cases specified in Article 300 in order to enable flat-rate farmers to offset at a fixed rate the input VAT charged;

(8) 'flat-rate compensation' means the amount arrived at by applying the flat-rate compensation percentage to the turnover of the flat-rate farmer in the cases specified in Article 300.

2. Where a farmer processes, using means normally employed in an agricultural, forestry or fisheries undertaking, products deriving essentially from his agricultural production, such processing activities shall be treated as agricultural production activities, as listed in Annex VII.

Simon's Tax Cases—*Finanzamt Rendsburg v Harbs* [2006] STC 340*; *Slaby v Minster Finansow / Kuc and anor v Dyrektor Izby Skarbowej w Warszawie* (Cases C-180/10 and C-181/10) [2011] STC 2230.

Article 296

1. Where the application to farmers of the normal VAT arrangements, or the special scheme provided for in Chapter 1, is likely to give rise to difficulties, Member States may apply to farmers, in accordance with this Chapter, a flat-rate scheme designed to offset the VAT charged on purchases of goods and services made by the flat-rate farmers.
2. Each Member State may exclude from the flat-rate scheme certain categories of farmers, as well as farmers for whom application of the normal VAT arrangements, or of the simplified procedures provided for in Article 281, is not likely to give rise to administrative difficulties.
3. Every flat-rate farmer may opt, subject to the rules and conditions to be laid down by each Member State, for application of the normal VAT arrangements or, as the case may be, the simplified procedures provided for in Article 281.

Article 297

Member States shall, where necessary, fix the flat-rate compensation percentages. They may fix varying percentages for forestry, for the different sub-divisions of agriculture and for fisheries.

Member States shall notify the Commission of the flat-rate compensation percentages fixed in accordance with the first paragraph before applying them.

Article 298

The flat-rate compensation percentages shall be calculated on the basis of macro-economic statistics for flat-rate farmers alone for the preceding three years.

The percentages may be rounded up or down to the nearest half-point. Member States may also reduce such percentages to a nil rate.

Article 299

The flat-rate compensation percentages may not have the effect of obtaining for flat-rate farmers refunds greater than the input VAT charged.

Article 300

The flat-rate compensation percentages shall be applied to the prices, exclusive of VAT, of the following goods and services:

(1) agricultural products supplied by flat-rate farmers to taxable persons other than those covered, in the Member State in which these products were supplied, by this flat-rate scheme;

(2) agricultural products supplied by flat-rate farmers, in accordance with the conditions specified in Article 138, to non-taxable legal persons whose intra-Community acquisitions of goods are subject to VAT, pursuant to Article 2(1)(*b*), in the Member State in which dispatch or transport of those agricultural products ends;

(3) agricultural services supplied by flat-rate farmers to taxable persons other than those covered, in the Member State in which these services were supplied, by this flat-rate scheme.

Article 301

1. In the case of the supply of agricultural products or agricultural services specified in Article 300, Member States shall provide that the flat-rate compensation is to be paid either by the customer or by the public authorities.
2. In respect of any supply of agricultural products or agricultural services other than those specified in Article 300, the flat-rate compensation shall be deemed to be paid by the customer.

Article 302

If a flat-rate farmer is entitled to flat-rate compensation, he shall not be entitled to deduction of VAT in respect of activities covered by this flat-rate scheme.

VAT EC

Article 303

1. Where the taxable customer pays flat-rate compensation pursuant to Article 301(1), he shall be entitled, in accordance with the conditions laid down in Articles 167, 168 and 169 and Articles 173 to 177 and the procedures laid down by the Member States, to deduct the compensation amount from the VAT for which he is liable in the Member State in which his taxed transactions are carried out.

2. Member States shall refund to the customer the amount of the flat-rate compensation he has paid in respect of any of the following transactions:

(*a*) the supply of agricultural products, carried out in accordance with the conditions specified in Article 138, to taxable persons, or to non-taxable legal persons, acting as such in another Member State within the territory of which their intra-Community acquisitions of goods are subject to VAT pursuant to Article 2(1)(*b*);

(*b*) the supply of agricultural products, carried out in accordance with the conditions specified in Articles 146, 147, 148 and 156, Article 157(1)(*b*) and Articles 158, 160 and 161, to a taxable customer established outside the Community, in so far as the products are used by that customer for the purposes of the transactions referred to in Article 169(*a*) and (*b*) or for the purposes of supplies of services which are deemed to take place within the territory of the Member State in which the customer is established and in respect of which VAT is payable solely by the customer pursuant to Article 196;

(*c*) the supply of agricultural services to a taxable customer established within the Community but in another Member State or to a taxable customer established outside the Community, in so far as the services are used by the customer for the purposes of the transactions referred to in Article 169(*a*) and (*b*) or for the purposes of supplies of services which are deemed to take place within the territory of the Member State in which the customer is established and in respect of which VAT is payable solely by the customer pursuant to Article 196.

3. Member States shall determine the method by which the refunds provided for in paragraph 2 are to be made. In particular, they may apply the provisions of Directives 79/1072/EEC and 86/560/EEC.

Article 304

Member States shall take all measures necessary to verify payments of flat-rate compensation to flat-rate farmers.

Article 305

Whenever Member States apply this flat-rate scheme, they shall take all measures necessary to ensure that the supply of agricultural products between Member States, carried out in accordance with the conditions specified in Article 33, is always taxed in the same way, whether the supply is effected by a flat-rate farmer or by another taxable person.

CHAPTER 3

SPECIAL SCHEME FOR TRAVEL AGENTS

Article 306

1. Member States shall apply a special VAT scheme, in accordance with this Chapter, to transactions carried out by travel agents who deal with customers in their own name and use supplies of goods or services provided by other taxable persons, in the provision of travel facilities. This special scheme shall not apply to travel agents where they act solely as intermediaries and to whom point (*c*) of the first paragraph of Article 79 applies for the purposes of calculating the taxable amount.

2. For the purposes of this Chapter, tour operators shall be regarded as travel agents.

Simon's Tax Cases—*Secret Hotels2 Ltd (formerly Med Hotels Ltd) v R&C Comrs* [2014] UKSC 16, [2014] STC 937.

Article 307

Transactions made, in accordance with the conditions laid down in Article 306, by the travel agent in respect of a journey shall be regarded as a single service supplied by the travel agent to the traveller.

The single service shall be taxable in the Member State in which the travel agent has established his business or has a fixed establishment from which the travel agent has carried out the supply of services.

Article 308

The taxable amount and the price exclusive of VAT, within the meaning of point (8) of Article 226, in respect of the single service provided by the travel agent shall be the travel agent's margin, that is to say, the difference between the total amount, exclusive of VAT, to be paid by the traveller and the actual cost to the travel agent of supplies of goods or services provided by other taxable persons, where those transactions are for the direct benefit of the traveller.

Article 309

If transactions entrusted by the travel agent to other taxable persons are performed by such persons outside the Community, the supply of services carried out by the travel agent shall be treated as an intermediary activity exempted pursuant to Article 153.

If the transactions are performed both inside and outside the Community, only that part of the travel agent's service relating to transactions outside the Community may be exempted.

Article 310

VAT charged to the travel agent by other taxable persons in respect of transactions which are referred to in Article 307 and which are for the direct benefit of the traveller shall not be deductible or refundable in any Member State.

CHAPTER 4
SPECIAL ARRANGEMENTS FOR SECOND-HAND GOODS, WORKS OF ART, COLLECTORS' ITEMS AND ANTIQUES

SECTION 1
Definitions

Article 311

1. For the purposes of this Chapter, and without prejudice to other Community provisions, the following definitions shall apply:

(1) 'second-hand goods' means movable tangible property that is suitable for further use as it is or after repair, other than works of art, collectors' items or antiques and other than precious metals or precious stones as defined by the Member States;

(2) 'works of art' means the objects listed in Annex IX, Part A;

(3) 'collectors' items' means the objects listed in Annex IX, Part B;

(4) 'antiques' means the objects listed in Annex IX, Part C;

(5) 'taxable dealer' means any taxable person who, in the course of his economic activity and with a view to resale, purchases, or applies for the purposes of his business, or imports, second-hand goods, works of art, collectors' items or antiques, whether that taxable person is acting for himself or on behalf of another person pursuant to a contract under which commission is payable on purchase or sale;

(6) 'organiser of a sale by public auction' means any taxable person who, in the course of his economic activity, offers goods for sale by public auction with a view to handing them over to the highest bidder;

(7) 'principal of an organiser of a sale by public auction' means any person who transmits goods to an organiser of a sale by public auction pursuant to a contract under which commission is payable on a sale.

2. Member States need not regard as works of art the objects listed in points (5), (6) or (7) of Annex IX, Part A.

3. The contract under which commission is payable on a sale, referred to in point (7) of paragraph 1, must provide that the organiser of the sale is to put up the goods for public auction in his own name but on behalf of his principal and that he is to hand over the goods, in his own name but on behalf of his principal, to the highest bidder at the public auction.

Commentary—*De Voil Indirect Tax Service* **V3.532.**

Simon's Tax Cases—Art 311, *Direktsia 'Obzhalvane I upravlenie na izpalnenieto' Varna v Auto Nikolovi OOD* (Case C-203/10) [2011] STC 1294; *Bawaria Motors Sp z oo v Minister Finansow* (C-160/11) [2012] STC 2088.

Art 311(1)(5), *Jyske Finans A/S v Skatteministeriet (Nordania Finans A/S and BG Factoring A/S intervening)* [2006] STC 1744*.

SECTION 2
Special arrangements for taxable dealers

SUBSECTION 1
Margin scheme

Article 312

For the purposes of this Subsection, the following definitions shall apply:

(1) 'selling price' means everything which constitutes the consideration obtained or to be obtained by the taxable dealer from the customer or from a third party, including subsidies directly linked to the transaction, taxes, duties, levies and charges and incidental expenses such as commission, packaging, transport and insurance costs charged by the taxable dealer to the customer, but excluding the amounts referred to in Article 79;

(2) 'purchase price' means everything which constitutes the consideration, for the purposes of point (1), obtained or to be obtained from the taxable dealer by his supplier.

Article 313

1. In respect of the supply of second-hand goods, works of art, collectors' items or antiques carried out by taxable dealers, Member States shall apply a special scheme for taxing the profit margin made by the taxable dealer, in accordance with the provisions of this Subsection.

VAT EC

2. Pending introduction of the definitive arrangements referred to in Article 402, the scheme referred to in paragraph 1 of this Article shall not apply to the supply of new means of transport, carried out in accordance with the conditions specified in Article 138(1) and (2)(*a*).

Simon's Tax Cases—Art 315, *Bawaria Motors Sp z oo v Minister Finansow* (C-160/11) [2012] STC 2088.

Article 314

The margin scheme shall apply to the supply by a taxable dealer of second-hand goods, works of art, collectors' items or antiques where those goods have been supplied to him within the Community by one of the following persons:

(*a*) a non-taxable person;

(*b*) another taxable person, in so far as the supply of goods by that other taxable person is exempt pursuant to Article 136;

(*c*) another taxable person, in so far as the supply of goods by that other taxable person is covered by the exemption for small enterprises provided for in Articles 282 to 292 and involves capital goods;

(*d*) another taxable dealer, in so far as VAT has been applied to the supply of goods by that other taxable dealer in accordance with this margin scheme.

Simon's Tax Cases—Art 314, *Direktsia 'Obzhalvane I upravlenie na izpalnenieto' Varna v Auto Nikolovi OOD* (Case C-203/10) [2011] STC 1294; *Bawaria Motors Sp z oo v Minister Finansow* (C-160/11) [2012] STC 2088.

Article 315

The taxable amount in respect of the supply of goods as referred to in Article 314 shall be the profit margin made by the taxable dealer, less the amount of VAT relating to the profit margin.

The profit margin of the taxable dealer shall be equal to the difference between the selling price charged by the taxable dealer for the goods and the purchase price.

Simon's Tax Cases—Art 315, *Bawaria Motors Sp z oo v Minister Finansow* (C-160/11) [2012] STC 2088.

Article 316

1. Member States shall grant taxable dealers the right to opt for application of the margin scheme to the following transactions:

(*a*) the supply of works of art, collectors' items or antiques, which the taxable dealer has imported himself;

(*b*) the supply of works of art supplied to the taxable dealer by their creators or their successors in title;

(*c*) the supply of works of art supplied to the taxable dealer by a taxable person other than a taxable dealer where the reduced rate has been applied to that supply pursuant to Article 103.

2. Member States shall lay down the detailed rules for exercise of the option provided for in paragraph 1, which shall in any event cover a period of at least two calendar years.

Article 317

If a taxable dealer exercises the option under Article 316, the taxable amount shall be determined in accordance with Article 315.

In respect of the supply of works of art, collectors' items or antiques which the taxable dealer has imported himself, the purchase price to be taken into account in calculating the profit margin shall be equal to the taxable amount on importation, determined in accordance with Articles 85 to 89, plus the VAT due or paid on importation.

Article 318

1. In order to simplify the procedure for collecting the tax and after consulting the VAT Committee, Member States may provide that, for certain transactions or for certain categories of taxable dealers, the taxable amount in respect of supplies of goods subject to the margin scheme is to be determined for each tax period during which the taxable dealer must submit the VAT return referred to in Article 250.

In the event that such provision is made in accordance with the first subparagraph, the taxable amount in respect of supplies of goods to which the same rate of VAT is applied shall be the total profit margin made by the taxable dealer less the amount of VAT relating to that margin.

2. The total profit margin shall be equal to the difference between the following two amounts:

(*a*) the total value of supplies of goods subject to the margin scheme and carried out by the taxable dealer during the tax period covered by the return, that is to say, the total of the selling prices;

(*b*) the total value of purchases of goods, as referred to in Article 314, effected by the taxable dealer during the tax period covered by the return, that is to say, the total of the purchase prices.

3. Member States shall take the measures necessary to ensure that the taxable dealers referred to in paragraph 1 do not enjoy unjustified advantage or sustain unjustified harm.

Article 319

The taxable dealer may apply the normal VAT arrangements to any supply covered by the margin scheme.

Article 320

1. Where the taxable dealer applies the normal VAT arrangements to the supply of a work of art, a collectors' item or an antique which he has imported himself, he shall be entitled to deduct from the VAT for which he is liable the VAT due or paid on the import.

Where the taxable dealer applies the normal VAT arrangements to the supply of a work of art supplied to him by its creator, or the creator's successors in title, or by a taxable person other than a taxable dealer, he shall be entitled to deduct from the VAT for which he is liable the VAT due or paid in respect of the work of art supplied to him.

2. A right of deduction shall arise at the time when the VAT due on the supply in respect of which the taxable dealer opts for application of the normal VAT arrangements becomes chargeable.

Simon's Tax Cases—Art 320, *Direktsia 'Obzhalvane I upravlenie na izpalnenieto' Varna v Auto Nikolovi OOD* (Case C-203/10) [2011] STC 1294.

Article 321

If carried out in accordance with the conditions specified in Articles 146, 147, 148 or 151, the supply of second-hand goods, works of art, collectors' items or antiques subject to the margin scheme shall be exempt.

Article 322

In so far as goods are used for the purpose of supplies carried out by him and subject to the margin scheme, the taxable dealer may not deduct the following from the VAT for which he is liable:

(*a*) the VAT due or paid in respect of works of art, collectors' items or antiques which he has imported himself;

(*b*) the VAT due or paid in respect of works of art which have been, or are to be, supplied to him by their creator or by the creator's successors in title;

(*c*) the VAT due or paid in respect of works of art which have been, or are to be, supplied to him by a taxable person other than a taxable dealer.

Article 323

Taxable persons may not deduct from the VAT for which they are liable the VAT due or paid in respect of goods which have been, or are to be, supplied to them by a taxable dealer, in so far as the supply of those goods by the taxable dealer is subject to the margin scheme.

Article 324

Where the taxable dealer applies both the normal VAT arrangements and the margin scheme, he must show separately in his accounts the transactions falling under each of those arrangements, in accordance with the rules laid down by the Member States.

Article 325

The taxable dealer may not enter separately on the invoices which he issues the VAT relating to supplies of goods to which he applies the margin scheme.

SUBSECTION 2

Transitional arrangements for second-hand means of transport

Article 326

Member States which, at 31 December 1992, were applying special tax arrangements other than the margin scheme to the supply by taxable dealers of second-hand means of transport may, pending introduction of the definitive arrangements referred to in Article 402, continue to apply those arrangements in so far as they comply with, or are adjusted to comply with, the conditions laid down in this Subsection.

Denmark is authorised to introduce tax arrangements as referred to in the first paragraph.

Article 327

1. These transitional arrangements shall apply to supplies of second-hand means of transport carried out by taxable dealers, and subject to the margin scheme.

2. These transitional arrangements shall not apply to the supply of new means of transport carried out in accordance with the conditions specified in Article 138(1) and (2)(*a*).

3. For the purposes of paragraph 1, the land vehicles, vessels and aircraft referred to in point (*a*) of Article 2(2) shall be regarded as 'second-hand means of transport' where they are second-hand goods which do not meet the conditions necessary to be regarded as new means of transport.

Article 328

The VAT due in respect of each supply referred to in Article 327 shall be equal to the amount of VAT that would have been due if that supply had been subject to the normal VAT arrangements, less the amount of VAT regarded as being incorporated by the taxable dealer in the purchase price of the means of transport.

Article 329

The VAT regarded as being incorporated by the taxable dealer in the purchase price of the means of transport shall be calculated in accordance with the following method:

(*a*) the purchase price to be taken into account shall be the purchase price within the meaning of point (2) of Article 312;

(*b*) that purchase price paid by the taxable dealer shall be deemed to include the VAT that would have been due if the taxable dealer's supplier had applied the normal VAT arrangements to the supply;

(*c*) the rate to be taken into account shall be the rate applicable, pursuant to Article 93, in the Member State in the territory of which the place of the supply to the taxable dealer, as determined in accordance with Articles 31 and 32, is deemed to be situated.

Article 330

The VAT due in respect of each supply of means of transport as referred to in Article 327(1), determined in accordance with Article 328, may not be less than the amount of VAT that would be due if that supply were subject to the margin scheme.

Member States may provide that, if the supply is subject to the margin scheme, the margin may not be less than 10% of the selling price within the meaning of point (1) of Article 312.

Article 331

Taxable persons may not deduct from the VAT for which they are liable the VAT due or paid in respect of second-hand means of transport supplied to them by a taxable dealer, in so far as the supply of those goods by the taxable dealer is subject to VAT in accordance with these transitional arrangements.

Article 332

The taxable dealer may not enter separately on the invoices he issues the VAT relating to supplies to which he applies these transitional arrangements.

SECTION 3

Special arrangements for sales by public auction

Article 333

1. Member States may, in accordance with the provisions of this Section, apply special arrangements for taxation of the profit margin made by an organiser of a sale by public auction in respect of the supply of second-hand goods, works of art, collectors' items or antiques by that organiser, acting in his own name and on behalf of the persons referred to in Article 334, pursuant to a contract under which commission is payable on the sale of those goods by public auction.

2. The arrangements referred to in paragraph 1 shall not apply to the supply of new means of transport, carried out in accordance with the conditions specified in Article 138(1) and (2)(*a*).

Article 334

These special arrangements shall apply to supplies carried out by an organiser of a sale by public auction, acting in his own name, on behalf of one of the following persons:

(*a*) a non-taxable person;

(*b*) another taxable person, in so far as the supply of goods, carried out by that taxable person in accordance with a contract under which commission is payable on a sale, is exempt pursuant to Article 136;

(*c*) another taxable person, in so far as the supply of goods, carried out by that taxable person in accordance with a contract under which commission is payable on a sale, is covered by the exemption for small enterprises provided for in Articles 282 to 292 and involves capital goods;

(*d*) a taxable dealer, in so far as the supply of goods, carried out by that taxable dealer in accordance with a contract under which commission is payable on a sale, is subject to VAT in accordance with the margin scheme.

Article 335

The supply of goods to a taxable person who is an organiser of sales by public auction shall be regarded as taking place when the sale of those goods by public auction takes place.

Article 336

The taxable amount in respect of each supply of goods referred to in this Section shall be the total amount invoiced in accordance with Article 339 to the purchaser by the organiser of the sale by public auction, less the following:

(*a*) the net amount paid or to be paid by the organiser of the sale by public auction to his principal, as determined in accordance with Article 337;

(*b*) the amount of the VAT payable by the organiser of the sale by public auction in respect of his supply.

Article 337

The net amount paid or to be paid by the organiser of the sale by public auction to his principal shall be equal to the difference between the auction price of the goods and the amount of the commission obtained or to be obtained by the organiser of the sale by public auction from his principal pursuant to the contract under which commission is payable on the sale.

Article 338

Organisers of sales by public auction who supply goods in accordance with the conditions laid down in Articles 333 and 334 must indicate the following in their accounts, in suspense accounts:

(*a*) the amounts obtained or to be obtained from the purchaser of the goods;

(*b*) the amounts reimbursed or to be reimbursed to the vendor of the goods.

The amounts referred to in the first paragraph must be duly substantiated.

Article 339

The organiser of the sale by public auction must issue to the purchaser an invoice itemising the following:

(*a*) the auction price of the goods;

(*b*) taxes, duties, levies and charges;

(*c*) incidental expenses, such as commission, packing, transport and insurance costs, charged by the organiser to the purchaser of the goods.

The invoice issued by the organiser of the sale by public auction must not indicate any VAT separately.

Article 340

1. The organiser of the sale by public auction to whom the goods have been transmitted pursuant to a contract under which commission is payable on a public auction sale must issue a statement to his principal. The statement issued by the organiser of the sale by public auction must specify separately the amount of the transaction, that is to say, the auction price of the goods less the amount of the commission obtained or to be obtained from the principal.

2. The statement drawn up in accordance with paragraph 1 shall serve as the invoice which the principal, where he is a taxable person, must issue to the organiser of the sale by public auction in accordance with Article 220.

Article 341

Member States which apply the arrangements provided for in this Section shall also apply these arrangements to supplies of second-hand means of transport, as defined in Article 327(3), carried out by an organiser of sales by public auction, acting in his own name, pursuant to a contract under which commission is payable on the sale of those goods by public auction, on behalf of a taxable dealer, in so far as those supplies by that taxable dealer would be subject to VAT in accordance with the transitional arrangements for second-hand means of transport.

SECTION 4

Measures to prevent distortion of competition and tax evasion

Article 342

Member States may take measures concerning the right of deduction in order to ensure that the taxable dealers covered by special arrangements as provided for in Section 2 do not enjoy unjustified advantage or sustain unjustified harm.

Article 343

Acting unanimously on a proposal from the Commission, the Council may authorise any Member State to introduce special measures to combat tax evasion, pursuant to which the VAT due under the margin scheme may not be less than the amount of VAT which would be due if the profit margin were equal to a certain percentage of the selling price.

The percentage of the selling price shall be fixed in the light of the normal profit margins made by economic operators in the sector concerned.

CHAPTER 5
SPECIAL SCHEME FOR INVESTMENT GOLD

SECTION 1
General provisions

Article 344

1. For the purposes of this Directive, and without prejudice to other Community provisions, 'investment gold' shall mean:

(1) gold, in the form of a bar or a wafer of weights accepted by the bullion markets, of a purity equal to or greater than 995 thousandths, whether or not represented by securities;

(2) gold coins of a purity equal to or greater than 900 thousandths and minted after 1800, which are or have been legal tender in the country of origin, and are normally sold at a price which does not exceed the open market value of the gold contained in the coins by more than 80%.

2. Member States may exclude from this special scheme small bars or wafers of a weight of 1 g or less.

3. For the purposes of this Directive, the coins referred to in point (2) of paragraph 1 shall not be regarded as sold for numismatic interest.

Article 345

Starting in 1999, each Member State shall inform the Commission by 1 July each year of the coins meeting the criteria laid down in point (2) of Article 344(1) which are traded in that Member State. The Commission shall, before 1 December each year, publish a comprehensive list of those coins in the 'C' series of the *Official Journal of the European Union*. Coins included in the published list shall be deemed to fulfil those criteria throughout the year for which the list is published.

SECTION 2
Exemption from VAT

Article 346

Member States shall exempt from VAT the supply, the intra-Community acquisition and the importation of investment gold, including investment gold represented by certificates for allocated or unallocated gold or traded on gold accounts and including, in particular, gold loans and swaps, involving a right of ownership or claim in respect of investment gold, as well as transactions concerning investment gold involving futures and forward contracts leading to a transfer of right of ownership or claim in respect of investment gold.

Article 347

Member States shall exempt the services of agents who act in the name and on behalf of another person, when they take part in the supply of investment gold for their principal.

SECTION 3
Taxation option

Article 348

Member States shall allow taxable persons who produce investment gold or transform gold into investment gold the right to opt for the taxation of supplies of investment gold to another taxable person which would otherwise be exempt pursuant to Article 346.

Article 349

1. Member States may allow taxable persons who, in the course of their economic activity, normally supply gold for industrial purposes, the right to opt for the taxation of supplies of gold bars or wafers, as referred to in point (1) of Article 344(1), to another taxable person, which would otherwise be exempt pursuant to Article 346.

2. Member States may restrict the scope of the option provided for in paragraph 1.

Article 350

Where the supplier has exercised the right under Articles 348 and 349 to opt for taxation, Member States shall allow the agent to opt for taxation of the services referred to in Article 347.

Article 351

Member States shall lay down detailed rules for the exercise of the options provided for in this Section, and shall inform the Commission accordingly.

SECTION 4
Transactions on a regulated gold bullion market

Article 352

Each Member State may, after consulting the VAT Committee, apply VAT to specific transactions relating to investment gold which take place in that Member State between taxable persons who are members of a gold bullion market regulated by the Member State concerned or between such a taxable person and another taxable person who is not a member of that market. However, the Member State may not apply VAT to supplies carried out in accordance with the conditions specified in Article 138 or to exports of investment gold.

Article 353

Member States which, pursuant to Article 352, tax transactions between taxable persons who are members of a regulated gold bullion market shall, for the purposes of simplification, authorise suspension of the tax to be collected and relieve taxable persons of the accounting requirements in respect of VAT.

SECTION 5

Special rights and obligations for traders in investment gold

Article 354

Where his subsequent supply of investment gold is exempt pursuant to this Chapter, the taxable person shall be entitled to deduct the following:

(*a*) the VAT due or paid in respect of investment gold supplied to him by a person who has exercised the right of option under Articles 348 and 349 or supplied to him in accordance with Section 4;

(*b*) the VAT due or paid in respect of a supply to him, or in respect of an intra-Community acquisition or importation carried out by him, of gold other than investment gold which is subsequently transformed by him or on his behalf into investment gold;

(*c*) the VAT due or paid in respect of services supplied to him consisting in a change of form, weight or purity of gold including investment gold.

Article 355

Taxable persons who produce investment gold or transform gold into investment gold shall be entitled to deduct the VAT due or paid by them in respect of the supply, intra-Community acquisition or importation of goods or services linked to the production or transformation of that gold, as if the subsequent supply of the gold exempted pursuant to Article 346 were taxed.

Article 356

1. Member States shall ensure that traders in investment gold keep, as a minimum, accounts of all substantial transactions in investment gold and keep the documents which enable the customers in such transactions to be identified.

Traders shall keep the information referred to in the first subparagraph for a period of at least five years.

2. Member States may accept equivalent obligations under measures adopted pursuant to other Community legislation, such as Directive 2005/60/EC of the European Parliament and of the Council of 26 October 2005 on the prevention of the use of the financial system for the purpose of money laundering and terrorist financing [1], to comply with the requirements under paragraph 1.

3. Member States may lay down obligations which are more stringent, in particular as regards the keeping of special records or special accounting requirements.

[1] OJ L 309, 25.11.2005, p. 15.

CHAPTER 6

[SPECIAL SCHEMES FOR NON-ESTABLISHED TAXABLE PERSONS SUPPLYING TELECOMMUNICATIONS SERVICES, BROADCASTING SERVICES OR ELECTRONIC SERVICES TO NON-TAXABLE PERSONS.]

Amendments—Heading to Chapter 6 substituted by Council Directive 2008/8/EC art 5(6) with effect from 1 January 2015 (OJ L 44, 20.2.2008 p 11). Heading previously read "Special scheme for non-established taxable persons supplying electronic services to non-taxable persons".

SECTION 1

General provisions

Article 357

This Chapter shall apply until 31 December 2014.[1]

Amendments—[1] Article 357 repealed by Council Directive 2008/8/EC art 5(7) with effect from 1 January 2015 (OJ L 44, 20.2.2008 p 11).

[Article 358

For the purposes of this Chapter, and without prejudice to other Community provisions, the following definitions shall apply:

1. "telecommunications services" and "broadcasting services" mean the services referred to in points (a) and (b) of the first paragraph of Article 58;

2. "electronic services" and "electronically supplied services" mean the services referred to in point (c) of the first paragraph of Article 58;

VAT EC

3. "Member State of consumption" means the Member State in which the supply of the telecommunications, broadcasting or electronic services is deemed to take place according to Article 58;
4. "VAT return" means the statement containing the information necessary to establish the amount of VAT due in each Member State.][1]

Cross-references—See VATA 1994 Sch 3BA (electronic, telecommunication and broadcasting services: Union scheme, from 1 January 2015).

Amendments—[1] Article 358 substituted by Council Directive 2008/8/EC art 5(8) with effect from 1 January 2015 (OJ L 44, 20.2.2008 p 11). Article 358 previously read as follows—

> "For the purposes of this Chapter, and without prejudice to other provisions, the following definitions shall apply:
>
> (1) "non-established taxable person" means a taxable person who has not established his business in the territory of the Community and who has no fixed establishment there and who is not otherwise required to be identified pursuant to Article 214;
>
> (2) "electronic services" and "electronically supplied services" mean the services referred to in point (k) of the first paragraph of Article 59;
>
> (3) "Member State of identification" means the Member State which the non-established taxable person chooses to contact to state when his activity as a taxable person within the territory of the Community commences in accordance with the provisions of this Chapter;
>
> (4) "Member State of consumption" means the Member State in which, pursuant to Article 58, the supply of the electronic services is deemed to take place;
>
> (5) "VAT return" means the statement containing the information necessary to establish the amount of VAT due in each Member State.".

SECTION 2

[Special scheme for telecommunications, broadcasting or electronic services supplied by taxable persons not established within the Community]

Amendments—Heading to Section 2 substituted by Council Directive 2008/8/EC art 5(9) with effect from 1 January 2015 (OJ L 44, 20.2.2008 p 11). Heading previously read "Special scheme for electronically supplied services".

[Article 358a

For the purposes of this Section, and without prejudice to other Community provisions, the following definitions shall apply:
1. "taxable person not established within the Community" means a taxable person who has not established his business in the territory of the Community and who has no fixed establishment there and who is not otherwise required to be identified for VAT purposes;
2. "Member State of identification" means the Member State which the taxable person not established within the Community chooses to contact to state when his activity as a taxable person within the territory of the Community commences in accordance with the provisions of this Section.][1]

Amendments—[1] Article 358a inserted by Council Directive 2008/8/EC art 5(10) with effect from 1 January 2015 (OJ L 44, 20.2.2008 p 11).

[Article 359

Member States shall permit any taxable person not established within the Community supplying telecommunications, broadcasting or electronic services to a non-taxable person who is established in a Member State or has his permanent address or usually resides in a Member State, to use this special scheme. This scheme applies to all those services supplied within the Community.][1]

Cross-references—See VATA 1994 Sch 3BA (electronic, telecommunication and broadcasting services: Union scheme, from 1 January 2015).

Amendments—[1] Articles 359–365 substituted by Council Directive 2008/8/EC art 5(11) with effect from 1 January 2015 (OJ L 44, 20.2.2008 p 11). Article 359 previously read as follows—

> **Article 359**
>
> "Member States shall permit any non-established taxable person supplying electronic services to a non-taxable person who is established in a Member State or who has his permanent address or usually resides in a Member State, to use this special scheme. This scheme applies to all electronic services supplied in the Community.".

[Article 360

The taxable person not established within the Community shall state to the Member State of identification when he commences or ceases his activity as a taxable person, or changes that activity in such a way that he no longer meets the conditions necessary for use of this special scheme. He shall communicate that information electronically.][1]

Cross-references—See VATA 1994 Sch 3BA (electronic, telecommunication and broadcasting services: Union scheme, from 1 January 2015).

Amendments—[1] Articles 359–365 substituted by Council Directive 2008/8/EC art 5(11) with effect from 1 January 2015 (OJ L 44, 20.2.2008 p 11). Article 360 previously read as follows—

Article 360

"The non-established taxable person shall state to the Member State of identification when he commences or ceases his activity as a taxable person, or changes that activity in such a way that he no longer meets the conditions necessary for use of this special scheme. He shall communicate that information electronically.".

[Article 361

1. The information which the taxable person not established within the Community must provide to the Member State of identification when he commences a taxable activity shall contain the following details:

(a) name;

(b) postal address;

(c) electronic addresses, including websites;

(d) national tax number, if any;

(e) a statement that the person is not identified for VAT purposes within the Community.

2. The taxable person not established within in the Community shall notify the Member State of identification of any changes in the information provided.][1]

Cross-references—See VATA 1994 Sch 3BA (electronic, telecommunication and broadcasting services: Union scheme, from 1 January 2015).

Amendments—[1] Articles 359–365 substituted by Council Directive 2008/8/EC art 5(11) with effect from 1 January 2015 (OJ L 44, 20.2.2008 p 11). Article 361 previously read as follows—

"Article 361

1. The information which the non-established taxable person must provide to the Member State of identification when he commences a taxable activity shall contain the following details:

name;

postal address;

electronic addresses, including websites;

national tax number, if any;

a statement that the person is not identified for VAT purposes within the Community.

2. The non-established taxable person shall notify the Member State of identification of any changes in the information provided.".

[Article 362

The Member State of identification shall allocate to the taxable person not established within the Community an individual VAT identification number and shall notify him of that number by electronic means. On the basis of the information used for that identification, Member States of consumption may have recourse to their own identification systems.][1]

Cross-references—See VATA 1994 Sch 3BA (electronic, telecommunication and broadcasting services: Union scheme, from 1 January 2015).

Amendments—[1] Articles 359–365 substituted by Council Directive 2008/8/EC art 5(11) with effect from 1 January 2015 (OJ L 44, 20.2.2008 p 11). Article 362 previously read as follows—

"Article 362

The Member State of identification shall allocate to the non-established taxable person an individual VAT identification number and shall notify him of that number by electronic means. On the basis of the information used for that identification, Member States of consumption may have recourse to their own identification systems.".

[Article 363

The Member State of identification shall delete the taxable person not established within the Community from the identification register in the following cases:

(a) if he notifies that Member State that he no longer supplies telecommunications, broadcasting or electronic services;

(b) if it may otherwise be assumed that his taxable activities have ceased;

(c) if he no longer meets the conditions necessary for use of this special scheme;

(d) if he persistently fails to comply with the rules relating to this special scheme.][1]

Cross-references—See VATA 1994 Sch 3BA (electronic, telecommunication and broadcasting services: Union scheme, from 1 January 2015).

Amendments—[1] Articles 359–365 substituted by Council Directive 2008/8/EC art 5(11) with effect from 1 January 2015 (OJ L 44, 20.2.2008 p 11). Article 363 previously read as follows—

"Article 363

The Member State of identification shall strike the non-established taxable person from the identification register in the following cases:

if he notifies that Member State that he no longer supplies electronic services;

if it may otherwise be assumed that his taxable activities have ceased;

if he no longer meets the conditions necessary for use of this special scheme;

if he persistently fails to comply with the rules relating to this special scheme.".

[Article 364

The taxable person not established within the Community shall submit by electronic means to the Member State of identification a VAT return for each calendar quarter, whether or not telecommunications, broadcasting or electronic services have been supplied. The VAT return shall be submitted within 20 days following the end of the tax period covered by the return.][1]

Cross-references—See VATA 1994 Sch 3BA (electronic, telecommunication and broadcasting services: Union scheme, from 1 January 2015).

Amendments—[1] Articles 359–365 substituted by Council Directive 2008/8/EC art 5(11) with effect from 1 January 2015 (OJ L 44, 20.2.2008 p 11). Article 364 previously read as follows—

> **"Article 364**
>
> The non-established taxable person shall submit by electronic means to the Member State of identification a VAT return for each calendar quarter, whether or not electronic services have been supplied. The VAT return shall be submitted within 20 days following the end of the tax period covered by the return.".

[Article 365

The VAT return shall show the identification number and, for each Member State of consumption in which VAT is due, the total value, exclusive of VAT, of supplies of telecommunications, broadcasting and electronic services carried out during the tax period and total amount per rate of the corresponding VAT. The applicable rates of VAT and the total VAT due must also be indicated on the return.][1]

Cross-references—See VATA 1994 Sch 3BA (electronic, telecommunication and broadcasting services: Union scheme, from 1 January 2015).

Amendments—[1] Articles 359–365 substituted by Council Directive 2008/8/EC art 5(11) with effect from 1 January 2015 (OJ L 44, 20.2.2008 p 11). Article 365 previously read as follows—

> **"Article 365**
>
> The VAT return shall show the identification number and, for each Member State of consumption in which VAT is due, the total value, exclusive of VAT, of supplies of electronic services carried out during the tax period and the total amount of the corresponding VAT. The applicable rates of VAT and the total VAT due must also be indicated on the return.".

Article 366

[1. The VAT return shall be made out in euro.

Member States which have not adopted the euro may require the VAT return to be made out in their national currency. If the supplies have been made in other currencies, the taxable person not established within the Community shall, for the purposes of completing the VAT return, use the exchange rate applying on the last day of the tax period.][1]

2. The conversion shall be made by applying the exchange rates published by the European Central Bank for that day, or, if there is no publication on that day, on the next day of publication.

Cross-references—See VATA 1994 Sch 3BA (electronic, telecommunication and broadcasting services: Union scheme, from 1 January 2015).

Amendments—[1] Para 1 substituted by Council Directive 2008/8/EC art 5(12) with effect from 1 January 2015 (OJ L 44, 20.2.2008 p 11). Para 1 previously read as follows—

> "1. The VAT return shall be made out in euro.
>
> Member States which have not adopted the euro may require the VAT return to be made out in their national currency. If the supplies have been made in other currencies, the non-established taxable person shall, for the purposes of completing the VAT return, use the exchange rate applying on the last day of the tax period.".

[Article 367

The taxable person not established within the Community shall pay the VAT, making reference to the relevant VAT return, when submitting the VAT return, at the latest, however, at the expiry of the deadline by which the return must be submitted.

Payment shall be made to a bank account denominated in euro, designated by the Member State of identification. Member States which have not adopted the euro may require the payment to be made to a bank account denominated in their own currency.][1]

Cross-references—See VATA 1994 Sch 3BA (electronic, telecommunication and broadcasting services: Union scheme, from 1 January 2015).

Amendments—[1] Articles 367, 368 substituted by Council Directive 2008/8/EC art 5(13) with effect from 1 January 2015 (OJ L 44, 20.2.2008 p 11). Article 367 previously read as follows—

> **"Article 367**
>
> The non-established taxable person shall pay the VAT when submitting the VAT return.
>
> Payment shall be made to a bank account denominated in euro, designated by the Member State of identification. Member States which have not adopted the euro may require payment to be made to a bank account denominated in their own currency.".

[Article 368

The taxable person not established within the Community making use of this special scheme may not deduct VAT pursuant to Article 168 of this Directive. Notwithstanding Article 1(1) of Directive 86/560/EEC, the taxable person in question shall be refunded in accordance with the said Directive. Articles 2(2) and (3) and Article 4(2) of Directive 86/560/EEC shall not apply to refunds relating to telecommunications, broadcasting or electronic services covered by this special scheme.][1]

Cross-references—See VATA 1994 Sch 3BA (electronic, telecommunication and broadcasting services: Union scheme, from 1 January 2015).

Amendments—[1] Articles 367, 368 substituted by Council Directive 2008/8/EC art 5(13) with effect from 1 January 2015 (OJ L 44, 20.2.2008 p 11). Article 368 previously read as follows—

> **"Article 368**
>
> The non-established taxable person making use of this special scheme may not deduct VAT pursuant to Article 168 of this Directive. Notwithstanding Article 1(1) of Directive 86/560/EEC, the taxable person in question shall be refunded in accordance with the said Directive. Articles 2(2) and (3) and Article 4(2) of Directive 86/560/EEC shall not apply to refunds relating to electronic services covered by this special scheme.".

Article 369

[1. The taxable person not established within the Community shall keep records of the transactions covered by this special scheme. Those records must be sufficiently detailed to enable the tax authorities of the Member State of consumption to verify that the VAT return is correct.][1]

2. The records referred to in paragraph 1 must be made available electronically on request to the Member State of identification and to the Member State of consumption.

Those records must be kept for a period of ten years from the end of the year during which the transaction was carried out.

Cross-references—See VATA 1994 Sch 3BA (electronic, telecommunication and broadcasting services: Union scheme, from 1 January 2015).

Amendments—[1] Para 1 substituted by Council Directive 2008/8/EC art 5(14) with effect from 1 January 2015 (OJ L 44, 20.2.2008 p 11). Para 1 previously read as follows—

> "1. The non-established taxable person shall keep records of the transactions covered by this special scheme. Those records must be sufficiently detailed to enable the tax authorities of the Member State of consumption to verify that the VAT return is correct.".

[SECTION 3

Special scheme for telecommunications, broadcasting or electronic services supplied by taxable persons established within the Community but not in the Member State of consumption

Article 369a

For the purposes of this Section, and without prejudice to other Community provisions, the following definitions shall apply:

1. "taxable person not established in the Member State of consumption" means a taxable person who has established his business in the territory of the Community or has a fixed establishment there but has not established his business and has no fixed establishment within the territory of the Member State of consumption;

2. "Member State of identification" means the Member State in the territory of which the taxable person has established his business or, if he has not established his business in the Community, where he has a fixed establishment.

Where a taxable person has not established his business in the Community, but has more than one fixed establishment therein, the Member State of identification shall be the Member State with a fixed establishment where that taxable person indicates that he will make use of this special scheme. The taxable person shall be bound by this decision for the calendar year concerned and the two calendar years following.][1]

Amendments—[1] Section 3 (articles 369a–369k) inserted by Council Directive 2008/8/EC art 5(15) with effect from 1 January 2015 (OJ L 44, 20.2.2008 p 11).

[Article 369b

Member States shall permit any taxable person not established in the Member State of consumption supplying telecommunications, broadcasting or electronic services to a non-taxable person who is established or has his permanent address or usually resides in that Member State, to use this special scheme. This special scheme applies to all those services supplied in the Community.][1]

Amendments—[1] Section 3 (articles 369a–369k) inserted by Council Directive 2008/8/EC art 5(15) with effect from 1 January 2015 (OJ L 44, 20.2.2008 p 11).

[Article 369c

The taxable person not established in the Member State of consumption shall state to the Member State of identification when he commences and ceases his taxable activities covered by this special scheme, or changes those activities in such a way that he no longer meets the conditions necessary for use of this special scheme. He shall communicate that information electronically.][1]

VAT EC

Amendments—[1] Section 3 (articles 369a–369k) inserted by Council Directive 2008/8/EC art 5(15) with effect from 1 January 2015 (OJ L 44, 20.2.2008 p 11).

[Article 369d

A taxable person making use of this special scheme shall, for the taxable transactions carried out under this scheme, be identified for VAT purposes in the Member State of identification only. For that purpose the Member State shall use the individual VAT identification number already allocated to the taxable person in respect of his obligations under the internal system.

On the basis of the information used for that identification, Member States of consumption may have recourse to their own identification systems.][1]

Amendments—[1] Section 3 (articles 369a–369k) inserted by Council Directive 2008/8/EC art 5(15) with effect from 1 January 2015 (OJ L 44, 20.2.2008 p 11).

[Article 369e

The Member State of identification shall exclude the taxable person not established in the Member State of consumption from this special scheme in any of the following cases:

(a) if he notifies that he no longer supplies telecommunications, broadcasting or electronic services;

(b) if it may otherwise be assumed that his taxable activities covered by this special scheme have ceased;

(c) if he no longer meets the conditions necessary for use of this special scheme;

(d) if he persistently fails to comply with the rules relating to this special scheme.][1]

Amendments—[1] Section 3 (articles 369a–369k) inserted by Council Directive 2008/8/EC art 5(15) with effect from 1 January 2015 (OJ L 44, 20.2.2008 p 11).

[Article 369f

The taxable person not established in the Member State of consumption shall submit by electronic means to the Member State of identification a VAT return for each calendar quarter, whether or not telecommunications, broadcasting or electronic services have been supplied. The VAT return shall be submitted within 20 days following the end of the tax period covered by the return.][1]

Amendments—[1] Section 3 (articles 369a–369k) inserted by Council Directive 2008/8/EC art 5(15) with effect from 1 January 2015 (OJ L 44, 20.2.2008 p 11).

[Article 369g

The VAT return shall show the identification number referred to in Article 369d and, for each Member State of consumption in which VAT is due, the total value, exclusive of VAT, of supplies of telecommunications, broadcasting or electronic services carried out during the tax period and the total amount per rate of the corresponding VAT. The applicable rates of VAT and the total VAT due must also be indicated on the return.

Where the taxable person has one or more fixed establishments, other than that in the Member State of identification, from which the services are supplied, the VAT return shall in addition to the information referred to in the first paragraph include the total value of supplies of telecommunications, broadcasting or electronic services covered by this special scheme, for each Member State in which he has an establishment, together with the individual VAT identification number or the tax reference number of this establishment, broken down by Member State of consumption.][1]

Amendments—[1] Section 3 (articles 369a–369k) inserted by Council Directive 2008/8/EC art 5(15) with effect from 1 January 2015 (OJ L 44, 20.2.2008 p 11).

[Article 369h

1. The VAT return shall be made out in euro. Member States which have not adopted the euro may require the VAT return to be made out in their national currency. If the supplies have been made in other currencies, the taxable person not established in the Member State of consumption shall, for the purposes of completing the VAT return, use the exchange rate applying on the last date of the tax period.

2. The conversion shall be made by applying the exchange rates published by the European Central Bank for that day, or, if there is no publication on that day, on the next day of publication.][1]

Amendments—[1] Section 3 (articles 369a–369k) inserted by Council Directive 2008/8/EC art 5(15) with effect from 1 January 2015 (OJ L 44, 20.2.2008 p 11).

[Article 369i

The taxable person not established in the Member State of consumption shall pay the VAT, making reference to the relevant VAT return, when submitting the VAT return, at the latest, however, at the expiry of the deadline by which the return must be submitted.

Payment shall be made to a bank account denominated in euro, designated by the Member State of identification. Member States which have not adopted the euro may require the payment to be made to a bank account denominated in their own currency.][1]

Amendments—[1] Section 3 (articles 369a–369k) inserted by Council Directive 2008/8/EC art 5(15) with effect from 1 January 2015 (OJ L 44, 20.2.2008 p 11).

[Article 369j

The taxable person not established in the Member State of consumption making use of this special scheme may not, in respect of his taxable activities covered by this scheme, deduct VAT pursuant to Article 168 of this Directive. Notwithstanding Article 2(1) and Article 3 of Directive 2008/9/EC, the taxable person in question shall be refunded in accordance with the said Directive.

If the taxable person not established in the Member State of consumption making use of this special scheme also carries out in the Member State of consumption activities not covered by this scheme in respect of which he is obliged to be registered for VAT purposes, he shall deduct VAT in respect of his taxable activities which are covered by this scheme in the VAT return to be submitted pursuant to Article 250.][1]

Amendments—[1] Section 3 (articles 369a–369k) inserted by Council Directive 2008/8/EC art 5(15) with effect from 1 January 2015 (OJ L 44, 20.2.2008 p 11).

[Article 369k

1. The taxable person not established in the Member State of consumption shall keep records of the transactions covered by this special scheme. Those records must be sufficiently detailed to enable the tax authorities of the Member State of consumption to verify that the VAT return is correct.

2. The records referred to in paragraph 1 must be made available electronically on request to the Member State of consumption and to the Member State of identification.

Those records must be kept for a period of 10 years from 31 December of the year during which the transaction was carried out.][1]

Amendments—[1] Section 3 (articles 369a–369k) inserted by Council Directive 2008/8/EC art 5(15) with effect from 1 January 2015 (OJ L 44, 20.2.2008 p 11).

TITLE XIII
DEROGATIONS

CHAPTER 1

DEROGATIONS APPLYING UNTIL THE ADOPTION OF DEFINITIVE ARRANGEMENTS

SECTION 1

Derogations for States which were members of the Community on 1 January 1978

Article 370

Member States which, at 1 January 1978, taxed the transactions listed in Annex X, Part A, may continue to tax those transactions.

Simon's Tax Cases—*Jetair NV and anor v FOD Financien* (Case C-599/12) [2014] STC 1088.

Article 371

Member States which, at 1 January 1978, exempted the transactions listed in Annex X, Part B, may continue to exempt those transactions, in accordance with the conditions applying in the Member State concerned on that date.

Commentary—*De Voil Indirect Tax Service* **V4.275**.

Simon's Tax Cases—*Norbury Developments Ltd v C&E Comrs* [1999] STC 511*; *Finanzamt Goslar v Breitsohl* [2001] STC 355*; *Idéal Tourisme SA v Belgian State* [2001] STC 1386*.

Article 372

Member States which, at 1 January 1978, applied provisions derogating from the principle of immediate deduction laid down in the first paragraph of Article 179 may continue to apply those provisions.

Article 373

Member States which, at 1 January 1978, applied provisions derogating from Article 28 or from point (*c*) of the first paragraph of Article 79 may continue to apply those provisions.

Article 374

By way of derogation from Articles 169 and 309, Member States which, at 1 January 1978, exempted, without deductibility of the VAT paid at the preceding stage, the services of travel agents, as referred to in Article 309, may continue to exempt those services. That derogation shall apply also in respect of travel agents acting in the name and on behalf of the traveller.

SECTION 2

Derogations for States which acceded to the Community after 1 January 1978

Article 375

Greece may continue to exempt the transactions listed in points (2), (8), (9), (11) and (12) of Annex X, Part B, in accordance with the conditions applying in that Member State on 1 January 1987.

VAT EC

Article 376

Spain may continue to exempt the supply of services performed by authors, listed in point (2) of Annex X, Part B, and the transactions listed in points (11) and (12) of Annex X, Part B, in accordance with the conditions applying in that Member State on 1 January 1993.

Article 377

Portugal may continue to exempt the transactions listed in points (2), (4), (7), (9), (10) and (13) of Annex X, Part B, in accordance with the conditions applying in that Member State on 1 January 1989.

Article 378

1. Austria may continue to tax the transactions listed in point (2) of Annex X, Part A.

2. For as long as the same exemptions are applied in any of the Member States which were members of the Community on 31 December 1994, Austria may, in accordance with the conditions applying in that Member State on the date of its accession, continue to exempt the following transactions:

(*a*) the transactions listed in points (5) and (9) of Annex X, Part B;

(*b*) with deductibility of the VAT paid at the preceding stage, all parts of international passenger transport operations, carried out by air, sea or inland waterway, other than passenger transport operations on Lake Constance.

Article 379

1. Finland may continue to tax the transactions listed in point (2) of Annex X, Part A, for as long as the same transactions are taxed in any of the Member States which were members of the Community on 31 December 1994.

2. Finland may, in accordance with the conditions applying in that Member State on the date of its accession, continue to exempt the supply of services by authors, artists and performers, listed in point (2) of Annex X, Part B, and the transactions listed in points (5), (9) and (10) of Annex X, Part B, for as long as the same exemptions are applied in any of the Member States which were members of the Community on 31 December 1994.

Article 380

Sweden may, in accordance with the conditions applying in that Member State on the date of its accession, continue to exempt the supply of services by authors, artists and performers, listed in point (2) of Annex X, Part B, and the transactions listed in points (1), (9) and (10) of Annex X, Part B, for as long as the same exemptions are applied in any of the Member States which were members of the Community on 31 December 1994.

Article 381

The Czech Republic may, in accordance with the conditions applying in that Member State on the date of its accession, continue to exempt the international transport of passengers, as referred to in point (10) of Annex X, Part B, for as long as the same exemption is applied in any of the Member States which were members of the Community on 30 April 2004.

Article 382

Estonia may, in accordance with the conditions applying in that Member State on the date of its accession, continue to exempt the international transport of passengers, as referred to in point (10) of Annex X, Part B, for as long as the same exemption is applied in any of the Member States which were members of the Community on 30 April 2004.

Article 383

Cyprus may, in accordance with the conditions applying in that Member State on the date of its accession, continue to exempt the following transactions:

(*a*) the supply of building land referred to in point (9) of Annex X, Part B, until 31 December 2007;

(*b*) the international transport of passengers, as referred to in point (10) of Annex X, Part B, for as long as the same exemption is applied in any of the Member States which were members of the Community on 30 April 2004.

Article 384

For as long as the same exemptions are applied in any of the Member States which were members of the Community on 30 April 2004, Latvia may, in accordance with the conditions applying in that Member State on the date of its accession, continue to exempt the following transactions:

(*a*) the supply of services by authors, artists and performers, as referred to in point (2) of Annex X, Part B;

(*b*) the international transport of passengers, as referred to in point (10) of Annex X, Part B.

Article 385

Lithuania may, in accordance with the conditions applying in that Member State on the date of its accession, continue to exempt the international transport of passengers, as referred to in point (10) of Annex X, Part B, for as long as the same exemption is applied in any of the Member States which were members of the Community on 30 April 2004.

Article 386

Hungary may, in accordance with the conditions applying in that Member State on the date of its accession, continue to exempt the international transport of passengers, as referred to in point (10) of Annex X, Part B, for as long as the same exemption is applied in any of the Member States which were members of the Community on 30 April 2004.

Article 387

For as long as the same exemptions are applied in any of the Member States which were members of the Community on 30 April 2004, Malta may, in accordance with the conditions applying in that Member State on the date of its accession, continue to exempt the following transactions:

(*a*) without deductibility of the VAT paid at the preceding stage, the supply of water by a body governed by public law, as referred to in point (8) of Annex X, Part B;

(*b*) without deductibility of the VAT paid at the preceding stage, the supply of buildings and building land, as referred to in point (9) of Annex X, Part B;

(*c*) with deductibility of the VAT paid at the preceding stage, inland passenger transport, international passenger transport and domestic inter-island sea passenger transport, as referred to in point (10) of Annex X, Part B.

Article 388

Poland may, in accordance with the conditions applying in that Member State on the date of its accession, continue to exempt the international transport of passengers, as referred to in point (10) of Annex X, Part B, for as long as the same exemption is applied in any of the Member States which were members of the Community on 30 April 2004.

Article 389

Slovenia may, in accordance with the conditions applying in that Member State on the date of its accession, continue to exempt the international transport of passengers, as referred to in point (10) of Annex X, Part B, for as long as the same exemption is applied in any of the Member States which were members of the Community on 30 April 2004.

Article 390

Slovakia may, in accordance with the conditions applying in that Member State on the date of its accession, continue to exempt the international transport of passengers, as referred to in point (10) of Annex X, Part B, for as long as the same exemption is applied in any of the Member States which were members of the Community on 30 April 2004.

[Article 390a

Bulgaria may, in accordance with the conditions applying in that Member State on the date of its accession, continue to exempt the international transport of passengers as referred to in point 10 of Annex X, Part B, for as long as the same exemption is applied in any of the Member States which were members of the Community on 31 December 2006.]

Amendments—Articles 390a, 390b inserted by Council Directive 2009/162/EU art 1(15) with effect from 15 January 2010 (OJ L 10, 15.1.2010, p 14).

[Article 390b

Romania may, in accordance with the conditions applying in that Member State on the date of its accession, continue to exempt the international transport of passengers, as referred to in point 10 of Annex X, Part B, for as long as the same exemption is applied in any of the Member States which were members of the Community on 31 December 2006.]

Amendments—Articles 390a, 390b inserted by Council Directive 2009/162/EU art 1(15) with effect from 15 January 2010 (OJ L 10, 15.1.2010, p 14).

SECTION 3

Provisions common to Sections 1 and 2

Article 391

Member States which exempt the transactions referred to in Articles 371, 375, 376 or 377, Article 378(2), Article 379(2) or [Articles 380 to 390b] may grant taxable persons the right to opt for taxation of those transactions.

Commentary—*De Voil Indirect Tax Service* **V4.275**.

Simon's Tax Cases—*Finanzamt Goslar v Breitsohl* [2001] STC 355*.

Amendments—Words substituted for "Articles 380 to 390" by Council Directive 2009/162/EU art 1(16) with effect from 15 January 2010 (OJ L 10, 15.1.2010, p 14).

VAT EC

Article 392

Member States may provide that, in respect of the supply of buildings and building land purchased for the purpose of resale by a taxable person for whom the VAT on the purchase was not deductible, the taxable amount shall be the difference between the selling price and the purchase price.

Article 393

1. With a view to facilitating the transition to the definitive arrangements referred to in Article 402, the Council shall, on the basis of a report from the Commission, review the situation with regard to the derogations provided for in Sections 1 and 2 and shall, acting in accordance with Article 93 of the Treaty decide whether any or all of those derogations is to be abolished.

2. By way of definitive arrangements, passenger transport shall be taxed in the Member State of departure for that part of the journey taking place within the Community, in accordance with the detailed rules to be laid down by the Council, acting in accordance with Article 93 of the Treaty.

CHAPTER 2
DEROGATIONS SUBJECT TO AUTHORISATION

SECTION 1
Simplification measures and measures to prevent tax evasion or avoidance

Article 394

Member States which, at 1 January 1977, applied special measures to simplify the procedure for collecting VAT or to prevent certain forms of tax evasion or avoidance may retain them provided that they have notified the Commission accordingly before 1 January 1978 and that such simplification measures comply with the criterion laid down in the second subparagraph of Article 395(1).

Article 395

1. The Council, acting unanimously on a proposal from the Commission, may authorise any Member State to introduce special measures for derogation from the provisions of this Directive, in order to simplify the procedure for collecting VAT or to prevent certain forms of tax evasion or avoidance.

Measures intended to simplify the procedure for collecting VAT may not, except to a negligible extent, affect the overall amount of the tax revenue of the Member State collected at the stage of final consumption.

2. A Member State wishing to introduce the measure referred to in paragraph 1 shall send an application to the Commission and provide it with all the necessary information. If the Commission considers that it does not have all the necessary information, it shall contact the Member State concerned within two months of receipt of the application and specify what additional information is required.

Once the Commission has all the information it considers necessary for appraisal of the request it shall within one month notify the requesting Member State accordingly and it shall transmit the request, in its original language, to the other Member States.

3. Within three months of giving the notification referred to in the second subparagraph of paragraph 2, the Commission shall present to the Council either an appropriate proposal or, should it object to the derogation requested, a communication setting out its objections.

4. The procedure laid down in paragraphs 2 and 3 shall, in any event, be completed within eight months of receipt of the application by the Commission.

[5. In cases of imperative urgency as set out in Article 199b(1), the procedure laid down in paragraphs 2 and 3 shall be completed within six months of receipt of the application by the Commission.]

Simon's Tax Cases—*C&E Comrs v Next plc* [1995] STC 651*; *Primback Ltd v C&E Comrs* [1996] STC 757*; *Finanzamt Bergisch Gladbach v Skripalle* (Case C-63/96) [1997] STC 1035*; *Finanzamt Sulingen v Sudholz* [2005] STC 747*.
Art 395(1), *Genius Holding BV v Staatssecretaris van Financiën* [1991] STC 239*; *'K' Line Air Service Europe BV v Eulaerts NV and Belgian State* (Case C-131/91) [1996] STC 597*.

Amendments—Para 5 inserted by Council Directive 2013/42/EU art 2 with effect from 15 August 2013 until 31 December 2018 (OJ L 201, 26.7.2013, p 1).

SECTION 2
International agreements

Article 396

1. The Council, acting unanimously on a proposal from the Commission, may authorise any Member State to conclude with a third country or an international body an agreement which may contain derogations from this Directive.

2. A Member State wishing to conclude an agreement as referred to in paragraph 1 shall send an application to the Commission and provide it with all the necessary information. If the Commission considers that it does not have all the necessary information, it shall contact the Member State concerned within two months of receipt of the application and specify what additional information is required.

Once the Commission has all the information it considers necessary for appraisal of the request it shall within one month notify the requesting Member State accordingly and it shall transmit the request, in its original language, to the other Member States.

3. Within three months of giving the notification referred to in the second subparagraph of paragraph 2, the Commission shall present to the Council either an appropriate proposal or, should it object to the derogation requested, a communication setting out its objections.

4. The procedure laid down in paragraphs 2 and 3 shall, in any event, be completed within eight months of receipt of the application by the Commission.

TITLE XIV
MISCELLANEOUS

CHAPTER 1
IMPLEMENTING MEASURES

Article 397

The Council, acting unanimously on a proposal from the Commission, shall adopt the measures necessary to implement this Directive.

CHAPTER 2
VAT COMMITTEE

Article 398

1. An advisory committee on value added tax, called 'the VAT Committee', is set up.
2. The VAT Committee shall consist of representatives of the Member States and of the Commission.

The chairman of the Committee shall be a representative of the Commission.

Secretarial services for the Committee shall be provided by the Commission.

3. The VAT Committee shall adopt its own rules of procedure.
4. In addition to the points forming the subject of consultation pursuant to this Directive, the VAT Committee shall examine questions raised by its chairman, on his own initiative or at the request of the representative of a Member State, which concern the application of Community provisions on VAT.

Simon's Tax Cases—*Stradasfalti Srl v Agenzia delle Entrate – Ufficio di Trento* [2007] STC 508*.

CHAPTER 3
CONVERSION RATES

Article 399

Without prejudice to any other particular provisions, the equivalents in national currency of the amounts in euro specified in this Directive shall be determined on the basis of the euro conversion rate applicable on 1 January 1999. Member States having acceded to the European Union after that date, which have not adopted the euro as single currency, shall use the euro conversion rate applicable on the date of their accession.

Article 400

When converting the amounts referred to in Article 399 into national currencies, Member States may adjust the amounts resulting from that conversion either upwards or downwards by up to 10%.

CHAPTER 4
OTHER TAXES, DUTIES AND CHARGES

Article 401

Without prejudice to other provisions of Community law, this Directive shall not prevent a Member State from maintaining or introducing taxes on insurance contracts, taxes on betting and gambling, excise duties, stamp duties or, more generally, any taxes, duties or charges which cannot be characterised as turnover taxes, provided that the collecting of those taxes, duties or charges does not give rise, in trade between Member States, to formalities connected with the crossing of frontiers.

Simon's Tax Cases—*KÖGÁZ rt and others v Zala Megyei Közigazgatàsi Hivatal Vezetoje, OTP Garancia Biztosító rt v Vas Megvei Közigazgatàsi Hivatal* [2008] STC 2367*; *Metropol Spielstatten Unternehmergesellschaft (haftungsbeschrankt) v Finanzamt Hamburg-Bergedorf* (Case C-440/12) [2014] STC 505.

TITLE XV
FINAL PROVISIONS

CHAPTER 1
TRANSITIONAL ARRANGEMENTS FOR THE TAXATION OF TRADE BETWEEN MEMBER STATES

Article 402

1. The arrangements provided for in this Directive for the taxation of trade between Member States are transitional and shall be replaced by definitive arrangements based in principle on the taxation in the Member State of origin of the supply of goods or services.

2. Having concluded, upon examination of the report referred to in Article 404, that the conditions for transition to the definitive arrangements are met, the Council shall, acting in accordance with Article 93 of the Treaty, adopt the provisions necessary for the entry into force and for the operation of the definitive arrangements.

Article 403

The Council shall, acting in accordance with Article 93 of the Treaty, adopt Directives appropriate for the purpose of supplementing the common system of VAT and, in particular, for the progressive restriction or the abolition of derogations from that system.

Article 404

Every four years starting from the adoption of this Directive, the Commission shall, on the basis of information obtained from the Member States, present a report to the European Parliament and to the Council on the operation of the common system of VAT in the Member States and, in particular, on the operation of the transitional arrangements for taxing trade between Member States. That report shall be accompanied, where appropriate, by proposals concerning the definitive arrangements.

CHAPTER 2
TRANSITIONAL MEASURES APPLICABLE IN THE CONTEXT OF ACCESSION TO THE EUROPEAN UNION

Article 405

For the purposes of this Chapter, the following definitions shall apply:

(1) 'Community' means the territory of the Community as defined in point (1) of Article 5 before the accession of new Member States;

(2) 'new Member States' means the territory of the Member States which acceded to the European Union after 1 January 1995, as defined for each of those Member States in point (2) of Article 5;

(3) 'enlarged Community' means the territory of the Community as defined in point (1) of Article 5 after the accession of new Member States.

Article 406

The provisions in force at the time the goods were placed under temporary importation arrangements with total exemption from import duty or under one of the arrangements or situations referred to in Article 156, or under similar arrangements or situations in one of the new Member States, shall continue to apply until the goods cease to be covered by these arrangements or situations after the date of accession, where the following conditions are met:

(*a*) the goods entered the Community or one of the new Member States before the date of accession;

(*b*) the goods were placed, on entry into the Community or one of the new Member States, under these arrangements or situations;

(*c*) the goods have not ceased to be covered by these arrangements or situations before the date of accession.

Article 407

The provisions in force at the time the goods were placed under customs transit arrangements shall continue to apply until the goods cease to be covered by these arrangements after the date of accession, where the following conditions are met:

(*a*) the goods were placed, before the date of accession, under customs transit arrangements;

(*b*) the goods have not ceased to be covered by these arrangements before the date of accession.

Article 408

1. The following shall be treated as an importation of goods where it is shown that the goods were in free circulation in one of the new Member States or in the Community:

(*a*) the removal, including irregular removal, of goods from temporary importation arrangements under which they were placed before the date of accession under the conditions provided for in Article 406;

(*b*) the removal, including irregular removal, of goods either from one of the arrangements or situations referred to in Article 156 or from similar arrangements or situations under which they were placed before the date of accession under the conditions provided for in Article 406;

(*c*) the cessation of one of the arrangements referred to in Article 407, started before the date of accession in the territory of one of the new Member States, for the purposes of a supply of goods for consideration effected before that date in the territory of that Member State by a taxable person acting as such;

(*d*) any irregularity or offence committed during customs transit arrangements started under the conditions referred to in point (*c*).

2. In addition to the case referred to in paragraph 1, the use after the date of accession within the territory of a Member State, by a taxable or non-taxable person, of goods supplied to him before the date of accession within the territory of the Community or one of the new Member States shall be treated as an importation of goods where the following conditions are met:

(*a*) the supply of those goods has been exempted, or was likely to be exempted, either under points (*a*) and (*b*) of Article 146(1) or under a similar provision in the new Member States;

(*b*) the goods were not imported into one of the new Member States or into the Community before the date of accession.

Article 409

In the cases referred to in Article 408(1), the place of import within the meaning of Article 61 shall be the Member State within whose territory the goods cease to be covered by the arrangements or situations under which they were placed before the date of accession.

Article 410

1. By way of derogation from Article 71, the importation of goods within the meaning of Article 408 shall terminate without the occurrence of a chargeable event if one of the following conditions is met:

(*a*) the imported goods are dispatched or transported outside the enlarged Community;

(*b*) the imported goods within the meaning of Article 408(1)(*a*) are other than means of transport and are redispatched or transported to the Member State from which they were exported and to the person who exported them;

(*c*) the imported goods within the meaning of Article 408(1)(*a*) are means of transport which were acquired or imported before the date of accession in accordance with the general conditions of taxation in force on the domestic market of

one of the new Member States or of one of the Member States of the Community or which have not been subject, by reason of their exportation, to any exemption from, or refund of, VAT.

2. The condition referred to in paragraph 1(*c*) shall be deemed to be fulfilled in the following cases:

(*a*) when the date of first entry into service of the means of transport was more than eight years before the accession to the European Union.

(*b*) when the amount of tax due by reason of the importation is insignificant.

VAT EC

CHAPTER 3
TRANSPOSITION AND ENTRY INTO FORCE

Article 411

1. Directive 67/227/EEC and Directive 77/388/EEC are repealed, without prejudice to the obligations of the Member States concerning the time-limits, listed in Annex XI, Part B, for the transposition into national law and the implementation of those Directives.

2. References to the repealed Directives shall be construed as references to this Directive and shall be read in accordance with the correlation table in Annex XII.

Article 412

1. Member States shall bring into force the laws, regulations and administrative provisions necessary to comply with Article 2 (3), Article 44, Article 59(1), Article 399 and Annex III, point (18) with effect from 1 January 2008. They shall forthwith communicate to the Commission the text of those provisions and a correlation table between those provisions and this Directive.

When Member States adopt those provisions, they shall contain a reference to this Directive or be accompanied by such a reference on the occasion of their official publication. Member States shall determine how such reference is to be made.

2. Member States shall communicate to the Commission the text of the main provisions of national law which they adopt in the field covered by this Directive.

Article 413

This Directive shall enter into force on 1 January 2007.

Article 414

This Directive is addressed to the Member States.

ANNEX I

LIST OF THE ACTIVITIES REFERRED TO IN THE THIRD SUBPARAGRAPH OF ARTICLE 13(1)

(1) Telecommunications services;

(2) supply of water, gas, electricity and thermal energy;

(3) transport of goods;

(4) port and airport services;

(5) passenger transport;

(6) supply of new goods manufactured for sale;

(7) transactions in respect of agricultural products, carried out by agricultural intervention agencies pursuant to Regulations on the common organisation of the market in those products;

(8) organisation of trade fairs and exhibitions;

(9) warehousing;

(10) activities of commercial publicity bodies;

(11) activities of travel agents;

(12) running of staff shops, cooperatives and industrial canteens and similar institutions;

(13) activities carried out by radio and television bodies in so far as these are not exempt pursuant to Article 132(1)(q).

ANNEX II

[INDICATIVE LIST OF THE ELECTRONICALLY SUPPLIED SERVICES REFERRED TO IN POINT (C) OF THE FIRST PARAGRAPH OF ARTICLE 58]

Amendments—Heading to Annex II substituted by Council Directive 2008/8/EC art 5(16) with effect from 1 January 2015 (OJ L 44, 20.2.2008 p 11). Heading previously read "Indicative list of the electronically supplied services referred to in article 58 and point (k) of the first paragraph of article 59".

(1) Website supply, web-hosting, distance maintenance of programmes and equipment;

(2) supply of software and updating thereof;

(3) supply of images, text and information and making available of databases;

(4) supply of music, films and games, including games of chance and gambling games, and of political, cultural, artistic, sporting, scientific and entertainment broadcasts and events;

(5) supply of distance teaching.

ANNEX III

LIST OF SUPPLIES OF GOODS AND SERVICES TO WHICH THE REDUCED RATES REFERRED TO IN ARTICLE 98 MAY BE APPLIED

(1) Foodstuffs (including beverages but excluding alcoholic beverages) for human and animal consumption; live animals, seeds, plants and ingredients normally intended for use in the preparation of foodstuffs; products normally used to supplement foodstuffs or as a substitute for foodstuffs;

(2) supply of water;

(3) pharmaceutical products of a kind normally used for health care, prevention of illnesses and as treatment for medical and veterinary purposes, including products used for contraception and sanitary protection;

(4) medical equipment, aids and other appliances normally intended to alleviate or treat disability, for the exclusive personal use of the disabled, including the repair of such goods, and supply of children's car seats;

(5) transport of passengers and their accompanying luggage;

[(6) supply, including on loan by libraries, of books on all physical means of support (including brochures, leaflets and similar printed matter, children's picture, drawing or colouring books, music printed or in manuscript form, maps and hydrographic or similar charts), newspapers and periodicals, other than material wholly or predominantly devoted to advertising;][1]

(7) admission to shows, theatres, circuses, fairs, amusement parks, concerts, museums, zoos, cinemas, exhibitions and similar cultural events and facilities;

(8) reception of radio and television broadcasting services;

(9) supply of services by writers, composers and performing artists, or of the royalties due to them;

(10) provision, construction, renovation and alteration of housing, as part of a social policy;

[(10a) renovation and repairing of private dwellings, excluding materials which account for a significant part of the value of the service supplied;
(10b) window-cleaning and cleaning in private households;][1]
(11) supply of goods and services of a kind normally intended for use in agricultural production but excluding capital goods such as machinery or buildings;
(12) accommodation provided in hotels and similar establishments, including the provision of holiday accommodation and the letting of places on camping or caravan sites;
[(12a) restaurant and catering services, it being possible to exclude the supply of (alcoholic and/or non-alcoholic) beverages;][1]
(13) admission to sporting events;
(14) use of sporting facilities;
(15) supply of goods and services by organisations recognised as being devoted to social wellbeing by Member States and engaged in welfare or social security work, in so far as those transactions are not exempt pursuant to Articles 132, 135 and 136;
(16) supply of services by undertakers and cremation services, and the supply of goods related thereto;
(17) provision of medical and dental care and thermal treatment in so far as those services are not exempt pursuant to points (*b*) to (*e*) of Article 132(1);
(18) supply of services provided in connection with street cleaning, refuse collection and waste treatment, other than the supply of such services by bodies referred to in Article 13.
[(19) minor repairing of bicycles, shoes and leather goods, clothing and household linen (including mending and alteration);
(20) domestic care services such as home help and care of young, elderly, sick or disabled;
(21) hairdressing.][1]

Simon's Tax Cases—*Finanzamt Rendsburg v Harbs* [2006] STC 340*.

(3), *European Commission v Spain* (Case C-360/11) [2013] STC 2236.

(4), *European Commission v Spain* (Case C-360/11) [2013] STC 2236.

(7), *Erotic Center BVBA v Belgium* [2010] STC 1018*.

Amendments—[1] Point 6 substituted, and points (10a), (10b), (12a), (19)–(21) inserted, by Council Directive 2009/47/EC art 1, Annex, with effect from 1 June 2009 (OJ L 116, 9.5.2009 p 18). Text previously read as follows—

"(6) supply, including on loan by libraries, of books (including brochures, leaflets and similar printed matter, children's picture, drawing or colouring books, music printed or in manuscript form, maps and hydrographic or similar charts), newspapers and periodicals, other than material wholly or predominantly devoted to advertising;".

ANNEX IV

LIST OF THE SERVICES REFERRED TO IN ARTICLE 106

(1) Minor repairing of:
(a) bicycles;
(b) shoes and leather goods;
(c) clothing and household linen (including mending and alteration);
(2) renovation and repairing of private dwellings, excluding materials which account for a significant part of the value of the service supplied;
(3) window-cleaning and cleaning in private households;
(4) domestic care services such as home help and care of the young, elderly, sick or disabled;
(5) hairdressing.[1]

Amendments—[1] Annex IV repealed by Council Directive 2009/47/EC art 1, Annex, with effect from 1 June 2009 (OJ L 116, 9.5.2009 p 18).

ANNEX V

CATEGORIES OF GOODS COVERED BY WAREHOUSING ARRANGEMENTS OTHER THAN CUSTOMS WAREHOUSING AS PROVIDED FOR UNDER ARTICLE 160(2)

	CN-code	*Description of goods*
(1)	0701	Potatoes
(2)	0711 20	Olives
(3)	0801	Coconuts, Brazil nuts and cashew nuts
(4)	0802	Other nuts
(5)	0901 11 00	Coffee, not roasted
	0901 12 00	

	CN-code	*Description of goods*
(6)	0902	Tea
(7)	1001 to 1005 1007 to 1008	Cereals
(8)	1006	Husked rice
(9)	1201 to 1207	Grains and oil seeds (including soya beans) and oleaginous fruits
(10)	1507 to 1515	Vegetable oils and fats and their fractions, whether or not refined, but not chemically modified
(11)	1701 11 1701 12	Raw sugar
(12)	1801	Cocoa beans, whole or broken, raw or roasted
(13)	2709 2710 2711 12 2711 13	Mineral oils (including propane and butane; also including crude petroleum oils)
(14)	Chapters 28 and 29	Chemicals in bulk
(15)	4001 4002	Rubber, in primary forms or in plates, sheets or strip
(16)	5101	Wool
(17)	7106	Silver
(18)	7110 11 00 7110 21 00 7110 31 00	Platinum (palladium, rhodium)
(19)	7402 7403 7405 7408	Copper
(20)	7502	Nickel
(21)	7601	Aluminium
(22)	7801	Lead
(23)	7901	Zinc
(24)	8001	Tin
(25)	ex 8112 92 ex 8112 99	Indium

ANNEX VI

LIST OF SUPPLIES OF GOODS AND SERVICES AS REFERRED TO IN POINT (D) OF ARTICLE 199(1)

(1) Supply of ferrous and non ferrous waste, scrap, and used materials including that of semi-finished products resulting from the processing, manufacturing or melting down of ferrous and non-ferrous metals and their alloys;

(2) supply of ferrous and non-ferrous semi-processed products and certain associated processing services;

(3) supply of residues and other recyclable materials consisting of ferrous and non-ferrous metals, their alloys, slag, ash, scale and industrial residues containing metals or their alloys and supply of selection, cutting, fragmenting and pressing services of these products;

(4) supply of, and certain processing services relating to, ferrous and non-ferrous waste as well as parings, scrap, waste and used and recyclable material consisting of cullet, glass, paper, paperboard and board, rags, bone, leather, imitation leather, parchment, raw hides and skins, tendons and sinews, twine, cordage, rope, cables, rubber and plastic;

(5) supply of the materials referred to in this annex after processing in the form of cleaning, polishing, selection, cutting, fragmenting, pressing or casting into ingots;

(6) supply of scrap and waste from the working of base materials.

ANNEX VII

LIST OF THE AGRICULTURAL PRODUCTION ACTIVITIES REFERRED TO IN POINT (4) OF ARTICLE 295(1)

(1) Crop production:

(*a*) general agriculture, including viticulture;

(*b*) growing of fruit (including olives) and of vegetables, flowers and ornamental plants, both in the open and under glass;

(*c*) production of mushrooms, spices, seeds and propagating materials;

(*d*) running of nurseries;

(2) stock farming together with cultivation:

(*a*) general stock farming;

(*b*) poultry farming;

(*c*) rabbit farming;

(*d*) beekeeping;

(*e*) silkworm farming;

(*f*) snail farming;

(3) forestry;

(4) fisheries:

(*a*) freshwater fishing;

(*b*) fish farming;

(*c*) breeding of mussels, oysters and other molluscs and crustaceans;

(*d*) frog farming.

ANNEX VIII

INDICATIVE LIST OF THE AGRICULTURAL SERVICES REFERRED TO IN POINT (5) OF ARTICLE 295(1)

(1) Field work, reaping and mowing, threshing, baling, collecting, harvesting, sowing and planting;

(2) packing and preparation for market, such as drying, cleaning, grinding, disinfecting and ensilage of agricultural products;

(3) storage of agricultural products;

(4) stock minding, rearing and fattening;

(5) hiring out, for agricultural purposes, of equipment normally used in agricultural, forestry or fisheries undertakings;

(6) technical assistance;

(7) destruction of weeds and pests, dusting and spraying of crops and land;

(8) operation of irrigation and drainage equipment;

(9) lopping, tree felling and other forestry services.

ANNEX IX

WORKS OF ART, COLLECTORS' ITEMS AND ANTIQUES, AS REFERRED TO IN POINTS (2), (3) AND (4) OF ARTICLE 311(1)

PART A

WORKS OF ART

(1) Pictures, collages and similar decorative plaques, paintings and drawings, executed entirely by hand by the artist, other than plans and drawings for architectural, engineering, industrial, commercial, topographical or similar purposes, hand-decorated manufactured articles, theatrical scenery, studio back cloths or the like of painted canvas (CN code 9701);

(2) original engravings, prints and lithographs, being impressions produced in limited numbers directly in black and white or in colour of one or of several plates executed entirely by hand by the artist, irrespective of the process or of the material employed, but not including any mechanical or photomechanical process (CN code 9702 00 00);

(3) original sculptures and statuary, in any material, provided that they are executed entirely by the artist; sculpture casts the production of which is limited to eight copies and supervised by the artist or his successors in title (CN code 9703 00 00); on an exceptional basis, in cases determined by the Member States, the limit of eight copies may be exceeded for statuary casts produced before 1 January 1989;

(4) tapestries (CN code 5805 00 00) and wall textiles (CN code 6304 00 00) made by hand from original designs provided by artists, provided that there are not more than eight copies of each;

(5) individual pieces of ceramics executed entirely by the artist and signed by him;

(6) enamels on copper, executed entirely by hand, limited to eight numbered copies bearing the signature of the artist or the studio, excluding articles of jewellery and goldsmiths' and silversmiths' wares;
(7) photographs taken by the artist, printed by him or under his supervision, signed and numbered and limited to 30 copies, all sizes and mounts included.

PART B
COLLECTORS' ITEMS

(1) Postage or revenue stamps, postmarks, first-day covers, pre-stamped stationery and the like, used, or if unused not current and not intended to be current (CN code 9704 00 00);
(2) collections and collectors' pieces of zoological, botanical, mineralogical, anatomical, historical, archaeological, palaeontological, ethnographic or numismatic interest (CN code 9705 00 00).

PART C
ANTIQUES

Goods, other than works of art or collectors' items, which are more than 100 years old (CN code 9706 00 00).

ANNEX X
LIST OF TRANSACTIONS COVERED BY THE DEROGATIONS REFERRED TO IN ARTICLES 370 AND 371 AND ARTICLES 375 TO 390B

Amendments—Annex X title substituted for "List of Transactions Covered By the Derogations Referred to in Articles 370 and 371 and Articles 375 to 390" by Council Directive 2009/162/EU art 1(17) with effect from 15 January 2010 (OJ L 10, 15.1.2010, p 14).

PART A
TRANSACTIONS WHICH MEMBER STATES MAY CONTINUE TO TAX

(1) The supply of services by dental technicians in their professional capacity and the supply of dental prostheses by dentists and dental technicians;
(2) the activities of public radio and television bodies other than those of a commercial nature;
(3) the supply of a building, or parts thereof, or of the land on which it stands, other than as referred to in point (*a*) of Article 12(1), where carried out by taxable persons who were entitled to deduction of the VAT paid at the preceding stage in respect of the building concerned;
(4) the supply of the services of travel agents, as referred to in Article 306, and those of travel agents acting in the name and on behalf of the traveller, in relation to journeys outside the Community.

PART B
TRANSACTIONS WHICH MEMBER STATES MAY CONTINUE TO EXEMPT

(1) Admission to sporting events;
(2) the supply of services by authors, artists, performers, lawyers and other members of the liberal professions, other than the medical and paramedical professions, with the exception of the following:
- (*a*) assignments of patents, trade marks and other similar rights, and the granting of licences in respect of such rights;
- (*b*) work, other than the supply of contract work, on movable tangible property, carried out for a taxable person;
- (*c*) services to prepare or coordinate the carrying out of construction work, such as services provided by architects and by firms providing on-site supervision of works;
- (*d*) commercial advertising services;
- (*e*) transport and storage of goods, and ancillary services;
- (*f*) hiring out of movable tangible property to a taxable person;
- (*g*) provision of staff to a taxable person;
- (*h*) provision of services by consultants, engineers, planning offices and similar services in scientific, economic or technical fields;
- (*i*) compliance with an obligation to refrain from exercising, in whole or in part, a business activity or a right covered by points (*a*) to (*h*) or point (*j*);
- (*j*) the services of forwarding agents, brokers, business agents and other independent intermediaries, in so far as they relate to the supply or importation of goods or the supply of services covered by points (*a*) to (*i*);

(3) the supply of telecommunications services, and of goods related thereto, by public postal services;
(4) the supply of services by undertakers and cremation services and the supply of goods related thereto;

(5) transactions carried out by blind persons or by workshops for the blind, provided that those exemptions do not cause significant distortion of competition;
(6) the supply of goods and services to official bodies responsible for the construction, setting out and maintenance of cemeteries, graves and monuments commemorating the war dead;
(7) transactions carried out by hospitals not covered by point (*b*) of Article 132(1);
(8) the supply of water by a body governed by public law;
(9) the supply before first occupation of a building, or parts thereof, or of the land on which it stands and the supply of building land, as referred to in Article 12;
(10) the transport of passengers and, in so far as the transport of the passengers is exempt, the transport of goods accompanying them, such as luggage or motor vehicles, or the supply of services relating to the transport of passengers;
(11) the supply, modification, repair, maintenance, chartering and hiring of aircraft used by State institutions, including equipment incorporated or used in such aircraft;
(12) the supply, modification, repair, maintenance, chartering and hiring of fighting ships;
(13) the supply of the services of travel agents, as referred to in Article 306, and those of travel agents acting in the name and on behalf of the traveller, in relation to journeys within the Community.

ANNEX XI

Simon's Tax Cases—Part B, (4), *Network Insurance Brokers Ltd v C&E Comrs* [1998] STC 742*.

Part B, (9), *Norbury Developments Ltd v C&E Comrs* (Case C-136/97) [1999] STC 511*.

PART A
REPEALED DIRECTIVES WITH THEIR SUCCESSIVE AMENDMENTS

(1) Directive 67/227/EEC (OJ 71, 14.4.1967, p. 1301)
Directive 77/388/EEC

(2) Directive 77/388/EEC (OJ L 145, 13.6.1977, p. 1)
Directive 78/583/EEC (OJ L 194, 19.7.1978, p. 16)
Directive 80/368/EEC (OJ L 90, 3.4.1980, p. 41)
Directive 84/386/EEC (OJ L 208, 3.8.1984, p. 58)
Directive 89/465/EEC (OJ L 226, 3.8.1989, p. 21)
Directive 91/680/EEC (OJ L 376, 31.12.1991, p. 1) — (except for Article 2)
Directive 92/77/EEC (OJ L 316, 31.10.1992, p. 1)
Directive 92/111/EEC (OJ L 384, 30.12.1992, p. 47)
Directive 94/4/EC (OJ L 60, 3.3.1994, p. 14) — (only Article 2)
Directive 94/5/EC (OJ L 60, 3.3.1994, p. 16)
Directive 94/76/EC (OJ L 365, 31.12.1994, p. 53)
Directive 95/7/EC (OJ L 102, 5.5.1995, p. 18)
Directive 96/42/EC (OJ L 170, 9.7.1996, p. 34)
Directive 96/95/EC (OJ L 338, 28.12.1996, p. 89)
Directive 98/80/EC (OJ L 281, 17.10.1998, p. 31)
Directive 1999/49/EC (OJ L 139, 2.6.1999, p. 27)
Directive 1999/59/EC (OJ L 162, 26.6.1999, p. 63)
Directive 1999/85/EC (OJ L 277, 28.10.1999, p. 34)
Directive 2000/17/EC (OJ L 84, 5.4.2000, p. 24)
Directive 2000/65/EC (OJ L 269, 21.10.2000, p. 44)
Directive 2001/4/EC (OJ L 22, 24.1.2001, p. 17)
Directive 2001/115/EC (OJ L 15, 17.1.2002, p. 24)
Directive 2002/38/EC (OJ L 128, 15.5.2002, p. 41)
Directive 2002/93/EC (OJ L 331, 7.12.2002, p. 27)
Directive 2003/92/EC (OJ L 260, 11.10.2003, p. 8)
Directive 2004/7/EC (OJ L 27, 30.1.2004, p. 44)
Directive 2004/15/EC (OJ L 52, 21.2.2004, p. 61)
Directive 2004/66/EC (OJ L 168, 1.5.2004, p. 35) — (only Point V of the Annex)
Directive 2005/92/EC (OJ L 345, 28.12.2005, p. 19)
Directive 2006/18/EC (OJ L 51, 22.2.2006, p. 12)
Directive 2006/58/EC (OJ L 174, 28.6.2006, p. 5)
Directive 2006/69/EC (OJ L 221, 12.8.2006, p. 9 — (only Article 1)
Directive 2006/98/EC (OJ L . . . , . . . , p. . . . (*) — (only point 2 of the Annex)

PART B
TIME LIMITS FOR TRANSPOSITION INTO NATIONAL LAW (REFERRED TO IN ARTICLE 411)

Directive	*Deadline for transposition*
Directive 67/227/EEC	1 January 1970
Directive 77/388/EEC	1 January 1978
Directive 78/583/EEC	1 January 1979
Directive 80/368/EEC	1 January 1979
Directive 84/386/EEC	1 July 1985
Directive 89/465/EEC	1 January 1990
	1 January 1991
	1 January 1992
	1 January 1993
	1 January 1994 for Portugal
Directive 91/680/EEC	1 January 1993
Directive 92/77/EEC	31 December 1992
Directive 92/111/EEC	1 January 1993
	1 January 1994
	1 October 1993 for Germany
Directive 94/4/EC	1 April 1994
Directive 94/5/EC	1 January 1995
Directive 94/76/EC	1 January 1995
Directive 95/7/EC	1 January 1996
	1 January 1997 for Germany and Luxembourg
Directive 96/42/EC	1 January 1995
Directive 96/95/EC	1 January 1997
Directive 98/80/EC	1 January 2000
Directive 1999/49/EC	1 January 1999
Directive 1999/59/EC	1 January 2000
Directive 1999/85/CE	—
Directive 2000/17/EC	—
Directive 2000/65/EC	31 December 2001
Directive 2001/4/EC	1 January 2001
Directive 2001/115/EC	1 January 2004
Directive 2002/38/EC	1 July 2003
Directive 2002/93/EC	—
Directive 2003/92/EC	1 January 2005
Directive 2004/7/EC	30 January 2004
Directive 2004/15/EC	—
Directive 2004/66/EC	1 May 2004
Directive 2005/92/EC	1 January 2006
Directive 2006/18/EC	—
Directive 2006/58/EC	1 July 2006
Directive 2006/69/EC	1 January 2008

ANNEX XII
CORRELATION TABLE

Directive 67/227/EEC	*Directive 77/388/EEC*	*Amending Directives*	*Other acts*	*This Directive*
Article 1, first paragraph				Article 1(1)
Article 1, second and third paragraphs				—
Article 2, first, second and third paragraphs				Article 1(2), first, second and third subparagraphs
Articles 3, 4 and 6				—
	Article 1			—
	Article 2, point (1)			Article 2(1)(a) and (c)
	Article 2, point (2)			Article 2(1)(d)
	Article 3(1), first indent			Article 5, point (2)
	Article 3(1), second indent			Article 5, point (1)
	Article 3(1), third indent			Article 5, points (3) and (4)
	Article 3(2)			—
	Article 3(3), first subparagraph, first indent			Article 6(2)(a) and (b)
	Article 3(3), first subparagraph, second indent			Article 6(2)(c) and (d)
	Article 3(3), first subparagraph, third indent			Article 6(2)(e), (f) and (g)
	Article 3(3) second subparagraph, first indent			Article 6(1)(b)
	Article 3(3) second subparagraph, second indent			Article 6(1)(c)
	Article 3(3), second subparagraph, third indent			Article 6(1)(a)
	Article 3(4), first subparagraph, first and second indents			Article 7(1)
	Article 3(4), second subparagraph, first second and third indents			Article 7(2)
	Article 3(5)			Article 8

Directive 67/227/EEC	*Directive 77/388/EEC*	*Amending Directives*	*Other acts*	*This Directive*
	Article 4(1) and (2)			Article 9(1), first and second subparagraphs
	Article 4(3)(a), first subparagraph, first sentence			Article 12(1)(a)
	Article 4(3)(a), first subparagraph, second sentence			Article 12(2), second subparagraph
	Article 4(3)(a), second subparagraph			Article 12(2), third subparagraph
	Article 4(3)(a), third subparagraph			Article 12(2), first subparagraph
	Article 4(3)(b), first subparagraph			Article 12(1)(b)
	Article 4(3)(b), second subparagraph			Article 12(3)
	Article 4(4), first subparagraph			Article 10
	Article 4(4), second and third subparagraphs			Article 11, first and second paragraphs
	Article 4(5), first, second and third subparagraphs			Article 13(1), first, second and third subparagraphs
	Article 4(5), fourth subparagraph			Article 13(2)
	Article 5(1)			Article 14(1)
	Article 5(2)			Article 15(1)
	Article 5(3)(a), (b) and (c)			Article 15(2)(a), (b) and (c)
	Article 5(4)(a), (b) and (c)			Article 14(2)(a), (b) and (c)
	Article 5(5)			Article 14(3)
	Article 5(6), first and second sentences			Article 16, first and second paragraphs
	Article 5(7)(a), (b) and (c)			Article 18(a), (b) and (c)
	Article 5(8), first sentence			Article 19, first paragraph
	Article 5(8), second and third sentences			Article 19, second paragraph
	Article 6(1), first subparagraph			Article 24(1)

Directive 67/227/EEC	*Directive 77/388/EEC*	*Amending Directives*	*Other acts*	*This Directive*
	Article 6(1), second subparagraph, first, second and third indents			Article 25(a), (b) and (c)
	Article 6(2), first subparagraph, points (a) and (b)			Article 26(1)(a) and (b)
	Article 6(2), second subparagraph			Article 26(2)
	Article 6(3)			Article 27
	Article 6(4)			Article 28
	Article 6(5)			Article 29
	Article 7(1)(a) and (b)			Article 30, first and second paragraphs
	Article 7(2)			Article 60
	Article 7(3), first and second subparagraphs			Article 61, first and second paragraphs
	Article 8(1)(a), first sentence			Article 32, first paragraph
	Article 8(1)(a), second and third sentences			Article 36, first and second paragraphs
	Article 8(1)(b)			Article 31
	Article 8(1)(c), first subparagraph			Article 37(1)
	Article 8(1)(c), second subparagraph, first indent			Article 37(2), first subparagraph
	Article 8(1)(c), second subparagraph, second and third indents			Article 37(2), second and third subparagraphs
	Article 8(1)(c), third subparagraph			Article 37(2), fourth subparagraph
	Article 8(1)(c), fourth subparagraph			Article 37(3), first subparagraph
	Article 8(1)(c), fifth subparagraph			—
	Article 8(1)(c), sixth subparagraph			Article 37(3), second subparagraph
	Article 8(1)(d), first and second subparagraphs			Article 38(1) and (2)

Directive 67/227/EEC	*Directive 77/388/EEC*	*Amending Directives*	*Other acts*	*This Directive*
	Article 8(1)(e), first sentence			Article 39, first paragraph
	Article 8(1)(e), second and third sentences			Article 39, second paragraph
	Article 8(2)			Article 32, second paragraph
	Article 9(1)			Article 43
	Article 9(2) introductory sentence			—
	Article 9(2)(a)			Article 45
	Article 9(2)(b)			Article 46
	Article 9(2)(c), first and second indents			Article 52(a) and (b)
	Article 9(2)(c), third and fourth indents			Article 52(c)
	Article 9(2)(e), first to sixth indents			Article 56(1)(a) to (f)
	Article 9(2)(e), seventh indent			Article 56(1)(l)
	Article 9(2)(e), eighth indent			Article 56(1)(g)
	Article 9(2)(e), ninth indent			Article 56(1)(h)
	Article 9(2)(e), tenth indent, first sentence			Article 56(1)(i)
	Article 9(2)(e), tenth indent, second sentence			Article 24(2)
	Article 9(2)(e), tenth indent, third sentence			Article 56(1)(i)
	Article 9(2)(e), eleventh and twelfth indents			Article 56(1)(j) and (k)
	Article 9(2)(f)			Article 57(1)
	Article 9(3)			Article 58, first and second paragraphs
	Article 9(3)(a) and (b)			Article 58, first paragraph, points (a) and (b)
	Article 9(4)			Article 59(1) and (2)

Directive 67/227/EEC	*Directive 77/388/EEC*	*Amending Directives*	*Other acts*	*This Directive*
	Article 10(1)(a) and (b)			Article 62, points (1) and (2)
	Article 10(2), first subparagraph, first sentence			Article 63
	Article 10(2), first subparagraph, second and third sentences			Article 64(1) and (2)
	Article 10(2), second subparagraph			Article 65
	Article 10(2), third subparagraph, first, second and third indents			Article 66(a), (b) and (c)
	Article 10(3), first subparagraph, first sentence			Article 70
	Article 10(3), first subparagraph, second sentence			Article 71(1), first subparagraph
	Article 10(3), second subparagraph			Article 71(1), second subparagraph
	Article 10(3), third subparagraph			Article 71(2)
	Article 11(A)(1)(a)			Article 73
	Article 11(A)(1)(b)			Article 74
	Article 11(A)(1)(c)			Article 75
	Article 11(A)(1)(d)			Article 77
	Article 11(A)(2)(a)			Article 78, first paragraph, point (a)
	Article 11(A)(2)(b), first sentence			Article 78, first paragraph, point (b)
	Article 11(A)(2)(b), second sentence			Article 78, second paragraph
	Article 11(A)(3)(a) and (b)			Article 79, first paragraph, points (a) and (b) Article 87(a) and (b)
	Article 11(A)(3)(c), first sentence			Article 79, first paragraph, point (c)

Directive 67/227/EEC	*Directive 77/388/EEC*	*Amending Directives*	*Other acts*	*This Directive*
	Article 11(A)(3)(c), second sentence			Article 79, second paragraph
	Article 11(A)(4),first and second subparagraphs			Article 81, first and second paragraphs
	Article 11(A)(5)			Article 82
	Article 11(A)(6), first subparagraph, first and second sentences			Article 80(1), first subparagraph
	Article 11(A)(6), first subparagraph, third sentence			Article 80(1), second subparagraph
	Article 11(A)(6), second subparagraph			Article 80(1), first subparagraph
	Article 11(A)(6), third subparagraph			Article 80(2)
	Article 11(A)(6), fourth subparagraph			Article 80(3)
	Article 11(A)(7), first and second subparagraphs			Article 72, first and second paragraphs
	Article 11(B)(1)			Article 85
	Article 11(B)(3)(a)			Article 86(1)(a)
	Article 11(B)(3)(b), first subparagraph			Article 86(1)(b)
	Article 11(B)(3)(b), second subparagraph			Article 86(2)
	Article 11(B)(3)(b), third subparagraph			Article 86(1)(b)
	Article 11(B)(4)			Article 87
	Article 11(B)(5)			Article 88
	Article 11(B)(6), first and second subparagraphs			Article 89, first and second paragraphs
	Article 11(C)(1), first and second subparagraphs			Article 90(1) and (2)

Directive 67/227/EEC	*Directive 77/388/EEC*	*Amending Directives*	*Other acts*	*This Directive*
	Article 11(C)(2), first subparagraph			Article 91(1)
	Article 11(C)(2), second subparagraph, first and second sentences			Article 91(2), first and second subparagraphs
	Article 11(C)(3), first and second indents			Article 92(a) and (b)
	Article 12(1)			Article 93, first paragraph
	Article 12(1)(a)			Article 93, second paragraph, point (a)
	Article 12(1)(b)			Article 93, second paragraph, point (c)
	Article 12(2), first and second indents			Article 95, first and second paragraphs
	Article 12(3)(a), first subparagraph, first sentence			Article 96
	Article 12(3)(a), first subparagraph, second sentence			Article 97(1)
	Article 12(3)(a), second subparagraph			Article 97(2)
	Article 12(3)(a), third subparagraph, first sentence			Article 98(1)
	Article 12(3)(a), third subparagraph, second sentence			Article 98(2), first subparagraph Article 99(1)
	Article 12(3)(a), fourth subparagraph			Article 98(2), second subparagraph
	Article 12(3)(b), first sentence			Article 102, first paragraph
	Article 12(3)(b), second, third and fourth sentences			Article 102, second paragraph
	Article 12(3)(c), first subparagraph			Article 103(1)
	Article 12(3)(c), second subparagraph, first and second indents			Article 103(2)(a) and (b)
	Article 12(4), first subparagraph			Article 99(2)

Directive 67/227/EEC	*Directive 77/388/EEC*	*Amending Directives*	*Other acts*	*This Directive*
	Article 12(4), second subparagraph, first and second sentences			Article 100, first and second paragraphs
	Article 12(4), third subparagraph			Article 101
	Article 12(5)			Article 94(2)
	Article 12(6)			Article 105
	Article 13(A)(1), introductory sentence			Article 131
	Article 13(A)(1)(a) to (n)			Article 132(1)(a) to (n)
	Article 13(A)(1)(o), first sentence			Article 132(1)(o)
	Article 13(A)(1)(o), second sentence			Article 132(2)
	Article 13(A)(1)(p) and (q)			Article 132(1)(p) and (q)
	Article 13(A)(2)(a), first to fourth indents			Article 133(a) to (d)
	Article 13(A)(2)(b), first and second indents			Article 134(a) and (b)
	Article 13(B), introductory sentence			Article 131
	Article 13(B)(a)			Article 135(1)(a)
	Article 13(B)(b), first subparagraph			Article 135(1)(l)
	Article 13(B)(b), first subparagraph, points (1) to (4)			Article 135(2), first subparagraph, points (a) to (d)
	Article 13(B)(b), second subparagraph			Article 135(2), second subparagraph
	Article 13(B)(c)			Article 136(a) and (b)
	Article 13(B)(d)			—
	Article 13(B)(d), points (1) to (5)			Article 135(1)(b) to (f)
	Article 13(B)(d), point (5), first and second indents			Article 135(1)(f)
	Article 13(B)(d), point (6)			Article 135(1)(g)

Directive 67/227/EEC	*Directive 77/388/EEC*	*Amending Directives*	*Other acts*	*This Directive*
	Article 13(B)(e) to (h)			Article 135(1)(h) to (k)
	Article 13(C), first subparagraph, point (a)			Article 137(1)(d)
	Article 13(C), first subparagraph, point (b)			Article 137(1)(a), (b) and (c)
	Article 13(C), second subparagraph			Article 137(2), first and second subparagraphs
	Article 14(1), introductory sentence			Article 131
	Article 14(1)(a)			Article 140(a)
	Article 14(1)(d), first and second subparagraphs			Article 143(b) and (c)
	Article 14(1)(e)			Article 143(e)
	Article 14(1)(g), first to fourth indents			Article 143(f) to (i)
	Article 14(1)(h)			Article 143(j)
	Article 14(1)(i)			Article 144
	Article 14(1)(j)			Article 143(k)
	Article 14(1)(k)			Article 143(l)
	Article 14(2), first subparagraph			Article 145(1)
	Article 14(2), second subparagraph, first, second and third indents			Article 145(2), first, second and third subparagraphs
	Article 14(2), third subparagraph			Article 145(3)
	Article 15, introductory sentence			Article 131
	Article 15, point (1)			Article 146(1)(a)
	Article 15, point (2), first subparagraph			Article 146(1)(b)
	Article 15, point (2), second subparagraph, first and second indents			Article 147(1), first subparagraph, points (a) and (b)

Directive 67/227/EEC	*Directive 77/388/EEC*	*Amending Directives*	*Other acts*	*This Directive*
	Article 15, point (2), second subparagraph, third indent, first part of the sentence			Article 147(1), first subparagraph, point (c)
	Article 15, point (2), second subparagraph, third indent, second part of the sentence			Article 147(1), second subparagraph
	Article 15, point (2), third subparagraph, first and second indents			Article 147(2), first and second subparagraphs
	Article 15, point (2), fourth subparagraph			Article 147(2), third subparagraph
	Article 15, point (3)			Article 146(1)(d)
	Article 15, point (4), first subparagraph, points (a) and (b)			Article 148(a)
	Article 15, point (4), first subparagraph, point (c)			Article 148(b)
	Article 15, point (4), second subparagraph, first and second sentences			Article 150(1) and (2)
	Article 15, point (5)			Article 148(c)
	Article 15, point (6)			Article 148(f)
	Article 15, point (7)			Article 148(e)
	Article 15, point (8)			Article 148(d)
	Article 15, point (9)			Article 148(g)
	Article 15, point (10), first subparagraph, first to fourth indents			Article 151(1), first subparagraph, points (a) to (d)
	Article 15, point (10), second subparagraph			Article 151(1), second subparagraph
	Article 15, point (10), third subparagraph			Article 151(2)
	Article 15, point (11)			Article 152
	Article 15, point (12), first sentence			Article 146(1)(c)

VAT EC

Directive 67/227/EEC	*Directive 77/388/EEC*	*Amending Directives*	*Other acts*	*This Directive*
	Article 15, point (12), second sentence			Article 146(2)
	Article 15, point (13)			Article 146(1)(e)
	Article 15, point (14), first and second subparagraphs			Article 153, first and second paragraphs
	Article 15, point (15)			Article 149
	Article 16(1)			—
	Article 16(2)			Article 164(1)
	Article 16(3)			Article 166
	Article 17(1)			Article 167
	Article 17(2), (3) and (4)			—
	Article 17(5), first and second subparagraphs			Article 173(1), first and second subparagraphs
	Article 17(5), third subparagraph, points (a) to (e)			Article 173(2)(a) to (e)
	Article 17(6)			Article 176
	Article 17(7), first and second sentences			Article 177, first and second paragraphs
	Article 18(1)			—
	Article 18(2), first and second subparagraphs			Article 179, first and second paragraphs
	Article 18(3)			Article 180
	Article 18(4), first and second subparagraphs			Article 183, first and second paragraphs
	Article 19(1), first subparagraph, first indent			Article 174(1), first subparagraph, point (a)
	Article 19(1), first subparagraph, second indent, first sentence			Article 174(1), first subparagraph, point (b)
	Article 19(1), first subparagraph, second indent, second sentence			Article 174(1), second subparagraph
	Article 19(1), second subparagraph			Article 175(1)

Directive 67/227/EEC	*Directive 77/388/EEC*	*Amending Directives*	*Other acts*	*This Directive*
	Article 19(2), first sentence			Article 174(2)(a)
	Article 19(2), second sentence			Article 174(2)(a) and (b)
	Article 19(2), third sentence			Article 174(3)
	Article 19(3), first subparagraph, first and second sentences			Article 175(2), first subparagraph
	Article 19(3), first subparagraph, third sentence			Article 175(2), second subparagraph
	Article 19(3), second subparagraph			Article 175(3)
	Article 20(1), introductory sentence			Article 186
	Article 20(1)(a)			Article 184
	Article 20(1)(b), first part of the first sentence			Article 185(1)
	Article 20(1)(b), second part of the first sentence			Article 185(2), first subparagraph
	Article 20(1)(b), second sentence			Article 185(2), second subparagraph
	Article 20(2), first subparagraph, first sentence			Article 187(1), first subparagraph
	Article 20(2), first subparagraph, second and third sentences			Article 187(2), first and second subparagraphs
	Article 20(2), second and third subparagraphs			Article 187(1), second and third subparagraphs
	Article 20(3), first subparagraph, first sentence			Article 188(1), first subparagraph
	Article 20(3), first subparagraph, second sentence			Article 188(1), second and third subparagraphs
	Article 20(3), first subparagraph, third sentence			Article 188(2)
	Article 20(3), second subparagraph			Article 188(2)

VAT EC

Directive 67/227/EEC	*Directive 77/388/EEC*	*Amending Directives*	*Other acts*	*This Directive*
	Article 20(4), first subparagraph, first to fourth indents			Article 189(a) to (d)
	Article 20(4), second subparagraph			Article 190
	Article 20(5)			Article 191
	Article 20(6)			Article 192
	Article 21			—
	Article 22			—
	Article 22a			Article 249
	Article 23, first paragraph			Article 211, first paragraph Article 260
	Article 23, second paragraph			Article 211, second paragraph
	Article 24(1)			Article 281
	Article 24(2)			Article 292
	Article 24(2)(a), first subparagraph			Article 284(1)
	Article 24(2)(a), second and third subparagraphs			Article 284(2), first and second subparagraphs
	Article 24(2)(b), first and second sentences			Article 285, first and second paragraphs
	Article 24(2)(c)			Article 286
	Article 24(3), first subparagraph			Article 282
	Article 24(3), second subparagraph, first sentence			Article 283(2)
	Article 24(3), second subparagraph, second sentence			Article 283(1)(a)
	Article 24(4), first subparagraph			Article 288, first paragraph, points (1) to (4)
	Article 24(4), second subparagraph			Article 288, second paragraph
	Article 24(5)			Article 289

Directive 67/227/EEC	*Directive 77/388/EEC*	*Amending Directives*	*Other acts*	*This Directive*
	Article 24(6)			Article 290
	Article 24(7)			Article 291
	Article 24(8)(a), (b) and (c)			Article 293, points (1), (2) and (3)
	Article 24(9)			Article 294
	Article 24a, first paragraph, first to twelfth indents			Article 287, points (7) to (16)
	Article 25(1)			Article 296(1)
	Article 25(2), first to eighth indents			Article 295(1), points (1) to (8)
	Article 25(3), first subparagraph, first sentence			Article 297, first paragraph, first sentence and second paragraph
	Article 25(3), first subparagraph, second sentence			Article 298, first paragraph
	Article 25(3), first subparagraph, third sentence			Article 299
	Article 25(3), first subparagraph, fourth and fifth sentences			Article 298, second paragraph
	Article 25(3), second subparagraph			Article 297, first paragraph, second sentence
	Article 25(4), first subparagraph			Article 272(1), first subparagraph, point (e)
	Article 25(5) and (6)			—
	Article 25(7)			Article 304
	Article 25(8)			Article 301(2)
	Article 25(9)			Article 296(2)
	Article 25(10)			Article 296(3)
	Article 25(11) and (12)			—
	Article 26(1) first and second sentences			Article 306(1), first and second subparagraphs
	Article 26(1) third sentence			Article 306(2)

VAT EC

Directive 67/227/EEC	*Directive 77/388/EEC*	*Amending Directives*	*Other acts*	*This Directive*
	Article 26(2), first and second sentences			Article 307, first and second paragraphs
	Article 26(2), third sentence			Article 308
	Article 26(3), first and second sentences			Article 309, first and second paragraphs
	Article 26(4)			Article 310
	Article 26a(A)(a), first subparagraph			Article 311(1), point (2)
	Article 26a(A)(a), second subparagraph			Article 311(2)
	Article 26a(A)(b) and (c)			Article 311(1), points (3) and (4)
	Article 26a(A)(d)			Article 311(1), point (1)
	Article 26a(A)(e) and (f)			Article 311(1), points (5) and (6)
	Article 26a(A)(g), introductory sentence			Article 311(1), point (7)
	Article 26a(A)(g), first and second indents			Article 311(3)
	Article 26a(B)(1)			Article 313(1)
	Article 26a(B)(2)			Article 314
	Article 26a(B)(2), first and second indents			Article 314(a) to (d)
	Article 26a(B)(3), first subparagraph, first and second sentences			Article 315, first and second paragraphs
	Article 26a(B)(3), second subparagraph			Article 312
	Article 26a(B)(3), second subparagraph, first and second indents			Article 312, points (1) and (2)
	Article 26a(B)(4), first subparagraph			Article 316(1)

Directive 67/227/EEC	*Directive 77/388/EEC*	*Amending Directives*	*Other acts*	*This Directive*
	Article 26a(B)(4), first subparagraph, points (a), (b) and (c)			Article 316(1)(a), (b) and (c)
	Article 26a(B)(4), second subparagraph			Article 316(2)
	Article 26a(B)(4), third subparagraph, first and second sentences			Article 317, first and second paragraphs
	Article 26a(B)(5)			Article 321
	Article 26a(B)(6)			Article 323
	Article 26a(B)(7)			Article 322
	Article 26a(B)(7)(a), (b) and (c)			Article 322(a), (b) and (c)
	Article 26a(B)(8)			Article 324
	Article 26a(B)(9)			Article 325
	Article 26a(B)(10) first and second subparagraphs			Article 318(1), first and second subparagraphs
	Article 26a(B)(10), third subparagraph, first and second indents			Article 318(2)(a) and (b)
	Article 26a(B)(10), fourth subparagraph			Article 318(3)
	Article 26a(B)(11), first subparagraph			Article 319
	Article 26a(B)(11), second subparagraph, point (a)			Article 320(1), first subparagraph
	Article 26a(B)(11), second subparagraph, points (b) and (c)			Article 320(1), second subparagraph
	Article 26a(B)(11), third subparagraph			Article 320(2)
	Article 26a(C)(1), introductory sentence			Article 333(1) Article 334
	Article 26a(C)(1), first to fourth indents			Article 334(a) to (d)
	Article 26a(C)(2), first and second indents			Article 336(a) and (b)

Directive 67/227/EEC	*Directive 77/388/EEC*	*Amending Directives*	*Other acts*	*This Directive*
	Article 26a(C)(3)			Article 337
	Article 26a(C)(4), first subparagraph, first, second and third indents			Article 339, first paragraph, points (a), (b) and (c)
	Article 26a(C)(4), second subparagraph			Article 339, second paragraph
	Article 26a(C)(5), first and second subparagraphs			Article 340(1), first and second subparagraphs
	Article 26a(C)(5), third subparagraph			Article 340(2)
	Article 26a(C)(6), first subparagraph, first and second indents			Article 338, first paragraph, points (a) and (b)
	Article 26a(C)(6), second subparagraph			Article 338, second paragraph
	Article 26a(C)(7)			Article 335
	Article 26a(D), introductory sentence			—
	Article 26a(D)(a)			Article 313(2) Article 333(2)
	Article 26a(D)(b)			Article 4(a) and (c)
	Article 26a(D)(c)			Article 35 Article 139(3), first subparagraph
	Article 26b(A), first subparagraph, point (i), first sentence			Article 344(1), point (1)
	Article 26b(A), first subparagraph, point (i), second sentence			Article 344(2)
	Article 26b(A), first subpara- *graph, point (ii), first to fourth* indents			Article 344(1), point (2)
	Article 26b(A), second subparagraph			Article 344(3)
	Article 26b(A), third subparagraph			Article 345

Directive 67/227/EEC	*Directive 77/388/EEC*	*Amending Directives*	*Other acts*	*This Directive*
	Article 26b(B), first subparagraph			Article 346
	Article 26b(B), second subparagraph			Article 347
	Article 26b(C), first subparagraph			Article 348
	Article 26b(C), second subparagraph, first and second sentences			Article 349(1) and (2)
	Article 26b(C), third subparagraph			Article 350
	Article 26b(C), fourth subparagraph			Article 351
	Article 26b(D)(1)(a), (b) and (c)			Article 354(a), (b) and (c)
	Article 26b(D)(2)			Article 355
	Article 26b(E), first and second subparagraphs			Article 356(1), first and second subparagraphs
	Article 26b(E), third and fourth subparagraphs			Article 356(2) and (3)
	Article 26b(F), first sentence			Article 198(2) and (3)
	Article 26b(F), second sentence			Articles 208 and 255
	Article 26b(G)(1), first subparagraph			Article 352
	Article 26b(G)(1), second subparagraph			—
	Article 26b(G)(2)(a)			Article 353
	Article 26b(G)(2)(b), first and second sentences			Article 198(1) and (3)
	Article 26c(A)(a) to (e)			Article 358, points (1) to (5)
	Article 26c(B)(1)			Article 359
	Article 26c(B)(2), first subparagraph			Article 360
	Article 26c(B)(2), second subparagraph, first part of the first sentence			Article 361(1)

Directive 67/227/EEC	*Directive 77/388/EEC*	*Amending Directives*	*Other acts*	*This Directive*
	Article 26c(B)(2), second subparagraph, second part of the first sentence			Article 361(1)(a) to (e)
	Article 26c(B)(2), second subparagraph, second sentence			Article 361(2)
	Article 26c(B)(3), first and second subparagraphs			Article 362
	Article 26c(B)(4)(a) to (d)			Article 363(a) to (d)
	Article 26c(B)(5), first subparagraph			Article 364
	Article 26c(B)(5), second subparagraph			Article 365
	Article 26c(B)(6), first sentence			Article 366(1), first subparagraph
	Article 26c(B)(6), second and third sentences			Article 366(1), second subparagraph
	Article 26c(B)(6), fourth sentence			Article 366(2)
	Article 26c(B)(7), first sentence			Article 367, first paragraph
	Article 26c(B)(7), second and third sentences			Article 367, second paragraph
	Article 26c(B)(8)			Article 368
	Article 26c(B)(9), first sentence			Article 369(1)
	Article 26c(B)(9), second and third sentences			Article 369(2), first and second subparagraphs
	Article 26c(B)(10)			Article 204(1), third subparagraph
	Article 27(1) first and second sentences			Article 395(1) first and second subparagraphs
	Article 27(2), first and second sentences			Article 395(2), first subparagraphs
	Article 27(2), third sentence			Article 395(2), second subparagraph

Directive 67/227/EEC	*Directive 77/388/EEC*	*Amending Directives*	*Other acts*	*This Directive*
	Article 27(3) and (4)			Article 395(3) and (4)
	Article 27(5)			Article 394
	Article 28(1) and (1a)			—
	Article 28(2), introductory sentence			Article 109
	Article 28(2)(a), first subparagraph			Article 110, first and second paragraphs
	Article 28(2)(a), second subparagraph			—
	Article 28(2)(a), third subparagraph, first sentence			Article 112, first paragraph
	Article 28(2)(a), third subparagraph, second and third sentences			Article 112, second paragraph
	Article 28(2)(b)			Article 113
	Article 28(2)(c), first and second sentences			Article 114(1), first and second subparagraphs
	Article 28(2)(c), third sentence			Article 114(2)
	Article 28(2)(d)			Article 115
	Article 28(2)(e), first and second subparagraphs			Article 118, first and second paragraphs
	Article 28(2)(f)			Article 120
	Article 28(2)(g)			—
	Article 28(2)(h), first and second subparagraphs			Article 121, first and second paragraphs
	Article 28(2)(i)			Article 122
	Article 28(2)(j)			Article 117(2)
	Article 28(2)(k)			Article 116
	Article 28(3)(a)			Article 370
	Article 28(3)(b)			Article 371
	Article 28(3)(c)			Article 391
	Article 28(3)(d)			Article 372

VAT EC

Directive 67/227/EEC	*Directive 77/388/EEC*	*Amending Directives*	*Other acts*	*This Directive*
	Article 28(3)(e)			Article 373
	Article 28(3)(f)			Article 392
	Article 28(3)(g)			Article 374
	Article 28(3a)			Article 376
	Article 28(4) and (5)			Article 393(1) and (2)
	Article 28(6), first subparagraph, first sentence			Article 106, first and second paragraphs
	Article 28(6), first subparagraph, second sentence			Article 106, third paragraph
	Article 28(6), second subparagraph, points (a), (b) and (c),			Article 107, first paragraph, points (a), (b) and (c)
	Article 28(6), second subparagraph, point (d)			Article 107, second paragraph
	Article 28(6), third subparagraph			Article 107, second paragraph
	Article 28(6), fourth subparagraph, points (a), (b) and (c)			Article 108(a), (b) and (c)
	Article 28(6), fifth and sixth subparagraphs			—
	Article 28a(1), introductory sentence			Article 2(1)
	Article 28a(1)(a), first subparagraph			Article 2(1)(b)(i)
	Article 28a(1)(a), second subparagraph			Article 3(1)
	Article 28a(1)(a), third subparagraph			Article 3(3)
	Article 28a(1)(*b*)			Article 2(1)(b)(ii)
	Article 28a(1)(c)			Article 2(1)(b)(iii)
	Article 28a(1a)(a)			Article 3(1)(a)
	Article 28a(1a)(b), first subparagraph, first indent			Article 3(1)(b)

Directive 67/227/EEC	Directive 77/388/EEC	Amending Directives	Other acts	This Directive
	Article 28a(1a)(b), first subparagraph, second and third indents			Article 3(2), first subparagraph, points (a) and (b)
	Article 28a(1a)(b), second subparagraph			Article 3(2), second subparagraph
	Article 28a(2), introductory sentence			—
	Article 28a(2)(a)			Article 2(2), point (a) (i), (ii), and (iii)
	Article 28a(2)(b), first subparagraph			Article 2(2), point (b)
	Article 28a(2)(b), first subparagraph, first and second indents			Article 2(2), point (b) (i), (ii), and (iii)
	Article 28a(2)(b), second subparagraph			Article 2(2), point (c)
	Article 28a(3), first and second subparagraphs			Article 20, first and second paragraphs
	Article 28a(4), first subparagraph			Article 9(2)
	Article 28a(4), second subparagraph, first indent			Article 172(1), second subparagraph
	Article 28a(4), second subparagraph, second indent			Article 172(1), first subparagraph
	Article 28a(4), third subparagraph			Article 172(2)
	Article 28a(5)(b), first subparagraph			Article 17(1), first subparagraph
	Article 28a(5)(b), second subparagraph,			Article 17(1), second subparagraph and (2), introductory sentence
	Article 28a(5)(b), second subparagraph, first indent			Article 17(2)(a) and (b)
	Article 28a(5)(b), second subparagraph, second indent			Article 17(2)(c)

Directive 67/227/EEC	*Directive 77/388/EEC*	*Amending Directives*	*Other acts*	*This Directive*
	Article 28a(5)(b), second subparagraph, third indent			Article 17(2)(e)
	Article 28a(5)(b), second subparagraph, fifth, sixth and seventh indents			Article 17(2)(f), (g) and (h)
	Article 28a(5)(b), second subparagraph, eighth indent			Article 17(2)(d)
	Article 28a(5)(b), third subparagraph			Article 17(3)
	Article 28a(6), first subparagraph			Article 21
	Article 28a(6), second subparagraph			Article 22
	Article 28a(7)			Article 23
	Article 28b(A)(1)			Article 40
	Article 28b(A)(2), first and second subparagraphs			Article 41, first and second paragraphs
	Article 28b(A)(2), third subparagraph, first and second indents			Article 42(a) and (b)
	Article 28b(B)(1), first subparagraph, first and second indents			Article 33(1)(a) and (b)
	Article 28b(B)(1), second subparagraph			Article 33(2)
	Article 28b(B)(2), first subparagraph			Article 34(1)(a)
	Article 28b(B)(2), first subparagraph, first and second indents			Article 34(1)(b) and (c)
	Article 28b(B)(2), second subparagraph, first and second sentences			Article 34(2), first and second subparagraphs
	Article 28b(B)(2), third subparagraph, first sentence			Article 34(3)
	Article 28b(B)(2), third subparagraph, second and third sentences			—

Directive 67/227/EEC	*Directive 77/388/EEC*	*Amending Directives*	*Other acts*	*This Directive*
	Article 28b(B)(3), first and second subparagraphs			Article 34(4), first and second subparagraphs
	Article 28b(C)(1), first indent, first subparagraph			Article 48, first paragraph
	Article 28b(C)(1), first indent, second subparagraph			Article 49
	Article 28b(C)(1), second and third indents			Article 48, second and third paragraphs
	Article 28b(C)(2) and (3)			Article 47, first and second paragraphs
	Article 28b(C)(4)			Article 51
	Article 28b(D)			Article 53
	Article 28b(E)(1), first and second subparagraphs			Article 50, first and second paragraphs
	Article 28b(E)(2), first and second subparagraphs			Article 54, first and second paragraphs
	Article 28b(E)(3), first and second subparagraphs			Article 44, first and second paragraphs
	Article 28b(F), first and second paragraphs			Article 55, first and second paragraphs
	Article 28c(A), introductory sentence			Article 131
	Article 28c(A)(a), first subparagraph			Article 138(1)
	Article 28c(A)(a), second subparagraph			Article 139(1), first and second subparagraphs
	Article 28c(A)(b)			Article 138(2)(a)
	Article 28c(A)(c), first subparagraph			Article 138(2)(b)
	Article 28c(A)(c), second subparagraph			Article 139(2)
	Article 28c(A)(d)			Article 138(2)(c)

Directive 67/227/EEC	*Directive 77/388/EEC*	*Amending Directives*	*Other acts*	*This Directive*
	Article 28c(B), introductory sentence			Articles 131
	Article 28c(B)(a), (b) and (c)			Article 140(a), (b) and (c)
	Article 28c(C)			Article 142
	Article 28c(D), first subparagraph			Article 143(d)
	Article 28c(D), second subparagraph			Article 131
	Article 28c(E), point (1), first indent, replacing Article 16(1)			
	— paragraph 1, first subparagraph			Article 155
	— paragraph 1, first subparagraph, point (A)			Article 157(1)(a)
	— paragraph 1, first subparagraph, point (B), first subparagraph, points (a), (b) and (c)			Article 156(1)(a), (b) and (c)
	— paragraph 1, first subparagraph, point (B), first subparagraph, point (d), first and second indents			Article 156(1)(d) and (e)
	— paragraph 1, first subparagraph, point (B), first subparagraph, point (e), first subparagraph			Article 157(1)(b)
	— paragraph 1, first subparagraph, point (B), first subparagraph, point (e), second subparagraph, first indent			Article 154

Directive 67/227/EEC	*Directive 77/388/EEC*	*Amending Directives*	*Other acts*	*This Directive*
	— paragraph 1, first subparagraph, point (B), first subparagraph, point (e), second subparagraph, second indent, first sentence			Article 154
	— paragraph 1, first subparagraph, point (B), first subparagraph, point (e), second subparagraph, second indent, second sentence			Article 157(2)
	— paragraph 1, first subparagraph, point (B), first subparagraph, point (e), third subparagraph, first indent			—
	— paragraph 1, first subparagraph, point (B), first subparagraph, point (e), third subparagraph, second, third and fourth indents			Article 158(1)(a), (b) and (c)
	— paragraph 1, first subparagraph, point (B), second subparagraph			Article 156(2)
	— paragraph 1, first subparagraph, point (C)			Article 159
	— paragraph 1, first subparagraph, point (D), first subparagraph, points (a) and (b)			Article 160(1)(a) and (b)
	— paragraph 1, first subparagraph, point (D), second subparagraph			Articles 160(2)

Directive 67/227/EEC	*Directive 77/388/EEC*	*Amending Directives*	*Other acts*	*This Directive*
	— paragraph 1, first subparagraph, point (E), first and second indents			Article 161(a) and (b)
	— paragraph 1, second subparagraph			Article 202
	— paragraph 1, third subparagraph			Article 163
	Article 28c(E), point (1), second indent, inserting paragraph 1a into Article 16			
	— paragraph 1a			Article 162
	Article 28c(E), point (2), first indent, amending Article 16(2)			
	— paragraph 2, first subparagraph			Article 164(1)
	Article 28c(E), point (2), second indent, inserting the second and third subparagraphs into Article 16(2)			
	— paragraph 2, second subparagraph			Article 164(2)
	— paragraph 2, third subparagraph			Article 165
	Article 28c(E), point (3), first to fifth indents			Article 141(a) to (e)
	Article 28d(1), first and second sentences			Article 68, first and second paragraphs
	Article 28d(2) and (3)			Article 69(1) and (2)
	Article 28d(4), first and second subparagraphs			Article 67(1) and (2)
	Article 28e(1), first subparagraph			Article 83
	Article 28e(1), second subparagraph, first and second sentences			Article 84(1) and (2)

Directive 67/227/EEC	*Directive 77/388/EEC*	*Amending Directives*	*Other acts*	*This Directive*
	Article 28e(2)			Article 76
	Article 28e(3)			Article 93, second paragraph, point (b)
	Article 28e(4)			Article 94(1)
	Article 28f, point (1) replacing Article 17(2), (3) and (4)			
	— paragraph 2(a)			Article 168(a)
	— paragraph 2(b)			Article 168(e)
	— paragraph 2(c)			Article 168(b) and (d)
	— paragraph 2(d)			Article 168(c)
	— paragraph 3(a), (b) and (c)			Article 169(a), (b) and (c) Article 170(a) and (b)
	— paragraph 4, first subparagraph, first indent			Article 171(1), first subparagraph
	— paragraph 4, first subparagraph, second indent			Article 171(2), first subparagraph
	— paragraph 4, second subparagraph, point (a)			Article 171(1), second subparagraph
	— paragraph 4, second subparagraph, point (b)			Article 171(2), second subparagraph
	— paragraph 4, second subparagraph, point (c)			Article 171(3)
	Article 28f, point (2) replacing Article 18(1)			
	— paragraph 1(a)			Article 178(a)
	— paragraph 1(b)			Article 178(e)
	— paragraph 1(c)			Article 178(b) and (d)
	— paragraph 1(d)			Article 178(f)
	— paragraph 1(e)			Article 178(c)
	Article 28f, point (3) inserting paragraph 3a into Article 18			

Directive 67/227/EEC	*Directive 77/388/EEC*	*Amending Directives*	*Other acts*	*This Directive*
	— paragraph 3a, first part of the sentence			Article 181
	— paragraph 3a, second part of the sentence			Article 182
	Article 28g replacing Article 21			
	— paragraph 1(a), first subparagraph			Article 193
	— paragraph 1(a), second subparagraph			Article 194(1) and (2)
	— paragraph 1(b)			Article 196
	— paragraph 1(c), first subparagraph, first, second and third indents			Article 197(1)(a), (b) and (c)
	— paragraph 1(c), second subparagraph			Article 197(2)
	— paragraph 1(d)			Article 203
	— paragraph 1(e)			Article 200
	— paragraph 1(f)			Article 195
	— paragraph 2			—
	— paragraph 2(a), first sentence			Article 204(1), first subparagraph
	— paragraph 2(a), second sentence			Article 204(2)
	— paragraph 2(b)			Article 204(1), second subparagraph
	— paragraph 2(c), first subparagraph			Article 199(1)(a) to (g)
	— paragraph 2(c), second, third and fourth subparagraphs			Article 199(2), (3) and (4)
	— paragraph 3			Article 205
	— paragraph 4			Article 201

Directive 67/227/EEC	*Directive 77/388/EEC*	*Amending Directives*	*Other acts*	*This Directive*
	Article 28h replacing Article 22			
	— paragraph 1(a), first and second sentences			Article 213(1), first and second subparagraphs
	— paragraph 1(b)			Article 213(2)
	— paragraph 1(c), first indent, first sentence			Article 214(1)(a)
	— paragraph 1(c), first indent, second sentence			Article 214(2)
	— paragraph 1(c), second and third indents			Article 214(1)(b) and (c)
	— paragraph 1(d), first and second sentences			Article 215, first and second paragraphs
	— paragraph 1(e)			Article 216
	— paragraph 2(a)			Article 242
	— paragraph 2(b), first and second indents			Article 243(1) and (2)
	— paragraph 3(a), first subparagraph, first sentence			Article 220, point (1)
	— paragraph 3(a), first subparagraph, second sentence			Article 220, points (2) and (3)
	— paragraph 3(a), second subparagraph			Article 220, points (4) and (5)
	— paragraph 3(a), third subparagraph, first and second sentences			Article 221(1), first and second subparagraphs
	— paragraph 3(a), fourth subparagraph			Article 221(2)
	— paragraph 3(a), fifth subparagraph, first sentence			Article 219

Directive 67/227/EEC	*Directive 77/388/EEC*	*Amending Directives*	*Other acts*	*This Directive*
	— paragraph 3(a), fifth subparagraph, second sentence			Article 228
	— paragraph 3(a), sixth subparagraph			Article 222
	— paragraph 3(a), seventh subparagraph			Article 223
	— paragraph 3(a), eighth subparagraph, first and second sentences			Article 224(1) and (2)
	— paragraph 3(a), ninth subparagraph, first and second sentences			Article 224(3), first subparagraph
	— paragraph 3(a), ninth subparagraph, third sentence			Article 224(3), second subparagraph
	— paragraph 3(a), tenth subparagraph			Article 225
	— paragraph 3(b), first subparagraph, first to twelfth indents			Article 226, points (1) to (12)
	— paragraph 3(b), first subparagraph, thirteenth indent			Article 226, points (13) and (14)
	— paragraph 3(b), first subparagraph, fourteenth indent			Article 226, point (15)
	— paragraph 3(b), second subparagraph			Article 227
	— paragraph 3(b), third subparagraph			Article 229
	— paragraph 3(b), fourth subparagraph			Article 230

Directive 67/227/EEC	*Directive 77/388/EEC*	*Amending Directives*	*Other acts*	*This Directive*
	— paragraph 3(b), fifth subparagraph			Article 231
	— paragraph 3(c), first subparagraph			Article 232
	— paragraph 3(c), second subparagraph, introductory sentence			Article 233(1), first subparagraph
	— paragraph 3(c), second subparagraph, first indent, first sentence			Article 233(1), first subparagraph, point (a)
	— paragraph 3(c), second subparagraph, first indent, second sentence			Article 233(2)
	— paragraph 3(c), second subparagraph, second indent, first sentence			Article 233(1), first subparagraph, point (b)
	— paragraph 3(c), second subparagraph, second indent, second sentence			Article 233(3)
	— paragraph 3(c), third subparagraph, first sentence			Article 233(1), second subparagraph
	— paragraph 3(c), third subparagraph, second sentence			Article 237
	— paragraph 3(c), fourth subparagraph, first and second sentences			Article 234
	— paragraph 3(c), fifth subparagraph			Article 235
	— paragraph 3(c), sixth subparagraph			Article 236
	— paragraph 3(d), first subparagraph			Article 244

Directive 67/227/EEC	*Directive 77/388/EEC*	*Amending Directives*	*Other acts*	*This Directive*
	— paragraph 3(d), second subparagraph, first sentence			Article 245(1)
	— paragraph 3(d), second subparagraph, second and third sentences			Article 245(2), first and second subparagraphs
	— paragraph 3(d), third subparagraph, first and second sentences			Article 246, first and second paragraphs
	— paragraph 3(d), fourth, fifth and sixth subparagraphs			Article 247(1), (2) and (3)
	— paragraph 3(d), seventh subparagraph			Article 248
	— paragraph 3(e), first subparagraph			Articles 217 and 241
	— paragraph 3(e), second subparagraph			Article 218
	— paragraph 4(a), first and second sentences			Article 252(1)
	— paragraph 4(a), third and fourth sentences			Article 252(2), first and second subparagraphs
	— paragraph 4(a), fifth sentence			Article 250(2)
	— paragraph 4(b)			Article 250(1)
	— paragraph 4(c), first indent, first and second subparagraphs			Article 251(a) and (b)
	— paragraph 4(c), second indent, first subparagraph			Article 251(c)
	— paragraph 4(c), second indent, second subparagraph			Article 251(d) and (e)

Directive 67/227/EEC	*Directive 77/388/EEC*	*Amending Directives*	*Other acts*	*This Directive*
	— paragraph 5			Article 206
	— paragraph 6(a), first and second sentences			Article 261(1)
	— paragraph 6(a), third sentence			Article 261(2)
	— paragraph 6(b), first subparagraph			Article 262
	— paragraph 6(b), second subparagraph, first sentence			Article 263(1), first subparagraph
	— paragraph 6(b), second subparagraph, second sentence			Article 263(2)
	— paragraph 6(b), third subparagraph, first and second indents			Article 264(1)(a) and (b)
	— paragraph 6(b), third subparagraph, third indent, first sentence			Article 264(1)(d)
	— paragraph 6(b), third subparagraph, third indent, second sentence			Article 264(2), first subparagraph
	— paragraph 6(b), fourth subparagraph, first indent			Article 264(1)(c) and (e)
	— paragraph 6(b), fourth subparagraph, second indent, first sentence			Article 264(1)(f)
	— paragraph 6(b), fourth subparagraph, second indent, second sentence			Article 264(2), second subparagraph
	— paragraph 6(b), fifth subparagraph, first and second indents			Article 265(1)(a) and (b)

Directive 67/227/EEC	*Directive 77/388/EEC*	*Amending Directives*	*Other acts*	*This Directive*
	— paragraph 6(b), fifth subparagraph, third indent, first sentence			Article 265(1)(c)
	— paragraph 6(b), fifth subparagraph, third indent, second sentence			Article 265(2)
	— paragraph 6(c), first indent			Article 263(1), second subparagraph
	— paragraph 6(c), second indent			Article 266
	— paragraph 6(d)			Article 254
	— paragraph 6(e), first subparagraph			Article 268
	— paragraph 6(e), second subparagraph			Article 259
	— paragraph 7, first part of the sentence			Article 207, first paragraph Article 256 Article 267
	— paragraph 7, second part of the sentence			Article 207, second paragraph
	— paragraph 8, first and second subparagraphs			Article 273, first and second paragraphs
	— paragraph 9(a), first subparagraph, first indent			Article 272(1), first subparagraph, point (c)
	— paragraph 9(a), first subparagraph, second indent			Article 272(1), first subparagraph, points (a) and (d)
	— paragraph 9(a), first subparagraph, third indent			Article 272(1), first subparagraph, point (b)
	— paragraph 9(a), second subparagraph			Article 272(1), second subparagraph
	— paragraph 9(b)			Article 272(3)

Directive 67/227/EEC	*Directive 77/388/EEC*	*Amending Directives*	*Other acts*	*This Directive*
	— paragraph 9(c)			Article 212
	— paragraph 9(d), first subparagraph, first and second indents			Article 238(1)(a) and (b)
	— paragraph 9(d), second subparagraph, first to fourth indents			Article 238(2)(a) to (d)
	— paragraph 9(d), third subparagraph			Article 238(3)
	— paragraph 9(e), first subparagraph			Article 239
	— paragraph 9(e), second subparagraph, first and second indents			Article 240, points (1) and (2)
	— paragraph 10			Articles 209 and 257
	— paragraph 11			Articles 210 and 258
	— paragraph 12, introductory sentence			Article 269
	— paragraph 12(a), first, second and third indents			Article 270(a), (b) and (c)
	— paragraph 12(b), first second and third indents			Article 271(a), (b) and (c)
	Article 28i inserting a third subparagraph into Article 24(3)			
	— paragraph 3, third subparagraph			Article 283(1)(b) and (c)
	Article 28j, point (1) inserting a second subparagraph into Article 25(4)			
	— paragraph 4, second subparagraph			Article 272(2)
	Article 28j, point (2) replacing Article 25(5) and (6)			

Directive 67/227/EEC	*Directive 77/388/EEC*	*Amending Directives*	*Other acts*	*This Directive*
	— paragraph 5, first subparagraph, points (a), (b) and (c)			Article 300, points (1), (2) and (3)
	— paragraph 5, second subparagraph			Article 302
	— paragraph 6(a), first subparagraph, first sentence			Article 301(1)
	— paragraph 6(a), first subparagraph, second sentence			Article 303(1)
	— paragraph 6(a), second subparagraph, first, second and third indents			Article 303(2)(a), (b) and (c)
	— paragraph 6(a), third subparagraph			Article 303(3)
	— paragraph 6(b)			Article 301(1)
	Article 28j, point (3) inserting a second subparagraph into Article 25(9)			
	— paragraph 9, second subparagraph			Article 305
	Article 28k, point (1), first subparagraph			—
	Article 28k, point (1), second subparagraph, point (a)			Article 158(3)
	Article 28k, point (1), second subparagraph, points (b) and (c)			—
	Article 28k, points (2), (3) and (4)			—
	Article 28k, point (5)			Article 158(2)
	Article 28l, first paragraph			—

Directive 67/227/EEC	*Directive 77/388/EEC*	*Amending Directives*	*Other acts*	*This Directive*
	Article 28l, second and third paragraphs			Article 402(1) and (2)
	Article 28l, fourth paragraph			—
	Article 28m			Article 399, first paragraph
	Article 28n			—
	Article 28o(1), introductory sentence			Article 326, first paragraph
	Article 28o(1)(a), first sentence			Article 327(1) and (3)
	Article 28o(1)(a), second sentence			Article 327(2)
	Article 28o(1)(b)			Article 328
	Article 28o(1)(c), first second and third indents			Article 329(a), (b) and (c)
	Article 28o(1)(d), first and second subparagraphs			Article 330, first and second paragraphs
	Article 28o(1)(e)			Article 332
	Article 28o(1)(f)			Article 331
	Article 28o(1)(g)			Article 4(b)
	Article 28o(1)(h)			Article 35 Article 139(3), second subparagraph
	Article 28o(2)			Article 326, second paragraph
	Article 28o(3)			Article 341
	Article 28o(4)			—
	Article 28p(1), first, second and third indents			Article 405, points (1), (2) and (3)
	Article 28p(2)			Article 406
	Article 28p(3), first subparagraph, first and second indents			Article 407(a) and (b)
	Article 28p(3), second subparagraph			—

Directive 67/227/EEC	*Directive 77/388/EEC*	*Amending Directives*	*Other acts*	*This Directive*
	Article 28p(4)(a) to (d)			Article 408(1)(a) to (d)
	Article 28p(5), first and second indents			Article 408(2)(a) and (b)
	Article 28p(6)			Article 409
	Article 28p(7), first subparagraph, points (a), (b) and (c)			Article 410(1)(a), (b) and (c)
	Article 28p(7), second subparagraph, first indent			—
	Article 28p(7), second subparagraph, second, third and fourth indents			Article 410(2)(a), (b) and (c)
	Article 29(1) to (4)			Article 398(1) to (4)
	Article 29a			Article 397
	Article 30(1)			Article 396(1)
	Article 30(2), first and second sentences			Article 396(2), first subparagraph
	Article 30(2), third sentence			Article 396(2), second subparagraph
	Article 30(3) and (4)			Article 396(3) and (4)
	Article 31(1)			—
	Article 31(2)			Article 400
	Article 33(1)			Article 401
	Article 33(2)			Article 2(3)
	Article 33a(1), introductory sentence			Article 274
	Article 33a(1)(a)			Article 275
	Article 33a(1)(b)			Article 276
	Article 33a(1)(c)			Article 277
	Article 33a(2), introductory sentence			Article 278
	Article 33a(2)(a)			Article 279

Directive 67/227/EEC	*Directive 77/388/EEC*	*Amending Directives*	*Other acts*	*This Directive*
	Article 33a(2)(b)			Article 280
	Article 34			Article 404
	Article 35			Article 403
	Articles 36 and 37			—
	Article 38			Article 414
	Annex A(I)(1) and (2)			Annex VII, point (1)(a) and (b)
	Annex A(I)(3)			Annex VII, points (1)(c) and (d)
	Annex A(II)(1) to (6)			Annex VII, points (2)(a) to (f)
	Annex A(III) and (IV)			Annex VII, points (3) and (4)
	Annex A(IV)(1) to (4)			Annex VII, points (4)(a) to (d)
	Annex A(V)			Article 295(2)
	Annex B, introductory sentence			Article 295(1), point (5)
	Annex B, first to ninth indents			Annex VIII, points (1) to (9)
	Annex C			—
	Annex D(1) to (13)			Annex I, points (1) to (13)
	Annex E(2)			Annex X, Part A, point (1)
	Annex E(7)			Annex X, Part A, point (2)
	Annex E(11)			Annex X, Part A, point (3)
	Annex E(15)			Annex X, Part A, point (4)
	Annex F(1)			Annex X, Part B, point (1)
	Annex F(2)			Annex X, Part B, points (2)(a) to (j)
	Annex F(5) to (8)			Annex X, Part B, points (3) to (6)
	Annex F(10)			Annex X, Part B, point (7)
	Annex F(12)			Annex X, Part B, point (8)
	Annex F(16)			Annex X, Part B, point (9)

Directive 67/227/EEC	*Directive 77/388/EEC*	*Amending Directives*	*Other acts*	*This Directive*
	Annex F(17), first and second subparagraphs			Annex X, Part B, point (10)
	Annex F(23)			Annex X, Part B, point (11)
	Annex F(25)			Annex X, Part B, point (12)
	Annex F(27)			Annex X, Part B, point (13)
	Annex G(1) and (2)			Article 391
	Annex H, first paragraph			Article 98(3)
	Annex H, second paragraph, introductory sentence			—
	Annex H, second paragraph, points (1) to (6)			Annex III, points (1) to (6)
	Annex H, second paragraph, point (7), first and second subparagraphs			Annex III, points (7) and (8)
	Annex H, second paragraph, points (8) to (17)			Annex III, points (9) to (18)
	Annex I, introductory sentence			—
	Annex I(a), first to seventh indents			Annex IX, Part A, points (1) to (7)
	Annex I(b), first and second indents			Annex IX, Part B, points (1) and (2)
	Annex I(c)			Annex IX, Part C
	Annex J, introductory sentence			Annex V, introductory sentence
	Annex J			Annex V, points (1) to (25)
	Annex K(1), first, second and third indents			Annex IV, points (1)(a), (b) and (c)
	Annex K(2) to (5)			Annex IV, points (2) to (5)
	Annex L, first paragraph, points (1) to (5)			Annex II, points (1) to (5)
	Annex L, second paragraph			Article 56(2)
	Annex M, points (a) to (f)			Annex VI, points (1) to (6)

Directive 67/227/EEC	*Directive 77/388/EEC*	*Amending Directives*	*Other acts*	*This Directive*
		Article 1, point (1), second subparagraph, of Directive 89/465/EEC		Article 133, second paragraph
		Article 2 of Directive 94/5/EC		Article 342
		Article 3, first and second sentences, of Directive 94/5/EC		Article 343, first and second paragraphs
		Article 4 of Directive 2002/38/EC		Article 56(3) Article 57(2) Article 357
		Article 5 of Directive 2002/38/EC		—
			Annex VIII(II), point (2)(a) of the Act of Accession of Greece	Article 287, point (1)
			Annex VIII(II), point (2)(b) of the Act of Accession of Greece	Article 375
			Annex XXXII(IV), point (3)(a), first indent and second indent, first sentence, of the Act of Accession of Spain and Portugal	Article 287, points (2) and (3)
			Annex XXXII(IV), point (3)(b), first subparagraph, of the Act of Accession of Spain and Portugal	Article 377
			Annex XV(IX), point (2)(b), first subparagraph, of the Act of Accession of Austria, Finland and Sweden	Article 104
			Annex XV(IX), point (2)(c), first subparagraph, of the Act of Accession of Austria, Finland and Sweden	Article 287, point (4)

Directive 67/227/EEC	*Directive 77/388/EEC*	*Amending Directives*	*Other acts*	*This Directive*
			Annex XV(IX), point (2)(f), first subparagraph, of the Act of Accession of Austria, Finland and Sweden	Article 117(1)
			Annex XV(IX), point (2)(g), first subparagraph, of the Act of Accession of Austria, Finland and Sweden	Article 119
			Annex XV(IX), point (2)(h), first subparagraph, first and second indents, of the Act of Accession of Austria, Finland and Sweden	Article 378(1)
			Annex XV(IX), point (2)(i), first subparagraph, first indent, of the Act of Accession of Austria, Finland and Sweden	—
			Annex XV(IX), point (2)(i), first subparagraph, second and third indents, of the Act of Accession of Austria, Finland and Sweden	Article 378(2)(a) and (b)
			Annex XV(IX), point (2)(j) of the Act of Accession of Austria, Finland and Sweden	Article 287, point (5)
			Annex XV(IX), point (2)(l), first subparagraph, of the Act of Accession of Austria, Finland and Sweden	Article 111(a)
			Annex XV(IX), point (2)(m), first subparagraph, of the Act of Accession of Austria, Finland and Sweden	Article 379(1)

Directive 67/227/EEC	Directive 77/388/EEC	Amending Directives	Other acts	This Directive
			Annex XV(IX), point (2)(n), first subparagraph, first and second indents, of the Act of Accession of Austria, Finland and Sweden	Article 379(2)
			Annex XV(IX), point (2)(x), first indent, of the Act of Accession of Austria, Finland and Sweden	Article 253
			Annex XV(IX), point (2)(x), second indent, of the Act of Accession of Austria, Finland and Sweden	Article 287, point (6)
			Annex XV(IX), point (2)(z), first subparagraph, of the Act of Accession of Austria, Finland and Sweden	Article 111(b)
			Annex XV(IX), point (2)(aa), first subparagraph, first and second indents, of the Act of Accession of Austria, Finland and Sweden	Article 380
			Protocol No 2 of the Act of Accession of Austria, Finland and Sweden concerning the Åland Islands	Article 6(1)(d)
			Annex V(5), point (1)(a) of the 2003 Act of Accession of the Czech Republic, Estonia, Cyprus, Latvia, Lithuania, Hungary, Malta, Poland Slovenia and Slovakia	Article 123
			Annex V(5), point (1)(b) of the 2003 Act of Accession	Article 381

VAT EC

Directive 67/227/EEC	*Directive 77/388/EEC*	*Amending Directives*	*Other acts*	*This Directive*
			Annex VI(7), point (1)(a) of the 2003 Act of Accession	Article 124
			Annex VI(7), point (1)(b) of the 2003 Act of Accession	Article 382
			Annex VII(7), point (1), first and second subparagraphs, of the 2003 Act of Accession	Article 125(1) and (2)
			Annex VII(7), point (1), third subparagraph, of the 2003 Act of Accession	—
			Annex VII(7), point (1), fourth subparagraph, of the 2003 Act of Accession	Article 383(a)
			Annex VII(7), point (1), fifth subparagraph, of the 2003 Act of Accession	—
			Annex VII(7), point (1), sixth subparagraph, of the 2003 Act of Accession	Article 383(b)
			Annex VIII(7), point (1)(a) of the 2003 Act of Accession	—
			Annex VIII(7), point (1)(b), second subparagraph, of the 2003 Act of Accession	Article 384(a)
			Annex VIII(7), point (1), third subparagraph, of the 2003 Act of Accession	Article 384(b)
			Annex IX(8), point (1) of the 2003 Act of Accession	Article 385
			Annex X(7), point (1)(a)(i) and (ii) of the 2003 Act of Accession	Article 126(a) and (b)
			Annex X(7), point (1)(c) of the 2003 Act of Accession	Article 386

Directive 67/227/EEC	*Directive 77/388/EEC*	*Amending Directives*	*Other acts*	*This Directive*
			Annex XI(7), point (1) of the 2003 Act of Accession	Article 127
			Annex XI(7), point (2)(a) of the 2003 Act of Accession	Article 387(c)
			Annex XI(7), point (2)(b) of the 2003 Act of Accession	Article 387(a)
			Annex XI(7), point (2)(c) of the 2003 Act of Accession	Article 387(b)
			Annex XII(9), point (1)(a) of the 2003 Act of Accession	Article 128(1) and (2)
			Annex XII(9), point (1)(b) of the 2003 Act of Accession	Article 128(3), (4) and (5)
			Annex XII(9), point (2) of the 2003 Act of Accession	Article 388
			Annex XIII(9), point (1)(a) of the 2003 Act of Accession	Article 129(1) and (2)
			Annex XIII(9), point (1)(b) of the 2003 Act of Accession	Article 389
			Annex XIV(7), first subparagraph, of the 2003 Act of Accession	Article 130(a) and (b)
			Annex XIV(7), second subparagraph, of the 2003 Act of Accession	—
			Annex XIV(7), third subparagraph, of the 2003 Act of Accession	Article 390

COUNCIL DIRECTIVE 2007/74/EC OF 20 DECEMBER 2007 ON THE EXEMPTION FROM VALUE ADDED TAX AND EXCISE DUTY OF GOODS IMPORTED BY PERSONS TRAVELLING FROM THIRD COUNTRIES

(2007/74/EC)

Note—See OJ L 346, 29.12.2007 p 6.

THE COUNCIL OF THE EUROPEAN UNION,

Having regard to the Treaty establishing the European Community, and in particular Article 93 thereof,

Having regard to the proposal from the Commission,

Having regard to the Opinion of the European Parliament,

Having regard to the Opinion of the European Economic and Social Committee,

Whereas:

(1) Council Directive 69/169/EEC of 28 May 1969 on the harmonisation of provisions laid down by law, regulation or administrative action relating to exemption from turnover tax and excise duty on imports in international travel[1] established a Community system of tax exemptions. While it remains necessary to maintain that system in order to prevent double taxation, as well as in cases where, in view of the conditions under which goods are imported, the usual need to protect the economy is absent, it should still apply only to non-commercial imports of goods in the personal luggage of travellers from third countries.

(2) However, given the number of amendments required, as well as the need to adapt Directive 69/169/EEC to enlargement and to the new external borders of the Community, and to restructure and simplify certain provisions for the sake of clarity, the complete revision and repeal and replacement of Directive 69/169/EEC is justified.

(3) The quantitative limits and monetary thresholds to which the exemptions are subject should meet the current needs of Member States.

(4) The monetary threshold should take account of changes in the real value of money since the last increase in 1994 and should also reflect the abolition of quantitative limits on goods subject to excise duties in some Member States which will now fall into the general threshold on VAT.

(5) The ease of shopping abroad could cause problems to Member States which share land-borders with third countries with significantly lower prices. It is justifiable, therefore, to set a lower monetary threshold for forms of travel other than air and sea travel.

(6) In the experience of the Commission, the quantities for tobacco products and alcoholic beverages have, in general, been shown to be appropriate and should therefore be maintained.

(7) The quantitative limits for the exemption of excise goods should reflect the current scheme of taxation of such goods in the Member States. Accordingly, it is appropriate to provide for a limit for beer whereas the limits for perfume, coffee and tea should be discontinued.

(8) It is appropriate to allow Member States to set lower limits with regard to the monetary threshold for children and to exclude under-aged persons from the exemptions for tobacco products and alcoholic beverages, in order to ensure a high level of health protection.

(9) Given the need to promote a high level of human health protection for Community citizens, it is appropriate to allow Member States to apply reduced quantitative limits for the exemption of tobacco products.

(10) In order to take account of the special situation of certain people with regard to their location or working environment, it should also be possible for Member States to apply narrower exemptions in the case of frontier workers, persons residing near Community frontiers and the crew of the means of transport used in international travel.

(11) It is to be recalled that Austria shares a land border with Samnauntal, a Swiss enclave where a specific tax system is applied which results in significantly lower taxation than that applicable under the rules applying in the rest of Switzerland and, indeed, in the Kanton of Graubünden of which Samnauntal forms part. In view of that special situation, which has led Austria to apply lower quantitative limits for tobacco products with respect to that enclave in accordance with Article 5(8) of Directive 69/169/EEC, it is appropriate to allow that Member State to apply the lower limit provided for tobacco products by this Directive only to Samnauntal.

(12) For Member States which have not introduced the euro, a mechanism should be set up to enable amounts expressed in national currencies to be converted into euro and thus ensure equal treatment in the Member States.

(13) The amount on which Member States are free not to levy taxes on the import of goods should be increased in order to reflect current monetary values,

Note—[1] OJ L 133, 4.6.1969 p 6. Directive as last amended by Directive 2005/93/EC (OJ L 346, 29.12.2005 p 16).

HAS ADOPTED THIS DIRECTIVE:

CHAPTER 1

SUBJECT-MATTER AND DEFINITIONS

Article 1

This Directive lays down rules relating to the exemption from value added tax (VAT) and excise duty of goods imported in the personal luggage of persons travelling from a third country or from a territory where the Community provisions on VAT or excise duty, or both, as defined in Article 3, do not apply.

Article 2

Where a journey involves transit through the territory of a third country, or begins in a territory as referred to in Article 1, this Directive shall apply if the traveller is unable to establish that the goods transported in his luggage have been acquired subject to the general conditions governing taxation on the domestic market of a Member State and do not qualify for any refunding of VAT or excise duty. Overflying without landing shall not be regarded as transit.

Article 3

For the purposes of this Directive, the following definitions shall apply:

1. "third country" means any country which is not a Member State of the European Union;

In view of the Fiscal Agreement between France and the Principality of Monaco dated 18 May 1963 and the Agreement of friendship and neighbourly relations between Italy and the Republic of San Marino dated 31 March 1939, Monaco shall not be regarded as a third country and San Marino shall not be regarded as a third country in respect of excise duty;

2. "territory where the Community provisions on VAT or excise duty, or both do not apply" means any territory, other than a territory of a third country, where Directives 2006/112/EC[1] or 92/12/EEC, or both do not apply;

In view of the Agreement between the Governments of the United Kingdom and the Isle of Man on Customs and Excise and associated matters dated 15 October 1979, the Isle of Man shall not be regarded as a territory where the Community provisions on VAT or excise duty, or both do not apply;

3. "air travellers" and "sea travellers" means any passengers travelling by air or sea other than private pleasure-flying or private pleasure-sea-navigation;

4. "private pleasure-flying" and "private pleasure-sea-navigation" means the use of an aircraft or a sea-going vessel by its owner or the natural or legal person who enjoys its use either through hire or through any other means, for purposes other than commercial and in particular other than for the carriage of passengers or goods or for the supply of services for consideration or for the purposes of public authorities;

5. "frontier zone" means a zone which, as the crow flies, does not extend more than 15 kilometres from the frontier of a Member State and which includes the local administrative districts part of the territory of which lies within the zone; Member States may grant exemptions therefrom;

6. "frontier-zone worker" means any person whose normal activities require that he should go to the other side of the frontier on his work days.

Note—[1] OJ L 347, 11.12.2006 p 1. Directive as amended by Directive 2006/138/EC (OJ L 384, 29.12. 2006 p 92).

CHAPTER 2

EXEMPTIONS

Section 1

COMMON PROVISIONS

Article 4

Member States shall, on the basis of either monetary thresholds or quantitative limits, exempt from VAT and excise duty goods imported in the personal luggage of travellers, provided that the imports are of a non-commercial character.

Article 5

For the purposes of the application of the exemptions, personal luggage shall be regarded as the whole of the luggage which a traveller is able to present to the customs authorities upon arrival, as well as luggage which he presents later to the same authorities, subject to proof that such luggage was registered as ac-companied luggage, at the time of his departure, with the company which has been responsible for conveying him. Fuel other than that referred to in Article 11 shall not be regarded as personal luggage.

Article 6

For the purposes of the application of the exemptions, imports shall be regarded as being of a non-commercial character if they meet the following conditions:

(a) they take place occasionally;

(b) they consist exclusively of goods for the personal or family use of the travellers, or of goods intended as presents.

The nature or quantity of the goods must not be such as to indicate that they are being imported for commercial reasons.

Article 7

1. Member States shall exempt from VAT and excise duty imports of goods, other than those referred to in Section 3, the total value of which does not exceed EUR 300 per person.

In the case of air and sea travellers, the monetary threshold specified in the first subparagraph shall be EUR 430.

2. Member States may lower the monetary threshold for travellers under 15 years old, whatever their means of transport. However, the monetary threshold may not be lower than EUR 150.

3. For the purposes of applying the monetary thresholds, the value of an individual item may not be split up.

4. The value of the personal luggage of a traveller, which is imported temporarily or is re-imported following its temporary export, and the value of medicinal products required to meet the personal needs of a traveller shall not be taken into consideration for the purposes of applying the exemptions referred to in paragraphs 1 and 2.

Section 3

QUANTITATIVE LIMITS

Article 8

1. Member States shall exempt from VAT and excise duty imports of the following types of tobacco product, subject either to the following higher or lower quantitative limits:

(*a*) 200 cigarettes or 40 cigarettes;

(*b*) 100 cigarillos or 20 cigarillos;

(*c*) 50 cigars or 10 cigars;

(*d*) 250g smoking tobacco or 50g smoking tobacco.

Each amount specified in points (*a*) to (*d*) shall represent, for the purposes of paragraph 4, 100% of the total allowance for tobacco products.

Cigarillos are cigars of a maximum weight of 3 grams each.

2. Member States may choose to distinguish between air travellers and other travellers by applying the lower quantitative limits specified in paragraph 1 only to travellers other than air travellers.

3. By derogation from paragraphs 1 and 2, Austria may, as long as the tax system in the Swiss enclave of Samnauntal differs from that applicable in the rest of the Kanton of Graubünden, limit the application of the lower quantitative limit to tobacco products brought into the territory of that Member State by travellers who enter its territory directly from the Swiss enclave of Samnauntal.

4. In the case of any one traveller, the exemption may be applied to any combination of tobacco products, provided that the aggregate of the percentages used up from the individual allowances does not exceed 100%.

Article 9

1. Member States shall exempt from VAT and excise duty alcohol and alcoholic beverages other than still wine and beer, subject to the following quantitative limits:

(*a*) a total of 1 litre of alcohol and alcoholic beverages of an alcoholic strength exceeding 22% vol, or un-denatured ethyl alcohol of 80% vol and over;

(*b*) a total of 2 litres of alcohol and alcoholic beverages of an alcoholic strength not exceeding 22% vol.

Each of the amounts specified in points (*a*) and (*b*) represent, for the purposes of paragraph 2, 100% of the total allowance for alcohol and alcoholic beverages.

2. In the case of any one traveller, the exemption may be applied to any combination of the types of alcohol and alcoholic beverage referred to in paragraph 1, provided that the aggregate of the percentages used up from the individual allowances does not exceed 100%.

3. Member States shall exempt from VAT and excise duty a total of 4 litres of still wine and 16 litres of beer.

Article 10

Exemptions under Articles 8 or 9 shall not apply in the case of travellers under 17 years of age.

Article 11

Member States shall exempt from VAT and excise duty, in the case of any one means of motor transport, the fuel contained in the standard tank and a quantity of fuel not exceeding 10 litres contained in a port-able container.

Article 12

The value of goods referred to in Articles 8, 9 or 11 shall not be taken into consideration for the purposes of applying the exemption provided for in Article 7(1).

CHAPTER 3
SPECIAL CASES

Article 13

1. Member States may lower the monetary thresholds or the quantitative limits, or both, in the case of travellers in the following categories:

(*a*) persons resident in a frontier zone;

(*b*) frontier-zone workers;

(*c*) the crew of a means of transport used to travel from a third country or from a territory where the Community provisions on VAT or excise duty, or both do not apply.

2. Paragraph 1 shall not apply where a traveller in one of the categories listed therein produces evidence to show that he is going beyond the frontier zone of the Member State or that he is not returning from the frontier zone of the neighbouring third country.

However, it shall apply where frontier-zone workers or the crew of the means of transport used in international travel import goods when travelling in the course of their work.

CHAPTER IV
GENERAL AND FINAL PROVISIONS

Article 14

Member States may choose not to levy VAT or excise duty on the import of goods by a traveller when the amount of the tax which should be levied is equal to, or less than, EUR 10.

Article 15

1. The euro equivalent in national currency which shall apply for the implementation of this Directive shall be fixed once a year. The rates applicable shall be those obtaining on the first working day of October. They shall be published in the Official Journal of the European Union and shall apply from 1 January of the following year.

2. Member States may round off the amounts in national currency resulting from the conversion of the amounts in euro provided for in Article 7, provided such rounding-off does not exceed EUR 5.

3. Member States may maintain the monetary thresholds in force at the time of the annual adjustment provided for in paragraph 1 if, prior to the rounding-off provided for in paragraph 2, conversion of the corresponding amounts expressed in euro would result in a change of less than 5% in the exemption expressed in national currency or in a lowering of this exemption.

Article 16

Every four years and for the first time in 2012 the Commission shall forward a report on the implementation of this Directive to the Council, where appropriate accompanied by a proposal for amendment.

Article 17

In Article 5(9) of Directive 69/169/EEC the date of 31 December 2007 shall be replaced by 30 November 2008.

Article 18

Directive 69/169/EEC shall be repealed and replaced by this Directive with effect from 1 December 2008.

References to the repealed Directive shall be construed as references to this Directive and shall be read in accordance with the correlation table in the Annex.

Article 19

1. Member States shall bring into force the laws, regulations and administrative provisions necessary to comply with Articles 1 to 15 of this Directive with effect from 1 December 2008. They shall forthwith communicate to the Commission the text of those measures.

When Member States adopt those measures, they shall contain a reference to this Directive or be accompanied by such reference on the occasion of their official publication. Member States shall determine how such reference is to be made.

2. Member States shall communicate to the Commission the text of the main provisions of national law which they adopt in the field covered by this Directive.

Article 20

This Directive shall enter into force on the day of its publication in the Official Journal of the European Union.

It shall apply with effect from 1 December 2008.

However, Article 17 shall apply with effect from 1 January 2008.

Article 21

This Directive is addressed to the Member States.

Done at Brussels, ... *20 December 2007.*

For the Council
The President
F. Nunes Correia

ANNEX

CORRELATION TABLE

Directive 69/169/EEC	*This Directive*
Article 1(1)	Article 7(1)
Article 1(2)	Article 7(2)
Article 1(3)	Article 7(3)
Article 2	–
Article 3, point one	Article 7(4)
Article 3, point two	Article 6
Article 3, point three, first subparagraph	Article 5
Article 3, point three, second subparagraph	Article 5 and 11
Article 4(1), introductory phrase	Article 8(1) introductory phrase, Article 9(1) introductory phrase
Article 4(1), second column	–
Article 4(1)(*a*), first column	Article 8(1)
Article 4(1)(*b*), first column	Article 9(1)
Article 4(1)(*c*), (*d*) and (*e*), first column	–
Article 4(2) first subparagraph	Article 10
Article 4(2) second subparagraph	–
Article 4(3)	Article 12
Article 4(4)	Article 2
Article 4(5)	–
Article 5(1)	–
Article 5(2)	Article 13(1)
Article 5(3)	–
Article 5(4)	Article 13(2)
Article 5(5)	–
Article 5(6), introductory phrase, first indent	Article 3(5)
Article 5(6), introductory phrase, second indent	Article 3(6)
Article 5(7)	–
Article 5(8)	–
Article 5(9)	–
Article 7(1)	–
Article 7(2)	Article 15(1)
Article 7(3)	Article 15(2)
Article 7(4)	Article 15(3)
Article 7(5)	–
Article 7a(1)	–
Article 7a(2)	Article 14
Article 7b	–
Article 7c	–
Article 7d	–
Article 8(1)	Article 19(1), first subparagraph
Article 8(2), first subparagraph	Article 19(1), first subparagraph
Article 8(2), second subparagraph	–

Directive 69/169/EEC	*This Directive*
Article 9	Article 21

COUNCIL DIRECTIVE 2008/9/EC
OF 12 FEBRUARY 2008
LAYING DOWN DETAILED RULES FOR THE REFUND OF VALUE ADDED TAX, PROVIDED FOR IN DIRECTIVE 2006/112/EC, TO TAXABLE PERSONS NOT ESTABLISHED IN THE MEMBER STATE OF REFUND BUT ESTABLISHED IN ANOTHER MEMBER STATE

(2008/9/EC)

Note—See OJ L 44, 20.02.2008 p 23.

THE COUNCIL OF THE EUROPEAN UNION,

Having regard to the Treaty establishing the European Community, and in particular Article 93 thereof,

Having regard to the proposal from the Commission,

Having regard to the opinion of the European Parliament,[1]

Having regard to the opinion of the European Economic and Social Committee,[2]

Whereas:

(1) Considerable problems are posed, both for the administrative authorities of Member States and for businesses, by the implementing rules laid down by Council Directive 79/1072/EEC of 6 December 1979 on the harmonisation of the laws of the Member States relating to turnover taxes – Arrangements for the refund of value added tax to taxable persons not established in the territory of the country.[3]

(2) The arrangements laid down in that Directive should be amended in respect of the period within which decisions concerning applications for refund are notified to businesses. At the same time, it should be laid down that businesses too must provide responses within specified periods. In addition, the procedure should be simplified and modernised by allowing for the use of modern technologies.

(3) The new procedure should enhance the position of businesses since the Member States shall be liable to pay interest if the refund is made late and the right of appeal by businesses will be strengthened.

(4) For clarity and better reading purposes, the provision concerning the application of Directive 79/1072/EEC, previously contained in Council Directive 2006/112/EC of 28 November 2006 on the common system of value added tax[4], should now be integrated in this Directive.

(5) Since the objectives of this Directive cannot be sufficiently achieved by the Member States and can therefore, by reason of the scale of the action, be better achieved at Community level, the Community may adopt measures, in accordance with the principle of subsidiarity as set out in Article 5 of the Treaty. In accordance with the principle of proportionality, as set out in that Article, this Directive does not go beyond what is necessary in order to achieve those objectives.

(6) In accordance with point 34 of the Interinstitutional Agreement on better law-making[5], Member States are encouraged to draw up, for themselves and in the interests of the Community, their own tables illustrating, as far as possible, the correlation between this Directive and the transposition measures, and to make them public.

(7) In the interest of clarity, Directive 79/1072/EEC should therefore be repealed, subject to the necessary transitional measures with respect to refund applications introduced before 1 January 2010,

Notes—

1 OJ C 285 E, 22.11.2006 p 122.
2 OJ C 28, 3.2.2006 p 86.
3 OJ L 331, 27.12.1979 p 11. Directive as last amended by Directive 2006/98/EC (OJ L 363, 20.12.2006 p 129).
4 OJ L 347, 11.12.2006 p 1. Directive as last amended by Directive 2007/75/EC (OJ L 346, 29.12.2007 p 13).
5 OJ C 321, 31.12.2003 p 1.

HAS ADOPTED THIS DIRECTIVE:

VAT EC

Article 1

This Directive lays down the detailed rules for the refund of value added tax (VAT), provided for in Article 170 of Directive 2006/112/EC, to taxable persons not established in the Member State of refund, who meet the conditions laid down in Article 3.

Article 2

For the purposes of this Directive, the following definitions shall apply:

1 "taxable person not established in the Member State of refund" means a taxable person within the meaning of Article 9(1) of Directive 2006/112/EC who is not established in the Member State of refund but established in the territory of another Member State;

2 "Member State of refund" means the Member State in which the VAT was charged to the taxable person not established in the Member State of refund in respect of goods or services supplied to him by other taxable persons in that Member State or in respect of the importation of goods into that Member State;

3 "refund period" means the period mentioned in Article 16 covered by the refund application;

4 "refund application" means the application for refund of VAT charged in the Member State of refund to the taxable person not established in the Member State of refund in respect of goods or services supplied to him by other taxable persons in that Member State or in respect of the importation of goods into that Member State;

5 "applicant" means the taxable person not established in the Member State of refund making the refund application.

Article 3

This Directive shall apply to any taxable person not established in the Member State of refund who meets the following conditions:

(*a*) during the refund period, he has not had in the Member State of refund, the seat of his economic activity, or a fixed establishment from which business transactions were effected, or, if no such seat or fixed establishment existed, his domicile or normal place of residence;

(*b*) during the refund period, he has not supplied any goods or services deemed to have been supplied in the Member State of refund, with the exception of the following transactions:

(i) the supply of transport services and services ancillary thereto, exempted pursuant to Articles 144, 146, 148, 149, 151, 153, 159 or 160 of Directive 2006/112/EC;

(ii) the supply of goods and services to a person who is liable for payment of VAT in accordance with Articles 194 to 197 and Article 199 of Directive 2006/112/EC.

Simon's Tax Cases—*Daimler AG and another v Skatteverket* (Joined cases C-318/11 and C-319/11) [2013] STC 670.

Article 4

This Directive shall not apply to:

(*a*) amounts of VAT which, according to the legislation of the Member State of refund, have been incorrectly invoiced;

(*b*) amounts of VAT which have been invoiced in respect of supplies of goods the supply of which is, or may be, exempt under Article 138 or Article 146(1)(*b*) of Directive 2006/112/EC.

Article 5

Each Member State shall refund to any taxable person not established in the Member State of refund any VAT charged in respect of goods or services supplied to him by other taxable persons in that Member State or in respect of the importation of goods into that Member State, insofar as such goods and services are used for the purposes of the following transactions:

(*a*) transactions referred to in Article 169(*a*) and (*b*) of Directive 2006/112/EC;

(*b*) transactions to a person who is liable for payment of VAT in accordance with Articles 194 to 197 and Article 199 of Directive 2006/112/EC as applied in the Member State of refund.

Without prejudice to Article 6, for the purposes of this Directive, entitlement to an input tax refund shall be determined pursuant to Directive 2006/112/EC as applied in the Member State of refund.

Article 6

To be eligible for a refund in the Member State of refund, a taxable person not established in the Member State of refund has to carry out transactions giving rise to a right of deduction in the Member State of establishment.

When a taxable person not established in the Member State of refund carries out in the Member State in which he is established both transactions giving rise to a right of deduction and transactions not giving rise to a right of deduction in that Member State, only such proportion of the VAT which is refundable in accordance with Article 5 may be refunded by the Member State of refund as is attributable to the former trans-actions in accordance with Article 173 of Directive 2006/112/EC as applied by the Member State of establishment.

Article 7

To obtain a refund of VAT in the Member State of refund, the taxable person not established in the Member State of refund shall address an electronic refund application to that Member State and submit it to the Member State in which he is established via the electronic portal set up by that Member State.

Article 8

1. The refund application shall contain the following information:

(*a*) the applicant's name and full address;

(*b*) an address for contact by electronic means;

(*c*) a description of the applicant's business activity for which the goods and services are acquired;

(*d*) the refund period covered by the application;

(*e*) a declaration by the applicant that he has supplied no goods and services deemed to have been sup-plied in the Member State of refund during the refund period, with the exception of transactions referred to in points (i) and (ii) of Article 3(*b*);

(*f*) the applicant's VAT identification number or tax reference number;

(*g*) bank account details including IBAN and BIC codes.

2. In addition to the information specified in paragraph 1, the refund application shall set out, for each Member State of refund and for each invoice or importation document, the following details:

(*a*) name and full address of the supplier;

(*b*) except in the case of importation, the VAT identification number or tax reference number of the supplier, as allocated by the Member State of refund in accordance with the provisions of Articles 239 and 240 of Directive 2006/112/EC;

(*c*) except in the case of importation, the prefix of the Member State of refund in accordance with Article 215 of Directive 2006/112/EC;

(*d*) date and number of the invoice or importation document;

(*e*) taxable amount and amount of VAT expressed in the currency of the Member State of refund;

(*f*) the amount of deductible VAT calculated in accordance with Article 5 and the second paragraph of Article 6 expressed in the currency of the Member State of refund;

(*g*) where applicable, the deductible proportion calculated in accordance with Article 6, expressed as a percentage;

(*h*) nature of the goods and services acquired, described according to the codes in Article 9.

Article 9

1. In the refund application, the nature of the goods and services acquired shall be described by the following codes:

1 = fuel;

2 = hiring of means of transport;

3 = expenditure relating to means of transport (other than the goods and services referred to under codes 1 and 2);

4 = road tolls and road user charge;

5 = travel expenses, such as taxi fares, public transport fares;

6 = accommodation;

7 = food, drink and restaurant services;

8 = admissions to fairs and exhibitions;

9 = expenditure on luxuries, amusements and entertainment;

10 = other.

If code 10 is used, the nature of the goods and services supplied shall be indicated.

2. The Member State of refund may require the applicant to provide additional electronic coded information as regards each code set out in paragraph 1 to the extent that such information is necessary because of any restrictions on the right of deduction under Directive 2006/112/EC, as applicable in the Member State of refund or for the implementation of a relevant derogation received by the Member State of refund under Articles 395 or 396 of that Directive.

Article 10

Without prejudice to requests for information under Article 20, the Member State of refund may require the applicant to submit by electronic means a copy of the invoice or importation document with the refund application where the taxable amount on an invoice or importation document is EUR 1000 or more or the equivalent in national currency. Where the invoice concerns fuel, the threshold is EUR 250 or the equivalent in national currency.

Article 11

The Member State of refund may require the applicant to provide a description of his business activity by using the harmonised codes determined in accordance with the second subparagraph of Article 34a(3) of Council Regulation (EC) No 1798/2003[1].

VAT EC

Note—[1] OJ L 264, 15.10.2003 p 1.

Article 12

The Member State of refund may specify which language or languages shall be used by the applicant for the provision of information in the refund application or of possible additional information.

Article 13

If subsequent to the submission of the refund application the deductible proportion is adjusted pursuant to Article 175 of Directive 2006/112/EC, the applicant shall make a correction to the amount applied for or already refunded.

The correction shall be made in a refund application during the calendar year following the refund period in question or, if the applicant makes no refund applications during that calendar year, by submitting a separate declaration via the electronic portal established by the Member State of establishment.

Article 14

1. The refund application shall relate to the following:
   (*a*) the purchase of goods or services which was invoiced during the refund period, provided that the VAT became chargeable before or at the time of the invoicing, or in respect of which the VAT became chargeable during the refund period, provided that the purchase was invoiced before the tax became chargeable;
   (*b*) the importation of goods during the refund period.

2. In addition to the transactions referred to in paragraph 1, the refund application may relate to invoices or import documents not covered by previous refund applications and concerning transactions completed during the calendar year in question.

Article 15

1. The refund application shall be submitted to the Member State of establishment at the latest on 30 September of the calendar year following the refund period. The application shall be considered submitted only if the applicant has filled in all the information required under Articles 8, 9 and 11.
[Refund applications which relate to refund periods in 2009 shall be submitted to the Member State of establishment on 31 March 2011 at the latest.][1]

2. The Member State of establishment shall send the applicant an electronic confirmation of receipt with-out delay.

Amendments—[1] In para 1, second sub-para inserted by Council Directive 2010/66 Art 1 with effect from 1 October 2010.

Article 16

The refund period shall not be more than one calendar year or less than three calendar months. Refund applications may, however, relate to a period of less than three months where the period represents the remainder of a calendar year.

Article 17

If the refund application relates to a refund period of less than one calendar year but not less than three months, the amount of VAT for which a refund is applied for may not be less than EUR 400 or the equivalent in national currency.

If the refund application relates to a refund period of a calendar year or the remainder of a calendar year, the amount of VAT may not be less than EUR 50 or the equivalent in national currency.

Article 18

1. The Member State of establishment shall not forward the application to the Member State of refund where, during the refund period, any of the following circumstances apply to the applicant in the Member State of establishment:
   (*a*) he is not a taxable person for VAT purposes;
   (*b*) he carries out only supplies of goods or of services which are exempt without deductibility of the VAT paid at the preceding stage pursuant to Articles 132, 135, 136, 371, Articles 374 to 377, Article 378(2)(*a*), Article 379(2) or Articles 380 to 390 of Directive 2006/112/EC or provisions providing for identical exemptions contained in the 2005 Act of Accession;
   (*c*) he is covered by the exemption for small enterprises provided for in Articles 284, 285, 286 and 287 of Directive 2006/112/EC;
   (*d*) he is covered by the common flat-rate scheme for farmers provided for in Articles 296 to 305 of Directive 2006/112/EC.

2. The Member State of establishment shall notify the applicant by electronic means of the decision it has taken pursuant to paragraph 1.

Article 19

1. The Member State of refund shall notify the applicant without delay, by electronic means, of the date on which it received the application.

2. The Member State of refund shall notify the applicant of its decision to approve or refuse the refund application within four months of its receipt by that Member State.

Article 20

1. Where the Member State of refund considers that it does not have all the relevant information on which to make a decision in respect of the whole or part of the refund application, it may request, by electronic means, additional information, in particular from the applicant or from the competent authorities of the Member State of establishment, within the four-month period referred to in Article 19(2). Where the additional information is requested from someone other than the applicant or a competent authority of a Member State, the request shall be made by electronic means only if such means are available to the recipient of the request.

If necessary, the Member State of refund may request further additional information.

The information requested in accordance with this paragraph may include the submission of the original or a copy of the relevant invoice or import document where the Member State of refund has reasonable doubts regarding the validity or accuracy of a particular claim. In that case, the thresholds mentioned in Article 10 shall not apply.

2. The Member State of refund shall be provided with the information requested under paragraph 1 within one month of the date on which the request reaches the person to whom it is addressed.

Article 21

Where the Member State of refund requests additional information, it shall notify the applicant of its decision to approve or refuse the refund application within two months of receiving the requested information or, if it has not received a reply to its request, within two months of expiry of the time limit laid down in Article 20(2). However, the period available for the decision in respect of the whole or part of the refund application shall always be at least six months from the date of receipt of the application by the Member State of refund.

Where the Member State of refund requests further additional information, it shall notify the applicant of its decision in respect of the whole or part of the refund application within eight months of receipt of the application by that Member State.

Article 22

1. Where the refund application is approved, refunds of the approved amount shall be paid by the Member State of refund at the latest within 10 working days of the expiry of the deadline referred to in Article 19(2) or, where additional or further additional information has been requested, the deadlines referred to in Article 21.

2. The refund shall be paid in the Member State of refund or, at the applicant's request, in any other Member State. In the latter case, any bank charges for the transfer shall be deducted by the Member State of refund from the amount to be paid to the applicant.

Article 23

1. Where the refund application is refused in whole or in part, the grounds for refusal shall be notified by the Member State of refund to the applicant together with the decision.

2. Appeals against decisions to refuse a refund application may be made by the applicant to the competent authorities of the Member State of refund in the forms and within the time limits laid down for appeals in the case of refund applications from persons who are established in that Member State.

If, under the law of the Member State of refund, failure to take a decision on a refund application within the time limits specified in this Directive is not regarded either as approval or as refusal, any administrative or judicial procedures which are available in that situation to taxable persons established in that Member State shall be equally available to the applicant. If no such procedures are available, failure to take a decision on a refund application within these time limits shall mean that the application is deemed to be rejected.

Article 24

1. Where a refund has been obtained in a fraudulent way or otherwise incorrectly, the competent authority in the Member State of refund shall proceed directly to recover the amounts wrongly paid and any penal-ties and interest imposed in accordance with the procedure applicable in the Member State of refund, without prejudice to the provisions on mutual assistance for the recovery of VAT.

2. Where an administrative penalty or interest has been imposed but has not been paid, the Member State of refund may suspend any further refund to the taxable person concerned up to the unpaid amount.

Article 25

The Member State of refund shall take into account as a decrease or increase of the amount of the refund any correction made concerning a previous refund application in accordance with Article 13 or, where a separate declaration is submitted, in the form of separate payment or recovery.

Article 26

Interest shall be due to the applicant by the Member State of refund on the amount of the refund to be paid if the refund is paid after the last date of payment pursuant to Article 22(1).

If the applicant does not submit the additional or further additional information requested to the Member State of refund within the specified time limit, the first paragraph shall not apply. It shall also not apply until the documents to be submitted electronically pursuant to Article 10 have been received by the Member State of refund.

Article 27

1. Interest shall be calculated from the day following the last day for payment of the refund pursuant to Article 22(1) until the day the refund is actually paid.

2. Interest rates shall be equal to the interest rate applicable with respect to refunds of VAT to taxable persons established in the Member State of refund under the national law of that Member State.

If no interest is payable under national law in respect of refunds to established taxable persons, the interest payable shall be equal to the interest or equivalent charge which is applied by the Member State of refund in respect of late payments of VAT by taxable persons.

Article 28

1. This Directive shall apply to refund applications submitted after 31 December 2009.

2. Directive 79/1072/EEC shall be repealed with effect from 1 January 2010. However, its provisions shall continue to apply to refund applications submitted before 1 January 2010.

References to the repealed Directive shall be construed as references to this Directive except for refund applications submitted before 1 January 2010.

Article 29

1. Member States shall bring into force the laws, regulations and administrative provisions necessary to comply with this Directive with effect from 1 January 2010. They shall forthwith inform the Commission thereof.

When such provisions are adopted by Member States, they shall contain a reference to this Directive or be accompanied by such reference on the occasion of their official publication. The methods of making such reference shall be laid down by Member States.

2. Member States shall communicate to the Commission the text of the main provisions of national law which they adopt in the field covered by this Directive.

Article 30

This Directive shall enter into force on the day of its publication in the Official Journal of the European Union.

Article 31

This Directive is addressed to the Member States.

Done at Brussels, ... *12 February 2008.*

For the Council
The President
A. Bajuk

COUNCIL DIRECTIVE 2009/132/EC OF 19 OCTOBER 2009 DETERMINING THE SCOPE OF ARTICLE 143(B) AND (C) OF DIRECTIVE 2006/112/EC AS REGARDS EXEMPTION FROM VALUE ADDED TAX ON THE FINAL IMPORTATION OF CERTAIN GOODS

2009/132/EC

THE COUNCIL OF THE EUROPEAN UNION,

Having regard to the Treaty establishing the European Community, and in particular Articles 93 and 94 thereof,

Having regard to the proposal from the Commission,

Having regard to the opinion of the European Parliamen,[1]

Having regard to the opinion of the European Economic and Social Committee,[2]

Whereas:

(1) Council Directive 83/181/EEC of 28 March 1983 determining the scope of Article 14(1)(d) of Directive 77/388/EEC as regards exemption from value added tax on the final importation of certain goods[3] has been substantially amended several times.[4] In the interests of clarity and rationality the said Directive should be codified.

(2) Pursuant to Article 131 and Article 143(b) and (c) of Council Directive 2006/112/EC of 28 November 2006 on the common system of value added tax,[5] Member States are, without prejudice to other Community provisions and under conditions which they shall lay down for the purpose, inter

alia, of preventing any possible evasion, avoidance or abuse, to exempt final importation of goods qualifying for exemption from customs duties other than as provided for in the Common Customs Tariff.

(3) Pursuant to Article 145 of Directive 2006/112/EC, the Commission is required to submit to the Council proposals designed to lay down Community tax rules clarifying the scope of the exemptions referred to in Articles 143 and 144 of that Directive and detailed rules for their implementation.

(4) While it is deemed desirable to achieve the greatest possible degree of uniformity between the system for customs duties and that for value added tax, account should be taken, nevertheless, in applying the latter system, of the differences as regards objective and structure between customs duties and value added tax.

(5) Separate arrangements for value added tax should be laid down for imported goods to the extent necessary to comply with the objectives of tax harmonisation. The exemptions on importation can be granted only on condition that they are not liable to affect the conditions of competition on the market.

(6) Certain reliefs applied in the Member States stem from conventions between those Member States and third countries which, given their purpose, concern only the signatory Member States. It is not expedient to define at Community level conditions for granting such reliefs. The Member States concerned need merely be authorised to retain them.

(7) This Directive should be without prejudice to the obligations of the Member States relating to the time limits for transposition into national law of the Directives set out in Annex II, Part B,

Notes[1] Opinion of 11 March 2009 (not yet published in the Official Journal).
[2] OJ C175, 28.7.2009, p 123.
[3] OJ L105, 23.4.1983, p 38.
[4] See Annex II, Part A.
[5] OJ L347, 11.12.2006, p 1.

HAS ADOPTED THIS DIRECTIVE:

TITLE I
SCOPE AND DEFINITIONS

Article 1

The scope of the exemptions from value added tax (hereinafter VAT) referred to in Article 143(b) and (c) of Directive 2006/112/EC and the rules for their implementation, referred to in Article 145 of that Directive, shall be defined by this Directive.

In accordance with Article 131 and Article 143(b) and (c) of Directive 2006/112/EC, the Member States shall apply the exemptions laid down in this Directive under the conditions fixed by them in order to ensure that such exemptions are correctly and simply applied and to prevent any evasion, avoidance or abuses.

Article 2

1. For the purposes of this Directive:
   (a) 'imports' means imports as defined in Article 30 of Directive 2006/112/EC and the entry for home use after being subject to one of the systems provided for in Article 157(1)(a) of that Directive or a system of temporary admission or transit;
   (b) 'personal property' means any property intended for the personal use of the persons concerned or for meeting their household needs, including household effects, cycles and motor-cycles, private motor vehicles and their trailers, camping caravans, pleasure craft and private aeroplanes, as well as household provisions appropriate to normal family requirements, and household pets and saddle animals;
   (c) 'household effects' means personal effects, household linen and furnishings and items of equipment intended for the personal use of the persons concerned or for meeting their household needs;
   (d) 'alcoholic products' means products (beer, wine, aperitifs with a wine or alcohol base, brandies, liqueurs and spirituous beverages, etc.) falling within CN codes 2203 to 2208;
   (e) 'Community' means the territory of the Member States where Directive 2006/112/EC applies.
2. The nature or quantity of personal property shall not reflect any commercial interest, nor shall they be intended for an economic activity within the meaning of Article 9(1) of Directive 2006/112/EC. However, portable instruments of the applied or liberal arts, required by the person concerned for the pursuit of his trade or profession, shall also constitute personal property.

TITLE II
IMPORTATION OF PERSONAL PROPERTY BELONGING TO INDIVIDUALS COMING FROM THIRD COUNTRIES OR THIRD TERRITORIES

CHAPTER 1
PERSONAL PROPERTY OF NATURAL PERSONS TRANSFERRING THEIR NORMAL PLACE OF RESIDENCE TO THE COMMUNITY

Article 3

Subject to Articles 4 to 11, exemption from VAT on importation shall be granted on personal property imported by natural persons transferring their normal place of residence from outside the Community to a Member State of the Community.

Article 4

Exemption shall be limited to personal property which:

(a) except in special cases justified by the circumstances, has been in the possession of and, in the case of non-consumable goods, used by the person concerned at his former normal place of residence for a minimum of six months before the date on which he ceases to have his normal place of residence outside the Community;

(b) is intended to be used for the same purpose at his new normal place of residence.

The Member States may in addition make exemption of personal property conditional upon such property having borne, either in the country of origin or in the country of departure, the customs and/or fiscal charges to which it is normally liable.

Article 5

Exemption may be granted only to persons whose normal place of residence has been outside the Community for a continuous period of at least 12 months.

However, the competent authorities may grant exceptions to this rule provided that the intention of the person concerned was clearly to reside outside the Community for a continuous period of at least 12 months.

Article 6

Exemption shall not be granted in respect of:

(a) alcoholic products;

(b) tobacco or tobacco products;

(c) commercial means of transport;

(d) articles for use in the exercise of a trade or profession, other than portable instruments of the applied or liberal arts.

Vehicles intended for mixed use for commercial or professional purposes may also be excluded from exemption.

Article 7

1. Except in special cases, exemption shall be granted only in respect of personal property entered for permanent importation within 12 months of the date of establishment, by the person concerned, of his normal place of residence in the Community.

2. The personal property may be imported in several separate consignments within the period referred to in paragraph 1.

Article 8

1. Until 12 months have elapsed from the date of the declaration for its final importation, personal property which has been imported exempt from tax may not be lent, given as security, hired out or transferred, whether for a consideration or free of charge, without prior notification to the competent authorities.

2. Any loan, giving as security, hiring out or transfer before the expiry of the period referred to in paragraph 1 shall entail payment of the relevant VAT on the goods concerned, at the rate applying on the date of such loan, giving as security, hiring out or transfer, on the basis of the type of goods and the customs value ascertained or accepted on that date by the competent authorities.

Article 9

1. By way of derogation from Article 7(1), exemption may be granted in respect of personal property permanently imported before the person concerned establishes his normal place of residence in the Community, provided that he undertakes actually to establish his normal place of residence there within a period of six months. Such undertaking shall be accompanied by a security, the form and amount of which shall be determined by the competent authorities.

2. Where use is made of paragraph 1, the period laid down in point (a) of the first paragraph of Article 4 shall be calculated from the date of importation into the Community.

Article 10

1. Where, owing to occupational commitments, the person concerned leaves the third country or third territory where he had his normal place of residence without simultaneously establishing his normal place of residence on the territory of a Member State the Community, although having the intention of ultimately doing so, the competent authorities may authorise exemption in respect of the personal property which he transfers into the said territory for this purpose.

2. Exemption in respect of the personal property referred to in paragraph 1 shall be granted in accordance with the conditions laid down in Articles 3 to 8, on the understanding that:

(a) the periods laid down in point (a) of the first paragraph of Article 4 and paragraph 1 of Article 7 shall be calculated from the date of importation;

(b) the period referred to in Article 8(1) shall be calculated from the date when the person concerned actually establishes his normal place of residence on the territory of the Community.

3. Exemption shall also be subject to an undertaking from the person concerned that he will actually establish his normal place of residence on the territory of the Community within a period laid down by the competent authorities in keeping with the circumstances. The latter may require this undertaking to be accompanied by a security, the form and amount of which they shall determine.

Article 11

The competent authorities may derogate from points (a) and (b) of the first paragraph of Article 4, points (c) and (d) of the first paragraph of Article 6 and Article 8 when a person has to transfer his normal place of residence to the territory of a Member State as a result of exceptional political circumstances.

CHAPTER 2
GOODS IMPORTED ON THE OCCASION OF A MARRIAGE

Article 12

1. Subject to Articles 13 to 16, exemption shall be granted in respect of trousseaux and household effects, whether or not new, belonging to a person transferring his or her normal place of residence to the territory of the Community on the occasion of his or her marriage.

Exemption shall also be granted in respect of presents customarily given on the occasion of a marriage which are received by a person fulfilling the conditions laid down in the first subparagraph from persons having their normal place of residence outside the Community. The exemption shall apply to presents of a value of not more than EUR 200. Member States may, however, grant exemption for more than EUR 200 provided that the value of each exempt present does not exceed EUR 1,000.

2. The Member State may make exemption of the goods referred to in the first subparagraph of paragraph 1 conditional on their having borne, either in the country or territory of origin or in the country or territory of departure, the customs and fiscal charges to which they are normally liable.

Article 13

The exemption may be granted only to persons:

(a) whose normal place of residence has been outside the Community for a continuous period of at least 12 months;

(b) who produce evidence of their marriage.

However, derogations from the rule referred to in the first subparagraph may be granted provided that the intention of the person concerned was clearly to reside outside the Community for a continuous period of at least 12 months.

Article 14

No exemption shall be granted for alcoholic products, tobacco or tobacco products.

Article 15

1. Save in exceptional circumstances, exemption shall be granted only in respect of goods permanently imported:

(a) not earlier than two months before the date fixed for the wedding; and

(b) not later than four months after the date of the wedding.

In the case referred to in point (a), exemption may be made subject to the lodging of appropriate security, the form and amount of which shall be determined by the competent authorities.

2. Goods to which exemption is granted may be imported in several separate consignments, within the period referred to in paragraph 1.

Article 16

1. Until 12 months have elapsed from the date of the declaration for their final importation, personal property which has been imported exempt from tax may not be lent, given as security, hired out or transferred, whether for a consideration or free of charge, without prior notification to the competent authorities.

2. Any loan, giving as security, hiring out or transfer before the expiry of the period referred to in paragraph 1 shall entail payment of the relevant VAT on the goods concerned, at the rate applying on the date of such loan, giving as security, hiring out or transfer, on the basis of the type of goods and the value ascertained or accepted on that date by the competent authorities.

CHAPTER 3
PERSONAL PROPERTY ACQUIRED BY INHERITANCE

Article 17

Subject to Articles 18, 19 and 20, exemption shall be granted in respect of personal property acquired by inheritance by a natural person having his normal place of residence in the Community.

Article 18

Exemption shall not be granted in respect of:

(a) alcoholic products;
(b) tobacco or tobacco products;
(c) commercial means of transport;
(d) articles for use in the exercise of a trade or profession, other than portable instruments of the applied or liberal arts, which were required for the exercise of the trade or profession of the deceased;
(e) stocks of raw materials and finished or semi-finished products;
(f) livestock and stocks of agricultural products exceeding the quantities appropriate to normal family requirements.

Article 19

1. Exemption shall be granted only in respect of personal property permanently imported not later than two years from the date on which the person becomes entitled to the goods (final settlement of the inheritance).

However, this period may be extended by the competent authorities on special grounds.

2. The goods may be imported in several separate consignments within the period referred to in paragraph 1.

Article 20

Articles 17, 18 and 19 shall apply *mutatis mutandis* to personal property acquired by inheritance by legal persons engaged in a non-profit-making activity who are established on the territory of the Community.

TITLE III
IMPORTATION OF SCHOOL OUTFITS, EDUCATIONAL MATERIALS AND RELATED HOUSEHOLD EFFECTS

Article 21

1. Exemption shall be granted in respect of outfits, educational materials and household effects representing the usual furnishings for a student's room and belonging to pupils or students coming to stay in the Community for the purposes of studying there and intended for their personal use during the period of their studies.

2. For the purposes of this Article:

(a) 'pupil or student' means any person enrolled in an educational establishment in order to attend, full-time, the courses offered therein;
(b) 'outfit' means underwear and household linen as well as clothing, whether or not new;
(c) 'educational materials' means articles and instruments (including calculators and typewriters) normally used by pupils or students for the purposes of their studies.

Article 22

Exemption shall be granted at least once per school year.

TITLE IV
IMPORTS OF NEGLIGIBLE VALUE

Article 23

Goods of a total value not exceeding EUR 10 shall be exempt on admission. Member States may grant exemption for imported goods of a total value of more than EUR 10, but not exceeding EUR 22.

However, Member States may exclude goods which have been imported on mail order from the exemption provided for in the first sentence of the first subparagraph.

Article 24

Exemption shall not apply to the following:

(a) alcoholic products;

(b) perfumes and toilet waters;
(c) tobacco or tobacco products.

TITLE V
CAPITAL GOODS AND OTHER EQUIPMENT IMPORTED ON THE TRANSFER OF ACTIVITIES

Article 25

1. Without prejudice to the measures in force in the Member State with regard to industrial and commercial policy, and subject to Articles 26 to 29, Member States may allow exemption, on admission, for imports of capital goods and other equipment belonging to undertakings which definitively cease their activity in the third country or third territory of origin in order to carry on a similar activity in the Community and which, in accordance with Article 213(1) of Directive 2006/112/EC, have given advance notice to the competent authorities of the Member State of importation of the commencement of such activity.

Where the undertaking transferred is an agricultural holding, its livestock shall also be exempt on admission.

2. For the purposes of paragraph 1:
   (a) 'activity' means an economic activity as referred to in Article 9(1) of Directive 2006/112/EC;
   (b) 'undertaking' means an independent economic unit of production or of the service industry.

Article 26

1. The exemption shall be limited to capital goods and equipment which:
   (a) except in special cases justified by the circumstances, have actually been used in the undertaking for a minimum of 12 months prior to the date on which the undertaking ceased to operate in the third country or third territory from which it is transferring its activity;
   (b) are intended to be used for the same purposes after the transfer;
   (c) are to be used for the purposes of an activity not exempted under Articles 132, 133, 135 and 136 of Directive 2006/112/EC;
   (d) are appropriate to the nature and size of the undertaking in question.

2. Pending entry into force of the common rules referred to in the first paragraph of Article 176 of Directive 2006/112/EC, Member States may exclude from the exemption, in whole or in part, capital goods in respect of which they have availed themselves of the second subparagraph of Article 176 of that Directive.

Article 27

No exemption shall be granted to undertakings established outside the Community and the transfer of which to the territory of the Community is consequent upon or is for the purpose of merging with, or being absorbed by, an undertaking established in the Community, without a new activity being set up.

Article 28

No exemption shall be granted for:
   (a) means of transport which are not in the nature of instruments of production or of the service industry;
   (b) supplies of all kinds intended for human consumption or for animal feed;
   (c) fuel and stocks of raw materials or finished or semi-finished products;
   (d) livestock in the possession of dealers.

Article 29

Except in special cases justified by the circumstances, the exemption shall be granted only in respect of capital goods and other equipment imported before the expiry of a period of 12 months from the date when the undertaking ceased its activities in the third country or third territory of origin.

TITLE VI
IMPORTATION OF CERTAIN AGRICULTURAL PRODUCTS AND PRODUCTS INTENDED FOR AGRICULTURAL USE

CHAPTER 1
PRODUCTS OBTAINED BY COMMUNITY FARMERS ON PROPERTIES LOCATED IN THIRD COUNTRIES OR THIRD TERRITORIES

Article 30

1. Subject to Articles 31 and 32, agricultural, stock-farming, bee-keeping, horticultural and forestry products from properties located in a third country or third territory adjoining the territory of the Community which are operated by agricultural producers having their principal undertaking in

the Community and adjacent to the country or territory concerned shall be exempt on admission. Pure-bred horses, not more than six months old and born in a third country or third territory of an animal covered in the Community and then exported temporarily to give birth, shall also be exempt on admission.
2. To be eligible for the exemption under the first subparagraph of paragraph 1, stock-farming products must be obtained from animals reared, acquired or imported in accordance with the general tax arrangements applicable in the Member State of importation.

Article 31

Exemption shall be limited to products which have not undergone any treatment other than that which normally follows their harvest or production.

Article 32

Exemption shall be granted only in respect of products imported by the agricultural producer or on his behalf.

Article 33

This Chapter shall apply *mutatis mutandis* to the products of fishing or fish-farming activities carried out in the lakes or waterways bordering the territory of the Community by fishermen established in the Community and to the products of hunting activities carried out on such lakes or waterways by sportsmen established in the Community.

CHAPTER 2

SEEDS, FERTILISERS AND PRODUCTS FOR THE TREATMENT OF SOIL AND CROPS

Article 34

Subject to Article 35, seeds, fertilisers and products for the treatment of soil and crops, intended for use on property located in the Community, and adjoining a third country or third territory and operated by agricultural producers having their principal undertaking in the said country or territory adjacent to the territory of the Community shall be exempt on admission.

Article 35

1. Exemption shall be limited to the quantities of seeds, fertilisers or other products required for the purpose of operating the property.
It shall be granted only for seeds, fertilisers or other products introduced directly into the Community by the agricultural producer or on his behalf.
2. Member States may make exemption conditional upon the granting of reciprocal treatment.

TITLE VII

IMPORTATION OF THERAPEUTIC SUBSTANCES, MEDICINES, LABORATORY ANIMALS AND BIOLOGICAL OR CHEMICAL SUBSTANCES

CHAPTER 1

LABORATORY ANIMALS AND BIOLOGICAL OR CHEMICAL SUBSTANCES INTENDED FOR RESEARCH

Article 36

1. The following shall be exempt on admission:
   (a) animals specially prepared and sent free of charge for laboratory use;
   (b) biological or chemical substances which are imported subject to the limits and conditions laid down in Article 60 of Council Regulation (EC) No 918/83 of 28 March 1983 setting up a Community system of reliefs from customs duty.[1]

2. The exemption referred to in paragraph 1 shall be limited to animals and biological or chemical substances which are intended for either of the following:
   (a) public establishments principally engaged in education or scientific research, including those departments of public establishments which are principally engaged in education or scientific research;
   (b) private establishments principally engaged in education or scientific research and authorised by the competent authorities of the Member States to receive such articles exempt from tax.

CHAPTER 2

THERAPEUTIC SUBSTANCES OF HUMAN ORIGIN AND BLOOD-GROUPING AND TISSUE-TYPING REAGENTS

Article 37

1. Without prejudice to the exemption provided for in Article 143(a) of Directive 2006/112/EC and subject to Article 38 of this Directive, the following shall be exempted:
   (a) therapeutic substances of human origin;

(b) blood-grouping reagents;
(c) tissue-typing reagents.

2. For the purposes of paragraph 1:
(a) 'therapeutic substances of human origin' means human blood and its derivatives (whole human blood, dried human plasma, human albumin and fixed solutions of human plasma protein, human immunoglobulin and human fibrinogen);
(b) 'blood-grouping reagents' means all reagents, whether of human, animal, plant or other origin used for blood-type grouping and for the detection of blood incompatibilities;
(c) 'tissue-typing reagents' means all reagents whether of human, animal, plant or other origin used for the determination of human tissue-types.

Article 38

Exemption shall be limited to products which:
(a) are intended for institutions or laboratories approved by the competent authorities, for use exclusively for noncommercial medical or scientific purposes;
(b) are accompanied by a certificate of conformity issued by a duly authorised body in the country or territory of departure;
(c) are in containers bearing a special label identifying them.

Article 39

Exemption shall include the special packaging essential for the transport of therapeutic substances of human origin or blood-grouping or tissue-typing reagents and also any solvents and accessories needed for their use which may be included in the consignments.

CHAPTER 3

REFERENCE SUBSTANCES FOR THE QUALITY CONTROL OF MEDICAL PRODUCTS

Article 40

Consignments which contain samples of reference substances approved by the World Health Organisation for the quality control of materials used in the manufacture of medicinal products and which are addressed to consignees authorised by the competent authorities of the Member States to receive such consignments free of tax shall be exempt on admission.

CHAPTER 4

PHARMACEUTICAL PRODUCTS USED AT INTERNATIONAL SPORTS EVENTS

Article 41

Pharmaceutical products for human or veterinary medical use by persons or animals participating in international sports events shall, within the limits necessary to meet their requirements during their stay in the Community, be exempt on admission.

Notes[1] OJ L105, 23.4.1983, p 1.

TITLE VIII

GOODS FOR CHARITABLE OR PHILANTHROPIC ORGANISATIONS

CHAPTER 1

GENERAL PROVISION

Article 42

Member States may impose a limit on the quantity or value of the goods, exempt under Chapters 2, 3 or 4 in order to remedy any abuse and to combat major distortions of competition.

CHAPTER 2

GOODS IMPORTED FOR GENERAL PURPOSES

Article 43

1. Subject to Articles 44, 45 and 46, the following shall be exempt on admission:
(a) basic necessities obtained free of charge and imported by State organisations or other charitable or philanthropic organisations approved by the competent authorities for distribution free of charge to needy persons;
(b) goods of every description sent free of charge, by a person or organisation established outside the Community, and without any commercial intent on the part of the sender, to State organisations or other charitable or philanthropic organisations approved by the competent authorities, to be used for fund-raising at occasional charity events for the benefit of needy persons;

(c) equipment and office materials sent free of charge, by a person or organisation established outside the Community, and without any commercial intent on the part of the sender, to charitable or philanthropic organisations approved by the competent authorities, to be used solely for the purpose of meeting their operating needs or carrying out their stated charitable or philanthropic aims.

2. For the purposes of paragraph 1(a) 'basic necessities' means those goods required to meet the immediate needs of human beings, such as food, medicine, clothing and bed-clothes.

Article 44

Exemption shall not be granted in respect of:

(a) alcoholic products;
(b) tobacco or tobacco products;
(c) coffee and tea;
(d) motor vehicles other than ambulances.

Article 45

Exemption shall be granted only to organisations accounting procedures of which enable the competent authorities to supervise their operations and which offer all the guarantees considered necessary.

Article 46

1. The organisation entitled to exemption may not lend, hire out or transfer, whether for a consideration or free of charge, the goods referred to in Article 43 for purposes other than those laid down in Article 43(1)(a) and (b), unless the competent authorities have been informed thereof in advance.

2. Should goods and equipment be lent, hired out or transferred to an organisation entitled to benefit from exemption pursuant to Articles 43 and 45, the exemption shall continue to be granted provided that the latter uses the goods and equipment for purposes which confer the right to such exemption. In other cases, loan, hiring out or transfer shall be subject to prior payment of VAT at the rate applying on the date of the loan, hiring out or transfer, on the basis of the type of goods and equipment and the value ascertained or accepted on that date by the competent authorities.

Article 47

1. Organisations referred to in Article 43 which cease to fulfil the conditions giving entitlement to exemption, or which are proposing to use goods and equipment exempt on admission for purposes other than those provided for by that Article, shall so inform the competent authorities.

2. Goods remaining in the possession of organisations which cease to fulfil the conditions giving entitlement to exemption shall be liable to the relevant import VAT at the rate applying on the date on which those conditions cease to be fulfilled, on the basis of the type of goods and equipment and the value as ascertained or accepted on that date by the competent authorities.

3. Goods used by the organisation benefiting from the exemption for purposes other than those provided for in Article 43 shall be liable to the relevant import VAT at the rate applying on the date on which they are put to another use on the basis of the type of goods and equipment and the value as ascertained on that date by the competent authorities.

CHAPTER 3

ARTICLES IMPORTED FOR THE BENEFIT OF HANDICAPPED PERSONS

Article 48

1. Articles specially designed for the education, employment or social advancement of blind or other physically or mentally handicapped persons shall be exempt on admission where:

(a) they are imported by institutions or organisations that are principally engaged in the education of or the provision of assistance to handicapped persons and are authorised by the competent authorities of the Member States to receive such articles exempt from tax; and
(b) they are donated to such institutions or organisations free of charge and with no commercial intent on the part of the donor.

2. Exemption shall apply to specific spare parts, components or accessories specifically for the articles in question and to the tools to be used for the maintenance, checking, calibration and repair of the said articles, provided that such spare parts, components, accessories or tools are imported at the same time as the said articles or, if imported subsequently, that they can be identified as being intended for articles previously exempt on admission or which would be eligible to be so exempt at the time when such entry is requested for the specific spare parts, components or accessories and tools in question.

3. Articles exempt on admission may not be used for purposes other than the education, employment or social advancement of blind or other handicapped persons.

Article 49

1. Goods exempt on admission may be lent, hired out or transferred, whether for a consideration or free of charge, by the beneficiary institutions or organisations on a non-profit-making basis to the persons referred to in Article 48 with whom they are concerned, without payment of VAT on importation.

2. No loan, hiring out or transfer may be effected under conditions other than those provided for in paragraph 1 unless the competent authorities have first been informed.

Should an article be lent, hired out or transferred to an institution or organisation itself entitled to benefit from this exemption, the exemption shall continue to be granted, provided the latter uses the article for purposes which confer the right to such exemption.

In other cases, loan, hiring out or transfer shall be subject to prior payment of VAT, at the rate applying on the date of the loan, hiring out or transfer, on the basis of the type of goods and the value ascertained or accepted on that date by the competent authorities.

Article 50

1. Institutions or organisations referred to in Article 48 which cease to fulfil the conditions giving entitlement to exemption, or which are proposing to use articles exempt on admission for purposes other than those provided for by that Article shall so inform the competent authorities.

2. Articles remaining in the possession of institutions or organisations which cease to fulfil the conditions giving entitlement to exemption shall be liable to the relevant import VAT at the rate applying on the date on which those conditions cease to be fulfilled, on the basis of the type of goods and the value ascertained or accepted on that date by the competent authorities.

3. Articles used by the institution or organisation benefiting from the exemption for purposes other than those provided for in Article 48 shall be liable to the relevant import VAT at the rate applying on the date on which they are put to another use on the basis of the type of goods and the value ascertained or accepted on that date by the competent authorities.

CHAPTER 4
GOODS IMPORTED FOR THE BENEFIT OF DISASTER VICTIMS

Article 51

Subject to Articles 52 to 57 goods imported by State organisations or other charitable or philanthropic organisations approved by the competent authorities shall be exempt on admission where they are intended:

(a) for distribution free of charge to victims of disasters affecting the territory of one or more Member States; or

(b) to be made available free of charge to the victims of such disasters, while remaining the property of the organisations in question.

Goods imported by disaster-relief agencies in order to meet their needs during the period of their activity shall also benefit upon admission from the exemption under the same conditions.

Article 52

No exemption shall be granted for materials and equipment intended for rebuilding disaster areas.

Article 53

Granting of the exemption shall be subject to a decision by the Commission, acting at the request of the Member State or States concerned in accordance with an emergency procedure entailing the consultation of the other Member States. This decision shall, where necessary, lay down the scope and the conditions of the exemption.

Pending notification of the Commission's decision, Member States affected by a disaster may authorise the suspension of any import VAT chargeable on goods imported for the purposes described in Article 51, subject to an undertaking by the importing organisation to pay such tax if exemption is not granted.

Article 54

Exemption shall be granted only to organisations the accounting procedures of which enable the competent authorities to supervise their operations and which offer all the guarantees considered necessary.

Article 55

1. The organisations benefiting from the exemption may not lend, hire out or transfer, whether for a consideration or free of charge, the goods referred to in the first paragraph of Article 51 under conditions other than those laid down in that Article without prior notification thereof to the competent authorities.

2. Should goods be lent, hired out or transferred to an organisation itself entitled to benefit from exemption pursuant to Article 51, the exemption shall continue to be granted, provided the latter uses the goods for purposes which confer the right to such exemption.

VAT EC

In other cases, loan, hiring out or transfer shall be subject to prior payment of VAT, at the rate applying on the date of the loan, hiring out or transfer, on the basis of the type of goods and the value ascertained or accepted on that date by the competent authorities.

Article 56

1. The goods referred to in point (b) of the first paragraph of Article 51, after they cease to be used by disaster victims, may not be lent, hired out or transferred, whether for a consideration or free of charge, unless the competent authorities are notified in advance.
2. Should goods be lent, hired out or transferred to an organisation itself entitled to benefit from exemption pursuant to Article 51 or, if appropriate, to an organisation entitled to benefit from exemption pursuant to Article 43(1)(a), the exemption shall continue to be granted, provided such organisations use the goods concerned for purposes which confer the right to such exemption.
In other cases, loan, hiring out or transfer shall be subject to prior payment of VAT, at the rate applying on the date of the loan, hiring out or transfer, on the basis of the type of goods and the value ascertained or accepted on that date by the competent authorities.

Article 57

1. Organisations referred to in Article 51 which cease to fulfil the conditions giving entitlement to exemption, or which are proposing to use the goods exempt on admission for purposes other than those provided for by that Article shall so inform the competent authorities.
2. In the case of goods remaining in the possession of organisations which cease to fulfil the conditions giving entitlement to exemption, when these are transferred to an organisation itself entitled to benefit from exemption pursuant to this Chapter or, if appropriate, to an organisation entitled to benefit from exemption pursuant to Article 43, the exemption shall continue to be granted, provided the organisation uses the goods in question for purposes which confer the right to such exemptions. In other cases, the goods shall be liable to the relevant import VAT at the rate applying on the date on which those conditions cease to be fulfilled, on the basis of the type of goods and the value ascertained or accepted on that date by the competent authorities.
3. Goods used by the organisation benefiting from the exemption for purposes other than those provided for in this Chapter shall be liable to the relevant import VAT at the rate applying on the date on which they are put to another use, on the basis of the type of goods and the value ascertained or accepted on that date by the competent authorities.

TITLE IX
IMPORTATION IN THE CONTEXT OF CERTAIN ASPECTS OF INTERNATIONAL RELATIONS

CHAPTER 1
HONORARY DECORATIONS OR AWARDS

Article 58

On production of satisfactory evidence to the competent authorities by the persons concerned, and provided the operations involved are not in any way of a commercial character, exemption shall be granted in respect of:

(a) decorations conferred by the government of a third country on persons whose normal place of residence is in the Community;

(b) cups, medals and similar articles of an essentially symbolic nature which, having been awarded in a third country or third territory to persons having their normal place of residence in the Community as a tribute to their activities in fields such as the arts, the sciences, sport or the public service or in recognition of merit at a particular event, are imported by such persons themselves;

(c) cups, medals and similar articles of an essentially symbolic nature which are given free of charge by authorities or persons established in a third country, to be presented on the territory of the Community for the same purposes as those referred to in point (b);

(d) awards, trophies and souvenirs of a symbolic nature and of limited value intended for distribution free of charge to persons normally resident in a third country or third territory, at business conferences or similar international events; their nature, unitary value or other features, must not be such as might indicate that they are intended for commercial purposes.

CHAPTER 2
PRESENTS RECEIVED IN THE CONTEXT OF INTERNATIONAL RELATIONS

Article 59

Without prejudice, where relevant, to the provisions applicable to the international movement of travellers, and subject to Articles 60 and 61, exemption shall be granted in respect of goods:

(a) imported by persons who have paid an official visit in a third country or third territory and who have received such goods on that occasion as gifts from the host authorities;

(b) imported by persons coming to pay an official visit in the Community and who intend to offer them on that occasion as gifts to the host authorities;
(c) sent as gifts, in token of friendship or goodwill, by an official body, public authority or group carrying on an activity in the public interest which is located in a third country or third territory, to an official body, public authority or group carrying on an activity in the public interest which is located in the Member State of importation and approved by the competent authorities to receive such goods exempt from tax.

Article 60

No exemption shall be granted for alcoholic products, tobacco or tobacco products.

Article 61

Exemption shall be granted only:
(a) where the articles intended as gifts are offered on an occasional basis;
(b) where they do not, by their nature, value or quantity, reflect any commercial interest;
(c) if they are not used for commercial purposes.

CHAPTER 3
GOODS TO BE USED BY MONARCHS OR HEADS OF STATE

Article 62

1. Exemption from tax, within the limits and under the conditions laid down by the competent authorities, shall be granted in respect of:
(a) gifts to reigning monarchs and heads of State;
(b) goods to be used or consumed by reigning monarchs and heads of State of a third country, or by persons officially representing them, during their official stay in the Community.

2. The exemption referred to in paragraph 1(b) may be made subject, by the Member State of importation, to reciprocal treatment.

3. The exemption referred to in paragraph 1 is also applicable to persons enjoying prerogatives at international level analogous to those enjoyed by reigning monarchs or heads of State.

TITLE X
IMPORTATION OF GOODS FOR THE PROMOTION OF TRADE

CHAPTER 1
SAMPLES OF NEGLIGIBLE VALUE

Article 63

1. Without prejudice to Article 67(1)(a), samples of goods which are of negligible value and which can be used only to solicit orders for goods of the type they represent shall be exempt on admission.

2. The competent authorities may require that certain articles, to qualify for exemption on admission, be rendered permanently unusable by being torn, perforated, or clearly and indelibly marked, or by any other process, provided such operation does not destroy their character as samples.

3. For the purposes of paragraph 1, 'samples of goods' means any article representing a type of goods whose manner of presentation and quantity, for goods of the same type or quality, rule out its use for any purpose other than that of seeking orders.

CHAPTER 2
PRINTED MATTER AND ADVERTISING MATERIAL

Article 64

Subject to Article 65, printed advertising matter such as catalogues, price lists, directions for use or brochures shall be exempt on admission provided that they relate to:
(a) goods for sale or hire by a person established outside the Community; or
(b) transport, commercial insurance or banking services offered by a person established outside the Community.

Article 65

1. The exemption shall be limited to printed advertisements which fulfil the following conditions:
(a) printed matter must clearly display the name of the undertaking which produces, sells or hires out the goods, or which offers the services to which it refers;
(b) each consignment must contain no more than one document or a single copy of each document if it is made up of several documents;
(c) printed matter must not be the subject of grouped consignments from the same consignor to the same consignee.

2. By way of derogation from paragraph 1(b), consignments comprising several copies of the same document may nevertheless be granted exemption provided their total gross weight does not exceed one kilogram.

Article 66

Articles for advertising purposes, of no intrinsic commercial value, sent free of charge by suppliers to their customers which, apart from their advertising function, are not capable of being used shall be exempt on admission.

CHAPTER 3

GOODS USED OR CONSUMED AT A TRADE FAIR OR SIMILAR EVENT

Article 67

1. Subject to Articles 68, 69, 70 and 71, the following shall be exempt on admission:
   (a) small representative samples of goods intended for a trade fair or similar event;
   (b) goods imported solely in order to be demonstrated or in order to demonstrate machines and apparatus displayed at a trade fair or similar event;
   (c) various materials of little value, such as paints, varnishes and wallpaper, which are to be used in the building, fitting-out and decoration of temporary stands at a trade fair or similar event, which are destroyed by being used;
   (d) printed matter, catalogues, prospectuses, price lists, advertising posters, calendars, whether or not illustrated, unframed photographs and other articles supplied free of charge in order to advertise goods displayed at a trade fair or similar event.
2. For the purposes of paragraph 1, 'trade fair or similar event' means:
   (a) exhibitions, fairs, shows and similar events connected with trade, industry, agriculture or handicrafts;
   (b) exhibitions and events held mainly for charitable reasons;
   (c) exhibitions and events held mainly for scientific, technical, handicraft, artistic, educational or cultural or sporting reasons, for religious reasons or for reasons of worship, trade union activity or tourism, or in order to promote international understanding;
   (d) meetings of representatives of international organisations or collective bodies;
   (e) official or commemorative ceremonies and gatherings;

However, that definition shall not cover exhibitions staged for private purposes in commercial stores or premises to sell goods.

Article 68

The exemption referred to in Article 67(1)(a) shall be limited to samples which:
   (a) are imported free of charge as such or are obtained at the exhibition from goods imported in bulk;
   (b) are exclusively distributed free of charge to the public at the exhibition for use or consumption by the persons to whom they have been offered;
   (c) are identifiable as advertising samples of low unitary value;
   (d) are not easily marketable and, where appropriate, are packaged in such a way that the quantity of the item involved is lower than the smallest quantity of the same item actually sold on the market;
   (e) in the case of foodstuffs and beverages not packaged as referred to in point (d), are consumed on the spot at the exhibition;
   (f) in their total value and quantity, are appropriate to the nature of the exhibition, the number of visitors and the extent of the exhibitor's participation.

Article 69

The exemption referred to in Article 67(1)(b) shall be limited to goods which are:
   (a) consumed or destroyed at the exhibition; and
   (b) appropriate, in their total value and quantity, to the nature of the exhibition, the number of visitors and the extent of the exhibitor's participation.

Article 70

The exemption referred to in Article 67(1)(d) shall be limited to printed matter and articles for advertising purposes which:
   (a) are intended exclusively to be distributed free of charge to the public at the place where the exhibition is held; and
   (b) in their total value and quantity, are appropriate to the nature of the exhibition, the number of visitors and the extent of the exhibitor's participation.

Article 71

The exemption referred to in Article 67(1)(a) and (b) shall not be granted for:

(a) alcoholic products;
(b) tobacco or tobacco products;
(c) fuels, whether solid, liquid or gaseous.

TITLE XI
GOODS IMPORTED FOR EXAMINATION, ANALYSIS OR TEST PURPOSES

Article 72

Subject to Articles 73 to 78, goods which are to undergo examination, analysis or tests to determine their composition, quality or other technical characteristics for purposes of information or industrial or commercial research shall be exempt on admission.

Article 73

Without prejudice to Article 76, the exemption shall be granted only on condition that the goods to be examined, analysed or tested are completely used up or destroyed in the course of the examination, analysis or testing.

Article 74

No exemption shall be granted in respect of goods used in examination, analysis or tests which in themselves constitute sales promotion operations.

Article 75

Exemption shall be granted only in respect of the quantities of goods which are strictly necessary for the purpose for which they are imported. These quantities shall in each case be determined by the competent authorities, taking into account the said purpose.

Article 76

1. The exemption shall cover goods which are not completely used up or destroyed during examination, analysis or testing, provided that the products remaining are, with the agreement and under the supervision of the competent authorities:
(a) completely destroyed or rendered commercially valueless on completion of examination, analysis or testing; or
(b) surrendered to the State without causing it any expense, where this is possible under national law; or
(c) in duly justified circumstances, exported outside the Community.

2. For the purposes of paragraph 1, 'products remaining' means products resulting from the examinations, analyses or tests or goods not actually used.

Article 77

Save where Article 76(1) is applied, products remaining at the end of the examinations, analyses or tests referred to in Article 72 shall be subject to the relevant import VAT, at the rate applying on the date of completion of the examinations, analyses or tests, on the basis of the type of goods and the value ascertained or accepted on that date by the competent authorities.

However, the interested party may, with the agreement and under the supervision of the competent authorities, convert products remaining to waste or scrap. In this case, the import duties shall be those applying to such waste or scrap at the time of conversion.

Article 78

The period within which the examinations, analyses or tests must be carried out and the administrative formalities to be completed in order to ensure the use of the goods for the purposes intended shall be determined by the competent authorities.

TITLE XII
MISCELLANEOUS IMPORTS

CHAPTER 1
CONSIGNMENTS SENT TO ORGANISATIONS PROTECTING COPYRIGHTS OR INDUSTRIAL AND COMMERCIAL PATENT RIGHTS

Article 79

Trademarks, patterns or designs and their supporting documents, as well as applications for patents for invention or the like, to be submitted to the bodies competent to deal with the protection of copyrights or the protection of industrial or commercial patent rights shall be exempt on admission.

CHAPTER 2
TOURIST INFORMATION LITERATURE

Article 80

The following shall be exempt on admission:

(a) documentation (leaflets, brochures, books, magazines, guidebooks, posters, whether or not framed, unframed photographs and photographic enlargements, maps, whether or not illustrated, window transparencies, and illustrated calendars) intended to be distributed free of charge and the principal purpose of which is to encourage the public to visit foreign countries, in particular in order to attend cultural, tourist, sporting, religious or trade or professional meetings or events, provided that such literature contains not more than 25 % of private commercial advertising and that the general nature of its promotional aims is evident;
(b) foreign hotel lists and yearbooks published by official tourist agencies, or under their auspices, and timetables for foreign transport services, provided that such literature is intended for distribution free of charge and contains not more than 25 % of private commercial advertising;
(c) reference material supplied to accredited representatives or correspondents appointed by official national tourist agencies and not intended for distribution, that is to say, yearbooks, lists of telephone or telex numbers, hotel lists, fairs catalogues, specimens of craft goods of negligible value, and literature on museums, universities, spas or other similar establishments.

CHAPTER 3
MISCELLANEOUS DOCUMENTS AND ARTICLES

Article 81

1. The following shall be exempt on admission:
(a) documents sent free of charge to the public services of Member States;
(b) publications of foreign governments and publications of official international bodies intended for distribution without charge;
(c) ballot papers for elections organised by bodies set up in countries outside the Community;
(d) objects to be submitted as evidence or for like purposes to the courts or other official agencies of the Member States;
(e) specimen signatures and printed circulars concerning signatures sent as part of customary exchanges of information between public services or banking establishments;
(f) official printed matter sent to the central banks of the Member States;
(g) reports, statements, notes, prospectuses, application forms and other documents drawn up by companies with headquarters outside the Community and sent to the bearers or subscribers of securities issued by such companies;
(h) recorded media (punched cards, sound recordings, microfilms, etc.) used for the transmission of information sent free of charge to the addressee, in so far as exemption does not give rise to abuses or to major distortions of competition;
(i) files, archives, printed forms and other documents to be used in international meetings, conferences or congresses, and reports on such gatherings;
(j) plans, technical drawings, traced designs, descriptions and other similar documents imported with a view to obtaining or fulfilling orders outside the Community or to participating in a competition held in the Community;
(k) documents to be used in examinations held in the Community by institutions set up outside the Community;
(l) printed forms to be used as official documents in the international movement of vehicles or goods, within the framework of international conventions;
(m) printed forms, labels, tickets and similar documents sent by transport undertakings or by undertakings of the hotel industry located outside the Community to travel agencies set up in the Community;
(n) printed forms and tickets, bills of lading, way-bills and other commercial or office documents which have been used;
(o) official printed forms from national or international authorities, and printed matter conforming to international standards sent for distribution by associations established outside the Community to corresponding associations located in the Community;
(p) photographs, slides and stereotype mats for photographs, whether or not captioned, sent to press agencies to newspaper or magazine publishers;
(q) articles listed in Annex I which are produced by the United Nations or one of its specialised agencies whatever the use for which they are intended;
(r) collectors' pieces and works of art of an educational, scientific or cultural character which are not intended for sale and which are imported by museums, galleries and other institutions approved by the competent authorities of the Member States for the purpose of duty-free admission of these goods;
(s) importations of official publications issued under the authority of the country or territory of export, international institutions, regional or local authorities and bodies under public law established in the country or territory of export, and printed matter distributed on the occasion

of elections to the European Parliament or on the occasion of national elections in the country in which the printed matter originates by foreign political organisations officially recognised as such in the Member States, in so far as such publications and printed matter have been subject to tax in the country or territory of export and have not benefited from remission of tax on export.

2. The exemption referred to in paragraph 1(r) is granted only on condition that the articles in question are imported free of charge or, if they are imported against payment, that they are not supplied by a taxable person.

CHAPTER 4
ANCILLARY MATERIALS FOR THE STOWAGE AND PROTECTION OF GOODS DURING THEIR TRANSPORT

Article 82

The various materials such as rope, straw, cloth, paper and cardboard, wood and plastics which are used for the stowage and protection — including heat protection — of goods during their transport on the territory of the Community, shall be exempt on admission, provided that:

(a) they are not normally reusable; and

(b) the consideration paid for them forms part of the taxable amount on importation as defined in Chapter 4 of Title VII of Directive 2006/112/EC.

CHAPTER 5
LITTER, FODDER AND FEEDINGSTUFFS FOR ANIMALS DURING THEIR TRANSPORT

Article 83

Litter, fodder and feedingstuffs of any description put on board the means of transport used to convey animals on the territory of the Community for the purpose of distribution to the said animals during the journey shall be exempt on admission.

CHAPTER 6
FUELS AND LUBRICANTS PRESENT IN LAND MOTOR VEHICLES AND SPECIAL CONTAINERS

Article 84

1. Subject to Articles 85, 86 and 87, the following shall be exempt on admission:

(a) fuel contained in the standard tanks of:

(i) private and commercial motor vehicles and motorcycles;

(ii) special containers;

(b) fuel contained in portable tanks carried by private motor vehicles and motorcycles, up to a maximum of 10 litres per vehicle and without prejudice to national provisions on the holding and transport of fuel.

2. For the purpose of paragraph 1:

(a) 'commercial motor vehicle' means any motorised road vehicle (including tractors with trailers) which, by its type of construction and equipment, is designed for, and capable of, transporting, whether for payment or not, more than nine persons including the driver, or goods, and any road vehicle for a special purpose other than transport as such;

(b) 'private motor vehicle' means any motor vehicle not covered by the definition set out in point (a);

(c) 'standard tanks' means:

(i) the tanks permanently fixed by, the manufacturer to all motor vehicles of the same type as the vehicle in question and whose permanent fitting enables fuel to be used directly, both for the purpose of propulsion and, where appropriate, for the operation, during transport, of refrigeration systems and other systems;

(ii) tanks permanently fixed by the manufacturer to all containers of the same type as the container in question and whose permanent fitting enables fuel to be used directly for the operation, during transport, of refrigeration systems and other systems with which special containers are equipped;

(d) 'special container' means any container fitted with specially designed apparatus for refrigeration systems, oxygenation systems, thermal insulation systems, or other systems.

In addition to the tanks referred to in point (c)(i) of the first subparagraph, gas tanks fitted to motor vehicles designed for the direct use of gas as a fuel and tanks fitted to ancillary systems with which the vehicle may be equipped shall also be considered to be standard tanks.

Article 85

Member States may limit the application of the exemption for fuel contained in the standard fuel tanks of commercial motor vehicles and special containers:

VAT EC

(a) when the vehicle comes from a third country or third territory, to 200 litres per vehicle and per journey;
(b) to 200 litres per special container and per journey.

Article 86

Member States may limit the amount of fuel exempt on admission in the case of:
(a) commercial motor vehicles engaged in international transport coming from third countries or third territories to their frontier zone, to a maximum depth of 25 kilometres as the crow flies, where such transport consists of journeys made by persons residing in that zone;
(b) private motor vehicles belonging to persons residing in the frontier zone, to a maximum depth of 15 km as the crow flies, contiguous with a third country or third territory.

Article 87

1. Fuel exempt on admission may not be used in a vehicle other than that in which it was imported nor be removed from that vehicle and stored, except during necessary repairs to that vehicle, or transferred for a consideration or free of charge by the person granted the exemption.
2. Non-compliance with paragraph 1 shall give rise to application of the import VAT relating to the products in question at the rate in force on the date of such non-compliance, on the basis of the type of goods and the value ascertained or accepted on that date by the competent authorities.

Article 88

The exemption shall also apply to lubricants carried in motor vehicles and required for their normal operation during the journey in question.

CHAPTER 7
GOODS FOR THE CONSTRUCTION, UPKEEP OR ORNAMENTATION OF MEMORIALS TO, OR CEMETERIES FOR, WAR VICTIMS

Article 89

Exemption from tax shall be granted in respect of goods imported by organisations authorised for that purpose by the competent authorities, for use in the construction, upkeep or ornamentation of cemeteries and tombs of, and memorials to, war victims of a third country who are buried in the Community.

CHAPTER 8
COFFINS, FUNERARY URNS AND ORNAMENTAL FUNERARY ARTICLES

Article 90

The following shall be exempt on admission:
(a) coffins containing bodies and urns containing the ashes of deceased persons, as well as the flowers, funeral wreaths and other ornamental objects normally accompanying them;
(b) flowers, wreaths and other ornamental objects brought by persons resident outside the Community, attending a funeral or coming to decorate graves on the territory of the Community provided these importations do not reflect, by either their nature or their quantity, any commercial intent.

TITLE XIII
GENERAL AND FINAL PROVISIONS

Article 91

Where this Directive provides that the granting of an exemption shall be subject to the fulfilment of certain conditions, the person concerned shall, to the satisfaction of the competent authorities, furnish proof that those conditions have been met.

Article 92

1. The exchange value in national currency of the euro to be taken into consideration for the purposes of this Directive shall be fixed once a year. The rates to be applied shall be those obtaining on the first working day in October and shall take effect on 1 January the following year.
2. Member States may round off the amounts in national currency arrived at by converting the amounts in euro.
3. Member States may continue to apply the amounts of the exemptions in force at the time of the annual adjustment provided for in paragraph 1, if conversion of the amounts of the exemptions expressed in euro leads, before the rounding-off provided for in paragraph 2, to an alteration of less than 5 % in the exemption expressed in national currency or to a reduction in that exemption.

Article 93

This Directive shall not prevent Member States from continuing to grant:

(a) the privileges and immunities granted by them under cultural, scientific or technical cooperation agreements concluded between Member States and third countries;
(b) the special exemptions justified by the nature of frontier traffic which are granted by them under frontier agreements concluded between Member States and third countries;
(c) exemptions in the context of agreements entered into on the basis of reciprocity with third countries that are Contracting Parties to the Convention on International Civil Aviation, signed at Chicago on 7 December 1944, for the purpose of implementing Recommended Practices 4.42 and 4.44 in Annex 9 to the Convention.

Article 94

Until the establishment of Community exemptions upon importation, Member States may retain the exemptions granted to:
(a) merchant-navy seamen;
(b) workers returning to their country of origin after having resided for at least six months outside the Community on account of their occupation.

Article 95

Member States shall inform the Commission of the measures which they adopt to give effect to this Directive, indicating, where the case arises, those measures which they adopt by simple reference to identical provisions of Regulation (EEC) No 918/83.

Article 96

Directive 83/181/EEC, as amended by the Directives listed in Annex II, Part A, is repealed, without prejudice to the obligations of the Member States relating to the time limits for transposition into national law of the Directives set out in Annex II, Part B.

References to the repealed Directive shall be construed as references to this Directive and shall be read in accordance with the correlation table in Annex III.

Article 97

This Directive shall enter into force on the 20th day following its publication in the *Official Journal of the European Union*.

Article 98

This Directive is addressed to the Member States.

Done at Luxembourg, ... 19 October 2009.

For the Council
The President
E. ERLANDSSON

ANNEX I

VISUAL AND AUDITORY MATERIALS OF AN EDUCATIONAL, SCIENTIFIC OR CULTURAL CHARACTER

CN code	Description
3704 00	Photographic plates, film, paper, paperboard and textiles, exposed but not developed:
ex 3704 00 10	– Plates and film:
	— Cinematograph film, positives, of an educational, scientific or cultural character
ex 3705	Photographic plates and film, exposed and developed, other than cinematograph film:
	— Of an educational, scientific or cultural character
3706	Cinematograph film, exposed and developed, whether or not incorporating sound track or consisting only of sound track:
3706 10	– Of a width of 35 mm or more:
	– – Other:
ex 3706 10 99	– – – Other positives:
	— Newsreels (with or without sound track) depicting events of current news value at the time of importation, and imported up to a limit of two copies of each subject for copying purposes

VAT EC

CN code	Description
	— Archival film material (with or without sound track) intended for use in connection with newsreel films — Recreational films particularly suited for children and young people — Other films of educational, scientific or cultural character
3706 90	– Other:
	– – Other:
	– – – Other positives:
ex 3706 90 51	— Newsreels (with or without sound track) depicting events of current news value at the time of importation, and imported up to a limit of two copies of each subject for copying purposes
ex 3706 90 91	— Archival film material (with or without sound track) intended for use in connection with newsreel films
ex 3706 90 99	— Recreational films particularly suited for children and young people — Other films of educational, scientific or cultural character
4911	Other printed matter, including printed pictures and photographs: – Other:
4911 99	– – Other:
ex 4911 99 00	– – Other: — Microcards or other information storage media required in computerised information and documentation services of an educational, scientific or cultural character — Wall charts designed solely for demonstration and education
ex 8523	Records, tapes and other recorded media for sound or other similarly recorded phenomena including matrices and masters for the production of records, but excluding products of Chapter 37: — Of an educational, scientific or cultural character
ex 9023 00	Instruments, apparatus and models, designed for demonstrational purposes (for example, in education or exhibitions), unsuitable for others uses: — Patterns, models and wall charts of an educational, scientific or cultural character, designed solely for demonstration and education — Mock-ups or visualisations of abstract concepts such as molecular structures or mathematical formulae
Various	Holograms for laser projection Multimedia kits Materials for programmed instructions, including materials in kit form with the corresponding printed materials

ANNEX II

PART A

REPEALED DIRECTIVE WITH THE LIST OF ITS SUCCESSIVE AMENDMENTS

(referred to in Article 96)

Council Directive 83/181/EEC

(OJ) L105, 23.4.1983, p 38)	
Council Directive 85/346/EEC	
(OJ L183, 16.7.1985, p 21)	
Council Directive 88/331/EEC	
(OJ L151, 17.6.1988, p 79)	
Commission Directive 89/219/EEC	
(OJ L92, 5.4.1989, p 13)	
Council Directive 91/680/EEC	only as regards Article 2(1) first indent
(OJ L376, 31.12.1991, p 1)	
1994 Act of Accession, Annex I, point XIII.B.4	
(OJ C241, 29.8.1994, p 276)	

PART B

LIST OF TIME LIMITS FOR TRANSPOSITION INTO NATIONAL LAW

(referred to in Article 96)

Directive	Time limit for transposition
83/181/EEC	30 June 1984
85/346/EEC	1 October 1985
88/331/EEC	1 January 1989
89/219/EEC	1 July 1989
91/680/EEC	31 December 1992

ANNEX III

CORRELATION TABLE

Directive 83/181/EEC	This Directive
—	Title I
Article 1(1)	Article 1(1), first and second subparagraphs
Article 1(2) introductory sentence	Article 2(1) introductory sentence
Article 1(2)(a)	Article 2(1)(a)
Article 1(2)(b) first subparagraph	Article 2(1)(b)
Article 1(2)(b) second subparagraph, first and second indents	Article 2(1)(b)
Article 1(2)(b) third subparagraph	Article 2(1)(b)
Article 1(2)(b) fourth subparagraph	Article 2(2)
Article 1(2)(c), (d) and (e)	Article 2(1)(c), (d) and (e)
Title I	Title II
Chapter I	Chapter 1
Articles 2 to 5	Articles 3 to 6
Article 6 first and second paragraphs	Article 7(1) and (2)
Articles 7 to 10	Articles 8 to 11
Chapter II	Chapter 2
Article 11(1) and (2)	Article 12(1), first and second subparagraphs
Article 11(3)	Article 12(2)
Article 12, introductory sentence	Article 13, first subparagraph, introductory sentence
Article 12(a), first sentence	Article 13, first subparagraph, point (a)
Article 12(a), second sentence	Article 13, second subparagraph
Article 12(b)	Article 13, first subparagraph, point (b)

VAT EC

Directive 83/181/EEC	This Directive
Article 13	Article 14
Article 14(1) introductory sentence	Article 15(1), first subparagraph, introductory sentence
Article 14(1) first indent, opening words	Article 15(1), first subparagraph, point (a)
Article 14(1) first indent, words in parentheses	Article 15(1), second subparagraph
Article 14(1), second indent	Article 15(1), first subparagraph, point (b)
Article 14(2)	Article 15(2)
Article 15	Article 16
Chapter III	Chapter 3
Articles 16 to 19	Articles 17 to 20
Title II	Title III
Articles 20 and 21	Articles 21 and 22
Title III	Title IV
Articles 22 and 23	Articles 23 and 24
Title IV	Title V
Article 24(1)	Article 25(1)
Article 24(2) introductory sentence	Article 25(2) introductory sentence
Article 24(2) first and second indents	Article 25(2)(a) and (b)
Article 25(1)	Article 26(1)
Article 25(2)	—
Article 25(3)	Article 26(2)
Articles 26, 27 and 28	Articles 27, 28 and 29
Title V	Title VI
Chapter I	Chapter 1
Article 29(1)	Article 30(1), first subparagraph
Article 29(2)	Article 30(2)
Article 29(3)	Article 30(1), second subparagraph
Articles 30, 31 and 32	Articles 31, 32 and 33
Chapter II	Chapter 2
Article 33	Article 34
Article 34(1) and (2)	Article 35(1), first and second subparagraphs
Article 34(3)	Article 35(2)
Title VI	Title VII
Chapter I	Chapter 1
Article 35(1) introductory sentence	Article 36(1) introductory sentence
Article 35(1)(a)	Article 36(1)(a)
Article 35(1)(b) introductory sentence	Article 36(1)(b)
Article 35(1)(b) first indent	—
Article 35(1)(b) second indent	Article 36(1)(b)
Article 35(2) introductory sentence	Article 36(2), introductory sentence
Article 35(2) first and second indents	Article 36(2)(a) and (b)
Chapter II	Chapter 2
Article 36(1)	Article 37(1)
Article 36(2) introductory sentence	Article 37(2) introductory sentence
Article 36(2) first, second and third indents	Article 37(2)(a), (b) and (c)
Articles 37 and 38	Articles 38 and 39
Chapter IIa	Chapter 3
Article 38a	Article 40
Chapter III	Chapter 4
Article 39	Article 41
Title VII	Title VIII

Directive 83/181/EEC	This Directive
—	Chapter 1
Article 40	Article 42
Chapter I	Chapter 2
Articles 41 to 45	Articles 43 to 47
Chapter II	Chapter 3
Articles 46, 47 and 48	Articles 48, 49 and 50
Chapter III	Chapter 4
Article 49(1) and (2)	Article 51, first and second paragraphs
Articles 50 to 55	Articles 52 to 57
Title VIII	Title IX
Chapter I	Chapter 1
Article 56	Article 58
Chapter II	Chapter 2
Articles 57 and 58	Articles 59 and 60
Article 59, introductory sentence	Article 61, introductory sentence
Article 59, first, second and third indents	Article 61(a), (b) and (c)
Chapter III	Chapter 3
Article 60 first paragraph, introductory sentence	Article 62(1), introductory sentence
Article 60, first paragraph, point (a)	Article 62(1)(a)
Article 60, first paragraph, point (b), first sentence	Article 62(1)(b)
Article 60, first paragraph, point (b), second sentence	Article 62(2)
Article 60, second paragraph	Article 62(3)
Title IX	Title X
Chapter I	Chapter 1
Article 61	Article 63
Chapter II	Chapter 2
Article 62, introductory sentence	Article 64, introductory sentence
Article 62(a)	Article 64(a)
Article 62(b)	—
Article 62(c)	Article 64(b)
Article 63, first paragraph, introductory sentence	Article 65(1), introductory sentence
Article 63, first paragraph, point (a)	Article 65(1)(a)
Article 63, first paragraph, point (b), first sentence	Article 65(1)(b)
Article 63, first paragraph, point (b), second sentence	Article 65(2)
Article 63, first paragraph, point (c)	Article 65(1)(c)
Article 63, second paragraph	—
Article 64	Article 66
Chapter III	Chapter 3
Article 65(1)	Article 67(1)
Article 65(2), introductory sentence	Article 67(2), first subparagraph, introductory sentence
Article 65(2)(a) to (e)	Article 67(2) first subparagraph, points (a) to (e)
Article 65(2), final sentence	Article 67(2), second subparagraph
Articles 66 to 69	Articles 68 to 71
Title X	Title XI

Directive 83/181/EEC	This Directive
Articles 70 to 73	Articles 72 to 75
Article 74(1) introductory sentence	Article 76(1) introductory sentence
Article 74(1), first, second and third indents	Article 76(1)(a), (b) and (c)
Article 74(2)	Article 76(2)
Articles 75 and 76	Articles 77 and 78
Title XI	Title XII
Chapter I	Chapter 1
Article 77	Article 79
Chapter II	Chapter 2
Article 78	Article 80
Chapter III	Chapter 3
Article 79(a) to (q)	Article 81(1)(a) to (q)
Article 79(r), first sentence	Article 81(1)(r)
Article 79(r), second sentence	Article 81(2)
Article 79(s)	Article 81(1)(s)
Chapter IV	Chapter 4
Article 80	Article 82
Chapter V	Chapter 5
Article 81	Article 83
Chapter VI	Chapter 6
Article 82(1) introductory sentence	Article 84(1) introductory sentence
Article 82(1)(a) first and second indents	Article 84(1)(a)(i) and (ii)
Article 82(1)(b)	Article 84(1)(b)
Article 82(2) introductory sentence	Article 84(2) first subparagraph, introductory sentence
Article 82(2)(a) first subparagraph, first and second indents and second subparagraph	Article 84(2), first subparagraph, point (a)
Article 82(2)(b)	Article 84(2), first subparagraph, point (b)
Article 82(2)(c) introductory sentence	Article 84(2), first subparagraph, point (c) introductory sentence
Article 82(2)(c) first indent, first subparagraph	Article 84(2), first subparagraph, point (c)(i)
Article 82(2)(c) first indent, second subparagraph	Article 84(2), second subparagraph
Article 82(2)(c), second indent	Article 84(2), first subparagraph, point (c)(ii)
Article 82(2)(d)	Article 84(2), first subparagraph, point (d)
Article 83 first paragraph introductory sentence	Article 85 introductory sentence
Article 83(a)	Article 85(a)
Article 83(b)	—
Article 83(c)	Article 85(b)
Article 83 second subparagraph	—
Article 84	Article 86
Article 85 first and second paragraphs	Article 87(1) and (2)
Article 86	Article 88
Chapter VII	Chapter 7
Article 87	Article 89
Chapter VIII	Chapter 8
Article 88	Article 90
Title XII	Title XIII
Articles 89, 90 and 91	Articles 91, 92 and 93
Article 92	Article 94

Directive 83/181/EEC	This Directive
Article 93(1)	—
Article 93(2)	Article 95
—	Article 96
—	Article 97
Article 94	Article 98
Annex	Annex I
—	Annex II
—	Annex III

COUNCIL DIRECTIVE 2010/24/EU OF 16 MARCH 2010 CONCERNING MUTUAL ASSISTANCE FOR THE RECOVERY OF CLAIMS RELATING TO TAXES, DUTIES AND OTHER MEASURES

2010/24/EU

Cross reference—See FA 2011 Sch 25 (mutual assistance for recovery of taxes).

THE COUNCIL OF THE EUROPEAN UNION,

Having regard to the Treaty on the Functioning of the European Union, and in particular Articles 113 and 115 thereof,

Having regard to the proposal from the European Commission,

Having regard to the opinion of the European Parliament [1],

Having regard to the opinion of the European Economic and Social Committee [2],

Acting in accordance with a special legislative procedure,

Whereas:

(1) Mutual assistance between the Member States for the recovery of each others' claims and those of the Union with respect to certain taxes and other measures contributes to the proper functioning of the internal market. It ensures fiscal neutrality and has allowed Member States to remove discriminatory protective measures in cross-border transactions designed to prevent fraud and budgetary losses.

(2) Arrangements for mutual assistance for recovery were first set out in Council Directive 76/308/EEC of 15 March 1976 on mutual assistance for the recovery of claims resulting from operations forming part of the system of financing the European Agricultural Guidance and Guarantee Fund, and of the agricultural levies and customs duties [3]. That Directive and the acts amending it were codified by Council Directive 2008/55/EC of 26 May 2008 on mutual assistance for the recovery of claims relating to certain levies, duties, taxes and other measures [4].

(3) Those arrangements, however, while providing a first step towards improved recovery procedures within the Union by approximating applicable national rules, have proved insufficient to meet the requirements of the internal market as it has evolved over the last 30 years.

(4) To better safeguard the financial interests of the Member States and the neutrality of the internal market, it is necessary to extend the scope of mutual assistance for recovery to claims relating to taxes and duties not yet covered by mutual assistance for recovery, whilst in order to cope with the increase in assistance requests and to deliver better results, it is necessary to make assistance more efficient and effective and to facilitate it in practice. In order to fulfil these objectives, important adaptations are necessary, whereby a mere modification of the existing Directive 2008/55/EC would not be sufficient. The latter should therefore be repealed and replaced by a new legal instrument which builds on the achievements of Directive 2008/55/EC but provides for clearer and more precise rules where necessary.

(5) Clearer rules would promote a wider information exchange between Member States. They would also ensure that all legal and natural persons in the Union are covered, taking into account the ever increasing range of legal arrangements, including not only traditional arrangements such as trusts and foundations, but any new instrument which may be set up by taxpayers in the Member States. They would furthermore make it possible to take account of all forms that claims of the public authorities relating to taxes, duties, levies, refunds and interventions may take, including all pecuniary claims against the taxpayer concerned or against a third party which substitute the original claim. Clearer rules are primarily necessary

VAT EC

to define better the rights and obligations of all the parties concerned.

(6) This Directive should not affect the Member States' competence to determine the recovery measures available under their internal legislation. However, it is necessary to ensure that neither disparities between national laws nor lack of coordination between competent authorities jeopardise the seamless operation of the mutual assistance system provided for in this Directive.

(7) Mutual assistance may consist of the following: the requested authority may supply the applicant authority with the information which the latter needs in order to recover claims arising in the applicant Member State and notify to the debtor all documents relating to such claims emanating from the applicant Member State. The requested authority may also recover, at the request of the applicant authority, the claims arising in the applicant Member State, or take precautionary measures to guarantee the recovery of these claims.

(8) The adoption of a uniform instrument to be used for enforcement measures in the requested Member State, as well as the adoption of a uniform standard form for notification of instruments and decisions relating to the claim, should resolve the problems of recognition and translation of instruments emanating from another Member State, which constitute a major cause of the inefficiency of the current arrangements for assistance.

(9) A legal basis for exchange of information without prior request on specific tax refunds should be created. For reasons of efficiency, it should also be rendered possible for tax officials of a Member State to attend or to participate in administrative enquiries in another Member State. Provision should also be made for more direct information exchange between services with a view to making assistance faster and more efficient.

(10) Given the increasing mobility within the internal market, and the restrictions imposed by the Treaty or other legislation on the guarantees that can be requested from taxpayers not established within the national territory, the possibilities for requesting recovery or precautionary measures in another Member State should be extended. As the age of a claim is a critical factor, it should be possible for Member States to make a request for mutual assistance, even though the domestic means of recovery have not yet been fully exhausted, inter alia, where recourse to such procedures in the applicant Member State would give rise to disproportionate difficulty.

(11) A general obligation to communicate requests and documents in a digital form and via an electronic network, and with precise rules on the use of languages for requests and documents, should allow Member States to handle requests faster and more easily.

(12) During the recovery procedure in the requested Member State, the claim, the notification made by the authorities of the applicant Member State or the instrument authorising its enforcement might be contested by the person concerned. It should be laid down that in such cases the person concerned should bring the action before the competent body of the applicant Member State and that the requested authority should suspend, unless the applicant authority requests otherwise, any enforcement proceedings which it has begun until a decision is taken by the competent body of the applicant Member State.

(13) To encourage Member States to devote sufficient resources to the recovery of other Member States' claims, the requested Member State should be able to recover the costs related to recovery from the debtor.

(14) Efficiency would be best achieved if, when executing a request for assistance, the requested authority could make use of the powers provided under its national laws applying to claims concerning the same or similar taxes or duties. In the absence of a similar tax or duty, the most appropriate procedure would be that provided under the laws of the requested Member State which applies to claims concerning the tax levied on personal income. This use of national legislation should not, as a general rule, apply with regard to the preferences accorded to claims arising in the requested Member State. However, it should be made possible to extend preferences to claims of other Member States based on an agreement between the Member States concerned.

(15) With regard to questions on limitation, it is necessary to simplify the existing rules, by providing that the suspension, interruption or prolongation of periods of limitation is in general determined according to the laws in force in the requested Member State, except where suspension, interruption or prolongation of the period of limitation is not possible under the laws in force in that State.

(16) Efficiency requires that information communicated in the course of mutual assistance may be used in the Member State receiving the information for purposes other than those provided for in this Directive, where this is allowed under the domestic legislation of both the Member State providing the information and the Member State receiving the information.

(17) This Directive should not prevent the fulfilment of any obligation to provide wider assistance ensuing from bilateral or multilateral agreements or arrangements.

(18) The measures necessary for the implementation of this Directive should be adopted in accordance with Council Decision 1999/468/EC of 28 June 1999 laying down the procedures

for the exercise of implementing powers conferred on the Commission[5].

(19) In accordance with point 34 of the Interinstitutional Agreement on better law-making, Member States are encouraged to draw up, for themselves and in the interest of the Union, their own tables illustrating, as far as possible, the correlation between this Directive and the transposition measures, and to make them public.

(20) Since the objectives of this Directive, namely the provision of a uniform system of recovery assistance within the internal market, cannot be sufficiently achieved by the Member States and can therefore, by reason of the uniformity, effectiveness and efficiency required, be better achieved at the level of the Union, the Union may adopt measures, in accordance with the principle of subsidiarity as set out in Article 5 of the Treaty. In accordance with the principle of proportionality, as set out in that Article, this Directive does not go beyond what is necessary in order to achieve those objectives.

(21) This Directive respects the fundamental rights and observes the principles which are recognised in particular by the Charter of Fundamental Rights of the European Union,

1 Opinion of 10 February 2010 (not yet published in the Official Journal).
2 Opinion of 16 July 2009 (not yet published in the Official Journal).
3 OJ L 73, 19.3.1976, p. 18.
4 OJ L 150, 10.6.2008, p. 28.
5 OJ L 184, 17.7.1999, p. 23.

HAS ADOPTED THIS DIRECTIVE:

CHAPTER I
GENERAL PROVISIONS

Article 1 Subject matter

This Directive lays down the rules under which the Member States are to provide assistance for the recovery in a Member State of any claims referred to in Article 2 which arise in another Member State.

Article 2 Scope

1. This Directive shall apply to claims relating to the following:
   (a) all taxes and duties of any kind levied by or on behalf of a Member State or its territorial or administrative subdivisions, including the local authorities, or on behalf of the Union;
   (b) refunds, interventions and other measures forming part of the system of total or partial financing of the European Agricultural Guarantee Fund (EAGF) and the European Agricultural Fund for Rural Development (EAFRD), including sums to be collected in connection with these actions;
   (c) levies and other duties provided for under the common organisation of the market for the sugar sector.
2. The scope of this Directive shall include:
   (a) administrative penalties, fines, fees and surcharges relating to the claims for which mutual assistance may be requested in accordance with paragraph 1, imposed by the administrative authorities that are competent to levy the taxes or duties concerned or carry out administrative enquiries with regard to them, or confirmed by administrative or judicial bodies at the request of those administrative authorities;
   (b) fees for certificates and similar documents issued in connection with administrative procedures related to taxes and duties;
   (c) interest and costs relating to the claims for which mutual assistance may be requested in accordance with paragraph 1 or point (a) or (b) of this paragraph.
3. This Directive shall not apply to:
   (a) compulsory social security contributions payable to the Member State or a subdivision of the Member State, or to social security institutions established under public law;
   (b) fees not referred to in paragraph 2;
   (c) dues of a contractual nature, such as consideration for public utilities;
   (d) criminal penalties imposed on the basis of a public prosecution or other criminal penalties not covered by paragraph 2(a).

Article 3 Definitions

For the purposes of this Directive:
   (a) 'applicant authority' means a central liaison office, a liaison office or a liaison department of a Member State which makes a request for assistance concerning a claim referred to in Article 2;
   (b) 'requested authority' means a central liaison office, a liaison office or a liaison department of a Member State to which a request for assistance is made;
   (c) 'person' means:
      (i) a natural person;

VAT EC

(ii) a legal person;
(iii) where the legislation in force so provides, an association of persons recognised as having the capacity to perform legal acts but lacking the legal status of a legal person; or
(iv) any other legal arrangement of whatever nature and form, which has legal personality or not, owning or managing assets which, including income derived therefrom, are subject to any of the taxes covered by this Directive;

(d) 'by electronic means' means using electronic equipment for the processing, including digital compression, and storage of data, and employing wires, radio transmission, optical technologies or other electromagnetic means;
(e) 'CCN network' means the common platform based on the common communication network (CCN) developed by the Union for all transmissions by electronic means between competent authorities in the area of customs and taxation.

Article 4 Organisation

1. Each Member State shall inform the Commission by 20 May 2010 of its competent authority or authorities (hereinafter respectively referred to as the 'competent authority') for the purpose of this Directive and shall inform the Commission without delay of any changes thereof.
The Commission shall make the information received available to the other Member States and publish a list of the competent authorities of the Member States in the Official Journal of the European Union.
2. The competent authority shall designate a central liaison office which shall have principal responsibility for contacts with other Member States in the field of mutual assistance covered by this Directive.
The central liaison office may also be designated as responsible for contacts with the Commission.
3. The competent authority of each Member State may designate liaison offices which shall be responsible for contacts with other Member States concerning mutual assistance with regard to one or more specific types or categories of taxes and duties referred to in Article 2.
4. The competent authority of each Member State may designate offices, other than the central liaison office or liaison offices, as liaison departments. Liaison departments shall request or grant mutual assistance under this Directive in relation to their specific territorial or operational competences.
5. Where a liaison office or a liaison department receives a request for mutual assistance requiring action outside the competence assigned to it, it shall forward the request without delay to the competent office or department, if known, or to the central liaison office, and inform the applicant authority thereof.
6. The competent authority of each Member State shall inform the Commission of its central liaison office and any liaison offices or liaison departments which it has designated. The Commission shall make the information received available to the Member States.
7. Every communication shall be sent by or on behalf or, on a case by case basis, with the agreement of the central liaison office, which shall ensure effectiveness of communication.

CHAPTER II
EXCHANGE OF INFORMATION

Article 5 Request for information

1. At the request of the applicant authority, the requested authority shall provide any information which is foreseeably relevant to the applicant authority in the recovery of its claims as referred to in Article 2.
For the purpose of providing that information, the requested authority shall arrange for the carrying-out of any administrative enquiries necessary to obtain it.
2. The requested authority shall not be obliged to supply information:
(a) which it would not be able to obtain for the purpose of recovering similar claims arising in the requested Member State;
(b) which would disclose any commercial, industrial or professional secrets;
(c) the disclosure of which would be liable to prejudice the security of or be contrary to the public policy of the requested Member State.
3. Paragraph 2 shall in no case be construed as permitting a requested authority of a Member State to decline to supply information solely because this information is held by a bank, other financial institution, nominee or person acting in an agency or a fiduciary capacity or because it relates to ownership interests in a person.
4. The requested authority shall inform the applicant authority of the grounds for refusing a request for information.

Article 6 Exchange of information without prior request

Where a refund of taxes or duties, other than value-added tax, relates to a person established or resident in another Member State, the Member State from which the refund is to be made may inform the Member State of establishment or residence of the upcoming refund.

Article 7 Presence in administrative offices and participation in administrative enquiries

1. By agreement between the applicant authority and the requested authority and in accordance with the arrangements laid down by the requested authority, officials authorised by the applicant authority may, with a view to promoting mutual assistance provided for in this Directive:
   (a) be present in the offices where the administrative authorities of the requested Member State carry out their duties;
   (b) be present during administrative enquiries carried out in the territory of the requested Member State;
   (c) assist the competent officials of the requested Member State during court proceedings in that Member State.

2. In so far as it is permitted under the legislation in force in the requested Member State, the agreement referred to in paragraph 1(b) may provide that officials of the applicant Member State may interview individuals and examine records.

3. Officials authorised by the applicant authority who make use of the possibilities offered by paragraphs 1 and 2 shall at all times be able to produce written authority stating their identity and their official capacity.

CHAPTER III

ASSISTANCE FOR THE NOTIFICATION OF DOCUMENTS

Article 8 Request for notification of certain documents relating to claims

1. At the request of the applicant authority, the requested authority shall notify to the addressee all documents, including those of a judicial nature, which emanate from the applicant Member State and which relate to a claim as referred to in Article 2 or to its recovery.

The request for notification shall be accompanied by a standard form containing at least the following information:
   (a) name, address and other data relevant to the identification of the addressee;
   (b) the purpose of the notification and the period within which notification should be effected;
   (c) a description of the attached document and the nature and amount of the claim concerned;
   (d) name, address and other contact details regarding:
      (i) the office responsible with regard to the attached document, and, if different;
      (ii) the office where further information can be obtained concerning the notified document or concerning the possibilities to contest the payment obligation.

2. The applicant authority shall make a request for notification pursuant to this article only when it is unable to notify in accordance with the rules governing the notification of the document concerned in the applicant Member State, or when such notification would give rise to disproportionate difficulties.

3. The requested authority shall forthwith inform the applicant authority of any action taken on its request for notification and, more especially, of the date of notification of the document to the addressee.

Article 9 Means of notification

1. The requested authority shall ensure that notification in the requested Member State is effected in accordance with the national laws, regulations and administrative practices in force in the requested Member State.

2. Paragraph 1 shall be without prejudice to any other form of notification made by a competent authority of the applicant Member State in accordance with the rules in force in that Member State. A competent authority established in the applicant Member State may notify any document directly by registered mail or electronically to a person within the territory of another Member State.

CHAPTER IV

RECOVERY OR PRECAUTIONARY MEASURES

Article 10 Request for recovery

1. At the request of the applicant authority, the requested authority shall recover claims which are the subject of an instrument permitting enforcement in the applicant Member State.

2. As soon as any relevant information relating to the matter which gave rise to the request for recovery comes to the knowledge of the applicant authority, it shall forward it to the requested authority.

Article 11 Conditions governing a request for recovery

1. The applicant authority may not make a request for recovery if and as long as the claim and/or the instrument permitting its enforcement in the applicant Member State are contested in that Member State, except in cases where the third subparagraph of Article 14(4) applies.

2. Before the applicant authority makes a request for recovery, appropriate recovery procedures available in the applicant Member State shall be applied, except in the following situations:

VAT EC

(a) where it is obvious that there are no assets for recovery in the applicant Member State or that such procedures will not result in the payment in full of the claim, and the applicant authority has specific information indicating that the person concerned has assets in the requested Member State;
(b) where recourse to such procedures in the applicant Member State would give rise to disproportionate difficulty.

Article 12 Instrument permitting enforcement in the requested Member State and other accompanying documents

1. Any request for recovery shall be accompanied by a uniform instrument permitting enforcement in the requested Member State.

This uniform instrument permitting enforcement in the requested Member State shall reflect the substantial contents of the initial instrument permitting enforcement, and constitute the sole basis for the recovery and precautionary measures taken in the requested Member State. It shall not be subject to any act of recognition, supplementing or replacement in that Member State.

The uniform instrument permitting enforcement shall contain at least the following information:

(a) information relevant to the identification of the initial instrument permitting enforcement, a description of the claim, including its nature, the period covered by the claim, any dates of relevance to the enforcement process, and the amount of the claim and its different components such as principal, interest accrued, etc.;
(b) name and other data relevant to the identification of the debtor;
(c) name, address and other contact details regarding:
    (i) the office responsible for the assessment of the claim, and, if different;
    (ii) the office where further information can be obtained concerning the claim or the possibilities for contesting the payment obligation.

2. The request for recovery of a claim may be accompanied by other documents relating to the claim issued in the applicant Member State.

Article 13 Execution of the request for recovery

1. For the purpose of the recovery in the requested Member State, any claim in respect of which a request for recovery has been made shall be treated as if it was a claim of the requested Member State, except where otherwise provided for in this Directive. The requested authority shall make use of the powers and procedures provided under the laws, regulations or administrative provisions of the requested Member State applying to claims concerning the same or, in the absence of the same, a similar tax or duty, except where otherwise provided for in this Directive.

If the requested authority considers that the same or similar taxes or duties are not levied on its territory, it shall make use of the powers and procedures provided under the laws, regulations or administrative provisions of the requested Member State which apply to claims concerning the tax levied on personal income, except where otherwise provided for in this Directive.

The requested Member State shall not be obliged to grant other Member States' claims preferences accorded to similar claims arising in that Member State, except where otherwise agreed between the Member States concerned or provided in the law of the requested Member State. A Member State which grants preferences to another Member State's claims may not refuse to grant the same preferences to the same or similar claims of other Member States on the same conditions.

The requested Member State shall recover the claim in its own currency.

2. The requested authority shall inform the applicant authority with due diligence of any action it has taken on the request for recovery.

3. From the date on which the recovery request is received, the requested authority shall charge interest for late payment in accordance with the laws, regulations and administrative provisions in force in the requested Member State.

4. The requested authority may, where the laws, regulations or administrative provisions in force in the requested Member State so permit, allow the debtor time to pay or authorise payment by instalment and it may charge interest in that respect. It shall subsequently inform the applicant authority of any such decision.

5. Without prejudice to Article 20(1), the requested authority shall remit to the applicant authority the amounts recovered with respect to the claim and the interest referred to in paragraphs 3 and 4 of this Article.

Article 14 Disputes

1. Disputes concerning the claim, the initial instrument permitting enforcement in the applicant Member State or the uniform instrument permitting enforcement in the requested Member State and disputes concerning the validity of a notification made by a competent authority of the applicant Member State shall fall within the competence of the competent bodies of the applicant Member State. If, in the course of the recovery procedure, the claim, the initial instrument permitting enforcement in the applicant Member State or the uniform instrument permitting enforcement in the

requested Member State is contested by an interested party, the requested authority shall inform that party that such an action must be brought by the latter before the competent body of the applicant Member State in accordance with the laws in force there.

2. Disputes concerning the enforcement measures taken in the requested Member State or concerning the validity of a notification made by a competent authority of the requested Member State shall be brought before the competent body of that Member State in accordance with its laws and regulations.

3. Where an action as referred to in paragraph 1 has been brought before the competent body of the applicant Member State, the applicant authority shall inform the requested authority thereof and shall indicate the extent to which the claim is not contested.

4. As soon as the requested authority has received the information referred to in paragraph 3, either from the applicant authority or from the interested party, it shall suspend the enforcement procedure, as far as the contested part of the claim is concerned, pending the decision of the body competent in the matter, unless the applicant authority requests otherwise in accordance with the third subparagraph of this paragraph.

At the request of the applicant authority, or where otherwise deemed to be necessary by the requested authority, and without prejudice to Article 16, the requested authority may take precautionary measures to guarantee recovery in so far as the laws or regulations in force in the requested Member State allow such action.

The applicant authority may, in accordance with the laws, regulations and administrative practices in force in the applicant Member State, ask the requested authority to recover a contested claim or the contested part of a claim, in so far as the relevant laws, regulations and administrative practices in force in the requested Member State allow such action. Any such request shall be reasoned. If the result of contestation is subsequently favourable to the debtor, the applicant authority shall be liable for reimbursing any sums recovered, together with any compensation due, in accordance with the laws in force in the requested Member State.

If a mutual agreement procedure has been initiated by the competent authorities of the applicant Member State or the requested Member State, and the outcome of the procedure may affect the claim in respect of which assistance has been requested, the recovery measures shall be suspended or stopped until that procedure has been terminated, unless it concerns a case of immediate urgency because of fraud or insolvency. If the recovery measures are suspended or stopped, the second subparagraph shall apply.

Article 15 Amendment or withdrawal of the request for recovery assistance

1. The applicant authority shall inform the requested authority immediately of any subsequent amendment to its request for recovery or of the withdrawal of its request, indicating the reasons for amendment or withdrawal.

2. If the amendment of the request is caused by a decision of the competent body referred to in Article 14(1), the applicant authority shall communicate this decision together with a revised uniform instrument permitting enforcement in the requested Member State. The requested authority shall then proceed with further recovery measures on the basis of the revised instrument.

Recovery or precautionary measures already taken on the basis of the original uniform instrument permitting enforcement in the requested Member State may be continued on the basis of the revised instrument, unless the amendment of the request is due to invalidity of the initial instrument permitting enforcement in the applicant Member State or the original uniform instrument permitting enforcement in the requested Member State.

Articles 12 and 14 shall apply in relation to the revised instrument.

Article 16 Request for precautionary measures

1. At the request of the applicant authority, the requested authority shall take precautionary measures, if allowed by its national law and in accordance with its administrative practices, to ensure recovery where a claim or the instrument permitting enforcement in the applicant Member State is contested at the time when the request is made, or where the claim is not yet the subject of an instrument permitting enforcement in the applicant Member State, in so far as precautionary measures are also possible, in a similar situation, under the national law and administrative practices of the applicant Member State.

The document drawn up for permitting precautionary measures in the applicant Member State and relating to the claim for which mutual assistance is requested, if any, shall be attached to the request for precautionary measures in the requested Member State. This document shall not be subject to any act of recognition, supplementing or replacement in the requested Member State.

2. The request for precautionary measures may be accompanied by other documents relating to the claim, issued in the applicant Member State.

Article 17 Rules governing the request for precautionary measures

In order to give effect to Article 16, Articles 10(2), 13(1) and (2), 14, and 15 shall apply *mutatis mutandis*.

Article 18 Limits to the requested authority's obligations

1. The requested authority shall not be obliged to grant the assistance provided for in Articles 10 to 16 if recovery of the claim would, because of the situation of the debtor, create serious economic or social difficulties in the requested Member State, in so far as the laws, regulations and administrative practices in force in that Member State allow such exception for national claims.

2. The requested authority shall not be obliged to grant the assistance provided for in Articles 5 and 7 to 16, if the initial request for assistance pursuant to Article 5, 7, 8, 10 or 16 is made in respect of claims which are more than 5 years old, dating from the due date of the claim in the applicant Member State to the date of the initial request for assistance.

However, in cases where the claim or the initial instrument permitting enforcement in the applicant Member State is contested, the 5-year period shall be deemed to begin from the moment when it is established in the applicant Member State that the claim or the instrument permitting enforcement may no longer be contested.

Moreover, in cases where a postponement of the payment or instalment plan is granted by the competent authorities of the applicant Member State, the 5-year period shall be deemed to begin from the moment when the entire payment period has come to its end.

However, in those cases the requested authority shall not be obliged to grant the assistance in respect of claims which are more than 10 years old, dating from the due date of the claim in the applicant Member State.

3. A Member State shall not be obliged to grant assistance if the total amount of the claims covered by this Directive, for which assistance is requested, is less than EUR 1 500.

4. The requested authority shall inform the applicant authority of the grounds for refusing a request for assistance.

Article 19 Questions on limitation

1. Questions concerning periods of limitation shall be governed solely by the laws in force in the applicant Member State.

2. In relation to the suspension, interruption or prolongation of periods of limitation, any steps taken in the recovery of claims by or on behalf of the requested authority in pursuance of a request for assistance which have the effect of suspending, interrupting or prolonging the period of limitation according to the laws in force in the requested Member State shall be deemed to have the same effect in the applicant Member State, on condition that the corresponding effect is provided for under the laws in force in the applicant Member State.

If suspension, interruption or prolongation of the period of limitation is not possible under the laws in force in the requested Member State, any steps taken in the recovery of claims by or on behalf of the requested authority in pursuance of a request for assistance which, if they had been carried out by or on behalf of the applicant authority in its Member State, would have had the effect of suspending, interrupting or prolonging the period of limitation according to the laws in force in the applicant Member State shall be deemed to have been taken in the latter State, in so far as that effect is concerned.

The first and second subparagraphs shall not affect the right of the competent authorities in the applicant Member State to take measures to suspend, interrupt or prolong the period of limitation in accordance with the laws in force in that Member State.

3. The applicant authority and the requested authority shall inform each other of any action which interrupts, suspends or prolongs the limitation period of the claim for which the recovery or precautionary measures were requested, or which may have this effect.

Article 20 Costs

1. In addition to the amounts referred to in Article 13(5), the requested authority shall seek to recover from the person concerned and retain the costs linked to the recovery that it incurred, in accordance with the laws and regulations of the requested Member State.

2. Member States shall renounce all claims on each other for the reimbursement of costs arising from any mutual assistance they grant each other pursuant to this Directive.

However, where recovery creates a specific problem, concerns a very large amount in costs or relates to organised crime, the applicant and requested authorities may agree reimbursement arrangements specific to the cases in question.

3. Notwithstanding paragraph 2, the applicant Member State shall remain liable to the requested Member State for any costs and any losses incurred as a result of actions held to be unfounded, as far as either the substance of the claim or the validity of the instrument permitting enforcement and/or precautionary measures issued by the applicant authority are concerned.

CHAPTER V

GENERAL RULES GOVERNING ALL TYPES OF ASSISTANCE REQUESTS

Article 21 Standard forms and means of communication

1. Requests pursuant to Article 5(1) for information, requests pursuant to Article 8(1) for notification, requests pursuant to Article 10(1) for recovery or requests pursuant to Article 16(1) for precautionary measures shall be sent by electronic means, using a standard form, unless this is impracticable for technical reasons. As far as possible, these forms shall also be used for any further communication with regard to the request.

The uniform instrument permitting enforcement in the requested Member State, the document permitting precautionary measures in the applicant Member State and the other documents referred to in Articles 12 and 16 shall also be sent by electronic means, unless this is impracticable for technical reasons.

Where appropriate, the standard forms may be accompanied by reports, statements and any other documents, or certified true copies or extracts thereof, which shall also be sent by electronic means, unless this is impracticable for technical reasons.

Standard forms and communication by electronic means may also be used for the exchange of information pursuant to Article 6.

2. Paragraph 1 shall not apply to the information and documentation obtained through the presence in administrative offices in another Member State or through the participation in administrative enquiries in another Member State, in accordance with Article 7.

3. If communication is not made by electronic means or with use of standard forms, this shall not affect the validity of the information obtained or of the measures taken in the execution of a request for assistance.

Article 22 Use of languages

1. All requests for assistance, standard forms for notification and uniform instruments permitting enforcement in the requested Member States shall be sent in, or shall be accompanied by a translation into, the official language, or one of the official languages, of the requested Member State. The fact that certain parts thereof are written in a language other than the official language, or one of the official languages, of the requested Member State, shall not affect their validity or the validity of the procedure, in so far as that other language is one agreed between the Member States concerned.

2. The documents for which notification is requested pursuant to Article 8 may be sent to the requested authority in an official language of the applicant Member State.

3. Where a request is accompanied by documents other than those referred to in paragraphs 1 and 2, the requested authority may, where necessary, require from the applicant authority a translation of such documents into the official language, or one of the official languages of the requested Member State, or into any other language bilaterally agreed between the Member States concerned.

Article 23 Disclosure of information and documents

1. Information communicated in any form pursuant to this Directive shall be covered by the obligation of official secrecy and enjoy the protection extended to similar information under the national law of the Member State which received it.

Such information may be used for the purpose of applying enforcement or precautionary measures with regard to claims covered by this Directive. It may also be used for assessment and enforcement of compulsory social security contributions.

2. Persons duly accredited by the Security Accreditation Authority of the European Commission may have access to this information only in so far as it is necessary for care, maintenance and development of the CCN network.

3. The Member State providing the information shall permit its use for purposes other than those referred to in paragraph 1 in the Member State receiving the information, if, under the legislation of the Member State providing the information, the information may be used for similar purposes.

4. Where the applicant or requested authority considers that information obtained pursuant to this Directive is likely to be useful for the purposes referred to in paragraph 1 to a third Member State, it may transmit that information to that third Member State, provided this transmission is in accordance with the rules and procedures laid down in this Directive. It shall inform the Member State of origin of the information about its intention to share that information with a third Member State. The Member State of origin of the information may oppose such a sharing of information within ten working days of the date at which it received the communication from the Member State wishing to share the information.

5. Permission to use information pursuant to paragraph 3 which has been transmitted pursuant to paragraph 4 may be granted only by the Member State from which the information originates.

6. Information communicated in any form pursuant to this Directive may be invoked or used as evidence by all authorities within the Member State receiving the information on the same basis as similar information obtained within that State.

CHAPTER VI
FINAL PROVISIONS

Article 24 Application of other agreements on assistance

1. This Directive shall be without prejudice to the fulfilment of any obligation to provide wider assistance ensuing from bilateral or multilateral agreements or arrangements, including for the notification of legal or extra-legal acts.

2. Where the Member States conclude such bilateral or multilateral agreements or arrangements on matters covered by this Directive other than to deal with individual cases, they shall inform the Commission thereof without delay. The Commission shall in turn inform the other Member States.

3. When providing such greater measure of mutual assistance under a bilateral or multilateral agreement or arrangement, Member States may make use of the electronic communication network and the standard forms adopted for the implementation of this Directive.

Article 25 Committee

1. The Commission shall be assisted by the Recovery Committee.

2. Where reference is made to this paragraph, Articles 5 and 7 of Decision 1999/468/EC shall apply. The period referred to in Article 5(6) of Decision 1999/468/EC shall be set at 3 months.

Article 26 Implementing provisions

The Commission shall adopt, in accordance with the procedure referred to in Article 25(2), detailed rules for implementing Article 4(2), (3) and (4), Article 5(1), Articles 8, 10, 12(1), Article 13(2), (3), (4) and (5), Articles 15, 16(1) and 21(1).

Those rules shall relate to at least the following:

(a) the practical arrangements with regard to the organisation of the contacts between the central liaison offices, the other liaison offices and the liaison departments, referred to in Article 4(2), (3) and (4), of different Member States, and the contacts with the Commission;

(b) the means by which communications between authorities may be transmitted;

(c) the format and other details of the standard forms to be used for the purposes of Article 5(1), Articles 8, 10(1), Article 12(1) and Article 16(1);

(d) the conversion of the sums to be recovered and the transfer of sums recovered.

Article 27 Reporting

1. Each Member State shall inform the Commission annually by 31 March of the following:

(a) the number of requests for information, notification and recovery or for precautionary measures which it sends to each requested Member State and which it receives from each applicant Member State each year;

(b) the amount of the claims for which recovery assistance is requested and the amounts recovered.

2. Member States may also provide any other information that may be useful for evaluating the provision of mutual assistance under this Directive.

3. The Commission shall report every 5 years to the European Parliament and the Council on the operation of the arrangements established by this Directive.

Article 28 Transposition

1. Member States shall adopt and publish, by 31 December 2011, the laws, regulations and administrative provisions necessary to comply with this Directive. They shall forthwith inform the Commission thereof.

They shall apply these provisions from 1 January 2012.

When these provisions are adopted by Member States, they shall contain a reference to this Directive or shall be accompanied by such a reference on the occasion of their official publication. The methods of making such reference shall be laid down by Member States.

2. Member States shall communicate to the Commission the text of the main provisions of national law which they adopt in the field covered by this Directive.

Article 29 Repeal of Directive 2008/55/EC

Directive 2008/55/EC is repealed with effect from 1 January 2012.

References to the repealed Directive shall be construed as references to this Directive.

Article 30 Entry into force

This Directive shall enter into force on the 20th day following its publication in the Official Journal of the European Union.

Article 31 Addressees

This Directive is addressed to the Member States.

Done at Brussels, 16 March 2010.

COUNCIL DIRECTIVE 2011/16/EU OF 15 FEBRUARY 2011 ON ADMINISTRATIVE COOPERATION IN THE FIELD OF TAXATION AND REPEALING DIRECTIVE 77/799/EEC

THE COUNCIL OF THE EUROPEAN UNION,

Having regard to the Treaty on the Functioning of the European Union, and in particular Articles 113 and 115 thereof,

Having regard to the proposal from the European Commission,

Having regard to the opinion of the European Parliament[1],

Having regard to the opinion of the European Economic and Social Committee[2],

Acting in accordance with a special legislative procedure,

Whereas:

(1) The Member States' need for mutual assistance in the field of taxation is growing rapidly in a globalised era. There is a tremendous development of the mobility of taxpayers, of the number of cross-border transactions and of the internationalisation of financial instruments, which makes it difficult for Member States to assess taxes due properly. This increasing difficulty affects the functioning of taxation systems and entails double taxation, which itself incites tax fraud and tax evasion, while the powers of controls remain at national level. It thus jeopardises the functioning of the internal market.

(2) Therefore, a single Member State cannot manage its internal taxation system, especially as regards direct taxation, without receiving information from other Member States. In order to overcome the negative effects of this phenomenon, it is indispensable to develop new administrative cooperation between the Member States' tax administrations. There is a need for instruments likely to create confidence between Member States, by setting up the same rules, obligations and rights for all Member States.

(3) Therefore, a completely new approach should be taken by creating a new text to give Member States the power to efficiently cooperate at international level to overcome the negative effects of an ever-increasing globalisation on the internal market.

(4) In such a context, the existing Council Directive 77/799/EEC of 19 December 1977 concerning mutual assistance by the competent authorities of the Member States in the field of direct taxation and taxation of insurance premiums[3] no longer provides for appropriate measures. Its deep weaknesses have been looked into by the Ad hoc Council Working Party on Tax Fraud in its report of 22 May 2000 and more recently by the Commission Communication on Preventing and Combating Corporate and Financial Malpractice of 27 September 2004 and the Commission Communication concerning the need to develop a coordinated strategy to improve the fight against fiscal fraud of 31 May 2006.

(5) Directive 77/799/EEC, even with its later amendments, was designed in a different context to current internal market requirements and is no longer able to meet the new requirements of administrative cooperation.

(6) Due to the number and the importance of adaptations to be made to Directive 77/799/EEC, a mere amendment thereof would not be sufficient to fulfil the objectives described above. Directive 77/799/EEC should therefore be repealed and replaced by a new legal instrument. That instrument should apply to direct taxes and indirect taxes that are not yet covered by other Union legislation. To this end, this new Directive is considered to be the proper instrument in terms of effective administrative cooperation.

(7) This Directive builds on the achievements of Directive 77/799/EEC but provides for clearer and more precise rules governing administrative cooperation between Member States where necessary, in order to establish, especially as regards the exchange of information, a wider scope of administrative cooperation between Member States. Clearer rules should also make it possible in particular to cover all legal and natural persons in the Union, taking into account the ever- increasing range of legal arrangements, including not only traditional arrangements such as trusts, foundations and investment funds, but any new instrument which may be set up by taxpayers in the Member States.

(8) There should be more direct contact between Member States' local or national offices in charge of administrative cooperation, with communication between central liaison offices being the rule. The lack of direct contacts leads to inefficiency, under-use of the arrangements for administrative cooperation and delays in communication. Provision should therefore be made to bring about more direct contacts between services with a view to making cooperation more efficient and faster. The assignment of competences to the liaison departments should be deferred to the national provisions of each Member State.

(9) Member States should exchange information concerning particular cases where requested by another Member State and should make the necessary enquiries to obtain such

VAT EC

information. The standard of 'foreseeable relevance' is intended to provide for exchange of information in tax matters to the widest possible extent and, at the same time, to clarify that Member States are not at liberty to engage in 'fishing expeditions' or to request information that is unlikely to be relevant to the tax affairs of a given taxpayer. While Article 20 of this Directive contains procedural requirements, those provisions need to be interpreted liberally in order not to frustrate the effective exchange of information.

(10) It is recognised that the mandatory automatic exchange of information without preconditions is the most effective means of enhancing the correct assessment of taxes in cross-border situations and of fighting fraud. To that end, a step-by-step approach should therefore be followed starting with the automatic exchange of available information on five categories and reviewing the relevant provisions after a report by the Commission.

(11) The spontaneous exchange of information between Member States should also be strengthened and encouraged.

(12) Time limits for the provision of information under this Directive should be laid down in order to ensure that the information exchange is timely and thus effective.

(13) It is important that officials of the tax administration of one Member State are allowed to be present in the territory of another Member State.

(14) Since the tax situation of one or more persons liable to tax established in several Member States is often of common or complementary interest, it should be made possible for simultaneous controls to be carried out on such persons by two or more Member States, by mutual agreement and on a voluntary basis.

(15) In view of the legal requirement in certain Member States that a taxpayer be notified of decisions and instruments concerning his tax liability and of the ensuing difficulties for the tax authorities, including cases where the taxpayer has relocated to another Member State, it is desirable that, in such circumstances, the tax authorities should be able to call upon the cooperation of the competent authorities of the Member State to which the taxpayer has relocated.

(16) Feedback on information sent will encourage administrative cooperation between Member States.

(17) Collaboration between the Member States and the Commission is necessary for the permanent study of cooperation procedures and the sharing of experience and best practices in the fields considered.

(18) It is important for the efficiency of administrative cooperation that information and documents obtained under this Directive could, subject to the restrictions laid down in this Directive, be used by the Member State that received them also for other purposes. It is also important that Member States could transmit that information to a third country, under certain conditions.

(19) The situations in which a requested Member State may refuse to provide information should be clearly defined and limited, taking into account certain private interests which should be protected as well as the public interest.

(20) However, a Member State should not refuse to transmit information because it has no domestic interest or because the information is held by a bank, other financial institution, nominee or person acting in an agency or fiduciary capacity or because it relates to ownership interests in a person.

(21) This Directive contains minimum rules and should therefore not affect Member States' right to enter into wider cooperation with other Member States under their national legislation or in the framework of bilateral or multilateral agreements concluded with other Member States.

(22) It should also be made clear that where a Member State provides a wider cooperation to a third country than is provided for under this Directive, it should not refuse to provide such wider cooperation to other Member States wishing to enter into such mutual wider cooperation.

(23) The exchange of information should be made through standardised forms, formats and channels of communication.

(24) An evaluation of the effectiveness of administrative cooperation should be made, especially on the basis of statistics.

(25) The measures necessary for the implementation of this Directive should be adopted in accordance with Council Decision 1999/468/EC of 28 June 1999 laying down the procedures for the exercise of implementing powers conferred on the Commission[4].

(26) In accordance with point 34 of the Interinstitutional Agreement on better law-making, Member States are encouraged to draw up, for themselves and in the interests of the Union, their own tables illustrating, as far as possible, the correlation between this Directive and the transposition measures, and to make them public.

(27) All exchange of information referred to in this Directive is subject to the provisions

implementing Directive 95/46/EC of the European Parliament and of the Council of 24 October 1995 on the protection of individuals with regard to the processing of personal data and on the free movement of such data[5] and to Regulation (EC) No 45/2001 of the European Parliament and of the Council of 18 December 2000 on the protection of individuals with regard to the processing of personal data by the Community institutions and bodies and on the free movement of such data[6]. However, it is appropriate to consider limitations of certain rights and obligations laid down by Directive 95/46/EC in order to safeguard the interests referred to in Article 13(1)(e) of that Directive. Such limitations are necessary and proportionate in view of the potential loss of revenue for Member States and the crucial importance of information covered by this Directive for the effectiveness of the fight against fraud.

(28) This Directive respects the fundamental rights and observes the principles which are recognised in particular by the Charter of Fundamental Rights of the European Union.

(29) Since the objective of this Directive, namely the efficient administrative cooperation between Member States to overcome the negative effects of the increasing globalisation on the internal market, cannot be sufficiently achieved by the Member States and can therefore, by reason of the uniformity and effectiveness required, be better achieved at the level of the Union, the Union may adopt measures, in accordance with the principle of subsidiarity as set out in Article 5 of the Treaty on the European Union. In accordance with the principle of proportionality, as set out in that Article, this Directive does not go beyond what is necessary in order to achieve that objective,

1 Opinion of 10 February 2010 (not yet published in the Official Journal).
2 Opinion of 16 July 2009 (not yet published in the Official Journal).
3 OJ L 336, 27.12.1977, p. 15.
4 OJ L 184, 17.7.1999, p. 23.
5 OJ L 281, 23.11.1995, p. 31.
6 OJ L 8, 12.1.2001, p. 1.

HAS ADOPTED THIS DIRECTIVE:

CHAPTER I
GENERAL PROVISIONS

***Article 1* Subject matter**

1. This Directive lays down the rules and procedures under which the Member States shall cooperate with each other with a view to exchanging information that is foreseeably relevant to the administration and enforcement of the domestic laws of the Member States concerning the taxes referred to in Article 2.
2. This Directive also lays down provisions for the exchange of information referred to in paragraph 1 by electronic means, as well as rules and procedures under which the Member States and the Commission are to cooperate on matters concerning coordination and evaluation.
3. This Directive shall not affect the application in the Member States of the rules on mutual assistance in criminal matters. It shall also be without prejudice to the fulfilment of any obligations of the Member States in relation to wider administrative cooperation ensuing from other legal instruments, including bilateral or multilateral agreements.

***Article 2* Scope**

1. This Directive shall apply to all taxes of any kind levied by, or on behalf of, a Member State or the Member State's territorial or administrative subdivisions, including the local authorities.
2. Notwithstanding paragraph 1, this Directive shall not apply to value added tax and customs duties, or to excise duties covered by other Union legislation on administrative cooperation between Member States. This Directive shall also not apply to compulsory social security contributions payable to the Member State or a subdivision of the Member State or to social security institutions established under public law.
3. In no case shall the taxes referred to in paragraph 1 be construed as including:
   (a) fees, such as for certificates and other documents issued by public authorities; or
   (b) dues of a contractual nature, such as consideration for public utilities.
4. This Directive shall apply to the taxes referred to in paragraph 1 levied within the territory to which the Treaties apply by virtue of Article 52 of the Treaty on the European Union.

***Article 3* Definitions**

For the purposes of this Directive the following definitions shall apply:

1. 'competent authority' of a Member State means the authority which has been designated as such by that Member State. When acting pursuant to this Directive, the central liaison office, a liaison department or a competent official shall also be deemed to be competent authorities by delegation according to Article 4;
2. 'central liaison office' means the office which has been designated as such with principal responsibility for contacts with other Member States in the field of administrative cooperation;

VAT EC

3. 'liaison department' means any office other than the central liaison office which has been designated as such to directly exchange information pursuant to this Directive;
4. 'competent official' means any official who is authorised to directly exchange information pursuant to this Directive;
5. 'requesting authority' means the central liaison office, a liaison department or any competent official of a Member State who makes a request for assistance on behalf of the competent authority;
6. 'requested authority' means the central liaison office, a liaison department or any competent official of a Member State who receives a request for assistance on behalf of the competent authority;
7. 'administrative enquiry' means all controls, checks and other action taken by Member States in the performance of their duties with a view to ensuring the proper application of tax legislation;
8. 'exchange of information on request' means the exchange of information based on a request made by the requesting Member State to the requested Member State in a specific case;

[9. "automatic exchange" means the systematic communication of predefined information on residents in other Member States to the relevant Member State of residence, without prior request, at pre-established regular intervals. In the context of Article 8, available information refers to information in the tax files of the Member State communicating the information, which is retrievable in accordance with the procedures for gathering and processing information in that Member State. In the context of Article 8(3a), Article 8(7a), Article 21(2) and Article 25(2) and (3) any capitalised term shall have the meaning that it has under the corresponding definitions set out in Annex I.][1]

10. 'spontaneous exchange' means the non-systematic communication, at any moment and without prior request, of information to another Member State;
11. 'person' means:
    (a) a natural person;
    (b) a legal person;
    (c) where the legislation in force so provides, an association of persons recognised as having the capacity to perform legal acts but lacking the status of a legal person; or
    (d) any other legal arrangement of whatever nature and form, regardless of whether it has legal personality, owning or managing assets, which, including income derived therefrom, are subject to any of the taxes covered by this Directive;
12. 'by electronic means' means using electronic equipment for the processing, including digital compression, and storage of data, and employing wires, radio transmission, optical technologies or other electromagnetic means;
13. 'CCN network' means the common platform based on the common communication network (CCN), developed by the Union for all transmissions by electronic means between competent authorities in the area of customs and taxation.

Amendments—[1] Para 9 substituted by Council Directive 2014/107/EU Art 1(1) with effect from 5 January 2015. See Art 2 for implementation provisions (deadline for implementation is 31 December 2015, with measures to apply from 1 January 2016) (OJ L 359, 16.12.2014, p 1).

Article 4 Organisation

1. Each Member State shall inform the Commission, within one month from 11 March 2011, of its competent authority for the purposes of this Directive and shall inform the Commission without delay of any change thereto.

The Commission shall make the information available to the other Member States and publish a list of the authorities of the Member States in the *Official Journal of the European Union*.

2. The competent authority shall designate a single central liaison office. The competent authority shall be responsible for informing the Commission and the other Member States thereof.

The central liaison office may also be designated as responsible for contacts with the Commission. The competent authority shall be responsible for informing the Commission thereof.

3. The competent authority of each Member State may designate liaison departments with the competence assigned according to its national legislation or policy. The central liaison office shall be responsible for keeping the list of liaison departments up to date and making it available to the central liaison offices of the other Member States concerned and to the Commission.

4. The competent authority of each Member State may designate competent officials. The central liaison office shall be responsible for keeping the list of competent officials up to date and making it available to the central liaison offices of the other Member States concerned and to the Commission.

5. The officials engaged in administrative cooperation pursuant to this Directive shall in any case be deemed to be competent officials for that purpose, in accordance with arrangements laid down by the competent authorities.

6. Where a liaison department or a competent official sends or receives a request or a reply to a request for cooperation, it shall inform the central liaison office of its Member State under the procedures laid down by that Member State.

7. Where a liaison department or a competent official receives a request for cooperation requiring action which falls outside the competence it is assigned according to the national legislation or policy of its Member State, it shall forward such request without delay to the central liaison office of its Member State and inform the requesting authority thereof. In such a case, the period laid down in Article 7 shall start the day after the request for cooperation is forwarded to the central liaison office.

CHAPTER II
EXCHANGE OF INFORMATION

SECTION I
EXCHANGE OF INFORMATION ON REQUEST

***Article 5* Procedure for the exchange of information on request**

At the request of the requesting authority, the requested authority shall communicate to the requesting authority any information referred to in Article 1(1) that it has in its possession or that it obtains as a result of administrative enquiries.

***Article 6* Administrative enquiries**

1. The requested authority shall arrange for the carrying out of any administrative enquiries necessary to obtain the information referred to in Article 5.
2. The request referred to in Article 5 may contain a reasoned request for a specific administrative enquiry. If the requested authority takes the view that no administrative enquiry is necessary, it shall immediately inform the requesting authority of the reasons thereof.
3. In order to obtain the requested information or to conduct the administrative enquiry requested, the requested authority shall follow the same procedures as it would when acting on its own initiative or at the request of another authority in its own Member State.
4. When specifically requested by the requesting authority, the requested authority shall communicate original documents provided that this is not contrary to the provisions in force in the Member State of the requested authority.

***Article 7* Time limits**

1. The requested authority shall provide the information referred to in Article 5 as quickly as possible, and no later than six months from the date of receipt of the request.
However, where the requested authority is already in possession of that information, the information shall be transmitted within two months of that date.
2. In certain special cases, time limits other than those provided for in paragraph 1 may be agreed upon between the requested and the requesting authorities.
3. The requested authority shall confirm immediately and in any event no later than seven working days from receipt, if possible by electronic means, receipt of a request to the requesting authority.
4. Within one month of receipt of the request, the requested authority shall notify the requesting authority of any deficiencies in the request and of the need for any additional background information. In such a case, the time limits provided for in paragraph 1 shall start the day after the requested authority has received the additional information needed.
5. Where the requested authority is unable to respond to the request by the relevant time limit, it shall inform the requesting authority immediately and in any event within three months of the receipt of the request, of the reasons for its failure to do so, and the date by which it considers it might be able to respond.
6. Where the requested authority is not in possession of the requested information and is unable to respond to the request for information or refuses to do so on the grounds provided for in Article 17, it shall inform the requesting authority of the reasons thereof immediately and in any event within one month of receipt of the request.

SECTION II
MANDATORY AUTOMATIC EXCHANGE OF INFORMATION

***Article 8* Scope and conditions of mandatory automatic exchange of information**

1. The competent authority of each Member State shall, by automatic exchange, communicate to the competent authority of any other Member State, information regarding taxable periods as from 1 January 2014 that is available concerning residents in that other Member State, on the following specific categories of income and capital as they are to be understood under the national legislation of the Member State which communicates the information:
   (a) income from employment;
   (b) director's fees;
   (c) life insurance products not covered by other Union legal instruments on exchange of information and other similar measures;
   (d) pensions;
   (e) ownership of and income from immovable property.

VAT EC

2. Before 1 January 2014, Member States shall inform the Commission of the categories listed in paragraph 1 in respect of which they have information available. They shall inform the Commission of any subsequent changes thereto.

[3. The competent authority of a Member State may indicate to the competent authority of any other Member State that it does not wish to receive information on one or several of the categories of income and capital referred to in paragraph 1. It shall also inform the Commission thereof.

A Member State may be considered as not wishing to receive information in accordance with paragraph 1, if it does not inform the Commission of any single category in respect of which it has information available.][1]

[3a. Each Member State shall take the necessary measures to require its Reporting Financial Institutions to perform the reporting and due diligence rules included in Annexes I and II and to ensure effective implementation of, and compliance with, such rules in accordance with Section IX of Annex I.

Pursuant to the applicable reporting and due diligence rules contained in Annexes I and II, the competent authority of each Member State shall, by automatic exchange, communicate within the deadline laid down in point (b) of paragraph 6 to the competent authority of any other Member State, the following information regarding taxable periods as from 1 January 2016 concerning a Reportable Account:

(a) the name, address, TIN(s) and date and place of birth (in the case of an individual) of each Reportable Person that is an Account Holder of the account and, in the case of any Entity that is an Account Holder and that, after application of due diligence rules consistent with the Annexes, is identified as having one or more Controlling Persons that is a Reportable Person, the name, address, and TIN(s) of the Entity and the name, address, TIN(s) and date and place of birth of each Reportable Person;

(b) the account number (or functional equivalent in the absence of an account number);

(c) the name and identifying number (if any) of the Reporting Financial Institution;

(d) the account balance or value (including, in the case of a Cash Value Insurance Contract or Annuity Contract, the Cash Value or surrender value) as of the end of the relevant calendar year or other appropriate reporting period or, if the account was closed during such year or period, the closure of the account;

(e) in the case of any Custodial Account:

(i) the total gross amount of interest, the total gross amount of dividends, and the total gross amount of other income generated with respect to the assets held in the account, in each case paid or credited to the account (or with respect to the account) during the calendar year or other appropriate reporting period; and

(ii) the total gross proceeds from the sale or redemption of Financial Assets paid or credited to the account during the calendar year or other appropriate reporting period with respect to which the Reporting Financial Institution acted as a custodian, broker, nominee, or otherwise as an agent for the Account Holder;

(f) in the case of any Depository Account, the total gross amount of interest paid or credited to the account during the calendar year or other appropriate reporting period; and

(g) in the case of any account not described in point (e) or point (f), the total gross amount paid or credited to the Account Holder with respect to the account during the calendar year or other appropriate reporting period with respect to which the Reporting Financial Institution is the obligor or debtor, including the aggregate amount of any redemption payments made to the Account Holder during the calendar year or other appropriate reporting period.

For the purposes of the exchange of information under this paragraph, unless otherwise foreseen in this paragraph or in the Annexes, the amount and characterisation of payments made with respect to a Reportable Account shall be determined in accordance with national legislation of the Member State which communicates the information.

The first and second subparagraphs of this paragraph shall prevail over point (c) of paragraph 1 or any other Union legal instrument, including Council Directive 2003/48/EC*, to the extent that the exchange of information at issue would fall within the scope of point (c) of paragraph 1 or of any other Union legal instrument, including Directive 2003/48/EC.

4. Before 1 July 2016, Member States shall provide the Commission on an annual basis with statistics on the volume of automatic exchanges and, to the extent possible, with information on the administrative and other relevant costs and benefits relating to exchanges that have taken place and any potential changes, for both tax administrations and third parties.

[5. Before 1 July 2017, the Commission shall submit a report that provides an overview and an assessment of the statistics and information received, on issues such as the administrative and other relevant costs and benefits of the automatic exchange of information, as well as practical aspects linked thereto. If appropriate, the Commission shall present a proposal to the Council regarding the categories and the conditions laid down in paragraph 1, including the condition that information concerning residents in other Member States has to be available, or the items referred to in paragraph 3a, or both.

When examining a proposal presented by the Commission, the Council shall assess further strengthening of the efficiency and functioning of the automatic exchange of information and raising the standard thereof, with the aim of providing that:

(a) the competent authority of each Member State shall, by automatic exchange, communicate to the competent authority of any other Member State, information regarding taxable periods as from 1 January 2017 concerning residents in that other Member State, on all categories of income and capital listed in paragraph 1, as they are to be understood under the national legislation of the Member State communicating the information; and

(b) the lists of categories and items laid down in paragraphs 1 and 3a be extended to include other categories and items, including royalties.][1]

[6. The communication of information shall take place as follows:

(a) for the categories laid down in paragraph 1: at least once a year, within six months following the end of the tax year of the Member State during which the information became available;

(b) for the information laid down in paragraph 3a: annually, within nine months following the end of the calendar year or other appropriate reporting period to which the information relates.][1]

7. The Commission shall adopt the practical arrangements for the automatic exchange of information, in accordance with the procedure referred to in Article 26(2), before the dates referred to in Article 29(1).

[7a. For the purposes of subparagraphs B.1(c) and C.17(g) of Section VIII of Annex I, each Member State shall, by 31 July 2015, provide to the Commission the list of entities and accounts that are to be treated, respectively, as Non-Reporting Financial Institutions and Excluded Accounts. Each Member State shall also inform the Commission if any changes in this respect occur. The Commission shall publish in the Official Journal of the European Union a compiled list of the information received and shall update the list as necessary.

Member States shall ensure that those types of Non-Reporting Financial Institutions and Excluded Accounts satisfy all the requirements listed in subparagraphs B.1(c) and C.17(g) of Section VIII of Annex I, and in particular that the status of a Financial Institution as a Non-Reporting Financial Institution or the status of an account as an Excluded Account does not frustrate the purposes of this Directive.][1]

8. Where Member States agree on the automatic exchange of information for additional categories of income and capital in bilateral or multilateral agreements which they conclude with other Member States, they shall communicate those agreements to the Commission which shall make those agreements available to all the other Member States

Cross-reference—See art 29 below: member states shall bring into force the laws, regulations and administrative provisions necessary to comply with Article 8 of this Directive with effect from 1 January 2015.

* Council Directive 2003/48/EC of 3 June 2003 on taxation of savings income in the form of interest payments (OJ L 157, 26.6.2003, p. 38).

Amendments—[1] Paras 3, 5, 6 substituted and paras 3a, 7a inserted, by Council Directive 2014/107/EU Art 1(2) with effect from 5 January 2015. See Art 2 for implementation provisions (deadline for implementation is 31 December 2015, with measures to apply from 1 January 2016) (OJ L 359, 16.12.2014, p 1).

VAT EC

SECTION III

SPONTANEOUS EXCHANGE OF INFORMATION

Article 9 Scope and conditions of spontaneous exchange of information

1. The competent authority of each Member State shall communicate the information referred to in Article 1(1) to the competent authority of any other Member State concerned, in any of the following circumstances:

(a) the competent authority of one Member State has grounds for supposing that there may be a loss of tax in the other Member State;

(b) a person liable to tax obtains a reduction in, or an exemption from, tax in one Member State which would give rise to an increase in tax or to liability to tax in the other Member State;

(c) business dealings between a person liable to tax in one Member State and a person liable to tax in the other Member State are conducted through one or more countries in such a way that a saving in tax may result in one or the other Member State or in both;

(d) the competent authority of a Member State has grounds for supposing that a saving of tax may result from artificial transfers of profits within groups of enterprises;

(e) information forwarded to one Member State by the competent authority of the other Member State has enabled information to be obtained which may be relevant in assessing liability to tax in the latter Member State.

2. The competent authorities of each Member State may communicate, by spontaneous exchange, to the competent authorities of the other Member States any information of which they are aware and which may be useful to the competent authorities of the other Member States.

***Article 10* Time limits**

1. The competent authority to which information referred to in Article 9(1) becomes available, shall forward that information to the competent authority of any other Member State concerned as quickly as possible, and no later than one month after it becomes available.

2. The competent authority to which information is communicated pursuant to Article 9 shall confirm, if possible by electronic means, the receipt of the information to the competent authority which provided the information immediately and in any event no later than seven working days.

CHAPTER III
OTHER FORMS OF ADMINISTRATIVE COOPERATION

SECTION I
PRESENCE IN ADMINISTRATIVE OFFICES AND PARTICIPATION IN ADMINISTRATIVE ENQUIRIES

***Article 11* Scope and conditions**

1. By agreement between the requesting authority and the requested authority and in accordance with the arrangements laid down by the latter, officials authorised by the requesting authority may, with a view to exchanging the information referred to in Article 1(1):

(a) be present in the offices where the administrative authorities of the requested Member State carry out their duties;

(b) be present during administrative enquiries carried out in the territory of the requested Member State.

Where the requested information is contained in documentation to which the officials of the requested authority have access, the officials of the requesting authority shall be given copies thereof.

2. In so far as this is permitted under the legislation of the requested Member State, the agreement referred to in paragraph 1 may provide that, where officials of the requesting authority are present during administrative enquiries, they may interview individuals and examine records.

Any refusal by the person under investigation to respect the inspection measures of the officials of the requesting authority shall be treated by the requested authority as if that refusal was committed against officials of the latter authority.

3. Officials authorised by the requesting Member State present in another Member State in accordance with paragraph 1 shall at all times be able to produce written authority stating their identity and their official capacity.

SECTION II
SIMULTANEOUS CONTROLS

***Article 12* Simultaneous controls**

1. Where two or more Member States agree to conduct simultaneous controls, in their own territory, of one or more persons of common or complementary interest to them, with a view to exchanging the information thus obtained, paragraphs 2, 3 and 4 shall apply.

2. The competent authority in each Member State shall identify independently the persons for whom it intends to propose a simultaneous control. It shall notify the competent authority of the other Member States concerned of any cases for which it proposes a simultaneous control, giving reasons for its choice.

It shall specify the period of time during which those controls are to be conducted.

3. The competent authority of each Member State concerned shall decide whether it wishes to take part in simultaneous controls. It shall confirm its agreement or communicate its reasoned refusal to the authority that proposed a simultaneous control.

4. The competent authority of each Member State concerned shall appoint a representative with responsibility for supervising and coordinating the control operation.

SECTION III
ADMINISTRATIVE NOTIFICATION

***Article 13* Request for notification**

1. At the request of the competent authority of a Member State, the competent authority of another Member State shall, in accordance with the rules governing the notification of similar instruments in the requested Member State, notify the addressee of any instruments and decisions which emanate from the administrative authorities of the requesting Member State and concern the application in its territory of legislation on taxes covered by this Directive.

2. Requests for notification shall indicate the subject of the instrument or decision to be notified and shall specify the name and address of the addressee, together with any other information which may facilitate identification of the addressee.

3. The requested authority shall inform the requesting authority immediately of its response and, in particular, of the date of notification of the instrument or decision to the addressee.

4. The requesting authority shall only make a request for notification pursuant to this Article when it is unable to notify in accordance with the rules governing the notification of the instruments concerned in the requesting Member State, or where such notification would give rise to disproportionate difficulties. The competent authority of a Member State may notify any document by registered mail or electronically directly to a person within the territory of another Member State.

SECTION IV
FEEDBACK

***Article 14* Conditions**

1. Where a competent authority provides information pursuant to Articles 5 or 9, it may request the competent authority which receives the information to send feedback thereon. If feedback is requested, the competent authority which received the information shall, without prejudice to the rules on tax secrecy and data protection applicable in its Member State, send feedback to the competent authority which provided the information as soon as possible and no later than three months after the outcome of the use of the requested information is known. The Commission shall determine the practical arrangements in accordance with the procedure referred to in Article 26(2).
2. Member States' competent authorities shall send feedback on the automatic exchange of information to the other Member States concerned once a year, in accordance with practical arrangements agreed upon bilaterally.

SECTION V
SHARING OF BEST PRACTICES AND EXPERIENCE

***Article 15* Scope and conditions**

1. Member States shall, together with the Commission, examine and evaluate administrative cooperation pursuant to this Directive and shall share their experience, with a view to improving such cooperation and, where appropriate, drawing up rules in the fields concerned.
2. Member States may, together with the Commission, produce guidelines on any aspect deemed necessary for sharing best practices and sharing experience.

CHAPTER IV
CONDITIONS GOVERNING ADMINISTRATIVE COOPERATION

***Article 16* Disclosure of information and documents**

1. Information communicated between Member States in any form pursuant to this Directive shall be covered by the obligation of official secrecy and enjoy the protection extended to similar information under the national law of the Member State which received it. Such information may be used for the administration and enforcement of the domestic laws of the Member States concerning the taxes referred to in Article 2.

Such information may also be used for the assessment and enforcement of other taxes and duties covered by Article 2 of Council Directive 2010/24/EU of 16 March 2010 concerning mutual assistance for the recovery of claims relating to taxes, duties and other measures[1], or for the assessment and enforcement of compulsory social security contributions.

In addition, it may be used in connection with judicial and administrative proceedings that may involve penalties, initiated as a result of infringements of tax law, without prejudice to the general rules and provisions governing the rights of defendants and witnesses in such proceedings.

2. With the permission of the competent authority of the Member State communicating information pursuant to this Directive, and only in so far as this is allowed under the legislation of the Member State of the competent authority receiving the information, information and documents received pursuant to this Directive may be used for other purposes than those referred to in paragraph 1. Such permission shall be granted if the information can be used for similar purposes in the Member State of the competent authority communicating the information.

3. Where a competent authority of a Member State considers that information which it has received from the competent authority of another Member State is likely to be useful for the purposes referred to in paragraph 1 to the competent authority of a third Member State, it may transmit that information to the latter competent authority, provided that transmission is in accordance with the rules and procedures laid down in this Directive. It shall inform the competent authority of the Member State from which the information originates about its intention to share that information with a third Member State. The Member State of origin of the information may oppose such a sharing of information within 10 working days of receipt of the communication from the Member State wishing to share the information.

4. Permission to use information pursuant to paragraph 2, which has been transmitted pursuant to paragraph 3, may be granted only by the competent authority of the Member State from which the information originates.

5. Information, reports, statements and any other documents, or certified true copies or extracts thereof, obtained by the requested authority and communicated to the requesting authority in accordance with this Directive may be invoked as evidence by the competent bodies of the requesting Member State on the same basis as similar information, reports, statements and any other documents provided by an authority of that Member State.

[1] OJ L 84, 31.3.2010, p. 1.

***Article 17* Limits**

1. A requested authority in one Member State shall provide a requesting authority in another Member State with the information referred to in Article 5 provided that the requesting authority has exhausted the usual sources of information which it could have used in the circumstances for obtaining the information requested, without running the risk of jeopardising the achievement of its objectives.
2. This Directive shall impose no obligation upon a requested Member State to carry out enquiries or to communicate information, if it would be contrary to its legislation to conduct such inquiries or to collect the information requested for its own purposes.
3. The competent authority of a requested Member State may decline to provide information where the requesting Member State is unable, for legal reasons, to provide similar information.
4. The provision of information may be refused where it would lead to the disclosure of a commercial, industrial or professional secret or of a commercial process, or of information whose disclosure would be contrary to public policy.
5. The requested authority shall inform the requesting authority of the grounds for refusing a request for information.

***Article 18* Obligations**

1. If information is requested by a Member State in accordance with this Directive, the requested Member State shall use its measures aimed at gathering information to obtain the requested information, even though that Member State may not need such information for its own tax purposes. That obligation is without prejudice to paragraphs 2, 3 and 4 of Article 17, the invocation of which shall in no case be construed as permitting a requested Member State to decline to supply information solely because it has no domestic interest in such information.
2. In no case shall Article 17(2) and (4) be construed as permitting a requested authority of a Member State to decline to supply information solely because this information is held by a bank, other financial institution, nominee or person acting in an agency or a fiduciary capacity or because it relates to ownership interests in a person.
3. Notwithstanding paragraph 2, a Member State may refuse the transmission of requested information where such information concerns taxable periods prior to 1 January 2011 and where the transmission of such information could have been refused on the basis of Article 8(1) of Directive 77/799/EEC if it had been requested before 11 March 2011.

***Article 19* Extension of wider cooperation provided to a third country**

Where a Member State provides a wider cooperation to a third country than that provided for under this Directive, that Member State may not refuse to provide such wider cooperation to any other Member State wishing to enter into such mutual wider cooperation with that Member State.

***Article 20* Standard forms and computerised formats**

1. Requests for information and for administrative enquiries pursuant to Article 5 and their replies, acknowledgements, requests for additional background information, inability or refusal pursuant to Article 7 shall, as far as possible, be sent using a standard form adopted by the Commission in accordance with the procedure referred to in Article 26(2).
The standard forms may be accompanied by reports, statements and any other documents, or certified true copies or extracts thereof.
2. The standard form referred to in paragraph 1 shall include at least the following information to be provided by the requesting authority:
(a) the identity of the person under examination or investigation;
(b) the tax purpose for which the information is sought.
The requesting authority may, to the extent known and in line with international developments, provide the name and address of any person believed to be in possession of the requested information as well as any element that may facilitate the collection of information by the requested authority.
3. Spontaneous information and its acknowledgement pursuant to Articles 9 and 10 respectively, requests for administrative notifications pursuant to Article 13 and feedback information pursuant to Article 14 shall be sent using the standard form adopted by the Commission in accordance with the procedure referred to in Article 26(2).

[4. The automatic exchange of information pursuant to Article 8 shall be sent using a standard computerised format aimed at facilitating such automatic exchange and based on the existing computerised format pursuant to Article 9 of Directive 2003/48/EC, to be used for all types of automatic exchange of information, adopted by the Commission in accordance with the procedure referred to in Article 26(2).][1]

[1] OJ L 157, 26.6.2003, p. 38.

Amendments—[1] Para 4 substituted by Council Directive 2014/107/EU Art 1(3) with effect from 5 January 2015. See Art 2 for implementation provisions (deadline for implementation is 31 December 2015, with measures to apply from 1 January 2016) (OJ L 359, 16.12.2014, p 1).

Article 21 Practical arrangements

1. Information communicated pursuant to this Directive shall, as far as possible, be provided by electronic means using the CCN network.

Where necessary, the Commission shall adopt practical arrangements necessary for the implementation of the first subparagraph in accordance with the procedure referred to in Article 26(2).

[2. The Commission shall be responsible for whatever development of the CCN network is necessary to permit the exchange of that information between Member States and for ensuring the security of the CCN network.

Member States shall be responsible for whatever development of their systems is necessary to enable that information to be exchanged using the CCN network and for ensuring the security of their systems.

Member States shall ensure that each individual Reportable Person is notified of a breach of security with regard to his data when that breach is likely to adversely affect the protection of his personal data or privacy.

Member States shall waive all claims for the reimbursement of expenses incurred in applying this Directive except, where appropriate, in respect of fees paid to experts.][1]

3. Persons duly accredited by the Security Accreditation Authority of the Commission may have access to that information only in so far as it is necessary for the care, maintenance and development of the CCN network.

4. Requests for cooperation, including requests for notification, and attached documents may be made in any language agreed between the requested and requesting authority.

Those requests shall be accompanied by a translation into the official language or one of the official languages of the Member State of the requested authority only in special cases when the requested authority states its reason for requesting a translation.

Amendments—[1] Para 2 substituted by Council Directive 2014/107/EU Art 1(4) with effect from 5 January 2015. See Art 2 for implementation provisions (deadline for implementation is 31 December 2015, with measures to apply from 1 January 2016) (OJ L 359, 16.12.2014, p 1).

Article 22 Specific obligations

1. Member States shall take all necessary measures to:
   (a) ensure effective internal coordination within the organisation referred to in Article 4;
   (b) establish direct cooperation with the authorities of the other Member States referred to in Article 4;
   (c) ensure the smooth operation of the administrative cooperation arrangements provided for in this Directive.

2. The Commission shall communicate to each Member State any general information concerning the implementation and application of this Directive which it receives and which it is able to provide.

CHAPTER V
RELATIONS WITH THE COMMISSION

Article 23 Evaluation

1. Member States and the Commission shall examine and evaluate the functioning of the administrative cooperation provided for in this Directive.

2. Member States shall communicate to the Commission any relevant information necessary for the evaluation of the effectiveness of administrative cooperation in accordance with this Directive in combating tax evasion and tax avoidance.

3. Member States shall communicate to the Commission a yearly assessment of the effectiveness of the automatic exchange of information referred to in Article 8 as well as the practical results achieved. The form and the conditions of communication of that yearly assessment shall be adopted by the Commission in accordance with the procedure referred to in Article 26(2).

4. The Commission shall, in accordance with the procedure referred to in Article 26(2), determine a list of statistical data which shall be provided by the Member States for the purposes of evaluation of this Directive.

5. Information communicated to the Commission under paragraphs 2, 3 and 4 shall be kept confidential by the Commission in accordance with the provisions applicable to Union authorities.

VAT EC

6. Information communicated to the Commission by a Member State under paragraphs 2, 3 and 4, as well as any report or document produced by the Commission using such information, may be transmitted to other Member States. Such transmitted information shall be covered by the obligation of official secrecy and enjoy the protection extended to similar information under the national law of the Member State which received it.
Reports and documents produced by the Commission referred to in this paragraph may only be used by the Member States for analytical purposes but shall not be published or made available to any other person or body without express agreement of the Commission.

CHAPTER VI

RELATIONS WITH THIRD COUNTRIES

Article 24 Exchange of information with third countries

1. Where the competent authority of a Member State receives from a third country information that is foreseeably relevant to the administration and enforcement of the domestic laws of that Member State concerning the taxes referred to in Article 2, that authority may, in so far as this is allowed pursuant to an agreement with that third country, provide that information to the competent authorities of Member States for which that information might be useful and to any requesting authorities.
2. Competent authorities may communicate, in accordance with their domestic provisions on the communication of personal data to third countries, information obtained in accordance with this Directive to a third country, provided that all of the following conditions are met:
  (a) the competent authority of the Member State from which the information originates have consented to that communication;
  (b) the third country concerned has given an undertaking to provide the cooperation required to gather evidence of the irregular or illegal nature of transactions which appear to contravene or constitute an abuse of tax legislation.

CHAPTER VII

GENERAL AND FINAL PROVISIONS

Article 25 Data protection

[1.] [1] All exchange of information pursuant to this Directive shall be subject to the provisions implementing Directive 95/46/EC. However, Member States shall, for the purpose of the correct application of this Directive, restrict the scope of the obligations and rights provided for in Article 10, Article 11(1), Articles 12 and 21 of Directive 95/46/EC to the extent required in order to safeguard the interests referred to in Article 13(1)(e) of that Directive.
[2. Reporting Financial Institutions and the competent authorities of each Member State shall be considered to be data controllers for the purposes of Directive 95/46/EC.
3. Notwithstanding paragraph 1, each Member State shall ensure that each Reporting Financial Institution under its jurisdiction informs each individual Reportable Person concerned that the information relating to him referred to in Article 8(3a) will be collected and transferred in accordance with this Directive and shall ensure that the Reporting Financial Institution provides to that individual all information that he is entitled to under its domestic legislation implementing Directive 95/46/EC in sufficient time for the individual to exercise his data protection rights and, in any case, before the Reporting Financial Institution concerned reports the information referred to in Article 8(3a) to the competent authority of its Member State of residence.
4. Information processed in accordance with this Directive shall be retained for no longer than necessary to achieve the purposes of this Directive, and in any case in accordance with each data controller's domestic rules on statute of limitations.][1]

Amendments—[1] Paras 2–4 inserted by Council Directive 2014/107/EU Art 1(5) with effect from 5 January 2015. See Art 2 for implementation provisions (deadline for implementation is 31 December 2015, with measures to apply from 1 January 2016) (OJ L 359, 16.12.2014, p 1).

Article 26 Committee

1. The Commission shall be assisted by a committee referred to as the 'Committee on Administrative Cooperation for Taxation'.
2. Where reference is made to this paragraph, Articles 5 and 7 of Decision 1999/468/EC shall apply. The period laid down in Article 5(6) of Decision 1999/468/EC shall be set at three months.

Article 27 Reporting

Every five years after 1 January 2013, the Commission shall submit a report on the application of this Directive to the European Parliament and to the Council.

Article 28 Repeal of Directive 77/799/EEC

Directive 77/799/EEC is repealed with effect from 1 January 2013.
References made to the repealed Directive shall be construed as references to this Directive.

Article 29 **Transposition**

1. Member States shall bring into force the laws, regulations and administrative provisions necessary to comply with this Directive with effect from 1 January 2013.

However, they shall bring into force the laws, regulations and administrative provisions necessary to comply with Article 8 of this Directive with effect from 1 January 2015.

They shall forthwith inform the Commission thereof.

When Member States adopt those measures, they shall contain a reference to this Directive or shall be accompanied by such a reference on the occasion of their official publication. The methods of making such reference shall be laid down by the Member States.

2. Member States shall communicate to the Commission the text of the main provisions of national law which they adopt in the field covered by this Directive.

Article 30 **Entry into force**

This Directive shall enter into force on the day of its publication in the *Official Journal of the European Union.*

Article 31 **Addressees**

This Directive is addressed to the Member States.

Done at Brussels, ...15 February 2011.

For the Council

The President

MATOLCSY Gy.

[ANNEX I

REPORTING AND DUE DILIGENCE RULES FOR FINANCIAL ACCOUNT INFORMATION

This Annex lays down the reporting and due diligence rules that have to be applied by Reporting Financial Institutions in order to enable the Member States to communicate, by automatic exchange, the information referred to in Article 8(3a) of this Directive. This Annex also describes the rules and administrative procedures that Member States shall have in place to ensure effective implementation of, and compliance with, the reporting and due diligence procedures set out below.

SECTION I

GENERAL REPORTING REQUIREMENTS

A Subject to paragraphs C through E, each Reporting Financial Institution must report to the competent authority of its Member State the following information with respect to each Reportable Account of such Reporting Financial Institution:

1. the name, address, Member State(s) of residence, TIN(s) and date and place of birth (in the case of an individual) of each Reportable Person that is an Account Holder of the account and, in the case of any Entity that is an Account Holder and that, after application of the due diligence procedures consistent with Sections V, VI and VII, is identified as having one or more Controlling Persons that is a Reportable Person, the name, address, Member State(s) and (if any) other jurisdiction(s) of residence and TIN(s) of the Entity and the name, address, Member State(s) of residence, TIN(s) and date and place of birth of each Reportable Person;

2. the account number (or functional equivalent in the absence of an account number);

3. the name and identifying number (if any) of the Reporting Financial Institution;

4. the account balance or value (including, in the case of a Cash Value Insurance Contract or Annuity Contract, the Cash Value or surrender value) as of the end of the relevant calendar year or other appropriate reporting period or, if the account was closed during such year or period, the closure of the account;

5. in the case of any Custodial Account:

(a) the total gross amount of interest, the total gross amount of dividends, and the total gross amount of other income generated with respect to the assets held in the account, in each case paid or credited to the account (or with respect to the account) during the calendar year or other appropriate reporting period; and

(b) the total gross proceeds from the sale or redemption of Financial Assets paid or credited to the account during the calendar year or other appropriate reporting period with respect to which the Reporting Financial Institution acted as a custodian, broker, nominee, or otherwise as an agent for the Account Holder;

6. in the case of any Depository Account, the total gross amount of interest paid or credited to the account during the calendar year or other appropriate reporting period; and

VAT EC

7. in the case of any account not described in subparagraph A(5) or (6), the total gross amount paid or credited to the Account Holder with respect to the account during the calendar year or other appropriate reporting period with respect to which the Reporting Financial Institution is the obligor or debtor, including the aggregate amount of any redemption payments made to the Account Holder during the calendar year or other appropriate reporting period.

B The information reported must identify the currency in which each amount is denominated.

C Notwithstanding subparagraph A(1), with respect to each Reportable Account that is a Pre-existing Account, the TIN(s) or date of birth is not required to be reported if such TIN(s) or date of birth is not in the records of the Reporting Financial Institution and is not otherwise required to be collected by such Reporting Financial Institution under domestic law or any Union legal instrument. However, a Reporting Financial Institution is required to use reasonable efforts to obtain the TIN(s) and date of birth with respect to Pre-existing Accounts by the end of the second calendar year following the year in which Pre-existing Accounts were identified as Reportable Accounts.

D Notwithstanding subparagraph A(1), the TIN is not required to be reported if a TIN is not issued by the relevant Member State or other jurisdiction of residence.

E Notwithstanding subparagraph A(1), the place of birth is not required to be reported unless:
(1) the Reporting Financial Institution is otherwise required to obtain and report it under domestic law or the Reporting Financial Institution is or has been otherwise required to obtain and report it under any Union legal instrument in effect or that was in effect on 5 January 2015; and
(2) it is available in the electronically searchable data maintained by the Reporting Financial Institution.

SECTION II
GENERAL DUE DILIGENCE REQUIREMENTS

A An account is treated as a Reportable Account beginning as of the date it is identified as such pursuant to the due diligence procedures in Sections II through VII and, unless otherwise provided, information with respect to a Repor

B The balance or value of an account is determined as of the last day of the calendar year or other appropriate reporting period.

C Where a balance or value threshold is to be determined as of the last day of a calendar year, the relevant balance or value must be determined as of the last day of the reporting period that ends with or within that calendar year.

D Each Member State may allow Reporting Financial Institutions to use service providers to fulfil the reporting and due diligence obligations imposed on such Reporting Financial Institutions, as contemplated in domestic law, but these obligations shall remain the responsibility of the Reporting Financial Institutions.

E Each Member State may allow Reporting Financial Institutions to apply the due diligence procedures for New Accounts to Pre-existing Accounts, and the due diligence procedures for High Value Accounts to Lower Value Accounts. Where a Member State allows New Account due diligence procedures to be used for Pre-existing Accounts, the rules otherwise applicable to Pre-existing Accounts continue to apply.

SECTION III
DUE DILIGENCE FOR PRE-EXISTING INDIVIDUAL ACCOUNTS

A Introduction. The following procedures apply for purposes of identifying Reportable Accounts among Pre-existing Individual Accounts.

B Lower Value Accounts. The following procedures apply with respect to Lower Value Accounts.
1. Residence Address. If the Reporting Financial Institution has in its records a current residence address for the individual Account Holder based on Documentary Evidence, the Reporting Financial Institution may treat the individual Account Holder as being a resident for tax purposes of the Member State or other jurisdiction in which the address is located for purposes of determining whether such individual Account Holder is a Reportable Person.
2. Electronic Record Search. If the Reporting Financial Institution does not rely on a current residence address for the individual Account Holder based on Documentary Evidence as set forth in subparagraph B(1), the Reporting Financial Institution must review electronically searchable data maintained by the Reporting Financial Institution for any of the following indicia and apply subparagraphs B(3) to (6):

(a) identification of the Account Holder as a resident of a Member State;

(b) current mailing or residence address (including a post office box) in a Member State;

(c) one or more telephone numbers in a Member State and no telephone number in the Member State of the Reporting Financial Institution;

(d) standing instructions (other than with respect to a Depository Account) to transfer funds to an account maintained in a Member State;

(e) currently effective power of attorney or signatory authority granted to a person with an address in a Member State; or

(f) a "hold mail" instruction or "in-care-of" address in a Member State if the Reporting Financial Institution does not have any other address on file for the Account Holder.

3. If none of the indicia listed in subparagraph B(2) are discovered in the electronic search, then no further action is required until there is a change in circumstances that results in one or more indicia being associated with the account, or the account becomes a High Value Account.

4. If any of the indicia listed in subparagraph B(2)(a) through (e) are discovered in the electronic search, or if there is a change in circumstances that results in one or more indicia being associated with the account, then the Reporting Financial Institution must treat the Account Holder as a resident for tax purposes of each Member State for which an indicium is identified, unless it elects to apply subparagraph B(6) and one of the exceptions in that subparagraph applies with respect to that account.

5. If a "hold mail" instruction or "in-care-of" address is discovered in the electronic search and no other address and none of the other indicia listed in subparagraph B(2)(a) through (e) are identified for the Account Holder, the Reporting Financial Institution must, in the order most appropriate to the circumstances, apply the paper record search described in subparagraph C(2), or seek to obtain from the Account Holder a self-certification or Documentary Evidence to establish the residence(s) for tax purposes of such Account Holder. If the paper search fails to establish an indicium and the attempt to obtain the self-certification or Documentary Evidence is not successful, the Reporting Financial Institution must report the account to the competent authority of its Member State as an undocumented account.

6. Notwithstanding a finding of indicia under subparagraph B(2), a Reporting Financial Institution is not required to treat an Account Holder as a resident of a Member State if:

(a) the Account Holder information contains a current mailing or residence address in that Member State, one or more telephone numbers in that Member State (and no telephone number in the Member State of the Reporting Financial Institution) or standing instructions (with respect to Financial Accounts other than Depository Accounts) to transfer funds to an account maintained in a Member State, and the Reporting Financial Institution obtains, or has previously reviewed and maintains, a record of:

(i) a self-certification from the Account Holder of the Member State(s) or other jurisdiction(s) of residence of such Account Holder that does not include that Member State; and

(ii) Documentary Evidence establishing the Account Holder's non-reportable status;

(b) the Account Holder information contains a currently effective power of attorney or signatory authority granted to a person with an address in that Member State, and the Reporting Financial Institution obtains, or has previously reviewed and maintains, a record of:

(i) a self-certification from the Account Holder of the Member State(s) or other jurisdiction(s) of residence of such Account Holder that does not include that Member State; or

(ii) Documentary Evidence establishing the Account Holder's non-reportable status.

C Enhanced Review Procedures for High Value Accounts. The following enhanced review procedures apply with respect to High Value Accounts.

1. Electronic Record search. With respect to High Value Accounts, the Reporting Financial Institution must review electronically searchable data maintained by the Reporting Financial Institution for any of the indicia described in subparagraph B(2).

2. Paper Record Search. If the Reporting Financial Institution's electronically searchable databases include fields for, and capture all of the information described in, subparagraph C(3), then a further paper record search is not required. If the electronic databases do not capture all of this information, then with respect to a High Value Account, the Reporting Financial Institution must also review the current customer master file and, to the extent not contained in the current customer master file, the following documents associated with the account and obtained by the Reporting Financial Institution within the last five years for any of the indicia described in subparagraph B(2):

(a) the most recent Documentary Evidence collected with respect to the account;

VAT EC

(b) the most recent account opening contract or documentation;

(c) the most recent documentation obtained by the Reporting Financial Institution pursuant to AML/KYC Procedures or for other regulatory purposes;

(d) any power of attorney or signature authority forms currently in effect; and

(e) any standing instructions (other than with respect to a Depository Account) to transfer funds currently in effect.

3. Exception To The Extent Databases Contain Sufficient Information. A Reporting Financial Institution is not required to perform the paper record search described in subparagraph C(2) to the extent the Reporting Financial Institution's electronically searchable information includes the following:

(a) the Account Holder's residence status;

(b) the Account Holder's residence address and mailing address currently on file with the Reporting Financial Institution;

(c) the Account Holder's telephone number(s) currently on file, if any, with the Reporting Financial Institution;

(d) in the case of Financial Accounts other than Depository Accounts, whether there are standing instructions to transfer funds in the account to another account (including an account at another branch of the Reporting Financial Institution or another Financial Institution);

(e) whether there is a current "in-care-of" address or "hold mail" instruction for the Account Holder; and

(f) whether there is any power of attorney or signatory authority for the account.

4. Relationship Manager Inquiry for Actual Knowledge. In addition to the electronic and paper record searches described in subparagraphs C(1) and (2), the Reporting Financial Institution must treat as a Reportable Account any High Value Account assigned to a relationship manager (including any Financial Accounts aggregated with that High Value Account) if the relationship manager has actual knowledge that the Account Holder is a Reportable Person.

5. Effect of Finding Indicia.

(a) If none of the indicia listed in subparagraph B(2) are discovered in the enhanced review of High Value Accounts described in paragraph C, and the account is not identified as held by a Reportable Person in subparagraph C(4), then further action is not required until there is a change in circumstances that results in one or more indicia being associated with the account.

(b) If any of the indicia listed in subparagraphs B(2)(a) through (e) are discovered in the enhanced review of High Value Accounts described in paragraph C, or if there is a subsequent change in circumstances that results in one or more indicia being associated with the account, then the Reporting Financial Institution must treat the account as a Reportable Account with respect to each Member State for which an indicium is identified unless it elects to apply subparagraph B(6) and one of the exceptions in that subparagraph applies with respect to that account.

(c) If a "hold mail" instruction or "in-care-of" address is discovered in the enhanced review of High Value Accounts described in paragraph C, and no other address and none of the other indicia listed in subparagraphs B(2)(a) through (e) are identified for the Account Holder, the Reporting Financial Institution must obtain from such Account Holder a self-certification or Documentary Evidence to establish the residence(s) for tax purposes of the Account Holder. If the Reporting Financial Institution cannot obtain such self-certification or Documentary Evidence, it must report the account to the competent authority of its Member State as an undocumented account.

6. If a Pre-existing Individual Account is not a High Value Account as of 31 December 2015, but becomes a High Value Account as of the last day of a subsequent calendar year, the Reporting Financial Institution must complete the enhanced review procedures described in paragraph C with respect to such account within the calendar year following the year in which the account becomes a High Value Account. If based on this review such account is identified as a Reportable Account, the Reporting Financial Institution must report the required information about such account with respect to the year in which it is identified as a Reportable Account and subsequent years on an annual basis, unless the Account Holder ceases to be a Reportable Person.

7. Once a Reporting Financial Institution applies the enhanced review procedures described in paragraph C to a High Value Account, the Reporting Financial Institution is not required to reapply such procedures, other than the relationship manager inquiry described in subparagraph C(4), to the same High Value Account in any subsequent year unless the account is undocumented where the Reporting Financial Institution should reapply them annually until such account ceases to be undocumented.

8. If there is a change of circumstances with respect to a High Value Account that results in one or more indicia described in subparagraph B(2) being associated with the account, then the Reporting Financial Institution must treat the account as a Reportable Account with respect to each Member State for which an indicium is identified unless it elects to apply subparagraph B(6) and one of the exceptions in that subparagraph applies with respect to that account.

9. A Reporting Financial Institution must implement procedures to ensure that a relationship manager identifies any change in circumstances of an account. For example, if a relationship manager is notified that the Account Holder has a new mailing address in a Member State, the Reporting Financial Institution is required to treat the new address as a change in circumstances and, if it elects to apply subparagraph B(6), is required to obtain the appropriate documentation from the Account Holder.

D Review of Pre-existing High Value Individual Accounts must be completed by 31 December 2016. Review of Preexisting Lower Value Individual Accounts must be completed by 31 December 2017.

E Any Pre-existing Individual Account that has been identified as a Reportable Account under this Section must be treated as a Reportable Account in all subsequent years, unless the Account Holder ceases to be a Reportable Person.

SECTION IV
DUE DILIGENCE FOR NEW INDIVIDUAL ACCOUNTS

The following procedures apply for purposes of identifying Reportable Accounts among New Individual Accounts.

A With respect to New Individual Accounts, upon account opening, the Reporting Financial Institution must obtain a self-certification, which may be part of the account opening documentation, that allows the Reporting Financial Institution to determine the Account Holder's residence(s) for tax purposes and confirm the reasonableness of such selfcertification based on the information obtained by the Reporting Financial Institution in connection with the opening of the account, including any documentation collected pursuant to AML/KYC Procedures.

B If the self-certification establishes that the Account Holder is resident for tax purposes in a Member State, the Reporting Financial Institution must treat the account as a Reportable Account and the self-certification must also include the Account Holder's TIN with respect to such Member State (subject to paragraph D of Section I) and date of birth.

C If there is a change of circumstances with respect to a New Individual Account that causes the Reporting Financial Institution to know, or have reason to know, that the original self-certification is incorrect or unreliable, the Reporting Financial Institution cannot rely on the original self-certification and must obtain a valid self-certification that establishes the residence(s) for tax purposes of the Account Holder.

SECTION V
DUE DILIGENCE FOR PRE-EXISTING ENTITY ACCOUNTS

The following procedures apply for purposes of identifying Reportable Accounts among Pre-existing Entity Accounts.

A Entity Accounts Not Required to Be Reviewed, Identified or Reported. Unless the Reporting Financial Institution elects otherwise, either with respect to all Pre-existing Entity Accounts or, separately, with respect to any clearly identified group of such accounts, a Pre-existing Entity Account with an aggregate account balance or value that does not exceed, as of 31 December 2015, an amount denominated in the domestic currency of each Member State that corresponds to USD 250 000, is not required to be reviewed, identified, or reported as a Reportable Account until the aggregate account balance or value exceeds that amount as of the last day of any subsequent calendar year.

B Entity Accounts Subject to Review. A Pre-existing Entity Account that has an aggregate account balance or value that exceeds, as of 31 December 2015, an amount denominated in the domestic currency of each Member State that corresponds to USD 250 000, and a Pre-existing Entity Account that does not exceed, as of 31 December 2015, that amount but the aggregate account balance or value of which exceeds such amount as of the last day of any subsequent calendar year, must be reviewed in accordance with the procedures set forth in paragraph D.

VAT EC

C Entity Accounts With Respect to Which Reporting Is Required. With respect to Pre-existing Entity Accounts described in paragraph B, only accounts that are held by one or more Entities that are Reportable Persons, or by Passive NFEs with one or more Controlling Persons who are Reportable Persons, shall be treated as Reportable Accounts.

D Review Procedures for Identifying Entity Accounts With Respect to Which Reporting Is Required. For Pre-existing Entity Accounts described in paragraph B, a Reporting Financial Institution must apply the following review procedures to determine whether the account is held by one or more Reportable Persons, or by Passive NFEs with one or more Controlling Persons who are Reportable Persons:

1. Determine Whether the Entity Is a Reportable Person.

(a) Review information maintained for regulatory or customer relationship purposes (including information collected pursuant to AML/KYC Procedures) to determine whether the information indicates that the Account Holder is resident in a Member State. For this purpose, information indicating that the Account Holder is resident in a Member State includes a place of incorporation or organisation, or an address in a Member State.

(b) If the information indicates that the Account Holder is resident in a Member State, the Reporting Financial Institution must treat the account as a Reportable Account unless it obtains a self-certification from the Account Holder, or reasonably determines based on information in its possession or that is publicly available, that the Account Holder is not a Reportable Person.

2. Determine Whether the Entity is a Passive NFE with One or More Controlling Persons who are Reportable Persons. With respect to an Account Holder of a Pre-existing Entity Account (including an Entity that is a Reportable Person), the Reporting Financial Institution must determine whether the Account Holder is a Passive NFE with one or more Controlling Persons who are Reportable Persons. If any of the Controlling Persons of a Passive NFE is a Reportable Person, then the account must be treated as a Reportable Account. In making these determinations the Reporting Financial Institution must follow the guidance in subparagraphs D(2)(a) through (c) in the order most appropriate under the circumstances.

(a) Determining whether the Account Holder is a Passive NFE. For purposes of determining whether the Account Holder is a Passive NFE, the Reporting Financial Institution must obtain a self-certification from the Account Holder to establish its status, unless it has information in its possession or that is publicly available, based on which it can reasonably determine that the Account Holder is an Active NFE or a Financial Institution other than an Investment Entity described in subparagraph A(6)(b) of Section VIII that is not a Participating Jurisdiction Financial Institution.

(b) Determining the Controlling Persons of an Account Holder. For the purposes of determining the Controlling Persons of an Account Holder, a Reporting Financial Institution may rely on information collected and maintained pursuant to AML/KYC Procedures.

(c) Determining whether a Controlling Person of a Passive NFE is a Reportable Person. For the purposes of determining whether a Controlling Person of a Passive NFE is a Reportable Person, a Reporting Financial Institution may rely on:

(i) information collected and maintained pursuant to AML/KYC Procedures in the case of a Pre-existing Entity Account held by one or more NFEs with an aggregate account balance or value that does not exceed an amount denominated in the domestic currency of each Member State that corresponds to USD 1 000 000; or

(ii) a self-certification from the Account Holder or such Controlling Person of the Member State(s) or other jurisdiction(s) in which the controlling person is resident for tax purposes.

E Timing of Review and Additional Procedures Applicable to Pre-existing Entity Accounts 1. Review of Pre-existing Entity Accounts with an aggregate account balance or value that exceeds, as of 31 December 2015, an amount denominated in the domestic currency of each Member State that corresponds to USD 250 000, must be completed by 31 December 2017.

2. Review of Pre-existing Entity Accounts with an aggregate account balance or value that does not exceed, as of 31 December 2015, an amount denominated in the domestic currency of each Member State that corresponds to USD 250 000 but exceeds that amount as of 31 December of a subsequent year, must be completed within the calendar year following the year in which the aggregate account balance or value exceeds such amount.

3. If there is a change of circumstances with respect to a Pre-existing Entity Account that causes the Reporting Financial Institution to know, or have reason to know, that the self-certification or other documentation associated with an account is incorrect or unreliable, the Reporting Financial Institution must re-determine the status of the account in accordance with the procedures set forth in paragraph D.

SECTION VI
DUE DILIGENCE FOR NEW ENTITY ACCOUNTS

The following procedures apply for purposes of identifying Reportable Accounts among New Entity Accounts.

Review Procedures for Identifying Entity Accounts With Respect to Which Reporting Is Required. For New Entity Accounts, a Reporting Financial Institution must apply the following review procedures to determine whether the account is held by one or more Reportable Persons, or by Passive NFEs with one or more Controlling Persons who are Reportable Persons:

1. Determine Whether the Entity Is a Reportable Person.

(a) Obtain a self-certification, which may be part of the account opening documentation, that allows the Reporting Financial Institution to determine the Account Holder's residence(s) for tax purposes and confirm the reasonableness of such self-certification based on the information obtained by the Reporting Financial Institution in connection with the opening of the account, including any documentation collected pursuant to AML/KYC Procedures. If the Entity certifies that it has no residence for tax purposes, the Reporting Financial Institution may rely on the address of the principal office of the Entity to determine the residence of the Account Holder.

(b) If the self-certification indicates that the Account Holder is resident in a Member State, the Reporting Financial Institution must treat the account as a Reportable Account, unless it reasonably determines based on information in its possession or that is publicly available that the Account Holder is not a Reportable Person with respect to such Member State.

2. Determine Whether the Entity is a Passive NFE with One or More Controlling Persons Who Are Reportable Persons. With respect to an Account Holder of a New Entity Account (including an Entity that is a Reportable Person), the Reporting Financial Institution must determine whether the Account Holder is a Passive NFE with one or more Controlling Persons who are Reportable Persons. If any of the Controlling Persons of a Passive NFE is a Reportable Person, then the account must be treated as a Reportable Account. In making these determinations the Reporting Financial Institution must follow the guidance in subparagraphs A(2)(a) through (c) in the order most appropriate under the circumstances.

a) Determining whether the Account Holder is a Passive NFE. For purposes of determining whether the Account Holder is a Passive NFE, the Reporting Financial Institution must rely on a self-certification from the Account Holder to establish its status, unless it has information in its possession or that is publicly available, based on which it can reasonably determine that the Account Holder is an Active NFE or a Financial Institution other than an Investment Entity described in subparagraph A(6)(b) of Section VIII that is not a Participating Jurisdiction Financial Institution.

(b) Determining the Controlling Persons of an Account Holder. For purposes of determining the Controlling Persons of an Account Holder, a Reporting Financial Institution may rely on information collected and maintained pursuant to AML/KYC Procedures.

(c) Determining whether a Controlling Person of a Passive NFE is a Reportable Person. For purposes of determining whether a controlling person of a Passive NFE is a Reportable Person, a Reporting Financial Institution may rely on a self-certification from the Account Holder or such Controlling Person.

SECTION VII
SPECIAL DUE DILIGENCE RULES

The following additional rules apply in implementing the due diligence procedures described above:

A Reliance on Self-Certifications and Documentary Evidence. A Reporting Financial Institution may not rely on a selfcertification or Documentary Evidence if the Reporting Financial Institution knows or has reason to know that the self-certification or Documentary Evidence is incorrect or unreliable.

B Alternative Procedures for Financial Accounts held by Individual Beneficiaries of a Cash Value Insurance Contract or an Annuity Contract and for a Group Cash Value Insurance Contract or Group Annuity Contract. A Reporting Financial Institution may presume that an individual beneficiary (other than the owner) of a Cash Value Insurance Contract or an Annuity Contract receiving a death benefit is not a Reportable Person and may treat such Financial Account as other than a Reportable Account unless the Reporting Financial Institution has actual knowledge, or reason to know, that the beneficiary is a Reportable Person. A Reporting Financial Institution has reason to know that a beneficiary of a Cash Value Insurance Contract or an Annuity Contract is a Reportable Person if the information collected by the Reporting Financial Institution and associated with the beneficiary contains indicia as described in paragraph B of Section III. If a Reporting Financial Institution has actual knowledge, or reason to know, that the beneficiary is a Reportable Person, the Reporting Financial Institution must follow the procedures in paragraph B of Section III.

A Reporting Financial Institution may treat a Financial Account that is a member's interest in a Group Cash Value Insurance Contract or Group Annuity Contract as a Financial Account that is not a Reportable Account until the date on which an amount is payable to the employee/certificate holder or beneficiary, if the Financial Account that is a member's interest in a Group Cash Value Insurance Contract or Group Annuity Contract meets the following requirements:

(i) the Group Cash Value Insurance Contract or Group Annuity Contract is issued to an employer and covers 25 or more employees/certificate holders;

(ii) the employee/certificate holders are entitled to receive any contract value related to their interests and to name beneficiaries for the benefit payable upon the employee's death; and

(iii) the aggregate amount payable to any employee/certificate holder or beneficiary does not exceed an amount denominated in the domestic currency of each Member State that corresponds to USD 1 000 000.

The term "Group Cash Value Insurance Contract" means a Cash Value Insurance Contract that (i) provides coverage on individuals who are affiliated through an employer, trade association, labour union, or other association or group; and (ii) charges a premium for each member of the group (or member of a class within the group) that is determined without regard to the individual health characteristics other than age, gender, and smoking habits of the member (or class of members) of the group.

The term "Group Annuity Contract" means an Annuity Contract under which the obligees are individuals who are affiliated through an employer, trade association, labour union, or other association or group.

C Account Balance Aggregation and Currency Rules

1. Aggregation of Individual Accounts. For purposes of determining the aggregate balance or value of Financial Accounts held by an individual, a Reporting Financial Institution is required to aggregate all Financial Accounts maintained by the Reporting Financial Institution, or by a Related Entity, but only to the extent that the Reporting Financial Institution's computerised systems link the Financial Accounts by reference to a data element such as client number or TIN, and allow account balances or values to be aggregated. Each holder of a jointly held Financial Account shall be attributed the entire balance or value of the jointly held Financial Account for purposes of applying the aggregation requirements described in this subparagraph.

2. Aggregation of Entity Accounts. For purposes of determining the aggregate balance or value of Financial Accounts held by an Entity, a Reporting Financial Institution is required to take into account all Financial Accounts that are maintained by the Reporting Financial Institution, or by a Related Entity, but only to the extent that the Reporting Financial Institution's computerised systems link the Financial Accounts by reference to a data element such as client number or TIN, and allow account balances or values to be aggregated. Each holder of a jointly held Financial Account shall be attributed the entire balance or value of the jointly held Financial Account for purposes of applying the aggregation requirements described in this subparagraph.

3. Special Aggregation Rule Applicable to Relationship Managers. For purposes of determining the aggregate balance or value of Financial Accounts held by a person to determine whether a financial account is a High Value Account, a Reporting Financial Institution is also required, in the case of any Financial Accounts that a relationship manager knows, or has reason to know, are directly or indirectly owned, controlled, or established (other than in a fiduciary capacity) by the same person, to aggregate all such accounts.

4. Amounts Read to Include Equivalent in Other Currencies. All amounts denominated in the domestic currency of each Member State shall be read to include equivalent amounts in other currencies, as determined by domestic law.

SECTION VIII
DEFINED TERMS

The following terms have the meanings set forth below:

A Reporting Financial Institution

1. The term "Reporting Financial Institution" means any Member State Financial Institution that is not a NonReporting Financial Institution. The term "Member State Financial Institution" means: (i) any Financial Institution that is resident in a Member State, but excludes any branch of that Financial Institution that is located outside that Member State; and (ii) any branch of a Financial Institution that is not resident in a Member State, if that branch is located in that Member State.

2. The term "Participating Jurisdiction Financial Institution" means (i) any Financial Institution that is resident in a Participating Jurisdiction, but excludes any branch of that Financial Institution that is located outside such Participating Jurisdiction; and (ii) any branch of a Financial Institution that is not resident in a Participating Jurisdiction, if that branch is located in such Participating Jurisdiction.
3. The term "Financial Institution" means a Custodial Institution, a Depository Institution, an Investment Entity, or a Specified Insurance Company.
4. The term "Custodial Institution" means any Entity that holds, as a substantial portion of its business, Financial Assets for the account of others. An Entity holds Financial Assets for the account of others as a substantial portion of its business if the Entity's gross income attributable to the holding of Financial Assets and related financial services equals or exceeds 20 % of the Entity's gross income during the shorter of: (i) the three-year period that ends on 31 December (or the final day of a non-calendar year accounting period) prior to the year in which the determination is being made; or (ii) the period during which the Entity has been in existence.
5. The term "Depository Institution" means any Entity that accepts deposits in the ordinary course of a banking or similar business.
6. The term "Investment Entity" means any Entity:

(a) which primarily conducts as a business one or more of the following activities or operations for or on behalf of a customer:

(i) trading in money market instruments (cheques, bills, certificates of deposit, derivatives, etc.); foreign exchange; exchange, interest rate and index instruments; transferable securities; or commodity futures trading;

(ii) individual and collective portfolio management; or

(iii) otherwise investing, administering, or managing Financial Assets or money on behalf of other persons;

or

(b) the gross income of which is primarily attributable to investing, reinvesting, or trading in Financial Assets, if the Entity is managed by another Entity that is a Depository Institution, a Custodial Institution, a Specified Insurance Company, or an Investment Entity described in subparagraph A(6)(a).

An Entity is treated as primarily conducting as a business one or more of the activities described in subparagraph A(6)(a), or an Entity's gross income is primarily attributable to investing, reinvesting, or trading in Financial Assets for the purposes of subparagraph A(6)(b), if the Entity's gross income attributable to the relevant activities equals or exceeds 50 % of the Entity's gross income during the shorter of: (i) the three-year period ending on 31 December of the year preceding the year in which the determination is made; or (ii) the period during which the Entity has been in existence. The term "Investment Entity" does not include an Entity that is an Active NFE because that Entity meets any of the criteria in subparagraphs D(8)(d) through (g).
This paragraph shall be interpreted in a manner consistent with similar language set forth in the definition of "financial institution" in the Financial Action Task Force Recommendations.
7. The term "Financial Asset" includes a security (for example, a share of stock in a corporation; partnership or beneficial ownership interest in a widely held or publicly traded partnership or trust; note, bond, debenture, or other evidence of indebtedness), partnership interest, commodity, swap (for example, interest rate swaps, currency swaps, basis swaps, interest rate caps, interest rate floors, commodity swaps, equity swaps, equity index swaps, and similar agreements), Insurance Contract or Annuity Contract, or any interest (including a futures or forward contract or option) in a security, partnership interest, commodity, swap, Insurance Contract, or Annuity Contract. The term "Financial Asset" does not include a non-debt, direct interest in real property.
8. The term "Specified Insurance Company" means any Entity that is an insurance company (or the holding company of an insurance company) which issues, or is obligated to make payments with respect to, a Cash Value Insurance Contract or an Annuity Contract.

B Non-Reporting Financial Institution

1. The term "Non-Reporting Financial Institution" means any Financial Institution which is:

(a) a Governmental Entity, International Organisation or Central Bank, other than with respect to a payment that is derived from an obligation held in connection with a commercial financial activity of a type engaged in by a Specified Insurance Company, Custodial Institution, or Depository Institution;

(b) a Broad Participation Retirement Fund; a Narrow Participation Retirement Fund; a Pension Fund of a Governmental Entity, International Organisation or Central Bank; or a Qualified Credit Card Issuer;

VAT EC

(c) any other Entity that presents a low risk of being used to evade tax, has substantially similar characteristics to any of the Entities described in subparagraphs B(1)(a) and (b), and is included in the list of Non-Reporting Financial Institutions referred to in Article 8(7a) of this Directive, provided that the status of such Entity as a Non-Reporting Financial Institution does not frustrate the purposes of this Directive;

(d) an Exempt Collective Investment Vehicle; or

(e) a trust to the extent that the trustee of the trust is a Reporting Financial Institution and reports all information required to be reported pursuant to Section I with respect to all Reportable Accounts of the trust.

2. The term "Governmental Entity" means the government of a Member State or other jurisdiction, any political subdivision of a Member State or other jurisdiction (which, for the avoidance of doubt, includes a state, province, county, or municipality), or any wholly owned agency or instrumentality of a Member State or other jurisdiction or of any one or more of the foregoing (each, a "Governmental Entity"). This category is comprised of the integral parts, controlled entities, and political subdivisions of a Member State or other jurisdiction.

(a) An "integral part" of a Member State or other jurisdiction means any person, organisation, agency, bureau, fund, instrumentality, or other body, however designated, that constitutes a governing authority of a Member State or other jurisdiction. The net earnings of the governing authority must be credited to its own account or to other accounts of the Member State or other jurisdiction, with no portion inuring to the benefit of any private person. An integral part does not include any individual who is a sovereign, official, or administrator acting in a private or personal capacity.

(b) A "controlled entity" means an Entity which is separate in form from the Member State or other jurisdiction or which otherwise constitutes a separate juridical entity, provided that:

(i) the Entity is wholly owned and controlled by one or more Governmental Entities directly or through one or more controlled entities;

(ii) the Entity's net earnings are credited to its own account or to the accounts of one or more Governmental Entities, with no portion of its income inuring to the benefit of any private person; and

(iii) the Entity's assets vest in one or more Governmental Entities upon dissolution.

(c) Income does not inure to the benefit of private persons if such persons are the intended beneficiaries of a governmental programme, and the programme activities are performed for the general public with respect to the common welfare or relate to the administration of some phase of government. Notwithstanding the foregoing, however, income is considered to inure to the benefit of private persons if the income is derived from the use of a Governmental Entity to conduct a commercial business, such as a commercial banking business, that provides financial services to private persons.

3. The term "International Organisation" means any international organisation or wholly owned agency or instrumentality thereof. This category includes any intergovernmental organisation (including a supranational organisation) (i) that is comprised primarily of governments; (ii) that has in effect a headquarters or substantially similar agreement with the Member State; and (iii) the income of which does not inure to the benefit of private persons.

4. The term "Central Bank" means an institution that is by law or government sanction the principal authority, other than the government of the Member State itself, issuing instruments intended to circulate as currency. Such an institution may include an instrumentality that is separate from the government of the Member State, whether or not owned in whole or in part by the Member State.

5. The term "Broad Participation Retirement Fund" means a fund established to provide retirement, disability, or death benefits, or any combination thereof, to beneficiaries who are current or former employees (or persons designated by such employees) of one or more employers in consideration for services rendered, provided that the fund:

(a) does not have a single beneficiary with a right to more than 5 % of the fund's assets;

(b) is subject to government regulation and provides information reporting to the tax authorities; and

(c) satisfies at least one of the following requirements:

(i) the fund is generally exempt from tax on investment income, or taxation of such income is deferred or taxed at a reduced rate, due to its status as a retirement or pension plan;

(ii) the fund receives at least 50 % of its total contributions (other than transfers of assets from other plans described in subparagraphs B(5) through (7) or from retirement and pension accounts described in subparagraph C(17)(a)) from the sponsoring employers;

(iii) distributions or withdrawals from the fund are allowed only upon the occurrence of specified events related to retirement, disability, or death (except rollover distributions to other retirement funds described in subparagraphs B(5) through (7) or retirement and pension accounts described in subparagraph C(17)(a)), or penalties apply to distributions or withdrawals made before such specified events; or

(iv) contributions (other than certain permitted make-up contributions) by employees to the fund are limited by reference to earned income of the employee or may not exceed, annually, an amount denominated in the domestic currency of each Member State that corresponds to USD 50 000, applying the rules set forth in paragraph C of Section VII for account aggregation and currency translation.

6. The term "Narrow Participation Retirement Fund" means a fund established to provide retirement, disability, or death benefits to beneficiaries who are current or former employees (or persons designated by such employees) of one or more employers in consideration for services rendered, provided that:

(a) the fund has fewer than 50 participants;

(b) the fund is sponsored by one or more employers that are not Investment Entities or Passive NFEs;

(c) the employee and employer contributions to the fund (other than transfers of assets from retirement and pension accounts described in subparagraph C(17)(a)) are limited by reference to earned income and compensation of the employee, respectively;

(d) participants that are not residents of the Member State in which the fund is established are not entitled to more than 20 % of the fund's assets; and

(e) the fund is subject to government regulation and provides information reporting to the tax authorities.

7. The term "Pension Fund of a Governmental Entity, International Organisation or Central Bank" means a fund established by a Governmental Entity, International Organisation or Central Bank to provide retirement, disability, or death benefits to beneficiaries or participants who are current or former employees (or persons designated by such employees), or who are not current or former employees, if the benefits provided to such beneficiaries or participants are in consideration of personal services performed for the Governmental Entity, International Organisation or Central Bank.

8. The term "Qualified Credit Card Issuer" means a Financial Institution satisfying the following requirements:

(a) the Financial Institution is a Financial Institution solely because it is an issuer of credit cards that accepts deposits only when a customer makes a payment in excess of a balance due with respect to the card and the overpayment is not immediately returned to the customer; and

(b) beginning on or before 1 January 2016, the Financial Institution implements policies and procedures either to prevent a customer from making an overpayment in excess of an amount denominated in the domestic currency of each Member State that corresponds to USD 50 000, or to ensure that any customer overpayment in excess of that amount is refunded to the customer within 60 days, in each case applying the rules set forth in paragraph C of Section VII for account aggregation and currency translation. For this purpose, a customer overpayment does not refer to credit balances to the extent of disputed charges but does include credit balances resulting from merchandise returns.

9. The term "Exempt Collective Investment Vehicle" means an Investment Entity that is regulated as a collective investment vehicle, provided that all of the interests in the collective investment vehicle are held by or through individuals or Entities that are not Reportable Persons, except a Passive NFE with Controlling Persons who are Reportable Persons.

An Investment Entity that is regulated as a collective investment vehicle does not fail to qualify under subparagraph B(9) as an Exempt Collective Investment Vehicle, solely because the collective investment vehicle has issued physical shares in bearer form, provided that:

(a) the collective investment vehicle has not issued, and does not issue, any physical shares in bearer form after 31 December 2015;

(b) the collective investment vehicle retires all such shares upon surrender;

(c) the collective investment vehicle performs the due diligence procedures set forth in Sections II through VII and reports any information required to be reported with respect to any such shares when such shares are presented for redemption or other payment; and

(d) the collective investment vehicle has in place policies and procedures to ensure that such shares are redeemed or immobilised as soon as possible, and in any event prior to 1 January 2018.

C Financial Account

1. The term "Financial Account" means an account maintained by a Financial Institution, and includes a Depository Account, a Custodial Account and:

(a) in the case of an Investment Entity, any equity or debt interest in the Financial Institution. Notwithstanding the foregoing, the term "Financial Account" does not include any equity or debt interest in an Entity that is an Investment Entity solely because it (i) renders investment advice to, and acts on behalf of; or (ii) manages portfolios for, and acts on behalf of, a customer for the purpose of investing, managing, or administering Financial Assets deposited in the name of the customer with a Financial Institution other than such Entity;

(b) in the case of a Financial Institution not described in subparagraph C(1)(a), any equity or debt interest in the Financial Institution, if the class of interests was established with the purpose of avoiding reporting in accordance with Section I; and

(c) any Cash Value Insurance Contract and any Annuity Contract issued or maintained by a Financial Institution, other than a non-investment-linked, non-transferable immediate life annuity that is issued to an individual and monetises a pension or disability benefit provided under an account that is an Excluded Account.

The term "Financial Account" does not include any account that is an Excluded Account.

2. The term "Depository Account" includes any commercial, checking, savings, time, or thrift account, or an account that is evidenced by a certificate of deposit, thrift certificate, investment certificate, certificate of indebtedness, or other similar instrument maintained by a Financial Institution in the ordinary course of a banking or similar business. A Depository Account also includes an amount held by an insurance company pursuant to a guaranteed investment contract or similar agreement to pay or credit interest thereon.

3. The term "Custodial Account" means an account (other than an Insurance Contract or Annuity Contract) which holds one or more Financial Assets for the benefit of another person.

4. The term "Equity Interest" means, in the case of a partnership that is a Financial Institution, either a capital or profits interest in the partnership. In the case of a trust that is a Financial Institution, an Equity Interest is considered to be held by any person treated as a settlor or beneficiary of all or a portion of the trust, or any other natural person exercising ultimate effective control over the trust. A Reportable Person will be treated as being a beneficiary of a trust if such Reportable Person has the right to receive directly or indirectly (for example, through a nominee) a mandatory distribution or may receive, directly or indirectly, a discretionary distribution from the trust.

5. The term "Insurance Contract" means a contract (other than an Annuity Contract) under which the issuer agrees to pay an amount upon the occurrence of a specified contingency involving mortality, morbidity, accident, liability, or property risk.

6. The term "Annuity Contract" means a contract under which the issuer agrees to make payments for a period of time determined in whole or in part by reference to the life expectancy of one or more individuals. The term also includes a contract that is considered to be an Annuity Contract in accordance with the law, regulation, or practice of the Member State or other jurisdiction in which the contract was issued, and under which the issuer agrees to make payments for a term of years.

7. The term "Cash Value Insurance Contract" means an Insurance Contract (other than an indemnity reinsurance contract between two insurance companies) that has a Cash Value.

8. The term "Cash Value" means the greater of (i) the amount that the policyholder is entitled to receive upon surrender or termination of the contract (determined without reduction for any surrender charge or policy loan); and (ii) the amount the policyholder can borrow under or with regard to the contract. Notwithstanding the foregoing, the term "Cash Value" does not include an amount payable under an Insurance Contract:

(a) solely by reason of the death of an individual insured under a life insurance contract;

(b) as a personal injury or sickness benefit or other benefit providing indemnification of an economic loss incurred upon the occurrence of the event insured against;

(c) as a refund of a previously paid premium (less cost of insurance charges whether or not actually imposed) under an Insurance Contract (other than an investment-linked life insurance or annuity contract) due to cancellation or termination of the contract, decrease in risk exposure during the effective period of the contract, or arising from the correction of a posting or similar error with regard to the premium for the contract;

(d) as a policyholder dividend (other than a termination dividend) provided that the dividend relates to an Insurance Contract under which the only benefits payable are described in subparagraph C(8)(b); or

(e) as a return of an advance premium or premium deposit for an Insurance Contract for which the premium is payable at least annually if the amount of the advance premium or premium deposit does not exceed the next annual premium that will be payable under the contract.

9. The term "Pre-existing Account" means:

(a) a Financial Account maintained by a Reporting Financial Institution as of 31 December 2015;

(b) any Financial Account of an Account Holder, regardless of the date such Financial Account was opened, if:

(i) the Account Holder also holds with the Reporting Financial Institution (or with a Related Entity within the same Member State as the Reporting Financial Institution) a Financial Account that is a Pre-existing Account under subparagraph C(9)(a);

(ii) the Reporting Financial Institution (and, as applicable, the Related Entity within the same Member State as the Reporting Financial Institution) treats both of the aforementioned Financial Accounts, and any other Financial Accounts of the Account Holder that are treated as Pre-existing Accounts under point (b), as a single Financial Account for purposes of satisfying the standards of knowledge requirements set forth in paragraph A of Section VII, and for purposes of determining the balance or value of any of the Financial Accounts when applying any of the account thresholds;

(iii) with respect to a Financial Account that is subject to AML/KYC Procedures, the Reporting Financial Institution is permitted to satisfy such AML/KYC Procedures for the Financial Account by relying upon the AML/KYC Procedures performed for the Pre-existing Account described in subparagraph C(9)(a); and

(iv) the opening of the Financial Account does not require the provision of new, additional or amended customer information by the Account Holder other than for the purposes of this Directive.

10. The term "New Account" means a Financial Account maintained by a Reporting Financial Institution opened on or after 1 January 2016 unless it is treated as a Pre-existing Account under subparagraph C(9)(b).

11. The term "Pre-existing Individual Account" means a Pre-existing Account held by one or more individuals.

12. The term "New Individual Account" means a New Account held by one or more individuals.

13. The term "Pre-existing Entity Account" means a Pre-existing Account held by one or more Entities.

14. The term "Lower Value Account" means a Pre-existing Individual Account with an aggregate balance or value as of 31 December 2015 that does not exceed an amount denominated in the domestic currency of each Member State that corresponds to USD 1 000 000.

15. The term "High Value Account" means a Pre-existing Individual Account with an aggregate balance or value that exceeds, as of 31 December 2015, or 31 December of any subsequent year, an amount denominated in the domestic currency of each Member State that corresponds to USD 1 000 000.

16. The term "New Entity Account" means a New Account held by one or more Entities.

17. The term "Excluded Account" means any of the following accounts:

(a) a retirement or pension account that satisfies the following requirements:

(i) the account is subject to regulation as a personal retirement account or is part of a registered or regulated retirement or pension plan for the provision of retirement or pension benefits (including disability or death benefits);

(ii) the account is tax-favoured (i.e., contributions to the account that would otherwise be subject to tax are deductible or excluded from the gross income of the Account Holder or taxed at a reduced rate, or taxation of investment income from the account is deferred or taxed at a reduced rate);

(iii) information reporting is required to the tax authorities with respect to the account;

(iv) withdrawals are conditioned on reaching a specified retirement age, disability, or death, or penalties apply to withdrawals made before such specified events; and

(v) either (i) annual contributions are limited to an amount denominated in the domestic currency of each Member State that corresponds to USD 50 000 or less; or (ii) there is a maximum lifetime contribution limit to the account of an amount denominated in the domestic currency of each Member State that corresponds to USD 1 000 000 or less, in each case applying the rules set forth in paragraph C of Section VII for account aggregation and currency translation.

A Financial Account that otherwise satisfies the requirement of subparagraph C(17)(a)(v) will not fail to satisfy such requirement solely because such Financial Account may receive assets or funds transferred from one or more Financial

Accounts that meet the requirements of subparagraph C(17)(a) or (b) or from one or more retirement or pension funds that meet the requirements of any of subparagraphs B(5) through (7);

(b) an account that satisfies the following requirements:

(i) the account is subject to regulation as an investment vehicle for purposes other than for retirement and is regularly traded on an established securities market, or the account is subject to regulation as a savings vehicle for purposes other than for retirement;

(ii) the account is tax-favoured (i.e., contributions to the account that would otherwise be subject to tax are deductible or excluded from the gross income of the Account Holder or taxed at a reduced rate, or taxation of investment income from the account is deferred or taxed at a reduced rate);

(iii) withdrawals are conditioned on meeting specific criteria related to the purpose of the investment or savings account (for example, the provision of educational or medical benefits), or penalties apply to withdrawals made before such criteria are met; and

(iv) annual contributions are limited to an amount denominated in the domestic currency of each Member State that corresponds to USD 50 000 or less, applying the rules set forth in paragraph C of Section VII for account aggregation and currency translation.

A Financial Account that otherwise satisfies the requirement of subparagraph C(17)(b)(iv) will not fail to satisfy such requirement solely because such Financial Account may receive assets or funds transferred from one or more Financial Accounts that meet the requirements of subparagraph C(17)(a) or (b) or from one or more retirement or pension funds that meet the requirements of any of subparagraphs B(5) through (7);

(c) a life insurance contract with a coverage period that will end before the insured individual attains age 90, provided that the contract satisfies the following requirements:

(i) periodic premiums, which do not decrease over time, are payable at least annually during the period the contract is in existence or until the insured attains age 90, whichever is shorter;

(ii) the contract has no contract value that any person can access (by withdrawal, loan, or otherwise) without terminating the contract;

(iii) the amount (other than a death benefit) payable upon cancellation or termination of the contract cannot exceed the aggregate premiums paid for the contract, less the sum of mortality, morbidity, and expense charges (whether or not actually imposed) for the period or periods of the contract's existence and any amounts paid prior to the cancellation or termination of the contract; and

(iv) the contract is not held by a transferee for value;

(d) an account that is held solely by an estate if the documentation for such account includes a copy of the deceased's will or death certificate;

(e) an account established in connection with any of the following:

(i) a court order or judgment.

(ii) a sale, exchange, or lease of real or personal property, provided that the account satisfies the following requirements:

— the account is funded solely with a down payment, earnest money, deposit in an amount appropriate to secure an obligation directly related to the transaction, or a similar payment, or is funded with a Financial Asset that is deposited in the account in connection with the sale, exchange, or lease of the property,

— the account is established and used solely to secure the obligation of the purchaser to pay the purchase price for the property, the seller to pay any contingent liability, or the lessor or lessee to pay for any damages relating to the leased property as agreed under the lease,

— the assets of the account, including the income earned thereon, will be paid or otherwise distributed for the benefit of the purchaser, seller, lessor, or lessee (including to satisfy such person's obligation) when the property is sold, exchanged, or surrendered, or the lease terminates,

— the account is not a margin or similar account established in connection with a sale or exchange of a Financial Asset, and

— the account is not associated with an account described in subparagraph C(17)(f);

(iii) an obligation of a Financial Institution servicing a loan secured by real property to set aside a portion of a payment solely to facilitate the payment of taxes or insurance related to the real property at a later time;

(iv) an obligation of a Financial Institution solely to facilitate the payment of taxes at a later time;

(f) a Depository Account that satisfies the following requirements:

(i) the account exists solely because a customer makes a payment in excess of a balance due with respect to a credit card or other revolving credit facility and the overpayment is not immediately returned to the customer; and

(ii) beginning on or before 1 January 2016, the Financial Institution implements policies and procedures either to prevent a customer from making an overpayment in excess of an amount denominated in the domestic currency of each Member State that corresponds to USD 50 000, or to ensure that any customer overpayment in excess of that amount is refunded to the customer within 60 days, in each case applying the rules set forth in paragraph C of Section VII for currency translation. For this purpose, a customer overpayment does not refer to credit balances to the extent of disputed charges but does include credit balances resulting from merchandise returns;

(g) any other account that presents a low risk of being used to evade tax, has substantially similar characteristics to any of the accounts described in subparagraphs C(17)(a) through (f), and is included in the list of Excluded Accounts referred to in Article 8(7a) of this Directive, provided that the status of such account as an Excluded Account does not frustrate the purposes of this Directive.

D Reportable Account

1. The term "Reportable Account" means a Financial Account that is maintained by a Member State Reporting Financial Institution and is held by one or more Reportable Persons or by a Passive NFE with one or more Controlling Persons that is a Reportable Person, provided it has been identified as such pursuant to the due diligence procedures described in Sections II through VII.

2. The term "Reportable Person" means a Member State Person other than: (i) a corporation the stock of which is regularly traded on one or more established securities markets; (ii) any corporation that is a Related Entity of a corporation described in clause (i); (iii) a Governmental Entity; (iv) an International Organisation; (v) a Central Bank; or (vi) a Financial Institution.

3. The term "Member State Person" with regard to each Member State means an individual or Entity that is resident in any other Member State under the tax laws of that other Member State, or an estate of a decedent that was a resident of any other Member State. For this purpose, an Entity such as a partnership, limited liability partnership or similar legal arrangement, which has no residence for tax purposes shall be treated as resident in the jurisdiction in which its place of effective management is situated.

4. The term "Participating Jurisdiction" with regard to each Member State means:

(a) any other Member State;

(b) any other jurisdiction (i) with which the Member State concerned has an agreement in place pursuant to which that jurisdiction will provide the information specified in Section I; and (ii) which is identified in a list published by that Member State and notified to the European Commission;

(c) any other jurisdiction (i) with which the Union has an agreement in place pursuant to which that jurisdiction will provide the information specified in Section I; and (ii) which is identified in a list published by the European Commission.

5. The term "Controlling Persons" means the natural persons who exercise control over an Entity. In the case of a trust, that term means the settlor(s), the trustee(s), the protector(s) (if any), the beneficiary(ies) or class(es) of beneficiaries, and any other natural person(s) exercising ultimate effective control over the trust, and in the case of a legal arrangement other than a trust, such term means persons in equivalent or similar positions. The term "Controlling Persons" must be interpreted in a manner consistent with the Financial Action Task Force Recommendations.

6. The term "NFE" means any Entity that is not a Financial Institution.

7. The term "Passive NFE" means any: (i) NFE that is not an Active NFE; or (ii) an Investment Entity described in subparagraph A(6)(b) that is not a Participating Jurisdiction Financial Institution.

8. The term "Active NFE" means any NFE that meets any of the following criteria:

(a) less than 50 % of the NFE's gross income for the preceding calendar year or other appropriate reporting period is passive income and less than 50 % of the assets held by the NFE during the preceding calendar year or other appropriate reporting period are assets that produce or are held for the production of passive income;

(b) the stock of the NFE is regularly traded on an established securities market or the NFE is a Related Entity of an Entity the stock of which is regularly traded on an established securities market;

(c) the NFE is a Governmental Entity, an International Organisation, a Central Bank, or an Entity wholly owned by one or more of the foregoing;

(d) substantially all of the activities of the NFE consist of holding (in whole or in part) the outstanding stock of, or providing financing and services to, one or more subsidiaries that engage in trades or businesses other than the business of a Financial Institution, except that an Entity does not qualify for this status if the Entity functions (or holds itself out) as an investment fund, such as a private equity fund, venture capital fund, leveraged buyout fund, or any investment vehicle whose purpose is to acquire or fund companies and then hold interests in those companies as capital assets for investment purposes;

(e) the NFE is not yet operating a business and has no prior operating history, but is investing capital into assets with the intent to operate a business other than that of a Financial Institution, provided that the NFE does not qualify for this exception after the date that is 24 months after the date of the initial organisation of the NFE;

(f) the NFE was not a Financial Institution in the past five years, and is in the process of liquidating its assets or is reorganising with the intent to continue or recommence operations in a business other than that of a Financial Institution;

(g) the NFE primarily engages in financing and hedging transactions with, or for, Related Entities that are not Financial Institutions, and does not provide financing or hedging services to any Entity that is not a Related Entity, provided that the group of any such Related Entities is primarily engaged in a business other than that of a Financial Institution; or

(h) the NFE meets all of the following requirements:

(i) it is established and operated in its Member State or other jurisdiction of residence exclusively for religious, charitable, scientific, artistic, cultural, athletic, or educational purposes; or it is established and operated in its Member State or other jurisdiction of residence and it is a professional organisation, business league, chamber of commerce, labour organisation, agricultural or horticultural organisation, civic league or an organisation operated exclusively for the promotion of social welfare;

(ii) it is exempt from income tax in its Member State or other jurisdiction of residence;

(iii) it has no shareholders or members who have a proprietary or beneficial interest in its income or assets;

(iv) the applicable laws of the NFE's Member State or other jurisdiction of residence or the NFE's formation documents do not permit any income or assets of the NFE to be distributed to, or applied for the benefit of, a private person or non-charitable Entity other than pursuant to the conduct of the NFE's charitable activities, or as payment of reasonable compensation for services rendered, or as payment representing the fair market value of property which the NFE has purchased; and

(v) the applicable laws of the NFE's Member State or other jurisdiction of residence or the NFE's formation documents require that, upon the NFE's liquidation or dissolution, all of its assets be distributed to a Governmental Entity or other non-profit organisation, or escheat to the government of the NFE's Member State or other jurisdiction of residence or any political subdivision thereof.

E Miscellaneous

1. The term "Account Holder" means the person listed or identified as the holder of a Financial Account by the Financial Institution that maintains the account. A person, other than a Financial Institution, holding a Financial Account for the benefit or account of another person as agent, custodian, nominee, signatory, investment advisor, or intermediary, is not treated as holding the account for purposes of this Directive, and such other person is treated as holding the account. In the case of a Cash Value Insurance Contract or an Annuity Contract, the Account Holder is any person entitled to access the Cash Value or change the beneficiary of the contract. If no person can access the Cash Value or change the beneficiary, the Account Holder is any person named as the owner in the contract and any person with a vested entitlement to payment under the terms of the contract. Upon the maturity of a Cash Value Insurance Contract or an Annuity Contract, each person entitled to receive a payment under the contract is treated as an Account Holder.

2. The term "AML/KYC Procedures" means the customer due diligence procedures of a Reporting Financial Institution pursuant to the anti-money laundering or similar requirements to which such Reporting Financial Institution is subject.

3. The term "Entity" means a legal person or a legal arrangement, such as a corporation, partnership, trust, or foundation.
4. An Entity is a "Related Entity" of another Entity if (i) either Entity controls the other Entity; (ii) the two Entities are under common control; or (iii) the two Entities are Investment Entities described in subparagraph A(6)(b), are under common management, and such management fulfils the due diligence obligations of such Investment Entities. For this purpose control includes direct or indirect ownership of more than 50 % of the vote and value in an Entity.
5. The term "TIN" means Taxpayer Identification Number (or functional equivalent in the absence of a Taxpayer Identification Number).
6. The term "Documentary Evidence" includes any of the following:
   (a) a certificate of residence issued by an authorised government body (for example, a government or agency thereof, or a municipality) of the Member State or other jurisdiction in which the payee claims to be a resident;
   (b) with respect to an individual, any valid identification issued by an authorised government body (for example, a government or agency thereof, or a municipality), that includes the individual's name and is typically used for identification purposes;
   (c) with respect to an Entity, any official documentation issued by an authorised government body (for example, a government or agency thereof, or a municipality) that includes the name of the Entity and either the address of its principal office in the Member State or other jurisdiction in which it claims to be a resident or the Member State or other jurisdiction in which the Entity was incorporated or organised;
   (d) any audited financial statement, third-party credit report, bankruptcy filing, or securities regulator's report.

With respect to a Pre-existing Entity Account, Reporting Financial Institutions may use as Documentary Evidence any classification in the Reporting Financial Institution's records with respect to the Account Holder that was determined based on a standardised industry coding system, that was recorded by the Reporting Financial Institution consistent with its normal business practices for purposes of AML/KYC Procedures or another regulatory purposes (other than for tax purposes) and that was implemented by the Reporting Financial Institution prior to the date used to classify the Financial Account as a Pre-existing Account, provided that the Reporting Financial Institution does not know or does not have reason to know that such classification is incorrect or unreliable. The term "standardised industry coding system" means a coding system used to classify establishments by business type for purposes other than tax purposes.

SECTION IX
EFFECTIVE IMPLEMENTATION

Pursuant to Article 8(3a) of this Directive, Member States must have rules and administrative procedures in place to ensure effective implementation of, and compliance with, the reporting and due diligence procedures set out above including:

(1) rules to prevent any Financial Institutions, persons or intermediaries from adopting practices intended to circumvent the reporting and due diligence procedures;

(2) rules requiring Reporting Financial Institutions to keep records of the steps undertaken and any evidence relied upon for the performance of the above procedures and adequate measures to obtain those records;

(3) administrative procedures to verify Reporting Financial Institutions' compliance with the reporting and due diligence procedures; administrative procedures to follow up with a Reporting Financial Institution when undocumented accounts are reported;

(4) administrative procedures to ensure that the Entities and accounts defined in domestic law as Non-Reporting Financial Institutions and Excluded Accounts continue to have a low risk of being used to evade tax; and

(5) effective enforcement provisions to address non-compliance.

SECTION X
IMPLEMENTATION DATES AS REGARDS REPORTING FINANCIAL INSTITUTIONS LOCATED IN AUSTRIA

In the case of Reporting Financial Institutions located in Austria, all references to "2016" and "2017" in this Annex should be read as references to "2017" and "2018" respectively.

In the case of Pre-existing Accounts held by Reporting Financial Institutions located in Austria, all references to "31 December 2015" in this Annex should be read as references to "31 December 2016".][1]

VAT EC

Amendments—[1] Annex I inserted by Council Directive 2014/107/EU Art 1(6), Annex, with effect from 5 January 2015. See Art 2 for implementation provisions (deadline for implementation is 31 December 2015, with measures to apply from 1 January 2016) (OJ L 359, 16.12.2014, p 1).

[ANNEX II

COMPLEMENTARY REPORTING AND DUE DILIGENCE RULES FOR FINANCIAL ACCOUNT INFORMATION

1 Change in circumstances

A "change in circumstances" includes any change that results in the addition of information relevant to a person's status or otherwise conflicts with such person's status. In addition, a change in circumstances includes any change or addition of information to the Account Holder's account (including the addition, substitution, or other change of an Account Holder) or any change or addition of information to any account associated with such account (applying the account aggregation rules described in subparagraphs C(1) through (3) of Section VII of Annex I) if such change or addition of information affects the status of the Account Holder.

If a Reporting Financial Institution has relied on the residence address test described in subparagraph B(1) of Section III of Annex I and there is a change in circumstances that causes the Reporting Financial Institution to know or have reason to know that the original Documentary Evidence (or other equivalent documentation) is incorrect or unreliable, the Reporting Financial Institution must, by the later of the last day of the relevant calendar year or other appropriate reporting period, or 90 calendar days following the notice or discovery of such change in circumstances, obtain a self-certification and new Documentary Evidence to establish the residence(s) for tax purposes of the Account Holder. If the Reporting Financial Institution cannot obtain the self-certification and new Documentary Evidence by such date, the Reporting Financial Institution must apply the electronic record search procedure described in subparagraphs B(2) through (6) of Section III of Annex I.

2 Self-certification for New Entity Accounts

With respect to New Entity Accounts, for the purposes of determining whether a Controlling Person of a Passive NFE is a Reportable Person, a Reporting Financial Institution may only rely on a self-certification from either the Account Holder or the Controlling Person.

3 Residence of a Financial Institution

A Financial Institution is "resident" in a Member State if it is subject to the jurisdiction of such Member State (i.e., the Member State is able to enforce reporting by the Financial Institution). In general, where a Financial Institution is resident for tax purposes in a Member State, it is subject to the jurisdiction of such Member State and it is, thus, a Member State Financial Institution. In the case of a trust that is a Financial Institution (irrespective of whether it is resident for tax purposes in a Member State), the trust is considered to be subject to the jurisdiction of a Member State if one or more of its trustees are resident in such Member State except if the trust reports all the information required to be reported pursuant to this Directive with respect to Reportable Accounts maintained by the trust to another Member State because it is resident for tax purposes in such other Member State. However, where a Financial Institution (other than a trust) does not have a residence for tax purposes (e.g., because it is treated as fiscally transparent, or it is located in a jurisdiction that does not have an income tax), it is considered to be subject to the jurisdiction of a Member State and it is, thus, a Member State Financial Institution if:

(a) it is incorporated under the laws of the Member State;

(b) it has its place of management (including effective management) in the Member State; or

(c) it is subject to financial supervision in the Member State.

Where a Financial Institution (other than a trust) is resident in two or more Member States, such Financial Institution will be subject to the reporting and due diligence obligations of the Member State in which it maintains the Financial Account(s).

4 Account maintained

In general, an account would be considered to be maintained by a Financial Institution as follows:

(a) in the case of a Custodial Account, by the Financial Institution that holds custody over the assets in the account (including a Financial Institution that holds assets in street name for an Account Holder in such institution);

(b) in the case of a Depository Account, by the Financial Institution that is obligated to make payments with respect to the account (excluding an agent of a Financial Institution regardless of whether such agent is a Financial Institution);

(c) in the case of any equity or debt interest in a Financial Institution that constitutes a Financial Account, by such Financial Institution;

(d) in the case of a Cash Value Insurance Contract or an Annuity Contract, by the Financial Institution that is obligated to make payments with respect to the contract.

5 Trusts that are Passive NFEs

An Entity such as a partnership, limited liability partnership or similar legal arrangement that has no residence for tax purposes, according to subparagraph D(3) of Section VIII of Annex I, shall be treated as resident in the jurisdiction in which its place of effective management is situated. For these purposes, a legal person or a legal arrangement is considered "similar" to a partnership and a limited liability partnership where it is not treated as a taxable unit in a Member State under the tax laws of such Member State. However, in order to avoid duplicate reporting (given the wide scope of the term "Controlling Persons" in the case of trusts), a trust that is a Passive NFE may not be considered a similar legal arrangement.

6 Address of Entity's principal office

One of the requirements described in subparagraph E(6)(c) of Section VIII of Annex I is that, with respect to an Entity, the official documentation includes either the address of the Entity's principal office in the Member State or other jurisdiction in which it claims to be a resident or the Member State or other jurisdiction in which the Entity was incorporated or organised. The address of the Entity's principal office is generally the place in which its place of effective management is situated. The address of a Financial Institution with which the Entity maintains an account, a post office box, or an address used solely for mailing purposes is not the address of the Entity's principal office unless such address is the only address used by the Entity and appears as the Entity's registered address in the Entity's organisational documents. Further, an address that is provided subject to instructions to hold all mail to that address is not the address of the Entity's principal office.][1]

Amendments—[1] Annex II I inserted by Council Directive 2014/107/EU Art 1(6), Annex, with effect from 5 January 2015. See Art 2 for implementation provisions (deadline for implementation is 31 December 2015, with measures to apply from 1 January 2016) (OJ L 359, 16.12.2014, p 1).

EU Regulations

COUNCIL REGULATION 2913/92/EEC OF 12 OCTOBER 1992 ESTABLISHING THE COMMUNITY CUSTOMS CODE

(2913/92/EEC)

Note—See OJ L302 19.10.1992, p 1.

Repeal—This Regulation was to be repealed by European Parliament and Council Regulation 450/2008/EU, Art 186. This repeal was to be effected by 23 June 2013 at the latest (See OJ L 145, 4.6.2008, p 1). However, Regulation 450/2008/EU was "recast" as the Union Customs Code (Regulation 952/2013/EU), which was adopted on 9 October 2013 and is likely to apply from 1 May 2016. Until that date, the provisions of the Community Customs Code and its implementing provisions will continue to apply.

Full details of the Community Customs Code, its implementing regulation (2454/93/EEC) and the Union Customs Code are available in *Tolley's Customs and Excise Duties Handbook*.

Contents

VAT EC

THE COUNCIL OF THE EUROPEAN COMMUNITIES

Having regard to the Treaty establishing the European Economic Community, and in particular Articles 28, 100a and 113 thereof,

Having regard to the proposal from the Commission,

In co-operation with the European Parliament,

Having regard to the opinion of the Economic and Social Committee,

Whereas the Community is based upon a customs union; whereas it is advisable, in the interests both of Community traders and the customs authorities, to assemble in a code the provisions of customs legislation that are at present contained in a large number of Community regulations and directives; whereas this task is of fundamental importance from the standpoint of this internal market;

Whereas such a Community Customs Code (hereinafter called "the Code") must incorporate current customs legislation; whereas it is, nevertheless, advisable to amend that legislation in order to make it more consistent, to simplify it and to remedy certain omissions that still exist with a view to adopting complete Community legislation in this area;

Whereas, based on the concept of an internal market, the code must contain the general rules and procedures which ensure the implementation of the tariff and other measures introduced at Community level in connection with trade in goods between the Community and third countries; whereas it must cover, among other things, the implementation of common agricultural and commercial policy measures taking into account the requirements of these common policies;

Whereas it would appear advisable to specify that this Code is applicable without prejudice to specific provisions laid down in other fields; whereas such specific rules may exist or be introduced in the context, *inter alia*, of legislation relating to agriculture, statistics, commercial policy or own resources;

Whereas, in order to secure a balance between the needs of the customs authorities in regard to ensuring the correct application of customs legislation, on the one hand, and the right of traders to be treated fairly, on the other, the said authorities must be granted, *inter alia*, extensive powers of control and the said traders a right of appeal; whereas the implementation of a customs appeals system will require the United Kingdom to introduce new administrative procedures which cannot be effected before 1 January 1995;

Whereas in view of the paramount importance of external trade for the Community, customs formalities and controls should be abolished or at least kept to a minimum;

Whereas it is important to guarantee the uniform application of this Code and to provide, to that end, for a Community procedure which enables the procedures for its implementation to be adopted within a suitable time; whereas a Customs Code Committee should be set up in order to ensure close and effective co-operation between the Member States and the Commission in this field;

Whereas in adopting the measures required to implement this Code, the utmost care must be taken to prevent any fraud or irregularity liable to affect adversely the General Budget of the European Communities,

HAS ADOPTED THIS REGULATION:

TITLE I: GENERAL PROVISIONS

CHAPTER 1—SCOPE AND BASIC DEFINITIONS

Article 1

Customs rules shall consist of this Code and the provisions adopted at Community level or nationally to implement them. The Code shall apply, without prejudice to special rules laid down in other fields

— to trade between the Community and third countries,

— to goods covered by the Treaty establishing the European Coal and Steel Community, the Treaty establishing the European Economic Community or the Treaty establishing the European Atomic Energy Community.

Article 2

1. Save as otherwise provided, either under international conventions or customary practices of a limited geographic and economic scope or under autonomous Community measures, Community customs rules shall apply uniformly throughout the customs territory of the Community.

2. Certain provisions of customs rules may also apply outside the customs territory of the Community within the framework of either rules governing specific fields or international conventions.

Article 3

[1 The customs territory of the Community shall comprise:

— the territory of the Kingdom of Belgium,
— the territory of the Kingdom of Denmark, except the Faroe Islands and Greenland,
— the territory of the Federal Republic of Germany, except the Island of Heligoland and the territory of Büsingen (Treaty of 23 November 1964 between the Federal Republic of Germany and the Swiss Confederation),
— the territory of the Kingdom of Spain, except Ceuta and Melilla,
— [the territory of the French Republic, except the overseas territories and Saint-Pierre and Miquelon and Mayette,][2]
— the territory of the Hellenic Republic,
— the territory of Ireland,
— the territory of the Italian Republic, except the municipalities of Livigno and Campione d'Italia and the national waters of Lake Lugano which are between the bank and the political frontier of the area between Ponte Tresa and Porto Ceresio,
— the territory of the Grand Duchy of Luxembourg,
— the territory of the Republic of Austria,
— the territory of the Kingdom of the Netherlands in Europe,
— the territory of the Portuguese Republic,
— [the territory of the Republic of Finland,][2]
— the territory of the Kingdom of Sweden,
— the territory of the United Kingdom of Great Britain and Northern Ireland and of the Channel Islands and the Isle of Man.][1]
[— the territory of the Republic of Bulgaria,
— the territory of Romania][4]
[— the territory of the Republic of Croatia][5]

[2. The following territories situated outside the territory of the Member States shall, taking the conventions and treaties applicable to them into account, be considered to be part of the customs territory of the Community:

(*a*) FRANCE

The territory of the principality of Monaco as defined in the Customs Convention signed in Paris on 18 May 1963 (Official Journal of the French Republic of 27 September 1963, p. 8679)

(*b*) CYPRUS

The territory of the United Kingdom Sovereign Base Areas of Akrotiri and Dhekelia as defined in the Treaty concerning the Establishment of the Republic of Cyprus, signed in Nicosia on 16 August 1960 (United Kingdom Treaty Series No 4 (1961) Cmnd. 1252).][3]

3. The customs territory of the Community shall include the territorial waters, the inland maritime waters and the airspace of the Member States, and the territories referred to in paragraph 2, except for the territorial waters, the inland maritime waters and the airspace of those territories which are not part of the customs territory of the Community pursuant to paragraph 1.

Amendments—

[1] Article 3(1) is substituted by the Act of Accession 1994, art 29, Annex I; see OJ L1, 1.1.95, p 181.
[2] Indents 5 and 13 are substituted by EC Regulation 82/97/EC with effect from 1 January 1997; see OJ L 17, 21.1.97, p 1.
[3] Article 3(2) is substituted by the 2003 Act of Accession Protocol No 3 Annex Part One para 1.
[4] Entries in article 3(1) inserted by Council Regulation 1791/2006/EC art 1, Annex Part 12.
[5] Entry for Republic of Croatia inserted by Council Regulation 517/2013/EU art 1, Annex.

Article 4

For the purposes of this Case, the following definitions shall apply:

(1) "Person" means:
— a natural person,
— a legal person,
— where the possibility is provided for under the rules in force, an association of persons recognised as having the capacity to perform legal acts but lacking the legal status of a legal person.

(2) "Persons established in the Community" means:
— in the case of a natural person, any person who is normally resident there,
— in the case of a legal person or an association of persons, any person that has in the Community its registered office, central headquarters or a permanent business establishment.

(3) "Customs authorities" means the authorities responsible *inter alia* for applying customs rules.

(4) "Customs office" means any office at which all or some of the formalities laid down by customs rules may be completed.

[(4a) "Customs office of entry" means the customs office designated by the customs authorities in accordance with the customs rules to which goods brought into the customs territory of the Community must be conveyed without delay and at which they will be subject to appropriate risk-based entry controls;][3]

[(4b) "Customs office of import" means the customs office designated by the customs authorities in accordance with the customs rules where the formalities for assigning goods brought into the customs territory of the Community to a customs-approved treatment or use, including appropriate risk-based controls, are to be carried out;][3]

[(4c) "Customs office of export" means the customs office designated by the customs authorities in accordance with the customs rules where the formalities for assigning goods leaving the customs territory of the Community to a customs-approved treatment or use, including appropriate risk-based controls, are to be completed;][3]

[(4d) "Customs office of exit" means the customs office designated by the customs authorities in accordance with the customs rules to which goods must be presented before they leave the customs territory of the Community and at which they will be subject to customs controls relating to the completion of exit formalities, and appropriate risk-based controls.][3]

(5) "Decision" means any official act by the customs authorities pertaining to customs rules giving a ruling on a particular case, such act having legal effects on one or more specific or identifiable persons; [this term covers *inter alia*, binding information within the meaning of Article 12.] [1]

(6) "Customs status" means the status of goods as Community or non-Community goods.

(7) "Community goods" means goods:

— [wholly obtained in the customs territory of the Community under the conditions referred to in Article 23 and not incorporating goods imported from countries or territories not forming part of the customs territory of the Community. Goods obtained from goods placed under a suspensive arrangement shall not be deemed to have Community status in cases of special economic importance determined in accordance with the committee procedure,][1]

— imported from countries or territories not forming part of the customs territory of the Community which have been released for free circulation,

— obtained or produced in the customs territory of the Community, either from goods referred to in the second indent alone or from goods referred to in first and second indents.

(8) "Non-Community goods" means goods other than those referred to in sub-paragraph 7.

Without prejudice to Articles 163 and 164, Community goods shall lose their status as such when they are actually removed from the customs territory of the Community.

(9) "Customs debt" means the obligation on a person to pay the amount of the import duties (customs debt on importation) or export duties (customs debt on exportation) which apply to specific goods under the Community provisions in force.

(10) "Import duties" means:

— customs duties and charges having an effect equivalent to customs duties payable on the importation of goods,

— . . . [1] import charges introduced under the common agricultural policy or under the specific arrangements applicable to certain goods resulting from the processing of agricultural products.

(11) "Export duties" means:

— customs duties and charges having an effect equivalent to customs duties payable on the exportation of goods,

— . . . [1] export charges introduced under the common agricultural policy or under the specific arrangements applicable to certain goods resulting from the processing of agricultural products.

(12) "Debtor" means any person liable for payment of a customs debt.

(13) "Supervision by the customs authorities" means action taken in general by those authorities with a view to ensuring that customs rules and, where appropriate, other provisions applicable to goods subject to customs supervision are observed.

[(14) "Customs controls" means specific acts performed by the customs authorities in order to ensure the correct application of customs rules and other legislation governing the entry, exit, transit, transfer and end-use of goods moved between the customs territory of the Community and third countries and the presence of goods that do not have Community status; such acts may include examining goods, verifying declaration data and the existence and authenticity of electronic or written documents, examining the accounts of undertakings and other records, inspecting means of transport, inspecting luggage and other goods carried by or on persons and carrying out official inquiries and other similar acts.][3]

(15) "Customs-approved treatment or use of goods" means:

(*a*) the placing of goods under a customs procedure;

(*b*) their entry into a free zone or free warehouse;

(*c*) their re-exportation from the customs territory of the Community;

(*d*) their destruction;
(*e*) their abandonment to the Exchequer.

(16) "Customs procedure" means:
(*a*) release for free circulation;
(*b*) transit;
(*c*) customs warehousing;
(*d*) inward processing;
(*e*) processing under customs control;
(*f*) temporary admission;
(*g*) outward processing;
(*h*) exportation.

(17) "Customs declaration" means the act whereby a person indicates in the prescribed form and manner a wish to place goods under a given customs procedure.

(18) "Declarant" means the person making the customs declaration in his own name or the person in whose name a customs declaration is made.

(19) "Presentation of goods to customs" means the notification to the customs authorities, in the manner laid down, of the arrival of goods at the customs office or at any other place designated or approved by the customs authorities.

(20) "Release of goods" means the act whereby the customs authorities make goods available for the purposes stipulated by the customs procedure under which they are placed.

(21) "Holder of the procedure" means the person on whose behalf the customs declaration was made or the person to whom the rights and obligations of the above mentioned person in respect of a customs procedure have been transferred.

(22) "Holder of the authorisation" means the person to whom an authorisation has been granted.

(23) "Provisions in force" means Community or national provisions.

[(24) "Committee procedure" means either the procedure referred to in Articles 247 and 247a, or in Articles 248 and 248a.][2]

[(25) "Risk" means the likelihood of an event occurring, in connection with the entry, exit, transit, transfer and end-use of goods moved between the customs territory of the Community and third countries and the presence of goods that do not have Community status, which—
— prevents the correct application of Community or national measures, or
— compromises the financial interests of the Community and its Member States, or
— poses a threat to the Community's security and safety, to public health, to the environment or to consumers.][3]

[(26) "Risk management" means the systematic identification of risk and implementation of all measures necessary for limiting exposure to risk. This includes activities such as collecting data and information, analysing and assessing risk, prescribing and taking action and regular monitoring and review of the process and its outcomes, based on international, Community and national sources and strategies.][3]

Amendments—[1] Article 4(5), (7),(10),(11) are amended by EC Regulation 82/97/EC with effect from 1 January 1997; see at L 17, 21.10.97, p 10.
[2] Article 4(24) replaced by EC Regulation 2700/2000/EC with effect from 19 December 2000; see OJ L 311, 12.12.2000, p 17.
[3] Article 4(4a)–(4d), (25), (26) inserted, and article 4(14) substituted, by Parliament and Council Regulation (EC) 648/2005 art 1(1); see OJ L 117; 04.05.2005, p 13.

CHAPTER 2—SUNDRY GENERAL PROVISIONS RELATING IN PARTICULAR TO THE RIGHTS AND OBLIGATIONS OF PERSONS WITH REGARD TO CUSTOMS RULES

SECTION 1
RIGHT OF REPRESENTATION

Article 5

1. Under the conditions set out in Article 64(2) and subject to the provisions adopted within the framework of Article 243(2)(*b*), any person may appoint a representative in his dealings with the customs authorities to perform the acts and formalities laid down by customs rules.

2. Such representation may be:
— direct, in which case the representative shall act in the name of and on behalf of another person, or
— indirect, in which case the representative shall act in his own name but on behalf of another person.

A Member State may restrict the right to make customs declarations:
— by direct representation, or
— by indirect representation,

so that the representative must be a customs agent carrying on his business in that country's territory.

3. Save in the cases referred to in Article 64(2)(*b*) and (3), a representative must be established within the Community.

VAT EC

4. A representative must state that he is acting on behalf of the person represented, specify whether the representation is direct or indirect and be empowered to act as a representative.
A person who fails to state that he is acting in the name of or on behalf of another person or who states that he is acting in the name of or on behalf of another person without being empowered to do so shall be deemed to be acting in his own name and on his own behalf.
5. The customs authorities may require any person stating that he is acting in the name of or on behalf of another person to produce evidence of his powers to act as a representative.

Simon's Tax Cases—Art 5(4), *TNT (UK) Ltd v R&C Comrs* [2012] UKUT 49 (TCC), [2012] STC 1232.

[SECTION 1A

AUTHORISED ECONOMIC OPERATORS][1]

Amendments—[1] Section 1a and Article 5a inserted by Parliament and Council Regulation (EC) 648/2005 art 1(2); see OJ L 117; 04.05.2005, p 13.

Article 5a

1. Customs authorities, if necessary following consultation with other competent authorities, shall grant, subject to the criteria provided for in paragraph 2, the status of "authorised economic operator" to any economic operator established in the customs territory of the Community.
An authorised economic operator shall benefit from facilitations with regard to customs controls relating to security and safety and/or from simplifications provided for under the customs rules.
The status of authorised economic operator shall, subject to the rules and conditions laid down in paragraph 2, be recognised by the customs authorities in all Member States, without prejudice to customs controls. Customs authorities shall, on the basis of the recognition of the status of authorised economic operator and provided that the requirements relating to a specific type of simplification provided for in Community customs legislation are fulfilled, authorise the operator to benefit from that simplification.
2. The criteria for granting the status of authorised economic operator shall include:
— an appropriate record of compliance with customs requirements,
— a satisfactory system of managing commercial and, where appropriate, transport records, which allows appropriate customs controls,
— where appropriate, proven financial solvency, and
— where applicable, appropriate security and safety standards.

The committee procedure shall be used to determine the rules:
— for granting the status of authorised economic operator,
— for granting authorisations for the use of simplifications,
— for establishing which customs authority is competent to grant such status and authorisations,
— for the type and extent of facilitations that may be granted in respect of customs controls relating to security and safety, taking into account the rules for common risk management,
— for consultation with, and provision of information to, other customs authorities;

and the conditions under which:
— an authorisation may be limited to one or more Member States,
— the status of authorised economic operator may be suspended or withdrawn, and
— the requirement of being established in the Community may be waived for specific categories of authorised economic operator, taking into account, in particular, international agreements.][1]

Amendments—[1] Section 1a and Article 5a inserted by Parliament and Council Regulation (EC) 648/2005 art 1(2); see OJ L 117; 04.05.2005, p 13.

SECTION 2

DECISIONS RELATING TO THE APPLICATION OF CUSTOMS RULES

Article 6

1. Where a person requests that the customs authorities take a decision relating to the application of customs rules that person shall supply all the information and documents required by those authorities in order to take a decision.
2. Such decision shall be taken and notified to the applicant at the earliest opportunity.
Where a request for a decision is made in writing, the decision shall be made within a period laid down in accordance with the existing provisions, starting on the date on which the said request is received by the customs authorities. Such a decision must be notified in writing to the applicant.
However, that period may be exceeded where the customs authorities are unable to comply with it. In that case, those authorities shall so inform the applicant before the expiry of the above mentioned period, stating the grounds which justify exceeding it and indicating the further period of time which they consider necessary in order to give a ruling on the request.

3. Decisions adopted by the customs authorities in writing which either reject requests or are detrimental to the persons to whom they are addressed shall set out the grounds on which they are based. They shall refer to the right of appeal provided for in Article 243.

4. Provision may be made for the first sentence of paragraph 3 to apply likewise to other decisions.

Article 7

Save in the cases provided for in the second sub-paragraph of Article 244, decisions adopted shall be immediately enforceable by customs authorities.

Article 8

1. A decision favourable to the person concerned shall be annulled if it was issued on the basis of incorrect or incomplete information and:

— the applicant knew or should reasonably have known that the information was incorrect or incomplete, and

— such decision could not have been taken on the basis of correct or complete information.

2. The persons to whom the decision was addressed shall be notified of its annulment.

3. Annulment shall take effect from the date on which the annulled decision was taken.

Article 9

1. A decision favourable to the person concerned, shall be revoked or amended where, in cases other than those referred to in Article 8, one or more of the conditions laid down for its issue were not or are no longer fulfilled.

2. A decision favourable to the person concerned may be revoked where the person to whom it is addressed fails to fulfil an obligation imposed on him under that decision.

3. The person to whom the decision is addressed shall be notified of its revocation or amendment.

4. The revocation or amendment of the decision shall take effect from the date of notification. However, in exceptional cases where the legitimate interests of the person to whom the decision is addressed so require, the customs authorities may defer the date when revocation or amendment takes effect.

Article 10

Articles 8 and 9 shall be without prejudice to national rules which stipulate that decisions are invalid or become null and void for reasons unconnected with customs legislation.

SECTION 3
INFORMATION

Article 11

1. Any person may request information concerning the application of customs legislation from the customs authorities.

Such a request may be refused where it does not relate to an import or export operation actually envisaged.

2. The information shall be supplied to the applicant free of charge. However, where special costs are incurred by the customs authorities, in particular as a result of analyses or expert reports on goods, or the return of the goods to the applicant, he may be charged the relevant amount.

Article 12

Note—Article 12 is outside the scope of this work.

SECTION 4
OTHER PROVISIONS

[Article 13

1. Customs authorities may, in accordance with the conditions laid down by the provisions in force, carry out all the controls they deem necessary to ensure that customs rules and other legislation governing the entry, exit, transit, transfer and end-use of goods moved between the customs territory of the Community and third countries and the presence of goods that do not have Community status are correctly applied. Customs controls for the purpose of the correct application of Community legislation may be carried out in a third country where an international agreement provides for this.

2. Customs controls, other than spot-checks, shall be based on risk analysis using automated data processing techniques, with the purpose of identifying and quantifying the risks and developing the necessary measures to assess the risks, on the basis of criteria developed at national, Community and, where available, international level.

The committee procedure shall be used for determining a common risk management framework, and for establishing common criteria and priority control areas.

Member States, in cooperation with the Commission, shall establish a computer system for the implementation of risk management.

3. Where controls are performed by authorities other than the customs authorities, such controls shall be performed in close coordination with the customs authorities, wherever possible at the same time and place.
4. In the context of the controls provided for in this Article, customs and other competent authorities, such as veterinary and police authorities, may communicate data received, in connection with the entry, exit, transit, transfer and end-use of goods moved between the customs territory of the Community and third countries and the presence of goods that do not have Community status, between each other and to the customs authorities of the Member States and to the Commission where this is required for the purposes of minimising risk.
Communication of confidential data to the customs authorities and other bodies (eg security agencies) of third countries shall be allowed only in the framework of an international agreement and provided that the data protection provisions in force, in particular Directive 95/46/EC of the European Parliament and of the Council of 24 October 1995 on the protection of individuals with regard to the processing of personal data and on the free movement of such data and Regulation (EC) No 45/2001 of the European Parliament and of the Council of 18 December 2000 on the protection of individuals with regard to the processing of personal data by the Community institutions and bodies and on the free movement of such data are respected.][1]

Amendments—[1] Article 13 substituted by Parliament and Council Regulation (EC) 648/2005 art 1(3); see OJ L 117; 04.05.2005, p 13.

Article 14

For the purposes of applying customs legislation, any person directly or indirectly involved in the operations concerned for the purposes of trade in goods shall provide the customs authorities with all the requisite documents and information, irrespective of the medium used, and all the requisite assistance at their request and by any time limit prescribed.

[Article 15

All information which is by nature confidential or which is provided on a confidential basis shall be covered by the duty of professional secrecy. It shall not be disclosed by the competent authorities without the express permission of the person or authority providing it. The communication of information shall, however, be permitted where the competent authorities are obliged to do so pursuant to the provisions in force, particularly in connection with legal proceedings. Any disclosure or communication of information shall fully comply with prevailing data protection provisions, in particular Directive 95/46/EC and Regulation (EC) No 45/2001.][1]

Amendments—[1] Article 15 substituted by Parliament and Council Regulation (EC) 648/2005 art 1(4); see OJ L 117; 04.05.2005, p 13.

Article 16

The persons concerned shall keep the documents referred to in Article 14 for the purposes of [customs controls][1], for the period laid down in the provisions in force and for at least three calendar years, irrespective of the medium used. That period shall run from the end of the year in which:

(*a*) in the case of goods released for free circulation in circumstances other than those referred to in (*b*) or goods declared for export, from the end of the year in which the declarations for release for free circulation or export are accepted;

(*b*) in the case of goods released for free circulation at a reduced or zero rate of import duty on account of their end-use, from the end of the year in which they cease to be subject to customs supervision;

(*c*) in the case of goods placed under another customs procedure, from the end of the year in which the customs procedure concerned is completed;

(*d*) in the case of goods placed in a free zone or free warehouse, from the end of the year on which they leave the undertaking concerned.

Without prejudice to the provisions of Article 221(3), second sentence, where a check carried out by the customs authorities in respect of a customs debt shows that the relevant entry in the accounts has to be corrected, the documents shall be kept beyond the time limit provided for in the first paragraph for a period sufficient to permit the correction to be made and checked.

Amendments—[1] Words substituted by Parliament and Council Regulation (EC) 648/2005 art 1(5); see OJ L 117; 04.05.2005, p 13.

Article 17

Where a period, date or time limit is laid down pursuant to customs legislation for the purpose of applying legislation, such period shall not be extended and such date or time limit shall not be deferred unless specific provision is made in the legislation concerned.

[Article 18

1. The value of the ecu in national currencies to be applied for the purposes of determining the tariff classification of goods and import duties shall be fixed once a month. The rates to be used for this conversion shall be those published in the *Official Journal of the European Communities* on the penultimate working day of the month. Those rates shall apply throughout the following month.

However, where the rate applicable at the start of the month differs by more than 5% from that published on the penultimate working day before the 15th of that same month, the latter rate shall apply from the 15th until the end of the month in question.

2. The value of the ecu in national currencies to be applied within the framework of customs legislation in cases other than those referred to in paragraph 1 shall be fixed once a year. The rates to be used for this conversion shall be those published in the *Official Journal of the European Communities* on the first working day of October, with effect from 1 January of the following year. If no rate is available for a particular national currency, the rate applicable to that currency shall be that obtaining on the last day for which a rate was published in the *Official Journal of the European Communities.*

3. The customs authorities may round up or down the sum resulting from the conversion into their national currency of an amount expressed in ecus for purposes other than determining the tariff classification of goods or import or export duties.

The rounded-off amount may not differ from the original amount by more than 5%.

The customs authorities may retain unchanged the national-currency value of an amount expressed in ecus if, at the time of the annual adjustment provided for in paragraph 2, the conversion of that amount, prior to the above mentioned rounding-off, results in a variation of less than 5% in the national-currency value or a reduction in that value.][1]

Amendment—[1] Article 18 is substituted by EC regulation 82/97/EC with effect from 1 January 1997; see OJ L 17, 21.1.97.

Article 19

The procedure of the Committee shall be used to determine in which cases and under which conditions the application of customs legislation may be simplified.

TITLE II

FACTORS ON THE BASIS OF WHICH IMPORT DUTIES OR EXPORT DUTIES AND THE OTHER MEASURES PRESCRIBED IN RESPECT OF TRADE IN GOODS ARE APPLIED

Articles 20–26

Note—Articles 20–26 are outside the scope of this work.

CHAPTER 2—ORIGIN OF GOODS

SECTION 2

Article 27 Preferential origin of goods

The rules on preferential origin shall lay down the conditions governing acquisition of origin which goods must fulfil in order to benefit from the measures referred to in Article 20(3)(*d*) or (*e*).

Those rules shall:

(*a*) in the case of goods covered by the agreements referred to in Article 20(3)(*d*), be determined in those agreements;

(*b*) in the case of goods benefiting from the preferential tariff measures referred to in Article 20(3)(*e*), be determined in accordance with the Committee procedure.

CHAPTER 3—VALUE OF GOODS FOR CUSTOMS PURPOSES

Article 28

The provisions of this Chapter shall determine the customs value for the purposes of applying the Customs Tariff of the European Communities and non-tariff measures laid down by Community provisions governing specific fields relating to trade in goods.

Article 29

1. The customs value of imported goods shall be the transaction value, that is, the price actually paid or payable for the goods when sold for export to the customs territory of the Community, adjusted, where necessary, in accordance with Articles 32 and 33, provided:

(*a*) that there are no restrictions as to the disposal or use of the goods by the buyer, other than restrictions which:

— are imposed or required by a law or by the public authorities in the Community,

— limit the geographical area in which the goods may be resold, or

— do not substantially affect the value of the goods;

(*b*) that the sale or price is not subject to some condition or consideration for which a value cannot be determined with respect to the goods being valued;

(*c*) that no part of the proceeds of any subsequent resale, disposal or use of the goods by the buyer will accrue directly or indirectly to the seller, unless an appropriate adjustment can be made in accordance with Article 32; and

(*d*) that the buyer and seller are not related, or, where the buyer and seller are related, that the transaction value is acceptable for customs purposes under paragraph 2.

VAT EC

(*a*) In determining whether the transaction value is acceptable for the purposes of paragraph 1, the fact that the buyer and the seller are related shall not in itself be sufficient grounds for regarding the transaction value as unacceptable. Where necessary, the circumstances surrounding the sale shall be examined and the transaction value shall be accepted provided that the relationship did not influence the price. If, in the light of information provided by the declarant or otherwise, the customs authorities have grounds for considering that the relationship influenced the price, they shall communicate their grounds to the declarant and he shall be given a reasonable opportunity to respond. If the declarant so requests, the communication of the grounds shall be in writing.

(*b*) In a sale between related persons, the transaction value shall be accepted and the goods valued in accordance with paragraph 1 wherever the declarant demonstrates that such value closely approximates to one of the following occurring at or about the same time:

(i) the transaction value in sales, between buyers and sellers who are not related in any particular case, of identical or similar goods for export to the Community;

(ii) the customs value of identical or similar goods, as determined under Article 30(2)(*c*);

(iii) the customs value of identical or similar goods, as determined under Article 30(2)(*d*).

In applying the foregoing tests, due account shall be taken of demonstrated differences in commercial levels, quantity levels, the elements enumerated in Article 32 and costs incurred by the seller in sales in which he and the buyer are not related and where such costs are not incurred by the seller in sales in which he and the buyer are related.

(*c*) The tests set forth in sub-paragraph (*b*) are to be used at the initiative of the declarant and only for comparison purposes. Substitute values may not be established under the said sub-paragraph.

3

(*a*) The price actually paid or payable is the total payment made or to be made by the buyer to or for the benefit of the seller for the imported goods and includes all payments made or to be made as a condition of sale of the imported goods by the buyer to the seller or by the buyer to a third party to satisfy an obligation of the seller. The payment need not necessarily take the form of a transfer of money. Payment may be made by way of letters of credit or negotiable instrument and may be made directly or indirectly.

(*b*) Activities, including marketing activities, undertaken by the buyer on his own account, other than those for which an adjustment is provided in Article 32, are not considered to be an indirect payment to the seller, even though they might be regarded as of benefit to the seller or have been undertaken by agreement with the seller, and their cost shall not be added to the price actually paid or payable in determining the customs value of imported goods.

Simon's Tax Cases—*R&C Comrs v Asda Stores Ltd* [2014] EWCA Civ 317, [2014] STC 1649.

Article 30

1. Where the customs value cannot be determined under Article 29, it is to be determined by proceeding sequentially through sub-paragraphs (*a*), (*b*), (*c*) and (*d*) of paragraph 2 to the first sub-paragraph under which it can be determined, subject to the proviso that the order of application of sub-paragraphs (*c*) and (*d*) shall be reversed if the declarant so requests; it is only when such value cannot be determined under a particular sub-paragraph that the provisions of the next sub-paragraph in a sequence established by virtue of this paragraph can be applied.

2. The customs value as determined under this Article shall be:

(*a*) the transaction value of identical goods sold for export to the Community and exported at or about the same time as the goods being valued;

(*b*) the transaction value of similar goods sold for export to the Community and exported at or about the same time as the goods being valued;

(*c*) the value based on the unit price at which the imported goods for identical or similar imported goods are sold within the Community in the greatest aggregate quantity to persons not related to the sellers;

(*d*) the computed value, consisting of the sum of:

— the cost or value of materials and fabrication or other processing employed in producing the imported goods,

— an amount for profit and general expenses equal to that usually reflected in sales of goods of the same class or kind as the goods being valued which are made by producers in the country of exportation for export to the Community,

— the cost or value of the items referred to in Article 32(1)(*e*).

3. Any further conditions and rules for the application of paragraph 2 above shall be determined in accordance with the committee procedure.

Article 31

1. Where the customs value of imported goods cannot be determined under Articles 29 or 30, it shall be determined, on the basis of data available in the Community, using reasonable means consistent with the principles and general provisions of:

— the agreement on implementation of Article VII of the General Agreement on Tariffs and Trade, [of 1994] [1]
— Article VII of the General Agreement on Tariffs and Trade, [of 1994] [1]
— the provisions of this chapter.

2. No customs value shall be determined under paragraph 1 on the basis of:
 (*a*) the selling price in the Community of goods produced in the Community;
 (*b*) a system which provides for the acceptance for customs purposes of the higher of two alternative values;
 (*c*) the price of goods on the domestic market of the country of exportation;
 (*d*) the cost of production, other than computed values which have been determined for identical or similar goods in accordance with Article 30(2)(*d*);
 (*e*) prices for export to a country not forming part of the customs territory of the Community;
 (*f*) minimum customs values; or
 (*g*) arbitrary or fictitious values.

Amendment—[1] Words added to first and second indents by EC Regulation 82/97/EC with effect from 1 January 1997; see OJ L 17, 21.1.97, p 1.

Article 32

1. In determining the customs value under Article 29, there shall be added to the price actually paid or payable for the imported goods:
 (*a*) the following, to the extent that they are incurred by the buyer but are not included in the price actually paid or payable for the goods:
  (i) commissions and brokerage, except buying commissions,
  (ii) the cost of containers which are treated as being one, for customs purposes, with the goods in question,
  (iii) the cost of packing, whether for labour or materials;
 (*b*) the value, apportioned as appropriate, of the following goods and services where supplied directly or indirectly by the buyer free of charge or at reduced cost for use in connection with the production and sale for export of the imported goods, to the extent that such value has not been included in the price actually paid or payable:
  (i) materials, components, parts and similar items incorporated in the imported goods,
  (ii) tools, dies, moulds and similar items used in the production of the imported goods,
  (iii) materials consumed in the production of the imported goods,
  (iv) engineering, development, artwork, design work, and plans and sketches undertaken elsewhere than in the Community and necessary for the production of the imported goods;
 (*c*) royalties and licence fees related to the goods being valued that the buyer must pay, either directly or indirectly, as a condition of sale of the goods being valued, to the extent that such royalties and fees are not included in the price actually paid or payable;
 (*d*) the value of any part of the proceeds of any subsequent resale, disposal or use of the imported goods that accrues directly or indirectly to the seller;
 (*e*)
  (i) the cost of transport and insurance of the imported goods, and
  (ii) loading and handling charges associated with the transport of the imported goods

 to the place of introduction into the customs territory of the Community.

2. Additions to the price actually paid or payable shall be made under this Article only on the basis of objective and quantifiable data.
3. No additions shall be made to the price actually paid or payable in determining the customs value except as provided in this Article.
4. In this Chapter, the term "buying commissions" means fees paid by an importer to his agent for the service of representing him in the purchase of the goods being valued.
5. Notwithstanding paragraph 1(*c*):
 (*a*) charges for the right to reproduce the imported goods in the Community shall not be added to the price actually paid or payable for the imported goods in determining the customs value; and
 (*b*) payments made by the buyer for the right to distribute or resell the imported goods shall not be added to the price actually paid or payable for the imported goods if such payments are not a condition of the sale for export to the Community of the goods.

Simon's Tax Cases—Art 32(3), *Umbro International Ltd v R&C Comrs* [2009] STC 1345.

Article 33

1. Provided that they are shown separately from the price actually paid or payable, the following shall not be included in the customs value:
 (*a*) charges for the transport of goods after their arrival at the place of introduction into the customs territory of the Community;

(*b*) charges for construction, erection, assembly, maintenance or technical assistance, undertaken after importation of imported goods such as industrial plant, machinery or equipment;

(*c*) charges for interest under a financing arrangement entered into by the buyer and relating to the purchase of imported goods, irrespective of whether the finance is provided by the seller or another person, provided that the financing arrangement has been made in writing and where required, the buyer can demonstrate that:

— such goods are actually sold at the price declared as the price actually paid or payable, and

— the claimed rate of interest does not exceed the level for such transactions prevailing in the country where, and at the time when, the finance was provided;

(*d*) charges for the right to reproduce imported goods in the Community;

(*e*) buying commissions;

(*f*) import duties or other charges payable in the Community by reason of the importation or sale of the goods.

Article 34

Specific rules may be laid down in accordance with the procedure of the committee to determine the customs value of carrier media for use in data processing equipment and bearing data or instructions.

Article 35

[Where factors used to determine the customs value of goods are expressed in a currency other than that of the Member State where the valuation is made, the rate of exchange to be used shall be that duly published by the authorities competent in the matter][1].

Such rate shall reflect as effectively as possible the current value of such currency in commercial transactions in terms of the currency of such Member State and shall apply during such period as may be determined in accordance with the procedure of the committee.

Where such a rate does not exist, the rate of exchange to be used shall be determined in accordance with the procedure of the committee.

Amendment—[1] First paragraph of Article 35 replaced by. EC Regulation 2700/2000/EC with effect from 19 December 2000 with effect from 19 December 2000; see OJ L 311, 12.12.2000, p 17.

Article 36

1. The provisions of this chapter shall be without prejudice to the specific provisions regarding the determination of the value for customs purposes of goods released for free circulation after being assigned a different customs-approved treatment or use.

2. By way of derogation from Articles 29, 30 and 31, the customs value of perishable goods usually delivered on consignment may, at the request of the declarant, be determined under simplified rules drawn up for the whole Community in accordance with the committee procedure.

TITLE III

PROVISIONS APPLICABLE TO GOODS BROUGHT INTO THE CUSTOMS TERRITORY OF THE COMMUNITY UNTIL THEY ARE ASSIGNED A CUSTOMS-APPROVED TREATMENT OR USE

CHAPTER 1—ENTRY OF GOODS INTO THE CUSTOMS TERRITORY OF THE COMMUNITY

[Article 36a

1. Goods brought into the customs territory of the Community shall be covered by a summary declaration, with the exception of goods carried on means of transport only passing through the territorial waters or the airspace of the customs territory without a stop within this territory.

2. The summary declaration shall be lodged at the customs office of entry.

Customs authorities may allow the summary declaration to be lodged at another customs office, provided that this office immediately communicates or makes available electronically the necessary particulars to the customs office of entry.

Customs authorities may accept, instead of the lodging of the summary declaration, the lodging of a notification and access to the summary declaration data in the economic operator's computer system.

3. The summary declaration shall be lodged before the goods are brought into the customs territory of the Community.

4. The committee procedure shall be used to establish:

— the time limit by which the summary declaration is to be lodged before the goods are brought into the customs territory of the Community,

— the rules for exceptions from, and variations to, the time limit referred to in the first indent, and

— the conditions under which the requirement for a summary declaration may be waived or adapted, in accordance with the specific circumstances and for particular types of goods traffic, modes of transport and economic operators and where international agreements provide for special security arrangements.][1]

Amendments—[1] Articles 36a–36c inserted by Parliament and Council Regulation (EC) 648/2005 art 1(6); see OJ L 117; 04.05.2005, p 13.

[Article 36b

1. The committee procedure shall be used to establish a common data set and format for the summary declaration, containing the particulars necessary for risk analysis and the proper application of customs controls, primarily for security and safety purposes, using, where appropriate, international standards and commercial practices.

2. The summary declaration shall be made using a data processing technique. Commercial, port or transport information may be used, provided that it contains the necessary particulars.

Customs authorities may accept paper-based summary declarations in exceptional circumstances, provided that they apply the same level of risk management as that applied to summary declarations made using a data processing technique.

3. The summary declaration shall be lodged by the person who brings the goods, or who assumes responsibility for the carriage of the goods into the customs territory of the Community.

4. Notwithstanding the obligation of the person referred to in paragraph 3, the summary declaration may be lodged instead by:

(*a*) the person in whose name the person referred to in paragraph 3 acts; or

(*b*) any person who is able to present the goods in question or to have them presented to the competent customs authority; or

(*c*) a representative of one of the persons referred to in paragraph 3 or points (*a*) or (*b*).

5. The person referred to in paragraphs 3 and 4 shall, at his request, be authorised to amend one or more particulars of the summary declaration after it has been lodged. However, no amendment shall be possible after the customs authorities:

(*a*) have informed the person who lodged the summary declaration that they intend to examine the goods; or

(*b*) have established that the particulars in questions are incorrect; or

(*c*) have allowed the removal of the goods.][1]

Amendments—[1] Articles 36a–36c inserted by Parliament and Council Regulation (EC) 648/2005 art 1(6); see OJ L 117; 04.05.2005, p 13.

[Article 36c

1. The customs office of entry may waive the lodging of a summary declaration in respect of goods for which, before expiry of the time limit referred to in Article 36a(3) or (4), a customs declaration is lodged. In such case, the customs declaration shall contain at least the particulars necessary for a summary declaration and, until such time as the former is accepted in accordance with Article 63, it shall have the status of a summary declaration.

Customs authorities may allow the customs declaration to be lodged at a customs office of import different from the customs office of entry, provided that this office immediately communicates or makes available electronically the necessary particulars to the customs office of entry.

2. Where the customs declaration is lodged other than by use of data processing technique, the customs authorities shall apply the same level of risk management to the data as that applied to customs declarations made using a data processing technique.][1]

Amendments—[1] Articles 36a–36c inserted by Parliament and Council Regulation (EC) 648/2005 art 1(6); see OJ L 117; 04.05.2005, p 13.

Article 37

1. Goods brought into the customs territory of the Community shall, from the time of their entry, be subject to customs supervision. They may be subject to [customs controls][1] in accordance with the provisions in force.

2. They shall remain under such supervision for as long as necessary to determine their customs status, if appropriate, and in the case of non-Community goods and without prejudice to Article 82(1), until their customs status is changed, they enter a free zone or free warehouse or they are re-exported or destroyed in accordance with Article 182.

Amendments—[1] Words in para (1) substituted by Parliament and Council Regulation (EC) 648/2005 art 1(7); see OJ L 117; 04.05.2005, p 13.

Article 38

1. Goods brought into the customs territory of the Community shall be conveyed by the person bringing them into the Community without delay, by the route specified by the customs authorities and in accordance with their instructions, if any:

(*a*) to the customs office designated by the customs authorities or to any other place designated or approved by those authorities; or,

(*b*) to a free zone, if the goods are to be brought into that free zone direct:

— by sea or air, or

VAT EC

— by land without passing through another part of the customs territory of the Community, where the free zone adjoins the land frontier between a Member State and a third country.

2. Any person who assumes responsibility for the carriage of goods after they have been brought into the customs territory of the Community, *inter alia* as a result of transhipment, shall become responsible for compliance with the obligation laid down in paragraph 1.

3. Goods which, although still outside the customs territory of the Community, may be subject to [customs controls by][1] a Member State under the provisions in force, as a result of *inter alia* an agreement concluded between that Member State and a third country, shall be treated in the same way as goods brought into the customs territory of the Community.

4. Paragraph 1(*a*) shall not preclude implementation of any provisions in force with respect to tourist traffic, frontier traffic, postal traffic or traffic of negligible economic importance, on condition that customs supervision and customs control possibilities are not thereby jeopardised.

[5 Paragraphs 1 to 4 and Articles 36a to 36c and 39 to 53 shall not apply to goods which temporarily leave the customs territory of the Community while moving between two points in that territory by sea or air, provided that the carriage is effected by a direct route and by regular air or shipping services without a stop outside the customs territory of the Community.][2]

6. Paragraph 1 shall not apply to goods on board vessels or aircraft crossing the territorial sea or airspace of the Member States without having as their destination a port or airport situated in those Member States.

Amendments—[1] Words in para (3) substituted by Parliament and Council Regulation (EC) 648/2005 art 1(7); see OJ L 117; 04.05.2005, p 13.

[2] Para (5) substituted by Parliament and Council Regulation (EC) 648/2005 art 1(8); see OJ L 117; 04.05.2005, p 13.

Article 39

1. Where, by reason of unforeseeable circumstances or force majeure, the obligation laid down in Article 38(1) cannot be complied with, the person bound by that obligation or any other person acting in his place shall inform the customs authorities of the situation without delay. Where the unforeseeable circumstances or force majeure do not result in total loss of the goods, the customs authorities shall also be informed of their precise location.

2. Where, by reason of unforeseeable circumstances or force majeure, a vessel or aircraft covered by Article 38(6) is forced to put into port or land temporarily in the customs territory of the Community and the obligation laid down in Article 38(1) cannot be complied with, the person bringing the vessel or aircraft into the customs territory of the Community or any other person acting in his place shall inform the customs authorities of the situation without delay.

3. The customs authorities shall determine the measures to be taken in order to permit customs supervision of the goods referred to in paragraph 1 as well as those on board a vessel or aircraft in the circumstances specified in paragraph 2 and to ensure, where appropriate, that they are subsequently conveyed to a customs office or other place designated or approved by the authorities.

CHAPTER 2—PRESENTATION OF GOODS TO CUSTOMS

[Article 40

Goods entering the customs territory of the Community shall be presented to customs by the person who brings them into that territory or, if appropriate, by the person who assumes responsibility for carriage of the goods following such entry, with the exception of goods carried on means of transport only passing through the territorial waters or the airspace of the customs territory of the Community without a stop within this territory. The person presenting the goods shall make a reference to the summary declaration or customs declaration previously lodged in respect of the goods.][1]

Amendments—[1] Article 40 substituted by Parliament and Council Regulation (EC) 648/2005 art 1(9); see OJ L 117; 04.05.2005, p 13.

Article 41

Article 40 shall not preclude the implementation of rules in force relating to goods:

(*a*) carried by travellers;

(*b*) placed under a customs procedure but not presented to customs.

Article 42

Goods may, once they have been presented to customs, and with the permission of the customs authorities, be examined or samples may be taken, in order that they may be assigned a customs-approved treatment or use. Such permission shall be granted, on request, to the person authorised to assign the goods such treatment or use.

CHAPTER 3—[UNLOADING OF GOODS PRESENTED TO CUSTOMS][1]

Amendments—[1] Title substituted by Parliament and Council Regulation (EC) 648/2005 art 1(10); see OJ L 117; 04.05.2005, p 13.

Articles 43–45

Amendments—Articles 43–45 repealed by Parliament and Council Regulation (EC) 648/2005 art 1(11); see OJ L 117; 04.05.2005, p 13.

Article 46

1. Goods shall be unloaded or transhipped from the means of transport carrying them solely with the permission of the customs authorities in places designated or approved by those customs authorities. However, such permission shall not be required in the event of the imminent danger necessitating the immediate unloading of all or part of the goods. In that case, the customs authorities shall be informed accordingly forthwith.
2. For the purpose of inspecting goods and the means of transport carrying them, the customs authorities may at any time require goods to be unloaded and unpacked.

Article 47

Goods shall not be removed from their original position without the permission of the customs authorities.

Articles 48–57

Note—Articles 48–57 are outside the scope of this work.

TITLE IV
CUSTOMS—APPROVED TREATMENT OR USE

CHAPTER 1—GENERAL

Article 58

1. Save as otherwise provided, goods may at any time, under the conditions laid down, be assigned any customs-approved treatment or use irrespective of their nature or quantity, or their country of origin, consignment or destination.
2. Paragraph 1 shall not preclude the imposition of prohibitions or restrictions justified on grounds of public morality, public policy or public security, the protection of health and life of humans, animals or plants, the protection of national treasures possessing artistic, historic or archaeological value or the protection of industrial and commercial property.

CHAPTER 2—CUSTOMS PROCEDURES

SECTION 1
PLACING OF GOODS UNDER A CUSTOMS PROCEDURE

Article 59

1. All goods intended to be placed under a customs procedure shall be covered by a declaration for that customs procedure.
2. Community goods declared for an export, outward processing, transit or customs warehousing procedure shall be subject to customs supervision from the time of acceptance of the customs declaration until such time as they leave the customs territory of the Community or are destroyed or the customs declaration is invalidated.

Article 60

Insofar as Community customs legislation lays down no rules on the matter, Member States shall determine the competence of the various customs offices situated in their territory, account being taken, where applicable, of the nature of the goods and the customs procedure under which they are to be placed.

Article 61

The customs declaration shall be made:

(*a*) in writing; or

(*b*) using a data-processing technique where provided for by provisions laid down in accordance with the committee procedure or where authorised by the customs authorities; or

(*c*) by means of a normal declaration or any other act whereby the holder of the goods expresses his wish to place them under a customs procedure, where such a possibility is provided for by the rules adopted in accordance with the committee procedure.

A
DECLARATIONS IN WRITING
I
Normal procedure

Article 62

1. Declarations in writing shall be made on a form corresponding to the official specimen prescribed for that purpose. They shall be signed and contain all the particulars necessary for implementation of the provisions governing the customs procedure for which the goods are declared.
2. The declaration shall be accompanied by all the documents required for implementation of the provisions governing the customs procedure for which the goods are declared.

Article 63

Declarations which comply with the conditions laid down in Article 62 shall be accepted by the customs authorities immediately, provided that the goods to which they refer are presented to customs.

Article 64

1. Subject to Article 5, a customs declaration may be made by any person who is able to present the goods in question or to have them presented to the competent customs authority, together with all the documents which are required to be produced for the application of the rules governing the customs procedure in respect of which the goods were declared.
2. However,
   (*a*) where acceptance of a customs declaration imposes particular obligations on a specific person, the declaration must be made by that person or on his behalf;
   (*b*) the declarant must be established in the Community.
   However, the condition regarding establishment in the Community shall not apply to persons who:
   — make a declaration for transit or temporary importation;
   — declare goods on an occasional basis, provided that the customs authorities consider this to be justified.
3. Paragraph 2(*b*) shall not preclude the application by the Member States of bilateral agreements concluded with third countries, or customary practices having similar effect, under which nationals of such countries may make customs declarations in the territory of the Member States in question, subject to reciprocity.

Article 65

The declaration shall, at his request, be authorised to amend one or more of the particulars of the declaration after it has been accepted by customs. The amendment shall not have the effect of rendering the declaration applicable to goods other than those it originally covered.
However, no amendment shall be permitted where authorisation is requested after the customs authorities:
   (*a*) have informed the declarant that they intend to examine the goods; or,
   (*b*) have established that the particulars in question are incorrect; or,
   (*c*) have released the goods.

Article 66

1. The customs authorities shall, at the request of the declarant, invalidate a declaration already accepted where the declarant furnishes proof that goods were declared in error for the customs procedure covered by that declaration or that, as a result of special circumstances, the placing of the goods under the customs procedure for which they were declared is no longer justified.
Nevertheless, where the customs authorities have informed the declarant of their intention to examine the goods, a request for invalidation of the declaration shall not be accepted until after the examination has taken place.
2. The declaration shall not be invalidated after the goods have been released, except in cases defined in accordance with the committee procedure.
3. Invalidation of the declaration shall be without prejudice to the application of the penal provisions in force.

Article 67

Save as otherwise expressly provided, the date to be used for the purposes of all the provisions governing the customs procedure for which the goods are declared shall be the date of acceptance of the declaration by the customs authorities.

Article 68

For the verification of declarations which they have accepted, the customs authorities may:

(*a*) examine the documents covering the declaration and the documents accompanying it. The customs authorities may require the declarant to present other documents for the purpose of verifying the accuracy of the particulars contained in the declaration;

(*b*) examine the goods and take samples for analysis or for detailed examination.

Article 69

1. Transport of the goods to the places where they are to be examined and samples are to be taken, and all the handling necessitated by such examination or taking of samples, shall be carried out by or under the responsibility of the declarant. The costs incurred shall be borne by the declarant.

2. The declarant shall be entitled to be present when the goods are examined and when samples are taken. Where they deem it appropriate, the customs authorities shall require the declarant to be present or represented when the goods are examined or samples are taken in order to provide them with the assistance necessary to facilitate such examination or taking of samples.

3. Provided that samples are taken in accordance with the provisions in force, the customs authorities shall not be liable for payment of any compensation in respect thereof but shall bear the costs of their analysis or examination.

Article 70

1. Where only part of the goods covered by a declaration are examined, the results of the partial examination shall be taken to apply to all the goods covered by that declaration.

However, the declarant may request a further examination of the goods if he considers that the results of the partial examination are not valid as regards the remainder of the goods declared.

2. For the purposes of paragraph 1, where a declaration form covers two or more items, the particulars relating to each item shall be deemed to constitute a separate declaration.

Article 71

1. The results of verifying the declaration shall be used for the purposes of applying the provisions governing the customs procedure under which the goods are placed.

2. Where the declaration is not verified, the provisions referred to in paragraph 1 shall be applied on the basis of the particulars contained in the declaration.

Article 72

1. The customs authorities shall take the measures necessary to identify the goods where identification is required in order to ensure compliance with the conditions governing the customs procedure for which the said goods have been declared.

2. Means of identification affixed to the goods or means of transport shall be removed or destroyed only by the customs authorities or with their permission unless, as a result of unforeseeable circumstances or force majeure, their removal or destruction is essential to ensure the protection of the goods or means of transport.

Article 73

1. Without prejudice to Article 74, where the conditions for placing the goods under the procedure in question are fulfilled and provided the goods are not subject to any prohibitive or restrictive measures, the customs authorities shall release the goods as soon as the particulars in the declaration have been verified or accepted without verification. The same shall apply where such verification cannot be completed within a reasonable period of time and the goods are no longer required to be present for verification purposes.

2. All the goods covered by the same declaration shall be released at the same time.

For the purposes of this paragraph, where a declaration form covers two or more items, the particulars relating to each item shall be deemed to constitute a separate declaration.

Article 74

1. Where acceptance of a customs declaration gives rise to a customs debt, the goods covered by the declaration shall not be released unless the customs debt has been paid or secured. However, without prejudice to paragraph 2, this provision shall not apply to the temporary importation procedure with partial relief from import duties.

2. Where, pursuant to the provisions governing the customs procedure for which the goods are declared, the customs authorities require the provision of a security, the said goods shall not be released for the customs procedure in question until such security is provided.

Article 75

Any necessary measures, including confiscation and sale, shall be taken to deal with goods which:

(*a*) cannot be released because:

— it has not been possible to undertake or continue examination of the goods within the period prescribed by the customs authorities for reasons attributable to the declarant; or,

— the documents which must be produced before the goods can be placed under the customs procedure requested have not been produced; or,

VAT EC

— payments or security which should have been made or provided in respect of import duties or export duties, as the case may be, have not been made or provided within the period prescribed; or
— they are subject to bans or restrictions;
(*b*) are not removed within a reasonable period after their release.

II.
Simplified procedures

Article 76

1. In order to simplify completion of formalities and procedures as far as possible while ensuring that operations are conducted in a proper manner, the customs authorities shall, under conditions laid down in accordance with the committee procedure, grant permission for:
(*a*) the declaration referred to in Article 62 to omit certain of the particulars referred to in paragraph 1 of that Article for some of the documents referred to in paragraph 2 of that Article not to be attached thereto;
(*b*) a commercial or administrative document, accompanied by request for the goods to be placed under the customs procedure in question, to be lodged in place of the declaration referred to in Article 62;
(*c*) the goods to be entered for the procedure in question by means of an entry in the records; in this case, the customs authorities may waive the requirement that the declarant presents the goods to customs.

The simplified declaration, commercial or administrative document or entry in the records must contain at least the particulars necessary for identification of the goods. Where the goods are entered in the records, the date of such entry must be included.
2. Except in cases to be determined in accordance with the committee procedure, the declarant shall furnish a supplementary declaration which may be of a general, periodic or recapitulative nature.
3. Supplementary declarations and the simplified declarations referred to in sub-paragraphs 1(*a*), (*b*) and (*c*), shall be deemed to constitute a single, indivisible instrument taking effect on the date of acceptance of the simplified declarations; in the cases referred to in sub-paragraph 1(*c*), entry in the records shall have the same legal force as acceptance of the declaration referred to in Article 62.
4. Special simplified procedures for the Community transit procedure shall be laid down in accordance with the committee procedure.

B
OTHER DECLARATIONS

Article 77

[1] [1] Where the customs declaration is made by means of a data-processing technique within the meaning of Article 61(*b*), or by an oral declaration or any other act within the meaning of Article 61(*c*), Articles 62 to 76 shall apply *mutatis mutandis* without prejudice to the principles set out therein.
[2 Where the customs declaration is made by means of a data-processing technique, the customs authorities may allow accompanying documents referred to in Article 62(2) not to be lodged with the declaration. In this case the documents shall be kept at the customs authorities' disposal][1]

Amendments—[1] Paragraph numbered, and Article 77(2) added by EC Regulation 2700/2000/EC with effect from 19 December 2000; see OJ L 311, 12.12.2000, p 17.

C
POST-CLEARANCE EXAMINATION OF DECLARATIONS

Article 78

1. The customs authorities may, on their own initiative or at the request of the declarant, amend the declaration after release of the goods.
2. The customs authorities may, after releasing the goods and in order to satisfy themselves as to the accuracy of the particulars contained in the declaration, inspect the commercial documents and data relating to the import or export operations in respect of the goods concerned or to subsequent commercial operations involving those goods. Such inspections may be carried out at the premises of the declarant, of any other person directly or indirectly involved in the said operations in a business capacity or of any other person in possession of the said document and data for business purposes. Those authorities may also examine the goods where it is still possible for them to be produced.
3. Where revision of the declaration or post-clearance examination indicates that the provisions governing the customs procedure concerned have been applied on the basis of incorrect or incomplete information, the customs authorities shall, in accordance with any provisions laid down, take the measures necessary to regularise the situation, taking account of the new information available to them.

Simon's Tax Cases—Art 78(3) *Terex Equipment Ltd and others v R&C Comrs* [2010] STC 575.

SECTION 2

RELEASE FOR FREE CIRCULATION

Article 79

Release for free circulation shall confer on non-Community goods the customs status of Community goods.

It shall entail application of commercial policy measures, completion of the other formalities laid down in respect of the importation of goods and the charging of any duties legally due.

Article 80

1. By way of derogation from Article 67, provided that the import duty chargeable on the goods is one of the duties referred to in the first indent of Article 4(10) and that the rate of duty is reduced after the date of acceptance of the declaration for release for free circulation but before the goods are released, the declarant may request application of the more favourable rate.

2. Paragraph 1 shall not apply where it has not been possible to release the goods for reasons attributable to the declarant alone.

Article 81

Where a consignment is made up of goods falling within different tariff classifications, and dealing with each of those goods in accordance with its tariff classification for the purpose of drawing up the declaration would entail a burden of work and expense disproportionate to the import duties chargeable, the customs authorities may, at the request of the declarant, agree that import duties be charged on the whole consignment on the basis of the tariff classification of the goods which are subject to the highest rate of import duty.

Article 82

1. Where goods are released for free circulation at a reduced or zero rate of duty on account of their end-use, they shall remain under customs supervision. Customs supervision shall end when the conditions laid down for granting such a reduced or zero rate of duty cease to apply, where the goods are exported or destroyed or where the use of the goods for purposes other than those laid down for the application of the reduced or zero rate of duty is permitted subject to payment of the duties due.

2. Articles 88 and 90 shall apply *mutatis mutandis* to the goods referred to in paragraph 1.

Article 83

Goods released for free circulation shall lose their customs status as Community goods where:

(*a*) the declaration for release for free circulation is invalidated after release [. . .], or

(*b*) the imported duties payable on those goods are repaid or remitted:

— under the inward processing procedure in the form of the drawback system; or

— in respect of defective goods or goods which fail to comply with the terms of the contract, pursuant to Article 238; or

— in situations of the type referred to in Article 239 where repayment or remission is conditional upon the goods being exported or re-exported or being assigned an equivalent customs-approved treatment or use.

Amendment—Words in sub-para(*a*) repealed by EC Regulation 82/97/EC with effect from 1 January 1997; see OJ L17, 21.1.97

SECTION 3

SUSPENSIVE ARRANGEMENTS AND CUSTOMS PROCEDURES WITH ECONOMIC IMPACT

A PROVISIONS COMMON TO SEVERAL PROCEDURES

Article 84

1. In Articles 85 to 90:

(*a*) where the term "procedure" is used, it is understood as applying, in the case of non-Community goods, to the following arrangements:

— external transit;

— customs warehousing;

— inward processing in the form of a system of suspension;

— processing under customs control;

— temporary importation;

(*b*) where the term "customs procedure with economic impact" is used, it is understood as applying to the following arrangements:

— customs warehousing;

— inward processing;

— processing under customs control;

— temporary importation;
— outward processing.

2. "Import goods" means goods placed under a suspensive procedure and goods which, under the inward processing procedure in the form of the drawback system, have undergone the formalities for release for free circulation and the formalities provided for in Article 125.

3. "Goods in the unaltered state" means import goods which, under the inward processing procedure or the procedures for processing under customs control, have undergone no form of processing.

Article 85

The use of any customs procedure with economic impact shall be conditional upon authorisation being issued by the customs authorities.

Article 86

Without prejudice to the additional special conditions governing the procedure in question, the authorisation referred to in Article 85 and that referred to in Article 100(1) shall be granted only:

— to persons who offer every guarantee necessary for the proper conduct of the operations;
— where the customs authorities can supervise and monitor the procedure without having to introduce administrative arrangements disproportionate to the economic needs involved.

Article 87

1. The conditions under which the procedure in question is used shall be set out in the authorisation.

2. The holder of the authorisation shall notify the customs authorities of all factors arising after the authorisation was granted which may influence its continuation or content.

[Article 87a

In the cases referred to in the second sentence of the first indent of Article 4 (7), any products or goods obtained from goods placed under a suspensive arrangement shall be considered as being placed under the same arrangement][1]

Amendment—[1] This article was inserted by EC Regulations 82/97/EC with effect from 1 January 1997; see OJ L 21.1.97. p 1.

Article 88

The customs authorities may make the placing of goods under a suspensive arrangement conditional upon the provision of security in order to ensure that any customs debt which may be incurred in respect of those goods will be paid.

Special provisions concerning the provision of security may be laid down in the context of a specific suspensive arrangement.

Article 89

1. A suspensive arrangement with economic impact shall be discharged when a new customs-approved treatment or use is assigned either to the goods placed under that arrangement or to compensating or processed products placed under it.

2. The customs authorities shall take all the measures necessary to regularise the position of goods in respect of which a procedure has not been discharged under the conditions prescribed.

Article 90

The rights and obligations of the holder of a customs procedure with economic impact may, on the conditions laid down by the customs authorities, be transferred successively to other persons who fulfil any conditions laid down in order to benefit from the procedure in question.

Articles 91–200

Note—Articles 91–200 are outside the scope of this work.

CHAPTER 2—INCURRENCE OF A CUSTOMS DEBT

Article 201

1. A customs debt on importation shall be incurred through:

(*a*) the release for free circulation of goods liable to import duties, or
(*b*) the placing of such goods under the temporary importation procedure with partial relief from import duties.

2. A customs debt shall be incurred at the time of acceptance of the customs declaration in question.

3. The debtor shall be the declarant. In the event of indirect representation, the person on whose behalf the customs declaration is made shall also be a debtor.

Where a customs declaration in respect of one of the procedures referred to in paragraph 1 is drawn up on the basis of information which leads to all or part of the duties legally owed not being collected, the persons who provided the information required to draw up the declaration and who knew, or who ought reasonably to have known that such information was false, may also be considered debtors in accordance with the national provisions in force.

Article 202

1. A customs debt on importation shall be incurred through:

(*a*) the unlawful introduction into the customs territory of the Community of goods liable to import duties, or

(*b*) the unlawful introduction into another part of that territory of such goods located in a free zone or free warehouse.

For the purpose of this Article, unlawful introduction means any introduction in violation of the provisions of Articles 38 to 41 and the second indent of Article 177.

2. The customs debt shall be incurred at the moment when the goods are unlawfully introduced.

3. The debtors shall be:

— the person who introduced such goods unlawfully,

— any persons who participated in the unlawful introduction of the goods and who were aware or should reasonably have been aware that such introduction was unlawful, and

— any persons who acquired or held the goods in question and who were aware or should reasonably have been aware at the time of acquiring or receiving the goods that they had been introduced unlawfully.

Article 203

1. A customs debt on importation shall be incurred through:

— the unlawful removal from customs supervision of goods liable to import duties.

2. The customs debt shall be incurred at the moment when the goods are removed from customs supervision.

3. The debtors shall be:

— the person who removed the goods from customs supervision,

— any persons who participated in such removal and who were aware or should reasonably have been aware that the goods were being removed from customs supervision,

— any persons who acquired or held the goods in question and who were aware or should reasonably have been aware at the time of acquiring or receiving the goods that they had been removed from customs supervision, and

— where appropriate, the person required to fulfil the obligations arising from temporary storage of the goods or from the use of the customs procedure under which those goods are placed.

Simon's Tax Cases—Art 78(3) *Terex Equipment Ltd and others v R&C Comrs* [2010] STC 575.

Article 204

1. A customs debt on importation shall be incurred through:

(*a*) non-fulfilment of one of the obligations arising, in respect of goods liable to import duties, from their temporary storage or from the use of the customs procedure under which they are placed, or

(*b*) non-compliance with a condition governing the placing of the goods under that procedure or the granting of a reduced or zero rate of import duty by virtue of the end-use of the goods,

in cases other than those referred to in Article 203 unless it is established that those failures have no significant effect on the correct operation of the temporary storage or customs procedure in question.

2. The customs debt shall be incurred either at the moment when the obligation whose non-fulfilment gives rise to the customs debt ceases to be met or at the moment when the goods are placed under the customs procedure concerned where it is established subsequently that a condition governing the placing of the goods under the said procedure or the granting of a reduced or zero rate of import duty by virtue of the end-use of the goods was not in fact fulfilled.

3. The debtor shall be the person who is required, according to the circumstances, either to fulfil the obligations arising, in respect of goods liable to import duties, from their temporary storage or from the use of the customs procedure under which they have been placed, or to comply with the conditions governing the placing of the goods under that procedure.

Article 205

1. A customs debt on importation shall be incurred through:

— the consumption or use, in a free zone or a free warehouse, of goods liable to import duties, under conditions other than those laid down by the legislation in force.

Where goods disappear and where their disappearance cannot be explained to the satisfaction of the customs authorities, those authorities may regard the goods as having been consumed or used in the free zone or the free warehouse.

2. The debt shall be incurred at the moment when the goods are consumed or are first used under conditions other than those laid down by the legislation in force.

3. The debtor shall be the person who consumed or used the goods and any persons who participated in such consumption or use and who were aware or should reasonably have been aware that the goods were being consumed or used under conditions other than those laid down by the legislation in force.

Where customs authorities regard goods which have disappeared as having been consumed or used in the free zone or the free warehouse and it is not possible to apply the preceding paragraph, the person liable for payment of the customs debt shall be the last person known to these authorities to have been in possession of the goods.

Article 206

1. By way of derogation from Articles 202 and 204(1)(*a*), no customs debt on importation shall be deemed to be incurred in respect of specific goods where the person concerned proves that the non-fulfilment of the obligations which arise from:

— the provisions of Articles 38 to 41 and the second indent of Article 177, or
— keeping the goods in question in temporary storage, or
— the use of the customs procedure under which the goods have been placed,

results from the total destruction or irretrievable loss of the said goods as a result of the actual nature of the goods or unforeseeable circumstances or *force majeure*, or as a consequence of authorisation by the customs authorities.

For the purposes of this paragraph, goods shall be irretrievably lost when they are rendered unusable by any person.

2. Nor shall a customs debt on importation be deemed to be incurred in respect of goods released for free circulation at a reduced or zero rate of import duty by virtue of their end-use, where such goods are exported or re-exported with the permission of the customs authorities.

Article 207

Where, in accordance with Article 206(1), no customs debt is deemed to be incurred in respect of goods released for free circulation at a reduced or zero rate of import duty on account of their end-use, any scrap or waste resulting from such destruction shall be deemed to be non-Community goods.

Article 208

Where in accordance with Article 203 or 204 a customs debt is incurred in respect of goods released for free circulation at a reduced rate of import duty on account of their end-use, the amount paid when the goods were released for free circulation shall be deducted from the amount of the customs debt.

This provision shall apply *mutatis mutandis* where a customs debt is incurred in respect of scrap and waste resulting from the destruction of such goods.

Article 209

1. A customs debt on exportation shall be incurred through:

— the exportation from the customs territory of the Community, under cover of a customs declaration, of goods liable to export duties.

2. The customs debt shall be incurred at the time when such customs declaration is accepted.

3. The debtor shall be the declarant. In the event of indirect representation, the person on whose behalf the declaration is made shall also be a debtor.

Article 210

1. A customs debt on exportation shall be incurred through:

— the removal from the customs territory of the Community of goods liable to export duties without a customs declaration.

2. The customs debt shall be incurred at the time when the said goods actually leave that territory.

3. The debtor shall be:

— the person who removed the goods, and
— any persons who participated in such removal and who were aware or should reasonably have been aware that a customs declaration had not been but should have been lodged.

Article 211

1. A customs debt on exportation shall be incurred through:

— failure to comply with the conditions under which the goods were allowed to leave the customs territory of the Community with total or partial relief from export duties.

2. The debt shall be incurred at the time when the goods reach a destination other than that for which they were allowed to leave the customs territory of the Community with total or partial relief from export duties or, should the customs authorities be unable to determine that time, the expiry of the time limit set for the production of evidence that the conditions entitling the goods to such relief have been fulfilled.

3. The debtor shall be the declarant. In the event of indirect representation, the person on whose behalf the declaration is made shall also be a debtor.

Article 212

The customs debt referred to in Articles 201 to 205 and 209 to 211 shall be incurred even if it relates to goods subject to measures of prohibition or restriction on importation or exportation of any kind whatsoever. However, no customs debt shall be incurred on the unlawful introduction into the customs territory of the Community of counterfeit currency or of narcotic drugs and psychotropic substances which do not enter into the economic circuit strictly supervised by the competent authorities with a view to their use for medical and scientific purposes. For the purposes of criminal law as applicable to customs offences, the customs debt shall nevertheless be deemed to have been incurred where, under a Member State's criminal law, customs duties provide the basis for determining penalties, or the existence of a customs debt is grounds for taking criminal proceedings.

[Article 212a

Where customs legislation provides for favourable tariff treatment of goods by reason of their nature or end-use or for relief or total or partial exemption from import or export duties pursuant to Articles 21, 82, 145 or 184 to 187, such favourable tariff treatment, relief or exemption shall also apply in cases where a customs debt is incurred pursuant to Articles 202 to 205, 210 or 211, on condition that the behaviour of the person concerned involves neither fraudulent dealing nor obvious negligence and he produces evidence that the other conditions for the application of favourable treatment, relief or exemption have been satisfied.]

Amendments—This Article replaced by EC Regulation 2700/2000/EC with effect from 19 December 2000; see OJ L 311, 12.12.2000, p 17.

Article 213

Where several persons are liable for payment of one customs debt, they shall be jointly and severally liable for such debt.

Article 214

1. Save as otherwise expressly provided by this Code and without prejudice to paragraph 2, the amount of the import duty or export duty applicable to goods shall be determined on the basis of the rules of assessment appropriate to those goods at the time when the customs debt in respect of them is incurred.

2. Where it is not possible to determine precisely when the customs debt is incurred, the time to be taken into account in determining the rules of assessment appropriate to the goods concerned shall be the time when the customs authorities conclude that the goods are in a situation in which a customs debt is incurred.

However, where the information available to the customs authorities enables them to establish that the customs debt was incurred prior to the time when they reached that conclusion, the amount of the import duty or export duty payable on the goods in question shall be determined on the basis of the rules of assessment appropriate to the goods at the earliest time when existence of the customs debt arising from the situation may be established from the information available.

3. Compensatory interest shall be applied, in the circumstances and under the conditions to be defined in the provisions adopted under the committee procedure, in order to prevent the wrongful acquisition of a financial advantage through deferment of the date on which the customs debt was incurred or entered into the accounts.

[Article 215

1. A customs debt shall be incurred—
   - — at the place where the events from which it arises occur,
   - — if it is not possible to determine that place, at the place where the customs authorities conclude that the goods are in a situation in which a customs debt is incurred,
   - — if the goods have been entered for a customs procedure which has not been discharged, and the place cannot be determined pursuant to the first or second indent within a period of time determined, if appropriate, in accordance with the committee procedure, at the place where the goods were either placed under the procedure concerned or were introduced into the Community customs territory under that procedure.

2. Where the information available to the customs authorities enables them to establish that the customs debt was already incurred when the goods were in another place at an earlier date, the customs debt shall be deemed to have been incurred at the place which may be established as the location of the goods at the earliest time when existence of the customs debt may be established.

3. The customs authorities referred to in Article 217(1) are those of the Member State where the customs debt is incurred or is deemed to have been incurred in accordance with this Article.][1]

[4 If a customs authority finds that a customs debt has been incurred under Article 202 in another Member State and the amount of that debt is lower than EUR 5000, the debt shall be deemed to have been incurred in the Member State where the finding was made.][2]

Amendment—[1] This Article was substituted by European Parliament and Council Regulation (EC) 955/1999, Art 1, para 7; see OJ L 119, 7.5.99, p 1.

[2] This paragraph added by EC Regulation 2700/2000/EC with effect from 19 December 2000; see OJ L 311, 12.12.2000, p 17.

Article 216

1. In so far as agreements concluded between the Community and certain third countries provide for the granting on importation into those countries of preferential tariff treatment for goods originating in the Community within the meaning of such agreements, on condition that, where they have been

VAT EC

obtained under the inward processing procedure, non-Community goods incorporated in the said originating goods are subject to payment of the import duties payable thereon, the validation of the documents necessary to enable such preferential tariff treatment to be obtained in third countries shall cause a customs debt on importation to be incurred.

2. The moment when such customs debt is incurred shall be deemed to be the moment when the customs authorities accept the export declaration relating to the goods in question.

3. The debtor shall be the declarant. In the event of indirect representation, the person on whose behalf the declaration is made shall also be a debtor.

4. The amount of the import duties corresponding to this customs debt shall be determined under the same conditions as in the case of a customs debt resulting from the acceptance, on the same date, of the declaration for release for free circulation of the goods concerned for the purpose of terminating the inward processing procedure.

Articles 217–232

Note—Articles 217–232 are outside the scope of this work.

CHAPTER 4—EXTINCTION OF CUSTOMS DEBT

Article 233

Without prejudice to the provisions in force relating to the time-barring of a customs debt and non-recovery of such a debt in the event of the legally established insolvency of the debtor, a customs debt shall be extinguished:

(*a*) by payment of the amount of duty;

(*b*) by remission of the amount of duty;

(*c*) where, in respect of goods declared for a customs procedure entailing the obligation to pay duties:

— the customs declaration is invalidated[. . .][1],

— the goods, before their release, are either seized and simultaneously or subsequently confiscated, destroyed on the instructions of the customs authorities, destroyed or abandoned in accordance with Article 182, or destroyed or irretrievably lost as a result of their actual nature or of unforeseeable circumstances or *force majeure*;

(*d*) where goods in respect of which a customs debt is incurred in accordance with Article 202 are seized upon their unlawful introduction and are simultaneously or subsequently confiscated.

In the event of seizure and confiscation, the customs debt shall, nonetheless for the purposes of the criminal law applicable to customs offences, be deemed not to have been extinguished where, under a Member State's criminal law, customs duties provide the basis for determining penalties or the existence of a customs debt is grounds for taking criminal proceedings.

Amendment—[1] Words in sub-para (*c*) first indent were repealed by EC Regulation 82/97/EC with effect from 1 January 1997; see OJ L17, 21.1.97, p 1.

Article 234

A customs debt, as referred to in Article 216, shall also be extinguished where the formalities carried out in order to enable the preferential tariff treatment referred to in Article 216 to be granted are cancelled.

Articles 235–242

Note—Articles 235–242 are outside the scope of this work.

TITLE VIII
APPEALS

Article 243

1. Any person shall have the right to appeal against decisions taken by the customs authorities which relate to the application of customs legislation, and which concern him directly and individually.

Any person who has applied to the customs authorities for a decision relating to the application of customs legislation and has not obtained a ruling on that request within the period referred to in Article 6(2) shall also be entitled to exercise the right of appeal.

The appeal must be lodged in the Member State where the decision has been taken or applied for.

2. The right of appeal may be exercised:

(*a*) initially, before the customs authorities designated for that purpose by the Member States;

(*b*) subsequently, before an independent body, which may be a judicial authority or an equivalent specialised body, according to the provisions in force in the Member States.

Article 244

The lodging of an appeal shall not cause implementation of the disputed decision to be suspended.

The customs authorities shall, however, suspend implementation of such decision in whole or in part where they have good reason to believe that the disputed decision is inconsistent with customs legislation or that irreparable damage is to be feared for the person concerned.
Where the disputed decision has the effect of causing import duties or export duties to be charged, suspension of implementation of that decision shall be subject to the existence or lodging of a security. However, such security need not be required where such a requirement would be likely, owing to the debtor's circumstances, to cause serious economic or social difficulties.

Article 245

The provisions for the implementation of the appeals procedure shall be determined by the Member States.

Article 246

This title shall not apply to appeals lodged with a view to the annulment or revision of a decision taken by the customs authorities on the basis of criminal law.

TITLE IX
FINAL PROVISIONS
CHAPTER 1—CUSTOMS CODE COMMITTEE

[Article 247

The measures necessary for the implementation of this Regulation, including implementation of the Regulation referred to in Article 184, except for Title VIII and subject to Articles 9 and 10 of Regulation (EEC) No 2658/87(7) and to Article 248 of this Regulation shall be adopted in accordance with the regulatory procedure referred to in Article 247a(2) in compliance with the international commitments entered into by the Community.][1]

Amendments—[1] Articles 247, 247a, 248, 248a, 249 substituted for Articles 247, 248, and 249 by EC Regulation 2700/2000/EC with effect from 19 December 2000; see OJ L 311, 12.12.2000, p 17.

[Article 247a

1. The Commission shall be assisted by a Customs Code Committee (hereinafter referred to as 'the Committee').
2. Where reference is made to this paragraph, Articles 5 and 7 of Decision 1999/468/EC shall apply, having regard to the provisions of Article 8 thereof.
The period laid down in Article 5(6) of Decision 1999/468/EC shall be set at three months.
3. The Committee shall adopt its rules of procedure.][1]

Amendments—[1] Articles 247, 247a, 248, 248a, 249 substituted for Articles 247, 248, and 249 by EC Regulation 2700/2000/EC with effect from 19 December 2000; see OJ L 311, 12.12.2000, p 17.

[Article 248

The measures necessary for implementing Articles 11, 12 and 21 shall be adopted in accordance with the management procedure referred to in Article 248a(2).][1]

Amendments—[1] Articles 247, 247a, 248, 248a, 249 substituted for Articles 247, 248, and 249 by EC Regulation 2700/2000/EC with effect from 19 December 2000; see OJ L 311, 12.12.2000, p 17.

[Article 248a

1. The Commission shall be assisted by a Customs Code Committee, hereinafter referred to as 'the Committee'.
2. Where reference is made to this paragraph, Articles 4 and 7 of Decision 1999/468/EC shall apply.
The period laid down in Article 4(3) of Decision 1999/468/EC shall be set at three months.
3. The Committee shall adopt its rules of procedure.][1]

Amendments—[1] Articles 247, 247a, 248, 248a, 249 substituted for Articles 247, 248, and 249 by EC Regulation 2700/2000/EC with effect from 19 December 2000; see OJ L 311, 12.12.2000, p 17.

[Article 249

The Committee may examine any question concerning customs legislation which is raised by its chairman, either on his own initiative or at the request of a Member State's representative.][1]

Amendments—[1] Articles 247, 247a, 248, 248a, 249 substituted for Articles 247, 248, and 249 by EC Regulation 2700/2000/EC with effect from 19 December 2000; see OJ L 311, 12.12.2000, p 17.

CHAPTER 2—LEGAL EFFECTS IN A MEMBER STATE OF MEASURES TAKEN, DOCUMENTS ISSUED AND FINDINGS MADE IN ANOTHER MEMBER STATE

Article 250

Where a customs procedure is used in several Member States,

— the decisions, identification measures taken or agreed on, and the documents issued by the customs authorities of one Member State shall have the same legal effects in other Member States as such decisions, measures taken and documents issued by the customs authorities of each of those Member States;

— the findings made at the time controls are carried out by the customs authorities of a Member State shall have the same conclusive force in the other Member States as the findings made by the customs authorities of each of those Member States.

CHAPTER 3—OTHER FINAL PROVISIONS

Article 251

1. The following Regulations and Directives are hereby repealed:

— Council Regulation (EEC) No 1224/80 of 28 May 1980 on the valuation of goods for customs purposes, as last amended by the Regulation (EEC) No 4046/89;

— Council Regulation (EEC) No 2151/84 of 23 July 1984 on the customs territory of the Community, as last amended by the Act of Accession of Spain and Portugal.

Note—Repeals within the scope of this work only are mentioned: other repeals have been omitted.

Article 252

Note—Article 252 is outside the scope of this work.

Article 253

This Regulation shall enter into force on the third day following that of its publication in the *Official Journal of the European Communities.*

It shall apply from 1 January 1994.

Title VIII shall not apply to the United Kingdom until 1 January 1995.

However, Article 161 and, in so far as they concern re-exportation, Articles 182 and 183 shall apply from 1 January 1993. In so far as the said Articles make reference to provisions in this Code and until such time as such provisions enter into force, the references shall be deemed to allude to the corresponding provisions in the Regulations and Directives listed in Article 251.

Before 1 October 1993, the Council shall, on the basis of a Commission progress report on discussions regarding the consequences to be drawn from the monetary conversion rate used for the application of common agricultural policy measures, review the problem of trade in goods between the Member States in the context of the internal market. This report shall be accompanied by Commission proposals if any, on which the Council shall take a decision in accordance with the provisions of the Treaty.

Before 1 January 1998, the Council shall, on the basis of a Commission report, review this Code with a view to making such adaptations as may appear necessary taking into account in particular the achievement of the internal market. This report shall be accompanied by proposals, if any, on which the Council shall take a decision in accordance with the provisions of the Treaty.

Note—This Regulation was published in OJ L302, 19.10.92.

This Regulation shall be binding in its entirety and directly applicable in all Member States.

COMMISSION REGULATION 2454/93/EEC OF 2 JULY 1993 LAYING DOWN PROVISIONS FOR THE IMPLEMENTATION OF COUNCIL REGULATION NO 2913/92/EEC ESTABLISHING THE COMMUNITY CUSTOMS CODE

(2454/93/EEC)

Note—See OJ L253 11.11.1993, p 1.

PART I: GENERAL IMPLEMENTING PROVISIONS

TITLE I: GENERAL

THE COMMISSION OF THE EUROPEAN COMMUNITIES,

Having regard to the Treaty establishing the European Economic Community,

Having regard to Council Regulation (EEC) No 2913/92 of 12 October 1992 establishing the Community Customs Code, hereinafter referred to as the "Code", and in particular Article 249 thereof,

Whereas the Code assembled all existing customs legislation in a single legal instrument; whereas at the same time the Code made certain modifications to this legislation to make it more coherent, to simplify it and to plug certain loopholes; whereas it therefore constitutes complete Community legislation in this area;

Whereas the same reasons which led to the adoption of the Code apply equally to the customs implementing legislation; whereas it is therefore desirable to bring together in a single regulation those customs implementing provisions which are currently scattered over a large number of Community regulations and directives;

Whereas the implementing code for the Community Customs Code hereby established should set out existing customs implementing rules; whereas it is nevertheless necessary, in the light of experience:

— to make some amendments in order to adapt the said rules to the provisions of the Code,

— to extend the scope of certain provisions which currently apply only to specific customs procedures in order to take account of the Code's comprehensive application,

— to formulate certain rules more precisely in order to achieve greater legal security in their application;

Whereas the changes made relate mainly to the provisions concerning customs debt;

Whereas it is appropriate to limit the application of Article 791(2) until 1 January 1995 and to review the subject matter in the light of experience gained before that time;

Whereas the measures provided for by this Regulation are in accordance with the opinion of the Customs Code Committee,

HAS ADOPTED THIS REGULATION:

PART ONE

GENERAL IMPLEMENTING PROVISIONS

TITLE I—GENERAL

CHAPTER 1—DEFINITIONS

Article 1

For the purposes of this Regulation:

1. *Code means*:
   Council Regulation (EEC) No 2913/92 of 12 October 1992 establishing a Community Customs Code;

[2 *ATA carnet means*:
   the international customs document for temporary importation established by virtue of the ATA Convention or the Istanbul Convention;][1]

[3. *Committee means:*
   the Customs Code Committee established by Articles 247a and 248a of the Code;][2]

4. *Customs Co-operation Council means:*
   the organisation set up by the Convention establishing a Customs Co-operation Council, done at Brussels on 15 December 1950;

5. *Particulars required for identification of the goods means:*
   on the one hand, the particulars used to identify the goods commercially allowing the customs authorities to determine the tariff classification and, on the other hand, the quantity of the goods;

6. *Goods of a non-commercial nature means:*
   goods whose entry for the customs procedure in question is on an occasional basis and whose nature and quantity indicate that they are intended for the private, personal or family use of the consignees or persons carrying them, or which are clearly intended as gifts;

7. *Commercial policy measures means:*
   non-tariff measures established, as part of the common commercial policy, in the form of Community provisions governing the import and export of goods, such as surveillance or safeguard measures, quantitative restrictions or limits and import or export prohibitions;

8. *Customs nomenclature means:*
   one of the nomenclatures referred to in Article 20(6) of the Code;

9. *Harmonised System means:*
   the Harmonised Commodity Description and Coding System;

[10. *Treaty means:*
   the Treaty establishing the European Community;][2]

[11. *Istanbul Convention means:*
   the Convention on Temporary Admission agreed at Istanbul on 26 June 1990.][1]

[12. *Economic operator means*:
   a person who, in the course of his business, is involved in activities covered by customs legislation.][3]

Amendments—[1] Point 2 replaced and point 11 added by Commission Regulation 1762/95/EC (see OJ L171, 21.7.95, p 8).

[2] Points 3, 10 replaced by Commission Regulation 444/2002 art 1(1) (OJ L 68; 12.3.2002 p 11).

[3] Point 12 added by Commission Regulation 1875/2006/EC (OJ L 360, 19.12.2006, p 64).

[Article 1a

For the purposes of applying Articles 291 to 300, the countries of the Benelux Economic Union shall be considered as a single Member State.][1]

Amendments—[1] Article 1a substituted by Commission Regulation 1602/2000/EC with effect from 1 January 2001; see OJ L 188, 26.08.2000, p 1.

CHAPTER 2—DECISIONS

Article 2

Where a person making a request for a decision is not in a position to provide all the documents and information necessary to give a ruling, the customs authorities shall provide the documents and information at their disposal.

Article 3

A decision concerning security favourable to a person who has signed an undertaking to pay the sums due at the first written request of the customs authorities, shall be revoked where the said undertaking is not fulfilled.

Article 4

A revocation shall not affect goods which, at the moment of its entry into effect, have already been placed under a procedure by virtue of the revoked authorisation.

However, the customs authorities may require that such goods be assigned to a permitted customs-approved treatment or use within the period which they shall set.

[Article 4a

1. Under the conditions and in the manner which they shall determine, and with due regard to the principles laid down by customs rules, the customs authorities may provide that formalities shall be carried out by a data-processing technique.

For this purpose:

— "a data-processing technique" means:

(*a*) the exchange of EDI standard messages with the customs authorities;

(*b*) thc introduction of information required for completion of the formalities concerned into customs data-processing systems;

— "EDI" (electronic data interchange) means, the transmission of data structured according to agreed message standards, between one computer system and another, by electronic means,

— "standard message" means a predefined structure recognised for the electronic transmission of data.

2. The conditions laid down for carrying out formalities by a data-processing technique shall include inter alia measures for checking the source of data and for protecting data against the risk of unauthorised access, loss, alteration or destruction.

Article 4b

Where formalities are carried out by a data-processing technique, the customs authorities shall determine the rules for replacement of the handwritten signature by another technique which may be based on the use of codes.][1]

Amendments—[1] Articles 4a and 4b added by Commission Regulation 3665/93/EEC; see OJ L335, 31.12.93, p 1.

[Article 4c

For test programmes using data-processing techniques designed to evaluate possible simplifications, the customs authorities may, for the period strictly necessary to carry out the programme, waive the requirement to provide the following information—

(*a*) the declaration provided for in Article 178(1);

(*b*) by way of derogation from Article 222(1), the particulars relating to certain boxes of the Single Administrative Document which are not necessary for the identification of the goods and which are not the factors on the basis of which import or export duties are applied.

However, the information shall be available on request in the framework of a control operation.

The amount of import duties to be charged in the period covered by a derogation granted pursuant to the first subparagraph shall not be lower than that which would be levied in the absence of a derogation.

Member States wishing to engage in such test programmes shall provide the Commission in advance with full details of the proposed test programme, including its intended duration. They shall also keep the Commission informed of actual implementation and results. The Commission shall inform all the other Member States.][1]

Amendments—[1] Article 4c added by Commission Regulation 2787/2000/EC with effect from 3 January 2001; see OJ L 330 27.12.2000, p 1.

Articles 4d–140

Note—Articles 4d–140 are outside the scope of this work; please refer to Tolley's *Customs Duties Handbook*.

TITLE V—CUSTOMS VALUE

CHAPTER 1—GENERAL PROVISIONS

Article 141

1. In applying the provisions of Articles 28 to 36 of the Code and those of this title, Member States shall comply with the provisions set out in Annex 23.

The provisions as set out in the first column of Annex 23 shall be applied in the light of the interpretative note appearing in the second column.

2. If it is necessary to make reference to generally accepted accounting principles in determining the customs value, the provisions of Annex 24 shall apply.

Article 142

1. For the purposes of this title:

(*a*) "the Agreement" means the Agreement on implementation of Article VII of the General Agreement on Tariffs and Trade concluded in the framework of the multilateral trade negotiations of 1973 to 1979 and referred to in the first indent of Article 31(1) of the Code;

(*b*) "produced goods" includes goods grown, manufactured and mined;

VAT EC

(*c*) "identical goods" means goods produced in the same country which are the same in all respects, including physical characteristics, quality and reputation. Minor differences in appearance shall not preclude goods otherwise conforming to the definition from being regarded as identical;

(*d*) "similar goods" means goods produced in the same country which, although not alike in all respects, have like characteristics and like component materials which enable them to perform the same functions and to be commercially interchangeable; the quality of the goods, their reputation and the existence of a trademark are among the factors to be considered in determining whether goods are similar;

(*e*) "goods of the same class or kind" means goods which fall within a group or range of goods produced by a particular industry or industry sector, and includes identical or similar goods.

2. "Identical goods" and "similar goods", as the case may be, do not include goods which incorporate or reflect engineering, development, artwork, design work, and plans and sketches for which no adjustment has been made under Article 32(1)(*b*)(iv) of the Code because such elements were undertaken in the Community.

Article 143

1. [For the purposes of Title II, Chapter 3 of the Code and of this Title, persons shall be deemed to be related only if—][1]

(*a*) they are officers or directors of one another's businesses;

(*b*) they are legally recognised partners in business;

(*c*) they are employer and employee;

(*d*) any person directly or indirectly owns, controls or holds 5% or more of the outstanding voting stock or shares of both of them;

(*e*) one of them directly or indirectly controls the other;

(*f*) both of them are directly or indirectly controlled by a third person;

(*g*) together they directly or indirectly control a third person; or

(*h*) they are members of the same family. Persons shall be deemed to be members of the same family only if they stand in any of the following relationships to one another;

— husband and wife,

— parent and child,

— brother and sister (whether by whole or half blood),

— grandparent and grandchild,

— uncle or aunt and nephew or niece,

— parent-in-law and son-in-law or daughter-in-law,

— brother-in-law and sister-in-law.

2. For the purposes of this title, persons who are associated in business with one another in that one is the sole agent, sole distributor or sole concessionaire, however described, of the other shall be deemed to be related only if they fall within the criteria of paragraph 1.

Amendments—[1] In para 1 words substituted by Commission Regulation (EC) 46/1999, Art 1, para 8; see OJ L 10, 15.01.99, p 1.

Article 144

1. For the purposes of determining customs value under Article 29 of the Code of goods in regard to which the price has not actually been paid at the material time for valuation for customs purposes, the price payable for settlement at the said time shall as a general rule be taken as the basis for customs value.

2. The Commission and the Member States shall consult within the Committee concerning the application of paragraph 1.

[Article 145

1. Where goods declared for free circulation are part of a larger quantity of the same goods purchased in one transaction, the price actually paid or payable for the purposes of Article 29(1) of the Code shall be that price represented by the proportion of the total price which the quantity so declared bears to the total quantity purchased.

Apportioning the price actually paid or payable shall also apply in the case of the loss of part of a consignment or when the goods being valued have been damaged before entry into free circulation.

2. After release of the goods for free circulation, an adjustment made by the seller, to the benefit of the buyer, of the price actually paid or payable for the goods may be taken into consideration for the determination of the customs value in accordance with Article 29 of the Code, if it is demonstrated to the satisfaction of the customs authorities that:

(*a*) the goods were defective at the moment referred to by Article 67 of the Code;

(*b*) the seller made the adjustment in performance of a warranty obligation provided for in the contract of sale, concluded before release for free circulation of the goods;

(*c*) the defective nature of the goods has not already been taken into account in the relevant sales contract.

3. The price actually paid or payable for the goods, adjusted in accordance with paragraph 2, may be taken into account only if that adjustment was made within a period of 12 months following the date of acceptance of the declaration for entry to free circulation of the goods.][1]

Amendments—[1] Substituted by Commission Regulation (EC) 444/2002, Art 1, para 6; see OJ L68, 12.03.2002, p 11.

Article 146

Where the price actually paid or payable for the purposes of Article 29(1) of the Code includes an amount in respect of any internal tax applicable within the country of origin or export in respect of the goods in question, the said amount shall not be incorporated in the customs value provided that it can be demonstrated to the satisfaction of the customs authorities concerned that the goods in question have been or will be relieved therefrom for the benefit of the buyer.

Article 147

1. For the purposes of Article 29 of the Code, the fact that the goods which are the subject of a sale are declared for free circulation shall be regarded as adequate indication that they were sold for export to the customs territory of the Community. [In the case of successive sales before valuation, only the last sale, which led to the introduction of the goods into the customs territory of the Community, or a sale taking place in the customs territory of the Community before entry for free circulation of the goods shall constitute such indication.

Where a price is declared which relates to a sale taking place before the last sale on the basis of which the goods were introduced into the customs territory of the Community, it must be demonstrated to the satisfaction of the customs authorities that this sale of goods took place for export to the customs territory in question.

The provisions of Articles 178 to 181a shall apply.][1]

2. . . . [1] where goods are used in a third country between the time of sale and the time of entry into free circulation the customs value need not be the transaction value.

3. The buyer need satisfy no condition other than that of being a party to the contract of sale.

Amendments—[1] Words in para 1 replaced and words omitted from para 2 deleted by Commission Regulation 1762/95/EC; see OJ L171, 21.7.95, p 8.

Article 148

Where, in applying Article 29(1)(*b*) of the Code, it is established that the sale or price of imported goods is subject to a condition or consideration the value of which can be determined with respect to the goods being valued, such value shall be regarded as an indirect payment by the buyer to the seller and part of the price actually paid or payable provided that the condition or consideration does not relate to either:

(*a*) an activity to which Article 29(3)(*b*) of the Code applies; or

(*b*) a factor in respect of which an addition is to be made to the price actually paid or payable under the provisions of Article 32 of the Code.

Article 149

1. For the purposes of Article 29(3)(*b*) of the Code, the term "marketing activities" means all activities relating to advertising and promoting the sale of the goods in question and all activities relating to warranties or guarantees in respect of them.

2. Such activities undertaken by the buyer shall be regarded as having been undertaken on his own account even if they are performed in pursuance of an obligation on the buyer following an agreement with the seller.

Article 150

1. In applying Article 30(2)(*a*) of the Code (the transaction value of identical goods), the customs value shall be determined by reference to the transaction value of identical goods in a sale at the same commercial level and in substantially the same quantity as the goods being valued. Where no such sale is found, the transaction value of identical goods sold at a different commercial level and/or in different quantities, adjusted to take account of differences attributable to commercial level and/or to quantity, shall be used, provided that such adjustments can be made on the basis of demonstrated evidence which clearly establishes the reasonableness and accuracy of the adjustment, whether the adjustment leads to an increase or a decrease in the value.

2. Where the costs and charges referred to in Article 32(1)(*e*) of the Code are included in the transaction value, an adjustment shall be made to take account of significant differences in such costs and charges between the imported goods and the identical goods in question arising from differences in distances and modes of transport.

3. If, in applying this Article, more than one transaction value of identical goods is found, the lowest such value shall be used to determine the customs value of the imported goods.

4. In applying this Article, a transaction value for goods produced by a different person shall be taken into account only when no transaction value can be found under paragraph 1 for identical goods produced by the same person as the goods being valued.

5. For the purposes of this Article, the transaction value of identical imported goods means a customs value previously determined under Article 29 of the Code, adjusted as provided for in paragraphs 1 and 2 of this Article.

Article 151

1. In applying Article 30(2)(*b*) of the Code (the transaction value of similar goods), the customs value shall be determined by reference to the transaction value of similar goods in a sale at the same commercial level and in substantially the same quantity as the goods being valued. Where no such sale is found, the transaction value of similar goods sold at a different commercial level and/or in different quantities, adjusted to take account of differences attributable to commercial level and/or to quantity, shall be used, provided that such adjustments can be made on the basis of demonstrated evidence which clearly establishes the reasonableness and accuracy of the adjustment, whether the adjustment leads to an increase or a decrease in the value.
2. Where the costs and charges referred to in Article 32(1)(*e*) of the Code are included in the transaction value, an adjustment shall be made to take account of significant differences in such costs and charges between the imported goods and the similar goods in question arising from differences in distances and modes of transport.
3. If, in applying this Article, more than one transaction value of similar goods is found, the lowest such value shall be used to determine the customs value for the imported goods.
4. In applying this Article, a transaction value for goods produced by a different person shall be taken into account only when no transaction value can be found under paragraph 1 for similar goods produced by the same person as the goods being valued.
5. For the purposes of this Article, the transaction value of similar imported goods means a customs value previously determined under Article 29 of the Code, adjusted as provided for in paragraphs 1 and 2 of this Article.

Article 152

1

(*a*) If the imported goods or identical or similar imported goods are sold in the Community in the condition as imported, the customs value of imported goods, determined in accordance with Article 30(2)(*c*) of the Code, shall be based on the unit price at which the imported goods or identical or similar imported goods are so sold in the greatest aggregate quantity, at or about the time of the importation of the goods being valued, to persons who are not related to the persons from whom they buy such goods, subject to deductions for the following:

(i) either the commissions usually paid or agreed to be paid or the additions usually made for profit and general expenses (including the direct and indirect costs of marketing the goods in question) in connection with sales in the Community of imported goods of the same class or kind;

(ii) the usual costs of transport and insurance and associated costs incurred within the Community;

(iii) the import duties and other charges payable in the Community by reason of the importation or sale of the goods.

[(*aa*) The customs value of certain perishable goods imported on consignment may be directly determined in accordance with Article 30(2)(*c*) of the Code. For this purpose the unit prices shall be notified to the Commission by the Member States and disseminated by the Commission via TARIC in accordance with Article 6 of Council Regulation (EEC) No 2658/87.

The unit prices shall be calculated and notified as follows:

(i) After the deductions provided for in point (*a*), a unit price per 100 kg net for each category of goods shall be notified by the Member States to the Commission. The Member States may fix standard amounts for the costs referred to in point (*a*)(ii) which shall be made known to the Commission.

(ii) The unit price may be used to determine the customs value of the imported goods for periods of 14 days, each period beginning on a Friday.

(iii) The reference period for determining the unit prices shall be the preceding period of 14 days which ends on the Thursday preceding the week during which new unit prices are to be established.

(iv) The unit prices shall be notified by the Member States to the Commission in euro not later than 12 noon on the Monday of the week in which they are disseminated by the Commission. If that day is a non-working day, notification shall be made on the working day immediately preceding that day. Unit prices shall only apply if this notification is disseminated by the Commission.][1]

(*b*) If neither the imported goods nor identical nor similar imported goods are sold at or about the time of importation of the goods being valued, the customs value of imported goods determined under this Article shall, subject otherwise to the provisions of paragraph 1(*a*), be based on the unit price at which the imported goods or identical or similar imported goods are sold in the Community in the condition as imported at the earliest date after the importation of the goods being valued but before the expiration of 90 days after such importation.

2. If neither the imported goods nor identical nor similar imported goods are sold in the Community in the condition as imported, then, if the importer so requests, the customs value shall be based on the unit price at which the imported goods, after further processing, are sold in the greatest aggregate quantity to persons in the Community who are not related to the persons from whom they buy such goods, due allowance being made for the value added by such processing and the deductions provided for in paragraph 1(*a*).

3. For the purposes of this Article, the unit price at which imported goods are sold in the greatest aggregate quantity is the price at which the greatest number of units is sold in sales to persons who are not related to the persons from whom they buy such goods at the first commercial level after importation at which such sales take place.

4. Any sale in the Community to a person who supplies directly or indirectly free of charge or at reduced cost for use in connection with the production and sale for export of the imported goods any of the elements specified in Article 32(1)(*b*) of the Code should not be taken into account in establishing the unit price for the purposes of this Article.

5. For the purposes of paragraph 1(*b*), the "earliest date" shall be the date by which sales of the imported goods or of identical or similar imported goods are made in sufficient quantity to establish the unit price.

Amendments—[1] Para (*aa*) inserted by Council Regulation (EC) 215/2006 art 1(1); see OJ L 038; 9.2.2006, p 11.

Article 153

1. In applying Article 30(2)(*d*) of the Code (computed value), the customs authorities may not require or compel any person not resident in the Community to produce for examination, or to allow access to, any account or other record for the purposes of determining this value. However, information supplied by the producer of the goods for the purposes of determining the customs value under this Article may be verified in a non-Community country by the customs authorities of a Member State with the agreement of the producer and provided that such authorities give sufficient advance notice to the authorities of the country in question and the latter do not object to the investigation.

2. The cost or value of materials and fabrication referred to in the first indent of Article 30(2)(*d*) of the Code shall include the cost of elements specified in Article 32(1)(*a*)(ii) and (iii) of the Code. It shall also include the value, duly apportioned, of any product or service specified in Article 32(1)(*b*) of the Code which has been supplied directly or indirectly by the buyer for use in connection with the production of the imported goods. The value of the elements specified in Article 32(1)(*b*)(iv) of the Code which are undertaken in the Community shall be included only to the extent that such elements are charged to the producer.

3. Where information other than that supplied by or on behalf of the producer is used for the purposes of determining a computed value, the customs authorities shall inform the declarant, if the latter so requests, of the source of such information, the data used and the calculations based on such data, subject to Article 15 of the Code.

4. The "general expenses" referred to in the second indent of Article 30(2)(*d*) of the Code, cover the direct and indirect costs of producing and selling the goods for export which are not included under the first indent of Article 30(2)(*d*) of the Code.

Article 154

Where containers referred to in Article 32(1)(*a*)(ii) of the Code are to be the subject of repeated importations, their cost shall, at the request of the declarant, be apportioned, as appropriate, in accordance with generally accepted accounting principles.

Article 155

For the purposes of Article 32(1)(*b*)(iv) of the Code, the cost of research and preliminary design sketches is not to be included in the customs value.

Article 156

Article 33(*c*) of the Code shall apply *mutatis mutandis* where the customs value is determined by applying a method other than the transaction value.

[Article 156a

1. The customs authorities may, at the request of the person concerned, authorise:

— by derogation from Article 32(2) of the Code, certain elements which are to be added to the price actually paid or payable, although not quantifiable at the time of incurrence of the customs debt,

— by derogation from Article 33 of the Code, certain charges which are not to be included in the customs value, in cases where the amounts relating to such elements are not shown separately at the time of incurrence of the customs debt,

to be determined on the basis of appropriate and specific criteria.

VAT EC

In such cases, the declared customs value it not to be considered as provisional within the meaning of the second indent of Article 254.

2. The authorisation shall be granted under the following conditions:

(*a*) the carrying out of the procedures provided for by Article 259 would, in the circumstances, represent disproportionate administrative costs;

(*b*) recourse to an application of Articles 30 and 31 of the Code appears to be inappropriate in the particular circumstances;

(*c*) there are valid reasons for considering that the amount of import duties to be charged in the period covered by authorisation will not be lower than that which would be levied in the absence of an authorisation;

(*d*) competitive conditions amongst operators are not distorted.]

Amendment—This article is added by Commission Regulation 1676/96/EC; see OJ L 218 28.8.96, p1.

CHAPTER 2—PROVISIONS CONCERNING ROYALTIES AND LICENCE FEES

Article 157

1. For the purposes of Article 32(1)(*c*) of the Code, royalties and licence fees shall be taken to mean in particular payment for the use of rights relating:

— to the manufacture of imported goods (in particular, patents, designs, models and manufacturing know-how), or

— to the sale for exportation of imported goods (in particular, trade marks, registered designs), or

— to the use or resale of imported goods (in particular, copyright, manufacturing processes inseparably embodied in the imported goods).

2. Without prejudice to Article 32(5) of the Code, when the customs value of imported goods is determined under the provisions of Article 29 of the Code, a royalty or licence fee shall be added to the price actually paid or payable only when this payment:

— is related to the goods being valued, and

— constitutes a condition of sale of those goods.

Article 158

1. When the imported goods are only an ingredient or component of goods manufactured in the Community, an adjustment to the price actually paid or payable for the imported goods shall only be made when the royalty or licence fee relates to those goods.

2. Where goods are imported in an unassembled state or only have to undergo minor processing before resale, such as diluting or packing, this shall not prevent a royalty or licence fee from being considered related to the imported goods.

3. If royalties or licence fees relate partly to the imported goods and partly to other ingredients or component parts added to the goods after their importation, or to post-importation activities or services, an appropriate apportionment shall be made only on the basis of objective and quantifiable data, in accordance with the interpretative note to Article 32(2) of the Code in Annex 23.

Article 159

A royalty or licence fee in respect of the right to use a trade mark is only to be added to the price actually paid or payable for the imported goods where:

— the royalty or licence fee refers to goods which are resold in the same state or which are subject only to minor processing after importation,

— the goods are marketed under the trade mark, affixed before or after importation, for which the royalty or licence fee is paid, and

— the buyer is not free to obtain such goods from other suppliers unrelated to the seller.

Article 160

When the buyer pays royalties or licence fees to a third party, the conditions provided for in Article 157(2) shall not be considered as met unless the seller or a person related to him requires the buyer to make that payment.

Article 161

Where the method of calculation of the amount of a royalty or licence fee derives from the price of the imported goods, it may be assumed in the absence of evidence to the contrary that the payment of that royalty or licence fee is related to the goods to be valued.

However, where the amount of a royalty or licence fee is calculated regardless of the price of the imported goods, the payment of that royalty or licence fee may nevertheless be related to the goods to be valued.

Article 162

In applying Article 32(1)(*c*) of the Code, the country of residence of the recipient of the payment of the royalty or licence fee shall not be a material consideration.

CHAPTER 3—PROVISIONS CONCERNING THE PLACE OF INTRODUCTION INTO THE COMMUNITY

Article 163

1. For the purposes of Article 32(1)(*e*) and Article 33(*a*) of the Code, the place of introduction into the customs territory of the Community shall be:

(*a*) for goods carried by sea, the port of unloading, or the port of transhipment, subject to transhipment being certified by the customs authorities of that port;

(*b*) for goods carried by sea and then, without transhipment, by inland waterway, the first port where unloading can take place either at the mouth of the river or canal or further inland, subject to proof being furnished to the customs office that the freight to the port of unloading is higher than that to the first port;

(*c*) for goods carried by rail, inland waterway, or road, the place where the first customs office is situated;

(*d*) for goods carried by other means, the place where the land frontier of the customs territory of the Community is crossed.

[2. The customs value of goods introduced into the customs territory of the Community and then carried to a destination in another part of that territory through the territories of Belarus, Russia, Switzerland, Bosnia and Herzegovina, the Federal Republic of Yugoslavia or the former Yugoslav Republic of Macedonia shall be determined by reference to the first place of introduction into the customs territory of the Community, provided that goods are carried direct through the territories of those countries by a usual route across such territory to the place of destination.][1]

3. The customs value of goods introduced into the customs territory of the Community and then carried by sea to a destination in another part of that territory shall be determined by reference to the first place of introduction into the customs territory of the Community, provided the goods are carried direct by a usual route to the place of destination.

[4. Paragraphs 2 and 3 of this Article shall also apply where the goods have been unloaded, transhipped or temporarily immobilised in the territories of Belarus, Russia, Switzerland, Bosnia and Herzegovina, the Federal Republic of Yugoslavia or the former Yugoslav Republic of Macedonia for reasons related solely to their transport.][1]

5. For goods introduced into the customs territory of the Community and carried directly from one of the French overseas departments to another part of the customs territory of the Community or vice versa, the place of introduction to be taken into consideration shall be the place referred to in paragraphs 1 and 2 situated in that part of the customs territory of the Community from which the goods came, if they were unloaded or transhipped there and this was certified by the customs authorities.

6. When the conditions specified at paragraphs 2, 3 and 5 are not fulfilled, the place of introduction to be taken into consideration shall be the place specified in paragraph 1 situated in that part of the customs territory of the Community to which the goods are consigned.

Amendments—[1] Paras 2, 4 replaced by Commission Regulation 519/2013/EU art 1 Annex (OJ L 158, 10.6.2013, p. 74).

CHAPTER 4—PROVISIONS CONCERNING TRANSPORT COSTS

Article 164

In applying Article 32(1)(*e*) and 33(*a*) of the Code:

(*a*) where goods are carried by the same mode of transport to a point beyond the place of introduction into the customs territory of the Community, transport costs shall be assessed in proportion to the distance covered outside and inside the customs territory of the Community, unless evidence is produced to the customs authorities to show the costs that would have been incurred under a general compulsory schedule of freight rates for the carriage of the goods to the place of introduction into the customs territory of the Community;

(*b*) where goods are invoiced at a uniform free domicile price which corresponds to the price at the place of introduction, transport costs within the Community shall not be deducted from that price. However, such deduction shall be allowed if evidence is produced to the customs authorities that the free-frontier price would be lower than the uniform free domicile price;

(*c*) where transport is free or provided by the buyer, transport costs to the place of introduction, calculated in accordance with the schedule of freight rates normally applied for the same modes of transport, shall be included in the customs value.

Article 165

1. All postal charges levied up to the place of destination in respect of goods sent by post shall be included in the customs value of these goods, with the exception of any supplementary postal charge levied in the country of importation.

2. No adjustment to the declared value shall, however, be made in respect of such charges in determining the value of consignments of a non-commercial nature.

VAT EC

3. Paragraphs 1 and 2 are not applicable to goods carried by the express postal services known as EMS-Datapost (in Denmark, EMS-Jetpost, in Germany, EMS-Kurierpostsendungen, in Italy, CAI-Post).

Article 166

The air transport costs to be included in the customs value of goods shall be determined by applying the rules and percentages shown in Annex 25.

CHAPTER 5—VALUATION OF CERTAIN CARRIER MEDIA FOR USE IN ADP EQUIPMENT

Article 167

. . . [1]

Amendments—[1] Repealed by Commission Regulation (EC) 444/2002, Art 1, para 7; see OJ L68, 12.03.2002, p 11.

CHAPTER 6—PROVISIONS CONCERNING RATES OF EXCHANGE

Article 168

For the purposes of Articles 169 to 171 of this chapter:

(*a*) "rate recorded" shall mean:

— the latest selling rate of exchange recorded for commercial transactions on the most representative exchange market or markets of the Member State concerned, or

— some other description of a rate of exchange so recorded and designated by the Member State as the "rate recorded" provided that it reflects as effectively as possible the current value of the currency in question in commercial transactions;

(*b*) "published" shall mean made generally known in a manner designated by the Member State concerned;

(*c*) "currency" shall mean any monetary unit used as a means of settlement between monetary authorities or on the international market.

Article 169

1. Where factors used to determine the customs value of goods are expressed at the time when that value is determined in a currency other than that of the Member State where the valuation is made, the rate of exchange to be used to determine that value in terms of the currency of the Member State concerned shall be the rate recorded on the second-last Wednesday of a month and published on that or the following day.

2. The rate recorded on the second-last Wednesday of a month shall be used during the following calendar month unless it is superseded by a rate established under Article 171.

3. Where a rate of exchange is not recorded on the second-last Wednesday indicated in paragraph 1, or, if recorded, is not published on that or the following day, the last rate recorded for the currency in question published within the preceding 14 days shall be deemed to be the rate recorded on that Wednesday.

Article 170

Where a rate of exchange cannot be established under the provisions of Article 169, the rate of exchange to be used for the application of Article 35 of the Code shall be designated by the Member State concerned and shall reflect as effectively as possible the current value of the currency in question in commercial transactions in terms of the currency of that Member State.

Article 171

1. Where a rate of exchange recorded on the last Wednesday of a month and published on that or the following day differs by 5% or more from the rate established in accordance with Article 169 for entry into use the following month, it shall replace the latter rate from the first Wednesday of that month as the rate to be applied for the application of Article 35 of the Code.

2. Where in the course of a period of application as referred to in the preceding provisions, a rate of exchange recorded on a Wednesday and published on that or the following day differs by 5% or more from the rate being used in accordance with this Chapter, it shall replace the latter rate and enter into use on the Wednesday following as the rate to be used for the application of Article 35 of the Code. The replacement rate shall remain in use for the remainder of the current month, provided that this rate is not superseded due to operation of the provisions of the first sentence of this paragraph.

3. Where, in a Member State, a rate of exchange is not recorded on a Wednesday or, if recorded, is not published on that or the following day, the rate recorded shall, for the application in that Member State of paragraphs 1 and 2, be the rate most recently recorded and published prior to that Wednesday.

Article 172

When the customs authorities of a Member State authorise a declarant to furnish or supply at a later date certain details concerning the declaration for free circulation of the goods in the form of a periodic declaration, this authorisation may, at the declarant's request, provide that a single rate be used for conversion into that Member State's currency of elements forming part of the customs value as expressed in a particular currency. In this case, the rate to be used shall be the rate, established in accordance with this Chapter, which is applicable on the first day of the period covered by the declaration in question.

CHAPTER 7—SIMPLIFIED PROCEDURES FOR CERTAIN PERISHABLE GOODS

Articles 173–177

Amendments—Articles 173–177 repealed by Council Regulation (EC) 215/2006 art 1(2); see OJ L 038; 9.2.2006, p 11.

CHAPTER 8—DECLARATIONS OF PARTICULARS AND DOCUMENTS TO BE FURNISHED

Article 178

1. Where it is necessary to establish a customs value for the purposes of Articles 28 to 36 of the Code, a declaration of particulars relating to customs value (value declaration) shall accompany the customs entry made in respect of the imported goods. The value declaration shall be drawn up on a form D.V.1 corresponding to the specimen in Annex 28, supplemented where appropriate by one or more forms D.V.1 *bis* corresponding to the specimen in Annex 29.

[2. The value declaration provided for in paragraph 1 shall be made only by a person established in the Community and in possession of the relevant facts. The second indent of Article 64(2)(b) and Article 64(3) of the Code shall apply *mutatis mutandis*.][1]

3. The customs authorities may waive the requirement of a declaration on the form referred to in paragraph 1 where the customs value of the goods in question cannot be determined under the provisions of Article 29 of the Code. In such cases the person referred to in paragraph 2 shall furnish or cause to be furnished to the customs authorities such other information as may be requested for the purposes of determining the customs value under another Article of the said Code; and such other information shall be supplied in such form and manner as may be prescribed by the customs authorities.

4. The lodging with a customs office of a declaration required by paragraph 1 shall, without prejudice to the possible application of penal provisions, be equivalent to the engagement of responsibility by the person referred to in paragraph 2 in respect of:

— the accuracy and completeness of the particulars given in the declaration,
— the authenticity of the documents produced in support of these particulars, and
— the supply of any additional information or document necessary to establish the customs value of the goods.

5. This Article shall not apply in respect of goods for which the customs value is determined under the simplified procedure system established in accordance with the provisions of Articles 173 to 177.

Amendments—[1] Article 178(2) is replaced by Commission Regulation 1677/98 art 1(1); OJ L 212, 30.07.98, p 18–22 with effect from 6 August 1998.

Article 179

1. Except where it is essential for the correct application of import duties, the customs authorities shall waive the requirement of all or part of the declaration provided for in Article 178(1):

(*a*) where the customs value of the imported goods in a consignment does not exceed [EUR 10000][1], provided that they do not constitute split or multiple consignments from the same consignor to the same consignee; or

(*b*) where the importations involved are of a non-commercial nature; or

(*c*) where the submission of the particulars in question is not necessary for the application of the Customs Tariff of the European Communities or where the customs duties provided for in the Tariff are not chargeable pursuant to specific customs provisions.

2. The amount in ecu referred to in paragraph 1(*a*) shall be converted in accordance with Article 18 of the Code. The customs authorities may round-off upwards or downwards the sum arrived at after conversion.

The customs authorities may maintain unamended the exchange value in national currency of the amount determined in ecu if, at the time of the annual adjustment provided for in Article 18 of the Code, the conversion of this amount, before the rounding-off provided for in this paragraph, leads to an alteration of less than 5% in the exchange value expressed in national currency or to a reduction thereof.

3. In the case of continuing traffic in goods supplied by the same seller to the same buyer under the same commercial conditions, the customs authorities may waive the requirement that all particulars under Article 178(1) be furnished in support of each customs declaration, but shall require them whenever the circumstances change and at least once every three years.

4. A waiver granted under this Article may be withdrawn and the submission of a D.V.1 may be required where it is found that a condition necessary to qualify for that waiver was not or is no longer met.

Amendments—[1] Figure substituted by Commission Regulation (EC) 444/2002, Art 1, para 8; see OJ L68, 12.03.2002, p 11.

Article 180

Where computerised systems are used, or where the goods concerned are the subject of a general, periodic or recapitulative declaration, the customs authorities may authorise variations in the form of presentation of data required for the determination of customs value.

Article 181

1. The person referred to in Article 178(2) shall furnish the customs authorities with a copy of the invoice on the basis of which the value of the imported goods is declared. Where the customs value is declared in writing this copy shall be retained by the customs authorities.
2. In the case of written declarations of the customs value, when the invoice for the imported goods is made out to a person established in a Member State other than that in which the customs value is declared, the declarant shall furnish the customs authorities with two copies of the invoice. One of these copies shall be retained by the customs authorities; the other, bearing the stamp of the office in question and the serial number of the declaration at the said customs office, shall be returned to the declarant for forwarding to the person to whom the invoice is made out.
3. The customs authorities may extend the provisions of paragraph 2 to cases where the person to whom the invoice is made out is established in the Member State in which the customs value is declared.

[Article 181a

1. The customs authorities need not determine the customs valuation of imported goods on the basis of the transaction value method if, in accordance with the procedure set out in paragraph 2, they are not satisfied, on the basis of reasonable doubts, that the declared value represents the total amount paid or payable as referred to in Article 29 of the Code.
2. Where the customs authorities have the doubts described in paragraph 1 they may ask for additional information in accordance with Article 178(4). If those doubts continue, the customs authorities must, before reaching a final decision, notify the person concerned, in writing if requested, of the grounds for those doubts and provide him with a reasonable opportunity to respond. A final decision and the grounds therefor shall be communicated in writing to the person concerned.][1]

Amendments—[1] Article 181a is inserted by Commission Regulation 3254/94/EC; see OJ L346, 31.12.94, p 1.

Articles 181b–197

Note—Articles 181b–197 are outside the scope of this work.

TITLE VII—CUSTOMS DECLARATIONS—NORMAL PROCEDURE

Articles 198–856a

Note—Articles 198–856a are outside the scope of this work.

PART FOUR
CUSTOMS DEBT

Articles 857–912

Note—Articles 857–912g are outside the scope of this work.

PART FIVE
FINAL PROVISIONS

Article 913

The following Regulation and Directives shall be repealed:

— Commission Regulation (EEC) No 1494/80 of 11 June 1980 on interpretative notes and generally accepted accounting principles for the purposes of customs value,

— Commission Regulation (EEC) No 1495/80 of 11 June 1980 implementing certain provisions of Council Regulation (EEC) No 1224/80 on the valuation of goods for customs purposes, as last amended by Regulation (EEC) No 558/91,

— Commission Regulation (EEC) No 1496/80 of 11 June 1980 on the declaration of particulars relating to customs value and on documents to be furnished, as last amended by Regulation (EEC) No 979/93,

— Commission Regulation (EEC) No 3177/80 of 5 December 1980 on the place of introduction to be taken into consideration in applying Article 14(2) of Council Regulation (EEC) No 1224/80 on the valuation of goods for customs purposes, as last amended by Regulation (EEC) No 2779/90,

— Commission Regulation (EEC) No 3179/80 of 5 December 1980 on postal charges to be taken into consideration when determining the customs value of goods sent by post, as last amended by Regulation (EEC) No 1264/90,

— Commission Regulation (EEC) No 1577/81 of 12 June 1981 establishing a system of simplified procedures for the determination of the customs value of certain perishable goods, as last amended by Regulation (EEC) No 3334/90,

— Commission Regulation (EEC) No 3158/83 of 9 November 1983 on the incidence of royalties and licence fees in customs value,

— Commission Regulation (EEC) No 1766/85 of 27 June 1985 on the rates of exchange to be used in the determination of customs value, as last amended by Regulation (EEC) No 593/91,
— Commission Regulation (EEC) No 3903/92 of 21 December 1992 on air transport costs.

Note—Repeals within the scope of this work only are mentioned: other repeals have been omitted.

Article 914

References to the provisions repealed shall be understood as referring to this Regulation.

Article 915

This Regulation shall enter into force on the third day following its publication in the *Official Journal of the European Communities*.
It shall apply from 1 January 1994.

. . .

This Regulation shall be binding in its entirety and directly applicable in all Member States.

Note—Words omitted are outside the scope of this work.

ANNEX 23

INTERPRETATIVE NOTES ON CUSTOMS VALUE

First column	*Second column*
Reference to provisions of the Customs Code	*Notes*
Article 29(1)	The price actually paid or payable refers to the price for the imported goods. Thus the flow of dividends or other payments from the buyer to the seller that do not relate to the imported goods are not part of the customs value.
Article 29(1)(*a*) third indent	An example of such restriction would be the case where a seller requires a buyer of automobiles not to sell or exhibit them prior to a fixed date which represents the beginning of a model year.
Article 29(1)(*b*)	Some examples of this include: (*a*) the seller establishes the price of the imported goods on condition that the buyer will also buy other goods in specified quantities; (*b*) the price of the imported goods is dependent upon the price or prices at which the buyer of the imported goods sells other goods to the seller of the imported goods; (*c*) the price is established on the basis of a form of payment extraneous to the imported goods, such as where the imported goods are semi-finished goods which have been provided by the seller on condition that he will receive a specified quantity of the finished goods. However, conditions or considerations relating to the production or marketing of the imported goods shall not result in rejection of the transaction value. For example, the fact that the buyer furnishes the seller with engineering and plans undertaken in the country of importation shall not result in rejection of the transaction value for the purposes of Article 29(1).
Article 29(2)	**1** Paragraphs 2(*a*) and (*b*) provide different means of establishing the acceptability of a transaction value. **2** Paragraph 2(*a*) provides that where the buyer and the seller are related, the circumstances surrounding the sale shall be examined and the transaction value shall be accepted as the customs value provided that the relationship did not influence the price. It is not intended that there should be an examination of the circumstances in all cases where the buyer and the seller are related. Such examination will only be required where there are doubts about the acceptability of the price. Where the customs authorities have no doubts about the acceptability of the price, it should be accepted without requesting further information from the declarant. For example, the customs authorities may have previously examined the relationship, or it may already have detailed information concerning the buyer and the seller, and may already be satisfied from such examination or information that the relationship did not influence the price.

VAT EC

3 Where the customs authorities are unable to accept the transaction value without further inquiry, it should give the declarant an opportunity to supply such further detailed information as may be necessary to enable it to examine the circumstances surrounding the sale. In this context, the customs authorities should be prepared to examine relevant aspects of the transaction, including the way in which the buyer and seller organise their commercial relations and the way in which the price in question was arrived at, in order to determine whether the relationship influenced the price. Where it can be shown that the buyer and seller, although related under the provisions of Article 143 of this Regulation, buy from and sell to each other as if they were not related, this would demonstrate that the price had not been influenced by the relationship. As an example of this, if the price had been settled in a manner consistent with the normal pricing practices of the industry in question or with the way the seller settles prices for sales to buyers who are not related to him, this would demonstrate that the price had not been influenced by the relationship. As a further example, where it is shown that the price is adequate to ensure recovery of all costs plus a profit which is representative of the firm's overall profit realised over a representative period of time (eg on an annual basis) in sales of goods of the same class or kind, this would demonstrate that the price had not been influenced.

4 Paragraph 2(*b*) provides an opportunity for the declarant to demonstrate that the transaction value closely approximates to a "test" value previously accepted by the customs authorities and is therefore acceptable under the provisions of Article 29. Where a test under paragraph 2(*b*) is met, it is not necessary to examine the question of influence under paragraph 2(*a*). If the customs authorities already have sufficient information to be satisfied, without further detailed inquiries, that one of the tests provided in paragraph (2)(*b*) has been met, there is no reason for them to require the declarant to demonstrate that the test can be met.

Article 29(2)(*b*) A number of factors must be taken into consideration in determining whether one value "closely approximates" to another value. These factors include the nature of the imported goods, the nature of the industry itself, the season in which the goods are imported, and, whether the difference in values is commercially significant. Since these factors may vary from case to case, it would be impossible to apply a uniform standard such as a fixed percentage, in each case. For example, a small difference in value in a case involving one type of goods could be unacceptable while a large difference in a case involving another type of goods might be acceptable in determining whether the transaction value closely approximates to the "test" values set forth in Article 29(2)(*b*).

Article 29(3)(*a*) An example of an indirect payment would be the settlement by the buyer, whether in whole or in part, of a debt owed by the seller.

Article 30(2)(*a*), (*b*) **1** In applying these provisions, the customs authorities shall, wherever possible, use a sale of identical or similar goods, as appropriate, at the same commercial level and in substantially the same quantity as the goods being valued. Where no such sale is found, a sale of identical or similar goods, as appropriate, that takes place under any one of the following three conditions may be used:

(*a*) a sale at the same commercial level but in a different quantity;

(*b*) a sale at a different commercial level but in substantially the same quantity; or

(*c*) a sale at a different commercial level and in a different quantity.

2 Having found a sale under any one of these three conditions adjustments will then be made, as the case may be, for:

(*a*) quantity factors only;

(*b*) commercial level factors only; or

(*c*) both commercial level and quantity factors.

3 The expression "and/or" allows the flexibility to use the sales and make the necessary adjustments in any one of the three conditions described above.

4 A condition for adjustment because of different commercial levels or different quantities is that such adjustment, whether it leads to an increase or a decrease in the value, be made only on the basis of demonstrated evidence that clearly establishes the reasonableness and accuracy of the adjustment, eg valid price lists containing prices referring to different levels or different quantities. As an example of this, if the imported goods being valued consist of a shipment of 10 units and the only identical or similar imported goods, as appropriate, for which a transaction value exists involved a sale of 500 units, and it is recognised that the seller grants quantity discounts, the required adjustment may be accomplished by resorting to the seller's price list and using that price applicable to a sale of 10 units. This does not require that a sale had to have been made in quantities of 10 as long as the price list has been established as being bona fide through sales at other quantities. In the absence of such an objective measure, however, the determination of a customs value under the provisions of Article 30(2)(*a*) and (*b*) is not appropriate.

Article 30(2)(*d*)

1 As a general rule, customs value is determined under these provisions on the basis of information readily available in the Community. In order to determine a computed value, however, it may be necessary to examine the costs of producing the goods being valued and other information which has to be obtained from outside the Community. Furthermore, in most cases the producer of the goods will be outside the jurisdiction of the authorities of the Member States. The use of the computed value method will generally be limited to those cases where the buyer and seller are related, and the producer is prepared to supply to the authorities of the country of importation the necessary costings and to provide facilities for any subsequent verification which may be necessary.

2 The "cost or value" referred to in Article 30(2)(*d*), first indent, is to be determined on the basis of information relating to the production of the goods being valued supplied by or on behalf of the producer. It is to be based upon the commercial accounts of the producer, provided that such accounts are consistent with the generally accepted accounting principles applied in the country where the goods are produced.

3 The "amount for profit and general expenses" referred to in Article 30(2)(*d*), second indent, is to be determined on the basis of information supplied by or on behalf of the producer unless his figures are inconsistent with those usually reflected in sales of goods of the same class or kind as the goods being valued which are made by producers in the country of exportation for export to the country of importation.

4 No cost or value of the elements referred to in this Article shall be counted twice in determining the computed value.

5 It should be noted in this context that the "amount for profit and general expenses" has to be taken as a whole. It follows that if, in any particular case, the producer's profit figure is low and his general expenses are high, his profit and general expenses taken together may nevertheless be consistent with that usually reflected in sales of goods of the same class or kind. Such a situation might occur, for example, if a product were being launched in the Community and the producer accepted a nil or low profit to offset high general expenses associated with the launch. Where the producer can demonstrate that he is taking a low profit on his sales of the imported goods because of particular commercial circumstances, his actual profit figures should be taken into account provided that he has valid commercial reasons to justify them and his pricing policy reflects usual pricing policies in the branch of industry concerned. Such a situation might occur, for example, where producers have been forced to lower prices temporarily because of an unforeseeable drop in demand, or where they sell goods to complement a range of goods being produced in the country of importation and accept a low profit to maintain competitivity. Where the producer's own figures for profit and general expenses are not consistent with those usually reflected in sales of goods of the same class or kind as the goods being valued which are made by producers in the country of exportation for export to the country of importation, the amount for profit and general expenses may be based upon relevant information other than that supplied by or on behalf of the producer of the goods.

6 Whether certain goods are "of the same class or kind" as other goods must be determined on a case-by-case basis with reference to the circumstances involved. In determining the usual profits and general expenses under the provisions of Article 30(2)(*d*), sales for export to the country of importation of the narrowest group or range of goods, which includes the goods being valued, for which the necessary information can be provided, should be examined. For the purposes of Article 30(2)(*d*), "goods of the same class or kind" must be from the same country as the goods being valued.

Article 31(1)

1 Customs values determined under the provisions of Article 31(1) should, to the greatest extent possible, be based on previously determined customs values.

2 The methods of valuation to be employed under Article 31(1) should be those laid down in Articles 29 and 30(2), but a reasonable flexibility in the application of such methods would be in conformity with the aims and provisions of Article 31(1).

3 Some examples of reasonable flexibility are as follows:

(*a*) *Identical goods*—the requirement that the identical goods should be exported at or about the same time as the goods being valued could be flexibly interpreted; identical imported goods produced in a country other than the country of exportation of the goods being valued could be the basis for customs valuation; customs values of identical imported goods already determined under the provisions of Article 30(2)(*c*) and (*d*) could be used.

(*b*) *Similar goods*—the requirement that the similar goods should be exported at or about the same time as the goods being valued could be flexibly interpreted; similar imported goods produced in a country other than the country of exportation of the goods being valued could be the basis for customs valuations; customs values of similar imported goods already determined under the provisions of Article 30(2)(*c*) and (*d*) could be used.

(*c*) *Deductive method*—the requirement that the goods shall have been sold in the "condition as imported" in Article 152(1)(*a*) could be flexibly interpreted; the "90 days" requirement could be administered flexibly.

Article 32(1)(*b*)(ii)

1 There are two factors involved in the apportionment of the elements specified in Article 32(1)(*b*)(ii) to the imported goods—the value of the element itself and the way in which that value is to be apportioned to the imported goods. The apportionment of these elements should be made in a reasonable manner appropriate to the circumstances and in accordance with generally accepted accounting principles.

2 Concerning the value of the element, if the buyer acquires the element from a seller not related to him at a given cost, the value of the element is that cost. If the element was produced by the buyer or by a person related to him, its value would be the cost of producing it. If the element had been previously used by the buyer, regardless of whether it had been acquired or produced by him, the original cost of acquisition or production would have to be adjusted downwards to reflect its use in order to arrive at the value of the element.

3 Once a value has been determined for the element, it is necessary to apportion that value to the imported goods. Various possibilities exist. For example, the value might be apportioned to the first shipment, if the buyer wishes to pay duty on the entire value at one time. As another example, he may request that the value be apportioned over the number of units produced up to the time of the first shipment. As a further example, he may request that the value be apportioned over the entire anticipated production where contracts of firm commitments exist for the production. The method of apportionment used will depend upon the documentation provided by the buyer.

4 As an illustration of the above, a buyer provides the producer with a mould to be used in the production of the imported goods and contracts with him to buy 10,000 units. By the time of arrival of the first shipment of 1,000 units, the producer has already produced 4,000 units. The buyer may request the customs authorities to apportion the value of the mould over 1,000, 4,000 or 10,000 units.

Article 32(1)(*b*)(iv)	**1** Additions for the elements specified in Article 32(1)(*b*)(iv) should be based on objective and quantifiable data. In order to minimise the burden for both the declarant and customs authorities in determining the values to be added, data readily available in the buyer's commercial record system should be used in so far as possible. **2** For those elements supplied by the buyer which were purchased or leased by the buyer, the addition would be the cost of the purchase or the lease. No addition shall be made for those elements available in the public domain, other than the cost of obtaining copies of them. **3** The ease with which it may be possible to calculate the values to be added will depend on a particular firm's structure and management practice, as well as its accounting methods. **4** For example, it is possible that a firm which imports a variety of products from several countries maintains the records of its design centre outside the country of importation in such a way as to show accurately the costs attributable to a given product. In such cases, a direct adjustment may appropriately be made under the provisions of Article 32. **5** In another case, a firm may carry the cost of the design centre outside the country of importation as a general overhead expense without allocation to specific products. In this instance, an appropriate adjustment could be made under the provisions of Article 32 with respect to the imported goods by apportioning total design centre costs over total production benefiting from the design centre and adding such apportioned cost on a unit basis to imports. **6** Variations in the above circumstances will, of course, require different factors to be considered in determining the proper method of allocation. **7** In cases where the production of the element in question involves a number of countries and over a period of time, the adjustment should be limited to the value actually added to that element outside the country of importation.
Article 32(1)(*c*)	The royalties and licence fees referred to in Article 32(1)(*c*) may include, among other things, payments in respect of patents, trademarks and copyrights.
Article 32(2)	Where objective and quantifiable data do not exist with regard to the additions required to be made under the provisions of Article 32, the transaction value cannot be determined under the provisions of Article 29. As an illustration of this, a royalty is paid on the basis of the price in a sale in the importing country of a litre of a particular product that was imported by the kilogram and made up into a solution after importation. If the royalty is based partially on the imported goods and partially on other factors which have nothing to do with the imported goods (such as when the imported goods are mixed with domestic ingredients and are no longer separately identifiable, or when the royalty cannot be distinguished from special financial arrangements between the buyer and the seller), it would be inappropriate to attempt to make an addition for the royalty. However, if the amount of this royalty is based only on the imported goods and can be readily quantified, an addition to the price actually paid or payable can be made.

Reference to provisions of the Customs Code Implementing Provisions	*Notes*
Article 143(1)(*e*)	One person shall be deemed to control another when the former is legally or operationally in a position to exercise restraint or direction over the latter.
Article 150(1) Article 151(1)	The expression "and/or" allows the flexibility to use the sales and make the necessary adjustments in any one of the three conditions described in paragraph 1 of the interpretative notes to Articles 30(2)(*a*) and (*b*).
Article 152(1)(*a*)(i)	**1** The words "profit and general expenses" should be taken as a whole. The figure for the purposes of this deduction should be determined on the basis of information supplied by the declarant unless his figures are inconsistent with those obtaining in sales in the country of importation of imported goods of the same class or kind. Where the declarant's figures are inconsistent with such figures, the amount for profit and general expenses may be based upon relevant information other than that supplied by the declarant.

2 In determining either the commissions or the usual profits and general expenses under this provision, the question whether certain goods are of the same class or kind as other goods must be determined on a case-by-case basis by reference to the circumstances involved. Sales in the country of importation of the narrowest group or range of imported goods of the same class or kind, which includes the goods being valued, for which the necessary information can be provided, should be examined. For the purposes of this provision, "goods of the same class or kind" includes goods imported from the same country as the goods being valued as well as goods imported from other countries.

Article 152(2) **1** Where this method of valuation is used, deductions made for the value added by further processing shall be based on objective and quantifiable data relating to the cost of such work. Accepted industry formulas, recipes, methods of construction, and other industry practices would form the basis of the calculations.

2 This method of valuation would normally not be applicable when, as a result of the further processing, the imported goods lose their identity. However, there can be instances where, although the identity of the imported goods is lost, the value added by the processing can be determined accurately without unreasonable difficulty.

On the other hand, there can also be instances where the imported goods maintain their identity but form such a minor element in the goods sold in the country of importation that the use of this valuation method would be unjustified. In view of the above, each situation of this type must be considered on a case-by-case basis.

Article 152(3) **1** As an example of this, goods are sold from a price list which grants favourable unit prices for purchases made in larger quantities.

Sale quantity	Unit price	Number of sales	Total quantity sold at each price
One to 10 units	100	10 sales of five units	65
		Five sales of three units	
11 to 25 units	95	Five sales of 11 units	55
Over 25 units	90	One sale of 30 units	80
		One sale of 50 units	

The greatest number of units sold at a price is 80; therefore, the unit price in the greatest aggregate quantity is 90.

2 As another example of this, two sales occur. In the first sale 500 units are sold at a price of 95 currency units each. In the second sale 400 units are sold at a price of 90 currency units each. In this example, the greatest number of units sold at a particular price is 500; therefore, the unit price in the greatest aggregate quantity is 95.

3 A third example would be the following situation where various quantities are sold at various prices.

(*a*) Sales

Sale quantity	*Unit price*
40 units	100
30 units	90
15 units	100
50 units	95
25 units	105
35 units	90
5 units	100

(*b*) Total

Total quantity sold	*Unit price*
65	90
50	95
60	100
25	105

In this example, the greatest number of units sold at a particular price is 65; therefore, the unit price in the greatest aggregate quantity is 90.

ANNEX 24

APPLICATION OF GENERALLY ACCEPTED ACCOUNTING PRINCIPLES FOR THE DETERMINATION OF CUSTOMS VALUE

1. "Generally accepted accounting principles" refers to the recognised consensus or substantial authoritative support within a country at a particular time as to which economic resources and obligations should be recorded as assets and liabilities, which changes in assets and liabilities should be recorded, how the assets and liabilities and changes in them should be measured, what information should be disclosed and how it should be disclosed, and which financial statements should be prepared. These standards may be broad guidelines of general application as well as detailed practices and procedures.

2. For the purposes of the application of the customs valuation provisions, the customs administration concerned shall utilise information prepared in a manner consistent with generally accepted accounting principles in the country which is appropriate for the Article in question. For example, the determination of usual profit and general expenses under the provisions of Article 152(1)(*a*)(i) of this Regulation would be carried out utilising information prepared in a manner consistent with generally accepted accounting principles of the country of importation. On the other hand, the determination of usual profit and general expenses under the provisions of Article 30(2)(*d*) of the Code would be carried out utilising information prepared in a manner consistent with generally accepted accounting principles of the country of production. As a further example, the determination of an element provided for in Article 32(1)(*b*)(ii) of the Code undertaken in the country of importation would be carried out utilising information in a manner consistent with the generally accepted accounting principles of that country.

[ANNEX 25

AIR TRANSPORT COSTS TO BE INCLUDED IN THE CUSTOMS VALUE

1. The following table shows—

(*a*) third countries listed by continents and zones[1] (column 1).

(*b*) the percentages which represent the part of the air transport costs from a given third country to the EC to be included in the customs value (column 2).

Notes—

[1] The percentages are valid for all airports in a given country unless specific airports of departure are indicated.

2. When goods are shipped from countries or from airports not included in the following table, other than the airports referred to in paragraph 3, the percentage given for the airport nearest to that of departure shall be taken.

3. As regards the French overseas departments of Guadeloupe, Guyana, Martinique and Reunion, of which territories the airports are not included in the table, the following rules shall apply—

(*a*) for goods shipped direct to those departments from third countries, the whole of the air transport cost is to be included in the customs value;

(*b*) for goods shipped to the European part of the Community from third countries and transhipped or unloaded in one of those departments, only the air transport costs which would have been incurred for carrying the goods only as far as the place of transhipment or unloading are to be included in the customs value;

(*c*) for goods shipped to those departments from third countries and transhipped or unloaded in an airport in the European part of the Community, the air transport costs to be included in the customs value are those which result from the application of the percentages given in the following table to the costs which would have been incurred for carrying the goods from the airport of departure to the airport of transhipment or unloading.

The transhipment or unloading shall be certified by an appropriate endorsement by the customs authorities on the air waybill or other air transport document, with the official stamp of the office concerned; failing this certification the provisions of the last subparagraph of Article 163(6) of this Regulation shall apply.

1	2
Zone (country) of departure (third country)	*Percentages of the air transport costs to be included in the customs value for zone of arrival EC*
America	

VAT EC

Zone A **Canada:**	70
Gander, Halifax, Moncton, Montreal, Ottawa, Quebec, Toronto, (other airports see zone B) **Greenland**	
United States of America: Akron, Albany, Atlanta, Baltimore, Boston, Buffalo, Charleston, Chicago, Cincinnati, Columbus, Detroit, Indianapolis, Jacksonville, Kansas City, Lexington, Louisville, Memphis, Milwaukee, Minneapolis, Nashville, New Orleans, New York, Philadelphia, Pittsburgh, St Louis, Washington DC, (other airports see zones B and C)	
Zone B **Canada:** Edmonton, Vancouver, Winnipeg, (other airports see zone A) **United States of America:** Albuquerque, Austin, Billings, Dallas, Denver, Houston, Las Vegas, Los Angeles, Miami, Oklahoma, Phoenix, Portland, Puerto Rico, Salt Lake City, San Francisco, Seattle, (other airports see zones A and C) **Central America** (all countries) **South America** (all countries)	78
Zone C **United States of America:** Anchorage, Fairbanks, Honolulu, Juneau, (other airports see zones A and B)	89
Africa	
Zone D Algeria, Egypt, Libya, Morocco, Tunisia	33
Zone E Benin, Burkina Faso, Cameroon, Cape Verde, Central African Republic, Chad, Côte d'Ivoire, Djibouti, Ethiopia, Gambia, Ghana, Guinea, Guinea-Bissau, Liberia, Mali, Mauritania, Niger, Nigeria, Senegal, Sierra Leone, Sudan, Togo	50
Zone F Burundi, Democratic Republic of Congo, Congo (Brazzaville), Equatorial Guinea, Gabon, Kenya, Rwanda, São Tomé and Principe, Seychelles, Somalia, St. Helena, Tanzania, Uganda	61
Zone G Angola, Botswana, Comoros, Lesotho, Madagascar, Malawi, Mauritius, Mozambique, Namibia, Republic of South Africa, Swaziland, Zambia, Zimbabwe	74
Asia	
Zone H Armenia, Azerbaijan, Georgia, Iran, Iraq, Israel, Jordan, Kuwait, Lebanon, Syria	27
Zone I Bahrain, Muscat and Oman, Qatar, Saudi Arabia, United Arab Emirates, Yemen (Arab Republic)	43

Zone J Afghanistan, Bangladesh, Bhutan, India, Nepal, Pakistan.	46
Zone K Kazakhstan, Kyrgyzstan, Tajikistan, Turkmenistan, Uzbekistan, Russia: Novosibirsk, Omsk, Perm, Sverdlovsk, (other airports see zones L, M, and O)	57
Zone L Brunei, China, Indonesia, Kampuchea, Laos, Macao, Malaysia, Maldives, Mongolia, Myanmar, Philippines, Singapore, Sri Lanka, Taiwan, Thailand, Vietnam Russia: Irkutsk, Kirensk, Krasnoyarsk, (other airports see zones K, M and O)	70
Zone M Japan, Korea (North), Korea (South) Russia: Khabarovsk, Vladivostok, (other airports see zones K, L and O)	83
Australia and Oceania	
Zone N Australia and Oceania	79
Europe	
Zone O Iceland, Russia: Gorky, Kuibishev, Moscow, Orel, Rostov, Volgograd, Voronej, (other airports see zones K, L and M), Ukraine	30
Zone P Albania, Belarus, Bosnia-Herzegovina, . . .[2], Faroe Islands, Former Yugoslav Republic of Macedonia, Moldova, Norway, . . .[2], Serbia and Montenegro, Turkey	15
Zone Q . . .[3] Switzerland][1]	5

Amendments—

[1] Annex 25 replaced by Commission Regulation (EC) 881/2003 Annex III (L 134; 29.05.2003 p 1) with effect from 1 May 2004.

[2] Words repealed by Commission Regulation 1792/2006/EC art 1, Annex Part 11(45) (OJ L 362, 20.12.2006, p 1).

[3] Word "Croatia" repealed from Zone Q by Commission Regulation 519/2013/EU art 1, Annex (OJ L 158, 10.6.2013, p. 74).

ANNEX 28

Note—Form DV1, European Community—Declaration of Particulars Relating to Customs Value, is not reproduced here.

ANNEX 29

Note—Form DV1 BIS, European Community—Continuation Sheet, is not reproduced here.

COUNCIL REGULATION 1798/2003/EC OF 7 OCTOBER 2003 ON ADMINISTRATIVE COOPERATION IN THE FIELD OF VALUE ADDED TAX AND REPEALING REGULATION (EEC) NO 218/92

(1798/2003/EC)

Notes—See OJ L 264; 15.10.2003 p 1.

This Regulation to be repealed by Council Regulation 904/2010/EU with effect from 1 January 2012. However, the effects of Article 2(1) of this Regulation shall be maintained until the date of publication by the Commission of the list of competent authorities referred to in Article 3 of Regulation 904/2010/EU. Chapter V, with the exception of Article 27(4), of this Regulation shall remain applicable until 31 December 2012. References made to the repealed Regulation shall be construed as references to Regulation 904/2010/EU.

Cross references—See Council Directive 2003/93 art 2 (OJ L 264; 15.10.2003 p 23): references made to Directive 77/799/EEC in relation to value added tax shall be construed as references to Council Regulation (EC) 1798/2003 (OJ L 264; 15.10.2003 p 1).

Simon's Tax Cases—*Silversafe Ltd (in liquidation) and another v Hood and others* [2007] STC 871; *EC Commission v EU Council (supported by Ireland, Portuguese Republic and United Kingdom)* [2007] STC 1121.

THE COUNCIL OF THE EUROPEAN UNION,

Having regard to the Treaty establishing the European Community, and in particular Article 93 thereof,

Having regard to the proposal from the Commission,

Having regard to the opinion of the European Parliament,

Having regard to the opinion of the European Economic and Social Committee,

Whereas:

(1) Tax evasion and tax avoidance extending across the frontiers of Member States lead to budget losses and violations of the principle of fair taxation and are liable to bring about distortions of capital movements and of the conditions of competition. They therefore affect the operation of the internal market.

(2) Combating value added tax (VAT) evasion calls for close cooperation between the administrative authorities in each Member State responsible for the application of the provisions in that field.

(3) The tax harmonisation measures taken to complete the internal market should therefore include the establishment of a common system for the exchange of information between the Member States whereby the Member States' administrative authorities are to assist each other and cooperate with the Commission in order to ensure the proper application of VAT on supplies of goods and services, intra-Community acquisition of goods and importation of goods.

(4) Electronic storage and transmission of certain data for VAT control purposes is indispensable for the proper functioning of the VAT system.

(5) The conditions for the exchange of, and direct access of Member States to, electronically stored data in each Member State should be clearly defined. Operators should have access to certain of such data where required for the fulfilment of their obligations.

(6) The Member State of consumption has primary responsibility for assuring that non-established suppliers comply with their obligations. To this end, the application of the temporary special scheme for electronically supplied services that is provided for in Article 26c of Sixth Council Directive 77/388/EEC of 17 May 1977 on the harmonisation of the laws of Member States relating to turnover taxes, Common system of value added tax: uniform basis of assessment, requires the definition of rules concerning the provision of information and transfer of money between the Member State of identification and the Member State of consumption.

(7) Council Regulation (EEC) No 218/92 of 27 January 1992 on administrative cooperation in the field of indirect taxation (VAT) established in this respect a system of close cooperation amongst the Member States' administrative authorities and between those authorities and the Commission.

(8) Regulation (EEC) No 218/92 supplements Council Directive 77/799/EEC of 19 December 1977 concerning mutual assistance by the competent authorities of the Member States in the field of direct and indirect taxation.

(9) Those two legal instruments have proved to be effective but are no longer able to meet the new requirements of administrative cooperation resulting from the ever closer integration of economies within the internal market.

(10) The existence of two separate instruments for cooperation on VAT has, moreover, hampered effective cooperation between tax administrations.

(11) The rights and obligations of all parties concerned are currently ill-defined. Clearer and binding rules governing cooperation between Member States are therefore necessary.

(12) There is not enough direct contact between local or national anti-fraud offices, with communication between central liaison offices being the rule. This leads to inefficiency, under-use of the arrangements for administrative cooperation and delays in communication. Provision should therefore be made to bring about more direct contacts between services with a view to making cooperation more efficient and faster.

(13) Cooperation is also not intensive enough, in that, apart from the VAT information exchange system (VIES), there are not enough automatic or spontaneous exchanges of information between Member States. Exchanges of information between the respective administrations as well as between administrations and the Commission should be made more intensive and swifter in order to combat fraud more effectively.

(14) The provisions on VAT administrative cooperation of Regulation (EEC) No 218/92 and of

Directive 77/799/EEC should therefore be joined and strengthened. For reasons of clarity this should be done in a single new instrument which replaces Regulation (EEC) No 218/92.

(15) This Regulation should not affect other Community measures which contribute to combating VAT fraud.

(16) For the purposes of this Regulation, it is appropriate to consider limitations of certain rights and obligations laid down by Directive 95/46/EC of the European Parliament and of the Council of 24 October 1995 on the protection of individuals with regard to the processing of personal data and on the free movement of such data in order to safeguard the interests referred to in Article 13(1)(*e*) of that Directive.

(17) The measures necessary for the implementation of this Regulation should be adopted in accordance with Council Decision 1999/468/EC of 28 June 1999 laying down the procedures for the exercise of implementing powers conferred on the Commission.

(18) This Regulation respects the fundamental rights and observes the principles which are recognised in particular by the Charter of Fundamental Rights of the European Union,

HAS ADOPTED THIS REGULATION:

CHAPTER I—GENERAL PROVISIONS

Article 1

1. This Regulation lays down the conditions under which the administrative authorities in the Member States responsible for the application of the laws on VAT on supplies of goods and services, intra-Community acquisition of goods and importation of goods are to cooperate with each other and with the Commission to ensure compliance with those laws.

To that end, it lays down rules and procedures to enable the competent authorities of the Member States to cooperate and to exchange with each other any information that may help them to effect a correct assessment of VAT.

This Regulation also lays down rules and procedures for the exchange of certain information by electronic means, in particular as regards VAT on intra-Community transactions.

[This Regulation also lays down rules and procedures for the exchange by electronic means of value added tax information on services in accordance with the special schemes provided for in Chapter 6 of Title XII of Directive 2006/112/EC and also for any subsequent exchange of information and, as far as services covered by those special schemes are concerned, for the transfer of money between Member States' competent authorities.][1]

2. This Regulation shall not affect the application in the Member States of the rules on mutual assistance in criminal matters.

Amendments—[1] In para 1, fourth sub-para substituted by Council Regulation 143/2008/EC of 12 February 2008, art 2(1) with effect from 1 January 2015. That para previously read as follows—

"For the period provided for in Article 357 of Council Directive 2006/112/EC of 28 November 2006 on the common system of value added tax, it also lays down rules and procedures for the exchange by electronic means of value added tax information on services supplied electronically in accordance with the special scheme provided for in Chapter 6 of Title XII of that Directive and also for any subsequent exchange of information and, as far as services covered by that special scheme are concerned, for the transfer of money between Member States' competent authorities.".

Article 2

For the purposes of this Regulation:

1. "competent authority of a Member State", means:

— *in Belgium:*

Le ministre des finances

De Minister van financiën,

[— in Bulgaria:

Изпълнителният директор на Националната ауенция за приходите,][2]

[— *in the Czech Republic:*

Ministerstvo financí,][1]

— *in Denmark:*

Skatteministeren,

— *in Germany:*

Bundesministerium der Finanzen,

[— *in Estonia:*

Maksuamet,][1]

— *in Greece:*

Υπονρειο Οικονομίαζ και Οικονομικων

— *in Spain:*

El Secretario de Estado de Hacienda,

— *in France:*

le ministre de l'économie, des finances et de l'industrie,

VAT EC

— *in Ireland:*
The Revenue Commissioners,
— *in Italy:*
il Capo del Dipartimento delle Politiche Fiscali,
[— *in Cyprus:*
Υπουργός Οικονομικών ή εξουσιοδοτημένος αντιπρόσωπος του,
— *in Latvia:*
Valsts ienemumu dienests,
— *in Lithuania:*
Valstybine mokesciu inspekcija prie Finansu ministerijos,][1]
— *in Luxembourg:*
L'Administration de l'Enregistrement et des Domaines,
[— in Hungary:
Adó- és Pénzügyi Ellenorzési Hivatal Központi Kapcsolattartó Irodája,
— in Malta:
Dipartiment tat-Taxxa fuq il-Valur Mizjud fil-Ministeru tal-Finanzi u Affarijiet Ekonomici,][1]
— *in the Netherlands:*
De minister van Financiën,
— *in Austria:*
Bundesminister für Finanzen,
[— in Poland:
Minister Finansów,][1]
[— in Romania:
Agentia Nationala de Administrare Fiscala,][2]
— *in Portugal:*
O Ministro das Finanças,
[— *in Slovenia:*
Ministrstvo za finance,
— *in Slovakia:*
Ministerstvo financií][1]
— *in Finland:*
Valtiovarainministeriö
Finansministeriet,
— *in Sweden:*
Chefen för Finansdepartementet,
— *in the United Kingdom:*
The Commissioners of Customs and Excise;

2. "central liaison office", means the office which has been designated under Article 3(2) with principal responsibility for contacts with other Member States in the field of administrative cooperation;
3. "liaison department", means any office other than the central liaison office with a specific territorial competence or a specialised operational responsibility which has been designated by the competent authority pursuant to Article 3(3) to exchange directly information on the basis of this Regulation;
4. "competent official", means any official who can directly exchange information on the basis of this Regulation for which he has been authorised pursuant to Article 3(4);
5. "requesting authority", means the central liaison office, a liaison department or any competent official of a Member State who makes a request for assistance on behalf of the competent authority;
6. "requested authority", means the central liaison office, a liaison department or any competent official of a Member State who receives a request for assistance on behalf of the competent authority;
7. "intra-Community transactions", means the intra-Community supply of goods or services;
[8. "intra-Community supply of goods" means any supply of goods which must be declared in the recapitulative statement provided for in Article 262 of Directive 2006/112/EC;
9. "intra-Community supply of services" means any supply of services which must be declared in the re-capitulative statement provided for in Article 262 of Directive 2006/112/EC;
10. "intra-Community acquisition of goods" means the acquisition of the right under Article 20 of Directive 2006/112/EC to dispose as owner of moveable tangible property;
11. "VAT identification number" means the number provided for in Articles 214, 215 and 216 of Directive 2006/112/EC;][3]
12. "administrative enquiry", means all the controls, checks and other action taken by Member States in the performance of their duties with a view to ensuring proper application of VAT legislation;
13. "automatic exchange", means the systematic communication of predefined information to another Member State, without prior request, at pre-established regular intervals;
14. "structured automatic exchange", means the systematic communication of predefined information to another Member State, without prior request, as and when that information becomes available;

15. "spontaneous exchange", means the irregular communication without prior request of information to another Member State;
16. "person", means:
(*a*) a natural person;
(*b*) a legal person; or
(*c*) where the legislation in force so provides, an association of persons recognised as having the capacity to perform legal acts but lacking the legal status of a legal person;
17. "to grant access", means to authorise access to the relevant electronic database and to obtain data by electronic means;
18. "by electronic means", means using electronic equipment for the processing (including digital compression) and storage of data, and employing wires, radio transmission, optical technologies or other electromagnetic means;
19. "CCN/CSI network", means the common platform based on the common communication network (CCN) and common system interface (CSI), developed by the Community to ensure all transmissions by electronic means between competent authorities in the area of customs and taxation.

Note—See OJ L 264; 15.10.2003 p 1.

Amendments—[1] Entries inserted by Council Regulation 885/2004 art 1, Annex Part IV para 2 (OJ L 168; 1.5.2004 p 1).
[2] Entries inserted by Council Regulation 1791/2006/EC art 1, Annex Part 7 (OJ L 363, 20.12.2006, p 1).
[3] Points 8–11 substituted by Council Regulation 143/2008/EC of 12 February 2008, art 1(2) with effect from 1 January 2010. Text previously read as follows—

"8. "intra-Community supply of goods", means any supply of goods which must be declared in the recapitulative statement provided for in Article 22(6)(*b*) of Directive 77/388/EEC;
9. "intra-Community supply of services", means any supply of services covered by Article 28b(C), (D), (E) and (F) of Directive 77/388/EEC;
10. "intra-Community acquisition of goods", means acquisition of the right to dispose as owner of movable tangible property under Article 28a(3) of Directive 77/388/EEC;
11. "VAT identification number", means the number provided for in Article 22(1)(*c*), (*d*) and (*e*) of Directive 77/388/EEC;".

Further amendments—Existing first para renumbered as para 1, and new para 2 to be inserted by Council Regulation 143/2008/EC of 12 February 2008, art 2(2) with effect from 1 January 2015. New para 2 reads "2. The definitions contained in Articles 358, 358a and 369a of Directive 2006/112/EC shall also apply for the purposes of this Regulation.".
It is not clear how it was intended that these amendments should be made to the text of this Article.

Article 3

1. The competent authorities referred to in point 1 of Article 2 are the authorities in whose name this Regulation is to be applied, whether directly or by delegation.
2. Each Member State shall designate a single central liaison office to which principal responsibility shall be delegated for contacts with other Member States in the field of administrative cooperation. It shall inform the Commission and the other Member States thereof.
3. The competent authority of each Member State may designate liaison departments. The central liaison office shall be responsible for keeping the list of those departments up to date and making it available to the central liaison offices of the other Member States concerned.
4. The competent authority of each Member State may in addition designate, under the conditions laid down by it, competent officials who can directly exchange information on the basis of this Regulation. When it does so, it may limit the scope of such designation. The central liaison office shall be responsible for keeping the list of those officials up to date and making it available to the central liaison offices of the other Member States concerned.
5. The officials exchanging information under Articles 11 and 13 shall in any case be deemed to be competent officials for this purpose, in accordance with conditions laid down by the competent authorities.
6. Where a liaison department or a competent official sends or receives a request or a reply to a request for assistance, it shall inform the central liaison office of its Member State under the conditions laid down by the latter.
7. Where a liaison department or a competent official receives a request for assistance requiring action outside its territorial or operational area, it shall forward such request without delay to the central liaison office of its Member State and inform the requesting authority thereof. In such a case, the period laid down in Article 8 shall start the day after the request for assistance has been forwarded to the central liaison office.

Article 4

1. The obligation to give assistance as provided for in this Regulation shall not cover the provision of information or documents obtained by the administrative authorities referred to in Article 1 acting with the authorisation or at the request of the judicial authority.

2. However, where a competent authority has the powers in accordance with national law to communicate the information referred to in paragraph 1, it may be communicated as a part of the administrative cooperation provided for in this Regulation. Any such communication must have the prior authorisation of the judicial authority if the necessity of such authorisation derives from national law.

CHAPTER II—EXCHANGE OF INFORMATION ON REQUEST

SECTION 1—REQUEST FOR INFORMATION AND FOR ADMINISTRATIVE ENQUIRIES

Article 5

1. At the request of the requesting authority, the requested authority shall communicate the information referred to in Article 1, including any information relating to a specific case or cases.
2. For the purpose of forwarding the information referred to in paragraph 1, the requested authority shall arrange for the conduct of any administrative enquiries necessary to obtain such information.
[3. The request referred to in paragraph 1 may contain a reasoned request for a specific administrative enquiry. If the Member State takes the view that no administrative enquiry is necessary, it shall immediately inform the requesting authority of the reasons thereof.
Notwithstanding the first subparagraph and without prejudice to Article 40 of this Regulation, an enquiry into the amounts declared by a taxable person in connection with the supply of telecommunications services, broadcasting services and electronically supplied services which are taxable in the Member State in which the requesting authority is situated and for which the taxable person makes use or opts not to make use of the special scheme provided for in Section 3 of Chapter 6 of Title XII of Directive 2006/112/EC, may only be refused by the requested authority if information on the same taxable person obtained in an administrative enquiry held less than two years previously, has already been supplied to the requesting authority.
However, with respect to the requests referred to in the second subparagraph made by the requesting authority and assessed by the requested authority in conformity with a Statement of Best Practices concerning the interaction of this paragraph and Article 40(1) to be adopted in accordance with the procedure referred to in Article 44(2), a Member State which refuses to hold an administrative enquiry on the basis of Article 40 shall provide to the requesting authority the dates and values of any relevant supplies made over the last two years by the taxable person in the Member State of the requesting authority.][1]
4. In order to obtain the information sought or to conduct the administrative enquiry requested, the requested authority or the administrative authority to which it has recourse shall proceed as though acting on its own account or at the request of another authority in its own Member State.

Amendments—[1] Para 3 substituted by Council Regulation 143/2008/EC of 12 February 2008, art 2(3) with effect from 1 January 2015. Para 3 previously read as follows—

> "3. The request referred to in paragraph 1 may contain a reasoned request for a specific administrative enquiry. If the Member State takes the view that no administrative enquiry is necessary, it shall immediately inform the requesting authority of the reasons thereof.".

Article 6

Requests for information and for administrative enquiries pursuant to Article 5 shall, as far as possible, be sent using a standard form adopted in accordance with the procedure referred to in Article 44(2).

Article 7

1. At the request of the requesting authority, the requested authority shall communicate to it any pertinent information it obtains or has in its possession as well as the results of administrative enquiries, in the form of reports, statements and any other documents, or certified true copies or extracts thereof.
2. Original documents shall be provided only where this is not contrary to the provisions in force in the Member State in which the requested authority is established.

SECTION 2—TIME LIMIT FOR PROVIDING INFORMATION

Article 8

The requested authority shall provide the information referred to in Articles 5 and 7 as quickly as possible and no later than three months following the date of receipt of the request.
However, where the requested authority is already in possession of that information, the time limit shall be reduced to a maximum period of one month.

Article 9

In certain special categories of cases, time limits different from the ones provided for in Article 8 may be agreed between the requested and the requesting authorities.

Article 10

Where the requested authority is unable to respond to the request by the deadline, it shall inform the requesting authority in writing forthwith of the reasons for its failure to do so, and when it considers it would be likely to be able to respond.

SECTION 3—PRESENCE IN ADMINISTRATIVE OFFICES AND PARTICIPATION IN ADMINISTRATIVE ENQUIRIES

Article 11

1. By agreement between the requesting authority and the requested authority and in accordance with the arrangements laid down by the latter, officials authorised by the requesting authority may, with a view to exchanging the information referred to in Article 1, be present in the offices where the administrative authorities of the Member State in which the requested authority is established carry out their duties. Where the requested information is contained in documentation to which the officials of the requested authority have access, the officials of the requesting authority shall be given copies of the documentation containing the requested information.

2. By agreement between the requesting authority and the requested authority, and in accordance with the arrangements laid down by the latter, officials designated by the requesting authority may, with a view to exchanging the information referred to in Article 1, be present during the administrative enquiries. Administrative enquiries shall be carried out exclusively by the officials of the requested authority. The requesting authority's officials shall not exercise the powers of inspection conferred on officials of the requested authority. They may, however, have access to the same premises and documents as the latter, through their intermediary and for the sole purpose of the administrative enquiry being carried out.

3. The officials of the requesting authority present in another Member State in accordance with paragraphs 1 and 2 must at all times be able to produce written authority stating their identity and their official capacity.

SECTION 4—SIMULTANEOUS CONTROLS

Article 12

With a view to exchanging the information referred to in Article 1, two or more Member States may agree to conduct simultaneous controls, in their own territory, of the tax situation of one or more taxable persons who are of common or complementary interest, whenever such controls would appear to be more effective than controls carried out by only one Member State.

Article 13

1. A Member State shall identify independently the taxable persons whom it intends to propose for a simultaneous control. The competent authority of that Member State shall notify the competent authority in the other Member States concerned of the cases proposed for simultaneous controls. It shall give reasons for its choice, as far as possible, by providing the information which led to its decision. It shall specify the period of time during which such controls should be conducted.

2. The Member States concerned shall then decide whether they wish to take part in the simultaneous controls. On receipt of a proposal for a simultaneous control, the competent authority of the Member State shall confirm its agreement or communicate its reasoned refusal to its counterpart authority.

3. Each competent authority of the Member States concerned shall appoint a representative to be responsible for supervising and coordinating the control operation.

CHAPTER III—REQUEST FOR ADMINISTRATIVE NOTIFICATION

Article 14

The requested authority shall, at the request of the requesting authority and in accordance with the rules governing the notification of similar instruments in the Member State in which it is established, notify the addressee of all instruments and decisions which emanate from the administrative authorities and concern the application of VAT legislation in the territory of the Member State in which the requesting authority is established.

Article 15

Requests for notification, mentioning the subject of the instrument or decision to be notified, shall indicate the name, address and any other relevant information for identifying the addressee.

Article 16

The requested authority shall inform the requesting authority immediately of its response to the request for notification and notify it, in particular, of the date of notification of the decision or instrument to the addressee.

CHAPTER IV—EXCHANGE OF INFORMATION WITHOUT PRIOR REQUEST

Article 17

Without prejudice to the provisions of Chapters V and VI, the competent authority of each Member State shall, by automatic or structured automatic exchange, forward the information referred to in Article 1 to the competent authority of any other Member State concerned, in the following cases:

1. Where taxation is deemed to take place in the Member State of destination and the effectiveness of the control system necessarily depends on the information provided by the Member State of origin;
2. Where a Member State has grounds to believe that a breach of VAT legislation has been committed or is likely to have been committed in the other Member State;
3. Where there is a risk of tax loss in the other Member State.

[For the purposes of the first paragraph, each Member State of establishment shall cooperate with each Member State of consumption so as to make it possible to ascertain whether the taxable persons established on its territory declare and pay correctly the VAT due with regard to telecommunications services, broadcasting services and electronically supplied services for which the taxable person makes use or opts not to make use of the special scheme provided for in Section 3 of Chapter 6 of Title XII of Directive 2006/112/EC. The Member State of establishment shall inform the Member State of consumption of any discrepancies of which it becomes aware.][1]

Amendments—[1] Final para inserted, by Council Regulation 143/2008/EC of 12 February 2008, art 2(4) with effect from 1 January 2015.

Article 18

The following shall be determined in accordance with the procedure referred to in Article 44(2):

1. The exact categories of information to be exchanged;
2. The frequency of the exchanges;
3. The practical arrangements for the exchange of information.

[Each Member State shall determine whether it will take part in the exchange of a particular category of information, as well as whether it will do so in an automatic or structured automatic way. However, each Member State shall take part in exchanges of the information available to it with regard to telecommunications services, broadcasting services and electronically supplied services for which the taxable person makes use or opts not to make use of the special scheme provided for in Section 3 of Chapter 6 of Title XII of Directive 2006/112/EC.][1]

Amendments—[1] Second para substituted by Council Regulation 143/2008/EC of 12 February 2008, art 2(5) with effect from 1 January 2015. That para previously read as follows—

> "Each Member State shall determine whether it will take part in the exchange of a particular category of information, as well as whether it will do so in an automatic or structured automatic way.".

Article 19

The competent authorities of the Member States may, in any case by spontaneous exchange, forward to each other, any information referred to in Article 1 of which they are aware.

Article 20

Member States shall take the necessary administrative and organisational measures to facilitate the exchanges provided for in this Chapter.

Article 21

A Member State cannot be obliged, for the purposes of implementing the provisions of this Chapter, to impose new obligations on persons liable for VAT with a view to collecting information nor to bear disproportionate administrative burdens.

CHAPTER V—STORAGE AND EXCHANGE OF INFORMATION SPECIFIC TO INTRA-COMMUNITY TRANSACTIONS

Article 22

[1. Each Member State shall maintain an electronic database in which it stores and processes the information which it collects pursuant to Chapter 6 of Title XI of Directive 2006/112/EC.][1]

To enable that information to be used in the procedures provided for in this Regulation, the information shall be stored for at least five years from the end of the calendar year in which access to the information is to be granted.

2. Member States shall ensure that their databases are kept up to date, and are complete and accurate. Criteria shall be defined, in accordance with the procedure referred to in Article 44(2), to determine which changes are not pertinent, essential or useful and therefore need not be made.

Note—This Regulation to be repealed by Council Regulation 904/2010/EU with effect from 1 January 2012. However, Chapter V, with the exception of Article 27(4), shall remain applicable until 31 December 2012. References made to the repealed Regulation shall be construed as references to Regulation 904/2010/EU

Amendments—[1] Para substituted by Council Regulation 143/2008/EC of 12 February 2008, art 1(3) with effect from 1 January 2010. Text previously read as follows—

> "1. Each Member State shall maintain an electronic database in which it shall store and process the information that it collects in accordance with Article 22(6)(*b*) in the version given in Article 28h of Directive 77/388/EEC.".

Article 23

On the basis of the data stored in accordance with Article 22, the competent authority of a Member State shall have communicated to it automatically and without delay by any other Member State the following information, to which it may also have direct access:

1. VAT identification numbers issued by the Member State receiving the information;

[2. the total value of all intra-Community supplies of goods and the total value of all intra-Community supplies of services to persons holding a VAT identification number by all operators identified for the purposes of VAT in the Member State providing the information.][1]

[The values referred to in point 2 of the first paragraph shall be expressed in the currency of the Member State providing the information and shall relate to the periods for submission of the recapitulative statements specific to each taxable person which are established in accordance with Article 263 of Directive 2006/112/EC.][2]

Amendments—[1] In point 2, first sub-para substituted by Council Regulation 143/2008/EC of 12 February 2008, art 1(4) with effect from 1 January 2010. Text previously read as follows—

> "2. the total value of all intra-Community supplies of goods to persons holding a VAT identification number by all operators identified for the purposes of VAT in the Member State providing the information.".

[2] Second para substituted by Council Regulation (EC) No 37/2009 of 16 December 2008, art 1(1) with effect from 1 January 2010. Text previously read as follows—

> "The values referred to in point 2 shall be expressed in the currency of the Member State providing the information and shall relate to calendar quarters.".

Article 24

[On the basis of the data stored in accordance with Article 22 and solely in order to prevent a breach of VAT legislation, the competent authority of a Member State shall, wherever it considers it necessary for the control of intra-Community acquisitions of goods or intra-Community supplies of services taxable in its territory, obtain directly and without delay, or have direct access to by electronic means, any of the following information:

1. the VAT identification numbers of the persons who carried out the supplies of goods and services referred to in point 2 of the first paragraph of Article 23;

2. the total value of supplies of goods and services from each such person to each person holding a VAT identification number referred to in point 1 of the first paragraph of Article 23.][1]

[The values referred to in point 2 of the first paragraph shall be expressed in the currency of the Member State providing the information and shall relate to the periods for submission of the recapitulative statements specific to each taxable person which are established in accordance with Article 263 of Directive 2006/112/EC.][2]

Amendments—[1] First para substituted by Council Regulation 143/2008/EC of 12 February 2008, art 1(5) with effect from 1 January 2010. Text previously read as follows—

> "On the basis of the data stored in accordance with Article 22 and solely in order to prevent a breach of VAT legislation, the competent authority of a Member State shall, wherever it considers it necessary for the control of intra-Community acquisitions of goods, obtain directly and without delay, or have direct access to by electronic means, any of the following information:
>
> 1. The VAT identification numbers of the persons who effected the supplies referred to in point 2 of Article 23; and
> 2. The total value of such supplies from each such person to each person holding a VAT identification number referred to in point 1 of Article 23.".

[2] Second para substituted by Council Regulation (EC) No 37/2009 of 16 December 2008, art 1(2) with effect from 1 January 2010. Text previously read as follows—

> "The values referred to in point 2 shall be expressed in the currency of the Member State providing the information and shall relate to calendar quarters.".

Article 25

[1. Where the competent authority of a Member State is obliged to grant access to information under Articles 23 and 24, it shall do so as soon as possible and, at the latest, within one month of the end of the period to which the information relates.

2. By way of derogation from paragraph 1, where information is added to a database in the circumstances provided for in Article 22, access to such additional information shall be granted as quickly as possible and no later than one month after the end of the period in which it was collected.][1]

3. The conditions under which access to the corrected information may be granted shall be laid down in accordance with the procedure referred to in Article 44(2).

Amendments—[1] Paras 1, 2 substituted by Council Regulation (EC) No 37/2009 of 16 December 2008, art 1(3) with effect from 1 January 2010. Text previously read as follows—

> "1. Where the competent authority of a Member State is obliged to grant access to information under Articles 23 and

VAT EC

24, it shall do so as soon as possible and within three months at the latest of the end of the calendar quarter to which the information relates.

2. By way of derogation from paragraph 1, where information is added to a database in the circumstances provided for in Article 22, access to such additional information shall be granted as quickly as possible and no later than three months from the end of the quarter in which it was collected.".

Article 26

Where, for the purposes of Articles 22 to 25, the competent authorities of the Member States store information in electronic databases and exchange such information by electronic means, they shall take all measures necessary to ensure compliance with Article 41.

Article 27

1. Each Member State shall maintain an electronic database containing a register of persons to whom VAT identification numbers have been issued in that Member State.

2. At any time the competent authority of a Member State may obtain directly or have communicated to it, from the data stored in accordance with Article 22, confirmation of the validity of the VAT identification number under which a person has effected or received an intra-Community supply of goods or services.

On specific request, the requested authority shall also communicate the date of issue and, where appropriate, the expiry date of the VAT identification number.

3. On request, the competent authority shall also provide without delay the name and address of the person to whom the number has been issued, provided that such information is not stored by the requesting authority with a view to possible use at some future time.

[4. The competent authorities of each Member State shall ensure that persons involved in the intra-Community supply of goods or of services and non-established taxable persons supplying telecommunication services, broadcasting services and electronically supplied services, in particular those referred to in Annex II of Directive 2006/112/EC, are allowed to obtain confirmation of the validity of the VAT identification number of any specified person.

The Member States shall provide such confirmation by electronic means in accordance with the procedure referred to in Article 44(2) of this Regulation.][1]

5. Where, for the purposes of paragraphs 1 to 4, the competent authorities of the Member States store information in electronic databases and exchange such information by electronic means, they shall take all measures necessary to ensure compliance with Article 41.

Amendments—[1] Para 4 substituted by Council Regulation 143/2008/EC of 12 February 2008, art 2(6) with effect from 1 January 2015. Para 4 previously read as follows—

"4. The competent authorities of each Member State shall ensure that persons involved in the intra-Community supply of goods or of services and, for the period provided for in Article 357 of Directive 2006/112/EC, non-established taxable persons supplying electronically supplied services, in particular those referred to in Annex II of that Directive, are allowed to obtain confirmation of the validity of the VAT identification number of any specified person.

During the period provided for in Article 357 of Directive 2006/112/EC, the Member States shall provide such confirmation by electronic means in accordance with the procedure referred to in Article 44(2) of this Regulation.".

CHAPTER VI—[PROVISIONS CONCERNING THE SPECIAL SCHEMES IN CHAPTER 6 OF TITLE XII OF DIRECTIVE 2006/112/EC]

Amendments—Heading substituted by Council Regulation 143/2008/EC of 12 February 2008, art 2(7) with effect from 1 January 2015. Text previously read "Provisions concerning the special scheme in Chapter 6 of Title XII of Directive 2006/112/EC".

[Article 28

The following provisions shall apply concerning the special schemes provided for in Chapter 6 of Title XII of Directive 2006/112/EC.][1]

Amendments—[1] Article 28 substituted by Council Regulation 143/2008/EC of 12 February 2008, art 2(8) with effect from 1 January 2015. Text previously read as follows—

"The following provisions shall apply concerning the special scheme provided for in Chapter 6 of Title XII of Directive 2006/112/EC. The definitions contained in Article 358 of that Directive shall also apply for the purpose of this Chapter.".

[Article 29

1. The information provided by the taxable person not established in the Community to the Member State of identification when his activities commence pursuant to Article 361 of Directive 2006/112/EC shall be submitted in an electronic manner. The technical details, including a common electronic message, shall be determined in accordance with the procedure provided for in Article 44(2) of this Regulation.

2. The Member State of identification shall transmit the information referred to in paragraph 1 by electronic means to the competent authorities of the other Member States within 10 days from the end of the month during which the information was received from the taxable person not established within the Community. Similar details for the identification of the taxable person applying the special scheme under Article 369b of Directive 2006/112/EC shall be transmitted within 10 days from the

end of the month during which the taxable person stated that his taxable activities under that scheme commenced. In the same manner the competent authorities of the other Member States shall be informed of the allocated identification number. The technical details, including a common electronic message, by which this information is to be transmitted, shall be determined in accordance with the procedure provided for in Article 44(2) of this Regulation.

3. The Member State of identification shall without delay inform by electronic means the competent authorities of the other Member States if a taxable person not established in the Community or a taxable person not established in the Member State of consumption is excluded from the special scheme.][1]

Amendments—[1] Article 29 substituted by Council Regulation 143/2008/EC of 12 February 2008, art 2(9) with effect from 1 January 2015. Article 29 previously read as follows—

"Article 29

1. The information provided by the taxable person not established in the Community to the Member State of identification when his activities commence pursuant to Article 361 of Directive 2006/112/EC shall be submitted in an electronic manner. The technical details, including a common electronic message, shall be determined in accordance with the procedure provided for in Article 44(2) of this Regulation.

2. The Member State of identification shall transmit this information by electronic means to the competent authorities of the other Member States within 10 days from the end of the month during which the information was received from the non-established taxable person. In the same manner the competent authorities of the other Member States shall be informed of the allocated identification number. The technical details, including a common electronic message, by which this information is to be transmitted, shall be determined in accordance with the procedure provided for in Article 44(2).

3. The Member State of identification shall without delay inform by electronic means the competent authorities of the other Members States if a non-established taxable person is excluded from the identification register.".

Article 30

[The return with the details set out in Articles 365 and 369g of Directive 2006/112/EC is to be submitted in an electronic manner. The technical details, including a common electronic message, shall be determined in accordance with the procedure provided for in Article 44(2) of this Regulation. The Member State of identification shall transmit this information by electronic means to the competent authority of the Member State of consumption concerned at the latest 10 days after the end of the month in which the return was received. The information provided for in the second paragraph of Article 369g of Directive 2006/112/EC shall also be transmitted to the competent authority of the Member State of establishment concerned. Member States which have required the tax return to be made in a national currency other that euro, shall convert the amounts into euro using the exchange rate valid for the last date of the reporting period. The exchange shall be done following the exchange rates published by the European Central Bank for that day, or, if there is no publication on that day, on the next day of publication. The technical details by which this information is to be transmitted shall be determined in accordance with the procedure provided for in Article 44(2) of this Regulation.][1]

The Member State of identification shall transmit by electronic means to the Member State of consumption the information needed to link each payment with a relevant quarterly tax return.

Amendments—[1] First and second paras substituted by Council Regulation 143/2008/EC of 12 February 2008, art 2(10) with effect from 1 January 2015. Those paras previously read as follows—

"The return with the details set out in Article 365 of Directive 2006/112/EC is to be submitted in an electronic manner. The technical details, including a common electronic message, shall be determined in accordance with the procedure provided for in Article 44(2) of this Regulation.

The Member State of identification shall transmit this information by electronic means to the competent authority of the Member State concerned at the latest 10 days after the end of the month that the return was received. Member States which have required the tax return to be made in a national currency other than euro, shall convert the amounts into euro using the exchange rate valid for the last date of the reporting period. The exchange shall be done following the exchange rates published by the European Central Bank for that day, or, if there is no publication on that day, on the next day of publication. The technical details by which this information is to be transmitted shall be determined in accordance with the procedure provided for in Article 44(2).".

[Article 31

The provisions in Article 22 of this Regulation shall apply also to information collected by the Member State of identification in accordance with Articles 360, 361, 364, 365, 369c, 369f and 369g of Directive 2006/112/EC.][1]

Amendments—[1] Article 31 substituted by Council Regulation 143/2008/EC of 12 February 2008, art 2(11) with effect from 1 January 2015. Article 31 previously read as follows—

"The provisions in Article 22 of this Regulation shall apply also to information collected by the Member State of identification in accordance with Articles 360, 361, 364 and 365 of Directive 2006/112/EC.".

Article 32

The Member State of identification shall ensure that the amount the non-established taxable person has paid is transferred to the bank account denominated in euro, which has been designated by the Member State of consumption to which the payment is due. Member States which required the payments in a national currency other than euro, shall convert the amounts into euro using the exchange rate valid for the last date of the reporting period. The exchange shall be done following the exchange rates published by the European Central Bank for that day, or, if there is no publication on that day, on the next day of publication. The transfer shall take place at the latest 10 days after the end of the month that the payment was received.

If the non-established taxable person does not pay the total tax due, the Member State of identification shall ensure that the payment is transferred to the Member States of consumption in proportion to the tax due in each Member State. The Member State of identification shall inform by electronic means the competent authorities of the Member States of consumption thereof.

[Concerning the payments to be transferred to the Member State of consumption in accordance with the special scheme provided for in Section 3 of Chapter 6 of Title XII of Directive 2006/112/EC, the Member State of identification shall, of the amounts referred to in the first and second paragraphs, be entitled to retain:

(a) from 1 January 2015 until 31 December 2016 — 30 %,
(b) from 1 January 2017 until 31 December 2018 — 15 %,
(c) from 1 January 2019 — 0 %.][1]

Amendments—[1] Para to be inserted at end by Council Regulation 143/2008/EC of 12 February 2008, art 2(12) with effect from 1 January 2015.

Article 33

Member States shall notify by electronic means the competent authorities of the other Member States of the relevant bank account numbers for receiving payments according to Article 32.

Member States shall without delay notify by electronic means the competent authorities of the other Member States and the Commission of changes in the standard tax rate.

Article 34

Articles 28 to 33 of this Regulation shall apply for the period provided for in Article 357 of Directive 2006/112/EC.[1]

Amendments—[1] Article 34 repealed by Council Regulation 143/2008/EC of 12 February 2008, art 2(13) with effect from 1 January 2015.

CHAPTER VIA—PROVISIONS CONCERNING THE EXCHANGE AND CONSERVATION OF INFORMATION IN THE CONTEXT OF THE PROCEDURE PROVIDED FOR IN DIRECTIVE 2008/9/EC

Article 34a

1. Where the competent authority of the Member State of establishment receives an application for refund of value added tax under Article 5 of Directive 2008/9/EC of 12 February 2008 laying down detailed rules for the refund of value added tax, provided for in Directive 2006/112/EC, to taxable persons not established in the Member State of refund but established in another Member State* and Article 18 of that Directive is not applicable, it shall, within 15 calendar days of its receipt and by electronic means, forward the application to the competent authorities of each Member State of refund concerned with confirmation that the applicant as defined in Article 2(5) of Directive 2008/9/EC is a taxable person for the purposes of value added tax and that the identification or registration number given by this person is valid for the refund period.

2. The competent authorities of each Member State of refund shall notify by electronic means the competent authorities of the other Member States of any information required by them under Article 9(2) of Directive 2008/9/EC. The technical details, including a common electronic message by which this information is to be transmitted, shall be determined in accordance with the procedure provided for in Article 44(2) of this Regulation.

3. The competent authorities of each Member State of refund shall notify by electronic means the competent authorities of the other Member States if they want to make use of the option to require the applicant to provide the description of business activity by harmonised codes as referred to in Article 11 of Directive 2008/9/EC.

The harmonised codes referred to in the first subparagraph shall be determined in accordance with the procedure provided for in Article 44(2) of this Regulation on the basis of the NACE classification established by Regulation (EEC) No 3037/90.]

Note—* OJ L 44, 20.2.2008 p 23.

Amendments—Chapter VIa inserted by Council Regulation 143/2008/EC of 12 February 2008, art 1(13) with effect from 1 January 2010.

CHAPTER VII—RELATIONS WITH THE COMMISSION

Article 35

1. The Member States and the Commission shall examine and evaluate how the arrangements for administrative cooperation provided for in this Regulation are working. The Commission shall pool the Member States' experience with the aim of improving the operation of those arrangements.
2. The Member States shall communicate to the Commission any available information relevant to their application of this Regulation.
3. A list of statistical data needed for evaluation of this Regulation shall be determined in accordance with the procedure referred to in Article 44(2). The Member States shall communicate these data to the Commission in so far as they are available and the communication is not likely to involve administrative burdens which would be unjustified.
4. With a view to evaluating the effectiveness of this system of administrative cooperation in combating tax evasion and tax avoidance, Member States may communicate to the Commission any other information referred to in Article 1.
5. The Commission shall forward the information referred to in paragraphs 2, 3 and 4 to the other Member States concerned.

CHAPTER VIII—RELATIONS WITH THIRD COUNTRIES

Article 36

1. When the competent authority of a Member State receives information from a third country, that authority may pass the information on to the competent authorities of Member States which might be interested in it and, in any event, to all those which request it, in so far as permitted by assistance arrangements with that particular third country.
2. Provided the third country concerned has given an undertaking to provide the assistance required to gather evidence of the irregular nature of transactions which appear to contravene VAT legislation, information obtained under this Regulation may be communicated to that third country, with the consent of the competent authorities which supplied the information, in accordance with their domestic provisions applying to the communication of personal data to third countries.

CHAPTER IX—CONDITIONS GOVERNING THE EXCHANGE OF INFORMATION

Article 37

Information communicated pursuant to this Regulation shall, as far as possible, be provided by electronic means under arrangements to be adopted in accordance with the procedure referred to in Article 44(2).

Article 38

Requests for assistance, including requests for notification, and attached documents may be made in any language agreed between the requested and requesting authority. The said requests shall only be accompanied by a translation into the official language or one of the official languages of the Member State in which the requested authority is established, in special cases when the requested authority gives a reason for asking for such a translation.

Article 39

[The Commission and the Member States shall ensure that such existing or new communication and information exchange systems which are necessary to provide for the exchanges of information described in Articles 29 and 30 are operational. The Commission will be responsible for whatever development of the common communication network/common system interface (CCN/CSI) is necessary to permit the exchange of this information between Member States. Member States will be responsible for whatever development of their systems is necessary to permit this information to be exchanged using the CCN/CSI.][1]

Member States shall waive all claims for the reimbursement of expenses incurred in applying this Regulation except, where appropriate, in respect of fees paid to experts.

Amendments—[1] First para substituted by Council Regulation 143/2008/EC of 12 February 2008, art 2(14) with effect from 1 January 2015. Text previously read as follows—

> "For the period provided for in Article 357 of Directive 2006/112/EC, the Commission and the Member States shall ensure that such existing or new communication and information exchange systems which are necessary to provide for the exchanges of information described in Articles 29 and 30 of this Regulation are operational. The Commission will be responsible for whatever development of the common communication network/common system interface (CCN/CSI) is necessary to permit the exchange of this information between Member States. Member States will be responsible for whatever development of their systems is necessary to permit this information to be exchanged using the CCN/CSI.".

Article 40

1. The requested authority in one Member State shall provide a requesting authority in another Member State with the information referred to in Article 1 provided that:

(*a*) the number and the nature of the requests for information made by the requesting authority within a specific period do not impose a disproportionate administrative burden on that requested authority;

(*b*) that requesting authority has exhausted the usual sources of information which it could have used in the circumstances to obtain the information requested, without running the risk of jeopardising the achievement of the desired end.

2. This Regulation shall impose no obligation to have enquiries carried out or to provide information if the laws or administrative practices of the Member State which would have to supply the information do not authorise the Member State to carry out those enquiries or collect or use that information for that Member State's own purposes.

3. The competent authority of a Member State may refuse to provide information where the Member State concerned is unable, for legal reasons, to provide similar information. The Commission shall be informed of the grounds of the refusal by the requested Member State.

4. The provision of information may be refused where it would lead to the disclosure of a commercial, industrial or professional secret or of a commercial process, or of information whose disclosure would be contrary to public policy.

5. The requested authority shall inform the requesting authority of the grounds for refusing a request for assistance.

6. A minimum threshold triggering a request for assistance may be adopted in accordance with the procedure referred to in Article 44(2).

Article 41

1. Information communicated in any form pursuant to this Regulation shall be covered by the obligation of official secrecy and enjoy the protection extended to similar information under both the national law of the Member State which received it and the corresponding provisions applicable to Community authorities.

Such information may be used for the purpose of establishing the assessment base or the collection or administrative control of tax for the purpose of establishing the assessment base.

The information may also be used for the assessment of other levies, duties, and taxes covered by Article 2 of Council Directive 76/308/EEC of 15 March 1976 on mutual assistance for the recovery of claims relating to certain levies, duties, taxes and other measures.

In addition, it may be used in connection with judicial proceedings that may involve penalties, initiated as a result of infringements of tax law without prejudice to the general rules and legal provisions governing the rights of defendants and witnesses in such proceedings.

2. Persons duly accredited by the Security Accreditation Authority of the European Commission may have access to this information only in so far as it is necessary for care, maintenance and development of the CCN/CSI network.

3. By way of derogation from paragraph 1, the competent authority of the Member State providing the information shall permit its use for other purposes in the Member State of the requesting authority, if, under the legislation of the Member State of the requested authority, the information can be used for similar purposes.

4. Where the requesting authority considers that information it has received from the requested authority is likely to be useful to the competent authority of a third Member State, it may transmit it to the latter authority. It shall inform the requested authority thereof in advance. The requested authority may require that the transmission of the information to a third party be subject to its prior agreement.

5. Member States shall, for the purpose of the correct application of this Regulation, restrict the scope of the obligations and rights provided for in Article 10, Article 11(1), Articles 12 and 21 of Directive 95/46/EC to the extent required in order to safeguard the interests referred to in Article 13(e) of that Directive.

Article 42

Reports, statements and any other documents, or certified true copies or extracts thereof, obtained by the staff of the requested authority and communicated to the requesting authority under the assistance provided for by this Regulation may be invoked as evidence by the competent bodies of the Member State of the requesting authority on the same basis as similar documents provided by another authority of that country.

Article 43

1. For the purpose of applying this Regulation, Member States shall take all necessary measures to:

(*a*) ensure effective internal coordination between the competent authorities referred to in Article 3;

(*b*) establish direct cooperation between the authorities authorised for the purposes of such coordination;

(*c*) ensure the smooth operation of the information exchange arrangements provided for in this Regulation.

2. The Commission shall communicate to each Member State, as quickly as possible, any information which it receives and which it is able to provide.

CHAPTER X—GENERAL AND FINAL PROVISIONS

Article 44

1. The Commission shall be assisted by the Standing Committee on Administrative Cooperation, (hereinafter referred to as the Committee).

2. Where reference is made to this paragraph, Articles 5 and 7 of Decision 1999/468/EC shall apply, having regard to the provisions of Article 8 thereof.

The period laid down in Article 5(6) of Decision 1999/468/EC shall be set at three months.

3. The Committee shall adopt its rules of procedure.

Article 45

1. Every three years from the date of entry into force of this Regulation, the Commission shall report to the European Parliament and the Council on the application of this Regulation.

2. Member States shall communicate to the Commission the text of any provisions of national law, which they adopt in the field covered by this Regulation.

Article 46

1. The provisions of this Regulation shall be without prejudice to the fulfilment of any wider obligations in relation to mutual assistance ensuing from other legal acts, including bilateral or multilateral agreements.

2. Where the Member States conclude bilateral arrangements on matters covered by this Regulation other than to deal with individual cases, they shall inform the Commission without delay. The Commission shall in turn inform the other Member States.

Article 47

Regulation (EEC) No 218/92 is hereby repealed.

References made to the repealed Regulation shall be construed as references to this Regulation.

Article 48

This Regulation shall enter into force on 1 January 2004.

This Regulation shall be binding in its entirety and directly applicable in all Member States.

REGULATION 638/2004/EC OF THE EUROPEAN PARLIAMENT AND OF THE COUNCIL OF 31 MARCH 2004 ON COMMUNITY STATISTICS RELATING TO THE TRADING OF GOODS BETWEEN MEMBER STATES AND REPEALING COUNCIL REGULATION (EEC) NO 3330/91

(638/2004/EC)

THE EUROPEAN PARLIAMENT AND THE COUNCIL OF THE EUROPEAN UNION,

Having regard to the Treaty establishing the European Community, and in particular Article 285(1) thereof,

Having regard to the proposal from the Commission,

Having regard to the opinion of the European Economic and Social Committee,

Acting in accordance with the procedure laid down in Article 251 of the Treaty,

Whereas:

(1) Council Regulation (EEC) No 3330/91 of 7 November 1991 on the statistics relating to the trading of goods between Member States(3) introduced a completely new system of data collection, which has been simplified on two occasions. In order to improve the transparency of this system and to make it easier to understand, Regulation (EEC) No 3330/91 should be replaced by this Regulation.

(2) This system should be retained, as a sufficiently detailed level of statistical information is still required for the Community policies involved in the development of the internal market and for Community enterprises to analyse their specific markets. Aggregated data also need to be available quickly in order to analyse the development of the Economic and Monetary Union. Member States should have the possibility of collecting information which meets their specific needs.

(3) There is, however, a need to improve the wording of the rules on compiling statistics relating to the trading of goods between Member States so that they can be more easily understood by the companies responsible for providing the data, the national services collecting the data and users.

(4) A system of thresholds should be retained, but in a simplified form, in order to provide a satisfactory response to users' needs whilst reducing the burden of response on the parties responsible for providing statistical information, particularly small and medium-sized enterprises.

(5) A close link should be maintained between the system for collecting statistical information and

the fiscal formalities which exist in the context of trade of goods between Member States. This link makes it possible, in particular, to check the quality of the information collected.

(6) The quality of the statistical information produced, its evaluation by means of common indicators and transparency in this field are important objectives, which call for regulation at Community level.

(7) Since the objective of the planned action, namely the creation of a common legal framework for the systematic production of Community statistics relating to the trading of goods between Member States, cannot be sufficiently achieved at national level and can be better achieved at Community level, the Community may adopt measures, in accordance with the principle of subsidiarity as set out in Article 5 of the Treaty. In accordance with the principle of proportionality, as set out in that Article, this Regulation does not go beyond what is required to achieve this objective.

(8) Council Regulation (EC) No 322/97 of 17 February 1997 on Community statistics provides a reference framework for this Regulation. However, the very detailed level of information in the field of statistics relating to the trading of goods requires specific rules with regard to confidentiality.

(9) It is important to ensure the uniform application of this Regulation and, in order to do so, to make provision for a Community procedure to help determine the implementing arrangements within an appropriate timescale and to make the necessary technical adaptations.

(10) The measures necessary for implementation of this Regulation should be adopted in accordance with Council Decision 1999/468/EC of 28 June 1999 laying down the procedures for the exercise of implementing powers conferred on the Commission,

HAVE ADOPTED THIS REGULATION:

Article 1 Subject matter

This Regulation establishes a common framework for the systematic production of Community statistics relating to the trading of goods between Member States.

Article 2 Definitions

For the purpose of this Regulation, the following definitions shall apply:

(*a*) "goods": all movable property, including electric current;

(*b*) "specific goods or movements": goods or movements which, by their very nature, call for specific provisions, and in particular industrial plants, vessels and aircraft, sea products, goods delivered to vessels and aircraft, staggered consignments, military goods, goods to or from offshore installations, spacecraft, motor vehicle and aircraft parts and waste products;

(*c*) "national authorities": national statistical institutes and other bodies responsible in each Member State for producing Community statistics relating to the trading of goods between Member States;

(*d*) "Community goods":

(i) goods entirely obtained in the customs territory of the Community, without addition of goods from third countries or territories which are not part of the customs territory of the Community;

(ii) goods from third countries or territories which are not part of the customs territory of the Community, which have been released for free circulation in a Member State;

(iii) goods obtained in the customs territory of the Community either from the goods referred to exclusively in point (ii) or from the goods referred to in points (i) and (ii);

(*e*) "Member State of dispatch": the Member State as defined by its statistical territory from which goods are dispatched to a destination in another Member State;

(*f*) "Member State of arrival": the Member State as defined by its statistical territory in which goods arrive from another Member State;

(*g*) "goods in simple circulation between Member States": Community goods dispatched from one Member State to another, which, on the way to the Member State of destination, travel directly through another Member State or stop for reasons related only to the transport of the goods.

Article 3 Scope

1. Statistics relating to the trading of goods between Member States shall cover dispatches and arrivals of goods.

2. Dispatches shall cover the following goods leaving the Member State of dispatch for a destination in another Member State:

(*a*) Community goods, except goods which are in simple circulation between Member States;

(*b*) goods placed in the Member State of dispatch under the inward processing customs procedure or the processing under customs control procedure.

3. Arrivals shall cover the following goods entering the Member State of arrival, which were initially dispatched from another Member State:

(*a*) Community goods, except goods which are in simple circulation between Member States;

(*b*) goods formerly placed in the Member State of dispatch according to the inward processing customs procedure or the processing according to customs control procedure, which are maintained according to the inward processing customs procedure or the processing according to customs control procedure or released for free circulation in the Member State of arrival.

[4. The Commission shall be empowered to adopt delegated acts in accordance with Article 13a relating to different or specific rules applying to specific goods or movements.';][1]

5. Some goods, a list of which shall be drawn up in accordance with the procedure referred to in Article 14(2), shall be excluded from the statistics for methodological reasons.

Amendments—[1] Para 4 substituted by Regulation 659/2014/EU Art 1(1) with effect from 17 July 2014 (OJ L 189, 27.6.2014, p 128).

Article 4 Statistical territory

1. The statistical territory of the Member States shall correspond to their customs territory as defined in Article 3 of Council Regulation (EEC) No 2913/92 of 12 October 1992 establishing the Community Customs Code.

2. By way of derogation from paragraph 1, the statistical territory of Germany shall include Heligoland.

Article 5 Data sources

1. A specific data collection system, hereinafter referred to as the "Intrastat" system, shall apply for the provision of the statistical information on dispatches and arrivals of . . .[1] goods which are not the subject of a single administrative document for customs or fiscal purposes.

[2. The statistical information on dispatches and arrivals of goods which are the subject of a single administrative document for customs or fiscal purposes shall be provided directly by customs to the national authorities, at least once a month.][1]

[2a. The customs administration responsible in each Member State shall, on its own initiative or at the request of the national authority, provide the national authority with any available information to identify the person who carries out dispatches and arrivals of goods covered by the customs procedures of inward processing or processing under customs control.][1]

3. For specific goods or movements, sources of information other than the Intrastat system or customs declarations may be used.

4. Each Member State shall organise the way Intrastat data is supplied by the parties responsible for providing information. To facilitate the task of these parties, the conditions for increased use of automatic data processing and electronic data transmission shall be promoted by the Commission (Eurostat) and the Member States.

Amendments—[1] In para 1, word "Community" repealed, para 2 substituted, and para 2a inserted, by Regulation 659/2014/EU Art 1(2) with effect from 17 July 2014 (OJ L 189, 27.6.2014, p 128).

[Article 6 Reference period

The reference period for the information to be provided in accordance with Article 5 shall be:

(a) the calendar month of dispatch or arrival of the goods;

(b) the calendar month during which the chargeable event occurs for the Community goods on which VAT becomes chargeable on intra-Community acquisitions and supplies; or

(c) the calendar month during which the declaration is accepted by customs where the customs declaration is used as data sources.][1]

Amendments—[1] Article 6 substituted by Regulation 659/2014/EU Art 1(3) with effect from 17 July 2014 (OJ L 189, 27.6.2014, p 128).

Article 7 Parties responsible for providing information

[1. The parties responsible for providing the information for the Intrastat system shall be:

(*a*) the taxable person as defined in Title III of Council Directive 2006/112/EC of 28 November 2006 on the common system of value added tax, in the Member State of dispatch, who:

(i) has concluded the contract, with the exception of transport contracts, giving rise to the dispatch of goods or, failing that;

(ii) dispatches or provides for the dispatch of the goods or, failing that;

(iii) is in possession of the goods which are the subject of the dispatch;

or its tax representative in accordance with Article 204 of Directive 2006/112/EC; and

(*b*) the taxable person as defined in Title III of Directive 2006/112/EC, in the Member State of arrival, who:

(i) has concluded the contract, with the exception of transport contracts, giving rise to the delivery of goods or, failing that;

(ii) takes delivery or provides for delivery of the goods or, failing that;

(iii) is in possession of the goods which are the subject of the delivery;

or its tax representative in accordance with Article 204 of Directive 2006/112/EC.][1]

2. The parties responsible for providing information may transfer the task to a third party, but such transfer shall in no way reduce the responsibility of the said party.

3. Failure by any party responsible for providing information to fulfil his/her obligations under this Regulation shall render him/her liable to the penalties which the Member States shall lay down.

Amendments—[1] Para 1 substituted by Parliament and Council Regulation 222/2009 of 11 March 2009 art 1(3) with effect from 1 January 2010. Text previously read as follows—

"1. The parties responsible for providing the information for the Intrastat system shall be:

(*a*) the natural or legal person registered for VAT in the Member State of dispatch who:

(i) has concluded the contract, with the exception of transport contracts, giving rise to the dispatch of goods or, failing that,

(ii) dispatches or provides for the dispatch of the goods or, failing that,

(iii) is in possession of the goods which are the subject of the dispatch;

(*b*) the natural or legal person registered for VAT in the Member State of arrival who:

(i) has concluded the contract, with the exception of transport contracts, giving rise to the delivery of goods or, failing that,

(ii) takes delivery or provides for delivery of the goods or, failing that,

(iii) is in possession of the goods which are the subject of the delivery.".

Article 8 Registers

1. National authorities shall set up and manage a register of intra-Community operators containing at least the consignors, upon dispatch, and the consignees, upon arrival.

2. In order to identify the parties responsible for providing information referred to in Article 7 and to check the information which is provided, the tax administration responsible in each Member State shall furnish the national authority:

[(*a*) at least once a month, with the lists of taxable persons who have declared that, during the period in question, they have supplied goods to other Member States or acquired goods from other Member States. The lists shall show the total values of the goods declared by each taxable person for fiscal purposes;][1]

(*b*) on its own initiative or at the request of the national authority, with any information provided for fiscal purposes which could improve the quality of statistics.

The arrangements for the communication of the information shall be determined in accordance with the procedure referred to in Article 14(2).

This information shall be treated by the national authority in accordance with the rules applied to it by the tax administration.

3. The tax administration shall bring to the attention of VAT-registered traders the obligations which they may incur as parties responsible for providing the information required by Intrastat.

Amendments—[1] Para 2(*a*) substituted by Parliament and Council Regulation 222/2009 of 11 March 2009 art 1(3) with effect from 1 January 2010. Text previously read as follows—

"(*a*) at least once a month, with the lists of natural or legal persons who have declared that, during the period in question, they have supplied goods to other Member States or acquired goods from other Member States. The lists shall show the total values of the goods declared by each natural or legal person for fiscal purposes;".

Article 9 Intrastat information to be collected

1. The following information shall be collected by the national authorities:

[(*a*) the individual identification number allocated to the party responsible for providing information in accordance with Article 214 of Directive 2006/112/EC;][1]

(*b*) the reference period;

(*c*) the flow (arrival, dispatch);

(*d*) the commodity, identified by the eight-digit code of the Combined Nomenclature as defined in Council Regulation (EEC) No 2658/87 of 23 July 1987 on the tariff and statistical nomenclature and on the Common Customs Tariff;

(*e*) the partner Member State;

(*f*) the value of the goods;

(*g*) the quantity of the goods;

(*h*) the nature of the transaction.

[Definitions of the statistical data referred to in points (e) to (h) are laid down in the Annex. The Commission shall adopt, by means of implementing acts, the arrangements to collect that information, in particular the codes and the format to be employed.

Those implementing acts shall be adopted in accordance with the examination procedure referred to in Article 14(2).][2]

2. Member States may also collect additional information, for example:

(*a*) the identification of the goods, at a more detailed level than the Combined Nomenclature;

(*b*) the country of origin, on arrival;

(*c*) the region of origin, on dispatch, and the region of destination, on arrival;

(*d*) the delivery terms;

(*e*) the mode of transport;

(*f*) the statistical procedure.

[Definitions of the statistical data referred to in points (*e*) to (*h*) are given in the Annex. Where necessary, the Commission shall determine the arrangements for the collection of that information, particularly the codes to be employed. Those measures, designed to amend non-essential elements of this Regulation, inter alia, by supplementing it, shall be adopted in accordance with the regulatory procedure with scrutiny referred to in Article 14(3).][1]

Amendments—[1] Para 1(*a*), and final para, substituted by Parliament and Council Regulation 222/2009 of 11 March 2009 art 1(3) with effect from 1 January 2010. Text previously read as follows—

"(*a*) the identification number allocated to the party responsible for providing information in accordance with Article 22(1)(*c*) of the Sixth Council Directive 77/388/EEC of 17 May 1977 on the harmonisation of the laws of the Member States relating to turnover taxes-common system of value added tax: uniform basis of assessment, in the version given in Article 28h thereof;".

"Definitions of the statistical data referred to in points (*b*) to (*f*) are given in the Annex. Where necessary, the arrangements for the collection of this information, particularly the codes to be employed, shall be determined in accordance with the procedure referred to in Article 14(2).".

[2] In para (1), paras substituted by Regulation 659/2014/EU Art 1(4) with effect from 17 July 2014 (OJ L 189, 27.6.2014, p 128).

[Article 9a Exchange of confidential data

The exchange of confidential data, as defined in Article 3(7) of Regulation (EC) No 223/2009 of the European Parliament and of the Council*, may take place for statistical purposes only, between the national authorities responsible in each Member State, where the exchange serves the efficient development, production and dissemination of European statistics relating to the trading of goods between Member States or improves their quality.

National authorities that have obtained confidential data shall treat that information confidentially and shall use it exclusively for statistical purposes in accordance with Chapter V of Regulation (EC) No 223/2009.

* Regulation (EC) No 223/2009 of the European Parliament and of the Council of 11 March 2009 on European statistics and repealing Regulation (EC, Euratom) No 1101/2008 of the European Parliament and of the Council on the transmission of data subject to statistical confidentiality to the Statistical Office of the European Communities, Council Regulation (EC) No 322/97 on Community Statistics, and Council Decision 89/382/EEC, Euratom establishing a Committee on the Statistical Programmes of the European Communities (OJ L 87, 31.3.2009, p. 164).

Amendments—[1] Article 9a inserted by Regulation 659/2014/EU Art 1 (5) with effect from 17 July 2014 (OJ L 189, 27.6.2014, p 128).

Article 10 Simplification within the Intrastat system

1. In order to satisfy users' needs for statistical information without imposing excessive burdens on economic operators, Member States shall define each year thresholds expressed in annual values of intra-Community trade, below which parties are exempted from providing any Intrastat information or may provide simplified information.

2. The thresholds shall be defined by each Member State, separately for arrivals and dispatches.

[3. The thresholds below which parties are exempted from providing any Intrastat information shall be set at a level that ensures that the value of at least 97 % of the total dispatches and at least [93%][2] of the total arrivals of the relevant Member State's taxable persons is covered.

[The Commission shall be empowered to adopt delegated acts in accordance with Article 13a to adapt those Intrastat coverage rates to technical and economic developments whenever it is possible to reduce them, while maintaining statistics which meet the quality indicators and standards in force.][3]][1]

4. Member States may define other thresholds below which parties may benefit from the following simplification:

(*a*) exemption from providing information about the quantity of the goods;

(*b*) exemption from providing information about the nature of the transaction;

(*c*) possibility of reporting a maximum of 10 of the detailed relevant subheadings of the Combined Nomenclature, that are the most used in terms of value, and regrouping the other products in accordance with rules determined in accordance with the procedure referred to in Article 14(2).

[The Commission shall be empowered to adopt delegated acts in accordance with Article 13a to specify the conditions for defining those thresholds.][3]

[5. Member States may, under certain conditions that meet quality requirements, simplify the information to be provided for small individual transactions provided that such simplification has no detrimental effects on the quality of the statistics. The Commission shall be empowered to adopt delegated acts in accordance with Article 13a to specify those conditions.][3]

6. The information on the thresholds applied by the Member States shall be sent to the Commission (Eurostat) no later than 31 October of the year preceding the year to which they apply.

Amendments—[1] Para 3 substituted by Parliament and Council Regulation 222/2009 of 11 March 2009 art 1(6) with effect from 1 January 2010.

[2] In para 3, "93%" substituted for "95%" by Commission Regulation 1093/2013/EU art 1 with effect from 26 November 2013 (OJ L 294, 6.11.2013, p 28).

[3] In paras 3, 4, paras substituted, and para 5 substituted, by Regulation 659/2014/EU Art 1 (6) with effect from 17 July 2014 (OJ L 189, 27.6.2014, p 128).

[Article 11 Statistical confidentiality

Only where the party or parties that have provided information so request shall the national authorities decide whether statistical results which may make it possible to identify the said provider(s) are to be disseminated or are to be amended in such a way that their dissemination does not prejudice statistical confidentiality.][1]

Amendments—[1] Article 11 substituted by Parliament and Council Regulation 222/2009 of 11 March 2009 art 1(7) with effect from 1 January 2010. Text previously read as follows—

> **"Article 11**
>
> **Statistical confidentiality**
>
> Where the parties who have provided information so request, the national authorities shall decide whether statistical results which make it possible indirectly to identify the said provider(s) are to be disseminated or are to be amended in such a way that their dissemination does not prejudice statistical confidentiality.".

Article 12 Transmission of data to the Commission

1. Member States shall transmit to the Commission (Eurostat) the monthly results of their statistics relating to the trading of goods between Member States no later than:

[(*a*) 40 calendar days after the end of the reference month for the aggregated data to be defined by the Commission. The Commission shall be empowered to adopt delegated acts in accordance with Article 13a to define those aggregated data. Those delegated acts shall take into account the relevant economic and technical developments.][2]

(*b*) 70 calendar days after the end of the reference month in the case of detailed results including the information referred to in Article 9(1), first subparagraph, points (*b*) to (*h*).

As regards the value of the goods, the results shall include the statistical value only, as defined in the Annex.

Member States shall transmit to the Commission (Eurostat) the data which are confidential.

[2. Member States shall provide the Commission (Eurostat) with monthly results which cover their total trade in goods by using estimates, where necessary. The Commission shall by means of implementing acts, determine the breakdown for such estimates. Those implementing acts shall be adopted in accordance with the examination procedure referred to in Article 14(2).][2]

3. Member States shall transmit the data to the Commission (Eurostat) in electronic form, in accordance with an interchange standard. The practical arrangements for the transmission of data shall be determined in accordance with the procedure referred to in Article 14(2).

[4. Member States shall transmit to the Commission (Eurostat) annual statistics on trade by business characteristics, namely economic activity carried out by the enterprise according to the section or two-digit level of the common statistical classification of economic activities in the European Community (NACE), as established by Regulation (EC) No 1893/2006 of the European Parliament and of the Council, and size-class measured in terms of number of employees.

Those statistics shall be compiled by linking data on business characteristics recorded according to Regulation (EC) No 177/2008 of the European Parliament and of the Council of 20 February 2008 establishing a common framework for business registers for statistical purposes with the statistics referred to in Article 3 of this Regulation.

[The Commission shall adopt, by means of implementing acts, technical provisions for compiling those statistics in the most economical way.

Those implementing acts shall be adopted in accordance with the examination procedure referred to in Article 14(2).][2]][1]

Amendments—[1] Para 4 inserted by Parliament and Council Regulation 222/2009 of 11 March 2009 art 1(8) with effect from 1 January 2010.

[2] In para 1, point (a) substituted, para 2 substituted, and in para 4, paras substituted, by regulation 659/2014/EU Art 1 (7) with effect from 17 July 2014 (OJ L 189, 27.6.2014, p 128).

[Article 13 Quality

1. For the purposes of this Regulation, the following quality criteria shall apply to the statistics to be transmitted:

(*a*) "relevance", which refers to the degree to which statistics meet current and potential needs of the users;

(*b*) "accuracy", which refers to the closeness of estimates to the unknown true values;

(*c*) "timeliness", which refers to the period between the availability of the information and the event or phenomenon it describes;

(*d*) "punctuality", which refers to the delay between the date of release of the data and the target date (the date by which the data should have been delivered);

(*e*) "accessibility" and "clarity", which refer to the conditions and modalities by which users can obtain, use and interpret data;

(*f*) "comparability", which refers to the measurement of the impact of differences in applied statistical concepts, measurement tools and procedures where statistics are compared between geographical areas, sectoral domains or over time;
(*g*) "coherence", which refers to the adequacy of the data to be reliably combined in different ways and for various uses.

2. Member States shall provide the Commission (Eurostat) with an annual report on the quality of the statistics transmitted.

3. In applying the quality criteria laid down in paragraph 1 to the statistics covered by this Regulation, the modalities and structure of the quality reports shall be defined in accordance with the regulatory procedure referred to in Article 14(2).

The Commission (Eurostat) shall assess the quality of the statistics transmitted.

[4. The Commission shall adopt, by means of implementing acts, any measures necessary to ensure the quality of the statistics transmitted in accordance with the quality criteria, avoiding excessive costs for the national authorities.

Those implementing acts shall be adopted in accordance with the examination procedure referred to in Article 14(2).][2]][1]

Amendments—[1] Article 13 substituted by Parliament and Council Regulation 222/2009 of 11 March 2009 art 1(9) with effect from 1 January 2010.

[2] Para 4 substituted by regulation 659/2014/EU Art 1 (8) with effect from 17 July 2014 (OJ L 189, 27.6.2014, p 128).

[Article 13a Exercise of the delegation

1. The power to adopt delegated acts is conferred on the Commission subject to the conditions laid down in this Article.

2. When exercising the power delegated in Article 3(4), Article 10(3), (4) and (5) and point (a) of Article 12(1) of this Regulation, the Commission shall act in accordance with Article 14(3) of Regulation (EC) No 223/2009, ensuring, inter alia, that the delegated acts do not impose a significant additional burden on the Member States and on the respondents.

It is of particular importance that the Commission follow its usual practice and carry out consultations with experts, including Member States' experts, before adopting those delegated acts.

3. The power to adopt delegated acts referred to in Article 3(4), Article 10(3), (4) and (5) and point (a) of Article 12(1) shall be conferred on the Commission for a period of five years from 17 July 2014. The Commission shall draw up a report in respect of the delegation of power not later than nine months before the end of the fiveyear period. The delegation of power shall be tacitly extended for periods of an identical duration, unless the European Parliament or the Council opposes such extension not later than three months before the end of each period.

4. The delegation of power referred to in Article 3(4), Article 10(3), (4) and (5) and point (a) of Article 12(1) may be revoked at any time by the European Parliament or by the Council. A decision to revoke shall put an end to the delegation of the power specified in that decision. It shall take effect the day following the publication of the decision in the Official Journal of the European Union or at a later date specified therein. It shall not affect the validity of any delegated acts already in force.

5. As soon as it adopts a delegated act, the Commission shall notify it simultaneously to the European Parliament and to the Council

6. A delegated act adopted pursuant to Article 3(4), Article 10(3), (4) and (5) and point (a) of Article 12(1) shall enter into force only if no objection has been expressed either by the European Parliament or the Council within a period of three months of notification of that act to the European Parliament and the Council or if, before the expiry of that period, the European Parliament and the Council have both informed the Commission that they will not object. That period shall be extended by three months at the initiative of the European Parliament or the Council.][1]

Amendments—[1] Article 13a inserted by regulation 659/2014/EU Art 1 (9) with effect from 17 July 2014 (OJ L 189, 27.6.2014, p 128).

[Article 14 Committee procedure

1. The Commission shall be assisted by the European Statistical System Committee established by Regulation (EC) No 223/2009. That committee shall be a committee within the meaning of Regulation (EU) No 182/2011 of the European Parliament and of the Council*.

2. Where reference is made to this paragraph, Article 5 of Regulation (EU) No 182/2011 shall apply.][1]

* Regulation (EU) No 182/2011 of the European Parliament and of the Council of 16 February 2011 laying down the rules and general principles concerning mechanisms for control by Member States of the Commission's exercise of implementing powers (OJ L 55, 28.2.2011, p. 13).

Amendments—[1] Article 14 substituted by regulation 659/2014/EU Art 1 (10) with effect from 17 July 2014 (OJ L 189, 27.6.2014, p 128).

Article 15 Repeal

1. Regulation (EEC) No 3330/91 is hereby repealed.

2. References to the repealed regulation shall be construed as being made to this Regulation.

VAT EC

Article 16 Entry into force

This Regulation shall enter into force on the 20th day following that of its publication in the Official Journal of the European Union.

It shall apply from 1 January 2005.

This Regulation shall be binding in its entirety and directly applicable in all Member States.

ANNEX

DEFINITIONS OF STATISTICAL DATA

1. PARTNER MEMBER STATE

(*a*) The partner Member State is the Member State of consignment, on arrival. This means the presumed Member State of dispatch in cases where goods enter directly from another Member State. Where, before reaching the Member State of arrival, goods have entered one or more Member States in transit and have been subject in those States to halts or legal operations not inherent in their transport (eg change of ownership), the Member State of consignment shall be taken as the last Member State where such halts or operations occurred.

(*b*) The partner Member State is the Member State of destination, on dispatch. This means the last Member State to which it is known, at the time of dispatch, that the goods are to be dispatched.

2. QUANTITY OF THE GOODS

The quantity of the goods can be expressed in two ways:

(*a*) the net mass, which means the actual mass of the goods excluding all packaging;

(*b*) the supplementary units, which mean the possible units measuring quantity other than net mass, as detailed in the annual Commission regulation updating the Combined Nomenclature.

3. VALUE OF THE GOODS

The value of the goods can be expressed in two ways:

[(*a*) the taxable amount, which is the value to be determined for taxation purposes in accordance with Directive 2006/112/EC;][1]

[(*b*) the statistical value, which is the value calculated at the national borders of the Member States. It shall be based on the taxable amount or, where applicable, the value replacing it. It includes only incidental expenses (freight, insurance) incurred, in the case of dispatches, in the part of the journey located on the territory of the Member State of dispatch and, in the case of arrivals, in the part of the journey located outside the territory of the Member State of arrival. It is said to be a fobvalue (free on board) for dispatches, and a cifvalue (cost, insurance, freight) for arrivals.][2]

Amendments—[1] Para (*a*) substituted by Parliament and Council Regulation 222/2009 of 11 March 2009 art 1(11) with effect from 1 January 2010. Text previously read as follows—

"(*a*) the taxable amount, which is the value to be determined for taxation purposes in accordance with Directive 77/388/EEC;".

[2] Para (*b*) substituted by regulation 659/2014/EU Art 1 (11) with effect from 17 July 2014 (OJ L 189, 27.6.2014, p 128).

4. NATURE OF THE TRANSACTION

The nature of transaction means the different characteristics (purchase/sale, work under contract, etc.) which are deemed to be useful in distinguishing one transaction from another.

5. COUNTRY OF ORIGIN

(*a*) The country of origin, on arrivals only, means the country where the goods originate.

(*b*) Goods which are wholly obtained or produced in a country originate in that country.

(*c*) Goods whose production involved more than one country shall be deemed to originate in the country where they underwent their last, substantial, economically justified processing or working in a company equipped for that purpose, resulting in the manufacture of a new product or representing an important stage of manufacture.

6. REGION OF ORIGIN OR DESTINATION

(*a*) The region of origin, on dispatch, means the region of the Member State of dispatch where the goods were produced or were erected, assembled, processed, repaired or maintained; failing that, the region of origin is the region where the goods were dispatched, or, failing that, the region where the commercial process took place.

(*b*) The region of destination, on arrival, means the region of the Member State of arrival where the goods are to be consumed or erected, assembled, processed, repaired or maintained; failing that, the region of destination is the region to which the goods are to be dispatched, or, failing that, the region where the commercial process is to take place.

7. DELIVERY TERMS

The delivery terms mean those provisions of the sales contract which lay down the obligations of the seller and the buyer respectively, in accordance with the Incoterms of the International Chamber of Commerce (cif, fob, etc.).

8. MODE OF TRANSPORT

The mode of transport is determined by the active means of transport by which the goods are presumed to be going to leave the statistical territory of the Member State of dispatch, on dispatch, and by the active means of transport by which the goods are presumed to have entered the statistical territory of the Member State of arrival, on arrival.

9. STATISTICAL PROCEDURE

The statistical procedure means the different characteristics which are deemed to be useful in distinguishing different types of arrivals/dispatches for statistical purposes.

REGULATION 450/2008/EC OF THE EUROPEAN PARLIAMENT AND OF THE COUNCIL OF 23 APRIL 2008 LAYING DOWN THE COMMUNITY CUSTOMS CODE (MODERNISED CUSTOMS CODE)

(450/2008/EC)

Note—See OJ L 145, 04.06.2008 p 1.

The Modernised Customs Code was "recast", before it became applicable, as the Union Customs Code (Regulation 2013/952/EU)which was adopted on which was adopted on 9 October 2013.

Contents

ANNEX

CORRELATION TABLES

1.

REGULATION (EEC) NO 2913/92

Regulation (EEC) No 2913/92	*This Regulation*
Article 1	Article 4
Article 2	Article 1
Article 3	Article 3
Article 4	Article 4
Article 4, points (4a) to (4d)	–
Article 5	Articles 11 and 12
Article 5a	Articles 13, 14 and 15
Article 6	Article 16
Article 7	Article 16
Article 8	Article 18
Article 9	Article 19
Article 10	Article 16
Article 11	Articles 8 and 30
Article 12	Article 20
Article 13	Articles 25 and 26
Article 14	Article 9
Article 15	Article 6
Article 16	Article 29
Article 17	Article 32
Article 18	Article 31
Article 19	Articles 116 and 183
Article 20	Articles 33 and 34
Article 21	Article 33
Article 22	Article 35
Article 23	Article 36
Article 24	Article 36
Article 25	–
Article 26	Article 37

VAT EC

Article 27	Article 39
Article 28	Article 40
Article 29	Article 41
Article 30	Article 42
Article 31	Article 42
Article 32	Article 43
Article 33	Article 43
Article 34	Article 43
Article 35	Article 31
Article 36	Article 41
Article 36a	Article 87
Article 36b	Articles 5, 88 and 89
Article 36c	Article 90
Article 37	Article 91
Article 38	Articles 92 and 93
Article 39	Article 94
Article 40	Article 95
Article 41	Article 95
Article 42	Article 91
Article 43	–
Article 44	–
Article 45	–
Article 46	Article 96
Article 47	Article 96
Article 48	Article 97
Article 49	–
Article 50	Articles 98 and 151
Article 51	Articles 151 and 152
Article 52	Article 152
Article 53	Article 151
Article 54	Article 99
Article 55	Article 100
Article 56	Article 125
Article 57	Article 126
Article 58	Articles 91 and 97
Article 59	Article 104
Article 60	Article 105
Article 61	Article 107
Article 62	Article 108
Article 63	Article 112
Article 64	Article 111
Article 65	Article 113
Article 66	Article 114
Article 67	Article 112
Article 68	Article 117
Article 69	Article 118
Article 70	Article 119
Article 71	Article 120
Article 72	Article 121
Article 73	Article 123
Article 74	Article 124
Article 75	Article 126

Article 76	Articles 108, 109, 110 and 112
Article 77	Articles 107 and 108
Article 78	Article 27
Article 79	Article 129
Article 80	–
Article 81	Article 115
Article 82	Article 166
Article 83	Article 102
Article 84	Article 135
Article 85	Article 136
Article 86	Article 136
Article 87	Article 136
Article 87a	–
Article 88	Article 136
Article 89	Article 138
Article 90	Article 139
Article 91	Articles 140 and 144
Article 92	Article 146
Article 93	Article 147
Article 94	Articles 62, 63, 136 and 146
Article 95	Articles 136 and 146
Article 96	Article 146
Article 97	Article 143
Article 98	Articles 143, 148 and 153
Article 99	Article 153
Article 100	Article 136
Article 101	Article 149
Article 102	Article 149
Article 103	–
Article 104	Article 136
Article 105	Article 137
Article 106	Articles 137 and 154
Article 107	Article 137
Article 108	Article 150
Article 109	Articles 141 and 143
Article 110	Article 153
Article 111	Article 140
Article 112	Article 53
Article 113	–
Article 114	Articles 142 and 168
Article 115	Articles 142 and 143
Article 116	Article 136
Article 117	Article 136
Article 118	Article 169
Article 119	Article 167
Article 120	Article 143
Article 121	Articles 52 and 53
Article 122	Articles 52 and 53
Article 123	Article 170
Article 124	–
Article 125	–
Article 126	–

Article 127	–
Article 128	–
Article 129	–
Article 130	Article 168
Article 131	Article 143
Article 132	Article 136
Article 133	Article 136
Article 134	–
Article 135	Article 53
Article 136	Article 53
Article 137	Article 162
Article 138	Article 136
Article 139	Article 162
Article 140	Article 163
Article 141	Article 164
Article 142	Articles 143 and 164
Article 143	Articles 47 and 165
Article 144	Articles 47, 52 and 53
Article 145	Articles 48 and 171
Article 146	Articles 143 and 171
Article 147	Article 136
Article 148	Article 136
Article 149	Article 171
Article 150	Article 171
Article 151	Article 171
Article 152	Article 172
Article 153	Article 171
Article 154	Articles 173 and 174
Article 155	Article 173
Article 156	Article 173
Article 157	Article 174
Article 158	–
Article 159	–
Article 160	–
Article 161	Articles 176, 177 and 178
Article 162	Article 177
Article 163	Article 145
Article 164	Articles 103 and 145
Article 165	Article 143
Article 166	Article 148
Article 167	Articles 155 and 156
Article 168	Article 155
Article 168a	–
Article 169	Articles 157 and 158
Article 170	Articles 157 and 158
Article 171	Article 150
Article 172	Article 156
Article 173	Articles 141 and 159
Article 174	–
Article 175	Article 159
Article 176	Article 137
Article 177	Article 160

Article 178	Article 53
Article 179	–
Article 180	Article 161
Article 181	Article 160
Article 182	Articles 127, 168 and 179
Article 182a	Article 175
Article 182b	Article 176
Article 182c	Articles 176, 179 and 180
Article 182d	Articles 5, 180 and 181
Article 183	Article 177
Article 184	–
Article 185	Articles 130 and 131
Article 186	Article 130
Article 187	Article 132
Article 188	Article 133
Article 189	Article 56
Article 190	Article 58
Article 191	Article 56
Article 192	Articles 57 and 58
Article 193	Article 59
Article 194	Article 59
Article 195	Article 61
Article 196	Article 60
Article 197	Article 59
Article 198	Article 64
Article 199	Article 65
Article 200	-
Article 201	Article 44
Article 202	Article 46
Article 203	Article 46
Article 204	Articles 46 and 86
Article 205	Article 46
Article 206	Articles 46 and 86
Article 207	Article 86
Article 208	Article 47
Article 209	Article 48
Article 210	Article 49
Article 211	Article 49
Article 212	Article 50
Article 212a	Article 53
Article 213	Article 51
Article 214	Articles 52 and 78
Article 215	Articles 55 and 66
Article 216	Article 45
Article 217	Articles 66 and 69
Article 218	Article 70
Article 219	Article 70
Article 220	Articles 70 and 82
Article 221	Articles 67 and 68
Article 222	Article 72
Article 223	Article 73
Article 224	Article 74

Article 225	Article 74
Article 226	Article 74
Article 227	Article 75
Article 228	Article 76
Article 229	Article 77
Article 230	Article 73
Article 231	Article 73
Article 232	Article 78
Article 233	Article 86
Article 234	Article 86
Article 235	Article 4
Article 236	Articles 79, 80, and 84
Article 237	Articles 79 and 84
Article 238	Articles 79, 81 and 84
Article 239	Articles 79, 83, 84, and 85
Article 240	Article 79
Article 241	Article 79
Article 242	Article 79
Article 243	Article 23
Article 244	Article 21
Article 245	Article 23
Article 246	Article 22
Article 247	Article 183
Article 247a	Article 184
Article 248	Article 183
Article 248a	Article 184
Article 249	Article 185
Article 250	Articles 17, 120 and 121
Article 251	Article 186
Article 252	Article 186
Article 253	Article 187

2.

REGULATIONS (EEC) NO 3925/91 AND (EC) NO 1207/2001

Repealed Regulation	*This Regulation*
Regulation (EEC) No 3925/91	Article 28
Regulation (EC) No 1207/2001	Article 39

COUNCIL REGULATION 904/2010/EU OF 7 OCTOBER 2010 ON ADMINISTRATIVE COOPERATION AND COMBATING FRAUD IN THE FIELD OF VALUE ADDED TAX (RECAST)

THE COUNCIL OF THE EUROPEAN UNION,

Having regard to the Treaty on the Functioning of the European Union, and in particular Article 113 thereof,

Having regard to the proposal from the European Commission,

Having regard to the opinion of the European Parliament[1],

Having regard to the opinion of the European Economic and Social Committee[2],

Acting in accordance with a special legislative procedure,

Whereas:

(1) Council Regulation (EC) No 1798/2003 of 7 October 2003 on administrative cooperation in the field of value added tax[3] has been substantially amended several times. Since further amendments are to be made, it should be recast in the interests of clarity.

(2) The instruments to combat fraud in the field of value added tax (hereinafter 'VAT') in Regulation (EC) No 1798/2003 should be improved and supplemented subsequent to the Council Conclusions of 7 October 2008; the Communication from the Commission to the Council, the European Parliament and the European Economic and Social Committee on a coordinated strategy to improve the fight against VAT fraud in the European Union; and the Report from the Commission to the Council and the European Parliament on the application of Council Regulation (EC) No 1798/2003 concerning administrative cooperation in the field of VAT (hereinafter the 'Commission's report'). Editorial and practical clarifications of the provisions of Regulation (EC) No 1798/2003 are also required.

(3) Tax evasion and tax avoidance extending across the frontiers of Member States lead to budget losses and violations of the principle of fair taxation. They are also liable to bring about distortions of capital movements and of the conditions of competition. They thus affect the operation of the internal market.

(4) Combating VAT evasion calls for close cooperation between the competent authorities in each Member State responsible for the application of the provisions in that field.

(5) The tax harmonisation measures taken to complete the internal market should include the establishment of a common system for cooperation between the Member States, in particular as concerns exchange of information, whereby the Member States' competent authorities are to assist each other and to cooperate with the Commission in order to ensure the proper application of VAT on supplies of goods and services, intra-Community acquisition of goods and importation of goods.

(6) Administrative cooperation should not lead to an undue shift of administrative burdens between Member States.

(7) For the purposes of collecting the tax owed, Member States should cooperate to help ensure that VAT is correctly assessed. They must therefore not only monitor the correct application of tax owed in their own territory, but should also provide assistance to other Member States for ensuring the correct application of tax relating to activity carried out on their own territory but owed in another Member State.

(8) Monitoring the correct application of VAT on cross-border transactions taxable in a Member State other than that where the supplier is established depends in many cases on information which is held by the Member State of establishment or which can be much more easily obtained by that Member State. Effective supervision of such transactions is therefore dependent on the Member State of establishment collecting, or being in a position to collect, that information.

(9) In order to establish the one-stop shop scheme provided for by Council Directive 2006/112/EC of 28 November 2006 on the common system of value added tax[4], and to apply the refund procedure for taxable persons not established in the Member State of refund provided for in Council Directive 2008/9/EC of 12 February 2008 laying down detailed rules for the refund of value added tax, provided for in Directive 2006/112/EC, to taxable persons not established in the Member State of refund but established in another Member State[5], rules on the exchange and storage of information by Member States are required.

(10) In cross-border situations, it is important to specify the obligations of each Member State so that the tax can be effectively monitored in the Member State in which it is owed.

(11) Electronic storage and transmission of certain data for VAT control purposes are indispensable for the proper functioning of the VAT system. They allow for rapid information exchange and automated access to information, which strengthen the fight against fraud. That can be achieved by enhancing the databases on VAT-taxable persons and their intra-Community transactions through the inclusion in those databases of a range of information on the taxable persons and their transactions.

(12) The Member States should implement proper verification procedures to ensure that the information is up-to-date, comparable and of good quality, thereby increasing its reliability. The conditions for the exchange of, and the automated access of Member States to, electronically stored data should be clearly defined.

(13) In order to fight fraud effectively, it is necessary to provide for information exchange without prior request. To facilitate the exchange of information, the categories for which an automatic exchange needs to be established should be specified.

(14) As indicated in the Commission's report, feedback is an appropriate means to ensure continual improvement of the quality of the information exchanged. A framework for the provision of feedback should therefore be put in place.

(15) For the effective monitoring of VAT on cross-border transactions, it is necessary to

provide for the possibility of simultaneous controls by Member States and of the presence of officials of one Member State in the territory of another Member State, within the framework of administrative cooperation.

(16) Online confirmation of the validity of VAT identification numbers is a tool which is increasingly used by operators. The system for confirming the validity of VAT identification numbers should provide automated confirmation of the relevant information to operators.

(17) Some taxable persons are subject to specific obligations which are different from those in force in the Member State in which they are established, particularly as regards invoicing, when they supply goods or services to customers established on the territory of another Member State. A mechanism should be established to make information on such obligations readily available for those taxable persons.

(18) Recent practical experience of the application of Regulation (EC) No 1798/2003 in the fight against carrousel fraud has shown that in some cases it is essential to establish a much faster mechanism for the exchange of information, covering much more, and better targeted, information in order to combat fraud effectively. In accordance with the Council Conclusions of 7 October 2008, a decentralised network without legal personality, to be called Eurofisc, should be established within the framework of this Regulation for all the Member States, to promote and facilitate multilateral and decentralised cooperation permitting targeted and swift action to combat specific types of fraud.

(19) The Member State of consumption has primary responsibility for assuring that non-established suppliers comply with their obligations. To this end, the application of the temporary special scheme for electronically supplied services that is provided for in Chapter 6 of Title XII of Directive 2006/112/EC requires the definition of rules concerning the provision of information and transfer of money between the Member State of identification and the Member State of consumption.

(20) Information obtained by a Member State from third countries may be very useful to other Member States. Likewise information obtained by a Member State from other Member States may be very useful to third countries. The conditions for the exchange of such information should therefore be specified.

(21) National rules on banking secrecy should not stand in the way of the application of this Regulation.

(22) This Regulation should not affect other measures adopted at Union level which contribute to combating VAT fraud.

(23) In the interests of effectiveness and speed and on grounds of cost, it is essential that the information communicated under this Regulation should be provided by electronic means wherever possible.

(24) In view of the repetitive nature of certain requests and the linguistic diversity within the Union, it is important to enhance the use of standard forms in the exchange of information so that information requests can be more rapidly processed.

(25) The time limits laid down in this Regulation for the provision of information are to be understood as maximum periods not to be exceeded, the principle being that, in order for cooperation to be effective, information already available to the requested Member State should be provided without further delay.

(26) For the purposes of this Regulation, it is appropriate to consider limitations of certain rights and obligations laid down by Directive 95/46/EC of the European Parliament and of the Council of 24 October 1995 on the protection of individuals with regard to the processing of personal data and on the free movement of such data[6] in order to safeguard the interests referred to in Article 13(1)(e) of that Directive. Such limitations are necessary and proportionate in view of the potential loss of revenue for Member States and the crucial importance of information covered by this Regulation for the effectiveness of the fight against fraud.

(27) As the measures necessary to implement this Regulation are measures of general scope within the meaning of Article 2 of Council Decision 1999/468/EC of 28 June 1999 laying down the procedures for the exercise of implementing powers conferred on the Commission[7], they must be adopted in conformity with the regulatory procedure provided for in Article 5 of that Decision,

HAS ADOPTED THIS REGULATION:

[1] Opinion of 5 May 2010 (not yet published in the Official Journal).
[2] Opinion of 17 February 2010 (not yet published in the Official Journal).
[3] OJ L 264, 15.10.2003, p. 1.
[4] OJ L 347, 11.12.2006, p. 1.
[5] OJ L 44, 20.2.2008, p. 23.
[6] OJ L 281, 23.11.1995, p. 31.
[7] OJ L 184, 17.7.1999, p. 23.

CHAPTER I
GENERAL PROVISIONS

Article 1

1. This Regulation lays down the conditions under which the competent authorities in the Member States responsible for the application of the laws on VAT are to cooperate with each other and with the Commission to ensure compliance with those laws.

To that end, it lays down rules and procedures to enable the competent authorities of the Member States to cooperate and to exchange with each other any information that may help to effect a correct assessment of VAT, monitor the correct application of VAT, particularly on intra-Community transactions, and combat VAT fraud. In particular, it lays down rules and procedures for Member States to collect and exchange such information by electronic means.

2. This Regulation lays down the conditions under which the authorities referred to in paragraph 1 are to assist in the protection of VAT revenue in all the Member States.

3. This Regulation shall not affect the application in the Member States of the rules on mutual assistance in criminal matters.

4. This Regulation also lays down rules and procedures for the exchange by electronic means of VAT information on services supplied electronically in accordance with the special scheme provided for in Chapter 6 of Title XII of Directive 2006/112/EC and also for any subsequent exchange of information and, as far as services covered by that special scheme are concerned, for the transfer of money between Member States' competent authorities.

Article 2

1. For the purposes of this Regulation, the following definitions shall apply:

(a) 'central liaison office' means the office which has been designated pursuant to Article 4(1) with principal responsibility for contacts with other Member States in the field of administrative cooperation;

(b) 'liaison department' means any office other than the central liaison office which has been designated as such by the competent authority pursuant to Article 4(2) to exchange directly information on the basis of this Regulation;

(c) 'competent official' means any official who can directly exchange information on the basis of this Regulation for which he has been authorised pursuant to Article 4(3);

(d) 'requesting authority' means the central liaison office, a liaison department or any competent official of a Member State who makes a request for assistance on behalf of the competent authority;

(e) 'requested authority' means the central liaison office, a liaison department or any competent official of Member State who receives a request for assistance on behalf of the competent authority;

(f) 'intra-Community transactions' means the intra-Community supply of goods or services;

(g) 'intra-Community supply of goods' means any supply of goods which must be declared in the recapitulative statement provided for in Article 262 of Directive 2006/112/EC;

(h) 'intra-Community supply of services' means any supply of services which must be declared in the recapitulative statement provided for in Article 262 of Directive 2006/112/EC;

(i) 'intra-Community acquisition of goods' means the acquisition of the right pursuant to Article 20 of Directive 2006/112/EC to dispose as owner of moveable tangible property;

(j) 'VAT identification number' means the number provided for in Articles 214, 215 and 216 of Directive 2006/112/EC;

(k) 'administrative enquiry' means all the controls, checks and other action taken by Member States in the performance of their duties with a view to ensuring proper application of VAT legislation;

(l) 'automatic exchange' means the systematic communication of predefined information to another Member State, without prior request;

(m) 'spontaneous exchange' means the non-systematic communication, at any moment and without prior request, of information to another Member State;

(n) 'person' means:

(i) a natural person;

(ii) a legal person;

(iii) where the legislation in force so provides, an association of persons recognised as having the capacity to perform legal acts but lacking the legal status of a legal person; or

(iv) any other legal arrangement of whatever nature and form, which has legal personality or not, and conducts transactions which are subject to VAT;

(o) 'automated access' means the possibility of access without delay to an electronic system in order to consult certain information contained therein;

(p) 'by electronic means' means using electronic equipment for the processing (including digital compression) and storage of data, and employing wires, radio transmission, optical technologies or other electromagnetic means;

(q) 'CCN/CSI network' means the common platform based on the common communication network (hereinafter the 'CCN') and common system interface (hereinafter the 'CSI'), developed by the Union to ensure all transmissions by electronic means between competent authorities in the area of customs and taxation;

(r) 'simultaneous control' means coordinated checks on the tax situation of a taxable person or related taxable persons, organised by two or more participating Member States with common or complementary interests.

2. From 1 January 2015, the definitions contained in Articles 358, 358a and 369a of Directive 2006/112/EC shall also apply for the purposes of this Regulation.

Article 3

The competent authorities are the authorities in whose name this Regulation is to be applied, whether directly or by delegation.

Each Member State shall inform the Commission by 1 December 2010 of its competent authority for the purposes of this Regulation and shall subsequently inform the Commission without delay about any change thereof.

[Croatia shall inform the Commission by 1 July 2013 of its competent authority for the purposes of this Regulation and of the subsequent changes as mentioned in the second paragraph.][1]

The Commission shall make available to the Member States a list of all competent authorities and publish this information in the *Official Journal of the European Union.*

Amendments—[1] Paragraph relating to the accession of Croatia inserted by Council Regulation 517/2013/EU art 1, Annex with effect from 1 July 2013 (OJ L 158, 10.6.2013, p. 1).

Article 4

1. Each Member State shall designate a single central liaison office to which principal responsibility shall be delegated for contacts with other Member States in the field of administrative cooperation. It shall inform the Commission and the other Member States thereof. The central liaison office may also be designated as responsible for contacts with the Commission.

2. The competent authority of each Member State may designate liaison departments. The central liaison office shall be responsible for keeping the list of those departments up-to-date and making it available to the central liaison offices of the other Member States concerned.

3. The competent authority of each Member State may in addition designate, under the conditions laid down by it, competent officials who can directly exchange information on the basis of this Regulation. When it does so, it may limit the scope of such designation. The central liaison office shall be responsible for keeping the list of those officials up-to-date and making it available to the central liaison offices of the other Member States concerned.

4. The officials exchanging information pursuant to Articles 28, 29 and 30 shall in any case be deemed to be competent officials for this purpose, in accordance with conditions laid down by the competent authorities.

Article 5

Where a liaison department or a competent official sends or receives a request or a reply to a request for assistance, it shall inform the central liaison office of its Member State under the conditions laid down by the latter.

Article 6

Where a liaison department or a competent official receives a request for assistance requiring action outside its territorial or operational area, it shall forward such request without delay to the central liaison office of its Member State and inform the requesting authority thereof. In such a case, the period laid down in Article 10 shall start the day after the request for assistance has been forwarded to the central liaison office.

CHAPTER II
EXCHANGE OF INFORMATION ON REQUEST

SECTION 1

REQUEST FOR INFORMATION AND FOR ADMINISTRATIVE ENQUIRIES

Article 7

1. At the request of the requesting authority, the requested authority shall communicate the information referred to in Article 1, including any information relating to a specific case or cases.

2. For the purpose of forwarding the information referred to in paragraph 1, the requested authority shall arrange for the conduct of any administrative enquiries necessary to obtain such information.

3. Until 31 December 2014, the request referred to in paragraph 1 may contain a reasoned request for an administrative enquiry. If the requested authority takes the view that the administrative enquiry is not necessary, it shall immediately inform the requesting authority of the reasons thereof.

4. As from 1 January 2015, the request referred to in paragraph 1 may contain a reasoned request for a specific administrative enquiry. If the requested authority takes the view that no administrative enquiry is necessary, it shall immediately inform the requesting authority of the reasons thereof.
Notwithstanding the first subparagraph, an enquiry into the amounts declared by a taxable person in connection with the supplies of goods or services listed in Annex I, which are made by a taxable person established in the Member State of the requested authority and are taxable in the Member State of the requesting authority, may be refused solely:
- (a) on the grounds provided for in Article 54(1), assessed by the requested authority in conformity with a statement of best practices concerning the interaction of this paragraph and Article 54(1), to be adopted in accordance with the procedure provided for in Article 58(2);
- (b) on the grounds provided for in paragraphs 2, 3 and 4 of Article 54; or
- (c) on the grounds that the requested authority had already supplied the requesting authority with information on the same taxable person as a result of an administrative enquiry held less than two years previously.

Where the requested authority refuses an administrative enquiry referred to in the second subparagraph on the grounds set out in points (a) or (b), it shall nevertheless provide to the requesting authority the dates and values of any relevant supplies made by the taxable person in the Member State of the requesting authority over the previous two years.
5. In order to obtain the information sought or to conduct the administrative enquiry requested, the requested authority or the administrative authority to which it has recourse shall proceed as though acting on its own account or at the request of another authority in its own Member State.

Article 8

Requests for information and for administrative enquiries pursuant to Article 7 shall be sent using a standard form adopted in accordance with the procedure provided for in Article 58(2), except in the cases referred to in Article 50 or in exceptional cases where the request includes the reasons for which the requesting authority considers the standard form not to be appropriate.

Article 9

1. At the request of the requesting authority, the requested authority shall communicate to it any pertinent information it obtains or has in its possession as well as the results of administrative enquiries, in the form of reports, statements and any other documents, or certified true copies or extracts thereof.
2. Original documents shall be provided only where this is not contrary to the provisions in force in the Member State in which the requested authority is established.

SECTION 2
TIME LIMIT FOR PROVIDING INFORMATION

Article 10

The requested authority shall provide the information referred to in Articles 7 and 9 as quickly as possible and no later than three months following the date of receipt of the request.
However, where the requested authority is already in possession of that information, the time limit shall be reduced to a maximum period of one month.

Article 11

In certain special categories of cases, time limits which are different from those provided for in Article 10 may be agreed between the requested and the requesting authorities.

Article 12

Where the requested authority is unable to respond to the request by the deadline, it shall inform the requesting authority in writing forthwith of the reasons for its failure to do so, and when it considers it would be likely to be able to respond.

CHAPTER III
EXCHANGE OF INFORMATION WITHOUT PRIOR REQUEST

Article 13

1. The competent authority of each Member State shall, without prior request, forward the information referred to in Article 1 to the competent authority of any other Member State concerned, in the following cases:
- (a) where taxation is deemed to take place in the Member State of destination and the information provided by the Member State of origin is necessary for the effectiveness of the control system of the Member State of destination;
- (b) where a Member State has grounds to believe that a breach of VAT legislation has been committed or is likely to have been committed in the other Member State;
- (c) where there is a risk of tax loss in the other Member State.

2. The exchange of information without prior request shall either be automatic, in accordance with Article 14, or spontaneous, in accordance with Article 15.

3. The information shall be forwarded by means of standard forms adopted in accordance with the procedure provided for in Article 58(2).

Article 14

1. The following shall be determined in accordance with the procedure provided for in Article 58(2):
   (a) the exact categories of information subject to automatic exchange;
   (b) the frequency of the automatic exchange for each category of information; and
   (c) the practical arrangements for the automatic exchange of information.

A Member State may abstain from taking part in the automatic exchange of information with respect to one or more categories where the collection of information for such exchange would require the imposition of new obligations on persons liable for VAT or would impose a disproportionate administrative burden on the Member State.

The results of the automatic exchange of information for each category shall be reviewed once a year by the Committee referred to in Article 58(1), so as to ensure that this type of exchange takes places only where it is the most efficient means for the exchange of information.

2. As from 1 January 2015, the competent authority of each Member State shall, in particular, exchange information automatically in order to enable Member States of consumption to ascertain whether taxable persons not established in their territory declare and correctly pay the VAT due with regard to telecommunication services, broadcasting services and electronically supplied services, regardless of whether those taxable persons make use of the special scheme provided for in Section 3 of Chapter 6 of Title XII of Directive 2006/112/EC. The Member State of establishment shall inform the Member State of consumption of any discrepancies of which it becomes aware.

Article 15

The competent authorities of the Member States shall, by spontaneous exchange, forward to the competent authorities of the other Member States any information referred to in Article 13(1) which has not been forwarded under the automatic exchange referred to in Article 14 of which they are aware and which they consider may be useful to those competent authorities.

CHAPTER IV
FEEDBACK

Article 16

Where a competent authority provides information pursuant to Article 7 or 15, it may request the competent authority which receives the information to give feedback thereon. If such request is made, the competent authority which receives the information shall, without prejudice to the rules on tax secrecy and data protection applicable in its Member State, send feedback as soon as possible, provided that this does not impose a disproportionate administrative burden on it. Practical arrangements shall be determined in accordance with the procedure provided for in Article 58(2).

CHAPTER V
STORAGE AND EXCHANGE OF SPECIFIC INFORMATION

Article 17

1. Each Member State shall store in an electronic system the following information:
   (a) information which it collects pursuant to Chapter 6 of Title XI of Directive 2006/112/EC;
   (b) data on the identity, activity, legal form and address of persons to whom it has issued a VAT identification number, collected pursuant to Article 213 of Directive 2006/112/EC, as well as the date on which that number was issued;
   (c) data on VAT identification numbers it has issued which have become invalid, and the dates on which those numbers became invalid; and
   (d) information which it collects pursuant to Articles 360, 361, 364 and 365 of Directive 2006/112/EC as well as, from 1 January 2015, information which it collects pursuant to Articles 369c, 369f and 369g of that Directive.

2. The technical details concerning the automated enquiry of the information referred to in points (b), (c) and (d) of paragraph 1 shall be adopted in accordance with the procedure provided for in Article 58(2).

Article 18

To enable the information referred to in Article 17 to be used in the procedures provided for in this Regulation, that information shall be available for at least five years from the end of the first calendar year in which access to the information is to be granted.

Article 19

Member States shall ensure that the information available in the electronic system referred to in Article 17 is kept up-to-date, and is complete and accurate.

Criteria shall be defined, in accordance with the procedure provided for in Article 58(2), to determine which changes are not pertinent, essential or useful and therefore need not be made.

Article 20

1. The information referred to in Article 17 shall be entered into the electronic system without delay.

2. By way of derogation from paragraph 1, the information referred to in Article 17(1)(a) shall be entered into the electronic system no later than one month after the end of the period to which that information relates.

3. By way of derogation from paragraphs 1 and 2, where information is to be corrected in, or added to, the electronic system pursuant to Article 19, the information must be entered no later than one month after the period in which it was collected.

Article 21

1. Every Member State shall grant the competent authority of any other Member State automated access to the information stored pursuant to Article 17.

2. With respect to the information referred to in Article 17(1)(a), at least the following details shall be accessible:

(a) VAT identification numbers issued by the Member State receiving the information;

(b) the total value of all intra-Community supplies of goods and the total value of all intra-Community supplies of services to persons holding a VAT identification number referred to in point (a) by all operators identified for the purposes of VAT in the Member State providing the information;

(c) the VAT identification numbers of the persons who carried out the supplies of goods and services referred to in point (b);

(d) the total value of the supplies of goods and services referred to in point (b) from each person referred to in point (c) to each person holding a VAT identification number referred to in point (a);

(e) the total value of the supplies of goods and services referred to in point (b) from each person referred to in point (c) to each person holding a VAT identification number issued by another Member State under the following conditions:

(i) access is in connection with an investigation into suspected fraud;

(ii) access is through a Eurofisc liaison official, as referred to in Article 36(1), who holds a personal user identification for the electronic systems allowing access to this information; and

(iii) access is only granted during general working hours.

The values referred to in points (b), (d) and (e) shall be expressed in the currency of the Member State providing the information and shall relate to the periods for submission of the recapitulative statements specific to each taxable person which are established in accordance with Article 263 of Directive 2006/112/EC.

Article 22

1. In order to provide a reasonable level of assurance to tax administrations with regard to the quality and reliability of the information available through the electronic system referred to in Article 17, Member States shall adopt the measures necessary to ensure that the data provided by taxable persons and non-taxable legal persons for their identification for VAT purposes in accordance with Article 214 of Directive 2006/112/EC, are, in their assessment, complete and accurate.

Member States shall implement procedures for checking these data as determined by the results of their risk assessment. The checks shall be carried out, in principle, prior to identification for VAT purposes or, where only preliminary checks are conducted before such identification, no later than six months from such identification.

2. The Member States shall inform the Committee referred to in Article 58(1) of the measures implemented at national level to ensure the quality and reliability of the information in accordance with paragraph 1.

Article 23

Member States shall ensure that the VAT identification number, referred to in Article 214 of Directive 2006/112/EC, is shown as invalid in the electronic system referred to in Article 17 of this Regulation at least in the following situations:

(a) where persons identified for VAT purposes have stated that their economic activity, as defined in Article 9 of Directive 2006/112/EC, has ceased or where the competent tax administration considers that they have ceased such activity. A tax administration may presume in particular that a person has ceased economic activity when, despite being required to do so, that person has failed to submit VAT returns and recapitulative statements for a year after expiry of the deadline for submission of the first return or statement missed. The person shall have the right to prove the existence of an economic activity by other means;

(b) where persons have declared false data in order to obtain VAT identification or have failed to communicate changes to their data and, had the tax administration known, the latter would have refused identification for VAT purposes or withdrawn the VAT identification number.

Article 24

Where, for the purposes of Articles 17 to 21, the competent authorities of the Member States exchange information by electronic means, they shall take all measures necessary to ensure compliance with Article 55.

Member States shall be responsible for all necessary developments to their systems to permit the exchange of that information using the CCN/CSI network.

CHAPTER VI

REQUEST FOR ADMINISTRATIVE NOTIFICATION

Article 25

The requested authority shall, at the request of the requesting authority and in accordance with the rules governing the notification of similar instruments in the Member State in which the requested authority is established, notify the addressee of all instruments and decisions which emanate from the competent authorities and concern the application of VAT legislation in the territory of the Member State in which the requesting authority is established.

Article 26

Requests for notification, mentioning the subject of the instrument or decision to be notified, shall indicate the name, address and any other relevant information for identifying the addressee.

Article 27

The requested authority shall inform the requesting authority immediately of its response to the request for notification and notify it, in particular, of the date of notification of the decision or instrument to the addressee.

CHAPTER VII

PRESENCE IN ADMINISTRATIVE OFFICES AND PARTICIPATION IN ADMINISTRATIVE ENQUIRIES

Article 28

1. By agreement between the requesting authority and the requested authority, and in accordance with the arrangements laid down by the latter, officials authorised by the requesting authority may, with a view to exchanging the information referred to in Article 1, be present in the offices of the administrative authorities of the requested Member State, or any other place where those authorities carry out their duties. Where the requested information is contained in documentation to which the officials of the requested authority have access, the officials of the requesting authority shall be given copies thereof.

2. By agreement between the requesting authority and the requested authority, and in accordance with the arrangements laid down by the latter, officials authorised by the requesting authority may, with a view to exchanging the information referred to in Article 1, be present during the administrative enquiries carried out in the territory of the requested Member State. Such administrative enquiries shall be carried out exclusively by the officials of the requested authority. The officials of the requesting authority shall not exercise the powers of inspection conferred on officials of the requested authority. They may, however, have access to the same premises and documents as the latter, through the intermediation of the officials of the requested authority and for the sole purpose of carrying out the administrative enquiry.

3. The officials of the requesting authority present in another Member State in accordance with paragraphs 1 and 2 must at all times be able to produce written authority stating their identity and their official capacity.

CHAPTER VIII

SIMULTANEOUS CONTROLS

Article 29

Member States may agree to conduct simultaneous controls whenever they consider such controls to be more effective than controls carried out by only one Member State.

Article 30

1. A Member State shall identify independently the taxable persons which it intends to propose for a simultaneous control. The competent authority of that Member State shall notify the competent authority of the other Member States concerned of the cases proposed for a simultaneous control. It shall give reasons for its choice, as far as possible, by providing the information which led to its decision. It shall specify the period of time during which such controls should be conducted.

2. The competent authority of the Member State that receives the proposal for a simultaneous control shall confirm its agreement or communicate its reasoned refusal to its counterpart authority, in principle within two weeks of receipt of the proposal, but within a month at the latest.

3. Each competent authority of the Member States concerned shall appoint a representative to be responsible for supervising and coordinating the control operation.

CHAPTER IX
PROVIDING INFORMATION TO TAXABLE PERSONS

Article 31

1. The competent authorities of each Member State shall ensure that persons involved in the intra-Community supply of goods or of services and non-established taxable persons supplying telecommunication services, broadcasting services and electronically supplied services, in particular those referred to in Annex II to Directive 2006/112/EC, are allowed to obtain, for the purposes of such transactions, confirmation by electronic means of the validity of the VAT identification number of any specified person as well as the associated name and address. This information shall correspond to the data referred to in Article 17.
2. Each Member State shall provide confirmation by electronic means of the name and address of the person to whom the VAT identification number has been issued in accordance with its national data protection rules.
3. During the period provided for in Article 357 of Directive 2006/112/EC, paragraph 1 of this Article shall not apply to non-established taxable persons supplying telecommunication services and radio and television broadcasting services.

Article 32

1. The Commission shall, on the basis of the information provided by the Member States, publish on its website the details of the provisions approved by each Member State which transpose Chapter 3 of Title XI of Directive 2006/112/EC.
2. The details and format of the information to be submitted shall be decided in accordance with the procedure provided for in Article 58(2).

CHAPTER X
EUROFISC

Article 33

1. In order to promote and facilitate multilateral cooperation in the fight against VAT fraud, this Chapter establishes a network for the swift exchange of targeted information between Member States hereinafter called 'Eurofisc'.
2. Within the framework of Eurofisc, Member States shall:
   (a) establish a multilateral early warning mechanism for combating VAT fraud;
   (b) coordinate the swift multilateral exchange of targeted information in the subject areas in which Eurofisc will operate (hereinafter 'Eurofisc working fields');
   (c) coordinate the work of the Eurofisc liaison officials of the participating Member States in acting on warnings received.

Article 34

1. Member States shall participate in the Eurofisc working fields of their choice and may also decide to terminate their participation therein.
2. Member States having chosen to take part in a Eurofisc working field shall actively participate in the multilateral exchange of targeted information between all participating Member States.
3. Information exchanged shall be confidential, as provided for in Article 55.

Article 35

The Commission shall provide Eurofisc with technical and logistical support. The Commission shall not have access to the information referred to in Article 1, which may be exchanged over Eurofisc.

Article 36

1. The competent authorities of each Member State shall designate at least one Eurofisc liaison official. Eurofisc liaison officials shall be competent officials within the meaning of Article 2(1)(c) and shall carry out the activities referred to in Article 33(2). They shall remain answerable only to their national administrations.
2. The liaison officials of the Member States participating in a particular Eurofisc working field (hereinafter 'participating Eurofisc liaison officials') shall designate a coordinator (hereinafter 'Eurofisc working field coordinator'), among the participating Eurofisc liaison officials, for a limited period of time. Eurofisc working field coordinators shall:
   (a) collate the information received from the participating Eurofisc liaison officials and make all information available to the other participating Eurofisc liaison officials. The information shall be exchanged by electronic means;
   (b) ensure that the information received from the participating Eurofisc liaison officials is processed, as agreed by the participants in the working field, and make the result available to the participating Eurofisc liaison officials;
   (c) provide feedback to the participating Eurofisc liaison officials.

Article 37

Eurofisc working field coordinators shall submit an annual report of the activities of all working fields to the Committee referred to in Article 58(1).

CHAPTER XI
PROVISIONS CONCERNING THE SPECIAL SCHEMES IN CHAPTER 6 OF TITLE XII OF DIRECTIVE 2006/112/EC

SECTION 1
PROVISIONS APPLICABLE UNTIL 31 DECEMBER 2014

Article 38

The following provisions shall apply concerning the special scheme provided for in Chapter 6 of Title XII of Directive 2006/112/EC. The definitions contained in Article 358 of that Directive shall also apply for the purpose of this Chapter.

Article 39

1. The information provided by the taxable person not established in the Community to the Member State of identification, when his activities commence pursuant to Article 361 of Directive 2006/112/EC, shall be submitted by electronic means. The technical details, including a common electronic message, shall be determined in accordance with the procedure provided for in Article 58(2) of this Regulation.
2. The Member State of identification shall transmit this information by electronic means to the competent authorities of the other Member States within 10 days from the end of the month during which the information was received from the non-established taxable person. In the same manner the competent authorities of the other Member States shall be informed of the allocated identification number. The technical details, including a common electronic message, by which this information is to be transmitted, shall be determined in accordance with the procedure provided for in Article 58(2).
3. The Member State of identification shall without delay inform by electronic means the competent authorities of the other Members States if a non-established taxable person is excluded from the identification register.

Article 40

1. The return with the details set out in Article 365 of Directive 2006/112/EC is to be submitted by electronic means. The technical details, including a common electronic message, shall be determined in accordance with the procedure provided for in Article 58(2) of this Regulation.
2. The Member State of identification shall transmit this information by electronic means to the competent authority of the Member State concerned at the latest 10 days after the end of the month during which the return was received. Member States which have required the tax return to be made in a national currency other than euro, shall convert the amounts into euro using the exchange rate valid for the last date of the reporting period. The exchange shall be done following the exchange rates published by the European Central Bank for that day, or, if there is no publication on that day, on the next day of publication. The technical details by which this information is to be transmitted shall be determined in accordance with the procedure provided for in Article 58(2).
3. The Member State of identification shall transmit by electronic means to the Member State of consumption the information needed to link each payment with a relevant quarterly tax return.

Article 41

1. The Member State of identification shall ensure that the amount the non-established taxable person has paid is transferred to the bank account denominated in euro which has been designated by the Member State of consumption to which the payment is due. Member States which required the payments in a national currency other than euro shall convert the amounts into euro using the exchange rate valid for the last date of the reporting period. The exchange shall be done following the exchange rates published by the European Central Bank for that day, or, if there is no publication on that day, on the next day of publication. The transfer shall take place at the latest 10 days after the end of the month during which the payment was received.
2. If the non-established taxable person does not pay the total tax due, the Member State of identification shall ensure that the payment is transferred to the Member States of consumption in proportion to the tax due in each Member State. The Member State of identification shall inform by electronic means the competent authorities of the Member States of consumption thereof.

Article 42

Member States shall notify by electronic means the competent authorities of the other Member States of the relevant bank account numbers for receiving payments according to Article 41.
Member States shall without delay notify by electronic means the competent authorities of the other Member States and the Commission of changes in the standard tax rate.

SECTION 2
PROVISIONS APPLICABLE FROM 1 JANUARY 2015

Article 43

The following provisions shall apply concerning the special schemes provided for in Chapter 6 of Title XII of Directive 2006/112/EC.

Article 44

1. The information provided by the taxable person not established in the Community to the Member State of identification when his activities commence pursuant to Article 361 of Directive 2006/112/EC shall be submitted by electronic means. The technical details, including a common electronic message, shall be determined in accordance with the procedure provided for in Article 58(2) of this Regulation.

2. The Member State of identification shall transmit the information referred to in paragraph 1 by electronic means to the competent authorities of the other Member States within 10 days from the end of the month during which the information was received from the taxable person not established within the Community. Similar details for the identification of the taxable person applying the special scheme pursuant to Article 369b of Directive 2006/112/EC shall be transmitted within 10 days from the end of the month during which the taxable person stated that his taxable activities under that scheme commenced. In the same manner the competent authorities of the other Member States shall be informed of the allocated identification number.

The technical details, including a common electronic message, by which this information is to be transmitted, shall be determined in accordance with the procedure provided for in Article 58(2) of this Regulation.

3. The Member State of identification shall without delay inform by electronic means the competent authorities of the other Member States if a taxable person not established in the Community or a taxable person not established in the Member State of consumption is excluded from the special scheme.

Article 45

1. The return with the details set out in Articles 365 and 369g of Directive 2006/112/EC is to be submitted by electronic means. The technical details, including a common electronic message, shall be determined in accordance with the procedure provided for in Article 58(2) of this Regulation.

2. The Member State of identification shall transmit this information by electronic means to the competent authority of the Member State of consumption concerned at the latest 10 days after the end of the month during which the return was received. The information provided for in the second paragraph of Article 369g of Directive 2006/112/EC shall also be transmitted to the competent authority of the Member State of establishment concerned. Member States which have required the tax return to be made in a national currency other that euro, shall convert the amounts into euro using the exchange rate valid for the last date of the reporting period. The exchange shall be done following the exchange rates published by the European Central Bank for that day, or, if there is no publication on that day, on the next day of publication. The technical details by which this information is to be transmitted shall be determined in accordance with the procedure provided for in Article 58(2) of this Regulation.

3. The Member State of identification shall transmit by electronic means to the Member State of consumption the information needed to link each payment with a relevant quarterly tax return.

Article 46

1. The Member State of identification shall ensure that the amount the non-established taxable person has paid is transferred to the bank account denominated in euro which has been designated by the Member State of consumption to which the payment is due. Member States which required the payments in a national currency other than euro shall convert the amounts into euro using the exchange rate valid for the last date of the reporting period. The exchange shall be done following the exchange rates published by the European Central Bank for that day, or, if there is no publication on that day, on the next day of publication. The transfer shall take place at the latest 10 days after the end of the month during which the payment was received.

2. If the non-established taxable person does not pay the total tax due, the Member State of identification shall ensure that the payment is transferred to the Member States of consumption in proportion to the tax due in each Member State. The Member State of identification shall inform by electronic means the competent authorities of the Member States of consumption thereof.

3. Concerning the payments to be transferred to the Member State of consumption in accordance with the special scheme provided for in Section 3 of Chapter 6 of Title XII of Directive 2006/112/EC, the Member State of identification shall, of the amounts referred to in paragraphs 1 and 2 of this Article, be entitled to retain:

(a) from 1 January 2015 until 31 December 2016 — 30 %;
(b) from 1 January 2017 until 31 December 2018 — 15 %;

(c) from 1 January 2019 — 0 %.

Article 47

Member States shall notify by electronic means the competent authorities of the other Member States of the relevant bank account numbers for receiving payments in accordance with Article 46.

Member States shall without delay notify by electronic means the competent authorities of the other Member States and the Commission of changes in the tax rate applicable for supplies of telecommunication services, broadcasting services and electronically supplied services.

CHAPTER XII

EXCHANGE AND CONSERVATION OF INFORMATION IN THE CONTEXT OF THE PROCEDURE FOR THE REFUND OF VAT TO TAXABLE PERSONS NOT ESTABLISHED IN THE MEMBER STATE OF REFUND BUT ESTABLISHED IN ANOTHER MEMBER STATE

Article 48

1. Where the competent authority of the Member State of establishment receives an application for refund of VAT pursuant to Article 5 of Directive 2008/9/EC, and Article 18 of that Directive is not applicable, it shall, within 15 calendar days of its receipt and by electronic means, forward the application to the competent authorities of each Member State of refund concerned with confirmation that the applicant as defined in Article 2(5) of Directive 2008/9/EC is a taxable person for the purposes of VAT and that the identification or registration number given by this person is valid for the refund period.

2. The competent authorities of each Member State of refund shall notify by electronic means the competent authorities of the other Member States of any information required by them pursuant to Article 9(2) of Directive 2008/9/EC. The technical details, including a common electronic message by which this information is to be transmitted, shall be determined in accordance with the procedure provided for in Article 58(2) of this Regulation.

3. The competent authorities of each Member State of refund shall notify by electronic means the competent authorities of the other Member States if they want to make use of the option to require the applicant to provide the description of business activity by harmonised codes as referred to in Article 11 of Directive 2008/9/EC.

The harmonised codes referred to in the first subparagraph shall be determined in accordance with the procedure provided for in Article 58(2) of this Regulation on the basis of the NACE classification established by Regulation (EC) No 1893/2006 of the European Parliament and of the Council of 20 December 2006 establishing the statistical classification of economic activities NACE Revision 2[1].

[1] OJ L 393, 30.12.2006, p. 1.

CHAPTER XIII

RELATIONS WITH THE COMMISSION

Article 49

1. The Member States and the Commission shall examine and evaluate how the arrangements for administrative cooperation provided for in this Regulation are working. The Commission shall pool the Member States' experience with the aim of improving the operation of those arrangements.

2. The Member States shall communicate to the Commission any available information relevant to their application of this Regulation.

3. A list of statistical data needed for evaluation of this Regulation shall be determined in accordance with the procedure provided for in Article 58(2). The Member States shall communicate these data to the Commission in so far as they are available and the communication is not likely to involve administrative burdens which would be unjustified.

4. With a view to evaluating the effectiveness of this system of administrative cooperation in combating tax evasion and tax avoidance, Member States may communicate to the Commission any other information referred to in Article 1.

5. The Commission shall forward the information referred to in paragraphs 2, 3 and 4 to the other Member States concerned.

6. Where necessary, in addition to what is required by other provisions in this Regulation, the Commission shall send to the competent authorities of each Member State any information that might enable them to combat fraud in the field of VAT as soon as it obtains such information.

7. The Commission may, at the request of a Member State, provide its expert opinions, technical or logistical assistance, or any other support with a view to attaining the objectives of this Regulation.

CHAPTER XIV
RELATIONS WITH THIRD COUNTRIES

Article 50

1. When the competent authority of a Member State receives information from a third country, that authority may pass the information on to the competent authorities of Member States which might be interested in it and, in any event, to all those which request it, in so far as permitted by assistance arrangements with that particular third country.

2. Competent authorities may communicate, in accordance with their domestic provisions on the communication of personal data to third countries, information obtained in accordance with this Regulation to a third country, provided that the following conditions are met:

(a) the competent authority of the Member State from which the information originates has consented to that communication; and

(b) the third country concerned has given an undertaking to provide the cooperation required to gather evidence of the irregular nature of transactions which appear to contravene VAT legislation.

CHAPTER XV
CONDITIONS GOVERNING THE EXCHANGE OF INFORMATION

Article 51

1. Information communicated pursuant to this Regulation shall, as far as possible, be provided by electronic means under arrangements to be adopted in accordance with the procedure provided for in Article 58(2).

2. Where the request has not been lodged completely through the electronic system referred to in paragraph 1, the requested authority shall confirm receipt of the request by electronic means without delay and, in any event, no later than five working days after receipt.

Where an authority has received a request or information of which it is not the intended recipient, it shall send a message by electronic means to the sender without delay and, in any event, no later than five working days after receipt.

Article 52

Requests for assistance, including requests for notification, and attached documents may be made in any language agreed between the requested and requesting authority. The said requests shall be accompanied by a translation into the official language or one of the official languages of the Member State in which the requested authority is established only in special cases when the requested authority gives a reason for asking for such a translation.

Article 53

The Commission and the Member States shall ensure that such existing or new communication and information exchange systems which are necessary to provide for the exchanges of information described in this Regulation are operational. A service level agreement ensuring the technical quality and quantity of the services to be delivered by the Commission and the Member States for the functioning of those communication and information exchange systems shall be decided in accordance with the procedure provided for in Article 58(2). The Commission shall be responsible for whatever development of the CCN/CSI network is necessary to permit the exchange of this information between Member States. Member States shall be responsible for whatever development of their systems is necessary to permit this information to be exchanged using the CCN/CSI network. Member States shall waive all claims for the reimbursement of expenses incurred in applying this Regulation except, where appropriate, in respect of fees paid to experts.

Article 54

1. The requested authority in one Member State shall provide a requesting authority in another Member State with the information referred to in Article 1 provided that:

(a) the number and the nature of the requests for information made by the requesting authority within a specific period do not impose a disproportionate administrative burden on that requested authority;

(b) that requesting authority has exhausted the usual sources of information which it could have used in the circumstances to obtain the information requested, without running the risk of jeopardising the achievement of the desired end.

2. This Regulation shall impose no obligation to have enquiries carried out or to provide information on a particular case if the laws or administrative practices of the Member State which would have to supply the information do not authorise the Member State to carry out those enquiries or collect or use that information for that Member State's own purposes.

3. The competent authority of a requested Member State may refuse to provide information where the requesting Member State is unable, for legal reasons, to provide similar information. The Commission shall be informed of the grounds of the refusal by the requested Member State.

4. The provision of information may be refused where it would lead to the disclosure of a commercial, industrial or professional secret or of a commercial process, or of information whose disclosure would be contrary to public policy.
5. Paragraphs 2, 3 and 4 should on no account be interpreted as authorising the requested authority of a Member State to refuse to supply information on a taxable person identified for VAT purposes in the Member State of the requesting authority on the sole grounds that this information is held by a bank, other financial institution, nominee or person acting in an agency or fiduciary capacity or because it relates to ownership interests in a legal person.
6. The requested authority shall inform the requesting authority of the grounds for refusing a request for assistance.
7. A minimum threshold triggering a request for assistance may be adopted in accordance with the procedure provided for in Article 58(2).

Article 55

1. Information communicated or collected in any form pursuant to this Regulation, including any information to which an official has had access in the circumstances set out in Chapters VII, VIII and X, and in the cases referred to in paragraph 2 of this Article, shall be covered by the obligation of official secrecy and enjoy the protection extended to similar information under both the national law of the Member State which received it and the corresponding provisions applicable to Union authorities. Such information shall be used only in the circumstances provided for in this Regulation.
Such information may be used for the purpose of establishing the assessment base or the collection or administrative control of tax for the purpose of establishing the assessment base.
The information may also be used for the assessment of other levies, duties, and taxes covered by Article 2 of Council Directive 2008/55/EC of 26 May 2008 on mutual assistance for the recovery of claims relating to certain levies, duties, taxes and other measures[1].
In addition, it may be used in connection with judicial proceedings that may involve penalties, initiated as a result of infringements of tax law without prejudice to the general rules and legal provisions governing the rights of defendants and witnesses in such proceedings.
2. Persons duly accredited by the Security Accreditation Authority of the Commission may have access to this information only in so far as it is necessary for care, maintenance and development of the CCN/CSI network.
3. By way of derogation from paragraph 1, the competent authority of the Member State providing the information shall permit its use for other purposes in the Member State of the requesting authority, if, under the legislation of the Member State of the requested authority, the information can be used for similar purposes.
4. Where the requesting authority considers that information it has received from the requested authority is likely to be useful to the competent authority of a third Member State, it may transmit it to the latter authority. It shall inform the requested authority thereof in advance. The requested authority may require that the transmission of the information to a third party be subject to its prior agreement.
5. All storage or exchange of information referred to in this Regulation is subject to the provisions implementing Directive 95/46/EC. However, Member States shall, for the purpose of the correct application of this Regulation, restrict the scope of the obligations and rights provided for in Article 10, Article 11(1) and Articles 12 and 21 of Directive 95/46/EC to the extent required in order to safeguard the interests referred to in Article 13(1)(e) of that Directive.

Article 56

Reports, statements and any other documents, or certified true copies or extracts thereof, obtained by the staff of the requested authority and communicated to the requesting authority under the assistance provided for by this Regulation may be invoked as evidence by the competent bodies of the Member State of the requesting authority on the same basis as similar documents provided by another authority of that country.

Article 57

1. For the purpose of applying this Regulation, Member States shall take all necessary measures to:
   (a) ensure effective internal coordination between the competent authorities;
   (b) establish direct cooperation between the authorities authorised for the purposes of such coordination;
   (c) ensure the smooth operation of the information exchange arrangements provided for in this Regulation.
2. The Commission shall communicate to each Member State, as quickly as possible, any information which it receives and which it is able to provide.

[1] OJ L 150, 10.6.2008, p. 28.

CHAPTER XVI
FINAL PROVISIONS

Article 58

1. The Commission shall be assisted by the Standing Committee on Administrative Cooperation.
2. Where reference is made to this paragraph, Articles 5 and 7 of Decision 1999/468/EC shall apply, having regard to the provisions of Article 8 thereof.
The period laid down in Article 5(6) of Decision 1999/468/EC shall be set at three months.

Article 59

1. By 1 November 2013 and thereafter every five years, the Commission shall report to the European Parliament and the Council on the application of this Regulation.
2. Member States shall communicate to the Commission the text of any provisions of national law which they adopt in the field covered by this Regulation.

Article 60

1. This Regulation shall be without prejudice to the fulfilment of any wider obligations in relation to mutual assistance ensuing from other legal acts, including bilateral or multilateral agreements.
2. Where the Member States conclude bilateral arrangements on matters covered by this Regulation, in particular pursuant to Article 11, other than to deal with individual cases, they shall inform the Commission without delay. The Commission shall in turn inform the other Member States.

Article 61

Regulation (EC) No 1798/2003 shall be repealed with effect from 1 January 2012. However, the effects of Article 2(1) of that Regulation shall be maintained until the date of publication by the Commission of the list of competent authorities referred to in Article 3 of this Regulation.
Chapter V, with the exception of Article 27(4), of that Regulation shall remain applicable until 31 December 2012.
References made to the repealed Regulation shall be construed as references to this Regulation.

Article 62

This Regulation shall enter into force on the 20th day following its publication in the *Official Journal of the European Union*.
It shall apply from 1 January 2012.
However, Articles 33 to 37 shall apply from 1 November 2010;
Chapter V, with the exception of Articles 22 and 23, shall apply from 1 January 2013;
— Articles 38 to 42 shall apply from 1 January 2012 until 31 December 2014; and
— Articles 43 to 47 shall apply from 1 January 2015.
This Regulation shall be binding in its entirety and directly applicable in all Member States.

Done at Luxembourg, ... 7 October 2010.

For the Council
The President
S. VANACKERE

ANNEX I

List of supplies of goods and services to which Article 7(3) and (4) applies:

1. distance selling (Articles 33 and 34 of Directive 2006/112/EC);
2. services connected with immovable property (Article 47 of Directive 2006/112/EC);
3. telecommunication services, radio and television broadcasting services and electronically supplied services (Article 58 of Directive 2006/112/EC);
4. hiring, other than short-term hiring, of a means of transport to a non-taxable person (Article 56 of Directive 2006/112/EC).

ANNEX II

Repealed Regulation and successive amendments

Council Regulation (EC) No 1798/2003	OJ L 264, 15.10.2003, p. 1.
Council Regulation (EC) No 885/2004	OJ L 168, 1.5.2004, p. 1.
Council Regulation (EC) No 1791/2006	OJ L 363, 20.12.2006, p. 1.
Council Regulation (EC) No 143/2008	OJ L 44, 20.2.2008, p. 1.
Council Regulation (EC) No 37/2009	OJ L 14, 20.1.2009, p. 1.

VAT EC

ANNEX III
CORRELATION TABLE

Regulation (EC) No 1798/2003	This Regulation
First and second subparagraphs of Article 1(1)	First and second subparagraphs of Article 1(1)
Third subparagraph of Article 1(1)	—
Fourth subparagraph of Article 1(1)	Article 1(4)
Article 1(2)	Article 1(3)
Article 2(1)(1)	Article 3
Article 2(1)(2)	Article 2(1)(a)
Article 2(1)(3)	Article 2(1)(b)
Article 2(1)(4)	Article 2(1)(c)
Article 2(1)(5)	Article 2(1)(d)
Article 2(1)(6)	Article 2(1)(e)
Article 2(1)(7)	Article 2(1)(f)
Article 2(1)(8)	Article 2(1)(g)
Article 2(1)(9)	Article 2(1)(h)
Article 2(1)(10)	Article 2(1)(i)
Article 2(1)(11)	Article 2(1)(j)
Article 2(1)(12)	Articlo 2(1)(k)
Article 2(1)(13)	Article 2(1)(l)
Article 2(1)(14)	—
Article 2(1)(15)	Article 2(1)(m)
Article 2(1)(16)	Article 2(1)(n)
Article 2(1)(17)	—
Article 2(1)(18)	Article 2(1)(p)
Article 2(1)(19)	Article 2(1)(q)
Article 2(2)	Article 2(2)
Article 3(1)	—
Article 3(2)	Article 4(1)
Article 3(3)	Article 4(2)
Article 3(4)	Article 4(3)
Article 3(5)	Article 4(4)
Article 3(6)	Article 5
Article 3(7)	Article 6
Article 4	—
Article 5(1)	Article 7(1)
Article 5(2)	Article 7(2)
Article 5(3)	Up to 31 December 2014: Article 7(3) From 1 January 2015: Article 7(4)
Article 5(4)	Article 7(5)
Article 6	Article 8
Article 7	Article 9
Article 8	Article 10
Article 9	Article 11
Article 10	Article 12
Article 11	Article 28
Article 12	Article 29
Article 13	Article 30
Article 14	Article 25
Article 15	Article 26
Article 16	Article 27

Regulation (EC) No 1798/2003	This Regulation
Article 17 first subparagraph	Article 13(1)
Article 17 second subparagraph	Article 14(2)
Article 18	First subparagraph of Article 14(1)
Article 19	—
Article 20	—
Article 21	Second subparagraph of Article 14(1)
First subparagraph of Article 22(1)	Article 17(1)(a)
Second subparagraph of Article 22(1)	Article 18
Article 22(2)	Article 19
First paragraph of Article 23	Article 21(2)(a) and (b)
Second paragraph of Article 23	Second subparagraph of Article 21(2)
First paragraph of Article 24, point (1)	Article 21(2)(c)
First paragraph of Article 24, point (2)	Article 21(2)(d)
Second paragraph of Article 24	Second subparagraph of Article 21(2)
Article 25(1)	Article 20(1)
Article 25(2)	Article 20(2)
Article 25(3)	—
Article 26	Article 24 first subparagraph
Article 27(1)	Article 17(1)(b)
Article 27(2)	Article 17(1)(b) and Article 21(1)
Article 27(3)	Article 17(1)(b) and Article 21(1)
Article 27(4)	Article 31
Article 27(5)	Article 24
Article 28	Up to 31 December 2014: Article 38 From 1 January 2015: Article 43
Article 29	Up to 31 December 2014: Article 39 From 1 January 2015: Article 44
Article 30	Up to 31 December 2014: Article 40 From 1 January 2015: Article 45
Article 31	Article 17(1)(d)
Article 32	Up to 31 December 2014: Article 41 From 1 January 2015: Article 46
Article 33	Up to 31 December 2014: Article 42 From 1 January 2015: Article 47
Article 34	—
Article 34a	Article 48
Article 35	Article 49
Article 36	Article 50
Article 37	Article 51(1)
Article 38	Article 52
Article 39	Article 53
Article 40	Article 54
Article 41	Article 55
Article 42	Article 56
Article 43	Article 57
Article 44	Article 58
Article 45	Article 59
Article 46	Article 60
Article 47	Article 61
Article 48	Article 62

COUNCIL IMPLEMENTING REGULATION 282/2011/EU OF 15 MARCH 2011 LAYING DOWN IMPLEMENTING MEASURES FOR DIRECTIVE 2006/112/EC ON THE COMMON SYSTEM OF VALUE ADDED TAX

(recast)

THE COUNCIL OF THE EUROPEAN UNION,

Having regard to the Treaty on the Functioning of the European Union,

Having regard to Council Directive 2006/112/EC of 28 November 2006 on the common system of value added tax [1], and in particular Article 397 thereof,

Having regard to the proposal from the European Commission,

Whereas:

(1) A number of substantial changes are to be made to Council Regulation (EC) No 1777/2005 of 17 October 2005 laying down implementing measures for Directive 77/388/EEC on the common system of value added tax [2]. It is desirable, for reasons of clarity and rationalisation, that the provisions in question should be recast.

(2) Directive 2006/112/EC contains rules on value added tax (VAT) which, in some cases, are subject to interpretation by the Member States. The adoption of common provisions implementing Directive 2006/112/EC should ensure that application of the VAT system complies more fully with the objective of the internal market, in cases where divergences in application have arisen or may arise which are incompatible with the proper functioning of such internal market. These implementing measures are legally binding only from the date of the entry into force of this Regulation and are without prejudice to the validity of the legislation and interpretation previously adopted by the Member States.

(3) Changes resulting from the adoption of Council Directive 2008/8/EC of 12 February 2008 amending Directive 2006/112/EC as regards the place of supply of services [3] should be reflected in this Regulation.

(4) The objective of this Regulation is to ensure uniform application of the current VAT system by laying down rules implementing Directive 2006/112/EC, in particular in respect of taxable persons, the supply of goods and services, and the place of taxable transactions. In accordance with the principle of proportionality as set out in Article 5(4) of the Treaty on European Union, this Regulation does not go beyond what is necessary in order to achieve this objective. Since it is binding and directly applicable in all Member States, uniformity of application will be best ensured by a Regulation.

(5) These implementing provisions contain specific rules in response to selective questions of application and are designed to bring uniform treatment throughout the Union to those specific circumstances only. They are therefore not conclusive for other cases and, in view of their formulation, are to be applied restrictively.

(6) If a non-taxable person changes residence and transfers a new means of transport, or a new means of transport returns to the Member State from which it was originally supplied exempt of VAT to the non-taxable person returning it, it should be clarified that such a transfer does not constitute the intra-Community acquisition of a new means of transport.

(7) For certain services, it is sufficient for the supplier to demonstrate that the customer for these services, whether or not a taxable person, is located outside the Community for the supply of those services to fall outside the scope of VAT.

(8) It should be specified that the allocation of a VAT identification number to a taxable person who makes or receives a supply of services to or from another Member State, and for which the VAT is payable solely by the customer, does not affect the right of that taxable person to benefit from non-taxation of his intra- Community acquisitions of goods. However, if the taxable person communicates his VAT identification number to the supplier in respect of an intra- Community acquisition of goods, he is in any event deemed to have opted to make those transactions subject to VAT.

(9) The further integration of the internal market has led to an increased need for cooperation by economic operators established in different Member States across internal borders and the development of European economic interest groupings (EEIGs), constituted in accordance with Council Regulation (EEC) No 2137/85 of 25 July 1985 on the European Economic Interest Grouping (EEIG) [4]. It should therefore be clarified that EEIGs are taxable persons where they supply goods or services for consideration.

(10) It is necessary to clearly define restaurant and catering services, the distinction between the two, and the appropriate treatment of these services.

(11) In order to enhance clarity, the transactions identified as electronically supplied services should be listed without the lists being definitive or exhaustive.

(12) It is necessary, on the one hand, to establish that a transaction which consists solely of assembling the various parts of a machine provided by a customer must be considered as a supply of services, and, on the other hand, to establish the place of such supply when the service is supplied to a non-taxable person.

(13) The sale of an option as a financial instrument should be treated as a supply of services separate from the underlying transactions to which the option relates.

(14) To ensure the uniform application of rules relating to the place of taxable transactions, concepts such as the place where a taxable person has established his business, fixed establishment, permanent address and the place where a person usually resides should be clarified. While taking into account the case law of the Court of Justice, the use of criteria which are as clear and objective as possible should facilitate the practical application of these concepts.

(15) Rules should be established to ensure the uniform treatment of supplies of goods once a supplier has exceeded the distance selling threshold for supplies to another Member State.

(16) It should be clarified that the journey of the means of transport determines the section of a passenger transport operation effected within the Community, and not the journey of the passengers within it.

(17) In the case of intra-Community acquisition of goods, the right of the Member State of acquisition to tax the acquisition should remain unaffected by the VAT treatment of the transaction in the Member States of departure.

(18) The correct application of the rules governing the place of supply of services relies mainly on the status of the customer as a taxable or non-taxable person, and on the capacity in which he is acting. In order to determine the customer's status as a taxable person, it is necessary to establish what the supplier should be required to obtain as evidence from his customer.

(19) It should be clarified that when services supplied to a taxable person are intended for private use, including use by the customer's staff, that taxable person cannot be deemed to be acting in his capacity as a taxable person. Communication by the customer of his VAT identification number to the supplier is sufficient to establish that the customer is acting in his capacity as a taxable person, unless the supplier has information to the contrary. It should also be ensured that a single service acquired for the business but also used for private purposes is only taxed in one place.

(20) In order to determine the customer's place of establishment precisely, the supplier of the service is required to verify the information provided by the customer.

(21) Without prejudice to the general rule on the place of supply of services to a taxable person, where services are supplied to a customer established in more than one place, there should be rules to help the supplier determine the customer's fixed establishment to which the service is provided, taking account of the circumstances. If the supplier of the services is not able to determine that place, there should be rules to clarify the supplier's obligations. Those rules should not interfere with or change the customer's obligations.

(22) The time at which the supplier of the service must determine the status, the capacity and the location of the customer, whether a taxable person or not, should also be specified.

(23) Without prejudice to the general application of the principle with respect to abusive practices to the provisions of this Regulation, it is appropriate to draw specific attention to its application to certain provisions of this Regulation.

(24) Certain specific services such as the assignment of television broadcasting rights in respect of football matches, the translation of texts, services for claiming VAT refunds, and services as an intermediary to a non- taxable person involve cross-border scenarios or even the participation of economic operators established outside the Community. The place of supply of these services needs to be clearly determined in order to create greater legal certainty.

(25) It should be specified that services supplied by an intermediary acting in the name and on behalf of another person who takes part in the provision of accommodation in the hotel sector are not governed by the specific rule for the supply of services connected with immovable property.

(26) Where various services supplied in the framework of organising a funeral form part of a single service, the rule on the place of supply should also be determined.

(27) In order to ensure uniform treatment of supplies of cultural, artistic, sporting, scientific, educational, entertainment and similar services, admission to such events and ancillary services which are related to admission need to be defined.

(28) It is necessary to clarify the treatment of restaurant services and catering services supplied on board a means of transport when passenger transport is being carried out on the territory of several countries.

(29) Given that particular rules for the hiring of a means of transport depend on the duration of its possession or use, it is necessary not only to establish which vehicles should be

considered means of transport, but also to clarify the treatment of such a supply where one successive contract follows another. It is also necessary to determine the place where a means of transport is actually put at the disposal of the customer.

(30) In certain specific circumstances a credit or debit card handling fee which is paid in connection with a transaction should not reduce the taxable amount for that transaction.

(31) It is necessary to clarify that the reduced rate may be applied to the hiring out of tents, caravans and mobile homes installed on camping sites and used as accommodation.

(32) Vocational training or retraining should include instruction relating directly to a trade or profession as well as any instruction aimed at acquiring or updating knowledge for vocational purposes, regardless of the duration of a course.

(33) Platinum nobles should be treated as being excluded from the exemptions for currency, bank notes and coins.

(34) It should be specified that the exemption of the supply of services relating to the importation of goods the value of which is included in the taxable amount of those goods should cover transport services carried out during a change of residence.

(35) Goods transported outside the Community by the purchaser thereof and used for the equipping, fuelling or provisioning of means of transport used for non- business purposes by persons other than natural persons, such as bodies governed by public law and associations, should be excluded from the exemption for export transactions.

(36) To guarantee uniform administrative practices for the calculation of the minimum value for exemption on exportation of goods carried in the personal luggage of travellers, the provisions on such calculations should be harmonised.

(37) It should be specified that the exemption for certain transactions treated as exports should also apply to services covered by the special scheme for electronically supplied services.

(38) A body to be set up under the legal framework for a European Research Infrastructure Consortium (ERIC) should only qualify as an international body for the purposes of exemption from VAT where it fulfils certain conditions. The features necessary for it to benefit from exemption should therefore be identified.

(39) Supplies of goods and services under diplomatic and consular arrangements, or to recognised international bodies, or to certain armed forces are exempt from VAT subject to certain limits and conditions. In order that a taxable person making such a supply from another Member State can establish that the conditions and limits for this exemption are met, an exemption certificate should be established.

(40) Electronic import documents should also be admitted to exercise the right to deduct, where they fulfil the same requirements as paper-based documents.

(41) Where a supplier of goods or services has a fixed establishment within the territory of the Member State where the tax is due, the circumstances under which that establishment should be liable for payment of VAT should be specified.

(42) It should be clarified that a taxable person who has established his business within the territory of the Member State where the tax is due must be deemed to be a taxable person established in that Member State for the purposes of liability for the tax, even when that place of business is not involved in the supply of goods or services.

(43) It should be clarified that every taxable person is required to communicate his VAT identification number, as soon as he has one, for certain taxable transactions in order to ensure fairer collection of the tax.

(44) Weights for investment gold which are definitely accepted by the bullion market should be named and a common date for establishing the value of gold coins be determined to ensure equal treatment of economic operators.

(45) The special scheme for taxable persons not established in the Community, supplying services electronically to non- taxable persons established or resident within the Community, is subject to certain conditions. Where those conditions are no longer fulfilled, the consequences thereof should, in particular, be made clear.

(46) Certain changes result from Directive 2008/8/EC. Since those changes concern, on the one hand, the taxation of the long-term hiring of means of transport as from 1 January 2013 and, on the other, the taxation of electronically supplied services as from 1 January 2015, it should be specified that the corresponding Articles of this Regulation apply only as from those dates,

[1] OJ L 347, 11.12.2006, p. 1.
[2] OJ L 288, 29.10.2005, p. 1.
[3] OJ L 44, 20.2.2008, p. 11.
[4] OJ L 199, 31.7.1985, p. 1.

HAS ADOPTED THIS REGULATION:

CHAPTER I
SUBJECT MATTER

Article 1

This Regulation lays down measures for the implementation of certain provisions of Titles I to V, and VII to XII of Directive 2006/112/EC.

CHAPTER II
SCOPE
(TITLE I OF DIRECTIVE 2006/112/EC)

Article 2

The following shall not result in intra-Community acquisitions within the meaning of point (b) of Article 2(1) of Directive 2006/112/EC:

(a) the transfer of a new means of transport by a non-taxable person upon change of residence provided that the exemption provided for in point (a) of Article 138(2) of Directive 2006/112/EC could not apply at the time of supply;

(b) the return of a new means of transport by a non-taxable person to the Member State from which it was initially supplied to him under the exemption provided for in point (a) of Article 138(2) of Directive 2006/112/EC.

Article 3

Without prejudice to point (b) of the first paragraph of Article 59a of Directive 2006/112/EC, the supply of the following services is not subject to VAT if the supplier demonstrates that the place of supply determined in accordance with Subsections 3 and 4 of Section 4 of Chapter V of this Regulation is outside the Community:

(a) from 1 January 2013, the service referred to in the first subparagraph of Article 56(2) of Directive 2006/112/EC;

(b) from 1 January 2015, the services listed in Article 58 of Directive 2006/112/EC;

(c) the services listed in Article 59 of Directive 2006/112/EC.

Article 4

A taxable person who is entitled to non-taxation of his intra- Community acquisitions of goods, in accordance with Article 3 of Directive 2006/112/EC, shall remain so where, pursuant to Article 214(1)(d) or (e) of that Directive, a VAT identification number has been attributed to that taxable person for the services received for which he is liable to pay VAT or for the services supplied by him within the territory of another Member State for which VAT is payable solely by the recipient. However, if that taxable person communicates this VAT identification number to a supplier in respect of an intra-Community acquisition of goods, he shall be deemed to have exercised the option provided for in Article 3(3) of that Directive.

VAT EC

CHAPTER III
TAXABLE PERSONS
(TITLE III OF DIRECTIVE 2006/112/EC)

Article 5

A European Economic Interest Grouping (EEIG) constituted in accordance with Regulation (EEC) No 2137/85 which supplies goods or services for consideration to its members or to third parties shall be a taxable person within the meaning of Article 9(1) of Directive 2006/112/EC.

CHAPTER IV
TAXABLE TRANSACTIONS
(ARTICLES 24 TO 29 OF DIRECTIVE 2006/112/EC)

Article 6

1. Restaurant and catering services mean services consisting of the supply of prepared or unprepared food or beverages or both, for human consumption, accompanied by sufficient support services allowing for the immediate consumption thereof. The provision of food or beverages or both is only one component of the whole in which services shall predominate. Restaurant services are the supply of such services on the premises of the supplier, and catering services are the supply of such services off the premises of the supplier.

2. The supply of prepared or unprepared food or beverages or both, whether or not including transport but without any other support services, shall not be considered restaurant or catering services within the meaning of paragraph 1.

[Article 6a

1. Telecommunications services within the meaning of Article 24(2) of Directive 2006/112/EC shall cover, in particular, the following:

(a) fixed and mobile telephone services for the transmission and switching of voice, data and video, including telephone services with an imaging component (videophone services);
(b) telephone services provided through the internet, including voice over internet Protocol (VoIP);
(c) voice mail, call waiting, call forwarding, caller identification, three-way calling and other call management services;
(d) paging services;
(e) audiotext services;
(f) facsimile, telegraph and telex;
(g) access to the internet, including the World Wide Web;
(h) private network connections providing telecommunications links for the exclusive use of the client.

2. Telecommunications services within the meaning of Article 24(2) of Directive 2006/112/EC shall not cover the following:
(a) electronically supplied services;
(b) radio and television broadcasting (hereinafter "broadcasting") services.][1]

Amendments—[1] Articles 6a, 6b inserted by Council Implementing Regulations 1042/2013/EU art 1(1)(a) with effect from 1 January 2015 (OJ L 284, 26.10.2013, p 1).

[Article 6b

1. Broadcasting services shall include services consisting of audio and audiovisual content, such as radio or television programmes which are provided to the general public via communications networks by and under the editorial responsibility of a media service provider, for simultaneous listening or viewing, on the basis of a programme schedule.

2. Paragraph 1 shall cover, in particular, the following:
(a) radio or television programmes transmitted or retransmitted over a radio or television network;
(b) radio or television programmes distributed via the internet or similar electronic network (IP streaming), if they are broadcast simultaneous to their being transmitted or retransmitted over a radio or television network.

3. Paragraph 1 shall not cover the following:
(a) telecommunications services;
(b) electronically supplied services;
(c) the provision of information about particular programmes on demand;
(d) the transfer of broadcasting or transmission rights;
(e) the leasing of technical equipment or facilities for use to receive a broadcast;
(f) radio or television programmes distributed via the internet or similar electronic network (IP streaming), unless they are broadcast simultaneous to their being transmitted or retransmitted over a radio or television network.][1]

Amendments—[1] Articles 6a, 6b inserted by Council Implementing Regulations 1042/2013/EU art 1(1)(a) with effect from 1 January 2015 (OJ L 284, 26.10.2013, p 1).

Article 7

1. 'Electronically supplied services' as referred to in Directive 2006/112/EC shall include services which are delivered over the Internet or an electronic network and the nature of which renders their supply essentially automated and involving minimal human intervention, and impossible to ensure in the absence of information technology.

2. Paragraph 1 shall cover, in particular, the following:
(a) the supply of digitised products generally, including software and changes to or upgrades of software;
(b) services providing or supporting a business or personal presence on an electronic network such as a website or a webpage;
(c) services automatically generated from a computer via the Internet or an electronic network, in response to specific data input by the recipient;
(d) the transfer for consideration of the right to put goods or services up for sale on an Internet site operating as an online market on which potential buyers make their bids by an automated procedure and on which the parties are notified of a sale by electronic mail automatically generated from a computer;
(e) Internet Service Packages (ISP) of information in which the telecommunications component forms an ancillary and subordinate part (i.e. packages going beyond mere Internet access and including other elements such as content pages giving access to news, weather or travel reports; playgrounds; website hosting; access to online debates etc.);
(f) the services listed in Annex I.

3. [Paragraph 1 shall not cover the following:][1]
[(a) broadcasting services;][1]
(b) telecommunications services;
(c) goods, where the order and processing is done electronically;

(d) CD-ROMs, floppy disks and similar tangible media;
(e) printed matter, such as books, newsletters, newspapers or journals;
(f) CDs and audio cassettes;
(g) video cassettes and DVDs;
(h) games on a CD-ROM;
(i) services of professionals such as lawyers and financial consultants, who advise clients by e-mail;
(j) teaching services, where the course content is delivered by a teacher over the Internet or an electronic network (namely via a remote link);
(k) offline physical repair services of computer equipment;
(l) offline data warehousing services;
(m) advertising services, in particular as in newspapers, on posters and on television;
(n) telephone helpdesk services;
(o) teaching services purely involving correspondence courses, such as postal courses;
(p) conventional auctioneers' services reliant on direct human intervention, irrespective of how bids are made;
(q) . . .[1]
(r) . . .[1]
(s) . . .[1]
[(t) tickets to cultural, artistic, sporting, scientific, educational, entertainment or similar events booked online;
(u) accommodation, car-hire, restaurant services, passenger transport or similar services booked online.][1]

Amendments—[1] In para 3, words substituted for words "Paragraph 1 shall not, in particular, cover the following:", sub-para (a) substituted, sub-paras (q), (r), (s) repealed, and sub-paras (t), (u) inserted, by Council Implementing Regulations 1042/2013/EU art 1(1)(b) with effect from 1 January 2015 (OJ L 284, 26.10.2013, p 1).

Article 8

If a taxable person only assembles the various parts of a machine all of which were provided to him by his customer, that transaction shall be a supply of services within the meaning of Article 24(1) of Directive 2006/112/EC.

Article 9

The sale of an option, where such a sale is a transaction falling within the scope of point (f) of Article 135(1) of Directive 2006/112/EC, shall be a supply of services within the meaning of Article 24(1) of that Directive. That supply of services shall be distinct from the underlying transactions to which the services relate.

[Article 9a

1. For the application of Article 28 of Directive 2006/112/EC, where electronically supplied services are supplied through a telecommunications network, an interface or a portal such as a marketplace for applications, a taxable person taking part in that supply shall be presumed to be acting in his own name but on behalf of the provider of those services unless that provider is explicitly indicated as the supplier by that taxable person and that is reflected in the contractual arrangements between the parties.

In order to regard the provider of electronically supplied services as being explicitly indicated as the supplier of those services by the taxable person, the following conditions shall be met:

(a) the invoice issued or made available by each taxable person taking part in the supply of the electronically supplied services must identify such services and the supplier thereof;
(b) the bill or receipt issued or made available to the customer must identify the electronically supplied services and the supplier thereof.

For the purposes of this paragraph, a taxable person who, with regard to a supply of electronically supplied services, authorises the charge to the customer or the delivery of the services, or sets the general terms and conditions of the supply, shall not be permitted to explicitly indicate another person as the supplier of those services.

2. Paragraph 1 shall also apply where telephone services provided through the internet, including voice over internet Protocol (VoIP), are supplied through a telecommunications network, an interface or a portal such as a marketplace for applications and are supplied under the same conditions as set out in that paragraph.

3. This Article shall not apply to a taxable person who only provides for processing of payments in respect of electronically supplied services or of telephone services provided through the internet, including voice over internet Protocol (VoIP), and who does not take part in the supply of those electronically supplied services or telephone services.][1]

Amendments—[1] Article 9a inserted by Council Implementing Regulations 1042/2013/EU art 1(1)(c) with effect from 1 January 2015 (OJ L 284, 26.10.2013, p 1).

VAT EC

CHAPTER V
PLACE OF TAXABLE TRANSACTIONS

SECTION 1
CONCEPTS

Article 10

1. For the application of Articles 44 and 45 of Directive 2006/112/EC, the place where the business of a taxable person is established shall be the place where the functions of the business's central administration are carried out.

2. In order to determine the place referred to in paragraph 1, account shall be taken of the place where essential decisions concerning the general management of the business are taken, the place where the registered office of the business is located and the place where management meets.

Where these criteria do not allow the place of establishment of a business to be determined with certainty, the place where essential decisions concerning the general management of the business are taken shall take precedence.

3. The mere presence of a postal address may not be taken to be the place of establishment of a business of a taxable person.

Article 11

1. For the application of Article 44 of Directive 2006/112/EC, a 'fixed establishment' shall be any establishment, other than the place of establishment of a business referred to in Article 10 of this Regulation, characterised by a sufficient degree of permanence and a suitable structure in terms of human and technical resources to enable it to receive and use the services supplied to it for its own needs.

2. For the application of the following Articles, a 'fixed establishment' shall be any establishment, other than the place of establishment of a business referred to in Article 10 of this Regulation, characterised by a sufficient degree of permanence and a suitable structure in terms of human and technical resources to enable it to provide the services which it supplies:

(a) Article 45 of Directive 2006/112/EC;
(b) from 1 January 2013, the second subparagraph of Article 56(2) of Directive 2006/112/EC;
(c) until 31 December 2014, Article 58 of Directive 2006/112/EC;
(d) Article 192a of Directive 2006/112/EC.

3. The fact of having a VAT identification number shall not in itself be sufficient to consider that a taxable person has a fixed establishment.

Article 12

For the application of Directive 2006/112/EC, the 'permanent address' of a natural person, whether or not a taxable person, shall be the address entered in the population or similar register, or the address indicated by that person to the relevant tax authorities, unless there is evidence that this address does not reflect reality.

Article 13

The place where a natural person 'usually resides', whether or not a taxable person, as referred to in Directive 2006/112/EC shall be the place where that natural person usually lives as a result of personal and occupational ties.

Where the occupational ties are in a country different from that of the personal ties, or where no occupational ties exist, the place of usual residence shall be determined by personal ties which show close links between the natural person and a place where he is living.

[Article 13a

The place where a non-taxable legal person is established, as referred to in the first subparagraph of Article 56(2) and Articles 58 and 59 of Directive 2006/112/EC, shall be:

(a) the place where the functions of its central administration are carried out; or
(b) the place of any other establishment characterised by a sufficient degree of permanence and a suitable structure in terms of human and technical resources to enable it to receive and use the services supplied to it for its own needs.][1]

Amendments—[1] Article 13a inserted by Council Implementing Regulations 1042/2013/EU art 1(2)(a) with effect from 1 January 2015 (OJ L 284, 26.10.2013, p 1).

[Article 13b

For the application of Directive 2006/112/EC, the following shall be regarded as "immovable property":

(a) any specific part of the earth, on or below its surface, over which title and possession can be created;
(b) any building or construction fixed to or in the ground above or below sea level which cannot be easily dismantled or moved;

(c) any item that has been installed and makes up an integral part of a building or construction without which the building or construction is incomplete, such as doors, windows, roofs, staircases and lifts;

(d) any item, equipment or machine permanently installed in a building or construction which cannot be moved without destroying or altering the building or construction.]

Prospective amendments—Article 13b to be inserted by Council Implementing Regulations 1042/2013/EU art 1(2)(a) with effect from 1 January 2017 (OJ L 284, 26.10.2013, p 1).

SECTION 2

PLACE OF SUPPLY OF GOODS

(ARTICLES 31 TO 39 OF DIRECTIVE 2006/112/EC)

Article 14

Where in the course of a calendar year the threshold applied by a Member State in accordance with Article 34 of Directive 2006/112/EC is exceeded, Article 33 of that Directive shall not modify the place of supplies of goods other than products subject to excise duty carried out in the course of the same calendar year which are made before the threshold applied by the Member State for the calendar year then current is exceeded provided that all of the following conditions are met:

(a) the supplier has not exercised the option provided for under Article 34(4) of that Directive;

(b) the value of his supplies of goods did not exceed the threshold in the course of the preceding calendar year.

However, Article 33 of Directive 2006/112/EC shall modify the place of the following supplies to the Member State in which the dispatch or transport ends:

(a) the supply of goods by which the threshold applied by the Member State for the calendar year then current was exceeded in the course of the same calendar year;

(b) any subsequent supplies of goods within that Member State in that calendar year;

(c) supplies of goods within that Member State in the calendar year following the calendar year in which the event referred to in point (a) occurred.

Article 15

The section of a passenger transport operation effected within the Community referred to in Article 37 of Directive 2006/112/EC, shall be determined by the journey of the means of transport and not by the journey completed by each of the passengers.

SECTION 3

PLACE OF INTRA-COMMUNITY ACQUISITIONS OF GOODS

(ARTICLES 40, 41 AND 42 OF DIRECTIVE 2006/112/EC)

Article 16

Where an intra-Community acquisition of goods within the meaning of Article 20 of Directive 2006/112/EC has taken place, the Member State in which the dispatch or transport ends shall exercise its power of taxation irrespective of the VAT treatment applied to the transaction in the Member State in which the dispatch or transport began.

Any request by a supplier of goods for a correction in the VAT invoiced by him and reported by him to the Member State where the dispatch or transport of the goods began shall be treated by that Member State in accordance with its own domestic rules.

SECTION 4

PLACE OF SUPPLY OF SERVICES

(ARTICLES 43 TO 59 OF DIRECTIVE 2006/112/EC)

SUBSECTION 1

STATUS OF THE CUSTOMER

Article 17

1. If the place of supply of services depends on whether the customer is a taxable or non-taxable person, the status of the customer shall be determined on the basis of Articles 9 to 13 and Article 43 of Directive 2006/112/EC.

2. A non-taxable legal person who is identified or required to be identified for VAT purposes under point (b) of Article 214(1) of Directive 2006/112/EC because his intra-Community acquisitions of goods are subject to VAT or because he has exercised the option of making those operations subject to VAT shall be a taxable person within the meaning of Article 43 of that Directive.

Article 18

1. Unless he has information to the contrary, the supplier may regard a customer established within the Community as a taxable person:

(a) where the customer has communicated his individual VAT identification number to him, and the supplier obtains confirmation of the validity of that identification number and of the associated name and address in accordance with Article 31 of Council Regulation (EC) No 904/2010 of 7 October 2010 on administrative cooperation and combating fraud in the field of value added tax [a];

(b) where the customer has not yet received an individual VAT identification number, but informs the supplier that he has applied for it and the supplier obtains any other proof which demonstrates that the customer is a taxable person or a non-taxable legal person required to be identified for VAT purposes and carries out a reasonable level of verification of the accuracy of the information provided by the customer, by normal commercial security measures such as those relating to identity or payment checks.

2. Unless he has information to the contrary, the supplier may regard a customer established within the Community as a non-taxable person when he can demonstrate that the customer has not communicated his individual VAT identification number to him.

[However, irrespective of information to the contrary, the supplier of telecommunications, broadcasting or electronically supplied services may regard a customer established within the Community as a non-taxable person as long as that customer has not communicated his individual VAT identification number to him.][1]

3. Unless he has information to the contrary, the supplier may regard a customer established outside the Community as a taxable person:

(a) if he obtains from the customer a certificate issued by the customer's competent tax authorities as confirmation that the customer is engaged in economic activities in order to enable him to obtain a refund of VAT under Council Directive 86/560/EEC of 17 November 1986 on the harmonization of the laws of the Member States relating to turnover taxes – Arrangements for the refund of value added tax to taxable persons not established in Community territory [b];

(b) where the customer does not possess that certificate, if the supplier has the VAT number, or a similar number attributed to the customer by the country of establishment and used to identify businesses or any other proof which demonstrates that the customer is a taxable person and if the supplier carries out a reasonable level of verification of the accuracy of the information provided by the customer, by normal commercial security measures such as those relating to identity or payment checks.

[a] OJ L 268, 12.10.2010, p. 1.

[b] OJ L 326, 21.11.1986, p. 40.

Amendments—[1] Words in para 2 inserted by Council Implementing Regulations 1042/2013/EU art 1(2)(b) with effect from 1 January 2015 (OJ L 284, 26.10.2013, p 1).

SUBSECTION 2

CAPACITY OF THE CUSTOMER

Article 19

For the purpose of applying the rules concerning the place of supply of services laid down in Articles 44 and 45 of Directive 2006/112/EC, a taxable person, or a non-taxable legal person deemed to be a taxable person, who receives services exclusively for private use, including use by his staff, shall be regarded as a non-taxable person.

Unless he has information to the contrary, such as information on the nature of the services provided, the supplier may consider that the services are for the customer's business use if, for that transaction, the customer has communicated his individual VAT identification number.

Where one and the same service is intended for both private use, including use by the customer's staff, and business use, the supply of that service shall be covered exclusively by Article 44 of Directive 2006/112/EC, provided there is no abusive practice.

SUBSECTION 3

LOCATION OF THE CUSTOMER

Article 20

Where a supply of services carried out for a taxable person, or a non-taxable legal person deemed to be a taxable person, falls within the scope of Article 44 of Directive 2006/112/EC, and where that taxable person is established in a single country, or, in the absence of a place of establishment of a business or a fixed establishment, has his permanent address and usually resides in a single country, that supply of services shall be taxable in that country.

The supplier shall establish that place based on information from the customer, and verify that information by normal commercial security measures such as those relating to identity or payment checks.

The information may include the VAT identification number attributed by the Member State where the customer is established.

Article 21

Where a supply of services to a taxable person, or a non-taxable legal person deemed to be a taxable person, falls within the scope of Article 44 of Directive 2006/112/EC, and the taxable person is established in more than one country, that supply shall be taxable in the country where that taxable person has established his business.

However, where the service is provided to a fixed establishment of the taxable person located in a place other than that where the customer has established his business, that supply shall be taxable at the place of the fixed establishment receiving that service and using it for its own needs.

Where the taxable person does not have a place of establishment of a business or a fixed establishment, the supply shall be taxable at his permanent address or usual residence.

Article 22

1. In order to identify the customer's fixed establishment to which the service is provided, the supplier shall examine the nature and use of the service provided.

Where the nature and use of the service provided do not enable him to identify the fixed establishment to which the service is provided, the supplier, in identifying that fixed establishment, shall pay particular attention to whether the contract, the order form and the VAT identification number attributed by the Member State of the customer and communicated to him by the customer identify the fixed establishment as the customer of the service and whether the fixed establishment is the entity paying for the service.

Where the customer's fixed establishment to which the service is provided cannot be determined in accordance with the first and second subparagraphs of this paragraph or where services covered by Article 44 of Directive 2006/112/EC are supplied to a taxable person under a contract covering one or more services used in an unidentifiable and non-quantifiable manner, the supplier may legitimately consider that the services have been supplied at the place where the customer has established his business.

2. The application of this Article shall be without prejudice to the customer's obligations.

Article 23

1. From 1 January 2013, where, in accordance with the first subparagraph of Article 56(2) of Directive 2006/112/EC, a supply of services is taxable at the place where the customer is established, or, in the absence of an establishment, where he has his permanent address or usually resides, the supplier shall establish that place based on factual information provided by the customer, and verify that information by normal commercial security measures such as those relating to identity or payment checks.

2. Where, in accordance with Articles 58 and 59 of Directive 2006/112/EC, a supply of services is taxable at the place where the customer is established, or, in the absence of an establishment, where he has his permanent address or usually resides, the supplier shall establish that place based on factual information provided by the customer, and verify that information by normal commercial security measures such as those relating to identity or payment checks.

[Article 24

Where services covered by the first subparagraph of Article 56(2) or Articles 58 and 59 of Directive 2006/112/EC are supplied to a non-taxable person who is established in more than one country or who has his permanent address in one country and his usual residence in another, priority shall be given:

(a) in the case of a non-taxable legal person, to the place referred to in point (a) of Article 13a of this Regulation, unless there is evidence that the service is used at the establishment referred to in point (b) of that article;

(b) in the case of a natural person, to the place where he usually resides, unless there is evidence that the service is used at his permanent address.][1]

Amendments—[1] Article 24 substituted by Council Implementing Regulations 1042/2013/EU art 1(2)(c) with effect from 1 January 2015 (OJ L 284, 26.10.2013, p 1).

[SUBSECTION 3A

PRESUMPTIONS FOR THE LOCATION OF THE CUSTOMER

Article 24a

1. For the application of Articles 44, 58 and 59a of Directive 2006/112/EC, where a supplier of telecommunications, broadcasting or electronically supplied services provides those services at a location such as a telephone box, a telephone kiosk, a wi-fi hot spot, an internet café, a restaurant or a hotel lobby where the physical presence of the recipient of the service at that location is needed for the service to be provided to him by that supplier, it shall be presumed that the customer is established, has his permanent address or usually resides at the place of that location and that the service is effectively used and enjoyed there.

2. If the location referred to in paragraph 1 of this Article is on board a ship, aircraft or train carrying out a passenger transport operation effected within the Community pursuant to Articles 37 and 57 of Directive 2006/112/EC, the country of the location shall be the country of departure of the passenger transport operation.][1]

Amendments—[1] Subsections 3a–3c inserted by Council Implementing Regulations 1042/2013/EU art 1(2)(d)(i) with effect from 1 January 2015 (OJ L 284, 26.10.2013, p 1).

[Article 24b

For the application of Article 58 of Directive 2006/112/EC, where telecommunications, broadcasting or electronically supplied services are supplied to a non-taxable person:

(a) through his fixed land line, it shall be presumed that the customer is established, has his permanent address or usually resides at the place of installation of the fixed land line;

(b) through mobile networks, it shall be presumed that the place where the customer is established, has his permanent address or usually resides is the country identified by the mobile country code of the SIM card used when receiving those services;

(c) for which the use of a decoder or similar device or a viewing card is needed and a fixed land line is not used, it shall be presumed that the customer is established, has his permanent address or usually resides at the place where that decoder or similar device is located, or if that place is not known, at the place to which the viewing card is sent with a view to being used there;

(d) under circumstances other than those referred to in Article 24a and in points (a), (b) and (c) of this Article, it shall be presumed that the customer is established, has his permanent address or usually resides at the place identified as such by the supplier on the basis of two items of non-contradictory evidence as listed in Article 24f of this Regulation.][1]

Amendments—[1] Subsections 3a–3c inserted by Council Implementing Regulations 1042/2013/EU art 1(2)(d)(i) with effect from 1 January 2015 (OJ L 284, 26.10.2013, p 1).

[Article 24c

For the application of Article 56(2) of Directive 2006/112/EC, where the hiring, other than short-term hiring, of means of transport is supplied to a non-taxable person, it shall be presumed that the customer is established, has his permanent address or usually resides at the place identified as such by the supplier on the basis of two items of non- contradictory evidence as listed in Article 24e of this Regulation.][1]

Amendments—[1] Subsections 3a–3c inserted by Council Implementing Regulations 1042/2013/EU art 1(2)(d)(i) with effect from 1 January 2015 (OJ L 284, 26.10.2013, p 1).

[SUBSECTION 3B

REBUTTAL OF PRESUMPTIONS

Article 24d

1. Where a supplier supplies a service listed in Article 58 of Directive 2006/112/EC, he may rebut a presumption referred to in Article 24a or in point (a), (b) or (c) of Article 24b of this Regulation on the basis of three items of non-contradictory evidence indicating that the customer is established, has his permanent address or usually resides elsewhere.

2. A tax authority may rebut presumptions that have been made under Article 24a, 24b or 24c where there are indications of misuse or abuse by the supplier.][1]

Amendments—[1] Subsections 3a–3c inserted by Council Implementing Regulations 1042/2013/EU art 1(2)(d)(i) with effect from 1 January 2015 (OJ L 284, 26.10.2013, p 1).

[SUBSECTION 3C

EVIDENCE FOR THE IDENTIFICATION OF THE LOCATION OF THE CUSTOMER AND REBUTTAL OF PRESUMPTIONS

Article 24e

For the purposes of applying the rules in Article 56(2) of Directive 2006/112/EC and fulfilling the requirements of Article 24c of this Regulation, the following shall, in particular, serve as evidence:

(a) the billing address of the customer;

(b) bank details such as the location of the bank account used for payment or the billing address of the customer held by that bank;

(c) registration details of the means of transport hired by the customer, if registration of that means of transport is required at the place where it is used, or other similar information;

(d) other commercially relevant information.][1]

Amendments—[1] Subsections 3a–3c inserted by Council Implementing Regulations 1042/2013/EU art 1(2)(d)(i) with effect from 1 January 2015 (OJ L 284, 26.10.2013, p 1).

[Article 24f

For the purpose of applying the rules in Article 58 of Directive 2006/112/EC and fulfilling the requirements of point (d) of Article 24b or Article 24d(1) of this Regulation, the following shall, in particular, serve as evidence:

(a) the billing address of the customer;

(b) the internet Protocol (IP) address of the device used by the customer or any method of geolocation;

(c) bank details such as the location of the bank account used for payment or the billing address of the customer held by that bank;

(d) the Mobile Country Code (MCC) of the International Mobile Subscriber Identity (IMSI) stored on the Subscriber Identity Module (SIM) card used by the customer;

(e) the location of the customer's fixed land line through which the service is supplied to him;

(f) other commercially relevant information.][1]

Amendments—[1] Subsections 3a–3c inserted by Council Implementing Regulations 1042/2013/EU art 1(2)(d)(i) with effect from 1 January 2015 (OJ L 284, 26.10.2013, p 1).

SUBSECTION 4

COMMON PROVISION REGARDING DETERMINATION OF THE STATUS, THE CAPACITY AND THE LOCATION OF THE CUSTOMER

Article 25

For the application of the rules governing the place of supply of services, only the circumstances existing at the time of the chargeable event shall be taken into account. Any subsequent changes to the use of the service received shall not affect the determination of the place of supply, provided there is no abusive practice.

SUBSECTION 5

SUPPLY OF SERVICES GOVERNED BY THE GENERAL RULES

Article 26

A transaction whereby a body assigns television broadcasting rights in respect of football matches to taxable persons, shall be covered by Article 44 of Directive 2006/112/EC.

Article 27

The supply of services which consist in applying for or receiving refunds of VAT under Council Directive 2008/9/EC of 12 February 2008 laying down detailed rules for the refund of value added tax, provided for in Directive 2006/112/EC, to taxable persons not established in the Member State of refund but established in another Member State [1] shall be covered by Article 44 of Directive 2006/112/EC.

Article 28

In so far as they constitute a single service, the supply of services made in the framework of organising a funeral shall fall within the scope of Articles 44 and 45 of Directive 2006/112/EC.

Article 29

Without prejudice to Article 41 of this Regulation, the supply of services of translation of texts shall fall within the scope of Articles 44 and 45 of Directive 2006/112/EC.

[1] OJ L 44, 20.2.2008, p. 23.

SUBSECTION 6

SUPPLY OF SERVICES BY INTERMEDIARIES

Article 30

The supply of services of intermediaries as referred to in Article 46 of Directive 2006/112/EC shall cover the services of intermediaries acting in the name and on behalf of the recipient of the service procured and the services performed by intermediaries acting in the name and on behalf of the provider of the services procured.

Article 31

Services supplied by intermediaries acting in the name and on behalf of another person consisting of the intermediation in the provision of accommodation in the hotel sector or in sectors having a similar function shall fall within the scope of:

(a) Article 44 of Directive 2006/112/EC if supplied to a taxable person acting as such, or a non-taxable legal person deemed to be a taxable person;

(b) Article 46 of that Directive, if supplied to a non-taxable person.

[SUBSECTION 6A

SUPPLY OF SERVICES CONNECTED WITH IMMOVABLE PROPERTY

Article 31a

1. Services connected with immovable property, as referred to in Article 47 of Directive 2006/112/EC, shall include only those services that have a sufficiently direct connection with that property. Services shall be regarded as having a sufficiently direct connection with immovable property in the following cases:

(a) where they are derived from an immovable property and that property makes up a constituent element of the service and is central to, and essential for, the services supplied;

(b) where they are provided to, or directed towards, an immovable property, having as their object the legal or physical alteration of that property.

2. Paragraph 1 shall cover, in particular, the following:

(a) the drawing up of plans for a building or parts of a building designated for a particular plot of land regardless of whether or not the building is erected;

(b) the provision of on site supervision or security services;

(c) the construction of a building on land, as well as construction and demolition work performed on a building or parts of a building;

(d) the construction of permanent structures on land, as well as construction and demolition work performed on permanent structures such as pipeline systems for gas, water, sewerage and the like;

(e) work on land, including agricultural services such as tillage, sowing, watering and fertilisation;

(f) surveying and assessment of the risk and integrity of immovable property;

(g) the valuation of immovable property, including where such service is needed for insurance purposes, to determine the value of a property as collateral for a loan or to assess risk and damages in disputes;

(h) the leasing or letting of immovable property other than that covered by point (c) of paragraph 3, including the storage of goods for which a specific part of the property is assigned for the exclusive use of the customer;

(i) the provision of accommodation in the hotel sector or in sectors with a similar function, such as holiday camps or sites developed for use as camping sites, including the right to stay in a specific place resulting from the conversion of timeshare usage rights and the like;

(j) the assignment or transfer of rights other than those covered by points (h) and (i) to use the whole or parts of an immovable property, including the licence to use part of a property, such as the granting of fishing and hunting rights or access to lounges in airports, or the use of an infrastructure for which tolls are charged, such as a bridge or tunnel;

(k) the maintenance, renovation and repair of a building or parts of a building, including work such as cleaning, tiling, papering and parqueting;

(l) the maintenance, renovation and repair of permanent structures such as pipeline systems for gas, water, sewerage and the like;

(m) the installation or assembly of machines or equipment which, upon installation or assembly, qualify as immovable property;

(n) the maintenance and repair, inspection and supervision of machines or equipment if those machines or equipment qualify as immovable property;

(o) property management other than portfolio management of investments in real estate covered by point (g) of paragraph 3, consisting of the operation of commercial, industrial or residential real estate by or on behalf of the owner of the property;

(p) intermediation in the sale, leasing or letting of immovable property and in the establishment or transfer of certain interests in immovable property or rights in rem over immovable property (whether or not treated as tangible property), other than intermediation covered by point (d) of paragraph 3;

(q) legal services relating to the transfer of a title to immovable property, to the establishment or transfer of certain interests in immovable property or rights in rem over immovable property (whether or not treated as tangible property), such as notary work, or to the drawing up of a contract to sell or acquire immovable property, even if the underlying transaction resulting in the legal alteration of the property is not carried through.

3. Paragraph 1 shall not cover the following:

(a) the drawing up of plans for a building or parts of a building if not designated for a particular plot of land;

(b) the storage of goods in an immovable property if no specific part of the immovable property is assigned for the exclusive use of the customer;

(c) the provision of advertising, even if it involves the use of immovable property;

(d) intermediation in the provision of hotel accommodation or accommodation in sectors with a similar function, such as holiday camps or sites developed for use as camping sites, if the intermediary is acting in the name and on behalf of another person;

(e) the provision of a stand location at a fair or exhibition site together with other related services to enable the exhibitor to display items, such as the design of the stand, transport and storage of the items, the provision of machines, cable laying, insurance and advertising;
(f) the installation or assembly, the maintenance and repair, the inspection or the supervision of machines or equipment which is not, or does not become, part of the immovable property;
(g) portfolio management of investments in real estate;
(h) legal services other than those covered by point (q) of paragraph 2, connected to contracts, including advice given on the terms of a contract to transfer immovable property, or to enforce such a contract, or to prove the existence of such a contract, where such services are not specific to a transfer of a title on an immovable property.]

Prospective amendments—Articles 31a, 31b inserted by Council Implementing Regulations 1042/2013/EU art 1(2)(d)(ii) with effect from 1 January 2017 (OJ L 284, 26.10.2013, p 1).

[Article 31b

Where equipment is put at the disposal of a customer with a view to carrying out work on immovable property, that transaction shall only be a supply of services connected with immovable property if the supplier assumes responsibility for the execution of the work.

A supplier who provides the customer with equipment together with sufficient staff for its operation with a view to carrying out work shall be presumed to have assumed responsibility for the execution of that work. The presumption that the supplier has the responsibility for the execution of the work may be rebutted by any relevant means in fact or law.]

Prospective amendments—Articles 31a, 31b inserted by Council Implementing Regulations 1042/2013/EU art 1(2)(d)(ii) with effect from 1 January 2017 (OJ L 284, 26.10.2013, p 1).

[Article 31c

For the purpose of determining the place of supply of telecommunications, broadcasting or electronically supplied services provided by a taxable person acting in his own name together with accommodation in the hotel sector or in sectors with a similar function, such as holiday camps or sites developed for use as camping sites, those services shall be regarded as being supplied at those locations.][1]

Amendments—[1] Article 31c inserted by Council Implementing Regulations 1042/2013/EU art 1(2)(d)(ii) with effect from 1 January 2015 (OJ L 284, 26.10.2013, p 1).

SUBSECTION 7

SUPPLY OF CULTURAL, ARTISTIC, SPORTING, SCIENTIFIC, EDUCATIONAL, ENTERTAINMENT, AND SIMILAR SERVICES

Article 32

1. Services in respect of admission to cultural, artistic, sporting, scientific, educational, entertainment or similar events as referred to in Article 53 of Directive 2006/112/EC shall include the supply of services of which the essential characteristics are the granting of the right of admission to an event in exchange for a ticket or payment, including payment in the form of a subscription, a season ticket or a periodic fee.

2. Paragraph 1 shall apply in particular to:
(a) the right of admission to shows, theatrical performances, circus performances, fairs, amusement parks, concerts, exhibitions, and other similar cultural events;
(b) the right of admission to sporting events such as matches or competitions;
(c) the right of admission to educational and scientific events such as conferences and seminars.

3. Paragraph 1 shall not cover the use of facilities such as gymnastics halls and suchlike, in exchange for the payment of a fee.

Article 33

The ancillary services referred to in Article 53 of Directive 2006/112/EC shall include services which are directly related to admission to cultural, artistic, sporting, scientific, educational, entertainment or similar events and which are supplied separately for a consideration to a person attending an event.

Such ancillary services shall include in particular the use of cloakrooms or sanitary facilities but shall not include mere intermediary services relating to the sale of tickets.

[Article 33a

The supply of tickets granting access to a cultural, artistic, sporting, scientific, educational, entertainment or similar event by an intermediary acting in his own name but on behalf of the organiser or by a taxable person, other than the organiser, acting on his own behalf, shall be covered by Article 53 and Article 54(1) of Directive 2006/112/EC.][1]

Amendments—[1] Article 33a inserted by Council Implementing Regulations 1042/2013/EU art 1(2)(d)(iii) with effect from 1 January 2015 (OJ L 284, 26.10.2013, p 1).

SUBSECTION 8
SUPPLY OF ANCILLARY TRANSPORT SERVICES AND VALUATIONS OF AND WORK ON MOVABLE PROPERTY

Article 34

Except where the goods being assembled become part of immovable property, the place of the supply of services to a non-taxable person consisting only of the assembly by a taxable person of the various parts of a machine, all of which were provided to him by his customer, shall be established in accordance with Article 54 of Directive 2006/112/EC.

SUBSECTION 9
SUPPLY OF RESTAURANT AND CATERING SERVICES ON BOARD MEANS OF TRANSPORT

Article 35

The section of a passenger transport operation effected within the Community as referred to in Article 57 of Directive 2006/112/EC shall be determined by the journey of the means of transport and not by the journey completed by each of the passengers.

Article 36

Where restaurant services and catering services are supplied during the section of a passenger transport operation effected within the Community, that supply shall be covered by Article 57 of Directive 2006/112/EC.

Where restaurant services and catering services are supplied outside such a section but on the territory of a Member State or a third country or third territory, that supply shall be covered by Article 55 of that Directive.

Article 37

The place of supply of a restaurant service or catering service carried out within the Community partly during a section of a passenger transport operation effected within the Community, and partly outside such a section but on the territory of a Member State, shall be determined in its entirety according to the rules for determining the place of supply applicable at the beginning of the supply of the restaurant or catering service.

SUBSECTION 10
HIRING OF MEANS OF TRANSPORT

Article 38

1. 'Means of transport' as referred to in Article 56 and point (g) of the first paragraph of Article 59 of Directive 2006/112/EC shall include vehicles, whether motorised or not, and other equipment and devices designed to transport persons or objects from one place to another, which might be pulled, drawn or pushed by vehicles and which are normally designed to be used and actually capable of being used for transport.

2. The means of transport referred to in paragraph 1 shall include, in particular, the following vehicles:

(a) land vehicles, such as cars, motor cycles, bicycles, tricycles and caravans;
(b) trailers and semi-trailers;
(c) railway wagons;
(d) vessels;
(e) aircraft;
(f) vehicles specifically designed for the transport of sick or injured persons;
(g) agricultural tractors and other agricultural vehicles;
(h) mechanically or electronically propelled invalid carriages.

3. Vehicles which are permanently immobilised and containers shall not be considered to be means of transport as referred to in paragraph 1.

Article 39

1. For the application of Article 56 of Directive 2006/112/EC, the duration of the continuous possession or use of a means of transport which is the subject of hiring shall be determined on the basis of the contract between the parties involved.

The contract shall serve as a presumption which may be rebutted by any means in fact or law in order to establish the actual duration of the continuous possession or use.

The fact that the contractual period of short-term hiring within the meaning of Article 56 of Directive 2006/112/EC is exceeded on grounds of force majeure shall have no bearing on the determination of the duration of the continuous possession or use of the means of transport.

2. Where hiring of one and the same means of transport is covered by consecutive contracts between the same parties, the duration shall be that of the continuous possession or use of the means of transport provided for under the contracts as a whole.

For the purposes of the first subparagraph a contract and its extensions shall be consecutive contracts. However, the duration of the short-term hire contract or contracts preceding a contract which is regarded as long-term shall not be called into question provided there is no abusive practice.

3. Unless there is abusive practice, consecutive contracts between the same parties for different means of transport shall not be considered to be consecutive contracts for the purposes of paragraph 2.

Article 40

The place where the means of transport is actually put at the disposal of the customer as referred to in Article 56(1) of Directive 2006/112/EC, shall be the place where the customer or a third party acting on his behalf takes physical possession of it.

SUBSECTION 11

SUPPLY OF SERVICES TO NON-TAXABLE PERSONS OUT SIDE THE COMMUNITY

Article 41

The supply of services of translation of texts to a non-taxable person established outside the Community shall be covered by point (c) of the first paragraph of Article 59 of Directive 2006/112/EC.

CHAPTER VI

TAXABLE AMOUNT

(TITLE VII OF DIRECTIVE 2006/112/EC)

Article 42

Where a supplier of goods or services, as a condition of accepting payment by credit or debit card, requires the customer to pay an amount to himself or another undertaking, and where the total price payable by that customer is unaffected irrespective of how payment is accepted, that amount shall constitute an integral part of the taxable amount for the supply of the goods or services, under Articles 73 to 80 of Directive 2006/112/EC.

CHAPTER VII

RATES

Article 43

'Provision of holiday accommodation' as referred to in point (12) of Annex III to Directive 2006/112/EC shall include the hiring out of tents, caravans or mobile homes installed on camping sites and used as accommodation.

CHAPTER VIII

EXEMPTIONS

SECTION 1

EXEMPTIONS FOR CERTAIN ACTIVITIES IN THE PUBLIC INTEREST

(ARTICLES 132, 133 AND 134 OF DIRECTIVE 2006/112/EC)

Article 44

Vocational training or retraining services provided under the conditions set out in point (i) of Article 132(1) of Directive 2006/112/EC shall include instruction relating directly to a trade or profession as well as any instruction aimed at acquiring or updating knowledge for vocational purposes. The duration of a vocational training or retraining course shall be irrelevant for this purpose.

SECTION 2

EXEMPTIONS FOR OTHER ACTIVITIES

(ARTICLES 135, 136 AND 137 OF DIRECTIVE 2006/112/EC)

Article 45

The exemption provided for in point (e) of Article 135(1) of Directive 2006/112/EC shall not apply to platinum nobles.

SECTION 3

EXEMPTIONS ON IMPORTATION

(ARTICLES 143, 144 AND 145 OF DIRECTIVE 2006/112/EC)

Article 46

The exemption provided for in Article 144 of Directive 2006/112/EC shall apply to transport services connected with the importation of movable property carried out as part of a change of residence.

SECTION 4
EXEMPTIONS ON EXPORTATION
(ARTICLES 146 AND 147 OF DIRECTIVE 2006/112/EC)

Article 47

'Means of transport for private use' as referred to in point (b) of Article 146(1) of Directive 2006/112/EC shall include means of transport used for non-business purposes by persons other than natural persons, such as bodies governed by public law within the meaning of Article 13 of that Directive and associations.

Article 48

In order to determine whether, as a condition for the exemption of the supply of goods carried in the personal luggage of travellers, the threshold set by a Member State in accordance with point (c) of the first subparagraph of Article 147(1) of Directive 2006/112/EC has been exceeded, the calculation shall be based on the invoice value. The aggregate value of several goods may be used only if all those goods are included on the same invoice issued by the same taxable person supplying goods to the same customer.

SECTION 5
EXEMPTIONS RELATING TO CERTAIN TRANSACTIONS TREATED AS EXPORTS
(ARTICLES 151 AND 152 OF DIRECTIVE 2006/112/EC)

Article 49

The exemption provided for in Article 151 of Directive 2006/112/EC shall also apply to electronic services where these are provided by a taxable person to whom the special scheme for electronically supplied services provided for in Articles 357 to 369 of that Directive applies.

Article 50

1. In order to qualify for recognition as an international body for the application of point (g) of Article 143(1) and point (b) of the first subparagraph of Article 151(1) of Directive 2006/112/EC a body which is to be set up as a European Research Infrastructure Consortium (ERIC), as referred to in Council Regulation (EC) No 723/2009 of 25 June 2009 on the Community legal framework for a European Research Infrastructure Consortium (ERIC) [1] shall fulfil all of the following conditions:

(a) it shall have a distinct legal personality and full legal capacity;
(b) it shall be set up under and shall be subject to European Union law;
(c) its membership shall include Member States and, where appropriate, third countries and intergovernmental organisations, but exclude private bodies;
(d) it shall have specific and legitimate objectives that are jointly pursued and essentially non-economic in nature.

2. The exemption provided for in point (g) of Article 143(1) and point (b) of the first subparagraph of Article 151(1) of Directive 2006/112/EC shall apply to an ERIC referred to in paragraph 1 where it is recognised as an international body by the host Member State.

The limits and conditions of such an exemption shall be laid down by agreement between the members of the ERIC in accordance with point (d) of Article 5(1) of Regulation (EC) No 723/2009. Where the goods are not dispatched or transported out of the Member State in which the supply takes place, and in the case of services, the exemption may be granted by means of a refund of the VAT in accordance with Article 151(2) of Directive 2006/112/EC.

Article 51

1. Where the recipient of a supply of goods or services is established within the Community but not in the Member State in which the supply takes place, the VAT and/or excise duty exemption certificate set out in Annex II to this Regulation shall, subject to the explanatory notes set out in the Annex to that certificate, serve to confirm that the transaction qualifies for the exemption under Article 151 of Directive 2006/112/EC.

When making use of that certificate, the Member State in which the recipient of the supply of goods or services is established may decide to use either a common VAT and excise duty exemption certificate or two separate certificates.

2. The certificate referred to in paragraph 1 shall be stamped by the competent authorities of the host Member State. However, if the goods or services are intended for official use, Member States may dispense the recipient from the requirement to have the certificate stamped under such conditions as they may lay down. This dispensation may be withdrawn in the case of abuse.

Member States shall inform the Commission of the contact point designated to identify the services responsible for stamping the certificate and the extent to which they dispense with the requirement to have the certificate stamped. The Commission shall inform the other Member States of the information received from Member States.

3. Where direct exemption is applied in the Member State in which the supply takes place, the supplier shall obtain the certificate referred to in paragraph 1 of this Article from the recipient of the goods or services and retain it as part of his records. If the exemption is granted by means of a refund of the VAT, pursuant to Article 151(2) of Directive 2006/112/EC, the certificate shall be attached to the request for refund submitted to the Member State concerned.

[1] OJ L 206, 8.8.2009, p. 1.

CHAPTER IX
DEDUCTIONS
(TITLE X OF DIRECTIVE 2006/112/EC)

Article 52

Where the Member State of importation has introduced an electronic system for completing customs formalities, the term 'import document' in point (e) of Article 178 of Directive 2006/112/EC shall cover electronic versions of such documents, provided that they allow for the exercise of the right of deduction to be checked.

CHAPTER X
OBLIGATIONS OF TAXABLE PERSONS AND CERTAIN NON-TAXABLE PERSONS
(TITLE XI OF DIRECTIVE 2006/112/EC)

SECTION 1
PERSONS LIABLE TO PAY THE VAT
(ARTICLES 192A TO 205 OF DIRECTIVE 2006/112/EC)

Article 53

1. For the application of Article 192a of Directive 2006/112/EC, a fixed establishment of the taxable person shall be taken into consideration only when it is characterised by a sufficient degree of permanence and a suitable structure in terms of human and technical resources to enable it to make the supply of goods or services in which it intervenes.

2. Where a taxable person has a fixed establishment within the territory of the Member State where the VAT is due, that establishment shall be considered as not intervening in thesupply of goods or services within the meaning of point (b) of Article 192a of Directive 2006/112/EC, unless the technical and human resources of that fixed establishment are used by him for transactions inherent in the fulfilment of the taxable supply of those goods or services made within that Member State, before or during this fulfilment.

Where the resources of the fixed establishment are only used for administrative support tasks such as accounting, invoicing and collection of debt-claims, they shall not be regarded as being used for the fulfilment of the supply of goods or services.

However, if an invoice is issued under the VAT identification number attributed by the Member State of the fixed establishment, that fixed establishment shall be regarded as having intervened in the supply of goods or services made in that Member State unless there is proof to the contrary.

Article 54

Where a taxable person has established his place of business within the territory of the Member State where the VAT is due, Article 192a of Directive 2006/112/EC shall not apply whether or not that place of business intervenes in the supply of goods or services he makes within that Member State.

SECTION 2
MISCELLANEOUS PROVISIONS
(ARTICLES 272 AND 273 OF DIRECTIVE 2006/112/EC)

Article 55

For the transactions referred to in Article 262 of Directive 2006/112/EC, taxable persons to whom a VAT identification number has been attributed in accordance with Article 214 of that Directive and non-taxable legal persons identified for VAT purposes shall be required, when acting as such, to communicate their VAT identification number forthwith to those supplying goods and services to them.

The taxable persons referred to in point (b) of Article 3(1) of Directive 2006/112/EC, who are entitled to non-taxation of their intra-Community acquisitions of goods in accordance with the first paragraph of Article 4 of this Regulation, shall not be required to communicate their VAT identification number to those supplying goods to them when a VAT identification number has been attributed to them in accordance with Article 214(1)(d) or (e) of that Directive.

CHAPTER XI
SPECIAL SCHEMES

SECTION 1

SPECIAL SCHEME FOR INVESTMENT GOLD (ARTICLES 344 TO 356 OF DIRECTIVE 2006/112/EC)

Article 56

'Weights accepted by the bullion markets' as referred to in point (l) of Article 344(1) of Directive 2006/112/EC shall at least cover the units and the weights traded as set out in Annex III to this Regulation.

Article 57

For the purposes of establishing the list of gold coins referred to in Article 345 of Directive 2006/112/EC, 'price' and 'open market value' as referred to in point (2) of Article 344(1) of that Directive shall be the price and open market value on 1 April of each year. If 1 April does not fall on a day on which those values are fixed, the values of the next day on which they are fixed shall be used.

[SECTION 2

SPECIAL SCHEMES FOR NON-ESTABLISHED TAXABLE PERSONS SUPPLYING TELECOMMUNICATIONS SERVICES, BROADCASTING SERVICES OR ELECTRONIC SERVICES TO NON-TAXABLE PERSONS (ARTICLES 358 TO 369K OF DIRECTIVE 2006/112/EC)

Amendments—Section 2 (Articles 57a–63c) substituted by Council Regulation 967/2012/EU with effect from 1 January 2015 (OJ L 290, 20.10.2012, p. 1).
Wording of previous version of Section 2 is reproduced after Article 63c below.

SUBSECTION 1

DEFINITIONS

Article 57a

For the purposes of this Section, the following definitions shall apply:

(1) "non-Union scheme" means the special scheme for telecommunications services, broadcasting services or electronic services supplied by taxable persons not established within the Community provided for in Section 2 of Chapter 6 of Title XII of Directive 2006/112/EC;

(2) "Union scheme" means the special scheme for telecommunications services, broadcasting services or electronic services supplied by taxable persons established within the Community but not established in the Member State of consumption provided for in Section 3 of Chapter 6 of Title XII of Directive 2006/112/EC;

(3) "special scheme" means the "non-Union scheme" and/or the "Union scheme" as the context requires;

(4) "taxable person" means a taxable person not established within the Community as defined in point (1) of Article 358a of Directive 2006/112/EC, or a taxable person not established in the Member State of consumption, as defined in point (1) of the first paragraph of Article 369a of that Directive.

Amendments—Section 2 (Articles 57a–63c) substituted by Council Regulation 967/2012/EU with effect from 1 January 2015 (OJ L 290, 20.10.2012, p. 1).
Wording of previous version of Section 2 is reproduced after Article 63c below.

SUBSECTION 2

APPLICATION OF THE UNION SCHEME

Article 57b

Where a taxable person using the Union scheme has established his business within the Community, the Member State in which his place of business is established shall be the Member State of identification.

Where a taxable person using the Union scheme has established his business outside the Community, but has more than one fixed establishment in the Community, he may choose any Member State in which he has a fixed establishment as the Member State of identification, in accordance with the second paragraph of Article 369a of Directive 2006/112/EC.

Amendments—Section 2 (Articles 57a–63c) substituted by Council Regulation 967/2012/EU with effect from 1 January 2015 (OJ L 290, 20.10.2012, p. 1).
Wording of previous version of Section 2 is reproduced after Article 63c below.

SUBSECTION 3

SCOPE OF THE UNION SCHEME

Article 57c

The Union scheme shall not apply to telecommunications, broadcasting or electronic services supplied in a Member State where the taxable person has established his business or has a fixed establishment. The supplies of those services shall be declared to the competent tax authorities of that Member State in the VAT return as provided for under Article 250 of Directive 2006/112/EC.

Amendments—Section 2 (Articles 57a–63c) substituted by Council Regulation 967/2012/EU with effect from 1 January 2015 (OJ L 290, 20.10.2012, p. 1).

Wording of previous version of Section 2 is reproduced after Article 63c below.

SUBSECTION 4

IDENTIFICATION

Article 57d

When a taxable person informs the Member State of identification that he intends to make use of one of the special schemes, that special scheme shall apply as from the first day of the following calendar quarter.

However, where the first supply of services to be covered by that special scheme takes place before the date referred to in the first paragraph, the special scheme shall apply as from the date of that first supply, provided the taxable person informs the Member State of identification of the commencement of his activities to be covered by the scheme no later than the tenth day of the month following that first supply.

Amendments—Section 2 (Articles 57a–63c) substituted by Council Regulation 967/2012/EU with effect from 1 January 2015 (OJ L 290, 20.10.2012, p. 1).

Wording of previous version of Section 2 is reproduced after Article 63c below.

Article 57e

The Member State of identification shall identify the taxable person using the Union scheme by means of his VAT identification number as referred to in Articles 214 and 215 of Directive 2006/112/EC.

Amendments—Section 2 (Articles 57a–63c) substituted by Council Regulation 967/2012/EU with effect from 1 January 2015 (OJ L 290, 20.10.2012, p. 1).

Wording of previous version of Section 2 is reproduced after Article 63c below.

Article 57f

1. Where a taxable person using the Union scheme ceases to meet the conditions of the definition laid down in point (2) of the first paragraph of Article 369a of Directive 2006/112/EC, the Member State in which he has been identified shall cease to be the Member State of identification. Where that taxable person still fulfils the conditions for using that special scheme, he shall, to continue using that scheme, indicate as the new Member State of identification the Member State in which he has established his business or, if he has not established his business in the Community, a Member State where he has a fixed establishment.

2. Where the Member State of identification changes in accordance with paragraph 1, that change shall apply as from the date on which the taxable person ceases to have a business establishment or a fixed establishment in the Member State previously indicated as the Member State of identification.

Amendments—Section 2 (Articles 57a–63c) substituted by Council Regulation 967/2012/EU with effect from 1 January 2015 (OJ L 290, 20.10.2012, p. 1).

Wording of previous version of Section 2 is reproduced after Article 63c below.

Article 57g

A taxable person using a special scheme may cease using that special scheme regardless of whether he continues to supply services which can be eligible for that special scheme. The taxable person shall inform the Member State of identification at least 15 days before the end of the calendar quarter prior to that in which he intends to cease using the scheme. Cessation shall be effective as of the first day of the next calendar quarter.

VAT obligations relating to supplies of telecommunications, broadcasting or electronic services arising after the date on which the cessation became effective shall be discharged directly with the tax authorities of the Member State of consumption concerned.

Where a taxable person ceases using a special scheme in accordance with the first paragraph, he shall be excluded from using that scheme in any Member State for two calendar quarters from the date of cessation.

Amendments—Section 2 (Articles 57a–63c) substituted by Council Regulation 967/2012/EU with effect from 1 January 2015 (OJ L 290, 20.10.2012, p. 1).

Wording of previous version of Section 2 is reproduced after Article 63c below.

SUBSECTION 5

REPORTING OBLIGATIONS

Article 57h

1. A taxable person shall, no later than the tenth day of the next month, inform the Member State of identification by electronic means of:

— the cessation of his activities covered by a special scheme,

— any changes to his activities covered by a special scheme whereby he no longer meets the conditions necessary for using that special scheme, and

— any changes to the information previously provided to the Member State of identification.

2. Where the Member State of identification changes in accordance with Article 57f, the taxable person shall inform both relevant Member States of the change no later than the tenth day of the month following the change of establishment. He shall communicate to the new Member State of identification the registration details required when a taxable person makes use of a special scheme for the first time.

Amendments—Section 2 (Articles 57a–63c) substituted by Council Regulation 967/2012/EU with effect from 1 January 2015 (OJ L 290, 20.10.2012, p. 1).

Wording of previous version of Section 2 is reproduced after Article 63c below.

SUBSECTION 6

EXCLUSION

Article 58

Where at least one of the criteria for exclusion laid down in Article 363 or Article 369e of Directive 2006/112/EC applies to a taxable person using one of the special schemes, the Member State of identification shall exclude that taxable person from that scheme.

Only the Member State of identification can exclude a taxable person from using one of the special schemes.

The Member State of identification shall base its decision on exclusion on any information available, including information provided by any other Member State.

The exclusion shall be effective as from the first day of the calendar quarter following the day on which the decision on exclusion is sent by electronic means to the taxable person.

However where the exclusion is due to a change of place of business or fixed establishment, the exclusion shall be effective as from the date of that change.

Amendments—Section 2 (Articles 57a–63c) substituted by Council Regulation 967/2012/EU with effect from 1 January 2015 (OJ L 290, 20.10.2012, p. 1).

Wording of previous version of Section 2 is reproduced after Article 63c below.

Article 58a

A taxable person using a special scheme who has, for a period of eight consecutive calendar quarters, made no supplies of services covered by that scheme in any Member State of consumption, shall be assumed to have ceased his taxable activities within the meaning of point (b) of Article 363 or point (b) of Article 369e of Directive 2006/112/EC respectively. This cessation shall not preclude him from using a special scheme if he recommences his activities covered by either scheme.

Amendments—Section 2 (Articles 57a–63c) substituted by Council Regulation 967/2012/EU with effect from 1 January 2015 (OJ L 290, 20.10.2012, p. 1).

Wording of previous version of Section 2 is reproduced after Article 63c below.

Article 58b

1. Where a taxable person is excluded from one of the special schemes for persistent failure to comply with the rules relating to that scheme, that taxable person shall remain excluded from using either scheme in any Member State for eight calendar quarters following the calendar quarter during which the taxable person was excluded.

2. A taxable person shall be regarded as having persistently failed to comply with the rules relating to one of the special schemes, within the meaning of point (d) of Article 363 or point (d) of Article 369e of Directive 2006/112/EC, in at least the following cases:

(a) where reminders pursuant to Article 60a have been issued to him by the Member State of identification, for three immediately preceding calendar quarters and the VAT return has not been submitted for each and every one of these calendar quarters within 10 days after the reminder has been sent;

(b) where reminders pursuant to Article 63a have been issued to him by the Member State of identification, for three immediately preceding calendar quarters and the full amount of VAT declared has not been paid by him for each and every one of these calendar quarters within 10 days after the reminder has been sent, except where the remaining unpaid amount is less than EUR 100 for each calendar quarter;

(c) where following a request from the Member State of identification or the Member State of consumption and one month after a subsequent reminder by the Member State of identification, he has failed to make electronically available the records referred to in Articles 369 and 369k of Directive 2006/112/EC.

Amendments—Section 2 (Articles 57a–63c) substituted by Council Regulation 967/2012/EU with effect from 1 January 2015 (OJ L 290, 20.10.2012, p. 1).

Wording of previous version of Section 2 is reproduced after Article 63c below.

Article 58c

A taxable person who has been excluded from one of the special schemes shall discharge all VAT obligations relating to supplies of telecommunications, broadcasting or electronic services arising after the date on which the exclusion became effective directly with the tax authorities of the Member State of consumption concerned.

Amendments—Section 2 (Articles 57a–63c) substituted by Council Regulation 967/2012/EU with effect from 1 January 2015 (OJ L 290, 20.10.2012, p. 1).

Wording of previous version of Section 2 is reproduced after Article 63c below.

SUBSECTION 7

VAT RETURN

Article 59

1. Any return period within the meaning of Article 364 or Article 369f of Directive 2006/112/EC shall be a separate return period.

2. Where, in accordance with the second paragraph of Article 57d, a special scheme applies from the date of the first supply, the taxable person shall submit a separate VAT return for the calendar quarter during which the first supply took place.

3. Where a taxable person has been registered under each of the special schemes during a return period, he shall submit VAT returns and make the corresponding payments to the Member State of identification for each scheme in respect of the supplies made and the periods covered by that scheme.

4. Where the Member State of identification changes in accordance with Article 57f after the first day of the calendar quarter in question, the taxable person shall submit VAT returns and make corresponding payments to both the former and the new Member State of identification covering the supplies made during the respective periods in which the Member States have been Member State of identification.

Amendments—Section 2 (Articles 57a–63c) substituted by Council Regulation 967/2012/EU with effect from 1 January 2015 (OJ L 290, 20.10.2012, p. 1).

Wording of previous version of Section 2 is reproduced after Article 63c below.

Article 59a

Where a taxable person using a special scheme has supplied no services in any Member State of consumption under that special scheme during a return period, he shall submit a VAT return indicating that no supplies have been made during that period (a nil-VAT return).

Amendments—Section 2 (Articles 57a–63c) substituted by Council Regulation 967/2012/EU with effect from 1 January 2015 (OJ L 290, 20.10.2012, p. 1).

Wording of previous version of Section 2 is reproduced after Article 63c below.

Article 60

Amounts on VAT returns made under the special schemes shall not be rounded up or down to the nearest whole monetary unit. The exact amount of VAT shall be reported and remitted.

Amendments—Section 2 (Articles 57a–63c) substituted by Council Regulation 967/2012/EU with effect from 1 January 2015 (OJ L 290, 20.10.2012, p. 1).

Wording of previous version of Section 2 is reproduced after Article 63c below.

Article 60a

The Member State of identification shall remind, by electronic means, taxable persons who have failed to submit a VAT return under Article 364 or Article 369f of Directive 2006/112/EC, of their obligation to submit such a return. The Member State of identification shall issue the reminder on the tenth day following that on which the return should have been submitted, and shall inform the other Member States by electronic means that a reminder has been issued.

Any subsequent reminders and steps taken to assess and collect the VAT shall be the responsibility of the Member State of consumption concerned.

Notwithstanding any reminders issued, and any steps taken, by a Member State of consumption, the taxable person shall submit the VAT return to the Member State of identification.

Amendments—Section 2 (Articles 57a–63c) substituted by Council Regulation 967/2012/EU with effect from 1 January 2015 (OJ L 290, 20.10.2012, p. 1).

Wording of previous version of Section 2 is reproduced after Article 63c below.

Article 61

1. Changes to the figures contained in a VAT return shall, after its submission, be made only by means of amendments to that return and not by adjustments to a subsequent return.
2. The amendments referred to in paragraph 1 shall be submitted electronically to the Member State of identification within three years of the date on which the initial return was required to be submitted.

However, the rules of the Member State of consumption on assessments and amendments shall remain unaffected.

Amendments—Section 2 (Articles 57a–63c) substituted by Council Regulation 967/2012/EU with effect from 1 January 2015 (OJ L 290, 20.10.2012, p. 1).
Wording of previous version of Section 2 is reproduced after Article 63c below.

Article 61a

If a taxable person:

(a) ceases to use one of the special schemes;
(b) is excluded from one of the special schemes; or
(c) changes the Member State of identification in accordance with Article 57f;

he shall submit his final VAT return and the corresponding payment, and any corrections to or late submissions of previous returns, and the corresponding payments, to the Member State which was the Member State of identification at the time of the cessation, exclusion or change.

Amendments—Section 2 (Articles 57a–63c) substituted by Council Regulation 967/2012/EU with effect from 1 January 2015 (OJ L 290, 20.10.2012, p. 1).
Wording of previous version of Section 2 is reproduced after Article 63c below.

SUBSECTION 8

CURRENCY

Article 61b

Where a Member State of identification whose currency is not the euro determines that VAT returns are to be made out in its national currency, that determination shall apply to the VAT returns of all taxable persons using the special schemes.

Amendments—Section 2 (Articles 57a–63c) substituted by Council Regulation 967/2012/EU with effect from 1 January 2015 (OJ L 290, 20.10.2012, p. 1).
Wording of previous version of Section 2 is reproduced after Article 63c below.

SUBSECTION 9

PAYMENTS

Article 62

Without prejudice to the third paragraph of Article 63a, and to Article 63b, a taxable person shall make any payment to the Member State of identification.

Payments of VAT made by the taxable person under Article 367 or Article 369i of Directive 2006/112/EC shall be specific to the VAT return submitted pursuant to Article 364 or Article 369f of that Directive. Any subsequent adjustment to the amounts paid shall be effected by the taxable person only by reference to that return and may neither be allocated to another return, nor adjusted on a subsequent return. Each payment shall refer to the reference number of that specific return.

Amendments—Section 2 (Articles 57a–63c) substituted by Council Regulation 967/2012/EU with effect from 1 January 2015 (OJ L 290, 20.10.2012, p. 1).
Wording of previous version of Section 2 is reproduced after Article 63c below.

Article 63

A Member State of identification which receives a payment in excess of that resulting from the VAT return submitted under Article 364 or Article 369f of Directive 2006/112/EC shall reimburse the overpaid amount directly to the taxable person concerned.

Where a Member State of identification has received an amount in respect of a VAT return subsequently found to be incorrect, and that Member State has already distributed that amount to the Member States of consumption, those Member States of consumption shall each reimburse their respective part of any overpaid amount directly to the taxable person.

However, where overpayments relate to periods up to and including the last return period in 2018, the Member State of identification shall reimburse the relevant portion of the corresponding part of the amount retained in accordance with Article 46(3) of Regulation (EU) No 904/2010 and the Member State of consumption shall reimburse the overpayment less the amount that shall be reimbursed by the Member State of identification.

The Member States of consumption shall, by electronic means, inform the Member State of identification of the amount of those reimbursements.

Amendments—Section 2 (Articles 57a–63c) substituted by Council Regulation 967/2012/EU with effect from 1 January 2015 (OJ L 290, 20.10.2012, p. 1).

Wording of previous version of Section 2 is reproduced after Article 63c below.

Article 63a

Where a taxable person has submitted a VAT return under Article 364 or Article 369f of Directive 2006/112/EC, but no payment has been made or the payment is less than that resulting from the return, the Member State of identification shall, by electronic means on the tenth day following the latest day on which the payment should have been made in accordance with Article 367 or Article 369i of Directive 2006/112/EC, remind the taxable person of any VAT payment outstanding. The Member State of identification shall by electronic means inform the Member States of consumption that the reminder has been sent.

Any subsequent reminders and steps taken to collect the VAT shall be the responsibility of the Member State of consumption concerned. When such subsequent reminders have been issued by a Member State of consumption, the corresponding VAT shall be paid to that Member State.

The Member State of consumption shall, by electronic means, inform the Member State of identification that a reminder has been issued.

Amendments—Section 2 (Articles 57a–63c) substituted by Council Regulation 967/2012/EU with effect from 1 January 2015 (OJ L 290, 20.10.2012, p. 1).

Wording of previous version of Section 2 is reproduced after Article 63c below.

Article 63b

Where no VAT return has been submitted, or where the VAT return has been submitted late or is incomplete or incorrect, or where the payment of VAT is late, any interest, penalties or any other charges shall be calculated and assessed by the Member State of consumption. The taxable person shall pay such interests, penalties or any other charges directly to the Member State of consumption.

Amendments—Section 2 (Articles 57a–63c) substituted by Council Regulation 967/2012/EU with effect from 1 January 2015 (OJ L 290, 20.10.2012, p. 1).

Wording of previous version of Section 2 is reproduced after Article 63c below.

SUBSECTION 10

RECORDS

Article 63c

1. In order to be regarded as sufficiently detailed within the meaning of Articles 369 and 369k of Directive 2006/112/EC, the records kept by the taxable person shall contain the following information:

(a) the Member State of consumption to which the service is supplied;
(b) the type of service supplied;
(c) the date of the supply of service;
(d) the taxable amount indicating the currency used;
(e) any subsequent increase or reduction of the taxable amount;
(f) the VAT rate applied;
(g) the amount of VAT payable indicating the currency used;
(h) the date and amount of payments received;
(i) any payments on account received before the supply of service;
(j) where an invoice is issued, the information contained on the invoice;
(k) the name of the customer, where known to the taxable person;
(l) the information used to determine the place where the customer is established or has his permanent address or usually resides.

2. The information referred to in paragraph 1 shall be recorded by the taxable person in such a way that it can be made available by electronic means without delay and for each single service supplied.'

Amendments—Section 2 (Articles 57a–63c) substituted by Council Regulation 967/2012/EU with effect from 1 January 2015 (OJ L 290, 20.10.2012, p. 1).

CHAPTER XII

FINAL PROVISIONS

Article 64

Regulation (EC) No 1777/2005 is hereby repealed.

References made to the repealed Regulation shall be construed as references to this Regulation and shall be read in accordance with the correlation table set out in Annex IV.

Article 65

This Regulation shall enter into force on the 20th day following its publication in the *Official Journal of the European Union*.

It shall apply from 1 July 2011.

However:

— point (a) of Article 3, point (b) of Article 11(2), Article 23(1) and Article 24(1) shall apply from 1 January 2013,
— point (b) of Article 3 shall apply from 1 January 2015,
— point (c) of Article 11(2) shall apply until 31 December 2014.

This Regulation shall be binding in its entirety and directly applicable in all Member States.

Done at Brussels, ...15 March 2011.

For the Council
The President
MATOLCSY Gy.

ANNEX I

ARTICLE 7 OF THIS REGULATION

(1) Point (1) of Annex II to Directive 2006/112/EC:
(a) Website hosting and webpage hosting;
(b) automated, online and distance maintenance of programmes;
(c) remote systems administration;
(d) online data warehousing where specific data is stored and retrieved electronically;
(e) online supply of on-demand disc space.

(2) Point (2) of Annex II to Directive 2006/112/EC:
(a) Accessing or downloading software (including procurement/accountancy programmes and anti-virus software) plus updates;
(b) software to block banner adverts showing, otherwise known as Bannerblockers;
(c) download drivers, such as software that interfaces computers with peripheral equipment (such as printers);
(d) online automated installation of filters on websites;
(e) online automated installation of firewalls.

(3) Point (3) of Annex II to Directive 2006/112/EC:
(a) Accessing or downloading desktop themes;
(b) accessing or downloading photographic or pictorial images or screensavers;
(c) the digitised content of books and other electronic publications;
(d) subscription to online newspapers and journals;
(e) weblogs and website statistics;
(f) online news, traffic information and weather reports;
(g) online information generated automatically by software from specific data input by the customer, such as legal and financial data, (in particular such data as continually updated stock market data, in real time);
(h) the provision of advertising space including banner ads on a website/web page;
(i) use of search engines and Internet directories.

(4) Point (4) of Annex II to Directive 2006/112/EC:
(a) Accessing or downloading of music on to computers and mobile phones;
(b) accessing or downloading of jingles, excerpts, ringtones, or other sounds;
(c) accessing or downloading of films;
(d) downloading of games on to computers and mobile phones;
(e) accessing automated online games which are dependent on the Internet, or other similar electronic networks, where players are geographically remote from one another.
[(f) receiving radio or television programmes distributed via a radio or television network, the internet or similar electronic network for listening to or viewing programmes at the moment chosen by the user and at the user's individual request on the basis of a catalogue of programmes selected by the media service provider such as TV or video on demand;
(g) receiving radio or television programmes distributed via the internet or similar electronic network (IP streaming) unless they are broadcast simultaneous to their being transmitted or retransmitted over a radio and television network;
(h) the supply of audio and audiovisual content via communications networks which is not provided by and under the editorial responsibility of a media service provider;
(i) the onward supply of the audio and audiovisual output of a media service provider via communications networks by someone other than the media service provider.][1]

(5) Point (5) of Annex II to Directive 2006/112/EC:
(a) Automated distance teaching dependent on the Internet or similar electronic network to function and the supply of which requires limited or no human intervention, including virtual classrooms, except where the Internet or similar electronic network is used as a tool simply for communication between the teacher and student;

(b) workbooks completed by pupils online and marked automatically, without human intervention.

Amendments—[1] In para (4), sub-paras (f)–(i) inserted by Council Implementing Regulations 1042/2013/EU art 1(3) with effect from 1 January 2015 (OJ L 284, 26.10.2013, p 1).

ANNEX II

ARTICLE 51 OF THIS REGULATION

The form from Annex II can be found at www.eur-lex.europa.eu/LexUriServ/LexUriServ.do?uri=OJ:L:2011:077:0001:0022:EN:PDF.

EXPLANATORY NOTES

1. For the supplier and/or the authorised warehousekeeper, this certificate serves as a supporting document for the tax exemption of the supplies of goods and services or the consignments of goods to the eligible bodies/individuals referred to in Article 151 of Directive 2006/112/EC and Article 13 of Directive 2008/118/EC. Accordingly, one certificate shall be drawn up for each supplier/warehousekeeper. Moreover, the supplier/warehousekeeper is required to keep this certificate as part of his records in accordance with the legal provisions applicable in his Member State.

2.

(a) The general specification of the paper to be used is as laid down in the *Official Journal of the European Communities* C 164 of 1.7.1989, p. 3.

The paper is to be white for all copies and should be 210 millimetres by 297 millimetres with a maximum tolerance of 5 millimetres less or 8 millimetres more with regard to their length.

For an exemption from excise duty the exemption certificate shall be drawn up in duplicate:

— one copy to be kept by the consignor,

— one copy to accompany the movement of the products subject to excise duty.

(b) Any unused space in box 5.B. is to be crossed out so that nothing can be added.

(c) The document must be completed legibly and in a manner that makes entries indelible. No erasures or overwriting are permitted. It shall be completed in a language recognised by the host Member State.

(d) If the description of the goods and/or services (box 5.B of the certificate) refers to a purchase order form drawn up in a language other than a language recognised by the host Member Stale, a translation must be attached by the eligible body/individual.

(e) On the other hand, if the certificate is drawn up in a language other than a language recognised by the Member State of the supplier/warehousekeeper, a translation of the information concerning the goods and services in box 5.B must be attached by the eligible body/individual.

(f) A recognised language means one of the languages officially in use in the Member State or any other official language of the Union which the Member State declares can be used for this purpose.

3. By its declaration in box 3 of the certificate, the eligible body/individual provides the information necessary for the evaluation of the request for exemption in the host Member State.

4. By its declaration in box 4 of the certificate, the body confirms the details in boxes 1 and 3(a) of the document and certifies that the eligible individual is a staff member of the body.

5.

(a) The reference to the purchase order form (box 5.B of the certificate) must contain at least the date and order number. The order form should contain all the elements that figure at box 5 of the certificate. If the certificate has to be stamped by the competent authority of the host Member State, the order form shall also be stamped.

(b) The indication of the excise identification number as defined in Article 22(2)(a) of Council Regulation (EC) No 2073/2004 of 16 November 2004 on administrative cooperation in the field of excise duties is optional; the VAT identification number or tax reference number must be indicated.

(c) The currencies should be indicated by means of a three-letter code in conformity with the ISO code 4217 standard established by the International Standards Organisation [1].

6. The abovementioned declaration by the eligible body/individual; shall be authenticated at box 6 by the stamp of the competent authority of the host Member State. That authority can make its approval dependent on the agreement of another authority in its Member State. It is up to the competent tax authority to obtain such an agreement.

7. To simplify the procedure, the competent authority can dispense with the obligation on the eligible body to ask for the stamp in the case of exemption for official use. The eligible body should mention this dispensation at box 7 of the certificate.

[1] As an indication, some codes relating to currencies currently used: EUR (euro), BGN (lev), CZK (Czech koruna), DKK (Danish krone), GBP (pound sterling), HUF (forint), LTL (litas), PLN (zloty), RON (Romanian leu), SEK (Swedish krona), USD (United States dollar).

ANNEX III

ARTICLE 56 OF THIS REGULATION

Unit	Weights traded
Kg	12,5/1
Gram	500/250/100/50/20/10/5/2,5/2
Ounce (1 oz = 31,1035 g)	100/10/5/1/½/¼
Tael (1 tael = 1,193 oz) [1]10	10/5/1
Tola (10 tolas = 3,75 oz) [2]	10

[1] Tael = a traditional Chinese unit of weight. The nominal fineness of a Hong Kong tael bar is 990 but in Taiwan 5 and 10 tael bars can be 999,9 fineness.

[2] Tola = a traditional Indian unit of weight for gold. The most popular sized bar is 10 tola, 999 fineness.

ANNEX IV

CORRELATION TABLE

Regulation (EC) No 1777/2005	This Regulation
Chapter I	Chapter I
Article 1	Article 1
Chapter II	Chapters III and IV
Section 1 of Chapter II	Chapter III
Article 2	Article 5
Section 2 of Chapter II	Chapter IV
Article 3(1)	Article 9
Article 3(2)	Article 8
Chapter II	Chapter V
Section 1 of Chapter III	Section 4 of Chapter V
Article 4	Article 28
Section 2 of Chapter III	Section 4 of Chapter V
Article 5	Article 34
Article 6	Articles 29 and 41
Article 7	Article 26
Article 8	Article 27
Article 9	Article 30
Article 10	Article 38(2)(b) and (c)
Article 11(1) and (2)	Article 7(1) and (2)
Article 12	Article 7(3)
Chapter IV	Chapter VI
Article 13	Article 42
Chapter V	Chapter VIII
Section 1 of Chapter V	Section 1 of Chapter VIII
Article 14	Article 44
Article 15	Article 45
Section 2 of Chapter V	Section 4 of Chapter VIII
Article 16	Article 47
Article 17	Article 48
Chapter VI	Chapter IX

Regulation (EC) No 1777/2005	This Regulation
Article 18	Article 52
Chapter VII	Chapter XI
Article 19(1)	Article 56
Article 19(2)	Article 57
Article 20(1)	Article 58
Article 20(2)	Article 62
Article 20(3), first subparagraph	Article 59
Article 20(3), second subparagraph	Article 60
Article 20(3), third subparagraph	Article 63
Article 20(4)	Article 61
Chapter VIII	Section 3 of Chapter V
Article 21	Article 16
Article 22	Article 14
Chapter IX	Chapter XII
Article 23	Article 65
Annex I	Annex I
Annex II	Annex III

COMMISSION IMPLEMENTING REGULATION 79/2012/EU OF 31 JANUARY 2012 LAYING DOWN DETAILED RULES FOR IMPLEMENTING CERTAIN PROVISIONS OF COUNCIL REGULATION (EU) NO 904/2010 CONCERNING ADMINISTRATIVE COOPERATION AND COMBATING FRAUD IN THE FIELD OF VALUE ADDED TAX

(recast)

THE EUROPEAN COMMISSION,

Having regard to the Treaty on the Functioning of the European Union,

Having regard to Council Regulation (EU) No 904/2010 of 7 October 2010 on administrative cooperation and combating fraud in the field of value added tax[1] and, in particular Articles 14, 32, 48 and 49 and Article 51(1) thereof,

Whereas:

(1) To improve and supplement the instruments to combat fraud, Council Regulation (EC) No 1798/2003 of 7 October 2003 on administrative cooperation in the field of value added tax and repealing Regulation (EEC) No 218/92[2] has been recast and repealed by Regulation (EU) No 904/2010. The rules as they can be found in Regulation (EU) No 904/2010 should be reflected at the level of the acts implementing Regulation (EU) No 904/2010.

(2) Commission Regulation (EC) No 1925/2004 of 29 October 2004 laying down detailed rules for implementing certain provisions of Council Regulation (EC) No 1798/2003 concerning administrative cooperation in the field of value-added tax[3] has been substantially amended. Since further amendments are to be made following the adoption of Regulation (EU) No 904/2010 and in order to have a single set of rules on the exchange of information it should be recast in the interests of clarity together with Commission Regulation (EC) No 1174/2009 of 30 November 2009 laying down rules for the implementation of Articles 34a and 37 of Council Regulation (EC) No 1798/2003 as regards refunds of value added tax under Council Directive 2008/9/EC[4].

(3) In order to facilitate the exchange of information between Member States it is necessary to specify the exact categories of information to be exchanged without prior request, as well as the frequency with which those exchanges are to be made, and the relevant practical arrangements. To the extent that Member States intend to abstain from such exchange, they should notify it to the Commission in accordance with Article 14(1) of Regulation (EU) No 904/2010.

(4) Pursuant to Article 51 of Regulation (EU) No 904/2010 information shall be communicated between tax au-thorities as far as possible by electronic means. Consequently, the practical arrangements and technical details should be laid down.

(5) Practical arrangements should be determined for the provision of information relating to invoicing rules, value added tax (VAT) rates applicable in the context of the special schemes applicable to non-established taxable persons and the additional electronic coded information referred to in Article 9(2) of Council Directive 2008/9/EC of 12 February 2008 laying down detailed rules for the refund of value added tax, provided for in Directive 2006/112/EC, to taxable persons not established in the Member State of refund but established in another Member State[5].

(6) In order to ensure that Member States are able to effectively make use of the possibilities to require the in-formation foreseen by certain provisions of Directive 2008/9/EC, it is necessary to specify the relevant har-monised codes to be applied when exchanging the relevant information, including the means through which such exchange should take place, in accordance with Regulation (EU) No 904/2010.

(7) Article 9(2) of Directive 2008/9/EC provides that the Member State of refund may require the applicant to provide additional electronic coded information supplementing the codes set out in Article 9(1) of Directive 2008/9/EC, to the extent that such information is necessary due to any restrictions on the right of deduction under Council Directive 2006/112/EC of 28 November 2006 on the common system of value added tax[6], or for the implementation of a derogation received by the Member State of refund under Article 395 or 396 of that Directive.

(8) Pursuant to Article 48(2) of Regulation (EU) No 904/2010, the competent authorities of the Member State of refund are to notify by electronic means the competent authorities of the other Member States of any infor-mation required by them under Article 9(2) of Directive 2008/9/EC.

(9) For that purpose, the technical details for the transmission of the additional information required by Member States under Article 9(2) of Directive 2008/9/EC should be determined. In particular, the codes to be used for the transmission of this information should be specified. The codes set out in Annex III to this Regulation have been developed by the Standing Committee on Administrative Cooperation (SCAC) on the basis of the information required by Member States for the purposes of applying Article 9(2) of Directive 2008/9/EC.

(10) Applicants may be required according to Article 11 of Directive 2008/9/EC to provide a description of their business activity using harmonised codes. For that purpose, the commonly used codes provided for in Article 2(1)(d) of Regulation (EC) No 1893/2006 of the European Parliament and of the Council of 20 December 2006 establishing the statistical classification of economic activities NACE Revision 2 and amending Council Regulation (EEC) No 3037/90 as well as certain EC Regulations on specific statistical domains[7] should be employed.

(11) Article 25 of Regulation (EU) No 904/2010 states that the requested authority shall, at the request of the re-questing authority, notify the addressee of all instruments and decisions emanating from the administrative authorities and concerning the application of VAT legislation in the Member State in which the requesting authority is established.

(12) Where a Member State of refund requests the Member State of establishment to notify the applicant of its decisions and instruments for the purposes of the application of Directive 2008/9/EC, for reasons of data protection, it should be possible that such notification be made via the common communication net-work/common system interface (CCN/CSI) as defined in Article 2(1)(q) of Regulation (EU) No 904/2010.

(13) Rules should be laid down implementing, inter alia, Article 48 of Regulation (EU) No 904/2010 as regards the introduction of administrative cooperation and the exchange of information concerning the rules relating to the place of supply of services, the special schemes and the refund procedure for value added tax.

(14) Finally, it is necessary to establish a list of the statistical data needed for the evaluation of Regulation (EU) No 904/2010.

(15) The measures provided for in this Regulation are in accordance with the opinion of the Standing Committee on Administrative Cooperation,

1 OJ L 268, 12.10.2010, p. 1.
2 OJ L 264, 15.10.2003, p. 1.
3 OJ L 331, 5.11.2004, p. 13.
4 OJ L 314, 1.12.2009, p. 50.
5 OJ L 44, 20.2.2008, p. 23.
6 OJ L 347, 11.12.2006, p. 1.
7 OJ L 393, 30.12.2006, p. 1.

HAS ADOPTED THIS REGULATION:

Article 1 Subject matter

This Regulation lays down detailed rules for implementing Articles 14, 32, 48 and 49 and Article 51(1) of Regulation (EU) No 904/2010.

Article 2 Categories of information to be exchanged without prior request
The categories of information subject to automatic exchange, in accordance with Article 13 of Regulation (EU) No 904/2010, shall be the following:
(1) information on non-established traders;
(2) information on new means of transport.

Article 3 Subcategories of infor-mation to be exchanged without prior request
1. In respect of non-established traders the information subject to automatic exchange shall be the following: (a) information on the allocation of VAT identification numbers to taxable persons established in another Member State; (b) information on VAT refunds to taxable persons not established in the Member State of refund but estab-lished in another Member State pursuant to Council Directive 2008/9/EC. 2. In respect of new means of transport, the information subject to automatic exchange shall be the following: (a) information on supplies exempted in accordance with Article 138(2)(a) of Directive 2006/112/EC, of new means of transport as defined in Article 2(2), (a) and (b)of that Directive, by persons regarded as taxable persons pursuant to Article 9(2) of that Directive who are identified for VAT purposes; (b) information on supplies exempted in accordance with Article 138(2)(a) of Directive 2006/112/EC, of new vessels and aircraft as defined in Article 2(2), (a) and (b) of that Directive, by taxable persons identified for VAT purposes, other than those referred to in point (a), to persons not identified for VAT purposes; (c) information on supplies exempted in accordance with Article 138(2)(a) of Directive 2006/112/EC, of new motorised land vehicles as defined in Article 2(2), (a) and (b) of that Directive, by taxable persons identified for VAT purposes, other than those referred to in point (a), to persons not identified for VAT purposes.

Article 4 Notification of abstention from participation in the exchange of information without prior request
By 20 May 2012 each Member State shall notify the Commission in writing of its decision, taken in accordance with the second subparagraph of Article 14(1) of Regulation (EU) No 904/2010, as to whether it is going to abstain from taking part in the automatic exchange of one or more categories or subcategories of information referred to in Articles 2 and 3 of this Regulation.
[Croatia shall notify the Commission of its decision, referred to in the previous sentence, to abstain from taking part in the automatic exchange of information by 1 July 2013.][1]
The Commission shall inform the other Member States accordingly of the categories for which a Member State has abstained.

Amendments—[1] Sentence relating to Croatia inserted by Commission Regulation 519/2013/EU art 1, Annex with effect from 1 July 2013 (OJ L 158, 10.6.2013, p. 74).

Article 5 Frequency of the transmission of the information
In cases where the automatic exchange system is being used, information concerning the categories and subcategories referred to respectively in Articles 2 and 3 shall be provided as soon as it becomes available, and in any event within 3 months of the end of the calendar quarter during which that information has become available.

Article 6 Transmission of communications
1. Information communicated pursuant to Regulation (EU) No 904/2010 shall, as far as possible, be transmitted only by electronic means via the CCN/CSI network, with the exception of the following: (a) the request for notification referred to in Article 25 of Regulation (EU) No 904/2010 and the instrument or decision of which notification is requested; (b) original documents provided pursuant to Article 9 of Regulation (EU) No 904/2010. 2. The competent authorities of the Member States may agree to communicate the information referred to in points (a) and (b) of paragraph 1 by electronic means.

Article 7 Information to taxable persons
1. Member States shall provide the details on invoicing listed in Annex I to this Regulation in accordance with Article 32 of Regulation (EU) No 904/2010 via the web portal established by the Commission. 2. The Commission shall make the web portal referred to in paragraph 1 available for those Member States choosing to publish the following additional information: (a) the information on storage of invoices listed in Annex II; (b) the additional electronic coded information required by Member States pursuant to Article 9(2) of Directive 2008/9/EC; (c) until 31 December 2014 the standard tax rate referred to in the second paragraph of Article 42 of Regulation (EU) No 904/2010; (d) as from 1 January 2015 the tax rate applicable for supplies of telecommunication services, broad-casting services and electronically supplied services referred to in the second paragraph of Article 47 of Regulation (EU) No 904/2010.

Article 8 Information exchanged in the framework of VAT refund
Where a Member State of refund notifies other Member States that it requires additional electronic coded information as provided for in Article 9(2) of Directive 2008/9/EC, the codes specified in Annex III to this Regulation shall be used for the purposes of transmitting this information.

Article 9 Description relating to the business activity exchanged in the framework of VAT refund

Where a Member State of refund requires a description of the applicants business activity as provided for in Article 11 of Directive 2008/9/EC, such information shall be given at the fourth level of the NACE Rev. 2 codes, as provided for in Article 2(1)(d) of Regulation (EC) No 1893/2006.

Article 10 Notification of instruments and decisions relating to a VAT refund

Where a Member State of refund requests a Member State of establishment of an addressee to notify in-struments and decisions relating to a refund under Directive 2008/9/EC to the addressee, that notification request may be transmitted via the CCN/CSI network as defined in Article 2(1)(q) of Regulation (EU) No 904/2010.

Article 11 Statistical data

The list of statistical data referred to in Article 49(3) of Regulation (EU) No 904/2010 is set out in Annex IV. Each Member State shall, before 30 April each year by electronic means, communicate to the Commission the statistical data referred to in the first paragraph, using the model set out in Annex IV.

Article 12 Communication of national measures

Member States shall communicate to the Commission the text of any laws, regulations or administrative pro-visions which they apply in the field covered by this Regulation. The Commission shall communicate those measures to the other Member States.

Article 13 Repeal

Regulations (EC) No 1925/2004 and (EC) No 1174/2009 are repealed. References to the repealed Regulations shall be construed as references to this Regulation and shall be read in accordance with the correlation table in Annex VI.

Article 14 Entry into force

This Regulation shall enter into force on the 20th day following its publication in the Official Journal of the European Union. This Regulation shall be binding in its entirety and directly applicable in all Member States.

Done at Brussels, 31 January 2012.

For the Commission

The President

José Manuel Barroso

ANNEX 1

THE DETAILS ON INVOICING IN ACCORDANCE WITH BY ARTICLE 32 OF REGULATION (EU) NO 904/2010

1. Issuance of invoices

Article 221(1) of Directive 2006/112/EC - option to require invoices to be issued

Q1. In what other circumstances are invoices required?

Q2. If required, are the invoices simplified invoices or full invoices?

Article 221(2) of Directive 2006/112/EC - option for invoices for exempt financial and insurance services

Q3. Is an invoice required for exempted financial and insurance services?

Q4. If yes, is a simplified or full invoice required? Article 221(3) of Directive 2006/112/EC - option not to require an invoice for exempt supplies

Q5. For which, if any, exempt supplies is an invoice not required?

2. Time of issue of an invoice

Article 222 of Directive 2006/112/EC - option to impose time limits on when invoices are issued.

Q6. Is there a time limit for issuing invoices other than that for intra-Community supplies or cross-border supplies of services subject to the reverse charge?

Q7. If yes, by when must an invoice be issued?

3. Summary invoices

Article 223 of Directive 2006/112/EC - time period for issuing summary invoices

Q8. Can summary invoices be issued for supplies becoming chargeable to tax during a period of more than 1 calendar month? This excludes intra-Community supplies and cross-border supplies of services subject to the reverse charge.

Q9. If yes, what is the time period?

4. Self-billed invoices

Article 224 of Directive 2006/112/EC - option for self-billed invoices to be issued in the name and on behalf of the taxable person

Q10. Is there a requirement for self-billed invoices to be issued in the name of and behalf of the taxable person making the supply?

5. Outsourcing of invoices to non-EU third parties

Article 225 of Directive 2006/112/EC - option to impose conditions on non-EU third parties issuing invoices on behalf of EU suppliers

Q11. Are any conditions imposed on outsourcing of invoices to third parties established outside the EU?

Q12. If yes, what conditions are imposed?

6. Content of invoices

Article 227 of Directive 2006/112/EC - requirement to mention the customer's VAT identification number

Q13. Other than for intra-Community supplies of goods or reverse charge supplies is the customer's VAT identification number required on the invoice?

Q14. If yes, in what circumstances is the customer's VAT identification number required on an invoice?

Article 230 of Directive 2006/112/EC - currency on the VAT invoice

Q15. Where the VAT amount is converted to the national currency using the exchange rate from the European Central Bank, is notification required?

Article 239 of Directive 2006/112/EC - use of a tax reference number

Q16. Is a VAT identification number issued if the supplier or customer does not make intra-Community acquisitions, distance sales or intra-Community supplies?

Article 240 of Directive 2006/112/EC - use of a VAT identification number and a tax reference number

Q17. Where both a VAT identification number and a tax reference number are issued, in what circumstance is one or both required to be mentioned on the invoice?

7. Paper and electronic invoices

Article 235 of Directive 2006/112/EC - electronic invoices issued from outside of the EU

Q18. Are there any conditions for electronic invoices issued from a third country?

Q19. If yes, what are those conditions?

8. Simplified invoices

Article 238 of Directive 2006/112/EC - use of simplified invoices

Q20. In what circumstances are simplified invoices allowed?

Article 226b of Directive 2006/112/EC - details required on a simplified invoice

Q21. What details are required for simplified invoices?

ANNEX 2

THE INFORMATION ON STORAGE OF INVOICES THAT MEMBER STATES MAY PROVIDE VIA THE WEB PORTAL

Article 245 of Council Directive 2006/112/EC - place of storage

Q1. If the place of storage is outside the Member State, is the notification of the place of storage required?

Q2. If yes, how is this notification to be done?

Q3. Can paper invoices be stored outside the Member State?

Article 247(1) of Council Directive 2006/112/EC - storage period

Q4. What are the periods of storage for invoices?

Article 247(2) of Council Directive 2006/112/EC - form of storage

Q5. Can paper invoices be stored electronically?

Q6. Can electronic invoices be stored in paper form?

Q7. Must the data guaranteeing the authenticity of the origin and integrity of the content of invoices stored electronically be kept in the case when e-signatures or EDI are used?

Article 247(3) of Council Directive 2006/112/EC - storage in a third country

Q8. Can invoices be stored in a third country?

Q9. If yes, are there any conditions?

ANNEX 3

CODES FOR USE IN THE TRANSMISSION OF INFORMATION UNDER ARTICLE 48(2) OF REGULATION (EU) NO 904/2010

(Not reproduced – see www.eur-lex.europa.eu/LexUriServ/LexUriServ.do?uri=OJ:L:2012:029:0013:0032:EN:PDF)

VAT EC

ANNEX 4

MODEL FOR THE COMMUNICATION FROM THE MEMBER STATES TO THE COMMISSION REFERRED TO IN ARTICLE 49(3) OF REGULATION (EU) NO 904/2010

(Not reproduced – see www.eur-lex.europa.eu/LexUriServ/LexUriServ.do?uri=OJ:L:2012:029:0013:0032:EN:PDF)

ANNEX 5

REPEALED REGULATIONS

Commission Regulation (EC) No 1925/2004 (OJ L 331, 5.11.2004, p. 13)

Commission Regulation (EC) No 1792/2006 (OJ L 362, 20.12.2006, p. 1)

Commission Regulation (EC) No 1174/2009 (OJ L 314, 1.12.2009, p. 50)

COMMISSION IMPLEMENTING REGULATION 815/2012/EU OF 13 SEPTEMBER 2012 LAYING DOWN DETAILED RULES FOR THE APPLICATION OF COUNCIL REGULATION (EU) NO 904/2010, AS REGARDS SPECIAL SCHEMES FOR NON-ESTABLISHED TAXABLE PERSONS SUPPLYING TELECOMMUNICATIONS, BROADCASTING OR ELECTRONIC SERVICES TO NON-TAXABLE PERSONS

(815/2012/EU)

THE EUROPEAN COMMISSION,

Having regard to the Treaty on the Functioning of the European Union,

Having regard to Council Regulation (EU) No 904/2010 of 7 October 2010 on administrative cooperation and combating fraud in the field of value added tax,[1] and in particular Article 44(1), second subparagraph of Article 44(2), Article 45(1) and (2), and Article 51(1) thereof,

Whereas:

(1) Regulation (EU) No 904/2010 lays down the rules for the administrative cooperation and the fight against fraud in the field of value added tax (VAT). Articles 44 and 45 of Regulation (EU) No 904/2010 specifically concern the exchange of information relating to the special schemes for telecommunications, broadcasting or electronic services provided for in Chapter 6 of Title XII of Council Directive 2006/112/EC of 28 November 2006 on the common system of value added tax.[2] Those special schemes involve a taxable person established outside the Member State of consumption declaring the VAT due on relevant sales in the Member State of consumption via an electronic interface in the Member State of identification (one-stop shop).

(2) Certain information relating to transactions carried out under those special schemes is to be collected and exchanged between Member States. Specifically, that relates to the exchange of identification and the collection and exchange of VAT return details, including corrections to those VAT returns, between Member States.

(3) To ensure that information is exchanged in a uniform manner, it is necessary to adopt the technical details for such exchange, including a common electronic message. This would also allow for the uniform development of the technical and functional specifications, as they would follow a regulated framework.

(4) Certain information relating to changes to the identification details such as the exclusion from the special schemes, the voluntary cessation or the change of Member State of identification should also be exchanged, without delay, in a uniform manner in order to allow Member States to monitor the correct application of the special schemes and to combat fraud. To that end, common arrangements for the electronic exchange of such information should be provided.

(5) In order to keep the administrative burden to a minimum, it is necessary to establish certain requirements for the electronic interface that facilitate submission of identification information and VAT returns by taxable persons. Member States should not be prevented from providing additional functionalities to further reduce administrative burdens.

(6) In order to ensure that the information relating to registration into the scheme, and VAT returns rendered under the scheme, can be transmitted and processed effectively Member States should develop their electronic interface in a uniform manner. It is therefore necessary to establish the common electronic message for the transmission of that information.

(7) It is necessary to clarify the information to be submitted in cases where no sales under the special schemes are made in a particular period in one or all Member States.

(8) With a view to enabling Member States and taxable persons to refer to the VAT returns in an

unequivocal way in their subsequent communications, including on the payment of the tax, the Member State of identification should allocate a unique reference number to each VAT return.

(9) This Regulation should apply from the same day from which Articles 44 and 45 of Regulation (EU) No 904/2010 apply.

(10) The measures provided for in this Regulation are in accordance with the opinion of the Standing Committee on Administrative Cooperation,

Notes[1] OJ L268, 12.10.2010, p 1.
[2] OJ L347, 11.12.2006, p 1.

HAS ADOPTED THIS REGULATION:

Article 1 Definitions

For the purposes of this Regulation, the following definitions apply:

(1) 'non-Union scheme' means the special scheme for telecommunications services, broadcasting services or electronic services supplied by taxable persons not established within the Community provided for in Section 2 of Chapter 6 of Title XII of Directive 2006/112/EC;

(2) 'Union scheme' means the special scheme for telecommunications services, broadcasting services or electronic services supplied by taxable persons established within the Community but not in the Member State of consumption provided for in Section 3 of Chapter 6 of Title XII of Directive 2006/112/EC;

(3) 'special schemes' means non-Union scheme and Union scheme.

Article 2 Functionalities of the electronic interface

The electronic interface in the Member State of identification by which a taxable person registers the use of one of the special schemes, and via which that person submits the value added tax (VAT) returns under that scheme to the Member State of identification, shall have the following functionalities:

(a) it must offer the facility to save the identification details pursuant to Article 361 of Directive 2006/112/EC, or the VAT return pursuant to Articles 365 and 369g of Directive 2006/112/EC, before they are submitted;

(b) it must allow for the taxable person to submit the relevant information relating to the VAT returns via an electronic file transfer in accordance with conditions laid down by the Member State of identification.

Article 3 Transmission of identification information

1. The Member State of identification shall transmit the following to the other Member States, via the CCN/CSI network:

(a) information to identify the taxable person using the non- Union scheme;

(b) similar details to identify the taxable person using the Union scheme;

(c) allocated identification number.

The common electronic message set out in Annex I shall be used to transmit the information referred to in the first subparagraph. Column B of the common electronic message set out in Annex I shall be used for the non-Union scheme and column C of that common electronic message shall be used for the Union scheme.

2. The Member State of identification shall without delay inform the other Member States via the CCN/CSI network, using the common electronic message set out in Annex II to this Regulation, where the taxable person:

(a) is excluded from one of the special schemes;

(b) voluntarily ceases to use one of the special schemes;

(c) changes the Member State of identification within the Union scheme.

Article 4 Submission of VAT return by the taxable person

1. The taxable person shall submit the VAT returns with the details pursuant to Articles 365 and 369g of Directive 2006/112/EC to the Member State of identification using the common electronic message set out in Annex III to this Regulation. Column B of the common electronic message set out in Annex III shall be used for the non-Union scheme and column C of that common electronic message shall be used for the Union scheme.

2. Where a taxable person makes no supplies of services under the special schemes in any Member State during a return period, a nil VAT return shall be completed. For that purpose, only boxes 1, 2 and 21 of the common electronic message set out in Annex III shall be completed for the Union scheme and boxes 1, 2 and 11 for the non-Union scheme.

3. The taxable person shall only be required to insert the supplies relating to a Member State of consumption and from a Member State of establishment if supplies of services under the special schemes have been made in or from that Member State respectively within the return period.

Article 5 Transmission of information contained in VAT return

The information contained in the VAT return referred to in Article 4(1) shall be sent by the Member State of identification to each Member State of consumption and establishment mentioned on the VAT return, via the CCN/CSI network, using the common electronic message set out in Annex III to this Regulation.

For the purpose of the first paragraph, the Member State of identification shall transmit to the Member State of consumption and establishment in which or from which supplies have been made, the general information contained in part 1 of the common electronic message set out in Annex III, together with the information in part 2 of that common electronic message relating to that particular Member State of consumption or establishment.

The Member State of identification shall transmit the information contained in the VAT return only to those Member States which have been indicated on that VAT return.

Article 6 Unique reference number

The information transmitted pursuant to Article 5 shall contain a reference number allocated by the Member State of identification which is unique to the specific VAT return.

Article 7 Corrections to VAT returns

The Member State of identification shall allow the taxable person to correct any VAT returns via the electronic interface referred to in Article 2. The Member State of identification shall transmit information on corrections to the Member State(s) of consumption and establishment concerned in accordance with Article 5, and allocate a timestamp to that information.

Article 8 Entry into force

This Regulation shall enter into force on the twentieth day following that of its publication in the *Official Journal of the European Union*.

It shall apply from 1 January 2015.

This Regulation shall be binding in its entirety and directly applicable in all Member States.

Done at Brussels, ...13 September 2012.

For the Commission

The President

José Manuel BARROSO

ANNEX I

IDENTIFICATION DETAILS

Column A	Column B	Column C
Box number	The non-Union scheme	The Union scheme
1	Individual VAT identification number allocated by the Member State of identification in accordance with Article 362 of Directive 2006/112/EC[1]	Individual VAT identification number allocated by the Member State of identification in accordance with Article 369d of Directive 2006/112/EC, including the country code
2	The national tax number, if any	
3	The company name	The company name
4	The trading name(s) of the company if different from the company name	The trading name(s) of the company if different from the company name
5	The full postal address[2]	The full postal address[3]
6	The country in which the taxable person has his place of business	The country in which the taxable person has his place of business if not in the Union
7	The e-mail address of the taxable person	The e-mail address of the taxable person
8	The website(s) of the taxable person where available	The website(s) of the taxable person where available
9	Contact name	Contact name
10	Telephone number	Telephone number
11	IBAN or OBAN number	IBAN number
12	BIC number	BIC number

Column A	Column B	Column C
Box number	The non-Union scheme	The Union scheme
13.1		Individual VAT identification number(s) or if not available, tax reference number(s) allocated by the Member State(s) in which the taxable person has a fixed establishment(s)[4] other than in the Member State of identification
14.1		Full postal address(es) and trading name(s) of fixed establishments[5] other than in the Member State of identification
15.1		VAT identification number(s) allocated by Member State(s) as a non-established taxable person[6]
16	Electronic declaration that the taxable person is not registered for VAT within the Union	
17	Date of commencement of using the scheme[7]	Date of commencement of using the scheme[8]
18	Date of request to be registered under the scheme by the taxable person	Date of request to be registered under the scheme by the taxable person
19	Date of registration decision by the Member State of identification	Date of registration decision by the Member State of identification
20		Indicator of whether the taxable person is a VAT group[9]
21	Individual VAT identification number(s) allocated by the Member State of identification in accordance with Articles 362 or 369d of Directive 2006/112/EC if they have previously used either scheme	Individual VAT identification number(s) allocated by the Member State of identification in accordance with Articles 362 or 369d of Directive 2006/112/EC if they have previously used either scheme

Notes

1 To follow format: EUxxxyyyyyz where: xxx is the 3-digit ISO numeric of the MSI; yyyyy is the 5-digit number assigned by MSI; and z is a check digit.

2 Postcode to be indicated if there is one.

3 Postcode to be indicated if there is one.

4 Where there is more than one fixed establishment, use box 13.1, 13.2, etc.

5 Where there is more than one fixed establishment, use box 14.1, 14.2, etc.

6 Where there is more than one VAT identification number allocated by Member State(s) as a non-established taxable person, use box 15.1, 15.2 etc.

7 This can be in certain limited cases prior to the date of registration onto the scheme.

8 This can be in certain limited cases prior to the date of registration onto the scheme.

9 This is a simple yes/no tick box.

ANNEX II

DETAILS RELATING TO THE STATUS OF A TAXABLE PERSON IN THE REGISTER OF A MEMBER STATE OF IDENTIFICATION

Individual VAT identification number allocated by the Member State of identification, including country code	
Date from which the change is effective	Reason for changing the status of the taxable person in the register by using the following codes: (1) The taxable person has notified the Member State of identification that he no longer supplies telecommunications, broadcasting or electronic services; (2) It is assumed by the Member State of identification that the taxable activities of the taxable person covered by the special scheme have ceased;

VAT EC

Individual VAT identification number allocated by the Member State of identification, including country code	
	(3) The taxable person no longer meets the conditions necessary for the use of the special scheme; (4) The taxable person persistently fails to comply with the rules of the special scheme; (5) The taxable person has requested to voluntarily leave the scheme; (6) The taxable person has requested to be identified in a new Member State of identification.

ANNEX III

VAT RETURNS

Part 1: General information		
Column A	Column B	Column C
Box number	The non-Union scheme	The Union scheme
Unique reference number:[1]		
1	Individual VAT identification number allocated by the Member State of identification, in accordance with Article 362 of Directive 2006/112/EC	Individual VAT identification number allocated by the Member State of identification, in accordance with Article 369d of Directive 2006/112/EC, including country code
2	VAT period[2]	VAT period[3]
2a	Start date and end date of period[4]	Start date and end date of period[5]
3	Currency	Currency
Part 2: For each Member State of consumption in which VAT is due[6]		
		2(a) **Supplies carried out from the place of business or fixed establishment in the Member State of identification**
4.1	Country code of the Member State of consumption	Country code of the Member State of consumption
5.1	Standard VAT rate in the Member State of consumption	Standard VAT rate in the Member State of consumption
6.1	Reduced VAT rate in the Member State of consumption	Reduced VAT rate in the Member State of consumption
7.1	Taxable amount at standard rate	Taxable amount at standard rate
8.1	VAT amount at standard rate	VAT amount at standard rate
9.1	Taxable amount at reduced rate	Taxable amount at reduced rate
10.1	VAT amount at reduced rate	VAT amount at reduced rate
11.1	Total VAT amount payable	Total VAT amount payable for supplies of services carried out from the place of business or fixed establishment in the Member State of identification
		2(b) **Supplies carried out from fixed establishments not in Member State of identification**[7]
12.1		Country code of the Member State of consumption
13.1		Standard VAT rate in the Member State of consumption
14.1		Reduced VAT rate in the Member State of consumption

15.1		Individual VAT identification number, or if not available tax reference number, allocated by the Member State of fixed establishment, including country code
16.1		Taxable amount at the standard rate
17.1		VAT amount payable at the standard rate
18.1		Taxable amount at the reduced rate
19.1		VAT amount payable at the reduced rate
20.1		Total VAT amount payable for supplies of services carried out from fixed establishment not in Member State of identification.
		2(c) **Grand total for the place of business or fixed establishment in the Member State of identification, and all fixed establishments in all other Member States**
21.1		Total VAT amount payable by all establishments (Box 11.1 + Box 11.2 . . . + Box 20.1 + Box 20.2 . . .)

Notes

1 Unique reference number as allocated by the Member State of identification shall consist of country code of MSI/VAT number/period – i.e. GB/xxxxxxxxx/Q1.yy + add timestamp for each version. The number shall be attributed by the Member State of identification before transmission of the return to the other Member States concerned.

2 Relates to calendar quarters: Q1.yyyy – Q2.yyyy – Q3.yyyy Q4.yyyy.

3 Relates to calendar quarters: Q1.yyyy – Q2.yyyy – Q3.yyyy Q4.yyyy.

4 To be completed only in cases where the taxable person submits more than one VAT return for the same quarter. Relates to calendar days: dd.mm.yyyy – dd.mm.yyyy.

5 To be completed only in cases where the taxable person submits more than one VAT return for the same quarter. Relates to calendar days: dd.mm.yyyy – dd.mm.yyyy.

6 Where there is more than one Member State of consumption (or if in a single Member State of consumption there has been a VAT rate change in the middle of a quarter), use box 4.2, 5.2, 6.2 etc.

7 Where there is more than one establishment, use box 12.1.2, 13.1.2 14.1.2 etc.

COMMISSION IMPLEMENTING REGULATION 1156/2012/EU OF 6 DECEMBER 2012 LAYING DOWN DETAILED RULES FOR IMPLEMENTING CERTAIN PROVISIONS OF COUNCIL DIRECTIVE 2011/16/EU ON ADMINISTRATIVE COOPERATION IN THE FIELD OF TAXATION

(1156/2012/EU)

THE EUROPEAN COMMISSION,

Having regard to the Treaty on the Functioning of the European Union,

Having regard to Council Directive 2011/16/EU of 15 February 2011 on administrative cooperation in the field of taxation and repealing Directive 77/799/EEC (1), and in particular Articles 20(1), 20(3) and 21(1) thereof,

Whereas:

(1) Directive 2011/16/EU replaced Council Directive 77/799/EEC of 19 December 1977 concerning mutual assistance by the competent authorities of the Member States in the field of direct taxation (2). A number of important adaptations of the rules concerning administrative cooperation in the field of taxation were made, in particular as regards the exchange of information between Member States with a view to enhancing the efficiency and the effectiveness of cross-border exchange of information.

(2) In order to facilitate the exchange of information, Directive 2011/16/EU requires that such exchange take place on the basis of standard forms. Accordingly and with a view to ensuring the appropriateness of the data exchanged and the efficiency of the exchange itself, detailed rules should be laid down in this regard, for the purposes of the exchange of information on request, spontaneous

exchange of information, notifications and feedback information. The form to be used should contain a number of fields that are sufficiently diversified, so as to allow Member States to easily deal with all relevant cases, using the fields appropriate for each case.

(3) According to Directive 2011/16/EU, the information should be communicated using the Common Communication Network (CCN) as far as possible. For the other cases, the practical arrangements for the communication should be specified.

(4) The measures provided for in this Regulation are in accordance with the opinion of the Committee on Administrative Cooperation for Taxation,

HAS ADOPTED THIS REGULATION:

Article 1

1. In regard to the forms to be used, 'field' means a location in a form where information to be exchanged pursuant to the Council Directive may be recorded.
2. The form to be used for requests for information and for administrative enquiries pursuant to Article 5 of Directive 2011/16/EU and their replies, acknowledgments, requests for additional background information, inability or refusal pursuant to Article 7 of that Directive shall comply with Annex I to this Regulation.
3. The form to be used for spontaneous information and its acknowledgment pursuant to Articles 9 and 10 respectively of Directive 2011/16/EU shall comply with Annex II to this Regulation.
4. The form to be used for requests for administrative notification pursuant to Article 13(1) and (2) of Directive 2011/16/EU and their responses pursuant to Article 13(3) of that Directive shall comply with Annex III to this Regulation.
5. The form to be used for feedback information pursuant to Article 14(1) of Directive 2011/16/EU shall comply with Annex IV to this Regulation.

[Article 1a

The computerised format to be used for the mandatory automatic exchange of information pursuant to Article 8(1) of Directive 2011/16/EU shall comply with Annex V to this Regulation.][1]

Amendments—[1] Article 1a inserted by Commission Implementing Regulation 1353/2014/EU Art 1(1) with effect from 1 January 2015 (OJ L 365, 19.12.2014, p 70).

Article 2

1. The reports, statements and other documents referred to in the information communicated pursuant to Directive 2011/16/EU may be sent using means of communication other than the CCN network.
2. Where the information referred to in Directive 2011/16/EU is not exchanged by electronic means using the CCN network, and unless otherwise agreed bilaterally, the information shall be provided under cover of a letter describing the information communicated and duly signed by the competent authority communicating the information.

Article 3

This Regulation shall enter into force on the third day following that of its publication in the *Official Journal of the European Union*.
It shall apply from 1 January 2013.
This Regulation shall be binding in its entirety and directly applicable in all Member States.

Done at Brussels, ...*6 December 2012.*

For the Commission
The President
José Manuel BARROSO

ANNEX I

Form referred to in Article 1(2)

The form for requests for information and for administrative enquiries pursuant to Article 5 of Directive 2011/16/EU and their replies, acknowledgments, requests for additional background information, inability or refusal pursuant to Article 7 of Directive 2011/16/EU contains the following fields:

— Legal basis
— Reference number
— Date
— Identity of the requesting and requested authorities
— Identity of the person under examination or investigation

— General case description and, if appropriate, specific background information likely to allow assessing the foreseeable relevance of the information requested to the administration and enforcement of the domestic laws of the Member States concerning the taxes referred to in Article 2 of Directive 2011/16/EU
— Tax purpose for which the information is sought
— Period under investigation
— Name and address of any person believed to be in possession of the requested information
— Fulfilment of the legal requirement imposed by Article 16(1) of Directive 2011/16/EU
— Fulfilment of the legal requirement imposed by Article 17(1) of Directive 2011/16/EU
— Reasoned request for a specific administrative enquiry and reasons for refusal to undertake the requested specific administrative enquiry
— Acknowledgement of the request for information
— Request for additional background information
— Reasons for inability or refusal to provide information
— Reasons for a failure to respond by the relevant time limit and date by which the requested authority considers it might be able to respond.

ANNEX II

Form referred to in Article 1(3)

The form for spontaneous information and its acknowledgment pursuant to Articles 9 and 10 respectively of Directive 2011/16/EU contains the following fields:

— Legal basis
— Reference number
— Date
— Identity of the sending and receiving authorities
— Identity of the person subject to the spontaneous exchange of information
— Period covered by the spontaneous exchange of information
— Fulfilment of the legal requirement imposed by Article 16(1) of Directive 2011/16/EU
— Acknowledgement of the spontaneous information.

ANNEX III

Form referred to in Article 1(4)

The form for request for notification pursuant to Article 13(1) and (2) of Directive 2011/16/EU and their responses pursuant to Article 13(3) of that Directive contains the following fields:

— Legal basis
— Reference number
— Date
— Identity of the requesting and requested authorities
— Name and address of the addressee of the instrument or decision
— Other information which may facilitate the identification of the addressee
— Subject of the instrument or decision
— Response of the requested authority, in accordance with Article 13(3) of Directive 2011/16/EU, including the date of notification of the instrument or decision to the addressee.

ANNEX IV

Form referred to in Article 1(5)

The form for feedback pursuant to Article 14(1) of Directive 2011/16/EU contains the following fields:

— Reference number
— Date
— Identity of the competent authority issuing the feedback
— General feedback on the information provided
— Results directly related to the information provided.

[ANNEX V

COMPUTERISED FORMAT REFERRED TO IN ARTICLE 1A

The computerised formats for the mandatory automatic exchange of information pursuant to Article 8 of Directive 2011/16/EU complies with the following tree structure and contains the following classes of elements*:

(a) As regards the overall message:

— A 'HEADER' containing:

— An 'ORIGINATING COUNTRY',

— A 'DESTINATION COUNTRIES',

— A unique 'MESSAGE ID',

— A 'CORRELATION ID',

— A 'TIMESTAMP' and

— A 'MESSAGE TYPE INDIC';

— And a 'BODY' following the tree structure and classes of elements of any one of the bodies included in this annex under points (b) to (g) depending on the nature of the information to be exchanged automatically.

(b) As regards the body for communicating information on income from employment or director's fees:

— An 'APPLICATION ID' stating the nature of the information exchanged,

— A 'TAX YEAR' and

— One or more building blocks containing:

— One or more 'RECIPIENTS' providing information on each recipient and containing:

— One or more 'PAYERS' providing information on each payer and containing:

— One or more 'RELATIONSHIPS' providing information on the nature of each relationship between the recipient and the payer and containing: **— One or more 'WORKPLACE' where the relationship is carried out and — One or more 'INCOMES' providing information on each income or fee under the relationship and containing:— The 'QUANTITY' of the days spent or worked by the recipient;**

— And/or one or more 'RECIPIENT INVALIDATIONS' in the case of a correction or cancellation of previously exchanged information.

(c) As regards the body for communicating information on pensions:

— An 'APPLICATION ID' stating the nature of the information exchanged,

— A 'TAX YEAR' and

— One or more building blocks containing:

— One or more 'RECIPIENTS' providing information on each recipient and containing:

— One or more 'PAYERS' providing information on each payer and containing:

— One or more 'SCHEMES' providing information on each pension and containing:**— One or more 'SCHEME REFERENCE INFOS', — One or more 'CAPITAL VALUES', — An 'ADMINISTRATOR', — One or more 'OWNERS', — One or more 'EVENTS' providing general information on each event under the scheme and containing:— One or more 'EVENT INFO' containing detailed information on the event and one or more 'FINANCIAL INFO' and/or — One or more 'TAX INFO' containing detailed information on the taxes and one or more 'FINANCIAL INFO';**

— And/or one or more 'RECIPIENT INVALIDATIONS' in the case of a correction or cancellation of previously exchanged information.

(d) As regards the body for communicating information on life insurance products:

— An 'APPLICATION ID' stating the nature of the information exchanged,

— A 'TAX YEAR' and

— One or more building blocks containing:

— One or more 'POLICIES' providing information on each product and containing:

— A 'CONTRIBUTION DURATION',

— A 'BENEFIT DURATION',

— A 'POLICY OPTIONS',

— One or more 'POLICY CAPITAL VALUES',

— An 'INSURER/PAYING AGENT',

— One or more 'BENEFICIARIES',

— One or more 'LIFE INSURED',

— One or more 'PAYERS OF PREMIUMS',

— One or more 'POLICY OWNERS',

— One or more 'EVENTS' providing general information on each event under the policy and containing:

— One or more 'EVENT INFO' containing detailed information on the event and one or more 'FINANCIAL INFO' and/or

— One or more 'TAX INFO' containing detailed information on the taxes and one or more 'FINANCIAL INFO';

— And/or one or more 'POLICY INVALIDATIONS' in the case of a correction or cancellation of previously exchanged information.

(e) As regards the body for communicating information on ownership of and income from immovable property:

— An 'APPLICATION ID' stating the nature of the information exchanged,

— A 'TAX YEAR' and One or more building blocks containing:

— One or more 'PARTIES' providing information on each recipient and containing:

— A 'PARTNER' providing information on the spouse and

— Option 1 when the information relates to an income which cannot be linked (even indirectly) to one or more identified property: one or more 'INCOMES' or

— Option 2 when the information relates either to another information than an income or to an income which can be linked (even indirectly) to one or more identified property: one or more 'PROPERTIES' providing information on each property and containing:

— One or more 'OWNERSHIPS' and its associated 'RIGHT' providing information on each ownership and associated right in the property and containing: **— One or more 'TRANSACTIONS' providing information on each transaction relating to the property, — One or more 'INCOMES' providing information on each income relating to the property;**

— And/or one or more 'PARTY INVALIDATIONS' in the case of a correction or cancellation of previously exchanged information.

(f) As regards the body in case no information is to be communicated in relation to a specific category:

— An 'APPLICATION ID' stating the nature of the information exchanged,

— A 'DETAIL' stating the reason for the absence of data and

— A 'YEAR'.

(g) As regards the body for an acknowledgement of receipt of the information for a specific category:

— An 'APPLICATION ID' stating the nature of the information exchanged,

— A 'STATUS' providing information on the acceptance or rejection of a message received and

— One or more 'ERROR' providing information on the errors identified in a message received.][1]

* However, only the fields actually available and applicable in a given case need to appear in the computerised format used in that case.

Amendments—[1] Annex V inserted by Commission Implementing Regulation 1353/2014/EU Art 1(2), Annex, with effect from 1 January 2015 (OJ L 365, 19.12.2014, p 70).

REGULATION 952/2013/EU OF THE EUROPEAN PARLIAMENT AND OF THE COUNCIL OF 9 OCTOBER 2013 LAYING DOWN THE UNION CUSTOMS CODE

(952/2013/EU)

(recast)

THE EUROPEAN PARLIAMENT AND THE COUNCIL OF THE EUROPEAN UNION,

Having regard to the Treaty on the Functioning of the European Union, and in particular Articles 33, 114 and 207 thereof,

Having regard to the proposal from the European Commission,

After transmission of the draft legislative act to the national parliaments,

Having regard to the opinion of the European Economic and Social Committee,[1]

Acting in accordance with the ordinary legislative procedure,[2]

Whereas:

(1) A number of amendments are to be made to Regulation (EC) No 450/2008 of the European Parliament and of the Council of 23 April 2008 laying down the Community Customs Code (Modernised Customs Code).[3] In the interests of clarity, that Regulation should be recast.

(2) It is appropriate to ensure that Regulation (EC) No 450/2008 is consistent with the Treaty on the Functioning of the European Union (TFEU), in particular Articles 290 and 291 thereof. It is also appropriate that the Regulation take account of the evolution of Union law and that some of its provisions are adapted in order to facilitate their application.

(3) In order to supplement or amend certain non-essential elements of this Regulation, the power to adopt delegated acts in accordance with Article 290 TFEU should be delegated to the Commission. It is of particular importance that the Commission carry out appropriate consultations during its preparatory work, including at expert level. The Commission, when preparing and drawing up delegated acts, should ensure a simultaneous, timely and appropriate transmission of relevant documents to the European Parliament and to the Council.

(4) In particular, when preparing and drawing up delegated acts, the Commission should ensure that Member States' experts and the business community are consulted in a transparent manner, and well in advance.

(5) In order to ensure uniform conditions for the implementation of this Regulation, implementing powers should be conferred on the Commission in order: to specify the format and code of the common data requirements for the purpose of the exchange of information between the customs authorities and between economic operators and customs authorities and the storage of such information and the procedural rules on the exchange and storage of information which can be made by means other than electronic data-processing techniques; to adopt decisions allowing one or several Member States to use means for the exchange and storage of information other than electronic data-processing techniques; to specify the customs authority which is responsible for the registration of economic operators and of other persons; to specify the technical arrangements for developing, maintaining and employing electronic systems; to specify the procedural rules on the conferral and proving of the entitlement for a customs representative to provide services in a Member State other than the one where he or she is established; the procedural rules on the submission and acceptance of an application for a decision relating to the application of the customs legislation, and on the taking and the monitoring of such a decision; the procedural rules on the annulment, revocation and amendment of favourable decisions; the procedural rules on the use of a decision relating to binding information after it ceases to be valid or is revoked; the procedural rules on the notification to the customs authorities that the taking of such decisions is suspended and on the withdrawal of such suspension; to adopt decisions requesting Member States to revoke decisions relating to binding information; to adopt the modalities for the application of the criteria for the granting of the status of authorised economic operator; to adopt measures to ensure uniform application of customs controls, including the exchange of risk information and analysis,

common risk criteria and standards, control measures and priority control areas; to determine the ports or airports where customs controls and formalities are to be carried out on cabin and hold baggage; to lay down the rules on currency conversion; to adopt measures on the uniform management of tariff quota and tariff ceilings and the management of the surveillance of the release for free circulation or export of goods; to adopt measures to determine the tariff classification of goods; to specify the procedural rules on the provision and the verification of the proof of non-preferential origin; the procedural rules on the facilitation of the establishment in the Union of the preferential origin of goods; to adopt measures to determine the origin of specific goods; the granting of a temporary derogation from the rules on preferential origin of goods benefiting from preferential measures adopted unilaterally by the Union; the determination of the origin of specific goods;

to specify the procedural rules on the determination of the customs value of goods; to specify the procedural rules on the provision of a guarantee, the determination of its amount, its monitoring and release and the revocation and cancellation of an undertaking given by a guarantor; to specify the procedural rules regarding temporary prohibitions of the use of comprehensive guarantees; to adopt measures to ensure mutual assistance between the customs authorities in the event of the incurrence of a customs debt; to specify the procedural rules on repayment and remission of an amount of import or export duty and the information to be provided to the Commission; to adopt decisions on repayment or remission of an amount of import or export duty; to specify the procedural rules on the lodging, amendment and invalidation of an entry summary declaration; to specify the time-limit within which a risk analysis is to be carried out on the basis of the entry summary declaration; to specify the procedural rules on the notification of arrival of sea-going vessels and aircraft and on the conveyance of goods to the appropriate place; to specify the procedural rules on the presentation of goods to customs; the procedural rules on the lodging, amendment and invalidation of the temporary storage declaration and on the movement of goods in temporary storage; the procedural rules for the provision and verification of the proof of the customs status of Union goods; the procedural rules on the determination of competent customs offices and on the lodging of the customs declaration where other means than electronic data processing techniques are used; the procedural rules on the lodging of a standard customs declaration and on the making available of supporting documents; the procedural rules on the lodging of a simplified declaration and a supplementary declaration; the procedural rules on the lodging of a customs declaration prior to the presentation of goods to customs, the acceptance of the customs declaration and the amendment of the customs declaration after the release of the goods; to adopt measures for the determination of the tariff subheading of the goods which are subject to the highest rate of import or export duty where a consignment is made of goods falling under different tariff subheadings; to specify the procedural rules on centralised clearance and on the waiver from the obligation for goods to be presented in that context; the procedural rules on entry in the declarant's records; the procedural rules on the customs formalities and controls to be carried out by the holder of the authorisation in the context of self-assessment; to adopt measures on the verification of the customs declaration, the examination and sampling of goods and the results of the verification;

the procedural rules on the disposal of goods; the procedural rules on the provision of information establishing that the conditions for relief from import duty for returned goods are fulfilled and on the provision of evidence that the conditions for relief from import duty for products of sea-fishing and other products taken from the sea are fulfilled; the procedural rules on the examination of the economic conditions in the context of special procedures; the procedural rules on the discharge of a special procedure; the procedural rules on the transfer of rights and obligations and the movement of goods in the context of special procedures; the procedural rules on the use of equivalent goods in the context of special procedures; the procedural rules for the application of the provisions of international transit instruments in the customs territory of the Union; the procedural rules on the placing of goods under the Union transit procedure and on the end of that procedure, on the operation of the simplifications of that procedure and on the customs supervision of goods passing through the territory of a country or territory outside the customs territory of the Union under the external Union transit procedure; the procedural rules on the placing of goods under the customs warehousing or free zone procedure; to lay down the time-limit within which risk analysis is to be carried out on the basis of the pre-departure declaration; to specify the procedural rules on the exit of goods;

the procedural rules on the lodging, amendment and invalidation of the exit summary declaration; the procedural rules on the lodging, amendment and invalidation of the re-export notification; to adopt a work programme supporting the development of related electronic systems and governing the setting up of transitional periods; to adopt decisions authorising Member States to test simplifications in the application of the customs legislation, especially when those simplifications are information technology (IT) related. Those powers should be exercised in accordance with Regulation (EU) No 182/2011 of the European Parliament and of the Council of 16 February 2011 laying down the rules and general principles concerning mechanisms for control by Member States of the Commission's exercise of implementing powers.[4]

(6) Considering the cooperation which is needed between the Member States and the Commission to develop, maintain and employ the electronic systems required for the implementation of the Union Customs Code (the Code), the Commission should not adopt the work programme supporting that development and governing the setting up of transitional periods where no opinion is delivered by the committee examining the draft implementing act.

(7) The advisory procedure should be used for the adoption of: decisions allowing one or several Member States to use means for the exchange and storage of information other than electronic data-processing techniques, given that those decisions do not affect all Member States; decisions requesting Member States to revoke decisions relating to binding information, given that those decisions affect only one Member State and aim at ensuring compliance with the customs legislation; decisions on repayment or remission of an amount of import or export duty given that those decisions directly affect the applicant for that repayment or remission.

(8) In duly justified cases, where imperative grounds of urgency so require, the Commission should adopt immediately applicable implementing acts relating to: measures to ensure uniform application of customs controls, including the exchange of risk information and analysis, common risk criteria and standards, control measures and priority control areas; the determination of the tariff classification of goods; the determination of the origin of specific goods; measures temporarily prohibiting the use of comprehensive guarantees.

(9) The Union is based upon a customs union. It is advisable, in the interests both of economic operators and of the customs authorities in the Union, to assemble current customs legislation in a code. Based on the concept of an internal market, that code should contain the general rules and procedures which ensure the implementation of the tariff and other common policy measures introduced at Union level in connection with trade in goods between the Union and countries or territories outside the customs territory of the Union, taking into account the requirements of those

common policies. Customs legislation should be better aligned on the provisions relating to the collection of import charges without change to the scope of the tax provisions in force.

(10) In order to ensure effective administrative simplification, the views of economic operators should be taken into account when the customs legislation is further modernised.

(11) In accordance with the Commission Communication of 9 August 2004 entitled "Protecting the Communities' financial interests – Fight against fraud – Action Plan for 2004-2005", it is appropriate to adapt the legal framework for the protection of the financial interests of the Union.

(12) Council Regulation (EEC) No 2913/92 of 12 October 1992 establishing the Community Customs Code[5] was based upon integration of the customs procedures applied separately in the respective Member States during the 1980s. That Regulation has been repeatedly and substantially amended since its introduction, in order to address specific problems such as the protection of good faith or the taking into account of security requirements. Further amendments to that Regulation were introduced by Regulation (EC) No 648/2005 of the European Parliament and of the Council of 13 April 2005[6] – and subsequently included in Regulation (EC) No 450/2008 – as a consequence of the important legal changes which have occurred in recent years, at both Union and international level, such as the expiry of the Treaty establishing the European Coal and Steel Community and the entry into force of the 2003, 2005 and 2011 Acts of Accession, as well as the amendment to the International Convention on the simplification and harmonisation of customs procedures (the Revised Kyoto Convention), the Union's accession to which was approved by Council Decision 2003/231/EC of 17 March 2003.[7]

(13) It is appropriate to introduce in the Code a legal framework for the application of certain provisions of the customs legislation to trade in Union goods between parts of the customs territory to which the provisions of Council Directive 2006/112/EC of 28 November 2006 on the common system of value added tax[8] or Council Directive 2008/118/EC of 16 December 2008 concerning the general arrangements for excise duty[9] apply and parts of that territory where those provisions do not apply, or to trade between parts where those provisions do not apply. Considering the fact that the goods concerned are Union goods and considering the fiscal nature of the measures at stake in that intra-Union trade, it is justified to introduce, appropriate simplifications to the customs formalities to be applied to those goods.

(14) In order to take into account the special fiscal regime of certain parts of the customs territory of the Union, the power to adopt delegated acts in accordance with Article 290 TFEU should be delegated to the Commission in respect of the customs formalities and controls to be applied to the trade in Union goods between those parts and the rest of the customs territory of the Union.

(15) The facilitation of legitimate trade and the fight against fraud require simple, rapid and standard customs procedures and processes. It is therefore appropriate, in line with the Commission Communication of 24 July 2003 entitled "A simple and paperless environment for customs and trade", to simplify customs legislation, to allow the use of modern tools and technology and to promote further the uniform application of customs legislation and modernised approaches to customs control, thus helping to ensure the basis for efficient and simple clearance procedures. Customs procedures should be merged or aligned and the number of procedures reduced to those that are economically justified, with a view to increasing the competitiveness of business.

(16) The completion of the internal market, the reduction of barriers to international trade and investment and the reinforced need to ensure security and safety at the external borders of the Union have transformed the role of customs authorities giving them a leading role within the supply chain and, in their monitoring and management of international trade, making them a catalyst to the competitiveness of countries and companies. The customs legislation should therefore reflect the new economic reality and the new role and mission of customs authorities.

(17) The use of information and communication technologies, as laid down in Decision No 70/2008/EC of the European Parliament and of the Council of 15 January 2008 on a paperless environment for customs and trade,[10] is a key element in ensuring trade facilitation and, at the same time, the effectiveness of customs controls, thus reducing costs for business and risk for society. It is therefore necessary to establish in the Code the legal framework within which that Decision can be implemented, in particular the legal principle that all customs and trade transactions are to be handled electronically and that information and communication systems for customs operations are to offer, in each Member State, the same facilities to economic operators.

(18) In order to ensure a paperless environment for customs and trade, the power to adopt delegated acts in accordance with Article 290 TFEU should be delegated to the Commission in respect of common data requirements for the purpose of the exchange and storage of information using electronic data processing techniques, cases where other means may be used for such exchange and storage and registration of persons. Means other than electronic data processing techniques could be used in particular on a transitional basis, where the necessary electronic systems are not yet operational, but not beyond 31 December 2020. Insofar as centralised clearance is concerned, those transitional measures would consist, until the necessary electronic systems are operational, in maintaining the procedure currently known as the 'single authorisation for simplified procedures'.

(19) Use of information and communication technologies should be accompanied by harmonised and standardised application of customs controls by the Member States, to ensure an equivalent level

of customs control throughout the Union so as not to give rise to anti-competitive behaviour at the various Union entry and exit points.

(20) In the interests of facilitating business, while at the same time providing for the proper levels of control of goods brought into or taken out of the customs territory of the Union, it is desirable that the information provided by economic operators be shared, taking account of the relevant data-protection provisions, between customs authorities and with other agencies involved in that control. Those controls should be harmonised, so that the economic operator need give the information only once and that goods are controlled by those authorities at the same time and at the same place.

(21) In the interests of facilitating business, all persons should continue to have the right to appoint a representative in their dealings with the customs authorities. However, it should no longer be possible for that right of representation to be reserved under a law laid down by one of the Member States. Furthermore, a customs representative who complies with the criteria for the granting of the status of authorised economic operator for customs simplifications should be entitled to provide his or her services in a Member State other than the Member State where he or she is established. As a general rule, a customs representative should be established in the customs territory of the Union. That obligation should be waived where the customs representative acts on behalf of persons who are not required to be established within the customs territory of the Union or in other justified cases.

(22) All decisions relating to the application of the customs legislation, including to binding information, should be covered by the same rules. Any such decisions should be valid throughout the Union and should be capable of being annulled, amended except where otherwise stipulated, or revoked where they do not conform to the customs legislation or its interpretation.

(23) The streamlining of customs procedures within an electronic environment requires the sharing of responsibilities between the customs authorities of different Member States. It is necessary to ensure an appropriate level of effective, dissuasive and proportionate penalties throughout the internal market.

(24) Compliant and trustworthy economic operators should enjoy the status of 'authorised economic operator' subject to the granting of an authorisation for customs simplifications or an authorisation for security and safety, or both. Depending on the type of authorisation granted, authorised economic operators should be able to take maximum advantage of widespread use of customs simplifications or benefit from facilitations relating to security and safety. They should also be given more favourable treatment in respect of customs controls, such as fewer physical and document-based controls.

(25) Compliant and trustworthy economic operators should benefit from international mutual recognition of the status of 'authorised economic operator'.

(26) In order to secure a balance between, on the one hand, the need for customs authorities to ensure the correct application of the customs legislation and, on the other, the right of economic operators to be treated fairly, the customs authorities should be granted extensive powers of control and economic operators a right of appeal.

(27) In accordance with the Charter of Fundamental Rights of the European Union, it is necessary, in addition to the right of appeal against any decision taken by the customs authorities, to provide for the right of every person to be heard before any decision is taken which would adversely affect him or her. However, restrictions to that right may be justified in particular where the nature or the level of the threat to the security and safety of the Union and its residents, to human, animal or plant health, to the environment or to consumers so requires.

(28) In order to minimise the risk to the Union, its citizens and its trading partners, the harmonised application of customs controls by the Member States should be based upon a common risk management framework and an electronic system for its implementation. The establishment of a risk management framework common to all Member States should not prevent them from controlling goods by random checks.

(29) In order to ensure a consistent and equal treatment of persons concerned by customs formalities and controls, the power to adopt delegated acts in accordance with Article 290 TFEU should be delegated to the Commission in respect of determining other cases where the customs representative is not obliged to be established in the customs territory of the Union and rules relating to decisions taken by the customs authorities, including those relating to binding information, authorised economic operator and simplifications.

(30) It is necessary to establish the factors on the basis of which import or export duty and other measures in respect of trade in goods are applied. It is also appropriate to lay down more detailed provisions for issuing proofs of origin in the Union, where the exigencies of trade so require.

(31) In order to supplement the factors on the basis of which import or export duty and other measures are applied, the power to adopt delegated acts in accordance with Article 290 TFEU should be delegated to the Commission in respect of rules on origin of goods.

(32) It is desirable to group together all cases of incurrence of a customs debt on import, other than following the submission of a customs declaration for release for free circulation or temporary admission with partial relief, in order to avoid difficulties in determining the legal basis on which the customs debt was incurred. The same should apply in cases of incurrence of a customs debt on export.

(33) It is appropriate to establish the place where the customs debt is incurred and where the import or export duty should be recovered.

(34) The rules for special procedures should allow for the use of a single guarantee for all categories of special procedures and for that guarantee to be comprehensive, covering a number of transactions.

(35) A comprehensive guarantee with a reduced amount, including for customs debts and other charges which have been incurred, or a comprehensive guarantee with a guarantee waiver, should be authorised under certain conditions. A comprehensive guarantee with a reduced amount for customs debts and other charges which have been incurred should be equivalent to the provision of a guarantee for the whole amount of import or export duty payable, in particular for the purposes of the release of the goods concerned and of the entry in the accounts.

(36) In order to ensure better protection of the financial interests of the Union and of the Member States, a guarantee should cover non-declared or incorrectly declared goods included in a consignment or in a declaration for which it is provided. For the same reason, the undertaking of the guarantor should also cover amounts of import or export duty which fall to be paid following post-release controls.

(37) In order to safeguard the financial interests of the Union and of the Member States and to curb fraudulent practices, arrangements involving graduated measures for the application of a comprehensive guarantee are advisable. Where there is an increased risk of fraud it should be possible to prohibit temporarily the application of the comprehensive guarantee, taking account of the particular situation of the economic operators concerned.

(38) It is appropriate to take account of the good faith of the person concerned in cases where a customs debt is incurred through non-compliance with the customs legislation and to minimise the impact of negligence on the part of the debtor.

(39) In order to protect the financial interests of the Union and of the Member States and to supplement the rules concerning the customs debt and the guarantees, the power to adopt delegated acts in accordance with Article 290 TFEU should be delegated to the Commission in respect of the place of incurrence of the customs debt, the calculation of the amount of import and export duty, the guarantee of that amount and the recovery, repayment, remission and extinguishment of the customs debt.

(40) It is necessary to lay down the principle of how to determine the customs status of Union goods and the circumstances pertaining to the loss of such status, and to provide a basis for determining when that status remains unaltered in cases where goods are temporarily taken out of the customs territory of the Union.

(41) In order to ensure free movement of Union goods in the customs territory of the Union and customs treatment of non-Union goods brought into that territory, the power to adopt delegated acts in accordance with Article 290 TFEU should be delegated to the Commission in respect of the determination of the customs status of goods, the loss of the customs status of Union goods, the preservation of that status for goods temporarily leaving the customs territory of the Union and the duty relief for returned goods.

(42) It is appropriate, where an economic operator has provided, in advance, the information necessary for risk-based controls on the admissibility of the goods, to ensure that quick release of goods is then the rule. Fiscal and trade policy controls should primarily be performed by the customs office competent in respect of the premises of the economic operator.

(43) The rules for customs declarations and for the placing of goods under a customs procedure should be modernised and streamlined, in particular by requiring that, as a rule, customs declarations be made electronically and by providing for only one type of simplified declaration and for the possibility to lodge a customs declaration in the form of an entry in the declarant's records.

(44) Since the Revised Kyoto Convention favours the lodging, registering and checking of the customs declaration prior to the arrival of the goods and, furthermore, the dissociation of the place where the declaration is lodged from the place where the goods are physically located, it is appropriate to provide for centralised clearance at the place where the economic operator is established.

(45) It is appropriate to lay down at Union level the rules governing the destruction or disposal otherwise of goods by the customs authorities, since these are matters which previously required national legislation.

(46) In order to supplement the rules regarding the placing of goods under a customs procedure and ensure equal treatment of the persons concerned, the power to adopt delegated acts in accordance with Article 290 TFEU should be delegated to the Commission in respect of the rules relating to the customs declaration and the release of goods.

(47) It is appropriate to lay down common and simple rules for the special procedures, supplemented by a small set of rules for each category of special procedure, in order to make it simple for the operator to choose the right procedure, to avoid errors and to reduce the number of post-release recoveries and repayments.

(48) The granting of authorisations for several special procedures with a single guarantee and a single supervising customs office should be facilitated and there should be simple rules on the

incurrence of a customs debt in these cases. The basic principle should be that goods placed under a special procedure, or the products made from them, are to be assessed at the time when the customs debt is incurred. However, it should also be possible, where economically justified, to assess the goods at the time when they were placed under a special procedure. The same principles should apply to usual forms of handling.

(49) In view of increased security-related measures, the placing of goods into free zones should become a customs procedure and the goods should be subject to customs controls at entry and with regard to records.

(50) Given that the intention of re-export is no longer necessary, the inward processing suspension procedure should be merged with processing under customs control and the inward processing drawback procedure abandoned. This single inward processing procedure should also cover destruction, except where destruction is carried out by, or under the supervision of, customs.

(51) In order to supplement the rules on special procedures and ensure equal treatment of the persons concerned, the power to adopt delegated acts in accordance with Article 290 TFEU should be delegated to the Commission in respect of the rules relating to cases where goods are placed under special procedures, movements, usual forms of handling and equivalence of those goods and discharge of those procedures.

(52) Security-related measures relating to Union goods taken out of the customs territory of the Union should apply equally to the re-export of non-Union goods. The same rules should apply to all types of goods, with the possibility of exceptions where necessary, such as for goods only transiting through the customs territory of the Union.

(53) In order to ensure the customs supervision of goods brought into and taken out of the customs territory of the Union and the application of security-related measures, the power to adopt delegated acts in accordance with Article 290 TFEU should be delegated to the Commission in respect of the rules relating to entry summary declaration and pre-departure declarations.

(54) In order to explore further customs and trade facilitation, in particular by making use of the most recent tools and technology, Member States should be authorised, under certain conditions and upon application, to test for a limited period of time simplifications in the application of the customs legislation. That possibility should not jeopardise the application of the customs legislation or create new obligations for economic operators, who may take part in these tests on a purely voluntary basis.

(55) In accordance with the principle of proportionality, as set out in Article 5 of the Treaty on European Union (TEU), it is necessary and appropriate, for the achievement of the basic objectives of enabling the customs union to function effectively and implementing the common commercial policy, to lay down the general rules and procedures applicable to goods brought into or taken out of the customs territory of the Union. In accordance with the first subparagraph of Article 5(4) TEU, this Regulation does not go beyond what is necessary in order to achieve those objectives.

(56) In order to simplify and rationalise customs legislation, a number of provisions contained in autonomous Union acts have, for the sake of transparency, been incorporated into the Code. Council Regulation (EEC) No 3925/91 of 19 December 1991 concerning the elimination of controls and formalities applicable to the cabin and hold baggage of persons taking an intra-Community flight and the baggage of persons making an intra- Community sea crossing,[11] Regulation (EEC) No 2913/92, Council Regulation (EC) No 1207/2001 of 11 June 2001 on procedures to facilitate the issue or the making out in the Community of proofs of origin and the issue of certain approved exporter authorisations under the provisions governing preferential trade between the European Community and certain countries,[12] and Regulation (EC) No 450/2008 should therefore be repealed.

(57) The provisions of this Regulation setting out the delegation of power and the conferral of implementing powers and the provisions on charges and costs should apply from the date of entry into force of this Regulation. The other provisions should apply from 1 May 2016.

(58) This Regulation should be without prejudice to existing and future Union rules on access to documents adopted in accordance with Article 15(3) TFEU. It should also be without prejudice to national rules on access to documents.

(59) The Commission should make every effort to ensure that the delegated and implementing acts provided for in this Regulation enter into force sufficiently in advance of the application date of the Code to allow its timely implementation by Member States,

Notes[1] OJ C229, 31.7.2012, p 68.

[2] Position of the European Parliament of 11 September 2013 (not yet published in the Official Journal) and decision of the Council of 27 September 2013.

[3] OJ L145, 4.6.2008, p 1.

[4] OJ L55, 28.2.2011, p 13.

[5] OJ L302, 19.10.1992, p 1.

[6] OJ L117, 4.5.2005, p 13.

[7] OJ L86, 3.4.2003, p 21.

[8] OJ L347, 11.12.2006, p 1.

[9] OJ L9, 14.1.2009, p 12.

[10] OJ L23, 26.1.2008, p 21.

[11] OJ L374, 31.12.1991, p 4.

[12] OJ L165, 21.6.2001, p 1.

HAVE ADOPTED THIS REGULATION:

TITLE I

GENERAL PROVISIONS

CHAPTER 1

SCOPE OF THE CUSTOMS LEGISLATION, MISSION OF CUSTOMS AND DEFINITIONS

Article 1 Subject matter and scope

1. This Regulation establishes the Union Customs Code (the Code), laying down the general rules and procedures applicable to goods brought into or taken out of the customs territory of the Union.

Without prejudice to international law and conventions and Union legislation in other fields, the Code shall apply uniformly throughout the customs territory of the Union.

2. Certain provisions of the customs legislation may apply outside the customs territory of the Union within the framework of legislation governing specific fields or of international conventions.

3. Certain provisions of the customs legislation, including the simplifications for which it provides, shall apply to the trade in Union goods between parts of the customs territory of the Union to which the provisions of Directive 2006/112/EC or of Directive 2008/118/EC apply and parts of that territory where those provisions do not apply, or to trade between parts of that territory where those provisions do not apply.

Article 2 Delegation of power

The Commission shall be empowered to adopt delegated acts in accordance with Article 284 specifying the provisions of the customs legislation and the simplifications thereof with respect to the customs declaration, the proof of the customs status, the use of the internal Union transit procedure insofar as it does not affect a proper application of the fiscal measures at stake, which apply to the trade in Union goods referred to in Article 1(3). Those acts may address particular circumstances pertaining to the trade in Union goods involving only one Member State.

Article 3 Mission of customs authorities

Customs authorities shall be primarily responsible for the supervision of the Union's international trade, thereby contributing to fair and open trade, to the implementation of the external aspects of the internal market, of the common trade policy and of the other common Union policies having a bearing on trade, and to overall supply chain security. Customs authorities shall put in place measures aimed, in particular, at the following:

(a) protecting the financial interests of the Union and its Member States;

(b) protecting the Union from unfair and illegal trade while supporting legitimate business activity;

(c) ensuring the security and safety of the Union and its residents, and the protection of the environment, where appropriate in close cooperation with other authorities; and

(d) maintaining a proper balance between customs controls and facilitation of legitimate trade.

Article 4 Customs territory

1. The customs territory of the Union shall comprise the following territories, including their territorial waters, internal waters and airspace:

— the territory of the Kingdom of Belgium,

— the territory of the Republic of Bulgaria,

— the territory of the Czech Republic,

— the territory of the Kingdom of Denmark, except the Faroe Islands and Greenland,

— the territory of the Federal Republic of Germany, except the Island of Heligoland and the territory of Büsingen (Treaty of 23 November 1964 between the Federal Republic of Germany and the Swiss Confederation),

— the territory of the Republic of Estonia,

— the territory of Ireland,

— the territory of the Hellenic Republic,

— the territory of the Kingdom of Spain, except Ceuta and Melilla,

— the territory of the French Republic, except the French overseas countries and territories to which the provisions of Part Four of the TFEU apply,

— the territory of the Republic of Croatia,

— the territory of the Italian Republic, except the municipalities of Livigno and Campione d'Italia and the national waters of Lake Lugano which are between the bank and the political frontier of the area between Ponte Tresa and Porto Ceresio,

— the territory of the Republic of Cyprus, in accordance with the provisions of the 2003 Act of Accession,

— the territory of the Republic of Latvia,
— the territory of the Republic of Lithuania,
— the territory of the Grand Duchy of Luxembourg,
— the territory of Hungary,
— the territory of Malta,
— the territory of the Kingdom of the Netherlands in Europe,
— the territory of the Republic of Austria,
— the territory of the Republic of Poland,
— the territory of the Portuguese Republic,
— the territory of Romania,
— the territory of the Republic of Slovenia,
— the territory of the Slovak Republic,
— the territory of the Republic of Finland,
— the territory of the Kingdom of Sweden, and
— the territory of the United Kingdom of Great Britain and Northern Ireland and of the Channel Islands and the Isle of Man.

2. The following territories, including their territorial waters, internal waters and airspace, situated outside the territory of the Member States shall, taking into account the conventions and treaties applicable to them, be considered to be part of the customs territory of the Union:

(a) FRANCE

The territory of Monaco as defined in the Customs Convention signed in Paris on 18 May 1963 (Journal officiel de la République française (Official Journal of the French Republic) of 27 September 1963, p. 8679);

(b) CYPRUS

The territory of the United Kingdom Sovereign Base Areas of Akrotiri and Dhekelia as defined in the Treaty concerning the Establishment of the Republic of Cyprus, signed in Nicosia on 16 August 1960 (United Kingdom Treaty Series No 4 (1961) Cmnd. 1252).

Article 5 Definitions

For the purposes of the Code, the following definitions shall apply:

(1) "customs authorities" means the customs administrations of the Member States responsible for applying the customs legislation and any other authorities empowered under national law to apply certain customs legislation;

(2) "customs legislation" means the body of legislation made up of all of the following:

(a) the Code and the provisions supplementing or implementing it adopted at Union or national level;

(b) the Common Customs Tariff;

(c) the legislation setting up a Union system of reliefs from customs duty;

(d) international agreements containing customs provisions, insofar as they are applicable in the Union;

(3) "customs controls" means specific acts performed by the customs authorities in order to ensure compliance with the customs legislation and other legislation governing the entry, exit, transit, movement, storage and end-use of goods moved between the customs territory of the Union and countries or territories outside that territory, and the presence and movement within the customs territory of the Union of non-Union goods and goods placed under the end-use procedure;

(4) "person" means a natural person, a legal person, and any association of persons which is not a legal person but which is recognised under Union or national law as having the capacity to perform legal acts;

(5) "economic operator" means a person who, in the course of his or her business, is involved in activities covered by the customs legislation;

(6) "customs representative" means any person appointed by another person to carry out the acts and formalities required under the customs legislation in his or her dealings with customs authorities;

(7) "risk" means the likelihood and the impact of an event occurring, with regard to the entry, exit, transit, movement or end-use of goods moved between the customs territory of the Union and countries or territories outside that territory and to the presence within the customs territory of the Union of non-Union goods, which would:

(a) prevent the correct application of Union or national measures;

(b) compromise the financial interests of the Union and its Member States; or

(c) pose a threat to the security and safety of the Union and its residents, to human, animal or plant health, to the environment or to consumers;

(8) "customs formalities" means all the operations which must be carried out by a person and by the customs authorities in order to comply with the customs legislation;
(9) "entry summary declaration" means the act whereby a person informs the customs authorities, in the prescribed form and manner and within a specific time-limit, that goods are to be brought into the customs territory of the Union;
(10) "exit summary declaration" means the act whereby a person informs the customs authorities, in the prescribed form and manner and within a specific time-limit, that goods are to be taken out of the customs territory of the Union;
(11) "temporary storage declaration" means the act whereby a person indicates, in the prescribed form and manner, that goods are in temporary storage;
(12) "customs declaration" means the act whereby a person indicates, in the prescribed form and manner, a wish to place goods under a given customs procedure, with an indication, where appropriate, of any specific arrangements to be applied;
(13) "re-export declaration" means the act whereby a person indicates, in the prescribed form and manner, a wish to take non-Union goods, with the exception of those under the free zone procedure or in temporary storage, out of the customs territory of the Union;
(14) "re-export notification" means the act whereby a person indicates, in the prescribed form and manner, a wish to take non-Union goods which are under the free zone procedure or in temporary storage out of the customs territory of the Union;
(15) "declarant" means the person lodging a customs declaration, a temporary storage declaration, an entry summary declaration, an exit summary declaration, a re- export declaration or a re-export notification in his or her own name or the person in whose name such a declaration or notification is lodged;
(16) "customs procedure" means any of the following procedures under which goods may be placed in accordance with the Code:

(a) release for free circulation;
(b) special procedures;
(c) export;

(17) 'temporary storage' means the situation of non-Union goods temporarily stored under customs supervision in the period between their presentation to customs and their placing under a customs procedure or re-export;
(18) "customs debt" means the obligation on a person to pay the amount of import or export duty which applies to specific goods under the customs legislation in force;
(19) "debtor" means any person liable for a customs debt;
(20) "import duty" means customs duty payable on the import of goods;
(21) "export duty" means customs duty payable on the export of goods;
(22) "customs status" means the status of goods as Union or non-Union goods;
(23) "Union goods" means goods which fall into any of the following categories:

(a) goods wholly obtained in the customs territory of the Union and not incorporating goods imported from countries or territories outside the customs territory of the Union;
(b) goods brought into the customs territory of the Union from countries or territories outside that territory and released for free circulation;
(c) goods obtained or produced in the customs territory of the Union, either solely from goods referred to in point (b) or from goods referred to in points (a) and (b);

(24) "non-Union goods" means goods other than those referred to in point 23 or which have lost their customs status as Union goods;
(25) "risk management" means the systematic identification of risk, including through random checks, and the implementation of all measures necessary for limiting exposure to risk;
(26) "release of goods" means the act whereby the customs authorities make goods available for the purposes specified for the customs procedure under which they are placed;
(27) "customs supervision" means action taken in general by the customs authorities with a view to ensuring that customs legislation and, where appropriate, other provisions applicable to goods subject to such action are observed;
(28) "repayment" means the refunding of an amount of import or export duty that has been paid;
(29) "remission" means the waiving of the obligation to pay an amount of import or export duty which has not been paid;
(30) "processed products" means goods placed under a processing procedure which have undergone processing operations;
(31) "person established in the customs territory of the Union" means:

(a) in the case of a natural person, any person who has his or her habitual residence in the customs territory of the Union;

(b) in the case of a legal person or an association of persons, any person having its registered office, central headquarters or a permanent business establishment in the customs territory of the Union;

(32) "permanent business establishment" means a fixed place of business, where both the necessary human and technical resources are permanently present and through which a person's customs-related operations are wholly or partly carried out;

(33) "presentation of goods to customs" means the notification to the customs authorities of the arrival of goods at the customs office or at any other place designated or approved by the customs authorities and the availability of those goods for customs controls;

(34) "holder of the goods" means the person who is the owner of the goods or who has a similar right of disposal over them or who has physical control of them;

(35) "holder of the procedure" means:

(a) the person who lodges the customs declaration, or on whose behalf that declaration is lodged; or

(b) the person to whom the rights and obligations in respect of a customs procedure have been transferred;

(36) "commercial policy measures" means non-tariff measures established, as part of the common commercial policy, in the form of Union provisions governing international trade in goods;

(37) "processing operations" means any of the following:

(a) the working of goods, including erecting or assembling them or fitting them to other goods;

(b) the processing of goods;

(c) the destruction of goods;

(d) the repair of goods, including restoring them and putting them in order;

(e) the use of goods which are not to be found in the processed products, but which allow or facilitate the production of those products, even if they are entirely or partially used up in the process (production accessories);

(38) "rate of yield" means the quantity or percentage of processed products obtained from the processing of a given quantity of goods placed under a processing procedure;

(39) "decision" means any act by the customs authorities pertaining to the customs legislation giving a ruling on a particular case, and having legal effects on the person or persons concerned;

(40) "carrier" means:

(a) in the context of entry, the person who brings the goods, or who assumes responsibility for the carriage of the goods, into the customs territory of the Union. However,

(i) in the case of combined transportation, "carrier" means the person who operates the means of transport which, once brought into the customs territory of the Union, moves by itself as an active means of transport;

(ii) in the case of maritime or air traffic under a vessel- sharing or contracting arrangement, "carrier" means the person who concludes a contract and issues a bill of lading or air waybill for the actual carriage of the goods into the customs territory of the Union;

(b) in the context of exit, the person who takes the goods, or who assumes responsibility for the carriage of the goods, out of the customs territory of the Union. However:

(i) in the case of combined transportation, where the active means of transport leaving the customs territory of the Union is only transporting another means of transport which, after the arrival of the active means of transport at its destination, will move by itself as an active means of transport, 'carrier' means the person who will operate the means of transport which will move by itself once the means of transport leaving the customs territory of the Union has arrived at its destination;

(ii) in the case of maritime or air traffic under a vessel- sharing or contracting arrangement, "carrier" means the person who concludes a contract, and issues a bill of lading or air waybill, for the actual carriage of the goods out of the customs territory of the Union;

(41) "buying commission" means a fee paid by an importer to an agent for representing him or her in the purchase of goods being valued.

CHAPTER 2
RIGHTS AND OBLIGATIONS OF PERSONS WITH REGARD TO THE CUSTOMS LEGISLATION

SECTION 1
PROVISION OF INFORMATION

Article 6 Means for the exchange and storage of information and common data requirements

1. All exchanges of information, such as declarations, applications or decisions, between customs authorities and between economic operators and customs authorities, and the storage of such information, as required under the customs legislation, shall be made using electronic data-processing techniques.

2. Common data requirements shall be drawn up for the purpose of the exchange and storage of information referred to in paragraph 1.

3. Means for the exchange and storage of information, other than the electronic data-processing techniques referred to in paragraph 1, may be used as follows:

(a) on a permanent basis where duly justified by the type of traffic or where the use of electronic data-processing techniques is not appropriate for the customs formalities concerned;

(b) on a temporary basis, in the event of a temporary failure of the computerised system of the customs authorities or of the economic operators.

4. By way of derogation from paragraph 1, the Commission may adopt in exceptional cases decisions allowing one or several Member States to use means for the exchange and storage of information other than electronic data-processing techniques.

Such a decision on a derogation shall be justified by the specific situation of the Member State requesting it and the derogation shall be granted for a specific period of time. The derogation shall be reviewed periodically and may be extended for further specific periods of time upon further application by the Member State to which it is addressed. It shall be revoked where no longer justified.

The derogation shall not affect the exchange of information between the Member State to which it is addressed and other Member States nor the exchange and storage of information in other Member States for the purpose of the application of the customs legislation.

Article 7 Delegation of power

The Commission shall be empowered to adopt delegated acts, in accordance with Article 284, in order to determine the following:

(a) the common data requirements referred to in Article 6(2), taking into account the need to accomplish the customs formalities laid down in the customs legislation and the nature and purpose of the exchange and storage of information referred to in Article 6(1);

(b) the specific cases where means for the exchange and storage of information, other than electronic data-processing techniques, may be used in accordance with point (a) of Article 6(3);

(c) the type of information and the particulars that are to be contained in the records referred to in Articles 148(4) and 214(1).

Article 8 Conferral of implementing powers

1. The Commission shall specify, by means of implementing acts:

(a) where necessary, the format and code of the common data requirements referred to in Article 6(2);

(b) the procedural rules on the exchange and storage of information which can be made by means other than the electronic data-processing techniques referred to in Article 6(3).

Those implementing acts shall be adopted in accordance with the examination procedure referred to in Article 285(4).

2. The Commission shall adopt the decisions on derogations referred to in Article 6(4) by means of implementing acts.

Those implementing acts shall be adopted in accordance with the advisory procedure referred to in Article 285(2).

Article 9 Registration

1. Economic operators established in the customs territory of the Union shall register with the customs authorities responsible for the place where they are established.

2. In specific cases, economic operators which are not established in the customs territory of the Union shall register with the customs authorities responsible for the place where they first lodge a declaration or apply for a decision.

3. Persons other than economic operators shall not be required to register with the customs authorities unless otherwise provided.

Where persons referred to in the first subparagraph are required to register, the following shall apply:

(a) where they are established in the customs territory of the Union, they shall register with the customs authorities responsible for the place where they are established;
(b) where they are not established in the customs territory of the Union, they shall register with the customs authorities responsible for the place where they first lodge a declaration or apply for a decision.

4. In specific cases, the customs authorities shall invalidate the registration.

Article 10 Delegation of power

The Commission shall be empowered to adopt delegated acts in accordance with Article 284, in order to determine:

(a) the cases referred to in Article 9(2), where economic operators which are not established in the customs territory of the Union are required to register with the customs authorities;
(b) the cases referred to in the first subparagraph of Article 9(3), where persons other than economic operators are required to register with the customs authorities;
(c) the cases referred to in Article 9(4) where the customs authorities invalidate a registration.

Article 11 Conferral of implementing powers

The Commission shall specify, by means of implementing acts, the customs authority responsible for the registration referred to in Article 9.

Those implementing acts shall be adopted in accordance with the examination procedure referred to in Article 285(4).

Article 12 Communication of information and data protection

1. All information acquired by the customs authorities in the course of performing their duty which is by its nature confidential or which is provided on a confidential basis shall be covered by the obligation of professional secrecy. Except as provided for in Article 47(2), such information shall not be disclosed by the competent authorities without the express permission of the person or authority that provided it.

Such information may, however, be disclosed without permission where the customs authorities are obliged or authorised to do so pursuant to the provisions in force, particularly in respect of data protection, or in connection with legal proceedings.

2. Confidential information referred to in paragraph 1 may be communicated to the customs authorities and other competent authorities of countries or territories outside the customs territory of the Union for the purpose of customs cooperation with those countries or territories in the framework of an international agreement or Union legislation in the area of the common commercial policy.

3. Any disclosure or communication of information as referred to in paragraphs 1 and 2 shall ensure an adequate level of data protection in full compliance with data protection provisions in force.

Article 13 Exchange of additional information between customs authorities and economic operators

1. Customs authorities and economic operators may exchange any information not specifically required under the customs legislation, in particular for the purpose of mutual cooperation in the identification and counteraction of risk. That exchange may take place under a written agreement and may include access to the computer systems of economic operators by the customs authorities.

2. Any information provided by one party to the other in the course of the cooperation referred to in paragraph 1 shall be confidential unless both parties agree otherwise.

Article 14 Provision of information by the customs authorities

1. Any person may request information concerning the application of the customs legislation from the customs authorities. Such a request may be refused where it does not relate to an activity pertaining to international trade in goods that is actually envisaged.

2. Customs authorities shall maintain a regular dialogue with economic operators and other authorities involved in international trade in goods. They shall promote transparency by making the customs legislation, general administrative rulings and application forms freely available, wherever practical without charge, and through the Internet.

Article 15 Provision of information to the customs authorities

1. Any person directly or indirectly involved in the accomplishment of customs formalities or in customs controls shall, at the request of the customs authorities and within any time-limit specified, provide those authorities with all the requisite documents and information, in an appropriate form, and all the assistance necessary for the completion of those formalities or controls.

2. The lodging of a customs declaration, temporary storage declaration, entry summary declaration, exit summary declaration, re-export declaration or re-export notification by a person to the customs authorities, or the submission of an application for an authorisation or any other decision, shall render the person concerned responsible for all of the following:

(a) the accuracy and completeness of the information given in the declaration, notification or application;

(b) the authenticity, accuracy and validity of any document supporting the declaration, notification or application;
(c) where applicable, compliance with all of the obligations relating to the placing of the goods in question under the customs procedure concerned, or to the conduct of the authorised operations.

The first subparagraph shall also apply to the provision of any information in any other form required by, or given to, the customs authorities.

Where the declaration or notification is lodged, the application is submitted, or information is provided, by a customs representative of the person concerned, as referred to in Article 18, that customs representative shall also be bound by the obligations set out in the first subparagraph of this paragraph.

Article 16 Electronic systems

1. Member States shall cooperate with the Commission to develop, maintain and employ electronic systems for the exchange of information between customs authorities and with the Commission and for the storage of such information, in accordance with the Code.

2. Member States to which a derogation has been granted in accordance with Article 6(4) shall not be required to develop, maintain and employ within the scope of that derogation the electronic systems referred to in paragraph 1 of this Article.

Article 17 Conferral of implementing powers

The Commission shall specify, by means of implementing acts, the technical arrangements for developing, maintaining and employing the electronic systems referred to in Article 16(1).

Those implementing acts shall be adopted in accordance with the examination procedure referred to in Article 285(4).

SECTION 2
CUSTOMS REPRESENTATION

Article 18 Customs representative

1. Any person may appoint a customs representative.

Such representation may be either direct, in which case the customs representative shall act in the name of and on behalf of another person, or indirect, in which case the customs representative shall act in his or her own name but on behalf of another person.

2. A customs representative shall be established within the customs territory of the Union.

Except where otherwise provided, that requirement shall be waived where the customs representative acts on behalf of persons who are not required to be established within the customs territory of the Union.

3. Member States may determine, in accordance with Union law, the conditions under which a customs representative may provide services in the Member State where he or she is established. However, without prejudice to the application of less stringent criteria by the Member State concerned, a customs representative who complies with the criteria laid down in points (a) to (d) of Article 39 shall be entitled to provide such services in a Member State other than the one where he or she is established.

4. Member States may apply the conditions determined in accordance with the first sentence of paragraph 3 to customs representatives not established within the customs territory of the Union.

Article 19 Empowerment

1. When dealing with the customs authorities, a customs representative shall state that he or she is acting on behalf of the person represented and shall specify whether the representation is direct or indirect.

Persons who fail to state that they are acting as a customs representative or who state that they are acting as a customs representative without being empowered to do so shall be deemed to be acting in their own name and on their own behalf.

2. The customs authorities may require persons stating that they are acting as a customs representative to provide evidence of their empowerment by the person represented.

In specific cases, the customs authorities shall not require such evidence to be provided.

3. The customs authorities shall not require a person acting as a customs representative, carrying out acts and formalities on a regular basis, to produce on every occasion evidence of empowerment, provided that such person is in a position to produce such evidence on request by the customs authorities.

Article 20 Delegation of power

The Commission shall be empowered to adopt delegated acts, in accordance with Article 284, in order to determine:

(a) the cases where the waiver referred to in the second subparagraph of Article 18(2) does not apply;

(b) the cases where the evidence of empowerment referred to in the first subparagraph of Article 19(2) is not required by the customs authorities.

Article 21 Conferral of implementing powers

The Commission shall specify, by means of implementing acts, the procedural rules on the conferral and proving of the entitlement referred to in Article 18(3).

Those implementing acts shall be adopted in accordance with the examination procedure referred to in Article 285(4).

SECTION 3

DECISIONS RELATING TO THE APPLICATION OF THE CUSTOMS LEGISLATION

Article 22 Decisions taken upon application

1. Where a person applies for a decision relating to the application of the customs legislation, that person shall supply all the information required by the competent customs authorities in order to enable them to take that decision.

A decision may also be applied for by, and taken with regard to, several persons, in accordance with the conditions laid down in the customs legislation.

Except where otherwise provided, the competent customs authority shall be that of the place where the applicant's main accounts for customs purposes are held or accessible, and where at least part of the activities to be covered by the decision are to be carried out.

2. Customs authorities shall, without delay and at the latest within 30 days of receipt of the application for a decision, verify whether the conditions for the acceptance of that application are fulfilled.

Where the customs authorities establish that the application contains all the information required in order for them to be able to take the decision, they shall communicate its acceptance to the applicant within the period specified in the first subparagraph.

3. The competent customs authority shall take a decision as referred to in paragraph 1, and shall notify the applicant without delay, and at the latest within 120 days of the date of acceptance of the application, except where otherwise provided

Where the customs authorities are unable to comply with the time-limit for taking a decision, they shall inform the applicant of that fact before the expiry of that time-limit, stating the reasons and indicating the further period of time which they consider necessary in order to take a decision. Except where otherwise provided, that further period of time shall not exceed 30 days.

Without prejudice to the second subparagraph, the customs authorities may extend the time-limit for taking a decision, as laid down in the customs legislation, where the applicant requests an extension to carry out adjustments in order to ensure the fulfilment of the conditions and criteria. Those adjustments and the further period of time necessary to carry them out shall be communicated to the customs authorities, which shall decide on the extension.

4. Except where otherwise specified in the decision or in the customs legislation, the decision shall take effect from the date on which the applicant receives it, or is deemed to have received it. Except in the cases provided for in Article 45(2), decisions adopted shall be enforceable by the customs authorities from that date.

5. Except where otherwise provided in the customs legislation, the decision shall be valid without limitation of time.

6. Before taking a decision which would adversely affect the applicant, the customs authorities shall communicate the grounds on which they intend to base their decision to the applicant, who shall be given the opportunity to express his or her point of view within a period prescribed from the date on which he or she receives that communication or is deemed to have received it. Following the expiry of that period, the applicant shall be notified, in the appropriate form, of the decision.

The first subparagraph shall not apply in any of the following cases:

(a) where it concerns a decision referred to in Article 33(1);
(b) in the event of refusal of the benefit of a tariff quota where the specified tariff quota volume is reached, as referred to in the first subparagraph of Article 56(4);
(c) where the nature or the level of a threat to the security and safety of the Union and its residents, to human, animal or plant health, to the environment or to consumers so requires;
(d) where the decision aims at securing the implementation of another decision for which the first subparagraph has been applied, without prejudice to the law of the Member State concerned;
(e) where it would prejudice investigations initiated for the purpose of combating fraud;
(f) in other specific cases.

7. A decision which adversely affects the applicant shall set out the grounds on which it is based and shall refer to the right of appeal provided for in Article 44.

Article 23 Management of decisions taken upon application

1. The holder of the decision shall comply with the obligations resulting from that decision.

VAT EC

2. The holder of the decision shall inform the customs authorities without delay of any factor arising after the decision was taken, which may influence its continuation or content.
3. Without prejudice to provisions laid down in other fields which specify the cases in which decisions are invalid or become null and void, the customs authorities which took a decision may at any time annul, amend or revoke it where it does not conform to the customs legislation.
4. In specific cases the customs authorities shall carry out the following:
(a) re-assess a decision;
(b) suspend a decision which is not to be annulled, revoked or amended.
5. The customs authorities shall monitor the conditions and criteria to be fulfilled by the holder of a decision. They shall also monitor compliance with the obligations resulting from that decision. Where the holder of the decision has been established for less than three years, the customs authorities shall closely monitor it during the first year after the decision is taken.

Article 24 Delegation of power

The Commission shall be empowered to adopt delegated acts in accordance with Article 284, in order to determine:
(a) the exceptions to the third subparagraph of Article 22(1);
(b) the conditions for the acceptance of an application, referred to in Article 22(2);
(c) the time-limit to take a specific decision, including the possible extension of that time-limit, in accordance with Article 22(3);
(d) the cases, referred to in Article 22(4), where the decision takes effect from a date which is different from the date on which the applicant receives it or is deemed to have received it;
(e) the cases, referred to in Article 22(5), where the decision is not valid without limitation of time;
(f) the duration of the period referred to in the first subparagraph of Article 22(6);
(g) the specific cases, referred to in point (f) of the second subparagraph of Article 22(6), where the applicant is given no opportunity to express his or her point of view;
(h) the cases and the rules for re-assessing and suspending decisions in accordance with Article 23(4);

Article 25 Conferral of implementing powers

The Commission shall specify, by means of implementing acts, the procedural rules for:
(a) the submission and the acceptance of the application for a decision, referred to in Article 22(1) and (2);
(b) taking the decision referred to in Article 22, including, where appropriate, the consultation of the Member States concerned;
(c) monitoring a decision, in accordance with Article 23(5).
Those implementing acts shall be adopted in accordance with the examination procedure referred to in Article 285(4).

Article 26 Union-wide validity of decisions

Except where the effect of a decision is limited to one or several Member States, decisions relating to the application of the customs legislation shall be valid throughout the customs territory of the Union.

Article 27 Annulment of favourable decisions

1. The customs authorities shall annul a decision favourable to the holder of the decision if all the following conditions are fulfilled:
(a) the decision was taken on the basis of incorrect or incomplete information;
(b) the holder of the decision knew or ought reasonably to have known that the information was incorrect or incomplete;
(c) if the information had been correct and complete, the decision would have been different.
2. The holder of the decision shall be notified of its annulment.
3. Annulment shall take effect from the date on which the initial decision took effect, unless otherwise specified in the decision in accordance with the customs legislation.

Article 28 Revocation and amendment of favourable decisions

1. A favourable decision shall be revoked or amended where, in cases other than those referred to in Article 27:
(a) one or more of the conditions for taking that decision were not or are no longer fulfilled; or
(b) upon application by the holder of the decision.
2. Except where otherwise provided, a favourable decision addressed to several persons may be revoked only in respect of a person who fails to fulfil an obligation imposed under that decision.
3. The holder of the decision shall be notified of its revocation or amendment.
4. Article 22(4) shall apply to the revocation or amendment of the decision.
However, in exceptional cases where the legitimate interests of the holder of the decision so require, the customs authorities may defer the date on which revocation or amendment takes effect up to one year. That date shall be indicated in the revoking or amending decision.

Article 29 Decisions taken without prior application

Except when a customs authority acts as a judicial authority, Article 22(4), (5), (6) and (7), Article 23(3) and Articles 26, 27 and 28 shall also apply to decisions taken by the customs authorities without prior application by the person concerned.

Article 30 Limitations applicable to decisions on goods placed under a customs procedure or in temporary storage

Except where the person concerned so requests, the revocation, amendment or suspension of a favourable decision shall not affect goods which, at the moment where the revocation, amendment or suspension takes effect, have already been placed and are still under a customs procedure or in temporary storage by virtue of the revoked, amended or suspended decision.

Article 31 Delegation of power

The Commission shall be empowered to adopt delegated acts, in accordance with Article 284, in order to determine:

(a) the cases, referred to in Article 28(2), where a favourable decision addressed to several persons may be revoked also in respect of persons other than the person who fails to fulfil an obligation imposed under that decision;

(b) the exceptional cases, in which the customs authorities may defer the date on which revocation or amendment takes effect in accordance with the second subparagraph of Article 28(4).

Article 32 Conferral of implementing powers

The Commission shall specify, by means of implementing acts, the procedural rules for annulling, revoking or amending favourable decisions.

Those implementing acts shall be adopted in accordance with the examination procedure referred to in Article 285(4).

Article 33 Decisions relating to binding information

1. The customs authorities shall, upon application, take decisions relating to binding tariff information (BTI decisions), or decisions relating to binding origin information (BOI decisions).

Such an application shall not be accepted in any of the following circumstances:

(a) where the application is made, or has already been made, at the same or another customs office, by or on behalf of the holder of a decision in respect of the same goods and, for BOI decisions, under the same circumstances determining the acquisition of origin;

(b) where the application does not relate to any intended use of the BTI or BOI decision or any intended use of a customs procedure.

2. BTI or BOI decisions shall be binding, only in respect of the tariff classification or determination of the origin of goods:

(a) on the customs authorities, as against the holder of the decision, only in respect of goods for which customs formalities are completed after the date on which the decision takes effect;

(b) on the holder of the decision, as against the customs authorities, only with effect from the date on which he or she receives, or is deemed to have received, notification of the decision.

3. BTI or BOI decisions shall be valid for a period of three years from the date on which the decision takes effect.

4. For the application of a BTI or BOI decision in the context of a particular customs procedure, the holder of the decision shall be able to prove that:

(a) in the case of a BTI decision, the goods declared correspond in every respect to those described in the decision;

(b) in the case of a BOI decision, the goods in question and the circumstances determining the acquisition of origin correspond in every respect to the goods and the circumstances described in the decision.

Article 34 Management of decisions relating to binding information

1. A BTI decision shall cease to be valid before the end of the period referred to in Article 33(3) where it no longer conforms to the law, as a result of either of the following:

(a) the adoption of an amendment to the nomenclatures referred to in points (a) and (b) of Article 56(2);

(b) the adoption of measures referred to in Article 57(4);

with effect from the date of application of such amendment or measures.

2. A BOI decision shall cease to be valid before the end of the period referred to in Article 33(3) in any of the following cases:

(a) where a regulation is adopted or an agreement is concluded by, and becomes applicable in, the Union, and the BOI decision no longer conforms to the law thereby laid down, with effect from the date of application of that regulation or agreement;

VAT EC

(b) where it is no longer compatible with the Agreement on Rules of Origin established in the World Trade Organisation (WTO) or with the explanatory notes or an origin opinion adopted for the interpretation of that Agreement, with effect from the date of their publication in the *Official Journal of the European Union*.

3. BTI or BOI decisions shall not cease to be valid with retroactive effect.

4. By way of derogation from Article 23(3) and Article 27, BTI and BOI decisions shall be annulled where they are based on inaccurate or incomplete information from the applicants.

5. BTI and BOI decisions shall be revoked in accordance with Article 23(3) and Article 28. However, such decisions shall not be revoked upon application by the holder of the decision.

6. BTI and BOI decisions may not be amended.

7. The customs authorities shall revoke BTI decisions:

(a) where they are no longer compatible with the interpretation of any of the nomenclatures referred to in points (a) and (b) of Article 56(2) resulting from any of the following:

(i) explanatory notes referred to in the second indent of point (a) of Article 9(1) of Council Regulation (EEC) No 2658/87 of 23 July 1987 on the tariff and statistical nomenclature and on the Common Customs Tariff,[1] with effect from the date of their publication in the *Official Journal of the European Union*;

(ii) a judgment of the Court of Justice of the European Union, with effect from the date of publication of the operative part of the judgment in the *Official Journal of the European Union*;

(iii) classification decisions, classification opinions or amendments of the explanatory notes to the Nomenclature of the Harmonized Commodity Description and Coding System, adopted by the Organization set-up by the Convention establishing a Customs Co-operation Council, done at Brussels on 15 December 1950, with effect from the date of publication of the Commission Communication in the 'C' series of the *Official Journal of the European Union*; or

(b) in other specific cases.

8. BOI decisions shall be revoked:

(a) where they are no longer compatible with a judgment of the Court of Justice of the European Union, with effect from the date of publication of the operative part of the judgment in the *Official Journal of the European Union*; or

(b) in other specific cases.

9. Where point (b) of paragraph 1 or paragraphs 2, 7 or 8 apply, a BTI or BOI decision may still be used in respect of binding contracts which were based upon that decision and were concluded before it ceased to be valid or was revoked. That extended use shall not apply where a BOI decision is taken for goods to be exported.

The extended use referred to in the first subparagraph shall not exceed six months from the date on which the BTI or BOI decision ceases to be valid or is revoked. However, a measure referred to in Article 57(4) or in Article 67 may exclude that extended use or lay down a shorter period of time. In the case of products for which an import or export certificate is submitted when customs formalities are carried out, the period of six months shall be replaced by the period of validity of the certificate.

In order to benefit from the extended use of a BTI or BOI decision, the holder of that decision shall lodge an application to the customs authority that took the decision within 30 days of the date on which it ceases to be valid or is revoked, indicating the quantities for which a period of extended use is requested and the Member State or Member States in which goods will be cleared under the period of extended use. That customs authority shall take a decision on the extended use and notify the holder, without delay, and at the latest within 30 days of the date on which it receives all the information required in order to enable it to take that decision.

10. The Commission shall notify the customs authorities where:

(a) the taking of BTI and BOI decisions, for goods whose correct and uniform tariff classification or determination of origin is not ensured, is suspended; or

(b) the suspension referred to in point (a) is withdrawn.

11. The Commission may adopt decisions requesting Member States to revoke BTI or BOI decisions, to ensure a correct and uniform tariff classification or determination of the origin of goods.

Notes[1] OJ L256, 7.9.1987, p 1.

Article 35 Decisions relating to binding information with regard to other factors

In specific cases, the customs authorities shall, upon application, take decisions relating to binding information with regard to other factors referred to in Title II, on the basis of which import or export duty and other measures in respect of trade in goods are applied.

Article 36 Delegation of power

The Commission shall be empowered to adopt delegated acts, in accordance with Article 284, in order to determine:

(a) the specific cases referred to in point (b) of Article 34(7) and point (b) of Article 34(8), where BTI and BOI decisions are to be revoked;

(b) the cases referred to in Article 35, where decisions relating to binding information are taken with regard to other factors on the basis of which import or export duty and other measures in respect of trade in goods are applied.

Article 37 Conferral of implementing powers

1. The Commission shall adopt, by means of implementing acts, the procedural rules for:
   (a) using a BTI or BOI decision after it ceases to be valid or is revoked, in accordance with Article 34(9);
   (b) the Commission to notify the customs authorities in accordance with points (a) and (b) of Article 34(10);
   (c) using decisions referred to in Article 35 and determined in accordance with point (b) of Article 36 after they cease to be valid;
   (d) suspending decisions referred to in Article 35 and determined in accordance with point (b) of Article 36 and notifying the suspension or the withdrawal of the suspension to the customs authorities.

Those implementing acts shall be adopted in accordance with the examination procedure referred to in Article 285(4).

2. The Commission shall adopt, by means of implementing acts, the decisions requesting Member States to revoke:
   (a) decisions referred to in Article 34(11);
   (b) decisions referred to in Article 35 and determined in accordance with point (b) of Article 36.

Those implementing acts shall be adopted in accordance with the advisory procedure referred to in Article 285(2).

Where the opinion of the committee referred to in Article 285(1) is to be obtained by written procedure, Article 285(6) shall apply.

SECTION 4

AUTHORISED ECONOMIC OPERATOR

Article 38 Application and authorisation

1. An economic operator who is established in the customs territory of the Union and who meets the criteria set out in Article 39 may apply for the status of authorised economic operator.

The customs authorities shall, following consultation with other competent authorities if necessary, grant that status, which shall be subject to monitoring.

2. The status of authorised economic operator shall consist in the following types of authorisations:
   (a) that of an authorised economic operator for customs simplifications, which shall enable the holder to benefit from certain simplifications in accordance with the customs legislation; or
   (b) that of an authorised economic operator for security and safety that shall entitle the holder to facilitations relating to security and safety.

3. Both types of authorisations referred to in paragraph 2 may be held at the same time.

4. The status of authorised economic operator shall, subject to Articles 39, 40 and 41, be recognised by the customs authorities in all Member States.

5. Customs authorities shall, on the basis of the recognition of the status of authorised economic operator for customs simplifications and provided that the requirements related to a specific type of simplification provided for in the customs legislation are fulfilled, authorise the operator to benefit from that simplification. Customs authorities shall not re-examine those criteria which have already been examined when granting the status of authorised economic operator.

6. The authorised economic operator referred to in paragraph 2 shall enjoy more favourable treatment than other economic operators in respect of customs controls according to the type of authorisation granted, including fewer physical and document-based controls.

7. The customs authorities shall grant benefits resulting from the status of authorised economic operator to persons established in countries or territories outside the customs territory of the Union, who fulfil conditions and comply with obligations defined by the relevant legislation of those countries or territories, insofar as those conditions and obligations are recognised by the Union as equivalent to those imposed to authorised economic operators established in the customs territory of the Union. Such a granting of benefits shall be based on the principle of reciprocity unless otherwise decided by the Union, and shall be supported by an international agreement or Union legislation in the area of the common commercial policy.

Article 39 Granting of status

The criteria for the granting of the status of authorised economic operator shall be the following:
   (a) the absence of any serious infringement or repeated infringements of customs legislation and taxation rules, including no record of serious criminal offences relating to the economic activity of the applicant;

(b) the demonstration by the applicant of a high level of control of his or her operations and of the flow of goods, by means of a system of managing commercial and, where appropriate, transport records, which allows appropriate customs controls;

(c) financial solvency, which shall be deemed to be proven where the applicant has good financial standing, which enables him or her to fulfil his or her commitments, with due regard to the characteristics of the type of business activity concerned;

(d) with regard to the authorisation referred to in point (a) of Article 38(2), practical standards of competence or professional qualifications directly related to the activity carried out; and

(e) with regard to the authorisation referred to in point (b) of Article 38(2), appropriate security and safety standards, which shall be considered as fulfilled where the applicant demonstrates that he or she maintains appropriate measures to ensure the security and safety of the international supply chain including in the areas of physical integrity and access controls, logistical processes and handling of specific types of goods, personnel and identification of his or her business partners.

Article 40 Delegation of power

The Commission shall be empowered to adopt delegated acts, in accordance with Article 284, in order to determine the following:

(a) the simplifications referred to in point (a) of Article 38(2);

(b) the facilitations referred to in point (b) of Article 38(2);

(c) the more favourable treatment referred to in Article 38(6).

Article 41 Conferral of implementing powers

The Commission shall adopt, by means of implementing acts, the modalities for the application of the criteria referred to in Article 39.

Those implementing acts shall be adopted in accordance with the examination procedure referred to in Article 285(4).

SECTION 5

PENALTIES

Article 42 Application of penalties

1. Each Member State shall provide for penalties for failure to comply with the customs legislation. Such penalties shall be effective, proportionate and dissuasive.

2. Where administrative penalties are applied, they may take, inter alia, one or both of the following forms:

(a) a pecuniary charge by the customs authorities, including, where appropriate, a settlement applied in place of and in lieu of a criminal penalty;

(b) the revocation, suspension or amendment of any authorisation held by the person concerned.

3. Member States shall notify the Commission, within 180 days from the date of application of this Article, as determined in accordance with Article 288(2), of the national provisions in force, as envisaged in paragraph 1 of this Article, and shall notify it without delay of any subsequent amendment affecting those provisions.

SECTION 6

APPEALS

Article 43 Decisions taken by a judicial authority

Articles 44 and 45 shall not apply to appeals lodged with a view to the annulment, revocation or amendment of a decision relating to the application of the customs legislation taken by a judicial authority, or by customs authorities acting as judicial authorities.

Article 44 Right of appeal

1. Any person shall have the right to appeal against any decision taken by the customs authorities relating to the application of the customs legislation which concerns him or her directly and individually.

Any person who has applied to the customs authorities for a decision and has not obtained a decision on that application within the time-limits referred to in Article 22(3) shall also be entitled to exercise the right of appeal.

2. The right of appeal may be exercised in at least two steps:

(a) initially, before the customs authorities or a judicial authority or other body designated for that purpose by the Member States;

(b) subsequently, before a higher independent body, which may be a judicial authority or an equivalent specialised body, according to the provisions in force in the Member States.

3. The appeal shall be lodged in the Member State where the decision was taken or was applied for.

4. Member States shall ensure that the appeals procedure enables the prompt confirmation or correction of decisions taken by the customs authorities.

Article 45 Suspension of implementation

1. The submission of an appeal shall not cause implementation of the disputed decision to be suspended.
2. The customs authorities shall, however, suspend implementation of such a decision in whole or in part where they have good reason to believe that the disputed decision is inconsistent with the customs legislation or that irreparable damage is to be feared for the person concerned.
3. In the cases referred to in paragraph 2, where the disputed decision has the effect of causing import or export duty to be payable, suspension of implementation of that decision shall be conditional upon the provision of a guarantee, unless it is established, on the basis of a documented assessment, that such a guarantee would be likely to cause the debtor serious economic or social difficulties.

SECTION 7

CONTROL OF GOODS

Article 46 Risk management and customs controls

1. The customs authorities may carry out any customs controls they deem necessary.
Customs controls may in particular consist of examining goods, taking samples, verifying the accuracy and completeness of the information given in a declaration or notification and the existence, authenticity, accuracy and validity of documents, examining the accounts of economic operators and other records, inspecting means of transport, inspecting luggage and other goods carried by or on persons and carrying out official enquiries and other similar acts.
2. Customs controls, other than random checks, shall primarily be based on risk analysis using electronic data- processing techniques, with the purpose of identifying and evaluating the risks and developing the necessary counter- measures, on the basis of criteria developed at national, Union and, where available, international level.
3. Customs controls shall be performed within a common risk management framework, based upon the exchange of risk information and risk analysis results between customs administrations and establishing common risk criteria and standards, control measures and priority control areas.
Controls based upon such information and criteria shall be carried out without prejudice to other controls carried out in accordance with paragraph 1 or with other provisions in force.
4. Customs authorities shall undertake risk management to differentiate between the levels of risk associated with goods subject to customs control or supervision and to determine whether the goods will be subject to specific customs controls, and if so, where.
The risk management shall include activities such as collecting data and information, analysing and assessing risk, prescribing and taking action and regularly monitoring and reviewing that process and its outcomes, based on international, Union and national sources and strategies.
5. Customs authorities shall exchange risk information and risk analysis results where:
   (a) the risks are assessed by a customs authority as being significant and requiring customs control and the results of the control establish that the event triggering the risks has occurred; or
   (b) the control results do not establish that the event triggering the risks has occurred, but the customs authority concerned considers the threat to present a high risk elsewhere in the Union.
6. For the establishment of the common risk criteria and standards, the control measures and the priority control areas referred to in paragraph 3, account shall be taken of all of the following:
   (a) the proportionality to the risk;
   (b) the urgency of the necessary application of the controls;
   (c) the probable impact on trade flow, on individual Member States and on control resources.
7. The common risk criteria and standards referred to in paragraph 3 shall include all of the following:
   (a) a description of the risks;
   (b) the factors or indicators of risk to be used to select goods or economic operators for customs control;
   (c) the nature of customs controls to be undertaken by the customs authorities;
   (d) the duration of the application of the customs controls referred to in point (c).
8. Priority control areas shall cover particular customs procedures, types of goods, traffic routes, modes of transport or economic operators which are subject to increased levels of risk analysis and customs controls during a certain period, without prejudice to other controls usually carried out by the customs authorities.

VAT EC

Article 47 Cooperation between authorities

1. Where, in respect of the same goods, controls other than customs controls are to be performed by competent authorities other than the customs authorities, customs authorities shall, in close cooperation with those other authorities, endeavour to have those controls performed, wherever possible, at the same time and place as customs controls (one-stop-shop), with customs authorities having the coordinating role in achieving this.

2. In the framework of the controls referred to in this Section, customs and other competent authorities may, where necessary for the purposes of minimising risk and combating fraud, exchange with each other and with the Commission data received in the context of the entry, exit, transit, movement, storage and end-use of goods, including postal traffic, moved between the customs territory of the Union and countries or territories outside the customs territory of the Union, the presence and movement within the customs territory of the Union of non-Union goods and goods placed under the end- use procedure, and the results of any control. Customs authorities and the Commission may also exchange such data with each other for the purpose of ensuring a uniform application of the customs legislation.

Article 48 Post-release control

For the purpose of customs controls, the customs authorities may verify the accuracy and completeness of the information given in a customs declaration, temporary storage declaration, entry summary declaration, exit summary declaration, re-export declaration or re-export notification, and the existence, authenticity, accuracy and validity of any supporting document and may examine the accounts of the declarant and other records relating to the operations in respect of the goods in question or to prior or subsequent commercial operations involving those goods after having released them. Those authorities may also examine such goods and/or take samples where it is still possible for them to do so.

Such controls may be carried out at the premises of the holder of the goods or of the holder's representative, of any other person directly or indirectly involved in those operations in a business capacity or of any other person in possession of those documents and data for business purposes.

Article 49 Intra-Union flights and sea crossings

1. Customs controls or formalities shall be carried out in respect of the cabin and hold baggage of persons either taking an intra-Union flight, or making an intra-Union sea crossing, only where the customs legislation provides for such controls or formalities.

2. Paragraph 1 shall apply without prejudice to either of the following:
   - (a) security and safety checks;
   - (b) checks linked to prohibitions or restrictions.

Article 50 Conferral of implementing powers

1. The Commission shall adopt, by means of implementing acts, measures to ensure uniform application of the customs controls, including the exchange of risk information and risk analysis results, the common risk criteria and standards, the control measures and the priority control areas referred to in Article 46(3).

Those implementing acts shall be adopted in accordance with the examination procedure referred to in Article 285(4).

On imperative grounds of urgency relating to such measures, duly justified by the need to rapidly update the common risk management framework and adapt the exchange of risk information and analysis, common risk criteria and standards, control measures and priority control areas to the evolution of risks, the Commission shall adopt immediately applicable implementing acts in accordance with the procedure referred to in Article 285(5).

Where the opinion of the committee referred to in Article 285(1) is to be obtained by written procedure, Article 285(6) shall apply.

2. The Commission shall determine, by means of implementing acts, the ports or airports where, in accordance with Article 49, customs controls and formalities are applied to the following:
   - (a) the cabin and hold baggage of persons:
     - (i) taking a flight in an aircraft which comes from a non- Union airport and which, after a stopover at a Union airport, continues to another Union airport;
     - (ii) taking a flight in an aircraft which stops over at a Union airport before continuing to a non-Union airport;
     - (iii) using a maritime service provided by the same vessel and comprising successive legs departing from, calling at or terminating in a non-Union port;
     - (iv) on board pleasure craft and tourist or business aircraft;
   - (b) cabin and hold baggage:
     - (i) arriving at a Union airport on board an aircraft coming from a non-Union airport and transferred at that Union airport to another aircraft proceeding on an intra-Union flight;

(ii) loaded at a Union airport onto an aircraft proceeding on an intra-Union flight for transfer at another Union airport to an aircraft whose destination is a non- Union airport.

Those implementing acts shall be adopted in accordance with the examination procedure referred to in Article 285(4).

SECTION 8
KEEPING OF DOCUMENTS AND OTHER INFORMATION, AND CHARGES AND COSTS

Article 51 Keeping of documents and other information

1. The person concerned shall, for the purposes of customs controls, keep the documents and information referred to in Article 15(1) for at least three years, by any means accessible by and acceptable to the customs authorities.

In the case of goods released for free circulation in circumstances other than those referred to in the third subparagraph, or goods declared for export, that period shall run from the end of the year in which the customs declarations for release for free circulation or export are accepted.

In the case of goods released for free circulation duty-free or at a reduced rate of import duty on account of their end-use, that period shall run from the end of the year in which they cease to be subject to customs supervision.

In the case of goods placed under another customs procedure or of goods in temporary storage, that period shall run from the end of the year in which the customs procedure concerned has been discharged or temporary storage has ended.

2. Without prejudice to Article 103(4), where a customs control in respect of a customs debt shows that the relevant entry in the accounts has to be corrected and the person concerned has been notified of this, the documents and information shall be kept for three years beyond the time- limit provided for in paragraph 1 of this Article.

Where an appeal has been lodged or where court proceedings have begun, the documents and information shall be kept for the period provided for in paragraph 1 or until the appeals procedure or court proceedings are terminated, whichever is the later.

Article 52 Charges and costs

1. Customs authorities shall not impose charges for the performance of customs controls or any other application of the customs legislation during the official opening hours of their competent customs offices.

2. Customs authorities may impose charges or recover costs where specific services are rendered, in particular the following:

(a) attendance, where requested, by customs staff outside official office hours or at premises other than customs premises;

(b) analyses or expert reports on goods and postal fees for the return of goods to an applicant, particularly in respect of decisions taken pursuant to Article 33 or the provision of information in accordance with Article 14(1);

(c) the examination or sampling of goods for verification purposes, or the destruction of goods, where costs other than the cost of using customs staff are involved;

(d) exceptional control measures, where these are necessary due to the nature of the goods or to a potential risk.

CHAPTER 3
CURRENCY CONVERSION AND TIME-LIMITS

Article 53 Currency conversion

1. The competent authorities shall publish and/or make available on the Internet the rate of exchange applicable where the conversion of currency is necessary for one of the following reasons:

(a) because factors used to determine the customs value of goods are expressed in a currency other than that of the Member State where the customs value is determined;

(b) because the value of the euro is required in national currencies for the purposes of determining the tariff classification of goods and the amount of import and export duty, including value thresholds in the Common Customs Tariff.

2. Where the conversion of currency is necessary for reasons other than those referred to in paragraph 1, the value of the euro in national currencies to be applied within the framework of the customs legislation shall be fixed at least once a year.

Article 54 Conferral of implementing powers

The Commission shall lay down, by means of implementing acts, rules on currency conversions for the purposes referred to in Article 53(1) and (2).

Those implementing acts shall be adopted in accordance with the examination procedure referred to in Article 285(4).

Article 55 Periods, dates and time-limits

1. Unless otherwise provided, where a period, date or time- limit is laid down in the customs legislation, such period shall not be extended or reduced and such date or time-limit shall not be deferred or brought forward.

2. The rules applicable to periods, dates and time-limits set out in Regulation (EEC, Euratom) No 1182/71 of the Council of 3 June 1971 determining the rules applicable to periods, dates and time-limits[1] shall apply, except where otherwise provided for in the customs legislation.

Notes[1] OJ L124, 8.6.1971, p 1.

TITLE II

FACTORS ON THE BASIS OF WHICH IMPORT OR EXPORT DUTY AND OTHER MEASURES IN RESPECT OF TRADE IN GOODS ARE APPLIED

CHAPTER 3

VALUE OF GOODS FOR CUSTOMS PURPOSES

Article 69 Scope

The customs value of goods, for the purposes of applying the Common Customs Tariff and non-tariff measures laid down by Union provisions governing specific fields relating to trade in goods, shall be determined in accordance with Articles 70 and 74.

Article 70 Method of customs valuation based on the transaction value

1. The primary basis for the customs value of goods shall be the transaction value, that is the price actually paid or payable for the goods when sold for export to the customs territory of the Union, adjusted, where necessary.

2. The price actually paid or payable shall be the total payment made or to be made by the buyer to the seller or by the buyer to a third party for the benefit of the seller for the imported goods and include all payments made or to be made as a condition of sale of the imported goods.

3. The transaction value shall apply provided that all of the following conditions are fulfilled:

(a) there are no restrictions as to the disposal or use of the goods by the buyer, other than any of the following:

(i) restrictions imposed or required by a law or by the public authorities in the Union;

(ii) limitations of the geographical area in which the goods may be resold;

(iii) restrictions which do not substantially affect the customs value of the goods;

(b) the sale or price is not subject to some condition or consideration for which a value cannot be determined with respect to the goods being valued;

(c) no part of the proceeds of any subsequent resale, disposal or use of the goods by the buyer will accrue directly or indirectly to the seller, unless an appropriate adjustment can be made;

(d) the buyer and seller are not related or the relationship did not influence the price.

Article 71 Elements of the transaction value

1. In determining the customs value under Article 70, the price actually paid or payable for the imported goods shall be supplemented by:

(a) the following, to the extent that they are incurred by the buyer but are not included in the price actually paid or payable for the goods:

(i) commissions and brokerage, except buying commissions;

(ii) the cost of containers which are treated as being one, for customs purposes, with the goods in question; and

(iii) the cost of packing, whether for labour or materials;

(b) the value, apportioned as appropriate, of the following goods and services where supplied directly or indirectly by the buyer free of charge or at reduced cost for use in connection with the production and sale for export of the imported goods, to the extent that such value has not been included in the price actually paid or payable:

(i) materials, components, parts and similar items incorporated into the imported goods;

(ii) tools, dies, moulds and similar items used in the production of the imported goods;

(iii) materials consumed in the production of the imported goods; and

(iv) engineering, development, artwork, design work, and plans and sketches undertaken elsewhere than in the Union and necessary for the production of the imported goods;

(c) royalties and licence fees related to the goods being valued that the buyer must pay, either directly or indirectly, as a condition of sale of the goods being valued, to the extent that such royalties and fees are not included in the price actually paid or payable;

(d) the value of any part of the proceeds of any subsequent resale, disposal or use of the imported goods that accrues directly or indirectly to the seller; and

(e) the following costs up to the place where goods are brought into the customs territory of the Union:

(i) the cost of transport and insurance of the imported goods; and
(ii) loading and handling charges associated with the transport of the imported goods.

2. Additions to the price actually paid or payable, pursuant to paragraph 1, shall be made only on the basis of objective and quantifiable data.

3. No additions shall be made to the price actually paid or payable in determining the customs value except as provided in this Article.

Article 72 Elements not to be included in the customs value

In determining the customs value under Article 70, none of the following shall be included:

(a) the cost of transport of the imported goods after their entry into the customs territory of the Union;
(b) charges for construction, erection, assembly, maintenance or technical assistance, undertaken after the entry into the customs territory of the Union of the imported goods such as industrial plants, machinery or equipment;
(c) charges for interest under a financing arrangement entered into by the buyer and relating to the purchase of the imported goods, irrespective of whether the finance is provided by the seller or another person, provided that the financing arrangement has been made in writing and, where required, the buyer can demonstrate that the following conditions are fulfilled:
  (i) such goods are actually sold at the price declared as the price actually paid or payable;
  (ii) the claimed rate of interest does not exceed the level for such transactions prevailing in the country where, and at the time when, the finance was provided;
(d) charges for the right to reproduce the imported goods in the Union;
(e) buying commissions;
(f) import duties or other charges payable in the Union by reason of the import or sale of the goods;
(g) notwithstanding point (c) of Article 71(1), payments made by the buyer for the right to distribute or resell the imported goods, if such payments are not a condition of the sale for export to the Union of the goods.

Article 73 Simplification

The customs authorities may, upon application, authorise that the following amounts be determined on the basis of specific criteria, where they are not quantifiable on the date on which the customs declaration is accepted:

(a) amounts which are to be included in the customs value in accordance with Article 70(2); and
(b) the amounts referred to in Articles 71 and 72.

Article 74 Secondary methods of customs valuation

1. Where the customs value of goods cannot be determined under Article 70, it shall be determined by proceeding sequentially from points (a) to (d) of paragraph 2, until the first point under which the customs value of goods can be determined.

The order of application of points (c) and (d) of paragraph 2 shall be reversed if the declarant so requests.

2. The customs value, pursuant to paragraph 1, shall be:

(a) the transaction value of identical goods sold for export to the customs territory of the Union and exported at or about the same time as the goods being valued;
(b) the transaction value of similar goods sold for export to the customs territory of the Union and exported at or about the same time as the goods being valued;
(c) the value based on the unit price at which the imported goods, or identical or similar imported goods, are sold within the customs territory of the Union in the greatest aggregate quantity to persons not related to the sellers; or
(d) the computed value, consisting of the sum of:
  (i) the cost or value of materials and fabrication or other processing employed in producing the imported goods;
  (ii) an amount for profit and general expenses equal to that usually reflected in sales of goods of the same class or kind as the goods being valued which are made by producers in the country of export for export to the Union;
  (iii) the cost or value of the elements referred to in point (e) of Article 71(1).

3. Where the customs value cannot be determined under paragraph 1, it shall be determined on the basis of data available in the customs territory of the Union, using reasonable means consistent with the principles and general provisions of all of the following:

(a) the agreement on implementation of Article VII of the General Agreement on Tariffs and Trade;
(b) Article VII of the General Agreement on Tariffs and Trade;
(c) this Chapter.

Article 75 Delegation of power

The Commission shall be empowered to adopt delegated acts, in accordance with Article 284, in order to determine the conditions for granting the authorisation referred to in Article 73.

Article 76 Conferral of implementing powers

The Commission shall specify, by means of implementing acts, the procedural rules for:

(a) determining the customs value in accordance with Articles 70(1) and (2) and Articles 71 and 72, including those for adjusting the price actually paid or payable;

(b) the application of the conditions referred to in Article 70(3);

(c) determining the customs value referred to in Article 74.

Those implementing acts shall be adopted in accordance with the examination procedure referred to in Article 285(4).

TITLE III
CUSTOMS DEBT AND GUARANTEES

CHAPTER 1
INCURRENCE OF A CUSTOMS DEBT

SECTION 1
CUSTOMS DEBT ON IMPORT

Article 77 Release for free circulation and temporary admission

1. A customs debt on import shall be incurred through the placing of non-Union goods liable to import duty under either of the following customs procedures:

(a) release for free circulation, including under the end-use provisions;

(b) temporary admission with partial relief from import duty.

2. A customs debt shall be incurred at the time of acceptance of the customs declaration.

3. The declarant shall be the debtor. In the event of indirect representation, the person on whose behalf the customs declaration is made shall also be a debtor.

Where a customs declaration in respect of one of the procedures referred to in paragraph 1 is drawn up on the basis of information which leads to all or part of the import duty not being collected, the person who provided the information required to draw up the declaration and who knew, or who ought reasonably to have known, that such information was false shall also be a debtor.

Article 78 Special provisions relating to non-originating goods

1. Where a prohibition of drawback of, or exemption from, import duty applies to non-originating goods used in the manufacture of products for which a proof of origin is issued or made out in the framework of a preferential arrangement between the Union and certain countries or territories outside the customs territory of the Union or groups of such countries or territories, a customs debt on import shall be incurred in respect of those non-originating goods, through the acceptance of the re-export declaration relating to the products in question.

2. Where a customs debt is incurred pursuant to paragraph 1, the amount of import duty corresponding to that debt shall be determined under the same conditions as in the case of a customs debt resulting from the acceptance, on the same date, of the customs declaration for release for free circulation of the non-originating goods used in the manufacture of the products in question for the purpose of ending the inward processing procedure.

3. Article 77(2) and (3) shall apply. However, in the case of non-Union goods as referred to in Article 270 the person who lodges the re-export declaration shall be the debtor. In the event of indirect representation, the person on whose behalf the declaration is lodged shall also be a debtor.

Article 79 Customs debt incurred through non-compliance

1. For goods liable to import duty, a customs debt on import shall be incurred through non-compliance with any of the following:

(a) one of the obligations laid down in the customs legislation concerning the introduction of non-Union goods into the customs territory of the Union, their removal from customs supervision, or the movement, processing, storage, temporary storage, temporary admission or disposal of such goods within that territory;

(b) one of the obligations laid down in the customs legislation concerning the end-use of goods within the customs territory of the Union;

(c) a condition governing the placing of non-Union goods under a customs procedure or the granting, by virtue of the end-use of the goods, of duty exemption or a reduced rate of import duty.

2. The time at which the customs debt is incurred shall be either of the following:

(a) the moment when the obligation the non-fulfilment of which gives rise to the customs debt is not met or ceases to be met;

(b) the moment when a customs declaration is accepted for the placing of goods under a customs procedure where it is established subsequently that a condition governing the placing of the goods under that procedure or the granting of a duty exemption or a reduced rate of import duty by virtue of the end-use of the goods was not in fact fulfilled.

3. In cases referred to under points (a) and (b) of paragraph 1, the debtor shall be any of the following:

(a) any person who was required to fulfil the obligations concerned;

(b) any person who was aware or should reasonably have been aware that an obligation under the customs legislation was not fulfilled and who acted on behalf of the person who was obliged to fulfil the obligation, or who participated in the act which led to the non-fulfilment of the obligation;

(c) any person who acquired or held the goods in question and who was aware or should reasonably have been aware at the time of acquiring or receiving the goods that an obligation under the customs legislation was not fulfilled.

4. In cases referred to under point (c) of paragraph 1, the debtor shall be the person who is required to comply with the conditions governing the placing of the goods under a customs procedure or the customs declaration of the goods placed under that customs procedure or the granting of a duty exemption or reduced rate of import duty by virtue of the end-use of the goods.

Where a customs declaration in respect of one of the customs procedures referred to in point (c) of paragraph 1 is drawn up, and any information required under the customs legislation relating to the conditions governing the placing of the goods under that customs procedure is given to the customs authorities, which leads to all or part of the import duty not being collected, the person who provided the information required to draw up the customs declaration and who knew, or who ought reasonably to have known, that such information was false shall also be a debtor.

Article 80 Deduction of an amount of import duty already paid

1. Where a customs debt is incurred, pursuant to Article 79(1) in respect of goods released for free circulation at a reduced rate of import duty on account of their end-use, the amount of import duty paid when the goods were released for free circulation shall be deducted from the amount of import duty corresponding to the customs debt.

The first subparagraph shall apply where a customs debt is incurred in respect of scrap and waste resulting from the destruction of such goods.

2. Where a customs debt is incurred, pursuant to Article 79(1) in respect of goods placed under temporary admission with partial relief from import duty, the amount of import duty paid under partial relief shall be deducted from the amount of import duty corresponding to the customs debt.

SECTION 2
CUSTOMS DEBT ON EXPORT

Article 81 Export and outward processing

1. A customs debt on export shall be incurred through the placing of goods liable to export duty under the export procedure or the outward processing procedure.

2. The customs debt shall be incurred at the time of acceptance of the customs declaration.

3. The declarant shall be the debtor. In the event of indirect representation, the person on whose behalf the customs declaration is made shall also be a debtor.

Where a customs declaration is drawn up on the basis of information which leads to all or part of the export duty not being collected, the person who provided the information required for the declaration and who knew, or who should reasonably have known, that such information was false shall also be a debtor.

Article 82 Customs debt incurred through non-compliance

1. For goods liable to export duty, a customs debt on export shall be incurred through non-compliance with either of the following:

(a) one of the obligations laid down in the customs legislation for the exit of the goods;

(b) the conditions under which the goods were allowed to be taken out of the customs territory of the Union with total or partial relief from export duty.

2. The time at which the customs debt is incurred shall be one of the following:

(a) the moment at which the goods are actually taken out of the customs territory of the Union without a customs declaration;

(b) the moment at which the goods reach a destination other than that for which they were allowed to be taken out of the customs territory of the Union with total or partial relief from export duty;

(c) should the customs authorities be unable to determine the moment referred to in point (b), the expiry of the time-limit set for the production of evidence that the conditions entitling the goods to such relief have been fulfilled.

3. In cases referred to under point (a) of paragraph 1, the debtor shall be any of the following:

(a) any person who was required to fulfil the obligation concerned;

(b) any person who was aware or should reasonably have been aware that the obligation concerned was not fulfilled and who acted on behalf of the person who was obliged to fulfil the obligation;

(c) any person who participated in the act which led to the non-fulfilment of the obligation and who was aware or should reasonably have been aware that a customs declaration had not been lodged but should have been.

4. In cases referred to under point (b) of paragraph 1, the debtor shall be any person who is required to comply with the conditions under which the goods were allowed to be taken out of the customs territory of the Union with total or partial relief from export duty.

SECTION 3

PROVISIONS COMMON TO CUSTOMS DEBTS INCURRED ON IMPORT AND EXPORT

Article 83 Prohibitions and restrictions

1. The customs debt on import or export shall be incurred even if it relates to goods which are subject to measures of prohibition or restriction on import or export of any kind.

2. However, no customs debt shall be incurred on either of the following:

(a) the unlawful introduction into the customs territory of the Union of counterfeit currency;

(b) the introduction into the customs territory of the Union of narcotic drugs and psychotropic substances other than where strictly supervised by the competent authorities with a view to their use for medical and scientific purposes.

3. For the purposes of penalties as applicable to customs offences, the customs debt shall nevertheless be deemed to have been incurred where, under the law of a Member State, import or export duty or the existence of a customs debt provide the basis for determining penalties.

Article 84 Several debtors

Where several persons are liable for payment of the amount of import or export duty corresponding to one customs debt, they shall be jointly and severally liable for payment of that amount.

Article 85 General rules for calculating the amount of import or export duty

1. The amount of import or export duty shall be determined on the basis of those rules for calculation of duty which were applicable to the goods concerned at the time at which the customs debt in respect of them was incurred.

2. Where it is not possible to determine precisely the time at which the customs debt is incurred, that time shall be deemed to be the time at which the customs authorities conclude that the goods are in a situation in which a customs debt has been incurred.

However, where the information available to the customs authorities enables them to establish that the customs debt had been incurred prior to the time at which they reached that conclusion, the customs debt shall be deemed to have been incurred at the earliest time that such a situation can be established.

Article 86 Special rules for calculating the amount of import duty

1. Where costs for storage or usual forms of handling have been incurred within the customs territory of the Union in respect of goods placed under a customs procedure or in temporary storage, such costs or the increase in value shall not be taken into account for the calculation of the amount of import duty where satisfactory proof of those costs is provided by the declarant.

However, the customs value, quantity, nature and origin of non- Union goods used in the operations shall be taken into account for the calculation of the amount of import duty.

2. Where the tariff classification of goods placed under a customs procedure changes as a result of usual forms of handling within the customs territory of the Union, the original tariff classification for the goods placed under the procedure shall be applied at the request of the declarant.

3. Where a customs debt is incurred for processed products resulting from the inward processing procedure, the amount of import duty corresponding to such debt shall, at the request of the declarant, be determined on the basis of the tariff classification, customs value, quantity, nature and origin of the goods placed under the inward processing procedure at the time of acceptance of the customs declaration relating to those goods.

4. In specific cases, the amount of import duty shall be determined in accordance with paragraphs 2 and 3 of this Article without a request of the declarant in order to avoid the circumvention of tariff measures referred to in point (h) of Article 56(2).

5. Where a customs debt is incurred for processed products resulting from the outward processing procedure or replacement products as referred to in Article 261(1), the amount of import duty shall be calculated on the basis of the cost of the processing operation undertaken outside the customs territory of the Union.

6. Where the customs legislation provides for a favourable tariff treatment of goods, or for relief or total or partial exemption from import or export duty pursuant to points (d) to (g) of Article 56(2), Articles 203, 204, 205 and 208 or Articles 259 to 262 of this Regulation or pursuant to Council Regulation (EC) No 1186/2009 of 16 November 2009 setting up a Community system of reliefs from

customs duty[1] such favourable tariff treatment, relief or exemption shall also apply in cases where a customs debt is incurred pursuant to Articles 79 or 82 of this Regulation, on condition that the failure which led to the incurrence of a customs debt did not constitute an attempt at deception.

Notes[1] OJ L324, 10.12.2009, p 23.

Article 87 Place where the customs debt is incurred

1. A customs debt shall be incurred at the place where the customs declaration or the re-export declaration referred to in Articles 77, 78 and 81 is lodged.

In all other cases, the place where a customs debt is incurred shall be the place where the events from which it arises occur.

If it is not possible to determine that place, the customs debt shall be incurred at the place where the customs authorities conclude that the goods are in a situation in which a customs debt is incurred.

2. If the goods have been placed under a customs procedure which has not been discharged or when a temporary storage did not end properly, and the place where the customs debt is incurred cannot be determined pursuant to the second or third subparagraphs of paragraph 1 within a specific time- limit, the customs debt shall be incurred at the place where the goods were either placed under the procedure concerned or were introduced into the customs territory of the Union under that procedure or were in temporary storage.

3. Where the information available to the customs authorities enables them to establish that the customs debt may have been incurred in several places, the customs debt shall be deemed to have been incurred at the place where it was first incurred.

4. If a customs authority establishes that a customs debt has been incurred under Article 79 or Article 82 in another Member State and the amount of import or export duty corresponding to that debt is lower than EUR 10,000, the customs debt shall be deemed to have been incurred in the Member State where the finding was made.

Article 88 Delegation of power

The Commission shall be empowered to adopt delegated acts, in accordance with Article 284, in order to determine:

(a) the rules for the calculation of the amount of import or export duty applicable to goods for which a customs debt is incurred in the context of a special procedure, which supplement the rules laid down in Articles 85 and 86;

(b) the cases referred to in Article 86(4);

(c) the time-limit referred to in Article 87(2).

CHAPTER 2

GUARANTEE FOR A POTENTIAL OR EXISTING CUSTOMS DEBT

Article 89 General provisions

1. This Chapter shall apply to guarantees both for customs debts which have been incurred and for those which may be incurred, unless otherwise specified.

2. Where the customs authorities require a guarantee for a potential or existing customs debt to be provided, that guarantee shall cover the amount of import or export duty and the other charges due in connection with the import or export of the goods where:

(a) the guarantee is used for the placing of goods under the Union transit procedure; or

(b) the guarantee may be used in more than one Member State.

A guarantee which may not be used outside the Member State where it is required shall be valid only in that Member State and shall cover at least the amount of import or export duty.

3. Where the customs authorities require a guarantee to be provided, it shall be required from the debtor or the person who may become the debtor. They may also permit the guarantee to be provided by a person other than the person from whom it is required.

4. Without prejudice to Article 97, the customs authorities shall require only one guarantee to be provided in respect of specific goods or a specific declaration.

The guarantee provided for a specific declaration shall apply to the amount of import or export duty corresponding to the customs debt and other charges in respect of all goods covered by or released against that declaration, whether or not that declaration is correct.

If the guarantee has not been released, it may also be used, within the limits of the secured amount, for the recovery of amounts of import or export duty and other charges payable following post-release control of those goods.

5. Upon application by the person referred to in paragraph 3 of this Article, the customs authorities may, in accordance with Article 95(1), (2) and (3), authorise the provision of a comprehensive guarantee to cover the amount of import or export duty corresponding to the customs debt in respect of two or more operations, declarations or customs procedures.

6. The customs authorities shall monitor the guarantee.

7. No guarantee shall be required from States, regional and local government authorities or other bodies governed by public law, in respect of the activities in which they engage as public authorities.

8. No guarantee shall be required in any of the following situations:
   (a) goods carried on the Rhine, the Rhine waterways, the Danube or the Danube waterways;
   (b) goods carried by a fixed transport installation;
   (c) in specific cases where goods are placed under the temporary admission procedure;
   (d) goods placed under the Union transit procedure using the simplification referred to in point (e) of Article 233(4) and carried by sea or air between Union ports or between Union airports.

9. The customs authorities may waive the requirement for provision of a guarantee where the amount of import or export duty to be secured does not exceed the statistical value threshold for declarations laid down in Article 3(4) of Regulation (EC) No 471/2009 of the European Parliament and of the Council of 6 May 2009 on Community statistics relating to external trade with non-member countries.[1]

Notes[1] OJ L152, 16.6.2009, p 23

Article 90 Compulsory guarantee

1. Where it is compulsory for a guarantee to be provided, the customs authorities shall fix the amount of such guarantee at a level equal to the precise amount of import or export duty corresponding to the customs debt and of other charges where that amount can be established with certainty at the time when the guarantee is required.

Where it is not possible to establish the precise amount, the guarantee shall be fixed at the maximum amount, as estimated by the customs authorities, of import or export duty corresponding to the customs debt and of other charges which have been or may be incurred.

2. Without prejudice to Article 95 where a comprehensive guarantee is provided for the amount of import or export duty corresponding to customs debts and other charges which vary in amount over time, the amount of such guarantee shall be set at a level enabling the amount of import or export duty corresponding to customs debts and other charges to be covered at all times.

Article 91 Optional guarantee

Where the provision of a guarantee is optional, such guarantee shall in any case be required by the customs authorities if they consider that the amount of import or export duty corresponding to a customs debt and other charges are not certain to be paid within the prescribed period. Its amount shall be fixed by those authorities so as not to exceed the level referred to in Article 90.

Article 92 Provision of a guarantee

1. A guarantee may be provided in one of the following forms:
   (a) by a cash deposit or by any other means of payment recognised by the customs authorities as being equivalent to a cash deposit, made in euro or in the currency of the Member State in which the guarantee is required;
   (b) by an undertaking given by a guarantor;
   (c) by another form of guarantee which provides equivalent assurance that the amount of import or export duty corresponding to the customs debt and other charges will be paid.

2. A guarantee in the form of a cash deposit or any other equivalent means of payment shall be given in accordance with the provisions in force in the Member State in which the guarantee is required.

Where a guarantee is given by making a cash deposit or any other equivalent means of payment, no interest thereon shall be payable by the customs authorities.

Article 93 Choice of guarantee

The person required to provide a guarantee may choose between the forms of guarantee laid down in Article 92(1).

However, the customs authorities may refuse to accept the form of guarantee chosen where it is incompatible with the proper functioning of the customs procedure concerned.

The customs authorities may require that the form of guarantee chosen be maintained for a specific period.

Article 94 Guarantor

1. The guarantor referred to in point (b) of Article 92(1) shall be a third person established in the customs territory of the Union. The guarantor shall be approved by the customs authorities requiring the guarantee, unless the guarantor is a credit institution, financial institution or insurance company accredited in the Union in accordance with Union provisions in force.

2. The guarantor shall undertake in writing to pay the secured amount of import or export duty corresponding to a customs debt and other charges.

3. The customs authorities may refuse to approve the guarantor or the type of guarantee proposed where either does not appear certain to ensure payment within the prescribed period of the amount of import or export duty corresponding to the customs debt and of other charges.

Article 95 Comprehensive guarantee

1. The authorisation referred to in Article 89(5) shall be granted only to persons who satisfy all of the following conditions:
   (a) they are established in the customs territory of the Union;

(b) they fulfil the criteria laid down in point (a) of Article 39;
(c) they are regular users of the customs procedures involved or operators of temporary storage facilities or they fulfil the criteria laid down in point (d) of Article 39.

2. Where a comprehensive guarantee is to be provided for customs debts and other charges which may be incurred, an economic operator may be authorised to use a comprehensive guarantee with a reduced amount or to have a guarantee waiver, provided that he or she fulfils the criteria laid down in points (b) and (c) of Article 39.

3. Where a comprehensive guarantee is to be provided for customs debts and other charges which have been incurred, an authorised economic operator for customs simplification shall, upon application, be authorised to use a comprehensive guarantee with a reduced amount.

4. The comprehensive guarantee with a reduced amount referred to in paragraph 3 shall be equivalent to the provision of a guarantee.

Article 96 Temporary prohibitions relating to the use of comprehensive guarantees

1. In the context of special procedures or temporary storage, the Commission may decide to temporarily prohibit recourse to any of the following:
(a) the comprehensive guarantee for a reduced amount or a guarantee waiver referred to in Article 95(2);
(b) the comprehensive guarantee referred to in Article 95, in respect of goods which have been identified as being subject to large-scale fraud.

2. Where point (a) or point (b) of paragraph 1 of this Article applies, recourse to the comprehensive guarantee for a reduced amount or a guarantee waiver or recourse to the comprehensive guarantee referred to in Article 95 may be authorised where the person concerned fulfils either of the following conditions:
(a) that person can show that no customs debt has arisen in respect of the goods in question in the course of operations which that person has undertaken in the two years preceding the decision referred to in paragraph 1;
(b) where customs debts have arisen in the two years preceding the decision referred to in paragraph 1, the person concerned can show that those debts were fully paid by the debtor or debtors or the guarantor within the prescribed time-limit.

To obtain authorisation to use a temporarily prohibited comprehensive guarantee, the person concerned must also fulfil the criteria laid down in points (b) and (c) of Article 39.

Article 97 Additional or replacement guarantee

Where the customs authorities establish that the guarantee provided does not ensure, or is no longer certain or sufficient to ensure, payment within the prescribed period of the amount of import or export duty corresponding to the customs debt and other charges, they shall require any of the persons referred to in Article 89(3) either to provide an additional guarantee or to replace the original guarantee with a new guarantee, according to his choice.

Article 98 Release of the guarantee

1. The customs authorities shall release the guarantee immediately when the customs debt or liability for other charges is extinguished or can no longer arise.

2. Where the customs debt or liability for other charges has been extinguished in part, or may arise only in respect of part of the amount which has been secured, a corresponding part of the guarantee shall be released accordingly at the request of the person concerned, unless the amount involved does not justify such action.

Article 99 Delegation of power

The Commission shall be empowered to adopt delegated acts, in accordance with Article 284, in order to determine:
(a) the specific cases, referred to in point (c) of Article 89(8), where no guarantee is required for goods placed under the temporary admission procedure;
(b) the form of the guarantee, referred to in point (c) of Article 92(1), and the rules concerning the guarantor referred to in Article 94;
(c) the conditions for the granting of an authorisation to use a comprehensive guarantee with a reduced amount or to have a guarantee waiver referred to in Article 95(2);
(d) time-limits for the release of a guarantee.

Article 100 Conferral of implementing powers

1. The Commission shall specify, by means of implementing acts, the procedural rules:
(a) for determining the amount of the guarantee, including the reduced amount referred to in Article 95(2) and (3);
(b) regarding the provision and the monitoring of the guarantee referred to in Article 89, the revocation and cancellation of the undertaking given by the guarantor referred to in Article 94, and the release of the guarantee referred to in Article 98;
(c) regarding the temporary prohibitions referred to in Article 96.

VAT EC

Those implementing acts shall be adopted in accordance with the examination procedure referred to in Article 285(4).
2. The Commission shall adopt the measures referred to in Article 96 by means of implementing acts.
Those implementing acts shall be adopted in accordance with the examination procedure referred to in Article 285(4).
On imperative grounds of urgency relating to such measures, duly justified by the need to rapidly enhance the protection of the financial interests of the Union and of its Member States, the Commission shall adopt immediately applicable implementing acts in accordance with the procedure referred to in Article 285(5).
Where the opinion of the committee referred to in Article 285(1) is to be obtained by written procedure, Article 285(6) shall apply.

CHAPTER 3
RECOVERY, PAYMENT, REPAYMENT AND REMISSION OF THE AMOUNT OF IMPORT OR EXPORT DUTY

SECTION 1
DETERMINATION OF THE AMOUNT OF IMPORT OR EXPORT DUTY, NOTIFICATION OF THE CUSTOMS DEBT AND ENTRY IN THE ACCOUNTS

Article 101 Determination of the amount of import or export duty
1. The amount of import or export duty payable shall be determined by the customs authorities responsible for the place where the customs debt is incurred, or is deemed to have been incurred in accordance with Article 87, as soon as they have the necessary information.
2. Without prejudice to Article 48, the customs authorities may accept the amount of import or export duty payable determined by the declarant.
3. Where the amount of import or export duty payable does not result in a whole number, that amount may be rounded.
Where the amount referred in the first subparagraph is expressed in euros, rounding may not be more than a rounding up or down to the nearest whole number.
A Member State whose currency is not the euro may either apply mutatis mutandis the provisions of the second subparagraph or derogate from that subparagraph, provided that the rules applicable on rounding do not have a greater financial impact than the rule set out in the second subparagraph.

Article 102 Notification of the customs debt
1. The customs debt shall be notified to the debtor in the form prescribed at the place where the customs debt is incurred, or is deemed to have been incurred in accordance with Article 87.
The notification referred to in the first subparagraph shall not be made in any of the following cases:
(a) where, pending a final determination of the amount of import or export duty, a provisional commercial policy measure taking the form of a duty has been imposed;
(b) where the amount of import or export duty payable exceeds that determined on the basis of a decision made in accordance with Article 33;
(c) where the original decision not to notify the customs debt or to notify it with an amount of import or export duty at a figure less than the amount of import or export duty payable was taken on the basis of general provisions invalidated at a later date by a court decision;
(d) where the customs authorities are exempted under the customs legislation from notification of the customs debt.
2. Where the amount of import or export duty payable is equal to the amount entered in the customs declaration, release of the goods by the customs authorities shall be equivalent to notifying the debtor of the customs debt.
3. Where paragraph 2 does not apply, the customs debt shall be notified to the debtor by the customs authorities when they are in a position to determine the amount of import or export duty payable and take a decision thereon.
However, where the notification of the customs debt would prejudice a criminal investigation, the customs authorities may defer that notification until such time as it no longer prejudices the criminal investigation.
4. Provided that payment has been guaranteed, the customs debt corresponding to the total amount of import or export duty relating to all the goods released to one and the same person during a period fixed by the customs authorities may be notified at the end of that period. The period fixed by the customs authorities shall not exceed 31 days.

Article 103 Limitation of the customs debt
1. No customs debt shall be notified to the debtor after the expiry of a period of three years from the date on which the customs debt was incurred.

2. Where the customs debt is incurred as the result of an act which, at the time it was committed, was liable to give rise to criminal court proceedings, the three-year period laid down in paragraph 1 shall be extended to a period of a minimum of five years and a maximum of 10 years in accordance with national law.

3. The periods laid down in paragraphs 1 and 2 shall be suspended where:

(a) an appeal is lodged in accordance with Article 44; such suspension shall apply from the date on which the appeal is lodged and shall last for the duration of the appeal proceedings; or

(b) the customs authorities communicate to the debtor, in accordance with Article 22(6), the grounds on which they intend to notify the customs debt; such suspension shall apply from the date of that communication until the end of the period within which the debtor is given the opportunity to express his or her point of view.

4. Where a customs debt is reinstated pursuant to Article 116(7), the periods laid down in paragraphs 1 and 2 shall be considered as suspended from the date on which the application for repayment or remission was submitted in accordance with Article 121, until the date on which the decision on the repayment or remission was taken.

Article 104 Entry in the accounts

1. The customs authorities referred to in Article 101 shall enter in their accounts, in accordance with the national legislation, the amount of import or export duty payable as determined in accordance with that Article.

The first subparagraph shall not apply in cases referred to in the second subparagraph of Article 102(1).

2. The customs authorities need not enter in the accounts amounts of import or export duty which, pursuant to Article 103, correspond to a customs debt which could no longer be notified to the debtor.

3. Member States shall determine the practical procedures for the entry in the accounts of the amounts of import or export duty. Those procedures may differ according to whether, in view of the circumstances in which the customs debt was incurred, the customs authorities are satisfied that those amounts will be paid.

Article 105 Time of entry in the accounts

1. Where a customs debt is incurred as a result of the acceptance of the customs declaration of goods for a customs procedure, other than temporary admission with partial relief from import duty, or of any other act having the same legal effect as such acceptance, the customs authorities shall enter the amount of import or export duty payable in the accounts within 14 days of the release of the goods.

However, provided that payment has been guaranteed, the total amount of import or export duty relating to all the goods released to one and the same person during a period fixed by the customs authorities, which may not exceed 31 days, may be covered by a single entry in the accounts at the end of that period. Such entry in the accounts shall take place within 14 days of the expiry of the period concerned.

2. Where goods may be released subject to certain conditions which govern either the determination of the amount of import or export duty payable or its collection, entry in the accounts shall take place within 14 days of the day on which the amount of import or export duty payable is determined or the obligation to pay that duty is fixed.

However, where the customs debt relates to a provisional commercial policy measure taking the form of a duty, the amount of import or export duty payable shall be entered in the accounts within two months of the date of publication in the *Official Journal of the European Union* of the Regulation establishing the definitive commercial policy measure.

3. Where a customs debt is incurred in circumstances not covered by paragraph 1, the amount of import or export duty payable shall be entered in the accounts within 14 days of the date on which the customs authorities are in a position to determine the amount of import or export duty in question and take a decision.

4. Paragraph 3 shall apply with regard to the amount of import or export duty to be recovered or which remains to be recovered where the amount of import or export duty payable has not been entered in the accounts in accordance with paragraphs 1, 2 and 3, or has been determined and entered in the accounts at a level lower than the amount payable.

5. The time-limits for entry in the accounts laid down in paragraphs 1, 2 and 3 shall not apply in unforeseeable circumstances or in cases of force majeure.

6. The entry in the accounts may be deferred in the case referred to in the second subparagraph of Article 102(3), until such time as the notification of the customs debt no longer prejudices a criminal investigation.

Article 106 Delegation of power

The Commission shall be empowered to adopt delegated acts, in accordance with Article 284, in order to determine the cases referred to in point (d) of Article 102(1) where the customs authorities are exempted from notification of the customs debt.

Article 107 Conferral of implementing powers

The Commission shall adopt, by means of implementing acts, measures to ensure mutual assistance between the customs authorities in case of incurrence of a customs debt.

Those implementing acts shall be adopted in accordance with the examination procedure referred to in Article 285(4).

SECTION 2

PAYMENT OF THE AMOUNT OF IMPORT OR EXPORT DUTY

Article 108 General time-limits for payment and suspension of the time-limit for payment

1. Amounts of import or export duty, corresponding to a customs debt notified in accordance with Article 102, shall be paid by the debtor within the period prescribed by the customs authorities.

Without prejudice to Article 45(2), that period shall not exceed 10 days following notification to the debtor of the customs debt. In the case of aggregation of entries in the accounts under the conditions laid down in the second subparagraph of Article 105(1), it shall be so fixed as not to enable the debtor to obtain a longer period for payment than if he or she had been granted deferred payment in accordance with Article 110.

The customs authorities may extend that period upon application by the debtor where the amount of import or export duty payable has been determined in the course of post-release control as referred to in Article 48. Without prejudice to Article 112(1), such extensions shall not exceed the time necessary for the debtor to take the appropriate steps to discharge his or her obligation.

2. If the debtor is entitled to any of the payment facilities laid down in Articles 110 to 112, payment shall be made within the period or periods specified in relation to those facilities.

3. The time-limit for payment of the amount of import or export duty corresponding to a customs debt shall be suspended in any of the following cases;

(a) where an application for remission of duty is made in accordance with Article 121;

(b) where goods are to be confiscated, destroyed or abandoned to the State;

(c) where the customs debt was incurred pursuant to Article 79 and there is more than one debtor.

Article 109 Payment

1. Payment shall be made in cash or by any other means with similar discharging effect, including by adjustment of a credit balance, in accordance with national legislation.

2. Payment may be made by a third person instead of the debtor.

3. The debtor may in any case pay all or part of the amount of import or export duty without awaiting expiry of the period he or she has been granted for payment.

Article 110 Deferment of payment

The customs authorities shall, upon application by the person concerned and upon provision of a guarantee, authorise deferment of payment of the duty payable in any of the following ways:

(a) separately in respect of each amount of import or export duty entered in the accounts in accordance with the first subparagraph of Article 105(1), or Article 105(4);

(b) globally in respect of all amounts of import or export duty entered in the accounts in accordance with the first subparagraph of Article 105(1) during a period fixed by the customs authorities and not exceeding 31 days;

(c) globally in respect of all amounts of import or export duty forming a single entry in accordance with the second subparagraph of Article 105(1).

Article 111 Periods for which payment is deferred

1. The period for which payment is deferred under Article 110 shall be 30 days.

2. Where payment is deferred in accordance with point (a) of Article 110, the period shall begin on the day following that on which the customs debt is notified to the debtor.

3. Where payment is deferred in accordance with point (b) of Article 110, the period shall begin on the day following that on which the aggregation period ends. It shall be reduced by the number of days corresponding to half the number of days covered by the aggregation period.

4. Where payment is deferred in accordance with point (c) of Article 110, the period shall begin on the day following the end of the period fixed for release of the goods in question. It shall be reduced by the number of days corresponding to half the number of days covered by the period concerned.

5. Where the number of days in the periods referred to in paragraphs 3 and 4 is an odd number, the number of days to be deducted from the 30-day period pursuant to those paragraphs shall be equal to half the next lowest even number.

6. Where the periods referred to in paragraphs 3 and 4 are weeks, Member States may provide that the amount of import or export duty in respect of which payment has been deferred is to be paid on the Friday of the fourth week following the week in question at the latest.

If those periods are months, Member States may provide that the amount of import or export duty in respect of which payment has been deferred is to be paid by the 16th day of the month following the month in question.

Article 112 Other payment facilities

1. The customs authorities may grant the debtor payment facilities other than deferred payment on condition that a guarantee is provided.

2. Where facilities are granted pursuant to paragraph 1, credit interest shall be charged on the amount of import or export duty.

For a Member State whose currency is the euro, the rate of credit interest shall be equal to the interest rate as published in the *Official Journal of the European Union*, C series, which the European Central Bank applied to its main refinancing operations, on the first day of the month in which the due date fell, increased by one percentage point.

For a Member State whose currency is not the euro, the rate of credit interest shall be equal to the rate applied on the first day of the month in question by the National Central Bank for its main refinancing operations, increased by one percentage point, or, for a Member State for which the National Central Bank rate is not available, the most equivalent rate applied on the first day of the month in question on the Member State's money market, increased by one percentage point.

3. The customs authorities may refrain from requiring a guarantee or from charging credit interest where it is established, on the basis of a documented assessment of the situation of the debtor, that this would create serious economic or social difficulties.

4. The customs authorities shall refrain from charging credit interest where the amount for each recovery action is less than EUR 10.

Article 113 Enforcement of payment

Where the amount of import or export duty payable has not been paid within the prescribed period, the customs authorities shall secure payment of that amount by all means available to them under the law of the Member State concerned.

Article 114 Interest on arrears

1. Interest on arrears shall be charged on the amount of import or export duty from the date of expiry of the prescribed period until the date of payment.

For a Member State whose currency is the euro, the rate of interest on arrears shall be equal to the interest rate as published in the *Official Journal of the European Union*, C series, which the European Central Bank applied to its main refinancing operations, on the first day of the month in which the due date fell, increased by two percentage points.

For a Member State whose currency is not the euro, the rate of interest on arrears shall be equal to the rate applied on the first day of the month in question by the National Central Bank for its main refinancing operations, increased by two percentage points, or, for a Member State for which the National Central Bank rate is not available, the most equivalent rate applied on the first day of the month in question on the Member State's money market, increased by two percentage points.

2. Where the customs debt is incurred on the basis of Article 79 or 82, or where the notification of the customs debt results from a post-release control, interest on arrears shall be charged over and above the amount of import or export duty, from the date on which the customs debt was incurred until the date of its notification.

The rate of interest on arrears shall be set in accordance with paragraph 1.

3. The customs authorities may refrain from charging interest on arrears where it is established, on the basis of a documented assessment of the situation of the debtor, that to charge it would create serious economic or social difficulties.

4. The customs authorities shall refrain from charging interest on arrears where the amount for each recovery action is less than EUR 10.

Article 115 Delegation of power

The Commission shall be empowered to adopt delegated acts, in accordance with Article 284, in order to determine the rules for the suspension of the time-limit for payment of the amount of import or export duty corresponding to a customs debt referred to in Article 108(3) and the period of suspension.

VAT EC

CHAPTER 4
EXTINGUISHMENT OF A CUSTOMS DEBT

Article 124 Extinguishment

1. Without prejudice to the provisions in force relating to non-recovery of the amount of import or export duty corresponding to a customs debt in the event of the judicially established insolvency of the debtor, a customs debt on import or export shall be extinguished in any of the following ways:

(a) where the debtor can no longer be notified of the customs debt, in accordance with Article 103;

(b) by payment of the amount of import or export duty;

(c) subject to paragraph 5, by remission of the amount of import or export duty;

(d) where, in respect of goods declared for a customs procedure entailing the obligation to pay import or export duty, the customs declaration is invalidated;

(e) where goods liable to import or export duty are confiscated or seized and simultaneously or subsequently confiscated;
(f) where goods liable to import or export duty are destroyed under customs supervision or abandoned to the State;
(g) where the disappearance of the goods or the non-fulfilment of obligations arising from the customs legislation results from the total destruction or irretrievable loss of those goods as a result of the actual nature of the goods or unforeseeable circumstances or force majeure, or as a consequence of instruction by the customs authorities; for the purpose of this point, goods shall be considered as irretrievably lost when they have been rendered unusable by any person;
(h) where the customs debt was incurred pursuant to Article 79 or 82 and where the following conditions are fulfilled:
  (i) the failure which led to the incurrence of a customs debt had no significant effect on the correct operation of the customs procedure concerned and did not constitute an attempt at deception;
  (ii) all of the formalities necessary to regularise the situation of the goods are subsequently carried out;
(i) where goods released for free circulation duty-free, or at a reduced rate of import duty by virtue of their end-use, have been exported with the permission of the customs authorities;
(j) where it was incurred pursuant to Article 78 and where the formalities carried out in order to enable the preferential tariff treatment referred to in that Article to be granted are cancelled;
(k) where, subject to paragraph 6, the customs debt was incurred pursuant to Article 79 and evidence is provided to the satisfaction of the customs authorities that the goods have not been used or consumed and have been taken out of the customs territory of the Union.

2. In the cases referred to in point (e) of paragraph 1, the customs debt shall, nevertheless, for the purposes of penalties applicable to customs offences, be deemed not to have been extinguished where, under the law of a Member State, import or export duty or the existence of a customs debt provide the basis for determining penalties.
3. Where, in accordance with point (g) of paragraph 1, a customs debt is extinguished in respect of goods released for free circulation duty-free or at a reduced rate of import duty on account of their end-use, any scrap or waste resulting from their destruction shall be deemed to be non-Union goods.
4. The provisions in force pertaining to standard rates for irretrievable loss due to the nature of goods shall apply where the person concerned fails to show that the real loss exceeds that calculated by applying the standard rate for the goods in question.
5. Where several persons are liable for payment of the amount of import or export duty corresponding to the customs debt and remission is granted, the customs debt shall be extinguished only in respect of the person or persons to whom the remission is granted.
6. In the case referred to in point (k) of paragraph 1, the customs debt shall not be extinguished in respect of any person or persons who attempted deception.
7. Where the customs debt was incurred pursuant to Article 79, it shall be extinguished with regard to the person whose behaviour did not involve any attempt at deception and who contributed to the fight against fraud.

Article 125 Application of penalties

Where the customs debt is extinguished on the basis of point (h) of Article 124(1), Member States shall not be precluded from the application of penalties for failure to comply with the customs legislation.

Article 126 Delegation of power

The Commission shall be empowered to adopt delegated acts, in accordance with Article 284, in order to determine the list of failures with no significant effect on the correct operation of the customs procedure concerned and to supplement point (i) of point (h) of Article 124(1).

TITLE IV

GOODS BROUGHT INTO THE CUSTOMS TERRITORY OF THE UNION

CHAPTER 1

ENTRY SUMMARY DECLARATION

Article 127 Lodging of an entry summary declaration

1. Goods brought into the customs territory of the Union shall be covered by an entry summary declaration.
2. The obligation referred to in paragraph 1 shall be waived:
(a) for means of transport and the goods carried thereon only passing through the territorial waters or the airspace of the customs territory of the Union without a stop within that territory; and

(b) in other cases, where duly justified by the type of goods or traffic, or where required by international agreements.

3. The entry summary declaration shall be lodged at the customs office of first entry within a specific time-limit, before the goods are brought into the customs territory of the Union.

Customs authorities may allow the entry summary declaration to be lodged at another customs office, provided that the latter immediately communicates or makes available electronically the necessary particulars to the customs office of first entry.

4. The entry summary declaration shall be lodged by the carrier.

Notwithstanding the obligations of the carrier, the entry summary declaration may be lodged instead by one of the following persons:

(a) the importer or consignee or other person in whose name or on whose behalf the carrier acts;

(b) any person who is able to present the goods in question or have them presented at the customs office of entry.

5. The entry summary declaration shall contain the particulars necessary for risk analysis for security and safety purposes.

6. In specific cases, where all the particulars referred to in paragraph 5 cannot be obtained from the persons referred to in paragraph 4, other persons holding those particulars and the appropriate rights to provide them may be required to provide those particulars.

7. Customs authorities may accept that commercial, port or transport information systems are used for the lodging of an entry summary declaration provided such systems contain the necessary particulars for such declaration and those particulars are available within a specific time-limit, before the goods are brought into the customs territory of the Union.

8. Customs authorities may accept, instead of the lodging of the entry summary declaration, the lodging of a notification and access to the particulars of an entry summary declaration in the economic operator's computer system.

Article 128 Risk analysis

The customs office referred to in Article 127(3) shall, within a specific time-limit, ensure that a risk analysis is carried out, primarily for security and safety purposes, on the basis of the entry summary declaration referred to in Article 127(1) or the particulars referred to in Article 127(8) and shall take the necessary measures based on the results of that risk analysis.

Article 129 Amendment and invalidation of an entry summary declaration

1. The declarant may, upon application, be permitted to amend one or more particulars of the entry summary declaration after it has been lodged.

No amendment shall be possible after any of the following:

(a) the customs authorities have informed the person who lodged the entry summary declaration that they intend to examine the goods;

(b) the customs authorities have established that the particulars of the entry summary declaration are incorrect;

(c) the goods have already been presented to customs.

2. When the goods for which an entry summary declaration has been lodged are not brought into the customs territory of the Union, the customs authorities shall invalidate that declaration in either of the following cases:

(a) upon application by the declarant;

(b) within 200 days after the lodging of the declaration.

Article 130 Declarations lodged instead of an entry summary declaration

1. The customs office referred to in Article 127(3) may waive the lodging of an entry summary declaration in respect of goods for which, prior to the expiry of the time-limit for lodging that declaration, a customs declaration is lodged. In that case, the customs declaration shall contain at least the particulars necessary for the entry summary declaration. Until such time as the customs declaration is accepted in accordance with Article 172, it shall have the status of an entry summary declaration.

2. The customs office referred to in Article 127(3) may waive the lodging of an entry summary declaration in respect of goods for which, prior to the expiry of the time-limit for lodging that declaration, a temporary storage declaration is lodged. That declaration shall contain at least the particulars necessary for the entry summary declaration. Until such time as the goods declared are presented to customs in accordance with Article 139, the temporary storage declaration shall have the status of an entry summary declaration.

Article 131 Delegation of power

The Commission shall be empowered to adopt delegated acts in accordance with Article 284, in order to determine:

(a) the cases where the obligation to lodge an entry summary declaration is waived, in accordance with point (c) of Article 127(2);

(b) the specific time-limit referred to in Article 127(3) and (7), within which the entry summary declaration is to be lodged before the goods are brought into the customs territory of the Union, taking into account the type of goods or traffic;
(c) the cases referred to in Article 127(6) and the other persons who may be required to provide particulars of the entry summary declaration in those cases.

Article 132 Conferral of implementing powers
The Commission shall specify, by means of implementing acts:
(a) the procedural rules for lodging the entry summary declaration referred to in Article 127;
(b) the procedural rules and the provision of particulars of the entry summary declaration by the other persons referred to in Article 127(6);
(c) the time-limit within which a risk analysis is to be carried out and the necessary measures to be taken, in accordance with Article 128;
(d) the procedural rules for amending the entry summary declaration, in accordance with Article 129(1);
(e) the procedural rules for invalidating the entry summary declaration in accordance with Article 129(2), taking into account the proper management of the entry of the goods.
Those implementing acts shall be adopted in accordance with the examination procedure referred to in Article 285(4).

CHAPTER 2
ARRIVAL OF GOODS

SECTION 1
ENTRY OF GOODS INTO THE CUSTOMS TERRITORY OF THE UNION

Article 133 Notification of arrival of a sea-going vessel or of an aircraft
1. The operator of a sea-going vessel or of an aircraft entering the customs territory of the Union shall notify the arrival to the customs office of first entry upon arrival of the means of transport.
Where information on arrival of a sea-going vessel or of an aircraft is available to the customs authorities they may waive the notification referred to in the first subparagraph.
2. Customs authorities may accept that port or airport systems or other available methods of information be used to notify the arrival of the means of transport.

Article 134 Customs supervision
1. Goods brought into the customs territory of the Union shall, from the time of their entry, be subject to customs supervision and may be subject to customs controls. Where applicable, they shall be subject to such prohibitions and restrictions as are justified on grounds of, inter alia, public morality, public policy or public security, the protection of the health and life of humans, animals or plants, the protection of the environment, the protection of national treasures possessing artistic, historic or archaeological value and the protection of industrial or commercial property, including controls on drug precursors, goods infringing certain intellectual property rights and cash, as well as to the implementation of fishery conservation and management measures and of commercial policy measures.
They shall remain under such supervision for as long as is necessary to determine their customs status and shall not be removed therefrom without the permission of the customs authorities.
Without prejudice to Article 254, Union goods shall not be subject to customs supervision once their customs status is established.
Non-Union goods shall remain under customs supervision until their customs status is changed, or they are taken out of the customs territory of the Union or destroyed.
2. The holder of goods under customs supervision may, with the permission of the customs authorities, at any time examine the goods or take samples, in particular in order to determine their tariff classification, customs value or customs status.

Article 135 Conveyance to the appropriate place
1. The person who brings goods into the customs territory of the Union shall convey them without delay, by the route specified by the customs authorities and in accordance with their instructions, if any, to the customs office designated by the customs authorities, or to any other place designated or approved by those authorities, or into a free zone.
2. Goods brought into a free zone shall be brought into that free zone directly, either by sea or air or, if by land, without passing through another part of the customs territory of the Union, where the free zone adjoins the land frontier between a Member State and a third country.
3. Any person who assumes responsibility for the carriage of goods after they have been brought into the customs territory of the Union shall become responsible for compliance with the obligations laid down in paragraphs 1 and 2.

4. Goods which, although still outside the customs territory of the Union, may be subject to customs controls by the customs authority of a Member State as a result of an agreement concluded with the relevant country or territory outside the customs territory of the Union, shall be treated in the same way as goods brought into the customs territory of the Union.
5. Paragraphs 1 and 2 shall not preclude application of special rules with respect to goods transported within frontier zones or in pipelines and wires as well as for traffic of negligible economic importance such as letters, postcards and printed matter and their electronic equivalents held on other media or to goods carried by travellers, provided that customs supervision and customs control possibilities are not thereby jeopardised.
6. Paragraph 1 shall not apply to means of transport and goods carried thereon only passing through the territorial waters or the airspace of the customs territory of the Union without a stop within that territory.

Article 136 Intra-Union air and sea services

Articles 127 to 130 and 133, Article 135(1) and Articles 137, 139 to 141, and 144 to 149 shall not apply to non-Union goods and goods referred to in Article 155, which have temporarily left the customs territory of the Union while moving between two points in that territory by sea or air, provided they have been carried by direct route without a stop outside the customs territory of the Union.

Article 137 Conveyance under special circumstances

1. Where, by reason of unforeseeable circumstances or force majeure, the obligation laid down in Article 135(1) cannot be complied with, the person bound by that obligation or any other person acting on that person's behalf shall inform the customs authorities of the situation without delay. Where the unforeseeable circumstances or force majeure do not result in total loss of the goods, the customs authorities shall also be informed of their precise location.
2. Where, by reason of unforeseeable circumstances or force majeure, a vessel or aircraft covered by Article 135(6) is forced to put into port or to land temporarily in the customs territory of the Union and the obligation laid down in Article 135(1) cannot be complied with, the person who brought the vessel or aircraft into the customs territory of the Union, or any other person acting on that person's behalf, shall inform the customs authorities of the situation without delay.
3. The customs authorities shall determine the measures to be taken in order to permit customs supervision of the goods referred to in paragraph 1, or of the vessel or aircraft and any goods thereon in the circumstances specified in paragraph 2, and to ensure, where appropriate, that they are subsequently conveyed to a customs office or other place designated or approved by the authorities.

Article 138 Conferral of implementing powers

The Commission shall specify, by means of implementing acts, the procedural rules on:
(a) the notification of arrival referred to in Article 133;
(b) the conveyance of goods referred to in Article 135(5).

Those implementing acts shall be adopted in accordance with the examination procedure referred to in Article 285(4).

SECTION 2

PRESENTATION, UNLOADING AND EXAMINATION OF GOODS

Article 139 Presentation of goods to customs

1. Goods brought into the customs territory of the Union shall be presented to customs immediately upon their arrival at the designated customs office or any other place designated or approved by the customs authorities or in the free zone by one of the following persons:
(a) the person who brought the goods into the customs territory of the Union;
(b) the person in whose name or on whose behalf the person who brought the goods into that territory acts;
(c) the person who assumed responsibility for carriage of the goods after they were brought into the customs territory of the Union.
2. Goods which are brought into the customs territory of the Union by sea or air and which remain on board the same means of transport for carriage, shall be presented to customs only at the port or airport where they are unloaded or transhipped. However, goods brought into the customs territory of the Union which are unloaded and reloaded onto the same means of transport during its voyage in order to enable the unloading or loading of other goods, shall not be presented to customs at that port or airport.
3. Notwithstanding the obligations of the person described in paragraph 1, presentation of the goods may be effected instead by one of the following persons:
(a) any person who immediately places the goods under a customs procedure;
(b) the holder of an authorisation for the operation of storage facilities or any person who carries out an activity in a free zone.

VAT EC

4. The person presenting the goods shall make a reference to the entry summary declaration or, in the cases referred to in Article 130, the customs declaration or temporary storage declaration which has been lodged in respect of the goods, except where the obligation to lodge an entry summary declaration is waived.
5. Where non-Union goods presented to customs are not covered by an entry summary declaration, and except where the obligation to lodge such declaration is waived, one of the persons referred to in Article 127(4) shall, without prejudice to Article 127(6), lodge immediately such declaration or shall instead lodge a customs declaration or temporary storage declaration.
6. Paragraph 1 shall not preclude application of special rules with respect to goods transported within frontier zones or in pipelines and wires as well as for traffic of negligible economic importance such as letters, postcards and printed matter and their electronic equivalents held on other media or to goods carried by travellers, provided that customs supervision and customs control possibilities are not thereby jeopardised.
7. Goods presented to customs shall not be removed from the place where they have been presented without the permission of the customs authorities.

Article 140 Unloading and examination of goods

1. Goods shall be unloaded or trans-shipped from the means of transport carrying them solely with the authorisation of the customs authorities in places designated or approved by those authorities.
However, such authorisation shall not be required in the event of an imminent danger necessitating the immediate unloading of all or part of the goods. In that case, the customs authorities shall immediately be informed accordingly.
2. The customs authorities may at any time require goods to be unloaded and unpacked for the purpose of examining them, taking samples or examining the means of transport carrying them.

Article 141 Goods moved under transit

1. Article 135(2) to (6) and Articles 139, 140 and 144 to 149 shall not apply when goods already under a transit procedure are brought into the customs territory of the Union.
2. Articles 140 and 144 to 149 shall apply to non-Union goods moved under a transit procedure, once such goods have been presented to the customs office of destination in the customs territory of the Union in accordance with the rules governing the transit procedure.

Article 142 Delegation of power

The Commission shall be empowered to adopt delegated acts in accordance with Article 284, in order to determine the conditions for approving the places referred to in Article 139(1).

Article 143 Conferral of implementing powers

The Commission shall specify, by means of implementing acts, the procedural rules regarding the presentation of goods to customs referred to in Article 139.
Those implementing acts shall be adopted in accordance with the examination procedure referred to in Article 285(4).

SECTION 3
TEMPORARY STORAGE OF GOODS

Article 144 Goods in temporary storage

Non-Union goods shall be in temporary storage from the moment they are presented to customs.

Article 145 Temporary storage declaration

1. Non-Union goods presented to customs shall be covered by a temporary storage declaration containing all the particulars necessary for the application of the provisions governing temporary storage.
2. Documents related to goods in temporary storage shall be provided to the customs authorities where Union legislation so requires or where necessary for customs controls.
3. The temporary storage declaration shall be lodged by one of the persons referred to in Article 139(1) or (2) at the latest at the time of the presentation of the goods to customs.
4. The temporary storage declaration shall, unless the obligation to lodge an entry summary declaration is waived, include a reference to any entry summary declaration lodged for the goods presented to customs, except where they have already been in temporary storage or have been placed under a customs procedure and have not left the customs territory of the Union.
5. Customs authorities may accept that the temporary storage declaration also takes one of the following forms:
(a) a reference to any entry summary declaration lodged for the goods concerned, supplemented by the particulars of a temporary storage declaration;
(b) a manifest or another transport document, provided that it contains the particulars of a temporary storage declaration, including a reference to any entry summary declaration for the goods concerned.

6. Customs authorities may accept that commercial, port or transport information systems are used to lodge a temporary storage declaration provided that they contain the necessary particulars for such declaration and these particulars are available in accordance with paragraph 3.
7. Articles 188 to 193 shall apply to the temporary storage declaration.
8. The temporary storage declaration may be used also for the purpose of:
(a) the notification of arrival referred to in Article 133; or
(b) the presentation of the goods to customs referred to in Article 139, insofar as it fulfils the conditions laid down in those provisions.
9. A temporary storage declaration shall not be required where, at the latest at the time of the presentation of the goods to customs, their customs status as Union goods is determined in accordance with Articles 153 to 156.
10. The temporary storage declaration shall be kept by, or be accessible to, the customs authorities for the purpose of verifying that the goods to which it relates are subsequently placed under a customs procedure or re-exported in accordance with Article 149.
11. For the purpose of paragraphs 1 to 10, where non- Union goods moved under a transit procedure are presented to customs at an office of destination within the customs territory of the Union, the particulars for the transit operation concerned shall be deemed to be the temporary storage declaration, provided they meet the requirements for that purpose. However, the holder of the goods may lodge a temporary storage declaration after the end of the transit procedure.

Article 146 Amendment and invalidation of a temporary storage declaration

1. The declarant shall, upon application, be permitted to amend one or more particulars of the temporary storage declaration after it has been lodged. The amendment shall not render the declaration applicable to goods other than those which it originally covered.
No amendment shall be possible after any of the following:
(a) the customs authorities have informed the person who lodged the declaration that they intend to examine the goods;
(b) the customs authorities have established that particulars of the declaration are incorrect.
2. Where the goods for which a temporary storage declaration has been lodged are not presented to customs, the customs authorities shall invalidate that declaration in either of the following cases:
(a) upon application by the declarant;
(b) within 30 days after the lodging of the declaration.

Article 147 Conditions and responsibilities for the temporary storage of goods

1. Goods in temporary storage shall be stored only in temporary storage facilities in accordance with Article 148 or, where justified, in other places designated or approved by the customs authorities.
2. Without prejudice to Article 134(2), goods in temporary storage shall be subject only to such forms of handling as are designed to ensure their preservation in an unaltered state without modifying their appearance or technical characteristics.
3. The holder of the authorisation referred to in Article 148 or the person storing the goods in the cases where the goods are stored in other places designated or approved by the customs authorities, shall be responsible for all of the following:
(a) ensuring that goods in temporary storage are not removed from customs supervision;
(b) fulfilling the obligations arising from the storage of goods in temporary storage.
4. Where, for any reason, goods cannot be maintained in temporary storage, the customs authorities shall without delay take all measures necessary to regularise the situation of the goods in accordance with Articles 197, 198 and 199.

Article 148 Authorisation for the operation of temporary storage facilities

1. An authorisation from the customs authorities shall be required for the operation of temporary storage facilities. Such authorisation shall not be required where the operator of the temporary storage facility is the customs authority itself.
The conditions under which the operation of temporary storage facilities is permitted shall be set out in the authorisation.
2. The authorisation referred to in paragraph 1 shall be granted only to persons who satisfy all of the following conditions:
(a) they are established in the customs territory of the Union;
(b) they provide the necessary assurance of the proper conduct of the operations; an authorised economic operator for customs simplifications shall be deemed to fulfil that condition insofar as the operation of temporary storage facilities is taken into account in the authorisation referred to in point (a) of Article 38(2);
(c) they provide a guarantee in accordance with Article 89.
Where a comprehensive guarantee is provided, compliance with the obligations attached to that guarantee shall be monitored by appropriate audit.

3. The authorisation referred to in paragraph 1 shall be granted only where the customs authorities are able to exercise customs supervision without having to introduce administrative arrangements which are disproportionate to the economic needs involved.
4. The holder of the authorisation shall keep appropriate records in a form approved by the customs authorities.
The records shall contain the information and the particulars which enable the customs authorities to supervise the operation of the temporary storage facilities, in particular with regard to the identification of the goods stored, their customs status and their movements.
An authorised economic operator for customs simplifications shall be deemed to comply with the obligation referred to in the first and second subparagraphs, insofar as his or her records are appropriate for the purpose of the operation of temporary storage.
5. The customs authorities may authorise the holder of the authorisation to move goods in temporary storage between different temporary storage facilities under the condition that such movements would not increase the risk of fraud, as follows:
- (a) such movement takes place under the responsibility of one customs authority;
- (b) such movement is covered by only one authorisation, issued to an authorised economic operator for customs simplifications; or
- (c) in other cases of movement.

6. The customs authorities may, where an economic need exists and customs supervision will not be adversely affected, authorise the storage of Union goods in a temporary storage facility. Those goods shall not be regarded as goods in temporary storage.

Article 149 End of temporary storage

Non-Union goods in temporary storage shall be placed under a customs procedure or re-exported within 90 days.

Article 150 Choice of a customs procedure

Except where otherwise provided, the declarant shall be free to choose the customs procedure under which to place the goods, under the conditions for that procedure, irrespective of their nature or quantity, or their country of origin, consignment or destination.

Article 151 Delegation of power

The Commission shall be empowered to adopt delegated acts, in accordance with Article 284, in order to determine:
- (a) the conditions for approving the places referred to in Article 147(1);
- (b) the conditions for granting the authorisation for the operation of temporary storage facilities, referred to in Article 148;
- (c) the cases of movement referred to in point (c) of Article 148(5).

Article 152 Conferral of implementing power

The Commission shall specify, by means of implementing acts, the procedural rules for:
- (a) lodging the temporary storage declaration referred to in Article 145;
- (b) amending the temporary storage declaration, in accordance with Article 146(1);
- (c) invalidating the temporary storage declaration, in accordance with Article 146(2);
- (d) the movement of goods in temporary storage referred to in Article 148(5).

Those implementing acts shall be adopted in accordance with the examination procedure referred to in Article 285(4).

TITLE V
GENERAL RULES ON CUSTOMS STATUS, PLACING GOODS UNDER A CUSTOMS PROCEDURE, VERIFICATION, RELEASE AND DISPOSAL OF GOODS

CHAPTER 1
CUSTOMS STATUS OF GOODS

Article 153 Presumption of customs status of Union goods

1. All goods in the customs territory of the Union shall be presumed to have the customs status of Union goods, unless it is established that they are not Union goods.
2. In specific cases, where the presumption laid down in paragraph 1 does not apply, the customs status of Union goods shall need to be proven.
3. In specific cases, goods wholly obtained in the customs territory of the Union do not have the customs status of Union goods if they are obtained from goods in temporary storage or placed under the external transit procedure, a storage procedure, the temporary admission procedure or the inward processing procedure.

Article 154 Loss of customs status of Union goods

Union goods shall become non-Union goods in the following cases:
- (a) where they are taken out of the customs territory of the Union, insofar as the rules on internal transit do not apply;

(b) where they have been placed under the external transit procedure, a storage procedure or the inward processing procedure, insofar as the customs legislation so allows;
(c) where they have been placed under the end-use procedure and are either subsequently abandoned to the State, or are destroyed and waste remains;
(d) where the declaration for release for free circulation is invalidated after release of the goods.

Article 155 Union goods leaving the customs territory of the Union temporarily
1. In the cases referred to in points (b) to (f) of Article 227(2), goods shall keep their customs status as Union goods only if that status is established under certain conditions and by means laid down in the customs legislation.
2. In specific cases, Union goods may move, without being subject to a customs procedure, from one point to another within the customs territory of the Union and temporarily out of that territory without alteration of their customs status.

Article 156 Delegation of power
The Commission shall be empowered to adopt delegated acts, in accordance with Article 284, in order to determine:
(a) the cases where the presumption laid down in Article 153(1) does not apply;
(b) the conditions for granting facilitation in the establishment of the proof of customs status of Union goods;
(c) the cases where the goods referred to in Article 153(3) do not have the customs status of Union goods;
(d) the cases where the customs status of goods referred to in Article 155(2) is not altered.

Article 157 Conferral of implementing powers
The Commission shall specify, by means of implementing acts, the procedural rules for the provision and verification of the proof of the customs status of Union goods.
Those implementing acts shall be adopted in accordance with the examination procedure referred to in Article 285(4).

CHAPTER 2
PLACING GOODS UNDER A CUSTOMS PROCEDURE

SECTION 1
GENERAL PROVISIONS

Article 158 Customs declaration of goods and customs supervision of Union goods
1. All goods intended to be placed under a customs procedure, except for the free zone procedure, shall be covered by a customs declaration appropriate for the particular procedure.
2. In specific cases, other than those referred to in Article 6(2), a customs declaration may be lodged using means other than electronic data-processing techniques.
3. Union goods declared for export, internal Union transit or outward processing shall be subject to customs supervision from the time of acceptance of the declaration referred to in paragraph 1 until such time as they are taken out of the customs territory of the Union or are abandoned to the State or destroyed or the customs declaration is invalidated.

Article 159 Competent customs offices
1. Except where Union legislation provides otherwise, Member States shall determine the location and competence of the various customs offices situated in their territory.
2. Member States shall ensure that official opening hours are fixed for those offices that are reasonable and appropriate, taking into account the nature of the traffic and of the goods and the customs procedures under which they are to be placed, so that the flow of international traffic is neither hindered nor distorted.
3. Except where otherwise provided, the competent customs office for placing the goods under a customs procedure shall be the customs office responsible for the place where the goods are presented to customs.

Article 160 Delegation of power
The Commission shall be empowered to adopt delegated acts, in accordance with Article 284, in order to determine the cases where a customs declaration may be lodged using means other than electronic data-processing techniques in accordance with Article 158(2).

Article 161 Conferral of implementing powers
The Commission shall specify, by means of implementing acts, the procedural rules for:
(a) determining the competent customs offices other than the one referred to in Article 159(3), including customs offices of entry and customs offices of exit;
(b) lodging the customs declaration in the cases referred to in Article 158(2).

VAT EC

Those implementing acts shall be adopted in accordance with the examination procedure referred to in Article 285(4).

SECTION 2
STANDARD CUSTOMS DECLARATIONS

Article 162 Content of a standard customs declaration

Standard customs declarations shall contain all the particulars necessary for application of the provisions governing the customs procedure for which the goods are declared.

Article 163 Supporting documents

1. The supporting documents required for the application of the provisions governing the customs procedure for which the goods are declared shall be in the declarant's possession and at the disposal of the customs authorities at the time when the customs declaration is lodged.
2. Supporting documents shall be provided to the customs authorities where Union legislation so requires or where necessary for customs controls.
3. In specific cases, economic operators may draw up the supporting documents provided they are authorised to do so by the customs authorities.

Article 164 Delegation of power

The Commission shall be empowered to adopt delegated acts, in accordance with Article 284, laying down the rules for granting the authorisation referred to in Article 163(3).

Article 165 Conferral of implementing powers

The Commission shall specify, by means of implementing acts, the procedural rules:

(a) for lodging the standard customs declaration referred to in Article 162;
(b) on the making available of the supporting documents referred to in Article 163(1).

Those implementing acts shall be adopted in accordance with the examination procedure referred to in Article 285(4).

SECTION 3
SIMPLIFIED CUSTOMS DECLARATIONS

Article 166 Simplified declaration

1. The customs authorities may accept that a person has goods placed under a customs procedure on the basis of a simplified declaration which may omit certain of the particulars referred to in Article 162 or the supporting documents referred to in Article 163.
2. The regular use of a simplified declaration referred to in paragraph 1 shall be subject to an authorisation from the customs authorities.

Article 167 Supplementary declaration

1. In the case of a simplified declaration pursuant to Article 166 or of an entry in the declarant's records pursuant to Article 182, the declarant shall lodge a supplementary declaration containing the particulars necessary for the customs procedure concerned at the competent customs office within a specific time-limit.

In the case of a simplified declaration pursuant to Article 166, the necessary supporting documents shall be in the declarant's possession and at the disposal of the customs authorities within a specific time-limit.

The supplementary declaration may be of a general, periodic or recapitulative nature.

2. The obligation to lodge a supplementary declaration shall be waived in the following cases:

(a) where the goods are placed under a customs warehousing procedure;
(b) in other specific cases.

3. The customs authorities may waive the requirement to lodge a supplementary declaration where the following conditions apply:

(a) the simplified declaration concerns goods the value and quantity of which is below the statistical threshold;
(b) the simplified declaration already contains all the information needed for the customs procedure concerned; and
(c) the simplified declaration is not made by entry in the declarant's records.

4. The simplified declaration referred to in Article 166 or the entry in the declarant's records referred to in Article 182, and the supplementary declaration shall be deemed to constitute a single, indivisible instrument taking effect, respectively, on the date on which the simplified declaration is accepted in accordance with Article 172 and on the date on which the goods are entered in the declarant's records.
5. The place where the supplementary declaration is to be lodged shall be deemed, for the purposes of Article 87, to be the place where the customs declaration has been lodged.

Article 168 Delegation of power

The Commission shall be empowered to adopt delegated acts in accordance with Article 284, in order to determine:

(a) the conditions for granting the authorisation referred to in Article 166(2);
(b) the specific time-limit referred to in the first subparagraph of Article 167(1) within which the supplementary declaration is to be lodged;
(c) the specific time-limit referred to in the second subparagraph of Article 167(1) within which supporting documents are to be in the possession of the declarant;
(d) the specific cases where the obligation to lodge a supplementary declaration is waived in accordance with point (b) of Article 167(2).

Article 169 Conferral of implementing powers

The Commission shall specify, by means of implementing acts, the procedural rules for lodging:
(a) the simplified declaration referred to in Article 166;
(b) the supplementary declaration referred to in Article 167.
Those implementing acts shall be adopted in accordance with the examination procedure referred to in Article 285(4).

SECTION 4
PROVISIONS APPLYING TO ALL CUSTOMS DECLARATIONS

Article 170 Lodging a customs declaration

1. Without prejudice to Article 167(1), a customs declaration may be lodged by any person who is able to provide all of the information which is required for the application of the provisions governing the customs procedure in respect of which the goods are declared. That person shall also be able to present the goods in question or to have them presented to customs.
However, where acceptance of a customs declaration imposes particular obligations on a specific person, that declaration shall be lodged by that person or by his or her representative.
2. The declarant shall be established in the customs territory of the Union.
3. By way of derogation from paragraph 2, the following declarants shall not be required to be established in the customs territory of the Union:
(a) persons who lodge a customs declaration for transit or temporary admission;
(b) persons, who occasionally lodge a customs declaration, including for end-use or inward processing, provided that the customs authorities consider this to be justified;
(c) persons who are established in a country the territory of which is adjacent to the customs territory of the Union, and who present the goods to which the customs declaration refers at a Union border customs office adjacent to that country, provided that the country in which the persons are established grants reciprocal benefits to persons established in the customs territory of the Union.
4. Customs declarations shall be authenticated.

Article 171 Lodging a customs declaration prior to the presentation of the goods

A customs declaration may be lodged prior to the expected presentation of the goods to customs. If the goods are not presented within 30 days of lodging of the customs declaration, the customs declaration shall be deemed not to have been lodged.

Article 172 Acceptance of a customs declaration

1. Customs declarations which comply with the conditions laid down in this Chapter shall be accepted by the customs authorities immediately, provided that the goods to which they refer have been presented to customs.
2. The date of acceptance of the customs declaration by the customs authorities shall, except where otherwise provided, be the date to be used for the application of the provisions governing the customs procedure for which the goods are declared and for all other import or export formalities.

Article 173 Amendment of a customs declaration

1. The declarant shall, upon application, be permitted to amend one or more of the particulars of the customs declaration after that declaration has been accepted by customs. The amendment shall not render the customs declaration applicable to goods other than those which it originally covered.
2. No such amendment shall be permitted where it is applied for after any of the following events:
(a) the customs authorities have informed the declarant that they intend to examine the goods;
(b) the customs authorities have established that the particulars of the customs declaration are incorrect;
(c) the customs authorities have released the goods.
3. Upon application by the declarant, within three years of the date of acceptance of the customs declaration, the amendment of the customs declaration may be permitted after release of the goods in order for the declarant to comply with his or her obligations relating to the placing of the goods under the customs procedure concerned.

Article 174 Invalidation of a customs declaration

1. The customs authorities shall, upon application by the declarant, invalidate a customs declaration already accepted in either of the following cases:

VAT EC

(a) where they are satisfied that the goods are immediately to be placed under another customs procedure;
(b) where they are satisfied that, as a result of special circumstances, the placing of the goods under the customs procedure for which they were declared is no longer justified.

However, where the customs authorities have informed the declarant of their intention to examine the goods, an application for invalidation of the customs declaration shall not be accepted before the examination has taken place.

2. The customs declaration shall not be invalidated after the goods have been released unless where otherwise provided.

Article 175 Delegation of power

The Commission shall be empowered to adopt delegated acts, in accordance with Article 284, in order to determine the cases where the customs declaration is invalidated after the release of the goods, as referred to in Article 174(2).

Article 176 Conferral of implementing powers

The Commission shall specify, by means of implementing acts, the procedural rules for:
(a) lodging a customs declaration in accordance with Article 171;
(b) accepting a customs declaration as referred to in Article 172, including the application of those rules in the cases referred to in Article 179;
(c) amending the customs declaration after the release of the goods in accordance with Article 173(3).

Those implementing acts shall be adopted in accordance with the examination procedure referred to in Article 285(4).

SECTION 5
OTHERS IMPLIFICATIONS

Article 177 Simplification of the drawing-up of customs declarations for goods falling under different tariff subheadings

1. Where a consignment is made up of goods falling within different tariff subheadings, and dealing with each of those goods in accordance with its tariff subheading for the purpose of drawing-up the customs declaration would entail a burden of work and expense disproportionate to the import or export duty chargeable, the customs authorities may, upon application by the declarant, agree that import or export duty be charged on the whole consignment on the basis of the tariff subheading of the goods which are subject to the highest rate of import or export duty.

2. Customs authorities shall refuse the use of the simplification referred to in paragraph 1 to goods subject to prohibitions or restrictions or excise duty where the correct classification is necessary to apply the measure.

Article 178 Conferral of implementing powers

The Commission shall adopt, by means of implementing acts, measures for the determination of the tariff subheading for the application of Article 177(1).

Those implementing acts shall be adopted in accordance with the examination procedure referred to in Article 285(4).

Article 179 Centralised clearance

1. The customs authorities may, upon application, authorise a person to lodge at a customs office responsible for the place where such person is established, a customs declaration for goods which are presented to customs at another customs office.

The requirement for the authorisation referred to in the first subparagraph may be waived where the customs declaration is lodged and the goods presented to customs offices under the responsibility of one customs authority.

2. The applicant for the authorisation referred to in paragraph 1 shall be an authorised economic operator for customs simplifications.

3. The customs office at which the customs declaration is lodged shall:
(a) supervise the placing of the goods under the customs procedure concerned;
(b) carry out the customs controls for the verification of the customs declaration, referred to in points (a) and (b) of Article 188;
(c) where justified, request that the customs office at which the goods are presented carry out the customs controls for the verification of the customs declaration referred to in points (c) and (d) of Article 188; and
(d) carry out the customs formalities for the recovery of the amount of import or export duty corresponding to any customs debt.

4. The customs office at which the customs declaration is lodged and the customs office at which the goods are presented shall exchange the information necessary for the verification of the customs declaration and for the release of the goods.

5. The customs office at which the goods are presented shall, without prejudice to its own controls pertaining to goods brought into or taken out of the customs territory of the Union, carry out the customs controls referred to in point (c) of paragraph 3 and provide the customs office at which the customs declaration is lodged with the results of these controls.
6. The customs office at which the customs declaration is lodged shall release the goods in accordance with Articles 194 and 195, taking into account:
(a) the results of its own controls for the verification of the customs declaration;
(b) the results of the controls carried out by the customs office at which the goods are presented for the verification of the customs declaration and the controls pertaining to goods brought into or taken out of the customs territory of the Union.

Article 180 Delegation of power
The Commission shall be empowered to adopt delegated acts, in accordance with Article 284, in order to determine the conditions for granting the authorisation referred to in the first subparagraph of Article 179(1).

Article 181 Conferral of implementing powers
The Commission shall specify, by means of implementing acts, the procedural rules concerning:
(a) the centralised clearance, including the relevant customs formalities and controls, referred to in Article 179;
(b) the waiver from the obligation for goods to be presented referred to in Article 182(3) in the context of centralised clearance.
Those implementing acts shall be adopted in accordance with the examination procedure referred to in Article 285(4).

Article 182 Entry in the declarant's records
1. The customs authorities may, upon application, authorise a person to lodge a customs declaration, including a simplified declaration, in the form of an entry in the declarant's records, provided that the particulars of that declaration are at the disposal of the customs authorities in the declarant's electronic system at the time when the customs declaration in the form of an entry in the declarant's records is lodged.
2. The customs declaration shall be deemed to have been accepted at the moment at which the goods are entered in the records.
3. The customs authorities may, upon application, waive the obligation for the goods to be presented. In that case, the goods shall be deemed to have been released at the moment of entry in the declarant's records.
That waiver may be granted where all of the following conditions are fulfilled:
(a) the declarant is an authorised economic operator for customs simplifications;
(b) the nature and flow of the goods concerned so warrant and are known by the customs authority;
(c) the supervising customs office has access to all the information it considers necessary to enable it to exercise its right to examine the goods should the need arise;
(d) at the time of the entry into the records, the goods are no longer subject to prohibitions or restrictions, except where otherwise provided in the authorisation.
However, the supervising customs office may, in specific situations, request that the goods be presented.
4. The conditions under which the release of the goods is allowed shall be set out in the authorisation.

Article 183 Delegation of power
The Commission shall be empowered to adopt delegated acts, in accordance with Article 284, in order to determine the conditions for granting the authorisation referred to in Article 182(1).

Article 184 Conferral of implementing powers
The Commission shall specify, by means of implementing acts, the procedural rules on entry in the declarant's records referred to in Article 182, including the relevant customs formalities and controls.
Those implementing acts shall be adopted in accordance with the examination procedure referred to in Article 285(4).

Article 185 Self-assessment
1. Customs authorities may, upon application, authorise an economic operator to carry out certain customs formalities which are to be carried out by the customs authorities, to determine the amount of import and export duty payable, and to perform certain controls under customs supervision.
2. The applicant for the authorisation referred to in paragraph 1 shall be an authorised economic operator for customs simplifications.

Article 186 Delegation of power
The Commission shall be empowered to adopt delegated acts in accordance with Article 284, in order to determine:

(a) the conditions for granting the authorisation referred to in Article 185(1);
(b) the customs formalities and the controls to be carried out by the holder of the authorisation referred to in Article 185(1).

Article 187 Conferral of implementing powers
The Commission shall specify, by means of implementing acts, the procedural rules regarding the customs formalities and the controls to be carried out by the holder of the authorisation in accordance with Article 185(1).
Those implementing acts shall be adopted in accordance with the examination procedure referred to in Article 285(4).

CHAPTER 3
VERIFICATION AND RELEASE OF GOODS

SECTION 1
VERIFICATION

Article 188 Verification of a customs declaration
The customs authorities may, for the purpose of verifying the accuracy of the particulars contained in a customs declaration which has been accepted:
(a) examine the declaration and the supporting documents;
(b) require the declarant to provide other documents;
(c) examine the goods;
(d) take samples for analysis or for detailed examination of the goods.

Article 189 Examination and sampling of goods
1. Transport of the goods to the places where they are to be examined and where samples are to be taken, and all the handling necessitated by such examination or taking of samples, shall be carried out by or under the responsibility of the declarant. The costs incurred shall be borne by the declarant.
2. The declarant shall have the right to be present or represented when the goods are examined and when samples are taken. Where the customs authorities have reasonable grounds for so doing, they may require the declarant to be present or represented when the goods are examined or samples are taken or to provide them with the assistance necessary to facilitate such examination or taking of samples.
3. Provided that samples are taken in accordance with the provisions in force, the customs authorities shall not be liable for payment of any compensation in respect thereof but shall bear the costs of their analysis or examination.

Article 190 Partial examination and sampling of goods
1. Where only part of the goods covered by a customs declaration is examined, or samples are taken, the results of the partial examination, or of the analysis or examination of the samples, shall be taken to apply to all the goods covered by the same declaration.
However, the declarant may request a further examination or sampling of the goods if he or she considers that the results of the partial examination, or of the analysis or examination of the samples taken, are not valid as regards the remainder of the goods declared. The request shall be granted provided that the goods have not been released or, if they have been released, that the declarant proves that they have not been altered in any way.
2. For the purposes of paragraph 1, where a customs declaration covers goods falling under two or more items, the particulars relating to goods falling under each item shall be deemed to constitute a separate declaration.

Article 191 Results of the verification
1. The results of verifying the customs declaration shall be used for the application of the provisions governing the customs procedure under which the goods are placed.
2. Where the customs declaration is not verified, paragraph 1 shall apply on the basis of the particulars contained in that declaration.
3. The results of the verification made by the customs authorities shall have the same conclusive force throughout the customs territory of the Union.

Article 192 Identification measures
1. The customs authorities or, where appropriate, economic operators authorised to do so by the customs authorities, shall take the measures necessary to identify the goods where identification is required in order to ensure compliance with the provisions governing the customs procedure for which those goods have been declared.
Those identification measures shall have the same legal effect throughout the customs territory of the Union.

2. Means of identification affixed to the goods, packaging or means of transport shall be removed or destroyed only by the customs authorities or, where they are authorised to do so by the customs authorities, by economic operators, unless, as a result of unforeseeable circumstances or force majeure, their removal or destruction is essential to ensure the protection of the goods or the means of transport.

Article 193 Conferral of implementing powers

The Commission shall specify, by means of implementing acts, measures on the verification of the customs declaration, the examination and sampling of goods and the results of the verification.

Those implementing acts shall be adopted in accordance with the examination procedure referred to in Article 285(4).

SECTION 2
RELEASE

Article 194 Release of the goods

1. Where the conditions for placing the goods under the procedure concerned are fulfilled and provided that any restriction has been applied and the goods are not subject to any prohibition, the customs authorities shall release the goods as soon as the particulars in the customs declaration have been verified or are accepted without verification.

The first subparagraph shall also apply where verification as referred to in Article 188 cannot be completed within a reasonable period of time and the goods are no longer required to be present for verification purposes.

2. All the goods covered by the same declaration shall be released at the same time.

For the purposes of the first subparagraph, where a customs declaration covers goods falling under two or more items the particulars relating to goods falling under each item shall be deemed to constitute a separate customs declaration.

Article 195 Release dependent upon payment of the amount of import or export duty corresponding to the customs debt or provision of a guarantee

1. Where the placing of goods under a customs procedure gives rise to a customs debt, the release of the goods shall be conditional upon the payment of the amount of import or export duty corresponding to the customs debt or the provision of a guarantee to cover that debt.

However, without prejudice to the third subparagraph, the first subparagraph shall not apply to temporary admission with partial relief from import duty.

Where, pursuant to the provisions governing the customs procedure for which the goods are declared, the customs authorities require the provision of a guarantee, those goods shall not be released for the customs procedure in question until such guarantee is provided.

2. In specific cases, the release of the goods shall not be conditional upon the provision of a guarantee in respect of goods which are the subject of a drawing request on a tariff quota.

3. Where a simplification as referred to in Articles 166, 182 and 185 is used and a comprehensive guarantee is provided, release of the goods shall not be conditional upon a monitoring of the guarantee by the customs authorities.

Article 196 Delegation of power

The Commission shall be empowered to adopt delegated acts, in accordance with Article 284, in order to determine the cases referred to in Article 195(2).

CHAPTER 4
DISPOSAL OF GOODS

Article 197 Destruction of goods

Where the customs authorities have reasonable grounds for so doing, they may require goods which have been presented to customs to be destroyed and shall inform the holder of the goods accordingly. The costs of the destruction shall be borne by the holder of the goods.

Article 198 Measures to be taken by the customs authorities

1. The customs authorities shall take any necessary measures, including confiscation and sale, or destruction, to dispose of goods in the following cases:

(a) where one of the obligations laid down in the customs legislation concerning the introduction of non-Union goods into the customs territory of the Union has not been fulfilled, or the goods have been withheld from customs supervision;

(b) where the goods cannot be released for any of the following reasons:

(i) it has not been possible, for reasons attributable to the declarant, to undertake or continue examination of the goods within the period prescribed by the customs authorities;

(ii) the documents which must be provided before the goods can be placed under, or released for, the customs procedure requested have not been provided;

VAT EC

(iii) payments or a guarantee which should have been made or provided in respect of import or export duty, as the case may be, have not been made or provided within the prescribed period;

(iv) the goods are subject to prohibitions or restrictions;

(c) where the goods have not been removed within a reasonable period after their release;

(d) where after their release, the goods are found not to have fulfilled the conditions for that release; or

(e) where goods are abandoned to the State in accordance with Article 199.

2. Non-Union goods which have been abandoned to the State, seized or confiscated shall be deemed to be placed under the customs warehousing procedure. They shall be entered in the records of the customs warehousing operator, or, where they are held by the customs authorities, by the latter.

Where goods to be destroyed, abandoned to the State, seized or confiscated are already subject to a customs declaration, the records shall include a reference to the customs declaration. Customs authorities shall invalidate that customs declaration.

3. The costs of the measures referred to in paragraph 1 shall be borne:

(a) in the case referred to in point (a) of paragraph 1, by any person who was required to fulfil the obligations concerned or who withheld the goods from customs supervision;

(b) in the cases referred to in points (b) and (c) of paragraph 1, by the declarant;

(c) in the case referred to in point (d) of paragraph 1, by the person who is required to comply with the conditions governing the release of the goods;

(d) in the case referred to in point (e) of paragraph 1, by the person who abandons the goods to the State.

Article 199 Abandonment

Non-Union goods and goods placed under the end-use procedure may with prior permission of the customs authorities be abandoned to the State by the holder of the procedure or, where applicable, the holder of the goods.

Article 200 Conferral of implementing powers

The Commission shall specify, by means of implementing acts, the procedural rules on:

(a) the destruction of goods, referred to in Article 197;

(b) the sale of goods, referred to in Article 198(1);

(c) abandonment of goods to the State in accordance with Article 199.

Those implementing acts shall be adopted in accordance with the examination procedure referred to in Article 285(4).

TITLE VI

RELEASE FOR FREE CIRCULATION AND RELIEF FROM IMPORT DUTY

CHAPTER 1

RELEASE FOR FREE CIRCULATION

Article 201 Scope and effect

1. Non-Union goods intended to be put on the Union market or intended for private use or consumption within the customs territory of the Union shall be placed under release for free circulation.

2. Release for free circulation shall entail the following:

(a) the collection of any import duty due;

(b) the collection, as appropriate, of other charges, as provided for under relevant provisions in force relating to the collection of those charges;

(c) the application of commercial policy measures and prohibitions and restrictions insofar as they do not have to be applied at an earlier stage; and

(d) completion of the other formalities laid down in respect of the import of the goods.

3. Release for free circulation shall confer on non-Union goods the customs status of Union goods.

Article 202 Commercial policy measures

1. Where processed products obtained under inward processing are released for free circulation and the calculation of the amount of import duty is made in accordance with Article 86(3), the commercial policy measures to be applied shall be those applicable to the release for free circulation of the goods which were placed under inward processing.

2. Paragraph 1 shall not apply to waste and scrap.

3. Where processed products obtained under inward processing are released for free circulation and the calculation of the amount of import duty is made in accordance with Article 85(1), the commercial policy measures applicable to those goods shall be applied only where the goods which were placed under inward processing are subject to such measures.

4. Where Union legislation establishes commercial policy measures on release for free circulation, such measures shall not apply to processed products released for free circulation following outward processing where:

(a) the processed products retain their Union origin within the meaning of Article 60;

(b) the outward processing involves repair, including the standard exchange system referred to in Article 261; or

(c) the outward processing follows further processing operations in accordance with Article 258.

TITLE VII
SPECIAL PROCEDURES
CHAPTER 1
GENERAL PROVISIONS

Article 210 Scope

Goods may be placed under any of the following categories of special procedures:

(a) transit, which shall comprise external and internal transit;

(b) storage, which shall comprise customs warehousing and free zones;

(c) specific use, which shall comprise temporary admission and end-use;

(d) processing, which shall comprise inward and outward processing.

Article 211 Authorisation

1. An authorisation from the customs authorities shall be required for the following:

(a) the use of the inward or outward processing procedure, the temporary admission procedure or the end-use procedure;

(b) the operation of storage facilities for the customs warehousing of goods, except where the storage facility operator is the customs authority itself.

The conditions under which the use of one or more of the procedures referred to in the first subparagraph or the operation of storage facilities is permitted shall be set out in the authorisation.

2. The customs authorities shall grant an authorisation with retroactive effect, where all of the following conditions are fulfilled:

(a) there is a proven economic need;

(b) the application is not related to attempted deception;

(c) the applicant has proven on the basis of accounts or records that:

(i) all the requirements of the procedure are met;

(ii) where appropriate, the goods can be identified for the period involved;

(iii) such accounts or records allow the procedure to be controlled;

(d) all the formalities necessary to regularise the situation of the goods can be carried out, including, where necessary, the invalidation of the customs declarations concerned;

(e) no authorisation with retroactive effect has been granted to the applicant within three years of the date on which the application was accepted;

(f) an examination of the economic conditions is not required, except where an application concerns renewal of an authorisation for the same kind of operation and goods;

(g) the application does not concern the operation of storage facilities for the customs warehousing of goods;

(h) where an application concerns renewal of an authorisation for the same kind of operation and goods, the application is submitted within three years of expiry of the original authorisation.

Customs authorities may grant an authorisation with retroactive effect also where the goods which were placed under a customs procedure are no longer available at the time when the application for such authorisation was accepted.

3. Except where otherwise provided, the authorisation referred to in paragraph 1 shall be granted only to persons who satisfy all of the following conditions:

(a) they are established in the customs territory of the Union;

(b) they provide the necessary assurance of the proper conduct of the operations; an authorised economic operator for customs simplifications shall be deemed to fulfil this condition, insofar as the activity pertaining to the special procedure concerned is taken into account in the authorisation referred to in point (a) of Article 38(2);

(c) where a customs debt or other charges may be incurred for goods placed under a special procedure, they provide a guarantee in accordance with Article 89;

(d) in the case of the temporary admission or inward processing procedure, they use the goods or arrange for their use or they carry out processing operations on the goods or arrange for them to be carried out, respectively.

4. Except where otherwise provided and in addition to paragraph 3, the authorisation referred to in paragraph 1 shall be granted only where all of the following conditions are fulfilled:

(a) the customs authorities are able to exercise customs supervision without having to introduce administrative arrangements disproportionate to the economic needs involved;
(b) the essential interests of Union producers would not be adversely affected by an authorisation for a processing procedure (economic conditions).

5. The essential interests of Union producers shall be deemed not to be adversely affected, as referred to in point (b) of paragraph 4, except where evidence to the contrary exists or where the economic conditions are deemed to be fulfilled.

6. Where evidence exists that the essential interests of Union producers are likely to be adversely affected, an examination of the economic conditions shall take place at Union level.

Article 212 Delegation of power

The Commission shall be empowered to adopt delegated acts, in accordance with Article 284, in order to determine:

(a) the conditions for granting the authorisation for the procedures referred to in Article 211(1);
(b) the exceptions to the conditions referred to in Article 211(3) and (4);
(c) the cases in which the economic conditions are deemed to be fulfilled as referred to in Article 211(5).

Article 213 Conferral of implementing powers

The Commission shall specify, by means of implementing acts, the procedural rules for examining the economic conditions referred to in Article 211(6).

Those implementing acts shall be adopted in accordance with the examination procedure referred to in Article 285(4).

Article 214 Records

1. Except for the transit procedure, or where otherwise provided, the holder of the authorisation, the holder of the procedure, and all persons carrying on an activity involving the storage, working or processing of goods, or the sale or purchase of goods in free zones, shall keep appropriate records in a form approved by the customs authorities.

The records shall contain the information and the particulars which enable the customs authorities to supervise the procedure concerned, in particular with regard to identification of the goods placed under that procedure, their customs status and their movements.

2. An authorised economic operator for customs simplifications shall be deemed to comply with the obligation laid down in paragraph 1 insofar as his or her records are appropriate for the purpose of the special procedure concerned.

Article 218 Transfer of rights and obligations

The rights and obligations of the holder of a procedure with regard to goods which have been placed under a special procedure other than transit may be fully or partially transferred to another person who fulfils the conditions laid down for the procedure concerned.

TITLE IX
ELECTRONIC SYSTEMS, SIMPLIFICATIONS, DELEGATION OF POWER, COMMITTEE PROCEDURE AND FINAL PROVISIONS

CHAPTER 1
DEVELOPMENT OF ELECTRONIC SYSTEMS

Article 278 Transitional measures

Means for the exchange and storage of information, other than the electronic data-processing techniques referred to in Article 6(1), may be used on a transitional basis, until 31 December 2020 at the latest, where the electronic systems which are necessary for the application of the provisions of the Code are not yet operational.

Article 279 Delegation of power

The Commission shall be empowered to adopt delegated acts in accordance with Article 284 specifying the rules on the exchange and storage of data in the situation referred to in Article 278.

Article 280 Work programme

1. In order to support the development of the electronic systems referred to in Article 278 and govern the setting up of transitional periods, the Commission shall, by 1 May 2014, draw up a work programme relating to the development and deployment of the electronic systems referred to in Article 16(1).

2. The work programme referred to in paragraph 1 shall have the following priorities:

(a) the harmonised exchange of information on the basis of internationally accepted data models and message formats;
(b) the reengineering of customs and customs related processes in view of enhancing their efficiency, effectiveness and uniform application and reducing compliance costs; and

(c) the offering to economic operators of a wide range of electronic customs services, enabling them to interact in the same way with the customs authorities of any Member State.

3. The work programme referred to in paragraph 1 shall be updated regularly.

Article 281 Conferral of implementing powers

The Commission shall adopt, by means of implementing acts, the work programme referred to in Article 280.

Those implementing acts shall be adopted in accordance with the examination procedure referred to in Article 285(4).

Where the committee delivers no opinion, the Commission shall not adopt the implementing acts referred to in paragraph 1 and the third subparagraph of Article 5(4) of Regulation (EU) No 182/2011 shall apply.

CHAPTER 2

SIMPLIFICATIONS IN THE APPLICATION OF THE CUSTOMS LEGISLATION

Article 282 Tests

The Commission may authorise one or more Member States, upon application, to test for a limited period of time simplifications in the application of the customs legislation, especially when IT-related. The test shall not affect the application of the customs legislation in those Member States that are not participating in such test and shall be evaluated periodically.

Article 283 Conferral of implementing powers

The Commission shall adopt, by means of implementing act, the decisions referred to in Article 282.

Those implementing acts shall be adopted in accordance with the examination procedure referred to in Article 285(4).

CHAPTER 3

DELEGATION OF POWER AND COMMITTEE PROCEDURE

Article 284 Exercise of the delegation

1. The power to adopt delegated acts is conferred on the Commission subject to the conditions laid down in this Article.

2. The power to adopt delegated acts referred to in Articles 2, 7, 10, 20, 24, 31, 36, 40, 62, 65, 75, 88, 99, 106, 115, 122, 126, 131, 142, 151, 156, 160, 164, 168, 175, 180, 183, 186, 196, 206, 212, 213, 221, 224, 231, 235, 253, 265, and 279 shall be conferred on the Commission for a period of five years from 30 October 2013. The Commission shall draw up a report in respect of the delegation of power not later than nine months before the end of the five-year period. The delegation of power shall be tacitly extended for periods of an identical duration, unless the European Parliament or the Council opposes such extension not later than three months before the end of each period.

3. The delegation of power referred to in Articles 2, 7, 10, 20, 24, 31, 36, 40, 62, 65, 75, 88, 99, 106, 115, 122, 126, 131, 142, 151, 156, 160, 164, 168, 175, 180, 183, 186, 196, 206, 212, 213, 221, 224, 231, 235, 253, 265, and 279 may be revoked at any time by the European Parliament or by the Council. A decision to revoke shall put an end to the delegation of the power specified in that decision. It shall take effect the day following the publication of the decision in the *Official Journal of the European Union* or at a later date specified therein. It shall not affect the validity of any delegated acts already in force.

4. As soon as it adopts a delegated act, the Commission shall notify it simultaneously to the European Parliament and to the Council.

5. A delegated act adopted pursuant to Articles 2, 7, 10, 20, 24, 31, 36, 40, 62, 65, 75, 88, 99, 106, 115, 122, 126, 131, 142, 151, 156, 160, 164, 168, 175, 180, 183, 186, 196, 206, 212, 213, 221, 224, 231, 235, 253, 265, or 279 shall enter into force only if no objection has been expressed either by the European Parliament or the Council within two months of notification of that act to the European Parliament and the Council or if, before the expiry of that period, the European Parliament and the Council have both informed the Commission that they will not object. That period shall be extended by two months at the initiative of the European Parliament or of the Council.

Article 285 Committee procedure

1. The Commission shall be assisted by the Customs Code Committee. That committee shall be a committee within the meaning of Regulation (EU) No 182/2011.

2. Where reference is made to this paragraph, Article 4 of Regulation (EU) No 182/2011 shall apply.

3. Where reference is made to this paragraph, Article 8 of Regulation (EU) No 182/2011 in conjunction with Article 4 thereof shall apply.

4. Where reference is made to this paragraph, Article 5 of Regulation (EU) No 182/2011 shall apply.

5. Where reference is made to this paragraph, Article 8 of Regulation (EU) No 182/2011 in conjunction with Article 5 thereof shall apply.

6. Where the opinion of the committee is to be obtained by written procedure and reference is made to this paragraph, that procedure shall be terminated without result only when, within the time-limit for delivery of the opinion, the chair of the committee so decides.

CHAPTER 4
FINAL PROVISIONS

Article 286 Repeal and amendment of legislation in force

1. Regulation (EC) No 450/2008 is repealed.
2. Regulation (EEC) No 3925/91, Regulation (EEC) No 2913/92 and Regulation (EC) No 1207/2001 are repealed from the date referred to in Article 288(2).
3. References to the repealed Regulations shall be construed as references to this Regulation and shall be read in accordance with the correlation tables set out in the Annex.
4. In the sixth indent of Article 3(1) of Regulation (EEC) No 2913/92, the phrase 'and Mayotte' is deleted as from 1 January 2014.
5. The first indent of point (a) of Article 9(1) of Regulation (EEC) No 2658/87 is deleted from the date referred to in Article 288(2).

Article 287 Entry into force

This Regulation shall enter into force on the twentieth day following that of its publication in the *Official Journal of the European Union*.

Article 288 Application

1. Articles 2, 7, 8, 10, 11, 17, 20, 21, 24, 25, 31, 32, 36, 37, 40, 41, 50, 52, 54, 58, 62, 63, 65, 66, 68, 75, 76, 88, 99, 100, 106, 107, 115, 122, 123, 126, 131, 132, 138, 142, 143, 151, 152, 156, 157, 160, 161, 164, 165, 168, 169, 175, 176, 178, 180, 181, 183, 184, 186, 187, 193, 196, 200, 206, 207, 209, 212, 213, 216, 217, 221, 222, 224, 225, 231, 232, 235, 236, 239, 253, 265, 266, 268, 273, 276, 279, 280, 281, 283, 284, 285 and 286 shall apply as from 30 October 2013.
2. Articles other than those referred to in paragraph 1 shall apply as from 1 May 2016.

This Regulation shall be binding in its entirety and directly applicable in all Member States.

Done at Strasbourg, ...9 October 2013.

ANNEX
CORRELATION TABLE

Regulation (EC) No 450/2008	This Regulation
Article 1(1) and (2)	Article 1(1) and (2)
Article 1(3), first subparagraph	Article 1(3)
Article 1(3), second subparagraph	Article 2
Article 2	Article 3
Article 3	Article 4
Article 4, points 1 to 8	Article 5, points 1 to 8
Article 4, point 9	Article 5, points 9 and 10
Article 4, point 10	Article 5, point 12
Article 4, points 11 and 12	Article 5, points 15 and 16
Article 4, points 13 to 17	Article 5, points 18 to 22
Article 4, point 18(a), first sentence	Article 5, point 23(a)
Article 4, point 18(a), second sentence	Article 130(3)
Article 4, point 18(b) and (c)	Article 5, point 23(b) and (c)
Article 4, points 19 to 26	Article 5, points 24 to 31
Article 4, point 27 to 32	Article 5, points 33 to 38
Article 4, point 33	—
Article 5(1), first subparagraph	Article 6(1)
Article 5(1), second and third subparagraphs	Articles 6(3) and 7(b)
Article (5)(2)	Articles 6(2), 7(a) and 8(1)(a)
Article 6	Article 12
Article 7	Article 13
Article 8	Article 14
Article 9	Article 15

Regulation (EC) No 450/2008	This Regulation
Article 10(1)	Articles 9 and 16(1)
Article 10(2)	Articles 10, 11 and 17
Article 11(1), first and second subparagraphs	Article 18
Article 11(1), third subparagraph	Article 18(2), first subparagraph
Article 11(2)	Article 18(3)
Article 11(3)(a)	Article 18(2), second subparagraph and Article 21
Article 11(3)(b)	Article 21
Article 11(3)(c)	—
Article 12(1)	Article 19(1)
Article 12(2), first subparagraph	Article 19(2), first subparagraph
Article 12(2), second subparagraph	Article 19(2), second subparagraph and Article 20(b)
Article 13(1)	Article 38(1)
Article 13(2)	Article 38(2) and (3)
Article 13(3)	Article 38(4)
Article 13(4)	Article 38(5), first sentence
Article 13(5)	—
Article 13(6)	Article 23(2)
Article 14	Article 39
Article 15(1)(a)	Article 22, Article 24(a) to (g) and Article 25(a) and (b)
Article 15(1)(b)	Articles 23(4)(b) and 24(h)
Article 15(1)(c)	—
Article 15(1)(d)	Article 22(1), third subparagraph and 24(a)
Article 15(1)(e)	Article 40(b)
Article 15(1)(f)	Article 25(b)
Article 15(1)(g)	Articles 23(4)(b), 24(h), 24(c), 28, 31(b) and 32
Article 15(1)(h)	—
Article 15(2)	—
Article 16(1)	Article 22(1), first and second subparagraphs
Article 16(2)	Article 22(3), first and second subparagraphs
Article 16(3)	Article 22(2)
Article 16(4), first subparagraph	Article 22(6), first subparagraph, first sentence
Article 16(4), second subparagraph	Article 22(6), first subparagraph, second sentence and Article 22(7)
Article 16(5)(a)	Article 22(6), second subparagraph and Article 24(g)
Article 16(5)(b)	Article 24(f)
Article 16(6)	Article 23(3)
Article 16(7)	Article 29
Article 17	Article 26
Article 18(1) to (3)	Article 27
Article 18(4)	Article 32
Article 19(1)	Article 28(1)(a)
Article 19(2) and (3)	Article 28(2) and (3)
Article 19(4)	Article 28(4), first subparagraph and second subparagraph, first sentence

VAT EC

Regulation (EC) No 450/2008	This Regulation
Article 19(5)	Article 31(a)
Article 20(1) to (4)	Article 33
Article 20(5)	Article 34(4)
Article 20(6), first subparagraph	Article 34(5), first sentence
Article 20(6), second subparagraph	Article 34(6)
Article 20(7)	Articles 22, 23, 24, 25 and 32
Article 20(8)(a)	Article 34(1) to (3)
Article 20(8)(b)	Article 34(9) and Article 37(1)(a)
Article 20(8)(c)	Article 34(11) and 37(2)
Article 20(9)	Articles 35, 36(b) and 37(1)(c) and (d)
Article 21	Article 42
Article 22	Article 43
Article 23	Article 44
Article 24(1) and (2)	Article 45(1) and (2)
Article 24(3), first subparagraph	Article 45(3)
Article 24(3), second subparagraph	—
Article 25(1)	Article 46(1)
Article 25(2), first subparagraph	Article 46(2)
Article 25(2), second and third subparagraphs	Article 46(3)
Article 25(3)	Article 46(4) to (8) and Article 50(1)
Article 26	Article 47
Article 27	Article 48
Article 28(1) and (2)	Article 49
Article 28(3)	Article 50(2)
Article 29	Article 51
Article 30(1)	Article 52
Article 30(2)	—
Article 31(1)	Article 53(1)
Article 31(2)	Article 53(3)
Article 31(3)	Article 54
Article 32	Article 55
Article 33(1) to (4)	Article 56(1) to (4)
Article 33(5)	Articles 56(5) and 58(1)
Article 34	Article 57(1),(2) and (3)
Article 35	Article 59
Article 36	Article 60
Article 37	Article 61
Article 38	Articles 62, 63, 67 and 68
Article 39(1) and (2)	Article 64(1) and (2)
Article 39(3)	Article 64(3), first subparagraph
Article 39(4) and (5)	Article 64(4) and (5)
Article 39(6)	Article 64(3), second subparagraph, Article 64(6) and Articles 63 to 68
Article 40	Article 69
Article 41	Article 70
Article 42(1)	Article 74(1)
Article 42(2)	Article 74(2)(a) to (c) and the introductory sentence of point (d)
Article 42(3)	Article 74(3)
Article 43(a)	Articles 71, 72 and 76(a)

Regulation (EC) No 450/2008	This Regulation
Article 43(b)	Article 74(2)(d), points (i), (ii) and (iii)
Article 43(c)	—
Article 43(d)	Articles 73 and 75 and Article 76(b) and (c)
Article 44	Article 77
Article 45	Article 78
Article 46	Article 79
Article 47	Article 80
Article 48	Article 81
Article 49	Article 82
Article 50	Article 83
Article 51	Article 84
Article 52	Article 85
Article 53(1) to (3)	Article 86(1) to (3)
Article 53(4)	Article 86(6)
Article 54(a) and (b)	Article 86(5) and Article 88(a)
Article 54(c)	Article 86(4) and Article 88(b)
Article 55(1)	Article 87(1)
Article 55(2), first subparagraph	Article 87(2)
Article 55(2), second subparagraph	Article 88(c)
Article 55(3) and (4)	Article 87(3) and (4)
Article 56(1) to (5)	Article 89(1) to (5)
Article 56(6)	Article 89(7)
Article 56(7)	Article 89(9)
Article 56(8)	Article 89(2), second subparagraph
Article 56(9), first indent	Article 100(1)(b)
Article 56(9), second indent	Articles 89(8) and 99(a)
Article 56(9), third indent	Article 89(2), second subparagraph
Article 57(1) and (2)	Article 90
Article 57(3)	Article 100(1)(a)
Article 58, first paragraph	Article 91
Article 58, second paragraph	—
Article 59(1), first subparagraph	Article 100(1)
Article 59(1), second subparagraph	Article 99(b)
Article 59(2)	Article 92(2)
Article 60	Article 93
Article 61	Article 94
Article 62(1) and (2)	Article 95(1) and (2)
Article 62(3)	Article 22, Article 24(a) to (g), Article 25(a) and (b) and Article 99(c)
Article 63(1) and (2)	—
Article 63(3)(a)	—
Article 63(3)(b)	Articles 96(1)(a), 96(2), 100(1)(c) and 100(2)
Article 63(3)(c)	Article 96(1)(b), 96(2), 100(1)(c) and 100(2)
Article 64	Article 97
Article 65(1) and (2)	Article 98
Article 65(3)	Articles 99(d) and 100(1)(b)
Article 66	Article 101(1) and (2)
Article 67(1), first and second subparagraphs	Article 102(1)

VAT EC

Regulation (EC) No 450/2008	This Regulation
Article 67(1), third subparagraph	Article 106
Article 67(2) and (3)	Article 102(2) and (3), first subparagraph
Article 68(1) and (2)	Article 103(1) and (2)
Article 68(3)	Article 103(3)(a)
Article 68(4)	Article 103(4)
Article 69	Article 104
Article 70	Article 105(1) to (5)
Article 71	Article 105(6)
Article 72(1) and (2)	Article 108(1) and (2)
Article 72(3)	Articles 108(3) and 115
Article 73	Article 109
Article 74	Article 110
Article 75	Article 111
Article 76	—
Article 77(1), first subparagraph	Article 112(1)
Article 77(1), second and third subparagraphs	Article 112(2)
Article 77(2)	Article 112(3)
Article 77(3)	Article 112(4)
Article 78(1), first subparagraph	Article 113
Article 78(1), second subparagraph	Articles 99(d) and 100(1)(b)
Article 78(2) to (4)	Article 114(1) to (3)
Article 78(5)	Article 114(4)
Article 79(1)	Article 116(1)
Article 79(2) to (5)	Article 116(4) to (7)
Article 80	Article 117(1)
Article 81(1) and (2)	Article 118(1) and (2)
Article 81(3)	Article 118(4)
Article 82(1)	Article 119(1)
Article 82(2)	Article 119(3)
Article 83	Article 120(1)
Article 84(1)	Article 121(1)
Article 84(2)	Article 121(3)
Article 85, first sentence	Articles 116(2), 117(2), 118(3), 119(2), 120(2), 121(2) and 123(1)
Article 85, second sentence	Articles 106(3), 122 and 123(2)
Article 86(1) introductory sentence	Article 124(1) introductory sentence and point (a)
Article 86(1) (a) to (c)	Article 124(1) (b) to (d)
Article 86(1) (d) and (e)	Article 124(1) (e)
Article 86(1) (f) to (k)	Article 124(1) (f) to (k)
Article 86(2) and (3)	Article 124(2) and (3)
Article 86(4) to (6)	Article 124(5) to (7)
Article 86(7)	Article 126
Article 87(1)	Articles 127(1) and 127(2)(a)
Article 87(2), first subparagraph	Article 127(3), first subparagraph
Article 87(2), second subparagraph	Article 127(8)
Article 87(3), first subparagraph, point (a)	Articles 127(2)(b) and 131(a)
Article 87(3), first subparagraph, points (b) and (c)	Article 131(b)
Article 87(3), first subparagraph, point (d)	Articles 127(3) and 161(a)

Regulation (EC) No 450/2008	This Regulation
Article 87(3), second subparagraph	—
Article 88(1), first subparagraph, first sentence	Article 6(1)
Article 88(1), first subparagraph, second sentence	Article 127(7)
Article 88(1), second subparagraph	Article 6(2)
Article 88(2)	Article 127(4), first subparagraph
Article 88(3)	Article 127(4), second subparagraph and (6)
Article 88(4), first subparagraph	Article 133(1), first subparagraph
Article 88(4), second and third subparagraphs	Articles 6(2) and 7(a)
Article 89(1)	Article 129(1)
Article 89(2)	—
Article 90	Article 130(1)
Article 91	Article 134
Article 92(1), first subparagraph	Article 135(1)
Article 92(1), second subparagraph	Article 135(2)
Article 92(1), third subparagraph	—
Article 92(2) to (5)	Article 135(3) to (6)
Article 93(1)	Article 136
Article 93(2)	—
Article 94	Article 137
Article 95(1)	Article 139(1)
Article 95(2) and (3)	Article 139(3) and (4)
Article 95(4)	Article 139(6)
Article 96(1) and (2)	Article 140
Article 96(3)	Article 139(7)
Article 97(1)	Article 149
Article 97(2)	Article 150
Article 98(1)	Article 144
Article 98(2)	Article 139(5)
Article 99	Article 141(1)
Article 100	Article 141(2)
Article 101(1)	Article 153(1)
Article 101(2)(a)	Articles 153(2) and 156(a)
Article 101(2)(b)	Articles 156(b) and 157
Article 101(2)(c)	Articles 153(3) and 156(c)
Article 102	Article 154
Article 103	Articles 155(2) and 156(d)
Article 104(1)	Article 158(1)
Article 104(2)	Article 158(3)
Article 105(1)	Article 159(1) and (2)
Article 105(2)(a) and (b)	Articles 159(3) and 161(a)
Article 105(2)(c)	Articles 22(1), third subparagraph, and 25(c)
Article 106(1), first subparagraph, first sentence	Article 179(1), first subparagraph
Article 106(1), first subparagraph, second sentence	—
Article 106(2)	Article 179(3) and (6)
Article 106(3)	Article 179(5)

VAT EC

Regulation (EC) No 450/2008	This Regulation
Article 106(4), first subparagraph, point (a)	Article 22, Article 24(a) to (g) and Article 25(a) and (b)
Article 106(4), first subparagraph, point (b)	Articles 23(4)(a) and 24(h)
Article 106(4), first subparagraph, point (c)	Article 179(1), second subparagraph, Article 179(2) and Article 180
Article 106(4), first subparagraph, point (d)	Article 22(1), third subparagraph and 24(a)
Article 106(4), first subparagraph, point (e)	Article 25(b)
Article 106(4), first subparagraph, point (f)	Articles 23(4)(b), 24(h), 28, 31(b) and 32
Article 106(4), first subparagraph, points (g) and (h)	Article 181
Article 106(4), second subparagraph	—
Article 107(1), first sentence	Article 6(1)
Article 107(1), second sentence	Article 182(1)
Article 107(2)	Article 158(2)
Article 107(3)	Articles 160, 161(b), 182(2) to (4), 183 and 184
Article 108(1), first subparagraph, first sentence	Article 162
Article 108(1), first subparagraph, second and third sentences	Article 170(4)
Article 108(1), second subparagraph	Articles 6(2), 7(a) and 8(1)(a)
Article 108(2)	Article 163(1) and (2)
Article 108(3), first subparagraph	Article 6(1)
Article 108(3), second subparagraph	—
Article 108(4)	Articles 163(3), 164 and 165(b)
Article 109(1)	Article 166(1)
Article 109(2)	Articles 166(2) and 168 (a)
Article 109(3)	Articles 6(2), 7(a), 8(1)(a) and 165(a)
Article 110(1), first subparagraph	Article 167(1), first subparagraph
Article 110(1), second subparagraph	Article 167(1), third subparagraph
Article 110(1), third subparagraph	Article 167(2) and (3) and Article 168(d)
Article 110(2) and (3)	Article 167(4) and (5)
Article 111(1)	Article 170(1)
Article 111(2), first sentence	Article 170(2)
Article 111(2), second sentence	Article 170(3)(a) and (b)
Article 111(3)	Articles 170(3)(c)
Article 112(1), first subparagraph	Article 172(1)
Article 112(1), second subparagraph, first sentence	Article 182(2)
Article 112(1), second subparagraph, second sentence	Article 182(3)
Article 112(2)	—
Article 112(3)	Article 172(2)
Article 112(4)	Articles 176(b)
Article 113(1) and (2)	Article 173(1) and (2)
Article 113(3)	Articles 173(3) and 176(c)
Article 114(1)	Article 174(1)
Article 114(2), first subparagraph	Article 174(2)
Article 114(2), second subparagraph	Article 175
Article 115, first paragraph	Article 177(1)
Article 115, second paragraph	Articles 177(2) and 178
Article 116(1)	Article 185(1)

Regulation (EC) No 450/2008	This Regulation
Article 116(2), first subparagraph, point (a)	Article 22, Article 24(a) to (g) and Article 25(a) and (b)
Article 116(2), first subparagraph, point (b)	Articles 23(4)(a), 23(5), 24(h) and 25(c)
Article 116(2), first subparagraph, points (c) and (d)	Articles 185(2) and 186(a)
Article 116(2), first subparagraph, point (e)	Article 22(1), third subparagraph and 24(a)
Article 116(2), first subparagraph, point (f)	Article 25(b)
Article 116(2), first subparagraph, point (g)	Articles 23(4)(b), 24(h), 28, 31(b) and 32
Article 116(2), first subparagraph, points (h) and (i)	Articles 186(b) and 187
Article 116(2), second subparagraph	—
Article 117	Article 188
Article 118	Article 189
Article 119(1) and (2)	Article 190
Article 119(3)	Article 193
Article 120	Article 191
Article 121	Article 192
Article 122	Article 193
Article 123(1) and (2)	Article 194
Article 123(3)	Article 179(4)
Article 124(1)	Article 195(1)
Article 124(2)	Article 195(2) and (3) and Article 196
Article 125	Article 197
Article 126(1)	Article 198(1)
Article 126(2)	Article 198(2), first subparagraph, first sentence
Article 127(1)	Article 199
Article 127(2)	Article 198(3)(d)
Article 128	Article 198(2), first subparagraph, second sentence and second subparagraph, Article 198(3)(a) to (c) and Article 200
Article 129	Article 201
Article 130(1)	Article 203(1), first subparagraph
Article 130(2) to (5)	Article 203(2) to (5)
Article 131(a)	—
Article 131(b)	Article 204
Article 132	Article 205
Article 133	Article 208(1)
Article 134	Articles 202, 203(1), second subparagraph, 203(6), 206, 207 and 209
Article 135	Article 210
Article 136(1)	Article 211(1)
Article 136(2), first subparagraph, point (a)	Article 22, Article 24(a) to (g) and Article 25(a) and (b)
Article 136(2), first subparagraph, point (b)	Articles 23(4)(a) and 24(h)
Article 136(2), first subparagraph, point (c)	Article 212(a)
Article 136(2), first subparagraph, point (d)	Article 22(1), third subparagraph and 24(a)
Article 136(2), first subparagraph, point (e)	Article 25(b)
Article 136(2), first subparagraph, point (f)	Articles 23(4)(b), 24(h), 28, 31(b) and 32
Article 136(2), first subparagraph, point (g)	—
Article 136(2), first subparagraph, point (h)	—

Regulation (EC) No 450/2008	This Regulation
Article 136(2), second subparagraph	—
Article 136(3), first subparagraph, point (a)	Article 211(3), first subparagraph, point (a)
Article 136(3), first subparagraph, point (b)	Article 211(3), first subparagraph, points (b) and (c)
Article 136(3), first subparagraph, point (c)	Article 211(3), first subparagraph, point (d)
Article 136(3), second subparagraph	Article 212(b)
Article 136(4), first subparagraph	Article 211(4)
Article 136(4), second subparagraph	Article 211(5)
Article 136(4), third subparagraph	Article 211(6)
Article 136(4), fourth subparagraph, points (a) and (b)	Article 213
Article 136(4), fourth subparagraph, point (c)	Article 212(c)
Article 136(5)	Article 23(2)
Article 137(1)	Article 214(1)
Article 137(2)	Article 214(2) and Article 7(c)
Article 138	Article 215(1) to (3)
Article 139	Article 218
Article 140(1)	Article 219
Article 140(2)	Articles 221(a) and 222(b)
Article 141	Article 220
Article 142(1), first, second and third subparagraphs	Article 223(1)
Article 142(1), fourth subparagraph	Article 224(a)
Article 142(2), first subparagraph, point (a)	Article 223(2), first subparagraph, point (a)
Article 142(2), first subparagraph, points (b) and (c)	Article 223(2), first subparagraph, points (c) and (d)
Article 142(2), second subparagraph	Article 223(2), first subparagraph, point (b) and Article 224(c)
Article 142(3), first subparagraph	Article 223(3)
Article 142(3), second subparagraph	Article 224(d)
Article 142(4)	Article 223(4)
Article 143	Articles 211(2), 216, 217, 221(b), 222(b), 224(b), 225, 228, 229, 230, 231(b), 232, 233(4), 235, 236, 243(2), 251(4), 254(2), (3), (6) and (7) and 257(4)
Article 144(1)	Article 226(1)
Article 144(2)	Articles 226(2) and 231(a)
Article 144(3)	Article 226(3)
Article 144(4)	—
Article 145(1) and (2)	Article 227
Article 145(3), first subparagraph	Article 155(1)
Article 145(3), second subparagraph	Article 157
Article 146	Article 233(1) to (3)
Article 147	Article 234
Article 148(1)	Article 237(1)
Article 148(2), first subparagraph	Article 237(2)
Article 148(2), second subparagraph	Articles 237(3) and 239
Article 149	Article 242
Article 150(1)	Article 238(1)
Article 150(2)(a)	—
Article 150(2)(b)	Article 238(2)
Article 150(3)	—

Regulation (EC) No 450/2008	This Regulation
Article 151(1), first subparagraph	Article 144
Article 151(1), second subparagraph	Article 145(3)
Article 151(2)	Article 145(5) and (11)
Article 151(3)	—
Article 151(4)	Article 147(4)
Article 151(5)	Article 145(1), (2), (4) and (6) to (10), Article 146, Article 147(3) and (4) and Article 148 and 151
Article 152	Article147(1) and (2)
Article 153	Article 240
Article 154(1)(a)	Article 237(3), first sentence
Article 154(1)(b)	Article 241(1)
Article 154(2)	Article 237(3), second sentence and Article 241(2)
Article 155(1)	Article 243(1)
Article 155(2) and (3)	Article 243(3) and (4)
Article 156	Article 244
Article 157	Article 245
Article 158	Article 246
Article 159	Article 247
Article 160	Article 248
Article 161	Article 249
Article 162	Article 250
Article 163	Article 251(1) to (3)
Article 164, first paragraph	Article 253
Article 164, second paragraph	—
Article 165	Article 252
Article 166(1)	Article 254(1)
Article 166(2) and (3)	Article 254(4) and (5)
Article 167	Article 255
Article 168	Article 256
Article 169	Article 257(1) to (3)
Article 170	Article 258
Article 171(1) and (2)	Article 259(1) and (2)
Article 171(3)	Article 86(5)
Article 171(4)	Article 259(3)
Article 172	Article 260
Article 173	Article 261
Article 174	Article 262
Article 175(1), first subparagraph	Article 263(1)
Article 175(1), second subparagraph	Article 263(2)(a)
Article 175(2) and (3)	Article 263(3) and (4)
Article 176(1)(a) and (b)	Article 263(2)(b) and Article 265(b)
Article 176(1)(c) and (d)	Article 265(b)
Article 176(1)(e)	Article 161(a)
Article 176(2)	—
Article 177(1) and (2)	Article 267(1) and (3)
Article 177(3)	Article 267(2)
Article 177(4)	Article 267(2)
Article 177(5)	Article 268
Article 178(1)	Article 269(1)

Regulation (EC) No 450/2008	This Regulation
Article 178(2)(a)	Article 269(2)(a) and (b)
Article 178(2)(b)	Article 269(2)(d) and (e)
Article 178(3)	Articles 269(3)
Article 179	Article 270
Article 180(1)	Article 271(1), first subparagraph
Article 180(2), first sentence	Article 6(1)
Article 180(2), second sentence	Article 271(3)
Article 180(3), first subparagraph	Article 6(2)
Article 180(3), second subparagraph	Article 271(4)
Article 180(4)	Article 271(2)
Article 181, first and second paragraphs	Article 272(1)
Article 181, second paragraph and third paragraph	—
Article 182(1)	Article 277
Article 182(2)	—
Article 183(1)	Articles 16(1) and 17
Article 183(2)(a) and (b)	—
Article 183(2)(c)	Articles 280 and 283
Article 184	Article 285
Article 185	—
Article 186	Article 286(2) and (3)
Article 187	Article 287
Article 188(1)	Article 288(1)
Article 188(2)	Article 288(2)
Article 188(3)	Article 288(1)

COUNCIL IMPLEMENTING REGULATION 1042/2013/EU OF 7 OCTOBER 2013 AMENDING IMPLEMENTING REGULATION (EU) NO 282/2011 AS REGARDS THE PLACE OF SUPPLY OF SERVICES

(No 1042/2013/EU)

THE COUNCIL OF THE EUROPEAN UNION,

Having regard to the Treaty on the Functioning of the European Union,

Having regard to Council Directive 2006/112/EC of 28 November 2006 on the common system of value added tax,[1] and in particular Article 397 thereof,

Having regard to the proposal from the European Commission,

Whereas:

(1) Directive 2006/112/EC provides that as from 1 January 2015, all telecommunications, radio and television broadcasting and electronically supplied services supplied to a non-taxable person are to be taxed in the Member State in which the customer is established, has his permanent address or usually resides, regardless of where the taxable person supplying those services is established. Most other services supplied to a non- taxable person continue to be taxed in the Member State in which the supplier is established.

(2) In order to determine which services must be taxed in the Member State of the customer, it is essential to define telecommunications, radio and television broadcasting and electronically supplied services. In particular, the concept of radio and television broadcasting (hereinafter 'broadcasting') services should be clarified, drawing from definitions laid down in Directive 2010/13/EU of the European Parliament and of the Council.[2]

(3) To clarify matters, transactions identified as electronically supplied services have been listed in Council Implementing Regulation (EU) No 282/2011,[3] without the list being exhaustive. The list should be updated, and similar lists should be drawn up for telecommunications and broadcasting services.

(4) It is necessary to specify who is the supplier for value added tax (VAT) purposes where

electronically supplied services, or telephone services provided through the internet, are supplied to a customer through telecommunications networks or via an interface or a portal.

(5) To ensure the uniform application of the rules governing the place of supply of hiring of means of transport and the place of supply of telecommunications, broadcasting and electronically supplied services, it is necessary to specify where a non-taxable legal person should be considered to be established.

(6) With a view to determining who is liable for payment of the VAT on the supply of telecommunications, broadcasting or electronically supplied services, and taking into account that the place of taxation is the same regardless of whether the customer is a taxable or a non-taxable person, the supplier should be able to determine the status of a customer solely based on whether the customer communicates his individual VAT identification number. This status must, in accordance with the general rules, be amended if such a communication is subsequently made by the customer. If no such communication is received, the supplier should remain liable for payment of the VAT.

(7) Where a non-taxable person is established in more than one country or has his permanent address in one country but usually resides in another, priority is to be given to the place that best ensures taxation at the place of actual consumption. To avoid conflicts concerning jurisdiction between Member States, the place of actual consumption should be specified.

(8) Rules should be established in order to clarify the tax treatment of the supply of hiring of means of transport and telecommunications, broadcasting and electronically supplied services to a non-taxable person whose place of establishment, permanent address or usual residence is practically impossible to determine or which cannot be determined with certainty. It is appropriate for those rules to be based on presumptions.

(9) Where information is available to determine the actual location at which the customer is established, has his permanent address or usually resides, it is necessary to provide for a presumption to be rebuttable.

(10) In certain cases where the service is occasional, habitually involves small amounts and requires the physical presence of the customer, such as the supply of telecommunications, broadcasting or electronically supplied services at a wi-fi hot spot or an internet café, or habitually does not give rise to payment receipts or other evidence of the service provided, as is the case with telephone boxes, the provision and control of evidence with respect to the place of establishment of the customer or his permanent address or usual residence would impose a disproportionate burden, or could pose problems of data protection.

(11) As the tax treatment of the supply of hiring of means of transport and telecommunications, broadcasting and electronically supplied services to a non-taxable person depends on where the customer is established, has his permanent address or usually resides, it is necessary to clarify, in cases for which no specific presumptions are established or for the rebuttal of presumptions, what evidence the supplier should have to identify the location of the customer. To that end an indicative, non-exhaustive list of evidence should be drawn up.

(12) In order to ensure the uniform tax treatment of supplies of services connected with immovable property, the concept of immovable property needs to be defined. The proximity required for there to be a connection with an immovable property should be specified, and a non-exhaustive list of examples of transactions identified as services connected with immovable property should also be provided.

(13) It is also necessary to clarify the tax treatment of the supply of services putting equipment at a customer's disposal with a view to carrying out work on immovable property.

(14) For practical reasons, it should be clarified that telecommunications, broadcasting or electronically supplied services provided by a taxable person acting in his own name in connection with the provision of accommodation in the hotel sector or sectors with a similar function should be regarded, for the purpose of determining the place of supply, as being supplied at those locations.

(15) In accordance with Directive 2006/112/EC, admission to cultural, artistic, sporting, scientific, educational, entertainment or similar events must in all circumstances be taxed at the place where the event actually takes place. It should be made clear that this also applies where tickets to such events are not sold directly by the organiser, but are distributed through intermediaries.

(16) Under Directive 2006/112/EC, VAT can become chargeable prior to, at the time of or soon after the supply of goods or services. In relation to telecommunications, broadcasting or electronically supplied services supplied during the period of transition to the new rules on the place of supply, conditions linked to the supply or differences in application between Member States could result in double taxation or non-taxation. In order to avoid that, and to ensure uniform application in Member States, it is necessary to lay down transitional provisions.

(17) For the purposes of this Regulation, it may be appropriate for Member States to adopt legislative measures limiting certain rights and obligations laid down by Directive 95/46/EC of

VAT EC

the European Parliament and of the Council[4] in order to safeguard an important economic or financial interest of a Member State or of the European Union, including monetary, budgetary and taxation matters, where such measures are necessary and proportionate in view of the risk of tax fraud and tax evasion in Member States, and in view of the need to ensure the correct collection of VAT covered by this Regulation.

(18) The concept of immovable property should be introduced in order to ensure a uniform tax treatment by Member States of supplies of services connected with immovable property. The introduction of that concept could have a considerable impact on the legislation and administrative practices in Member States. Without prejudice to such legislation or practices already applied in Member States and in order to ensure a smooth transition, that concept should be introduced at a later date.

(19) Implementing Regulation (EU) No 282/2011 should therefore be amended accordingly,

Notes[1] OJ L347, 11.12.2006, p 1.

[2] Directive 2010/13/EU of the European Parliament and of the Council of 10 March 2010 on the coordination of certain provisions laid down by law, regulation or administrative action in Member States concerning the provision of audiovisual media services (Audiovisual Media Services Directive) (OJ L95, 15.4.2010, p 1).

[3] Council Implementing Regulation (EU) No 282/2011 of 15 March 2011 laying down implementing measures for Directive 2006/112/EC on the common system of value added tax (OJ L77, 23.3.2011, p 1).

[4] Directive 95/46/EC of the European Parliament and of the Council of 24 October 1995 on the protection of individuals with regard to the processing of personal data and on the free movement of such data (OJ L281, 23.11.1995, p 31).

HAS ADOPTED THIS REGULATION:

Article 1

(*amends* Implementing Regulation (EU) No 282/2011)

Article 2

For telecommunications, radio and television broadcasting or electronically supplied services supplied by a supplier established within the Community to a non-taxable person who is established, has his permanent address or usually resides there, the following shall apply:

(a) the place of supply in respect of each chargeable event that occurs before 1 January 2015 shall be the place where the supplier is established, as provided for in Article 45 of Directive 2006/112/EC, regardless of when the supply, or continuous supply, of those services is completed;

(b) the place of supply in respect of each chargeable event that occurs on or after 1 January 2015 shall be the place where the customer is established, has his permanent address or usually resides, regardless of when the supply, or continuous supply, of those services commenced;

(c) where the chargeable event occurred before 1 January 2015 in the Member State where the supplier is established, no tax shall become chargeable in the Member State of the customer on or after 1 January 2015 in relation to the same chargeable event.

Article 3

This Regulation shall enter into force on the twentieth day following that of its publication in the *Official Journal of the European Union*.

It shall apply from 1 January 2015.

However, Articles 13b, 31a and 31b of Implementing Regulation (EU) No 282/2011, as inserted by this Regulation, shall apply from 1 January 2017.

This Regulation shall be binding in its entirety and directly applicable in all Member States.

Done at Luxembourg, ... 7 October 2013.

REGULATION 1286/2013/EU OF THE EUROPEAN PARLIAMENT AND OF THE COUNCIL OF 11 DECEMBER 2013 ESTABLISHING AN ACTION PROGRAMME TO IMPROVE THE OPERATION OF TAXATION SYSTEMS IN THE EUROPEAN UNION FOR THE PERIOD 2014-2020 (FISCALIS 2020) AND REPEALING DECISION NO 1482/2007/EC

(No 1286/2013/EU)

THE EUROPEAN PARLIAMENT AND THE COUNCIL OF THE EUROPEAN UNION,

Having regard to the Treaty on the Functioning of the European Union, and in particular Articles 114 and 197 thereof,

Having regard to the proposal from the European Commission,
After transmission of the draft legislative act to the national parliaments,
Having regard to the opinion of the European Economic and Social Committee,[1]
Acting in accordance with the ordinary legislative procedure,
Whereas:

(1) The multi-annual action programme for taxation which applied before 2014 has significantly contributed to facilitating and enhancing cooperation between tax authorities within the Union. The added value of that programme, including to the protection of the financial interests of Member States of the Union and of taxpayers, has been recognised by the tax administrations of the participating countries. The challenges identified for the next decade cannot be tackled if Member States do not look beyond the borders of their administrative territories or cooperate intensively with their counterparts. The Fiscalis programme, implemented by the Commission in cooperation with the participating countries, offers Member States a Union framework within which to develop those cooperation activities, and which is more cost-effective than if each Member State were to set up individual cooperation frameworks on a bilateral or multilateral basis. It is therefore appropriate to ensure the continuation of that programme by establishing a new programme in the same area.

(2) The programme established under this Regulation, "Fiscalis 2020", and its success are vital in the present economic situation and should support cooperation in fiscal matters.

(3) The activities under Fiscalis 2020, namely the European information systems as defined in this Regulation (European Information Systems), the joint actions for officials of tax authorities and the common training initiatives, are expected to contribute to the realisation of the Europe 2020 Strategy for smart, sustainable and inclusive growth by strengthening the functioning of the internal market, providing a framework within which to support activities enhancing the administrative capacity of tax authorities and advancing technical progress and innovation. In providing a framework for activities which strive for more efficient tax authorities, strengthen the competitiveness of businesses, promote employment and contribute to the protection of the financial and economic interests of the Member States of the Union and of taxpayers, Fiscalis 2020 will actively strengthen the functioning of the taxation systems in the internal market, while contributing to the gradual elimination of existing barriers and distortions within the internal market.

(4) The scope of Fiscalis 2020 should be brought into line with current needs so as to focus on all taxes harmonised at Union level and other taxes in so far as they are relevant for the internal market and for administrative cooperation between the Member States.

(5) To support the process of accession and association by third countries, Fiscalis 2020 should be open to the participation of acceding and candidate countries and to potential candidate countries and partner countries of the European Neighbourhood Policy if certain conditions are fulfilled and their participation supports only activities under Fiscalis 2020 which are aimed at fighting against tax fraud and tax evasion, and addressing aggressive tax planning. Considering the increasing level of interconnection of the world economy, Fiscalis 2020 should continue to provide for the possibility of inviting external experts to contribute to activities under Fiscalis 2020. External experts, such as representatives of governmental authorities, economic operators and their organisations or representatives of international organisations should be invited only where their contribution is considered to be essential for achieving the objectives of Fiscalis 2020.

(6) The objectives and priorities of Fiscalis 2020 take into account the problems and challenges identified for taxation in the next decade. Fiscalis 2020 should continue to play a role in vital areas such as the coherent implementation of Union law in the field of taxation, securing the exchange of information and supporting administrative cooperation and enhancing the administrative capacity of tax authorities. Given the problem dynamics of new challenges identified, additional emphasis should be put on supporting the fight against tax fraud, tax evasion and aggressive tax planning. Emphasis should also be placed on reducing the administrative burden for tax authorities and the compliance costs for tax payers and preventing instances of double taxation.

(7) At an operational level, Fiscalis 2020 should implement, operate and support the European Information Systems and administrative cooperation activities, reinforce the skills and competences of tax officials, enhance the understanding and implementation of Union law in the field of taxation, and support the improvement of administrative procedures and the sharing and dissemination of good administrative practices. Those objectives should be pursued with an emphasis on supporting the fight against tax fraud, tax evasion and aggressive tax planning.

(8) The programme tools which applied before Fiscalis 2020 should be supplemented in order to respond adequately to challenges awaiting tax authorities in the next decade and to remain in line with developments in Union law. Fiscalis 2020 should cover bilateral or multilateral controls and other forms of administrative cooperation as established in the relevant Union law on administrative cooperation; expert teams; public administration capacity–building actions providing specific and specialised coaching in the field of taxation to Member States facing particular and exceptional circumstances that justify such targeted actions; and, where necessary, studies and common communication activities in order to support the implementation of Union law in the field of taxation.

(9) The European Information Systems play a vital role in interconnecting tax authorities and thus

VAT EC

in reinforcing the taxation systems within the Union and should therefore continue to be financed and improved under Fiscalis 2020. In addition, it should be made possible to include in Fiscalis 2020 new tax-related information systems established under Union law. The European Information Systems should, where appropriate, be based on shared development models and IT architecture.

(10) In the context of improving administrative cooperation more widely and supportig the fight against tax fraud, tax evasion and aggressive tax planning, it may be useful for the Union to conclude agreements with third countries in order to allow those countries to use the Union components of the European Information Systems to support a secure exchange of information between them and the Member States in the framework of bilateral tax agreements.

(11) Common training activities should also be carried out under Fiscalis 2020. Fiscalis 2020 should continue to support participating countries in strengthening professional skills and knowledge relating to taxation through enhanced jointly developed training content that targets tax officials and economic operators. To that end, the current common training approach of the Fiscalis 2020, which was mainly based on central eLearning development, should develop into a multi-facetted training support programme for the Union.

(12) Fiscalis 2020 should cover a period of seven years to align its duration with that of the multiannual financial framework laid down in Council Regulation (EU, Euratom) No 1311/2013.[2]

(13) This Regulation lays down a financial envelope for the entire duration of Fiscalis 2020 which is to constitute the prime reference amount, within the meaning of Point 17 of the Interinstitutional Agreement of 2 December 2013 between the European Parliament, the Council and the Commission on budgetary discipline, on cooperation in budgetary matters and on sound financial management,[3] for the European Parliament and the Council during the annual budgetary procedure.

(14) In line with the Commission's commitment, set out in its Communication on the Budget Review of 2010, to coherence and simplification of funding programmes, resources should be shared with other Union funding instruments if the envisaged activities under Fiscalis 2020 pursue objectives which are common to various funding instruments, excluding however double financing.

(15) The measures necessary for the financial implementation of this Regulation should be adopted in accordance with Regulation (EU, Euratom) No 966/2012 of the European Parliament and of the Council,[4] and with Commission Delegated Regulation (EU) No 1268/2012.[5]

(16) Participating countries should bear the cost of national elements of Fiscalis 2020 which would include, inter alia, the non-Union components of the European Information Systems, and any training which is not part of the common training initiatives.

(17) Considering the importance of full participation of participating countries in joint actions, a co-financing rate of 100% of the eligible costs in respect of travel and accomodation costs, costs linked to organisation of events and daily allowances is possible where it is necessary to achieve fully the objectives of Fiscalis 2020.

(18) The financial interests of the Union should be protected through appropriate measures throughout the expenditure cycle, including the prevention, detection and investigation of irregularities, the recovery of funds lost, unduly paid or incorrectly used and, where appropriate, penalties.

(19) In order to ensure uniform conditions for the implementation of this Regulation, implementing powers should be conferred on the Commission in respect of the establishment of annual work programmes. Those powers should be exercised in accordance with Regulation (EU) No 182/2011 of the European Parliament and of the Council.[6]

(20) Since the objective of this Regulation, namely establishing a multi-annual programme to improve the operation of the taxation systems in the internal market, cannot be sufficiently achieved by the Member States as they cannot efficiently perform the cooperation and coordination necessary to achieve that objective, the Union may adopt measures in accordance with the principle of subsidiarity as set out in Article 5 of the Treaty on European Union. In accordance with the principle of proportionality, as set out in that Article, this Regulation does not go beyond what is necessary in order to achieve that objective.

(21) The Commission should be assisted by the Fiscalis 2020 Committee for the implementation of Fiscalis 2020.

(22) To facilitate the evaluation of Fiscalis 2020, a proper framework for monitoring the results achieved by Fiscalis 2020 should be put in place from the very beginning. The Commission, together with participating countries, should establish adjustable indicators and set pre-defined baselines for monitoring the results of activities under Fiscalis 2020. A mid-term evaluation looking at the achievement of the objectives of Fiscalis 2020, its efficiency and its added value at the European level should be carried out. A final evaluation should, in addition, deal with the long-term impact and the sustainability effects of Fiscalis 2020. Full transparency with regular reporting on monitoring and with the submission of evaluation reports to the European Parliament and to the Council should be ensured.

(23) Directive 95/46/EC of the European Parliament and of the Council[7] governs the processing of personal data carried out in the Member States in the context of this Regulation and under the supervision of the Member States competent authorities, in particular the public independent authorities designated by the Member States. Regulation (EC) No 45/2001 of the European Parliament and of the Council[8] governs the processing of personal data carried out by Commission within the

framework of this Regulation and under the supervision of the European Data Protection Supervisor. Any exchange or transmission of information by competent authorities should be in accordance with the rules on the transfer of personal data as laid down in Directive 95/46/EC and any exchange or transmission of information by the Commission should be in accordance with the rules on the transfer of personal data as laid down in Regulation (EC) No 45/2001.

(24) This Regulation replaces Decision No 1482/2007/EC of the European Parliament and of the Council.[9] That Decision should therefore be repealed,

Notes[1] OJ C143, 22.5.2012, p 48 and OJ C11, 15.1.2013, p 84.

[2] Council Regulation (EU, Euratom) No 1311/2013 of 2 December 2013 laying down the multiannual financial framework for the year 2014-2020 (see page 884 of this Official Journal).

[3] OJ C37, 20.12.2013, p 1.

[4] Regulation (EU, Euratom) No 966/2012 of the European Parliament and of the Council of 25 October 2012 on the financial rules applicable to the general budget of the Union and repealing Council Regulation (EC, Euratom) No 1605/2002 (OJ L298, 26.10.2012, p 1).

[5] Commission Delegated Regulation (EU) No 1268/2012 of 29 October 2012 on the rules of application of Regulation (EU, Euratom) No 966/2012 of the European Parliament and of the Council on the financial rules applicable to the general budget of the Union (OJ L362, 31.12.2012, p 1).

[6] Regulation (EU) No 182/2011 of the European Parliament and of the Council of 16 February 2011 laying down the rules and general principles concerning mechanisms for control by the Member States of the Commission's exercise of implementing powers (OJ L55, 28.2.2011, p 13).

[7] Directive 95/46/EC of the European Parliament and of the Council of 24 October 1995 on the protection of individuals with regard to the processing of personal data and on the free movement of such data (OJ L281, 23.11.1995, p 31).

[8] Regulation (EC) No 45/2001 of the European Parliament and of the Council of 18 December 2000 on the protection of individuals with regard to the processing of personal data by the Community institutions and bodies and on the free movement of such data (OJ L8, 12.1.2001, p 1).

[9] Decision No 1482/2007/EC of the European Parliament and of the Council of 11 December 2007 establishing a Community programme to improve the operation of taxation systems in the internal market (Fiscalis 2013) and repealing Decision No 2235/ 2002/EC (OJ L330, 15.12.2007, p 1).

HAVE ADOPTED THIS REGULATION:

CHAPTER I
GENERAL PROVISIONS

Article 1 Subject matter

1. A multi-annual action programme "Fiscalis 2020" ("the programme") is hereby established to improve the operation of the taxation systems in the internal market and to support cooperation in relation thereto.
2. The programme shall cover the period 1 January 2014 to 31 December 2020.

Article 2 Definitions

For the purpose of this Regulation, the following definitions shall apply:

(1) "tax authorities" means the public authorities and other bodies in the participating countries which are responsible for administering taxation or tax-related activities;

(2) "external experts" means:

(a) representatives of governmental authorities, including those from countries not participating in the programme pursuant toArticle 3(2);

(b) economic operators and organisations representing economic operators;

(c) representatives of international and other relevant organisations;

(3) "taxation" means the following:

(a) value added tax provided for in Council Directive 2006/112/EC;[1]

(b) excise duties on alcohol provided for in Council Directive 92/83/EEC;[2]

(c) excise duties on tobacco products provided for in Council Directive 2011/64/EU;[3]

(d) taxes on energy products and electricity provided for in Council Directive 2003/96/EC;[4]

(e) other taxes falling within the scope of Article 2(1)(a) of Council Directive 2010/24/EU[5] in so far as they are relevant for the internal market and for administrative cooperation between the Member States;

(4) "bilateral or multilateral controls" means the coordinated checking of the tax liability of one or more related taxable persons organised by two or more participating countries with common or complementary interests, which include at least two Member States.

Notes[1] Council Directive 2006/112/EC of 28 November 2006 on the common system of value added tax (OJ L347, 11.12.2006, p 1).

[2] Council Directive 92/83/EEC of 19 October 1992 on the harmonization of the structures of excise duties on alcohol and alcoholic beverages (OJ L316, 31.10.1992, p 21).

[3] Council Directive 2011/64/EU of 21 June 2011 on the structure and rates of excise duty applied to manufactured tobacco (OJ L176, 5.7.2011, p 24).

[4] Council Directive 2003/96/EC of 27 October 2003 restructuring the Community framework for the taxation of energy products and electricity (OJ L283, 31.10.2003, p 51).

[5] Council Directive 2010/24/EU of 16 March 2010 concerning mutual assistance for the recovery of claims relating to taxes, duties and other measures (OJ L84, 31.3.2010, p 1).

Article 3 Participation in the programme

1. Participating countries shall be the Member States and the countries referred to in paragraph 2, provided the conditions set out in that paragraph are met.

2. The programme shall be open to participation by any of the following countries:

(a) acceding countries, candidate countries and potential candidate countries benefiting from a pre-accession strategy, in accordance with the general principles and general terms and conditions for the participation of those countries in Union programmes established in the respective framework agreements, Association Council decisions or similar agreements;

(b) partner countries of the European Neighbourhood Policy provided that those countries have reached a sufficient level of approximation of the relevant legislation and administrative methods to those of the Union.

The partner countries referred to in point (b) of the first subparagraph shall participate in the programme in accordance with provisions to be determined with those countries following the establishment of framework agreements concerning their participation in Union programmes. Their participation shall support only activities under the programme which are aimed at fighting tax fraud and tax evasion and addressing aggressive tax planning.

Article 4 Participation in activities under the programme

External experts may be invited to contribute to selected activities organised under the programme wherever essential for the achievement of the objectives referred to in Articles 5 and 6. The external experts shall be selected by the Commission together with the participating countries, on the basis of their skills, experience and knowledge relevant to the specific activities, taking into account any potential conflict of interest, and striking a balance between business representatives and other civil society experts. A list of selected external experts shall be made public and shall be regularly updated.

Article 5 Overall objective and specific objective

1. The overall objective of the programme shall be to improve the proper functioning of the taxation systems in the internal market by enhancing cooperation between participating countries, their tax authorities and their officials.

2. The specific objective of the programme shall be to support the fight against tax fraud, tax evasion and aggressive tax planning and the implementation of Union law in the field of taxation by ensuring exchange of information, by supporting administrative cooperation and, where necessary and appropriate, by enhancing the administrative capacity of participating countries with a view to assisting in reducing the administrative burden on tax authorities and the compliance costs for taxpayers.

3. The achievement of the objectives referred to in this Article shall be measured on the basis, in particular, of the following:

(a) the availability of, and full access to, the common communication network for the European Information Systems;

(b) the feedback from participating countries on the results of actions under the programme.

Article 6 Operational objectives and priorities of the programme

1. The operational objectives and priorities of the programme shall be the following:

(a) to implement, improve, operate and support the European Information Systems for taxation;

(b) to support administrative cooperation activities;

(c) to reinforce the skills and competence of tax officials;

(d) to enhance the understanding and implementation of Union law in the field of taxation;

(e) to support the improvement of administrative procedures and the sharing of good administrative practices.

2. The objectives and priorities referred to in paragraph 1 shall be pursued with a particular emphasis on supporting the fight against tax fraud, tax evasion and aggressive tax planning.

CHAPTER II
ELIGIBLE ACTIONS

Article 7 Eligible actions

1. The programme shall provide, under the conditions set out in the annual work programme referred to in Article 14, financial support for the following:

(a) joint actions:

(i) seminars and workshops;

(ii) project groups, generally composed of a limited number of countries, operational during a limited period of time to pursue a predefined objective with a precisely described outcome;

(iii) bilateral or multilateral controls and other activities provided for in Union law on administrative cooperation, organised by two or more participating countries, which include at least two Member States;
(iv) working visits organised by the participating countries or another country to enable officials to acquire or increase their expertise or knowledge in tax matters;
(v) expert teams, namely structured forms of cooperation, with a non-permanent character, pooling expertise to perform tasks in specific domains, in particular in the European Information Systems, possibly with the support of online collaboration services, administrative assistance and infrastructure and equipment facilities;
(vi) public administration capacity-building and supporting actions;
(vii) studies;
(viii) communication projects;
(ix) any other activity in support of the overall, specific and operational objectives and priorities set out in Articles 5 and 6, provided that the necessity for such other activity is duly justified;

(b) European Information Systems building: the development, maintenance, operation and quality control of Union components of the European Information Systems set out in point A of the Annex and new European Information Systems established under Union law, with a view to interconnecting tax authorities efficiently;
(c) common training activities: jointly developed training actions to support the necessary professional skills and knowledge relating to taxation.

Working visits referred to in point (a)(iv) of the first subparagraph shall not exceed one month. For working visits organised within third countries, only travel and subsistence (accommodation and daily allowance) costs shall be eligible under the programme.

Expert teams referred to in point (a)(v) of the first subparagraph shall be organised by the Commission in cooperation with the participating countries and, unless duly justified, shall not exceed one year.

2. The resources for the eligible actions referred to in this Article shall be allocated in a balanced manner and in proportion to the real needs of those actions.

3. When evaluating the programme, the Commission shall assess the need for introducing budgetary ceilings for the various eligible actions.

Article 8 Specific implementation provisions for joint actions

1. Participation in joint actions referred to in point (a) of the first subparagraph of Article 7(1) shall be on a voluntary basis.

2. Participating countries shall ensure that officials with an appropriate profile and qualifications, including language skills, are nominated to participate in the joint actions.

3. Participating countries shall, where appropriate, take the necessary measures to raise awareness of the joint actions and to ensure that use is made of the outputs generated.

Article 9 Specific implementation provisions for the European Information Systems

1. The Commission and the participating countries shall ensure that the European Information Systems referred to in point A of the Annex are developed, operated and appropriately maintained.

2. The Commission shall coordinate, in cooperation with the participating countries, those aspects of the establishment and functioning of the Union and non-Union components of the European Information Systems referred to in point A of the Annex which are necessary to ensure their operability, interconnectivity and continuous improvement.

3. The use of the Union components of the European Information Systems referred to in point A of the Annex by non-participating countries shall be subject to agreements with those countries to be concluded in accordance with Article 218 of the Treaty on the Functioning of the European Union.

Article 10 Specific implementation provisions for common training activities

1. Participation in common training activities referred to in point (c) of the first subparagraph of Article 7(1) shall be on a voluntary basis.

2. Participating countries shall ensure that officials with an appropriate profile and qualifications, including language skills, are nominated to participate in the common training activities.

3. Participating countries shall integrate, where appropriate, jointly developed training content, including e-learning modules, training programmes and commonly agreed training standards into their national training programmes.

CHAPTER III

FINANCIAL FRAMEWORK

Article 11 Financial framework

1. The financial envelope for the implementation of the programme shall be EUR 223,366,000 in current prices.

2. The financial allocation for the programme may also cover expenses pertaining to preparatory, monitoring, checking, audit and evaluation activities which are required on a regular basis for the management of the programme and the achievement of its objectives; in particular, studies, meetings of experts, information and communication activities related to the objectives laid down in this Regulation, expenses linked to IT networks focusing on information processing and exchange, together with all other technical and administrative assistance expenses incurred by the Commission for the management of the programme.
The share of administrative expenditure shall, in general, not exceed 5% of the overall cost of the programme.

Article 12 Types of intervention

1. The Commission shall implement the programme in accordance with Regulation (EU, Euratom) No 966/2012.
2. Union financial support for activities provided for in Article 7 shall take the form of:
(a) grants;
(b) public procurement contracts;
(c) the reimbursement of costs incurred by external experts referred to in Article 4.
3. The co-financing rate for grants shall be up to 100% of the eligible costs in the case of travel and accommodation costs, costs linked to the organisation of events and daily allowances.
That rate shall apply to all eligible actions with the exception of expert teams referred to in point (a)(v) of the first subparagraph of Article 7(1). The applicable co-financing rate for expert teams, where those actions require the awarding of grants, shall be set out in the annual work programmes.
4. The Union components of the European Information Systems shall be financed by the programme. Participating countries shall, in particular, bear the costs of the acquisition, development, installation, maintenance and day-to-day operation of the non-Union components of the European Information Systems.

Article 13 Protection of the financial interests of the Union

1. The Commission shall take appropriate measures to ensure that, where actions financed under this Regulation are implemented, the financial interests of the Union are protected by the application of preventive measures against fraud, corruption and any other illegal activities by effective checks and, if irregularities are detected, by the recovery of the amounts unduly paid and, where appropriate, by effective, proportionate and dissuasive administrative and financial penalties.
2. The Commission or its representatives and the Court of Auditors shall have the power of audit, on the basis of documents and on the spot, over all grant beneficiaries, contractors and subcontractors who have received Union funds under this Regulation.
3. The European Anti-fraud Office (OLAF) may carry out investigations, including on-the-spot checks and inspections, in accordance with the provisions and procedures laid down in Regulation (EC) No 1073/1999 of the European Parliament and of the Council[1] and Council Regulation (Euratom, EC) No 2185/96[2] with a view to establishing whether there has been fraud, corruption or any other illegal activity affecting the financial interests of the Union in connection with a grant agreement or grant decision or a contract funded under this Regulation.

Notes[1] Regulation (EC) No 1073/1999 of the European Parliament and of the Council of 25 May 1999 concerning investigations conducted by the European Anti-fraud Office (OLAF) (OJ L136, 31.5.1999, p 1).

[2] Council Regulation (Euratom, EC) No 2185/96 of 11 November 1996 concerning on-the-spot checks and inspections carried out by the Commission in order to protect the European Communities' financial interests against fraud and other irregularities (OJ L292, 15.11.1996, p 2).

CHAPTER IV
IMPLEMENTING POWERS

Article 14 Work programme

In order to implement the programme, the Commission shall, by means of implementing acts, adopt annual work programmes, which shall set out the objectives pursued, the expected results, the method of implementation and their total amount. They shall also contain a description of the actions to be financed, an indication of the amount allocated to each action type and an indicative implementation timetable. The annual work programmes shall include for grants the priorities, the essential evaluation criteria and the maximum rate of co-financing. Those implementing acts shall be based on the results of previous years and shall be adopted in accordance with the examination procedure referred to in Article 15(2).

Article 15 Committee procedure

1. The Commission shall be assisted by a committee. That committee shall be a committee within the meaning of Regulation (EU) No 182/2011.
2. Where reference is made to this paragraph, Article 5 of Regulation (EU) No 182/2011 shall apply.

CHAPTER V
MONITORING AND EVALUATION

Article 16 Monitoring of actions under the programme

1. The Commission shall, in cooperation with the participating countries, monitor the programme and actions under it.
2. The Commission and participating countries shall establish qualitative and quantitative indicators and, where necessary, add new indicators during the course of the programme. The indicators shall be used to measure the effects of the programme against pre-defined baselines.
3. The Commission shall make public the outcome of the monitoring referred to in paragraph 1 and the indicators referred to in paragraph 2.
4. The outcome of the monitoring shall be used for the evaluation of the programme in accordance with Article 17.

Article 17 Evaluation and review

1. The Commission shall submit to the European Parliament and to the Council mid-term and final evaluation reports regarding the matters referred to in paragraphs 2 and 3. The results of those evaluations shall be integrated into decisions on possible renewal, modification or suspension of the programme for subsequent periods. Those evaluations shall be carried out by an independent external evaluator.
2. The Commission shall, by 30 June 2018, draw up a mid-term evaluation report on the achievement of the objectives of the actions under the programme, the efficiency of the use of resources and the added value at the European level of the programme. That report shall, additionally, address the simplification and the continued relevance of the objectives, as well as the contribution of the programme to the Union priorities of smart, sustainable and inclusive growth.
3. The Commission shall, by 31 December 2021, draw up a final evaluation report on the matters referred to in paragraph 2, and on the long-term impact and the sustainability of effects of the programme.
4. Upon request from the Commission, the participating countries shall provide it with all available data and information relevant for the purpose of contributing to its mid-term and final evaluation reports.

CHAPTER VI
FINAL PROVISIONS

Article 18 Repeal

Decision No 1482/2007/EC is repealed with effect from 1 January 2014.

However, financial obligations related to actions pursued under that Decision shall continue to be governed by it until their completion.

Article 19 Entry into force

This Regulation shall enter into force on the third day following that of its publication in the *Official Journal of the European Union*.

It shall apply from 1 January 2014.

This Regulation shall be binding in its entirety and directly applicable in all Member States.

Done at Strasbourg, ... *11 December 2013.*

For the European Parliament

The President

M. SCHULZ

For the Council

The President

V. LEŠKEVIČIUS

ANNEX
EUROPEAN INFORMATION SYSTEMS ETC

A. The European Information Systems are the following:

(1) the common communications network / common systems interface (CCN/CSI -CCN2), CCN mail3, the CSI bridge, the http bridge, CCN LDAP and related tools, CCN web portal, CCN monitoring;

(2) supporting systems, in particular the application configuration tool for CCN, the activity reporting tool (ART2), Taxud electronic management of project online (TEMPO), service management tool (SMT), the user management system (UM), the BPM system, the availability dashboard and AvDB, IT service management portal, directory and user access management;

(3) Programmes information and communication space (PICS);

(4) the VAT-related systems, in particular, the VAT information exchange system (VIES) and the VAT refund, including the VIES initial application, the VIES monitoring tool, the Taxation

VAT EC

statistical system, VIES-on-the-web, VIES-on-the-web configuration tool, the VIES and VAT refund test tools, the VAT number algorithms, the VAT exchange of e–forms, VAT on e-Services (VoeS); VoeS test tool, VAT e–forms test tool, mini one-stop-shop (MoSS);

(5) recovery-related systems, in particular eforms for recovery of claims, eforms for uniform instrument permitting enforcement (UIPE) and for uniform notification form (UNF);

(6) direct taxation-related systems, in particular taxation on savings system, taxation on savings test tool, e–forms for direct taxation, tax identification number TIN-on-the-web, the exchanges related to the Article 8 of Council Directive 2011/16/EU[1] and associated test tools;

(7) other taxation-related systems, in particular, the Taxes in Europe database (TEDB);

(8) the excise systems, in particular the system for exchange of excise data (SEED), the Excise Movement and Control System (EMCS), MVS eforms, test application (TA);

(9) other central systems, in particular, the Member States' Taxation Information and Communication system (TIC), the self-service testing system (SSTS), taxation-related statistics system, the central application for web forms, the central services / management information system for Excise (CS/MISE).

B. The Union components of the European Information Systems are:

(1) IT assets such as the hardware, the software and the network connections of the systems, including the associated data infrastructure;

(2) IT services necessary to support the development, the maintenance, the improvement and the operation of the systems; and

(3) any other elements which, for reasons of efficiency, security and rationalisation, are identified by the Commission as common to participating countries.

Notes[1] Council Directive 2011/16/EU of 15 February 2011 on administrative cooperation in the field of taxation and repealing Directive 77/799/EEC (OJ L64, 11.3.2011, p 1).

COMMISSION IMPLEMENTING REGULATION 17/2014/EU OF 10 JANUARY 2014

LAYING DOWN THE STANDARDISED FORM FOR THE NOTIFICATION FOR A SPECIAL MEASURE UNDER THE QUICK REACTION MECHANISM AGAINST VAT FRAUD

(No 17/2014/EU)

THE EUROPEAN COMMISSION,

Having regard to the Treaty on the Functioning of the European Union,

Having regard to Council Directive 2006/112/EC of 28 November 2006 on the common system of value added tax,[1] and in particular Article 199b(4) thereof,

Whereas:

(1) Directive 2006/112/EC, as amended by Council Directive 2013/42/EU,[2] introduces a Quick Reaction Mechanism for combatting value added tax (VAT) fraud.

(2) The Quick Reaction Mechanism allows Member States to notify the adoption of a special measure derogating from the general rule provided for in Directive 2006/112/EC concerning the person liable for the payment of VAT. That measure consists of applying VAT reverse charge for the purposes of combatting sudden and massive forms of fraud liable to lead to considerable and irreparable financial losses.

(3) In order to facilitate the processing of the notification of Quick Reaction Mechanism special measures, a standardised form of notification should be adopted, describing and structuring the required information from a notifying Member State.

(4) In order to shorten and streamline the notification procedure such forms should be submitted electronically to the Commission.

(5) The measures provided for in this Regulation are in accordance with the opinion of the Standing Committee on Administrative Cooperation,

Notes[1] OJ L347, 11.12.2006, p 1.

[2] Council Directive 2013/42/EU of 22 July 2013 amending Directive 2006/112/EC on the common system of value added tax as regards a Quick Reaction Mechanism against VAT fraud (OJ L201, 26.7.2013, p 1).

HAS ADOPTED THIS REGULATION:

Article 1

1. Member States shall use the standardised form set out in the Annex to this Regulation to notify the Commission of the adoption of a Quick Reaction Mechanism special measure provided for in Article 199b of Directive 2006/112/EC.
2. The notification referred to in paragraph 1 shall be submitted electronically to a dedicated e-mail address communicated by the Commission to the Standing Committee on Administrative Cooperation.

Article 2

This Regulation shall enter into force on the third day following that of its publication in the *Official Journal of the European Union*.
This Regulation shall be binding in its entirety and directly applicable in all Member States.

Done at Brussels, ...10 January 2014.

For the Commission

The President

José Manuel BARROSO

ANNEX

QUICK REACTION MECHANISM (QRM)[1]

NOTIFICATION FORM

1. **Notifying Member State**

Name of the Member State:

2. **Sector(s) to be covered**

Sector(s) concerned:

Description of the goods or services for which a QRM special measure is notified:[2]

3. **VAT fraud already detected in the sector(s) for which the notification is made (if more than one sector is concerned, please provide separate answers for each of the sectors concerned)**

Description of the type and features of the fraud (including (an estimate of) the number of persons alleged to be committing such fraud:[3]

The date on which (or period during which) the first case of fraud in this sector was detected:[3]

Actual or estimated VAT losses incurred over the past three months (in (or converted into) million EUR):[3]

Actual or estimated VAT losses incurred over the last calendar year (in (or converted into) million EUR):[3]

Actual or estimated VAT losses incurred over the year preceding the last calendar year (in (or converted into) million EUR):[3]

Latest available figure of total yearly national net VAT receipts:

4. **Anticipated future development of the fraud in the sector for which the notification is made (if more than one sector is involved, please provide separate answers for each sector concerned)**

Description of the type and features of the risk of fraud:

Member State assessment of how the fraud will develop and any evidence in support of that conclusion:

Estimate of the annual potential losses (in (or converted into) million EUR):

5. **Brief description of the urgency (e.g. reasons why other means — conventional anti-fraud measures, a derogation in accordance with Article 395 of Directive 2006/112/EC not entailing notification under Article 199b of that Directive, any legislative initiative . . . — cannot be used to combat the described fraud or risk of fraud)**

6. Describe briefly, if applicable, any envisaged accompanying measures

7. Any other comments or information

8. Person notifying the QRM special measure on behalf of the Member State concerned

Name of the person signing the notification:

Capacity of the person signing the notification:

Signature:

Date[1]:

[1] The date is the one when the electronic notification, referred to in Article 1(2) of this Regulation, is made.

[2] Use could be made for goods of the Combined Nomenclature classification.

[3] To be left blank if no VAT losses have occurred yet. Details on future developments are to be indicated in box 4.

Notes[1] See Article 199b of Directive 2006/112/EC.

EU Decisions

AUTHORISATION

APPLICATION OF ARTICLE 27 OF THE SIXTH COUNCIL DIRECTIVE OF 17 MAY 1977 ON VALUE ADDED TAX AUTHORISATION OF A DEROGATION REQUESTED BY THE GOVERNMENT OF THE UNITED KINGDOM

In its request dated 27 June 1986 and supplemented on 3 September 1986 following a request from the Commission for further information, the United Kingdom Government informed the Commission, pursuant to the above provisions, of its intention to introduce a measure derogating from the Sixth Directive.

The purpose of the measure, which replaces a previously notified derogation the scope of which was too broad, remains that of simplifying calculation of VAT in respect of long stays in hotels by assessing on a flat-rate basis the part of the service deemed to correspond to a letting of immovable property exempt under Article 13(B)(*b*)(1) of Sixth VAT Directive (77/388/EEC). However, the measure will henceforth apply only to hotel services provided to individuals themselves occupying the accommodation in question. Accordingly, the previous provision is repealed.

The Commission informed the other Member States, by letter dated 9 October 1986, of the request submitted by the United Kingdom Government.

In accordance with Article 27(4) of the Sixth Directive, the Council Decision authorising this derogation will be deemed to have been adopted if, within two months of the other Member States being informed as described above, neither the Commission nor any Member State has requested that the matter be discussed by the Council.

As neither the Commission nor any Member State has raised the matter within the prescribed time, the Council Decision is deemed to have been adopted on 10 December 1986.

Note—See OJ L359, 19.12.1986, p 59.

AUTHORISATION

APPLICATION OF ARTICLE 27 OF THE SIXTH COUNCIL DIRECTIVE OF 17 MAY 1977 ON VALUE ADDED TAX AUTHORISATION FOR A DEROGATION MEASURE REQUESTED BY THE UNITED KINGDOM GOVERNMENT

In its request dated 6 January 1987 the United Kingdom Government informed the Commission, pursuant to the above provisions, of its intention to introduce measures derogating from the sixth Directive with effect from 1 April 1987.

The purpose of the proposed anti-avoidance measures is to prevent taxable persons artificially reducing the price for supplies or imports of goods or for supplies of services to totally or partially exempt persons with whom they have certain family, legal or business ties specified in national legislation. In such circumstances, the free market value may be taken as the consideration for the transaction, irrespective of whether the latter is actually taxed or not, where otherwise there would be loss of tax.

The Commission informed the other Member States, by letter dated 10 February 1987, of the request submitted by the United Kingdom Government.

In accordance with Article 27(4) of the sixth Directive, the Council's decision will be deemed to have been adopted if, within two months of the other Member States being informed, as described above, neither the Commission nor any Member State has requested that the matter be raised by the Council.

As neither the Commission nor any Member State has requested such action within that period, the Council's decision is deemed to have been adopted on 11 April 1987.

Note—See OJ L132, 21.5.1987, p 22.

COUNCIL DECISION OF 18 JULY 1989 AUTHORISING THE UNITED KINGDOM TO APPLY A MEASURE DEROGATING FROM ARTICLE 11(A)(1)(*B*) OF THE SIXTH DIRECTIVE 77/388/EEC ON THE HARMONISATION OF THE LAWS OF THE MEMBER STATES RELATING TO TURNOVER TAXES

(89/466/EEC)

Note—See OJ L226 03.08.1989, p 23.

THE COUNCIL OF THE EUROPEAN COMMUNITIES

Having regard to the Treaty establishing the European Economic Community,

Having regard to the Sixth Council Directive 77/388/EEC of 17 May 1977 on the harmonisation of the laws of the Member States relating to turnover taxes—Common system of value added tax: uniform basis of assessment (OJ No L145, 13.6.1977, p 1), as last amended by the Act of Accession of Spain and Portugal, and in particular Article 27 thereof,

Having regard to the proposal from the Commission,

Whereas, under Article 27(1) of the Sixth Directive, the Council, acting unanimously on a proposal from the Commission, may authorise any Member State to introduce special measures for derogation from that Directive in order to simplify the procedure for charging the tax or to prevent certain types of tax evasion or avoidance;

Whereas the United Kingdom, by letter addressed to the Commission and registered on 9 January 1989, requested authorisation to introduce a special measure derogating from Article 11 of the said Directive;

Whereas the other Member States were informed of the United Kingdom's request on 9 February 1989;

Whereas, by letter dated 10 April 1989, the Commission, having decided that it had fundamental objections to the United Kingdom Government's request, asked, in accordance with Article 27(4) of the Sixth Directive, that the matter be raised by the Council;

Whereas, by a note dated 10 May 1989, the United Kingdom informed the Council that it was modifying and narrowing the scope of the derogation notified to the Commission on 9 January 1989;

Whereas the United Kingdom currently exempts all building land under Article 28(3)(*b*), read in conjunction with point 16 of Annex F to the Sixth Directive;

Whereas, in order to comply with the spirit of the Court of Justice ruling in Case 416/85, the United Kingdom wishes to tax supplies of buildings and the land on which they stand where these are used for commercial or industrial purposes, while retaining zero rating for supplies of residential buildings and exemption for supplies of building land;

Whereas, in order to simplify the procedure for charging the tax and to prevent certain types of tax evasion or avoidance, the United Kingdom wishes to apply the tax to transactions relating to commercial or industrial buildings and to the land on which they stand before first occupation on the basis of the open market value at the time they are taken into use; whereas, in the case of supply or letting with the developer option for taxation under Article 13(C)(*a*) of the Sixth Directive, this objective is achieved because the price of the supply or the rent necessarily reflects the value of the land at the time of such supply or letting;

Whereas, in order to achieve the objective in question where the building is to be occupied by a taxable person who has constructed it and who is not entitled to full deduction of the tax or where the same taxable person lets the building on an exempt basis under Article 13(B)(*b*) of the Sixth Directive, the United Kingdom intends to make use of the option provided for in Article 5(7)(*a*) and (*b*) of the said Directive to tax such occupation or letting of the property on the basis of its open market value;

Whereas, as a result of the taxable amount being determined by reference to the open market value in this way, the amended request derogates from Article 11(A)(1)(*b*) of the Sixth Directive, which stipulates that, in respect of supplies referred to in Article 5(6) and (7), the taxable amount is the purchase price of the goods or of similar goods or, in the absence of a purchase price, the cost price, determined at the time of supply;

Whereas it is appropriate to accede to the request of the United Kingdom pending deletion of point 16 of Annex F to the Sixth Directive, which permits Member States to exempt temporarily supplies of new buildings and building land;

Whereas the said special measure will not have a negative effect on the European Communities' own resources accruing from value added tax,

HAS ADOPTED THIS DIRECTIVE:

Article 1

By way of derogation from Article 11(A)(1)(*b*) of the Sixth Directive, the United Kingdom is hereby authorised to use the open market value as the taxable amount for the supply, within the meaning of Article 5(7)(*a*) and (*b*) of the said Directive, of buildings or parts of buildings before first occupation and of the land on which they stand.

Article 2

This authorisation shall be granted pending the deletion of point 16 of Annex F to the Sixth Directive.

Article 3

This Directive is addressed to the United Kingdom.

COUNCIL DECISION
OF 29 SEPTEMBER 1989
APPLICATION OF ARTICLE 27 OF THE SIXTH COUNCIL DIRECTIVE OF 17 MAY 1977 ON VALUE ADDED TAX AUTHORISING THE UNITED KINGDOM TO APPLY, IN RESPECT OF CERTAIN SUPPLIES TO UNREGISTERED RESELLERS, A MEASURE DEROGATING FROM ARTICLE 11A(1)(A) OF THE SIXTH DIRECTIVE 77/388/EEC ON THE HARMONISATION OF THE LAWS OF THE MEMBER STATES RELATING TO TURNOVER TAXES

(89/534/EEC)

Note—See OJ L280 29.09.1989, p 54.

THE COUNCIL OF THE EUROPEAN COMMUNITIES

Having regard to the Treaty establishing the European Economic Community,

Having regard to the Sixth Council Directive 77/388/EEC of 17 May 1977 on the harmonisation of the laws of the Member States relating to turnover taxes—Common system of value added tax: uniform basis of assessment, as last amended by the Act of Accession of Spain and Portugal, and in particular Article 27 thereof,

Having regard to the proposal from the Commission,

Whereas, under Article 27(1) of the Sixth Directive, the Council, acting unanimously on a proposal from the Commission, may authorise any Member State to introduce special measures for derogation from that Directive, in order to simplify the procedure for charging the tax or to prevent certain types of tax evasion or avoidance;

Whereas the United Kingdom was authorised by Council Decision 85/369/EEC, deemed to have been adopted on 13 June 1985, in accordance with the procedure laid down by Article 27(4) of the Sixth Directive, to introduce for a two-year period a derogation from the Sixth Directive to combat tax avoidance;

Whereas certain marketing structures based on sales of goods effected by taxable persons to non-taxable persons with a view to their resale at the retail stage result in avoidance of tax at the stage of final consumption;

Whereas, in order to prevent such tax avoidance, the United Kingdom applies a measure permitting the tax authorities to adopt administrative decisions the effect of which is to tax supplies made by the taxable persons operating such marketing structures on the basis of the open market value of the goods at the retail stage;

Whereas that measure constitutes a derogation from Article 11A(1)(*a*) of the Sixth Directive, which stipulates that, within the territory of the country, the taxable amount in respect of supplies of goods is everything which constitutes the consideration which has been, or is to be, obtained by the supplier from the purchaser or a third party for such supplies;

Whereas the United Kingdom was authorised by the Council Decision deemed to have been adopted on 25 May 1987 to extend for two years the derogation authorised by Decision 85/369/EEC;

Whereas the United Kingdom's application for that extension was limited to two years because of the proceedings in Joined Cases 138 and 139/86: reference to the Court of Justice by the "London Value Added Tax Tribunal" for a preliminary ruling in the proceedings pending before that Tribunal between "Direct Cosmetics Ltd" and "Laughtons Photographs Ltd" against "Commissioners of Customs and Excise" on the interpretation of Article 27 of the Sixth Directive and on the validity of Decision 85/369/EEC; whereas, in its judgement of 12 July 1988, the Court of Justice confirmed the validity of that Decision;

Whereas the United Kingdom, by letter received by the Commission on 24 February 1989, requested authorisation to extend the said measure for an indefinite period;

Whereas, in its judgement of 12 July 1988, the Court of Justice ruled *inter alia* that Article 27 of the Sixth Directive permitted the adoption of a derogating measure such as that at issue on condition that the resultant difference in treatment was justified by objective circumstances;

Whereas, in order to satisfy itself that this condition is met, the Commission must be informed of any administrative decisions adopted by the tax authorities in connection with the derogation in question;

Whereas the other Member States were notified of the United Kingdom's request on 22 March 1989; whereas the Council Decision is deemed to have been adopted if, within two months of the other Member States being informed, neither the Commission nor any Member State has requested that the matter be raised by the Council; whereas no such request has been made; whereas the Council's Decision is thus deemed to have been adopted on 24 May 1989;

Whereas the said measure will not have a negative effect on the European Communities' own resources accruing from value added tax,

HAS ADOPTED THIS DECISION:

Article 1

By way of derogation from Article 11A(1)(*a*) of the Sixth Directive, the United Kingdom is hereby authorised to prescribe, in cases where a marketing structure based on the supply of goods through non-taxable persons results in non-taxation at the stage of final consumption, that the taxable amount for supplies to such persons is to be the open market value of the goods as determined at that stage.

Article 2

The United Kingdom shall inform the Commission of any administrative decisions subsequently adopted in connection with the derogation.

Article 3

This Decision is addressed to the United Kingdom.

COUNCIL DECISION OF 21 DECEMBER 1992 AUTHORISING THE UNITED KINGDOM TO APPLY A PARTICULAR MEASURE IN ACCORDANCE WITH ARTICLE 22(12)(B) OF DIRECTIVE 77/388/EEC

(92/621/EEC)

Note—See OJ L408 31.12.1992, p 17.

THE COUNCIL OF THE EUROPEAN COMMUNITIES

Having regard to the Treaty establishing the European Economic Community,

Having regard to the Sixth Council Directive, 77/388/EEC, of 17 May 1977 on the harmonisation of the laws of the Member States relating to turnover taxes—Common system of value added tax: uniform basis of assessment, and in particular Article 22 thereof,

Having regard to the proposal from the Commission,

Whereas, under Article 22(12) of Directive 77/388/EEC, the Council, acting unanimously on a proposal from the Commission, may authorise any Member State to introduce particular measures to simplify the statement obligations laid down in paragraph 6(*b*) of Article 22; whereas Article 22(12) further stipulates that such simplification measures may not jeopardise the proper monitoring of intra-Community transactions, and may take the forms outlined in subparagraphs (*a*) and (*b*) of Article 22(12);

Whereas the United Kingdom, by letter received by the Commission on 22 May 1992, has requested authorisation for a simplification measure which takes the form laid down in subparagraph (*b*) of Article 22(12);

Whereas the authorisation will be temporary;

Whereas the particular measure will not affect the European Communities' own resources arising from value added tax,

HAS ADOPTED THIS DECISION:

Article 1

As provided for by Article 22(12) of Directive 77/388/EEC, the United Kingdom is hereby authorised, with effect from 1 January 1993 until 31 December 1996 or until the end of the transitional arrangements in the unlikely event that this is later, to introduce a particular measure in accordance with subparagraph (*b*) of Article 22(12), to simplify the obligations laid down in paragraph 6(*b*) of Article 22 regarding recapitulative statements.

Article 2

This Decision is addressed to the United Kingdom.

COUNCIL DECISION
OF 22 NOVEMBER 1993
AUTHORISING THE UNITED KINGDOM TO APPLY A PARTICULAR MEASURE IN ACCORDANCE WITH ARTICLE 22(12)(A) OF THE SIXTH DIRECTIVE 77/388/EEC ON THE HARMONISATION OF THE LAWS OF THE MEMBER STATES RELATING TO TURNOVER TAXES

(93/609/EC)

Note—See OJ L292 26.11.1993, p 51.

THE COUNCIL OF THE EUROPEAN UNION,

Having regard to the Treaty establishing the European Community,

Having regard to the Sixth Council Directive 77/388/EEC of 17 May 1977 on the harmonisation of the laws of the Member States relating to turnover taxes—Common system of value added tax: uniform basis of assessment, and in particular Article 22 thereof,

Having regard to the proposal from the Commission,

Whereas, pursuant to Article 22(12) of the Sixth Directive 77/388/EEC, the Council, acting unanimously on a proposal from the Commission, may authorise any Member State to introduce particular measures to simplify the statement obligations laid down in paragraph 6(*b*) of Article 22; whereas Article 22(12) further stipulates that such simplification measures may not jeopardise the proper monitoring of intra-Community transactions, and may take the forms outlined in subparagraphs (*a*) and (*b*) of Article 22(12);

Whereas the United Kingdom, by letter received by the Commission on 27 April 1993, has requested authorisation of a simplification measure which takes the form laid down in sub-paragraph (*a*) of Article 22(12);

Whereas the authorisation will be temporary;

Whereas the particular measure will not effect the European Communities' own resources arising from value added tax,

HAS ADOPTED THIS DECISION:

Article 1

As provided for by Article 22(12) of the Sixth Directive 77/388/EEC, the United Kingdom is hereby authorised, with effect from 1 January 1993 until 31 December 1996 or until the end of the transitional arrangements, should this be later, to introduce a particular measure in accordance with sub-paragraph (*a*) of Article 22(12), to simplify the obligations laid down in paragraph 6(*b*) of Article 22 regarding recapitulative statements.

Article 2

This Decision is addressed to the United Kingdom.

COUNCIL DECISION
OF 29 JUNE 1995
AUTHORISING THE UNITED KINGDOM TO APPLY A MEASURE DEROGATING FROM ARTICLES 6 AND 17 OF THE SIXTH COUNCIL DIRECTIVE (77/388/EEC) ON THE HARMONISATION OF THE LAWS OF THE MEMBER STATES RELATING TO TURNOVER TAXES

(95/252/EC)

Note—See OJ L159 11.07.1995, p 19.

VAT EC

THE COUNCIL OF THE EUROPEAN UNION,

Having regard to the Treaty establishing the European Community,

Having regard to the Sixth Council Directive (77/388/EEC) of 17 May 1977 on the harmonisation of the laws of the Member States relating to turnover taxes—Common system of value added tax: uniform basis of assessment and in particular Article 27 thereof,

Having regard to the proposal from the Commission,

Whereas, pursuant to Article 27(1) of the Directive 77/388/EEC, the Council, acting unanimously on a proposal from the Commission, may authorise any Member State to introduce special measures for derogation from that Directive, in order to simplify the procedure for charging the tax or to prevent certain types of tax evasion or avoidance;

Whereas, by registered letter to the Commission dated 22 March 1995, the United Kingdom requested authorisation to introduce a measure derogating from Articles 6(2) and 17 of the said Directive;

Whereas, in accordance with Article 27(3) of the said Directive, the other Member States were informed on 20 April 1995 of the request made by the United Kingdom;

Whereas the derogation in question, which forms part of a thorough recasting of the legislation governing the deduction of input tax on cars, aims, firstly, to restrict to 50 per cent the right of the hirer or lessee to deduct input tax on passenger car hire or leasing transactions where the car is used for private purposes and, secondly, to waive the value added tax payable on the private use of the car in question;

Whereas the objective of this input tax restriction is to introduce a flat-rate tax for the private use of cars hired or leased by taxable persons;

Whereas the measure, by reducing the administrative burden on traders, who are not required to keep records of private mileage, constitutes a simplification of the procedure for charging the tax within the meaning of Article 27 of Directive 77/388/EEC;

Whereas the authorisation requested by the United Kingdom can be granted only temporarily, either until the entry into force of the Community rules determining what expenditure will not be eligible for a deduction of value added tax pursuant to the first subparagraph of Article 17(6) of the said Directive or by 31 December 1997 at the latest;

Whereas the derogation in question has no adverse impact on the European Communities' own resources accruing from value added tax,

HAS ADOPTED THIS DECISION:

Article 1

By way of derogation from Article 17(2) and (3) of Directive 77/388/EEC, the United Kingdom is hereby authorised to restrict to 50 per cent the right of the hirer or lessee to deduct input tax on charges for the hire or lease of a passenger car where the car is used for private purposes.

Article 2

By way of derogation from Article 6(2)(*a*) of Directive 77/388/EEC, the United Kingdom is hereby authorised not to treat as supplies of services for consideration the private use of a business car hired or leased by a taxable person.

Article 3

This authorisation shall expire on the date of the entry into force of the Community rules determining what expenditure is not to be eligible for a deduction of value added tax, pursuant to the first subparagraph of Article 17(6) of Directive 77/388/EEC, but not later than 31 December 1997.

Article 4

This Decision is addressed to the United Kingdom.

COUNCIL DECISION OF 25 SEPTEMBER 2006 AUTHORISING THE UNITED KINGDOM TO INTRODUCE A SPECIAL MEASURE DEROGATING FROM ARTICLES 5(6) AND 11(A)(1)(*B*) OF DIRECTIVE 77/388/EEC ON THE HARMONISATION OF THE LAWS OF THE MEMBER STATES RELATING TO TURNOVER TAXES

(2006/659/EC)

Note—See OJ L 272, 03.10.2006 p 15.

THE COUNCIL OF THE EUROPEAN UNION,

Having regard to the Treaty establishing the European Community,

Having regard to the sixth Council Directive 77/388/EEC of 17 May 1977 on the harmonisation of the laws of the Member States relating to turnover taxes — Common system of value added tax: uniform basis of assessment[1], and in particular Article 27(1) thereof,

Having regard to the proposal from the Commission,

Whereas:

(1) By letter registered by the Secretariat-General of the Commission on 7 April 2005, the United Kingdom requested authorisation to derogate from Articles 5(6) and 11(A)(1)(*b*) of Directive 77/388/EEC.

(2) In accordance with Article 27(2) of Directive 77/388/EEC, the Commission informed the other Member States by letter dated 26 October 2005 of the request made by the United Kingdom. By letter dated 27 October 2005, the Commission notified the United Kingdom that it had all the information it considered necessary for appraisal of the request.

(3) The United Kingdom wishes to replace the derogation, provided for by Council Decision 86/356/EEC of 21 July 1986 authorising the United Kingdom to apply flat-rate measures in respect of the non-deductible value added tax charged on fuel expenditure in company cars[2], which authorised special simplification measures in order to determine on a flat-rate basis the proportion of value added tax (VAT) relating to expenditure on fuel in business cars partly used for private purposes. This procedure relieves taxable persons of the need to keep detailed mileage records in order to calculate, for each car, the exact amount of VAT related to private and business motoring. Like this system, the proposed new system will be optional for taxable persons.

(4) The current system is based on the type of fuel used and the engine size of the car. The United Kingdom wishes to amend this system and base it on the level of carbon dioxide (CO2) emissions from the car, as there is a proportional correlation between emissions and fuel consumption and therefore with expenditure on fuel. This means that a flat-rate scale system based on CO2 emissions could achieve the same objective of taxing fuel expenditure incurred by a business for private motoring. At the same time, the United Kingdom also expects to achieve greater accuracy in determining the charge for private consumption by increasing, and therefore refining, the number of scale bands in comparison with the existing bands.

(5) This arrangement has effectively enabled the United Kingdom to simplify the procedure for charging tax in relation to expenditure on fuel for business cars and the proposed system, based on CO2 emissions, will have a similar effect. Private consumption should be more accurately reflected under the new system.

(6) The authorisation should be limited in time, so that in the light of the experience gained up to that date an assessment may be made as to whether or not the derogation is still justified.

(7) Decision 86/356/EEC should be repealed after a certain period but in any case at the entry into force of the national provisions introducing the new special measure, in order to avoid a situation in which authorisations for both systems exist at the same time.

(8) The United Kingdom should inform the Commission of the national provisions introducing the new special measure as soon as they have been adopted and should ensure that this measure will not enter into force before 30 April 2007.

(9) The derogation has no negative impact on the Community's own resources accruing from VAT,

Note—[1] OJ L 145, 13.6.1977, p. 1. Directive as last amended by Directive 2006/69/EC (OJ L 221, 12.8.2006, p. 9).
[2] OJ L 212, 2.8.1986, p. 35.

HAS ADOPTED THIS DECISION:

Article 1

By way of derogation from Articles 5(6) and 11(A)(1)(*b*) of Directive 77/388/EEC, the United Kingdom is authorised, from 1 May 2007 until 31 December 2015, to fix on a flat-rate basis the proportion of value added tax relating to expenditure on fuel used for private purposes in business cars.

Article 2

The proportion of the tax referred to in Article 1 shall be expressed in fixed amounts, established on the basis of the CO2 emissions level of the type of vehicle, that reflect fuel consumption. The United Kingdom shall adjust these fixed amounts annually to reflect changes in the average cost of fuel.

Article 3

The system set up on the basis of this Decision shall be optional for taxable persons.

Article 4

Decision 86/356/EEC is repealed on 30 April 2007.

The United Kingdom shall inform the Commission of the national provisions referred to in Article 1 as soon as they have been adopted.

Article 5

This Decision is addressed to the United Kingdom of Great Britain and Northern Ireland.
Done at Brussels, 25 September 2006.

COUNCIL DECISION OF 5 MAY 2009 AMENDING DECISION 2007/250/EC AUTHORISING THE UNITED KINGDOM TO INTRODUCE A SPECIAL MEASURE DEROGATING FROM ARTICLE 193 OF DIRECTIVE 2006/112/EC ON THE COMMON SYSTEM OF VALUE ADDED TAX

(2009/439/EC)

Note—See OJ L 148, 11.6.2009 p 14.

THE COUNCIL OF THE EUROPEAN UNION,

Having regard to the Treaty establishing the European Community,

Having regard to Council Directive 2006/112/EC of 28 November 2006 on the common system of value added tax, and in particular Article 395(1) thereof,

Having regard to the proposal from the Commission,

Whereas:

(1) In a letter registered by the Secretariat-General of the Commission on 28 July 2008, the United Kingdom requested authorisation to continue to apply a special measure derogating from Article 193 of Directive 2006/112/EC as regards the person liable for the payment of value added tax (VAT) to the tax authorities and previously provided for by Council Decision 2007/250/EC of 16 April 2007.

(2) In accordance with Article 395(2) of Directive 2006/112/EC, the Commission informed the other Member States by letter of 17 March 2009 of the request made by the United Kingdom. By letter dated 20 March 2009, the Commission notified the United Kingdom that it had all the information it considered necessary for the appraisal of the request.

(3) The person liable for the payment of VAT under Article 193 of Directive 2006/112/EC is the taxable person supplying the goods. However, the derogating measure enabled the United Kingdom to apply, until 30 April 2009 and under certain conditions, a reverse charge mechanism which implied that the liability for the payment of VAT shifted to the taxable person to whom certain supplies of mobile phones and integrated circuit devices were made, provided the taxable amount of the supply was equal to, or higher than, GBP 5000.

(4) The purpose of that derogating measure was to deal with certain aggressive forms of tax evasion, and in particular with "carousel" schemes whereby goods are supplied several times without VAT being paid to the tax authorities while leaving customers with a valid invoice for VAT deduction. The application of the reverse charge, without actual payment of VAT from the customer to the supplier, removes the possibility of that form of tax evasion.

(5) Given the apparent seriousness of VAT fraud in the United Kingdom, as attested by the information submitted by the United Kingdom, and given the measure's expected preventive effect, the measure remains proportionate since the extension of the derogation is limited to a reasonable period and the measure remains targeted in scope. Furthermore, it does not form the basis of an overall measure for a generalised reverse charge system.

(6) The derogation has no negative impact on the Community's own resources accruing from VAT.

(7) Legal continuity of the measure should be ensured,

HAS ADOPTED THIS DECISION:

Article 1

Article 4 of Council Decision 2007/250/EC is replaced by the following:

> **"Article 4**
>
> This Decision shall expire on 30 April 2011."

Article 2

This Decision shall apply from 1 May 2009.

Article 3

This Decision is addressed to the United Kingdom of Great Britain and Northern Ireland.
Done at Brussels, 5 May 2009.

COMMISSION DECISION

(2012/C 198/05)
of 3 July 2012

setting up the EU VAT forum

THE EUROPEAN COMMISSION,

Having regard to the Treaty on the Functioning of the European Union,

Whereas:

(1) In its Communication of December 2008,[1] the Commission presented a short-term action plan for combating VAT fraud. It also suggested a reflection on a longer-term approach that could take into account technological developments and new strategies regarding compliance and monitoring, with the overall aim of reducing the involvement of tax authorities and reducing the administrative burden on business.

(2) Furthermore, given the taxpayers' crucial role in making the VAT system work, and the fact that their relationship with the tax authorities should be based on trust, which could have a considerable influence on the cost of administering the system, the Commission put forward the idea of devising a new approach based on voluntary compliance, risk assessment and monitoring. This approach called upon the expertise of business representatives to contribute to this reflection on the longer-term strategy.

(3) In March 2010, the business experts group on a smooth functioning of the VAT in the EU, hereinafter referred to as 'the business expert group on VAT' (BEGV), was set up in order to discuss at EU level the actual practical problems that arise from managing the VAT system as it is implemented in the Member States, as well as suggestions for possible solutions for reducing the administrative burden.

(4) On 23 February 2011, Member States agreed on setting up a new ad hoc expert group, known as the 'tax authorities dialogue platform' (TADP). The much-changed business environment prompted some Member States to develop a customer-led business strategy which is based on understanding the different groups of tax payers/customers, their behaviours and the difficulties they experience when dealing with tax authorities — from the individual filing of a tax return to the needs of large business. The aim of this approach was to create a level playing field for compliant business for fairer competition and it allowed the tax authorities to allocate resources to combat fraud more efficiently.

(5) Both experts groups have been set up to prepare the dialogue between tax authorities and business experts which is due to take place at EU level in a new forum.

(6) With a view to improving the governance of VAT at EU level, in line with the Communication from the Commission on the future of VAT — Towards a simpler, more robust and efficient VAT system tailored to the single market[2] —, stakeholders have also advocated setting up a channel of communication at EU level, where tax authorities, business representatives and the Commission would be able to exchange views on the practical aspects of VAT administration.

(7) Identifying best practices on both sides could contribute to streamlining the management of the VAT system, and thereby to reducing compliance costs, while at the same time securing VAT revenue. It is therefore appropriate to set up the EU VAT forum (comprising Member States and stakeholders, and chaired by the Commission) and to define its tasks and its structure.

(8) The EU VAT forum is a structured platform for dialogue, aimed at improving the relationship between business and tax authorities in order to create the conditions for a smoother functioning of the current VAT system in the EU, thereby reducing costs and administrative burden on both sides. Real practical problems arising from managing the VAT system are due to be discussed, as well as suggestions for possible solutions.

(9) The forum should be chaired by the Commission and consist of the Member States' tax authorities and of organisations representing business or tax practitioners; authorities and organisations in the Member States will nominate their representatives.

(10) Rules on disclosure of information by members of the forum should be provided for, without prejudice to the Commission's rules on security as set out in the Annex to Commission Decision 2001/844/EC, ECSC, Euratom.[3]

(11) Personal data should be processed in accordance with Regulation (EC) No 45/2001 of the European Parliament and of the Council of 18 December 2000 on the protection of individuals with regard to the processing of personal data by the Community institutions and bodies and on the free movement of such data,[4]

Notes[1] Communication from the Commission to the Council, the European Parliament, the European Economic and Social Committee on a coordinated strategy to improve the fight against VAT fraud in the European Union, COM(2008) 807 final of 1 December 2008.

2 COM(2011) 851, 6.12.2011.

3 OJ L317, 3.12.2001, p 1.

VAT EC

[4] OJ L8, 12.1.2001, p 1.

HAS DECIDED AS FOLLOWS:

Article 1 Subject matter

The group of experts called the 'EU VAT forum', hereinafter referred to as 'the forum', is hereby set up.

Article 2 Tasks

The forum's tasks shall be:

(a) to create a platform where business and national tax authorities' experts can informally discuss tax administration issues in the field of VAT with which both parties are currently confronted in a cross-border environment;

(b) to discuss practical insights provided by tax authorities, as well as business experts, and to elaborate on possible ways to manage the current VAT system more efficiently, including by combating fraud, in the interest of both parties with a view to achieving a smoother functioning of the current VAT system;

(c) to assist the Commission in promoting good practice including the use of IT, which could culminate in a more efficient, secure, fairer and cost-effective VAT system in the interests of both parties;

(d) to work, where necessary, in cooperation with any other appropriate bodies or committees dealing with VAT and administrative cooperation in the tax field.

Article 3 Consultation

The Commission may consult the forum on any matter relating to tax administration in the field of VAT.

Article 4 Membership — Appointment

1. The forum shall be composed of a maximum of 45 members.
2. The forum shall comprise:
   (a) one representative from each Member State;
   (b) representatives of maximum 15 organisations representing business or tax practitioners.
3. The tax authorities of each Member State shall nominate one representative from among the officials dealing with tax administration issues, compliance and services to users in the European VAT environment.
4. The Director-General for Taxation and Customs Union shall appoint organisations referred to in Article 4.2(b) with competence in the areas referred to in Article 2 and which have responded to a call for applications.
5. Organisations shall nominate one representative and an alternate to replace a representative who is absent or indisposed. The Director-General for Taxation and Customs Union may refuse a representative or an alternate proposed by an organisation on the basis that he or she does not meet the profile required in the call for applications. In such cases, the organisation concerned shall be asked to appoint another representative or another alternate.
6. Alternates shall be appointed on the same conditions as members; alternates automatically replace any members who are absent or indisposed.
7. Organisations are appointed for three years, unless they are replaced or excluded pursuant to paragraph 9. Their term of office may be renewed after they have responded to a further call for applications.
8. Organisations deemed suitable for membership, but not appointed, may be placed on a reserve list to be kept for three years, which the Commission shall use to appoint replacements.
9. Organisations referred to in Article 4.2(b) or their representatives may be replaced or excluded for the remainder of their term of office in any of the following cases:
   (a) where the organisation or its representative is no longer capable of contributing effectively to the forum's deliberations;
   (b) where the organisation or its representative does not comply with the condition set out in Article 339 of the Treaty on the Functioning of the European Union;
   (c) where the organisation or its representative is not independent of any outside influence;
   (d) where the organisation or its representative has failed to inform the Commission in good time of a conflict of interest;
   (e) where the organisation or its representative resigns;
   (f) where it is desirable in order to maintain a balanced representation of relevant areas of expertise and areas of interest.

The Director-General for Taxation and Customs Union may ask an organisation to appoint another representative or another alternate on the basis of one or more of the conditions set out in paragraph 9 of this Article.

10. The names of organisations and their representatives shall be published in the Register of Commission expert groups and other similar entities, hereinafter referred to as 'Register', as well as on a dedicated website.
11. Personal data shall be collected, processed and published in accordance with Regulation (EC) No 45/2001.

Article 5 Operation

1. The forum shall be chaired by a representative of the Commission.
2. In agreement with the Commission services, the forum may set up sub-groups to examine specific questions on the basis of terms of reference defined by the forum. Such sub- groups shall be disbanded as soon as their mandate is fulfilled.
3. The Chairperson may, on an ad hoc basis, invite experts from outside the forum with specific competence on a subject on the agenda to participate in the work of the forum or sub- group. In addition, the Chairperson may grant observer status to individuals or organisations as defined in Rule 8(3) of the horizontal rules on expert group[1] and candidate countries. In particular, representatives of accession countries and from international organisations may be invited as observers.
4. Members and their representatives, as well as invited experts and observers, shall comply with the obligation of professional secrecy laid down by the Treaties and their implementing rules, as well as with the Commission rules on security regarding the protection of EU classified information, laid down in the Annex to Decision 2001/844/EC, ECSC, Euratom. Should they fail to respect these obligations, the Commission may take all appropriate measures.
5. The meetings of the forum and its sub-groups shall in principle be held on Commission premises. The Commission shall provide secretarial services. Other Commission officials with an interest in the proceedings may attend meetings of the forum and its sub-groups.
6. The forum shall adopt its rules of procedure on the basis of the standard rules of procedure for expert groups.
7. The Commission publishes relevant documents on the activities carried out by the forum either in the Register or via a link from the Register to a dedicated website. A document shall not be published where its disclosure would undermine the protection of a public or private interest as defined in Article 4 of Regulation (EC) No 1049/2001.[2]

Notes[1] Communication from the President to the Commission — Framework for Commission expert groups: horizontal rules and public register, C(2010) 7649 final.
[2] These exceptions are intended to protect public security, military affairs, international relations, financial, monetary or economic policy, privacy and integrity of the individual, commercial interests, court proceedings and legal advice, inspections/investigations/audits and the institution's decision-making process.

Article 6 Meeting expenses

1. Participants in the activities of the forum shall not be remunerated for the services they render.
2. Travel and, where appropriate, subsistence expenses incurred by participants in the activities of the forum shall be reimbursed by the Commission in accordance with the provisions in force within the Commission.
3. Those expenses shall be reimbursed within the limits of the available appropriations allocated under the annual procedure for the allocation of resources.

Article 7 Applicability

This Decision shall apply until 30 September 2018.

Done at Brussels, ... 3 July 2012.

For the Commission
Algirdas ŠEMETA
Member of the Commission

COUNCIL DECISION 2013/52/EU OF 22 JANUARY 2013 AUTHORISING ENHANCED COOPERATION IN THE AREA OF FINANCIAL TRANSACTION TAX

(2013/52/EU)

THE COUNCIL OF THE EUROPEAN UNION,

Having regard to the Treaty on the Functioning of the European Union, and in particular Article 329(1) thereof,

Having regard to the requests made by the Kingdom of Belgium, the Federal Republic of Germany, the Republic of Estonia, the Hellenic Republic, the Kingdom of Spain, the French Republic, the Italian Republic, the Republic of Austria, the Portuguese Republic, the Republic of Slovenia and the Slovak Republic,

VAT EC

Having regard to the proposal from the European Commission,

Having regard to the consent of the European Parliament,

Whereas:

(1) In accordance with Article 3(3) of the Treaty on European Union (TEU), the Union shall establish an internal market.

(2) Pursuant to Article 113 of the Treaty on the Functioning of the European Union (TFEU) the Council shall adopt provisions for the harmonisation of legislation concerning turnover taxes, excise duties and other forms of indirect taxation to the extent that such harmonisation is necessary to ensure the establishment and the functioning of the internal market and to avoid distortion of competition.

(3) In 2011, the Commission took note of a debate which was ongoing at all levels on additional taxation of the financial sector. This debate originates from the desire to ensure that the financial sector fairly and substantially contributes to the costs of the crisis and that it is taxed in a fair way vis-à-vis other sectors for the future, to disincentivise excessively risky activities by financial institutions, to complement regulatory measures aimed at avoiding future crises and to generate additional revenue for general budgets or specific policy purposes.

(4) Against this background, on 28 September 2011, the Commission adopted a proposal for a Council Directive on a common system of financial transaction tax and amending Directive 2008/7/EC (1). The main objective of that proposal was to ensure the proper functioning of the internal market and to avoid distortion of competition.

(5) At the Council meeting of 22 June 2012, it was ascertained that there was no unanimous support for a common system of financial transaction tax (FTT) as proposed by the Commission. The European Council concluded on 29 June 2012 that the proposed Directive would not be adopted by the Council within a reasonable period. At the Council meeting of 10 July 2012, reference was made to persisting and essential differences in opinion as regards the need to establish a common system of FTT at the Union level and it was confirmed that the principle of harmonised taxation on financial transactions will not receive unanimous support within the Council in the foreseeable future.

(6) In these circumstances, 11 Member States, namely Belgium, Germany, Estonia, Greece, Spain, France, Italy, Austria, Portugal, Slovenia and Slovakia, addressed requests to the Commission by letters received between 28 September and 23 October 2012 indicating that they wished to establish enhanced cooperation between themselves in the area of FTT. These Member States requested that the scope and objectives of the enhanced cooperation be based on the Commission proposal for a Directive of 28 September 2011. Reference was also made in particular to the need to avoid evasive actions, distortions and transfers to other jurisdictions.

(7) The enhanced cooperation should provide the necessary legal framework for the establishment of a common system of FTT in the participating Member States and ensure that the basic features of the tax are harmonised. To the extent possible, incentives for tax arbitrage and allocation distortions between financial markets, as well as possibilities for double or non-taxation, as well as evasive actions, should thereby be avoided.

(8) The conditions laid down in Article 20 TEU and Articles 326 and 329 TFEU are fulfilled.

(9) It was recorded at the Council meeting on 29 June 2012 and confirmed on 10 July 2012 that the objective to adopt a common system of FTT cannot be attained within a reasonable period by the Union as a whole. Consequently, the requirement set out in Article 20(2) TEU that enhanced cooperation may be adopted only as a last resort is fulfilled.

(10) The substantive area within which enhanced cooperation would take place, namely, the establishment of a common system of FTT within the Union, is an area covered by Article 113 TFEU and therefore by the Treaties.

(11) Enhanced cooperation in the area of the establishment of a common system of FTT aims at ensuring the proper functioning of the internal market. At the scale of this cooperation, it avoids the coexistence of differing national regimes and thus an undue fragmentation of the market, as well as ensuing problems in the form of distortions of competition, deflections of trade between products, actors and geographical areas, and incentives for operators to avoid taxation through operations with little economic value. Such issues are of particular relevance in the area concerned, which is marked by highly mobile tax bases. Thus, it furthers the objectives of the Union, protects its interests and reinforces its integration process in accordance with Article 20(1) TEU.

(12) The establishment of a common harmonised system of FTT is not included in the list of areas of exclusive competence of the Union set out in Article 3(1) TFEU. Since it serves the functioning of the internal market, in accordance with Article 113 TFEU, it falls under the shared competences of the Union within the meaning of Article 4 TFEU and is thus within the framework of the Union's non-exclusive competence.

(13) Enhanced cooperation in the area concerned complies with the Treaties and Union law, in accordance with the first paragraph of Article 326 TFEU. In line with the second paragraph of Article 326 TFEU, it will not undermine the internal market or economic, social and territorial

cohesion, nor constitute a barrier to or discrimination in trade between Member States or distort competition between them.

(14) Enhanced cooperation in the area concerned respects the competences, rights and obligations of non-participating Member States, in accordance with Article 327 TFEU. Such system would not affect the possibility for non-participating Member States to keep or introduce an FTT on the basis of non-harmonised national rules. The common system of FTT would attribute taxing rights to the participating Member States only on the basis of appropriate connecting factors.

(15) Subject to compliance with any conditions of participation laid down in this Decision, enhanced cooperation in the area referred to therein is open at any time to all Member States willing to comply with the acts already adopted within this framework in accordance with Article 328 TFEU,

HAS ADOPTED THIS DECISION:

Article 1

The Kingdom of Belgium, the Federal Republic of Germany, the Republic of Estonia, the Hellenic Republic, the Kingdom of Spain, the French Republic, the Italian Republic, the Republic of Austria, the Portuguese Republic, the Republic of Slovenia and the Slovak Republic are hereby authorised to establish enhanced cooperation between themselves in the area of the establishment of a common system of financial transaction tax, by applying the relevant provisions of the Treaties.

Article 2

This Decision shall enter into force on the day of its adoption.

Done at Brussels, ...22 January 2013.

For the Council
The President
M Noonan

Commission Recommendation

RECOMMENDATION

(2012/771/EU)

of 6 December 2012

regarding measures intended to encourage third countries to apply minimum standards of good governance in tax matters

THE EUROPEAN COMMISSION,

Having regard to the Treaty on the Functioning of the European Union, and in particular Article 292 thereof,

Whereas:

(1) In an international context, the existence of differing tax legislation is generally accepted as a consequence of fiscal sovereignty. In this context, some, typically small, third countries with limited financial needs have opted for a low level of income tax which applies generally, both to individuals and to companies, or even no income tax at all. Such tax policies are not necessarily undesirable as such, as long as the State participates in international cooperation in order to allow other States to enforce their tax policy.

(2) However, policies which entail a low level of income tax or none at all often go along with a lack of transparency or exchange of information with other States. The States concerned attract investment by offering non-residents a shelter for some types of mobile income or capital and allowing them to conceal the existence of such income or capital from the tax administration of their State of residence.

(3) Various initiatives have been taken in international forums, such as the Organisation for Economic Cooperation and Development or G20, to address these concerns. Moreover, the Global Forum on Transparency and Exchange of Information for Tax Purposes (hereinafter 'the Global Forum') has developed standards of transparency and exchange of information for tax purposes. In 2009, the Global Forum agreed to review the implementation of those standards. It has engaged in a comprehensive peer review process and many traditional low tax jurisdictions have agreed to conclude bilateral agreements on exchange of information on tax matters.

(4) Within the Union, issues of transparency and exchange of information are addressed by Council Directive 2011/16/EU of 15 February 2011 on administrative cooperation in the field of taxation and repealing Directive 77/799/EEC.[1] Moreover, there is a consensus in the Union, expressed in the Code of conduct for business taxation referred to in Annex 1 to Conclusions of the Ecofin Council meeting on 1 December 1997 concerning taxation policy,[2] that harmful tax measures are not acceptable, which makes it difficult for Member States to maintain or introduce such measures. In addition, a number of measures potentially falling under the Code of conduct are subject to scrutiny under the rules on State aid set out in the Treaty on the Functioning of the European Union (TFEU).

(5) In its relations with third countries the Union has sought to convince them to subscribe to the Union principles concerning transparency and exchange of information (similar to the broadly accepted international standards for transparency and exchange of information) and the abolition of harmful tax measures as described in Commission Communication on promoting good governance in tax matters[3] and Commission Communication on tax and development cooperation with developing countries on promoting good governance in tax matters.[4]

(6) Member States whose tax base has been negatively affected by a lack of transparency or by harmful tax measures on the part of third countries have taken steps to remedy that situation. However, taxpayers respond to such measures by routing business or transactions through another jurisdiction with a lower level of protection. This risk is particularly relevant within the Union given the freedom of economic operators to do business anywhere in the Union. Consequently, the level of protection available within the Union against such erosion of the tax base tends to correspond to the lowest level of protection offered by any Member State.

(7) The distortions that this situation brings about within the Union can lead to artificial capital flows and movements of taxpayers within the internal market and thus harm its proper functioning, as well as erode Member States' tax bases. Such distortions should be remedied through an approach shared by all Member States.

(8) Therefore, it is necessary to clearly spell out minimum standards of good governance in tax

matters, both in regard to transparency and exchange of information and in regard to harmful tax measures, and a number of measures to be taken vis-à-vis third countries, with a view to encouraging those countries to comply with those standards.

(9) In regard to transparency and exchange of information, an internationally recognised standard has been set out in the Terms of Reference agreed by the Global Forum in 2009. Those terms should therefore form the basis of this Recommendation. As far as harmful tax measures are concerned, the Code of conduct for business taxation has proven to be a pertinent reference within the Union. Member States have committed themselves to promoting principles of that Code in third countries. It is therefore appropriate to refer to the criteria of that Code for the purposes of this Recommendation. In this regard, it is also appropriate to refer to the work of the Code of Conduct Group (business taxation), set up within the framework of the Council to asses the tax measures that may fall within scope of the Code of conduct for business taxation.[5] The cases assessed by this group can be of assistance when it comes to examine whether a given measure is to be considered as harmful.

(10) This Recommendation should indicate a set of measures to be applied in relation to third countries that do not meet the minimum standards of good governance in tax matters. By applying these measures together, Member States would significantly increase the overall effectiveness of the measures taken by each of them. Losses of tax revenues could therefore be reduced, along with administrative costs for tax administrations and the compliance burden on taxpayers.

(11) In order to promote the application of the minimum standards of good governance in tax matters, it is also necessary to indicate positive measures to encourage third countries that meet these standards or that are committed to meeting them but need assistance to achieve this.

(12) The measures indicated in this Recommendation and applied by Member States must be compatible with Union law, in particular with the fundamental freedoms enshrined in the TFEU,

Notes[1] OJ L64, 11.3.2011, p 1.
[2] OJ C2, 6.1.1998, p 1.
[3] COM(2009) 201 final of 28 April 2009.
[4] COM(2010) 163 final of 21 April 2010.
[5] OJ C99, 1.4.1998, p 1.

HAS ADOPTED THIS RECOMMENDATION:

1. Subject matter

This Recommendation provides criteria making it possible to identify third countries which do not meet minimum standards of good governance in tax matters. It also lists a series of actions that Member States may take in relation to third countries that do not meet those standards and in favour of third countries that do comply with them.

This Recommendation concerns income taxation.

2. Definitions

For the purpose of this Recommendation, the following definitions apply:

(a) 'income tax' means any tax on income, whether levied from individuals or from legal entities and irrespective of the manner in which it is levied, imposed on behalf of a State, its political subdivisions or its local authorities;

(b) 'third country' means any jurisdiction that is not a Member State;

(c) 'national blacklist' means a list adopted by a Member State which identifies other jurisdictions in regard to whom the Member State applies predefined tax measures or tax policies.

3. Minimum standards of good governance in tax matters

A third country only complies with minimum standards of good governance in tax matters where:

(a) it has adopted legal, regulatory and administrative measures intended to comply with the standards of transparency and exchange of information set out in the Annex, and effectively applies those measures;

(b) it does not operate harmful tax measures in the area of business taxation.

Tax measures which provide for a significantly lower effective level of taxation, including zero taxation, than those levels which generally apply in the third country in question are to be regarded as potentially harmful. Such a level of taxation may operate by virtue of the nominal tax rate, the tax base or any other relevant factor.

When assessing whether such measures are harmful, account should be taken of inter alia:

(a) whether advantages are accorded only to non-residents or in respect of transactions carried out with non-residents; or

(b) whether advantages are ring-fenced from the domestic market, so they do not affect the national tax base; or

(c) whether advantages are granted even without any real economic activity and substantial economic presence within the third country offering such tax advantages; or

VAT EC

(d) whether the rules for profit determination in respect of activities within a multinational group of companies departs from internationally accepted principles, notably the rules agreed upon within the Organisation for Economic Cooperation and Development; or

(e) whether the tax measures lack transparency, including where legal provisions are relaxed at administrative level in a non-transparent way.

When applying those criteria, Member States should take account of the conclusions reached in the Code of Conduct Group (business taxation) in regard to tax measures it has assessed as harmful.

4. Measures directed against third countries not complying with minimum standards set out in point 3

4.1. Member States should publish blacklists of third countries not complying with minimum standards set out in point 3, with a view to the application of point 4.3. Those blacklists should make reference to this Recommendation.

4.2. Member States that have adopted national blacklists should include in such lists third countries not complying with minimum standards set out in point 3.

4.3. Each Member State having concluded a double taxation convention with a third country not complying with minimum standards as set out in point 3 should, as most appropriate with a view to improve compliance by that third country with these standards, either seek to renegotiate the convention, suspend or terminate the convention.

5. Measures in favour of third countries complying with minimum standards set out in point 3

5.1. Member States should remove third countries which comply with minimum standards set out in point 3 from the blacklists referred to in point 4.1.

5.2. Member States should consider removing third countries which comply with minimum standards set out in point 3 from any existing national blacklists referred to in point 4.2.

5.3. Member States should consider initiating bilateral negotiations for the conclusion of double tax conventions with third countries which comply with minimum standards set out in point 3.

6. Measures in favour of third countries which are committed to comply with minimum standards set out in point 3.

6.1. Member States should consider offering closer cooperation and assistance to third countries, especially developing ones, which are committed to complying with minimum standards set out in point 3, in order to assist those third countries in fighting effectively against tax evasion and aggressive tax planning. To this end, they could second tax experts to such countries for a limited period of time.

When judging third countries' commitment to complying with those minimum standards, Member States should take into account all concrete indications to this effect, in particular steps towards compliance already taken by the third country concerned.

6.2. As long as a third country benefits from assistance in accordance with point 6.1 and accomplishes the expected progress towards compliance with the said minimum standards, Member States should abstain from applying the measures referred to in point 4, except for the renegotiation of double tax conventions.

7. Follow-up

Member States should inform the Commission on the measures taken in order to comply with the present Recommendation, as well as any changes made to such measures.

The Commission will publish a report on the application this Recommendation within three years after its adoption.

8. Addressees

This Recommendation is addressed to the Member States.

Done at Brussels, ... 6 December 2012.

For the Commission

Algirdas ŠEMETA

Member of the Commission

ANNEX

STANDARDS OF TRANSPARENCY AND EXCHANGE OF INFORMATION

A. AVAILABILITY OF INFORMATION

A.1. The third country concerned ensures that ownership and identity information for all relevant entities and arrangements is available to its competent authorities.

A.2. The third country concerned ensures that reliable accounting records are kept for all relevant entities and arrangements.

A.3. Banking information is available for all account holders.

B. ACCESS TO INFORMATION

B.1. Competent authorities of the third country concerned have the power to obtain and provide information that is the subject of a request under an agreement on exchange of information, from any person within their territorial jurisdiction who is in possession or control of such information.

B.2. The rights and safeguards that apply to persons in the requested third country concerned are compatible with effective exchange of information.

C. EXCHANGING INFORMATION

C.1. Mechanisms for the exchange of information with Member States are such that this exchange is carried out in an effective manner.

C.2. The network of information exchange mechanisms of the third country concerned covers all Member States.

C.3. The mechanisms for exchange of information of the third country concerned contain adequate provisions to ensure the confidentiality of information received from Member States.

C.4. The exchange of information mechanisms of the third country concerned respect the rights and safeguards of taxpayers and third parties.

C.5. The third country concerned provides information under its network of agreements with Member States in a timely manner.

Value Added Tax
Extra-statutory Concessions

List of concessions

International field

ESC 2.1 VAT, excise and customs duties: goods and services
ESC 2.2 VAT, excise and customs duties: UK-manufactured alcoholic liquor and tobacco products purchased by diplomats — Obsolete. Overtaken by legislation - Customs & Excise (Personal Reliefs for Special Visitors) Order 1992.
ESC 2.3 VAT, excise and customs duties: United States Air Force
ESC 2.4 VAT and customs duty—gifts
ESC 2.5 VAT: American war graves
ESC 2.6 VAT: Supplies to diplomatic missions, international organisations, NATO forces etc in other EC countries
ESC 2.7 VAT and customs duty: certain aircraft ground and security equipment
ESC 2.8 Relief from UK excise duty on alcoholic drinks supplied duty-paid in another Member State for consumption on Eurostar trains which are in UK territory.

Concessions designed to remove inequities or anomalies in administration

ESC 3.1 VAT: VAT on purchase of road fuel — Obsolete. Legislated Finance Act 2013.
ESC 3.2 VAT: Group supplies using an overseas member: anticipation of legislative changes — Obsolete. Legislated FA 1997 and FA 2012.
ESC 3.3 VAT: Zero rating of supplies of certain goods used in connection with collection of monetary donations
ESC 3.4 VAT: Misunderstanding by a VAT trader – obsolete – withdrawn with effect from 1 January 2012
ESC 3.5 VAT: Misdirection (obsolete)
ESC 3.6 VAT: Coin-operated machines
ESC 3.7 VAT: VAT on minor promotional items supplied in linked supplies schemes
ESC 3.8 VAT: Use of margin scheme for vehicle sales when incomplete records have been kept – obsolete – withdrawn with effect from 1 April 2010
ESC 3.9 VAT: Recoveries under the VAT Act 1994 Schedule 11 paragraph 5
ESC 3.10 VAT: VAT on necessary meals and accommodation provided by recognised representative sporting bodies to amateur sports persons chosen to represent that body in a competition
ESC 3.11 VAT: Incorrect customer declaration
ESC 3.12 VAT: Buses with special facilities for carrying disabled persons – obsolete – due to changes introduced in SI 2009/217
ESC 3.13 VAT: Repayment of import VAT to shipping agents and freight forwarders
ESC 3.14 VAT: Zero-rating of certain supplies of free zone goods
ESC 3.15 VAT: Printed matter published in instalments
ESC 3.16 VAT: Connection to the gas or electricity mains supply — Obsolete - withdrawn with effect from 1 January 2012.
ESC 3.17 VAT: Zero-rating of supplies of training for foreign governments
ESC 3.18 VAT: Exemption for all domestic service charges
ESC 3.19 VAT: Supplies of "relevant goods" to charities
ESC 3.20 VAT: Disapplication of repayment of input tax (Value Added Tax Act 1994 s 36(4A) and the VAT Regulations 1995
ESC 3.21 VAT: Sales of poor quality goods
ESC 3.22 VAT: Valuation of the refurbishment or fitting out of a building for the purposes of the capital goods scheme — Obsolete - withdrawn with effect from 1 January 2011.
ESC 3.23 VAT: Supplies by Financial Ombudsman Services Ltd to ombudsman authorities
ESC 3.24 VAT: Charities who provide care in an institution and also supply goods to disabled persons resident in their own and other institutions.
ESC 3.25 VAT: Resuscitation training models supplied to charities and other eligible bodies for use in first aid training
ESC 3.26 VAT: Works of art, antiques and collectors' items
ESC 3.27 VAT: Use of the Auctioneers' Scheme for sales of goods at auction on behalf of non-taxable persons
ESC 3.28 VAT: Supplies by Financial Services Authority to self-regulating organisations
ESC 3.29 VAT: Charitable buildings – obsolete – withdrawn with effect from 1 April 2010
ESC 3.30 VAT: Retail pharmacists

ESC 3.31 VAT: Supplies by the Financial Services Compensation Scheme Ltd (FSCS) to compensation scheme authorities

ESC 3.32 VAT: Electronic face value vouchers — Obsolete.

ESC 3.33 VAT: Supplies previously made by the Post Office – obsolete – due to changes in Group 3 of Schedule 9 to the VAT Act 1994 and the Postal Services Act 2011

ESC 3.34 VAT: Tax reclaimed by museums and galleries covered by Section 33A of the Value Added Tax Act 1994

ESC 3.35 VAT: Apportionment of certain membership subscriptions to non-profit making bodies

ESC 3.36 VAT: Imported works of art, antiques etc — Obsolete. Legislated SI 2009/730.

ESC 3.37 VAT: Exemption for supplies of welfare services by private welfare agencies pending registration – obsolete – withdrawn with effect from 9 December 2010

Insurance Premium Tax—Concessions designed to remove inequities or anomalies in administration

See *Insurance Premium Tax* post for Concessions 4.1 to 4.6.

Landfill Tax—Concessions designed to remove inequities or anomalies in administration

See *Landfill Tax* post for Concession 5.1.

Climate Change Levy—Concessions designed to remove inequities or anomalies in administration

See *Climate Change Levy* post for Concessions 7.1 to 7.4.

Facilitation of exports

ESC 8.1 VAT: Sailaway boats — Obsolete - withdrawn with effect from 1 January 2012.

Non-commercial transactions

ESC 9.1 VAT: VAT on goods supplied at duty-free and tax-free shops

ESC 9.2 VAT: Marine fuel

ESC 9.3 VAT and excise duties: Personal reliefs for goods permanently imported from third countries

ESC 9.4 VAT and excise duties: Personal reliefs for goods permanently imported from third countries

ESC 9.5 VAT and excise duties: Personal reliefs for goods permanently imported from third countries

ESC 9.6 VAT and excise duties: Personal reliefs for goods permanently imported from third countries

ESC 9.7 VAT and excise duties: Personal reliefs for goods permanently imported from third countries

VAT Notice 48: Extra-statutory Concessions

SECTION 1 INTRODUCTION

21 May 2015.

This notice cancels and replaces Notice 48 (March 2012). Details of any changes to the previous version can be found in paragraph 1.1 of this notice.

1.1 WHAT IS THIS NOTICE ABOUT?

This notice gives details of all HM Revenue and Customs (HMRC) Extra-Statutory Concessions (ESCs) in force at the time of going to print.

This notice has been updated to include details of ESCs that have been granted, or become obsolete. ESCs 2.2, 3.1, 3.2, 3.32, 3.36, 4.2, 4.3, 4.5, 6.4, 6.5, 6.6 and 6.7 are obsolete.

1.2 WHAT IS AN EXTRA-STATUTORY CONCESSION?

In certain circumstances where remission or repayment of revenue is not provided for by law, the department may allow relief on an extra-statutory basis. ESCs are remissions of revenue that allow relief in specific sets of circumstances to all businesses falling within the relevant conditions. They are authorised when strict application of the law would create a disadvantage or the effect would not be the one intended.

1.3 HOW ARE ESCS APPLIED?

HMRC ESCs are of general application. That is, a concession may be exercised by anyone to whom the circumstances set out in the concession apply without reference to HMRC. However, where an attempt is made to use an ESC for tax avoidance, the Commissioners may withdraw or restrict its application.

1.4 AGREEMENTS WITH TRADE BODIES

In certain trades, particular arrangements for applying VAT and other charges have been agreed with the appropriate trade association. These are not ESCs and are listed in VAT Notice 700/57: *administrative agreements entered into with trade bodies.*

1.5 FORMER INLAND REVENUE ESCS

Former Inland Revenue ESCs are published in Extra-Statutory Concessions: www.gov.uk/government/publications/extra-statutory-concessions-ex-inland-revenue.

SECTION 2 INTERNATIONAL FIELD

2.1 VAT, EXCISE AND CUSTOMS DUTIES: GOODS AND SERVICES

Duty (which includes all import and excise duties) and VAT are remitted or refunded in accordance with agreements with the authorities concerned on:

- goods and services imported by or supplied to visiting forces and their instrumentalities, for the official use of the force, or their instrumentalities;
- goods and services imported by or supplied to NATO military headquarters, organisations or agencies, for their official use;
- United States and Canadian Government expenditure on mutual defence or mutual aid contracts; and
- temporary importations of equipment required by contractors for fulfilling NATO infrastructure contracts or in connection with the provision and maintenance of US forces defence facilities in the United Kingdom.

2.2 VAT, EXCISE AND CUSTOMS DUTIES: UK-MANUFACTURED ALCOHOLIC LIQUOR AND TOBACCO PRODUCTS PURCHASED BY DIPLOMATS

Obsolete. Overtaken by legislation - Customs & Excise (Personal Reliefs for Special Visitors) Order 1992.

2.3 VAT, EXCISE AND CUSTOMS DUTIES: UNITED STATES AIR FORCE

Relief from VAT and /or excise duty is allowed, in accordance with conditions agreed with the United States Air Force, on:

- charges for admission to air shows and open days; and
- goods sold by US forces organisations during air shows and open days to persons not entitled to receive / consume them unless customs charges have been paid.

2.4 VAT AND CUSTOMS DUTY: GIFTS

Duty and VAT are remitted on gifts (whether imported or purchased in the United Kingdom) from United States forces to charitable organisations.

2.5 VAT: AMERICAN WAR GRAVES

In order to place inland purchases on the same footing as imported goods, VAT is remitted on the supply of goods and services to the American Battle Monuments Commission for the maintenance of the American Military Cemetery and Memorial at Maddingley, Cambridge and Brookwood, Surrey.

2.6 VAT: SUPPLIES TO DIPLOMATIC MISSIONS, INTERNATIONAL ORGANISATIONS, NATO FORCES ETC IN OTHER EC COUNTRIES

A VAT registered trader can zero rate supplies of goods, (other than new means of transport), or services made to entitled persons and bodies resident or situated in other EC countries provided:

- the goods or services are for either the official use of the entitled bodies or for the personal use of entitled members etc thereof
- the supplier obtains from the customer an application for exemption from VAT under Article 15.10 of the Sixth VAT Directive (or, if not available, a written order/certificate confirming eligibility under that Article)
- in the case of goods, they are removed to another EC country; and
- the supplier obtains and keeps proof of removal of the goods to another EC country within three months of the time of supply. This should be the commercial proof of export or removal normally acceptable for VAT zero rating purposes

2.7 VAT AND CUSTOMS DUTY: CERTAIN AIRCRAFT GROUND AND SECURITY EQUIPMENT

The Convention on International Civil Aviation (Chicago Convention) allows relief from duty and VAT for certain ground and security equipment imported into the territory of one Contracting State by an airline of another Contracting State operating an international service. The United Kingdom is a signatory to the Chicago Convention.

Additionally, the United Kingdom has concluded a number of Air Service Agreements which allow, on a reciprocal basis, the various reliefs detailed in the Convention, including the one mentioned above.

We have become aware that end-use relief may be being claimed erroneously in these cases. Aircraft ground and security equipment does not qualify for end-use relief. We are in the process of drawing up a new procedure to enable the relief to be correctly claimed.

In the interim period an extra-statutory concession has been agreed to allow relief for ground and security equipment to be claimed. The following list details those goods which qualify for relief and who is eligible to claim it.

2.7.1 Qualifying goods

The following ground and security equipment for aircraft—

(a) Repair, maintenance and servicing equipment—

- material for airframes, engines and instruments;
- specialised aircraft repair kits;
- starter batteries and carts;
- maintenance platforms and steps;
- test equipment for aircraft, aircraft engines, and instruments;
- aircraft engine heaters and coolers; and
- ground radio equipment.

(b) Passenger-handling equipment—

- passenger-loading steps;
- specialised passenger-weighing devices; and
- specialised catering equipment.

(c) Cargo-loading equipment—

- vehicles for moving or loading of baggage, cargo, equipment or supplies;
- specialised cargo-loading devices; and
- specialised cargo-weighing devices.

(d) Component parts for incorporation into ground equipment including the items listed above.

(e) Security equipment:

- weapon-detecting devices;
- explosives-detecting devices; and
- intrusion detecting devices.

(f) component parts for incorporation into security equipment.

Claims for relief of duty and VAT under this concession should be addressed to the Entry Processing Unit where the goods will be cleared with a copy of this advice.

Press releases etc—Concession announced in Business Brief 18/97, 22-8-97.

2.8 RELIEF FROM UK EXCISE DUTY ON ALCOHOLIC DRINKS SUPPLIED DUTY PAID IN ANOTHER MEMBER STATE FOR CONSUMPTION ON EUROSTAR TRAINS WHICH ARE IN UK TERRITORY

The measure provides a scheme to tax alcohol supplied for consumption on Eurostar trains. The basis for the scheme is that alcoholic drinks loaded in France or Belgium duty paid on journeys commencing from those member states and destined for the UK will not incur a liability to UK duty when entering the UK. Conversely, such goods loaded for journeys commencing from the UK will be UK duty paid, but will not attract reimbursement when consumed outside UK territory. The revenue effect will therefore be broadly neutral.

3 VALUE ADDED TAX: CONCESSIONS DESIGNED TO REMOVE INEQUITIES OR ANOMALIES IN ADMINISTRATION

3.1 VAT: VAT ON PURCHASE OF ROAD FUEL

Obsolete. Legislated Finance Act 2013.

3.2 VAT: GROUP SUPPLIES USING AN OVERSEAS MEMBER: ANTICIPATION OF LEGISLATIVE CHANGES

3.2.1 First part of concession

Obsolete. Legislated Finance Act 1997.

3.2.2 Second part of concession

Obsolete. Legislated Finance Act 2012.

Commentary—*De Voil Indirect Tax Service* **V3.267.**

3.3 VAT: ZERO RATING OF SUPPLIES OF CERTAIN GOODS USED IN CONNECTION WITH COLLECTION OF MONETARY DONATIONS

This concession applies to supplies to a charity of the following goods—

(a) lapel stickers or attachments designed to be worn on the lapel, which are of no intrinsic value, low cost to the charity and are given as a token in acknowledgement of a donation;
(b) component parts of items described in (a) above when supplied for self assembly;
(c) any form of receptacle which—
 - is manufactured specifically for the purpose of collecting donated money;
 - is used solely for collecting money for charity;
 - is, or will be, clearly marked as collecting for a named charity; and
 - can be secured by lock or tamper evident seal.

(d) bucket lids, designed to fit buckets and provide a secure seal, for use solely in connection with collecting money for charity;
(e) pre-printed letters the primary purpose of which is to appeal for money for charity (not necessarily including the addressees' particulars);
(f) envelopes used in conjunction with letters described (e) above for forwarding donations, provided that they are over-printed with an appeal request related to that contained in the letter;
(g) outer envelopes used in conjunction with letters described in (e) above, provided that they are over-printed with an appeal request related to that contained in the letter;
(h) pre-printed collecting envelopes appealing for money (of the type used by the welfare charities and which are usually hand delivered to domestic premises);
(i) stewardship envelopes used for planned giving which, as a minimum requirement, are pre-printed with the name of the relevant place of worship or other charity

Where this concession applies, the supply may be treated as if it were a zero-rated supply.

This concession applies from 1 April 2000.

The Commissioners may withdraw or restrict the application of this concession if they have reasonable cause to believe it is being abused.

3.4 VAT: MISUNDERSTANDING BY A VAT TRADER

Obsolete - withdrawn with effect from 1 January 2012.

3.5 VAT: MISDIRECTION

Obsolete.

3.6 VAT: COIN-OPERATED MACHINES

The tax point for supplies made from coin-operated machines is the date the machine is used. As an accounting convenience, however, operators may delay accounting for VAT until the takings are removed from a machine.

For all other purposes the normal tax point rules apply. Therefore in the event of a theft of takings from a machine, VAT must still be accounted for in full on any supplies that have been made from the machine.

3.7 VAT ON MINOR PROMOTIONAL ITEMS SUPPLIED IN LINKED SUPPLIES SCHEMES

These are schemes in which a minor article is linked, although not necessarily physically linked, with a main article (of either goods or services) and sold with it at a single price. The price paid should normally be apportioned to reflect any difference where the items are liable to VAT at different rates.

However, if the minor article:

(a) is not charged to the customer at a separate price;
(b) costs the supplier no more than 20 per cent of the total cost of the combined supply (excluding VAT); and
(c) costs the supplier no more than:
 - £1 (excluding VAT) if included with goods intended for retail sale, or
 - £5 (excluding VAT) otherwise,

the supplier may account for VAT on the minor article at the same rate as the main article – that is, no apportionment is necessary.

3.8 VAT: USE OF MARGIN SCHEME FOR VEHICLE SALES WHEN INCOMPLETE RECORDS HAVE BEEN KEPT

Obsolete - withdrawn with effect from 1 April 2010.

3.9 VAT: RECOVERIES UNDER VATA 1994 SCH 11 PARA 5

Where an amount is shown or represented as VAT on an invoice issued by a person who is neither registered nor required to be registered for VAT at the time when the invoice is issued, the provisions of VATA 1994 Sch 11 para 5 (formerly VATA 1983 Sch 7 para 6) enable the Commissioners to require that person to pay an equivalent amount to them. The Act does not provide any relief in respect of related VAT incurred by such a person. On the grounds of equity, a person making such a payment may be permitted to deduct from it the amount of VAT incurred on supplies to him of goods and services that were directly attributable to any invoiced supply in respect of which such payment is required.

Where such a person has made a supply to a taxable person and, on the invoice, showed or represented an amount as VAT, the recipient of the supply has no logical entitlement to treat that amount as his input tax. If it is clear that the taxable person who received the supply has treated such an amount as input tax in good faith, action to recover the amount so deducted may be remitted on grounds of equity.

3.10 VAT ON NECESSARY MEALS AND ACCOMMODATION PROVIDED BY RECOGNISED REPRESENTATIVE SPORTING BODIES TO AMATEUR SPORTS PERSONS CHOSEN TO REPRESENT THAT BODY IN A COMPETITION

The Value Added Tax (Input Tax) Order 1992 (SI 1992/3222) (formerly the Value Added Tax (Special Provisions) Order 1981 (SI 1981/1741) as amended by the VAT (Special Provisions) (Amendment) Order 1988 (SI 1988/1124)) prevents input tax deduction where goods or services have been provided for the purposes of business entertainment except where this entertainment is of an employee. The effect of this provision is to produce different treatment as between, for example, professional football teams and amateur football teams. This is because the professional players are employees of their clubs and input tax is deductible, while the amateur players are, by definition, not employees and input tax is blocked. This distinction between amateur and professional sportsmen has led to inequity in the VAT treatment of certain amateur representative bodies who are registered for VAT and account for output tax on "gate money" in the same way as professional clubs, but cannot recover VAT on some of their genuine business expenses.

With the overwhelming number of clubs this has provided no problem as members' subscriptions are regarded as being payment, in part, for any accommodation or meals that they may receive when playing for that club. However, problems have been encountered with certain bodies that choose, from affiliated clubs, individual amateur sports persons to represent their country or county. These persons so selected are not full subscribing members of the representational body. They pay a very small nominal subscription, or no subscription at all so the provision in VAT Notice 700/65: *business entertainment* - cannot apply. To remove this inequity of treatment as between professional and amateur bodies, it has been agreed that input tax necessarily incurred on the provision of accommodation and meals for team members selected by such representative bodies may be deductible as input tax. This concession not only applies to selected players but also to the committee members of the body who are to be treated as "persons engaged in the management of a company and deemed to be employees of that company". The concession does not cover alcoholic drinks and tobacco (including cigarettes and cigars) provided for consumption by players and committee members.

3.11 VAT: INCORRECT CUSTOMER DECLARATION

Where a customer provides an incorrect declaration claiming eligibility for zero rating under Groups 2, 4, 5, 6, 8, 12 or 15 of the zero rate Schedule of VATA 1994, or eligibility for a reduced rate under Group 1 of Sch 7A for the qualifying use of fuel and power, and where a supplier, despite having taken all reasonable steps to check the validity of the declaration, nonetheless fails to identify the inaccuracy and in good faith makes the supplies concerned at the zero rate, or a reduced rate, HMRC will not seek to recover the tax due from the supplier.

3.12 VAT: BUSES WITH SPECIAL FACILITIES FOR CARRYING DISABLED PERSONS

Obsolete - due to changes introduced in SI 2009/217 - The Value Added Tax (Input Tax) (Amendment) Order 2009.

3.13 VAT: REPAYMENT OF IMPORT VAT TO SHIPPING AGENTS AND FREIGHT FORWARDERS

Import VAT may be paid directly to shipping agents and freight forwarders where importers go into liquidation, or where an administrator or administrative receiver has been appointed who certifies that, in his or her opinion, ordinary unsecured creditors would receive nothing in a liquidation, leaving the agents unable to recover VAT paid on their behalf. The importers must have gone into a formal state of insolvency or receivership within six months of the date of lodgement of the Customs entry, and the goods must have remained under the agents' control throughout their stay in the UK and have been re-exported unused from the European Community.

3.14 VAT: ZERO RATING OF CERTAIN SUPPLIES OF FREE ZONE GOODS

From 1 August 1991 the supply of goods subject to import VAT which are free zone goods in the UK may be zero rated on condition that there is an agreement between the supplier and the customer that the customer will clear the goods for removal from the zone and will take responsibility for payment of the import VAT.

3.15 VAT: PRINTED MATTER PUBLISHED IN INSTALMENTS

Books are zero rated for VAT under item 1 of Group 3 of Schedule 8 to the VAT Act 1994 (formerly item 1 of Group 3 of Schedule 5 to the VAT Act 1983). However, there is a specialist area of the market known as continuity publishing or part-works where the product is supplied in parts over varying periods but builds up into a greater whole, such as, a loose-leaf book. Unless such items, when viewed independently, are books etc at the time of supply, they are not entitled to zero rating under the present law.

From 1 February 1993 by way of concession, if, at the time of supply, an article is or was no by itself regarded as a book, including a loose-leaf book, qualifying for zero rating under VATA 1994 Sch 8 Group 3 item 1, but is or was a part of a larger finite work which itself would fall under Sch 8 Group 3 item 1 as a book, then the individual component parts may also be zero rated where they are or were being supplied either direct by the publisher or through a distribution chain to the final consumer.

From 26 October 1993 by way of further concession in relation to card-based boxed continuity series publications, such publications, even though not bound or held together other than in or by their container, and having all the other characteristics of a book, will for VAT purposes be treated as a book.

3.16 VAT: CONNECTION TO THE GAS OR ELECTRICITY MAINS SUPPLY

Obsolete - withdrawn with effect from 1 January 2012.

3.17 VAT: ZERO RATING OF SUPPLIES OF TRAINING FOR FOREIGN GOVERNMENTS

From 1 October 1993 the services of training (not being services comprised in any Group of Sch 9 to VATA 1994, formerly VATA 1983 Sch 6), supplied to a foreign government in furtherance of its sovereign activities (and not its business activities), is liable to VAT at the zero rate provided the supplier retains a statement in writing from that government (or its accredited representative), that the trainees are employed in furtherance of its sovereign activities.

3.18 VAT: EXEMPTION FOR ALL DOMESTIC SERVICE CHARGES

The concession exempts form 1 April 1994 all mandatory service charges or similar charges paid by the occupants of residential property towards the upkeep of the dwellings or block of flats in which they reside and towards the provision of a warden, caretakers, and people performing a similar function for those occupants. The concession does not exempt service charges paid in respect of holiday accommodation as defined in VATA 1994 Sch 9 Group 1 Notes 11-13 para 1(*e*) (formerly VATA 1983 Sch 6 Group 1 Notes (10), (10A) and (10B) para 1(*d*)).

3.19 VAT: SUPPLIES OF "RELEVANT GOODS" TO CHARITIES

Where "relevant goods" of a kind described in VATA 1994 Group 15 Note 3 are supplied to a charity—

(a) whose sole purpose and function is to provide a range of care services to meet the personal needs of handicapped people (of which transport might form a part); or
(b) which provides transport services predominantly to handicapped people,

then by concession, the supply of those goods will be zero rated, as will the repair and maintenance of those goods and the supply of any further goods in connection with that repair and maintenance.

"Handicapped" means chronically sick or disabled.

In order to be eligible for this concession, a charity must demonstrate that it meets the requirements of sub-paragraphs (a) or (b) above by way of—

- its charitable aims and objectives;
- its publicity and advertising material;
- any documents which it has issued for the purpose of obtaining funding from a third party such as a local authority;
- its day-to-day operations; and
- any other evidence that may be relevant.

3.20 VAT: DISAPPLICATION OF REPAYMENT OF INPUT TAX (VATA 1994 S 36(4A)) AND SI 1995/2518 (AS AMENDED BY THE VAT (AMENDMENT) REGULATIONS, SI 1997/1086)

(1) Subject to paragraphs 3 and 4 below, VATA 1994 s 36(4A) will not apply to any person where—
   (a) an insolvency procedure has commenced in relation to that person under VATA 1994 s 81(4B), (4C), and (5);
   (b) the claimant's notification of his claim for bad debt relief in accordance with regulation 166A of the VAT Regulations 1995 (SI 1995/2518), is received after the insolvency procedure has commenced; and
   (c) each relevant supply upon which the claim for bad debt relief is based, was made prior to the commencement of the insolvency procedure.

(2) Paragraph 1 above applies whether or not the business of the person who is the subject of the insolvency procedure continues to be carried on.

(3) Paragraph 1 above does not apply unless the Commissioners have received notification on Form VAT 769: *notification of insolvency details*, or such other notification as the Commissioners may require, in respect of the insolvency procedure referred to in that paragraph.

(4) Paragraph 1 above does not apply in circumstances where its application would give rise to tax avoidance.

The insolvency procedures to which the extra-statutory concession applies

The insolvency procedures included in VATA 1994 s 81 for the purposes of this concession are—

- bankruptcy;
- compulsory liquidation (winding up);
- creditors' voluntary liquidation (voluntary winding up);
- members' voluntary liquidation (voluntary winding up);
- administrative receivership;
- administrative order;
- individual Voluntary Arrangement;
- company Voluntary Arrangement;
- Scottish Trust Deed; and
- deed of Arrangement.

After further consultations with representatives of insolvency practitioners, and colleagues within Customs who deal with insolvency policy, it has been agreed that the application of this concession should be extended to a number of other types of insolvencies that are not included in the strict application of VATA 1994 s 81. Accordingly this concession will apply to the following types of insolvency that are not included in s 81.

- Partnership Voluntary Arrangement.
  (Insolvent Partnerships Order 1994).

VAT ESC

(Insolvent Partnerships Order (Northern Ireland) 1995).

- Partnership Liquidation.
(Insolvent Partnerships Order 1994).
(Insolvent Partnerships Order (Northern Ireland) 1995).
- Partnership Administration Order
(Insolvent Partnerships Order 1994).
(Insolvent Partnerships Order (Northern Ireland) 1995).
- Sequestration.
(Bankruptcy (Scotland) Act 1985).
(Bankruptcy (Scotland) Act 1993).
- County Court Administration Order.
(County Court Act 1984). Scheme of Arrangement.
(Companies Act 1985).
- Deceased Persons Administration Order
(Administration of Insolvent Estates of Deceased Persons Order 1986).
(Administration of Insolvent Estates of Deceased Persons Order (Northern Ireland 1991).

Application of extra-statutory concession

The effective date for the application of the concession will be the date of Customs claim in the insolvency. This will be the relevant date of the insolvency and the insolvency meeting date (if applicable).

In Administration Order cases the effective date will be the date of the Administration Order.

Where there is a subsequent insolvency the concession will also apply to that subsequent insolvency.

If an insolvency arrangement fails the insolvency is annulled and the requirement to account for clawback will be reinstated.

The concession will only apply to a provisional liquidation if it is followed by a permanent liquidation. In these circumstances the clawback concession will take effect from the date of the provisional liquidation.

3.21 VAT: SALES OF POOR QUALITY GOODS

By concession, the supply by a charity of any goods which have been donated for sale or the supply of such goods by a taxable person who is covenanted by deed to give all the profits of that supply to a charity, shall be treated as zero rated, provided that—

(a) the supply is a sale of goods donated to that charity or taxable person; but
(b) the goods, although of a kind which the charity or taxable person makes available to the general public for purchase (whether in a shop or elsewhere) are by reason of their poor quality not fit to be so made available.

3.22 VAT: VALUATION OF THE REFURBISHMENT OR FITTING OUT OF A BUILDING FOR THE PURPOSES OF THE CAPITAL GOODS SCHEME

Obsolete - withdrawn with effect from 1 January 2011.

3.23 VAT: SUPPLIES BY FINANCIAL OMBUDSMAN SERVICES LTD TO OMBUDSMAN AUTHORITIES

This concession provides that payments from eight ombudsman authorities for the performance by the Financial Ombudsman Services Ltd (FOS) of the complaint handling duties of the authorities shall not be treated as consideration for any supply in the course of furtherance of any business by FOS.

The payment of any amount at any time by the—

- Office of the Building Societies Ombudsman (OBSO)
- Office of the Banking Ombudsman (OBO)
- Insurance Ombudsman Bureau (IOB)
- Personal Assurance Arbitration Service (PAAS)

- PIA Ombudsman Bureau (PIAOB)
- Office of the Investment Ombudsman Bureau (OIOB)
- SFA Complaints Bureau and Arbitration Service (SFACBAS)
- FSA Independent Investigator (FSAII)

to FOS for the supply of services by FOS in connection with the ombudsman and complaint handing scheme duties by OBSO, OBO, IOB, PAAS, PIAOB, OIOB, SFACBAS and FSAII (as the case may be) between 1 April 2000 and 1 October 2000 shall not be treated as consideration for any supply in the course of any business carried on by FOS.

3.24 VAT: CHARITIES WHO PROVIDE CARE IN AN INSTITUTION AND ALSO SUPPLY GOODS TO DISABLED PERSONS RESIDENT IN THEIR OWN AND OTHER INSTITUTIONS

(1) This concession applies in relation to a supply of goods which, apart from VATA 1994 Sch 8 Group 12 Note (5B), would fall within para (g) of item 2 of that Group, where—
  (a) the goods are goods other than spectacles or contact lenses, and are designed solely for use by a visually handicapped person;
  (b) the goods are supplied by a charity at or below cost;
  (c) the recipient of the supply is a resident or is attending the premises of a relevant institution as defined in Note (5I) to the said Group 12; and
  (d) the charity is not actively engaged in supplying goods within paragraph (a) above solely to handicapped persons who are resident in or attending the premises of a relevant institution as defined by Note (5I) to the said Group 12 operated, managed or controlled by the charity.

(2) Where this concession applies, the supply of the goods may be treated as if it were a zero-rated supply.

(3) The Commissioners may withdraw or restrict the application of this concession if they have reasonable cause to believe it is being abused.

3.25 VAT: RESUSCITATION TRAINING MODELS SUPPLIED TO CHARITIES AND OTHER ELIGIBLE BODIES FOR USE IN FIRST AID TRAINING

(1) The concession shall operate to include in VATA 1994 Sch 8 Group 15 Note (3), the following—
  (a) human resuscitation training models acquired for use in first aid training in either or both cardiopulmonary resuscitation and defibrillation techniques; and
  (b) parts and accessories for use in or with the goods described in paragraph (a) above, where the parts and accessories are for use in the training of either or both cardiopulmonary resuscitation and defibrillation techniques.

(2) In this concession resuscitation training model means a model which includes a head and torso designed for use in the training of cardiopulmonary resuscitation or defibrillation techniques.

(3) In this concession cardiopulmonary resuscitation means a combination of expired air ventilation and chest compression.

(4) The Commissioners may withdraw or restrict the application of this concession if they have reasonable cause to believe that it is being abused.

3.26 VAT: WORKS OF ART, ANTIQUES AND COLLECTORS' ITEMS

The VAT (Treatment of Transactions) Order 1995 (SI 1995/958) relieves from VAT certain transactions by treating them as neither a supply of goods nor a supply of services. This Order may also be applied, in the same way that it applies to works of art, to the following goods—

(a) all works of art falling within paragraph (*a*) of Annex I to Council Directive 77/388/EEC (inserted by Council Directive 94/5/EC) which do not already fall within the said order;
(b) collectors' items falling within paragraph (*b*) of the said Annex I; and
(c) antiques falling within paragraph (*c*) of the said Annex I.

3.27 VAT: USE OF THE AUCTIONEERS' SCHEME FOR SALES OF GOODS AT AUCTION ON BEHALF OF NON-TAXABLE PERSONS

From 1 January 1999, an auctioneer selling, on behalf of a third party vendor who is a non-taxable person, goods which have been grown, made or produced (including bloodstock or

VAT ESC

livestock reared from birth) by that person, may enter the goods into the auctioneers' scheme provided he holds a certificate from the vendor which includes—

(a) vendor's full name and address;
(b) description of goods and date of sale;
(c) declaration that the vendor is not registered nor required to be registered for VAT;
(d) signature of vendor and date;
(e) signature of auctioneer and date,

and all other conditions of the scheme must be met. The completed certificate must be retained with the relevant records for VAT purposes.

An example of an acceptable certificate is set out below:

AUCTIONEERS' SCHEME FOR SECOND-HAND GOODS, WORKS OF ART, ANTIQUES AND COLLECTORS' ITEMS

Extra-statutory concession number xx

Vendor's Certificate for goods grown, made or produced and sold at auction on behalf of non-taxable persons

I (full name)

of (address)

declare that I am not registered or required to be registered for VAT and that the goods detailed below are to be sold at auction on my behalf by (auctioneer's name)

Description of goods

Date of sale (to be completed by auctioneer)

Signature of vendor

Signature of auctioneer

Date

3.28 VAT: SUPPLIES BY FINANCIAL SERVICES AUTHORITY TO SELF-REGULATING ORGANISATIONS

The payment of any amount at any time by the Investment Management Regulatory Organisation (IMRO), the Personal Investment Authority (FSA) or the Securities and Futures Authority (SFA) to the Financial Services Authority (FSA) for the supply by the FSA in the carrying out of the regulatory functions of IMRO, PIA or SFA (as the case may be) between 1 April 1998 and the coming in to effect of the Financial Services and Markets Act 2000 and similar payments by the Registrar of Friendly Societies (RFS) and the Insurance Directorate of HM Treasury (ID) for the supply by FSA in the carrying out of regulatory functions of RFS or ID (as the case may be) between 1 January 1999 and the coming into effect of the Financial Services and Markets Act 2000 shall not be treated as consideration for any supply in the course or furtherance of any business carried on by FSA

3.29 VAT: CHARITABLE BUILDINGS

Obsolete - withdrawn with effect from 1 April 2010.

3.30 VAT: RETAIL PHARMACISTS

(1) This concession applies in relation to a supply of goods which, apart from VATA 1984 Sch 8 Group 12 Note (5A), would fall within Item 1 of that Group, when—

(a) the goods supplied are dispensed to an individual for his/ her personal use while he/she is an inpatient or resident or while h/she is attending a relevant institution which is a hospital or nursing home;

(b) the goods are ordered in accordance with the National Health Service Act 1977 s 41, the National Health Service (Scotland) Act 1978 s 27 or the Health and Personal Social Services (Northern Ireland) Order 1972 art 63;
(c) the goods are dispensed in accordance with the National Health Service (Pharmaceutical Services) Regulations 1992 Sch 1 to the National Health Service (Pharmaceutical Services) (Scotland) Regulations 1995 or the Pharmaceutical Services Regulations (Northern Ireland) 1997; and
(d) the person dispensing the goods is paid for doing so by—
- the Prescription Pricing Authority;
- the Prescription Information and Pricing Services Division of the Welsh Health Common Services Authority;
- the Pharmacy Practice Division of the Common Services Agency; or
- the Central Services Agency.

(2) Where this concession applies, the supply may be treated as if it were a zero-rated supply.
(3) The Commissioners may withdraw or restrict the application of the concession if they have reasonable cause to believe that it is being abused.

3.31 VAT: SUPPLIES BY THE FINANCIAL SERVICES COMPENSATION SCHEME LTD (FSCS) TO COMPENSATION SCHEME AUTHORITIES

The payment of any amount at any time by the Investors Compensation Scheme (ICS), the Deposit Protection Scheme (DPS), the Building Societies Investor Protection Scheme (BSIPS), the Policyholders Protection Scheme (PPS), the Friendly Societies Protection Scheme (FSPS), and the Section 43 Scheme (S43S) for the supply of services by FSCS in carrying out the compensatory scheme functions of ICS, DPS, BSIPS, PPS, FSPS, and S43S (as the case may be) between 1 February 2001 and the coming into effect of the Financial Services & Markets Act 2000 shall not be treated as consideration for any supply in the course of any business carried on by FSCS.

3.32 VAT: ELECTRONIC FACE VALUE VOUCHERS

Obsolete.

3.33 VAT: SUPPLIES PREVIOUSLY MADE BY THE POST OFFICE

Obsolete - due to changes in Group 3 of Schedule 9 to the VAT Act 1994 and the Postal Services Act 2011.

3.34 VAT: TAX RECLAIMED BY MUSEUMS AND GALLERIES COVERED BY SECTION 33A OF THE VALUE ADDED TAX ACT 1994

1. Scope of this extra-statutory concession

1.1 The Government is committed to free public access to the main national museums and galleries. Ordinarily, when a museum or gallery moves from charging taxable entrance charges to free admission, it loses its entitlement to recover the VAT incurred on the related goods and services it purchases. This is because admitting the public free of charge is not a business activity and thus there is no entitlement to recover input tax in relation to it. The purpose of the scheme in Section 33A of the Value Added Tax Act 1994 ("the Act") is to refund this irrecoverable VAT to the bodies listed in an Order made under Section 33A(9). The entitlement to such refunds will commence from the date the Order takes effect in relation to the museum or gallery listed in it.

1.2 When a person recovers input tax on goods or services and subsequently transfers or uses them for a non-business purpose, a supply of the goods or services is deemed to have been made under paragraphs 5(1) or 5(4) of Schedule 4 to the Act (goods), or under Article 3 of the Value Added Tax (Supply of Services) Order 1993 (SI 1993/1507) (services).

1.3 Furthermore, where input tax had been recovered in relation to a capital item as defined in regulation 113 of the Value Added Tax Regulations 1995, a move from taxable admission charges to non-business free access can have an effect on the proportion of taxable as opposed to exempt use of the capital item. This would result in adjustments of the input tax recovered under the normal operation of the capital goods scheme.

1.4 This extra-statutory concession aims to ensure that the museums and galleries specified in an Order made under Section 33A(9) of the Act are not required to repay input tax, properly

VAT ESC

recovered at the time on goods and services used in connection with taxable supplies of admitting the public for payment, solely on account of the move to free admission.

1.5 The concession will not be extended to any situation where it appears to the Commissioners that its use will assist in avoiding VAT, and where it appears to them that the concession has been so used it will be treated as never having applied.

2. Operation of this extra-statutory concession

2.1 Each of the following descriptions of transactions shall be treated as neither a supply of goods nor a supply of services, namely:

(a) goods which after purchase are subsequently put to a non-business use giving rise otherwise to a supply under paragraphs 5(1) or 5(4) of Schedule 4 to the Act; and
(b) services which after purchase are subsequently put to a non-business use giving rise otherwise to a supply under Article 3 of the Value Added Tax (Supply of Services) Order 1993.

This is providing in each case, that the change in use of the goods and services arose solely as a direct result of a body listed in an Order made under Section 33A(9) of the Act using the goods or services for the purpose of offering free rights of admission to the museum or gallery to which the Order specifies.

2.2 This paragraph applies to adjustments to the deduction of input tax on capital items under Part XV of the Value Added Tax Regulations 1995. Adjustment will not be required in so far as a change in use of a capital item relates to free admission with related refunds of VAT under Section 33A of the Act. Otherwise, adjustments are not affected. Where this paragraph applies, the owner of a capital item shall in each subsequent interval adjust the total input tax on the capital item and the extent of taxable use of the capital item for the purposes of Part XV as follows:

(a) the total input tax on the capital item shall be deemed to be the proportion that would have been input tax if admissions which have subsequently become free had been free at the time the VAT was incurred; and
(b) the extent of taxable use of the capital item at the time the original entitlement to deduction was determined shall be deemed to be the extent of taxable use at that time if admissions which have subsequently become free had been free at that time.

3. Dates when this extra-statutory concession has effect

3.1 This extra-statutory concession takes effect for each museum or gallery specified in an Order made under Section 33A(9) of the Act on the day appointed in the Order for that museum or gallery, whether or not the day appointed was before the date of publication of this concession.

3.35 VAT: APPORTIONMENT OF CERTAIN MEMBERSHIP SUBSCRIPTIONS TO NON-PROFIT MAKING BODIES

Where a membership body supplies, in return for its membership subscription, a principal benefit, together with one or more ancillary benefits, it will normally have to treat the subscription as being in return for that principal benefit. This means that the body will have to ignore the liability to the VAT of the ancillary benefits and account for VAT on the whole subscription based on the liability to VAT of that principal benefit.

However bodies that are non-profit making and supply a mixture of zero rated, exempt and/or standard-rated benefits to their members in return for their subscriptions, may apportion such subscriptions to reflect the value and VAT liability of those individual benefits, without regard to whether there is one principal benefit. This concession may not be used for the purpose of tax avoidance.

3.36 VAT: IMPORTED WORKS OF ART, ANTIQUES ETC

Obsolete. Legislated SI 2009/730.

3.37 VAT: EXEMPTION FOR SUPPLIES OF WELFARE SERVICES BY PRIVATE WELFARE AGENCIES PENDING REGISTRATION

Obsolete - withdrawn with effect from 9 December 2010.

SECTION 8 FACILITATION OF EXPORTS

8.1 VAT: SAILAWAY BOATS

Obsolete — withdrawn with effect from 1 January 2012.

SECTION 9 NON-COMMERCIAL TRANSACTIONS

9.1 VAT—VAT ON GOODS SUPPLIED AT DUTY-FREE AND TAX-FREE SHOPS

The supplier of goods which are liable to VAT and which are supplied to intending passengers at duty-free and tax-free shops approved by the Commissioners may, for those goods which are exported directly to a place outside the VAT territory of the member states, be regarded as the exporter and zero rate the supply.

9.2 VAT: MARINE FUEL

Commercial vessels engaged on voyages within UK territorial waters (or within the limits of a port), may receive certain types of marine fuel VAT free providing the conditions set out in Notice 703 *VAT: Exports and removals of goods from the United Kingdom* are met.

This relief extends only to those supplies of fuel which were zero rated prior to 1 July 1990 under the Value Added Tax Act 1983 Schedule 5 Group 7 item 4. It does not apply to petrol, DERV or lubricating oil.

9.3 VAT AND EXCISE DUTIES: PERSONAL RELIEFS FOR GOODS PERMANENTLY IMPORTED FROM THIRD COUNTRIES

Where property (including motor vehicles) which has been purchased in accordance with the terms of Directive 77/388/EEC art 15.10 and which otherwise qualifies for relief from payment of customs charges under the HM Revenue & Customs Duties (Personal Reliefs for Goods Permanently Imported) Order 1992 art 11, relief is not to be refused solely by reason of art 11.2 of that Order.

9.4 VAT AND EXCISE DUTIES: PERSONAL RELIEFS FOR GOODS PERMANENTLY IMPORTED FROM THIRD COUNTRIES

Where property (including motor vehicles) which has been purchased by members of UK forces (or by the civilian staff accompanying them) in countries outside the area of the European Community and which otherwise qualifies for relief from payment of customs charges under the HM Revenue & Customs Duties (Personal Reliefs for Goods Permanently Imported) Order 1992 art 11, relief is not to be refused solely by reason of art 11.2 of that Order.

9.5 VAT AND EXCISE DUTIES: PERSONAL RELIEFS FOR GOODS PERMANENTLY IMPORTED FROM THIRD COUNTRIES

Where property (including motor vehicles) which has been purchased under a UK export scheme by members of the UK diplomatic service, by members of UK forces or by civilian staff accompanying them or by members of international organisations and which otherwise qualifies for relief from payment of customs charges under the HM Revenue & Customs Duties (Personal Reliefs for Goods Permanently Imported) Order 1992 art 11, relief is not to be refused solely by reason of art 11.2 of that Order.

9.6 VAT AND EXCISE DUTIES: PERSONAL RELIEFS FOR GOODS PERMANENTLY IMPORTED FROM THIRD COUNTRIES

Where personal belongings otherwise qualify for relief under the HM Revenue & Customs Duties (Personal Reliefs for Goods Permanently Imported) Order 1992 art 11 save only that the property has not been possessed and used for the specified period, then just as relief can be granted from customs duties as "special cases justified by the circumstances" under Council Regulation 918/83 art 3, similar consideration shall apply in respect of VAT and excise duties and relief may be granted accordingly.

9.7 VAT AND EXCISE DUTIES: PERSONAL RELIEFS FOR GOODS PERMANENTLY IMPORTED FROM THIRD COUNTRIES

Where personal belongings otherwise qualify for relief under the HM Revenue & Customs Duties (Personal Reliefs for Goods Permanently Imported) Order 1992 art 11 save only that the property is declared for relief outside the specific periods, then just as relief can be granted from customs duties as special cases under art 6, or under art 9 of Council Regulation 918/83, similar consideration shall apply in respect of VAT and excise duties and relief may be granted accordingly.

SECTION 10 CONCESSIONS OBSOLETE SINCE LAST EDITION OF UPDATE 1 TO NOTICE 48 (PUBLISHED IN OCTOBER 2000)

10.1 VAT: GROUP SUPPLIES USING AN OVERSEAS MEMBER: TRANSITIONAL RELIEF

10.1.1 General

With effect from 26 November 1996, a resolution under the Provisional Collection of Taxes Act has created a new tax charge for the representative member of a VAT group, where supplies of a type set out in Schedule 5 to the VAT Act 1994 are purchased by an overseas group member and used for making Schedule 5 supplies to a UK group member. This new tax charge was made permanent when the Finance Act 1997 was passed on 19 March 1997. The new tax charge is given effect by section 41 of the Finance Act, which inserts the new rules into section 43 of the VAT Act 1994 at paragraphs (2A) to (2E).

The time of the supply which is taxed under section 41 is the time when the supply is paid for or, if the consideration is not in money, on the last day of the prescribed accounting period in which the services are performed. Under this concession, taxpayers may treat the introduction of the new charge under section 41 as though it were a change in the rate of VAT, and covered by section 88 of the VAT Act 1994.

This means that, where the UK group member has on, or after 26 November 1996, paid for services affected by section 41, but performance of those services took place to any extent before that date, the group may account for tax only on that proportion of the services which were performed on or after 26 November 1996. Further details are contained in VAT Notice 700: the VAT guide.

10.1.2 Telecommunications services

Telecommunications services are not currently affected by section 41 because they do not fall within Schedule 5 of the VAT Act 1994. However, it is possible that relevant telecommunications services will be so included shortly. When that happens, appropriate rules will be introduced to determine whether and when VAT should be accounted for on these telecommunications services provided by suppliers outside the UK, but received by customers within the UK. Accordingly, this concession does not apply to telecommunications services.

Commentary—*De Voil Indirect Tax Service* **V3.193.**

10.2 VAT: DEVELOPER'S SELF-SUPPLY ON 1 MARCH 1997

1. The developer's self-supply on 1 March 1997 under paragraph 5(1)(*b*) of Schedule 10 to the Value Added Tax Act 1994 need not be treated as made where—

(a) construction of a building or civil engineering work is still in progress on 1 March 1997 and the value of the developer's potential self-supply including those construction costs in paragraph 6(2)(*b*) of Schedule 10 to the Value Added Tax Act 1994 incurred both before and on or after 28 February 1997, would be less than £100,000; or

(b) a building or civil engineering work was completed before 1 March 1995 and either—

   (i) the building is fully occupied or the civil engineering work is used by a "developer" who is a taxable person for non-business purposes, rather than in connection with making any exempt supplies of goods or services, and consequently the "developer" under paragraph 5(5) of Schedule 10 to the Value Added Tax Act 1994 would have been a taxable person under paragraph 5(4)(*b*) of that Schedule; or

(ii) the building has been fully occupied or the civil engineering work has been fully used before 1 March 1997; or

(iii) the building or civil engineering work is the subject of an election to waive exemption, and input tax has been provisionally recovered in the anticipation of granting a taxable interest in it.

2. Examples of buildings or civil engineering works which might be within paragraph 1(*b*)(i) above are non-business NHS hospitals, government offices, and buildings and civil engineering works occupied or used by a local authority or similar body pursuant to its statutory non-business activities.

3. If a "developer"—

(a) has completed the construction of a building or civil engineering work before 1 March 1995; and

(b) considers that the building or work would not have been subject to the developer's self-supply had the provisions in paragraph 5(1)(*a*) of Schedule 10 to the Value Added Tax Act 1994 continued after 28 February 1997, but the situation is not described in paragraphs 1(a) to 1(b) above,

then that person may make an individual request in writing to the Commissioners of HMRC not to be treated as making a developer's self-supply on 1 March 1997.

Any reference in this concession to a building or civil engineering work includes a building or work which has been or is being reconstructed, enlarged or extended.

Commentary—*De Voil Indirect Tax Service* **V3.244.**

VAT Notices

Contents

VAT Notices in current issue

Notice No	*Title*
48	Extra-statutory concessions (2015) [see *Extra-statutory concessions* ante]
60	The Intrastat general guide (January 2015)
101	Deferring duty, VAT and other charges (2009)
160	Compliance checks into indirect tax matters (2011)
179	Motor and heating fuels–general information and accounting for excise and VAT (2015)
252	Valuation of imported goods for customs purposes, VAT and trade statistics (2013)
372	Importing commercial samples free of duty and VAT (February 2015)
700	The VAT guide (2015) [part reproduced]
700/1	Should I be registered for VAT? (2014)
700/2	Group and divisional registration (2014)
700/7	Business promotions (2012)
700/8	Disclosure of VAT avoidance schemes (2013) [reproduced]
700/9	Transfer of a business as a going concern (2012) [reproduced]
700/11	Cancelling your registration (2015)
700/12	Filling in your VAT return (2014)
700/14	Video cassette films: rental and part-exchange (2014)
700/17	Funded pension schemes (2012)
700/18	Relief from VAT on bad debts (2013)
700/21	Keeping VAT records (2015)
700/24	Postage, delivery charges and direct marketing (2015)
700/25	Taxis and hire-cars (2002)
700/34	Staff (2012)
700/41	Late registration penalty (2012)
700/42	Misdeclaration penalty and repeated misdeclaration penalty (2012)
700/43	Default interest (2010)
700/44	Barristers and advocates (2014)
700/45	How to correct VAT errors and make adjustments or claims (2015)
700/46	Agricultural flat rate scheme (2012)
700/50	Default surcharge (2013)
700/56	Insolvency (2015)
700/57	Administrative agreements entered into with trade bodies (2014 with Update 1) [summary table reproduced]
700/58	Treatment of VAT repayment returns and VAT repayment supplement (2010)
700/60	Payments on account (2014)
700/62	Self billing (2014)
700/63	Electronic invoicing (2015)
700/64	Motoring expenses (2014)
700/65	Business entertainment (2012)
700/67	Registration scheme for racehorse owners (2002)
701/1	Charities (2014 with Updates 1 and 2)
701/2	Welfare (2011)
701/5	Clubs and associations (2013)
701/6	Charity-funded equipment for medical, veterinary, etc uses (2014 with Update 1 and Supplement issued in 1997)

Notice No	*Title*
701/7	VAT reliefs for disabled people (2015)
701/8	Postage stamps and philatelic supplies (2003)
701/9	Commodities and terminal markets (2011)
701/10	Zero-rating of books etc (2015)
701/12	Disposals of antiques, works of art etc from historic houses (2011)
701/14	Food (2014)
701/15	Animals and animal food (2011)
701/16	Water and sewerage services (2014 with Update 1)
701/18	Woman's sanitary protection products (2011)
701/19	Fuel and power (2012)
701/20	Caravans and houseboats (2014)
701/21	Gold (2013) [part reproduced]
701/21A	Investment gold coins (2012) [reproduced]
701/22	Tools for the manufacture of goods for export (2002)
701/23	Protective equipment (2011)
701/29	Betting, gaming and lotteries (2013)
701/30	Education and vocational training (2014)
701/31	Health institutions (2014)
701/32	Burial, cremation and the commemoration of the dead (2012)
701/35	Youth clubs (2011)
701/36	Insurance (2013) [part reproduced]
701/38	Seeds and plants (2011)
701/40	Food processing services (2011)
701/41	Sponsorship (2002)
701/45	Sport (2011)
701/47	Culture (2011)
701/48	Corporate purchasing cards (2014) [part reproduced]
701/49	Finance (2013)
701/57	Health professionals (2014)
701/58	Charity advertising and goods connected with collecting donations (2002 with Update 1)
702	Imports (2014) [reproduced]
702/7	Import VAT relief for goods supplied onward to another country in the EC (2013)
702/8	Fiscal warehousing (2012)
702/9	Imports customs procedures (2012)
702/10	Tax warehousing (2012)
703	Exports of goods from the UK (2014) [reproduced]
703/1	Supply of freight containers for export or removal from the UK (2010) [part reproduced]
703/2	Sailaway boats supplied for export outside the EC (2012) [reproduced]
703/3	*Sailaway boat scheme* (cancelled: see Notice 703/2)
704	VAT retail exports (2014 with Update 1) [reproduced]
704/1	Tax free shopping in the UK (2012) [reproduced]
706	Partial exemption (2011)
706/2	Capital goods scheme (2011) [reproduced]
707	VAT personal export scheme (2014)
708	Buildings and construction (2014) [part reproduced]
708/6	Energy-saving materials (2014)
709/1	Catering and take-away food (2013)
709/3	Hotels and holiday accommodation (2013)

Notice No	Title
709/5	Tour operators' margin scheme (2009) [reproduced]
709/6	Travel agents and tour operators (2002)
714	Zero rating young children's clothing and footwear (2015)
718	The VAT Margin Scheme and global accounting (2011) [reproduced]
718/1	The VAT Margin Scheme on second-hand cars and other vehicles (2011) [reproduced]
718/2	The VAT Auctioneer's Scheme (2011) [reproduced]
719	*VAT refunds for 'do-it-yourself' builders and converters* (2009, now withdrawn)
723A	Refunds of VAT in the European Community for EC and non-EC businesses (2014)
725	The single market (2014) [reproduced]
726	Joint and several liability for unpaid VAT (2008)
727	Retail schemes (2012) [reproduced]
727/2	Bespoke retail schemes (2011)
727/3	Retail schemes: how to work the point of sale scheme (2013) [reproduced]
727/4	Retail schemes: how to work the apportionment schemes (2013) [reproduced]
727/5	Retail schemes: how to work the direct calculation schemes (2013) [reproduced]
728	New means of transport (2013) [reproduced]
731	Cash accounting (2015) [reproduced]
732	Annual accounting (2014)
733	Flat rate scheme for small businesses (2014) [reproduced]
735	VAT domestic reverse charge on specified goods and services (2015)
741	Place of supply of services (before 1 January 2010) (2010)
741A	Place of supply of services (2010) [reproduced]
742	Land and property (2012)
742/3	Scottish land law terms (2013)
742A	Opting to tax land and buildings (2015) [reproduced]
744A	Passenger transport (2009)
744B	Freight transport and associated services (2009)
744C	Ships, aircraft and associated services (2011)
747	VAT notices having the force of law (2003) [reproduced]
749	Local authorities and similar bodies (2002)
998	VAT refund scheme for National museums and galleries (2013)
999	Catalogue of publications (2015)
1001	VAT refund scheme for certain charities (2015)
SIVA 1	Simplified Import VAT Accounting (April 2010)

VAT Information sheets

3/96	Tour operators' margin scheme—practical implementation of the "airline charter option" following the changes which came into effect on 1 January 1996
4/96	Tour operators' margin scheme—practical implementation of the "agency option" following the changes which came into effect on 1 January 1996
1/97	Tour operators' margin scheme—practical implementation of the "trader to trader (wholesale) option" following the changes which came into effect on 1 January 1996
3/98	Local authorities and NHS—joint stores depots
5/98	Local authorities—supplies to new unitary authorities under local government reorganisation (transitional arrangements)
6/98	Local authority pension funds—VAT treatment and administrative concession

8/98	Charities—supply, repair and maintenance of relevant goods (and correction)
2/99	Local Authorities—agreement of s 33 methods
3/99	VAT—New Deal programme
6/99	Charities—liability of routine domestic tasks
8/99	Opticians—apportionment of charges for supplies of spectacles and dispensing
9/99	Imported works of art, antiques and collectors' pieces—changes to the reduced rate of VAT
12/99	VAT on business cars—changes to take effect on 1 December 1999
2/00	Exports and removals—conditions for zero-rating
3/00	Supplies through undisclosed agents—revised VAT treatment
2/01	Single or multiple supplies: how to decide
4/02	Budget 2002: VAT—partial exemption – standard method override
1/03	Electronically supplied services and broadcasting services: New EU place of supply rules
3/03	Modernisation of Face Value Vouchers
4/03	Electronically supplied services: A guide to interpretation
5/03	Electronically supplied services: evidence of customer location and status
6/03	Tribunal decision on VAT treatment of repossessed and voluntarily returned cars
7/03	Electronically supplied services: special scheme for non-EU businesses
10/03	Electronically supplied services: supplementary information on the Special Scheme for non-EU businesses
11/03	Electronic Point of Sale (EPOS) systems
12/03	Face value vouchers
13/03	Electronically supplied services: special scheme for non-EU businesses—currency exchange rates for reporting period ending 30 September 2003
14/03	New time of supply rules for on-going supplies
1/04	Electronically supplied services: special scheme for non-EU businesses—currency exchange rates for reporting period ending 31 December 2003
3/04	Electronically supplied services: EU Enlargement
4/04	Electronically supplied services: special scheme for non-EU businesses—currency exchange rates for reporting period ending 31 March 2004
5/04	Claims made in the light of GMAC High Court decision: VAT treatment of returned cars and other goods
6/04	Electronically supplied services: special scheme for non-EU businesses—currency exchange rates for reporting period ending 30 June 2004
7/04	Eligibility rules for VAT grouping
8/04	Electronically supplied services: special scheme for non-EU businesses—currency exchange rates for reporting period ending 30 September 2004
10/04	Changes to the place of supply of natural gas and electricity
11/04	Electronically supplied services: special scheme for non-EU businesses—currency exchange rates for reporting period ending 31 December 2004
1/05	E-supplied services: special scheme non-EU businesses—exchange rates
2/05	Electronically supplied services: changes to Greece VAT rate
3/05	Electronically supplied services: Special scheme for non-EU businesses
4/05	Electronically supplied services: change to Portugal VAT rate
5/05	Electronically supplied services: Special scheme for non-EU businesses Sep 2005
6/05	Business travel agents
8/05	Recovery of VAT by businesses on fuel purchased by employees on their behalf
1/06	Electronically supplied services: currency exchange rates—period ending 12–05
2/06	Electronically supplied services: changes to Hungary VAT rate
3/06	Dispensing Doctors and VAT Registration
5/06	Supplies of goods under finance agreements
8/06	Electronically supplied services: Special scheme for non-EU businesses
9/06	Electronically supplied services: Special scheme for non-EU businesses

10/06	Electronically supplied services: Special scheme for non-EU businesses
11/06	Guidance on the VAT treatment of certain Islamic products
12/06	Further information for dispensing doctors
1/07	Electronically supplied services: Special scheme for non-EU businesses
2/07	Electronically supplied services: Special scheme for non-EU businesses: VAT rates
3/07	Electronically supplied services: Special scheme for non-EU businesses: Germany
4/07	Electronically supplied services: Special scheme for non-EU businesses
5/07	Health professionals affected by changes to exemption for medical services
6/07	Reverse charge for purchases and sales of mobile phones and computer chips
7/07	Electronically supplied services: special scheme for non-EU businesses
8/07	Reverse charge for purchases and sales of mobile phones and computer chips
9/07	Electronically supplied services: special scheme for non-EU businesses
10/07	Changes to VAT invoicing with effect from October 2007
11/07	Accounting for VAT on standard-rated prescription products
12/07	Transfer of a Going Concern (TOGC): Changes to VAT record-keeping requirements
14/07	HMRC guidance: assets used partly for non-business purposes
15/07	Supply of parts and equipment for qualifying ships and aircraft
1/08	Electronically supplied services: Special Scheme for non-EU businesses
2/08	Electronically supplied services: Special Scheme for non-EU businesses
4/08	Supplies of government grant funded research
5/08	Electronically supplied services: currency exchange rates to June 2008
6/08	Electronically supplied services: Special scheme for non-EU businesses—changes
7/08	VAT: Partial Exemption—adjustments when house builders let their dwellings
9/08	Special scheme for non-EU businesses — exchange rates for period ending Sept 08
11/08	Electronically supplied services: changes to VAT rates
12/08	Electronically supplied services: Special scheme for non-EU businesses: Latvia
1/09	Electronically supplied services: Special scheme for non-EU businesses: changes
2/09	Special scheme for non-EU businesses: exchange rates for period ending Dec 2008
3/09	Withdrawal of the VAT Staff Hire Concession on 1 April 2009
4/09	VAT: Partial Exemption – changes to the standard method
5/09	Special scheme for non-EU businesses – exchange rates for period ending March 2009
7/09	Private use charge: manufacturer's company, dealer demonstrators & rental cars
8/09	Changes to the zero rate used for buildings used for a charitable use
9/09	Special Scheme for non-EU businesses – exchange rates for period ending Jun 2009
10/09	Electronically supplied services: Special scheme for non-EU businesses: changes
11/09	Electronically supplied services: Special scheme for non-EU businesses: changes
13/09	Electronically supplied services: Special scheme for non-EU businesses
14/09	Changes to the operation of the option to tax on supplies of land and build
15/09	Special Scheme for non-EU businesses — exchange rates for period ending Sept 09
16/09	Electronically supplied services: Special scheme for non-EU businesses: UK rate change from 1 January 2010
17/09	Electronically supplied services: Special scheme for non-EU businesses: changes
1/10	Special Scheme for non-EU businesses — exchange rates for period ending December 2010
3/10	VAT status of university trading companies: new guidelines
4/10	VAT: Partial Exemption — changes to the de minimis rules
5/10	Electronically supplied services: Special scheme for non-EU businesses
6/10	Electronically supplied services: Special scheme for non-EU businesses
9/10	Special Scheme for non-EU businesses — exchange rates for period ending March 20
11/10	Electronically supplied services: Special scheme for non-EU businesses — Spain
13/10	Calculating qualifying use for a charitable or a communal residential building

14/10	Electronically supplied services: Special scheme for non-EU businesses — Finland
15/10	Electronically supplied services: Special scheme for non-EU businesses — Greek VAT rate
16/10	Electronically supplied services: Special scheme for non-EU businesses — Romanian VAT rate
17/10	Special Scheme for non-EU businesses, exchange rates for period ending June 2010
18/10	Change to the Portuguese VAT rate from 1 July 2010
19/10	Special Scheme for non-EU businesses, exchange rates for period ending Sept 2010
20/10	Special scheme for non-EU businesses — change to UK VAT rate from 4 January 2011
21/10	Place of supply of natural gas and electricity (also heat and cooling)
22/10	Change to the Polish VAT rate, from 1 January 2011
23/10	Change to the Portuguese VAT rate, from 1 January 2011
01/11	Change to the VAT rate in Latvia from 1 January 2011
02/11	Special Scheme for non-EU businesses — exchange rates for period ending Dec 2010
03/11	Change to the Slovak VAT rate from 1 January 2011
04/11	Change in use provisions
05/11	Dispensing doctors (Scotland) and VAT registration
06/11	Implementing the VAT Technical Directive and changes to the partial exemption and capital goods scheme rules
07/11	Special Scheme for non-EU businesses — exchange rates for period ending Mar 2011
08/11	Motor manufacturer's company cars, dealer demonstrators, daily rental cars
09/11	VAT Refund Scheme for academies
10/11	Special Scheme for non-EU businesses - exchange rates period ending June 2011
11/11	Change to the Italian VAT rate from 17 September 2011
12/11	Special Scheme for non-EU businesses - exchange rates for period ending September 2011
13/11	Change to the VAT rate in Ireland from 1 January 2012
01/12	VAT Information Sheet - Electronically supplied services
02/12	Change to the VAT rate in Hungary from 1 January 2012
03/12	Electronically supplied services: Special Scheme for non-EU businesses - change to the Cyprus VAT rate
04/12	Special Scheme for non-EU businesses – exchange rates for period ending March 2012
05/12	Special Scheme for non-EU businesses – exchange rates for period ending June 2012
06/12	Special scheme for non-EU businesses – Latvia VAT rate change from 1 July 2012
07/12	Guidance on the Cost Sharing Exemption – from 17 July 2012
08/12	Change to the Spanish VAT rate from 1 September 2012
09/12	Anti-forestalling for approved alterations to listed buildings
10/12	Approved alterations to listed buildings
11/12	Taxing holiday caravans
12/12	Hot food and premises
13/12	Hairdressers' chair rental
14/12	Self storage
15/12	Sports nutrition drinks
16/12	Electronically supplied services: Special scheme for non-EU businesses - change to Netherlands VAT rate from 1 October 2012
17/12	Special Scheme for non-EU businesses - exchange rates for period ending September 2012
18/12	New means of transport: revised Form VAT 411
19/12	Special scheme for non-EU businesses - Finland VAT rate change from January 2013
01/13	Special Scheme for non-EU businesses - exchange rates for period ending December 2012

02/13	Special scheme for non-EU businesses - Cyprus VAT rate change from 14 January 2013
03/13	Special scheme for non-EU businesses - Czech Republic VAT rate change from 1 January 2013
04/13	Taxing holiday caravans
05/13	Special Scheme for non-EU businesses - exchange rates for period ending Mar 2013
06/13	Notification of Vehicle Arrivals (NOVA)
07/13	Special scheme for non-EU businesses - Slovenia VAT rate change from 1 July 2013
08/13	Special scheme for non-EU businesses - VAT rate in Croatia
09/13	Special Scheme for non-EU businesses - exchange rates for period ending June 2013
10/13	Provision of storage facilities
11/13	Supplies of research between eligible bodies
12/13	Electronically supplied services: special scheme for non-EU businesses
13/13	Electronically supplied services: special scheme for non-EU businesses
14/13	Electronically supplied services: special scheme for non-EU businesses
15/13	Electronically supplied services: special scheme for non-EU businesses
16/13	Electronically supplied services: special scheme for non-EU businesses
1/14	Special scheme for non-EU businesses - Cyprus VAT rate change from 13 January 2014
2/14	VAT on buildings that are dwellings and used for a relevant residential purpose
3/14	VAT Treatment of refunds made by manufacturers
4/14	Special Scheme for non-EU businesses - exchange rates for period ending March 2014
5/14	Electronically supplied services - Special scheme for non-EU businesses and changes to the VAT rate
6/14	Cross-border VAT refunds - Republic of Serbia
7/14	Special Scheme for non-EU businesses - exchange rates for period ending June 2014
8/14	VAT place of supply of services/Mini-One Stop Shop
9/14	Special Scheme for non-EU businesses
10/14	Special Scheme for non-EU businesses
1/15	Refund claims by sports clubs for exempt supplies made to non-members
2/15	VAT MOSS exchange rates - March 2015
3/15	VAT MOSS exchange rates - June 2015

VAT Notices with the force of law

NOTICE 747
VAT NOTICES HAVING THE FORCE OF LAW

June 2003

Under certain provisions of the Value Added Tax Act 1994, HMRC have the power to determine the detailed requirements of VAT. These provisions and conditions are set out either in regulations made by statutory instrument (secondary legislation) or in notices which also have, in whole or in part, statutory authority (tertiary legislation). The notices which contain provisions having the force of law, cross-referenced to the relevant enabling powers, are listed [and reproduced] below.

Notice	*Part having the force of law and its purpose*	*Enabling powers*
Notice 700: The VAT Guide	Paragraph 7.7—values expressed in foreign currency.	VATA 1994 Sch 6 para 11
Notice 701/21: Gold	Section 3—para 3.1: notification.	VATA 1994 ss 26, 31
	Section 4—paras 4.3–4.5: further notification requirements; para 4,6: invoicing requirements.	VAT regs 1995 reg 31A
	Section 6—paras 6.2–6.4: further invoicing requirements.	VAT (Investment Gold) Order 1999 (SI 1999/3116)
	Section 7—paras 7.1–7.7: record-keeping requirements.	
Notice 701/21A: Investment Gold Coins	Section 3—list of investment gold coins.	VATA 1994 Sch 9, Group 15
		VAT regs 1995 reg 31A
		VAT (Investment Gold) Order 1999 (SI 1999/3116)
Notice 701/36: Insurance	Paragraph 11.3.1: requirement to keep records	VATA 1994 Sch 11 para 6(1)
	Paragraph 11.3.2: relevant VAT invoice to be used when supplying goods or services under a VAT margin scheme	VAT Regs 1995 regs 31(1) and 31(2)
		VATA 1994 Legal Note (4)(*c*)(iii) to Item 4 of Group 2, Schedule 9
Notice 701/48: Corporate purchasing cards	Para 4.2—Line Item Detail (LID) invoices.	VATA 1994 Sch 11 para 2
	Para 4.3—the Summary VAT invoice.	VAT Regs 1995 regs 13 and 14
Notice 703: Exports and removals of goods from the United Kingdom	Principally paras 2.2 and 8.4 but specific conditions relating to the zero-rating of particular types of supplies of goods for export outside the EC, or removal to another EC Member State, are contained throughout the Notice.	VATA 1994 ss 30(6), (8) and (10) VAT Regs 1995 regs 127, 129 and 134
Notice 703/1: Supply of freight containers for export or removal from the United Kingdom	Paragraphs 4 and 5 contain the conditions which must be met in full in order to zero-rate supplies (by way of sale) of freight containers for export outside the EC or for removal to another EC Member State	VATA 1994 ss 30(6), (8) and (10) VAT Regs 1995 regs 128, 134

Notice	*Part having the force of law and its purpose*	*Enabling powers*
Notice 703/2: Sailaway boats supplied for export outside the European Community	Principally section 3 which sets out the conditions to be complied with, but other paras outline additional conditions which must be met.	VATA 1994 s 30(8) VAT Regs 1995 reg 129
Notice 704: Retail exports	Principally paragraph 1.1 but the notice expands on the conditions for the retailer to supply goods that can be zero-rated to entitled customers	VATA 1994 s 30(8) VAT Regs 1995 regs 130 and 131
Notice 704/1: VAT refunds for travellers departing from the European Community	Principally paragraph 1.2 but the notice expands on the conditions for travellers departing from the European Community and how they may be able to get a refund on some goods bought by using the Retail Export Scheme	VATA 1994 s 30(8) VAT Regs 1995 regs 130 and 131
Notice 707: VAT Personal Export Scheme	[Provisions included in boxes within the text].	VATA 1994 s 30(8) and 30(10) VAT Regs 1995 regs 132 and 133
Notice 708: Buildings and construction	Section 17, para 17.1—Zero-rated and reduced-rated building work 17.2—Zero-rated sales and long leases	VATA 1994 Sch 7A, Group 6 para 8(2)(b), Group 7, para 4A(1)(b); Sch 8 Group 5 Note (12)(b)
Notice 709/5: Tour operators' margin scheme	The notice provides that certain goods and services which would otherwise be covered by the Margin Scheme are excluded, and specifies the method of calculation for the Margin Scheme	VATA 1994 s 53 VAT (Tour Operators) Order 1987 SI 1987/1806 arts 3 and 7 as amended by the VAT (Tour Operators) Orders of 1990, 1992 and 1995
Notice 718: Margin Schemes for second-hand goods, works of art, antiques and collectors' items	Section 3: Records and Accounts. Section 6: Global Accounting—records and accounts. Para 6.2—all apart from final sentence.	VATA 1994 s 50A. VAT (Cars) Order 1992 (SI 1992/3122) as amended
	Para 6.3. Para 6.4—final sentence. Para 6.5—all apart from final sub-para. Para 6.6—all apart from final sentence.	VAT (Special Provisions) Order 1995 (SI 1995/1268) as amended VAT (Input Tax) Order 1992 (SI 1992/3222) as amended
	Para 6.7; Para 6.9. Section 7: The Auctioneers' Scheme—basic principles. Para 7.3—final sentence. Section 8: The Auctioneers' Scheme—records and accounts. Para 8.1; Para 8.2 Section 22: Horses and ponies. Para 22.7—final sub-para.	
Notice 725: VAT: The Single Market	[Provisions included in boxes within the text].	VATA 1994 s 30(8) VATA 1994 Sch 7 para 4
Notice 727: VAT: Retail schemes	Section 2.1: When should I use a retail scheme?	VATA 1994 Sch 11 para 2(6)
	Section 2.2: What if my business makes retail and non-retail sales?	VAT Regs 1995 Part IX (regs 66–75)

Notice	*Part having the force of law and its purpose*	*Enabling powers*
	Section 2.4: Can I use a retail scheme for sales to other VAT registered businesses?	
	Section 3.4: How does the Point of Sale scheme work?	
	Section 3.7: What factors should I consider before choosing Apportionment Scheme (1)?	
	Section 3.9: What factors should I consider before using Apportionment Scheme (2)?	
	Section 3.12: What factors should I consider before using Direct Calculation scheme(1)?	
	Section 4.1: Can I use a mixture of schemes?	
	Section 4.2. Can I change schemes?	
	Section 4.4: Do I need to keep a record of my Daily Gross Takings?	
	Section 5.1: What is a bespoke scheme?	
	Section 6.1: What must I do when I cease using a retail scheme?	
	Section 6.2: Are there any other rules when ceasing to use a scheme?	
	Section 8.3: What are the conditions for using the catering adaptation? schemes or Apportionment Scheme (1)?	
	Section 8.5: How do I start to use the adaptation?	
	Section 8.6: Do I have to maintain any records?	
	Section 8.7: How do I calculate my output tax under the catering adaptation?	
	Section 8.8: How do I calculate the percentage of my standard-rated sales?	
	Section 9.4: How does the adjustment work if I use the Direct Calculation?	
	Section 9.5: How do I estimate the percentage of zero-rated supplies?	
Notice 727/3: Retail schemes: How to work the Point of Scale scheme	Section 2: General rules—paras 2.3–2.5.	VATA 1994 Sch 11 para 2(6)
	Section 3: The Point of Sale Scheme—paras 3.2–3.4.	VAT Regs 1995 Part IX (SI 1995/2518) (regs 66–75)
	Section 4: Mechanics of the Point of Sale Scheme—para 4.2.	
	Section 5: Daily Gross Takings (DGT) checklist—paras 5.1–5.5.	
	Section 6: Special transactions.	
	Section 7: Business promotions—paras 7.2–7.6.	
Notice 727/4: Retail schemes. How to work the Apportionment Schemes	Section 2: General rules—paras 2.3–2.5.	VATA 1994 Sch 11 para 2(6)
	Section 3: Basic principles of Apportionment Schemes 1 and 2—paras 3.2–3.6.	VAT Regs 1995 Part IX (SI 1995/2518) (regs 66–75)
	Section 4: Mechanics of Apportionment Scheme 1—paras 4.2–4.3.	
	Section 5: Mechanics of Apportionment Scheme 2—paras 5.2–5.4.	
	Section 6: Daily Gross Takings (DGT) checklist—paras 6.1–6.5.	
	Section 7: Special transactions.	
	Section 8: Business promotions.	

Notice	*Part having the force of law and its purpose*	*Enabling powers*
Notice 727/5: Retail schemes. How to work the Direct Calculation schemes	Section 2: General rules—paras 2.3–2.5.	VATA 1994 Sch 11 para 2(6)
	Section 3: Basic Principles of Direct Calculation Schemes 1 and 2—paras 3.1–3.7.	VAT Regs 1995 Part IX (SI 1995/2518) (regs 66–75)
	Section 4: Mechanics of the Direct Calculation Schemes (1 and 2)—paras 4.2–4.5.	
	Section 5: Daily Gross Takings (DGT) checklist—paras 5.1–5.5.	
	Section 6: Special transactions.	
	Section 7: Business promotions.	
Notice 728: New Means of Transport	Para 6.1—What happens when I buy an NMT in the UK for removal to another member state? and para 3.6—rate of exchange used to calculate the value of an NMT. Other conditions and procedures to be complied with are set out elsewhere in the Notice	VATA 1994 s 30(8); Sch 7 para 4(2) VAT Regs 1995 reg 155
Notice 731: Cash accounting	Section 2: Basics of cash accounting.	VATA 1994 s 25(1) and Sch 11 para. 2(7)
	Para 2.1—final sub-para.	
	Para 2.3—first sub-para.	VAT Regs 1995 regs 56–65 as amended by VAT (Amendment) (No 3) Regulations 1997
	Para 2.5—final sub-para.	
	Section 3: Records and accounting for VAT.	
	Para 3.2.2—first sub-para.	
	Para 3.3—final sub-para.	
	Para 3.4.1—final sub-para.	
	Para 3.4.2—final sub-para.	
	Section 4: Special rules for particular transactions.	
	Para 4.2—first sub-para.	
	Para 4.3—first sub-para.	
	Para 4.5—first sub-para.	
	Para 4.7—second sub-para.	
	Para 4.8—final sub-para.	
	Section 5: Leaving the cash accounting scheme.	
	Para 5.3—first line, second sub-para.	
	Para 5.6—final sub-para.	
	Para 5.7.2—first sub-para.	
	Para 5.9—final sub-para.	
Notice 733: Flat rate scheme for small businesses	Para 6.4: Records to be kept.	The primary legislation is contained in the VATA 1994 s 26B, as amended by FA 2002
	Para 7.11: Stock adjustment.	
	Para 9.4: Time of payment.	
	Para 9.5: Value of payment.	This is supplemented by more detailed rules in Regs 55A to 55V to the VAT Regulations 1995
	Para 9.6: Value of Supply.	
	Para 9.7: Ceasing to use the cash-based method.	
	Para 10.3: Value of Daily Gross Takings.	
	Para 10.4: Value of Daily Gross Takings.	
	Para 10.6: Adjustment to Daily Gross Takings.	
Notice 742A:Opting to tax land and buildings	The text within boxes in paragraphs 2.7.5, 3.4.2, 3.6.2, 5.6, 6.3.6, 6.3.8, 8.1.4, 8.1.6, 8.3.4, 8.3.7 and 14.9, which explains how to make a notification or application and what information it should contain.	[VATA 1994 Sch 10]
	The text within boxes A-L in paragraphs 2.7.2, 3.4.3, 3.6.3, 5.2, 6.3.5, 8.1.2, 8.3.3, 13.8.6, 13.9.1, 14.8.3 and 14.9 and 14.12.	

NOTICE 700
THE VAT GUIDE

1 April 2015

7. OUTPUT TAX: INTRODUCTION AND TAX VALUE

. . . .

7.7 Values expressed in a foreign currency

> Paragraph 7.7 in this notice has the force of law under the VAT Act 1994, Schedule 6, Paragraph 11.

For VAT purposes, amounts of money must always be expressed in sterling. If you need to convert an amount from a foreign currency into sterling, you must do so on the following basis:

(a) unless you have adopted one of the alternatives set out below, you must use the UK market selling rate at the time of the supply. The rates published in national newspapers will be acceptable as evidence of the rates at the relevant time

(b) as an alternative, you may use the period rate of exchange published by HMRC for customs purposes - our VAT Helpline can give you details of particular period rates, you may adopt this alternative for all your supplies or for all supplies of a particular class or description - if you opt for only a particular class or description, you should make a note of the details in your records at the time of adoption

You do not need to notify us in advance if you wish to adopt this alternative, but having made such an option, you cannot then change it without first getting the agreement of the VAT Written Enquiries Team or:

(c) you may apply in writing to the VAT Written Enquiries Team to use a rate - or method of determining a rate - which you use for commercial purposes but which is not covered by (a) or (b) above

In considering whether to allow such applications, local VAT offices will take into account:

- whether the proposed rate or method is determined by reference to the UK currency market
- whether it is objectively verifiable
- the frequency with which it is proposed to update it (forward rates or methods deriving from forward rates are not acceptable)

Whatever rate or method you adopt, the appropriate rate for any supply is that current at the time of the supply.

If you make supplies that fall within the Tour Operators' Margin Scheme (TOMS), see VAT Notice 709/5: *tour operators margin scheme* for details of how to convert the value of your purchases.

Commentary—*De Voil Indirect Tax Service* **V3.103.**

NOTICE 700/8
DISCLOSURE OF VAT AVOIDANCE SCHEMES

October 2013.

This notice cancels and replaces Notice 700/8 (February 2006). Details of any changes to the previous version can be found in paragraph 1.2 of this notice.

Paragraphs 5.2, 5.4, 8.2 and 8.7 of this notice, which explain how to make a notification and where to send it, have the force of law under the VAT (Disclosure of Avoidance Schemes) Regulations 2004, regulation 3. These paragraphs are indicated by being placed in a box.

1 INTRODUCTION

1.1 What is this notice about?

This notice is about what to do when you enter into arrangements or transactions that are intended to give you or any other person a VAT advantage when compared to adopting a different course of action.

This notice does not cover the rules for notifying arrangements relating to Income Tax, Corporation Tax, Capital Gains Tax or Stamp Duty Land Tax. The rules for these taxes are explained in guidance available on our website, at www.hmrc.gov.uk the Anti Avoidance Group's page or phone the Anti Avoidance Group on 0207 438 6733.

1.2 What's changed?

This notice has been revised to include legislative changes made since the last version to the meaning of "tax advantage", the "duty to notify" rules, and the range of 'listed schemes' and 'hallmarks'. It also corrects some minor errors and expands on the guidance to help you identify the schemes that must be notified.

This notice has been revised to include legislative changes made since the last version to the meaning of 'tax advantage', the 'duty to notify' rules, and the range of 'listed schemes' and 'hallmarks'. It also corrects some minor errors and expands on the guidance to help you identify the schemes that must be notified.

You can access details of any changes since February 2006 from our website, go to www.hmrc.go-v.uk or telephone our Helpline on 0300 200 3700.

This notice and others mentioned are available both on paper and on our website.

1.3 Who should read this notice?

You should read this notice if you are, or are liable to be, registered for VAT in the UK, and either:

(a) enter into one of 10 specific arrangements (known in this notice as 'listed schemes') that the Treasury have designated as having been, or might be, entered into for the purpose of enabling any person to obtain a VAT advantage, or

(b) enter into, or knowingly become a party to, any other arrangements or transactions that are intended to give you or any other person a VAT advantage and which include, or are associated with, one of 8 'hallmarks' of tax avoidance.

More detailed criteria on whether the rules for 'listed schemes' or 'hallmarked' schemes affect you can be found from paragraphs 4.1 and 7.1 respectively.

In general, you will not need to read this notice if you, or where you are a member of a corporate group, the whole group, make taxable and exempt supplies totalling below £150,000 per quarterly VAT accounting period or £50,000 if you submit monthly returns.

It is suggested you also read this notice if you devise or sell VAT avoidance, planning or mitigation schemes, arrangements or devices.

1.4 WHAT LAW COVERS THIS NOTICE?

The main relevant law is as follows—

- The meaning of "tax advantage" and "notifiable scheme", and the duty to notify and penalty provisions, are prescribed in: Schedule 11A to the VAT Act 1994 (as inserted by section 19 and Schedule 2 to the Finance Act 2004 with effect from 1 August 2004; and amended by section 6 and Schedule 1 to the Finance (No. 2) Act 2005 with effect from 1 August 2005).
- Transitional provisions relating to changes in 2005 to the meaning of "tax advantage" and the duty to notify provisions are found in: The Finance (No. 2) Act 2005, section 6, (Appointed Day and Savings Provisions) Order 2005 (SI 2005/2010).
- The "listed schemes" and "hallmarks" are described in: The VAT (Disclosure of Avoidance Schemes) (Designations) Order 2004 (SI 2004/1933) (as amended by The VAT

(Disclosure of Avoidance Schemes) (Designations) (Amendment) Order 2005 (SI 2005/1724) with effect from 1 August 2005).

– The time of notification, and information to be notified, is prescribed in: The VAT (Disclosure of Avoidance Schemes) Regulations 2004 (SI 2004/1929) (as amended by The VAT (Disclosure of Avoidance Schemes) (Amendment) Regulations 2005 (SI 2005/2009) with effect from 1 August 2005).

Commentary—*De Voil Indirect Tax Service* **V5.213.**

2 OBTAINING A VAT ADVANTAGE

2.1 Can I structure my affairs so as to obtain a VAT advantage?

Yes, provided what you do is not dishonest. However, under the rules explained in this notice, you may need to formally tell us about what you are doing; and we might decide to challenge whether the structure achieves the intended advantage (see also paragraph 3.10).

Note: If you are required to tell us what you are doing, you may be liable to a *penalty* if you do not provide us on time with the information explained in this notice

2.2 Can I get a ruling on the arrangements and transactions I'm planning to do?

CAP1 - *Clearances and Approvals 1* (www.hmrc.gov.uk/cap/nscg.htm) explains how you can normally obtain our view on how transactions should be treated for VAT. However, we will not 'approve' tax planning arrangements and will refuse to give rulings where we suspect that the transactions are part of a tax avoidance scheme.

2.3 What happens if I obtain a VAT advantage dishonestly?

The matter could be investigated as either a criminal investigation or under the civil investigation of fraud procedures. Civil investigations are undertaken in accordance with Code of Practice 9 (www.hmrc.gov.uk/leaflets/cop9-2005.htm).

Commentary—*De Voil Indirect Tax Service* **V5.213.**

3 ABOUT NOTIFYING HMRC

3.1 What must I tell HMRC about?

You must tell us about—

– certain arrangements that are named and described in the relevant law (referred to in this notice as "listed schemes") – see paragraph 3.4 below and sections 4 to 6; and

– arrangements and transactions that include or are associated with at least one of a range of designated provisions that are often linked with avoidance (referred to in this notice as "hallmarks" and "hallmarked schemes") – see paragraph 3.6 below and sections 7, 8 and 10.

3.2 Does everyone have to notify?

No. Only taxable persons (ie, those who are, or are liable to be, registered for VAT in the UK) have to notify.

Even then, various filters, or tests, may mean you do not have to notify. For example, your turnover may be below the relevant threshold. The detailed rules are explained in sections 4 and 7 for listed schemes and hallmarked schemes respectively.

There is also a voluntary facility that allows any person to register a hallmarked scheme with us. Businesses using one of these registered schemes may be exempt from having to separately notify (see paragraph 7.8 and section 9).

3.2.1 VAT groups

The representative member of a VAT Group is responsible for notifying schemes involving group members - see also paragraph 3.3.2.

3.3 Does only the beneficiary of the VAT advantage have to notify?

No. Any taxable person (see paragraph 3.2 above) who is a party to a notifiable scheme may have to tell us about the scheme.

3.3.1 "A party to a scheme"

You are a party to a scheme if you knowingly take part in it.

You are not a party to a scheme if you—

(a) are unwittingly involved in any of the steps of the scheme (ie, you have no knowledge of either the existence of the scheme or the role you play in it); or
(b) act purely in an advisory capacity.

3.3.2 VAT groups

Where a member of a VAT Group is a contractual party in a notifiable scheme, the duty to disclose falls on the representative member of the group.

The notification should provide the name of the group member who is involved in the scheme as well as the name and registration number of the representative member - see paragraphs 5.2 and 8.2.

3.3.3 What if another party to the scheme has already made a notification?

You must still notify us.

3.3.4 Joint notifications

Where more than one party is obliged to notify us, the parties concerned can make a joint notification. The notification should make it clear that it is a joint notification, who all the parties are that are making the notification, and provide the information set out in paragraph 5.3 or 8.3 as appropriate.

3.4 What are the listed schemes?

The schemes are—

- Scheme 1 – The first grant of a major interest in a building (see paragraphs 6.1 and 6.2);
- Scheme 2 – Payment handling services (see paragraphs 6.1 and 6.3);
- Scheme 3 – Value shifting (see paragraphs 6.1 and 6.4);
- Scheme 4 – Leaseback agreements (see paragraphs 6.1 and 6.5);
- Scheme 5 – Extended approval periods (see paragraphs 6.1 and 6.6);
- Scheme 6 – Groups: third party suppliers (see paragraphs 6.1 and 6.7);
- Scheme 7 – Education and training by a non-profit making body (see paragraphs 6.1 and 6.8);
- Scheme 8 – Education and training by a non-eligible body (see paragraphs 6.1 and 6.9); and
- Scheme 9 – Cross-border face-value vouchers (see paragraphs 6.1 and 6.10); and
- Scheme 10 – Surrender of a relevant lease (see paragraphs 6.1 and 6.11).

3.5 New listed schemes

The range of listed schemes may be updated periodically by the making of a new Treasury Statutory Instrument. We will give one month's notice of the intention to list a new scheme, so that interested parties can let us have their views on the proposals. Notice of such proposed changes will be given on our website at www.hmrc.gov.uk.

3.6 What are the hallmarks?

The hallmarks are—

- Confidentiality condition agreements (see paragraphs 10.1 and 10.2);
- Agreements to share a tax advantage (see paragraphs 10.1 and 10.3);

- Contingent fee agreements (see paragraphs 10.1 and 10.4);
- Prepayments between connected parties (see paragraphs 10.1 and 10.5);
- Funding by loans, share subscriptions or subscriptions in securities (see paragraphs 10.1 and 10.6);
- Off-shore loops (see paragraphs 10.1 and 10.7);
- Property transactions between connected persons (see paragraphs 10.1 and 10.8); and
- The issue of face-value vouchers (see paragraphs 10.1 and 10.9).

3.7 What if HMRC already know I am using a notifiable scheme?

You must still notify us under the rules set out in this notice.

3.8 What don't I have to notify?

There is no "white list" of schemes that do not require notification. If you have a liability to notify us about a scheme, you should do so even if you believe we already know about the type of scheme you are using.

Section 11 explains our view on some frequently encountered issues to do with hallmarked schemes.

3.9 Will my notification be made public?

Notifications are subject to the normal rules of taxpayer confidentiality found in the Commissioners for Revenue & Customs Act 2005 and, other than in the exceptional circumstances allowed for, are not made public. However, if we challenge what you are doing and the matter progresses to the Courts the hearing is likely to be held in public.

3.10 Are all notified arrangements regarded as avoidance and challenged?

No. Whilst we have tried to keep the burden to a minimum, you may have to tell us about arrangements that we do not consider to be avoidance.

We will examine all notifications sent to us and might decide to investigate further, challenging the arrangements where appropriate. This may mean that you are issued with an assessment for an amount of tax that we believe has been incorrectly declared. Should the arrangements give rise to a tax liability over and above what would have been due if the arrangements had not been entered into, an assessment may also be issued for this additional amount.

As well as the notified arrangements, an investigation may include an examination of other arrangements that you use in your business.

Commentary—*De Voil Indirect Tax Service* **V5.213.**

4 LISTED SCHEMES – DECIDING WHETHER YOU MUST NOTIFY

4.1 Decision chart

You must notify use of a listed scheme when *all* of the following tests are met—

Test	*Description*	*Further information*
1	You are a *taxable person*	Paragraph 3.2
2	You are a *party* to a *listed scheme*	Paragraph 3.3 and section 6
3	A *relevant event* occurs	Paragraph 4.2
4	Your *turnover* exceeds either of the minimum thresholds	Paragraphs 4.3
5	You have *not already notified* HM Revenue & Customs, as required under the rules set out in this notice, that you are using the scheme	Paragraph 4.4

Section 5 explains by when you must make your notification, the information it should contain and where to send it.

4.2 Relevant events that trigger notification

The requirement for you to notify is triggered when one of the following events occurs to you:

- You show in a VAT return, in respect of any VAT accounting period starting on or after 1 August 2004, a higher or lower net amount of VAT than would be the case but for the listed scheme.
- You make a claim (such as by submitting a voluntary disclosure), in respect of any VAT accounting period starting on or after 1 August 2004 for which a VAT return has been submitted, for the repayment of output tax over-declared or input tax credit under-claimed that is greater than would be the case but for the listed scheme.
- The amount of non-deductible VAT (see paragraph 4.2.1 below) you incur, in respect of any VAT accounting period starting on or after 1 August 2005, would have been higher but for the listed scheme.

4.2.1 Non-deductible VAT incurred

VAT is, or would have been, incurred by you when it is, or would have been:

- VAT on the supply to you of any goods or services (including VAT on reverse charges).
- VAT on the acquisition by you from another Member State of any goods, or
- VAT paid or payable by you on the importation of any goods from a place outside the EU.

It is, or would have been, non-deductible VAT when it is, or would have been—

- VAT that is input tax, but for which you are not entitled to credit; or
- VAT that is not input tax, and for which you are not entitled to a refund under any provision of VATA 1994.

Commentary—*De Voil Indirect Tax Service* **V5.213.**

4.3 The minimum turnover thresholds

The turnover threshold is measured by reference to the *total* amount of *taxable and exempt* supplies made by—

- you; or
- where you are a member of a corporate group, *the whole group*, made up of the ultimate holding company (or entity) and all its subsidiaries, including you. For this purpose UK company law definitions used for preparing group accounts apply (section 259 of the Companies Act 1985). As a result the group will normally be made up of all the companies shown as subsidiaries in the ultimate parent's consolidated group accounts, plus any companies that are excluded from the consolidation but are subsidiaries for UK company law purposes.

For the purpose of calculating turnover, intra-corporate group transactions are included. However, intra-VAT Group transactions are ignored.

4.3.1 The threshold

Your turnover exceeds the minimum threshold when the total amount of *taxable and exempt* supplies made by you (or the wider corporate group as explained above) is, or is greater than:

(a) £600,000 in the year immediately prior to the VAT accounting period that triggers notification (see paragraph 4.2); or

(b) the appropriate proportion of £600,000 in the VAT accounting period immediately prior to the VAT accounting period that triggers notification. (For example, the "appropriate proportion" is one twelfth of £600,000 (ie £50,000) where the VAT accounting period is one month; and one quarter of £600,000 (ie £150,000) where the VAT accounting period is three months.)

4.3.2 Disaggregation

Should we find that a taxable person's business has been split in an attempt to avoid the requirement to make a notification, we will use our powers to direct that the separate entities be treated as one. If it is found later that other entities should have been included in that direction, a supplementary direction can be made to include them. The effect a supplementary direction has on the timing of a notification is explained in paragraph 5.1.5.

Commentary—*De Voil Indirect Tax Service* **V2.190C.**

4.4 Exemption for previously notified schemes

4.4.1 General

The use of some schemes will only trigger one relevant event (see paragraph 4.2). Others, such as a payment handling service, are designed to give an ongoing VAT benefit over time. Consequently, more than one relevant event may occur. The use of such a scheme only has to be notified once.

However, a listed scheme may be used more than once. For example, listed scheme 1 (first grant of a major interest) may be used to remove the VAT cost of refurbishing more than one property. Where this happens, each adoption of the scheme must be notified, but you only need tell us once about each case.

Paragraph 5.3 explains what information to provide.

4.4.2 Listed schemes notified under the rules for hallmarked schemes

The range of listed schemes may change (see paragraph 3.5). If you have previously notified your use of a listed scheme under the rules for hallmarked schemes, you are not required to make a new notification when the scheme becomes "listed".

If the scheme is used again, you must notify the new arrangements – see paragraph 4.4.1.

Commentary—*De Voil Indirect Tax Service* **V5.213.**

5 LISTED SCHEMES – HOW TO NOTIFY HMRC

5.1 By what date must I notify HMRC?

Your notification must be made to HMRC within 30 days of:

- in the case of the net amount of VAT shown in a VAT return being different to what would otherwise be the case (see the first bullet at paragraph 4.2), the due date for making the return
- in the case of a claim being made that is greater than would otherwise be the case (see the second bullet at paragraph 4.2), the making of the claim; or
- in the case of the amount of your non-deductible VAT in respect of a VAT accounting period being less than would otherwise be the case (see the third bullet at paragraph 4.2), the due date for making a return in respect of that accounting period.

For examples of when a notification is due see paragraphs 5.1.3 to 5.1.4.

5.1.1 Early notifications

HMRC will accept early notifications, such as before the relevant event has taken place, provided the scheme has been implemented.

5.1.2 Transitional rules for newly listed schemes

Use of listed schemes 1 to 8 need only be notified when a relevant event takes place in relation to an accounting period starting on or after 1 August 2004.

Use of listed schemes 9 and 10 need only be notified when a relevant event takes place in relation to an accounting period starting on or after 1 August 2005.

5.1.3 Examples of due date for notifying when a return is affected (for listed schemes 1 to 8)

Examples of the notification due date, when the net amount of VAT shown on a return is affected by the scheme, include:

Period of affected VAT return	*Due date for submitting return*	*Notification due*
1 June 2004 to 31 August 2004	30 September 2004	No notification required (return starts before 1 August 2004)
1 August 2004 to 31 August 2004	30 September 2004	30 October 2004

Period of affected VAT return	*Due date for submitting return*	*Notification due*
1 August 2004 to 31 October 2004	30 November 2004	30 December 2004
1 September 2004 to 30 November 2004	31 December 2004	30 January 2005
1 October 2004 to 31 December 2004	31 January 2005	2 March 2005

If you pay VAT due on a return by an approved electronic method you may be entitled to an extension to the due date for submitting your return. If this is the case, the due date for notifying a scheme is 30 days after the extended due date for submitting the return.

5.1.4 Examples of due date for notifying when a claim is affected (for listed schemes 1 to 8)

Examples of the notification due date, when the amount of VAT being claimed is affected by use of the scheme, include—

VAT return period covered by affected claim	*Date claim is made*	*Notification due*
1 August 2004 to 31 August 2004	27 November 2004	27 December 2004
1 July 2004 to 30 September 2004	14 January 2005	No notification required (return starts before 1 August 2004)
1 October 2004 to 31 December 2004	29 August 2005	28 September 2005

5.1.5 Directions that taxpayers are treated as one

Where HM Revenue & Customs issue a direction that a number of taxpayers should be treated as one (see paragraph 4.3.2), the due date is determined by reference to the first relevant event (see paragraph 4.2) that takes place following the issue of the direction.

5.2 How do I notify HMRC?

The following rule has the force of law

> You must notify us either in writing or by email to the relevant address given at paragraph 5.4. The notification should be prominently headed:
>
> – Disclosure of use of listed scheme - Notification under paragraph 6(2) of Schedule 11A to the VAT Act 1994.
>
> and give your:
>
> – business name (if you are the representative member of a VAT Group, notifying as a result of a group member being involved in a notifiable scheme, also tell us the name of the member)
> – address; and
> – VAT registration number.

5.3 What information must I provide?

The only information you must provide is the number of the scheme, which can be found in section 6. Your obligation to notify is fulfilled on receipt of the required information at one of the addresses given in paragraph 5.4.

On some occasions you may use more than one scheme at the same time (see paragraph 4.4). Where this happens you must tell us about all of the schemes of each type that are being used and haven't previously been reported.

For joint notifications, see paragraph 3.3.4.

5.4 Where do I send my notification?

The following rule has the force of law

> You must send your notification to either of the addresses given below.
>
> Post to:
>
> Anti-Avoidance Group (Intelligence)
> VAT Avoidance Disclosures Unit
> CTIAA Intelligence S0528
> PO Box 194
> Bootle L69 9AA
>
> Or e-mail to:
>
> vat.avoidance.disclosures.bst@hmrc.gsi.gov.uk

5.5 What if I send my notification to another address?

If you send your notification to an address other than those given in paragraph 5.4 (for example to another office or the VAT Written Enquiries Team), you will not have made a proper notification. Failure to make a proper notification will make you liable to a penalty as explained in section 12.

5.6 How will HMRC deal with my notification?

We will acknowledge receipt of all notifications received at the addresses given in paragraph 5.4, and consider whether we wish to investigate - see paragraph 3.10. If we do not contact you, this does not mean the arrangements are acceptable to us.

If we are already investigating your use of the notified scheme, that investigation will continue as appropriate.

Commentary—*De Voil Indirect Tax Service* **V5.213.**

6 THE LISTED SCHEMES

6.1 Descriptions of the listed schemes

The listed schemes are described in paragraphs 6.2 to 6.9 below. (Note: Arrangements that are not covered by a listed scheme may need to be notified as a hallmarked scheme - see section 7.)

The descriptions are intended only as a guide and are not a substitute for the descriptions contained in the relevant law (see paragraph 1.4). For each scheme there is:

- a list of the identifying features of the scheme;
- an example of arrangements that are covered by the listed scheme; and
- in some cases, examples of ones that are not.

6.1.1 Whether the features of a scheme are present

A feature of a scheme is regarded as being present when it is either—

- present as a matter of fact; or
- a taxable person treats it as being present for the purpose of making a VAT return or voluntary disclosure, even if it is not actually present (whether as a matter of law or for any other reason). For example, a feature of a scheme may rely on a transaction being a supply for VAT purposes. If, for the purpose of making a return, a taxable person treats the transaction as being such a supply, then the feature is regarded as being present (for

the purposes of deciding whether disclosure is required), even if it is subsequently found, say by the Courts, that there has been no supply as a matter of law.

6.1.2 Connected persons

For the purposes of the scheme descriptions a person is connected with another where:

– one of them is an undertaking in relation to which the other is a group undertaking as defined by s 259 of the Companies Act 1985 (essentially, one is the parent or subsidiary undertaking of the other, or both are subsidiaries of a common parent undertaking); or
– both of them are connected to the same trust.

A person is connected to a trust where he:

– is the settlor of the trust, or a trustee or beneficiary of it; or
– holds any shares in a company in accordance with the terms of the trust, or is a person on whose behalf such shares are held.

Commentary—*De Voil Indirect Tax Service* **V5.213.**

6.2 Scheme 1 – The first grant of a major interest in a building

This scheme aims to remove the VAT cost of extending, enlarging, repairing, refurbishing or servicing buildings that are zero-rated when sold by developers.

Examples of the buildings concerned are houses, student halls of residence and buildings used by charities for non-business activities.

6.2.1 The scheme's features

The scheme comprises or includes the following features—

(a) a zero-rated major interest grant is made in the building (see Notice 708 "Buildings and construction") to a connected person (see paragraph 6.1.2); and
(b) the following input tax is attributed to the grant:
  – input tax in respect of a service charge relating to the building; or
  – input tax in connection with any extension, enlargement, repair, maintenance or refurbishment of the building (other than for remedying defects In the original construction).

6.2.2 Examples of arrangements included in the listed scheme

A housing landlord may seek to use this scheme to recover input tax on the renovation of houses that he had constructed several years earlier. Having decided that some of the houses require major refurbishment, the landlord leases or sells them to a subsidiary in such a way that he attributes to that zero-rated disposal the VAT on the refurbishment, which may be undertaken either before or after the grant. The subsidiary may then simply lease the houses back to the landlord so that he can then let them on again to tenants.

By way of another example, the builder of new halls of residence may try to recover future input tax on repairs and maintenance of the buildings, even though his income from the property at that time will be exempt, by building into the initial zero-rated lease or sale a payment for, and agreement to provide, repairs and maintenance in the future.

6.2.3 Examples of arrangements not included in the listed scheme

This listed scheme does not include arrangements where—

(a) the zero-rated grant is made under VATA 1994, Sch 8, Group 5, Item 1(b) (person converting a non-residential building);
(b) the zero-rated grant is made under VATA 1994, Sch 8, Group 6, Item 1 (substantial reconstruction of a protected building); or
(c) there is no zero-rated grant made to a connected person.

Commentary—*De Voil Indirect Tax Service* **V5.213.**

6.3 Scheme 2 – Payment handling services

This scheme aims to reduce the VAT due on the advertised price of retail goods or services by transforming an element of the price into an exempt payment handling service (such as credit/debit card or cash handling).

6.3.1 The scheme's features

The scheme comprises or includes the following features—

- a retail supply of goods or services;
- a linked supply to the same customer, by the retailer or any person, that relates to the means of payment used for the retail supply and is a supply of a description falling within the VAT Act 1994, Schedule 9, Group 5 (finance), and
- the total consideration due for the retail supply and linked supply is no different, or not significantly different, from what it would be for the retail supply alone.

6.3.2 Example of arrangements included in the listed scheme

When a customer presents his goods at the till, and decides to pay by credit or debit card rather than cash, he may be informed that part of the ticket price is being paid to a separate company and is in consideration for processing or accepting his credit card as the means of payment. Agreements signed or agreed by the customer at the point of sale may be alleged to support this.

The total amount paid by the customer remains the same whether or not the handling service is actually used or needed by the customer but is separated into a reduced value for the taxable goods and an exempt amount paid to the separate company. There is no comparable reduction in the value for the goods if he chooses to pay by cash.

Commentary—*De Voil Indirect Tax Service* **V5.213.**

6.4 Scheme 3 – Value shifting

This scheme aims to transfer value from standard-rated retail supplies into linked zero-rated or exempt supplies.

6.4.1 The schemes features

The scheme comprises or includes the following features—

(a) a standard-rated retail supply of goods or services;
(b) a linked zero-rated or exempt supply by any person to the same customer;
(c) the linked supply is treated as a separate supply under the terms of an agreement made by the customer;
(d) the terms of the agreement attribute part of the consideration for the retail supply and linked supply to the linked supply; and
(e) the total consideration due for the retail supply and linked supply is no different, or not significantly different, from what it would be for the retail supply alone.

6.4.2 Example of arrangements included in the listed scheme

A retail customer making a large purchase may find that, at the point of sale, he is offered an insurance product with the goods. Rather than paying an additional amount for this cover, the customer will be informed that the ticket price has now been apportioned to cover both the goods and the insurance. If the customer then says he does not want the insurance, there is no reduction of the ticket price to reflect this. The overall price paid by the customer remains the same whether he takes the insurance or not.

6.4.3 Examples of arrangements not included in the listed scheme

Notification is not required when the linked goods or services are supplied free, with no part of the price being attributed to that supply.

Additionally notification is not required for normal business promotion arrangements. For example: a retailer offers a 'meal deal' where customers can buy a sandwich, a soft drink and packet of crisps for a single price that is lower than the normal combined price of the three items. When apportioning the cost between the zero-rated and standard-rated items the retailer spreads the discount across all the goods supplied. These arrangements are unlikely to be notifiable as each linked supply would not normally be subject to a separate agreement with the customer; and the total amount payable is likely to be significantly different from what it would be for the standard rated element alone.

Commentary—*De Voil Indirect Tax Service* **V5.213.**

6.5 Scheme 4 – Leaseback agreements

This scheme aims to defer or reduce the VAT cost of acquiring goods by a business that cannot recover all of the input tax on those goods were it to directly buy them itself.

6.5.1 The scheme's features

The scheme comprises or includes the following features—

(a) a person (the "relevant person") receives a supply of goods, or the leasing or letting on hire of goods;

(b) he uses the goods in his business, but is not entitled to full input tax credit for the VAT on the supply to him;

(c) the supply to him is made by a person connected with him (see paragraph 6.1.2);

(d) the supplier, or a person connected with him, is entitled to full input tax credit on the purchase of the goods; and

(e) the relevant person (or a person connected with him) funds (directly or indirectly) more than 90 per cent of the cost of the goods.

For the purposes of this scheme, goods do not include land transactions.

6.5.2 Examples of arrangements included in the listed scheme

A partly exempt trader, such as a bank, requires new computer equipment. The decision is taken that the bank's corporate group will purchase the equipment outright. However, in order to reduce or remove the VAT effect of the irrecoverable input tax, the group acquires the computers in a subsidiary, which then leases them to the bank. Depending on the values and length of the lease, the intention is to spread the irrecoverable VAT cost, or to avoid a proportion of it altogether.

6.5.3 Example of arrangements not included in the listed scheme

Notification is not required for leasing arrangements that are between unconnected parties. For example:

Company "A", an insurance business, requires a new computerised telephone system for its call centres. Rather than buy the equipment outright it decides to lease it. It contracts with Company "B", an unconnected commercial leasing business, to lease the equipment for a five-year period. As Company "B" has no expertise in sourcing the equipment required, it is agreed that Company "A" will purchase the equipment from its usual supplier. Company "A" then sells the equipment to Company "B" who leases it back to Company "A".

Commentary—*De Voil Indirect Tax Service* **V5.213.**

6.6 Scheme 5 – Extended approval periods

This scheme aims to defer accounting for output tax on retail (including mail order) supplies of goods.

6.6.1 The scheme's features

The scheme comprises or includes the following features:

(a) a retail supply of goods where the goods are sent or taken on approval, sale or return, or similar terms;

(b) a requirement that the customer pays in full before any approval, return or similar period expires; and

(c) for the purposes of accounting for VAT, the supplier treats the goods as supplied on a date after the date on which payment is received in full.

6.6.2 Example of arrangements included in the listed scheme

A customer orders goods from an Internet retailer. The retailer is paid on-line when the customer places the order and delivery follows shortly thereafter. The retailer, either due to various guarantees, or specific terms and conditions, seeks to account for VAT on the transaction at a later date, claiming the supply was on "approval" or "sale or return". This is despite the fact that payment has been received, delivery has taken place and, in some cases, the goods have been consumed or used by the customer before the retailer regards the customer as having accepted the goods.

Commentary—*De Voil Indirect Tax Service* **V5.213.**

6.7 Scheme 6 – Groups: third party suppliers

These are schemes that aim to reduce or remove the VAT incurred on bought in taxable services (including outsourced services) by a user that cannot recover all of the input tax charged to it for those services.

6.7.1 The scheme's features

The scheme description is linked to legislation that took effect from 1 August 2004 and which only applies to businesses that are in VAT Groups or intend to join a VAT Group where the VAT Group concerned has a turnover exceeding £10 million a year. Notification of this scheme only applies to bodies affected by that legislation. VAT Information Sheet 07/04 Eligibility Rules for VAT Grouping gives guidance on the linked legislation.

The scheme comprises or includes the following features:

(a) supplies made to one or more VAT Group members by a body that is a specified body for the purposes of the VAT (Groups: eligibility) Order 2004 (SI 2004/1931), and
(b) the benefits condition of the VAT (Groups: eligibility) Order 2004 (SI 2004/1931) is not satisfied.

6.7.2 Example of arrangements included in the listed scheme

A partly exempt business, say company A an insurance company, wants to buy in computer services from third party company B, but wants to reduce the irrecoverable VAT cost of doing this. Companies A and B establish company C, in which A owns 51% of C's shares. Company A includes C in its VAT Group. Company B owns the remaining shares in C, but these shares confer rights to 99% of the dividends declared by C and 99% of the assets on winding up.

Company C holds the contract to provide the computer services required by company A from company B and employs the staff to provide the service. Besides the dividends, B also receives benefits from C in the form of a management charge for managing C's activity of providing computer services. As a result almost all of the benefits of company C's activity accrue to company B. Thus company B has access to the profits and benefits of the computer service activity, and company A hopes to avoid a large VAT cost as there will be no VAT charged within the VAT Group.

Commentary—*De Voil Indirect Tax Service* **V5.213.**

6.8 Scheme 7—education and training by a non-profit making body

This scheme aims to allow a business providing education or training to avoid charging VAT on supplies to customers by arranging for those supplies to be made through a non-profit making body.

6.8.1 The scheme's features

The scheme comprises or includes the following features:

(a) a non-profit making body conducts a business whose activities consist wholly or mainly of the supply of VAT exempt education or vocational training to persons who are not taxable persons
(b) it receives any of the following 'key supplies', for use in that business, from a connected taxable person (see paragraph 6.1.2) who is not eligible for the exemption (see the VAT Act 1994, Schedule 9, Group 6, note 1)–

- a capital item (including leasing or letting on hire of a capital item),
- staff,
- management services,
- administration services, or
- accountancy services; and

(c) in any one VAT return accounting period the value of those key supplies comprise 20% or more of the non-profit making body's costs.

"Non-profit making body" means a body within VATA 1994, Sch 9, Group 6, Note (1)(e), which is not otherwise within Note 1.

"Vocational training" has the meaning given by VATA 1994, Sch 9, Group 6, Note (3) but does not include vocational training of a description falling within item 5 or 5A of that Group.

6.8.2 Example of arrangements included in the listed scheme

A training company such as a driving instruction business, which normally trains private individuals and accounts for VAT out of its income, decides to set up a new non-profit making body to provide the training in the future, exempt from VAT. However, being a non-profit making body it is unable to distribute its profits, and the shareholders of the existing business will lose out. Various agreements may therefore be put in place to act as a mechanism to return those profits to the original training company. For example, the business premises may be leased, the rent for which may be set at a rate directly related to the turnover or profit of the non-profit making body.

Commentary—*De Voil Indirect Tax Service* **V5.213**.

6.9 Scheme 8 – Education and training by a non-eligible body

This scheme aims to enable "eligible bodies" that would otherwise make exempt supplies to make taxable supplies and so avoid incurring irrecoverable input tax. The typical customers involved would be bodies such as NHS Trusts and Local Authorities, but can also include normal commercial bodies.

6.9.1 The scheme's features

This scheme comprises or includes the following features:

(a) a body that is not an eligible body for the purposes of the exemption (see VATA 1994, Sch 9, Group 6, note 1) is connected (see paragraph 6.1.2) to a body that is an eligible body; and

(b) the non-eligible body conducts a business whose activities consist wholly or mainly of the taxable supply of education or vocational training.

In addition, either:

(a) the non-eligible body benefits or intends to benefit the eligible body by way of gift, dividend or otherwise;
or both—

(b) the eligible body makes to the non-eligible body, for use in the non-eligible body's business, any supply (including the leasing or letting on hire) of any of the following "key supplies"–
- a capital item (including the leasing or letting on hire of a capital item),
- staff,
- management services,
- administration services, or
- accountancy services; and

(c) in any one VAT return accounting period the value of those key supplies comprise 20 per cent or more of the non-eligible body's costs.

6.9.2 Example of arrangements included in the listed scheme

An institution, such as a university, has a contract to provide training to employees of a NHS Trust. Normally, the training would be exempt from VAT and thus the VAT on costs involved in providing it would not be recoverable. In order to provide this training, the university needs to build a new facility, but would like to reduce the cost of the irrecoverable VAT on the building.

The university may establish a subsidiary that is expressly allowed to distribute its profits, claiming exemption for its training supplies. The subsidiary may have few or no resources, so will need to be provided with those resources by the university under various contracts and agreements. It is also likely that the university would want to access any profits from this activity and may choose to do this by having the subsidiary gift those profits to it under the Gift Aid relief. Thus the university may hope to transform the training into a fully taxable activity and recover the input tax on the new facility in the subsidiary, together with other taxable costs.

Commentary—*De Voil Indirect Tax Service* **V5.213.**

6.10 Scheme 9 – Cross-border face-value vouchers

This scheme aims to avoid paying VAT anywhere in the EU on "relevant services" originating from UK suppliers and provided to UK residents who use face-value vouchers (such as phone cards) to pay for them.

"Relevant services" are telecommunication services, radio and television broadcasting services, and electronically supplied services (such as software, images, music and games supplied over the internet).

6.10.1 The scheme's features

This scheme comprises or includes the following features:

(a) the supply of a "relevant service" from a UK supplier (S) to someone (A) in another EU member state;
(b) a person (B) in another member state B, who may be the same person as A or a different person, uses S's service to supply a "relevant service" to a customer in the UK (the "retail supply");
(c) S (the UK supplier) and B (the person making the retail supply) are connected persons (see paragraph 6.1.2);
(d) the customer is not a taxable person and uses a face-value voucher issued by a non-UK person (C), who may be the same person as B or a different person, to obtain the supply;
(e) B (the person making the retail supply) does not account for VAT on that supply in the UK or any other EU member state.

6.10.2 Example of arrangements included in the listed scheme

A company, UK Supplier Ltd, contracts to supply telecommunication services to a related company, Redeemer Ltd, in another EU Member State, such as Ireland.

A second related Irish company, Issuer Ltd, issues phone cards and sells them to UK retailers. The retailers sell the cards to UK customers, who use them to obtain telecommunication services from Redeemer Ltd. The cards say that, when they are used, Redeemer Ltd will provide the telecommunication services. Redeemer Ltd does this by buying in the services under its contract with UK Supplier Ltd.

Redeemer Ltd and Issuer Ltd argue that no VAT is due in Ireland or the UK.

NB only taxable persons in the UK who are party to the scheme, such as UK Supplier Ltd, are required to notify. UK retailers who are not party to the scheme (because they have no knowledge of their involvement in it), and parties who are not taxable persons in the UK, are not required to notify - see paragraphs 3.2 and 3.3.

6.10.3 Examples of arrangements not included in the listed scheme

Not included are any arrangements where the person that makes the retail supplies to the final consumer belongs outside the EU or where no UK supplier of a relevant service is involved in the scheme.

Commentary—*De Voil Indirect Tax Service* **V5.213.**

6.11 Scheme 10 – Surrender of a relevant lease

This scheme aims to allow a person to escape, or substantially reduce, the VAT incurred on opted lease rentals whilst remaining in occupation of the building.

6.11.1 The scheme's features

This scheme comprises or includes the following features:

(a) an occupier of a building (or part of a building) agrees with the landlord to the surrender or other early termination of his lease, tenancy or licence to occupy a building;

(b) the building is a capital item within the meaning of the Capital Goods Scheme (whether or not the adjustment period has expired);

(c) the occupier, or any person connected with him, is a person who–
- is a landlord of the building,
- owns it for the purposes of the Capital Goods Scheme, and
- has elected to waive exemption (also known as "opting to tax") in relation to it;

(d) before the surrender–
- the occupier paid VAT on the rent of the building (or part of the building), and
- was unable to recover this VAT in full; and

(e) following the surrender—
- the occupier continues to occupy at least 80 per cent of the area previously occupied, and
- pays no VAT on the rent, or pays less than 50 per cent of the amount of VAT previously paid (comparing similar rental periods).

6.11.2 Examples of arrangements included in the listed scheme

Included are arrangements whereby:

- the occupier surrenders or terminates a taxable lease early and, despite the existence of an option to tax, the connected landlord makes a grant of a new lease that is exempt from VAT by reason of the option to tax disapplication rules
- the occupier surrenders or terminates a taxable lease early and, despite the existence of an option to tax, the connected landlord sells the building to the occupier as an exempt from VAT by reason of the option to tax disapplication rules
- the occupier, who is also a landlord further back in a chain of leases, arranges for all of the leases to be surrendered, leaving the occupier with the building (possibly paying a small amount of taxable ground rent to the ultimate freeholder).

Commentary—*De Voil Indirect Tax Service* **V5.213.**

7 HALLMARKED SCHEMES – DECIDING WHETHER YOU MUST NOTIFY

7.1 Decision chart

You are liable to notify use of a hallmarked scheme when all of the following tests are met:

Test	*Description*	*Further information*
1	You are a taxable person	Paragraph 3.2
2	You are a party to a scheme	Paragraphs 3.3 and 7.3
3	That scheme is not a listed scheme	Paragraph 3.4 and section 6
4	The main purpose, or one of the main purposes, of the scheme is for any person to obtain a tax advantage	Paragraph 7.4
5	A relevant event occurs	Paragraph 7.5
6	Your turnover exceeds either of the minimum thresholds	Paragraphs 7.6
7	Your scheme contains one or more hallmarks of avoidance	Paragraph 3.6 and section 10
8	You have not already notified HMRC, under the rules set out in this notice, that you are using the scheme	Paragraph 7.7
9	You have not been provided with a scheme number by someone who has registered the scheme with HMRC	Paragraph 7.8

Section 8 explains by when you must make your notification, the information it should contain and where to send it.

7.2 Protective notifications

If you are unsure whether you meet all of the relevant tests for notification, you may make a protective notification. In doing so you should explain which test, or tests, is causing you difficulty and why.

7.3 What is a scheme?

A scheme is any planned action entered into and includes any arrangements, transaction or series of transactions.

Engaging someone to ensure you claim all the input tax to which you are entitled, utilising an extra-statutory concession or trade facilitation measure open to all, using the grouping provisions, "opting to tax" a property, or negotiating a new partial exemption method are not in themselves schemes. This is the case even if they involve a hallmark of avoidance (see paragraph 3.6 and section 10). However, these features may form part of a scheme. You can find more on this and further examples in Section 11.

7.4 Schemes used for the purpose of obtaining a tax advantage

A scheme is potentially notifiable if the main purpose or one of the main purposes of it is for any person, who might not be you, to obtain a tax advantage. You may be liable to notify before that advantage is obtained (see paragraph 7.5 below for information on the events that trigger notification), or if you are not the person obtaining the advantage.

You are only required to notify if you are a party to the scheme. If the advantage accrues to another person and you are unaware that this will happen or of your role in the scheme then you are not required to notify - see paragraph 3.3.

7.4.1 What is a "tax advantage"?

A tax advantage happens when, as a result of the scheme:

(a) any taxable person accounts, or will account, for a lower net amount of VAT than would otherwise be the case in respect of a VAT return for any VAT accounting period starting on or after 1 August 2004;

(b) any taxable person obtains, or will obtain, in respect of any VAT accounting period starting on or after 1 August 2004, a VAT repayment that—
- he would not otherwise obtain,
- is larger than would otherwise be the case, or
- is earlier than would otherwise be the case;

(c) any taxable person recovers, or will recover, in respect of any VAT accounting period starting on or after 1 August 2004, input tax before the supplier has to account for the corresponding output tax, and the period between the two events is longer than would otherwise be the case;

(d) the amount of any taxable person's non-deductible VAT (see paragraph 7.4.2), in respect of any VAT accounting period starting on or after 1 August 2005, is less than would otherwise be the case; or

(e) in relation to any person who is not a taxable person, the amount of his non-refundable VAT (see paragraph 7.4.3), at any time on or after 1 August 2005, is less than would otherwise be the case.

7.4.2 Non-deductible VAT

VAT is non-deductible VAT when, in relation to a taxable person, it is:

- VAT that is input tax, but for which he is not entitled to credit; or
- VAT incurred by him that is not input tax and for which he is not entitled to a refund under any provision of VATA 1994.

VAT is incurred by a taxable person when it is:

- VAT on the supply to him of any goods or services (including VAT on reverse charges);
- VAT on the acquisition by him from another member state of any goods; or
- VAT paid or payable by him on the importation of any goods from a place outside the member states.

7.4.3 Non-refundable VAT

VAT is non-refundable VAT when, in relation to a person who is not a taxable person:

(a) it is:
- VAT on the supply to him of any goods or services;
- VAT on the acquisition by him from another member state of any goods; or
- VAT paid or payable by him on the importation of any goods from a place outside the member states; and

(b) it is not VAT that he is entitled to be refunded under any provision of VATA 1994.

7.4.4 Is the obtaining of a tax advantage a main purpose of the scheme?

There is no one factor that determines whether the obtaining of a tax advantage is the main, or one of the main, purposes of a scheme. All surrounding circumstances need to be taken into consideration. They include:

- the overall objectives of the arrangements and transactions (including the objectives of any wider corporate or VAT Group to which the parties to the scheme belong; and the objectives of any persons or businesses who control the parties), and
- whether the introduction of any unnecessary, complex or costly steps would have taken place were it not for the tax advantage that can be obtained.

In general, it is likely the main purpose test would be met where, more likely than not, were it not for any VAT advantage arising, the arrangements would either have not been implemented or would have been implemented in a different manner.

Similarly, where there are two or more ways of carrying out a genuine commercial objective and the choice is determined on grounds other than the potential VAT saving but a VAT advantage (when compared to adopting one or more of the alternatives) nevertheless arises; it is unlikely the main purpose test would be met.

7.5 Relevant events that trigger notification

The requirement for you to notify is triggered when one of the following events occurs *to you*:

- You show in a VAT return, in respect of any VAT accounting period starting on or after 1 August 2004 (or 1 August 2005 when the scheme involves only hallmark 8 (face-value vouchers) and no other hallmark), a higher or lower net amount of VAT than would be the case but for the scheme.
- You make a claim (such as by submitting a voluntary disclosure), in respect of any VAT accounting period starting on or after 1 August 2004 for which a VAT return has been submitted (or 1 August 2005 when the scheme involves only hallmark 8 (face-value vouchers) and no other hallmark), for the repayment of output tax over declared or input tax credit under claimed that is greater than would be the case but for the scheme.
- The amount of non-deductible VAT (see paragraph 7.5.1 below) you incur, in respect of any VAT accounting period starting on or after 1 August 2005, would have been higher but for the scheme.

7.5.1 Non-deductible VAT incurred

VAT is, or would have been, incurred by you when it is, or would have been:

- VAT on the supply to you of any goods or services (including VAT on reverse charges);
- VAT on the acquisition by you from another member state of any goods; or
- VAT paid or payable by you on the importation of any goods from a place outside the EU.

It is, or would have been, non-deductible VAT when it is, or would have been:

- VAT that is input tax, but for which you are not entitled to credit; or
- VAT that is not input tax, and for which you are not entitled to a refund under any provision of VATA 1994.

7.6 The minimum turnover thresholds

The turnover threshold is measured by reference to the *total* amount of *taxable and exempt* supplies made by—

- you; or
- where you are a member of a corporate group, *the whole group*, made up of the ultimate holding company (or entity) and all its subsidiaries, including you. For this purpose UK company law definitions used for preparing group accounts apply (section 259 of the Companies Act 1985). As a result the group will normally be made up of all the companies shown as subsidiaries in the ultimate parent's consolidated group accounts, plus any companies that are excluded from the consolidation but are subsidiaries for UK company law purposes.

For the purpose of calculating turnover, intra-corporate group transactions are included. However, intra-VAT Group transactions are ignored.

7.6.1 The threshold

Your turnover exceeds the minimum threshold when the total amount of *taxable and exempt* supplies made by you (or the wider corporate group as explained above) is, or is greater than—

(a) £10 million in the year immediately prior to the VAT return period that triggers notification (see paragraph 7.5); or

(b) the appropriate proportion of £10 million in the VAT return period immediately prior to the VAT return period that triggers notification. (For example, the "appropriate proportion" is one twelfth of £10 million (ie, £833,334) where the VAT return period is one month; and one quarter of £10 million (ie, £2.5 million) where the VAT return period is three months.)

7.6.2 Disaggregation

Should we find that a taxable person's business has been split in an attempt to avoid the requirement to make a notification, we will use our powers to direct that the separate entities be treated as one. If it is found later that other entities should have been included in that direction, a supplementary direction can be made to include them. The effect a supplementary direction has on the timing of a notification is explained in paragraph 8.1.2.

7.7 What if I have already notified HM Revenue & Customs?

You need only notify a scheme once.

If you enter into new arrangements that are structured in the same way as a previously notified scheme you need not notify these new arrangements. (By "structured in the same way", we mean that the details of the scheme required to be notified under paragraph 8.4 and 8.6 are the same. The parties to the scheme and the hallmarks may be different.)

However, if you enter into new arrangements that are structured in a materially different way to a previously notified scheme, you will, subject to the necessary conditions being met (such as the turnover threshold, etc), have to notify use of that scheme irrespective of whether the hallmarks are the same.

For hallmarked schemes that become listed schemes, see paragraph 4.4.2.

7.8 Hallmarked schemes already registered with HM Revenue & Customs

You are not required to notify us about your use of a hallmarked scheme if someone has registered it with us under the Voluntary Registration Scheme (see section 9), and they have advised you of the scheme reference number we have allocated to it (prefixed by the letters VRS).

In addition, there is no requirement to enter the reference number on a VAT return or to tell us in advance of any enquiries we wish to make that you hold the number. You should, however, keep a record of when you were advised of it.

We do not publish details of the schemes that have been registered with us, or who have registered them.

Commentary—*De Voil Indirect Tax Service* **V5.213.**

8 HALLMARKED SCHEMES – HOW TO NOTIFY HMRC

8.1 By what date must I notify HMRC?

Your notification must be made to HMRC within 30 days of:

- in the case of the net amount of VAT shown in a VAT return being different to what would otherwise be the case (see the first bullet at paragraph 7.5), the due date for making the return;
- in the case of a claim being made that is greater than would otherwise be the case (see the second bullet at paragraph 7.5), the making of the claim; or
- in the case of the amount of your non-deductible VAT in respect of a VAT accounting period being less than would otherwise be the case (see the third bullet at paragraph 7.5), the due date for making a return in respect of that accounting period.

For examples of when a notification is due see paragraphs 5.1.3 to 5.1.4.

8.1.1 Early notifications

HMRC will accept early notifications, such as before the relevant event has taken place, provided the scheme has been implemented.

8.1.2 Directions that taxpayers are treated as one

Where HMRC issue a direction that a number of taxpayers should be treated as one (see paragraph 7.6.2), the due date is determined by reference to the first relevant event (see paragraph 7.5) that takes place following the issue of the direction.

Commentary—*De Voil Indirect Tax Service* **V5.213.**

8.2 How do I notify HMRC?

The following rule has the force of law

You must notify us either in writing or by email to the relevant address given at paragraph 8.7. The notification should be prominently headed:

- Disclosure of use of hallmarked scheme – Notification under paragraph 6(3) of Sch 11A to VATA 1994.

and give your:

- business name (if you are the representative member of a VAT group, notifying as a result of a group member being involved in a notifiable scheme, also tell us the name of the member);
- address; and
- VAT registration number.

Commentary—*De Voil Indirect Tax Service* **V5.213.**

8.3 What information must I provide?

When notifying a hallmarked scheme you *must* provide *all* the following information, to the extent that it is known to you, and explain what information you are unable to provide and why—

- information demonstrating how the scheme works – see paragraph 8.4;
- a statement as to which hallmark or hallmarks are included in or associated with the scheme you are notifying to us – see paragraph 8.5; and
- a statement as to which specific legislation you rely upon for the tax advantage – see paragraph 8.6.

For joint notifications, see paragraph 3.3.4.

Commentary—*De Voil Indirect Tax Service* **V5.213.**

8.4 The workings of the scheme

To make a valid notification you must provide sufficient information to show:

- how the scheme works; and

- how the involvement of any party to the scheme contributes to the obtaining of the tax advantage, including, to the extent that it is material to the obtaining of the tax advantage:
- a description of each arrangement, transaction or series of transactions – see paragraph 8.4.1;
- their sequence – see paragraph 8.4.2;
- their timing, or the intervals between them – see paragraph 8.4.3; and
- the goods or services involved – see paragraph 8.4.1.

You are *not required* to quantify the amount or expected amount of the tax advantage.

8.4.1 Describing the scheme

You must provide sufficient information so that HMRC can understand how the tax advantage is obtained. The degree of information to be provided will vary from scheme to scheme and the extent to which you have knowledge of other parties' intentions and circumstances.

For most notifications we recommend you include, along with the description of how the beneficiary obtains the tax advantage:

- a summary of the scheme (ie what the beneficiaries' tax position would be without the scheme, and whether the scheme provides them with an absolute saving or a deferral of a tax burden); and
- a diagrammatic representation of its structure (showing the participants, transaction flows, and so on.).

The scheme description need only provide generic information; you do not need to provide the detail that is specific to your circumstances. For example, a step of the scheme could be described as, "building is leased to Company A" rather than, "1 High Street is leased to Bank plc." It follows that you do not need to submit copies of contracts and other documents. However, if you find it easier to explain the scheme by referring to the specific detail of your case, you may do so. You may also submit supplementary documentation if you wish.

Remember, to the extent that it is known to you, you will need to explain how the involvement of any party to the scheme contributes to the obtaining of the tax advantage. In the example given, you should go on and say whether the lease is taxed and, if so, whether any of the tax charged is recoverable by Company A/Bank plc.

8.4.2 Sequence

Where the order of the arrangements or transactions is critical to the workings of the scheme, this should be explained. You should make it clear what the precise sequence is. We recommend listing these as "Step 1", "Step 2", etc.

8.4.3 Timing and interval

Where the timing of, or interval between, arrangements or transactions are critical to the workings of the scheme, this should be explained.

For example, you should explain if the interval between transactions are due to take place within a short period of time of each other to take advantage of a VAT rule; over a long period to cause a VAT "drip feed" effect; or timed to miss or bridge accounting periods.

Commentary—*De Voil Indirect Tax Service* **V5.213.**

8.5 Declaration of hallmarks

This need not be a standalone part of your notification; it can be included as part of your general explanation of the working of the scheme. If you are unsure whether a feature is a hallmark, say why you are unsure.

8.6 The statutory provision

You must let us know the law that you believe gives rise to the tax advantage (see paragraph 7.4.1) derived from use of the scheme. This could be:

- UK law;

- the law of another country, such as where you rely on a different tax treatment; or
- EU law, such as where you rely on the principle of "direct effect" (ie that EU law has effect, irrespective of the provisions of UK VAT law).

Commentary—*De Voil Indirect Tax Service* **V5.213.**

8.7 Where do I send my notification?

The following rule has the force of law

> Your must send your notification to either of the following addresses:
>
> Post to:
>
> Anti-Avoidance Group (Intelligence)
> VAT Avoidance Disclosures Unit
> HM Revenue & Customs
> CTIAA Intelligence S0528
> PO Box 194
> Bootle L69 9AA
>
> Or e-mail to:
>
> vat avoidance.disclosures.bst@hmrc.gsi.gov.uk

8.8 What if I send my notification to another address?

If you send your notification to an address other than those given in paragraph 8.7 (for example to another office or the VAT Written Enquiries Team), you will not have made a proper notification. Failure to make a proper notification will make you liable to a penalty as explained in Section 12.

8.9 How will HMRC deal with my notification?

We will acknowledge receipt of all notifications received at the addresses given in paragraph 8.7. However, the acknowledgement is not a confirmation that you have met your statutory obligation.

If your notification does not contain all the information set out in paragraphs 8.3 to 8.6, you may be contacted and asked to provide the required information or explain why you are unable to provide it. Only when the information (to the extent that you are able) has been provided will your obligation be discharged. If this is not done within the time limit for making a notification, you will be liable to a penalty as explained in Section 12.

Once the required information has been provided, we will consider whether we wish to investigate further at that time - see paragraph 3.10. If we do not contact you, this does not mean the arrangements are acceptable to us.

If we are already investigating your use of the notified scheme, that action will continue as appropriate.

Commentary—*De Voil Indirect Tax Service* **V5.213.**

9 HALLMARKED SCHEMES – VOLUNTARY REGISTRATION SCHEME

9.1 Why use the Voluntary Registration Scheme?

The principal objective of the rules for hallmarked schemes is to allow HMRC to find out about new and innovative schemes. The Voluntary Registration Scheme allows us to learn about these schemes whilst reducing the burdens on business - they are exempted from having to notify us of their use of the scheme (see paragraph 7.8).

The Voluntary Registration Scheme does not exempt a person from notifying a listed scheme.

9.2 Is it an approval system?

No. Acceptance of an application to register the details of a hallmarked scheme does not mean that we agree with the analysis that has been provided.

9.3 How do I know whether a scheme has already been registered?

We do not publish details of schemes that have been registered with us. If you apply to register a scheme that is the same as, or a variant of, a scheme that somebody else has already registered with us, we will issue you with your own unique reference number.

9.4 Who can register a scheme?

Anyone, including advisers, promoters and trade bodies, can apply to register a scheme; you need not have devised or marketed it yourself.

However, in some cases we may decide not to issue you with a reference number (see paragraph 9.9).

9.5 How do I register a scheme?

You should write or send an email to the address shown in paragraph 8.7, giving us the details of the scheme you wish to register. Please make it clear in your notification that you are applying for a reference number under the Voluntary Registration Scheme.

9.6 Information to be provided

When applying to register a hallmarked scheme, you *must* provide the same information that anyone required to make a notification would. The information required is explained in paragraphs 8.3 to 8.6.

You can apply to register variations of a scheme at the same time, although we may decide to issue different reference numbers for each variation.

9.7 Will HMRC acknowledge my application?

Yes, we will acknowledge your application upon receipt.

9.8 How quickly are reference numbers issued?

Subject to paragraph 9.9 below, we aim to examine applications and issue reference numbers (prefixed by the letters VRS) within ten working days of receipt.

9.9 Will a reference number always be issued?

No, the issue of a reference number is discretionary. Whilst we will normally issue reference numbers in relation to schemes, whether we agree that they work or not, we will not normally issue a reference number in relation to applications that are unclear or ambiguous, or appear to cover several different schemes rather than just one. We will also not issue a reference number for a scheme that appears to be an existing listed scheme.

9.10 What happens if a VRS reference number is not issued?

The normal rules for hallmarked schemes apply – see section 7.

Commentary—*De Voil Indirect Tax Service* **V5.213.**

10 THE HALLMARKS

10.1 Descriptions of the "hallmarks"

The hallmarks are described in paragraphs 10.2 to 10.8 below.

These descriptions are intended to help you decide if they appear in the scheme you are using, so that you will know whether you have to notify your use of the scheme to us. The descriptions are not a substitute for the descriptions contained in the law (see paragraph 1.4). It is your responsibility to decide whether or not a particular hallmark occurs in your scheme.

10.1.1 Connected persons

For the purposes of the hallmark descriptions a person is connected with another where:

- one of them is an undertaking in relation to which the other is a group undertaking as defined by s 259 of the Companies Act 1985 (essentially, one is the parent or subsidiary undertaking of the other, or both are subsidiaries of a common parent undertaking); or
- both of them are connected to the same trust.

A person is connected to a trust where he:

- is the settlor of the trust, or a trustee or beneficiary of it; or
- holds any shares in a company in accordance with the terms of the trust, or is a person on whose behalf such shares are held.

10.2 Confidentiality condition agreements

There is a "confidentiality condition" hallmark when there is an agreement that prevents or limits a person from giving others details of how a scheme gives rise to a tax advantage (see paragraph 7.4.1).

The hallmark is aimed at confidentiality conditions that are intended to protect the competitive advantage of a promoter or creator of the scheme over other promoters, say because it is an innovative scheme, and is often made before a potential user has the full details of the scheme explained to them. It, therefore, applies where:

- a specific condition of confidentiality is imposed; or
- a client specifically undertakes (either in writing or verbally) not to reveal details of how a particular scheme gives rise to a tax advantage.

10.2.1 General confidentiality clauses

It is standard practice for advisers to include a "general confidentiality condition" within their terms of engagement, prohibiting the client from passing on advice to third parties.

You need not regard a general confidentiality clause as being a confidentiality condition hallmark if it is simply imposed in relation to all advice, not merely the scheme in question. However, it is regarded as a hallmark where:

- it is introduced specifically in order to prevent or limit a person from revealing details of how a particular scheme gives rise to a tax advantage; or
- it is specifically drawn to a client's attention by an adviser when introducing a scheme to the client in order to prevent or limit him from revealing details of how the particular scheme gives rise to a tax advantage.

10.3 Agreements to share a tax advantage

There is a "sharing a tax advantage" hallmark when there is an agreement that the tax advantage (see paragraph 7.4.1) accruing from the scheme be shared, to any extent, between the person to whom it accrues and the promoter or any other person who is a party to the scheme.

A "promoter" is anyone who, in the course of their trade, profession or business of providing taxation services, designs or sells the arrangements entered into.

10.4 Contingent fee agreements

There is a "contingent fee" hallmark when there is an agreement that payment to a promoter of a scheme is partly or wholly contingent on the tax advantage (see paragraph 7.4.1) accruing from use of the scheme.

A "promoter" is anyone who, in the course of their trade, profession or business of providing taxation services, designs or sells the arrangements entered into.

10.5 Prepayments between connected persons

There is a "prepayment" hallmark when the operation of a scheme involves a prepayment being made for supplies between connected persons (see paragraph 10.1.1). The prepayment may be of any amount and the time between the prepayment and the actual provision of the goods or services may be of any duration.

10.6 Funding by loans, share subscriptions or subscriptions in securities

This hallmark applies when a supply of goods or services made between two connected persons is funded (in whole or in part):

- by a loan between connected persons;
- by one person subscribing for shares in another with whom he is connected; or
- by one person subscribing in securities issued by another with whom he is connected.

"Connected persons" is explained at paragraph 10.1.1.

10.7 Off-shore loops

This hallmark applies when certain exported services (which allow the exporter to recover related input tax) are used to provide other services to UK persons, and these 'imported' services are not subject to VAT.

In detail it applies when:

(a) a person makes a supply of services covered by—
- art 3(a) of the VAT (Input Tax) (Specified Supplies) Order 1999 (exempt financial and insurance services supplied to a person who belongs outside the member states of the EU),
- art 3(b) of the VAT (Input Tax) (Specified Supplies) Order 1999 (services directly linked to the export of goods to a place outside the member states), insofar as they are supplies of a description falling within item 2 of Group 5 of Sch 9 to the VATA 1994 (the making of any advance or any credit),
- art 3(c) of the VAT (Input Tax) (Specified Supplies) Order 1999 (the provision of certain intermediary insurance or financial services), or
- paras 1 to 8 of Sch 5 to VATA 1994 (services supplied where received), and the recipient belongs in a country, other than the Isle of Man, which is not a member state of the EU; and

(b) the service is used or intended to be used, in whole or in part, directly or indirectly, in making to a person belonging in the UK a supply which is:
- zero-rated,
- exempt, or
- treated as made in another country (and not the UK) by virtue of s 7(10) of VATA 1994.

10.8 Property transactions between connected persons

This hallmark applies when:

(a) a grant, which is not a zero-rated grant, is made of:
- any interest in, right over or licence to occupy land, or
- in relation to land in Scotland, any personal right to call for or be granted any such interest or right;

(b) the grantor or grantee of the interest or right is a person who cannot recover input tax in full;

(c) a work of any construction, alteration, demolition, repair, maintenance or civil engineering has been or is to be carried out on the land; and

(d) the grant is made to a person connected with the grantor (see paragraph 10.1.1).

10.9 Issue of face-value vouchers

This hallmark applies when:

(a) face-value vouchers are issued for consideration; and

(b) either—

- the issuer does not expect at least 75 per cent of the vouchers to be redeemed within three years of them being issued, or
- whatever the expected redemption rate, the vouchers are issued to a connected person (see paragraph 10.1.1) outside of any VAT group to which the issuer belongs.

10.9.1 Expected redemption rates

The expected redemption rate is measured by reference to the face value of the vouchers taken together, for example:

- A business issues £1m worth of vouchers and expects £900,000 worth of those vouchers to be redeemed. That is a 90 per cent expected redemption rate, irrespective of whether the expectation is actually met.
- A business issues vouchers that can be partly redeemed, such as may happen with certain electronic vouchers, and expects 100 per cent of them to be redeemed but on average only 30 per cent of the value to be redeemed. That would be a 30 per cent expected redemption rate, again irrespective of whether the expectation is actually met.

Commentary—*De Voil Indirect Tax Service* **V5.213.**

11 HALLMARKED SCHEMES—FREQUENTLY ASKED QUESTIONS

11.1 Use of extra statutory concessions

Q: I am using an extra statutory concession (ESC). When I use the ESC I could be seen as obtaining a tax advantage. Do I have to notify HMRC under the new rules?

A: No. An ESC is not, in itself, a scheme. It is a remission of revenue that allows relief in specific sets of circumstances to all businesses falling within the relevant conditions. It is authorised when strict application of the law would create an undue disadvantage or the effect would not be the one intended. However, you should remember that if an ESC is used as part of a tax avoidance scheme that use is likely to be challenged by HMRC. HMRC may also consider withdrawing or restricting the ESC's application.

11.2 Use of partial exemption special methods

Q: I have negotiated a new partial exemption special method (PESM). It gives me a higher rate of input tax recovery compared with my previous method. Do I notify HMRC under the new rules?

A: No, a PESM is not a scheme. When a PESM is agreed with HMRC it is a fair and reasonable estimate of input tax recovery.

11.3 Changes to VAT group structures

Q: On occasions we add or remove a company from our VAT Group. Changes to our group generally affect the amount of VAT declared by the group on its returns. Do we notify HMRC under these rules?

A: No. Making such a change does not, in itself, constitute a scheme as it can only be done on application to HMRC.

11.4 VAT audits

Q: I do not have the staff or expertise to check all my purchase invoices to make sure I claim all the input tax I am entitled to. I am therefore going to engage someone to do this for me, who charges a fee contingent on the amount of VAT claimed. This is not being done in conjunction with any other arrangements or transactions. Contingent fees are a hallmark of tax avoidance. Do I notify HMRC under the new rules?

A: No. Simply claiming all input tax to which you are entitled is not a "scheme". You are not implementing arrangements or transactions to gain a tax advantage. You are simply seeking to recover the correct amount of tax.

11.5 Identifying use of hallmarks

Q: I am using a scheme, and am not sure whether it contains any hallmarks of avoidance. Should I notify my use of this scheme to protect myself from the possible imposition of a penalty at a later date?

A: You may make a protective notification if you wish. There is further information on this at paragraph 7.2. Remember, however, the presence of a hallmark of avoidance is not the only test for having to notify a scheme. A scheme is notifiable only if *all* the tests in paragraph 7.1 are met.

If your turnover is below £10 million, for example, you do not have to notify us.

11.6 Subsidiaries funded by share capital or loans

Q: My Company is forming a subsidiary company that will supply it with goods and services. The subsidiary will be funded by share capital or a loan. For the purposes of the law we are connected persons. This is the funding by share subscriptions or loans hallmark. I will have to investigate whether this results in a tax advantage. It is difficult for me to do this, so to be safe should I notify HMRC under the new rules?

A: Not unless all the tests listed in paragraph 7.1 are met. In relation to the tax advantage test, the obtaining a tax advantage has to be a main purpose. The presence of a tax advantage does not automatically cause the test to be met.

12 PENALTIES

Commentary—*De Voil Indirect Tax Service* **V5.213.**

12.1 The penalties

The penalties for failing to make a full notification to us at the correct time are—

- 15 per cent of the VAT saved (see paragraph 12.2 below) for listed schemes; and
- £5,000 for hallmarked schemes.

12.2 What is the VAT saved?

The VAT saved by a taxable person is the aggregate of:

- the amount by which the amount of VAT he has shown as payable in relevant VAT returns is less than the amount that he would have shown were it not for the scheme;
- the amount by which the amount of VAT he has shown as repayable in relevant VAT returns exceeds the amount that he would have shown were it not for the scheme;
- the amount by which the amount he has claimed (for example in a voluntary disclosure) exceeds the amount that he would have claimed were it not for the scheme; and,
- the amount by which the amount of non-deductible VAT (see paragraph 7.4.2) that he would have incurred were it not for the scheme exceeds that which has been incurred (to the extent that it is not already represented in the calculation).

12.2.1 Relevant VAT returns

Relevant VAT Returns begin with that in which a tax advantage (see paragraph 7.4.1) first arose and end with the VAT Return covering:

- the date on which the person complied with the requirement to notify; or, if earlier,
- the VAT Return for the period immediately before HMRC notify the penalty assessment to the taxpayer.

If it is unclear which VAT returns are to be used for the calculation, we will use best judgement to determine which apply and advise you accordingly.

12.3 Will a penalty always be issued?

No, there are a number of circumstances where a penalty will not be issued. We will not issue a penalty if you:

- can demonstrate that you had a reasonable excuse for failing to notify us;

- as a result of the actions which triggered your requirement to notify you:
- are convicted of an offence under VATA 1994 or other legislation; or
- are assessed for a penalty for conduct involving dishonesty under the rules relating to VAT evasion.

Civil investigations into VAT evasion are undertaken in accordance with Code of Practice 9, which can be accessed at: www.hmrc.gov.uk/leaflets/c11.htm

Commentary—*De Voil Indirect Tax Service* **V5.335.**

12.4 Reasonable excuse

No penalty will be payable if you are able to satisfy us, or on appeal, the VAT and Duties Tribunal, that there is a reasonable excuse for your failure to notify us that you are using a scheme. Notice 700/42 "Misdeclaration penalty and repeated misdeclaration penalty" gives more guidance on the term "reasonable excuse". If reasonable excuse does not apply, there may still be grounds for mitigation.

Commentary—*De Voil Indirect Tax Service* **V5.335.**

12.5 Mitigation

A penalty can be reduced if there are mitigating circumstances that fall short of a reasonable excuse.

The law does not define the grounds for mitigation but it specifically *excludes*.

- your lack of funds to pay any tax or penalty due;
- the fact that little or no tax has been lost; and
- the fact that you acted in good faith.

When we consider mitigation we will consider all the facts that led to the failure to notify us. The amount of mitigation allowed will depend on the specific circumstances of your case.

Commentary—*De Voil Indirect Tax Service* **V5.334.**

12.6 Issuing a penalty assessment

If you are liable to a penalty we will notify you in writing of your liability to the penalty and explain:

- the amount of the penalty;
- the reasons for the imposition of the penalty;
- how the penalty has been calculated; and
- the amount of any mitigation allowed.

An assessment for a penalty that is due will be issued even if, before that happens, the taxable person concerned ceases to be a party to the scheme that gave rise to the requirement to notify. Any penalty due is treated as recoverable as if it were VAT due from the assessed person. The penalty cannot be claimed as input tax.

Commentary—*De Voil Indirect Tax Service* **V5.333.**

12.7 Time period for issuing a penalty

No assessment to a penalty can be issued more than two years after we had sufficient facts to enable us to issue one.

13 RECONSIDERATIONS AND APPEALS

13.1 What if I disagree with a penalty or direction?

If you disagree with:

- your liability to a penalty;
- the amount of a penalty; or
- a direction issued in the circumstances explained in paragraphs 4.3.2 and 7.6.2,

you may ask for a reconsideration to be undertaken or appeal to the VAT and Duties Tribunal.

13.2 Reconsiderations

You should write to us within 30 days of the date of the letter in which we notified our decision to you, and ask for a reconsideration to be undertaken if you think that:

– you have a reasonable excuse for the failure to notify (see paragraph 0); or
– there are mitigating circumstances which warrant reduction of the penalty (see paragraph 12.5).

The notification letter will give the address to which you should write asking for a reconsideration to be undertaken.

13.3 Appeals

You also have the right to appeal to an independent VAT and duties tribunal.

You can find further information about appeals and reviews on the HMRC website (www.hmrc.gov.uk/complaints-appeals/how-to-appeal/) or you can phone the number on the letter telling you of the decision you disagree with. You can find out more about tribunals on the Tribunals Service website (www.justice.gov.uk/tribunals/tax) or you can telephone them on 0845 223 8080.

The tribunal can consider whether there is a reasonable excuse and can also increase as well as decrease any amount of mitigation that we have allowed.

Commentary—*De Voil Indirect Tax Service* **V5.262, V5.4.**

700/9
TRANSFER OF A BUSINESS AS A GOING CONCERN

December 2012

This notice cancels and replaces the April 2008 edition. The main change is the inclusion of a link to form VAT 68 "Request for transfer of a registration number" in new section 11.

1 INTRODUCTION

1.1 What is this notice about?

This notice explains whether the transfer of a business should be treated as a "Transfer of a business as a going concern" (TOGC) for VAT purposes, or not. It also explains the VAT treatment in each circumstance. It is intended to help you ensure that the correct amount of VAT, when chargeable, is correctly accounted for and paid.

You should read this notice if you are selling or otherwise transferring a business, or part of a business. It will also be of interest to you if you are acquiring a business. In certain circumstances special TOGC rules apply and the sale will not be treated as a supply for VAT purposes, so no VAT should be charged. The sales affected will typically be those where a business is sold as a "going concern" or where the sale is of part of a business which can be operated separately.

It is important to note that the transfer of a business which does not qualify to be treated as a TOGC may very well still render the purchaser liable for VAT registration. Further information on this is contained in Notice 700/1 Should I be registered for VAT?

The law refers to the transferor (the person selling the business) and the transferee (the person buying the business). To avoid confusion this notice refers to these as the "seller" and the "purchaser" respectively.

This notice and others mentioned are available both on paper and on our internet website at www.hmrc.gov.uk.

1.1.1 Changes from previous edition of this notice

This revised notice replaces the April 2008 edition. It has been revised to include an example of the VAT 68 form – Transfer of a Going Concern.

You can access details of any changes to this notice since it was published either on our website at www.hmrc.gov.uk or by phoning the VAT Helpline on 0845 010 9000.

1.1.2 Use of examples in this notice

It should be noted that in the interests of readability it has been decided to only include examples of scenarios which help to illustrate a point or an area of potential confusion. We are aware that many of the examples of transfer set out in this notice are those involving property, premises, or property rental business whereas there are not many on other trades or situations. This reflects a certain level of complexity in these types of business that continue to give rise to issues and requests for clarification and guidance. In our view the inclusion of all permutations of transfers by all the different types of business would be impractical and make this notice excessively large and less user friendly for the range of customers that it is intended to inform.

It is important that each transfer is considered individually for TOGC on the basis of its facts and circumstances so a "one size fits all" approach is not appropriate. Further examples of the application of the TOGC conditions are contained in HM Revenue & Customs (HMRC) internal guidance which is accessible through our website.

1.2 What is a Transfer of a business as a going concern (TOGC) for VAT purposes?

Normally the sale of the assets of a VAT registered or VAT registerable business will be subject to VAT at the appropriate rate. A transfer of a business as a going concern for VAT purposes (TOGC) however is the sale of a business including assets which must be treated as a matter of law, as "neither a supply of goods nor a supply of services" by virtue of meeting certain conditions. Where the sale meets the conditions then the supply is outside the scope of VAT and therefore VAT is not chargeable.

It is important to be aware that the TOGC rules are mandatory and not optional. So it is important to establish from the outset whether the sale is or is not a TOGC.

The main UK law concerning TOGCs is The VAT (Special Provisions) Order 1995 (SI 1995/1268 Art 5). The UK law is derived from Articles 19 and 29 of the Principal VAT Directive (Directive 2006/112/EC). But there are several other legal provisions relating to TOGC. These are sections 44, 49, 94(6) and para 8 Schedule 4 VAT Act 1994. Extracts of UK VAT law are shown at section 10.

We see the main conditions as being:

- the assets must be sold as part of the transfer of a "business" as a "going concern"
- the assets are to be used by the purchaser with the intention of carrying on the same kind of "business" as the seller (but not necessarily identical)
- where the seller is a taxable person, the purchaser must be a taxable person already or become one as the result of the transfer
- in respect of land which would be standard rated if it were supplied, the purchaser must notify HMRC that he has opted to tax the land by the relevant date, and must notify the seller that their option has not been disapplied by the same date
- where only part of the "business" is sold it must be capable of operating separately
- there must not be a series of immediately consecutive transfers of "business"

Our view of what these mean in practice as well as other rules and effects of TOGC treatment are dealt with in this Notice and in our Internal Guidance.

Note: For the purposes of this paragraph the word "business" has the meaning set out in section 94 VAT Act 1994 and "going concern" has the meaning that at the point in time to which the description applies, the business is "live or operating" and "has all parts and features necessary to keep it in operation, as distinct from its being only an inert aggregation of assets". (However also see sub-paragraph 2.3.1).

1.3 What is not a TOGC?

Examples of situations that do not fall under the TOGC provisions include;

- There is no transfer of a business as a going concern through changes in the constitution of a partnership.
- If there has been no transfer of assets there is nothing to which the TOGC provisions can apply.
- When there is a transfer of shares in a limited company from one person to another, the assets still belong to the limited company. Thus there is no change in the ownership of the assets so no supplies to which the TOGC provisions could apply.

- Where a VAT registered farmer transfers his business as a "going concern" to a farmer who is certified under the Agricultural Flat Rate Scheme there can be no TOGC for VAT since the purchaser is not registered or registerable for VAT (see notice 700/46).

If you are registered for VAT but you have not yet made taxable supplies, the transfer of your business might not be the transfer of a "going concern". However, where sufficient preparatory work has been undertaken prior to making taxable supplies there may be a business capable of being transferred as a going concern. Section 6 gives examples of transfers of property, some of which are transfers of businesses as a going concern.

1.4 Business assets

For there to be a transfer capable of being treated as a TOGC it must include the transfer of business assets. Business assets can include stock in trade, machinery, goodwill, premises and fixtures and fittings. Where the assets are transferred from one person to another the transfer may, subject to the meeting of the conditions, be covered by the TOGC provisions. For TOGC provisions to apply it is important that the assets, whatever they are and however many are to be transferred, put the purchaser in possession of a business, rather than simply assets. The assets of a business may be transferred in a number of situations. Below are examples of common transfers, but the list is not exhaustive:

- the assets may be bought by another person and the existing business may cease to trade
- the existing owner may die or retire and the business assets be taken over by another person
- part of an existing business may be sold to another person and
- the assets may be transferred to a new legal entity, for example, a sole proprietor may take on a partner, or form a limited company.

1.5 Why have the TOGC rules?

The TOGC provisions are intended to simplify accounting for VAT when a business changes hands. They have the following main purposes:

- to relieve the buyer of a business from the burden of funding any VAT on the purchase. Thereby helping businesses by improving their cash flow and avoiding the need to separately value assets which may be liable at different rates or are exempt and which have been sold as a whole, and;
- to protect Government revenue by removing a charge to tax and entitlement to input tax where the output tax may not be paid to HMRC. For example, where a business charges tax, which is claimed as input tax by the new business but never declared or paid by the old business.

2 HOW TO APPLY THE TOGC RULES

2.1 What is this section about?

This section deals with the special rules which apply to a transfer of a business so that the transfer of some, or all of the assets, should be treated as a TOGC and not as a taxable supply.

2.2 Why it is important to get the tax treatment right

The TOGC rules are compulsory. You cannot choose to 'opt out'. So, it is very important that you establish from the outset whether the business is being sold as a TOGC. Incorrect treatment could result in corrective action by HMRC which may attract a penalty and or interest.

If all the conditions in paragraphs 1.2 and 2.3 are met, the TOGC rules apply and VAT must not be charged or accounted for on the assets transferred (except, in certain circumstances, on the premises ie, land and/or property used in the business. Details of the circumstances in which you must charge VAT on the premises are set out in paragraph 2.4).

If VAT is charged when it should not have been the—

- purchaser will not be able to reclaim this amount as input tax, because there was no taxable supply and
- seller will have to cancel any tax invoice issued and provide the new owner with a refund of the VAT charged. Normally this will be by issue of a credit note or document giving similar effect.

The relevant law is reproduced at section 10.

2.3 What conditions need to be met to treat a transfer as a TOGC?

If all of the conditions listed at paragraph 1.2 above and expanded below are met, the transfer of the assets of the business, other than premises, is a TOGC. It is not a taxable supply and you, as the seller, must not charge VAT. Paragraph 2.4 explains whether you need to charge tax on the transfer of premises.

2.3.1 Business Activities

The effect of the transfer must be to put the new owner in possession of a business which can be operated as such. The term 'business' means a business activity recognised as such in VAT law. For example, some of the activities of charities or local authorities are not considered to be business (see Notice 700 The VAT Guide for more information). A sale of "capital assets" is not in itself a transfer of a business as a going concern. However, if the effect of the sale is to put the purchaser in possession of a business, it is a TOGC, even if the assets are transferred on different dates.

The business, or part business, must be a "going concern" at the time of the transfer. It can still be a "going concern" even though it is unprofitable, or is trading under the control of a liquidator or administrative receiver, or a trustee in bankruptcy, or an administrator appointed under the Insolvency Act 1986.

2.3.2 Use of Assets – Same kind of business

The assets you are transferring must be intended for use by the new owner in carrying on the same kind of business. If the purchaser intends to use the assets to carry on a different kind of business you must charge VAT in the normal way.

If the purchaser intends in due course to carry on a different kind of business using the assets purchased, the sale may still be a TOGC if the purchaser continues the old business initially.

The test is whether the purchaser intends to carry on the business he has bought. This test does not lend itself to a set time-span, because 'continuation of a business' can vary between different types of activity.

See section 7 for examples.

2.3.3 Consecutive transfers of business

There must not be a series of immediately consecutive transfers of the business. Where A sells its assets to B who immediately sells those assets on to C, because B has not carried on the business the TOGC provisions do not apply to any of the transactions. This means that the sales take their normal VAT liability (taxable or exempt). Such immediate transfers often occur in property transactions where A contracts to sell property to B, and B "sub-sells" the property to C with both contracts being completed by a single transfer from A to C. Different rules apply in Scotland, however, to the transfer of a property rental business. Under Scottish law the disposition of the 'ownership of the property' ('dominium utile') may been seen to be direct from A to C, and the TOGC provisions may apply, subject to meeting the other conditions in this paragraph and paragraph 2.4.

2.3.4 VAT registration

Where the seller of the business or part of the business is registered for VAT, the purchaser must be registered or at the date of the transfer be required to be registered for VAT because all of the conditions for compulsory registration are met, or have been accepted for voluntary registration. This condition is not met if the purchaser is not registered and is not required to be registered for VAT. This could be either because:

(a) at the date the transfer takes place, the purchaser does not expect the value of their taxable supplies in the next 12 months to be above the deregistration limit, for example the purchaser intends to reduce trading by introducing shorter working hours; or

(b) the seller was not required to be registered but was registered voluntarily at the date of the transfer. Thus, at that date, the purchaser is not required to register because the value of their taxable supplies in the 12 month period then ended is not above the registration limit.

In such circumstances, unless the purchaser has been accepted for voluntary registration, the conditions for the transfer to be treated as a TOGC are not met and the sale takes its normal liability. Where only part of the business is being transferred, the purchaser must look at the turnover of this part to determine whether he must be registered. Further details about registration can be found in "Notice 700/1 *Should I be registered for VAT?*" The supplement to "Notice 700/1 *Should I be registered for VAT?*" gives details of registration limits.

2.3.5 Seller not VAT registered

There can be a TOGC where the seller is not registered for VAT. For example, because the seller is trading below the registration limit or making wholly exempt supplies. A TOGC is possible in both these circumstances. Thus the sale of a non-VAT registered business which includes trading stock, the value of which might otherwise take the trader over the registration limit, will not do so because it can be treated as a TOGC and therefore not a supply.

However, where the transfer of assets is a relevant supply for VAT registration purposes, the unregistered seller will have to register and account for VAT on the transfer of assets. Further information about relevant supplies can be found in Notice 700/1 Should I be registered for VAT?

2.3.6 No significant break in trading

There must be no significant break in the normal trading pattern before or immediately after the transfer. The 'break in trade' needs to be considered in the context of the type of business concerned, this might vary between different types of trade or activity. For example, HMRC do not consider that where a 'seasonal' business has closed for the 'off-season' as normal at the time of sale, that there has necessarily been a break in trade. In addition, a short period of closure that does not significantly disrupt the existing trading pattern, for example, for redecoration, will not prevent the business from being transferred as a TOGC.

2.3.7 Transfer of part of your business

If you are transferring only part of your business, that part must be able to operate alone. It does not matter whether it will, in fact, be operated separately from any other businesses the purchaser carries on. An 'in-house' function is not a 'business' for TOGC condition purposes when it only operates internally. The assets of the part of the business you transfer must have been used to make supplies, they must not merely be used for the overheads of your business (see also paragraph 7.2).

2.3.8 Transfers involving land and property

If the transfer of the land or property would normally be a taxable supply, both the seller and the purchaser may need to meet certain conditions for it to be included as part of the TOGC. This is explained in more detail at paragraph 2.4 below.

2.4 Should VAT be charged when land or buildings are transferred as part of a TOGC?

A TOGC will often involve the transfer of land and buildings. There are extra rules to determine whether VAT should be charged on the transfer of land and buildings even if the rest of the transfer does qualify for TOGC treatment.

If all the conditions in paragraph 2.3 are met and the purchaser has complied with the following requirements, the transfer of land and buildings can be part of a TOGC and therefore not subject to VAT.

If the seller is transferring land or buildings:

- on which he has elected to waive exemption (opted to tax) or
- which are new (less than three years old) or unfinished buildings or civil engineering works which would ordinarily be standard-rated

and the purchaser,

- has notified to HMRC his election to tax the land or buildings by the "relevant date" and
- has notified the seller by the relevant date that their election will not be disapplied then

then the transfer of the land or buildings can be included in the TOGC (see 2.4.1 regarding option to tax and "relevant date").

If the seller is transferring land or buildings on which there is no election to tax, and the supply would not be otherwise standard-rated, in other words, if the supply is zero-rated or exempt then the purchaser is not required to opt to tax and there ceases to be a requirement to notify that the option has not been disapplied. In these circumstances the transfer of the land or buildings can be included in the TOGC.

Note on responsibility for applying correct treatment – option to tax by the purchaser

The seller is responsible for applying the correct VAT treatment and may be required to support their decision. If the transaction is to be treated as a TOGC the seller must be satisfied that the purchaser's election to tax is in place by the relevant date. They may therefore consider asking the purchaser for evidence of this, such as a copy of the notification letter. The seller must have the purchaser's notification of the nondisapplication of the election to tax and may find it prudent to obtain this in writing.

2.4.1 Election to waive exemption (option to tax)

The option to tax by the purchaser, referred to above, must be notified to HMRC in writing no later than the relevant date and must apply from that time. You should note that the relevant date is the time of the supply. For VAT purposes the time of supply is normally the date of the transfer, but will also include receipt of a deposit that may otherwise have created a tax point. A tax point is not created by the receipt of a deposit by a third party acting as an independent stakeholder (as opposed to an agent of the seller) until the money is released to the vendor. Further information on tax points this can be found in Notice 700 The VAT Guide.

Where the written notification of the option to tax is sent to HMRC by mail, the notification must be properly addressed, pre-paid and posted on or before the relevant date. Notice 742A Opting to tax land and buildings fully explains the option to tax.

2.4.2 Disapplication of the purchaser's option to tax – the anti-avoidance measure

An option to tax can be disapplied as a result of an anti-avoidance measure. Where an option is disapplied this means it will cease to have effect in respect of certain supplies. The anti-avoidance measure only has effect where land and buildings are occupied for something other than fully taxable business purposes and where the land or building is a capital item for the purposes of Capital Goods Scheme (see Notices 706 Partial Exemption and 706/2 Capital Goods Scheme). The measure is explained fully in Notice 742A Opting to tax land and buildings.

Changes were made to the measure from 18 March 2004. From the same date the TOGC rules were also amended. Under the new rules for freehold transfers of new buildings and civil engineering works (less than three years old) and land and buildings on which the seller has exercised an option to tax, can only be included within a TOGC where:

(1) the purchaser confirms that an option to tax has been made and notified by the relevant date, and
(2) the purchaser makes a declaration to the seller that his option will not be disapplied by the anti-avoidance provisions (see Notice 742A).

Where the purchaser fails to do either of the above the transfer will fall outside of the TOGC provisions and the supply will be subject to VAT. However, the transfer of other business assets may still qualify to be treated as a TOGC.

The following tables will help you decide on whether land and buildings can be included in the transfer of assets as part of a TOGC

Commercial land or building, ordinarily exempt

Has seller opted to tax (building over 3 years old)?	*Has the purchaser opted to tax?*	*Will the purchaser's option to tax be disapplied?*	*Transfer of a going concern provisions met?*
Yes	Yes	Yes	No
Yes	No	N/A	No

Commercial land or building, ordinarily exempt

Has seller opted to tax (building over 3 years old)?	*Has the purchaser opted to tax?*	*Will the purchaser's option to tax be disapplied?*	*Transfer of a going concern provisions met?*
Yes	Yes	No	Yes
No	No	N/A	Yes
No	Yes	Yes	Yes
No	Yes	No	Yes

New building (less than 3 years old), ordinarily standard-rated

Has seller opted to tax?	*Has the purchaser opted to tax?*	*Will the purchaser's option to tax be disapplied?*	*Transfer of a going concern provisions met?*
Yes	Yes	Yes	No
Yes	No	N/A	No
Yes	Yes	No	Yes
No	No	N/A	No
No	Yes	Yes	No
No	Yes	No	Yes

2.5 What are the rules when a "property rental business" is transferred?

Section 6 gives examples of circumstances concerning the transfer of land/property where there may (or may not) be a transfer of a business of "property rental" as a "going concern". In those cases where there has been such a transfer, the conditions of paragraphs 2.3 and 2.4 must still be met for there to be a TOGC and for the supply of assets to be ignored for VAT purposes.

An optional statement of practice is available where a property rental business is being transferred to a nominee acquiring title for a named beneficial owner. See section 8.

Where only the beneficial ownership of a property rental business is transferred and the legal title is retained by the seller there may be a TOGC. If the seller's ownership is reduced to being no more than that of a bare trustee, it is accepted that the property, together with its lettings may be transferred as a "going concern".

Where there is a transfer of a beneficial interest from A to B to C on the same day this is seen as a series of consecutive transfers, even where the legal title is transferred directly from A to C. The condition as per sub-paragraph 2.3.3 is not met and TOGC does not apply to any of the transactions. Different rules apply in Scotland, however, to the transfer of a property rental business, where it is possible to "dispone" ownership. Under Scottish law the disposition of the 'ownership of the property' may been seen to be direct from A to C, and the TOGC provisions may apply, subject to meeting the other conditions in paragraph 2.3 and paragraph 2.4.

When a tenanted building is sold or a lease is assigned mid-way through a rent period, an adjustment is normally made to the consideration at the point of completion. These adjustments may be for rent collected, or for water and power paid for in advance prior to the sale or assignment. They are not consideration for any supply and are outside the scope of VAT. For VAT purposes the consideration for the sale of the building or the assignment of the lease is the full value of the supply before any adjustment is made (see Notice 742 Land and Property).

2.6 Deduction of VAT on expenses incurred on the transfer

Although there is no supply for VAT purposes where there is a TOGC, this does not prevent the deduction, subject to the usual rules, of input tax on related expenses (for example solicitors' fees and estate agents' costs). There is, however, a distinction between the extent to which the seller and the purchaser can deduct such input tax.

2.6.1 Purchaser (Transferee)

If the purchaser acquires assets by way of a TOGC and the assets are to be used exclusively to make taxable supplies, the VAT incurred on the cost of acquiring those assets should be attributed to those taxable supplies and can be recovered in full. If the assets of the acquired business are to be used exclusively to make exempt supplies, none of the input tax on the cost of acquiring those assets can be recovered. However, if the assets are to be used in making both taxable and exempt supplies, any input tax incurred is residual input tax and must be apportioned in accordance with the purchaser's VAT partial exemption method.

2.6.2 Seller (Transferor)

The sale of the business as a TOGC is not a supply and the input tax incurred on the cost of selling the business cannot be attributed to it by the seller. These costs are, therefore, treated as a general business overhead. Where the seller's business is partly exempt the costs, having a direct and immediate link with the whole of the seller's business activity, are to be apportioned by reference to the seller's partial exemption method. However, where part of a business is transferred as a TOGC, and those expenses can be shown to have a direct and immediate link with the transferred part of the business, then those expenses form part of the overheads of that part of the business. Where that part of the business made only taxable supplies then tax is deductible on those expenses. Where that part of the business made only exempt supplies the tax is not deductible. However, where taxable and exempt supplies were made by that part of the business, then the tax is residual input tax and is attributable to taxable supplies by reference to the seller's partial exemption method.

In instances, either at 2.6.1 or 2.6.2 where the existing partial exemption method fails to achieve a fair and reasonable result, then we would be prepared to approve the use of another method, as long as that method provides for a fair and reasonable recovery of input tax. See Notice 706 Partial Exemption for further guidance.

3 RULES FOLLOWING A TOGC

3.1 What is this section about?

This section explains the rules following a TOGC in relation to:

– capital goods scheme considerations
– de-registration and goods still owned by the original business
– transfer of the previous owner's registration number
– business records
– giving away goods or services owned by the previous business
– Intrastat rules.
– Customs authorisations and Excise and Inland Customs approvals

3.2 The Capital Goods Scheme (CGS) and how it interacts with the TOGC provisions

The scheme applies where the value of taxable (other than zero-rated) supplies received in connection with the acquisition or creation of any of the items listed below is £250,000 or more. In the case of computers and computer equipment the scheme only applies where the value of the supply is £50,000 or more. The scheme applies to the following:

– The interest supplied to an owner in land, a building or part of a building
– A building or part of a building which is subject to a self-supply
– Goods and services received in constructing a building
– Goods and services received in altering a building or constructing an extension or annex
– The interest supplied to the owner, or the goods and services received in constructing a civil engineering work
– Capital expenditure on supplies of services and of goods affixed to the building in refurbishing or fitting out a building
– A computer or an item of computer equipment; and, if relevant
– related self-supplies.

Items that fall within the scheme are called "capital items".

3.2.1 How the CGS works

Further details of how the CGS operates can be found in Notice 706/2 Capital Goods Scheme. A summary of the CGS to aid in understanding this section is that the scheme requires that adjustments are made to the input tax claimed in relation to a capital item if within a period of ten successive intervals (each interval normally corresponds with your partial exemption tax year) there is a change in the extent to which the item is used to make taxable supplies. This period is called the adjustment period. For computers, items of computer equipment and in cases where the interest supplied in the land and buildings etc. has less than 10 years to run at the time it is supplied to you, then the adjustment period is only 5 years.

3.2.2 Capital item is transferred as part of a transfer of a going concern

If a capital item is transferred to you as part of a TOGC then you, as the new owner, assume responsibility for any adjustments of input tax required under the scheme for the remainder of the adjustment period. Purchasers should therefore confirm with the seller whether any of the assets being transferred are covered by the scheme and details of the adjustments already made. It is important to be aware that if the purpose to which the asset has been put changes at or after the transfer, the purchaser may need to repay some of the input tax claimed by the original owner. Similarly, he may be entitled to recover more tax than that originally claimed.

If the seller has been fully taxable since the acquisition of the capital item and the purchaser is and remains fully taxable until the expiry of the adjustment period, then no adjustments are required under the scheme. It is only when there is a change in the extent to which the capital item is used in making taxable and exempt supplies, within the adjustment period, that adjustments have to be made.

3.2.3 Partial Exemption clawback/payback and how it interacts with the TOGC provisions.

There may be occasions where the intended use of goods or services on which you based your claim to input tax changes. Where you change your intention before you use the goods or services, or, where you actually use the goods or services for a different purpose, the 'clawback' or 'payback' provisions may apply. If a business is transferred as a TOGC the new owner becomes responsible for any payback or clawback adjustments that become necessary.

Clawback applies where:

(a) you have claimed input tax on goods or services because:
- you intended to use them in making taxable supplies but in the event you use them, or form an intention to use them, in making either exempt supplies or both taxable and exempt supplies; or

(b) you have claimed input tax on goods or services because:
- you intended to use them in making both taxable and exempt supplies but in the event you use them, or form an intention to use them, in making only exempt supplies.

And for both (a) and (b) above where the change of intention occurs within six years of the beginning of the period covered by the VAT return in which the original intention was formed.

Payback applies where:

(a) you have not claimed input tax on goods and services because;
- you intended to use them in making exempt supplies but in the event you use them, or form an intention to use them, in making taxable supplies or both taxable and exempt supplies; or

(b) you have not claimed input tax on goods or services because:
- you intended to use them in making both taxable and exempt supplies but in the event you use them, or form an intention to use them, in making only taxable supplies.

And for both (a) and (b) above where the change of intention occurs within six years of the beginning of the period covered by the VAT return in which the original intention was formed.

Further details on payback and clawback can be found in Notice 706 Partial Exemption.

3.3 How should I treat business assets that are not transferred if I am de-registering from VAT?

If you transfer your business as a TOGC and are not going to continue trading in another capacity you will need to cancel your VAT registration using Form VAT 7. However if you are cancelling your registration and have any goods which you have claimed input tax on and are not transferring with the business, you will normally have to account for VAT on these assets. Notice 700/11 Cancelling your registration tells you more about this. You should be aware that if you fail to notify HMRC of any changes affecting your registration details within 30 days of them occurring you may become liable to a financial penalty.

If, when you cancel your registration, you have a capital item covered by the scheme and which is still within its adjustment period you will need to make a final adjustment. Notice 706/2 Capital goods scheme tells you more about this.

3.4 Reallocation of the VAT registration number from seller to purchaser

In certain circumstances the purchaser can apply to keep the seller's VAT registration number. As part of that application both the seller and the purchaser must agree to the consequences of reallocation.

The transfer of a VAT registration number can be requested using HMRC's online services or by a completing Form VAT 68.

Online application

The purchaser of the business can view the consequences of requesting the transfer a VAT registration number when they register for VAT using the online tax registration service.

The seller can view the consequences of requesting the transfer of a VAT registration number when they complete the relevant details in the online service - Change Customer Details

If either the purchaser or seller do not want to use the online service then they should complete the relevant sections of Form VAT 68.

VAT 68

If the purchaser and/or seller wish to complete a VAT 68 they can download it from our website hmrc.gov.uk.

The consequences of reallocation for both the purchaser and seller are set on the form.

The purchaser will also need to complete a VAT 1- Application for registration.

If the seller completes a VAT 68 agreeing to transfer their VAT registration number they must not complete a VAT 7.

An example of the form VAT 68 is contained in Section 11.

If you fail to notify HMRC of any changes affecting your registration details within 30 days of them occurring you may become liable to a financial penalty.

Consequences of transferring a VAT registration number are legally binding on both parties and include the transfer of any VAT liability to the purchaser. The purchaser is liable for any outstanding VAT from the seller's registration including VAT on stocks and assets kept by the seller. However the seller is no longer entitled to any repayments of VAT or unclaimed input tax whether these amounts refer to periods before or after the transfer.

The consequences also include the transfer of entitlement to unclaimed VAT bad debt relief on debts incurred by the seller of the business. However, the purchaser also takes the requirement to repay input tax claimed by the seller on supplies he received and which have subsequently become the subject of a bad debt relief claim made by the supplier or if the supplies remain unpaid after six months.

Further details about bad debt relief can be found in Notice 700/18 Relief from VAT on bad debts.

If the registration number is reallocated, the seller must still follow the procedure set out in Notice 700/11 Cancelling your registration.

3.4.1 Special VAT arrangements applying to the seller's registration

If any special arrangements apply to the seller's registration -for example, self-billing, a partial exemption special method, or a Notice of Direction for sale by retail at open market value - they may need to end when the business is transferred. In such cases, or if the use of a retail scheme or Excise and Inland Customs registration or approval is involved, you should ask our advice service or your allocated point of contact for guidance. In any case where a simplification scheme is in use both the seller and purchaser of a business are advised to check the published rules for such schemes to ensure that treatment is correct.

Further guidance can be found in:

Notice 718 "Margin Scheme for second hand goods".
Notice 727 "Retail Schemes and the relevant Notice for the Retail Scheme in use"
Notice 731 "Cash accounting"
Notice 732 "Annual accounting"
Notice 742A "Opting to tax land and buildings"
Notice 706/2 "Capital Goods Scheme"
See also VAT Information Sheet 14/07 on assets used partly for non-business purposes.

3.5 VAT registration number not reallocated from seller to purchaser

Where the VAT registration number of the seller of a business or part of a business is not transferred to the purchaser, there is no transfer of VAT liability to the purchaser and the purchaser is not liable for any outstanding VAT from the seller's registration.

There is also no transfer of entitlement to unclaimed VAT bad debt relief on debts incurred by the seller of the business because the supplies to which the relief might apply were not made by the purchaser.

The seller retains the requirement to repay input tax claimed by him on supplies he received and which have subsequently become the subject of a bad debt relief claim made by the supplier or if they remain unpaid after six months. Further details about bad debt relief can be found in Notice 700/18 Relief from VAT on bad debts.

If the seller is continuing to trade then he is still subject to the requirement to notify HMRC of the sale or transfer of the business (Notice 700 Section 26).

If the seller is ceasing to trade or is no longer registerable as a result of the transfer then he must follow the procedure set out in Notice 700/11 Cancelling your registration. See also 3.3 above.

3.5.1 Special VAT arrangements applying to the seller's registration

If any special arrangements apply to the seller's registration -for example, self-billing, a partial exemption special method, or a Notice of Direction for sale by retail at open market value - they may in many cases end when the business to which they relate is transferred. In such cases, or if the use of a retail scheme or Excise and Inland Customs registration or approval is involved, you should ask our advice service or your allocated officer for guidance. See 3.4.1 for reference to further guidance on specific potential situations.

3.6 What should happen to the business records?

This will depend on whether the purchaser has taken on the seller's VAT registration number.

In respect of all transfer contracts entered into before 1 September 2007

The business records that had to be kept for VAT purposes by the seller had to be transferred to the new owner. The purchaser took over the obligation to keep and preserve them. However, if the seller needed to retain the records he could apply to HMRC for permission to do so. If permission was granted, he should still have made available to the purchaser the information needed to comply with his duties under the VAT Act.

In respect of all transfer contracts entered into on or after 1 September 2007

The seller of a business (or part business) sold as a TOGC retains the business records, unless the VAT registration number is also transferred. However, the seller must make available to the purchaser the information necessary for the purchaser to comply with his duties under the VAT Act.

If the purchaser is unable to obtain this information from the seller, then HMRC can disclose to the purchaser the information HMRC holds that is necessary for the purchaser to comply with duties under the VAT Act. HMRC will advise the seller of its intention to disclose information to the purchaser thereby providing the opportunity to identify any confidentiality issues.

3.7 What if I give away goods or services owned by the previous business?

The purchaser may be liable for VAT on the deemed supply of assets taken into private use or disposed of as gifts where the assets where transferred to him and the seller originally reclaimed input tax on the purchase of those assets - see Notice 700 Section 9 Output tax: business and non-business use.

Under the normal rules, when a business gives away goods or services on which input tax has been recovered, VAT is due on that disposal. Business gifts costing £50 or less or free samples are exceptions to this rule. Where goods and services are transferred as part of a TOGC, and a previous business has had entitlement to input tax on those supplies, output tax is still due on any subsequent free supply of those goods or services by the purchaser.

3.8 Intrastat Rules

VAT registered businesses are required to complete statistical Supplementary Declarations (SDs) if their intra-EC trade exceeds annually set value thresholds for either dispatches (exports) or acquisitions (imports) of goods.

When the VAT registration of a trader responsible for providing SDs is amended as a result of a change of ownership, name, address, legal status or similar change that does not significantly affect their intra-Community operations, then the new VAT registered trader keeps the legal responsibilities and obligations to continue to provide SDs

3.9 TOGC interaction with Customs authorisations

It is important to note that the treatment of a transfer of a business as a TOGC for VAT purposes may well give rise to registration issues for Customs authorisation and Excise and Inland Customs approvals. The transfer of the VAT registration number by VAT 68 as per section 3.4 above does not mean that registration for other duties or taxes has similarly been transferred. Generally Customs or EICS registrations or approvals will need to be applied for again. If you are a seller or a purchaser of a business and are subject to these regimes you are advised to contact your issuing authority within HMRC or contact our advice service for advice on the effect.

4 VAT GROUPS AND TOGCS

4.1 Transfers of businesses between members of the same VAT group

The formation of a VAT group creates a single person for VAT purposes and as such any supply by a member of a VAT group is considered to be made by the representative member of the group. Therefore any assets transferred by a group member as part of the transfer of a going concern are considered to be transferred by the representative member.

The transfer of assets within a VAT group, like most supplies between the members of a VAT group, is disregarded for VAT purposes.

4.2 Transfers made to persons outside the VAT group

There cannot be a TOGC when the sole activity of the business transferred is the making of supplies from one group member to another. However, if supplies are also being made to businesses outside of the VAT group, a TOGC is possible.

4.3 Transfers made to a VAT Group

Where a business is sold and the purchaser is part of a VAT group and uses the new acquisition simply to make supplies to VAT group members, the business has effectively ceased and it cannot be treated as a TOGC. However, if supplies are also being made to businesses outside of the VAT group, a TOGC is possible. For example:

Situation	*Status*
The purchaser of a property rental business is a member of the same VAT group as the existing tenant	Not a TOGC
A VAT group member sells a property currently being rented to a another group member to a third party	Not a TOGC
A property rental business is sold where the tenant who is a member of the outgoing landlord's VAT group is only one of a number of tenants	Can be a TOGC
A property rental business is sold where the tenant who is a member of the purchaser's VAT group is only one of a number of tenants	Can be a TOGC

5 MEMBERS OF A PARTLY EXEMPT VAT GROUP

5.1 What is this section about?

This section provides information on the requirements for a new owner who is a member of a partly exempt VAT group acquiring a business as a TOGC.

5.2 General rules for partly exempt VAT groups

If you are a member of a partly exempt VAT group and you acquire business assets as part of a TOGC, you must treat these assets as being both supplied to the group and supplied by the group - that is, a self-supply is triggered. In practice this means that the representative member must account for output tax in relation to the supply by the group and recover the input tax incurred in relation to the supply to the group in accordance with the partial exemption method in operation. However, the input tax cannot be attributed to the self-supply itself.

5.2.1 Exclusions

The self-supply will not be triggered in relation to:

— Any assets which were assets of the previous owner more than three years before the date of the transfer.

— Goodwill (eg, unidentifiable goodwill, use of a trade mark or trading name, the sole right to trade in a particular area, etc.)

— Any assets which are zero-rated or exempt (for example zero-rated or exempt freehold or leasehold interests in land).

— Or items which fall within the Capital Goods Scheme. For further details of items covered by the capital goods scheme see paragraph 3.2 and Notice 706/2 Capital goods scheme.

The above self-supply made by the representative member must not be taken into account when working out how much input tax the VAT group is entitled to recover.

5.3 What is the value for VAT purposes of the supply made to and by the representative member?

The value of the supply by, and to, the representative member, is its open market value. If the previous owner is unconnected with your group, this will normally be the consideration you paid for the assets on which tax is due. If VAT is not due on some of the assets, the consideration must be apportioned fairly between the standard-rated assets and other assets. The paragraph on mixed supplies in Notice 700 The VAT Guide tells you how to do this.

5.4 Can this VAT due be reduced in any circumstances?

HMRC can reduce the VAT chargeable in relation to the self-supply if you can produce satisfactory evidence to show that the previous owner did not recover all of the input tax incurred on the original purchase (for example, if he was partly exempt or the input tax was 'blocked' eg, on the purchase of a car).

In a case where the seller's partial exemption recovery rate (during the partial exemption tax year in which the assets were purchased) is equal to or less than the purchaser's recovery rate (during the partial exemption tax year in which the assets were acquired) the VAT charge will be reduced to nil, although no tax will be refunded.

If you consider that you have evidence to show that the tax due should be reduced you should consult our advice service.

6 TRANSFERRING A PROPERTY BUSINESS AS A TOGC

6.1 What is this section about?

This section provides guidance on when a property can be transferred as a TOGC.

6.2 Examples of when a property business can be transferred as a TOGC

If you:

- Own the freehold of a property which you let to a tenant and sell the freehold with the benefit of the existing lease, a business of property rental is transferred to the purchaser. This is a business transferred as a TOGC even if the property is only partly tenanted. Similarly, if you own the lease of a property (which is subject to a sub-lease) and you assign your lease with the benefit of the sub-lease, this is a business transferred as a TOGC
- Own a building where there is a contract to pay rent in the future but where the tenants are enjoying an initial rent free period, even if the building is sold during the rent free period, you are carrying on a business of property rental
- Granted a lease in respect of a building but the tenants are not yet in occupation, you are carrying on a property rental business
- Own a property and have found a tenant but not actually entered into a lease agreement when you transfer the freehold to a third party (with the benefit of a contractual agreement for a lease but before the lease has been signed), there is sufficient evidence of intended economic activity for there to be a property rental business capable of being transferred
- Are a property developer selling a site as a package (to a single buyer) which is a mixture of let and unlet, finished or unfinished properties, and the sale of the site would otherwise have been standard rated, then subject to the purchaser opting to tax for the whole site, the whole site can be regarded as a business transferred as a going concern.
- Own a number of let freehold properties, and you sell one of them, the sale of this single let or partly let property can be a TOGC of a property rental business.
- Have a partially-let building this is capable of being a property rental business, providing that the letting constitutes economic activity. This may include electricity sub-stations or space for advertising hoardings providing that there is a lease in place.
- Purchase the freehold and leasehold of a property from separate sellers without the interests merging and the lease has not been extinguished, providing you continue to exploit the asset by receiving rent from the tenant, then such a transaction can be a TOGC.

6.3 Examples where there is not a TOGC

If you:

- Are a property developer and have built a building and you allow someone to occupy temporarily (without any right to occupy after any proposed sale) or you are "actively marketing" it in search of a tenant, there is no property rental business being carried on
- Own the freehold of a property and grant a lease, even a 999year lease, you are not transferring a business as a going concern. You are creating a new asset (the lease) and selling it while retaining your original asset (the freehold). This is true regardless of the length of the lease. Similarly, if you own a headlease and grant a sub-lease you are not transferring your business as a going concern.
- Sell a property where the lease you granted is surrendered immediately before the sale, your property rental business ceases and so cannot be transferred as a going concern -even if tenants under a sublease remain in occupation When the lease is brought to an end the property rental business carried on by the former freeholder has ceased and cannot be transferred.

- Sell a property freehold to the existing tenant who leases the whole premises from you, this cannot be a transfer of a going concern because the tenant cannot carry on the same business of property rental. This would remain the case even if the new freeholder vacated the property on acquisition and found a new tenant since when the lease is brought to an end the property rental business carried on by the former freeholder has ceased.
- Have granted a lease in respect of a building and the tenant is running a business from the premises. The tenant then sells the assets of his business as a going concern and surrenders his lease to you. You grant the new owner of the business a lease in respect of the building. This is not a transfer by you of a property rental business.

6.4 Additional points on the transfer of property and TOGCs

6.4.1 Transfers of a number of sites or buildings

The transfer of a number of sites or buildings where some of the sites or buildings are let, or partially let and some are unlet, needs to be considered on a case by case basis. The nature of the sites or building and their use are all factors for consideration. It is important to look at whether the assets can be identified as a single business or an identifiable part of a business. In addition all the conditions as set out at sections 1.2 and 2.3 of this notice would need to be met. For example the sale of a chain of shops or pubs could be a TOGC whereas the sale of a grouping of disparate properties might not.

7 WHAT IS THE "SAME KIND OF BUSINESS"?

7.1 Trading activities after a business is transferred

When selling your business assets, you must check that the purchaser intends to carry on the same kind of business before the sale can be ignored for VAT purposes under the TOGC rules.

Common areas of difficulty include companies which have more than one trading activity. For example, a brewery is in business selling beers, wines and spirits to the public via their managed house outlets. It is also in business renting properties to tenants (where the tenants are selling to the public). So, for example, if a brewery was leasing a pub to tenants, and then sold the business to someone who was to run the pub themselves, then it would not be a TOGC: the brewery had a business of renting the property, the new owner has a business of running a pub, although the new owner may need to be registered for VAT from the date the pub was sold to them by the brewery -see Notice 700/1 for further information.

You must therefore check whether the person buying your assets intends to operate the business in the same way as you.

7.2 Examples of the same kind of business:

If you sell:

- a restaurant and/or bar but the purchaser is to immediately alter the style of the business, the same kind of business is still being carried on, eg, an Italian restaurant becoming a Mexican restaurant is still a restaurant
- your business to someone who intends to restructure it such that it will not be the same but they actually continue with your business, even if for a very short period of time, they will have carried on the same kind of business.

7.3 Examples of different types of business

If you:

- grant franchises to operate trading sites, as opposed to operating the actual trading activity of the business, the transferee is not carrying on the same kind of business as you, or
- sell your business to a customer who will only use "your" product to support his existing business and will not be making any supplies of "your" product to any third parties, the purchaser will not be carrying on the same kind of business.

8 PROPERTY LETTING BUSINESS—STATEMENT OF PRACTICE

8.1 What is this section about?

See also paragraph 2.5.

This section reproduces the contents of Business Brief 10/96 dated 5 June 1996.

This statement of practice about nominee purchasers acquiring legal title is optional and may only be applied by persons transferring an interest in land to a person who is a nominee for a named beneficial owner. The option is not available if the nominee is acting for an undisclosed beneficial owner.

Where the legal title in land is to be held by a nominee for a named beneficial owner, HMRC will, for the purpose of establishing the transfer of a property letting business as a going concern, from 1 June 1996, consider the named beneficial owner of the land and not the nominee acquiring legal title to be the transferee.

The new optional practice allows a person transferring an interest in land to a nominee for a named beneficial owner, with the agreement of that nominee and beneficial owner, to treat the named beneficial owner as the transferee for the purposes of establishing whether there has been a transfer of a going concern. This Business Brief contains an example format that the parties can use to record agreement if they so wish.

Persons transferring an interest in land to a person who is a nominee for a named beneficial owner will be expected to check the VAT registration and where necessary the VAT elections made by the beneficial owner.

Examples of where a nominee might exist to hold the legal title in property for a beneficial owner are -where the legal title is held by four or fewer persons on trust for a partnership (this example does not arise in Scottish law); where the legal title is held on trust for an unincorporated association; and where the legal title is held on trust for a pension fund.

8.2 Background

HMRC have reviewed their policy whereby the passing of title in property between legal owners solely determined whether Article 5 of the VAT (Special Provisions) Order 1995 (SI 1995 No. 1268) applied in the circumstances above.

Strictly, a transfer of a going concern cannot occur where the transferee is a nominee for a beneficial owner because the beneficial owner will be the person carrying on the business, not the nominee. The optional treatment above does not disturb any transactions prior to 1 June 1996, but from that date allows a more relaxed approach to be adopted. It is deregulatory and should reduce business costs in the circumstances described.

The option does not need to apply to transactions where the nominee is the transferor of the legal title. In these cases, Paragraph 8 of Schedule 10 to the VAT Act 1994 deems the beneficial owner to be the transferor.

The above principles, which are based upon English land law, may also be applied to similar transactions in Scotland and Northern Ireland as necessary.

8.3 Suggested Format of Notice of Agreement

The following Notice of Agreement is optional and other clear written evidence of agreement will be accepted by HMRC. The transferor, transferee beneficial owner and nominee should each retain a copy of any written evidence.

8.3.1 Notice of Agreement to adopt Statement of Practice

Property: (Address)

Transferor/vendor: (X)

Nominee/purchaser: (Y)

Future Beneficial Owner: (Z)

X, Y and Z confirm that they have agreed to adopt the optional practice set out in Customs & Excise Business Brief 10/96 in relation to the purchase of the Property pursuant to an agreement dated () between X and Y.

Following the transfer of the Property Y will hold the legal title as nominee for Z, the beneficial owner.

SIGNED for and on behalf of X:

SIGNED for and on behalf of Y:

SIGNED for and on behalf of Z:

DATE:

9 FURTHER ADVICE

9.1 HMRC rulings on transfers of business

HMRC do give further advice as outlined and in particular where an unusual aspect has been identified in a potential TOGC. Normally the seller should make the request as it is their responsibility to determine whether VAT is chargeable or not. It is important that any request for is made in writing, and contains in full all relevant facts and information and also a clear indication of what aspects of the arrangement give rise to doubt or uncertainty.

There are, however, circumstances where we do not give VAT clearances, including on TOGC cases. These circumstances are listed in CAP1 and HMRC's clearance service for businesses.'

10 UK VAT LAW CONCERNING TOGCS

10.1 Extract from the Value Added Tax (Special Provisions) Order 1995 – SI 1995/1268

"5(1) Subject to paragraph (2) below, there shall be treated as neither a supply of goods nor a supply of services the following supplies by a person of assets of his business

(a) their supply to a person to whom he transfers his business as a going concern where
   (i) the assets are to be used by the transferee in carrying on the same kind of business, whether or not as part of any existing business, as that carried on by the transferor, and
   (ii) in a case where the transferor is a taxable person, the transferee is already, or immediately becomes as a result of the transfer, a taxable person or a person defined as such in section 3(1) of the Manx Act;

(b) their supply to a person to whom he transfers part of his business as a going concern where
   (i) that part is capable of separate operation,
   (ii) the assets are to be used by the transferee in carrying on the same kind of business, whether or not as part of any existing business, as that carried on by the transferor in relation to that part, and
   (iii) in a case where the transferor is a taxable person, the transferee is already or immediately becomes as a result of the transfer, a taxable person or a person defined as such in section 3(1) of the Manx Act.

(2) A supply of assets shall not be treated as neither a supply of goods nor a supply of services by virtue of paragraph (1) above to the extent that it consists of

(a) a grant which would, but for an election which the transferor has made, fall within item 1 of group 1 of Schedule 9 to the Act; or

(b) a grant of a fee simple which falls within paragraph (a) of item 1 of group 1 of Schedule 9 to the Act,

unless the transferee has made an election in relation to the land concerned which has effect on the relevant date and has given any written notification of the election required by paragraph 3(6) of Schedule 10 to the Act, no later than the relevant date.

(3) In paragraph (2) of this article

"election" means an election having effect under paragraph 2 of Schedule 10 to the Act;

"relevant date" means the date upon which the grant would have been treated as having been made or, if there is more than one such date, the earliest of them;

"transferor" and "transferee" include a relevant associate of either respectively as defined in paragraph 3(7) of Schedule 10 to the Act.

(a) Schedule 10 was amended by the Value Added Tax (Buildings and Land) Order 1995 (S.I. 1995/279)

10.2 Extracts from the Value Added Tax Act 1994

44(1) Subject to subsections (2) to (4) below, subsection (5) below applies where

(a) a business, or part of a business, carried on by a taxable person is transferred as a going concern to a body corporate treated as a member of a group under section 43;
(b) on the transfer of the business or part, chargeable assets of the business are transferred to the body corporate; and
(c) the transfer of the assets is treated by virtue of section 5(3)(c) as neither a supply of goods nor a supply of services.

(2) Subsection (5) below shall not apply if the representative member of the group is entitled to credit for the whole of the input tax on supplies to it and importations by it

(a) during the prescribed accounting period in which the assets are transferred, and
(b) during any longer period to which regulations under section 26(3)(b) relate and in which the assets are transferred.

(3) Subsection (5) below shall not apply if the Commissioners are satisfied that the assets were assets of the taxable person transferring them more than three years before the day on which they are transferred.

(4) Subsection (5) below shall not apply to the extent that the chargeable assets consist of capital items in respect of which regulations made under section 26(3) and (4), and in force when the assets are transferred, provide for adjustment to the deduction of input tax.

(5) The chargeable assets shall be treated for the purposes of this Act as being, on the day on which they are transferred, both supplied to the representative member of the group for the purpose of its business and supplied by that member in the course or furtherance of its business.

(6) A supply treated under subsection (5) above as made by a representative member shall not be taken into account as a supply made by him when determining the allowance of input tax in his case under section 26.

(7) The value of a supply treated under subsection (5) above as made to or by a representative member shall be taken to be the open market value of the chargeable assets.

(8) For the purposes of this section, the open market value of any chargeable assets shall be taken to be the price that would be paid on a sale (on which no VAT is payable) between a buyer and a seller who are not in such a relationship as to affect the price.

(9) The Commissioners may reduce the VAT chargeable by virtue of subsection (5) above in a case where they are satisfied that the person by whom the chargeable assets are transferred has not received credit for the full amount of input tax arising on the supply to or acquisition, or importation by him of the chargeable assets.

(10) For the purposes of this section, assets are chargeable assets if their supply in the United Kingdom by a taxable person in the course or furtherance of his business would be a taxable supply (and not a zero-rated supply)."

49(1) Where a business carried on by a taxable person is transferred to another person as a going concern, then

(a) for the purpose of determining whether the transferee is liable to be registered under this Act he shall be treated as having carried on the business before as well as after the transfer and supplies by the transferor shall be treated accordingly; and
(b) [omitted by FA 2007, s. 100(2)(c) and repealed by FA 2007, s. 114 and sch. 27, Pt. 6(2).]

(2) Without prejudice to subsection (1) above, the Commissioners may by regulations make provision for securing continuity in the application of this Act in cases where a business carried on by a taxable person is transferred to another person as a going concern and the transferee is registered under this Act in substitution for the transferor.

(2A) Regulations under subsection (2) above may, in particular, provide for the duties under this Act of the transferor to preserve records relating to the business or part of the business for any period after the transfer to become duties of the transferee unless the Commissioners, at the request of the transferor, otherwise direct.

(3) Regulations under subsection (2) above may, in particular, provide

(a) for liabilities and duties under this Act (excluding sections 59 to 70) of the transferor (other than the duties mentioned in subsection 2A above) to become, to such extent as may be provided by the regulations, liabilities and duties of the transferee; and

(b) for any right of either of them to repayment or credit in respect of tax to be satisfied by making a repayment or allowing a credit to the other

but no such provision as is mentioned in paragraph (a) or (b) of this subsection shall have effect in relation to any transferor and transferee unless an application in that behalf has been made by them under the regulations."

11 VAT 68 – TRANSFER OF A BUSINESS AS GOING CONCERN

The VAT 68 form is published here by the Commissioners under Regulation 6(1)(d) of the VAT Regulations 1995. It is the form which must be completed if the seller and purchaser of a business want to apply to transfer a VAT registration number.

VAT 68 – Request for transfer of a registration number – www.hmrc.gov.uk/forms/vat68.pdf

700/62
SELF-BILLING

September 2014

This notice cancels and replaces Notice 700/62 (July 2013).

1 INTRODUCTION

1.1 What is this notice about?

This notice is about the VAT treatment of self-billing. Self-billing is a commercial arrangement between a supplier and a customer in which the customer prepares the supplier's invoice and forwards a copy to the supplier with the payment.

You may only issue self-billed invoices to your suppliers if—

- they have agreed to this method of accounting
- you can meet all the conditions in section 3 and paragraph 4.1

You do not need to seek HM Revenue and Customs' (HMRC's) authorisation to operate self-billing.

Commentary—*De Voil Indirect Tax Service* **V3.523**.

1.2 What's changed

HMRC has made changes to the July 2013 edition to make the notice suitable for publication on GOV.UK.

1.3 Who should read this notice?

This notice is written for customers who operate, or wish to operate, self-billing with their suppliers and for suppliers who accept, or wish to accept, self-billed invoices from their customers.

If you are a . . .	*I see especially sections . . .*
customer who issues, or who wants to start issuing self-billed invoices to your suppliers (in other words, you are a *self-biller*).	2-5 and 7-8
supplier who has a customer that issues, or wants to issue, you with self-billed invoices (in other words, you are a *self-billee*).	6 and 7-8

1.4 What law covers this notice?

The relevant law is—

- VATA 1994, s 29 and
- the VAT Regulations, regs 13(3) and (13)(3A) to 13(3F).

Part of this notice has the force of law under these regulations. It is indicated by being placed in a box.

2 ADVANTAGES OF BEING A SELF-BILLER AND POINTS TO WATCH

2.1 Advantages

The advantages of self-billing are—

- your accounting staff will be working with uniform purchase documentation; and
- it may make invoicing easier if you (rather than your supplier) determine the value of your purchase after the goods have been delivered or the services supplied.

Commentary—*De Voil Indirect Tax Service* **V3.523**.

2.2 Points to watch

Before you begin self-billing, you should consider the following points—

— You can only recover the VAT shown on self-billed invoices if you meet the conditions explained in this notice.

— You may find it difficult to set up self-billing arrangements with your suppliers, or burdensome to maintain them.

— You will be responsible for ensuring that the self-billed invoices you raise carry the correct VAT liability for the goods or services supplied to you.

— If you are raising *electronic* self-billed invoices to large numbers of suppliers, you will need to ensure that your accounting system is robust and accurate enough to handle the demands you will be placing on it. There is more information about this in section 8 of Notice 700/63 "Electronic Invoicing".

3 SELF-BILLING AGREEMENTS

Commentary—*De Voil Indirect Tax Service* **V3.523**.

3.1 Contents of agreements

A self-billed invoice can only be issued under an agreement with your supplier. The following table summarises what the VAT regulations say about what makes a valid self-billing agreement.

No.	*A valid self-billing agreement must . . .*
1	include the supplier's agreement for the self-biller to raise invoices in respect of his (the self-billee's) supplies.
2	specify that the supplier agrees not to raise VAT invoices for supplies covered by the agreement.
3	contain a start date and expiry date, though the expiry date can be related to the term of any contract between the supplier and customer.
4	bind both you and your supplier. This means it should be in writing either on paper or in electronic form.
5	be produced if you are asked to produce it by one of our visiting officers.

You can't claim the VAT back on a self-billed invoice you have raised if the supplier is not VAT-registered, so it is advisable for the agreement to include—

6 the supplier's agreement that he will notify the self-biller if he ceases to be registered, transfers his business as a going concern or becomes registered under another VAT number.

Your self-billed invoice replaces your supplier's sales invoice it is helpful for the agreement to—

7 make it clear if you intend to outsource responsibility for issuing the self-bills to a third party, such as an accounting bureau.

Remember, any invoice must conform with the rules for a self-billed VAT invoice in paragraph 4.2.

3.2 How to prepare an agreement

To help you prepare an agreement, we have provided an example at section 8 of this notice. You may use this and complete it with your own and your supplier's details if you wish.

If you prefer, you can prepare your own agreement or make it part of the contract with your supplier. But if you do this, remember to include *all* the information required in an agreement.

3.3 Reviewing agreements

A self-billing agreement will specify the period that the agreement is to run for. If you want to carry on self-billing at the end of that period—

- you will need to review the agreement so that you can provide HMRC with evidence to show that your supplier has agreed to accept the invoices you raise on his behalf for a further period, and
- you and your supplier will need to agree a new period for self-billing.

However, if you have a business contract with your supplier, you may not need to make separate self-billing agreements. In these circumstances the self-billing agreement is included in the terms of the contract, the agreement will last until the end date of the contract. In these circumstances, you would need to review the self-billing agreement until the contract had expired.

Reviewing agreements is important, because it allows you to confirm that your supplier is—

- still VAT-registered; and
- happy to continue the VAT self-billing arrangement with you for a further period.

For this reason it is advisable to carry out a review every 12 months.

3.3.1 If I have made VAT self-billing agreements with individual suppliers on different dates, do I have to review them all on the same date?

No. If you have a large number of suppliers, and you have made agreements with them on different dates, you will review each agreement when the expiry date for each agreement occurs.

If you do make individual agreements with your suppliers on the same date, and the agreements all expire on the same date (for example, you have agreed with all of your suppliers to operate VAT self-billing for a period of 12 months from today's date) you may find it difficult to review all of the agreements on the same date. In such a situation you may, if you wish, review them on a rolling basis spread over 6 to 12 months.

If you do this, take care when setting time limits on your original agreements. Please remember, you must avoid self-billing a supplier at any time when you do not have his written agreement to do so.

3.3.2 What if I self-bill one of my suppliers for less than 12 months?

If you are providing self-billed invoices to a supplier for a period of less than 12 months, you will not normally need to review the agreement.

3.4 What if I fail to set up an agreement?

Without an agreement, the self-billed invoices you have issued are not evidence of your entitlement to input tax, and you may be assessed for tax and a penalty if you have claimed input tax on them.

4 RULES FOR SELF-BILLERS

This section covers the rules that apply when you have a formal agreement with your supplier to self-bill.

Commentary—*De Voil Indirect Tax Service* **V3.514, 523**.

4.1 Main rules for self-billers

If you are a self-biller you must—

- raise self-billed invoices for all transactions with the supplier named on the document for the period of the agreement between you and your supplier; or, if you have a contract with your supplier, for the duration of that contract;
- complete self-billed documents showing the supplier's name, address and VAT registration number, together with all the other details that make up a full VAT invoice. For more information, see paragraph 4.2;
- set up a new agreement if your supplier transfers his business as a going concern, and both you and the individual who has bought the business want to continue operating self-billing;
- keep the names, addresses and VAT registration numbers of the suppliers who have agreed to you self-billing them, and be able to produce them for HMRC to inspect if they ask you to. We recommend that you review these details regularly so that you can be sure that you are only claiming VAT on invoices you have issued to suppliers who have valid VAT registration numbers. The simplest way of doing this is to keep a list of the suppliers you self-bill.

You must *not* issue self-billed VAT invoices—

- — on behalf of suppliers who are not registered, or who have deregistered;
- on behalf of a supplier who has changed his VAT registration number until you have drawn up a new self-billing agreement with him.

One way that you can check whether the VAT registration number and address provided by your supplier is valid is by entering the VAT registration number on the European Commission VIES VAT registration number validation page at VIES VAT number validation (http://ec.europa.eu/taxation_customs/vies/)

4.2 What information must self-billed invoices contain?

The invoices must contain all the data elements listed in paragraph 16.3 of Notice 700 "The VAT Guide".

The following rule has the force of law

You must clearly mark each self-billed invoice you raise with the reference: "SELF-BILLING"

HMRC advises that you should also include the following statement on each self-billed invoice you raise:
"THE VAT SHOWN IS YOUR OUTPUT TAX DUE TO HMRC".

This will help to prevent your suppliers claiming the VAT back on these invoices by mistake.

4.3 What if I buy a business from somebody who has been self-billing?

You may carry on self-billing if this method of accounting suits both you and your suppliers. If you do decide to continue self-billing, you must make a new self-billing agreement with each supplier.

If you are not sure whether you want to self-bill your suppliers, section 2 will help you to weigh up the advantages and disadvantages.

4.4 What if I use a third party to issue my self-billed invoices?

If you use a third party service provider to issue self-billed invoices on your behalf, you are still responsible for ensuring that invoices are issued.

This is because your suppliers will have agreed to accept the invoices that *you* issue on their behalf. So, you will still be responsible for:

- setting up and reviewing self-billing agreements with your suppliers;
- keeping copies of those agreements;
- keeping the names, addresses and registration details of your suppliers; and
- producing the copy agreements or your suppliers' details for inspection when HMRC asks you to.

4.5 What if I need to correct a self-billed invoice?

You should not reduce the value of a supply for which you have already raised a self-billed invoice by reducing the total you show on a subsequent invoice. Instead, you should issue a debit note for the amount by which the value of the supply has been changed.

4.6 What happens if I break the self-billing rules?

If this happens the self-billed invoices you issue will not be proper invoices. They will not be evidence of your right to deduct input tax and your supplier will have to issue his own invoices.

4.7 What if I have claimed input tax incorrectly?

Claiming input tax incorrectly can result in an assessment, which may carry a penalty and interest.

To help avoid this, please remember that you cannot claim input tax—

- when your supplier is not registered for VAT, or has deregistered; or
- on any sales invoices from your supplier to whom you have already issued a self-billed invoice for the same supply.

If you find that you have claimed input tax incorrectly, please see Notice 700/45 "How to correct VAT errors and make adjustments or claims" (Part V8). This will tell you how to correct the error and how you can avoid a penalty.

5 TAX POINTS FOR SELF-BILLED SUPPLIES

5.1 What is the tax point for supplies I self-bill?

The normal tax point rules described in sections 14 and 15 of Notice 700 "The VAT Guide" apply, apart from those linked to the issue of a VAT invoice. This is because issuing a self-billed invoice does not normally create a tax point in the same way as happens when a supplier issues its own VAT invoice.

The one exception to this is where you issue a self-billed invoice within 14 days of the basic tax point as described in paragraph 14.2.2(b) of Notice 700 "The VAT Guide" (Part V8). This creates a tax point in the same way as a normal VAT invoice.

Commentary—*De Voil Indirect Tax Service* **V3.523**.

5.2 When can I claim the input tax?

You can claim input tax on a self-billed invoice in the accounting period in which the tax point falls (in line with paragraph 5.1 above).

Where you issue a self-billed invoice with payment to the supplier, you may use a notional tax point for the purposes of claiming back input tax. The notional tax point is the day after the date the self-bill invoice was issued.

6 INFORMATION FOR SELF-BILLEES (SUPPLIERS)

6.1 How will I know if one of my customers is intending to self-bill?

The customer will seek your agreement in writing. We have provided an example of a written agreement at section 8. The agreement that your customer asks you to sign will be similar to this.

The rules for agreements are explained in paragraph 3.1.

You will need to keep a copy of any self-billing agreement you make. You may keep this in either a paper or electronic format, but must be able to produce it if one of HMRC's visiting officers asks you to.

Once you have given your agreement, the main rules that apply to you as a self-billee are explained in paragraph 6.3.

Commentary—*De Voil Indirect Tax Service* **V3.523**.

6.2 What if I do not want to agree to self-billing?

HMRC will not insist that you agree to self-billing. But your customer may make self-billing a condition of doing business with you.

6.3 Main rules for self-billees (suppliers)

If you are a self-billee, you must—

- *not* raise sales invoices for any transactions with your self-biller for the period of your self-billing agreement with him. The agreement will last either for a specified period agreed between you *or*, if you have a contract with your customer, for the duration of that contract;
- agree to accept the invoices your customer raises on your behalf for the duration of the agreement; and
- agree to notify your customer at once if your VAT registration status changes. This is because a new agreement will have to be drawn up.

6.4 How should I treat the self-bills I receive for VAT purposes?

The self-billed invoice relates to supplies you have made to your customer, and the VAT figure on it is your output tax. You need to account for this on the VAT payable side of your VAT Account (see section 6 of Notice 700/21 "Keeping Records and Accounts").

Self-billees sometimes make the mistake of treating their self-billed invoices as purchase invoices. If you have treated the VAT on a self-billed invoice as your input tax, this is an error. Section 2 of Notice 700/45 "How to correct VAT errors and make adjustments or claims", tells you how to correct the error.

Remember, you must not issue your own sales invoices in respect of any transactions covered by the self-billing agreement.

6.5 When do I have to account for the output tax on self-bills?

This is governed by the tax point in the normal way. The rules are described in sections 14 and 15 of Notice 700 "The VAT Guide". There is more information on the effect these rules have on self-billed supplies in section 5 of this notice.

Your customer is required to show the tax point on the self-billed invoice. You need to be aware that, under the normal tax point rules, you may still be required to account for output tax even if you have not yet—

- received the self-billed invoice; or
- been paid for the supply.

6.6 What if I can't meet the self-billing conditions?

If you—

- are unable to meet the conditions for self-billing in this notice
- fail to meet them

you will have to tell your customer/s and arrange to issue your own invoices for the supplies you make to them.

7 SELF-BILLING OUTSIDE THE UK

7.1 Can I self-bill outside the UK?

Yes. Self-billing is not restricted to domestic supplies. You may hold self-billing agreements with businesses in EC member states and in countries outside the EU.

7.2 What are the rules for intra-EC self-billing?

Individual member states cannot impose additional conditions for VAT self-billing, so there will not be any additional conditions or procedures for self-billing in the member states in whose territory the goods or services are supplied.

7.3 Supplies of goods

The following table tells you what you will need to bear in mind if you have self-billing agreements for supplies of goods with non-UK businesses.

If you are a . . .	*Then you need to . . .*
self-biller being supplied with goods from another member state	be aware that the self-billed invoice may establish the time of acquisition in the same way as an invoice issued by the supplier. You will find more about the time of acquisition in section 4 of Notice 725 "The Single Market".
self-billee supplying goods to another member state	be able to meet the conditions in paragraph 3.1 of Notice 725 "The Single Market" so that you have evidence to support the zero-rating of that supply. Remember that, when you negotiate the agreement, you will be agreeing to accept *all* the invoices that your customer issues on your behalf. Remember also that the terms of this agreement may be different from those in the agreements you have signed with your UK customers for the reason given in paragraph 7.2.
self-biller being supplied with goods from a country outside the EU	familiarise yourself with the rules on import VAT in Notice 702 "Imports". You may also need to check what information your supplier will need you to include in the invoices you raise on his behalf so that they will be acceptable to his own tax authorities as evidence of export.
self-billee making supplies of goods to a country outside the EU	meet the requirements for documentary evidence of export. These are explained in section 2 of Notice 703 "Exports and removals of goods from the United Kingdom".

7.4 Supplies of services

If you have self-billing agreements for supplies of services with non-UK businesses, you will need to—

- be familiar with the rules in Notice 741 "Place of supply of services"; and
- agree the correct VAT treatment of the supply with the other party from the outset.

8 EXAMPLE SELF-BILLING AGREEMENT

What follows is an example of an acceptable self-billing agreement (www.hmrc.gov.uk/publicnotices/self-billing-agreement.pdf). You may use it if you wish to, but you do not have to word your agreement in exactly this way as long as the agreement you do use contains all the relevant information, as explained in section 3.

Self-Billing Agreement

This is an agreement to a self-billing procedure between

Customer name VAT number
And
Supplier name VAT number

The self-biller (the customer) agrees:

(1) To issue self-billed invoices for all supplies made to them by the self-billee (the supplier) until ______/______/______ *(insert either an end date for the agreement or the date your contract ends).*
(2) To complete self-billed invoices showing the supplier's name, address and VAT registration number, together with all the other details which constitute a full VAT invoice.
(3) To make a new self-billing agreement in the event that their VAT registration number changes.
(4) To inform the supplier if the issue of self billed invoices will be outsourced to a third party.

The self-billee agrees:

(1) To accept invoices raised by the self-biller on their behalf until ______/______/______ *(insert either an end date for the agreement or the date your contract ends).*
(2) Not to raise sales invoices for the transactions covered by this agreement.
(3) To notify the customer immediately if they
- change their VAT registration number;
- cease to be VAT registered; or
- sell their business, or part of their business.

Signed by Signed by
On behalf of On behalf of
Date Date

NOTICE 701/21
GOLD

2013

Commentary—*De Voil Indirect Tax Service* **V4.186.**

Note—Certain paragraphs within the following extracts have the force of law and these are enclosed within boxes.

3 THE NEED TO NOTIFY EXEMPT SUPPLIES OF INVESTMENT GOLD

3.1 When and how do I have to notify?

The first time that you make an exempt supply of investment gold which exceeds £5,000, or when the value of your supplies of exempt investment gold to any one customer is over £10,000 in any 12 month period, you must notify us within 28 days at the following address—

HM Revenue & Customs
Written Enquiries Section
Alexander House
Victoria Avenue
Southend
Essex SS99 1BD

If you are required to notify that you trade in investment gold and you are not registered for VAT, you must also provide the following information—

(1) Name of company, partnership or sole proprietor.
(2) Company incorporation number or details of partners.
(3) Address(es).
(4) Phone number.
(5) Contact name.
(6) Accountant's name, address and phone number.
(7) Associated VAT registration numbers.

The Gold Team will send you an acknowledgement. If, however, you do not receive this within 28 days, you must check that they have received your notification.

You do not need to notify us of subsequent supplies.

4 OPTING TO TAX INVESTMENT GOLD

. . .

4.3 What if I produce or transform gold into investment gold?

As long as you are a taxable person you may opt to tax any supply of investment gold to another taxable person.

You must notify your local Business Advice Centre if you intend to opt to tax. If you do not receive an acknowledgement within 28 days, you must check that they have received the notification.

4.4 What if I supply gold for industrial purposes?

If you are a taxable person, who as a normal part of your business supplies gold for industrial purposes, you may only opt to tax certain supplies of investment gold, *but you need to get our agreement first*.

To get our agreement to you opting to tax your supplies of investment gold, you must write to your local Business Advice Centre, giving your VAT registration number and confirming that you normally trade in gold for industrial purposes. If they agree they will send you a letter of approval within 28 days. They will normally impose conditions and the letter will also explain what these are and tell you when you can start opting.

We will accept that you normally supply investment gold for industrial purposes if you can show that you do so on a regular basis.

Once you have received our agreement, you may opt to tax supplies of investment gold bars or wafers you make to other taxable persons.

We may however withdraw our approval for the protection of the revenue.

4.5 What if I act as an agent?

If you are acting for a named principal and your principal has opted to tax, you may opt to tax your services in so far as they are related to your principal's "opted" supplies of investment gold.

> You must inform your local Business Advice Centre that you intend to opt to tax your services. If you do not receive an acknowledgement within 28 days, you must check that they have received the notification.

4.6 Do I need to alter my invoices?

As opting to tax a transaction is simple—once you have fulfilled the conditions in paragraph 4.3, 4.4 and 4.5, all you need to do is to include the following statement on your invoice.

> "We have opted to tax this transaction."

But please note that once you have opted to tax a particular supply you cannot change your mind and exempt it.

. . .

6 INVOICING REQUIREMENTS FOR TRADING IN EXEMPT INVESTMENT GOLD

. . .

6.2 When do I need to issue an invoice for sales of exempt investment gold?

> You *must* issue an invoice for—
>
> – each sale involving exempt investment gold which exceeds £5,000;
> – smaller transactions if the total value of sales to that customer has exceeded £10,000 in the last twelve months.
>
> You must also give each invoice a unique identifying number.

But please note that you do not need to produce the invoice or keep the records described in this section or section 7 or notify us that you trade in investment gold (section 3) if every supply of investment gold you make is for less than £5,000, unless the total value of supplies to an individual customer over the previous twelve months was above £10,000.

6.3 Do I need to raise an invoice if I buy investment gold from a person who does not trade in investment gold?

> Yes—you *must* issue an invoice on behalf of the seller if—
>
> – the value of the purchase is more than £5,000; or
> – you make more than one purchase from the same supplier and the total value of your purchases from that supplier has gone over £10,000 in the last twelve months.
>
> It must contain all of the relevant details specified in paragraph 6.4.
>
> Also, the invoice must include the following declaration which must be signed by the seller—
>
> "I declare that to the best of my knowledge the details shown on this invoice are correct." (Signature and name).

6.4 What must I show on the invoice for sales of exempt investment gold?

Each invoice *must* contain the following details if appropriate—

- name and address of seller; your name and address (if different to the seller); name and address of the purchaser; delivery address (if different); unique customer reference (see paragraph 7.1(b)).
- date of invoice; delivery date; type of supply (for example, sale).
- your VAT registration number if you, or your principal are registered for VAT, or the seller's VAT registration number (if you are not the seller); and
- a description of the gold supplied;
  - *for bars and wafers*—form, weight and purity, any other identifying feature (including any proprietary mark, hallmark and serial number where applicable); *or*
  - *for investment gold coins*—the coin type, country of origin and whether or not the coin is included on the list of gold coins reproduced in Notice 701/21A "Investment gold coins".
- the number of items; and
- the total amount payable.

. . .

7 RECORDS TO BE KEPT

7.1 Records to be kept for gold delivered or taken away by your customer

If you sell exempt investment gold which is delivered or available to be taken away by your customer, you must keep the following information as part of your business records. These requirements do not apply if you make supplies described within paragraphs 7.2, 7.3(a), 7.6 and 8.2.

This applies whether or not you are registered for VAT.

(a) Accounting record

You must keep and maintain a record showing the following details—

- invoice number;
- invoice date;
- customer reference number;
- customer's VAT registration number (if applicable);
- description of the gold (form, quantity and purity);
- name and address of the agent (if applicable);
- name and address of the purchaser; and
- transaction value.

(b) Customer record

You must keep and maintain a record identifying customers who purchase exempt investment gold. This record must have a unique reference number and contain the following information—

- name;
- date of birth;
- current address; and
- phone number (if available).

You must take reasonable steps to make sure that your customer has given you correct information. In order to do this, you must ask for and examine at least one document from each of the following lists.

List 1	*List 2*
Passport	phone bill
Full driving licence	Other utility bill
National Insurance card	Deeds
Birth certificate	Tenancy lease
National identity card	Council tax bill
	Hotel key card (for non-UK residents only)

You may agree alternative satisfactory evidence with your local Business Advice Centre.

If possible, you should keep a copy of the documents you see. You should write on each copy "certified as original document". You must sign and date this declaration.

If it is not possible to keep a copy of the document you see, you must record, as part of your customer record, sufficient details to let us to obtain a copy if we ask. As a minimum you should record—

- the name of the document;
- the reference number; and
- the name and address of the issuing authority.

You must insist that your customer produces the original document. You must keep the record up to date.

(c) Method of keeping the required particulars

Where you are required to keep and maintain the records specified in parts (a) and (b) of this paragraph you may, as an alternative, keep and maintain the details required in a manner which is convenient for your business provided—

- all the details specified are accessible for inspection by a VAT officer; and
- you have agreed the format with your local Business Advice Centre.

7.2 Banks and other financial service businesses

If you are a bank or other financial service business which, for the purposes of the Money Laundering Regulations, SI 1993/1933, is a "relevant financial business" you may, as an alternative to the customer record set out in paragraph 7.1(b), keep and maintain the records specified in those regulations.

Relevant financial businesses to which this applies must conduct the appropriate identification procedures and keep the required records in the case of all transactions in investment gold where the value of a one-off transaction exceeds 15,000 euro or, where one-off transactions appear linked and their value together exceeds 15,000 euro.

For the purposes of this notice the exchange rate between the euro and the United Kingdom Pound sterling shall be the annual rate published in the Official Journal of the European Communities (OJEC).

7.3 Auctioneers and other agents of investment gold

(a) Were you are acting in your own name

If, as an agent or auctioneer, you invoice goods in your own name for goods sold on behalf of a third party vendor, the goods are treated for VAT purposes as supplies both to and by you. Auctioneers are treated as agents for VAT purposes. For more information about the VAT treatment of transactions by agents see Notice 700 "The VAT guide".

You are considered to be making a supply of services to the vendor in return for commission charged, and if a buyer's premium is charged, you are also making a further supply of services to the buyer.

It is important not to confuse the supply of the goods with the supply of services to the seller or the buyer.

As an agent or auctioneer, you are treated as if you were supplying the goods yourself. The special scheme applies to you in the same way as it would apply to a principal. Supplies involving investment gold or investment gold coins will be exempt, unless you are selling gold upon which an option to tax has been exercised. For more information about opting to tax see section 4. The auctioneer will also have the same rights of deduction (see section 5) and is bound by the same notification, record keeping and accounting obligations (see sections 6, 7, and 8).

It is important that you check with the vendor before the sale whether the gold being sold is investment gold. If you are an auctioneer you should also remember that investment gold coins are not eligible for the Auctioneers' Scheme.

If you are an agent or auctioneer acting in your own name, your supply of services to either the buyer or the seller will be taxable.

(b) Where you are acting in the name of your principal

If, as an agent or auctioneer, you sell and invoice the goods in the name of your principal, your supply will be exempt (see paragraph 2.2). You may opt to tax these services, if you are registered for VAT and your principal also opts to tax his onward supply of the investment gold (see paragraph 4.5).

7.4 Internet and mail order sales

If you sell investment gold over the internet or by mail order and you fulfil the conditions at (a) or (b) below, you may, instead of keeping the customer record set out at paragraph 7.1(b), keep and maintain the following record—

(a) if your supply is paid for by credit card and the delivery address is also the card holder's address, you must record the name of your customer, the credit card issuer and the card number; or

(b) if your supply is paid for by cheque, you must record the name of your customer, the name of the bank and the account number of your customer.

You must also keep proof of despatch of the investment gold to your customer's address.

7.5 Sales by VAT registered businesses

If you are registered for VAT and you are—

- authorised to opt to tax supplies of investment gold; or
- a producer or transformer of investment gold;

you must keep and maintain with your VAT account, in addition to the records set out in paragraphs 3.1, 6.2, 6.3, and 7.3(a) and 7.6, a record of any supply of investment gold made to another taxable person where you have delivered or otherwise made the gold available to them, and on which you have not opted to tax.

7.6 Sales to VAT registered businesses

If you sell investment gold to another VAT registered business you may, instead of keeping the customer record described at paragraph 7.1(b), ask your customer for their VAT registration number. However, you must check with your local Business Advice Centre that the VAT registration number provided is authentic.

7.7 How long must I keep my records?

You must keep all the documents and records specified in this section for at least six years from the date of the transaction. In the case of regular customers, you must keep your customer record for six years following the most recent supply of investment gold.

> If you purchase investment gold you must keep the purchase invoice you receive for at least six years from the date of the transaction.

NOTICE 701/21A
INVESTMENT GOLD COINS

February 2012.

This notice cancels and replaces Notice 701/21A (February 2011).

1 INTRODUCTION

1.1 What does this notice cover?

This notice:

— explains that an investment gold coin is exempt from Value Added Tax (VAT) and explains which coins can be considered as investment gold coins (see section 2), and

— provides revised lists of investment gold coins whose supply is exempt from VAT (in section 3). Readers are advised that, because there are several changes from previous lists, they should refer directly to the lists for qualifying coins.

You should read this notice alongside Notice 701/21 "Gold" which gives further information about dealing in gold coins.

You can access details of any changes to this notice since January 2010 on our website, go to www.hmrc.gov.uk or by phoning the VAT Helpline on 0845 010 9000.

Commentary—*De Voil Indirect Tax Service* **V4.186.**

1.2 Who should read this notice?

Traders dealing in investment gold coins.

2 INVESTMENT GOLD COINS

2.1 What is an investment gold coin?

An investment gold coin is:

(a) gold coin minted after 1800 that:
— is of a purity of not less than 900 thousandths
— is, or has been, legal tender in its country of origin, and
— is of a description of coin that is normally sold at a price that does not exceed 180 per cent of the open market value of the gold contained in the coin, or

(b) a gold coin on the lists in Section 3.

A coin not on the lists can still be exempt from VAT if it falls within the description at (a) above. But you must be able to show from your business records that any such coin meets the criteria.

You should treat coins that do not fall within (a) or (b) above as subject to VAT at the standard rate.

Commentary—*De Voil Indirect Tax Service* **V4.186.**

2.2 Coin types

All gold coins that have the same denomination (face value), size and gold fineness as those described at paragraph 2.1 and section 3, are exempt from VAT.

The definition for VAT purposes is wider than the one which coin experts (numismatists) normally use. This is because changes of superficial design do not alter the gold coin type or description.

So, a gold coin type may be a single issue for one year, or have been produced for almost two centuries, as in the case of the British sovereign.

Commentary—*De Voil Indirect Tax Service* **V4.186.**

2.3 Selling price

Of the three criteria in paragraph 2.1(a), only the selling price of the coin is subjective.

Coins are minted in various finishes and will be sold at a variety of prices. If exemption depended on the actual selling price of an individual coin this would lead to inconsistency. Administration of the exemption would become burdensome for traders and HM Revenue & Customs (HMRC) alike. For this reason, exemption depends on the normal selling price.

Commentary—*De Voil Indirect Tax Service* **V4.186.**

2.4 What is the "normal" selling price?

This is the price that can most usually be demanded for a particular type of coin.

It does not matter that an individual coin is of special interest to collectors; if the usual price of the coin type falls within 180 per cent of the value of the gold contained therein, all coins of that type will be exempt.

Similarly, if a coin type is usually valued at more than 180 per cent of the gold value, because of its interest to collectors, but an individual coin is in such poor condition that it is worth less than 180 per cent of its gold value, that coin (like others of its type), will be subject to VAT at the standard rate.

Commentary—*De Voil Indirect Tax Service* **V4.186.**

2.5 Conditions affecting the normal selling price

The finish influences the normal selling price of coins. Investment gold coins fall into two broad classes.

The first consists of relatively older issues made to circulate as currency.

These will normally be worn from circulation.

The second, generally more recent, are primarily produced as a store of wealth. These may have been issued in a number of finishes and if the majority of a type of coin are in for example "brilliant uncirculated" condition then, other things being equal, the brilliant uncirculated value will reflect the normal selling price.

On the other hand, if the majority of a particular coin are in "proof" condition, then the value of the proof coin is more likely to reflect the normal selling price. The test of normal selling price must take into account these factors and be based on the condition in which the gold coin type is most frequently traded.

Commentary—*De Voil Indirect Tax Service* **V4.186.**

2.6 Can I use the Margin Scheme for investment gold coins?

No. You cannot sell investment gold coins (see paragraph 2.1) under the Margin Scheme.

If you have mistakenly included investment gold coins as purchases in Margin Scheme stock records, delete the entry and note it accordingly.

If you have included the coins in Global Accounting purchases, remove the items from the scheme and adjust the total purchases in the period. You must also deduct the value you have attributed to the items from your Global Accounting purchase record.

Guidance on correcting errors is in Notice 700/45 "How to correct VAT errors and make adjustments or claims".

Further guidance on the Margin Scheme is in Notice 718 "The VAT margin scheme and global accounting".

Commentary—*De Voil Indirect Tax Service* **V4.186.**

2.7 Record keeping requirements for dealers in investment gold coins

There are specific record keeping and notification rules for dealers in investment gold and investment gold coins. These are in Notice 701/21 "Gold".

3 LISTS OF INVESTMENT GOLD COINS

The European Commission publish annually a list of gold coins which must be treated as investment gold coins in all EU member states. **The list has legal force and supplements the law.**

HMRC have added an additional list of gold coins alongside the European Commission list. These are gold coins that HMRC recognise as falling within the exemption for investment gold coins.

This second list does not have legal force.

These lists are valid for the year 2012. They are set in alphabetical order, by names of countries and denominations of coins. Within the same category of coins, the list follows the increasing value of the currency.

The denomination of each coin reflects the currency shown on the coins. However, where the currency on the coin is not shown in roman script, where possible its denomination in the list is shown in brackets.

Commentary—*De Voil Indirect Tax Service* **V4.186.**

Table 1: The European Commission List

Country of issue	*Denomination of the coins*
AFGHANISTAN	(20 AFGHANI)
	10 000 AFGHANI
	(½ AMANI)
	(1 AMANI)
	(2 AMANI)
	(4 GRAMS)
	(8 GRAMS)
	1 TILLA
	2 TILLAS
ALBANIA	20 LEKE
	50 LEKE
	100 LEKE
	200 LEKE
	500 LEKE
ALDERNEY	5 POUNDS
	25 POUNDS
	1 000 POUNDS
ANDORRA	50 DINERS
	100 DINERS
	250 DINERS
	1 SOVEREIGN
ANGUILLA	5 DOLLARS
	10 DOLLARS
	20 DOLLARS
	100 DOLLARS
ARGENTINA	1 ARGENTINO
ARUBA	10 FLORIN
	25 FLORIN
AUSTRALIA	5 DOLLARS
	15 DOLLARS
	25 DOLLARS
	50 DOLLARS
	100 DOLLARS
	150 DOLLARS
	200 DOLLARS

Country of issue	*Denomination of the coins*
	250 DOLLARS
	500 DOLLARS
	1 000 DOLLARS
	2 500 DOLLARS
	3 000 DOLLARS
	10 000 DOLLARS
	½ SOVEREIGN (= ½ POUND)
	1 SOVEREIGN (= 1 POUND)
AUSTRIA	10 CORONA (= 10 KRONEN)
	100 CORONA (= 100 KRONEN)
	1 DUCAT
	(4 DUCATS)
	10 EURO
	25 EURO
	50 EURO
	100 EURO
	4 FLORIN = 10 FRANCS (= 4 GULDEN)
	8 FLORIN = 20 FRANCS (= 8 GULDEN)
	25 SCHILLING
	100 SCHILLING
	200 SCHILLING
	200 SCHILLING/ 10 EURO
	500 SCHILLING
	1 000 SCHILLING
	2 000 SCHILLING
BAHAMAS	10 DOLLARS
	20 DOLLARS
	25 DOLLARS
	50 DOLLARS
	100 DOLLARS
	150 DOLLARS
	200 DOLLARS
	250 DOLLARS
	2 500 DOLLARS
BELGIUM	10 ECU
	20 ECU
	25 ECU
	50 ECU
	100 ECU
	50 EURO GOLD
	100 EURO
	20 FRANCS
	5 000 FRANCS
BELIZE	25 DOLLARS
	50 DOLLARS
	100 DOLLARS
	250 DOLLARS
BERMUDA	10 DOLLARS
	25 DOLLARS
	30 DOLLARS
	50 DOLLARS

Country of issue	*Denomination of the coins*
	60 DOLLARS
	100 DOLLARS
	200 DOLLARS
	250 DOLLARS
BHUTAN	1 SERTUM
	2 SERTUMS
	5 SERTUMS
BOLIVIA	4 000 PESOS BOLIVIANOS
BOTSWANA	5 PULA
	150 PULA
	10 THEBE
BRAZIL	300 CRUZEIROS
	(4 000 REIS)
	(5 000 REIS)
	(6 400 REIS)
	(10 000 REIS)
	(20 000 REIS)
BRITISH VIRGIN ISLES	100 DOLLARS
BULGARIA	(1 LEV)
	(5 LEVA)
	(10 LEVA)
	(20 LEVA)
	(100 LEVA)
	(125 LEVA)
	(1 000 LEVA)
	(10 000 LEVA)
	(20 000 LEVA)
BURUNDI	10 FRANCS
	25 FRANCS
	50 FRANCS
	100 FRANCS
CANADA	1 DOLLAR
	2 DOLLARS
	5 DOLLARS
	10 DOLLARS
	20 DOLLARS
	50 DOLLARS
	100 DOLLARS
	175 DOLLARS
	200 DOLLARS
	350 DOLLARS
	1 SOVEREIGN
CAYMAN ISLANDS	25 DOLLARS
	50 DOLLARS
	100 DOLLARS
	250 DOLLARS
CHAD	3 000 FRANCS
	5 000 FRANCS
	10 000 FRANCS
	20 000 FRANCS
CHILE	2 PESOS

Country of issue	Denomination of the coins
	5 PESOS
	10 PESOS
	20 PESOS
	50 PESOS
	100 PESOS
	200 PESOS
CHINA	5/20 YUAN (1/20 oz)
	10/50 YUAN (1/10 oz)
	25/100 YUAN (1/4 oz)
	50/200 YUAN (½ oz)
	100/500 YUAN (1 oz)
	5 (YUAN)
	10 (YUAN)
	20 (YUAN)
	25 (YUAN)
	50 (YUAN)
	100 (YUAN)
	150 (YUAN)
	200 (YUAN)
	250 (YUAN)
	300 (YUAN)
	400 (YUAN)
	450 (YUAN)
	500 (YUAN)
	1 000 (YUAN)
COLOMBIA	1 PESO
	2 PESOS
	2 ½ PESOS
	5 PESOS
	10 PESOS
	20 PESOS
	100 PESOS
	200 PESOS
	300 PESOS
	500 PESOS
	1 000 PESOS
	1 500 PESOS
	2 000 PESOS
	15 000 PESOS
CONGO	10 FRANCS
	20 FRANCS
	25 FRANCS
	50 FRANCS
	100 FRANCS
COOK ISLANDS	100 DOLLARS
	200 DOLLARS
	250 DOLLARS
COSTA RICA	5 COLONES
	10 COLONES
	20 COLONES
	50 COLONES

Country of issue	*Denomination of the coins*
	100 COLONES
	200 COLONES
	1 500 COLONES
	5 000 COLONES
	25 000 COLONES
CUBA	4 PESOS
	5 PESOS
	10 PESOS
	20 PESOS
	50 PESOS
	100 PESOS
CYPRUS	50 POUNDS
CZECH REPUBLIC	1 000 KORUN (1 000 Kc)
	2 000 KORUN (2 000 Kc)
	2 500 KORUN (2 500 Kc)
	5 000 KORUN (5 000 Kc)
	10 000 KORUN (10 000 Kc)
CZECHOSLOVAKIA	1 DUKAT
	2 DUKAT
	5 DUKAT
	10 DUKAT
DENMARK	10 KRONER
	20 KRONER
	1 000 KRONER
DOMINICAN REPUBLIC	30 PESOS
	100 PESOS
	200 PESOS
	250 PESOS
ECUADOR	1 CONDOR
	10 SUCRES
EL SALVADOR	25 COLONES
	50 COLONES
	100 COLONES
	200 COLONES
	250 COLONES
EQUATORIAL GUINEA	250 PESETAS
	500 PESETAS
	750 PESETAS
	1 000 PESETAS
	5 000 PESETAS
ETHIOPIA	400 BIRR
	600 BIRR
	10 (DOLLARS)
	20 (DOLLARS)
	50 (DOLLARS)
	100 (DOLLARS)
	200 (DOLLARS)
FIJI	5 DOLLARS
	10 DOLLARS
	200 DOLLARS
	250 DOLLARS

Country of issue	*Denomination of the coins*
FINLAND	100 EURO
	1 000 MARKKAA
	2 000 MARKKAA
FRANCE	¼ EURO
	10 EURO
	20 EURO
	50 EURO
	100 EURO
	200 EURO
	250 EURO
	500 EURO
	1 000 EURO
	5 000 EURO
	5 FRANCS
	10 FRANCS
	20 FRANCS
	40 FRANCS
	50 FRANCS
	100 FRANCS
	500 FRANCS
	655, 97 FRANCS
GABON	10 FRANCS
	25 FRANCS
	50 FRANCS
	100 FRANCS
	1 000 FRANCS
	3 000 FRANCS
	5 000 FRANCS
	10 000 FRANCS
	20 000 FRANCS
GAMBIA	200 DALASIS
	500 DALASIS
	1 000 DALASIS
GERMANY	1 DM
	100 EURO
GIBRALTAR	1/25 CROWN
	1/10 CROWN
	1/5 CROWN
	1/2 CROWN
	1 CROWN
	2 CROWNS
	50 PENCE
	1 POUND
	5 POUNDS
	25 POUNDS
	50 POUNDS
	100 POUNDS
	1/25 ROYAL
	1/10 ROYAL
	1/5 ROYAL
	½ ROYAL

Country of issue	*Denomination of the coins*
	1 ROYAL
GUATEMALA	5 QUETZALES
	10 QUETZALES
	20 QUETZALES
GUERNSEY	1 POUND
	5 POUNDS
	10 POUNDS
	25 POUNDS
	50 POUNDS
	100 POUNDS
GUINEA	1 000 FRANCS
	2 000 FRANCS
	5 000 FRANCS
	10 000 FRANCS
HAITI	20 GOURDES
	50 GOURDES
	100 GOURDES
	200 GOURDES
	500 GOURDES
	1 000 GOURDES
HONDURAS	200 LEMPIRAS
	500 LEMPIRAS
HONG KONG	1 000 DOLLARS
HUNGARY	1 DUKAT
	4 FORINT = 10 FRANCS
	8 FORINT = 20 FRANCS
	50 FORINT
	100 FORINT
	200 FORINT
	500 FORINT
	1 000 FORINT
	5 000 FORINT
	10 000 FORINT
	20 000 FORINT
	50 000 FORINT
	100 000 FORINT
	500 000 FORINT
	10 KORONA
	20 KORONA
	100 KORONA
ICELAND	500 KRONUR
	10 000 KRONUR
INDIA	1 MOHUR
	15 RUPEES
	1 SOVEREIGN
INDONESIA	2 000 RUPIAH
	5 000 RUPIAH
	10 000 RUPIAH
	20 000 RUPIAH
	25 000 RUPIAH
	100 000 RUPIAH

Country of issue	*Denomination of the coins*
	200 000 RUPIAH
IRAN	(1/2 AZADI)
	(1 AZADI)
	(1/4 PAHLAVI)
	(1/2 PAHLAVI)
	(1 PAHLAVI)
	(2 1/2 PAHLAVI)
	(5 PAHLAVI)
	(10 PAHLAVI)
	50 POUND
	500 RIALS
	750 RIALS
	1 000 RIALS
	2 000 RIALS
IRAQ	(5 DINARS)
	(50 DINARS)
	(100 DINARS)
ISLE OF MAN	1/20 ANGEL
	1/10 ANGEL
	1/4 ANGEL
	1/2 ANGEL
	1 ANGEL
	5 ANGEL
	10 ANGEL
	15 ANGEL
	20 ANGEL
	1/25 CROWN
	1/10 CROWN
	1/5 CROWN
	1/2 CROWN
	1 CROWN
	50 PENCE
	1 POUND
	2 POUNDS
	5 POUNDS
	50 POUNDS
	(1/2 SOVEREIGN)
	(1 SOVEREIGN)
	(2 SOVEREIGNS)
	(5 SOVEREIGNS)
ISRAEL	20 LIROT
	50 LIROT
	100 LIROT
	200 LIROT
	500 LIROT
	1 000 LIROT
	5 000 LIROT
	5 NEW SHEQALIM
	10 NEW SHEQALIM
	20 NEW SHEQALIM
	5 SHEQALIM

Country of issue	*Denomination of the coins*
	10 SHEQALIM
	500 SHEQEL
ITALY	20 EURO
	50 EURO
IVORY COAST	10 FRANCS
	25 FRANCS
	50 FRANCS
	100 FRANCS
JAMAICA	100 DOLLARS
	250 DOLLARS
JERSEY	1 POUND
	2 POUNDS
	5 POUNDS
	10 POUNDS
	20 POUNDS
	25 POUNDS
	50 POUNDS
	100 POUNDS
	1 SOVEREIGN
JORDAN	2 DINARS
	5 DINARS
	10 DINARS
	25 DINARS
	50 DINARS
	60 DINARS
KATANGA	5 FRANCS
KENYA	100 SHILLINGS
	250 SHILLINGS
	500 SHILLINGS
KIRIBATI	150 DOLLARS
LATVIA	100 LATU
LESOTHO	1 LOTI
	2 MALOTI
	4 MALOTI
	10 MALOTI
	20 MALOTI
	50 MALOTI
	100 MALOTI
	250 MALOTI
	500 MALOTI
LITHUANIA	100 LITU
	200 LITU
LUXEMBOURG	5 EURO
	10 EURO
	20 FRANCS
	40 FRANCS
MACAU	250 PATACAS
	500 PATACAS
	1 000 PATACAS
	10 000 PATACAS
MALAWI	250 KWACHA

Country of issue	*Denomination of the coins*
MALAYSIA	100 RINGGIT
	200 RINGGIT
	250 RINGGIT
	500 RINGGIT
MALI	10 FRANCS
	25 FRANCS
	50 FRANCS
	100 FRANCS
MALTA	50 EURO
	5 (LIRI)
	10 (LIRI)
	20 (LIRI)
	25 (LIRI)
	50 (LIRI)
	100 (LIRI)
	LM 25
MARSHALL ISLANDS	20 DOLLARS
	50 DOLLARS
	200 DOLLARS
MAURITIUS	100 RUPEES
	200 RUPEES
	250 RUPEES
	500 RUPEES
	1 000 RUPEES
MEXICO	1/20 ONZA
	1/10 ONZA
	¼ ONZA
	½ ONZA
	1 ONZA
	2 PESOS
	2½ PESOS
	5 PESOS
	10 PESOS
	20 PESOS
	50 PESOS
	250 PESOS
	500 PESOS
	1 000 PESOS
	2 000 PESOS
MONACO	10 EURO
	20 EURO
	100 EURO
	20 FRANCS
	100 FRANCS
	200 FRANCS
MONGOLIA	750 (TUGRIK)
	1 000 (TUGRIK)
NEPAL	1 ASARPHI
	1 000 RUPEES
NETHERLANDS	(1 DUKAAT)
	(2 DUKAAT)

Country of issue	*Denomination of the coins*
	10 EURO
	20 EURO
	50 EURO
	1 GULDEN
	5 GULDEN
	10 GULDEN
NETHERLANDS ANTILLES	5 GULDEN
	10 GULDEN
	50 GULDEN
	100 GULDEN
	300 GULDEN
NEW ZEALAND	5 DOLLARS
	10 DOLLARS
	150 DOLLARS
	1,56 grammes/1/20 ounce
	3,11 grammes/1/10 ounce
	7,77 grammes/1/4 ounce
	15,56 grammes/1/2 ounce
	31,1 grammes/1 ounce
NICARAGUA	50 CORDOBAS
NIGER	10 FRANCS
	25 FRANCS
	50 FRANCS
	100 FRANCS
NORWAY	1 500 KRONER
OMAN	25 BAISA
	50 BAISA
	100 BAISA
	1/4 OMANI RIAL
	1/2 OMANI RIAL
	OMANI RIAL
	5 OMANI RIALS
	10 OMANI RIALS
	15 OMANI RIALS
	20 OMANI RIALS
	25 OMANI RIALS
	75 OMANI RIALS
PAKISTAN	3 000 RUPEES
PANAMA	100 BALBOAS
	500 BALBOAS
PAPUA NEW GUINEA	100 KINA
PERU	1/5 LIBRA
	1/2 LIBRA
	1 LIBRA
	5 SOLES
	10 SOLES
	20 SOLES
	50 SOLES
	100 SOLES
PHILIPPINES	1 000 PISO
	1 500 PISO

Country of issue	*Denomination of the coins*
	5 000 PISO
POLAND	50 ZLOTY (orzel bielik)
	50 ZLOTY
	100 ZLOTY (orzel bielik)
	(exception 100 Zlotych "Beatyfikacja Jana Pawla II 1 V 2011")
	100 ZLOTY
	200 ZLOTY (orzel bielik)
	200 ZLOTY
	500 ZLOTY (orzel bielik)
PORTUGAL	1 ESCUDO
	100 ESCUDOS
	200 ESCUDOS
	500 ESCUDOS
	5 EURO
	8 EURO
	10 000 REIS
RHODESIA	1 POUND
	5 POUNDS
	10 SHILLINGS
RUSSIA	1 (Chervonet)
	15 (ROUBLES)
	25 (ROUBLES)
	50 (ROUBLES)
	100 (ROUBLES)
	200 (ROUBLES)
	1 000 (ROUBLES)
	10 000 (ROUBLES)
RWANDA	10 FRANCS
	25 FRANCS
	50 FRANCS
	100 FRANCS
SAN MARINO	20 EURO
	50 EURO
	1 SCUDO
	2 SCUDI
	5 SCUDI
	10 SCUDI
SAUDI ARABIA	1 GUINEA (= 1 SAUDI POUND)
SENEGAL	10 FRANCS
	25 FRANCS
	50 FRANCS
	100 FRANCS
	250 FRANCS
	500 FRANCS
	1 000 FRANCS
	2 500 FRANCS
SERBIA	10 DINARA
	20 DINARA
SEYCHELLES	1 000 RUPEES
	1 500 RUPEES

Country of issue	*Denomination of the coins*
SIERRA LEONE	20 DOLLARS
	50 DOLLARS
	100 DOLLARS
	250 DOLLARS
	500 DOLLARS
	2 500 DOLLARS
	1/4 GOLDE
	1/2 GOLDE
	1 GOLDE
	5 GOLDE
	10 GOLDE
	1 LEONE
SINGAPORE	1 DOLLAR
	2 DOLLARS
	5 DOLLARS
	10 DOLLARS
	20 DOLLARS
	25 DOLLARS
	50 DOLLARS
	100 DOLLARS
	150 DOLLARS
	250 DOLLARS
	500 DOLLARS
SLOVAKIA	100 EURO
	5 000 KORUN (5 000 sk)
	10 000 KORUN (10 000 sk)
SLOVENIA	100 EURO
	5 000 TOLARS
	20 000 TOLARS
	25 000 TOLARS
SOLOMON ISLANDS	10 DOLLARS
	25 DOLLARS
	50 DOLLARS
	100 DOLLARS
SOMALIA	20 SHILLINGS
	50 SHILLINGS
	100 SHILLINGS
	200 SHILLINGS
	500 SHILLINGS
	1 500 SHILLINGS
SOUTH AFRICA	1/10 KRUGERRAND
	1/4 KRUGERRAND
	1/2 KRUGERRAND
	1 KRUGERRAND
	1/10 oz NATURA
	1/4 oz NATURA
	1/2 oz NATURA
	1 oz NATURA
	1/2 POND
	1 POND
	1/10 PROTEA

Country of issue	*Denomination of the coins*
	1 PROTEA
	1 RAND
	2 RAND
	5 RAND
	25 RAND
	½ SOVEREIGN (= ½ POUND)
	1 SOVEREIGN (= 1 POUND)
SOUTH KOREA	2 500 WON
	20 000 WON
	25 000 WON
	30 000 WON
	50 000 WON
SPAIN	2 (ESCUDOS)
	10 (ESCUDOS)
	20 EURO
	100 EURO
	200 EURO
	400 EURO
	10 PESETAS
	20 PESETAS
	25 PESETAS
	5 000 PESETAS
	10 000 PESETAS
	20 000 PESETAS
	40 000 PESETAS
	80 000 PESETAS
	100 REALES
SUDAN	25 POUNDS
	50 POUNDS
	100 POUNDS
SURINAME	20 DOLLARS
	50 DOLLARS
	100 GULDEN
SWAZILAND	2 EMALANGENI
	5 EMALANGENI
	10 EMALANGENI
	20 EMALANGENI
	25 EMALANGENI
	50 EMALANGENI
	100 EMALANGENI
	250 EMALANGENI
	1 LILANGENI
SWEDEN	5 KRONOR
	10 KRONOR
	20 KRONOR
	1 000 KRONOR
	2 000 KRONOR
SWITZERLAND	10 FRANCS
	20 FRANCS
	50 FRANCS
	100 FRANCS

Country of issue	Denomination of the coins
SYRIA	(½ POUND)
	(1 POUND)
TANZANIA	1 500 SHILINGI
	2 000 SHILINGI
THAILAND	(150 BAHT)
	(300 BAHT)
	(400 BAHT)
	(600 BAHT)
	(800 BAHT)
	(1 500 BAHT)
	(2 500 BAHT)
	(3 000 BAHT)
	(4 000 BAHT)
	(5 000 BAHT)
	(6 000 BAHT)
TONGA	½ HAU
	1 HAU
	5 HAU
	¼ KOULA
	½ KOULA
	1 KOULA
TRISTAN DE CUHNA	2 POUNDS
	5 POUNDS
	QUARTER SOVEREIGN
	HALF SOVEREIGN
	SOVEREIGN
TUNISIA	2 DINARS
	5 DINARS
	10 DINARS
	20 DINARS
	40 DINARS
	75 DINARS
	10 FRANCS
	20 FRANCS
	100 FRANCS
	5 PIASTRES
TURKEY	(25 KURUSH) (= 25 PIASTRES)
	(50 KURUSH) (= 50 PIASTRES)
	(100 KURUSH) (= 100 PIASTRES)
	(250 KURUSH) (= 250 PIASTRES)
	(500 KURUSH) (= 500 PIASTRES)
	½ LIRA
	1 LIRA
	500 LIRA
	1 000 LIRA
	10 000 LIRA
	50 000 LIRA
	100 000 LIRA
	200 000 LIRA
	1 000 000 LIRA
	60 000 000 LIRA

Country of issue	*Denomination of the coins*
TURKS & CAICOS ISLANDS	100 CROWNS
TUVALU	50 DOLLARS
UGANDA	50 SHILLINGS
	100 SHILLINGS
	500 SHILLINGS
	1 000 SHILLINGS
UNITED ARAB EMIRATES	(500 DIRHAMS)
	(750 DIRHAMS)
	(1 000 DIRHAMS)
UNITED KINGDOM	(1/3 GUINEA)
	($^1/_2$ GUINEA)
	50 PENCE
	2 POUNDS
	5 POUNDS
	10 POUNDS
	25 POUNDS
	50 POUNDS
	100 POUNDS
	QUARTER SOVEREIGN
	($^1/_2$ SOVEREIGN) (= $^1/_2$ POUND)
	(1 SOVEREIGN) (= 1 POUND)
	(2 SOVEREIGNS)
	(5 SOVEREIGNS)
URUGUAY	5 000 NUEVO PESOS
	20 000 NUEVO PESOS
	5 PESOS
USA	1 DOLLAR
	2.5 DOLLARS
	5 DOLLARS
	10 DOLLARS (AMERICAN EAGLE)
	20 DOLLARS
	25 DOLLARS
	50 DOLLARS
VATICAN	20 EURO
	50 EURO
	10 LIRE GOLD
	20 LIRE
	100 LIRE GOLD
VENEZUELA	(10 BOLIVARES)
	(20 BOLIVARES)
	(100 BOLIVARES)
	1 000 BOLIVARES
	3 000 BOLIVARES
	5 000 BOLIVARES
	10 000 BOLIVARES
	5 VENEZOLANOS
WESTERN SAMOA	50 TALA
	100 TALA
YUGOSLAVIA	20 DINARA
	100 DINARA
	200 DINARA

Country of issue	Denomination of the coins
	500 DINARA
	1 000 DINARA
	1 500 DINARA
	2 000 DINARA
	2 500 DINARA
	5 000 DINARA
	1 DUCAT
	4 DUCATS
ZAIRE	100 ZAIRES
ZAMBIA	250 KWACHA

Table 2: UK list of additional coins recognised as investment gold coins

Country of issue	Denomination of the coins
AUSTRIA	20 CORONA (= 20 KRONEN)
FINLAND	10 MARKKAA
	20 MARKKAA
GERMANY	10 MARK
	20 MARK
	200 EURO
GREECE	20 DRACHMAI
	2 500 DRACHMAI
	5 000 DRACHMAI
	100 EURO
ITALY	10 LIRE
	20 LIRE
	40 LIRE
	80 LIRE
	100 LIRE
LIBERIA	12 DOLLARS
	20 DOLLARS
	25 DOLLARS
	30 DOLLARS
	100 DOLLARS
	200 DOLLARS
	250 DOLLARS
	500 DOLLARS
	2 500 DOLLARS
NORWAY	10 KRONER
	20 KRONER
POLAND	10 ZLOTYCH
	20 ZLOTYCH
ROMANIA	12½ LEI
	20 LEI
	25 LEI
	50 LEI
	100 LEI
	500 LEI
	1 000 LEI
	2 000 LEI

Country of issue	*Denomination of the coins*
	5 000 LEI
RUSSIA	5 (ROUBLES)
	7½ (ROUBLES)
	10 (ROUBLES)
SLOVENIA	180 EURO
	2 500 TOLARS

NOTICE 701/36
INSURANCE

2013

Note—This notice cancels and replaces Notice 701/36 (May 2012).

> Paragraph 11.3.1 in this Notice has the force of law under VATA 1994 Sch 11 para 6(1), VAT Regulations, SI 1995/2518 reg 31(1), (2), VATA 1994 Sch 9 Group 2 Item 4, Note (4)(*c*)(iii).

11.3 DISCLOSURE PROVISIONS

There are special provisions in UK VAT legislation requiring suppliers to disclose to their customers any amount they charge, in addition to the insurance premium, for arranging the insurance. These provisions are as follows.

If you are:

- a supplier of taxable (but not zero rated) goods or services; and
- insurance is supplied to your customers in connection with the supply of those goods or services; and
- a supply of related services is made in connection with that insurance by either; you, the supplier of the goods or services, or by someone connected to you (as defined by section 993 of the Income Tax Act 2007 and section 1122 of the Corporation Tax Act 2010).

then for any additional amount charged for arranging the insurance to be exempt:

- the amounts of the premium and also of any fee charged in addition to the premium must be identified in writing on a document; and
- that document must be issued to the customer at or before the time the insurance transaction is entered into.

If these conditions are not met, there will continue to be no VAT chargeable on the amount collected by you and passed onto the insurer for the supply of insurance. Any fees or commission you receive for your services of arranging the insurance, however, will be liable to tax at the same rate as the goods or services themselves.

11.3.1 Disclosure procedures for insurance sold over the phone, Internet and so on

We realise that the disclosure provisions laid out in paragraph 11.3 may cause problems for businesses that effect transactions over the phone, or by some other means of electronic communication, whereby the customer and the salesperson are not physically together when the sale takes place.

Obviously in these circumstances it would not be possible for a document containing the required statements to be given to the customer at or before the time the transaction is entered into.

To overcome this problem, we require a person selling insurance with taxable goods and/or services by electronic means to keep additional records as detailed under step 4 in the table below. VAT legislation allows us to specify which records a taxable business is required to keep and also allows us to supplement, by means of a notice (in this case, this notice), the list of those records.

For an additional fee charged by a supplier selling insurance with other goods or services by electronic means to be exempt, therefore, the following procedure must be implemented:

Step	Procedure
1	The supplier must make full disclosure at the time the insurance transaction takes place. For example, if holidays are being sold over the phone, the salesperson must inform the customer orally of the amounts in sterling due for the premium and any additional fee charged in connection with the insurance.
2	The supplier must have in place a system whereby sales staff annotate a document (even if this only involves ticking a box) at the time they make oral or electronic disclosure to the customer to indicate that they have done so.
3	The supplier must comply with the legal requirement to prepare a document containing the details laid out in paragraph 11.3 and issue it to the customer (albeit after the insurance transaction has been entered into).
4	The supplier must retain a copy of these records as they would their normal VAT records.

11.3.2 Insurance sold with goods or services under a VAT margin scheme

The legislation states that we may set out in a notice the form of the document to be used for making the disclosure detailed in paragraph 11.3.

Using this notice, therefore, we require a person supplying goods or services under one of the VAT margin schemes to make the required disclosure on the relevant VAT invoice issued by that person.

Information on margin schemes can be found in Notices 718/1 The VAT Margin Scheme on second-hand cars and other vehicles and 709/5 Tour operators' margin scheme.

Commentary—*De Voil Indirect Tax Service* **V4.121**.

NOTICE 701/48
CORPORATE PURCHASING CARDS

2014

4.2 THE LINE ITEM DETAIL VAT INVOICE

Commentary—*De Voil Indirect Tax Service* **V3.415, V3.421**.
Note—This paragraph has the force of law under the VAT Regulations 1995, SI 1995/2518 regs 13, 14.

As the invoice report is issued by the card company or bank to the purchaser, the supplier will not know when it is actually issued. But as the date is normally only relevant for tax point purposes (which have been specially provided for, see paragraph 2.3), we have agreed to waive the requirement to show the date of issue contained in regulation 14(1)(c) of the Value Added Tax Regulations 1995.

The invoice report issued to the purchaser must, however, show the transmission date for each transaction, so the purchaser will know the date from which input tax can be claimed. The invoice report is, therefore, acceptable as evidence for input tax recovery, subject to the normal rules governing entitlement.

In order to fulfil the requirements of regulation 31(1)(c) of the Value Added Tax Regulations 1995, suppliers must retain the invoice data transmitted and any invoices from their normal systems which they have produced but not issued.

4.3 WHAT IS A SUMMARY VAT INVOICE

Commentary—*De Voil Indirect Tax Service* **V3.415, V3.421**.
Note—This paragraph has the force of law under SI 1995/2518 regs 14 and 15.

Some suppliers do not have accounting systems capable of transmitting LID invoices but are able to provide summary VAT information. As a general rule, we will accept summary VAT invoice reports in support of input tax claims.

The summary VAT invoice reports must contain the following information—

- value of the supply;
- VAT amount charged;
- VAT rate;
- time of supply;
- description of the goods;
- supplier's name, address and VAT number; and
- customer's name and address.

If you are capable of transmitting only summary VAT data you must, for purchasing card transactions, continue to generate VAT invoices at the same time for output tax accounting purposes. However, you may discharge your obligation to issue an invoice where single transactions have a value of not more than £5,000 by transmitting the summary VAT information to your bank or card company.

Where the value of a single transaction exceeds £5,000 you must issue a VAT invoice. A single transaction is the total value of purchases made using a card at any one time, for example from one "swipe" of the card. You must also issue a copy of your normal VAT invoice, for any transaction where the value does not exceed £5,000, if you are specifically requested to do so by your customer. In such a case the invoice must be clearly endorsed with the words "Paid by purchasing card—Supplementary VAT invoice".

702
IMPORTS

October 2014

This Notice cancels and replaces the April 2014 edition.

1 INTRODUCTION

1.1 What is this notice about?

It explains how imported goods are treated for VAT purposes.

The VAT treatment of goods entering the UK from other parts of the EC territory (see section 9) is set out in Notice 725 "The Single Market" and Notice 728 "New means of transport".

The VAT treatment of goods imported under Customs Procedures with Economic Impact and end use is set out in Notice 702/9 "Imports Customs procedures".

The VAT treatment of goods imported into Fiscal warehouses is set out in Notice 702/8 "VAT: Fiscal Warehousing".

1.2 What's changed?

Amendments have been made to paragraphs 4.2 the C18 team have moved from Grimsby to National Clearance Hub (NCH) Salford and 8.8 Isle of Man VAT registered importers has been deleted.

1.3 Who should read this notice?

It will be of interest to anyone importing goods into the UK from outside the fiscal (VAT) territory of the European Union (EU). You can find out the extent of the fiscal territory in section 9.

1.4 What law covers this notice?

The EU law relating to Import VAT is contained in the EU Principal VAT Directive (2006/112/EC).

The primary UK VAT law is contained in VATA 1994. The effect of VATA 1994 s 16 is that most HM Revenue & Customs (HMRC) legislation applies to import VAT except where specifically disapplied through secondary legislation.

Secondary legislation concerning import VAT is mainly contained in regulations, notably the VAT Regulations 1995 (SI 1995/2518), and orders made under the powers contained in VATA 1994. Regulations 118, 119, 120 and 121 of the VAT Regulations 1995 specify the EU and HMRC legislation disapplied.

This notice is not the law. It is our view of the law and nothing in this notice takes the place of the law.

1.5 What is import VAT?

Import VAT is the transaction tax levied on imported goods. Goods are treated as imported when—

— they arrive in the UK directly from outside the EU and are entered to free circulation in the UK or customs duty otherwise becomes chargeable on them, *or*

— they have been placed under one of the customs suspensive arrangements listed in Notice 702/9 "Import Customs Procedures" and the goods are being removed to free circulation in the UK or customs duty otherwise becomes chargeable.

1.6 What is the territory of the EU?

Unless otherwise qualified, the term "EU" is used in this notice to refer to the VAT (fiscal) territory of the EU, which is different from the customs territory of the EU. The countries and territories, which make up the VAT (fiscal) territory of the EC are listed in section 9.

1.7 How to treat transactions with the Isle of Man

Goods removed from the Isle of Man to the UK are not treated as an importation provided that—

— any VAT due has been accounted for in the Isle of Man; *or*

— if the goods were relieved of VAT in the Isle of Man, the conditions of that relief have not been broken.

1.8 Goods imported from the special territories including the Channel Islands

Section 9 lists the territories inside/outside the EU for customs duty and VAT purposes.

The Channel Islands and special territories listed in Section 9 are part of the EU for customs purposes but are not part of the VAT territory.

If you import goods from the Channel Islands or special territories you will be liable for import VAT in the same way as you would for those imports detailed in paragraph 1.5.

1.9 How to treat transactions with countries which join the EU

Goods received from countries joining the EU may be subject to accessionary rates of EU customs duties. Unlike goods from other EU member states, therefore, some frontier formalities may remain for duty purposes. However, for VAT purposes, such goods will not be subject to the import VAT treatment described in this notice. Instead, for registered traders, the arrangements set out in Notice 725 "The Single Market" will apply. You will not have to pay Import VAT at the time the goods are entered for Customs purposes.

1.10 How to treat services received from outside the EU

If you receive any of the services from outside the EU where the place of supply is the customer's country, for example, the UK, you may be required to account for any VAT due on them under the reverse charge provisions. You will find more information in Notice 741 "Place of supply of services" (before 1 January 2010) and Notice 741A "Place of supply of services".

2 IMPORTATION – GENERAL

Economic Operator Registration and Identification (EORI) scheme

Economic Operator Registration and Identification (EORI) scheme was implemented in the European Union (EU) UK 1 July 2009. You will require an EORI number if you import from or export to countries outside of the EU. Full details about EORI including the EORI application forms can be found at the following link

customs.hmrc.gov.uk/channelsPortalWebApp/channelsPortalWebApp.portal?_nfpb=true &_pageLabel=pageVAT_ShowContent&id=HMCE_PROD1_028517&propertyType=document

2.1 VAT rate at importation

VAT is charged on the importation of goods at the same rate as if the goods had been supplied in the UK.

2.2 How import VAT is charged and collected

Goods are declared to Customs using form C88 Single administrative document (SAD) that in most cases is presented in an electronic format. Import VAT is dealt with in the same way as a Customs duty. You can pay it outright at importation, or under the duty deferment arrangements explained in Notice 101 "Deferring duty, VAT and other charges". Notice 101 also covers Simplified Import VAT Accounting (SIVA). This is a scheme that reduces the level of financial security required to guarantee the payment of import VAT through the duty deferment system. Traders must be authorised to operate SIVA. See Notice SIVA 1 for application details on the HMRC website.

If you wish to apply for, or have any queries about deferment, you should contact:

HM Revenue & Customs
Banking Operations
Central Deferment Office
6th Floor NW
Alexander House
21 Victoria Avenue
Southend-on-Sea
Essex SS99 1AA

Telephone: 03000 593075, 593551, 593095, 593434

Fax: 03000 594280

Note: You cannot use the Cash accounting* scheme for imported goods.

* The Cash accounting scheme should not be confused with the Flexible Accounting Scheme (FAS). FAS may be used (by Director Trader (DTI) agents) to pay charges due on imported goods using an immediate payment method.

Details about the FAS scheme can be found in Notice 100.

2.3 Who can reclaim import VAT as input tax?

Subject to the normal rules, you can claim as input tax any import VAT you pay on goods, provided those goods are imported for the purpose of your business. Your claim must normally be made on the VAT return for the accounting period during which the importation took place.

The normal evidence of payment of import VAT is the import VAT certificate (form C79), which is issued monthly. Section 8 gives more information about the C79, as well as the acceptable evidence for those types of importation that at present do not appear on a C79. It also explains what to do if you lose a certificate or have any queries about items missing from certificates.

If you are partly exempt and are unsure about the amount of tax that you may reclaim, you should consult the Helpline on 0300 200 3700.

2.4 Can a shipping or forwarding agent reclaim input tax?

If you act as a shipping or forwarding agent for an importer and pay or defer VAT on their behalf, it is a commercial arrangement between you and your principal. You cannot claim the VAT as input tax because the goods are not imported for the purpose of your business. Although HMRC usually deal with agents in relation to the importation and clearance of goods, it is the importer's responsibility to ensure that goods are properly entered, and that any

Import VAT and other charges due are paid. Only the importer has the legal right to reclaim the VAT paid on imported goods as input tax, subject to the normal conditions being met.

2.5 What can I do as a shipping or forwarding agent if an importer does not pay me the import VAT?

If an importer fails to pay you import VAT you paid on their behalf, your only recourse is to the importer, except where—

— the importer has gone into liquidation; *or*
— an administrator or administrative receiver has been appointed, who certifies that in their opinion, ordinary unsecured creditors will receive nothing in the liquidation.

In such cases you may be able to recover amounts paid as tax from HMRC. All of the following conditions must be met—

— the interval between the date of the import entry for the goods and the date the importer became insolvent is no more than six months.
— you entered the goods in accordance with instructions from the importer.
— during their stay in the UK the goods were under your control and were not used; and
— the goods have been re-exported in the same state as they were imported.

To claim repayment you should write to the National Duty Repayment Centre at Dover, enclosing—

evidence that the import VAT has been paid to HMRC
— a certificate from the person in charge, for example, the liquidator, that the VAT has not been, and will not be, reclaimed as input tax
— within six months of confirmation from the person in charge that the importer became formally insolvent the date the entry was lodged with HMRC
— a declaration that you will not recover the relevant VAT in whole or in part from the insolvency; and
— evidence to satisfy HMRC that you have acted in accordance with the importer's instructions.

HM Revenue & Customs
National Duty Repayments Centre
Priory Court
St John's Road
Dover CT17 9SH.
Telephone: 03000 582687
Fax: 03000 583027

Email: NDRC Enquiries ndrcenquiries@hmrc.gsi.gov.uk

If you need any further advice you should contact the Helpline on 0300 200 3700.

2.6 Claiming repayment of overpaid import VAT

Method of claiming repayment of overpaid import VAT – VAT registered, non VAT registered and non-fully taxable traders

Non VAT registered and non fully taxable traders can claim overpaid customs duties and import VAT using form C285 Application for repayment/remission.

VAT registered traders can use form C285 to claim repayment of overpaid customs duties but must claim the equivalent of any overpaid import VAT as input tax on their VAT return subject to the normal VAT rules.

Current Month Adjustments (CMA)

Where the overpayment of customs duty or import VAT is made via your deferment account, you may (regardless of your VAT status) apply to have your deferment account adjusted to reflect the correct amount of duty or import VAT. Your request for CMA must be made on form C285 and sent to the National Duty Repayment Centre (NDRC) at the address quoted under paragraph 2.5.

Current month adjustments can only be made in the month that the error occurs and therefore you must make your application for adjustment before the last day of the month in which the overpayment was made. Please ensure that you submit all supporting documents with your claim as there will be no time for further enquires to be made. If your application is received after the month end or without all supporting documentation it will be dealt with as a standard repayment. This means that if you are a VAT registered trader requesting the adjustment of overpaid import VAT your claim will be refused and you will have to claim the equivalent amount as input tax on your VAT return as explained above.

Repayments to agents

If an importer fails to pay you the import VAT that you paid on their behalf, your only recourse is to the importer, except in the circumstances set out in paragraph 2.5. If you need any further advice please contact the NDRC.

2.7 Non-UK traders with a UK establishment and their agents

Appointing an agent to import and supply goods

If you

— import goods for onward supply in the UK; and
— you do not supply any other supplies in the UK

you can arrange for an agent who is resident in the UK, and who is registered for VAT purposes, to import and supply goods on your behalf. If you do this, you will not need to register for VAT in the UK. You must agree with the agent that they will issue proper tax invoices for the supplies of the goods.

If you adopt this arrangement the place of supply of your agent's supply of services to you may be where you belong, or where the underlying supply of the goods is made. See Notice 741 "Place of supply of services" (before 1 January 2010) and Notice 741A "Place of supply of services".

UK agent's responsibilities

If you act as an agent for a non-UK trader under the arrangement referred to above, you will be treated as importing and supplying the goods as the principal. You must make any necessary customs entries as importer, pay or defer the VAT and take delivery of the goods. You can reclaim the import VAT as input tax, subject to the normal rules, but you must treat the transactions as a supply by you and charge and account for VAT on the onward sale in the normal way.

The place of supply of your services to the non-UK trader may be supplied where the non-UK trader belongs or where the underlying supply of the goods is made. See Notice 741 "Place of supply of services" (before 1 January 2010) and Notice 741A "Place of supply of services".

Registering for VAT in the UK

If you do not wish to use the arrangements referred to above, but you make taxable supplies in the UK, you will have to register for VAT here. There is more information about the liability to register for UK VAT in Notice 700/1 "Should I be registered for VAT?".

You may choose one of three options. You may—

— appoint a tax representative to deal with your tax affairs;
— appoint an agent to deal with your tax affairs; or
— deal with your VAT obligations yourself.

You will find more information in Notice 700/4 "Registration for VAT: Non-established taxable persons" and Notice 725 "The Single Market".

2.8 Non-UK traders without a UK establishment and their agents

Appointing an agent to import and supply goods

If you

— import goods for onward supply in the UK, and
— do not make any other taxable supplies in the UK

you can arrange for an agent who is resident in the UK, and who is registered for VAT purposes, to import and supply goods on your behalf. If you do this, you will not need to register for VAT in the UK. You must agree with the agent that they will issue proper tax invoices for the supplies of the goods.

If you adopt this arrangement the place of supply of your agent's supply of services to you may be where you belong, or where the underlying supply of the goods is made. See Notice 741 "Place of supply of services".

UK agent's responsibilities

If you act as an agent for a non-UK trader under the arrangement referred to above, you will be treated as importing and supplying the goods as the principal. You must make any necessary Customs entries as importer, pay or defer the VAT and take delivery of the goods. You can reclaim the import VAT as input tax, subject to the normal rules, but you must treat the transactions as a supply by you and charge and account for VAT on the onward sale in the normal way.

The place of supply of your services to the non-UK trader may be supplied where the non-UK trader belongs or where the underlying supply of the goods is made. See Notice 741 "Place of supply of services".

Registering for VAT in the UK

If you do not wish to use the arrangements referred to above, but you make taxable supplies in the UK, you will have to register for VAT here. There is more information about the liability to register for UK VAT in Notice 700/1 "Should I be registered for VAT?"

You may choose one of three options. You may—

— appoint a tax representative to deal with your tax affairs
— appoint an agent to deal with your tax affairs, or
— deal with your VAT obligations yourself.

2.9 Goods not wholly owned by the importer

If you import goods that belong wholly or partly to another person, and the goods are to be used for your own or other person's private purposes, you cannot recover the import VAT paid as input tax. This situation will arise; for example, if a VAT registered marine repair trader imports a privately owned yacht for repair, where the yacht is to be used after repair for private purposes. If such treatment results in VAT being charged twice, you should apply to your local VAT office for a repayment. You should write giving full details of the goods and the reasons for your claim. You should enclose the VAT copy of the customs declaration or a copy of the import VAT certificate (form C79) and a copy of any sales invoice for the goods.

2.10 Goods lost or destroyed

Where imported goods are lost or destroyed before they are released from official control you can apply to HMRC at the place where the import entry was presented for repayment or remission of the Import VAT paid or due, using Form C285 "*Application for repayment/remission*" (see paragraph 2.6). Where imported goods are lost or destroyed after release from official control, you can deduct the VAT paid as input tax, subject to the normal rules, provided the goods were to be used for the purposes of your business. You need not account for output tax unless you supplied the goods to someone else before the loss or destruction occurred. You will find more about this in Notice 700 "*The VAT Guide*".

2.11 Goods supplied before delivery of an import entry

If:

— you make a supply of imported goods between the time of their arrival in the UK and the time when an import entry is delivered to HMRC; and
— the new owner of the goods is required to make the import entry;

then you should zero-rate the supply.

2.12 What to do when the precise amount of duty is not known

When the precise amount of Import Duty due cannot be assessed at the time the declaration is presented, release of the goods can usually be allowed on payment of a deposit or the provision of security to cover the amount of duty considered to be in dispute (see Notice 252: "Valuation of imported goods for customs purposes, VAT and trade statistics").

If you are VAT registered you may pay the import VAT outright, based on the value for VAT that includes the highest potential duty amount. An import VAT certificate (Form C79) will be issued and you can claim repayment on your VAT return under the normal rules. Alternatively, you may provide security for the disputed amount of VAT. However, you should be aware that this might not be to your advantage. If you choose to secure the disputed element of VAT, a C79 will not be issued until after the duty amount has been adjusted. The adjustment may not take place until some weeks after the deposit has been made, depending on how long it takes you or your agent to produce the necessary evidence. Input tax recovery may be delayed accordingly.

If you are not VAT registered you must secure the amount of VAT in dispute.

3 VALUATION OF IMPORTED GOODS FOR VAT PURPOSES

3.1 Value for import VAT

General

The value for VAT of imported goods is their customs value, determined according to the customs rules described in Notice 252 "Valuation of imported goods for customs purposes, VAT and trade statistics", *plus*, if not already included in the price—

— all incidental expenses such as commission, packing, transport and insurance costs incurred up to the goods' first destination in the UK; *plus*
— all such incidental expenses where they result from transport to a further place of destination in the EU if that place is known at the time of importation; *plus*
— any customs duty or levy payable on importation into the UK; *plus*
— any excise duty or other charges payable on importation into the UK (except the VAT itself).

Note: Some goods are entitled to a reduced valuation at import. See paragraph 3.4 for details.

Incidental expenses

In addition to the examples given above (such as transport), the term "incidental expenses" also covers such items as customs clearance charges, quay rent, entry fees, demurrage, handling, loading and storage costs. Generally, where supplies of services qualify for zero-rating because they are supplied in connection with an importation of goods, the cost of those services should be included in the value for import VAT.

Certain costs, for example, royalties and licence fees, should not be included in the value for import VAT as they are taxable under the reverse charge/international service arrangements (see Notice 741 "Place of supply of services" (before 1 January 2010) and Notice 741A "Place of supply of services" for details).

First destination

"First destination" is the place mentioned on the consignment note or any other commercial document relating to the imported goods. In the absence of such documentation, it means the place of the first transfer of the goods in the UK.

Further destination

If a further destination in the UK or another EU member state is known at the time the goods are imported, costs relating to the transport of the goods to that place must be included in the import VAT value.

Calculation of the amount for incidental expenses

The following three methods may be used to calculate the "incidental expenses" element of the import VAT value. The first method requires actual costs to be declared, whilst methods two and three provide ways of estimating the incidental expenses. Use of the three methods is non-hierarchical and individual importers or agents may use whichever method best suits their particular circumstances.

Method one

This method requires the actual costs to be declared at the time the goods are imported. The time of importation is the time when the customs debt is incurred or would have been incurred if the goods were subject to duty. In cases where the costs are later found to be incorrect (eg if additional storage costs are incurred) the amount(s) paid will need to be adjusted after importation.

Method two

The following nationally agreed rates may be used to estimate the incidental expenses to be included in the import VAT value. The rates are intended only for international movements of goods, which terminate in the UK, and represent average costs of handling, storage, customs declarations and transport to destination. Values for other consignments, including those destined for delivery in other member states, should be based on methods one or three. If importers/agents use the method two rates, post importation adjustments are not required. Additionally, where it is found that the amount of import VAT based on actual costs exceeds the amount declared on the basis of method two rates, HMRC will not seek to collect the arrears of import VAT unless the importer concerned is not registered for VAT, or if registered, is restricted in the amount of import VAT that can be claimed as input tax.

Group A Airfreight	—40p per chargeable kilo or a minimum amount of £100 to be added to the value at the time of importation, whichever is the greater.
Group B Surface freight groupage/consolidation consignments by trailer, rail wagon or container	—Delivery and handling combination of £90 per gross weight tonne plus a flat "other ancillaries" rate of £80 per consignment, minimum £170, to be added to the value at the time of importation.
Group C Surface freight full load consignments by trailer, rail wagon or container	—£550 per full load consignment to be added to the value at the time of importation.

Method three

In cases where methods one and two are considered inappropriate or impractical to use, individual agreements may be negotiated with your Entry Processing Unit, or with the importers local Excise and Inland Customs office. Importers or agents interested in this method, who are uncertain about which office to approach should contact the Helpline, telephone 0300 200 3700. Once a method three rate is used, post importation adjustments are not required.

3.2 How Customs calculate import VAT

HMRC data processing system (The Customs Handling of Import and Export Freight (CHIEF)) calculates the value for VAT by adding any duties, levies and additional costs to be included in the VAT value to the value declared in Box 22 of the import declaration (the SAD). Where any of these additional costs, which need to be included in the VAT value, are not included in the total invoice value (Box 22) or the other value build-up boxes (63–67), you must declare them in the Adjustment For import VAT Value box (68).

If the value for VAT is less than that which CHIEF would normally calculate for customs duty purposes, you must calculate the amount of VAT payable manually. Except at manual locations, you must enter the code "VAT" in the Rate column of Box 47. You must enter the calculated payment in the amount column.

3.3 Value declaration

If goods are liable to ad valorem customs duty (that is, a duty chargeable on the basis of value), a declaration on Form C105 (Valuation Declaration) made for duty purposes, will also generally be acceptable for VAT. However, the declaration will only provide information which helps determine the customs value of the goods, and it should not be regarded as establishing their full value for VAT purposes (see paragraph 3.1).

Where goods are not liable to ad valorem duty but are liable to VAT at the standard rate, a valuation declaration for import VAT is only to be completed when requested by customs and—

— the value exceeds £6,500; and
— the importer is not registered for VAT; or
— the importer is registered for VAT; and
— the goods are not for the purpose of the business; or
— deduction of input tax would not be allowed; or
— the value of the goods is not being determined under customs valuation method 1 (see Notice 252 "Valuation of imported goods for customs purposes, VAT and trade statistics").

There are no arrangements for registering a General Valuation Statement for VAT only entries. Individual valuation declarations must be submitted where necessary.

Whether or not a valuation declaration is required for the goods, evidence of value must be produced. Acceptable evidence is a copy of the seller's invoice or other document against which payment will be made. This will include telex or similar messages used instead of invoices.

Further information on valuation declarations is given in Notice 251 "Valuation declarations and statements" and Notice 252 "Valuation of imported goods for customs purposes, VAT and trade statistics".

3.4 Imported works of art, antiques and collectors' items

Certain works of art, antiques and collectors' items are entitled to a reduced valuation at importation. This is reached by calculating a value for duty using the appropriate duty method, adding any additional costs (see paragraph 3.1) and multiplying the total by 25 per cent. Applying the 20 per cent rate to this value gives an effective VAT rate of 5 per cent.

3.5 Which works of art, antiques and collectors' items are eligible for the reduced valuation?

Section 11 contains definitions of the works of art, antiques and collectors' items that will be eligible for the reduced valuation.

You can find details of the entry procedure in HMRC Tariff. The following Customs Procedure Codes (CPCs) apply:

— 40 00 200 (imports from third countries);
— 49 00 029 (imports from special territories).

Previously exported works of art, antiques and collectors' items

An imported work of art, antique or collectors' item, as defined in section 11, will be eligible for the reduced rate provided that it had not been exported from the United Kingdom less than 12 months before the date of importation.

You can find details of the declaration procedure in HMRC Tariff. The following CPCs apply:

— 61 00 F03/4 (from third countries);
— 49 23 F01, 49 00 F03/4 (from special territories).

Further details can be found in:

— Notice 718 "The VAT Margin Scheme and global accounting"; and
— The Tariff, Volume 3, Appendix E4.

3.6 Treatment of auctioneer's commissions in valuing goods for import VAT purposes

As explained in paragraph 3.1, commissions connected with an importation of goods are normally included as part of the overall value of goods for import VAT purposes. However this general rule no longer applies in respect of certain imports of works of art, antiques and collector's pieces.

Where works of art, antiques and collector's pieces are temporarily imported into the UK and sold by auction while subject to the temporary admission (TA) regime, the auctioneer will charge commission to the buyer. This commission is known as buyer's premium. Where auctioned goods have been removed from TA and finally imported into the United Kingdom the buyer's premium has always been included in the value of the goods for import VAT purposes. However because the goods attract an effective reduced rate of VAT (equivalent to 5 per cent), the premium was also taxed at this effective reduced rate. The European Court of Justice has ruled that the commission should in fact be taxed at the standard rate of VAT and the UK has therefore introduced the following arrangement with effect from 1 September 2006.

From this date buyer's premium is not to be included in the value for import VAT purposes of works of art, antiques and collectors items sold at auction under Temporary Admission and subsequently finally imported into the United Kingdom. This is because arrangements have been made for the commission to be taxed under the normal rules as a standard rated domestic supply. Auctioneers should consult Notice 718/2 "Margin schemes for second hand goods, works of art, antiques and collectors' items" for further details of the new arrangements.

4 IMPORT ENTRY PROCEDURE

You will find details of the declaration procedure in Volume 3 of HMRC Tariff.

The following paragraphs give particular information about the import VAT aspects.

4.1 Normal procedure

Unless the goods are placed under excise warehousing or one of the customs arrangements listed in Public Notice 702/9 "Imports Customs procedures", the payment of the import VAT due must normally be made either at the time of importation, or be deferred together with any duty due, provided you or your agent are approved to use the deferment scheme (see paragraph 2.2). As an alternative to deferring the payment of all the import charges on an entry to either the importer's or the agent's deferment account, payment of the VAT may be deferred to the importer's account and all other charges to the agent's. Volume 3 of the HMRC Tariff explains how to do this. Further information can also be found in Notice: 101 "Deferring Duty, VAT and other charges".

The import entry must be presented at the National Clearance Hub. If the consignment is covered by a single commodity code for customs purposes, but includes goods liable to VAT at both the standard and zero rate (such as clothing for adults and children), the importer or agent must complete a separate item on the entry for the goods liable to each rate of VAT. Special rules apply to the completion of the tax lines in the calculation of taxes box (Box 47) depending on whether the entry is presented at a manual or customs computerised location.

4.2 Amendment of the declaration

Where an amendment of the declaration is made after the goods have been released out of official charge and this results in less import VAT being payable than was originally declared and paid, you can reclaim the higher amount of tax as input tax in the normal way. You can also use the procedure described in paragraph 2.6. Where amendment of a declaration results in more import VAT being payable, you must submit the additional payment, and a completed form C18 to the NCH office (see address below). The additional payment will appear on the import VAT certificate (form C79), which is the official evidence for input tax deduction (see section 8).

C18 Team
NCH
HMRC
Ralli Quays
3 Stanley Sreet
Salford
M60 9HL

4.3 Postal imports

Consignments not exceeding £2000 in value

If you are registered for VAT and are importing goods in the course of your business Royal Mail/Parcelforce will ask you for payment of VAT when the package is delivered. You must keep the charge label which was attached to the package to support any claim to input tax.

Note: To support your claim to import tax you should keep the charge label, postal wrapper and any Customs declaration (that is, form CN22 or form CN23) that was attached to the package.

Consignments exceeding £2000 in value entered to home use and free circulation

For postal imports with a value greater than £2,000 you must lodge a declaration on form C88 Single Administrative Document (SAD) which will be sent to you for completion. You should return it to Customs with an invoice and/or other acceptable evidence of the value of the goods. You will have to pay the import VAT and any other charges due at importation before the goods can be released to you. This may be done by use of your deferment account if you are approved to do so. After payment you will be sent a copy of the declaration to support any claim to input tax deduction. For further information regarding postal imports you should refer to Notices 143 "A guide for international post users" and 144 "Trade imports by post: how to complete Customs documents".

4.4 Goods imported from outside the EU which are destined for another EU member state

If you import goods from outside the EU which are then consigned to a destination in another EU member state you must normally either—

— put the goods into free circulation in the UK, through the payment of any customs duty and/or import VAT due; or
— place the goods under the external Community Transit arrangements, in which case any duty and/or import VAT will be payable in the EU member state of destination. See European Commission Transit Manual, and the UK Supplement to the Transit Manual for further information on the community transit procedure.

In short, you will not normally be able to put goods into free circulation in one EU member state and pay import VAT in another. However, you may wish to take advantage of a VAT relief for goods you import and put into free circulation in the course of a zero-rated supply of those goods to a taxable person in another member state (see Notice 702/7 "Import VAT relief for goods supplied onward to another country in the EC").

4.5 ATA Carnets

An ATA Carnet is an international customs document that simplifies the customs formalities for goods temporarily imported or exported.

Further information can be found in Notice 104 "ATA Carnets" and 702/9 "Imports: Customs procedures".

4.6 Goods Imported under Temporary Admission (TA)

Temporary Admission (TA) enables you to obtain relief from import VAT and customs duties on a range of goods temporarily admitted for use from outside the EU, provided that they are intended for re-export after use (in most cases use can be for up to a maximum of two years).

Further information can be found in Section 3 of Notice 702/9 "Import Customs procedures", Notice 200 "Temporary Admission", Notice 306 "Temporary Admission — temporarily importing non-EC containers and pallets" and Notice 308 "Temporary admission – temporarily importing non-EC means of transport for private or commercial use".

5 RELIEF FROM IMPORT VAT

5.1 Imports to free circulation without payment of import VAT

Subject to certain conditions, you can import some types of goods without payment of import VAT. The VAT relief follows the customs duty reliefs that are explained in the notices listed below.

Notice	*No.*
317	Imports by charities free of duty and VAT
340	Importing scientific instruments free of duty and VAT
341	Importing donated medical equipment free of duty and VAT
342	Importing miscellaneous documents and other related articles free of duty and VAT
343	Importing capital goods free of duty and VAT
361	Importing museum and gallery exhibits free of duty and VAT
362	Imported antiques
364	Importing decorations and awards: free of duty and VAT
365	Importing animals for scientific research free of import duties and VAT
366	Importing biological and chemical substances for research free of duty and VAT
367	Importing commercial samples of negligible value: free of duty and VAT
368	Importing inherited goods free of duty and VAT
369	Importing blood grouping, tissue typing and certain therapeutic substances – free of duty and VAT
371	Importing goods for disabled people free of duty and VAT
373	Importing visual and auditory materials free of duty and VAT
374	Importing goods for test free of duty and VAT

5.2 Goods under a customs suspensive arrangement

If you import goods from outside the EU, and place them under one of the customs arrangements listed in Notice 702/9 "Import Customs procedures", the importation for VAT purposes is not regarded as having taken place until you declare the goods for free circulation in the UK. Import VAT is then chargeable. All the conditions applicable to the appropriate customs duty procedure, including the declaration and provision of entry, security etc, will apply for VAT purposes, even where import VAT is the only charge due.

You can move goods from one suspensive regime to another, for example, from customs warehousing to Inward Processing Relief suspension, without payment of import VAT.

However for goods entered to Inward Processing Relief under the drawback system, End-Use relief (other than the continental shelf), Temporary Importation with partial relief or outward processing relief you must pay the import VAT at the time of importation. See Notices 221 "Inward processing relief", 200 "Temporary Importation", 235 "Outward Processing Relief", and 770 "End-Use Relief" for further information.

Further information is contained in Notice 702/9 "Import Customs procedures".

5.3 Re-importation of goods temporarily exported for process or repair

If you re-import goods that were temporarily exported outside the EU territory for repair, service, making up or processing see Notice 702/9 "Import Customs procedures", section 7. You can find the duty relief procedures and entry procedures in Notice 235 "Outward processing Relief".

5.4 Goods re-imported in the same state

If you re-import your own goods in the same state as they were exported, you need not pay import VAT provided—

- — the goods were last exported from the EU by you, and
- — the goods meet conditions 2-5 in the checklist for customs duty Returned Goods Relief in section 5 of Notice 236 "Importing returned goods free of duty and VAT"; and
- — any import VAT chargeable on the goods was accounted for or paid and neither has been, nor will be reclaimed; *and*
- — the goods were *not* exported with a view to avoiding or abusing the normal VAT supply rules by using Returned Goods Relief.

This relief is intended primarily to avoid import VAT having to be paid and reclaimed, perhaps several times, for example, on goods taken outside the EU on approval and brought back unsold or on tools and equipment returned after use outside the EU.

There are various returned goods reliefs, each of which has its set of limiting conditions, and in certain circumstances you may have a choice of more than one. A complete list of returned goods relief Customs Procedure Codes detailing the type of procedure for which goods may be entered can be found in Volume 3, Appendix E of HMRC Tariff. You will find details of the entry procedures for claiming relief on reimported goods in Notice 236 "Importing returned goods free of duty and tax".

5.5 Where can I find more information about import VAT reliefs?

Import VAT reliefs are described fully in Volume 3 of the Tariff. The main VAT reliefs fall within the following CPC headings:

CPC heading	*Code*
Temporary admission	53
IP suspension	51
Conditional (free circulation import) reliefs	40
Returned goods	61
Outward Processing Relief	61
Processing under Customs Control	91
Zero-rated onward supplies	42

6 UNREGISTERED PERSONS

Unless otherwise indicated in this, or other sections, all the procedures in this notice also apply to unregistered persons.

6.1 Goods imported for business purposes

You must declare goods on importation and pay or defer the import VAT in the same way as anyone who is registered for VAT. However, as you are not entitled to reclaim the import VAT you pay as input tax, you do not receive an import VAT certificate (C79 –see section 8). However you can claim import VAT paid on goods when—

- — VAT was overpaid at importation. You should make a written request on form C285 "Application for repayment/remission" as explained in paragraph 2.6 for direct repayment through the duty adjustment system; or
- — the goods are not what you ordered or are otherwise not in accordance with contract. You will find details of the procedure you must follow in Notice 266 "Rejected imports: repayment or remission of duty and VAT".

6.2 Goods imported for non-business purposes

You do not have to complete a declaration on Form C88 Single administrative document (SAD) unless you are importing the goods as freight, you are claiming one of the relief's listed in paragraph 5.1 or you are claiming an exemption. If these reliefs are not applicable, you can only claim any import VAT paid in the circumstances explained in paragraph 6.1.

6.3 Personal reliefs

As well as the reliefs described in parag 5.4 and some of the reliefs described in para 5.1, you can also claim relief from import VAT on specific categories of goods. These reliefs are explained in the notices listed below—

— Notice 3 "Bringing your belongings and private motor vehicle to the UK from outside the European Community".
— Notice 8 "Sailing your pleasure craft to and from the United Kingdom".

7 IMPORTING COMPUTER SOFTWARE

7.1 How do I arrive at the Customs value?

The customs value of imported software has to be determined according to the normal valuation rules. Where the customs value is declared on the basis of the transaction value, under Art 29 of Council Regulation No 2913/92, the value should be based on the price actually paid or payable for both the carrier medium and the data and instructions (the software) on it. For customs valuation purposes, no distinction is made between normalised or specific software.

7.2 What is "normalised" software?

Products containing "normalised" software are mass produced items which are freely available to all customers and usable by them independently after installation and limited training in a standard form to carry out the same applications or functions. They are made up of a coherent set of programs and support material and often include the service of installation, training and maintenance. Personal computer software, home computer software and game packages are in this category. Also included are standard packages adapted at the supplier's instigation to include security or similar devices.

7.3 What if the normalised software is supplied free of charge?

If the software is supplied to you free of charge, for example in an inter-company transaction, you will pay VAT on the value in accordance with the valuation rules in paragraph 3.1.

7.4 What is "specific" software?

"Specific" products are—

— items made to customers' special requirements, either as unique programs or adaptations from standard programs;
— inter-company information data and accounts;
— enhancements and updates of existing "specific" programs; and
— enhancements and updates of existing "normalised" programs supplied under contractual obligation to customers who have bought the original program.

7.5 What is the basis of the value for import VAT?

Under VATA 1994 s 21(1), the value of imported goods shall be determined according to the rules applicable in the case of Community Customs duties. (See paragraph 7.1). For a full description of Place of Supply of services see Public Notice 741 (before 1 January 2010) and Notice 741A.

— *Normalised software*. Import VAT is due on the Customs value of the software, For example, the total value of the carrier medium and the data and instructions (the software) on it, adjusted where appropriate in accordance VATA 1994 s 21(2).
— *Specific software*. No import VAT is due. The total amount of the value of both software and carrier medium is treated as the consideration for the supply of services and is taxed accordingly within the member state concerned.

7.6 Transmission and provision of information by satellite, telephone, telex, fax etc

The transmission and provision of information by satellite, phone, telex, facsimile etc. is treated as a service. You will find more information on this in Notice 741 "Place of supply of services" (before 1 January 2010) and Notice 741A "Place of supply of services".

8 IMPORT VAT CERTIFICATE (C79)

(Referred to in paragraphs 2.3, 4.2 and 6.1)

8.1 What this section is about

This section explains the current arrangements for the issue of evidence that import VAT has been paid.

8.2 Basic information about import VAT certificates

You need to hold official evidence of VAT paid on imported goods before you can recover the VAT as input tax. The normal evidence is the monthly certificate, known as form C79. It does not in itself allow you to claim back the VAT you have paid which must, in all cases, be deductible under the normal input tax rules.

We send the certificates (form C79) to the VAT/EORI registered person whose VAT registration number is shown in Box 8 of the import declaration. You must take great care to use the correct EORI number. If not, the VAT you have paid may not appear on your certificate and may even end up on another person's certificate. Similarly, you may find someone else's import VAT on your certificate.

WARNING: We will take action against agents/importers who persistently quote incorrect EORI numbers. This may include prosecution.

8.3 What does the certificate cover?

The C79 certificate is issued in connection with most import procedures, and also post importation corrections and removals from a customs warehouse. These are listed in paragraph 8.17. There are some types of importation that do not appear on the certificate. These are listed in paragraph 8.18 together with the acceptable evidence of payment shown against each type.

8.4 What does the C79 certificate look like and what information is on it?

The certificate is made up of twin sided A4 sheets with a blue print background. A specimen of the format of a certificate is reproduced in paragraph 8.5.

Flexible Accounting System (FAS) paid VAT transactions will be shown under your EORI number.

Neither the agent's VAT number nor the agent's reference number appears on the certificate for immediate payment and FAS paid transactions. If this causes you particular difficulties you may wish to consider arranging duty deferment facilities.

The accounting date will be shown against each item on the certificate, and transactions will appear on the certificate for the month covering that accounting date – for example, transactions bearing an accounting date of October will normally appear on the October C79 certificates. For transactions paid by duty deferment the accounting date is normally the date of clearance of the goods. For immediate payment and FAS items the accounting date may, in some instances, be later than the date of the declaration. So some goods cleared in late October may have a November accounting date, and will therefore appear on the November certificate.

Transactions that are the subject of an accounting query will appear on the first certificate issued after the query has been dealt with.

A single total of VAT for the period will appear at the end of the final page.

8.5 Example of a certificate

(Referred to in paragraph 8.4)

8020/01210/I/00003	H.M. CUSTOMS AND EXCISE MONTHLY VAT CERTIFICATE	VC 0001	
DATE PRODUCED 12/11/90	***DO NOT DESTROY***		PAGE 1

PLEASE NOTE 123 MESSAGE BOX

VAT IMPORTS
LTD 60 PENDENNIS
ROAD BRISTOL BS8
4TQ

1/00002

VAT REGISTRATION
NO. 101222233

PERIOD ENDING
. . . .OCTOBER 90

A/C date	ENTRY NO.	AGENT'S REF.	WARE-HOUSE CODE NO.	WARR NO. /CONSEC NO.	AGENT'S VAT NO.	VAT AMOUNT
DECLARED TURN 101222233 000						
CARDIFF						
01.10.90	051061	974			176716142	4943.88
01.10.90	051062	977			176716142	2523.22
14.10.90	052137	9104			254213733	261.47
16.10.90	052245	991			176716142	1910.19
16.10.90	052246	997			176716142	839.29
21.10.90	053678	9111			254213733	1021.07
21.10.90	053679	9112			254212733	415.93
22.10.90	054379	102			266109875	3391.60
23.10.90	055378	9220			254213733	944.02
24.10.90	055469	9244			254213733	1033.85
25.10.90	056893	166			266109875	1124.94
28.10.90	059784	193			266109875	724.01
DECLARED TURN 101222233 110						
LIVERPOOL						
01.10.90	095766	1130			163356465	3398.92
05.10.90	095932	1140			163356465	216.09
05.10.90	095933	1141			163356465	3610.36
14.10.90	097839	1232			163356465	5569.59
15.10.90	099145	1556			163356465	812.43
15.10.90	099146	1557			163356465	3465.95
23.10.90	100162	2018			163356465	2021.37
25.10.90	101387	2118			163356465	1027.44
TOTAL VAT FOR THE PERIOD						**39305.64**

****YOU MUST KEEP THIS CERTIFICATE TO SUPPORT YOUR CLAIM TO INPUT TAX****

8.6 When can I expect my C79 certificate?

Certificates cover accounting transactions made in each calendar month should be received around the 24th of each month following imports logged the previous month. For example,

October certificates (certificates covering transactions with accounting dates in October) should be received on or about the 24 November. We post the certificates direct to your address as shown on the main VAT register. This means that, for VAT group registrations, a single certificate is issued to the address of the representative member of the group. Certificates cannot be sent to an address other than that on the main VAT register.

8.7 How to use the C79 certificate

The original certificate or Customs issued replacement is the prime evidence for claiming input tax deduction. However, you may copy and distribute certificates as required for internal accounting purposes. We will also allow a self-accounting branch to use a photocopy of the certificate as an accounting document for the purpose of input tax deduction, provided the original is made available for inspection if requested by the control officer.

The date when the VAT shown on the certificate may be treated as input tax is normally the accounting date alongside each item, not the date when the certificate is issued. So, for example, if your VAT return period ends 31 October, you may treat as input tax for that period, subject to the normal rules, VAT paid shown on your October certificate (issued 12 November).

If you have non-standard tax periods and the issue date of the 12th of the month causes you difficulties, you may wish to consider applying to your local VAT office (LVO) for permission to estimate input tax.

8.8 Health authorities and government departments

We do not issue certificates to health authorities and government departments whose TURNs begin with HA or GD.

When VAT is paid at the point of importation and the authority or department is entitled to input tax deduction, a HMRC authenticated copy of the declaration will be issued as evidence.

8.9 Negative amounts on certificates

Negative amounts may appear on your certificate. These are either repayments of import VAT (see paragraph 8.11) or corrections of errors.

8.10 Lost or missing certificates

We keep for a period of six years, microfiche copies of all monthly certificates issued. You can get replacements of lost or missing certificates from:

HM Revenue & Customs
VAT Central Unit, Microfilm Section
8th Floor, Alexander House
Victoria Avenue
Southend-on-Sea SS99 1AU

You need to request them in writing, by faxing your request to – fax no. 03000 594271 on business headed paper, quoting your VAT registration number and the month(s) for which replacement is required. Replacement certificates will be issued to your VAT registered address. Duplicates take approximately two-three weeks to issue.

Before you request replacement certificates, you need to be sure that a certificate should, in fact, have been issued (see paragraph 8.16).

VCU Microfilm section cannot answer general queries about certificates. You should contact the Helpline, telephone 0300 200 3700.

If there is not enough time for you to get a replacement certificate before your VAT return is due, contact your LVO to arrange use of alternative evidence or estimation of input tax.

8.11 Newly registered traders

If you are newly registered for VAT you will need to apply for an EORI number completing parts A and C of the C220 EORI application form – form C220 electronic application. A certificate cannot be produced without a UK EORI number.

8.12 Queries about additional items on certificates

Paragraph 8.2 explains how someone else's import VAT can appear on your certificate. If you discover such an item you must not deduct as input tax the amount shown. If you or the agent who made the import declaration later corrects the error, a negative amount will appear on your next certificate. If you have already wrongly deducted the VAT shown, you must show the negative amount as a credit on the VAT deductible side of your account. This will reduce the amount of input tax you are able to claim in that period.

8.13 Queries about items missing from certificates

If you consider that any VAT amounts paid or deferred are missing from a certificate ask yourself—

— Could the item be outside the scope of the certificate?
Paragraph 8.18 explains which imports do not appear on certificates. Where this is so, you will receive the form of evidence listed.

— Am I newly registered?
If "yes" follow the action in paragraph 8.13

— Is the item likely to have an accounting date within the month covered by the certificate?
If "no" wait for the item to appear on your next certificate (see paragraph 8.4).

If none of these explanations apply, you or your agent may have entered your EORI number incorrectly on the entry and you should contact the centralised processing unit dealing with post-clearance non-revenue amendments. Their address is Custom House, Ralli Quays, Salford, M60 9LA. Telephone: 03000 587641 Fax: 03000 588482 Email: nchtechnical@hmrc.gsi.gov.uk

However where there is a revenue implication you should contact the centralised processing unit dealing with such matters. Their address and telephone is the same as above.

8.14 Further help or advice

If you need further help or advice on the C79 certificate system you should contact our Helpline, telephone 0300 200 3700.

8.15 Importations which appear on the certificate

(Referred to in paragraph 8.3)

Import procedure	*Previous evidence for input tax deduction*
A: Air/sea imports	
The Single Administrative Document (SAD)	
—manually processed	SAD – authenticated copy 8
—trader input / computer processed	Weekly VAT certificate issued by Customs computer report TW-AH or TW-BH
—input / computer processed	Weekly VAT certificate issued by Customs computer report TW-AH or TW-BH
B: Post entry correction	Form C18
C: Removals from warehouse	
Customs warehouse	Form C259 – authenticated copy 4
Excise or Customs warehouse	Duty payment Form W5, W6 or W20 or Duty deferment Form W5D, W6D or W20D
Hydrocarbon oils	Duty payment W50
	Duty deferment VAT 908

8.16 Importations which do not appear on the certificate

(Referred to in paragraph 8.3)

Import procedure	*Previous evidence for input tax deduction*
A: Air/sea imports	
Bulked entries – Single Administrative Document (SAD)	Customs authenticated invoices
Registered consignees	Customs authenticated invoices
SAD (simplified)	PE33 (not authenticated by Customs)
Transit Shed Register (TSR) – imports not exceeding £600 (non-DTI)	Customs authenticated commercial invoice (or local variations of procedure) certified by Customs. The concession allowing use of copies of agents' disbursement invoices in certain circumstances will continue.
B: Postal imports	
—Exceeding £2000 – SAD	SAD – authenticated copy 8
—Not exceeding £2000 (Customs declaration Form CN22/CN23)	No input tax evidence issued. Importers must retain evidence of payment of import charges by retaining the customs charge label and declaration that is on the front of the parcel.

9 VAT TERRITORY OF THE EUROPEAN UNION (EU)

(Referred to in paragraphs 1.1, 1.6 and 7.3)

VAT TERRITORY OF THE EUROPEAN Union (EU)

Member state	including...	*but excluding...*
Austria	Jungholtz and Mittelberg	
Belgium		
Bulgaria		
Croatia		
Cyprus	the British Sovereign Base Areas of Akrotiri and Dhekelia	the United Nations buffer zone and the part of Cyprus to the north of the buffer zone, where the Republic of Cyprus does not exercise effective control
Czech Republic		
Denmark		the Faroe Islands, and Greenland
Estonia		
Hungary		
Finland		the Aland Islands
France	Monaco	Martinique, French Guiana, Guadeloupe, Reunion, Mayotte and Saint-Martin (French Republic)
Germany		the island of Heligoland, and Büsingen
Greece		Mount Athos (also known as Agion Oros)
Ireland		
Italy		Campione d'Italia, the Italian Waters of Lake Lugano and Lvigno
Latvia		

Member state	including...	*but excluding...*
Lithuania		
Luxembourg		
Malta		
Netherlands		Antilles
Poland		
Portugal	the Azores, and Madeira	
Romania		
Slovakia		
Slovenia		
Spain	the Balearic Islands	the Canary Islands, Ceuta and Melilla
Sweden		
United Kingdom	the Isle of Man	the Channel Islands, and Gibraltar

Goods entering the UK from the "special territories" will, for VAT purposes, be treated as imported goods.

Note: Liechtenstein, the Vatican City, Andorra and San Marino are not within the EU for VAT purposes.

10 CUSTOMS SUSPENSIVE ARRANGEMENTS

(Referred to in paragraphs 4.1 and 5.2)

Details of Customs suspensive arrangements are now contained in Public Notice 702/9 "Import Customs procedures".

11 DEFINITION OF ARTICLES WHICH ARE ELIGIBLE FOR IMPORTATION AT A REDUCED VALUATION GIVING AN EFFECTIVE VAT RATE OF 5 PER CENT

(Referred to in paragraph 3.5)

This section applies only to VAT.

11.1 Works of art

— Pictures, collages and similar decorative plaques, paintings and drawings, executed entirely by hand by the artist, other than plans and drawings for architectural, engineering, industrial, commercial, topographical or similar purposes, hand-decorated manufactured articles, theatrical scenery, studio back cloths or the like of painted canvas (Tariff heading 9701).

— Original engravings, prints and lithographs, being impressions produced in limited numbers directly in black and white or in colour of one or several plates executed entirely by hand by the artist, irrespective of the process or of the material employed by him, but not including any mechanical or photomechanical process (Tariff code 9702 00 00).

— Original sculptures and statuary, in any material, provided that they are executed entirely by the artist; sculpture casts (Tariff code 9703 00 00). See Notice 718 "The VAT Margin scheme and global accounting" for the definition of sculpture casts.

— Tapestries (Tariff code 5805 00 00) and wall textiles, made by hand from original designs provided by artists, provided that there are not more than eight copies of each.

— Individual pieces of ceramics executed entirely by the artist and signed by him.

— Enamels on copper, executed entirely by hand, limited to eight numbered copies bearing the signature of the artist or the studio, excluding articles of jewellery and goldsmiths' and silversmiths' wares.

— Photographs taken by the artist, printed by him or under his supervision, signed and numbered and limited to 30 copies, all sizes and mounts included.

11.2 Antiques

— Objects other than works of art or collectors' items, which are more than 100 years old (tariff code 9706 00 00).

11.3 Collectors' items

— Postage or revenue stamps, postmarks, first-day covers, pre-stamped stationery and the like, franked or if unfranked not being of legal tender and not being intended for use as legal tender (tariff code 9704 00 00).
— Collections and collectors' pieces of zoological, botanical, mineralogical, anatomical, historical, archaeological, palaeontological, ethnographic or numismatic interest (tariff code 9705 00 00).

11.4 Items of historical significance

An article which is not 100 years old may be eligible for the scheme under this heading if it is of historical significance because of it's uniqueness, or by having a direct association with an historical person or event, or is a rare example marking an important change in technical or artistic development in a particular field. Items, which were mass-produced or are merely the products of a bygone age, are unlikely to be eligible.

The list of examples shown is by no means exhaustive but gives general guidelines on the types of article eligible under this heading.

Postage stamps: Issued by a country to mark its independence.

Motor vehicles which—

— possess a certain scarcity value;
— are not normally used for their original purpose;
— are the subject of transactions outside the normal trade in similar utility vehicles;
— are of high value; and
— illustrate a significant step in the evolution of human achievements or a period of that evolution.

In view of the fact that a motor vehicle is basically a utility article with a relatively short life, and subject to constant technical development, then the foregoing preconditions underlying the above judgments, in so far as they are not obviously contradicted by the facts, can be taken to apply in respect of—

— Vehicles in their original state, without substantial changes to the chassis, steering or breaking system, engine etc, at least 30 years old and of a model or type which is no longer in production.

Also included as collectors' pieces of historical interest are—

(a) motor vehicles, irrespective of their date of manufacture, which can be proved to have been used in the course of an historic event;
(b) motor-racing vehicles, which can be proved to be designed, built and used solely for competition and have scored significant sporting successes at prestigious national or international events.

The above notes and criteria also apply to motorcycles.

If you wish to import a vehicle covered by the guidelines above, you are advised to phone the Classification Advice Line on telephone: 03000 513777 Option 2, before making a purchase to ensure that your vehicle will be eligible for the reduced rate of VAT at import.

Products designed by famous historical craftsmen.

Such as—

— De Morgan or William Morris tiles and ceramics;
— Peter Waals desks and tables;
— Mcintosh and William Morris home furnishings (eg carpets, curtains, vases, clocks, chairs);
— decorative glassware produced by Galle, Lalique and Tiffany.

Medals (Military)

- All military medals awarded up to and including World War 1;
- medals awarded after World War 1 which are inscribed with the recipients name;
- individual military medals awarded after World War 1 for an act of gallantry, outstanding service etc whether or not they bear the recipients name.

(Civilian)

- All civil medals awarded individually which bear the recipients name.

Militaria

- General military items up to and including World War 1 such as weapons, badges etc; items of militaria which belonged to, or were used by, a famous person who won a gallantry award.

11.5 What if I disagree with any of your decisions?

If you do not agree with any decision issued to you there are three options available. Within 30 days of the date of the decision you can either—

- send new information or arguments to the decision maker,
- request a review of the decision by someone not involved in making the disputed decision.

Your request must be in writing and should set out the reasons why you do not agree with the decision.

Please write to:

Customs and International
Review and Appeals Team
7th Floor South West
Alexander House
21 Victoria Avenue
Southend-on-Sea
Essex SS99 1AA

or appeal direct to the Tribunal who are independent of HMRC.

If you opt to have your case reviewed you will still be able to appeal to the tribunal if you disagree with the outcome.

Further information relating to reviews and appeals is contained in leaflet HMRC1 which can be obtained from our website or by phoning 0300 200 3700.

There are penalties for failing to comply with HMRC requirements. Serious breaches can lead to the imported goods being seized and criminal prosecution.

In your own interests, if you are unsure about something please ask for advice by contacting the Helpline on 0300 200 3700.

11.6 Where can I get more information?

You can find more information about reviews and appeals from our guide "Appeals against HM Revenue & Customs decisions" or our fact sheet, HMRC 1, "HMRC decisions – what to do if you disagree". You can download copies of these information sheets by visiting our website, go to www.hmrc.gov.uk or telephone the Helpline on 0300 200 3700.

702/7

IMPORT VAT RELIEF FOR GOODS SUPPLIED ONWARD TO ANOTHER COUNTRY IN THE EC

February 2013

This notice cancels and replaces Notice 702/7 (April 2010). Details of any changes to the previous version can be found in paragraph 1.2 of this notice.

VAT Regulations 1995 reg 123 gives the Commissioners power to impose conditions on the relief. Those conditions have the force of law. Where those conditions appear in this notice, they are placed in a box headed: "the following text has the force of law".

1 INTRODUCTION

1.1 What is this notice about?

This notice explains how VAT registered traders who receive goods from outside the European Union (EU) may claim "onward support relief" from the import VAT that would otherwise be chargeable.

Commentary—*De Voil Indirect Tax Service* V3.337.

1.2 What's changed?

This notice has been changed to make it clearer that a VAT-registered importer acting as agent in an onward supply must be "acting in his own name" in relation to that supply. It has also been changed to address changes to the way VAT identification numbers are entered in box 44 of the import declaration.

1.3 Who should read this notice?

This notice is of interest to anyone who is or will be importing goods from outside the European Union (EU) (whether on their own behalf or on behalf of another person) in the course of a supply to a person in another EU country (or "member state"*).

*For a full list of member states in VAT territory of the Single Market see Notice 725, section 2.4.

1.4 What law covers this notice?

OSR relief is provided by:

- Directive 2006/112/EC (The Principal VAT Directive) art 143
- VATA 1994 s 47
- VAT Regulations 1995 reg 123
- VAT Regulations 1995 reg 134

2 ONWARD SUPPLY RELIEF (OSR)

2.1 Who is eligible to use OSR?

A UK VAT registered person who imports goods then—

(a) makes an onward supply of those goods that is zero rated in accordance with reg 134 of the VAT Regulations 1995 (supplies to persons taxable in another member state), or
(b) acts as agent for a non-taxable person in relation to an onward supply of those goods that is zero rated in accordance with reg 134 of the VAT Regulations 1995 provided that the agent "acts in his own name" in relation to that supply.

The zero rating of supplies to persons taxable in another member state is dealt with in Notice 725.

Commentary—*De Voil Indirect Tax Service* V3.337.

2.2 Can an agent use OSR?

Yes, they can, provided that—

(a) they are the importer of the goods (which they will be if they have submitted the import declaration in their won name), and
(b) they act in their own name in relation to the onward supply.

An agent acts in his own name in the onward supply if he acts as though he were the vendor. We would not consider an agent to be acting in his own name if—

- the contract for sale is between his principal name and the purchaser, or

- if the invoice for the purchase price is issued in the principal's name, or
- if the agent represents to the buyer that he is acting, in the sale, on behalf of a named principal.

VATA 1994 s 47 applies in particular.

Note: An agent not fulfilling the above and acting purely as the freight forwarder would not meet the conditions of OSR, retrospective amendment of the Customs declaration at that point would not be possible. Such traders should have used an alternative system such as (but not restricted to) External Community Transit.

Prior to the use of any Customs procedures you must make sure that you meet all the conditions for actually submitting the Customs declaration as well as conditions applying subsequently.

2.3 What are the conditions of OSR?

The following text has the force of law

You must enter in box 44 of the import SAD—

- your VAT identification number (beginning Y040GB if you are importing the goods on your own behalf and Y042GB if you are importing them as an agent for someone else)
- if known, the expected place and date of onward consignment
- if known, the particulars of the onward transport
- the name, address and VAT identification number (including the Y041 prefix followed by the two-digit country code) of the purchaser in the member state of destination.

You must also—

(a) despatch the goods in the same state as they were when imported (without processing them in any way)
(b) remove the goods to another member state within one month of the date of importation (which is the date on which they are released to free circulation). If you cannot meet this deadline, you can apply to the National Import Relief Unit (NIRU) for an extension (see below for contact details)
(c) complete EU sales lists and record EU trade figures in your VAT returns
(d) comply with all the obligations of a person making a zero rated supply (see Notice 725).

National Import Relief Unit
Abbey House
Head Street
Enniskillen
Co. Fermanagh
N. Ireland BT74 7JL
Tel: 028 66344557
Fax: 028 66344571
Email: niru@hmrc.gsi.gov.uk

2.4 other details required on Single Administrative Document (SAD)

Enter the appropriate Customs Procedure Code (CPC) in box 37.

By using the CPC you are making a declaration that you—

- have met the conditions of the relief at paragraphs 2.1–2.3
- will produce, if asked by one of our officers, commercial evidence that the goods have been supplied onward to another EU country, and
- will pay on demand any import charges due if the conditions of the relief are not met.

Although the law allows us to, we do not normally require you to provide security for VAT.

What are the CPCs?

The CPC applicable to your particular OSR importation (and the conditions that apply) can be found by referencing the—

Integrated Tariff of the United Kingdom, Volume 3, Appendix E2.

Note—when goods are imported make sure the correct import CPC is used. Failure to do so may result in OSR being refused.

2.5 What happens if you do not comply with the conditions of OSR?

If you do not comply with the OSR conditions we will normally issue a C18 demand for the import VAT.

If you do not have to pay the import VAT, you may be able to reclaim it as input tax on your VAT return. However, import VAT can only be recovered as input tax where the goods, on which the import VAT has been charged, are used in the making of taxable supplies. In practice this requires that the business makes the onward supply as principal or undisclosed agent (please see paragraphs 2.1–2.2).

For further details please refer to Notice 702.

3 HOW DO YOU APPEAL AGAINST A DECISION?

If you do not agree with any decision issued to you there are other options available. Within 30 days of the date of the decision you can either:

- send new information or arguments to the decision maker, or
- request a review of the decision by someone not involved in making the disputed decision.

Your request must be in writing and should set out the reasons why you do not agree with the decision.

Please write to:

ECSM
Review and Appeals Team
7th Floor South West
Alexander House
21 Victoria Avenue
Essex
SS99 1AA

Or, appeal direct to the Tribunal who are independent of HMRC.

If you opt to have your case reviewed you will still be able to appeal to the tribunal if your disagree with the outcome.

Further information relating to reviews and appeals is contained in leaflet HMRC1 which can be obtained from our website or by phoning 0845 900 0404.

Commentary—*De Voil Indirect Tax Service* **V3.337.**

702/8
FISCAL WAREHOUSING

October 2012

This notice contains information previously contained in Notice 702/9 "Warehouses and Free Zones" which has been cancelled and replaced by Notice 702/9 "VAT: Import Customs Procedures".

Paragraphs 5.1 and 5.2 have the force of law under the VAT Regulations 1995 regs 145B(1) and 145C.

1 INTRODUCTION

1.1 What is this notice about?

This notice gives information on the VAT treatment of goods entered into, supplied within and removed from fiscal warehouses.

Commentary—*De Voil Indirect Tax Service* **V1.216–V1.218, V3.384, Division V5.4.**

1.2 What's changed?

This notice has been updated to reflect the legal status of the certificates reproduced at paragraphs 5.1 and 5.2.

1.3 Who should read this notice?

You should read this notice if you trade in any of the eligible commodities listed in paragraph 2.3 of this notice, or if you provide storage facilities for any of these commodities.

1.4 Fiscal warehouse law

— *EC Law* – Directive 2006/112 – art 160(2) and Annex V
— *UK Primary Law* – VATA 1994 – ss 18A, B, C, D, E and F
— *UK Secondary Law* – VAT Regulations 1995 – regs 145A to 145J.

1.5 What is a fiscal warehouse?

A fiscal warehouse is a regime where certain commodities in free circulation within the EC can be traded VAT-free, subject to the conditions described in section 2. Goods are in free circulation if they are produced in the EC or, in the case of imported goods, all duties taxes and levies due at importation have been paid.

1.6 Commodities eligible for fiscal warehousing in the UK

Goods	*What is suspended*
Specified commodities that are in free circulation (see paragraph 2.3)	Supply VAT — this is VAT which is charged on the supply of any goods or services that takes place in the UK, made by a taxable person in the course of any business carried out by that person.

Supply of VAT is normally paid when the goods are removed from the regime.

1.7 The territory of the EC

The term "EC" as used in this notice refers to the VAT territory of the European Community, which is different from its customs territory. The countries and territories which make up the VAT territory of the EC are listed in section 3.

1.8 Treatment of transactions with the Isle of Man

Goods removed from the Isle of Man to the UK are not treated as an importation as long as—

- any VAT due has been accounted for in the Isle of Man, or
- if the goods were relieved of VAT in the Isle of Man, the conditions of that relief have not been broken.

1.9 Treatment of transactions with the Channel Islands

The Channel Islands are part of the customs territory of the EC but not part of its VAT territory. The territories which share this status are often called "special territories" and they are listed in section 3.

Goods you receive from the Channel Islands or other special territories are imports for VAT purposes and are, in principle, treated in the same way as other imports at the time of importation. You will find further information about import procedures (including some simplified procedures) for goods received from the Channel Islands and other special territories in the Customs and Excise Integrated Tariff and Notice 702 "VAT: Imports" (Part V8).

1.10 Right of appeal

If you disagree with any decision made by Revenue & Customs you can ask for it to be reconsidered by the office where that decision was made. You should certainly do so if you can provide further relevant information, or if there are facts which you think may not have been fully taken into account. If you are still not satisfied, you may be able to appeal to an independent Tribunal. There are limits for doing this.

If you do not agree with the result of our reconsideration you can appeal to the First-Tier Tribunal to decide the matter. There is more information about what you can do if you disagree with our decision in a HMRC factsheet and customer guidance which can be found on the HMRC website.

2 SUPPLIES OF GOODS AND SERVICES WITHIN FISCAL WAREHOUSES

Commentary—*De Voil Indirect Tax Service* **V3.138, V3.176, V3.366, V3.370, V3.384, V3.388, V3.396, V4.209, V5.132B, V5.141A, V5.404.**

2.1 What this section covers

Fiscal warehousing provides a regime which enables certain EC goods to be traded VAT free, subject to the conditions described in the rest of this notice. The relevant law is set out in paragraph 1.4.

This section explains in detail what the regime is intended to achieve, and gives guidance on—

- who may use the regime;
- what goods are eligible;
- the treatment of goods entering, sold within and removed from a fiscal warehouse;
- the treatment of services within a fiscal warehouse;
- how you can become authorised to operate a fiscal warehouse;
- when VAT becomes due on removing goods from a fiscal warehouse and how to account for it.

2.2 The purpose of fiscal warehousing

Fiscal warehousing is a regime under which certain specified commodities may be placed in a notified warehouse and traded by businesses which are not required to be VAT registered if that is their only business activity within the UK.

VAT on the supplies of commodities both—

— entering a fiscal warehouse, and
— made whilst within the warehouse,

is relieved and accounted for when the commodities are removed from the regime.

VAT on certain services made within a fiscal warehousing regime are also relieved and accounted for when commodities are removed (see paragraph 2.17).

Both EC origin and non-EC origin commodities in free circulation are eligible for the regime.

Fiscal warehousing creates a trading environment for eligible EC commodities compatible with the VAT-free trading available in excise warehouses and customs warehouses. Excise and customs warehouse premises may also be used for fiscal warehousing, but separate authorisation is needed for the fiscal warehousing regime. Retail sales are not allowed within a fiscal warehousing regime.

2.3 Eligible commodities

Any of the commodities contained in the following table are eligible to be placed in a fiscal warehouse. These commodities are eligible for trading in and transfer between EC fiscal warehousing regimes.

Description of goods	*Combined nomenclature code of the European Communities (Commodity Code)*
Tin	8001
Copper	7402740374057408
Zinc	7901
Nickel	7502
Aluminium	7601
Lead	7801
Indium	ex 8112 91ex 8112 99
Cereals	1001 to 1005
	1006: unprocessed rice only
	1007 to 1008
Oil seeds and oleaginous fruit	1201 to 1207
Coconuts, Brazil nuts and cashew nuts	0801
Other nuts	0502
Olives	0711 20
Grains and seeds (including Soya beans)	1201 to 1207
Coffee, not roasted	0901 11 00
	0901 12 00
Tea	0902
Cocoa beans, whole or broken, raw or roasted	1801
Raw sugar	1701 11
	1701 12
Rubber, in primary forms or in plates, sheets or strip	4001
	4002
Wool	5101
Chemicals in bulk	Chapters 28 and 29
Mineral oils (including propane and butane; also including crude petroleum oils)	2709
	2710
	2711 12
	2711 13
Silver	7106
Platinum (Palladium, Rhodium)	7110 11 00
	7110 21 00
	7110 31 00
Potatoes	0701
Vegetable oils and fats and their fractions, whether or not refined, but not chemically modified	1507 to 1515

2.4 Principal criteria for eligibility for fiscal warehousing

- The commodity in question should be commonly traded in large quantities on a recognised international market.
- All commodities entered to fiscal warehousing must be in free circulation within the EC. That means all duties, taxes and levies must have been either paid or deferred, including customs duty, import VAT, excise duty and any CAP charges due on the goods.

Non-eligible commodities may be stored in a place which is a fiscal warehouse, but such goods cannot be subject to a fiscal warehousing regime or benefit from the conditions of fiscal warehousing.

2.5 What authorisation is needed?

Before you can operate a fiscal warehouse you must apply to HM Revenue & Customs for authorisation. You will have to be able to satisfy certain criteria to ensure that your revenue record and internal accounting procedures are of a sufficiently high order to guarantee the integrity of the regime. If you currently operate any Departmentally approved warehousing system you must still apply for a separate authorisation for fiscal warehousing, although satisfactory operation of an existing warehouse will be taken into account when assessing your application for fiscal warehousing authorisation.

2.6 Method of application

You must complete a letter of application as described in section 6. You can get the address to send it to from our VAT Helpline – see paragraph 1.2. Once we are satisfied that you can fully comply with fiscal warehousing requirements we will send you a letter of authorisation, which will be conditional on your acceptance of any conditions we believe to be appropriate. The authorisation will be granted without a time limit, except in the case of provisional authorisations (see paragraph 2.9).

Once you are authorised, you may request a change of approval conditions by contacting our VAT Helpline well in advance, explaining the reason for the required change. In particular you should notify Customs of any new premises you intend to use for fiscal warehousing. If we agree to your request we will confirm it in writing. You should keep this confirmation together with your original letter of authorisation. We may also change the authorisation conditions ourselves, if we consider that a change in your circumstances merits this. We will of course notify you in advance of any authorisation changes we may consider appropriate, and you have an automatic right of appeal.

2.7 Basic criteria for authorisation as a fiscal warehousekeeper

Before we can approve any application to operate fiscal warehousing, the following criteria must be met—

- You must be VAT registered in the UK.
- The revenue record of your business must be of a high standard (for example VAT returns and payments must be up to date).
- If you are already authorised to operate any authorised UK duty suspensive regime you must have a proven satisfactory record of operation.
- You must be able to comply with the conditions of authorisation and with such regulations as may be laid down for the operation of the regime. This is particularly important as penalties can be imposed for failure to comply.
- The administration and organisation of your business must be sound and strictly managed.
- You must provide a list of the addresses of all storage sites which will form part of the fiscal warehouse you intend to operate and any other premises where records will be held. Retail premises cannot be used as fiscal warehouse premises. All notified premises should meet the requirements of health and safety legislation. This also applies to any third party premises you intend to use.
- Your accounts and stock control records must be capable of meeting the requirements set out in paragraph 2.22. In particular, they must be able to differentiate between fiscally warehoused goods and other non-fiscally warehoused goods. The records must also be capable of identifying the location and quantity of any given item held within a fiscal warehousing regime at any stage.

2.8 Refusal and appeal against refusal

We may refuse authorisation where any of the required criteria are not met. If we do we will write to you setting out the reasons for our refusal and explaining how you can appeal against our decision. This allows for an initial local review of the decision and then, if necessary, an appeal to a VAT and Duties Tribunal. If you disagree with the decision and wish it to be reviewed locally by a member of staff not connected with the decision, you should apply in writing within 28 days of receiving the letter of refusal. This review does not affect your right to appeal to a VAT and Duties Tribunal.

If you wish to appeal directly to the Tribunal you should telephone our VAT Helpline. You also have the right to appeal against any conditions which we may have imposed on your application for authorisation.

2.9 Provisional authorisation

Where we cannot approve your request for authorisation immediately, for example because you have not yet secured the necessary premises, we may give you a letter of provisional consent to establish a fiscal warehouse as long as the outstanding criteria are met within a specified period of time. If any condition is not met within the deadline, the application will lapse and a fresh application must be submitted.

2.10 Transferring an authorisation

Once you are authorised to operate a fiscal warehouse, you cannot transfer your authorisation to another person or company. If you sell your business as a going concern, the prospective new owner must apply for authorisation in their own right and we will consider this on its merits. The new owner's application must be accompanied by a written declaration from you confirming the date on which your authorisation will cease (the date of the transfer of going concern).

2.11 Cancelling or revoking an authorisation

To cancel your authorisation you must give us advance notice in writing, stating the date by which all goods will cease to be traded and removed from the warehousing arrangements. You must ensure that VAT is accounted for on all such removals in accordance with paragraph 2.19.

We can revoke your authorisation at any time for any reasonable cause, for example if you do not comply with any of the conditions of the authorisation. Except in very exceptional circumstances we will notify you in advance of any intended revocation, and you will always have a right to appeal. Where we withdraw your authorisation, any goods held in your regime will be treated as though they had been removed by the proprietor at the time of withdrawal and VAT will be due in accordance with paragraph 2.19.

2.12 Warehousekeepers' responsibilities

As a fiscal warehousekeeper you—

- must keep a record of all eligible commodities that are entered to your warehousing regime whether you are the depositor or not
- must keep separate records of non-eligible goods entered to the warehouse for storage
- are responsible for the physical security of eligible commodities and may be held liable for VAT on any unexplained stock discrepancies other than through natural wastage or other legitimate causes.

  The amount due on such losses will be assessed on the basis of the VAT due on a sale of those goods at their highest open market value, or at the highest rate of VAT applying during the time the goods were in the fiscal warehouse. There is a right of appeal where such an assessment is made.
- must, before any commodities can be removed from the regime,
  - obtain sufficient evidence to be satisfied that the remover:
  - is the owner of the goods
  - is either VAT registered or has presented Form VAT 150 (see paragraph 2.19) and paid any VAT due at the local Entry Processing Unit.

  Note: Failure to ensure that VAT has been properly accounted for on such removals can render you jointly liable with the owner for any unpaid VAT.

2.13 VAT treatment of goods intended to be entered into fiscal warehouse

Any supply of goods, or acquisition of goods from another member state, destined for entry to a fiscal warehouse may be relieved from VAT.

If you are the purchaser and wish to obtain the relief, you must provide the seller of the goods with a certificate stating that you intend to place the goods in a fiscal warehouse.

If you are the acquirer you must produce and retain a certificate stating that the acquired goods are to be fiscally warehoused. Section 5 shows examples of what is required.

2.14 Goods entered into a fiscal warehouse

To be eligible for fiscal warehousing, commodities must be of a kind described in paragraph 2.3, and must be in free circulation as set out in paragraph 2.4.

2.15 Goods sold within a fiscal warehouse

Supplies of goods which are in a fiscal warehouse are outside the scope of UK VAT. There is no requirement to account for VAT to Revenue & Customs on such transactions, nor is there any direct Customs control over movements or transfers of goods whilst within the fiscal warehouse regime.

When goods are removed from the regime the amount of VAT payable will correspond—

- to the amount which would have been due on the transaction that caused the goods to be entered to the warehouse, or
- if they have been sold within the warehouse, to the amount which would have been due on the value of the last supply, subject to paragraph 2.17.

Any VAT due must be accounted for in accordance with paragraph 2.19. In order to be eligible for relief, supplies of unallocated goods (commodities warehoused in bulk storage containers that cannot be readily identified to a particular owner) within, or intended to be placed within a fiscal warehousing regime are treated as supplies of goods and not as supplies of services.

2.16 Treatment of services within a fiscal warehouse

Services which may be zero-rated are supplies of allowable physical services within the fiscal warehouse which would otherwise be taxable at the standard rate, for example storage charges.

Services which may not be zero-rated are brokerage, agents fees and transport between warehouses. For goods held in a fiscal warehouse, supplies of the usual forms of handling that are available to goods in a customs warehouse, may be relieved from VAT (these are listed in section 4). You will need to obtain written authority by contacting our VAT Helpline if you wish to obtain relief on supplies of services which exceed these specified operations.

2.17 Accounting for VAT on services applied to goods within a fiscal warehouse

On removal of the goods from the warehouse, any VAT relieved on each supply of services relating to those commodities made after the last sale in warehouse of such commodities must be accounted for, together with the VAT due on the relieved supply of the commodities. For example the commodity may be divided up into smaller packages by a simple operation that does not change its nature. The value of the service that is performed whilst the commodity is still relieved from VAT in the warehouse, must be added to the value of the supply when it is finally sold and removed from the warehouse.

For example:

Value of re-packaging service		£50
Value of final supply of commodity on removal from warehouse		£100
Value of total final supply		**£150**
VAT due on total final supply	**£150 × 20% =**	**£30**

Where, as a result of an operation carried out on eligible commodities, the resulting commodities are no longer eligible for fiscal warehousing, they are treated as having been removed and VAT will become due in accordance with paragraph 2.19.

2.18 Registration for VAT

If your only business activity is the supply of goods within a fiscal warehousing regime you have no liability to register for VAT, but you may do so voluntarily if you wish under VATA 1994 Sch 1(10). Your liability to register for other business activities is not affected by either the value of supplies made in a fiscal warehouse or the value of deemed supplies of relieved services accounted for by the remover of the goods.

2.19 Accounting for VAT due on goods removed from a fiscal warehouse

VAT becomes due when commodities finally leave the fiscal warehousing regime. The amount of VAT due corresponds to the amount of tax which would otherwise have been due on the final supply of goods in the warehouse, plus the amount of tax which would have been applied to any of the relieved supplies of services relating to those goods effected after that final supply.

The person liable to pay the VAT on removal is the person who causes the goods to cease to be covered by the regime.

- If you are VAT registered you should account for the VAT on your VAT return covering the period of the removal.
- If you are not registered, you must complete Form VAT 150: Advice of removals from fiscal warehouse by persons unregistered for VAT and present it to the local Entry Processing Unit (EPU) even when no VAT is due on removal. Payment of any VAT due on removal must be made in cash or by cheque. For all removals, proof of ownership and either a stamped copy of form VAT 150 or a VAT registration number is required by the warehousekeeper before the goods can be released.

Where goods are acquired from another member state and subsequently removed from warehouse without being sold within the warehouse, acquisition VAT must be accounted for in the normal way as explained in Notice 725 "The single market" (Part V8).

2.20 When VAT is not due on removal

If you remove your goods from a fiscal warehouse in any of the following situations, VAT is not due on the removal of the goods.

(a) Removals to home use:

- of zero-rated goods that have not been subject to relieved supplies of services whilst warehoused
- of your own goods (that either you produced or purchased VAT paid) which you entered to the fiscal warehouse and that have not been sold, nor have they been subject to relieved supplies of services whilst warehoused.

(b) Exports

Where goods are exported outside the EC, standard export procedures apply. Such removals must be supported by normal evidence of export. Any associated relieved supplies of services do not become taxable where goods have been exported.

(c) Despatches to other member states

Where goods are removed in the course of an intra-EC supply, normal Intrastat and intra-EC supply/acquisition rules apply for VAT registered traders. Relieved services are not taxed on removal to another member state but should be reflected in the value of the supply.

(d) Transfer to another UK fiscal warehouse

Such transfers can only be relieved from VAT where effective control over the goods is exercised by the despatching warehousekeeper. The warehousekeeper must obtain from the receiving warehousekeeper a written undertaking that they will comply with the regulations concerning transfers, and a certificate confirming that those regulations have been complied with (see paragraph 2.22(e)).

(e) Temporary removals

Authorisations (either general or specific) must be obtained through our VAT Helpline. Goods must be returned to the original site or another covered by the authorisation. In order to obtain authorisation, the remover must state the length of time the goods will need to be removed for and for what purpose the removal is required. Such removals must be notified to the warehousekeeper who is responsible for ensuring that any temporary removals meet the prescribed conditions.

(f) VAT-free sampling

Small quantities of commodities of a negligible commercial value can be removed for this purpose under a simplified removal scheme. The amount and approximate value of the commodity to be removed must be detailed in the authorisation given by our VAT Helpline. Such removals must be notified to the warehousekeeper, who is responsible for ensuring that they meet the prescribed conditions.

2.21 Input tax

Subject to the normal rules, you can reclaim as input tax any VAT paid as a result of the removal of goods from the fiscal warehouse, provided those goods are used for the purpose of your business. This claim for input tax is normally made on the same VAT return on which the VAT due on the removal is declared as output tax.

2.22 Other accounting requirements: the fiscal warehousing record

(a) Receipts into a fiscal warehouse

The warehousekeeper must allocate a unique reference number to each consignment received and record the nature and quantity of goods on entry and the date of receipt. The record must also show delivery note details for all goods received in warehouse. Non-eligible goods entered for storage must also be identified in the records.

(b) Stock records

Your system (manual or electronic) must be able to show the location of the goods at any given time. Where fiscally warehoused goods are co-located with other goods held under other warehousing regimes and other goods in free circulation, the stock records must be capable of separately identifying the different regimes.

(c) Removals from warehouse

For all removals from warehouse, stock records must contain details of the owner, quantity and type of commodities, the date of removal and details of either the remover's VAT registration number or a stamped copy of form VAT 150 (see paragraph 2.12). Before removal, and in order to establish both value and ownership, unregistered proprietors must produce to the local Entry Processing Unit a copy of the invoice or warrant used to purchase the commodities. In the case of a series of purchases, the most recent purchase should be used. They must then produce to the fiscal warehousekeeper, a stamped copy of form VAT 150 and the necessary commercial documentation to establish ownership. Registered removers must also establish ownership but need only give an undertaking to account for the VAT payable on any removal on the appropriate return. In the case of a temporary removal, details *must* be kept of the approval given by Customs and of the removal and return of goods. Similar details are also needed for removal of goods of negligible value. With the written permission given by Customs, damaged or outdated goods held under fiscal warehousing can be destroyed and the stock record adjusted accordingly. VAT is due on the removal of any scrap or waste which still has an economic use, based on the open market value of the goods removed.

(d) Removal in the course of an export or intra EC supply

The warehousekeeper must obtain proof of ownership and the VAT registration number of the remover in the normal way. The remover is entitled to zero rate the removal in both cases, but *must* include the value of any relieved supply of services in the value of a removal in the course of an intra EC supply. The warehousekeeper's records *must* include documentary evidence to show the goods have been exported.

(e) Transfer of goods from one fiscal warehouse in the UK to another

In order to exercise effective control over goods transferred from one fiscal warehouse in the UK to another, the despatching warehousekeeper remains responsible for the goods until receipted documentation is received from the receiving warehousekeeper acknowledging receipt of, and liability for, the goods. The records *must* also show the address of the fiscal warehouse to which the goods in question are transferred.

(f) Transfer of goods from a fiscal warehouse in the UK to one in another member state

Similar controls to those maintained for goods transferred to another fiscal warehouse in the UK must be exercised by warehousekeepers when goods are transferred to a fiscal warehouse in another member state. Such transfers can only be relieved from VAT where a corresponding regime exists in the member state of destination. The warehousekeeper's records *must* show the address of the place in the other member state to which the goods in question are transferred.

(g) Failure to provide documentation

Where the proper documentation is either not received by the warehousekeeper:

- within 30 days of a removal of goods from the warehouse in the course of transfer to another fiscal warehouse in the UK, or
- within 60 days in the case of either transfer to corresponding arrangements in another member state or export to a place outside the EC,

the warehouse record must be adjusted to show the goods as having been removed from the regime on the day they left the fiscal warehouse premises. The record must also show the remover as being the person on whose instructions the warehousekeeper allowed the goods to leave the warehouse.

(h) Deficiencies of goods

Where in any approved warehouse a deficiency is discovered in the stock approved for fiscal warehousing, VAT becomes due on the deficient goods as if they had been removed to home use. This depends on whether the goods were entered VAT paid or not and whether they were subsequently sold in the warehouse or not. See paragraphs 2.19 and 2.20.

3 THE FISCAL (VAT) TERRITORY OF THE EUROPEAN COMMUNITY

The following countries and territories are within the EC fiscal (VAT) area—

- Austria
- Belgium
- Bulgaria
- Cyprus
- The Czech Republic
- Denmark, excluding the Faroe Islands and Greenland
- Estonia
- Finland
- France including Monaco
- Germany, except Busingen and the Isle of Heligoland
- Greece
- Hungary
- The Republic of Ireland
- Italy, except the communes of Livigno and Campione d'Italia and the Italian waters of Lake Lugano
- Latvia
- Lithuania
- Luxembourg
- Malta
- The Netherlands
- Poland
- Portugal, including the Azores and Madeira
- Romania
- Slovakia
- Slovenia
- Spain, including the Balearic Islands, but excluding, Ceuta and Melilla
- Sweden
- United Kingdom and the Isle of Man.

There are some special territories which are within the EC customs area but outside the EC fiscal (VAT) area—

— Andorra

— Channel Islands
— Gibraltar
— Mount Athos (Greece)
— San Marino
— The Åland Islands (Finland)
— The Canary Islands (Spain)
— The overseas departments of France (Guadeloupe, Martinique, Reunion, St Pierre and Miquelon, and French Guiana)
— The Vatican City.

Goods entering the UK from these places are treated for VAT purposes as imported goods (paragraph 1.9).

Commentary—*De Voil Indirect Tax Service* **V1.213.**

4 USUAL FORMS OF HANDLING THAT MAY BE CARRIED OUT IN A FISCAL WAREHOUSE

Unless otherwise specified, none of the following forms of handling may give rise to a different eight-digit tariff commodity code (that means they must not produce new product).

Commentary—*De Voil Indirect Tax Service* **V3.386.**

4.1 Simple operations to ensure the preservation of the commodities in good condition during storage

(a) Ventilation, spreading out, drying, removal of dust, simple cleaning operations, repair of packing, elementary repairs of damage incurred during transport or storage insofar as it concerns simple operations, application and removal of protective coating for transport.
(b) Stocktaking, sampling and weighing of the goods.
(c) Removal of damaged or contaminated components.
(d) Conservation by means of irradiation or the addition of preservatives.
(e) Treatment against parasites.
(f) Any treatment by lowering the temperature, even if this results in a different eight-digit tariff commodity code.

4.2 Operations improving the presentation or marketability of the commodities

(a) Stemming and/or pitting of fruit.
(b) Assembly and mounting of goods, only if this concerns the mounting onto a complete product of accessories which do not play an essential role in the manufacture of the product, even if this results in a different eight-digit tariff commodity code for the mounted goods or accessories.
(c) Desalination, cleaning and butting of hides.
(d) Addition of goods, of one or more different types of goods, in as long as this addition is relatively small and does not change the nature of the original goods, even if this results in a different eight-digit tariff commodity code for the added goods; the added goods could also be products which were placed under the warehousing regime, or which were placed in the free zone or free warehouse.
(e) The dilution of fluids, even if the result is a different eight-digit tariff commodity code.
(f) The mixing between them of the same kind of goods, with a different quality, in order to obtain a constant quality or a quality which is requested by the customer, without changing the nature of the goods.
(g) Dividing the goods if only simple operations are involved.

4.3 Operations preparing the commodities for distribution or resale

(a) Sorting, mechanical filtering, classification and shifting.
(b) Adjusting and regulation.
(c) Packing, unpacking, change of packing, decanting and simple transfer into containers, even if this results in a different eight-digit tariff commodity code.
(d) The affixing and altering of marks including seals, labels, price tags or other similar distinguishing signs – however this operation must not change the apparent origin of the goods.
(e) Testing, adjusting and putting into working order of machines, apparatus and vehicles, if only simple operations are involved.

(f) Testing in order to control the compliance with European technical standards.
(g) Cutting up and breaking down of dried fruits or vegetables.
(h) Anti-rust treatment.
(i) Reconstruction of the goods after transport.
(j) The raising of temperature in order to allow the goods to be transported.
(k) The ironing of textiles.
(l) Electrostatic treatment of textiles.

5 CERTIFICATES

Commentary—*De Voil Indirect Tax Service* **V3.176, V4.209, V5.141A.**

5.1 Certificate required to secure relief from VAT on goods intended to be placed within a fiscal warehousing regime

Information to be indicated:

I. . . . . (full name)

. . . . (status in company) of

. . . . (name and address of company)

declare that . . . . (name of company) intends to enter to the fiscal warehousing regime at the fiscal warehouse shown below on (date), or within days commencing today, the goods indicated below:

- name and address of fiscal warehouse;
- authorisation number of the fiscal warehousekeeper;
- description of goods;
- quantity of goods.

I certify that the supply of goods/acquisition is eligible to be relieved from VAT under the following provisions of the VAT Act 1994 [delete as appropriate]:

sections 18B(2)(d)/18B(3) (purchases) or sections 18B(1)(d)/18B(3) (acquisitions).

. . . . (signature)

. . . . (date)

Note: You should be aware that there are severe penalties for making a false declaration. If there is any doubt about the eligibility of the goods or about the fiscal warehouse to which they are being sent, you should contact our VAT Helpline on 0845 010 9000.

A copy of the above declaration should be filed with the supplier's invoice and a copy of the delivery note.

5.2 Certificate required to secure zero-rating of services (other than the supply of warehousing) performed within a fiscal warehouse

Information to be indicated:

I . . . . (full name)

. . . . (status in company) of

. . . . (name and address of company) declare that the goods shown below are subject to a fiscal warehousing regime at the place indicated below:

— description of goods;
— quantity of goods;
— warehouse stock number;
— name and address of fiscal or other warehouse;
— authorisation number of the relevant warehousekeeper/warehouse.

and that the following services are to be performed on the goods in the fiscal warehouse:

— description of services.

I certify that the supply of services is eligible to be zero-rated for VAT purposes under section 18C(1) of the VAT Act 1994.

. . . . (signature)

. . . . (date)

Note: You should be aware that there are severe penalties for making a false declaration. If there is any doubt about a supply being entitled to zero-rating you should contact our VAT Helpline on 0845 010 9000 before signing and sending in the certificate to Customs.

A copy of the certificate should be filed with the supplier's invoice which should refer to s 18C(1) of the VAT Act 1994 to be eligible for zero-rating.

6 SPECIMEN APPLICATION FOR AUTHORISATION TO OPERATE A FISCAL WAREHOUSE

You *must* provide the following details where appropriate—

(a) Name or Business Name, Address & VAT Number (see Note 1).
(b) Address(es) & Description(s) of storage facilities. The Commissioners may, in considering your application, take into account the suitability of notified premises.
(c) Details of any authorised UK duty suspensive regime which you operate.
(d) Brief description of stock records and accounting system and place where stock records will be kept (see Note 2).
(e) Nature of the goods to be stored, either specific goods or "all eligible goods". Details of eligible goods are set out in paragraph 2.3
(f) Details of common storage of different categories of goods which may be in free circulation or under other customs procedures.
(g) Details of temporary removals or possible VAT free sampling. You must also indicate whether general authorisation will be required or whether an application will be made each time goods are to be temporarily removed.
(h) Details of documents you are attaching, for example, supplementary papers detailing records that will be kept.
(i) The application must be signed by a director, proprietor, partner or duly authorised person.

Notes

(1) Not required if application is on company headed notepaper giving these particulars.
(2) Please give details of—
  (a) documentation to be used to enter goods to the regime.
  (b) Stock control system.
  (c) Point at which goods will be deemed to have left the fiscal warehousing regime and are therefore liable to VAT on removal.
  (d) Documentation to be used to transfer goods to another UK fiscal warehouse.
  (e) Documentation to be used to transfer goods to a fiscal warehouse in another EC member state.

702/9
VAT—IMPORTS CUSTOMS PROCEDURES WITH ECONOMIC IMPACT AND END-USE RELIEF

October 2012

This notice cancels and replaces Notice 702/9 (November 2005).

1 INTRODUCTION AND OVERVIEW

1.1 What is this notice about?

This notice explains the import VAT treatment of goods which are—

- entered into and removed from customs suspensive regimes;
- supplied within Customs Warehouses;

- entered into and removed from end-use relief;
- re-imported under OPR after process/repair or replacement;
- placed under transit.

In addition it gives guidance on the treatment of supplies of goods whilst within the above regimes and supplies of services associated with these goods.

For general guidance concerning import VAT, entry procedures, valuation for import VAT and exceptions to the normal rules for charging import VAT you should consult Notice 702 "VAT Imports" (Part V8).

This notice does not include guidance on Fiscal warehouses (or Tax Warehouses) which can be found in Notice 702/8. The only warehousing regime covered in this book is therefore Customs Warehouses.

The meaning of the terms and abbreviations used can be found in the glossary at Section 15.

Commentary—*De Voil Indirect Tax Service* **V3.302.**

1.2 What has changed?

This notice has been rewritten to improve readability and to update the technical information. The main change concerns the removal of Free Zones. The information on certificates for zero-rating of services in section 12 has been changed to show that it has the force of law.

This notice replaces the previous version dated November 2005.

1.3 What is import VAT?

Import VAT is the transaction tax levied on imported goods. Goods are treated as imported when—

- they arrive in the UK directly from outside the EU and are entered to free circulation in the UK or customs duty otherwise becomes chargeable on them, *or*
- they have been placed under one of the customs suspensive arrangements listed in paragraph 2.1 in the EU and the goods are being removed to free circulation in the UK or customs duty otherwise becomes chargeable.

1.4 What law concerns this notice

EU law on Import VAT relief is contained in Council Directive 2006/112/EU which is interpreted into UK law in VATA 1994 under which authority for the VAT Regulations 1995 were made. Other national provisions and VAT directives may also apply. You should note that OPR is accepted from UK VAT law therefore there is no concept of "VAT only OPR" in the UK.

The majority of this notice is our view of the law and does not take the place of the law. The exception is the certificate reproduced at section 12 which has the force of law under reg 145C of the VAT Regulations 1995.

1.5 Goods from the Isle of Man

If you remove goods from the Isle of Man to the UK they are not treated as an import provided that—

— any import VAT due has been accounted for in the Isle of Man; or
— if the goods were relieved of import VAT in the Isle of Man, the conditions of the relief are still applicable.

1.6 Goods imported from the special territories including the Channel Islands

Section 11 lists the territories inside/outside the EU for customs duty and VAT purposes.

The Channel Islands and Special Territories listed in paragraph 11.2 are part of the EU for customs purposes but are not part of the VAT territory.

If you import goods from the Channel Islands or Special Territories you will be liable for import VAT in the same way as you would for imports under paragraph 1.3.

1.7 What rights do I have in relation to a customs decision

If you do not agree with any decision issued to you there are three options available.

Receiving an adverse Customs decision from HMRC – Right to be Heard

When you receive an adverse customs decision from HMRC you will first be issued with a Pre-Notification Communication explaining the reasons why the adverse decision has been made. This Pre-Notification is called your "Right to be Heard" and once issued, you will have a period of 30 calendar days in which you may make further representations or provide further information to HMRC concerning the decision.

Within 30 days of the date of the decision you can either—

- request a review of the decision by someone not involved in making the disputed decision. Your request must be in writing and should set out the reasons why you do not agree with the decision. Please write to:

Customs and International
Review and Appeals Team
7th Floor South West
Alexander House
21 Victoria Avenue
SS99 1AA, or

- appeal direct to the Tribunal who are independent of HM Revenue & Customs.

If you opt to have your case reviewed you will still be able to appeal to the tribunal if you disagree with the outcome.

Further information relating to reviews and appeals is contained in leaflet HMRC1 HM Revenue & Customs decisions – what to do if you disagree which can be obtained from our website or by phoning 0845 010 9000.

1.8 Obtaining more information

This notice sets out the general principles on import VAT for goods/processes specified in paragraph 1.1. It does not attempt to explain every aspect in detail.

You can get more information either on our internet website at www.hmrc.gov.ukor by contacting our VAT, Helpline on 0845 010 9000.

You may also find the following Notices useful—

- Notice 104 "ATA Carnets";
- Notice 200 "Temporary Importation";
- Notice 221 "Inward processing relief";
- Notice 232 "Customs Warehousing";
- Notice 235 "Outward Processing Relief";
- Notice 237 "Processing under Customs Control";
- Notice 306 "Temporary Admission containers and pallets";
- Notice 702 "VAT Imports";
- Notice 702/7 "Import VAT relief for goods supplied onward to another country in the EU";
- Notice 702/8 "Fiscal warehousing";
- Notice 703 "VAT—exports of goods from the UK";
- Notice 725 "VAT—Single Market";
- Notice 770 "End-Use relief".

2 IMPORTATION UNDER CUSTOMS SUSPENSIVE PROCEDURES OR END-USE RELIEF

Commentary—*De Voil Indirect Tax Service* **V3.331–338.**

2.1 General

For import VAT purposes goods are generally treated as imported when they arrive in the UK and are entered to free circulation. This can be either by direct import (from a place outside the customs territory of the EU) or indirect import (removal to the UK via another member state within the EU).

However, if you place your goods under one of the following suspensive arrangements, duty and import VAT will only become due when you remove the goods to free circulation in the UK.

The suspensive arrangements are—

- IP-Suspension;
- Temporary admission with total relief from customs duties;
- Processing under customs control;
- Customs warehousing;
- External transit (T1) arrangements or internal transit – (T2) arrangements (although internal transit is not a customs suspensive procedure it is included here as import VAT may become due if the goods are subsequently removed to free circulation);
- Temporary storage (although such goods are not strictly under customs arrangements, goods arriving from outside the EC have the status of temporary storage until they are entered and cleared to free circulation or another procedure).

Suspension of import VAT does not apply to goods entered to—

- IP Drawback;
- TA with partial relief from customs duty;
- End-use relief (other than goods for the continental shelf, see paragraph 2.1.1);
- Outward processing relief.

2.1.1 Goods for the Continental Shelf

Certain goods imported for the continental shelf are eligible for end-use relief (see paragraph 5.4). Import VAT is also relieved for these goods under reg 120 of the VAT Regulations 1995.

2.2 Treatment for import VAT

While your goods are held under customs suspensive procedures the import VAT remains suspended. All relevant Customs legislation, including EU Regulations, apply for import VAT purposes. This includes any authorisation, transfer, discharge, or security requirements as detailed in your authorisation for the procedure concerned.

2.3 Third country goods subject to VAT only

Any non-Community goods you import from outside the customs territory of the EC which are not subject to a positive duty rate may be placed under IP (Suspension), TI (total relief), Customs Warehousing or under external transit for import VAT purposes only.

Any goods you import which are liable for import VAT only are not entitled to be entered for relief under OPR, TA Partial relief or IP (drawback). If you wish to enter goods to PCC for VAT purposes only see paragraph 7.3.

2.4 Goods imported from special territories

Any goods you import from one of the special territories outside the customs territory of the EU may be imported to a customs suspensory relief/end-use relief for import VAT purposes subject to the exceptions listed in paragraph 2.3.

2.5 Valuation

The valuation rules that apply to imports are also applicable to any of the reliefs mentioned in this notice with the exception of certain goods entered to Temporary Admission relief (see paragraph 3.1). See Notice 252 "Valuation of imported goods for customs purposes, VAT and trade statistics" (Part V8) and Notice 702 "VAT Import" (Part V8) for further details.

Commentary—*De Voil Indirect Tax Service* **V3.321–329.**

2.6 Onward Supply Relief

Any goods that you import under IP Suspension, Processing Under Customs Control, Temporary Importation, Customs Warehousing arrangements, imported in the course of an onward supply to a taxable person in another member state may be put into Free Circulation in the UK without the payment of import VAT. VAT is accounted for on the supply/acquisition by the purchaser in the EU country of destination.

Any goods that you import for processing and supply to a customer in another member state under IP Suspension or Processing under customs control may claim onward supply relief once the imported goods are entered to Free Circulation in the UK and dispatched to the member state unprocessed or altered.

Also any goods that you import under OPR or IP Drawback cannot be entered to onward supply relief.

Further information on Onward Supply Relief can be found in Notice 702/7 "Import VAT relief for goods supplied onward to another country in the EU" (Part V8).

Commentary—*De Voil Indirect Tax Service* **V3.337.**

2.7 Transfer of goods under suspensory regimes

You may transfer goods from one suspensive regime to another, for example customs warehousing to IP without the payment of import VAT. For details of the arrangements for transferring goods between regimes you should consult the relevant regime Notice.

2.8 Acquisitions of goods held under customs suspensive regimes

If you receive goods held in one of the arrangements at paragraph 2.1 from a taxable person in another member state you must normally account for VAT on the acquisition in accordance with the normal rules, even though the import VAT remains suspended.

2.9 Supplies of goods under suspensive arrangements

If you supply goods held under one of the arrangements at paragraph 2.1 you must charge VAT in the normal way subject to the following special rules—

- Goods in temporary storage – If you supply the imported goods between the arrival of the goods in the UK but prior to a customs entry being made and the purchaser is required to make the import entry you may zero rate the supply.
- goods under Temporary Admission relief – if you supply the imported goods to persons established outside the EU – you may disregard the supply provided that the goods remain eligible for TA arrangements and the person is established outside the EU.
- Second-hand goods and works of art under Temporary Admission relief – you may disregard the supply provided;
  - the second hand goods were imported with a view to their sale by auction, or
  - the "works of art" were imported for an exhibition with a view to a possible sale.

If you sell any of the second hand goods (provided it is by auction) or the works of art (as long as they are still subject to TA relief with total relief from import duties) you may disregard the sale for VAT purposes.

Any services relating to such supplies eg auctioneers charges can be similarly disregarded but you must include them in the value for VAT at importation.

When the supply involves a change of ownership you may also disregard the supply for VAT purposes. For goods held under the customs warehousing regime see paragraph 4.3.

2.10 Security

We will not normally require security, (with the exception of certain goods entered to temporary importation – see Notice 200 or transfers of certain goods considered to bear increased risks). See Section 14 for further details. Where required, security must be provided for the potential duty and import VAT on the imported goods either by cash deposit or in the form of a guarantee issued by a recognised provider, such as a bank.

2.11 Authorising a third party to act on your behalf

You can use a third party for example an agent or freight forwarder to complete entries on your behalf. However you must make sure that you give clear written instructions to your agent about the goods to be entered to the particular regimes/relief's you are authorised for.

Direct representation – the third party makes an entry in your name and on your behalf but you are still responsible for any customs debt that may arise if an entry is incorrectly made.

Indirect representation – the third party makes an entry in their own name and they are jointly and severally liable with you for any customs debt that may arise if an entry is incorrectly made.

The third party must quote your authorisation number (if applicable) on the import C88 (SAD) declaration forms.

Always make sure that your third party sends you copies of the customs declarations for your records, and check that the correct CPC has been used and that the duty calculations are correct.

A third party may not enter goods on your behalf using the Customs Freight Simplified Procedures (CFSP) unless the third party and use of the simplified procedures are included in your authorisation.

When you renew your authorisation, remember to tell the third party your new number. If you do not do this, your imports may be delayed, or we may require security for the release of the goods.

Note: Third parties who enter to reliefs/regimes but fail to state in whose name they are acting shall be deemed to be acting in their own name and therefore liable for any customs debt that may arise.

2.12 Evidence for input tax deduction

You normally need to hold official evidence of VAT paid on imported goods before you can recover the VAT as input tax. The normal evidence is the monthly certificate, known as Form C79. It does not in itself allow you to claim back the VAT you have paid which must, in all cases, be deductible under the normal input tax rules.

The certificates are sent to the VAT registered person whose VAT registration number, plus a three digit suffix, is shown in Box 8 of the import entry. The whole number is known as the Economic Operator Registration Identification Number (EORI). You must take great care to use the correct EORI. If not, the VAT you have paid may not appear on your certificate and may even end up on another person's certificate. Similarly, you may find someone else's import VAT on your certificate.

Certificates cover accounting transactions made in each calendar month and are issued on or about the 12th day of the following month. For example, October certificates (certificates covering transactions with accounting dates in October) are issued on or about 12 November. Further information concerning evidence for input tax and C79's can be found in Notice 702 "VAT: Imports" (Part V8).

Where security for VAT has been provided, this does not entitle you to claim the VAT back. VAT can only be reclaimed when it has been paid to release the goods to free circulation.

Commentary—*De Voil Indirect Tax Service* **V3.426.**

3 GOODS IMPORTED UNDER TEMPORARY ADMISSION RELIEF (TA) AND ATA CARNETS

Commentary—*De Voil Indirect Tax Service* **V3.336–338.**

3.1 General

Temporary Admission Relief (TA) allows you to obtain total or partial relief from import duties on a range of goods imported from outside the EU, providing they are intended for re-export within a specified time (usually a maximum of two years).

Notices 200 "Temporary Importations", 306 "Temporary Admission containers and pallets" and 308 "Temporary Admission Means of Transport" detail the procedures to be followed for entering goods to TA relief. Any security will include the value for import VAT.

Import VAT is suspended for goods entered to TA total relief. However under TA partial relief, import VAT must be paid at the time of entry. Therefore goods which are free of customs duty and subject only to import VAT cannot be entered to TA partial relief.

3.2 Supplies of goods under temporary admission to persons established outside the EU

If you supply goods held under TA to persons established outside the EU and the goods remain eligible for TA relief, the supply may be disregarded for VAT purposes. Notice 200 explains how to discharge TA arrangements where goods are exported from the EU.

3.3 Retention of TA goods in the UK

When you place goods entered to temporary importation to free circulation in the UK, duty, import VAT and compensatory interest will become due. Compensatory interest is not applicable to the import VAT liability of such diversions and is not applicable to–

- works of art, collectors items and antiques diverted to free circulation (Commission Regulation 2454/93 Art 576(3a));
- personal effects (Commission Regulation 2454/93 Art 563);
- disaster relief material (Commission Regulation 2454/93 Art 565);
- sound image or data carrying media / publicity material (Commission Regulation 2454/93 Art 568);
- goods subject to satisfactory acceptance tests (Commission Regulation 2454/93 Art 573(b));
- goods for exhibition or use at a public event (Commission Regulation 2454/93 Art 576(1));
- goods for approval (Commission Regulation 2454/93 Art 576(2));
- goods other than newly manufactured imported with a view to sale by auction (Commission Regulation 2454/93 Art 576(3b)).

For certain works of art, antiques and collectors' items reduced valuation rules can apply which, in effect, reduces the VAT rate applicable to the goods, (see Notice 702 for further information).

Compensatory interest is also not due when—

- the period for interest is less than one month;
- the amount of interest that would be due *is less than* 20;
- duty was secured by cash deposit at least equal to the amount of duty due;
- goods are imported to TA with *partial relief* from import duties;
- the TA goods are diverted to free circulation to allow export preference to be claimed (for example on products produced using TA goods);
- you are diverting to free circulation waste and/or scrap from the destruction of TA goods (see Notice 200); or you can prove it has become impossible or uneconomic to re-export TA goods,

you will need to complete a C88 (SAD) entry to divert the goods in the normal way and place the amount of compensatory interest that will become due on deposit. Your written evidence to support your claim (for example a note of confirmation from the supplier refusing to accept the goods on return), should accompany your diversion entry. You must ensure that the evidence demonstrates that the circumstances did not arise from negligence or deception and that it is impossible or uneconomic to carry out the re-exportation of the goods. You should also explain how the circumstances have changed since the goods were imported.

Further information can be found in Notice 200.

3.4 Re-exporting goods from TA relief

If you re-export any goods you entered to TA relief you must retain evidence of the export in order to discharge your liability and to reclaim any security. Notice 200 explains in detail how to discharge TAI and the required forms of evidence.

3.5 ATA Carnets

An ATA Carnet is an internationally recognised booklet of vouchers which replace the normal customs declarations. It avoids the need to provide security for customs duty when you temporarily import goods, which simplifies the customs formalities for goods temporarily exported or imported.

In the UK, Chambers of Commerce and Industry issue ATA Carnets. As the Chambers provide a guarantee to cover any customs duty and other charges that become payable on the goods covered by the ATA Carnet (through the International Guarantee Chain), they may make a charge for the issue of an ATA Carnet and require the ATA Carnet holder to provide them, in turn, with a guarantee or other security for the duty and charges.

Any goods you import on an ATA carnet will not be liable to either customs duty or import VAT providing you export the goods prior to expiry of the carnet. Further information concerning ATA carnets can be found in Notice 104.

4 GOODS IMPORTED UNDER CUSTOMS WAREHOUSING AND SUPPLIES AND REMOVALS OF GOODS UNDER CUSTOMS WAREHOUSING

Customs warehousing permits the payment of import duties and/or VAT to be suspended or delayed for non-Community goods which are stored in premises or under an inventory system authorised as a customs warehouse.

Commentary—*De Voil Indirect Tax Service* **V3.332.**

4.1 Import VAT treatment of goods placed in a customs warehouse

No import VAT will be due when you place your goods in a customs warehouse. Import VAT will only become due when you remove the goods from the warehouse to free circulation. It is normally payable together with any customs or excise duty suspended by the person removing the goods.

4.2 Receipts into warehouse

You can store the following goods in a customs warehouse—

— non-Community goods liable to customs duties and/or VAT (whether or not eligible for preference) and/or excise duties;
— non-Community goods for which necessary supporting documents (such as BIS licence) are not available at the time of import;
— non-Community goods imported to another suspensive regime (such as IP or TA) warehoused for export from the Community;
— non Community PCC products;
— non-Community goods that are not subject to a positive rate of customs duty in the tariff, but are liable to import VAT;
— Cmmunity produced goods or non-Community goods released to free circulation, eligible for CAP refunds on export. These goods should be warehoused in a specially approved warehouse under the CAP pre financing arrangements; and
— non-Community goods in free circulation that are subject to a claim under the Rejected Imports arrangements.

4.3 Supplies of goods within customs warehouses

Supplies of goods within a customs warehouse are treated as taking place outside the UK. Therefore any such supplies are usually disregarded for VAT. Import VAT will become due when you remove the goods from the warehouse to free circulation and is normally payable together with any customs duty due.

4.3.1 What goods can I warehouse?

Warehouse regime	*Goods*	*Customs Duty (inc CAP charges)*	*Import VAT*	*Supply VAT*	*Excise duty*
Customs Warehouse	Third country goods of any kind whether subject to a positive rate of duty or not.	Suspended	Suspended	Suspended	Suspended

Warehouse regime	*Goods*	*Customs Duty (inc CAP charges)*	*Import VAT*	*Supply VAT*	*Excise duty*
Tax Warehouse (includes both manufacturing premises and storage premises)	Third country goods on which customs duty has been paid; Community goods; UK goods – mineral (hydrocarbon oils), alcohol and alcoholic beverages, manufactured tobacco	Paid	Paid	Suspended	Suspended
Fiscal Warehouse	Certain specified goods that are in free circulation (see Notice)	N/A	N/A	Suspended	N/A

While your goods are under the respective warehouse regime you do not need to pay either Customs duty, Excise duty or Import VAT. These will normally be paid when you remove the goods from the warehouse regime.

4.3.2 Are there any circumstances in which supplies are not disregarded for VAT purposes?

Yes, VAT will be due if you sell warehoused goods to unregistered distributors who retail the goods on to the final consumers, or use the goods themselves. In these circumstances, the VAT due on such supplies is in addition to import VAT which remains due when the goods are removed from the warehouse. See paragraph 4.5.

For fiscal warehouses see Notice 702/8.

4.4 Removal of goods from customs warehouses to free circulation

When you remove non-Community goods from a customs warehouse to free circulation import VAT will become due and is normally payable by the person who removes the goods. The VAT due will be based upon the import value of the goods (see paragraph 4.5).

When you remove imported goods from a customs warehouse to free circulation in the UK you must complete an entry at the time of removal. You must pay (or defer) any import VAT / customs duty due by completing a C88 (SAD) unless—

- they have also been warehoused for excise duty in a customs warehouse, in which case excise duty may be suspended if the goods are now to be placed in a tax warehouse but any duty and VAT must be paid when the goods are removed from the customs warehouse; or
- they qualify for relief from import VAT; or
- the goods are removed to another member state and Onward Supply Relief is claimed; or
- the goods are ex IPR drawback and import VAT has already been paid.

Further information concerning removal of goods from customs warehouses can be found in Notice 232.

4.5 Value for VAT of goods removed from customs warehouses

Any goods you remove from customs warehouses are subject to the normal valuation rules contained in Notice 702 "VAT: Imports" (Part V8), Notice 725 "VAT: Single Market"

(Part V8) and Notice 700 "The VAT guide" (Part V8). You must include any customs and/or excise duty due in the value unless excise duty is to be suspended by placing the goods in a tax warehouse but any duty and import VAT must be paid when the goods are removed from the customs warehouse.

The value on which import VAT is payable is based on the value for customs purposes, plus if not already included—

— all incidental expenses such as commission, packing, transport and insurance costs incurred up to the goods' removal from the customs warehousing arrangements; plus
— all such incidental costs where they result from transport to a further place of destination in the UK or another member state if that place is known at the time the goods are removed from customs warehousing arrangements; plus
— storage charges and usual forms of handling in certain circumstances; plus
— any customs duty, levy, excise duty or other charges payable on removal to free circulation.

If you operate a Type D customs warehouse you may find you have to enter different values for customs duty purposes and import VAT.

4.6 Removal of goods from a customs warehouse other than to free circulation

If you supply goods for export or supply goods to a taxable person in another EC member state where the goods move outside the customs warehouse arrangements you may zero rate that supply. If you are removing the goods directly to a customs warehouse in another EC member state under the customs warehouse transfer arrangements you may disregard the supply, for UK VAT purposes. However, in both cases you must enter any supplies made in this way on an EU Sales list (VAT 101) covering the time of removal and in Box 8 of your VAT return (VAT 100). For more information see Notices 60 and 725 You must ensure that you retain evidence of export as detailed in Notice 232 to discharge your liability.

4.7 Onward supply relief

If you remove non-Community goods into free circulation in the course of an onward zero rated supply to another member state they may qualify for onward supply relief subject to meeting the conditions set out in paragraph 2.6 and Notice 702/7.

4.8 Acquisitions from other member states

If you are VAT registered and acquire goods held in one of the suspensive arrangements listed in paragraph 2.1 from a taxable person in another EU member state you must normally account for VAT on the acquisition in accordance with the normal rules.

4.9 Transfers from customs warehouses to another customs suspensive procedure

If you remove goods from a customs warehouse for entry to another customs suspensive procedure, or export you must present a full entry on Form C88 unless you have been approved to use simplified procedures. Goods entered to transit must be declared on the NCTS unless UK simplified transit is used. Where goods are transferred to another customs suspensive procedure the import VAT and customs duty remain suspended under the new procedure.

4.10 Services which can be zero rated in a customs warehouse

You may zero rate any storage charges and usual forms of handling carried out on goods under the customs warehouse arrangements. However services such as brokerage, agent's fees and transport between warehouses are not eligible for zero rating. Services which are exempt from VAT when supplied outside the warehouse will remain exempt. Any VAT or customs duty due in respect of previously zero rated services should be accounted for together with any import VAT and customs duty payable when the goods are removed from the warehouse using a C88. The value of the services to be taxed should be entered in Box 47 of the C88.

4.11 Conditions for zero rating

To qualify for zero rating the following conditions must be met—

— a taxable person makes the supply of specified services;

- those services are wholly performed on or in relation to goods while those goods are subject to the customs warehousing regime;
- except where the services are the supply by an occupier of a customs warehouse (storage charges), the person to whom the supply is made must give the supplier a certificate, in such form as the Commissioners may specify, that the services are performed;
- the supply of services would (apart from this paragraph) be taxable and not zero-rated; and
- the supplier issues to the person to whom the supply is made an invoice in such form as the Commissioners may specify, that the supply is zero-rated.

4.12 How to relieve supplies of services

4.12.1 Owner of the goods

If as owner of the goods the usual forms of handling are supplied to you by a third party, you may have the services zero rated by the supplier. To do this you should issue the supplier a certificate before the services are supplied, stating the goods are under customs warehousing and the services you order to be carried out are eligible for zero rating. An example of the certificate is at Section 12. You may create your own version of the certificate but all the information shown in the example must be provided.

You should retain a copy of the certificate with your records as evidence to support the zero-rating of supplies.

4.12.2 Supplier of the service

If you receive a certificate you should issue a VAT invoice to your customer in the usual way, at the usual time, but VAT should be shown as zero-rated "in accordance with Section 18C(1) VAT Act 1994" and no VAT should be charged.

The certificate you receive from the owner should be kept with your records to support the zero-rating of your supplies. If you do not receive a certificate from the owner of the goods, you should issue your invoice in the usual way including VAT at the standard rate.

4.12.3 Warehouse storage charges

A certificate is not required to zero-rate warehouse keepers storage charges. Such supplies of services are normally automatically zero rated. The invoice issued by the warehouse keeper to enable zero rating should include the words "in accordance with Section 18C(1) VAT Act 1994" and no VAT should be charged. If as owner of the goods, you decide you want the storage charges standard rated you should notify the warehousekeeper in writing.

4.13 Deficiencies of warehouse goods

Any deficiencies of warehoused goods are deemed to be removed from the customs warehousing regime. Where deficiencies of imported goods are charged with duty, import VAT not already paid on the imported goods will also become due. Similarly, any acquisition VAT on goods from other member states which has not been accounted for will also be payable. In any case, you may deduct the VAT as input tax subject to the normal rules.

5 END-USE RELIEF

Commentary—*De Voil Indirect Tax Service* **V3.335B.**

5.1 General

End-use relief is a trade facilitation regime which assists certain industries and trades (including agriculture) within the EU by allowing reduced or nil rates of Customs duty (or agricultural charge) on certain goods imported from non-EU countries, provided the goods are put to a prescribed use.

End-use relief does not affect liability to import VAT, which you must pay or account for in the normal way, unless one of the reliefs listed in Notice 702 applies. End-use relief does not give relief from Excise or anti-dumping duties which, if due, must be paid.

Further information on end-use relief can be found in Notice 770.

5.2 VAT relief on aircraft end-use goods

Schedule 8, Group 8 of VATA 1994 allows zero-rating of aircraft or their parts providing those items are only applied to "qualifying aircraft".

A "qualifying aircraft" is any aircraft of a weight of not less than 8,000 kilogrammes which is neither designed nor adapted for use for recreation or pleasure.

Any import VAT due must be paid at the time of importation along with the customs duty on Form C88 (SAD).

The relief does not apply to any parts and equipment supplied to a Government Department unless—

— they are installed or incorporated in the course of a supply which is treated as being made in the course or furtherance of a business carried on by the department; or
— the parts and equipment are to be installed or incorporated in ships or aircraft used for the purposes of providing rescue or assistance at sea.

5.3 VAT relief on shipwork end-use goods

VATA 1994 Sch 8, Group 8 allows zero-rating of ships or their parts providing those items are only applied to "qualifying ships".

A "qualifying ship" is any ship of a gross tonnage of not less than 15 tons which is neither designed nor adapted for use for recreation or pleasure.

Any import VAT due must be paid at the time of importation along with the customs duty on Form C88 (SAD).

The relief does not apply to any parts and equipment supplied to a Government Department unless—

- they are installed or incorporated in the course of a supply which is treated as being made in the course or furtherance of a business carried on by the department; or
- the parts and equipment are to be installed or incorporated in ships or aircraft used for the purposes of providing rescue or assistance at sea.

5.4 Goods for the continental shelf

Any goods you import intended for—

— incorporation in offshore drilling or production platforms/workpoints for the purpose of their construction, repair, maintenance, fitting out, conversion; or
— equipping those platforms/workpoints; or
— downhole well construction;
— subsequent shipment to a platform/workpoint which are required to be tested before use; or
— training, provided that at the end of the programme, the goods are shipped to a platform/workpoint;

are eligible for shipwork end-use relief for the Continental Shelf. This covers offshore fixed drilling or production platforms within sub heading 8430 49 and floating or submersible drilling or production platforms of Tariff sub heading 8905 20 irrespective of whether the fixed or floating platforms are located within or outside UK territorial waters and tubes, pipes, cables and connection pieces linking drilling or production platforms to the mainland.

If the goods are to be used as above you may claim relief from import VAT under reg 120 of the VAT Regulations 1995.

5.5 VAT relief on goods entered under the military end-use scheme

Council Regulation No EC 150/2003 lays down the conditions for the suspension of import duties on certain weapons and military equipment when they are used by, or on behalf of, the military forces of a member state, for defending the territorial integrity of the member state or participating in international peace keeping or support operations or for other military purposes.

The relief under this regulation does not apply to import VAT which, if due should be paid at the time of importation. However relief from import VAT may be allowable under paras 6.2 to 6.4 above. It may also be available to UK contractors who import goods as agents of International Collaboration Defence Projects authorities under Sch 8 Group 13 item 2 of VATA 1994.

6 GOODS RE IMPORTED AFTER PROCESS/REPAIR OR REPLACEMENT (OPR)

Under Outward Processing Relief it may be possible to obtain relief from customs duties when re-importing Community goods that have previously been exported from the EU for processing or for repair.

Commentary—*De Voil Indirect Tax Service* **V3.326.**

6.1 General

Import VAT is normally due on the full value of re-imported goods unless relief is available under regs 124, 125 or 126 of the VAT Regulations 1995.

6.2 Goods re-imported after process or repair

You may reduce the amount of import VAT chargeable on goods you import from outside the EU if the goods have been previously exported for process or repair from the UK or any other member state providing you meet the following conditions—

- the goods were temporarily exported from the EU;
- at the time of exportation the goods were intended to be re-imported after completion of the treatment or process outside the EU;
- the goods are re imported after having undergone repair, process or adaptation outside the EU or having been made up or re-worked outside the EU;
- ownership of the goods was not transferred to any other person at exportation or during the time they were outside the EU; and
- a declaration is made at the time of re-importation that the above conditions have been fulfilled.

Further details can be found in Notice 235.

6.3 Calculation of import VAT on goods re-imported after process or repair

Provided the re-imported goods meet the conditions of paragraph 6.2 above you should calculate import VAT on the following value—

— the price charged for the process, repair or service, including any charge made for parts and materials; *plus*

— any freight and other charges (excluding insurance) paid for the transport of the goods to and from the processor's premises; *plus*

— any customs or excise duties or other import charges payable in the UK.

You must pay import VAT on the full VAT value of the compensating products unless the conditions for claiming VAT relief are satisfied.

You may recover the import VAT as input tax, subject to the normal rules. (see paragraph 2.12). However, if you are unable to reclaim input tax, for example because you are not registered for VAT, you should contact Customs at the point of importation as soon as you know the goods are to be replaced. If you are not aware of the details until after the goods have been imported you should contact our VAT Helpline on 0845 010 9000 and ask for Notice 266 and Form C&E 1179.

6.4 Zero-rated supplies and processes carried out free of charge

If the process is carried out free of charge, for example because the goods are covered by a warranty, guarantee or service agreement, or where the compensating products are zero-rated in the UK no import VAT will be due on re-importation of the compensating products.

If the supply of the goods themselves is normally zero rated they are not liable to import VAT on return from any repair or process carried out whilst outside the EU.

6.5 Replacement goods under OPR

All replacement goods are considered to be new imports and import VAT is therefore payable in accordance with the normal valuation rules. This applies regardless of whether any duty relief can be claimed under OPR.

6.6 Triangulation under OPR

Triangulation movements between member states normally involve a change in title to the exported goods and therefore the compensating products will not normally qualify for VAT relief.

6.7 Goods re imported after process or repair on which VAT relief only will be claimed- VAT only OPR

Any goods you re- import after process or repair on which VAT relief only will be claimed are not eligible for OPR authorisation and therefore the goods are *not under* OPR relief. You may be able to claim relief under reg 126 of VAT regulations 1995 by exporting the goods under CPC 22 00 00 and entering the re-imported goods to CPC 40 00 65.

6.8 Goods re imported in the same state

If you re import goods into the UK without them having been altered whilst outside the EU other than any necessary running repairs that did not increase their value you will be able to claim relief from import VAT under returned goods relief. Full details can be found in Notice 236.

7 PROCESSING UNDER CUSTOMS CONTROL (PCC)

Commentary—*De Voil Indirect Tax Service* **V3.335.**

7.1 General

The customs tariff is organised in such a way that, in most cases, imported goods carry higher rates of duty than the raw materials or components from which they are manufactured. In some cases however, processed products attract a lower rate of duty than the goods from which they are made. In some cases these tariff anomalies tend to make it more economical to import finished products directly from outside the EC, than to import the raw materials and manufacture the products in the Community.

The PCC procedure is a trade facilitation measure, intended to encourage processing in the Community by allowing certain raw materials or components to be imported under duty suspension arrangements. After processing, the finished products may be declared to free circulation at the lower rate that applies to them rather than the rate which applies to the raw materials.

Import VAT is similarly suspended until the goods are processed and declared to free circulation. Upon release to free circulation you will pay import VAT based on the value of the processed products, not the value at importation.

7.2 Calculation of import VAT upon discharge of PCC

Once you have processed the imported goods you must declare them to free circulation. Customs duty and import VAT become due when the free circulation declaration is made. The free circulation entry must be made prior to you removing the goods from the premises by completing a C88 or using CFSP LCP procedures. There are four valuation methods that you can use to declare your goods to free circulation. For further details see Notice 237.

Import VAT will be due on the customs value of the goods declared plus the amount of customs duty payable.

Any import VAT paid may be reclaimed as input tax in the usual way subject to the normal domestic VAT rules. (See paragraph 2.12.)

7.3 VAT only PCC

Under PCC the value of the goods released to free circulation is broadly the import value plus processing costs. Given the increase in value there would be no benefit in VAT only PCC since the processed goods would be subject to the same rate of VAT as if the processed products had been imported. Consequently applications to use PCC for VAT only purposes will not be accepted.

7.4 Transfers to other member states – Onward Supply Relief

Goods may be imported to PCC and supplied to another member state under the Onward Supply rules. Any customs duty is paid in the UK but the payment of import VAT is relieved using CPC 42 91 00. The consignee in the country of receipt then accounts for the import VAT.

Further details can be found in Notice 702/7.

8 INWARD PROCESSING RELIEF (IPR)

Commentary—*De Voil Indirect Tax Service* **V3.334.**

8.1 General

IPR provides relief to promote exports from the EU and assist Community processors to compete on an equal footing in the world market. Duty is relieved on imports of non-EU goods which are processed in the Community and re-exported providing the trade does not harm the essential interests of Community producers of similar goods. Under IP drawback you must pay the import VAT at the time of entry. However under IP suspension, the payment of import VAT is suspended and only becomes due if you subsequently divert the goods to free circulation.

Further information can be found in Notice 221.

8.2 Calculation of Import VAT

Import VAT is payable at diversion to free circulation. It is based on the value of the diverted goods, inclusive of duty, at first entry to IP in the EU and the rate to be applied is that of the member state of diversion at the date of diversion. No account is to be taken of changes in the value of goods following transfer from other IP traders, as this will have been accounted for under the normal VAT supply rules.

If you (as authorisation holder) are diverting a single item or several items with the same duty rate bought from another member state, the import VAT due can be calculated as follows:

Duty rate = 10%

Duty suspended at first entry to IP in the EU (as shown on Form INF1) = £400

Value for duty is £400 × 10 = £4000

Total = £4400

VAT is £4400 × 17½% = £770

If you are diverting several items with different duty rates, the EU supplier should be asked, by the authorisation holder to confirm the value for VAT of the diverted goods at import to that country.

If you divert suspension goods on their sale to a taxable person in another member state you may be eligible for relief from import VAT under the onward supply relief provisions. (See Notice 702/7.)

Compensatory interest charges are not included in the value for VAT purposes.

The authorisation holder making the diversion should produce an INF1 which has already been endorsed by the Customs authority in the first member state. If the authorisation holder does not have an endorsed INF1, you should send one to the first member state to obtain details of the amounts due.

8.3 Calculation of compensatory Interest

When you divert goods entered to IP Suspension to free circulation in the UK, customs duty, import VAT and compensatory interest will be due. Compensatory interest is not applicable to the import VAT liability of such diversions.

8.4 Transfers to other member states – Onward Supply Relief

If you import goods for processing and supply them to another member state you cannot claim onward supply relief. However you may be able to claim relief if the goods originally intended for process and re-export are diverted to free circulation in the UK with payment of customs duty and compensatory interest using CPC 42 51 00.

If you are a taxable person in the UK and your goods are held under IP Suspension you may claim onward supply relief providing the goods are—

- eligible for zero rating under of VATA 1994 s 30(8);
- the goods *so imported* are the subject to that supply under reg 123 of the VAT Regulations 1995; and
- the goods are removed to another member states within one month of the date of importation.

The effect of this is that *import* VAT is not paid anywhere, but VAT on the supply/acquisition is accounted for by the purchaser in the EU country of destination.

8.5 VAT only IP

If you import goods upon which there is no duty liability "VAT only" inward processing may be authorised. This can arise where—

- the rate of import duty is nil by way of the tariff rate or preferential rate being applied; or
- the goods are imported from one of the territories listed in paragraph 11.2. Import VAT will become due if the goods are diverted to free circulation (including end use).

The applicant is not required to be registered for VAT.

Further details can be found in Notice 221 "Inward Processing Relief".

9 EXTERNAL AND INTERNAL TRANSIT

Commentary—*De Voil Indirect Tax Service* **V3.333.**

9.1 General

Transit is a customs procedure which enables you to move goods within the customs territory of the European Union (EU) without the payment of import duties and other charges until they reach their final destination. Transit may take place under any of the following procedures/documents—

- Community transit (CT) procedure. (CT is also used for movements to/from EFTA and is then known as "common transit");
- TIR carnet;
- ATA carnet used as a transit document;
- Rhine manifest;
- NATO form 302;
- By post.

Further information can be found in the Commission Transit Manual.

9.2 External transit (T1)

The external transit procedure allows the movement of mainly non-Union goods within the customs territory of the EU without their being subject to import duties and other charges or to commercial policy measures. Community goods that are subject to a Community measure involving their export to third countries may also have to move under external transit. The external procedure ends and the obligations of the holder are met when the goods placed under the procedure and the required documents are produced at the office of destination in accordance with the provisions of the relevant customs procedure.

9.3 Internal transit (T2 or T2F)

The internal transit procedure allows the movement of Community goods from one point to another within the customs territory of the EU to pass through the territory of a third country without any change in their customs status. In the case of internal Community transit this is also sometimes used in other circumstances.

9.4 When must I use transit?

External transit must be used for movements of—

— Non-Union goods that have not been put into free circulation or another customs procedure which permits movement within the Union; and
— Union goods which have been placed under the common transit procedure and are travelling to or via an EFTA country and subject to a Union measure involving their export to a third country, eg Common Agricultural Policy (CAP) goods (see Notice 800);

Internal transit must be used for movements of Union goods when they are—

— travelling from one point in the EU customs territory to another through one or more EFTA countries. Use of the T2 procedure for direct transport by air or sea to or from an EFTA country is not required;
— travelling to, from or between the "special territories" of the Community except for direct movements between the UK and the Channel Islands;
— goods in Chapters 25-97 of the Harmonised System (HS) which are travelling to or from the Principality of Andorra. Although Andorra is not part of the EU, a special customs union exists with the EU for the above-mentioned goods. Goods in Chapters 1-24 of the HS are treated as non-Community goods.

Internal transit may also be used for Community goods when they are—

— travelling to or from San Marino. Although San Marino is not part of the EU, a special Customs union exists with the EU but it excludes goods coming under the Treaty establishing the European Coal and Steel Community, (Chapters 72 and 73). These are treated as non-Community goods when arriving in the Community from San Marino.

Further information on the CT procedure can be found in the Commission Transit Manual.

9.5 Treatment for import VAT

Any goods you place under external transit have the customs duty and import VAT suspended. Import VAT and customs duty will only become due if you subsequently remove the goods to free circulation in the UK.

Goods placed under internal transit may have the import VAT suspended in particular circumstances (eg the "T2F" procedure for movements to/from special territories).

9.6 Third country goods subject to VAT only

Any goods you import from outside the EU that are not subject to a positive duty rate may be placed under external transit for import VAT purposes only.

All the normal procedures for discharging transit apply.

9.7 Goods imported from special territories

Goods imported from one of the special territories listed in paragraph 11.2 must be imported under internal transit for import VAT purposes. (Internal T2F procedure.)

10 RECORDS

10.1 Keeping records

You must keep records of all the goods you import for any of the reliefs/regimes listed in this Notice.

These must show—

— the type of goods imported;
— the processes which are carried out;
— what the products are; and
— how you dispose of them or any unprocessed goods.

You should be able to use your normal commercial records, but we may ask you to adapt them to show the information needed to support your claims to duty/VAT relief.

10.2 Can I keep my records on computer?

If you wish to keep your records on a computer system or other electronic media, you must advise us when you apply for authorisation for any of the regimes in this Notice. We will need to ensure that the system meets our requirements. You may also have to provide technical information and assistance to our staff if they require it.

10.3 Retention of records

You must keep all records relating to your transactions for four years after your authorisation expires. We may still visit you even after your authorisation has expired. You must make your records available to our officers for examination if you are asked to do so.

11 LIST OF TERRITORIES INSIDE/OUTSIDE THE EU FOR CUSTOMS DUTY AND VAT PURPOSES

(referred to in paragraphs 1.6, 8.5 and 9.7)

(The customs territory of the EU includes the territorial waters, inland maritime waters and airspace of member states.)

11.1 Territories considered to be inside the EU for Customs duty and VAT purposes

Austria
Azores
Balearic Islands
Belgium
Bulgaria
Cyprus in accordance with the provisions of the Act of Succession (those areas under the control of the Government of the Republic of Cyprus and including UK Sovereign Base areas of Akrotiri and Dhekelia in Cyprus)
Czech Republic
Denmark
Estonia
Finland
France
Germany
Greece
Hungary
Republic of Ireland
Italy
Latvia
Lithuania
Luxembourg
Madeira
Malta
Monaco
Netherlands
Poland
Portugal
Romania
Slovakia
Slovenia
Spain
Sweden
United Kingdom of Great Britain and Northern Ireland and the Isle of Man

11.2 Territories considered to be inside the EU for Customs duty purposes (not VAT)

Åland Islands;
Andorra (only Tariff Chapters 25 onwards);
Canary Islands
Channel Islands
French Guyana
Guadeloupe
Martinique
Mount Athos (agion Poros)
Reunion
San Marino

11.3 Territories considered to be outside the EU for Customs duty and VAT purposes

Andorra (only Tariff Chapters 1–24)
Busingen
Ceuta
Commune of Livigno
Cyprus (those areas not under the control of the Government of the Republic of Cyprus
Faroe Islands
French overseas territories
Greenland
Heligoland
Lake Lugano
Melilla

Also all other territories not listed in this section.

12 CERTIFICATE TO SECURE ZERO RATING OF SERVICES (OTHER THAN THE SUPPLY OF WAREHOUSING) PERFORMED IN A FISCAL OR OTHER WAREHOUSE

(referred to in paragraph 4.12)

The following text has the force of law

Information to be indicated:

I (full name)
(status in company)
Of (name and address of company)

declare that the goods shown below are subject to a fiscal or other warehousing regime at the place indicated below—

— description of goods;
— quantity of goods;
— warehouse stock number;
— name and address of fiscal or other warehouse; and
— authorisation number of the relevant warehousekeeper/warehouse;

And that the following services are to be performed on the goods in the fiscal or other warehouse:

. . . .

I certify that the supply of services is eligible to be zero-rated for VAT purposes under VATA 1994 s 18C(1).

. . . . (signature)
. . . . (date)

NOTE: You should be aware that there are severe penalties for making a false declaration. If there is any doubt about a supply being entitled to zero-rating you should consult the VAT Helpline before signing and giving the certificate.

A copy of the certificate should be filed with the suppliers' invoice which should refer to s 18C(1) of VATA 1994 to be eligible for zero-rating.

Commentary—*De Voil Indirect Tax Service* **V3.138.**

13 CHART SHOWING TREATMENT OF GOODS FOR CUSTOMS AND VAT PURPOSES (IMPORT VAT AND SUPPLY VAT)

13.1 Receipt of goods into a UK Customs Warehouse and their removal to free circulation in the UK

	1. Non Community goods received direct from a third country placed in a customs warehouse	*2. Non–Community goods received direct from a third country or via another member state in which there is a nil rate of customers duty – VAT only customs warehousing*	*3. Non-Community received from a third country via another member state.*	*4. Goods imported from special territories*
Customs Duty	Suspended on entry into Customs warehouse. To be paid on removal.	n/a	Suspended on entry into Customs warehouse. To be paid on removal.	n/a
Excise Duty	Duty not due and suspended whilst in warehouse.	Duty not due and suspended whilst in warehouse.	Duty not due and suspended whilst in warehouse.	Duty not due and suspended whilst in warehouse.
Import VAT	Suspended on entry to customs warehouse. To be paid on removal.	Suspended on entry to customs warehouse. To be paid on removal. Any VAT due in respect of zero rated services should be paid on removal.	Suspended on entry to customs warehouse. To be paid on removal.	Suspended on entry to customs warehouse. To be paid on removal. Any VAT due in respect of zero rated services should be paid on removal.
Acquisition VAT	n/a	n/a	If the goods are the subject of an acquisition on arrival in the warehouse VAT is to be accounted for on the acquirer's VAT return for the period in which the acquisition tax point falls.	n/a
Supply VAT				
Extra EC Trade statistics	Due on arrival in the UK, and on removal from the warehouse to UK free circulation	n/a	Due on arrival in the UK, and on removal from the warehouse to UK free circulation	n/a
Intrastat Declaration	n/a	n/a	n/a	n/a
EC Boxes on VAT return	n/a	n/a	n/a	n/a

13.2 RECEIPT OF GOODS FROM INTO A UK CUSTOMS WAREHOUSE AND THEIR REMOVAL OTHER THAN TO FREE CIRCULATION IN THE UK

	1. Non-Community goods for direct export to a country outside the EU	*2. Non-Community goods for indirect export to a country outside the EU*	*3. Goods transferred to another member state under a duty suspensive regime*	*4. Non-Community goods moved to another Member State on which customs duty is paid on removal*	*5. Non-Community goods transferred to IP suspension in the UK from a customs warehouse.*	*6. Non-Community goods transferred to IP drawback in the UK from a customs warehouse*
Customs Duty	Not paid	Not paid, Goods must move under CPEI arrangements or transit.	Not paid, Goods must move under CPEI arrangements or transit.	Paid on removal from customs warehouse.	Continues to be suspended to be paid on final removal from IP if IP if not discharged.	To be paid on removal from warehouse.
Excise Duty	Not paid	Not paid	Not paid		Continues to be suspended if IP is not discharged.	To be paid on removal from warehouse.
Import VAT	n/a	Any VAT which would be due on removal to UK free circulation is not payable.	Any VAT which would be due on removal to UK free circulation is not payable. Otherwise outward movements of goods may be zero rated subject to the normal conditions for intra EU trade.	VAT is payable but may be relieved. If the goods are removed in the course of an onward zero rated supply, see paragraph 5.6.	Any import VAT due is to be paid with the customs duty.	Any import VAT due is to be paid with the customs duty.
Supply VAT	Supplies of goods removed from the UK may be zero-rated as exports (subject to the normal rules)	Supplies of goods removed from the UK may be zero-rated as exports (subject to the normal rules)	Supplies direct into a customs warehouse in another member state are outside the scope of UK VAT.		Supplies of goods under IP are subject to domestic VAT rules.	Declaration of goods under IP are subject to domestic VAT rules.

	1. Non-Community goods for direct export to a country outside the EU	*2. Non-Community goods for indirect export to a country outside the EU*	*3. Goods transferred to another member state under a duty suspensive regime*	*4. Non-Community goods moved to another Member State on which customs duty is paid on removal*	*5. Non-Community goods transferred to IP suspension in the UK from a customs warehouse.*	*6. Non-Community goods transferred to IP drawback in the UK from a customs warehouse*
Extra-EC Trade Statistics	Export declaration	Export declaration	Export declaration	Declaration required on removal from customs warehouse	Declaration required on removal from customs warehouse.	Declaration required on removal from customs warehouse.
Intrastat	n/a	n/a	n/a	n/a	n/a	n/a
EU boxes on VAT Return	n/a	n/a	n/a	Boxes 6 & 8	n/a	n/a
EU Sale Listings	n/a	n/a	Completion required	Completion required	n/a	n/a

14 GOODS REQUIRING A GUARANTEE WHEN TRANSFERRED

(referred to in paragraph 2.10)

Note: Where no figure appears in the minimum rate of guarantee column (column 5), security should be taken on basis of the actual customs charges that may become due.

1	2	3	4	5
CN code	*Description of goods*	*Minimum quantity guarantee*	*Sensitive goods code*	*Minimum rate of guarantee (Euro/tonne)*
		required only when the quantity exceeds the minimum quantity shown	Where the CN code is insufficient to identify goods concisely the CN code and sensitive goods code should be used	
0207 12 0207 14	Meat and edible offal, of the poultry of heading 0105, of fowls of the species Gallus Domesticus, Frozen	3000 Kg		
1701 11 1701 12 1701 91 1701 99	Cane or beet sugar and chemically pure sucrose in solid form	7000 Kg		

1 *CN code*	2 *Description of goods*	3 *Minimum quantity guarantee*	4 *Sensitive goods code*	5 *Minimum rate of guarantee (Euro/tonne)*
2208 20 2208 30 2208 40 2208 50 2208 60 2208 70 ex 2208 90	Spirits, liquors, other spirituous beverages	5hl		€2,500/hl pure alcohol
2402 20	Cigarettes containing tobacco	35000 pieces		€120/1000
2403 10	Smoking tobacco, whether or not containing tobacco substitutes in any proportion	35 Kg		

15 GLOSSARY

(referred to in paragraphs 1.1 and 1.2)

Acquisition VAT — Goods purchased from a VAT-registered business in another EU country and removed to the UK VAT in the UK may be applicable on the acquisition of the goods. This VAT is recovered as input tax on the same VAT return, subject to the normal rules for reclaiming input tax.

ATA Carnet — An international customs document for temporary importation and exportation regulated under the terms of the ATA or Istanbul Convention.

C88 — The UK version of the Single Administrative Document (SAD) for making import, export and transfer declarations.

CFSP — Customs Freight Simplified Procedures Simplified procedures for the importation of third country goods including the simplified declaration procedure and local clearance procedure.

Union Goods — Goods which are:

(a) entirely obtained or produced in the Customs territory of the Union, without the addition of goods from third countries or territories that are not part of the Customs territory of the Community;

(b) imported from countries or territories not forming part of the Customs territory of the Union which have been released for free circulation in a member state;

obtained or produced in the Customs territory of the community either wholly from those referred to at (b) or partly from (a) and (b).

Community Transit (CT)
Documents used for exports from the UK to or via other member states.

Compensating Products
All products obtained from processing operations.

Compensatory interest
Interest charged when certain TA/IP goods are diverted to Free Circulation.

Customs Procedure
Release for free circulation, Community Transit (Notice 750), Customs Warehousing (Notice 232) IP (Notice 221), Processing under Customs Control (PCC) (Notice 237), TA relief (Notice 200), Outward Processing Relief (OPR) (Notice 235), Exportation (Notice 275).

Customs procedure with economic impact
These are—

—customs warehousing;

—inward processing;

—processing under customs control;

temporary Admission, and

—outward processing.

Customs Procedure Code (CPC)
A seven-digit code used on entries on import, export and warehouse declarations, to identify the type of procedure for which the goods are entered and from which they came. Details of CPCs can be found in Volume 3 of the Tariff.

Customs duties
An indirect tax that provides protection for Community Industries raised on import goods. This includes duty, agricultural charges and other import charges provided for under CAP. It does not include Excise duty or VAT.

Customs warehouse
A system or place authorised by Customs for the storage of non-community goods under duty and import VAT suspension. See Notice 232.

EFTA
European Free Trade Association. A group of countries comprising Iceland, Norway and the Swiss Confederation.

End Use
Arrangements which allow certain imported goods to be declared to free circulation in the Union at a reduced or "nil" rate of duty, provided they are put to a prescribed use under Customs control. (See Notice 770 for full details.)

Excise Warehouse
A warehouse approved for the deposit of goods subject to excise duty see Tax warehouse.

Free circulation
Goods imported from outside the EU are in free circulation when—

—all the import formalities have been complied with; and

—all import duties, levies and equivalent charges payable
have been paid and have not been wholly or partly refunded.

Goods that originate in the Community are also in free circulation.

Import VAT	When goods are imported into the UK from outside the EU, VAT is normally due at the same rate as on a supply of those goods in the UK.
Input tax	Input tax is the VAT paid or payable by taxable persons on goods or services supplied to them (or acquired by them from another member state) used or to be used for the purposes of their business.
Inward Processing Relief (IP)	A customs procedure providing import duty relief for goods imported into the EU or removed from a customs warehouse, for process and export outside the Union. See Notice 221.
Member state	A member state of the European Union.
Non-Community Countries — also known as "third countries"	Countries which are not members of the European Union.
Non-Community goods	Goods which are not of Union origin or imported goods which have not been released into free circulation.
Outward Processing Relief	Allows temporarily export of Union goods for processing or repair, and re-importation of the compensating products with total or partial relief from import duties. See Notice 235.
Processing	Any operation which changes the condition of imported goods. This includes both the manufacture and assembly of goods.
Processing under Customs control (PCC)	A system of duty relief for goods imported or transferred from another customs regime for processing into products on which less or no duty is payable. See Notice 237.
SAD	Single Administrative Document used throughout the EU for making import and export declarations – the UK version is Form C88.
SI Statutory Instrument	Secondary legislation, also known as delegated or subordinate legislation, can take the form of Orders, Regulations or Rules. These all have the force of law. A Statutory Instrument (SI) is the form in which most secondary legislation is made.
Special Territory	A territory within the EU for customs purposes but outside for fiscal (VAT) purposes.
Supply VAT	VAT payable on the supply of goods or services.
Tax Warehouse	An authorised place where goods subject to excise duty are produced, processed, held, received or despatched under duty suspension arrangements by an authorised warehouse keeper in the course of his business and includes excise warehouses, registered premises, distilleries and refineries.
Third Country	Any country that is outside the Customs Territory of the European Union.
TA relief	Temporary Admission – a customs procedure which allows goods to be used in the Union without payment of duty or VAT under certain conditions and re-exported afterwards in the same state as they were in at import.
VATA 1994	VAT Act 1994
VAT	Value Added Tax

702/10
VAT—TAX WAREHOUSING

October 2012

This notice has been updated to reflect the legal status of the certificate reproduced at section 7.

1 INTRODUCTION AND OVERVIEW

1.1 What is this notice about?

This new notice gives information on the VAT treatment of goods entered into, supplied within, and removed from tax warehouses in the UK, together with the treatment of supplies of services associated with those goods.

Information on the VAT treatment of goods acquired from countries outside the European Community (EC) and removed to home use from customs warehouses and free zones can be found in Notice 702/9 "VAT: Imports Customs procedures with economic impact, End-Use Relief and Free Zones".

1.2 VAT warehousing law

Article 155 of Directive 2006/112 gives member states the option of not charging VAT on supplies of goods and services whilst within warehousing regimes. The UK has implemented this option within VATA 1994 s 18.

1.3 What is a tax warehouse?

A tax warehouse is an authorised place where goods subject to Excise Duty are produced, processed, held, received or dispatched under duty suspension arrangements by an authorised warehousekeeper in the course of their business. They include—

— excise warehouses
— registered premises and stores
— distilleries, and
— refineries.

Note: If you are supplying goods in, or removing them from a tax warehouse in another member state, the rules and procedures may be different to those that apply in the UK. You should therefore consult the authorities in that member state if you are in any doubt.

1.4 Warehouse keeper's responsibilities

The warehouse keeper's responsibilities are set out in detail within Notice 197 "Excise Goods: Receipt into and Removal from an excise warehouse of excise goods".

1.5 The territory of the European Community (EC)

1.6 The legal status of this notice

The majority of this notice is our view of the law and does not take the place of the law. The exception is the certificate reproduced at section 7 which has the force of law under reg 145C of the VAT Regulations 1995.

Unless otherwise qualified, the term "EC" is used in this notice to refer to the VAT territory of the EC, which is different from the customs territory of the EC. The countries and territories which make up the VAT territory of the EC are listed in section 8.

Commentary—*De Voil Indirect Tax Service* **V3.332.**

2 TRADING IN A TAX WAREHOUSE

2.1 Registration for VAT

If your only business activity is the supply of goods within a tax warehousing regime you have no liability to register for VAT, but you may do so voluntarily if you wish under VATA 1994 Sch 1(10). Your liability to register for other business activities is not affected by the value of supplies of goods or services made in a tax warehouse.

2.2 VAT implications of placing goods in a tax warehouse

No VAT is payable when excisable goods subject to a warehousing regime are placed in a tax warehouse approved for those goods. VAT may be due when goods are removed from the warehouse to home use and is payable together with any suspended duty by the person who is removing the goods (or by the person liable to pay the duty).

2.3 Supplies in a tax warehouse of Community and home produced goods

No VAT is due on a supply of goods made in a tax warehouse provided that supply is followed by another supply of the goods while they are still warehoused. This means that the last purchaser of the goods (or someone acting on their behalf) accounts for and pays (or defers) the VAT on their purchase together with the excise duty when the goods are removed to home use. Section 4 provides guidance on the VAT treatment of goods removed to a destination outside the UK.

2.4 VAT due on removals from tax warehouses

VAT is due on the last supply of goods in warehouse and must be accounted for and paid (or deferred) when the goods are removed from the warehousing regime to home use (this is usually the point at which duty becomes payable on the goods). The VAT due will depend on the origin of the goods and whether any subsequent supplies take place whilst in the tax warehouse in the UK. VAT may also be due on certain services associated with goods held in a tax warehouse (see Section 5).

Origin of goods ...	*Supplied in warehouse in the UK?*	*VAT due on removal from warehouse to home use in the UK*
Received from a warehouse in another EC member state. Supplier is VAT registered in another member state.	No.	Acquisition VAT is due. If you are VAT registered in the UK you should use your VAT return (form VAT 100) for the period covering the date of removal to account for the VAT on the goods removed. You may recover this VAT as input tax on the same return, subject to the normal rules. The appropriate removal declaration – see paragraph 3.2 – must also be completed, showing the value of the goods, the date of removal and, if the declarant is VAT registered in the UK, "ACQVAT" written in place of the VAT amount. Your copy of the form provides the necessary audit trail linking the warehouse removal and the declaration on the VAT return. For details of the reporting requirements for oils removed from warehouse see Notice 179 "Motor & heating fuels: General information and accounting for Excise Duty & VAT".

Origin of goods ...	*Supplied in warehouse in the UK?*	*VAT due on removal from warehouse to home use in the UK*
Received from a warehouse in another EC member state. Supplier is VAT registered in another member state.	Yes	Supply VAT. Where goods are acquired from another member state but supplied on whilst in the warehouse in the UK, the requirement to account for acquisition VAT is extinguished. Instead, VAT becomes due on the last supply made in warehouse. This is accounted for on the appropriate removal declaration – see paragraph 3.2.
Home produced	No	No VAT is due when the goods are removed from warehouse
Home produced	Yes	Supply VAT is due on the last supply made in warehouse

2.5 What is the VAT value of goods removed from UK tax warehouses?

Normal VAT valuation rules apply. If–

— acquisitions VAT is due see the valuation rules in Notice 725 "VAT The single market".
— supply VAT is due see the valuation rules in Notice 700 "The VAT Guide".

You must include any excise duty in the value.

Commentary—*De Voil Indirect Tax Service* **V3.332.**

3 ACCOUNTING FOR VAT ON REMOVALS FROM TAX WAREHOUSES

Commentary—*De Voil Indirect Tax Service* **V5.141, V5.141A.**

3.1 Responsibility for paying the VAT

VAT is due on the last supply of goods in the warehouse regime. It must be accounted for and paid (or deferred) when the goods—

— are removed from the warehouse regime to home use (this is usually the point at which duty becomes payable on the goods).

VAT due on goods acquired from another member state is accounted for on the acquirer's VAT return (form VAT 100) covering the period in which they are removed from the warehousing regime. If the acquirer is not registered for VAT in the UK, acquisition VAT is accounted for and paid (or deferred) using the removal document.

Any VAT due in respect of previously zero-rated services (see section 5) must be accounted for together with the VAT due on the relevant goods.

The person removing the goods from the tax warehouse is responsible for ensuring that the correct amount of VAT is paid at the time of entry to home use.

3.2 Removal documents

When goods are removed from an excise warehouse any VAT due should be accounted for as follows—

Product	*Duty/VAT due*	*Immediate payment*	*Deferred payment*
Alcoholic beverages	Excise duty and VAT	W5	W5D
Tobacco products	Excise duty and VAT	W6	W6D
Mineral oil products	Excise duty VAT	W50	HO10
		W50	VAT908

For details of the reporting requirements for oils removed from warehouse see Notice 179 "Motor & heating fuels: General information and accounting for Excise Duty and VAT".

For goods removed from registered premises/stores, the VAT is accounted for on these documents—

Product	*Duty/VAT due*	*Immediate payment*	*Deferred payment*
Beer	VAT	EX46(VAT)	EX46(VAT)
Cider, perry, wine and made wine	VAT	EX606(VAT)	EX606(VAT)
Tobacco products	Excise duty and VAT	TP7	TP7

Whether the goods are removed from an excise warehouse or registered premises/stores, there is no requirement to separate the VAT due on the supply of goods from that due on the supply of services. Only a total is required. However, a separate record of all zero-rated services received in warehouse will have to be kept by the recipient of these services.

3.3 Evidence for input tax deduction

You can reclaim VAT as input tax, subject to normal rules, provided you hold evidence to support that entitlement. The owner of the goods whose liability it is to pay any VAT due on removal from warehouse will be issued with a certificate (C79) during the month after payment. This document is the official evidence needed to claim the VAT paid on warehouse removals as input tax. Where a C79 is not received in time for you to complete your VAT return, you may use alternative evidence of removal or payment to claim input tax. If you do this you should ensure that when the C79 certificate is received, it agrees with the input tax previously claimed.

You must also avoid making a duplicate claim. If you remove goods on behalf of the owner using the owner's behalf, you will not receive an import VAT certificate. You must not use alternative evidence, as this is not your input tax, but you should charge the VAT you have paid as a disbursement to the owner.

3.4 Deficiencies of warehoused goods

Any deficiencies of warehoused goods are treated as though they have been removed from the warehousing regime. Where deficiencies of goods are charged with duty, VAT not already paid on those goods is also to be charged. Similarly, any acquisition VAT on goods from another member state which has not been accounted for should be accounted for when deficiencies occur. Deficiencies of home produced goods are not to be charged with VAT unless the goods have been supplied in warehouse before the loss. In each case, the VAT may be deducted as input tax, subject to the normal rules.

4 REMOVALS OF GOODS FROM A TAX WAREHOUSE TO A PLACE OUTSIDE THE UK

4.1 Goods removed from warehouse to a place outside the UK

Commentary—*De Voil Indirect Tax Service* **V3.332, V5.141.**

If goods are removed from a tax warehouse in the UK to a destination outside the UK, you will not have to pay the VAT normally due on removal to home use. In such circumstances, either the person making the final supply in warehouse or the person removing the goods can zero rate that transaction provided certain conditions are met (see table below). Liability to meet the zero rating conditions must be clearly established before the goods are delivered to avoid any doubt as to where responsibility lies.

The following table provides an overview of the VAT implications when goods are removed to a place outside the UK—

A country outside the EC	Any VAT which would be due on removal to UK home use is not payable. Supplies of goods removed from the UK may be zero-rated as exports subject to meeting the conditions in Notice 703 "VAT: Export of goods from the United Kingdom".

A VAT registered customer in a another member state	You may zero-rate a supply of goods to a customer who is VAT registered in another EC country where the goods are moving outside the warehousing system provided the conditions in Notice 725 "The Single Market" are met.
A tax warehouse in another EC member state	You may disregard, for UK VAT purposes, any supply of the goods provided you are removing them directly to a registered tax warehouse in another EC country.

4.2 Reporting requirements when removing goods to a place outside the UK

When goods are removed from a tax warehouse in the UK to a place outside the UK you may also be obliged to fulfil certain other reporting requirements which are explained below.

4.2.1 Goods exported to a destination outside the EC

You must lodge a customs declaration if you are exporting goods to a country outside the EC. Full information on how to complete a customs declaration is contained in Notice 275 "Export procedures". You should also declare the value of the goods in box 6 of your VAT Return (unless you are transferring your own goods to a destination outside the EC – see paragraph 4.3.1).

4.2.2 Goods removed to another EC member state

If you are supplying a VAT registered customer in another EC member state you must enter such supplies on an EC sales list covering the time of the removal and include them in box 8 of your VAT Return. If the value of your trade with other EC member states exceeds a legally set threshold you will also be required to complete a supplementary declaration for intra-EC statistical purposes (Intrastat). These requirements must be met whether you are removing goods outside the warehousing system or under duty suspension to a warehouse in another EC country. Full information on completing an EC sales list and a supplementary declaration are contained in Notice 725 The Single Market and Notice 60 "Intrastat General Guide".

4.3 Removal of own goods to a place outside the UK

Where you remove your own goods to another EC member state (see paragraphs 4.3.2 and 4.3.3), the reporting requirements explained at paragraph 4.2.2 must also be met.

4.3.1 Exports to destinations outside the EC

Transfer of own goods to a destination outside the EC is not deemed to be a supply for VAT purposes and there is no requirement to declare the value of such goods as an output in box 6 of your VAT Return. However, if you are the owner of goods in warehouse and you are removing those goods for export to a destination outside the EC, proof of export must be retained to show that the goods have been transferred.

4.3.2 Removals to destinations in other EC member states

Transfer of own goods to another member state is deemed to be a supply for VAT purposes. Such supplies may be zero-rated (see paragraph 4.1) subject to meeting conditions set out in Notice 725 "VAT: The single market".

4.3.3 Removals under duty suspension to a tax warehouse in another EC member state

Transfer of own goods in these circumstances are deemed to take place outside the UK and such transfers are disregarded for VAT purposes – see paragraph 4.1.

4.4 Removal of goods from customs warehouses to free circulation

UK duty paid excise goods which have been destroyed or removed to a destination outside the UK may be eligible for drawback (that is, a refund) of the duty paid. Detailed information on claiming drawback is contained in Notice 207 "Excise Duty: drawback". Where drawback is claimed because the goods in question are either—

— removed to a VAT registered customer in another member state (whether the goods go to a tax warehouse or not), or
— exported to a destination outside the EC.

the supply does not fall within a warehousing regime for VAT purposes. However, such supplies may be zero-rated provided the conditions in Notice 725 "The single market" (for removals to other member states) or in Notice 703 "VAT: Export of goods from the United Kingdom" (for exports outside the EC) are met.

5 SUPPLIES OF SERVICES IN TAX WAREHOUSES

Commentary—*De Voil Indirect Tax Service* **V3.332, V5.141, V5.141A.**

5.1 Treatment of services associated with goods held in tax warehouses

Some services associated with goods held in tax warehouses can be relieved from VAT at the time they are supplied. In certain circumstances VAT will become due on such services when the goods concerned are subsequently removed from the regime to home use. While this is intended to assist businesses we also recognise that some may prefer, for administrative purposes, to continue to have such services taxed at the time they are supplied.

5.2 Services which may be zero-rated in tax warehouses

The services eligible for zero rating are restricted to those physical services that take place in the warehouse and are directly associated with the goods held in the warehouse. These will include those processes that create a new product, and others such as storage or secondary packaging. Charges made, for example, for brokerage, acting as an agent or for transport between warehouses in the UK are not eligible. Again, services exempt when supplied outside the warehouse remain exempt when supplied inside the warehouse.

5.3 How supplies of services may be relieved

(a) For the owner of the goods

If, as owner of the goods, any of the eligible services described in paragraph 5.2 (except the warehouse storage charges – see paragraph 5.4) are supplied to you by a third party, you may have the services zero-rated by the supplier. To do this you need to issue to the supplier a certificate, stating the goods are under duty suspension arrangements at the time the services are to be carried out (an example of such a certificate is shown at section 7).

(b) For the supplier of the service

Before you perform the service you might obtain from the owner of the goods a certificate as described in (a) above. If you do receive such a certificate you should issue a VAT invoice to your customer in the usual way, and at the usual time, but VAT should be shown as zero-rated "in accordance with section 18C(1) VAT Act 1994" and no VAT should be charged. The certificate you receive from the owner should be kept with your records as it provides you with the evidence needed to support the zero rating of your supplies. If you do not receive a certificate from the owner of the goods, you should issue your invoice in the usual way including VAT (as necessary) at the standard rate.

5.4 Warehouse storage charges

The certificate mentioned in paragraph 5.3 is not required for warehouse keepers' storage charges. Such supplies of services are normally automatically zero-rated. The invoice that is to be issued by the warehouse keeper to enable zero rating should include the words "in accordance with section 18C(1) VAT Act 1994" and no VAT should be charged. If, as the owner of the goods, you decide you want the storage standard-rated, you should notify the warehouse keeper of this in writing. The ware housekeeper will then issue an invoice and include VAT at the standard rate.

5.5 Subsequent taxation of previously zero-rated services

(a) When tax will be due

Services which are zero-rated at the time of supply will subsequently be taxed either when the goods with which they are associated are removed from the warehousing regime to home use, or at the duty point, in the following circumstances—

— when the service has not created new goods (see paragraph 5.6), or
— when the goods themselves have not been the subject of a supply (whilst still warehoused) after the service was provided.

(b) When tax will not be due

— the service creates new goods
— the goods are supplied (whilst still warehoused) after the service was provided
— the goods are exported under duty suspension arrangements directly from the warehouse to a non-EC country, or
— the goods are sent under duty suspension arrangements to a tax warehouse in another member state.

5.6 Services that change the nature of the product and create new UK product

Some services or processes applied to existing goods can change their nature to the extent that a new product is considered to have been created (for example, refining crude oil into motor spirit). The new product is then treated as having been produced in the UK. A list of processes undertaken in tax warehouses which are regarded as creating new UK product can be found in section 6. In addition to these processes, a new product is created when home-produced goods are mixed or blended with Community or non-Community goods resulting in the original goods losing their identity.

If the original goods were acquired or supplied before processing, any VAT that would have been due on the goods if they had not been processed is extinguished.

5.7 Treatment of services that create new UK product

If a service is carried out on goods, whether acquired, supplied or home produced and the service changes the nature of the product, no VAT is due in respect of that service, nor on the acquisition or supply. This is because the goods upon which the process has been carried out have ceased to exist and therefore can never be removed from the warehouse. VAT will only be due if the new goods are subsequently supplied or have a further service carried out on them that does not create new UK product (for example, secondary packaging).

6 LIST OF PROCESSES THAT CHANGE THE CHARACTER OF GOODS HELD IN A TAX WAREHOUSE

Commentary—*De Voil Indirect Tax Service* **V5.141A.**

The following processes change the character of goods and create a new UK product when they are performed in a tax warehouse.

Excise warehouse

Alcoholic liquids

— Fortifying made-wine.
— Fortifying wine.
— Mixing beer or wine with made-wine to produce made-wine.
— Producing beverages/foodstuffs of low alcoholic strength qualifying for duty relief.
— Rectifying and compounding spirits.
— "Rendering" made-wine sparkling (that is, aerating/carbonating made-wine).
— The maturation and processing of plain spirits until they can legally be defined as whisky.
— The blending or marrying of different whiskies.

Registered Premises

Beer, Wine, Cider & Perry

— Blending
— Mixing (including making shandy and low alcohol drinks).
— Dilution.
— Pasteurisation.

— Carbonation.
— Sterile filtration.
— De-alcoholisation.
— Fortification.
— Fortification.
— The fermentation and processing of fresh grapes, or the must of fresh grapes, until they can legally be defined as wine.
— Rendering wine sparkling, including disgorging.
— Rendering cider sparkling.

Mineral Oil production plant

Refining processes including

— Synthesis (chemical refineries where hydrocarbon oil is produced as a by-product of the plant process).
— Oil to oil (oil refineries where crude and other feedstock is processed to produce a range of hydrocarbon products).

Examples of specific processes which constitute refining can be found in Notice 179 "Motor and Heating Fuels: General Information and Accounting for Excise Duty and VAT".

Tobacco manufacturing

Cigarettes

— Leaf to rag.
— Rag to cigarette.

Hand rolling tobacco

— Leaf to finished product.

Pipe tobacco

— Leaf to blended and flavoured rag (prior to pressing).
— Blended and flavoured rag (prior to pressing) to finished product.

Cigars

— Leaf to filler.
— Filler to cigar.

7 ZERO RATING OF SERVICES (OTHER THAN THE SUPPLY OF WAREHOUSING) PERFORMED WITHIN A TAX WAREHOUSE

Commentary—*De Voil Indirect Tax Service* **V3.138, V5.141, V5.141A**.

"The following text has the force of law"

(Referred to in paragraph 5.3(a).)

Information to be indicated:

I	(full name)
. . . .	(status in company)
Of	(name and address of company)

declare that the goods shown below are subject to a warehousing regime at the place indicated below—

— description of goods
— quantity of goods
— warehouse stock number
— name and address of warehouse
— authorisation number of the relevant warehouse keeper and/or warehouse

I certify that the supply of services is eligible to be zero-rated for VAT purposes under section 18C(1) of the VAT Act 1994.

. . . . (signature)

. . . . (date)

Note: You should be aware that there are severe penalties for making a false declaration. If there is any doubt about a supply being entitled to zero rating you should consult the Helpline on 0845 010 9000 before signing and giving the certificate.

A copy of the certificate should be filed with the suppliers' invoice which should refer to s 18 C (1) of the VAT Act 1994 to be eligible for zero rating.

8 THE FISCAL (VAT) TERRITORY OF THE EUROPEAN COMMUNITY

Commentary—*De Voil Indirect Tax Service* **V1.213.**

(Referred to in paragraph 1.5)

— Austria
— Belgium
— Bulgaria
— Cyprus
— Czech Republic
— Denmark, except the Faroe Islands and Greenland
— Estonia
— Finland
— France, including Monaco
— Germany, except Busingen and the Isle of Heligoland
— Greece
— Hungary
— The Republic of Ireland
— Italy, except the communes of Livigno and Campione d'Italia and the Italian waters of Lake Lugano
— Latvia
— Lithuania
— Luxembourg
— Malta
— The Netherlands
— Poland
— Portugal, including the Azores and Madeira
— Romania
— Slovakia
— Slovenia
— Spain, including the Balearic Islands but excluding Cueta and Melilla
— Sweden
— United Kingdom, including the Isle of Man.

There are some "special territories" which are within the EC customs area but outside the EC fiscal (VAT) area—

— Andorra
— Gibraltar
— Mount Athos (Greece)
— San Marino
— The Aland Islands (Finland)
— The Canary Islands
— The Channel Islands
— The overseas departments of France (Guadeloupe, Martinique, Renuion and French Guiana)
— The Vatican City

Goods entering the UK from these "special territories" are treated for VAT purposes as imported goods.

NOTICE 703
EXPORT OF GOODS FROM THE UNITED KINGDOM

April 2014.

This notice cancels and replaces Notice 703 (November 2013). Details of any changes to the previous version can be found in paragraph 1.2 of this notice.

Parts of this notice have the force of law under section 30(6) of the VAT Act 1994 and regulation 129 of the VAT Regulations 1995. These parts are indicated by being placed in a box as in the example shown below.

> **The following rule has the force of law**
>
> The evidence you obtain as proof of export, whether official or commercial or supporting must clearly identify: the supplier, the consignor (where different from the supplier) the customer, the goods, an accurate value, the export destination, and mode of transport and route of the export movement.

1 INTRODUCTION

Commentary—*De Voil Indirect Tax Service* **Division V4.3**.

1.1 What is this notice about?

This notice explains the conditions for zero-rating VAT on an export of goods, that is, when the goods leave the European Community (EC). It also provides guidance on what you should do when you export goods in specific circumstances. Goods delivered from the United Kingdom (UK) to a destination elsewhere in the EC are not exports for VAT purposes. Such transactions are called removals. You can find out more about removals in Notice 725 The Single Market.

For information on zero-rating of services performed on goods for export see Notice 741A Place of supply of services.

1.2 What's changed?

The following changes to the November 2013 version have been made:

- Paragraph 2.8 – Which countries and territories are part of the EC Fiscal (VAT) area? Cyprus was amended to reflect which areas are included or excluded.
- The fifth bullet point in Paragraph 2.9 – Countries and territories outside the EC Fiscal (VAT) area was amended to reflect the changes made to the French outermost regions by the Council Directive 2013/61/EU which came into effect from 1 January 2014.

You can access details of any changes since February 2014 from our website, go to www.hmrc.gov.uk or phone our Helpline on 0300 200 3700.

This notice and others mentioned are available and our website.

1.3 Who should read this notice?

You should read this notice if you are a VAT registered person and you intend to export goods or if you are involved in the exportation of goods from the UK to a destination outside the EC as a customs clearing agent, freight forwarder, haulier, warehousekeeper, shipping company or airline.

1.4 What EC law is covered by this notice?

Article 146 of the EC Directive 2006/112 provides the legal basis for exempting goods dispatched or transported out of the EC. Amongst other things it states that Member States shall lay down conditions 'for the purpose of ensuring the correct and straightforward application of such exemptions and preventing any evasion, avoidance or abuse'. The UK uses the term 'zero-rating' rather than 'exemption' used in EC law to avoid confusion with the use of exemption elsewhere in UK law.

1.5 Why do we refer to the EC and not the European Union (EU) throughout the notice?

The EU is a collective term. It does not, strictly speaking, have a legal personality. Where we speak of Community law it is correct to speak of the EC. We have, therefore, retained the term EC throughout the notice.

1.6 What is the UK law relating to exports?

The UK VAT law relating to the zero-rating of exports of goods for VAT purposes can be found in:

– VATA 1994 s 30(6) for direct exports.
– VATA 1994 s 30(8) and reg 129 of the VAT Regulations (SI 1995/2518) for indirect exports.
– VATA 1994 s 30(10) for circumstances where the conditions for zero-rating are not met.

Additional legislation and Extra Statutory Concessions (ESCs) exist to allow relief from taxation in specific circumstances.

1.7 What is the legal status of this notice?

Under UK VAT law, HM Revenue & Customs (HMRC) may specify conditions to prevent evasion, avoidance or abuse. This notice lays down the conditions, which must be met in full, for goods exported outside the EC to be zero-rated. Plain English has been used wherever possible but as these conditions have legal status, some legal wording has been necessary.

Text shown in boxes has the force of law.

2 THE BASICS

2.1 What is meant by VAT zero-rating?

A zero-rated VAT supply is one which is subject to VAT but where the VAT is at 0 per cent.
Commentary—*De Voil Indirect Tax Service* **V4.201–202, 207**.

2.2 Why does zero-rating apply to exports?

VAT is a tax levied on goods and services consumed in the EC. When goods are exported they are "consumed" outside the EC and to impose VAT on such goods would be contrary to the purpose of the tax. Therefore, the supply of exported goods is zero-rated provided certain conditions are met.

2.3 Who is the "exporter" for VAT zero-rating purposes?

The exporter is the person who, for VAT purposes either—

– supplies or owns goods and exports or arranges for them to be exported to a destination outside the EC, or
– supplies goods to an overseas person, who arranges for the goods to be exported to a destination outside the EC.

Special rules exist if an export is preceded by multiple transactions (see paragraph 4.1).
Commentary—*De Voil Indirect Tax Service* **V4.201–202, 207**.

2.4 What is meant by "an overseas person"?

This means a person or company who is not resident in the UK or has no business establishment in the UK from which taxable supplies are made, or is an overseas authority.
Commentary—*De Voil Indirect Tax Service* **V4.326**.

2.5 Can I appoint someone to handle my export transactions?

Yes. You can appoint a freight forwarder, shipping company, airline or other person to handle export transactions and produce the necessary customs export declarations on your behalf. Information on customs procedures is contained in Notice 275 Customs: export procedures.

2.6 What are an agent's obligations?

The freight forwarder, shipping company, airline or other person appointed by you, the exporter, or your overseas customer must—

- take reasonable steps to make sure that the goods are as described by the exporter
- make sure that the necessary pre- or post-shipment customs formalities are completed
- make sure that the goods are exported within the time limits specified by the exporter
- keep records of each export transaction
- obtain or provide valid evidence of export (see sections 6 and 7) and send it to the exporter once the goods have been exported.

2.7 Which countries are part of the UK for VAT purposes?

The UK consists of England, Scotland, Wales, Northern Ireland and the waters within 12 nautical miles of their coastlines. Although the Isle of Man has its own VAT authority, sales to the Isle of Man are treated as any other sale within the UK.

The Channel Islands are part of the Customs territory of the EC, but are *outside* the EC, including the UK, for fiscal (VAT) purposes. Supplies of goods sent to the Channel Islands are regarded as exports for VAT purposes and may be zero-rated if the conditions set out in paragraph 3.3 or 3.4 are met. See paragraph 7.12 for information about evidence of export of goods to the Channel Islands.

Commentary—*De Voil Indirect Tax Service* **V1.215**.

2.8 Which countries and territories are part of the EC Fiscal (VAT) area?

- Austria
- Belgium
- Bulgaria
- Croatia
- Cyprus, including the British Sovereign Base Areas of Akrotiri and Dhekelia (but excluding the United Nations buffer zone and the part of Cyprus to the north of the buffer zone, where the Republic of Cyprus does not exercise effective control)
- Czech Republic
- Denmark, except the Faroe Islands and Greenland
- Estonia
- Finland
- France, including Monaco
- Germany, except Busingen and the Isle of Heligoland
- Greece
- Hungary
- The Republic of Ireland
- Italy, except the communes of Livigno and Campione d'Italia and the Italian waters of Lake Lugano
- Latvia
- Lithuania
- Luxembourg
- Malta
- The Netherlands
- Poland
- Portugal, including the Azores and Madeira
- Romania
- Slovakia
- Spain, including the Balearic Islands but excluding Ceuta and Melilla
- Slovenia
- Sweden
- United Kingdom and the Isle of Man.

2.9 Countries and territories outside the EC fiscal (VAT) area

- The Aland Islands
- Andorra
- The Canary Islands
- The Channel Islands
- The outermost regions of France (Guadeloupe, French Guiana, Martinique, Mayotte, Réunion and Saint-Martin (French Republic))
- Gibraltar
- Mount Athos
- San Marino
- The Vatican City
- All other countries which do not appear in paragraph 2.8.

Commentary—*De Voil Indirect Tax Service* **V1.213**.

2.10 What is meant by direct exports?

For VAT purposes a direct export occurs when you the supplier send goods to a destination outside the EC, and you are responsible either for arranging the transport yourself or appointing a freight agent. The goods may be exported by any of the following means:

- in your baggage
- in your own transport
- by rail, post or courier service, or
- by a shipping line, airline or freight forwarder employed by you and not by your customer.

Commentary—*De Voil Indirect Tax Service* **V4.311**.

2.11 What is meant by indirect exports?

An indirect export occurs when your overseas customer (as defined in paragraph 2.4) or their agent collects or arranges for the collection of the goods from you the supplier within the UK and then takes them outside the EC. This includes goods collected ex-works (see paragraph 6.6 for further information).

Commentary—*De Voil Indirect Tax Service* **V4.326**.

2.12 What happens if I supply goods to an overseas customer who is also established in the UK?

(a) Where you supply goods for export outside the EC, and your customer has an establishment in the UK from where they make taxable supplies, you may zero-rate the supply as a direct export provided:

- you or your representative arranges for the goods to be sent directly to a non-EC country
- the overseas delivery address for the goods is shown on the invoice even if the invoice is made out or sent to the address of the UK establishment, or a UK Shared Service Centre for administrative reasons, and
- the conditions, time limits and evidential requirements for direct exports are met—see paragraph 3.3.

(b) But where your customer or their representative arranges for the goods to be exported outside the EC, this is an indirect export. As the customer is established in the UK, it is not an 'overseas person' for VAT zero-rating purposes – see paragraph 2.4. This means that the conditions for zero-rating an indirect export (see paragraph 3.4) are not met and the supply cannot be zero-rated. VAT is due at the appropriate UK rate.

Note: if your customer does not have a business establishment in the UK the supply is eligible for zero-rating as an indirect export even if that customer is VAT registered in the UK.

Commentary—*De Voil Indirect Tax Service* **V4.326**.

2.13 What is the time of supply of exported goods?

The time of supply determines when a supply of goods or services is treated as taking place. This is called the tax point. In most cases the time of supply will be the earlier of either the date you:

- send the goods to your customer or your customer takes them away, or

– receive full payment for the goods.

For the treatment of deposits and progress payments see paragraph 11.5.

Commentary—*De Voil Indirect Tax Service* **V3.131, V4.307**.

2.14 How do I treat exports where there is no taxable supply?

You need not account for VAT if you—

- supply and export goods which you are to install outside the EC for your customer (the supply takes place in the country where the goods are installed)
- export goods outside the EC temporarily for exhibition or processing, or
- export goods outside the EC on sale or return, where the goods remain your property until they are sold.

However, you must still hold valid proof of export (see sections 6 and 7) to demonstrate to us how you disposed of the goods. You must also declare to us any goods returned to the UK.

2.15 How do I treat transfer of my own goods?

When transferring goods from your UK business to your branch outside the EC you need proof of export as evidence that you have transferred your goods.

Transfer of goods from your UK business to a branch outside the EC is not a supply but you must declare to us any goods returned to the UK, and retain the details. You can deduct any related input tax subject to the normal rules but do not include the value of any transferred goods as an output in Box 6 of your VAT return.

2.16 Goods accidentally lost, destroyed or stolen before export

You must account for VAT on goods destined for export outside the EC which have been accidentally lost, destroyed or stolen in the UK as follows:

- before you supplied them – no VAT is due
- you supplied them for direct export - no VAT is due provided that evidence of loss, destruction or theft is held, for example an insurance claim, police investigation and so on
- you supplied them for indirect export – VAT is due at the appropriate rate if the goods have been delivered to or collected by the overseas person, or their agent, in the UK.

Commentary—*De Voil Indirect Tax Service* **V4.339**.

3 CONDITIONS AND TIME LIMITS FOR ZERO-RATING

3.1 General

You must meet certain conditions before you can zero-rate supplies of goods for export. These conditions cover the—

- evidence (either official or commercial) you must hold to prove entitlement to zero-rating
- time limits in which the goods must be physically exported from the EC
- time limits in which you must obtain evidence of export to support zero-rating.

Only exports that comply with these conditions are eligible for zero-rating.

Commentary—*De Voil Indirect Tax Service* **V4.307**.

3.2 Why are conditions necessary?

The conditions set out in regulations and this notice are necessary to make sure only genuine exports are zero-rated whilst keeping VAT export procedures as simple as possible.

3.3 Conditions for zero-rating direct exports

The text in this box has the force of law

A supply of goods sent to a destination outside the EC is liable to the zero rate as a direct export where you—

- make sure that the goods are exported from the EC within the specified time limits (see paragraph 3.5)
- obtain official or commercial evidence of export as appropriate (see paragraphs 6.2 and 6.3) within the specified time limits
- keep supplementary evidence of the export transaction (see paragraph 6.4), *and*
- comply with the law and the conditions of this notice.

You must not zero-rate a direct export where you—

- deliver or post the goods to a customer's address in the EC (including the UK), or
- allow the goods to be collected by or on behalf of your customer even if it is claimed they are for subsequent export. See paragraphs 3.6 and 7.4 for details of deliveries made to another UK trader for groupage, consolidation, processing or incorporation prior to export.

3.4 Conditions for zero-rating indirect exports

The text in this box has the force of law

A supply of goods to an overseas customer (see paragraph 2.4) sent to a destination outside the EC is liable to the zero rate as an indirect export where:

- overseas customer:
- exports the goods from the EC within the specified time limits (see paragraph 3.5), *and*
- obtains and gives you valid official or commercial evidence of export as appropriate (see paragraphs 6.2 and 6.3) within the specified time limits, and you:
- keeps supplementary evidence of export transactions (see paragraph 6.4), *and*
- complies with the law and the conditions of this notice,

and the goods are not used between the time of leaving your premises and export, except where specifically authorised elsewhere in this notice or any other VAT notice.

You must not zero-rate an indirect export where the goods are:

- supplied to a private individual who is resident in the UK, or
- supplied to a customer that has a place of business in the UK from which taxable supplies are made), or
- delivered to, or collected by, a UK customer at a UK address.

If your export transactions do not fit specifically into any of these categories or those listed in sections 3 and 4 contact our Helpline for advice prior to export, obtaining a written decision, if necessary.

3.5 What are the time limits for exporting the goods and obtaining evidence?

You must export the goods from the EC and obtain valid evidence of export within the time limits shown in the table below. In all cases the time limits are triggered by the time of supply (see paragraph 12.3).

The text in this box has the force of law

Type of export	*Time limit for exporting goods*	*Time limit for obtaining evidence*
Direct (under the control of the supplier) and indirect (ex-works) exports (see paragraphs 3.3 and 3.4)	3 months	3 months
Supplies of goods involved in groupage or consolidation prior to export (see paragraph 7.4)	3 months	3 months

Type of export	*Time limit for exporting goods*	*Time limit for obtaining evidence*
Exports through auctioneers (see paragraph 7.9)	3 months	3 months
Goods delivered to the Foreign & Commonwealth Office (FCO) for export through diplomatic channels (see paragraph 7.11)	3 months	3 months
Goods ordered by a responsible person of an installation situated outside UK territorial waters (see paragraph 4.8)	3 months	3 months
Goods ordered by the Ministry of Defence (MOD) and other Government Departments provided they are directly exported (see paragraphs 4.9 and 4.11)	3 months	3 months
Goods to be delivered to overseas authorities provided they are ordered through their embassies, High Commissions or UK purchasing agents (see paragraph 4.12)	3 months	3 months
Supplies of goods involved in processing or incorporation prior to export (see paragraph 3.6).	6 months	6 months
Thoroughbred racehorses (subject to conditions to be found in Notice 700/57 "Administrative Agreements entered into with trade bodies"). This notice also sets the conditions for extending the time limits to 12 months.	6 months	6 months

If you have not exported the goods within the time limits, or do not hold the necessary evidence to show that the goods have been physically exported, you must not zero-rate the supply and must account for VAT at the appropriate UK rate (see paragraphs 11.2 and 11.3).

3.6 Conditions for zero-rating goods for export after processing or incorporation

The text in this box has the force of law

> When you make a supply of goods to an overseas person for export, but deliver them to a third person in the UK who is also making a taxable supply of goods or services to that overseas person, you can zero-rate the supply provided—
>
> – the goods are only being delivered and *not supplied* to the third person in the UK
> – no use is made of the goods other than for processing or incorporation into other goods for export
> – the goods are exported from the EC and you obtain evidence of export within the specified time limits
> and your records show:
> – the name and address of the overseas person the invoice number and date
> – the description, quantity and value of the goods
> – the name and address of the third person in the UK to whom the goods were delivered
> – the date by which the goods must be exported and proof of export obtained, and
> – the date of actual exportation.

Your records must be able to show that the goods you supplied have been processed or incorporated into the goods exported.

Where such supplies are made, an extension to the normal time limits for exporting the goods and obtaining satisfactory evidence of export is allowed – see paragraph 3.5.

In cases where the third person is not in the UK but in another EC Member State the same conditions will generally apply to allow you to zero-rate your supply.

However, you should establish the full facts behind the particular supply in question before assuming that zero-rating is appropriate. If you intend to make such a supply and are unsure as to whether it may be zero-rated, you should contact our Helpline.

3.7 What if I can't meet all the conditions?

If you do not meet all the above conditions the supply cannot be zero-rated as an export and you must account for VAT at the appropriate UK rate (see paragraph 11.2).

It is therefore essential that you establish at the time of sale what type of export documentation will be sent to you to support the zero-rating of your supply.

3.8 Right of appeal

If you disagree with a decision we have given, you can ask for it to be reviewed. If you do not want a review or disagree with the review conclusion you can appeal to a tribunal. You can find out more about appeals procedures in factsheet 1 (HM Revenue & Customs decisions - what to do if you disagree (www.hmrc.gov.uk/factsheets/hmrc1.pdf)) available on the HMRC website.

4 CONDITIONS FOR ZERO-RATING IN SPECIFIC CIRCUMSTANCES

4.1 Multiple transactions leading to a single movement of goods

Where a single movement of goods is supported by two or more underlying transactions only the final transaction may be zero-rated.

This might happen where more than two businesses are involved. For example, in the scenario shown below three companies are involved in a chain of transactions.

- Company A (based outside the EC) orders goods from Company B (UK based).
- Company B purchases the goods from Company C (also UK based) but does not take delivery of the goods.
- Company C, at the request of Company B, sends the goods direct to Company A.

In this scenario there are 2 separate transactions which should be treated as follows:

- Supply of goods from Company C to Company B is a supply in the UK and must be invoiced at the appropriate rate of UK VAT.
- Supply of goods from Company B to Company A is zero-rated as an export subject to the relevant conditions being met.

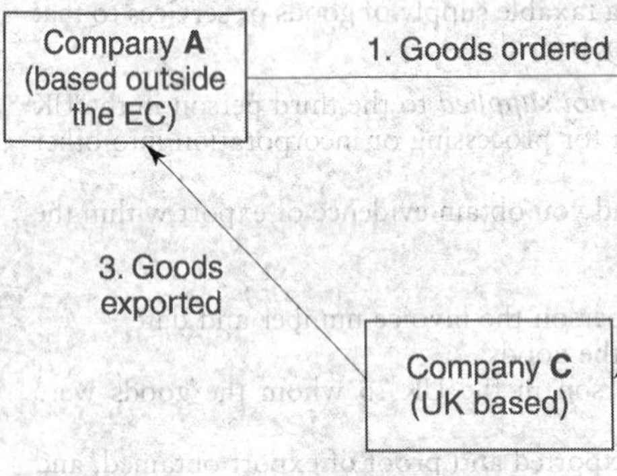

Commentary—*De Voil Indirect Tax Service* **V4.311**.

4.2 How are exports by members of a VAT Group treated?

Formation of a VAT Group is an arrangement that allows two or more corporate bodies to account for VAT as a single taxable person. A VAT group is treated in the same way as a single company registered for VAT on its own. The registration is made in the name of the representative member, who is responsible for completing and rendering the single return on behalf of the group. For further information on VAT groups please refer to VAT Notice 700/2 Group and divisional registration.

Where an exporter is part of a VAT group registration, purchases between VAT group members are not normally chargeable with VAT. Once a supply is made to an entity outside of the VAT Group the normal rules of export apply.

4.3 Exports from UK free zones

Free zones have no special status for VAT export purposes. You may zero-rate supplies of goods from a free zone for export outside the EC, provided the conditions explained in this notice are met. Supplies made to customers based within a UK free zone should be treated as normal domestic supplies.

4.4 Exports of containers

Supplies of new or second-hand freight containers for export are treated as supplies of goods and can be zero-rated provided that the conditions for export are met. The containers may be used to carry other goods for export during the export movement. The definition of the term 'container' and the conditions to be met before you can zero-rate the supply of a container may be found in Notice 703/1 Supply of Freight containers for export or removal from the United Kingdom.

Commentary—*De Voil Indirect Tax Service* **V4.323**.

4.5 Exports of computer software

Exports of standard ("normalised") computer software packages are regarded as supplies of goods, which may be zero-rated on export from the EC, subject to the conditions in this notice.

Supplies of—

- specific items of software tailored to the individual requirements of a company, and
- software transmitted by phone or other data network

are generally regarded as supplies of services and are therefore outside the scope of this notice. You can find further information in Notice 741A Place of supply of services.

4.6 Exports of hydrocarbon oils

Hydrocarbon oils are subject to UK excise duty and are normally held in warehouses approved by HMRC until the time of delivery. Sales within these warehouses prior to delivery are disregarded for VAT purposes. See paragraph 7.10 for evidence of export from the EC.

4.7 Exports to oil rigs, etc. and other continental shelf installations

This paragraph applies to the export of goods to structures such as oil rigs, drilling units, accommodation platforms and similar oil or gas exploration / exploitation structures. It also applies to mobile floating structures such as drill ships, tankers, jack-up rigs, semi submersible rigs and Floating Production Storage and Offloading (FPSO) vessels which are often stationed at fixed locations.

Exports to installations outside EC territorial waters

(a) Goods supplied and exported by you to an installation not owned by you

You can zero-rate the supply as a direct export provided that the goods are exported and you obtain valid proof of export within three months of the time of supply.

(b) Goods sent to an installation owned by you

There is no supply as this is a transfer of your own goods (see paragraphs 2.14 and 2.15). However, you must still hold valid proof of export to demonstrate how you disposed of the goods.

(c) Goods sent to replenish your own stocks on an installation not owned by you.

The supply position is the same as at (b) above.

Commentary—*De Voil Indirect Tax Service* **V4.337**.

4.8 Goods supplied for sale on installations which are situated outside UK territorial waters

UK territorial waters consists of the waters within twelve nautical miles of the coastlines of England, Scotland, Wales and Northern Ireland.

The text in this box has the force of law

You can zero-rate these supplies provided:

- you obtain a written order for the goods from a responsible person on the installation to which the goods are to be sent
- the goods are supplied either direct to the installation or through an agent for consolidation followed by direct delivery to the installation, and
- you obtain a receipt for the goods, signed by a responsible person on the installation, within three months of the time of supply.

Commentary—*De Voil Indirect Tax Service* **V4.337**.

4.9 Supplies to the Ministry of Defence (MOD) and overseas military establishments

The MOD is registered for VAT in the UK and all supplies to them, or to any military establishment in the UK on their behalf, should include VAT at the appropriate rate.

Direct exports to overseas military and similar installations may be zero-rated provided you comply with the conditions set out in this notice. See paragraphs 4.10 and 10.7 for further information.

4.10 Supplies to regimental shops

Special conditions exist to allow the zero-rating of supplies of goods where the Regiment (or equivalent military unit) is about to be posted to a location outside the EC.

The text in this box has the force of law

You can zero-rate the supply of goods (except new and second-hand motor vehicles) to Regimental shops provided:

- each written order received from the President of the Regimental Institute (PRI) states that the Regiment is about to take up an overseas posting and that the goods ordered will be exported from the EC
- the goods are delivered to the PRI ready packed for shipment no more than 48 hours before the Regiment is due to depart for the overseas posting
- the goods are exported outside the EC, *and*
- you retain a certificate of receipt signed by the PRI which clearly identifies the goods, gives full shipment details and states the date on which they were exported from the EC.

The PRI will keep a full record of such transactions for reference purposes for a period of not less than six years.

Commentary—*De Voil Indirect Tax Service* **V4.336**.

4.11 Supplies to Government Departments other than the Foreign and Commonwealth office (FCO)

You can zero-rate the supply of goods to Government Departments only if you arrange for their direct export to a destination outside the EC and comply with the conditions set out in this notice. For supplies to the FCO see paragraph 7.11.

You must not zero-rate goods for export delivered to Government Departments in the UK even if the goods are ordered for, or by, overseas establishments.

4.12 Supplies to overseas authorities

If you do not meet *all* of the conditions below the supply cannot be zero-rated as an export and you must account for VAT on the supply at the appropriate UK rate.

The text in this box has the force of law

You may zero-rate supplies of goods to overseas authorities which are ordered through their embassies, High Commissions or purchasing agents in the UK, provided:

- you keep a separate record of each transaction (see section 11), including evidence that the supply has been made to an overseas authority, for example the order for the goods, sales invoice made out to the overseas authority, evidence of payment from the overseas authority and so on
- the goods are exported and proof of export obtained within three months, as detailed on the form at section 12, and
- the goods are not used between the time of leaving your premises and export, either for their normal purpose or for display, exhibition or copying.

Commentary—*De Voil Indirect Tax Service* **V4.326**.

4.13 Export of motor vehicles

You can zero-rate the supply of any motor vehicle, new or second hand:

- as a direct export under the conditions specified in paragraph 3.3, provided that the vehicle is not used or delivered in the EC before it is exported
- as an indirect export under the conditions specified in paragraph 3.4 provided that the vehicle is not subsequently used except for the trip to the place of departure from the EC, or
- if the vehicle is sold to a private individual under the terms of the Personal Export Scheme – see paragraph 9.1.

Commentary—*De Voil Indirect Tax Service* **V4.334**.

4.14 Tools used in the UK to manufacture goods for export

Notice 701/22 "Tools for manufacture of goods for export" explains the conditions for zero-rating supplies of jigs, patterns, templates, dies, moulds, punches and similar tools used in the UK to manufacture goods for export.

Commentary—*De Voil Indirect Tax Service* **V4.283**.

5. CUSTOMS DECLARATIONS VIA THE NATIONAL EXPORT SYSTEM (NES) AND THE NEW COMPUTERISED TRANSIT SYSTEM (NCTS)

Commentary—*De Voil Indirect Tax Service* **V4.308**.

5.1 What is NES?

NES is a system used by freight agents, importers and exporters, to declare import or export entries electronically. If you export goods including those goods that are leaving the EC via other EC Member States, you should refer to the procedures and customs requirements described in detail in Notice 275 Customs: export procedures.

5.2 How does NES work?

The NES operates via a computer system known as 'Customs Handling of Import Export Freight' or CHIEF. When an export declaration is entered to CHIEF it must go through a number of stages before the export procedure is finalised. The stages are:

- Pre-lodgement of data.
- Acceptance of data.
- Arrival message.
- Departure message.

At each stage the Status of Entry code and the ICS (Indicate Clearance Status) code will change, and a message showing the current status is generated by NES to the person who submitted the electronic declaration.

5.3 What will NES produce as evidence of export?

Official evidence of export cannot be obtained until the export declaration has been fully discharged. This happens when a departure message is input to CHIEF by either the port inventory system, a nominated loader, or, in some cases, by Customs. Official evidence will be either:

– a copy of the final goods departed message (see 5.4), or
– a screen print from CHIEF showing the appropriate status codes (see 5.5).

5.4 Goods Departed Message (GDM)

At UK air and seaports a computerised system is used to follow the goods through the port area. Where these systems are linked to NES, an electronic message known as a Goods Departed Message (GDM) will be generated and should be received by the person submitting the export declaration. The GDM is official evidence of export *only* when goods leave the EC from the UK.

If you, as an exporter or supplier, do not input export declarations yourself, you will not receive the appropriate messages to confirm the goods have been exported from the EC. You should ask your agent or the person who declares the goods on your behalf to supply you with a copy of the final goods departed message appropriate for your exports.

Similarly, if your overseas customer or their agent inputs the export declaration, you should ask for a paper copy of the final goods departed message appropriate to the goods you supplied. If official evidence of export cannot be obtained, you will need to rely on commercial transport evidence as described in paragraphs 6.3 and 6.6.

5.5 Screen print from CHIEF

If you or your agent make your electronic export declarations via CHIEF or the WEB declaration option, an alternative to the Goods Departed Message can be obtained by printing a copy of the screen "DEVD option 2" in CHIEF. This screen print will provide official proof of export *only* when it shows:

– a Status of Entry code 8, *and*
– ICS Code 60.

These codes mean that the goods have actually departed from the EC.

5.6 Assumed Departure Message

When goods have arrived at the port but for some reason a departure message is not input, CHIEF will issue an Assumed Departure Message within a specified timescale. This message is not accepted as evidence for VAT zero-rating. Alternative commercial transport evidence as described in paragraph 6.3 must be produced.

5.7 What happens where goods leave from a port or airport where no computerised system is in place?

Where no computerised system is in place at the port or airport, you or your agent or forwarder can arrange with Customs to manually enter a departure message when the goods are exported. In this scenario you or your agent should ask the Customs Officer for a printed copy of the DEVD option 2 screen showing the ICS code 60 (see 5.5) to use as official proof of export. This, together with the supporting supplementary evidence will be accepted as evidence for zero-rating.

5.8 What happens if the goods are not exported?

If for any reason the goods are not exported and an export declaration has been made, the Customs Officer at the declared port of export must be formally advised and the export declaration cancelled. Where goods are supplied in the UK instead, VAT must be accounted for at the appropriate UK rate.

5.9 What is the New Computerised Transit System (NCTS)?

NCTS is a European wide system, based upon electronic declaration and processing, designed to provide better management and control of goods under Community/Common Transit (CT) procedures. In some circumstances you may be required to enter the goods to the CT procedure if the goods you export transit the UK or one or more other Member States before leaving the EC. Further details about NCTS and CT requirements can be found in Notice 275 Customs: export procedures.

5.10 How does NCTS work?

The system automatically produces a Transit Accompanying Document (TAD) containing a unique Movement Reference Number (MRN) and bar code. The TAD moves with the goods. If the goods are presented intact, together with the TAD, at the office of destination, a message is sent to the office where the NCTS declaration was made. The CT procedure is then discharged electronically. There is no requirement to return a paper document to the exporter.

5.11 What will NCTS produce as evidence of export?

Where goods have been entered to NCTS, official evidence of export will be confirmation that the CT procedure has been discharged. The exporter or agent can obtain this confirmation from NCTS by entering the unique Movement Reference Number.

(When NCTS is used the Goods Departed Message (GDM) generated by NES is not accepted as evidence for VAT zero-rating. This is because in these circumstances the GDM only confirms that the goods have left the UK, not that the goods have left the EC.)

5.12 What additional documents are required before export of restricted goods?

The export of certain goods is prohibited or restricted. Where the export is one of restricted goods you will need to obtain a licence in addition to the official and commercial transport documentary evidence.

- Under NES the licence must be referenced on the declaration and produced when requested by Customs.
- With a non-NES declaration the licence must accompany the customs declaration.

Further advice on restricted goods may be obtained from—

- Export Control Organisation, 3rd Floor, 1 Victoria Street, London, SW1H 0ET; email address: eco.help@dti.gsi.gov.uk
- Specialist Service Centre for Exports, Animal Health and Veterinary Agency (AHVLA), Hadrian House, Wavell Drive, Carlisle, CA1 2TB
- Department for Culture Media and Sport, 100 Parliament Street, London SW1A 2BQ.

6 PROOF OF EXPORT

6.1 What does this section cover?

This section explains the evidence that is required for a supply of goods exported outside the EC to be zero-rated for VAT.

For VAT zero-rating purposes you must produce either official evidence as described in paragraph 6.2 or commercial evidence as described in paragraph 6.3. Equal weight is put on official and commercial transport evidence but both must be supported by supplementary evidence to show that a transaction has taken place, and that the transaction relates to the goods physically exported. If the evidence of export provided is found to be unsatisfactory, VAT zero-rating will not be allowed and the supplier of the goods will be liable to account for the VAT due (see paragraph 11.2).

Commentary—*De Voil Indirect Tax Service* **V4.306**.

6.2 Official evidence

Official evidence is produced by Customs systems, for example Goods Departed Messages (GDM) generated by NES. See section 5 for more detail on how official evidence of export is produced.

6.3 Commercial transport evidence

This describes the physical movement of the goods, for example:

- Authenticated sea-waybills.

- Authenticated air-waybills.
- PIM/PIEX International consignment notes.
- Master air-waybills or bills of lading.
- Certificates of shipment containing the full details of the consignment and how it left the EC, or
- International Consignment Note/Lettre de Voiture International (CMR) fully completed by the consignor, the haulier and the receiving consignee, or Freight Transport Association (FTA) own account transport documents fully completed and signed by the receiving customer.

Further details on the purpose of these documents can be found in Notice 275 Customs: export procedures.

Photocopy certificates of shipment are not normally acceptable as evidence of export, nor are photocopy bills of lading, sea-waybills or air-waybills (unless authenticated by the shipping or air line).

6.4 What supplementary evidence is available?

You are likely to hold, within your accounting system some or all of the following:

- customer's order
- sales contract
- inter-company correspondence
- copy of export sales invoice
- advice note
- consignment note
- packing list
- insurance and freight charges documentation
- evidence of payment, and/or
- evidence of the receipt of the goods abroad.

You must hold sufficient evidence to prove that a transaction has taken place, though it will probably not be necessary for you to hold all of the items listed.

6.5 What must be shown on export evidence?

The text in this box has the force of law

The evidence you obtain as proof of export, whether official or commercial, or supporting must clearly identify:

- the supplier
- the consignor (where different from the supplier)
- the customer
- the goods
- an accurate value
- the export destination, *and*
- the mode of transport and route of the export movement.

Vague descriptions of goods, quantities or values are not acceptable. For instance, "various electrical goods" must not be used when the correct description is "2000 mobile phones (Make ABC and Model Number XYZ2000)". An accurate value, for example, £50,000 must be shown and not excluded or replaced by a lower or higher amount.

If the evidence is found to be unsatisfactory you as the supplier will become liable for the VAT due.

6.6 What evidence will I need to obtain to substantiate VAT zero-rating when I do not arrange shipment of the goods?

Typically this occurs when goods are supplied ex-works. If your overseas customer arranges for the goods to be collected from your premises and exported to a place outside the EC

Member States it can be difficult for you, as the supplier, to obtain adequate proof of export as the carrier is contracted to your overseas customer. For this type of transaction the standard of evidence required to substantiate VAT zero-rating is high.

Before zero-rating the supply and releasing the goods to your customer, you must confirm what evidence of export is to be provided.

If the evidence of export:

- does not show that the goods have left the EC within the appropriate time limits, or
- is found, upon examination, to be unsatisfactory

you, the supplier, *will* become liable for payment of the VAT.

For these reasons you should consider whether to:

- include the requirement for the buyer to provide export evidence as part of the sales contract between you and your customer, and/or
- secure against the possibility that your buyer will fail to provide the proper export evidence by, for example, taking a deposit from your customer equal to the amount of VAT you will be liable to pay if the evidence is not sent to you.

The deposit can be refunded when you obtain evidence that proves the goods were exported.

Evidence must show the goods you supplied have left the EC. Copies of transport documents alone will not be sufficient. Information held must identify the date and route of the movement and the mode of transport involved. It should include the following:

- a written order from your customer which shows their name and address, and the address where the goods are to be delivered
- copy sales invoice showing the invoice number, customer's name and a description of the goods
- delivery address for the goods
- date of departure of goods from your premises and from the EC
- name and address of the haulier collecting the goods; registration number of the vehicle collecting the goods and the name and signature of the driver
- where the goods are to be taken out of the EC by an alternative haulier or vehicle, the name and address of that haulier, the registration number of the vehicle and a signature for the goods
- route, for example, Channel Tunnel, port of exit
- copy of travel tickets, and
- name of ferry or shipping company and date of sailing or airway number and airport.

The information held should also include (if applicable):

- the trailer number
- full container number, and
- the name and address for consolidation, groupage or processing.

At the time when the goods leave the EC the above information could be obtained from your customer, the haulier, the freight forwarder or the documents listed in paragraph 6.4.

See paragraph 7.3 for goods that your customer intends to export in his baggage or his private motor vehicle.

6.7 How long must I retain export documentation?

To substantiate zero-rating a transaction you *must* make sure that the proof of export is:

- kept for six years, and
- made readily available to any visiting VAT Officer to substantiate the zero-rating of your exports.

6.8 What happens if I do not hold the correct export evidence?

If you do not hold the correct export evidence, within the appropriate time limits, then the goods supplied become subject to VAT at the appropriate UK rate. See paragraph 11.2 for details of procedures to follow in these circumstances.

6.9 If I am an overseas customer arranging my own export what do I need to do to make sure that I get the benefit of zero-rating?

Once you have collected the goods or arranged for the goods to be taken to the port or airport, for export, you should provide the supplier of the goods with all of the documentary evidence you hold to prove that the goods have been physically exported. You should make sure that the supplier is in possession of this evidence to allow them to meet the time limits for export.

6.10 What if I have lost or mislaid export evidence?

If you have lost or mislaid the official or commercial evidence of export supplied by the ship owner or carrier, duplicate evidence of export may be obtained. The replacement evidence of export must be clearly marked "DUPLICATE EVIDENCE OF EXPORT" and be authenticated and dated by an official of the issuing company.

7 PROOF OF EXPORT FOR ZERO-RATING IN SPECIFIC CIRCUMSTANCES

This section covers the specific evidence of export that you must obtain according to the method of export used. In all cases the official or commercial transport evidence you obtain must be supported by the supplementary information set out in paragraph 6.4 to show that the transaction has taken place.

Commentary—*De Voil Indirect Tax Service* **V4.306, 326.**

7.1 Air and sea freight

If you are using commercial transport documents as proof of export for goods exported outside the EC by:

- Air – you must obtain and keep an authenticated master or house air-waybill endorsed with the flight prefix and number, and the date and place of departure.
- Sea – you must keep one of the copies of the shipped bill of lading or sea-waybill (certifying actual shipment) or, where a shipping company does not issue these, a certificate of shipment given by a responsible official of that company.

7.2 Road freight

The International Consignment Note (CMR) provides evidence of the identity of the contracting parties when goods are transferred by road. It is in three parts and is completed and signed by the sender of the goods, the carrier and the person receiving the goods. Where the overseas customer arranges for the goods to be collected ex-works the CMR alone is not conclusive evidence that the goods in question have left the EC but, where the CMR is used as part of the evidence, it is important that the information is complete and all the details legible.

7.3 Merchandise in Baggage (MIB)

Commercial or business goods exported in accompanied baggage are known as MIB. Commercial evidence of export is normally only available where goods are shipped as manifested freight, as individual consignments or as part of groupage consignments. Currently MIB is outside the scope of the National Export System and you will need to complete a non-electronic paper Single Administrative Document (SAD) Form C88 and follow the procedures below.

Provided the goods and correctly completed SAD copies 2 and 3 are presented to the MIB officer, official certification of copy 3 of the SAD can be obtained for the following:

- Merchandise in Baggage.
- Re-export of temporarily imported goods.
- Transfers of own goods (see paragraph 2.15).
- Purchases by overseas persons.
- Exports where commercial documents are not available (for example where an ATA carnet has been lost).

In all these cases the certified copy 3 of the SAD (Form C88) is your evidence of export.

(a) Where you export the goods

If you export goods in baggage or in a private motor vehicle, you must:

- Include "MIB" in box 44 of the export SAD (C88).

- Arrive well before your scheduled departure time and present copy 2 and copy 3 (marked "for VAT purposes only") of the SAD, with the goods, to the MIB officer at the UK place of export from the EC for the reverse of copy 3 to be certified that goods have been shipped.

Copy 3 will be handed back to you as evidence of export for retention in your records.

(b) Where your customer exports the goods

Where your overseas customer collects the goods from your premises and arranges transportation in baggage or in a private motor vehicle you must:

- Give your customer a completed SAD with your name and VAT number shown in box 2. (This will make sure that your overseas customer does not include your supplies on a single SAD covering goods purchased from a number of UK suppliers. If they did this, they would be unable to provide you with an original officially certified copy 3 for your records).

Your overseas customer must:

- Arrive well before their scheduled departure time and present copy 2 and copy 3 (marked "for VAT purposes only") of the SAD (Form C88) with the goods, to the MIB officer at the UK place of export from the EC. The MIB officer will certify the reverse of copy 3 to show that goods have been shipped and hand it back to your overseas customer.
- Send you copy 3 as evidence of export for retention in your records.

(c) Leaving the EC via another member state

If you or your customer depart the EC via another Member State copy 3 of the SAD (Form C88) will be certified by Customs at the place you leave the EC.

Full details of the MIB procedures are given in Notice 6 Merchandise in Baggage.

7.4 Groupage or consolidation transactions

If you use a freight forwarder, consignments (often coming from several consignors) may be aggregated into one load, known as groupage or consolidation cargo. The freight forwarder must keep copies of the original bill of lading, sea-waybill or air-waybill, and all consignments in the load must be shown on the container or vehicle manifest. You will be issued with a certificate of shipment by the freight forwarder, often supported by an authenticated photocopy of the original bill of lading, a sea-waybill or a house air-waybill. Where such consignments are being exported, the forwarder is usually shown as the consignor in the shipping documents.

(a) Certificate of shipment

Certificates of shipment are usually produced by packers and consolidators involved in road, rail and sea groupage consignments when they themselves receive only a single authenticated transport document from the carrier. The certificate of shipment is an important document, which should be sent to you as soon as the goods have been exported from the EC.

The certificate of shipment must be an original and authenticated by an official of the issuing company unless it is computer produced, on a once-only basis, as a by-product of the issuing company's accounting system.

A properly completed certificate of shipment will help you to meet the evidential requirements described in paragraph 6.1.

(b) What information must be shown?

Although the certificate of shipment can be in any format, it must be an original and will usually contain the following information:

- the name and address of the issuing company
- a unique reference number or issuer's file reference
- the name of the exporter (and VAT number, if known)
- the place, port or airport of loading

- the place, port or airport of shipment
- the name of the export vessel or the aircraft, flight prefix and number
- the date of sailing or flight
- the customer's name
- the destination of the goods
- a full description of the goods exported (including quantity, weight and value)
- the number of packages
- the exporter's invoice number and date if known
- the bill of lading or air-waybill number (if applicable), and
- the identifying number of the vehicle, container or railway wagon.

7.5 Postal exports

Goods exported by post may be zero-rated if they are direct exports and you hold the necessary evidence of posting to an address outside the EC.

(a) Evidence of posting for letter post or airmail (packages up to 2kg)

A fully completed certificate of posting form, presented with the goods for export, and stamped by the Post Office will be your evidence of export. Acceptable forms are:

- Form C&E 132 (www.hmrc.gov.uk/forms/ce132.pdf) for single or multiple packages taken to the Post Office. Blank forms may be obtained from our Helpline or from our Internet site.
- Form P326 available from the Post Office and used for single packages taken to the Post Office.

Also acceptable is:

- A Certificate of Posting for International Mail, or a Royal Mail Collection Manifest, available from a Royal Mail sales advisor, for use by customers using their Business Collections Service, where the Royal Mail collection driver signs the certificate.

You can find further information on Royal Mail international services on their website at www.royalmail.com.

(b) Evidence of posting for parcels

Parcelforce Worldwide operates a range of international parcel services. If you use any of these services for a non-EC destination, you will use a bar-coded service label and customs declaration. The customs declaration may either be a paper "despatch pack", or an online version. The information required for both formats is the same. Whichever version you use, you should be aware of the following points:

- A fully completed customs declaration is required for every parcel (even if you are sending a multiple item consignment) as every parcel may be inspected by Customs on an individual basis.
- A full and clear description of all the items within the parcel is required including quantity, weight, and value of the goods.
- If you arrange for the parcel to be collected from your premises, the collection driver will provide a despatch pack for you to complete (if you have not already completed the declaration) and will then sign the receipt copy. If you have completed and printed your declaration online, the collection driver will sign your online receipt or manifest.
- If the parcel is taken to a Post Office the completed receipt copy from the despatch pack will be handed back to you, together with a printed proof of shipment from the Post Office SmartPost system. This will show the overseas delivery address, date of despatch and unique consignment number (which will match the unique consignment number on your despatch pack customer receipt.) You should keep *both* the proof of shipment and the customer receipt.

In addition to the individual parcel declarations described above, account customers of Parcelforce Worldwide who export on a regular basis also have two additional potential sources of information listing multiple export parcels:

- Worldwide Despatch Manager (WDM) – online users can print a manifest, which lists all despatched parcels.
- Statement of account.

All of the individual parcel declarations, plus either the manifest or the statement of account listing each export will provide proof of export for VAT purposes.

You can find further information on Parcelforce Worldwide International Services, on their website at www.parcelforce.com.

7.6 Exports by courier and fast parcel services

Courier and fast parcel operators specialise in the shipment of small consignments to overseas destinations within guaranteed times.

(a) Operators who do not issue separate certificates of shipment

Most courier and fast parcel operators do not issue separate certificates of shipment.

The invoice for moving small consignments for export from the EC, which routinely bears details of the unique air-waybill numbers for each shipment, represents normal commercial evidence of export. In addition, many express companies are able to offer a track and trace service via their websites where the movement of consignments can be traced through to the final destination. This information can be printed and can also be used to confirm that the goods have left the EC.

(b) Operators who use the system based upon a Despatch Pack

A few companies still use a documentary system based upon a Despatch Pack containing accounting data, a Customs export declaration and receipt copies of a house airway bill or consignment note. These packs are issued to customers to complete for each export shipment.

Goods being exported outside the EC must be fully and clearly described with the value shown on the export declaration. A Despatch Pack must be completed for each overseas address and consignee. The driver collecting the parcels will endorse the receipt copy and return it to the consignor. This, plus the statement of account issued by the express operator, listing each export shipment, will provide commercial proof of export.

(c) Use of more than one courier/fast parcel company

Due to the complexities of the movement of consignments within the courier/fast parcel environment, there is often more than one company involved in the handling and ultimate export of the goods. You as the UK supplier may not be certain as to which courier/fast parcel company has made the export declaration to Customs. Consequently it may be difficult to obtain official proof of export, leaving you to rely on the commercial evidence of export as described above. If the operator makes a bulk declaration when exporting the goods via another Member State, it may not be possible to print a travelling Copy 3 for the individual consignments of the SAD referred to in paragraph 7.3.

In these circumstances, you must use commercial evidence of export, typically fully completed transport documents.

However, where you, as the supplier, are certain that the export declaration has been made by a specific courier/fast parcel company you may rely on either commercial or official evidence as detailed in paragraphs 6.2 and 6.3.

(d) Overseas customer arranging the export by courier

If your overseas customer arranges for the goods to be exported by courier you should find out what proof of export they will be providing to allow you to zero-rate the supply. More information on what you should do is contained in paragraph 6.6.

7.7 Exports by rail

Rail contractors offer services by rail for parcels and full loads.

(a) Parcels

If you intend to export parcels by rail, you should establish what evidence of export will be provided to you by the rail contractor. This will normally be a consignment note such as a 5-part PIM/PIEX - International Consignment Note, copy 4 is the exporter's copy and receipt for the goods.

These receipted forms plus the railway statement of account listing each export provide your evidence of export for VAT purposes.

(b) Bulk cargo services

Rail contractors offer services for the movement of full loads in wagons, containers and swap bodies. Containers and swap bodies are handled by intermediaries who use their own consignment documentation. Full loads in wagons use the 5-part "Convention International des Marchandises par Chemin de Fer" (CIM) consignment note. This contains the "Uniform Rules concerning the contract for International Carriage of goods by rail".

In all cases, the exporter's copy of the consignment note endorsed with a railway stamp is your evidence of export.

7.8 Exports through packers

For goods exported under groupage arrangements, you must obtain a certificate of shipment (see paragraph 7.4) signed by the packer showing a full description of the goods packed for export - including quantity, weight, value, destination, and so on.

For single consignments you must obtain commercial evidence of shipment by road, rail, sea or air and a certificate of posting or equivalent evidence of export when exported by other means.

7.9 Exports through auctioneers

Auctioneers act in a number of ways. It is important that you check with the auctioneer before you sell your goods whether they are acting in their own name. You can find further information on the role of auctioneers in Notice 700 The VAT Guide and Notice 718/2 The VAT Auctioneers' Scheme.

(a) Auctioneer acting in your name

If you sell goods through an auctioneer who:

- is not acting in their own name, and
- exports the goods.

you may zero-rate your supply provided that you obtain a certificate of export from the auctioneer, in the form set out in paragraph 12.2 or paragraph 12.3 within three months of the date of the auction. The auctioneer must hold valid evidence of export for the goods.

(b) Auctioneer acting in own name

If you sell goods through an auctioneer who is acting in their own name, the goods are treated as being supplied to the auctioneer and must not be zero-rated by you as an export. The auctioneer will be able to zero-rate the onward supply in the normal way.

7.10 Exports from Customs, Excise and/or fiscal warehouses

A warehousekeeper who holds valid commercial transport evidence that the goods delivered from the warehouse have been exported may provide the registered owner of the goods with a signed and dated document certifying export. It must include the following information:

- name and address of the warehousekeeper
- order number, invoice number and date of transaction
- name and address of the owner of the goods
- details of the stock exported (description, quantity, value, and so on)
- name of the export vessel or aircraft flight prefix and number
- port or airport of loading
- date of sailing or departure
- destination of the goods
- bill of lading or air-waybill number (where appropriate)
- identifying number of the container or railway wagon (if used), and
- signature of the warehousekeeper and date.

7.11 Supplies to the Foreign and Commonwealth Office (FCO)

You can zero-rate the supply of goods ordered by British Embassies, High Commissions and diplomats abroad that are delivered to the FCO for export through diplomatic channels within three months of the time of supply. You as the supplier must keep a separate record of each transaction.

To evidence that the supply was made to an overseas person, you must be able to identify the destination of the goods. You should therefore retain documents which contain this information, for example the order. You must also obtain a certificate of receipt from the FCO within three months of the time of the supply of goods. The certificate may be on a copy of the sales invoice or on an itemised list, which you must keep to support your claim to zero-rating.

You must not zero-rate the supply of any other goods ordered by and delivered to the FCO for stock or general distribution.

7.12 Exports to the Channel Islands

Excise goods or goods subject to Customs controls (for example restricted goods) being exported to the Channel Islands will always require a SAD (Form C88) declaration. This may be made using the National Export System (NES).

In the case of goods not subject to Customs or Excise controls one of the following declaration procedures may be used:

- a bulk NES declaration by the shipping line supported by individual Consignment Note and Customs Declarations (CNCD), or
- individual NES declarations by exporters.

Further details may be found in Notice 275 Customs: export procedures.

At south coast ferry ports a combined CNCD with a supporting itemised schedule of goods exported may be used in place of the SAD and sea waybill for manifested freight.

A CNCD may be on an approved standard commercial document or a partly completed SAD.

Evidence of export for goods sent to the Channel Islands is made up of the following (as appropriate):

- official proof of export produced by NES – see section 5
- goods shipped by air – an authenticated master air-waybill or house air-waybill (see paragraph 7.1)
- goods carried as Merchandise in Baggage – a Customs certified copy 3 of the SAD (Form C88) (see paragraph 7.3)
- goods shipped through a freight forwarder – a certificate of shipment issued by the freight forwarder (see paragraph 7.4) or an authenticated copy of the CNCD
- goods shipped through a fast parcel or courier service – evidence as per paragraph 7.6, or
- goods shipped directly by the south coast ferry companies – an authenticated copy of the CNCD as described above.

7.13 Exports via EC member states

Where you send goods by road via for example Dover, across the EC before final export, or where you move goods from the UK to an airport in another Member State before final export, this is an export via an EC Member State.

If you export to non-EC countries via other EC Member States, you will require either official proof of export for VAT purposes (see paragraph 6.2) or commercial transport evidence (see paragraph 6.3) that the goods have left the EC to substantiate the zero-rating of the supplies.

7.14 Channel tunnel

The evidence of export procedures outlined above for exports via other EC Member States apply equally to goods transported via the Channel Tunnel.

The arrangements outlined in paragraph 7.7 cover goods carried on through-rail freight services through the Tunnel.

There are Merchandise in Baggage facilities at both the Waterloo International Terminal (for foot passengers) and at Ashford Inland Clearance Depot (for car and coach passengers joining the Tunnel at Cheriton).

8 EXTRA-STATUTORY CONCESSIONS (ESCS)

Two extra-statutory concessions exist which allow zero-rating of VAT on supplies of goods in specific circumstances. Further details may be found in Notice 48 Extra-Statutory Concessions.

8.1 Duty or tax-free shops (ESC 9.1)

(a) Can I zero-rate the supply of goods made from my "airside" duty or tax-free shop?

ESC 9.1 allows zero-rating of the supply of goods to be carried in the personal luggage of passengers flying directly out of the UK to a non-EC country.

If you operate a duty or tax-free shop at an airport, you can zero-rate the supply of goods for immediate export by travellers departing on flights to destinations outside the EC. Although it is the intending passenger who is exporting the goods, it is the retailer who is treated as the exporter for VAT purposes and therefore needs to evidence that the goods have been exported.

To zero-rate the supply you must provide us with evidence of the sale to an intending passenger for export to a third country.

At the point of sale you should check that:

- the traveller is departing directly to a destination outside the EC, and
- the goods are to be exported.

We must be able to verify the transaction. Acceptable evidence showing that the sale is to an entitled passenger is obtained from the airline boarding card or travel document. This clearly shows the names of passengers, the date of travel and the flight number/destination. Information from the boarding cards or travel documents presented by entitled passengers should be retained by retailers as part of their export evidence.

If you, as a retailer, are unsure about the acceptability of the evidence you propose to use you should contact our Helpline. Large businesses controlled by the Large Business Service (LBS) should contact their Customer Relationship Manager. Any agreement reached on acceptability of alternative evidence should be confirmed in writing.

(b) If the customer returns goods as defective can I zero-rate the replacement goods?

If, following the sale, the customer returns the goods as defective and you as the retailer are required to replace them, whether you charge VAT on the value of the replacement goods will depend upon their ultimate destination. If the replacement goods are to be exported they may be zero-rated, subject to the normal export rules. If they are delivered to an address within the UK or EC Member State the original zero-rate sale must be cancelled and the supply is subject to VAT at the appropriate rate.

You can find information on when you may zero-rate supplies to customers registered for VAT in another EC Member State in Notice 725 The Single Market.

Commentary—*De Voil Indirect Tax Service* **V4.338**.

8.2 Relief for marine fuel (ESC 9.2)

Extra Statutory Concession (ESC) 9.2 allows vessels engaged on commercial voyages within UK territorial waters (or within the limits of a port) to receive certain types of marine fuel VAT free.

You can zero-rate such supplies as ships' stores providing:

- you obtain, from the person to whom the marine fuel is to be supplied, a written declaration that the goods are for use as stores on a non-private voyage
- you obtain written confirmation from the master, owner or duly authorised agent of the vessel declaring that the fuel is solely for use on a named ship
- the fuel is sent direct to the ship or addressed and delivered to the master of a named vessel c/o the shipping line or agent, and

– you hold a receipt confirming delivery of the fuel on board the ship, signed by the master or other responsible officer.

The concession described above extends only to those supplies of fuel, which were zero-rated prior to 1 July 1990. It does not apply to petrol, Ultra Low Sulphur Diesel (ULSD) or lubricating oil.

Commentary—*De Voil Indirect Tax Service* **V4.321**.

9 EXPORTS BY RETAILERS

9.1 Export schemes for retailers

There are a number of exports schemes for retailers selling goods for export by private individuals.

(a) Retail Export Scheme (RES)

The Retail Export Scheme allows participating retailers to refund VAT on goods purchased by entitled customers. You should refer to the conditions laid down in Notice 704 VAT Retail exports.

(b) Personal Export Scheme for vehicles (PES)

You can zero-rate the supply of a new or second hand motor vehicle for export by your customer in certain circumstances. You should refer to the conditions in Notice 707 (VAT Personal Export Scheme).

(c) Sailaway Boat Scheme

The Sailaway Boat Scheme allows boats exported to final destinations outside the EC to be zero-rated for VAT purposes. You can find more details in Notice 703/2 Sailaway boats supplied for export outside the EC.

9.2 Retail exports shipped as freight or household effects

(a) Direct exports

If you, as retailer, arrange for goods to be exported outside the EC you may zero-rate the supply provided all the conditions in paragraph 3.3 are met.

(b) Indirect exports

If your overseas customer arranges for the export of the goods outside the EC you may zero-rate the supply provided all the conditions in paragraph 3.4 are met.

Commentary—*De Voil Indirect Tax Service* **V4.331–335**.

10 STORES FOR USE IN SHIPS, AIRCRAFT OR HOVERCRAFT TO DESTINATIONS OUTSIDE UK

Commentary—*De Voil Indirect Tax Service* **V4.321–322**.

10.1 What is meant by the term "stores"?

Stores are goods for use in a ship, aircraft or hovercraft and include:

- fuel
- goods for running repairs or maintenance, for example lubricants, spare and replacement parts
- goods for general use on board by the crew
- goods for sale by retail to passengers carried on the voyage or flight who intend to use the stores on board only.

10.2 What supplies are eligible for zero-rating?

You can zero-rate supplies of goods classed as "stores" under paragraph 10.1 for the fuelling and provisioning of vessels and aircraft providing:

- They are for use on a voyage or flight with a non-private purpose and with an eventual destination outside the UK. See paragraph 8.2 for details of an Extra Statutory Concession (ESC) covering supplies of marine fuel to vessels for voyages in home waters.
- They are shipped from the UK within three months of supply.
- The conditions outlined in paragraph 10.4 are met.

10.3 Supplies to registered shipping companies etc

If you make supplies to VAT registered shipping lines or airline operators they can choose to have:

- All supplies, including goods for shipment as stores on their ships or aircraft, delivered to their premises.
  In these circumstances you must charge VAT at the appropriate rate. The shipping or airline company can deduct input tax subject to the normal rules. (The subsequent transfer of the goods from their premises to the ship or aircraft for use as stores is not then a supply for VAT purposes).
- Supplies of stores made direct to foreign-going craft.
  You can zero-rate such supplies provided the goods are eligible for stores relief under paragraph 10.2, and the conditions in paragraph 10.4 are met.

When you receive an order for goods to be shipped as stores you must make sure that you receive clear instructions on how to deal with the supply.

10.4 Conditions for zero-rating supplies to foreign-going vessels and aircraft

Unless *all* these conditions are met there is no eligibility for zero-rating and you must account for VAT at the appropriate UK rate.

The text in this box has the force of law

You can zero-rate eligible supplies of goods to foreign-going vessels and aircraft providing:

- The person to whom the goods are supplied is the end user for example master of the vessel.
- The person to whom the goods are to be supplied declares in writing that the goods are for use as stores on a voyage or flight which is to be made for a non-private purpose.
- You obtain and hold a written order or confirmation given by the master, commander, owner or duly authorised agent of the ship or aircraft. This must include a declaration that the goods are solely for use as stores on a named ship or aircraft that is entitled to receive duty-free stores for the voyage in question, which is to an eventual destination outside the UK. Aircraft making through international flights are eligible to receive VAT-free stores even if the aircraft makes one or more stops in the UK in the course of such a flight.
- You send the goods—
  - direct to the ship or aircraft
  - through freight forwarders for consolidation and delivery direct to the ship or aircraft, or
  - addressed and delivered to the master of a named vessel c/o the shipping line or agent.
- You obtain and hold a receipt confirming delivery of the goods on board the ship or aircraft, signed by the master, commander or other responsible officer of the ship or aircraft. You can accept such a receipt signed by a responsible official of the airline concerned. However airlines using this facility must obtain prior written agreement from HM Revenue & Customs. They must confirm that the signatory is in a position to provide the receipt based on personal knowledge of flight details and that the airline will maintain documentation enabling HM Revenue & Customs staff to verify entitlement to relief.
- You have a certificate of export as described in paragraph 7.10 where your supplies are made direct from a warehouse not operated or owned by you to an eligible vessel or aircraft. The advice note issued by the warehousekeeper normally serves

this purpose.

Please note the conditions for zero-rating in the following specific circumstances:

- Where there is a supply chain, intermediaries must account for VAT at the appropriate rate.
- If you supply goods to a shore-side storage tank you may not zero-rate the supply *unless* your customer is the exporter of the goods and you hold the necessary evidence.

10.5 Supplies for sale in ships' shops and on board aircraft and for ships' slop chests

The arrangements in paragraphs 10.2, 10.3 and 10.4 apply to goods supplied for sale in ships' shops, and so on even though there may be no taxable supply at the time of shipment (for example transfer of own goods, supply on sale or return terms). Where goods have been shipped on a foreign-going ship or aircraft, any later sale of the goods will be a supply outside the UK and there will be no further VAT liability unless they are re-landed in the UK (see paragraph 10.6).

VAT is chargeable on goods sold on board a vessel on a coastwise journey or aircraft on an internal flight.

10.6 Re-landed stores

Where stores are supplied and subsequently re-landed in the UK these are treated as imports and you should follow the procedures in VAT Notice 702 Imports.

10.7 Supplies of mess and canteen stores for HM ships

(a) Conditions for zero-rating

The text in this box has the force of law

> You can zero-rate supplies of goods for use as mess and canteen stores on HM Ships which are about to leave for a foreign port or a voyage outside UK territorial waters of more than fifteen days duration. The goods must be ordered for the general use on board by members of the ship's company. The Commanding Officer must certify each order: "HMS. . . . . is deploying from the United Kingdom for service abroad on . . . . (date) calling at a foreign port or on a voyage outside territorial waters of more than fifteen days' duration and these stores are for use by members of the crew during the deployment".
>
> You must deliver the goods direct to the ship for loading on board, obtain a receipt for them on board and keep it to support your claim for zero-rating.

(b) Sale or return

If you supply duty-free goods on sale or return to messes in HM Ships you cannot zero-rate them for VAT purposes when they are sent out to the ship, as there is no taxable supply at that time. The taxable supply occurs only when the goods are adopted, that is when the customer pays for the goods or otherwise indicates his wish to keep them; or at the end of 12 months or any shorter period you have agreed for the goods to be bought or returned (see Notice 700 The VAT Guide). You are responsible for ensuring that the messes inform you promptly of when the adoption of the goods took place. If adoption occurs when the vessel is in UK territorial waters the supply is taxable, if outside there is no supply for VAT purposes. Commanders of HM Ships will provide suppliers with this information.

(c) Sales of goods in canteens and shops

Where there is no supply at the time of delivery on board, VAT is chargeable at the appropriate rate on sales of goods in canteens and shops on board HM Ships in UK ports or on coastwise voyages. If the ship is outside UK territorial waters any sale of goods is outside the scope of VAT and is taxable only if the goods are re-landed in the UK. Notice 700 The VAT Guide explains how to deal with this in your records and accounts.

11 RECORDS AND ACCOUNTING FOR VAT

11.1 What records do I need to keep?

Notice 700 The VAT Guide contains details of the records and accounts you should keep. In addition you should retain evidence of export as described in sections 6 and 7. It is important that you follow the accounting instructions explained in this section if you do not hold the evidence of export from the EC by the due date.

If you do not follow these rules, you will be liable to be assessed for VAT due on the supplies and may incur default interest and financial penalties as a result.

Commentary—*De Voil Indirect Tax Service* **V4.306, V5.201–211**.

11.2 How do I adjust my accounts if I do not receive evidence of export or if goods are not exported?

If you make an export you can zero-rate the supply in your records when the goods are supplied to your customer. But if you do not:

– obtain and hold the required evidence of export, or
– make sure the goods have been exported within the relevant time limit for the supply.

You must amend your VAT records and account for VAT on the taxable proportion of the invoiced amount or consideration you have received. For a VAT rate of 20 per cent the VAT element would be calculated at 1/6th.

When you amend your VAT records, you must make an entry equal to the tax on the supplies concerned on the "VAT PAYABLE" side of your VAT account. You must include this amount in Box 1 of your VAT return *for the period in which the relevant time limit expires*.

11.3 What if the goods are exported or I obtain evidence of export after I have accounted for VAT?

If the goods are subsequently exported and/or you later obtain evidence of export you can then zero-rate the supply and adjust your VAT account *for the period in which you obtained the evidence*. This is provided that the goods have not been used in the UK prior to export (unless specifically authorised by HM Revenue & Customs) and in the case of an *indirect export* – see paragraph 2.11 – the goods have been supplied to an overseas person (as defined in paragraph 2.4).

11.4 How do I account for exported goods, which are subsequently returned damaged?

Where export goods damaged after shipment are relanded in the UK they must be declared to HMRC. If you or a member of a salvage association subsequently sell the goods, the seller must account for VAT, at the appropriate UK rate, on the sale price.

Commentary—*De Voil Indirect Tax Service* **V4.339**.

11.5 How do I account for VAT on deposits and progress payments?

Deposits and progress payments are part payments towards the total cost of a supply received in advance of its completion and have the same VAT liability as the final supply. If the final supply is to be zero-rated as an export, these payments may also be zero-rated.

However, if the goods are not eventually exported or you fail to obtain valid evidence of export you must account for VAT on the total value of the supply, including any deposit, progress or stage payments, on your next VAT return.

VAT Notices

12 FORMS

12.1 Example of a certificate of shipment for embassies, High Commissions etc

Certificate of shipment

Date of issue:
Reference:

Supplier
VAT number
Supplier's invoice number and date
Port of loading
Port of shipment
Flight/sailing
Destination
AWB No
HAWB No
Bill of lading No
Sea-waybill No
Number of packages

Description of export goods	**Quantity**	**Weight**	**Value**

(Authorised Signatory)

12.2 Example of a Certificate of export for goods sold at auction and exported direct by the auctioneer as air or sea freight

I, ... (full name of signatory) certify that the article(s) detailed below and sold as Lot No(s) . . . . at auction by me on . . . . (date of sale) has/have* been exported from the EC on the undermentioned vessel/aircraft*:

Description of article(s)	*LOT No*	*Value £'s*

Name of export vessel, or aircraft flight prefix and number

Port or airport of loading . . . .

Date of sailing or departure . . . .

Destination . . . .

Bill of lading or air-waybill number (where appropriate) . . . .

Identifying number of container or railway wagon (if used) . . . .

. . . . (Signature of auctioneer)

Date . . . .

*Delete as necessary

12.3 Certificate of export for goods sold at auction and exported direct by the auctioneer by parcel post or courier service

I, ... (full name of signatory) certify that the article(s) detailed below and sold as Lot No(s) . . . . at auction by me on . . . . (date of sale) has/have* been exported from the EC by post/courier service*:

Description of article(s)	*LOT No*	*Value £'s*

Place of posting . . . .

Method of posting (parcel/letter and so on) . . . .

Date of posting . . . .

Destination . . . .

Certificate(s) of posting numbers held by me . . . .

. . . . (Signature of auctioneer)

Date . . . .

*Delete as necessary

13 TRADE ASSOCIATION CONTACT DETAILS

You can get further guidance about the commercial aspects of specific exports from freight forwarders, shipping companies or airlines at the appropriate ports or airports.

The Trade Associations listed below may also provide advice:

Automated Customs and International Trade Association (ACITA)
20-22 Richfield Avenue
Reading
Berkshire RG1 8EQ

Association of International Courier and Express Services (AICES)
Global Logistics Centre
Horton Road
Colnbrook
Berkshire SL3 0DL

British Exporters Association (BEXA)
Broadway House
Tothill Street
London SW1H 9NQ

British International Freight Association (BIFA)
Redfern House
Browells Lane
Feltham
Middlesex W13 7EP

Customs Practitioners Group
100 New Bridge Street
London EC4V 6JA

Electronic Data Interchange Association
148 Buckingham Palace Road
London SW1W 9TR

Freight Transport Association (FTA)
Hermes House
St John's Road
Tunbridge Wells
Kent TN4 9UZ

The Institute of Export
Minerva Business Park
Lynch Wood
Peterborough
Cambridgeshire PE2 6FT

Business Information
British Standards Institution
389 Chiswick High Road
London W4 4AL

United Kingdom Oil Industry Taxation Committee (UKOITC)
Total House
4 Lancer Square
London W8 4EW

NOTICE 703/1
SUPPLY OF FREIGHT CONTAINERS FOR EXPORT OR REMOVAL FROM THE UNITED KINGDOM

February 2010

Commentary—*De Voil Indirect Tax Service* **V4.323**.

3.2 CONDITIONS FOR ZERO-RATING THE SALE OF A CONTAINER IN THE UK FOR INDIRECT EXPORT FROM THE EC

For VAT purposes, an indirect export occurs when an overseas customer or their agent collects, or arranges for the collection of the container from the supplier and then exports it outside the EC.

The following requirement has the force of law

To zero-rate the sale of a freight container for indirect export, you must obtain a written undertaking from your customer that:

- the container will be exported from the EC, and
- will not be used within the EC except for:
  - a single domestic journey before export of the container, on which inland freight may be carried between two points within the UK. This is allowable only if the route brings the container reasonably directly from the point of supply to the place where it is to be loaded with export cargo or exported;
  - international movements of goods, which may include a journey within the UK for the purpose of loading or unloading the goods;
- records accounting for the use of the container will be maintained, as specified in paragraph 3.3.

The above conditions, where met, allow a chain of supplies to be zero-rated.

3.3 RECORDS YOU NEED TO KEEP IF YOU ARE SUPPLIED WITH A ZERO-RATED CONTAINER FOR EXPORT

The following requirement has the force of law

If you are supplied with a zero-rated container you must keep sufficient records to satisfy HM Revenue & Customs that:

- the container has not been used in the EC (except as allowed under paragraph 3.2)
- it has been exported, or
- you have sold or leased it to someone else and have obtained the undertaking referred to in paragraph 3.2.

4. CONDITIONS FOR ZERO-RATING THE SALE OF CONTAINERS TO VAT REGISTERED CUSTOMERS IN OTHER MEMBER STATES

This section should be read in conjunction with Notice 725 "The Single Market".

The following requirement has the force of law

The supply of a container for removal to another EC Member State is zero-rated provided that all the following conditions are met:

- you obtain your EC customer's VAT registration number (with a 2- digit country code prefix) which you must show on your VAT invoice
- the container is sent from the UK to a destination in another EC Member State, and
- within three months of the date of supply, you obtain and hold valid commercial documentary evidence that the container has been removed from the UK. Examples of acceptable evidence are listed in Notice 725 The Single Market.

If your customer is not registered for VAT in another EC Member State, or all of the above conditions are not met, you cannot zero-rate your supply and you must account for tax on the container in the UK.

If your EC customer collects or arranges for the collection of the container and its removal from the UK, you should confirm with your customer how the container is to be removed, and what evidence of removal will be available to you. You may also wish to consider taking a deposit from your customer (equal to the amount of VAT you will have to account for if the conditions for zero-rating are not met) if you believe you will not be able to obtain evidence of the type listed in Notice 725.

WHERE BOTH YOU AND YOUR CUSTOMER BELONG IN THE UK

You must treat the supply as being made in the UK and must charge VAT on it. Your customer may then recover input tax subject to the normal rules (see Notice 700 The VAT Guide).

The following requirement has the force of law

However, if your customer is to export the container from the EC, you may zero-rate the lease of the container provided that you, as the supplier, obtain from your customer a written undertaking (as set out in paragraph 3.2).

NOTICE 703/2
SAILAWAY BOATS SUPPLIED FOR EXPORT OUTSIDE THE EC

January 2012

This notice cancels and replaces Notices 703/2 (May 2010). Details of any changes to those notices can be found in paragraph 1.1.

1 SAILAWAY BOATS SUPPLIED FOR EXPORT OUTSIDE THE EUROPEAN UNION

1.1 What is this notice about?

This notice explains the procedures for zero-rating the supply of a "sailaway" boat. It includes information that was previously contained in Notice 703/3 Sailaway boat scheme which is cancelled. The notice has been changed because UK residents can no longer purchase a boat using the scheme

Commentary—*De Voil Indirect Tax Service* **V4.335**.

1.2 What is the scheme?

It is a way for an entitled person to buy a boat for export from the European Union (EU) without paying VAT. Paragraphs 1.3 and 1.4 explain which boat purchases are eligible and who is an entitled person respectively.

1.3 What is the definition of a "sailaway boat"?

A "sailaway" boat is defined as one which is to be—

– delivered to the buyer or their authorised skipper within the EU, and
– exported under its own power to a destination outside the VAT territory of the EU.

1.4 Who can use this scheme?

The scheme can only be used for the private purchase of a boat for private purposes by—

– An overseas visitor who intends to export the boat under its own power to a destination outside the EU within six months of the date of delivery. This is normally the date the boat leaves the manufacturer or supplier.

This scheme must not be used to purchase boats used for commercial purchases.

Before 1 January 2012 UK residents who intended to export the boat to a destination outside the EU could also use the scheme, but they are no longer eligible. However, UK residents may be able to purchase a boat VAT-free provided that the seller arranges the direct export of the boat to a destination outside the EU. See paragraph 1.6 and Notice 703 Exports and removals of goods from the United Kingdom for conditions.

1.5 Are all the boat purchases eligible under the scheme?

No. The scheme cannot be used for—

– Boats exported on a trailer or for exporting parts or accessories.
– Commercial supplies. Commercial sales may still be zero-rated for VAT purposes but under different arrangements – see Notice 703 "Exports and removals of goods from the UK".
– A new boat to be taken to another EU Member State. See Notice 728 "New means of transport". Or
– Or boats whose final destination is one of the EU Member States listed below:
  – Austria, Belgium, Bulgaria, Cyprus*, The Czech Republic, Denmark, Estonia, Finland, France including Monaco, Germany, Greece, Hungary, Republic of Ireland, Italy, Latvia, Lithuania, Luxembourg, Malta, The Netherlands, Poland, Portugal including the Azores and Madeira, Romania, The Slovak Republic, Slovenia, Spain and the Balearic Islands, Sweden, and the United Kingdom including the Isle of Man.

* The European Commission in December 2003 advised that the application of the 6th VAT Directive (Directive 77/388/EEC of 17 May 1977) shall be suspended in those areas of Cyprus

in which the Government of the Republic of Cyprus does not exercise effective control. From 1 May 2004 goods to these destinations continue to be eligible for zero-rating as exports.

1.6 Can direct exports be included in this scheme?

If the seller arranges delivery of a boat either on a trailer or by using a skipper employed by them to a destination outside the EU, then they must not use this scheme. If the boat is not to be used in the EU before it is exported, the seller can arrange for the boat to be delivered direct to a destination outside the EU free of VAT. For further information about direct exports see Notice 703 Exports and removals of goods from the United Kingdom.

1.7 Does the scheme include boats that are taken to other Member States of the EU?

No. Boats supplied for private use that are removed from the UK to another EU country cannot be supplied under the scheme described in this notice. For details of how they can be supplied free of VAT see Notice 728 "New means of transport".

1.8 Does the scheme cover parts and accessories?

No. But parts and accessories may be supplied under the Retail Export Scheme. Notice 704 "Retail Exports" explains how to deal with sales made under the Retail Export Scheme.

2 INFORMATION FOR SELLERS

2.1 What do I have to do prior to the boat being supplied?

Before a boat is supplied you must—

- ensure that the buyer is entitled to use the scheme (see paragraph 1.4)
- ensure that the buyer intends to export the boat from the EU within the permitted six month time limit as outlined in paragraph 1.4
- give the buyer a copy of this notice and an application form VAT436, and
- ensure the form VAT436 is fully completed by you and the buyer, and Part 2 is submitted to the Personal Transport Unit (PTU) at least two weeks before the boat is delivered to the customer.

All notifications should be serially numbered in the top right hand corner and submitted to the PTU at the following address:

HM Revenue & Customs
Personal Transport Unit
Priory Court
St John's Road
Dover
CT17 9SH
Phone: 01304 664171
Fax: 01304 664179

Please ensure that notifications are correct and complete before you accept them. An incorrect or incomplete notification will be returned for correction, and this may delay the delivery of the boat.

The PTU will be pleased to provide any help or advice on the purchase of a sailaway boat.

Commentary—*De Voil Indirect Tax Service* **V4.335**.

2.2 What should I do at the time of sale?

At the time of sale you must—

- ensure that the buyer knows that he/she must not dispose, or attempt to dispose of the boat in the EU by hire, pledge as security*, sale, gift or any other means:
  - keep a separate record of the sale, and
  - agree how any refund of the deposited VAT will be paid (see paragraph 2.6).

*The boat's documents may only be used as security that is required by the finance house for the purchase of the boat. The boat must not be pledged as security for a separate purchase, for example a car, flat or house.

2.3 What forms have to be used?

You will need to prove that the boat has been removed from the EU before you can zero-rate the sale. The uses of the forms vary according to whether a boat departs to a destination outside the EU directly from the UK or via another Member State, see paragraphs 3.3 and 3.4.

The forms needed are:

Form VAT436 "Notification of VAT-free purchase of a Sailaway boat and buyer's declaration".

Original copy 1	– copy for certification by a Customs officer
Copy 2	– Customs copy
Copy 3	– buyer's copy
Copy 4	– seller's copy
Form C88 "Single Administrative Document	– copies 1 to 3
Copy 1	– Community transit copy where applicable (seller to take a copy for their own records)
Copy 2	for UK Customs
Copy 3	– for certification when the boat finally leaves the EU.
Form C1331 "Notice of intended departure	– to advise departure from the UK".

2.4 What will happen if the order is cancelled?

If, after the notification is processed, the order for the boat is cancelled by the buyer before delivery, you should immediately notify the PTU of—

- the name of the buyer
- details of the boat, and
- the reference number shown on the form VAT436.

2.5 How do I account for VAT?

You must keep a separate record of all boats sold under the scheme. The sales invoice must clearly show that the supply of the boat was made under the Sailaway boat scheme.

If you do not obtain and hold evidence to show that the boat was exported within the six month time limit (see paragraph 1.4), you must account for VAT accordingly:

- if you have taken a deposit of the VAT due, then it should be brought to account, or
- if you have not taken a deposit you must amend your VAT records and account for VAT on the taxable proportion of the invoiced amount of consideration you have received, for a VAT rate of 20 per cent the VAT element is calculated at 1/6.

When you amend your VAT records you must make an entry equal to the tax on the supplies concerned on the "VAT payable" side of your account. You include this amount in box 1 of your VAT return for the period in which the time limit expires.

2.6 Should I take a deposit of VAT?

The boat is not eligible for zero-rated VAT status until you receive form VAT436 certified by the Customs office at the place of final departure from the EU. You are, therefore, strongly advised to treat any sale of a boat under the scheme as liable to VAT until you have received the certified form VAT436. You may wish to ask the buyer for a deposit equal to the amount of VAT, to be returned when the required evidence of export is received.

If you do not receive the necessary evidence of export you will have to account for the VAT due – *even if you did not charge it at the point of sale.*

2.7 What do I do when I receive the certified evidence of export?

When you receive the Customs certified evidence of export, you should refund any deposit to the buyer by the method agreed, and account for the sale in your VAT records as explained in paragraph 2.5.

2.8 What if I receive evidence of export after I have accounted for VAT?

If you later obtain evidence that the boat was exported from the EU within the permitted time limits, you can zero-rate the supply and refund any deposit and adjust your VAT account for the period in which you obtained the evidence. You should treat the transaction as a credit in your VAT records. See Notice 700 "The VAT Guide".

2.9 Can I use the scheme for supplies destined for the Channel Islands?

The Channel Islands are outside the EU VAT area and therefore qualify as a final destination for boats supplied VAT-free for export. EU residents who register VAT-free boats in the Channel Islands cannot claim VAT-free temporary importation of such boats into an EU Member State. VAT is payable on these importations. However subject to their meeting the conditions for temporary importation, private persons resident in the Channel Islands may be entitled to import their own boats for their own personal use for up to 18 months, without payment of import VAT.

3 INFORMATION FOR BUYERS

3.1 How do I use the scheme?

Before purchasing the boat you should make sure that the seller operates the scheme. The seller will check that you are entitled to use the scheme and ask you to complete form VAT436.

Commentary—*De Voil Indirect Tax Service* **V4.335**.

3.2 Can I use the boat before it is exported?

Yes, but you must not—

- hire the boat
- give it away
- offer it for sale
- use it as security, except as part of any financial arrangement for the purchase of the boat, or
- dispose of it in any other way while in the EU.

If the boat is re-imported or returns to the EU at any time, you must inform the nearest Customs office of its arrival.

3.3 What must I do if I am leaving the UK directly for a destination outside the EU?

You must—

- Ensure that the boat is exported within six months of the date of delivery (see paragraph 1.4).
- Complete form C1331 Notice of intended departure.
- Make the boat available for inspection by Customs at exportation. Where possible this should be arranged in advance with the Customs at the port of exportation. Contact details can be found in Notice 8 "Sailing your pleasure craft to and from the United Kingdom".
- Take the completed form VAT436 and C1331 to the Customs office nearest the place of departure. Customs will retain the form C1331 and sign and stamp form VAT436 to show that the boat has been declared for exportation. The certified form will be returned to you.
- Return the certified form VAT436 to the seller. If the seller has given you a stamped addressed envelope, Customs may agree to return the form on your behalf.

3.4 What must I do if I am calling into another Member State before finally exporting the boat from the EU?

You must:

- Ensure that the boat is exported within six months of the date of delivery (see paragraph 1.4).
- Take the completed forms C88 (copies 2 and 3) and VAT436 to the UK Customs office nearest the place of departure from the UK. Customs will keep copy 2 of the form C88 and return copy 3, together with form VAT436, to you.

- Take copy 3 of the form C88 and the form VAT436 to the Customs office at the place of final departure from the EU for certification.
- Return the certified form C88 and form VAT436 to the seller.

The seller should ensure that you understand that they cannot zero-rate the supply of the boat and make the refund of VAT until they have received the Customs certified documents.

3.5 How do I get the deposit for VAT back?

The seller will refund any deposit of VAT by the method that they have agreed with you. They will be able to do this as soon as they have received the certified forms VAT436 and C88.

3.6 What should I do if I do not receive the deposit back?

If you do not receive the refund within a reasonable period of time, you should contact the seller. HM Revenue & Customs (HMRC) is not responsible for refunding the deposit for VAT.

3.7 What if I want to re-import a VAT-free boat into the EU?

If a boat that was supplied tax free at purchase is brought back to the EU it must be declared to Customs in the Member State of importation. The seller should ensure that you are fully aware of the need to make an import declaration. VAT will be payable unless some other relief is available.

YOUR RIGHTS AND OBLIGATIONS

Your Charter explains what you can expect from us and what we expect from you. For more information go to www.hmrc.gov.uk/charter/.

PUTTING THINGS RIGHT

If you are unhappy with our service, please contact the person or office you have been dealing with. They will try to put things right. If you are still unhappy, they will tell you how to complain.

If you want to know more about making a complaint go to www.hmrc.gov.uk and under quick links, select Complaints.

HOW WE USE YOUR INFORMATION

HMRC is a Data Controller under the Data Protection Act 1998. We hold information for the purposes specified in our notification to the Information Commissioner, including the assessment and collection of tax and duties, the payment of benefits and the prevention and detection of crime, and may use this information for any of them.

We may get information about you from others, or we may give information to them. If we do, it will only be as the law permits to—

- check the accuracy of information
- prevent or detect crime
- protect public funds.

We may check information we receive about you with what is already in our records. This can include information provided by you, as well as by others, such as other government departments or agencies and overseas tax and customs authorities. We will not give information to anyone outside HMRC unless the law permits us to do so. For more information go to www.hmrc.gov.uk and look for Data Protection Act within the Search facility.

NOTICE 704
VAT: RETAIL EXPORTS

2004 *(with Update 1)*.

This notice cancels and replaces Notice 704 (July 2003). Details of any changes to the previous version can be found in paragraph 1.2 of this notice.

Regulation 131 of the VAT Regulations 1995 sets out conditions for using the Retail Export Scheme. This regulation also gives the Commissioners power to impose further conditions which must be met to allow a supply to be zero-rated. Parts of this notice have the force of law under that regulation. These paragraphs are indicated by three asterisks (***) at the beginning and end of the paragraph.

EXAMPLE:

The following text has the force of law

There is no facility to have your refund document stamped in your country of destination

. . .

Commentary—*De Voil Indirect Tax Service* **V4.331**.

1 INTRODUCTION

1.1 What is this notice about?

This notice explains when supplies of goods sold by VAT registered retailers to entitled persons for personal use and exported as accompanied baggage can be zero-rated. In particular, it sets out the conditions that must be complied with by retailers and entitled customers using the VAT Retail Export Scheme.

1.2 What's changed?

The notice has been rewritten to improve readability. In addition, the scheme and conditions have been reviewed and changed and you are strongly recommended to read through this notice to understand where changes have been made. The main changes have been introduced to:

- take account of European Community (EC) enlargement from 1 May 2004 (covered in update 1, issued February 2004);
- limit purchases under the scheme by overseas students and migrant workers to the end of their stay in the EC;
- include the new invoicing requirements arising from implementation of the EC VAT Invoicing Directive; and
- set out conditions for retailers who complete refund forms after the date of sale.

You can access details of any changes to this notice since November 2004 either on our Internet website at www.hmce.gov.uk or by telephoning the Helpline on 0300 200 3700.

This notice and others mentioned are available both on paper and on our website.

1.3 Who should read this notice?

This notice is intended for retailers and entitled customers.

1.4 What is the legal status of this notice?

Article 15 of the EC Sixth VAT Directive states that Member States shall lay down conditions "for the purpose of ensuring the correct and straightforward application of such exemptions (zero-rating) and preventing any evasion, avoidance or abuse". Under United Kingdom VAT law, the Commissioners of Customs and Excise may specify conditions in regulations or otherwise impose conditions to meet this requirement.

The VAT Regulations 1995 and this notice lay down the conditions for the VAT Retail Export Scheme which must be met in full for a supply of goods for export outside the EC to be zero-rated. As these conditions have legal status, some legal wording has been necessary but plain English has been used wherever possible.

Text with three asterisks at the beginning and end of the paragraph has the force of law.

1.5 Where can travellers obtain further information?

Retailers and travellers may obtain further information and advice from the Helpline on: 0300 200 3700; or +44 20 8929 0152 for international callers.

See "Further help and advice" on the inside front cover for full details. This notice and others mentioned are available in hard copy from the National Advice Service and on our website.

A simplified notice aimed specifically at travellers, Notice 704/1 Tax Free Shopping: VAT Refunds for travellers departing from the European Community (EC) highlights the main aspects of the scheme. Notice 704/1 is available in various languages.

Tourist and travel organisations as well as the VAT refund companies distribute information about the VAT Retail Export Scheme.

(Please note that whilst retail export schemes operate throughout the EC they are regulated by the laws of the individual Member States and may differ in significant details from the scheme in the UK. Travellers wishing to purchase goods in another EC Member State should contact the Customs or tax authorities of the Member State for detailed information and advice.)

2 GENERAL PRINCIPLES

2.1 What is the VAT Retail Export Scheme?

The VAT Retail Export Scheme allows:

- certain customers (see paragraph 2.4) to receive a refund of VAT paid on goods exported to destinations outside the European Community (EC) subject to conditions detailed at paragraph 2.3; and
- retailers to zero-rate goods sold to entitled customers when they have the necessary evidence of export and have refunded the VAT to the customer.

This is a voluntary scheme and retailers do not have to operate it. Those who do must ensure that all the conditions set out in this notice are met.

2.2 Is there a minimum sales value?

No. Although retailers may set a minimum sales value below which they will not operate the scheme.

2.3 What conditions apply to the scheme?

The following text has the force of law

***Retailers and refund companies (see paragraph 5.5) may only operate the VAT Retail Export Scheme when they comply with the conditions set out in this notice. Briefly these are:

- the customer must be entitled to use the scheme (see paragraph 2.4);
- the goods must be eligible to be purchased under the scheme (see paragraph 2.6);
- the customer must make the purchase in person and complete the form at the retailer's premises in full (see paragraph 3.1 and 7.4.2);
- the goods must be exported from the EC by the last day of the third month following that in which the goods were purchased;
- the customer must send the retailer or the refund company evidence of export stamped by Customs on an official version of Form VAT 407, an approved version of Form VAT 407 or an officially approved invoice (see Section 4); and
- the retailer or the refund company must not zero-rate the supply until the VAT has been refunded to the customer (see paragraph 5.2).***

2.3.1 Can the time limit for export be extended?

No. The goods must be exported from the EC by the last day of the third month following that in which the goods were purchased.

The following text has the force of law

Retailers and refund companies must not zero-rate goods exported after the last day of the third month following the month in which the goods were purchased-even if the VAT refund document has been stamped in error by a UK or other EC Customs officer.

2.4 Who can buy goods under the scheme?

2.4.1 Overseas visitors

An overseas visitor is a traveller (including a member of the crew of a ship or aircraft) who is not established in the EC. This means a person:

– whose domicile or habitual place of residence is not situated within the EC. A person's "domicile or habitual residence" is the place entered as such on their valid passport, identity card or other acceptable document, such as a driving licence. *The customer must prove their eligibility to use the scheme by providing one or more of these documents;* and
– who intends to leave the UK for a final destination outside the EC, with the goods, by the last day of the third month following that in which the goods were purchased (for example, goods purchased on 1 June must be exported by 30 September); and
who exports the goods having produced them, their receipts, and the VAT refund document to a Customs officer at the point of departure from the EC.

2.4.2 Overseas visitors studying or working in the UK

Overseas visitors (see paragraph 2.4.1) entering the UK as students or migrant workers are only entitled to purchase goods under the scheme during the last 4 months of their stay in the UK. Such visitors will have been issued with a pre-entry visa from the UK and in the case of work periods of 6 months or more a separate work permit document is issued in the UK. The visa is contained in the overseas person's passport and shows the start and end date for the study or work period authorised. *Retailers should ask to see the visa or work permit before selling goods under the scheme.*

The customer most prove their eligibility to use the scheme by providing evidence that the period of their visit is ending and must:

– intend to leave the EC with the goods by the last day of the third month following that in which the goods were purchased; and
– having left the EC remain outside the EC for a minimum period of 12 months; and
– export the goods having produced them, their receipts, and the VAT refund document to a Customs officer at the point of departure from the EC.

2.4.3 Entitled EC residents

For the purposes of this scheme only, a customer who is established in the EC but intends to permanently leave the EC for a minimum period of 12 months may also be treated as an overseas visitor. To qualify under this provision, the customer must:

– intend to leave the UK with the goods by the last day of the third month following that in which the goods were purchased for an immediate destination outside the EC; and
– remain outside the EC for a period of at least 12 months. The customer must prove their eligibility to use the scheme by providing evidence of their intention to remain outside the EC for at least 12 months. Typically this evidence would be one of the following: overseas work permit, approved visa application, residency permit; and
– export the goods having produced them, their receipts, and the VAT refund document to a Customs officer at the point of departure from the EC.

2.5 Which countries are in the EC?

The VAT territory of the EC is made up of 25 Member States [(27 from 1 January 2007)], including some territories with which certain countries have links. Goods cannot be purchased under this scheme for removal to another Member State. Details of the fiscal (VAT) territory of the EC and of the special territories that are outside the EC for VAT purposes are in Section 9 of this notice.

Note—Para 2.5 amended by Update 1, January 2007.

2.6 What goods can be sold under the scheme?

The following text has the force of law

***Standard-rated goods and lower-rated goods with the exception of those listed below may be sold under the scheme:

- new and second hand motor vehicles for personal export (see Notice 705 Buyer's guide to personal exports of motor vehicles to destinations outside the EC);
- boats sold to visitors who intend to sail them to a destination outside the EC (see Notice 703/2 Sailaway boats supplied for export outside the EC);
- goods over £600 (excluding VAT) in value exported for business purposes (see Notice 703 Export of goods from the United Kingdom);
- goods that will be exported as freight or unaccompanied baggage (see Notice 703 Export of goods from the United Kingdom);
- goods requiring an export licence (but antiques can be sold under the scheme even if they require an export licence);
- unmounted gemstones;
- bullion (over 125g, 2.75 troy ounces or 10 Tolas);
- goods for consumption in the EC-no certification of export will be given for used consumable items, for example, perfume which is wholly or partly consumed in the EC; and
- goods purchased by mail order including those purchased over the Internet (see paragraph 2.8).

Zero-rated goods such as books and children's clothing cannot be sold under the scheme.***

2.7 Can retailers exclude certain goods from the scheme?

Yes, they can if they wish. They do not have to operate the scheme for all lines of goods that they sell.

2.8 Can the scheme be used for sales by mail order or goods sold over the Internet?

No. Goods sold to entitled persons by mail order or over the Internet will fall within the export rules set out in Notice 703 Export of goods from the United Kingdom. However, a mail order company or an Internet retailer with a retail outlet can use the scheme for goods sold from that outlet provided they comply with all the conditions set out in this notice.

2.9 Can the scheme be used for services?

No. The scheme is for the sale of goods only. The scheme cannot be used for services supplied to customers such as hotel accommodation, meals and car hire. This applies even where services are sold with the goods, for example labour costs for fitting spare parts to a motor vehicle. Where a vehicle brought into the UK for the use of the overseas visitor requires repairs, the sale of the spare parts only and not the cost of fitting can be included in the scheme.

But see Notice 703 Export of goods from the United Kingdom for guidance on what to do in the case of a vehicle owned by an overseas person and temporarily imported for work. Extended warranty work may not be zero-rated under the VAT Retail Export Scheme.

3 MAKING A SALE UNDER THE VAT RETAIL EXPORT SCHEME

As a retailer, you are strongly advised to keep a stock of VAT Notices 704 and 704/1 to help you explain the scheme to customers who may not have obtained a notice for themselves.

3.1 What to do at the time of sale

Please note that for you to comply with the conditions of the scheme your customer must attend in person at the time of the sale although a third party may pay for the goods. There is no facility under this scheme for a representative to attend in place of the entitled person at the time of the sale.

When customers ask to use the scheme you must:

Step	*Procedure*
1	Check that they are entitled to use the scheme (see paragraph 2.4);
2	Check that the goods are eligible for the scheme (see paragraph 2.6);
3	Check that the customer intends to leave the EC with the goods for a final destination outside the EC by the last day of the third month following that in which the goods were purchased;

Step	*Procedure*
4	Fill in a VAT refund document. A responsible member of staff should complete the document. Ensure all sections are fully completed, unused lines are ruled through and the customer and retailer declarations are signed at the time of the sale (see paragraph 4.2 for full details).

In addition give your customer a copy of Notice 704/1 and:

– agree with your customer how the refund will be made. (It would be useful to provide your customer with a reply paid envelope for the refund document to be returned after stamping by Customs);
– explain about any administrative fees;
– mark your customer's sales receipt to indicate that the goods have been included on a VAT refund document. For example: "VAT Export";
– explain that no refunds will be made on items (such as perfume) wholly or partly consumed in the EC;
– advise them to produce their refund document to the Customs officer for stamping at the point of departure from the EC. Explain that failure to do so will mean that a refund will not be paid. The goods and receipts must also be available for inspection if required. (See paragraph 3.4 if the customer is departing the EC on a through (transit) flight);
– advise them to allow plenty of time in which to produce their goods and refund form prior to departure. This is particularly important if they are exporting goods in hold baggage as they may need to allow up to two hours in addition to their advised check in time in case of queues;
– advise them to carry items of high value, for example, jewellery, furs, cameras, watches, silverware, laptop computers and small antiques in their hand baggage; and
– you may also wish to advise your customer to take a photocopy of the VAT refund document once it has been stamped by Customs.

3.2 Refund documents

When you make a sale under the scheme to an entitled person going to a final destination outside the EC you must complete a VAT refund document. The document can be a Form VAT 407 or an officially approved invoice that both you and your customer must sign at the time of the sale.

The document must be the original signed by you or your representative and by your customer-photocopies will not be accepted by Customs at export.

3.3 Issuing VAT 407 Forms

Blank VAT 407 forms must not be issued to members of the public. They must only be issued to VAT registered retailers who operate the VAT Retail Export Scheme.

3.4 Producing goods and refund documents to Customs

You should give customers a copy of Notice 704/1 and advise them that:

– they must produce the VAT refund document to the Customs officer at the point of departure from the EC. The goods and receipts must also be available for inspection if required. The Customs officer will stamp the refund document to show that the goods have been exported and return it to the customer; and
– they should send back to you or to the refund company the refund documents stamped by the UK or EC Customs officer. They should use the reply paid envelope you provide, or hand the documents to the cash refund booth, if appropriate (see paragraph 6.4).

Remember, whilst a single refund document is acceptable, it is recommended that you issue separate VAT refund documents (but make only one administrative charge) if the customer intends to carry some goods in hand baggage and other goods in hold baggage. This is particularly important if the customer is leaving on a through (transit) flight via another EC airport because the goods in hold baggage must be declared before check in, whilst the goods in hand baggage must be declared at the final point of departure from the EC.

3.5 Goods not exported

When customers present the VAT refund documents to the UK or other EC Customs officer, they are making a declaration that all the goods shown on the document are being exported from the EC. Customers sometimes decide not to export goods purchased under the scheme.

You should inform your customer that any goods listed on the VAT refund document not exported from the EC must be clearly *deleted* from the document *before* it is presented to a UK or EC Customs officer for stamping. It is a Customs offence to make a false declaration.

3.6 Charging for administrative or handling expenses

If you intend to deduct an amount from the refund due, to cover administrative or handling expenses, the amount of the administration fee and net refund due must be shown clearly on the VAT refund document. You are strongly advised to explain this charge clearly to your customers when they buy the goods to avoid subsequent confusion or misunderstanding.

3.7 Refunds to customers

When you receive a VAT refund document stamped by UK or other EC Customs, check that all goods have been exported from the EC by the last day of the third month following that in which the goods were purchased.

Where they have, you should make any refund due to your customer by the method agreed at the time of sale.

You cannot zero-rate the sale unless you have a stamped VAT refund document showing that the goods have been exported within the time limit and can show that the refund has been made to your customer.

Refund forms stamped outside the EC are not to be accepted as evidence of export under any circumstances.

4 COMPLETION AND CONTROL OF REFUND FORMS

You may use a Form VAT 407 or adapted invoice for the scheme.

4.1 Form VAT 407

If you use the Form VAT 407 the following versions can be used:

- Form VAT 407 issued by Customs, available free of charge from the National Advice Service;
- your own version of the Form VAT 407, containing the same information as the Customs' version and approved beforehand by Customs; or
- a refund company's version of the Form VAT 407, containing the same information as the Customs' version and approved beforehand by Customs.

4.2 How to complete Form VAT 407

When completing a Form VAT 407 the following instructions must be followed.

PART	Completed by	Procedure
A	Customer	Make sure your customer completes this part legibly in full at the time of sale and signs the declaration.
B	Retailer	(a) Give a full and accurate description of the goods quoting identification numbers, serial numbers or other identifying marks for example hallmarks, together with the quantity (and weight in the case of jewellery) of goods sold. Descriptions such as stock numbers, "see invoice attached", "Jewellery" or "Designer goods" are not acceptable. The description must be clear enough to allow the UK or EC Customs officer to readily identify the goods. (b) Cross through any unused lines on the form.

PART	Completed by	Procedure
		(c) Show – the total amount payable including VAT in both words and figures; – the amount of VAT included in the price; – the amount of any administration fee that will be deducted from the refund; and – the amount of refund that will be paid to the customer.
C	Retailer	(a) Insert the full name of your business, address and VAT number; (b) Insert the date the goods were sold to the customer; and (c) the declaration must be signed either by yourself or another responsible person in your business.
D	Customs Officer	At the point of departure from the EC a Customs officer must stamp the form to validate the export. (Whilst desirable, it is not essential the Customs officer signs the form.)

Customs officers may refuse to stamp refund forms completed incorrectly or not completed in full. For example, forms showing inadequate descriptions of goods may be rejected.

4.3 Officially approved invoice

If you do not use one of the versions of Form VAT 407 described at paragraph 4.1 you may use an officially approved invoice. You should be aware that if you do use an officially approved invoice you must meet the requirements of invoicing legislation. The invoice must include the details set out at paragraph 4.3.1.

4.3.1 What general information is required on an invoice?

Where the total consideration for a supply (including VAT) is less than £250 a simplified invoice may be issued. Simplified invoices must show:

- your name, address and VAT registration number;
- the time of supply;
- a description sufficient to identify the goods supplied;
- the total amount payable including VAT; and
- for each rate of VAT chargeable, the gross amount payable including VAT and the VAT rate applicable.

Where the total consideration for a supply (including VAT) is £250 or more, the invoice must show:

- an identifying number;
- your name, address and VAT registration number;
- date of issue;
- time of supply (tax point-only needs to be shown if different from the date of issue);
- your customer's name (or trading name) and address*;
- a *description* identifying the goods . . . you are supplying;
- the gross total amount payable excluding VAT;
- the rate of any cash discount offered;
- the unit price (see Notice 700 The VAT guide); and
- the total amount of VAT charged, shown in sterling.

For each *description*, of goods . . . you must show the:

- quantity of goods . . . ;
- rate of VAT; and
- amount payable excluding VAT.

*Where an approved invoice is used for the scheme the usual address will be your customer's place of residence outside the EC.

Provided your customer agrees, a retailer may issue a modified VAT invoice showing the VAT inclusive amounts of each supply instead of the VAT exclusive values. However, in all other respects the modified invoice should show the details required for a full VAT invoice (see Notice 700 The VAT guide as amended by Update 2 issued February 2004

Remember, you cannot use the VAT Retail Export Scheme for services.

Note—Para 4.3.1 amended by Update 1, January 2007.

4.4 Design and size of own versions of VAT 407s or invoices

The following text has the force of law

- ***The VAT 407 or invoice must closely follow the design of the Customs and Excise version of Form VAT 407 . . .
- It must include the data protection statement shown on the face of the form and the information shown on the reverse side of the Customs and Excise version of Form VAT 407. This includes:
  - the heading "Retail Export Scheme";
  - providing spaces for the retailer's and the customer's declarations as stipulated on the Form VAT 407, including details of the customer's passport/identity number and country of issue, date of arrival in the EC, intended date of departure from the EC;
  - and a separate box not less than 5 cm by 3.5 cm for official stamping by a Customs officer at the customer's point of departure from the EC.
- The total amount payable must be shown in words as well as figures.
- Each VAT 407 or invoice must show the amount of any administrative charge and the net refund due to the customer.***

Note—Para 4.4 amended by Update 1, January 2007.

4.5 Prior approval of own versions of VAT 407s or invoices

You must seek approval beforehand from Customs and Excise if you wish to use your own adapted VAT 407 or invoice for sales made under the scheme.

Remember, if you use an officially approved VAT 407 or invoice you must still make sure that your customer is entitled to use the scheme and that the declarations are completed in full and signed by you (or another responsible person in your business) and your customer at the time of the sale.

4.6 How can I obtain approval from Customs and Excise?

If you do not intend to use the VAT 407 Form issued by Customs and Excise you must send a sample of your own invoice or version of the VAT 407 refund document for approval to Customs & Excise. Addresses can be obtained from the Helpline on 0300 200 3700 (see the "Further help and advice" section at the front of this notice for details), or via our Customs and Excise Internet home page by following the links from "contact us" through to Written Enquiries Teams.

4.7 Reply paid envelope

Each year several hundred VAT refund documents are returned to Customs at Heathrow airport for a variety of reasons. This is usually because the postage has not been paid and because the document contains a customs' stamp. Whether using a Form VAT 407, your own or a refund company's version, or an adapted invoice, give your customer the fully completed VAT refund document and a reply paid envelope addressed to either you or the refund company administering the refund. If you do not provide a reply paid envelope, you should make it clear that your customer is responsible for providing the envelope and paying the correct postage.

4.8 Can I complete the VAT refund form before export of the goods for past purchases?

Paragraph 3.2 states that refund forms must be completed at the time of sale. Customers may ask you to complete a refund form to cover past purchases. You may only agree to such requests provided you have adequate security procedures in place to prevent abuse of the scheme. This includes:

- stamping till receipts to show that the goods have been purchased under the Retail Export Scheme, for example "VAT Export".
- your till system allowing you to check that the receipts produced are genuine and can only appear once on a VAT 407 refund document;
- your system allowing you to check whether:
  - a refund for returned goods has already been made for a receipt now produced or
  - a VAT 407 refund document has been issued for goods where a refund for returned goods is now sought.

The following text has the force of law

Where you cannot show that you have adequate security procedures in place, you must continue to complete VAT refund documents at the time of the sale.

4.8.1 Completion of refund documents on production of receipts for past purchases

Where you do have adequate safeguards in place to prevent abuse of the scheme and a customer asks for a refund document to cover a series of purchases over a period of time, you must include only those goods that will be exported by the last day of the third month following that in which the goods were purchased. The purchase date entered on the refund document must be the date of the earliest purchase.

4.9 Control of blank or partly completed VAT refund documents

Whether you use:

- Form VAT 407 issued by Customs;
- a refund company's version of the form; or
- your own officially approved invoice,

you must:

- keep stocks of the blank documents secure;
- not issue blank or partly completed forms to any person outside your business.

4.10 Uncertified export documents

The following text has the force of law

If your customers send you VAT refund documents which have not been stamped by UK or other EC Customs, you cannot zero-rate the supply because export of the goods from the EC has not been certified as required by the scheme.

There are no exceptions to this rule.

4.11 Lost refund documents

4.11.1 Document lost before certification

If your customer has lost the VAT refund document before leaving the EC and asks for another, you can prepare a "DUPLICATE" *clearly marked* as such. The duplicate form and the goods must be produced to the Customs officer at the point of departure from the EC. You should take steps to ensure that should the original document appear it is not processed through your records.

When issuing a duplicate document, you must:

- make sure the original document has not been received and processed by you already;
- be satisfied that a sale took place by the production of till receipts or other information; and
- advise the traveller if they find the original refund document later, it is to be cancelled.

If you later receive the original document ensure it is cancelled.

4.11.2 Document lost after certification

If your customer has lost the VAT refund document after stamping by UK or other EC Customs, you may issue a duplicate only where a photocopy of the stamped original is produced. Duplicates of forms lost after Customs stamping must **not** be issued in any other circumstances.

The duplicate and the photocopy of the original document stamped by Customs must be sent to the Customs officer who stamped the original document. If satisfied, the Customs officer will stamp the duplicate and return it to you so that a refund may be made.

5 ACCOUNTING FOR VAT

5.1 Must I charge VAT at the point of sale?

You must treat any sale of standard-rated and lower-rated goods you make under the scheme as liable to VAT until you have received the VAT refund document appropriately stamped by a UK or other EC Customs officer. It is in your interest to charge VAT at the point of sale, and refund it to your customer only when you get valid evidence of export. Until you receive the necessary evidence of export and make the refund to your customer you will have to account for the VAT due.

5.2 What must I do before zero-rating the sale?

The following text has the force of law

You must obtain the stamped refund document and refund the VAT to your customer by the agreed method. You must retain the stamped refund document and evidence of the refund made to your customer to support the zero-rating of the supply.

If the certified VAT refund document arrives after you have accounted for VAT, you can refund the VAT and zero-rate the sale by reducing your output tax by the relevant amount in box 1 of your VAT return [for the period in which the evidence is received and the refund is made]—see Notice 700 The VAT Guide.

Note—Para 5.2 amended by Update 1, January 2007.

5.3 Retailers using a retail scheme

The individual retail schemes notices (in the 727 series) will explain how you should deal with sales and refunds under the VAT Retail Export Scheme in your retail scheme calculations.

5.4 Retailers not using a retail scheme

You must keep a record of all sales including VAT made under the VAT Retail Export Scheme. When you receive a VAT refund document stamped by a UK or other EC Customs officer and you have refunded the VAT, you can zero-rate the sale in your records.

5.5 Refund companies

You may contract with a refund company to administer the refund on your behalf. Refund companies usually provide an officially approved VAT refund document of their own design for use by retailers. If you use one of these companies, you still have to account for the VAT, as explained in paragraphs 5.1 and 5.2. You must retain the certified VAT refund documents and evidence that the VAT has been refunded in your records to support any zero-rating claimed.

5.6 Concession shops

Many larger stores operate concessions for other retailers within their own stores, where one counter or area sells goods from another retailer's range. Where the sale is rung through the main store tills it is acceptable for the VAT refund document to be issued by the host store (typically at the main customer service desk). In these circumstances the host store is responsible for complying with the conditions of the scheme as set out in this notice and for accounting for the VAT.

However, where the concession operates its own tills and issues receipts in its own right showing its own name and VAT number, any VAT refund documents relating to these purchases must be issued by the concession and not the host store. In these cases the concession is responsible for complying with the conditions of the scheme as set out in this notice and for accounting for the VAT.

5.7 Direct reclaim system

The direct reclaim system involves two distinct transactions. A retailer sells goods to a refund company who immediately sells them on to an eligible traveller. The accounting procedure is as follows:

– The retailer must invoice the sale to the refund company because this is a business-to-business supply, not a retail sale, and account for VAT on the supply. See paragraph 4.3.1 for the information that must be included on a VAT invoice.
– The refund company may use the invoice from the retailer to reclaim input tax on the purchase from the retailer. Notice 700 The VAT Guide provides information on the rules for invoices and claiming input tax.
– The refund company must also account for VAT on the sale to the traveller. It may subsequently zero-rate the supply *but only* where and when all the conditions of the VAT Retail Export Scheme set out in this notice are met.
– The retailer may include the sale to the refund company in their daily gross takings for retail scheme purposes if they wish.

5.8 Sales under the Margin Scheme for second-hand goods, works of art, antiques and collectors' items

If you make sales under the Margin Scheme for second-hand goods, accounting requirements will differ from those that must be fulfilled under the VAT Retail Export Scheme. You can use the two schemes for a single sale if you adapt the VAT refund document as follows:

– head it "Second-hand goods-this document is adapted in accordance with Notice 704, paragraph 5.8";
– leave the line "Amount of VAT included in the price" blank; and
– complete the refund due box.

See also Notice 718 "Margin Schemes for second-hand goods, works of art, antiques and collectors' items" [now "The VAT margin scheme and global accounting"].

5.9 Sales by auctioneers

If an auctioneer sells goods on your behalf to someone who is entitled to use the Retail Export Scheme and a VAT refund document is completed, you can zero-rate the sale when:

– the VAT refund document stamped by a UK or EC Customs officer is returned to you, and
– you have made the refund to your customer.

However, the VAT Retail Export Scheme can no longer be used for goods exported as freight (see paragraph 6.2). Exports of goods by freight should be made in accordance with the procedures described in Notice 703 Export of goods from the United Kingdom.

If auctioneers are registered for VAT and sell goods in their own name to someone who is entitled to use the scheme then, for VAT purposes, they may be treated as both receiving and making a supply of goods in accordance with Notice 700 The VAT Guide. They can zero-rate the sale provided they hold a VAT refund document stamped by a UK or EC Customs officer and have refunded the VAT to their customer.

5.10 VAT treatment of administration or handling fees

If you deduct an amount from the VAT refund due to cover administrative or handling expenses, the amount you deduct is a consideration for the supply of the service to your customers in connection with the export of goods to a destination outside the EC, and is zero-rated.

6 OTHER INFORMATION

6.1 Goods exported as hold baggage

Customers leaving by air may not always be able to export large or heavy items as hand baggage and customers buying such items should be advised to inform Customs before checking their baggage in. The airline enquiry desk can tell your customer of the Customs arrangements in force, as these vary from airport to airport.

Advise your customer that during busy periods queues are likely. Therefore they may need to allow up to two hours, prior to check in and the security procedures, to produce the goods and refund document. Long queues at the airport will not be accepted as a reason for failing to obtain a Customs stamp on the refund form.

6.2 Goods exported as freight

The concession allowing the Retail Export Scheme to be used for goods exported by travellers as freight (including unaccompanied baggage, courier and post) was withdrawn on 1 July 2003. The procedures for exporting goods by freight are described in Notice 703 Export of goods from the United Kingdom.

6.3 Supplies to diplomats, members of international organisations and NATO forces in other Member States

The scheme cannot be used for such supplies. There are special arrangements under Article 15(10) of the EC Sixth VAT Directive-see Notice 725 The Single Market.

6.4 Cash refund booths

Some refund companies have arrangements with refund booths at ports, airports and border crossing points from which cash refunds can be made to travellers before they leave the EC. In addition some refund companies will pay cash refunds to travellers in local currency at their destinations. The cash booth may charge your customer an additional administrative fee for these facilities. In all cases the customer will need to have their VAT refund document stamped by Customs at the place of departure from the EC.

6.5 Export licensing

Antiques may be exported only on production of a valid export licence to Customs at the point of departure from the UK. Further advice can be obtained from:

The Department for Culture, Media and Sport
2–4 Cockspur Street
LONDON SW1Y 5DH

If you sell goods that fall into this category you should explain this to your customers. They will probably need your assistance to obtain an export licence.

6.6 Information on other types of exports

Notice 703 Export of goods from the United Kingdom contains further guidance on zero-rating goods sent directly from the UK as freight or by courier or post.

7 INFORMATION FOR TRAVELLERS

7.1 What is the VAT Retail Export Scheme?

While you are in the United Kingdom (UK) you will pay Value Added Tax (VAT) on most goods that you buy. The VAT Retail Export Scheme allows you to claim a VAT refund on some of those goods by following the conditions summarised at paragraph 2.3 of this notice. Many shops in the UK will advertise the scheme as "Tax Free Shopping".

7.2 Do I qualify to use the scheme?

Paragraph 2.4 explains who is entitled to use the scheme.

7.3 Can I use the scheme for everything that I buy?

No. Not all shops operate the scheme; check before you buy. You cannot use the scheme to get a refund of VAT on meals and services such as hotel accommodation, car hire, taxi fares, etc, even though you may have been charged VAT on them.

The scheme may be used for any standard rated and lower-rated goods except those listed in paragraph 2.6 of this notice. There are different rules for these goods. You can get details and copies of the relevant notices from the National Advice Service. See the "Further help and advice" section at the front of this notice for details.

Under certain circumstances business travellers may obtain refunds of VAT paid on services provided and goods consumed in the EC. Notice 723 Refunds of VAT in the European Community for EC and non-EC businesses explains the conditions and how to make a claim. Customs officers at the place the traveller departs the UK are not involved in the refund of VAT on business expenses.

7.4 Making a purchase using the VAT Retail Export Scheme

7.4.1 What must I do before buying the goods?

Check that the retailer operates the scheme. Retailers do not have to operate the scheme, but those who do usually advertise the scheme as "Tax Free Shopping".

7.4.2 How do I buy tax-free goods?

Purchases must always be made by you personally although they may be paid for by a third party. There is no facility under this scheme for a representative to attend in your place at the time of sale.

7.4.3 When you buy the goods:

- tell the retailer that you want to use the scheme;
- ask the retailer to explain how the scheme works. You should make sure you understand what you have to do;
- tell the retailer your country of final destination. The retailer will ask you to provide proof that you are eligible to use the scheme (see paragraph 2.4);
- the retailer will ask you to complete and sign a VAT refund document at the time of sale in his presence. Make sure that you complete part A in full. Incomplete forms will not be stamped by Customs;
- make sure the retailer fully completes part B including an accurate description of the goods and signs the retailer's declaration in part C; and
- discuss with the retailer how the refund will be made, for example, cheque or credit card, how long it will take to receive the refund and any administration charges they will make.

The retailer will then give the completed VAT refund document to you. You may also be given a reply paid envelope. If the retailer does not give you one, you must provide an envelope and pay the postage for the return of the refund form after it has been stamped by Customs.

Remember, you must not allow anyone to sign the refund document on your behalf. If you do so, you will not be entitled to a VAT refund.

7.4.4 What VAT refund document will the retailer give me?

The retailer will give you one of the following documents:

- an official Customs Form VAT 407;
- a shop or refund company's own version of the VAT 407 form; or
- a sales invoice that is headed "Retail Export Scheme" and contains all the details that are shown on a Form VAT 407.

7.4.5 What happens if I return the goods to the shop for a refund or exchange?

If you wish to return goods that have been sold to you under the scheme, either for a full refund or for exchange you must also take your receipt and the VAT refund document back to the retailer. The retailer will delete the entry for the returned goods or cancel the VAT refund document and issue a new one as appropriate.

7.4.6 Can I use the scheme without an approved VAT refund document?

No. You cannot use the scheme without one of the refund documents described in Section 4. These forms are only available from VAT registered retailers who operate the scheme. They are not available to travellers at airports, ports or from Customs and Excise. *Till receipts alone are not acceptable for the scheme as operated in the UK.*

7.5 Exporting the goods

7.5.1 When must I export the goods?

You must export the goods from the EC by the last day of the third month following that in which the goods were purchased. For example, goods purchased on 3 February have to be exported by 31 May.

7.5.2 What must I do when I leave the EC?

(a) Leaving for an immediate destination outside the EC:

- If you **are not** travelling to any other country within the EC, you must present your refund document to Customs at your port or airport of departure when you leave the UK. The goods and receipts must also be available for inspection if required.
- If you are leaving by air and have goods that are too large or heavy to carry on board the aircraft you may pack them in your hold baggage. If you do this, you should contact the Customs officer *before you check in* and produce the goods for examination and the refund document for certification. However, you should always carry high value items in your hand baggage, this includes jewellery, furs, cameras, expensive watches, silverware, laptop computers and small antiques. Contact the airline or airport enquiry desk to check the arrangements in force as these vary from airport to airport.
- During busy periods, queues are likely and you should *allow yourself plenty of time* in which to produce the goods and refund document before departure. This is particularly important if you are exporting goods in your hold baggage as you may need to allow up to two hours in addition to your advised check in time. *Long queues will not be accepted as a reason for not obtaining a UK or EC Customs' stamp on the refund document.*
- If satisfied that all the conditions of the scheme have been met the Customs officer will stamp your VAT refund documents.

(b) Leaving the EC via another EC country:
If you are departing the EC via another EC country, you must present the goods and the refund document to the Customs authorities of that country.

(c) Leaving the EC on a through (transit) flight **via another EC airport:**
There are special rules for goods being carried on through flights leaving via another EC airport:

- *Hand Baggage*: Goods carried as hand baggage must be produced with the refund document to Customs in the last EC airport before leaving to return home.
- *Hold Baggage*: Goods carried as hold baggage must be produced with the refund document to UK Customs before you check in your baggage.

7.5.3 What should I do if there is no Customs presence?

In most cases you will be able to locate a Customs officer to stamp your refund document. However, some ports and airports do not have a 24-hour Customs presence and at others the Customs export offices are open only when there are departures for immediate destinations outside the EC. At such places there will either be a telephone to speak to Customs or a clearly marked post box to deposit your refund document. *You must ensure that your refund document is fully completed and that the reply paid envelope is not sealed before it is placed in the deposit box.* Customs will collect it and if satisfied that all the conditions of the scheme have been met, they will stamp it and send it to the retailer or refund company to arrange your refund.

Remember, if you are travelling to an EC airport where you will transfer to a flight out of the EC, you must produce the goods carried in your hand baggage and the refund form to Customs at the last point of transfer before departure from the EC.

The following text has the force of law

There is no facility to have your refund document stamped in your country of destination.

7.5.4 Am I making a declaration to Customs when I present the VAT refund document to the Customs officer?

Yes, you are making a declaration that:

- you are eligible to use the scheme; and
- that all the goods shown on the document are being exported from the EC by you.

It is a very serious offence to make a false declaration. This may involve you missing your flight or sailing and the misdeclared goods may be seized and penalties imposed.

7.5.5 What should I do if I decide not to export all of the goods bought under the scheme?

If you decide to leave goods bought under the scheme in the EC, you **must** clearly delete those items from any VAT refund document for certification when you finally leave the EC. This amendment *must be made before* you present the VAT refund document and the remaining goods to Customs for examination and stamping. The VAT refund document must show only the items being exported.

7.5.6 What happens if I cannot produce the goods and /or get the VAT refund document stamped before I leave the EC?

You will not receive any refund of VAT. If, however, you cannot produce the goods because, for example, your baggage has been lost or mislaid, you must tell the Customs officer at the port or airport of departure from the EC. The officer will tell you what action to take.

Your refund document must be stamped by a Customs officer when you leave the EC. Certification by anyone other than an EC Customs officer when you leave the EC is not acceptable. Long queues at the airport will not be accepted as a reason for not getting a UK or EC Customs' stamp on the form. Forms stamped outside the EC are not acceptable.

7.6 Obtaining your refund

Methods for the payment of refunds are set out at paragraphs 7.6.1 and 7.6.2. Whichever method is used, it should have been agreed between you and the retailer when you bought the goods.

Your refund may be reduced by an administration charge. This charge should be clearly shown on your refund document.

If you do not receive your refund within a reasonable time you should write to the retailer – not to Customs and Excise.

7.6.1 How do I obtain my refund?

After your VAT refund document has been stamped and returned to you by Customs you can either:

- post the refund document back to the retailer to arrange payment of your refund; or
- post the refund document back to a VAT refund company to arrange payment of your refund.

7.6.2 Can I obtain a cash refund at the airport?

Not all retailers and airports offer this "Cash Service". The retailer will advise you whether a cash refund is available. In such circumstances you will be advised to hand your refund document to a cash refund booth to arrange immediate payment.

The refund document will be passed to Customs by the cash refund booth. After stamping by Customs the form is sent to the retailer or refund company as evidence that the goods have been exported.

7.7 Lost refund documents

7.7.1 What should I do if I have lost the VAT refund document before stamping?

If the refund document is lost before stamping you should ask the retailer to provide a duplicate document. This must be clearly headed up "DUPLICATE". Produce the duplicate document with the goods to the Customs export officer when you leave the EC. If you find the original refund document later – destroy it.

7.7.2 What should I do if the VAT refund document is lost after stamping?

If the refund document is lost after stamping, unless you can produce a photocopy of the stamped refund document you will not receive a refund of VAT. If, however, you can provide a photocopy of the VAT refund document stamped by Customs at your final departure point from the EC, you can return this to the retailer and ask for a duplicate refund form to be issued and sent for stamping to the original Customs office. The document must be clearly headed up "DUPLICATE".

7.8 What should I do if I bring the goods back into the EC?

If the goods are brought back into the EC at any time they must be declared to Customs in the importing EC Member State-unless they are within the duty or tax-free traveller's allowance limits of that Member State.

However, if you purchased goods as an entitled EC resident (see paragraph 2.4.3) or as a student or migrant worker (see paragraph 2.4.2) and re-import them within 12 months of your departure from the EC, duty and tax free allowances will not apply to the goods as you will have failed to remain outside the EC for at least 12 months. You will have to pay any import duties, including VAT that are due.

8 INTRA EC CRUISES – SPECIAL ARRANGEMENT

8.1 Why is there a need for a special arrangement?

Non-EC passengers on wholly intra EC cruises may not have access to their luggage and purchases made under the VAT Retail Export Scheme from disembarkation until they arrive at their final non-EC destination. They cannot, therefore, produce their goods and VAT refund document to the Customs officer for stamping at their point of final departure from the EC.

Therefore, for wholly intra EC cruises which commence within the UK and where the final port of disembarkation is also within the UK, a special arrangement was introduced on 1 July 2003.

8.2 What is the special arrangement?

8.2.1 Individual purchases below £1000

Cruise operators may produce an omnibus bulk refund document for all eligible goods, below £1000 per item, purchased on board by entitled individual passengers.

The omnibus refund document must accompany the individual passenger's luggage to the airport of departure.

If satisfied the Customs officer will stamp the bulk refund form and return it to the cruise operator. On receipt of the certified bulk refund form, the cruise operator must account for the sales in their VAT records, as explained in Section 5.

The following has the force of law

However, the cruise operator must account for VAT on any goods on the bulk refund form not exported from the EC within the prescribed limits.

8.2.2 Bulk refund documents

The format of the bulk refund document must be approved beforehand by Customs. (See paragraph 4.6 for details).

It must be clearly headed "**Retail Export Scheme**" and must only include those goods that:

- were sold on board the vessel;
- are eligible to be supplied under the VAT Retail Export Scheme (see paragraph 2.6); and
- were supplied to entitled customers (see paragraph 2.4).

It must also give the following details:

- your name, address and VAT registration number;
- your customer's name and usual address;
- your customer's passport number and country of issue;
- a description which clearly identifies the goods and the quantity involved; and
- the amount payable per item. (Where this includes VAT, the amount payable inclusive of VAT and the amount of VAT included in the total price should be shown).

In addition, it must include a retailer declaration as stipulated on the Form VAT 407 signed by a responsible ship's officer, and a separate box not less than 5 cm by 3.5 cm for official certification by Customs and Excise.

8.2.3 Individual purchases £1000 and above

The normal VAT 407 form or equivalent (see paragraph 4.1) must be completed for purchases of £1000 or more per item. The customer must produce the goods and the form for stamping to the Customs officer at the point of final departure from the EC.

9 FISCAL (VAT) TERRITORY OF THE EUROPEAN COMMUNITY

9.1 Countries and territories within the EC fiscal (VAT) area

The following countries and territories are within the EC fiscal (VAT) area:

- Austria
- Belgium
- Cyprus*
- The Czech Republic
- Denmark, except the Faroe Islands and Greenland
- Estonia
- Finland
- France, including Monaco
- Germany, except Busingen and the Isle of Heligoland
- Greece
- Hungary
- The Republic of Ireland
- Italy, except the communes of Livigno and Campione d'Italia and the Italian waters of Lake Lugano
- Latvia
- Lithuania
- Luxembourg
- Malta
- The Netherlands
- Poland
- Portugal, including the Azores and Madeira
- The Slovak Republic
- Slovenia
- Spain, including the Balearic Islands but excluding Ceuta and Melilla
- Sweden
- United Kingdom and the Isle of Man

[**Plus, from 1 January 2007—**

- Bulgaria,
- Romania.]

* The European Commission has advised that the application of the 6th VAT Directive (Directive 77/388/EEC of 17 May 1977) shall be suspended in those areas of Cyprus in which the Government of the Republic of Cyprus does not exercise effective control. Eligible goods to entitled customers going to these destinations may be sold under this scheme.

Note—Para 9.1 amended by Update 1, January 2007.

9.2 Countries and territories outside the EC fiscal (VAT) area

The following countries and territories are outside the EC fiscal (VAT) area:

- The Channel Islands
- Andorra
- San Marino
- The Aland Islands
- The Canary Islands
- The overseas departments of France (Guadeloupe, Martinique, Réunion, St Pierre and Miquelon and French Guiana)
- Mount Athos
- Gibraltar
- The Vatican City

If you need more information on the VAT territory of the EC, please contact the Helpline on 0300 200 3700. (See the inside front cover for details).

NOTICE 704/1
TAX FREE SHOPPING IN THE UK

2012

1 INTRODUCTION

This Notice tells you how you can get the VAT back on goods you buy in the United Kingdom (UK) from shops that offer Tax Free Shopping (also known as the VAT Retail Export Scheme).

Commentary—*De Voil Indirect Tax Service* **V4.331**.

2 WHAT IS TAX FREE SHOPPING?

In the UK, Value Added Tax (VAT) is charged on many goods and services. Tax Free Shopping allows travellers leaving the European Union (EU) to get a VAT refund on goods they buy here and take home. It cannot be used for services.

In most cases, the shop or refund company will charge you a fee for using Tax Free Shopping. They will take the money out of your VAT refund.

3 CAN I USE THE SCHEME?

an overseas visitor

- your home, or the place you live, is outside the EU *and*
- you plan to take the goods out of the EU by the last day of the third month after the one in which you bought them (see section 6)

an overseas resident studying or working in the UK, *or*

a resident of the EU

- you plan to take the goods out of the EU by the last day of the third month after the one in which you bought them (see section 6) *and*
- you can show that you will be staying outside the EU for at least 12 months

If you belong to one of these categories, you must be able to prove this to the shop assistant and to customs when you leave the EU by showing your passport, visa or other documents. If you cannot prove this when you leave, your claim will not be approved.

4 CAN I USE THE SCHEME FOR EVERYTHING I BUY?

No. Not all shops offer Tax Free Shopping – check before you buy the goods.

You can use Tax Free Shopping for any goods on which you have paid VAT except:

- goods (for example, perfume or chocolates) which you have used, or partly used, in the EU

- motor vehicles and boats
- goods over £600 in value that will be exported for business purposes (you have to use a form C88 for these)
- goods that will be exported as freight and goods that need an export licence (except antiques)
- unmounted gemstones and bullion (over 125g, 2.75 troy ounces or 10 Tolas)
- mail order goods including Internet sales
- any services, for example, hotel bills.

5 HOW DO I SHOP TAX FREE?

Step	Details
1.	Find a shop that offers Tax Free Shopping. You have to be in the shop yourself when you buy the goods (although somebody else can pay for them).
2.	Tell the shop assistant that you want to use Tax Free Shopping and show your passport or national ID card.
3.	Ask the shop assistant to explain the scheme to you. Discuss: — how the refund will be made — when you will get it — what the charge is – this should be written on your refund form. Make sure that you are allowed to shop tax free (see section 3) and that you understand what you need to do.
4.	The shop assistant will give you the form. Fill in and sign the customer sections of the VAT refund form in the presence of the shop assistant. You must sign the form yourself. The only exception to this rule is for people who are not able to sign the form themselves for reasons directly related to disability.
5.	The shop assistant must also fill in and sign the form while you are in the shop. They may give you a reply paid envelope so you can post the form back after you have had it stamped by a customs officer.
6.	Take — the form (and the envelope) — the goods and — all your receipts with you to show to customs when you leave the EU. You will not get your VAT back if you only have till receipts.

6 WHEN DO I HAVE TO EXPORT THE GOODS?

You must export the goods (that is, take them out of the EU with you) by the last day of the third month after the one in which you buy them.

For example, if you bought the goods on the 3rd of February, you would have to export them by the 31st of May.

7 WHAT DO I HAVE TO DO WHEN I LEAVE THE EU?

You must get your form checked and stamped by a customs officer *in the EU*: you can't have this done when you get home.

7.1.1 I'm leaving the UK for a destination outside the EU:

Show your goods, till receipts and refund form to a UK customs officer. If you're going to carry any of the goods in your hold baggage, you must be prepared to show those goods to a customs officer *before* you check your baggage in. See paragraph 7.2.

7.1.2 I'm leaving the UK for another EU country:

Show your goods, till receipts and refund form to customs in the last EU country you visit. The deadline for exporting the goods stays the same regardless of how many countries you visit.

7.1.3 I'm leaving the UK by air and will change flights in another EU country before leaving the EU:

Show your goods, refund form and till receipts

- to a UK customs officer before you check in if the goods are in your hold baggage. See paragraph 7.2.
- to a customs officer in the last EU country you pass through if the goods are in your hand baggage.

7.2 Submitting your claim

Step	Details
1.	Allow plenty of time at the port or airport. There can be long queues to get your VAT refund processed. At Heathrow airport, to save time, you can get your form checked at a VAT refunds desk before it is stamped by a customs officer.
2.	Take your goods with the form and receipts to a VAT refunds desk at the airport or port. Remember, your form must be fully completed. You must hold all receipts for any goods you are exporting. If no officer is available, there will be: — a phone to ring the officer and you will be advised what to do, or — a clearly marked customs post box. Post your form (with its unsealed envelope) in the box.
Note:	When you show your refund form to the officer, you are declaring that: — you are eligible to use the scheme — you are exporting all the goods out of the EU. If you cannot prove this, you may miss your flight (or sailing) and customs can take the goods away from you. **It is a serious offence to make a false declaration.**
3.	When the officer is satisfied that you have met all the conditions of the scheme, they will stamp your refund form.
4.	Put the checked and stamped form in the post to: — the shop, or — a commercial refund company so that they can pay your refund. The address will be on the form. (If you posted your form in the customs post box, the customs officer will do this for you.) The refund will be made by the method agreed between you and the shop (see Section 5). Some companies offer an immediate cash refund. They will check your form, keep it and give you a cash refund before you leave the UK. There is a charge for this service.
5.	If you do not get your refund within a reasonable time you should write to the shop. Please **do not** write to HM Revenue and Customs or UK Border Agency (UKBA).

8 WHAT MUST I DO WHEN I LEAVE THE UK?

If	then
you **take the goods back** to the shop for a full refund or exchange	you must take your receipts and the VAT refund document with you. The shop will: — delete the entry for the returned goods or — cancel the VAT refund document and issue a new one.
you decide to **leave behind** any of the things you bought under the scheme	you must cross those items off your refund form before you present it, with any remaining goods, to customs.
you **lose** your refund form	ask the shop to provide a replacement document If you find the original later, destroy it.

9 IMPORTANT THINGS TO REMEMBER

- You and the shop assistant must fill in and sign the VAT refund form *when you buy the goods* (see section 5)
- Give yourself plenty of time when you leave the EU (see section 7)
- You *must* be prepared to show the goods, the till receipts *and* the VAT refund document to a customs officer when you leave the EU, or you won't get a refund (see step 2 in section 7.2 for what to do if you can't find a customs officer)
- Your refund will probably be reduced by an administration charge (see section 2). Make sure you understand how much the charge will be *before* you buy the goods
- If you don't export the goods by the deadline, you won't get a refund (see section 6)
- Your refund form *must* be checked and stamped *in the EU*: you can't have this done in the country you're travelling to (see section 7).

YOUR RIGHTS AND OBLIGATIONS

Your Charter explains what you can expect from us and what we can expect from you. For more information go to www.hmrc.gov.uk/charter.

PUTTING THINGS RIGHT

If you are unhappy with our service, please contact the person or office you have been dealing with. They will try to put things right. If you are still unhappy, they will tell you how to complain.

If you want to know more about making a complaint go to hmrc.gov.uk and under quick links, select Complaints and appeals.

Commentary—*De Voil Indirect Tax Service* **V4.331.**

706/2
CAPITAL GOODS SCHEME

October 2011

This notice cancels and replaces Notice 706/2 (January 2002)

1 INTRODUCTION

1.1 What is this notice about?

This notice explains how the Capital Goods Scheme works and which items are covered by the scheme.

1.2 Who should read this notice?

You should read this notice if you acquire, create or construct capital items for use in your business and you incur VAT on those items. The aim of this scheme is to provide a fair and reasonable attribution of input tax to taxable supplies and other supplies with the right to recover VAT. Capital items can be used in your business over a period of years. Over the years the extent to which you use these in making taxable supplies can vary.

If you make, or intend to make exempt supplies, it is important to read Notice 706 "Partial Exemption" in conjunction with this Notice.

This notice has been revised to improve readability and incorporates changes to the Capital Goods Scheme which took effect from 1 January 2011.

1.3 How does the scheme work?

The scheme allows for adjustments to be made to the initial amount of input tax claimed. This reflects the differences in the use of capital goods over a period of time. This period is known as the "adjustment period". If, during the adjustment period there is any change in the proportion of taxable use then you must make an adjustment to your input tax to take account of this.

1.4 When does the scheme not apply?

The scheme does not apply if—

— the assets are acquired solely for resale; or
— you spend money on assets which are solely for resale; or
— assets are acquired, or you spend money on assets, which are wholly used for non-business purposes.

1.5 What if I make only taxable supplies?

You do not have to be partly exempt or (for capital costs incurred after 1 January 2011) have non-business activities when you incurred the costs for the CGS to apply. For example, you may use a building purchased for £300,000 plus VAT for wholly taxable purposes for six years. In year seven you diversify into an exempt activity – for example insurance – and base your new insurance team in this building. The building remains subject to theCGS and CGS adjustments may now be required.

2 RECORD KEEPING

2.1 What records do I need to keep?

In addition to those records shown in Notice 700 "The VAT Guide", your records should include the following—

- description of the capital item;
- value of the capital item;
- the amount of VAT incurred on the capital item;
- the amount of input tax reclaimed by you on the capital item;
- the start and end date of each interval, including the first;
- when adjustments are due; and
- the date and value of disposal (if the item was disposed of or partly disposed of before the end of the adjustment period).

2.2 How long do I need to keep them?

You are not required to keep VAT records for longer than six years. However the CGS allows you to make adjustments up to ten years later. We would recommend that you keep records long enough to show us how you calculated each adjustment.

3 SCOPE OF THE CAPITAL GOODS SCHEME

3.1 What items are covered by the scheme?

Assets covered by the scheme are known as "capital items".
The CGS applies to capital expenditure on land and buildings with a value of £250,000 or more (exclusive of VAT) which was subject to VAT at the standard or reduced rate. The purchases in question are—

- an interest supplied to an owner in land, a building or part of a building or a civil engineering work. Civil engineering work should be given its everyday meaning. It includes such items as roads, bridges, golf courses, running tracks and installation of pipes for connection to mains services;
- expenditure incurred in the construction of a building, part of a building or a civil engineering work;
- alterations, extensions and annexes to buildings which increase the existing floor space by 10 per cent or more (for input tax incurred on or after 1 January 2011 the CGS definition relating to expenditure in this category has been simplified by removing the floor space element of the definition);
- for input tax incurred on or after 1 January 2011, the CGS has been extended to include alterations, extensions and annexes to civil engineering works;
- capital expenditure on services, and goods affixed to the building in the course of refurbishing or fitting out a building (for input tax incurred on or after 1 January 2011 it no longer matters whether goods are affixed to a structure or not, only whether the expenditure has been capitalised);

– for input tax incurred on or after 1 January 2011 the CGS has been extended to include refurbishments of civil engineering works.

The CGS also applies to—

— any computer with a VAT exclusive value of £50,000 or more. "Computer" means a single item of equipment rather than a complete network. Computer software and computerised equipment such as a computerised phone exchange or computer controlled blast furnace are not included;
— With effect from 1 January 2011 the CGS has been extended to apply to capital expenditure on aircraft, ships, boats and other vessels with a VAT exclusive value of £50,000 or more. As well as VAT incurred in respect of the purchase of such assets, the scheme also includes VAT incurred in the course of their manufacture, refurbishment, fitting out, alteration or extension.

4 VALUES AND DEFINITIONS

4.1 What is meant by "capital expenditure"?

This is normally expenditure capitalised for accounting purposes. We will not normally challenge your capitalisation policy for the purposes of the CGS, except in cases of avoidance or abuse.

In some cases charities may incur expenditure of a capital nature on land and property which is not capitalised in their accounts (eg certain heritage buildings, churches etc). This is generally because the charity does not have unfettered freedom to exploit or dispose of the land or property concerned. This will not prevent expenditure that is essentially capital in nature from being adjusted under the CGS.

4.2 What is the value of a capital item?

This is the VAT-exclusive value of the item. Only the value of standard or reduced-rated taxable supplies is considered.

Before 1 January 2011, the value of a capital item was determined by reference to the business-related expenditure. With effect from 1 January 2011, the value is determined by reference to total expenditure on an asset. This includes both business and non-business expenditure on an asset.

EXAMPLE

A business purchases a building for £1 million and incurs £200,000 VAT. The building is to be used for 60 per cent business purposes and 40 per cent non-business purposes (eg charitable use). Before 1 January 2011, £600,000 (60 per cent of £1 million) determined the value for CGS purposes. Under the new rules that took effect from 1 January 2011, all of the expenditure on the building (£1 million) is the value for CGS purposes. As the CGS threshold for buildings remains at £250,000, the building is a capital item in both scenarios.

4.3 What about expenditure incurred on a capital item before and after 1 January 2011?

It will be necessary to determine the amount of business-related expenditure incurred on the asset up to 31 December 2010 and the total amount of expenditure (business and non-business) incurred on or after 1 January 2011. If the sum of these amounts exceeds the relevant CGS threshold, the asset falls within the CGS.

4.4 What is the adjustable amount of VAT?

Prior to 1 January 2011, only VAT on the business-related expenditure on an asset (ie input tax) fell within the CGS. With effect from 1 January 2011, all of the VAT on an asset (in this instance input tax and non-business VAT) falls within the CGS.

EXAMPLE

Following on from the above example; prior to 1 January 2011, input tax of £105,000 (17.5 per cent of £600,000) fell within the CGS. With effect from 1 January 2011, VAT of £175,000 (17.5 per cent of £1 million) falls within the CGS (£200,000 after the increase in the standard rate of VAT to 20 per cent on 4 January 2011).

If expenditure is incurred both before and after 1 January 2011, the VAT on the business related expenditure incurred up to 31 December 2010 and the total VAT incurred on the asset on or after 1 January 2011 fall within the CGS.

4.5 What if I have to estimate the value?

If you do not know whether a project exceeds the value threshold for the CGS until all invoices have been received you will need to estimate the value of the supplies you have received. This may happen with construction projects and refurbishments where VAT is incurred over a period of time and also with contracts that include a retention clause. A retention clause involves a proportion of the contract price being held back and only paid when the work has been satisfactorily completed.

If, when you start the CGS, you estimate that the value of relevant supplies will exceed the value threshold, the item will become a capital item. Even if you find later on that the value does not reach the threshold, the item remains in the scheme and you should continue to make adjustments as necessary.

If you do estimate the value of a capital item you will need to keep all the documents you based your estimation on, such as a contract, as our officer may ask to see it.

4.6 What should I include in the value of land or buildings that I acquire?

Only include the value of the interest in the land and/or building supplied to you, if the supply was taxable and not zero-rated. Do not include any associated costs such as legal or estate agency fees.

In calculating the value of the interest supplied to you in the land and/or building, you do not need to include the value of any rent or service charges unless—

– it has been paid or is payable more than 12 months in advance; or
– is invoiced by the supplier for a period of more than 12 months. In that case, you should include the value of rent/service charges when calculating the value of the capital item.

4.7 What should I include in the value of a constructed building or civil engineering work?

You should include the total VAT-exclusive cost of any of the following supplies made to you—

– the interest in the land, if the supply to you was taxable (other than zero-rated); and
– taxable (other than zero-rated) goods and services supplied for, or in connection with, the construction of the building or civil engineering work.

You should include all the costs involved in making the building ready, such as—

– professional and managerial services including architects, surveyors and site management;
– demolition and site clearance;
– building and civil engineering contractors' services;
– materials used in the construction;
– security;
– equipment hire;
– haulage;
– landscaping; and
– fitting out, including the value of any fixtures.

4.8 If I have purchased land and constructed a building on it, do I have two capital items?

No, this is treated as one capital item.

4.9 What should I include in the value of an alteration, extension or annex where the value of the goods and services received is £250,000 or more?

You should include the total value of all taxable (other than zero-rated) goods or services supplied to you for, or in connection with, the alteration, extension or annex.

You should include all the costs involved in making the building or civil engineering work ready. See examples at paragraph 4.7.

4.10 What should I include in the value if a capital item is refurbished or fitted out?

You should only include the value of capital expenditure on the taxable (other than zero-rated) supply of services and of goods affixed to the building or civil engineering work supplied to you for or in connection with the refurbishment or fit out.

However, for capital items where the costs are incurred on or after 1 January 2011 there is no longer a requirement for goods used for the refurbishment to be affixed to the building.

You should include all the costs involved in making the refurbished or fitted out building ready. See examples at paragraph 4.7.

4.11 What are "goods affixed" to the building?

These are goods which become part of the fabric of the building. Generally these are items that are sold with the property and are not portable or easily removed.

"Goods affixed" does not include items secured for safety or security reasons or computers or computer equipment. These may be subject to the CGS in their own right.

The following lists will help you to decide whether an item is "affixed".

This list is not exhaustive and the deciding factor is usually whether the item becomes part of the fabric of the building. Common inclusions are—

- materials to build;
- internal and external walls;
- roofs and ceilings;
- floors and hard flooring;
- permanent partitioning;
- windows;
- lifts;
- "built in" storage such as cupboards or shelving;
- air conditioning;
- lighting; and
- decorative features.

Common exclusions are—

- office furniture;
- storage unless it is "built in";
- carpets;
- computers and computer equipment; and
- factory and office machinery.

Again, this list is not exhaustive.

For capital items where the capital costs are incurred on or after 1 January 2011 there is no longer a requirement for goods used for a refurbishment to be affixed to a building. For capital items where the capital costs were incurred before 1 January 2011, this treatment is already allowed in relation to the "goods affixed" condition by concession and is adopted by most businesses.

4.12 What if the refurbishment is in phases?

If you do this you will need to decide whether the work should be treated as a whole for CGS purposes or whether there is more than one refurbishment. If you think that each phase is really a separate refurbishment then they should be treated separately for CGS purposes.

Normally there is more than one refurbishment when—

- there are separate contracts for each phase of the work; or
- a contract where each phase is a separate option which can be selected; and
- each phase of work is completed before work on the next phase starts.

A refurbishment which is only undertaken in phases because the building is occupied and where the contractors work on one floor at a time is normally considered to be only one refurbishment.

4.13 What about regular refurbishments?

These are sometimes referred to as "rolling refurbishments".

Problems may occur if successive refurbishments begin before each adjustment period has expired. If this happens you should either—

- treat the original refurbishment as "destroyed" (see paragraph 9.8) if there is nothing left of the earlier refurbishment or this earlier work is stripped out or replaced. The effect of this is that no further adjustments would be required to the input tax on the previous refurbishment; or
- continue to make adjustments for the remainder of the adjustment period if elements of the earlier refurbishment are retained.

4.14 What should I include in the value of computers?

You should include any delivery and installation costs, unless these are supplied separately. If you import a computer you should use the value for VAT at importation. This will include any import duty payable.

5 CAN I OPT TO HOLD ALL OR PART OF AN ASSET OUTSIDE THE VAT SYSTEM?

5.1 What is this option?

You may make a choice, when acquiring an asset, to exclude all or part of it from your business's assets, by holding it privately or as a non-business asset. If such an option is made, the excluded element never forms part of your business assets. The option is only available if you have private or non-business activities.

If all or part of an asset is excluded from your business assets because you hold it for private or non-business use, the costs and related VAT are also excluded from the VAT system. Expenditure relating to the element that has been excluded from your business does not count towards the CGS threshold, but the related VAT is always non-deductible and will not benefit from adjustment if taxable use increases.

5.2 When and how is the option made?

The choice to exclude any part of an asset from your business's assets must be made at the time when the relevant expenditure is incurred and should be recorded to avoid the risk of future disputes. Evidence might include minutes of a board meeting, a note in your VAT file or similar contemporaneous material to evidence your decision.

5.3 How does an option to hold part of an asset outside the business interact with the CGS?

The CGS will only apply to that part of the asset that forms part of your business assets, and you will need to take into account the business/non-business use and taxable/exempt use of that part in the CGS adjustment period, as described in section 6.

"First use" will be the first time that any part of a constructed, altered, extended, refurbished or fitted out building is used.

5.4 Do the CGS rules apply to expenditure initially allocated entirely to non-business activities?

No, VAT on costs allocated entirely to non-business purposes is not eligible for adjustment under the CGS rules.

6 INTERVALS AND THE ADJUSTMENT PERIOD?

6.1 What is an adjustment period?

An adjustment period is the time over which you review the extent to which a capital item is used in making taxable supplies.

6.2 How long are the adjustment periods?

These are—

- five intervals for computers;

– five intervals for ships and aircraft; and
– ten intervals for all other capital items.

For capital items where the period of adjustment (under the old rules) had not started before 1 January 2011 there are new rules which align the period of adjustment with the owner's interest in the asset (see below).

For capital items where the period of adjustment (under the old rules) had started before 1 January 2011 there were five intervals for an interest in land, buildings or civil engineering works which had less than ten years to run when they were acquired.

6.3 Aligning the period of adjustment with your interest in an asset

In some cases, the period of time that you have an interest in an asset is less than the normal period of adjustment under the CGS (ten years for land and buildings, five years for ships and aircraft). From 1 January 2011 the adjustment period is aligned with your interest in the asset.

Where the number of intervals comprising the normal period of adjustment (five or ten intervals) exceeds the number of complete years that you have an interest in the asset by more than 1, the period of adjustment is reduced to a number of intervals equal to the number of complete years plus one, down to a minimum of three intervals.

The period of adjustment is reduced to the number of whole years plus one to cater for any residual interest (in this instance any remaining interest after whole years have been taken into account) in the Capital item to help ensure a fair recovery of VAT.

Example: A business acquires a seven-year interest in a building that falls within the CGS

The normal period of adjustment for a building is ten intervals. However, the business only has a seven-year interest in the asset. As ten exceeds seven by more than one, the period of adjustment for the building is reduced to the number of complete years plus one, ie eight intervals.

If your interest in an asset is for fewer than three intervals then the asset does not fall within the CGS. This is because the CGS only deals with capital expenditure, which is generally expenditure that will be used by a business for a minimum of two years and this normally equates to three intervals under the CGS.

6.4 What is the first interval?

For capital items for which the period of adjustment (under the old rules) had not started before 1 January 2011 the first interval is a period of time that starts with first use of the asset. This is a common start date for all categories of capital items.

For capital items for which the period of adjustment (under the old rules) had started before 1 January 2011 the first interval is a period of time that starts on—

– the date of purchase, importation or acquisition;
– the date the owner first uses the item where the item is constructed, altered, extended, refurbished or fitted out; or
– the date of registration (or inclusion into an existing VAT group), where the owner is not a registered person when they first use the item.

"Use" includes any use in the business.

First use will correspond with the first time that a Capital item or part of such asset is used for business or non-business purposes. In the case of a building, this would normally correspond with the earlier of the granting of a lease/licence or physical occupation. The only pre-condition is that first use can only start when input tax has been incurred on the asset.

6.5 When does the first interval end?

The first interval ends on the day before the start of your next partial exemption tax year.

With effect from 3 July 1997, if there is no change of use between the first and the second interval and the length of the two intervals combined is less than 12 months, the two intervals are rolled together and treated as the first interval.

6.6 Do I need to make any adjustments to the first interval?

You do not need to make any adjustment after the end of the first interval. Your normal partial exemption (and/or business/non-business calculation if applicable) will determine the amount of VAT you can recover at the end of the first interval. CGS adjustments are only made after the end of subsequent intervals.

6.7 What is a subsequent interval?

The intervals following the first interval are called *subsequent intervals* and are normally in line with the partial exemption tax year.

6.8 When could an adjustment be required?

If, in any subsequent interval, the extent to which you use an item in making taxable supplies increases or decreases when compared to your initial use, you will have to make a CGS adjustment. You only make CGS adjustments to subsequent intervals. No adjustments are made after the end of the first interval.

6.9 What happens when the adjustment period ends?

If you continue to use a capital item in your business for the whole of the adjustment period, the period will usually end after the 5th or the 10th interval as explained in paragraphs 6.2 and 6.3. You should make your adjustment for the final interval in the normal way (see Section 8) on the return for the second prescribed accounting period after the end of the interval and from then on no further adjustments are needed.

6.10 What do I do about changes in use after the final interval?

You do not need to make any further adjustments for changes in use after the final interval.

7 HOW DO I WORK OUT THE ADJUSTMENTS?

7.1 How do I work out how much input tax I can initially reclaim?

You can initially reclaim VAT that is used or to be used to make taxable supplies. This involves the following steps—

Step 1 is to establish the extent to which the asset is used or to be used for business purposes. The proportion of VAT on the cost of the asset that relates to business activities is counted as input tax and is carried forward to step 2 (VAT relating to nonbusiness activities is known as "non-business VAT" and is not deductible). This is known as a business/non-business (BNB) calculation and you are required to select your own fair and reasonable calculation.

Step 2 is to establish the extent to which input tax carried forward from step 1 is used or to be used to make taxable supplies.

- If the asset is used only to make taxable supplies, all of the input tax is deductible.
- If the asset is used only to make exempt supplies, none of the input tax is deductible.
- If the asset is used to make taxable and exempt supplies, you will need to carry out a partial exemption calculation. A partial exemption calculation is normally carried out in accordance with a partial exemption method and, unlike the BNB calculation, is normally subject to an annual adjustment – see Notice 706 "Partial Exemption" for further details.

EXAMPLE

Following on from the example at paragraphs 4.2 and 4.4 (building cost £1 million and 60 per cent business use intended), the building has 60 per cent business use involving only the making of taxable supplies in the year of acquisition (the first interval under the CGS).
Initially the business needs to calculate how much of the VAT incurred on the building is deductible following the steps above. As the building will be used for 60% business purposes, £120,000 VAT can be treated as input tax. As the business activities involve only making taxable supplies, all of this input tax is deductible.

The default position for determining how much VAT is deductible on costs is as set out above. Step 1 requires you to select your own fair and reasonable BNB calculation. Step 2 requires you to determine recoverable VAT in accordance with a partial exemption method, assuming you are partly exempt – either the turnoverbased standard method which is set out in legislation or, alternatively, a special method which must be approved by HMRC.

However, for VAT incurred on or after 1 January 2011, HMRC is now able to approve a method covering BNB calculations. Where you are also required to carry out partial exemption calculations, HMRC can also approve use of one single agreement covering the business's BNB and partial exemption calculations. This is known as the combined method. See Notice 706 "Partial Exemption" for further details.

7.2 What is the "baseline" recovery of VAT established at the end of the first interval?

With effect from 1 January 2011, you need to calculate the amount of deductible VAT on the asset following the two steps in paragraph 7.1 (or your approved combined method). The baseline recovery percentage is the amount of deductible input tax on the asset expressed as a percentage of the total VAT on the asset, in this instance Input Tax and non-business VAT.

Before 1 January 2011, you were required to calculate an amount of input tax that was deductible on a capital item following the two steps in paragraph 7.1. However, the baseline recovery percentage for the CGS was established by the amount of deductible Input Tax, expressed as a percentage of the total Input Tax on the capital item.

7.3 What happens if I make an incorrect initial claim for VAT in the first interval?

The "baseline" recovery of VAT on a capital item is the amount that is deductible in the tax year or years that it was incurred in. This is then adjusted up or down with changes of use in subsequent intervals. If there were errors in the initial deduction then—

- they can be corrected only by adjustments to that initial deduction, not by making adjustments under the CGS that treat that initial deduction as if it had been correct; and
- if they are outside the capping limits, they cannot be corrected at all.

For more information on capping, see section 14 of Notice 706.

Whether or not any errors in the initial deduction can actually be corrected, subsequent interval adjustments will always refer back to the corrected baseline. This may lead to situations where adjustments are due that common sense would say should not be. As an overriding consideration, however, adjustments should not be made or allowed where they would result in the claiming of more than all, or less than none, of the input tax effectively adjusted in that interval. An example follows—

EXAMPLE

A business buys a capital item and recovers 70 per cent of the VAT incurred. More than four years later it is discovered that this deduction is in error and only 30 per cent should have been recovered. This error cannot be corrected as it is capped. In interval 6 the business uses the asset 50 per cent for taxable purposes. Despite the fact that it has already recovered 70 per cent of the VAT on the item it is still entitled to use an adjustment percentage of plus 20 per cent in the interval 6 adjustment.

7.4 How do I measure the extent of taxable use in subsequent intervals?

You are required to review the extent to which VAT is deductible on the asset in each subsequent interval. To do this you must imagine that you have incurred all of the VAT on the asset again and repeat the steps in paragraph 7.1 taking account of any changes in use.

For capital items whose adjustment period started on or after 1 January 2011 you need to review your BNB calculation in addition to your partial exemption calculation for the capital item in each subsequent interval and account for any required adjustment in the normal way.

In each of the subsequent intervals (between two and nine depending on the individual item and when it was acquired) the extent of taxable use (and/or nonbusiness use if the item was purchased after 1 January 2011) determined under the longer period partial exemption calculation (and/or business/non-business calculation if applicable) is compared with the "baseline" recovery. The difference is called the "adjustment percentage".

7.5 How do I calculate the actual adjustment I must make?

The actual input tax adjustment (if any) required in a subsequent interval is calculated by dividing the total input tax (or total VAT if incurred after 1 January 2011) on the capital item by the total number of intervals in the adjustment period (usually either five or ten). You then multiply by the adjustment percentage. Thus the calculation is:

For capital items whose adjustment period begins before 1 January 2011—

$$\frac{\text{Total input tax on the capital item}}{\text{Number of intervals in the adjustment period}} \times \text{the adjustment percentage}$$

For capital items whose adjustment period begins on or after 1 January 2011—

$$\frac{\text{Total VAT on the capital item}}{\text{Number of intervals in the adjustment period}} \times \text{the adjustment percentage}$$

EXAMPLE

Following on from the example at paragraphs 4.2, 4.4 and 7.1

Subsequent year adjustments

With effect from 1 January 2011, all of the expenditure on the building falls within the CGS. The baseline recovery percentage needs to be determined by reference to the amount of deductible input tax on the asset expressed as a percentage of the total VAT on the asset—

120,000/200,000 = 60%

In each subsequent interval the business is then required to imagine that it has incurred all of the VAT (£200,000) again and repeat the steps in paragraph 7.1. As the building will be used entirely for taxable business purposes, the CGS recovery percentage will be 100% in the remaining intervals. This means that the business will be able to reclaim—

(100% – 60%) x £200,000/10 = £8,000

at the end of each of the remaining 9 intervals under the wider CGS – reflecting the increased taxable business use of the building.

Prior to 1 January 2011, only the expenditure allocated to business activities and related input tax fell within the scope of the CGS. The baseline recovery percentage was determined by reference to the amount of deductible input tax expressed as a percentage of total input tax, which is 100 per cent in this example. The business was then required to imagine that it had incurred all of the input tax (£120,000) again and review the extent to which it had been used to make taxable supplies in each subsequent interval. In this case, the input tax was used only to make taxable supplies in each subsequent interval and so no further adjustments were necessary under the old CGS rules, even though business use of the building had increased.

If you incur expenditure on your capital asset both before and after 1 January 2011 you will have a "split" capital item. Input tax incurred up to 31 December 2010 must be reviewed in light of any change in the mix of taxable and exempt supplies made. VAT incurred on or after 1 January 2011 must be reviewed separately in light of both changes in business use in the mix of taxable and exempt supplies made.

Where the period of adjustment is reduced so that it aligns with your interest in an asset (see paragraph 6.3), the denominator in the fraction used to determine CGS adjustments also needs to be reduced to ensure that all of the VAT incurred on the asset is reviewed over the period of time that you have an interest in the asset. This helps to ensure a fair recovery of VAT.

Example: A business acquires a seven-year interest in a building that falls within the CGS

One-eighth of total VAT on the capital item would be reviewed at the end of the subsequent seven intervals.

7.6 How do I deal with VAT incurred before the first interval?

If you incur VAT before the first interval you will need to work out the overall initial percentage you can claim against which you can measure the percentage of taxable use in any subsequent interval.

If you have incurred VAT before the first interval you could, for example, work out the percentage of total input tax to which you were originally entitled, by expressing the total input tax recovered as a percentage of the total VAT incurred on the capital item.

AN EXAMPLE OF THIS IS SHOWN BELOW.

A partly exempt business constructs a new headquarters building. It incurs £600,000 of input tax on the building in the tax year ending 31 March 2012. Its partial exemption reclaimable percentage for the year as a whole is 75 per cent so it reclaims £450,000.

In the following tax year, the year ending 31 March 2013, it incurs another £400,000 of input tax on the building and reclaims £320,000 because its partial exemption reclaimable percentage for the year is 80 per cent.
It occupies the building for use in its partly exempt business on 1 September 2012 so the first interval runs from 1 September 2012 to 31 March 2013 (the day before the start of the next tax year, which is 1 April 2013).
The business has therefore incurred some VAT before the first interval and will need to work out an overall average reclaimable percentage to measure against for future subsequent intervals—

$$\frac{\text{Total input tax reclaimed}}{\text{Total VAT incurred}} \times \text{Average reclaimable percentage}$$

$$\frac{£770{,}000}{£1{,}000{,}000 \text{ x } 100\% = 77\%}$$

Therefore, 77 per cent is the "baseline" against which future adjustments are measured.

7.7 How do I deal with VAT incurred after the first interval?

This can happen with construction projects and refurbishments where the work is carried out over a period of time and also where contracts include a retention clause.
If you incur VAT in the first interval, you reclaim it using the normal rules. This is subject to adjustment from the end of the second interval. If you also incur VAT in the second interval, this will not form part of the CGS adjustment in interval 2, but will be adjusted from the third interval onwards.
Examples for dealing with theses two amounts of input tax are shown below—
There are two options shown below that you may wish to use to deal with input tax incurred on a capital item after the first interval. The two options are known as—

- combined adjustments; and
- parallel adjustments.

(All the figures in the combined adjustments and parallel adjustments tables are in thousands.)

7.8 Example of dealing with VAT incurred after the first interval

This example considers a constructed building which was first occupied for fully business purposes by a partly exempt business on 1 August 2013. At the first interval £8,000,000 input tax was incurred on the capital item of which 75 per cent was recovered using the business' partial exemption reclaimable percentage. Additional amounts of input tax were incurred in subsequent intervals in completing the construction as below:

Dates	*Interval*	*VAT incurred on building*	*Partial Exemption (PE) percentage*	*Input tax claimed on building*
1/8/13 to 31/3/14	1	£8,000,000	75%	£6,000,000
1/4/14 to 31/3/15	2	£4,000,000	90%	£3,600,000
1/4/15 to 31/3/16	3	£3,000,000	75%	£2,250,000
1/4/16 to 31/3/17	4	£2,500,000	72%	£1,800,000
1/4/17 to 31/3/18	5	£0	80%	£0
1/4/18 to 31/03/19	6	£0	84%	£0
1/4/19 to 31/3/20	7	£0	88%	£0
1/4/20 to 31/3/21	8	£0	74%	£0
1/4/21 to 31/3/22	9	£0	72%	£0
1/4/22 to 31/3/23	10	£0	70%	£0
	Total £17,500,000			

Remember

To work out the amount of adjustment for an interval, you divide the total VAT incurred on the capital item by the total number of intervals in the adjustment period (usually either 5 or 10). You then multiply by the adjustment percentage:

$$\frac{\text{Total input tax on the capital item}}{\text{Number or intervals in the adjustment period}} \times \text{the adjustment percentage}$$

Combined adjustments (figures in table are in thousands)

This approach involves rolling together the adjustment calculations for the remaining intervals.

Each time an additional amount of input tax is incurred the overall initial recovery percentage, the "baseline", should be re-evaluated and used to measure against for future intervals. The baseline can be calculated by determining what percentage of input tax has been reclaimed over the expired intervals, using the formula—

$$\frac{\text{Input tax reclaimed}}{\text{Input tax incurred}} \times 100\% = \text{Average reclaimable}\%$$

Interval	*VAT incurred*	*PE %*	*Input tax reclaimed*	*Capital Goods Scheme baseline*	*VAT to be adjusted*	*Capital Goods Scheme adjustment*	
				%		*%*	*Amount*
1	£8,000	75	£6,000	75	n/a	0	0
2	£4,000	90	£3,600	75	£8,000	15	£120
3	£3,000	75	£2,250	80	£12,000	(5)	(£60)
4	£2,500	72	£1,800	79	£15,000	(7)	(£105)
5	£0	80	£0	78	£17,500	2	£35
6	£0	84	£0	78	£17,500	6	£105
7	£0	88	£0	78	£17,500	10	£175
8	£0	74	£0	78	£17,500	(4)	(£70)
9	£0	72	£0	78	£17,500	(6)	(£105)
10	£0	70	£0	78	£17,500	(8)	(£140)
Totals	£17,500		£13, 650				(£45)

At the end of interval 2 the business had reclaimed—

$$\frac{9{,}600}{12000} \times 100 = 80\%$$

This becomes the CGS baseline percentage for interval 3.

At the end of interval 3 the business had reclaimed—

$$\frac{11{,}850}{15{,}000} \times 100 = 79\%$$

This becomes the CGS baseline percentage for interval 4.

Note— You should round special method percentages to two decimal places. If you are using the standard method you must round up to the next whole number unless you incur more than £400,000 of residual input tax each month on average in which case you must round to two decimal places.

This method produces a net adjustment figure of £45,000 due to HMRC over the ten-year adjustment period.

When deducted from the input tax initially reclaimed of £13,650,000 (over four years), the business' total amount of input tax reclaimed is £13,605,000.

Against total VAT incurred of £17,500,000 this is a reclaimable percentage of 77.74 per cent.

Parallel adjustments (figures in table are in thousands)

This approach involves carrying out separate, but simultaneous adjustments for the remaining intervals of the CGS adjustment period.

Interval	*Input tax incurred*	*PE %*	*Input tax reclaimed*	*Adj. of Interval 1 input tax incurred**		*Adj. of Interval 2 input tax incurred**	
				%	*Amount*	*%*	*Amount*
1	£8,000	75	£6,000	n/a	n/a	n/a	n/a
2	£4,000	90	£3,600	15	£120	n/a	n/a
3	£3,000	75	£2,250	0	0	(15)	(£60)
4	£2,500	72	£1,800	(3)	(£24)	(18)	(£72)
5	£0	80	£0	5	£40	(10)	(£40)
6	£0	84	£0	9	£72	(6)	(£24)
7	£0	88	£0	13	£104	(2)	(£8)
8	£0	74	£0	(1)	(£8)	(16)	(£64)
9	£0	72	£0	(3)	(£24)	(8)	(£72)
10	£0	70	£0	(5)	(£40)	(20)	(£80)
Totals	£17,500		£13,650		£240		(£420)

Interval	*Adj. of Interval 3 input tax incurred**		*Adj. of Interval 4 input tax incurred**		*Totals*
	%	*Amount*	*%*	*Amount*	
1	n/a	n/a	n/a	n/a	£0
2	n/a	n/a	n/a	n/a	£120
3	n/a	n/a	n/a	n/a	(£60)
4	(3)	(£9)	n/a	n/a	(£105)
5	5	£15	8	£20	£35
6	9	£27	12	£30	£105
7	13	£39	16	£40	£175
8	(1)	(£3)	2	£5	(£70)
9	(3)	(£9)	0	£0	(£105)
10	(5)	(£15)	(2)	(£5)	(£140)
Totals		£45		£90	(45)

*Figure is divided by the amount of intervals in the adjustment period. In this case divided by 10.

This method also produces a net adjustment figure of £45,000 due to HMRC over the ten-year adjustment period.

When deducted from the input tax initially reclaimed of £13,650,000 (over four years), the business' total amount of input tax reclaimed is £13,605,000.

Against total VAT incurred of £17,500,000 this is a reclaimable percentage of 77.74 per cent.

7.9 Changing method

If you do not think your normal partial exemption method gives a fair reflection of how your capital item will be used in making taxable supplies in subsequent intervals you can apply for an alternative CGS method to determine this. Any calculation that achieves a fair result is acceptable. You must obtain HMRC's agreement before using such an alternative method.

7.10 Can I always use the method I choose?

No, we can insist that you use a particular method to calculate the extent of taxable use of the capital item in subsequent intervals. We will only insist on this if we are unable to reach an agreement on the method you should use. We will write to you if we think you should use our method. If you do not agree with our decision you can ask for either of the following—

- a review of our decision;
- an appeal to be heard by an independent tribunal.

There is more information about what you can do if you disagree with our decision in a HMRC factsheet and customer guidance which can be found at: "Factsheet HMRC1 HM Revenue & Customs decisions – what to do if you disagree".

7.11 Can I take account of the partial exemption de minimis limit when calculating my CGS adjustments?

In any subsequent interval where the longer period calculation finds you to be de minimis any exempt business use in that period is generally ignored for CGS purposes. If, however, the Standard Method Override (See Notice 706 "Partial Exemption") would have been triggered had all the input tax on the item been incurred in the year in question and treated as de minimis, this is not the case.

If we have agreed or directed you to use an alternative method for calculating the extent of taxable use of a capital item in subsequent intervals then you should not take account of the partial exemption de minimis limit unless the method specifies otherwise.

Note: in subsequent intervals, you should not include input tax arising from adjustments under the CGS when applying the partial exemption de minimis limit.

You can find out more about the partial exemption de minimis limit in Notice 706 "Partial Exemption". If you have an agreed combined business/non-business and PE method you will not be able to benefit from the de minimis rules.

7.12 What if a capital item is not used for a while?

Once the CGS has started, even if a capital item is not being used, it is treated as being used for the purpose for which it is made available. For example, if you have a computer which you take out of use for repair or overhaul it is treated, while it is out of use, as still being used for the same purpose as it was used before the overhaul.

If you dispose of a capital item without ever having used it, see Section 9.

8 ACCOUNTING FOR ADJUSTMENTS

8.1 In which accounting period do I make the adjustment?

You should enter your CGS adjustment amount on your VAT account for the second tax period after the end of the relevant subsequent interval in question. This is the period after the one in which you make your partial exemption annual adjustment for the year (unless you have chosen to make your annual adjustment in the last period of your tax year – see Notice 706 "Partial Exemption"). You should include the CGS adjustment amount in box 4 of your VAT return.

For example—

- if your tax periods end on the last day of March, June, September and December, your tax year is the twelve months ending 31 March. You should make your CGS adjustment in the period ending 30 September;
- if you are on monthly returns your tax year is the twelve months ending 31 March. You should make your CGS adjustment in the period ending 31 May; and
- if you make payments on account, this will not effect the timing of your adjustment, which you would make as described above.

If your registration is cancelled, you enter the adjustment amount on your final VAT return for the period ending on the effective date of deregistration.

8.2 Whose responsibility is it to carry out Capital Goods Scheme adjustments?

The person responsible for accounting for an adjustment for a given interval is the person who is treated as owner at the point immediately prior to the end of that interval. The "owner" of a capital item is a person who has or who acquires an interest in the item in question and will be the person who incurs the VAT charged on the capital item.

8.3 Who is treated as owner of a capital item following a TOGC?

The purchaser is treated as the owner for CGS purposes and is also treated as having done everything that the seller has done in respect of the capital item.

8.4 Who is treated as owner of a capital item in the case of a VAT group?

The representative member is treated as the owner of the capital item for CGS purposes whilst the real owner of the asset is in the representative member's VAT group. The representative member is also treated as having done everything that a group member has done in respect of the asset.

9 DISPOSAL OF CAPITAL ITEMS DURING THE ADJUSTMENT PERIOD

9.1 Sale of a capital item during an adjustment period

If you sell a capital item before the end of the adjustment period, your adjustment for the interval in which you sell it will be your final adjustment for that item, and must include all adjustment amounts for any remaining intervals.

To work out the final adjustment—

(1) For the interval in which you sell the item you should work out the adjustment amount (or in the first interval the initial reclaim of input tax) in the normal way as explained in Section 7.

(2) For any remaining complete intervals in the adjustment period, the capital item is treated as being used, taxable (at 100 per cent) if the sale was a taxable supply and exempt (0 per cent) if the sale was an exempt supply.

You should make your final disposal adjustment, including all adjustment amounts for remaining complete intervals, on your VAT return for the second accounting period after the end of the interval in which you sold the capital item. If you have a capital item and the adjustment period ends, see Section 6.9.

9.2 Are there any other rules on disposals?

If you dispose of a capital item as a transfer of a going concern (TOGC) – see VAT Leaflet 700/9 "Transfer of a Business as a Going Concern" – you will need to give the new owner the details of to the capital item so that future CGS adjustments can be made. As a future new owner you should ask the seller for information on the capital item being sold as a TOGC which relates to the CGS "status". The new owner must continue making the CGS adjustments for any remaining intervals.

The examples in paragraphs 9.3 and 9.4 explain this in more detail.

9.3 Example 1 of dealing with a TOGC

A fully taxable company constructs a new business premises for £1 million plus VAT. The company recovers the input tax at 100 per cent and uses it as intended in the business for two years. In the following year the company decides to let a specific area of the 4th floor. The company does not opt to tax – the supply is exempt. The company is aware of the CGS and makes an appropriate adjustment.

After a further two years the company decides to move the taxable operations and sells the building (NB, the building is no longer new) with the benefit of an existing tenant to a VAT registered property company. This supply is treated as a TOGC. (Neither party has to opt to tax in these circumstances.)

The new owner does not opt to tax and continues to let the premises to the existing and new tenants. The supplies are exempt and during the period covered by the CGS the use has changed from fully taxable to exempt.

The new owner must repay a percentage of the input tax originally claimed by the previous owner. This can be as much as 1/10th for each remaining interval.

9.4 Example 2 of dealing with a TOGC

A hotel chain incurs £3 million plus VAT on a total refurbishment of one of its prestigious hotels. It only makes taxable supplies from the hotel and recovers 100 per cent of the tax incurred. After five years the hotel is sold as a TOGC to another hotel chain. Neither party has opted to tax the premises.

The new owners decide that in addition to the normal B & B there is a market for supplying conferences and bare room hire. As they have not opted to tax the supplies are exempt – the total income from this venture representing 5 per cent of their turnover.

As the refurbishment is still covered by the scheme the new owner is liable to repay an amount of the original input tax incurred for each of remaining intervals that the item is used in making mixed supplies.

The timing of intervals may change on transfer of the business, depending on whether the new owner of the business is also taking over the seller's VAT registration number.

9.5 What if I am the seller or new owner of a capital item?

If you are taking over the seller's VAT registration number then—

- the interval during which the business is transferred continues without a break;
- the seller does not need to make any adjustments for that interval;
- you, as the new owner are responsible for any adjustments as if you had owned the capital item for the whole of that interval and for any remaining intervals in the normal way.

If you are not taking over the seller's VAT registration number then—

If you are the owner—

- the interval in which the seller transfers the business ends on the day before the transfer takes place;
- each subsequent interval then ends on successive anniversaries of that date irrespective of whether there are any future transfers of the item.

If you are the seller—

- you should make any adjustment for that interval on your VAT return for the 2nd period after the end of your tax year in the normal way;
- if you are cancelling your registration you should make any adjustment on your final return; and
- the new owner is responsible for the next interval which runs from the date of transfer to the anniversary date and any other remaining intervals which run for 12 months from each anniversary date.

Subsequent intervals applicable to the transferred item may coincide with the new owner's partial exemption tax year. If they do not the new owner (who has to carry out successive anniversary adjustments) will need to agree a way of calculating subsequent intervals with HMRC.

Where you transfer a business as a going concern, you do not treat any capital item included as part of the transfer as "sold" for the purposes of the scheme.

9.6 What if I cancel my registration?

If you are cancelling your registration, you may have to account for VAT on some of your business assets on hand depending on why you are cancelling your registration and what happened when you obtained them. If, when you cancel your registration, you have a capital item covered by the scheme which is still within its adjustment period and you find that you must account for VAT on your business assets, you will need to make a final adjustment.

If you are not required to account for VAT on your business assets because the VAT on the supply would be less than the monetary limit specified in Notice 700/11 "Cancelling your registration", you will still be treated as having made a supply and you will need to make a final adjustment. This also applies if the supply was exempt or zero-rated.

You should make your adjustment in exactly the same way as in paragraph 9.1, except that you include any adjustment for the remainder of the adjustment period on your final VAT return.

9.7 What if I sell a capital item without ever having used it?

If you have never used the item in the course or furtherance of your business, it is not regarded as a capital item for the purposes of the scheme.

If you have a capital item, which has not been used for a while, see Section 7.12.

9.8 What if a capital item is lost, stolen or destroyed?

If a capital item is lost, stolen or destroyed you should check your records to see how much the item was used in the interval in which this occurred. Calculate the CGS adjustment as if you had used the item for the whole of that interval. This is your final adjustment for the item. You do not need to make any adjustments for remaining complete intervals in the adjustment period. You should make your final adjustment on your VAT return for the second accounting period after the end of the tax year in which the item was lost, stolen or destroyed.

You will need to keep all documents which relate to the loss or destruction in case our officers wish to see them.

10 PART DISPOSALS OF CGS ITEMS

10.1 How do I deal with part disposals

Before 1 January 2011 the CGS period of adjustment was only brought to an end when the owner disposed of the whole of its interest in the asset. So, for example, if part of your refurbishment was destroyed or part of your building was sold, you would in theory still have been required to perform CGS adjustments on all of the VAT incurred on the asset including that part that had been destroyed. With effect from 1 January 2011 a business that makes a part disposal carries out a final adjustment in relation to the VAT on the part disposal and is only required to carry out adjustments in relation to that part of the capital item still in existence or which it still owns.

If you make a part disposal of an asset you will be required to carry out a final adjustment in relation to the VAT incurred on that part of the asset that is sold or destroyed. If the sale is a taxable supply, that part of the VAT will be attributable to taxable supplies for each remaining complete interval; if the sale is an exempt supply, that part of the VAT will be attributable to exempt supplies for each remaining complete interval. The remaining part of the VAT on the asset that is retained by you will continue to be subject to adjustments in the normal way.

10.2 How is the amount of VAT relating to a part disposal established?

The VAT attributable to the part disposal should be calculated on a fair basis. For example, where part of a building is sold, the VAT relating to the part disposal might be determined by reference to the market value of the part of the building sold as a proportion of the total market value of the building. Alternatively, it might be determined by reference to amount of the floor space sold as a proportion of the total floor space of the building. As long as the proportion of VAT attributable to the part disposal is fair, it will not be challenged by HMRC.

EXAMPLE

A business acquires a building for £1,000,000 + £200,000 VAT and first uses it on 1 April 2011. It uses the building for exempt purposes until 31 March 2016. It then decides to sell 50 per cent (by floor area) of the building on 30 September 2016 by way of a taxable supply for £750,000 + £150,000 VAT. It retains the remaining 50 per cent of the building and continues to use it to make exempt supplies.

When the business first acquires the building, it intends using it to make exempt supplies and so none of the £200,000 VAT on the purchase is deductible. Therefore the CGS baseline recovery percentage is nil. As use does not change during the following four intervals, no adjustment is due. However, in interval 6 it disposes of 50 per cent of the building and this is considered by the business to be a fair reflection of the VAT attributable to that part disposal ie £100,000.

In interval 6, which runs from 1 April 2016 to 31 March 2017, the business uses the building to make a taxable supply (the part disposal) and for exempt purposes. Therefore the total VAT on the building falls to be residual. If we assume that the partial exemption recovery percentage for this part of the business is 25 per cent, it can recover £200,000/10 x (25% – 0%) = £5,000 in this interval.

For the remaining four intervals, the VAT on the part disposal (£100,000) is treated as relating to taxable supplies. Therefore, a final adjustment of £100,000/10 (100% – 0%) x 4 = £40,000 is due to the business.

The business is required to account for output tax of £150,000 to HMRC on the part disposal in 2016. Both the interval 6 adjustment and the final adjustment for the part of the building disposed of are claimable on the second return after the end of interval 6 (ie in the period ending 30 September 2017).

The business also needs to carry out adjustments in relation to the part of the Capital item that it retains. Assuming it continues to be used to make exempt supplies for the remaining four intervals, no adjustments will be due.

10.3 How is part disposal by TOGC, loss or destruction dealt with?

In these circumstances, there is no supply for VAT purposes and so no final adjustment is made for remaining complete intervals in relation to the VAT on the part of the capital item that has been transferred, lost or destroyed. However, adjustments are still required in relation to that part of the capital item that is retained in accordance with the normal rules (even if related expenditure on the asset falls below the CGS threshold).

If the part disposal is by TOGC the capital item is split into two parts and adjustments in relation to the element transferred are continued by the transferee.

11 ARE THERE ANY OTHER RULES ON DISPOSALS?

If you dispose of a capital item before the end of its adjustment period we may apply the disposal test. The disposal test has been updated to deal with part disposals.

11.1 How does the disposal test work?

When a capital item is moved with a company into or out of a VAT group, the responsibility for the capital item is transferred. This means that the new owner must continue making the Capital Goods Scheme adjustments for any remaining intervals.

- the input tax initially recovered on the capital item;
- any adjustments already made under the CGS; and
- any final adjustment that is required as a result of the sale of the item.

If the total input tax exceeds the output tax due on the disposal of the item then, in principle, it may be necessary to adjust the amount of input tax recovered in relation to the capital item.

11.2 When does the disposal test apply?

The disposal test will only apply if you sell a capital item before the end of the adjustment period and benefit from an unjustified tax advantage because of the early sale. An unjustified tax advantage is normally one arising from an avoidance scheme where the owner seeks to secure an amount of input tax that would still be subject to adjustment under the CGS, were it not for the sale of the item, less any output tax due on the sale. We have published a Statement of Practice about the application of the disposal test.

We have the discretion to exclude certain disposals from the test and therefore from any disposal test adjustment.

For example, it will not be applied—

- to sales of computer equipment;
- where an owner disposes of an item at a loss due to market conditions (such as a general downturn in property prices);
- where the value of the item has depreciated;
- where the value of the item is reduced for other legitimate reasons (such as accepting a lower price to effect a quick sale);
- where the amount of output tax on disposal is less than the total input tax claimed only due to a reduction in the VAT rate; and
- where the item is used only for taxable (including zero-rated) purposes throughout the adjustment period (which includes the final disposal).

11.3 What disposal test adjustment should be made?

In cases where you gain an unjustified tax advantage you will need to calculate the amount of tax to be adjusted. To do this you will—

- have to calculate the net tax advantage; and
- then the net tax advantage that is unjustified.

Some form of apportionment needs to be applied to work out how much of the net tax advantage is unjustified. This might be achieved using the ratio that the value of the final taxable sale bears to the value of both the exempt supply and the final taxable sale (refer to example 4 in the Statement of Practice).

12 MOVEMENTS OF CAPITAL ITEMS INTO AND OUT OF VAT GROUPS

12.1 Item moves with a company

When a capital item is moved with a company into or out of a VAT group, the responsibility for the capital item is transferred. This means that the new owner must continue making the CGS adjustments for any remaining intervals.

12.2 Owner of a capital item moves into a VAT group

If you are the owner of a capital item and you move into a VAT group, the relevant interval terminates a day before the move takes place.

Each subsequent interval will end on successive anniversaries of that date, irrespective of whether there are any future movements into or out of VAT groups.

12.3 Company leaves a VAT group taking capital item bought during group membership with it

If a capital item is obtained by a company while it is a member of a VAT group, and the company moves out of the group, the relevant interval terminates on the day the move takes place. Each subsequent interval shall end on successive anniversaries of that date, again irrespective of whether there are any future movements into or out of VAT groups.

The previous owner of the capital item should make any adjustment for that interval on the VAT return for the second period after the end of the tax year in the normal way. The new owner then becomes responsible for the next interval, which runs from the date of the transfer to the anniversary date, and any other remaining intervals, which run for 12 months from each anniversary date.

Subsequent intervals applicable to the transferred item may coincide with the new owner's partial exemption tax year. However, if they do not, the new owner (who has to carry out successive anniversary adjustments) will need to agree a way of calculating subsequent intervals with HMRC.

13 VAT INCURRED BEFORE REGISTRATION

13.1 How does the present legislation work?

The present legislation applies if you register, or apply to register, on or after 1 January 2011 – even in cases where registration is backdated to an earlier date.

Under the present legislation, expenditure incurred on assets of a description falling within the CGS by an unregistered business counts towards the CGS threshold. If the threshold is met, the related VAT is brought into the CGS.

When you register for VAT, you deduct one complete interval from the period of adjustment (normally ten years for land and buildings) for each complete year (12-month period) that has elapsed between the date of first use of the asset (see paragraph 11.3) and the date of registration.

VAT that you incurred on the asset while you were unregistered is non-deductible and so the baseline recovery percentage for the CGS is nil.

The first interval applicable to the asset will run from the date of first use (see paragraph 11.3) to the day before the start of your first tax year (ie finishing at the same time as the registration period – see Notice 706 "Partial Exemption"). The legislation treats this as a subsequent interval and so any taxable use of the asset during the registration period will enable you to make an adjustment in your favour. Because pre-registration use is accounted for by a (potential) decrease in the number of intervals, only use in the registration period needs to be taken into account in considering the first interval adjustment. You then need to monitor taxable use over remaining subsequent intervals, making adjustments in the normal way.

EXAMPLE

A business purchased a building while it was unregistered for £250,000 and incurred VAT of £50,000 (assuming a 20 per cent rate of VAT for simplicity). It first used the building on 1 October 2009. On 1 January 2011, it registers for VAT and its first tax year starts on 1 April 2011. It uses the building entirely for making taxable supplies after it registers for VAT.

The CGS period of adjustment for the building is ten intervals and the baseline recovery percentage is nil. However, as 1 complete year has elapsed between first use of the building and the date the business registered for VAT, the CGS period of adjustment is reduced by 1 to 9 intervals. The first interval runs from 1 October 2009 to the day before the business's first VAT tax year which, in this example, is 31 March 2011. As the legislation treats this interval as a subsequent interval, the business needs to establish the recovery percentage for its first interval.

As the business only makes taxable supplies in the first interval, it is entitled to recover 100 per cent of 50,000/10 = £5,000 in relation to the first interval. The definition of the first interval covers all the way back from first use but this simply sets the CGS running. As exempt pre-registration use is reflected by the number of intervals being reduced (in this case from 10 to 9) that use does not need to be taken into account again in the first interval adjustment. So it is only the use while registered that is taken into account.

Assuming the building is used entirely for taxable purposes in subsequent intervals, the business will also be entitled to recover 100 per cent of 50,000/10 = £5,000 in respect of the remaining eight intervals (as the period of adjustment has been reduced to 9 to reflect use of the asset when the business was unregistered).

13.4 Can I still reclaim VAT on capital items under regulation 111?

No, pre-registration VAT incurred on capital items can only now be deducted in accordance with the CGS rules, to prevent duplicate claims.

NOTICE 707
VAT PERSONAL EXPORT SCHEME

January 2014.

Revised Notice January 2014. This notice cancels and replaces Notice 707 (October 2011). Details of any changes to the previous version can be found in paragraph 1.2 of this notice.

EXAMPLE:

The following rule has the force of law

> If you receive a net payment you must include the full value before such deductions (and including VAT) in your scheme turnover. This will usually be the value shown on your sales invoice.

1 Introduction

1.1 What is this Notice about?

This notice describes the Personal Export Scheme (PES). The scheme allows motor vehicles to be supplied in the United Kingdom free of Value Added Tax (VAT) if they will soon be exported to a destination outside the European Union (EU). This notice sets out the conditions you must follow if you want to use the scheme, either as a buyer or a seller.

1.2 What's changed?

This new notice contains the information which was previously in Notices 705 and 705A. We have combined the notices to reduce duplication and make it easier for buyers and sellers to find all the information they need.

You can access details of any changes to this notice on our website at www.hmrc.gov.uk or by phoning the VAT helpline on 0300 200 3700.

This notice and others mentioned are available both on paper and on our website.

1.3 Who should read this notice?

This notice is intended for:

– overseas visitors and EU residents who intend to remain outside the EU for at least six months and
– businesses who wish to sell vehicles under the Personal Export Scheme

1.4 Force of law

The legal provisions that cover the Personal Export Scheme are contained in:

– the VAT Act 1994 section 30(8) and 30(10)
– regulations 132 and 133 of the VAT Regulations 1995. These regulations allow for specific conditions that have the force of law.

The VAT Regulations 1995 and this notice lay down the conditions which must be met in full for a motor vehicle to be supplied free of VAT under the Personal Export Scheme.

2 Basic principles

2.1 What is the Personal Export Scheme?

The Personal Export Scheme (PES) allows entitled customers to buy a motor vehicle in the UK free of VAT for export outside the European Union (EU). Subject to some restrictions, the vehicle can be used for a limited period in the EU before it is exported.

Warning: It may be difficult to import motor vehicles into some countries. If you are thinking of buying a vehicle under the scheme, you should check with the relevant Embassy or High Commission in the UK because additional restrictions, paperwork and costs may apply.

2.2 Who can buy a vehicle under the scheme?

The scheme can be used by:

(a) overseas visitors. An overseas visitor is somebody *who has not been* in the EU for more than either:
– 365 days in the two years before the date when they apply to use the scheme or
– 1095 days in the six years before the date when they apply to use the scheme.
They must also:
– intend to leave, and stay outside, the EU with the motor vehicle for at least six months and
– comply with all the other conditions of the scheme.

(b) entitled EU residents. An entitled EU resident *has been* in the EU for more than either:
– 365 days in the two years before the date when they apply to use the scheme *or*
– 1095 days in the six years before the date when they apply to use the scheme.
They must also:
– intend to leave, and stay outside, the EU with the motor vehicle for at least six months; and
– comply with all the other conditions of the scheme.

2.3 What type of vehicle can be supplied under the scheme?

The scheme can be used to supply a new or used:

– motor vehicle

- motorcycle
- motor caravan.

It can not be used to supply:

- pedal cycles
- trailer caravans.

2.4 What if VAT is shown on the customer's invoice?

A vehicle purchased at a price including VAT will *not* be eligible for a refund even if the customer later exports it to a destination outside the EU.

2.5 Can the scheme be used to buy a motor vehicle to take to another EU country?

No. The scheme can only be used for vehicles which will be exported *outside* the EU.

Note: If the price of the vehicle *when purchased* included VAT, your customer will *not* be eligible for a refund even if the vehicle is later exported to a destination outside the EC.

Notice 728 *New means of transport* explains the VAT rules for removing a vehicle from the UK to another EU Member State.

2.6 Which countries belong to the European Union?

The VAT territory of the EU is made up of 27 Member States including some territories with which they have links. There is a list of:

- the fiscal (VAT) territory of the EU and
- the special territories which are outside the EU for VAT purposes in section 14.

2.7 Direct Exports

There is no need to use the scheme if the vehicle is *not* going to be used in the UK before it is exported from the EU. If the vehicle is going to be exported directly, you should read Notice 703 Exports and removals of goods from the UK.

If the customer drives their vehicle to the EU port or airport of departure, they will be using the vehicle in the EU.

3. Buying a vehicle under the scheme: basic information

3.1 Where can I buy the vehicle?

You can only buy the vehicle from a business which operates the Personal Export Scheme.

If	*Then*
order:	
a new vehicle with factory-fitted /dealer-fitted extras, or	those extras can only be supplied to you VAT-free if they are included on the invoice for the vehicle itself.
a used vehicle with dealer-fitted extras	So, if you don't order them at the same time that you buy the vehicle, you will be charged VAT on them.

3.2 How do I apply to use the scheme?

The business you are buying the vehicle from will give you a VAT 410 application form.

You must fill in the form and sign the declaration. You are signing to say that you have read and understand sections 1–7 of this notice and that you will meet *all* the conditions of the scheme. You must give the completed VAT 410 form back to the business. They will give you back the customer copy, which you should keep.

Warning: it is an offence to give incorrect information on the VAT 410 form. If you do this, you will be liable to prosecution.

3.3 When can I apply to use the scheme?

You can apply to use the scheme if you are	*and you intend to leave the EU in*
an overseas visitor (see paragraph 2.2)	15 months or less
an entitled EU resident (see paragraph 2.2)	9 months or less

3.4 How long can I use the vehicle in the UK before I export it?

If you are	*you may take delivery and use the vehicle in the UK*
an overseas visitor	during the last *12 months* of your stay in the EU.
an entitled EU resident	during the last *6 months* before you finally leave the EU.

3.5 Who can take delivery of the vehicle?

The vehicle can only be delivered to the person who applied to use the scheme.

When you take delivery of the vehicle, you will have to sign a certificate of receipt.

If you need somebody else to take delivery of the vehicle for you, you must ask our Personal Transport Unit for written permission (see paragraph 6.1 for contact details).

4 Buying a vehicle under the scheme: using the vehicle before exporting it from the EU

4.1 Do I have to insure the vehicle?

Yes. You should insure the vehicle for its *full* purchase price, including VAT.

If	*Then*
you can't export the vehicle because it has:	the VAT you didn't pay when you bought it will become due.
been stolen, or	
involved in an accident and written-off	

4.2 Can anybody else drive the vehicle while it is in the EU?

Yes, but only if *you* are still in the EU.

The vehicle can only be driven by another person:

– who has your permission and

– is an entitled person (see paragraph 2.2)

or who is

– your wife, husband or civil partner; or
– a chauffeur.

4.3 Can I visit another EU country with the vehicle?

Yes. But you can only bring the vehicle back to the UK if:

– you bring it back before the due date for exporting it; and
– you still plan to export it and leave the EU by the due date.

If you are thinking about visiting another EU country with the vehicle, you should check with that country's VAT authorities before you go. Your vehicle has been supplied free of VAT, so you need to find out whether the country you plan to visit has any tax or customs requirements which you will need to meet.

4.4 What if I take the vehicle to a country outside the EU?

If	*Then*
you take the vehicle out of the EU before its final date for export, and then re-import it into either the UK or another EU country	you must declare the vehicle to customs at the place you re-import it into the EU. You must show the customs officer the following document: for a new vehicle – the pink registration book (VX302); for a second-hand vehicle – the VAT 410 form.

5 Buying a vehicle under the scheme: exporting your vehicle

5.1 When must I export the vehicle?

If	*you must export the vehicle*
an overseas visitor	within 12 months of the date it was delivered to you.
an entitled EU resident	within 6 months of the date it was delivered to you.

5.2 Where can I find the last possible date by which I must export the vehicle?

If the vehicle is	*its final date for exportation will be on*
new	the pink registration book (VX302).
second-hand	the Form VAT 410.

5.3 What do I need to do when I export the vehicle?

You must tell:

- in England, Scotland and Wales, your Driver Vehicle Licensing Agency Local Office (DVLA LO)
- in Northern Ireland, the Driver Vehicle Agency (DVA)
- in the Isle of Man, the Vehicle and Driving Administrator

Contact details for these offices are listed in section 15.

If your vehicle is	*you must*
new	fill in the tear-off section of the pink registration certificate (VX302) and send it to the office which serves your location. The address will be on the document.
second-hand	fill in the relevant section of the vehicle registration certificate (V5C) to notify change of keeper, then send the whole document to the office which serves your location. The address will be on the document.

The office will send you a registration certificate. This will allow you to re-register the vehicle in the country you are taking it to.

Note: If you plan to leave the UK less than 14 days after buying the vehicle, you should tell the motor dealer before you buy so that they can tell the DVLA/DVA about the export. You will need to take the vehicle registration certificate (which will be in the previous keeper's name) with you when you leave.

You need to make your shipping arrangements in good time so that you can be sure that your vehicle is exported by the due date.

5.4 What if I don't export the vehicle?

If	*Then*
you don't export the vehicle by the due date	the VAT you didn't pay when you bought the vehicle will become payable *and* we can take the vehicle away from you.

You must not dispose of, or try to dispose of, the vehicle in the EU by:

- hire
- pledge
- as security
- sale
- gift, or
- any other means.

6 Buying a vehicle under the scheme: change of circumstances

6.1 What must I do if my plans change while the vehicle is in the UK?

f your plans change, you must contact our Personal Transport Unit (PTU) at once. Their contact details are:

HM Revenue & Customs
Personal Transport Unit
Priory Court
St John's Road
Dover
Kent CT17 9SH

Phone: 01304 664171

If	*Then*
after buying the vehicle, you find that:	
you can not export it by the due date or	you can no longer use the vehicle VAT-free.
either you or the vehicle will not be staying outside the EU for at least six consecutive months from the date of export	You will have to pay the full amount of VAT that you did not pay when you bought the vehicle. The PTU will tell you how to do this.

6.2 What must I do if I change my plans while the vehicle is in another EU country?

If, while you are visiting another EU country, you decide to stay there with the vehicle, then the vehicle will not be exported from the EU by the due date.

If this happens, you must notify the VAT authorities in the EU country in which you are staying at once. They will tell you how you can pay the VAT and any other local taxes which are due.

7 Buying a vehicle under the scheme: re-importing a vehicle

7.1 What if I bring a vehicle back to the UK after exporting it?

If you bring a vehicle back into the UK after exporting it outside the EU, you will ordinarily have to pay taxes at importation.

7.2 How much VAT will I be charged when I bring the vehicle back to the UK?

If you are eligible for relief from duty and tax as explained in Notice 3 Bringing your belongings and private motor vehicle to the United Kingdom from outside the European Community, then you will not be charged any VAT.

If you are *not* eligible for relief from duty and tax, you will be charged VAT as follows:

If	*Then*
you re-import the vehicle six months or more after the due date for export (see paragraph 5.2) or you can show that you and the vehicle have remained outside the EU for at least six consecutive months	you will be charged VAT on the vehicle's value at the time you re-import it.

In all other cases, you will be charged the VAT you did not pay when you bought the vehicle.

7.3 Must I license and register the vehicle once it is permanently back in the UK?

Yes. The only exception to this is if you are not going to use, or keep, the vehicle on the public roads.

When you arrive in the UK you must apply at once to the nearest licensing and registration office (see section 15). You will need to produce proof of either:

- payment of, or
- exemption from

VAT in order to re-license or re-register the vehicle.

7.4 What should I do if I re-import the vehicle into another EU country?

You should contact the VAT authority in the EU country you will be staying in so that you can find out how to pay the VAT and any other local taxes which are due.

8 Selling a vehicle under the scheme: basic information

8.1 Do I have to use the scheme?

No. The scheme is optional.

8.2 When can I take an order for a vehicle under the scheme?

You can take an order under the scheme if your customer intends to leave the EU in:

- 15 months or less, if they are an overseas visitor (see paragraph 2.2), or
- 9 months or less, if they are an entitled EU resident (see paragraph 2.2).

8.3 What do I have to do at the time of sale?

You should make sure that your customer is entitled to use the scheme (see paragraph 2.2).

If your customer is entitled to use the scheme, you must give them a copy of:

- sections 1 – 7 of this notice
- an application form VAT 410.

You should explain the conditions of the scheme to the customer and give them time to read sections 1 – 7 of this notice.

By completing Form VAT 410, the applicant declares that they:

- have received, read and understood sections 1 – 7 of this notice and
- will comply with all the conditions of the scheme which are listed on the back of the VAT 410 form.

Warning: it is an offence for applicants to give incorrect information on the VAT 410 form: you should advise them that, if they do so, they will be liable to prosecution.

You can obtain supplies of VAT 410 forms from our Helpline: see paragraph 1.2 for contact details.

8.4 The VAT 410 form

The VAT 410 form is carbonated and consists of 4 copies:

- Part 1 - (blue) HMRC copy
- Part 2 - (green) customer copy
- Part 3 - (pink) supplier copy and
- Part 4 - (yellow) DVLA/DVA copy.

All completed application forms must be serially-numbered in the top right hand corner. Each separate franchise at the same location will require a separate series of numbers.

You should forward the blue HMRC copy of the form to the Personal Transport Unit (PTU) at least two weeks before the date of delivery of the vehicle. Their address is:

HM Revenue & Customs Personal Transport Unit
Priory Court
St John's Road
DOVER
Kent CT17 9SH
Phone: 01304 664171
Fax: 01304 664179

Please make sure that your customers have completed the application forms fully and correctly before you accept them.

If	*Then*
the form is incomplete or inaccurate	the PTU will return it to you for correction. This may delay the delivery of the vehicle.
the form is completed accurately	the PTU will send you a VAT 412 form. You must not zero-rate the sale in your records until you have received the VAT 412.
— the form is completed accurately and	the PTU can phone you with the approval number once they have received the VAT 410.
— you need to supply the vehicle urgently	Once you have the number, you may release the vehicle. But you must not zero-rate the sale in your records until you have received the VAT 412.

8.5 Invoicing vehicles and supplying extras

You must supply and invoice the VAT-free vehicle direct to the applicant.

Note: you can only supply any factory-fitted or dealer-fitted extras VAT-free if they are included on the initial invoice for the supply of the vehicle at the time it is purchased.

8.6 Insuring the vehicle

You should advise the customer to insure the vehicle for its full *VAT-inclusive* value at the time of purchase for the reasons explained in paragraph 4.1.

8.7 What should I do if an order is cancelled?

If, after the application has been approved, the customer cancels it before delivery, you should contact the PTU immediately at the address given in paragraph 8.4. They will need the following details:

- the customer's name
- the serial number of the VAT 410 application form
- in the case of a new vehicle, the make and model ordered
- in the case of a second-hand vehicle, the registration number.

8.8 What should I do if I find out that the scheme's conditions have been breached?

If you find out that:

- a vehicle you supplied under the scheme has been retained in the United Kingdom beyond the due date for export or
- any other condition of the scheme has been breached

you must let the PTU know immediately.

9 Selling a vehicle under the scheme: registering and licensing vehicles

9.1 How do I register a new vehicle?

You must:

- submit an application Form V55 headed prominently in block letters "PERSONAL EXPORT (VAT FREE) VEHICLE"
- attach it to the yellow copy (part 4) of the Form VAT 410; and
- send both documents to the licensing office in the list at section 15 which is closest to you.

9.2 What if I sell a second-hand vehicle under the scheme?

These vehicles will already have been registered, so you must.

- notify the DVLA/DVA of the change of keeper, and
- apply for a special tax disc.

If there is a current tax disc in force, you must surrender it to the DVLA/DVA before the application to use the scheme can proceed. Only the registered keeper can apply to the DVLA/DVA for a tax refund on the disc.

Send the following documents to the DVLA/DVA:

- the yellow copy (part 4) of the Form VAT 410
- the completed V5C registration certificate
- Form V10 (application to license the vehicle)
- insurance certificate
- MoT certificate, if applicable
- Form VX304 (exemption from Vehicle Excise Duty), if applicable.

If the customer intends to export the vehicle within 14 days of buying it, you should give them the V5C Registration Certificate (which will be in the previous keeper's name). You must then notify the DVLA/DVA of the export.

10 Selling a vehicle under the scheme: procedures for delivery

10.1 What do I need to do before I deliver the vehicle?

New vehicles

Before you deliver the vehicle, you must complete the details required on pages 5 and 8 of the pink registration book, showing:

- the amount of VAT which has been remitted (in other words, not paid)
- the delivery date
- the final date for export.

Second-hand vehicles

If you have followed the procedures in paragraphs 9.2 and 12.2, you do not need to do anything else.

10.2 Delivery receipts

You must retain a dated certificate of receipt for the vehicle with your records. It must be signed by the applicant.

10.3 What is the procedure for an urgent delivery?

You may allow delivery within two weeks of the VAT 410 form being completed, but only if an overseas visitor or an entitled EU resident intends to leave the UK within one month of their application to buy a vehicle under the scheme.

For all urgent delivery requests, you must complete a Certificate for Urgent Delivery (see section 11). You should send a copy of the certificate by fax to the Personal Transport Unit at least three working days before the date you deliver the vehicle to the applicant. The certificate must be authorised by a

- sole proprietor
- partner
- director
- company secretary or
- a duly authorised person at a responsible level.

When you fax the certificate to the PTU, you must also fax a copy of the VAT 410 form plus, for new vehicles, the V55 Form. You should then post the original papers to the PTU (see paragraph 8.4).

*Note: You must **not** use this procedure if either*

- the initial application by the customer has been rejected or returned for amendment; or
- the customer has made more than one application in any period of 6 months.

10.4 Queries

If you have any doubts or questions before or after delivery of the vehicle which can *not* be resolved by our Helpdesk (see paragraph 1.2 for contact details), you should consult the PTU at the address shown in paragraph 8.4.

11 Format for certificate for urgent delivery

Certificate for urgent delivery

Applicant's Details:
Name: . . . . Invoice no: . . . .
Address: . . . .
. . . .
. . . .
. . . .
. . . .
Post Code: . . . .
Vehicle Details:
Make: . . . . Model: . . . .
Chassis No: . . . . Registration No: . . . .
I hereby certify that I have this day personally interviewed . . . . (*name of applicant)* who assures me that he/she has not applied for or acquired a VAT-free motor vehicle under the Personal Export Scheme, as described in Notice 705, within the last 6 months.

Applicant's Details:

I have also inspected his/her passport number . . . . . . issued by . . . . *(name of authority)* and the following documents: *(see * below)* . . . .

. . . .

I have no reason to doubt his/her status as an overseas visitor/entitled EU resident (delete as appropriate) or his/her declared intention to leave the European Union with the vehicle on *(date)* . . . . *(see ** below)* and to remain abroad with the vehicle for at least six consecutive months.

Signed: . . . .

Position in company: . . . .

Date: . . . .

* Example: details of car ferry tickets; overseas residence permit; return tickets; confirmatory letters or such evidence as was seen.
** This date must not be later than one month from the date of application.

12 What records must I keep?

12.1 Vehicles on which you were charged VAT

You must keep:

- the normal VAT records as set out in Notice 700 The VAT Guide and
- your pink copy of the VAT 410 form for inspection by our officers:

You must also keep a separate record of each vehicle you have supplied under the Scheme, showing:

- the date of delivery
- the applicant's name and UK address
- particulars of the vehicle supplied, including type, chassis number and registration number
- the amount of VAT remitted (i.e. not paid) on the delivery price. This must include the price of any accessories or extras and any delivery charges, less any discount allowed
- a certificate of receipt of the vehicle, signed and dated by the applicant. This must include the chassis number and the registration number.

12.2 Margin Scheme vehicles

You should already have a record of these in your Margin Scheme stock book.

When you sell a Margin Scheme vehicle under the Personal Export Scheme, you *must* close its stock book entry *and* include a cross-reference to the serial number of the VAT 410 form. Insert "zero-rate" in the VAT rate column of your stock book and "Nil" in the VAT due column.

You must then record the sale separately and include the details listed in paragraph 12.1.

12.3 How long must I keep the records?

You must keep records of all the vehicles you have sold for a period of six years as specified in Notice 700 The VAT Guide.

13 Suppliers Checklist

Have you checked?		*Tick if yes*
1	the customer is eligible to use the Personal Export Scheme (see paragraph 2.2)	
2	the customer has received and read a copy of sections 1 - 7 of Notice 705 (see paragraph 8.3)	
3	the customer agrees to comply with all the conditions of the scheme (see paragraph 8.3)	
4	the customer will personally take delivery of the vehicle in the UK (see paragraph 3.5)	
5	you have informed the customer that they will be liable to prosecution if the information they have given on the VAT 410 application form is incorrect (see paragraph 8.3)	
6	you have advised the customer to insure the vehicle for the full VAT-inclusive value at the time of purchase (see paragraph 8.6)	
7	the customer knows that the vehicle must be removed from the EU by the final date for exportation (see paragraph 5.1)	
8	you have informed the customer that: —if their order is cancelled or —they change their plans and the vehicle is to remain in the UK/EU they must immediately contact either the PTU at Dover, (see paragraph 6.1) or the VAT fiscal authority in the EU country in which they are to remain.	
9	you have kept a separate record of the vehicle (see paragraph 12.1)	
10	you have completed the VAT 410 form. Copies to be distributed as follows: —copy 1 (blue) - HMRC copy —copy 2 (green) - customer's copy —copy 3 (pink) - your copy —copy 4 (yellow) - DVLA/DVA copy, with the following documents attached: *For new vehicles:* Form V55 authorising the issue of a pink log book (see paragraph 9.1) *For second-hand vehicles:* —Completed V5C Registration Document; —V10 form (Vehicle licence application), and —VX304 if the purchaser is entitled to claim exemption from payment of vehicle excise duty (see paragraph 9.2)	
11	the vehicle has been delivered directly to the person who signed the VAT 410 Form (see paragraph 3.5)	
12	the applicant has signed a dated certificate of receipt for the vehicle, and you have retained a copy in your records (see paragraph 12.1)	

14 Fiscal (VAT) territory of the European Union

14.1 VAT territory of the Single Market

From 1 January 2007, the VAT territory of the EU is made up of 28 Member States. The following table shows the Member States and their territories which are included or excluded for VAT purposes.

Member State	*including*	*but excluding*
Austria	Jungholtz and Mittelberg	
Belgium		
Bulgaria		
Croatia		
Cyprus	the British Sovereign Base Areas of Akrotiri and Dhekelia	the United Nations buffer zone and the part of Cyprus to the north of the buffer zone where the republic of Cyprus does not exercise effective control
Czech Republic		
Denmark		the Faroe Islands, Greenland
Estonia		
Finland		the Aland islands
France	Monaco	Martinique, French Guiana, Guadeloupe, Reunion, St Pierre and Miquelon
Germany		the island of Heligoland, Busingen
Greece		Mount Athos (also known as Agion Oros)
Hungary		
Ireland		
Italy		Campione d'Italia, the Italian Waters of Lake Lugano, Livigno
Latvia		
Lithuania		
Luxembourg		
Malta		
Netherlands		Antilles
Poland		
Portugal	the Azores, Madeira	
Romania		
Slovakia		
Slovenia		
Spain	the Balearic Islands	The Canary Islands, Ceuta, Melilla
Sweden		
United Kingdom	the Isle of Man	The Channel Islands, Gibraltar

14.2 The following countries and territories are outside the EC fiscal (VAT) area

– Liechtenstein;
– Andorra;
– San Marino;
– The Vatican City.

If you need more information about the VAT territory of the EC, please contact our Helpline (see paragraph 1.2 for contact details).

15 Contact details for vehicle licensing offices

DVLA office	*Address*
Beverley	Crosskill House Mill Lane Beverley HU17 9JB

Birmingham	30 Granby Avenue Garretts Green Birmingham B33 0SD
Bristol	Northleigh House Lime Kiln Close Stoke Gifford Bristol BS34 8SR
Chelmsford	Swift House 18 Hoffmanns Way Chelmsford Essex CM1 1GU
Glasgow	46 West Campbell Street Glasgow G2 6TT
Leeds	Unit 9 Finch Drive Temple Point Leeds LS15 9JQ
Lincoln	Firth Court Firth Road Lincoln LN5 7WD
London Wimbledon	Connect House 133 to 137 Alexandra Road Wimbledon SW19 7JY
Maidstone	Coronet House 11 Queen Anne Road Maidstone ME14 1XB
Manchester	Trafford House Chester Road Manchester M32 0SL
Northampton	Ground Floor Riverside House Riverside Way Bedford Road Northampton NN1 5PE
Norwich	11 Prince of Wales Road Norwich NR1 1UP
Oxford	Ground Floor 3 Cambridge Terrace Oxford OX1 1RW
Stockton	St Marks House St Marks Court Thornaby Stockton on Tees TS17 6QR

The phone number for the DVLA is 0300 7906 802. For textphone minicom users, the number is 0300 123 1279.

If you are in Northern Ireland or the Isle of Man, vehicle licensing is carried out by different offices. Please use the one which is appropriate to you.

DVLA office	*Address*

Northern Ireland	DVA Licensing County Hall Castlerock Road Coleraine BT51 3TB 0845 402 4000
Isle of Man	Vehicle & Driving Administrator Sea Terminal Building Douglas Isle of Man IM1 2RF 01624 686825

NOTICE 708
BUILDINGS AND CONSTRUCTION

2014

18. THE CERTIFICATES

18.1 Zero-rated and reduced-rated building work

This certificate has the force of law

Certificate for zero-rated and reduced-rated building work.

1. Address of the building:

2. Name and address of organisation receiving the building work:

VAT Registration number (if registered):

Charity registration (if registered):

3. Date of completion (or estimated date of completion) of

the work:

Value (or estimated value) of the supply: £

Name, address and VAT registration number of building contractor:

4. I have read the relevant parts of Notice 708 Buildings and construction and certify that this organisation (in conjunction with any other organisation where applicable) will use the building, or the part of the building, for which zero-rating or reduced-rating is being sought **solely** for (tick as appropriate):

a relevant charitable purpose, namely by a charity in either or both of the following ways:

otherwise than in the course or furtherance of business ☑ or

as a village hall or similarly in providing social or recreational facilities for a local community ☑

a relevant residential purpose, namely as:

(a) a home or other institution providing residential accommodation for children ☑

(b) a home or other institution providing residential accommodation with personal care for persons in need of personal care by reason of old age, disablement, past or present dependence on alcohol or drugs or past or present mental disorder ☑

a hospice ☑

residential accommodation for students or school pupils ☑

residential accommodation for members of any of the armed forces ☑

a monastery, nunnery or similar establishment ☑ or

an institution which is the sole or main residence of at least 90 per cent of its residents ☑

and will not be used as a hospital, prison or similar institution or an hotel, inn or similar establishment.

5 I certify that the information given is complete and accurate and acknowledge that if the building, or the part of the building, for which zero-rated supplies have been obtained, within a period of 10 years from the date of its completion:

ceases to be used solely for a relevant residential purpose and/or a relevant charitable purpose;

is no longer used to the same extent for a relevant residential purpose and/or a relevant charitable purpose decreases; or

is disposed of,

a taxable supply will have been made, on which this organisation will have to account for VAT at the standard rate. .

Name (print):
Position held:
Date:
Signed:

General warning

1. HMRC reserves the right to alter the format of the certificate through the publication of a new notice. You must ensure that the certificate used is current at the time of issue.

Warnings for the issuer

2. You may be liable to a penalty if you issue a false certificate.

3. You are responsible for the information provided on the completed certificate.

Warnings for the contractor

4. You must take all reasonable steps to check the validity of the declaration given to you on this certificate.

5. This certificate does not automatically confer zero-rating or reduced-rating on your supplies. You must check that you meet all the conditions for zero-rating or reduced-rating your supply – see *Notice 708 Buildings and construction*.

18.2 Zero-rated sales and long leases

This certificate has the force of law

Certificate for sales and long leases of zero-rated buildings
1. Address of the building:
2. Name and address of organisation buying, or entering into a long lease on, the building (or part of the building): VAT Registration number (if registered): Charity registration (if registered):
3. Date (or estimated date) of purchase or commencement of the lease: Value (or estimated value) of the supply: £ Name, address and VAT registration number of the developer:
4. I have read the relevant parts of Notice 708 Buildings and construction and certify that the building, or the part of the building, for which zero-rating is being sought will be used **solely** for (tick as appropriate ☑): a relevant charitable purpose, namely by a charity in either or both of the following ways: (a) otherwise than in the course or furtherance of business ☑ or (b) as a village hall or similarly in providing social or recreational facilities for a local community. ☑ a relevant residential purpose, namely as: a home or other institution providing residential accommodation for children ☑

a home or other institution providing residential accommodation with personal care for persons in need of personal care by reason of old age, disablement, past or present dependence on alcohol or drugs or past or present mental disorder ☑

a hospice ☑

residential accommodation for students or school pupils ☑

residential accommodation for members of any of the armed forces ☑

a monastery, nunnery or similar establishment or ☑

an institution which is the sole or main residence of at least 90 per cent of its residents ☑

and will not be used as a hospital, prison or similar institution or an hotel, inn or similar establishment.

5. I certify that the information given is complete and accurate and acknowledge that if the building, or the part of the building, for which zero-rated supplies have been obtained, within a period of 10 years from the date of its completion:

ceases to be used solely for a relevant residential purpose and/or a relevant charitable purpose;

is no longer used to the same extent for a relevant residential purpose and/or a relevant charitable purpose decreases; or

is disposed of,

a taxable supply will have been made, on which this organisation will have to account for VAT at the standard rate. .

Name (print):
Position held:
Date:
Signed:

General warning

1. HMRC reserves the right to alter the format of the certificate through the publication of a new notice. You must ensure that the certificate used is current at the time of issue.

Warnings for the issuer

2. You may be liable to a penalty if you issue a false certificate.

3. You are responsible for the information provided on the completed certificate.

Warnings for the developer

4. You must take all reasonable steps to check the validity of the declaration given to you on this certificate.

5. This certificate does not automatically confer zero-rating on your sale or long-lease. You must also check that you meet all the conditions for zero-rating your supply – see Notice 708 Buildings and construction

NOTICE 709/5
TOUR OPERATORS' MARGIN SCHEME

November 2009

This notice cancels and replaces Notice 709/5 (August 2004)

The legal basis for the Tour Operators' Margin Scheme is VATA 1994 s 53 and the VAT (Tour Operators) Order 1987, SI 1987/1806. Sections 8 to 13 of this notice, contained in boxes, have the force of law under this Order.

EXAMPLE

This section has the force of law

Step	**Working out the total sales of margin scheme packages**
1	Total the VAT-inclusive selling prices of your designated travel services and margin scheme packages supplied during the financial year.

1 INTRODUCTION

1.1 What is this notice about?

This notice explains how you must account for VAT if you buy in and resell travel facilities as a principle or undisclosed agent (that is, acting in your own name).

It assumes that you have a knowledge of the basic principles of VAT that are explained in Notice 700 "The VAT Guide".

This notice should be read in conjunction with Notice 709/6 "Travel agents and tour operators".

This updated version of the notice has been produced primarily to include important changes to TOMS legislation and practice which come into effect from 1 January 2010. These changes have already been published in Revenue & Customs Brief 27/09. The sections of this notice which have been altered to take account of these changes are:

2.13, 3.1, 3.2, 3.3, 3.4, 3.5, 5.2, 5.3, 5.4, 5.5, 5.6, 5.11, 5.14, 6.2, 6.12, 6.13, plus the sections which have force of law, 8, 9, 10, 11, 12 and 13.

The changes relate to removal of the opt-in to the TOMS for wholesale supplies (previously detailed in section 3.2), removal of the opt-out for travel supplies consumed by businesses (previously detailed in section 3.3) and the introduction of a new market value calculation (annual adjustment), which is set out in a new section 8.

In addition to these changes the following sections have been changed:

Section 4.15 has been amended to clarify the tax point rules under method 2.

Section 4.20 has been amended to reflect the new invoicing regulations for TOMS supplies made to business customers after 1 October 2007.

Section 6.1 has been amended to update what should be included in the total selling price for the annual calculations.

Section 6.4 has been amended to add another typical example of overhead finance charges.

Commentary—*De Voil Indirect Tax Service* **V3.591**.

1.2 Where can I find the law that is relevant to this notice?

The relevant VAT law is in the

- VATA 1994 s 53; and Sch 8 Group 8 item 12; and
- Value Added Tax (Tour Operators) Order 1987, SI 1987/1806 as amended by the Value Added Tax (Tour Operators) (Amendment) Orders of 1990, 1992, 1995 and 2009.
- VAT Regulations 1995, SI 1995/2518 s 14(1)(n).

Under this law, HM Revenue & Customs have certain powers, including powers to specify—

- how to work out the value of supplies covered by the Tour Operators Margin Scheme (see sections 5, 8, 9, 10, 11, 12 and 13), and

therefore the whole of Sections 8 to 12 of this notice have the force of law. Other parts of this notice represent HM Revenue & Customs' interpretation of the law, but are not law in themselves.

2 INTRODUCTIONS TO THE TOUR OPERATORS' MARGIN SCHEME (TOMS)

2.1 What is the Tour Operators' Margin Scheme?

It is a special scheme for businesses that buy-in and resell travel, accommodation and certain other services (see paragraph 2.9) as a principal or undisclosed agent (that is, acting in your own name). In the UK this scheme is known by the abbreviated term "the TOMS".

The TOMS is a simplification measure. In many cases it enables VAT to be accounted for on travel supplies without businesses having to register and account for tax in each member state where the services and goods are enjoyed.

Commentary—*De Voil Indirect Tax Service* **V3.591, V3.592, V3.594**.

2.2 Does the TOMS only apply to "traditional" tour operators?

No, it covers anyone who is making the type of supplies detailed in paragraph 2.1, even if this is not your main business activity, or you do not view yourself as a "traditional" tour operator. For example—

- a hotelier who buys in coach passenger transport to collect its guests at the start and end of their stay;
- a coach operator who buys in hotel accommodation in order to put together a package;
- a company that arranges conferences, including providing hotel accommodation for delegates.

2.3 Must I use the TOMS?

It depends what you do. If you are an undisclosed agent (that is, acting in your own name) or a principal (see Notice 709/6 "Travel agents and tour operators") in making—

— margin scheme supplies (see paragraph 2.7); *or*
— other types of supply (for example an in-house supply) packaged/supplied with margin scheme supplies (see paragraphs 2.9 and 2.11),

then you are a tour operator and must account for VAT using the TOMS – see also paragraph 2.4.

2.4 Does the TOMS cover all my supplies?

Not necessarily, the TOMS does *not* apply to—

— supplies you have arranged as a disclosed agent/intermediary and your commission is readily identifiable (see paragraphs 2.14 and 6.7);
— in-house or agency supplies you make which are *not* packaged/supplied with margin scheme supplies (see paragraphs 2.12 and 2.13);
— supplies you make to business customers for subsequent resale by them (that is, wholesale supplies); or
— supplies that are incidental to your other supplies (see paragraph 3.6).

If you are unsure as to whether or not you must use the TOMS, you should contact your local VAT Business Advice Centre for advice. To help us decide, we may ask you to write in with copies of your contracts, brochures, booking terms and conditions, and other sales literature.

2.5 Is the TOMS affected by where the supplies are enjoyed?

No, the TOMS applies to travel services that are enjoyed—

— within the UK;
— within the EU (that is, other than the UK);
— outside the EU.

2.6 How does the TOMS work?

If you are registered for VAT, you must normally account for tax on the full selling price of your supplies, but you can reclaim the VAT charged on purchases (subject to the normal rules).

Under the TOMS, you cannot reclaim any UK or EC VAT charged on the travel services and goods you buy in and re-supply – the tax on such goods or services is accounted for in the relevant member state by the providers of those services (hotels, airlines and so on).

However as a tour operator based in the UK, you only account for VAT on the *margin* you make on your margin scheme supplies (see paragraph 2.7), that is, the difference between the amount you receive from your customer (including any amounts paid on behalf of your customer by third parties) and the amount you pay your suppliers.

Section 5 explains how to work out your output tax using the TOMS and the value of your outputs by using the appropriate calculation in sections 8, 9, 10, 11 and 12.

You can still reclaim, subject to the normal rules, VAT on overheads outside the TOMS (see paragraph 4.3).

2.7 What is a margin scheme supply?

A margin scheme supply is defined in law (see paragraph 1.2) as a "designated travel service".

This means it is a supply of goods or services which is—

— bought in from another person and re-supplied without material alteration or further processing; and
— supplied by a tour operator from an establishment in the UK, for the direct benefit of a traveller – see paragraph 2.8.

See also paragraphs 2.9, 2.10 and 2.11.

2.8 What is meant by the term "traveller"?

A person, including a business or local authority, who receives a supply of a designated travel service, other than for the purpose of re-supply.

2.9 What type of supplies fall within the TOMS?

The following are *always* margin scheme supplies—

— accommodation;
— passenger transport;
— hire of a means of transport;
— trips or excursions;
— services of tour guides;
— use of special lounges at airports.

See also paragraphs 2.10, 2.11 and 2.12.

2.10 Can any other supplies become margin scheme supplies?

Yes, supplies such as catering, admission tickets and sports facilities fall within this category, if they are—

— bought in and sold on without material alteration, for the direct benefit of a traveller; and
— provided as part of a package with one or more of the supplies listed in paragraph 2.9.

2.11 What is a margin scheme package?

It is a single transaction, which may include one or more margin scheme supplies, or it may also include margin scheme supplies sold together with an in-house supply and/or an agency supply.

2.12 What about supplies of services similar to those at paragraph 2.9 that are not bought-in?

These are described as "in-house" supplies and are defined as—

— a supply made from your *own resources*; or
— resulting from purchases that you have bought in but materially altered or further processed, so that what you eventually supply is different from what you purchased.

2.13 How do I account for VAT on in-house supplies?

If supplied on their own (that is, not with margin scheme supplies) in-house supplies are taxed under the normal VAT rules, that is, they are not subject to the TOMS.

You can find examples of in-house supplies in section 7 of this notice.

If you make a mixture of in-house supplies and bought-in margin scheme supplies, they must *all* be accounted for using the TOMS; the in-house supplies will need to be quantified so they can be accounted for under the normal rules. There are two different TOMS methods. The cost based method and the market value method. These are fully explained in sections 5, 8 and 9 of this notice.

To determine which method is appropriate for your business to use you will need to consider the following—

If you . . .	*Then you . . .*
can calculate the market value of an in-house supply in a package	must follow the market value calculation in section 8 for those in-house supplies.
can calculate the market value of in-house supplies but the cost based method is an accurate reflection of your package	may ignore the market value method and follow the cost based method in section 9.
cannot calculate a market value for an in-house supply in a package	follow the cost based method in section 9 for those in-house supplies.

Note: if you can calculate a market value for some in-house supplies and not others you may have to use a mixture of the apportionment methods.

For example:

Package 1: includes an in-house supply A for which a market value can be established – the market value method will be used for the in-house supply.

Package 2: includes an in-house supply B for which a market value cannot be established – the cost-based method will be used for the in-house supply.

Package 3: includes both the in-house supplies A and B – the market value method must be used to extract A from the package and the cost-based method used for remaining parts of the package.

However, if the structure of the package is such that the cost-based method is an accurate reflection of the package, then the figures for A can be included in the cost-based calculation and the market value method ignored.

2.14 Must agency supplies be included in the TOMS?

If you act as a disclosed agent in the making of margin scheme supplies (that is, you name the provider of the margin scheme supplies), you are not yourself making margin scheme supplies and so you must normally account for any VAT on your commission under the normal rules (that is, not using the TOMS) – see Notice 709/6 "Travel Agents and Tour Operators".

However, if you...	*Then you . . .*
— use the TOMS because you make margin scheme supplies in your own name; and — also receive *variable* commission (or commission which is otherwise not readily identifiable) as a disclosed agent	must include your agency income and directly related costs in your TOMS calculations (see paragraph 6.6 and Section 8).

2.15 Does it matter where my business is established?

If your supplies are made from an establishment in another member state you may have to register and account for tax under that country's equivalent of the TOMS (see paragraph 4.8).

3 SUPPLIES TO BUSINESSES

Commentary—*De Voil Indirect Tax Service* **V3.592.**

3.1 What happens if I make supplies to business customers?

Whether your supplies to business customers must be accounted for under the TOMS will depend on whether your supplies are to be resold or consumed by that business customer.

If your supplies are to business customers . . .	*These supplies do...*
which are for subsequent resale (wholesale supplies).	not fall within the TOMS – see paragraph 3.2.
for consumption by those customers.	fall within the TOMS (provided they meet the definition of margin scheme supplies) – see paragraph 3.3.

3.2 Can I include wholesale supplies in the TOMS?

If you act as a disclosed agent in the making of margin scheme supplies (that is, you name the provider of the margin scheme supplies), you are not yourself making margin scheme supplies and so you must normally account for any VAT on your commission under the normal rules (that is, not using the TOMS) – see Notice 709/6 "Travel Agents and Tour Operators".

My supply is . . .	*The place of supply is where it...*
passenger transport.	takes place.
accommodation.	is situated.

live entertainment.	is physically performed.

Further guidance and more examples can be found in Notice 741 "Place of supply of services".

3.3 Can I exclude supplies to business customers for their consumption from the TOMS?

No. Supplies which are consumed by a business or its employees fall within the scope of the TOMS and must be accounted for using the scheme. Up until 1 January 2010 businesses were able to exclude certain supplies made to business customers for their own consumption, however from that date such exclusions are no longer permitted. This means that businesses will no longer be entitled to receive a VAT invoice for supplies made to them using the TOMS – see section 4.20 for further details on invoicing requirements.

3.4 What if I supply educational school trips which include margin scheme supplies?

From 1 January 2010 the arrangement which allowed certain supplies to local authorities for educational school trips to be excluded from the TOMS has been withdrawn. These must now be accounted for using the TOMS (unless the body they are supplied to will re-sell them as wholesale supplies – see paragraph 3.1). If you are unsure whether or not your supply will be re-supplied, then you should use the TOMS to account for VAT.

3.5 What if I supply the teaching of English as a foreign language?

If you make supplies of this nature (either in-house or bought-in) in a package with one or more of the supplies listed in paragraph 2.9 you should refer to Business Briefs 18/99 and 27/99.

3.6 What if my TOMS supplies form only an incidental part of my business?

You need not use the TOMS if you—

- do not buy in any supplies of accommodation or passenger transport for resale (a definition of passenger transport can be found in Notice 744A "Passenger Transport"; *and*
- buy in for resale some other supplies which are normally margin scheme supplies; and
- do not expect your gross total turnover from these supplies to be more than 1 per cent of your total gross turnover.

EXAMPLES

I am a hotelier who buys in	*My supplies . . .*
occasional car hire for guests, the income is less than 1 per cent of my gross annual turnover.	can be outside the TOMS.
occasional taxi trips for my guests, the income is less than 1 per cent of my gross annual turnover.	are within the TOMS. Although the turnover from these supplies is less than 1 per cent, the resupply of taxi trips is considered to be passenger transport.
the services of guides for my guests, the gross income from this is 1 per cent of my gross turnover. I also buy in car hire, the income from this is also 1 per cent of my gross annual turnover.	are within the TOMS. Although both types of supply are eligible for exclusion, the total income from both is greater than 1 per cent of the total business turnover.

4 SPECIAL RULES

4.1 What is my taxable turnover for VAT registration or deregistration purposes?

If you are considering whether you must register for VAT, or whether you may deregister, your taxable turnover is regarded as the—

- total *margin* on your taxable (including zero-rated) margin scheme supplies; plus
- full value of taxable (including zero-rated) in-house supplies; plus

— full value of taxable agency commission; plus
— full value of any other taxable (including zero-rated) supplies you make in the UK.

Commentary—*De Voil Indirect Tax Service* **V3.594**.

4.2 Can I make TOMS supplies from within a VAT Group?

Yes, however, if you make margin scheme supplies, you cannot belong to a VAT group if any other member of the group—

— has an overseas establishment; and
— makes supplies outside the UK, which would be taxable (including zero-rated) supplies if made in the UK; and
— supplies goods and services which will become, or are intended to become, margin scheme supplies (that is, which are for resale, whether or not by the other member concerned).

4.3 What VAT can I reclaim on my purchases?

You *may* reclaim (outside the TOMS)—

— UK VAT incurred on your overheads and on purchases relating to your in-house supplies, subject to the normal rules – see Notice 700 "The VAT Guide".
— VAT incurred in other member states on your overheads and on purchases relating to your in house supplies, subject to the conditions set out in Notice 723 "Refunds of VAT in the European Community for EC and non-EC traders". Please note you must reclaim any such VAT from the appropriate VAT authorities in the other member state(s) concerned – do not reclaim such VAT on your UK VAT returns. However, if you make supplies in any other member state, you may have to register and account for VAT in that country, in which case this refund procedure may not be appropriate.

4.4 What VAT can't I reclaim?

You *cannot* reclaim VAT on purchases that you make to resell as margin scheme supplies, whether incurred in the UK or another member state.

4.5 What type of supply am I making?

When you sell a margin scheme package you are regarded as making a *single* supply of services for VAT purposes. The nature of your service is that of putting together the package or organising the travel services.

Example:

You buy in hotel accommodation and transport to provide a tour. You are making a single supply of the tour rather than two separate supplies of transport and accommodation.

4.6 Where is the place of supply of margin scheme services?

The place of supply of your *margin scheme supplies* depends on where your business is established.

I have an establishment in . . .	*The place of supply is . . .*
the UK and nowhere else.	the UK.
many countries, but I have sold this package from my establishment in the UK.	the UK.
many countries, but I have sold this package from my establishment in another member state.	outside of the UK. This supply is outside the scope of UK VAT, but is within the scope of taxation in the member state where the establishment is.
many countries, but I have sold this package from my establishment outside the EC.	outside of the UK and also outside of the EU. The TOMS does not apply.

4.7 Where is the place of supply of in-house supplies?

Whether or not in-house supplies are part of a package, normal place of supply VAT rules always apply, for example—

My supply is. . .	*The place of supply is where it . . .*
passenger transport.	takes place.
accommodation.	is situated.
live entertainment.	is physically performed.

Further guidance and more examples can be found in Notice 741 "Place of supply of services".

4.8 What happens if my place of supply is in another member state?

If you are making either margin scheme (see paragraph 4.6) or in-house supplies (see paragraph 4.7) where the place of supply is in another member state, you may need to register for VAT in that member state. In order to verify this, you should check that country's VAT registration threshold. Further information can be obtained directly from the VAT authorities in that country. The addresses can be found in Notice 725 "The Single Market".

4.9 What is the VAT liability of margin scheme supplies?

Your *margin scheme supplies* are—

— standard-rated when enjoyed in the EC (for a list of EC territories see Notice 725 "The Single Market"); or

— zero-rated when enjoyed outside the EC.

The VAT liability of in-house supplies included within a margin scheme package is not affected by these rules. You should also see the options described in—

— VAT Information Sheet 3/96: Practical implementation of the airline charter option following the changes which came into effect on 1 January 1996;

— VAT Information Sheet 4/96: Practical implementation of the agency option following the changes which came into effect on 1 January 1996;

— VAT Information Sheet 1/97: Tour Operators' Margin Scheme: Practical implementation of the trader to trader (wholesale) option following the changes which came into effect on 1 January 1996.

4.10 What happens when I make a margin scheme supply of transport that is partly inside the EU?

It depends on whether the journey has stops or not – see paragraphs 4.11 and 4.12.

4.11 How do I treat a journey without stops?

If a journey begins or ends outside the EC, it may be treated as being enjoyed wholly outside the EC. Temporary stops for refuelling or "comfort" breaks are not regarded as stops, providing that passengers are not able to break their journey at these times. The return trip is treated the same way unless any material difference occurs between the two legs, such as a stop. See also paragraph 4.12.

4.12 How do I treat a journey with stops?

Generally where a journey involves travel in both EC and non-EC countries, which involve a stop or stops, within the EC, the journey cannot be regarded as either being enjoyed wholly inside or outside of the EC. In order to account for this type of journey within the TOMS, it is necessary to apportion between the EC and non-EC elements of the journey. There are several ways of doing this (for example using a mileage based split or a nights spent in/out of the EC split), but whatever the method used it should produce a fair and reasonable result. See also paragraph 4.13.

4.13 How do I treat cruises and connected flights?

Transport used	*Treatment*
Cruises	Apportionment on the basis of "days in and days out" of the EC, based on the itinerary, is acceptable. For this purpose, the days on which the vessel leaves a non-EC port until it arrives in an EC port are regarded as outside the EC, and the days on which a vessel leaves an EC port until it reaches a non-EC port are regarded as inside the EC.
Connected flights	If a second or subsequent flight is an international flight, it will not be regarded as a separate journey provided the connection is made within 24 hours of the scheduled arrival of the first flight. If the second or subsequent flight is domestic, it will not be regarded as a separate journey provided the connection is made within six hours of the scheduled arrival of the first flight.

4.14 What is the time of my supply (the tax point)?

You must use one of the two methods detailed below to work out the tax point for your margin scheme supplies *and* any in-house supplies sold within a margin scheme package.

You cannot change from one tax point method to another without written permission from your local VAT Office. A change of method will be allowed only in exceptional circumstances, and will not normally be allowed mid-way through a financial year.

Method	*The tax point is . . .*
One	—the date of departure of the traveller; or —the first date on which the traveller occupies any accommodation, whichever happens first.
Two	—the same as method one; or —the date of receipt of payment of a certain size, whichever happens first (the date of receipt of money includes receipt by a travel agent on your behalf).

See also paragraph 4.15.

4.15 What else should I consider?

If you receive a single payment that covers the whole of your selling price in respect of a particular supply or package there is a single tax point when you receive payment.

If you receive more than one payment, you may have more than one tax point. Each time you receive a payment *exceeding 20 per cent* of the selling price, a tax point for that amount is created. A tax point is also created each time the payments you have received to date (and not already accounted for) exceed 20 per cent when added together.

Any amount left outstanding at the time of departure of the traveller or the first date the traveller occupies any accommodation must be accounted for on the earlier of these dates.

Example (to show how method two works):

A traveller books a package holiday for a total selling price of £1,200.

I have received . . .	*Has a tax point been created?*
a deposit of £120 on booking, three months before departure.	No – payment is less than 20 per cent of the selling price.
a further £200, two months before departure.	Yes – the total received (£320) amounts to more than 20 per cent of the selling price.

a further £100, one month before departure.	Yes – the total received is more than 20 per cent of the selling price.
the traveller departs and pays the balance on return.	Yes – the tax point for the balance remaining £780 is created on the date of departure.

4.16 Can I use the Cash Accounting Scheme for the TOMS?

No, because of the special tax point rules detailed above you cannot use Cash Accounting for any supplies accounted for under the TOMS.

4.17 Can I use the Annual Accounting Scheme for the TOMS?

Yes, you should include the figures from your annual TOMS calculation on the VAT return for the year in which the supplies were made, for example:

Your financial year ends on 31 December 2008 and your Annual Accounting VAT return also covers a period ending on 31 December 2008. Immediately after your financial year-end you must carry out your annual TOMS calculation and declare the figures from it on your VAT return for the period ending 31 December 2008. You can find further information in Notice 731 "Cash accounting".

4.18 Can I use the flat-rate scheme for new businesses for the TOMS?

No, TOMS supplies are specifically excluded from the flat-rate scheme – see Notice 733 "Flat rate scheme for small businesses".

4.19 What about self-billing?

Services provided to you by an agent/intermediary in arranging *any* UK margin scheme supply are standard-rated, even if those supplies are enjoyed outside the EC, or consist of transport alone (see Notice 709/6 "Travel agents and tour operators"). If you are authorised to self-bill the commission paid to the agent (see Notice 700 "The VAT Guide") you must ensure that VAT is added as appropriate.

4.20 Can I issue a VAT invoice for TOMS sales?

No, VAT invoices *cannot* be issued for supplies accounted under the TOMS. This is because the amount of output tax charged on a supply will not usually be known at the time the supply is made. VAT can only be determined following the end of your financial year, when the end of year TOMS calculation has been performed.

With effect from 1 October 2007 changes were made to the VAT invoicing regulations. These only affect TOMS supplies made to business customers.

From that date, when a TOMS supply is sold to a business for use in its business (for example travel supplies used by its employees) the invoice has to include a reference to indicate that the TOMS has been applied. It is suggested that the reference either refers to the relevant EC Directive or the relevant UK legislation.

Examples of acceptable indications will include the following:

— This is a Tour Operators' Margin Scheme supply.
— This supply falls under the Value Added Tax (Tour Operators) Order 1987.

More information about the VAT invoicing regulation changes can be found in VAT Information Sheet 10/07.

5 TOMS – THE CALCULATIONS

Commentary—*De Voil Indirect Tax Service* **V3.593**.

5.1 What is the purpose of the year-end calculation?

The year-end calculation will—

— work out the total margin achieved;

— apportion the total margin between different types of supplies, that is: margin scheme, in-house, agency;
— apportion the total margin between supplies with different VAT liabilities, for example standard-rated, zero-rated, outside the scope or exempt;
— work out the output tax due on margin scheme supplies and packages; and
— work out net values for supplies with different VAT liabilities.

5.2 How does the year-end calculation work?

The formula is at Section 8 and it covers every type of supply which might be accountable for via the TOMS.

Market value calculation

Where the market value calculation is used, it is necessary to follow through to the cost-based calculation, as it is possible that packages could consist of in-house supplies with both a market value and without a market value. Many parts of the market value calculation are common to the cost-based method.

The market value calculation is set out at section 8 of this notice and works on the basis of extracting from a package a selling value for the bought-in designated travel services. This is done by deducting the market value of in-house supplies from the full package price, leaving the selling value of the bought-in designated travel services on which a margin is then calculated using the formula set out in section 9.

Cost-based calculation

The formula for this calculation is at section 9 of this notice and it covers every type of supply which might be accountable for via the TOMS. You only need to use the steps that are applicable to your business.

The apportionment of the total margin calculated is based on the *direct* costs of your supplies, that is, not indirect/overhead costs (see examples of indirect costs at paragraph 6.4).

It works on the principle that you achieve the same percentage margin on all the elements of your packages.

You will find the calculation easier if you record your direct costs according to type and liability.

EXAMPLE

If the purchase prices of your standard-rated margin scheme supplies amount to 30 per cent of your total direct costs, the calculation will determine that 30 per cent of your total margin relates to standard-rated margin scheme supplies.

5.3 Must I use the market value method?

If you are using the cost-based method for any package you should, in principle, immediately change to the market value method where you can establish a market value for that package. However, if you are satisfied that the cost-based method is an accurate reflection of the structure of any package, that is, you achieve the same percentage mark-up on all components, you may use the cost-based method instead.

5.4 Can I change between the market value and cost-based methods?

You should not change back and forward between the two methods simply because at any given time one method or the other results in less tax being due.

However, if you are using the market value method for any package, you should immediately change to the cost-based method if it is no longer possible to establish a market value for that package.

5.5 Is there a simpler version of this calculation?

Yes, if the component supplies of *all* your margin scheme packages are liable to VAT at the standard rate, you *must* use the simplified calculation in section 11. This achieves the same result as the full calculation at section 8 and 9, but avoids the need to work out the costs of in-house supplies (if included in packages).

You *cannot* use the simplified calculation if all of your supplies are zero-rated.

EXAMPLE

You supply margin scheme packages, consisting of in-house hotel accommodation in the UK and bought-in coach transport (to collect and return guests). Both the in-house supply of accommodation and the margin scheme supply of passenger transport are standard-rated, which means the simplified calculation must be used.

5.6 What records do I need to keep?

To do the market value calculation you must have . . .	*and . . .*
a record of the market value for each in-house supply (where used);	in addition to the figure, you will need to be able to show how it was calculated and why it is the market value of the supplies in question.
To do either the full or simplified calculation, you must have . . .	*and . . .*
a record of the total selling price for margin scheme supplies and/or packages;	separate records of the *direct* costs for margin scheme supplies and the different types of supplies within margin scheme packages, that is— —standard-rated and zero-rated margin scheme supplies; —standard-rated, zero-rated, exempt and outside the scope in-house supplies; —standard-rated, zero-rated, exempt and outside the scope agency supplies, for which your commission is not readily identifiable.

5.7 When must I do the year-end calculation?

The information is given in TL4 of section 13, which has the force of law. This means that the full or simplified calculation *must* be done immediately after your financial year-end and any output tax adjustment entered on the VAT return for the first VAT period ending *after* your financial year-end.

If you fail to make the calculation/adjustment when you should have done, you must use the voluntary disclosure procedure (see Notice 700/45 "How to correct VAT errors and make adjustments or claims").

If you use the Annual Accounting scheme see paragraph 4.17.

Example Your financial year ends on 31 March. Any adjustment *must* be entered on the VAT return for periods ending April, May or June, whichever applies to you.

5.8 Can I await audited accounts before carrying out the year-end calculation/adjustment?

No, although they will assist, you *must not* wait for the production of audited accounts before doing the year-end calculation/adjustment.

If the audit identifies errors in the calculation after you have submitted the relevant VAT return, you must rework the calculation and then follow the procedures outlined in Notice 700/45 "How to correct VAT errors and make adjustments on your claims".

If you submit quarterly returns, you will find it useful to bring your VAT periods into line with your financial year-end, both for convenience and to allow you the maximum time in which to make the calculation and any adjustment. You will need to apply in writing to—

HM Revenue & Customs
VAT Written Enquiries Team
4th Floor West
Alexander House
21 Victoria Avenue
Southend-on-Sea
Essex SS99 1BD.

5.9 Can I do separate calculations for EC and non-EC supplies?

Yes, if you make supplies (including packages), which are enjoyed outside the EU, you may elect to do separate year-end and provisional calculations, for those supplies.

If you choose to make separate calculations, you must include in the non-EC calculation, *all* supplies which are enjoyed wholly outside the EC. However, if you supply a package that is enjoyed partly within the EC and partly outside the EC, the *entire* package must be included in the calculation for *EC only* supplies. The related direct costs being entered to standard-rated or zero-rated steps within the *EC only* calculation depending on where the supplies are enjoyed.

5.10 What if I want to change between the full and separate EC/non-EC methods?

This information is given in TL1 of Section 13, *which has the force of law*. You can only switch to separate calculations (or revert to a single calculation) at the *start* of your financial year; that is, no later than the due date of your first VAT return for that financial year. Permission to do this must be requested, in writing and *in advance of the financial year in question*, from your local VAT Business Advice Centre. Permission will *not* be granted retrospectively.

Permission to switch to separate calculations will only be granted if your local VAT Business Advice are satisfied that your records for direct costs and sales are adequate to calculate accurate but separate sets of margins.

5.11 How do I account for VAT during the year?

Once you have completed one of the year-end calculations at sections 8 and 9, you will have percentages enabling you to provisionally account for output tax and enter net sales values on your VAT returns for the next financial year. Section 10 shows you how to do this. If you have not yet completed your year-end calculation because it is the first year that you have been required to use the TOMS, see paragraph 5.13.

Revised provisional percentages *must* be calculated at the end of each year.

If you have used the simplified method at section 11 the provisional percentage calculation is described in section 12.

5.12 Can I account for VAT on each package instead?

No, this is because precise figures are not usually known at the time your VAT returns are due, for example, you may not know what discounts you have given or received, what refunds may be due to your customers, how many places you can fill, etc.

The TOMS requires you to account for output tax on a *provisional* basis on your VAT returns during the year, with a year-end calculation and any adjustment to be done during the next VAT return period.

5.13 What if I have just started to use the TOMS?

If you have just registered for VAT, or have only just started to make margin scheme supplies, you must work out a *provisiona* l percentage to use during the first relevant financial year.

This may be based on—

— previous trading figures; or
— projected costings and margins; or
— actual monthly/quarterly figures during the first year (but not for subsequent years).

Whatever method you choose, the first year-end calculation and appropriate adjustment will correct any under/over payment of VAT during this first year.

If in doubt, you should contact the Helpline for further guidance.

5.14 Is it necessary for me to always carry out the TOMS calculations?

If you make any TOMS supplies (even if you make no profit or all your supplies are zero-rated) you must carry out the TOMS calculations specified in this notice.

6 THE YEAR-END TOMS CALCULATION – SELLING PRICE AND COSTS

Commentary—*De Voil Indirect Tax Service* **V3.593**.

6.1 How do I work out the selling price of my TOMS supplies?

The first step is to add up the selling prices of your supplies with tax points (see paragraph 4.14) during the financial year.

The selling price should include . . .	*The selling price should not include . . .*
The total VAT inclusive selling price of all your margin scheme supplies. If you make a charge for payment by credit card this is also part of your total selling price and must be included in this total.	Any refunds made to customers for unsatisfactory service.
The total VAT-inclusive selling price of any in-house supplies which you have supplied together with margin scheme supplies.	The value of any packages of supplies which do not include any margin scheme supplies – you should account for VAT on these in the normal way.
Amounts received relating to any supplies, packaged with margin scheme supplies which you arrange as an agent, if your commission is *not* readily identified.	Amounts collected by you as an agent, if your commission *is* readily identified.
Monies received from customers who fail to turn up.	Forfeited deposits and cancellation fees received from customers who cancel a booking.
If you sell through an agent, the full amount paid by, or on account of, the customer (even if the agent deducts a commission and you receive only the balance). If the agent grants a discount to the customer and makes good this discount, your selling price is the amount paid by the customer *plus* the "top-up" amount added by the agent.	Any discount *you* agree with your customer.
Any surcharges made.	
Any Air Passenger Duty (APD) payable by the customer.	

The resulting total should be recorded at *step 1* of your year-end TOMS calculations (see sections 8, 9 and 10).

6.2 How do I work out the market value of my margin scheme supplies?

The market value method is used to apportion the selling price of your package in order to determine the selling price of your in-house supplies.

There is no set way to calculate a market value for your in-house supplies but there are some general principles that must be considered—

— The market value must reflect the reality of your business, use of third party comparators must truly reflect your business model.
— Market values may be averaged across a range of packages but must be properly weighted and reviewed regularly.
— The calculation of the market value must accommodate child and other discounted packages.
— You should keep full details of the business model used to calculate the market value for verification by HM Revenue & Customs.

6.3 How do I work out the purchase price of my margin scheme supplies?

The first step is to add up the total VAT-inclusive purchase prices of the goods and services that you have bought in for resale as margin scheme supplies. You must only include purchases that relate to the supplies that are included at step 1 of the year-end TOMS calculation (see paragraph 6.1) for that financial year.

The cost must—

— take into account any discounts or price reductions received from your supplier, even if they are received at a later date;
— include any Air Passenger Duty payable;
— *not* include the cost of any supplies you make which do not include margin scheme supplies; and
— *not* include any indirect costs (see paragraph 6.4).

6.4 What are indirect costs?

Indirect costs are general business costs, which are *not* directly and specifically incurred in order to make margin scheme or in-house supplies. Only the direct costs of making your supplies should be included in the calculations.

Some examples of indirect costs are—

— brochures;
— advertising;
— inspection trips made to research resorts, facilities etc;
— office expenses (telephone, IT equipment, office stationery, rent etc);
— accountancy, legal and other similar professional services;
— hiring or employing representatives at airports or resorts (see paragraph 6.9);
— financial services (including bank, credit card transaction fees and foreign exchange charges);
— HP, leasing and finance charges for the purchase of assets (including those used in making in-house supplies);
— market research; and
— commission paid to agents.

The above list does not of itself have the force of law, however Sections 8, 9, 10, 11, 12 and 13 of this notice do.

6.5 What about the direct costs of making in-house supplies?

You must include in your year-end TOMS calculations the VAT-exclusive direct costs incurred in making your in-house supplies, but *only* to the extent that they are supplied with margin scheme supplies as part of a package. Examples of the types of in-house direct costs that you might incur and advice on what to do if the costs also relate to non-TOMS supplies can be found in section 7 of this notice.

If all your margin scheme package supplies are liable to VAT at the same rate (see paragraph 5.5 of this notice) you do *not* need to work out these costs.

6.6 What if I am billed for my direct costs in a foreign currency?

If any of the supplies that you buy to resell as TOMS supplies are billed to you in a foreign currency you will need to convert the cost into sterling to work out your margin. There are five methods available to do this. They are reproduced in part TL2 of section 13.

You must keep documentary evidence relating to the purchase of the currency to show which rate you have used.

Once you have decided which method you want to use, you will only be allowed to change to a different method at the *start of your next financial year*; that is, no later than the due date of your first VAT return for that financial year. Permission will not be granted retrospectively.

All these methods represent tertiary law (see part TL2 of section 129). No other options can be used.

6.7 How do I treat commissions I receive for agency supplies arranged as part of a margin scheme?

Agency supplies, where the commission is . . .	*must be . . .*
readily identifiable	excluded from your TOMS calculations (so you must exclude your commission and all monies for the supply that you have arranged).
not readily identifiable	included in the TOMS calculations (at step 1) so you must include the gross amount paid by the traveller and the net amount paid to your principal (at steps 8 or 9). This ensures that the VAT payable on your commission is calculated (at step 22 of the end of year you must exclude your commission and all monies for the supply that you have arranged).

6.8 What if I supply insurance in a margin scheme package?

Travel and holiday insurance can be supplied as part of a margin scheme package, very often, but not always, as an optional extra. The way in which this insurance must be treated for VAT purposes will depend upon the contractual arrangements, and whether it is the traveller or you (the tour operator) who is the insured person.

If, as normally would be the case, the insurance policy issued by the insurer makes it clear that a *named* traveller, and not you (the tour operator), is the insured person, there is a supply of insurance from the permitted insurer to the traveller. If you arrange for insurance to be supplied by a named company to the traveller under this type of arrangement, you do so as an agent.

If your commission for such a supply is readily identifiable, the full amount paid by the traveller for the insurance must be excluded from the selling price at step 1 of the year-end TOMS calculation. Similarly, the net premium passed on by you to the insurance company must be excluded from the costs. However, if the commission value is not readily identifiable, values relating to the insurance must be included in the year-end TOMS calculation (see paragraph 6.7).

If the insurance is being offered "free" by you as part of a package, the full amount paid by the traveller for the package must be included in the selling price at step 1 of the year-end TOMS calculations.

Any costs you incur in relation to such insurance are not to be included in your year-end TOMS calculations.

You may sometimes enter into an agreement with an insurer under which *you* (the tour operator) are the insured person. The insurer agrees to reimburse you in respect of claims made by travellers for delay compensation, medical costs and so on. This is an indirect cost and therefore outside the TOMS. If any charge (including Insurance Premium Tax) is passed onto the traveller, this should be included at Step 1 of the year-end TOMS calculations.

You can find out more about insurance in Notice 701/36 "Insurance".

6.9 What if I suffer bad debts?

The rules for claiming bad debt relief are detailed in Notice 700/18 "Relief from VAT on bad debts". The procedures for reclaiming VAT on bad debts incurred within the TOMS are exactly as those detailed in that notice, with the following exception. Under the TOMS, bad debt relief is restricted to a maximum of the VAT fraction of the profit margin of the bad debt.

To calculate the amount of the relief due, you should refer to the calculation that you should have performed to calculate the provisional amount of output tax due (see paragraph 5.11 of this notice). Step 2 of section 10 (or step 1 of section 11) of this calculation gives the percentage of your total sales for that year which were liable to VAT. You should multiply the amount of the bad debt by this percentage and then by the VAT fraction (current at the time the supplies were made) to arrive at the amount of bad debt relief claimable.

6.10 Can the cost of representatives and guides be included in the calculation?

The services of your representatives at airports and resorts are not normally supplies in their own right and are not regarded as in-house supplies. The costs incurred in providing these services (whether bought in or in-house) are indirect costs for the purposes of the TOMS.

However, personnel providing *specialist* services (whether bought in or in-house), for example: guiding is often a supply in its own right.

If the supply is made in-house (see section 7 of this notice) the place of supply and liability will depend on the exact nature of the service (see paragraph 4.7 of this notice).

6.11 What if I incur unforeseen costs?

If you have to buy in additional accommodation, transport, meals and so on as a result of delays, breakdowns or other unforeseen circumstances, these usually should be treated as margin scheme supplies unless the cost of the additional items is—

— ultimately met by someone else; or
— a direct cost of your in-house supplies.

EXAMPLES

You have an agreement with an airline from which you buy in air transport that any additional costs arising from flight delays will be met by the airline. This cost has been met by someone else. Your coach breaks down and you have to hire a replacement vehicle (with or without a driver). This is a direct cost of your in-house supply.

6.12 What happens if I don't use the market value method?

HM Revenue & Customs officers will first ask you to explain why it is not possible to establish a market value. If it is possible, then they will ask you to confirm that the cost-based method is an accurate reflection of the actual structure of the package. If it is not an accurate reflection and it is possible to establish a market value, then you will have to calculate and apply that market value as part of the calculation.

6.13 What happens if my market value is not accepted by HM Revenue & Customs?

If an officer of HM Revenue & Customs does not believe your market value is reasonable, the officer will first consider whether it is actually possible to calculate a market value and, if so, what that market value is. If he considers it is possible, then the revised market value will be applied to the calculation. If an officer does not believe it is possible to calculate a market value, then the cost-based calculation method will be used.

7 TYPES OF IN-HOUSE SUPPLIES

Commentary—*De Voil Indirect Tax Service* **V3.592**.

7.1 What is an in-house supply of coach or rail transport?

As mentioned at paragraph 2.12, an in-house supply is one made from your own resources or one where what has been purchased has been materially altered when it is supplied on.

You make an in-house supply of coach/rail passenger transport if you (or a member of your VAT group) own or hire a coach/train, provide a driver, fuel, road licences, repairs, and so on. This is because you have put together these separate components, which become passenger transport.

This passenger transport has *not* been acquired and re-supplied by you to the traveller without material alteration or further processing and so *cannot* be a margin scheme supply.

7.2 Is it possible to make in-house supplies of air transport?

Yes, if you make supplies using aircraft owned by you or a member of your VAT group.

Also, if you...	*then . . .*
—charter an entire aircraft for a whole season, for example Slot 1 every Wednesday for May to October inclusive; and —put your own catering facilities on board or buy them in from a separate source; and —buy in transfer journeys from a separate source	your supply of passenger transport will be in-house and not margin scheme.

Further details on this type of in-house supply can be found in VAT Information Sheet 3/96 Practical implementation of the airline charter option, following the changes which came into effect on 1 January 1996.

7.3 Can cruises be considered as in-house supplies?

Yes, if you or a member of your VAT group, own the vessel on which the cruise is supplied.

Also, if you . . .	*then . . .*
—charter a vessel from the owner for a period of two years or more, whether only with deck/engine crew or with both deck/engine crew and "hotel" /domestic/catering staff (the vessel need not be in service continuously throughout the period, but the owner must not have the right to use the vessel to make supplies to any other customer, during the charter period; *or* —hire a vessel including deck/engine crew, but employ or engage your own "hotel"/domestic/catering staff.	your supplies of cruises on that vessel will be regarded as in-house passenger transport.

7.4 What if vehicles, aircraft, vessels, are used to provide transport both inside and outside the TOMS?

Only in-house passenger transport supplied *with* margin scheme supplies can be included in TOMS calculations.

If your in-house transport is also used to supply passenger transport outside the TOMS (for example coach hire), the direct cost of your in-house transport must be apportioned to take account of this. Thus income and costs relating to your (non-TOMS) in-house supplies must be excluded from your end of year TOMS calculation/adjustment.

Form of transport	*Method of apportionment will*
road or rail	normally be made on a mileage basis
air	usually be based on hours flown
sea	normally be made on the basis of days used on types of supply

If you wish to adopt any other basis for apportionment you should submit your proposed method in writing to your local VAT Business Advice Centre in advance of when your year-end calculation/adjustment is due.

7.5 What are the usual direct costs of supplying in-house passenger transport?

In order to undertake the end of year TOMS calculation, you will need to work out the direct costs of in-house supplies that are provided as part of a margin scheme package (see paragraphs 6.5 and 7.4).

The following list of items has been provided in order to assist you in calculating the value of these costs. The following list does not of itself have the force of law, however section 8, 9, 10, 11, 12 and 13 of this notice do.

Form of transport	*Details*
General	—depreciation on vehicles, aircraft, vessels, (which you or a member of your VAT group own **must be calculated on the same basis as your audited accounts** – including, for example, being spread over a number of years)
	—rental or leasing of vehicles, aircraft or vessels (see also paragraph 6.4 regarding HP, leasing and finance charges)
	—crew/drivers costs (including employer's National Insurance contributions)
	—subsistence paid to crew/drivers
	—fuel
	—insurance
	—repair and maintenance of vehicles, aircraft or vessels
Road or rail transport	—garaging and parking
	—bridge and road tolls
	—ferry costs
	—road fund licences
Air transport	—Air Passenger Duty (APD)
	—landing fees
Cruises	—berthing fees
Chartering an aircraft (see paragraph 7.2)	—charter fee
	—catering charges
	—transfer journeys
Chartering a vessel (see paragraph 7.3)	—charter fee
	—"hotel"/domestic/catering staff

7.6 How is an in-house supply of accommodation made?

If you own a hotel and supply accommodation within it, you are making an in-house supply of accommodation.

If you hire, lease or rent accommodation under an agreement whereby you take responsibility for the upkeep of the property and you are required to undertake any maintenance to the fabric of the building (that is, not just cleaning and changing towels/bed linen and so on), you are making an in-house supply of accommodation.

Also, if you buy in accommodation and provide catering staff from separate sources, for example a ski chalet with a chalet-maid, you are making an in-house supply, commonly referred to as "catered accommodation".

7.7 What are the usual direct costs of supplying in-house accommodation?

In order to undertake the end of year TOMS calculation, you will need to work out the direct costs of in-house supplies that are provided as part of a margin scheme package (see paragraphs 6.5 and 7.8).

The following list of items has been provided in order to assist you in calculating the value of these costs.

This list itself does not have the force of law, however sections 8, 9, 10, 11, 12 and 13 of this notice do.

— depreciation of buildings, fixtures and fittings, for which you or a member of your VAT group are liable (calculated on the same basis as your audited accounts);

— catering purchases;
— heating and lighting;
— rates;
— building insurance;
— rental of equipment/furniture;
— repairs, maintenance and cleaning for which you are liable;
— staff costs (including wages and employer's National Insurance contributions).

7.8 What if premises are used to provide accommodation both inside and outside the TOMS?

Only the income and costs relating to in-house accommodation supplied *with* margin scheme supplies can be included in the TOMS calculations (the law relating to this is contained within the steps of the TOMS calculation – see sections 8, 9 and 11 and paragraph 1(e) of TL5 in section 13).

If your premises are also used to provide accommodation outside the TOMS, the annual direct cost of your accommodation *must* be apportioned to take account of this.

This apportionment should normally be on the basis of the number of guests/days booked for each type of supply.

It is also likely that some of the costs will relate to the whole premises (for example, rates, insurance, heating and lighting) even though certain parts of your premises are probably not used specifically to provide hotel accommodation (for example, administrative offices, public bars, private accommodation and so on). If so, these costs should be apportioned on the basis of the floor area for the various parts of the building. If you wish to adopt any other basis for the apportionment you should submit your proposed method in writing to your local VAT Business Advice Centre in advance of when your year-end calculation/adjustment is due.

7.9 Can supplies on camp/caravan sites be in-house accommodation?

Yes, if you rent space on a site, install your own tents or caravans, then sell accommodation in these tents or caravans, your supply is of in-house accommodation.

If however, you buy in accommodation in a tent or caravan for resale, from a third party who provides the tent/caravan as well as the site, your supply is of margin scheme accommodation, that is, not in-house accommodation.

Similarly, if you buy in space on a site and sell it to customers for use with their own tent/caravan, you are making a margin scheme supply.

7.10 What if I sell an asset for which depreciation has been entered as an in-house cost?

You will need to make an appropriate adjustment to in-house costs, within the year-end TOMS calculation, for the year in which the sale takes place.

This adjustment will be—

— a reduction to the relevant in-house costs, in respect of any profit made on disposal, based on "book values" in your accounts; or
— an increase to the relevant in-house costs, in respect of a loss made on disposal, based on "book values" in your accounts.

7.11 How is in-house training supplied?

If you organise a training or tuition course by putting together a number of elements, for example: teachers, classrooms, lecture rooms, projectors, lighting, your supply of training is in-house.

This is because you have—

— not bought in training as such, only the constituent parts; and
— changed the nature of the supplies bought in, to create a training package.

However, if you simply purchase a place on a course from a third party, and sell it on as part of a package with one of the supplies listed in paragraph 2.9 (for example, passenger transport or accommodation), your supply of this place is a margin scheme supply.

If you make exempt supplies of training (education), you will need to read Notice 706 "Partial Exemption".

7.12 What if I organise conferences that do not include margin scheme supplies?

If you hire a room at a hotel or conference centre, provide necessary equipment (for example microphones, projectors and other audio-visual aids, manuals/handouts for delegates) and reception staff, your supply of an organised conference will be in-house rather than margin scheme.

This is because although some of the supplies above are bought in by you, they will not be re-supplied in the same state, but put to use as ingredients of a different supply, that is, the organised conference.

Refreshments served at the conference venue during the conference hours are *not* regarded as separate supplies, even if you purchase them from an outside caterer, as they form part of the in-house supply of the conference.

If however, you simply buy in a place at a conference from a third party, and sell it on as part of a package with one of the supplies listed in paragraph 2.9 (for example, passenger transport or accommodation), your supply of this place is a margin scheme supply.

See also paragraph 7.13.

7.13 What if I organise conferences that do include margin scheme supplies?

If you also supply overnight accommodation and/or passenger transport for conference delegates, these do *not* form part of your in-house organised conference. If they are bought in and re-supplied to a business customer, they must normally be accounted for *under the TOMS*, unless re-supplied by the business customer (see paragraph 3.2).

Other supplies, for example restaurant meals (outside the conference hours), theatre tickets or excursions will also be margin scheme supplies, if supplied as part of the conference package with accommodation and/or passenger transport.

7.14 How are organised shoots accounted for within the TOMS?

If you organise a shooting event (including clay pigeons), by putting together a number of elements, for example the right to use the land, host services, beaters, clays, etc your supply of the event will be an in-house supply.

If you organise a shoot as above, but create a package that includes one or more margin scheme supplies, for example passenger transport or accommodation, your supply of the shooting event *only* will be an in-house supply, whilst the passenger transport and/or accommodation will be margin scheme supplies.

However, if you simply buy in and sell on the right to participate in a shoot organised by someone else, this will be a normal (non-TOMS) VAT supply, unless it is provided in a package with one or more of the supplies in paragraph 2.9).

In some circumstances, shoots are not organised in the course or furtherance of a business, and are therefore outside the scope of VAT. If you are unsure about whether your shoot is outside the scope of VAT please contact the Helpline.

8 MARKET VALUE CALCULATIONS (ANNUAL ADJUSTMENT)

Commentary—*De Voil Indirect Tax Service* **V3.593**.

This section has the force of law and is referred to in paragraphs 2.6, 2.13, 2.14, 5.2, 5.5 and 7.5.

Only use this section if you have packages or parts of packages being apportioned by the market value of the in-house element of the package. On completion of all the steps M1–M5 you must then follow the steps in the cost-based calculation in section 9, taking forward the figures from this section as instructed.

Step Boxes requiring "raw data" entry are in white, boxes which "process" that data are in grey.

Calculate the value of sales of margin scheme packages

M1 Total the VAT-inclusive selling prices of your designated travel services and margin scheme packages supplied during the financial year including any that are not "market value" packages.

Working out the market value

M2 Total the VAT-inclusive purchase prices of the standard-rated designated travel services included in the total at M1: **carry forward this figure to step 21 of section 9**.

M3 Total the VAT inclusive market value of the zero-rated and outside the scope in-house travel services at M1: **carry forward this figure to step 26 of section 9**.

M4 Total the VAT-exclusive direct costs to you of the standard-rated in-house supplies at step M2 + step M3.

Working out selling value of designated travel services and non-market value in-house supplies

M5 Deduct the total at step M4 from the total at step M1: **carry forward this figure to step 1 of section 9**.

9 COST-BASED CALCULATIONS (ANNUAL ADJUSTMENT)

This section has the force of law and is referred to in paragraphs 2.6, 5.2, 5.10, 6.1, 6.4, 6.8, 6.9, 7.5, 7.7 and 7.8.

Commentary—*De Voil Indirect Tax Service* **V3.593**.

This section applies to packages being apportioned by reference to the costs of the in-house element of the package, and imports the figures calculated by the market value method in section 8, where that method is used for all or some of the travel packages. Do not include values already entered in section 8 unless explicitly instructed.

Step

Working out the total sales of margin scheme packages

1 Bring forward the total calculated at step M5 of section 8. If section 8 is not used then enter the VAT-inclusive selling prices of your designated travel services and margin scheme packages supplied during the financial year.

Working out the purchase prices of margin scheme supplies

2 Total the VAT-inclusive purchase prices of the standard-rated designated travel services included in the total at step 1.

3 Total the VAT-inclusive purchase prices of the non standard-rated designated travel services (supplies enjoyed outside the EC) included in the total at step 1.

Working out the direct costs of in-house supplies. Steps 4 to 7 can be ignored where a market value is applied to all in-house supplies under section 8

4 Total the VAT-exclusive direct costs to you of the standard-rated in-house supplies included in step 1. Add a percentage of that amount equivalent to the standard rate of VAT.

5 Total the VAT-exclusive direct costs to you of the zero-rated in-house supplies included in step 1.

6 Total the VAT-inclusive direct costs to you of the exempt in-house supplies included in step 1. Deduct any input tax that you are entitled to recover on these costs.

7 Total the direct costs to you of the in-house supplies included in step 1 that are supplied outside the UK, exclusive of any VAT incurred on these costs that you are entitled to recover. Add to the total an uplift equivalent to the percentage VAT rate applicable to such supplies if you have accounted for VAT on these supplies to the VAT authorities in another member state.

Working out the "costs" of agency supplies

8 Total the VAT-inclusive amounts paid by you to your principals in respect of the agency supplies included in step 1 for which the consideration you receive is standard-rated.

9 Total the VAT-inclusive amounts paid by you to your principals in respect of the agency supplies included in step 1 for which the consideration you receive is not standard-rated.

Working out the total margin

10 Add the totals of costs at steps 2 to 9 inclusive.

11 Calculate the total margin for all the supplies included in step 1 by deducting the total at step 10 from the total at step 1.

Apportioning the margin

12 Calculate the margin for the standard-rated designated travel services by applying the following formula: total at step 2 / total at step 10 × total at step 11

13 Calculate the margin for the zero-rated designated travel services by applying the following formula:

total at step 3 / total at step 10 × total at step 11

14 Calculate the margin for the standard-rated in-house supplies by applying the following formula:

total at step 4 / total at step 10 × total at step 11

15 Calculate the margin for the zero-rated in-house supplies by applying the following formula:

total at step 5 / total at step 10 × total at step 11

16 Calculate the margin for the exempt in-house supplies by applying the following formula:

total at step 6 / total at step 10 × total at step 11

17 Calculate the margin for the supplies made outside the UK by applying the following formula:

total at step 7 / total at step 10 × total at step 11

18 Calculate the consideration for the standard-rated agency supplies by applying the following formula:

total at step 8 / total at step 10 × total at step 11

19 Calculate the consideration for the non-standard-rated agency supplies by applying the following formula:

total at step 9 / total at step 10 × total at step 11

Working out your output tax

20 Calculate the output VAT due on the designated travel services by applying the following formula:

total at step 12 × the VAT fraction

21 Calculate the output VAT due on the standard-rated in-house supplies by applying the following formula:

(total at step 4 + total at step 14 + total calculated at step M2 of section 0) × the VAT fraction.

22 Calculate the output VAT due on the standard-rated agency supplies by applying the following formula:

total at step 18 × the VAT fraction

Working out sales values

23 Calculate the VAT-exclusive value of the standard-rated designated travel services by deducting the total at step 20 from the total at step 12.

24 Note the value of the zero-rated designated travel services at step 13.

25 Calculate the VAT-exclusive value of your standard-rated in-house supplies by applying the following formula:

(total at step 4 + total at step 14 + total calculated at step M2 of section 0) – total at step 21

26 Calculate the value of the zero-rated supplies made within the scheme by applying the following formula:

total at step 5 + total at step 15 + total calculated at step M3 of section 0

27 Calculate the value of your exempt in-house supplies made by applying the following formula:

total at step 6 + total at step 16

28 Calculate the value of your in-house supplies which are supplied outside the UK by applying the following formula:

total at step 7 + total at step 17

29 Calculate the total VAT exclusive value of the supplies:

total of steps 23 to 28. Include this total in box 6 of your VAT return.

Working out the annual adjustment

30 Calculate the total output VAT due on your designated travel services and margin scheme packages by adding the totals at steps 20 to 22 inclusive.

31 Total the provisional output VAT which has been accounted for during the financial year on the supplies included in the total at step 1.

32 Deduct the total at step 31 from the total at step 30. Include the resulting total in box 1 of your VAT return, either as a payable amount where the amount is positive or as a deductible amount where the amount is negative.

10 ACCOUNTING FOR VAT ON THE PROVISIONAL VALUE OF DESIGNATED TRAVEL SERVICES AND MARGIN SCHEME PACKAGES

Commentary—*De Voil Indirect Tax Service* **V3.593**.

This section has the force of law and is referred to in paragraphs 1.2, 2.6, 5.10, 6.4, 6.9, 7.5 and 7.7.

Step **Working out the provisional percentage**

1 Calculate the VAT-inclusive amount of your standard-rated supplies of designated travel services and margin scheme packages for the preceding financial year by adding the totals from steps 4, 12, 14 and 18 of section 9, together with the total M2 in the market value calculation in section 8.

2 Calculate the VAT-inclusive standard-rated percentage of the total selling price of all your designated travel services and margin scheme packages for the preceding tax year by applying the following formulae:

If you have used a market value to value in-house supplies

total at step 1 of section 10/total at step M1 of section 8 x100

If you have not used a market value to value in-house supplies

total at step 1 of section 10/total at step 1 of section 9 x 100

Working out the VAT return figures

3 Total the VAT-inclusive selling prices of the designated travel services and margin scheme packages supplied during the prescribed accounting period.

4 Calculate the provisional VAT-inclusive amount of your standard-rated supplies of designated travel services and margin scheme packages made during the prescribed accounting period by applying the following formula:

total at step 3 × percentage at step 2

5 Calculate the provisional amount of output VAT due for the prescribed accounting period by applying the following formula:

total at step 4 × the VAT fraction

11 SIMPLIFIED END-OF-YEAR CALCULATION (ANNUAL ADJUSTMENT)

Commentary—*De Voil Indirect Tax Service* **V3.593**.

This section has the force of law and is referred to in paragraphs 1.2, 2.6, 5.4, 5.10, 6.1, 6.4, 6.8, 6.9, 7.5, 7.7 and 7.8.

Step	
1	Total the VAT-inclusive selling prices of your designated travel services and margin scheme packages supplied during the financial year.
2	Total the VAT-inclusive purchase prices of the designated travel services included in the total at step 1.
3	Calculate the VAT-inclusive amount of the supplies included in step 1 by deducting the total at step 2 from the total at step 1.
4	Calculate the total output VAT due on your designated travel services and margin scheme packages by applying the following formula: total at step 3 x the VAT fraction.
5	Calculate the VAT-exclusive value of your designated travel services and margin scheme packages by deducting the total at step 4 from the total at step 3.
6	Total the provisional output VAT which has been accounted for during the financial year on the supplies included in the total at step 1.
7	Deduct the total at step 6 from the total at step 4. Include the resulting total in box 1 of your VAT return, either as a payable amount where the amount is positive or as a deductible amount where the amount is negative.

12 ACCOUNTING FOR VAT ON THE PROVISIONAL VALUE OF DESIGNATED TRAVEL SERVICES AND MARGIN SCHEME PACKAGES WHEN THE SIMPLIFIED CALCULATION APPLIES (ALL SUPPLIES STANDARD-RATED)

Commentary—*De Voil Indirect Tax Service* **V3.593**.

This section has the force of law and is referred to in paragraphs 1.2, 2.6, 5.10, 6.4, 7.5 and 7.7.

Step	
1	Calculate the VAT-inclusive standard-rated percentage of the total selling price of all your designated travel services and margin scheme packages for the preceding tax year by applying the following formula: total at step 3 of section 11/total at step 1 of section 11 x 100
2	Total the VAT-inclusive selling prices of all of your designated travel services and margin scheme packages supplied during the prescribed accounting period.
3	Calculate the provisional VAT-inclusive amount of your standard-rated supplies of designated travel services and margin scheme packages made during the prescribed accounting period by applying the following formula: total at step 2 × percentage at step 1.
4	Calculate the provisional amount of output VAT due for the prescribed accounting period by applying the following formula: total at step 3 × the VAT fraction.
5	Calculate the provisional VAT-exclusive value of all of your designated travel services and margin scheme packages made during the prescribed accounting period by deducting the total at step 4 from the total at step 3.

13 TERTIARY LAW

This section has the force of law and is referred to in paragraphs 1.1, 1.2, 3.2, 5.8, 6.4, 6.4, 7.5, 7.7 and 7.8.

Commentary—*De Voil Indirect Tax Service* **V3.593**.

TL1

(1) This Section shall come into effect on 1 January 1998.

(2) Where a tour operator, in the same financial year, supplies—

(a) designated travel services or margin scheme packages which are to be enjoyed wholly outside the European Community; and

(b) designated travel services or margin scheme packages which are to be enjoyed wholly or partly within the European Community,

the Commissioners of HM Revenue & Customs may, on being given written notification by the tour operator no later than the due date for rendering his first VAT return for the financial year in which the supplies are to be made, allow the supplies under sub-paragraph (a) to be valued separately from those under sub-paragraph (b).

(3) Where a tour operator, under paragraph 2 above, has separately valued supplies of designated travel services or margin scheme packages enjoyed wholly outside the European Community from supplies of designated travel services or margin scheme packages enjoyed wholly or partly within the European Community, the Commissioners of HM Revenue & Customs may, on being given written notification by the tour operator no later than the due date for rendering his first VAT return for any subsequent financial year, allow supplies to be made in such subsequent financial year to be valued using the method specified at section 8 of this notice.

TL2

(1) This section shall come into effect on 1 January 1998.

(2) Where—

(a) a supply of goods or services is acquired by a tour operator for the purpose of supplying a designated travel service; and

(b) the value of the supply to the tour operator is expressed in a currency other than sterling;

the tour operator must convert such value into sterling for the purposes of steps 2 and 3 of section 8 of this notice or step 2 of section 11 of this notice.

(3) For the purposes of paragraph 2 above, the tour operator must use:

(a) the rate of exchange published in the Financial Times using the Federation of Tour Operators' base rate current at the time such supplies were costed by the person from whom the tour operator has acquired the goods or services; or

(b) the commercial rate of exchange current at the time that the supplies in his brochure were costed; or

(c) the rate published in the Financial Times on the date that the tour operator pays for the supplies; or

(d) the rate of exchange which was applicable to the purchase by the tour operator of the foreign currency which he used to pay for those supplies; or

(e) the period rate of exchange published by HM Revenue & Customs for customs purposes in force at the time the tour operator pays for those supplies.

(4) Where the methods at paragraph 3(a) or (b) above are used, the tour operator must publish the rate in any brochure or leaflet in which these supplies are held out for sale.

(5) The Commissioners of HM Revenue & Customs may, on being given written notification by a tour operator no later than the due date for rendering his first return of his financial year, allow a different method to be used in that financial year from that used in the previous financial year.

TL3

(1) This section shall come into effect on 1 October 2010.

(2) Where possible the value of any in-house supplies shall be valued by reference to their market value and the value of designated travel services and agency supplies

shall be determined by applying the formula set out in section 8 of this notice (hereinafter referred to as the "market value calculation"), unless during the relevant period all such supplies are liable to VAT at the same rate, in which case the value shall be determined by applying the formula set out in section 11 of this notice (hereinafter referred to as "the simplified calculation").

(3) On completing the steps in the market value calculation the figures produced must be entered into the cost-based calculation as detailed in section 9 together with any packages, or parts of packages, for which the market value calculation is not being done.

(4) Where the cost-based calculation in TL4 accurately reflects the structure of the package holidays you may opt to use the cost-based calculation for all packages regardless of whether a market value can be established for some or all of the packages and section 8 calculation may be ignored.

(5) Where the market value calculation has been used a tour operator may only cease to use that method where it becomes impossible to continue to determine a market value of the supply in question or where the cost-based calculation accurately reflects the structure of the package.

A change of method to gain a more favourable VAT outcome is not permitted.

TL4

(1) Subject to sections TL1 and TL3 of section 13 of this Notice, the value of designated travel services, in-house supplies and agency supplies shall be determined by applying the formula set out in section 9 of this notice (hereinafter referred to as the "cost-based calculation"), unless during the relevant period all such supplies are liable to VAT at the same rate, in which case the value shall be determined by applying the formula set out in section 11 of this notice (hereinafter referred to as "the simplified calculation").

(2) The provisional value of designated travel services, in-house supplies and agency supplies shall be determined in accordance with the formula set out in—
- (a) section 10 of this notice, where the cost-based calculation applies; or
- (b) section 12 of this notice, where the simplified calculation applies.

(3) A tour operator shall be required to account for VAT on the provisional value of his supplies of designated travel services, in-house supplies and agency supplies on the VAT return for the prescribed accounting period in which the supplies are made.

(4) The difference between the amount of VAT due on the value of designated travel services, in-house supplies and agency supplies supplied during a tour operator's financial year, and the amount of VAT paid on the provisional value of those supplies, shall be adjusted by the tour operator on the VAT return for the first prescribed accounting period ending after the end of the financial year during which the supplies were made.

TL5

(1) For the purpose of sections 8 to 13 of this notice—
- (a) "in-house supply" means a supply by a tour operator which is neither a designated travel service nor an agency supply;
- (b) "market value" means the selling price of the in-house element of a "margin scheme package" were it to be sold independent of the package in an arm's-length transaction to an unconnected person;
- (c) "cost-based method" means the calculation in section 9 of this notice;
- (d) "agency supply" means a supply arranged by a tour operator between two other persons, in the capacity of an agent or intermediary for either person, for which the tour operator receives a consideration, the value of which is not readily identifiable;

(e) "margin scheme package" means a single transaction which includes one or more designated travel services;
(f) "financial year" means a period corresponding to a tour operator's financial year for accounting purposes;
(g) "direct costs" means costs which are directly and specifically attributable to the provision of in-house supplies, to the extent that they are so attributable;
(h) "VAT fraction" has the same meaning as in Notice 700 "The VAT Guide".

NOTICE 718
THE VAT MARGIN SCHEME AND GLOBAL ACCOUNTING

April 2011

This notice cancels and replaces Notice 733 (January 2011). Details of the changes to the previous version can be found in paragraph 1.2 of this notice.

1 INTRODUCTION

1.1 What is this notice about?

This notice explains when you may use the margin scheme for second-hand goods, works of art, antiques and collectors' items, or the global accounting scheme, to account for VAT on your sales of goods.

It explains—

— which goods you can sell under the schemes;
— how the schemes work;
— how you must calculate the margin; and
— what records you must keep.

This notice assumes that you have a working knowledge of basic VAT principles, as outlined in Notice 700 "The VAT Guide".

If, after reading this notice, you need any further help or advice, contact our VAT Helpline.

1.2 What's changed

We have rewritten this notice to make it easier for you to find the information you need. General information in sections 2 to 13 applies to both schemes. In the later sections, we describe the global accounting scheme, the conditions for its use, and the impact the margin schemes have on particular business sectors.

We have removed—

— the information which is relevant to people who buy and sell motor vehicles; and
— the information about the Auctioneers' Scheme

and have put it in two separate notices.

The rules about margin scheme declarations on invoices have changed: please see the paragraphs 5.3 (margin scheme) and 15.5 (global accounting) for details.

We have updated the Notice to reflect the VAT rate of 20%.

This notice and others mentioned are available on our website.

1.3 Who should read this notice

You should read this notice if you make supplies of—

— second-hand goods;
— works of art;
— antiques; or

— collectors' items.

1.4 Force of law

In UK law, VATA 1994 s 50A allows the Treasury to make Orders to introduce second-hand schemes.

The VAT (Special Provisions) Order 1995 (as amended) covers all goods other than cars.

Parts of this notice have the force of law under the order. All of sections 4 and 5 have legal force and supplement the law. Certain paragraphs within other parts of the notice also have the force of law. Those paragraphs are indicated by a statement and by having been placed in a box.

2 BASIC PRINCIPLES

2.1 What are margin schemes?

A margin scheme is an optional method of accounting which allows you to calculate VAT on the value you add to the goods you sell, rather than on the full selling price.

There are three margin schemes for goods—

— The margin scheme for second-hand goods, works of art, antiques and collectors' items (referred to throughout this notice as the margin scheme);
— global accounting;
— The VAT Auctioneers' Scheme (see Notice 718/2 "The VAT Auctioneers' Scheme").

Commentary—*De Voil Indirect Tax Service* **V3.531**.

2.2 Why would I want to use a margin scheme?

Using a margin scheme will reduce the VAT you have to pay if you sell—

— second-hand goods;
— works of art;
— antiques; or
— collectors' items
— on which you could not claim back any VAT when you purchased them

Without a margin scheme, you would have to account for VAT on the full selling price of each item.

Using a margin scheme allows you to account for VAT on the difference between the price you paid for an item and the price you sold it for.

If you sell an item for less than you paid for it, you won't have any VAT to account for on the sale.

Commentary—*De Voil Indirect Tax Service* **V3.531**.

2.3 What are the conditions for using the schemes?

You don't have to use the margin schemes: they're optional.

If you do decide to use one, there are a number of conditions you will have to meet. If you can't meet all the conditions, you can't use the scheme.

The detailed conditions are explained throughout this notice. The main ones are—

— *the goods must be eligible* (see paragraph 2.7);
— *you must have acquired the goods in eligible circumstances.* In most cases, this means that you obtained the goods for resale in circumstances where you could not claim any VAT back (see paragraph 2.9);
— *you must calculate the margin in accordance with the rules of the scheme.* There are special rules about how to calculate your buying price, your selling price and your margin under the schemes. The margin you calculate under the scheme may not be the same as your profit margin (see paragraph 3.3);
— *you must meet the record keeping rules of the scheme.* There are special rules about invoicing and stock records (see sections 5 and 6).

Commentary—*De Voil Indirect Tax Service* **V3.531–537**.

2.4 Why are the conditions so strict?

The conditions about eligibility of goods are strict to ensure that—

— only those goods which the law permits; and
— on which there was no VAT to recover
— are sold under the margin schemes. They prevent businesses from declaring less VAT than is due on goods which are not covered by the schemes.

2.5 What if I can't meet all the conditions?

If you sell an eligible item, but cannot meet all the record-keeping, invoicing and accounting requirements, you cannot use a margin scheme.

Even though that item would otherwise have been eligible for onward sale under a margin scheme, you must deal with the sale in the normal way, accounting for VAT on the full selling price.

Commentary—*De Voil Indirect Tax Service* **V3.532**.

2.6 What if I have claimed VAT?

If you have—

— reclaimed; or
— were entitled to reclaim

VAT on an item you have purchased, you cannot use a margin scheme when you sell it. You must account for VAT on the full selling price under the normal rules, with the exception detailed below.

The only exception to this rule is where you opt to use one of the margin schemes for imported works of art, antiques and collectors' items and for works of art obtained from creators or their heirs (see section 10).

You cannot make an item eligible for the schemes by refraining from claiming the VAT back on it. Any item on which you were charged VAT will be ineligible.

2.7 Which categories of goods can I sell under the margin schemes?

This is a quick guide to the goods which are eligible to be sold under the scheme. You should refer to section 20 at the end of this notice, where we have reproduced the law on eligible goods, if you are in any doubt.

Second-hand goods

The legal definition of second-hand goods is goods which are suitable for further use as they are, or after repair. In most cases, goods which are second-hand in the ordinary usage of the term will be eligible for the margin schemes.

For the special rules about the legal definition of a second-hand motor vehicle, see Notice 718/1 "The VAT Margin Scheme on second-hand cars and other vehicles".

Works of art

The legal definition of works of art includes pictures, paintings, collages and drawings executed by hand by the artist. Craft items and items produced in a technical or industrial context may not be eligible to be sold under the margin schemes. If you are in any doubt, please check the list in paragraph 20.1.

Antiques and collectors' items

The legal definition of an antique is an item, other than a work of art or a collectors' item, which is over 100 years old.

Not everything which somebody might collect will be included in the legal definition of a collectors' item for margin scheme purposes. If you are in any doubt, check the list in paragraph 20.1.

Commentary—*De Voil Indirect Tax Service* **V3.532.**

2.8 Are there any categories of goods I can't sell under the schemes?

Yes. You must not use a margin scheme to account for sales of—

— precious metals;
— investment gold; or
— precious stones.

There is more information about these categories of goods in paragraph 20.2.

There is more information about these categories of goods in paragraph 20.2. You can only use a margin scheme to account for sales of air guns if you are registered under the Firearms Act 1968.

There are special rules about types of goods you must not sell under global accounting. See paragraph 14.5 for more information.

Commentary—*De Voil Indirect Tax Service* **V3.532, 534, 535.**

2.9 Can I sell all eligible goods under the schemes?

No. You can only use a margin scheme if both—

— the item; and
— the circumstances in which you bought it

are eligible. Eligible circumstances are those in which you were not charged VAT when you purchased the item.

The most common ones are:

— where you buy the goods from a private individual or an unregistered business which does not have to charge VAT to you; and
— where you buy the goods from another business which is selling them on to you under a margin scheme.

If you have bought an item and VAT is shown separately on the purchase invoice, you can't sell that item on under a margin scheme, even if you haven't claimed the VAT back, with the exception detailed below.

The only exception to this rule is where you opt to use one of the margin schemes for imported works of art, antiques and collectors' items and for works of art obtained from creators or their heirs (see section 10).

Commentary—*De Voil Indirect Tax Service* **V3.532, 534, 535.**

2.10 What if I make sales under the normal VAT rules as well?

You can use a margin scheme for some of your sales and the normal rules for others.

But, if you have sold an item under the normal VAT rules (that is, you charged VAT on the full selling price), you can't go back and apply a margin scheme to that sale later.

Commentary—*De Voil Indirect Tax Service* **V3.532, 534, 535.**

2.11 How do the margin schemes affect VAT on my overheads?

You can reclaim VAT you are charged on any business overheads, repairs, parts or accessories, as usual. But you must not add any of these costs to the purchase price of the goods you sell under the scheme.

For example, if you purchase new parts and fit them to a second-hand clock, you cannot add the cost of those parts to the purchase price you use when you calculate your margin.

Commentary—*De Voil Indirect Tax Service* **V3.532, 534, 535.**

3. MAKING YOUR MARGIN SCHEME CALCULATIONS

3.1 How do I calculate my selling price?

Your selling price is everything which you are to receive for the goods, whether from the buyer or a third party. It includes incidental expenses directly linked to the sale, for example—

— commission;
— packaging;
— transport; and
— insurance costs

which you have charged to the customer.

Optional extras charged to the buyer, including any insurance provided by a third party, and disbursements do not form part of the selling price: you should account for these separately outside the margin scheme. You can find more information about disbursements in section 25 of Notice 700 "The VAT Guide".

If	*Then*
the buyer is charged by another business for, for example, delivering the item	that is a separate supply of services between the courier and the buyer: it will not form part of your selling price.

The consideration you receive for the goods may not be wholly in money: if that is the case, the normal rules about value in Notice 700 "The VAT Guide" will apply.

3.2 How do I calculate my purchase price?

Your purchase price is everything which you had to pay for the goods: it will mirror the rules for the selling price described in paragraph 3.1. It includes incidental expenses directly linked to the purchase, for example—

— commission;
— packaging;
— transport; and
— insurance costs

which you have charged by your supplier.

You must not include any cost to you of bringing the goods to sale. Your purchase price does not include the cost of repair, refurbishment or your business overheads.

For example, if you purchase an antique table, and have it restored prior to putting it up for sale, you must not add the cost of the restoration to the purchase price of the table. You must use the original price you paid for the table when you calculate the margin for the purposes of the scheme.

Remember: the margin schemes tax the difference between what you paid for the item and what you sold it for, not the overall profit you have made on it.

3.3 How do I calculate the margin?

Under the margin schemes, you only have to account for VAT when you sell an item for more than you paid for it.

To work out the VAT due on an individual Margin Scheme sale, follow the steps in the example below—

(a)	Purchase price	£1,500	
(b)	Selling price		2,000
(c)	Gross Margin (b – a)	£500	
(d)	VAT payable (c x $^1/_6$ths)	£83.33	

The calculation to work out the VAT due depends on the VAT rate in force.

The VAT fraction allows you to calculate the amount of VAT included in a given sum of money.

A standard rate of VAT of 20 per cent gives a VAT fraction of $^1/_6$ths. When you have worked out your gross margin, multiply the figure by 1, then divide by 6.

For more information about how to calculate your margin if you are using global accounting, see paragraph 14.8.

Commentary—*De Voil Indirect Tax Service* **V3.532, 534, 535**.

4 BUYING AND SELLING GOODS UNDER THE MARGIN SCHEME

The rules in this section have the force of law.

4.1 What must I do when I buy goods?

Step	*Action*	*Details*
1	Check that the goods are eligible for the scheme.	See section 2 for these rules.
2	Obtain a purchase invoice.	If you are buying from a private individual or an unregistered business, you must make out the invoice yourself and include all of the details in paragraph 5.3.
3	Enter the purchase details of the goods in your stock book under the appropriate headings.	The purchase price must be the one you agreed with the seller. You must not alter this price and you must not add the cost of repair, refurbishment or business overheads to it. If you buy a number of items as a single lot but intend to sell them separately, you must allocate a purchase price to each one.

4.2 What must I do when I sell goods?

The table below lists the steps you must follow when you sell goods under the margin scheme.

Step	*Action*	*Details*
1	Check first that you have followed all of the rules relating to the purchase of the item.	See paragraph 4.1. If you have not, you cannot use the margin scheme.
2	Make out a sales invoice.	The invoice must include all of the details in paragraph 5.3.
4	Enter the sales details in your stock book under the appropriate headings.	
5	Issue the invoice to your customer and keep a copy for your records.	If you include more than one item on the same sales invoice, you must allocate a selling price to each one.

5 RECORDS AND ACCOUNTS

The detailed rules in this section have the force of law

Commentary—*De Voil Indirect Tax Service* **V3.536**.

5.1 What records must I keep?

Notice 700/21 "Keeping VAT Records" gives guidance on the general records you must keep if you are registered for VAT.

If you use the margin scheme, there are some additional record keeping rules which apply to your stock book and invoices – paragraphs 5.2 to 5.3 give details.

These additional rules exist so that there will be a clear audit trail of the margin you have achieved on each item you have sold. It's important that you keep to these rules so that you can continue using the margin scheme. If we can't check the margins you have declared from your records, VAT will be due on the full selling price of the goods you've supplied, even if they were otherwise eligible for the scheme. If you are not sure whether your records meet the margin scheme rules, please contact our Helpline.

5.2 What are the rules for stock books?

You must keep your stock book up to date and it must include all of the information in the table below. This applies to each item you purchase for resale under the margin scheme. You may, if you wish, include further information for your own accounting purposes.

Purchase details	*Sales details*
Stock number in numerical sequence	
Date of purchase	Date of sale
Purchase invoice number (unless you made out the purchase invoice yourself – see 5.3)	Sales invoice number
Purchase price	Selling price or method of disposal
Name of seller	Name of buyer
Description of the item	
	Margin on sale (sales price minus purchase price)
	VAT due (margin x $^{1}/_{6}$)

You must include your margin scheme calculations under the appropriate headings in your stock book. No VAT will be due if your purchase price is higher than, or the same as, your selling price. In these circumstances you should show the VAT due as 'Nil' in your stock book.

You must not offset any VAT on goods which you sold at a loss against VAT on goods which you have sold at a profit. The exception to this is if you use global accounting. For more information about global accounting, see section 14.

An example of a margin scheme stock book is included at section 6.

5.3 What are the rules for margin scheme invoices?

The information in the table below must always appear on the invoices you receive, or issue.

Remember: if you are buying from a private individual or an unregistered business, you must make out the purchase invoice yourself.

Purchase invoices	*Sales invoices*
seller's name and address	your name, address and VAT registration number
your name and address	the buyer's name and address
a means of cross-referencing between the sales system and the stock book, for example, the stock book number	a means of cross-referencing between the sales system and the stock book, for example, the stock book number
invoice number (unless you made out the purchase invoice yourself)	invoice number
date of transaction date of	date of transaction
a description of the item	a description of the item
total price – you must not add any other costs to this price	total price – you must not show VAT separately
if you bought the item from another VAT-registered business, any of the following—	any of the following—
—Margin Scheme - second hand goods, or	—Margin Scheme - second hand goods, or
—Margin Scheme - works of art or	—Margin Scheme - works of art or
—Margin Scheme - collectors' items and antiques.	—Margin Scheme - collectors' items and antiques.

Note: If the purchase invoice shows a separate VAT amount, the item is not eligible to be sold under the margin scheme.

5.4 Filling in your VAT return

You will need to fill in a VAT return at the end of each tax period. Here are the special rules you must follow for any goods which you have bought or sold under a margin scheme during the tax period—

— *Box 1*. Include the output tax due on all eligible goods sold in the period covered by the return.
— *Box 6*. Include the full selling price of all eligible goods sold in the period, less any VAT due on the margin.
— *Box 7*. Include the full purchase price of eligible goods bought in the period.

There is no requirement to include margin scheme purchases or sales in boxes 8 and 9 of your VAT return.

Further guidance on how to fill in VAT returns is available in Notice 700/12 "Filling in your VAT return".

5.5 How long must I keep records?

Generally, you must keep all your business records for VAT purposes for at least six years. If the six-year rule causes you serious storage problems or undue expense, then you should consult our Helpline. We may be able to allow you to keep some records for a shorter period.

But if your current stock includes items which you obtained more than six years ago, you must retain all the evidence which will show their eligibility for margin scheme treatment when you eventually sell them.

5.6 Do I need to keep records for goods on sale or return?

If your stock includes goods supplied to you on a sale or return basis (see Notice 700 "The VAT Guide", paragraph 14.4), you must include, in your stock book or in a separate record, the following details for each item—

— the date of transfer of the item;
— description of the item;
— the name and address of the person transferring the item to you; and
— the date of sale or return.

Similarly, if any goods are removed from your stock on a sale or return basis to another business's premises, you should note your stock record with the date and details of the business to whom you have transferred the goods.

5.7 How do I treat invoices in foreign currencies?

If you are buying and selling eligible goods in a foreign currency (including euro), you must convert the price into sterling in order to calculate your margin.

Invoice	
Purchase invoices	If you buy a number of items at an inclusive price and do not intend to sell them as one lot, you must convert the price to sterling and then apportion this amount between the items. You must then enter the sterling amounts in your stock record on an item by item basis.
Sales invoices	If you issue a sales invoice in a foreign currency, the invoice must also show the sterling equivalent of the selling price. If the invoice covers more than one item, it must show the price, both in foreign currency and sterling, for each item. You must then enter the sterling amounts in your stock record on an item by item basis. If, however, you are selling as one lot goods which you bought as one lot, you need only show a total foreign currency and sterling value for that lot.

To convert amounts in foreign currencies you must use one of the methods outlined in Notice 700 "The VAT Guide". Whichever method you choose, you must use the exchange rate which was current at the time the transaction took place.

6 EXAMPLE OF A MARGIN SCHEME STOCK BOOK

6.1 How do I complete my stock book?

EXAMPLE

Purchase details

1	2	3	4	5	6
Stock no	Date of purchase	Purchase invoice no	Purchase price	Name of seller	Description of item
100	01/02/08	50	£2,500	Mr J. Smith	Clarice Cliff tea service, Crocus pattern

Sales details

7	8	9
Date of sale	Sales invoice no	Name of buyer
31/03/08	150	Mrs F. Bloggs

Accounting details

10	11	12
Selling price	Margin (11 – 4)	VAT Due
£3,000	£500	£83.33

7. THE MARGIN SCHEMES AND BUYING AND SELLING WITHIN THE EC

7.1 Can I use the schemes for goods I buy from within the EC?

All member states operate a margin scheme but you can only use one of the UK margin schemes for the onward sale of goods in the following circumstances—

7.1.1 You buy goods from a private individual

There will be no VAT due on these goods when they are brought into the UK. You can use a margin scheme for the onward sale of these goods, provided you can meet all the conditions of the scheme.

7.1.2 You buy goods from a registered business under a margin scheme

As with transactions between UK VAT-registered dealers, you can use a margin scheme if one was used when the goods were supplied to you.

All member states operate a margin scheme. Margin scheme invoices must include one of the following:

— a reference to Arts 313, 326 or 333 of Directive 2006/112/EC;
— a reference to the corresponding part of the relevant national VAT legislation; or
— another declaration to indicate that the goods have been sold under the margin scheme.

7.2 How should I treat invoices from EC businesses?

Some member states require invoices for supplies made in their country to include the VAT registration number of the customer.

If *Then*

you receive an invoice for a supply from another member state which shows: —one of the margin scheme indications listed in 7.1.2 above; and —your VAT registration number	if you are sure that the supply has been made under a margin scheme, you can enter the details into your scheme records.
you receive an invoice for a supply from another member state and it —shows your VAT number; but —does not show one of the margin scheme indications listed in 7.1.2 above	it is likely that the goods have not been supplied under a margin scheme. You must account for acquisition tax in the UK and charge VAT on the full selling price of the goods when you sell them. There is more information about such transactions in Notice 725 "The Single Market".

If you are in any doubt about whether the supply was made under a margin scheme, you should check with your supplier before entering the details into your records.

7.3 How do I treat sales to other member states?

Sales made under a margin scheme to other EC member states are treated in exactly the same way as sales within the UK..

This means that VAT is due on the margin in the UK and you must issue a normal margin scheme sales invoice (see paragraph 5.3).

If	*Then*
you are selling goods under the scheme to a registered business in another member state	there is no requirement to obtain that business's VAT registration number. If you prefer, you can, in agreement with that dealer, treat the sale outside the margin scheme. If you do that, you can zero-rate the sale under the normal EC supply rules. You will have to obtain the dealer's VAT registration number and show it on your invoice. For detailed information about the rules, see Notice 725 "The Single Market".
you are selling eligible goods to EC private individuals you can either use—	—one of the margin schemes; or —the normal VAT arrangements, that is you charge VAT on the full selling price.

Paragraph 7.5 explains the procedures for dealing with the purchase and sale of new means of transport.

7.4 How do I treat the transfer of my own goods?

The transfer of goods within the same legal entity from one EC member state to another is deemed to be a supply of goods for VAT purposes. See section 9 of Notice 725 "The Single Market".

If	*Then*
—you transfer your own goods to another EC member state using one of the margin schemes; and	—you will not have to account for any VAT on the transfer in the UK, and
—you supply the goods to yourself at the price for which you obtained them	—you will not have to account for acquisition VAT in the other member state. If you sell the goods on after you transferred them, that sale will be subject to the VAT rules of the member state in which you make the sale.

7.5 Can I use the margin schemes for the purchase and sale of new means of transport?

No. New means of transport are always liable to VAT in the member state of destination. This means that any new means of transport that you purchase from, or sell to, another member state will not be eligible for the margin scheme.

You can find more information in Notice 728 "New Means of Transport".

7.6 Do I have to complete EC sales lists and Intrastat?

No.

VAT-registered businesses in the UK who make supplies of goods to VAT-registered businesses in other EC member states are required to complete lists (form VAT 101) of their EC supplies.

But you should not include any margin schemes transactions on an EC sales list because they will be subject to VAT in the UK and therefore not eligible for zero-rating.

Intrastat is the system for collecting statistics on the trade in goods between EC member states. But, because margin scheme goods are subject to VAT in the country of origin, there is no requirement either—

— to include margin scheme purchases or sales in boxes 8 and 9 of your VAT return; or
— to complete a supplementary declaration.

You can find guidance on completion of your VAT return in paragraph 5.4.

You can find further information on intra-EC transactions in the following publications—

Notice 723 "Refunds of VAT in the EC for EC and non-EC businesses"

Notice 725 "The Single Market"

Notice 60 "Intrastat General Guide"

8. THE MARGIN SCHEMES AND IMPORTS AND EXPORTS

8.1 Can I use the margin schemes when I sell goods I have imported?

Not usually, no.

You will be charged VAT on the full value of any goods you import from countries outside the European Community. This means you can't use a margin scheme when you sell those goods on, even if you haven't reclaimed the VAT on the purchase.

Also, you can't use a margin scheme when you sell goods which have been imported into other EC member states, and which you have got somebody to collect on your behalf.

There is one exception to this rule, and it relates to imported works of art, antiques and collectors' items. You can opt to use the margin scheme (or the VAT auctioneers' scheme) for such items provided you comply with the conditions in section 10.

8.2 What should I do if I export goods?

If	*Then*
you export eligible goods (see paragraph 20) to a destination outside the European Community	you may zero-rate the sale, provided you can meet the conditions set out in Notice 703 "VAT Exports and removals of goods from the United Kingdom".
you can meet the conditions	you should insert "nil" in the VAT due column of your stock book. You should refer in your stock book to the reason why you have closed the entry.

8.2.1 What if someone is selling the goods on my behalf?

You cannot usually zero-rate an export if you sell the goods through an auctioneer or dealer who acts as an agent in their own name.

This is because the sale of the goods is treated as two separate supplies: the first from you to the agent, and the second from the agent to the purchaser. Your sale of the goods is a supply to the agent, rather than a supply to the final purchaser. So it can only be treated as a zero-rated export if the agent is located outside the EC.

8.2.2 What if I am an auctioneer?

If you	*then*
—are acting in your own name;	—you will be making a combined supply of goods and services, with VAT due on the profit margin
—can meet the conditions for zero-rating in Notice 703, and;	—the liability of your services will follow that of the goods, with the result that the whole supply will be zero-rated.
—sell the exported goods under the auctioneers' scheme	However, you must obtain proof of export, as described in Notice 703, when you apply zero-rating to the margin.
sell the exported goods under the margin scheme	the liability of your services will not follow that of the goods because your services are charged and invoiced outside the scheme. You will be able to sell the goods at the zero-rate outside the scheme if you can meet the conditions in Notice 703, but your services will normally be standard-rated.

8.2.3 What about the retail export scheme?

The retail export scheme allows certain overseas visitors to get a VAT refund on goods they buy and export in their personal luggage. You can use the retail export scheme together with the margin scheme or the auctioneers' scheme but, if you do, you must account for VAT on the sale until—

— you receive a refund document stamped by UK or EC Customs; and
— you have made the refund to your customer.

You can find more information about the retail export scheme in Notice 704 "VAT retail exports".

9. TRANSFERS OF GOING CONCERNS AND ASSIGNMENTS OF RIGHTS

9.1 What if I take over a business as a going concern (TOGC)?

If you obtain goods under a transfer of a going concern (TOGC), no VAT will be chargeable on the transfer. But this does not necessarily mean that you will be able to sell the goods on under a margin scheme.

You will only be able to use the scheme if the last person to obtain the goods – other than by way of a TOGC or an assignment of rights – would have been entitled to use a margin scheme to sell them.

Where there has been—

— a succession of TOGCs or assignments; or
— a mixture of both

it is the first person in that chain who must have been entitled to use the margin scheme himself.

9.2 What about the records?

From 1 September 2007, the seller in a TOGC retains the records. However—

— the seller must make available to the buyer any information the buyer needs to comply with his duties under VATA 1994; and

— where the buyer applies to HMRC for permission to take on the seller's VAT number, the seller is required to transfer the records to the buyer. If the seller needs to retain the records, he may apply to HMRC for permission to do so.

The records will include the purchase invoices for stock on hand. You will be able to tell from these invoices whether or not the goods are eligible to be sold under the scheme.

If	*then*
the transferor of the goods bought them on margin scheme invoices	you will be able to sell them under the scheme.
the transferor bought them on invoices showing VAT	they are not eligible for the scheme and you will have to account for VAT on the full selling price when you sell them.

So it is in your own interest when you buy a business as a TOGC to—

— check the position with the seller; and
— make sure that you have all the records you need if you intend to sell eligible goods on under a margin scheme.

9.3 What will my margin scheme purchase price be?

Your purchase price will be the price paid when the eligible item was bought by the person in the chain who was entitled to use a margin scheme to sell it himself.

You will be able to identify the original purchase price from the purchase invoices which will form part of the business records.

If	*then*
—you have obtained goods under a TOGC from a bank or financial institution; and —goods when they were assigned the rights in a hire purchase or conditional sale agreement	the records that are usually kept in relation to these transactions should provide the information you need.

9.4 What are the rules for banks and finance houses?

If	*then*
—a bank or a financial institution; and —you have acquired eligible goods as a result of having been assigned the rights to them in hire purchase or conditional sale agreements	you can only use the margin scheme to sell those goods if the last person to obtain them – other than by way of an assignment of rights or a TOGC – would have been entitled to use the margin scheme.

Where there has been—

— a succession of assignments or TOGCs; or
— a mixture of both

it is therefore the first person in that chain who must have been entitled to use the margin scheme.

10 THE MARGIN SCHEMES IN PARTICULAR CIRCUMSTANCES: WORKS OF ART, ANTIQUES AND COLLECTORS' ITEMS ON WHICH VAT HAS BEEN CHARGED

10.1 What is this section about?

When you obtain goods which have had VAT charged on their full value, they are not normally eligible for the margin schemes.

However, you may opt to use the margin scheme or global accounting for—

— works of art, antiques and collectors' items which you have imported from countries outside the European Community; and
— works of art you have obtained (that is, which were supplied in the UK or acquired from another Member State) from creators or their heirs, whether or not VAT was charged on their purchase or acquisition.

If	*then*
—you don't opt to use a margin scheme; or —you can't meet the conditions described in paragraph 10.2	you must sell the goods under the normal VAT rules.

You can find details of import procedures and special arrangements for supplies of temporarily admitted (TA) goods in Notice 702 "Imports".

10.2 What are the conditions for using this option?

If you want to use the margin scheme or global accounting in any of these circumstances, you must meet the following conditions—

— you must inform our VAT Written Enquiries Team, 4th Floor West, Alexander House, 21 Victoria Street, Southend-on-Sea, Essex, SS99 1BD, in writing that you are going to take up the option, and you must specify the date from which you will be applying it;
— you must exercise the option for a period of at least two years, after which you must inform the VAT Written Enquiries Team (please see address above) in writing as and when you wish to stop using the scheme;
— you must use the scheme in respect of all transactions and goods listed in paragraph 10.1, not just in respect of certain categories of transactions or certain categories of goods; and
— if, having exercised the option, you decide to sell any goods covered by the option outside the scheme (for example, if you export the goods), you are not entitled to recover any input tax on those goods until the period in which you account for VAT on their sale.

10.3 What is my purchase price when I use this option?

10.3.1 Imported works of art, antiques and collectors' items

When you opt to use a margin scheme for imported works of art, antiques or collectors' items, those goods will carry a reduced VAT rate of 5 per cent.

Your purchase price will be the value for VAT at import, plus the import VAT.

— You must not reclaim the import VAT as input tax.
— Notice 702 "VAT Imports" contains detailed guidance about the valuation of imported goods for VAT purposes.

EXAMPLE

VAT-registered dealer using the Margin Scheme option for an imported antique item

Example

(a)	Value for VAT at import	£1,000
(b)	Import VAT (a x 5%)	£50
(c)	Purchase price for margin scheme (a +b)	£1,050
(d)	Selling price	£1,500
(e)	Margin (d – c)	£450
(f)	VAT due (e x $^1/_6$ths)	£75

10.3.2 Works of art obtained from the creator or their heirs

When you opt to use a margin scheme for works of art obtained (that is supplied in the UK, or acquired from another member state) from artists or their heirs, you must not recover any VAT you are charged. Under the margin scheme, your purchase price will be the total price of the work of art inclusive of any VAT.

If the work of art is an acquisition from another EC member state you should—

— account for acquisition tax in box 2 of your VAT return;
— not recover the corresponding acquisition tax in box 4 (input tax), and;
— add this unrecoverable acquisition tax to the net purchase price for margin scheme purposes.

EXAMPLE

VAT-registered dealer using the margin scheme for goods from an artist or his heirs acquired from another member state.

Example

(a)	Value of acquisition	£1,000
(b)	Acquisition VAT accounted for in box 2 of your VAT return	£175
(c)	Purchase price for margin scheme (a +b)	£1,175
(d)	Selling price	£2,000
(e)	Margin (d – c)	£825
(f)	VAT due (e x $^{1}/_{6}$ths)	£137.50

If the work of art was supplied in the UK, you must not reclaim any VAT charged by the supplier.

Note—The duplicate numbering of para 10.2 and 10.2.1 appears in the original of this Notice as at the time of printing.

11. THE MARGIN SCHEMES AND BUYING AND SELLING AT AUCTION

11.1 Who should read this section?

You should read this section if—

— you sell goods under the margin scheme or global accounting, and
— you buy or sell at auction.

11.2 What should I do if I buy goods at auction?

If you intend to use the margin scheme or global accounting for the onward sale of goods you have bought at auction, you must check whether the goods are eligible.

You should be able to find this out from the auctioneer's sales catalogue.

If the auctioneer charges VAT separately on the hammer price of goods you buy, you won't be able to use a margin scheme for your onward sale.

11.3 What is the purchase price of eligible goods I buy at auction?

Your purchase price will be the hammer price of the goods plus charges for services.

The invoice you get from the auctioneer will itemise, for each lot you have bought, the hammer price of the goods and any charges for services (for example, buyer's premium). These charges must not show VAT separately.

This will be your purchase price for the purposes of the Margin Scheme or Global Accounting, and is the amount that you must show in your stock book. It should be clearly identified on the invoice you get from the auctioneer.

If the auctioneer bills you for any other services, and charges VAT on them separately, you can reclaim the VAT under the normal rules. You must not add those charges to your own margin scheme purchase price. To avoid confusion, you may want to ask the auctioneer to provide you with a separate invoice for such charges.

If you are in any doubt about what your margin scheme purchase price should be for goods you have bought at auction, you should check with the auctioneer.

11.4 What is the selling price of eligible goods I sell at auction?

Before the sale is due to take place, you should discuss with the auctioneer whether you want it to be treated under the auctioneers' scheme or under the normal margin scheme. (The auctioneer's scheme is a special variation on the normal margin scheme. It works by creating a margin which is equal to the auctioneer's charge for his services to both the vendor and the purchaser. See Notice 718/2 "The Auctioneers' Scheme" for more information.)

If the auctioneer uses	*the invoice will include*	*your margin scheme selling price will be*
the auctioneers' scheme	—the hammer price of the goods —his commission charges, and —the net amount payable to you. None of these amounts should show VAT separately.	the hammer price less the commission charge.
the margin scheme	the hammer price of the goods. VAT must not be shown separately on this amount.	the hammer price.

Your selling price for margin scheme purposes should be easy to identify from the invoice you receive. You should check with the auctioneer if you are in any doubt.

If the auctioneer's scheme is used, you will get a separate invoice for any charges other than the auctioneer's commission.

If the margin scheme is used, you will be invoiced separately for—

— the auctioneer's commission; and
— any other charges.

You can reclaim the VAT on these invoices under the normal rules but you must not deduct the charges from your margin scheme selling price.

12. THE MARGIN SCHEMES AND JOINT PURCHASES AND SHARES

12.1 What is this section about?

This section tells you how to account under the margin schemes for goods

— in which shares have been sold; or
— which are jointly owned.

If your specific circumstances are not covered in this section, you should contact our Helpline.

12.2 How do I treat shares?

If	*then*
—you have an eligible item in stock; and —you sell a share in it	—this is a supply of an undivided share in goods and therefore a supply of services —the sale is not eligible to be accounted for under a margin scheme, so you must account for VAT under the normal rules.
you sell an item in which the title to the goods is shared	you must —account for the VAT due on the whole of the sale, not just on your own share, and —issue the other shareholders with statements which show their share of the proceeds of the sale, but which don't show any VAT.

12.3 How do I treat joint purchases?

If—

— you and other dealer(s) jointly buy an eligible item for resale; and
— it is you who makes the purchase
— you should follow the steps in the table below:

Step	*Action*	*Details*
1	Keep the purchase invoice.	The invoice must show all the details set out in paragraph 5.3.
2	Enter the purchase details of the item in your stock book.	The purchase price for the purposes of calculating the margin will be the full joint purchase price.
3	Invoice the other joint buyers for their contribution towards the cost of the item.	There must be no VAT on the invoices and you must endorse each invoice along the following lines: "This payment is your contribution towards the purchase of the above article. I shall be accounting for the full amount of VAT due under the scheme when it is sold".
4	Keep copies of those invoices and enter the details in your stock book.	You won't use these sales figures when you calculate the overall margin achieved on the final sale.

12.4 What if I then sell the goods?

If—

— you bought the item; and
— you are also the one who sells it

you should follow the steps in the table below—

Step	*Action*	*Details*
1	Issue a sales invoice and keep a copy of it.	Your invoice must show all the details set out in paragraph 5.3.
2	Enter the details of the sale in your stock book.	For the purposes of calculating the margin on the sale, your selling price is the full joint selling price, not just your share of the proceeds.
3	Issue statements to the other joint buyers showing their shares of the proceeds of the sale.	There must be no VAT on the statements and you must endorse each invoice along the following lines: "This payment is your share of the proceeds of the sale of . . . . I am accounting for the full amount of VAT due on the sale under the scheme."

12.5 What if one of the other joint owners sells the goods?

If—

— you bought the item; but
— one of the other joint owners sells it

you should follow the steps in the table below—

Step	*Action*	*Details*

1	Obtain the purchase invoice for the goods from you.	
2	Issue a sales invoice and keep a copy of it.	Their invoice must show all the details set out in paragraph 5.3.
3	Complete their own stock book, treating the purchase and sale of the article as having being made entirely by themself.	For the purposes of calculating the margin on the sale, the purchase price is the full joint purchase price and the selling price is the full joint selling price.
4	Issue statements to the other joint owners showing their shares of the proceeds of the sale	There must be no VAT on the statements and he must endorse each invoice along the following lines: "This payment is your share of the proceeds of the sale of . . . . I am accounting for the full amount of VAT due on the sale under the scheme."

Having passed the purchase invoice on to whoever made the sale, you must close down the entry for it in your own stock book, and make a note that VAT has been accounted for by another joint owner. (You do not have to account for any VAT on the transaction.)

You should then cross-refer that entry in your stock book to the sale statement you receive from the other person – step 4 in the above table.

12.6 What if I sell the goods but I didn't buy them?

If—

— you didn't buy the item; but
— you are the one selling it

you should follow the steps in the table below—

Step	*Action*	*Details*
1	Obtain the purchase invoice for the goods from the joint owner who bought them.	
2	Issue a sales invoice and keep a copy of it.	Yours invoice must show all the details set out in paragraph 5.3.
3	Complete your stock book, treating the purchase and sale of the article as having being made entirely by yourself.	For the purposes of calculating the margin on the sale, the purchase price is the full joint purchase price and the selling price is the full joint selling price.
4	Issue statements to the other joint owners showing their shares of the proceeds of the sale.	There must be no VAT on the statements and he must endorse each invoice along the following lines: "This payment is your share of the proceeds of the sale of . . . . I am accounting for the full amount of VAT due on the sale under the scheme."

Having passed the purchase invoice on to you, the purchaser must close down the entry for it in their stock book, and make a note that VAT has been accounted for by another joint owner.

13 ANSWERS TO COMMON QUESTIONS

Commentary—*De Voil Indirect Tax Service* **V3.532**.

13.1 Can I get relief from bad debts?

If you supply goods and do not receive payment within certain time limits you may claim relief from VAT on the "bad debt". You will find full details of the time limits and conditions for claiming in VAT Notice 700/18 "Relief from VAT on bad debts".

If you sold the goods under a margin scheme, the amount of VAT on which you claim relief cannot be higher than the amount of VAT you accounted for on the margin.

To explain, here are two examples based on the following figures—

Goods purchased for:	£400
Goods sold for:	£500
Margin:	£100
VAT payable (£100 x $^1/_6$):	£16.66

Example 1. The customer only pays £350 leaving a debt of £150.
The debt is greater than the margin so the potential bad debt relief is £100 (margin) x $^1/_6$ths = £16.66.
Example 2. The customer pays £450 leaving a debt of only £50 then this debt is less than the margin so the potential bad debt relief is £50 (debt) x $^1/_6$ths = £8.33.
If you receive payment from your customer after making a claim for bad debt relief, you must refund the appropriate amount to us.

13.2 What if I sell insurance with a margin scheme supply?

If you sell insurance with a standard-rated product (such as a domestic appliance) the insurance will be exempt from VAT provided—

— it is supplied under a contract between an insurer and your customer;
— it is the customer's own risk which is being insured, that is, the individual customer's risk is referred to in the policy. It is not necessary for the customer to be specifically named. If you and the customer are the insured, it is sufficient for the policy to refer to, for example, "J. Smith and customers"; and
— you disclose the amount of the premium, and any fee (or commission) charged over and above that premium on your sales invoice at the time of sale.

If you do not meet these requirements, the insurance element of your supply will be standard-rated.

While insurance is exempt from VAT, it is subject to insurance premium tax (IPT), which is usually accounted for by the insurer. IPT is due on the gross premium. In most cases, this is the amount the customer pays for the insurance. It will include—

— the premium due to the insurer; plus
— any commission or fee that you may charge on top.

If you do make additional charges, you should disclose these amounts to the insurer so that they can account for the correct amount of IPT.

Additionally, where—

— the insurance is subject to the higher rate of IPT (17.5 per cent), and
— you charge a fee in connection with that insurance

you may be liable to register and account for IPT on the fee.

You can find further information in Notice 701/36 "Insurance" and Notice IPT 1 "A General Guide to IPT". Guidance on Mechanical Breakdown Insurance (MBI) and warranties is in Notice 718/1 "The VAT Margin Scheme on second-hand cars and other vehicles".

13.3 How do I deal with gifts?

If	*then*
you *sell* an item which was given to you in the course of your business	you cannot use a margin scheme. You must account for VAT on the full selling price.
you *give away* an item which would have been eligible for sale under a margin scheme	no VAT is due.

	You must include full details of the person you gave the item to in your stock book.

13.4 How do I deal with private sales?

The private sale of goods which are not assets of your business is usually outside the scope of VAT and no VAT is due.

However if—

— you are a sole proprietor; and
— you sell an eligible item (see paragraph 2.7) which you transfer to your business from your private holdings

you can use the margin scheme for the sale of that item.

You must be able to produce evidence of what the purchase price was when you bought it for your private use. If you cannot do this, you must account for VAT on the full sales value.

13.5 How do I deal with hire-purchase sales?

13.5.1 Who is my customer?

If	*then*
you sell an eligible item and arrange hire-purchase (HP) terms with a finance company on behalf of your customer	you are deemed to be selling the item to the finance company.

No VAT is due on the finance charges, provided these are itemised separately.

13.5.2 What sales records do I need to keep?

You must transfer the sales price of the item from the HP agreement to your stock book.

If	*then*
—you have issued your own sales invoice to your customer; and —you have a copy of the HP agreement	either— —attach a copy of the completed HP agreement to the sales invoice; or —include a cross-reference to the HP agreement in your sales records.
the finance company holds the HP agreement and you don't get a copy of it for your records	keep a copy of— —the agreed quotation; or —the agreed proposal documents together with— —the name of the finance company; —the date; and —the reference number of the final agreement in your sales records.

You may use a copy of the HP agreement as your sales invoice provided it shows—

— all the identifying details of the item; and
— the cash price of the item as the gross price payable.

(The gross price is the amount borrowed plus any cash deposit paid, plus any amount allowed for a part-exchange item.)

Remember, VAT must not be shown separately on either

— the HP agreement; or
— the customer's sales invoice.

13.6 How do I treat part-exchange goods?

If you—

— sell eligible goods; and
— take others in part-exchange

the selling price on which you calculate your margin must include the value of the part-exchanged goods.

For example, you sell a boat for £2,500 for which you paid £1,500. However, you also take a boat in part-exchange which you value at £500 so the customer actually only hands over a balance of £2,000. The selling price you insert in your stock book must be £2,500 and you must account for VAT on the full margin of £1,000.

At the same time, you must use the value at which you part-exchanged an item as its purchase price in your stock book. In the example above, your purchase price would be £500. You must not alter this purchase price.

If you buy from	*then*
another VAT-registered dealer	you must obtain a purchase invoice for the goods.
a private person or unregistered dealer	you may include details of part-exchange items on your sales invoice provided all the requirements of paragraph 5.3 are met.

13.7 How do I deal with occasional sales of eligible goods?

If	*then*
you are not in business to buy and sell second-hand goods; but—	you need not comply with the full record keeping requirements in section 4 and 5, provided you—
—you very occasionally find yourself with an eligible item to sell; and	—meet the other conditions of the scheme; and
—you would like to use a margin scheme for the sale	—hold evidence of both the purchase and selling price.

13.8 How should finance companies treat the sale of second-hand repossessed goods?

Repossessed goods which have been—

— voluntarily returned under an HP agreement;
— repossessed under the terms of a finance agreement; or
— returned by a customer under the Consumer Credit Act once they have made 50 per cent of the total payments due.

If	*then*
—a finance company sells repossessed second-hand goods, originally sold under a margin scheme; and	they do not have to account for VAT on the sale.
—the goods are in the same condition as when they were repossessed	The condition of the goods is generally unaffected by— —cleaning; or —inclusion of instruction manuals if they are otherwise missing.
—a finance company sells repossessed second-hand goods, originally sold under a margin scheme; and	they may sell those goods under a margin scheme.

—the condition of the goods has changed	The purchase price for margin scheme purposes will be the original price the finance company paid to the dealer. The condition of the goods will have changed if any— —improvements; —repairs; —replacement parts; or —general making good of damage have been carried out.

13.9 What if I buy goods from an insurance company or finance house?

If you buy eligible goods from either—

— an insurance company which has acquired them as a result of an insurance claim; or
— a finance house which has repossessed them

the company/finance house will not charge you VAT if—

— the goods are sold on in exactly the same state as they were in when they were acquired; and
— the goods were obtained by the company/finance house from a person who would not themselves have charged VAT on their sale, for example, a private individual.

You can re-sell such goods under a margin scheme provided you can meet the conditions of the scheme.

13.10 How do I treat Artist's Resale Right charges?

Artist's Resale Right (sometimes known as Droit de Suite) is a royalty which is charged, in certain circumstances, when original works of art are re-sold. It was introduced into the UK in 2006. The charges are outside the scope for VAT purposes. They have no impact on margin scheme calculations. You must not reduce your margin by the cost of the charges.

14 GLOBAL ACCOUNTING

Commentary—*De Voil Indirect Tax Service* **V3.535**.

14.1 What is global accounting?

Global accounting is an optional simplified variation of the normal margin scheme.

14.2 How does it differ from the margin scheme?

Under	*you account for VAT on*
the standard margin scheme	the margin you achieve on the sale of individual eligible items.
global accounting	the margin you achieve between your total eligible purchases and total eligible sales in an accounting period.

14.3 Would I benefit from using global accounting?

If you—

— buy and sell bulk volume, low value eligible goods; and
— are unable to maintain the detailed records required of businesses who use the standard margin scheme

global accounting will suit your business and will reduce the amount of VAT you have to pay.

14.4 Which goods can I use global accounting for?

You can include most items which would be eligible for sale under the margin scheme (see paragraph 20.1) as long as they have a purchase price of *£500 or less per item.* The exceptions to this are listed in paragraph 14.5 below.

14.5 Which goods can I not use global accounting for?

You cannot sell any of the following goods under Global Accounting, regardless of their purchase price—

— aircraft;
— boats and outboard motors;
— caravans and motor caravans;
— horses and ponies; and
— motor vehicles including motorcycles—except those broken up for scrap (see paragraph 14.9).

14.6 What do I need to consider when I start using the scheme?

When you start using global accounting you may find that you already have eligible stock on hand.

If that is the case, you may include the value of this stock when you calculate your total purchases at the end of the first period. (Paragraph 14.7 explains how to value your stock on hand.)

If you don't take your stock on hand into account, you will have to pay VAT on the full price, rather than on the margin you have achieved, when you sell it.

14.7 How do I value my stock on hand?

You must be able to identify—

— stock which is eligible for global accounting; and
— its purchase value.

You would normally establish the value from the original purchase invoices.

But if—

— you are newly registered; and
— don't have original purchase invoices

you may determine the purchase value using another method.

There is no set way of doing this, but you must be able to demonstrate satisfactorily to us that the method you have used has produced a fair and reasonable total. You must retain evidence of this method with the rest of your global accounting records for six years.

Remember, any goods you bought on an invoice which shows a separate VAT figure are *not* eligible for resale under the scheme.

14.8 How do I work out the VAT due under global accounting?

Under global accounting, VAT is calculated at the end of each tax period. Because you can take account of opening stock in your scheme calculations, you may find that you produce a negative margin at the end of several periods. In other words, your total purchases may exceed your total sales. In such cases, no VAT is due. But you *must* carry the negative margin forward to the next period as in the following example:—

Period one

(a)	total purchase value of stock on hand	£10,000
(b)	total purchases from your purchase summary	£2,000
(c)	total sales from your sales summary	£8,000

(d)	margin = c – (a + b) sales minus (purchases plus stock on hand) £8,000 – (£10,000 + £2,000)	(£4,000)

Because the margin you have produced is negative, there is no VAT for you to pay. However, you must carry this negative margin forward into the next period as follows—

Period two

(a)	negative margin from previous period	£4,000
(b)	total purchases for this period	£1,000
(c)	total sales for this period	£7,000
(d)	margin = c – (a + b) sales minus (purchases plus negative margin) £7,000 – (£1,000 + £4,000)	(£2,000)
(e)	VAT due = margin (£2,000) x VAT fraction (1/6ths)	£333.33

There is no negative margin to carry forward this time. Therefore, in the third period, you would calculate VAT on the margin between total sales and total purchases.

You may only offset a negative margin against your next global accounting margin. You cannot offset it against any other figure or record.

You must keep copies of these calculations with your other global accounting records for six years.

14.9 Can I use global accounting for the sale of scrap?

Yes. You may include motor vehicles which would be eligible for sale under the margin scheme in global accounting if you break them up and sell them on as scrap.

You must keep the normal commercial documentation to show that the vehicle no longer exists and that the scrap parts are therefore eligible for global accounting.

If	*then*
the vehicle has already been entered into your second-hand stock book	you should close the entry and transfer the details to your global accounting purchase records.
you buy a scrap motor vehicle for more than £500	you can still use the global accounting scheme for disposal of the components. However, any individual component valued at over £500 must be excluded from global accounting.
you are charged VAT separately when you buy a vehicle	you cannot use either global accounting or the margin scheme when you sell any scrap parts from that vehicle.

14.10 Can I use global accounting for bulk purchases and collections?

Yes, you can, even if the combined purchase price is over £500.

However, if any individual item has a purchase value of over £500, you must not sell it on under global accounting.

You may sell it under the normal margin scheme if you can meet the record keeping conditions detailed in sections 4 and 5. If you intend to do this, you will have to make sure that the item is identified and fully described on your purchase invoice.

Alternatively, you may sell the item under the normal VAT rules.

14.11 Global accounting in other situations

If	*then*
you split collections of items, such as stamp collections, and either— —sell the items separately; or —use them to form other collections	you can account for those sales under global accounting, provided all the items are eligible.
you purchase an eligible item for £500 or more; and —the item is made up of several components valued at less than £500; but —you sell the component items individually (For example, you purchase a tea set for £600 and you sell the cups and saucers individually for £50 each.)	you can account for the sales under global accounting.
you purchase an eligible item for £500 or more, and —the item is made up of several components valued at less than £500; and —you sell the item in the same state as it was purchased (For example, you purchase the tea set for £600, but you sell it on as a tea set.)	you can *not* account for the sale under global accounting. You may account for the sale under the margin scheme, provided you can meet the record- keeping requirements.
you combine two or more items to produce only one item for resale (For example, you use one item as a spare part for another.)	you can account for the sale under global accounting.
you buy eligible items and use them to produce something which is *not* eligible (For example, you buy second-hand fabrics and trimmings and make them into cushion covers.)	—you can *not* account for the sale under either global accounting or the margin scheme; —you must sell the item under the normal rules and account for VAT on the full selling price.

15 GLOBAL ACCOUNTING—RECORDS AND ACCOUNTS

15.1 What records do I need to keep?

You do not need to keep all the detailed records which are required under the normal margin scheme—for instance, you do not have to maintain a detailed stock book. Global accounting records do not have to be kept in any set way but they must be complete, up to date and clearly distinguishable from any other records.

You must keep records of purchases and sales as described in the following paragraphs together with the workings you used to calculate the VAT due. You must keep all your records for six years.

If we can't check the margins you have declared from your records, VAT will be due on the full selling price of the goods you've supplied, even if they were otherwise eligible for the scheme. If you are not sure about how to maintain your global accounting records, please contact our Helpline.

Commentary—*De Voil Indirect Tax Service* **V3.536**.

15.2 What must I do when buying goods under Global Accounting?

The boxed text below has the force of law

When you buy goods which you intend to sell under Global Accounting you must—

- check that the goods are eligible for global accounting;
- obtain a purchase invoice. If you buy from a private person or an unregistered dealer, you should make out the invoice at the time you buy the goods. If you buy from another VAT-registered dealer, the dealer must make out the invoice at the time of sale; and
- enter the purchase details of the goods in your global accounting purchase records. The purchase price must be the price on the invoice which has been agreed between you and the seller.

You cannot use the scheme if an amount of VAT is shown on the invoice.

15.3 What details must be included on purchase invoices?

The following rule/requirement/paragraph has the force of law

Purchase invoices must include—

- your name and address;
- the seller's name and address;
- invoice number;
- date of transaction;
- description of goods (this must be sufficient to enable us to verify that the goods are eligible for global accounting, for example "four tables, ten chairs" – "assorted goods" is not acceptable);
- total price, you must not show VAT separately; and

for goods purchased from another VAT-registered dealer, any of the following—

- the statement "Global Accounting Invoice"

15.4 What must I do when selling goods under global accounting?

If you have complied with the purchase conditions above, you may use global accounting for the sale of the goods by—

- recording the sale in your usual way, for example, by using a cash register;
- issuing a sales invoice for sales to other VAT-registered dealers and keeping a copy of the invoice; and
- transferring your daily takings for eligible goods and/or totals of copy invoices to your global accounting sales record or summary (see paragraph 15.6).

The following rule/requirement/paragraph has the force of law

You must be able to distinguish at the point of sale between sales made under global accounting and other types of transactions.

15.5 What details must I include on sales invoices?

The following rule/requirement/paragraph has the force of law

You must issue a sales invoice to other VAT-registered dealers. These invoices and any other global accounting sales invoice you issue must show the following details—

- your name, address and VAT registration number;
- the buyer's name and address;

— invoice number;
— date of sale;
— description of goods (this must be sufficient to enable us to verify that the goods are eligible for global accounting, for example "four tables, ten chairs" – "assorted goods" is not acceptable);
— total price – you must not show VAT separately; and
— the statement "Global Accounting Invoice"
— you are selling an item for more than £500 and you don't want the purchaser to know that you bought it under Global Accounting, you may use one of the Margin Scheme sales invoice statements listed in paragraph 5.3.

15.6 What details should I include in my purchase and sales summaries?

The following rule/requirement/paragraph has the force of law

Although you do not have to keep your purchase and sales records or summaries in any particular way, they must include the following details taken from your purchase invoices and any sales invoices you may issue—

— invoice number (where the purchase invoice shows one);
— date of purchase/sale;
— description of goods (this must be sufficient to enable us to verify that the goods are eligible for global accounting, for example "four tables, ten chairs" – "assorted goods" is not acceptable); and
— total price.

Paragraph 14.8 gives an example of how you should work out the VAT due at the end of each period.

15.7 What if I stop using the scheme or transfer goods as a going concern?

The following rule/requirement/paragraph has the force of law

If you stop using global accounting for any reason – for example, you deregister for VAT – you must make a closing adjustment to take account of purchases for which you have taken credit, but which have not been sold (in other words, your closing stock on hand). The adjustment required in this paragraph does not apply if the total VAT due on your stock on hand is £1,000 or less. In the final period for which you are using the scheme, you must add the purchase value of your closing stock to your sales figure for that period. In this way you will pay VAT (at cost price) on the stock for which you previously had credit under the scheme.

Here is an example of a closing adjustment under global accounting: At the end of the period calculate:

— Value of purchases during the period— £5,000
— Value of sales during the period—£10,000
— Purchase value of closing stoc— £8,000
— Add purchase value of closing stock to sales for period (c + b)—£18,000
— Subtract purchases in this period from sales (d – a)—£13,000
— VAT due on margin (e x $^1/_6$ths)—£2,166.66

You must make a similar adjustment if you transfer goods as part of a transfer of a going concern (TOGC). In that case you should add the purchase value of goods included in the scheme to your sales figure for the period in which the TOGC takes place. This adjustment is separate from the TOGC itself, which is not subject to VAT.

15.8 What must I do if I sell items outside the scheme?

If you sell goods which you had included in your global accounting purchase records outside the scheme (for example, you export them), you must adjust your records accordingly.

You do this by subtracting the purchase value of the goods you have sold outside the scheme from your total purchases at the end of the period.

If you do not know the exact purchase value – for example, the goods may have been part of a bulk purchase – you must apportion a value. There is no set way of doing this, but your method must be fair and reasonable and you must be able to demonstrate to us how you determined the value.

You must retain any such evidence and calculations with your records for six years.

15.9 How do I treat stolen or destroyed goods?

The following rule/requirement/paragraph has the force of law

If you lose any goods through breakage, theft or destruction, you must subtract their purchase price from your global accounting purchase record.

15.10 How do I treat repairs and restoration costs?

You can reclaim the VAT you are charged on any business overheads, repairs, restoration costs, etc. But you must not add any of these costs to the purchase price of the goods you sell under the scheme.

15.11 How do I treat global accounting invoices in foreign currencies?

15.11.1 Purchases

Global accounting invoices will normally only show a total price for the goods you buy and sell under the scheme.

If the individual purchase price of each item on the invoice is below £500, you need to convert the invoice total to sterling before you enter it into your purchase records.

Because individual items with a purchase value over £500 are not eligible for this scheme, you must deduct the value of any such items from the purchase invoice total.

You do this by—

— converting the total value in foreign currency (including euro) into sterling; and
— apportioning this figure so as to exclude the item, or items, with individual purchase values over £500.

You then enter the net purchase amount in sterling in your purchase records.

To convert amounts in foreign currencies you must use one of the methods outlined in Notice 700 "The VAT Guide". Whichever method you adopt, you must use the exchange rate which is current at the time the supply is made to you.

15.11.2 Sales

If you issue a global accounting sales invoice in a foreign currency, you must show the sterling equivalent of the total value of the goods. Even if you sell more than one item on the same invoice, you need only show the total foreign currency and sterling price on that invoice. You must enter the sterling price in your sales record.

To convert amounts into foreign currencies you must use one of the methods outlined in Notice 700, "The VAT Guide". Whichever method you adopt, you must use the exchange rate which is current at the time you make the supply.

16. THE MARGIN SCHEME IN PARTICULAR TRADE SECTORS: DEALERS IN SECOND-HAND HORSES AND PONIES

16.1 What do I need to know?

This section deals with the special rules you need to follow if you want to sell second-hand horses and ponies under the margin scheme. It doesn't give you detailed information about how to use the scheme: that information is in sections 2 to 13.

You can only sell horses and ponies which are second-hand under the margin scheme.

A horse or pony which has previously been owned by somebody else is second-hand.

A horse or pony which you have bred and are selling for the first time is not second-hand, regardless of how much work or expense you have put in to preparing it for sale.

If VAT is shown separately on the purchase invoice for a horse or pony you have bought, you can't use the margin scheme when you sell the animal on.

Paragraphs 16.2 to 16.6 of this section tell you what records you must keep if you use the special three-part forms supplied by The British Equestrian Trade Association (BETA).

Paragraph 16.7 tells you what records you must keep if you don't use the special three-part forms.

16.2 What is the three-part form?

The three-part form is a document you can use to account for VAT on the sale of horses and ponies under the margin scheme. It is an alternative to keeping the normal margin scheme records. The three-part forms come in numbered sets, with a VAT summary sheet at the back. They are sold by—

The British Equestrian Trade Association (BETA)
Stockeld Park
Wetherby
West Yorkshire LS22 4AW

If you use the three-part form each time you sell a second-hand horse or pony, it will provide you with all the stock and sales records you need to keep for the margin scheme. You won't need to keep a stock book or invoices as described in section 5.

This is how the form creates your records—

Part	*becomes*
A of the form (white)	your stock record
B of the form (pink)	your copy sales invoice
C of the form (yellow)	your customer's purchase invoice

You must not alter the serial number on the form.

The following paragraphs tell you how to complete the form. If you don't complete it correctly, our officers won't be able to confirm the margin you have achieved and you will have to account for VAT on the full selling price.

As with all your other VAT books and records, you must keep your parts of the form for six years after the date of sale of the animal.

16.3 Buying a second-hand horse or pony, using the three-part form

16.3.1 What if I buy a horse or pony from a private individual?

Step	*Action*	*Details*
1	Complete the "Description" and "Written Description" sections of Parts A, B and C of the form.	

2	Write the unique identifying number of the horse's passport in the space for "Reg. No".	If the horse or pony doesn't have a passport, you and a vet must sign Parts A, B and C of the form to certify that the horse or pony is the one described on the form. If the purchase price of the horse or pony is £500 or less, the vet's signature is not necessary.
3	Give the form a stock number in numerical sequence	
4	Complete the Purchase Record section on the reverse of Part A	
5	Keep all three parts of the form	You will need them when you resell the horse or pony.

When you are completing the "Description" and "Written Description" at Step 1 of the table, you must do this in accordance with the standard laid down by the Royal College of Veterinary Surgeons in the booklet "Verification of horses: instructions for veterinary surgeons". The booklet is published by the Weatherbys Group in conjunction with the RCVS and the British Equine Veterinary Association.

You can buy a copy from:

www.weatherbys-bookshop.com or:—

Weatherbys Bookshop
Sanders Road
Wellingborough
Northants NN8 4BX

16.3.2 What if I buy from someone who is selling under the scheme?

You should follow the rules in the table above.

If the seller is using the three-part form—

— they will give you Part C of their form, and you must keep that with your own partially completed form;
— they will not have to sign the declaration on the reverse of Part A; and
— if the horse or pony doesn't have a passport and has a purchase price of £500 or more, the Part C you are given should already have been signed by a vet. You need only copy the details of the vet's name, practice, etc on to your form – you need not get the vet to sign it.

16.4 Selling a horse or pony, using the three-part form

Step	*Action*	*Details*
1	Check that the horse or pony is eligible to be sold under the margin scheme.	The animal must— —be second-hand; and —have been bought under eligible circumstances. If it doesn't meet these conditions, you must account for VAT on the full selling price.
2	Check that you followed the procedure in paragraph 16.3.1 when you bought the horse or pony.	If you haven't, you can't use the three-part form when you sell the horse or pony on under the margin scheme.
3	Complete the sales record sections on the reverse of Parts A, B and C.	
4	Complete the VAT Record section on the reverse of Part A.	Paragraph 3.3 tells you how to work out the VAT due on the sale.

5	CKeep Parts A and B.
6	Give Part C to the buyer.
7	Complete the VAT summary sheet.

You will need them when you resell the horse or pony.

16.5 Buying a horse or pony at auction, using the three-part form

You should follow the steps in the table at paragraph 16.3.

If the horse or pony is being sold under the scheme, the auctioneer will give you Part C of the seller's form (you must keep this part with your own partially completed form).

If the horse or pony is sold by a private person, you must get the auctioneer to complete details of his name, address and Lot number on the reverse of Part A of your form.

16.6 Selling a horse or pony at auction, using the three-part form

You should tell the auctioneer that your horse or pony is being sold under the scheme and give the auctioneer Parts B and C of your form, which must already be completed as per paragraph 16.4.

After the sale—

— the auctioneer will complete the sales details on the reverse of Parts B and C, adding their name and address;
— Part C will be given to the buyer;
— Part B will be returned to you; and
— you should complete the Sales and VAT Records sections on your Part A.

16.7 What records do I have to keep if I don't use the three-part form?

If you prefer not to use the three-part form available from BETA, you can maintain the normal records and accounts detailed in sections 4 and 5.

If you purchase a horse or pony from a VAT-registered dealer who uses the three-part form, either direct or at auction, you will be given Part C of the form.

You may use this as your purchase invoice and enter the details in your stock book. You must include sufficient details in your stock book to identify the horse or pony.

If you do decide to keep normal margin scheme records, you must include enough information in your stock book to identify the horse or pony, such as—

— unique identifying passport number;
— colour;
— sex; and
— type or breed (for example, cob or thoroughbred);
— age (if known);
— height;
— stable name (if known); and
— distinctive markings.

17 THE MARGIN SCHEME IN PARTICULAR TRADE SECTORS: AGENTS

17.1 What is an agent?

Dealers often sell goods for, or on behalf of, other dealers or private sellers. They may—

— retain a percentage of the selling price; or
— make a separate charge to the owner.

In these circumstances, the seller is acting as the agent of the person who owns the goods. Both parties will need to follow the rules about agents in this section.

17.2 I am the owner of the goods: how do I calculate my margin?

If—

— you own eligible goods;

— you are registered for VAT; and
— an agent sells the goods on your behalf in his own name

you can still account for your own sale under a margin scheme.

Your purchase price will be calculated in the normal way (see paragraph 3.2). Your selling price will depend on the way your agent has accounted for his sale and will be the same as the agent's purchase price (see paragraphs 17.4 and 17.5 below). Ask the agent if you are not sure what your selling price should be.

17.3 I am an agent: can I use a margin scheme?

Yes. If you are an agent acting in your own name (sometimes known as an undisclosed agent), you can use a margin scheme when you sell eligible goods (see section 2).

Your margin will be equal to the charges you make for your services as an agent. The way you calculate your margin will depend on how you have decided to account for those charges. You can find more information about agents and VAT, and about the options you have for accounting for your charges, in Notice 700 "The VAT Guide".

The following paragraphs explain how your choice of accounting method will affect your margin scheme calculations.

17.4 I am an agent and I invoice my charges separately to the seller

If you do this, you have to issue—

— an invoice for your charges with VAT on it; and
— another, separate invoice for the goods you have sold under the margin scheme.

You calculate your margin on the sale of the goods like this—

Purchase price	The total price you receive for the goods, *not* including any charges made to the buyer. (If the seller is using a margin scheme for their sale of the goods to you, this figure will also be their selling price for margin scheme purposes.)
Selling price	The total price you receive for the goods *including* any incidental expenses and commission you charge to the buyer. (If you charge the buyer for any optional services which are not directly linked to the goods, you should invoice for these outside the margin scheme.)
Margin	The difference between the purchase price and the selling price.
VAT due	Apply the VAT fraction to the margin (see paragraph 3.3).

17.4.1 How does using a margin scheme help me?

If you	*then*
—use a margin scheme; and	you will pay VAT on—
—invoice your charges separately to the seller	—the invoice for your charges to the seller; and
	—your margin, which will be equal to any charges you make to the buyer
	but—
	—you *won't* pay any VAT on the goods.
— *don't* use a margin scheme; and	you will pay VAT on—
—invoice your charges separately to the seller	—your charges to both the seller and the buyer; *and* the goods.

17.5 I am an agent and I include my charges to the seller in the sale of the goods

If you include your charges to the seller in the sale of the goods, you calculate your margin like this—

Purchase price	The total sum you receive for the transaction *less* your charges to the seller. (If the seller is using a margin scheme for their sale of the goods to you, this figure will also be their selling price for margin scheme purposes.)
Selling price	The total sum you receive for the transaction *inclusive of* any incidental charges you make to the buyer. (If you charge the buyer for any optional services which are not directly linked to the goods, you should invoice for these outside the margin scheme.)
Margin	The difference between the purchase price and the selling price.
VAT due	Apply the VAT fraction to the margin (see paragraph 3.3).

This method mirrors the method used by auctioneers to calculate their purchase and selling prices under the auctioneers' scheme (see Notice 718/2 "The Auctioneers' Scheme").

17.5.1 How does using a margin scheme help me?

If you	*then*
—use a margin scheme; and	you will pay VAT on—
—include your charges to the seller in the sale of the goods	—your margin, which will be equal to the charges you make to the buyer and the seller *but*— —you *won't* pay any VAT on the goods.
— *don't* use a margin scheme; and	you will pay VAT on—
—include your charges to the seller in the sale of the goods	—your charges to both the seller and the buyer; *and* the goods.

17.6 What if I sell zero-rated goods?

If	*then*
you are an agent acting in your own name and—	your charges will fall outside the margin scheme and will be standard-rated for VAT, regardless of the liability of the goods.
—you use a margin scheme; and	
—you invoice your charges separately to the seller	
you are an agent acting in your own name and—	the VAT liability of your services will follow that of the goods.
—you use a margin scheme; and	This means that if you sell zero-rated goods, for example, antique books, your margin will also be zero-rated.
—you include your charges to the seller in the sale of the goods	In the VAT due column of your stock record, you should insert "nil".

17.7 What records do I need to keep?

If you issue invoices in your own name for the margin scheme sales you make as an agent, you must keep the records described in section 5.

If you sell goods on behalf of someone who:

— is registered for VAT; and
— who is using a margin scheme themselves

you must make sure they give you an invoice which includes all the details described at paragraph 5.3. That person's selling price should follow the rules at 17.4 and 17.5 above.

If you sell goods on behalf of someone who is not registered for VAT, you must make out the invoice yourself.

18. THE MARGIN SCHEME IN PARTICULAR TRADE SECTORS: PAWNBROKERS

18.1 Can I use a margin scheme when I sell unredeemed pawns?

Yes, in specific circumstances.

If—

— the loan is for £75 or less; and
— you adopt the statutory six month redemption period

ownership of the pledge passes to you if it is not redeemed within that time limit.

If you dispose of the goods to a third party, there will be VAT on the sale.

If—

— the goods are eligible; and
— you can meet all the other conditions of the scheme

you may account for the sale under the margin scheme or global accounting.

18.2 What is my purchase price for the margin scheme?

If you use a margin scheme for goods described in paragraph 18.1, your purchase price will be the amount which would be needed to redeem the pawn, that is—

— the amount of the loan; plus
— the initial six months' interest payable; minus
— any payments received from the pledgor.

You must not add any interest relating to the three-month period of grace or other items such as—

— cleaning;
— repair charges;
— storage and other overhead expenses

to the purchase price.

18.3 What should I use as my purchase invoice?

You may use the "Credit Agreement and Pawn Receipt" as your purchase invoice, if you wish, provided—

— the contract number is entered in your pledge stock record and cross refers to the agreement; and
— a copy of the interest calculations and total purchase value for margin scheme purposes is attached, if it differs from the amount shown on the receipt.

18.4 Under what circumstances can I not use a margin scheme?

18.4.1 Pledges restored during the period of grace

If you restore the pledge to the pledgor during the period of grace, there will be no VAT on the supply provided you—

— record the redemption in your pledge stock records; and
— stamp the "Credit Agreement and Pawn Receipt" with the date of redemption and keep it for inspection by HMRC.

You cannot account for the restoration of the pledge under the margin scheme or global accounting, so you will need to adjust your purchase record if you have already entered the items in your scheme records.

18.4.2 Pledges where ownership of the goods does not pass to you

If	*then*
—the loan exceeds £75; or	ownership of the pledge does not pass to you at the end of the redemption period.
—the redemption period has been agreed for a time longer than the usual six months	There will be no VAT on the sale of the pledged goods if you dispose of them to a third party, so you cannot use a margin scheme when you sell them.

You may sell these goods at auction on the pledgor's behalf, and the auctioneer can use the auctioneers' scheme provided that—

— the pledgor is not VAT-registered;
— the goods are eligible; and
— the conditions are met.

However, it is important to be aware that, if—

— the pledgor is registered for VAT; and
— the pledge is something he acquired in the course of business

there will be VAT on the sale. You must follow the procedures for accounting for VAT on goods sold in satisfaction of a debt described in Notice 700 "The VAT Guide".

19 THE MARGIN SCHEME IN PARTICULAR TRADE SECTORS: DEALERS IN SECOND-HAND CARAVANS AND HOUSEBOATS

19.1 Can I use the margin scheme?

It depends on the VAT liability of the caravan or houseboat you are selling.

If	*then*
you sell a second-hand caravan or house-boat which is zero-rated	You may use the Margin Scheme for the sale of any standard-rated fixtures or removable contents.
	You may, though, use the margin scheme for the sale of any standard-rated fixtures or removable contents.
you sell— —second-hand boats which are not house-boats; or —second-hand caravans which do not meet the criteria for zero-rating	you may use the margin scheme to account for VAT on the sale.

You can find—

— information about the VAT liability of caravans and houseboats;
— guidance on how to calculate a value for standard-rated fixtures or contents; and
— guidance on how to calculate the margin

in Notice 701/20 "Caravans and houseboats".

20 DEFINITIONS

Commentary—*De Voil Indirect Tax Service* V3.532.

20.1 Definitions of eligible goods

For the purposes of the schemes in this notice, the words and phrases below have the following meaning—

Second-hand goods

Tangible moveable property that is suitable for further use as it is or after repair, other than works of art, collectors' items or antiques and other than precious metals and precious stones.

Works of art

(1) "Work of art" means, subject to subsections 2 and 3 below—
- (a) any mounted or unmounted painting, drawing, collage, decorative plaque or similar picture that was executed by hand;
- (b) any original engraving, lithograph or other print which—
  - (i) was produced from one or more plates executed by hand by an individual who executed them without using any mechanical or photomechanical process; and
  - (ii) either is the only one produced from the plate or plates or is comprised in a limited edition;
- (c) any original sculpture or statuary, in any material;
- (d) any sculpture cast which—
  - (i) was produced by or under the supervision of the individual who made the mould or became entitled to it by succession on the death of that individual; and
  - (ii) either is the only cast produced from the mould or is comprised in a limited edition;
- (e) any tapestry or other hanging which—
  - (i) was made by hand from an original design; and
  - (ii) either is the only one made from the design or is comprised in a limited edition;
- (f) any ceramic executed by an individual and signed by him;
- (g) any enamel on copper which—
  - (i) was executed by hand;
  - (ii) is signed either by the person who executed it or by someone on behalf of the studio where it was executed;
  - (iii) either is the only one made from the design in question or is comprised in a limited edition; and
  - (iv) is not comprised in an article of jewellery or an article of a kind produced by goldsmiths or silversmiths;
- (h) any mounted or unmounted photograph which—
  - (i) was printed by or under the supervision of the photographer;
  - (ii) is signed by him; and
  - (iii) either is the only print made from the exposure in question or is comprised in a limited edition;

(2) The following do not fall within the definition of works of art—
- (a) any technical drawing, map or plan;
- (b) any picture comprised in a manufactured article that has been hand-decorated; or
- (c) anything in the nature of scenery, including a backcloth.

(3) An item comprised in a limited edition shall be taken to be so comprised for the purposes of subsection 1(d) to (h) above only if—
- (a) in the case of sculpture casts—
  - (i) the edition is limited so that the number produced from the same mould does not exceed eight; or
  - (ii) the edition comprises a limited edition of nine or more casts made before 1 January 1989 which the Commissioners have directed should be treated, in the exceptional circumstances of the case, as a limited edition for the purposes of subsection 1(d) above;
- (b) in the case of tapestries and hangings, the edition is limited so that the number produced from the same design does not exceed eight;
- (c) in the case of enamels on copper—
  - (i) the edition is limited so that the number produced from the same design does not exceed eight; and
  - (ii) each of the enamels in the edition is numbered and is signed as mentioned in subsection 1(g)(ii) above;
- (d) in the case of photographs—

(i) the edition is limited so that the number produced from the same exposure does not exceed 30; and
(ii) each of the prints in the edition is numbered and is signed as mentioned in subsection 1(h)(ii) above.

Collectors' items

Collections and collectors' pieces of zoological, botanical, mineralogical, anatomical, historical, archaeological, palaeontological, ethnographic, numismatic or philatelic interest.

A collector's piece is of philatelic interest if—

(a) it is a postage or revenue stamp, a postmark, a first-day cover or an item of pre-stamped stationery; and
(b) it is franked or (if unfranked) it is not legal tender and is not intended for use as such.

Note: unfranked stamps which are valid for postage are not collectors' items and cannot be included in the margin schemes: that is, stamps on which the value is—

— in decimal currency; or
— currently valid for 1st or 2nd class postage; or
— £1, or a multiple of £1, of the present monarch's reign.

Antiques

Antiques means objects other than works of art or collectors' items which are more than 100 years old.

20.2 Definitions of ineligible goods

Precious metals

Goods (including coins) consisting in precious metals or any supply of goods containing precious metals where the consideration for the supply (excluding any VAT) is, or is equivalent to an amount which does not exceed the open market value of the metal contained in the goods.

For gold coins sold at or below the open market value (that is the daily "fix" price) the special accounting and payment system for gold transactions applies. Further details can be found in Notice 701/21 "Gold".

Investment gold

Gold coins which meet the definition of investment gold are not considered of numismatic interest and are not eligible for the margin schemes. Further details about investment gold can be found in Notice 701/21A "Investment Gold Coins".

Precious stones

Precious stones of any age which are not mounted, set or strung. For the purposes of the margin scheme, precious stones are diamonds, rubies, sapphires and emeralds.

NOTICE 718/1
THE VAT MARGIN SCHEME ON SECOND-HAND CARS AND OTHER VEHICLES

9 March 2011

This notice replaces the December 2009 version and has been updated to reflect the change in the standard rate of VAT to 20% from January 2011.T

1 INTRODUCTION

1.1 What is this notice about?

This notice explains when you may use the Second-Hand Margin Scheme to account for VAT on your sales of second-hand vehicles.

It explains—

— which vehicles you can sell under the scheme;
— how the scheme works;
— how to calculate the margin; and
— what records you must keep.

This notice assumes that you have a working knowledge of basic VAT principles, as outlined in Notice 700 "The VAT Guide".

If, after reading this notice, you need any further help or advice, please contact our VAT Helpline.

1.2 What's changed

The information in this notice used to be contained in Notice 718 "Margin schemes for second-hand goods, works of art, antiques and collectors' items". We have moved the things which are relevant to businesses who deal in second-hand motor vehicles into this separate, shorter notice so that you can find what you need more easily.

The rules about Margin Scheme declarations on invoices have changed: please see the table in section 5.3 for details.

We have updated the Notice to reflect the VAT rate of 20%.

1.3 Who should read this notice

You should read this notice if you are registered for VAT and you make, or intend to make, supplies of second-hand vehicles.

1.4 Force of law

The VAT (Cars) Order 1992 requires businesses who sell vehicles under the Margin Scheme to keep the records and accounts detailed in sections 4 and 5 of this notice. All of sections 4 and 5 have legal force and supplement the law.

Commentary—*De Voil Indirect Tax Service* **V3.531**.

2 BASIC PRINCIPLES

2.1 Why would I want to use the Margin Scheme?

If you sell second-hand vehicles on which you weren't charged VAT, using the Margin Scheme will save you money.

Without the Margin Scheme, you would have to account for VAT on the full selling price of each vehicle.

But, if you use the Margin Scheme, you can account for VAT on the difference between the price you pay for a second-hand vehicle and the price you sell it for.

If you sell a vehicle for less than you paid for it, you won't have to account for any VAT on the sale.

2.2 What are the conditions for using the Scheme?

You don't have to use the Margin Scheme: it's optional.

If you decide to use it, there are a number of conditions you will have to meet. If you can't meet all the conditions, you can't use the scheme.

The detailed conditions are explained throughout this notice. The main ones are—

— the vehicles must be eligible (see paragraph 2.3);
— you must have acquired the vehicles in eligible circumstances. In most cases, this means that you have obtained eligible vehicles for resale in circumstances where VAT was not chargeable (see paragraph 2.4);
— you must calculate the margin in accordance with the rules of the scheme. There are special rules about how to calculate your buying price, your selling price and your margin under the scheme. Your margin may not be the same as your profit margin (see paragraph 3.3);

— you must meet the record keeping rules of the scheme. There are special rules about invoicing and stock records (see sections 4 and 5).

2.3 What makes a vehicle eligible?

Only second-hand vehicles can be sold under the Margin Scheme. Under the legal definition of second-hand goods, a second-hand motor vehicle is one which—

— has been driven on the road for business or pleasure purposes; and
— is suitable for further use as it is or after repair.

2.4 Can I sell all second-hand vehicles under the scheme?

No. You can only use the Margin Scheme if both—

— the vehicle; and
— the circumstances in which you bought it

are eligible.

The table below explains which vehicles are eligible for the Margin Scheme.

You can use the Margin Scheme for second-hand vehicles you have bought from . . .	*You can't use the Margin Scheme for . . .*
private individuals in the UK or another EC member state.	—new vehicles (registration and delivery mileage do not make a vehicle "used" for margin scheme purposes); or —new means of transport purchased from other member states. New means of transport are always liable to VAT in the member state of destination. You can find more information in Notice 728 "New Means of Transport".
businesses not registered for VAT.	any vehicle purchased on an invoice which shows VAT separately – regardless of whether you reclaim the VAT.
dealers or businesses who were unable to reclaim the input VAT on purchase.	vehicles bought from registered dealers in other member states which have not been supplied under a margin scheme.
VAT-registered dealers, if sold to you under the Margin Scheme (this should be clear from the invoice you receive).	imported vehicles – including vehicles collected on your behalf.
VAT-registered dealers in other Member States, if supplied to you under a margin scheme.	category A and B write-off vehicles, or any vehicle which is subject to the End Of Life Directive.
Motability – for which you have an invoice showing VAT charged at the zero-rate.	

2.5 What if I make sales under the normal VAT rules as well?

You can use the Margin Scheme for some of your sales and the normal rules for others.

But, if you have sold a vehicle under the normal VAT rules (that is, you have charged VAT on the full selling price), you cannot go back and apply the Margin Scheme to that sale later.

2.6 How does the Margin Scheme affect VAT on my overheads?

You can reclaim the VAT you are charged on any business overheads, repairs, parts or accessories. But you must not add any of these costs to the purchase price of the vehicles you sell under the scheme.

See paragraph 3.2 for more detailed information on how to calculate your purchase price.

2.7 What if I buy vehicles from online auction sites?

If you buy a second-hand vehicle from an online auction site, you are responsible for finding out—

— whether the person selling the vehicle is VAT-registered; and
— whether the vehicle is eligible to be sold under the Margin Scheme.

If the vehicle is eligible, and you want to sell it under the scheme, you must keep all the records described in section 5.

2.8 What if I was charged VAT?

If you have—

— reclaimed; or
— were entitled to reclaim

VAT on a second-hand vehicle, you cannot use the Margin Scheme when you sell it. You must account for VAT on the full selling price under the normal rules.

This includes—

— import VAT charged on vehicles purchased from a third country; and
— acquisition tax chargeable on purchases from dealers in other EC member states.

Commentary—*De Voil Indirect Tax Service* **V3.534**.

3. MAKING YOUR MARGIN SCHEME CALCULATIONS

3.1 How do I calculate my selling price?

Your selling price is everything which you are to receive for the vehicle, whether from the buyer or a third party. It includes—

— incidental expenses directly linked to the sale, for example, where you have had to pay for an MOT to make the vehicle saleable; and
— accessories fitted prior to the sale.

Disbursements do *not* form part of the selling price: these should be accounted for separately outside the Margin Scheme. Section 9 contains information on how you should treat linked insurance products and warranties.

The consideration you receive may not be wholly in money: if that is the case, the normal rules about value in Notice 700 "The VAT Guide" will apply.

3.2 How do I calculate my purchase price?

Your purchase price is everything which you had to pay for the vehicle: it will mirror the rules for the selling price described in paragraph 3.1.

You must not include any cost to you of bringing the vehicle to sale. Your purchase price does not include the cost of any repairs, refurbishment, accessories or your business overheads.

For example, if you purchase new parts and fit them to a car, you must not add the cost of those parts to the purchase price of the car. You must use the original price you paid for the car when you calculate the margin for the purposes of the scheme.

Remember: the Margin Scheme taxes the difference between what you paid for the vehicle and what you sold it for, not the overall profit you have made on it.

3.3 How do I calculate the margin?

Under the margin schemes, you only have to account for VAT when you sell an item for more than you paid for it.

To work out the VAT due on an individual Margin Scheme sale, follow the steps in the example below—

Term	*Description*
(a) Purchase price	£1,500
(b) Selling price	2,000
(c) Gross Margin (b – a)	£500
(d) VAT payable (c x 1/6ths)	£83.33

The VAT fraction allows you to calculate the amount of VAT included in a given sum of money.

A standard rate of VAT of *20 per cent* gives a VAT fraction of 1/6ths. When you have worked out your gross margin, multiply the figure by 1, then divide by 6.

Commentary—*De Voil Indirect Tax Service* **V3.534**.

4 BUYING AND SELLING GOODS UNDER THE MARGIN SCHEME

The rules in this section have the force of law.

4.1 What must I do when I buy a vehicle?

The table below lists the steps you must follow when you buy a vehicle for resale under the Margin Scheme.

Step	*Action*	*Details*
1	Check that the goods are eligible for the scheme.	See section 2 for these rules.
2	Obtain a purchase invoice.	If you are buying from a private individual or an unregistered business, you must make out the invoice yourself and include all of the details in paragraph 5.3.
3	Enter the purchase details of the goods in your stock book under the appropriate headings.	The purchase price must be the one you agreed with the seller. You must not alter this price and you must not add the cost of repair, refurbishment or business overheads to it.
		If you buy a number of vehicles as a single lot but intend to sell them separately, you must allocate a purchase price to each one.

4.2 What must I do when I sell a vehicle?

The table below lists the steps you must follow when you buy a vehicle for resale under the Margin Scheme.

Step	*Action*	*Details*
1	Check first that you have followed all of the rules relating to the purchase of the item.	See paragraph 4.1. If you have not, you cannot use the Margin Scheme.
2	Make out a sales invoice.	The invoice must include all of the details in paragraph 5.3.
4	Enter the sales details in your stock book under the appropriate headings.	
5	Issue the invoice to your customer and keep a copy for your records.	If you include more than one item on the same sales invoice, you must allocate a selling price to each one.

Commentary—*De Voil Indirect Tax Service* **V3.534**.

5 RECORDS AND ACCOUNTS

The detailed rules in this section have the force of law.

5.1 What records must I keep?

Notice 700/21 "Keeping VAT Records" gives guidance on the general records you must keep if you are registered for VAT.

If you use the Margin Scheme, there are some additional record keeping rules which apply to your stock book and invoices – paragraphs 5.2 to 5.3 give details.

These additional rules exist so that our officers can use your records to check the margin you have achieved on each vehicle you have sold. It's important that you keep to these rules so that you can continue using the Margin Scheme. If we can't check the margins you have declared from your records, VAT will be due on the full selling price of the vehicles you've supplied, even if they were otherwise eligible for the scheme. If you are not sure whether your records meet the Margin Scheme rules, please contact our VAT Helpline.

5.2 What are the rules for stock books?

You must keep your stock book up to date and it must include all of the information in the table below. This applies to each vehicle you purchase for resale under the Margin Scheme. You may, if you wish, include further information for your own accounting purposes.

Purchase details	*Sales details*
Stock number in numerical sequence	
Date of purchase	Date of sale
Purchase invoice number	Sales invoice number
Purchase price	Selling price or method of disposal
Name of seller	Name of buyer
Vehicle registration number	
Description of the item (for example, make and model)	
	Margin on sale (sales price minus purchase price)
	VAT due (margin x VAT fraction – $^1/_6$)

You must include your Margin Scheme calculations under the appropriate headings in your stock book. If your purchase price is higher than, or the same as, your selling price, then no VAT will be due. In these circumstances you should show the VAT due as "Nil" in your stock book.

You must not offset any VAT on vehicles which are sold at a loss against VAT on vehicles which you have sold at a profit.

An example of a Margin Scheme stock book is included at section 6.

5.3 What are the rules for Margin Scheme invoices?

The information in the table below must always appear on the invoices you receive, or issue.

Remember: if you are buying from a private individual or an unregistered business, you must make out the purchase invoice yourself.

Purchase invoices	*Sales invoices*
seller's name and address	your name, address and VAT registration number
your name and address	the buyer's name and address
a means of cross-referencing between the sales system and the stock book, for example, the stock book number	a means of cross-referencing between the sales system and the stock book, for example, the stock book number
invoice number (unless you made out the purchase invoice yourself)	invoice number
date of transaction	date of transaction

a description of the vehicle, including its registration number	a description of the vehicle, including its registration number
total price – you must not add any other costs to this price	total price – you must not show VAT separately
if you have bought the vehicle from another VAT-registered business,:	Margin Scheme - second hand goods
Margin Scheme - second hand goods	

Note: If you have received a purchase invoice which shows that VAT has been charged on the vehicle, then the vehicle is not eligible to be sold under the Margin Scheme – regardless of whether you have claimed the VAT.

5.4 Filling in your VAT return

You will need to fill in a VAT return at the end of each tax period. Here are the special rules you must follow for any vehicles which you have bought or sold under the Margin Scheme during the tax period—

— *Box 1.* Include the output tax due on all eligible vehicles sold in the period covered by the return.
— *Box 6.* Include the full selling price of all eligible vehicles sold in the period, less any VAT due on the margin.
— *Box 7.* Include the full purchase price of eligible vehicles bought in the period.

There is no requirement to include Margin Scheme purchases or sales in boxes 8 and 9 of your VAT return.

Further guidance on how to fill in VAT returns is available in Notice 700/12 "Filling in your VAT return".

5.5 How long must I keep records?

Generally, you must keep all your business records for VAT purposes for at least six years. If the six year rule causes you serious storage problems or undue expense, then you should consult our VAT Helpline. We may be able to allow you to keep some records for a shorter period.

But if your current stock includes vehicles which you obtained more than six years ago, you must retain all the evidence which will show their eligibility for Margin Scheme treatment when you eventually sell them.

5.6 Do I need to keep records for goods on sale or return?

If your stock includes goods supplied to you on a sale or return basis (see Notice 700 "The VAT Guide", paragraph 14.4), you must include, in your stock book or in a separate record, the following details for each vehicle—

— the date of transfer of the vehicle;
— description of the vehicle, including its registration number;
— the name and address of the dealer/person transferring the vehicle; and
— the date of sale or return.

Similarly, if any vehicles are removed from your stock on a sale or return basis to another dealer's premises, you should note your stock record with the date and details of the dealer to whom you have transferred the vehicles.

If you sell a vehicle on behalf of a third party, and you issue an invoice for that vehicle in your own name, you are acting as an agent for VAT purposes and you must account for any output tax on the sale. You can find out more about agents and the Margin Scheme in Notice 718 "The VAT Margin Scheme and Global Accounting".

5.7 How do I treat invoices in foreign currencies?

If you are buying and selling an eligible vehicle in a foreign currency (including euro), you must convert the price into sterling in order to calculate your margin.

Term	*Description*
Purchase invoices	If you buy a number of vehicles at an inclusive price and do not intend to sell them as one lot, you must convert the price to sterling and then apportion this amount between the vehicles. You must then enter the sterling amounts in your stock record on a vehicle by vehicle basis.
Sales invoices	If you issue a sales invoice in a foreign currency, the invoice must also show the sterling equivalent of the selling price. If the invoice covers more than one vehicle, it must show the price, both in foreign currency and sterling, for each vehicle. You must then enter the sterling amounts in your stock record on a vehicle by vehicle basis. If, however, you are selling as one lot vehicles which you bought as one lot, you need only show a total foreign currency and sterling value for that lot.

To convert amounts in foreign currencies you must use one of the methods outlined in Notice 700 "The VAT Guide". Whichever method you choose, you must use the exchange rate which was current at the time the transaction took place.

Commentary—*De Voil Indirect Tax Service* **V3.536**.

6 EXAMPLE OF A MARGIN SCHEME STOCK BOOK

6.1 How do I complete my stock book?

EXAMPLE

Purchase details

1 Stock no	2 Date of purchase	3 Purchase invoice no	4 Purchase price	5 Name of seller	6 Vehicle registration no	7 Description of vehicle
100	01/02/08	50	£2,500	Mr J. Smith	R123ABC	Ford Fiesta 1.4L

Sales details

8 Date of sale	9 Sales invoice no	10 Name of buyer
31/03/08	150	Mrs F. Bloggs

Accounting details

11 Selling price	12 Margin (11 – 4)	13 VAT Due
£3,000	£500	£83.33

Commentary—*De Voil Indirect Tax Service* **V3.536**.

7. THE GLOBAL ACCOUNTING SCHEME

7.1 What is the Global Accounting scheme?

Global Accounting is an optional, simplified variation of the normal Margin Scheme. Under Global Accounting, VAT is accounted for on the margin achieved on total eligible sales less total eligible purchases in each VAT period.

Individual items sold under Global Accounting must have a purchase price of £500 or less.

This notice does not deal with the general rules for using Global Accounting. For detailed information on the Global Accounting scheme, including the record keeping requirements, please see Notice 718.

7.2 Can I sell vehicles under Global Accounting?

No. Motor vehicles are excluded from being sold under the Global Accounting scheme.

7.3 What about sales of scrap?

Motor vehicles which would be eligible for sale under the Margin Scheme may be included in the Global Accounting scheme if they are sold on as scrap.

You must keep the normal commercial documentation to show that the vehicle no longer exists and that the parts are therefore eligible for Global Accounting.

If . . .	*then . . .*
the vehicle has already been entered into your second-hand stock book	you should close the entry and transfer the details to your Global Accounting purchase records.
you buy a scrap motor vehicle for more than £500	you can still use the Global Accounting scheme for disposal of the components. However, any individual component valued at over £500 must be excluded from Global Accounting.
you are charged VAT separately when you buy a vehicle	you cannot sell any scrap parts from that vehicle under either Global Accounting or the Margin Scheme.

Commentary—*De Voil Indirect Tax Service* **V3.535**.

8. BUYING AND SELLING VEHICLES AT AUCTION

8.1 Who should read this section?

You should read this section if—

— you sell second-hand vehicles under the Margin Scheme; and
— you buy or sell vehicles through auctions.

8.2 What should I do if I buy eligible vehicles at auction?

If you want to use the Margin Scheme (or Global Accounting, if you are buying vehicles for scrap) for the onward sale of a vehicle you have bought at auction, you must check whether the vehicle you want to buy is eligible for onward sale under the scheme.
You should be able to find this out from the auctioneer's sales catalogue.

If the auctioneer charges VAT separately on the hammer price of a vehicle you buy, you won't be able to use the Margin Scheme or Global Accounting for your onward sale.

8.3 What is the purchase price of eligible vehicles I buy at auction?

Your purchase price will be the hammer price of the vehicle plus charges for services.

The invoice you get from the auctioneer will itemise, for each lot you have bought, the hammer price of the goods and any charges for services (for example, buyer's premium). These charges must not show VAT separately.

This will be your purchase price for the purposes of the Margin Scheme or Global Accounting, and is the amount that you must show in your stock book. It should be clearly identified on the invoice you get from the auctioneer.

If the auctioneer bills you for any other services, and charges VAT on them separately, you can reclaim the VAT under the normal rules. You must not add those charges to your own Margin Scheme purchase price. To avoid confusion, you may want to ask the auctioneer to provide you with a separate invoice for such charges.

If you are in any doubt about what your Margin Scheme purchase price should be for a vehicle you have bought at auction, you should check with the auctioneer.

8.4 What is an indemnity fee?

When you buy a vehicle at auction, you will usually be charged an indemnity fee. This is a charge which ensures that you will have compensation or indemnity if the vehicle you have bought is later found to have been stolen or to have finance outstanding on it.

You must not include the indemnity fee in your purchase price for Margin Scheme purposes.

8.5 What is the selling price of eligible vehicles I sell at auction?

Before the sale is due to take place, you should discuss with the auctioneer whether you want it to be treated under the Auctioneers' Scheme or under the normal Margin Scheme. (The Auctioneers' Scheme is a special variation on the normal Margin Scheme. It works by creating a margin which is equal to the auctioneer's charge for his services to both the vendor and the purchaser.)

If the auctioneer uses	*the invoice will include*	*your Margin Scheme selling price will be*
the Auctioneers' Scheme	—the hammer price of the goods —his commission charges, and —the net amount payable to you. None of these amounts should show VAT separately.	the hammer price less the commission charge.
the Margin Scheme	the hammer price of the goods. VAT must not be shown separately on this amount. The auctioneer's commission and any other charges for services must be invoiced separately.	the hammer price.

Your selling price for Margin Scheme purposes should be easy to identify from the invoice you receive. You should check with the auctioneer if you are in any doubt.

If the Auctioneers' Scheme is used, you will be invoiced separately for any other charges.

If the Margin Scheme is used, you will be invoiced separately for—

— the auctioneer's commission; and
— any other charges.

You can reclaim the VAT on these invoices under the normal rules but you must not deduct the charges from your Margin Scheme selling price.

Commentary—*De Voil Indirect Tax Service* **V3.533, V3.534**.

9. LINKED INSURANCE PRODUCTS AND WARRANTIES

9.1 What are linked insurance products and warranties?

A *linked insurance product* is a contract of insurance between an insurer (usually someone other than yourself) and the purchaser of a vehicle. The contract will provide cover against particular risks.

Linked insurance products include—

— Mechanical Breakdown Insurance (MBI);
— Guaranteed Asset Protection (GAP);
— key, wheel and tyre cover; and
— paint and fabric damage cover.

A *warranty* is an undertaking, or guarantee, which you give to your customer that, if goods should prove to be faulty within a specified time or mileage limit, you will bear the cost of providing the appropriate repairs or replacement parts.

The situations which can commonly arise are described below, together with the appropriate VAT treatment.

If you arrange linked insurance products for your customers, you should read Notice 701/36 "Insurance" in addition to the rest of this section.

In addition, insurance-backed warranties or MBI policies etc., are subject to the Higher Rate of Insurance Premium Tax (IPT). Generally, insurers account for IPT. However, if you make a charge in connection with this type of insurance, you may need to register and account for IPT on those charges. We have included some specific information in this section and you can find further information on the higher rate of IPT in Notice IPT1 "A General Guide to IPT".

9.2 What if I don't make a separate charge?

If you provide your customer with a "free"

— linked insurance product, or
— warranty,

then the selling price of the vehicle for Margin Scheme purposes includes the cost to you of supplying the product.

Any mention of the linked insurance product on your invoice must show that no separate charge is being made.

The price of the vehicle shown on the sales invoice to the customer must be the same as that entered in your stock book.

9.3 What if I make a separate charge for a linked insurance product?

If you arrange linked insurance products for your customer to purchase, you are acting as an agent of the insurance company. The VAT treatment depends on whether any risk covered by the insurance policy is yours or your customer's.

9.3.1 When is the charge exempt?

The supply of the linked insurance product is exempt if it satisfies the following conditions—

— it is supplied under a contract of insurance between an insurer and your customer
— it is your customer's risks which are insured
— your customer is entirely free to purchase the vehicle without the insurance product, and
— you disclose the insurance premium and any other amount (fees or commission) being charged (see Notice 701/36 "Insurance") to the customer.

Under these conditions, there are separate supplies of the vehicle and the insurance, each with its own consideration.

Your selling price for the purposes of calculating the margin on the vehicle must not include the charge for the insurance product.

9.3.2 When is the charge standard-rated?

If the insurance contract is between you and the insurer, and only your risk of having to repair defective items is covered, then the supply is standard-rated.

You must account for—

— VAT on the margin (if there is one) on the vehicle under the Margin Scheme; and
— VAT on the standard-rated "insurance" charge outside the Margin Scheme.

9.3.3 What if the circumstances are more complicated?

The table below gives you the rules you must follow in other situations.

If . . .	*then . . .*
you subsequently negotiate with the customer a reduced price for the vehicle (including the linked insurance product)	the exempt premium payable for the linked insurance product remains unchanged.

negotiations with the customer result in the supply of an upgraded linked insurance product with an increased premium due from the customer	you must itemise the product separately and show the increased exempt premium.
you advertise the vehicle and the linked insurance product at a single price, that is you do not disclose to the customer the amount of the premium	any fee or commission income you receive in relation to this insurance is standard-rated. The net premium paid to and retained by the insurer remains exempt. You must only show the selling price of the vehicle, net of the insurance, in your stock book. See paragraph 9.6, example 2.

In all cases, the value shown on the sales invoice for the vehicle itself must be the same as that entered in your stock book.

You can find further information on the implications of these arrangements for Insurance Premium Tax in Notice IPT1 "A General Guide to IPT".

9.4 What if I make a separate charge for a warranty?

If you provide a warranty, and make a separate charge for it, that charge will be standard-rated.

Your selling price for the purposes of calculating the margin on the vehicle must not include the charge for the warranty.

You must account for—

— VAT on the margin (if there is one) on the vehicle under the Margin Scheme; and
— VAT on the standard-rated charge for the warranty outside the Margin Scheme.

The value shown on the sales invoice for the vehicle must be the same as that entered in your stock book.

9.5 What about supplies made under other schemes?

The supply of a warranty or a linked "insurance" product under any other type of scheme is standard-rated.

For example, a dealer may set up a "fund" into which amounts charged to customers for warranties are paid, and from which repair claims are met. The dealer may obtain insurance cover against any deficiency in the fund. These policies are covered by arrangements commonly known as "stop-loss". In such circumstances, there is no contract of insurance between the insurer and the customer purchasing an item. Only the dealer's risk is insured, so any charge to the customer will be taxable at the standard rate.

9.6 How does this work in practice?

Example 1

In this example, the amount due under the contract of insurance is £200 (the net amount payable to the insurer is £120 and the commission you retain is £80).

If	*then the VAT treatment is*
the gross premium (£200) is disclosed to the customer	£200 exempt, consisting of— —£120 net exempt premium which you, as agent, pass to the insurance provider; and —£80 exempt commission, which you keep.
the gross premium is not disclosed to customer	—£120 net exempt premium which you, as agent, pass to the insurance provider, and —£80 standard-rated commission, which you keep. You must account for the VAT on this outside the Margin Scheme.

In this example, IPT is due on the gross premium of £200.

If	*then*
you disclose the gross premium to the insurance provider	they will account for the IPT.
you choose not to disclose the commission (£80) to the insurance provide	you may be liable to register and account for the higher rate of IPT (17.5%) on this amount in addition to any VAT that may be due.

Example 2

In addition to the £200 in the example above, you charge the customer a fee of £50 for arranging the insurance-backed product.

If	*then the VAT treatment is*
the value of both—	£250 exempt, consisting of—
—the amount due under the contract and	—£120 net exempt premium which you, as agent, pass to the insurance provider; and
—the fee	—£80 exempt commission and.
are disclosed to the customer	—£50 exempt fee, both of which you keep.
either—	—£120 net exempt premium which you, as agent, pass to the insurance provider; and
—only the value of the amount due under the contract of insurance is disclosed, and not the fee, or	—£80 standard rated commission and
—only the fee is disclosed and not the amount due under the contract of insurance	—£50 standard-rated fee, both of which you keep.
	You must account for the VAT on these charges outside the Margin Scheme.

In this example, IPT is due on £250.

If	*then*
—the whole charge is made under the contract of insurance, and	they will account for the IPT.
—you disclose the gross premium to the insurance provider	
—you do not disclose the commission (£80) to the insurance provider, and/or	you must register and account for IPT on these amounts in addition to any VAT that may be due.
—the £50 fee is charged under a separate contract between you and your customer	

If you receive a lot of VAT-exempt income from providing linked insurance products, there is a possibility that your business may be partially exempt. See Notice 706 “Partial Exemption” for more information.

10. OTHER ISSUES WHICH MAY AFFECT YOUR MARGIN SCHEME CALCULATIONS

10.1 Can I claim relief for bad debts?

If you supply goods and do not receive payment within certain time limits, you may claim relief from VAT on the “bad debt”. You will find full details of the time limits and conditions for claiming in Notice 700/18 “Relief from VAT” on bad debts.

Under the Margin Scheme, the amount of VAT on which you claim relief cannot exceed the amount of VAT previously accounted for on the margin. This is best explained by two examples based on the following figures—

Vehicle purchased for: £400
Vehicle sold for: £500

Margin on which VAT is paid to Customs: £100

VAT payable (£100 x $^1/_6$ths): £16.66

Example 1. The customer only pays £350 leaving a debt of £150. The debt is greater than the margin so the potential bad debt relief is £100 (the margin) x $^1/_6$ths = £16.66.

Example 2. The customer pays £450 leaving a debt of only £50. This debt is less than the margin so the potential bad debt relief is £50 (the debt) x $^1/_6$ths = £8.33.

If you receive payment from your customer after making a claim for bad debt relief, you must refund the appropriate amount to HMRC.

10.2 How should I treat MOTs?

If you sell a second-hand car with an MOT, you are making a single supply.

You should not deduct the value of the MOT from your Margin Scheme selling price.

You should record the full selling price, including the MOT, in your stock book, and you should use this figure for calculating the margin on the sale.

10.3 How should I treat road fund licences?

If you . . .	*then . . .*
buy a vehicle for resale under the Margin Scheme and you surrender its unexpired road fund licence for a refund	you must not adjust the purchase price of the vehicle by the amount of that refund.
—sell a vehicle with an unexpired licence; or	you are making a single supply.
—offer a road fund licence as part of an agreed sale price	You must include the value of the licence in the selling price entered in your stock book.
agree to obtain the licence on behalf of the customer, after negotiating the sale of a car	you may treat the licence as a separate supply, provided you can meet the conditions for a disbursement as explained in Notice 700 "The VAT Guide". If you cannot meet those conditions, the car and licence are treated as a single supply and you must calculate your margin on the total, combined value.

10.4 How should I treat vehicles I take in part-exchange?

10.4.1 Selling price

If . . .	*then . . .*
you sell an eligible vehicle and take another in part-exchange	you must not reduce the selling price on which you calculate your margin by the value of the part-exchanged vehicle.

For example, you sell a car for £2,500 which you bought for £1,500.

You take a car in part-exchange which you value at £200. The customer pays the balance of £2,300.

The selling price you insert in your stock book must be £2,500 and you must account for VAT on the full margin of £1,000.

10.4.2 Purchase price

When you take a second-hand commercial vehicle in part-exchange, it is important to check whether your customer is VAT-registered. If your customer is registered for VAT, he must issue you with a sales invoice.

As with all vehicles you plan to sell, you must check whether the vehicle you take in part-exchange is eligible to be sold on under the Margin Scheme (see paragraph 2.4).

If the vehicle is eligible for the Margin Scheme, you must include its details on the purchase side of your stock book. In the example above, your purchase price would be £200. You must not alter this purchase price.

If you over-allow on the value of the vehicle you have taken in part-exchange, your purchase price for the purposes of the Margin Scheme must be the one you agreed with your customer and which appears on the sales invoice.

For example, you sell a car for £3,500 which you bought for £2,000.

You take a car in part-exchange for which you allow £800, so the customer pays the balance of £2,700. However, the book value of the part-exchange is only £600.

The purchase price in your Margin Scheme stock book must be £800.

10.4.3 Points to watch

If you buy from a private person, or from a business which is not registered for VAT, you may include the details of the part-exchange vehicle on your sales invoice provided all the requirements of paragraph 5.3 are met.

If you take a low value car in part-exchange, and sell it for parts (either useable parts, or parts as scrap metal), you cannot account for those sales under the Margin Scheme.

If you sell it for useable parts, you must account for VAT on the full selling price of each item sold.

See section 7 for the rules to follow when you sell an entire vehicle to be broken into scrap or break a vehicle into parts.

10.5 How should I treat hire-purchase sales?

10.5.1 Who is my customer?

If . . .	*then . . .*
you sell an eligible vehicle and arrange hire-purchase (HP) terms with a finance company on behalf of your customer	you are deemed to be selling the vehicle to the finance company.

10.5.2 What sales records do I need to keep?

You must transfer the sales price of the item from the HP documentation to your stock book.

If	*Then you must*
—you have issued your own sales invoice to your customer; and —you have a copy of the HP agreement	either —attach a copy of the completed HP agreement to the sales invoice; or —include a cross-reference to the HP agreement in your sales records.
the finance company holds the HP agreement and you don't get a copy of it for your records	keep a copy of —the agreed quotation; or —the agreed proposal documents together with: together with: —the name of the finance company; —the date; and —the reference number of the final agreement

in your sales records.

You may use a copy of the HP agreement as your sales invoice provided it shows:

— all the identifying details of the item; and
— the cash price of the item as the gross price payable.

(The gross price is the amount borrowed plus any cash deposit paid, plus any amount allowed for a part-exchange item.)

Remember, VAT must not be shown separately on either—

— the HP agreement; or
— the customer's sales invoice.

10.5.3 What is my selling price for a hire-purchase vehicle?

The values shown on any documentation raised to the finance company must always be the same as the values declared to HMRC in your books and records. This includes the value of any part-exchange vehicle or cash deposit paid by the customer.

10.6 What if I rebuild a vehicle?

If	*Then you must*
—you build a vehicle from one or more used vehicles which you acquired under eligible circumstances; and	you can sell it under the Margin Scheme.
—the Driver and Vehicle Licensing Agency (DVLA) does not require it to be re-registered	The purchase price you enter in your stock book is the price you paid for the vehicle for which the registration number is carried forward.
—you construct a vehicle from the used components and parts of other vehicles; and	you cannot use the Margin Scheme.
the DVLA gives it a new registration number	You must account for VAT on the full selling price.

10.7 What if I buy an eligible vehicle from an insurance company or finance house?

If you buy an eligible vehicle from	*you will not be charged VAT provided*
—an insurance company which has acquired it as a result of an insurance claim; or	the vehicle is sold on to you in exactly the same state; and
—a finance house which has repossessed it	it was obtained by the insurance company/finance house from a person who would not have charged VAT on its supply, for example, a private individual.

You can resell such vehicles using the Margin Scheme provided you meet the conditions in paragraph 2.2.

10.8 What if I sell a vehicle which has been adapted for a disabled person?

Notice 701/59 "Motor Vehicles for disabled people" explains when a vehicle which has been adapted for use by a disabled person will be zero-rated.

There would be no benefit to you in selling a zero-rated vehicle under the Margin Scheme. You can sell the vehicle outside the Margin Scheme by closing its entry in your Margin Scheme stock book. You should refer in your stock book to the reason why you have closed the entry. You can then raise an invoice for the vehicle in the usual way, as you would do for any sale you make outside the Margin Scheme.

10.9 What if I sell high value vehicles for cash?

Accepting cash payments for the second-hand vehicles you sell won't affect your Margin Scheme calculations. However, if you sell a vehicle for the equivalent of 15,000 euro or more, and take payment for it in cash, you will need to register with HMRC as a High Value Dealer. See Notice MLR6 Registration guide for High Value Dealers for more information.

10.10 How do I deal with gifts?

You cannot use the Margin Scheme when you sell a vehicle which was given to you. You must account for VAT on the full selling price.

If you give away a vehicle which would have been eligible for sale under the Margin Scheme, no VAT is due. But you must include full details of the person you gave the car to in your stock book.

10.11 What if I sell a vehicle privately?

The private sale of goods which are not assets of your business is usually outside the scope of VAT and no VAT is due.

However, if

— you are a sole proprietor; and
— you sell an eligible vehicle (see paragraph 2.3) which you transfer to your business from your private holdings

you can use the Margin Scheme for the sale of that item.

You must be able to produce evidence of what the purchase price was when you bought it for your private use. If you cannot do this, you must account for VAT on the full sales value.

10.12 What if I only make occasional sales of eligible vehicles?

If	*Then*
you are not in business to buy and sell second-hand vehicles; but	you need not comply with the full record keeping requirements in section 5, provided you:
—you very occasionally find yourself with an eligible one to sell; and	—meet the other conditions of the scheme; and
—you would like to use the Margin Scheme for the sale	—hold evidence of both the purchase and selling price.

10.13 What is the Personal Export Scheme?

The Personal Export Scheme allows entitled customers to buy a new or used motor vehicle in the UK free of VAT for export outside the European Community. If you want to sell vehicles under the scheme, you will need to read Notice 705A "VAT: Supplies of vehicles under the Personal Export Scheme for removal from the European Community".

Commentary—*De Voil Indirect Tax Service* **V3.534**.

11. TRANSFERS OF GOING CONCERNS AND ASSIGNMENTS OF RIGHTS

11.1 What if I take over a business as a going concern (TOGC)?

If you obtain vehicles under a transfer of a going concern (TOGC), no VAT will be chargeable on the transfer. However, this does not necessarily mean that you will be able to sell the vehicles on under the Margin Scheme.

You will only be able to use the scheme if the last person to obtain the vehicles – other than by way of a TOGC or an assignment of rights – would have been entitled to use the Margin Scheme to sell them.

Where there has been—

— a succession of TOGCs or assignments; or

— a mixture of both

it is the first person in that chain who must have been entitled to use the Margin Scheme himself.

11.2 What about the records?

From 1 September 2007, the seller of a TOGC retains the records. However—

— the seller must make available to the buyer any information the buyer needs to comply with his duties under VATA 1994; and
— where the buyer applies to HMRC for permission to take on the seller's VAT number, the seller is still required to transfer the records to the buyer. If the seller needs to retain the records, he may apply to HMRC for permission to do so.

The records will include the purchase invoices for stock on hand. You will be able to tell from these invoices whether or not the vehicles are eligible to be sold the scheme.

If	*then*
the transferor of the vehicles bought them on Margin Scheme invoices	you will be able to sell them under the scheme.
the transferor bought them on invoices showing VAT	they are not eligible for the scheme and you will have to account for VAT on the full selling price when you sell them.

So it is in your own interest when you buy a business as a TOGC to—

— check the position with the seller; and
— make sure that you have the records you need if the vehicles are eligible to be sold under the Margin Scheme.

11.3 What are the rules for banks and finance houses?

If you are	*then*
—a bank; or —a financial institution; and you have acquired eligible vehicles as a result of having been assigned the rights to them in hire purchase or conditional sale agreements	you can only use the Margin Scheme to sell those vehicles if the last person to obtain them – other than by way of an assignment of rights or a TOGC – would have been entitled to use the Margin Scheme.

Where there has been—

— a succession of assignments or TOGCs; or
— a mixture of both

it is therefore the first person in that chain who must have been entitled to use the Margin Scheme.

11.4 What will my Margin Scheme purchase price be?

Your purchase price will be the price paid when the eligible vehicle was bought by the person in the chain who was entitled to use the Margin Scheme to sell it himself.

You will be able to identify the original purchase price from the purchase invoices which will form part of the business records.

When you buy a business as a TOGC, you must ensure that you have the necessary records to enable you to calculate a margin. You will always need the purchase invoices. You may enter the vehicles obtained under a TOGC into your own stock record if the original stock record is retained by the transferor of the business.

If—

— you have obtained goods under a TOGC from a bank or financial institution; and

— that body had obtained those goods when they were assigned the rights in a hire purchase or conditional sale agreement

the records which are usually kept in relation to these transactions should provide the necessary information.

Commentary—*De Voil Indirect Tax Service* **V3.534**.

NOTICE 718/2
VAT AUCTIONEERS' SCHEME

March 2011

This notice replaces the December 2009 version. It has been updated to reflect the change in the standard rate of VAT to 20% from January 2011. Section 4 has also been updated to reflect the fact that declarations on Auctioneers' Scheme invoices are no longer required to contain references to the relevant EU or UK legislation.

1 INTRODUCTION

1.1 What is this notice about?

This notice is about the Auctioneers' Scheme, which is a variation on the VAT Margin Scheme for second-hand goods, antiques, works of art and collectors' items. It tells you when you may use the Auctioneers' Scheme to account for VAT on the supplies you make.

It explains—

— which goods you can include under the scheme;
— how the scheme works;
— how you must calculate the margin; and
— what records you must keep.

This notice assumes that you have a working knowledge of basic VAT principles, as outlined in Notice 700 "The VAT Guide".

If, after reading this notice, you need any further help or advice, contact our VAT Helpline on 0845 010 9000.

1.2 What's changed

The information in this notice used to be contained in Notice 718 "Margin schemes for second-hand goods, works of art, antiques and collectors' items". We have moved the information which is relevant to auctioneers who opt to use the Auctioneers' Scheme into this separate, shorter notice so that you can find what you need more easily.

The rules about declarations on Auctioneers' Scheme invoices have changed: see section 4 for details.

We have updated the Notice to reflect the VAT rate of 20%.

1.3 Who should read this notice

You should read this notice if you are an auctioneer and you want to know about the Auctioneers' Scheme.

1.4 Force of law

In UK law, VATA 1994 s 50A allows the Treasury to make Orders to introduce second-hand schemes.

The VAT (Cars) Order 1992 covers cars.

The VAT (Special Provisions) Order 1995 (as amended) covers all goods other than cars.

Parts of this notice have the force of law under the orders. Paragraphs which have the force of law are indicated by a statement and by having been placed in a box.

Commentary—*De Voil Indirect Tax Service* **V3.531–V3.538.**

2 BASIC PRINCIPLES

2.1 I am an auctioneer: how do I account for VAT?

If you—

— invoice in your own name; and
— sell goods which would be eligible for sale under the Margin Scheme

there are several options you can choose from to account for VAT on your sales.

You may—

— use the Auctioneers' Scheme;
— use the Margin Scheme;
— apply the rules for invoicing as an agent.

You do not have to apply the same option to all your sales. This notice is about the Auctioneers' Scheme. Please see Notice 718 "The VAT Margin Scheme and Global Accounting" for more about using the standard margin scheme, and for more general information about margin schemes.

2.2 What is the Auctioneers' Scheme?

The Auctioneers' Scheme is a variation on the standard margin scheme for second-hand goods, works of art, antiques and collectors' items. It allows you to account for VAT on a margin which is equal to the value of the services you have supplied to the seller and the buyer.

Using a margin scheme means that you don't have to account for VAT on the hammer price of the goods.

2.3 How does the scheme work?

When you calculate the margin under the scheme, you—

— add the value of your services to the buyer to the hammer price; and
— subtract the value of your services to the seller from the hammer price.

Section 3 provides full guidance on how to calculate the VAT due under the scheme.

2.4 What are the conditions for using the scheme?

You don't have to use any of the margin schemes: they're optional.

If you do decide to use one, there are a number of conditions you will have to meet. If you can't meet all the conditions, you can't use the scheme.

The detailed conditions for using the Auctioneers' Scheme are explained throughout this notice. The main ones are:

— *the goods must be eligible* (see paragraph 2.6)
— *you must have acquired the goods in eligible circumstances.* In most cases, this means that you obtained the goods for resale in circumstances where you could not claim any VAT back (see paragraph 2.5)
— *you must calculate the margin in accordance with the rules of the scheme.* There are special rules about how to calculate your buying price, your selling price and your margin under the scheme. The margin you calculate under the scheme may not be the same as your profit margin (see section 3)
— *you must meet the record keeping rules of the scheme.* There are special rules about invoicing and stock records (see section 4).

2.5 When can I use the scheme?

You can use the scheme if—

— the goods are eligible

and the seller is *one* of the following—

— not registered for VAT;
— a VAT-registered person supplying goods under the standard margin scheme or Global Accounting;
— an insurance company selling eligible margin scheme goods which it has acquired as the result of an insurance claim (provided the goods are sold at auction in the same state); or
— a finance house selling eligible margin scheme goods which it has repossessed (provided the goods are sold at auction in the same state).

2.6 Which goods are eligible to be sold under the scheme?

This is a quick guide to the goods which are eligible to be sold under the margin schemes. If you are in any doubt, you should refer to section 20 at the end of Notice 718 "The VAT Margin Scheme and Global Accounting", where we have reproduced the law on eligible goods.

Second-hand goods

The legal definition of second-hand goods is goods which are suitable for further use as they are, or after repair. In most cases, goods which are second-hand in the ordinary usage of the term will be eligible for the margin schemes.

For the special rules about the legal definition of a second-hand motor vehicle, see Notice 718/1 "The VAT Margin Scheme on second-hand cars and other vehicles".

Works of art

The legal definition of works of art includes pictures, paintings, collages and drawings executed by hand by the artist. Craft items and items produced in a technical or industrial context may not be eligible to be sold under the margin schemes. If you are in any doubt, check the list at the end of Notice 718.

Antiques and collectors' items

The legal definition of an antique is an item, other than a work of art or a collectors' item, which is over 100 years old.

Not everything which somebody might collect will be included in the legal definition of a collectors' item for margin scheme purposes. If you are in any doubt, check the list at the end of Notice 718.

2.7 Are there any categories of goods I can't sell under the scheme?

Yes. You must not use the scheme to account for sales of—

— precious metals;
— investment gold; or
— precious stones.

There is more information about these categories of goods at the end of Notice 718.

You can only use the scheme to account for sales of air guns if you are registered under the Firearms Act 1968.

2.8 What if I make sales under the normal VAT rules as well?

You can use a margin scheme for some of your sales and the normal rules for others.

But, if you have sold an item under the normal VAT rules (that is, you charged VAT on the full selling price), you can't go back and apply any of the margin schemes to that sale later.

2.9 What if I can't meet all the conditions?

If you sell an eligible item, but cannot meet all the record keeping, invoicing and accounting requirements, you cannot use either the Auctioneers' Scheme or the standard margin scheme.

You will have to pay VAT on the hammer price as well as on your services to the vendor and the purchaser under the normal VAT rules for undisclosed agents. You can find further information about those rules in Notice 700 "The VAT Guide".

It is important to check with the seller whether the goods are eligible for inclusion in the Auctioneers' Scheme before you auction them.

Commentary—*De Voil Indirect Tax Service* **V3.533.**

3. MAKING YOUR AUCTIONEERS' SCHEME CALCULATIONS

3.1 How do I calculate VAT on goods I sell under the Auctioneers' Scheme?

As explained in paragraph 2.2, you calculate your margin by taking into account charges for the services you make to the seller and the buyer.

When you are calculating the amount of VAT due on an individual sale, you must work from the hammer price, as follows—

Scenario	*Solution*
Your purchase price is	the hammer price *less* any commission charges you make to the seller. You must not include any other services which you supply to the seller.
Your selling price is	the hammer price *plus* any charges for services you make to the buyer. (For example, buyer's premium or other commission; incidental expenses such as packing, transport and insurance costs.)
To calculate your margin	you subtract the purchase price from the selling price.
To calculate the VAT on the sale	you multiply the margin by $^1/_6$ (the VAT fraction).

Paragraph 3.2 explains which charges can be included in your scheme calculations.

There are detailed examples of calculations at section 8.

3.2 Which charges must I include in my Auctioneers' Scheme calculations?

When you calculate your buying and selling prices under the Auctioneers' Scheme, you must always include—

— seller's commission;
— buyer's premium; and
— any other charges you make to the buyer for incidental expenses such as packing, transport and insurance costs.

You must *not* include—

— services which are a separate supply in their own right, for example, providing illustrations in the auction catalogue; or
— indemnity fees, if an approved insurance company is providing the insurance policy.

For more information about insurance provided by a third party, see Notice 718.

You must make sure that—

— the charges included in your scheme calculations do not show VAT separately; and
— your invoices clearly show (for the benefit of both seller and buyer) the respective selling and purchase prices they will need for their own scheme calculations.

If you have made any charges which are not included in your scheme calculations, you must—

— invoice for them separately; and
— charge VAT on them under the normal rules.

3.3 How do I work out the time of supply?

If you are acting in your own name, the goods you sell are deemed, for VAT purposes, to be both a supply *to* you and a supply *from* you.

Because these two supplies happen at the same time, they share a common tax point. This is determined by reference to the actual sale of the goods at auction. The tax point for both supplies will be the earlier of—

— you handing the goods over to the buyer; or
— you receiving payment.

3.4 What if I sell zero-rated goods?

Under the Auctioneers' Scheme, a margin is created from the supply of services made to the seller and the buyer. These services are not separately charged with VAT.

If you sell zero-rated goods, for example antique books, your margin will also be zero-rated.

In the VAT due column of your stock record, you should insert "nil".

3.5 How do I treat sales to other EC member states?

Sales made under the Auctioneers' Scheme to other Member States are treated in the same way as sales within the UK. The sales are liable to VAT in the UK.

The goods will not be subject to acquisition VAT when they are taken into another EC Member State, so you should not include them on—

— EC sales lists; or
— boxes 8 and 9 of your VAT returns.

See Notice 718 for more detailed information for businesses which use margin schemes about buying and selling within the EC.

3.6 How do I treat goods supplied for export?

If you	*then*
—are acting in your own name;	you will be making a combined supply of goods and services, with VAT due on the profit margin.
—can meet the conditions for zero-rating in Notice 703 "Exports and removals of goods from the UK", and; —sell the exported goods under the Auctioneers' Scheme	The liability of your services will follow that of the goods, with the result that the whole supply will be zero-rated. However, you must obtain proof of export, as described in Notice 703, when you apply zero-rating to the margin.
sell the exported goods under the Margin Scheme	the liability of your services will *not* follow that of the goods because your services are charged and invoiced outside the scheme. You will be able to sell the goods at the zero-rate outside the scheme if you can meet the conditions in Notice 703, but your services will normally be standard-rated.

3.7 What about the Retail Export Scheme?

The retail export scheme allows certain overseas visitors to get a VAT refund on goods they buy and export in their personal luggage. You can use the retail export scheme together with the Auctioneers' Scheme but, if you do, you must account for VAT on the sale until—

— you receive a refund document stamped by UK or EC Customs; and
— you have made the refund to your customer.

You can find more information about the retail export scheme in Notice 704 "VAT retail exports".

Commentary—*De Voil Indirect Tax Service* **V3.533**.

4 THE AUCTIONEERS' SCHEME – RECORDS AND ACCOUNTS

4.1 What records must I keep?

Notice 700/21 "Keeping VAT Records" gives guidance on the general records you must keep if you are registered for VAT.

If you use the Auctioneers' Scheme, there are some additional record keeping rules which apply to your stock record and invoices – paragraphs 4.2 to 4.8 give details.

These additional rules exist so that there will be a clear audit trail of the margin you have achieved on each item you have sold. It's important that you keep to these rules so that you can continue using the Auctioneers' Scheme. If we can't check the margins you have declared from your records, VAT will be due on the full selling price of the goods you've supplied, even if they were otherwise eligible for the scheme.

4.2 What sort of stock record must I keep?

The boxed text below has the force of law.

The following requirements has the force of law

Although you must always keep stock records, you don't have to maintain a stock book which is strictly in accordance with the requirements set out in Notice 718.

However, if you don't maintain a stock book, you *must* retain sufficient alternative records which provide the information required in Notice 718.

Examples may include—

— entry forms;
— sales catalogues;
— copies of lots and sales of the day, and copies of sales and purchase invoices.

4.3 What are the rules about invoices for the Auctioneers' Scheme?

The following requirements has the force of law

When you sell an item under the scheme, you must issue an invoice to both the buyer and the seller.

You must—

— issue the *seller* with an invoice or statement which includes all the details in the table below; and
— issue the *buyer* with an invoice or other document which includes all the details in the table below.

Purchase Invoice/statement	*Sales invoice*
seller's name and address	your name, address and VAT registration number
your name and address	the buyer's name and address
a means of cross-referencing between the sales system and the stock book, for example, the stock book number	a means of cross-referencing between the sales system and the stock book, for example, the stock book number
invoice number	invoice number
date of transaction	date of transaction
a description of the item	a description of the item
the hammer price of the goods	the hammer price of the goods
any commission charges you made to the seller.	any charges for services made in connection with the sale of the goods (see paragraph 3.2).
You must not show a separate amount of VAT on these charges	You must not show a separate amount of VAT on these charges
the net amount due to the seller.	the amount due from the buyer.
This amount will form—	This amount will form—

Purchase Invoice/statement	*Sales invoice*
—your purchase price; and	—your selling price; and
—the selling price for a vendor who is VAT-registered and is using the Margin Scheme.	—the purchase price for a seller who is VAT-registered and is using the Margin Scheme.

If either the seller or the buyer is using a margin scheme, their respective selling and purchase prices *must* be clear from the invoices you issue. This means that you should allocate any charges included under the scheme against each separate lot.

In other words, if you are selling several items on behalf of one seller, you must not put the total commission charged to that seller on the invoice for one of the items.

Note: If the purchase invoice shows a separate VAT amount, the item is not eligible to be sold under the scheme.

4.4 May I include scheme and non-scheme supplies on one invoice?

To avoid causing the buyer confusion, we recommend that you issue separate invoices if you sell goods to the same buyer under both the Auctioneers' Scheme and normal accounting. However, you may, if you wish, include all those goods on the same invoice.

If you choose to do this, you *must* ensure that each supply can be clearly distinguished. The buyer must be able to establish the sales price for those items which were sold under the Auctioneers' Scheme. This amount will form the purchase price for a VAT-registered dealer who will be selling the item on using a margin scheme.

4.5 Can I re-invoice for goods under the normal rules?

If	*Then*
—you have sold goods under the Auctioneers' Scheme, and —the buyer subsequently decides that they wish to treat the transaction outside the scheme, preferring to pay VAT separately on the hammer price and other charges	you may re-invoice for the transaction under the normal VAT rules, provided that —you are able to comply with all the relevant VAT regulations for the substitute transaction, and —at the time of the amendment, both you and the buyer hold all the original records relating to the transaction
—you can meet these conditions, and —you are willing to re-invoice	you must cancel the first entry in your records and cross-refer to the amended transaction.

The replacement invoice which you issue to the buyer must—

— refer clearly to the original transaction; and
— state that it is cancelled and that the buyer should amend their VAT account accordingly.

There is a limit to how long after the due date of the VAT return on which you accounted for the original supply you may issue a replacement invoice. This is because the capping rules prevent input tax being claimed on invoices over a particular age. For up-to-date information about the capping time limits, see Notice 700/45 "How to correct VAT errors and make adjustments or claims".

4.6 How do I treat Auctioneers' Scheme invoices in foreign currencies?

If	*then*
currency – including the euro – under the Auctioneers' Scheme	you must show the sterling equivalent for *each element* of the supply – for example, the hammer price of the goods; the amount of commission; other charges due – and *not* just for the total value of the sale.

To convert amounts into foreign currencies you must use one of the methods outlined in Notice 700 The VAT Guide. Whichever method you adopt, you must use the exchange rate which is current at the time you make the supply.

4.7 Filling in your VAT return

At the end of each tax period you will need to fill in a VAT return. Here are the special rules you must follow for any goods which you have bought or sold under a margin scheme during the tax period—

— *Box 1* Include the output tax due on all eligible goods sold in the period covered by the return.
— *Box 6* Include the full selling price of all eligible goods sold in the period, less any VAT due on the margin.
— *Box 7* Include the full purchase price of eligible goods bought in the period.

There is no requirement to include margin scheme purchases or sales in boxes 8 and 9 of your VAT return.

Further guidance on how to fill in VAT returns is available in Notice 700/12 "Filling in your VAT return".

4.8 How long must I keep records?

Generally, you must keep all your business records for VAT purposes for at least six years. If the six year rule causes you serious storage problems or undue expense, then you should consult our VAT Helpline. We may be able to allow you to keep some records for a shorter period.

Commentary—*De Voil Indirect Tax Service* **V3.536**.

5. THE AUCTIONEERS' SCHEME IN PARTICULAR CIRCUMSTANCES

5.1 Can I use the scheme to sell goods on behalf of a pawnbroker?

If	*then*
—the goods are eligible; —the value of the pawn is greater than £75; —the pawn has not been redeemed; and —the pledgor is not VAT-registered	you may use the Auctioneers' Scheme to sell the goods on behalf of the pawnbroker.

5.2 What if I sell a horse or pony and use the three-part form?

The three-part form is a document which can be used to account for VAT on the sale of horses and ponies under the standard margin scheme. The three-part forms come in numbered sets, with a VAT summary sheet at the back. They are sold by the British Equestrian Trade Association (BETA).

When you sell a horse or pony on behalf of a person who is selling it under the standard margin scheme and is using the three-part form, they will give you Parts B (pink) and C (yellow) of the partially-completed form.

After the sale you should—

— complete the reverse of Parts B and C;
— give Part C to the buyer;
— return Part B to the seller.

When you sell a horse or pony on behalf of a person who is not registered for VAT to a person who is registered, you should complete your name, address and Lot number on the reverse of Part A (white) of the buyer's form.

For more information about the special three-part form for the sale of horses and ponies under the standard margin scheme, see Notice 718.

5.3 Can I use the Auctioneers' Scheme for the sale of new goods on behalf of nontaxable persons?

An Extra Statutory Class Concession (ESCC), introduced with effect from 1 January 1999, allows the Auctioneers' Scheme to be used for the sale of all goods grown, made or produced (including bloodstock or livestock reared from birth) by non-taxable persons.

As a condition of using the concession, you must obtain—

— a signed certificate from the vendor giving the vendor's name and address;
— a description of the goods; and
— confirmation that he/she is not registered for VAT nor required to be registered for VAT.

You may incorporate the certificate into your existing sales entry in agreement with our Helpline. See section 6 for an example of the certificate.

Commentary—*De Voil Indirect Tax Service* **V3.533**.

6. EXAMPLE OF VENDOR'S CERTIFICATE FOR GOODS SOLD UNDER THE AUCTIONEERS' SCHEME ON BEHALF OF NON-TAXABLE PERSONS

Referred to in paragraph 5.3.

AUCTIONEERS' SCHEME FOR SECOND-HAND GOODS, WORKS OF ART, ANTIQUES AND COLLECTORS' ITEMS

Extra statutory concession number 3.27

Vendor's Certificate for goods grown, made or produced and sold at auction on behalf of non-taxable persons

I (full name) . . . .

of (address) . . . .

declare that I am not registered or required to be registered for Value Added Tax and that the goods detailed below are to be sold at auction on my behalf by (auctioneer's name).

Description of Goods . . . .

Date of Sale (to be completed by auctioneer) . . . .

Signature of vendor . . . .

Signature of Auctioneer . . . .

Date . . . .

---

7. THE AUCTIONEERS' SCHEME OPTION FOR GOODS ON WHICH VAT HAS BEEN CHARGED

7.1 When can I use this option?

When you obtain goods which have had VAT charged on their full value, they are not normally eligible for the Auctioneers' Scheme.

However,

If	*then*
—you are an auctioneer; and —you act in your own name;	you may opt to use the Auctioneers' Scheme for —works of art, antiques and collectors' items which you have imported yourself (as principal on behalf of a third party) for onward sale in your own name; and —works of art you have obtained (that is, which were supplied in the UK or acquired from another Member State) from creators or their heirs, for onward sale in your own name, whether or not VAT was charged on their purchase or acquisition.
—you don't opt to use the Auctioneers' Scheme or the Margin Scheme (see Notice 718); or —you can't meet the conditions described in paragraph 7.2	you must account for VAT in accordance with the general rules for auctioneers.

You can find details of import procedures and special arrangements for supplies of temporarily admitted (TA) goods in Notice 702 "Imports".

7.2 What are the conditions for using this option?

If you want to take up the Auctioneers' Scheme option in any of these circumstances, you must meet the following conditions—

— you must inform our *VAT Written Enquiries Team*, 4th Floor West, Alexander House, 21 Victoria Street, Southend-on- Sea, Essex, SS99 1BD, in writing that you are going to take up the option, and you must specify the date from which you will be applying it;

— you must exercise the option for a period of at least two years, after which you must inform the *VAT Written Enquiries Team* (please see address above) in writing as and when you wish to stop using the scheme;

— you must use the scheme in respect of all transactions and goods listed in paragraphs 7.1, not just in respect of certain categories of transactions or certain categories of goods, and;

— if, having exercised the option, you decide to sell any goods covered by the option outside the scheme (for example, if you export the goods), you are not entitled to recover any input tax on those goods until the period in which you account for VAT on their sale.

7.3 What are the rules about goods held under Temporary Admission (TA)?

Works of art, antiques, and collectors' items imported into the UK from places outside the EC Member States qualify for a reduced rate of import VAT (currently 5 per cent).

Such goods are often entered for relief under Temporary Admission (previously known as Temporary Importation) in order to be sold at auction. See Notice 200 "Temporary importation".

Once the auction has taken place, the goods are—

— re-exported from the EU;

— declared to another Customs procedure, for example Customs Warehousing (see Notice 232) or Inward Processing Relief (see Notice 221); or

— finally imported.

If imported, the goods qualify for the reduced rate of VAT but the buyer's premium does not. You may use the Auctioneers' Scheme to account for sales of such items by auction, but you must charge VAT on the buyer's premium at the appropriate rate.

If the goods are	*then*
—finally *imported*; or —declared for entry to Customs Warehousing or Inward Processing Relief after the auction	you must charge VAT on the buyer's premium at the standard rate.
—directly *re-exported* from TA following the auction	you may charge VAT on the buyer's premium at the zero rate.

Paragraph 7.5 explains the procedures for dealing with the purchase and sale of new means of transport.

7.4 What is my purchase price when I use this option?

7.4.1 Imported works of art, antiques and collectors' items

When you opt to use the Auctioneers' Scheme for imported works of art, antiques or collectors' items on behalf of an overseas seller, the option will apply to imports at a reduced rate of 5 per cent.

You must not—

— reclaim the import VAT as input tax; or

— include it in your Auctioneers' Scheme calculations.

(You may, however, wish to recoup the amount from the seller outside the scheme.)

You must calculate your purchase price in accordance with the rules in paragraph 3.1

7.4.2 Works of art obtained from the creator or their heirs

When you opt to use the Auctioneers' Scheme for works of art obtained from the creator or his heirs you must not reclaim any VAT charged by the supplier.

If the work of art is an acquisition you should—

— account for acquisition tax in box 2 of your VAT return; and
— not recover the corresponding acquisition tax in box 4 (Input Tax).

You must calculate your purchase price in accordance with the rules in paragraph 3.1.

The creator, or their heir, will have to account for output tax on the full hammer price, so they may ask you to sell the item under the option for the standard margin scheme (see Notice 718), rather than the Auctioneers' Scheme.

If you account for the sale under the standard margin scheme, you must show VAT separately on any invoice/statement you issue for charges for your services. This is so that the seller will be able to reclaim the input tax on those charges.

Your purchase price under the standard margin scheme option will be the hammer price *only*.

See section 8 for example calculations for the Auctioneers' Scheme.

Commentary—*De Voil Indirect Tax Service* **V3.533**.

8. EXAMPLE CALCULATIONS FOR THE AUCTIONEERS' SCHEME

8.1 What is this section for?

We have included this section to help you understand the effect that different scenarios will have on the total VAT you would owe us for the same transaction.

In all of the examples—

— the hammer price is £1,000;
— the rate of VAT is 20 per cent and the VAT fraction is $^{1}/_{6}$ths;
— the commission is a VAT-inclusive rate of 12 per cent, that is, 10 per cent plus VAT; and
— buyer's premium is a VAT-inclusive rate of 18 per cent, that is, 15 per cent plus VAT.

8.2 Example 1

You sell the item under the Auctioneers' Scheme.

You charge commission to the seller.

You don't charge buyer's premium or any other charges to the buyer.

Section	*Description*	*Value*
(a)	*Hammer price*	£1,000
(b)	*Commission* charged to seller:	
	Commission rate times hammer price 12 % × 1,000	£120
(c)	*Purchase price*	
	Hammer price less commission (a – b) 1,000 – 120	£880
(d)	*Selling Price* =	
	Hammer price (a)	£1,000
(e)	*Margin*	
	Selling Price less purchase price (d – c) 1,000.00 – 880	£120
(f)	*VAT on sale*	
	Margin (e) times VAT fraction 120 × $^{1}/_{6}$ths	£20

8.3 Example 2

You sell the item under the Auctioneers' Scheme.

You charge commission to the seller.

You charge buyer's premium.

Section	Description	Value
(a)	*Hammer price*	£1,000
(b)	*Commission* charged to seller:	
	Commission rate times hammer price 12% × 1,000	£120
(c)	*Purchase price*	
	Hammer price less commission (a – b) 1,000 – 120	£880
(d)	*Buyer's premium*	
	Rate of buyer's premium times hammer price 18% × 1,000	£180
(e)	*Selling Price*	
	Hammer price plus buyer's premium (a + d) 1,000 + 180	£1,180
(f)	*Margin*	
	Selling Price less purchase price (e – c) 1,180 – 880	£300
(g)	*VAT on sale*	
	Margin (f) times VAT fraction 300 × 1/6ths	£50

8.4 Example 3

You sell the item under the Auctioneers' Scheme.

The item you are selling is for export outside the European Community.

You charge commission to the seller.

You charge buyer's premium.

Note: You must obtain proof of export before you can apply zero-rating to the sale. See Notice 703 "Exports and removals of goods from the United Kingdom" for more information.

Section	Description	Value
(a)	*Hammer price*	£1,000
(b)	*Commission* charged to seller:	
	Commission rate times hammer price 12% × 1,000	£120
(c)	*Buyer's premium*	
	Rate of buyer's premium times hammer price 18% × 1,000	£180
(d)	*Purchase price*	
	Hammer price less commission (a – b) 1,000 – 120	£880
(e)	*Selling Price*	
	Hammer price plus buyer's premium (a + c) 1,000 + 180	£1,180
(f)	*Margin*	
	Selling Price less purchase price (e – d) 1,180 – 880	£300
(g)	*VAT on sale*	
	Zero-rated	Nil

8.5 Example 4

You sell the item under the Margin Scheme.

You charge commission to the seller.

You charge buyer's premium.

Section	Description	Value
(a)	*Hammer price*	£1,000
(b)	*Buyer's premium*	

	Rate of buyer's premium times hammer price 20% × 1,000	£180
(c)	*Purchase price* (a)	£1,000
(d)	*Selling Price*	
	Hammer price plus buyer's premium (a + b)	£1,180
(e)	*Margin*	
	Selling Price less purchase price (d – c)	£180
(f)	*VAT on sale*	
	Margin (e) times VAT fraction 118 × $^1/_6$ths	£30

If you sell the item under the Margin Scheme, you must charge commission to the seller on a separate invoice, and account for VAT on the full amount.

Using the figures from this example, the commission to the seller is £100. VAT at 20 per cent on that amount gives a total charge for commission of £120.

Note: the total VAT you declare to us on the sale of this item under the Margin Scheme will be the same as it would have been if you had used the Auctioneers' Scheme in Example 2. (£30 + £30 = £50.)

If the vendor is VAT-registered, he will be able to reclaim the VAT on the separate commission invoice if you have used the Margin Scheme for the sale.

8.6 Example 5

You sell the item under the Auctioneers' Scheme option for imported works of art, antiques or collectors' items.

The item is valued at import at £500. You pay import VAT at 5 per cent on this value (£25)

You charge commission to the seller.

You charge buyer's premium.

Section	*Description*	*Value*
(a)	*Hammer price*	£1,000
(b)	*Buyer's premium*	
	Rate of buyer's premium times hammer price 18% × 1,000	£180
(c)	*Commission* charged to seller	
	Commission rate times hammer price 12% × 1,000	£120
(d)	*Purchase price*	
	(Hammer price less commission, a – c)	£880
(e)	*Selling Price*	
	Hammer price plus buyer's premium (a + b)	£1,180
(f)	*Margin*	
	Selling Price less purchase price (e – d)	£300
(g)	*VAT on sale*	
	Margin (f) times VAT fraction 300 × $^1/_6$ths	£50

Note: you can recoup the £25 import VAT you had to pay when the item entered the UK from the seller in the USA, but you must not include it in your Auctioneers' Scheme calculations.

8.7 Example 6

You sell zero-rated goods (such as antique books) under the Auctioneers' Scheme.

You charge commission to the seller.

You charge buyer's premium.

Section	*Description*	*Value*

(a)	*Hammer price*	£1,000
(b)	*Commission* charged to seller (exclusive of VAT)	£100
(c)	*Buyer's premium* (exclusive of VAT)	£150
(d)	*Purchase price*	£900
	Hammer price less commission (a – b) 1,000 – 100	£1,150
(e)	*Selling Price*	
	Hammer price plus buyer's premium (a + c) 1,000 + 150	£1,150
(f)	*Margin*	
	Selling Price less purchase price (e – d) 1,150 – 900	£250
(g)	*VAT on sale*	
	Zero-rated	Nil

723A
REFUNDS OF VAT IN THE EUROPEAN COMMUNITY FOR EC AND NON-EC BUSINESSES

December 2014

This notice cancels and replaces Notice 723A (October 2011).

1 INTRODUCTION

Commentary—*De Voil Indirect Tax Service* **V5.151A, V5.152.**

1.1 What is this notice about?

This notice explains the schemes for claiming a refund of VAT incurred in—

either . . .	*Section*
European Union (EU) countries if you are established in another EU member state	2 – gives an overview of the scheme
	3 – explains how UK and Isle of Man businesses can claim from other member states
	4 – explains how businesses in other EU member states can claim from the UK
or	5 – gives an overview of the refund scheme in the UK for non-EU businesses
the United Kingdom (UK) if you are established outside the EU	6 – explains how non-EU businesses can claim from the UK
	7 – explains where you can get more information about the schemes
	8 – provides contact details for Tax Authorities in other EU member states

It has been restructured and rewritten to reflect the changes required by the EU Council Directive 2008/9.

1.2 What law applies to this notice?

UK law	— VATA 1994 s 39
	— VAT Regulations 1995, SI 1995/2518, Parts XX and XXI
EC law	— EC Council Directive 2008/9 Thirteenth VAT Directive (86/560/EEC)

1.3 Isle of Man

For VAT purposes, the Isle of Man is treated as part of the UK. VAT is chargeable in the Isle of Man under Manx legislation, which is broadly similar to UK legislation. The schemes described in this notice apply equally to refunds of VAT incurred in the Isle of Man. Any references to the UK in this notice are to be taken to include the Isle of Man.

2 REFUNDS OF VAT FOR EU BUSINESSES: OVERVIEW OF THE EUROPEAN UNION REFUND SCHEME

Commentary—*De Voil Indirect Tax Service* **V5.151A.**

2.1 Introduction

The electronic cross-border refund system enables a business that incurs VAT on expenditure in a member state where it is not established and makes no supplies, to recover that VAT directly from that member state (the member state of Refund). The previous system, known as the 8th VAT Directive refund system, was a lengthy, burdensome, paper-based system.

Following agreement between EU Finance Ministers, EU legislation to reform the system was adopted in February 2008, as part of the VAT package of legislation. The electronic system will apply to all claims submitted on or after 1/1/2010.

Requests for refunds will continue to be dealt with by the member state of refund. The amount refundable will also continue to be determined under the deduction rules of the member state of refund and the relevant repayment will be made directly by that member state to the business. The system will be an electronic one, with specified timescales and interest payable if these are not met.

2.2 The Refund Scheme – general rules

Electronic claims will be completed and submitted via the competent authorities in the member state in which the claimant is established.

2.3 Who can make the application

The applicant must be a taxable person established in a member state other than the member state of refund, or their authorised agent.

The applicant must meet the following conditions.

(a) The applicant must not be registered, liable or eligible to be registered in the member state from which they are claiming the refund.
(b) The applicant must have no fixed establishment, seat of economic activity, place of business or other residence there.
(c) During the refund period the applicant must not have supplied any goods or services in the member state of refund with the exception of:
  (i) transport services and services ancillary thereto
  (ii) supplies of goods or services where VAT is payable by the person to whom the supply is made.

2.4 Checks by the member state of establishment

Basic registration checks will be carried out by the member state of establishment before the application is forwarded electronically to the member state from which the refund is being claimed.

The member state of establishment will not forward the application to the member state of refund where during the period of refund any of the following apply.

(a) The applicant is not a taxable person for VAT purposes.
(b) The applicant makes only exempt supplies.
(c) The applicant is covered by the exemption for small enterprises.
(d) The applicant is operating the flat-rate scheme for farmers.

If the member state of establishment decides not to forward the application it must notify the applicant of this decision.

2.5 Applications

A separate application must be completed for each member state. Applications can be commenced and stored in an incomplete state on the system and may be recalled and finalised to be submitted at a later date.

2.6 Application periods

The refund period must not be more than one calendar year or less than three calendar months unless the period covered represents the remainder of a calendar year (for example where interim applications have already been submitted earlier in the year, or if the applicant has recently become VAT registered).

2.7 Minimum applications

If the refund application relates to a period of less than a calendar year, but not less than three months the minimum amount claimable is EUR 400 or the equivalent in national currency.

If the refund application relates to a period of a calendar year or the remainder of a calendar year the minimum amount claimable is EUR 50 or the equivalent in national currency.

2.8 Time limits for making an application

Properly completed applications must be submitted to the member state of establishment at the latest on 30 September of the calendar year following the refund year. If you deregister for VAT during the refund year you should submit your application as soon as possible following deregistration.

Deadline for 2009 EU Cross-Border VAT Refund Claims

The deadline for businesses to submit their 2009 EU VAT Cross-Border refund claims is to be extended from 30 September 2010 to 31 March 2011.

The European Commission has proposed a six month extension to the deadline, which was previously 30 September 2010, because of technical problems with a number of other member states' portals. The Commission proposal has been unanimously supported by member states.

Please note: If you make a refund claim during this extended period the HMRC VAT EU Refund service will display the following warning message:

"The refund period start month cannot be before January of this year".

Please ignore this message. Your claim will be processed and forwarded to the member state of refund for consideration.

2.9 Scope of application

Supplies of goods or services received with a tax point during the period of the refund application.

Goods imported into the member state of refund during the period of the refund application.

In addition, the application may include supplies or imports not included in a previous application as long as they relate to the same calendar year.

The application may not include:

(a) amounts of VAT that have been incorrectly invoiced
(b) amounts of VAT that have been invoiced in respect of goods despatched to other member states or exported outside the EU.

2.10 Partial exemption

A restriction to the amount of VAT claimable is to be applied if you make taxable and exempt supplies.

2.11 Standard fields

The use of standard fields of information and expense codes will aid completion and are mandatory. Failure to include all standard information will result in rejection in the member state of establishment. It is important to note that if a fully completed application is not received by the 30 September of the year following the refund period this will render it out of time.

Standard fields

(1) Applicants name and full address.
(2) An address for contact by electronic means (email address).
(3) A description of the applicant's business activity for which the goods and services are acquired.
(4) Period dates to which the refund application relates.
(5) A declaration by the applicant that they have supplied no goods and services in the member state of refund during the period of the application, with the exception of transactions relating to:
    (i) transport services and services ancillary thereto
    (ii) the supply of good or services where VAT is payable by the person to whom the supply is made.
(6) The applicants VAT identification number or tax reference number.
(7) Bank account details including IBAN and BIC codes.

2.12 Standard fields for invoices or importations included in the refund application

(1) Name and address of the supplier.
(2) Except in cases of importation the VAT identification number or tax reference number of the supplier.
(3) Except in the case of importation, the prefix of the member state of refund.
(4) Date and number of the invoice or importation document.
(5) Taxable amount and amount of VAT expressed in the currency of the member state of refund.
(6) The amount of deductible VAT expressed in the currency of the member state of refund. This is the amount of VAT recoverable taking account of any partial exemption restriction, and any restriction on the recovery of input tax applying in the member state of refund.
(7) Where applicable the deductible proportion calculated in accordance with the rules applying in the member state of establishment.
(8) Nature of the goods and services acquired, described according to the following expenditure codes.

2.13 Expenditure codes

(1) Fuel.
(2) Hiring of means of transport.
(3) Expenditure relating to means of transport.
(4) Road tolls and road user charge.
(5) Travel expenses, such as taxi fares, public transport fares.
(6) Accommodation.
(7) Food, drink and restaurant services.
(8) Admissions to fairs and exhibitions.
(9) Expenditure on luxuries, amusements and entertainment.
(10) Other.

Member states may require further sub codes to be used in respect of each of the above to the extent that such information is necessary due to any restrictions on the right to deduct in that member state.

If code 10 is used without an accompanying sub code, a narrative description of the goods and services must be provided.

Full details of expenditure codes required by each member state can be obtained from its tax authority, and may also be available through the electronic claim system.

2.14 Invoices required to be scanned and submitted electronically with the application

Member states may require invoices with a value of EUR 1,000 or more (EUR 250 in the case of fuel) – or the equivalent in national currency – to be scanned and submitted electronically with the application. All other invoices should be retained as they may be requested at a later date by the member state of refund.

2.15 Language

Free text fields will now have more choice of language to be used. Some member states allow the use of a second language with English being a common option.

Full details of languages required by each member state can be obtained from its Tax Authority, and may also be available through the electronic claim system.

2.16 Communication Applicants will be informed at the following key stages of the process

(a) When the member state of establishment forwards the application to the member state of refund.
(b) When the member state of refund receives the application.
(c) If the member state of refund requires further information.
(d) When the member state of refund makes its decision.

It is essential that the email address provided on the application is correct and if this changes at any time before the application is decided it must be amended at the earliest opportunity.

2.17 Method of payment

The payment will be made in the member state of refund or, at the applicant's request, in any other member state. In the latter case, any bank charges for the transfer will be deducted by the member state of refund from the amount to be paid to the applicant.

If incorrect bank details are submitted by the claimant and they result in further bank charges being incurred these may also be deducted from the amount payable on the current or subsequent applications. It is extremely important therefore that you ensure that the bank details you supply are absolutely correct.

2.18 Time Limits for processing an application

The member state of refund must notify the applicant of the decision to approve or refuse the application within four months of the date they first received the application.

If the member state of refund requires additional information in order to process the application, it can request this from the applicant, the applicant's tax authority, or a third party before the expiry of the four month period.

The additional information must be provided by the person to whom the request is made within one month of receiving the request.

Once the member state of refund has received the additional information it has two further months in which to notify its decision.

If further additional information is requested by the member state of refund the final deadline for making a decision can be extended up to a maximum of eight months from the date they received the application. Payment must be made within 10 working days following expiry of the appropriate decision deadline.

2.19 Incorrect application/payment errors

If an applicant discovers that it has made an error on an application, a corrected application can be submitted. The correction procedures allows existing lines on the application to be amended or deleted (by reducing to "nil"), but does not allow new lines to be added. The correction procedure can also be used to amend incorrect bank details, email addresses etc. If an application is found to be incorrect any overpayment will be recovered, normally by deducting it from any refund due.

All member states take a very serious view of incorrect applications. Refunds obtained on the basis of any incorrect application can be recovered, penalties and interest may be imposed and further refund applications suspended.

2.20 Refused applications

If the member state of refund refuses an application fully or partly they must also notify the applicant of the reasons for refusal.

If this happens the applicant can appeal against the decision using the appeals procedure of that member state. This means that the normal VAT appeals rules of that member state on time limits, form of appeal etc, will apply.

If the member state of refund has not notified its decision within the appropriate decision deadline the applicant should consider that the application has been rejected unless any alternative procedures apply in that member state.

The applicant's own VAT authority cannot intervene on its behalf.

2.21 Interest

Interest may be payable by the member state of refund to the applicant if payment is made after the final payment deadline set out above.

If applicable it will be paid from the day following that deadline up to the date the refund is actually paid.

Interest rates must be the same as those applied to refunds of VAT to taxable persons established in the member state of refund under the national law of that member state.

If no interest is payable under national law in respect of refunds to established taxable persons, the interest payable will be equal to the interest or equivalent charge which is applied by that member state in respect of late payments of VAT by taxable persons.

3 REFUNDS OF VAT FOR UK AND ISLE OF MAN BUSINESSES CLAIMING FROM OTHER MEMBER STATES

How do I make an application under the Refund procedure?

All applications made on or after 1 January 2010 regardless as to whether they cover periods prior to 1 January 2010 must be submitted using the electronic online system. In order to be able to make an electronic application for refund of VAT you first need to register for VAT Online Services (https://www.gov.uk/send-vat-return).

Commentary—*De Voil Indirect Tax Service* **V5.151A.**

3.1 How do I register for online services?

You will need to have your VAT 4 Certificate of Registration and a copy of your last VAT return to hand and follow the on screen instructions.

An activation PIN number will be mailed to the business address registered with HMRC within set time limits (currently 7–10 days). Once this is received you will have 28 days from the date of the letter to activate the service.

3.2 Can I use an agent?

Yes – Agents can register to enable them to make refund applications on behalf of their clients and additional security procedures have been built in to their online application process. Full instructions are available here (https://www.gov.uk/appoint-tax-agent).

As a security measure the activation PIN number will be mailed to the business. The 28 days activation period will still apply therefore the business should forward the PIN to their agent in time for them to complete the activation process within 28 days otherwise the PIN will expire and the process will have to be repeated.

In order to preserve agent/client confidentiality HMRC's Customer Contact staff cannot discuss applications with an agent who does not provide the full application reference number. If no application reference is quoted, only the client can discuss that application with HMRC.

The claim form has been largely standardised but the member state of Refund retain the ability to decide preferences such as language required for any free text areas. Some member states now accept more than one language with English being a common option.

3.3 Who is eligible to claim?

You must be a taxable person registered for VAT in the UK or in the Isle of Man.

For VAT purposes the Isle of Man is treated as part of the UK. VAT is chargeable in the Isle of Man under MANX legislation, which is broadly similar to UK legislation. The schemes described in this notice apply equally to refunds of VAT incurred in the Isle of Man. Any references to the UK in this notice are taken to include the Isle of Man.

You must meet the following conditions:

(a) you must not be registered, liable or eligible to be registered in the member state of refund

(b) you must not have any fixed establishment, seat of economic activity, place of business or other residence in the member state of refund

(c) during the refund period you must not have supplied any goods or services in the member state of refund with the exception of:

  (i) transport services and services ancillary thereto

  (ii) any goods or services where VAT is payable by the person to whom the supply is made.

If you are registered as a VAT group, and the group has member companies in the member state of refund, you may only use the refund scheme to claim VAT incurred by companies who are not established in – and do not make supplies in – the member state of refund.

By submitting your application through HMRC you are declaring that you meet these conditions.

3.4 Will I need to prove my taxable person status?

Applications will be subjected to automated registration verifications by HMRC before being forwarded electronically to the member state from which the refund is being claimed.

Certificates of Status (VAT 66) are therefore no longer required for refund applications from other member states.

Applications will only be forwarded to the member state of refund if these checks are satisfactory.

If the checks are not satisfactory the application will be rejected by the electronic portal and you will receive an appropriate error message.

Deregistered applicants must submit their applications as soon as possible, and not later than three months from their date of deregistration.

In respect of VAT group registrations, the application will be forwarded in the name of the representative member. Where the application relates to VAT incurred by other group members, it may be accompanied by a covering note explaining that these companies are members of the same VAT group. This note can be sent using the “attachment” facility for invoices (explained further below), and may reduce requests for additional information from the member state of refund.

3.5 How do I claim?

A separate online application is required for each member state from which you wish to claim. In order to start an application you must access the relevant online services section using your unique PID and password and enter your standard data into the required fields, along with invoice or importation details for expenditure you wish to reclaim.

Applications can be commenced and saved if incomplete and can be recalled for completion and submission at a later date. This facility is available for applications relating to each member state.

3.6 What period must my application cover?

The refund period must not be more than one calendar year or less than three calendar months (unless the period covered represents the remainder of a calendar year, for example, where interim applications have already been submitted earlier in the year covering more than nine months, or if you have recently become VAT registered).

Generally refund periods do not have to cover strict calendar quarters. For example, you may submit two applications covering five months each, and a final one covering two months. However, some member states have their own requirements, and details of these can be obtained from the relevant tax authority.

Generally refund periods may not overlap. For example, you may not submit an application covering 1 January to 31 March and another for 1 March to 31 May. However you may submit a further application covering the whole refund year after the year end. This enables you to claim for any purchases which you have missed in earlier periods.

3.7 Is there a minimum amount that can be claimed?

If the refund application relates to a period of less than a calendar year, but not less than three months the minimum amount claimable is EUR 400 or the equivalent in national currency.

If the refund application relates to a period of a calendar year or the remainder of a calendar year the minimum amount claimable is EUR 50 or the equivalent in national currency.

3.8 What invoices can be included on the application?

Invoices relating to supplies of goods or services with a tax point during the period of the refund application.

Invoices relating to an importation of goods into the member state of refund during the period of the refund application.

In addition you may claim for invoices or imports not included in a previous application as long as they relate to the same calendar year.

The application may not include amounts of VAT that have been:

(a) incorrectly invoiced
(b) invoiced in respect of goods despatched to another member state or exported outside the EU
(c) incurred in respect of non business activities.

3.9 What information is covered by the Standard information fields?

(1) Name.
(2) Electronic contact address (email address).
(3) Description of your business activity to which the goods and services to be claimed relates.
(The electronic portal will permit up to three business activities to be entered).
(4) Period of application.
(5) Declaration of eligibility to claim, (in the UK the making of an application is considered to be the declaration.
(6) VAT registration number.
(7) Specified bank account details to include IBAN and BIC codes.

3.10 What information is required in respect of invoices being claimed?

(1) Name and address of your supplier.
(2) Except in cases of importation the VAT identification number or tax reference number of the supplier.
(3) Date and number of the invoice or importation document.
(4) Taxable amount and amount of VAT expressed in the currency of the member state of refund.
(5) The amount of deductible VAT expressed in the currency of the member state of refund. This is the amount of VAT recoverable taking account of any partial exemption restriction, and any restriction on the recovery of input tax applying in the member state of refund.
(6) Where applicable the deductible proportion calculated in accordance with the rules applying in the member state of establishment.
(7) Nature of the goods and services acquired, described according to the following expenditure codes.
    (1) Fuel.
    (2) Hiring of means of transport.
    (3) Expenditure relating to means of transport.
    (4) Road tolls and road user charge.
    (5) Travel expenses, such as taxi fares, public transport fares.

(6) Accommodation.
(7) Food, drink and restaurant services.
(8) Admissions to fairs and exhibitions.
(9) Expenditure on luxuries, amusements and entertainment.
(10) Other.

Many member states will require sub-codes in addition to the main codes set out above, to the extent that such information is necessary due to restrictions on the right to deduct in those member states. Where applicable, these sub-codes will appear as completion options on the electronic portal. Where code 10 is used, without an accompanying sub-code, a narrative description of the goods or services must be entered in a free text box, using the language(s) required by the member state of refund.

If an invoice includes items covering more than one expenditure code the code relating to the highest proportion of expenditure is the one that should be used.

3.11 Do I have to restrict applications in respect of partial exemption?

Yes – you must apply the appropriate recovery rate for the goods or services purchased against each invoice or importation on your application, and show the amount of VAT recoverable in the appropriate box. The recovery rate to be applied is the last percentage appropriate to the refund period covering the invoice date. For example, if the claimable percentage for the March 2010 period is 5 per cent and the application is submitted in April before the annual adjustment is calculated the claim should be restricted to 5 per cent. However if you only make one application at the year end and have already calculated that the annual adjustment covering the March 2010 quarter is 3 per cent then you may only claim 3 per cent.

Following your annual adjustment, you will not be required to amend refund applications already submitted. The invoices can only be entered once and the percentage to be used is that covering the invoice date.

3.12 Do I have to restrict applications in respect of non-business expenses?

Yes – expenditure incurred in another member state that relates to non-business activities is not claimable under the refund scheme.

3.13 What Language do I need to use on the application?

Member states generally require the application to be in their own language but with effect from 1 January 2010 they may allow the use of a second language in the free text fields, and English is a common option. The language(s) required by the member state of refund will be displayed on the electronic portal as you complete the application.

3.14 What invoices may be required to be scanned and submitted electronically?

Subject to the rules of the member state of refund you may be requested to submit invoices with values of EUR 1,000 or more (EUR 250 or more in the case of fuel) – or the equivalent in national currency – with the application. All other invoices should be retained as they may be requested at a later date by the member state of refund.

If you have imported goods, you must have the VAT copy of the import entry or other Customs document showing the amount of VAT that you have paid.

The documents must be scanned and saved as files of PDF, TIFF, or JPEG format, and the total attachment size per application must not exceed five megabytes. In order to keep your attachment size within this limit, you should scan the documents at the lowest resolution that still provides a legible copy, and you may include the document files in a “zip” file. You may not, however, include “zip” files within “zip” files.

Where the UK tax authorities receive an attachment larger than five megabytes, containing “zip” files within “zip” files, or infected by a virus, they will remove and destroy the attachment. They will notify you if this happens.

3.15 How will I know what is happening with my application?

You will be informed electronically at the following key stages of the process.

(a) If your application fails basic validation checks by the electronic portal (by an error message).
(b) When HMRC forwards your application to the member state of refund.
(c) When the member state of refund receives the application.
(d) If the member state of refund requires additional information from you.
(e) When the member state of refund makes its decision.

It is essential that the email address you provide is correct and if this changes at any time before the application is decided it must be amended at the earliest opportunity using the application correction procedures.

3.16 What are the time limits for submitting an application?

Applications must be submitted to HMRC at the latest by 30 September of the calendar year following the refund year and will only be considered submitted if the applicant has completed *all of the required standing data fields* (see above). Properly completed applications will be forwarded to the member state of refund who will be responsible for deciding the application.

3.17 What are the time limits for the member state of refund to process an application?

The member state of refund must notify the applicant of its decision to approve or refuse the application within four months of the date they first received the application.

Where the member state of refund requires more information in order to decide the application this will be requested by electronic means either from the claimant, from the competent authorities of the member state of establishment, or from third parties. Any request for additional information must be made within the four month period referred to above.

Where additional information is requested it should be supplied within one month of the date on which the request reaches the person to whom it is addressed.

Once the member state of refund has received the additional information it has a further two months in which to notify its decision.

If further additional information is requested by the member state of refund the final deadline for making a decision can be extended up to a maximum of eight months from the date they received the application. Payment must be made within 10 working days following expiry of the appropriate decision deadline.

3.18 How will I receive my payment?

The refund will be paid in the member state of refund or, at the applicant's request, in any other member state. In the latter case, any bank charges for the transfer will be deducted by the member state of refund from the amount to be paid to the applicant.

If incorrect bank details are submitted by the claimant and they result in further bank charges being incurred these will also be deducted from the amount payable on the current or subsequent applications. It is extremely important therefore that you ensure that the bank details you supply are correct. If you change bank accounts whilst an application is pending you must ensure that these details are amended.

3.19 What do I do if I discover that I have made an error on my application?

The electronic portal provides a correction facility whereby you can recall the original application and amend existing details (including contact and bank details) and invoice lines. You may reduce an existing line to "nil" (effectively deleting it), or substitute new invoice details for the existing ones. You may not, however, add new lines.

3.20 Will I be penalised for the error?

All member states take a very serious view of incorrect or false applications. Refunds claimed incorrectly on the basis of incorrect or false information can be recovered and penalties and interest may be imposed and further refund applications suspended.

HMRC will not be able to intervene – this is a matter for the member state of refund. If your application is found to be incorrect after the refund has been paid, any overpayment will be recovered, normally by deducting it from any subsequent refund.

3.21 Can my application be refused?

If the member state of refund refuses an application fully or partly they must also notify you of the reasons for refusal.

If this happens you can appeal against the decision using the appeals procedure of that member state. This means that the normal VAT appeals rules of that member state on time limits, form of appeal etc, will apply.

If the member state of refund has not notified its decision within the appropriate decision deadline you should consider that the application has been rejected unless any alternative procedures apply in that member state.

HMRC cannot intervene on your behalf.

3.22 Will I be able to claim interest if my application is delayed?

Interest may be payable to you by the member state of refund if payment is made after the deadline.

If applicable it will be paid from the day following the deadline up to the date the refund is actually paid.

Interest rates must be the same as those applied to refunds of VAT to taxable persons established in the member state of refund under the national law of that member state.

If no interest is payable under national law in respect of refunds to established taxable persons, the interest payable will be equal to the interest or equivalent charge which is applied by that member state in respect of late payments of VAT by taxable persons.

4 REFUNDS OF VAT IN THE UK FOR EU BUSINESSES

Who can make the application?

You must be a taxable person established in a member state other than the UK.

You must meet the following conditions:

- you must not be registered, liable or eligible to be registered in the UK
- you must not have any place of business in the UK or in the Isle of Man
- you must not make any supplies in the UK (other than transport services related to the international carriage of goods, or goods and services where VAT is payable by the person to whom the supply is made).

If you use an agent to submit your application and/or receive payment of refunds on your behalf, you must submit a letter of authority, in hard copy, to the UK Overseas Repayment Unit (ORU). Contact details for the ORU, and an acceptable form of words for the letter of authority, are given at section 6.5.

Commentary—*De Voil Indirect Tax Service* **V5.151A.**

4.1 How do I submit my application?

You must submit your application through the electronic facility provided by the tax authority in your own member state. For more information about this facility, you should contact your own tax authority.

4.2 What period must my application cover?

The period covered by your application is known as the "refund period". This must not be more than one calendar year or less than three calendar months (unless it covers the remainder of a calendar year, for example, where applications have already been submitted covering more than nine months). Refund periods do not have to cover strict calendar quarters. For example, you may submit two applications covering five months each, and a final one covering two months. Generally, refund periods may not overlap. For example, you may not submit an application covering 1 January to 31 March, and another for 1 March to 31 May. However, you may submit a further application covering the whole of the refund year after the year end. This enables you to claim for any purchases or imports which you have missed in earlier periods.

4.3 When must my application be submitted?

Your application must be submitted via the electronic facility in your own member state, at the latest by 30 September of the year following that in which the VAT was incurred. So, for VAT incurred during 2010, you must submit your application by 30 September 2011.

4.4 Is there a limit to how much I can claim?

There is no maximum limit, but there are minimum limits below which you can not submit an application. These are:

- £295 where the application covers less than a calendar year but not less than three calendar months, and
- £35 where the application covers a calendar year or the remainder of a calendar year.

4.5 What VAT can I claim on my application?

You can claim VAT on goods and services purchased during the refund period, and VAT on goods imported *into the UK* during the refund period.

You may not claim:

- Amounts of VAT that have been incorrectly invoiced, or where VAT has been charged on the despatch of goods to another member state, or the export of goods outside the EU (you must take this up with the supplier).
- VAT on the purchase of a motor car.
- VAT on goods and services used for business entertainment. As an exception, VAT on entertainment for overseas customers may be reclaimed but only if it is of a very basic nature.
- VAT on goods and services used for non-business activities.

In addition, where you incur VAT on charges for hiring or leasing a motor car, you may only claim 50 per cent of the total VAT charged.

4.6 What happens if I make both taxable and exempt supplies?

You must apply the appropriate restriction to the VAT you reclaim, following the rules that apply in your own member state.

If your own member state operates the "pro-rata" system in respect of taxable and exempt supplies, and your pro-rata rate changes from one year to the next, you should submit a pro-rata adjustment through your tax authority's electronic facility.

4.7 What information must I show on my application?

The electronic facility provided by your tax authority will contain fields for completion, and you should direct any detailed queries about input of data to the facility to your tax authority. However, as a guide, the following information is required on each refund application:

- your name and address
- an address for contact by electronic means (an email address)
- a description, using NACE codes, of the your business activity for which you have purchased the goods and services
- the start and end dates of the refund period covered by the application
- a declaration that you have not made any supplies of goods or services in the UK during the refund period (except for those specified in paragraph 4.1 above)
- your VAT identification number or tax reference number
- your bank details including your IBAN and BIC codes.

In addition, you must provide the following details for each purchase or importation included in your application:

- the name and full address of the supplier
- the VAT registration number of the supplier in the UK, including the prefix "GB" (except in the case of imports)
- the date and number of the supplier's invoice or the importation document

- the taxable amount and the amount of VAT on the invoice, expressed in pounds sterling
- the amount of VAT deductible in respect of the purchase or importation, expressed in pounds sterling
- where applicable under the rules of your member state, the appropriate pro-rata rate
- a description of the goods and services purchased or goods imported, using the codes in paragraph 4.8 below.

4.8 What goods and services codes and subcodes will the UK require on refund applications?

Code	*Sub code*
Code 1. Fuel	
1.6 Fuel purchased for resale	
Code 2. Hiring of means of transport	
2.2 Hiring of means of transport with a mass less than or equal to 3.500kg other than means of transport for paying passengers	
2.4 Hiring of means of goods transport	
2.5 Hiring of passenger and multipurpose cars	2.5.1 Used exclusively for business purposes
	2.5.2 Used partly for commercial passenger transport or driving instruction
2.6 Hiring of motorcycles, caravans and vessels for recreational or sports purposes, and aircraft with a mass less than 1.550kg	2.6.1 Used for commercial passenger transport or driving instruction
	2.6.2 Used for other business purposes
2.7 Hiring of passenger cars of the M1 category	
2.9 Hiring of means of passenger transport with less than 9 spaces	2.9.1 Used for commercial operations
	2.9.2 Used for other than commercial operations
Code 3. Expenditure relating to means of transport (other than goods and services referred to under codes 1 and 2)	
3.2 Expenditure relating to means of transport with a mass less than or equal to 3.500kg other than means of transport for paying passengers	3.2.1 Purchase of means of transport with a mass less than or equal to 3.500kg other than means of transport for paying passengers
	3.2.2 Maintenance of a means of transport with a mass less than or equal to 3.500kg other than means of transport for paying passengers
	3.2.3 Purchase and installation of accessories for a means of transport with a mass less than or equal to 3.500kg other than means of transport for paying passengers
3.4 Expenditure relating to means of goods transport	3.4.1 Purchase of a means of goods transport
	3.4.2 Maintenance of a means of goods transport
3.5 Maintenance of passenger and multi-purpose cars	3.5.1 Used exclusively for business purposes
	3.5.2 Used partly for commercial passenger transport, driving instruction, or rental purposes
3.6 Maintenance, of motorcycles, caravans and vessels for recreational and sports purposes, and aircrafts with a mass greater than 1.550kg	3.6.1 Used for commercial passenger transport, driving instruction, rental purposes

	3.6.2 Used for other business purposes
3.7 Expenditure, other than maintenance, garaging and parking relating to passenger and multipurpose cars	3.7.1 Used exclusively for business purposes
	3.7.2 Used partly for commercial passenger transport, driving instruction or rental purposes
3.8 Expenditure, other than maintenance, garaging and parking relating to motorcycles, caravans and vessels for recreational and sports purposes, and aircrafts with a mass greater than 1.550kg.	3.8.1 Used for commercial passenger transport, driving instruction, rental purposes or resale
	3.8.2 Used for other business purposes
3.9 Purchase of passenger car of "M1" category	
3.10 Purchase of accessories for passenger cars of "M1" category, including their assembly and installation	
3.12 Expenditure relating to means of passenger transport with less than 9 places used for commercial operations	
Code 5. Travel expenses, such as taxi fares, public transport fares	
5.1 For the taxable person or an employee of the taxable person	
5.2 For someone other than the taxable person, or an employee of the taxable person	
5.3 For the taxable person or an employee of the taxable person in the context of a conference, fair, exhibition or congress	5.3.1 For the organiser of the event
	5.3.2 For a participant in the event, where the expenditure is directly charged by the organiser
Code 6. Accommodation	
6.1 Expenditure on lodging and accommodation for the taxable person, or an employee of the taxable person	
6.2 Expenditure on lodging and accommodation for someone other than the taxable person or an employee of the taxable person	
6.4 Expenditure on lodging and accommodation for the taxable person or an employee of the taxable person in the context of a conference, fair, exhibition or congress	6.4.1 For the organiser of the event
	6.4.2 For a participant in the event, where the expenditure is directly charged by the organiser
6.6 Expenditure on lodging and accommodation for onward supply	
Code 7. Food, drink and restaurant services	
7.1 Food and drink provided by hotels, bars, restaurants and boarding houses, including breakfast	7.1.1 For the taxable person or an employee of the taxable person
	7.1.2 For someone other than the taxable person or an employee of the taxable person
7.2 Food and drink provided in the context of a conference, fair, exhibition or congress	7.2.1 For the organiser of the event
	7.2.2 For a participant in the event, where the expenditure is directly charged by the organiser
7.4 Restaurant services purchased for onward supply	

Code 8. Admissions to fairs and exhibitions	
8.1 For the taxable person or an employee of the taxable person	
8.2 For someone other than the taxable person or an employee of the taxable person	
Code 9. Expenditure on luxuries, amusements and entertainment	
9.1 Purchase of alcohol	
9.2 Purchase of manufactured tobacco	
9.3 Expenditure on receptions and entertainment.	9.3.1 For publicity purposes
	9.3.2 Not for publicity purposes
9.4 Expenditure on maintenance of pleasure craft	
9.5 Expenditure on works of art, collectors' items and antiques	
9.6 Expenditure on luxuries, amusements and entertainment for advertising	
9.7 Expenditure on luxuries, amusements and entertainment other than 9.1, 9.2 and 9.3	
10. Other	
10.1 Tools	
10.2 Repairs within a warranty period	
10.3 Services connected with education	
10.4 Work on property	10.4.1 Work on immoveable property
	10.4.2 Work on immoveable property used as a dwelling
	10.4.3 Work on moveable property other than code 3
10.5 Purchase or hiring of property	10.5.1 Purchase or hiring of immoveable property
	10.5.2 Purchase or hiring of immoveable property used as a dwelling
	10.5.3 Purchase or hiring of moveable property other than code 2
10.6 Provision of water, gas or electricity through a distribution network	
10.7 Gifts of a small value	
10.8 Office expenses	
10.9 Participation in fairs and seminars, education or training	10.9.1 Fairs
	10.9.2 Seminars
	10.9.3 Education
	10.9.4 Training
10.10 Flat rate additions on livestock and agricultural produce	
10.11 Expenditure on postage of mail to countries outside the EU	
10.12 Expenditure on fax and phone in connection with accommodation	
10.13 Goods and services acquired by a travel organiser for the direct benefit of the traveller	
10.14 Goods purchased for resale other than 1.6	

10.15 services purchased for resale other than 6.6 and 7.4	
10.16 Work on property	10.16.1 Work on immoveable property used as a residence, recreational or leisure facility
	10.16.2 Work on immoveable property other than 10.16.1
	10.16.3 Work on moveable property connected with or use of an immoveable property in 10.16.1
	10.16.4 Work on moveable property other than 10.16.3

Where you have entered code 10, with no accompanying sub-code, you must provide a free text description of the goods or services in English.

4.9 What scanned documents must I send with my application?

You must attach scanned copies of all invoices and import documents where the taxable amount exceeds:

- £200 in the case of fuel, and
- £750 in the case of all other goods and services.

The documents must be scanned and saved as files of PDF, TIFF or JPEG format, and the total attachment size per application must not exceed *five* megabytes. In order to keep your attachment size within this limit, you should scan the documents at the lowest resolution that still provides a legible copy, and you may include the document files in a "zip" file. You may not, however, include "zip" files within "zip" files.

Where the UK tax authorities receive an attachment larger than five megabytes, containing "zip"' files within "zip" files, or infected by a virus, they will remove and destroy the attachment. They will notify you if this happens. To prevent this happening, if the attachment size would exceed five megabytes, please remove lower value invoices to reduce the attachment size to an acceptable limit for submitting. If we require copies of further invoices, we will ask for them separately. The UK recommends TIFF or PDF format at 200 DPI.

4.10 What happens once the UK receives my application?

The UK tax authority will notify you of the date on which it received your application. Within four months of that date, the UK tax authority will advise you whether your application has been accepted, partly or wholly rejected, or further information is required. If the UK tax authority requests further information (which may take the form of original invoices or other documents) you must supply this within one month of the date on which you receive the request. The UK tax authority will then have a maximum period of eight months from the date it received your application, to notify you of its decision.

4.11 When will I receive payment?

Unless your application has been wholly rejected, you will receive payment of any amount due to you within ten working days of the decision deadlines set out in paragraph 4.10 above. Payment will be made in pounds sterling, to the bank account detailed in your application, so it is important that the account details are correct.

4.12 Will I receive interest if payment is made late?

Where the UK tax authority fails to make payment to you by the deadlines set out in paragraph 4.11 above (and provided you have supplied any additional information requested within the required timescales) you will be paid interest. Interest will be calculated at the same rate applied to taxable persons within the UK, and the interest calculation period will run from the date payment was due until the date it is made.

4.13 Can my application be refused?

Yes. But we will tell you why we have refused it.

If you do not agree with the decision to refuse your application, you can:

- ask for the decision to be reviewed by an HMRC officer not previously involved in the matter, or
- appeal to an independent tribunal.

If you opt for a review you can still appeal to the tribunal after the review has finished.

If you want a review you should write to the address given in the decision letter within 30 days of the date of the letter, giving your reasons why you do not agree with the decision. We will not take any action to collect the disputed tax while the review of the decision is being carried out.

If you want to appeal to the tribunal you should send them your appeal within 30 days of the date of the decision letter.

You can find further information about appeals and reviews on the HMRC website (https://www.gov.uk/tax-appeals).

You can find out more about tribunals on the Tribunals Service website (http://www.justice.gov.uk/tribunals/tax) or you can phone them on 0845 223 8080.

4.14 Can I correct an application after it has been submitted?

The UK will accept corrected applications, but you should seek advice from your tax authority about how these should be submitted through the electronic facility in your own member state. The UK may impose penalties for applications which are found to be incorrect, so if you realise that you have made an error on an application after it has been submitted, you should submit a correction as soon as possible. You can use the correction procedure to amend existing claim lines, you can not delete a claim line but you can reduce the VAT value to zero, and you may not insert additional lines. If you have missed an invoice from an application, you should include it on a later one. You should also use the claims procedure to amend your email address or bank details, if these change after you have submitted your application. Corrected applications must be submitted by the same deadline as original applications, that is, by 30 September of the year following the year in which the VAT was incurred.

5 REFUNDS OF VAT IN THE UK FOR NON-EU BUSINESSES: OVERVIEW OF THE REFUND SCHEME

What is the scheme for?

If you are registered for business purposes in a country, which is not a member state of the EU and you buy goods or services in the UK, you may have to pay VAT. This need not happen if you buy goods for export, but it may apply if what you buy is used in the UK – for example, if you take part in a trade fair.

If you are not registered for VAT in the UK you cannot treat this VAT as input tax, but you may be able to use this scheme to reclaim VAT charged on imports into the UK or purchases of goods and services used in the UK.

For VAT purposes the Isle of Man is treated as part of the UK. VAT is chargeable in the Isle of Man under MANX legislation which is broadly similar to UK legislation. This scheme applies equally to refunds of VAT incurred in the Isle of Man. Any references to the UK in this notice are to be taken to include the Isle of Man.

5.1 Who can use the scheme?

If you are registered for business purposes in a non-EU country, you can use the scheme to reclaim VAT paid in the UK, provided that you:

- are not registered, liable or eligible to be registered for VAT in the UK; you will find more about this in Notice 700/1 "Should I be registered for VAT?"
- have no place of business or other residence in the EU, and

- do not make any supplies in the UK (other than transport services related to the international carriage of goods, or services where VAT is payable by the person in the UK to whom the supply is made).
- it is a condition of the scheme that your own country allows similar concessions to UK traders in respect of its own turnover taxes. But your application will only be refused on these grounds if your own country has a scheme for refunding these taxes, but refuses to allow UK traders to use it.

VAT Retail Export Scheme

There is also a VAT Retail Export Scheme which allows non-EU visitors a refund of VAT on certain goods that they buy in the EU. For more details of the Scheme (as it operates in the UK) see Notice 704 "VAT Retail Exports".

Commentary—*De Voil Indirect Tax Service* **V5.152.**

5.2 Can I reclaim VAT on all the goods and services I buy?

No. You cannot use the scheme to reclaim VAT on:

- non-business supplies. However, if a supply covers both business and non-business use, VAT can be reclaimed on the business element of the supply
- any supply used or to be used to make a supply in the United Kingdom
- the supply or importation of most ordinary business cars. Only 50 per cent of the VAT incurred on the hire of lease of a car for mixed business and private purposes is allowed
- certain second-hand goods, such as cars and antiques for which no tax invoice will be issued
- business entertainment/hospitality expenses. As an exception, VAT on entertainment for overseas customers may be reclaimed but only if it is of a very basic nature.
- export of goods – but these will be zero-rated, provided the supplier has the necessary evidence, or
- goods and services, such as hotel accommodation, you have bought for resale which are for the direct benefit of travellers
- any supply used or to be used to make an exempt supply outside the United Kingdom. (For this purpose an exempt supply is a supply described as exempt in Sch 9 to VATA 1994, whether or not the place of the supply is in the UK.)

5.3 Partial exemption

In most cases where goods and services are used to make both taxable and exempt supplies you can only recover VAT to the extent that they are used to make taxable supplies. For further information see Public Notice 706 "Partial Exemption".

5.4 What about VAT paid on imports?

If you have to arrange for goods to be imported into the UK you can reclaim any VAT due, *provided there is no other VAT relief available at import*. But you must remember that you will not be able to use the scheme if, as a result of importing the goods, you become liable to register for VAT in the UK. If you are importing goods into the UK you will find more about this in VAT Notice 702 "Imports".

5.5 How much can I claim?

There is no maximum amount you can claim but the UK has set minimum claim amounts that can be refunded.

Your application should cover any VAT you are reclaiming over a period of at least three months but not more than the full prescribed year. When your application is for a period covering less than 12 months the total amount of VAT claimed must not be less than £130. The application can cover less than three months if this is all that remains of the prescribed year. In that case, or when the application is for the full 12 months of the prescribed year, the amount of VAT claimed must not be less than £16. You can also include items missed on earlier applications as long as they related to VAT charged in the year of the application.

5.6 Is there a time limit for making an application?

You *must* make any claim no later than six months after the end of the "prescribed year" in which you incurred the VAT. The prescribed year is the twelve months from 1 July to 30 June of the following calendar year, so you must make your application no later than 31 December. *Please note that, to ensure fair treatment for all claimants, applications are dealt with on a 'first come, first served' basis and that the time limit is applied strictly.*

6 REFUNDS OF VAT IN THE UK FOR NON-EU BUSINESSES

6.1 Application form

You make your application on form VAT 65A (https://www.gov.uk/government/uploads/system/uploads/attachment_data/file/389937/vat65a.pdf), which is available from the HMRC website.

The following statement has the force of law.

> Applications by non-EU businesses for refunds of VAT incurred in the UK (under the terms of VAT Regulations 1995, SI 1995/2518 s 1919(1)(a)) may be made on form VAT 65A and must contain the information requested on that form.

The legislation also permits use of a similar form if it is produced by an official authority and contains the same information and declaration set out in the VAT 65A.

You must fill in the form in English, using block capitals, and send it with the original copy of all invoices included on the application to:

HM Revenue & Customs
VAT Overseas Repayment Unit
P O Box 34
Foyle House
Duncreggan Road
Londonderry
BT48 7AE

6.2 Certificate proving proof of business activity

When you make your first application you must also include a certificate from the official authority in your own country showing that you are registered for business purposes in that country. When you apply for the certificate, make sure you ask for it to show all the information that the UK authorities will need to process your application. For example, if the invoices are made out in your company's trading style, the certificate must show this as well as the name of the person registered.

The certificate must contain:

- the name, the address and official stamp of the authorising body
- your own name and address
- the nature of your business, and
- your business registration number.

It must be an original certificate, a photocopy is not acceptable.

You may use form VAT 66A (http://www.hmrc.gov.uk/forms/vat66a.pdf).

The following statement has the force of law.

> The certificate of status for non-EU businesses required under the terms of VAT Regulations 1995, SI 1995/2518 s 191(1)(b)(i) may be made on form VAT 66A and must contain the information requested on that form.
>
> The legislation also provides for use of a similar form if it is produced by an official authority and contains the same information set out in the VAT 66A.

6.3 How long is the certificate valid?

Each certificate is valid for twelve months from its date of issue and will cover any applications you make during that year. Once the certificate has expired you will need to send a new one with your next application.

6.4 Must I have proof of the VAT I have paid?

Yes. You must have correctly completed invoices, vouchers or receipts from your suppliers showing:

— an identifying number
— your supplier's name, address and VAT registration number
— your name and address
— details of goods or services supplied
— the date of supply
— the cost of the goods or services (excluding VAT)
— the rate of VAT, and
— the amount of VAT charged.

If the value of a supply is £250 or less (including VAT), the invoice need only show:

— your supplier's name, address and VAT registration number
— the date of supply
— details of goods or services supplied
— the cost of the goods or services (including VAT), and
— the rate of VAT.

If you have imported goods, you must have the VAT copy of the import entry or other Customs document showing the amount of VAT that you have paid.

You must provide the originals of all invoices and import documents with your application. Copies are not acceptable.

6.5 Must I make the application myself?

It's up to you. You can prepare and send in your own application or have this done by an agent. Your agent will need either a Power of Attorney or letter of authority before acting for you, and receive money on your behalf.

The following is an example of the format of a letter of authority, which is acceptable to HMRC:

The following is an example of the format of a letter of authority, which is acceptable to Customs:

'I [name and address of claimant] hereby appoint [name and address of agent] to act on my behalf in connection with any application I make to the Commissioners of HM Revenue and Customs under the Value Added Tax Regulations 1995 as from time to time amended or replaced. Any repayment of VAT to which I am entitled pursuant to any such application made on my behalf by my above named agent shall be paid to [name and address of payee].

Date Signed [by the claimant]'

6.6 When will I be paid?

The refund will be made within six months of receiving a satisfactory application. If your application is in order, the invoices showing that you have paid the VAT will be returned to you as soon as your application is authorised for payment. If you have a query about an application you have made please contact the UK VAT Overseas Repayment Unit.

HM Revenue and Customs
VAT Overseas Repayment Unit
PO Box 34
Foyle House
Duncreggan Road
Londonderry
BT48 7AE

Phone: 03000 537 402
Fax: 03000 537 405
Email: enq.oru.ni@hmrc.gsi.gov.uk

Warning! If your application is found to be incorrect after the refund has been paid, any overpayment will normally be deducted from your next refund.

The UK authorities take a very serious view of false applications. Refunds obtained by means of a false application can be recovered, and penalties may be imposed.

6.7 Method of Payment

Payment can be made directly to your own bank through:

- SWIFT (Society for Worldwide Inter-Bank Financial Telecommunications)
- to a UK bank or
- by Payable Order in sterling directly to yourself or to your appointed agent.

As payment by SWIFT is faster, less expensive and more secure, you are encouraged to use this method of payment. If you opt for payment by SWIFT you must ensure that you provide the following information, together with a copy of a bank credit slip:

- bank account number
- currency of account
- bank identification code
- bank account name
- bank name
- bank address.

Payments to bank accounts will be made in £ Sterling. If you opt for payment by Payable Order you should cash it at your own bank. Payable Orders are computer generated and, unlike cheques, they are not signed. They should not be returned to HMRC for encashment.

6.8 Can my application be refused?

Yes. But we will tell you why we have refused it.

If you do not agree with the decision to refuse your application, you can:

- ask for the decision to be reviewed by an HMRC officer not previously involved in the matter, or
- appeal to an independent tribunal.

If you opt for a review you can still appeal to the tribunal after the review has finished.

If you want a review you should write to the address given in the decision letter within 30 days of the date of the letter, giving your reasons why you do not agree with the decision. We will not take any action to collect the disputed tax while the review of the decision is being carried out.

If you want to appeal to the tribunal you should send them your appeal within 30 days of the date of the decision letter.

You can find further information about appeals and reviews on the HMRC website

You can find out more about tribunals on the Tribunals Service website (www.tribunals.gov.uk/tax) or you can phone them on 0845 223 8080.

Commentary—*De Voil Indirect Tax Service* **V5.152.**

7 WHERE CAN I GET MORE INFORMATION ABOUT THE SCHEMES?

For general information about the schemes please check our website at www.hmrc.gov.uk or phone our VAT Helpline on 0300 200 3700 (callers from outside the UK should call +44 208 929 0152).

If you have a query about a application you have sent to the UK VAT Overseas Repayment Unit please contact:

HM Revenue and Customs
VAT Overseas Repayment Unit
PO Box 34
Foyle House
Duncreggan Road
Londonderry
BT48 7AE
Phone: 03000 537 402
Fax: 03000 537 405
Email: enq.oru.ni@hmrc.gsi.gov.uk

8 CONTACT DETAILS FOR TAX AUTHORITIES IN OTHER EU MEMBER STATES

The following link provides contact details for the Tax Authorities in other member states: http://ec.europa.eu/taxation_customs/resources/documents/taxation/vat/traders/vat_refunds/refund-_contact_details_table_en.pdf

NOTICE 725
THE SINGLE MARKET

January 2014

This notice cancels and replaces Notice 725 (June 2013).

Parts of this notice have force of law. The items concerned are flagged accordingly and the text appears in a box as follows.

Example of "force of law" text

Text shown in boxes has the force of law.

1 INTRODUCTION

1.1 What is this notice about?

This notice explains the way VAT is charged and accounted for on movements of goods within the EC Single Market and how businesses should account for VAT on goods they buy from other EC Member States.

1.2 What's changed?

This notice has been revised to reflect the following changes.

Paragraph 16.19 - VAT registration numbers in other Member States. Introduction of Croatia with effect from 1 July 2013 and changes to Ireland

1.3 Who should read it?

You should read this notice if you are involved in the movement of goods between EC member states or make supplies to diplomatic missions, consulates, international organisations or NATO visiting forces.

1.4 Legal status of this notice

Paragraphs 4.3, 4.4, 4.5, 5.2, 8.5, 17.10 have force of law. The items concerned are flagged accordingly and the text appears in a box as follows.

Example of "force of law" text

Text shown in boxes has the force of law.

Commentary—*De Voil Indirect Tax Service* **V3.1, V3.3, V4.3, V5.2.**

2 VAT IN THE EC

2.1 What is the Single Market?

The Single Market is a term that has applied since 1 January 1993 to trading between member states. This covers intra-EC supplies of goods.

Commentary—*De Voil Indirect Tax Service* **V1.210, V3.361–V3.398, V4.341–V4.361, V5.271–V5.276.**

2.2 Are goods arriving in the UK from other member states referred to as imports?

With the introduction of the Single Market, goods coming into the UK from other member states are no longer called imports, but are referred to as acquisitions or arrivals. The term "import" is only used for goods coming into the UK from countries outside the EC. For further information on imports, see Notice 702 Imports.

2.3 Are goods leaving the UK to go to other member states referred to as exports?

With the introduction of the Single Market, goods leaving the UK to go to other member states are no longer called exports, but are referred to as dispatches or removals. The term "export" is only used for goods leaving the UK to go to countries outside the EC. For information about exports, see Notice 703 VAT Export of goods from the United Kingdom.

2.4 VAT territory of the Single Market

From 1 May 2004, the VAT territory of the EC is made up of 28 member states. The following table shows the member states and their territories which are included or excluded for VAT purposes. For further information about the territory of the EC for Intrastat purposes, see Notice 60 "Intrastat General Guide". From 1 January 2007 Bulgaria and Romania will join the EC.

Member state	*including . . .*	*but excluding . . .*
Austria	Jungholtz and Mittelberg	
Belgium		
Bulgaria		
Croatia		
Cyprus	the British Sovereign Base Areas of Akrotiri and Dhekelia,	the United Nations buffer zone and the part of Cyprus to the north of the buffer zone, where the Republic of Cyprus does not exercise effective control.
Czech Republic		
Denmark		the Faroe Islands, and Greenland.
Estonia		
Hungary		the Åland Islands.
Finland		
France	Monaco,	Martinique, French Guiana, Guadeloupe, Reunion, and St Pierre and Miquelon.
Germany		the island of Heligoland, and Büsingen.
Greece		Mount Athos (also known as Agion Oros).

Ireland		
Italy		Campione d'Italia, the Italian Waters of Lake Lugano and Lvigno
Latvia		
Lithuania		
Luxembourg		
Malta		
Netherlands		Antilles
Poland		
Portugal	the Azores, and Madeira	
Romania		
Slovakia		
Slovenia		
Spain	the Balearic Islands,	the Canary Islands, Ceuta, and Melilla.
Sweden		
United Kingdom	the Isle of Man,	the Channel Islands, and Gibraltar.

Commentary—*De Voil Indirect Tax Service* **V1.213**.

2.5 Other areas not within the EC

Liechtenstein, the Vatican City, Andorra and San Marino are not within the EC for VAT purposes.

Commentary—*De Voil Indirect Tax Service* **V1.213**.

2.6 Why do I need to know the status of the territories?

You need to know which territories are included, or excluded, from a member state because—

– movements of goods between the UK and any of the above countries, or their *included* territories, are treated as intra-EC supplies for VAT purposes; whereas
– movements of goods between the UK and any of the *excluded* territories are treated as imported or exported goods for VAT purposes.

Commentary—*De Voil Indirect Tax Service* **V3.362, V4.301**.

2.7 How is VAT collected on goods moving between member states?

VAT on goods traded between Member States is not collected at the frontier. The way VAT is accounted for on intra-EC supplies largely depends on whether the recipient of the supply is registered for VAT in the Member State of arrival. For further information see sections 3 and 6. For these purposes movements of goods between Member States within the same legal entity (often referred to as a transfers of own goods) are treated as supplies (see section 9). Special rules apply in the case of natural gas and electricity, along with heat and cooling (see VAT Information Sheet 21/10 "Place of supply of natural gas and electricity (also heat and cooling)").

2.8 How is VAT collected on supplies of excise goods?

For information about the VAT treatment of supplies involving excise goods, see paragraph 15.4.

2.9 Trade statistics on goods moving between member states

The system for collecting statistics on the trade in goods between member states is known as Intrastat. All businesses carrying out trade with other member states must declare the totals of their sales and acquisitions on their VAT return. Traders whose EC trade exceeds a legally set threshold have to complete additional statistical information called Supplementary Declarations. Statistics are compiled from the Supplementary Declarations and information supplied on the VAT return. For further information on this, see section 18 and Notice 60 "Intrastat General Guide".

Commentary—*De Voil Indirect Tax Service* **V5.276**.

2.10 Are the VAT rules and Intrastat the same in other member states?

Yes. But there may be some small variations. If you want to check the position in another member state you should contact the relevant VAT authority (see paragraph 2.11).

2.11 VAT in other member states

Details of contact addresses and other useful information provided by the VAT authorities in other member states can be found on the following EC website:

europa.eu.int/comm/taxation_customs/taxation/vat/traders/vat_community/index_en.htm

2.12 Equivalent of "value added tax" & "VAT" in other member states

The equivalent in each member state is:

Member state	*VAT equivalent*
Austria	Mehrwertsteuer (Mwst) Umsatzsteuer (Umst)
Belgium	Belasting over de Toegevoegde Waarde (BTW) Taxe sur la Valeur Ajoutée (TVA)
Bulgaria	*Данък Добавена Стойност* or Данък Добавена Стойност
Croatia	PDV Id. Broj (PDV-1D)
Cyprus	Φόρος ΠροστιΘέμενης Αξίας (ΦΠΑ)
Czech Republic	Daň z přidané hodnoty (DPH)
Denmark	Omsaetningafgift
Estonia	Käibemaks
Finland	Arvonlisavero (ALV)
France	Taxe sur la Valeur Ajoutée (TVA)
Germany	Mehrwertsteuer (Mwst), Umsatzsteuer (Umst)
Greece	Arithmos Forologikou Mitroou (FPA)
Hungary	Általános Forgalmi Adó (ÁFA)
Ireland	Value Added Tax
Italy	Imposta sul valore Aggiunto (IVA)
Latvia	Pievienotās vértîbas nodoklis
Lithuania	Pridetines vertes mokestis (PVM)
Luxembourg	Taxe sur la Valeur Ajoutée (TVA)
Malta	Value Added Tax
Netherlands	Omzetbelasting (OB) Belasting over de Toegevoegde Waarde (BTW)
Poland	Podatek od towarów i uslug
Portugal	Imposto sobre o Valor Acrescentado (IVA)
Romania	Tăxa pe valoarea adăugată
Slovakia	Daň z přidanej hodnoty (DPH)
Slovenia	Davek na dodano vrednost (DDV)
Spain	Impuesto sobre el Valor Anadidio (IVA)
Sweden	Mervardeskatt (MOMS)

2.13 Normal rules for claiming input tax

The amount you can reclaim as input tax is subject to the "normal rules". These include the evidence you must obtain and any additional partial exemption calculations you are required to carryout. For further information about this see dealing with input tax in Notice 700 "The VAT Guide" and Notice 706 "Partial Exemption".

3 SUPPLIES TO CUSTOMERS REGISTERED FOR VAT IN ANOTHER MEMBER STATE

3.1 How is VAT accounted for?

The normal VAT treatment of goods supplied between VAT-registered traders in different member states is as follows—

- the supply in the member state of dispatch is zero-rated (how this applies in the UK is explained in more detail in section 4), and
- VAT is due on the acquisition of the goods in the member state of arrival and is accounted for by the customer on their VAT return at the rate in force in that member state (how this applies in the UK is explained in more detail in section 7).

Commentary—*De Voil Indirect Tax Service* **V3.137, V4.341–V4.361, V5.271–V5.276**.

3.2 Special rules

There are various special rules that apply in particular circumstances. These are explained in the following sections of this notice—

Section	*Subject*
9	Transfers of own goods
10	Temporary movements of goods
11	Installed or assembled goods
12	Intra-EC processing, repair, etc
13	Triangulation
14	Supplies to diplomatic missions, consulates, international organisations and NATO visiting forces
15	Other intra-EC movements of goods

3.3 Supplies to the Isle of Man and the Channel Islands

Goods sent to the Isle of Man from the UK are treated as domestic supplies for VAT purposes. Consequently the rules described in this notice do not apply and VAT must be charged at the appropriate UK rate in the normal way. On the other hand, goods sent to the Channel Islands are treated as exports from the EC for VAT purposes. For further information about exports, see Notice 703 "Export of goods from the United Kingdom".

3.4 Time of supply (tax point) for goods supplied to other member states

The tax point for a supply of goods to a VAT registered customer in another member state is the earlier of either—

- the fifteenth day of the month following the one in which you send the goods to your customer (or your customer takes them away); or
- the date you issue a VAT invoice for the supply.

3.5 Why do I need to know the tax point for my supplies?

You should use the tax point as the reference date for including the supplies on your VAT return, EC Sales Lists and, normally, your Intrastat Supplementary Declarations.

However, if it is more convenient, you may use the calendar month during which the goods arrive in, or are dispatched from the UK for your Intrastat Supplementary Declaration, see Notice 60 "Intrastat General Guide".

3.6 Payments received in advance of invoicing or delivery

The receipt of a payment in these circumstances does not create a tax point for your intra-EC supply. However, you must issue a VAT invoice to your customer for the amount paid to you (see paragraph 16.9) and the date of issue of the VAT invoice will be the tax point.

Where you issue a series of invoices relating to the same supply of goods, the time limit for obtaining valid evidence of removal begins from the date of the final invoice (see paragraph 4.4).

3.7 Reporting requirements

Type of movement	*VAT return*	*EC Sales List (see section 17)*	*Supplementary declaration (see section 18)*
Goods supplied to VAT registered customers in other member states where zero-rating conditions in paragraph 4.3 are met.[1]	*Boxes 6 and 8* – value of supply	Yes—customer's VAT number and value of supply	Yes—as a dispatch (value of supply).
Goods supplied to customers in other member states if the zero-rating conditions in paragraph 4.3 are not met.[2]	*Box 1* – output tax* *and 6* – value of supply. (*see also paragraph 16.10 in cases where the time limits for removal and obtaining evidence are not met)	No	Yes—as a dispatch. See also paragraphs 0 and 6.17 for distance sales and Notice 60 "Intrastat General Guide".

1 Supply may be zero-rated.
2 UK VAT charged at appropriate rate. (But see paragraph 6.4 about distance selling).

3.8 What happens if goods are lost, destroyed, or stolen?

As the supplier your liability to account for VAT depends on the circumstances.

Where goods are lost, destroyed or stolen and this occurs . . .	*then . . .*
in the UK before you have supplied them (eg whilst in storage awaiting delivery or collection),	if there has been no supply, no VAT is due.
while being transported in the UK by either you or your customer	VAT is due *unless* you hold evidence of loss, destruction or theft (eg an insurance claim or police investigation).

while being transported outside the UK by either you or your customer	the goods may continue to be zero-rated (see paragraph 4.3) *provided* you have valid proof of removal of the goods from the UK and the VAT registration number of your customer. (NB Your customer may still be liable to account for acquisition tax. Also there may be additional VAT liabilities if the loss, destruction or theft occurs en route through a member state. In that event you should check on the position with the VAT authority in the member state concerned – see paragraph 2.11).

4 ZERO-RATING OF SUPPLIES TO VAT REGISTERED CUSTOMERS IN ANOTHER MEMBER STATE – GENERAL REQUIREMENTS

Commentary—*De Voil Indirect Tax Service* **V4.341–361**.

4.1 EC law covered by this section

Article 28C(A) of the EC Sixth Directive (77/388/EEC) states that member states shall exempt certain supplies subject to conditions laid down for the purpose of ensuring the correct and straightforward application of such exemptions (zero-rating) and preventing any evasion, avoidance or abuse. The UK uses the term "zero-rating" rather than "exemption" used in EC law to avoid confusion with the use of exemption elsewhere in UK law.

4.2 UK law on removals

The UK VAT law relating to the zero-rating of removals of goods for VAT purposes can be found in VATA 1994 ss 30(8), 30(10) and the VAT Regulations 1995 reg 134.

4.3 When can a supply of goods be zero-rated?

The text in this box has the force of law

A supply from the UK to a customer in another EC member state is liable to the zero rate where—

– you obtain and show on your VAT sales invoice your customer's EC VAT registration number, including the two-letter country prefix code; and
– the goods are sent or transported out of the UK to a destination in another EC member state; and
– you obtain and keep valid commercial evidence that the goods have been removed from the UK within the time limits set out at paragraph 4.4.

You must not zero-rate a sale, even if the goods are subsequently removed to another member state, if you—

– supply the goods to a UK VAT registered customer (unless that customer is also registered for VAT in another member state. In such cases they must provide their EC VAT registration number and the goods must be removed to another EC member state);
– deliver to, or allow the goods to be collected by, a UK customer at a UK address; or
– allow the goods to be used in the UK in the period between supply and removal, except where specifically authorised to do so.

Paragraph 4.9 covers the checks that you must undertake to ensure that your customer's EC VAT number is valid.

Commentary—*De Voil Indirect Tax Service* **V4.305–V4.306**.
Simon's Tax Cases—*R (on the application of Corkteck Ltd) v R&C Comrs* [2009] STC 1681*; *N2J v R&C Comrs* [2009] STC 2193*.

4.4 Time limits for removal of goods and obtaining evidence of removal

The text in this box has the force of law

In all cases the time limits for removing the goods and obtaining valid evidence of removal will begin from the time of supply. For goods removed to another EC member state the time limits are as follows—

— three months (including supplies of goods involved in groupage or consolidation prior to removal); or
— six months for supplies of goods involved in processing or incorporation prior to removal.

4.5 Goods removed to customers in other member states after processing or incorporation

The text in this box has the force of law

When you make a supply of goods to a VAT registered customer in another member state, but have to deliver them to a third person in the UK who is also making a taxable supply of goods or services to that customer, you can zero-rate the supply provided—

– you obtain and show on your VAT sales invoice your customer's EC VAT registration number, including the two-letter country prefix code;
– the goods are only being delivered and *not* supplied to the third person in the UK;
– no use is made of the goods other than for processing or incorporation into other goods for removal; and
– you obtain and keep valid commercial evidence that the goods have been removed from the UK within the time limits set out at paragraph 4.4;

and your records show—

– the name, address and VAT number of the customer in the EC;
– the invoice number and date;
– the description, quantity and value of the goods;
– the name and address of the third person in the UK to whom the goods were delivered;
– the date by which the goods must be removed;
– proof of removal obtained from the person responsible for transporting the goods out of the UK; and
– the date the goods were actually removed from the UK.

Your records must be able to show that the goods you supplied have been processed or incorporated into the goods removed from the UK.

In cases where the third person is not in the UK but in another EC member state, the same conditions will generally apply to allow you to zero-rate your supply.

4.6 What should I do if I cannot meet all the conditions in paragraphs 4.3, 4.4 or 4.5?

If you cannot obtain and show a valid EC VAT registration number on your sales invoice you must charge and account for tax in the UK at the appropriate UK rate.

If the goods are not removed or you do not have the evidence of removal within the time limits you must account for VAT as described in paragraph 16.10. No VAT is due on goods which would normally be zero rated when supplied in the UK. You may wish to consider taking a deposit for the VAT (see paragraph 5.5) if you have reason to doubt that the goods will be removed. Extra caution may be advisable if your customer:

– is not previously known to you;
– arranges to collect and transport the goods, or their transport arrives without advance correspondence or notice;
– pays in cash; or

– purchases types or quantities of goods inconsistent with their normal commercial practice.

4.7 How can I obtain my EC customer's VAT registration number?

You should carry out normal commercial checks such as bank and trade credit worthiness references before you start making supplies to an EC customer. As part of these checks you should ask your customer to supply you with their EC VAT number. We strongly recommend that you obtain confirmation of their EC VAT registration number in writing. You should retain the letter or advice received from your customer for future reference because one of the conditions for zero-rating your supply, is that you hold a valid EC VAT number for your customer. For further information on normal commercial checks, please see section 6 of Notice 726. Joint and several liability for unpaid VAT

4.8 How can I make sure my EC customers give me their VAT registration numbers?

When you write to your customer, ask them to provide you with the number which has been allocated to them for intra-EC trade. In certain countries for example. Spain and Italy, businesses are required to register their VAT number for Intra -EC use and if they don't do this, the number will show as invalid on the Europa website.(see below). If they do not supply you with their VAT number then you are obliged to charge UK VAT on any supplies of goods. If you are supplying services and your customer cannot supply you with a VAT number then you must make sure you have sufficient evidence to show that your supply is to a business in order to zero rate the supply.

4.9 Checking the validity of an EC customer's VAT registration number

You should check the validity of the number you have been given by making sure it follows the format at paragraph 16.19. Further checks on the validity of a customer's number should be made using the Europa website (ec.europa.eu/taxation_customs/taxation/vat/traders/vat_number/index_en.htm).

All Member States share these arrangements and businesses in other Member States can verify a UK VAT registration number in the same way.

When making an enquiry on the Europa website you must identify yourself by entering your own VAT registration number and print out a record of the date and time that the enquiry was made and the result of the enquiry. If it later turns out that the customer's number was invalid, for example. the tax authorities database was not up to date, you will be able to rely on the validation record as one element to demonstrate your good faith as a compliant business and, in the UK, to justify why you should not be held jointly and severally liable for any VAT fraud and revenue losses which occur.

You must also regularly check your EC customer's VAT registration number to make sure that the details are still valid and that the number has not been recently deregistered.

Alternatively you can contact the VAT Helpline on 0300 200 3700 to validate your customer's VAT registration number and to verify that the name and address is correct.

4.10 Will I have to account for VAT if my customer's VAT number turns out to be invalid?

No. But only if you have genuinely done everything you can to check the validity of the VAT number, can demonstrate you have done so, have taken heed of any indications that something might be wrong and have no other reason to suspect the VAT number is invalid.

4.11 What is meant by "reasonable steps"?

HMRC does not expect you to go beyond what is reasonable but will be seeking to identify what actions you took to check the validity of your customer's EU VAT registration number. This will focus on the due diligence checks you undertook and, most importantly, the actions taken by you in response to the results of those checks.

We would consider "reasonable steps" to be, you genuinely doing everything you can to check the integrity of the VAT registration number, being able to demonstrate you have done so and taking heed of any indications that the number may be invalid.

Some examples of *not* having taken "reasonable steps" would be

- using a VAT number that does not conform to the published format for your customer's Member State as shown in paragraph 16.19, or
- using a VAT number that you have not regularly checked using the Europa website or with HMRC
- using a VAT number which you have already been informed is invalid, or
- using a VAT number which you know does not belong to your customer.

4.12 Will VAT be chargeable if reasonable steps are not considered to have been taken?

Yes. You will have to account for VAT at the appropriate UK rate.

4.13 Intra-EC supplies of freight containers

For information about the conditions for zero-rating the sale of a container to a VAT registered customer in another member state, see Notice 703/1 "Supply of freight containers for export or removal from the United Kingdom".

5 ZERO-RATING OF SUPPLIES TO VAT REGISTERED CUSTOMERS IN ANOTHER MEMBER STATE – EVIDENCE OF REMOVAL

Commentary—*De Voil Indirect Tax Service* **V4.343**.

5.1 Evidence of removal

A combination of these documents must be used to provide clear evidence that a supply has taken place, and the goods have been removed from the UK—

- the customer's order (including customer's name, VAT number and delivery address for the goods);
- inter-company correspondence;
- copy sales invoice (including a description of the goods, an invoice number and customer's EC VAT number etc.);
- advice note;
- packing list;
- commercial transport document(s) from the carrier responsible for removing the goods from the UK, for example an International Consignment Note (CMR) fully completed by the consignor, the haulier and signed by receiving consignee;
- details of insurance or freight charges;
- bank statements as evidence of payment;
- receipted copy of the consignment note as evidence of receipt of goods abroad;
- any other documents relevant to the removal of the goods in question which you would normally obtain in the course of your intra-EC business.

Photocopy certificates of shipment or other transport documents are not normally acceptable as evidence of removal unless authenticated with an original stamp and dated by an authorised official of the issuing office.

5.2 What must be shown on documents used as proof of removal?

The text in this box has the force of law

The documents you use as proof of removal must clearly identify the following—

- the supplier;
- the consignor (where different from the supplier);
- the customer;
- the goods;
- an accurate value;
- the mode of transport and route of movement of the goods; and
- the EC destination.

Vague descriptions of goods, quantities or values are not acceptable. For instance, "various electrical goods" must not be used when the correct description is "2000 mobile phones (Make ABC and Model Number XYZ2000)". An accurate value, for example, £50,000 must be shown and not excluded or replaced by a lower or higher amount.

If the evidence is found to be unsatisfactory *you* as the supplier could become *liable* for the VAT due.

5.3 Evidence of removal of goods to the Republic of Ireland across the Irish Land Boundary

The evidence you obtain must clearly show that the goods have left the UK. The types of documentary evidence required are explained in paragraphs 5.1 and 5.2. See also paragraph 5.5 for advice when goods are collected by your customer. Depending on the circumstances of the removal, we recommend that you obtain the following types of evidence to meet the conditions for zero-rating—

If the goods are...	*then commercial evidence should include...*
removed by road by an independent carrier	a copy of the carrier's invoice or consignment note, supported by evidence that the goods have been delivered to a destination in the Republic of Ireland (eg a receipted copy of the consignment note).
removed by rail	the consignor's copy of the consignment note signed by the railway official accepting the goods for delivery to your customer.
removed in your own transport	a copy of the delivery note showing your customer's name, address, EC VAT number and actual delivery address in the Republic of Ireland if different, and a signature of your customer, or their authorised representative, confirming receipt of the goods.
collected by your customer or their authorised representative	a written order completed by your customer, which shows their name, address, EC VAT number, the name of the authorised representative collecting the goods, the address in the Republic of Ireland where the goods are to be delivered, the vehicle registration number of the transport used, and a signature of your customer, or their authorised representative, confirming receipt of the goods.

Where you sell a motor vehicle, which is collected by your customer or their representative, it may be difficult to obtain satisfactory evidence of removal from the UK. In these circumstances, a copy of the vehicle registration document issued by the authorities in the Republic of Ireland will normally provide satisfactory evidence of removal if supported by other evidence described above and in paragraph 5.1.

5.4 What if I deliver the goods to my customer in another EC member state?

In addition to the examples of acceptable documents relating to the sale listed in paragraph 5.1, travel tickets can also be used to demonstrate that an intra-EC journey took place for the purpose of removing the goods from the UK.

5.5 What if my customer collects the goods or arranges for their collection and removal from the UK?

If your VAT registered EC customer is arranging removal of the goods from the UK it can be difficult for you as the supplier to obtain adequate proof of removal as the carrier is contracted to your EC customer. For this type of transaction the standard of evidence required to substantiate VAT zero-rating is high.

Before zero-rating the supply you must ascertain what evidence of removal of the goods from the UK will be provided. You should consider taking a deposit equivalent to the amount of VAT you would have to account for if you do not hold satisfactory evidence of the removal of the goods from the UK. The deposit can be refunded when you obtain evidence that proves the goods were removed within the appropriate time limits.

Evidence must show that the goods you supplied have left the UK. Copies of transport documents alone will not be sufficient. Information held must identify the date and route of the movement of goods and the mode of transport involved. It should include the following:

Item	*Description*
1	Written order from your customer which shows their name, address and EC VAT number and the address where the goods are to be delivered.
2	Copy sales invoice showing customer's name, EC VAT number, a description of the goods and an invoice number.
3	Date of departure of goods from your premises and from the UK.
4	Name and address of the haulier collecting the goods.
5	Registration number of the vehicle collecting the goods and the name and signature of the driver and, where the goods are to be taken out of the UK by a different haulier or vehicle, the name and address of that haulier, that vehicle registration number and a signature for the goods.
6	Route, for example, Channel Tunnel, port of exit.
7	Copy of travel tickets.
8	Name of ferry or shipping company and date of sailing or airway number and airport.
9	Trailer number (if applicable).
10	Full container number (if applicable).
11	Name and address for consolidation, groupage, or processing (if applicable).

5.6 How long must I retain evidence of removal?

You must make sure that the proof of removal is—

- retained for six years; and
- made readily available so that any VAT assurance officer is able to substantiate the zero-rating of your removals.

5.7 Can I use an agent?

You, as the supplier of the goods, or your customer can appoint a freight forwarder, shipping company, airline or other person to handle your intra-EC supplies and produce the necessary evidence of removal.

However, you remain legally responsible for ensuring that the conditions for zero-rating supplies of goods to other EC member states, as set out in paragraphs 4.3, 4.4 and 4.5, are met. This includes obtaining and holding evidence of removal of the goods from the UK.

5.8 Groupage or consolidation transactions

If you use a freight forwarder, consignments (often coming from several consignors) may be aggregated into one load, known as groupage or consolidation cargo. The freight forwarder must keep copies of the original bill of lading, sea-waybill or air-waybill, and all consignments in the load must be shown on the container or vehicle manifest. You will be issued with a certificate of shipment by the freight forwarder, often supported by an authenticated photocopy of the original bill of lading, a sea-waybill or a house air-waybill. Where such consignments are being removed, the forwarder may be shown as the consignor in the shipping documents.

(a) Certificate of shipment

Certificates of shipment are usually produced by packers and consolidators involved in road, rail and sea groupage consignments when they themselves receive only a single authenticated transport document from the carrier. It is an important document, which should be sent to you as soon as the goods have been removed from the UK.

The certificate of shipment must be an original and authenticated by an official of the issuing company unless it is computer produced, on a once-only basis, as a by-product of the issuing company's accounting system. A properly completed certificate of shipment will help you to meet the evidential requirements described in paragraph 5.1.

(b) What information must be shown?

Although the certificate of shipment can be in any format, it must be an original and will usually contain the following information—

- the name and address of the issuing company;
- a unique reference number or issuer's file reference;
- the name of the supplier of the goods (and VAT number if known);
- the place, port or airport of loading;
- the place, port or airport of shipment;
- the name of the ship or the aircraft flight prefix and number;
- the date of sailing or flight;
- the customer's name;
- the destination of the goods;
- a full description of the goods removed to another member state (including quantity, weight and value);
- the number of packages;
- the supplier's invoice number and date if known;
- the bill of lading or air-waybill number (if applicable);
- the identifying number of the vehicle, container or railway wagon.

5.9 Postal services

Goods sent by post may be zero-rated if they are sent directly to your customer registered for VAT in another EC member state, and you hold the necessary evidence of posting. The receipted forms described in the table below, plus the Parcelforce Worldwide statement of account or parcel manifest listing each parcel or multi-parcel, will provide evidence of removal.

Method of posting	*Evidence required*
Letter post or airmail	A fully completed certificate of posting form presented with the goods, and stamped by the Post Office. Acceptable forms are: —Form C&E 132 for single or multiple packages taken to the Post Office. Blank forms may be obtained from our website go to, www.hmrc.gov.uk or by phoning the VAT Helpline on 0300 200 3700. —Form P326 available from the Post Office and used for single packages taken to the Post Office; or —a Certificate of Posting for International Mail Only, or a Royal Mail Collection Manifest, available from a Royal Mail sales advisor, for use by customers using their Business Collections Service, where the Royal Mail collection driver signs the certificate. Further information on Royal Mail international services is available on their website at www.royalmail.com
Parcels	Parcelforce Worldwide operates a range of international parcel services. If you use any of these services you will be provided with: —a service specific barcoded label; —a customs export declaration (for non-EC destinations only); —a copy of the Parcelforce Worldwide conditions of carriage; and —a printed receipt, which is your proof of shipment for all destinations.

An individual barcode label must be affixed to every parcel. You do not need to complete the customs export declaration for goods being sent to another EC member state.

If you arrange for the parcel to be collected from your premises the collecting driver will sign your printed receipt. This is your proof of shipment for EC destinations.

If the parcel is taken to a Post Office, the counter clerk will provide you with a printed proof of shipment from the Post Office SmartPost system. This will show the overseas delivery address, date of dispatch and unique consignment number. You should keep this printed proof of shipment as your evidence of removal.

In addition to the individual parcel declarations described above, account customers of Parcelforce Worldwide have two further potential sources of information listing multiple parcel dispatches. These are—

—Worldwide Dispatch manager (WDM) – online users can print a manifest which lists all dispatched parcels; and

—a Statement of Account.

All of the individual parcel declarations, plus either the manifest or the statement of account listing each dispatch will provide proof of removal for VAT purposes. You can find further information on Parcelforce Worldwide International services on their website at www.parcelforce.com

5.10 Couriers and fast parcel services

Courier and fast parcel operators specialise in the shipment of goods to overseas destinations within guaranteed timescales.

(a) Operators who do not issue separate certificates of shipment

Most courier and fast parcel operators do not issue separate certificates of shipment. The invoice for moving goods from the UK, which bears details of the unique airway bill numbers for each shipment, represents normal commercial evidence of removal. In addition, many express companies are able to offer a track and trace service via their websites where the movement of goods can be traced through to the final destination. This information can be printed and also be used to confirm removal from the UK.

(b) Operators who use the system based upon a Dispatch Pack

A few companies still use a documentary system based upon a Dispatch Pack containing accounting data, a Customs export declaration and receipt copies of the relevant house airway bill or consignment note. These packs are issued to customers to complete for each removal from the UK.

An export declaration does not need to be completed for goods being sent to another EC member state but a Dispatch Pack must be completed for each overseas address and consignee. The driver collecting the parcels will endorse the receipt copy and return it to the consignor. This, plus the statement of account listing each removal, will provide evidence of removal from the UK.

(c) Use of more than one courier/fast parcel company

Due to the complexities of the movement of goods within the courier/fast parcel environment, there is often more than one company involved in the handling and ultimate removal of the goods. Ultimately, you as the UK supplier may not be certain as to which courier/fast parcel company has removed the goods. If you are aware that this may happen you will need to establish what proof of removal you will receive from the company to whom you give your goods. The proof available is described in (a) and (b) above.

(d) Overseas customer arranging the removal by courier

If your EC customer arranges for the goods to be removed by courier you should ascertain what proof of removal they will be providing to allow you to zero-rate the supply. You should consider taking a deposit equivalent to the amount of VAT you would have to account for if you do not hold satisfactory evidence of the removal of the goods from the UK. The deposit can be refunded when you obtain evidence that proves the goods were removed within the appropriate time limits.

6 SUPPLIES TO CUSTOMERS (INCLUDING PRIVATE INDIVIDUALS) WHO ARE NOT REGISTERED FOR VAT

6.1 How is VAT accounted for?

For supplies to unregistered customers, or private individuals, VAT is normally accounted for by the supplier as a domestic supply in the member state from which the goods are dispatched.

Commentary—*De Voil Indirect Tax Service* **V2.171, V3.172, V4.352, V5.271–V5.276**.

6.2 Tax point for supplies where UK VAT is chargeable

As a domestic supply, liable to UK VAT, the normal tax point rules apply. For further information about the normal rules, see the sections dealing with time of supply in Notice 700 "The VAT Guide".

6.3 Special arrangements for supplies of goods to private individuals or non-registered persons

Special arrangements apply to the following—

— supplies to non-registered persons of new means of transport including boats, aircraft and motor vehicles (for further information, see Notice 728 "New means of transport");
— supplies of excise goods for private purposes (for further information see section 15.4);
— distance sales (for further information see paragraph 6.4 and Notice 700/1 "Should I be registered for VAT?"); and
— purchases by exempt bodies and non-taxable organisations (for further information about how this can make the purchaser liable to register for VAT, see Notice 700/1 "Should I be registered for VAT?").

6.4 Distance selling

Distance selling occurs when a taxable person in one member state supplies and delivers goods to a customer in another member state who is not registered or liable to be registered for VAT. These customers are known as non-taxable persons and will include private individuals, public bodies, charities and businesses which are not VAT registered because their turnover is below the registration threshold or whose activities are entirely exempt. The most common examples of distance sales are goods supplied by mail order or ordered over the internet.

6.5 How do I treat distance sales from the UK to other member states?

(a) Accounting for VAT

If you are registered for VAT in the UK and make distance sales to customers in another EC member state, you should charge UK VAT until—

– the value of your supplies in a calendar year exceed the distance selling threshold in that country; or
– you exercise the option described in paragraph 6.10.

Once the value of your distance sales exceeds this threshold, you will be liable to register and account for VAT in that member state.

(b) Intrastat

If you trade above the UK Intrastat threshold you must report your distance sales to all non-taxable persons on your Intrastat Supplementary Declaration, even when your distance sales from the UK are below the distance selling threshold in the member state of arrival. For further information, see Notice 60 "Intrastat General Guide".

6.6 What is the distance selling threshold for each member state?

Each member state is responsible for setting its own threshold, which is set in its own currency. The level of the threshold in a particular member state can be found on the website mentioned at paragraph 2.11 or by contacting the VAT authority in the member state concerned.

6.7 Distance sales of excise goods

If you make any distance sales of excise goods to another EC member state you will be required to register and account for VAT in that member state, irrespective of the value involved.

6.8 Should I keep a record of my distance sales to each member state?

You must keep a separate record of your distance sales to each member state. This will allow you to monitor any liability to register for VAT there.

6.9 Will I be required to appoint someone to act on my behalf in another member state?

If you are required to register in another member state, you may need to appoint someone to act on your behalf there. You should check this with the relevant VAT authority (see paragraph 2.11). Alternatively, you may be able to register personally and deal with your tax obligations yourself.

6.10 Opting to account for VAT on supplies in the member state to which the goods are sent

If your distance sales are below the threshold you may, nevertheless, opt to register and account for VAT in the member state of destination of the goods. But this does mean you will have to account for VAT on all supplies below the distance selling threshold in that member state.

6.11 What should I do to exercise this option?

If you decide to exercise the option you must do the following:

Step	*Action*
1	Notify HMRC by writing to the appropriate written enquiries team details of which can be found on our website go to www.hmrc.gov.uk or by phoning the VAT Helpline on 0300 200 3700.
2	Contact the VAT authority for the member state to which the goods are supplied. (You will need to do this at least 30 days before making the first supply you intend to be covered by the option and must register from that date. You will also need to provide them with written evidence that you have informed HMRC in the UK).

You will then be subject to, and must comply with, the VAT rules in that member state.

6.12 How will this affect my UK VAT registration?

Once you have taken up the option to account for VAT in another member state, you will no longer charge UK VAT.

6.13 When can I cancel the option?

You will normally be required to remain registered in that Member State for at least two calendar years from the date of the first supply following registration there. After this time, if the value of your supplies remains below the threshold and you decide to cancel your option, you must notify HMRC by writing to the appropriate written enquiries team. Details can be found on our website go to, www.hmrc.gov.uk or by phoning the VAT Helpline on 0300 200 3700. This should not be less than 30 days before the date of the first supply you intend to make after the cancellation.

6.14 What should I do if I am required to register for VAT in another member state?

The registration requirements in each member state vary. If you are required to register for VAT in another member state, you must notify the appropriate VAT authority (see paragraph 2.11). You are responsible for ensuring that you register at the correct time and that you account for tax to the correct VAT authority.

6.15 How do the distance selling rules apply to group registrations?

Group treatment is a facility which allows two or more corporate bodies controlled by the same person, to account for VAT as a single VAT registration. Although each VAT group member is, and remains, a legal entity in its own right, it is treated as a single taxable person in the UK. However, UK VAT groups are not recognised in other member states.

Group members must therefore individually monitor the value of their own distance sales to each member state. Where the value of sales in a calendar year exceeds a member state's distance selling threshold, that group member will be liable to register for VAT there in its own right.

A group member is entitled to exercise the option described at paragraph 6.10.

6.16 What should I do if I am making distance sales to the UK?

If you make distance sales to the UK, and the value of these sales in a calendar year exceeds the UK threshold of £70,000, you will be liable to register for VAT in the UK. You must then charge and account for UK VAT on your sales. However, any supplies involving goods subject to excise duty are not subject to the threshold and you must register for VAT immediately you make a supply of this kind. You can also register in the UK under the option described in paragraph 6.10.

For more information about registering for VAT in the UK for distance sales, see Notice 700/1 "Should I be registered for VAT?"

6.17 Reporting requirements

Type of movement	*VAT return*	*EC Sales List (see Section 17)*	*Supplementary Declaration (see Section 18)*	*Notes*
Distance sales from UK below threshold in member state of arrival.	*Box 1* – output tax. *Box 6* – value of supply.	No.	Yes – as a dispatch (use VAT exclusive value). (See Notice 60 "Intrastat General Guide")	Treated as a UK domestic supply for VAT purposes, but must still be declared on your Supplementary Declaration.
Distance sales from UK on or above threshold in the member state of arrival (or where option to register there has been exercised – see paragraph 6.10).	*Boxes 6 and 8* – value of supply.	No.	Yes – as a dispatch (value of supply).	Although VAT is chargeable on the supply in the member state of the arrival, the value must still be declared on your UK VAT return and Supplementary Declaration.

Distance sales to UK above UK distance selling threshold (or where option to register here has been exercised – see paragraph 6.16).	*Box 1* – output tax. *Box 6* – value of supply.	No.	Yes – as an arrival (value of supply) if the Intrastat threshold for arrivals has been exceeded. (See Notice 60 "Intrastat General Guide") for details of the current Intrastat threshold.)	Treated as a supply in UK and supplier required to register here.
Distance sales to UK below UK distance selling threshold.	No.	No.	No.	No.

7 UK ACQUISITION OF GOODS FROM ANOTHER MEMBER STATE

Commentary—*De Voil Indirect Tax Service* **V3.361–V3.398, V5.271–V5.276.**

7.1 What is an acquisition?

An acquisition in the UK occurs where

- there is an intra-EC movement of goods to the UK;
- the goods are received here by a VAT registered trader; and
- the supplier is registered for VAT in the member state of departure.

In which case the recipient is required to account for VAT on the goods acquired in the UK.

7.2 How do I account for acquisition tax in the UK?

You must account for any tax due on your VAT return for the period in which the tax point occurs (see paragraph 7.3) and you may treat this as input tax on the same VAT return subject to the normal rules (see paragraph 2.13).

7.3 Time of acquisition

The time of acquisition is the earlier of either—

- the 15th day of the month following the one in which the goods were sent to you; or
- the date your supplier issued their invoice to you.

7.4 Rate of VAT on acquisitions in the UK

Acquisitions are liable at the same rate as domestic supplies of identical goods in the UK. So, for example, no tax is due on acquisitions of goods which are currently zero-rated in the UK.

7.5 Do I account for acquisition tax if I make a part or full payment for the goods?

No, part or full payment for an intra-EC supply of goods does not create a tax point for the acquisition.

7.6 What should I do if my supplier sends me an invoice for the amount I paid?

You should account for the acquisition tax, provided the date of issue of the invoice is earlier than the 15th day of the month following the one in which the goods were sent to you.

7.7 Is acquisition tax always due where the goods are received?

The VAT on an acquisition is always due in the member state where the goods are received. However, there is a "fallback" provision that applies where the VAT registration number quoted to the supplier to secure zero rating has been issued in a different member state. In that event the acquisition tax must be accounted for in the member state of registration, but the customer also remains liable to account for acquisition VAT in the member state to which the goods have been sent.

7.8 Do I have to account for acquisition tax whenever I give my UK VAT number to an EC supplier?

You are liable to account for acquisition tax in the UK unless you can demonstrate that you have already accounted for acquisition VAT in the member state to which the goods were dispatched where this is different (see paragraph 7.7 above).

7.9 Refund of UK acquisition tax if VAT is also accounted for in the member state of arrival

You can obtain a refund of any UK acquisition tax accounted for in the circumstances described in paragraph 7.8. But you should only do this where you have not claimed, or have been unable to claim, full input tax credit for that acquisition.

7.10 Changes to your VAT registration

(a) Group registrations

If you are part of a VAT group, you must notify the National Registration Service in writing of any changes to the membership of the group. The address for this can be found on our website at www.hmrc.gov.uk

It is in your own interests to do this promptly, as it allows us to make sure that our records are kept up to date at all times. We can then reply correctly and without delay to any enquiries made about your registration number.

(b) Other registrations

Remember, if you acquire goods from other member states you will need to inform your EC suppliers of any changes to your VAT registration number. Otherwise they will have to charge you VAT on their supplies.

7.11 Reporting requirements

Type of movement	*VAT return*	*EC Sales List (see Section 17)*	*Supplementary Declaration (see Section 18)*	*Notes*
Acquisitions of goods from VAT registered suppliers in other EC member states.	*Box 2* – acquisition VAT for goods positive-rated in UK. *Box 4* – input tax subject to normal rules (see paragraph 2.13) *Boxes 7 & 9* – value of acquisition.	No.	Yes – as an arrival (value of supply).	You must provide your EC supplier with your VAT number to quote on the sales invoice.

8 TAX VALUE OF ACQUISITIONS

8.1 Calculating the amount of tax due on an acquisition

The amount of tax due on an acquisition is the tax value multiplied by the appropriate VAT rate.

Commentary—*De Voil Indirect Tax Service* **V3.390–V3.392**.

8.2 What is the tax value of an acquisition?

This is, usually, what you pay for the goods, it is also called the "consideration".

Commentary—*De Voil Indirect Tax Service* **V3.390**.

8.3 What is consideration?

Consideration is any form of payment in money or in kind, including anything which is itself a supply. The consideration includes any payment which you make to cover your supplier's costs in making the supply, such as packing, transport or insurance for which they are responsible under their contract with you.

8.4 Establishing the tax value of an acquisition

The tax value of your acquisition can be established as follows:

Where . . .	*then the tax value of your acquisition is . . .*
the consideration is wholly in money,	the amount paid.
the consideration is non-monetary, for example the supply is made in return for payment in goods or services, or is monetary and non-monetary,	the monetary equivalent of the consideration calculated by reference to the price, excluding VAT, which you would have to pay if the consideration were monetary.
the consideration involves a discounted amount and you pay the discounted amount,	based on the discounted amount.
the consideration includes the offer of a conditional discount which is dependent upon some future event, for example on condition that you buy more from your supplier, or make payment within a specified period of time,	based on the full amount paid. If you later earn the discount, the tax value is reduced and you can adjust the amount of tax accounted for (but you should only do this where you have not claimed, or have been unable to claim, full input tax credit for that acquisition).
there is no consideration, for example a transfer of own goods (see section 9), or when goods are supplied without charge,	in either case, what it would cost you, or the person transferring the goods to you, to purchase the goods in question at the time of the acquisition.

8.5 What should I do if the value of an acquisition is in a foreign currency?

Where the value of your acquisition is in a foreign currency, you should convert it to sterling as follows

The text in this box has the force of law.

For VAT purposes, amounts of money must always be expressed in sterling. If you need to convert an amount from a foreign currency into sterling, you must do so on the following basis:

(a) Unless you have adopted one of the alternatives set out below, you must use the UK market selling rate at the time of the acquisition. The rates published in national newspapers will be acceptable as evidence of the rates at the relevant time.

(b) As an alternative you may use the period rate of exchange published by HMRC for customs purposes. The VAT Helpline can give details of particular period rates. You may adopt this alternative in respect of all your acquisitions or in respect of all acquisitions of a particular class or description. If you opt in respect only of a particular class or description you should make a note in your records at the time of adoption of the class or description to which your option relates.
You do not need to notify HMRC in advance if you wish to adopt this alternative, but if you make such an option you cannot then change it without first obtaining HMRC agreement.

(c) You may apply in writing to HMRC for the use of a rate or of a method of determining a rate which you use for commercial purposes but which is not covered by (a) or (b) above. In considering whether to allow such applications

> HMRC will take into account whether the proposed rate or method is determined by reference to the UK currency market, whether it is objectively verifiable, and the frequency with which the applicant proposes to update it. Forward rates or methods deriving from forward rates are not acceptable.

Before 1 January 1993 you may have used a rate authorised in writing by HM Revenue & Customs under the concessionary arrangements for supplies which applied up to that date. By concession you may extend this to acquisitions without further notification, unless the rate you use wholly derives from currency markets other than in the UK. Your continued use of these concessionary rates is subject to review by HMRC.

The text in this box has the force of law.

> Whatever rate or method you adopt, the appropriate rate for any supply is the one current at the time of supply.

8.6 Do I include any excise duty in the tax value of an acquisition?

Yes. For goods subject to excise duty or, in the case of EC accessionary states, customs duty or agricultural levy, the value of the acquisition is the value determined according to the principles outlined in this chapter plus the duty and/or levy arising from the removal to the UK.

9 TRANSFERS OF OWN GOODS BETWEEN MEMBER STATES

9.1 What is the position if I transfer of my own goods?

A transfer of your own goods from one member state to another within the same legal entity, for example between branches of the same company, is deemed to be a supply of goods for VAT purposes.

Commentary—*De Voil Indirect Tax Service* **V3.213**.

9.2 Is the supply liable to VAT?

The transfer of your own goods is liable to VAT in the same way as other intra-EC supplies of goods described in this notice.

9.3 Can the supply be zero-rated?

The supply may be zero-rated subject to the conditions in paragraph 4.3.

9.4 Is acquisition tax due?

You will normally be liable to account for acquisition VAT in the member state to which the goods are transferred.

9.5 Registering for VAT in the member state to which the goods are sent

You may need to be registered for VAT in the member state to which the goods were dispatched in order to meet your obligations to account for acquisition tax and also to account for VAT if you subsequently supply the goods there. You will also be able to use that VAT registration number to support zero-rating of the deemed supply in the UK (see paragraph 4.3).

9.6 What do I do if I am not registered in the member state to which the goods are sent?

If you are not registered for VAT in the member state to which you transfer your own goods, you should treat the supply as a domestic supply (see paragraph 6.1). You must account for VAT on the transfer at the appropriate UK rate.

9.7 Do I need to register for VAT in the UK if I transfer my own goods from another member state?

This will depend on whether you exceed the UK VAT registration thresholds. For further information about registering for VAT in the UK, see Notice 700/1 "Should I be registered for VAT?".

9.8 Are there any exceptions to this rule?

There are some exceptions which are covered in sections 10 and 11.

9.9 Reporting requirements

Type of movement	*VAT Return*	*EC Sales List (see Section 17)*	*Supplementary Declaration (see Section 18)*	*Notes*
Transfers from the UK to other member states.	*Boxes 6 & 8* – value based on cost of goods.	Yes – value based on cost of goods.	Yes – as a dispatch (value based on cost of goods).	A deemed supply in the UK. It may be zero-rated subject to the conditions in paragraph 4.3.
Transfers from other member states to the UK.	*Box 2* – acquisition VAT for positive-rated goods in UK. *Box 4* – input tax subject to normal rules (see paragraph 2.13). *Boxes 7 and 9* – value based on cost of goods.	No.	Yes – as an arrival (value based on cost of goods).	There is an acquisition in the UK by the owner of the goods.

10 TEMPORARY MOVEMENT OF GOODS

10.1 Are temporary movements of goods treated as a transfer of my own goods?

The following temporary movements are *not* treated as deemed supplies of goods as described in section 9:

– goods transferred temporarily to another member state in order to make a supply of services there provided *all* of the conditions at paragraph 10.2 are met, and
– goods transferred to another member state for temporary use there provided *all* of the conditions at paragraph 10.4 are met.

In each case no acquisition VAT is due in the member state to which the goods are transferred.

10.2 Conditions for the temporary movement of goods used to make a supply of services

You must meet *all* of the following conditions:

Condition	*Description*
1	You do not have a place of business in the member state to which the goods are temporarily transferred.
2	You have a specific contract to fulfil.
3	You intend to return the goods to the member state from which they were dispatched.

10.3 In what circumstances might this apply?

This can apply to your tools and equipment which you take to another member state to use there, for example to repair or service machinery. It also applies to goods that are loaned or leased to somebody in another member state.

10.4 Conditions for goods transferred for temporary use in another member state

You must meet *both* of the following conditions:

Condition	*Description*
1	The goods would be eligible for temporary importation relief if they were imported from outside the EC
2	They are to remain in the other member state for no longer than two years.

10.5 Which goods are eligible for temporary import relief?

For further information about this, see Notice 200 Temporary Admission.

10.6 What happens if circumstances change?

The conditions described at paragraphs 10.2 or 10.4 may later cease to be met (for example, in the case of paragraph 10.2, where the goods are disposed of locally rather than returned to the UK or, in the case of paragraph 10.4, they are to remain in the other member state for more than two years). In that event the original movement should be treated belatedly as a deemed supply and acquisition, as described in section 9.

10.7 Do I need to hold evidence of removal and return to the UK?

Although these transfers of your own goods are not treated as supplies for VAT purposes, you still need commercial evidence that the goods left the UK and have later returned. You must also maintain a register of temporary movements of goods, as described in paragraph 16.7.

10.8 Reporting requirements

Type of movement	*VAT return*	*EC Sales List (see Section 17)*	*Supplementary Declaration (see Section 18)*	*Notes*
Goods sent from the UK used in making a supply of services in another member state that remain out of the UK for LESS than 2 years.	No.	No.	No.	Requirement to keep a register of goods moved temporarily (see paragraph 16.7).

Goods sent from the UK used in making a supply of services in another member state that remain out of the UK for MORE than 2 years.	No.	No.	Yes – as a dispatch (value based on cost of goods).	Requirement to keep a register of goods moved temporarily (see paragraph 16.7).
Temporary transfer of goods from UK which would be eligible for temporary importation relief if sent from outside EC that remain out of the UK for *less* than 2 years.	No.	No.	No.	Requirement to keep a register of goods moved temporarily (see paragraph 16.7).

11 INSTALLED OR ASSEMBLED GOODS

Commentary—*De Voil Indirect Tax Service* **V3.213, V3.376 V3.379, V3.384, V4.343, V5.271–V5.276.**

11.1 What is covered by the term installed or assembled goods?

A supply of installed or assembled goods occurs when you supply goods and there is a contractual obligation for you to install or assemble the goods for your customer. For example a supplier of studio recording equipment where the supply involves installation at the customer's studio.

11.2 Place of supply of installed or assembled goods

The supply takes place where the installation or assembly of the goods is carried out.

11.3 Registering for VAT for supplies of installed or assembled goods

You are liable to register for VAT in any member state in which you are supplying installed or assembled goods. However, some member states operate a simplified procedure which permits the VAT-registered customer to account for the VAT due. You are not required to register in a member state which has this facility.

11.4 Which member states operate the simplified procedure?

Adoption of the simplified procedure is optional for member states. To find out if it is available in a particular member state you should contact the VAT authority there (see paragraph 2.11).

11.5 Are installed or assembled goods liable to acquisition tax?

The movement of the goods (eg the component parts) between member states as part of a supply of installed or assembled goods is not treated as a supply of own goods. Consequently there is no acquisition in the member state of installation or assembly.

11.6 Accounting for VAT on goods installed or assembled in the UK

If you supply goods from outside the UK to be installed or assembled here (the goods may be sourced from another member state or a third country) your supply is liable to VAT in the UK and you may be required to register here. However, the UK operates the simplified procedure mentioned in paragraph 11.3. You may use that simplified procedure provided—

– your customer is registered for VAT in the UK;
– you are registered for VAT in another member state, and
– you are not required to be registered here for any other reason.

11.7 How does the simplified procedure work?

Under the simplified procedure your UK customer is treated as acquiring the goods in the UK and must account for acquisition VAT on the full value of your supply. As a result you are no longer liable to account for VAT.

11.8 Using the simplified procedure

If you are a supplier in another member state and you wish to use these simplified arrangements you must do *all* of the following:

Step	*Action*
1	Issue your customer with a VAT invoice.
2	Issue that invoice within 15 days of the date on which your supply would otherwise have taken place under normal UK time of supply rules for goods. (For further information about this, see the sections dealing with time of supply in Notice 700 "The VAT Guide".) These include receipt of a payment, or completion of the installation or assembly.
3	Tell us you intend to use this arrangement. You should write to: The Non Established Taxable Persons Unit (NETPU) HM Revenue & Customs Ruby House 8 Ruby Place Aberdeen AB10 1ZP and include the following information: —your name, address and EC VAT registration number; —the name, address and VAT registration number of your UK customer (you must make a separate notification for each customer no later than the date of issue of the first invoice to the customer concerned); and —the date on which you began, or will begin, the installation or assembly of the goods.
4	Send a copy of the notification to your UK customer to advise them that you are using the simplified arrangements and so they are required to account for the VAT. You must send this no later than the date you issue the first invoice to your customer.

11.9 Do I have to send a notification for further supplies to the same customer?

No. But you will have to make further notifications for any new UK customers.

11.10 Receiving installed or assembled goods from a supplier using the simplified procedure

As the UK customer you should account for VAT on the supply to you as an acquisition by including the tax in Box 2 of your VAT return. You may also include this as input tax on the same VAT return subject to the normal rules (see paragraph 2.13).

11.11 Reporting requirements

Type of movement	*VAT return*	*EC Sales List (see Section 17)*	*Supplementary Declaration (see Section 18)*

Goods sent from UK for installation or assembly in another member state.	*Box 6* – value of supply.	No.	Yes – as a dispatch (value based on cost of goods if known, otherwise open market value).
	Box 8 – value based on cost of goods at time of dispatch.		
Goods sent from another member state for installation or assembly in UK where supplier registers for VAT in UK.	*Box 1* – output tax.	No.	Yes – as an arrival (value based on cost of goods if known, otherwise open market value).
	Box 6 – value of supply.		
Goods installed or assembled in the UK where supplier elects to use simplification procedure.[1]	*Box 2* – acquisition VAT.	No.	Yes – as an arrival (value based on cost of goods if known, otherwise open market value).
	Box 4 – input tax (subject to normal rules see paragraph 2.13).		
	Boxes 7 & 9 – value of acquisition.		

1 Customer is responsible for reporting requirements.

12 MOVEMENTS OF GOODS FOR PROCESS, REPAIR, ETC

12.1 What is covered by this section?

This section outlines the VAT treatment of goods that are moved between member states in circumstances where some form of service is to be applied to those goods. The services can include things like processing, repair and valuation.

12.2 Goods sent from the UK for work to be carried out elsewhere in the EC

This can include goods sent to more than one service provider in the other member state or in different member states *provided*, in all cases, the goods are returned to the UK after the services have been completed. Where it applies there is no deemed supply of own goods as described in section 9.

You are, however, required to:

Step	*Action*
1	Record the movement of the goods in your temporary movements register (see paragraph 16.7).
2	Hold commercial documentary evidence that the goods have been removed from the UK.
3	Account for VAT on each of the supplies of services you have received as a reverse charge. (For further information about the reverse charge, as it applies to work carried out on goods, see Notice 741A "Place of supply of services".)
4	Where applicable complete an Intrastat Supplementary Declaration (see paragraph 12.7). For more information about Intrastat, see Notice 60 "Intrastat General Guide"

12.3 Goods sent to the UK for work to be carried out

As the supplier of the service there is no requirement for you to account for VAT on the movement of the goods *provided* you return them to your customer when the work has been completed. Similarly, provided your customer is registered for VAT elsewhere within the EC, you are not required to charge VAT on the supply of your services. Your customer will account for this as a reverse charge. For further information about the reverse charge, as it applies to work carried out on goods, see Notice 741A "Place of supply of services".

You are, however, required to:

Step	*Action*
1	Record the arrival and return of the goods in your temporary movements register (see paragraph 16.7).
2	Hold commercial documentary evidence that the goods have been removed from the UK.
3	Where applicable complete an Intrastat Supplementary Declaration (see paragraph 12.7). For more information about Intrastat, see Notice 60 "Intrastat General Guide"

12.4 What happens if goods are not returned to the member state of departure?

These arrangements do not apply if, for any reason, the goods are not eventually returned to the member state from which they were originally sent. In that event they become subject to the normal intra-EC supply and acquisition rules and the owner of the goods may be liable to register for VAT in the member state concerned.

12.5 Work performed on goods in another member state before removal to the UK

This can occur where you buy goods from another member state and have work performed on them before they are removed to the UK. The work may be performed by more than one supplier and they may be located in different member states. Whatever the position you are required to:

Step	*Action*
1	Account for acquisition VAT on the supply of the goods in the normal way.
2	Account for VAT on each of the supplies of services you have received as a reverse charge. For more information about the reverse charge, as it applies to work carried out on goods, see Notice 741A "Place of supply of services".
3	Where applicable complete an Intrastat Supplementary Declaration (see paragraph 12.7). For more information about Intrastat, see Notice 60 "Intrastat General Guide".

12.6 Work performed on goods before removal from the UK

This can occur if you make an intra-EC supply of goods and your customer has work performed on them before they leave the UK. In this situation you can continue to treat the supply under the normal rules described in section 3 *provided* you meet all the relevant conditions. You will therefore need to make sure that your customer provides you with evidence of removal of the goods from the UK once the work has been completed (see paragraph 4.5).

12.7 Reporting requirements

Repaired goods:

Type of movement	*VAT return*	*EC Sales List (see Section 17)*	*Supplementary Declaration (see Section 18)*	*Notes*
Goods sent to another member states for repair – owner's reporting requirements.	No.	No.	No.	
Goods received back in the UK by owner after repair in another member state – UK owner's reporting requirements.	*Box 1* – output tax* *Box 4* – input tax, subject to normal rules (see paragraph 2.13). *Box 6* – value of repair services.	No.	No.	*Output tax accounted for on repair services as a reverse charge (see paragraph 12.2).
Goods for repair received in the UK from other member states – UK repairer's reporting requirements.	No.	No.	No.	
Repaired goods returned to customer in another member state – UK repairer's reporting requirements	*Boxes 6* – value of repair service.	No.	No.	VAT on repair services accounted for by EC customer as a reverse charge (see paragraph 12.3).

Processed goods:

Type of movement	*VAT return*	*EC Sales List (see Section 17)*	*Supplementary Declaration (see Section 18)*
Goods sent from UK for process in another member state – UK owner's reporting requirements.	No.	No.	Yes – as a dispatch (value based on cost of goods).
Goods returned to UK from EC processor – UK owner's reporting requirements.[1]	*Box 1*– output tax[1] *Box 4* – input tax subject to normal rules (see paragraph 2.13) *Box 6* – value of the processing services.	No	Yes – as an arrival (value based on cost of goods and cost of process).
Goods received for process in UK from EC customer – UK processor's reporting requirements.	No.	No.	Yes – as an arrival (value based on cost of goods if known, otherwise open market value).
Goods returned after process in UK to EC customer — UK processor's reporting requirements[2].	*Box 6* – value of process.	No.	Yes – as a dispatch (value based on cost of goods, if known, otherwise, open market value and cost of process).

1 Output tax accounted for on processor's services as a reverse charge (see paragraph 12.2).

2 VAT on processing services accounted for by EC customer as a reverse charge (see paragraph 12.3).

13 TRIANGULATION

Commentary—*De Voil Indirect Tax Service* **V3.380**.

13.1 What is triangulation?

Triangulation is the term used to describe a chain of intra-EC supplies of goods involving three parties. But, instead of the goods physically passing from one to the other, they are delivered directly from the first to the last party in the chain.

For example:

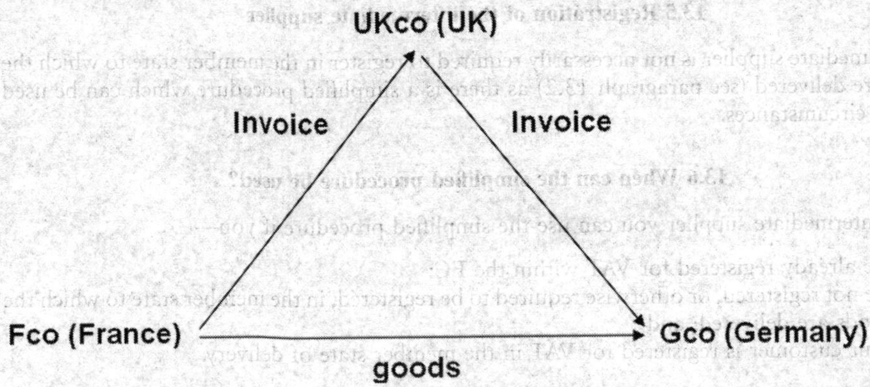

Here a UK company receives an order from a customer in Germany. To fulfil the order the UK supplier in turn orders goods from their own supplier in France. The goods are delivered from France to Germany.

13.2 What is the supply position?

There is a supply of goods by the . . .	*and this means that . . . .*
French company to the UK company	the French company can zero-rate the supply subject to the conditions described in paragraph 4.3.
UK company to the German company	the UK company is acquiring and supplying those goods in Germany and is liable to register for VAT there unless the simplified procedure described at paragraph 13.5 is used.

13.3 How might I become involved in triangulation?

You might become involved in triangulation as either—

– the first supplier of the goods (the French company in the example above);
– the intermediate supplier (the UK company in the example above); or
– the final customer (the German company in the example above).

13.4 Treatment of supplies for VAT purposes

The VAT treatment within the EC is normally as follows:

If you are the . . .	*you may . . .*
first supplier	zero-rate your supply of the goods subject to the conditions in paragraph 4.3.

intermediate supplier	be liable to register for VAT in the member state to which the goods are delivered and account for VAT on the acquisition and on your supply.
the final customer	not need to do anything as you are receiving a domestic supply (but see the simplified procedure described in paragraph 13.5).

13.5 Registration of the intermediate supplier

An intermediate supplier is not necessarily required to register in the member state to which the goods are delivered (see paragraph 13.2) as there is a simplified procedure which can be used in these circumstances.

13.6 When can the simplified procedure be used?

As the intermediate supplier you can use the simplified procedure if you—

- are already registered for VAT within the EC;
- are not registered, or otherwise required to be registered, in the member state to which the goods are delivered; and
- your customer is registered for VAT in the member state of delivery.

13.7 Use of the simplified procedure as a UK intermediate supplier

To use the simplified procedure if you are a UK intermediate supplier making supplies of goods to a customer in another member state, you must do *all* of the following:

Step	*Action*
1	Use your UK VAT registration number to allow your EC supplier to zero-rate the supply of goods in the member state from which the goods were dispatched.
2	Issue a VAT invoice to your customer containing all the details normally required for intra-EC supplies.
3	Include the supply on your EC Sales List (see Section 17), quoting the VAT number of your customer in the member state of destination of the goods.
4	Enter the total value of triangular supplies to each EC customer in that quarter on your EC Sales List on a single line separately from any other intra-EC supplies to that customer.
5	Identify your triangular transactions by inserting the figure 2 in the indicator box (the notes on the reverse of the EC Sales List give further details).
6	Omit details of triangular transactions on your UK VAT return and Intrastat Supplementary Declaration (see Section 18).

13.8 Submitting a UK EC Sales List if your intra-EC supplies only involve triangular contracts

EC Sales Lists (Forms VAT 101 & 101A) can be submitted—

- using the EC Sales List online service (see paragraph 17.4);
- by downloading the forms from the HMRC website; or
- by contacting the VAT Helpline who will arrange for EC Sales Lists to be sent to you automatically.

13.9 Use of the simplified procedure as an intermediate supplier in another member state

If you are an intermediate supplier in another member state making supplies to a customer in the UK you can avoid having to register for VAT in the UK by using the simplified procedure. To do so you must do *all* of the following:

Step	*Action*
1	Issue a VAT invoice to your customer containing all the details required by the member state in which you are VAT-registered.
2	Issue that invoice within 15 days of the date on which your supply would otherwise have taken place under normal UK tax point rules for supplies of goods (for further information about tax points, see the sections sealing with time of supply in Notice 700 "The VAT guide".
3	Tell us you intend to use this arrangement. You should write to: The Non Established Taxable Persons Unit (NETPU) HM Revenue & Customs Ruby House 8 Ruby Place Aberdeen AB10 1ZP and include the following information: —your name, address and EC VAT registration number you used, or will use, to obtain zero-rating of the initial supply of the goods; —the name, address and VAT registration number of your UK customer (you must make a separate notification for each customer no later than the date of issue of the first invoice to the customer concerned); and —the date the goods were first delivered, or are intended to be delivered, to your customer under these arrangements
4	Send a copy of the notification to your UK customer to advise them that you are using the simplified arrangements and so they are required to account for the VAT. You must send this no later than the date you issue the first invoice to your customer.

13.10 Do I have to make further notifications for the same customer?

No, but you will have to make further notifications for any other UK customers.

13.11 Goods received from a supplier using the simplified procedure

As a UK customer whose supplier is using the simplified procedure you should do the following:

Step	*Action*
1	On receipt of your copy of your supplier's notification to HMRC (see paragraph 13.9 – step 4), account for VAT on the goods supplied to you under the simplified procedure as an acquisition (see section 7).
2	Submit supplementary declarations for goods supplied to you under these simplified arrangements (see section 18).

13.12 Triangulation involving a non-EC intermediate supplier

The VAT treatment will depend on the VAT registered status of the intermediate supplier as follows:

If the intermediate supplier is . . .	*then . . .*
already registered for VAT within the EC	the procedures described earlier in this section will apply.

not registered for VAT within the EC	the first supplier will be making a domestic supply (see section 6). However, in acquiring/supplying the goods involved, the intermediate supplier may be required to register in either the member state of dispatch or arrival.

13.13 Triangulation where the movement of the goods is to a place outside the EC

Triangulation in these circumstances is not an issue. The supplier may, regardless of the location of the other parties, treat the supply as an export (see Notice 703 "Exports of goods from the United Kingdom").

13.14 Triangulation where the movement of goods is from a place outside the EC

The triangulation simplification arrangements do not apply in these circumstances and it may be necessary for the first supplier or the intermediary supplier to register for VAT in the Member State where the supply takes place, depending on who imports the goods.

14 SUPPLIES TO PRIVILEGED PERSONS IN OTHER EC MEMBER STATES

14.1 Arrangements for diplomatic missions, consulates, international organisations and NATO visiting forces in other EC member states

Under international agreements, some people and bodies working in the international arena and hosted by other EC member states may make purchases free of VAT. This section explains when you may zero-rate supplies under these agreements. The host government determines what bodies and persons qualify, and it may impose limitations. If your customer has any doubts about their status they should contact their host VAT authority for advice (see paragraph 2.11).

Qualifying bodies and persons have a duty to abide by the law and agreements underlying their entitlement to make purchases free of VAT (including limitations imposed by their host member state), and to observe policies controlling abuse of those entitlements.

These arrangements apply only to supplies that would otherwise be subject to UK VAT at a positive rate. They do not apply to new means of transport. For further information about the zero-rating of new means of transport, see Notice 728 "New means of transport".

14.2 What is an "international organisation"?

For the purposes of this relief, "international organisation" means an organisation established by a treaty between sovereign governments. An organisation formed by agreement between non-governmental bodies such as limited companies or charities is not an international organisation; nor is a body set up by a single state or government, for example a government department. Well known international organisations include the institutions of the European Union, the United Nations and its various subsidiary organisations, and the North Atlantic Treaty Organisation (NATO).

14.3 What is a "NATO visiting force"?

For the purposes of this relief, a "NATO visiting force" means an armed force contingent that—

– belongs to a NATO member state;
– is stationed in an EC member state, and
– does not belong to the state in which it is stationed.

14.4 Zero-rating supplies of goods

A supply qualifies for zero-rating if it satisfies the following conditions:

Step *Description*

1	You must receive a certificate of entitlement (see paragraph 14.6).
2	The goods must be for the official use of: —an embassy; —a high commission; —a consulate; —an international organisation; —a NATO visiting force; or —a British armed force contingent based in Cyprus; or for the personal use of a member of staff of one of these bodies. "Official use" includes goods the body receives for distribution (including sale) to its members and their accompanying dependants. "Personal use" includes distributing goods to their accompanying dependants for no reward.
3	You, or a forwarder acting on your behalf, must remove the goods to an official address of the embassy, high commission, consulate, international organisation or force in another EC member state or in one of the Sovereign Base Areas in Cyprus. You may consign goods to the post or to a courier or fast parcel service, including the British Forces Post Office (BFPO). If your customer is a British embassy or high commission in another member state, you may consign goods to the Foreign and Commonwealth Office for delivery through diplomatic channels.
4	You must obtain and keep proof of the removal of the goods from the UK to the customer's address in the host country. Proof of posting is sufficient.
5	If the supply is for a contingent of British forces in Cyprus or its staff, or for a NATO visiting force in Germany or its staff, the order must be placed by an Official Procurement Agency for the force, such as the NAAFI or a regimental purchasing officer.

14.5 Zero rating supplies of services

A supply of services qualifies for zero rating if it satisfies the following conditions:

Step	*Description*
1	You must receive a certificate of entitlement (see paragraph 14.6).
2	The supply of services must be made to an international organisation, a NATO visiting force, or a British force in Cyprus, for the official use of the force or organisation.
3	The person placing the order must be based in an office of the force or international organisation in an EC member state other than the UK.
4	A supply of services to British forces must in addition satisfy the following conditions: —the service must consist of training, software development, a supply of staff, or goods forwarding; —for training, the trainees must all be members of a British contingent based in an EC member state other than the UK, or members of British forces Cyprus; —for software development, the software must be for the use of the force, and not for use in the UK; —for a supply of staff, the staff must work exclusively for the force in the visiting force's host country or in a Sovereign Base Area in Cyprus, and

—if the service is goods forwarding, the goods must all be forwarded to or from the force's premises in the other member state or in a Sovereign Base Area in Cyprus.

14.6 What is a "certificate of entitlement"?

You must obtain and keep documentation uniquely identifying the supply and claiming entitlement under Art 15(10) of EC Council Directive 77/388/EEC. This must be either—

- a certificate bearing the original signature of the head or acting head of the embassy, high commission, consulate, visiting force contingent or international organisation, with evidence of the qualifying status of the signatory; or
- any other form of certificate specified by their host government.

Exceptionally in the case of a supply for the British force in Cyprus or its members, or for a visiting force in Germany or its members, you must obtain and keep a certificate from the person placing the order uniquely identifying the supply for which relief is claimed, and claiming entitlement as follows:

- for British forces in Cyprus – under Art 14(1)(g) of EC Council Directive 77/388/EEC, or
- for a visiting force in Germany – under Art 15(10) of EC Council Directive 77/388/EEC.

14.7 Should I include these supplies on my EC Sales Lists?

Entries on EC Sales Lists are not required for these supplies.

14.8 Should I include these supplies on my Supplementary Declarations?

Certain supplies of goods under these arrangements must be included on your Supplementary Declarations. For further information see Notice 60 "The Intrastat General Guide".

14.9 Do these supplies count towards distance selling thresholds?

In general, these transactions are not regarded as distance sales and do not count towards distance selling thresholds. Exceptionally supplies to Germany, do count towards your distance selling threshold in that country.

14.10 When should I seek further advice?

If you, as a supplier, receive a certificate claiming VAT relief for any goods or services that fail the requirements of this Notice, or if you have any doubts about the documentation you receive, contact the VAT Helpline on 0300 200 3700 for advice.

15 OTHER INTRA-EC MOVEMENTS OF GOODS

Commentary—*De Voil Indirect Tax Service* **V3.213, V3.315**.

15.1 What does this section cover?

This section gives information about:

Subject	*Location*
Call-off stocks	Paragraph 15.2
Consignment stocks	Paragraph 15.3
Excise goods	Paragraph 15.4
Goods supplied on sale or return, or similar terms	Paragraph 15.5
Samples	Paragraph 15.6
Goods sent for testing	Paragraph 15.7

15.2 Call-off stocks

Call-off stocks are goods transferred by the supplier between member states, to be held for an individual customer in the member state of arrival pending "call-off" for use by the customer as they need them. In the meantime title and ownership of the goods remains with the supplier.

This only applies in cases where the goods are destined for a single identified customer either—

- for consumption within their business (eg as part of a manufacturing process), or
- to make onward supplies to their own customers.

Movements of goods to maintain the suppliers own stocks in another member state, or where they are available for call-off by more than one customer, are to be dealt with as consignment stocks (see paragraph 15.3).

(a) Does the location of storage facilities affect treatment as call-off stocks?

The goods will normally be stored by the supplier at the customers premises. However, goods delivered to storage facilities operated by the supplier can still be treated as call-off goods provided the conditions described in paragraph 15.2 are met and the customer is aware of the details of deliveries into storage. Otherwise the goods should be treated as consignment stocks (see paragraph 15.3).

(b) VAT treatment of call-off stocks

If you . . .	*then . . .*
send goods from the UK to be held as call-off stock in another member state,	the normal intra-EC rules apply so that your supply is treated as taking place in the UK and may be zero-rated subject to the conditions described in paragraph 4.3.
receive goods held in the UK as call-off stock by a supplier in another member state,	the normal intra-EC rules apply and you should account for acquisition tax as described in section 7.

(c) Reporting requirements

Type of movement	*VAT return*	*EC Sales List (see Section 17)*	*Supplementary Declaration (see Section 18)*	*Notes*
Goods sent as call-off stocks from the UK to another member state.	*Boxes 6 and 8* – value based on cost of goods.	Yes – value based on cost of goods.	Yes – as a dispatch, (value based on cost of goods).	The supply may be zero-rated.
Goods received in the UK as call-off stocks.	*Box 2* –acquisition VAT for positive-rated goods in UK. *Box 4* – input tax subject to normal rules. *Boxes 7 and 9* – value based on cost of goods.	No.	Yes – as an arrival (value based on cost of goods).	There is an acquisition by the UK customer.

15.3 Consignment stocks

Consignment stocks are goods you transfer between member states to meet future supplies to be made by you, or on your behalf, in the member state of arrival. The important feature is that the movement of the goods occurs before a customer has been found for them. This can include goods not meeting the conditions necessary for treatment as call-off stocks (see paragraph 15.2).

Consignment stocks are treated as a transfer of own goods for VAT accounting and reporting purposes (see section 9).

15.4 Movements of excise goods between member states

All excisable goods must travel with an accompanying document. There are two types of accompanying document:

– an Administrative Accompanying Document (AAD), and
– a Simplified Administrative Accompanying Document (SAAD).

Examples of the circumstances in which they are used are as follows.

If the movement of goods is between warehouses and . . .	*then . . .*
they are moving under authorised duty suspension arrangements (for example an excise warehouse)	the consignor must complete an AAD. There must also be a financial guarantee to cover all excise duty liabilities during the movement. The consignee must complete a certificate of receipt for the goods on the reverse of Copy 3 of the AAD and return it to the consignor.
UK excise duty has already been paid	the goods should travel with SAAD. The customer must also provide evidence that the excise duty has been paid in the member state of destination or secured to the satisfaction of the VAT authorities there, *before the supplier dispatches the goods.*

For further information on the use of AADs and SAADs, see Notice 197 Excise Goods: receipt into and removal from an excise warehouse of excise goods.

(a) Supply of excise goods to persons not registered for VAT

You can zero-rate an intra-EC supply of excise goods to persons not registered for VAT in another member state, provided *all* the following three conditions are met—

Condition	*Description*
1	The goods are not for private use.
2	They are removed or dispatched from the UK to a destination in another member state by or on behalf of the customer.
3	Within fifteen days of the end of the month in which they are moved, you must obtain (and keep) a receipted copy 3 of the AAD, (see paragraph 15.4). This must be certified by the consignee or VAT authority in the member state of destination. The movement of goods must be completed as soon as possible and the certificate of receipt for the goods must be issued within four months of the time of supply.

(b) Payment of excise duty and VAT in the member state of arrival

If the conditions in sub-paragraph (a) above are not met, the customer is liable for the excise duty and VAT. If duty suspended goods go missing in transit then the person who supplied the movement guarantee will be liable for the duty, along with any person who may be jointly and severally liable.

(c) VAT treatment for excise goods supplied to a VAT registered customer

Excise goods sold to somebody who is registered for VAT in another member state are treated in the same way as any other type of goods.

(d) Excise goods supplied for private purposes

Excise goods supplied for private purposes where you arrange delivery to a customer in another member state are covered by the special VAT arrangements for distance selling (see paragraph 6.4). Also the vendor must pay the duty in the member state of destination at the time the goods are delivered. You may therefore have to register for excise purposes with the VAT authorities in the member state concerned (see paragraph 2.11). In the UK, people receiving goods under Distance Selling arrangements, must appoint a Duty Representative to account for UK excise duty, before the goods are dispatched.

15.5 VAT treatment of goods removed from a warehouse to a place outside the UK

If goods are removed from a tax warehouse in the UK to a destination outside the UK, you will not have to pay the VAT normally due on removal to home use. In such circumstances, either the person making the final supply in warehouse or the person removing the goods can zero rate that transaction provided certain conditions are met (see table below). Liability to meet the zero rating conditions must be clearly established before the goods are delivered to avoid any doubt as to where responsibility lies.

The following table provides an overview of the VAT implications when goods are removed to a place outside the UK:

Where goods are removed from warehouse to	*the VAT treatment is*
A country outside the EC	Any VAT which would be due on removal to UK home use is not payable. Supplies of goods removed from the UK may be zero-rated as exports subject to meeting the conditions in Notice 703 VAT: Export of goods from the United Kingdom. An ESL is not required
A VAT registered customer in another Member State	You may zero-rate a supply of goods to a customer who is VAT registered in another EC country where the goods are moving outside the warehousing system provided the conditions in Notice 725 The Single Market An ESL and an entry in box 8 of the VAT return is required
A tax warehouse in another EC Member State	You may disregard, for UK VAT purposes, any supply of the goods provided you are removing them directly to a registered tax warehouse in another EC country. An ESL, or an entry in Box 8 of the VAT return is not required

15.6 Goods sent on sale or return, approval or similar terms

These are goods which are not supplied until they are adopted by the customer. Adoption occurs when the customer indicates that they are going to keep the goods. Until then the customer has an unqualified right to return them at any time, unless there is an agreed time limit after which the goods are to be automatically treated as accepted.

(a) Accounting for VAT

If you send goods . . .	*then . . .*
from the UK on sale or return, approval or similar terms to somebody in another member state	you should treat this as a transfer of own goods (see section 9). This means that: —you will be making an acquisition of the goods in the member state to which the goods are sent;

	—a supply of those goods in that member state if, and when, the goods are eventually adopted by your customer; and —you may need to register there to account for any VAT due on the acquisition and supply of the goods.
to the UK from another member state on sale or return, approval or similar terms	you should treat this as a transfer of own goods (see section 9). This means that: —you will be making an acquisition of the goods in the UK; —a supply of those goods in the UK if, and when, the goods are eventually adopted by your customer; and —you will also be liable to register for VAT in the UK; to account for any VAT due on the acquisition and supply of the goods.

(b) Reporting requirements

Type of movement	*VAT return*	*EC Sales List (see Section 17)*	*Supplementary Declaration (see Section 18)*	*Notes*
Goods sent from UK to another member state.	*Boxes 6 & 8* – value based on cost of goods.	Yes – value based on cost of goods.	Yes – as a despatch (value based on cost of goods).	See section 9 (transfers of own goods). This assumes sender of goods is registered for VAT in member state of arrival.
Goods sent to UK from another member state.	*Box 2* – acquisition VAT for positive-rated goods in UK. *Box 4* – input tax subject to normal rules. *Boxes 7 & 9* – Value based on cost of goods.	No.	Yes as an arrival (value based on cost of goods).	There is an acquisition in the UK by the owner of the goods. This assumes sender of goods is registered for VAT in the UK.

15.7 Samples

Movements of goods that qualify as samples are disregarded for intra-EC supply and acquisition purposes. Details of the conditions that must be met to treat something as a sample can be found in Notice 700 "The VAT Guide".

Reporting requirements

Type of movement	*VAT return*	*EC Sales List (see Section 17)*	*Supplementary Declaration (see Section 18)*	*Notes*

Samples sent to, or received from, another member state.	No.	No.	No (when the goods are supplied free of charge).	

15.8 Goods sent for testing

Goods sent to, or received from, another member state for testing are disregarded provided that:

— ownership remains unchanged; and
— the goods are either returned to the member state of departure or are destroyed.

Reporting requirements

Type of movement	*VAT return*	*EC Sales List (see Section 17)*	*Supplementary Declaration (see Section 18)*	*Notes*
Goods sent to, or received from, another member states for testing.	No.	No.	No (unless it is known at time of dispatch that they will be tested to destruction – if so value based on cost of goods).	

16 ACCOUNTING AND RECORD KEEPING

Commentary—*De Voil Indirect Tax Service* **V5.271–V5.276**.

16.1 Do I have to complete any returns in addition to my VAT return?

Yes, in addition to the VAT return you may have to complete the following:

– an EC Sales List – listing goods that you have sent to VAT registered businesses in other member states; and services you have supplied that are subject to the reverse charge procedure in your customer's member state; and
– an Intrastat Supplementary Declaration – which is completed for supplies of goods by larger businesses.

For further information see sections 17 and 18 respectively.

16.2 Completion of VAT returns, EC Sales Lists & Supplementary Declaration

The reporting requirements for the various types of intra-EC transaction covered by this notice are described in each section.

16.3 Which boxes do I complete on my VAT return?

On the VAT return (Form VAT 100) there are a number of boxes to gather information on the value of goods sold to, or bought from, other member states and two boxes for VAT due on acquisitions. These are:

Box Number	*Description*
2	Total VAT due on EC acquisitions in the period.
4	Amount of VAT deductible on any business purchase including acquisitions of goods and related costs from other EC member states (subject to the normal input tax rules).

6	Total value of supplies of all your business sales including supplies to other EC member states.
7	Total value of purchases including acquisitions from VAT registered suppliers in other EC member states.
8	Total value of supplies of goods and directly related costs (such as freight and insurance charges) to member states in the period (excluding VAT). The value you enter in box 8, should be the total of all intra-EC supplies of goods made in that reporting period (excluding VAT) and not just the value of payments received. (Figures entered in this box must also be included in the box 6 total.)
9	Total value of acquisitions and directly related costs (such as freight and insurance charges) from member states in the period (excluding VAT). (Figures entered in this box must also be included in the box 7 total.)

For further information about Form VAT 100, see Notice 700/12 "Filling in your VAT return".

16.4 I account for VAT using the cash accounting scheme how should I complete box 8 of the VAT return?

The value you enter in box 8, should be the total of all intra-EC supplies of goods made in that reporting period (excluding VAT) and not the value of payments received in that period. The total value of entries on your ESL should agree with the value entered in box 8 of your VAT Return (see Notice 731 Cash Accounting).

16.5 In which VAT accounting period should I account for VAT on my acquisitions?

You must account for any VAT due on your VAT return for the period in which the tax becomes due. This is the period when the time of acquisition (tax point) occurs. Paragraph 7.3 provides further information on this. You may also treat this tax as input tax on the same VAT return, subject to the normal rules for claiming input tax (see paragraph 2.13).

16.6 Do I include the value of intra-EC supplies of services in box 8 of the VAT return?

No. The value of services supplied or acquired should not be included in boxes 8 or 9 of your VAT Return. These boxes should only be used to record intra-EC supplies / acquisitions of goods and related costs.

16.7 What records do I have to keep in order to account for tax on my acquisitions?

In addition to the normal VAT records you are required to keep, you must, if you are involved in buying goods from VAT registered traders in other member states, keep all of the following records:

Item	*Description*
1	VAT invoices issued to you by suppliers in other member states
2	Documents relating to goods acquired by you from other member states
3	Copies of your completed EC Sales Lists (your EC Sales List account) (see section 17).
4	Copies of your Intrastat Supplementary Declarations if applicable (see section 18).

16.8 Recording the tax due on acquisitions in your VAT account

You must calculate the VAT due on the acquisition of goods from other member states (see section 7) and enter the total on the 'VAT payable' side of your VAT account under the heading "VAT due on acquisitions".

You may then deduct the VAT due on these acquisitions as input tax on the "VAT deductible" side of your VAT account, under the heading 'VAT deductible on acquisitions', subject to the normal rules for claiming input tax (see paragraph 2.13).

16.9 Records of goods sent to another member state on a temporary basis

If you are a taxable person and you move goods to, or receive goods from, other member states on a temporary basis, you must:

Step	*Action*
1	Keep a register of temporary movements of goods. The register need not be kept in any particular format (see paragraph 16.8) but it must be readily available for all goods temporarily moved to and from the UK.
2	Include in the register all goods moved between the UK and other member states where they are to be returned within a period of two years after their first removal or receipt. It would also be advisable to include any goods for which you are not sure of the date of return

16.10 What information should I record in my temporary movement register?

You should record the following:

Item	*Information*
1	For goods you are sending out of the UK – the date the goods were removed.
2	For goods received from another member state – the date the goods arrived.
3	The date the goods are returned.
4	A description of the goods.
5	The reason for the movement (for example process work).
6	The consideration for the supply, if applicable.

16.11 What records do I need to keep for removals?

If you remove goods to another EC member state you must keep the records and detailed accounts described in Notice 700 "The VAT Guide". Your records must provide a clear link with the evidence required in this notice. It is important that you follow the accounting instructions explained in paragraph 16.10 if the goods are not removed or you do not hold evidence to show removal of the goods within the time limits.

16.12 How do I adjust my accounts if goods are not removed or I do not receive evidence of removal?

Whether you or your VAT registered EC customer arranges for the removal of goods to another EC member state, you can only zero-rate the supply in your records when the goods are supplied to your customer and you meet the conditions set out in paragraphs 4.3 and 4.4.

If the goods have not been removed or you do not have satisfactory evidence of removal within three months (six months for goods involved in processing or incorporation before removal) and the goods would be subject to VAT in the UK, you must account for VAT. You must amend your VAT records and account for VAT on the invoiced amount or consideration you have received. For a VAT rate of 17.5 per cent the VAT element would be calculated at 7/47 and for the 20 per cent rate (from 4 January 2011) at 1/6..

To amend your VAT records, you must make an entry equal to the tax on the supplies concerned on the "VAT Payable" side of your VAT account. Include this amount in Box 1 of your VAT return *for the period in which the time limit expires*. If you do not, you are likely to be assessed for tax due on the supplies and may incur default interest and a financial penalty.

16.13 What do I do if the goods are later removed or I receive evidence of removal after I have accounted for VAT?

If the goods are subsequently removed from the UK and/or you later obtain evidence showing that the goods were removed, you may zero-rate the supply and adjust your VAT account *for the period in which you obtain the evidence*. This is provided that the goods have not been used in the UK before removal, unless specifically authorised.

16.14 When do I have to issue a VAT invoice?

You must normally issue a VAT invoice within 30 days of making the supply of—

- standard-rated goods or services to a registered person in the UK;
- goods or services, other than exempt supplies, to a person in another member state;
- goods or services to a non-taxable person in another member state (such as a public body, a charity or an unregistered business);
- distance sales of goods (for example mail order) to unregistered persons in other member states); or
- new means of transport (motor vehicles, boats or planes) to persons in other member states.

You should also issue a VAT invoice within 30 days of receiving a payment on account from a customer in another member state.

If you wish or need to invoice outside this 30 day period you should contact the VAT Helpline explaining the full circumstances. However, permission may be refused.

16.15 Do I always have to issue a full VAT invoice to a VAT-registered customer in another member state?

A full VAT invoice must always be issued if you wish to zero-rate a supply to a customer registered for VAT in another member state.

16.16 What information should I show on a VAT invoice?

If you make supplies to a customer in another EC country, the VAT invoice you issue must show the following details in addition to the information normally required on a VAT invoice issued to a UK customer:

Item	*Information*
1	The letters "GB" (the "country identifier" for the UK) as a prefix to your VAT registration number.
2	The VAT registration number, if any, of your customer in the other member state, including the country identifier as a prefix (see paragraph 16.19).
3	In the case of a new means of transport, a description which identifies it as such.
4	A reference to indicate that the supply is a zero-rated intra-EC supply of goods.

For further information about information normally required to be included on a VAT invoice, see the sections dealing with VAT invoices in Notice 700 "The VAT Guide".

16.17 Do I always have to invoice in sterling?

You can invoice in any currency when you issue VAT invoices for supplies where the customer in the other member state is registered for VAT and their registration number is quoted on the invoice.

Where UK VAT is chargeable (for example on distance sales) the sterling equivalent of the amount of VAT, if any, at each rate must always be shown. For further information about this, see the sections dealing with VAT invoices in Notice 700 "The VAT Guide". See also paragraph 8.5 for information about the exchange rates which may be used.

16.18 Typical VAT invoice for supplies to another member state

This is an example of a VAT invoice issued for supplies made to a customer in Germany.

Sales Invoice No. 174				
Foundation Trading (UK) Ltd, Bowman Street, Chester				
		VAT Regd No. GB 987 6543 21		
To—EIN ANDER		VAT Regd No. DE 99345195 5		
HOCHSTRASSE				
BONN		Time of supply 15/02/2006		
		Date of issue 19/02/2006		
Sale				
Quantity	Description and price	Amount exclusive of VAT	VAT Rate	VAT Net
		£	%	£
6	RADIOS, SW15 @ £25.20	151.20		
4	P/C SM1993 @ £319.20	1276.80		
6	LAMPS T77 @ £15.55	93.30		
		1521.30	0	0.00
	Terms—Cash discount of 5% if paid within 30 days	1521.30		
		VAT	0.00	
	"Zero-rated intra-EC supply" *	TOTAL	1521.30	

* This wording is not prescriptive. Similar wording or a reference to the relevant EC or UK law is acceptable.

16.19 Country codes and VAT registration numbers in the other Member States

The following table shows:

- the format of VAT registration numbers in each member state, and
- the country codes which you should use as a prefix to those VAT registration numbers for your EC customers.

Customer's VAT registration numbers should be verified using the Europa website VIES VAT number validation or by contacting the VAT Helpline on 0300 200 3700.

In certain countries for example Spain and Italy, businesses are required to register their VAT number for Intra -EC use and if they don't do this, the number will show as invalid on the VIES VAT number validation checker. You may need to contact your customer and advise them to register the number for intra-EC use.

Remember — the country code to use as a prefix to your UK VAT registration number is GB.

Member state	*Country code*	*Format of VAT number*	*Number of characters*
Austria[1]	AT	U12345678	9
Belgium[2]	BE	0123456789	10
Bulgaria	BG	0123456789 or 0123456789	9 or 10
Croatioa	HR	12345678901	11
Republic of Cyprus (see paragraph 2.4 for extent of VAT territory)[3]	CY	12345678X	9
Czech Republic[4]	CZ	12345678 or 123456789 or 1234567890	8, 9 or 10
Denmark	DK	12345678	8

Estonia	EE	123456789	9
Finland	FI	12345678	8
France[5]	FR	12345678901 or X1234567890 or 1X123456789 or XX123456789	11
Germany[6]	DE	123456789	9
Greece	EL	012345678	9
Hungary	HU	12345678	8
Ireland[7]	IE	1234567X or 1X23456X or 1234567XX	Second character can also be '+' or '*' 9
Italy	IT	12345678901	11
Latvia	LV	12345678901	11
Lithuania	LT	123456789 123456789012	9 or 12
Luxembourg	LU	12345678	8
Malta	MT	12345678	8
Netherlands[8]	NL	123456789B01	12
Poland	PL	1234567890	10
Portugal	PT	123456789	9
Romania	RO	01234567890	2 to 10 digits
Slovakia (Slovak Rep)	SK	1234567890	10
Slovenia	SI	12345678	8
Spain[9]	ES	X12345678 or 12345678X or X1234567X	9
Sweden	SE	123456789001	12

1 First character is always U.
2 Nine digits prior to 1 April 2005. Prefix any 9 digit numbers with "0".
3 Last character must be a letter.
4 Where 11, 12 or 13 numbers are quoted – delete the first 3 as these are a tax code.
5 May include alpha character(s), either first, second or first & second.
All alpha characters except I and O are valid.
Must be the 11 alpha numeric TVA number, not the 14 digit SERIT number.
6 Must be the nine character Umsatzsteuer Identifikationsnummer (ust — Id Nr), not the ten character Umsatzsteuer nummer.
7 Includes one or two alpha characters – either last, or second & last.
8 The tenth digit is always B
Three digit suffix will always be in the range B01 to B99
9 Includes one or two alpha characters – first or last, or first & last.

17 EC SALES LISTS (ESL)

Commentary—*De Voil Indirect Tax Service* **V5.271–V5.273, V5.346, V5.355**.

17.1 Why are ESLs necessary?

All businesses registered for VAT have to submit ESLs for their EC supplies of goods and/or services subject to the reverse charge in their customer's member state. The information provided on the ESL is used in the UK and by other member states to make sure that VAT has been correctly accounted for. It is a condition of zero-rating for intra-EC supplies of goods that you have a valid VAT registration number for your EC customer. The following EUROPA website—

ec.europa.eu/taxation_customs/taxation/vat/traders/vat_number/index provides an electronic checking facility for all member states VAT registration numbers (see paragraph 4.9).

17.2 Do other member states have ESLs?

Yes. But they are called "recapitulative statements" or "summary statements".

17.3 Who must complete an ESL?

You must complete an ESL if you:

– make supplies of goods to a business registered for VAT in another Member State, including transfer of your own goods, (see section 9), or
– are the intermediary in triangular transactions between VAT registered traders in other Member States, (see section 13) or
– make supplies of services subject to the reverse charge in your customer's Member State.

You do not need to complete an ESL if you:

– are involved in triangulation and the goods are exported to a final customer outside the EU, (See VAT Notice 703 paragraph 4.1 for more information). The triangulation simplification measures do not apply in these circumstances.

17.4 How do I submit my ESL?

(a) Electronically

You may submit an ESL electronically using—

– an online form;
– an upload facility for large data (CSV or XML) files;
– UN-EDIFACT (to use this method send an e-mail to ecu@hmrc.gsi.gov.uk to register); or
– visit the Electronic Data Capture Services section of the HMRC website for the Trade Specification.

The benefits of submitting data electronically include—

– a user friendly system;
– front end validation of data (ie identification of errors on screen);
– a facility to view past Internet submissions;
– a secure system using SSL encryption technology; and
– time stamped acknowledgement of data submitted.

The service is free with registration and enrolment via the HMRC website or Government Gateway using PIN and password.

Submitting electronically will help your business by reducing—

– paperwork;
– manual entry delays;
– manual entries;
– time spent on correcting errors;
– your administration and thereby your costs.

For further information please visit our website at www.hmrc.gov.uk, selecting the EC Sales List option from the Online Services page. For assistance with the online service you should contact Specialist e-Customer Support on 0300 200 3701.

(b) Paper format

You can also submit your ESLs via the paper form VAT 101.

17.5 How do I obtain a form VAT 101 or VAT 101A?

You can obtain a VAT 101 in various ways.

Option	*Source*
1	You will automatically be sent an ESL (Form VAT 101) if at any time you have completed Box 8 of your VAT return. The form will be sent to you separately from your VAT return and should be returned separately.
2	If you have Internet access you can download copies from our website (see paragraph 17.6).
3	Forms can be obtained from the VAT Helpline, phone 0300 200 3700.
4	If you have a low level of EC sales you may be eligible to complete a simplified ESL annually (see paragraph 17.7).

If you run out of space ESL Continuation Sheets (VAT 101A) are available from our website go to, www.hmrc.gov.uk or by phoning the VAT Helpline on 0300 200 3700.

17.6 What is available from our website?

You can complete your ESLs online, download forms and find help on how to complete them on our website, go to www.hmrc.gov.uk as follows—

– EC Sales List (Form VAT 101). (An example, including notes on completion, can be found at paragraph 17.10);
– ESL Continuation Sheet (Form 101A);
– ESL Correction Sheet (Form 101B);
– EC Sales List: How to complete one box-by-box;
– Reporting your EU sales using the EC Sales List (ESL); and
– other VAT notices referred to in this notice.

17.7 How often must I submit my ESL?

This will depend on whether you supply goods or services and for goods the quarterly value (excluding VAT) of those supplies. However there is no requirement to submit nil ESLs.

If you . . .	*you will . . .*
make supplies of services only	be required to submit an ESL for each calendar quarter ending 31 March, 30 June, 30 September and 31 December but may choose to submit monthly if you prefer (see also paragraph 17.9).
make supplies of goods and the value of those supplies has not exceeded £35,000 (excl. VAT) in the current, or four previous quarters, for the period 1 Jan 2010 until 31 Dec 2011	be required to submit an ESL for each calendar quarter ending 31 March, 30 June, 30 September, and 31 December but may choose to submit monthly if you prefer (see also paragraph 17.9).
make supplies of goods and the value of those supplies has exceeded £35,000 (excl. VAT) in the current, or four previous quarters, for the period 1 Jan 2010 until 31 Dec 2011	be required to submit ESLs calendar monthly. (If you submit separate ESLs for branches within your business and the total value of goods supplied from all the branches is more than £35,000, each branch will have to submit a monthly ESL.)
make supplies of goods and services and because the value of the supplies of goods is above the quarterly threshold, you are required to submit monthly ESLs for goods	have the choice to either— —report both goods and services in each month, (using indicator 3 to identify supplies of services); or —report only goods in months 1 & 2, and in month 3 report goods for the month and services for the whole quarter (using indicator 3 to identify supplies of services).

supply goods or services, make annual VAT returns and —your total annual taxable turnover does not exceed £145,000; and —the annual value of your supplies to other member states is not more than £11,000; and —the supplies do not include new means of transport (boats, aircraft and motorised land vehicles – for further information about this, see Notice 728 "New Means of Transport")	be able to apply to the VAT Helpline for approval to submit your ESL once a year and agree the due date for sending in your annual ESL.
supply goods only (including triangular transactions – see paragraph 13.8), have a low level of EC Sales and —your total taxable turnover does not exceed the VAT registration threshold plus £25,500; —the annual value of your supplies to other member states is not more than £11,000; —the supplies do not include new means of transport (boats, aircraft and motorized land vehicles – for further information about this see Notice 728 "New Means of Transport"	be able to apply to the VAT Helpline for approval to submit a simplified annual ESL and agree the due date for sending in your annual ESL. If you receive approval you will be allowed to complete a less detailed ESL, showing only the VAT registration numbers of your EC customers. Actual values are not required but you must enter a nominal value of £1 for each entry on the ESL form.

17.8 What is the due date for submitting an ESL?

The deadlines for submitting an ESL to HMRC, for all frequencies of submissions and for goods and services are—

— for paper ESLs – within 14 days of the end of the reporting period; and
— for electronic (online) ESLs – within 21 days of the end of the reporting period.

17.9 Changing VAT return periods to coincide with calendar quarterly ESL periods

You can apply to the National Registration Service (NRS) to change your VAT return periods to coincide with your calendar quarterly ESL period. Advice on how to contact the NRS can be obtained from our website go to www.hmrc.gov.uk or by phoning the VAT Helpline on 0300 200 3700.

17.10 Copy of the ESL (Form VAT 101)

The following rule has the force of law.

> The Form VAT 101 is specified in this section of this notice for the purposes of VAT Regulations (SI 1995/2518), Regulation 22A(2)(a).

HM Revenue & Customs

Value Added Tax EC Sales List

If blank, please enter your name and address here

Please enter the following details. If you don't, we won't be able to use the information you give on the rest of this form.

VAT Registration Number

Branch/subsidiary identifier

Period reference ***MM YY***

To avoid a penalty, please make sure this form reaches HMRC **within 14 days** of the period end date.

Enter the dates in the format DD MM YYYY

to

Period for services from to

If you move, transfer, supply or sell goods or supply services to other EU countries you have to complete an EC sales list. If you have not been involved in any such transactions during this period, you **do not** need to complete this form.

If you file your EC Sales List online, you will get an extra seven days to do so. To find out more go to **www.hmrc.gov.uk** and under *do it online* select *VAT online*.

Before you start, please enter your details at the top of this page. When we receive this form we will scan it, so please write clearly in black ink and leave blank any boxes that don't apply to you. The notes on page 2 will help you complete the rest of this form. If you have more than eight transactions to record, please use a VAT101A *Continuation sheet*. See page 2 for details.

For further advice go to **www.hmrc.gov.uk** or phone our Helpline on **0845 010 9000** (Monday to Friday, 8am to 8pm)

	Country code	Customer VAT Registration Number	Total value of supplies In pound sterling	Indicator
1			£ . 00	
2			£ . 00	
3			£ . 00	
4			£ . 00	
5			£ . 00	
6			£ . 00	
7			£ . 00	
8			£ . 00	

Declaration You, or someone on your behalf, must sign below.

I declare that the information given on this form and any continuation sheets is correct and complete to the best of my knowledge.

Signature

Contact number *in case we need to speak to you*

Full name of signatory in capital letters

Date DD MM YYYY

Number of pages to this list

VAT101MAN **PAGE 1** **HMRC 10/09**

Before you start

Monthly Sales Lists

If you supply goods and services and are required to file your EC Sales List for goods monthly:

- you may report **goods only** in months 1 and 2 and report **goods** for the month and **services** for the whole quarter in month 3, or
- you can report goods and services each month.

Simplified annual EC Sales List (ESL) for supplies of goods

If HM Revenue & Customs has given you approval to submit a simplified annual ESL because you have low levels of supplies of goods to other EC countries, you are not required to enter the actual value of supplies.

Instead, enter a nominal total value of £1. Then follow the rest of the guidance about the VAT Registration Number and the indicator box.

How to fill in this form

- Write inside the boxes. Use black ink and capital letters.
- If you make a mistake, please cross it out and write the correct information below it.
- Leave blank any boxes that don't apply to you – please don't strike through them. Do not write 'none'.
- Only include your sales for the period(s) shown on page 1.
- Enter each type of sale on a separate line.

Country code

Enter your customer's country code. This is made up of two letters. It can only be one of the codes shown below.

EC country codes							
Austria	AT	Germany	DE	Netherlands	NL		
Belgium	BE	Greece	EL	Poland	PL		
Bulgaria	BG	Hungary	HU	Portugal	PT		
Cyprus	CY	Ireland	IE	Romania	RO		
Czech Republic	CZ	Italy	IT	Slovak Republic	SK		
Denmark	DK	Latvia	LV	Slovenia	SI		
Estonia	EE	Lithuania	LT	Spain	ES		
Finland	FI	Luxembourg	LU	Sweden	SE		
France	FR	Malta	MT				

Customer's VAT Registration Number

Enter your customer's VAT Registration Number starting from the left hand side.

Please do not include the country code in this column, or any spaces, dashes or comma. If you need to, refer to Notice 725 *The Single Market* to check how VAT numbers for each of the EC countries are formatted.

One of the conditions for zero-rating supplies of goods and services to other EC countries is that you must provide a **valid** VAT Registration Number for each of your customers.

You can check that a number is valid on the Europa website.

Go to www.ec.europa.eu/taxation_customs/vies

Total values of supplies and the indicator box

In all cases, enter the total, rounded down to the nearest pound sterling. Enter each amount starting from the right hand side. We have already added the zero pence and decimal point for you. Please **do not** add commas.

If you have a minus figure to enter because the value of credit notes is greater than the total value of supplies, enter a minus sign in a white box **before** each value.

Please note that you may need up to three lines for each customer. This is because the total value of **each type of sale** needs to be entered. For example, if you have supplied goods direct **and** as a triangulated sale **and** have supplied a service, you must complete three lines for that customer. Further guidance is given below.

- If you supplied goods, enter the value (including related costs) of all the goods supplied to that customer (deducting credit notes where appropriate). Leave the indicator column **blank**.

  Related costs include services which form part of the **goods**, such as freight and insurance charges.
- If you were an intermediate supplier in a triangulated sale, enter the total value of the supplies to each customer on a separate line from any other supplies made to that customer. Enter 2 in the indicator column.
- If you have supplied services which were subject to the reverse charge in the customer's member state, enter the total value of these supplies on a separate line. Enter 3 in the indicator column.

Other forms you may need

If you need more space please do not add lines to this form. Please use the form VAT101A *Continuation sheet*.

If you need to correct any data supplied in a previous period or supply previously omitted data, please do so on form VAT101B *Correction to EC Sales List*.

To obtain any of these forms, please go to www.hmrc.gov.uk select Find a Form and enter the form number (for example, *VAT101A* or *VAT101B*). Or phone the Helpline on **0845 010 9000** and ask for copies.

What to do next

When you have completed and signed this form please send it in the addressed envelope to:

HM Revenue & Customs
Comben House
Farriers Way
Liverpool
L75 1AY

To avoid penalty, please make sure this form reaches us on time.

Need help?

If you need further guidance on EC Sales Lists please refer to Notice 725 *The Single Market* which is available online.

Go to **www.hmrc.gov.uk** or phone the Helpline on **0845 010 9000** Monday to Friday, 8am to 8pm.

VAT101MAN **PAGE 2**

17.11 What information must I provide on my ESL?

You must provide *all* of the following information:

Information	*Description*
Country code	The two letter prefix which identifies your customer's country code, as shown in paragraph 16.19.

Information	*Description*
Customer's VAT registration number	The VAT registration number of your customer in the other member state. The table in paragraph 16.19 shows the only acceptable format of EC VAT numbers. We recommend that you check your customer's VAT registration numbers regularly using the Europa website (see paragraph 17.1).
Total value of supplies in £s sterling	The total value for the appropriate period of— —the goods and related services which you have supplied to each customer, leaving the indicator column blank (related services are services which form part of the price of the goods such as freight charges and insurance.); —triangular transactions, entered on a separate line for each customer and using code '2' in the indicator column, and —supplies of services subject to the reverse charge in your customer's member state, entered on a separate line for each customer and using code '3' in the indicator column. If you make a supply of services to a business which is not registered for VAT in their member state because it is below the registration threshold, but which has provided you with evidence that it is in business (for place of supply purposes), you should not include these supplies on your ESL. If you are completing a simplified annual ESL you must insert £1 in the value column for each entry.

17.12 Will I be penalised if I fail to submit my ESL, send it in late, or make mistakes?

If you fail to submit your ESL by the due date (see paragraph 17.8) you may be liable to a penalty of 5, £10 or £15 for each day that you are late, subject to a maximum of 100 days. The rate applied will depend on the number of times you have been late. You will remain liable to penalties without notice until 12 months have elapsed without further default.

If you submit an ESL that contains a material inaccuracy and you fail to tell us, you may be liable to a penalty of £100. Material inaccuracies fall into three main categories—

- data is missing from the ESL;
- there are factually incorrect lines on the ESL; or
- an invalid VAT number is used.

You will not be liable to a penalty if you can satisfy us that you have a reasonable excuse (see paragraph 17.3).

17.13 What is meant by "reasonable excuse"?

There is no legal definition of reasonable excuse but we will look closely at the circumstances of each case. If you can show that your conduct was that of a conscientious business person who accepted the need to comply with VAT requirements, then there may be a reasonable excuse.

Genuine mistakes, honesty and acting in good faith are not accepted as reasonable excuses for penalty purposes. The law provides specifically that you do not have a reasonable excuse if you relied on some other person to perform any task for you.

In addition, the fact that you have:

— quoted a VAT number for your customer that does not conform to the published format for your customer's EC member state as shown in paragraph 16.19; or
— used a VAT number which HMRC has informed you is invalid;

will not be accepted as a reasonable excuse for the material inaccuracy. In such cases you may also be liable to account for the VAT on any supplies where you have not met the requirements for zero-rating (see paragraph 4.3).

17.14 What will happen in the event of errors?

If you submit a paper ESL we will notify you of any errors that we identify on a Form VAT 104 (ESL Error Report). The computer-generated form is sent to you with a copy of our "Helpful Hints" document. The form will show the error lines and the reasons for the errors. Please correct the errors in the spaces provided and return the form within 21 days of receipt to the address shown. Alternatively, you can voluntarily submit a VAT 101B to notify HMRC of any errors made.

If you submit your ESL online using the ECSL service, any errors are highlighted onscreen as you complete the form, allowing you to correct them prior to submission. If you choose to submit the ESL with some errors still remaining, you will be able to correct these errors online, up to 21 days after the date of submission. After that date, the facility will no longer be available and any outstanding errors will be notified to you in writing, as described above.

If you submit by CSV or XML you can still use the online correction service to correct error lines identified at the time of submission. Alternatively, if you decide to submit a new file, you must delete the error lines from your original submission within 21 days, using the "Correct declaration errors" page on the ECSL Online Service, to avoid receiving correspondence on this subject.

17.15 How can I avoid making errors?

When completing your ESL please make sure that—

- you check the validity of your customer's VAT number (see paragraph 4.9);
- the country code and customer number match the format for the relevant member state (see paragraph 16.19);
- the value of supplies is in £'s sterling, rounded *down* to the nearest £, starting from the right hand side of the box (the decimal point and pence have already been entered on the form);
- you enter the total value of each type of sale one entry per customer, per period of submission;
- if you supplied goods, you enter the value (including related costs such as freight and insurance charges) of all the goods supplied to that customer (deducting credit notes where appropriate) and leave the indicator column blank;
- if you were an intermediate supplier in a triangular sale, you enter the total value of the supplies to each customer (deducting credit notes where appropriate) on a separate line from any other supplies made to that customer and enter 2 in the indicator column;
- if you supplied services which were subject to the reverse charge in the customer's member state, you enter the total value of these supplies to each customer, (deducting credit notes where appropriate) on a separate line from any other supplies made to that customer and enter 3 in the indicator column;
- you enter your customer's VAT registration number (starting from the left hand side of the box;
- you complete the bottom of the ESL form with the number of pages you are submitting ("Number of pages to this list" box) and your declaration including your contact phone number, signature and date;
- you retain a copy of the completed ESL for your records; and
- advise us if you will no longer be making any EC supplies by contacting the VAT Helpline.

Please *do not*:

- put the country code in the Customer VAT Registration Box;
- enter dashes, spaces, commas or slashes;
- enter details for the Canaries, the Channel Islands, Gibraltar, Norway and Switzerland, or any other countries which are outside the EC (see paragraph 2.4);
- enter EC customer VAT registration numbers that you think may be correct – check them using the Europa website (see paragraph 4.9.);
- alter any of the details on your printed EC Sales VAT 101 form — if any of the details are wrong, or you have a query, please contact the VAT Helpline;

– send a "nil" return – ESLs are not required if you have not made any supplies of goods to the [*sic*], or
– include supplies to UK customers as these are not EC transactions.

17.16 What should I do if I have made errors?

You must tell us about all errors and omissions on your ESL where:
– errors exceed £100;
– an incorrect VAT registration number has been quoted; or
– you have used the wrong transaction type indicator when completing the ESL.

You can download a form VAT 101B (ESL Corrections) from the HMRC website to notify of any errors made. For help on the correction of errors please contact the VAT Helpline or e-mail the esl.helpdesk@hmrc.gsi.gov.uk

17.17 Can I submit separate ESLs for different parts of my business?

You can choose to submit separate ESLs on paper or online if you have—

— individual branches of your business;
— individual companies within a group VAT registration; or
— self accounting branches within a group VAT registration.

You should contact HMRC to arrange to do this. You will be given a three-digit code for each branch or company in your business. You will need to use this as an identifier when you complete the separate ESLs. If you wish to submit data online for individual Branches you must register each one separately with HMRC's Online Services.

Please note that if the total value of goods supplied from all the branches of your business is more than £70,000 (excluding VAT) in the current or previous four quarters, each branch will have to submit a monthly ESL.

17.18 Can I use an agent to send in my ESL?

You may use an agent to act on your behalf, but remember the legal responsibility for the accurate and timely completion and submission of an ESLremains with you.

Any agent can submit an online EC Sales List on behalf of a client but the agent must be registered for VAT and appointed online by the client to act on their behalf.

The client should enrol online, as an organisation, for the EC Sales service through www.hmrc.gov.uk. An activation pin will be issued (by post) and once the client has activated the service, they should login to www.gateway.gov.uk and select 'Manage services', then 'Appoint agent', They should then enter the agents reference number, in order to link their VAT number to the agents online account.

17.19 Do I need to complete an ESL if my only EC supplies are triangular transactions?

Yes. If your only EC supplies are part of a triangular transaction, you are still required to submit an ESL and this can be submitted online, or by downloading a form from our website go to, www.hmrc.gov.uk or by phoning the VAT Helpline on 0300 200 3700 who will arrange for ESLs to be sent to you automatically.

17.20 Do I need to complete an ESL if my only EC supplies are services?

Yes. If your only EC supplies are services subject to the reverse charge in your customer's member state, you are still required to submit an ESL (see paragraph 17.21).

17.21 Do I have to include supplies of goods on the ESL that would be zero-rated if supplied within the UK?

Yes, you must complete an ESL if you make supplies of goods to a trader registered for VAT in another member state, including the transfer of your own goods and goods that would be zero-rated if supplied within the UK.

17.22 Do I include goods supplied free of charge to a customer in another member state?

You are making a deemed supply of goods and you must include it on your ESL. The value you show is the cost to you of the goods. Samples or gifts may be excluded provided you meet the conditions described in the section dealing with output tax in Notice 700 "The VAT Guide".

17.23 Distance selling

If you make supplies of goods to customers who are not VAT-registered in other member states and you are responsible for delivery of the goods (distance selling – see section 6) do *not* enter these supplies on your ESL.

17.24 Do I include temporary movements of my own goods to another member state?

Not unless the conditions relating to the transfer change (see section 10).

17.25 How do I account for credit notes?

Deduct the value of the credit note from the value of the supplies made to your customer. If the value of credit notes exceeds the value of supplies show the resulting negative figure using a minus sign.

17.26 How do I determine the liability of a supply of services in my customer's member state?

The law requires that businesses report supplies of services that are taxable in the customer's member state (from 1 January 2010) and the onus is on businesses to comply with the law. If reasonable attempts, which may include discussing with the customer, or the customer's tax authority, have failed to ascertain what the VAT treatment is in the other member state(s), businesses may wish to assume that the UK VAT treatment will apply to those supplies. This is on the basis that it should be consistent with the EC Principal VAT Directive and therefore with the law in other member states.

If subsequently it becomes clear that a supply categorised and reported as taxable is in fact exempt, or vice versa, the business must submit a VAT 101B ESL Correction sheet. This form can be downloaded from the HMRC website or requested from the VAT Helpline.

Once the business has knowledge that a VAT treatment of a supply in a member state is different to that in the UK, it should adopt this treatment in their reporting of such supplies to that jurisdiction in the future.

17.27 Should I record supplies to a "taxable person" in another member state if they do not have a VAT registration number?

No, you should only record on an ESL supplies to businesses in other Member States that are VAT registered and can provide a valid VAT registration number. If you make a supply to a business which is not registered for VAT in their Member State because it is below the registration threshold, but which has provided you with evidence that it is in business (for place of supply purposes), you should not include these supplies on your ESL. This is because the absence of a VAT registration number would cause it to be rejected. However, in some cases receipt of the supply will result in the business being required to register in their Member State. If this is the case and a VAT registration number is subsequently given to you, an amendment should be made to the ESL using form VAT 101B ESL Correction sheet. This form can be downloaded from our website go to, www.hmrc.gov.uk or by phoning the VAT Helpline on 0300 200 3700.

17.28 When is an intra-EC supply of services to be included on an ESL?

The date on which a transaction should be included on the ESL is dependent on the time of supply rules in the customer's MS. On the basis that other member states rules are, like the UK's, consistent with the adopted EC legislation, the time of supply will be either the date of payment or performance (completion), whichever is the earlier. There is no requirement for a business to confirm with the customer that the ESL period and the VAT period on which they declare the transaction as a reverse charge match. For the purposes of completing an ESL, where it is evident that for certain types of supply the date of performance or date of payment is almost the same as "date of invoice", the "invoice date"' may be used. As a general principle we will accept reliance on an invoice date or any other reasonable methodology provided it does not produce a manifestly inaccurate overall result. Ultimately it is up to individual businesses to identify the most appropriate methodology for their particular circumstances.

17.29 Can I use the quarterly invoice date to complete my ESL for continuous supplies of management services?

Yes.

17.30 Is an ESL required if the supply of services is subject to a "zero rate" in the customer's member state?

No, ESLs are only required for taxable supplies where the recipient is liable to account for VAT under the reverse charge provisions. For zero-rated supplies there is no reverse charge so there is no ESL requirement.

18 INTRASTAT

Commentary—*De Voil Indirect Tax Service* **V5.276**.

18.1 What is Intrastat?

Intrastat is the name given to the system for collecting statistics on the trade in goods between member states. Intrastat replaced customs declarations as a source of trade statistics within the EC. It exists throughout the EC and requirements are similar in all member states.

18.2 Are supplies of services included in Intrastat?

Supplies of services are excluded from Intrastat except where they are related charges such as freight and insurance and form part of the contract to supply goods.

18.3 How are the Intra-EC trade statistics collected?

All businesses carrying out trade with other member states must declare the totals of their sales and acquisitions on their VAT returns. Those businesses over a legally set threshold are also required to provide more detailed information on Intrastat Supplementary Declarations. Intra-EC trade statistics are compiled from the Supplementary Declarations and estimations made using the information on the VAT Returns. For details of the current Intrastat threshold see Notice 60 "Intrastat General Guide".

18.4 How are values of EC trade declared on a VAT return?

All businesses registered for VAT must complete two boxes on their VAT returns showing the total value of goods supplied to other member states and the total value of goods acquired from other member states, see paragraph 16.3. For further information about this, see Notice 700/12 "Filling in your VAT return".

18.5 Which larger businesses complete Supplementary Declarations?

Those businesses with a value of trade in goods with other member states above the Intrastat threshold for either acquisitions or supplies of goods must complete Supplementary Declarations each month. For further information about this, see Notice 60 "Intrastat General Guide".

18.6 How are goods described for Intrastat purposes?

For Intrastat purposes, goods received into the UK are called arrivals and goods consigned to another member state from the UK are called dispatches. This is because the Intrastat system developed separately from the VAT system and there are some differences in coverage between the two systems. For further information about this, see Notice 60 "Intrastat General Guide".

18.7 Where can I obtain further information or help?

For further information about Intrastat requirements, see Notice 60 "Intrastat General Guide". If you cannot find the answer to your questions there, the VAT Helpline will assist you. You should make it clear that your enquiry concerns Intrastat.

Detailed guidance and updates on Intrastat matters can also be obtained on the Intrastat pages at: www.uktradeinfo.com

18.8 Can I make Intrastat declarations electronically?

If you are interested in making Intrastat declarations electronically, please contact HM Revenue & Customs, uktradeinfo Customer Services by phone on 01702 367485. Guidance on submitting your forms electronically can also be found on the Intrastat pages of

www.uktradeinfo.com

NOTICE 727
RETAIL SCHEMES

2012

1 INTRODUCTION

This notice cancels and replaces Notice 727 (January 2011).

1.2 What are retail schemes?

The retail schemes are methods you can use to arrive at the value of your taxable retail sales and to determine what proportion of those sales are taxable at the different rates of VAT. As at 4 January 2011 the VAT rates are—

- standard rate (20 per cent);
- lower rate (5 per cent); and
- zero rate (0 per cent).

Most VAT-registered businesses take these details from tax invoices issued to customers. These schemes provide an alternative if you are a retailer and you find it difficult to issue invoices for a large number of supplies made direct to the public. Each scheme has a turnover limit.

The boxed text below has the force of law.

> The turnover limits for the schemes apply to the whole of your VAT registration.

Commentary—*De Voil Indirect Tax Service* **V3.551**.

. . .

1.4 Force of law

Parts of this notice have the force of law under the VAT Regulations 1995, Part IX (regs 66–75). All of Sections 7 and 10 have legal force and supplement the law. Certain paragraphs within other parts of the notice also have legal force and supplement the law. The text of those paragraphs is indicated by a statement and has been placed in a box.

Commentary—*De Voil Indirect Tax Service* **V3.552**.

2 USING RETAIL SCHEMES

2.1 When should I use a retail scheme?

The schemes are intended for businesses who cannot reasonably be expected to account for VAT in the normal way. Under normal accounting there is no requirement for you to issue a tax invoice to customers who are not registered for VAT. But normal accounting does require you to identify, for each supply you make, the tax exclusive value and the VAT, and to be able to produce periodic totals of those amounts.

The boxed text below has the force of law.

The schemes can be used for retail sales only.

Retail sales are generally low in value and made to a large number of customers in small quantities.

Commentary—*De Voil Indirect Tax Service* **V3.551**.

2.2 What if my business makes retail and non-retail sales?

This paragraph has the force of law.

If you make a mixture of retail and non retail sales you can use a retail scheme to calculate the tax due on your retail sales only. You must account for non-retail sales using the normal method of accounting.

Commentary—*De Voil Indirect Tax Service* **V3.551**.

2.3 How do I choose a retail scheme?

Sections 3 and 5 explain briefly the way in which the different schemes work and how they suit different types of business. You will find further information about individual schemes in the specific retail scheme notice.

If, after reading Sections 3 and 5, you find that you are eligible for more than one scheme you will need to choose the one best suited to your particular business. You should also consider other factors too, such as the complexity of the calculation and the amount of paperwork, record-keeping or stock taking you will need to undertake, relative to the other schemes.

Section 11 shows a comparison in table form. Remember, the valuation of the tax due may vary from scheme to scheme.

Commentary—*De Voil Indirect Tax Service* **V3.561**.

2.4 Can I use a retail scheme for sales to other VAT registered businesses?

This paragraph has the force of law.

Sales to other VAT-registered businesses must not be included in a retail scheme. The exception to this is *occasional cash sales*, for example a—

- garage supplying petrol to a VAT registered customer; or
- retail DIY store supplying building materials to a VAT-registered builder.

Commentary—*De Voil Indirect Tax Service* **V3.551**.

3 STANDARD SCHEMES

. . .

3.4 How does the Point of Sale scheme work?

Under the Point of Sale scheme you calculate the tax due on your sales by identifying the correct VAT liability at the time you make the sale.

This usually means using a till system which is capable of distinguishing between goods sold at different rates of VAT. But you can use the scheme if you can separate your sales in another way, for example by using separate tills for different rates.

Once your system has produced the total value of sales at each rate you calculate your output tax by applying the appropriate VAT fraction to the relevant portion of your Daily Gross Takings (see para 4.6).

The boxed text below has the force of law.

> If you make only standard or only lower-rated sales, you must use this scheme.

Commentary—*De Voil Indirect Tax Service* **V3.571**.

. . .

3.7 What factors should I consider before choosing Apportionment scheme (1)?

The scheme is relatively simple. However, if on average, you achieve a higher mark-up for your zero-rated goods than your lower or standard-rated goods, you may find that you pay more VAT if you use Apportionment scheme (1) than you would using another scheme.

The boxed text below has the force of law.

> You can only use the scheme if your total tax exclusive turnover from retail sales does not exceed *£1 million*;
>
> You cannot use the scheme for supplies of services, or for supplies of goods which you have made or grown yourself, or for supplies of catering.

You can find further information about the Apportionment schemes in Notice 727/4 "How to work the Apportionment Schemes".

Commentary—*De Voil Indirect Tax Service* **V3.572**.

. . .

3.9 What factors should I consider before choosing Apportionment scheme (2)?

The scheme can be complex to operate but if you use it properly, it will provide you with a more accurate valuation of your supplies over a period of time.

The boxed text below has the force of law.

> You can only use the scheme if your total tax exclusive turnover from retail sales does not exceed *£130 million*;
>
> You must be able to work out the Expected Selling Prices (ESPs) of your stock on hand when you start to use the scheme;
>
> You cannot use the scheme for supplies of services or catering.

You can find further information about the Apportionment schemes in Notice 727/4 "How to work the Apportionment Schemes".

Commentary—*De Voil Indirect Tax Service* **V3.572**.

. . .

3.12 What factors should I consider before choosing Direct Calculation scheme (1)?

Direct Calculation scheme (1) can be relatively simple if you have a small proportion of sales at one rate of VAT. But the scheme can produce inaccuracies if ESP are not calculated accurately. Additionally it can be complex to work out if you sell goods at three rates of VAT, though it may be possible to account for a small number of goods at a third rate outside the scheme.

You should also consider the following—

The boxed text below has the force of law.

- You cannot use Direct Calculation scheme (1) if your annual tax exclusive retail turnover exceeds £1 *million.*;
- if your minority sales are zero-rated you may not use the scheme for zero-rated services;
- if your minority sales are standard-rated you may not use the scheme for standard-rated services;
- the scheme may not be used for supplies of catering.

You can find further information about the schemes in Notice 727/5 "How to work the Direct Calculation schemes".

Commentary—*De Voil Indirect Tax Service* **V3.573**.

4 SPECIAL RULES ABOUT THE STANDARD SCHEMES

4.1 Can I use a mixture of schemes?

The boxed text below has the force of law.

Normally the retail scheme calculation will be a single calculation for the whole of your VAT registration. You can, if you wish, use the same scheme separately at a number of distinct business locations. But, if you use a scheme other than the Point of Sale scheme (see para 3.4), there may be a need to make adjustments to account for transfers between different parts of the business. You must agree the details of such adjustments with your local VAT Business Advice Centre.

You may find that you need to use different schemes in different parts of your business. Provided you are eligible for the schemes, you can mix the Point of Sale scheme (see para 3.4) with either a Direct Calculation (see paras 3.10 to 3.13) or an Apportionment scheme (see paras 3.6 to 3.9). But, you cannot use different versions of the Direct Calculation or Apportionment schemes and you must not use an Apportionment scheme in some parts of your business and a Direct Calculation scheme in other parts.

Remember, you can always use the normal method of accounting together with any scheme or any allowable mixture for which you are eligible.

Commentary—*De Voil Indirect Tax Service* **V3.562**.

4.2 Can I change schemes?

The boxed text below has the force of law.

You can change schemes at the end of a complete year reckoned from the beginning of the tax period in which you first adopted the scheme. You must use the scheme for 12 months, unless—

- you become ineligible for the scheme you are using; or
- we allow or require an earlier change.

If you become ineligible you must cease to use the scheme from the end of the next complete accounting period.

For example, if you account for VAT by reference to quarters ending March, June, September and December and your turnover makes you ineligible for a scheme during February, you must cease to use that scheme to account for supplies made on or after 1 July.

Some schemes require adjustments when you cease to use them, see para 6.1.

Commentary—*De Voil Indirect Tax Service* **V3.563**.

. . .

4.4 Do I need to keep a record of my Daily Gross Takings (DGT)?

This paragraph has the force of law.

Yes. All the retail schemes require a record of the value of your retail sales called the Daily Gross Takings or DGT. From the day you start to use a scheme you must keep a record of your DGT. You must include in this record—

- all payments for your retail supplies as they are received by you from cash customers;
- the full value, including VAT, of all your credit or other non cash retail sales at the time you make the supply; and
- details of any adjustments made to this record.

Commentary—*De Voil Indirect Tax Service* **V3.556**.

. . .

5 BESPOKE SCHEMES

5.1 What is a bespoke scheme?

The boxed text below has the force of law.

If your annual turnover of retail sales, excluding VAT, is above *£130 million* you cannot use the published standard schemes.

If you think your annual turnover is about to exceed £130 million you should contact HMRC as soon as possible to agree a bespoke scheme.

A bespoke scheme will be tailored to meet the particular requirements of your business and is likely to be an adaptation, to a greater or lesser extent, of one of the published schemes.

You can find further information about bespoke schemes in Notice 727/2 "VAT: Bespoke retail schemes".

Commentary—*De Voil Indirect Tax Service* **V3.552, 574.**

6 CEASING TO USE A RETAIL SCHEME

6.1 What must I do when I cease using a retail scheme?

Depending on the scheme you use, you must follow the rules in the table below. *This paragraph has the force of law.*

Scheme	*Procedure*
Point of Sale	No adjustment on ceasing to use for all or part of a VAT registration.
Apportionment (1)	You must perform a closing adjustment, as for the annual adjustment, even if you leave before the anniversary of starting to use the scheme.
Apportionment (2)	Normally no adjustment is necessary. However, if you are ceasing to use this scheme in part of your business but are continuing to use it in other parts of the registration, make sure that the rolling calculation reflects the ESP of stock now excluded from the Apportionment calculation.

Scheme	Procedure
Direct Calculation (1)	Normally no adjustment is necessary.
Direct Calculation (2)	You must make a closing adjustment, as for the annual adjustment, even if you leave before the anniversary of starting to use the scheme. The adjustment must take account of any disposals made during the year which were not by way of retail sale. This is done by excluding from the figures used in the calculation, the value of any goods which were previously part of the scheme calculation but were not a retail sale.

Commentary—*De Voil Indirect Tax Service* **V3.563**.

6.2 Are there any other rules when ceasing to use a scheme?

Apart from these special rules under the retail scheme, you should also remember—

- only goods sold by retail can be included in the retail scheme. If you cease to use a scheme because you transfer part or all of your business as a going concern, the value of stock transferred will have to be excluded from your retail scheme; and
- if you cease to trade, VAT may become due on the value of your stocks and assets (see Notice 700/11 "Cancelling your registration").

We may require additional adjustments where unusual patterns of trade prevent your scheme from producing a fair and reasonable result.

For these reasons you must always tell your local VAT Business Advice Centre if—

The boxed text below has the force of law.

- you buy or sell part of a business; or
- the legal entity of your business changes (for example, from sole proprietor to partnership); or
- you are registered as a group and the composition of the group is to change.

Commentary—*De Voil Indirect Tax Service* **V3.261**.

. . .

8 CATERING ADAPTATION

This section supplements the rules in the "How to work" notices.

. . .

8.3 What are the conditions for using the catering adaptation?

This paragraph has the force of law.

You may use the catering adaptation described in paras 8.7 and 8.8 provided—

- you can satisfy us that you are unable to operate the Point of Sale scheme;
- yyou have reasonable grounds for believing that the tax-exclusive value of your taxable retail catering sales (standard and zero-rated sales) will not exceed *£1 million* in the next 12 months; and
- your use of the catering adaptation produces a fair and reasonable result in any period.

Commentary—*De Voil Indirect Tax Service* **V3.565**.

8.4 What happens if I do not comply with the conditions?

If you do not comply with the conditions of the catering adaptation we may—

- assess for the underdeclared VAT arising from unsatisfactory use of the catering adaptation; and/or
- refuse use of the catering adaptation for future periods.

Commentary—*De Voil Indirect Tax Service* **V3.565**.

8.5 How do I start to use the adaptation?

This paragraph has the force of law.

If you wish to use the adaptation and meet the conditions detailed in para 8.3 you must notify your local VAT Business Advice Centre. Generally we will do no more than acknowledge your letter. You may begin to use the adaptation as soon as you receive our acknowledgement.

Commentary—*De Voil Indirect Tax Service* **V3.565**.

8.6 Do I have to maintain any records?

The boxed text below has the force of law.

Yes. To use the catering adaptation you must maintain a record of Daily Gross Takings (DGT).

The DGT is not simply a record of cash on hand. Details of the DGT requirements are given in paras 4.4 to 4.6.

Commentary—*De Voil Indirect Tax Service* **V3.565**.

8.7 How do I calculate my output tax under the catering adaptation?

To calculate your output tax on catering sales, follow the procedure in the table below for each tax period. *This paragraph has the force of law.*

Step	*Procedure*	*Result*
1	Establish your Daily Gross Takings (DGT) in accordance with paras 4.4 to 4.6 and the rules contained in the relevant scheme notice.	£ ______
2	Calculate the percentage of your total catering sales made at the standard rate. See the rules covering the making of the calculation in para 8.8.	= %
3	Apply the percentage at Step 2 to the DGT at Step 1.	£ ______
4	Total at Step 3 x VAT fraction. (1/6th for VAT at 20 per cent.)	£ ______ This is your output tax on catering sales for this period.

Commentary—*De Voil Indirect Tax Service* **V3.565**.

8.8 How do I calculate the percentage of my standard-rated sales?

This paragraph has the force of law.

Your method of calculation must be able to satisfy us when we visit that the catering adaptation gives a fair and reasonable result in any period. Whichever way you choose to make your calculation you must always—

- base the calculation on a sample of your actual sales for a representative period. The representative period will depend on the nature of your business but you must be able to satisfy us that it takes account of hourly, daily and seasonal fluctuations;
- retain details of the sample, including the dates and times it took place; and
- carry out a new calculation in each tax period. You must not use a calculation that has been established by a previous owner of the business.

Commentary—*De Voil Indirect Tax Service* **V3.565**.

8.9 What is the legal basis for the catering adaptation?

The catering adaptation is published under VAT Regulations 1995, reg 67.

Commentary—*De Voil Indirect Tax Service* **V3.565**.

9 RETAIL CHEMIST ADJUSTMENT

This section supplements the rules in the "How to work" notices.

9.1 What is the liability of goods supplied on prescription?

The supply of goods dispensed by a registered chemist on the prescription of a medical practitioner is zero-rated under Group 12 of the Zero-Rated Schedule of the VAT Act 1994. You can find further information in Notice 701/31 "Health".

Commentary—*De Voil Indirect Tax Service* **V3.566**.

9.2 Why is an adjustment necessary?

Most Group 12 goods dispensed on prescription are standard-rated when purchased by the chemist but zero-rated when supplied to the patient. A number of items supplied on prescription such as gluten free bread, are zero-rated at purchase and some items, such as smoking cessation products, are charged at the reduced rate at purchase. Consequently, a further adjustment is necessary.

Commentary—*De Voil Indirect Tax Service* **V3.566**.

9.3 Does the adjustment apply to all the retail schemes?

No. If you are using a *Point of Sale scheme* you will be accounting for VAT at the correct rate. This is because you identify the correct rate of VAT at the time the supply is made and no adjustment is necessary. Also, the Retail Chemist adjustment cannot be used with *Apportionment scheme (2)*.

Other retail schemes require the adjustments explained in para 9.4 in order to reduce the output tax which the scheme would otherwise produce.

If you use a direct calculation scheme, you must normally calculate Expected Selling Prices (ESPs) for your "minority" goods (see paras 3.10 and 3.13). However, if your minority goods are standard-rated sales, you may calculate ESPs on the basis of the zero-rated goods received for resale if this would be simpler for your business.

Commentary—*De Voil Indirect Tax Service* **V3.566**.

9.4 How does the adjustment work if I use the Direct Calculation schemes or Apportionment scheme (1)?

Whether you are using the first or the second Direct Calculation scheme or Apportionment scheme (1) you must make the following adjustment. *This paragraph has the force of law.*

Step	*Procedure*	*Result*
1	Calculate your DGT including the total amount from your prescription charges and NHS cheque (less the value of any exempt supplies such as rota payments).	£ ________
2	Work out the output tax as explained in the Direct Calculation schemes notice or Apportionment schemes notice.	£ ________

Step	Procedure	Result
3	Add up the payments received in the period for all Group 12 goods - even if you did not supply the goods in the period. Remember your NHS cheque may include payments for supplies not zero-rated under Group 12, but exempt or standard-rated. Such amounts must not be included in this total.	£ ____________
4	Estimate the value of goods included in step 3 that were zero-rated when you received them (see para 9.5 below).	£ ____________
5	Estimate the value of goods included in step 3 that were charged at the reduced rate when you received them (see para 9.6 below)	£ ____________
6	Add the totals at step 4 and step 5	£ ____________
7	Subtract the total at step 6 from the total at step 3.	£ ____________
8	To work out the VAT you will have included in step 2 from Group 12 goods, which were standard rated when you received them, multiply the total at step 7 by the VAT fraction (1/6 for VAT at 20%).	£ ____________
9	To work out the VAT you will have included in step 2 from Group 12 goods, which were charged at the reduced rate when you received them, multiply the total at step 5 by the VAT fraction (1/21 for VAT at 5%).	£ ____________
10	To work out the total VAT you will have included in step 2 from Group 12 goods add the totals at step 8 and step 9	£ ____________
11	The output tax is the total at step 2 minus the notional output tax at step 10.	£ ____________

Commentary—*De Voil Indirect Tax Service* **V3.566**.

9.5 How do I estimate the percentage of zero-rated supplies?

This paragraph has the force of law.

One of the adjustments set out at paragraph 9.4 requires you to estimate a value for payments for all Group 12 goods that were zero-rated when you received them (see steps 3 and 4 of para 9.4). You must be able to satisfy us if we visit you that your estimation gives a fair and reasonable valuation in any period. Whichever way you choose to make your estimation you must always—

- base the estimation on a sample of your actual purchases for a representative period. The representative period will depend on the nature of your business but you must take account of seasonal fluctuations etc;
- retain details of the sample; and
- carry out a new estimation in each tax period. You must not use an estimation that has been established by a previous owner of the business.

Commentary—*De Voil Indirect Tax Service* **V3.566**.

10 SPECIAL ARRANGEMENTS FOR FLORISTS

10.1 About this section

This section applies to florists or other retailers who are members of organisations such as Interflora, Teleflorist and Flowergram which facilitate the purchase and delivery of flowers. It—

– supplements the rules in the "How to work" notices;
– replaces Notice 727/1 "Retail florists"; and
– has the force of law under regulation 67 of the VAT Regulations 1995 (SI 1995/2518).

Commentary—*De Voil Indirect Tax Service* **V3.567**.

10.2 Is an adjustment necessary for sales made by florists?

Yes. The adjustments you make will depend on your retail scheme and whether or not you are the member of an organisation such as one of those referred to in para 10.1 who—

– receives payment direct from the customer (the sending member); or
– delivers the flowers and receives payment from the organisation (the executing member).

Commentary—*De Voil Indirect Tax Service* **V3.567**.

10.3 How must I treat invoices issued by the agency?

The documents you receive from the agency may show the output tax which you must pay to us. This is known as "self-billed" output tax because the agency issues the invoice for the sales you make. You should check your agency documentation carefully and bring any tax shown to account outside your retail scheme. You do this by adding the self-billed output tax to any VAT calculated in accordance with your retail scheme.

You should find more about self-billed output tax in your agency documentation. You can find further information in Notice 700 "The VAT Guide" or you can ask your local VAT Business Advice Centre.

Commentary—*De Voil Indirect Tax Service* **V3.567**.

10.4 How does the adjustment work?

Depending on the scheme you use, you should follow the rules in the table below—

	As sending member you must . . .	*As executing member you must . . .*
Point of Sale	include the payments received in your DGT when you take the order. (No adjustment is necessary.)	not include payments received from the agency in your Daily Gross Takings; account for any tax due outside your retail scheme.
Apportionment (1) and (2)	identify from agency documentation the value of the sales you make as a sending member and account for any tax due outside your retail scheme; not include the payments for these sales in your DGT under the retail scheme calculation.	account for any tax due outside your retail scheme on the basis of the agency documentation; not include the agency payments in your Daily Gross Takings; exclude the value of flowers from your purchase records if you use the simple scheme-Apportionment scheme (1); adjust your Expected Selling Prices for the value of flowers sent as executing member and accounted for outside the retail scheme if you use Apportionment scheme (2).
Direct Calculation (1) and (2)	identify from agency documentation the value of the sales you make as a sending member and account for any tax due on those amounts outside your retail scheme;	account for any tax due outside your retail scheme on the basis of the agency documentation;

	As sending member you must . . .	*As executing member you must . . .*
	not include the payments for these sales in your DGT under the retail scheme calculation.	not include agency payments in your Daily Gross Takings; adjust your Expected Selling Prices for the value of flowers sent as executing member and accounted for outside the retail scheme.

Commentary—*De Voil Indirect Tax Service* **V3.567**.

. . .

NOTICE 727/3
RETAIL SCHEMES—HOW TO WORK THE POINT OF SALE SCHEME

January 2013

This notice cancels and replaces Notice 727/3 (January 2011).

1 INTRODUCTION

1.1 WHAT IS THIS NOTICE ABOUT?

This notice tells you about the Point of Sale Scheme, one of the standard Retail Schemes. It explains the general rules applicable to the scheme, how the scheme works (including the calculation of VAT), and what records you should keep-especially your Daily Gross Takings (DGT) records.

The changes are:

– paragraph 2.6 - updated to reflect the current "capping" regulations
– paragraph 8.2 - change of address

You can access details of any changes to this notice since March 2002 either online, go to at www.hmrc.gov.uk or by phoning the VAT Helpline on 0300 200 3700.

Commentary—*De Voil Indirect Tax Service* **V3.551–V3.576.**

1.2 WHO SHOULD READ THIS NOTICE?

You should read this if—

— you are a VAT registered business making retail sales;
— you are unable to account for VAT on those sales in the normal way (see para 2.1); and
— — your annual turnover, excluding VAT, does not exceed £130 million.

1.3 ARE THERE OTHER RETAIL SCHEMES?

Yes. Other standard retail schemes are the Apportionment Schemes and Direct Calculation Schemes. There are also Bespoke Retail Schemes. Businesses whose annual retail turnover exceeds £130 million cannot use a standard scheme. Instead they can agree a bespoke retail scheme (see para 2.7).

1.4 FORCE OF LAW

Parts of this notice have the force of law under the VAT Regulations 1995, Part IX (regulations 66–75). All paragraphs in Section 6 and certain paragraphs in other sections have legal force and supplement the law. The text of these paragraphs is placed in a box and indicated by a statement.

Commentary—*De Voil Indirect Tax Service* **V3.552.**

1.5 WHERE CAN I FIND OUT ABOUT THE OTHER SCHEMES?

You will find a general introduction to retail schemes as well as guidance on choosing a retail scheme in Notice 727 "VAT Retail Schemes" (Part V8).

Details of the other schemes can be found in—

Notice 727/2 *Bespoke Retail Schemes.*

Notice 727/4 *How to work the Apportionment Schemes*; and

Notice 727/5 *How to work the Direct Calculation Schemes.*

1 INTRODUCTION

. . .

2 GENERAL RULES

All boxed text in this section has the force of law (see para 1.4).

2.1 WHO CAN USE A RETAIL SCHEME?

Any retailer who would find it difficult to account for VAT in the normal way can use a retail scheme. Accounting in the normal way does not require you to issue a tax invoice to unregistered customers. But it does require you to identify, for each sale, the tax exclusive value and the VAT and to be able to produce periodic totals of those amounts.

Commentary—*De Voil Indirect Tax Service* **V3.551.**

2.2 CAN I USE ANY RETAIL SCHEME?

No. Some of the schemes have turnover limits (see para 3.2 for guidance on when to use the Point of Sale Scheme).

Otherwise, provided your chosen retail scheme produces a fair and reasonable result you may choose a scheme which suits your business best. Notice 727 *VAT Retail* schemes tells you more about choosing a retail scheme.

Commentary—*De Voil Indirect Tax Service* **V3.571, 574.**

2.3 CAN I USE THE SCHEME TO ACCOUNT FOR ALL MY RETAIL AND NON-RETAIL SUPPLIES?

> The following text has the force of law.
>
> No. Retail schemes can be used for retail supplies only.
>
> If you make a mixture of retail and non-retail sales you must only use a retail scheme to calculate the tax due on your retail sales. You must account for non-retail sales using the normal method of accounting.

2.4 WHAT IF MY BUSINESS MAKES SALES TO OTHER VAT REGISTERED BUSINESSES?

> The following text has the force of law.
>
> Sales to other VAT registered businesses must not be included in a retail scheme.
>
> The exception to this are occasional cash sales, for example—
>
> – a garage supplying petrol to a VAT registered customer; or
> – a retail DIY store supplying building materials to a VAT registered builder.

Commentary—*De Voil Indirect Tax Service* **V3.551.**

2.5 CAN I CHANGE SCHEMES?

Yes. You can change schemes at the end of a complete year, reckoned from the beginning of the tax period in which you first adopted the scheme. You must use the scheme for 12 months, unless—

- you become ineligible for the scheme you are using; or
- we allow or require an earlier change.

If you become ineligible you must cease using the scheme from the end of the next complete accounting period.

For example, if you account for VAT by reference to quarters ending March, June, September and December and your turnover makes you ineligible for a scheme during February, you must cease to use that scheme to account for supplies made on or after 1 July.

Commentary—*De Voil Indirect Tax Service* **V3.563.**

2.6 CAN I CHANGE SCHEMES RETROSPECTIVELY?

No. Retrospective changes to retail schemes are not normally allowed. The VAT and Duty Tribunals have repeatedly confirmed the principle that where you operate a scheme according to the published rules (or an agreed variation), the tax which is due under that scheme is the correct VAT for the period. You cannot change schemes retrospectively simply because another scheme produces a lower or different valuation.

We may allow retrospective change in exceptional cases. If you think you have exceptional grounds for a retrospective change you should write to your local VAT Business Advice Centre giving as much detail as possible.

The maximum period for recalculation following a retrospective change of scheme is four years and you must have been, and remain, eligible to use the new scheme during the full period for which you apply.

Commentary—*De Voil Indirect Tax Service* **V3.563.**

2.7 WHAT SHOULD I DO IF I EXCEED THE TURNOVER LIMIT?

If you think your annual retail turnover (excluding VAT) is about to exceed £130 million you should contact your local HMRC as soon as possible to agree a bespoke scheme. A bespoke scheme will be tailored to meet the particular requirements of your business and is likely to be a variation of one of the published standard schemes. For further information see Notice 727/2 *Bespoke retail schemes*.

3 The Point of Sale Scheme

All boxed text in this section has the force of law (see para 1.4).

3.1 HOW DOES THE POINT OF SALE SCHEME WORK?

The Point of Sale scheme works by identifying the VAT liability of the goods or services you sell at the time you make the sale. This usually means using a till system which can distinguish between goods sold at different rates of VAT. However, we accept any system provided you can separate your sales, for example by using separate tills for different rates.

Commentary—*De Voil Indirect Tax Service* **V3.571.**

3.2 CAN I USE THE POINT OF SALE SCHEME RATHER THAN ANY OTHER RETAIL SCHEME?

The following text has the force of law.

Yes. You can use the Point of Sale scheme if you are a retailer making supplies at two or more rates and you can identify the correct liability of the supplies at the time you make them (see para 2.2 for guidance on how to choose a retail scheme).

However, you must use the Point of Sale scheme rather than any other retail scheme if you make supplies at only one positive rate (that is, all lower-rated or all standard-rated).

Commentary—*De Voil Indirect Tax Service* **V3.562.**

3.3 CAN I USE OTHER SCHEMES WITH THE POINT OF SALE SCHEME?

The following text has the force of law.

Provided you are eligible to use the schemes, you can mix the Point of Sale scheme with either a Direct Calculation or an Apportionment Scheme.

However, you cannot use different versions of the Apportionment Scheme and you must not mix a Direct Calculation Scheme with an Apportionment Scheme.

NB Normally, the retail scheme uses a single calculation for the whole of your VAT registration. However, it is acceptable if you wish to use the same scheme separately at a number of distinct business locations. Then you may need to make adjustments to account for transfers between different parts of the business and you must agree the details of such adjustments with your local VAT Business Advice Centre.

You can always use the normal method of accounting together with any scheme or any allowable mixture for which you are eligible.

Commentary—*De Voil Indirect Tax Service* **V3.556.**

3.4 DO I NEED TO KEEP ANY RECORDS?

The following text has the force of law.

You must keep—

- a record of your Daily Gross Takings (DGT) and of how those gross takings are made up, as described in the DGT Checklist in Section 5; and
- any working papers you use to calculate your output tax.

The normal record keeping requirements also apply. Notice 700 *The VAT Guide* tells you what is needed.

3.5 WHAT IF I OPERATE THE SCHEME INCORRECTLY?

Any staff you employ need to be able to operate your system correctly, even at the busiest times. If you operate the scheme incorrectly you could underdeclare your output tax and be subject to an assessment and even a financial penalty.

4 MECHANICS OF THE POINT OF SALE SCHEME

4.1 HOW DO I CALCULATE VAT UNDER THE POINT OF SALE SCHEME?

The Point of Sale scheme works by applying the appropriate VAT fraction to your total of positive-rated daily gross takings (DGT) to establish the amount of tax that is due on your eligible retail sales. This gives you your scheme output tax. Section 5 explains the DGT rules in detail.

The VAT fraction is simply a way of calculating the amount of VAT contained in the total gross takings. Notice 700 *The VAT Guide* tells you more about the VAT fraction.

Commentary—*De Voil Indirect Tax Service* **V3.571.**

4.2 CAN YOU EXPLAIN THE SCHEME CALCULATIONS STEP BY STEP?

The boxed text below has the force of law (see para 1.4).

The following table is a step-by-step guide to how you must calculate your VAT using this scheme.

(a) Starting to use the scheme		
From the day you start to use the scheme keep a record of your Daily Gross Takings (DGT) at each rate of VAT		
(b) At the end of each tax period—		
Step 1	Add up your DGT for standard-rated supplies for this tax period	£______
Step 2	Add up your DGT for lower-rated supplies for this tax period, if you have any	£______
(c) To calculate your scheme output tax—		
Step 3	Multiply step 1 by 7/47 (VAT at 17.5%)	£______
Step 4	Multiply step 2 by 1/21 (VAT at 5%)	£______
Step 5	Add step 3 to step 4 to get the scheme output tax	£______

Commentary—*De Voil Indirect Tax Service* **V3.571.**

4.3 HOW DO I COMPLETE MY VAT RETURN?

Your output tax figure is used to complete Box 1 of your VAT return (Form VAT 100). If you are using more than one scheme you must add together the output tax calculated by each scheme as well as any other amounts of output tax due and put the total in Box 1.

To help you fill in your VAT return see Notice 700/12 *Filling in your VAT return.* You can get a copy by contacting our National Advice Service.

Commentary—*De Voil Indirect Tax Service* **V3.571.**

5 DAILY GROSS TAKINGS (DGT) CHECKLIST

All boxed text in this section has the force of law (see para 1.4).

The DGT is a record of your retail supplies and is a crucial part of your retail scheme records. It is important that you follow the guidance in this section on how to calculate your DGT.

5.1 WHAT MUST I INCLUDE IN MY DAILY GROSS TAKINGS (DGT)?

From the day you start using the scheme you must keep a record of your DGT. You must include in your DGT record—

- all payments as they are received by you or on your behalf from cash customers for your retail supplies;
- the full value, including VAT, of all your credit or other non cash retail sales at the time you make the supply; and
- details of any adjustments made to this record.

The DGT record will normally be a till roll or copies of sales vouchers. It is this record and not simply cash on hand which constitutes your DGT.

Commentary—*De Voil Indirect Tax Service* **V3.556, 557.**

5.2 ARE ALL FORMS OF CASH PAYMENT INCLUDED IN MY DGT?

Yes. You must include and record the following in your DGT as they are received from your customers—

- Cash;
- Cheques;
- Debit or credit card vouchers;
- Switch, Delta or similar electronic transactions; and
- Electronic cash.

Commentary—*De Voil Indirect Tax Service* **V3.556, 557.**

5.3 IS MY DGT SIMPLY A RECORD OF CASH RECEIPTS?

No. You must also include the following in your DGT on the day you make the supply—

- the full value of credit sales (excluding any disclosed exempt charge for credit);
- the value of any goods taken out of the business for your own use;
- the cash value of any payment in kind for retail sales;
- the face value of gift, book and record vouchers redeemed (subject to para 6.17); and
- any other payments for retail sales.

Commentary—*De Voil Indirect Tax Service* **V3.556, 557.**

5.4 WHAT TRANSACTIONS MAY REDUCE MY DGT?

Your till roll or other record of sales constitutes your DGT and it is this figure which you must use when calculating output tax due under your retail scheme.

However, you may reduce your DGT for the following—

The following text has the force of law

- Counterfeit notes;
- Customer overspends using Shopacheck;
- Illegible credit card transactions (where a customer's account details are not legible on the credit card voucher and therefore cannot be presented and redeemed at the bank);
- Inadvertent acceptance of a cheque guarantee card as a credit card;
- Inadvertent acceptance of foreign currency (where discovered at a later time, for example when cashing up);
- Inadvertent acceptance of out of date coupons which have previously been included in your DGT but which are not honoured by promoters;
- Instalments in respect of credit sales;
- Receipts recorded for exempt supplies;
- Receipts recorded for supplies which are to be accounted for outside the scheme;
- Refunds to customers for overcharges or faulty/unsuitable goods;
- Supervisor's float discrepancies;
- Till breakdowns (where incorrect till readings are recorded due to mechanical faults, for example till programming error, false reading and till reset by engineer);
- Unsigned or dishonoured cheques from cash customers (but not from credit customers);
- Use of training tills (where the till used by staff for training has been returned to the sales floor without the zeroing of figures); and
- Void transactions (where an incorrect transaction has been voided at the time of the error).

Commentary—*De Voil Indirect Tax Service* **V3.556, 557.**

5.5 HOW MAY I REDUCE MY DGT FOR TRANSACTIONS LISTED IN PARAGRAPH 5.4?

The following text has the force of law.

You must be able to provide evidence to support any adjustments to your DGT figure.

If you make an adjustment but subsequently receive a payment, you must include that payment in your DGT.

You must not reduce your DGT for till shortages which result from theft of cash, fraudulent refunds and voids or poor cash handling by staff. See para 6.31 for further details.

Commentary—*De Voil Indirect Tax Service* **V3.557.**

5.6 WHAT IF I AM INVOLVED IN TRANSACTIONS NOT COVERED IN THIS SECTION?

If you have a particular type of transaction which is not covered in this section, you may find further help in Section 6. There is also advice on the treatment of business promotions in Section 7.

Commentary—*De Voil Indirect Tax Service* **V3.557.**

6 SPECIAL TRANSACTIONS

All boxed text in this section has the force of law (see para 1.4).

If you have a particular type of transaction which is not covered in this section, obtain advice from your local VAT Business Advice Centre. The address and telephone number are in the phone book under "Customs and Excise".

6.1 ACQUISITIONS FROM OTHER EC MEMBER STATES

The following text has the force of law.

Notice 725 *VAT—The Single Market* explains how you account for VAT on goods purchased (acquisitions) from other EC Member States.

Suppliers from elsewhere in the EC will not charge VAT on their sales to you but you will have to account for VAT at the rate applicable to the goods in the UK.

For retail scheme purposes, references in this notice to zero-rated goods apply only to goods which are zero-rated in the UK; goods which you acquire from other EC member states at zero-rate, but which are standard-rated in the UK, must be treated as standard-rated in your retail scheme calculations.

6.2 AMUSEMENT AND GAMING MACHINES

The following text has the force of law.

Add the "taxable take" of the machine to your standard-rated Daily Gross Takings on the day you remove the cash and/or tokens from the machine.

For details of how to work out the taxable take, see Notice 701/13 *Gaming and amusement machines*.

Commentary—*De Voil Indirect Tax Service* **V3.557.**

6.3 BT PHONECARDS

The following text has the force of law.

The sale of BT phonecards is outside the scope of VAT (provided they are not sold for more than their face value). Exclude these sales from your Daily Gross Takings. Account for any commission received from BT outside your retail scheme.

If you deal in other types of phonecards you should consult your local VAT Business Advice Centre. The address and telephone number are in the phone book under "Customs and Excise".

Commentary—*De Voil Indirect Tax Service* **V3.557.**

6.4 BUSINESS ENTERTAINMENT / GIFTS

The following text has the force of law.

If you purchase goods specifically to consume in the course of business entertainment or to supply as gifts, or you supply such goods from your normal stock, you must account for any tax due by adding the value of the goods to your Daily Gross Takings at the relevant rate.

Commentary—*De Voil Indirect Tax Service* **V3.557.**

6.5 BUSINESS OVERHEADS

The following text has the force of law.

Exclude from your scheme any purchases of goods or services which are not for resale, for example your business overheads such as gas, electricity and rent.

Commentary—*De Voil Indirect Tax Service* **V3.557.**

6.6 BUSINESS PROMOTIONS

The following text has the force of law.

See Section 7 of this notice.

6.7 CASH DISCOUNTS

The following text has the force of law.

If you offer goods on cash discount or early settlement include the discounted value in your Daily Gross Takings at the time of the supply.

6.8 CATERING SUPPLIES

The following text has the force of law.

See catering supplies in Notice 727 *VAT Retail schemes*.

6.9 CREDIT TRANSACTIONS

The following text has the force of law.

Account for output tax on credit retail supplies by including the full value of the goods in your Daily Gross Takings (DGT) at the time you make the supply. Do not wait until you are paid and do not include the instalments in the DGT when they are received.

Additional rules apply depending on the way the credit sales are financed—

Supplies involving a finance company	If you arrange credit for your customer through a finance company you should include the full amount paid by the customer in your DGT at the time you make the supply.
Self-financed credit supplies	If you make a separate charge for credit (additional to the cash price) and you disclose it to the customer this is exempt from VAT and should be excluded from your DGT. NB. If your turnover is less than £1 million and you run a business where your customers do not pay for the goods when they receive them (for example you may be a milkman or newsagent) you may take account of opening and closing debtors in your scheme calculations. Notice 727 *VAT Retail Schemes* provides an example of how to do this.

Commentary—*De Voil Indirect Tax Service* **V3.557.**

6.10 DELIVERY CHARGES

The following text has the force of law.

If, in order to fulfil your contract for the sale of the goods, you also deliver them, then there is a single supply of delivered goods. It does not matter whether the charge you make for delivery is separately itemised or invoiced. Examples of supplies of delivered goods are doorstep deliveries of milk and newspapers. The liability of the delivery charge follows the liability of the goods. In this case include the full amount charged in your Daily Gross Takings.

If you supply goods under a contract that does not require delivery but where, nevertheless, you agree to deliver the goods and make a separate charge, then that charge is for a standard-rated supply of services and any tax due must be accounted for outside your retail scheme.

Commentary—*De Voil Indirect Tax Service* **V3.557.**

6.11 DEPOSITS

The following text has the force of law.

Most deposits are an advance payment for a supply and must be included in your Daily Gross Takings (DGT).

However, if you take a deposit for another reason, for example as security to ensure the safe return of goods, you should exclude this amount from your DGT (regardless of whether it is eventually refunded or forfeited).

Commentary—*De Voil Indirect Tax Service* **V3.557.**

6.12 DISHONOURED CHEQUES / COUNTERFEIT NOTES

The following text has the force of law.

See the entry entitled "Unsigned or dishonoured cheques" in para 5.4.

6.13 DISPOSAL OF BUSINESS ASSETS

The following text has the force of law.

If you dispose of a business asset, such as a cash register or a van, you should account for VAT on the sale outside your retail scheme.

Commentary—*De Voil Indirect Tax Service* **V3.557.**

6.14 EXEMPT SUPPLIES

The following text has the force of law.

Any payments received for supplies which are exempt from VAT must be excluded from your scheme calculations.

If you make exempt supplies, for example the sale of National Lottery tickets or financial services, you will need to consider the rules on partial exemption explained in Notice 706 *Partial exemption* and Notice 706/2 *The capital goods scheme*.

Commentary—*De Voil Indirect Tax Service* **V3.557.**

6.15 EXPORTS TO COUNTRIES OUTSIDE THE EUROPEAN COMMUNITY

The following text has the force of law.

Retail Exports	If you make supplies under the terms of the retail export scheme as described in Notice 704 "VAT Retail exports", you should account for tax as follows— (a) Include in your Daily Gross Takings (DGT) all amounts, including VAT, for goods sold for retail export. Do not deduct the refunds which you expect to make to customers.

	(b) At the end of each tax period add up the amounts for standard-rated goods which have actually been exported. This will be the total of the amounts shown on the officially certified forms returned to you during the period. (c) Calculate notional tax on the total amount at (b), using the VAT fraction that applied at the time when you included the amounts in your DGT. (d) Subtract the notional tax at (c) from your retail scheme output tax.
Direct and Indirect Exports	If you export goods direct, or supply goods in the UK to overseas traders for subsequent indirect export by them, as described in Notice 703 "Exports and removals of goods from the UK", you should exclude these goods (which are supplied as direct or indirect exports) from your retail scheme calculations.

Commentary—*De Voil Indirect Tax Service* **V3.557.**

6.16 Florists

The following text has the force of law.

If you are a member of an organisation such as Interflora, Teleflorist and Flowergram, see Notice 727 *VAT Retail schemes*.

6.17 GIFT, BOOK AND RECORD VOUCHERS

If you . . .	*then . . .*
sell gift vouchers at a value higher than their face value	the excess is consideration for a supply of services and VAT should be accounted for outside the retail scheme. When you redeem the vouchers you must include their face value in your DGT.
sell gift vouchers at their face value	do not include the amount in your DGT. But, when you redeem the vouchers you must include their face value in your DGT.
sell gift vouchers at a price lower than their face value	do not include the amount in your DGT. When you redeem the voucher, if you have evidence to prove that the voucher was supplied at a discount, then you may include the discounted amount in your DGT. Otherwise you must include the full face value of the voucher in your DGT.
include gift vouchers with other products for a single charge	the supply of the goods and voucher is treated as a multiple supply. This means VAT is only due on that portion of the payment which relates to the goods. You should omit from your DGT that part of the payment which relates to the gift voucher, usually the face value. But you must include in your DGT the face value of the voucher when redeemed by the customer.
issue gift vouchers free of charge	no VAT is due on issue. When the voucher is redeemed for goods no VAT is due unless the cost of the goods exceeds £50. If the cost exceeds £50, VAT is due on the full amount. However, if you also sell such vouchers and are unable to distinguish between the two types at redemption, then you must include the full face value of the voucher in your DGT when it is redeemed.

If you . . .	*then . . .*
have purchased a third party's gift vouchers which you intend to issue free of charge (for example in your own promotion)	you normally have not been charged VAT. Equally, you do not have to account for any VAT when you give them away.
redeem gift vouchers and issue tax invoices to VAT registered businesses	you must account for these sales outside your retail scheme.

Commentary—*De Voil Indirect Tax Service* **V3.557.**

6.18 GOODS BOUGHT AT ONE RATE AND SOLD AT ANOTHER

The following text has the force of law.

For some goods the rate of tax you charge depends on how they are offered for sale. For example, meat is zero-rated when sold for human consumption but the same meat becomes standard-rated when sold as pet food. If you—

- are a chemist see Notice 727 *VAT Retail schemes.*
- sell take-away food see Notice 709/1 *Catering and take-away food and the Catering Adaptation* in Notice 727 *VAT Retail schemes.*
- sell young children's clothing see Notice 714 *Young children's clothing and footwear.*

As the retailer, you are responsible for ensuring that the correct liability for VAT is applied when you sell goods. If you make a mistake you may underdeclare the amount of tax due, and so may be liable to an assessment and interest to correct the error.

Commentary—*De Voil Indirect Tax Service* **V3.557.**

6.19 GOODS SOLD ON "SALE OR RETURN" OR SIMILAR TERMS

The following text has the force of law.

You should keep a separate record of goods supplied on a "sale or return" basis. You should only include the amount due for these in your Daily Gross Takings (DGT) when the customer has adopted the goods. If the customer pays a deposit see para 6.11.

Commentary—*De Voil Indirect Tax Service* **V3.557.**

6.20 IMPORTS

The following text has the force of law.

If you import goods from countries outside the European Community, you should read Notice 702 *Imports.*

6.21 PART-EXCHANGE

The following text has the force of law.

When you accept goods or services in part-exchange, you should include in your Daily Gross Takings the full selling price, including VAT, of the goods you supply.

If you resell goods you have accepted in part-exchange you may be able to use the Second-hand margin scheme see Notice 718 *Margin scheme for second-hand goods, works of art, antiques and collectors' items.* If, however, you are unable to use that scheme you should include the part exchange goods in your retail scheme.

Commentary—*De Voil Indirect Tax Service* **V3.557.**

6.22 PRIVATE OR PERSONAL USE OF GOODS

The following text has the force of law.

Tax is due on any positive-rated goods purchased for resale but which you take out of your business for private or personal use. You must add the value of such goods to your Daily Gross Takings.

Commentary—*De Voil Indirect Tax Service* **V3.557.**

6.23 REFUNDS

The following text has the force of law.

You may deduct amounts which are refunded or credited to customers from your Daily Gross Takings, to a maximum of the amount originally charged.

Commentary—*De Voil Indirect Tax Service* **V3.557.**

6.24 RENTED PAYPHONES

The following text has the force of law.

If you rent a payphone from BT or another supplier you are making supplies to users of the telephone and VAT is due on these supplies. Include the money from the payphone in your standard-rated Daily Gross Takings.

Commentary—*De Voil Indirect Tax Service* **V3.557.**

6.25 RETAIL SALES TO PERSONS FROM OTHER EC MEMBER STATES

The following text has the force of law.

Supplies made in the UK to persons from other EC member states should be accounted for as normal domestic retail sales.

Special arrangements apply to Distance Selling. This is where goods are sold to unregistered persons in other EC member states and the supplier is responsible for delivery to the customer. You can find out more about it in Notice 725 *VAT—The Single Market*.

Commentary—*De Voil Indirect Tax Service* **V3.557.**

6.26 ROAD FUEL

The following text has the force of law.

If you use road fuel for private motoring you must account for VAT on this outside the retail scheme, using the rules set out in Notice 700/64 *Motoring expenses.*

Commentary—*De Voil Indirect Tax Service* **V3.557.**

6.27 SALE OF DISCOUNT VOUCHERS OR CARDS

The following text has the force of law.

If you sell discount vouchers or cards entitling the holder to discounts on purchases from you, you must include the payment received in your Daily Gross Takings (DGT).

For example, if the voucher or card can only be used for purchases of zero-rated goods, you should add the payments received for the voucher or card to your zero-rated DGT.

If you sell discount vouchers or cards entitling the holder to discounts at several traders, this is a standard-rated supply and you must add the payments received to your standard-rated DGT.

Commentary—*De Voil Indirect Tax Service* **V3.557.**

6.28 SAVING STAMPS, TRAVEL CARDS AND POOLS COUPONS

The following text has the force of law.

These should be dealt with outside your scheme.

Commentary—*De Voil Indirect Tax Service* **V3.557.**

6.29 SALE OR ASSIGNMENT OF DEBTS

The following text has the force of law.

If you sell or assign debts due from your customers, no adjustment to your VAT account is necessary since you will already have included the correct amount when you made the supply.

Commentary—*De Voil Indirect Tax Service* **V3.557.**

6.30 SECOND-HAND GOODS

The following has the force of law.

You may be able to use the special scheme for second-hand goods see Notice 718 *Margin scheme for second-hand goods, works of art, antiques and collectors' items.* Alternatively, sales of second-hand goods should be accounted for within your retail scheme in the same way as new goods.

Commentary—*De Voil Indirect Tax Service* **V3.557.**

6.31 THEFT, SHRINKAGE, LEAKAGE AND STOCK LOSSES

The following text has the force of law.

If you find that there are unexplained accounting discrepancies between stock and sales, you must consider the extent to which this is attributable to unrecorded sales, such as to the theft of cash by staff, and add the value back to your Daily Gross Takings.

Where possible these adjustments should be allocated to the specific VAT period in which the theft took place. Otherwise, such shrinkage should be apportioned across relevant tax periods on a fair and reasonable basis.

Unless you have evidence of the liability of the unaccounted supplies, adjustments must be in line with the usual proportion of standard against zero-rated supplies.

Commentary—*De Voil Indirect Tax Service* **V3.557.**

7 BUSINESS PROMOTIONS

All boxed text in this section has the force of law (see para 1.4).

7.1 ABOUT BUSINESS PROMOTION SCHEMES IN GENERAL

The general guidelines on the business promotion schemes covered in this section are given in Notice 700/7 *Business promotion schemes.*

The VAT treatment under your retail scheme depends on whether the promotion is funded solely by you as the retailer or by, or together with, a third party such as the manufacturer.

If you wish to operate a particular promotion scheme which is not covered here you should contact your local VAT Business Advice Centre. The address and telephone number are in the phone book under "Customs and Excise". The timing of this adjustment should follow the rule in para 7.6(c).

Commentary—*De Voil Indirect Tax Service* **V3.166, V3.556, V3.557.**

7.2 DISCOUNT VOUCHERS

As part payment	When you take a discount voucher as part payment, you should include only the amount of money received from your customer in your DGT. If you subsequently receive payment for the coupon from another source you must include the extra amount in your DGT.
Handling charges	If you make a further charge to a manufacturer for handling the coupons, this is payment for a supply which is exempt from VAT and should be excluded from your DGT.
Sale	If you sell discount vouchers—see para 6.27 of this notice.

Commentary—*De Voil Indirect Tax Service* **V3.557.**

7.3 VOUCHERS WITH NO VALUES OR AMOUNTS BUT REDEEMABLE FOR WHOLE ITEMS

Vouchers issued by you to customers making a specific purchase or purchases	No VAT is due upon issue and no further VAT is due when the voucher is used by the customer to obtain the reward goods.
Vouchers issued freely by you	No VAT is due upon issue. When the voucher is redeemed for goods no VAT is due unless the cost of the goods is over £50. VAT is then due on the value of those goods.
	See also para 6.4 regarding business gifts.
Vouchers issued by another person but redeemable with you	They are likely to be subject to the terms and conditions of that person's promotion. For example, you may be given certain stocks to give away on behalf of that person.

	Notice 700/7 *Business promotion schemes* contains further information. Alternatively, contact your local VAT Business Advice Centre. The address and phone number are in the phone book under "Customs and Excise".

Commentary—*De Voil Indirect Tax Service* **V3.557.**

7.4 VOUCHERS REDEEMED FOR CASH WITH YOU

> The following text has the force of law.
>
> If you redeem vouchers for cash, the cash payment is outside the scope of VAT. You must not alter your Daily Gross Takings (DGT) by the cash paid out.

Commentary—*De Voil Indirect Tax Service* **V3.557.**

7.5 GIFT VOUCHERS

> The following text has the force of law.
>
> See para 6.17 of this notice.

Commentary—*De Voil Indirect Tax Service* **V3.557.**

7.6 Goods linked in a promotion

These include promotions where—

Two different articles are sold for a single price in a combined offer, for example—

- a washing machine with an iron; or
- a jar of coffee with a packet of chocolate biscuits.

A number of same articles are sold in a multibuy offer, for example—

- "buy two and get a third free".

> (a) If both articles are liable at the same rate of tax (as the washing machine/iron combined offer and the multibuy examples above), then there are no additional rules to follow under the Point of Sale scheme.
>
> (b) If the articles are liable at different rates of tax (as the coffee/ biscuits combined offer in the examples above), then there are additional rules to apportion the selling price—
>
> - you may use the method explained in Notice 700 *The VAT Guide*; or
> - in the case of goods linked by the manufacturer, you may treat the articles in accordance with the information shown on the supplier's invoice. For example, if the invoice shows separate prices and amounts of tax, you may apportion your selling price on the same basis.
>
> As a concession, where the minor article satisfies the criteria set out in Notice 700/7 *Business promotion schemes*, you may account for VAT on the minor item at the same rate as the main article.
>
> If an apportionment of the selling price is necessary, you must separate the amount allocated to the zero-rated article from your standard-rated takings before carrying out your scheme calculation.
>
> (c) If a manufacturer or joint sponsor contributes towards payment for goods, then strictly speaking, when you receive a contribution from a manufacturer or joint sponsor representing partial payment for goods supplied to a customer, you should account for this in the period the goods are supplied.

However, as a concession, you may account for such contributions in the period you receive them from the manufacturer or joint sponsor.

(d) If a manufacturer or joint sponsor contributes, for example towards advertising, then you have made a separate supply of services and this must be dealt with outside your retail scheme.

Commentary—*De Voil Indirect Tax Service* **V3.557.**

...

727/4

RETAIL SCHEMES—HOW TO WORK THE APPORTIONMENT SCHEMES

January 2013

Update 1 (December 2002) and Update 2 (April 2009) have been incorporated in this notice. This notice cancels and replaces Notice 727/4 (January 2011).

1 INTRODUCTION

1.1 What is this notice about?

This notice tells you about Apportionment Schemes 1 and 2, two of the standard Retail Schemes. It explains the general rules applicable to the schemes, how the schemes work (including the calculation of AT), and what records you should keep - especially your Daily Gross Takings (DGT) records and, for Apportionment Scheme 2, your Expected Selling Prices (ESPs) records.

- paragraph 2.6 - updated to reflect the current "capping" regulations
- paragraph 9.2 - change of address

You can access details of any changes to this notice since March 2002 either online, go to www.hmrc.gov.uk or by phoning the VAT Helpline on 0845 010 9000. This notice and others mentioned are available both on paper and online.

Commentary—*De Voil Indirect Tax Service* **V3.551–V3.576**.

1.2 Who should read this notice?

You should read this if—

- you are a VAT registered business making retail sales;
- you are unable to account for VAT on those sales in the normal way (see para 2.1); and
- your annual retail turnover, excluding VAT, does not exceed £130 million.

1.3 Are there other retail schemes?

Yes. Other standard retail schemes are the Point of Sale Scheme and the Direct Calculation Schemes.

Businesses whose annual retail turnover exceeds £130 million cannot use a standard scheme. Instead they can agree a bespoke retail scheme (see para 3.4.2).

1.4 Force of law

Parts of this notice have the force of law under the VAT Regulations 1995, Part IX (regulations 66–75). All paragraphs in Section 7 and certain paragraphs in other sections have legal force and supplement the law.

The text of these paragraphs is placed in a box and indicated by a statement.

1.5 Where can I find out about the other schemes?

You will find a general introduction to retail schemes as well as guidance on choosing a retail scheme in Notice 727 "VAT Retail Schemes".

Details of the other schemes can be found in—

- Notice 727/2 "Bespoke Retail Schemes";
- Notice 727/3 "How to work the Point of Sale Scheme"; and
- Notice 727/5 "How to work the Direct Calculation Schemes".

2 GENERAL RULES

All boxed text in this section has the force of law (see para 1.4).

2.1 Who can use a retail scheme?

Any retailer who would find it difficult to account for VAT in the normal way can use a retail scheme.

Accounting in the normal way does not require you to issue a tax invoice to unregistered customers. But it does require you to identify, for each sale, the tax exclusive value and the VAT and to be able to produce periodic totals of those amounts.

Commentary—*De Voil Indirect Tax Service* **V3.551–V3.576**.

2.2 Can I use any retail scheme?

No. Some of the schemes have turnover limits (see para 3.4 for guidance on the Apportionment Schemes).

Otherwise, provided your chosen retail scheme produces a fair and reasonable result you may choose the scheme which suits your business best. Notice 727 "VAT Retail schemes" tells you more about choosing a retail scheme.

2.3 Can I use the scheme to account for all my retail and non-retail supplies?

The following rule/requirement/paragraph has the force of law.

> No. Retail schemes can be used for retail supplies only.
>
> If you make a mixture of retail and non-retail sales you must only use a retail scheme to calculate the tax due on your retail sales. You must account for non-retail sales using the normal method of accounting.

2.4 What if my business makes sales to other VAT registered businesses?

The following rule/requirement/paragraph has the force of law.

> Sales to other VAT registered businesses must not be included in a retail scheme.
>
> The exception to this is occasional cash sales, for example—
>
> - a garage supplying petrol to a VAT registered customer; or
> - a retail DIY store supplying building materials to a VAT registered builder.

2.5 Can I change schemes?

The following rule/requirement/paragraph has the force of law.

> Yes. You can change schemes at the end of a complete year, reckoned from the beginning of the tax period in which you first adopted the scheme. You must use the scheme for 12 months, unless—

> – you become ineligible for the scheme you are using; or
> – we allow or require an earlier change.
>
> If you become ineligible you must cease using the scheme from the end of the next complete accounting period.

For example, if you account for VAT by reference to quarters ending March, June, September and December and your turnover makes you ineligible for a particular scheme during February, you must cease to use that scheme to account for supplies made on or after 1 July.

Some schemes require adjustments when you cease using them (see paras 3.5 for guidance on the Apportionment Schemes).

2.6 Can I change schemes retrospectively?

No. Retrospective changes to retail schemes are not normally allowed. The VAT and Duty Tribunals have repeatedly confirmed the principle that where you operate a scheme according to the published rules (or an agreed variation), the tax due under that scheme is the correct VAT for the period. You cannot change schemes retrospectively simply because another scheme produces a lower or different valuation.

We may allow retrospective change in exceptional cases. If you think you have exceptional grounds for a retrospective change you should write to HMRC giving as much detail as possible.

The maximum period for recalculation following a retrospective change of scheme is four years and you must have been, and remain, eligible to use the new scheme during the full period for which you apply.

3 BASIC PRINCIPLES OF APPORTIONMENT SCHEMES 1 AND 2

All boxed text in this section has the force of law (see para 1.4).

Unless stated otherwise, this section applies to both Apportionment Schemes 1 and 2.
Commentary—*De Voil Indirect Tax Service* **V3.572**.

3.1 How do the Apportionment Schemes work?

3.1.1 Apportionment Scheme 1

Apportionment Scheme 1 is the simpler scheme designed for smaller businesses with a tax exclusive turnover not exceeding £1 million. You work out the value of your purchases for retail sale at different rates of VAT and apply the proportions of those purchase values to your sales.

For example, if—

– 50 per cent of the value of your goods purchased for retail sale are standard rated;
– 30 per cent are lower-rated; and
– 20 per cent zero-rated,

your takings are treated as standard-rated, lower-rated and zero-rated in the same proportions. You then calculate your output tax by applying the relevant VAT fraction (or fractions if more than one positive rate is used) to these positive-rated takings figures.

Once a year you make a similar calculation based on your purchases for the year. This is compared with the tax you have paid to correct any over or under payment.

This scheme is relatively simple. However, if, on average, you achieve a higher mark-up for your zero-rated goods than your lower or standard-rated goods, you may find that you pay more tax if you use the simple Apportionment scheme than you would using another scheme.

3.1.2 Apportionment Scheme 2

Apportionment Scheme 2 is available to businesses with an annual retail turnover, excluding VAT, not exceeding £130 million. You calculate the Expected Selling Prices (ESPs) of standard and lower-rated goods you receive for retail sale (para 5.3). You then work out the ratio of these to the ESPs of all goods received for retail sale and apply this ratio to your takings.

For example, if—

– 60 per cent of the ESPs of all goods you receive for retail sale are standard-rated; and
– 40 per cent are zero-rated,
– then 60 per cent of your takings are treated as standard-rated and 40 per cent as zero-rated. You then calculate your output tax by applying the relevant VAT fraction to these figures for takings.

This scheme can be complex to operate but, if worked properly, will provide a more accurate valuation of your supplies over a period of time.

3.2 Can I use other schemes with the Apportionment Schemes?

The following rule/requirement/paragraph has the force of law.

Yes. Provided you are eligible to use the schemes—

– you can mix the Point of Sale scheme with either of the Apportionment Schemes; but
– you cannot mix different versions of the Apportionment Schemes and you must not use an Apportionment Scheme in some parts of your business and a Direct Calculation Scheme in others.

Note. Normally, the retail scheme uses a single calculation for the whole of your VAT registration. However, if you wish you can use the same scheme separately at a number of distinct business locations. But you may then need to make adjustments to account for transfers between different parts of the business and you must agree the details of such adjustments with HMRC.

You can always use the normal method of accounting together with any scheme or any allowable mixture for which you are eligible.

3.3 Do I need to keep any records?

The following rule/requirement/paragraph has the force of law.

Yes. For both Apportionment Schemes 1 and 2 you must keep—

– a record of your Daily Gross Takings (DGT) and of how those gross takings are made up, as described in the DGT Checklist in Section 6; and
– any working papers you use to calculate your output tax.

Additionally, for Apportionment Scheme 2, you must keep—

— a record of your Expected Selling Prices (ESPs) as explained in para 5.3.

The normal record keeping requirements also apply. Notice 700 "The VAT Guide" tells you what is needed.

3.4 What should I do if I exceed the turnover limit?

The following rule/requirement/paragraph has the force of law.

The turnover limit for the scheme applies to the whole of your VAT registration.

3.4.1 Apportionment Scheme 1

If you think your annual tax exclusive turnover is about to exceed £1 million you should consider Apportionment Scheme 2 or any of the other standard retail schemes (para 2.2).

3.4.2 Apportionment Scheme 2

If you think your annual retail turnover, excluding VAT, is about to exceed £130 million you should contact HMRC as soon as possible to agree a bespoke scheme. A bespoke scheme will be tailored to meet the particular requirements of your business and is likely to be a variation of one of the published standard schemes. For further information see Notice 727/2 "Bespoke retail schemes".

3.5 What must I do when I cease to use the Apportionment Schemes?

3.5.1 Apportionment Scheme 1

The following rule/requirement/paragraph has the force of law.

> When you cease to use Scheme 1, you must perform a closing adjustment, as for the annual adjustment (see para 4.3.2), even if you leave before your scheme's first anniversary.

3.5.2 Apportionment Scheme 2

The following rule/requirement/paragraph has the force of law.

> When you cease to use Scheme 2, no adjustment is normally required. However, if you cease to use the scheme in one part of your business but continue to use it in other parts, make sure that the rolling calculation reflects the stock/Expected Selling Prices (ESPs) now excluded from the apportionment calculation.

3.6 Are there any other rules when I cease to use the Apportionment Schemes?

Apart from making the adjustments as explained in para 3.5, you should also remember—

- you can only include goods sold by retail in your scheme. If you transfer part or all of your business as a going concern and you cease to use the scheme, you will have to exclude the value of the stock which has been transferred from your retail scheme;
- if you cease to trade, VAT may become due on the value of your stocks and assets (see Notice 700/11 "Cancelling your registration"); and
- we may require additional adjustments where unusual patterns of trade prevent your chosen scheme from producing a fair and reasonable result.

The following rule/requirement/paragraph has the force of law.

> For these reasons you must always tell your VAT Business Advice Centre if you are—
>
> - intending to buy or sell part of a business; or
> - changing the legal entity of your business (for example, from sole proprietor to partnership); or
> - registered as a group and the composition of the group is to change.

4 MECHANICS OF APPORTIONMENT SCHEME 1

All boxed text in this section has the force of law (see para 1.4).

4.1 How do I calculate VAT under Apportionment Scheme 1?

The scheme works by applying the appropriate VAT fraction(s) to your total of positive-rated Daily Gross Takings (DGT) to establish the amount of tax that is due on your eligible retail sales. This gives you your scheme output tax. Section 6 explains the DGT rules in detail.

The VAT fraction is simply a way of calculating the amount of VAT contained in the total gross takings. Notice 700 "The VAT Guide" tells you more about the VAT fraction.

Commentary—*De Voil Indirect Tax Service* **V3.572.**

4.2 Starting to use Apportionment Scheme 1

The following rule/requirement/paragraph has the force of law.

When you start to use the scheme remember—

- you must not include goods you have in stock as goods received in the period. However, if you have stock items which you intend to sell and not restock, you may include these in your calculation, unless these goods have already been allowed for by you in a previous scheme;
- the scheme is only for goods bought for retail sale. If you sell goods you have made or grown yourself, you will need to account for them outside the scheme; and
- if you supply services or catering, you will need to account for them outside the scheme.

4.3 Apportionment Scheme 1 calculations

The following is a step-by-step guide to how you must calculate your VAT using this scheme.

4.3.1 Your VAT calculations for Scheme 1

For each tax period—

Step 1	Add up your Daily Gross Takings (DGT) for this tax period (see Section 6)	£______
Step 2	Add up the cost, including VAT, of all goods received in the period for retail sale at the standard rate	£______
Step 3	Add up the cost, including VAT, of all goods received in the period for retail sale at the lower rate	£______
Step 4	Add up the cost, including VAT, of all goods received in the period for retail sale at standard, lower and zero rates.	£______

At the end of each tax period, use these figures to work out what proportion of your DGT comes from sales at the different rates by performing the following calculation—

Step 5	Total at step 1 x 1/6 (VAT at 20%) ×	Total at step 2 / Total at step 4
	Output tax on sales at the standard rate	£______
Step 6	Total at step 1 x 1/21 (VAT at 5%) x	Total at step 3 / Total at step 4
	Output tax on sales at the lower rate	£______

Step 7	Add the totals at step 5 and step 6 This is your output tax for Apportionment Scheme 1	£_______

4.3.2 Annual adjustment for Scheme 1

You must make an annual adjustment to your calculations to cover any over or underpayment of tax that you have made during the retail scheme year—

Step 1	Add up the Daily Gross Takings (DGT) for the year	£___________
Step 2	Add up the cost to you, including VAT, of goods at the standard rate of VAT received for retail sale during the year	£___________
Step 3	Add up the cost to you, including VAT, of goods at the lower rate of VAT received for retail sale during the year	£___________
Step 4	Add up the cost to you including VAT of all goods, standard, lower and zero-rated, received for retail sale during the year	£___________

To work out what proportion of your DGT comes from sales at the positive rates—

Step 5	Total at step 1 × 1/6 (VAT at 20%) ×	Total at step 2 / Total at step 4	£___________
Step 6	Total at step 1 × 1/21 (VAT at 5%) ×	Total at step 3 / Total at step 4	£___________
Step 7	Add together totals at step 5 and step 6		£___________
Step 8	Add together the amount of output tax calculated under the retail scheme in the tax periods during the year		£___________
Step 9	If the total at step 7 is more than the total at step 8 you have paid too little tax and you should show the difference in the VAT PAYABLE side of your VAT account for the period covering the adjustment. If the total at step 7 is less than the total at step 8 you have paid too much tax and you should show the difference in the VAT DEDUCTIBLE side of your VAT account for the period covering the adjustment.		

4.3.3 Annual adjustment timetable for Scheme 1

The following rule/requirement/paragraph has the force of law

You must make this annual adjustment on—

31 March	if your tax periods end on the last day of June, September, December or March.
30 April	if your tax periods end on the last day of July, October, January or April.
31 May	if your tax periods end on the last day of August, November, February or May.

If you make monthly returns you must make the adjustment on 31 March.

If you have been using the scheme for one tax period or less, you do not have to make the first adjustment until the following year—

—The first adjustment must include all tax periods since you started to use the scheme; and

—For all later adjustments you include only tax periods since your last adjustment.

4.4 How do I complete my VAT return?

Your output tax figure is used to complete Box 1 of your VAT return (Form VAT 100). If you are using more than one scheme you must add together the output tax calculated from each scheme as well as any other amounts of output tax which are due, and put the total in Box 1.

To help you fill in your VAT return see VAT Notice 700/12 "Filling in your VAT return". You can get a copy by contacting our National Advice Service.

5 MECHANICS OF APPORTIONMENT SCHEME 2

All boxed text in this section has the force of law (see para 1.4).

5.1 How do I calculate VAT under Apportionment Scheme 2?

The scheme works by applying the appropriate VAT fraction(s) to your total of positive-rated Daily Gross Takings (DGT) to establish the amount of tax that is due on your eligible retail sales. This gives you your scheme output tax. Section 6 explains the DGT rules in detail.

The VAT fraction is simply a way of calculating the amount of VAT contained in the total gross takings. Notice 700 "The VAT Guide" tells you more about the VAT fraction.

Commentary—*De Voil Indirect Tax Service* **V3.572.**

5.2 Starting to use Apportionment Scheme 2

The following rule/requirement/paragraph has the force of law.

When you start to use the scheme remember—

- you will need to work out the Expected Selling Prices (ESPs) of goods in stock at each rate of tax and to use a rolling calculation as described in para 5.3; and
- if you supply services or catering, you will need to account for them outside the scheme.

5.3 Expected Selling Prices (ESPs) calculations for Scheme 2

To use this scheme you need to calculate ESPs and make adjustments to them as detailed here.

5.3.1 How do I calculate ESPs for Scheme 2?

The following rule/requirement/paragraph has the force of law.

How you calculate your ESPs has a direct effect on the tax you pay under the scheme. You must therefore calculate your ESPs as realistically and accurately as possible to reflect factors which might prevent you from achieving the price.

For example—

- price changes—increases and decreases, for example, sell by date reductions;
- special offers and promotion schemes;
- wastage;
- freezer breakdowns;
- breakages;
- shrinkage-pilferage and loss of stock; and
- bad debts that have been written off in the period.

The list is not exhaustive. If you are aware of other factors which affect your ESPs you must make the appropriate adjustments.

You can calculate your ESPs in any way that produces a fair and reasonable result but you must always be consistent in the method you use (both within one period and from one period to another). You must also record any adjustments and keep the working papers with your retail scheme calculations.

5.3.2 What must I not include in my ESP calculations for Scheme 2?

ESPs are used to calculate the value of your retail sales at different rates. Therefore, you must not include in your calculation—

- wholesale sales;
- goods bought for private use; or
- disposals of stock resulting from a sale of all or part of the business.

5.3.3 What if I have difficulty in making ESP adjustments for Scheme 2?

If you have difficulty in making these adjustments, you may need to use another scheme. However, your local office may—

- agree a method of sampling where reductions cannot be established accurately; or
- agree to the omission of certain adjustments where the effect does not distort your retail scheme.

5.4 Apportionment Scheme 2 calculations

The following is a step-by-step guide to how you must calculate your VAT using this scheme.

5.4.1 Expected Selling Prices (ESPs) of your opening stock

When you start to use the scheme you must establish the ESPs of your opening stock of goods for retail sale at each rate as follows—

Step 1	Work out the ESPs, including VAT, of standard-rated goods for retail sale in stock.	£______ Standard-rated stock
Step 2	Work out the ESPs, including VAT, of lower-rated goods for retail sale in stock.	£______ Low-rated stock
Step 3	Work out the ESPs, including VAT, of all goods for retail sale in stock.	£______ Total stock

If possible, you should carry out physical stock taking. Otherwise, you may use the ESP values of the goods you received for retail sale in the three months before you started to use the scheme.

5.4.2 Quarterly returns: Output tax for your first three periods

For each of your first three tax periods calculate your output tax for the period as follows—

Step 1	Add up your Daily Gross Takings for this tax period only	£______
Step 2	Add up the Expected Selling Prices (ESPs), including VAT, of the standard-rated goods— —received, made or grown for retail sale since you started to use the scheme;	£______

—acquired from other European Community (EC) States since you started to use the scheme; plus

—your standard-rated stock figure at 5.4.1.

Step 3 Add up the ESPs, including VAT, of lower-rated goods— £______

—received, made or grown for retail sale since you started to use the scheme;

—acquired from other EC States since you started to use the scheme; plus

—your lower-rated stock figure at 5.4.1.

Step 4 Add up the ESPs, including VAT, of all goods-standard, lower and zero-rated— £______

—received, made or grown for retail sale since you started the scheme;

—acquired from other EC States since you started to use the scheme; plus

—your total stock figure at 5.4.1.

At the end of each tax period use these figures to work out what proportion of your Daily Gross Takings comes from sales at the positive rates of VAT—

Step 5 Total at step 1 × 1/6 (VAT at 20%) × $\frac{\text{Total at step 2}}{\text{Total at step 4}}$ £______

Step 6 Total at step 1 × 1/21 (VAT at 5%) × $\frac{\text{Total at step 3}}{\text{Total at step 4}}$ £______

Step 7 Total at steps 5 and 6 £______

This is your output tax for Apportionment Scheme 2

5.4.3 Quarterly returns—Output tax for your fourth and subsequent periods

For the fourth quarterly and all later quarterly periods you calculate your output tax for the period as follows—

Ignore the stock that you had in hand when you started to use the scheme

Step 1 Add up the Daily Gross Takings for this tax period only £______

Step 2 Add up the Expected Selling Prices (ESPs), including VAT, of standard-rated goods— £______

—received, made or grown for resale; or

—acquired from other EC States, in this period and the three previous tax periods

Step 3 Add up the ESPs, including VAT, of lower-rated goods— £______

—received, made or grown for resale; or

—acquired from other EC States in this period and the three previous tax periods

Step 4 Add up the ESPs, including VAT, of all goods, standard, lower and zero-rated—

—received, made or grown for resale; or

—acquired from other EC States, in this period and the three previous tax periods

At the end of each tax period, use these figures to work out what proportion of your Daily Gross Takings comes from sales at the positive rates of VAT—

Step 5 Total at step 1 x 1/6 (VAT at 20%) x $\frac{\text{Total at step 2}}{\text{Total at step 4}}$ £______

Step 6	Total at step 1 × 1/21 (VAT at 5%) x	Total at step 3 / Total at step 4	£________
Step 7	Total at steps 5 and 6 This is your output tax for Apportionment Scheme 2		£________

5.4.4 Monthly returns: Output tax for your first eleven periods

> The method at para 5.4.2 applies for working out your output tax for the first eleven monthly returns.

5.4.5 Monthly returns—Output tax for your twelfth and subsequent periods

The following rule/requirement/paragraph has the force of law.

> The method at para 5.4.3 applies for working out your output tax for the twelfth and later monthly returns. But as you make 12 returns in a year, you must include the previous 11 tax periods.

5.5 How do I complete my VAT return?

Your output tax figure is used to complete Box 1 of your VAT return (Form VAT 100). If you are using more than one scheme you must add together the output tax calculated by each scheme as well as any other amounts of output tax due and put the total in Box 1.

To help you fill in your VAT return see VAT Notice 700/12 "Filling in your VAT return". You can get a copy by contacting our VAT Helpline.

6 DAILY GROSS TAKINGS (DGT) CHECKLIST

All boxed text in this section has the force of law (see para 1.4).

The DGT is a record of your retail supplies and is a crucial part of your retail scheme records. It is important that you follow the guidance in this section on how to calculate your DGT.

6.1 What must I include in my Daily Gross Takings (DGT)?

The following rule/requirement/paragraph has the force of law.

> From the day you start using the scheme you must keep a record of your DGT. You must include in your DGT record—
>
> – all payments as they are received by you or on your behalf from cash customers for your retail supplies;
> – the full value, including VAT, of all your credit or other non cash retail sales at the time you make the supply; and
> – details of any adjustments made to this record.

The DGT record will normally be a till roll or copies of sales vouchers. It is this record and not simply cash on hand which constitutes your DGT.

Commentary—*De Voil Indirect Tax Service* **V3.556, V3.557.**

6.2 Are all forms of cash payment included in my DGT?

Yes. You must include and record the following in your DGT as they are received from your customers—

- Cash;
- Cheques;
- Debit or credit card vouchers;
- Switch, Delta or similar electronic transactions; and
- Electronic cash

6.3 Is my DGT simply a record of cash receipts?

No. You must also include the following in your DGT on the day you make the supply—

- the full value of credit sales (excluding any disclosed exempt charge for credit);
- the value of any goods taken out of the business for your own use;
- the cash value of any payment in kind for retail sales;
- the face value of gift, book and record vouchers redeemed (subject to para 7.18); and
- any other payments for retail sales.

6.4 What transactions may reduce my DGT?

Your till roll or other record of sales constitutes your DGT and it is this figure which you must use when calculating output tax due under your retail scheme.

The following rule/requirement/paragraph has the force of law.

However, you may reduce your DGT for the following—

- Counterfeit notes;
- Customer overspends using Shopacheck;
- Illegible credit card transactions (where a customer's account details are not legible on the credit card voucher and therefore cannot be presented and redeemed at the bank);
- Inadvertent acceptance of a cheque guarantee card as a credit card;
- Inadvertent acceptance of foreign currency (where discovered at a later time, for example when cashing up);
- Inadvertent acceptance of out of date coupons which have previously been included in your DGT but which are not honoured by promoters;
- Instalments in respect of credit sales;
- Receipts recorded for exempt supplies;
- Receipts recorded for goods or services which are to be accounted for outside the scheme;
- Refunds to customers for overcharges or faulty/unsuitable goods;
- Supervisor's float discrepancies;
- Till breakdowns (where incorrect till readings are recorded due to mechanical faults, for example till programming error, false reading and till reset by engineer);
- Unsigned or dishonoured cheques from cash customers (but not from credit customers);
- Use of training tills (where the till used by staff for training has been returned to the sales floor without the zeroing of figures); and

– Void transactions (where an incorrect transaction has been voided at the time of the error).

6.5 How may I reduce my DGT for transactions listed in para 6.4?

The following rule/requirement/paragraph has the force of law.

> You must be able to provide evidence to support any adjustments to your DGT figure.
>
> If you make an adjustment but subsequently receive a payment, you must include that payment in your DGT.
>
> You must not reduce your DGT for till shortages which result from theft of cash, fraudulent refunds and voids or poor cash handling by staff. See para 7.34 for further details.

6.6 What if I am involved in transactions not covered in this section?

If you have a particular type of transaction which is not covered in this section, you must check Sections 7 and 8 to see if any of the rules there apply to your business before using the Apportionment Schemes to calculate your tax.

7 SPECIAL TRANSACTIONS

All boxed text in this section has the force of law (see para 1.4).

If you have a particular type of transaction which is not covered in this section, you should ask for advice from HMRC. The address and telephone number are in the phone book under "Customs and Excise".

7.1 Acquisitions from other EC member states

The following rule/requirement/paragraph has the force of law.

> Notice 725 "VAT—The Single Market" explains how you account for VAT on goods purchased (acquisitions) from other EC member states.
>
> Suppliers from elsewhere in the EC will not charge VAT on their sales to you but you will have to account for VAT at the rate applicable to the goods in the UK.
>
> For retail scheme purposes, references in this notice to zero-rated goods apply only to goods which are zero-rated in the UK; goods which you acquire from other EC member states at zero-rate, but which are standard-rated in the UK, must be treated as standard-rated in your retail scheme calculations.

Commentary—*De Voil Indirect Tax Service* **V3.556, V3.557, V3.567** .

7.2 Amusement and gaming machines

The following rule/requirement/paragraph has the force of law.

> If you are using either of the Apportionment Schemes, you should exclude from your Daily Gross Takings the takings from the machines and account for the VAT due as explained in VAT Notice 701/13 "Gaming and amusements machines".

7.3 BT Phonecards

The following rule/requirement/paragraph has the force of law.

> The sale of BT unused phonecards is outside the scope of VAT (provided they are not sold for more than their face value). Exclude these sales from your Daily Gross Takings. Account for any commission received from BT outside your retail scheme.
>
> If you deal in other types of phonecards you should consult HMRC.

7.4 Business entertainment / gifts

The following rule/requirement/paragraph has the force of law.

> If you purchase goods specifically to consume in the course of business entertainment or to supply as gifts, you must account for any tax due outside your scheme.
>
> If you supply these goods from your normal stock and operate—
>
> – Apportionment Scheme 1, include the full value of the item in your Daily Gross Takings (DGT).
>
> – Apportionment Scheme 2, include the full value of the item in your DGT and make the necessary adjustment to your ESPs for such goods.

7.5 Business overheads

The following rule/requirement/paragraph has the force of law.

> Exclude from your scheme any purchases of goods or services which are not for resale, for example your business overheads such as gas, electricity and rent.

7.6 Business promotions

> See Section 8.

7.7 Cash discounts

The following rule/requirement/paragraph has the force of law.

> If you offer goods on cash discount or early settlement include the discounted value in your Daily Gross Takings at the time of the supply.

7.8 Catering supplies

> See catering supplies in Notice 727 "VAT Retail schemes".

7.9 Chemists

See VAT Notice 727 "VAT Retail schemes".

7.10 Credit transactions

The following rule/requirement/paragraph has the force of law.

Account for output tax on credit retail supplies by including the full value of the goods in your Daily Gross Takings (DGT) at the time you make the supply. Do not wait until you are paid and do not include the instalments in the DGT when they are received.

Additional rules apply depending on the way the credit sales are financed—

Supplies involving a finance company	If you arrange credit for your customer through a finance company, our view is that in most cases you should include the full amount paid by the customer in your DGT at the time you make the supply. However, in some circumstances VAT may only be due on the amount you receive from the finance company. Business Brief 15/96 explains the circumstances in which this treatment may be appropriate.
Self-financed credit supplies	If you make a separate charge for credit (additional to the cash price) and you disclose it to the customer, this is exempt from VAT and should be excluded from your DGT. NB If your turnover is less than £1 million and you run a business where your customers do not pay for the goods when they receive them (for example, you may be a milkman or newsagent), you may take account of opening and closing debtors in your scheme calculations. Notice 727 "VAT Retail Schemes" provides an example of how to do this.

7.11 Delivery charges

The following rule/requirement/paragraph has the force of law.

If, in order to fulfil your contract for the sale of goods, you also deliver them, then there is a single supply of delivered goods. It does not matter whether the charge you make for delivery is separately itemised or invoiced. Examples of supplies of delivered goods are doorstep deliveries of milk or newspapers. The liability of the delivery charge follows the liability of the goods. In this case include the full amount charged in your Daily Gross Takings.

If you supply goods under a contract that does not require delivery but where, nevertheless, you agree to deliver the goods and make a separate charge, then that charge is for a standard-rated supply of services and any tax due must be accounted for outside your retail scheme.

7.12 Deposits

The following rule/requirement/paragraph has the force of law.

Most deposits are advance payments for supplies and must be included in your Daily Gross Takings (DGT).

However, if you take a deposit for another reason, for example as security to ensure the safe return of goods you have hired out and you either refund it when the goods are returned safely or you forfeit it to compensate you for loss or damage, you should exclude this amount from your DGT.

7.13 Dishonoured cheques / counterfeit notes

See the entry entitled "Unsigned or dishonoured cheques" in para 6.4.

7.14 Disposal of business assets

The following rule/requirement/paragraph has the force of law.

If you dispose of a business asset, such as a cash register or a van, you should account for VAT on the sale outside your retail scheme.

7.15 Exempt supplies

The following rule/requirement/paragraph has the force of law.

Any payments received for supplies which are exempt from VAT must be excluded from your scheme calculations.

If you make exempt supplies, for example the sale of National Lottery tickets or financial services, you will need to consider the rules on partial exemption explained in Notice 706 "Partial exemption" and Notice 706/2 "The capital goods scheme".

7.16 Exports to countries outside the European Community

The following rule/requirement/paragraph has the force of law.

For—

– Retail Exports, if you make supplies for retail exports (including supplies to UK residents going abroad and to crew of ships and aircraft), under the terms of the retail export scheme as described in Notice 704 "VAT Retail exports"; and
– Direct and Indirect Exports, if you export goods direct, or supply goods in the UK to overseas traders for subsequent indirect export by them, as described in VAT Notice 703 "Exports and removals of goods from the UK",

you must allow for those exports in your scheme calculation as follows—

For either Retail Exports or Direct and Indirect Exports—

(a) Include in your Daily Gross Takings (DGT) all amounts, including VAT, for goods sold for retail export or sent for export.
(b) At the end of each tax period add up the amounts for standard-rated goods which have actually been exported or sent for export.

(c) Calculate notional tax on the total amount at (b), using the VAT fraction that applied at the time when you included the amounts in your DGT.
(d) Subtract the notional tax at (c) from your scheme output tax.

For Direct and Indirect Exports only—

(e) where you do not obtain proof of shipment within three months of the date on which you supplied the goods for export, you must enter the notional tax on those goods already calculated at (b) as an addition to the VAT PAYABLE side of your VAT account for the current tax period.

7.17 Florists

If you are a member of an organisation such as Interflora, Teleflorist or Flowergram, see Notice 727 "VAT Retail schemes".

7.18 Gift, book and record vouchers

The following rule/requirement/paragraph has the force of law.

If you . . .	*then . . .*
sell gift vouchers at a value higher than their face value	the excess is consideration for a supply of services and VAT should be accounted for on it outside the retail scheme. When you redeem the vouchers you must include their face value in your Daily Gross Takings (DGT).
sell gift vouchers at their face value	do not include the amount in your DGT. But, when you redeem the vouchers you must include their face value in your DGT.
sell gift vouchers at a price lower than their face value	do not include the amount in your DGT. When you redeem the voucher, if you have evidence to prove that that voucher was supplied at a discount, then you may include the discounted amount in your DGT. Otherwise you must include the full face value of the voucher in your DGT.
include gift vouchers with other products for a single charge	the supply of the goods and voucher is treated as a multiple supply. This means VAT is only due on that portion of the payment which relates to the goods. You should omit from your DGT that part of the payment which relates to the gift voucher, usually the face value. But you must include in your DGT the face value of the voucher when redeemed by the customer.
issue gift vouchers free of charge	no VAT is due on the issue. When the voucher is redeemed for goods no VAT is due unless the cost of the goods exceeds £50. If the cost exceeds £50, VAT is due on the full amount. However, if you also sell such vouchers and are unable to distinguish between the two types at redemption, then you must include the full face value of the voucher in your DGT when it is redeemed.
have purchased a third party's gift vouchers which you intend to issue free of charge (for example in your own promotion)	you will not normally have been charged VAT. Equally, you do not have to account for any VAT when you give them away.
redeem gift vouchers and issue tax invoices to VAT registered businesses	you must account for these sales outside your retail scheme.

7.19 Goods bought at one rate and sold at another

The following rule/requirement/paragraph has the force of law.

For some goods the rate of tax you charge depends on how they are offered for sale. For example, meat is zero-rated when sold for human consumption but the same meat becomes standard-rated when sold as pet food.

If you are a chemist see Notice 727 "VAT Retail schemes".

If you sell take-away food see VAT Notice 709/2 "Catering and take-away food and the Catering Adaptation" in Notice 727 "VAT Retail schemes".

If you sell young children's clothing see Notice 714 "Young children's clothing and footwear".

All other goods you buy at one rate of tax and sell at another should be treated as follows—

You must keep separate stocks of the goods that you put up or hold out for sale at the different tax rates. When they are received you must enter them in your records of goods received for resale at the tax rate that will apply when they are sold.

If you hold a common stock of those goods that you draw on to sell at different tax rates, depending on the scheme you are using, you must enter in your scheme records their cost to you or their ESP, at the tax rate that applied when you received them. But, when they are put up or held out for sale at the other tax rate, you must—

(a) deduct the appropriate amounts from your scheme records at the tax rate that applied when you received the goods; and

(b) enter the corresponding amounts in your scheme records at the tax rate that applies when you sell them.

As the retailer, you are responsible for ensuring that the correct liability for VAT is applied when you sell goods. If you make a mistake you may underdeclare the amount of tax due, and so may be liable to an assessment and interest to correct the error.

7.20 Goods bought from unregistered suppliers

The following rule/requirement/paragraph has the force of law.

If you buy goods for retail sale from suppliers who are not registered for VAT, you must include these goods in your scheme calculation at the appropriate rate.

7.21 Goods sold on "sale or return" or similar terms

The following rule/requirement/paragraph has the force of law.

You should keep a separate record of goods supplied on a "sale or return" basis. You should only include the amount due for these in your Daily Gross Takings (DGT) when the customer has adopted the goods.

7.22 Imports

If you import goods from countries outside the European Community, you should read Notice 702 "Imports".

7.23 Part-exchange

The following rule/requirement/paragraph has the force of law.

When you accept goods or services in part-exchange, you should include in your Daily Gross Takings the full selling price, including VAT, of the goods you supply.

If you resell goods you have accepted in part-exchange you may be able to use the Second-hand Margin Scheme (see Notice 718 "Margin Scheme for second-hand goods, works of art, antiques and collectors' items"). If, however, you are unable to use that scheme you should include the goods previously taken in part exchange in your retail scheme.

7.24 Private or personal use of goods

The following rule/requirement/paragraph has the force of law.

Tax is due on any positive-rated goods purchased for retail sale but which you take out of your business for private or personal use (see Notice 700 "The VAT Guide"). You must add the value of such goods to your Daily Gross Takings.

If you operate—

- Apportionment scheme 1, include the full value of the item in your DGT.
- Apportionment scheme 2, include the full value of the item in your DGT and make any necessary adjustments to your ESPs.

7.25 Recall of goods by manufacturers

The following rule/requirement/paragraph has the force of law.

If a manufacturer recalls contaminated or otherwise faulty goods you must adjust your—

- purchase records if you use Apportionment Scheme 1; or
- ESP records if you use Apportionment Scheme 2.

7.26 Refunds to customers

The following rule/requirement/paragraph has the force of law.

You may deduct from your Daily Gross Takings amounts which are refunded or credited to customers in respect of taxable supplies of goods to a maximum of the amount originally charged.

7.27 Rented payphones

The following rule/requirement/paragraph has the force of law.

> If you rent a payphone from BT or another supplier, you are making supplies to users of the payphone and VAT is due on these supplies. As this is a service the supplies must be dealt with outside the Apportionment Schemes.

7.28 Retail sales to persons from other EC member states

The following rule/requirement/paragraph has the force of law.

> Supplies made in the UK to persons from other EC member states should be accounted for as normal domestic retail sales.
>
> Special arrangements apply to Distance Selling. This is where goods are sold to unregistered persons in other EC member states and the supplier is responsible for delivery to the customer. You can find out more about it in Notice 725 "VAT—The Single Market" and Notice 700/1A "Distance Selling".

7.29 Road fuel

The following rule/requirement/paragraph has the force of law.

> If you use road fuel for private motoring you must account for VAT on this outside the retail scheme, using the rules set out in Notice 700/64 "Motoring expenses".

7.30 Sale of discount vouchers or cards

The following rule/requirement/paragraph has the force of law.

> If you sell discount vouchers or cards entitling the holder to discounts on purchases—
>
> — from you, you must include the payment received in your Daily Gross Takings; or
> — with several traders, this is a separate standard-rated supply of services and must be dealt with outside your scheme.

7.31 Sale or assignment of debts

The following rule/requirement/paragraph has the force of law.

> If you sell or assign debts due from your customers, no adjustment to your VAT account is necessary since you will already have included the correct amount when you made the supply.

7.32 Saving stamps, travel cards and pools coupons

The following rule/requirement/paragraph has the force of law.

These should be dealt with outside your scheme.

7.33 Second-hand goods

The following rule/requirement/paragraph has the force of law.

You may be able to use the special scheme for second-hand goods (see Notice 718 "Margin scheme for second-hand goods, works of art, antiques and collectors' items").

Alternatively, sales of second-hand goods should be accounted for within your retail scheme in the same way as new goods.

7.34 Theft, shrinkage, leakage and stock losses

The following rule/requirement/paragraph has the force of law.

If you find that there are unexplained accounting discrepancies between stock and sales, you must consider the extent to which this is attributable to unrecorded sales, such as to the theft of cash by staff, and add the value back to your Daily Gross Takings.

Where possible these adjustments should be allocated to the specific VAT period in which the theft took place. Otherwise, such shrinkage should be apportioned across relevant tax periods on a fair and reasonable basis.

Unless you have evidence of the liability of the unaccounted supplies, adjustments must be in line with the usual proportion of standard against zero-rated supplies.

When you do this exercise, you will need to consider whether the shrinkage for which you have adjusted your DGT requires you to further adjust your ESPs.

8 BUSINESS PROMOTIONS

All boxed text in this section has the force of law (see para 1.4).

The general guidelines on the business promotion schemes covered in this section are given in Notice 700/7 "Business promotion schemes".

The VAT treatment under your retail scheme depends on whether the promotion is funded solely by you as the retailer or by, or together with, a third party such as the manufacturer.

If you wish to operate a particular promotion scheme which is not covered here you should contact HMRC. The address and telephone number are in the phone book under "Customs and Excise".

Commentary—*De Voil Indirect Tax Service* **V3.166, V3.556, V3.557.**

8.1 Discount vouchers

The following rule/requirement/paragraph has the force of law.

As part payment	When you take a discount voucher as part payment, you should include only the amount of money received from your customer in your Daily Gross Takings (DGT). If you subsequently receive payment for the voucher from another source you must include the extra amount in your DGT.

	The timing of the adjustment should follow the rule under the heading "When to account for manufacturer's contributions" in para 8.5.
Handling charges	If you make a further charge to a manufacturer for handling the vouchers, this is payment for a supply which is exempt from VAT and should be excluded from your DGT.
Sale	If you sell discount vouchers—see para 7.30.

8.2 Vouchers with no values or amounts but redeemable for whole items

The following rule/requirement/paragraph has the force of law.

	Description
Vouchers issued by you to customers making a specific purchase or purchases	No VAT is due upon issue and no further VAT is due when the voucher is used by the customer to obtain the reward goods. However, under Apportionment Scheme 2, you must adjust your ESPs for the reward goods.
Vouchers issued freely by you	—No VAT is due upon issue. —When the voucher is redeemed for goods no VAT is due unless the cost of the goods is over £50. VAT is then due on the value of those goods at the time you give them away and you must add that value to your DGT. You must also adjust the ESPs of the goods concerned under Apportionment scheme 2.
Vouchers issued by another person but redeemable with you	They are likely to be subject to the terms and conditions of that person's promotion. For example, you may be given certain stocks to give away on behalf of that person. These stocks must not be included in your retail scheme calculations. Notice 700/7 "Business promotion schemes" contains further information. Alternatively, contact HMRC. The address and telephone number are in the phone book under 'Customs and Excise'.

8.3 Vouchers redeemed for cash with you

The following rule/requirement/paragraph has the force of law.

> If you redeem vouchers for cash, the cash payment is outside the scope of VAT. You must not alter your Daily Gross Takings by the cash paid out.

8.4 Gift vouchers

> See para 7.18.

8.5 Goods linked in a promotion

These include promotions where—

Two different articles are sold for a single price in a combined offer, for example—

– a washing machine with an iron; or
– a jar of coffee with a packet of chocolate biscuits.

A number of same articles are sold in a multibuy offer, for example—

—"buy two and get a third free".

The following rule/requirement/paragraph has the force of law.

It is necessary to distinguish between business promotions where the supplier or sponsor contributes in whole or in part to the cost of the promotion, and those which are wholly sponsored by the retailer. This affects both how you treat your Daily Gross Takings (DGT) and how you carry out the rest of the calculation.

Apportionment Scheme 1

Where such a contribution is received, it must be included in the DGT. No adjustment to purchases will be necessary for these promotions.

Apportionment Scheme 2

Where such a contribution is received, it must be included in the DGT. You may also have to make appropriate adjustments to your Expected Selling Prices (ESPs).

If the supplier/ manufacturer or sponsor makes—

A full contribution	You should not make any ESP adjustments.
A partial contribution	You should adjust ESPs for the appropriate goods to the extent of the amount not supported by the manufacturer or sponsor.
No contribution	you will have to make an appropriate adjustment to the ESPs of the promotion goods.

If the promotion goods are liable at different rates of tax (as in the example of linked coffee and chocolate biscuits), there are additional rules to reflect the variation in your ESPs. You may—

—use the method explained in Notice 700 "The VAT Guide"; or

—in the case of goods linked by the manufacturer, treat the articles in accordance with the information shown on the supplier's invoice.

For example, if the invoice shows separate prices and amounts of tax, you may apportion the ESPs of the linked goods on the same basis.

As a concession, where the minor article satisfies the criteria set out in Notice 700/7 "Business promotion schemes", you may account for VAT on the minor article at the same rate as the main article. If you wish to take advantage of this concession, you will need to adjust the record of purchases or the ESPs of the promotion goods as appropriate.

When to account for manufacturer's contributions

Strictly speaking, when you receive a contribution from a manufacturer or joint sponsor representing partial payment for goods supplied to a customer, you should account for this in the period the goods are supplied.

However, as a concession, you may account for such contributions in the period they are received from the manufacturer or joint sponsor.

If a manufacturer or joint sponsor contributes, for example towards advertising, you have made a separate supply of services and this must be dealt with outside your retail scheme.

9 APPEALS

9.1 What if I disagree with a decision made by you?

If you disagree with a decision made by us, you can ask for it to be reconsidered.

Commentary—*De Voil Indirect Tax Service* **V5.4**.

9.2 Is there anything else I can do if I am still not satisfied?

You can also appeal to an independent VAT and Duties Tribunal if you are still not satisfied.

You will find out more about the appeal procedure in—

– the leaflet Appeals and Applications to the Tribunals issued by the President of the VAT and Duties Tribunal. Copies of the leaflet and the forms for making an appeal can be obtained by contacting VAT Helpline; and

– Notice 700 "The VAT Guide".

NOTICE 727/5
RETAIL SCHEMES—HOW TO WORK THE DIRECT CALCULATION SCHEMES

January 2013

This notice cancels and replaces Notice 727/5 (January 2011). Details of any changes to the previous version can be found in paragraph 1.1 of this notice.

1 INTRODUCTION

1.1 What is this notice about?

This notice tells you about Direct Calculation Schemes 1 and 2, two of the standard Retail Schemes. It explains the general rules applicable to the schemes, how the schemes work (including the calculation of VAT), and what records you should keep - especially your Daily Gross Takings (DGT) and your Expected Selling Prices (ESPs) records.

The changes are:

– paragraph 2.6 – updated to reflect the current "capping" regulations
– paragraph 8.2 – change of address

You can access details of any changes to this notice since March 2002 either online, go to www.hmrc.gov.uk or by phoning the VAT Helpline on 0300 200 3700.

Commentary—*De Voil Indirect Tax Service* **V3.571.**

1.2 Who should read this notice?

You should read this if—

– you are a VAT registered business making retail sales;
– you are unable to account for VAT on those sales in the normal way (see para 2.1); and
– your annual retail turnover, excluding VAT, does not exceed £130 million.

Commentary—*De Voil Indirect Tax Service* **V3.571.**

1.3 Are there other retail schemes?

Yes. Other standard retail schemes are the Point of Sale Scheme and the Apportionment Schemes. Businesses whose annual retail turnover exceeds £130 million cannot use a standard scheme. Instead they can agree a bespoke retail scheme (see para 3.5).

Commentary—*De Voil Indirect Tax Service* **V3.552.**

1.4 Force of law

Parts of this notice have the force of law under the VAT Regulations 1995, Part IX (regs 66–75). All paragraphs in Section 6 and certain paragraphs in other sections have legal force and supplement the law. The text of these paragraphs is placed in a box and indicated by a statement.

Commentary—*De Voil Indirect Tax Service* **V3.552.**

1.5 Where can I find out about the other schemes?

You will find a general introduction to retail schemes as well as guidance on choosing a retail scheme in Notice 727 *VAT Retail Schemes*.

Details of the other schemes can be found in—

Notice 727/2 *Bespoke Retail Schemes*;

Notice 727/3 *How to work the Point of Sale Scheme*; and

Notice 727/4 *How to work the Apportionment Schemes*.

VAT Notices

2 GENERAL RULES

All boxed text in this section has the force of law (see para 1.4).

2.1 Who can use a retail scheme?

Any retailer who would find it difficult to account for VAT in the normal way can use a retail scheme. Accounting in the normal way does not require you to issue a tax invoice to unregistered customers. But it does require you to identify, for each sale, the tax exclusive value and the VAT and to be able to produce periodic totals of those amounts.

Commentary—*De Voil Indirect Tax Service* **V3.573.**

2.2 Can I use any retail scheme?

No. Some of the schemes have turnover limits (see para 3.5 for guidance on the Direct Calculation Schemes).

Otherwise, provided your chosen retail scheme produces a fair and reasonable result you may choose the scheme which suits your business best. Notice 727 *VAT Retail schemes* tells you more about choosing a retail scheme.

Commentary—*De Voil Indirect Tax Service* **V3.571, 574.**

2.3 Can I use the scheme to account for all my retail and non-retail supplies?

The following has the force of law

> No. Retail schemes can be used for retail supplies only.
>
> If you make a mixture of retail and non-retail sales you must only use a retail scheme to calculate the tax due on your retail sales. You must account for non-retail sales using the normal method of accounting.

2.4 What if my business makes sales to other VAT registered businesses?

The following has the force of law

> Sales to other VAT registered businesses must not be included in a retail scheme.
>
> The exception to this are occasional cash sales, for example—
>
> – a garage supplying petrol to a VAT registered customer; or
> – a retail DIY store supplying building materials to a VAT registered builder.

Commentary—*De Voil Indirect Tax Service* **V3.551.**

2.5 Can I change schemes?

The following has the force of law

> Yes. You can change schemes at the end of a complete year, reckoned from the beginning of the tax period in which you first adopted the scheme. You must use the scheme for 12 months, unless—
>
> – you become ineligible for the scheme you are using; or
> – we allow or require an earlier change.
>
> If you become ineligible you must cease using the scheme from the end of the next complete accounting period.

For example, if you account for VAT by reference to quarters ending March, June, September and December and your turnover makes you ineligible for a scheme during February, you must cease to use that scheme to account for supplies made on or after 1 July. Some schemes require adjustments when you cease using them (see para 3.6 for guidance on the Direct Calculation Schemes).

Commentary—*De Voil Indirect Tax Service* **V3.563.**

2.6 Can I change schemes retrospectively?

No. Retrospective changes to retail schemes are not normally allowed. The VAT and Duty Tribunals have repeatedly confirmed the principle that where you operate a scheme according to the published rules (or an agreed variation), the tax due under that scheme is the correct VAT for the period. You cannot change schemes retrospectively simply because another scheme produces a lower or different valuation.

We may allow retrospective change in exceptional cases. If you think you have exceptional grounds for a retrospective change you should write to your local VAT Business Advice Centre giving as much detail as possible.

The maximum period for recalculation following a retrospective change of scheme is four years and you must have been, and remain, eligible to use the new scheme during the full period for which you apply.

Commentary—*De Voil Indirect Tax Service* **V3.563.**

3 BASIC PRINCIPLES OF DIRECT CALCULATION SCHEMES 1 AND 2

All boxed text in this section has the force of law (see para 1.4).

Unless stated otherwise, this section applies to both Direct Calculation Schemes 1 and 2.

3.1 How do the Direct Calculation Schemes work?

The schemes work by calculating the Expected Selling Price (ESPs) of goods for retail sale at one or two rates of VAT in order to establish the proportion of your Daily Gross Takings (DGT) on which VAT is due.

The following has the force of law

> You must always calculate the Expected Selling Prices of your "minority goods". These are the goods at the rate of tax which forms the smallest proportion of your retail supplies. But see an exception to this rule in 4.2.1.

For example, if you make—

- 60 per cent standard-rated sales; and
- 40 per cent zero-rated sales,

your minority goods are your zero-rated goods. You therefore calculate the Expected Selling Prices (ESPs) for your zero-rated goods received, made or grown for retail sale and then deduct this from your Daily Gross Takings. This gives you your figure for standard-rated sales, to which you apply the VAT fraction to arrive at your output tax liability.

On the other hand, if you make—

- 60 per cent zero-rated sales; and
- 40 per cent standard-rated sales,

your minority goods are your standard-rated goods. You calculate the ESPs for your standard-rated goods received, made or grown for retail sale. You then apply the VAT fraction to this figure to arrive at your output tax liability.

Commentary—*De Voil Indirect Tax Service* **V3.573.**

3.2 What other rules are there when using the Direct Calculation Schemes?

Both schemes work mainly on the premise that you supply goods at two rates of tax (standard and zero). For calculation purposes, if you supply goods at all three rates (standard, lower and zero), the lower-rated supplies are always assumed to be the second minority goods (see Section 4).

Scheme 2 operates in the same way as Scheme 1, but requires an annual stock adjustment to correct any under or overpayment of VAT during the year (see para 4.5).

You should also note—

- if your minority goods are zero-rated you cannot use the schemes for zero-rated supplies of services;
- if your minority goods are standard-rated you cannot use the schemes for standard-rated supplies of services; and
- you may not use the schemes for supplies of catering.

If you set Expected Selling Prices (ESPs) for standard-rated goods and your standard-rated stock has a slow turnover you should be aware that the scheme may not be the best suited to your business, as you will pay VAT in the period in which the goods are received and not necessarily when they are sold.

The Direct Calculation scheme can be relatively simple if you have a small proportion of supplies at one rate. But the scheme can produce significant inaccuracies if Expected Selling Prices are not calculated accurately. Additionally it can be complex to work if you sell goods at three rates of tax, though it may be possible to account for a small number of goods at a third rate outside the scheme.

Commentary—*De Voil Indirect Tax Service* **V3.573.**

3.3 Can I use other schemes with the Direct Calculation Schemes?

The following has the force of law

Yes. Provided you are eligible to use the schemes—

- you can mix the Point of Sale Scheme with either of the Direct Calculation Scheme; but
- you cannot mix different versions of the Direct Calculation Schemes and you must not use a Direct Calculation Scheme in some parts of your business and an Apportionment Scheme in others.

NB Normally, the retail scheme uses a single calculation for the whole of your VAT registration. However, if you wish you can use the same scheme separately at a number of distinct business locations. But you may then need to make adjustments to account for transfers between different parts of the business and you must agree the details of such adjustments with your local VAT Business Advice Centre.

You can always use the normal method of accounting together with any scheme or any allowable mixture for which you are eligible.

Commentary—*De Voil Indirect Tax Service* **V3.562.**

3.4 Do I need to keep any records?

The following has the force of law

Yes. You must keep—

- a record of your Daily Gross Takings (DGT) and how those gross takings are made up, as described in the DGT Checklist in Section 5;
- any working papers you use to calculate your output tax; and
- a record of your Expected Selling Prices (ESPs) as explained in para 4.3.

The normal record keeping requirements also apply. Notice 700 *The VAT Guide* tells you what is needed.

Commentary—*De Voil Indirect Tax Service* **V3.566.**

3.5 What should I do if I exceed the turnover limits?

Direct Calculation Scheme 1 is available to businesses with an annual tax exclusive retail turnover not exceeding £1 million. If you think your annual tax exclusive turnover is about to exceed £1 million you should consider Direct Calculation Scheme 2 or any of the other standard retail schemes (para 2.2).

Direct Calculation Scheme 2 is available to businesses with an annual retail turnover, excluding VAT, between £1 million and £130 million. If you think your annual retail turnover, excluding VAT, is about to exceed £130 million you should contact HM Revenue & Customs (HMRC) as soon as possible to agree a bespoke scheme.

The following has the force of law

For both Schemes 1 and 2, the turnover limits apply to the whole of your VAT registration.

If your turnover is over £1 million and you wish to use a Direct Calculation scheme you must operate Scheme 2.

3.6 What must I do when I cease to use the Direct Calculation Schemes?

The following has the force of law

Direct Calculation Scheme 1—No adjustment is normally required.

Direct Calculation Scheme 2—You must do a closing adjustment, as for the annual adjustment (para 4.5), even if you leave before the anniversary of starting to use the scheme. The adjustment must include the tax periods since your last adjustment and must take account of any disposals made during the year which were not by way of retail sale. You do this by excluding from the figures used in your calculation the value of any goods which were previously part of the retail scheme but have not been sold by way of retail. You must also make an adjustment if a part of your business leaves the scheme.

Commentary—*De Voil Indirect Tax Service* **V3.573.**

3.7 Are there any other rules when I cease to use the schemes?

Apart from making the adjustments as explained in para 3.6, you should also remember—

- You can only include retail sale of goods in your scheme. If you transfer part or all of your business as a going concern and you cease to use the scheme, you will have to exclude the value of the stock which has been transferred from your retail scheme.
- If you cease to trade, VAT may become due on the value of your stocks and assets (see Notice 700/11 *Cancelling your registration*).
- And we may require additional adjustments where unusual patterns of trade prevent your chosen scheme from producing a fair and reasonable result.

The following has the force of law

For these reasons you must always tell your VAT Business Advice Centre if you are—

- intending to buy or sell part of a business; or
- changing the legal entity of your business (for example, from sole proprietor to partnership); or
- registered as a group and the composition of the group is to change.

Commentary—*De Voil Indirect Tax Service* **V3.261.**

4 MECHANICS OF THE DIRECT CALCULATION SCHEMES (1 AND 2)

All boxed text in this section has the force of law (see para 1.4).

Apart from the requirement under Scheme 2 to carry out a stock-take and to make an annual adjustment (para 4.5), both Direct Calculation Schemes work in very much the same way. Unless stated otherwise, the rules in this section apply to both schemes.

The calculations (for both zero- and standard-rated minority goods detailed here) assume that the second minority goods are liable to tax at the lower rate.

4.1 How do I calculate VAT under the Direct Calculation Schemes?

The Direct Calculation Schemes work by applying the appropriate VAT fraction(s) to your total of positive-rated Daily Gross Takings (DGT) to establish the amount of tax that is due on your eligible retail sales. This gives you your scheme output tax. Section 5 explains the DGT rules in detail.

The VAT fraction is simply a way of calculating the amount of VAT contained in the total gross takings. Notice 700 "*The VAT Guide* tells you more about the VAT fraction.

Commentary—*De Voil Indirect Tax Service* **V3.573.**

4.2 Starting to use the Direct Calculation Schemes

4.2.1 Before you start to use the Direct Calculation Schemes

Before you start to use a Direct Calculation scheme you have to decide which goods you are going to set Expected Selling Prices (ESPs) for. You will have to estimate whether the larger portion of your sales is standard-rated or zero-rated. If you also make lower-rated supplies you will have to consider these in making your estimate.

The following has the force of law

You must calculate your ESPs for the goods forming the smallest proportion (your minority goods) of your supplies. (See the example in para 3.1).

Once you have started to set ESPs for minority goods, you must continue to set ESPs for that rate of goods for the whole of the retail scheme year.

However, retailers using Direct Calculation Scheme 1 may mark up the "majority" goods if it is more straightforward for them to do so.

For example, newsagents will probably find it easier to set ESPs for their majority sales of magazines and newspapers. There will be fewer purchase records for these than for their minority standard rated sales of tobacco and confectionery which may come from a variety of sources.

4.2.2 When you start to use the Direct Calculation Schemes

The following has the force of law

When you start to use the scheme remember:

for Direct Calculation Schemes 1 or 2, you must not include goods you have in stock as goods received in the period. However, if you have stock items which you intend to sell and not restock, you may include these in your calculation for the first period, unless these goods have already been allowed for by you in a previous scheme; and

additionally for Direct Calculation Scheme 2, you must know the ESPs of the minority goods in stock, although you will not need to use this information until the annual adjustment is due.

Commentary—*De Voil Indirect Tax Service* **V3.573.**

4.3 Expected Selling Prices (ESPs)

To use this scheme you need to calculate ESPs and make adjustments to them as detailed here.

4.3.1 How do I calculate ESPs?

The following has the force of law

How you calculate your ESPs has a direct effect on the tax you pay under the scheme. You must therefore calculate your ESPs as accurately as possible.

You can calculate your ESPs in any way that produces a fair and reasonable result. However, you must always use the same method and you must also make the adjustments described in para 4.3.3.

The most common methods of calculating ESPs are—

(a) mark up each line of goods—this is the most accurate method; or
(b) mark up classes of goods—for example vegetables or confectionery; or
(c) use recommended retail prices.

The following has the force of law

You can only use method (b) if—

- you are unable to mark up each line, as in (a) above;
- the variation in mark up within the group is no more than 10 per cent;
- the mark up is reviewed each quarter; and
- the class of goods has a commercial basis and is not constructed artificially.

You can only use method (c) if—

- you are able to record the recommended retail selling price (RRP) on receipt of the goods; and
- your invoices or other supplier documentation show the tax inclusive RRP of each separate line of goods, distinguish standard-rated, lower-rated and zero-rated sales and total goods at each rate of tax.

4.3.2 What must I not include in my ESP calculations?

The following has the force of law

ESPs are used to calculate the value of your retail sales at different rates. Therefore, you must not include in your calculation—

- wholesale sales;
- goods bought for private use; or
- disposals of stock resulting from a sale of all or part of the business.

4.3.3 ESP Adjustment

The following has the force of law

As ESPs will rarely be fully achieved in your retail scheme you must make adjustments at the end of each tax period to take account of factors which might affect the selling price.

For example—

- price changes—increases and decreases, for example, sell by date reductions;
- special offers and promotion schemes;
- wastage;
- freezer breakdowns;
- breakages;
- shrinkage—pilferage and loss of stock; and
- bad debts that have been written off in the period.

This list is not exhaustive; if you are aware of other factors which affect your ESPs you must make the appropriate adjustment.

How you make these adjustments is up to you but you must always be consistent in the method you use (both within one period and from one period to another). You must also record any adjustments and keep the working papers with your retail scheme calculations.

4.3.4 What if I have difficulty in making ESP adjustments?

If you have difficulty in making these adjustments, you may need to use another scheme. However, your local office may:

- agree a method of sampling where reductions cannot be established accurately; or
- agree to the omission of certain adjustments where the effect does not distort your retail scheme.

Commentary—*De Voil Indirect Tax Service* **V3.573.**

4.4 Direct Calculation Schemes 1 and 2 calculations

The following has the force of law

If you are using Direct Calculation Scheme 2 you must also make the adjustment described in para 4.5 after you have calculated your output tax for the fourth quarter, and you must account for any difference on your return for that quarter.

The following is a step-by-step guide to how you must calculate your VAT using Schemes 1 or 2.

4.4.1 Setting ESPs for zero-rated goods

The calculation assumes that the second minority goods are liable to tax at the lower rate.

If you set ESPs for zero-rated goods then you should make your scheme calculation as follows—

Step 1	Add up your Daily Gross Takings (DGT) for this tax period (see Section 5)	£______
Step 2	Add up the Expected Selling Prices (ESPs) of your zero-rated goods received, made or grown for retail sale in the tax period (adjusted as in para 4.3.3)	£______
Step 3	Deduct the total at step 2 from the total at step 1 to work out the standard-rated element of your takings	
Step 4	Multiply the total at step 3 by 1/6 (VAT at 20 per cent) If you make supplies at only two rates of tax, this is your Scheme 1 or 2 output tax	
If you also make supplies at the lower rate you will need to make the following additional calculation—		
Step 5	Add up the Expected Selling Prices (ESPs) of your lower rated goods received, made or grown for retail sale in the tax period (adjusted as in para 4.3.3)	£______
Step 6	Multiply the figure at step 5 by 1/21 (VAT at 5 per cent)	£______
Step 7	Multiply the figure at step 5 by 1/6 (VAT at 20 per cent)	£______
Step 8	Deduct the tax figure at step 6 from the tax figure at step 7	£______
Step 9	Reduce the figure for output tax at step 4 by the figure at step 8 to arrive at your scheme output tax	£______

4.4.2 Setting ESPs for standard-rated goods

The calculation assumes that the second minority goods are liable to tax at the lower rate.

The following has the force of law

If you set ESPs for standard-rated goods then you should make your scheme calculation as follows—		
Step 1	Add up your Daily Gross Takings (DGT) for this tax period (see para 5). Although this is not used in this calculation, it is still a requirement of operating the scheme and is also used in completing your VAT return	£______
Step 2	Add up the Expected Selling Prices (ESPs) of your standard-rated goods received, made or grown for retail sale in the tax period (adjusted as in para 4.3.3)	£______

Step 3	Multiply the figure at step 2 by 1/6 (VAT at 20 per cent) If you make supplies at only two rates of tax, this is your Scheme 1 or 2 output tax	£__________
If you also make supplies at the lower rate you will need to make the following additional calculation—		
Step 4	Add up the ESPs of your lower-rated goods received, made or grown for retail sale in the tax period (adjusted as in para 4.3.3)	£__________
Step 5	Multiply the figure at step 4 by 1/21 (VAT at 5 per cent)	£__________
Step 6	Add the tax figure at step 5 to the tax figure at step 3	£__________

Commentary—*De Voil Indirect Tax Service* **V3.573.**

4.5 Annual adjustment (for Direct Calculation Scheme 2 only)

This sub-section details the annual adjustment required if you use Direct Calculation Scheme 2.

Scheme 2 is based on your retail trade over a full year. This year runs from the beginning of the first tax period in which you use the scheme.

At the end of each year you make an adjustment to reflect the actual sales made by your retail outlets during the year. It compares the movement in stock and levels of goods received, made or grown for retail resale, with what has been accounted for under the scheme calculations for the year.

The following has the force of law

> Once you have calculated your output tax due under the retail scheme for the fourth quarter, as in para 4.4, you must carry out the annual adjustment as described below.

4.5.1 If you set ESPs for zero-rated goods

The adjustment assumes that the second minority goods are liable to tax at the lower rate.

The adjustment must take account of any disposals since the last adjustment which were not made by way of retail sale. You do this by excluding from the figures used in the calculation the value of any goods which were previously part of the scheme calculation, or included in the opening stock figure, but have not been sold by way of retail.

The adjustment is also required if a part of your business leaves the scheme.

Step 1	When you begin to use the scheme establish the Expected Selling Prices (ESPs) of your opening stock of zero-rated goods for retail sale making any necessary adjustments as in para 4.3.3	£__________
Step 2	Add up your Daily Gross Takings (DGT) for the four quarters	£__________

Step 3	Total the ESPs of your zero-rated goods received, made or grown for retail sale in the four quarters, adjusted as in para 4.3.3, and add the opening zero-rated stock figure at step 1	£________
Step 4	At the end of the scheme year, or when you cease to use the scheme, establish the ESPs of your closing stock of zero-rated goods for retail sale. (This becomes your opening zero-rated stock figure for the next year)	£________
Step 5	Deduct the figure at step 4 from the figure at step 3. This gives the ESPs for the zero-rated goods you have sold by retail in the year	£________
If you make supplies at only two rates of tax complete steps 6–9. If you make supplies at three rates of tax, omit steps 6–9 and go to step 10.		
Step 6	Deduct the figure at step 5 from the figure at step 2. This gives you your standard-rated takings for the year	£________
Step 7	Multiply the figure at 6 by 1/6 (VAT at 20 per cent)	£________
Step 8	Add up the output tax you have paid under the retail scheme in the four quarters	£________
Step 9	If the figure at step 7 is greater than the figure at step 8 you have paid too little tax and you should add the difference to your output tax in the fourth quarter.	£________
	If the figure at step 7 is smaller than the figure at step 8 you have paid too much tax and you should deduct the difference from your output tax in the fourth quarter.	
Steps 10–20 are only necessary if you make supplies at three rates of tax.		
Step 10	When you begin to use the scheme establish the ESPs of your opening stock of lower-rated goods for retail sale, making any necessary adjustments as in para 4.3.3	£________
Step 11	Total the ESPs of your lower-rated goods received, made or grown for retail sale in the four quarters, adjusted as in para 4.3.3, and add the opening lower-rated stock figure at step 10	£________

Step 12	At the end of the scheme year, or when you cease to use the scheme, establish the ESPs of your closing stock of lower-rated goods for retail sale (this becomes your opening lower-rated stock for next year)	£
Step 13	Deduct the figure at step 12 from the figure at step 11. This gives the ESPs for the lower-rated goods you have sold by retail in the year	£
Step 14	Multiply the figure at step 13 by 1/21 (VAT at 5 per cent)	£
Step 15	Add together the figure for total ESPs for zero-rated goods you have sold by retail in the year at step 5 and the figure at step 13	£
Step 16	Deduct the figure at step 15 from the figure at step 2. This gives you your standard-rated takings for the year	£
Step 17	Multiply the figure at step 16 by 1/6 (VAT at 20 per cent)	£
Step 18	Add together the figures at step 14 and step 17 to arrive at the output tax due under the retail scheme	£
Step 19	Add up the output tax you have paid under the retail scheme in the four quarters	£
Step 20	If the figure at step 18 is greater than the figure at step 19 you have paid too little tax and you should add the difference to your output tax in the fourth quarter. If the figure at step 18 is smaller than the figure at step 19 you have paid too much tax and you should deduct the difference from your output tax in the fourth quarter.	

4.5.2 If you set ESPs for standard-rated goods

The adjustment assumes that the second minority goods are liable to tax at the lower rate.

The following has the force of law

The adjustment must take account of any disposals since the last adjustment which were not made by way of retail sale. You do this by excluding from the figures used in the calculation the value of any goods which were previously part of the scheme calculation, or included in the opening stock figure, but have not been sold by way of retail.

The adjustment is also required if a part of your business leaves the scheme.

Step 1	When you begin to use the scheme establish the Expected Selling Prices (ESPs) of your opening stock of standard-rated goods for retail sale, making any necessary adjustments as in para 4.3.3	£

Step 2	Total the ESPs of your standard-rated goods received, made or grown for retail sale in the four quarters, adjusted as in para 4.3.3	£________
Step 3	Add together the totals at step 1 and step 2	£________
Step 4	At the end of the scheme year, or when you cease to use the scheme, establish the ESPs of your closing stock of standard-rated goods for retail sale. (This becomes your standard-rated opening stock figure for the next year)	£________
Step 5	Deduct the figure at step 4 from the figure at step 3. This gives the ESPs for the standard-rated goods you have sold by retail sale in the year	£________
Step 6	Multiply the figure at step 5 by 1/6 (VAT at 20 per cent)	£________
Step 7	Add up the output tax you have paid under the retail scheme in the four quarters	£________
Step 8	If the figure at step 6 is greater than the figure at step 7 you have paid too little tax for your standard-rated supplies of goods and you should add the difference to your output tax in the fourth quarter. If the figure at step 6 is smaller than the figure at step 7 you have paid too much tax for your standard-rated supplies of goods and you should deduct the difference from your output tax in the fourth quarter.	

If you also make supplies at the lower rate repeat steps 1–8 substituting "lower-rated" for "standard-rated", and at step 6 "1/21" for "1/6".

Commentary—*De Voil Indirect Tax Service* **V3.573.**

4.6 How do I complete my VAT return?

Your output tax figure is used to complete Box 1 of your VAT return (Form VAT 100). If you are using more than one scheme you must add together the output tax calculated from each scheme as well as any other amounts of output tax which are due, and put the total in Box 1.

To help you fill in your VAT return see VAT Notice 700/12 *Filling in your VAT return*. You can get a copy by contacting our National Advice Service.

Commentary—*De Voil Indirect Tax Service* **V3.573.**

5 DAILY GROSS TAKINGS (DGT) CHECKLIST

All boxed text in this section has the force of law (see para 1.4).

The DGT is a record of your retail supplies and is a crucial part of your retail scheme records. It is important that you follow the guidance in this section on how to calculate your DGT.

5.1 What must I include in my Daily Gross Takings (DGT)?

The following has the force of law

From the day you start using the scheme you must keep a record of your DGT. You must include in your DGT record—

- all payments as they are received by you or on your behalf from cash customers for your retail supplies;
- the full value, including VAT, of all your credit or other non cash retail sales at the time you make the supply; and
- details of any adjustments made to this record.

The DGT record will normally be a till roll or copies of sales vouchers. It is this record and not simply cash on hand which constitutes your DGT.

Commentary—*De Voil Indirect Tax Service* **V3.556, 557.**

5.2 Are all forms of cash payment included in my DGT?

The following has the force of law

Yes. You must include and record the following in your DGT as they are received from your customers—

- Cash;
- Cheques;
- Debit or credit card vouchers;
- Switch, Delta or similar electronic transactions; and
- Electronic cash.

Commentary—*De Voil Indirect Tax Service* **V3.557.**

5.3 Is my DGT simply a record of cash receipts?

No. You must also include the following in your DGT on the day you make the supply—

- the full value of credit sales (excluding any disclosed exempt charge for credit);
- the value of any goods taken out of the business for your own use;
- the cash value of any payment in kind for retail sales;
- the face value of gift, book and record vouchers redeemed (subject to para 6.17); and
- any other payments for retail sales.

5.4 What transactions may reduce my DGT?

The following has the force of law

Your till roll or other record of sales constitutes your DGT and it is this figure which you must use when calculating output tax due under your retail scheme.

However, you may reduce your DGT for the following—

- Counterfeit notes;
- Customer overspends using Shopacheck;

- Illegible credit card transactions (where a customer's account details are not legible on the credit card voucher and therefore cannot be presented and redeemed at the bank);
- Inadvertent acceptance of a cheque guarantee card as a credit card;
- Inadvertent acceptance of foreign currency (where discovered at a later time, for example when cashing up);
- Inadvertent acceptance of out of date coupons which have previously been included in your DGT but which are not honoured by promoters;
- Instalments in respect of credit sales;
- Receipts recorded for exempt supplies;
- Receipts recorded for goods or services which are to be accounted for outside the scheme;
- Refunds to customers for overcharges or faulty / unsuitable goods;
- Supervisor's float discrepancies;
- Till breakdowns (where incorrect till readings are recorded due to mechanical faults, for example till programming error, false reading and till reset by engineer);
- Unsigned or dishonoured cheques from cash customers (but not from credit customers);
- Use of training tills (where the till used by staff for training has been returned to the sales floor without the zeroing of figures); and
- Void transactions (where an incorrect transaction has been voided at the time of the error).

Commentary—*De Voil Indirect Tax Service* **V3.557.**

5.5 How may I reduce my DGT for transactions listed in para 5.4?

The following has the force of law

You must be able to provide evidence to support any adjustments to your DGT figure.

If you make an adjustment but subsequently receive a payment, you must include that payment in your DGT.

You must not reduce your DGT for till shortages which result from theft of cash, fraudulent refunds and voids or poor cash handling by staff. See para 6.33 for further details.

Commentary—*De Voil Indirect Tax Service* **V3.557.**

5.6 What if I am involved in transactions not covered in this section?

If you have a particular type of transaction which is not covered in this section, you must check Sections 6 and 7 to see if any of the rules there apply to your business before using the Direct Calculation Schemes to calculate your tax.

Commentary—*De Voil Indirect Tax Service* **V3.557.**

6 SPECIAL TRANSACTIONS

All boxed text in this section has the force of law (see para 1.4).

If you have a particular type of transaction which is not covered in this section, you should ask for advice from your local VAT Business Advice Centre. The address and telephone number are in the phone book under "Customs and Excise".

6.1 Acquisitions from other EC member states

The following has the force of law

Notice 725 *VAT—The Single Market* explains how you account for VAT on goods purchased (acquisitions) from other EC member states.

Suppliers from elsewhere in the EC will not charge VAT on their sales to you but you will have to account for VAT at the rate applicable to the goods in the UK.

For retail scheme purposes, references in this notice to zero-rated goods apply only to goods which are zero-rated in the UK; goods which you acquire from other EC member states at zero-rate, but which are standard-rated in the UK, must be treated as standard-rated in your retail scheme calculations.

Commentary—*De Voil Indirect Tax Service* **V3.556, V3.557, V3.567**

6.2 Amusement and gaming machines

The following has the force of law

Where your minority goods are—

- zero-rated (and lower-rated where applicable, as described in para 4.4.1), add the cash and/or tokens from the machine to your Daily Gross Takings on the day that you remove them from the machine; or
- standard-rated (and lower-rated where applicable, as described in para 4.4.2), exclude the takings from your scheme calculations and account for the tax as explained in VAT Notice 701/13 *Gaming and amusement machines*.

Commentary—*De Voil Indirect Tax Service* **V3.557.**

6.3 BT Phonecards

The following has the force of law

The sale of unused BT phonecards is outside the scope of VAT (provided they are not sold for more than face value). Exclude these sales from your Daily Gross Takings. Account for any commission received from BT outside your retail scheme.

If you deal in other types of phonecards you should consult your local VAT Business Advice Centre.

Commentary—*De Voil Indirect Tax Service* **V3.557.**

6.4 Business entertainment / gifts

The following has the course of law

If you purchase goods specifically to consume in the course of business entertainment or to supply as gifts, you must account for any tax due outside your scheme.

If you use or supply these goods from your normal stock you can account for any tax due under your retail scheme as follows—

- if the goods are lower or standard-rated and your minority goods are zero-rated, you must add the value of the supply to your Daily Gross Takings (DGT); or
- if your minority goods are lower or standard-rated, no addition to the DGT is necessary but you must adjust the ESP to reflect the value to be accounted for.

Commentary—*De Voil Indirect Tax Service* **V3.557.**

6.5 Business overheads

The following has the force of law

Exclude from your scheme any purchases of goods or services which are not for resale, for example your business overheads such as gas, electricity and rent.

6.6 Business promotions

The following has the force of law

See Section 7.

6.7 Catering supplies

The following has the force of law

See catering supplies in Notice 727 *VAT Retail schemes.*

6.8 Chemists

The following has the force of law

See VAT Notice 727 *VAT Retail schemes.*

6.9 Credit transactions

The following has the force of law

Account for output tax on credit retail supplies by including the full value of the goods in your Daily Gross Takings (DGT) at the time you make the supply. Do not wait until you are paid and do not include the instalments in the DGT when they are received.

Additional rules apply depending on the way the credit sales are financed:

Supplies involving a finance company	If you arrange credit for your customer through a finance company, our view is that in most cases you should include the full amount paid by the customer in your DGT at the time you make the supply. However, in some circumstances VAT may only be due on the amount you receive from the finance company. Business Brief 15/96 explains the circumstances in which this treatment may be appropriate.
Self-financed credit supplies	If you make a separate charge for credit (additional to the cash price) and you disclose it to the customer, this is exempt from VAT and should be excluded from your DGT.

NB If your turnover is less than £1 million and you run a business where your customers do not pay for the goods when they receive them (for example, you may be a milkman or newsagent), you may take account of opening and closing debtors in your scheme calculations. Notice 727 *VAT Retail Schemes* provides an example of how to do this.

Commentary—*De Voil Indirect Tax Service* **V3.557.**

6.10 Delivery charges

The following has the force of law

If, in order to fulfil your contract for the sale of the goods, you also deliver them, then there is a single supply of delivered goods. It does not matter whether the charge you make for delivery is separately itemised or invoiced. Examples of supplies of delivered goods are doorstep deliveries of milk or newspapers. The liability of the delivery charge follows the liability of the goods. In this case include the full amount charged in your Daily Gross Takings and also allow for the delivery charge element in the ESP calculation.

If you supply goods under a contract that does not require delivery but where, nevertheless, you agree to deliver the goods and make a separate charge, then that charge is for a standard-rated supply of services. You can include the supply of goods in your Daily Gross Takings (DGT) but how you treat the delivery charges depends on which rate of goods you are marking up. For:

- zero-rated minority goods, include the delivery charges in your DGT; or
- standard-rated minority goods, you can add back as part of your standard rated sales figure the service which will not be included in your ESP calculation. If you do not do this, you must account for the tax due on the charges outside your retail scheme.

You will find more about delivery charges and delivered goods in Notice 700 *The VAT Guide* and Notice 700/24 *Postage and delivery charges*.

Commentary—*De Voil Indirect Tax Service* **V3.557.**

6.11 Deposits

The following has the force of law

Most deposits are advance payments for supplies and must be included in your Daily Gross Takings (DGT).

However, if you take a deposit for another reason, for example as security to ensure the safe return of goods you have hired out and you either refund it when the goods are returned safely or you forfeit it to compensate you for loss or damage, you should exclude this amount from your DGT.

Commentary—*De Voil Indirect Tax Service* **V3.557.**

6.12 Dishonoured cheques / counterfeit notes

The following has the force of law

See the entry entitled "Unsigned or dishonoured cheques" in para 5.4.

6.13 Disposal of business assets

The following has the force of law

If you dispose of a business asset, such as a cash register or a van, you should account for VAT on the sale outside your retail scheme.

Commentary—*De Voil Indirect Tax Service* **V3.557.**

6.14 Exempt supplies

The following has the force of law

Any payments received for supplies which are exempt from VAT must be excluded from your scheme calculations.

If you make exempt supplies, for example the sale of National Lottery tickets or financial services, you will need to consider the rules on partial exemption explained in Notice 706 *Partial exemption* and Notice 706/2 *The capital goods scheme.*

Commentary—*De Voil Indirect Tax Service* **V3.557.**

6.15 Exports to countries outside the European Community

You must allow for the following exports in your scheme calculations (as set out in 6.15.1 and 6.15.2)—

- Retail Exports: If you make supplies for retail exports (including supplies to UK residents going abroad and to crew of ships and aircraft), under the terms of the retail export scheme as described in Notice 704 *VAT Retail exports*; and
- Direct and Indirect Exports: If you export goods direct, or supply goods in the UK to overseas traders for subsequent indirect export by them, as described in VAT Notice 703 *Exports and removals of goods from the UK*.

NB For Direct Exports, if you are unable to supply the evidence of exportation, you will be held accountable for the tax. Therefore, if you do not arrange the exportation yourself, you should consider asking your customer for a deposit (equal to the amount of tax for which you will be accountable if your customer does not supply the evidence).

If you make retail sales to persons from other EC member states see para 6.27.

6.15.1 Scheme 1 or 2 calculation for zero-rated minority goods

The following has the force of law

You must follow the normal scheme rules but—

For either Retail Exports or Direct and Indirect Exports—

(a) Include in your Daily Gross Takings (DGT) all amounts, including VAT, for goods sold for retail export or sent for export.

(b) At the end of each tax period add up the amounts for standard-rated goods which have actually been exported or sent for export.

(c) Calculate notional tax on the total amount at (b), using the VAT fraction that applied at the time when you included the amounts in your DGT.

(d) Subtract the notional tax at (c) from your scheme output tax.

For Direct and Indirect Exports only—

(e) where you do not obtain proof of shipment within three months of the date on which you supplied the goods for export, you must enter the notional tax on those goods already calculated at (b) as an addition to the VAT PAYABLE side of your VAT account for the current tax period.

6.15.2 Scheme 1 or 2 calculation for standard-rated minority goods

The following has the force of law

Follow the method set out in para 4.4, but at the end of each tax period—

For either Retail Exports or Direct and Indirect Exports—

(a) Add up the original Expected Selling Prices (ESPs) including VAT, of the standard-rated goods sold for retail export or sent for export.
(b) Calculate notional tax on the total at (a) using the VAT fraction that applied at the time when you included the amounts in your scheme calculations.
(c) Subtract the notional tax at (b) from your scheme output tax.

For Direct Exports only—

(d) Where you do not obtain proof of shipment within three months of the date on which you supplied any goods for export, you must include the notional tax on those goods already calculated at (b) as an addition to the VAT PAYABLE side of your VAT account for the current tax period.

6.16 Florists

The following has the force of law

If you are a member of an organisation such as Interflora, Teleflorist and Flowergram, see Notice 727 *VAT Retail schemes*.

6.17 Gift, book and record vouchers

The following has the force of law

If you . . .	*then . . .*
sell gift vouchers at a value higher than their face value	the excess is consideration for a supply of services and VAT should be accounted for on it outside the retail scheme. When you redeem the vouchers you must include their face value in your Daily Gross Takings (DGT).
sell gift vouchers at their face value	do not include the amount in your DGT. But, when you redeem the vouchers you must include their face value in your DGT.
sell gift vouchers at a price lower than their face value	do not include the amount in your DGT. When you redeem the voucher, if you have evidence to prove that that voucher was supplied at a discount, then you may include the discounted amount in your DGT. Otherwise you must include the full face value of the voucher in your DGT.

include gift vouchers with other products for a single charge	the supply of the goods and voucher is treated as a multiple supply. This means VAT is only due on that portion of the payment which relates to the goods. You should omit from your DGT that part of the payment which relates to the gift voucher, usually the face value. But you must include in your DGT the face value of the voucher when redeemed by the customer.
issue gift vouchers free of charge	No VAT is due on the issue. When the voucher is redeemed for goods no VAT is due unless the cost of the goods exceeds £50. If the cost exceeds £50, VAT is due on the full amount. However, if you also sell such vouchers and are unable to distinguish between the two types at redemption, then you must include the full face value of the voucher in your DGT when it is redeemed.
have purchased a third party's gift vouchers which you intend to issue free of charge (for example in your own promotion)	you will not normally have been charged VAT. Equally, you do not have to account for any VAT when you give them away.
redeem gift vouchers and issue tax invoices to VAT registered businesses	You must account for these sales outside your retail scheme.

Commentary *De Voil Indirect Tax Service* **V3.557.**

6.18 Goods bought at one rate and sold at another

The following has the force of law

For some goods the rate of tax you charge depends on how they are offered for sale. For example, meat is zero-rated when sold for human consumption but the same meat becomes standard-rated when sold as pet food.

If you are a chemist see Notice 727 *VAT Retail schemes.*

If you sell take-away food see VAT Notice 709/2 *Catering and take-away food* and the Catering Adaptation in Notice 727 *VAT Retail schemes.*

If you sell young children's clothing see Notice 714 *Young children's clothing and footwear.*

All other goods you buy at one rate of tax and sell at another should be treated as follows—

– You must keep separate stocks of the goods that you put up or hold out for sale at the different tax rates. When they are received you must enter them in your records of goods received for resale at the tax rate that will apply when they are sold.

– If you hold a common stock of those goods that you draw on to sell at different tax rates, depending on the scheme you are using, you must enter in your scheme records their cost to you or their ESP, at the tax rate that applied when you received them. But, when they are put up or held out for sale at the other tax rate, you must—

(a) deduct the appropriate amounts from your scheme records at the tax rate that applied when you received the goods; and

(b) enter the corresponding amounts in your scheme records at the tax rate that applies when you sell them.

As the retailer, you are responsible for ensuring that the correct liability for VAT is applied when you sell goods. If you make a mistake you may underdeclare the amount of tax due, and so may be liable to an assessment and interest to correct the error.

Commentary—*De Voil Indirect Tax Service* **V3.557.**

6.19 Goods bought from unregistered suppliers

The following has the force of law

> If you buy goods for retail sale from suppliers who are not registered for VAT, you must include in your ESP calculation only those goods which are taxable at your minority rate.

Commentary—*De Voil Indirect Tax Service* **V3.557.**

6.20 Goods sold on "sale or return" or similar terms

The following has the force of law

> You should keep a separate record of goods supplied on a "sale or return" basis. You should only include the amount due for these in your Daily Gross Takings when the customer has adopted the goods.
>
> If the customer pays a deposit see 6.11.

Commentary—*De Voil Indirect Tax Service* **V3.557.**

6.21 Imports

The following has the force of law

> If you import goods from countries outside the European Community, you should read Notice 702 *Imports*.

6.22 Part-exchange

The following has the force of law

> When you accept goods or services in part-exchange, you should include in your Daily Gross Takings the full selling price, including VAT, of the goods you supply.
>
> If you resell goods you have accepted in part-exchange you may be able to use the Second-hand Margin Scheme (see Notice 718 *Margin scheme for second-hand goods, works of art, antiques and collectors' items*). If, however, you are unable to use that scheme you should include the goods previously taken in part exchange in your retail scheme.

Commentary—*De Voil Indirect Tax Service* **V3.557.**

6.23 Private or personal use of goods

The following has the force of law

> Tax is due on any positive-rated goods purchased for retail sale but which you take out of your business for personal or private use (see Notice 700 *The VAT Guide*). You must add the value of such goods—

- to your Daily Gross Takings (DGT), if your minority goods are zero-rated; or
- to your ESPs and DGT to reflect the value due, if your minority goods are lower or standard-rated.

Commentary—*De Voil Indirect Tax Service* **V3.557.**

6.24 Recall of goods by manufacturers

The following has the force of law

If a manufacturer recalls contaminated or otherwise faulty goods, you must adjust your ESP records.

Commentary—*De Voil Indirect Tax Service* **V3.557.**

6.25 Refunds to customers

The following has the force of law

You may deduct from your Daily Gross Takings amounts which are refunded or credited to customers in respect of taxable supplies of goods or services to a maximum of the amount originally charged.

Commentary—*De Voil Indirect Tax Service* **V3.557.**

6.26 Rented payphones

The following has the force of law

If you rent a payphone from BT or another supplier, you make supplies to users of the payphone and VAT is due on these supplies. You must account for the VAT as follows—

- for zero or lower-rated minority goods, include the money removed from the payphone in your Daily Gross Takings; or
- for standard-rated minority goods, deal with the money received from the payphone outside your Direct Calculation scheme.

Commentary—*De Voil Indirect Tax Service* **V3.557.**

6.27 Retail sales to persons from other EC member states

The following has the force of law

Supplies made in the UK to persons from other EC member states should be accounted for as normal domestic retail sales.

Special arrangements apply to Distance Selling. This is where goods are sold to unregistered persons in other EC Member States and the supplier is responsible for delivery to the customer. You can find out more about it in Notice 725 *VAT—The Single Market* and Notice 700/1A *Distance Selling*.

Commentary—*De Voil Indirect Tax Service* **V3.557.**

6.28 Road fuel

The following has the force of law

> If you use road fuel for private motoring you must account for VAT on this outside the retail scheme, using the rules set out in Notice 700/64 *Motoring expenses.*

Commentary—*De Voil Indirect Tax Service* **V3.557.**

6.29 Sale of discount vouchers or cards

The following has the force of law

> If you sell discount vouchers or cards entitling the holder to discounts on purchases—
>
> – from you, you must include the payment received in your Daily Gross Takings; or
> – with several traders, this is a separate standard-rated supply of services and must be dealt with outside your scheme.

Commentary—*De Voil Indirect Tax Service* **V3.557.**

6.30 Sale or assignment of debts

The following has the force of law

> If you sell or assign debts due from your customers, no adjustment to your VAT account is necessary since you will already have included the correct amount when you made the supply.

Commentary—*De Voil Indirect Tax Service* **V3.557.**

6.31 Saving stamps, travel cards and pools coupons

The following has the force of law

> These should be dealt with outside your scheme.

Commentary—*De Voil Indirect Tax Service* **V3.557.**

6.32 Second-hand goods

The following has the force of law

> You may be able to use the special scheme for second-hand goods (see Notice 718 *Margin scheme for second-hand goods, works of art, antiques and collectors' items*).
>
> Alternatively, sales of second-hand goods should be accounted for within your retail scheme in the same way as new goods.

Commentary—*De Voil Indirect Tax Service* **V3.557.**

6.33 Theft, shrinkage, leakage and stock losses

The following has the force of law

> If you find that there are unexplained accounting discrepancies between stock and sales, you must consider the extent to which this is attributable to unrecorded sales, such as to the theft of cash by staff, and add the value back to your Daily Gross Takings.
>
> Where possible these adjustments should be allocated to the specific VAT period in which the theft took place. Otherwise, such shrinkage should be apportioned across relevant tax periods on a fair and reasonable basis;
>
> Unless you have evidence of the liability of the unaccounted supplies, adjustments must be in line with the usual proportion of standard against zero-rated supplies; and
>
> When you do this exercise, you will need to consider whether the shrinkage for which you have adjusted your DGT requires you to further adjust your ESPs.

Commentary—*De Voil Indirect Tax Service* **V3.557.**

7 BUSINESS PROMOTIONS

All boxed text in this section has the force of law (see para 1.4).

The general guidelines on the business promotion schemes covered in this section are given in Notice 700/7 *Business promotion schemes*.

The VAT treatment under your retail scheme depends on whether the promotion is funded solely by you as the retailer or by, or together with, a third party such as the manufacturer.

If you wish to operate a particular promotion scheme which is not covered here you should contact your local VAT Business Advice Centre. The address and telephone number are in the phone book under "Customs and Excise".

7.1 Discount vouchers

The following has the force of law

As part payment	When you take a discount voucher as part payment, you should include only the amount of money received from your customer in your Daily Gross Takings (DGT). If you subsequently receive payment for the voucher from another source you must include the extra amount in your DGT. The timing of the adjustment should follow the rule under the heading "When to account for manufacturer's contributions " in para 7.5.
Handling charges	If you make a further charge to a manufacturer for handling the vouchers, this is payment for a supply which is exempt from VAT and should be excluded from your DGT.
Sale	If you sell discount vouchers—see para 6.29.

Commentary—*De Voil Indirect Tax Service* **V3.166, V3.556, V3.557.**

7.2 Vouchers with no values or amounts but redeemable for whole items

The following has the force of law

Vouchers issued by you to customers making a specific purchase or purchases	No VAT is due upon issue and no further VAT is due when the voucher is used by the customer to obtain the reward goods.

	However, you must adjust your ESPs for the reward goods.
Vouchers issued freely by you	No VAT is due upon issue. When the voucher is redeemed for goods no VAT is due unless the cost of the goods is over £50. VAT is then due on the value of those goods at the time you give them away and you must add that value to your DGT. See also para 6.4 regarding business gifts.
Vouchers issued by another person but redeemable with you	They are likely to be subject to the terms and conditions of that person's promotion. For example, you may be given certain stocks to give away on behalf of that person. These stocks must not be included in your retail scheme calculations. Notice 700/7 *Business promotion schemes* contains further information. Alternatively, contact your local VAT Business Advice Centre. The address and telephone number are in the phone book under "Customs and Excise".

Commentary—*De Voil Indirect Tax Service* **V3.557.**

7.3 Vouchers redeemed for cash with you

The following has the force of law

> If you redeem vouchers for cash, the cash payment is outside the scope of VAT. You must not alter your Daily Gross Takings by the cash paid out.

Commentary—*De Voil Indirect Tax Service* **V3.557.**

7.4 Gift vouchers

> See para 6.17.

7.5 Goods linked in a promotion

These include promotions where—

Two different articles are sold for a single price in a combined offer, for example—

– a washing machine with an iron; or
– a jar of coffee with a packet of chocolate biscuits.

A number of same articles are sold in a multibuy offer, for example—

– buy two and get a third free.

> If both articles are liable at the same rate of tax (as in the examples of linked washing machine/iron and same article multibuy), there are no additional rules to follow under the Direct Calculation Schemes.
>
> If the articles are liable at different rates of tax (as in the example of linked coffee and chocolate biscuits), there are additional rules to apportion the selling price—
> –you may use the method explained in Notice 700 "The VAT Guide"; or

–in the case of goods linked by the manufacturer, you may treat the articles in accordance with the information shown on the supplier's invoice. For example, if the invoice shows separate prices and amounts of tax, you may apportion your Expected Selling Price (ESPs) on the same basis. As a concession, where the minor article satisfies the criteria set out in Notice 700/7 "Business promotion schemes", you may account for VAT on the minor item at the same rate as the main article.
If an apportionment of the selling price is necessary, you must separate the amount allocated to the lower or zero-rated article from your standard-rated takings before carrying out your scheme calculation.
When to account for manufacturer's contributions Strictly speaking, when you receive a contribution from a manufacturer or joint sponsor representing partial payment for goods supplied to a customer, you should account for this in the period the goods are supplied. However, as a concession, you may account for such contributions in the period they are received from the manufacturer or joint sponsor.
Correcting ESPs You will need to adjust your ESPs if the contribution is for the class of goods which you have marked up in your retail scheme. If you receive from the supplier or sponsor— –a full contribution, do not adjust your ESPs; –a partial contribution, adjust your ESPs for the appropriate goods to the extent of the amount not supported by the sponsor or manufacturer; or –no contribution, make an appropriate adjustment to the ESPs of the promotion goods.
If a manufacturer or joint sponsor contributes, for example towards advertising, you have made a separate supply of services and this must be dealt with outside your scheme.

Commentary—*De Voil Indirect Tax Service* **V3.557.**

NOTICE 728
NEW MEANS OF TRANSPORT

April 2013.

This notice cancels and replaces Notice 728 (October 2012). Details of any changes to the previous version can be found in paragraph 1.2 of this notice.

Paragraph 3.6 of this notice has the force of law under the VAT Act 1994, Schedule 6, Item 11(2). Paragraph 6.1 of this notice has the force of law under the VAT Regulations 1995, Regulation 155. Section 11 of this notice has the force of law under the VAT Regulations 1995, Regulation 22. These paragraphs are indicated by being placed in a box.

EXAMPLE:

The following rule has the force of law If you receive a net payment you must include the full value before such deductions (including VAT) in your scheme turnover. This will usually be the value shown on your sales invoice.

1 INTRODUCTION

1.1 What is the notice about?

It explains how VAT applies to new means of transport.

In the EU most goods are charged with VAT in the country in which they are purchased. However for a new land vehicle, ship or aircraft, VAT will be due in the Member State of destination if:

- it falls within the definition of "New Means of Transport" (NMT), and
- it is sold to a customer who intends to take it to another Member State.

The definition of a Means of Transport within this notice and when it is "New" is common to all EU Member States and is only for the purpose of determining when VAT is due. Other agencies, for example the Driver and Vehicle Licensing Agency (DVLA), may have different definitions.

References to the Driver and Vehicle Licensing Agency (DVLA) should be read as including The Driver and Vehicle Agency (DVA) in Northern Ireland.

References to "ship" includes "boat" or "vessel".

This notice also provides information on how to notify HMRC about the arrival of any NMT into the UK.

1.2 What's changed?

Most of the changes that have been made to this notice since the October 2012 edition reflect the introduction of a new legal requirement to notify HMRC about land vehicles being brought into the UK from 15 April 2013.

These vehicle arrivals will need to be notified using the Notification of Vehicle Arrivals (NOVA) system. Please refer to the NOVA Information Sheet, available from www.hmrc.gov.uk/thelibrary/notices for further information. Sections 3, 5 and 8 all include changes relating to the introduction of NOVA and how to notify HMRC of the arrival of a land vehicle in the UK.

Paragraph 2.1 clarifies the meaning of "Means of Transport" for this notice only.

Paragraph 3.2 includes changes to the deadlines for notifying HMRC about a vehicle's arrival in the UK. Please note: the changes to the notification deadlines apply to ships and planes being brought into the UK as well as land vehicles.

You can access details of any changes to this notice since October 2012 on our website at www.hmrc.gov.uk or by phoning the VAT Helpline on 0845 010 9000.

This notice and others mentioned are available both on paper and on our website.

1.3 Who should read this notice?

This notice should be read by anyone considering obtaining a land vehicle, ship or aircraft in another Member State with the intention of bringing it into the UK and vice versa.

2 HOW TO IDENTIFY AND DEAL WITH NEW MEANS OF TRANSPORT

2.1 What is a "means of transport" for the purposes of this notice?

A "means of transport" for the purposes of this notice is any of the following when it is intended for the transport of passengers or goods:

- a ship more than 7.5 metres long (about 24.6 feet)
- an aircraft with a take-off weight of more than 1550 kilograms (about 4417lb), *or*
- a motorised land vehicle which:
  - has an engine with a displacement or cylinder capacity of more than 48 cubic centimetres, or
  - is constructed or adapted to be electrically propelled using more than 7.2 kilowatts (about 9.65 horsepower).

Commentary—*De Voil Indirect Tax Service* **V1.294.**

2.2 When is a means of transport not new?

A ship or aircraft or a motorised land vehicle is *not* new when *all* the following conditions are met:

A ship or aircraft is not new	—when more than three months have elapsed since the date of its first entry into service (see paragraph 2.3), and

	—it has, since its first entry into service, travelled under its own power for more than —100 hours if it is a ship, or —40 hours if it is an aircraft.
A motorised land vehicle is not new	—when more than six months have elapsed since the date of its first entry into service (see paragraph 2.3), and —it has, since its first entry into service, travelled under its own power for more than 6000 kilometres.

Commentary—*De Voil Indirect Tax Service* **V1.294.**

2.3 What does "first entered into service" mean?

For ships or aircraft it is the earlier of

- the date it was delivered from its manufacturer to its first purchaser or owner, or
- the date it was first made available to its first purchaser or owner, or
- the date it was first taken into use for demonstration purposes, by the manufacturer.

For motorised land vehicles it is the earlier of

- the date it was first registered for road use in the member state of manufacture, or
- the date when it was first liable to be registered for road use there.

For motorised land vehicles which are removed from Member State of supply without being registered for the road, it is the earlier of

- the date it was made available to the first purchaser, or
- the date it was taken into use for demonstration purposes by its manufacturer or sole concessionaire

See also paragraph 2.4.

Commentary—*De Voil Indirect Tax Service* **V1.294.**

2.4 What happens if HM Revenue & Customs is not satisfied with the date of first entry?

If we are not satisfied that a date of first entry into service has been established in accordance with the guidelines at paragraph 2.3, the NMT may be treated as having first entered into service on the date when the invoice relating to its first supply was issued.

Commentary—*De Voil Indirect Tax Service* **V1.294.**

2.5 Is your land vehicle, ship or aircraft an NMT?

If your answer is yes then go to paragraph 2.6 or if it is no then go to section 5.

2.6 How should I treat the acquisition or supply of an NMT?

This depends on whether you are VAT-registered or a person/business not registrable for VAT – see table below.

Persons not registrable for VAT	*VAT-registered person/business*
—Purchasing an NMT in another member state and bringing it to the UK (see section 3)	—Purchase of an NMT in another member state and bringing it to UK (see section 8)
—Bringing back an NMT to the UK by members of NATO forces (see section 4)	—Supply of an NMT in the UK for removal to other member state (see section 9)
—Bringing means of transport which are not new to the UK (see section 5)	—Purchase of an NMT in the UK for removal to another member state by a registered business in another member state (see section 9).
—Purchasing an NMT in the UK for removal to another member state (see section 6)	
—VAT refunds for non-registrable persons of an NMT for removal to other member state (see section 7)	

Persons not registrable for VAT	*VAT-registered person/business*
—Registration, licensing, type approval and Insurance (see section 10).	

3 PURCHASING AN NMT IN ANOTHER MEMBER STATE AND BRINGING IT TO THE UK (PERSONS NOT REGISTERED FOR VAT)

3.1 When is the VAT due?

VAT is due at the time of acquisition. This is either:

– the fifteenth day of the month following the one in which the NMT was made available to, or taken away by, the customer (sometimes referred to as the date of removal), *or*
– the date of issue of the tax invoice, whichever is earlier.

Note: the date the VAT is due is a legal point and maybe different from the date of arrival of the NMT, the date notification of arrival must be made by and the date payment of the VAT must be made.

Please see Para 3.2 for information on when a notification must be made and Paras 3.8 and 3.9 for information on when the VAT due must be paid.

Commentary—*De Voil Indirect Tax Service* **V3.388.**

3.2 When do I notify HMRC about the NMT I have brought to the UK?

If you purchase an NMT in another Member State to bring to the UK, you *must* notify us *within 14 days of its arrival in the UK or its acquisition, whichever is the later*. You may be liable to a financial penalty if you do not notify us within the 14 days.

Commentary—*De Voil Indirect Tax Service* **V5.127.**

3.3 How do I notify HMRC about a NMT land vehicle I have brought to the UK?

You must notify HMRC of any land vehicle brought into the UK by using the Notification of Vehicle Arrivals (NOVA) system. If you do not already have access to any of HMRC's online services you will need to register through HMRC's website.

The NOVA system allows HMRC to assess whether or not any VAT is due on a vehicle, and if so, make sure it is paid and accounted for correctly. You will not be able to register the vehicle with the DVLA until HMRC has been notified and are satisfied that any VAT due has been accounted for.

For more information on NOVA and how to notify HMRC please refer to the NOVA Information Sheet, available from www.hmrc.gov.uk/thelibrary/notices.

3.4 How do I notify HMRC about an NMT ship or an aircraft I have brought to the UK?

To make the notification about a ship or aircraft you must use Form VAT 415, which is available from our VAT Helpline or can be downloaded from our website. The notification must be in English.

To process your notification the Form VAT 415 should be accompanied by a copy of the final purchase invoice, showing:

– the hull/aircraft number
– the price paid, and
– any invoices for accessories purchased with the ship or aircraft.

We can process your notification more quickly if it is accompanied by these documents.

The completed form should be sent by post to:

HMRC
Personal Transport Unit
Priory Court

St Johns Road
Dover
Kent
CT17 9SH

Please note: that the Personal Transport Unit only accepts postal notifications, as there are no public enquiry counters.

Commentary—*De Voil Indirect Tax Service* **V5.127.**

3.5 How is the VAT that is due calculated?

The VAT is calculated on the total amount you have paid for the NMT (excluding all trade-ins, part-exchanges or special discounts not freely available to the general public), including any extras you had fitted to it at the time it was supplied, plus any delivery or incidental charges made by your supplier.

For land vehicles, NOVA will automatically calculate how much VAT is due on the NMT. If you are notifying online, NOVA will inform you at the end of the notification process how much VAT is due. If you notify us by using the VAT NOVA1 paper form, we will write to you telling you how much VAT is due.

For ships and aircraft, we will *only* calculate how much VAT you owe when the documents stated in paragraph 3.4 are received.

Commentary—*De Voil Indirect Tax Service* **V3.390.**

3.6 What rate of exchange is used in the calculation?

This information has the force of law.

For VAT purposes, amounts of money must always be expressed in sterling. If the invoice for your NMT is in another currency, including the Euro, HMRC will convert it into sterling using the rate of exchange current at time of acquisition.

This is normally done using the HM Revenue & Customs' period rate of exchange, which closely reflects the UK market rate. However, you may make a specific request in writing at the time of notification to use the actual market rate applicable on the date of acquisition. The rates published in national newspapers will be acceptable as evidence of the rate at the relevant time. Rates obtained before the acquisition date are not acceptable. If you do not request the use of market rate at the time of your notification, the HM Revenue & Customs' period rate will be used automatically.

Commentary—*De Voil Indirect Tax Service* **V3.393.**

3.7 Can I obtain an estimate of the VAT due on the NMT first?

Yes, you can obtain an estimate if you wish to know in advance how much VAT you would have to pay. You should contact the VAT Helpline, but *please note* that the final charges may differ because of exchange rate fluctuations or changes to the value of the NMT.

3.8 When do I actually pay the VAT on my NMT land vehicle?

NOVA will calculate the amount of VAT due and notify you, either automatically through the NOVA online system or by letter if you submitted a paper form (VAT NOVA1) notification. You will also receive instructions on how to pay. Please do not send any payment before NOVA has confirmed how much VAT is due.

You will need to pay HMRC the VAT due before you can apply for a UK vehicle registration.

Commentary—*De Voil Indirect Tax Service* **V5.127.**

3.9 When do I actually pay the VAT on my NMT ship or aircraft?

We will calculate the amount of VAT you owe and send you a demand for payment together with instructions on how to pay. Please do not send any payment before you receive the demand, because the amount you calculate could vary due to the different exchange rates used. You must pay the amount of VAT on demand *within 30 days* of the date on which it was issued.

3.10 What if I fail to notify HMRC or fail to pay the VAT due?

For land vehicles, failure to notify within 14 days of arrival into the UK may result in a late notification penalty being applied – regardless of whether any VAT is due on the vehicle. If a penalty is due HMRC will confirm in writing the amount due and how it has been calculated.

Please note: you must notify HMRC and pay any VAT due before the vehicle can be registered and licensed with the DVLA or DVA.

For ships and aircraft you may be liable to a financial penalty in addition to the VAT due

- if you fail to notify us within 14 days that you have brought an NMT to the UK; or
- if you provide incomplete or inaccurate information on form VAT 415.

You can avoid financial penalties by notifying HMRC in time and by taking care to complete the forms fully and accurately.

You will have a right to appeal if we impose any of the above penalties.

Commentary—*De Voil Indirect Tax Service* **V5.349.**

3.11 Under what circumstances may VAT not be payable?

All movements of NMT to the UK are liable to VAT, except where the NMT is a land vehicle constructed or adapted for a disabled person. For more information on VAT relief for people with disabilities see Notice 701/7 "VAT reliefs for disabled people" and the HMRC help sheet "VAT1615 About purchasing zero-rated adapted vehicles (Guidance for Customers)". See also paragraph 3.12.

Commentary—*De Voil Indirect Tax Service* **V4.281.**

3.12 Are there any more circumstances when VAT may not be payable?

Yes, you may be entitled to claim relief from VAT that is due when you remove your NMT to the UK if you meet the conditions below.

If you	*and*
are —a diplomat, or —a member of an officially recognised international organisation, or —a member of NATO or the civilian staff accompanying them	you are returning from service in another member state. Section 4 has more information on whether you qualify for the relief.
or —have paid VAT in the Member State of supply	You have brought the NMT to the UK on change of residence, which was not contemplated at the time of purchase.

3.13 Can I use another person to obtain and bring the NMT to the UK?

Yes, you can use another person, as an intermediary or agent, to assist you in obtaining your NMT and bringing it to the UK. See also paragraph 3.14.

3.14 Who is then responsible for notifying HMRC and for paying the VAT?

If you use an agent or intermediary to obtain and bring the NMT to the UK and the supplier's invoice is raised in your name and given to you by the intermediary, *you* are still the person responsible for notifying HMRC that the NMT has been brought to the UK and for paying the VAT that is due.

If bringing a land vehicle into the UK, anyone may act as your agent in notifying and paying HMRC using NOVA (see Para 3.3 (above) for information on where to find out more about NOVA). Any penalties, which result from late notification or payment, will be due from you even if your intermediary caused the delay.

If bringing a ship or aircraft into the UK, the declaration on the notification of acquisition (Form VAT 415) should, at all times, be completed by you (the acquirer) and not the intermediary.

Agents who are VAT registered and acting in their own name in relation to the supply of the NMT should use the procedure in section 8.

3.15 Must I keep a record of my NMT purchase?

You must keep your NMT purchase invoice and proof that you have paid the VAT for six years from the date of purchase. You could be asked to demonstrate that the VAT on your NMT has been paid.

If you decide to sell your NMT within the six-year period you are advised to pass your proof of VAT payment to the new owner.

Commentary—*De Voil Indirect Tax Service* **V5.202.**

3.16 What if I bought the NMT from a non-taxable person and it was already tax paid in that member state?

The supply of the NMT should be zero-rated. The supplier of the NMT should seek a refund of taxes paid from their own member state's fiscal authority and acquisition tax will be due in the UK.

3.17 What if I paid tax in the Member State of supply?

The supply of the NMT should be zero-rated and the Member State of supply will have rules in place similar to those in the Notice. You will need to confirm the exact procedures to be followed with the supplier. Note that in some Member States the supplier may take a refundable deposit equivalent to the VAT which is refunded once you have paid the VAT in the destination state.

If you have been incorrectly charged VAT or are having difficulty in obtaining a refund of a deposit taken in another Member State this does no affect the liability to pay VAT in the UK on the acquisition. Recovery of the "overpayment" will need to be taken up with the suppler or the relevant tax authority in that Member State of supply.

4 NATO FORCES AND DIPLOMATS BRINGING NMTS TO THE UK FROM ANOTHER MEMBER STATE

4.1 As a returning member of the NATO forces/civilian staff, can I claim relief from VAT when I bring my NMT back to the UK?

You can only claim entitlement to VAT relief if you comply with the notification requirements described in section 3. If you meet these requirements you can claim relief at the end of your tour on permanent posting back to the UK. You *must* be in possession of Form BFG NOVA1 if returning from Germany or Form BFC 414 from Cyprus, in order to register your vehicle.

These forms are available from (respectively):

Customs and Immigration
British Forces Liaison
Germany, BFPO40

or

SBA Customs
RAF Akrotiri BFPO57

If you are returning from any other Member State you must provide HMRC with evidence to show that the host authority relieved the tax. If returning with a land vehicle use form NOVA1, if returning with a ship/aircraft use VAT Form 415.

4.2 I am a diplomat returning to the UK from another Member State with my Means of Transport. Can I claim relief from VAT?

You can claim relief if you produce *both* evidence of your tax-free status from your head of mission *and* confirmation that the host Member State has granted you relief on your NMT. If you are returning with a land vehicle form NOVA1 should be used, if you are returning with a ship/aircraft that is a new means of transport form VAT 415 should be used.

5. VISITING THE UK OR BRINGING MEANS OF TRANSPORT WHICH ARE NOT NEW TO THE UK

5.1 What if I live in another Member State but bring my means of transport on temporary visits to the UK?

If you are normally resident (see paragraph 5.2) in another Member State and you bring your means of transport with you on a temporary visit to the UK, you do not have to notify HMRC or pay VAT on it.

5.2 What does "normally resident" mean?

Where you have spent at least 185 days in the last twelve months because of your work and personal connections. But if:

– you have no work connections, *or*
– your work and personal connections are in different countries,

then you will usually be considered to be resident in the country where your personal connections are.

5.3 What should I do if I decide to stay and keep my means of transport in the UK?

If your plans change, and you decide to stay in the UK and keep your ship or boat here, you do not need to notify HMRC unless either:

– it was supplied to you tax-free because of your special status in the member state in which you have been living or working, *and*
– the supply took place within the three months prior to your arrival in the UK, *or*
– it was supplied to you tax-free for removal from the member state of supply, and no EU taxes have been paid on it.
– at the time you brought a land vehicle into the UK, it was not required to be registered for road use here (because you were intending to remain here for less than 6 months in a 12 month period), but you now intend to remain and register and license the vehicle with the DVLA, you must notify the vehicle using the VAT NOVA1 form within 14 days of the change of intention. For more information on NOVA and how to notify HMRC please refer to the NOVA Information Sheet, available from www.hmrc.gov.uk/thelibrary/notices.

5.4 What if I am bringing a land vehicle, ship or aircraft, which is not an NMT into the UK?

If you bring the means of transport to the UK from another Member State, you will not have to pay UK VAT if:

– you did not purchase it with the intention of acquiring it into the UK – see paragraph 3.1 *or*
– it is no longer a "New Means of Transport" as defined in section 2, *and*
– you have paid VAT on its purchase in the Member State of supply.

However, please note that if bringing a land vehicle into the UK you must notify HMRC of its arrival through the NOVA system regardless of whether it is new or otherwise.

You will not be able to license and register your vehicle with the DVLA until HMRC have received notification of its arrival from you and confirmed that no VAT is due.

If you are a VAT registered business bringing a land vehicle which is not an NMT into the UK, you may have to account for VAT on your VAT return under the normal rules for intra-EU supplies (see Para 8.1). If VAT is due, the vehicle will be known as a "qualifying vehicle" for NOVA purposes.

Please see Para 3.3 for where to find more information about NOVA, including information on "qualifying vehicles".

Any land vehicle used on public roads in the UK,will be subject to UK licensing, registration and insurance requirements, which are explained in section 10.

6 PURCHASING AN NMT IN THE UK FOR REMOVAL TO ANOTHER MEMBER STATE

Commentary—*De Voil Indirect Tax Service* **V4.356.**

6.1 What happens when I buy an NMT in the UK for removal to another member state?

This information is given in the box below.

This information has the force of law.

> If you buy an NMT in the UK to take to another Member State, you will be liable for the VAT on the value of the NMT when you arrive there. To make sure that the purchase of the NMT is free of UK VAT, you must comply with certain conditions. These are:
>
> – the means of transport must be "new"
> – you or your authorised chauffeur, pilot or skipper must personally take delivery of the new means of transport in the UK
> – you must remove it from the UK to the member state of destination within two months of the date of supply to you, *and*
> – you must complete and sign a declaration on a Form VAT 411, stating your intention to remove the NMT from the UK and pay any VAT due in the member state of destination. Your supplier must complete their part of the form.

6.2 Can an NMT be purchased using a Finance House?

Yes, but normally this will mean the dealer is selling the means of transport to the finance house who in turn sell it to you. If that is the case then you must make sure it is the finance house that is shown as the supplier and the dealer must send the second copy of Form VAT 411 to the finance house for their retention.

6.3 What is Form VAT 411?

Form VAT 411 is your declaration that you will take the NMT to another member state within two months and pay the VAT there. It is also your supplier's declaration that they have supplied an NMT to you for removal from the UK.

6.4 How is the Form VAT 411 used?

The form is made up of an original (the top sheet) and three copies. When it has been properly completed, your supplier will send the original copy to us (see paragraph 9.5) and give the first copy to you. The supplier will keep the second copy of the form as part of their business records, and, if the NMT is a land vehicle, they will use the third copy to register it for road use if you are going to drive it out of the UK.

6.5 What if I am VAT registered in another Member State but buy an NMT in the UK for removal?

If you are registered for VAT in another EU Member State and you buy an NMT from a VAT registered person in the UK for removal to that State your supplier may zero-rate the supply under normal rules – see Notice 725 *The Single Market*.

To benefit from zero-rating you must remove the NMT from the UK within two months of the time of supply. You must account for any tax due on the acquisition in the Member State of destination, under the laws of that State.

6.6 Can I use the land vehicle on UK roads before removal to another Member State?

You must not use your land vehicle on UK roads unless it has been licensed and registered, and is properly insured. Section 10 contains more information on this.

6.7 What if I am unable to remove the NMT due to circumstances beyond my control?

If you purchase an NMT and then find that because of circumstances beyond your control, you are unable to remove it, you should inform us immediately by writing to the address given in paragraph 3.4. See also paragraph 6.8.

When we receive your letter we will calculate the VAT due and send you a demand, which you must pay immediately.

6.8 What happens if I fail to or am unable to remove the NMT within the period allowed?

If you fail or are unable to remove your NMT from the UK within the two-month period allowed, you should inform HMRC and pay the VAT, which is due. Failure to do so may make your NMT liable to forfeiture.

6.9 Are these NMT exempt from "type approval"?

You can find more information on "type approval" and how it affects NMTs that are land vehicles from paragraphs 10.7 onwards.

6.10 Should I insure the NMT that I purchased in the UK for removal to another Member State?

If you buy an NMT in the UK for removal to another Member State you should consider insuring it for its *full value* including UK VAT. If for any reason (for example, an accident) it is not removed from the UK, you will be liable for any UK VAT which was not charged at the time the NMT was supplied to you.

It is a legal requirement that you must be insured against third-party liabilities before you drive a land vehicle on UK roads. If your vehicle is registered in the UK, its use must be covered by a policy of insurance issued by an authorised insurer (a member of the Motor Insurers Bureau).

6.11 Is there anything else I must do?

When an NMT (that is a vehicle) is finally removed from the UK, the DVLA require the tear-off portion of the VX302. In the case of a temporary removal to another EU Member State, say for a holiday, the VX302 is not required to be completed. If it is then it can cause problems on return to the UK as the licence is cancelled.

7 VAT REFUNDS FOR NON-REGISTRABLE PERSONS OF AN NMT FOR REMOVAL TO OTHER MEMBER STATES

7.1 Who is entitled to a refund?

This section will normally apply where a consumer purchases a new land vehicle, ship or aircraft which they then resell while it is still within the definition of a New Means of Transport. You may be entitled to a refund of VAT if you satisfy *all* the following conditions:

- you are not registrable for VAT in the UK
- you are selling your NMT to another person, and that person intends to remove the NMT to another member state within two months of the date of supply, *and*
- you can demonstrate that you have paid UK VAT on your NMT.

7.2 How do I claim my refund?

To claim your refund you should write to the PTU (address at paragraph 3.4) at least 14 days (but no more than one month) before you expect to sell your NMT. You can use the form at section 12 to do this.

When we receive your notification (see also paragraph 7.3) we will advise you if we want to examine the NMT before you sell it, to confirm its eligibility for refund.

7.3 What documents should I submit with the claim form?

Before any refund is made we will need to see *all* the following documents:

- proof of your original purchase (normally the invoice or import entry)

- evidence that you have paid VAT
- proof of your sale, normally this would be your bill of sale and evidence that you have received payment, *and*
- that the NMT has been removed to another member state.

7.4 What happens if I cannot produce the documents listed at paragraph 7.3?

No refund will be given until you have produced documents showing all these things. (Your documents will be returned to you promptly.)

7.5 How will my VAT refund be calculated?

The amount of VAT refunded to you will depend on the value of the supply you make to your customer, but it cannot exceed that amount of VAT, which you have already paid when you obtained the NMT.

8 ACQUISITION OF NMTS BY VAT REGISTERED PERSONS AND BUSINESSES

Commentary—*De Voil Indirect Tax Service* **V3.366–V3.398; V4.341–V4.361; V5.272.**

8.1 How do I obtain an NMT from another member state?

You should provide the supplier or vendor with your UK VAT registration number to enable them to zero-rate the supply of the means of transport to you. In reality the intra-EU supplies of NMT between VAT registered persons are treated the same as for any other good (see Notice 725 *The Single Market*); in this case the good happens to be a means of transport' that happens to be "new". The rest of this section needs to be read in that context.

8.2 How do I account for VAT on an NMT purchased in another member state for removal to the UK?

If you are registered for VAT in the UK and you buy a VAT-free NMT from a person registered in another EU Member State, you should account for VAT due on your normal VAT return for the period in which you acquired the NMT. See also paragraph 8.3

8.3 Do I have to do anything else?

If the NMT is a land vehicle, it must be licensed and registered before it is used on public roads.

However, please note that you will not be able to license and register the vehicle with DVLA until you have notified HMRC about the vehicle's arrival through the NOVA system and HMRC have confirmed that the notification has been accepted.

8.4 Do I still account for acquisition VAT if I make an onward supply of the NMT in the UK?

Yes, you must account for acquisition tax on the vehicles you acquire. If they form part of your stock in trade, you may recover input tax equal to the amount of acquisition tax you declared. You must charge output tax on the full value of the supply to your customer.

8.5 What if I arrange the supply of an NMT from an EU supplier direct to a customer in the UK?

If you arrange the supply of an NMT from a supplier in another EU Member State direct to a customer in the UK, you are acting as an intermediary. If you act in this way for a person who is not registered for VAT in the UK, you may as part of your service (and subject to your customer's authorisation) notify HMRC about the acquisition of the NMT on behalf of your principal using the procedures described in section 3, but see also paragraph 8.6.

8.6 Who will be responsible for the declaration and payment of VAT?

For land vehicles:

Please refer to the NOVA Information Sheet, available from www.hmrc.gov.uk/thelibrary/notices for further information.

For ships and aircraft:

The customer, or acquirer if he is the principal, is responsible for the declaration you make on their behalf and for the payment of the VAT, which is due.

You may however make the payment on their behalf. When you trade as an intermediary you must make sure that the customer is provided with the sales invoice from the supplier and the invoice clearly shows the name and address of the acquirer of the NMT and the amount they have paid to the supplier. You should also distinguish clearly between:

- transactions in which you act as an intermediary, *and*
- the transactions in which you acquire and supply an NMT to the order of a person in the UK, in which case the provisions of paragraph 8.2 may apply.

8.7 If I am not the acquirer of a land vehicle into the UK then who should complete the notification at the time of registration?

For land vehicles:

Please refer to the NOVA Information Sheet, available from www.hmrc.gov.uk/thelibrary/notices for further information.

9. SUPPLY OF NMTS BY A VAT REGISTERED PERSON

9.1 What are the conditions for zero-rating the supply of NMT in the UK for removal to another Member State?

Assuming you are registered for VAT in the UK, these depend on whether:

- your customer is VAT registered in the Member State of destination – see paragraph 9.2, *or*
- your customer is not VAT registered in the Member State of destination – see paragraph 9.3.

9.2 What conditions should I meet if my customer is not VAT registered in the member state of destination?

You must meet *all* the conditions in order to zero-rate the supply to your customer who will be liable for any VAT in their member state:

- you must show on your VAT invoice your customer's VAT registration number (with the two-digit country code prefix, see *Notice 725 The Single Market*), *and*
- the NMT must be despatched or transported to another Member State within two months of the date you issue the invoice for the supply, *and*
- you must hold valid commercial documentary evidence, which confirms that the NMT has been removed from the UK
- you should also see paragraph 9.4.

9.3 What conditions should I meet if my customer is not VAT registered in the Member State of destination?

You must meet all the conditions in order to zero-rate the supply to your customer who will be liable for any VAT in their Member State:

- the means of transport must qualify as "new", see section 2 *and*
- you and your customer must make a joint declaration about the transaction on a Form VAT 411. If this form is not completed properly, you will not be entitled to zero-rate the supply – see paragraphs 6.2 & 6.7.

9.4 Should I complete the EC Sales List (ESL) form for this transaction?

You should only complete the ESL form when your customers are registered for VAT in another Member State showing the customer's registration number and value of supplies made in the reporting period. For more information please see Notice 725 *The Single Market*.

9.5 Where should I send the completed VAT 411?

You must send all originals to:

HMRC
Personal Transport Unit
Priory Court
St Johns Road
Dover
Kent CT17 9SH

See also paragraph 9.6.

9.6 Must I submit the Form VAT 411 within a certain deadline?

Yes, you must submit this within six weeks of the end of the calendar quarter in which you have made the supply.

9.7 I have purchased an unregistered NMT from a UK VAT registered supplier. Who is responsible for declaring acquisition tax?

The first acquirer of the vehicle into the UK is responsible for declaring acquisition tax on his VAT return. The onward supply of the vehicle to business is a standard-rated supply in the UK for which a normal VAT invoice should be issued.

10. REGISTRATION, LICENSING, TYPE APPROVAL OF LAND VEHICLES

10.1 Must I license and register a land vehicle that I brought to the UK from another Member State?

All vehicles used on the UK roads *must* be licensed and registered. If you purchase an NMT in another member state and bring it to the UK, the vehicle must be registered and licensed as soon as possible after arrival. You are not legally entitled to use or keep the vehicle on UK public roads until it has been licensed and registered in the UK.

10.2 Do I need to register a land vehicle purchased in the UK for removal to another Member State?

If you purchase a land vehicle in the UK for removal to another EU Member State and the vehicle is not already registered for road use in the UK, it will be allocated a registration number in a special 'VAT-free' series of numbers. This allows it to be identified as tax-free for the length of time it remains in the UK prior to removal.

The supplier of the vehicle will obtain the number for you by presenting copy 3 of the Form VAT 411 at one of the DVLA Local Offices (VROs).

10.3 List of DVLA local offices

Please refer to the links below for updated list of DVLA local offices; the first link is for offices in the UK and the second link is for DVA in Northern Ireland.

DVLA UK: www.gov.uk/dvla-offices

DVA Northern Ireland: www.dvani.gov.uk

10.4 In what other circumstances do I need to register a land vehicle?

If you are VAT registered in another EU Member State and have purchased an unregistered land vehicle that will be used on the road before removal from the UK, you should register the vehicle for road use. Form VAT 411A should be completed and be presented to the DVLA Local Office (see paragraph 10.3) who will allocate a registration mark in the tax-free series.

10.5 What if I decide to keep the land vehicle in the UK permanently?

If your plans change and you decide to keep the land vehicle in the UK permanently, you cannot retain the 'VAT Free' registration mark. In these circumstances you should contact the Personal Transport Unit (PTU) for advice.

10.6 What if I am a visitor to the UK?

If you are a visitor to the UK you need no further insurance if your vehicle is:

– covered by a valid "Green Card", *or*
– normally based and currently insured in another member state.

10.7 What is "type approval"?

"Type approval" is the official recognition that a land vehicle has satisfied certain international safety standards. You cannot licence and register a vehicle in the UK unless it is type-approved or otherwise exempt. For type approval purposes a motor vehicle is:

– a passenger vehicle with four or more wheels, or three wheels if it has a maximum gross weight of more than 1,000 kilograms, intended to carry no more than eight passengers, excluding the driver, *or*
– a three-wheeled passenger vehicle with a maximum gross weight of under 1,000 kilograms, if it has either a maximum speed of more than 50 kilometres per hour or an engine capacity of more than 50 cubic centimetres, *or*
– a goods vehicle.

10.8 What happens if I supply in the UK for removal to another Member State a land vehicle which is not "type approved"?

If you supply in the UK for removal to another Member State a land vehicle, which is *not* type approved, and your customer changes their mind about removal and keeps the vehicle in the UK, it may not be licensed and registered here.

10.9 Are NMT land vehicles exempt from type approval?

NMT vehicles supplied in the UK are exempted from UK type approval requirements for as long as they are relieved from VAT whilst awaiting removal from the UK. If the vehicle is not removed and as a consequence becomes liable to UK VAT, the exemption from type approval is withdrawn. The absence of type approval may affect your ability to register the vehicle in the UK for permanent use on UK roads.

10.10 Where can I find more information on type approval?

You can find out more about type approval from the Vehicle Certification Agency:

www.dft.gov.uk/vca

11 A COPY OF FORM VAT 411

This section has the force of law and is referred to in paragraphs 1.3, 3.9, 6.1, 6.2, 6.3, 6.4, 9.3, 9.5, 9.6 and 10.2

> **This information has the force of law . . .**
> The Form VAT 411 is specified in this section of this notice for the purposes of VAT Regulations (SI 1995/2518) Regulation 22C(3)(a).

To download a copy of the form please use the following link VAT411: www.hmrc.gov.uk/forms/vat411.pdf

12 APPLICATION FOR A REFUND OF VAT

Information on completing this form is given in section 7.

NEW MEANS OF TRANSPORT: APPLICATION FOR A REFUND OF VAT
Your details
Surname (Mr/Mrs/Miss/Dr) . . . .

Forenames . . . .

Full Address . . . .

. . . .

. . . .

Telephone . . . .

Details of the original supply to you

Name and address of supplier . . . .

. . . .

. . . .

The price paid by you (exclusive of VAT) . . . .

The amount of VAT paid . . . .

Details of the proposed sale by you

Name and address of proposed purchaser . . . .

. . . .

. . . .

Name of the EU Member State to which the New Means of Transport is to be removed: . . . .

. . . .

Date of proposed sale by you . . . .

Sale price . . . .

DETAILS OF THE NEW MEANS OF TRANSPORT

	Motorised Land Vehicle	*Ship*	*Aircraft*
Make			
Model			
Colour			
Registration No.			
Engine No			
Length in metres	xxxxxxxxxxx		xxxxxxxxxx
Take off weight (kg)	xxxxxxxxxxx	xxxxxxxxxxx	
Chassis/Hull/Airframe No			
Mileage since first entry into service		xxxxxxxxxxx	xxxxxxxxxx
Cubic centimetres/kilowatts		xxxxxxxxxxx	xxxxxxxxxx
Hours of use since first entry into service	xxxxxxxxxxx		

Place in the UK where the New Means of Transport is currently kept

. . . .

. . . .

. . . .

Dates and times when the New Means of Transport may be inspected

. . . .

. . . .

. . . .

Amount of refund being claimed . . . .

I declare that the information I have given and the documents relating to this claim are true and complete.

Signature . . . .

Date . . . .

Please note: no repayment will be considered until Customs have examined your proof of purchase, evidence of payment of VAT, proof of the sale in question and evidence of removal from the UK.

13 GLOSSARY

Throughout this notice the following terms have the meanings shown:

Term	*Meaning*
EU	The European Community: Austria, Belgium, Bulgaria, *Cyprus, Czech Republic, Denmark (except the Faroe Islands and Greenland), Estonia, Finland, France (including Monaco), Germany, Greece, Hungary, Ireland, Italy, Latvia, Lithuania, Luxembourg, Malta, Netherlands, Poland, Portugal (including Azores and Maderia), Romania, Slovakia, Slovinia, Spain (not the Canary Islands), Sweden, and the UK. Croatia will become a Member State with effect from 1 July 2013. *The European Commission has advised that, as the situation stands at present, the application of the Principal VAT Directive shall be suspended in those area of Cyprus in which the Government of the Republic of Cyprus does not exercise effective control. Transactions with those areas will continue from 1 May 2004 to be treated as non-EU transactions.
UK	The United Kingdom: England, Scotland, Wales, Northern Ireland, (including the Isle of Man but not the Channel Islands).
Another member state	Any member state of the European Community other than the UK.
NMT	New Means of Transport (see the definition in paragraph 2.1).
First entry into service	See paragraph 2.3.

NOTICE 731
CASH ACCOUNTING

24 March 2015.

This notice cancels and replaces Notice 731 (November 2013). Details of any changes to the previous version can be found in paragraph 1.2 of this notice.

The legal basis for the Cash Accounting Scheme is in the VAT Regulations 1995, regulations 56 to 65. Parts of this notice have the force of law under these regulations. These parts are indicated by being placed in a box.

Example: The following text has the force of law

> You cannot retrospectively apply the cash accounting scheme to your business.

1 INTRODUCTION

1.1 What is this notice about?

This notice explains how the cash accounting scheme works and the conditions you must meet if you want to use it.

Commentary—*De Voil Indirect Tax Service* **V2.199.**

1.2 What's changed?

Amendments to this notice were required to make it suitable for publication on GOV.UK and to update guidance on what to do if you disagree with a decision made by HM Revenue and Customs (HMRC) (see paragraph 6.8).

1.3 What is the cash accounting scheme?

The scheme allows you to account for VAT (*output tax*) on your sales on the basis of payments you receive, rather than on tax invoices you issue. This is different from the normal rules that require you to account for VAT on your sales when you issue a VAT invoice, even if your customer has not paid you.

However, if you choose to use the scheme, you can only reclaim the VAT incurred on your purchases (*input tax*) once you pay your supplier. Under the normal method of accounting for VAT you can reclaim VAT on purchases you make as soon as you receive a VAT invoice even if you have not paid your supplier.

1.4 Is the scheme suitable for my business?

The scheme could help your cash flow, because in general you do not have to pay VAT to HMRC until your customer has paid you. The scheme will be especially helpful if you give your customers extended credit or suffer a lot of "bad debts".

However, the scheme may not give you any benefit if you:

- are usually paid as soon as you make a sale;
- regularly reclaim more VAT than you pay; or
- make continuous supplies of services.

If you find the scheme is of no benefit, you can stop using it at the end of a VAT accounting period and return to the normal method of accounting for VAT, for more information see paragraph 6.1.

1.5 Additional rules which have force of law

The rules about cash accounting are set out in the VAT Regulations 1995. Some additional rules made under Regulations 57 and 59 are included in this notice. Their inclusion means that they have the force of law. The text relating to those rules have been placed in a box.

2 BASICS OF CASH ACCOUNTING

2.1 Am I eligible to use the scheme?

You are eligible to start using the scheme if you meet the following conditions:

- you expect the value of your taxable supplies in the next year will be £1,350,000 or less - to work out the value of your taxable supplies, see paragraph 2.2
- you have no VAT returns outstanding
- you have not been convicted of a VAT offence in the last year
- you have not accepted an offer to compound proceedings in connection with a VAT offence in the last year
- you have not been assessed to a penalty for VAT evasion involving dishonest conduct in the last year
- you do not owe HMRC any money or if you do, you have made arrangements with them to clear the total amount of your outstanding VAT payments (including surcharges and/or penalties)
- HMRC has not written to you withdrawing use of the scheme during the last year
- HMRC has not written to you and denied you access to the scheme
- you comply with the conditions set out in this notice

Commentary—*De Voil Indirect Tax Service* **V2.199.**

2.2 How do I work out the value of my taxable supplies for joining the scheme?

Your taxable supplies are the value excluding VAT, of standard, lower and zero-rated supplies you expect to make. Do not include the value of any exempt supplies or the value of any expected sale of capital assets.

2.3 How do I estimate what my future taxable supplies will be?

If you have been registered for less than 12 months, the simplest way is to estimate in the same way you did when you completed Form VAT 1 VAT: *application for registration*. If you have been registered for 12 months or more, you can use the value of your past year's taxable supplies as a guide.

If you believe these methods are not a good indicator of your future taxable supplies, you can make the estimate in any reasonable way.

You might use:

- your business plans;
- information relating to pre-registration business activity; or
- business information from a previous owner.

2.4 What if I estimate that my VAT turnover will not exceed £1,350,000 in the coming year and I am wrong?

HMRC will not penalise you for this provided you can show that there were reasonable grounds for your estimate.

If your estimate of turnover had no reasonable estimate HMRC will immediately remove you from the scheme. So it is sensible to keep a record of how the estimate was made.

2.5 What do I do if the value of my taxable supplies exceeds £1,350,000?

Once you have joined the scheme you may continue to use it until the annual value of your taxable supplies including the disposal of stock and capital assets, but excluding VAT, reaches £1,600,000.

If this figure is exceeded, you will have to leave the scheme at the end of your current tax period and use the normal method of accounting in future. For example:

If your VAT quarter ends on	*and your taxable supplies in the 12 months then ending*	*you must leave the scheme on*
30 November	Exceeded £1,600,000	30 November and begin normal VAT accounting from 1 December.

An exception to this rule for one-off sales is explained in paragraph 2.6.

You should monitor the amount of your taxable supplies regularly so that you have time to modify your books and records if you have to leave the scheme.

If you do leave the scheme, you must bring all outstanding VAT to account in accordance with paragraph 6.4.

2.6 What if my taxable supplies exceed £1,600,000 because of a "one-off" increase in sales?

If you exceed the £1,600,000 limit because of a one-off increase in sales, you may be able to remain on cash accounting on condition that you meet *all* of the following criteria:

- the "one off" increase has not happened before and is not expected to happen again, for example, the sale of a capital asset
- the sale arose from a genuine commercial activity
- there are reasonable grounds for believing that the value of your taxable supplies in the next 12 months will be below £1,350,000.

You must keep a record of how you came to your decision to remain on the scheme. If HMRC finds that you do not meet all the conditions then they may exclude you from the scheme immediately, or from the date your ineligible use began.

2.7 Must I use the scheme for all aspects of my business?

The following text has force of law

Subject to the exceptions listed below you must use the Cash Accounting Scheme for the whole of your VAT-registered business.

The transactions below are excluded from cash accounting both to simplify the scheme and assist the cash flow of small businesses:

- goods that you buy or sell under lease purchase, hire purchase, conditional sale or credit sale agreements
- goods imported or acquired from another European Community (EC) member state (or goods removed from a Customs warehouse or free zone), for further information see paragraph 5.5
- certain goods on which the purchaser must account for output tax on his VAT return on the suppliers behalf due to the reverse charge (for further information see VAT Notice 735: *VAT reverse charge on specified goods and services*)

The transactions below are excluded from cash accounting to prevent abuse of the scheme:

- supplies where you issue a VAT invoice and payment of that invoice is not due in full within 6 months of the date it was issued
- supplies of goods or services where you issue a VAT invoice in advance of making the supply or providing the goods.

Transactions excluded from the scheme must be accounted for under the normal VAT accounting rules as explained in VAT Notice 700: *the VAT Guide*.

2.8 Can I use any other schemes when I am on the cash accounting scheme?

If you use the Cash Accounting Scheme you may also be able to use the Annual Accounting Scheme. This scheme allows you to even out your VAT payments as you pay monthly or quarterly instalments based on an estimate of your annual VAT liability. At the end of the year you complete a single VAT Return and pay any balance due. For further information see VAT Notice 732: *annual accounting*.

The Flat Rate Scheme cannot be used with cash accounting but it does have its own cash based method. For more information see VAT Notice 733: *Flat Rate Scheme for small businesses*.

3 STARTING TO USE THE CASH ACCOUNTING SCHEME

3.1 How do I start to use the cash accounting scheme?

The following text has force of law

You cannot retrospectively apply the cash accounting scheme to your business.

If your business is already registered for VAT and you are eligible to use the scheme (see paragraph 2.1) you may use the scheme from the start of your next VAT period. There is no need to apply to use the scheme but you must avoid accounting for VAT twice on any supplies made or received before you began to use the scheme.

The following text has force of law and is designed to avoid you paying (or claiming) VAT twice when you change your method of accounting

In order to do this you must, from the date you start to use the scheme, identify and separate in your records any payments you receive or make for transactions already accounted for under the normal method of VAT accounting. Exclude such payments from your scheme records.

Commentary—*De Voil Indirect Tax Service* **V2.199.**

3.2 I am a new VAT registration, how do I calculate my VAT due?

If you use the scheme from the first date of your VAT registration you may be eligible to reclaim, as though it was input tax, VAT on certain purchases made prior to being registered. For more information see VAT Notice 700: *the VAT Guide*.

For example, you may be able to reclaim VAT on:

- initial stocks
- tools
- machinery
- office furniture
- other capital equipment

If you choose to use the scheme from the date of your VAT registration, you must recover the VAT on such purchases as follows:

The following text has force of law

> If you have already paid for the qualifying goods and services, reclaim the VAT as though it was input tax on your first VAT return.
>
> If you pay for the goods or services after you have registered for VAT, claim the VAT, as though it was input tax, in the tax period in which you pay for them.

4 RECORDS AND ACCOUNTING FOR VAT

4.1 Record keeping

Most of the rules about record keeping are the same whether or not you use the scheme. The normal requirements are contained in VAT Notice 700: *the VAT Guide* and VAT Notice 700/21: *keeping VAT records*. However, there are some extra rules that apply only to the Cash Accounting Scheme and these are explained below.

Note: This section contains only the general rules that apply to all businesses using the scheme. You must check Section 5 for details of special rules that apply to particular transactions.

Commentary—*De Voil Indirect Tax Service* **V2.199, V5.201.**

4.2 Are there any special rules for invoices?

If you receive payment in coins or notes from a customer you must, if asked, endorse the customer's copy of your sales invoice with the amount that they have paid and the date it was paid.

Similarly, *if you pay a supplier in coins or notes,* you must make sure that they endorse your copy of the purchase invoice with the amount you have paid and the date it was paid.

4.3 Do I have to keep any other records?

The following text has force of law

In order to operate the cash accounting scheme, your records must clearly cross-refer payments:

– *received* by you, or on your behalf, to your corresponding sales invoice;
– *made* by you to the corresponding purchase invoice;
– *made or received* to the normal commercial evidence (such as bank statements, cheque stubs, paying-in slips.

The easiest way to do this is to keep a cash book summarising all payments made and received, with separate columns for VAT. Whatever form your records take, they should always be complete and up to date.

If you are in any doubt about how to keep your records, contact the VAT Helpline on Telephone: 0300 200 3700.

4.4 When must I account for the VAT on my sales?

VAT on your sales (*output tax*) must be accounted for on the VAT return for the accounting period in which you receive a payment from your customer. For the purposes of the scheme, the date you are paid depends on the way in which your customer pays you. The rules are as follows:

If you are paid by	*Then the date you receive payment is*
cash (coins or notes)	the date you receive the money
giro, standing order or direct debit	the date your bank account is credited with such a payment

The following text has force of law

If you are paid by credit or debit card: you receive payment on the date you make out a sales voucher for the payment (not when you actually receive payment from the card provider).

If the credit or debit card payment is not honoured, then you do not have to account for the VAT. If you have already accounted for the VAT you can adjust your VAT account, or make a refund claim in line with VAT Notice 700/45: *How to correct VAT errors and make adjustments or claims*. If you later receive a payment for the supply, then you must account for the VAT due on that payment.

If you are paid by cheque: you receive payment on the date you receive the cheque, or the date on the cheque, whichever is later.

If the cheque is not honoured, then you do not have to account for the VAT. If you have already accounted for the VAT you can adjust your VAT account, or make a refund claim in line with VAT Notice 700/45: *how to correct VAT errors and make adjustments or claims*. If you later receive a payment for the supply, then you must account for the VAT due on that payment.

Commentary—*De Voil Indirect Tax Service* **V5.109.**

4.5 When can I reclaim VAT incurred on my purchases and expenses?

Once you start to use the scheme you claim the VAT you incur on your purchases and expenses (*input tax*) on the VAT return for the tax period in which you make a payment to your supplier. For the purposes of the scheme the date you pay depends on the way in which you make a payment. The rules are as follows:

If you pay by	*Then the date you make payment is*
cash (coins or notes)	the date you pay the money. But remember - you need a receipted invoice to claim back VAT on purchases you have paid for in this way (see paragraph 4.2).
Giro, standing order or direct debit	the date your bank account is debited with such a payment.

The following text has force of law

If you pay by credit or debit card: the date of payment is the date a sales voucher is made out for the payment.

If you pay by cheque: the date of payment is the date you send the cheque, or the date on the cheque, whichever is later. If your cheque is not honoured, you cannot reclaim the VAT. If you have already accounted for the VAT you should adjust your VAT account, or make a voluntary disclosure in line with VAT Notice 700/45: *how to correct VAT errors and make adjustments or claims.*

Paragraphs 5.7, 5.8, 5.9 and 5.10 contain further information relating to payments.

Commentary—*De Voil Indirect Tax Service* **V3.418.**

4.6 Partial exemption

If you incur input tax on goods and services that you use or intend to use in the making of exempt supplies, you may not be able to claim all your input tax. This is known as partial exemption. If you are partly exempt, you should see VAT Notice 706: *partial exemption.*

Under the normal method of accounting for VAT, businesses who are partly exempt will usually make a calculation to establish the correct amount of input tax claimable, based on purchases and sales made during a tax period.

Partly exempt businesses who use the scheme must base such a calculation on payments made and received in a tax period.

4.7 How do I fill in my VAT return?

When you fill in your VAT return remember that the amounts of VAT due and deductible are based on payments received and made, not on invoices issued. For the purposes of the scheme the "Value of Outputs" and the "Value of Inputs" are the amounts of payments you have received or made exclusive of VAT.

Remember, if you make supplies to other EC Member States the amount you put in Box 8 of the VAT return should be the total value of all supplies of goods and services made, exclusive of VAT, and not the total of payments received.

5 SPECIAL RULES FOR PARTICULAR TRANSACTIONS

5.1 Deposits

The rules about deposits are in VAT Notice 700: *the VAT Guide*. If you receive or pay a deposit which serves as an advance payment, you must account for it in accordance with the rules in paragraphs 4.4 and 4.5.

VAT does not apply to deposits taken as a security to make sure the safe return of goods, whether you refund it upon return of the goods or retain it to compensate you for loss or damage.

Commentary—*De Voil Indirect Tax Service* V2.199.

5.2 Payments collected by agents on your behalf

The following text has force of law

If an agent collects payments on your behalf, you must account for VAT on the supply in the VAT period in which your agent collects payment from your customer.

The value on which VAT is due, is the amount of the taxable debt that the agent collects from your customer, not the amount of credit given to you by the agent (see paragraph 5.8 for more information).

5.3 Factoring

The following text has force of law

Recourse agreements (that is where you remain responsible for bearing any loss resulting from an unpaid debt).

If you have assigned to a factor a debt in respect of a taxable supply you have made while using the cash accounting scheme, you must account for output tax on the supply in the VAT period in which your factor collects payment from your customer.

The value, on which VAT is due, is the amount that the factor collects from your customer in relation to taxable supplies, not any lesser amount paid to you by the factor (see paragraph 5.8). If the factor is unable to collect all (or part) of the debt, then you must account for that amount under the normal rules, in line with paragraph 4.4.

Non-recourse agreements (that is where the factor accepts the risk of any loss resulting from your customer's debt).

If you have assigned to a factor a debt in respect of a taxable supply you have made while using the cash accounting scheme, you must account for output tax on the supply in the VAT period in which your factor collects payment from your customer.

The value, on which VAT is due, is the amount that the factor collects from your customer in relation to taxable supplies, not any lesser amount paid to you by the factor (see paragraph 5.8).

> If the factor is unable to collect all (or part) of the debt on your behalf, then you must account for output tax on the uncollected element of the debt, in the period in which any advance made against that debt is written off by the factor.
>
> If, however, the factor re-assigns all or part of the debt back to you under a recourse clause, then you may be able to claim bad debt relief, subject to paragraph 6.6.

Commentary—*De Voil Indirect Tax Service* **V5.156.**

5.4 Selling debts

The following text has force of law

> If you sell a debt for a taxable supply you made while using the cash accounting scheme, you must account for VAT on the supply in the VAT period in which the debt is sold.
>
> You must account for the output tax on the full value of the supply, to which the debt relates, not on any lesser amount which you receive when you sell the debt.

5.5 Imports and EC acquisitions

The following text has force of law

> You cannot use the cash accounting scheme for goods you import, acquire from a business registered in another EC Member State or remove from a Customs warehouse or free zone.

You must account for VAT on such purchases under the normal VAT rules as explained in VAT Notice 700: *the VAT Guide*. You can, however, use the scheme to account for VAT on the onward supply of such goods.

Full details of the VAT import and warehouse requirements are in VAT Notice 702: *imports*.

5.6 Exports and supplies to other EC member states

If you use the scheme and export goods or despatch them to another EC Member State but don't receive the evidence of export/supply within the time limits allowed, you must account for the VAT that becomes due. This means that you account for VAT on any payments already received.

If you receive further payments for such goods you must account for VAT on these payments when you receive them.

If you later obtain evidence of export/supply you can then zero rate the supply and adjust your VAT account for the tax period in which you obtained the evidence.

Full details of the VAT documentary evidence of export requirements are in VAT Notice 703: *export of goods from the UK* or, for retail exports, VAT Notice 704: *retail exports*.

Further information regarding acquisitions from, and despatches to, other EC member states can be found in VAT Notice 725: *the single market*.

5.7 Part payments

This paragraph explains what to do if you receive part payment for an invoice in circumstances where you still expect to receive the rest of the payment. Paragraph 5.8 deals with part payments where your customer has made a deduction before paying your invoice.

The following text has force of law

> If you make or receive payments which:
>
> - are a partial payment of an invoice; or
> - cover more than one invoice; or
> - relate to an invoice for supplies at different rates of tax.
>
> you must allocate the payment to the invoices in the order in which you issue or receive them.
>
> Where you make or receive partial payment of an invoice and VAT is not identified separately you must treat the payment as VAT inclusive. Where you make or receive payments which relate to an invoice for supplies at different rates of tax you must apportion the amount paid or received between the different rates and treat the amounts on which VAT is due at the standard or lower rate as VAT inclusive.

Examples of how this can be done are shown in Section 8.

5.8 Payments received net of deductions

The following text has force of law

> If you receive a net payment you must account for VAT on the full value of taxable supplies made by you before such deductions. This will usually be the value shown on your VAT invoice - remember not to include any amounts that are for supplies that do not attract VAT.

Some examples of payments that you may receive that are net of deductions are payments:

- where commission has been deducted by your customer
- where commission or payment for expenses has been deducted by a factor or agent collecting money on your behalf (see paragraph 5.2 and paragraph 5.3 for more information)
- where commission or payment for expenses has been deducted by an auctioneer selling goods on your behalf
- made by an employer/contractor who has deducted income tax

5.9 Payments in kind (for example, barter, part exchange)

The general rules about payments in kind are in VAT Notice 700: *the VAT Guide*.

If you pay or are paid fully or partly in kind, such as by barter or part exchange, you must still account for VAT each time you make or receive a "payment". You receive/make "payment" on the date you receive/supply the goods or services agreed in lieu of money.

You must account for VAT on the full tax value of the supply which is usually the price, excluding VAT, which a customer would have to pay for the supply if they had paid for it with money only.

5.10 Payments received and made in a foreign currency

If you issue VAT invoices in a foreign currency, including euro, you must follow the rules in the relevant paragraphs of VAT Notice 700: *the VAT Guide*. If the invoice is paid in full, you will not need to convert the foreign currency payment into sterling for the purposes of the scheme. You must always declare the sterling amount of VAT due on the supply as shown on the invoice.

5.11 What about partial payments?

If you receive a partial payment in a foreign currency against an invoice expressed in:

Both a foreign currency and sterling

You will need to calculate the amount of VAT included in the payment by determining what proportion of the total amount due on the invoice is being paid and applying that proportion to the total VAT due.

For example, if the payment in the foreign currency represents half of the total foreign currency amount due on an invoice, you must declare half of the sterling VAT figure as shown on the invoice.

Sterling only

You will need to convert the foreign currency payment into sterling using one of the methods outlined in VAT Notice 700: *the VAT Guide*. For the purposes of the scheme, you must be consistent in the method used. But whatever method you adopt, the exchange rate to be used is that current at the time of the supply by you. This may not be the same as the exchange rate which applies at the time you receive payment. Once you have established what the sterling equivalent of the foreign currency payment is and what proportion of the total sterling amount due this represents, you can then determine how much of the payment is VAT.

The above rules also apply if you pay for supplies from other UK businesses in a foreign currency.

Note. This section cannot deal with all the possible situations you may encounter. If you have difficulty in dealing with a transaction, please do not guess the answer. Contact the VAT Helpline on Telephone: 0300 200 3700.

5.12 What do I do if the price agreed for a supply changes?

Any increase or decrease in the price must be evidenced by the issue of a credit or debit note. Where a further payment or refund is then received or made, this should be recorded in your payment record as normal.

For information on credit notes see VAT Notice 700: *the VAT Guide*.

6 LEAVING THE SCHEME

6.1 What if I want to leave the scheme?

The following text has force of law

You can only leave the scheme at the end of a tax period.

You must then use the normal method of accounting for VAT from the beginning of the next tax period. You must bring all outstanding VAT to account in accordance with paragraph 6.4.

Commentary—*De Voil Indirect Tax Service* **V2.199, V5.102.**

6.2 When must I stop using the scheme?

You must stop using the scheme if:

- you cannot comply with the record keeping requirements set out in this notice
- during a period of one year (ending at the end of a tax period) the value of your taxable supplies, including disposal of stock and capital assets but excluding VAT, exceeds £1,600,000
- •HMRC write to you withdrawing use of the scheme
- you are convicted of a VAT offence
- you accept an offer to compound proceedings in connection with a VAT offence
- you are assessed to a penalty for VAT evasion involving dishonest conduct

6.3 May I re-join the scheme after leaving it?

If you leave the scheme voluntarily or because the value of your taxable supplies exceeded £1,600,000, you may begin to use the scheme again from the start of a tax period, provided you are eligible to do so as detailed in paragraph 2.1.

6.4 How do I account for VAT if I leave the scheme voluntarily or because my turnover has exceeded the ceiling?

When you leave the scheme there may be supplies that you have made for which you have not been paid and as a result you have not accounted for any VAT. You will need to account for this VAT even if you have not been paid by the customer. There may also be cases where you have not paid your suppliers and you have not yet claimed your input tax. You are entitled to claim this input tax subject to the normal VAT rules. You may choose either to:

account for all your outstanding VAT due in the period in which you stop using the scheme. This may be simpler but could have a serious effect on your cash flow if the amounts of unpaid VAT on supplies you have made are high. As an alternative you can opt for a further six months in which to account for the outstanding VAT.

Please note that you cannot opt for a further six months in which to account for the outstanding VAT if:

- HMRC has withdrawn use of the scheme from you
- the value of your taxable supplies has exceeded £1,600,000 and the value of your supplies made in the previous 3 months totalled more than £1,350,000

You do not need to notify HMRC which method you have chosen.

6.5 How do I account for VAT if I use the 6-month option?

To avoid double accounting you will need to keep your normal cash accounting records for the supplies you made and received while you used the scheme. In particular you will need to keep a record of payments you make and receive during the 6 months. In addition, you will need to keep separate records required under normal VAT accounting for new supplies you make and receive after you left the scheme.

Commentary—*De Voil Indirect Tax Service* **V5.103.**

6.6 Do I have to account for outstanding VAT on "bad" debts when I leave the scheme?

One advantage of the Cash Accounting Scheme is that you do not have to account for VAT on bad debts. However, if you stop using cash accounting, you have to account for VAT on supplies you have made and received even if they have not been paid for (see paragraph 6.4).

If you have not received any payment then you may be able to claim relief for your bad debts which meet the conditions of the bad debt relief scheme.

The key conditions are:

- that it is 6 months from the date on which the debt became due and payable or the supply was made, whichever is later
- you can provide evidence that the bad debt has been written off in your "refunds for bad debts" account
- for supplies made prior to 1 January 2003, where your customer is registered for VAT, you have notified your customer of your claim for bad debt relief

For more information see VAT Notice 700/18: *relief from VAT on bad debts.*

Commentary—*De Voil Indirect Tax Service* **V5.156.**

6.7 What do I do if use of the scheme is withdrawn or I am told I cannot use the scheme?

You will be advised in writing if HMRC decide to deny you access or withdraw use of the scheme from you. If you are using the scheme the letter will specify when you must stop using the scheme and when you must account for the outstanding tax due on supplies made and received while using the scheme (further details on how to do this are in paragraph 6.4).

If you disagree with the decision to deny you access to the scheme or withdraw use of the scheme, you may ask HMRC to reconsider.

You should do this within 30 days of the date of the decision and you should let HMRC know if you:

- think that there are facts that may not have been fully considered; or

- can provide further information.

6.8 Is there anything else I can do?

You can also appeal to an independent Tribunal.

The leaflet HM Revenue and Customs decisions (www.gov.uk/government/publications/hm-revenue-and-customs-decisions-what-to-do-if-you-disagree): what to do if you disagree tells you what to do.

6.9 I've appealed to a VAT Tribunal. May I continue to use the scheme?

If you have appealed to a VAT tribunal about a decision to:

- deny you access to use the scheme;
- withdraw use of the scheme on the grounds of protection of the revenue; or
- not to allow you to continue to use the scheme once you have exceeded the tolerance

You must not use the scheme until your appeal is resolved.

If you have appealed against any other matter, then HMRC will normally allow continued use of the scheme, pending the outcome of the appeal. However, if HMRC considers that an appeal facilitates manipulation of the scheme, they may withdraw use of the scheme for the protection of the revenue and you will not be able to use it until the appeal is settled.

Contact the VAT Helpline on Telephone: 0300 200 3700 for further guidance on this matter.

6.10 What do I do if I cease trading?

If you cease trading, you may continue to use the scheme while you dispose of any remaining stocks or assets. Once your VAT registration is cancelled you must follow the rules in paragraph 6.12.

Commentary—*De Voil Indirect Tax Service* **V2.199.**

6.11 What happens if my business becomes insolvent?

If your business becomes insolvent, you will need to account on your pre-insolvency VAT return for all VAT on supplies made and received by you before the date of your insolvency which has not yet been accounted for under the scheme.

Where trading continues after the relevant date, the office holder responsible for the business may continue to use the scheme subject to the rules set out in this notice.

The following text has force of law

> If the office holder does continue to use the cash accounting scheme they must, from the date of insolvency, separate in the business records any payments the business receives or makes for transactions already accounted for on the pre-insolvency VAT return.

Further details relating to insolvency matters are in VAT Notice 700/56: *Insolvency*.

Commentary—*De Voil Indirect Tax Service* **V2.199.**

6.12 What if I deregister?

You will have 2 months to submit your final return after you deregister. On this return you must account for all outstanding VAT on supplies made and received prior to deregistration.

This applies even if you have not been paid, but you can also reclaim any VAT provided that you have the VAT invoices. If some of the outstanding VAT relates to bad debts you may claim relief as detailed in paragraph 6.6.

You may also need to account for VAT on the value of any stocks and assets you still have. For further information see VAT Notice 700/11: *cancelling your registration*.

Commentary—*De Voil Indirect Tax Service* **V2.199.**

7 TRANSFER OF A GOING CONCERN

7.1 What if I sell or buy a business as a going concern and the VAT registration number has not been transferred?

Where the whole of a business which uses the scheme is transferred as a going concern and the existing owner cancels the VAT registration of that business, he must follow the rules in paragraph 6.12. The new owner can then choose, subject to eligibility, whether or not to use the scheme.

7.2 What if I sell or buy as a going concern a business which is using the scheme and the VAT registration number has been transferred?

The following text has force of law

> If you sell your business as a going concern and the new owner takes over your VAT registration number, you must advise the new owner that you are using the cash accounting scheme.

The new owner must continue to operate the scheme and account for payments for supplies and purchases made by the previous owner, as if the new owner had made them.

If the new owner does not want to continue to use the scheme, they must leave the scheme as soon as possible and follow the rules in paragraph 6.4.

Remember, outstanding VAT must be accounted for on the return for the tax period in which the new owner stopped using the scheme.

If only part of a business is transferred as a going concern, you should contact the VAT Helpline on Telephone: 0300 200 3700.

Commentary—*De Voil Indirect Tax Service* **V2.199.**

8 ACCOUNTING FOR PART PAYMENTS

(referred to in paragraph 5.7)

8.1 Accounting for VAT when a part payment is made against one invoice

Invoice A	
Standard-rated goods	£1,000.00
VAT	£200.00
Total	**£1,200.00**

Step	*Action*
Step 1	If a payment of £780.00 is made against invoice A, determine what percentage of that payment represents VAT as follows—

$$\frac{\text{Amount of money received}}{\text{Total invoice amount}} \times 100 = \text{Percentage of VAT due}$$

for example

$$\frac{£780.00}{£1,200.00} \times 100 = 64\%$$

Step 2 Multiply the amount of VAT charged by the percentage calculated at *Step 1.*

for example

£200.00 × 65% = £130.00

In this example £130.00 of the £780.00 payment received should be accounted for as VAT. The remaining £70.00 VAT still due to HMRC (£200.00 - £130.00 = £70.00) should be accounted for when further payment is received.

8.2 Accounting for VAT on a single payment made against more than one invoice, or against invoices for supplies at different rates of tax

Invoice B		*Invoice C*	
Standard-rated goods	£1,000.00	Standard-rated goods	£2,000.00
VAT	£200.00	Zero-rated goods	£1,000.00
		VAT	£400.00
Total	**£1,200.00**	**Total**	**£3,400.00**

If a payment of £2,730.00 is made against invoices B and C which does not relate to any particular supply you should allocate it as follows:

Step	*Action*
Step 1	Allocate £1,200.00 of the £2,730.00 to the earliest supply ie invoice B and account for VAT of £200.00. The balance of the payment of £1,530.00 (£2,730.00 - £1,200.00 = £1,530.00) should then be allocated against the later supply, ie invoice C, as follows:
Step 2	Calculate what percentage of the remaining £1,530.00 represents VAT against invoice C. (Remaining amount of money available ÷ Total amount still owed to you (that is invoice C) × 100 = Percentage of invoice paid. for example (£1,530.00 ÷ £3,400.00) x 100 = 45%
Step 3	Multiply the amount of VAT due on invoice C by the percentage calculated at Step 2 for example £400.00 x 45% = £180.00

In this example £380.00 (£200.00 + £180.00 = £380.00) of the £2,730.00 payment should be accounted for as VAT against the £600.00 VAT due. (£200.00 + £400.00 = £600.00).

The remaining £220.00 VAT still due (£600.00 – £380.00) should be accounted for when you receive further payment.

NOTICE 733
FLAT RATE SCHEME FOR SMALL BUSINESSES

April 2014

This notice cancels and replaces Notice 733 (May 2013). Details of the changes to the previous version can be found in paragraph 1.2 of this notice.

The legal basis for the flat rate scheme is in the VAT Regulations 1995, regs 55A–55V, 57A and 69A. Parts of this notice have the force of law under those regulations. These parts are indicated by being placed in a box as in the example shown below.

The following rule has the force of law

If you receive a net payment, you must include the full value before such deductions (and including VAT) in your scheme turnover. This will usually be the value shown on your sales invoice.

1 INTRODUCTION

1.1 What is this notice about?

This notice describes the flat rate scheme for small businesses.

Section 2 gives an overview to help you decide whether the scheme can help your business.

If you decide the scheme may help your business the rest of the notice contains the detailed rules on operating the scheme and explains how to apply.

Many of the normal VAT rules apply to the flat rate scheme. So if you can't find the answer to your question in this notice, remember the basics of VAT can be found in Notice 700 *The VAT Guide*.

Commentary—*De Voil Indirect Tax Service* **V2.199B–V2.199D.**

1.2 What has changed?

This revised notice replaces the May 2013 edition. The changes are:

– Paragraph 5.2 - change of email address

You can get details of any changes to this notice since March 2007 either on our website, go to www.hmrc.gov.uk or by phoning our VAT Helpline on 0300 200 3700.

This notice and any others mentioned in the text are available both on paper and on our website.

Those parts of this notice that have the force of law are marked clearly.

2 BASICS OF THE FLAT RATE SCHEME

2.1 What is the flat rate scheme?

The flat rate scheme is designed to help small businesses by taking some of the work out of recording VAT sales and purchases. If you use the scheme you apply a single percentage to your turnover in a VAT period. The result is the VAT you pay to HM Revenue & Customs (HMRC).

Commentary—*De Voil Indirect Tax Service* **V2.199B–V2.199D.**

2.2 How will it help me?

The main benefit of the scheme is the time saved recording VAT on sales and purchases. This can also take some of the stress out of completing VAT returns at the quarter end. And because you can easily calculate how much VAT you owe on takings, it can help you to manage cash flow.

2.3 Will all businesses benefit?

Not every business will enjoy all the benefits of the scheme. For example, if your customers are VAT registered you will have to calculate the VAT and issue VAT invoices in the normal way. Businesses who buy and sell goods from outside the UK can find the scheme more complex and if you do this make sure you understand the rules in 6.4.

Also, as the flat rates are averages, some businesses using the flat rate scheme may pay more VAT than they would on normal accounting.

2.4 What about input tax?

Input tax is the VAT charged to you by other businesses. Under normal VAT accounting, you claim this back from us on your quarterly VAT return. If you use the flat rate scheme, you do not recover input tax or VAT on imports or acquisitions. This is because the flat rates are calculated to represent the net VAT you need to pay to us. In other words, an allowance for input tax is built into the flat rates.

There are special rules when you buy high value capital goods. Section 15 explains how you can claim back the VAT on these purchases.

2.5 Who can join the scheme?

The scheme is for businesses with a turnover no more than £150,000 a year, *excluding* VAT. There are some additional rules to stop abuse of the scheme. If you want to know more, section 3 explains the joining conditions in more detail.

The flat rate scheme is a simpler method of working out the VAT you have to pay to us and so is unsuitable where you regularly receive repayments from us.

2.6 How do I join?

You can apply by post, telephone, or email. Section 5 gives full details.

2.7 Can I combine the flat rate scheme with other schemes?

The table below shows which other schemes you can use with the flat rate scheme.

Scheme	*May be used with flat rate scheme?*	*Further information*
Annual accounting	Yes	Combining the annual accounting scheme with the flat rate scheme can mean you: —spend less time working out how much VAT you owe —avoid a big bill by evening out your VAT over the year —submit only one VAT return a year. If you wish to join both schemes, Notice 732 *Annual accounting* contains a joint application form. If you are already using one of the schemes and wish to use the other, complete the form for the scheme you have not yet joined.
Cash accounting	No but	the flat rate scheme has its own cash based method that is very similar to the cash accounting scheme. See section 9
Retail schemes	No but	the flat rate scheme has its own retail based method that is very similar to ordinary retail schemes. If you want to leave a retail scheme to join the flat rate scheme, simply follow the rules about ceasing to use the retail scheme in Notice 727 *Retail schemes*.
Margin scheme for second-hand goods	No	If you sell a significant proportion of second-hand goods using margin schemes or the auctioneers' scheme, the flat rate scheme will be of limited value to your business. This is because the flat rate scheme calculates VAT on the total received for your sale rather than on the margin.

3 ELIGIBILITY AND CONDITIONS OF THE SCHEME

Commentary—*De Voil Indirect Tax Service* **V2.199B–V2.199D.**

3.1 Who can join?

The flat rate scheme is for small businesses. You can apply to use the scheme if there are reasonable grounds for believing that your taxable turnover (excluding VAT) in the next year will be £150,000 or less.

3.2 How do I work out my taxable turnover?

Leave out any anticipated sales of capital assets but include all of the following:

- the value of your standard rate, zero rate and reduced rate supplies
- your turnover from the sale of second-hand goods sold outside the margin scheme. See Notice 718 *Margin schemes* and
- any sales of investment gold that are covered by VATA s 55. See Notice 701/21 *Gold*

Remember to *leave out* any VAT when doing this test.

3.3 How do I know what my future turnover is going to be?

You may forecast this in any reasonable way. If you have been registered for VAT for 12 months or more, the turnover declared on your returns may be a reasonable guide but take into account any expected changes. If you are not VAT registered when you apply for the scheme, you may forecast your turnover by looking at—

- any period of trading before you apply
- the turnover of the previous business owner or
- information on business plans or loan applications.

3.4 What if my future turnover rises above my forecast?

If your forecast turns out to be too low, we will not penalise you provided there were reasonable grounds for what you forecast. So it is sensible to keep a record of the figures you used to calculate your future turnover.

If your forecast had no reasonable basis, we may exclude you from the scheme immediately, or from the date your ineligible use began.

3.5 What if my turnover rises once I have joined the scheme?

You may stay in the scheme provided your total turnover (including VAT) for the year just gone does not rise above £230,000. Make this check on each anniversary of your business joining the flat rate scheme. You must leave the scheme if your turnover increases so that there are grounds for believing that the total value of your income will rise above £230,000 in the next 30 days alone.

Important note. you become eligible for the scheme based on the level of your taxable turnover, but the test of continuing eligibility for the scheme is based on all income (including exempt income). This could mean that, if you have a very high level of exempt income, in extreme cases you could be eligible to join but have to leave immediately. This is unlikely to happen in practice because the scheme is not suitable for businesses with high levels of exempt turnover. See paragraph 6.2 for further details.

See section 12 for further details about leaving the scheme.

3.6 Who cannot join the scheme?

You cannot join the scheme if *any* of the following apply—

- you are not registered for VAT
- you use the second-hand margin scheme or the auctioneers' scheme
- you are required to use the tour operator's margin scheme
- you are required to operate the Capital Goods Scheme for certain capital items (see paragraph 15.6)

- you have stopped using the flat rate scheme in the 12 months before the date of your new application
- in the 12 months before your application you have either—
  - accepted a compound penalty offer or been convicted of an offence in connection with VAT or
  - been assessed with a penalty for conduct involving dishonesty
- you are, or within the past 24 months have been, registered for VAT in the name of either a—
  - VAT group (see paragraph 3.7) or
  - division
- you are, or within the past 24 months have been, eligible for VAT group treatment (see paragraph 3.7)
- your business is "associated" with another one in the special way explained in paragraph 3.8.

3.7 Can I use the scheme if I am in a VAT group?

VAT groups are for incorporated businesses which are linked to other incorporated businesses by common control or ownership. If you are eligible to be in a VAT group, even if you are not currently in one, then you cannot use the flat rate scheme. If you become eligible to join a VAT group after you join the scheme, then you must leave the scheme with effect from the date you become eligible.

For details of eligibility to join a group see Notice 700/2 *Group and divisional registration.*

If your business has been eligible to join a VAT group in the last two years, but is not eligible at the time you apply, we can let you use the scheme if we agree in writing that your former eligibility is not a risk to the revenue.

3.8 What if my business is closely linked with another business?

There is a rule which stops "associated" businesses joining the flat rate scheme. Paragraph 3.9 explains some exceptions to this rule.

If you are unsure whether the particular relationship between your business and another constitutes "association" then please contact our VAT Helpline.

You are associated with another business in this special sense if—

- one business is under the dominant influence of another
- two businesses are closely bound by financial, economic and organisational links or
- another company has the right to give directions to you
- in practice your company habitually complies with the directions of another. The test here is a test of the commercial reality rather than of the legal form.

If your business has been associated in this way with another in the last two years, but is not associated at the time you apply, we can let you use the scheme if we agree in writing that your former association is not a risk to the revenue.

3.9 I have a close connection with another business – does this mean we are "associated"?

Not necessarily. Businesses are not generally "associated" in this special sense where a normal commercial relationship exists.

EXAMPLE 1

A business is not associated with its customer's company just because it supplies them with the goods they request in the form they request them.

EXAMPLE 2

A husband and wife are each separately VAT registered in different types of business. Even if they share premises, provided this is charged at a market rate, they will not be "associated".

4 DETERMINING YOUR FLAT RATE PERCENTAGE

Commentary—*De Voil Indirect Tax Service* **V2.199C.**

4.1 Which flat rate applies to my business?

The flat rate you use depends on the business sector that you belong in. All the sectors can be found at the link in paragraph 4.3. The correct sector is the one that most closely describes what your business will be doing in the coming year. Sections FRS7200 and FRS7300 of the Flat Rate Scheme Guidance show you which businesses we think belong in each sector.

The following steps may help you select the most appropriate sector for your business.

Step	*What you need to do*	*Please remember*
1	See if your business is mentioned at the link in paragraph 4.3 or in the guidance mentioned in paragraph 4.1	The descriptions of the sectors are not technical and use ordinary English. So if there is a match or a close fit, use that sector.
2	Check to make sure your business is not mentioned in a composite sector	Some of the sectors refer to more than one business type.
3	If there is no sector that mentions your business, look at the sectors for "Businesses not mentioned elsewhere"	There is one for retail, one for business services and one for manufacturing.
4	If you still haven't found a sector you can use "Any other activity not listed elsewhere". However, if you are still unsure, or unhappy with your choice, you can phone our VAT Helpline on 0300 200 3700.	Tell the VAT Helpline that you have followed Steps 1 to 3 above.

4.2 What if I get the sector wrong?

We will not normally check your choice of sector when we process your application. So if you have made a mistake you may pay too much tax or too little. Paying too little could mean that you are faced with an unexpected VAT bill at a later date.

However, if we approve you to join the scheme, we will not change your choice of sector retrospectively as long as your choice was reasonable. It will be sensible to keep a record of why you chose your sector in case you need to show us that your choice was reasonable.

Note: Some business activities can reasonably fit into more than one sector. So changing your sector does not automatically make your original choice unreasonable.

4.3 The trade sectors and flat rates

Information regarding the trade sectors and flat rate percentages can be found on the website www.hmrc.gov.uk/manuals/frsmanual/FRS7300.htm.

4.4 Business activities that are the source of common enquiry

The table below gives the trade sector for particular business activities, which have been the subject of common enquiries to our VAT Helpline.

Business activity	*Trade sector*	*Flat rate percentage*
Engineering consultants and designers	—Architects, civil and structural engineers	12.5
Agents	—Business services that are not listed elsewhere	11
Barristers	—Lawyers or legal services	13
Florists	—Retailing that is not listed elsewhere	6
Agronomists	—Management consultancy	12.5

Note: If you act as a consultant and you do not fit into another specific sector, you should choose Management Consultancy. This sector is not restricted to businesses that fit the traditional idea of management consultant.

4.5 Reduction of 1 % for new VAT registrations

If you are in your first year of VAT registration you get a 1 % reduction in flat rate. This means you can take 1 % off the flat rate you apply to your turnover, until the day before your first anniversary of becoming VAT registered. Note that the entitlement to apply the reduction runs for the 12 months following the date of registration for VAT and not the date you join the FRS.

You will not be entitled to apply the 1 % reduction if you register for VAT 12 months after you were required to do so.

If your business is a transfer of a going concern, you will be entitled to apply the 1 % reduction from the date of the transfer.

EXAMPLE 1

A business registers for VAT on 1 December 2008 and uses the flat rate scheme from that date with a flat rate of 10 %. From 1 December 2008 to 30 November 2009 it can use 9 % if there are no changes to the business during this time.

EXAMPLE 2

A business registers for VAT on 6 January 2009 but does not join the flat rate scheme until 1 July 2009 at a rate of 6 %. From 1 July 2009 to 5 January 2010 it may use 5 % if there are no changes to the business during this time.

EXAMPLE 3

A business registers for VAT on 1 March 2009 but does not join the flat rate scheme until 1 May 2010. As the business has been registered for VAT for more than 12 months, it cannot apply the 1 % reduction to its flat rate percentage.

EXAMPLE 4

A business becomes liable to be registered for VAT on 1 March 2009 but HMRC does not become aware of this liability until 1 June 2010. It cannot apply the 1 % reduction to its flat rate percentage.

EXAMPLE 5

A business becomes liable to be registered for VAT on 1 April 2009 but HMRC does not become aware of this liability until 1 September 2009. The business can apply the 1 % reduction from the date it joins the FRS until 31 March 2010. If it joins the scheme with a start date of later than 31 March 2010, it cannot apply the reduction.

4.6 What if my business fits into more than one sector?

If your business includes supplies in two or more sectors, you must apply the percentage appropriate to your main business activity as measured by turnover. Choose the sector for which your business gets the greater part of its turnover. Do not split your turnover, or apply more than one percentage.

EXAMPLE:

If a taxi business does some car repairs, it will have to decide which of the two activities will generate the larger amount of turnover and apply the appropriate flat rate percentage to the whole of its VAT inclusive turnover.

If the taxi part of the business . . .	*and the car repair part of the business . . .*	*the business*
expects to generate turnover of £40,000 (including VAT) in the next year	expects to generate turnover (including VAT) of £15,000 in the next year	should apply the flat rate percentage for a taxi business to the total VAT inclusive turnover for both parts of the business.

4.7 What if the balance between parts of my business changes?

If the balance changes but you continue to do all the same activities, carry on using the percentage that was appropriate at the start of the year until the anniversary of you joining the scheme. Review the balance between the parts of the business each year. Make this review for the first day of the VAT period in which the anniversary of you joining the scheme falls. If on that date the balance has changed, or you expect it to change over the year ahead, switch to the trade sector for the larger portion of your expected business.

This may also mean that your flat rate changes. If this occurs use the new flat rate from the start of the VAT period in which your anniversary falls; not just from the anniversary to the end of the period.

4.8 What if I start or stop a business activity during the year?

If you stop a business activity or start a new one during the year, you will need to check if the flat rate scheme is still the better way to calculate your VAT. The change may mean you are no longer eligible to use the scheme – see paragraph 12.2. If you are still eligible to use the scheme, consider which business activity forms the larger part of your expected business. Do this in the way described in paragraph 4.7. Apply the appropriate percentage from the date of the change in your business until your next anniversary of joining the scheme, or the next change to your business – whichever comes first.

If you change flat rate percentages you must write and tell us within 30 days of the change taking place. You should write to: National Registration Service HM Revenue & Customs Imperial House 77 Victoria Street Grimsby Lincolnshire DN31 1DB

4.9 What if the Table of flat rates changes?

If the flat rate for your trade sector changes, you must use the new rate from the date of the change. A new Table will be published in advance, which will be found at the link in paragraph 4.3. In these circumstances you do not have to write and tell us that you have started to use a different rate.

4.10 How do I deal with two flat rates in one VAT period?

Where a change in flat rate occurs in the middle of your VAT accounting period you will have to do two calculations for that period. The first calculation will be from the beginning of the period to the day before the start date for the new flat rate and the other from the start date to the end of the period.

4.11 What if the change of rate coincides with changes to my business?

If the introduction of a new flat rate coincides with the day you would otherwise make a change to your business under the rules in paragraph 4.8, you should make the change as normal but use the new flat rate at the link in paragraph 4.3. If there is more than one change of flat rate in your accounting period (more likely for annual accounters), then you will need more than two VAT calculations for the period. Do each in the way outlined in paragraph 4.8.

5 APPLYING FOR THE SCHEME

5.1 When can I apply?

You can apply at the time you register for VAT, or any later time. If you apply near the time of your VAT registration, you can start using the scheme from the date you are registered for VAT. Try not to delay your application if you wish to use the scheme from your date of registration.

Commentary—*De Voil Indirect Tax Service* **V2.199B.**

5.2 How can I apply?

By post

There is an application form VAT 600 FRS Flat rate scheme application from the HMRC website.

Postal applications should be sent to our National Registration Service at the following address:

National Registration Service

HM Revenue & Customs

Imperial House

77 Victoria Street

Grimsby

Lincolnshire

DN31 1DB

If you are registering for VAT, you can enclose the form with your Form VAT 1 Application for Registration.

By email

Download a VAT 600 FRS Flat rate scheme application.

Fill it in on your computer and send it to: frsapplications.vrs@hmrc.gsi.gov.uk.

Please send questions or correspondence to our VAT Helpline, not this address.

By phone

Call our VAT Helpline on 0300 200 3700.

5.3 How do I fill in the application form?

The table below will help you to fill in the form. If you are in doubt please telephone our VAT Helpline.

Section A	
Business name	Use your normal business name. If you are already registered for VAT, this should be the name on your VAT Certificate of Registration.
Business Address	This is your principal place of business. Again, if you are already registered for VAT, this should be the address on your VAT Certificate of Registration.
Phone number	You do not have to give this, but it may help us to process your application more quickly if we can phone you to clear up questions about your application
VAT registration number	If you have not been advised of a VAT registration number, leave this blank. Make sure you send the scheme application to the same office as you sent the VAT 1 Notification of VAT registration.
Section B	
Main business activity	Decide which of the sectors in section 4 most accurately describes your business. If your business covers more than one sector, use the sector that is the main part of your business. Decide which is the main part by the amount of turnover each makes.
Flat rate percentage	This is the percentage for your sector as shown at the link in paragraph 4.3. Insert the full flat rate for your sector even if you are entitled to the 1 % reduction.
Section B	
Start date	This will normally be from the beginning of the VAT period after we receive your application. We will confirm your actual start date in writing.

Section A	—If you would prefer to start using the scheme from another date, write the date and reason in the box provided – see paragraph 5.5 for further information.
Section C Signature and date	The form should be signed and dated by the owner, a partner, or a director of the business that is applying. A signature is not required on an electronic application. Just type your name in the box.

If your accountant or other representative applies by phone for you to use the scheme, we will send you a copy of the application form completed by us for your records. If there are any errors on it please contact us immediately.

5.4 Do I need to keep a copy of my application?

Yes. This is a good idea and will help if you have to contact us about your application. Please also note the office to which you send it.

5.5 When can I start to use the scheme?

We will notify you in writing if your application is successful. The letter will tell you the date you can start to use the scheme. This will normally be from the start of the VAT period following receipt of your application. Earlier or later start dates can be agreed. When considering an earlier or later start date, we will consider all the facts including the timing of your application and your compliance record. We will not normally allow you to go back and use the scheme for periods for which you have already calculated your VAT liability.

5.6 What if I don't receive a reply to my application?

We will deal with your application under our Taxpayer's Charter standards. If you do not hear from us within 30 calendar days, please contact the office to which you sent the application to check that it has been received.

6 DETERMINING YOUR FLAT RATE TURNOVER

Commentary—*De Voil Indirect Tax Service* **V2.199B.**

6.1 How do I work out my flat rate turnover?

It is important to get this right. If you include items that are not part of the turnover, you will pay too much VAT. If you leave out items, you will pay too little VAT and could be assessed and have to pay a penalty and interest.

The turnover to which you apply the flat rate is *all* that you receive including the VAT.

There are three ways of calculating your turnover. They are:

Method	*Description*
Basic turnover	This is principally for those who deal mainly with other VAT registered businesses. If you are used to accounting for VAT on an invoice basis, this can be the simplest to operate. For details see section 8.
Cash based turnover	This method is the flat rate scheme equivalent of cash accounting. It is based, not on the time you make the supply, but on the time you are paid for your goods or services. This can be helpful if you give extended credit or your customers pay you late. For details see section 9.

Retailer's turnover	This is essentially the same as a retail scheme and is best if you are a retailer selling goods to the public. For details see section 10.

Whichever method you use, you must use that method for at least 12 months.

6.2 What must I include in my flat rate turnover?

Your flat rate turnover is all the supplies your business makes, including VAT. This means *all* of the following—

- the *VAT inclusive* sales and takings for standard rate, zero rate and reduced rate supplies
- the value of exempt income, such as any rent or lottery commission. These examples are not exhaustive and you can find out more about exempt income in Notice 700 *The VAT Guide*.
- supplies of capital expenditure goods, unless they are supplies on which VAT has to be calculated outside the flat rate scheme in accordance with paragraph 15.9 and
- the value of any despatches to other member states of the EC if you are making intra EC supplies. For details see Notice 725 *The Single Market*.

Note: as exempt and zero rate supplies are included in your flat rate turnover you apply the flat rate percentage to the exempt and zero rate turnover. You may pay more VAT by being on the scheme if these supplies are a larger proportion of your business turnover than the average for your trade sector.

6.3 What income do I exclude from my flat rate turnover?

You exclude from your flat rate turnover—

- private income, for example income from shares
- bank interest
- the proceeds from the sale of goods you own but which have not been used in your business
- any sales of gold that are covered by VATA s 55 – see Notice 701/21 *Gold*
- non-business income and any supplies outside the scope of UK VAT and
- sales of capital expenditure goods on which you have claimed input tax.

6.4 Special circumstances

Depending on the specific details of your business before you work out your flat rate turnover you may also need to take account of the following—

If your business	*Then*
sells goods to other member states of the EU	include this income in your flat rate turnover. If your business has a higher proportion of this type of sale than others in your trade sector you may find that operating the flat rate scheme puts you at a disadvantage compared to your competitors.
sells services to other member states of the EU	if your supplies are outside the scope of VAT, leave them out of your flat rate turnover. This will depend on the place of supply of the services – see Notice 741A *Place of supply of services*.
buys goods from other member states of the EU	you must account for VAT on these acquisitions in box 2 of your VAT return. Acquisition tax is payable at the standard rate of VAT and not at the flat rate. For full details about intra-Community trade see Notice 725 *The Single Market*.

purchases services from outside the UK to which the reverse charge applies	these supplies should be dealt with outside of the FRS. Exclude them from your flat rate turnover but record them in boxes 1 and 4 of your VAT return, as you would under normal accounting. For more information about reverse charges, see Notice 700 *The VAT Guide*.
is partly exempt	you are treated on the scheme as fully taxable and do not have to make any partial exemption calculations. You must, however, include your exempt income in your flat rate turnover.
incurs motoring expenses	you do not have to pay any road fuel scale charges since you are not reclaiming any input tax on the road fuel your business uses.
sells second-hand goods	you can include these sales in your flat rate turnover, but you will pay more VAT than if you leave the scheme and use the second hand margin scheme. Including second hand sales is the simplest option and if you only make occasional sales of second-hand goods you may consider this simplicity is worth the extra expense. You cannot, however, use the flat rate scheme and the margin scheme at the same time. You can find more about the second hand margin scheme in Notice 718 *Margin schemes for second-hand goods, works of art, antiques and collectors' items*.
is acting as an agent	if you pay amounts to third parties as an agent and debit your client with the precise amounts paid out, you may be able to treat them as disbursements. If you are making such disbursements, then the money received for them is not part of your flat rate turnover. For further information about disbursements see Notice 700 *The VAT Guide*.

7 KEEPING RECORDS AND FILLING IN YOUR VAT RETURN

Commentary—*De Voil Indirect Tax Service* **V2.199D.**

7.1 Must I keep a VAT account?

Yes. If the only VAT to be accounted for is the VAT calculated under the flat rate scheme, just record that in the VAT payable portion of your VAT account. For further details of the VAT account see Notice 700 *The VAT Guide*.

In some cases, however, you may have VAT to account for outside the flat rate scheme, for example the single purchase or disposal of capital expenditure goods of more than £2,000 in value. You should enter this in your VAT account in the normal way, in addition to your flat rate VAT.

7.2 Do I need to keep any special records?

Yes.

This rule has the force of law

You must keep a record of your flat rate calculation showing—

– your flat rate turnover for the VAT accounting period
– the flat rate percentage you have used
– the tax calculated as due.

This record must be kept with your VAT account.

7.3 Do I still need to issue VAT invoices?

Yes. You must still issue VAT invoices to your VAT registered customers. Your customers will treat these as normal VAT invoices. When you come to calculate the scheme turnover, do not forget to include the VAT inclusive total of any invoices you have issued into the method of working out turnover that you are using (see paragraph 6.2). You must keep copies of all sales invoices that you issue to your VAT registered customers.

7.4 How do I calculate the VAT on these invoices?

Record VAT on your sales invoices using the normal rate for the supply (standard, reduced or zero rate or exempt) and not the flat rate percentage assigned to your trade sector. At the end of the VAT period you add up the VAT inclusive total of all your supplies whether you gave a VAT invoice or not and apply the flat rate percentage to this total to give the amount of VAT you must pay to us.

7.5 How do I fill in my VAT return?

Filling in your VAT return is different on the scheme from the normal VAT rules because you are calculating net tax without reference to output tax and input tax. Follow the rules in the Table below where they differ from those on the VAT return form. If the value for any box is none, write none in the box. Do not leave any box blank.

Filling in your VAT return

Box 1	Use this for the VAT due under the flat rate scheme (see box 6 below). You may have other output tax to include in the box such as the sale of capital expenditure goods on which you have claimed input tax separately while using the flat rate scheme. See paragraph 15.9.
Box 2	In this box you must account for VAT on any goods you buy from other EC member states at the standard rate of VAT and not at your flat rate.
Box 3	Will be the sum of boxes 1 + 2 in the normal way.
Box 4	Will usually be none. If you are filling in a paper VAT return write "none". If you are filling in an online return, leave as "£0.00". However, there may be a claim if you— —make a single purchase of capital expenditure goods of more than £2,000 in value (inc VAT), see paragraph 15.2; —can recover VAT on stocks and assets on hand at registration, see paragraph 7.6; or —are making a claim for bad debt relief. You should also use this box to record transactions that are subject to the reverse charge – cancelling out the figure recorded in box 1. As with goods and services you buy from suppliers in the UK, you must not normally claim VAT on any acquisitions of goods and related services from other EC member states. However, you can normally claim for any single purchase of capital expenditure goods of £2,000 or more value, including VAT. For more details, see paragraph 15.2.
Box 5	Will be the result of box 3 minus box 4 in the normal way.
Box 6	Enter the turnover to which you applied the flat rate scheme percentage, *including* VAT. You should also include the value, excluding VAT, of any supplies accounted for outside the flat rate scheme, such as the sale of capital expenditure goods. For example: if your VAT inclusive turnover is £10,000 and your flat rate is 8 % put the £10,000 in this box and include the £800 in box 1.

Box 7	Will usually be none, except where— —you made a single purchase of capital expenditure goods costing more than £2,000 (including VAT) and you are claiming the input tax in box 4 or —you have acquired goods from other member states of the EU. Put the VAT exclusive value in this box.
Boxes 8 and 9	Use in the normal way.

7.6 Can I recover VAT paid before registration on goods and services?

Yes. Record the claim for eligible VAT in your VAT account for your first VAT return.

For details of the rules for claims, see Notice 700/1 *Should I be registered for VAT?*

If you do claim VAT on capital assets on hand at registration and dispose of them later, you must account for VAT at the standard rate of VAT under the normal VAT rules.

7.7 Common errors made on VAT returns

— Failure to include any VAT on EC acquisitions in box 2.
— Failure to account for VAT on EC acquisitions in box 2 at the standard rate.
— "None" (or "£0.00" for online returns) missed out of box 4.
— Forgetting to include rental income, such as rent, in the turnover to which the flat rate is applied.
— VAT-exclusive figure is put in box 6, meaning that the flat rate is applied to the net, rather than the gross turnover.
— The 1 % reduction is applied by businesses that have been registered for more than 12 months.

7.8 How do I prepare business accounts for income tax purposes while I am using the flat rate scheme?

It is expected that accounts for businesses who are using the scheme will be prepared using gross receipts, less the flat rate VAT percentage, for turnover and that expenses will include the irrecoverable input VAT.

For both VAT and income tax purposes, there is a requirement to keep a record of sales and purchases. But, for businesses using the scheme, that record does not have to analyse gross, VAT and net separately. The records need only be complete, orderly and easy to follow.

See Notice 700/12 *Filling in your return* for further details.

7.9 How do I pay my return?

You can pay by cheque, postal order or electronic means. You may get extra time to pay and submit your return if you pay by electronic means.

If you use the flat rate scheme and annual accounting scheme together, then you must pay by electronic means. For further details on payment see Notice 700 *The VAT Guide*.

7.10 Online VAT returns

Paper VAT returns are being phased out and we will notify you in writing if you have to submit your return online and pay any VAT due electronically. Even if you are not required to submit your return online, you may do so if you wish.

If you send us your VAT return online you must also pay any VAT due by electronic means. To submit your return online you must register and enrol through our website at www.hmrc.gov.uk and choose to use the VAT Online Returns Service or commercially available software.

7.11 Can penalties apply to flat rate scheme users?

Yes. Surcharge is applied in the normal way if you send your return in late or pay any VAT due after the due date. For details see Notice 700/50 *Default surcharge*.

Businesses with a turnover up to £150,000 are issued with a letter offering help and advice on how to avoid late returns and payments the first time they pay late.

If you make errors on your VAT return, then you may be liable to a misdeclaration penalty as well as being assessed for any VAT and default interest due. See Notice 700/42 *Misdeclaration penalty and repeated misdeclaration penalty* and Notice 700/43 *Default Interest.*

8 THE BASIC TURNOVER METHOD

Commentary—*De Voil Indirect Tax Service* **V2.199B.**

8.1 How do I use the basic turnover method?

Apply the flat rate percentage for your business to the VAT inclusive total of the supplies that have their tax point in the VAT accounting period.

Tax points are worked out using the normal VAT rules for time of supply. If you issue VAT invoices, this is often the date you issue an invoice. But in some circumstances it will be the date you receive payment, or the date you complete a service or make goods available to your customer.

The detailed rules which you must follow are in Notice 700 *The VAT Guide.*

9 THE CASH BASED TURNOVER METHOD

Commentary—*De Voil Indirect Tax Service* **V2.199B.**

9.1 How do I use the cash based turnover method?

Apply the flat rate percentage to the VAT inclusive supplies for which you have been *paid* in the accounting period.

The following rule has the force of law

Cash (coins or notes): you receive payment on the date you receive the money.

Cheques: you receive payment on the date you receive the cheque, or the date on the cheque, whichever is the later. If the cheque is not honoured you do not need to account for the VAT. If you have already accounted for the VAT you can adjust your records accordingly.

Giro, standing order or direct debit: you receive payment on the date your bank account is credited with such a payment.

Credit or debit card: you receive payment on the date you make out a sales voucher for a credit/debit card payment (not when you actually get paid by the card provider).

9.2 Change of tax rate or insolvency

In these special circumstances, the *basic* turnover method tax point will determine the treatment of your supplies.

9.3 What if I used Cash accounting before joining the flat rate scheme?

You carry on as before. There is no need to pay the VAT your customers owe you when you change schemes. Include any payments you receive whilst using the flat rate scheme in the total to which you apply your flat rate percentage. Notice 731 *Cash accounting* gives information about the Cash accounting scheme.

9.4 What if I receive a payment "net of deductions"?

The following rule has the force of law.

If you receive a net payment, you must include the full value before such deductions (and including the relevant VAT) in your scheme turnover. This will usually be the value shown on your sales invoice.

Some examples of payments that you may receive that are net of deductions are:

- where commission has been deducted by your customer
- where commission or payment for expenses has been deducted by a factor or agent collecting money on your behalf
- where commission or payment for expenses has been deducted by an auctioneer selling goods on your behalf
- payments made by an employer/contractor who has deducted income tax.

9.5 What if I receive payments in kind (for example, barter, part exchange)?

The following rule has the force of law.

If you are paid fully or partly in kind, such as by barter or part exchange, you must include the value including VAT in your flat rate turnover each time you make or receive a "payment". You receive "payment" on the date you receive the goods or services agreed in lieu of money.

You must account for VAT on the full value of the supply, which is the price, including VAT, which a customer would have to pay for the supply if they had paid for it with money only.

The general rules about payments in kind are in Notice 700 *The VAT Guide*.

9.6 What if I want to stop using the cash based method?

The following rule has the force of law.

If at any time you stop using the cash based accounting method, you must account for VAT on all the supplies made by you while you were using the method for which payment has not been received.

The supplies must be included in your scheme turnover in the return for the period in which you cease to use the cash based method.

The only exception to this is if you cease to use the FRS, but immediately start to use the cash accounting scheme described in Notice 731 *Cash accounting*. Any business that leaves the Flat Rate Scheme and immediately starts to use the Cash Accounting Scheme should apply the appropriate flat rate percentage to any supplies made while part of the Flat Rate Scheme when payment for those supplies is received

You may be able to balance this adjustment with a claim for relief for stocks on hand (paragraph 12.8), or a claim for bad debts (section 14).

10 THE RETAILER'S TURNOVER METHOD

Commentary—*De Voil Indirect Tax Service* **V2.199B.**

10.1 What is the retailer's turnover method?

This method is based on your daily takings. You record payments from your customers as you receive them (for example, through your till) and total the takings daily.

You calculate your daily takings using the guidance at 10.2 to 10.7 below.

To work out your flat rate turnover, you then add to your takings any other items of income your business receives, including those from outside the retail environment. You may find it helpful to make weekly and monthly totals.

At the end of your VAT accounting period, you apply the flat rate percentage to your flat rate turnover for that period.

Examples of other items of income your business receives might be—

— rent from a flat above the shop
— installation or callout charges if they are invoiced for, rather than going through your till
— disclosed exempt charge for credit.

10.2 What do I include in daily takings?

The following rule has the force of law.

You must include and record the following in your daily takings as they are received from your customers—

– cash
– cheques
– debit or credit card vouchers
– Switch, Delta or similar electronic transactions
– electronic cash.

10.3 What non-cash sales do I include in daily takings?

The following rule has the force of law.

In addition to cash payments you must add the following to, and record in, your daily takings, on the day you make the supply—

– the full value of credit sales
– the cash value of any payment in kind for retail sales
– the face value of gift, book and record vouchers redeemed
– any other payments for retail sales.

10.4 May I make any deductions from my daily takings?

Yes. Your till roll or other record of sales together with the additions explained above constitutes your daily takings and it is this figure which you must start with when calculating your flat rate VAT. You may, however, reduce this daily takings figure with the amount of any of the following—

– void transactions – where an incorrect transaction has been voided at the time of the error
– illegible credit card transactions – where a customer's account details are unclear on the credit card voucher and therefore cannot be presented and redeemed at the bank
– unsigned or dishonoured cheques from cash customers – but not from credit customers
– counterfeit notes
– where a cheque guarantee card is accepted incorrectly as a credit card
– acceptance of out of date coupons which have previously been included in the daily takings but which are not honoured by promoters
– supervisor's float discrepancies
– till breakdowns – where incorrect till readings are recorded due to mechanical faults, for example a till programming error, false reading and till reset by engineer
– use of training tills – where the till used by staff for training has been returned to the sales floor without the zeroing of figures

- customer overspends using Shopacheck
- inadvertent acceptance of foreign currency – where discovered at a later time, for example when cashing up
- receipts for goods or services which are to be accounted for outside the flat rate scheme
- refunds given to customers in respect of taxable supplies to cover accidental overcharges or where goods are unsuitable or faulty
- instalments for credit sales.

10.5 What are the rules for making adjustments to my daily takings?

If you wish to adjust your daily takings, the following rules apply.

The following rule has the force of law.

- you must be able to provide evidence to support any adjustments to your daily takings figure
- if you make an adjustment but receive a payment later, the amount must be included in your daily takings
- you must not make any reductions from daily takings for till shortages that result from theft of cash, fraudulent refunds and voids or poor cash handling by staff.

For further details about cash handling, see Notice 727/3 *Retail schemes: How to work the Point of Sale scheme*.

10.6 Are there other rules about daily takings?

Yes. If you are involved in part-exchange, sale or return, credit sales, deposits, vouchers, coupons, or other special transactions, you will have to make other adjustments to your daily takings. Notice 727/3 *Retail schemes: How to work the Point of Sale scheme* will help. The rules for these adjustments apply to businesses using the flat rate scheme in the same way that they apply to businesses using the normal VAT system. If you are in doubt then please contact our VAT Helpline.

10.7 Special rules for florists

Special rules apply if you are a member of organisations such as Interflora, Teleflorist or Flowergram.

- When you receive payment direct from your customer, you are the sending member and must include the amount the customer pays you in your daily gross takings.
- When you deliver flowers ordered by customers at another florist, you are the executing member and you must add the order value and the VAT shown, from the monthly Agency self billed invoice, to your flat rate turnover. This will be the gross figure.
- When orders taken by you are delivered by other florists, the invoice from the agency will show the value of these orders as a purchase figure plus VAT. The figures shown may be net or gross depending on which agency is used. *The input tax is always shown but this amount cannot be reclaimed under the flat rate scheme.*

11 CHANGES TO YOUR BUSINESS

Commentary—*De Voil Indirect Tax Service* **V2.199B–V2.199D.**

11.1 What if my business grows?

If your business grows but you remain eligible to use the flat rate scheme you do not need to take any further action. You must check your turnover at least once a year on your anniversary of joining the scheme. If you are expecting sales of £230,000 or more in the next month you should check that you do not exceed the "forward look" test in paragraph 12.2(b).

11.2 What if the increase in my turnover is a one-off?

If, when you do your annual check you find that your turnover has gone above the £230,000 limit but you expect that your turnover in the next year will fall below £191,500 in the next year, you may be able to remain on the scheme with our agreement. If you wish to remain on the scheme in those circumstances, apply in writing to:

HMRC

VAT Written Enquiries Team

4th Floor West

Alexander House

21 Victoria Avenue

Southend On Sea

Essex

SS99 1BD.

You will need to demonstrate that:

– Your VAT inclusive total turnover in the coming year will not exceed £191,500.
– The increase was the result of unexpected business activity which has not occurred before and is not expected to recur – if you successfully tender for an annual contract that takes you over the threshold, this cannot be classed as unexpected.
– The increase arose from genuine commercial activity.

If, however, the increase occurred in such a way that you must leave the scheme in the circumstances described in paragraph 12.2(b), then you cannot remain on the scheme even if the three conditions above are met.

11.3 What if the nature of my business changes?

If you change the nature of your business but remain eligible to use the flat rate scheme, apply the appropriate flat rate percentage for the trade sector for the new type of business from the date of the change. You must write and tell us about the change within 30 days of the date of the change. This should be recorded with your VAT account as explained in paragraph 7.2.

11.4 What if a business change makes me ineligible to use the flat rate scheme?

If the change in your business results in you becoming ineligible to use the flat rate scheme you must write and tell us and start accounting for VAT in the standard way.

See paragraph 12.2 for the rules on what makes you ineligible to continue using the scheme and when you must leave.

12 LEAVING THE SCHEME

Commentary—*De Voil Indirect Tax Service* **V2.199D.**

12.1 When can I leave the scheme?

If you wish to leave the scheme you must write and tell us. We would expect that most businesses will leave at the end of an accounting period. However, you may leave voluntarily at any time during an accounting period. We will confirm the date you left the scheme in writing.

12.2 When must I leave the scheme?

The table below details circumstances that can cause you to become ineligible to continue using the scheme and the date on which you must leave the scheme.

Ref	*If you become ineligible because*	*then you must leave the scheme with effect from*
(a)	At the anniversary of your start date your total income (including VAT) in the year then ending (excluding sales of capital assets) is more than £230,000. Note: your total income is determined by —the value of invoices you have issued (if you use the basic turnover method) —the actual payments you have received (if you use the cash based turnover method)	for businesses on quarterly VAT returns: —the end of the VAT period containing your anniversary; or for annual accounters: —the end of the month after the month containing your FRS anniversary, or the end of your current annual VAT period, whichever comes first.
(b)	there are reasonable grounds to believe the total value of your turnover for the next 30 days alone will be more than £230,000 (excluding sales of capital assets).	the beginning of the period of 30 days.
(c)	you become a tour operator and have to account for VAT using the Tour Operator's Margin Scheme.	the date you became a tour operator.
(d)	you intend, or expect, to buy assets that are covered by the capital goods scheme (see paragraph 15.6).	the date your intention or expectation occurred.
(e)	you become eligible for VAT group treatment, or register in the name of divisions	the date you become eligible or registered in divisions.
(f)	you become associated with another business in the way described in paragraph 3.9.	the date you become associated.
(g)	you decide to account for VAT using the second hand margin scheme or the auctioneer's scheme.	the beginning of the VAT period in which you decide to use either scheme.

12.3 How often do I have to check my turnover?

You have to make sure that your turnover has not risen above the limit in paragraph 12.2(a) and (b) each year, on your anniversary of joining the scheme.

If your business is growing rapidly, you will need to check at least monthly that you do not become ineligible by virtue of the rule in 12.2(b).

12.4 What must I do if I deregister?

If you deregister you leave the scheme the day before your deregistration date. You must account for output tax on your final VAT return for:

- sales made on the last day of registration (which must be accounted for outside of the scheme)
- the value of any capital expenditure goods or any pre-registration stock, on which you recovered input tax at the time of registration and which are still on hand at the date of deregistration.

Note: if you use the cash based turnover method you must follow the rules at 9.6.

12.5 Can you withdraw the scheme from me?

Yes. We may withdraw the scheme at any time for the protection of the revenue. We will specify the date of withdrawal in our notice of withdrawal.

Additionally, if we withdraw the scheme because you were never eligible to use it, we will backdate the withdrawal to the time when you started to use the scheme and you will have to account normally for VAT from then.

12.6 Can I rejoin the scheme?

Yes. If you meet the requirements again, you can rejoin. But you will not be eligible to rejoin for a period of 12 months.

12.7 What must I do after leaving the scheme?

If you are deregistering refer to paragraph 12.4. In general, moving to the normal VAT rules is straightforward but in some circumstances you may need to make extra adjustments to ensure your VAT returns are accurate. The table below gives details.

If	*Then*
you stop using the scheme in the middle of a VAT accounting period,	you must do two calculations when you complete your next VAT return: —the first calculation will be for the portion of the period you used the scheme —the other calculation will be for the rest of the period, using normal VAT rules. This will give you two sets of figures for the period you stop using the scheme. Add these together when you complete your VAT return.
you use the cash based method under the flat rate scheme and you do *not* move immediately to the cash accounting scheme (see Notice 731 *Cash accounting*).	when you leave the scheme you must follow the rule described in paragraph 9.6
you use the cash based method under the flat rate scheme and you move immediately to the cash accounting scheme (see *Notice 731 Cash accounting*).	when you leave the scheme you must follow the rule described in paragraph 9.6
the value of your stock has increased while you have been on the scheme	you may be eligible to recover additional VAT on stock which you have on hand when you leave the scheme – see paragraph 12.8.

12.8 What do I do about stock on hand when I leave the scheme?

You may be able to make a stock adjustment and claim input tax when you leave the scheme. Follow the steps in the table at paragraph 12.9 below to find out if and how, you need to make an adjustment. To do this you will need to value your stock. You do not need to do a formal stock-take for the purpose of valuing your stock, but your figures must be reasonable. It makes sense to keep a record of how you valued your stock in case we query the figures.

12.9 How do I make the stock adjustment?

Paragraph 12.8 explains circumstances in which you may be able to recover additional input tax when you leave the scheme if your stock of standard rated items has increased. This is voluntary. The following table explains how you make the adjustment.

This table has the force of law.

Step	*What you need to do*	*Example*

1	Work out the VAT exclusive value of stock on hand on which you had recovered input tax before you joined the flat rate scheme. (Remember, if you were previously on cash accounting, this will be based on stock for you had paid for which you had paid.)	£10,000
2	Work out the VAT exclusive value of stock on hand on which you will be unable to recover input tax after you stop using the flat rate scheme.	£20,000
3	Subtract the figure at Step 1 from the figure at Step 2. (If the figure at Step 1 is larger than the figure at Step 2, you will not be entitled to the adjustment. No further action is necessary.)	£20,000 – £10,000 = £10,000
4	Multiply the result of Step 3 by the standard rate of VAT.	£10,000 x 20% = £2,000
5	Claim the VAT calculated at Step 4 in the VAT recoverable portion of your VAT account in the first return you make after leaving the flat rate scheme.	£2,000 recoverable from us as a result of FRS stock adjustment.

13 BARRISTERS

13.1 Can barristers use the flat rate scheme?

Barristers whose chambers use any of the methods of accounting for common expenses may use the scheme. However, those chambers using method 3 (sometimes known as the combination method) must follow the rules below if they have any members using the flat rate scheme. Chambers must ensure that input tax claims are apportioned and only relate to those barristers who are not on the scheme.

EXAMPLE:

- A chambers has ten barristers, two of whom use the flat rate scheme. The common fund has paid £12,000.00, including VAT, on goods purchased. If none of the barristers were using the scheme, they could have claimed £2,000.00 input tax.
- However, as two of them use the flat rate scheme the chambers must apportion the input tax. If 30 %t of the input tax is apportioned to the two barristers on the flat rate scheme, the chambers, through the nominated member of the common fund, can only claim 70 % (£1,400.00) of the VAT paid on the goods. This is the input tax relating to the eight barristers not using the scheme.
- The remaining 30 % cannot be claimed as the two barristers using the flat rate scheme have already had their input tax taken into account in their flat rate percentage.

13.2 Do barristers using the scheme have to keep special records?

Chambers choosing to use the adaptation of method 3 explained above, must ensure that barristers do not claim input tax while they use the scheme.

They must put in place a system that monitors the input tax claimed for common expenses. This system must contain records that show—

- The value of the original VAT invoice.
- The amount and percentage of input tax claimed back by the nominated member for each VAT invoice.
- How the input tax is apportioned to the individual barristers.
- How the input tax reclaimed is calculated for each VAT invoice.

The records of all members of chambers using the flat rate scheme must be made available during a visit to the chambers by an officer from HMRC.

Barristers on the flat rate scheme whose chambers use method 3 must ensure that the nominated member does not claim input tax on their behalf.

14 BAD DEBT RELIEF

Commentary—*De Voil Indirect Tax Service* **V1.156.**

14.1 Can I claim bad debt relief if I use the flat rate scheme?

Bad debt relief arises if you account for and pay output tax on supplies for which you are not paid later. The rules are explained in Notice 700/18 *Relief from VAT on bad debts* and these will apply to you.

If you use the *basic* or *retailer's* turnover methods of flat rate accounting, you can claim relief on eligible supplies at the standard rate of VAT, rather than the flat rate. This is because the flat rate includes an allowance for input tax which only occurs if you have been paid by your customer. As you will not have been paid, you will not have had full credit for any input tax.

If you are using the cash turnover method, the rule for claiming bad debt relief are different, as explained at paragraph 14.2 below.

14.2 What if I use the cash turnover method of accounting?

If you use the cash turnover method of accounting you may be eligible for bad debt relief if—

- you have not been paid by your customer and it has been six months since you made the supplies
- you have not accounted for and paid tax on the supply
- you have written off the debt in your accounts.

If you meet all these conditions, your claim will be for the difference between the VAT you charged to your customer and the amount you would have declared to us had you been paid. As with businesses that use the basic and retailer's methods, this is because your flat rate takes account of input tax that you would otherwise have been entitled to, if you had been paid by your customer.

You can make the adjustment as follows:

Step	*What you need to do*	*Example*
1	Identify the VAT in the unpaid supply	Total price = £1,2000 VAT= £175
2	Calculate the VAT that would have been paid under the flat rate scheme if your customer had paid you. That is the total owed (including VAT) multiplied by your flat rate scheme percentage.	£1,200 x (say) 10% = £120
3	Subtract the sum of step 2 from the sum of step 1	£200 – £120 = £80
4	Step 3 is your special allowance under the flat rate scheme. Include it in your VAT account in your next return.	£80 is added to the VAT deductible portion of your VAT account and creates a claim or reduces the VAT payable.

Note: If you apply for bad debt relief on a supply made while using the FRS you should make the adjustment as above, even if you have withdrawn from the scheme.

15 CAPITAL EXPENDITURE GOODS

Commentary—*De Voil Indirect Tax Service* **V2.199B.**

15.1 Definition of "capital expenditure goods" on which input tax can be claimed

Normally, capital goods are those goods which are bought to be used in the business but are not used up by it, except through normal wear and tear over a number of years – for example a van, a computer or a bottling machine but not the fuel, printer paper or bottles that go into them.

Capital expenditure goods in the flat rate scheme are capital goods that would fall into the above definition, but also specifically exclude any goods bought to—

- resell

- incorporate into other goods for onward supply
- consume (or completely use) within one year
- generate business income by being leased, let or hired
- goods covered by the capital goods scheme (see paragraph 15.6).

Nothing in this section allows a business using the flat rate scheme to reclaim VAT on goods which it would not be able to claim under the normal VAT rules.

15.2 Reclaim of VAT on capital expenditure goods

If you use the flat rate scheme, you can reclaim the VAT you have been charged on a single purchase of capital expenditure goods where the amount of the purchase, including VAT, is £2,000 or more.

You deal with these capital expenditure goods outside the flat rate scheme. This means that you claim the input tax in box 4 of your VAT return.

If the supply is—

- more than one purchase
- under £2,000 including VAT or
- of services

then no VAT is claimable, as this input tax is already taken into account in the calculation of your flat rate percentage.

15.3 What counts as a single purchase of capital goods?

The normal VAT rules are used to determine whether any particular supply is one, or more than one, purchase and whether supplies are of goods or services.

Examples of a single purchase are—

- *A computer package* (computer, printer, camera, scanner, speakers etc.) bought as one package is one purchase of capital expenditure goods. If the package costs £2,000 or more (incl. VAT) then input tax can be claimed.
- *Items of kitchen equipment* (a pizza oven, a fridge and a dishwasher) bought for a restaurant. If all the items are from one supplier at one time, then they count as one purchase of capital expenditure goods. If they are from three different suppliers, or at three different times then they will be three purchases and each must be £2,000 or more (inc VAT) to qualify for a reclaim of VAT.

15.4 What counts as goods and services?

- *A van leased/hired to your business*, counts as one continuous supply of services, as ownership will never transfer to your business. For more information on "lease, let, or hire" see paragraph 15.7.
- *A van bought on hire purchase* is a supply of capital expenditure goods because ownership will eventually transfer to your business. If this cost £2,000 or more (incl VAT) then input tax can be claimed.
- *A builder builds an extension* to his business premises supplying all materials himself and including their cost in his final bill. No VAT is claimable, as this construction is a supply of services, not of capital expenditure goods.

15.5 What counts as capital or non-capital goods?

- *A shopkeeper buys bricks, cement and fittings* from his local builder's merchant intending to employ a builder to convert them into an extension of the business premises. No VAT is reclaimable as bricks etc. are not capital expenditure goods.
- *A shop is bought freehold for a retail business* to operate from. If a former owner has opted to tax the property, VAT will be payable on the purchase of these capital expenditure goods and input tax can be claimed.

15.6 What if I intend, or expect, to buy assets that are covered by the capital goods scheme?

If you intend, or expect, to buy such goods you must leave the flat rate scheme and write and tell us immediately. The capital goods scheme applies to—

- computers and items of computer equipment with a VAT exclusive value of £50,000 or more
- land and buildings, civil engineering works and refurbishments of a VAT-exclusive value of £250,000 or more.

For more information, see Notice 706/2 *Capital goods scheme.*

15.7 What if goods are bought to "lease, let or hire"

Where capital goods are bought with the intention of generating income from them either directly (for example boats for hire on a boating lake, hire of bouncy castles or marquees) or indirectly (for example company van used for deliveries during week and hired out at weekends), then they are not capital expenditure goods no matter how much they cost.

15.8 Apportionments for private use

To help simplify the flat rate scheme, where VAT on capital expenditure goods is reclaimable, the intended use of those items is treated as wholly for taxable supplies.

This means that you do not apportion input tax to cover any planned private or exempt use of the goods. This is different to the normal VAT rules.

EXAMPLE

- if employees are allowed free use of the company van at weekends to move goods or
- a business video camera is used free by a friend of the proprietor to video a family wedding,

then there is no restriction of input tax or payment of output tax under the flat rate scheme.

15.9 Output tax due on disposal of capital expenditure goods

Where you have reclaimed input tax on capital expenditure goods then, when they are eventually sold out of the business, you must account for output tax at the appropriate VAT rate for the sale (not at the flat rate).

EXAMPLE

A business on the scheme buys a delivery van for £6,000 including VAT of £1,000 and it is not used for anything else. As the van is capital expenditure goods, VAT can be reclaimed. When the business later sells or part exchanges the van, say for £2,000, it must account for the VAT on this amount at 20 %, not at the flat rate.

Note: If you have not claimed input tax on capital items, either by choice or because it was not allowed, you must include the sale of those items in your flat rate turnover.

16 APPEALS

Commentary—*De Voil Indirect Tax Service* **Division V5.4.**

16.1 What if I disagree with your decision about my use of the flat rate scheme?

You can ask us to reconsider our decision. Write to the office with whose decision you disagree saying why you disagree. A different officer will review the decision.

You can ask an independent Tribunal to decide the matter if—

- we refuse to authorise your use of the scheme
- we remove you from the scheme
- you disagree the category and the flat rate percentage that applies to your business.

Further information about what to do if you disagree with an HMRC decision can be found on HMRC's website: www.hmrc.gov.uk/complaints-appeals/how-to-appeal/indirect-tax.htm.

16.2 Can I carry on using the scheme if I have appealed?

If you have appealed about our decision to withdraw or refuse use of the scheme, you must not use the scheme until your appeal is resolved.

If you have appealed against any other matter, such as an assessment, we will normally allow you to continue to use the scheme pending the outcome of the appeal.

17 FORM VAT 600 FRS

Not reproduced here: (www.hmrc.gov.uk/forms/vat600frs.pdf)

741A
PLACE OF SUPPLY OF SERVICES

January 2010

This notice cancels and replaces Notice 741 (May 2008) with effect from 1 January 2010. Details of the changes to the previous version can be found in paragraph 1.3 of this notice.

1 INTRODUCTION

1.1 Who should read this notice?

You should read this notice if you make supplies of services to customers in other member states of the European Community (EC) or to customers outside the EC or if you receive services from suppliers that belong outside the UK.

1.2 What is this notice about?

This notice explains how to determine the place of supply of your services. It also explains how to deal with supplies of services which you *receive* from outside the United Kingdom (UK).

1.3 What has changed?

1 January 2010 saw the introduction of substantial changes to the place of supply of services rules. These changes include a new basic rule ("the general rule") for business to business (B2B) supplies and a reduction in the number of exceptions to the general rule. Further changes are due to come into effect on 1 January 2011, 1 January 2013 and 1 January 2015. This notice has been updated to provide guidance on the changes up to and including 1 January 2013.

The 2015 changes introduce new place of supply of services rules for business to consumer (B2C) supplies of telecommunications and broadcasting services. Guidance on these changes will be published at a later date.

1.4 What VAT law covers this notice?

UK VAT law covering this notice is contained in VATA 1994, as amended, which is referred to in this notice as VATA:

– A new s 7A of VATA defines a "relevant business person" for supplies of services. It also covers the general rule for business to business (B2B) and business to consumer (B2C) supplies of services. See paragraph 2.4 and section 5 of this notice.
– Section 8 of VATA covers the reverse charge procedure. See section 18 of this notice.
– Section 9 of VATA covers place of belonging. See section 3 of this notice.
– Schedule 3B of VATA covers the special scheme for non-EC suppliers making supplies of electronically supplied services to consumers in the EC. See section 20 of this notice.
– Schedule 4A of VATA covers the exceptions to the general rule. See table 1 in paragraph 2.4.3.
– Schedule 6 para 8 of VATA covers the valuation of reverse charge services. See section 18 of this notice.
– Schedule 8 Group 7 of VATA covers the zero-rating provisions for international services. See sections 4, 8, 10, 11 and 13 of this notice.

EC VAT law covering this notice is contained in Council Directive 2006/112/EC (Principal VAT Directive) and Council Regulation (EC) No. 1777/2005 (Implementing Regulation). The Implementing Regulation has direct effect.

1.5 How to use this notice

This notice assumes you have a knowledge of the principles of VAT explained in Notice 700 "The VAT Guide" and have read Notice 700/15 "The ins and outs of VAT".

It is unlikely that all the information in this notice will apply to you, so you do not need to read it all from cover to cover. The table at paragraph 2.4 will help you identify which sections are appropriate to you. There is a contents list and also an index in section 22 which covers popular areas. You should take care to read the beginning of appropriate sections and remember that lists of examples are not exhaustive.

1.6 What to do if you disagree with a decision made by HMRC

If you disagree with any decision made by HMRC you can ask for it to be reconsidered. You should certainly do so if you can provide further relevant information, or if there are facts which you think may not have been fully taken into account. If you are still not satisfied, you may be able to appeal to an independent Tribunal. There are time limits for doing this.

If you do not agree with the result of our reconsideration you can appeal to the First-Tier Tribunal to decide the matter. There is more information about what you can do if you disagree with our decision in a HMRC fact sheet and customer guidance which can be found on our website.

2 PLACE OF SUPPLY OF SERVICES

2.1 What is "place of supply of services"?

For VAT purposes, the *place of supply of services* is the place where a service is treated as being supplied. This is the place where it is liable to VAT (if any). There are a number of place of supply rules for determining where services of different kinds are made:

- where the place of supply of services is in a member state of the European Community (EC), that supply is subject to the VAT rules of that member state and not those of any other country. If the member state is not the UK, such supplies are said to be "outside the scope" of UK VAT;
- where the place of supply of services is outside the EC, that supply is made outside the EC and is therefore not liable to VAT in any member state (although local taxes may apply). Such supplies are said to be "outside the scope" of both UK and EC VAT.

2.2 What does "place of supply" mean for UK suppliers?

If the place of supply of your services is the UK, you must charge any UK VAT due and account for it to HMRC regardless of where your customer belongs. If the place of supply of your services is another member state, you or your customer may be liable to account for any VAT due to the tax authorities of that country. See paragraph 2.12.

Where the place of supply of your services is outside the UK, you should ensure that your records demonstrate that this is the case. See paragraph 2.7.

2.3 What services are being supplied?

To begin with, it is essential that you think carefully about the nature of any services that you supply (or receive). You must identify the real nature of a supply of services where general or generic descriptions are used, because it may affect which place of supply rule applies.

Although reference to your own costs may suggest the nature of your services, you should ask yourself "what am I supplying?". Your invoices should explain the type of services you are actually providing.

2.4 How do I determine the place of supply of services?

From 1 January 2010 there are two general rules for the place of supply of services, one for business to business (B2B) and one for business to consumer (B2C) supplies. There are also special place of supply rules for certain services. Services covered by the special place of supply rules are detailed in table 1 below.

To identify whether someone is a business customer or a consumer see paragraphs 2.5 and 2.6. To decide where a supplier or a customer belongs see section 3.

2.4.1 The B2B general rule

The B2B general rule for supplies of services is that the supply is made where the customer belongs (see section 5).

2.4.2 The B2C general rule

The B2C general rule for supplies of services is that the supply is made where the supplier belongs (see section 5).

2.4.3 Table 1 Services covered by the special place of supply rules

There are special rules for:	*For further information refer to:*
services relating to land and property;	section 6;
services of short-term hire of means of transport;	section 7;
services of B2C long-term hire of means of transport made on or after 1 January 2013;	section 7;
services of B2C long-term hire of pleasure boats made on or after 1 January 2013	section 7;
services involving physical performance. For example artistic, cultural, education and training, sporting, entertainment services, exhibitions, conferences, meetings;	section 8;
ancillary transport, valuation of/work on goods	sections 5 (B2B supplies) and 8 (B2C supplies)
valuation of, or work on, goods for an EC VAT registered customer where the goods are subsequently removed to another country;	section 8 and diagram 1 at 8.5;
restaurant and catering services;	section 9
passenger transport;	section 10
B2C freight transport;	section 11
certain intermediary services;	section 12
B2C supplies of certain services which are mainly "intangible" in character, supplied to customers belonging outside the EC.	sections 14 and 15.

2.5 What does "B2B supplies"mean?

For place of supply of services purposes "B2B supplies" means supplies to businesses whose activities are wholly of a business nature. It also includes supplies to entities which have both business and non-business activities such as charities and government departments.

2.6 What does "B2C supplies" mean?

For place of supply of services purposes "B2C supplies" means supplies to:

– a private individual
– a charity, government department or other body which has no business activities, or
– a "person" who receives a supply of services wholly for private purposes.

2.7 How do I satisfy myself that I make B2B supplies?

To satisfy yourself that this section applies you should obtain commercial evidence showing that your customer belongs outside the UK and does not receive your supply for a wholly private purpose.

For some supplies of services it will be clear that the supply would not be purchased by anyone for a wholly private purpose.

VAT registration numbers are the best evidence that the supply is not received for a wholly private purpose and should be requested. If your customer is unable to provide a VAT number, you can accept alternative evidence. This includes certificates from fiscal authorities, business letterheads or other commercial documents indicating the nature of the customer's activities. Such evidence should be kept as part of your records. Where VAT numbers are available, they should be shown on your invoice.

Some customers may be VAT registered but have non-business as well as business activities. Examples of such customers are government departments and municipal authorities or similar bodies. In such circumstances provided your customer receives the services for the purpose of their business or non-business activities (such as statutory duties or charitable activities) the place of supply is determined by where the customer belongs. If the services you are supplying to your customer are being used for a wholly private purpose, it is not a B2B supply. Instead you will need to decide whether the B2C general rule or one of the other place of supply rules applies.

See section 19 for the additional requirements for suppliers of electronically supplied services.

2.8 Why isn't there just one place of supply rule for all services?

There is not one place of supply rule for all services because, where the customer belongs in one country and the supplier in a different country, rules are needed to determine the correct place of supply of the services in question.

Where the place of supply is in a member state, rules are necessary to avoid the possibility of supplies being taxed more than once, or not at all.

2.9 VAT liability

This notice does not cover VAT liability. There is no general relief for the export of services as there is for goods. Services supplied in the UK may be exempt, zero-rated, standard-rated or liable to VAT at a reduced rate. For information on the VAT liability of supplies see Notice 701/39.

2.10 Tour operators' margin scheme

If you buy, from a third party, travel, hotel, holiday and certain other supplies of a kind enjoyed by travellers and resell them as principal and in your own name, there are different place of supply rules. See Notice 709/5 "Tour operators' margin scheme".

2.11 What are the territorial limits of the UK?

The UK consists of Great Britain, Northern Ireland and the waters within 12 nautical miles of their coastlines. The Isle of Man is treated as part of the UK for VAT purposes and VAT is chargeable in the Isle of Man (under Manx law which generally parallels UK legislation). There is no VAT in the Channel Islands, which are outside the UK and EC for VAT purposes.

The territorial limits of the EC, which are important in establishing where particular types of service are supplied, are shown in section 21.

2.12 Can I recover input tax?

If you supply services, you may recover (subject to the normal rules) input tax related to:

- taxable supplies
- supplies made outside the UK which would be taxable if they were made in the UK, or
- supplies of exempt insurance services and certain exempt financial services, and supplies made outside the UK which would have been exempt supplies if they had been made in the UK, where they are:
  - made to a person who belongs outside the EC
  - supplies directly linked to the export of goods to a place outside the EC, or
  - the making of arrangements for such supplies.

See also Notice 706 "Partial exemption".

2.14 Can businesses recover VAT incurred in other member states?

A business customer who incurs VAT in other member states may be able to claim a refund of VAT incurred on services supplied in the UK. See Notice 723 "Refunds of VAT in the EC for EC and non-EC businesses".

Information about registering for VAT in the UK is given in Notice 700/1 "Should I be registered for VAT?"

2.15 How do I fill in my UK VAT return?

If you are registered for VAT in the UK you must complete a VAT return for each tax period and submit it to HMRC by the due date. Guidance on how to fill in your VAT return is contained in Notice 700/12 "Filling in your VAT return". If you receive supplies of services that are made in the UK and where you are responsible for accounting for any UK VAT due under the reverse charge procedure see paragraph 18.3.

2.16 Could I be liable to register for VAT in other member states?

If you supply services whose place of supply is in another member state, you may be liable to register for VAT in that country (subject to its VAT registration rules). If you do not have an establishment in that member state, you may need to appoint a local tax representative to account for VAT there on your behalf.

Details of contact addresses and other useful information provided by the VAT authorities in other member states can be found on the Commission website.

3 PLACE OF BELONGING

The law on place of belonging is in VATA s 9.

UK VAT law refers to "belonging" whereas EC VAT law refers to "establishment". These two terms have the same meaning for VAT purposes.

3.1 Why are "belonging" rules necessary?

For certain types of supply the place where a supplier or customer belongs determines where services are supplied and who accounts for any VAT due. Rules are needed to ensure that the correct place of supply is identified.

You can find out more information about this in sections:

- 5 – B2B general rule services (supplied where the customer belongs) and B2C general rule services (supplied where the supplier belongs)
- 14 – B2C services supplied where the customer belongs
- 16 – Use and enjoyment of hire of means of transport, letting on hire of goods, telecommunications services and radio and television broadcasting services, and
- 17 – Use and enjoyment of electronically supplied services.

The place of supply of land-related services is where the land is located. See section 6. The place of supply of "where performed" services is generally the place of performance. See section 8. Therefore the place of belonging of either the supplier or the customer does not affect the place of supply of these services.

3.2 When do I belong in the UK?

You belong in the UK for the purposes of either making or receiving supplies of services when any of the following apply:

- you have a *business establishment* (see paragraph 3.3) or some other *fixed* establishment (see paragraph 3.4) in the UK and none elsewhere;
- you have a business establishment in the UK and fixed establishments in other countries, but the UK establishment is most directly connected with making or receiving the supplies in question;
- you have a fixed establishment in the UK and a business establishment and/or fixed establishments overseas, but the UK establishment is most directly connected with making or receiving the supplies in question; or
- you have no business or fixed establishment anywhere, but your *usual place of residence* is the UK. See paragraph 3.5.

3.3 What is a business establishment?

The business establishment is the principal place of business and is usually the head office, headquarters or "seat" from which the business is run. There can be only one such place which may be an office, showroom or factory.

3.3.1 Examples of business establishment

- A business has its headquarters in the UK and branches in France, Italy and Germany. Its business establishment is the headquarters in the UK.

– A company is incorporated in the UK but trades entirely from its head office in Bermuda. Its business establishment is the head office in Bermuda.

3.4 What is a fixed establishment?

A fixed establishment is an establishment other than the business establishment, which has the technical and human resources necessary for providing or receiving services permanently present. A business may have several fixed establishments, which may include a branch of a business or an agency.

If you have a temporary presence of human and technical resources, this does not create a fixed establishment in the UK. For example, an overseas television company sending staff and equipment to the UK to film for a week does not constitute a fixed establishment in the UK.

Where you have establishments in more than one country, you will need to decide which one is most directly connected with a supply. See paragraph 3.6.

3.4.1 Examples of fixed establishment

– An overseas business sets up a branch comprising staff and offices in the UK to provide services. The UK branch is a fixed establishment.
– A company with a business establishment overseas owns a property in the UK which it leases to tenants. The property does not in itself create a fixed establishment. However, if the company has UK offices and staff or appoints a UK agency to carry on its business by managing the property, this creates a fixed establishment in the UK.
– An overseas business contracts with UK customers to provide services. It has no human or technical resources in the UK and therefore sets up a UK subsidiary to act in its name to provide those services. The overseas business has a fixed establishment in the UK created by the agency of the subsidiary.
– A company is incorporated in the UK but trades entirely overseas from its head office in the USA, which is its business establishment. The UK registered office is a fixed establishment.
– A UK company acts as the Operating Member of a consortium for offshore exploitation of oil or gas using a fixed production platform. The rig is a fixed establishment of the Operating Member.

3.5 What is the usual place of residence?

If a limited company or other corporate body has neither a business establishment nor other fixed establishment in any country, its usual place of residence (in other words, its place of belonging) is where it is legally constituted.

Individuals receiving supplies in a private capacity are treated as belonging in the country where they have their usual place of residence. An individual has only one usual place of residence at any point in time. Individuals are normally resident in the country where they have set up home with their family and are in full time employment. They are not resident in a country they are only visiting as a tourist.

3.5.1 Examples of usual place of residence

– The board of directors of a company incorporated in Bermuda, which has no business or fixed establishment anywhere in the world, meet from time to time in different countries, including the UK. The company belongs in Bermuda where it is incorporated.
– A person lives in the UK, but commutes to France daily for work. He belongs in the UK.
– Overseas forces personnel on a tour of duty in the UK live in rented accommodation with their families. They have homes overseas to which they periodically return on leave. They belong in the UK throughout their tour of duty.

3.5.2 What is the usual place of residence of a person with no right to remain in the UK?

For VAT purposes, persons who have not been granted a right or permission to remain in the UK should be treated as belonging in their country of origin. This will apply to, for example, asylum seekers and those entering without permission.

In these circumstances, the country in which individuals have their usual or permanent place of residence can only reasonably be seen to be their country of origin unless and until they are granted the right to remain in the UK.

Once an individual has been granted leave or permission to remain in the UK, he belongs in the UK.

3.6 I have more than one establishment. Where do I belong?

If, as either the supplier or the recipient of services, you have establishments in more than one country, the supplies you make from, or receive at, each establishment have to be looked at separately. For each supply of services, you are regarded as belonging in the country where the establishment most directly connected with that particular supply is located.

To decide which establishment is most directly connected with the supply, you should consider all the facts, including:

- for suppliers, from which establishment the services are actually provided;
- for recipients, at which establishment the services are actually consumed, effectively used or enjoyed;
- which establishment appears on the contracts, correspondence and invoices;
- where the directors or others who entered into the contract are permanently based; *and*
- at which establishment decisions are taken and controls are exercised over the performance of the contracts.

Normally it is the establishment actually providing or receiving the supply of services which is the establishment most directly connected with the supply, even if the contractual position is different.

3.6.1 Examples where a business has more than one establishment

Where a *supplier* has more than one establishment:

- a company whose business establishment is in France contracts with a UK bank to supply French speaking staff for the bank's international desk in London. The French company also has a fixed establishment in the UK created by a branch, which provides staff to other customers. The French establishment deals directly with the UK bank without any involvement of the UK branch. The staff are supplied by the French establishment;
- an overseas business establishment contracts with private customers in the UK to provide information. The services are provided and invoiced by its UK branch. Customers' day to day contact is with the UK branch and they pay the UK branch. The services are actually supplied from the UK branch which is a fixed establishment.

Where a *recipient* has more than one establishment:

- a UK supplier contracts to supply advertising services. Its customer has its business establishment in Austria and a fixed establishment in the UK created by its branch. Although day-to-day contact on routine administrative matters is between the supplier and the UK branch, the Austrian establishment takes all artistic and other decisions about the advertising. The supplies are received at the overseas establishment;
- a UK accountant supplies accountancy services to a UK incorporated company which has its business establishment abroad. However, the services are received in connection with the company's UK tax obligations and therefore the UK fixed establishment, created by the registered office, receives the supply;
- a customer has a business establishment in the UK and a fixed establishment in the USA created by its branch. The UK establishment contracts a UK company to provide staff to the USA branch. The supplier invoices the UK establishment and is paid by them. The services are most directly used by the USA branch and therefore are received at the overseas establishment.

3.7 What if I am unsure where my customer belongs?

If you are unsure where your customer belongs you should refer to paragraphs 3.6 and 3.6.1 for help in determining which of your customer's establishments receives your services. Further factors which may help you decide this include:

- obvious use of your services at a particular establishment (for example, the lease of equipment for use at that establishment);
- taking your instructions from a particular establishment;
- the service relating to business being conducted by your customer in an establishment in a particular country (such as written reports or accounts); *and*

– delivering any "products" (like a mastertape) to a particular establishment.

However, it is always necessary to consider all the facts.

If you are a supplier it is your responsibility to find out at which establishment your customer receives your supplies and therefore whether or not UK VAT is chargeable. If you have established the facts about your customer but are still unsure about where your services are received, you should contact our Helpline for guidance.

3.8 Securities

There is a special rule, known as the "easement" for supplies of securities, where the identity of the purchaser is not known (see paragraph 15.6.4).

4 INTERNATIONAL SERVICES: ZERO-RATING

The law on zero-rating of certain international services is in Group 7 (International services) of Schedule 8 (Zero-Rate) of VATA

Zero-rating (under an extra-statutory concession) also applies to training services supplied to overseas governments. See paragraph 8.2.

Zero-rated supplies are taxable supplies on which the rate of VAT is nil. Related input tax you incur may be recovered subject to the normal rules.

4.1 When does zero-rating apply?

Zero-rating under Group 7 of Sch 8 of VATA can apply to certain international services where the place of supply is the UK. Zero-rating under Group 7 does *not* cover services where the place of supply is outside the UK and consequently outside the scope of UK VAT.

4.2 Which international services can zero-rating apply to?

If the place of supply of the international services is the UK *and* certain conditions are met, zero-rating may apply to the following types of service:

– work on goods for export from the EC. See paragraph 8.6; *and*
– intermediary services. See section 13.

4.2.1 Do I need to keep evidence for zero-rating?

You must keep evidence (for example, commercial documentation) to substantiate the zero-rating of supplies you make.

4.2.2 What if my services do not qualify for zero-rating?

If the place of supply of your services is the UK and they do not qualify for zero-rating, then you should charge UK VAT in the normal way.

5 GENERAL RULE SERVICES

The law on general rule services is in VATA s 7A.

5.1 Why are there two different general rules for the place of supply of services?

From 1 January 2010 there are two different general rules for business to business (B2B) and business to consumer (B2C) supplies of services to better achieve taxation where services are consumed.

5.2 What is the B2B rule for supplies of services?

If you supply B2B services, other than those covered by the special rules described in the other sections of this notice, the place of supply of your services is the place where your customer belongs for the purposes of making your supply (see section 3).

This is known as the B2B general rule. If you supply services that fall under this section and your customer belongs outside the UK, your supply is outside the scope of UK VAT. If your customer belongs outside the EC there may be local taxes which apply.

If your supply is taxable at a standard or reduced rate of VAT (that is to say that the supply is not exempt or zero-rated) and is made to a customer belonging in another member state who is VAT registered there, with effect from 1 January 2010 you may need to complete and submit an EC Sales List. See Notice 725 "The single market".

If however, your customer belongs in the UK, you must account for any UK VAT due.

To decide if you make B2B supplies see paragraph 2.5.

If you provide bought-in supplies of hired means of transport for the direct benefit of a traveller see paragraph 2.10.

If you supply B2B intermediary services where the place of supply is the UK, but the arranged supply is supplied outside the EC you may be able to zero-rate your supply. See section 13.

5.3 What is the B2C general rule for supplies of services?

If you supply B2C services, other than those covered by the special rules described in the other sections of this notice, the place of supply of your services is the place where you belong for the purposes of making your supply (see section 3).

This is known as the B2C general rule. If you supply services that fall under this section and you belong in the UK, you must account for any UK VAT due, no matter where your customer belongs.

To decide if you make B2C supplies see paragraph 2.6.

If you provide bought-in supplies of hired means of transport for the direct benefit of a traveller see paragraph 2.10.

5.4 How do I decide if services fall under the B2C or B2B general rules?

It is not possible to give a conclusive definition of B2C and B2B general rule services. The B2C and B2B general rules will only apply if a supply of services cannot be seen to fall under any of the other rules. Before deciding that a supply falls under the B2C or B2B general rules, you should identify the exact nature of your services and consider them against the other rules.

5.5 Additional rules for supplies of hire of a means of transport, letting on hire of goods, telecommunications services, radio and TV broadcasting services and electronically supplied services

In addition to the rules in this section and section 18 (which covers B2B supplies received in the UK), there are additional rules for supplies of letting on hire of a means of transport, letting on hire of goods, telecommunications services, radio and TV broadcasting services and electronically supplied services, depending on where they are used and enjoyed. See sections 16 and 17.

6 SERVICES RELATING TO LAND

The law on land-related services is in VATA Sch 4A para 1.

6.1 What is the place of supply of services relating to land?

If you supply services that relate to land or property, the place of supply of those services is where the land itself is located, irrespective of where you or your customer belong.

If you supply bought-in supplies of land-related services, such as hotel accommodation, or provide land-related services together with other bought-in supplies (for example, passenger transport), for the direct benefit of a traveller, see paragraph 2.10.

6.2 What is the VAT liability of supplies relating to UK land or property?

This notice deals only with the place of supply of land-related services. Once you have identified a supply of services relating to UK land or property, you then need to determine its VAT liability by referring to Notice 708 "Buildings and construction" and Notice 742 "Land and property".

6.3 What is "land" for the purposes of this section?

For the purposes of this section "land" includes all forms of land and property; growing crops, buildings, walls, fences, civil engineering works or other structures fixed permanently to the land or seabed. It also covers plant, machinery or equipment which is an installation or edifice in its own right, for example, a refinery or fixed oil/gas production platform. Machinery installed in buildings other than as a fixture is normally not regarded as "land" but as "goods".

6.4 Examples of land-related services?

- The supply of hotel accommodation.
- The provision of a site for a stand at an exhibition where the exhibitor obtains the right to a defined area of the exhibition hall. See section 8 where sites are not defined.
- Services supplied in the course of construction, conversion, enlargement, reconstruction, alteration, demolition, repair or maintenance (including painting and decorating) of any building or civil engineering work.
- The supply of plant or machinery, together with an operator, for work on a construction site.
- Services of estate agents, auctioneers, architects, solicitors, surveyors, engineers and similar professional people relating to land, buildings or civil engineering works. This includes the management, conveyancing, survey or valuation of property by a solicitor, surveyor or loss adjuster.
- Services connected with oil/gas/mineral exploration or exploitation relating to specific sites of land or the seabed. See sections 7 and 13 where such services do not relate to specific sites.
- The surveying (such as seismic, geological or geomagnetic) of land or seabed, including associated data processing services to collate the required information.
- Legal services such as conveyancing or dealing with applications for planning permission.
- Packages of property management services which may include rent collection, arranging repairs and the maintenance of financial accounts.
- The supply of warehouse space.

6.5 What if my services are not directly land-related?

This place of supply rule applies only to services which relate *directly* to a specific site(s) of land or property. It does not apply if a supply of services has only an indirect connection with land, or if the land-related service is only an incidental component of a more comprehensive supply of services.

For example, the services of an interior designer contracted to redesign the decor of a particular hotel would be land-related. However, if the same supplier was contracted to create a "corporate" colour scheme/style for a hotel chain to use in their own properties, those design services would not be land-related. See section 5 if you make B2B supplies and sections 14 and 15 if you make B2C supplies of such services.

6.5.1 Examples of services which are not land-related

- Repair and maintenance of machinery which is not installed as a fixture. This is work on goods. See section 5 if you make B2B supplies of such services. See section 8 if you make B2C supplies of such services.
- The hiring out of civil engineering plant on its own, which is the letting on hire of goods.
- The secondment of staff to a building site, which is a supply of staff.
- The legal administration of a deceased person's estate which happens to include property. These are lawyers' services.
- Advice or information relating to land prices or property markets because they do not relate to specific sites.
- Feasibility studies assessing the potential of particular businesses or business potential in a geographic area. Such services do not relate to a specific property or site.
- Provision of a recording studio where technicians are included as part of the supply. These are engineering services.
- Services of an accountant in simply calculating a tax return from figures provided by a client, even where those figures relate to rental income.

See section 5 if you make B2B supplies of such services. See sections 14 and 15 if you make B2C supplies of such services.

6.6 UK customers receiving services relating to UK land

If you are a UK VAT registered recipient of these services and you receive them for business purposes you may be required to account for the reverse charge if your supplier belongs outside the UK. See section 16.

6.7 Non-UK suppliers of services relating to UK land

If you are a supplier who does not belong in the UK, and your customer is not registered for UK VAT, you, as the supplier, are responsible for accounting for any UK VAT due on your supply. If you are not already registered in the UK, you may be liable to register. See paragraph 2.14.

6.8 Liability to register for VAT in other member states

If you supply services relating to land in another member state, you may be liable to register for VAT in that member state. See paragraph 2.16.

7 SERVICES OF THE HIRING OF MEANS OF TRANSPORT

The law on services of hiring of means of transport is in VATA Sch 4A paras 3 and 13A (para 13A is effective on and after 1 January 2013).

Hire of a means of transport does not cover supplies which include the services of a driver, pilot, operator or crew. The place of supply of such transport-related services depends on the nature of the services supplied. See section 11.

For the letting on hire of other goods, see section 5 if you make B2B supplies and sections 14 and 15 if you make B2C supplies.

However, there are additional rules for all hired goods (including letting on hire or leasing means of transport), depending on where they are used and enjoyed (see section 16).

7.1 What is a "means of transport"?

To decide whether goods that you hire are means of transport, you must consider the actual structure and design of the hired goods. This objective consideration applies even where the intended, or actual, use of the hired goods may not be as a means of transport. For example, a yacht is a means of transport even if it is to be used for racing, as is a train which may be leased to a transport museum.

7.1.1 Examples of means of transport

- Ships, boats, yachts, hovercraft, barges or dracones (bulk liquid barges).
- Aircraft.
- Cars, trucks, lorries.
- Motorcycles, cycles.
- Touring caravans and trailers.
- Trailers and semi-trailers.
- Railway wagons.

7.1.2 Examples of goods which are not a means of transport

- Freight containers.
- Static caravans.
- Racing cars where the provision of the car forms part of a supply of sporting services (see section 8).

7.2 What are the rules for the place of supply of services of hiring out means of transport?

There are different rules for the place of supply of services of hiring out means of transport depending on who receives the supply and how long the means of transport is hired for.

7.2.1 What is the place of supply of B2B and B2C services of short-term hire of means of transport?

B2B and B2C short-term hiring of means of transport are supplied where the means of transport is put at the disposal of the hiree.

To decide whether you make B2B or B2C supplies see paragraphs 2.5 and 2.6.

7.2.2 What does "place where the means of transport is put at the disposal of the customer" mean?

The "place where the means of transport is put at the disposal of the customer" means the place where the customer takes actual physical control of the means of transport.

7.2.3 What is short-term and long-term hire of means of transport?

Short-term hire of means of transport is hiring for a continuous period not exceeding 90 days if the means of transport is a vessel and not exceeding 30 days for any other means of transport.

Any hire beyond this period is a long-term hire of means of transport.

To decide whether a particular hire is short or long-term hire you should look at the hire contract(s). See table 2.

7.2.4 Table 2 Short-term or long-term hire of means of transport

When . . .	*if...*
two or more separate contracts for the hire of the same means of transport follow each other with two days or less between them, the term of the first contract needs to be considered in order to decide whether the second term is short-term or long-term.	the two contracts together exceed 30 days (or 90 days for vessels) then the second and subsequent consecutive contracts are treated as long-term hires. If the first contract is genuinely of a short-term hire it will remain so.
there is a second separate contract for short-term hire between the same two parties.	that second separate hire contract relates to a different means of transport or the terms of the hire differ significantly, the contracts will need to be considered separately.
a short-term hire contract is extended.	that extension means that it exceeds the 30 or 90 day period the place of supply is determined by the long-term hire rule, unless it can be satisfactorily demonstrated that the circumstances leading to the events were outside the control of the parties involved.

7.2.5 What is the place of supply of B2B services of long-term hire of means of transport?

B2B supplies of long-term hiring of means of transport are subject to the general rule for the place of supply of services and supplied where the recipient/customer belongs. See section 5.

7.2.6 What is the place of supply of B2C services of long-term hire of means of transport?

From 1 January 2010 to 31 December 2012 inclusive, B2C supplies of the long-term hire of means of transport are subject to the B2C general rule for the place of supply of services and are made where the supplier belongs. See section 5.

On or after 1 January 2013 B2C supplies of the long-term hire of means of transport are made where the recipient/customer belongs, unless the hire is long-term hire of a pleasure boat.

7.2.7 On or after 1 January 2013 what is the place of supply of B2C services of long-term hire of a pleasure boat?

On or after 1 January 2013 the place of supply of B2C services of long-term hire of a pleasure boat will be the place where the pleasure boat is put at the disposal of the customer where the service is provided from the supplier's place of business or fixed establishment in that place.

7.3 Additional rules for hire of means of transport

There are additional rules for any hire of means of transport depending on where the supply is used and enjoyed. See section 16.

7.4 Zero-rating of hired means of transport made in the UK

When supplied in the UK, the hire of certain ships and aircraft is zero rated. See Notice 744C "Ships, aircraft and associated services".

8 SERVICES SUPPLIED "WHERE PERFORMED"

The law on "where performed" services is in the VATA Sch 4A paras 4, 9A, 13, 14 and 14A.

8.1 What services are supplied "where performed"?

The changes to the place of supply rules for services supplied "where performed" are being introduced in two phases. Table 2 below sets out the changes for B2B and B2C supplies.

8.1.1 Table 3 Changes effective from 1 January 2010 and 1 January 2011

Service description	*Place of supply from 1 January 2010*	*Place of supply from 1 January 2011*
Services of work on, or valuation of moveable goods; and ancillary transport services.	B2B supplies are subject to the B2B general rule. See section 5. B2C supplies are made where the services are physically performed.	
Services relating to cultural, artistic, sporting, scientific, educational, entertainment or similar activities (including fairs and exhibitions); and ancillary services relating to such activities, including services of organisers of such activities.	B2B and B2C supplies are made where the services are physically carried out.	B2B supplies are subject to the B2B general rule and the place of supply is where the customer belongs. See section 5. B2C supplies are made where the activities actually take place.
B2B supplies of services in respect of admission to cultural, artistic, sporting, scientific, educational, entertainment or similar events (including fairs and exhibitions); and B2B supplies of ancillary services relating to admission to such events.	Supplied where services physically carried out.	The place of supply is where the events actually take place.

Services covered by this section generally relate to a live event or physical activity. You will need to consider the nature of services that you supply, as terms such as entertainment, sponsorship, or scientific may apply to services which fall under other sections.

If you resell services covered by this section, particularly educational services and services connected with conferences and meetings, together with accommodation or travel, see paragraph 2.10.

8.1.2 Examples of services supplied "where performed"

If you supply these services you should look carefully to see if your supplies are subject to the new B2B general rule, unless your supplies are of admissions services or services related to admissions in which case this section applies. If you make B2C supplies of these services table 3 in paragraph 8.1.1 shows whether your supplies will be affected by the changes effective from 1 January 2010 and 1 January 2011.

– Services of sportspersons appearing in exhibition matches, races or other forms of competition. However, where you receive sponsorship or prize money, you will need to determine whether or not these moneys are received as consideration for a supply. If they are consideration for a supply, the nature of your supply must be determined, see paragraph 8.1.3 and Notice 701/41 "Sponsorship".

- Provision of race prepared cars. Such packages include the hire of the car and support services to ensure optimum maintenance and operation of the car throughout a series of races.
- Scientific services of technicians carrying out tests or experiments in order to obtain data. The final compilation of your record of results, carried out in the UK, will not make the supply liable to UK VAT provided your services were otherwise performed outside the UK.
- Services of an actor or singer, whether or not in front of a live audience.
- Services relating to conferences or meetings.
- Services of an oral interpreter at an event, such as a meeting. For other forms of translation services, see paragraph 8.1.3.
- The right to participate in an exhibition or the provision of an undefined site for a stand at an exhibition. See section 6 for defined sites.
- Services relating to a specific exhibition. This includes carpenters and electricians erecting and fitting out stands at exhibition venues.
- Educational and training services. Such services may be exempt when made in the UK, see Notice 701/30 "Education and vocational training". See paragraph 8.2 for zero-rating of training performed in the UK for overseas Governments. The following interpretive note determines where flying or sailing training is performed.

Note: Flying training is treated as supplied wholly outside the UK provided the trainer aircraft leaves UK airspace and proceeds directly to a destination abroad, and at least 12 hours' training is provided at that place. Sailing training is treated as supplied wholly outside the UK provided all of the training is carried out on a vessel which clears UK territorial waters for a foreign destination. Also, it must remain outside UK territorial waters for the whole of the period of training (except for proceeding directly from and returning directly to the UK).

8.1.3 Examples of services that are not supplied "where performed"

- Services of sportspersons receiving sponsorship money as consideration for product endorsement or publicity appearances. These are advertising services rather than participation in a sporting event.
- Written translation services or interpreters' services which do not take place at an event. These are consultancy services.
- The hire of goods without any additional services, even if the customer uses those goods at an exhibition or concert.

For B2B supplies of such services see section 5. For B2C supplies of such services see sections 14 and 15.

- The provision of a defined site for a stand at an exhibition, which is land-related. See section 6.
- Scientific services which include a recommendation or conclusion. These are services of consultancy or provision of information (for B2B supplies of such services see section 5, for B2C supplies of such services see section 14 and paragraph 15.5; or, if connected with oil/gas/mineral exploration or exploitation of specific sites of land or the seabed, they are land-related see section 6).
- Veterinary services. These are general rule services. See section 5.

8.2 Training performed in the UK for overseas Governments

Non-exempt training services supplied in the UK to overseas Governments for the purposes of their sovereign activities can be zero-rated under an extra-statutory concession.

The relief does not apply if services are received for business purposes. It therefore excludes the training of personnel from Government owned industries or sponsored commercial organisations such as state airlines or nationalised industries.

However, such businesses may be able to claim a refund of VAT paid in the UK, see Notice 723 "Refunds of VAT in the EC for EC and non-EC businesses".

If you supply training services to foreign or overseas Governments your supply will be zero-rated provided both of the following conditions are met:

- the services must be used by the foreign or overseas Government for the furtherance of its sovereign activities (that is not for business purposes), and

- you must obtain and retain a written statement from the foreign or overseas Government concerned, or its accredited representative, certifying that the trainees are employed in furtherance of its sovereign activities.

8.2.1 What do we mean by "foreign or overseas Government"?

"Foreign or overseas Government" includes overseas Government officials, public servants and members of organisations such as the armed forces, the police, the emergency services and similar bodies answerable to the Government concerned.

8.2.2 When are training services not zero-rated?

Training services are not zero-rated:

- when the conditions in paragraph 8.2 are not met
- when the training services are provided to personnel from Government-owned businesses or sponsored commercial organisations such as state airlines or nationalised industries, or
- when the training services are exempt from VAT. See Notice 701/30 "Education and vocational training" for further details.

8.2.3 Does zero-rating extend to associated services?

Zero-rating only applies to the supply of the actual training and does not extend to any associated services which are supplied separately, such as accommodation or transport.

8.3 Exhibition organising

If you supply these services you should look carefully to see if your supplies are subject to the new B2B general rule, unless your supplies are of admissions services or services related to admissions in which case this section applies. If you make B2C supplies of these services table 3 shows whether your supplies will be affected by the changes effective from 1 January 2010 and 1 January 2011.

"Exhibition organiser" is a very general description. It covers a variety of services which are performed in different ways. It is important to establish the nature of services rather than relying on how the supply is described. For example:

- if you are an exhibition owner, your services will be of the event itself. Your supplies are likely to be of stand sites, visitor admission or advertising services (such as space in an event publication). Your services will not be ancillary exhibition services as they would not be of organising the event. See sections 5, 6, 14 and 15;
- if you act as an organiser for an exhibition owner in making all the arrangements for the event on behalf of the owner, your services are ancillary to exhibition services. See table 3;
- if you are a representative body assisting exhibitors to attend exhibitions by providing a single package of various services which may include exhibition space obtained from the owner, consultancy, design, provision of displays, transport and stand construction, your services are supplied where they are physically carried out and from a January 2011 where the activities or events take place. See table 2.

8.3.1 Representative bodies and exhibitions held in other member states

If you supply a comprehensive package of services for an exhibition in another member state, you are supplying services which are performed at the venue. You may be required to account for VAT in that member state. If you are not required to account for VAT in that member state and your services are otherwise physically carried out in the UK, your services are supplied in the UK.

8.4 Ancillary services

If you supply these services you should look carefully to see if your supplies are subject to the new B2B general rule from 1 January 2011, unless your supplies are of admissions services or services related to admissions in which case this section applies. If you make B2C supplies of these services table 2 shows whether your supplies will be affected by the changes effective from 1 January 2010 and 1 January 2011.

The place of supply of services which are ancillary to:

- cultural, artistic, sporting, scientific, educational entertainment activities, and
- exhibitions, conferences or meetings

is where those ancillary services are physically carried out and from 1 January 2011 is where the activities actually take place. Ancillary services include the services of organising such supplies.

8.4.1 Examples of ancillary services

- Services of a co-ordinator in administering arrangements for a sporting event on behalf of a promoter.
- Services of lighting or sound technicians at a concert. This also covers the hire of equipment included as part of the same supply. Where equipment is hired separately, see section 5 if you make B2B supplies of such services and sections 14 and 15 if you make B2C supplies of such services.

8.4.2 Examples of services not included as ancillary services

- A supply of advertising services to a sponsor by the promoter/owner of a sporting event.
- The simple hiring of equipment for use at a concert, without the services of technicians or operators.

See section 5 if you make B2B supplies and sections 14 and 15 if you make B2C supplies of such services.

- Certain services which may be described as "exhibition organising". See paragraph 8.3.

8.4.3 Ancillary transport services

See section 5 if you make B2B supplies of ancillary transport services. If you make B2C supplies of such services see section 11.

8.5 Valuation of, or work carried out on, goods

From 1 January 2010 B2C supplies of valuations of, or work on, another person's goods are supplied where those services are physically performed. B2B supplies of such services are subject to the B2B general rule. See section 5.

For the purposes of these place of supply provisions, goods must constitute tangible moveable property. See paragraph 8.5.1.

8.5.1 What are "goods"?

"Goods" include all forms of tangible moveable property, covering both finished commodities and raw materials but does not include immoveable property such as permanently installed goods and fixtures. See paragraph 6.3.

8.5.2 What does "work carried out on goods" mean?

Work carried out on goods is essentially any physical service carried out on another person's goods. Examples include:

- processing, manufacturing or assembling
- repairs, cleaning or restoration
- alterations, calibrations, insulating, lacquering, painting, polishing, resetting (of jewellery), sharpening, varnishing, waterproofing, and
- nominations to stallions/covering (that is, attempting to secure the pregnancy of mares).

8.5.3 Examples of valuation services or work on goods

- Services of a sub-contractor installing machinery supplied by another person.
- Simple valuation of goods by loss adjusters, average adjusters, motor assessors, surveyors and other experts in connection with an insurance proposal or claim. The final compilation of a related report in a different country from the goods will not change the

place of supply from the country where valuation work is performed. However, where valuation forms only a part of your professional services your supplies are of consultancy. See section 5 if you make B2B supplies and sections 14 and 15 if you make B2C supplies of such services.

8.5.4 Examples of supplies which are not valuation services or work on goods

- Work which is not mainly physical work performed on the goods themselves. For example, where inspection, is not "work on goods". It can be "valuation", but only if that is the purpose of the inspection. However, such activities may form part of a consultancy service.
- Testing and analysis of goods. The physical work simply provides data for the required analysis.

See section 5 if you make B2B supplies and sections 14 and 15 if you make B2C supplies of such services.

- Valuation of, or work carried out on, land or property. See section 6.
- Veterinary services. See section 5.

8.5.5 Does zero-rating apply for work on goods?

Certain supplies of work on goods (but not valuation of goods) for export from the EC are zero-rated when made in the UK. See section 4 and paragraph 8.6. Zero-rating is also available for certain processing services relating to zero-rated goods.

8.6 Zero-rating of work on goods for export from the EC

The law relating to the zero-rating of work on goods for export from the EC is in VATA, Sch 8, Group 7 Item 1.

Work on goods for export from the EC is zero-rated provided that all of the following conditions are met:

- the goods on which the work is to be carried out, must have been obtained, acquired within, or imported into the EC for the purposes of being worked on, and
- the goods must not be used in the UK between the time of leaving the supplier's premises and exportation, and
- on completion of the work, the goods are intended to be and, in fact are, exported from the EC either:
  - by you, the supplier of the service, (or someone acting on your behalf), or
  - if your customer belongs outside the EC, by your customer (or someone acting on your customer's behalf). See section 3 for guidance on place of belonging.

8.6.1 Examples of work on goods which may qualify for zero-rating under this section

- Alterations and repairs, calibrations, cleaning, insulating, lacquering, painting, polishing, resetting (jewellery), cutting (of precious stones), sharpening, varnishing and waterproofing.
- The repair of freight containers.
- Services relating directly to the "covering" (that is, attempting to secure the pregnancy) of a mare, provided the mare is exported before the birth of the foal.
- The gelding and/or breaking in of young horses (for example training yearling racehorses to the stage where they can be ridden safely in races). However, actual racing is not accepted as training and if any horse is acquired or temporarily imported with the intention of racing it in the EC before re-export, zero-rating will not apply.
- The restoration of classic cars.

8.6.2 Examples of services which do not qualify for zero-rating under this section

- Work which is not physical work carried out on the goods themselves (for example, mere inspection of goods or testing and analysis of goods is not "work on goods").
- Repair or other work which becomes necessary in the EC after acquisition or importation of goods, such as incidental running repairs, while the goods are being used (even though they may be subsequently exported).

– Valuation services.

8.6.3 How do I treat goods supplied with my services?

Any goods used in conjunction with the work performed, such as spare parts, paint, and so on, should be treated as part of the supply of services.

8.6.4 What export evidence do I need?

In order to zero-rate a supply of such services you must obtain and keep satisfactory official or commercial evidence of the export of the goods to a place outside the EC.

Examples of acceptable evidence of export are contained in Notice 703 "VAT: Export of goods from the United Kingdom".

If, in anticipation of export to a place outside the EC, you zero-rate your supply under this item but, in the event, the goods are used in the EC before export or export does not take place, you will need to reconsider both the place of supply of your services and, if it is the UK, the appropriate VAT rate that applies.

8.7 UK customers receiving "where performed" services made in the UK

If you are a UK VAT registered recipient of a "where performed" service which is performed in the UK you may be required to account for any UK VAT due under the reverse charge procedure if your supplier belongs outside the UK. See section 18.

8.8 Non-UK suppliers of "where performed" services made in the UK

If you are a supplier who does not belong in the UK, and your customer is not registered for UK VAT, you, as the supplier, are responsible for accounting for any UK VAT due on your "where performed" supply if it is supplied in the UK. If you are not already registered in the UK, you may be liable to register. See paragraph 2.14.

8.9 Could I be liable to register in other member states?

If you supply "where performed" services and the place of supply is in another member state, you may be liable to register for VAT in that member state. See paragraph 2.16.

9 RESTAURANT AND CATERING SERVICES

The law on the place of supply of restaurant and catering services is in VATA Sch 4A paras 5 and 6.

9.1 Place of supply of restaurant and catering services

The place of supply of restaurant and catering services is where the services are physically carried out.

There is a separate rule for EC on-board restaurant and catering services. See paragraph 9.2.

9.2 Place of supply of EC on-board restaurant and catering services

The place of supply of EC on-board restaurant and catering services supplied on a ship, aircraft or train for the transportation of passengers on an intra-EC journey is the member state of departure.

10 PASSENGER TRANSPORT

The law on place of supply of passenger transport is in VATA Sch 4A, para 2.

10.1 Place of supply of passenger transport

The place of supply of passenger transport is where it takes place. Therefore where passenger transport takes place in the UK, the UK is the place of supply. Special rules apply to some transport by sea or air. See paragraph 10.2.

To the extent that such transport takes place outside the UK, it is outside the scope of UK VAT, except where paragraph 10.2 applies. However, if a journey involves travel through another member state, the supply of passenger transport will be made in that member state to the extent that the transport takes place there.

See Notice 744A "Passenger Transport" for detailed guidance on the VAT treatment of passenger transport.

This notice also describes the VAT treatment of passenger transport supplied in the UK by non-UK suppliers.

If you supply bought-in supplies of passenger transport, or provide passenger transport together with *other* bought-in supplies, such as hotel accommodation, for the direct benefit of a traveller, see paragraph 2.10.

10.2 What are the special rules for passenger transport that leaves and re-enters the UK?

The special rules are that provided the ship, aircraft or vehicle does not put in, land or stop (except in an emergency or involuntarily) in any other country, journeys which begin and end in the same country, but take place partly outside that country, are treated as taking place wholly within that country. This applies even if the journey is part of a longer journey involving travel to or from another country.

10.3 Zero-rating of intermediary services made in the UK

Some supplies of intermediaries are zero-rated when supplied in the UK. See section 12 and Notices:

– 744A "Passenger Transport"; *and*
– 709/6 "Travel agents and tour operators".

11 B2C SUPPLIES OF FREIGHT TRANSPORT, RELATED SERVICES AND CHARTER PARTY CONTRACTS

The law on fB2C supplies of reight transport and related services is in VATA Sch 4A paras 11 and 12.

11.1 What does this section cover?

This section is intended to give only a basic overview of the VAT treatment of B2C supplies of freight transport and related services. B2B supplies of freight transport and related services fall under the B2B general rule (see section 5). The table below outlines the main categories of these types of services and gives a general indication as to where the place of supply is. However, for full and detailed guidance on the VAT treatment of such services you should refer to Notice 744B "Freight transport and associated services".

If the type of supply is:	*the place of supply will be:*
B2C domestic freight transport (which takes place wholly within one country);	where the transport takes place.
B2C international freight transport (between the EC and non-EC countries, or wholly outside the EC);	where the transport takes place.
B2C intra-EC freight transport (from one member state to another);	the member state in which the transportation begins.
B2C ancillary transport services relating to domestic, international freight transport or intra-EC freight transport;	where the services are physically performed.
making arrangements for or facilitation of B2C domestic or international freight transport;	where the transport takes place.
making arrangements for or facilitation of B2C intra-EC freight transport;	the member state in which the transportation begins.
making arrangements for or facilitation of related B2C ancillary services;	where the ancillary services are physically performed.

11.2 Ship and aircraft charter party contracts

If you supply the whole of a ship or aircraft with crew under a formal written charter party contract, the place of supply is subject to the general rule. B2B supplies are made where the customer belongs. B2C supplies are made where you belong. See section 5. But if:

- you supply a whole ship or aircraft without crew under a written charter party agreement, your supply is the hire of a means of transport (see sections 5 and 7);
- you supply a whole ship or aircraft with crew but without a written charter party contract, or of part of the seating capacity in a ship or aircraft, the place of supply of such transport-related services depends on the nature of the services supplied.

See Notice 744C "Ships, aircraft and associated services" for further information.

11.3 Zero-rating of intermediary services made in the UK

Some supplies of intermediary services are zero-rated when supplied in the UK. See section 13 and Notices:

- 744B "Freight transport and associated services"; and
- 744C "Ships, aircraft and associated services".

12 B2C INTERMEDIARIES

The law on B2C intermediary services covered by this section is in VATA Sch 4A para 10. Most B2B intermediary services fall under the B2B general rule, see section 5.

12.1 When am I an intermediary for the purposes of this section?

You are an intermediary for the purposes of this section if you act as a third party in arranging, or even simply facilitating, the making of supplies. An intermediary arranges supplies between two other parties; a supplier and that supplier's customer. Intermediaries may be referred to as brokers, buying or selling agents, go-betweens, commissionaires or agents acting in their own name (undisclosed agents). Payments for their services are often described as commission.

In this section, your customer is the person to whom you supply your intermediary services. This can be either the supplier or the recipient of the arranged supply (and in some cases may even be both).

12.2 Are all intermediary services covered by this section?

Not all intermediary services are covered by this section. Most B2B intermediary services fall under the B2B general rule and are supplied where the customer belongs, see section 5.

12.3 What determines the place of supply of intermediary services in this section?

The place of supply of your intermediary services is where the underlying arranged supply is made.

12.4 How do I establish the place of supply of arranged supplies of services?

You can establish the place of supply of arranged supplies of services by referring to the appropriate section of this notice.

Type of arranged supply:	*For further information see:*
hired means of transport;	sections 5 and 7;
land-related services;	section 6;
"where performed" services;	section 8;
passenger transport, B2C domestic or international freight transport;	sections 10 and 11;
B2C services supplied where the customer belongs;	sections 14 and 15;
general rule services.	section 5.

12.5 How do I establish the place of supply of arranged goods?

The place of supply of arranged supplies of goods is determined by the place of supply of the underlying supply of goods. The place of supply of goods is generally where the goods are located when they are supplied. However, there are special rules for imported goods (from outside the EC) and installed or assembled goods:

- the place of supply of goods imported by *the supplier* is the member state of importation;
- the place of supply of goods imported by *the customer* is outside the EC;
- the place of supply of installed or assembled goods is where they are installed or assembled.

12.6 Intermediary services supplied in the UK

If you are an intermediary and the place of supply of your arranging service is the UK, but the place of supply of the service being arranged is outside the EC, your supply in the UK can be zero-rated. See section 13. This does not include banking, financial and insurance services which are exempt in the UK.

13 ZERO-RATING OF INTERMEDIARY SERVICES MADE IN THE UK

The law on zero-rating of certain intermediary services made in the UK is in VATA Sch 8 Group 7 Item 2.

13.1 When should I consider whether zero-rating applies to my intermediary services?

If you have established that the place of supply of your intermediary services is the UK you should then consider whether zero-rating applies.

You can zero-rate the supply of the making of arrangements for:

- the export of any goods to a place outside the member states
- a supply of services which is itself zero-rated as work on goods for export from the EC. See paragraph 8.6, or
- any supply of services which is made outside the member states.

Zero-rating under these provisions only applies to the actual making of arrangements for eligible supplies. It does not extend to services which simply facilitate supplies.

For further information see section 4, paragraph 8.6 and Notices:

- 744A "Passenger Transport";
- 744B "Freight transport and associated services";
- 744C "Ships, aircraft and associated services"; and
- 709/6 "Travel agents and tour operators".

13.1.1 Examples of zero-rated intermediary services

- If you obtain an order from an overseas buyer of UK-produced goods, and those goods are actually exported from the EC, your supply of services to the UK exporter or the overseas buyer is zero-rated. You must obtain suitable commercial evidence of export. See Notice 703 "Export of goods from the United Kingdom" (**Part V8**).
- If you arrange for a person in the UK to provide a repair service, which is itself zero-rated under VATA 1994, Sch 8, Group 7, Item 1, your supply is also zero-rated. See paragraph 8.6.
- If you arrange for a person who belongs in the UK to supply consultancy services to a person who belongs in Canada, your supply to the UK consultant is zero-rated. This is because the place of supply of the consultancy service is outside the EC – where the customer belongs – Canada. Therefore, you are arranging a supply that is made outside the member states. See sections 5,14 and 15 for guidance on the place of supply of consultancy type services.

13.1.2 Examples of intermediary services which are not zero-rated

- The making of arrangements for the supply of exempt insurance or finance. See Notices 701/36 "Insurance" and 701/49 "Finance and Securities".

- The making of arrangements for a supply of freight transport is not zero-rated under this provision. However, it may be eligible for zero-rating under a different provision, see Notice 744B "Freight transport and associated services".
- Services supplied by a person acting as a principal, even if their trading title or classification includes the word "agent" or "agency".
- If you act as an intermediary in arranging a supply of services within the EC.
- If you arrange for a supply of goods which are supplied within the EC, and those goods remain in the EC. See Notice 700 "The VAT Guide" for information on the place of supply of goods and Notice 725 "The single market".

13.2 Am I liable to register for VAT if the place of supply of my services is the UK?

If you make taxable supplies in the UK above the registration threshold, you are liable to register for VAT. However, if all of your supplies are zero-rated you may apply for exemption from registration. If the value of your supplies is below the threshold you may also register on a voluntary basis. Further information on all matters relating to VAT registration can be found in Notice 700/1 "Should I be registered for VAT?"

13.3 Non-UK intermediaries arranging supplies made in the UK

If you are a non-UK intermediary arranging a supply which is supplied in the UK and your customer is not UK VAT registered, you, as the supplier, are responsible for accounting for any UK VAT due on your supply. If you are not already registered in the UK, you may be liable to register. See paragraph 2.14.

13.4 Liability to register in other member states

If you supply services of arranging a supply which is supplied in another member state and your customer is not EC VAT registered, you may be liable to register for VAT in that member state. See paragraph 2.16.

14 B2C SERVICES SUPPLIED WHERE THE CUSTOMER BELONGS

The law on B2C services supplied in a customer's country is in VATA Sch 4A para 16

14.1 When do I need to refer to this section?

You need to refer to this section if you belong in the UK and supply services in section 15. If you are unsure whether you belong in the UK, see section 3.

See section 20 for electronically supplied services where the supplier belongs outside the EC.

14.2 What do I need to know to decide if my services fall under this section?

You need to know:

- whether your services are covered by section 15;
- who your customer is (that is, who is the recipient of your supply); and
- where your customer belongs for the purposes of receiving your supply. See section 3.

14.3 What is the place of supply of my services if my customer belongs outside the EC?

If, as a UK supplier, you supply any of the services in section 15 to a customer who belongs outside the EC, your services are supplied in your customer's country and are outside the scope of UK and VAT. B2C supplies are explained in paragraph 2.6.

However, there are additional rules for the B2C letting on hire of goods, telecommunications services, radio and television broadcasting services (see section 16).

14.3.1 Example of a supply of services supplied outside the EC

- If you supply accountancy services to a business or private individual who belongs in the Channel Islands, the place of supply of your services is outside the EC. This is because your customer belongs outside the EC. You should not charge VAT.

14.4 How do I satisfy myself that this section applies?

To satisfy yourself that this section applies you should obtain commercial evidence showing that your customer belongs outside the EC.

14.5 When does this section not apply?

This section does not apply if:

- you cannot determine where your customer belongs;
- your customer belongs in the UK; or
- your customer belongs in another member state.

In such cases and provided the additional rules for the letting on hire of goods, telecommunications services and radio and television broadcasting services do not apply (see paragraph 14.6) your supplies are subject to the B2C general rule and are supplied in the UK. See section 5.

14.6 What are the additional place of supply rules for letting on hire of goods, telecommunications services, radio and television broadcasting services?

Paragraphs 14.3 and 14.4 apply to B2C supplies of letting on hire of goods, telecommunications services and radio and television broadcasting services unless these services are:

- received by a customer belonging outside the EC but the services are used in the UK; or
- received by a UK customer, or a customer in another member state, but the services are used outside the EC.

In these cases you can establish the place of supply by referring to the appropriate section of this notice.

Description of service:	*Dealt with in:*
letting on hire of goods;	sections 16 and 22;
telecommunications services;	sections 16 and 22;
radio and television broadcasting services;	sections 16 and 22;

14.7 Zero-rating of intermediary services made in the UK

If your services of the making of arrangements for supplies of services (which are themselves made outside the EC) are supplied in the UK, they can be zero-rated. See section 13. This does not include banking, financial and insurance services which are exempt in the UK.

15 SCHEDULE 4A, PARAGRAPH 16(2)(A)-(K) – B2C SERVICES THAT CAN BE SUPPLIED IN A CUSTOMER'S COUNTRY

The law which lists the services that can be supplied in a customer's country is in the VATA, Sch 4A, para 16(2)(a)-(k).

Remember, this section covers a list of services. It does not determine where supplies of these services are made.

When these services are made by UK suppliers, see section 14.

15.1 What kind of services are covered by this section?

The common feature of services covered by this section is that their place of performance can be indeterminate or variable and they are easily undertaken in a different place to where a supplier has established a business. They are often intangible in nature.

15.2 Paragraph 16(2)(a) of Sch 4A: Transfers and assignments of copyright, patents, licences, trademarks and similar rights

15.2.1 What types of services fall within para 16(2)(a)?

This paragraph covers transfers, assignments and grants of copyright, patents, licences, trademarks and other similar rights. Similar rights are intellectual property rights which are capable of being legally enforced. Payments for these intellectual rights are often known as "royalties". They can be made on a regular and continuing basis or take the form of a single, one-off fee. Services which do not involve intellectual property are not covered even though they may be described as a right or licence.

15.2.2 Examples of services within para 16(2)(a)

- The granting of a licence to use computer software.
- The transfer of permission to use a logo.
- The granting of a right by a photographer for one of his photographs to be published in a magazine article. This includes material which is digitally downloaded to the customer.

15.2.3 Examples of exclusions from para 16(2)(a)

- The supply of individual shares in goods, for example an animal or yacht, even though certain rights may be included in the supply.
- The supply of a right to obtain reduced rates for admission to conferences and meetings as well as similar discounts on facilities available to members of clubs, associations or societies in return for a subscription.
- The supply of the right to occupy land or property including hotel accommodation. See section 6.
- The granting of a right to a future supply of a service. The place of supply of that right will be the same place as the underlying supply to which the right relates. This will be the case even in situations where the right is never exercised. A right to services includes a reference to any right, option or priority with respect to the supply of services and to the supply of an interest deriving from any right to services.

15.3 Paragraph 16(2)(b) of Sch 4A: Acceptance of any obligation to refrain from pursuing or exercising, in whole or part, any business activity or any such rights as are referred to in para 16(2)(a) above

15.3.1 What types of services fall within para 16(2)(b)?

This paragraph covers entering into agreements not to pursue or undertake any business activity and refraining from exercising, or relinquishing, those rights covered by para 16(2)(a) of Sch 4A. See paragraph 15.2.

15.3.2 Examples of services within para 16(2)(b)

- The vendor of a business accepting an undertaking not to compete with the purchaser.
- Agreement by the owner of a trademark to refrain from using it.

15.4 Paragraph 16(2)(c) of Sch 4A: Advertising services

15.4.1 What types of services fall within para 16(2)(c)?

This paragraph covers all services of publicising another person's name or products with a view to encouraging their sale. It includes supplies of advertising services in the established media: for example, of radio or television advertising time; of the right to place an advertisement on a hoarding; or of advertising space in any publication. It also covers newer promotional methods such as an entry in a telephone enquiry directory or advertising space in any electronic location.

Advertising or promotional messages may be disseminated in numerous ways. This paragraph covers everything provided as part of an advertising campaign, even if elements of the campaign would have fallen under other place of supply rules had they been supplied in isolation.

15.4.2 Example of advertising services

- Website advertising.

15.4.3 Example of an exclusion from advertising services

- The provision of space or stands at a trade fair or exhibition. See sections 6 and 8.

15.5 Paragraph 16(2)(d) of Sch 4A: Services of consultants, engineers, consultancy bureaux, lawyers, accountants, and other similar services; data processing and provision of information, other than any services relating to land

15.5.1 What types of services fall within para 16(2)(d)?

This paragraph covers a wide range of services of different natures. It covers services of consultants, engineers, consultancy bureaux, lawyers and accountants as well as other services which are similar to them. Data processing services and the provision of information are also included. It does not matter how supplies of these services are delivered to a customer, which may be by electronic transmission, courier or mail. However, where any of these services relate to land or property they are excluded from para 16(2)(d) of Sch 4A. See section 6.

15.5.2 What are services of consultants and consultancy bureaux?

Services of consultants and consultancy bureaux cover the normal services of experts in all professional areas who act in an accepted professional or advisory capacity. Examples include:

- research and development
- market research
- written translation services or interpreters' services which do not take place at an event, such as interpreting services for a telephone conference. See section 8 for oral interpreting at an event
- testing and analysis of goods (for example, drugs, chemicals and domestic electrical appliances). The essential nature of such services is analysis by experts who use the results of the testing to reach a professional conclusion, such as whether goods meet specified standards
- writing scientific reports
- production of customised ("bespoke" or "specific") computer software, excluding digitally downloaded software, as well as the services of adapting existing packages. However, some "off-the-shelf" software packages are treated as supplies of goods, and
- software maintenance involving upgrades, advice and resolving any problems. The place of performance is not relevant as solutions may be provided by telephone conversations, remote links or attending a mainframe site. However, a contract for simply maintaining computer hardware relates to work on goods. See section 8.

15.5.3 Examples of exclusions from services of consultants and consultancy bureaux

- Services of consultants and consultancy bureaux are excluded from para 16(2)(d) of Sch 4A if they relate to specific land or property.
- Supplies described as management services, unless they can be shown to be essentially of consultancy services. However, such services may fall elsewhere within para 16(2)(d) of Sch 4A.
- Clerical or secretarial services, the provision of office facilities and archiving services. See section 5.
- Services provided by a consultant which are outside the supplier's

15.5.4 What are services of engineers?

Services of engineers cover engineering design or consultancy services. Engineers generally, but not always, possess formal qualifications. The services must be of a type expected of an expert or professional. Examples include:

- the provision of intellectual engineering advice or design. This includes overseeing the resultant physical work, provided that any such supervision is merely to ensure that the design or other advice is properly implemented, and
- services of engineers/technicians within the entertainment industry. This covers editors and sound engineers producing an edit master from which copies can be made (films, videos, compact discs or audio tapes) as well as those who exercise a degree of artistic control or influence over material.

15.5.5 Examples of exclusions from services of engineers

- Services of surveyors and consultants consisting primarily of work such as design, surveying, site supervision or valuation where these directly relate to land or property. See section 6.
- Services carried out by an engineer which consist wholly or mainly of physical work on goods, including installation of goods. See section 8.

15.5.6 What are services of lawyers and accountants?

Services of lawyers and accountants include services normally provided by lawyers, accountants, solicitors, barristers or auditors in their professional capacities, except where those services directly relate to land or property. See section 6. Examples include:

- legal and accountancy services in the *general* administration or winding up of a deceased's estate even if that estate includes land or property. Such supplies are not made to beneficiaries but to the estate. This is seen as whoever is appointed executor or administrator, although they may also be a beneficiary; and
- services described as management services, the essential nature of which comprise accountancy or legal services.

15.5.7 Examples of exclusions from services of lawyers and accountants

- Services consisting primarily of work which directly relates to land or property, such as:
  - property management,
  - conveyancing,
  - obtaining planning consent, or
  - a claim of ownership over a particular piece of land or property. See section 6.
- Clerical or secretarial services, which includes the keeping of financial records. See section 5.

15.5.8 What are similar services?

Similar services include services which are similar to those normally provided by consultants, consultancy bureaux, engineers, lawyers, and accountants. Examples include:

- services of loss adjusters and assessors in assessing the validity of claims (except when these services relate to land). Such services may include examination of goods to establish a value for damage or deterioration as well as negotiating a settlement amount;
- services of surveyors, providing opinions which do not relate to specific sites;
- architects' services where there is no specific site of land. See section 6;
- design services;
- services of specialists or technicians which are essentially creative or artistic in nature; and
- services of film directors or producers, where their services are not of rights already covered by para 16(2)(a) of Sch 4A. See paragraph 15.2.

15.5.9 Examples of exclusions from similar services

- Services provided by architects and surveyors which directly relate to land or property. This includes surveying, site supervision, conveyancing, valuation and obtaining planning consent. See section 6.
- Loss adjusting services in relation to claims on land or property (see section 6) and services provided by a loss adjuster which are simply the valuation of goods (see section 8).

15.5.10 What is data processing?

For the purposes of para 16(2)(d) of Sch 4A, data processing is the application of programmed instructions on existing data which results in the production of required information.

15.5.11 Examples of exclusions from data processing

- Services which simply include an element of data processing. Where this is simply required for a contract to be completed, the nature of the actual contracted services determines which section applies.

- Processing data from seismic surveys where the computer analysis relates to a specified area of land or seabed. See section 6.
- Simple re-formatting where there is no change to the meaning of the content.

15.5.12 What is provision of information?

Provision of information covers the supplying of knowledge of any type and in any form. Information includes facts, data, figures and other material. Examples include:

- tourist information;
- weather forecasts;
- information supplied by a private enquiry agent;
- telephone helpdesk services (such as for computer software);
- satellite, navigational and location services; and
- provision of on-line information.

15.5.13 Examples of exclusions from provision of information

- The delivery or transmission of another person's information by whatever means. See section 11 for transporting goods and for electronic delivery see paragraphs 15.10 and 15.12.
- Information relating to specific land or property. See section 6.

15.5.14 Does it matter which part of para16(2)(d) of Sch 4A applies to a service?

It does not matter which part of para 16(2)(d) of Sch 4A applies to a service. Provided a supply of services falls within para 16(2)(d) of Sch 4A it is not necessary to determine which part within para 16(2)(d) of Sch 4A best describes the supply as the place of supply will be the same.

15.6 Paragraph 16(2)(e) of Sch 4A: Banking, financial and insurance services (including reinsurance), other than the provision of safe deposit facilities

15.6.1 What types of services fall within para 16(2)(e)?

This paragraph covers all banking, financial and insurance services. Many, but not all, of these are exempt when made in the UK. See Notices 701/36 "Insurance" and 701/49 "Finance".

15.6.2 Examples of banking, financial and insurance services

- Granting of mortgages and loans; selling debts.
- The storage of gold bullion or gold coins by a bank or a dealer in gold who is a subsidiary of a bank.
- The sale of securities as principal.
- The sale of unallocated precious metals (gold, silver, platinum, palladium, rhodium, ruthenium, osmium and iridium) or of unallocated precious metal coins. (Goods are unallocated if they remain an unidentifiable part of a larger stock of goods held by the supplier).
- Debt collection services.
- Portfolio management services.
- The provision of insurance or reinsurance.
- The supply of financial futures and financial options.
- Trustee services.
- Commodity brokers' services of arranging transactions in futures and options.

15.6.3 Examples of exclusions from banking, financial and insurance services

- Services of physical safe custody – other than those in paragraph 15.6.2.
- Rent collection services. See section 6.

15.6.4 Securities

Where securities are sold by UK suppliers and the place where the purchaser cannot be determined, you may apply a special rule, known as the "easement". For full details on how this works, you should refer to Notice 701/49 "Finance".

15.7 Paragraph 16(2)(f) of Sch 4A: The provision of access to, and transport or transmission through, natural gas and electricity distribution systems and the provision of other directly linked services

15.7.1 What types of services fall within para 16(2)(f)?

This paragraph covers supplies of services which allow access to, and actual use of, the distribution networks. The distribution systems are the transmission networks of pipelines, cables and interconnectors, which enable the national and international transport of gas and electricity to be carried out. They provide the essential link between producers and consumers of natural gas and electricity within Europe.

Also included are "directly linked" services. These are services which, although not directly involving use of the systems, are clearly an adjunct to such usage.

15.7.2 Examples of services within para 16(2)(f)?

- Use of the gas National Transmission System.
- Use of the National Grid.
- Provision of data on network usage.
- Storage of gas within the natural gas distribution system.
- Services involving injection of gas into the system.

15.7.3 Examples of exclusions from para 16(2)(f)

- Balancing and imbalance charges.
- Contract termination payments.
- Fees/subscriptions for membership of regulatory or trade bodies.
- Brokerage fees.

15.8 Paragraph 16(2)(g) of Sch 4A: The supply of staff

15.8.1 What types of services fall within paragraph 16(2)(g)?

This paragraph covers the supply of staff. A supply of staff is the placing of personnel under the general control and guidance of another party as if they become employees of that other party. You must distinguish between a supply of staff and a supply of other services which you make by using the staff yourself. The latter is not a supply of staff even if you charge by the hour.

When a supplier uses employees to provide whatever service they are contracted to supply (under a contract for services) to a customer, it is not a supply of staff by the supplier but a supply of other services.

15.8.2 Examples of supplies of staff

- If you supply (which may be described as a secondment, transfer or placement) a typist to your customer and that typist comes under their general control and direction as an employee, your supply is of staff.
- The supply, secondment, loan, hire, lease or transfer *as principals* of personnel for a consideration by bodies such as employment and recruitment businesses, agencies or bureaux.
- The transfer for a fee by a sports club of a professional sportsman who has a contract of service with the club, such as a professional footballer.

15.8.3 Examples of exclusions from supplies of staff

- The supply by a freelancer or other person of a specific service or services under a contract for services. The place of supply will depend on the nature of the services provided.
- Supplies by employment or recruitment businesses or agencies, of making arrangements for the supply of staff between other parties (see section 12).
- If you are a company that employs typists and you supply *typing services* under a specific typing assignment for a third party using those typists, your service is not a supply of staff but of typing services. See section 5.

15.9 Paragraph 16(2)(h) of Sch 4A: The letting on hire of goods other than means of transport

15.9.1 What types of services fall within para 16(2)(h)?

This paragraph covers the letting on hire, or leasing, of all goods other than those which are a means of transport (see sections 5 and 7). Goods include all forms of movable property but exclude land and property or equipment and machinery installed as a fixture.

This paragraph does not cover supplies of the letting on hire or leasing of goods where the services of an operator or technician are included. In such cases the place of supply of such services depends on the nature of the services provided.

15.9.2 Examples of services of the letting on hire of goods other than means of transport

- The hire of mobile telephone handsets. See paragraph 15.11 if the supply is of telecommunications services.
- The hire of freight containers. See paragraph 15.9.5 for additional rules.
- The hire of computer and office equipment.
- The hire of exhibition stand furniture and equipment without any other services.

15.9.3 Examples of exclusions from services of the letting on hire of goods other than means of transport

- The hire of exhibition stand space. See sections 6 and 8.
- The hire of a means of transport – including the leasing or hiring out of cars. See sections 5 and 7.

15.9.4 Additional rules for goods on hire

In addition to the rules in section 14 covering supplies made to overseas customers, there are additional rules for the letting on hire of goods, depending on where they are used and enjoyed. See sections 16 and 22.

15.9.5 Zero-rating for container exports

Containers which are exported from the EC are zero-rated whether they are supplied on hire or by outright sale. See Notice 703/1 "Supply of freight containers for export or removal from the United Kingdom".

15.10 Paragraph 16(2)(i) of Sch 4A: Telecommunications services

15.10.1 What types of services fall within para 16(2)(i)?

Telecommunications services means services relating to the transmission, emission or reception of signals, writing, images and sounds or information of any nature by wire, radio, optical or other electromagnetic systems, including:

- the related transfer or assignment of the right to use capacity for such transmission, emission or reception, and
- the provision of access to global information networks.

This paragraph covers the sending or receiving of material by electronic or similar communications systems. This may be via cable, fibre optics, radio waves, microwaves, satellite, or copper wire and covers telephony (systems for transmission of speech and other sounds) and telegraphy (systems for providing distant reproduction of written, printed or pictorial matter) as well as the right to use such facilities.

If you simply supply the "content" of a transmission, you should identify the actual nature of the services provided. For example, a weather forecasting service where weather charts are faxed to the customer is a supply of delivered information and not transmission. See paragraph 15.5.12.

15.10.2 Examples of telecommunications services

- Telephone calls, calls delivered by cellular phones, paging, the transmission element of Electronic Data Interchange, teleconferencing and call-back services.
- Switching, completion of another provider's calls, the provision of leased lines and circuits or global networks.
- Telex, facsimile, multi-messaging.
- Email and access to the Internet.
- Satellite transmission services, covering transponder rental/hire and both space segments and earth segments, which includes uplinks and downlinks via land earth stations, coastal stations, outside broadcasting units, or similar.
- Transmission or delivery of another person's material by electronic means.

15.10.3 Examples of exclusions from telecommunications services

- Supplies of information ordered and delivered through the Internet. See paragraph 15.5.12.
- Travel information accessed by telephone. See paragraph 15.5.12.
- Granting copyright to use transmitted material. See paragraph 15.2.1.
- Processing of data. See paragraph 15.5.10.
- Broadcasting to subscribers. See paragraph 15.12.

15.10.4 Do Internet services constitute telecommunications services?

Access to the Internet and World Wide Web, the provision of email addresses and chatline facilities are telecommunications services. If you supply basic access to the Internet, even if related software, some information and customer support facilities are included, your supply is of telecommunications services.

However:

- if you supply a package of Internet services where the emphasis is on content rather than communication, your supply is **not** of pure telecommunications services. The place of supply of such a package depends on the nature of the services provided; or
- if you supply services separately or services which are simply delivered to a customer by electronic transmission, the place of supply depends on the nature of the services provided.

15.10.5 Additional rules for telecommunications services

In addition to the rules in section 14 covering B2C supplies made to overseas customers, there are additional rules for telecommunications services depending on where they are used and enjoyed. See sections 16 and 22.

15.11 Paragraph 16(2)(j) of Sch 4A: Radio and television broadcasting services

15.11.1 What types of services fall within para 16(2)(j)?

This paragraph covers services of broadcasting by audio and video signals, regardless of the means used (for example landline, line of sight or satellite link).

15.11.2 Example of radio and television broadcasting services

Subscription for satellite or cable television.

15.11.3 Example of exclusion from radio and television broadcasting services

Service of transmitting another person's material by electronic means.

15.11.4 Additional rules for radio and television broadcasting services

In addition to the rules in section 14 covering B2C supplies made to overseas customers, there are additional rules for radio and television broadcasting services, depending on where they are used and enjoyed. See sections 16 and 22.

15.12 Paragraph 16(2)(k) of Sch 4A: Electronically supplied services

15.12.1 What types of services fall within para 16(2)(k)?

This paragraph covers a service:

- delivered over the Internet or an electronic network (in other words is reliant on the Internet or similar network for its provision), and
- where the nature of the particular service means it is heavily dependent on information technology for its supply. In other words the service is essentially automated, involving minimal human intervention and in the absence of information technology does not have viability.

In general the use of the Internet or other electronic networks by parties to communicate with respect to transactions or to facilitate trading does not, any more than the use of a telephone or fax, affect the VAT treatment. For example, where parties simply use the Internet to convey information in the course of a business transaction (for example email), this does not change the nature of that transaction. This differs from a supply that is completely dependent on the Internet in order to be carried out (for example searching and retrieving information from a database with no human intervention).

15.12.2 Examples of electronically supplied services

- Website supply or web hosting services.
- Distance maintenance of programmes and equipment.
- Supplies of software and updating thereof.
- Supplies of images, text and information and making available of databases.
- Supply of music, films and games, including games of chance and gambling games and of political, cultural, artistic, sporting, scientific, educational or entertainment broadcasts of events.
- Supply of distance teaching.

15.12.3 Examples of exclusions from electronically supplied services

- Supplies of goods, where the order and processing is done electronically.
- Supplies of CD-Roms, games on a CD-Rom, floppy disks and similar tangible media.
- Supplies of printed matter, such as books, newsletters, newspapers or journals.
- Supplies of CDs, audio cassettes, videos cassettes, DVDs.
- Services of lawyers and financial consultants and so on, who advise clients through email.
- Teaching services, where the course content is delivered by a teacher over the Internet or an electronic network (in other words, via a remote link).
- Offline physical repair services of computer equipment.
- Offline data warehousing services.
- Advertising services, in particular as in newspapers, on posters and on television.
- Telephone helpdesk services.
- Teaching services purely involving correspondence courses, such as postal courses.
- Conventional auctioneers' services reliant on direct human intervention, irrespective of how bids are made.
- Telephone services with a video component, otherwise known as videophone services.
- Internet and worldwide web access services. See paragraph 15.10.4.
- Telephone services provided through the Internet.

15.12.4 VAT treatment of downloaded publications

For VAT and duty purposes, all supplies of downloaded publications are regarded as supplies of *services* and not goods. The UK VAT relief of zero-rating of supplies of printed matter does not apply because the relief is for goods and not services.

15.13 Emissions allowances

B2B supplies of trading in emissions allowances or instruments are subject to the B2B general rule, see section 5. B2C supplies of such services supplied by a UK supplier to a customer belonging outside the EC are supplied where the customer belongs under paragraph 16 of Sch

4A of the VATA. B2C supplies of such services supplied by a UK supplier to a customer belonging either in the UK or in another member state will continue to be taxed where the supplier belongs, under the B2C general rule, see section 5.

Emissions allowances under the EU Emissions Trading Scheme (EU ETS), and instruments representing emission reductions, carbon credits, and certificates that identify that the production of energy has been generated from renewable sources include, but are not limited to, Certified Emissions Reductions (CERs), Renewal Obligation Certificates (ROCs), Emission Reduction Units (ERUs), Levy Exemption Certificates (LECs), Assigned Amount Units (AAUs), EU Allowances (EUAs), Renewable Energy Certificates and Verified Emission Reductions (VERs).

Where certificates or instruments are sold with goods or services they will usually be viewed as incidental or ancillary to the main supply. An example of this is where a guarantee of origin is issued to customers purchasing electricity that certifies the electricity was generated from renewable sources.

16 USE AND ENJOYMENT OF LETTING ON HIRE OF GOODS, TELECOMMUNICATIONS SERVICES AND RADIO AND TELEVISION BROADCASTING SERVICES

The law on use and enjoyment of the letting on hire of goods, telecommunications services and radio and television broadcasting services is in VATA Sch 4A paras 3, 7 and 8.

For definitions of these services see:

- section 7 – means of transport;
- paragraph 15.9 – services of the letting on hire or leasing of goods other than means of transport;
- paragraph 15.10 – telecommunications services; and
- paragraph 15.11 – radio and television broadcasting services.

16.1 When do the additional rules for letting on hire of goods, telecommunications services and radio and television broadcasting services apply?

The additional rules for letting on hire of goods, telecommunications services and radio and television broadcasting services apply in either of the following situations:

- the place of supply would be the UK under another section (because the supplier or customer belongs in the UK) but the services are effectively used and enjoyed outside the EC; or
- the place of supply would be outside the EC under another section (because the supplier or customer belongs outside the EC) but the services are effectively used and enjoyed in the UK.

In these circumstances, the place of supply is where their effective use and enjoyment takes place. Where this is the UK, the services are subject to UK VAT.

16.2 What do I need to know to decide whether these rules apply?

In order to decide whether these rules apply you need to know:

- where the supplier and customer belong; *and*
- the place where the services are effectively used and enjoyed.

16.3 Does it always matter where the letting on hire of goods, telecommunications services and radio and television broadcasting services are effectively used and enjoyed?

It does not always matter where the letting on hire of goods, telecommunications services and radio and television broadcasting services are effectively used and enjoyed.

It only matters in the situations described in paragraph 16.1. The use and enjoyment provisions apply where the EC position would otherwise be distortive. Consequently, they do not apply where:

- the place of supply is the UK (because either the supplier or the customer belongs in the UK) and the service was effectively used and enjoyed in another member state; *or*

– the place of supply is another member state (because either the supplier or the customer belongs there) but the supply is effectively used and enjoyed in the UK.

16.4 What does effective use and enjoyment of the letting on hire of goods (including hired means of transport) mean?

Effective use and enjoyment takes place where the hired goods are used (in practice this will be where the goods are physically located) irrespective of contract, payment or beneficial interest.

16.5 Use and enjoyment of hired means of transport

If you (as lessor) hire out a means of transport where the place of supply would be the UK but the means of transport is used and enjoyed outside the EC during the hiring period, the place of supply of your services is outside the EC to the extent that the use and enjoyment takes place outside the EC. You will need to retain evidence to substantiate such use and enjoyment.

Similarly, if you (as lessor) hire out a means of transport where the place of supply would be outside the EC but the means of transport is used and enjoyed in the UK during the hiring period, the place of supply of your services is the UK to the extent that the use and enjoyment takes place within the UK.

16.5.1 Examples for hired means of transport

If you	*the place of supply of your services is*
hire out a means of transport where the place of supply is the UK which is used and enjoyed within the EC,	the UK.
hire out a means of transport where the place of supply is the UK which is used and enjoyed outside the EC throughout the hiring period,	outside the EC.
hire out a means of transport where the place of supply is the UK which is used and enjoyed partly within and partly outside the EC during the hiring period,	the UK to the extent that the means of transport is used and enjoyed in the EC.
hire out a means of transport where the place of supply is outside the EC which is used and enjoyed within the UK for the whole duration of the hiring period,	the UK.
hire out a means of transport where the place of supply is outside the EC which is used and enjoyed partly within the UK during the hiring period,	the UK to the extent that the means of transport is used and enjoyed in the UK.

16.6 Use and enjoyment of the letting on hire of goods (other than means of transport)

If the place of supply of your services would be the UK under sections 5 or 14, and the goods are used and enjoyed outside the EC during the hiring period, your services are supplied outside the EC to the extent that the effective use and enjoyment takes place outside the EC. You will need to retain evidence to substantiate such use and enjoyment. 56 If the place of supply of your services would be outside the EC under sections 5 or 14, and the goods are used and enjoyed in the UK during the hiring period, your services are supplied in the UK to the extent that the effective use and enjoyment takes place in the UK.

16.6.1 Examples for hired goods other than means of transport

- A Canadian company hires out recording equipment to a UK private individual who uses the equipment in his UK home. The place of supply is the UK. This is because the goods are used and enjoyed in the UK and the place of supply would otherwise have been outside the EC. See section 5.
- An Australian tourist hires a video camera from a UK provider during a visit to the UK. The place of supply is the UK. This is because the goods are used and enjoyed in the UK and the place of supply would otherwise have been outside the EC. See section 14.

- UK golf shop hires out a set of golf clubs to a UK customer for use on a holiday in the USA. The place of supply is outside the EC if the customer is able to demonstrate that the golf clubs are used and enjoyed only in the USA. This is because the goods are used and enjoyed outside the EC and the place of supply would otherwise have been the UK. See section 5.
- company belonging in Switzerland hires fax machines from a supplier in the USA. The fax machines are partly used and enjoyed at the Swiss company's London branch. The place of supply is the UK to the extent that the machines are used at the London branch. This is because the goods are used and enjoyed in the UK and the place of supply would otherwise have been outside the EC. See section 5.

16.7 What does effective use and enjoyment of telecommunications services and radio and television broadcasting services mean?

Effective use and enjoyment takes place where the customer actually consumes telecommunications services and radio and television broadcasting services (in practice this will be where the services are physically used) irrespective of contract, payment or beneficial interest.

16.7.1 Examples for telecommunications services

- A private individual whose usual place of residence is in the UK rents a telephone line for his holiday home in Florida from a UK supplier. The services are actually used and enjoyed in Florida. The place of supply is outside the EC because effective use and enjoyment takes place outside the EC and the services would otherwise be supplied in the UK. See section 5.
- A UK resident rents a telephone line for his elderly mother's house in Australia. He receives and pays the bills from his UK provider. The services are actually used and enjoyed in Australia by his mother. The place of supply is outside the EC because effective use and enjoyment takes place outside the EC and the services would otherwise be supplied in the UK. See section 5.
- The parents of a student travelling in the Far East accept a reverse charge call to their UK home from their daughter. The accepted call forms part of the service from their local provider and is actually used and enjoyed at the UK family home. The place of supply is the UK because the services are not effectively used and enjoyed outside the EC. See section 5.
- A business traveller makes a reservation at a Hong Kong hotel from his London office using a toll free number. The telecommunications services are supplied to, and used by, the Hong Kong hotel. The place of supply is outside the EC because the services are not effectively used and enjoyed in the UK. See section 5.

16.7.2 How do the extra rules apply to travellers?

Telecommunications services are subject to UK VAT when used in the UK by non-EC visitors. Examples include public pay-phones, fax shop services and charges for calls made from hotel rooms. However, elements of telecommunications services used in the UK are ignored if they are:

- simply an incidental part of an established telephone contract or account held by a customer who belongs outside the EC;
- used by a non-EC temporary visitor; *and*
- HMRC is satisfied that these conditions are not being abused.

If a UK resident uses telecommunications services outside the EC under such an account with a UK provider, those services will be outside the scope of UK VAT, provided that evidence is retained to substantiate the element of use and enjoyment that occurs outside the EC.

16.8 Do I have to apply different rules if I supply electronically supplied services as well as telecommunications services or radio and television broadcasting services?

HMRC recognises that in certain situations, the place of supply would be the same whether the rules for telecommunications services and radio and television broadcasting services, or those for electronically supplied services were applied. This is because most non-business customers use and enjoy services in the same country in which they belong. See paragraph 17.7.

16.9 Accounting procedures for UK suppliers of letting on hire of goods (other than means of transport), telecommunications services and radio and television broadcasting services

If your	*you*
customer belongs in the UK,	are not required to account for UK VAT to the extent that your customer uses and enjoys your services outside the EC.
non-business customer belongs in another member state,	are not required to account for UK VAT to the extent that your customer uses and enjoys your services outside the EC.
customer belongs outside the EC,	are required to account for UK VAT to the extent that your customer uses and enjoys your services in the UK.
customer belongs outside the EC and your customer uses and enjoys your services in another member state,	may be required to account for VAT in that member state because those services are supplied in that member state (see paragraph 16.14).

16.10 Accounting procedures for non-UK suppliers of the letting on hire of goods (including means of transport), telecommunications services and radio and television broadcasting services used and enjoyed in the UK

If you are a supplier who does not belong in the UK and your customer is registered for UK VAT and receives the supply for business purposes, your customer is responsible for accounting for any VAT due on the supply under the reverse charge procedure. See paragraph 18.11.

If you are a supplier who does not belong in the UK, and your customer is not registered for UK VAT, you, as the supplier, are responsible for accounting for any VAT due on your supply where the place of supply is the UK. See paragraph 18.11.6. If you are not already registered in the UK, you may be liable to register. See paragraph 2.14.

If you are a supplier who does not belong in the EC, you are required to register and account for UK VAT if you supply services that are used and enjoyed in the UK by UK private individuals and non-business organisations, subject to the normal rules. See Notice 700/1 "Should I be registered for VAT?"

16.11 Accounting procedures for UK VAT registered recipients of services of the letting on hire of goods (other than means of transport), telecommunications services and radio and television broadcasting services from a non-EC supplier where the place of supply is the UK

If you are a UK VAT registered recipient of these services and:

– you belong outside the EC for the purposes of receiving the supply;
– you use and enjoy the services in the UK; *and*
– your supplier belongs outside the UK

you are required to account for UK VAT using the reverse charge procedure. See paragraph 18.11. See paragraph 18.10 if you belong in the UK for the purposes of receiving such a supply.

16.12 Accounting procedures for UK VAT registered recipients of services of hired means of transport from a non-EC supplier where the place of supply is the UK

If you are a UK VAT registered recipient of these services, you are required to account for the reverse charge where your supplier belongs outside the EC (see paragraphs 18.10 and 18.11).

16.13 How do I account for VAT on the letting on hire of goods, telecommunications services and radio and television broadcasting services that are only partly liable to UK VAT because of the use and enjoyment provisions?

You are only required to account for UK VAT to the extent that the place of supply of services is the UK. Therefore you should seek to identify the location where the services are actually used.

HMRC will normally accept any records or documentation that demonstrates any division in the provision of services but, where such records do not exist, you should make a fair and reasonable assessment.

There is no prescribed method for determining the extent to which services are used in the UK. You may adopt whatever method is available to you that produces a fair and reasonable reflection of services that are liable to UK VAT. If you are in doubt you should contact our Helpline. Evidence of how the apportionment has been made should be retained and made available on request.

16.14 Liability to register in other member states

If you supply the letting on hire of any goods, telecommunications services or radio and television broadcasting services where the place of supply would be outside the EC under sections 5 or 14, and the services are effectively used and enjoyed by your customer in another member state, you may be liable to register for VAT in that member state (see paragraph 2.16).

16.15 Decision tables for hired goods (other than means of transport), telecommunications services and radio and television broadcasting services

Tables in section 22 contain further guidance for all suppliers to help in deciding the place of supply of hired goods (other than means of transport), telecommunications services and radio and television broadcasting services.

17 USE AND ENJOYMENT OF ELECTRONICALLY SUPPLIED SERVICES

The law on the additional rules for electronically supplied services is VATA Sch 4A para 9.

For a definition of electronically supplied services see paragraph 15.12.

17.1 What is the VAT liability of electronically supplied services?

Normally, electronically supplied services supplied in a member state will be taxable at the standard rate established by a member state in accordance with arts 97–98(2) of the Principal VAT Directive (formerly art 12(3)(a) of the VAT Sixth Directive), unless an exempting provision in a member state applies.

Particular care should be taken where a service includes both electronic and other elements. Such composite transactions must generally be considered on a case-by-case basis.

17.2 When do the additional rules for electronically supplied services apply?

The additional rules for electronically supplied services apply where there is a B2B supply in either of the following situations:

– the place of supply would be the UK (because the supplier or the customer belongs in the UK) but the services are effectively used and enjoyed outside the EC; *or*
– the place of supply would be outside the EC (because the supplier or the customer belongs outside the EC), but the services are effectively used and enjoyed in the UK.

In these circumstances, the place of supply of the electronically supplied services is where their effective use and enjoyment takes place. Where this is the UK, the services are subject to UK VAT.

17.3 How do suppliers of electronically supplied services determine if their customers are in business?

In addition to the guidance in paragraph 2.7, section 19 contains additional guidelines which will help suppliers of electronically supplied services determine if they make B2B supplies.

17.4 What do I need to know to decide whether these rules apply?

You need to know:

– where the supplier and customer belong; and
– the place where the services are effectively used and enjoyed.

17.5 Does it always matter where electronically supplied services are effectively used and enjoyed?

It does not always matter where electronically supplied services are effectively used and enjoyed. It only matters in the situations described in paragraph 17.2. The use and enjoyment provisions apply where the EC position would otherwise be distortive. Consequently, they do not apply in any situation where:

– B2C supplies of electronically supplied services are made. This is because most consumers are considered to use and enjoy the services in the same country in which they belong;
– the place of supply is the UK (because either the supplier or the customer belongs in the UK) and the service was effectively used and enjoyed in another member state; or
– the place of supply is in another member state (because either the supplier or the customer belongs there) but the supply is effectively used and enjoyed in the UK.

In such situations the rules set out in sections 5, 14 and 18 apply.

17.6 What does effective use and enjoyment of electronically supplied services mean?

Effective use and enjoyment takes place where the customer actually consumes the electronically supplied services irrespective of contract, payment or beneficial interest.

17.6.1 Examples for electronically supplied services

– A UK business purchases digitised software from an Irish supplier for use only in its branch in the Channel Islands. Although the supply is received in the UK where the business belongs, it is used outside the EC and is outside the scope of UK (and EC) VAT.
– A USA business purchases web-hosting services for its international business, including its UK branch. Although the supply is received in the USA, to the extent that it is used in the UK, it is subject to UK VAT.
– A UK business purchases downloaded information from another UK business for use in both its UK headquarters and its Canadian branch. Although the supply is received in the UK, to the extent it is used in Canada it is outside the scope of UK VAT. UK VAT is only due to the extent of use by the UK headquarters.

17.7 Do I have to apply different rules if I supply telecommunications services or radio and television broadcasting services as well as electronically supplied services?

HMRC recognises that in certain situations, the place of supply would be the same whether the rules for telecommunications services and radio and television broadcasting services, or those for electronically supplied services were applied. This is because most customers receiving B2C supplies use and enjoy services in the same country in which they belong.

Consequently, if you are:

– a UK business which supplies electronically supplied services;
– your services are B2C supplies, and
– your existing accounting systems are set up to tax supplies where they are effectively used and enjoyed;

you may, exceptionally, opt to apply the use and enjoyment rules to your supplies of electronically supplied services.

This is a simplification measure which prevents the need for businesses to adjust their systems. However, HMRC will not allow this simplification to be used in any case where we consider it leads to abuse.

17.8 Accounting procedures for UK suppliers of electronically supplied services

If your	*you are*
B2B supply is to a customer belonging in the UK,	not required to account for UK VAT to the extent that your business customer uses and enjoys your services outside the EC.
B2B supply is to a customer belonging outside the EC,	required to account for UK VAT to the extent that your customer uses and enjoys your services in the UK.

If your	*you are*
B2B supply is to a customer belonging outside the EC and your customer uses and enjoys your services in another member state.	not required to account for UK VAT as those services are supplied in that member state. See section 23.

17.9 Accounting procedures for non-UK suppliers of electronically supplied services used and enjoyed in the UK

17.9.1 Non-UK supplier supplying a customer registered for UK VAT

If you are a supplier who does not belong in the UK and you make B2B supplies to a customer belonging in the UK who is registered for UK VAT, your customer is responsible for accounting for any VAT due on the supply under the reverse charge procedure. See paragraph 18.11. If you are registered for VAT in the UK but do not belong in the UK see paragraph 17.10.

See paragraph 16.12.1.

17.9.2 Non-UK supplier supplying a customer not registered for UK VAT

If you are a supplier who does not belong in the UK, and you make B2B supplies but your customer is not registered for UK VAT, you, as the supplier, are responsible for accounting for any VAT due on your supply where the place of supply is the UK. See paragraph 18.11.6. If you are not already registered in the UK, you may be liable to register. See paragraph 2.14.

If you are a non-EC supplier of electronically supplied services providing B2C services to in the EC, you may be potentially required to register and account for VAT in every member state where you supply your services (according to the rules which apply in the various member states).

However, to relieve this burden, a simplified special scheme permits you to register electronically in the member state of your choice and account for EC VAT on an electronic VAT return. See section 20. This scheme does not apply to non-EC businesses supplying other services.

17.10 Accounting procedures for UK customers receiving electronically supplied services from a non-EC supplier where the place of supply is the UK

If you are a UK VAT registered recipient receiving a B2B supply and:

– you belong outside the EC for the purposes of receiving the supply;
– you use and enjoy the services in the UK; *and*
– your supplier belongs outside the UK;

you are required to account for VAT using the reverse charge procedure. See paragraph 18.11. If you belong in the UK for the purposes of receiving such a supply see paragraphs 17.9.1 and 18.10.

17.11 How do I account for VAT on electronically supplied services that are only partly liable to UK VAT because of the use and enjoyment provisions?

You are only required to account for UK VAT to the extent that the place of supply of services is the UK. Therefore you should seek to identify the location where the services are actually used.

HMRC will normally accept any records or documentation that demonstrates the extent to which services are used and enjoyed in the UK but, where such records do not exist, you should make a fair and reasonable assessment.

There is no prescribed method for determining the extent to which services are used in the UK. You may adopt whatever method is available to you that produces a fair and reasonable reflection of services that are liable to UK VAT. If you are in doubt you should contact our Helpline. Evidence of how the apportionment has been made should be retained to be made available on request.

17.12 Liability to register in other member states

If you supply B2B electronically supplied services where the place of supply would be outside the EC under section 5, and the services are effectively used and enjoyed by your customer in another member state, you may be liable to register for VAT in that member state. See paragraph 2.16.

17.13 Decision tables for electronically supplied services

Tables in section 23 contain further guidance for all suppliers to help in deciding the place of supply of electronically supplied services.

18 REVERSE CHARGE

The law on the reverse charge is in VATA 1994 s 8.

18.1 Who needs to refer to this section?

You will need to refer to this section if you belong, or are VAT registered, in the UK and receive the following types of services from an overseas supplier:

Types of services:	*Dealt with in:*
B2B general rule services;	paragraph 18.10;
any other services which are supplied in the UK.	paragraph 18.11.

It is important to refer to the appropriate paragraph because there are different conditions for each situation.

18.2 What is the "reverse charge"?

Normally, the supplier of a service is the person who must account, to the tax authorities, for any VAT due on the supply. However, in certain situations, it is the customer who must account for any VAT due. Although called reverse charge in this notice, the procedure may also be referred to as *tax shift.*

The reverse charge applies to almost all B2B supplies of services except those of a description in Schedule 9 of the VAT Act (Exemptions). It does not apply to land on which the option to tax has been exercised. Reverse charge is not a complicated accounting procedure. Where it applies to services which you receive, you, the customer, must act as if you are both the supplier and the recipient of the services.

18.3 How does the reverse charge work?

You simply credit your VAT account with an amount of output tax, calculated on the full value of the supply you have received, and at the same time debit your VAT account with the input tax to which you are entitled, in accordance with the normal rules. The partial exemption implications for reverse charge services are explained in Notice 706 "Partial exemption".

You then include in the relevant boxes of your VAT return:

- the amount of output tax in box 1 *VAT due on sales;*
- the amount of input tax in box 4 *VAT reclaimed on purchases;*
- the full value of the supply in box 6 *total value of sales;* and
- the full value of the supply in box 7 *total value of purchases.*

18.4 What is the effect of the reverse charge?

If you can attribute the input tax to taxable supplies, and can therefore reclaim it all, the reverse charge has no net cost to you. If you cannot, the effect is to make you pay VAT on the supply at the UK rate. This puts you in the same position as if you had received the supply from a UK supplier rather than from one outside the UK.

18.5 Valuation of supplies covered by the reverse charge

The amount payable to your overseas supplier for the services *excludes* UK VAT. The value of the transaction on which VAT must be accounted under the reverse charge is the total amount paid together with the value of any other form of consideration. This includes any taxes levied abroad. See Notice 700 "The VAT Guide" if you need to convert foreign currency into sterling.

18.6 Time of supply

The time of supply (tax point) for these services depends on whether you make a single supply of services or continuous supplies of services.

18.6.1 What is the time of supply for a single supply of services subject to the reverse charge?

The time of supply (tax point) for a single supply of services subject to the reverse charge is the date of completion of the service or, to the extent a payment for the service is made before completion, the date of payment.

18.6.2 What is the time of supply for a single supply of services subject to the reverse charge?

The time of supply (tax point) for continuous supplies of services subject to the reverse charge is the end of each periodic billing or payment period (or payment where this is earlier), with a compulsory tax point on 31 December each year in cases where a billing/payment period or payment has not arisen.

18.7 Can the reverse charge apply to services supplied by UK suppliers?

The reverse charge does not apply to supplies of services where both the supplier and the customer belong in the UK. It only applies where services are supplied in the UK by suppliers belonging overseas.

Services which, under the place of supply rules, are supplied in another country are outside the scope of UK VAT. Such services can only be subject to tax in that country.

18.8 International companies

The reverse charge does not apply to services provided by an overseas establishment to a customer belonging in the UK within the same legal entity as the overseas establishment, since this is not a supply for VAT purposes.

18.9 UK VAT incurred by non-UK suppliers

Suppliers who belong outside the UK, and whose customers account for UK VAT by means of the reverse charge, may be able to reclaim VAT incurred in the UK. See Notice 723 "Refunds of VAT in the EC for EC and non-EC businesses".

18.10 B2B general rule services

If you belong in the UK and receive supplies of any B2B general rule services (see section 5) where your supplier belongs outside the UK the reverse charge applies. If you are unsure whether you belong in the UK, see section 3.
the reverse charge applies. If you are unsure whether you belong in the UK, see section 3.

18.10.1 Examples

A UK business receives customised software from a USA business (B2B general rule service). The place of supply is the UK and the UK business must account for VAT under the reverse charge.

A UK charity with business and non-business activities receives a supply of legal services from a French business in relation to its non-business activities (B2B general rule service). The place of supply is the UK and the UK charity must account for VAT under the reverse charge.

18.10.2 What if I receive exempt or zero-rated services?

The reverse charge does not apply to exempt services or zero-rated services.

18.10.3 What if I am not already UK VAT registered and receive these services?

If you are not already UK VAT registered and you receive supplies of B2B general rule services which meet the conditions in paragraph 18.10 and are treated as supplied where the recipient belongs, the value of those supplies must be added to the value of your own taxable supplies in determining whether you should be registered for UK VAT. Even if you make no taxable supplies yourself you will still be a taxable person if the value of your imported services exceeds the registration limits.

18.10.4 What if the reverse charge does not apply to these services?

If the conditions in paragraph 18.10 are not met the reverse charge does not apply to these services and there is no UK VAT due on such supplies. However, see paragraph 18.11 if you receive:

- supplies of the letting on hire of goods;
- telecommunications services;
- radio and television broadcasting services; *or*
- electronically supplied services,

which are made in the UK under the additional rules for use and enjoyment of such supplies. See sections 16 and 17.

18.10.5 Group treatment

Where B2B general rule services (except services of a description in Sch 9 of VATA (Exemptions) and land on which the option to tax has been exercised) are purchased by an overseas member of a UK VAT group and provided to a UK member of that VAT group, its representative member is required to account for any UK VAT due under the intra-group reverse charge. See Notice 700/2 "Group and divisional registration".

18.11 Extension to other services supplied in the UK

The reverse charge also applies to the following services when they are made in the UK:

- services relating to land and property (see section 6);
- services supplied where performed (see section 8);
- passenger transport (see section 10);
- services covered by the additional rules for hired goods (including hired means of transport), telecommunications services, radio and television broadcasting services (see section 16), and
- services covered by the additional rules for electronically supplied services (see section 17).

18.11.1 When does the extension to the reverse charge apply?

The extension to the reverse charge applies if you are UK VAT registered and receive B2B supplies of the services listed in paragraph 18.11 which are supplied in the UK where your supplier belongs outside the UK.

18.11.2 Should I give my UK VAT registration number?

You should give your UK VAT registration number to your supplier as evidence that they are not liable to account for any UK VAT due.

18.11.3 What if I receive exempt or zero-rated services?

The reverse charge does not apply to exempt or zero-rated services.

18.11.4 What if I receive such supplies for wholly private purposes?

If you receive such supplies for wholly private purposes the reverse charge does not apply. You should not give a UK VAT registration number. Your supplier is liable to account for any UK VAT due.

18.11.5 What if I am not UK VAT registered and receive such services supplied in the UK?

If you are not UK VAT registered and receive such services supplied in the UK the reverse charge does not apply. Such supplies do not count as your taxable supplies for the purposes of determining whether you are liable to be registered as a taxable person. Your supplier is liable to account for any UK VAT due.

18.11.6 What if I am a non-UK supplier of these services but my customer does not give a UK VAT registration number?

If you are a non-UK supplier of these services but your customer does not give a UK VAT registration number you are responsible for accounting for any UK VAT due on your supply. If you are not already registered in the UK, you may be liable to register. See paragraph 2.16.

19 ELECTRONICALLY SUPPLIED SERVICES: EVIDENCE OF CUSTOMER LOCATION AND STATUS

For a definition of electronically supplied services see paragraph 15.12.

19.1 When do I need to refer to this section?

You need to refer to this section if you are a supplier of electronically supplied services. This is because you should identify the status and location of your customers in order to determine the place of supply of your services and thus the correct VAT treatment of such services.

19.2 How do I verify my customer's business status?

If you make B2B supplies within the EC the evidence required at the time of the transaction would normally be the customer's VAT registration number and country identification code prefix. The number must conform to the format for the registered person's member state. See Notice 725 "The single market".

Under normal trading practices you will often know your business customers. Therefore, in such cases, you will not need to routinely check all VAT numbers quoted, provided that the numbers conform to the correct country format.

However, where a relationship has not been established with a business customer the VAT number should be checked when:

— the VAT involved exceeds £500 on a single transaction; **or**
— the cumulative VAT on transactions for electronically supplied services to a single customer in a VAT quarter exceeds £500.

Similarly, if you supply downloaded music, games, films and so on of a kind normally supplied to a private consumer, you would not expect a VAT number to be quoted in such circumstances. However, where a VAT number is quoted in what is clearly a supply to a private consumer the use of that number should be challenged.

Full verification should be undertaken in *all* cases where you have any reason to believe that a VAT number quoted by a customer is false or is being used incorrectly.

If a customer claims to be in business but not to be VAT registered then alternative evidence should be obtained to support the claim. This can be in the form of other reasonable commercial evidence or records that should normally be available. Examples include contracts, business letterheads, a commercial website address, publicity material, certificates from fiscal authorities. A digital certificate from a reputable organisation can also be used for this purpose.

The VAT Information Exchange System (VIES) can support your decision-making process by providing an online verification system. The system can be accessed using the HMRC website or go direct to the Europa website.

You may also contact our Helpline to verify names and addresses as well as dates of registration and deregistration where appropriate.

Other member states may have similar systems by which it is possible to check the validity of VAT registration numbers.

If any of the above checks fail to confirm that your customer is in business or if there remains any doubt about the use of a VAT registration number, VAT should be charged as appropriate on all supplies to that customer including supplies that have already been made.

Any VAT that has been charged in error may be credited under the normal rules.

19.3 How do I identify my customer's country of residence?

Under normal trading practices you will often know your business customers and where they are located. However, this is less likely to be the case with B2C supplies and with lower value transactions to business customers. As technology cannot determine with certainty the place where such customers belong, *self-declaration by the customer combined with a reasonable level of verification* will be acceptable.

It is likely that you already have established procedures in place to identify and verify the country where your customer belongs. HMRC will rely as much as possible on those practices to ensure you are not burdened with unnecessary requirements. If the method you use is not included in the list of examples in the following paragraph, you are advised to contact HMRC.

Customer self-declaration will be acceptable (without prior approval from HMRC) in respect of electronically supplied services, where one or other of the following practices is followed:

(a) Use of your customer's postal address provided you have used it to send (for example) goods, catalogues, samples, CD-Roms, invoices, correspondence without these items having been returned, undelivered. (However, alternative means will have to be used if mail is returned undelivered).

(b) Acceptance of payment by credit/debit card where you compare the customer's home address with the billing address, but then rely on satisfactory alternative evidence if the match is unsuccessful.

(c) Acceptance of payment by credit/debit card and, using proprietary software, you compare the customer's country of residence with the location of the issuing bank but then rely on satisfactory alternative evidence if the match is unsuccessful.

(d) Use of geo-location or proprietary software to verify where your customer belongs but then rely on satisfactory alternative evidence if the match fails.

(e) Use of systems that are configured to identify where the service is used and enjoyed (for example telecommunications suppliers). HMRC will accept the arrangement as a proxy for identifying the country where the customer belongs.

If you use one or other of the above methods, you will need to demonstrate that HMRC's requirements have been met. For example, you may be asked to show how your system processes the relevant information.

19.4 What if the information provided by customers is found to be incorrect?

Where verification has been undertaken and the details provided were believed to be correct at that time, but subsequently the customer is found to have made a false declaration, HMRC will not seek to recover VAT from you, the supplier, where it was not charged to the customer. This does not apply if there was reasonable information at the time of the sale to indicate that the customer's information was incorrect. HMRC's treatment of such cases will be subject to periodic review.

20 ELECTRONICALLY SUPPLIED SERVICES: SPECIAL SCHEME FOR NON-EC BUSINESSES

The law on the special scheme for non-EC businesses supplying electronically supplied services is in VATA Sch 3B.

For a definition of electronically supplied services see paragraph 15.12.

20.1 When do I need to refer to this section?

You need to refer to this section if you are a non-EC business and you make B2C supplies of electronically supplied services to EC consumers. See paragraph 2.5 for an explanation of B2C supplies.

20.2 What is the special scheme for non-EC businesses?

The special scheme provides an optional, simplified means of registering and accounting electronically for EC VAT.

20.3 How does the scheme work?

Electronically supplied services, when supplied by non-EC businesses to EC consumers, are subject to VAT in the member state where the customer belongs.

This means that non-EC businesses would be required, under the normal rules, to register separately and account for VAT in each and every member state in which they make those supplies. For example, a Canadian business with customers in the UK, France and Spain would have to register in, and submit declarations to each of those member states.

As an alternative, the special scheme offers eligible non-EC businesses the option of registering electronically in a *single m* ember state of their choice and accounting for VAT on their sales of electronically supplied services to all EC consumers on a *single* quarterly electronic VAT declaration which provides details of VAT due in each member state. This is submitted with payment to the tax administration in the member state of registration which then distributes the VAT to the member states where the services are consumed.

20.3.1 Example

A USA business registers for the special scheme in the UK. Its customers are located in the UK, Germany and Italy. The USA business charges UK VAT to its UK customers, German VAT to its German customers and Italian VAT to its Italian customers. The business enters the VAT for each member state on the appropriate line of the electronic declaration. It sends the declaration electronically with payment to HMRC, who retain the UK VAT and pass on the German VAT to the German authorities and the Italian VAT to the Italian authorities.

20.4 Who may use the special scheme?

You are eligible to use the special scheme if:

— you make B2C supplies of electronically supplied services to consumers belonging in the EC
— you are not established within the EC, *and*
— you are not registered for VAT under the normal rules in any member state.

20.5 Can I use the special scheme if I make B2B supplies as well as B2C supplies to consumers in the EC?

You can use the special scheme for your B2C supplies to consumers in the EC even if you also make B2B supplies, subject to meeting the other conditions set out in paragraph 20.4.

You are not entitled to use the special scheme for B2B supplies. You are not required to charge and account for VAT on B2B cross-border supplies of electronically supplied services supplied in the EC because your customers account for any VAT due in their member state.

20.6 How do I register for the special scheme in the UK?

You can register in the UK for the special scheme from our website, go to About online services and select VAT on eServices (VoES).

From here you can access a secure site which automatically guides you through an electronic registration process. This will include selecting a user name and password to identify yourself for the purposes of completing and submitting declarations electronically (see paragraph 20.18).

This is a secure site which automatically guides you through an electronic registration process. This will include selecting a user name and password to identify yourself for the purposes of completing and submitting declarations electronically (see paragraph 18.18).

Remember: Subject to the conditions in paragraph 20.4, you can elect to register for the special scheme in a member state of your choice, but you can only register in that one member state.

20.7 What information must I provide to register?

You will only have to provide the following limited information to register:

– business name;
– postal address;
– electronic addresses including websites;
– national tax number (where applicable);
– a statement that you are not registered for VAT purposes within the EC; *and*
– the date on which you began, or intend to begin, making supplies of electronically supplied services to EC consumers.

HMRC will also ask you to provide a contact name and telephone number.

20.8 When will I receive a VAT identification number?

We will normally send your VAT identification number by email within five working days of us receiving your completed electronic registration request.

Identification numbers for the special scheme have their own unique format beginning with the prefix 'EU', followed by a nine-digit number. These are different from VAT registration numbers issued under the normal rules.

20.9 Must a business be making supplies before registering?

Subject to the other conditions, you are entitled to register for the special scheme even if you are not actually making supplies of electronically supplied services at the time but intend to do so at a later stage. You will need to complete "nil" VAT declarations for the period between the date you are registered until the time you begin to make supplies. See paragraph 20.18. However, you must advise HMRC if your intention to make supplies ceases. See paragraphs 20.15 and 20.16.

20.10 What if I am already registered for VAT in the EC under the normal rules but want to apply for the special scheme?

If you are required to be registered for VAT in the EC under the normal rules, for example, because you supply goods or services other than electronically supplied services, you are not eligible for the special scheme. You are required to account for VAT on electronically supplied services to EC consumers under the normal rules.

20.11 Are there any other conditions I must comply with if I apply for the special scheme?

If you apply for the special scheme you are required to comply with all its conditions. These include electronically registering, accounting for, and paying the VAT that is due at the correct time.

There are no penalties which apply under the special scheme. However, if you persistently fail to comply with its conditions, your registration may be cancelled. In that event, you would be required to register under the normal rules which apply in the various member states where your customers belong. You could then be subject to any penalties which those member states apply.

Similarly, if you are supplying electronic services to UK customers and you fail to register for VAT (either under the special scheme or under the normal rules), you may be compulsorily registered in the UK under the normal rules and may incur a late registration penalty.

20.12 Can I use an agent to deal with my VAT affairs?

Only a business may register for the special scheme. An agent, even an authorised one, is therefore not allowed to register for the special scheme on your behalf.

You may authorise an agent to submit declarations and, if necessary, payment on your behalf under the special scheme. However, rules regarding agents vary between the member states.

20.13 My sales of electronic services to EC consumers are small. Do I need to register for the special scheme?

There is no threshold for registration under the special scheme. Although your sales of electronically supplied services to EC consumers may be small or even occasional, the special scheme enables you to register, submit declarations and pay VAT in the *single* EC member state of your choice. If you choose not to register under the special scheme, the normal rules (including VAT registration thresholds) will apply. In contrast to the special scheme, these may require you to register and account for VAT in most member states where your customers belong.

20.14 Am I required to register if my services qualify for a VAT exemption in the EC?

Normally, electronically supplied services supplied in a member state will be taxable at the standard rate established by a member state, unless an exempting provision in a member state applies. If you think that your services may qualify for an exemption you should check with the member state(s) concerned.

However, if any of your services are taxable in your customer's member state, you may be required to register and account for VAT in the EC under either the normal rules or the special scheme.

20.15 What is the procedure if my business's circumstances change?

Once you are registered for the special scheme, you must notify us, using the dedicated website, if:

- there is any change in your business details as at paragraph 20.7 above;
- you cease to make, or cease to have the intention of making, electronically supplied services to EC consumers; *or*
- you cease to be eligible for the scheme (for example, you begin to supply goods in the EC and are consequently liable to register under the normal rules).

You must advise us within 30 days of the date of the changes, or of the date when your intention to make supplies ceased.

20.16 In what circumstances must I apply to cancel my registration under the special scheme?

You must apply to cancel your registration under the special scheme if at any time you cease to be eligible for it; for example, if you cease to supply electronically supplied services to EC consumers or if you establish your business within the EC.

We can also cancel your registration in certain circumstances if you do not meet the conditions of the special scheme, for example, because we discover you make supplies other than electronically supplied services in the EC and are therefore required to register under the normal rules.

20.17 What if I decide to switch from registration under the normal rules to the special scheme at a later date?

If you are required to be registered in the EC solely because you are supplying electronically supplied services to EC consumers, you may decide to register under the normal rules. For example, you might initially be making supplies of electronically supplied services to consumers in a single member state only. You may subsequently wish to register under the special scheme, for example, because you expand your market to consumers in other member states.

In these circumstances, you may apply to be registered for the special scheme in the UK provided you cancel your registration under the normal rules with the member state concerned.

20.18 What is the procedure for submitting declarations and payments?

Electronic declarations are due for each calendar quarter (30 September, 31 December, 31 March and 30 June) and should be submitted within 20 days after the end of the quarter to which it relates. For example, a declaration for the quarter ending 30 September should be submitted with full payment of the tax due, by 20 October. You must also submit "nil" declarations.

You complete the declaration by logging on to the dedicated website using your VAT identification number, user name and password to ensure security.

20.19 What details will be required on the VAT declaration?

For *each* member state in which your business has supplied electronically supplied services you must state on the declaration:

- the total value of all supplies in the period excluding any VAT;

– the VAT rate which applies; *and*
– the total amount of VAT payable.

You must also show the total amount of VAT payable in all member states.

20.20 Can I recover VAT on purchases under the special scheme?

You cannot recover VAT on purchases using the special scheme. The special scheme provides only for payment of the VAT due on sales to your EC customers without any deductions of EC VAT incurred on purchases. However, you may reclaim any VAT that you have paid on goods and services used for the purpose of your taxable activities falling under the special scheme from the member state where that VAT was paid, under the terms of the EC 13th Directive. See paragraphs 18.9 and 20.34.

20.21 How do I pay electronically?

You will need to arrange with your bank to make electronic payment to HMRC's bank account at the same time you submit the declaration. The bank account details can be found on the dedicated website. You should not use any other bank account.

20.22 In what currency must returns and payments be made?

Businesses registered for the special scheme in the UK are required to submit declarations and payments in sterling.

20.23 What exchange rate must I use when converting into sterling?

Businesses registered for the special scheme in the UK are required to submit declarations and payments to HMRC in sterling (GBP). Conversions from other currencies into sterling must be made using the exchange rates published by the European Central Bank (the ECB):

– for the last day of the reporting period to which the declaration relates; *or*
– if no such rate is published for that day, for the next day for which such a rate is published.

To avoid the need for businesses to calculate a conversion from the currency of sale into Euros and then from Euros into sterling, HMRC publishes online the exchange rates for some leading currencies direct into sterling. This includes dollars (USA, Canadian and Australian), rupees and yen.

Alternatively, you may calculate the conversion yourself using the exchange rates shown at the ECB's website www.ecb.int

20.24 What VAT rates apply in the member states?

Non-EC businesses supplying electronic services to EC consumers are required to charge VAT at the rate which applies in the customer's member state. These rates are published on the Commission's webpage //ec.europa.eu

20.25 How will I know that HMRC has received the declaration?

You will receive an on-line acknowledgment confirming that HMRC has received your declaration. If you do not immediately receive this, you should contact HMRC's Customer Services Team by email at voes@hmrc.gsi.gov.uk

This acknowledgment also provides a unique reference number for each declaration you submit. You should refer to this number if you need to contact HMRC with a query about a declaration.

20.26 What do I do if a business customer requests a refund of VAT?

The special scheme is intended for supplies to consumers who cannot recover VAT. Thus, a business customer who fails to provide a valid VAT registration number at the time of the transaction and is charged VAT, cannot deduct that VAT as input tax. However, if he subsequently produces a valid VAT registration number and requests a credit, you may refund the VAT.

20.27 What is the procedure for correcting an error in the VAT declared on the declaration?

If you submit a declaration and subsequently discover that you have made an error, for example, entering French VAT in the line for Spain or underdeclaring UK VAT, you should contact HMRC at voes@hmrc.gsi.gov.uk quoting your declaration acknowledgement number (see paragraph 20.25) and advising of the correct amount(s) due for the member state(s) concerned. You do not need to submit a supplementary declaration.

If you owe additional VAT as a result of your mistake, you will either be asked to send the payment to HMRC or advised that the member state(s) concerned will contact you to explain how you should pay the VAT due.

20.28 What do I do if I have paid an amount different to the VAT declared?

If you have declared the correct amount of tax, but discover that you have paid HMRC more or less than that amount in error, you should contact HMRC at voes@hmrc.gsi.gov.uk to obtain advice on what action to take.

20.29 What records should I maintain?

If you are registered for the special scheme you should maintain records of your transactions in sufficient detail to enable the tax administrations in your customers' member states to determine that the VAT declarations and payments you make are correct. These records include normal commercial data held for each transaction, for example, transaction number, date, type (credit or debit), customer name and location, currency and values including VAT.

These records should be made available electronically on request to either the tax administration where:

– you are registered for the special scheme; or
– where your customers belong.

20.30 How long must business records be retained?

Businesses must retain records relating to supplies made under the special scheme for a period of ten years.

20.31 Must I issue VAT invoices?

It is common practice for businesses supplying electronically supplied services to issue electronically an invoice or similar document which confirms the details of the sale. There are no special rules for issuing VAT invoices under the special scheme and consequently the normal rules apply. In the UK you are not required to issue VAT invoices for such supplies because your customers are not in business for the purposes of the special scheme and cannot deduct VAT on their purchases.

20.32 Can I appeal any aspects of the special scheme to a VAT Tribunal?

Under para 20(1) of Sch 3B to VATA 1994, you have the right to appeal to a VAT Tribunal about any decisions HMRC gives on the following aspects of the special scheme:

– registering or cancelling the registration of any person;
– a decision to give a formal notice of an amount underdeclared; or
– the amount of VAT stated as over or underdeclared in a formal notice.

20.33 What if I have a dispute with another member state?

UK VAT Tribunals cannot deal with VAT matters which fall within the jurisdiction of other member states. If you disagree with a decision taken by a member state about any aspect of the special scheme, for example the amount of VAT owed to you, you should raise the matter with them.

20.34 How do I make a claim under the 13th Directive for a refund of VAT paid in the UK?

Claims under the 13th Directive for a refund of VAT paid in the UK can be made on form VAT 65A. Claimants registered under the special scheme should state in s 9A of VAT 65A "ESS special scheme" and quote their special scheme identification number, and also indicate in section 10 of the form which expenditure relates to the special scheme.

Full details of the general requirements are in Notice 723 "Refunds of VAT in the EC for EC and non-EC businesses".

20.35 How do I recover VAT paid in other member states of the EC?

You must contact the responsible authorities in the other member states for information on how to reclaim VAT incurred in those countries. Details of the authorities are given in Notice 723 "Refunds of VAT in the EC for EC and non-EC businesses".

21 TERRITORY OF THE EUROPEAN COMMUNITY (THE EC)

From 1 January 2007, the VAT territory of the EC is made up of 27 member states. The following table shows the member states and their territories which are included or excluded for VAT purposes.

Member State	*Including*	*but excluding*
Austria	Jungholz and Mittelberg.	
Belgium		
Bulgaria		
Cyprus	the British Sovereign Base Areas of Akrotiri and Dhekelia,	the United Nations buffer zone and the part of Cyprus to the north of the buffer zone, where the Republic of Cyprus does not exercise effective control.
Czech Republic		
Denmark		the Faroe Islands and Greenland.
Estonia		
Finland		Aland Islands.
France	Monaco,	Martinique, French Guiana, Guadeloupe, Reunion and St Pierre and Miquelon.
Germany		the Island of Heligoland, and Büsingen.
Greece		Mount Athos (also known as Agion Oros).
Hungary		
Ireland		
Italy		Campione d'Italia, the Italian waters of Lake Lugano and Lvigno.
Latvia		
Lithuania		
Luxembourg		
Malta		
Netherlands		Antilles
Poland		
Portugal	the Azores, and Madeira.	
Romania		
Slovakia		
Slovenia		
Spain	the Balearic Islands,	the Canary Islands, Ceuta and Melilla.
Sweden		
United Kingdom	the Isle of Man,	the Channel Islands and Gibraltar.

21.1 Other areas not within the EC

Liechtenstein, the Vatican City, Andorra and San Marino are not within the EC for VAT purposes.

22 DECISION TABLES FOR TELECOMMUNICATIONS SERVICES, HIRED GOODS (OTHER THAN MEANS OF TRANSPORT), RADIO AND TELEVISION BROADCASTING SERVICES

(referred to in paragraphs 5.5, 15.9.4, 15.10.5, 15.11.4 and section 16).

22.1 What does this section cover?

This section provides more specific guidance through examples with explanations of place of supply, use and enjoyment implications and the UK VAT position.

It is important that you read each row in a table in its entirety.

Table 1	Paragraph 22.2 – gives examples where the supplier belongs in the UK.
Table 2	Paragraph 22.3 – gives examples where the supplier belongs in another member state.
Table 3	Paragraph 22.4 – gives examples where the supplier belongs outside the EC.

22.2 Table 1: Examples where the supplier belongs in the UK

Customer belongs (see section 3)	*UK VAT position is that***	*Additional rules: use and enjoyment provisions (see section 16)*
in the UK.	services are supplied in the UK and the supplier accounts for any UK VAT due.	Services used and enjoyed outside the EC are outside the scope of UK (and EC) VAT.
in another member state and receives a B2B supply of services.	services are supplied in the other member state and are outside the scope of UK VAT.	Do not apply.
in another member state and receives a B2C supply of services.	services are supplied in the UK and the supplier accounts for any UK VAT due.	Services used and enjoyed outside the EC are outside the scope of UK (and EC) VAT.
outside the EC.	services are supplied outside the EC and are outside the scope of UK (and EC) VAT.	Services used and enjoyed in the UK are supplied in the UK and the supplier accounts for any UK VAT due.

**This is the correct VAT treatment unless the additional rules shown in the last column apply.

22.3 Table 2: Examples where the supplier belongs in another member state

Customer belongs (see section 3)	*UK VAT position is that***	*Additional rules: use and enjoyment provisions (see section 16)*
in the UK and receives a B2B supply of services.	services are supplied in the UK and the customer accounts for UK VAT by applying the reverse charge (see section 18).	Services used and enjoyed outside the EC are outside the scope of UK (and EC) VAT.
in the UK and receives a B2C supply of services.	services are supplied in the supplier's member state and are outside the scope of UK VAT (invoices will show local VAT).	Do not apply.

Customer belongs (see section 3)	*UK VAT position is that***	*Additional rules: use and enjoyment provisions (see section 16)*
in another member state.	services are supplied in another member state and are outside the scope of UK VAT.	Do not apply.
outside the EC.	services are supplied outside the EC and are outside the scope of UK (and EC) VAT.	Services used and enjoyed in the UK are supplied in the UK and the supplier accounts for any UK VAT due, unless the customer provides a UK registration number and accounts for UK VAT by applying the reverse charge (see section 18).

** This is the correct VAT treatment unless the additional rules shown in the last column apply.

22.4 Table 3: Examples where the supplier belongs outside the EC

Customer belongs (see section 3)	*UK VAT position is that***	*Additional rules: use and enjoyment provisions (see section 16)*
in the UK and receives a B2B supply of services.	services are supplied in the UK and the customer accounts for any UK VAT by applying the reverse charge (see section 18).	Services used and enjoyed outside the EC are outside the scope of UK (and EC) VAT.
in the UK and receives a B2C supply of services.	services are supplied in the supplier's country and are outside the scope of UK (and EC) VAT – use and enjoyment provisions are likely to apply.	Services used and enjoyed in the UK are supplied in the UK and the supplier accounts for any UK VAT due.
in another member state and receives a B2B supply of services.	services are supplied in the other member state and are outside the scope of UK VAT.	Do not apply.
in another member state and receives a B2C supply of services.	services are supplied in the supplier's county and are outside the scope of UK (and EC) VAT.	Services used and enjoyed in the UK are supplied in the UK and the supplier accounts for any UK VAT due.
outside the EC.	services are supplied outside the EC and are outside the scope of UK (and EC) VAT.	Services used and enjoyed in the UK are supplied in the UK and the supplier accounts for any UK VAT due, unless the customer provides a UK registration number and accounts for UK VAT by applying the reverse charge (see section 18).

**This is the correct VAT treatment unless the additional rules shown in the last column apply.

23 DECISION TABLES FOR ELECTRONICALLY SUPPLIED SERVICES

(referred to in paragraph 5.5 and section 17)

23.1 What does this section cover?

This section provides more specific guidance through examples with explanations of place of supply, use and enjoyment implications and the UK VAT position.

It is important that you read each row in a table in its entirety.

Table 1	Paragraph 23.2 – gives examples where the supplier belongs in the UK.
Table 2	Paragraph 23.3 – gives examples where the supplier belongs in another member state.

Table 3	Paragraph 23.4 – gives examples where the supplier belongs outside the EC.

23.2 Table 1: Examples where the supplier belongs in the UK

Customer belongs (see section 3)	*UK VAT position is that***	*Additional rules: use and enjoyment provisions (see section 17)*
in the UK and receives a B2B supply of services.	services are supplied in the UK and the supplier accounts for any VAT due.	Services used and enjoyed outside the EC are outside the scope of UK (and EC) VAT.
in the UK and receives a B2C supply of services.	services are supplied in the UK and the supplier accounts for any VAT due.	Do not apply.
in another member state and receives a B2B supply of services.	services are outside the scope of UK VAT and the customer accounts for any VAT due.	Do not apply.
in another member state and receives a B2C supply of services.	services are supplied in the UK and the supplier accounts for any VAT due.	Do not apply.
outside the EC and receives a B2B supply of services.	if the services are not used and enjoyed in the EC the services are outside the scope of UK and EC VAT.	Services used and enjoyed in the UK are supplied in the UK and the supplier accounts for any VAT due. Services used and enjoyed in another member state are outside the scope of UK VAT but may be within the scope of VAT in the member state where they are used and enjoyed. Check with member state.
outside the EC and receives a B2C supply of services.	services are supplied outside the EC and outside the scope of UK (and EC) VAT.	Do not apply.

***This is the correct VAT treatment unless the additional rules shown in the last column apply.*

23.3 Table 2: Examples where the supplier belongs in the EC

Customer belongs (see section 3)	*UK VAT position is that***	*Additional rules: use and enjoyment provisions (see section 17)*
in the UK and receives a B2B supply of services.	services are supplied in the UK. Customer accounts for any UK VAT by applying the reverse charge (see section 18).	Services used and enjoyed outside the EC are outside the scope of UK VAT.
in the UK and receives a B2C supply of services.	services are supplied in the supplier's member state and the supplier accounts for any VAT due.	Do not apply.
in another member state.	services are outside the scope of UK VAT.	Do not apply.
outside the EC and receives a B2B supply of services.	if the services are not used and enjoyed in the EC the services are outside the scope of UK and EC VAT.	Services used and enjoyed in the UK are supplied in the UK. Supplier accounts for any VAT due unless the customer provides a UK VAT registration number and accounts for UK VAT using the reverse charge.

Customer belongs (see section 3)	UK VAT position is that**	Additional rules: use and enjoyment provisions (see section 17)
		Services used and enjoyed in another member state are outside the scope of UK VAT but may be within the scope of VAT in the member state where they are used and enjoyed. Check with member state.
outside the EC and receives a B2C supply of services.	services are supplied outside the EC and outside the scope of UK (and EC) VAT.	Do not apply.

***This is the correct VAT treatment unless the additional rules shown in the last column apply.*

23.4 Table 3: Examples where the supplier belongs outside the EC

Customer belongs (see section 3)	UK VAT position is that**	Additional rules: use and enjoyment provisions (see section 17)
in the UK and receives a B2B supply of services.	services are supplied in the UK. Customer accounts for any UK VAT by applying the reverse charge (see section 18).	Services used and enjoyed outside the EC are outside the scope of UK VAT.
in the UK and receives a B2C supply of services.	services are supplied in the UK. Supplier should account for any UK VAT due. (Supplier may opt to use the special scheme, subject to conditions.)	Do not apply.
in another member state.	services to customer in another member state are outside the scope of UK VAT.	Do not apply.
outside the EC and receives a B2B supply of services.	services are supplied outside the EC and are outside the scope of UK (and EC) VAT.	Services used and enjoyed in the UK are supplied in the UK. Supplier accounts for any UK VAT due unless the customer provides a UK VAT registration number and accounts for UK VAT using the reverse charge (see section 18). Services used and enjoyed in another member state are outside the scope of VAT but may be within the scope of VAT in the member state where they are used and enjoyed. Check with member state.
outside the EC and receives a B2C supply of services.	services are supplied outside the EC and are outside the scope of UK (and EC) VAT.	Do not apply.

***This is the correct VAT treatment unless the additional rules shown in the last column apply.*

NOTICE 742A
OPTING TO TAX LAND AND BUILDINGS

March 2015

This notice cancels and replaces Notice 742A (April 2014). Details of any changes to the previous version can be found in paragraph 1.2 of this notice.

The following areas of this notice have the force of law under Schedule 10 of the VAT Act 1994.

The text within boxes in paragraphs 2.7.5, 3.4.2, 3.6.2, 5.6, 6.3.6, 6.3.8, 8.1.4, 8.1.6, 8.3.4, 8.3.7 and 14.9, which explains how to make a notification or application and what information it should contain.

The text within boxes A–L in paragraphs 2.7.2, 3.4.3, 3.6.3, 5.2, 6.3.5, 8.1.2, 8.3.3, 13.8.6, 13.9.1, 14.8.3 and 14.9 and 14.12.

EXAMPLE:

The following statement has the force of the law.

Notification of the exclusion of a new building from the effect of an option to tax (*for the purpose of paragraph 27 of Sch 10 to VATA 1994*) must be made on form VAT 1614F and must contain the information requested on that form.

1 INTRODUCTION

1.1 What is this notice about?

This notice explains the effect of an option to tax and will help you to decide whether to exercise that option. It will tell you whether you need permission from HM Revenue and Customs (HMRC) before you can opt to tax, and how to notify HMRC of your decision. Prior to 1 June 2008, the option to tax was also referred to as the election to waive exemption. From 1 June 2008, it's only referred to as the option to tax.

HMRC recommends that you also read VAT Notice 742: land and property which gives basic information relating to supplies of land.

This notice assumes that you have a working knowledge of basic VAT principles as outlined in VAT Notice 700: the VAT Guide.

This notice is available both on paper and on the internet.

Commentary—*De Voil Indirect Tax Service* **V4.114–V4.116**.

1.2 What's changed?

This notice replaces the April 2014 edition of Notice 742A: Opting to tax land and buildings. The following boxes have been amended to accurately reflect the tertiary law:

— 5.2, 6.3, 8.1, 8.3, 14.9, 14.12 and
— Annex 1.

1.3 What effect does an option to tax have?

Supplies of land and buildings, such as freehold sales, leasing or renting, are normally exempt from VAT. This means that no VAT is payable, but the person making the supply cannot normally recover any of the VAT incurred on their own expenses.

However, you can opt to tax land. For the purposes of VAT, the term 'land' includes any buildings or structures permanently affixed to it. You don't need to own the land in order to opt to tax. Once you have opted to tax all the supplies you make of your interest in the land or buildings will normally be standard rated, and you will normally be able to recover any VAT you incur in making those supplies.

1.4 Who should read this notice?

You should read this notice if you make, or intend to make supplies of any interest in land, buildings or civil engineering works.

1.5 Note about terminology used in this notice

For the purpose of this notice:

— "property" means land (including buildings and civil engineering works), and

— an "interest in" property means any interest in, right over or licence to occupy property.

1.6 What law covers this notice?

The area of VAT law which specifies the supplies of land and buildings that are exempt from VAT is Group 1 of Sch 9 to VATA 1994. The law detailing the option to tax is found in Sch 10 to VATA 1994.

Some areas of this notice have force of law. Such areas are identified in the foreword to this notice.

2 THE SCOPE OF AN OPTION TO TAX

2.1 What am I opting to tax?

You are opting to tax land. For the purposes of VAT, the term 'land' includes buildings. When you opt to tax, you can specify an area of land or a 'building'. Commonly, you will specify a 'building' because that is the prominent feature of the land. If you specify:

— a building - the option to tax will continue to apply to the land on which the building stood if the building is demolished and to any future buildings constructed on the land
— land - the option will apply to any buildings on the land and future buildings constructed on the land

In both circumstances, you can specifically exclude new buildings from the effect of an option to tax if you wish to (see paragraph 2.7). Further details about the scope of an option to tax are in paragraph 2.4.

Commentary—*De Voil Indirect Tax Service* **V4.114–V4.116**.

2.2 What constitutes a "building"?

Usually it will be clear what constitutes a "building", for instance an office block or a factory. However in some instances the law treats more than one building as being a single "building" for the purpose of the option to tax. These are:

— buildings that are linked, or if not yet built are planned to be linked - see paragraph 2.3 for more information on links
— a complex consisting of a number of units grouped around a fully enclosed concourse, such as a shopping mall.

2.3 What is a "link"?

A link is an internal access or a covered walkway between buildings the purpose of which is to allow movement of goods and people.

It doesn't include:

— a car park, either above or below ground
— a public thoroughfare or
— a statutory requirement, such as a fire escape.

2.4 What is covered by the option to tax?

HMRC uses a number of basic principles to determine how far your option to tax extends over the land and associated buildings.

Option	*Principle*
Land	Your option to tax covers all the land, and any buildings or civil engineering works which are part of the land.
	Your option to tax will cover the discrete area of land that you specify, and will not affect any adjoining land.
	If you construct a new building on land that you have opted, the building will be covered by the option to tax unless you notify us that you wish to exclude the building from the effect of the option (paragraph 2.7 explains how to do this).

Option	*Principle*
Buildings	Your option to tax will cover the whole of the building, and the land under the building and within its curtilage (the land immediately around the building including, for example, forecourts and yards). If your interest in the building is restricted to one floor, your option to tax will still cover the remaining floors of the building. If the building stands in a large area of land, the extent of the curtilage (or how far the option to tax extends over the land) depends on how far the services of the building can be utilised. For example, a racecourse grandstand may provide electricity and shelter for stalls, or other facilities, within its peripheral area. An option to tax on the grandstand would extend over the whole area of land that uses the benefits. Equally, an option would normally extend to an area adjacent to a building which is put to a use that is ancillary to the use of the building, such as car parking. If the building is demolished or destroyed, your option to tax will still apply to the land on which the building stood and to any future buildings that are constructed on the land. However, if: —you opted to tax before 1 June 2008 —it is clear from your notification that the option was made on the building only (for example, you specified in your notification "Building at 1 High Street . . . ") you can, if you wish, treat the option as revoked once the building is demolished You don't need to notify us before revoking but you should retain evidence in case this is requested in the future.

2.5 Options exercised before 1 March 1995

Before 1 March 1995, slightly different rules applied to determine the scope of an option to tax. These rules will still apply to you if, before 1 March 1995, you opted to tax:

— agricultural land, or
— units within a parade, precinct or complex (such as a row of shops or a retail precinct).

If you have any queries about the scope of an option to tax exercised before 1 March 1995 in relation to agricultural land or a parade, precinct or complex, you should contact the Option to Tax National Unit (paragraph 4.2.3 shows how you may contact them).

2.6 What if I make changes to a building after I have opted to tax?

If you make changes to a building after you have opted to tax you will need to consider whether your option to tax covers those changes. This table below sets out the basic principles for the most common changes made.

Change	*Principle*
Extensions	If you have opted to tax a building and you extend it at a later date, upwards, downwards or sideways, your option to tax will apply to the whole of the extended building.
Linked buildings	If prior to their completion buildings are linked by an internal access or covered walkway (see paragraph 2.3 for more information on what is meant by a 'link') they are treated as a single building and an option to tax will apply to both parts. If a link is created after both buildings are completed, the option to tax will not flow through with the link.
Forming a complex	If you have a group of units that have been treated as separate buildings for the option to tax and you later decide to enclose them so as to form a complex which meets the description in paragraph 2.2, the option to tax will not spread to the un-opted units.

2.7 Excluding a new building from the effect of an option to tax

2.7.1 In what circumstances can I exclude a new building from the effect of an option?

If you construct a new building on opted land (and that building is not within the curtilage of an existing building - for the meaning of "curtilage", see paragraph 2.4) you may exclude the new building (and land within its curtilage) from the effect of the option to tax by notifying us of the exclusion.

If you decide to do this, the new building will be permanently excluded from the effect of your existing option to tax. But you may, if you wish, make a fresh option to tax in the future, subject to obtaining permission from us if appropriate - see Section 5.

If you choose to exclude a new building from the effect of an option to tax this may affect your entitlement to recover input tax on your costs. See Section 9 for further information about input tax.

2.7.2 What is the earliest time that I can exclude a building?

The earliest time that you can exclude a building from the effect of an option to tax is when construction begins. The time when construction of a building begins, for this purpose, is determined by box A.

Box A

The boxed text below has the force of law.

> The time at which the construction of a new building is taken to begin for the purposes of excluding it from the effect of an option to tax (for the purposes of para 27(7) of Sch 10 to VATA 1994).
>
> Construction of a building begins when it progresses above the level of the Notice 742A "Opting to tax land and buildings".

Usually, a building will have progressed above the level of the foundations at the point at which the first brick is laid.

2.7.3 When does exclusion have effect?

Exclusion has effect from the earliest of the following times, when:

— a grant of an interest in the building is first made
— the new building, or any part of it, is first used
— the new building is completed

2.7.4 When must I notify the exclusion?

An exclusion is only valid if it is notified to HMRC. Notification must be made after construction has begun (see paragraph 2.7.2) and, normally, within 30 days of the date the exclusion has effect (see paragraph 2.7.3). A longer period may be allowed in exceptional circumstances.

2.7.5 How do I notify you?

The following statement has the force of the law.

> Notification of the exclusion of a new building from the effect of an option to tax (*for the purpose of paragraph 27 of Sch 10 to VATA 1994*) must be made on form VAT 1614F and must contain the information requested on that form.

Form VAT1614F VAT: new buildings - exclusion from an option to tax (www.gov.uk/government/publications/vat-new-buildings-exclusion-from-an-option-to-tax-vat1614f) is available online or you can contact the VAT Helpline on Telephone: 0300 200 3700.

3 SUPPLIES NOT AFFECTED BY AN OPTION TO TAX

3.1 What supplies are not affected by an option to tax?

There are some supplies where, even if you have opted to tax, the option will not apply. *If you make any of the supplies described in this section your supplies will remain exempt from VAT even if you have opted to tax. This may have an impact on how much input tax you can claim or make it necessary for you to repay input tax that you have previously claimed.*

The table below summarises supplies on which the option to tax will have no effect and indicates where certificates are required.

Type of supply	Paragraph number (see below)	Evidence required
1. Buildings designed or adapted and intended for use as dwellings (for example existing houses and flats).	Paragraph 3.2	No certificate required. Recommend: evidence of intended use retained.
2. Buildings designed or adapted and intended for use for relevant residential purpose.	Paragraph 3.3	No certificate required, but purchasers or tenants must inform supplier of intended use. Recommend: Written confirmation of intended use is retained by supplier.
3. Buildings for conversion into dwellings etc (for example pub conversions).	Paragraph 3.4	Certificate (VAT1614D) must be given by recipient and retained by supplier.
4. Buildings intended to be used for a relevant charitable purpose.	Paragraph 3.5	No certificate required, but purchasers or tenants must inform supplier of intended use. Recommend: Written confirmation of intended use is retained by the supplier.
5. Land sold to a relevant housing association.	Paragraph 3.6	Certificate (VAT1614G) must be given by the recipient and retained by the supplier.
6. Land sold to an individual for construction of a dwelling	Paragraph 3.7	No certificate required.
7. Pitches for residential caravans.	Paragraph 3.8	No certificate required.
8. Moorings for residential houseboats.	Paragraph 3.9	No certificate required.
9. Supplies affected by the anti-avoidance measures.	Paragraph 3.11 and Section 13	No certificate required.

Commentary—*De Voil Indirect Tax Service* **V4.114–V4.116.**

3.2 Buildings designed or adapted and intended for use as dwellings

Your option to tax will not apply if you supply a building, or part of a building, that is designed or adapted and intended for use as a dwelling (such as a house), or as a number of dwellings (such as a block of flats). HMRC recommends that you retain evidence to show that the building is intended for use as a dwelling or number of dwellings. VAT Notice 708: buildings and construction explains what is meant by "designed as a dwelling".

3.3 Buildings designed or adapted and intended to be used for relevant residential purposes

Your option to tax will not apply if you supply a building, or part of a building that's designed or adapted for use for a relevant residential purpose (such as a nursing home) and the purchaser or tenant informs you before you make your supply that it is intended for use solely for a relevant residential purpose. Whilst there's no requirement for a formal certificate to be given, HMRC strongly recommends that you obtain confirmation of the intended use in writing and retain it with your VAT records.

Where part of a building is intended for use solely for a relevant residential purpose and part is not, your option to tax will not apply to the part to be used for a relevant residential purpose, but only where the different functions are to be carried out in clearly defined areas. In these circumstances the value of your supply should be fairly apportioned between the exempt and taxable elements.

A building used for a relevant residential purpose is one in which some of the facilities, such as dining rooms and bathrooms, are shared, but this doesn't include use as a hospital, prison, hotel or similar establishment. Examples include residential homes for children, the elderly or disabled persons and student halls of residence. See VAT Notice 708: buildings and construction for further details about the meaning of "solely for a relevant residential purpose".

3.4 Buildings for conversion into dwellings etc.

Your option to tax will not apply if you supply a building or part of a building that is not designed or adapted as a dwelling (or number of dwellings) or for a relevant residential purpose but you receive a certificate (VAT1614D) from the recipient of your supply (by the time described in paragraph 3.4.3 and paragraph 3.4.4) certifying that it is intended for use as a dwelling or number of dwellings or solely for a relevant residential purpose. This can apply where the building, or relevant part, is either intended for such use:

— without conversion work being undertaken
— after conversion.

3.4.1 In what circumstances can I issue a certificate?

As a recipient of a supply, you may certify that a building or part of a building is intended for use as a dwelling or solely for a relevant residential purpose only if you—

— intend to use the building (or part of the building) as a dwelling or solely for a relevant residential purpose,
— intend to convert the building (or part of a building) with a view to it being used as a dwelling or solely for a relevant residential purpose, or
— are a "relevant intermediary" (see paragraph 3.4.5)

You may not issue a certificate if the building is to be put to a non-qualifying use for a period before being used as a dwelling or solely for a relevant residential purpose. However, minor or incidental non-qualifying use (such as storing goods for a short period) is disregarded.

For the meaning of "solely for a relevant residential purpose", see paragraph 3.3 and VAT Notice 708: buildings and construction.

3.4.2 What form must the certificate take?

The following statement has the force of the law.

> Certification of intention to use a building (or part of a building) as a dwelling or dwellings or solely for a relevant residential purpose (*for the purpose of paragraph 6 of Sch 10 to VATA 1994*) must be made on form VAT 1614D and must contain the information requested on that form.

Form VAT1614D VAT: certificate to disapply the option to tax buildings for conversion into dwellings etc (www.gov.uk/government/publications/vat-certificate-to-disapply-the-option-to-tax-buildings-for-conversion-into-dwellings-etc-vat1614d) is available online or you can contact the VAT Helpline on Telephone: 0300 200 3700.

3.4.3 When should the certificate be provided?

As a supplier, if you receive a certificate by the time set out in Box B below, you *must* exempt your supply of the building or part of the building to which the certificate relates.

Box B

This boxed text below has the force of the law.

> Time by which a certificate of intended use as a dwelling (or dwellings) or solely for a relevant residential purpose must be given to the seller making the supply (*for the purpose of paragraph 6(2) of Sch 10 to VATA 1994*)

The certificate must be given before the price for the grant to the recipient by the seller is legally fixed, eg by exchange of contracts, letters or missives, or the signing of heads of agreement.

3.4.4 Can I accept a certificate after the time specified in Box B?

If you receive a certificate after the time the price for the grant has been legally fixed, you don't have to accept the certificate, but may do so at your discretion, but only in respect of supplies that arise after the certificate is given. For example, if you have granted a lease for periodic rental payments, you may only exempt the rental supplies that take place after you receive a certificate. If you sell the freehold, you may only exempt the supply if it takes place after you receive a certificate (in the case of freehold sales, the supply would typically take place at completion). It should be noted that it is the fixing of the price of the grant that establishes the time by which the certificate should be given. Care should be taken, particularly in relation to the signing of the heads of agreement, as this will not in all cases legally fix the price.

3.4.5 What is a "relevant intermediary"?

You're a "relevant intermediary" if you're purchasing an interest in a building or part of a building and—

— •you intend to dispose of the whole of the interest you are purchasing to another
— your prospective purchaser has given you a certificate certifying that they:
  — intend to convert the building (or part of it) with a view to it being used as a dwelling or solely for a relevant residential purpose
  — are a "relevant intermediary".

If you're a "relevant intermediary", the certificate you receive from your prospective purchaser serves 2 purposes.

(1) it allows you to issue a certificate to disapply your supplier's option to tax (so that your purchase of the building, or relevant part, is exempt).
(2) it will disapply your own option to tax (if you have made one) when you come to supply the building on to your purchaser (so that your sale of the building, or relevant part, is exempt).

3.4.6 What if only part of building is intended for use as a dwelling or for a relevant residential purpose?

If only part of the building is intended for use as a dwelling or solely for a relevant residential purpose, the certificate should make it clear that this is the case and must contain a description of the qualifying part. The option to tax will apply to the part of the building that is not intended for the qualifying use and the value of the supply should be fairly apportioned between the exempt and taxable elements. You can find out more about apportionment in VAT Notice 700: the VAT Guide.

3.4.7 What if I make more than one supply of an interest in the building?

If you make more than one supply of a relevant interest in a building to the person who has given you the certificate (for example, because you have granted a lease for periodic rental payments), your option will be disapplied in relation to all subsequent supplies that arise from the same grant in the building or parts of the building covered by the certificate. You should note that you're not obliged to accept a certificate if you receive it after the point at which the price for the grant is legally fixed. See paragraph 3.4.4.

3.5 Buildings to be used solely for a relevant charitable purpose

Your option to tax will not apply if you supply a building, or part of a building, and the purchaser or tenant informs you before you make your supply that they intend to use it solely for a relevant charitable purpose, other than as an office for general administration for example, head office functions of the charity. Whilst there's no requirement for a formal certificate to be given, HMRC strongly recommends that you obtain confirmation of the intended use in writing and retain it with your VAT records.

Where part of a building is intended to be used solely for a relevant charitable purpose (other than as an office) and part is not, your option to tax will not apply to the part used for a relevant charitable purpose, provided that the different functions are carried out in clearly defined areas. In these circumstances the value of your supply should be fairly apportioned between the exempt and taxable elements.

Relevant charitable purpose means use by a charity for its non-business activities, or as a village hall or similarly to provide social or recreational facilities for a local community. See VAT Notice 701/1: charities for more information on non-business activities carried out by such bodies and VAT Notice 708: buildings and construction for further details about the meaning of "solely for a relevant charitable purpose".

3.6 Land sold to a relevant housing association

Your option to tax will not apply if you supply land to a relevant housing association which provides you with a certificate (by the time described in paragraphs 3.6.3 and paragraph 3.6.4) certifying that, after any necessary demolition work, dwellings or relevant residential buildings will be constructed on the land. Where only part of the land is to be put to such use your option to tax will only be disapplied in relation to that part and you should therefore apportion the value of your supply between the exempt and taxable elements.

3.6.1 What is a relevant housing association?

A relevant housing association is a:

- registered social landlord within the meaning of Part 1 of the Housing Act 1996
- registered social landlord within the meaning of the Housing (Scotland) Act 2001 or
- registered housing association within the meaning of Part 2 of the Housing (Northern Ireland) Order 1992, or
- private registered provider of social housing within the meaning given by s 80(3) of the Housing and Regeneration Act 2008.

3.6.2 What form must the certificate take?

The following statement has the force of the law.

> Certification by a relevant housing association that land is to be used (after any necessary demolition work) for the construction of a building or buildings intended for use as a dwelling or number of dwellings or solely for a relevant residential purpose (*for the purpose of paragraph 10 of Sch 10 to VATA 1994*) must be made on certificate VAT 1614G and must contain the information requested on that form.

Form VAT1614G VAT: certificate to disapply the option to tax land sold to housing associations (www.gov.uk/government/publications/vat-certificate-to-disapply-the-option-to-tax-land-sold-to-housing-associations-vat1614g) is available online or you can contact the VAT Helpline on Telephone: 0300 200 3700.

3.6.3 When must the certificate be provided?

As a supplier, if you receive a certificate by the time set out in Box C below, you *must* exempt your supply of the land to which the certificate relates.

Box C

This boxed text below has the force of the law.

> Time by which a certificate of intended use of the land for constructing a dwelling, a number of dwellings, or solely for a relevant residential purpose must be given to the person making the supply (*for the purpose of paragraph 10(2) of Sch 10 to VATA 1994*)

The certificate must be given before the price for the grant to the recipient by the seller is legally fixed, eg exchange of contracts, by missives or letters, or the signing of heads of agreement.

3.6.4 Can I accept a certificate after the time specified in Box C?

If you receive a certificate after the time the price for the grant has been legally fixed, you don't have to accept the certificate, but may do so at your discretion, but only in respect of supplies that arise after the certificate is given. For example, if you have granted a lease for periodic rental payments, you may only exempt the rental supplies that take place after you receive a certificate. If you sell the freehold, you may only exempt the supply if it takes place after you receive a certificate (in the case of freehold sales, the supply would typically take place at completion). You should also note that the signing of the heads of agreement will not always fix the price of the grant.

3.7 Land sold to an individual for construction of a dwelling

Your option to tax will not apply if you supply land to someone who intends to build a dwelling on it for their own use, and not in the course or furtherance of any business carried on by them (no certificate is required). This includes cases where the purchaser intends to engage a builder to carry out the construction work on his behalf.

3.8 Pitches for residential caravans

Your option to tax will not apply if you supply a pitch for a permanent residential caravan (no certificate is required). A residential caravan is one where residence throughout the year is not prevented by covenant, planning consent or similar permission. See VAT Notice 701/20: caravans and houseboats for further information about caravan pitches.

3.9 Moorings for residential houseboats

Your option to tax will not apply if you supply facilities for the mooring or berthing of a residential houseboat (no certificate is required). A houseboat is a floating decked structure that is designed or adapted for use solely as a place of permanent habitation. A houseboat does not have the means of, nor is capable of being readily adapted for, self-propulsion. A residential houseboat is one where residence throughout the year is not prevented by covenant, planning consent or similar permission.

3.10 Building to be used for both commercial and residential purposes

If you supply a building that is intended to be used partly for commercial and partly for residential purposes, such as a shop with a flat above, you should apportion your supply between the taxable and exempt (or zero rated) elements. You may choose the method of apportionment but it must provide a fair and reasonable result. You can find out more about apportionment in VAT Notice 700: the VAT Guide.

A certificate might be required in order for you to treat the area intended for use as a dwelling as exempt. This depends on the status of that area of the building at the time of your supply if it is:

— already designed or adapted for use as a dwelling (for example, is already a flat), no certificate is required (see paragraph 3.2)
— not already designed or adapted as a dwelling at that time (for example, is office space intended for conversion into a flat), certificate VAT1614D is required (see paragraph 3.4)

3.11 Land or building affected by the anti-avoidance measures

The option to tax has no effect in relation to supplies resulting from a grant that falls within the anti-avoidance measures described within Section 13.

4 HOW TO OPT TO TAX

4.1 What do I need to do if I want to opt to tax?

There are 2 stages in opting to tax. The first stage is making the decision to opt. This may take place at a board meeting or similar, or less formally. However you reach your decision, HMRC recommends that you keep a written record, showing clear details of the land or buildings you are opting to tax, and the date you made your decision.

If you have previously made exempt supplies of the land or building you may need our permission before you can opt to tax. You can find more information about this in Section 5.

The second stage is to notify us of your decision in writing. Paragraph 4.2 explains how you should do this.

Commentary—*De Voil Indirect Tax Service* **V4.114–V4.116**.

4.2 Notification of an option to tax

4.2.1 When should I notify my option to tax?

For your option to tax to be valid you must normally make your notification within 30 days of your decision. You can ask HMRC to accept a notification made more than 30 days after your decision but we will not do so unless we are satisfied that you made your decision to opt at the relevant time. If you would like us to consider accepting a belated notification, you should enclose with your notification an explanation of your circumstances and any evidence that will help to show us that the decision was made at the relevant time.

We will normally accept a belated notification if you provide:

— direct documentary evidence that the decision was made at the relevant time (eg copies of correspondence with third parties referring to the option to tax)

— evidence that output tax has been charged and accounted for and input tax claimed in accordance with the option and a responsible person (such as a director) provides a written declaration that the decision to opt was made at the relevant time and that all relevant facts have been given

HMRC might accept a belated notification in other circumstances. This will depend on the facts of your case.

4.2.2 What should I include on my notification?

Your notification must state clearly what land or buildings you are opting to tax, and the date from which the option has effect (see paragraph 4.3). HMRC suggests you use the notification Form VAT1614A VAT: notification of an option to tax land and/or buildings is available online or you can contact the VAT Helpline on Telephone: 0300 200 3700.

If you're opting to tax discrete areas of land HMRC suggests that you send a map or plan clearly showing the opted land with your notification. If you're opting a building that has a postal address please give it in full including the postcode.

It would speed up our processing of your notification if you include your VAT registration number, or if your registration is pending, your VAT Registration Unit reference number.

It's important that an appropriate person signs the notification and any accompanying list or schedule. See Section 7 for more information.

4.2.3 Where should I send my notification?

If you're already registered for VAT, your notification should be made to our centralised Option to Tax Unit in writing, either by post to:

— by post to HM Revenue & Customs, Option to Tax National Unit, Cotton House, 7 Cochrane Street, Glasgow, G1 1GY or

— Fax to: 03000 529 807

— Scanning a signed letter or form and sending it by email to: optiontotaxnationalunit@hmrc.gsi.gov.uk

If you're not registered but need or wish to be registered for VAT as a result of your option to tax, your application to register for VAT and your notification of the option to tax should be submitted together to the appropriate VAT Registration Unit (see VAT Notice 700/1: should I be registered for VAT?). Information about registering for VAT is available on the GOV.UK website (www.gov.uk/vat-registration).

4.2.4 Will I receive an acknowledgement of my notification?

HMRC will normally acknowledge receipt of your notification within 15 working days, although this is not necessary for the option to tax to have legal effect. You should not delay charging VAT just because you have not received our acknowledgement.

4.2.5 What if I am notifying an option to tax in relation to land or buildings which are being transferred as a going concern?

You should read Section 11.

4.3 What is the effective date of my option to tax?

Your option to tax will have effect from the date of your decision, or any later date that you have specified, providing you notify HMRC in writing within the relevant time limits (see paragraph 4.2).

In no circumstances can an option to tax have effect from a date before you made your decision to opt.

4.4 Who is bound by the option to tax?

It's for you alone to decide whether to opt to tax any land or buildings. If you do decide to opt to tax and are not a member of a VAT group or intend to become one in the future, only the supplies you make of your interest in the land or building will be affected. Your option to tax will not affect supplies made by anyone else. For example, if you are selling an opted building the purchaser has the choice of whether to opt to tax or not. Similarly, if your tenant is sub-letting, they too have this same choice. For this reason, HMRC suggests that you inform your tenant of your decision at the earliest opportunity so that they may safeguard their right to recover input tax by opting to tax, should they wish to.

If you're a member of a VAT group your option to tax may affect other members. As "relevant associates" they may be bound by your option to tax (see paragraph 6.3).

4.5 What happens if I make an option but at the time of making it, intend to revoke it under the "cooling-off" period?

If, at the time of making an option you intend to revoke it during the 6 month "cooling-off" period (see paragraph 8.1), the option is treated as invalid from the outset.

5 PERMISSION TO OPT TO TAX

5.1 In what circumstances do I need permission from HMRC?

If you have made, or intend to make, any exempt supplies of the land or buildings within the 10 years prior to the date you wish your option to take effect, you will need our written permission to opt to tax unless you meet one or more of the automatic permission conditions set out below.

5.2 Automatic permission

You don't need to obtain our written permission before you opt to tax provided you meet the conditions HMRC have set out in a notice. The conditions have changed from time to time. Condition 3 was amended from 1 May 2009. If you meet any of the 4 conditions set out in box D below you do not need written permission before you opt to tax:

Box D

These conditions have the force of law.

Number	*Condition*
1.	It is a mixed-use development and the only exempt supplies have been in relation to the dwellings.
2.	You do not wish to recover any input tax in relation to the land or building incurred before your option to tax has effect; and —the consideration for your exempt supplies has, up to the date when your option to tax is to take effect, been solely by way of rents or service charges and excludes any premiums or payments in respect of occupation after the date on which the option takes effect. Regular rental and/or service charge payments can be ignored for the purposes of this condition. Payments are considered regular where the intervals between them are no more than a year and where each represents a commercial or genuine arms-length value; and —the only input tax relating to the land or building that you expect to recover after the option to tax takes effect will be on overheads, such as regular rental payments, service charges, repairs and maintenance costs. If you expect to claim input tax in relation to refurbishment or redevelopment of the building you will not meet this condition. Notes: When deciding whether you meet this condition you should disregard: —VAT refundable to local authorities and other bodies under s 33(2)(*b*) of VATA 1994; —any input tax you can otherwise recover by virtue of the partial exemption de minimis rules (Regulation 106, VAT Regulations 1995); and —any input tax you are entitled to recover on general business overheads not specifically related to the land or building, such as audit fees.
3.	You may opt to tax if you satisfy the first (outputs) requirement and (if applicable) the second (inputs) requirement. **Definitions** For the purposes of this condition: —"property" includes land, buildings and civil engineering works. —the question of whether a person is "connected" with another person is to be decided as it would be for the purposes of Part 1 of Sch 10 to VATA 1994 —"permissible exempt supplies" means the following exempt supplies arising from a grant in relation to the land: a. Supplies for which the consideration solely represents legal and/or valuation costs reimbursed under the agreement for the grant; or b. Supplies where: i. the consideration is provided by way of regular rents and/or service charges; and ii. the consideration relates to a period of occupation of the property and that period ends no later than 12 months from the date on which the option first takes effect; and iii. no opted supply, other than an opted supply relating solely to the same period of occupation as an exempt supply under point (ii) above, will be reduced in value as a result of the consideration payable for these exempt supplies. **First (outputs) requirement** You do not intend or expect that any supply which will be taxable as a result of you making your option to tax will either: 1. be made to a person connected with you; or 2. arise from an agreement under which you or another person has made or will make an exempt supply in respect of a right to occupy the property, where the right begins or continues after the date on which the option takes effect. **Application of the first (outputs) requirement** —You may disregard paragraph 1 of the requirement if the person connected with you is expected to be entitled to credit or refund of at least 80% of the VAT chargeable on the supply.

Number	Condition
	For the purposes of paragraph 2 of the requirement you may ignore permissible exempt supplies. **Second (inputs) requirement** 1. This requirement applies if you have been or expect to be entitled to credit for any part of the input tax incurred on your capital expenditure on the property as being wholly or partly attributable to supplies that are taxable supplies by virtue of your option to tax. 2. Where this requirement applies you must not intend or expect to use any part of the capital expenditure for either of the following purposes: a) making exempt supplies which do not confer a right to credit for input tax pursuant to s 26(2)(c) of VATA 1994; or b) for private or non-business purposes, other than purposes giving rise to a right to a refund of VAT on the supplies under ss 33, 33A or 41(3) of VATA 1994. **Application of the second (inputs) requirement** —For the purposes of the requirement, your capital expenditure is your expenditure on goods or services used in connection with the acquisition of, building works on, construction works on or the fitting out of, the property. Capital expenditure does not include expenditure on routine repairs and maintenance. —For the purposes of the requirement, "entitled to credit" includes a deduction or credit arising as a result of the application of Reg 109 or Part XV of the VAT Regulations 1995 (SI 1995/2518). —You may disregard paragraph 2a of the requirement if any of paragraphs a), b) or c) below apply: a) all the exempt supplies concerned are supplies which fulfil any of the following descriptions i. supplies within paras 5 to 11 of Sch 10 to VATA 1994 and made to a person who is not connected to you; ii. permissible exempt supplies; iii. supplies within Group 5 of Sch 9 to VATA 1994 which are incidental to one or more of your business activities; b) you make exempt supplies, but intend or expect the input tax incurred on your capital expenditure on the property that is attributed to those exempt supplies, including any subsequent adjustments to initial input tax deduction, will not exceed £5,000; c) you expect to be entitled to full credit for all the input tax incurred on your capital expenditure on the property as a result of the application of s 33(2) of VATA 1994.
4.	The exempt supplies have been incidental to the main use of the land or building. For example, where you have occupied a building for taxable purposes the following would be seen as incidental to the main use and the condition would be met: —allowing an advertising hoarding to be displayed; —granting space for the erection of a radio mast; —receiving income from an electricity sub-station. The letting of space to an occupying tenant, however minor, is not incidental.

5.3 Why is automatic permission condition 3 so long?

This condition has been written in a legally precise form in order to make sure it cannot be used for tax avoidance purposes. There is a flow diagram at Annex 2 of this notice which has been designed to assist in understanding this particular automatic permission condition.

5.4 What do I need to do if I meet one of the conditions?

If you meet one of the conditions and you decide that you want to opt to tax you still need to write to us to notify your option. You should state in your notification, preferably on Form VAT 1614A, that, although you have made previous exempt supplies of the land or building, you satisfy 1 of the conditions for automatic permission (clearly identifying which 1). Section 4 gives more information on notifying an option and the records you need to keep.

5.5 What if I don't meet any of the conditions?

If you don't meet any of the conditions for automatic permission you must obtain our written permission before you can opt to tax.

5.6 How do I apply for permission?

The following statement has the force of the law.

> An application for prior permission to opt to tax (*for the purpose of paragraphs 28 and 29 of Sch 10 to the VATA 1994*) must be made on form VAT 1614H and must contain the information requested on that form.

Form VAT 1614H: application for permission to opt (www.gov.uk/government/publications/vat-application-for-permission-to-opt-vat1614h) is available online or you can contact the VAT Helpline on Telephone: 0300 200 3700.

5.7 When will my option take effect?

Once permission is granted, your option will automatically take effect from your application date, or from any later date you request in your application. For applications made on or after 1 June 2008, there is no need for you to notify your option to tax separately once permission is granted.

If you wish your option to take effect from your application date, HMRC recommends you keep evidence of the date you submit the application form (such as a certificate of posting).

5.8 In what circumstances will you grant permission?

HMRC can't grant you permission to opt to tax until you provide all the information requested in application form VAT1614H and any additional information that we may ask for. Occasionally we will refuse permission if we are not satisfied that granting permission would result in a fair and reasonable attribution of input tax. If we are satisfied, we will write to you prior to granting permission and ask you to confirm that you still wish to proceed with your option to tax.

5.9 What if I fail to ask for permission?

If you notify HMRC of an option to tax without obtaining prior permission, in circumstances under which permission is required (see paragraph 5.1), your option to tax will be invalid. However, we have the discretion to treat the option as a valid option. HMRC will generally only exercise this discretion in cases where:

(a) tax would otherwise be at risk
(b) you took reasonable steps, before notifying the option, to determine whether permission was required, but failed to realise it was required due to a minor error or oversight - for example, you might have made a one off exempt supply which you had overlooked

If you think this should apply to you, please write to the Option to Tax National Unit (paragraph 4.2.3) shows how you may contact them) with details of your situation.

6 OPTION TO TAX AND VAT REGISTRATION

6.1 Liability to register for VAT

If you're not already registered for VAT, you should read VAT Notice 700/1: should I be registered for VAT? If you are required to or wish to register you should complete an application form and send it to the appropriate Registration Unit (listed in VAT Notice 700/1: Should I be registered for VAT?). The Registration Unit will need to be satisfied that you will be making taxable supplies, so you should send your option to tax notification with your application form. If you need HMRC's permission before opting to tax, you cannot register before we have given permission, so you should also enclose a copy of your written permission with your application.

If your turnover falls below the registration threshold and you deregister, the option to tax does not cease because you have deregistered. See Section 12 for more details.

Commentary—*De Voil Indirect Tax Service* **V2.144, V4.114–V4.116**.

6.2 How long must I keep records?

You must keep your correspondence and any record of your decision to opt to tax for a minimum of 6 years. An option to tax cannot normally be revoked until at least 20 years have passed - see Section 8. HMRC strongly recommends you keep your option to tax records for longer than 6 years.

Commentary—*De Voil Indirect Tax Service* **V5.201, V5.202**.

6.3 How does the option to tax affect group registrations?

6.3.1 What is a "relevant associate"?

An option to tax made by a member of a VAT group is generally binding upon other members of the same VAT group. A body corporate that is bound by another body corporate's option to tax under these rules is known as a "relevant associate" of the opter. If you're a relevant associate, you must normally charge VAT on any supplies you make of the opted property, even after you have left the VAT group.

For information about VAT groups, see VAT Notice 700/2: group and divisional registration.

You become a "relevant associate" if you are in the same VAT group as:

— the opter when the option first has effect
— the opter at any later time when the opter has an interest in the opted property
— another "relevant associate" of the opter when that relevant associate has an interest in the opted property

6.3.2 In what circumstances do I cease to be a "relevant associate"?

You cease to be a "relevant associate" in one of 3 ways, by:

— meeting the basic conditions explained below and automatically ceasing to be a relevant associate (see paragraph 6.3.3)
— meeting all of the specified conditions set out in box E below and notifying us on form VAT1614B (see paragraph 6.3.6)
— obtaining our permission (see paragraph 6.3.7)

6.3.3 Automatically ceasing to be a relevant associate

You will automatically cease to be a relevant associate in relation to an opted property if you meet *all* of the following conditions

— you're no longer in the VAT group in which you became a relevant associate, and
— you don't hold any interest in the opted property
— you have not disposed of the opted property on terms that may require the purchaser to make additional payment in the future, such payment is often referred to as an "overage" and can be contingent on such things as the purchaser obtaining planning permission
— you're not "connected" with any person who is the opter or relevant associate and who holds an interest in the land.

If you meet all of these conditions, you automatically cease to be a relevant associate from the time that all 4 conditions are met. There's no need for you to notify HMRC or to seek permission.

6.3.4 In what circumstances is a person connected with another?

See paragraph 13.7 of this notice.

6.3.5 Ceasing to be a relevant associate after 20 years

If you don't meet the basic conditions set out in paragraph 6.3.3, you will cease to be a relevant associate of an opter if you:

— meet all of the conditions specified in box E below
— notify us on form VAT1614B (see paragraph 6.3.6)

Box E

The boxed text below has the force of the law

Conditions for a body corporate to cease to be treated as a relevant associate of an opter (*for the purpose of paragraph 3(5)(a) of Sch 10 to VATA 1994* ("the VAT Act 1994")).

A body corporate ceases to be a relevant associate of an opter at the time when it meets all of the following conditions:

(1) **The grouping condition**
The body corporate has ceased to be treated as a member of the VAT group (see section 43 of the VAT Act 1994) by virtue of which it became a relevant associate of the opter.

(2) **The 20-year condition**
The body corporate has:
— held any relevant interest in the building or land acquired whilst a member of that VAT group for a period of at least 20 years; and
— been treated as a relevant associate of the opter for a period of at least 20 years.

(3) **The capital item condition**
Any land or building that is subject to the option is not, in relation to the body corporate, subject to input tax adjustment as a capital item under the capital goods scheme.

(4) **The valuation condition**
The body corporate, or a person connected with it, has not, within a period of ten years ending on the date that the body corporate ceases to be a relevant associate, made a supply of a relevant interest in the building or land that is subject to the option that:
– was for a consideration that was less than the open market value of that supply; or
– arose from a relevant grant.

(5) **The pre-payment condition**
No supply of goods or services has been made for a consideration to the body corporate (or to a person connected with it) which will be wholly or partly attributable to a supply or other use of the land or buildings made by that body (or by a person connected with it) more than 12 months later.

Explanatory Note 1

"Relevant interest in the building or land" means an interest in, right over or licence to occupy the building or land (or any part of it).

Explanatory Note 2

"Relevant grant" means a grant that the grantor intends or expects will give rise to a supply for a consideration significantly greater than any consideration for any earlier supply arising from the grant (except as a result of a rent review determined according to normal commercial practice).

Explanatory Note 3

For the purposes of conditions 4 and 5 above, any question whether a person is "connected" with another person is to be decided as it would be for the purposes of Part 1 of Sch 10 to the Act.

6.3.6 How do I notify you?

The following statement has the force of the law.

> Notification of cessation to be a relevant associate (*for the purpose of paragraph 4 of Sch 10 to VATA 1994*) must be made on form VAT 1614B and must contain the information requested on that form.

Form VAT1614B: ceasing to be a relevant associate in relation to an option to tax (www.gov.uk/government/publications/vat-ceasing-to-be-a-relevant-associate-in-relation-to-an-option-to-tax-vat1614b) is available online or you contact the VAT Helpline on Telephone: 0300 200 3700.

6.3.7 Applying for permission to cease to be a relevant associate

If you do not meet the all of the conditions set out in paragraph 6.3.2 or box E above, you may apply for permission to cease to be a relevant associate.

6.3.8 What form should my application take?

The following statement has the force of the law.

> Application for permission to cease to be a relevant associate (*for the purpose of paragraph 4 of Sch 10 to VATA 1994*) must be made on form VAT 1614B and must contain the information requested on that form.

You can download form VAT1614B from the HMRC website or obtain it from our VAT Helpline on Tel 0300 200 3700.

6.3.9 In what circumstances will you grant permission?

HMRC will not grant permission unless you meet conditions 1 and 2 of box E above.

In deciding whether or not to grant permission, we will give particular consideration to whether or not you or a third party has received a VAT benefit as a result of your actions.

6.3.10 If you grant permission, when will I cease to be a relevant associate?

You will cease to be a relevant associate from the date permission is granted, except in the circumstances specified below.

HMRC can only allow an earlier date if you previously gave a notification of ceasing to be a relevant associate believing, in error, that you met the conditions in box E above. If this is the case, we can allow you to cease to be a relevant associate from the date stated in the notification, but will not do so unless we are satisfied that the reasons for failing to meet the conditions are insignificant.

In granting permission, we can apply conditions. In cases where these are subsequently broken we may treat the original application for permission as invalid.

7 RESPONSIBILITY FOR OPTING TO TAX

7.1 Who is responsible for making the decision and notifying the option to tax?

The person responsible for making the decision and notifying the option to tax depends on the type of legal entity holding (or intending to hold) the interest in the land or building, and who within that entity has the authority to make decisions concerning VAT. In most cases it will be the sole proprietor, one or more partners (or trustees), a director or an authorised administrator. If you have appointed a third party to notify an option to tax on your behalf, HMRC require written confirmation that the third party is authorised to do so. We would also wish to be notified if you withdraw that authority. The following paragraphs explain who is responsible in other, slightly more unusual situations.

Commentary—*De Voil Indirect Tax Service* **V4.114–V4.116**.

7.2 Beneficial owners

In some cases there may be both a beneficial owner and a legal owner of land or buildings. An example of this is a bare trust, where a trustee is the legal owner but the benefit of the income from the land or building passes to the beneficial owner. For VAT purposes it is the beneficial owner who is making the supply of the land or building. It is the beneficial owner who should opt to tax, and who must account for any VAT due on the supply and claim any input tax that arises.

This is not the case, however, where the beneficiaries are numerous, such as unit trusts and pension funds. In such situations the person making the supply is the trustee who holds the legal interest and receives the immediate benefit of the consideration.

7.3 Joint owners

Joint ownership will arise if you and another person buy land or buildings together, or if you sell a part share of your land or building to someone else. If you are a joint owner it is likely that the only supply that can be made of the jointly owned land or building is by you and the other person together.

You and the other person should together notify a single option to tax if you want supplies of the jointly owned land or building to be standard rated. The taxable supply of the land or building is then made by both of you as one taxable person. To account for output tax and to be able to recover input tax, you and the other person should register for VAT together as if a partnership, even if you are not in partnership for any other purpose.

7.4 Limited partnerships

Under the Limited Partnership Act 1907 every limited partnership must be registered with the Registrar of Companies (Companies House). It follows that a limited partnership which is not registered with Companies House (such as an overseas limited partnership) cannot be treated as a limited partnership for VAT purposes and will normally be registered as a general partnership.

A limited partnership is made up of 1 or more "general" partners, who have unlimited liability, and one or more "limited" partners, who are not liable for debts and obligations of the firm. A limited partner is unable to take part in the management and running of the partnership business, and where HMRC finds that a limited partner is doing so, we will treat them as a general partner.

If there is only one general partner and one or more limited partners, the general partner is treated as a sole proprietor for VAT registration purposes. Likewise if there are 2 or more general partners and one or more limited partners, the general partners are treated as a partnership for VAT registration purposes. It is the general partner(s) who should opt to tax and account for any VAT due on the supply and claim any input tax that arises.

Where title to the land or building is held jointly in the names of the general partner(s) and the limited partner(s), only the titleholders can make any supplies of that land or building together. That suggests that the limited partner is involved in the management and running of the partnership, and as such HMRC treats them as a general partner and amend the VAT registration to reflect that. If the partnership decides to opt to tax, 1 or more of the partners should sign the notification.

7.5 Limited liability partnerships

A limited liability partnership has a separate legal status from its members and is able to enter into contracts in its own right. This means that the individual members of the limited liability partnership are protected from debts or liabilities arising from negligence, wrongful acts or conduct of another member, employee or agent of the partnership.

A limited liability partnership is a corporate body and is liable to register for VAT, subject to the normal registration rules. If the partnership decides to opt to tax, one or more members must sign the notification.

8 REVOKING AN OPTION TO TAX

8.1 Revoking an option to tax within the six-month "cooling-off" period

8.1.1 When can I revoke without prior permission?

If you change your mind within 6 months of the effective date of your option to tax, you can revoke your option to tax if you meet all the conditions set out in a) to d) in paragraph 8.1.2 together with 1 of the 3 conditions in box F below. You will not need our prior permission but you must notify us before the end of the 6 month period and your notification must be made on form VAT1614C (see paragraph 8.1.4).

Commentary—*De Voil Indirect Tax Service* **V4.114–V4.116**.

8.1.2 What are the conditions for revoking?

The conditions are:

(a) less than 6 months have passed since the day on which the option had effect
(b) no tax has become chargeable on a supply of the land as a result of the option
(c) no transfer of a going concern has occurred
(d) you have notified the revocation to HMRC on form VAT1614C (see paragraph 8.1.4)

Additional conditions are set out in box F below. To revoke your option to tax you must satisfy one of the 3 conditions in box F or obtain our permission. Where HMRC grants permission we may impose conditions.

Box F

The contents of this box have the force of the law.

Additional conditions for revoking an option to tax less than six months after the day on which it had effect (provision made under paragraph 23 (4) of Schedule 10 to the Value Added Tax Act 1994).

A revocation of an option to tax under paragraph 23 of Schedule 10 to the Value Added Tax Act 1994 is effective only if one of conditions (1) to (3) below is met in relation to the option, or if the taxpayer gets the prior permission of the Commissioners on an application made to them before the end of the six month period mentioned in paragraph 23(1)(a). Where the taxpayer seeks the prior permission of the Commissioners, they may specify conditions subject to which their permission is given and, if any of those conditions are broken, the Commissioners may treat the revocation as if it had not been made.

The conditions are that:

(1) neither the person who exercised the option to tax ('the opter') nor any relevant associate of the opter has recovered extra property input tax;
(2) by virtue of the revocation, the opter and all relevant associates of the opter would be liable to account to the Commissioners under regulation 107 or 108 of the Value Added Tax Regulations 1995 ('the VAT Regulations 1995') for all of the extra property input tax they have recovered, or
(3) extra property input tax has been recovered entirely on 1 capital item and amounts to less than 20 per cent of the total input tax incurred on that item.

Definition

"Extra property input tax" means input tax attributable to supplies which, if made at a time when the option has effect, would be taxable supplies by virtue of the option.

"Capital item" means a capital item to which part 15 of the VAT Regulations 1995 applies by virtue of regulation 113 of those Regulations.

8.1.3 Explanation of terms used in Box F

VAT Regulation 107 relates to the adjustment of partial exemption attribution at the end of a "longer period" (normally a year) and would apply where the property input tax credit was originally computed under a partial exemption method and revocation falls within the same "longer period".

VAT Regulation 108 (commonly called "clawback") requires adjustment of input tax credited as attributable to intended taxable supplies when the intended use of the inputs concerned changes before use starts. This will apply in most circumstances where revocation happens before the property is first used after incurring the input tax.

Information about "longer period" adjustments and "clawback" can be found in VAT Notice 706: partial exemption. Information about capital items can be found in VAT Notice 706/2: Capital Goods Scheme.

8.1.4 How do I notify you?

The following statement has the force of the law.

> Notification of revocation of an option to tax within the six month "cooling off" period (for the purpose of paragraph 23 of Schedule 10 to the VAT Act 1994) must be made on form VAT1614C and must contain the information requested on that form.

Form VAT1614C: revoking an option to tax within 6 month 'cooling off' period (www.gov.uk/government/publications/vat-revoking-an-option-to-tax-within-6-month-cooling-off-period-vat1614c) is available online or you contact the VAT Helpline on Telephone: 0300 200 3700.

8.1.5 When can I seek permission to revoke?

You can seek permission to revoke if you meet conditions a) to d) of paragraph 8.1.2 above but do not meet any of the three additional conditions specified in Box F.

8.1.6 How do I apply for permission?

The following statement has the force of the law.

> Application for permission to revoke an option to tax within the 6 month "cooling off period" (*for the purpose of paragraph 23 of Sch 10 to VATA 1994*) must be made on form VAT 1614C and must contain the information requested on that form.

Form VAT1614C: revoking an option to tax within 6 month 'cooling off' period (www.gov.uk/government/publications/vat-revoking-an-option-to-tax-within-6-month-cooling-off-period-vat1614c) is available online or you contact the VAT Helpline on Telephone: 0300 200 3700.

You must submit your application within 6 months of the effective date of your option to tax. Your application for permission will also be treated as notification of your revocation, so there is no requirement to make a separate notification once permission is granted.

When considering whether to grant permission, HMRC will give particular consideration to whether you or a third party has received a VAT benefit as a result of your actions.

8.1.7 When does the revocation take effect?

The revocation of an option to tax during its "cooling off" period has effect from the day on which the option was exercised. However, if HMRC set conditions when granting permission to revoke and any of these are broken, we may treat the revocation as invalid.

8.1.8 How should I adjust my input tax after I have revoked my option?

If you revoke an option to tax under the "cooling off" rules, you should adjust your input tax in accordance with the appropriate rules explained in VAT Notice 706: partial exemption and VAT Notice 706/2: Capital Goods Scheme (also see paragraph 8.1.3).

8.1.9 How does the "cooling off" period apply in relation to real estate elections?

If you choose, at the time of making a real estate election, to convert existing "global options" into separate options to tax, you cannot revoke these new separate options under the "cooling-off" period.

See Section 14 for information about real estate elections.

8.2 Automatic revocation of an option where no interest has been held for more than six years

8.2.1 In what circumstances does automatic revocation occur?

An option to tax is revoked where the opter has not held an interest in the opted building or land for a continuous period of six years commencing at any time after the option to tax has effect. The revocation is automatic and no notification is required. However, the revocation is subject to the rules described in paragraph 8.2.2 and will not be applicable in all cases.

8.2.2 Are there any circumstances in which the automatic revocation doesn't apply?

The automatic revocation will not occur where any of the following circumstances apply. All references to "relevant time" mean the time the option would otherwise be revoked:

(1) Where the opter has sold the property on terms that may require the purchaser to make additional payment after the "relevant time". Such payment is often referred to as an "overage" and can be contingent on such things as the purchaser obtaining planning permission.
The following 3 circumstances can only apply if the opter is or has been a member of a VAT group.

(2) Where a relevant associate of the opter in relation to the opted property (see paragraph 6.3) has sold the property on terms that may require the purchaser to make additional payment after the (see 1. above).

(3) Where before the "relevant time" a relevant associate of the opter in relation to the opted property (see paragraph 6.3) left the opter's VAT group and at the time of leaving any of the following applied:
   - (i) the relevant associate had an interest in the property
   - (ii) the relevant associate had, prior to leaving the VAT group, disposed of an interest on terms that might have required the purchaser to make additional payment at a later date (see 1. above)
   - (iii) the relevant associate was connected to the opter or another relevant associate of the opter and that person had an interest in the property

(1) Or where, at the "relevant time", a relevant associate of the opter in relation to the opted property (see paragraph 6.3) is member of the same VAT group and either currently holds an interest in the property or has held one during the previous 6 years.

8.3 Revoking an option where more than 20 years have elapsed since it first had effect

8.3.1 In what circumstances can I revoke without prior permission?

You may revoke an option to tax where more than 20 years have elapsed since the option first had effect if you meet either condition 1 or conditions 2 to 5 of box G below. You won't need HMRC's permission, but you must notify us on Form VAT1614J: revoking an option to tax after 20 years (see paragraph 8.3.4).

8.3.2 When does the option first have effect?

Your option first had effect on the day you exercised the option or any later day that you specified when opting to tax (see paragraph 4.3).

8.3.3 What are the conditions for revoking?

Box G

The following statement has the force of the law.

Conditions for revoking an option to tax when more than 20 years have elapsed since the option first had effect (for the purposes of para 25(1)(a) of Sch 10 to VATA 1994 ("the VAT Act 1994")).

A taxpayer may revoke an option to tax made by the taxpayer if either condition 1 below OR all of conditions 2 to 5 are met.

(1) **The relevant interest condition**
The taxpayer or a relevant associate connected to the taxpayer has no relevant interest in the building or land at the time when the option is revoked; and if the taxpayer or a relevant associate of the taxpayer has disposed of such an interest, no supply for the purpose of the charge to VAT in respect of the disposal—
(i) is yet to take place, or
(ii) would be yet to take place if one or more conditions (such as the happening of an event or the doing of an act) were to be met.

(2) **The 20-year condition**
The taxpayer or a relevant associate connected with the taxpayer held a relevant interest in the building or land—
— after the time from which the option has effect; and
— more than 20 years before the option is revoked.

(3) **The capital item condition**
Any land or building that is subject to the option at the time when it is revoked does not fall, in relation to the taxpayer or a relevant associate connected to the taxpayer, for input tax adjustment as a capital item under part 15 of the Value Added Tax Regulations 1995 (adjustments to the deduction of input tax on capital items).

(4) **The valuation condition**
The taxpayer or a relevant associate connected to the taxpayer has made no supply of a relevant interest in the building or land subject to the option in the 10 years immediately before revocation of the option that:
— was for a consideration that was less than the open market value of that supply, or
— arose from a relevant grant

(5) **The pre-payment condition**
No part of a supply of goods or services made for consideration to the taxpayer or a relevant associate connected to the taxpayer before the option is revoked will be attributable to a supply or other use of the land or buildings by the taxpayer more than 12 months after the option is revoked.

Explanatory Note 1

"Taxpayer" means—

(a) a person who exercised the option to tax or is treated as making that option by virtue of a real estate election pursuant to paragraph 21 of Sch 10 to the Act; and

(b) in relation to an option to tax treated as exercised by virtue of a real estate election made pursuant to paragraph 21 of Sch 10 to VATA 1994 by a body corporate treated as a member of a group under ss 43A to 43D of the Act other than the person described in (a) above, the body corporate whose relevant interest gave rise to the option to tax.

Explanatory Note 2

"Relevant interest in the building or land" means an interest in, right over or licence to occupy the building or land (or any part of it).

Explanatory Note 3

"Relevant grant" means a grant that the taxpayer intends or expects will give rise to a supply made after the option is revoked for a consideration significantly greater than any consideration for any supply arising from the grant before the revocation (except as a result of a rent review determined according to normal commercial practice).

Explanatory Note 4

In relation to condition 2 above, it does not matter whether, at the time the option is revoked, the taxpayer continues to hold the relevant interest in the building or land that meets the condition.

Explanatory Note 5

For the purpose of condition 3—

(1) land or buildings that fall for input tax adjustment as a capital item under Part 15 of the VAT Regulations shall not be regarded as so doing if the relevant amount does not exceed £10,000;

(2) the relevant amount is the total of the amounts that the taxpayer or a relevant associate connected with the taxpayer would be required to pay to the Commissioners pursuant to reg 115(2) of the VAT Regulations in respect of intervals ending after the revocation of the option if—

 (a) that person were a taxable person during such intervals; and

 (b) the land or building concerned were used, after the revocation of the option, only for making supplies that are not taxable supplies.

Explanatory Note 6

For the purposes of conditions 1 to 5 above, any question whether a person is "connected" with another person is to be decided as it would be for the purposes of Part 1 of Sch 10 to the Act.

Explanatory Note 7

"Relevant Associate" means — A body corporate as defined in para 3 of Sch 10 to the Act.

Further notes about Box G (these are for guidance only and do not have the force of law):

— The term "relevant associate" is explained in paragraph 6.3

— the second paragraph of condition 1 prevents revocation where the opter or a relevant associate has disposed of the property on terms which may require further payment to be made in the future - such payment is commonly referred to as an "overage" and can be contingent on such things as the granting of planning permission

— guidance on "connected" persons is in paragraph 13.7

8.3.4 How do I notify you?

The following statement has the force of the law.

Notification of revocation of an option to tax after 20 years (*for the purpose of paragraph 25 of Sch 10 to VATA 1994*) must be made on form VAT 1614J and must contain the information requested on that form.

Form VAT1614J (www.gov.uk/government/publications/vat-revoking-an-option-to-tax-after-20-years-vat1614j) is available online or you can contact the VAT Helpline on Telephone: 0300 200 3700.

8.3.5 When will my revocation take effect?

Your revocation will take effect from the day that you specify when you notify HMRC, but this cannot be any earlier than the day on which you notify us.

8.3.6 When can I seek permission to revoke?

If you don't meet the conditions in box G you may still seek our permission to revoke.

8.3.7 How do I apply for permission?

The following statement has the force of the law.

> Application for permission to revoke an option to tax after 20 years (*for the purpose of paragraph 25 of Sch 10 to VATA 1994*) must be made on form VAT 1614J and must contain the information requested on that form.

You can download form VAT1614J from the HMRC website or obtain it from our VAT Helpline on Tel 0300 200 3700.

8.3.8 In what circumstances will you grant permission?

HMRC will not grant permission unless you meet condition 2 of box G above.

In deciding whether or not to grant permission, we will give particular consideration to whether or not you or a third party has received a VAT benefit as a result of your actions.

8.3.9 If you grant permission, when will my revocation take effect?

If HMRC grants permission, revocation will take effect from the day we grant permission or such earlier or later day or time we specify. For this purpose, we may specify a time by reference to the happening of a particular event or meeting of a condition. For example, we may specify that revocation will take effect after the sale of a property has been completed.

We can only specify an earlier day if you previously gave notification of revocation believing, in error, that you met the conditions in box G above. In such cases we may allow the revocation to take effect from the day specified in your original notification, but we will only allow this where we are satisfied that the reasons for failing to meet the conditions are insignificant.

In granting permission HMRC may specify further conditions subject to which the permission is given. If any of these conditions are subsequently broken we may treat the revocation as if it had not been made.

9 INPUT TAX

9.1 Rules on reclaiming input tax

Your entitlement to recover any input tax you incur will depend on the liability of the supplies you make. This may be affected by your option to tax but you cannot assume that an option will allow input tax recovery and must still consider what supplies you will make and their liability.

If you make . . .	*then you will normally be . . .*
taxable supplies of the land or buildings	able to recover any input tax relating to those supplies
wholly exempt supplies of the land or building (see section 3)	unable to recover any input tax relating to those supplies
supplies that are both taxable and exempt, for example you may have opted to tax a building that is to be used for both commercial and residential purposes	able to recover only the input tax relating to the taxable supply, VAT Notice 706: partial exemption explains how to work out how much input tax relates to taxable supplies

General information about input tax can be found in VAT Notice 700: the VAT Guide (www.gov.uk/government/publications/vat-notice-700-the-vat-guide).

Commentary—*De Voil Indirect Tax Service* **V3.431, V4.463.**

9.2 What about input tax I incurred before I opted to tax?

9.2.1 May I recover input tax relating to supplies of land or buildings if the supplies are taxable in their own right?

Yes. For example, a freehold sale of a commercial building within 3 years of its completion is always standard rated. So if you construct a commercial building with the intention to make such a sale you may recover the input tax you incur.

But many supplies of land and buildings will only become taxable as a result of an option to tax. You may only recover input tax where you intend to make a taxable supply. For guidance on whether a taxable intention exists, see paragraphs 9.2.2, 9.2.3 and 9.2.4.

9.2.2 May I recover input tax now that relates to future supplies despite not having yet made my option?

Yes, in certain circumstances. Input tax incurred prior to the making of supplies can be recoverable where you have a clear intention, at the time the costs are incurred, that the supplies of the buildings or land will be taxable. *An option to tax is by far the best evidence of an intention to make taxable supplies for land and property transactions.*

Where, in exceptional circumstances, you wish to delay the making of the option until a future date you may still be able to recover the input tax relating to supplies which will follow the option. This will only be the case, however, where you are able to produce unequivocal documentary evidence, at the time you wish to reclaim your input tax, that you intend your supplies to be taxable.

9.2.3 What types of documents will be accepted as evidence that I intend to make taxable supplies?

A list of examples of the types of documents that may contain evidence of intention is shown below. The list is not intended to be exhaustive and whether a particular document provides the evidence will very much depend upon its content.

It's unlikely that any single document alone will provide sufficient evidence and you're advised to hold a number of separate documents to prove your intention. HMRC will normally consider evidence as satisfactory where it involves third parties and shows a firm commitment to the making of taxable supplies. For example:

- A signed agreement/contract that specifies that the vendor will opt to tax prior to the sale.
- An investment appraisal or business plan accepted by a bank, that confirms that supplies will be treated as taxable.
- Marketing literature that has been distributed to the public and where the scale and type of distribution, together with the nature of the advertisement itself, makes it clear that taxable supplies will be made.
- Instructions or advice from professional advisers that specifies the VAT treatment, together with confirmation of your acceptance of the advice.
- Any other similar document that shows that the intention is to make taxable supplies.

HMRC cannot give a list of unacceptable documents. However, any document that merely sets out an option or number of options will not be accepted as unequivocal documentary evidence of an intention to make taxable supplies.

9.2.4 Having recovered input tax relating to future taxable supplies, what action should I take?

Any documents used as evidence of intention must be retained and made available to HMRC on request.

Where the intention to make taxable supplies changes, a record must be kept of the date these changes occurred together with appropriate evidence. VAT previously deducted before the intention changed may need to be adjusted and repaid to HMRC - see VAT Notice 706: partial exemption for details.

If you have recovered input tax on the basis of an intention to opt to tax and wish to retain the input tax recovered, you must make an option to tax at the very latest before any supplies of the land or buildings are made, and notify the option as detailed in paragraph 4.2.

9.2.5 Are there any other circumstances in which input tax incurred prior to an option to tax can be recovered?

There are 3:

— where, prior to supplies being made, your intention to make exempt supplies changes to an intention to make taxable supplies you may be able to recover previously exempt input tax under the 'payback' rule - you will find more about the payback rule in VAT Notice 706: partial exemption - where, however, your change of intention is not accompanied by an option to tax you will need to retain suitable evidence of your new intention (see paragraph 9.2.3)

— where you made exempt supplies of the land or building before opting to tax and incurred exempt input tax you may be able to recover this under a longer period adjustment (see VAT Notice 706: partial exemption)

— if you have made exempt supplies and the initial attribution of your input tax has been finalised as exempt before you opt, you may be able to make adjustments under the Capital Goods Scheme in order to reflect your taxable use after the option (see paragraph 9.5)

In the circumstances described in the last 2 bullet points above, you may need to obtain our permission before you can opt to tax (see Section 5).

9.3 What about speculative and abortive costs?

As a developer you may spend time and effort investigating potential projects such as looking for sites and assessing their suitability. Where you have:

— a clear intention of what supplies you intend to make you must attribute the input tax incurred to the liability of the intended supply; or

— no firm intention of what supplies you will make, the input tax on the costs you incur is "residual" for partial exemption purposes.

Some potential projects are not followed through, and in the end no supplies are actually made. If costs are wasted then no adjustment to how input tax on them was attributed is needed. If up to the time of aborting the project you have no firm intention regarding the liability of the supplies you wish to make (and as a result are unable to attribute the input tax to the liability of the intended supply), the related input tax should be left as residual.

When you decide to proceed with a project you will have a clear intention as to what supplies you will make. (It is normally at this point that you decide whether to opt to tax for land and property supplies.) If you had not attributed the input tax previously you should then adjust the input tax accordingly under the "payback" and "clawback" rules. Input tax on the ongoing costs should be attributed to the expected taxable or exempt supplies.

You can find further information in VAT Notice 706: partial exemption.

9.4 What about the VAT I incurred prior to my registration?

You may find that you become registered for VAT as a result of opting to tax. Special rules apply to all newly registered persons under which they may be entitled to claim relief for VAT incurred on supplies they obtained before registration. Relief is restricted on supplies of services to those received not more than 6 months before your registration. This restriction may lead to inequitable treatment compared with a business carrying out similar activities, but who was already VAT registered when the tax was incurred. If you consider you have suffered because of this you should write to the Option to Tax National Unit (paragraph 4.2.3 shows how you may contact them) and explain your circumstances. But you should note that the Option to Tax National Unit will only consider cases where, had you been registered at the time the input tax was first incurred, the Capital Goods Scheme would have applied (see paragraph 9.5).

In all cases relief for VAT incurred before registration is restricted to tax which can be directly attributed to a taxable activity. If you incurred tax before registration that was attributable both to exempt supplies before registration as well as taxable supplies after registration, the relief will be restricted proportionately.

9.5 Capital goods scheme

If you acquire land or buildings which are considered to be capital items for the purposes of this scheme, you must review their use in your business over a series of intervals, normally lasting ten years. If there are changes in the extent to which they are used for making taxable supplies you must make input tax adjustments to take account of this. The Capital Goods Scheme will normally apply if you incur VAT on the purchase of the property, or on capital works, where VAT bearing costs, net of VAT, are £250,000 or more. But it will not apply where you have purchased property purely for the purpose of selling it on. You will find more information about how the scheme works in VAT Notice 706/2: Capital Goods Scheme.

Commentary—*De Voil Indirect Tax Service* **V3.470–V3.478**.

10 TIME OF SUPPLY (TAX POINT)

10.1 Normal tax point rules

The normal tax point rules apply to all supplies of land or buildings. These rules are explained in detail in VAT Notice 700: the VAT Guide.

Time of supply (tax point) 10.1 Normal tax point rules The normal tax point rules apply to all supplies of land or buildings. These rules are explained in detail in VAT Notice 700: the VAT Guide. If you make leasehold supplies and have opted to tax, a tax point will normally occur when you either issue a tax invoice or receive a payment, whichever is the earlier.

If you're selling the freehold of land or a building a basic tax point will normally occur at the time of legal completion under the terms of the contract, when the freehold is conveyed to the purchaser. The equivalent under Scottish land law is the time of delivery of the disposition. Any payments you receive after the basic tax point do not create a tax point. If you issue a VAT invoice within 14 days after the basic tax point, then the date of issue of that invoice becomes the tax point. If you issue a VAT invoice or receive a payment before the basic tax point, then an actual tax point will be created by whichever happens first, to the extent of the amount invoiced or payment received.

Commentary—*De Voil Indirect Tax Service* **V3.140A**.

10.2 Does a deposit create a tax point?

Often on the sale of land or buildings, the purchaser pays a deposit at exchange of contracts, followed by payment of the balance on the completion date. An independent stakeholder usually holds the deposit until completion, and the seller receives no payment until that time. In these circumstances, the deposit payment will not create a tax point. It follows that if the deposit is paid directly to the seller or their agent, the payment does create a tax point. In both cases, an earlier tax point arises if a tax invoice is issued before the seller receives any payment.

10.3 What if I receive arrears of rent following my option to tax?

In a tenanted building, a tax point might not occur until you receive payment. In these circumstances, if you opt to tax after the rent becomes due but before it is paid, you must account for output tax on the rental receipt. This is the case even if the payment covers a period before your option to tax took effect.

11 TRANSFER OF A BUSINESS AS A GOING CONCERN

11.1 What does "transferring a business as a going concern" mean?

VAT Notice 700/9: transfer of business as a going concern explains the VAT position if you're selling or transferring your business and its assets, or part of it. In certain circumstances, special transfer of a going concern (TOGC) rules apply, and the sale will not be treated as a supply for VAT purposes, so no VAT should be charged. The transfer of a businesses or part of a business is treated as a VAT free TOGC in the following circumstances, where:

— it's capable of separate operation after the sale has taken place
— it's sold as a going concern
— it's not part of a series of immediately consecutive transfers of a business
— the purchaser intends to carry on the same kind of business

— in relation to certain transfers of land and buildings, further conditions are met (see paragraph 11.2)

It's important to note that where the seller/transferor is a VAT-registered business the purchaser must also be a taxable person for VAT purposes or become one as a result of the transfer.

As the TOGC rules are mandatory and not optional, it's important to establish at the outset whether the sale or transfer of the business is or is not a TOGC.

Commentary—*De Voil Indirect Tax Service* **V2.226**.

11.2 What if I'm transferring land or buildings as part of a transfer of a going concern?

In order for the transfer to be treated as a VAT free TOGC you must meet all conditions specified in VAT Notice 700/9: transfer of business as a going concern.

In addition, however, you must meet 2 further conditions where you:

— have opted to tax the land or buildings being transferred and the option is not disapplied in relation to the transfer
— are transferring the freehold of a "new" building and the supply, but for the TOGC, would be subject to the standard rate of VAT

The additional conditions are that the purchaser must have:

— opted to tax or made a real estate election (these must have been both notified to HMRC and effective on or before the relevant date - paragraph 14.8 explains how to notify a real estate election)
— •notified you that their option to tax will not be disapplied under the anti-avoidance provision set out in VATA 1994, Schedule 10, paragraph 12 in respect of supplies they intend to make of the land or building (see Section 13)

The requirement for the purchaser to notify the seller that their option won't be disapplied is designed to deal with avoidance schemes making use of TOGC provisions. In deciding whether their option is disapplied, the transferee needs to consider whether there are any circumstances in which the building being transferred would become for them a capital item. This could be, for example, as a result of the building being treated as part of the TOGC or alternatively as a taxable supply.

In cases where prior permission for an option is required, the application must have been made on Form VAT1614H: application for permission to opt and HMRC must have granted permission before or on the relevant date (see Section 5).

Where land and buildings form part of a TOGC the transfer is treated as neither a supply of goods nor a supply of services for VAT purposes and no VAT should be charged.

11.2.1 What HMRC means by "notified"

By "notified to HMRC" we mean that the purchaser has properly addressed, pre-paid and posted the appropriate form or letter to us (or faxed it to us). The declaration that the option will not be disapplied must also be made by the relevant date.

11.2.2 What is the "relevant date"?

The relevant date is the time that the supply would be treated as taking place, if it were not for the special TOGC rules. This is normally the date of the transfer, but will also include receipt of a deposit if that is paid in advance of the date of the transfer (unless the deposit is paid to an independent stakeholder). Further information on time of supply can be found in Section 10 of this notice.

11.3 Can a transfer that would otherwise be exempt or zero rated be treated as a TOGC?

There's no requirement for the purchaser/transferee to opt to tax or notify the seller that their option is not disapplied where the sale would, apart from the TOGC provisions, be an exempt or zero-rated supply. In such instances the transfer of the land and buildings can be included in a TOGC regardless of whether the transferee has opted.

11.4 What if the conditions for TOGC are not met?

If you are transferring:

— •the freehold of land or buildings which are new (less than 3 years old) or unfinished buildings or civil engineering work which would normally be standard rated
— land or buildings on which you have opted to tax and the option is not disapplied and the purchaser has either:
— not opted to tax the property
— not notified you that the option to tax will not be disapplied then the conditions for a transfer of a going concern will not have been met in respect of the land or buildings. You will have to charge VAT on the sale of the land or building.

The following table will help you to decide whether the conditions for a transfer of a going concern have been met.

Commercial land or building, ordinarily exempt

Has seller opted to tax (building over three years old)?	Has the purchaser opted to tax?	Will the purchaser's option to tax be disapplied?	Transfer of a going concern provisions met?
Yes	Yes	Yes	No
Yes	No	N/A	No
Yes	Yes	No	Yes
No	No	N/A	Yes
No	Yes	Yes	Yes
No	Yes	No	Yes
Yes, but option disapplied	No	N/A	Yes

New building (less than three years old), ordinarily standard rated

Has seller opted to tax?	Has the purchaser opted to tax?	Will the purchaser's option to tax be disapplied?	Transfer of a going concern provisions met?
Yes	Yes	Yes	No
Yes	No	N/A	No
Yes	Yes	No	Yes
No	No	N/A	No
No	Yes	Yes	No
No	Yes	No	Yes

11.5 What about the input tax I incur on transfer expenses?

VAT incurred in making or receiving a TOGC is input tax. As with all input tax, it is recoverable to the extent that it will be used in making taxed supplies. The way you treat this input tax in practice will depend on whether you are the transferor (the person disposing of the business), or the transferee (the person acquiring the business).

11.5.1 Transferor

As a transferor of a going concern, the transfer of assets is neither a supply of goods nor a supply of services for VAT purposes (see VAT Notice 700/9: transfer of a business as a going concern). Costs incurred therefore cannot be related to the sale and are general costs of the business (ie overheads).

However, input tax on costs that relate wholly to the transfer of the business (for example legal fees) should be treated as an overhead of the specific property business being transferred rather than the whole VAT registration. Where that property business makes—

— only taxable supplies, the input tax is fully recoverable
— only exempt supplies, the input tax is wholly non-recoverable
— both taxable and exempt supplies, the input tax is residual and recoverable in accordance with the partial exemption method in place.

If you're partly exempt and your partial exemption method fails to achieve a fair and reasonable result, you may wish to discuss the matter with HMRC. In exceptional cases, where significant distortion and unfairness would otherwise arise, we may approve an alternative way of calculating recoverable input tax on the TOGC.

11.5.2 Transferee

If you're the transferee of a going concern and acquire assets for your business, the input tax on costs that relate wholly to the acquisition of those assets will be recoverable to the extent to which they will be used in making taxable supplies. Therefore, where they are to be used in making:

— only taxable supplies, the input tax is fully recoverable
— only exempt supplies, the input tax is wholly non-recoverable
— both taxable and exempt supplies, the input tax is residual and recoverable in accordance with the partial exemption method in place

Note: this guidance can only be applied to acquisitions of businesses by way of a transfer of a going concern. Any VAT incurred on costs related to any other form of acquisition, such as the acquisition of a controlling share interest in a business, should be considered under normal principles. If it's incurred for an economic purpose then it will be input tax. Its recoverability will depend on what supplies made or to be made it relates to.

11.5.3 Business acquired by a VAT group

If you acquire . . .	*and you . . .*	*your VAT group may . . .*
a business or its assets as a going concern	are a member of a VAT group registration that is partly exempt; or becomes partly exempt during the tax year in which the transfer takes place	have to account for VAT on certain assets as a supply both to and by the group. VAT Notice 700/9: transfer of business as a going concern gives full details

11.6 What if the land or buildings are in the capital goods scheme or have unused costs attaching to them?

Where assets are transferred without a supply occurring, any input tax rights and obligations go with them to the new owner. This means that the new owner may need to make Capital Goods Scheme adjustments (see VAT Notice: Capital Goods Scheme) or payback or clawback adjustments (see VAT Notice 706: partial exemption) that may fall due.

11.6.1 Capital goods scheme

If you are transferring land or buildings as part of a TOGC which are "capital items" items' for the purposes of the Capital Goods Scheme, you should make the purchaser aware of any Capital Goods Scheme adjustments you have made and provide sufficient information to allow the purchaser to carry out any future adjustments under the scheme that might be necessary.

If you have acquired land or buildings that are capital items, you're responsible for continuing the Capital Goods Scheme, and making any further adjustments of input tax required under the scheme, until the intervals are complete.

11.6.2 Payback or clawback adjustments

If you're transferring land or buildings as part of a TOGC and:

— you have incurred input tax on or related to the land or buildings
— that input tax has been attributed to taxable, exempt or mixed use based on an intention
— that intention has not been fulfilled as of the time of transfer

you should make the purchaser aware of this and provide them with sufficient information to allow them to carry out any future payback or clawback adjustments that might become necessary if they use the costs in making supplies differently to the intention you formed prior to the transfer.

If you have acquired land or buildings with unused costs attaching to them, you're responsible for monitoring whether you use the costs differently to the transferee's original intention and making any adjustments of input tax that may be required.

12 DEREGISTRATION

12.1 What happens to my option to tax if I deregister?

Your option to tax is not cancelled if you deregister. If you deregister due to a fall in turnover, and then at a later date your income increases above the VAT threshold, the option to tax will still have effect and you must apply to register again.

You might deregister because you're selling your business as a transfer of a going concern. If that is the case, and you're disposing of land or buildings that are capital items for the purposes of the Capital Goods Scheme as part of the transfer, you should inform the purchaser of any adjustments you have made under the scheme.

If the opted land or building is an asset on hand at deregistration you may have to account for output tax in respect of it. For more information please see VAT Notice 700/11: cancelling your registration.

Commentary—*De Voil Indirect Tax Service* **V3.261, V4.114–V4.116**.

13 ANTI-AVOIDANCE MEASURES

13.1 Why are the anti-avoidance measures needed?

Some businesses whose supplies are wholly or partly exempt are not entitled to recover all of the input tax they incur on the purchase of land or buildings, or on major construction projects. As a result, some of these organisations entered into arrangements designed to either increase the amount of input tax they could claim, or to spread the VAT cost of the purchase or construction over a number of years.

Commentary—*De Voil Indirect Tax Service* **V4.114–V4.116**.

To counter this, an anti-avoidance test was introduced. The test is applied each time a grant is made and if caught, the option to tax will not have effect (it will be "disapplied") in respect of the supplies that arise from that particular grant.

The anti-avoidance test may also impact on the VAT treatment of a TOGC of a property (see Section 11).

If you grant an interest in a building or land and the person that is to be in occupation makes predominantly taxable supplies and is able to receive credit for the majority of input tax they incur, you're unlikely to be affected by the anti-avoidance measure. Your option to tax may, however, be disapplied if any of the following situations arise (these are examples only), you:

— are a partly exempt business and grant a lease in a building that you intend to occupy at a later date
— are a partly exempt business and enter into a sale and leaseback of a property that you occupy
— construct a building and finance is provided by a bank that also intends to be in occupation
— purchase a building and finance is provided by a bank that also intends to be in occupation

Where your supplies of property become exempt supplies due to the disapplication of your option to tax, this may mean that you cannot recover input tax, or that you have to repay input tax that you have previously recovered.

13.2 What is the test?

The test is as follows:

If, at the time of the grant of land or buildings:

(1) The property is, or is expected to become, a capital item for the purposes of the Capital Goods Scheme, either for the grantor, a person to whom the property is transferred or a person treated as the grantor (see paragraph 13.3.3).
(2) It's the intention or expectation of the grantor or the person treated as the grantor (see paragraph 13.3.3) or a person responsible for financing the grantor's acquisition or development, that the building will be occupied by them or a person connected with them.

(3) The person occupying the property will be doing so other than wholly or substantially wholly for eligible purposes (see paragraph 13.9).

then the option to tax will not have effect in respect of supplies that arise from that particular grant.

The following paragraphs will explain what the test means and how it is to be applied to each grant.

13.3 Grants and supplies

13.3.1 What is a grant and who is the grantor?

The word "grant" refers to the act that transfers the interest in, or possession of, the land or building. Examples are a freehold sale of land or a building, the leasing or licensing of land or a building, or the assignment or surrender of that lease or licence.

The grantor is the person who sells, leases, licences or lets any of the land or buildings and can be anywhere in the "chain" of people who have an interest in the land or buildings concerned. For example, a freeholder (A) may sell land to another party (B) who constructs a new commercial building and then leases it to another business (C), who will occupy the building for its own use. In this case there are two grantors, A and B. It follows that if C goes on to sub-let part of the building to another business, there would then be three grantors. The test should be applied to each grant made.

13.3.2 What are supplies arising from a grant?

In the case of a freehold sale there is normally a single supply at the time of completion. For leases, however, it is usual for there to be a succession of supplies following the grant. These are treated as made when you either issue an invoice or receive payment (the earlier of the two). Payment would also include any non-monetary consideration.

13.3.3 What if I make supplies under a grant that was originally made by another person?

If you make a supply under a grant that was originally made by another person then, for the purposes of part 1 of the test in paragraph 13.2, you're treated as if you had made the grant. The grant is treated as made on the date of your first supply of the land.

Where, for the purposes of the test, you're treated as the person who made the grant, you will need to determine whether you satisfy the other elements of the anti-avoidance test. However, in such circumstances the test is still satisfied (and your option disapplied) where your grant is treated as made after the expiry of your Capital Goods Scheme adjustment period. For example, where there's an intention that the building will be occupied by someone connected with you and will not be used for eligible purposes, then even if your first supply (see paragraph 13.3.2) occurs after the building has ceased to be a capital item for the Capital Goods Scheme, your option to tax will still be disapplied. This overcomes an avoidance scheme that involved deferring the supplies made under the grant until the land is no longer a capital item.

13.4 How does HMRC establish a person's intention or expectation?

The option to tax has no effect in relation to the supplies arising from the grant if either the grantor, or the person responsible for financing the grantor's acquisition or development of that particular property, knows or expects at the time the grant is made that either one of them, or any party connected with them, will occupy it for other than eligible purposes (see paragraph 13.9). There doesn't have to be an intention to avoid VAT for the grant to be caught by the test.

We will consider commercial documents and other evidence such as minutes of meetings, business plans and finance requests to establish the intention and expectation of the businesses that are involved in the particular development or transaction.

13.5 What is meant by finance?

For the purpose of the anti-avoidance measure finance means directly or indirectly:

— providing all or part of the funds for the acquisition or development

— obtaining those funds from another person
— providing the funds for discharging all or part of the owner's borrowing for the acquisition or development
— procuring that such a liability will be discharged by another

Finance could take many different forms, such as loans, guaranteeing a loan, purchase of shares or securities which finance a development of land, share issues or premium deals.

13.6 When is someone responsible for financing an acquisition or development?

For the purposes of the anti-avoidance measure a person is only deemed to have been responsible for financing a development if two key conditions are met—

(a) at the time the finance is provided, or the agreement to provide the finance is entered into, the person providing the finance must intend or expect that he or the grantor, or somebody connected to either of them, will occupy the particular property for other than eligible purposes
(b) the funds must be for the purpose of financing the purchase, construction or refurbishment of that property

If either of these conditions is not met, a person will not be deemed to be responsible for providing finance, even if they have provided the funds to meet part or all of the cost of the acquisition or development.

13.7 What is the "connected" person test?

The test in s 1122 of the Corporation Tax Act 2010 applies to determine whether persons are connected. The following persons are treated as connected with you—

— your husband, wife or civil partner
— your relatives and their husbands, wives or civil partners
— your husband's or wife's or civil partner's relatives and their husbands, wives or civil partners
— if you're in business in a partnership, your partners and their husbands, wives, civil partners and relatives
— a company that you control, either by yourself or with any of the persons listed above, or
— the trustees of a settlement of which you are a settlor, or of which a person who is still alive and who is connected with you is a settlor.

Relative means a brother, sister, ancestor or lineal descendant. It doesn't include nephews, nieces, uncles and aunts.

A company is connected with another company if:

— the same person has control of both, or a person has control of one and persons connected with him (or he and persons connected with him) have control of the other
— a group of 2 or more persons have control of each company, and the groups either consist of the same persons or could be regarded as consisting of the same persons by treating (in one or more cases) a member of either group as replaced by a person with whom he is connected

13.7.2 Are there any exceptions to the normal "connected persons" rule?

For the purposes of the option to tax a company is not treated as "connected" to another company as a result of both being under the control of—

— the Crown
— a Minister of the Crown
— a government department, or
— a Northern Ireland department.

13.8 What does "occupation" mean?

13.8.1 When is a person in occupation of a building?

A person is in occupation of a building or land if they have—

— a physical presence, and
— the right to occupy the property as if they're the owner.

This means they will have actual possession and control of the land, together with the ability to exclude others from the enjoyment of such rights.

Normally a legal interest in or licence to occupy the land, will have been granted to them. However, occupation could also be by agreement or de facto and it is therefore necessary to take into account the day to day arrangements, particularly where these differ from the contractual terms. An exclusive right of occupation is not a requirement, an agreement might, for example, allow for joint occupation. It's also not necessary for a person to be utilising all of the land for all of the time for them to be considered as occupying it.

13.8.2 When is a person not in occupation for the purposes of the test?

A person is not "in occupation" where the interest they hold is subject to an inferior interest and they are prevented from having rights of occupation until the inferior interest expires. This can typically arise where a leaseholder has granted a sublease. However, an important feature of the test is that it is forward looking and takes account of the intended or expected occupation of the building or land throughout the Capital Goods Scheme adjustment period. As a result, a person who has granted an inferior interest but intends nevertheless to occupy the land during the adjustment period, would intend to be "in occupation" for the purposes of the anti-avoidance test.

13.8.3 In what circumstances can occupation be ignored?

A person can ignore the following types of occupation for the purposes of the test:

— occupation by a lessor which is purely for the purpose of making rental supplies under the grant - examples include
  — occupation by the grantor between the date of the grant and the start of occupation by the tenant which is for the purpose of undertaking refurbishment or repairs, and
  — occupation by maintenance, security, reception staff or similar, but not where it is for the purpose of providing ongoing services separate from the letting itself;
— occupation at a future date, but within the Capital Goods Scheme adjustment period, which is solely for the purpose of re-letting the property or making a fresh grant

13.8.4 What is the "10% occupation" rule?

Occupation of any part of the land or building (even a very small proportion) normally counts as occupation for the purposes of the anti-avoidance test. However, in respect of grants made on or after 1 April 2010, a person is not treated as being in occupation for the purposes of the test where the conditions of the '10% occupation rule' are met. The rule prevents disapplication of an option where the occupation is by a development financier (see paragraph 13.6) or a person connected to a development financier (except where such persons are connected to the grantor), and the part to be occupied is only a small proportion of any building included in the grant.

Following the introduction of the '10% occupation rule' a person who would otherwise be 'in occupation' for the purposes of the anti-avoidance test is treated as not occupying any part of the land if they satisfy a number of conditions.

13.8.5 How is the "10% occupation rule" applied?

The rule works as follows:

— the person(s) in occupation must not be the grantor or a person connected to the grantor
— there must be no intention or expectation at the time of the grant that the person(s) will occupy more than 10% of any building (or part of a building) included in the grant at

any time during the grantor's Capital Goods Scheme adjustment period - where the financier is in occupation together with persons connected to him, or alternatively, the occupation is by a number of persons connected to the financier, it is the combined occupation that counts towards the 10% threshold

— the proportion of the building occupied is to be calculated in relation to the whole of the single building or where the grantor holds an interest in only part of the building, that part in which an interest is held immediately prior to the grant being made (this includes any part of the building in which an interest is held by a person(s) connected to the grantor)

— where a number of buildings are included in the same grant the rule is applied to each building on an individual basis - where the 10% threshold is exceeded in relation to any of the buildings the conditions are not satisfied

— for the purposes of the rule a single building takes its meaning from VAT Act 1994 Schedule 10 sub-paragraphs 18(4) to (7) and includes some linked buildings and enclosed complexes (see paragraph 2.6)

— the conditions are not satisfied where the person(s) occupies any land included in the grant which is not a building - however, the occupation of land that falls within the curtilage of the building or is used for parking vehicles can be disregarded as long as such occupation is ancillary to that of the building

13.8.6 How do I calculate the proportion of the building occupied by a person for the purposes of the "10% occupation rule"?

For the purposes of calculating the percentage of the building occupied by a particular person the practices set out in the Royal Institution of Chartered Surveyors (RICS) 'Code of Measuring Practice' are to be used. Box H below sets out detailed rules about how the Code is to be applied. For example, the calculation must exclude any areas that are not available for exclusive occupation, such as (in most cases) walkways, stairwells and foyers. In addition, parts of buildings used for vehicle parking and parts which form the curtilage of the building are also excluded.

In most instances it will be clearly obvious that a tenant will be occupying less than 10% of a building. Where this is the case and HMRC have no reasons for believing that the 10% threshold will be exceeded at any time during the Capital Goods Scheme adjustment period, taxpayers will not be required to produce evidence of their RICS calculation. However, taxpayers should retain appropriate details with their VAT records about any parts of buildings to be occupied by development financiers (or persons connected to development financiers). In rare cases where the area occupied is close to 10% (plus or minus 5%) HMRC may ask to see evidence of RICS calculations.

The "10% occupation rule" is based on the intention or expectation of the grantor and development financier at the time the grant is made and involves a forward look over the 10-year period of the Capital Goods Scheme. The test, however, is a one-off test and where further occupation arises which was not intended or expected at the time of the original grant (and results in the 10% threshold being exceeded) the test is not reapplied to the original grant. However, in such cases (assuming other parts of the anti-avoidance test are met), the option will be disapplied in relation to the second and subsequent grants.

Box H

The boxed text below has the force of law.

Calculating the proportion of a "relevant building" occupied by a development financier or person connected to a development financier (for the purposes of para 15A(1)(b)(ii) of Sch 10 to VATA 1994).

The proportion of a 'relevant building' occupied by any person or persons for the purposes of paragraph 15A(1)(b)(ii) of Schedule 10 to the Value Added Tax Act 1994 is to be calculated using the recommended practices set out in the current version of the 'Code of Measuring Practice' published by the Royal Institution of Chartered Surveyors (the 'RICS Code'), but subject to the following:

(1) The following parts of the building must be excluded—

— any part which is not available for exclusive occupation;
— any part intended primarily for use for vehicle parking;
— any part which is land forming part of the curtilage of the building.

(2) Where in relation to any part of the "relevant building" the RICS Code either:
— does not specify a "core definition"; or
— specifies the use of more than one "core definition",

the "core definition" to be used is that applied or expected to be applied by the grantor for the purposes of calculating rent due from letting that part of the building or, if there is no such definition at the time of the grant, NIA (Net Internal Area).

Explanatory Note 1

Current version of the "Code of Measuring Practice" means the latest published version at the time the grant is made (ie, the grant that is subject to the anti-avoidance test).

13.9 When is occupation "wholly" or "substantially wholly" for eligible purposes?

13.9.1 What is "wholly" or "substantially wholly"?

The anti-avoidance measure examines whether the grantor or the person responsible for providing finance intends that the development will be occupied other than "wholly" or "substantially wholly" for eligible purposes.

The terms "wholly" or "substantially wholly" are defined in Box I below.

The boxed text below has the force of the law

Meaning of "wholly" and "substantially wholly" for eligible purposes (for the purpose of paragraph 15(5) of Sch 10 to VATA 1994)

Expression	*Meaning*
Occupation "wholly" for eligible purposes	Land occupied 100% for eligible purposes
Occupation "substantially wholly" for eligible purposes,	Land occupied at least 80% for eligible purposes

Box I

13.9.2 What are "eligible purposes"?

For someone to be in occupation of the development for eligible purposes they must be occupying it for the purpose of making taxable supplies, or for other supplies which entitle them to credit for their input tax.

Some organisations are always treated as occupying a development for eligible purposes and these include National Health Service Trusts and government departments. Occupation by local authorities or other bodies, such as police and fire authorities, are treated as eligible provided the occupation is for taxable or non-business purposes.

Occupation that arises only because of an automatic teller machine (ATM) fixed to the land is treated as for eligible purposes.

The following are examples of businesses and organisations that may occupy a development for other than eligible purposes:

— businesses, such as insurance companies and banks, making exempt supplies;
— someone who is not, or is not required to be, VAT registered.

Organisations, such as charities, who undertake non-business activities would **not** generally be in occupation for eligible purposes.

13.10 What land or buildings are covered by the capital goods scheme?

The anti-avoidance measure only applies to land and buildings that are, or are intended to become, capital items for the purpose of the capital goods scheme, either in the hands of the grantor or a person to whom the property is to be transferred. Generally, a capital item comes within the scheme when it is either bought, or first used.

The Capital Goods Scheme will normally apply if you incur VAT on the purchase of the property, or on capital works, where VAT bearing costs, net of VAT, are £250,000 or more. But it will not apply where you have purchased property purely for the purpose of selling it on. You will find more information about capital items and how the scheme works in VAT Notice 706/2: Capital Goods Scheme.

14 REAL ESTATE ELECTIONS ("REE")

14.1 Who should read this section?

Warning

This section is only likely to be of interest to you if you:

(a) intend to acquire a large number of properties and wish to opt to tax all of them
(b) have made a "global" option to tax in the past (see paragraph 14.13)

Commentary—*De Voil Indirect Tax Service* **V4.116**.

14.2 Note about terminology used in this section

For the purpose of this section—

— "property acquisition" means the acquisition of any interest in, right over, or licence to occupy land (including buildings and civil engineering works)
— "interest" means any interest in, right over or licence to occupy land (including buildings and civil engineering works).

14.3 What is a REE (introduction and overview)?

A REE is a formal decision to opt to tax all future property acquisitions.

If you make a REE, you will be treated as if you have made an option to tax in relation to every property in which you subsequently acquire an interest (there are some exceptions, which are explained in paragraph 14.7).

Each property you acquire will be treated as separately opted, with effect from the time of acquisition (see paragraph 14.5 below). Each of these options is capable of being separately revoked if the conditions for revocation are met. For example, if you acquire a property that you do not want to be opted, you may be able to revoke within 6 months of acquisition under the cooling off" provisions (see paragraph 8.1), but only if the relevant conditions are met.

For a REE to have legal effect, you need to notify the REE itself to HMRC (paragraph 14.9 explains how to do this), but once you have made a REE, there is no need for you to notify HMRC of an option to tax each time you acquire an interest in a property. You will, however, need to keep records and provide us with certain information if we request it (see paragraph 14.12).

14.4 Why were REEs introduced?

Some businesses with very large numbers of properties wish to opt to tax all (or nearly all) properties within their portfolios without having the administrative burden of having to notify HMRC of an individual option to tax each time they make a new acquisition. In the past, the only way to achieve this was to make a "global" option to tax. The REE was introduced as an alternative to the global option. It is designed to provide some of the advantages of a global option whilst providing greater flexibility. Information about global options is in paragraph 14.13.

14.5 When does an option to tax under a REE have effect?

Once you have made a REE, each property you subsequently acquire (subject to the exceptions explained in paragraph 14.7) will be treated as opted to tax with effect from the start of the day you acquire it.

For this purpose, you will be treated as acquiring the property at the time that the supply to you, for VAT purposes, is treated as made, or if there is more than one such time, the earliest of them. For further information about time of supply, see Section 10.

If you acquire a property as part of a VAT free transfer of a going concern (TOGC) (see Section 11), your option will have effect from the time that the supply to you would have been treated as made (or if there is more than one such time, the earliest of them) if the special TOGC rules had not applied.

14.6 an I opt to tax a property in which I don't hold an interest?

If, after making a REE, you wish to opt to tax a property before you acquire an interest in it, you may do so by making a separately notified option to tax under the normal rules (see Section 4).

14.7 What acquisitions are excluded from the effect of a REE?

The REE will not generate an option to tax for the following types of acquisitions—

1. Any acquisition of a property in respect of which you have already exercised an option to tax

If you acquire an interest in a property and you have (or a body corporate that was in your VAT group at the time, has) previously opted to tax the building or land, under the normal rules, with effect from a date prior to the acquisition date, the REE will have no effect in relation to that property.

2. Any acquisition of a property in respect of which you already hold an interest when acquiring another different interest

If the person who acquires an interest after the REE is made already held a different interest in the property before the REE was made and continues to hold that interest when acquiring the further, different interest, the REE will not generate an option to tax. This situation can typically arise where a leasehold interest is held prior to the purchase of the freehold. Alternatively, an interest in part of a building (for example, one floor) may be held at the time an interest in another part of the same building is acquired.

3. Any acquisition of a property for which permission to opt might ordinarily be required

The REE will not generate an option to tax for an acquisition if you have made exempt supplies of the property within the 10 years prior to the date of acquisition.

14.8 What happens to options to tax I made before making the REE?

14.8.1 Automatic revocation where no interest held

Any options to tax exercised by you (or by a person within your VAT group at the time) before making a REE will generally be revoked automatically when you make a REE if you don't hold an interest in the opted land or building at that time (and no one within your VAT group holds an interest). Details are in the table below. However, there are exceptions to this rule, which are explained in paragraph 14.8.2.

If...	*and...*	*then...*
You previously opted to tax a building (or part of a building)	you do not have a relevant interest in the building at the time you make a REE	your option is revoked (subject to paragraph 14.8.2)
You previously opted to tax land (without reference to a particular building or buildings)	you do not have a relevant interest in the land at the time you make a REE	your option is revoked (subject to paragraph 14.8.2)
You previously opted to tax land (without reference to a particular building or buildings)	you only have an interest in part of the land at the time you make a REE	your option is revoked in relation to the parts of land in which you do not hold a relevant interest (subject to paragraph 14.8.2)

14.8.2 What are the exceptions to automatic revocation?

Automatic revocation of an option will not occur at the time a REE is made in any of the following circumstances. All references to "relevant time" mean the time the REE is made or, in other words, the time the option would otherwise be revoked:

Option	Description
1.	Where the opter has sold the property on terms that may require the purchaser to make additional payment after the "relevant time". Such payments are often referred to as "overages" and can be contingent on such things as the purchaser obtaining planning permission.
	The following two circumstances can only apply if the person who opted to tax ("the opter") is or has been a member of a VAT group.
2.	Where a "relevant associate" of the opter in relation to the opted property (see paragraph 6.3) has sold the property on terms that may require the purchaser to make additional payment after the relevant time (see 1. above).
3.	you only have an interest in part of the land at the time you make a REE a. the relevant associate had an interest in or licence to occupy the property b. the relevant associate had, prior to leaving the VAT group, disposed of an interest on terms that might have required the purchaser to make additional payment at a later date (see 1. above) c. the relevant associate was connected to the opter or another relevant associate of the opter and that person had an interest in or licence to occupy the property

14.8.3 Conversion of single option (for example, a "global" option) into separate options

If, before you made a REE, you made a single option to tax in respect of land (without specifying a particular building or buildings) and that land is capable of being divided into separate parcels, you may convert the single option into separate options in respect of each of those parcels. This choice is only available in relation to land in which you have a relevant interest at the time you make the REE. Each parcel of land that is to be treated as being separately opted must meet the conditions set out in Box J below.

Box J

The boxed text below has the force of the law

Conversion of an option to tax land exercised before a real estate election into separate options to tax land in which a relevant interest is held at the time when the real estate election is made (for the purpose of para 22(6) of Sch 10 to VATA 1994.

A person making a real estate election may treat an option to tax made before the real estate election is made as though there were separate options to tax of individual parcels of that land. Each parcel of land that is to be treated as being separately opted must:

(1) be identified by at least one of the following—its postal address, land registry title number, map or plan or other description; and

(2) meet the conditions relating to the scope of an option contained in para 18 of Sch 10 to the VAT Act 1994.

If you choose to convert a single option into separate options, you should clearly identify the separate parcels of land when you notify your REE (see paragraph 14.9)

For the purpose of revocation, the new options are treated as having effect from the time that the original option had effect. These options cannot be revoked under the 6 month "cooling off" revocation.

If you're in a VAT group when you make a REE and you choose to convert a single option into separate options, you (that is, the person that has made the REE) will be treated as the opter for these new separate options, regardless of which VAT group member made the original option. For the purpose of revocation, the new separate options are treated as having effect from the time that the original option had effect. However, for the purpose of the "relevant associate" rules (see paragraph 6.3), they are treated as having effect from the date that the REE is made.

14.9 How do I notify a real estate election?

If you make a REE, you must notify it to HMRC within 30 days of having made it, or such longer period as we may allow.

The following statement has the force of the law.

> Notification of a real estate election (*for the purpose of paragraphs 21 and 22 of Sch 10 to VATA 1994*) must be made on form VAT 1614E and must contain the information requested on that form.

Form VAT1614E: notification of a real estate election is available online (www.gov.uk/government/publications/vat-notification-of-a-real-estate-election-vat1614e) or you can contact the VAT Helpline on Telephone: 0300 200 3700.

You must provide a list, with your notification, of properties in which you hold an interest at the time of making the REE (except for dwellings). If you have chosen to convert a single option into separate options (see paragraph 14.8.3), you must separately identify the separate parcels of land on this list. This list must contain the information specified in box K below.

Box K

The boxed text below has the force of the law.

> Information to be provided with a notification of a real estate election by a person holding one or more relevant interests in land or buildings (for the purpose of paragraph 21(7) of Sch 10 to VATA 1994 ("the VAT Act 1994")).
>
> The notification of a real estate election must contain the required information in relation to any land or buildings (other than buildings designed or adapted for use as a dwelling or a number of dwellings) in which the person making a real estate election holds a relevant interest at the time the REE is made.
>
> The required information must be provided by way of a list specifying the following in respect of each property (other than dwellings or buildings designed or adapted for use as a dwelling) in which the person holds a relevant interest—

Number	Condition
1.	a description of the land or buildings, identified by reference to postal address, land registry title number, map, plan or other description
2.	in the case of land or buildings in respect of which no option to tax made by the maker of a real estate election has effect, the date of acquisition of a relevant interest in that land or buildings
3.	in the case of land or buildings in respect of which an option to tax made by the maker of a real estate election has effect, the date when the relevant interest in the land or building was first acquired or, if later, the date when the option first had effect
4.	where an option has effect in relation to two or more separately listed parcels of land or buildings, they must be identified as being subject to the same option.

Explanatory Note 1

"Relevant interest" has the same meaning as in para 21(12) of Sch 10 to VATA 1994.

Explanatory Note 2

If the person making a real estate election has more than one relevant interest in a parcel of land or a building that were acquired at different times, only the date of acquisition of the most recently acquired relevant interest is to be provided.

Explanatory Note 3

If the person making a real estate election is required to provide the date when an option first had effect in relation to a parcel of land or a buildings and that date is unknown, that person should record that fact and enter an approximate date, using that person's best judgement, and provide a written explanation of why that date is considered reasonable.

14.10 What do I do if I have no record of the date an option to tax first had effect?

If you make a REE and don't have a record of the date when an option first had effect in relation to land or building, explanatory note 3 to box K allows you to provide an approximate date, using your best judgment. You also have to provide an explanation of why you consider that date is reasonable. HMRC will normally accept lists with such dates without further enquiry, but reserve the right to review them either as part of our general assurance and tax maintenance work, or as a result of a specific event (for example, notification of the revocation of an option to tax).

14.11 Incomplete or incorrect lists

If you submit an incomplete list or one which contains incorrect information, you should submit a revised and current updated list to your Client Relationship Manager or, if you do not have one, to the National Option to Tax Unit in Glasgow, (paragraph 4.2.3 shows how you may contact them) as soon as you identify the error.

14.12 What information must I provide after a real estate election has been made?

If you have made a REE, HMRC may, at any time, require you to provide within 30 days (or such longer period as we may allow) a list of all properties and parcels of land you hold at that time, together with details of all acquisitions, disposals and conversions to dwellings made since you last provided a list. In such a case, you have to provide the information set out in box L.

Box L

The boxed text below has the force of the law.

Information to be provided by the maker of a real estate election when required to do so by the Commissioners (under paragraph 21(8) of Sch 10 to VATA 1994 ("the VAT Act 1994")).

When required to do so, the maker of a real estate election must provide to the Commissioners the following information in relation to any land or buildings (other than buildings designed or adapted for use as a dwelling) in which that person or a relevant group member:

holds a relevant interest at the time of providing the required information; or
has ceased to hold a relevant interest since making a real estate election or, if later, since the last occasion on which the maker of the real estate election provided such information to the Commissioners

The information set out in Part A of this box is to be provided in respect of every such property; the information set out in Part B is to be provided in respect of every such property in which a relevant interest has been acquired or disposed of by the maker of the real estate election or a relevant group member since the date of the last such list, if any.

Part A.

In respect of any land or building in which the maker of a real estate election or a relevant group member holds a relevant interest or has ceased to hold such an interest as described above, the following information must be provided by way of a list specifying:

Number	Condition
1.	the description of the land or buildings identified by reference to its postal address, land registry title number, map, plan or other description
2.	in the case of land or buildings in respect of which no option to tax made by the maker of a real estate election or relevant group member has effect, the date of acquisition of the relevant interest in the land or buildings
3.	in the case of land or buildings in respect of which an option to tax made by the maker of a real estate election or a relevant group member has effect, the date when the relevant interest in the land or building was acquired or, if later, the date when the option first had effect
4.	where an option has effect in relation to two or more separately listed parcels of land or buildings, they must be identified as being subject to the same option

Part B

The following information must be provided in respect of every property in which a relevant interest has been acquired or disposed of by the maker or the real estate election or a relevant group member since the date of the last such list, if any, by way of a list specifying—

Number	Condition
1.	As appropriate, the date of the maker of the real estate election or a relevant group member—
	acquiring a relevant interest in land or buildings in which that person has no other relevant interest
	ceasing to hold a relevant interest in land or buildings without retaining another relevant interest in that property
	opting to tax land or buildings otherwise than by virtue of a real estate election
	converting a building or buildings into a dwelling or dwellings
	excluding a new building from the effect of an option, and
	revoking an option to tax in relation to land or buildings.
	identifying the land or building to which each occurrence relates.
2.	The VAT-exclusive value of the supply of a relevant interest acquired or disposed of by the maker of a real estate election or relevant group member.
3.	The VAT (if any) charged on the supply of a relevant interest by the maker of a real estate election or, where the supply occurred before its admission to the group, the relevant group member.

Explanatory Note 1

"*Relevant interest*" and "*relevant group member*" have the same meanings as they do in para 21(12) of Sch 10 to VATA 1994.

Explanatory Note 2

Where the maker of a real estate election or relevant group member has more than one relevant interest in the same land or building that were acquired at different times, only the date of acquisition of the most recently acquired relevant interest is to be provided.

Explanatory Note 3

In the case of land or a building in which an interest has been held before the date of a real estate election, the date of the occurrence of the making of an option to tax by the person making a real estate election or a relevant group member is the date when that option first has effect.

Explanatory Note 4

The date of the occurrence of the revocation of an option is the date from which the revocation has effect.

Explanatory Note 5

The requirement to provide the information set out in Parts A and B above does not apply to the revocation of an option to tax by virtue of paragraph 23 ("the cooling off" period) or paragraph 24 (lapse of six years since having a relevant interest) of Sch 10 to VATA 1994.

14.13 About global options to tax and REEs

14.13.1 What is a "global" option to tax?

A "global" option is a single option to tax which covers a large number of properties, such as "the whole of the UK" or "all current property holdings and all future acquisitions".

14.13.2 What are the disadvantages of a global option?

A global option is a single option to tax and therefore cannot be revoked on a property by property basis. A global option can only be revoked as a whole, and only if the relevant conditions are met for each property covered by the global option. Global options have caused particular problems for VAT groups, due to the relevant associate rules explained in paragraph 6.3.

14.13.3 Can I still make a global option instead of a REE?

You may still opt to tax a large area, such as the whole of the UK, if you wish to. However, you should be aware of the possible disadvantages described in paragraph 14.13.2. You can no longer exercise a global option in respect of "all current property holdings and future acquisitions".

14.13.4 I've made a global option in the past. Can I convert it into a REE?

If you have made a "global" option to tax in the past, you can, if you wish, make a REE. This will have the following implications for your existing global option—

- the global option will generally be revoked in respect of any land in which you don't hold a relevant interest when you make the REE (see paragraph 14.8.1)
- you can, if you wish, convert the remainder of the global option into separately opted parcels of land when you make a REE (see paragraph 14.8.3), each separate option will then be capable of being individually revoked, if the conditions for revocation are met

14.14 How are REEs treated in VAT groups?

14.14.1 Which member of a VAT Group can make a REE?

Any member of a VAT group can make a REE although HMRC expects that this will normally be done by the representative member of the VAT group.

14.14.2 What is the effect of a REE on properties acquired by other VAT group members?

If you're in a VAT group when you make a REE, or if you join one after you have made a REE, your REE will affect acquisitions of any members of your group, in addition to affecting your own acquisitions.

This means that where a body corporate in the same group as you acquires an interest in a property, you will be treated as having opted to tax that property at the time the interest is acquired (except for the circumstances described in paragraph 14.7).

You will be treated as the opter in these circumstances and the body corporate which has acquired the interest will be a "relevant associate" of you (see paragraph 6.3).

If a body corporate ceases to be a member of the same VAT group as you, any acquisitions it makes after ceasing to be a member of your VAT group will not be affected by the REE.

14.14.3 How does the REE effect an option to tax made by me (or by a body corporate within my VAT group at that time) before I made the REE?

If neither you nor any member of your VAT group holds an interest in the relevant opted property at the time of making the REE (or only holds an interest in part of it), the option might be automatically revoked (or partially revoked) (see paragraphs 14.8.1 and 14.8.2 for further information about this).

If the option is not automatically revoked (or if only part of it is revoked), and you choose to split the option into separately opted parcels of land (see paragraph 14.8.3), then you (that is, the person that has made the REE) will be treated as the opter for the new separately opted parcels of land, regardless of who made the original option (see paragraph 14.8.3 for further information about this).

For any other options to tax, the body corporate that originally made the option will remain the opter. Any further acquisitions that are made in relation to such opted property will not be affected by the REE.

14.15 Can I revoke a REE?

Once you have made a REE, you cannot revoke it but HMRC has the power to withdraw a REE if you do not comply with our requests for information (see paragraph 14.13).

If we withdraw your REE, you cannot make a further REE unless you obtain our permission first. Where a subsequent REE is made, you may not convert single options into separate options (see paragraph 14.8.3).

ANNEX 1

All the forms and certificates below have the force of law and must be used where appropriate. They're available on the www.hmrc.gov.uk website or from the VAT Helpline on Telephone: 0300 200 3700.

VAT1614B: ceasing to be a relevant associate in relation to an option to tax

VAT1614C: revoking an option to tax within 6 months "cooling off" period

VAT1614D: certificate to disapply the option to tax buildings for conversion into dwellings etc

VAT1614E: notification of a real estate election

VAT1614F: new buildings - exclusion from an option to tax

VAT 1614G: certificate to disapply the option to tax land sold to housing associations

VAT 1614H: application for permission to opt

VAT 1614J: revoking an option to tax after 20 years

ANNEX 2

For flow charts designed to assist with the application see the following link.www.gov.uk/government/uploads/system/uploads/attachment_data/file/372477/742A_Annex2.pdf

Notes

Note 1 – "Opted supplies" means supplies that will be taxable as a result of the option to tax. "Property" includes land, buildings and civil engineering works.

Note 2 – The question of whether a person is connected with another person is to be decided as it would be for the purposes of Part 1 of Schedule 10 to the VAT Act 1994. Guidance on connected persons is in paragraph 13.7.

Note 3 – "Permissible exempt supplies" means the following exempt supplies arising from a grant in relation to the land:

(a) supplies for which the consideration solely represents legal and/or valuation costs reimbursed under the agreement for the grant

(b) supplies where

  (i) the consideration received is rent and/or service charges which relates to a period of occupation of the property and that period ends no later than 12 months from the date on which the option first takes effect

  (ii) no taxable rents and service charges to be made after that 12-month period will be reduced in value as a result of the consideration payable for these exempt supplies.

Note 4 – For the purposes of the requirement, "entitled to credit" includes a deduction or credit arising as a result of the application of the "payback" provisions or the Capital Goods Scheme. Guidance on these terms can be found in VAT Notice 706: *partial exemption* and VAT Notice 706/2: *Capital Goods Scheme*.

Note 5 – For the purposes of the requirement, your "capital expenditure" is your expenditure on goods or services used in connection with the acquisition of, building works on, construction works on or the fitting out of, the property. Capital expenditure doesn't include expenditure on routine repairs and maintenance.

Note 6 – "Supplies conferring a credit to input tax" are supplies listed under the VAT (Input Tax) (Specified Supplies) Order 1999 (SI 1999/3121). These include:

(a) services made to a person outside the EU member states which are either:

  (i) directly linked to an export of goods to a place outside the member states

  (ii) certain intermediary services in connection with supplies of financial services which are exempt or would be exempt if made in the UK

(b) certain supplies of investment gold

Further details of these "specified supplies" is available in paragraph 8.2 of VAT Notice 706: *partial exemption*.

Note 7 – Paragraphs 5 –11 of Sch 10 to VATA 1994 deal with the following supplies:

(a) Para 5 - supplies of a building (or part of a building) designed or adapted and intended for use as a dwelling or solely for a relevant residential purpose (further information is in paragraph 3.2 and paragraph 3.3).

(b) Para 6 - supplies of a building (or part of a building) not designed or adapted as a dwelling or relevant residential building but intended for use as such, for example, following conversion (further information is in paragraph 3.4).

(c) Para 7 - supplies of a building (or part of a building) intended solely for a relevant charitable purpose other than as an office (further information is in paragraph 3.5).

(d) Para 8 - supplies of pitches for residential caravans (further information is in paragraph 3.8).

(e) Para 9 - moorings for residential houseboats (further information is in paragraph 3.9).

(f) Para 10 - supplies of land to housing associations (further information is in paragraph 3.6).

(g) Para 11 - supplies of land to individuals for the construction of dwellings (further information is in paragraph 3.7).

NOTICE 1001
VAT REFUND SCHEME FOR CERTAIN CHARITIES

28 April 2015

This new notice contains guidance on the VAT refund scheme for palliative care charities, air ambulance charities, search and rescue charities and medical courier charities, introduced by Finance Act 2015 with effect from 1 April 2015.

This notice explains the VAT rules that apply to charities eligible for refunds of VAT under sections 33C and 33D of the VAT Act 1994.

1. INTRODUCTION

1.1 WHAT IS THIS NOTICE ABOUT?

This notice only applies to those charities which are defined as a 'qualifying charity' in section 33D of the VAT Act 1994.

These are:

- palliative care charities
- air ambulance charities
- search and rescue charities
- medical courier charities

The notice explains which charities are eligible to use the refund scheme to claim a refund of VAT incurred on goods and services used for their non-business activities, what to do when circumstances change, what falls within the scope of the refund scheme and how to make a claim.

The notice assumes a working knowledge of basic VAT principles, as outlined in VAT Notice 700: the VAT guide.

For general guidance on VAT and charities, including details of certain reliefs, see VAT Notice 701/1: charities.

1.2 WHO SHOULD READ THIS NOTICE?

Palliative care charities, air ambulance charities, search and rescue charities and medical courier charities. For definitions of these charities see paragraph 1.7.

1.3 WHAT LAW COVERS THIS NOTICE?

The legislation covering VAT refunds to qualifying charities can be found in the VAT Act 1994 sections 33C and 33D.

1.4 WHAT IS THE DEFINITION OF A CHARITY?

A charity is defined for tax purposes in Schedule 6 to the Finance Act 2010.

In summary this means that a charity must be:

- based in the UK, EU, Iceland, Liechtenstein or Norway
- established for charitable purposes only
- registered with the Charity Commission for England and Wales or another regulator, if this applies to you
- run by 'fit and proper persons'

1.5 WILL I NEED TO EVIDENCE THAT I AM A CHARITY FOR TAX PURPOSES IN ORDER TO CLAIM A REFUND OF VAT?

You will need to be recognised as a charity for tax purposes by HM Revenue and Customs (HMRC) if you're either not already recognised in this way by HMRC or if you're not registered as a charity with the Charity Commission for England and Wales.

You can apply to be recognised by HMRC as a charity for tax purposes: www.gov.uk/charity-recognition-hmrc.

1.6 WHAT IS THE POSITION FOR CHARITIES THAT PROVIDE FREE GOODS OR SERVICES TO THE PUBLIC AND OTHER ORGANISATIONS?

If charities provide services free of charge to members of the public and other organisations they're not regarded as carrying out business activities for VAT purposes.

Supplies of goods free of charge can be business activities for VAT purposes in certain circumstances. For more information see VAT Notice 700: the VAT guide.

Such charities may, of course, have other activities that in their own right are business activities, for example, provision of training for a charge and sales of books and gifts.

Ordinarily, it's not possible to recover the VAT incurred on goods and services purchased to support non-business activities. In certain circumstances, however, there are schemes to reimburse this otherwise irrecoverable VAT. For this to be the case, the provisions of sections 33C and 33D of the VAT Act 1994 must apply.

For more information on non-business activities for VAT purposes see VAT Notice 701/1: charities.

1.7 WHAT CHARITIES ARE INCLUDED IN SECTIONS 33C AND 33D AND FROM WHEN?

It's not possible to provide an exhaustive list of the charities which are likely to benefit from the VAT refund scheme but the details below should help you decide if you're eligible.

There are 4 categories of qualifying charities in sections 33C and 33D:

(1) Palliative care charities - these are charities whose main purpose is the provision of palliative care under supervision of a medical professional to persons who are in need of such care because they have a terminal illness. Terminal illness means a progressive disease which will result in a person's death. This will mainly cover adult and children's hospices.

(2) Air ambulance charities - these are charities whose main purpose is to provide emergency medical air ambulance services. Their services must be arranged or requested by an NHS (National Health Service) body that delivers an NHS Ambulance Service. In England this is an NHS Trust, in Wales an NHS Foundation Trust, in Scotland a special Health Board and in Northern Ireland a Health and Social Care trust.

(3) Search and rescue charities - there are 2 types of search and rescue charities. The first type of search and rescue charities is those whose main purpose is to carry out coordinated search and rescue of persons who are, or may be, at risk of death or serious injury. Such charities include sea/shoreline rescue teams, mountain rescue teams, cave rescue teams, lowland search and rescue teams and rescue dog teams. The bodies coordinating search and rescue of persons are listed in section 33D of the VAT Act 1994. The second type of search and rescue charities is those whose main purpose is to support, develop and promote the first type of search and rescue charities. See paragraph 1.8 for what this means.

(4) Medical courier charities - there are 2 types of medical courier charities. The first type of medical courier charities is those whose main purpose is to provide services for the urgent transportation of items of a medical nature, for example blood, platelets, samples for analysis, drugs, patient notes, small medical instruments, donor breast milk and other medical supplies. The second type of medical courier charities is those whose main purpose is to support, develop and promote the first type of medical courier charities. See paragraph 1.8 for what this means. This will mainly cover 'blood bike' charities.

Qualifying charities can claim a refund of VAT incurred on most goods and services supplied to them on or after 1 April 2015 and which relate to their non-business activities. See paragraph 2.4.

1.8 WHAT DOES 'CHARITIES WHOSE MAIN PURPOSE IS TO SUPPORT, DEVELOP AND PROMOTE OTHER SEARCH AND RESCUE OR MEDICAL COURIER CHARITIES' MEAN?

You're a charity whose main purpose is to support, develop and promote other search and rescue charities or medical courier charities if you undertake one or more of the following:

- coordinate and provide support to such charities

- support and help with the establishment of such charities
- promote good practice for charitable search and rescue or medical courier activities - examples may include training, knowledge and information sharing
- arrange supplies of goods and services to such charities which are required for charitable search and rescue or medical courier activities
- represent such charities regionally and/or nationally

1.9 I AM A CHARITY BUT AM NOT INCLUDED IN SECTIONS 33C AND 33D. WHY CAN'T I ALSO CLAIM A REFUND OF VAT ON MY NON-BUSINESS ACTIVITIES?

In general charities can't recover VAT they incur on their non-business activities.

This refund scheme applies only to the 4 categories of qualifying charities in paragraph 1.7.

However, there are certain VAT reliefs for charities. For more information see VAT Notice 701/1: charities.

1.10 CAN SECTIONS 33C AND 33D CHARITIES JOIN VAT GROUPS?

If a sections 33C and 33D charity and its trading subsidiaries are VAT registered they can form a VAT group if they meet the requirements for VAT group treatment as set out in VAT Notice 700/2: group and divisional registration. HMRC will grant such requests only if they're satisfied that you're not seeking the arrangement for tax avoidance purposes.

If you're a VAT group which includes a qualifying charity (see paragraph 1.7), only the qualifying charity is eligible to claim a refund of VAT incurred on its non-business activities. The entitlement to refunds of VAT incurred on non-business activities doesn't extend to any residual rate for the VAT group as a whole.

2. WHAT VAT CAN I RECLAIM UNDER SECTIONS 33C AND 33D?

2.1 SCOPE OF THIS SECTION

This section explains what VAT you can reclaim under the scheme, if you're a qualifying charity. You can claim a refund of VAT you incur on most goods and services supplied to you on or after 1 April 2015 and which relate to your non-business activities.

This extends to UK VAT incurred on:

- the supply to you of goods or services
- goods imported from a country outside the EC or acquired from another member state of the EC

For further details on when you will incur VAT on goods imported from a country outside the EC or acquired from another member state of the EC you should read Notice 702: imports, VAT Notice 702/9: VAT - import customs procedures and VAT Notice 725: the single market.

It doesn't extend to supplies made to you before 1 April 2015.

2.2 MUST THE SUPPLY OF GOODS AND SERVICES BE MADE TO ME?

Yes. Whether or not you're registered for VAT, you can get refunds on goods and services you use or intend to use for your non-business activities only if you:

- place the order
- receive the supply
- receive a tax invoice addressed to you
- pay from your own funds (including funds awarded to you, for example, lottery funds)

'Non-business activities' doesn't mean purchases made for private purposes.

2.3 HOW FAR BACK CAN I CLAIM VAT?

VAT can only be claimed on supplies of goods and services you receive on or after 1 April 2015 and is subject to the time limits explained in paragraph 3.4 (if you're registered for VAT) and paragraph 4.3 (if you're not registered for VAT).

2.4 HOW DO I DECIDE IF I AM ELIGIBLE TO CLAIM A REFUND OF VAT INCURRED ON MY 'NON-BUSINESS ACTIVITIES'?

You're eligible to claim refunds of VAT where your main purpose is to carry out one of the following:

- coordinated search and rescue of persons
- coordinated emergency medical air ambulance activities
- palliative care activities
- medical courier activities

These will be services that you provide for no consideration - normally because they have been funded through grant-in-aid or voluntary donations. This means that you will be able to claim a refund of the VAT incurred on the purchases you make to support these, and any other activities that aren't carried on by way of business.

2.4.1 WHAT DO YOU MEAN BY 'MAIN PURPOSE'?

Main purpose means the primary function of the charity. Governing documents such as a charity's memorandum and articles of association, constitution, trust deed or declaration of trust and its annual report should refer to the main purpose of the charity.

2.4.2 I AM A HOSPICE CHARITY AND RECEIVE FUNDING FROM THE NHS, CLINICAL COMMISSIONING GROUP AND/OR LOCAL AUTHORITY TO SUPPORT MY PROVISION OF PALLIATIVE CARE. ARE MY ACTIVITIES NON-BUSINESS?

Provided one of the conditions below applies, you can treat the funding received as non-business income for VAT purposes. This means you can claim a refund of VAT incurred on supplies you use to provide palliative care:

- it must be grant funding you receive from any of the above bodies
- there must be no direct link between your palliative care activities and any consideration received for the provision of palliative care (for example funding under a standard NHS service level contract, such as a 2015/2016 contract in England or a service level agreement in Scotland, Wales or Northern Ireland)

If, however, you enter into arrangements that don't constitute a standard NHS service level contract because they cover requirements to care for referred or named individuals (in addition to requirements covering general outcomes), your activities under those arrangements may be a business activity. For more information on business activities and charities see VAT Notice 701/1: charities.

If you provide welfare services at significantly below cost to individuals you may be able to treat this as non-business income for VAT purposes. For more information see VAT Notice 701/1: charities.

2.4.3 SOME OF MY SUPPLIES ARE EXEMPT FROM VAT, IS THIS THE SAME AS NON-BUSINESS ACTIVITIES?

No, some supplies are exempt from VAT, which means that they're business activities for VAT purposes, but no tax is payable. Generally you're not able to recover VAT on costs you incur on exempt supplies. See paragraph 2.8.

2.4.4 SOME OF MY SUPPLIES ARE ZERO RATED FOR VAT, IS THIS THE SAME AS NON-BUSINESS ACTIVITIES?

No, some supplies are zero rated for VAT, which means VAT isn't payable on them. However, if you're VAT registered you can normally recover the VAT on expenses you incur on zero-rated supplies you make, subject to some restrictions.

For more information on zero-rated supplies see VAT Notice 700: the VAT guide.

2.4.5 I HAVE A MIXTURE OF BUSINESS AND NON-BUSINESS ACTIVITIES AND I INCUR OVERHEAD COSTS THAT RELATE TO BOTH. CAN I RECOVER ALL THE VAT I INCUR?

If you're a qualifying charity (see paragraph 1.7) and you carry out both business and non-business activities you will need to apportion any VAT you incur on overhead costs relating to both types of activity.

There are a number of methods a charity can use to apportion this VAT. Some methods are detailed in VAT Notice 700: the VAT guide. To claim a refund of VAT on the non-business proportion of overhead costs you will need to have a method in place.

If you're registered for VAT you can claim a refund of VAT incurred on your non-business activities and your taxable business activities on your VAT Return (see Section 3). If you make exempt supplies for VAT purposes see paragraph 2.8.

If you're not registered for VAT see Section 4 for how you can claim a refund of VAT on your non-business activities.

2.4.6 I RECHARGE COSTS TO OTHER CHARITIES/ORGANISATIONS. IS THIS A BUSINESS ACTIVITY?

If you recharge costs it may be a business activity. See VAT Notice 701/1: charities for more detailed information.

2.4.7 WHERE CAN I FIND MORE INFORMATION ON BUSINESS AND NON-BUSINESS ACTIVITIES AND CHARITIES?

For more information on business and non-business activities and charities see VAT Notice 701/1: charities.

2.5 CAN YOU GIVE MORE SPECIFIC EXAMPLES OF COSTS INCURRED ON NON-BUSINESS ACTIVITIES?

More specifically and where applicable, and provided the costs don't relate to any business activities, this might include the UK VAT you incur on:

- the purchase or lease of certain vehicles
- vehicle maintenance and storage
- the purchase of road fuel
- the purchase of drugs and medicines
- the purchase and maintenance of equipment
- uniforms, protective clothing and identity badges
- building costs including utilities, repairs and maintenance
- stationery and IT costs
- training
- fundraising costs

However, please see paragraph 2.7 which covers VAT where a refund can't be claimed.

2.6 AM I DISQUALIFIED FROM USING SECTIONS 33C AND 33D BECAUSE I CHARGE FOR SOME OF MY ACTIVITIES?

No. Provided your main purpose is one set out in paragraph 2.4 above it doesn't matter if you occasionally charge people for some of your activities. However, your claim under sections 33C and 33D is restricted to VAT incurred on your non-business activities as explained in paragraphs 2.2 to 2.4 above.

If you incur VAT on purchases made for your business activities for VAT purposes this VAT is input tax and is subject to the normal rules of input tax deduction, see VAT Notice 700: the VAT guide.

If you have exempt business activities see paragraph 2.4.3.

2.7 WHAT VAT CAN'T BE CLAIMED UNDER SECTIONS 33C AND 33D?

The provisions in sections 33C and 33D can't be used to reclaim any VAT you incur on any business activities such as:

- shops, catering outlets, commercial sponsorship (including commercially sponsored websites)
- educational courses that you provide for consideration

Additionally, sections 33C and 33D do not permit you to recover any VAT:

- which can't be recovered under the normal VAT rules, for example VAT incurred on business entertainment and, in certain circumstances, when you purchase or lease a car, see VAT Notice 700: the VAT guide
- incurred in another member state (for example, TVA (Taxe à la Valeur Ajoutée) incurred in France), in certain circumstances you can reclaim this VAT from the authorities in the

member state where you incurred the VAT, see VAT Notice 723A: refunds of VAT in the European Community for EC and non-EC businesses

2.8 WHAT OTHER VAT AM I ENTITLED TO RECOVER?

The provisions in sections 33C and 33D can't be used to recover VAT incurred in any circumstances other than those outlined in paragraphs 2.2 to 2.6.

However, if you're registered for VAT you can recover the VAT incurred on the supply to you of most goods and services, and the importation or acquisition by you of most goods that relate to your taxable business activities. See VAT Notice 700: the VAT guide.

You can't generally recover VAT incurred on supplies you make that are exempt from VAT, and you will need to operate a partial exemption method to determine whether, and how much, input tax will be restricted. For more information see VAT Notice 700: the VAT guide and VAT Notice 706: partial exemption.

If you're not registered for VAT, you can only reclaim VAT to the extent permitted under sections 33C and 33D.

3. I AM VAT REGISTERED. HOW DO I RECOVER THE VAT I HAVE INCURRED ON MY NON-BUSINESS ACTIVITIES?

3.1 SCOPE OF THIS SECTION

If you're a qualifying charity under sections 33C and 33D of the VAT Act 1994 and you're registered for VAT, this section explains how you can recover the VAT you have incurred in carrying out your non-business activities.

3.2 I'M NOT REGISTERED FOR VAT

If you're not registered for VAT and you don't need to register, you should read Section 4. You will still be able to claim a refund of the VAT you have incurred on the goods and services you have bought for your non-business activities.

3.3 I AM REGISTERED FOR VAT. HOW CAN I CLAIM THE VAT REFUNDS I AM ENTITLED TO?

You should claim your refund in Box 4 of the VAT Return. In that box you should include not only the value of the input tax you incurred in making your taxable business supplies, but also the amount of VAT you are reclaiming under sections 33C and 33D on those goods and services you have bought for your non-business activities. Be sure to include the net value of your claim in Box 7.

3.4 WHAT IF I DISCOVER VAT REFUNDS THAT I HAVE FAILED TO INCLUDE ON MY VAT RETURN?

You must make your claim within 4 years of the due date of your return for the prescribed accounting period in which the VAT became chargeable. The refund scheme applies to VAT incurred on supplies made to you on or after 1 April 2015 in relation to your non-business activities. It doesn't extend to supplies made to you before that date.

3.4.1 HOW DO I MAKE MY CLAIM FOR A REFUND OF VAT I HAVE FAILED TO INCLUDE ON MY VAT RETURN?

You must:

- make the claim in writing
- state the amount you are claiming
- state the periods covered
- explain the basis of your calculation
- hold evidence to support your claim

3.5 WHERE CAN I FIND MORE INFORMATION ON VAT REGISTRATION AND CHARITIES?

For more information on registering for VAT if you're a charity see VAT Notice 701/1: charities.

4. QUALIFYING CHARITIES WHICH ARE NOT REGISTERED FOR VAT

4.1 SCOPE OF THIS SECTION

If you're a qualifying charity under sections 33C and 33D of the VAT Act 1994 (see paragraph 1.7) and you're not registered for VAT, this section will help you make sure your claims for VAT refunds are valid. It also explains how to make them.

4.2 I AM IN SECTIONS 33C AND 33D BUT I'M NOT REGISTERED FOR VAT. I'M NOT SURE WHAT GOODS AND SERVICES I CAN RECOVER VAT ON. HOW CAN I FIND OUT?

Step	Action
1.	Read Section 2 of this notice to find out the main principles.
2.	Read Section 3 of this notice to see whether you can meet the various requirements set out there.
3.	Reclaim the VAT you have incurred only when you can attribute it to your non-business activities.
4.	Remember that, because you're not registered, you may neither charge VAT on your taxable business activities nor recover the VAT relating to them.

4.3 HOW CAN I CLAIM VAT REFUNDS I AM ENTITLED TO?

Step	Action
1.	Complete form VAT 126. Once completed send it to the address in paragraph 4.4.
2.	Make sure that your claim relates to a period of at least one calendar month - or at least 12 months if it is for less than £100.
3.	Make sure the period you choose ends on the last day of a calendar month.
4.	Make sure you make your claim within 4 years after the end of the month in which you received the supply, acquisition or importation eg, you receive a supply of goods in July 2015, so you must submit your claim by 31 July 2019.
5.	Keep the invoices and other records to support your claims for 6 years, unless you have applied in writing, and HMRC has agreed to you keeping them for a shorter period.
6.	If you obtain refunds by Bankers' Automated Clearing Service (Bacs), inform HMRC of any changes to the details of your bank account.

4.4 WHERE SHOULD I SEND MY CLAIM?

Send your claim to:

HM Revenue and Customs
DMB Banking 2
7th Floor
Regian House
James Street
Liverpool L75 1AD

4.5 WHAT WILL HMRC DO ONCE THEY RECEIVE MY CLAIM?

Normally, once HMRC receives your claim, they will:

(a) make your refund by BACS or payable order and
(b) give you a unique number to quote on all claims - but this doesn't mean that HMRC has registered you for VAT

From time to time HMRC will select claims for verification.

Administrative agreements with trade bodies

NOTICE 700/57
ADMINISTRATIVE AGREEMENTS ENTERED INTO WITH TRADE BODIES

2004 with Update 1

Note—HM Customs & Excise have made available details of a number of agreements made with trade bodies. These agreements permit members of the trade bodies to use procedures to meet their obligations under VAT law which take into account their individual circumstances.

The agreements made available, and covered by Notice 700/57, are listed in the table below.

Trade body	*Agreement*	*Remarks*
London Bullion Market Association	Supplies of bullion	
The Brewers' Society	Deduction of input tax incurred in respect of brewers' tenanted estate	
Association of British Factors and Discounters	Partial exemption and factors	
Finance Houses Association Ltd	Finance houses and partial exemption	
Association of British Insurers	Recovery of input tax incurred in UK in connection with supplies by branches outside the European Community	
Association of Investment Trust Companies	Partial exemption	
The British Printing Industries Federation	Apportionment of subsidy publishing supplies	
Marine, aviation and transport insurance underwriters	Claims related to input tax and associated imported services	
Association of British Insurers, Lloyd's of London, the Institute of London Underwriters, the British Insurance and Investment Association	Coding supplies of marine, aviation and transport (MAT) insurance services	
National Caravan Council Limited, British Holiday and Home Park Association Limited	Method of valuing removable contents sold with zero-rated caravans	
Association of Unit Trust and Investment Managers	VAT liability of charges made in connection with Personal Equity Plans (PEPs)	
British Bankers' Association	VAT liability of electronic banking/cash management services	
British Vehicle Rental and Leasing Association	Car leasing and repairs and maintenance services	Effective from 1 August 1995
Society of Motor Manufacturers and Traders	Calculating output tax on the self-supply of a motor vehicle	Effective from 1 August 1992
Gaming Board for Great Britain; British Casino Association	Competitions in card rooms	January 1998
British Phonographic Society	VAT liability of promotional samples given free of charge	March 1998

Trade body	*Agreement*	*Remarks*
Thoroughbred Breeders Association	Arrangements under which racehorse owners may register for VAT and the procedures that must be followed	March 1993
British Horseracing Board	Revised arrangements under which racehorse owners may register for VAT and the procedures that must be followed	January 1998
British Horseracing Board; Thoroughbred Breeders Association	Racehorses applied permanently to personal or other non-business use	
British Horseracing Board; Thoroughbred Breeders Association	Keeping of stallions at stud	
British Horseracing Board; Thoroughbred Breeders Association	Racehorses and time limits for exportation	
Meat and Livestock Commission	VAT treatment of levies collected (invoiced) from 1 October 1990 by the Commission from operators of slaughterhouses and exporters of live animals	
Society of Motor Manufacturers and Traders Ltd	How the one tonne payload test will be applied in practice to double cab pick-ups	
Society of Motor Manufacturers and Traders Ltd	Simplified method by which motor manufacturers, importers and wholesale distributors may calculate the VAT due on the private use of stock in trade cars provided to directors and employees free of charge	
Retail Motor Industry Federation	Simplified method by which retail motor dealers may calculate the VAT due on the private use of demonstrator cars provided to directors and employees free of charge	
British Vehicle Rental and Leasing Association	Simplified method which daily rental companies may use to calculate the VAT due on the incidental private use of their hire fleets	

VAT
Press Releases etc

Contents

VAT PRs etc

Company formation services with ancillary printed matter—clarification of treatment post CPP. Hotel conference/function facilities: revised interpretation of law on VAT treatment. *(18 January 2006. BB 1/06)*

Beauty procedures performed using class 3B or 4 lasers and/or intense pulse light (IPL) machines—clarification of liability. *(9 March 2006. BB 3/06)*

Off-street car parking provided by local authorities. *(24 March 2006. BB 4/06)*

Interim position following the Court of Session's decision in Edinburgh's Telford College. *(12 April 2006. BB 5/06)*

Exemption for the management of authorised collective investment schemes. *(27 June 2006. BB 7/06)*

Clarification of the treatment of travel agent funded discounts. *(7 July 2006. BB 8/06)*

Position following the Court of Appeal judgment in *Compass Contract Services Limited*. *(21 August 2006. BB 12/06)*

3-Year Cap on making claims—Court of Appeal Judgment in *Michael Fleming t/a Bodycraft*.
3-Year Cap on making claims—Court of Appeal Judgment in *Condé Nast Publications Ltd*. *(24 August 2006. BB 13/06)*

Gaming machines—accounting for VAT. The reduced value rule for long-stay guests in hotels—revised interpretation of the law on VAT treatment. *(27 September 2006. BB 15/06)*

Changes to VAT law in light of the Gambling Act. Publication of tax avoidance scheme disclosure statistics. Liability of private tuition. Liability of condoms supplied to charities providing care or medical treatment. *(13 October 2006. BB 16/06)*

Partial exemption: bookmakers—recovery of VAT on specialist television services and equipment. Disposable barbecues. *(19 October 2006. BB 17/06)*

Liability of agents' credit and debit card handling services. *(30 October 2006. BB 18/06)*

First grant of a major interest in residential property: attribution of input tax and the capital goods scheme. Final Business Brief. *(22 December 2006. BB 23/06)*

Further clarification of the treatment of foreign exchange transactions (forex) and transactions in other financial instruments. *(26 January 2007. HMRC Brief 05/07)*

Changes to the exemption for medical services from 1 May 2007. *(30 January 2007. HMRC Brief 06/07)*

Cash bingo: accounting for VAT on participation and session fees. *(1 February 2007. HMRC Brief 07/07)*

Manufacturers' "cash back" payments. *(6 February 2007. HMRC Brief 08/07)*

Liability of private tuition. *(6 February 2007. HMRC Brief 10/07)*

Fuel scale charge; new CO2 basis. *(12 February 2007. HMRC Brief 13/07)*

Changes to the rules on bad debt relief for goods supplied on credit terms. *(13 February 2007. HMRC Brief 14/07)*

Partial exemption: special method approvals. *(14 March 2007. HMRC Brief 23/07)*

Proposed reverse charge accounting for businesses trading in mobile telephones and computer chips: announcement of targeted implementation and details of how the rules will operate in practice; and exposure of draft legislation for comment. *(20 March 2007. HMRC Brief 24/07)*

Cultural exemption – clarification of "direct or indirect financial interest" [VATA 1994 Sch 9 Group 13 Note 2(c)]. *(22 March 2007. HMRC Brief 27/07)*

Partial exemption: VAT recovery on overhead costs relating to supplies of hire purchase. *(30 March 2007. HMRC Brief 31/07)*

VAT Strategy: Input tax deduction without a valid VAT invoice. *(10 April 2007. Statement of Practice)*

Partial exemption – VAT deduction by theatres on production costs. *(14 June 2007. HMRC Brief 45/07)*

Introduction of a reduced rate for the supply of smoking cessation products. *(28 June 2007. HMRC Brief 48/07)*

Changes to the VAT Invoicing Regulations with effect from 1 October 2007. *(24 July 2007. HMRC Brief 51/07)*

Revised treatment of VAT incurred on home computers made available by employers to their employees. *(14 August 2007. HMRC Brief 55/07)*

Place of supply of trading allowances in greenhouse gas emissions (update) *(22 August 2007. HMRC Brief 52/07)*

Claims in respect of fund management services. *(22 August 2007. HMRC Brief 58/07)*

Teleos and others (VAT—Intra-Community trade). *(11 October 2007. HMRC Brief 61/07)*

Withdrawal of zero-rating for adapted motor vehicles from 1 January 2012 *(19 December 2011. HMRC Brief 41/11)*
Withdrawal of zero-rating for adapted parts and accessories for boats from 1 January 2012 *(19 December 2011. HMRC Brief 42/11)*
Intrastat thresholds and changes to reporting procedures from 1 January 2012 *(23 December 2011. HMRC Brief 44/11)*
VAT – zero rate – extra care accommodation *(30 December 2011. HMRC Brief 47/11)*
Use of rebated fuel in vehicles undertaking snow clearance and gritting work *(5 January 2012. HMRC Brief 45/11)*
Use of rebated fuel in grass cutting vehicles *(5 January 2012. HMRC Brief 46/11)*
Pre-registration claims following de-registration of the same legal entity *(23 January 2012. HMRC Brief 1/12)*
Employment income - definition of mobile phone (treatment of smartphones) *(20 February 2012. HMRC Brief 2/12)*
VAT liability of caravan pitch rentals *(27 February 2012. HMRC Brief 5/12)*
VAT Tribunal decision in Paymex Limited v HMRC *(1 March 2012. HMRC Brief 3/12)*
VAT zero-rating of photo books – Harrier LLC case *(5 March 2012. HMRC Brief 4/12)*
Change to monthly deadline for Intrastat declarations *(16 March 2012. HMRC Brief 7/12)*
Changing VAT law on road fuel scale charges *(25 April 2012. HMRC Brief 11/12)*
Changes to the treatment of single purpose face value vouchers *(10 May 2012. HMRC Brief 12/12)*
Out-of-time claims for repayment of indirect taxes *(14 May 2012. HMRC Brief 13/12)*
Updated Senior Accounting Officer guidance *(11 June 2012. HMRC Brief 16/12)*
Place of supply of services connected to land *(2 August 2012. HMRC Brief 22/12)*
Withdrawal of reduced VAT rate for energy saving materials *(20 August 2012. HMRC Brief 26/12)*
VAT: addressing borderline anomalies – detailed information sheets published *(4 September 2012. HMRC Brief 27/12)*
Excise duty: increase in restoration fee for fuel offences *(26 October 2012. HMRC Brief 29/12)*
Removal of VAT registration threshold for businesses not established in the UK *(15 November 2012. HMRC Brief 31/12)*
Transfer of going concern in Robinson Family Limited case *(16 November 2012. HMRC Brief 30/12)*
Change in VAT treatment of insurance mis-selling reviews and helpline services *(5 December 2012. HMRC Brief 33/12)*
Motor vehicles for disabled people – new helpsheets *(12 December 2012. HMRC Brief 34/12)*
Voluntary scheme for adapted motor vehicles and boats *(12 December 2012. HMRC Brief 35/12)*
Consultation on withdrawal of VAT exemption for research services *(20 December 2012. HMRC Brief 38/12)*
VAT: Connection charges for water *(28 December 2012. HMRC Brief 40/12)*
VAT: Supplies made under finance leases following EON case *(2 January 2013. HMRC Brief 37/12)*
VAT: rooms provided in hotels or similar establishments with catering *(22 January 2013. HMRC Brief 2/13)*
SS/FS2a—Securities in respect of VAT at risk *(4 March 2013. HMRC Factsheet)*
SS/FS2b—Securities in respect of releasing a VAT credit *(4 March 2013. HMRC Factsheet)*
CC/FS12—Penalties for VAT and Excise wrongdoing *(March 2013. HMRC Factsheet)*
Changes to VAT place of supply rules and introduction of the "mini one-stop-shop" *(20 March 2013. HMRC Notice)*
Levy on "single-use" carrier bags in Northern Ireland *(2 April 2013. HMRC Brief 7/13)*
VAT treatment of services to employers in connection with group personal pensions *(17 April 2013. HMRC Brief 9/13)*
Update on withdrawal of exemption for supplies of research between eligible bodies *(26 April 2013. HMRC Brief 10/13)*
Portfolio management fees following ECJ decision in *Deutsche Bank (25 June 2013. HMRC Brief 11/13)*
Loss-adjusting services for marine and aviation insurance claims *(3 July 2013. HMRC Brief 13/13)*

Press Releases, etc

SETTLEMENT OF DISPUTES

19 November 1987. *Press Notice 82/87*

Customs & Excise have reviewed their policy on the VAT treatment of payments made under out-of-court settlements of disputes, after proceedings have been commenced by service of originating process (or appointment of an arbitrator).

They now take the view that, where such payments are in essence compensatory and do not relate directly to supplies of goods or services, they are outside the scope of VAT. This will be so even if the settlement is expressed in terms that the payment is consideration for the plaintiff's agreement to abandon his rights to bring legal proceedings. But payments will remain taxable if, and to the extent, that they are the consideration for specific taxable supplies by the plaintiff, eg where the dispute concerns payment for an earlier supply, or where the plaintiff grants future rights to exploit copyright material under the settlement.

These changes of policy may be applied from 19 November 1987.

NOTE

Customs & Excise had previously taken the view that all payments under out-of-court settlements were generally taxable. The revised VAT liability brings the VAT treatment of out-of-court settlements into line with the VAT treatment of payments under court orders.

Commentary—*De Voil Indirect Tax Service* **V3.102**.
Cross references—VATA 1994 s 5.

TREATMENT OF CERTAIN AGRICULTURAL GRANT SCHEMES

9 August 1989. *Press Notice 58/89*

Customs & Excise have been considering whether the voluntary surrender of right by landowners and farmers in return for the payment of certain grants should be liable to VAT at the standard rate, eg the surrender by a farmer of his milk quota in return for the payment of a grant by the Ministry of Agriculture, Fisheries and Food.

Customs have consulted other member states and the EC Commission. These discussions have not yet been finally concluded, and Treasury Ministers have therefore decided that VAT should not be applied in the meantime, and in any case not before 1 April 1991.

Customs' discussions have centred on grant payments to "outgoers" under the milk quota arrangements and the set-aside schemes but the same issues arise on other grant schemes.

The decision to suspend the application of VAT applies to these grant schemes and similar schemes, in particular those listed below:

MINISTRY OF AGRICULTURE, FISHERIES AND FOOD

Farm Woodland Schemes

Set Aside Scheme

Agriculture Act 1986 Section 18 (Environmentally Sensitive Areas)

Outgoers under the Milk (Cessation of Production) Act 1985

DEPARTMENT OF THE ENVIRONMENT

Nature Conservancy Council management agreements

Countryside Premium Scheme for Set Aside Land

Countryside Commission Community Forests Scheme

FORESTRY COMMISSION

Woodland Grant Scheme

Farm Woodland Scheme

Cross references—VATA 1994 s 5.

MESNE PROFITS

14 October 1992. *The Law Society*

Following an enquiry from a member of the profession, the Revenue Law Committee has been in correspondence with Customs as to what extent VAT is relevant to an award of mesne profits.

The Commissioners of Customs & Excise agree that mesne profits are damages for trespass (*Bramwell v Bramwell* [1942] 1 All ER 137). Such damages can only be recovered in respect of a defendant's continued occupation of premises after that right of occupation has expired. As such, an award of mesne profits is not consideration for a supply.

Where a landlord has elected to waive exemption from VAT under the provisions of [VATA 1994 Sch 10 paras 2–4], and arrears of rent accrue, in respect of which the landlord sues the tenant, in addition to a claim for mesne profits, the landlord will clearly have made a taxable supply, and non-payment of the rent by the tenant would not affect the landlord's liability to account for tax on the grant of the lease (the supply) subject to any cash accounting considerations.

If the landlord is not on cash accounting, tax points for the period in respect of which he is claiming arrears of rent will already have been determined under [the VAT Regulations SI 1995/2518 reg 85(1)(*b*) or (2) or 90(1)(*b*) or (2)] as the case may require.

If the landlord is on cash accounting, payments received both pursuant to and by way of settlement of litigation will be viewed by the Commissioners as referable in the first instance to being in satisfaction of rent (ie consideration for the grant). Therefore, if the total amount of the settlement is equal to or less than the arrears of rent, the whole of the settlement will be viewed by the Commissioners as payment received by the landlord in respect of the grant.

The Law Society's Gazette 14 October 1992 p 16.

Cross reference—VATA 1994 s 5.

VAT ON PRIVATE USE OF BUSINESS SERVICES

12 September 1994. *Business Brief 17/94*

An order exists to ensure that private or non-business use of services is taxed where initially the tax was recovered because the services were originally purchased wholly for business purposes. There is already a similar provision for goods.

The Value Added Tax (Supply of Services) Order 1983, SI 1983/1507 came into effect on 1 August 1993. The following information replaces and supplements the information in Business Brief 23/93 (26 July 1993) [not reproduced] in the light of comments received from business organisations.

AREAS AFFECTED

Most services by their nature are consumed at the point of delivery. However, some services are akin to goods in that they provide a tangible benefit that is used over time and whose use can therefore change. Examples are building construction and refurbishment, computer software and sporting rights.

A supply under the order occurs if the taxpayer has properly treated all the tax incurred as his input tax and no apportionment has been made under VATA 1994 s 24(5) and there is a subsequent permanent change of use to private or non-business use.

In principle a tax charge also arises if a taxpayer changes the nature of the use of services temporarily from business to non-business use. But a minor or occasional change of use should be ignored. In practice most supplies under the order will occur where the change of use is permanent.

There may also occasionally be circumstances where services are purchased by businesses for purposes similar to a business gift of goods. The taxpayer's purpose is a wholly business one but the services are used for a purpose unconnected with the business. One example is an employee's holiday paid for by the employer as an acknowledgment of exceptional performance.

In such cases a supply under the order occurs, parallel to that under VATA 1994 Sch 4 para 5 for business gifts of goods, where services are supplied to a business which are to be provided free of charge for private non-business use.

The order does not create a tax liability for expenditure that is used for the purposes of the business such as—the maintenance or running costs of a company car fleet, retraining prior to redundancy, subsistence, relocation expenses, information technology supplied for homeworking, domestic accommodation and outplacement.

Some businesses have asked how the order affects the private use of leased business cars. That is taxed by means of the blocking of input tax deduction on the purchase of the cars.

HOW IT WORKS

The point at which tax becomes due is at the end of each accounting period in which a supply under the order takes place.

If a taxpayer changes the use of services permanently from a business to a non-business use he should formally account for the full amount of tax due on the non-business use. There are no set rules about calculating this.

Although services are not subject to depreciation, a taxpayer can use his normal accounting convention for depreciating comparable business assets. Using the asset depreciation method, the value on which tax would be due could be—the cost of services multiplied by the projected period of non-business use, this total being divided by the total period over which comparable assets are normally depreciated.

Alternatively, he may use any other fair and reasonable basis to value the cost to him of the private or other non-business use.

The taxpayer should not account for tax beyond the point at which the asset is fully depreciated to nil value, or the accumulated tax accounted for equals the amount of the input tax on the service as has proved to be not attributable to business use, whichever is the earlier.

Commentary—*De Voil Indirect Tax Service* **V3.216**.
Cross-reference—VATA 1994 s 5.

VAT ON MILK QUOTAS

12 September 1994. *Business Brief 17/94*

Recent amendments to the Dairy Products Quotas Regulations allow the transfer of milk quotas without land in certain circumstances. This is a derogation from the general principle of quota attached to land. The supply or transfer of a milk quota without land qualifies as a supply of services, and is therefore standard rated.

However, when the transfer of a milk quota is linked with a supply of land under one agreement, this is regarded as one supply for VAT purposes. It doesn't matter if the land is sold freehold or as a leasehold transfer. The VAT liability of the quota will be the same as the VAT liability for the land, even if separate identifiable sums are paid for the land and the quota, or if the invoice details are split between the land and the quota.

If a milk quota is transferred with a grazing licence there are two separate supplies, one of animal feeding stuffs, through the grazing licence which is zero rated, and the other of the quota which is standard rated.

Commentary—*De Voil Indirect Tax Service* **V3.105; V4.111**.
Cross-reference—VATA 1994 Sch 9, Group 1.

SALE OF PROPERTY UNDER A POWER OF SALE—RECOVERY OF VAT ON COSTS INCURRED BY MORTGAGE LENDERS

8 December 1994. *Business Brief 24/94*

Customs & Excise have reconsidered the VAT treatment of costs incurred by mortgage lenders when selling property to realise their security in circumstances where a borrower has defaulted on a loan.

This Business Brief explains the reasons for this and sets out the arrangements which will apply for the future. It also sets out the position on payment of claims for past periods.

BACKGROUND

Business Brief 20/93 [30 June 1993] indicated that Customs were prepared to see lenders as agents of the borrower in arranging the sale of repossessed property, and hence allow them to claim bad debt relief (BDR), where appropriate, on the VAT incurred on selling costs.

However, Customs subsequently became aware that the order of attribution of the proceeds of sale under the Law of Property Act 1925 s 105 might override the Bad Debt Relief Regulations. This is because under s 105 the proceeds of sale are allocated first to costs such as those incurred in selling the property, which threw some considerable doubt over whether a bad debt was created on which relief could be claimed.

Doubts arose also about the status of lenders as agents and there was concern that some claims had included costs which went beyond the terms of the Business Brief. Customs therefore issued a further Business Brief 5/94 [1 March 1994] suspending the processing of claims, until such time as they could take legal advice and examine more fully the issues involved.

CURRENT POSITION

Having taken Counsel's advice, Customs are of the view that there is a good argument that in arranging the sale of repossessed property, mortgagees act under rights conferred by the mortgage agreement, and not as agents of the borrower. However, Customs believe they can rely on the wider interpretation of "agent" contained in the Sixth VAT Directive [Directive 77/388/EEC] in maintaining their current view on agency, as laid out in Business Brief 20/93. They face more difficulty with the Law of Property Act 1925 s 105, as it may override the order of attribution in the Bad Debt Relief Regulations, but again the matter is not free from doubt.

In the circumstances, Customs believe that the finely balanced nature of the legal advice allows some freedom of choice and they are re-introducing a form of easement.

NEW ARRANGEMENTS

General

The easement is strictly for the purposes of allowing a measure of relief for VAT on bad debts and depends crucially on Customs taking a relaxed view of the supply position. Lenders must not extend this treatment more widely in accounting for VAT within their businesses.

The new arrangements will apply to bad debt relief claims relating to supplies made on or after 1 July 1994. The overall aim is to provide relief to lenders where they suffer sticking tax on the costs of selling property in circumstances where borrowers have defaulted—in effect where the net proceeds of sale are reduced because the VAT element of the costs has not been recovered.

In principle, the easement covers costs incurred by lenders in arranging the sale of repossessed property and also to selling costs incurred when property is sold through a Law of Property Act receiver. It is emphasised that, with the single exception of build-out costs, the arrangements apply only to sale costs, and not to any incurred in relation to letting.

Although the Law of Property Act does not apply in Scotland, there are analogous provisions in the Conveyancing and Feudal Reform (Scotland) Act 1970 s 27. The arrangements therefore apply equally to Scotland.

Basic principle

Under the new arrangements, lenders can be seen as agents of the borrowers in relation to the costs of sale whether or not the mortgage deed specifies such a relationship, As an agent, the lender may treat the selling costs incurred as supplies made to them and by them under VATA 1994 s 47(3). The order of attribution of the sale proceeds in the Bad Debt Relief Regulations can then be applied and bad debt relief claimed as appropriate in accordance with normal rules.

These new arrangements apply only to costs relating directly to the sale of property, which would ordinarily have been incurred by the borrower had he arranged the sale himself. Examples of such costs include charges for professional services connected with the sale eg legal and estate agency fees.

The easement does not include costs incurred on services provided to, and used by, the lender as principal, even though they may be charged on to the borrower under the mortgage deed. Examples of such costs include legal fees associated with taking possession, and locksmiths' fees for securing the property. Costs incurred in pursuing claims against a valuer for negligence are also excluded.

OTHER EXPENSES

The position of certain other expenses incurred by lenders was discussed at recent meeting with trade representatives. Treatment of these under the new arrangements is outlined below.

LAW OF PROPERTY ACT RECEIVERS' CHARGES

Law of Property Act receivers' charges which relate specifically to the sale (not letting) of the property and any costs incurred by them in respect of the sale can be regarded as falling within the scope of the new arrangements, but only where the proceeds of sale received by lenders have been reduced by the VAT element of the charges. Where this happens, lenders may be regarded as acting as agents for the borrower in paying the costs.

This means that Customs are not prepared to apply this arrangement where the Law of Property Act receiver recovers the VAT incurred on behalf of a VAT registered borrower and this is reflected in the proceeds passed to the lender. This may occur, for example, where the Law of Property Act receiver has control of the borrower's VAT returns.

BUILD-OUT COSTS

These are expenses incurred on completion of a partly-completed building or major refurbishment of the property before sale. Customs' legal advice is that lenders incur such costs as principals and do not make any onward supplies to the borrower even though the costs are charged on under the terms of the mortgage deed. It was argued at the recent meetings with trade representatives that strict application of this line would create a hidden VAT charge in respect of buildings whose sale is zero-rated.

Customs are sympathetic to this view and are therefore prepared, very exceptionally, to treat the onward charge of the build-out costs as a supply by the lender as principal to the borrower, where the sale of the building by the borrower is the subject of a taxable supply or the transfer of a going concern for VAT purposes. In the case of build-out costs only, Customs are also prepared to see a supply where the property is the subject of a taxable let and output tax on the rents has been accounted for to Customs.

Customs are not prepared to see an onward supply (creating an entitlement to bad debt relief) when the sale of the building is exempt, where the VAT incurred on building costs would be sticking tax. Customs believe it would be quite wrong to allow recovery of tax by lenders in these circumstances. The arrangements will also not apply if the proceeds of sale or rent received by lenders reflect any input tax on build-out costs recovered by the borrower.

REPAIRS AND MAINTENANCE

Lenders can be seen as agents of the borrower in incurring these expenses and may use the VATA 1994 s 47(3) invoicing procedure to qualify for bad debt relief.

IN-HOUSE SERVICES

If lenders use their own in-house estate agencies or solicitors to deal with the sale, they may, exceptionally, be regarded as making a supply of those services as principal to the borrower under the new arrangements. However lenders may adopt this treatment in order to claim bad debt relief only where output tax has been accounted for on the supply to the borrower in accordance with normal rules.

RECORDS

There is no requirement on lenders to adopt the above arrangements but, if they wish to do so, the normal VAT invoicing and record keeping requirements must be followed for all supplies concerned.

PAST CLAIMS

The new arrangements outlined above are not being applied to claims in respect of supplies made on or before 30 June 1994. For past claims Customs are prepared to accept the wider application sought by lenders following Business Brief 20/93 and will allow relief in respect of all selling costs incurred before the above date, including build-out costs and Law of Property Act receivers' charges.

However, with the exception of build-out costs, those attributable to the letting out of property are excluded, as are those incurred by lenders in pursuing negligence claims against valuers. Customs do not accept that the latter are costs relating to the sale of property. In relation to in-house services, claims for past periods will be allowed only where a VAT charge to the borrower has been raised and output tax has been accounted for to Customs.

Any claims blocked as a result of Business Brief 5/94 will be released. Similarly, any claims held back by lenders because of the Business Brief may now be lodged in the normal way. Claimants are advised to contact their local VAT office to arrange the most suitable way to action their claims.

Commentary—*De Voil Indirect Tax Service* **V5.156.**
Cross-references—VATA 1994 ss 24, 36, 47 and Sch 4 para 7.

VAT ON VIABILITY STUDIES

28 March 1995. *Business Brief 6/95*

Both the trade and Customs have experienced difficulties in determining who receives the services of an investigating accountant and who is entitled to recover the VAT on those services.

Customs has therefore reviewed its policy and the following new arrangements have been agreed with the Society of Insolvency Practitioners, and will take effect from 1 May 1995.

CHANGES

From May 1, accountants who are engaged to conduct viability studies will be making supplies of their services to the person who has commissioned the work, instructed them, and who also receives the end product. The direction of the supply does not necessarily follow the direction of the payment for the services. The fact that the company may ultimately pay does not mean that the supply is received by the company. Accountants should issue invoices only to those persons to whom they are providing their services.

Where the company commissions the work and receives the report, the investigating accountant is making a supply to the company. The supply is received by the company for the purpose of its business and the company is entitled to recover the input tax subject to the normal rules. The accountant should therefore issue invoices to the company to allow this recovery. This will apply even if the bank or another third party receives a copy of the report. Acknowledgement of a separate duty of care to the bank by the accountant will not prejudice this supply route, or the ability of the company to recover the VAT on the costs of the viability study.

Where the bank commissions the work and receives the report, the investigating accountant is making a supply to the bank. The supply is received by the bank for the purpose of its business and the bank is entitled to recover the input tax subject to the normal rules. The accountant must issue invoices to the bank. This treatment will apply even if the company ultimately pays for the work, and receives copies of the report.

In some instances the bank receives one report and the company another. An example is where the bank requires a confidential security review as part of the investigation. The accountant might receive instructions only from the company, or separate instructions from both the company and the bank. In either case the accountant makes two separate supplies, one to the bank, and one to the company, and should issue two separate invoices.

Each supply is received for the purpose of the particular business, and both the bank and the company are entitled to recover the input tax invoiced to them subject to the normal rules.

If the company and bank issue joint instructions and both receive the same work product, the accountant's supply is made equally to both. The accountant should issue invoices to both the bank and the company, each for 50 per cent of the cost, and both recipients may recover input tax subject to the normal rules.

There may be circumstances where the company commissions the work, but does not receive any report. In this case the accountant's supply is made to the company, but is not used by the company for the purpose of its business. Therefore neither the bank nor the company is entitled to recover any input tax.

Commentary—*De Voil Indirect Tax Service* **V3.421**.
Cross reference—VATA 1994 s 24.

VAT EXEMPTION FOR SUPPLIES OF GOVERNMENT-FUNDED VOCATIONAL TRAINING

1 July 1996. *Business Brief 13/96*

Training providers and further education colleges should note that, with immediate effect, supplies of training, re-training or work experience paid for using Further Education Funding Council (FEFC) funds will qualify for VAT exemption under VATA 1994 Sch 9 Group 6 item 5.

Customs & Excise accept that, in these circumstances, the consideration payable is ultimately a charge to funds provided pursuant to arrangements made under the Employment and Training Act 1973 s 2. This maintains the VAT exempt status of vocational training, previously funded through the Department of Employment.

Similar supplies paid for by further education colleges in Scotland and Wales under parallel funding arrangements will also qualify for exemption under this item.

The exemption applies only to the extent that the consideration payable is ultimately a charge to such funds. This means that where a college pays for a particular training course using both FEFC funds and money available to it from other sources (for example a specific subsidy from industry, or accumulated tuition fees) then apportionment will be necessary to determine the extent to which exemption under item 5 applies. In such cases, where the training is purchased from a body that is not eligible as defined in Group 6 note 1, the single supply will comprise both exempt and standard-rated elements.

To ease this process of apportionment, colleges may opt to apply a global formula rather than perform a separate calculation each time they buy in a supply of vocational training. In other words, it is open for each college to express its annual FEFC allocation as a percentage of its total income for the year. It may then simply apply this percentage to each purchase of vocational training made in the subsequent year in order to arrive at the proportion that qualifies for exemption under item 5.

Commentary—*De Voil Indirect Tax Service* **V4.141**.
Cross reference—VATA 1994 Sch 9 Group 6 Item 5.

RECOVERY OF TAX INCURRED ON REPAIRS, MAINTENANCE, RENOVATION ETC TO FARMHOUSES

27 August 1996. *Business Brief 18/96*

Following a number of VAT tribunal decisions Customs & Excise have reviewed their approach to input tax claims made by sole proprietors and partnerships in relation to farmhouses. The following sets out guidelines which have been agreed with the National Farmers' Union.

However, it must be pointed out that this does not give an automatic entitlement to recover an amount of tax. Businesses should continue to consider their own particular circumstances, and use the guidelines below to assess the proportion of tax that is claimable.

THE GUIDELINES

In the case of a normal working farm where the VAT registered person is actively engaged in running it, 70% of tax incurred on repairs, maintenance and renovations, may be recovered as input tax. This position is in line with that adopted by VAT tribunals who have found that in those given circumstances the dominant purpose was to allow the farming business to be carried on, and allowed 70% of the tax to be claimed.

However, where the building work is more associated with an alteration, eg building an extension, the amount that may be recovered will depend on the purpose for the construction. If the circumstances are such that the dominant purpose is a business one then 70% can be claimed. But if the dominant purpose is a personal one we would expect the claim to be 40% or less, and in some cases, depending on the facts, none of the VAT incurred would be recoverable.

Where farming is not a full-time business and occupation for the VAT registered person, ie income is received from either full-time employment or other sources, the amount of tax that may be claimed will be considerably less. With these kind of cases VAT tribunals have accepted somewhere between 10% and 30% of tax incurred is claimable on the grounds that the dominant purpose is a personal one. Businesses should therefore assess their particular circumstances, and make claims within those parameters.

RETROSPECTIVE CLAIMS

Customs policy reflects the High Court judgment in the case of *The Victoria and Albert Museum Trustees v C & E Comrs* [1996] STC 1016. The museum wished to revisit past input tax claims on the grounds that it could have used a different and more favourable method to calculate its input tax. The court held there had been no error of law or fact, and consequently the museum were not permitted to revisit those earlier tax periods. The three year capping set out in News Release 42/96 [not reproduced] also has to be considered.

(a) Where a trader has claimed input tax of less than 70% without reference to Customs & Excise.
In this situation a retrospective claim is not allowable. The trader has assessed the input tax recovery position, and made a claim. There has been no error in law or fact to be corrected.

(b) Where a trader has claimed input tax based on an officer's decision, or has been assessed. In this instance a retrospective claim may be made but any claim will be subject to the three year capping. Where the business self-assessed its input tax at less than 70%, a refund claim will be allowed to the extent of the percentage self-assessed.

LIMITED COMPANIES

Where the occupant of the farmhouse is a director of the company, or a person connected with the director of the company, different legislation applies. This means that only tax on supplies that are used for other than domestic purposes is claimable as input tax. If a room is used partly for business and partly for domestic purposes, VAT will only be recoverable to the extent of the business use and suitable records will need to be kept to justify the proportion of tax being claimed.

Commentary—*De Voil Indirect Tax Service* **V3.408**.
Cross reference—VATA 1994 s 24.

MOT TEST CHARGES

17 October 1996. *Business Brief 21/96*

Following a review of their policy on the VAT treatment of Ministry of Transport (MOT) tests, Customs & Excise are introducing changes to operate from 1 November 1996, which will simplify the law in this area.

We are also clarifying the conditions which must be met, if the MOT test fee charged by the test centre to an unapproved garage and recharged to the latter's customer, is to be treated as a disbursement.

THE REVISED POSITION

The charge for an MOT test provided direct by a test centre to its customers is outside the scope of VAT, provided it does not exceed the statutory maximum.

The discount given by a test centre to an unapproved garage will be treated as a normal trade discount and will no longer be seen as consideration for a taxable supply by the unapproved garage either to the test centre or its customer.

Any amount charged by an unapproved garage to its customer over and above the amount charged by the test centre is consideration for its own service of arranging the test as agent of the customer and is taxable at the standard rate. Where the unapproved garage shows the exact amount charged by the test centre separately on the invoice to the customer, and meets the other conditions of para 10.8 of the VAT Guide, it may treat this element as a disbursement and also outside the scope of VAT.

If the unapproved garage chooses not to treat the amount charged by the test centre as a disbursement, or otherwise does not satisfy all the conditions set out in para 10.8 of the VAT Guide, it must account for VAT on the full invoiced amount.

We carried out the review because we recently became aware that our policy is creating difficulties for the trade and our own staff alike. Previous policy was formulated at a time when it was customary for test centres to charge the statutory fee and charge a lower amount only where an unapproved garage delivered a customer's vehicle for testing.

However, many test centres now offer discounts to all customers. Depending on the contractual situation, we have seen the discount as consideration either for a supply by the unapproved garage to the test centre of introducing a customer, or for a supply by the unapproved garage to its customer of arranging for the MOT test to be done. This has been the main difficulty because neither the trade nor local VAT audit staff have any easy way of knowing how much the test centre might normally charge.

We also found there was confusion about the procedures to be adopted where the unapproved garages were treating the charges raised by the test centre as a disbursement on behalf of their customers.

Commentary—*De Voil Indirect Tax Service* **V3.113**.
Cross reference—VATA 1994 s 5.

EXTENSION OF "CAPPING" TO CLAIMS FOR REFUNDS OTHER THAN FOR AMOUNTS OVERPAID AS VAT

27 March 1997. *Business Brief 9/97*

Customs and Excise laid secondary legislation on 26 March 1997 which introduces a three year time limit— "the cap"—for corrections and adjustments including refund claims for input tax not covered by FA 1997 [The VAT(Amendment) Regulations, SI 1997/1086].

On 18 July 1996, the then Paymaster General announced the introduction of a three year time limit on claims, mainly from payment traders, for refunds of amounts overpaid as VAT. However, no similar provisions were introduced for capping claims by way of secondary legislation, and there remained a number of methods of reclaiming VAT which were not subject to a three year cap. The legislation introduced on 26 March 1997 corrects this anomaly.

The changes will take effect on 1 May 1997 and will mainly affect repayment traders.

For ease of reference, any corrections and adjustments including refund claims for input tax are referred to as "claims" in the following text.

THE EFFECT OF THE CHANGES

The amendments extend a three year time limit to—

Late claims for input tax. If a business did not claim input tax on the proper return, it cannot claim input tax on a later return made more than three years after the date when the input tax should have been claimed.

Correction of errors. Errors cannot be corrected more than three years after the period in which the errors arose. This is regardless of whether the correction is made within the VAT account (for errors not exceeding £2,000 in net value) or by informing the local VAT office (net errors over £2,000). A transitional provision allows businesses to correct errors if they have not yet rendered the return in which they discovered the errors, that return is for a prescribed accounting period which begins before 1 May 1997, and it has not been made or required to have been made before 1 May 1997.

Adjustment to take account of an increase or decrease in consideration. Businesses cannot make an adjustment where the increase/decrease in consideration takes place more than three years after the end of the prescribed accounting period in which the original supply took place. A transitional provision allows businesses to adjust for increases/decreases without restriction if they have not yet rendered the return which they should make the adjustment, that return is for a prescribed accounting period which begins before 1 May 1997, and it has not been made or required to have been made before 1 May 1997.

Pre-registration expenses. Newly registered businesses can no longer reclaim VAT incurred on goods (including VAT on services performed on these goods) bought more than three years before the effective date on which they registered for VAT. This does not apply where someone registered before the regulations came into force and has yet to make their first return. Businesses must now also claim tax incurred before registration on the first return they are required to make rather than the first return they do make. Claims for VAT on pre-registration expenses must also be claimed within three years of the due date of the first return the business was required to make.

Post-deregistration expenses. Businesses which have deregistered from VAT can no longer reclaim VAT incurred after deregistration, if it was incurred more than three years before the claim. This does not apply to businesses which had deregistered and received the supply before these amendment regulations were made.

Adjustments under the capital goods scheme. Customs can no longer allow businesses to make belated adjustments to input tax incurred on capital goods items if the adjustment is made on a return for a prescribed accounting period which is more than three years after the end of the accounting period when the adjustment should have been made.

Claims for bad debt relief. Claims must now be made within three years six months of when the consideration for the supply was due or the date of supply, whichever was the later. This does not apply to claims for bad debt relief for any supplies where the consideration became due before the amendment regulations were made.

These changes take effect from 1 May 1997 and only affect claims or adjustments made on or after that date.

. . .

CLAIMS AND ADJUSTMENTS UNAFFECTED BY THE CHANGES

A number of claims dating back more than three years are not affected by the changes to the law. These include—

Returns following compulsory backdated registration for VAT. Where a business is registered for VAT with retrospective effect, it will be able to claim input tax on its first return and should account for output tax due even if the tax was incurred more than three years previously. (Businesses who choose to register for VAT voluntarily can only backdate their registration three years from the date of application).

Claims made under the regulations prior to 1 May 1997. These are not subject to the three year time limit, provided that—

(a) they were not claims for refunds of amounts overpaid as VAT — ie section 80 refund claims and;

(b) they were valid claims—eg it had been established that either United Kingdom law was ultra vires EC law, or that the Commissioners' interpretation of United Kingdom law was defective in some way, although it does not necessarily mean that Customs has agreed the claims; and

(c) that the claims were made in the proper form.

REVIEW

Customs will be reviewing the position of claims and adjustments in more detail to ensure that the three year time limit operates fairly and equitably.

. . .

Commentary—*De Voil Indirect Tax Service* **V3.404**.

TAXABLE ACQUISITION OF YACHTS IN THE UNITED KINGDOM

5 June 1997. *Business Brief 12/97*

Customs & Excise have agreed to introduce a temporary arrangement concerning the liability to account for VAT on the taxable acquisition of yachts in the United Kingdom, in certain limited circumstances. This follows representations made on behalf of owners of large yachts and is effective immediately.

Where a VAT-registered business in the United Kingdom buys a yacht from a supplier in another Member State, and the yacht is being removed from that Member State to the place where it will be hired on charter, acquisition VAT may be accounted for in the United Kingdom without the need for the yacht to actually come here. The normal rules will apply for recovery of any input tax that is incurred and for accounting for output tax on any supplies subsequently made.

This arrangement does not affect the VAT treatment of yachts being imported into the EU from third countries, and will be kept under review.

Commentary—*De Voil Indirect Tax Service* **V3.173**.

VAT CHANGES FOR BONUSES GIVEN BY CAR MANUFACTURES TO DEALERS OR FLEET BUYERS

21 July 1997. *Business Brief 16/97*

Fleet buyer bonuses are given by manufactures or sole concessionaires to customers who make bulk purchases of their vehicles. Dealer demonstrator bonuses are payments made, or credits allowed, by car manufactures or sole concessionaires to dealers, when the dealer agrees to adopt the car as a demonstrator vehicle.

In the past it has been common practice to treat the bonuses as the payment for a supply of services by dealers and customers, so VAT was due from the dealer or customer on this supply.

Following the decision by the European Court of Justice in Elida Gibbs Ltd, which established that discounts can be given by a supplier for his goods to someone other than his direct customer, we now accept that these bonus payments will normally be treated as discounts by manufacturers and sole concessionaires which reduce the value of their supplies. Values should also be adjusted by dealers in their second-hand stock books.

In many cases the net effect of this change will not alter the net tax due. However, if businesses believe that they have overpaid VAT in the past three years they should contact their local VAT Business Advice Centre listed under Customs & Excise in the telephone book.

Commentary—*De Voil Indirect Tax Service* **V3.103– 3.104**.

VACUUM CLEANERS, AIR PURIFICATION AND SIMILAR ANTI-ALLERGEN PRODUCTS

24 September 1997. *Business Brief 20/97*

Customs & Excise have undertaken and have completed a review of the VAT liability of vacuum cleaners, air purification products and similar allergy relief products. The review concluded that such products are standard-rated and not zero-rated under provisions relating to equipment "designed solely" for disabled people (Business Briefs 16/96 and 17/96).

Since 26 August 1996, all supplies of such products have been liable to VAT at the standard rate irrespective of to whom they are supplied.

This confirmation will help to provide certainty for suppliers and customers alike, and will prevent considerable distortion in the trade, particularly for vacuum cleaner suppliers. Previously VAT treatment of these products had been inconsistent. For further information traders and their advisers should contact their local VAT business advice centre listed under Customs & Excise in the telephone book.

HERBAL PRODUCT TO BE STANDARD-RATED

10 November 1997. *Business Brief 25/97*

From 1 February supplies of Khat (Catha edulis) are standard-rated. Previously this herbal stimulant had been zero-rated as a food product.

In the light of evidence suggesting that Khat is being increasingly used as a stimulant drug, it is now not regarded as a food product and is properly standard-rated.

. . . .

STATEMENT OF PRACTICE ON A BUDGET CHANGE TO THE CAPITAL GOODS SCHEME

19 December 1997. *Business Brief 30/97*

1 INTRODUCTION

1.1 Changes to the capital goods scheme announced at the time of the July 1997 budget included a test to be applied on the disposal of a capital item by the owner during the adjustment period. The test compares the total amount of input tax deducted or deductible on a capital item with the amount of output tax due on the disposal of that item. For the purposes of this Statement of Practice and the examples annexed, this test will be known as "the disposal test".

1.2 The policy objective underlying the disposal test is to ensure that partly exempt businesses such as banks, building societies, insurance companies, educational establishments, sports clubs, providers of private health care and the like, do not obtain an unjustified tax advantage by being able to recover the input tax they incur on land or property which is to be used for exempt purposes.

1.3 The change was announced as part of a package of anti-avoidance measures in the 1997 Budget. It was introduced by the Value Added Tax (Amendment) (No 3) Regulations, SI 1997/1614 and came into force with effect from 3 July 1997.

1.4 It is not intended that the disposal test should be applied to bona fide commercial transactions. The legislation gives Customs & Excise the power to exclude individual transactions and this power will be used either generally or specifically in cases that do not appear to Customs & Excise to involve unjustified tax advantage. So, for example, given the policy objective, the disposal test will not be applied to sales of computer equipment.

1.5 The purpose of this Statement of Practice is to clarify Customs & Excise policy in this area. It does not qualify the relevant legislation, nor does it affect a taxpayer's right of appeal to an independent VAT tribunal.

2 BACKGROUND

2.1 Generally, businesses making taxable supplies can recover VAT on goods and services they buy in for their business (input tax). Businesses making exempt supplies cannot normally recover their input tax. Businesses which make both taxable and exempt supplies can recover input tax to the extent that the goods and services on which it is incurred are used to make taxable supplies.

2.2 The capital goods scheme recognises that certain major capital assets (capital items) are not consumed immediately but are used by businesses over a number of years. It is designed to be fair to both businesses and the Exchequer. The scheme applies to—

- certain land and buildings where the VAT bearing costs of purchase or development (acquisition) amount to £250,000 or more, with an adjustment period of 10 intervals;
- items of computer equipment of a value of £50,000 or more, with an adjustment period of 5 intervals.

2.3 An interval normally equates with the partial exemption tax year. In the first interval the owner deducts input tax incurred on a capital item to the extent that the item is used or to be used in making taxable supplies. He must then review his use of the item over the relevant adjustment period. In each subsequent interval, if the extent of taxable use differs from that which governed the initial recovery of input tax, the owner must make an adjustment. The adjustment is calculated by comparing the percentage of taxable use in the subsequent interval with the initial recovery percentage.

2.4 For example, input tax is deducted in full when a property is acquired, because it is being used exclusively in making taxable supplies. In a subsequent interval the use to which it is put changes from fully taxable to fully exempt. The owner must pay back 1/10th of the input tax originally claimed. If the owner continues to use the property for exempt purposes, similar adjustments will have to be made (and amounts paid back) at the end of each interval for the remainder of the adjustment period.

2.5 The legal basis of the scheme is Part XV of the Value Added Tax Regulations [SI 1995/2518] (regs 112–116). Further information about the scheme can be found in VAT Leaflet 706/2/90 "Capital goods scheme—input tax on computers, land and buildings for use in your business".

3 DISPOSAL OF A CAPITAL ITEM

3.1 The period of adjustment is brought to an end by the outright disposal of the capital item during the adjustment period. In effect, on termination the item is treated as if it were used for the remainder of the adjustment period in making the supply which gives rise to the termination. So, where the capital item is sold and the sale is a taxable supply, the item is treated as being used in all remaining complete intervals for the making of taxable supplies. The owner must make a final adjustment in respect of all remaining intervals to reflect this.

3.2 Prior to 3 July 1997 businesses could acquire a new commercial building as a capital item and recover all of the input tax by putting the item to taxable use in the first interval. At the beginning of interval 2, the owner could make a very substantial exempt supply (say a 999 year lease—which is not an outright disposal because the freehold interest remains) and then immediately sell the freehold of the building—that sale being a compulsory taxable supply. Because there was an exempt lease, the value of the freehold sale was very low and there was output tax only on that very low value. The taxable sale of the capital item ensured the recovery of a high proportion of the input tax incurred while very little output tax was paid. The building then ceased to be a capital item. This results in an unjustified tax advantage and is the sort of arrangement that the new rule is designed to counter.

4 THE INTRODUCTION OF A TEST ON DISPOSAL

4.1 With effect from 3 July 1997 where the owner of a capital item disposes of it and the total input tax deducted is greater than the output tax due on the supply of the item, the owner is required to make an adjustment so that the input tax recoverable does not exceed the output tax chargeable on the supply of the item. The input tax recoverable is the aggregate of—

- the initial deduction of input tax incurred on the purchase or development of the item;
- any adjustments made previously in respect of the item under the scheme; and
- any adjustment that would otherwise be required due to the disposal of the item.

5 APPLICATION OF THE PROVISION

5.1 In principle the disposal test is wide ranging and impacts on many disposals of capital items. In practice it will only be applied where the owner of a capital item would otherwise gain an unjustified tax advantage, and then the tax charge will be limited to an adjustment amount that would ensure no unjustified tax advantage arises. The legislation includes a "save as the Commissioners otherwise allow" provision to enable Customs & Excise to exclude individual transcriptions. This power will be used to exclude the application of the disposal test in cases that do not appear to Customs & Excise to involve unjustified tax advantage. It will not be applied—

- to sales of computer equipment;
- where an owner disposes of an item at a loss due to market conditions (such as a general downturn in property prices);
- where the value of the item has depreciated;
- where the value of the item is reduced for other legitimate reasons (such as accepting a lower price to effect a quick sale);
- where the amount of output tax on disposal is less than the total input tax claimed only due to a reduction in the VAT rate;
- where the item is used only for taxable (including zero-rated) purposes throughout the adjustment period (which includes the final disposal).

VAT PRs etc

5.2 Where there is no unjustified tax advantage a business should not apply the disposal test and in such circumstances it is not necessary to apply to Customs & Excise for a specific ruling. A business need only apply the disposal test where it has entered into arrangements for tax mitigation affecting the particular capital item or its disposal. In cases of doubt or difficulty businesses should contact the local VAT office. Examples of where the disposal test should and should not be applied are set out in the annex.

5.3 Where there is an unjustified tax advantage businesses will need to work out the amount of tax to be adjusted. To do this, they will need to calculate the net tax advantage and then work out how much of the net tax advantage is unjustified. The net tax advantage is the overall benefit derived from the avoidance device. Normally the benefit is that the owner is able to secure the amount of input tax that would still be subject to adjustment under the scheme, were it not for the sale of the capital item. In order to achieve this benefit a taxable supply is made. The net tax advantage would therefore be the amount of input tax secured by the sale less any output tax due on the sale. Some form of apportionment needs to be applied to work out how much of the net tax advantage is unjustified.

Normally this could be achieved by using the ratio that the value of the final taxable sale bears to the value of both the exempt supply and the final taxable sale (see example 4 in the annex).

5.4 If Customs & Excise consider that the disposal of a capital item has resulted in an unjustified tax advantage to the owner the provision will be vigorously enforced. Implementation of the provision is to be closely monitored. For the next two years, where the provision is enforced and a business requests a review of that decision, any review will be carried out by the Partial Exemption Branch, Commercial Division, VAT Policy Directorate.

5.5 This Statement of Practice may be changed or disapplied if used for the purposes of avoidance of tax.

ANNEX 1—EXAMPLES

EXAMPLE 1

A business acquires the freehold of a newly constructed commercial property for £2 million plus VAT on 1 June 1995. The business immediately occupies the building for its own business purposes. The business is partly exempt with a recovery rate of 50 per cent and is therefore only able to deduct half of the input tax incurred under the normal partial exemption rules.

The business continues to use the building for taxable and exempt purposes for the remainder of the tax year ending on 30 April 1996 (the end of the first interval) and for the following tax year (the second interval) there is a small capital goods scheme adjustment made in respect of the second interval because the overall recovery rate increases.

During the third interval, on 1 August 1997, the business disposes of the property by way of a taxable supply (sold within three years of completion of the construction of the building) for £2 million plus VAT. As a consequence the business is required to carry out a final adjustment and is able to deduct 7/10ths of the input tax previously restricted. The disposal test does not affect the recovery of the 7/10ths because the output tax on disposal is greater than the input tax claimed in the adjustment period.

EXAMPLE 2

A business completes the construction of a £20 million office block, the whole cost of which had borne VAT, on 1 June 1995 and immediately occupies the building for its own business purposes. The business is partly exempt with a recovery rate of 50 per cent and is therefore only able to deduct half of the input tax incurred.

The business continues to use the building for taxable and exempt purposes for the remainder of the tax year ending on 30 April 1996 (the end of the first interval) and for the following tax year (the second interval). There is a small capital goods scheme adjustment made in respect of the second interval because the overall recovery rate increased.

During the third interval, on 1 August 1997, following a downturn in property prices, the business disposes of the property by way of a taxable supply (sold within three years of completion of construction of the building) for its open market value of £16 million plus VAT. As a consequence the business is required to carry out a final adjustment and is able to deduct 7/10ths of the input tax previously restricted. Since the output tax on disposal is less than the input tax claimed in the adjustment period, the disposal test applies. However, the owner is not required to pay any amount back to Customs & Excise because the building was sold at an open market price and not to obtain an unjustified tax advantage.

EXAMPLE 3

A business acquires the 20 year leasehold interest in an office block for a premium of £10 million plus VAT (the previous owner having opted to tax) on 1 June 1995. The business immediately occupies the building for its own business purposes. The business is partly exempt with a recovery rate of 65 per cent and is therefore only able to deduct that proportion of the input tax incurred. The business continues to use the building for taxable and exempt purposes for the remainder of the tax year ending on 31 March 1996 (the end of the first interval) and for the following six tax years (the second to the seventh intervals). There are some small capital goods scheme adjustments made in respect of the later intervals because the overall recovery rate increases or decreases as the case may be.

During the eighth interval, on 1 August 2003, following an expansion in their business, the business relocates to new premises and sells the remaining 12 years leasehold interest in the existing office block to a third party as an exempt supply (not having opted) at an open market price. As a consequence the business is required to carry out a final adjustment in respect of the ninth and tenth intervals and pay back 2/10ths of the input tax previously recovered in the first interval. In addition, since the output tax on disposal is less than the input tax claimed in the adjustment period, the disposal test applies. However, the owner is not required to pay any amount back to Customs & Excise because the building was sold at an open market price and there was no attempt to obtain an unjustified tax advantage. The capital goods scheme adjustments have adequately reflected the exempt use to which the property will be put for the remaining two complete intervals.

EXAMPLE 4

On 1 June 1997 a developer completes a £25 million commercial development, the whole cost of which had borne VAT (£4,375,000). The developer opts to tax the building and leases it out on a two year lease to a third party tenant at a market rent plus VAT. The developer is therefore able to deduct all the input tax incurred on the development under the normal partial exemption rules.

The business continues to let the building on a taxable lease for the remainder of the tax year ending on 31 March 1998 (the end of the first interval) and for the following tax year (the second interval). A capital goods scheme adjustment is therefore not required for the second interval.

On 1 June 1999 (part way through the third interval) the developer grants a 99 year lease at a premium of £24 million and a peppercorn rent to its wholly owned subsidiary. The subsidiary is wholly exempt. FA 1997 s 37 (VATA 1994 Sch 10 para 2(3AA)) operates so as to disapply the developer's option to tax so that the premium is not subject to VAT. At the end of the third interval there is therefore an adjustment in respect of 1/10th (£437,500) of the initial input tax incurred and a proportion of 1/10th (because there was some taxable use in the first part of the third interval) is paid back to Customs & Excise (assuming a recovery rate of 50%—£218,750).

On 1 May 2000 the developer sells the freehold, subject to the 99 year lease for £250,000 plus VAT, to the wholly owned subsidiary (a compulsory taxable supply). The sale effectively ends the fourth interval. Since the building is used for exempt purposes up to the sale there is an adjustment in respect of 1/10th of the initial input tax incurred. It is a full 1/10th that is restricted because the item is only used for exempt purposes up to the disposal of the item.

As a consequence of the low value taxable disposal, since there is no change in the extent of taxable use the business is not required to carry out a final adjustment. But since the output tax on disposal is less than the input tax claimed in the adjustment period, the disposal test applies. In this instance there is an unjustified tax advantage because the high value exempt grant in the third interval enables a low value taxable sale of the freehold. At the same time the taxable sale enables full recovery of input tax in respect of the remaining six intervals (the fifth to the tenth) while only 1/10th of the input tax is restricted (in the fourth interval) to reflect the exempt grant—

Interval	*Input tax claim*	*Output tax declared*	*Difference*
1–10	(4,375,000)		4,375,000
2–10			4,375,000
3–10	(218,750)		4,156,250
4–10	(437,500)	(43,750)	3,762,500
5–10			3,762,500

In principle £3,762,500 would be due. But the net tax advantage is that the owner is able to secure the amount of input tax that would still be subject to adjustment under the scheme (intervals 5–10), were it not for the sale of the capital item and in order to achieve this benefit a taxable supply is made.

The amount of input tax involved is 6/10ths of £4,375,000–£2,625,000. The amount of output tax involved is £43,750. The net tax advantage is therefore £2,581,250.

VAT PRs etc

Some form of fair and reasonable apportionment needs to be applied to work out how much of the net tax advantage is unjustified. This could be achieved by using the ratio that the value of the final taxable sale bears to the value of both the exempt supply and the final taxable sale—
Thus, in practice the disposal test would be applied, but the amount due to Customs & Excise would be the value of the unjustified tax advantage—£2,554,639.

. . . .

VAT CHANGES TO FLEET LEASING BONUSES

7 January 1998. *Business Brief 1/98*

This business brief explains a change in Customs & Excise's approach to the treatment of "fleet leasing bonus" payments—also known as fleet support payments.

BACKGROUND

A "fleet leasing bonus" is a payment made by a car manufacturer or dealer to a business who has leased a number of vehicles previously sold by the manufacturer or dealer to intermediaries. In the past it has been common practice to treat the bonus payment as the consideration for a supply of services by the customer, so VAT was due from the customer on this supply.

REVISED POSITION

Following the European Court of Justice judgment in Elida Gibbs, which established that discounts can be given by a supplier for his goods to someone other than his direct customer, we now accept that fleet leasing bonus payments will normally be treated as discounts. This interpretation follows that applied to bonus payments given by car manufacturers to businesses that buy fleets, detailed in Business Brief 16/97.

This change means that businesses that have received such payments will, in many cases, have overpaid VAT. Treating the payment as a discount rather than as the consideration for a supply of services will mean that no output tax can be due from the customer. However, as a discount the payment will also reduce the input tax recovered by the customer (if any) on the lease payments. For example where 50 per cent of the VAT incurred on the lease payments has been recovered, the bonus payment will reduce the VAT originally claimed by 7/47 × (50% × gross bonus payment).

If businesses believe that they have overpaid VAT in the past three years they should contact their local VAT business advice centre listed under Customs & Excise in the telephone book.

INSTALLATION OR ASSEMBLY OF IMPORTED GOODS

7 January 1998. *Business Brief 1/98*

Customs & Excise confirm that the place of supply concession which allows one-off supplies of installed or assembled goods in the UK to be treated as made outside the UK continues to operate.

The concession applies only where the supplier is not registered for VAT in the UK and the supply is a one off with no further UK business anticipated. In addition the goods must be imported into the UK from outside the EC, the customer must act as the importer of the goods and the full value including installation and assembly costs must be shown on the import entry.

VAT due will be collected at import thus avoiding the need for the supplier to register for VAT in respect of a one off supply.

Further information may be obtained from Bob Gilligan, Place of Supply Branch, 4th Floor East, New King's Beam House, 22 Upper Ground, London. Telephone number 0171 865 5397.

Commentary—*De Voil Indirect Tax Service* **V3.381**.

VAT PLACE OF SUPPLY RULES CHANGE FOR VETERINARY SERVICES

21 May 1998. *Business Brief 12/98*

This business brief explains the place of supply rules for supplies of veterinary services which are to be changed with effect from 1 June 1998.

BACKGROUND

Previously, veterinary services were supplied where they were performed. Therefore, if a UK veterinary surgeon supplied services to a French customer which were physically performed in Germany, the place of supply would have been Germany, and the supply would have been taxable there. However, the European Court of Justice (ECJ) has now ruled that veterinary services are supplied where the supplier belongs.

THE CHANGES

From 1 June 1998 the place of supply for veterinary services will be where the supplier belongs. Supplies of veterinary services by persons belonging in the UK are supplied in the UK and the UK VAT is due, subject to the normal registration rules.

Thus, a UK veterinary surgeon providing veterinary services to a French customer, which are physically performed in Germany, will be making supplies in the UK and UK VAT is due.

. . .

Commentary—*De Voil Indirect Tax Service* **V3.183.**

OVERSEAS BUSINESSES ESTABLISHED IN THE UK THROUGH AGENCIES

21 May 1998. *Business Brief 12/98*

This business brief explains the implications of decisions by the European Court of Justice (ECJ) in the case of *DFDS A/S* (C-260/95) ([1997] STC 384) and the High Court in *Chinese Channel (Hong Kong) Ltd* (CCHK) ([1998] STC 347) for businesses established overseas which carry on business in the UK through agencies.

BACKGROUND

Business Brief 26/96 outlined the case of *WH Payne & Co* ([1995] V & DR 490). The Tribunal commented that treating a person who carries on a business in a country through a branch or agency as having an establishment in that country (VATA 1994 s 9(5)(*a*)) was inconsistent with the EC Sixth VAT Directive (art 9). The Brief explained that Customs & Excise did not agree that the UK's "branch or agency" provisions were inconsistent with EC law. Customs & Excise would, therefore, continue to regard companies established overseas, which carried on a business through a branch or agency in the UK, as having a fixed establishment in the UK.

The subsequent case of CCHK looked at whether broadcasting services were supplied from its business establishment in Hong Kong or from a fixed establishment created by the agency of an associated company in the UK, Chinese Channel (UK) Ltd (CCUK). In finding that the supplies were made from Hong Kong, the Tribunal again cast doubt on the consistency of UK law (VATA 1994 s 9(5)(*a*)) with EC legislation (art 9) and held that "agency" could not extend to a separate company. Customs & Excise appealed to the High Court.

In the interim, the ECJ delivered its judgment in the case of *DFDS A/S*. The issue was whether a tour operator whose business was established in Denmark was supplying its services from a fixed establishment in the UK created by the agency of its UK subsidiary company (Sixth VAT Directive (art 26)).

COURT DECISIONS

In *DFDS A/S*, the ECJ stated that in determining whether DFDS A/S was established in the UK, it was necessary to ascertain whether or not the UK company, DFDS Ltd, was independent. The fact that DFDS Ltd was a separate legal entity with its own offices was insufficient to demonstrate independence. The ECJ found that there were several factors which showed DFDS Ltd was a mere auxiliary organ of its parent. In particular, DFDS Ltd was wholly owned by its parent and had various contractual obligations imposed upon it. The ECJ held that

DFDS Ltd was of the requisite minimum size in terms of its human and technical resources to provide the services, especially in view of the large number of employees and the terms under which it provided services to customers. It concluded that DFDS A/S had a fixed establishment in the UK from which the services were provided.

In *Chinese Channel*, the High Court relied upon the direct effect of the Sixth Directive in interpreting domestic law. It found that the Tribunal's struggle to find consistency between EC law (art 9(1) of the Sixth VAT Directive) and UK law (VATA 1994 s 9(5)(*a*)) was unnecessary and relied upon the ECJ's decision in *DFDS A/S*. The High Court held that because the establishment rules in the Sixth Directive's arts 9 and 26 were similar, DFDS A/S had application to services generally. The High Court said that although the typical agency was a subsidiary acting as a mere auxiliary organ of its overseas parent, it was not restricted to that description. The High Court stressed that what mattered was the reality, function and substance, and not any mere label or legal form. It added that since CCUK was an associate of CCHK, bore no financial risk and could not act for CCHK's competitors, the Tribunal might have concluded that CCUK was not independent had it not misdirected itself that its status as a separate legal entity precluded such a finding.

However, the High Court upheld the Tribunal's decision on the facts of the case. Customs & Excise were unable to impugn successfully the Tribunal's conclusion that, having assessed the contribution made by CCHK and CCUK, the service was supplied from Hong Kong. The High Court found that it was not just a matter of comparing the activities of the two establishments. Rather, it was necessary to consider the significance of those activities and the part they played in contributing to the service supplied. It did not follow that because CCUK had employed a far greater number of staff and spent more man hours than CCHK that CCUK made an equal or greater contribution to the service. It held that because most of the programmes originated in Hong Kong and by far the larger part of their broadcasting activity took place there, the Tribunal had been correct to conclude that the supplies had been made from the Hong Kong establishment.

WHEN AN OVERSEAS BUSINESS HAS A UK FIXED ESTABLISHMENT THROUGH AN AGENCY

Customs & Excise consider that these judgments support their existing policy that an agency creates a fixed establishment of its principal. However, these cases enable Customs & Excise to clarify the circumstances in which such agencies are treated as establishments of their principals.

A UK subsidiary or associate of an overseas business or a UK business unrelated to the overseas business is treated as the latter's UK fixed establishment if it meets the following criteria—

(1) it is of a certain minimum size with the permanent human and technical resources necessary for providing (or receiving) services;

(2) it is not, in function and substance, operating independently of the overseas business; and

(3) it actually supplies (or receives) the service.

If you are an overseas business carrying on business in the UK through such an agency, you are treated as having a fixed establishment here. The VAT implications of this are further explained in Notice 741 "VAT—place of supply of services".

When examining a specific case, our officers will have particular regard for the actual arrangements which exist between the prima facie agency and its principal, rather than any mere wording in contracts.

FURTHER ADVICE AND INFORMATION

If you are unsure whether you are making supplies through (or to) such agencies, you should contact your local VAT business advice centre.

Commentary—*De Voil Indirect Tax Service* **V3.221**.

REVIEW OF THE LIABILITY OF SWEETENED DRIED FRUIT

11 September 1998. *Business Brief 18/98*

Customs have completed a review of the VAT liability of sweetened dried fruit and the following areas have been clarified. Sweetened dried fruit sold as suitable for both snacking and home baking can be zero-rated irrespective of bag size.

Sweetened dried fruit sold as confectionery remains standard-rated. Dried fruit that is naturally sweet and has had no sweetening matter added to it remains zero-rated. An Update to VAT Notice 701/14: "Food", is available from local VAT business advice centres listed under Customs & Excise in the telephone directory.

Customs will not seek to recover VAT where a zero-rated ruling was originally given and this has changed to standard-rated as a result of the review, but in such cases the correct liability must be applied from 1 January 1999. Where a standard-rated ruling has changed to zero-rated, repayments will be subject both to capping and unjust enrichment considerations.

Commentary—*De Voil Indirect Tax Service* **V4.221, V4.226**.

LOCAL AUTHORITIES—WORKS IN DEFAULT

15 September 1998. *Business Brief 19/98*

In [*Glasgow City Council v C & E Comrs* (1998) VAT Decision 15491 (unreported),] the Edinburgh VAT and Duties Tribunal ruled on the liability of works in default and the subsequent recovery of costs under the Housing (Scotland) Act 1987 ss 108, 109.

This Act requires local authorities in Scotland to serve a repair notice to the owner of a property that they consider is in disrepair. If the owner does not comply with the notice the council is empowered to arrange for the work to be carried out and recover the cost of the work from the owner. The Tribunal decided that, in these specific circumstances there was no supply for VAT purposes by the Council.

The decision only applies to works in default carried out by Scottish local authorities under ss 108, 109 of the Act. However Customs are taking this opportunity to clarify their guidance on the treatment of all types of default works throughout the UK.

VAT LIABILITY OF WORKS IN DEFAULT

Local authorities are empowered, by specific legislative provisions, to issue notices requiring that works are carried out in a number of situations. The recipient of the notice may or may not comply.

When the recipient of the notice agrees to the work being carried out and arranges the work with either a contractor or with the authority then the supply of the contractor's services is to the recipient of the notice. If the authority arranges the contractor's supplies on the recipient's behalf they may treat these supplies as being to the authority and by the authority under VATA 1994 s 47(3).

If the recipient of the notice refuses to comply the authority may exercise its statutory powers, have the work carried out and recover the cost of the works from the recipient. In these circumstances the authority is not making a supply for VAT purposes.

RECOVERY OF VAT

Only when the supply of the works is to the local authority—as in the *Glasgow City Council* case—may it recover the VAT charged by the contractor. Where the authority makes an onward taxable supply in the course or furtherance of business, the VAT incurred will be recoverable as input tax under VATA 1994 s 25. Where the authority does not make a taxable supply but imposes the works under its statutory powers, as described above, VAT recovery will be under VATA 1994 s 33.

. . .

Commentary—*De Voil Indirect Tax Service* **V5.162, V2.108, V6.153A, V3.125, V3.221, V3.423**.

VAT PRs etc

VAT GROUPS AND TRANSFERS OF GOING CONCERNS (TOGCS)

18 December 1998. *Business Brief 26/98*

This Business Brief clarifies Customs' policy on whether there can be a transfer of a property rental business as a going concern where the landlord and the tenant or the purchaser and the tenant are members of the same VAT group.

BACKGROUND

In *C & E Comrs v Kingfisher plc* [1994] STC 19 the High Court found that members of a VAT group are to be considered a single taxable person for VAT purposes. The status of individual members of VAT groups has also been recently considered by the House of Lords in *C & E Comrs v Thorn Materials Supply Ltd and Thorn Resources Ltd* [1998] STC 725 which came to the same conclusion. A question raised by those decisions is whether there can be a TOGC when the sole business activity constitutes supplies from one group member to another. With property rental between group members, if the rental supply is disregarded under VATA 1994 s 43(1)*(a)*, it is simply as though the taxable person (the group) is occupying the property itself. Therefore, where a group member landlord sells a property which is tenanted by another group member, it is doubtful that a business exists which is making relevant supplies capable of transfer as a going concern. Conversely, where a landlord sells a property which is tenanted by a company that is a member of the new landlord's VAT group, the business ceases after the transfer because the tenant and the new landlord effectively become one taxable person.

Customs policy is as follows.

The following situations will not be considered to be TOGCs—

(1) Where the purchaser of the property rental business is a member of the same VAT group as the existing tenant.

(2) Where a member of a VAT group sells a property, which is being rented to another member of the group, to a third party.

The following situation will be considered to be a TOGC—

(3) Where the tenant who is a member of the landlord's VAT group is only one of a number of tenants. The presence of a tenant or tenants outside the group means that the whole transaction can still be treated as a TOGC.

IMPLEMENTATION DATE

This policy will take effect from 1 January 1999. Transactions prior to this date will not be affected. If transfers of the type described at (1) and (2) take place after 1 January 1999 they can still be treated as TOGCs if a deposit or other part-payment of the purchase price is received by the seller before that date. An amendment will be made to Notice No 700/9.

For further information businesses and their advisors should contact their local VAT business advice centre listed under Customs and Excise in the telephone book.

Commentary—*De Voil Indirect Tax Service* **V2.226**.

THE SINGLE CURRENCY (THE EURO)

13 January 1999. *Business Brief 1/99*

From 1 January 1999 eleven European countries adopted a single currency (the euro).

Although the UK is not one of the countries joining in the first wave, the introduction of the euro is likely to affect a wide range of UK businesses. This Business Brief explains the impact upon HM Customs & excise's requirements. There are two main issues, paying taxes and duties in euro and accounting and invoicing in euro.

1. PAYING TAXES AND DUTIES IN EURO

UK businesses can now pay Customs & excise taxes and duties (including arrears) in most cashless forms of the euro. Notes and coins will not be introduced until 2002. However, all declarations must continue to be made in sterling, including VAT returns and intrastat declarations.

Exchange Rate Fluctuations

When paying in euro, the exchange rate will fluctuate between the time payment is initiated or sent to Customs & excise and the time it is cleared. Businesses will be credited with the sterling value received by Customs and Excise. The repayment of overpayments to businesses and the payment of underpayments to Customs & Excise will be dealt with using existing debt management practices.

The shorter the delay between the time payment is made and the time it is cleared may help to minimise this fluctuation. Payments will be processed most quickly through the use of CHAPS euro (Clearing House Automated Payment System)-an electronic same day funds transfer system.

BACS direct debit

Most methods of payment can be used to pay in euro. One of the main exceptions is BACS direct debit. Although BACS direct credit is available, banks are not making BACS euro direct debit available at this time. The main impact of this is that importers who wish to use the duty deferment facility, of which one of the requirements is that direct debit be used, must continue to pay in sterling.

Conversion Costs

The costs incurred by Customs & Excise in converting euro tax and duty payments into sterling will not be passed on to businesses and will be borne by the Department.

Repayments

All repayments will continue to be made by Customs & Excise in sterling – the currency of the UK.

2. EURO ACCOUNTING AND INVOICING IN THE UK

Invoicing

Customs & Excise have simplified the current requirements for tax invoices issued in currencies other than sterling, in order to facilitate the euro.

If businesses issue tax invoices in euro the invoice must also show the sterling equivalent of the total net value of goods and services at each rate of VAT and the amount of VAT, if any, at each rate.

These rules are set out in HM Customs & Excise's Public Notice 700, paragraphs 6.3 and 3.1(f) but it is not now necessary to make line by line conversions.

The sterling VAT amount on tax invoices is to be used by both the supplier and the customer for VAT accounting purposes ie suppliers must declare the sterling VAT amounts on their sales invoices as output tax and their customers must use the same amounts for input tax purposes. These are necessary requirements in order to preserve the integrity of the tax. VAT and Duty accounts VAT and duty accounts must continue to be maintained in sterling.

Exchange Rates

There are 3 alternative methods that can be used to convert an amount from euro into sterling on invoices (Public notice 700, paragraph 3.1 (f)):

the UK market selling rate at the time of the supply – rates published in national newspapers are acceptable as evidence of the rates at the relevant time;

the period rate of exchange published by Customs & Excise for customs purposes; or—

you may apply in writing to the VAT Business Advice Centre for your area for the use of a rate or method of determining a rate which you use for commercial purposes but which is not covered by the two alternatives above.

Declarations

All declarations must continue to be made in sterling, including VAT returns and intrastat declarations. The one exception is Box 22 on the Single Administrative Document which is used for imports and exports, where euro values can be used.

SHIP DESIGN SERVICES

24 February 1999. *Business Brief 5/99*

This Business Brief gives Customs' position regarding ship design services. In June 1995, a tribunal (*Cholerton Ltd v C & E Comrs* (1995) VAT Decision 13387 unreported) held that, in certain circumstances, design services were integral to the modification of a ship, despite the fact that Cholerton did not carry out the modification services. The design services were found to be zero-rated. At the time, Customs accepted the decision and have since allowed businesses supplying design services in identical circumstances to zero-rate their supplies. However, we have now reviewed our policy. We consider that the tribunal failed to take into account that Cholerton was contracted to supply only design services and therefore made no supply of modification services to which the design services could be integral.

Accordingly, with effect from 1 July 1999, Customs will treat design services supplied in the UK as integral to the supply, modification or conversion of a qualifying ship only where a supplier specifically contracts with a customer to design and supply, modify or convert a qualifying ship. In other circumstances, design services will be standard-rated and deductible, subject to the normal rules.

For further information businesses and their advisors should contact their local VAT business advice centre listed under Customs and Excise in the telephone book.

Commentary—*De Voil Indirect Tax Service* **V4.251**.

THE THREE YEAR CAP AND PARTIAL EXEMPTION

31 March 1999. *Business Brief 8/99*

This Business Brief clarifies Customs' policy about how the three year cap affects businesses' partial exemption position, illustrated by a number of examples.

BACKGROUND

The purpose of the three year cap is to provide certainty and stability for both the Exchequer and the tax payer. The provisions are not intended to have any impact on the normal system of deduction and adjustments to deduction as set out in the VAT Regulations.

Any trader or business currently operating the partial exemption rules correctly will not be affected by the three year cap. This also applies to businesses which discover a mistake and make the necessary correction within the three year time limit. In other words, the three year cap only affects businesses who do not claim the input tax to which they were entitled or claim input tax to which they were not entitled, and fail to correct this within three years.

In addition, if a business fails to make an initial deduction of input tax (or gets the initial deduction wrong) and the error falls in a period which is more than three years old, the error cannot be corrected in the partial exemption annual adjustment even if the adjustment itself is not capped. However, even though the unclaimed amount of input tax cannot be reclaimed because it is capped, the annual adjustment itself should be based on the true amounts of input and output tax.

EXAMPLES

The effects of the three year cap are illustrated in the following examples—

(i) A partly exempt business (makes both exempt and taxable supplies) fails to use a partial exemption method and does not claim any input tax for a number of years. After an audit, the business submits a refund claim, in which the first quarter of the third tax year is "capped" (ie more than three years old) but the annual adjustment period itself is not "capped" (it falls within the three year period). Can the input tax in that period be recovered in the annual adjustment?

No—The trader, by failing to recover input tax in the relevant period, has failed to exercise the right to deduct. The trader is not able to claim this "capped" amount in the annual adjustment.

(ii) A partly exempt business calculates deductible input tax in accordance with his partial exemption method. In the first two quarters he fails the *de minimis* limits and so correctly restricts his exempt input tax. In the second two quarters he is able to benefit from the *de minimis* limits and so correctly recovers all his input tax in those quarters. At the end of the year he is able to benefit from the *de minimis* rules for the year as a whole but does not apply them. If he discovers this mistake within three years from the last day of the annual adjustment quarter is he able to correct it?

Yes—The partly exempt trader has correctly applied the *de minimis* rules to each quarter. Since it is at the time of the annual adjustment that the *de minimis* rules are applied to all the input tax incurred in the previous four quarters, it is at that time that any exempt input tax previously restricted may be recovered.

However, where a trader was entitled to apply the *de minimis* rules to a particular period but did not do so, and that period was "capped", any affected input tax falling in that period may not be recovered in the final *de minimis* calculation at the time of the annual adjustment (which itself is not "capped"). This is because the trader failed to exercise the right to deduct within the three year period.

(iii) A business with an agreed partial exemption method mistakenly treats taxable input tax as exempt. Can this input tax be recovered at the time of the annual adjustment if the input tax is proper to a period which is "capped" (but the annual adjustment is not "capped")?

No—We would not allow the trader to recover the exempt input tax at the time of the annual adjustment. The trader has mistakenly treated taxable input tax as exempt, and so he has failed to recover it.

Similarly, if the trader had incorrectly claimed exempt input tax and the input tax was proper to a period which was "capped", we would be unable to recover it under the assessment provisions in that period or the period of the annual adjustment (even if it was not "capped"). Customs are aware that, because of the complexity of the three year cap, we have agreed some claims and settled them as if the annual adjustment can be used to override the cap, effectively giving some claimants a repayment to which they were not entitled. We do not propose to revisit any of these claims, but all future claims will be treated on a proper basis.

. . .

Commentary—*De Voil Indirect Tax Service* **V3.405, V3.461–V3.466**.
Regulations—See VAT Regulations, SI 1995/2518 regs 99–111 (regulations made under VATA 1994 s 26(3)).
Cross references—See VATA 1994 s 26(3) (for powers to make regulations for securing a fair and reasonable attribution of input tax).
See also the VAT Regulations, SI 1995/2518 regs 29(1A), 34(1A) (time limit for claiming repayments).

CONTRACTING OUT OF VEHICLE REMOVAL/RECOVERY BY POLICE AUTHORITIES—TREATMENT OF STATUTORY FEES RETAINED BY CONTRACTORS

21 April 1999. *Business Brief 9/99*

The purpose of this business brief is to clarify the VAT treatment of statutory fees collected and retained by contractors who provide motor vehicle recovery services to police authorities.

Police forces have powers in various circumstances to remove and, where appropriate, store vehicles. Any associated statutory fees are outside the scope of VAT when levied by the police on the motorist or owner of the vehicle. However, the task of removing vehicles is now commonly contracted out by police authorities. These arrangements often include collection of fees by the contractors on behalf of the police. Where this occurs, the fees paid to the contractor are not consideration for any supply by the contractors to the motorist or vehicle owner, and are outside the scope of VAT.

However, under their agreements with the police authority or with an intermediary management company acting on behalf of the police authority, contractors may be entitled to retain some or all of the amounts which they have collected. Where this occurs the retained amount represents consideration for a supply of recovery services by the contractors to the police authority, and is liable to VAT at the standard rate. As well as accounting for VAT, the contractor should issue a VAT invoice to the police authority, who are entitled to recover the VAT charged subject to the normal rules.

ACTION FOR BUSINESSES

Customs have become increasingly aware that the VAT treatment of the retained fees is inconsistent, and that tax is not being accounted for properly in some cases. Therefore, any contractors engaged in vehicle recovery on behalf of a police authority should review their accounting procedures with the authority. Where VAT is not being accounted for in the manner set out above, arrangements should now be put in place for the future. In order to allow contractors time to re-organise their existing procedures, implementation of the correct VAT treatment is to take effect from 1 August 1999.

. . .

Commentary—*De Voil Indirect Tax Service* **V3.103**.

TOUR OPERATORS' MARGIN SCHEME (TOMS)

22 April 1999. *Business Brief, 10/99*

This business brief explains Customs' position in light of the ECJ decision in *C & E Comrs v Madgett & Baldwin t/a Howden Court Hotel* [[1998] STC 1189]. The hotel, in Torquay, supplies inclusive packages to tourists from the north of England. The packages comprise coach transport between the hotel and customers' home towns, a stay at the hotel for several days and coach excursions. The coach transport is bought-in by the hotel.

DEFINITION OF TOUR OPERATOR

The first issue before the ECJ was to determine whether the hotel's activities were those of a tour operator and therefore subject to VAT under the TOMS. The Court supported Customs' policy that the TOMS applies in principle to anyone who buys in and resells services for the direct benefit of a traveller, but added two new criteria to Customs' definition. The first was that the travel services must be bought in and resold "habitually". The second was that bought-in travel services which take up a small proportion of the package price are "ancillary" in relation to the main supply and would not justify a supplier being regarded as a tour operator. The Court's example of "ancillary" was a taxi ride between a hotel and a local railway station.

APPORTIONMENT OF PACKAGES WHICH INCLUDE IN-HOUSE SUPPLIES

The second issue before the ECJ related to the method of determining the value of the in-house element of the packages. In Madgett & Baldwin's case, the VAT on the margin of the bought-in element was the same whichever method was used. The Court held that, bearing this in mind, the operator was entitled to use a method based on the market value of the in-house supplies when the cost-based calculation required complex sub-apportionment exercises, and when it was possible to identify the in-house element of the package by a market value-based method.

THE WAY FORWARD

Customs see the decision as being primarily about simplification, rather than the amount of VAT paid by tour operators, and consider that the cost-based apportionment set out in Notice No 709/5 "Tour operators' margin scheme" remains a valid method of valuing in-house supplies. Customs intend to use the decision to simplify the TOMS and reduce the number of traders affected by it and will be consulting with the industry and other interested parties. A technical discussion document will be issued in May, exploring practical issues such as the interpretation and application of the terms "habitually", "ancillary" and "market value". Customs envisage this period of consultation running through to the autumn, with appropriate changes to the TOMS being made in due course.

The timing of these changes (and so any revision of Notice No 709/5) is uncertain at this stage, but they are unlikely to be implemented before April 2000. In the meantime, traders should continue to use the TOMS as set out in Notice No 709/5. Subject to capping, any changes which are beneficial to traders may be applied retrospectively. To protect themselves against the effects of capping, traders who consider that they have "overpaid" VAT may lodge a claim with their VAT business advice centre before changes are implemented.

Commentary—*De Voil Indirect Tax Service* **V3.591–593**.

PASSENGER TRANSPORT SERVICES WHICH INCLUDE CATERING

22 April 1999. *Business Brief 10/99*

This business brief explains Customs' position following the *Sea Containers* case which considered the VAT position of passenger transport supplied with catering on a railway train. There were a number of different types of supply all of which included in-house catering which was promoted as high quality in advertising material. The supplies included—

- charter of the whole train plus crew, with separately negotiated catering;
- charter of the whole train plus crew, with catering included in a single price;
- round trips sold to individual passengers which included high quality catering, such as five course meals and champagne lunches; and
- a stopping trip sold to individual passengers who could alight before the return journey, again including catering.

The issue for the tribunal was whether there were single supplies of zero-rated passenger transport, or separate supplies of transport and standard-rated catering. The tribunal found that in each case there were separate supplies.

Customs consider that this decision, in conjunction with the remarks of the European Court of Justice on single and multiple supplies in another recent case (*Card Protection Plan v C & E Comrs* (Case C–349/96) [1999] STC 270 confirms their current policy. Where an element of catering is included with scheduled passenger transport for no extra charge (such as a meal included in the price of an airline ticket) there is a single supply of passenger transport. Where catering, or other elements such as discos, receptions etc are included as a feature of leisure travel, there are separate supplies, and the catering and other extras are taxable at the standard rate.

. . .

Commentary—*De Voil Indirect Tax Service* **V3.105, V4.227, 251.**

TREATMENT OF EC GRANT AID FOR THE PROCESSING OF DRIED FODDER

22 December 1999. *Business Brief 28/99*

The purpose of this business brief is to notify a change to the VAT treatment of EC grants paid by the Intervention Board to processors of dried animal fodder.

DETAILS OF CHANGE

Until now the UK has not treated such payments as consideration for supplies by processors, but has regarded them as outside the scope of VAT. However, following an approach by the European Commission, the UK has agreed that these particular payments will be treated as falling within the scope of the tax. This does not involve a change in UK policy in relation to other EC grants.

ACTION FOR DRIED FODDER PROCESSORS

Since supplies of animal fodder are zero-rated no VAT is due on these grants. But processors who supply dried fodder must include the value of grants received in the total value of sales in box 6 of their VAT returns. This also applies to grants received where a business processes the grass of a third party and returns it to them after drying (although Customs understand that this does not happen at present in the UK). However, where the grants relate to fodder for the processors' own use, there is no supply by the processor for VAT purposes, and grants should continue to be treated as outside the scope of VAT. This change will take effect from 1 January 2000.

FURTHER ADVICE

For further advice and information, processors and their advisers should contact their local VAT office, listed under Customs & Excise in the telephone book.

Commentary—*De Voil Indirect Tax Service* **V4.221** (Zero-rating: animal feeding stuffs).

IMPORTED WORKS OF ART, ANTIQUES AND COLLECTORS' ITEMS

22 February 2000. *Business Brief 3/00*

With the change in the rate of import VAT on works of art, antiques and collectors' items in July 1999 [see Customs & Excise news release dated 2 July 1999, *Simon's Weekly Tax Intelligence* 1999 p 1156], an anti-avoidance measure was introduced to prevent the artificial movement of such items by people seeking to gain a tax advantage from the reduced rate of import VAT. This means that only qualifying imported goods, which have not been exported from the UK in the previous 12 months, are eligible for the 5% effective reduced rate of import VAT.

In practice, however, works of art and similar goods are sent outside the UK for various legitimate commercial reasons, and often return within 12 months. For instance, goods may be sent for exhibition, prior to auction in the UK, or sent on a sale or return basis and returned unsold. The anti-avoidance provision was not intended to disrupt businesses engaged legitimately in such activities and, in many cases, there are specific reliefs which override the "12 month" rule.

GOODS HELD IN TEMPORARY IMPORTATION (TI) ARRANGEMENTS

Goods which are held under a TI regime are not regarded, for VAT purposes, as having been "imported" into the UK. For VAT, goods are not treated as imported until the customs duty debt is incurred (for instance, on removal from TI to home use). Consequently, goods which are removed from TI and sent outside the EU are not considered to have been exported for VAT purposes, and therefore will not be caught by the "12 month" rule. This covers, for example, goods held under TI, intended for sale by auction in the UK, but sent to third countries for exhibition prior to auction.

GOODS NOT HELD IN TI ARRANGEMENTS

For goods sent outside the member states "on approval", or for goods exported for sale by auction, but which fail to sell and have to be returned to the UK within 12 months, "returned goods relief" may apply. Value Added Tax Regulations, SI 1995/2518 reg 125 allows such goods to be relieved from VAT at importation where they remain the property of the taxable person who exported them. Provided all the conditions of the relief are satisfied such goods qualify for full relief from VAT on importation, and will not be affected by the "12 month" rule.

For goods exported from the UK for repair or restoration work and returned to the UK within 12 months, "outward processing relief" may apply. Value Added Tax Regulations, SI 1995/2518 reg 126 allows the original value of the goods (ie the value at export) to be relieved from VAT at importation, where they have been sent outside the EU for process or repair and are subsequently returned without a change of ownership. Provided all the conditions of the relief are satisfied such goods will not be affected by the "12 month" rule. However, VAT at the standard rate is due on the price charged for the repair or restoration.

For goods which are exported from the EU, sold, and imported back into the UK within 12 months, there are no VAT reliefs available. Consequently they will normally attract VAT at 17.5% on importation. However, Customs have agreed that, if goods were exported from the UK prior to the introduction of the new rules on 28 July 1999, businesses should not be disadvantaged. Where businesses would not have known about the "12 month" rule at the time of exportation, then, where appropriate, goods will still qualify for import VAT at the 5% rate, following importation into the UK within the 12 month limit.

VAT AND CEMETERIES

17 March 2000. *Business Brief 4/00*

This business brief explains Customs' position following the tribunal decision in *Rhondda Cynon Taff County Borough Council* [(1999) VAT Decision 16496 unreported].

BACKGROUND

Since the inception of VAT local authorities have been able to recover the tax incurred in making insignificant exempt supplies under what is now VATA 1994, s 33. In this particular case the appellant argued that the provision and maintenance of cemeteries by local authorities, which Customs has always treated as exempt business activity, was non-business. As a result tax incurred by them in making such supplies did not count for partial exemption purposes and could be recovered as non-business under s 33. The tribunal agreed and concluded that the provision and maintenance of cemeteries by a local authority was not a business activity for VAT purposes, as it had been carried out by them under a special legal regime applicable to public authorities. In reaching this decision the tribunal considered the detailed legal structures which apply to local authorities who operate cemeteries. It also concluded that as there are so few privately owned cemeteries the non-business ruling would not distort competition.

NEW POSITION

Customs has concluded that the decision only applies to the provision and maintenance of local authority operated cemeteries. This includes the grant of a right to an exclusive burial, the right to place and maintain a tombstone, the keeping and storage of the plans and records of burials, general maintenance, and any actions intended to remove dangerous obstructions, eg collapsed vaults or broken headstones.

Local authority cemeteries may also offer further services, such as the provision of books of remembrance and the erection of headstones for which a charge is made. As the provision of these services is not covered by the special legal regime applicable to cemeteries, they remain business activities of the local authority.

CREMATORIA

Some local authorities also provide crematoria. While crematoria are governed by special legal provisions, similar to those which apply to cemeteries, the higher incidence of privately owned crematoria means that a distortion of competition would result if local authorities were allowed to treat these activities as non-business. Where local authorities operate sites which contain both cemeteries and crematoria and they have exceeded the partial exemption *de minimis* limits, a business/non-business apportionment will have be made between the activities.

For further advice and information, please contact your local business advice centre, listed under Customs and Excise in the telephone directory.

Commentary—*De Voil Indirect Tax Service* **V5.162**.

DEBT ENFORCEMENT SERVICES PROVIDED BY UNDER SHERIFFS AND SHERIFFS' OFFICERS

11 April 2000. *Business Brief 6/00*

This business brief explains changes with effect from 1 April 2000 to the VAT treatment of services provided by Under Sheriffs and Sheriffs' Officers in enforcing judgment debts.

BACKGROUND

Customs previously regarded services provided by Under Sheriffs and Sheriffs' Officers in enforcing High Court judgment debts and those of the County Court transferred to the High Court for enforcement as supplies to the High Sheriffs. As the High Sheriffs are not in business for VAT purposes, the tax on these services was not recoverable by them.

NEW VAT TREATMENT

Following an approach by the Under Sheriffs Association, and with the agreement of the Sheriffs' Officers' Association, Customs are now prepared to treat these debt enforcement services as supplies by Under Sheriffs to creditors. This means that, from 1 April 2000, where such creditors are registered for VAT, they will be able to recover tax charged by Under Sheriffs and Sheriffs' Officers, subject to the normal rules.

Therefore, while Under Sheriffs and Sheriffs' Officers may collect fees for their enforcement services from debtors, they should issue VAT invoices only to creditors in all cases. Any documents issued to debtors should make it clear that they are not VAT invoices.

For further information traders should contact their local Customs & Excise business advice centre listed under Customs & Excise in the telephone book.

Commentary—*De Voil Indirect Tax Service* **V5.173** (Enforcement: distress and diligence) and **V3.401** (Relief for tax chargeable, paid or payable.)

BLOODSTOCK—SALE OF ADDITIONAL NOMINATIONS BY STALLION SYNDICATES

28 September 2000. *Business Brief 13/00*

This business brief explains changes to the VAT treatment of additional nominations sold by stallion syndicates. The changes will take effect from 1 November 2000.

BACKGROUND

When a colt is to become a stallion standing at stud, it is often syndicated, usually into 40 shares. Each share entitles its owner to one nomination. This lets the owner nominate one mare to be covered by the stallion each breeding season. Each syndicate appoints a secretary, usually a bloodstock agency or a firm of solicitors, to deal with its financial and practical arrangements.

Until recently any additional nominations over and above the initial 40 have been sold through the secretary and the income has been distributed to the members. As the sums involved were low and likely to be below the VAT registration threshold, Customs accepted that these supplies could be treated as not subject to VAT. However, as stallions are now managing up to 100 coverings in a season, this VAT treatment is no longer appropriate.

NEW VAT TREATMENT

From 1 November 2000 the sale of additional stallion nominations will be treated as supplies in the course of business by the syndicates, which will render them liable to VAT registration. However, the bloodstock industry has said that the syndicates do not wish to be registered as partnerships. Customs are therefore prepared to treat syndicate secretaries as agents acting in their own names, but on behalf of the syndicates.

The accounting arrangements which follow have been discussed and agreed with the British Horseracing Board.

Secretaries will raise an invoice in their own name when the supply of an additional nomination is made. Where a secretary's turnover exceeds or is expected to exceed the current VAT registration threshold, the invoice should bear the secretary's own VAT registration number. It should be for the full value of the nomination plus VAT.

When secretaries pass money on to the syndicate members, the members will raise an invoice to the secretary for their share. This will be an invoice bearing the appropriate VAT if the member is registered. Any VAT charged may be treated as input VAT by the secretary.

Any money passed to members will count towards the calculation of their taxable turnover for VAT registration purposes.

The tax point for the supply by the member to the secretary will be the same as that of the supply by the secretary to the purchaser of the nomination.

The stud farm will raise a VAT invoice to the secretary for the keep of the stallion and the secretary will raise a VAT invoice to the stud for the nominations given in return for the keep. Any input tax incurred by the secretary on behalf of the syndicate may be recovered by the secretary. The secretary will pass these charges on in full to the members of the syndicate and raise a VAT invoice charging output tax on the onward supply.

Where a syndicate does not wish to use these arrangements, it will be required to register for VAT in its own right if its turnover exceeds or is expected to exceed the current VAT registration threshold.

For further information, traders and their advisers should contact their local VAT office, listed under Customs & Excise in the telephone directory.

Commentary—*De Voil Indirect Tax Service* **V6.114** (Bloodstock: syndicates).

20 FEBRUARY 2001. BUSINESS BRIEF 3/2001
VAT POSITION OF LIMITED LIABILITY PARTNERSHIPS

This business brief is to help businesses who are considering forming limited liability partnerships (LLPs) and outlines Customs' views on the VAT position of such partnerships. The contents of this business brief have been agreed with the Association of Partnership Practitioners and other interested parties.

WHAT IS A LIMITED LIABILITY PARTNERSHIP?

The Limited Liability Partnership Act 2000 received Royal Assent on 20 July 2000. LLPs can be formed with effect from 6 April 2001.

An LLP will have a legal status distinct from its members, and will be able to enter into contracts in its own right. This means that individual members of the LLP will be protected from debts or liabilities arising from negligence, wrongful acts or misconduct of another member, employee or agent of the LLP.

LIMITED LIABILITY PARTNERSHIPS AND VAT

The members of the LLP must prepare an incorporation document for the Registrar of Companies who, on acceptance, will issue a certificate of incorporation. This means that the LLP will be a corporate body, and that it, rather than the members, will be the legal entity for VAT purposes. The LLP itself then becomes liable for VAT registration, subject to the normal registration rules.

As with unlimited partnerships this does not normally mean that the members will be seen as supplying their services to the LLPs and they therefore will not normally have to register for VAT.

VAT LIABILITY IF AN EXISTING PARTNERSHIP CHANGES TO A LIMITED LIABILITY PARTNERSHIP

As the legal entity has changed from that of a partnership to a corporate body, the LLP may have to apply for VAT registration, subject to the normal rules. The normal transfer of a going concern rules will then also apply, including those relating to any option to tax. If the general partnership ceases to exist, it may be possible for the VAT number to be transferred to the LLP (Notice 700/9, "Transfer of a going concern", gives full details).

MEMBERSHIP OF A VAT GROUP

An LLP will be able to join a VAT group provided it meets the control conditions in VATA 1994 s 43A. This section allows two or more corporate bodies to apply for VAT grouping if each is established or has a fixed establishment in the UK and one of them controls the others; or one person controls all of them; or two or more individuals carrying on a business in partnership control all of them.

A corporate body is "controlled" by its "holding company". Individuals can fulfil the definition of a "holding company" without actually being a corporate body themselves. So, for VAT grouping purposes, individuals can "control" a corporate body. The terms "control" and "holding company" are defined in the Companies Act 1985 s 736.

Thus, if the LLP fulfils these control conditions with a number of subsidiary companies, it may form a VAT group with them. It is also possible that a group could be formed by two or more eligible companies and an LLP, where those eligible companies are controlling partners in the LLP.

Customs will also see the third of the above control conditions, ie two or more individuals carrying on a business in partnership control all of them, being met when the members of an LLP control all of the corporate bodies to be grouped.

[VATA 1994 ss 43C, 45]

COURT OF APPEAL DECISION RULES PENSION REVIEW SERVICES ARE VAT EXEMPT

20 February 2001. *Business Brief 3/01*

The Court of Appeal has ruled in the case of *Century Life plc* [[2001] STC 38] that the company's pension review services are exempt from VAT, because they are insurance related services provided by insurance agents. The supplies at issue were pension review services, carried out as a result of the Financial Services Authority (FSA)-inspired review of possible pension mis-selling.

Customs have decided not to seek leave to appeal to the House of Lords. This business brief explains the implications of the judgment for businesses which think they might be affected.

THE JUDGMENT

Before this judgment, Customs' view was that Century Life merely assisted an insurer, in this case Lincoln Assurance Limited, to comply with the regulatory requirements of the FSA. As a result, Customs believed that these services were not covered by the exemption as Century Life were not introducing or administering insurance contracts.

The Court said that Century Life's services were "intimately related to" insurance policies and that there was "a close nexus" between them and the insurance transaction concerned. And since Customs had accepted that the day to day business of Century Life could properly be characterised as that of "insurance agent", the Court judged the services in question to be exempt.

Since pension review services of the kind performed by Century Life have been ruled to be sufficiently closely "related to insurance", it follows that they are exempt when the "Century Life criteria" are met. However, the judgment does not necessarily apply to other services which are outsourced by insurers to insurance brokers or agents. Each case must be treated on its merits.

THE "CENTURY LIFE CRITERIA"

When someone reviews an insurer's personal pension policies for mis-selling, and during the course of this acts as an insurance broker or agent, having contact with insured persons on behalf of insurers, Customs will accept that the exemption applies to them.

If you think that your business meets these criteria, but you have already accounted for VAT on such services, you can make an adjustment to your VAT accounts as set out in Customs' Notice 700/45 "How to correct errors and make adjustments or claims" para 1.5. Alternatively, you can make a claim for repayment of the VAT taking into account any overclaimed input tax. Such claims will be paid subject to the conditions set out below—

- you must be able to produce suitable evidence that your case exactly fits the "Century Life criteria";
- you must be able to substantiate the amount claimed;
- you will need to look back at earlier attributions of input tax (any input tax incurred on goods and services used exclusively for these pension review services is now attributable to an exempt supply), substituting exempt values for taxable values in your partial exemption calculation and deducting the resulting "exempt input tax" from overpaid output tax in determining the amount of the claim.

Adjustments and refunds are subject to capping after three years.

If Customs can show that you effectively did not bear the burden of the tax, they may reject the claim on the grounds that it would unjustly enrich you. For example, this may have happened because you passed the tax on to someone else without losing profit by doing so, and are unable, or don't intend, to pass on the repayment.

A notification to Customs that you intend making a claim in the future is not a valid claim.

If you have been charged VAT by businesses whose supplies were exempt as a result of this decision, you cannot treat it as your input tax. You will need to make an adjustment to your VAT account to reverse any overclaimed input tax.

FURTHER INFORMATION

Further information can be found in Notice 700/45, entitled "How to correct VAT errors or make adjustments or claims". Businesses and their advisers can also contact their local VAT business advice centre, listed under Customs & Excise in the telephone directory.

Commentary—*De Voil Indirect Tax Service* **V3.221** (Supplies by and through agents).

OPTING TO TAX BUILDINGS TO BE CONVERTED TO DWELLINGS

2 July 2001. *Business Brief 8/01*

This business brief is about how Customs & Excise will implement a Tribunal decision on how the option to tax buildings applies to buildings, those which will be converted into dwellings (the VAT Duties Tribunal decision in the case of *SEH Holdings Ltd*, LON/98/1362).

TRIBUNAL DECISION

An option to tax cannot apply to a building or part of a building intended for use as a dwelling. The question for the tribunal was whether it could apply to the sale of a building (in this case a pub) that would eventually be converted into dwellings. However the sale was to someone who was not carrying out the conversion work but had the intention to sell the building to someone else another party on the same day.

The tribunal concluded that the option to tax did apply to the sale of the building. They decided that the person selling the building has only to consider the intended use of the building by the immediate purchaser, and that their intention has to be made known to the person selling the building at the time of the sale. This provides certainty for the person selling the building.

CUSTOMS POLICY

In the light of the tribunal's decision, Customs policy is that where the immediate purchaser of a building (which the vendor had opted to tax) does not intend to use the building himself as a dwelling nor to convert the building into dwellings for sale or rent, the vendor must account for VAT on the sale of the building.

As the previously published guidance by Customs on this type of transaction was not clear, we will not insist on this policy being applied to previous transactions. However, traders should apply this new policy to transactions taking place on or after 1 August 2001.

There is no change to policy in cases where the immediate purchaser of an opted building does intend to use the building as a dwelling or to convert it to dwellings for sale or rent. In these circumstances, the sale of the building remains exempt unless vendor and purchaser have agreed that the sale should be taxable.

AUCTION SALES

Customs are aware that there may be particular problems at auctions because the vendor is not normally aware of the purchaser prior to the auction day. The vendor may have difficulty in finding out what the purchaser intends to do with the building, at the time he has to decide whether to charge VAT or not if he has opted to tax the building. Similarly a purchaser who intends to convert a non-residential property into dwellings, and sell them zero-rated, may also find it difficult to agree with the vendor in writing, prior to the auction date, that the option to tax should still apply to the sale of the building.

Customs are currently reviewing this area of policy and will include the problems of auction sales. In the meantime we suggest that the purchaser should discuss any problem he is facing with the vendor or his representatives prior to the completion date so that they can agree to apply the correct VAT liability.

Customs recognise that in applying the decision strictly, there may be certain circumstances when the VAT charged becomes an additional cost and that this may discourage some developers from converting commercial property into dwellings. Consequently any business, which needs further advice on applying the decision, should contact their local VAT office.

Commentary—*De Voil Indirect Tax Service* **V4.115**.

PARTIAL EXEMPTION—SUPPLIES TO BE EXCLUDED FROM THE STANDARD METHOD CALCULATION

11 September 2001. *Business Brief 12/01*

This business brief provides further clarification of Customs & Excise policy previously outlined in Business Brief 8/99 following the House of Lords decision of 23 May 2001 in the *Liverpool Institute of Performing Arts* (LIPA) case (see [2001] STC 891).

WHAT WAS THE LIPA CASE ABOUT?

The LIPA case was about the scope of the partial exemption "standard method" (as described by reg 101 in VAT Regulations, SI 1995/2516) and what supplies should be included in it. Customs argued that the "standard method" calculation determines the deduction of VAT relating to supplies made within the UK and does not determine the deduction of VAT relating to supplies made outside the UK.

VAT PRs etc

WHAT DID THE HOUSE OF LORDS DECIDE?

The House of Lords agreed with Customs. It found that two separate regimes exist, under the VAT Regulations 1995, for determining the amount of VAT that a taxpayer can deduct—

- Regulation 101 (the "standard method") which determines the deduction of VAT relating to supplies made within the UK; and,
- Regulation 103(1) which determines the deduction of VAT relating to supplies made outside the UK.

Regulation 101 cannot therefore be used to determine the amount of VAT to be deducted relating to supplies made outside of the UK.

WHAT ARE THE SUPPLIES THAT FALL WITHIN REG 103(1)?

Regulation 103(1) supplies fall into two categories—

(a) Those that would be taxable if they were made within the UK (known as "foreign" supplies but referred to by the House of Lords as "out of country" supplies), eg advertising services; and,

(b) Those that would be exempt if they were made within the UK and which are specified in an Order under VATA 1994 s 26(2)(*c*) (known as "specified" exempt supplies) eg certain finance and insurance supplies made by a UK based business to a customer who "belongs" outside of the European Union.

HOW DOES REG 103(1) WORK?

Regulation 103(1) determines the amount of VAT that can be deducted on the basis of use. It is up to the taxpayer to decide how this can be achieved. Any method of calculation is acceptable to Customs provided the result is both fair and reasonable. If the result is not fair and reasonable Customs can raise an assessment to rectify the position.

IF REG 103(1) DEALS WITH "SPECIFIED" EXEMPT SUPPLIES HOW DO I DEAL WITH "NON-SPECIFIED" EXEMPT SUPPLIES?

"Non-specified" exempt supplies are those supplies made outside of the UK that would be exempt if they were made within the UK, but which are not specified in an Order under VATA 1994 s 26(2)(*c*).

The House of Lords confirmed that these supplies are to be given a similar treatment to exempt supplies made in the UK. Whilst the VAT incurred in making these supplies cannot be deducted, the value of these supplies must be included within the "standard method" calculation.

WHAT IF I MAKE SUPPLIES THAT FALL UNDER BOTH REGS 101 AND 103(1)?

If you make taxable and exempt supplies in the UK as well as making supplies outside of the UK, then both regs 101 and 103(1) need to be applied. Regulation 103(1) is always to be applied first. For example—

Step 1—determine the amount of VAT incurred that relates to "out of country" and "specified" exempt supplies. This is done on the basis of use in accordance with reg 103(1). This VAT may be deducted.

Step 2—the remaining VAT incurred that relates to taxable and exempt UK supplies and "non-specified" exempt supplies is dealt with under reg 101. The proportion that can be deducted equals the value of taxable supplies divided by the total value of taxable, and exempt UK supplies and "non-specified" exempt supplies (subject to the requirement to exclude the values of certain distorting supplies). Remember, the values of "out of country" and "specified" exempt supplies dealt with at step 1 are not to be included.

WHAT IF I USE A PARTIAL EXEMPTION "SPECIAL METHOD" INSTEAD OF THE "STANDARD METHOD"?

Customs can approve or direct that a partial exemption "special method" be used instead of the "standard method". Whilst Customs can approve a "special method" to deal with "out of country" and "specified" exempt supplies they cannot direct you to use one. If your approved "special method" already deals with "out of country" and "specified" exempt supplies then you need not take any action following the House of Lords decision. But, if your "special method" does not deal with these supplies then you need to deal with them under reg 103(1) before you apply your "special method".

If you have any further questions please telephone the National Advice Service on 0845 0109 000.

Commentary—*De Voil Indirect Tax Service* **V3.464**.

REDUCED RATE FOR SUPPLIES OF SMALL (DE MINIMIS) QUANTITIES OF FUEL OIL, GAS OIL OR KEROSENE

29 November 2001. *Business Brief 18/01*

This business brief article clarifies Customs' policy on supplies of small quantities of oil.

BACKGROUND

Provided it is not for use as road fuel, a supply to an end-user of a small quantity (not more than 2,300 litres) of fuel oil, gas oil or kerosene is treated as if it is for domestic use, and is subject to the reduced rate of VAT. There has been some confusion about how the reduced rate should apply when there is more than one delivery to the same site on the same day.

CUSTOMS' POLICY

In general, Customs regard a supply as comprising all deliveries to the same customer at the same site on the same day. This will be the case even if you raise separate delivery notes or invoices. Deliveries that take place on different days, or to different sites, are regarded as separate supplies, even if you issue a single invoice for more than one delivery.

The following examples help to explain these general principles—

SAME DAY DELIVERIES TO DIFFERENT TANKS

A business customer has two tanks on the same site. You fill both tanks on the same day and raise a separate invoice for each "drop". The amount supplied is the total amount delivered to both tanks. If this amount is above the 2,300 litre (*de minimis*) limit, your supply is standard-rated.

SEPARATE ORDERS ON DIFFERENT DAYS—SAME DAY DELIVERY

A customer places an order for 2,000 litres of gas oil but two days later, before it is delivered, orders a further 1,000 litres for delivery to a different tank on the same site at the same time. The amount supplied is the total amount delivered to both tanks. Your supply is standard-rated.

SEPARATE ORDERS ON THE SAME DAY

A customer places an order for 2,000 litres of gas oil. Later the same day the customer contacts you again and asks for a further delivery of 1,000 litres to a different tank on the same site. If both deliveries are made on the same day, the total amount of 3,000 litres is regarded as a single supply and is standard rated. If the orders are actually delivered on two different days the reduced rate could apply to both deliveries.

SHARED TANKS

You deliver oil to a group of farmers who share a common tank. Each farmer's part of the delivery is regarded as a separate supply and invoiced separately. Any supply to a farmer below the 2,300 litre (*de minimis*) limits will attract the reduced rate.

FURTHER INFORMATION

This clarification of the *de minimis* limit has been agreed with the oil industry. Businesses that have not been applying the *de minimis* limit in this way will be required to follow this policy from 1 June 2002. This will allow them time to make any necessary changes to their accounting systems.

Revised guidance will be included in VAT Notice 701/19 Fuel and power, which is currently being updated. For further advice contact our National Advice Service on 0845 010 9000.

Commentary—*De Voil Indirect Tax Service* **V4.406.**

BAD DEBT RELIEF ON GOODS SUPPLIED BY HIRE PURCHASE OR CONDITIONAL SALE

6 December 2001. *Business Brief 19/01*

This business brief announces changes to bad debt relief entitlement for goods supplied on hire purchase or conditional sale.

ATTRIBUTION OF PAYMENTS TO GOODS OR FINANCE

Bad debt relief can be claimed on supplies of goods made by way of hire purchase or conditional sale where the customer has defaulted.

Supplies made by hire purchase or conditional sale have two components—a supply of goods and a supply of associated finance.

When determining how much bad debt relief can be recovered, the supplier has had to allocate any payments received from their customer to the supply of the goods first and to the supply of finance only after the goods have been "paid in full". Finance companies have pointed out that this is unfair.

NEW TREATMENT

With immediate effect, suppliers can allocate each payment received from defaulting customers to goods and to finance in the same ratio as the total cost of goods and the total cost of finance to the customer. Further guidance is available in Annex 1 to this business brief.

Suppliers can re-calculate previous bad debt relief claims by applying this new policy and submitting a voluntary disclosure. All claims will be capped to three years starting six months from when the payment was due from the customer.

REPOSSESSED GOODS

In determining how much bad debt relief can be claimed, a supplier who has supplied goods by hire purchase or conditional sale has to deduct the proceeds from the disposal of any repossessed goods from the outstanding debt of their customer.

The disposal of these repossessed goods is subject to VAT where the customer has acquired the goods for a business purpose or where the supplier has changed their condition prior to re-selling them. Otherwise, the disposal of repossessed goods is relieved from VAT.

NEW TREATMENT

With immediate effect, where the disposal of the repossessed goods will be subject to VAT, suppliers no longer have to deduct the proceeds of the disposal from the outstanding debt of their customer, when claiming bad debt relief. Only the payments made by the customer have to be deducted.

There are no changes to the current policy where the disposal of repossessed goods will not be subject to VAT. In these cases the proceeds of the disposal, as well as the payments made by the customer must still be deducted from the outstanding debt. Further guidance is available in Annex 1 to this business brief.

Suppliers can re-calculate previous bad debt relief claims by applying this new policy and submitting a voluntary disclosure. All claims will be capped to three years starting six months from when the payment was due from the customer.

ANNEX 1—TECHNICAL DETAIL OF CHANGES TO BAD DEBT RELIEF

Attribution of payments in calculating entitlement to BDR

Current policy

A purchase made by a customer of goods by hire purchase ("HP") or conditional sale ("CS") consists of two supplies for VAT purposes. There is a supply of goods (taxable) and a supply of financial services (exempt). The time of supply for goods is typically when they are made available to the customer (VATA 1994 s 6) and the time of supply of the finance (VAT Regulations 1995 reg 90) is when payment is made.

Subject to meeting record keeping and timing conditions of the scheme, BDR arises when a customer defaults and the debt is unpaid. In determining how much BDR is recoverable, the supplier needs to allocate the payments received to the supply which occurred first (VAT Regulations 1995 reg 170(2)). In the case of HP and CS agreements, it will be the supply of goods that occurs first.

The impact of these rules has meant that suppliers have been allocating all the payments received against the goods in the first instance and only to the finance after the goods have been "paid in full".

Change in policy

While still believing the above analysis is correct in law, the Commissioners recognise that the outcome is not fair in relation to the commercial treatment of the transactions. Therefore with immediate effect, suppliers who make supplies under HP and CS agreements can apply the allocation rules set out in VAT Regulations 1995 reg 170(3). Now each payment can be allocated to interest and to goods in the same ratio as the total cost of the goods and total cost of the interest to the customer.

For example, if a car cost £8,000 and the interest over the life of the agreement is £2,000, each payment can be allocated 80% goods and 20% interest.

The Commissioners are currently considering whether a consequential amendment to the law is required to reinforce this new policy.

Treatment of repossessed goods

Current policy

The treatment of the sale of repossessed goods fall broadly into two groups—

- second hand goods (except cars); and
- cars.

While there are similarities, each group is dealt with by separate Orders. To remove the question of doubt, although goods may have originally been supplied new, by the time they are repossessed, they are considered to be second-hand within the meaning of these Orders.

Second-hand goods (except cars)

Subject to meeting the qualifying conditions below, the sale of repossessed second-hand goods (except cars) is treated as neither a supply of goods nor services ("de-supplied") under VAT (Special Provisions) Order, SI 1995/1268 art 4(1)(*a*). The qualifying conditions are that the goods are sold in the same condition as they were when repossessed and that, if the customer had sold them, they would not have been chargeable with VAT on the full price (eg because the customer had not acquired them for a business purpose or they were margin scheme supplies, etc).

If any goods do not qualify under art 4(1)(*a*) to be de-supplied because their condition has been changed or they would have been chargeable with VAT if disposed of by the customer, then their sale is a taxable supply. As the supplier never originally acquired the goods under any circumstances within VAT (Special Provisions) Order, SI 1995/1268 art 12(3), their disposal is not eligible as a margin scheme supply.

Cars

The treatment for cars is very similar to that of other goods. In the VAT (Cars) Order, SI 1992/3122 art 4(1)(*a*), the supply of a car which has been repossessed is de-supplied providing it is sold in the same condition and, under art 4(1A), providing the customer has not been able to deduct some or all of the input tax charged on the car.

If any cars do not qualify under art 4(1)(*a*) to be de-supplied because their condition has been changed or the customer has deducted some or all input tax charged upon it, its sale is a taxable supply. The disposal of these cars after repossession are not margin scheme supplies as the supplier never acquired them under any circumstances within art 8(2).

Recovery of bad debt relief

In determining how much BDR can be claimed, the supplier needs to identify how much consideration (which is attributable to the goods) has been received from the customer and the how much consideration (net of VAT if the sale is not de-supplied) has been received from the sale of the repossessed goods. These two amounts should be deducted from the original supply of the goods to the customer under the HP or CS agreement. Any outstanding balance that is attributable to the goods can, after applying the VAT fraction, be deducted as BDR.

For example, a car is supplied for £8,000 (including VAT of £1,191.49) plus £2,000 interest. It is repossessed and sold for £1,500. The customer has made payments totalling £3,000 (that is all attributable to supply of the goods). Providing six months have passed since the payment was due, a notification letter has been issued and the other record keeping requirements of the BDR scheme have been met, a BDR claim of £521.28 (£3,500 x 7/47) can be made.

If the sale of the repossessed car is a taxable supply, the net value raised from the sale will be £1,276.59 (the balance of £223.41 being VAT). As a result, the BDR claim would be will be £554.55 (£3,723.41 x 7/47).

Same condition

The condition of goods has been changed if any improvements, repairs, replacement parts or the generally making good of any damage has been carried out. The cleaning of goods generally does not affect the condition nor does the inclusion of instruction manuals if they are otherwise missing.

Change in policy

The policy change relates solely to conditions where the disposal of the repossessed goods is not de- supplied. There are no other policy changes in relation to repossessed goods.

With immediate effect, where the disposal of the repossessed goods will be subject to VAT, suppliers no longer have to deduct the proceeds of the disposal from the outstanding debt of their customer when claiming bad debt relief. BDR claims can now be based upon the amount actually paid by their customer providing the record keeping (including the notification letter) and time limit requirements of the scheme are met.

For example, a car is supplied for £8,000 (including VAT of £1,191.49) plus £2,000 interest. The customer has made payments totalling £3,000 that have been split £2,400 to the car and £600 to interest (following the new policy on attribution of payments). Providing six months have passed since the payment was due, a notification letter has been issued and the other record keeping requirements of the BDR scheme have been met, a BDR claim of £834.04 (£5,600 x 7/47) can be made. The sale of the repossessed car will be subject to VAT at 17.5%.

Retrospective application of these new policies

Suppliers can re-calculate previous BDR claims by applying the new policies for the attribution of payments and of the treatment of repossessed goods and submit a voluntary disclosure. Any claim will be capped to three years starting six months from when the consideration was due and payable by the customer.

Any suppliers who have not submitted any BDR claims can do so subject to being capped as above.

Commentary—*De Voil Indirect Tax Service* **V5.156, V3.117, V3.114**.

SINGLE AND MULTIPLE SUPPLIES—SALE OF SPECTACLES AND CONTACT LENSES

12 February 2002. *Business Brief 3/02*

Business Brief 2/01 set out Customs' policy as to whether a transaction consists of a single supply or two or more independent supplies for VAT purposes. The policy, which followed judgments of the European Court and House of Lords in the case of *Card Protection Plan*, has since been confirmed in a number of cases in the courts and VAT tribunal.

This Business Brief provides further clarification of Customs policy in this area, following the decision of the VAT Tribunal in the cases of *Southport Vision Plus* and *Leightons Ltd and Eye-Tech Ltd*. These cases concerned the sale of spectacles and contact lenses by dispensing opticians. The Tribunal found in favour of the appellants that this should be regarded as two separate supplies—one of standard rated goods and the other of exempt dispensing services. The supply of dispensed spectacles and contact lenses therefore continues to be treated in the same way as since 1995. The sight test and supplies of dispensing services independent of the supply of spectacles or contact lenses continue to be exempt.

The treatment of dispensed hearing aids, which is similar to that of dispensed spectacles and contact lenses, also remains unchanged.

Customs & Excise are not appealing this ruling. However, we wish to clarify our views on two aspects of the Tribunal's reasoning.

THE PROPORTION OF COST

The Tribunal took into account the existing agreement between Customs & Excise and opticians that dispensing services are a relatively high percentage of the total price of dispensed spectacles and contact lenses. *Card Protection Plan* established the principle that a single price is not a decisive indicator that there is a single supply. In the light of the Tribunal decision, Customs accept that if a distinct service element represents 50% or more of the price of a bundle of goods and services, it will be a strong indicator that this service is not ancillary to a principal supply of any other goods or services in that bundle and that the consideration may need to be apportioned accordingly.

However Customs also believe that this should not be allowed to open scope for avoidance. It will therefore not accept such an argument where it believes that there has been manipulation of values. It will continue to challenge the apportionment and any attempt to use manipulated values in a way that might distort a decision about whether a transaction is a single supply or multiple supplies.

ANCILLARY ELEMENTS

One of the tests established in *Card Protection Plan* is that a service should be regarded as ancillary to a principal supply if it does not constitute an aim in itself but a means of better enjoying the principal service supplied. In the opticians cases, the Tribunal concluded that the dispensing service cannot be regarded as a means of "better enjoying" the optical appliance, which, in the Tribunal's view, could not be enjoyed at all without the dispensing service.

If taken too widely, that line of reasoning would imply that a service would only be regarded as ancillary where it was, in effect, an optional part of the package. Customs continue to believe that the primary test remains what the customer thinks they are buying. A service can be regarded as an ancillary part of a single supply even where it is a compulsory part of the transaction.

Commentary—*De Voil Indirect Tax Service* **V3.106, V4.186**.

BAD DEBT RELIEF AND THE TREATMENT OF PROCEEDS FROM THE SALE OF REPOSSESSED CARS

9 May 2002. *Business Brief 13/02*

Business Brief 19/01 set out the Commissioners revised policy with respect to the treatment of proceeds from the sale of repossessed cars. The change in policy was introduced to alleviate the possibility of double taxation when new cars were repossessed and sold, where the sale after repossession was a taxable supply with VAT due on the full value. In such cases the proceeds from the sale of the repossessed car do not need to be deducted from the outstanding debt when calculating entitlement to bad debt relief. In case of any doubt this change only applies where the initial sale was of a new car.

Commentary—*De Voil Indirect Tax Service* **V3.117, V5.156.**

THREE YEAR CAP—MARKS & SPENCER—ECJ JUDGMENT, CASE C-62/00; [2002] STC 1036

5 August 2002. *Business brief 22/02*

BACKGROUND

Prior to 18 July 1996 if a trader discovered that he had paid more VAT to Customs & Excise than he ought to have, he had six years from the date on which the overpayment was made, or six years from the date on which he discovered his error, in which to make a claim to recover it from Customs. Where claims were made within six years of the date of discovery of an overpayment, they could go back to the inception of the tax in 1973.

On 18 July 1996, in the face of rising claims, the then Paymaster General announced that the time limit for claiming overpayments of VAT was to be reduced to three years. This meant that amounts overpaid more than three years before the date on which a claim was made could not be recovered. This change was applied to all claims made on or after 18 July 1996 and to all claims which had been made before that date but which had not yet been processed and paid. The capping legislation is contained in VATA 1994 s 80.

This change was enacted on 4 December 1996 by a resolution passed by Parliament under the Provisional Collection of Taxes Act 1968, which deemed the change to have had effect from 18 July 1996.

The manner in which this three year time limit was introduced, by FA 1997 s 47(2), was challenged in the courts by Marks and Spencer (M&S) and, during the course of this litigation the Court of Appeal sought the guidance of the ECJ on whether the manner of the introduction of the three year time limit was contrary to the principles of Community law.

Specifically, the Court of Appeal asked the ECJ whether it was permissible in Community law to shorten the time allowed for a person to claim repayment of amounts paid by way of VAT, which they overpaid in breach of directly effective rights conferred on them by the European 6th VAT Directive (the 6th Directive), to which the UK had not given effect in its domestic legislation and to do so with retrospective effect.

THE JUDGMENT OF THE ECJ

The ECJ delivered its judgment on 11 July 2002 and held that the UK had acted contrary to the principles of Community law in that it had failed to implement properly provisions of the 6th Directive, which conferred directly effective rights on taxpayers, and had then retrospectively shortened the time limit within which taxpayers could exercise their rights to repayment.

The ECJ held that when the UK introduced the new time limit they ought to have introduced it with a transitional period, beginning on the date on which the change was enacted, ie 4 December 1996. During this transitional period taxpayers who had directly effective rights under the 6th Directive, which had not been properly implemented in UK law, would have been able to exercise those rights before the new time limits were legitimately imposed.

The ECJ did not hold that it is contrary to Community law to impose time limits on the right to repayment of amounts paid by way of VAT contrary to directly effective provisions of the 6th Directive, but that it is contrary to Community law to impose those time limits with retrospective effect.

It is not the case that the UK capping legislation has been rendered invalid as a result of the fact that we failed to make provision for a transitional period when the three year time limit was introduced. A three year limitation period is, and remains, in force.

PRACTICAL EFFECTS OF THE JUDGMENT

Customs will now give effect, albeit retrospectively, to a transitional regime for when the three year time limit was introduced in 1996 to allow taxpayers to make the claims that they ought to have been able to make at the time. This transitional regime will apply from 4 December 1996 to 31 March 1997.

The judgment of the ECJ only actually requires that Customs give effect to this transitional period for those taxpayers who overpaid amounts by way of VAT in breach of directly effective rights of the 6th Directive as a result of the UK's failure to give proper effect to the Directive and were prevented, by the manner in which the three year time limit was introduced, from recovering those amounts.

However, if Customs had provided for a transitional regime at the time when the three year time limit was introduced, it would not have been applied in such a selective manner. Customs will not, therefore, restrict payment of claims only to those who would benefit from a strict interpretation of the ECJ's judgment in *Marks & Spencer*.

Taxpayers can now make claims under VATA 1994 s 80 for repayment of amounts overpaid, regardless of the cause of the overpayment, subject to the following criteria.

CLAIMS

Customs are now inviting all taxpayers to submit claims to their local VAT offices where—

- they made claims before 31 March 1997, which were capped (either by Customs or by them in expectation that no more than three years would be paid); or
- they made claims before 31 March 1997, which were repaid in full and amounts more than three years old were then clawed back by Customs by means of a recovery assessment; or
- they made no claim but can demonstrate that they discovered the error before 31 March 1997; and
- in all cases, the overpayments of VAT were made before 4 December 1996.

If you consider that you fall within the above parameters, you will have until 31 March 2003 to submit claims.

Claims may be refused in whole or in part if Customs are satisfied that repayment would lead to the unjust enrichment of the claimant.

CLAIMS WHICH DO NOT FALL WITHIN THE SCOPE OF THIS BUSINESS BRIEF

Claims made after 31 March 1997 will be subject to the three year time limit. For example, if between 1 April 1973 and 4 December 1996 you accounted for VAT at the standard rate on supplies, which ought to have been exempted from VAT, and you discovered the error on or after 1 April 1997, it will be limited to the amounts overpaid in the three years before the date on which the claim is made.

Claims relating to overpayments made after 4 December 1996 will be subject to the three year time limit. For example, a claim made after 5 December 1999 in respect of an overpayment made on 5 December 1996 will be out of time.

FORM OF CLAIM

Claims must be made in writing and must include—

- a statement of the amount being claimed and the method of calculation;
- the dates on which the overpayments were made;
- a copy of your original claim (where appropriate);
- copies of documents, schedules, etc. used in support of the application;
- the prescribed accounting periods in respect of which the claim for recovery of the overpayment was made;
- the reason for the claim;
- the reason why you will not be unjustly enriched if a repayment is now made; and
- any claim for interest that you consider you are entitled to make, and the reasons why you consider that your claim arose as the result of an error by Customs.

Claims should only be made for the net amount overpaid for any given prescribed accounting period. If you overpaid output tax during an accounting period on supplies which ought to have been exempted, and in the same accounting period you recovered more input tax than you ought, you should only submit a claim for that period for the amount of output tax over declared, less the amount of input tax over deducted ie the net overpayment.

ASSESSMENTS

When the time limit for making claims for overpaid VAT was reduced from six years to three, with effect from 18 July 1996, Customs' power to make assessments was also reduced by the same amount with effect from the same date. This remains unchanged.

Commentary—*De Voil Indirect Tax Service* **V5.159**.
Cross reference—See Business Brief 27/02 (extension of transitional period for capping limits).

ATTRIBUTION OF INPUT TAX INCURRED ON PROFESSIONAL SERVICES WHEN A COMPANY ACQUIRES SHARES IN ANOTHER COMPANY IN EXCHANGE FOR SHARES IN ITSELF

20 August 2002. *Business Brief 23/02*

BACKGROUND

This Business Brief article sets out Custom's policy following the decision of 24 June of the VAT and Duties Tribunal in the Southampton Leisure (LON/99/0466) appeal.

The appeal was concerned with the attribution of input tax incurred on certain professional services by the business, when it issued shares to the shareholders of Southampton Football Club Limited in exchange for their shares. Customs' view was that the services were used exclusively for the purposes of an exempt issue of shares, whereas the taxpayer's view was that the services were used in making both taxable and exempt supplies.

TRIBUNAL'S DECISION

The tribunal partly allowed the appeal. Whilst it supported Customs' view that the services relating to the public relations exercise was exclusively related to the issue of shares, the tribunal found that supplies of services, which included certain tasks namely—

- acting as financial advisor;
- the drafting of service contracts for the directors;
- the due diligence review of the target company's affairs—the investigation of title and/ or the valuation of that company's property;
- coordinating the transaction; and
- were not used exclusively in making the exempt supply of the issue of shares. As a result, the tax incurred on those supplies should be treated as residual input tax.

Customs have decided not to appeal the tribunal's decision.

IMPLICATIONS

Customs now accept that any taxed supplies of professional services, which include any of the above tasks in the circumstances of a merger and acquisition or management buy-out, has to some extent a direct and immediate link with the whole of the taxpayer's business. The tax incurred is residual input tax and is attributable to taxable supplies by reference to that person's partial exemption method. However, where a taxed supply of professional services is partly used in making an issue of shares to a person belonging outside the European Union, then the deductible proportion of tax is to be determined on a "use" basis under regulation 103(2) of the VAT Regulations 1995.

WHAT THE DECISION DOES NOT AFFECT

Customs take the view that the decision has no application where shares are issued for subscription. For example, an initial public offer or rights issue. In these instances, the taxed professional services relating to the offer are used exclusively for the purposes of the exempt supply of an issue of shares. But Customs do accept that any services providing general advice on the means of capital raising (provided it is just that) is part of the business' overheads and that the tax incurred on any such services should be treated as residual input tax. In most offers the decision to issue shares is taken at the outset and the question of any general advice simply does not arise.

CLAIMS

Customs will, subject to the normal capping rules, accept claims for overpaid tax. This will largely arise where a business, in the course of a merger or acquisition or management buy-out activity, has wholly attributed to exempt supplies and so treated as irrecoverable an amount of input tax incurred on a supply of professional services, but which following the tribunal's approach in Southampton Leisure ought to have been attributed to both taxable and exempt supplies. The amount of overpaid tax being the deductible proportion of (what is now accepted to be) residual input tax.

EXTENSION OF TRANSITIONAL PERIOD FOR CAPPING LIMITS—MARKS & SPENCER PLC V C&E COMRS, CJEC CASE C-62/00 [2002] STC 1036—ADDENDUM TO BUSINESS BRIEF 22/02—GRUNDIG ITALIANA SPA V MINISTERO DELLE FINANZE, CJEC CASE 255/00

8 October 2002. *Business Brief 27/02*

BACKGROUND

On 5 August 2002 Customs & Excise published Business Brief 22/02, which set out how we intended to give effect to the judgment of the European Court of Justice (ECJ) in *Marks & Spencer*. In that case, the ECJ held that when shortening the time limit for claiming amounts overpaid by way of tax in breach of Community law, member states must make provision for a transitional period during which taxpayers who have rights to make a claim under the "old" law can exercise those rights before they are finally extinguished by the "new" law.

Business Brief 22/02 recognised that there had been no transitional period when the three-year capping legislation was introduced in 1996. It went on to establish, retrospectively, a transitional period to run from 4 December 1996 (the date on which the resolution under the Provisional Collection of Taxes Act 1968 was passed by Parliament) until 31 March 1997 (90 days after 4 December, rounded up to the end of the month).

ECJ JUDGMENT IN GRUNDIG ITALIANA

The length of the transitional period was based on the opinion of the Advocate General in *Grundig Italiana*, a case in which the issue before the ECJ was whether a 90 day transitional period was reasonable where the time limit for submitting claims to recover amounts of overpaid tax is reduced from five years to three.

The Advocate General concluded that it was for the national courts to determine, as a question of fact, whether a transitional period rendered it impossible in practice or excessively difficult for a taxpayer to recover tax he had overpaid. The Advocate General held that the question was not one to which the ECJ could give an answer. However, he said nothing to suggest that the 90 day transitional period applied by the Italians was unreasonable.

On 24 September the ECJ handed down its judgment and, declining to follow the Advocate General, held that where time limits for claiming overpayments of tax are shortened from, for example, five or ten years to three, provision must be made for a transitional period of at least six months.

As a result, the transitional period set out in Business Brief 22/02 is extended by three months and will now be deemed to have run from 4 December 1996 to 30 June 1997 and taxpayers are now invited to submit, or resubmit, claims where:

– they made claims before 30 June 1997, which were capped (either by Customs or by them in expectation that no more than three years would be paid);
– or they made claims before 30 June 1997, which were repaid in full and amounts more than three years old were then clawed back by Customs by means of a recovery assessment;
– or they made no claim but can demonstrate that they discovered the error before 30 June 1997; and in all cases, the overpayments of VAT were made before 4 December 1996.

The deadline for making claims is also extended by three months to 30 June 2003. Requests for an extension will be given sympathetic consideration where taxpayers can demonstrate that they are experiencing real difficulties in meeting the deadline.

Both *Marks & Spencer* and *Grundig Italiana* are landmark cases in this area of Community law. Customs & Excise apologise for any inconvenience caused to taxpayers by the change contained in this Business Brief, but believe that it is right to give taxpayers the benefit of the current thinking of the European Court.

Commentary—*De Voil Indirect Tax Service* **V5.159**.

POLICY STATEMENT ON THE TREATMENT OF APPLICATIONS TO LEAVE A VAT GROUP

19 November 2002. *Business Brief 30/02*

This Business Brief is issued as a result of recent representations to Customs following the Court of Appeal decision in the case of *Customs and Excise v Barclays Bank PLC* [2001] EWCA Civ 1513, [2001] STC 1558. This article clarifies how Customs and Excise intend to deal with applications for a company to leave a VAT group.

The Court of Appeal ruled in October 2001 that Customs were not obliged to exclude a company from a VAT group as soon as the company ceased to be controlled by the group holding company. As a result of this ruling, Customs were able to prevent the company leaving the VAT group before FA 1995 s 25 came into effect on 1 March 1995. FA 1995 introduced an "exit charge" for companies leaving a VAT group in certain circumstances and would have applied in this case, increasing the amount of VAT due from Barclays.

Businesses and tax advisers are concerned that keeping a company in a VAT group after the company has been sold to a third party may cause commercial difficulties. In practice, it would be rare for Customs to set a later date for cases. Normally Customs policy will be to agree the date requested by the selling group. Customs will set a later date only if VAT avoidance is involved or is likely to arise through obtaining an earlier date.

Applications to leave a VAT group should continue to be made to Customs in the normal way as set out in Public Notice 700/2 Group treatment, indicating the date that the company wishes to leave the VAT group.

Commentary—*De Voil Indirect Tax Service* **V2.113**.

VAT GROUPS—PROTECTION OF THE REVENUE

19 November 2002. *Business Brief 30/02*

This article provides businesses with further guidance about VAT grouping structures. Customs will not use their revenue protection powers to challenge acceptable grouping structures.

VAT GROUPING RULES

The VAT grouping rules are a business facilitation measure. They allow members of a VAT group to disregard, for VAT purposes, any supplies between group members, with only one VAT return then being required for the whole VAT group. As a result, a company which decides to set up subsidiaries to carry on parts of its business will be treated for VAT purposes in the same way as if it had decided to carry on the business through branches of a single company.

Two companies can join a VAT group provided both are established (or have a fixed establishment) in the UK and both meet the control criteria, ie one of them controls the other, or they are both controlled by one person, or by two or more individuals carrying on business in a partnership.

Full details of the VAT grouping rules are in Public Notice 700/2.

REVENUE PROTECTION POWERS

The VAT grouping legislation gives Customs the power to prevent a company joining a VAT group and to remove an existing member from a VAT group where this is considered necessary for the protection of the revenue. (Business Briefs 15/99 and 01/01 provide more information about these powers.) One aim of these revenue protection powers is to prevent a company from using contrived structures which seek to extend the benefits of VAT grouping to supplies from what is, in effect, a third party supplier.

One example of a contrived structure which Customs have and will continue to challenge is the so-called A-B share scheme. This involves the setting up of a company where the VAT group holding company (the customer) will have "A" shares and a third party supplier, eg of IT services, will have "B" shares. Typically, while the "A" shares may attract some dividend, the "B" shares will entitle the third party supplier to all or the majority of the profits. The holding company will have the right to appoint the majority of the board of directors of the company, thus meeting the control criteria for eligibility to VAT grouping. The result is contrary to the VAT system and enables partly exempt VAT groups to avoid paying VAT on bought-in services.

ACCEPTABLE GROUPING STRUCTURES

As a general principle, Customs consider that the VAT grouping of two corporate bodies (A and B) is acceptable where A's corporate group either receives or has the ability to control 50% or more of the "economic benefits" of running B's business, provided that the determination of the "economic benefits" is not manipulated to divert benefits to a third party through, for example, high management charges; special dividend payments or other charges, payments or arrangements.

Customs will consider challenging any grouping structure which does not meet this general principle, unless the amount of VAT revenue at stake is nil or too low to justify action.

Examples of normal commercial structures which Customs consider acceptable and therefore would not be challenged are set out below. These are provided for guidance only. In all grouping cases, Customs will apply the principles set out above when determining whether to challenge any particular grouping scheme.

EXAMPLE 1: VAT GROUPING DOES NOT AFFECT THE NET VAT REVENUE TO A SIGNIFICANT EXTENT

A jointly owned supplier S is VAT grouped with one of its owners C, to whom it provides various taxable services. In the absence of VAT grouping, C would be able to recover all or substantially all the VAT it would pay on S's services. Customs would not take action under Business Brief 01/01 because such action would not be necessary for the protection of the revenue. The position would be similar if all of S's services to C were exempt or zero-rated.

EXAMPLE 2: 50:50 JOINT VENTURES

JV is jointly owned by companies P and Q, and has issued "A" shares to P and "B" shares to Q. It is VAT grouped with P by the "A" shares giving P a slim majority of the voting rights at general meetings. In reality, P and Q share approximately equally in the investment in JV and receive similar shares of its profits. JV is not a subsidiary of either P or Q for UK group accounts purposes. Customs would normally see such grouping as acceptable subject to the caveat under the general rule above that there were no arrangements for Q to obtain significantly more than 50% of the benefits from running JV's business, eg by levying management charges tailored to remove most of JV's profits.

Commentary—*De Voil Indirect Tax Service* **V2.113**.

EXEMPTION OF CALL CENTRE SERVICES IN THE INSURANCE SECTOR

1 July 2003. *Business Brief 7/03*

Following a recent VAT and Duties Tribunal decision, this article explains Customs' revised policy on the VAT treatment of call centre services where the call centre is attempting to sell insurance by cold calling and is able to put the insurer "on risk" at the point of sale.

THE TRIBUNAL DECISION

The appeal involved TeleTech, a company providing call centre and IT support services to a wide range of clients. The decision related to the services supplied to an insurance company. TeleTech cold called people using contact lists provided by the insurer and attempted to sell them health insurance products. The products were very straightforward and the telephone operatives were selected mainly for their expertise in call handling and selling. Only a small percentage of calls led to sales and TeleTech was paid on a flat fee rather than commission basis.

Customs ruled that TeleTech's services fell outside the exemption for insurance related services, arguing that TeleTech's services were principally of an advertising/promotional nature. The Tribunal allowed TeleTech's appeal on the grounds that TeleTech was selling or trying to sell insurance policies as agents. The decisive factor being that, where calls led to sales, TeleTech was able to put the insurer on risk and the customer on cover. The Tribunal Chairman also observed that the manner of remuneration (ie whether by flat fee or commission) had no bearing on the VAT treatment.

REVISED VAT TREATMENT

As a result of this decision, Customs now accept that call centre services, such as those supplied by TeleTech, are VAT exempt insurance related services where the call centre is able to put the insurer on risk at the point of sale without referral back to the insurer.

VAT PRs etc

Due to the unique nature of the insurance exemption, Customs see this decision as applying only to call centre services supplied in connection with insurance. Customs do not see the decision as having any implications for cases concerning the VAT liability of call centre services supplied to other sectors.

Businesses that think this decision applies to them, but have already accounted for VAT on such services, can make an adjustment to their VAT accounts for overpayments that total less than £2,000 net of any input tax over-claimed or for such overpayments exceeding £2,000. Claims must be submitted to your local Business Advice Centre for repayment, as set out in detail in Section 4 of Customs' Notice 700/45 "How to correct errors and make adjustments or claims".

All adjustments or claims must take into account any over-claimed input tax and are limited to a three-year period as explained in detail in Notice 700/45. Such claims will be paid subject to the conditions set out below—

- Businesses must be able to produce suitable evidence that the services in question qualify for exemption on the basis outlined above, and must be able to substantiate the amount claimed.
- Businesses will need to look back at earlier attributions of input tax (any input tax incurred on goods and services used exclusively for these call centre services is now attributable to an exempt supply), substituting exempt values for taxable values in the partial exemption calculation and deducting the resulting 'exempt input tax' from overpaid output tax in determining the amount of the claim.

If Customs can show that a business effectively did not bear the burden of the tax, it may reject the claim on the grounds that it would unjustly enrich a business. For example, this may have happened because a business passed the tax on to someone else without losing profit by doing so, and are unable, or don't intend, to pass on the repayment. Further details can be found in Notice 700/45 Section 14.

A notification to Customs that a business intends making a claim in the future is not a valid claim.

FURTHER INFORMATION

Further information can be found in Public Notice 700/45 "How to correct VAT errors or make adjustments or claims" or by contacting the National Advice Service on 0845 010 9000.

BUILDING AND CONSTRUCTION: GRANTS OF A MAJOR INTEREST BY MEMBERS OF VAT GROUPS

25 July 2003. *Business Brief 11/03*

The first grant of a major interest in a new dwelling, communal residential building or charitable building is zero-rated. "Grant of a major interest" means a freehold sale or a long lease in a building. This Business Brief article clarifies Customs' policy in relation to grants of major interest in zero-rated buildings by VAT groups in the rare situation when a group member makes more than one grant of a major interest in a building, the first of which is to another group member.

Where a major interest in a building is granted by one member of a VAT group to another, the grant should not be considered to be the "first grant of a major interest" in that building by that group member for the purpose of zero-rating.

In effect this means that the first grant of a major interest to a person outside the group can be zero-rated, regardless of the previous activity within the VAT group, so long as the group member making the grant is a person constructing (or converting) the building and it meets all the other criteria.

FURTHER INFORMATION

For further information please contact the National Advice Service on 0845 010 9000.

Commentary—*De Voil Indirect Tax Service* **V2.190; V4.233.**

TREATMENT OF COMMUNAL AREAS IN BLOCKS OF FLATS

25 July 2003. *Business Brief 11/03*

This Business Brief article announces Customs' new policy on communal areas in new buildings containing two or more dwellings. Typically these buildings are blocks of flats, which consist of individual dwellings and areas for the use of all residents, such as a lounge, laundry and refuse area. The first sale of each flat is zero-rated and the buyer also acquires a right to use the communal areas.

Where the communal areas are only used by residents and their guests, Customs accept that the construction of the whole building is zero-rated. Where the communal areas are partly used by others, for example if they contain leisure or gym facilities, whether or not for a charge, then the construction of the communal areas is standard-rated.

Where a building contains both a non-residential part and a dwelling, such as a shop with a flat above, zero-rating continues to apply only to the extent that the building is designed as a dwelling.

FURTHER INFORMATION

For further information please contact the National Advice Service on 0845 010 9000.

EXEMPTION OF INTERMEDIARY SERVICES PROVIDED IN THE FINANCE SECTOR

30 September 2003. *Business Brief 18/03*

Following a Court of Appeal decision, this article explains Customs' revised policy on the VAT treatment of services provided by a body that introduces its members, supporters or customers to a credit card provider and undertakes work preparatory to the provision of the credit card.

In a joined Court of Appeal hearing concerning co-branded (affinity) credit card schemes, both British Airports Authority (BAA) and Institute of Directors (IoD) successfully argued that their services of introducing members, supporters or customers to two different banks for the purposes of issuing a credit card were exempt from VAT as the negotiation of credit.

As part of its introductory service, BAA targeted suitable applicants, issued applications, assisted in the completion of the forms, and screened and processed them when they were returned. In the case of IoD, the introductory service supplied included providing a list of suitable members, encouraging members to apply, assisting them with their applications, and validating completed forms.

Customs argued that neither BAA nor IoD were financial intermediaries because they did not provide services that directly affected the underlying credit transactions. Rather they were providing a taxable marketing and promotional service to the banks.

LEGAL DECISIONS

BAA successfully challenged Customs' view in both the Tribunal and High Court. The IoD was defeated in the Tribunal. Both cases were heard jointly in the Court of Appeal.

In rejecting Customs' arguments, the Court of Appeal said that the deciding factor was how the services of BAA and IoD should be characterised and that the High Court had been correct in describing BAA's services as the negotiation of credit. There was an introduction of applicants to a source of credit, and the promotion and marketing element was just an "essential preliminary".

Customs has not appealed.

IMPLICATIONS

As a result of these judgments, a body that introduces its members, supporters or customers to a credit card provider and undertakes work preparatory to the provision of the credit card is providing exempt negotiation or intermediary services.

The decision clarifies UK law and, as a result, Customs accept that it is no longer necessary for the introducer to be capable of affecting the terms of the principal financial service for the exemption to apply.

Exemption, therefore, applies where an intermediary—

– stands between the parties to a contract in the performance of a distinct act of mediation;
– brings the two parties to the contract together; and
– undertakes "work preparatory" such as completing or assisting with the completion of application forms, forwarding forms to the credit card company, and making representations on behalf of either party.

Customs do not view marketing and promotional services supplied in isolation, nor the performing of clerical functions such as providing a list of names or access to a database as exempt intermediary services.

CHARITIES

Under a specific concession outlined in paragraph 11(a) of Public Notice 701/01/95 "Charities", Customs currently allows charities to treat part of their taxable income in respect of affinity credit cards as if it were outside the scope of VAT. However, as a result of the judgment in BAA and the IoD each charity will need to consider whether these supplies are now VAT exempt. Charities that continue to have taxable affinity credit card schemes can continue to treat their income as before.

INFORMATION ON MAKING CLAIMS OR ADJUSTMENTS

Businesses that think this Business Brief article applies to them but have already accounted for VAT on such services, may claim any resulting payment due to them from Customs by using one of the following methods, subject to statutory time limits.

(1) If the net value of the adjustments is £2000 or less, businesses may amend their VAT account and include the value of the adjustment on their current VAT return.
(2) If the net value of adjustments is more than £2000, a separate claim for payment should be submitted to the local Business Advice Centre. (Businesses cannot make this adjustment on their VAT return).

Both the above methods and how to make a claim are explained in detail in VAT Notice 700/45 "How to correct VAT errors and make adjustments or claims".

All adjustments or claims must take into account any over-claimed input tax and are limited to a three- year period as explained in detail in Notice 700/45. Such claims will be considered subject to the conditions set out below—

– Businesses must be able to produce suitable evidence that the services in question qualify for exemption on the basis outlined above, and must be able to substantiate the amount claimed.
– Businesses will need to look back at earlier attributions of input tax (any input tax incurred on goods and services used exclusively for these services is now attributable to an exempt supply), substituting exempt values for taxable values in the partial exemption calculation and deducting the resulting 'exempt input tax' from overpaid output tax in determining the amount of the claim.
– Businesses that have acquired a capital item (as defined in SI 1995/2518) and have undertaken an original deduction and/or interval adjustments over the last three years will need to recalculate those figures in order to compensate for the (potential) increased exempt use.

Customs may reject a claim on the grounds that payment would unjustly enrich a business. For example, this may have happened because a business passed the tax on to someone else and are unable, or do not intend, to pass on the repayment. Further details can be found in Notice 700/45 Section 14.

A notification to Customs that a business intends making a claim in the future is not a valid claim. The views expressed in this Business Brief article are those of HM Customs & Excise.

FURTHER INFORMATION

If taxpayers have any queries about the liability of their supplies they should contact Customs' National Advice Service on 0845 010 9000 (Text phone 0845 000 0200).

THE VAT POSITION OF TWO NEW PFI ARRANGEMENTS

30 September 2003. *Business Brief 18/03*

ISSUE

This Business Brief is intended to clarify the extent to which government departments and NHS bodies can recover the VAT they incur on two new types of PFI (Private Finance Initiative) arrangement, referred to respectively as "Composite Trade" ("Contract Debtor") and "NHS LIFT". What follows are general views, and they do not replace the need to look carefully at the circumstances of each case.

BACKGROUND

Under section 41(3) of the VAT Act 1994, government departments and health service bodies are eligible to recover VAT incurred on a range of services purchased in connection with their non-business activities.

The range of services which are eligible for section 41(3) refunds are listed in a Treasury direction published annually in the London, Edinburgh and Belfast Gazettes—the current Direction was published on 10 January 2003, having taken effect from 2 December 2002. It lists 75 different types of services as "Headings", in respect of which VAT may be recovered.

Headings 45 and 53 are relevant to the "Composite Trade" and "NHS LIFT" PFI arrangements. These state—

HEADING 45

Operation of hospitals, health care establishments and health care facilities and the provision of any related services.

HEADING 53

Provision under a PFI agreement of accommodation for office or other government use, together with management or other services in connection with that accommodation.

Both headings are concerned with PFI and PPP arrangements for buildings, which involve the transfer of risk to bodies outside government.

"COMPOSITE TRADE" ARRANGEMENTS

In most PFI arrangements concerning government real estate the property is acquired by the PFI contractor, with the government department or health service bodies having a lesser interest or a licence. This transfers risk in the property to the PFI contractor.

Under the "Composite Trade" structure, however, the main interest in the property remains vested in the government department or in the health service body, rather than passing to the PFI contractor.

This departure from the normal concept of transferring risk does not stop the PFI contractors' supplies to the government department or the health service body from falling within headings 45 or 53 of the Treasury direction. Provided the supply is of a description falling within either of those headings, then a government department or a health service body will be entitled to recover the VAT levied on the Facilities Management Charge, subject to the other rules laid down by the Treasury.

"NHS LIFT" ARRANGEMENTS

"NHS LIFT" (Local Improvement Finance Trusts) arrangements are intended to consolidate and deliver a wide range of local healthcare services from purpose built facilities. The services will primarily be made by local PCTs (Primary Care Trusts), local authority welfare services and GPs. But the intention is also to involve dentists, chemists etc.

To date, NHS LIFT arrangements have varied, which means that it is not possible to give a single, blanket piece of advice that applies to all such projects. However, Customs believe that in all cases, the question will generally be the extent to which the project qualifies for refunds under heading 45. The answer to this will depend upon the level of health related services that are provided in the building in question, otherwise than in the course of business, and the extent to which the NHS LIFT company is involved in the operation of a health care establishment.

In Customs' view the simple granting of a lease in a building is insufficient to qualify for refund under heading 45, even where it is the equivalent of a landlord repairing and maintaining lease. Customs consider that two requirements must be satisfied before heading 45 can apply. Firstly the building must either be a hospital, or be used to provide health care facilities. Secondly the supply by the PFI contractor to the health service body must be of the operation of that hospital or establishment.

For example, if the building is used for diagnostic work, treating patients and/or patient counselling, Customs accept that it is a health care establishment. Where the NHS LIFT company plays an active role in the operation of that establishment, providing in addition to cleaning and maintenance services, advice in deciding what healthcare services are needed for the local community, how to bring together these services, where to locate the building and, possibly, establishing links with the various health and care agencies, Customs would accept the requirements of heading 45 as being fully satisfied.

An NHS LIFT company would also be involved in the operation of the building if it provided and operated medical equipment.

These examples are nor exhaustive, and cases should be considered on their individual merits, paying regard to the two principles explained above.

TREATMENT OF CAGE ACCESSORIES FOR USE IN SPECIALISED LABORATORY CAGING

13 November 2003. *Business Brief 21/03*

This Business Brief article announces Customs' new policy on certain cage accessories supplied to eligible bodies for use in specialised laboratory caging following a Tribunal decision.

The zero rate applies to supplies of certain types of goods to eligible bodies such as not-for-profit research institutions. These goods include medical, scientific and laboratory equipment for use in medical or veterinary research and any parts or accessories for use in or with such laboratory equipment.

Following a recent VAT Tribunal decision (18247), Customs accept that cage and tray liners and research grade litter, bedding and nesting materials are accessories when designed for use in or with specialised laboratory caging. As a result supplies of these products will qualify for zero-rating when supplied to eligible bodies (see Notice 701/6 "Charity Funded Equipment for medical, veterinary etc uses" for a full list of eligible bodies).

Traders who have previously accounted for VAT on supplies to eligible bodies of these products for use in specialised laboratory caging, can make a claim to their local Business Advice Centre for repayment, as set out in detail in Section 4 of Notice 700/45 "How to correct errors and make adjustments or claims". All claims are limited to a three-year period and will be subject to unjust enrichment considerations as explained in detail in Notice 700/45.

OTHER PRODUCTS

The Tribunal also made some informal comments on the liability of certain other products, namely anaesthetic equipment; surgical instruments; autopsy equipment; surgical scissors; and operating lamps for surgery. These did not amount to a decision. In order to determine whether these goods will qualify for zero-rating when supplied to eligible bodies, a business must ask itself whether the criteria in Notice 701/6 have been met.

Other products, such as environmental enrichment products, were not considered by the Tribunal. Customs maintain that supplies of these products will not qualify for zero-rating when supplied to eligible bodies.

PARTIAL EXEMPTION—SPECIAL METHOD OVERRIDE NOTICE

10 December 2003. *Business Brief 27/03*

This Business Brief article describes the effect of the special method override Notice announced in today's pre-Budget Report and which comes into force from 1 January 2004.

SUMMARY

The special method override Notice (Notice) only affects partly exempt businesses that operate a partial exemption special method and where Customs have—

- served a Notice on the business; or,
- approved a Notice served by the business.

A Notice allows Customs or business to correct the results of an unfair special method until a replacement method is implemented.

No other businesses are affected by this measure.

BACKGROUND

A business that makes both taxable and exempt supplies is known as partly exempt and must apply a partial exemption method to calculate how much of the VAT it incurs on its costs and purchases it can deduct. A partial exemption method is supposed to ensure that the business can deduct a fair and reasonable amount of VAT on costs and purchases that are "used or will be used" in making taxable supplies ("the principle of use").

Most partly exempt businesses operate the standard method of partial exemption but some businesses, particularly the most complex ones, operate a special method that has been customised to their needs and approved or directed by Customs. Further details on partial exemption can be found in VAT Notice 706 "Partial Exemption" http://customs.hmrc.gov.uk/.

From time to time, for example when business circumstances change, a special method might no longer meet the principle of use and a new method must be found. Preparing a new special method can take time, especially for a large or complex business, and because a new method cannot normally be backdated Customs or the business can lose out as a result.

NEW MEASURE

A Notice allows either Customs or business to introduce an override with immediate effect, to correct the results of an unfair method until a replacement method is implemented. A business should then correct the results of its special method to ensure that VAT deducted fairly and reasonably reflects the principle of use. Corrections commence from a current or future date specified within the Notice and must continue each time the special method is applied (including any year end adjustment) until a replacement method is implemented. This means that neither Customs nor the business need be disadvantaged whilst a replacement special method is being prepared.

SITUATIONS COVERED BY THE NEW NOTICE

A Notice is intended to be a temporary measure and Customs expect its use to be rare. Customs will only issue or approve a Notice where—

- They have clear evidence that the current special method does not fairly and reasonably reflect the principle of use; and
- They are satisfied that preparing a replacement method will not conclude quickly and that Customs or business would otherwise lose out.

Customs will serve a Notice only when—

- They have attempted, unsuccessfully, to persuade the business to comply, and have the evidence to show this; and,
- They have decided that direction of a special method is not appropriate.

SERVING AND APPROVING A NOTICE

A Notice must specify—

- that it is a special method override notice;

- the current or future date from which it takes effect; and,
- the reasons why the current special method does not meet the principle of use.

When Customs serve a Notice they will also explain its practical effect, for example what a business must do to comply. When Customs approve a Notice served by a business, they will do so in writing as soon as possible and ideally within 30 days of receipt. Decisions on serving a Notice will be taken by a central team.

COMPLYING WITH A NOTICE

To comply with a Notice a business must for each VAT return period (including any year end adjustment)—

- determine the amount of deductible VAT using its current special method;
- determine the amount of deductible VAT in accordance with the principle of use; and,
- account for any difference between these amounts as a Notice correction.

In most cases the reasons given by Customs or business in the Notice will provide a basis for determining the Notice correction. However, a business must still consider its whole method and determine whether there are any other aspects that would otherwise give an unfair result. The Notice correction must therefore ensure that each time a VAT return is prepared, the amount of VAT deducted fairly and reasonably reflects the extent that costs and purchases are used or will be used in making taxable supplies (the principle of use).

If a business does not make corrections to the amount of VAT deducted, and Customs conclude that a Notice correction should have been made, then Customs will make the correction by way of VAT assessment.

RIGHT OF APPEAL

A business can appeal to the VAT and Duties Tribunal against—

- Customs' decision to serve a Notice;
- Customs' decision not to approve a Notice; and,
- any VAT assessments made under a Notice.

Commentary—*De Voil Indirect Tax Service* **V3.462**.

EXEMPTION OF "DEBT NEGOTIATION SERVICES"

24 December 2003. *Business Brief 30/03*

This Business Brief article has been issued to clarify Customs' change in policy on the VAT liability of "debt negotiation services", following the Tribunal decision in the case of *Debt Management Associates*. As a result of this change, the services of "debt negotiation", provided by an intermediary, will be exempt from VAT.

WHAT ARE "DEBT NEGOTIATION SERVICES"?

"Debt negotiation services" typically seek to acquire favourable repayment terms for a debtor who is experiencing difficulty in making repayments under terms already in place.

This type of service may include one or more of the following—

- taking details of income and expenditure, along with details of the creditor(s) and the amounts outstanding, and preparing and presenting a payment plan to the creditor;
- agreeing to act on behalf of such a debtor with the creditor in negotiating the payment plan; or
- agreeing to receive payments from the debtor and passing these payments on to the creditors (with or without first extracting a fee or commission for doing so).

Turning to what is meant by "negotiation", Customs considers that it refers to the activity of an intermediary providing a distinct act of mediation. The purpose of such intermediation is to do all that is necessary in order for two parties to enter into a contract, without the person who is acting as an intermediary having any interest of his own in the terms of the contract. Therefore, provided you bring together the two parties, act between those parties, and attempt to mediate a change to the payment terms you are "negotiating debts".

However, if you are merely providing a service typically undertaken by a company as part of its contract this will not be "negotiation of debts". For example—

- if you issue letters to the debtor on behalf of the creditor demanding payment; or
- if you seek to locate a debtor on behalf of the creditor; or
- if you provide accounting services to the creditor (ie you monitor the debtor's payment account and notify the creditor of any defaulted payments).

This list is not exhaustive.

If you provide a service containing both 'negotiation of debts' and one or more of the services listed above you will need to determine what element predominates. VAT Information Sheet 02/01: "Single or multiple supplies—how to decide" can assist you and is available online at www.hmce.gov.uk/forms/notices/info0201 If you have further questions please contact the National Advice Service on 0845 010 9000.

LIABILITY OF DEBT RE-NEGOTIATION SERVICES

Prior to the *Debt Management Associates* decision Customs' policy had been to tax the services of debt negotiation at the standard rate.

Customs now accept that where a business negotiates payment terms between two parties this is "negotiating debts" and within the scope of the finance exemption which applies to the provision of intermediary services by a person acting in an intermediary capacity and is thus exempt from VAT.

CLAIMS FOR REFUNDS OF VAT

Businesses that think this Business Brief article applies to them, but have already accounted for VAT on such services, may make a claim to their local Business Advice Centre for repayment, as set out in detail in Section 4 of Customs' Notice 700/45 "How to correct errors and make adjustments or claim" available from www.hmce.gov.uk/forms/notices/700-45. All claims are limited to a three-year period and will be subject to unjust enrichment considerations as explained in section 14 of Customs Notice 700/45.

All adjustments or claims must take into account any over-claimed input tax as well as any over declared output tax. Such claims will be considered subject to the conditions set out below—

- Businesses must be able to produce suitable evidence that the services in question qualify for exemption on the basis outlined above, and must be able to substantiate the amount claimed.
- Businesses will need to look back at earlier attributions of input tax to previously considered taxable supplies (including attributions to intended taxable supplies). This VAT will now directly relate to (revised) exempt supplies (or intended exempt supplies) and is therefore exempt input tax and fully restricted. In addition, where the business has apportioned VAT in accordance with the standard method, or a calculation under a special method, there must be a re-calculation of that method by substituting (reducing) the original taxable elements of the fraction by the revised (increased) exempt elements.

A notification to Customs that a business intends making a claim in the future is not a valid claim.

VAT – DEFINITION OF A MOTORCAR

9 June 2004. *Business Brief 16/04*

This Business Brief clarifies Customs' interpretation of the definition of a motorcar as contained in the Value Added Tax (Cars) Order 1992.

BACKGROUND

The UK operates a 'block' on the deduction of input tax on the purchase of a vehicle that is defined in VAT legislation as a motorcar. As a result of this block, most businesses that purchase motorcars are unable to recover the VAT they have incurred. In broad terms, the purpose of the block is to prevent recovery of input tax on vehicles whose physical attributes make them suitable for private motoring. It is important, therefore, for business to know the status of their vehicles under the terms of the legislation, as this will affect the deductibility of VAT on their purchase.

The clarification is necessary in the light of recent developments in the car-derived van market, which have resulted in the manufacture of vehicles that have blurred the distinction between cars and vans. This means that these vehicles are difficult to categorise in relation to the definition of motorcars in VAT legislation.

In response, Customs have issued new guidance, produced in consultation with manufacturers, which clarifies our treatment of car-derived vans and highlights the correct interpretation of the legal definition when considering combination vans. This guidance is available on request from the Customs' National Advice Service on 0845 010 9000.

VEHICLES AFFECTED AND THEIR VAT TREATMENT

The vehicles affected are certain car-derived vans and the combination van.

CAR-DERIVED VANS

Many car-derived vans pose no problem with regard to our current definition of a motor car, in that they are clearly vans or non-motor cars for VAT purposes eg they have no rear seats, metal side panels to the rear of the front seats, a load area which is highly unsuitable for carrying passengers etc.

However a number of models, where the vehicle starts off life as a car and is subsequently altered, cannot be so clearly defined. It is these vehicles which are the focus of this brief [and also an HMRC announcement of 27 October 2006].

On the exterior, these vehicles look like a motorcar but their interior has been altered to give the appearance and functionality of a van. The rear seats and seat belts along with their mountings have been completely removed and the rear area of the shell is fitted with a new floor panel to create a load area. In addition, the side 'windows' to the rear of the driver's seat are fitted with immovable opaque panels.

Customs will *not* view such a "car-derived" vehicle as a motorcar for VAT purposes, if:

— the technical criteria specified in Customs guidance are met by the manufacturer. The criteria relate to how any alterations to the vehicle have been effected
— the adaptations give the vehicle the functionality of a commercial vehicle. As such, the removal of a bench seat or similar from what is essentially a two-seater car would not automatically satisfy Customs' requirements and
— the space that remains behind the front row of seats is highly unsuitable for carrying passengers.

It may be difficult for businesses to satisfy themselves fully that all of the technical criteria have been met. At present, Customs, in partnership with the manufacturers, are developing a list of car-derived vans on which VAT can be deducted, subject to the normal rules. This list will be available shortly on the Customs' website. In the meantime, if businesses are in any doubt, they should obtain confirmation in writing from the vendor that the vehicle meets the technical criteria.

Customs consulted the manufacturers on the technical criterion in September 2003. As such, if businesses have bought such a car-derived van prior to 1 October 2003, it is unlikely that it will satisfy all of the technical criteria set out in Customs' guidance. However, where the vehicle has the appearance of a car-derived van as defined above, in such circumstances, Customs will allow that vehicle to be treated as a non-motor car for VAT purposes, and the VAT incurred can be recovered, subject to the normal rules.

COMBINATION VANS

While these vehicles have the appearance of vans, they are designed to be fitted with or include additional seats behind the front row of seats to enable the carriage of passengers.

Such vehicles are motorcars for VAT purposes except in the case of:

— larger vehicles which have a payload of more than one tonne (these vehicles are automatically excluded from becoming motor cars by the one tonne payload test contained in legislation) and
— those vehicles where the dedicated load area (ie that load area which is completely unaffected by the additional seating) is of a sufficient size compared to the passenger area to make the carriage of goods the predominant use of the vehicle.

— If businesses have previously bought a combination van, which does not fall within the exceptions above, it is a motorcar under VAT legislation. If businesses have recovered the VAT incurred on the purchase, they must make an adjustment to correct this overclaim.

Commentary—*De Voil Indirect Tax Service* **V3.443**.

Notes—See HMRC announcement of 27 October 2006 concerning clarification of the definition of car-derived vans. Also see Business Brief 13/06 with regard to retrospective claims for VAT overdeclared by motor retailers following the *Marks and Spencer* European Court decision.

GAS AND ELECTRICITY SUPPLIERS: NEW EXTRA-STATUTORY CONCESSION FOR BAD DEBTS

2 August 2004. *Business Brief 20/04*

This Business Brief article outlines a new Extra-Statutory Concession, enabling suppliers of gas and electricity to obtain relief from VAT on debts owed by domestic customers, after the suppliers have accepted the transfer of a domestic customer and their debt from another supply company.

BACKGROUND

The VAT Bad Debt Relief scheme enables VAT registered businesses to recover some or all of the VAT they have declared and paid in respect of their supplies, where their customer has failed to pay. Under the terms of the scheme, the person who makes the supply is the only person entitled to claim VAT Bad Debt Relief.

This concession supports Government policy to allow greater flexibility for domestic fuel and power consumers by enabling them to change suppliers even if they have a debt.

CHANGES

The ESC applies where a domestic customer who is in debt to one supplier changes supplier, and the debt is transferred to the new supplier. The new supplier may claim bad debt relief on any part of the debt that remains outstanding six months after the date of transfer.

TIMING

The ESC takes effect today, Monday 2 August 2004.

THE EXTRA-STATUTORY CONCESSION

(1) Where a contract for the supply of gas or electricity is substituted by a new contract ("novation") as a result of a domestic consumer transferring from one supplier to another, then, by concession, the new supplier may claim bad debt relief on a supply of gas or electricity made by the former supplier to that consumer, provided that all of the conditions in paragraph 2 below are satisfied.

(2) The conditions referred to in paragraph 1 above are:

(a) the whole or any part of the consideration for the supply is outstanding at the time of the novation

(b) the whole of the debt is transferred to the new supplier

(c) at the time of the novation, the former supplier (if he has not already done so) accounts for VAT on the supply at the appropriate rate or, if he has already received a refund upon a claim for bad debt relief in relation to that supply, repays to the Commissioners the amount of that refund

(d) the claim is not made until six months after payment for the novation and takes account

(e) both the former of any payments made by the customer after the date of the novation supplier and the new supplier have evidence of:

(i) the value of the debt (including the VAT amount) that has been transferred and

(ii) the date of payment for the novation

(f) the new supplier has a copy of the document issued by him to the consumer to recover the debt (not required if a pre-payment meter is in use).

(3) In this concession:

"domestic consumer" means a person to whom fuel or power is supplied for domestic use

VAT PRs etc

"domestic use" has the same meaning as in Group 1 of Schedule 7A to the Value Added Tax Act 1994

"gas" means gas that is conveyed through pipes to premises by a licensed gas transporter and

"licensed gas transporter" means any person authorised by a licence under section 7 of the Gas Act 1986 (as amended) to supply gas through pipes to any premises.

(4) This concession does not apply in circumstances where its application would give rise to tax avoidance.

VAT POSITION OF SHARE ISSUES AND PARTNERSHIP CONTRIBUTIONS FOLLOWING THE EUROPEAN COURT OF JUSTICE DECISION IN KAPHAG RENDITEFONDS

10 August 2004. *Business Brief 21/04*

This Business Brief clarifies Customs' position on two issues arising from the decision of the European Court of Justice in the German case of *KapHag Renditefonds v Finanzamt Charlottenburg* (Case C-442/01):

(A) Whether the issue of shares constitutes a supply for VAT purposes; and
(B) The VAT position of contributions to partnerships.

The case of KapHag concerned the admission of a new partner into a partnership on payment of a capital contribution. The European Court held that no supply was being made by either the individual partners or the partnership to the incoming partner in return for the capital contribution.

A WHETHER THE ISSUE OF SHARES CONSTITUTES A SUPPLY

The KapHag decision has been cited as authority for the view that an issue of shares by a company is similarly not a supply for VAT purposes. It is claimed that an issue of shares therefore falls outside the terms of Item 6 of Group 5 of Schedule 9 to the Value Added Tax Act 1994. That Item exempts from VAT:

"The issue, transfer or receipt of, or any dealing with, any security or secondary security . . . "

It is Customs' view that the formation or variation of a partnership arrangement is wholly distinguishable from the position where a company issues shares in return for consideration. KapHag was concerned solely with the issues surrounding a partnership. The VAT treatment of share issues has been considered by the Court of Appeal in Trinity Mirror plc ([2001] STC 192) where it was held that an issue of shares by a company did constitute a supply of services for VAT purposes and these fall to be exempt under Item 6 of Group 5 of Schedule 9 to the Act. In most circumstances there will then be a restriction of input tax under the partial exemption rules. Further information is available from VAT Notice 706 Partial Exemption.

B CONTRIBUTIONS TO PARTNERSHIPS

Partnerships to which this section applies include "normal" partnerships of individuals or corporate bodies, limited partnerships whose members are individuals or corporate bodies, overseas limited partnerships that are registered as "normal" partnerships or corporate bodies and limited liability partnerships.

Background

In KapHag, the incoming partner was contributing cash in return for admission into the partnership but it will often be the case that the contribution is in the form of other assets. For example, a new partner's contribution may comprise land or interests in land. The European Court's decision tacitly accepted the Advocate-General's Opinion that the same principles would apply whether the contribution consisted of cash or other assets. Whatever the nature of the assets comprising the contribution, there is no reciprocal supply from the partnership. However, where the assets are not cash, the making of the partnership contribution may have other VAT consequences.

The Advocate-General was satisfied that there was "no doubt that the new partner is effecting an act of disposal of his assets, for which the admission to the partnership is not the consideration" (Paragraph 33 of the Opinion). Such a disposal can therefore have VAT consequences when the partner contributing the assets is a VAT registered person. These consequences will vary depending on the nature of the assets being contributed.

KapHag establishes that nothing is provided by the partnership in return for the assets contributed, therefore any such disposal by the incoming partner is made for no consideration. The VAT Act provides that certain things are subject to VAT even when they are provided or done for no consideration. Customs' view is that all those provisions will still apply where there is no consideration when there is a contribution to partnership assets. A VAT registered person may therefore have to account for tax if he contributes assets to the partnership in the circumstances described in the Act. The VAT consequences can be considered under several main heads:

(i) Contribution to partnership comprising services;
(ii) Contribution to partnership comprising goods other than land;
(iii) Contribution to partnership comprising land or interests in land;
(iv) Whether contribution to partnership can constitute the transfer of a going concern;
(v) How the partnership can reclaim the output tax accounted for by an incoming partner on his contribution as its input tax;
(vi) Capital Goods Scheme consequences; and
(vii) Transfer of assets out of a partnership.

(i) Contribution to partnership comprising services

A partnership contribution may comprise services rather than goods – examples of this could be a trademark or trading logo or the use of an asset the ownership of which is retained by the incoming partner. Two legislative provisions set out the circumstances in which such a contribution may be regarded as a taxable supply, paragraph 5(4) of Schedule 4 to the VAT Act and the Value Added Tax (Supply of Services) Order 1993 (SI 1993/1507).

A supply can arise under paragraph 5(4) where a taxable person applies business goods to private use or makes them available for purposes other than those of his business. The taxable person or his predecessor must have been entitled to input tax under sections 25 and 26 of the VAT Act on the supply of those goods (or anything comprised in them) to him.

The Supply of Services Order similarly provides that a supply arises where a taxable person applies bought-in services to private or non-business use for no consideration where he has been entitled to input tax credit under sections 25 and 26. The value of such a supply cannot exceed the taxable person's input tax entitlement.

Where the above criteria are satisfied, a VAT registered incoming partner will have to account for tax on the supply of services that he is regarded as making in the disposal of the services from his existing business. The partnership may be able to recover this as its input tax where the contributed services are to be used for its business. The procedure for doing this is described at (v) below.

(ii) Contribution to partnership comprising goods other than land

If a partnership contribution comprises goods other than land that a taxable person (the transferor) held as assets, then a deemed supply will be generated as a result of Paragraph 5(1) of Schedule 4 to the VAT Act. This deemed supply does not require there to be consideration when the goods are transferred. It does however only apply where the taxable person disposing of the goods, or their predecessor, if for example they obtained the goods by way of a TOGC, was entitled to full or partial credit for the VAT charged when the goods were supplied to him. Where such a deemed supply arises, the incoming partner will have to account for VAT. The partnership may be able to recover this as its input tax where the contributed assets are to be used for its business. The procedure for doing this is described at (v) below.

(iii) Contribution to partnership comprising land or interests in land

The VAT treatment of land or interests in land also depends upon whether the incoming partner or his predecessor was entitled to deduct input tax in relation to the property that he is contributing to the partnership. For example, if he had opted to tax the property, or it was inherently taxable like new freehold commercial property, there may be a deemed supply as described at (ii) above. The incoming partner will then have to account for VAT on this supply.

As with other contributed goods, the partnership may be entitled to recover this as input tax where the property is to be used for the partnership's business. The procedure for doing this is described at (v) below.

Please note all submitted notifications of an option to tax need to be signed by "an authorised signatory" as described in paragraph 7.1 of VAT Notice 742A Opting to tax Land & Buildings.

(iv) Whether contribution to partnership can constitute the transfer of a going concern

It is possible that when assets are transferred by way of a partnership contribution that this could qualify to be treated as a transfer of a going concern (Section 49 of the VAT Act and Article 5 of the VAT (Special Provisions) Order 1995 (SI 1995/1268)). If the contribution meets the conditions to be treated as a transfer of a going concern no VAT will be due from the transferor.

(v) How the partnership can reclaim the output tax accounted for by an incoming partner on his contribution as its input tax

When an incoming partner contributes goods and/or services (on which VAT is due as described above) and the partnership uses them for its business purposes, the partnership can recover the VAT as input tax subject to the normal rules. The incoming partner cannot issue a tax invoice, but in order to provide the partnership with acceptable evidence to support a claim for recovery of input tax, he may use his normal invoicing documentation overwritten with the following statement:

> "Certificate for Tax on Partnership Contribution
>
> No payment is necessary for these goods/services. Output tax has been accounted for on the supply."

The incoming partner must show full details of the goods and/or services on the documentation and the amount of VAT shown must be the amount of output tax accounted for to Customs and Excise.

(vi) Capital Goods Scheme consequences

Where the capital contribution is in the form of an interest in land or a computer, it may be an existing capital item of the incoming partner under the Capital Goods Scheme (CGS). If the transfer to the partnership constitutes a supply which is a disposal of an existing CGS item, then this will wind up the existing CGS item and a disposal adjustment may be due. If the transfer constitutes a TOGC then this will end the current interval for the incoming partner and the partnership will then be responsible for making adjustments for any remaining intervals.

As transfers of assets capital contributions will always constitute either a supply or a TOGC, any existing CGS items will always either be subject to a disposal adjustment or continuing CGS adjustments.

Even if the asset transferred as a capital contribution is not a CGS item in the hands of the incoming partner, it may create a new CGS item for the partnership when its transfer constitutes a supply. If this happens the partnership will need to make adjustments in subsequent intervals in the normal way.

The CGS is further explained in VAT Notice 706/2 Capital Goods Scheme.

(vii) Transfer of assets out of a partnership

KapHag was only concerned with assets moving into a partnership in the form of a partnership contribution. It did not cover the reverse situation, where partnership assets are paid out to an outgoing partner or otherwise disposed of by the partnership for no consideration. Where a transfer of assets out of a partnership for no consideration occurs, one of the following sets of circumstances will apply.

(a) If the incoming partner accounted for output tax when he contributed the assets to the partnership and the partnership was entitled to recover all or part of this as its input tax, there will be a subsequent supply by the partnership when the same assets are transferred out unless the transfer out now satisfies the TOGC criteria.

(b) If no output tax was accounted for when the assets were contributed to the partnership because they constituted a TOGC, the transfer out of the same assets will be a deemed supply upon which the partnership will have to account for tax unless the TOGC criteria are again satisfied.

(c) The partnership may be transferring out more assets than those originally contributed to it. Although the original contribution to the partnership may not have been a TOGC, the subsequent transfer out may now satisfy the TOGC criteria. If it does, no VAT will be due from the partnership.

(d) The original contribution to the partnership may have been a TOGC but the partnership may now be transferring out less of the assets than were originally contributed. Unless the assets being transferred out still meet the TOGC criteria in their own right, there may be a deemed supply upon which the partnership will have to account for the appropriate tax. As explained at (ii) and (iii) above, the entitlement of the partnership or its predecessor to deduct input tax in relation to the items that are the subject of the transfer out will determine whether or not there is a supply.

Application of section 45 of the VAT Act 1994

In the past, there was uncertainty as to whether it was section 45(1) of the VAT Act that led to there being no supply from a partnership to an incoming partner. That section provides for the registration of partnerships in the following terms:

"45(1) The registration under this Act of persons—
(a) carrying on a business in partnership, or
(b) carrying on in partnership any other activities in the course or furtherance of which they acquire goods from other member States,
may be in the name of the firm; and no account shall be taken, in determining for any purpose of this Act whether goods or services are supplied to or by such persons or are acquired by such persons from another member State, of any change in the partnership."

Partnerships in England and Wales have no legal identity. A new partner joining a partnership, or old one leaving it, would result in a new partnership rather than change the composition of the existing one. Without s.45(1), deregistration and registration would be necessary every time a partner joined or left. The purpose of s.45(1) is to ensure continuity by providing that a business carried on in a firm's name is treated as a continuing business irrespective of changes in its composition. The situation addressed by s.45(1) is therefore entirely different to that considered in KapHag.

CUSTOMS' POLICY ON ASSESSMENTS FOLLOWING THE JUDGMENTS OF THE HIGH COURT IN C&E V LAURA ASHLEY AND THE COURT OF APPEAL IN DFS FURNITURE COMPANY V C&E

14 September 2004. *Business Brief 25/04*

This Business Brief clarifies Customs' policy on assessments following recent court judgments in Laura Ashley and DFS. Taxpayers are not asked to take any action as a consequence of this Business Brief.

GENERAL

The recent judgments in Laura Ashley, in the High Court, and DFS, in the Court of Appeal, are concerned with the validity of VAT recovery assessments, ie assessments made to recover money paid, repaid or credited to taxpayers in error. The judgments raised several points that Customs regarded as 'unsettled' and so we petitioned the House of Lords to hear a further appeal in the DFS case to clarify the position for the benefit of Customs and taxpayers alike. That petition was unsuccessful and so the DFS litigation is now at an end.

In dealing with the validity of recovery assessments, the court judgments, by implication, raise an issue of a more general nature about the effect of a finding that any assessment raised by Customs is invalid. It is Customs view that the proper course for a taxpayer to take if the taxpayer has been assessed and believes the assessment to be incorrect for any reason is to ask Customs to review the decision and, if still unsatisfied, to make a timely appeal to the VAT & Duties Tribunal.

Where an underdeclaration of tax has been correctly established but the related assessment, which has been paid but not appealed, is subsequently acknowledged to be technically flawed, for example where it was made for the wrong accounting period, Customs will not withdraw the assessment. There will not be any reason to do so. In addition, and subject always to the VAT appeal provisions, no repayment of money paid against a technically flawed but otherwise correct assessment will be made.

This general policy in no way alters Customs' obligation and commitment to make every effort to ensure that assessments for arrears of tax are correct in all respects.

The Laura Ashley and DFS judgments

The effect of these judgments, taken together, is that:

(a) assessment time limits cannot begin to run from the date of a court judgment, or its delivery;

but there is continuing uncertainty about:

(b) whether an assessment to recover money repaid or credited to a taxpayer as a result of a mistake of law is properly made under VATA 1994 s 80(4A) or s 73(2);

(c) whether, for a recovery assessment, time limits can run from the date a repayment is made; and

(d) which prescribed accounting period should be assessed when a recovery assessment is made under S73(2).

Customs future practice

1 Assessments time limits running from a court judgment

The law as currently interpreted by the courts in *C&E Comrs v DFS Furniture Company plc* [2004] STC 559 is that a court judgment, or its delivery, is not a fact for the purposes of the 'evidence of facts' time limit rules for making assessments. Customs now accept the DFS judgment on this point and will make no more assessments that rely solely on a court judgment as evidence of facts.

Where past recovery assessments have relied on a court judgment, it is probable that the repayment being recovered was made following a mistake of law. Any tax paid on the recovery assessment was properly due on remedy of the mistake of law.

Some appeals challenging the validity of recovery assessments have been lodged and stood over behind DFS. These appeals will now be reviewed by Customs and the appellants informed of the outcome as soon as possible.

2 Assessments made to recover money repaid or credited following a mistake of law

The judgment in *C&E Comrs v DFS Furniture Company plc* includes obiter dicta remarks which might be taken as suggesting that amounts repaid under VATA 1994 s (80)(1) following a mistake of law were only properly recoverable by assessment made under VATA 1994 s 73(2), subject to the time limits in VATA 1994 s 73(6)(*a*). Customs do not accept this approach.

For the time being, Customs will continue to make assessments under VATA 1994 s 80(4A) for recovery of amounts repaid under s 80(1). However, to protect the Exchequer in the event that the Court of Appeal in DFS is right, we will also assess in the alternative under s 73(2).

Whether past assessments were made under VATA 1994 s 80(4A) or s 73(2) it was appropriate for Customs to recover amounts repaid that ought not to have been repaid.

3 Recovery assessments time limits running from the date the incorrect repayment was made

The Court of Appeal in *C&E Comrs v DFS Furniture Company plc* appears to have taken the view that repayment is not itself a fact for the purposes of the 'evidence of facts' time limit rules for making assessments.

Customs do not think that many, if any, recovery assessments will have been made that rely on the fact of repayment to satisfy the evidence of facts time limit rules. Where at the time of considering a repayment claim Customs are already out of time to make a recovery assessment, we will take account of the obiter dicta remarks in *C&E Comrs v DFS Furniture Company plc* and not repay unless the claimant signs an undertaking to return any payment with interest in the event that the underlying issue is finally determined in Customs' favour.

4. The period to assess under s 73(2)

There are now three apparently conflicting judgments of the courts concerning the period Customs should assess when a recovery assessment is made under VATA 1994 s 73(2).

Customs have taken the period to assess as the period for which a return was made that contained the incorrect claim; or, following the judgment of the Court of Appeal in *C&E v Croydon Hotel and Leisure Co Ltd* [1996] STC 1105, the period in which a voluntary disclosure containing the incorrect claim was made. On this basis, the time limits applying to incorrect returns and to incorrect voluntary disclosures are consistent.

The judgment of the High Court in *C&E v Laura Ashley* [2004] STC 635 was that the period to assess should have been the period to which the relevant tax related, ie the assessment made under VATA 1994 s 73(2) to recover a repayment or credit wrongly given following a voluntary disclosure of an error in an earlier period should have been made for that earlier period.

Finally, the Court of Appeal in *C&E Comrs v DFS Furniture Company plc* [2004] STC 559 took the view that, in similar but not identical circumstances, the period to assess was the period current when the repayment was made.

Until these apparently conflicting judgments are resolved, Customs may in future need to protect tax in certain cases by making assessments in the alternative or by means of enforceable undertakings.

Where, following a court judgment against Customs on, for example, a liability point, Customs are appealing to have that judgment reversed, we would normally meet the claim of another taxpayer in a similar position and raise a recovery assessment to protect the revenue in the expectation that Customs' appeal will succeed. The Laura Ashley judgment may mean that such a protective assessment for an earlier period would be out of time under existing assessment time limit rules. In those circumstances, Customs will not pay a claim unless the claimant signs an undertaking to return any payment with interest in the event that the matter is finally determined in Customs' favour.

For the past, no corrective action is required, as any taxpayer who paid a recovery assessment made under VATA 1994 s 73(2) will have paid an amount that was properly due.

PLACE OF SUPPLY OF TRADING ALLOWANCES IN GREENHOUSE GAS EMISSIONS

26 October 2004. *Business Brief 28/04*

This Business Brief article announces Customs' policy in determining the place of supply of emissions allowances when traded across borders. This follows extensive discussions in Europe on the EU Emissions Trading Scheme (EU ETS) and ensures consistency with other member States, removing the possibility for double or no taxation.

BACKGROUND

The EU ETS sets out the rules for a scheme in greenhouse gas emission allowance trading within the Community. It is likely to come into force on 1 January 2005. However, in advance of that date all member States have agreed the rules for determining the place of supply of those allowances for VAT purposes. Whilst the UK initially considered that the place of supply of such supplies would come under the 'basic rule' (ie taxed in the country where the supplier is based), we have now agreed, as the result of representations made by businesses and discussions with other Member States, that for cross-border supplies of allowances, the place of supply should be the place where the customer belongs. This approach aligns our place of supply treatment with other Member States and therefore avoids instances of double taxation.

PLACE OF SUPPLY RULES

This only affects supplies of allowances when they are traded across borders; there is no change to the place of supply of supplies within a country (which continue to be taxed where the supplier is based, subject to the normal rules).

For supplies across borders, emissions trading in allowances will be treated as supplied where received (falling within Schedule 5 of the VAT Act 1994 and Article 9(2)(e) of the Sixth VAT Directive).

The place of supply of brokers' services needs to be determined separately. As the place of supply for cross-border transactions in allowances is where they are received, the broker's supply will take place where that broker's customer belongs, regardless of where the actual emissions allowances are sold. According to the normal rules, a broker is regarded as such when sufficient intermediation is performed.

Introduction is not sufficient-where the service is one of mere introduction, the supply will be seen in accordance with the basic rule ie where the introducer belongs.

EFFECTIVE DATE

This policy will be implemented from the date of this Business Brief. However, suppliers may continue to treat their supplies as basic rule for contracts entered into before this date.

CORRECTING LIABILITY ERRORS

26 October 2004. *Business Brief 28/04*

Business Brief 16/03 explained Customs' practice of announcing changes to policies and our interpretation of the law in Business Briefs. It went on to restate the policy set out in earlier Business Brief 14/94 concerning over- and underpayments arising when announced changes are not implemented by businesses. This Business Brief expands on that policy statement and deals more generally with the tax implications of changes in policy and in the interpretation of the law.

CHANGES IN POLICY

Generally, a change in Customs' policy is not applied retrospectively. Most changes will be announced in a Business Brief and in VAT Notes issued to all registered traders. They will be applied either from a current date or from some future date in order to give businesses time to prepare for the change or perhaps to provide for a transitional period so that businesses have an opportunity, for example, to benefit from an existing policy before a less beneficial policy is introduced.

CHANGES IN INTERPRETATION OF THE LAW

Significant changes in Customs' interpretation of the law will also be announced in a Business Brief and in VAT Notes issued to all registered traders. Unlike a prospective policy change, however, a change in our interpretation of the law, which will usually take place as a result of litigation, means that, in Customs' view, the relevant legislative provision should always have been applied in accordance with the revised interpretation.

For example, the High Court ruled in Kingscrest Associates Ltd [2002] STC 490 that the exemption in UK and EC law for care provided in hospitals and other similar establishments did not apply to non-medical care provided commercially in residential homes for children and young adults with learning difficulties. The effect of this decision was that certain supplies previously regarded as exempt were, and had always been, liable to VAT.

Changes in our interpretation of the law are therefore essentially retrospective. Where past declaration errors were made on returns on the basis of Customs' interpretation of the law, there are three general principles that will apply in correcting matters. These principles also reflect our views, supported by decisions in *Sunningdale Golf Club* [1997] V&DR 79 and *Barclays Bank PLC* LON/02/815 (decision number 18410) that businesses cannot take the benefit of a change in interpretation of the law without the burden.

(1) Customs will not expect or require businesses to correct past declaration errors, which were made on the basis of Customs interpretation of the law. Businesses will only be required to apply the new interpretation of the law from a current or future date, which we will announce. Where the new interpretation means that additional tax is due, this date will normally be after every registered trader has been informed of the change via VAT Notes.

(2) If, following a Customs announcement of its new interpretation of the law, a business chooses to correct historical errors we will accept the corrections provided the neutrality of the tax is respected and the business is no better off, and the Exchequer no worse off, than they would have been if the mistaken interpretation had not been made.

(3) Where Customs exercise a discretion not to collect arrears of tax due, including circumstances covered by the existing misdirection class concession, we shall do so in a manner consistent with the above principles.

Examples to illustrate how these general principles apply in particular circumstances are provided in an annexe to this Business Brief.

THE MISDIRECTION CLASS CONCESSION

The misdirection class concession says that:

> "If a Customs and Excise officer, with the full facts before him, has given a clear and unequivocal ruling on VAT in writing or, knowing the full facts, has misled a registered person to his detriment, any assessment of VAT due will be based on the correct ruling from the date the error was brought to the registered person's attention."

In operating the misdirection class concession Customs' policy is

- to apply the concession to net tax due in a period, ie output tax net of input tax and not to the tax undercharged;
- to apply the concession across periods so that where the output tax and the related input tax fall in different periods like consequences shall ensue as if the input tax and output tax fell in the same period; and
- not to apply the concession where the tax undercharged has or is to be charged on to customers.

This statement of practice applies to all cases where relief under the misdirection class concession is appropriate and is not limited to cases where there has been a mistaken interpretation of the law by Customs.

ANNEX

Example 1 Taxable supplies treated by Customs as exempt: businesses not previously registered for VAT

Where taxable supplies have been treated incorrectly by Customs as exempt, we will normally accept that the misdirection class concession applies and will only require the supplies to be taxable from a future date. This means that businesses will not usually be required to register in respect of previous supplies that were treated as exempt on the basis of Customs interpretation of the law at the time that the supply was made.

A business may choose, however, to register for VAT belatedly in respect of these supplies. In that event the business will normally be asked to complete a long first period return, covering the period from the effective date of registration to the end of the current period, or the date of deregistration if that is appropriate. This is the arrears period. Where taxable turnover is below the registration threshold, the backdating of any voluntary registration will be limited to three years and the long first period adjusted accordingly.

The long first period return must be completed showing any amounts due as output tax for the period covered as well as amounts claimed as input tax. Having chosen to register for VAT, the business must render accurate returns and declare the correct VAT liability. A return completed without fully accounting for output tax, on the basis that none was charged as a result of Customs' mistaken interpretation of the law, will be treated by Customs as a return in error.

Where the net tax position for the arrears period is that a repayment is due, Customs will repay this amount as a VAT credit due under section 25(3) of the VAT Act 1994.

Where the net tax position for the arrears period is that an amount is due to Customs and that amount has not been declared or not paid, we will remit the tax due under the misdirection class concession. The class concession here will be applied to net tax due (and not to output tax) and only across the whole of the arrears period.

A business that has registered belatedly may want to issue belated invoices to customers for VAT. Where, following the change in Customs' view of the law, a business issues additional invoices to recover undercharged VAT from his customers, the concession in the previous paragraph will not apply and he must account for and pay any VAT due. If additional invoices are issued to some customers and not others, relief under the misdirection class concession will only be available on amounts of VAT not charged, net of associated input tax.

Generally, then, there would in this example be no advantage to the taxpayer in being registered for VAT retrospectively unless large amounts of input tax were incurred in the arrears period on capital or overhead expenses.

Example 2 Taxable supplies treated as exempt; businesses registered for VAT

Where supplies have been incorrectly treated by Customs as exempt but are in fact taxable, once again we will normally accept that the misdirection class concession applies and only require that the supplies be treated as taxable from a future date.

However, a VAT registered trader may choose to correct the errors of the past by submitting a voluntary disclosure or repayment claim. Any such voluntary disclosure or repayment claim must be made in accordance with Customs' Notice 700/45 How to correct VAT errors and make adjustments or claims. All corrections must be made within time limits, and claims may be subject to an unjust enrichment defence, as detailed in the Notice.

Subject to the three year limitation period, any voluntary disclosure or repayment claim made should be for all prescribed accounting periods in which Customs' mistaken interpretation of the law has resulted in incorrect tax declarations or payments. Any voluntary disclosure or repayment claim must declare any amounts due as output tax as well as amounts being claimed as input tax and take account of all errors in the periods.

Should a voluntary disclosure for overdeclared tax or repayment claim fail to take into account all errors or all affected accounting periods, then Customs will set-off any amounts owed to us in other periods as a result of the same error.

Where the net tax position for all the periods is that a repayment is due, Customs will repay that amount.

Where, the net tax position is that an amount of VAT is due to us, which has not been paid, we will normally, by discretion, remit this tax, under the misdirection class concession. This means that where the errors are as a result of a taxable supply being treated as exempt, we will not assess for any net tax, ie the excess of output tax not charged over input tax that is deductible.

Where, despite Customs earlier view of the law, a business has treated the supplies all along as taxable and charged VAT to customers no corrective action will be appropriate. Where, following the change in Customs' view of the law, a business issues additional invoices to recover undercharged VAT from his customers, the concession in the previous paragraph will not apply and he must account for and pay any VAT due. If additional invoices are issued to some customers and not others, relief under the misdirection class concession will only be available on amounts of VAT not charged on additional invoices, net of associated input tax. The requirement that any corrections made must be made to all periods, will not apply where underdeclared tax is charged on and the underpayment voluntarily declared and paid to Customs.

Once again, it is likely that there is no material benefit to be gained by correcting the errors of the past unless the business has incurred substantial amounts of input tax on capital or overhead expenses.

Example 3 Exempt or taxable supplies treated as taxable at a higher rate, eg zero or lower rate treated as standard rate; voluntary disclosures from VAT registered traders.

Where supplies have been incorrectly treated by Customs as taxable but are in fact exempt, or are taxable at a lower rate, businesses may choose to correct the errors of the past. Any voluntary disclosure / repayment claim should be made as described in Customs' Notice 700/45 How to correct VAT errors and make adjustments or claims.

Subject to the three year limitation period, any voluntary disclosure / repayment claim should be for all prescribed accounting periods in which the liability error occurred, subject to time limits. When preparing a voluntary disclosure / repayment claim businesses must take account of all errors in the periods, declaring any input tax claimed in error and output tax overdeclared / overpaid.

Should a voluntary disclosure / repayment claim not take into account all errors or all affected accounting periods, then Customs will seek to set-off any amounts owed to us, for these periods against the amount claimed in other periods.

Where the net tax position for all the periods is that a repayment is due to the business, Customs will repay that amount, subject to repayment not unjustly enriching them. Unjust enrichment is dealt with in Notice 700/45 How to correct VAT errors and make adjustments or claims.

VAT AND PARTNERSHIP 'SHARES'

19 November 2004. *Business Brief 30/04*

BACKGROUND

Business Brief 21/04 clarified Customs' policy on share issues and partnership contributions following the European Court of Justice (ECJ) decision in KapHag Renditefonds (C-442/01). That Business Brief did not deal with the VAT position of transfers of partnership interests ('shares'). This Business Brief explains the VAT treatment of transactions involving the transfer of a partner's 'share'.

IS THE DISPOSAL OF A 'SHARE' IN A PARTNERSHIP A SUPPLY?

KapHag established that a partnership entity or the existing partners are making no supply when a new partner is admitted in return for making a capital contribution. The question arises whether the subsequent disposal by the partner of that 'share' in the partnership is a supply for VAT purposes. It is important to bear in mind that this 'share' is distinct from the assets that were contributed by the partner when they joined the partnership. Therefore, even though the selling price of the 'share' may be determined by the value of those assets, they are not the subject of the later sale, which has its own liability for VAT purposes.

Although the ECJ has not considered this type of transaction with respect to partnership 'shares', there have been a number of cases where it has given a decision in respect of transactions involving shares in companies. The cases of *Polysar* (C-60/90), *Harnas* and *Helm* (C-C-80/95), *Wellcome Trust* (C-155/94) and *Regie Dauphinoise* (C-306/94) have established that the mere acquisition and holding of shares in a company is not to be regarded as an economic activity. However, it has stated that transactions in shares or interests in companies and associations may constitute economic activity in three situations:

(a) Where the transactions constitute the direct, permanent and necessary extension of an economic activity.
(b) Where the transactions are effected in order to secure a direct or indirect involvement in the management of a company in which the holding is acquired.
(c) Where the transactions are effected as part of a commercial share-dealing activity.

Customs considers that the same principles apply to transactions involving partnership 'shares'. This means that in some circumstances the disposal of a partnership 'share' will not constitute a supply and in others it will.

Circumstances in which the disposal of a partnership 'share' will not constitute a supply

This list is not exhaustive. The most common situations in which the disposal of a partnership 'share' by a partner will not be a supply are likely to be:

(1) *The 'share' is disposed of for no consideration* – A 'share' in a partnership comprises services rather than goods. When services are transferred, assigned or otherwise disposed of for no consideration, they do not constitute any supply for VAT purposes.
(2) *The 'share' being sold was acquired simply as an investment* – Where a partner has acquired his 'share' merely to secure a share in any future profits and has had no involvement in running the partnership, the subsequent sale or assignment of that 'share' for consideration will not be an economic activity. This will not constitute any supply for VAT purposes.

Circumstances in which the disposal of a partnership 'share' will constitute a supply

Again, this list is not exhaustive. The most common situations in which the disposal of a partnership 'share' by a partner will be a supply are likely to be:

(1) *Where the partnership 'share' was acquired and disposed of as a direct extension of the partner's economic activities* – Where a partner is a taxable person in their own right, the

partnership 'share' may have been acquired in the course or furtherance of their own economic activities. If that is the case, the subsequent transfer or assignment of that 'share' for a consideration will also be economic activity of that taxable person. For example, the partner may have a business asset to be sold and, rather than selling the asset directly, may have contributed that asset into a partnership and sold the resultant partnership 'share' instead. The sale of that partnership 'share' will constitute a supply for VAT purposes.

(2) *Where the partnership 'share' was acquired in order to obtain an active role in the business of the partnership* – Where a partner is a taxable person in their own right and had acquired the partnership 'share' in order to actively participate in, or control, the business of the partnership, then the sale of that 'share' can be economic activity on the partner's part. The sale of the 'share' will constitute a supply for VAT purposes.

(3) *Where the partnership 'share' was acquired as part of a commercial partnership 'share-dealing' activity* – A partner who is a taxable person may have a business of dealing in partnership 'shares'. This will be economic activity on the partner's part. Sales or assignments of the partnership 'shares' that were acquired in the course of this activity that are for a consideration will constitute supplies for VAT purposes.

For the avoidance of any doubt, you should note that supplies of partnership 'shares' in the above circumstances cannot be disregarded by virtue of section 45(1) of the VAT Act 1994. As Business Brief 21/04 explained, the purpose of s.45 (1) is to ensure continuity by providing that changes in the composition of a partnership do not create the need for a partnership to deregister and re-register for VAT every time the partners change. It also makes it unnecessary to take account of any changes in the composition of the partnership when determining what supplies have been made or received by the partnership business. The section has no effect upon any supply that one of the partners may be making as a taxable person in their own right.

LIABILITY OF SUPPLIES OF PARTNERSHIP SHARES

In those circumstances where the disposal of a partnership 'share' is a supply, that supply will be an exempt financial service.

TREATMENT OF VAT ON ASSOCIATED PURCHASES

Where the disposal of an existing partnership 'share' is not a supply, the VAT incurred in connection with the disposal will normally not be input tax. Where the disposal is a supply, the related VAT will be input tax, but recovery will normally be fully restricted under the partial exemption rules as the supply is exempt. This is subject to the de minimis provisions (see VAT Notice 706 'Partial Exemption').

APPLICATION TO PAST TRANSACTIONS

This Business Brief clarifies existing policy and the above principles will be applied to all future transactions. Where a past transaction has been treated differently from the above and resulted in an underdeclaration Customs will take no further action. If a past transaction has been treated differently and resulted in an overdeclaration, businesses may use the voluntary disclosure procedure to reclaim the VAT. Any such claims will be subject to the 'three-year capping rules' and rules relating to the payment of statutory interest.

PARTIAL EXEMPTION: FLOOR-AREA BASED SPECIAL METHODS IN THE RETAIL SECTOR

15 December 2004. *Business Brief 34/04*

This Business Brief article sets out Customs' view on the use of floor-area based calculations in partial exemption special methods (special methods), particularly in the retail sector. No other businesses are affected.

This brief deals with questions put to Customs following the Tribunal's decision in the case of *Optika Ltd* VTD 18627 (Optika). There is no change of Customs' policy. Further information on partial exemption is available in Notice 706 'Partial Exemption'.

BACKGROUND

Optika, a retail optician, appealed against Customs' rejection of their proposed floor-area based special method. The Tribunal agreed with Customs because, in Optika's case, a floor-area based special method did not give a fair and reasonable result. A method is likely to be fair and reasonable if it:

- Can be operated by the business,
- Can be checked by Customs, and
- Produces a fair result.

In the right circumstances, floor-area based methods will meet all these conditions and Customs will approve them.

FLOOR-AREA BASED SPECIAL METHODS

Floor-area based special methods are likely to be acceptable when:

- Most of the business's VAT bearing costs relate to their premises, and
- Most of the floor-area of those premises is used for either wholly taxable or wholly exempt activities, with only minor areas relating to both.

FLOOR-AREA IN THE RETAIL SECTOR-THE IMPACT OF OPTIKA

Floor-area based special methods are seldom fair and reasonable for retailers. The following features from the Optika case illustrate this:

* NOTIONAL SPLITS OF 'MIXED USE' AREAS: Few areas of Optika's premises were exclusively used for taxable or exempt activities. Optika's proposals therefore required notional splits of mixed-use floor-areas in order to create any workable calculation. Methods that require significant notional splits are unacceptable due to the inherent uncertainties in making and checking them.

* WEIGHTING OF FLOOR AREAS: The method proposed by Optika required a weighting of floor areas with those at the front of the premises having far greater impact on the amount of tax deductible. Optika argued this reflected a system of weightings (known as zoning) commonly used by landlords to calculate rental charges. However, just because zoning is used to calculate an overall rent, this does not mean that more is charged for some areas than for others. Each rental is a single supply covering the entire premises.

* USE OF RETAIL AREAS: Optika's proposals assumed that the use made of the retail area and the shop front related to their taxable products. However the shop front attracted customers to purchase all of their products and much of the selling of exempt products took place in the retail area. Consequently the shop front and retail area are related to both taxable and exempt sales. Because the proposals were based on a mistaken assumption, they were unacceptable.

Many retailers share some or all of these features, either generally or in specific floor-area based special method proposals. Where this occurs floor-area based special methods will not be approved.

FLOOR-AREA IN THE RETAIL SECTOR—GENERAL

The sale of exempt products is often an important and consistent part of the trading activities of retailers, making a significant contribution to profits. For example when finance or insurance is standardly offered and actively marketed on goods being sold. Many retailers advertise and sell both taxable and exempt products in a large proportion of their premises. Where these factors are present, floor-area is unlikely to prove capable of providing a good basis for a special method.

Customs will refuse to approve any method that includes one or more of the features confirmed as unacceptable in the Optika case. Customs will seek to amend or replace any such existing methods that come to light. Businesses who feel that their current special method might not be fair and reasonable, based on the content of this brief, should contact their local VAT office or Customs' National Advice Service.

SUPPLIES OF NURSERY AND CRÈCHE FACILITIES BY A CHARITY

10 February 2005. *Business Brief 2/05*

This Business Brief article is issued to clarify Customs' position on the business status of supplies of nursery and crèche facilities where those supplies are made by a charity. This issue first arose as a result of the High Court case of *Yarburgh Children's Trust* (see Business Brief 4/03) and has recently been tested again in the High Court case of *St Paul's Community Project Ltd*.

In the earlier case of *Yarburgh*, the Court decided that the charity was not making supplies by way of business. Despite that decision, Customs' position remained that the provision of nursery and crèche facilities in such circumstances was a business activity for VAT purposes. However, in the more recent case of St Paul's, the Court's decision has again gone in favour of the charity. The Court found that the intrinsic nature of the enterprise was not the carrying on of a business, identifying the distinguishing features as the social concern for the welfare of disadvantaged children, lack of commerciality in setting fees and the overall intention simply to cover costs.

Customs do not agree that these features point to the activities being non-business because we consider that the charity is making supplies of services for consideration in much the same way as a commercial nursery. However, taking into account all the circumstances in this case, Customs have decided not to appeal further.

This means Customs will now accept that the provision of nursery and crèche facilities by charities, along the same lines as those in *Yarburgh Children's Trust* and *St Paul's Community Project Ltd*, is not a business activity for VAT purposes.

BACKGROUND

Both *Yarburgh Children's Trust* and *St Paul's Community Project Ltd* are charities which undertake to provide nursery and crèche facilities for pre-school age children as part of their charitable objectives. Both organisations charge fees for their services, which are set at a level designed to ensure that they merely cover their costs. They both undertook construction of new nursery premises. Such supplies would normally be subject to VAT but there are provisions in UK law which allow construction work to be zero-rated where buildings are used by a charity otherwise than in the course of business. Zero-rating can be beneficial to charities, if they undertake exempt activities and the amount of VAT they recover would be heavily restricted. Customs denied zero-rating on the grounds that these charities were making business supplies. The High Court has taken the opposing view that neither charity is in business for VAT purposes.

CUSTOMS' POLICY

It remains Customs' long standing policy that a business activity is possible even in the absence of a profit motive. Customs believe that this approach is consistent with UK and EC legislation and is supported by a number of decisions of the UK and European Courts. Many charities with activities not motivated by profit and whose fees are subsidised by public funds or donations benefit from such activities being business for VAT purposes, because they are able to recover VAT incurred in relation to those activities. It would not be beneficial for the charity sector as a whole if charitable activities were all regarded as non-business, as it would deny them recovery of input tax. In cases that are not broadly in line with *St Paul's* or *Yarburgh*, Customs shall continue to apply the business test, in order to determine whether the supplies concerned are being made by way of business.

WHAT CONSTITUTES A BUSINESS ACTIVITY FOR VAT PURPOSES?

As neither UK nor EC legislation has provided an exhaustive definition or test for determining if an activity is business, the meaning of business and economic activity has emerged from a body of case law. This has given rise to the business test, which consists of six elements or indicators that the Courts have seen as being characteristic of a business. These are not a checklist and a business may have some, but not all, of the features indicated. Instead they are a set of tools designed to help compare activities where there is some uncertainty about their nature with features of activities that are clearly business. In most cases, it will be clear that an activity is business but, where difficulties arise, Customs will apply this business test. The elements of this test were set out in Business Brief 4/03 and are reproduced below.

- Is the activity a serious undertaking earnestly pursued? (This considers whether the activity is carried on for business or daily work rather than pleasure or daily enjoyment.)
- Is the activity an occupation or function that is actively pursued with reasonable or recognisable continuity? (When considering this test one should consider how frequently the supplies will be made.)
- Does the activity have a certain measure of substance in terms of the quarterly or annual value of taxable supplies made?
- Is the activity conducted in a regular manner and on sound and recognised business principles?
- Is the activity predominately concerned with the making of taxable supplies for a consideration? (This has in many instances been seen as the most important and arguably the most problematic indicator. In the appeal of The Institute of Chartered Accountants England & Wales, the House of Lords found that the test must be read as asking 'what is the real nature of the activity' ie is the real nature of the activity the making of taxable supplies for consideration or is it something else?)
- Are the taxable supplies that are being made of a kind which, subject to differences of detail, are commonly made by those who seek to profit from them?

CLARIFICATION OF THE LIABILITY OF THE SUPPLY OF LIFTS TO EDUCATIONAL INSTITUTIONS

22 February 2005. *Business Brief 3/05*

This Business Brief sets out Customs' policy on the VAT treatment of lifts installed in educational institutions.

BACKGROUND

Educational institutions which have charitable status, such as grant-maintained schools and universities, can receive the supply and installation of lifts to facilitate the movement of disabled staff and pupils between floors in certain buildings at the zero rate of VAT. For such supplies to qualify for zero-rating, the building must be used by the educational institution for the provision of a permanent or temporary residence or a day-centre for disabled people. The relevant legislation is Items 17 and 18 to Group 12 of Schedule 8 of the VAT Act 1994.

As a consequence of comments made by the High Court in 1997 in the Help the Aged appeal (CO2399), Customs formed the view that educational institutions could be regarded as day-centres providing care for disabled people and therefore the installation of lifts in their non-residential buildings could be zero-rated under the above provisions, providing all other conditions were met.

Customs subsequently reconsidered our understanding of the comments made by the High Court, which concerned the interpretation of a different piece of legislation, and decided our original view of them was incorrect. Whilst having a duty of care, especially to disabled people, educational institutions, generally, do not provide care in a day-centre and the High Court's comments did not suggest that they do. Customs' policy therefore reverted to the scope of the zero-rating being limited to the supply of lifts installed in residential accommodation.

However, as a concession, where an educational institution could demonstrate that they had made a decision to proceed with the purchase and installation of a lift in non-residential accommodation before 1 January 2004, on the basis of our former policy, then zero-rating would apply. Additionally, Customs agreed that any lifts zero-rated in this way could also benefit from the zero-rating of their future repair and maintenance under the provisions of Item 5 of Group 12 to Schedule 8 of the VAT Act 1994.

Unfortunately, the changes in policy were not widely publicised at the time and we have recently been made aware that not all those concerned were aware of them. Customs have therefore decided to publicise the change of policy by means of this Business Brief. Customs have also decided to extend the transitional arrangements so that where a contract for the installation of a lift in non-residential accommodation has been entered into before 31 March 2005; we accept that the supply can be zero-rated providing all other conditions have been met. Where the installation of a lift has been zero-rated under these arrangements, subsequent supplies of repair and maintenance of that lift can also be zero-rated.

Where a contract for the installation of a lift in non-residential accommodation is entered into after that date the supply of installation services and any subsequent supplies of repair and maintenance will be standard-rated.

Where a supplier has accounted for VAT on past supplies and is satisfied that all other conditions have been met, subject to the statutory time limits, they may make a claim for the overpaid VAT in one of the following ways:

(1) If the net value of the total adjustments is £2,000 or less, suppliers may amend their VAT account and include the value of the adjustment on their current VAT return.

(2) If the net value of the total adjustments is more than £2,000, a separate claim for payment should be submitted to the local Business Advice Centre (suppliers cannot make this adjustment on their VAT returns).

Both of the above methods and how to make a claim are explained in VAT Notice 700/45 'How to correct VAT errors & make adjustments or claims'.

NB: Customs may reject a claim on the grounds that payment would unjustly enrich a supplier. For example, this may happen if the supplier is unable or does not intend to pass on the repayment to his customer. Further details can be found in VAT Notice 700/45.

This Business Brief does not apply to lift installations in those buildings where an educational institution provides permanent or temporary residence, which remains zero-rated, provided all other conditions are met.

HOT TAKE-AWAY FOOD

4 April 2005. *Business Brief 9/05*

This Business Brief clarifies Customs policy on the treatment of hot take-away food in light of recent VAT Tribunal decisions. It includes some minor amendments to policy, and replaces the guidance previously published in Business Brief 26/02.

Most food is zero-rated for VAT purposes. But hot take-away food and drink is standard-rated, whether sold from a traditional take-away, supermarket or any other outlet. Standard rating applies where the supplier's main intention in heating the food is to enable it to be consumed hot or warm (regardless of whether, in practice, the food is always consumed hot or warm). Standard rating applies irrespective of the customer's intention, the place of consumption or whether the food is collected or delivered.

CAN HOT FOOD BE ZERO-RATED?

You can only zero-rate hot food if your main purpose in heating the food is other than to enable it to be consumed hot or warm. For example, newly baked bread is often warm when sold, but is not normally heated for the purpose of enabling it to be consumed hot or warm.

In some cases suppliers have stated that they have other reasons for heating food and supplying it hot or warm. Supplies in such cases may qualify for zero-rating, but only where the circumstances (ie the nature of the product and the way in which it is stored, displayed, advertised, packaged and supplied) support the contention that the supplier's main purpose is other than to enable the food to be consumed hot. For example, items like chips, hot dogs, burgers and baked potatoes are always standard rated when sold hot because they are clearly intended to be eaten hot.

HOW DO I KNOW IF I CAN ZERO-RATE HOT FOOD?

You can only zero-rate hot food if your main reason for heating the food is other than to enable it to be consumed hot or warm. Any such claims must be consistent with the circumstances under which the hot food is supplied (see below). It is important to consider all of your reasons for heating the food before deciding on the VAT liability of your supplies. Often you may have more than one purpose in heating the food, in which case you must decide which is the dominant purpose.

On the basis of Tribunal and court findings, Customs consider the following to be relevant indicators:

Type of outlet—If advertised as a take-away food outlet, supplies of hot food will be standard-rated.

What happens to the food between the time it is cooked or heated and the time it is handed to the customer—If efforts are made to keep it hot, this may be an indicator for standard rating, whereas if it is left to cool naturally for a period of time this may be an indicator for zero-rating.

Type of packaging used—If food is packaged to retain heat, this would be an indicator for standard rating. However, the reverse does not necessarily apply, since food intended for immediate consumption will often be sold in packaging that is not heat retentive.

Availability of condiments, napkins and utensils-This would be an indicator for standard rating.

The way in which the food is advertised and promoted, including in-store signage and any wording shown on packaging.

Food hygiene regulations-Customs accept that in some cases food may be kept hot partly for the purpose of complying with food hygiene regulations. However, the requirement to comply with these regulations will often not be an aim in itself for the supplier, but merely a consequence of supplying food for consumption whilst hot or warm. If this is the case, then the supplies will be standard rated.

Palatability—If an item is generally accepted to be unpalatable when cold, this would be an indicator for standard rating. However, the reverse does not necessarily apply-The fact that an item remains palatable when cold does not preclude the possibility that it has been heated for the purpose of enabling it to be consumed hot.

JUDGMENT OF THE EUROPEAN COURT OF JUSTICE (ECJ) IN THE CASE OF ARTHUR ANDERSEN & CO ACCOUNTANTS (C-472/03)

18 May 2005. *Business Brief 11/05*

On 3 March 2005, the ECJ released its judgment in the case of Arthur Andersen. This Business Brief article outlines the findings of the Court, details how HM Revenue & Customs (HMRC) interpret these findings in relation to the current UK VAT exemption for insurance-related services and explains the position for businesses that consider they may be affected by the judgment.

The case, which was referred to the ECJ by the Netherlands Supreme Court, concerned the VAT liability of certain 'back office' services provided by Andersen Consulting Management Consultants (ACMC) to a life insurance company. ACMC used qualified personnel to undertake most of the activities related to insurance on behalf of the insurer including the issuing, management and cancellation of policies, the management of claims and, in most cases, taking decisions that bound the insurer to enter into insurance contracts.

The question put to the ECJ was whether such 'back office' activities carried out for an insurance company were exempt from VAT under Article 13B(a) of the Sixth Directive as "related services performed by insurance brokers and insurance agents".

To fall within the VAT exemption, ACMC had to qualify as either insurance brokers or insurance agents. The ECJ held that the essential characteristic of insurance brokers was that they had complete freedom as to choice of insurer for their clients and that, although insurance agents were tied to a particular insurer, their essential characteristic was that they introduced prospective customers to that insurer. As ACMC did not qualify on either count, their services were taxable at the standard rate.

HMRC's view is that the judgment means the UK VAT exemption for insurance-related services in Group 2 of Schedule 9 to the VAT Act 1994 is currently drawn too widely and, to bring it into line with the judgment, it will need to be amended.

UK law currently provides exemption for certain insurance administration and claims handling services including, for example, the provision of claims handling services by loss adjusters under delegated authority and the administration of policies on behalf of the insurer. Following the ECJ judgment, however, such services should only fall within the VAT exemption for insurance-related services where the provider had also previously introduced the policyholder to the insurer.

HMRC believe that the judgment does not preclude exemption where the provider does not itself have direct contact with the customer, provided that it sub-contracts the introductory service to a sub-agent, and there is a direct contractual link between the principal agent and the agent providing the introductory service. However, the power to bind the insurer to enter into contracts is not in itself enough to gain exemption.

Implementation of the judgment will lead to VAT becoming chargeable on many of the outsourced services currently provided to insurers. Where insurers use these outsourced services to provide exempt insurance services within the EU, this VAT will be irrecoverable.

HMRC are currently meeting insurance industry representative bodies and providers of the affected services to discuss the impact of this judgment. Following these preliminary discussions, there will be a 12 week formal consultation period on how the judgment is to be implemented in the UK, the proposed changes to UK legislation and the impact implementation will have on the affected industries. It is important to note, however, that the ECJ judgment is binding on member states and the consultation will therefore focus on how and when that implementation will take place. It is intended that the consultation document should be published in July 2005.

No action will be taken to change UK law or policy until formal consultation is complete. In the meantime, businesses can rely on UK law and policy on insurance-related services as it is currently explained in HMRC guidance and notices. There will be no change in the scope of the UK VAT exemption for insurance-related services until UK law has been amended.

If, however, you consider that your business is affected by the judgment, you do not have to wait for the UK law to be amended but are able to rely directly on EU law as outlined by the ECJ in its decision. This means that, whilst you do not have to do so, you can, if you wish:

– apply the revised VAT liability to your services from a current date; or
– make an adjustment retrospectively.

Information on how to make any adjustments to VAT previously paid can be found in VAT Notice 700/45 'How to correct VAT errors and make adjustments or claims'. Additional information on correcting VAT liability errors can be found in Customs' Business Brief 28/04

ZERO RATING FOR PROTECTED BUILDINGS—DEFINITION OF GARAGE

18 May 2005. *Business Brief 11/05*

This Business Brief article sets out HM Revenue & Customs' (HMRC) revised policy on what constitutes a "garage" for the purpose of the zero ratings relating to listed buildings which are dwellings.

It follows a decision of the VAT & Duties Tribunal in the case of *Grange Builders (Quainton) Ltd* (LON/02/982).

BACKGROUND

The law provides zero rating for approved alterations to a listed building designed to remain as or become a dwelling or number of dwellings and also for the first grant, by the person reconstructing such a building, of a major interest in the building or part of the building, or its site.

For the purpose of the zero rating, such a building can include a garage (occupied together with the dwelling), either constructed at the same time as the building or, where the building has been substantially reconstructed, at the same time as that reconstruction.

HMRC have always considered that in order for the alteration works to a garage to qualify for zero rating, it was necessary for the garage to have been constructed as a garage.

Therefore HMRC would not have seen the zero rate as applying to the alteration of a building (or part of a building) that was in use as a garage if it had not been constructed as a garage at the same time as the dwelling had been constructed (or substantially reconstructed).

THE TRIBUNAL DECISION

The Tribunal found that, for the alteration of a garage to qualify for zero rating, the building does not have to have been constructed as a garage or used as a garage since the time of the construction (or substantial reconstruction) of the dwelling. It held that a small timber-framed barn that was listed as part of the dwelling and in use as a garage was part of the listed dwelling for the purpose of the zero rating because:

- the barn had been constructed at the same time as the listed dwelling; and
- it had been used as a garage for a significant period before being altered.

HM REVENUE & CUSTOMS' REVISED POLICY

HMRC now accept that, provided a garage is in use as a garage before the alteration or reconstruction takes place and continues to be used as one afterwards, it is not necessary for the garage to have been constructed as a garage (ie as an enclosure for the storage of motor vehicles). It can also have been constructed as something different eg a barn.

The other criteria for zero rating must still be met; these are:

- listing (the garage must be listed, either in its own right or through the deeming provisions of planning law);
- occupation (the garage must be occupied together with the dwelling); and
- time of construction (the garage must have been either constructed at the same time as the listed dwelling or, where the dwelling has been substantially reconstructed, at the same time as that reconstruction).

VAT TREATMENT OF PAST SUPPLIES

Where a supplier has accounted for VAT on past supplies, they may make a claim for the overpaid VAT, subject to the three-year statutory time limits, in one of the following ways:

(a) If the net value of the total adjustments is £2,000 or less, suppliers may amend their VAT account and include the value of the adjustment on their current VAT return.

(b) If the net value of the total adjustments is more than £2,000, a separate claim for payment should be submitted to the local Business Advice Centre (suppliers cannot make this adjustment on their VAT returns).

Both of the above methods and how to make a claim are explained in VAT Notice 700/45 'How to correct VAT errors and make adjustments or claims'.

NB: HMRC may reject a claim on the grounds that payment would unjustly enrich a supplier. For example, this may happen if the supplier is unable or does not intend to pass on the repayment to his customer. Further details can be found in VAT Notice 700/45.

ALIGNING VAT ACCOUNTING PERIODS

15 June 2005. *Business Brief 12/05*

This Business Brief article explains and further publicises HM Revenue & Customs' existing policy on the use of the power to align VAT accounting periods.

BACKGROUND

HM Revenue & Customs continue to be concerned about situations in which businesses 'stagger' their VAT accounting periods in order to gain an unjustified and unintended cash flow benefit at the expense of the revenue.

One familiar example is the routing of export sales through a subsidiary which is outside the VAT group, or main VAT registration. In these cases, the export company has zero rated outputs and makes monthly repayment claims. By contrast, output tax on the supply to the subsidiary is standard rated and only brought to account by the parent or other associated company once a quarter. There is, accordingly, a cashflow benefit to the corporate group.

HM REVENUE & CUSTOMS' POLICY ON ALIGNMENT

HM Revenue & Customs have a discretionary power in Regulation 25 (VAT Regulations 1995) to align VAT periods between the associated businesses, thereby removing the cashflow benefit. They may exercise that power by either withdrawing existing permission for monthly periods or by directing a variation to accounting periods. HM Revenue & Customs intend to continue to exercise this power where there is little or no commercial rationale for the VAT period 'stagger' between the associated businesses besides obtaining the cashflow advantage. They may do so, notwithstanding that the usual policy for businesses expecting to make regular claims for repayment of VAT in other factual situations is to allow monthly returns.

There is no intention to use these powers except in cases where a significant cash flow advantage arises and there is a need to protect the revenue.

HM REVENUE & CUSTOMS' USE OF THE REGULATION 25 POWERS

There is no right of appeal to the VAT and Duties Tribunal against the use of the regulation 25 powers. However, the use of the power is subject to judicial review and new guidance shortly to be issued to staff will emphasise the need for exercise of the powers to be proportionate and to take into account all relevant information. That guidance will be available soon through the normal channels.

CLARIFICATION OF THE VAT POSITION OF SHARE ISSUES FOLLOWING THE EUROPEAN COURT OF JUSTICE DECISION IN KRETZTECHNIK

15 June 2005. *Business Brief 12/05*

Note—See also Business Brief 21/05, published 23 November 2005, for further information.

This Business Brief article is an update on HM Revenue & Customs' position on the VAT treatment of share issues and subsequent input tax recovery, following the decision in *Kretztechnik AG v Finanzamt Linz* (Case C-465/03).

THE DECISION

On 26 May 2005, the European Court of Justice (ECJ) gave its judgment in *Kretztechnik*. The ECJ had been asked to rule upon whether or not a first issue of shares by a public limited company is a supply and whether or not the VAT incurred on the costs of such an issue is deductible input tax. The judgment endorsed the earlier Opinion given by the Advocate General on 24 February 2005, ruling that such an issue is not a supply and that the VAT incurred on the costs is recoverable to the extent that the company's outputs are taxable transactions.

REVISED TREATMENT OF SHARE ISSUE TRANSACTIONS

Until now, HM Revenue & Customs' treatment of share issues has been guided by the Court of Appeal decision in *Trinity Mirror plc v C&E Commissioners* [2001] STC 192. This had established that the issue of shares in the UK by a company for the purpose of financing its business was an exempt supply under Item 6 of Group 5 of Schedule 9 to the VAT Act 1994. Any input tax that was attributable to the costs of making the issue was therefore generally not deductible. *Kretztechnik* has now established that this treatment is incorrect.

Companies that make a first issue of shares in circumstances that are the same as those in Kretztechnik's case are now entitled to recover the input tax incurred on the costs of the issue to the extent that they make taxable supplies. Therefore companies with wholly taxable outputs will be entitled to recover all of the relevant input tax, while those with both exempt and taxable outputs will be entitled to recover a proportion in accordance with their partial exemption method. Claims for input tax in respect of past share issues will be accepted subject to the three-year 'capping' rules. Notice 700/45 'How to correct VAT errors and make adjustments or claims' gives detailed guidance on capping and claim procedures.

There are a number of other situations in which a company may issue shares where the circumstances will differ greatly from those which existed in *Kretztechnik*. In particular, a share issue may take place as part of a company merger, demerger or other restructuring. HM Revenue & Customs are taking legal advice on the extent to which *Kretztechnik* applies to these other share issue situations and further guidance will be issued to businesses after this advice has been received. Any claims for repayment received in the interim will be acknowledged but not processed until this advice has been received.

TRANSACTIONS INVOLVING ISSUES OF FINANCIAL INSTRUMENTS AND SECURITIES OTHER THAN SHARES

Businesses may raise capital through the issue of financial instruments or securities other than shares, like bonds, debentures or loan notes. *Kretztechnik* was concerned solely with issues of shares and the ECJ did not comment upon the extent to which the same principles would apply to other types of issues. HM Revenue & Customs are obtaining legal advice on whether or not other issue transactions are affected and will issue further guidance after the position has been reviewed. Any claims for repayment received in the interim will be acknowledged but not processed until this advice has been received.

LANDLORD INDUCEMENTS TO TENANTS ENTERING LEASES

15 June 2005. *Business Brief 12/05*

This Business Brief article provides revised guidance on the VAT status of inducement payments by landlords to tenants. It replaces earlier guidance in Business Brief 04/03, dated 27 May 2003.

BUSINESS BRIEF 04/03

Business Brief 04/03 set out Customs' policy following the European Court of Justice (ECJ) and High Court decisions in the case of Trinity Mirror plc (formerly Mirror Group plc).

In paragraph 26 of the ECJ's judgment, it was held that a "tenant who undertakes, even in return for a payment from the landlord, solely to become a tenant and pay the rent does not, so far as that action is concerned, make a supply of services to the landlord". The High Court subsequently held that paragraph 26 of the ECJ judgment is narrowly drawn, and Business Brief 04/03 sought to give guidance on that.

In line with the High Court ruling, Business Brief 04/03 advised that "a prospective tenant receiving an inducement payment would make a taxable supply by affording the landlord the advantage of being bound by the lease obligations the tenant has to fulfil." In effect, this meant any such obligations other than to pay the rent (eg to redecorate the demised area every five years) would be sufficient to make the inducement payment consideration for a taxable supply.

CHANGE OF POLICY

Following representations from and detailed discussions with various bodies, HM Revenue & Customs now accept that lease obligations, to which tenants are normally bound, do not constitute supplies for which inducement payments on entering leases are consideration.

HM Revenue & Customs believe that the majority of such payments are therefore likely to be outside the scope of VAT as they are no more than inducements to tenants to take leases and to observe the obligations in them. There will be a taxable supply only where a payment is linked to benefits a tenant provides outside normal lease terms. However, merely putting such a benefit as an obligation in a lease will not mean it ceases to be a taxable transaction.

It is considered that this change of policy now effectively puts inducement payments on a similar VAT footing to rent free periods, in being mainly outside the scope of VAT and only a taxable consideration when directly linked to a specific benefit supplied by a tenant to a landlord.

Examples of taxable benefits by tenants that may be supplied in return for such inducements are:

- Carrying out building works to improve the property by undertaking necessary repairs or upgrading the property
- Carrying out fitting-out or refurbishment works for which the landlord has responsibility and is paying the tenant to undertake.
- Acting as anchor tenant

HM Revenue & Customs accept that this is a difficult area where the undertakings of landlords and tenants can change a number of times in the course of negotiating a tenancy. HM Revenue & Customs will therefore seek as much documentation as possible before reaching a decision. HM Revenue & Customs will not assume that there has been a supply and agree that less specific indicators do not determine the issue. For example, publicity indicating that Company X is to take a lease in a development does not, in itself, determine that the company is an anchor tenant.

Equally, undertakings to use improved materials as part of continuous repairs under a tenant repairing lease would not constitute a taxable benefit to the landlord under the first example above.

PAST TRANSACTIONS

The policy change referred to above may mean that there have been certain cases where tax has been charged wrongly in respect of landlord inducements under the guidelines in Business Brief 04/03.

Tenants who have wrongly declared output tax on inducements received are not obliged to adjust their VAT position. However, if they choose to, then, subject to the three-year capping provisions, they should proceed in accordance with VAT Notice 700/45 'How to Correct Errors and make adjustments or claims'.

Option 1

In accordance with paragraph 3.4 of Notice 700/45, where both the tenant and the landlord are registered for VAT, and provided they both agree, tenants may raise credit notes to their landlords and both parties would then adjust their VAT account.

Option 2

Alternatively where the landlord is not registered for VAT, tenants may choose to make a claim under Section 80 of the VAT Act 1994 for overpaid tax. Any such claim would be subject to the three-year capping provisions and the unjust enrichment defence. Sections 5 and 14 of Notice 700/45 refer.

Note that if past transactions are revisited there may be implications as regards deductible input tax-see below.

In all cases where tenants choose to correct past transactions it will be necessary to:

- review the attribution of any input tax incurred on costs, where that attribution was based on those costs being cost components of the taxable supply now being reversed out, and make any resultant adjustments, and
- revisit their partial exemption calculations for the prescribed and longer periods involved as necessary.

Whichever method tenants choose to correct the incorrect treatment of inducements as supplies, landlords must reduce their input tax deductions in respect of the inducements to the extent that they ultimately recovered or were entitled to recover input tax previously. This could also require partial exemption calculations to be revisited if an inputs based method is used or to determine whether de-minimis limits are exceeded.

Commentary—*De Voil Indirect Tax Service* **V4.111.**

BELATED NOTIFICATION OF AN OPTION TO TAX LAND AND BUILDINGS—CLARIFICATION OF HM REVENUE & CUSTOMS' POLICY

5 July 2005. *Business Brief 13/05*

This Business Brief clarifies HM Revenue & Customs' (HMRC) policy in relation to the exercise of their discretion to accept a belated notification of an option to tax land and buildings. In particular, it explains the distinction between a belated notification and a retrospective or backdated option. This clarification is given following a rise in the number of attempts to notify options to tax that are retrospective or backdated.

WHO IS AFFECTED?

All those who seek acknowledgement of a decision to opt to tax (sometimes known as an election to waive exemption) outside the 30-day time limit.

BACKGROUND

There are two distinct stages in the process of opting to tax. The first is making the decision to opt, the 'election'. The second is notifying HMRC of that decision, in writing, within 30 days of the date that the decision was made.

Of course, HMRC must be satisfied that the trader was legally entitled to opt to tax. If a trader has made previous exempt supplies of the property, they may require our prior written permission to opt to tax. If permission is required, the trader cannot make a valid election until our permission has been received. The circumstances when permission is required are detailed in VAT Notice 742A Opting to tax land and buildings, Section 5.

RETROSPECTIVE OR BACKDATED OPTIONS

The option has effect from the day on which the election is made or any later day specified in the election. This means that no option to tax can take effect from a date prior to the date on which the trader decided to make the election. This would be a backdated or retrospective option and HMRC has no discretion under the law to accept or acknowledge that it is valid.

BELATED NOTIFICATION OF AN OPTION

However, HMRC has discretion to accept a notification of an option to tax later than the prescribed time limit of 30 days after the decision to opt was made. The discretion is designed to cover situations where a trader has genuinely made the decision to opt to tax, but has failed to notify it to HMRC in time. Before considering whether to exercise this discretion, we would need to be satisfied that the decision was made on the date stated in the written notification.

EXERCISING THE DISCRETION

HMRC will usually accept a belated notification if a trader provides evidence, such as the minutes of a Board or management meeting, or correspondence referring to the decision. However, we accept that this is sometimes not available, so in its absence we would normally accept a statement from the responsible person, plus evidence that

- all the relevant facts have been given;
- output tax has been properly charged and accounted for from the date of the supposed election; and
- input tax recovery in respect of the land or building is consistent with the trader having made taxable supplies of it.

There may be other circumstances where we would accept a belated notification, but this would depend on the individual circumstances of the case.

Conversely, HMRC may not accept that a decision to opt was taken, even when the above conditions are met, if for example—

- there has been correspondence concerning or investigation into the liability of supplies of the property in question since the supposed date of the option, and no mention of the option to tax was made;
- the trader or his representative has previously put forward an alternative explanation for the charging of output tax (for example, that the supply was not of land and buildings, or was of a sports facility).

Moreover, HMRC reserves the right to refuse to accept the belated notification if to do so would produce an unfair result, or if the exercise of the discretion was sought in connection with a tax avoidance scheme.

PARTIAL EXEMPTION—TRIBUNAL DECISION IN NATIONAL PROVIDENT INSTITUTION (NPI)

28 July 2005. *Business Brief 14/05*

This Business Brief gives the Commissioners' views on the VAT and Duties Tribunal's decision in the *NPI* appeal (Decision No 18944) that was released on 18 February 2005.

The *NPI* case concerned recovery of input tax by an insurance company that made supplies of securities outside the EU. There is no change to the Commissioners' policy, which is explained below.

BACKGROUND

NPI made three sorts of supply for VAT purposes—

(a) taxable supplies of property (which it had opted to tax);

(b) exempt supplies of insurance (pensions, life assurance and annuities), exempt supplies of securities in the UK and in the EU; and
(c) specified supplies of securities outside the EU.

NPI was entitled to recover input tax on overheads that related to its taxable supplies and to its specified supplies. NPI used the standard method of partial exemption (PE), which determines the VAT recovery only in respect of taxable supplies. It is well established that the recovery of VAT on specified supplies has to be determined separately and before the recovery of VAT on taxable supplies.

Apportionment of input tax is therefore carried out in two stages—

(i) between specified supplies and other supplies (both taxable and exempt) on the basis of the relative use of input tax in making each category of supply; and
(ii) between taxable supplies and exempt supplies on the basis of the standard method or an approved special method.

Subject to the Commissioners' approval, these two stages can be combined into a single calculation, always provided that this achieves a fair and reasonable result.

NPI sought recovery of input tax through a single combined calculation on the basis of values. The Commissioners had not approved that calculation and did not consider that it achieved a fair and reasonable result. The Commissioners therefore applied a two-stage calculation using firstly a staff count and secondly values.

THE TRIBUNAL'S DECISION

The Tribunal reviewed the evidence presented and concluded that there was no demonstrable link between input tax on overheads and staff numbers because the main costs were consultant's fees and the like. It also found that the headcount had been estimated and was thus unreliable. The Tribunal therefore concluded that the Commissioners' method was unsafe. In the circumstances, since no other method had been put to the Tribunal, it held that the use of residual input tax in making specified supplies should be determined according to the proportion that the value of specified supplies bore to the value of all supplies.

THE COMMISSIONERS' VIEWS

The Commissioners have decided not to appeal because the decision was made on the facts of the case. They do not consider that it has any wider application for that reason.

Notwithstanding the Tribunal's views in the *NPI* case, the Commissioners consider that sales of securities will normally be distortive when they are included with other sorts of supply in a combined values-based calculation. This will, for example, be the case when the supplies of securities consume proportionately less by way of taxed overheads for each £1 in value than other supplies. This will work unfairly against the taxpayer when the recovery rate for securities transactions is less than that for insurance transactions and against HMRC when it is greater. For any values-based calculation to secure a fair and reasonable apportionment, there must be a proportionate and broadly similar link between the use of taxed overheads and the values of all the supplies in the PE calculation. Such a link would assume that, pound for pound, premium income consumed the same amount of taxed overheads as sales of securities. The Commissioners consider that will rarely be the true position.

USE OF VALUES-BASED PROXIES FOR "USE"

There is no change in the Commissioners' policy. Any proxy for use that secures a fair and reasonable apportionment of input tax to specified supplies is acceptable.

In the right circumstances, the Commissioners will not object to a values-based method for calculating recovery of input tax in respect of specified supplies. It will rarely however, be acceptable to mix securities with other different activities in a single outputs-based calculation. In such cases, a values-based approach will not give a fair and reasonable result because it is likely to significantly under- or over-state the extent to which input tax is used in making recoverable supplies.

FURTHER INFORMATION

Further information on partial exemption is available in VAT Notice 706 "Partial Exemption".

Commentary—*De Voil Indirect Tax Service* **V3.464.**

NEW CIVIL INVESTIGATION OF FRAUD PROCEDURES

16 September 2005. *Business Brief 18/05*

Both HM Customs & Excise and the Inland Revenue had procedures for tackling suspected serious tax fraud using civil powers. The former Inland Revenue's Hansard procedures and all former Customs & Excise Civil Evasion procedures are being replaced with a new single Civil Investigations of Fraud procedure for HMRC. (The only exception is the Customs Duties Civil Evasion Penalties applied to travellers at port and airport controls).

1 SEPTEMBER 2005 START AND NEW CODE OF PRACTICE 9 (2005)

The new Civil Investigation of Fraud procedure came into effect on 1 September 2005 for new cases with a new Code of Practice 9 (2005).

Existing cases will be worked to a conclusion under the old Hansard procedures (Code of Practice 9), New Approach or C&E Notice 730.

Initially the new procedure will only be used by officers serving in HMRC Special Civil Investigations. Use by other specialist teams within HMRC is under consideration.

THE CHANGES

- The new procedure is wholly civil, removing the threat of prosecution for the original tax offence—a change from the Inland Revenue's Hansard procedure.
- HMRC will retain the option to consider prosecution for a materially false disclosure or materially false statement with intent to deceive.
- Interviews will no longer be conducted under caution and tape-recorded.
- Investigations under the new Civil Investigation of Fraud procedure will cover both direct and indirect taxes where appropriate.

OUTLINE OF THE CIVIL INVESTIGATION OF FRAUD PROCEDURE

Where HMRC suspect serious tax fraud and decides to proceed via a civil rather than a criminal investigation, the taxpayer will be given one opportunity to secure maximum benefit by making a full disclosure of all irregularities within the direct and indirect tax regimes. If they take that opportunity the investigation will proceed more quickly, efficiently and advantageously for both the taxpayer and HMRC.

If a taxpayer decides not to make a full disclosure and co-operate, HMRC will conduct their own investigation, using statutory information powers if necessary. If irregularities are discovered they will issue formal assessments and pursue collection of unpaid tax with interest. Any penalties due are likely to be significantly higher to reflect the fact that the taxpayer did not take the opportunity given to them to disclose.

Once the decision by HMRC has been made to follow a civil route for investigation and the procedure is offered to the taxpayer, HMRC retain no underlying threat of prosecution for the original tax loss.

PROSECUTION FOR TAX FRAUD

HMRC reserve complete discretion to pursue a criminal investigation with a view to prosecution where they consider it necessary and appropriate. Where HMRC decide to use the Civil Investigation of Fraud procedure it will not prosecute for the original tax offence. However if materially false statements are made or materially false documents are provided with intent to deceive, HMRC may conduct a criminal investigation with a view to a prosecution of that conduct.

SINGLE MEETINGS TO DISCUSS INDIRECT AND DIRECT TAX MATTERS

Once the new procedure is introduced, where suspicions of irregularities cut across direct and indirect taxes, a single meeting will be held to cover all regimes. During this meeting it will be made clear to the taxpayer whether questions are relevant to direct taxes, indirect taxes or both.

DISCLOSURE REPORTS

Any disclosure reports prepared by professional advisers will now be expected to cover direct and indirect tax irregularities in the same document. We anticipate there will be cost savings and other benefits to the taxpayer in submitting a single disclosure report.

CIVIL INVESTIGATION OF FRAUD AND THE HUMAN RIGHTS ACT

We believe the new procedure is compliant with the Human Rights Act. The civil fraud processes previously operated by both departments have received considerable scrutiny in terms of Human Rights and, in particular, Article 6 "Right to a fair trial". The views of the courts in the lead Human Rights Act rulings of *Han & Yau* and *Gill & Gill* together with advice from leading counsel have provided the principles for designing the new procedure. The recent case of *Khan v C & E Comrs* (2005) has endorsed these principles and safeguards have been built into the new procedure.

CONSULTATION

This change is being made after consultation with relevant Representative Bodies.

Commentary—*De Voil Indirect Tax Service* **V5.224A, V5.311.**

HIGH COURT DECISION: CHURCH OF ENGLAND CHILDREN'S SOCIETY

10 October 2005. *Business Brief 19/05.*

This Business Brief outlines the decision of the High Court in *Church of England Children's Society (CECS)* [2005] EWHC 1692 (Ch) in favour of the charity, and how HM Revenue & Customs intend to apply the decision. HMRC have decided not to appeal.

BACKGROUND

CECS is a charity with a wide range of activities. To raise funds, it engages professional fundraisers to secure regular donations from members of the public. Those donating at least £5 per month receive a copy of the charity's newsletter three times a year.

The VAT Tribunal decided that—

- the fundraisers' fees related to the non-business activity of seeking donations, so the VAT incurred on them was not recoverable
- the newsletters were not zero-rated supplies of printed matter. However, they were deemed zero-rated gifts of business assets and input tax on their production and distribution costs was recoverable following the decision of the High Court in *West Herts College* [2001] STC 1245.

CECS appealed to the High Court against the first part of the Tribunal's decision and HMRC cross-appealed on the second part.

HIGH COURT DECISION

Fundraising fees

The High Court decided that if funds raised by donation by CECS were used to fund its taxable business activities, it was entitled to recover related input tax. It followed the recent judgment of the ECJ in *Kretztechnik AG v Finanzamt Linz* (Case C-465/03). In that case, the ECJ ruled that, where the capital-raising transaction to which costs most closely relate falls outside the scope of VAT because it is not a supply of goods or services, the costs can relate to the organisation as a whole. In other words, if the capital-raising transaction is for the purpose of the business's economic activity in general, the transaction has a direct and immediate link with the whole economic activity of the taxable person. VAT on the transaction is recoverable to the extent that the taxable person is making taxable supplies.

The CECS decision has wider implications than the use of professional fundraisers by charities. Subject to the guidance below, it could impact on the recovery of any VAT incurred in securing donations or legacies to support the work of a charity.

Deemed supplies

The Court also upheld the Tribunal's decision that the newsletter was a deemed zero-rated supply of printed matter and that input tax on the production and distribution costs could be recovered because it related to that taxable deemed supply.

THE WAY FORWARD

Fundraising costs

Where funds are raised solely for a restricted charitable purpose involving wholly non-business activities, the VAT incurred on raising those funds is not input tax and is not recoverable.

Conversely, where the funds raised are used wholly to support the making of business supplies, all of the VAT incurred on fundraising costs can be treated as input tax. The recovery of this input tax will depend upon whether these business supplies are taxable or exempt. Where fundraising input tax is wholly attributable to the making of taxable supplies by the charity, it can be recovered in full, subject to the normal rules. On the other hand, where fundraising input tax is wholly attributable to the making of exempt supplies by the charity, none of it will be recoverable, subject to the partial exemption de minimis limits.

So where a charity which has non-business and business activities incurs VAT on fundraising costs and the funds raised support various activities of the charity, the VAT incurred can only be recoverable input tax to the extent that the funds raised will support taxable business supplies. In practice this means that VAT incurred on fundraising costs must first be subject to an initial business/non-business apportionment to determine how much of the VAT incurred may be treated as input tax. Then, in circumstances where the charity has exempt business activities, this input tax is further subject to the partial exemption rules.

In some cases, a charity's existing business /non-business apportionment method and partial exemption method will produce a fair and reasonable basis by which input tax can be recovered. However, where this is not the case, HMRC will consider proposals for alternative methods. If exceptional circumstances exist, HMRC may allow alternative methods to be applied retrospectively, provided it is fair and reasonable for the charity as a whole.

Deemed supplies

The High Court decision has confirmed that input tax relating to a deemed supply is recoverable where the deemed supply is taxable.

However, in order for there to be a deemed supply, the gifted goods must first be business assets. This means that a charity purchasing or acquiring goods in order to give them away in the furtherance of its non-business charitable purposes would not be able to recover the VAT incurred on the purchase or acquisition of those goods. Following changes to the rules on gifts of business assets with effect from 1 October 2003, there is no longer a deemed supply where the total cost of production of newsletters provided to any donor does not exceed £50 in a twelve month period. Where input tax is incurred on business assets that are given away, but those gifts are not deemed supplies, the attribution of the input tax will be based on the business reasons behind making the gifts. Where input tax is incurred on business assets that are given away, and some of those gifts are deemed supplies whereas others are not, the attribution of the input tax will take both the deemed supplies and the underlying purpose behind making the gifts into account.

Examples

– If a religious charity incurs VAT producing and distributing bibles that it gifts to local hotels for use by guests, the VAT is not input tax and is not recoverable even if the bibles exceed the £50 cost rules that apply to deemed supplies. This is because giving away bibles is not a business activity and VAT incurred cannot therefore be input tax. However, if the charity produced bibles for gifts and for sale, then VAT incurred would be partly input tax.
– If the charity produces religious newsletters that advertise its business activities, VAT incurred will be input tax because of the advertisements. Furthermore, if the newsletters satisfy the deemed supply rules, then the input tax will be fully recoverable even if the charity's business activities are heavily exempt.

MAKING CLAIMS FOR REPAYMENT OF TAX

Charities that wish to make claims for input tax may do so by making a voluntary disclosure to their local VAT office in accordance with guidance in Notice 700/45 "How to correct VAT errors and make adjustments or claims", subject to the time limit in reg 29(1A) of the VAT Regulations 1995. This restricts late claims for input tax to three years from the due date of the return for the prescribed accounting period in which the input tax was chargeable.

Commentary—*De Voil Indirect Tax Service* **V3.211, 212.**

CLARIFICATION OF THE TREATMENT OF FOREIGN EXCHANGE TRANSACTIONS (FOREX)

23 November 2005. *Business Brief 21/05.*

This Business Brief clarifies HM Revenue and Customs' (HMRC) policy regarding forex transactions, following the Tribunal decision in *Willis Pension Fund Trustees Limited* (Willis) (2005) VAT Decision 19183. HMRC have decided not to appeal this decision.

BACKGROUND

Willis was the Trustee of the Willis Pension Fund, which was a pension scheme for the employees of the Willis Group Holding Limited group of companies. The scheme held various investments, including a number of overseas investments and equities. As a result, the sterling value of these assets was subject to exchange rate fluctuations. Willis entered into forex deals with various UK banks, using the services of a third party to conduct the transactions, in order to hedge or minimise the pension scheme's exposure to adverse exchange rate fluctuations. Willis did not offer a spread or charge a separate fee or commission, but relied on the movements in exchange rates in order to minimise their losses and, where possible, make a profit. The question before the Tribunal was whether in entering these transactions, Willis made a supply for VAT purposes.

Currently, HMRC's policy relies upon the European Court of Justice (ECJ) decision in *First National Bank of Chicago* (FNBC) C-172/96. FNBC entered forex transactions as a market maker. Although they did not charge a specific commission, they relied in part on the spread that they offered (that is, they set a buying price and selling price for each currency thereby offering a spread to the customer), in order to make a profit. The ECJ decided that the forex transactions entered into by FNBC were supplies of services and that the consideration for those services was the net result of the transactions over a period of time. HMRC applied this decision to all forex transactions and treated the supplies as exempt under VATA 1994 Sch 9 Group 5 item 1. As a result, businesses that entered into transactions with UK or EU institutions had a restriction placed on the recovery of any associated input tax. Conversely, businesses that entered into transactions with overseas institutions would have been entitled to recover the associated input tax in full under the VAT (Input Tax) (Specified Supplies) Order 1999.

THE DECISION

The Tribunal had to decide whether Willis provided any service to the counterparty when it entered into a foreign exchange transaction. Willis did not charge a fee or commission on the deal and did not factor a spread into its arrangements. Willis simply made the best deals it could from counterparties such as banks. The Tribunal decided that any "profit" retained by Willis from the forex transactions was not the consideration for a supply because it simply resulted from fluctuations in market rates. Willis entered into foreign exchange transactions solely to hedge against currency risks on its investment holdings.

HMRC now accept that there were no supplies made by Willis in respect of the hedging transactions and that this decision will apply to any business entering forex transactions on the same basis as Willis.

HMRC are considering whether this decision has wider application. Further guidance will be issued in due course.

INPUT TAX TREATMENT

HMRC now accept that any VAT paid on associated costs of forex hedging transactions such as those carried out by Willis relates to the business as a whole. It is residual input tax, which can be recovered subject to the partial exemption method used.

CLAIMS FOR OVERPAID INPUT TAX

Claims for input tax in respect of past forex transactions can be made subject to the three-year capping rules. Public Notice 700/45, "How to correct VAT errors and make adjustments or claims" provides further guidance on the capping rules and claim procedures. This will need to take into account any overclaim caused by recovery of the input tax relating to transactions with non-EU counterparties, under the specified supplies order.

Businesses that have recovered the associated input tax because they have entered into forex transactions in a similar way to Willis with non-EU counterparties, may need to consider whether all or part of that input tax should now be restricted following this decision.

Note—See also R&C Brief 5/07, published on 26-1-07.
Commentary—*De Voil Indirect Tax Service* **V3.152, V3.461, V6.126.**

FURTHER CLARIFICATION OF THE VAT POSITION OF SHARE ISSUES FOLLOWING THE EUROPEAN COURT OF JUSTICE'S DECISION IN KRETZTECHNIK

23 November 2005. *Business Brief 21/05*

Business Brief 12/05 explained HM Revenue and Customs' position on the VAT treatment of share issues and subsequent input tax recovery, following the decision in *Kretztechnik A.G. -v- Finanzamt Linz* (Case C-465/03). This Business Brief article contains additional guidance, with specific implementation dates underlined.

REVISED TREATMENT OF SHARE ISSUE TRANSACTIONS

Business Brief 12/05 advised that companies making a new issue of shares to raise capital for their business, in circumstances identical to those in *Kretztechnik's* case, were not making any supply but were entitled to treat the VAT on the costs of the issue as input tax. Companies that make both taxable and exempt supplies should recover a proportion of the input tax in accordance with their partial exemption method that applied at the time of the issue.

The following guidance explains the VAT position of share transactions where the circumstances differ from those in *Kretztechnik*.

TRANSACTIONS INVOLVING ISSUES OF OTHER TYPES OF SHARES

Businesses may issue shares of different types. For example, there may be an issue of preference shares, a special rights issue, a bonus issue or issue of scrip dividends. *Kretztechnik* principles are applicable to all such share issues and these are now to be regarded as non-supplies for VAT purposes.

TRANSACTIONS INVOLVING ISSUES BY DIFFERENT TYPES OF COMPANIES

Kretztechnik was a public limited company but the body issuing shares could be another type of company, a private company for example. Provided that the issuer's motivation is, like Kretztechnik's, the raising of capital, issues of shares by these other types of company will also be non-supplies for VAT purposes.

TRANSACTIONS INVOLVING THE ISSUE OF FINANCIAL INSTRUMENTS OR SECURITIES OTHER THAN SHARES

The issue of other types of security, such as bonds, debentures or loan notes, should also be treated as non-supplies when the purpose of the issue is to raise capital for the issuer's business. The input tax consequences will be the same as for an issue of shares. Similarly, the issue of shares or units in collective investment funds such as open-ended investment companies or authorised unit trusts will not be supplies for VAT purposes.

SHARES AND OTHER SECURITIES ISSUED IN OTHER SITUATIONS

An issue of shares or other securities may be one of several transactions that take place in the context of wider arrangements. For example, they may be issued in order to effect a company takeover or as part of a company restructuring through merger or demerger. When the issue does take place as part of such wider arrangements, it should still be regarded as a non-supply for VAT purposes.

MAKING CLAIMS

Claims for unrecovered input tax in respect of past issues of shares and other securities can be made subject to the three-year "capping" rules. Such claims need to take into account any input tax that has been over-claimed because it has been attributed to an issue of securities outside the EU. Public Notice 700/45 "How to correct VAT errors and make adjustments or claims" gives detailed guidance on capping and claim procedures.

TRANSFERS OF EXISTING SHARES

Transfers of existing shares for a consideration will continue to be exempt supplies provided that the supplies occur in the course of business activity. In such cases, the input tax that relates to the transfer will be exempt input tax and only recoverable to the extent that the shares have been sold to purchasers outside the EU.

LIABILITY CONSEQUENCES

There are no changes to the exemption for financial services arising from the judgment. Transactions that are no longer supplies, such as issues of shares, will no longer have a corresponding VAT liability such as exemption. However, intermediary and underwriting services in relation to such transactions will continue to be exempt.

CONSEQUENCES FOR THE VAT (INPUT TAX) (SPECIFIED SUPPLIES) ORDER 1999

Input tax on issues of shares made outside the EU

Prior to *Kretztechnik*, issues of shares and other securities to customers belonging outside the EU were treated as specified supplies. This meant that the input tax on related costs could be recovered. From the date of publication of this Business Brief this treatment will no longer apply unless—

(a) You have chosen to apply the *Kretztechnik* treatment to other issues before that date; or

(b) You are making a claim for retrospective recovery of input tax.

The changes announced in paragraph 2 of Business Brief 32/04 will still apply to other incidental financial transactions not affected by *Kretztechnik*.

Input tax incurred by intermediaries in share issues

The changes in this paragraph are effective only from 1 January 2006.

Previously, intermediaries could treat the following transactions as specified supplies—

(a) arranging an issue of shares or other securities on behalf of an issuer belonging outside the EU;

(b) arranging an issue of shares or other securities on behalf of an issuer (wherever they belonged) to recipients outside the EU.

This meant that the input tax on related costs could be recovered whether or not the intermediary's customer belonged outside the EU, provided the issue was made to someone belonging outside the EU. This was because this underlying issue of shares was treated as a supply for VAT purposes.

Following *Kretztechnik*, the situation has changed and, from 1 January 2006, only the services described at (*a*) above will be treated as specified supplies. This is because the underlying issue of shares by the intermediary's customer to the non-EU purchaser is no longer a supply. However, intermediary services to their own customers, as long as they belong outside the EU, is still a specified supply under the Specified Supplies Order.

There is no change to the position of intermediaries who arrange supplies of existing shares or other securities.

Impact of *Kretztechnik* upon the *Water Hall Group* decision

In *Water Hall Group plc*, a VAT Tribunal found that, when shares were issued to a UK company acting as nominee for purchasers belonging outside the EU, the input tax relating to those shares could not be reclaimed by the issuer because the supply was to the UK nominee rather than the non-EU purchasers. In Business Brief 02/05, HMRC announced that businesses should apply the Water Hall decision to issues of shares in the same circumstances. The situation would then be reviewed following release of the *Kretztechnik* decision.

This review has now been completed. HMRC's conclusion is that *Water Hall* no longer has any application. In *Kretztechnik*, an issue of shares was found not to be a supply for VAT purposes, so the question of who is making or receiving the supply no longer arises. We consider that transactions involving sales of existing shares are fundamentally different from share issues because they are capable of constituting supplies. Such transactions were not considered in Water Hall and that decision does not therefore apply to them. Supplies of existing shares are to be regarded as being made to or by the person who actually makes the purchase or sale of the shares. Where the actual purchaser is not known to the seller, the place of belonging of a nominee account for the purchaser, if known, may be used to determine the place of supply. If neither is known, you should treat the supply as made in the UK or refer to the special rules in paragraph 9.2 of Public Notice 701/49 "Finance and securities".

Note—See also Business Brief 22/05, 1 December 2005, below for further clarification on the VAT position of share issues made to customers outside the EU.

Commentary—*De Voil Indirect Tax Service* **V2.236, V3.464, V4.136E.**

JUDGMENT OF THE COURT OF APPEAL IN THE CASE OF IVOR JACOBS ([2005] EWCA CIV 930)

1 December 2005. *Business Brief 22/05.*

This Business Brief article sets out HM Revenue & Customs' (HMRC) revised policy on the recovery of VAT by those using the "VAT refunds for DIY builders and converters" scheme in cases where a mixed use building (used for non-residential and residential use) is converted into dwellings in light of the judgment of the Court of Appeal in the case of *Ivor Jacobs* (C3/2004/2457).

BACKGROUND

Mr Jacobs had converted a former residential school for boys into one large dwelling for his own occupation and three flats. His claim for a VAT refund under the provisions of the "VAT refunds for DIY builders and converters" scheme was rejected because none of the four resulting dwellings had been created exclusively from the conversion of the non-residential part of the school.

Mr Jacobs appealed against the above decision to a VAT Tribunal. The Tribunal found that, when looked at as a whole ie a "primary use" test, the school was entirely non-residential and its conversion qualified for the refund scheme.

HMRC appealed the Tribunal's decision to the High Court. The High Court rejected the Tribunal's "primary use" test and held that the school was in part residential and in part non-residential. However the High Court also rejected HMRC's view that any additional dwelling must be created entirely from the non-residential part. It held that the VAT incurred on converting the non-residential part used in creating the four dwellings was recoverable through the scheme. This is because converting the school had created additional dwellings, the school having contained one dwelling before conversion and four afterwards. The VAT incurred on the conversion of the residential part of the school was not recoverable.

The Court of Appeal unanimously dismissed HMRC's appeal and endorsed the High Court's judgment.

HM REVENUE & CUSTOMS' REVISED POLICY

HMRC now accept that, for the purposes of the DIY Refund Scheme, the conversion of a building that contains both a residential part and a non-residential part comes within the scope of the Scheme so long as the conversion results in an additional dwelling being created. It is no longer necessary for the additional dwelling to be created exclusively from the non-residential part. However, VAT recovery is restricted to the conversion of the non-residential part.

VAT PRs etc

BUILDERS AND DEVELOPERS

HMRC do not consider that the Court of Appeal decision has any impact in similar situations where a building, which is part residential/part non-residential, is being converted into a number of dwellings and the number of dwellings present post-conversion is greater than the number of dwellings present pre-conversion.

Items 1(b) and 3(a) of Group 5 to Schedule 8, VATA 1994 restrict the zero-rating to the dwelling(s) deriving from the conversion of the non-residential part. Our policy remains that the zero rate will not apply to any dwelling(s) deriving (whether in whole or in part) from the conversion of the residential part.

VAT TREATMENT OF PAST SUPPLIES

DIY house builders, who have converted property that was part residential/part non-residential and have increased the number of dwellings in the building overall, are invited to submit claims for VAT incurred on eligible expenditure in converting the non-residential part of the building into a part of the resulting dwellings.

HMRC will only entertain claims in respect of such conversions completed no later than three years prior to the date of this Business Brief.

Commentary—*De Voil Indirect Tax Service* **V4.232.**

FURTHER CLARIFICATION ON THE VAT POSITION OF SHARE ISSUES MADE TO CUSTOMERS OUTSIDE THE EU

1 December 2005. *Business Brief 22/05.*

We have had one or two enquiries on Business Brief 21/05 which explained HM Revenue and Customs' position on share issues following the decision in the European case of *Kretztechnik AG* (Case C-465/03). This item clarifies the situation regarding issues of shares and other securities made outside the EU.

CONSEQUENCES FOR THE VAT (INPUT TAX) (SPECIFIED SUPPLIES) ORDER 1999 INPUT TAX ON ISSUES OF SHARES MADE OUTSIDE THE EU

Prior to *Kretztechnik*, issues of shares and other securities to customers belonging outside the EU were treated as specified supplies. This meant that the input tax on related costs could be recovered under the Specified Supplies Order. From 29 November 2005, this treatment will no longer apply to new shares and securities issued outside the EU as they are no longer supplies, although input tax will still be recoverable on the related costs provided the issue is made for the purposes of a fully taxable business. If the issue is made for the purposes of a partly exempt business, then a proportion of the input tax will be recoverable under the business' normal partial exemption method.

The changes announced in paragraph 2 of Business Brief 32/04 will still apply to other incidental financial transactions not affected by *Kretztechnik*.

Commentary—*De Voil Indirect Tax Service* **V2.236, V3.464, V4.136E.**

VAT EXEMPTION FOR INSURANCE-RELATED SERVICES

5 December 2005. *Business Brief 23/05.*

The Government has considered responses to the HMRC consultation concerning VAT and insurance related services following the ECJ judgment in *Arthur Andersen & Co Accountants* (case C-472/03). The Government has noted that the VAT treatment of financial services and insurance will now be subject to review by the European Commission in the near future, and has decided to delay its decision regarding implementation of this ECJ judgment. The Government will monitor the progress of the review in deciding when to make the necessary changes to UK law and will provide industry with sufficient notice in advance of implementation.

Commentary—*De Voil Indirect Tax Service* **V4.123.**

COMPANY FORMATION SERVICES WITH ANCILLARY PRINTED MATTER—CLARIFICATION OF TREATMENT POST CPP

18 January 2006. *Business Brief 1/06*

The Commissioners are aware that traders providing company formation services may be incorrectly treating some supplies as separate zero-rated supplies of printed matter and standard-rated services.

This Business Brief article clarifies HMRC guidance previously issued. HMRC confirms its view, in the light of the Card Protection Plan case, on the correct treatment of these supplies. It aims to ensure that all traders providing such services treat them correctly for VAT purposes.

Furthermore there may be cases where traders have attempted to secure a competitive advantage over traders that have been treating the supplies correctly by using this incorrect treatment as a basis for value shifting by invoicing a breakdown of the package price.

BACKGROUND

Business Brief 2/01, issued on 16 February 2001, explained the ECJ and House of Lords decisions in the case of *Card Protection Plan (CPP)* (ECJ C-349/96). These decisions clarified how businesses are required to decide whether they are making single or multiple supplies for VAT purposes. The Business Brief required businesses to make necessary changes in treatment by 1 June 2001.

VAT Info Sheet 2/01 further advised businesses how to determine the proper VAT liability of supplies consisting of separately identifiable goods and services. It also advised affected businesses to review the VAT treatment of similar supplies against the tests set out in that sheet and to implement the necessary changes.

Despite this publicity, the company formation industry has in many cases failed to review such supplies post-CPP with the result that, in some cases, suppliers have continued incorrectly to zero-rate supplies of printed matter which are ancillary to supplies of company formation services.

TREATMENT OF COMPANY FORMATION SERVICE PACKAGES INCLUDING ANCILLARY PRINTED MATTER

HMRC's view is that where there is a single advertised price for a company formation package that includes some printed matter (for example a number of copies of the printed and perhaps bound Memorandum & Articles of Association), there is a single standard-rated supply of company formation services. This supply is the principal supply to which the supply of printed matter is ancillary.

The supply of the service by a registration agent of preparing and lodging the original Memorandum and Articles of Association with the Registrar of Companies is wholly standard-rated. In this situation, one or more copies of documents, such as the Certificates of Incorporation and the Memorandum and Articles of Association may be provided. Where these are provided in hard copy form (as opposed to digital format), the question arises as to whether there is a single supply of company registration services to which the supply of printed matter is ancillary, or separate supplies of zero-rated printed matter and standard-rated services.

The judgment in *Card Protection Plan* (ECJ C-349/96) set out a number of relevant criteria, namely:

– Where a transaction comprises a number of features or acts, regard must be had to all the circumstances in which it takes place.
– Where a supply is a single supply from an economic point of view, it should not be artificially split so as to distort the functioning of the VAT system.
– There is a single supply, in particular, in cases where one or more elements of a transaction are to be regarded as constituting the principal service, with other elements being ancillary to that principal service.
– While the charging of a single price is not decisive, the fact that several elements are supplied for a single price may indicate a single supply.

Therefore where a customer acquiring a registered company also receives hard copy documents as part of a fixed-price package, he would normally be seen as receiving a single supply of company formation services rather than separate supplies of company registration services and printed matter.

VAT PRs etc

Where additional copies of documentation are offered as an option for additional payment, there may be either a single supply or multiple supplies.

Action required by businesses making supplies of company formation service packages

Businesses to which this Business Brief applies must review their VAT treatment of these supplies and ensure that any necessary changes are implemented.

Where there has been historic incorrect treatment businesses should account for underpaid output tax by using one of the following methods:

- If the net value of all adjustments is £2000 or less, businesses may amend their VAT account and include the value of the adjustment on their current VAT return.
- If the net value of all adjustments is more than £2000, a separate payment should be submitted to the local Business Advice Centre. (Businesses may not make this adjustment on their VAT return).

Where there has been historic incorrect treatment but businesses can positively evidence misdirection by HMRC, then the correct treatment should be applied from a point not later than the date of this Business Brief.

In cases where misdirection is accepted, HMRC reserves the right to take action where it appears that the incorrect treatment has been used as the basis for value-shifting by invoicing an incorrect breakdown of the package price.

HOTEL CONFERENCE/FUNCTION FACILITIES: REVISED INTERPRETATION OF LAW ON VAT TREATMENT

18 January 2006. *Business Brief 1/06*

This Business Brief article announces changes in HM Revenue & Customs' interpretation of the law on the VAT treatment of hotel conference/function facilities. This change will be incorporated in an update to VAT Notice 709/3, "Hotels and Holiday Accommodation", to be issued in due course.

The change being made affects the liability of supplies of rooms by hotels that are to be used for meetings, conferences and similar functions. There is no change to the treatment of supplies of rooms where the primary use will be for the purpose of supplies of catering, such as dinner/dances, wedding receptions, etc. Supplies of rooms for such purposes are always taxable supplies.

BACKGROUND

Hotels and other establishments often provide rooms for meetings, conferences and similar functions organised by third parties. It is usual for them to make inclusive charges depending on the requirements of individual delegates. It is the general practice for hotels and similar providers to charge organisers on a delegate or attendee basis (referred to as the "delegate rate"), ie the charge will be determined according to the number of delegates requiring:

- use of conference room only;
- use of conference room plus meal(s) ('8 hour conference delegate rate'); or
- use of conference room plus meals and overnight sleeping accommodation ('24 hour conference delegate rate').

The supply of a conference/function room on its own in these circumstances is exempt from VAT (unless an option to tax has been made). Where, in addition to the use of the conference/function room, a meal is provided to delegates and an inclusive charge made (the 8 hour delegate rate), each element is treated as a separate supply, so whilst the conference room continues to be exempt from VAT (unless an option to tax has been made), the part of the consideration relating to the provision of food is taxable (unless the provision of refreshments is minimal, such as tea and biscuits). However; where the 24-hour conference delegate rate has been applied and an inclusive charge made, HMRC has until now seen the charge as consideration for a single taxable supply of use of the entire hotel's facilities including conference/function facilities, sleeping accommodation and food.

REVISED INTERPRETATION OF THE LAW

Where a room is provided for a meeting, conference or similar function organised by a third party (but not where the primary purpose is for a supply of catering—see above), HMRC now accepts that the provision of conference/function room hire, meals and sleeping accommodation under the 24 hour delegate rate, even where made in return for an inclusive charge, should be treated as separate supplies. These will be taxable supplies, with the exception of the conference/function room hire, which will be an exempt supply, unless the hotel has opted to tax its supplies. In cases where a single consideration is paid for supplies having different liabilities, for example where a charge for room hire is made under the 24-hour delegate rate by a hotel which has not opted to tax its room hire, a fair and reasonable apportionment of the consideration must be made.

There is no change to the treatment of 8-hour delegate charges.

Where hotels organise and run conferences or similar events themselves and charge for entry to delegates, their supplies are always taxable supplies.

MAKING CLAIMS OR ADJUSTMENTS

Hotels that have made an option to tax will be unaffected by the change and should continue to charge tax on their supplies. For other hotels and businesses, the change described above should be implemented from the date of this Business Brief and there is no requirement to make adjustments in respect of supplies made prior to this date. However, where hotels or other establishments wish to make a claim to HMRC for a repayment of output tax incorrectly paid, they may do so, subject to the conditions set out below, by using one of the following methods (full details are given in VAT Notice 700/45 How to correct VAT errors and make adjustments or claims):

- where the total of previous errors do not exceed £2000 net tax, an adjustment may be made to your current VAT return, or
- where the total previous errors exceed £2000 net tax a separate claim should be submitted to HMRC (in these cases the errors must not be corrected through your VAT returns). Details of where to send your claim can be obtained from the HM Revenue & Customs National Advice Service on 0845 010 9000.

All adjustments or claims are limited to a three-year period and will be subject to the following conditions:

- All claims must take into account input tax that has been claimed, but which under the revised interpretation will not relate to taxable supplies.
- Businesses must be able to produce evidence that they accounted for VAT in the circumstances described above, and must be able to substantiate the amount claimed.

Subject to the three-year limitation period, any claim should be for all prescribed accounting periods in which the liability error occurred.

Should a claim not take into account all errors or all affected accounting periods, then HMRC will seek to set-off amounts owed to us for these periods against amounts claimed in other periods.

HMRC may reject all or part of a claim if repayment would unjustly enrich the claimant. More details on 'unjust enrichment' can be found at part 14 of VAT Notice 700/45 "How to correct VAT errors and make adjustments or claims".

A notification to HMRC that a business intends making a claim in the future is not a valid claim.

FUTURE VAT IMPLICATIONS FOR HOTELS AND SIMILAR PROVIDERS

You should treat supplies in the way described above. Some hotels will now be making exempt supplies as a result of these changes. The input tax that they incur will, as a result, be subject to partial exemption rules and some restriction on the amount they can reclaim may follow. Details can be found in VAT Notice 706, "Partial Exemption". If hotels prefer, they can continue to treat their supplies as taxable (and thereby be entitled to continue claiming their input tax in full) by opting to tax. Details about how to do this are given in VAT Notice 742A, "Opting to tax land and buildings". Hotels that have already made exempt supplies of the meeting room may require permission for an option to tax and they will find further details in Section 5 of Notice 742A.

Where you are in any doubt about the correct treatment please contact the National Advice Service on the telephone number below.

Commentary—*De Voil Indirect Tax Service* **V4.113.**

BEAUTY PROCEDURES PERFORMED USING CLASS 3B OR 4 LASERS AND/OR INTENSE PULSE LIGHT (IPL) MACHINES—CLARIFICATION OF LIABILITY

9 March 2006. *Business Brief 3/06*

HMRC have become aware that some businesses providing beauty procedures using class 3B or 4 lasers and/or IPL machines may be incorrectly treating their supplies as VAT-exempt health services rather than standard rated supplies of beauty treatment. This Business Brief article is issued to assist those businesses to determine the correct liability of these services.

BACKGROUND

Following the establishment of the Healthcare Commission under the Care Standards Act 2000, certain procedures using prescribed techniques or prescribed technologies became regulated for the first time. Among these were the use of class 3B and 4 lasers and IPL machines.

This has led to establishments such as beauty salons, where class 3B and 4 lasers and/or IPL machines are used (for instance, for removing unwanted hair), being classified as independent hospitals for the purposes of the Care Standards legislation.

TREATMENT OF SUPPLIES MADE USING CLASS 3B AND 4 LASERS AND/OR IPL MACHINES

Where the procedure utilising this equipment is supplied as part of a treatment programme drawn up by a registered health professional following the diagnosis of a medical condition, this treatment is exempt from VAT.

But where it is carried out for a cosmetic reason rather than as an element of medical or surgical treatment, this service is taxable at the standard rate of VAT.

Action required by businesses making non-medical supplies using class 3B and 4 lasers and/or IPL machines

Businesses to which this Business Brief applies must review their VAT treatment of these supplies and ensure that any necessary changes are implemented.

Where businesses have previously been incorrectly treating non-medical supplies as exempt, they should account for any net tax underdeclared by using one of the following methods:

If the net value of all adjustments is £2000 or less, businesses may amend their VAT account and include the value of the adjustment on their current VAT return.

If the net value of all adjustments is more than £2000, a separate payment should be submitted to the local Business Advice Centre. (Businesses may not make this adjustment on their VAT return).

Both of the above methods and how to make a claim are explained in VAT Notice 700/45 'How to correct VAT errors and make adjustments or claims'.

If a voluntary disclosure is not made, and Customs discover the error, the taxpayer may be liable to a misdeclaration penalty.

Where there has been historic incorrect treatment but businesses can positively evidence misdirection by HMRC, then the correct treatment should be applied from a point not later than the date of this Business Brief. Further information can be found in Notice 700/6 "VAT rulings".

Commentary—*De Voil Indirect Tax Service* **V4.146.**

OFF-STREET CAR PARKING PROVIDED BY LOCAL AUTHORITIES

24 March 2006. *Business Brief 4/06*

The VAT and Duties Tribunal has decided that the Isle of Wight Council and three other local authorities do not have to charge VAT on car parking in their areas. This Business Brief article explains action that HM Revenue and Customs (HMRC) will be taking pending an appeal.

BACKGROUND

Under Article 4(5) of the EC Sixth VAT Directive, activities of public bodies are not regarded as being carried on by way of business for VAT purposes, if they do so under a statutory regime that is unique to the public sector ("special legal regime"), unless this would significantly distort competition with private sector bodies carrying on the same activity.

In an earlier decision (LON/00/653) dated 6 April 2004, the Tribunal found that the Isle of Wight Council provides off-street car parking spaces under such a special legal regime, and consequently this should not be regarded as a business activity for VAT purposes. However, because it considered that the UK has not properly implemented Article 4(5) into national law, the Tribunal did not consider whether such treatment would significantly distort competition (see Business Brief 18/04).

In November 2004 the High Court found that in assessing the applicability of Article 4(5) to a particular case, it is necessary to consider both the legal regime governing an activity and the issue of competition. Consequently the case was referred back to the Tribunal to consider arguments on competition.

THE TRIBUNAL'S DECISION

The Tribunal decided that the non-taxation of local authority off-street car parks does not significantly distort competition in the appellants' geographical areas. It concluded that distortion of the market by public authorities is generally inherent, because Article 4(5) provides that they do not have to charge VAT even though other providers of the same service might have to charge VAT. Consequently, taxation on the grounds of significant distortions of competition should be applied only in the most exceptional of circumstances. Additionally, it found that, in the case of car parking, competition must be looked at in the circumstances prevailing in individual local authorities and not on a nationwide basis.

HMRC'S RESPONSE

HMRC believes that the Tribunal has not taken full account of the EU case law that relates to the application of Article 4(5), including the principle of fiscal neutrality, which was argued at the hearing. Consequently, HMRC does not agree with this decision of the Tribunal and an appeal will accordingly be lodged with the High Court.

FURTHER ACTION

HMRC will consider making repayments to the 4 local authorities involved in the appeal. Any refunds would be subject to the unjust enrichment rules as summarised in the VAT Guide (Notice 700 paragraph 19.13).

As expressed the decision is confined to the circumstances of the four appellant local authorities in question. Theirs were the only circumstances that were considered by the Tribunal. It would be inappropriate for other local authorities to claim refunds of output tax declared on off-street parking simply on the basis of this decision, and any such claim will not be accepted. They should continue to account for VAT based on HMRC's view of the law. Where appropriate, HMRC will continue to make protective assessments or to disallow protective claims received. Should a higher court subsequently rule that HMRC's original decision was correct, we would seek repayment of any amounts previously paid. Interest and penalties will also be sought as appropriate. There is more information about this in para 8 of VAT Notice 700/45 and in Business Brief 28/04.

Commentary—*De Voil Indirect Tax Service* **V3.407.**

INTERIM POSITION FOLLOWING THE COURT OF SESSION'S DECISION IN EDINBURGH'S TELFORD COLLEGE

12 April 2006. *BB 5/06*

This Business Brief article explains that HM Revenue & Customs (HMRC) is currently considering the judgment of the Court of Session in the case of *Edinburgh's Telford College* (ETC) [2006] CSIH 13, XA18/05, XA 22/05, released on 22 February 2006, and a further Business Brief will be issued when this process is concluded.

BACKGROUND

ETC is a further education (FE) college, created by statute. It provides a mixture of further and higher education courses (Scottish Qualifications Framework Levels 4 to 8) which are funded under an agreement with the Scottish Education Funding Council (SEFC).

ETC incurred VAT on the construction of a campus building used for a mixture of non-business activities and activities which give rise to supplies that are either taxable or exempt from VAT. ETC argued that when it provides further and higher education courses, it engages as a public authority and consequently this activity is outside the scope of VAT under Article 4(5) of the Sixth VAT Directive—whether or not fees are charged.

On the basis of this argument, and following the judgments of the European Court of Justice in the cases of *Lennartz v Finanzamt Munchen III* (C-97/90) and *Seeling v Finanzamt Starnberg* (C-269/00) ("Lennartz accounting"), ETC wanted to recover in full the VAT incurred on the campus building. Under Lennartz accounting, when a taxable person incurs VAT on the purchase of an asset for mixed business and non-business use, they can recover the VAT attributable to taxable and non-business use in full and then account for output tax on the ongoing non-business use. In the case of land and buildings, output tax must be accounted for over a maximum period of 20 years.

THE TRIBUNAL FOUND THAT—

- ETC did not act as a public authority when delivering FE and HE courses funded by SEFC. This was because it considered ETC's educational supplies to be made under ordinary commercial contracts with its students.
- It is not necessary to exclude from Lennartz accounting any use of an asset to make supplies that are exempt from VAT. On this basis, the Tribunal upheld ETC's claim to recover all the VAT incurred on the construction of the campus building, even though it is used in part to make exempt supplies; and, as a result,
- HMRC was wrong not to have approved a proposed sectorised PE special method.

THE COURT OF SESSION'S FINDING

ETC appealed on the first point and HMRC cross-appealed on the second and third points. ETC did not contest HMRC's cross appeal, which was accepted by the Court, and thus the original claim was reduced to take into account the use of the campus building to make exempt supplies. The Court accepted ETC's argument that it engages as a public authority when delivering FE and HE courses. This was on the basis of the legal structure of ETC's managing body and of the legal requirements that relate to its funding stream. As such the Court held that this education was provided in a non-business capacity.

HMRC'S POSITION

The judgment of the Court of Session is currently being carefully considered, but HMRC are advised that—should it decide to appeal the case further—we have until 19 May 2006 in which to take the necessary action. A further Business Brief will be issued shortly, which will explain HMRC's response to the judgment and give any further guidance that may be necessary. However, the outcome of this case confirms HMRC's existing guidance that Lennartz accounting does not permit full recovery of VAT when an asset is partially used to make supplies which are exempt from VAT.

Note—See HMRC Brief 27/08, issued 22-5-08 (Interpretation of Article 13 of the Principal VAT Directive: "bodies governed by public law" and "special legal regime").

EXEMPTION FOR THE MANAGEMENT OF AUTHORISED COLLECTIVE INVESTMENT SCHEMES

27 June 2006. *Business Brief 7/06*

This Business Brief article announces changes to HMRC's policy concerning the VAT exemption for the management of authorised collective investment schemes, following the judgment of the European Court of Justice (ECJ) in case C-169/04, *Abbey National Plc & Inscape Investment Fund* ("Abbey"), on 4 May 2006.

It updates the section of Business Brief 10/03 headed 'What constitutes "management"?' and the changes apply from 1 October 2006.

BACKGROUND

Article 13B(d)(6) of the Sixth VAT Directive exempts "Management of special investment funds as defined by Member States". The United Kingdom applies this exemption to the management of authorised unit trusts (AUTs), and of the scheme property of open-ended investment companies (OEICs). The exemption is effected in UK law by items 9 and 10 of Group 5, Schedule 9 to the VAT Act 1994.

HMRC's policy has been to apply the exemption to fund management in a strict sense, ie where it involves the assessment of financial risks, the making of investment decisions as to both the selection and disposal of assets under management and a direct involvement in the transactions concerning the assets of the fund, mainly in securities. Services not comprising such investment management functions, such as fund accounting and administration services, were regarded as taxable.

Abbey challenged this interpretation and appealed to the VAT & Duties Tribunal against VAT charged to it on fund accounting and administration services and also against VAT charged to its funds on depository and trustee services. The case was referred to the ECJ, which delivered its judgment on 4 May 2006.

THE ABBEY JUDGMENT

Firstly, the court has ruled that "management" in Article 13B(d)(6) has its own independent meaning in Community law and Member States' discretion to define "management of special investment funds" relates only to the meaning of special investment funds and not to the activities which constitute "management" of such funds.

In considering the services at issue in the appeal, the court made reference to the UCITS Directive, as amended (European Council Directive 85/611/EEC, setting out common EU regulatory requirements for undertakings for collective investment in transferable securities—"UCITS").

It found that the services of trustees or depositories, such as those set out in Articles 7(1) and (3) and 14(1) and (3) of the UCITS Directive, are not covered by the concept of management and are therefore excluded from exemption. This affirms HMRC's policy in respect of such services and they continue to be subject to VAT.

For fund accounting and administration services, the court found that they would qualify as management of special investment funds for the purposes of the VAT exemption if, "viewed broadly, they form a distinct whole and are specific to, and essential for, the management of those funds".

REVISED INTERPRETATION OF THE LAW

Again by reference to the UCITS Directive, the court viewed that tasks, such as those set out in Annex II to the Directive under the heading 'Administration', and which are functions specific to special investment funds, are capable of coming within the scope of the exemption. Under this heading are:

(a) legal and fund management accounting services;
(b) customer inquiries;
(c) valuation and pricing (including tax returns);
(d) regulatory compliance monitoring;
(e) maintenance of unit-holder register;
(f) distribution of income;
(g) unit issues and redemptions;
(h) contract settlements (including certificate dispatch);
(i) record keeping.

The court also found that the exemption does not in principle preclude the management of special investment funds being broken down into a number of separate services which may come within the meaning of "management" for the purpose of the exemption.

HMRC accept that, to benefit from the exemption, it is not necessary that a third party provider of fund administration services performs all of the administration functions required by regulations such as those listed in Annex II to the UCITS Directive (and applicable to UK funds under Financial Services Authority sourcebook rules). It is, however, necessary that the services must, viewed broadly, form a distinct whole fulfilling in effect the specific essential functions of management. In other words, the service must be recognisable in its own right as a service of fund administration.

Just because a particular operation (such as each of those listed in Annex II) is a requirement of regulations it does not necessarily mean that it is exempt if provided in isolation. For example, legal services such as advice or drafting may be required to ensure that certain documents, eg a trust deed or fund prospectus, are valid and comply with the regulations, but this does not mean that the legal service is one of exempt fund administration. Similarly, an external audit of accounts does not of itself assume the characteristics of a fund administration service.

To be exempt, it is necessary for the service to be distinct as a fund administration service. This "distinctiveness" is normally attained by the bundling, into a single supply, of numerous operations that are typical of the administrative management of eg an OEIC. In deciding whether the overall service is distinct as fund administration, both the number of specific operations and their individual characteristics need to be taken into account.

For example, the daily valuation of assets is of particular importance and relevance to OEICs and AUTs in determining the price of shares or units and so this, together with related accounting and reporting functions would be sufficiently distinctive as a fund administration service. However, a service such as "price feeding" of information consisting of the market value of individual stocks, provided to the person carrying out the fund asset valuation, is not in itself a fund administration service.

As a further example, the maintenance of a register of shareholders does not, in isolation, represent a fund administration service. However, if the service is combined with the issue and redemption of the units or shares and collating the number of shares in issue for the purpose of establishing the daily price of the units, such a package takes on the distinct characteristics of fund administration and will be exempt.

HMRC are satisfied that the bundle of services provided by the Bank of New York in the Abbey case is exempt. This consisted of computing the amount of income and the price of units or shares, the valuation of assets, accounting, the preparation of statements for the distribution of income, the provision of information and documentation for periodic accounts, income forecasts and tax returns, as well as data processing, record-keeping and customer inquiries.

There are a number of businesses which provide specialist fund administration services in respect of AUTs and OEICs. In many cases, these services comprise a package of functions which, together, will satisfy the criteria for the exemption. However, as with some of the examples above, certain services or bundles of services cannot be viewed as a distinct service of fund administration. For instance, the legal services referred to above might be described as "specific to, and essential for", the management of the fund but they are not fund administration services.

If the criteria for exemption are satisfied, it should also be noted that a person providing such a package of services will generally be viewed as making a single exempt supply of fund administration services in respect of each fund where the manager has delegated the administrative functions. The fact that each element may be priced separately on a rate card does not affect this.

In summary, HMRC accept that, in accordance with the judgment, services which, viewed broadly, are distinct as fund administration services, and are specific to and essential for the management of AUTs or OEICs are exempt.

MAKING CLAIMS OR ADJUSTMENTS

Businesses that that have taxed fund administration services which satisfy the criteria above should exempt such services made from 1 October 2006. There is no requirement to make adjustments in respect of supplies made prior to this date. However, where businesses wish to make a claim to HMRC for a repayment of output tax incorrectly paid, they may do so, subject to the conditions set out below, by using one of the following methods (full details are given in VAT Notice 700/45 "How to correct VAT errors and make adjustments or claims"):

– Where the total of previous errors does not exceed £2000 net tax, an adjustment may be made to your current VAT return.

- Where the total of previous errors exceeds £2000 net tax, a separate claim should be submitted to HMRC (in these cases the errors must not be corrected through your VAT returns). Details of where to send your claim can be obtained from update 2 to VAT Notice 700/45 "How to correct VAT errors and make adjustments or claims" or the HM Revenue & Customs National Advice Service on 0845 010 9000.

All adjustments or claims are limited to a three-year period and will be subject to the following conditions:

- All claims must take into account input tax that has been claimed, but which under the revised interpretation will not relate to taxable supplies.
- Businesses must be able to produce evidence that they accounted for VAT in the circumstances described above, and must be able to substantiate the amount claimed.

Subject to the three-year limitation period, any claim should be for all prescribed accounting periods in which the liability error occurred.

Should a claim not take into account all errors or all affected accounting periods, then HMRC will seek to set-off amounts owed to us for these periods against amounts claimed in other periods.

HMRC may reject all or part of a claim if repayment would unjustly enrich the claimant. More details on 'unjust enrichment' can be found at part 14 of VAT Notice 700/45 "How to correct VAT errors and make adjustments or claims".

A notification to HMRC that a business intends making a claim in the future is not a valid claim.

Businesses that have lodged "protective" claims pending the judgments should review them to ensure that they comply with the criteria of the judgment explained in this Business Brief and satisfy the above conditions. In particular, any claims in respect of the services of trustees or depositories should be excluded, as the ECJ confirmed HMRC's view that the supply of these services is taxable at the standard rate.

Commentary—*De Voil Indirect Tax Service* **V4.136H**.

Note—See HMRC Brief 65/07: HMRC withdraw from the appeal in *JP Morgan Fleming Claverhouse Trust plc*.

VAT PRs etc

CLARIFICATION OF THE TREATMENT OF TRAVEL AGENT FUNDED DISCOUNTS

7 July 2006. *Business Brief 8/06*

This Business Brief article sets out the VAT treatment of supplies by tour operators in cases where agents offer discounts to the travelling customer, following the judgment in the case of First Choice Holidays plc (C-149/01). It also explains what action HM Revenue & Customs (HMRC) will take in relation to voluntary disclosures and assessments resulting from the application of Business Brief 33/02.

BACKGROUND

Within the travel industry it is common practice for tour operators to sell travel services (eg holidays) through travel agents and for travel agents to offer the traveller discounts on these services. The way discounts are operated can differ depending on the contractual obligations between the tour operator and travel agent. In some circumstances, tour operators agree to discounts being given by the travel agent on the understanding that the tour operator will only receive the discounted price the customer pays. In others, the travel agent itself subsidises the discount to the traveller and pays the tour operator the full advertised selling price of any travel services sold. This article affects only the latter circumstances and confirms that the tour operator must account for VAT on the full, advertised price.

In cases where the tour operator has offered the discount and receives only the reduced amount from the travel agent, that is the value to be used when calculating the selling price for VAT purposes. However, where the agent has subsidised the discount to the traveller, there has been some dispute as to the value of the selling price for VAT purposes.

THE COURT OF APPEAL DECISION

The Court of Appeal referred the case of First Choice Holidays to the ECJ which set down its judgment in June 2003, concluding that "the 'total amount to be paid by the traveller' . . .

includes the additional amount that a travel agent . . . must . . . pay to the tour operator on top of the price paid by the traveller and which corresponds in amount to the discount given by the travel agent to the traveller on the price of the holiday stated in the tour operator's brochure."

Now that litigation has been completed HMRC are able to set out the final position.

CONSEQUENCES OF THIS JUDGMENT

The judgment means that there is no change to HMRC's policy on discounts within the Tour Operators' Margin Scheme (TOMS), which is that the consideration for travel services is the total received by a tour operator, including any discount offered by a travel agent. As such, this is the amount that should be used to calculate the selling price for VAT purposes and, where applicable, entered into the TOMS calculation. It also confirms that there is no separate supply of a 'right to a discount', as found by the High Court.

BUSINESS BRIEF 32/02

Following the High Court's judgment in this case, Business Brief 33/02 explained how the High Court decision could be applied.

The Business Brief allowed tour operators to use the discounted price in their current TOMS calculations if they wished to, providing they took account of both parts of the High Court judgment. Those who did so were issued with protective preferred and alternative assessments, pending the final outcome of the litigation. The preferred assessments (payable immediately) calculated the additional VAT due if HMRC's view prevailed. The alternative assessments (payment suspended) calculated the additional VAT due on the separate 'top up' supplies if the High Court judgment stood.

The Business Brief also permitted tour operators and travel agents to submit protective voluntary disclosure claims for VAT they considered had been overpaid on previous VAT returns, as a result of tour operators calculating their TOMS on undiscounted holiday values and travel agents not having claimed input tax, on the supply of services to them, by the tour operator.

WAY FORWARD

Now the litigation is concluded, these arrangements need to be revisited. HMRC will be taking corrective action as follows: where tour operators have already declared and paid VAT in line with HMRC's view (either via their VAT returns or by paying the preferred protective assessments issued to them), the VAT paid should already be correct. Protective alternative assessments, issued to tour operators, based on the High Court view of transactions, will now be withdrawn and voluntary disclosure claims utilising the High Court decision will be formally rejected (if this has not already been done). Any protective assessments issued to travel agents who reclaimed input tax on separate 'top up' supplies made to them by tour operators will now be enforced, because it has been determined there were no such supplies and therefore there was no entitlement to input tax.

APPEALS

Businesses who have previously lodged appeals with the VAT and Duties Tribunal that were stayed pending the Court of Appeal decision in this case, are now invited to withdraw them.

FURTHER INFORMATION

Guidance can be found in VAT Notices 709/5 Tour Operators' Margin Scheme and 709/6 Travel Agents and Tour Operators.

Commentary—*De Voil Indirect Tax Service* **V3.591, V3.594**.

POSITION FOLLOWING THE COURT OF APPEAL JUDGMENT IN COMPASS CONTRACT SERVICES LIMITED

21 August 2006. *Business Brief 12/06*

This Business Brief article explains the position taken by HMRC following the judgment of the Court of Appeal in the case of *Compass Contract Services UK Limited ("Compass")*

([2006] EWCA Civ 730), released on 9 June 2006. HMRC have decided not to petition the House of Lords for leave to appeal against the judgment of the Court.

BACKGROUND

All supplies of food and drink in the course of catering are standard-rated. Catering is defined (VAT Act 1994 Schedule 8 Group 1) as including supplies of food or drink for consumption on the premises on which they are supplied (as well as hot take-away food), but it is not limited to such supplies.

Compass is a contract catering company that supplies food to staff working at BBC Television Centre. The VAT Tribunal found that the supply of cold food sold from Compass' retail outlets to those staff was zero-rated because there was no supply of catering and that the premises that Compass made their supplies from were the retail units occupied by them and not the whole BBC TV Centre site. The food was therefore not supplied for consumption on the premises on which it was supplied.

HMRC appealed directly to the Court of Appeal and its decision has addressed two main issues:

THE COURT OF APPEAL

"Catering per se"

The Court endorsed the approach set down in the *Safeway Stores plc* case ([1997] STC 163) to be taken in determining what a supply in the course of catering is.

Principally, this is that as no single factor is decisive in determining whether a supply is in the course of catering, all factors need to be considered when looking at the supplies being made.

This finding does not change the position that the sale of cold food by a retailer is standard-rated when sold in the course of catering (see VAT Notice 709/1 section 2). The decision of the Court re-emphasises the approach to take when looking at whether such a supply is being made in the course of catering.

"Premises"

VAT is always chargeable at the standard rate on the supply of food and drink for consumption on the premises on which they are supplied.

The Court of Appeal agreed with the Tribunal that Compass' premises consisted solely of their retail units and not BBC TV Centre as a whole (a restricted access premises). Therefore the sale of cold food to be taken for consumption away from Compass's retail units was zero-rated.

HMRC's previous policy on premises is set out in VAT Notice 709/1 section 3.1, and this advises that:

Premises fall within two categories, those to which the public has unrestricted access and those to which access is only allowed with permission of some sort.

Restricted access sites, such as secure office buildings, sports stadium, amusement parks and cinemas. Here, the premises are the whole of the building or site. This means that all supplies of food and drink will be standard-rated even if it is taken away from the point of sale.

Unrestricted access sites, such as restaurants, shopping malls, hospitals, bus stations and railway stations (including those with platform ticket barriers). Here, the premises are confined to the outlet itself plus any associated facilities, such as table and chairs outside a café, whether or not you provide these facilities.

However, the judgment in Compass states that:

> "the sandwiches were in fact supplied by Compass to retail customers at six particular outlets located at various points in the larger site, not everywhere or anywhere in the BBC Television Centre site. The geographical situation and the physical extent of the retail units under the control of Compass and to which customers have access are sufficiently identified to be regarded or recognisable as separate premises at which supplies of food are made to Compass customers within the meaning of Note (3)(a). No food is consumed in the Compass units themselves. That is where the supplies are made. It follows that the sandwiches supplied by Compass are not supplied for the purposes of being consumed on the premises on which they are supplied".

REVISED POLICY ON THE MEANING OF "PREMISES"

Following the Compass case HMRC have reconsidered their policy on "premises". The main change is that at restricted access sites a retailer will now be considered to occupy only that unit from which the sales of food have been made rather than the larger overall premises. However, the "premises" also includes any facilities provided to enable the purchasers to consume the food at the unit, such as areas of seating and tables within, and adjacent to, the retail unit, whether owned by the landlord or the retailer, but clearly for the use of the food retailer's customers.

This means that, unless the retailers supplies of cold food are in the course of catering (see section on Catering per se, above), the supply of cold food for consumption away from the immediate premises, elsewhere in the restricted access premises, will be zero-rated.

VAT NOTICE 709/1

An updated version of VAT Notice 709/1 will be released shortly to reflect this change to policy.

APPORTIONMENT

Where a retailer is unable to distinguish between standard-rated and zero-rated sales of cold food at the point of sale, the liability must be apportioned. However, the apportionment must be fair and reasonable and the retailer must be able to evidence and support the calculations made.

INFORMATION ON MAKING CLAIMS OR ADJUSTMENTS

Businesses making supplies of a similar nature to those made by Compass in this case will need to review the liability of the supplies that they have made. Businesses that have accounted for and paid VAT on supplies that they now consider to be zero-rated may submit claims for overpaid tax to their local Business Advice Centre. This will be subject to a three-year limitation period and unjust enrichment provisions.

Further information about claims can be found in VAT Notice 700/45 "How to correct VAT errors or make adjustments or claims" and Business Briefs 25/04 and 28/04.

3-YEAR CAP ON MAKING CLAIMS—COURT OF APPEAL JUDGMENT IN MICHAEL FLEMING T/A BODYCRAFT

24 August 2006. *Business Brief 13/06*

This Business Brief article explains HM Revenue & Customs' (HMRC) position following the judgment of the Court of Appeal in *Michael Fleming (t/a Bodycraft) v CRC (Condé Nast Publications Ltd intervening)* [2006] EWCA Civ 70; [2006] STC 864; [2006] All ER (D) 199 (Feb) (Fleming). The court decided the case against HMRC but has granted permission to appeal to the House of Lords and HMRC are doing so.

Pending the outcome of the appeal to the House of Lords, HMRC will give effect to the Court of Appeal's judgment for those who wish to make a claim, under the terms of this Business Brief, which includes a requirement to repay, with interest, in the event that this judgment is overturned. Many taxpayers may choose to await the final outcome of the litigation. In either event, claims arising out of this litigation will carry an entitlement to make a claim for statutory, simple interest (under VATA 1994 s 78).

BACKGROUND

In 1996 and 1997, the Government introduced a 3-year limitation period on claims for repayment of overpaid VAT, the correction of errors and late claims to input tax. It is now accepted, following the ECJ's judgment in *Marks & Spencer Plc v C&E Comrs* [2002] STC 1036 (M&S), that the statutory 3-year limitation periods (introduced with no express transitional periods during which taxpayers were able to make claims under the pre-existing rules) were, in certain cases, wrongly relied upon by HMRC against taxpayers.

Business Brief 22/02 invited claims under VATA 1994 s 80 for repayment of amounts paid incorrectly as VAT. Taxpayers were not, at that time, invited to submit or re-submit claims which had, or would have, been subject to the capping measures introduced, for example in the Value Added Tax Regulations 1995, SI 1995/2518 reg 29(1A), with effect from 1 May 1997.

The exclusion of claims (particularly those made under SI 1995/2518, reg 29 (input tax)) from the scope of Business Brief 22/02, and the refusal of claims made in accordance with it, led to a number of appeals to the VAT & Duties Tribunal challenging both the manner in which the relevant 3-year limitation periods were enacted and HMRC's response to the M&S judgment. Many of these appeals were decided in favour of HMRC but the Court of Appeal in Fleming found against them and held that persons whose right to deduct input tax arose before the date on which the new time limit was enacted, that is to say before 1 May 1997, should be allowed to claim without imposition of the 3-year cap.

IMPLICATIONS OF THE FLEMING JUDGMENT

The Court of Appeal's judgment has implications beyond late claims for input tax. HMRC accept, for present purposes, that any claim, under SI 1995/2518 regs 29, 34 or 35, or VATA 1994 s 80 arising before the enactment of the respective capping measures, is effectively uncapped. However, this does not mean that the 3-year time limits, as they operate currently since the date of their enactment, are themselves contrary to Community law or in any sense invalid.

MAKING A CLAIM

Taxpayers who believe that they are entitled to benefit from the Court of Appeal's judgment in Fleming, and who wish to claim without waiting until the matter is finally determined in the House of Lords, should proceed as follows—

Where a claim, relating to an event more than three years earlier, has already been made and remains "active", either because no appealable decision has yet been given by HMRC or because the matter is subject to appeal, taxpayers should write to HMRC (see the address below) asking for their claim to be considered in accordance with this Business Brief.

In all other cases, a fresh claim can be made where an amount—

– has been improperly paid as VAT before 4 December 1996;
– has been overdeclared as output tax in an accounting period ending before 4 December 1996; or
– became deductible as input tax on or before 30 April 1997 and has not yet been deducted.

In all cases, the claimant must sign an undertaking to the effect that, if the ultimate determination of litigation removes his entitlement, any credit given, or money paid, to him, will be returned to HMRC with interest. A copy of the undertaking is provided at the Annexe.

Claims falling within the scope of VATA 1994 s 80 will be paid only where HMRC are satisfied that to pay the claim will not result in the unjust enrichment of the claimant.

Form of claim

New claims must be made in writing and must include—

– a statement of the amount being claimed;
– the reason for the claim;
– the method of calculation in as much detail as possible;
– the prescribed accounting periods in respect of which claims are being made, allocating amounts to periods;
– the dates on which any overpayments, overdeclarations or underclaims were made and, if the overpayment was made pursuant to an assessment or voluntary disclosure, the date on which the assessment or disclosure was made;
– copies of all documents, schedules, etc. used in support of the claim;
– the reasons why you will not be unjustly enriched, where appropriate, if a credit is now given or a repayment made; and
– any claim for statutory, simple interest (under VATA 1994 s 78) that you consider you are entitled to make.

Claims (whether made under VATA 1994 s 80 or under SI 1995/2518, reg 29) will only be paid or credited on a net basis. For example, if you overdeclared output tax during a given accounting period on supplies which ought to have been exempt, and in the same accounting period you recovered more input tax than you ought, the input tax wrongly recovered will be set off against the overdeclared output tax and only the balance will be paid or credited. Conversely, if, in a given accounting period you have understated your input tax entitlement but you have also understated your output tax liability, your claim should be for any net credit due.

All claims are to be sent to the Voluntary Disclosure Team at—

HM Revenue & Customs, "Fleming" Claims Team (Leeds), Queens Dock, Liverpool, Merseyside, L74 4AA.

Telephone enquiries in relation to the submission of claims or to claims that have already been submitted to the Claims Team may be made on 0113 389 4432.

Commentary—*De Voil Indirect Tax Service* **V3.405.**
Note—See HMRC Brief 7/08 issued following the House of Lords decisions on *Michael Fleming* and *Condé Nast*.

3-YEAR CAP ON MAKING CLAIMS—COURT OF APPEAL JUDGMENT IN CONDÉ NAST PUBLICATIONS LTD

24 August 2006. *Business Brief 13/06*

This Business Brief article explains HMRC's position following the Court of Appeal judgment in *Condé Nast Publications Ltd v CRC* [2006] EWCA Civ 976 (Condé Nast).

Taxpayers need take no action as a consequence of this article. Any taxpayer who is likely to benefit from the Court of Appeal's judgment in Condé Nast will benefit from its judgment in Fleming and can lodge, or pursue, a claim as explained in the previous article in this Business Brief.

Like Fleming, Condé Nast concerned claims refused by HMRC on the basis that they were capped by a 3-year limitation period that, it is now accepted, should have been introduced with an express transitional period during which taxpayers ought to have been able to make claims under the pre-existing rules.

The Court of Appeal hearing Condé Nast was bound by, and followed, its majority judgment in Fleming and disposed of the appeal on that basis. However, the Condé Nast litigation raises an important issue not present on the facts of the Fleming case.

HMRC's view is that, in the absence of a transitional period expressly provided for in legislation, the capping provisions should only be disapplied to the extent necessary to give effect to a taxpayer's Community law rights, where, in individual cases, it was made impossible to exercise those rights by the manner in which the cap was introduced.

It should not be disapplied generally in respect of all claims arising before the capping legislation as was decided by the Court of Appeal. Consequently, HMRC argue that, if a taxpayer would not have put in a claim even had a transitional period been provided when the cap was introduced, the absence of a transitional period cannot be said to have infringed his Community law rights by preventing him from making his claim and the 3-year time limit should not be disapplied.

The Court of Appeal decided this point against HMRC. As it has significance in the event that the House of Lords overturns the judgment in Fleming, HMRC have now petitioned their Lordships for leave to appeal against the Court of Appeal's judgment in Condé Nast.

ANNEX

Undertaking to repay VAT and statutory interest

The Commissioners for HM Revenue and Customs ("the Commissioners") agree to credit the account of [] ("the Claimant") with the principal sum of VAT of £ [] without the need for any further court action by the Claimant. If that results in the Commissioners owing a net sum to the Claimant then the Commissioners agree to pay that net sum to the Claimant [with the appropriate amount of statutory interest].

In return, the Claimant agrees that, if the effect of the decision of the courts, in *Michael Fleming (t/a Bodycraft) v HMRC* [2006] EWCA Civ 70, *Condé Nast Publications Limited v HMRC* [2006]

EWCA Civ 976 or any other case, is that the Claimant was not entitled to the credit described above (or any part of the credit), the credit (or part of the credit) will be cancelled and the Claimant will repay all or the appropriate part of any net sum and statutory interest paid to it by the Commissioners.

The Claimant also agrees to pay simple interest, at the rate set under FA 1996 s 197, on any net sum and statutory interest repaid from the date it is paid to the Claimant by the Commissioners to the date it is repaid to the Commissioners.

The Claimant agrees to make the repayments described above, and pay interest thereon, within 28 days of a demand being made by the Commissioners.

Signed—

For the Commissioners for Her Majesty's Revenue & Customs

Name—

Signature—

Date—

For the Claimant

Name—

Signature—

Date—

Commentary—*De Voil Indirect Tax Service* **V3.405**.

Note—See HMRC Brief 7/08 issued following the House of Lords decisions on *Michael Fleming* and *Condé Nast*.

GAMING MACHINES—ACCOUNTING FOR VAT

27 September 2006. *Business Brief 15/06*

In Business Brief 23/05 (issued on 5 December 2005), we advised that the change to the definition of a gaming machine for VAT purposes created certainty by confirming that where the element of chance in the game is provided is not relevant. This followed attempts to avoid VAT by reconfiguring and developing machines so that the random number generator (RNG), which determined the outcome of the game, was sited outside the machine. HMRC consider that the majority of these machines were in fact gaming machines, even before the change in the definition in December 2005, despite having their RNGs fitted outside the main body of the machine. As such, VAT should have been accounted for, and the machines licensed as gaming machines.

It has come to our attention that some businesses failed to license or account for VAT on these machines or have submitted claims to HMRC requesting repayment of VAT that had been paid.

As VAT was correctly payable on these machines, repayments will not be made and, where tax has been underdeclared, assessments will be issued. If you consider you have been misdirected, you should advise your local Business Centre.

THE REDUCED VALUE RULE FOR LONG-STAY GUESTS IN HOTELS—REVISED INTERPRETATION OF THE LAW ON VAT TREATMENT

27 September 2006. *Business Brief 15/06*

This Business Brief article announces a change in HM Revenue & Customs' (HMRC) interpretation of the law regarding the application of the reduced value rule for long-stay guests in hotels. This change has been incorporated in an update to VAT Notice 709/3—Hotels and Holiday Accommodation, issued recently.

The change affects the treatment of supplies of overnight accommodation made by hotels (which includes inns, boarding houses and similar establishments), where the accommodation is provided to individuals for periods exceeding 28 days. Stays of up to and including 28 days are unaffected by the change and will continue to be subject to VAT at the standard rate.

BACKGROUND

Many people, for a variety of reasons, "live" in hotels or similar establishments for long periods. As the exemption from VAT for supplies of residential accommodation (for example in houses and flats) does not extend to the accommodation provided by hotels, such people would be disadvantaged. In order to provide greater consistency of treatment, a special valuation rule has the effect of treating supplies of accommodation by hotels as VAT-free from the 29th day of a person's stay. The rule (often referred to as "the reduced value rule") restricts the VAT charge to the part of the payment that is not for accommodation. As a result, where an inclusive charge is made, VAT continues to be due on the part of the charge that relates to meals and drinks, plus other services and facilities provided with the accommodation. Details of how to arrive at the part of the charge subject to tax are given in *Notice 709/03—Hotels and holiday accommodation*. The supply of the accommodation does not become an exempt supply, so there is no restriction to the amount of input tax the hotel can claim as a result of the rule.

It has been the view of HMRC that the rule only applies where the supply of the accommodation is made to the individual who will occupy it and that where the supply of the accommodation is to third parties, such as local authorities, VAT is applicable to the total charge regardless of the length of the individual's stay.

REVISED INTERPRETATION OF THE LAW

Following the recent decision of the Tribunal in the case of *Afro Caribbean Housing Association* [2006] SWTI 1374, HMRC now accepts that the reduced value rule is not limited to situations where the VAT supply is made to the individuals occupying the accommodation. This means, that where, for example, hotels contract with local authorities or other organisations for the provision of accommodation, for example to homeless people or asylum seekers, this can qualify for treatment under the reduced value rule.

However, there are no other changes to HMRC's interpretation of the rule, which means that it still only applies where the same individual is using the accommodation for a continuous period that exceeds 28 days (the first 28 days of each individual's stay is always subject to VAT on the full value). It does not apply, for example, where accommodation is block-booked by companies for periods over 28 days and is used by a number of different individuals for individual periods of less than 28 days. It also does not apply to holiday accommodation. *Notice 709/3—Hotels and holiday accommodation* describes in detail how the rule works.

MAKING CLAIMS OR ADJUSTMENTS

The change described above should be implemented from the date of this Business Brief and there is no requirement to make adjustments in respect of supplies made prior to this date. However, where hotels or other establishments wish to make a claim to HMRC for a repayment of output tax incorrectly paid, they may do so, subject to the conditions set out below, by using one of the following methods (full details are given in *VAT Notice 700/45—How to correct VAT errors and make adjustments or claims*)—

- where the total of previous errors do not exceed £2000 net tax, an adjustment may be made to your current VAT return; or
- where the total previous errors exceed £2000 net tax a separate claim should be submitted to HMRC (in these cases the errors must not be corrected through your VAT returns).

Details of where to send your claim can be obtained from update 2 to *VAT Notice 700/45—How to correct VAT errors and make adjustments or claims* or the HMRC National Advice Service on 0845 010 9000.

All adjustments or claims are limited to a three-year period and businesses must be able to produce evidence that they accounted for VAT in the circumstances described above, and must be able to substantiate the amount claimed. Subject to the three-year limitation period, any claim should also be for all prescribed accounting periods in which the error occurred. Should a claim not take into account all errors or all affected accounting periods, then HMRC will seek to set-off amounts owed to us for these periods against amounts claimed in other periods.

HMRC may reject all or part of a claim if repayment would unjustly enrich the claimant. More details on "unjust enrichment" can be found at part 14 of *VAT Notice 700/45—How to correct VAT errors and make adjustments or claims.*

A notification to HMRC that a business intends making a claim in the future is not a valid claim.

Where you are in any doubt about the correct treatment please contact the National Advice Service on 0845 010 9000.

Commentary—*De Voil Indirect Tax Service* **V4.113.**

CHANGES TO VAT LAW IN LIGHT OF THE GAMBLING ACT

13 October 2006. *Business Brief 16/06*

In Business Brief 23/05 (issued on 5 December 2005), we advised that the definition of "gaming machine" for VAT liability purposes in VATA 1994 Sch 9 Group 4 was to be amended by Treasury Order. This was intended to ensure that all gaming machines were excluded from the exemption, and so liable to VAT. In the process of doing this, we updated some of the elements of the definition by reference to GA 2005. VATA 1994 s 23, which includes a corresponding definition of a gaming machine in the provision which determines the value on which VAT is accounted for on gaming machine takings, was amended in FA 2006, with retrospective effect from 6 December 2005.

Two new Treasury Orders have been laid before Parliament that will come into effect on 1 November 2006. The new Orders continue to update VAT law in light of GA 2005, and will—

- remove the separate definition of "gaming machine" from Group 4, replacing it by a cross-reference to the identical definition in section 23;
- provide a new definition of "game of chance" in Group 4 and section 23, replacing the cross reference to the Gambling Act definition;
- ensure that the definition of "game of chance" is the same across the UK for both Group 4 and section 23;
- restore the application of VAT to pinball machines; and
- ensure that any game of chance which is not played for a prize does not fall within the exemption.

DEFINITION OF "GAMING MACHINE"

At present, section 23 and Group 4 contain identical definitions of "gaming machine". The new Group 4 Order replaces the definition of "gaming machine" in Group 4 with a cross-reference to the section 23 definition, which is itself amended by the other Order.

NEW DEFINITIONS OF "GAMBLING" AND "GAME OF CHANCE"

The definition of "gambling" was introduced into Group 4 and section 23 by inserting cross-references to the definitions of "betting" and "gaming" in the Gambling Act. The new Order amending section 23 replaces the cross-references to the Gambling Act with stand-alone definitions of "game of chance", based on provisions in GA 2005 s 6 and s 239. "Betting" is no longer to be defined. The new definition of "game of chance" in Group 4 applies for the use of the term in defining the scope of the exemption whether or not the game is played on a machine.

PINBALL MACHINES AND OTHER GAMES OF CHANCE NOT PLAYED FOR A PRIZE

The takings from pinball machines had inadvertently been brought within the scope of the exemption by the PBR Order, when the Gambling Act concept of gaming was imported into VAT legislation dealing with gaming machines. VAT exemption is currently available for the provision of facilities for playing a game of chance, whether or not for a prize. Gaming machines are excluded from the scope of this exemption. Before the PBR order was introduced, pinball machines were taxed as gaming machines as it was not a requirement for a gaming machine to offer a prize. However, the PBR order applied GA 2005 s 6(1), which provides that gaming is playing a game of chance for a prize, to the definition of gaming machines. Although this meant that pinball machines were excluded from the definition of gaming machines, as they do not offer prizes, they still qualified for VAT exemption as the provisions of facilities for playing a game of chance.

In future, only a game of chance played for a prize, whether or not played on a machine, will qualify for exemption in any event. "Prize" will be defined so as to exclude the opportunity to play the game again ("free plays").

Consequently, traders who have been accounting for VAT on pinball machines takings in the period from 6 December 2005 to 31 October 2006 may make a claim to HMRC for a repayment of output tax incorrectly paid, subject to the conditions set out below, by using one of the following (full details can be found in VAT Notice 700/45 *How to correct VAT errors or make adjustments or claims*—

– where the total of previous errors does not exceed £2000 net tax, an adjustment may be made to your current VAT return; and
– where the total of previous errors exceeds £2000 net tax a separate claim should be submitted to HMRC (in these cases the errors must not be corrected through your VAT returns).

Details of where to send your claim can be obtained from the HMRC National Advice Service on 0845 010 9000.

All adjustments or claims will be subject to the following conditions—

– all claims must take into account input tax that has been claimed, but which, while pinball machine takings were exempt, did not relate to taxable supplies; and
– businesses must be able to produce evidence that they accounted for VAT in the circumstances described above, and must be able to substantiate the amount claimed.

Any claim should be for all prescribed accounting periods in which the liability error occurred.

Should a claim not take into account all errors or all affected accounting periods, then HMRC will seek to set-off amounts owed to us for these periods against amounts claimed in other periods.

HMRC may reject all or part of a claim if repayment would unjustly enrich the claimant. More details on "unjust enrichment" can be found at part 14 of VAT Notice 700/45 *How to correct VAT errors and make adjustments or claims*.

Commentary—*De Voil Indirect Tax Service* **V4.131.**

PUBLICATION OF TAX AVOIDANCE SCHEME DISCLOSURE STATISTICS

13 October 2006. *Business Brief 16/06*

This Business Brief article announces HMRC's intention to publish the number of disclosures of tax avoidance schemes received.

BACKGROUND

In 2004 disclosure rules were introduced requiring promoters and users to notify details of certain direct tax and VAT arrangements to HMRC. The rules were extended to Stamp Duty Land Tax (SDLT) in 2005, and from 1 August 2006 to the whole of Income Tax, Corporation Tax and Capital Gains Tax.

Since the introduction of the rules, tax professionals, business and others have shown a great deal of interest in the total number of disclosures made, and have made many requests to HMRC for the information. These have included requests under the terms of FoIA 2000. As the disclosure rules were developed in collaboration with tax professionals and business, HMRC see making the information more accessible part of its continuing commitment to this collaboration. Publication of the information is not inconsistent with the strict rules on taxpayer confidentiality and the provisions of the FoIA 2000.

WHAT WILL BE PUBLISHED

Starting on 31 October 2006 HMRC will publish the total number of disclosures that have been made up to 30 September 2006. The information will appear in two tables, one for direct tax and SDLT and the other for VAT. The statistics will be updated in April and October of subsequent years.

Each tax within a table, with the exception of SDLT, is subdivided by category of scheme. For direct tax the categories are financial and employment up to 31 July 2006, and hallmark from 1 August 2006 onwards.

FOR VAT THE CATEGORIES ARE LISTED AND HALLMARK.

Within these categories the totals received will be given as six-monthly totals (for the six months ending 31 March and 30 September each year) and annual totals (for the financial year ending

31 March). An exception to giving a six-monthly total is for the six months ending 30 September 2006, as this covers the 1 August 2006 change of categories for direct tax disclosures. In this case the totals for each category will be for the period that they are applicable. The latest totals published will always be provisional, and will only be finalised when the statistics are next updated.

Information on the history of the disclosure rules and further details on interpreting the statistics will be published alongside the tables. The information note will give details of the total number of voluntary registration scheme (VAT hallmark) disclosures received to date.

WHERE TO FIND THE STATISTICS

The statistics will be published on HMRC's website—www.hmrc.gov.uk. Go to the home page and look for the link to the statistics under "What's New" (bottom of screen), otherwise from the home page use the link to the "Practitioner Zone" (top right hand corner) and then use the link under Library to "Anti Avoidance Group". From here follow further links to the statistics.

NEXT PUBLISHING DATE

The updated totals to 31 March 2007 will be published on 30 April 2007.

Commentary—*De Voil Indirect Tax Service* **V5.213.**

LIABILITY OF PRIVATE TUITION

13 October 2006. *Business Brief 16/06*

HMRC's policy on the liability of private tuition is set out in VAT Notice 701/30 *Education and vocational training*, section 6. This advises that the VAT exemption for private tuition only applies to sole proprietors and partnerships who teach a subject that is taught regularly in a number of schools or universities.

It has come to our attention that some businesses that supply private tuition have incorrectly exempted their supplies from VAT. This follows a Tribunal decision in the case of *Empowerment Enterprises Ltd*, which found that the exemption extended to tuition provided by directors of limited companies and those employed by sole proprietors, partnerships or limited companies.

HMRC appealed against the Tribunal's findings and the Court of Session, confirming that exemption is only available to sole proprietors and partnerships.

Therefore, all suppliers of private education should ensure that they are applying the correct liability to their supplies. Additionally, if you have been using the incorrect liability, you will need to account for any unpaid VAT as follows—

- where the total of previous errors does not exceed £2000 net tax, an adjustment may be made to your current VAT return; or
- where the total of previous errors exceeds £2000 net tax, a separate voluntary disclosure should be submitted to HMRC (in these cases the errors must not be corrected through your VAT returns).

Details of where to send your claim can be obtained from update 2 to VAT Notice 700/45—*How to correct VAT errors and make adjustments or claims* or from the HMRC National Advice Service on 0845 010 9000.

Commentary—*De Voil Indirect Tax Service* **V4.141.**
Simon's Tax Cases—*R&C Commissioners v Empowerment Enterprises Ltd* [2006] CSIH 46.

LIABILITY OF CONDOMS SUPPLIED TO CHARITIES PROVIDING CARE OR MEDICAL TREATMENT

13 October 2006. *Business Brief 16/06*

This business brief article explains HMRC's position as a result of the Tribunal's decision in the case of *Pasante Healthcare Ltd* [LON/06/118 (VTD 19724)].

BACKGROUND

The supply of a "medicinal product" to a charity providing care or medical or surgical treatment is zero-rated (VATA 1994, Sch 8, Group 15). Pasante Healthcare Ltd supplied condoms to a charity that provides free and confidential sexual health advice and contraception to young people. It contended that condoms are medicinal products within the terms of the Act, and therefore should be zero-rated when supplied to such a charity.

In order to qualify as a medicinal product the law requires that they be "administered". HMRC contended that the distribution of condoms by a charity did not meet the legal test.

DECISION

The Tribunal agreed with the appellant that a condom falls within the legal definition of a medicinal product as condoms distributed by a sexual health charity are administered within the terms of the legislation.

THE WAY FORWARD

HMRC have decided not to appeal the tribunal's decision. Businesses supplying condoms in similar circumstances to those of Pasante's should zero rate their supplies

The decision does not affect supplies of condoms to customers other than charities providing care, medical or surgical treatment. They will continue to be liable to the reduced rate of VAT, which applied to contraceptive products, with effect from 1 July 2006.

INFORMATION ON MAKING CLAIMS OR ADJUSTMENTS

Businesses that have accounted for and paid VAT on supplies of condoms that are now consider to be zero-rated may submit claims for overpaid tax to their local Business Advice Centre. These will be subject to a three-year limitation period and unjust enrichment provisions.

More information about claims can be found in VAT Notice 700/45 *How to correct VAT errors or make adjustments or claims* and Business Briefs 25/04 and 28/04.

FURTHER INFORMATION

For further information and advice, please contact HMRC Charity Helpline on 0845 302 0203.

Commentary—*De Voil Indirect Tax Service* **V4.146.**

PARTIAL EXEMPTION: BOOKMAKERS—RECOVERY OF VAT ON SPECIALIST TELEVISION SERVICES AND EQUIPMENT

19 October 2006. *Business Brief 17/06*

This Business Brief article clarifies HMRC policy on the recovery of VAT incurred by bookmakers on specialist TV services, following the Tribunal decision in the case of *Town and County Factors (TCF)*, VTD 19616 [but see Note below]. It uses a number of specialist terms, which are fully explained in Public Notice 706, Partial Exemption.

BACKGROUND

Betting shops often incur VAT on specialist TV services and equipment on which they screen racing and sporting events, including those for which exempt bets are accepted. TCF argued that VAT incurred on TV facilities was partly recoverable because they had a direct and immediate link with taxable supplies of gaming machines and refreshments, as well as exempt supplies of betting. HMRC's view was that the costs related wholly to exempt supplies so that no VAT was recoverable.

The Tribunal supported TCF, finding on the facts of the case that VAT incurred on specialist racing TV was residual because TCF added content to the broadcasts advertising their taxable services and because TV attracts customers into shops to play gaming machines. The Tribunal also found that VAT relating to Sky Sports was residual as the costs related to all of the activities of the betting shop even though the broadcasts did not carry adverts for their taxable services.

HMRC'S POLICY FOLLOWING TCF

HMRC are not appealing the decision. HMRC accept that bookmakers who add content to specialist racing TV to advertise their taxable services, may now treat the VAT as residual.

HMRC remain of the view that, where no such content is added, the VAT incurred is wholly related to exempt betting and is not recoverable.

HMRC accept that bookmakers may treat VAT incurred on Sky Sports as residual because the broadcasts are not exclusively related to exempt betting. VAT incurred on TV equipment is also residual provided it is used for broadcasts that relate to both taxable and exempt supplies. If the equipment is used wholly for specialist racing TV, then the VAT incurred is irrecoverable.

PARTIAL EXEMPTION METHODS

Even where VAT on specialist racing TV is residual, the amount of taxable use is likely to be very small compared with overhead costs such as lighting and heating. As a result existing Partial Exemption (PE) methods may no longer produce a fair and reasonable result and may need to be amended.

HMRC may seek to replace an unfair method or to prospectively amend its result. If you consider that your PE method is no longer fair and reasonable you should contact your Local Business Advice Centre with proposals for a new method.

CLAIMS FOR UNDER-RECOVERED INPUT TAX

Bookmakers may wish to claim input tax which, in the light of this Business Brief, was incorrectly treated as exempt. Claims should be submitted to the Local Business Advice Centre. They must use the PE method applicable to each accounting period unless there are exceptional circumstances as to why an alternative method is needed. All claims are subject to the relevant time limits.

Further information about making claims can be found in Public Notice 700/45 How to correct VAT errors or make adjustments or claims and Business Briefs 25/04 and 28/04.

Note—See now HMRC Brief 1/08 (following the decision in *Cheshire Racing Ltd*, HMRC now accept that SIS services have a direct and immediate link to gaming machine supplies made by bookmakers).

Commentary—*De Voil Indirect Tax Service* **V6.296.**

DISPOSABLE BARBECUES

19 October 2006. *Business Brief 17/06*

HM Revenue & Customs (HMRC) have been asked to clarify the VAT treatment of the sale of disposable barbecues. Some retailers have been treating such sales as reduced rate or mixed rate supplies (part standard-rated; part reduced-rated). The correct VAT treatment is that the sale of disposable barbecues is a single standard-rated supply, subject to VAT at 17.5 per cent.

Any errors made on previous VAT returns in respect of such supplies must be corrected in accordance with the conditions set out below, by using one of the following methods (full details are given in VAT Notice 700/45 How to correct VAT errors and make adjustments or claims):

- where the total of previous errors does not exceed £2000 net tax, an adjustment may be made to your current VAT return, or
- where the total of previous errors exceeds £2000 net tax a separate written disclosure should be submitted to HMRC (in these cases the errors must not be corrected through your VAT returns). Details of where to send your disclosure can be obtained from Update 2 to VAT Notice 700/45 How to correct VAT errors and make adjustments or claims or the HMRC National Advice Service on 0845 010 9000.

All adjustments are limited to a three-year period.

If in quantifying errors made, any business considers that the extra-statutory concessions relating to misdirection or misunderstanding apply, they should submit a complete report to HMRC. Details of these ESCs (3.4 and 3.5) and the circumstances under which HMRC will remit, or not assess, VAT undercharged are in Public Notice 48 Extra Statutory Concessions.

Where you are in any doubt about the correct treatment please contact the National Advice Service on 0845 010 9000.

Commentary—*De Voil Indirect Tax Service* **V3.103.**

LIABILITY OF AGENTS' CREDIT AND DEBIT CARD HANDLING SERVICES

30 October 2006. *Business Brief 18/06*

This Business Brief article announces HMRC's revised policy on the VAT liability of credit and debit card handling services supplied by agents, following the end of litigation in the cases of *Bookit Ltd* (Bookit) and *Scottish Exhibition Centre Ltd* (SEC).It replaces item 2 of Business Brief 21/05 and item 1 of Business Brief 17/98, both of which are now withdrawn. Public Notice 701/49, *Finance*, will be updated in due course.

SUMMARY

The House of Lords has refused HMRC's petition to appeal the Court of Appeal judgment in *Bookit* (EWCA Civ 550) [2006] STC 1367 and HMRC will not be seeking leave to appeal the judgment of the Court of Session in the case of *SEC* ([2006] Scot CS CSIH-42).The effect of the end of litigation in these two cases is that debit and credit card handling services provided by agents are VAT exempt where a key identified component is present in the service. Claims held pending the outcome of these cases will now be reviewed for payment and any assessments raised by HMRC for under-declared tax will be withdrawn where appropriate.

BACKGROUND

The Bookit case concerned the supply of Odeon cinema tickets. Customers wishing to purchase cinema tickets remotely, eg by phone or Internet, were redirected to Odeon's agent, Bookit, who charged the customer an additional fee over and above the price of the ticket for their service. Bookit contended this fee was for credit or debit card handling services and was VAT-exempt as a transaction concerning payments or transfers. The tribunal found that Bookit was providing a taxable card handling service to the customer in return for the additional fee. The High Court, in overturning the tribunal's decision, found that Bookit was carrying out an exempt card handling service. The Court of Appeal, in upholding the High Court judgment, found that the supply by Bookit to the customer included the following components:

- obtaining the card information with the necessary security information from the customer;
- transmitting that information to the card issuers;
- receiving the authorisation codes from the card issuers; and
- transmitting the card information with the necessary security information and the card issuers' authorisation codes to Girobank.

The Court found that the tribunal had been correct in finding components (i) to (iii) to be taxable, but because the fourth component was part of Bookit's service to the customer, and had the effect that funds were transferred to its account with Girobank, exemption was available to Bookit. The *SEC* case concerned the supply of tickets to events held in the Scottish Exhibition and Conference Centre in Glasgow. SEC acted as agent of the promoter in the selling of tickets and charged an additional fee to customers on tickets that were paid for by credit and debit card. SEC contended this fee was for card handling services and was VAT exempt. The tribunal found in HMRC's favour, stating that SEC was providing a single taxable booking service, with the taxable card handling service representing an ancillary aspect enhancing the main service. The Court of Session overturned the tribunal decision, finding that SEC was carrying out an exempt card handling service. The Court based its judgment on the decision of the Court of Appeal in Bookit and on an assumption of similar facts. HMRC do not therefore draw a distinction between the two judgments.

IMPLICATIONS OF THE JUDGMENTS

The judgments have provided further guidance on when a service of credit or debit card handling by an agent is VAT-exempt. If an agent, acting for the supplier of the goods or services, makes a charge to the customer over and above the price of the actual goods or services, for a separately identifiable service of handling payment by credit or debit card, and that service includes the fourth component listed above, then the additional charge will be exempt under item 1, Group 5 of Schedule 9 to the VAT Act 1994. However, where an agent provides some or all of the first three components without providing the fourth, the charge is taxable at the standard rate of VAT. Charges levied on the cardholder for payment by credit and debit card in any other circumstances will not fall within the exemption for financial services and the normal VAT treatment will apply. The judgments do not alter the general principle that the taxable amount for a supply of goods or services includes all payments which the supplier requires the customer to make as a condition of receiving the supply. If, for example, a supplier of goods or services requires a customer to pay an additional charge, above that of the price of the actual goods or services, for payment by credit or debit card, that charge is further consideration for the purchase of those goods or services and VAT is payable on that amount in accordance with the VAT treatment of the goods or services.

INFORMATION ON MAKING CLAIMS OR ADJUSTMENTS

Agents supplying card handling services that meet the criteria set out above, and who have been treating the charge as taxable at the standard rate, should exempt such services from the date of this Business Brief. Conversely, agents supplying card handling services that do not meet the criteria set out above, and have been treating those services as exempt, should now charge tax. There is no requirement to make adjustments in respect of earlier supplies. However, where businesses wish to make a claim to HMRC for a repayment of output tax incorrectly paid, they may do so, subject to the conditions set out below, by using one of the following methods (full details are given in VAT Notice 700/45 *How to correct VAT errors and make adjustments or claims*):

- where the total of previous errors does not exceed £2,000 net tax, an adjustment may be made to your current VAT return.
- where the total of previous errors exceeds £2,000 net tax, a separate claim should be submitted to HMRC (in these cases the errors must not be corrected through your VAT returns). Details of where to send your claim can be obtained from update 2 to VAT Notice 700/45 *How to correct VAT errors and make adjustments or claims* or the HM Revenue & Customs National Advice Service on 0845 010 9000.

All adjustments or claims are limited to a three-year period (subject to Business Brief 13/06) and will be subject to the following conditions:

- all claims must take into account input tax that has been claimed, but which under the revised interpretation will not relate to taxable supplies.
- businesses must be able to produce evidence that they accounted for VAT in the circumstances described above, and must be able to substantiate the amount claimed.

Subject to the three-year limitation period, any claim should be for all prescribed accounting periods in which the liability error occurred. Should a claim not take into account all errors or all affected accounting periods, then HMRC will seek to set-off amounts owed to us for these periods against amounts claimed in other periods. HMRC may reject all or part of a claim if repayment would unjustly enrich the claimant. More details on 'unjust enrichment' can be found at part 14 of VAT Notice 700/45 *How to correct VAT errors and make adjustments or claims*. A notification to HMRC that a business intends making a claim in the future is not a valid claim. HMRC will review claims by businesses for exemption of supplies of debit and credit card handling services, and businesses can expect requests to be challenged vigorously where there is evidence of underlying artificiality or abuse. If there is any doubt about the correct VAT treatment of your services, please contact the National Advice Service on 0845 010 9000.

Commentary—*De Voil Indirect Tax Service* **V4.136I.**

FIRST GRANT OF A MAJOR INTEREST IN RESIDENTIAL PROPERTY: ATTRIBUTION OF INPUT TAX AND THE CAPITAL GOODS SCHEME

22 December 2006. *Business Brief 23/06*

This Business Brief article confirms and explains HMRC policy regarding input tax incurred on the construction of residential property where the developer sells a long leasehold interest separately from the freehold interest.

BACKGROUND

The first grant of a major interest (freehold sale or lease exceeding 21 years) in residential property by its developer is zero-rated, under VAT Act 1994, Schedule 8, Group 5. However, all subsequent grants in the property are VAT exempt. VAT on costs relating to zero-rated supplies is fully recoverable whereas VAT relating to exempt supplies is not normally recoverable. Detailed rules on the liability of supplies of buildings are in Notice 708, on partial exemption in Notice 706 and on the capital goods scheme in Notice 706/2.

ATTRIBUTION OF INPUT TAX

When a residential property is constructed or results from the conversion of a non-residential property and the developer makes a first grant of a major interest in that property, any input tax incurred is recoverable in full. This is because the input tax is wholly attributed to that taxable first grant. This is the case even where the value of the first grant does not represent full equity in the property, such as in shared ownership schemes run by housing associations.

APPLICATION OF THE CAPITAL GOODS SCHEME (CGS)

Regulations 112(2) and 113 of the VAT Regulations 1995 set out when a building will be a capital item for the purposes of the CGS. If a developer constructs a residential property and the first grant of a major interest in the building is a long lease, he is using the building for a business purpose other than solely for the purpose of selling the building. As a result, the developer will have to treat the building as a capital item. The input tax incurred on the construction of the building and wholly attributed to the zero-rated long lease will have to be adjusted through the CGS should a subsequent exempt grant be made of the building. If a developer constructs a residential property and the first grant of a major interest is the sale of the freehold, the developer is using the building solely for the purpose of selling the building and will not have to treat the building as a capital item.

EXAMPLES

There are essentially three ways a developer might grant all the leases and the reversionary interest in the freehold of a residential property (typically a block of flats):

(a) All flats sold followed by the freehold—the sale of each individual flat will be zero-rated as first grant of a major interest. While the developer will hold a capital item, when the freehold is sold, we consider that this will only be exempt to the extent that it relates to those areas of the building that were previously the subject of the zero-rated grants of individual flats. Most of the sale of the freehold will be zero-rated because it relates to the common parts that have not been subject to any previous supply. These circumstances are part of the sale of new dwellings for which the zero-rating was designed. Furthermore any CGS adjustments would be negligible. Accordingly there is no need for CGS adjustments in this example.

(b) Freehold sold before any flats are sold—the sale of the freehold will be a zero-rated grant and since no leases had been granted, would not be a capital item (by virtue of Reg 112(2), VAT Regulations 1995). Since the freehold is zero-rated, all input tax incurred on the construction costs will be fully deductible. As the new freeholder, the purchaser will normally make any exempt grants of leases to buyers of flats. Even where the consideration for such sales accrues to the developer, so that VAT law treats the developer as the person supplying the flat, this will not impact on the initial deduction of input tax by the developer. It may, however, have implications for any input tax incurred on selling costs.

(c) Freehold sold after some flats have been sold—the flats sold before the freehold has been supplied will each be a zero-rated first grant of a major interest. While the developer will hold a capital item, when the freehold is sold, we consider that this will only be exempt to the extent that it relates to those areas of the building that were previously the subject of the zero-rated grants of individual flats. Most of the supply of the freehold will be zero-rated relating to the common parts and unsold flats that haven't been subject to any previous supply. As per example (a) above, no CGS adjustments are needed. If, under the agreement for sale, the developer has retained the right to receive the monies from the sale of the remaining unsold flats, the considerations set out in example (b) above apply.

OTHER RESIDENTIAL PROPERTY

The first grant of a major interest in a relevant residential property (eg a care home) is zero-rated. Under Reg 116(3), VAT Regulations 1995, in determining any CGS adjustments in subsequent years, the developer disregards any exempt supply arising directly from that grant (including all rents due under that lease). Even though the developer holds a capital item, providing he makes no exempt supplies other than those arising from that zero-rated grant, he will retain full deduction of the input tax on the construction of the development. However, if the developer makes a new grant, like selling the freehold, this is the second grant in the building and will be exempt. In this situation CGS adjustments are likely to be required and CGS calculations must be carried out.

Commentary—*De Voil Indirect Tax Service* **V3.470**.

FINAL BUSINESS BRIEF

22 December 2006. *Business Brief 23/06*

This is the last Business Brief that HMRC will issue. There has been a substantial decrease in demand for a paper product in recent years. When we consulted subscribers earlier this year their feedback was that a move to an online-only service was appropriate. An online-only service means that HMRC can get information published far more quickly. Business Briefs were originally published by the former HM Customs & Excise and dealt with changes in indirect tax policy. In the former Inland Revenue a similar publication 'Tax Bulletin' covered direct tax matters. HMRC are taking this opportunity to combine the two publications into a single online-only bulletin—'Revenue & Customs Brief'. Revenue & Customs Brief will appear in the Library section of our website at www.hmrc.gov.uk/library.htm, and will go live from 1 January 2007.

FURTHER CLARIFICATION OF THE TREATMENT OF FOREIGN EXCHANGE TRANSACTIONS (FOREX) AND TRANSACTIONS IN OTHER FINANCIAL INSTRUMENTS

26 January 2007. *HMRC Brief 5/07*

Business Brief 21/05 explained HMRC's position following the tribunal decision in *Willis Pension Fund Trustees Limited (Willis)* [VTD 19183] and the implications of the decision for other businesses conducting forex transactions. The Tribunal found that the forex transactions Willis entered into were not supplies for VAT purposes.

This Brief article sets out HMRC's view on when forex transactions are supplies for VAT purposes and the implications this has for VAT recovery. It also outlines HMRC's view on any wider application of the decision to transactions in other financial instruments.

DETERMINING IF YOUR FOREX TRANSACTIONS ARE SUPPLIES FOR VAT PURPOSES

The tribunal decision in Willis applied to a very specific set of circumstances and, whilst some general principles can be drawn from the decision, care needs to be taken when seeking to give it wider application. The European Court of Justice (ECJ) judgment in *First National Bank of Chicago (FNBC)* [C-172/96] is the leading authority on the VAT treatment of forex transactions.

In Willis, forex deals were entered into for the purposes of "hedging". This is a term that is variously defined, but "hedging" is about reducing exposure to risk of loss resulting from fluctuations in some commodity or financial market. What is relevant for VAT purposes is whether any underlying trade is performed to achieve that objective. "Hedging" is not in itself a test for determining whether or not there is a supply for VAT purposes.

In general, forex transactions are supplies for VAT purposes if you adopt a spread position over a period of time when buying and selling currency. This applies whether this is being done for your own account, in support of other areas of your business, or to reduce any exposure position in forex that you hold. A spread position means a difference between a bid price and a sell price from which you would expect to derive a profit. These forex transactions would include both "spot" and "forward" transactions, as envisaged by the FNBC judgment.

Most businesses actively involved in forex trading should readily be able to identify whether their forex transactions fall under the FNBC principle of adopting a spread position. If uncertainties remain, you should consider whether, in selling a currency, you are in a position to set the selling price. If so, you are able to determine the consideration you receive by setting a spread, even if only mimicking market movements, and your forex transactions are likely to be supplies for VAT purposes.

Where your forex transactions are supplies, the consideration will be the net result of all your forex transactions over a period of time and would be exempt under VATA 1994, Sch. 9, Group 5, Item 1. Any forex transactions, for which you charge an attributable fee or commission, would also be exempt supplies under Item 1.

The following are examples of circumstances when it is unlikely that your forex transactions would be seen as supplies for VAT purposes:

- a business simply exchanging one currency for another to realise foreign earnings into sterling, for example, or to acquire currency to settle liabilities incurred outside the UK, is unlikely to be seen as making supplies for VAT purposes provided such transactions are not part of a wider economic activity being carried out for an identifiable consideration
- a business entering into forward forex deals in order to limit its exposure to forex fluctuations in respect of future obligations is unlikely to be seen as making supplies for VAT purposes provided such transactions are not part of a wider economic activity being carried out for an identifiable consideration.

Businesses with a corporate treasury operation active in the financial markets may need to look carefully at their forex transactions. If no spread position is being taken and no profit being actively sought, it is unlikely that any forex transactions would be regarded as supplies. However, a number of larger businesses have corporate treasury operations that are much more pro-active, either externally or internally, within their commercial groups. For example, a business might typically run a "forex desk" in a similar manner to any other financial institution or market maker more traditionally associated with forex dealing. Such businesses are likely to be taking a spread position and would be making supplies. All their forex transactions, whether spot or forward and whether proprietary or in support of other activities or areas of the business, should be treated as forex supplies.

Intermediaries acting in relation to a forex transaction can exempt their intermediary services under item 5, Group 5 of Schedule 9. This applies whether or not the underlying forex transaction is a supply for VAT purposes.

HOW YOUR INPUT TAX RECOVERY WILL BE AFFECTED

The normal input tax recovery rules will apply. Businesses making exempt financial supplies cannot normally recover the VAT attributable to those supplies unless the recipient of those supplies is located outside the EU (in which case recovery is allowed under the VAT (Input Tax)(Specified Supplies) Order 1999). Businesses involved in forex transactions which are not seen as supplies for VAT purposes are able to recover the VAT attributable to those transactions as residual input tax, subject to the partial exemption method used. However, there is no right of recovery under the Specified Supplies Order for such transactions.

Supplies by financial intermediaries can attract recovery under the Specified Supplies Order if the recipient of the intermediaries' supply is based outside the EU, or if the underlying forex transaction is itself a supply which is made outside the EU. There is no right of recovery under the Specified Supplies Order, however, where the recipient of an intermediary's supply is based in the UK or elsewhere in the EU but the underlying transaction is not a supply for VAT purposes. Intermediaries arranging non-EU forex transactions will therefore need to determine whether the underlying transaction is a supply.

Businesses may wish to seek clarification on their present partial exemption methods, and some methods may need to be revised. There are provisions for excluding, in certain circumstances, incidental financial transactions from values-based calculations in partial exemption methods and the provisions of Regulation 106 of the VAT Regulations 1995 allow for de minimis levels of exempt input tax to be treated as attributable to taxable supplies. For further information on this, please refer to VAT Notice 706 *Partial exemption*. Whilst HMRC would wish to avoid disproportionate changes, any proposed changes will need to result in a fair and reasonable method.

WIDER APPLICATION IN RESPECT OF TRANSACTIONS IN OTHER FINANCIAL INSTRUMENTS

The Willis Tribunal made reference in its decision to interest rate swaps. It suggested that, in its view, there would only be a supply when it was possible to identify the consideration being obtained by a party entering into the contract.

There would appear to be nothing arising directly out of Willis that indicates a shortfall in HMRC's current approach to the VAT treatment of other financial instruments and it is, therefore, not intended to revise existing published policy. HMRC do, however, recognise that there may be particular circumstances where Willis principles could apply to transactions in other financial instrument transactions and HMRC would consider such cases on an individual basis.

CHANGES TO THE EXEMPTION FOR MEDICAL SERVICES FROM 1 MAY 2007

30 January 2007. *HMRC Brief 06/07*

This Revenue & Customs Brief announces the implementation of changes to the exemption from VAT for medical services, following the European Court of Justice (ECJ) decision in the case of *Dr Peter d'Ambrumenil and Dispute Resolution Services* (C-307/01). It follows on from earlier Business Briefs 29/03, 18/05 and 04/06.

The changes will take effect from 1 May 2007 subject to House of Commons approval. They affect certain services provided by health professionals registered on a statutory professional register who are registered for VAT. They will not impact on primary health care and core NHS services, which will remain free from VAT.

BACKGROUND

The ECJ decision concerned the VAT exemption for health services provided by health professionals registered on a statutory professional register. The court held that this exemption is restricted to "medical care", which it defined as those services **intended principally to protect (including maintain or restore) the health of an individual.** Medical services which are primarily for the purpose of enabling a third party to take a decision—many of which are currently exempt from VAT under UK law—are taxable. This means that VAT liability is dependent on the purpose for which the supply is made—referred to as the "purpose test".

Business Brief 18/05 issued on 16 September 2005 announced a three month consultation entitled "VAT: A review of the scope of the VAT exemption for medical services". This consultation primarily sought to gather information about the activities of health professionals, and the impact that the ECJ decision may have on the health sector and its clients. This consultation exercise has now been completed and a summary of responses received to this consultation is attached.

In response to the consultation responses and in conjunction with the British Medical Association and British Dental Association, HMRC have drawn up detailed guidance on the application of the purpose test to key services.

UK law will be amended with effect from 1 May 2007 in order to limit the exemption from VAT for health services to those services which constitute the provision of "medical care".

SERVICES AFFECTED

The services most affected by the changes are:

- witness testimony/reports for litigation, compensation or benefit purposes
- reports/medicals for the purpose of providing certain fitness certificates and
- some occupational health services.

These services will become liable to VAT at 17.5 per cent from 1 May 2007. However, this summary is not exhaustive, and health providers should consider the liability of all their services in conjunction with the guidance given in Notice 701/57 *Health professionals* (January 2007). If they remain uncertain as to the liability of any of their services having read the guidance, they should contact the National Advice Service on 0845 010 9000.

ACTION REQUIRED

The changes will affect health service providers registered on a statutory professional register who provide affected services and whose total taxable income is now over the VAT registration threshold, or who are already VAT registered.

Where the health provider is not already VAT registered, they will need to consider their turnover and if the value of all their taxable supplies, including the income from affected services, is over the registration threshold, they will need to register for VAT at the appropriate time in accordance with the guidelines on VAT registration, Notice 700/1 *Should I be registered for VAT?* They will then have to account for VAT on all their taxable supplies, but will be able to reclaim VAT on those purchases and expenses which relate to taxable supplies, in accordance with the normal VAT recovery rules and, in particular, the partial exemption regulations.

Registered health professionals who are already registered for VAT, for example, as a result of dispensing changes which took effect on 1 April 2006, will need to ensure that they account for VAT as appropriate on any affected services.

INSURANCE-RELATED MEDICAL SERVICES

Business Brief 29/03 issued in December 2003 gave details of certain services—such as conducting a medical to assess the level of insurance premiums—which were specifically considered by the ECJ and ruled to be outside the scope of the health exemption, and therefore taxable. The Business Brief explained that doctors and other health professionals were not required to take any action to register for VAT or charge VAT on these services until such time as HMRC formally implemented the changes.

Although such services will no longer qualify under the health exemption, in a recent tribunal case— *Morganash Ltd* (MAN/05/0749)—a ruling was given that medical services which were undertaken for the purpose of enabling a provider of life assurance to decide whether to accept a proposal for a policy fall within the scope of the UK exemption for insurance-related services, pending the implementation of the ECJ decision in the case of *Andersen* (C-472/03). HMRC have decided not to appeal this case and, as a result, accept that insurance-related medical services related to the setting up of contracts, the administration of policies or handling of claims, will remain exempt from VAT, pending any amendment of the UK exemption for insurance services.

Further, the following services will qualify as exempt under the health exemption as being principally for the purposes of protecting, maintaining or restoring the health of the individual concerned:

- health screening under private medical insurance policies—these are regular check-ups to detect early signs of disease;
- income/credit protection insurance—medical services where the policy holder has fallen ill (as opposed to losing their job) which are aimed at assisting the individual in returning to a normal life;
- motor insurance—where medical services are provided under a policy to assist in enabling an injured motorist to return to full health and/or work. (Note—this does not include medicals undertaken for DVLA purposes to ensure initial or continued fitness to drive which are liable to VAT at the standard rate);
- any other medical service provided in connection with an insurance policy where the principal aim is to assist in restoring the health of the individual.

Medical services provided for the purpose of valuing insurance policies for tax purposes, such as inheritance tax, will become liable to VAT at 17.5 per cent.

FURTHER ADVICE

HMRC will shortly be issuing an Information Sheet giving advice on VAT registration and accounting issues for those affected by the changes.

CASH BINGO: ACCOUNTING FOR VAT ON PARTICIPATION AND SESSION FEES

1 February 2007. *HMRC Brief 07/07*

This brief is about participation and session fees paid by cash bingo players. It clarifies HM Revenue & Customs' policy on how to calculate those fees for VAT purposes.

BACKGROUND

Participation and session fees charged for taking part in bingo played for cash prizes on premises licensed or registered under Part II of the Gaming Act 1968 (sometimes termed "mainstage" cash bingo) are consideration for standard-rated supplies. Stake money—the amount risked by the player, all of which must be returned as winnings—is not payment for a supply and so is outside the scope of VAT.

Where participation and session fees and stake money are received together in one composite amount charged to players, bingo promoters must work out how much of the payment is stake and how much is the participation and session fee in order to determine how much VAT is due. Section 3.2 of Notice 701/27 *Bingo* explains how to do this.

We have received enquiries from some bingo promoters performing the VAT calculation on a game-by-game basis, asking whether they are acting correctly and these have prompted the issue of this clarification.

CALCULATING THE VAT DUE

When a player pays to participate in all or part of a bingo session, the supply made by the promoter is the right to participate in the number of games during that session for which they have received payment. As a player cannot participate in further sessions unless they make further payment, the supply to the player is completed when the session ends. In these circumstances the amount of VAT due on participation and session charges should properly be calculated on a session-by-session basis by deducting the stake money arising in each individual session from the total amount (less any admission fees) paid by players to participate in that same session. Where money from other sources is added to the stake money received in the session in order to meet guaranteed prizes, that additional money cannot be used to reduce the value for VAT of the participation and session charges paid for taking part in that session.

Where a player pays to take part in an additional game ("flyer") that does not form part of the session charge, this is a separate supply of the right to participate in that further game. The VAT due on fees charged for participating in additional games should be calculated on a game-by-game basis.

Where a promoter provides facilities for participating in linked games or a national game, in which players located at more than one venue all participate in the same game, charges received at all the promoter's participating venues should be aggregated in order to calculate the amount of VAT due on par fees relating to the linked game or national game.

Promoters should not perform a single calculation for the whole of each VAT return period, aggregating stake money and receipts taken for all bingo played during that time.

Notice 701/27 *Bingo* will be updated.

MAKING CLAIMS OR ADJUSTMENTS

Bingo promoters that have calculated the VAT due on participation and session charges on a game-by-game basis, and who now find that they have done so incorrectly, may make a claim to HMRC for a repayment of any resulting overdeclaration, subject to the conditions set out in Notice 700/45 *How to correct VAT errors or make adjustments or claims*. In particular, businesses should note that:

- where the total of previous errors does not exceed £2000 net tax, an adjustment may be made to your current VAT return but
- where the total of previous errors exceeds £2000 net tax a separate claim should be submitted to HMRC (in these cases the errors must not be corrected through your VAT returns).

HMRC may reject all or part of a claim if repayment would unjustly enrich the claimant. More information about unjust enrichment can be found at part 14 of Notice 700/45.

Advice about where to send your claim can be obtained from HMRC's National Advice Service on 0845 010 9000.

MANUFACTURERS' "CASH BACK" PAYMENTS

6 February 2007. *HMRC Brief 08/07*

This Revenue and Customs Brief article explains the VAT treatment of "cash backs" and what businesses should do if they pay or receive "cash backs", or have paid or received them in the past.

BACKGROUND

The term "cash back" refers to a payment usually made by a manufacturer directly (or via a recovery agency) to the customer of a wholesaler or retailer—mostly in recognition of the volume of purchases. Similar payments may also be made under manufacturers' discount schemes, or may be referred to as volume bonuses or described in similar terms. Such payments occur outside the direct supply chain and as a result credit notes should not be used.

HMRC have become aware that some businesses have been accounting for "cash back" payments incorrectly. Some manufacturers have reduced their output tax, some have not. Some have made retrospective claims for overpaid output tax, but the recipients of those "cash backs" have not necessarily reduced their input tax.

VAT TREATMENT

The treatment of payments of this nature was laid down by the European Court of Justice (ECJ) in two cases: *Elida Gibbs* (C-317/94) and *Commission v Germany* (C-427/98). HMRC's policy is set out in VAT Notice 700/7 *Business Promotion Schemes* Section 7.5, which states that manufacturers are entitled to reduce the output tax on their sales in respect of the "cash backs", provided that they charged and accounted for VAT on their original supply.

If you are VAT-registered and you receive a "cash back" that relates to a taxable supply, this reduces the taxable value of your purchase, and you must reduce your input tax in the proportion in which you claimed it.

WAY FORWARD

Until 1 March 2007, providing—

– manufacturers have not reduced their output tax, and
– recipients have not reduced their input tax, and
– both parties have agreed to make no adjustments for the past, present and future,

HMRC will not require adjustments to be made in these circumstances, will not assess for over-claimed input tax, and will consider withdrawing any such assessments that have already been raised, subject to the usual three year limitation.

If manufacturers break the agreement, change their minds at a later date, and do adjust their output tax, HMRC will assess recipients in line with assessment time limits.

Where manufacturers have already adjusted their output tax and recipients have failed to adjust their input tax, HMRC will assess for over-claimed input tax, or defend assessments already issued.

In practice, where a manufacturer has not made a claim to reduce their output tax in respect to any "cash back" payments made prior to 1 March 2007, HMRC would assume an agreement between the parties. If however a manufacturer subsequently makes a claim for periods prior to 1 March 2007, HMRC continue to reserve the right to take action in respect to any failure to adjust input tax by the recipient.

A recipient of a "cash back" payment prior to 1 March 2007 remains responsible for identifying if there is a need to reduce their input tax. In cases of doubt they must determine the VAT treatment applied by the manufacturer and apply the guidance given.

From 1 March 2007, businesses should correctly make the necessary adjustments as outlined above. Businesses providing "cash backs" are entitled to reduce their output tax provided that they charged and accounted for VAT on their original supply.

If you are VAT-registered and you receive a "cash back", this reduces the taxable value of your purchase, and you must reduce your input tax accordingly. HMRC will assess for over-claimed input tax where these adjustments are not made.

Any "cash back" payment from manufacturer to customer, that does not affect the wholesaler, does not require the wholesaler to make any VAT adjustment.

CROSS BORDER "CASH BACKS"

Where "cash backs" are paid between businesses in different EU member states (MS), no VAT adjustments should be made. This means in practice:

- where a UK manufacturer pays a "cash back" to a recipient in another MS, the manufacturer cannot reduce his output tax; and
- where a UK recipient receives a "cash back" from a manufacturer in another MS, no input tax deduction is required by the recipient.

CHANGE OF LIABILITY IN THE SUPPLY CHAIN

Where the VAT liability of the goods changes in the supply chain (eg where a charity buys certain goods zero-rated from the wholesaler which were standard-rated for VAT when supplied by the manufacturer), manufacturers cannot reduce their output tax in relation to the "cash back" paid to the charity. Where the 'cash back' relates to goods that were supplied VAT-free to a business receiving the 'cash back', no adjustments should be made.

LIABILITY OF PRIVATE TUITION

6 February 2007. *HMRC Brief 10/07*

HMRC's policy on the liability of private tuition is set out in Notice 701/30 *(Education and vocational training)*, section 6. This advises that the VAT exemption for private tuition only applies to sole proprietors and partnerships who teach a subject that is taught regularly in a number of schools or universities.

It has come to our attention that some businesses that supply private tuition have incorrectly exempted their supplies from VAT. This follows a Tribunal decision in the case of *Empowerment Enterprises Ltd*, which found that the exemption extended to tuition provided by directors of limited companies and those employed by sole proprietors, partnerships or limited companies.

HMRC appealed against the Tribunal's findings and the Court of Session allowed the appeal, confirming that exemption is only available to sole proprietors and partnerships.

Therefore, all suppliers of private education should ensure that they are applying the correct liability to their supplies. Additionally, if you have been using the incorrect liability, you will need to account for any unpaid VAT as follows (full details are given in VAT Notice 700/45: *How to correct VAT errors and make adjustments or claims*):

- where the total of previous errors does not exceed £2000 net tax, an adjustment may be made to your current VAT return, or
- where the total of previous errors exceeds £2000 net tax, a separate voluntary disclosure should be submitted to HMRC (in these cases the errors must not be corrected through your VAT returns).

Details of where to send your claim can be obtained from update 2 to VAT Notice 700/45: *How to correct VAT errors and make adjustments or claims*, or from the HMRC National Advice Service.

FUEL SCALE CHARGE; NEW CO2 BASIS

12 February 2007. *HMRC Brief 13/07*

This Revenue and Customs Brief announces changes to the VAT fuel scale charge. These changes will come into effect on 1 May 2007 and businesses must use the new scales from the start of their first accounting period beginning on or after this date. We are announcing the change early to allow businesses time to familiarise themselves with the new charges and make any necessary IT system changes.

The existing VAT fuel scale charge, which is based on the engine size and fuel type of a car, will be replaced by a fuel scale charge based solely on the CO2 rating of a car. The new table, which mirrors that used for direct tax purposes, will have 21 bands with 5g/km increments. An outline of the bands is produced at **Annex A.**

The complete new table, which will be available following Budget 2007 as an amendment to Notice 700/64 *Motoring Expenses*, will provide business with the actual scale charge for a car within a particular band. Apart from the change to a CO2 basis, the system will operate in exactly the same way as the existing VAT fuel scale charge. We have provided an example with illustrative figures in **Annex A.**

VAT PRs etc

In keeping with the existing fuel scale charge, the CO2 based system will be subject to an annual review to ensure that the charge reflects changes in fuel prices. The figures produced at Budget 2007 will have been reviewed and, as with the current system, will be extant for one year. This change is not intended as a revenue raising measure and the switch to a CO2 basis will be revenue neutral overall.

Many businesses will already be aware of the underlying concept of the CO2 based system from using direct tax schemes (company car tax and company car fuel benefit) as well as the new system for Vehicle Excise Duty. For businesses unaware of their CO2 rating, a number of publicly available websites provide details on vehicles' official CO2 emission levels and we have included the details of one such site for ease of reference.

Vehicle Certification Agency—CO2 Database: www.vcacarfueldata.org.uk/search/search.asp

ANNEX A

Charge table:

Quarterly Returns

CO 2 emissions, g/km	*VAT Fuel Scale Charge*	*VAT on charge*	*Net amount*
140 or under			
145			
150			
155			
160			
165			
170			
175	£346.00*	£51.53*	£294.47*
180			
185			
190			
195			
200			
205			
210			
215			
220			
225			
230			
235			
240 or over			

* **Notional figures for illustrative purposes only.** The actual levels of new charges will be published at Budget 2007, and will reflect both the new structure and fuel prices at that time. The levels of the new charges will differ from those in the table above.

Example

Current Position

A business pays the current VAT fuel scale charge on a 2006 Vauxhall Vectra petrol 1.8i 4 door saloon; it pays a quarterly output tax charge of £51.53 and enters £294 in to the net outputs box on the return.

The CO2 rating for this vehicle is 175 g/km.

Following 1 May 2007 changes

The new fuel scale charge, which must be used from the start of your first accounting period beginning on or after 1 May 2007, can be found by looking along the band which covers 171 g/km – 175g/km. In this illustrative example, the new quarterly output tax charge is £51.53 and again the business enters £294 in to the net outputs box on the return.

The new system will determine the fuel scale charge by CO2 rating alone and there will be no adjustments for fuel type. The exception will be for vehicles too old to have an official CO2 rating; these businesses will be assigned a set band in the new system based on engine capacity alone.

CHANGES TO THE RULES ON BAD DEBT RELIEF FOR GOODS SUPPLIED ON CREDIT TERMS

13 February 2007. *HMRC Brief 14/07*

This article concerns changes to the bad debt relief provisions in respect of claims relating to goods supplied on credit terms, including hire-purchase, conditional sale and credit sale agreements. The new rules reflect existing commercial accounting methods and result in a more accurate bad debt relief figure for the supplier.

BACKGROUND

In VAT Information Sheet 05/04 we set out our policy on claims relating to overpaid VAT following conclusion of the litigation in the case of *General Motors Acceptance Corporation UK Ltd*. We then explained, in VAT Information Sheet 05/06, the changes we were making to close a loophole concerning goods sold, for a second time, by finance companies. We also announced in paragraph 6 of that Information Sheet that we intended to amend the bad debt relief rules to allow businesses to use the same basis for calculating bad debt relief as for the reduction of the original selling price. This article explains the changes we are now making to those rules.

WHY PAYMENTS FOR GOODS AND CREDIT AFFECT COMPUTATION OF BAD DEBT RELIEF

Where a business supplies goods on credit they make two supplies – goods (taxable) and credit (exempt). The supplier must account for VAT on the supply of goods at the outset (the normal time of supply rules apply). However, sometimes agreements are terminated because customers default.

If a customer makes some of the periodic payments before defaulting, these payments will cover both the goods and interest. In order to work out the amount of bad debt relief claimable on the goods, the supplier will need to look back at the payments the customer made before defaulting and allocate them between the goods and interest. They will then be able to calculate how much remains unpaid for the goods and so how much of the output tax they previously paid can be reclaimed as bad debt relief.

NEW LEGISLATION

The new rules will be contained in regulation 170A of the Value Added Tax Regulations 1995 (SI 1995/2518) (as amended) which, in addition to the existing rule, now contains another method of calculation.

INTERACTION WITH EXISTING COMMERCIAL PRACTICE

Previously, the legislation used a "straight-line" methodology. The new legislation will, for the first time, reflect existing commercial practice. Thus, for suppliers, the numbers you feed into the calculation will be based upon whatever commercial method you use, for example an actuarial method or the "Rule of 78". The ultimate purpose of the calculation is to arrive at the amount outstanding in respect of the goods element, which is used for calculating the amount of bad debt relief. The new method will result in a figure which accurately reflects the commercial basis of apportionment adopted by suppliers.

VOLUNTARY TERMINATION OF AGREEMENTS

These provisions apply only to situations where, upon default, customers still owe money. If your customer invokes a right, for example under consumer credit law, to end the agreement early (so-called "voluntary terminations"), they will not normally owe any money and bad debt relief should not apply.

BAD DEBT RELIEF CLAIMS FOR SUPPLIES MADE BEFORE 1 SEPTEMBER 2006

When allocating payments made by defaulting customers between capital and interest, the existing calculation at paragraph 5 of regulation 170A must be used.

BAD DEBT RELIEF CLAIMS FOR SUPPLIES MADE ON OR AFTER 1 SEPTEMBER 2006 AND BEFORE 1 SEPTEMBER 2007

For this transitional period, suppliers may choose between either the existing method (paragraph 5 of regulation 170A), or the new method (article 6 of regulation 170A). You do not have to notify your defaulting customers which method you have used, because they will continue to use the "straight-line" method.

You may if you wish calculate claims using the old method initially and then re-compute the claim using the new method. You can then adjust the difference. This is of course, subject to the normal capping rules.

BAD DEBT RELIEF CLAIMS FOR SUPPLIES MADE ON OR AFTER 1 SEPTEMBER 2007

When allocating payments made by defaulting customers between capital and interest, the new method of calculation at paragraph 6 of regulation 170A must be used.

INPUT TAX TO BE REPAID TO HMRC BY DEFAULTING CUSTOMERS

If you are a defaulting customer who must repay to HMRC VAT you previously reclaimed on the goods, you are unaffected by these changes – you must continue to use the "straight-line" method, whether the supplies were made before, on or after 1 September 2006.

PAYMENTS RECEIVED BY SUPPLIERS AFTER TERMINATION OF A CREDIT AGREEMENT

If you receive payments after the termination of a credit agreement, these should be allocated between the goods and credit according to the proportion of the balances due at the time payment is made. You will then need to re-visit any bad debt relief claim you previously made since the amount outstanding in respect of the goods will have changed.

REDUCTION IN THE PRICE OF A SUPPLY AFTER A BAD DEBT RELIEF REFUND

If you, as supplier, reduce your selling price after you have received a bad debt relief refund in relation to that supply, then you must repay the VAT element of the price reduction to HMRC. This is because, in reducing the selling price, you will be able to reduce the VAT you originally accounted for and therefore should not also receive bad debt relief as well.

PARTIAL EXEMPTION: SPECIAL METHOD APPROVALS

14 March 2007. *HMRC Brief 23/07*

This article provides further guidance on preparing and submitting the new Declaration that is required for all partial exemption special method applications that are approved on or after 1 April 2007. This article should be read in conjunction with the guidance at: [www.hmrc.gov.uk/ria/vat-partial-amendments-qa.pdf].

Further guidance on partial exemption is in Public Notice 706.

BACKGROUND

With effect from 1 April, HMRC will only approve a special method if the business has declared it to be fair and reasonable. The Declaration requires a reasonable person to take reasonable steps to ensure the proposed method is fair. If HMRC approves a method but subsequently discovers the person signing the Declaration did not act reasonably, it could override the method and require the business to recover VAT in accordance with the principle of use. This will improve equity between businesses and lessen the risk of unfair methods enabling HMRC to offer speedier approval increasing business certainty and reducing administrative costs.

HOW SHOULD THE DECLARATION BE MADE?

The Declaration can be made by completing the template in Annex A. It should clearly identify the business, the method to which it relates, and the signatory.

WHEN SHOULD THE DECLARATION BE MADE?

In most cases, the Declaration would accompany the special method proposal inviting HMRC to give approval. HMRC will review the method and unless problems are found, transpose it onto a special method letter adding standard clauses, glossary terms and routine references to ensure clarity, before returning it to the business. Provided the business is content that the method reflects its proposal, it can adopt it as agreed without further correspondence. There is no longer a requirement for the business to sign and return a copy of its finalised method, further saving administrative cost.

In some cases, the business will wish to discuss its draft special method before making a firm proposal to ensure it accords with guidance and partial exemption principles. In these cases, the Declaration should not be made until the special method has been fully developed, otherwise a new Declaration will be required before approval can be given. Similarly, if HMRC consider that a proposed method cannot be approved, despite the accompanying Declaration, it will discuss with the business giving reasons and invite a new proposal and Declaration.

ANNEX A

Partial Exemption—Special Method Declaration

Name of Business:

Address:

VAT Registration Number:

This Declaration is in accordance with paragraphs (9) and (10) of regulation 102 of the VAT Regulations 1995.

As

- [the taxable person (i.e. where the signatory is a sole proprietor)]
- [the person authorised by the taxable person to sign this declaration on its behalf][1]

, I hereby declare that to the best of my knowledge and belief, the proposed special method [state precisely where the method is set out] fairly and reasonably represents the extent to which goods or services are used or to be used in making taxable supplies.

I also confirm that I have taken reasonable steps to ensure that I am in possession of all relevant information before making this declaration.

Name (print):

Signed:

Position (print):

Date:

[1] Please delete as appropriate.

Commentary—*De Voil Indirect Tax Service* **V3.462**.

PROPOSED REVERSE CHARGE ACCOUNTING FOR BUSINESSES TRADING IN MOBILE TELEPHONES AND COMPUTER CHIPS: ANNOUNCEMENT OF TARGETED IMPLEMENTATION AND DETAILS OF HOW THE RULES WILL OPERATE IN PRACTICE; AND EXPOSURE OF DRAFT LEGISLATION FOR COMMENT

20 March 2007. *HMRC Brief 24/07*

WHO NEEDS TO READ THIS?

Businesses buying and/or selling any of the following goods:

(1) Mobile telephones; and
(2) Integrated circuit devices, such as microprocessors and central processing units, in a state prior to integration into end user products.

BACKGROUND

Business Briefs 10/06 and 14/06 gave notice of the Government's intention to implement reverse charge accounting arrangements for certain goods ("the reverse charge"), subject to an EU derogation. Business Brief 19/06 gave a commitment to provide UK business with about 8 weeks notice of the implementation of the reverse charge.

On 19 March 2007 the Government announced the **implementation of the reverse charge for mobile phones and computer chips with effect from 1 June 2007**. The reverse charge will **not apply** to the other goods mentioned in the earlier business Briefs.

The purpose of this Business Brief is to:

(A) provide:
 (i) confirmation of the timing of the introduction of the reverse charge, and of the goods to which it will apply;
 (ii) guidance on the application of reverse charge accounting to mobile phone contracts;
 (iii) guidance, to both retailers and wholesalers, on the operation of the de minimis rules;
 (iv) clarification of the proposed anti-disaggregation provisions;
 (v) guidance to certain customers, such as charities and Local Authorities, purchasing goods for business and non-business purposes;
 (vi) guidance on the impact of reverse charge accounting on Payments on Account;
 (vii) outline details of Reverse Charge Sales Lists, including notifying HMRC when the first supplies under the reverse charge are made;
 (viii) other details of how the new rules will operate in practice (completion of the VAT return; invoicing; the impact on the Cash Accounting Scheme, the Flat Rate Scheme and the second-hand margin scheme; and "light touch" on penalties); and
(B) expose the draft secondary legislation for urgent comment before it is laid in May 2007. Comments are invited by no later than 11 April 2007.

A. (I) TIMING AND SCOPE OF IMPLEMENTATION

Following negotiations with our European partners, the Government has decided to target the reverse charge accounting mechanism on mobile phones and computer chips only (detailed in categories 1 and 2 above) with effect from 1 June 2007. Reverse charge accounting will therefore not apply to electronic storage media used in connection with computers, mobile phones or certain other electronic devices, and electronic devices used for the storage, processing or recording of electronic data (categories 3 and 4 in Business Brief 14/06). Communication devices such as Blackberrys fall within the definition of a mobile phone and therefore will come within the scope of the reverse charge.

A. (II) APPLICATION OF REVERSE CHARGE ACCOUNTING TO MOBILE PHONE CONTRACTS

Mobile phones which are supplied with an airtime contract are excluded from the scope of reverse charge accounting. This includes replacement phones and upgrades supplied under the terms of an airtime contract. However, reverse charge accounting **will** apply to "Pay as You Go" ("Prepay") phones.

A. (III) OPERATION OF THE DE MINIMIS LIMIT

Business Brief 10/06 advised that the reverse charge would only apply to supplies of the specified goods with a VAT-exclusive value of £1000 or more, when made within the UK to a VAT-registered business and are to be used for business purposes. The Government has decided to raise this limit to £5000, which will apply to the total value of goods subject to the reverse charge supplied together and detailed on a single invoice. Normal VAT accounting continues to apply to supplies of these goods below that value.

Retailers, including internet retailers

The *de minimis* limit is intended to relieve retailers of the need to carry out the necessary checks to establish whether a customer is VAT-registered and is purchasing the goods for a business purpose. Raising the de minimis limit to £5000 should reduce the number of sales made by retailers to other businesses where reverse charge accounting could apply.

Nevertheless, we recognise that there will still be a limited number of cases where the value of a sale at the retail stage exceeds this de minimis threshold, and that in a retail environment it may be difficult to carry out the necessary checks. If, for a transaction over £5000 in value, a retailer is unable to carry out these checks to his satisfaction, then VAT should be charged in the normal way. Such a situation may also arise with internet sales from retail sites, which should be treated in the same way. However, retailers and internet suppliers already have their own checks, usually based on the value (for example, above £10,000) or quantity of the goods, to prevent fraud or money laundering. We would expect them to apply similar checks to prevent manipulation of the £5000 limit.

Wholesalers and other suppliers

Circumstances in other trading environments, such as the wholesale market, are different because suppliers normally have a more established relationship with their customers, which means that they are in a better position to carry out checks on their bona fides, including for the purpose of applying the reverse charge.

HMRC are often asked what additional checks businesses should make in order to demonstrate that they have taken reasonable steps to establish whether the reverse charge applies. It is very difficult to be specific because industries and relationships vary widely.

We are aware that legitimate businesses carry out several commercial checks on their suppliers and customers covering various risks, such as to ensure acceptable use of the goods by the customer. In most instances, these checks will be adequate for reverse charge purposes, provided they are properly evidenced, unless the supplier has doubts about the reliability of the customer.

Businesses selling goods under the reverse charge procedure need to obtain the VAT registration numbers of affected customers, as they will be required for the Reverse Charge Sales Lists. In general, there will be no need to verify VAT registration numbers of customers with an established trading relationship, unless there are specific doubts, but it may be prudent to verify the VAT registration number of new customers.

Where businesses trade with customers without satisfying themselves as to their bona fides, they may be liable to pay to HMRC any tax lost as a result.

A. (IV) ANTI-DISAGGREGATION PROVISIONS

In earlier consultation on the operation of the reverse charge, anti-disaggregation provisions had been suggested to prevent the possibility of manipulation of the de minimis limit, below which the reverse charge will not apply. However, the consultation process identified that businesses would have practical difficulties in implementing such provisions. In the light of these concerns, the Government has decided not to introduce anti-disaggregation provisions in relation to reverse charge accounting. However, any attempt to manipulate the de minimis limit of £5000 will be vigorously challenged.

A. (V) CHARITIES AND LOCAL AUTHORITIES

Some customers, such as charities and Local Authorities, may purchase goods to which the reverse charge applies which will be used partly for business and partly for non-business purposes. In such cases, the reverse charge applies: the customer should account for output tax under the reverse charge procedure and apply the appropriate restriction to the deduction of the resulting input VAT.

A. (VI) PAYMENTS ON ACCOUNT

The Payments on Account (POA) scheme requires businesses with a net VAT liability of £2 million per year or more to make monthly payments on account. Under the current POA rules, the introduction of the reverse charge would have the effect of bringing some businesses within the scope of the POA scheme, or increasing the monthly payments for some businesses already within the scheme. Legislation will be introduced to amend the POA scheme to allow affected businesses to apply to HMRC to exclude the output tax due under the reverse charge from the calculation to establish whether a business is in the POA scheme or the size of monthly payments a business in the scheme has to make.

A. (VII) REVERSE CHARGE SALES LISTS

The following is an outline of how Reverse Charge Sales Lists (RCSLs) will operate:

- the RCSL system will be web-based, accessed through the Government Gateway;
- businesses will have to notify HMRC within 30 days of making their first supply to which the reverse charge applies, and also when they cease to make such supplies;
- if they subsequently re-commence making such supplies, they will have to renotify HMRC;
- businesses making sales to which the reverse charge applied must submit a list for each period, or make a "nil declaration" for any period that the business did not make any relevant supplies but had not notified cessation of such supplies;
- RCSLs may be submitted by keying data on-line or submitting bulk data via a CSV (comma-separated value) file;
- RCSLs, covering the same period as the VAT return, must be submitted within 30 days of the end of the business's VAT return period in which the supplies are made; and
- the information required will be, for each customer, their VAT registration number and the total value of reverse charge supplies made each calendar month to that customer.

The technical specification for the RCSL CSV file for bulk upload is published on the HMRC website (via "VAT Reverse Charge for mobile phones, and computer chips" on the HMRC VAT internet page).

A. (VIII) OTHER PRACTICAL ISSUES

Completion of the VAT return

Suppliers of goods under reverse charge accounting must **not** enter in Box 1 of the VAT return any output tax on sales to which the reverse charge applies, but must enter the value of such sales in Box 6.

Customers must enter in Box 1 of the VAT return the output tax on purchases to which the reverse charge applies, but must **not** enter the value of such purchases in Box 6. They must reclaim the input tax on their reverse charge purchases in Box 4 of the VAT return and include the value of the purchases in Box 7, in the normal way.

Invoicing

When making a sale to which reverse charge accounting applies, suppliers must show all the information normally required to be shown on a VAT invoice and must also annotate the invoice to make it clear that the reverse charge applies and that the customer is required to account for the VAT. The amount of VAT due under the reverse charge rules must be clearly stated on the invoice but should not be included in the amount shown as total VAT charged. The precise wording is not prescribed in law and discussions with business have highlighted the need to keep the annotation short. Either of the following would be acceptable:

- customer to pay output tax of £X to HMRC;
- UK customer to pay O/T of £X to HMRC.

Alternatively, any of the following would also be acceptable, provided that the amount of tax is shown elsewhere on the invoice (but not in box for total output tax charged):

- VAT Act 1994 s 55A applies;
- s 55A VATA 1994 applies;
- customer to account for the VAT to HMRC;
- Reverse charge supply—customer to pay the VAT to HMRC;
- customer to pay VAT to HMRC;
- UK customer to pay VAT to HMRC.

Cash accounting scheme

Businesses using the cash accounting scheme which purchase or sell goods to which the reverse charge applies should exclude these transactions from the scheme and account for them under the reverse charge accounting provisions.

Flat rate scheme

It is unlikely that many businesses using the flat rate scheme will be involved in transactions of goods to which the reverse charge applies but, if they are, they should exclude these from the scheme and account for VAT in accordance with the reverse charge accounting provisions.

Second-hand margin scheme

Where relevant goods are sold under a second-hand margin scheme, the reverse charge will not apply.

Penalties—"light touch"

HMRC understand the difficulties businesses may have in implementing the reverse charge and will, where there is no loss of tax, apply a light touch in dealing with errors that occur in the first six months after introduction of the reverse charge.

B. DRAFT LEGISLATION

Section 19 Finance Act 2006 introduced a new s 55A and s 26AB into the VAT Act 1994, as well as amending other provisions of the Act. These will be brought into effect from 1 June 2007. Under the powers contained in these provisions and existing powers in the VAT Act, the following statutory instruments will be made:

(1) the Value Added Tax (Section 55A) (Specified Goods and Excepted Supplies) Order, which details the goods to which the reverse charge applies and supplies which will be excluded from the reverse charge [see now SI 2007/1417];
(2) the Value Added Tax (Payments on Account) (Amendment) Order, which amends the payment on account rules [see now SI 2007/1420];
(3) the Value Added Tax (Administration, Collection and Enforcement) Order to amend para 2(3B) of Schedule 11 to the VAT Act to allow regulations to be made to facilitate the introduction of reverse charge sales lists [see now SI 2007/1420];
(4) the Value Added Tax (Amendment) Regulations, which amend regulations relating to bad debt adjustments, the cash accounting and flat rate schemes and introduce the details of the reverse charge sales lists [see now SI 2007/313]. They also make consequential changes to the VAT accounting regulations.
(5) the Value Added Tax (Amendment) (No 2) Regulations implementing regulations relating to the cessation and recommencement of reverse charge sales lists [see now SI 2007/768].

A copy of the draft legislation is attached for information and any comment. Comments should be sent as soon as possible please (and by no later than 11 April 2007) by email to Anti VAT Fraud [see HMRC website for email form and draft legislation].

FURTHER DIALOGUE WITH BUSINESS

HMRC remain committed to working closely with affected businesses and their advisers – as well as the software developers that support those businesses – to facilitate a smooth implementation of the reverse charge.

Further guidance material will be issued before the end of March, and, as necessary, meetings and/or workshops will be organised (depending on need and demand).

VAT PRs etc

In the meantime any specific questions comments or concerns – about the terms of this Business Brief or more generally – can be sent by email to Anti VAT Fraud.

Commentary—*De Voil Indirect Tax Service* **V3.231, V3.233**.

CULTURAL EXEMPTION – CLARIFICATION OF "DIRECT OR INDIRECT FINANCIAL INTEREST" [VATA 1994 SCH 9 GROUP 13 NOTE 2(C)]

22 March 2007. *HMRC Brief 27/07*

This Brief provides guidelines, in the light of recent Court of Appeal Judgments in the cases of *Bournemouth Symphony Orchestra* (C3/2005/1681) and *Longborough Festival Opera* (C3/2006/0369), on how to interpret the term "direct or indirect financial interest". This is for the purpose of the exemption for cultural services contained in Group 13 of Schedule 9 to the VAT Act 1994. The term is relevant because one of the conditions for exemption for services provided by an "eligible body" under Item 2 of that Group is that the body "is managed and administered on a voluntary basis by persons who have no direct or indirect financial interest in its activities" (Note 2(c) refers).

This brief supersedes the advice given on this topic in paragraphs 4.9 to 4.11 of VAT Notice 701/47 Culture and paragraphs 2.2 and 2.3 of section 2 of chapter 28 of V1-7 (HMRC guidance). Update 1 to VAT Notice 701/47 will be available on our website shortly.

The key change from existing guidance is that any direct or indirect financial interest only affects entitlement to exemption if it is actual, not potential. It is now our view that a person who is managing and administering the cultural body can be seen to have a direct or indirect financial interest in its activities only when:

– the person receives any payments for services supplied to the cultural body above the market rate, paid as routine overheads, or receives any payments which are profit-related (whether below, at or above market rates); and
– there is a link between the payments and the person's participation in the direction of the cultural body's activities.

This means that payments to individuals for services of managing and administering the body are not financial interests if:

– they are allowed by the constitution;
– the recipient is excluded from any decision-making regarding the award of any contract to themselves;
– the payments are not above market rates; and
– are not linked to profits.

There is no financial interest where the only potential is for a financial loss – for example, where a risk is underwritten or guaranteed – so that the guarantor only stands to lose money and not gain money as a result.

It is not possible to give exhaustive guidance to cover every eventuality, and the advice given here is intended as a general guideline only.

Commentary—*De Voil Indirect Tax Service* **V4.176**.

PARTIAL EXEMPTION: VAT RECOVERY ON OVERHEAD COSTS RELATING TO SUPPLIES OF HIRE PURCHASE

30 March 2007. *HMRC Brief 31/07*

This article explains HMRC's policy on attributing VAT on overhead costs to supplies made under hire-purchase (HP) agreements. It affects businesses that make supplies under HP agreements to consumers, but does not apply to those who arrange such supplies and receive a commission. HMRC are aware that policy is not being applied consistently, so this article confirms the policy to be applied from 1 April 2007. This article also refers to the Tribunal decision *Royal Bank of Scotland* [VTD 19983] regarding VAT recovery and HP agreements.

BACKGROUND TO VAT RECOVERY

An HP transaction involves the supply of goods on credit terms. Provided the charge for credit is clearly identified to the customer, an HP transaction is treated as two supplies for VAT purposes, comprising:

– a supply of goods which is subject to VAT; and,
– a supply of credit which is exempt from VAT.

Businesses making both taxable and exempt supplies must apply a partial exemption method to apportion VAT on overhead costs (such as lighting and heating) to recover that VAT to the extent that the costs are 'used' for making taxable supplies.

The European Court of Justice (ECJ) has established the principles that apply to the recovery of input tax and the Court of Appeal in *Dial-a-phone* [2004] STC 987 confirmed that these principles also applied in UK law.

Costs are therefore "used" to make taxable supplies of goods or services within the meaning of the partial exemption regulations, if they:

– have a direct and immediate link with the taxable transaction (see *BLP* case C-4/94);
– are borne directly by the cost components of a taxable transaction (see *Midland Bank plc* case C-98/98);
– are costs of the various components of the price (see *DA and EA Rompelman* case C-268/83).

These are different aspects of a single test to determine whether VAT is recoverable.

In applying these ECJ principles, HMRC's view is that in order for costs to be a cost component of a taxable transaction, the costs should normally be reflected in the selling price of the taxable transaction. In other words, there is an objective test for determining VAT recovery, in that VAT on costs is not recoverable unless the costs are reflected in the selling price of the taxable supply.

VAT RECOVERY FOR HP TRANSACTIONS

Normally it is clear when VAT on costs is recoverable. This is because goods and services are either sold independently, each priced to reflect the costs incurred, or if they are supplied together, the price of each item reflects both direct costs and overheads.

In most HP transactions, the goods are resold at cost without any margin to cover overhead costs. As there is no margin on the HP goods, the cost of the overheads will normally be built into the price of the supply of credit. In this scenario, HMRC's view is that the overheads are purely cost components of the exempt supply. Otherwise the business would continually enjoy net VAT refunds despite:

– making no zero-rated or reduced rate supplies; and
– charging a total consideration under the HP agreement that fully recovers its costs and an element of profit.

Where overheads are used to make both HP transactions and other supplies on which VAT is charged (such as taxable purchase option fees or sales of repossessed goods), then some VAT on overhead costs is recoverable. In this scenario the partial exemption method should reflect the extent to which the overhead costs are a cost component of the prices of the supplies in question.

EXISTING METHODS

Businesses using special methods will need to review them to ensure that they are fair and reasonable in accordance with the above principles. If an existing method is not fair and reasonable, the business concerned should contact HMRC to discuss a new method going forward. In approving new methods, or reviewing existing methods, HMRC will ensure that methods fairly attribute VAT to taxable supplies taking account of this article.

HP businesses using the standard method will need to consider the standard method override provisions and, if necessary, apply for a special method. In doing this the above principles for HP transactions will need to be taken into account. Further guidance is available in VAT Notice 706 "Partial exemption".

ROYAL BANK OF SCOTLAND

In February, the Scottish Tribunal released its decision in the Royal Bank of Scotland (RBS) case regarding VAT recovery and HP transactions. RBS appealed HMRC's refusal to approve a replacement partial exemption method in which HP transactions would be treated as two transactions, one taxable and one exempt such that 50% of the VAT on related overhead costs would be recoverable. The Tribunal found for RBS. HMRC have lodged an appeal to the Court of Session. The cost component point was not tested because the appeal predated this Revenue and Customs Brief.

PARTIAL EXEMPTION – VAT DEDUCTION BY THEATRES ON PRODUCTION COSTS

14 June 2007. *HMRC Brief 45/07*

HMRC has revised its policy on input tax recovery on the costs of staging shows (production costs) for which the theatre's admissions are VAT exempt. It follows the judgment of the Court of Appeal in the case of *Mayflower Theatre Trust Ltd* ([2006] EWCA Civ 116) (MTT). It replaces the first article in Business Brief 12/06, which is now withdrawn. Further information on partial exemption can be found in Public Notice 706.

THE DISPUTE

MTT bought in performances (production services) under contract from touring companies. The supply of production services was a single supply for VAT purposes. HMRC maintained that none of the input tax was deductible because it related solely to supplies of exempt admission. MTT argued that the input tax was partly deductible (residual) because the production costs had a direct and immediate link not only to exempt admissions, but also to taxable supplies such as catering, programme sales and corporate sponsorship.

THE COURT OF APPEAL DECISION

The Tribunal found for HMRC but this was overturned in the High Court. The High Court allowed residual treatment concluding that the production costs were sufficiently linked to what the court described as "taxable tickets" which formed part of a single taxable supply of corporate sponsorship.

The Court of Appeal rejected the "taxable tickets" argument, and a further argument that the costs were overheads of the business as a whole. However, the Court of Appeal found that the production services included the provision of raw material that was essential for the printing of taxable programmes such as logos, photographs and casting information. Accordingly, the input tax was residual. HMRC has decided not to appeal this decision.

THE NEW HMRC POLICY

Theatres which receive single supplies of production services from touring companies, that include material essential for the printing of programmes, may treat the input tax as residual. This applies even where that programme material is a minor part of the contract.

Theatres that stage their own shows may receive supplies such as costumes or scenery. These supplies will not be residual. This is because the costs have a direct and immediate link with admissions and not with the printing of programmes even though costumes and scenery might be visible in subsequent programme photographs.

IMPACT ON THEATRES

The vast majority of theatres use the partial exemption standard method to apportion residual input tax between taxable and exempt supplies. This works well provided VAT bearing costs are used in proportion to the value of supplies made. However, residual production services are used almost entirely for exempt admissions with only a minimal link to taxable programmes. The Court of Appeal recognised that this led to an over-recovery of input tax.

Since 18 April 2002, if the standard method results in an over (or under) recovery of input tax which is classed as "substantial" then the recovery must be re-calculated in accordance with the "actual use" of the costs in question. This is known as the Standard Method Override (SMO). Further information on the SMO, including the definition of "substantial" can be found in the public notice.

Major theatres which buy in large numbers of shows are the ones most likely to trigger the SMO and thus need to undertake a "use-based" calculation for their costs.

A "use-based" calculation is any calculation that fairly reflects how costs are used. As production services only have a direct and immediate link with box office sales and programme sales, a fair calculation could be:

Recoverable input tax on production services =

$$\frac{\text{Value of programme sales}}{\text{Value of programme sales plus value of box office sales}} \times \text{Input tax incurred on production services}$$

Theatres operating the standard method which regularly receive production services that are residual may wish to seek approval for a special method to avoid the risk of triggering the SMO.

CLAIMS FOR UNDER-RECOVERED INPUT TAX

Theatres may wish to claim input tax which, in the light of this HMRC Brief, was incorrectly treated as exempt. They must use the partial exemption method in place when the input tax was incurred unless there are exceptional reasons why an alternative method is needed in which case full details should be submitted with the claim. Theatres using the standard method must consider the SMO when making a claim and all claims are subject to the normal three year time limit.

Theatres that have reclaimed input tax on the basis of the High Court's decision, but whose production costs exclude essential material for programmes, will now be subject to assessment with interest due.

Further information about making claims can be found in Public Notice 700/45 How to correct VAT errors and make adjustments or claims and in Business Briefs 25/04 and 28/04.

Commentary—*De Voil Indirect Tax Service* **V4.176**.

INTRODUCTION OF A REDUCED RATE FOR THE SUPPLY OF SMOKING CESSATION PRODUCTS

28 June 2007. *HMRC Brief 48/07*

With effect from 1 July 2007, the supply of smoking cessation products will be eligible for the reduced rate of VAT (5%).

This relief will be in force for a period of one year and its introduction will coincide with the ban on smoking in public places in England.

SCOPE OF THE REDUCED RATE

A new group will be added to Schedule 7A of the VAT Act 1994 to introduce the reduced rate to supplies of smoking cessation products, which are pharmaceutical products designed to help people to stop smoking tobacco.

The reduced rate will apply to non-prescribed sales of nicotine patches, nicotine gums, nicotine inhalators, lozenges and other pharmaceutical products held out for sale for the primary purpose of helping people to stop smoking.

The supply of smoking cessation products on a prescription by a medical practitioner will continue to be zero rated.

FURTHER ADVICE

Anyone who remains uncertain as to the liability of the supply of smoking cessation products should contact the National Advice Service.

CHANGES TO THE VAT INVOICING REGULATIONS WITH EFFECT FROM 1 OCTOBER 2007

24 July 2007. *HMRC Brief 51/07*

VAT regulation changes were made on 23 July 2007 and make minor modifications to the format of invoices which are effective from 1 October 2007.

The changes follow infraction proceedings begun by the European Commission. Consultation suggests that the effects on most UK businesses will be minor. Businesses most likely to be affected are those:

- using the margin scheme for second-hand goods, antiques, works of art, and collectors' items;
- involved in making travel related supplies that fall within the scope of the Tour Operators' Margin Scheme;
- involved in intra EU supplies of goods and services;
- making supplies where the customer accounts for the VAT.

THE CHANGES

1. The number on the invoice

Regulation 14(1)(*a*) will be amended to include a requirement for an invoice to bear a sequential number based on one or more series which uniquely identify the document.

Consultation supported the view of HMRC that this formal legal change will have little impact on the way invoices are numbered by the majority of businesses.

2. Reference to the second-hand margin schemes

Regulation 14 will be changed to add a requirement that invoices under the special arrangements for second-hand goods, antiques, works of art and collectors' items must include a reference to the nature of the treatment, which accords with the Directive. That means a reference to either the relevant EC or UK legislation, or including any other indication of the treatment.

3. Reference to the Tour Operators' Margin Scheme (TOMS)

Regulation 14 will be changed to add a requirement that invoices under TOMS must include a reference to the nature of the treatment, which accords with the Directive.

Businesses can include a reference to the relevant EC or UK legislation, or include any other indication of the treatment. The choice of legend is a matter for individual businesses to decide.

The new rule only applies to those occasions when an invoice is issued to another taxable person.

4. Reference to the reverse charge or exemption (including zero rate dispatches to other member States)

Regulations will be changed to add a requirement that zero rate dispatches and exempt or reverse charge invoices will require a reference to the grounds for the treatment when the supply is to a business customer based in another member State.

Businesses can include a reference to the relevant EC or UK legislation, or include any other indication of the treatment. The choice of legend is a matter for individual businesses to decide.

Regulation 14 will be amended to make it clear that the requirement also applies to UK supplies where the customer accounts for the VAT, such as the gold scheme (VATA 1994 s 55) or any reverse charge requirement introduced under Missing Trader Intra-Community (MTIC) rules in VATA 1994, s 55A.

The regulations make it clear that a requirement to issue invoices for exempt supplies only arises when the supply is business to business, across an EU border, and an invoice is required by the member State of receipt. Because practice varies widely across member States, HMRC guidance is that businesses should be guided by their customers.

5. References required

The regulations will be changed to make it clear that an invoice issued under the following procedures must contain a reference to the relevant EC or UK legislation, or include any other indication of the treatment. The choice of legend is a matter for individual businesses to decide:

- regulation17(2)(*b*) covering section 14(6) supplies to persons belonging in other member States
- regulation 18(2)(*d*) covering section 14(1) supplies by intermediate suppliers, and
- regulation 19(2)(*d*) covering section 14(2) supplies by persons belonging in other member States.

FURTHER INFORMATION

VAT Information Sheet 10/2007 provides additional details concerning the changes, together with a list of frequently asked questions (FAQs) that you may find helpful. Further information in relation to the consultation and the background to the changes can be found on the Joint VAT Consultative Committee (JVCC) page of the HMRC internet site, which includes two VAT invoicing consultation documents.

If you need further information about VAT invoicing, please ring the National Advice Service.

Commentary—*De Voil Indirect Tax Service* **V3.511**.

REVISED TREATMENT OF VAT INCURRED ON HOME COMPUTERS MADE AVAILABLE BY EMPLOYERS TO THEIR EMPLOYEES

14 August 2007. *HMRC Brief 55/07*

This Revenue and Customs Brief sets out HMRC's revised policy on the VAT treatment of computers made available by employers for use in their employee's homes; this follows withdrawal of the tax exemption which allowed employers to loan computer equipment to their employees tax free.

BACKGROUND

In April 1999 the Government introduced a direct tax exemption which enabled employers to loan a computer to their employees tax-free. The objective was to help increase access to computers and help employees increase their IT literacy skills. In January 2004 the Government launched the Home Computer Initiative which encouraged employers and employees to take advantage of the exemption and sought to make it as straightforward as possible for employers to lend computer equipment to their employees.

At that time the former HM Customs and Excise considered that, while there would undoubtedly be some private use of the computer—usually requiring some restriction on VAT recovery—in the circumstances of the HCI there would be wider benefits to the business and so the VAT treatment should mirror the approach taken for direct tax. Consequently, as long as there was some business use, any VAT incurred, could be deducted in full without any adjustment for private use.

Following a review of the HCI the direct tax exemption was withdrawn with effect from 6 April 2006. Consequently HMRC have now reviewed the VAT position.

HMRC'S REVISED POLICY

HMRC's policy to allow full VAT recovery without any adjustment for private use, in circumstances where there is any business use, is withdrawn from the date of this Revenue and Customs Brief.

With immediate effect businesses must consider why the computer is being provided to the employee to determine the level of VAT that can be claimed. Businesses will only be able to claim full VAT recovery without any requirement to account for VAT on any private use (subject of course to any restriction in respect of exempt supplies) where the provision of a computer is necessary for the employee to carry out the duties of his employment. In these circumstances HMRC's view is that it is unlikely that any private use will be significant when compared with the business need for providing the computer in the first place. This mirrors the approach taken for direct tax concerning exemptions for work related benefits in kind where there is no significant private use.

Where a business cannot demonstrate that it is necessary to provide an employee with a computer in order to carry out the duties of his employment then only a portion of the VAT incurred will be recoverable as input tax. HMRC will accept any method of apportioning the

VAT incurred as long as the result fairly and reasonably reflects the extent of business use. In order to minimise your administrative burdens you may be able to agree a set percentage with HMRC based on a representative period.

TRANSITIONAL PROVISIONS

Where a business continues to provide a computer under an existing HCI agreement full VAT recovery can continue until the agreement (normally 3 years) has expired. For further information on these transitional provisions please refer to direct tax guidance EIM2699.

WHAT IF THE BUSINESS IS NOT THE RECIPIENT OF THE SUPPLY?

Please note that it is a basic principle of the VAT system that VAT can only be recovered as input tax where the supply is to the taxable person or business. So, in circumstances where the supply of the computer is to the employee the business cannot recover the VAT incurred on that supply as input tax.

Commentary—*De Voil Indirect Tax Service* **V3.471**.

PLACE OF SUPPLY OF TRADING ALLOWANCES IN GREENHOUSE GAS EMISSIONS (UPDATE)

22 August 2007. *HMRC Brief 52/07*

Commentary—*De Voil Indirect Tax Service* **V3.193**.

Note—This Brief has been cancelled and incorporated into Notice 741 "Place of supply of services".

CLAIMS IN RESPECT OF FUND MANAGEMENT SERVICES

22 August 2007. *HMRC Brief 58/07*

BACKGROUND

The EC VAT Directive (formerly the Sixth Directive) exempts 'management of special investment funds as defined by member states'. The UK applies this exemption to the management of authorised unit trusts (AUTs), open-ended investment companies (OEICs) and trust-based schemes. The UK has not applied this exemption to the management of other funds, including investment trust companies (ITCs).

In 2004, JP Morgan Fleming Claverhouse Trust plc, an ITC, appealed to the VAT Tribunal against the VAT charged to it on investment management services. This appeal was joined by the Association of Investment Trust Companies (now the AIC) and the Tribunal referred 3 questions to the European Court of Justice (ECJ). In its judgment of 28 June 2007, the ECJ has given guidance to the Tribunal to determine whether the management of ITCs should be VAT exempt.

CLAIMS CONCERNING THE MANAGEMENT OF ITCS

We have received a number of claims for overpaid VAT on the management of ITCs since the litigation began in 2004. The claims concerning such services have been held over pending the final outcome in the litigation, and will be addressed in due course.

CLAIMS CONCERNING THE MANAGEMENT OF FUNDS OTHER THAN ITCS

Since the ECJ judgment, we have also received a number of claims for overpaid VAT in respect of the management of other funds not at issue in the litigation. Such claims have generally contained a request that they be held pending the final outcome in the *JP Morgan Fleming Claverhouse* case, using the ECJ judgment as support for the claims.

We take the view that this case does not concern the management of funds other than ITCs and that the ECJ judgment is clear in that it does not address the issues that arise concerning such other funds. There is thus no basis for HMRC to accept these claims, nor any current litigation against which to justify holding over the claims. Accordingly, any such claims in respect of the management of funds other than ITCs will be refused. This is in line with our existing published guidance (see paragraph 2.7 of "V1-33: VAT refunds – unjust enrichment – statutory interest – ex-gratia payments").

Commentary—*De Voil Indirect Tax Service* **V4.136H**.
Note—See HMRC Brief 65/07: HMRC withdraw from the appeal in *JP Morgan Fleming Claverhouse Trust plc*.

TELEOS AND OTHERS (VAT—INTRA-COMMUNITY TRADE)

11 October 2007. *HMRC Brief 61/07*

The European Court of Justice (ECJ) gave its judgement in this case (reference C-409/04; [2007] All ER (D) 160 (Sep)) on 27 September 2007.

The key points in the decision are:

– goods must physically leave the territory of the Member State of supply to qualify for zero rating;

If a supplier:

– acts in good faith and submits evidence establishing a right to zero-rate an intra Community transaction; and
– has no involvement in tax evasion and takes every reasonable measure in their power to ensure that the transaction did not lead to their participation in tax evasion,
– then the Member State cannot hold the supplier to account for the VAT on those goods if the information relied on subsequently proves to be false.

BACKGROUND

This case involved the purported removal of mobile phones to a VAT registered customer in Spain. No VAT is due in the UK on such transactions provided the supplier meets certain conditions set by HMRC. The principal conditions are that the supplier must obtain their customer's VAT registration number and they must obtain proof that the goods have been removed to another Member State.

Teleos treated all their supplies in this case as intra-EC transactions and did not account for any VAT (referred to as zero-rating for VAT purposes in the UK). To support their claim for VAT zero-rating they relied on commercial road transport documents as proof that the goods had been removed to another Member State. The documents subsequently proved to be false so HMRC disallowed VAT zero-rating and assessed. The ECJ decision is in response to a reference from the High Court following an application by Teleos (and others) to review the Commissioners decision on zero rating.

IMPACT IN THIS CASE

The case will go back to the administrative court to consider the taxpayer's application in the light of the ECJ's ruling. The Commissioners are examining their decision in that case and the case of the other parties to the litigation.

WIDER IMPLICATIONS OF THE DECISION

The Court ruled that EC law on intra-Community supply and intra-Community acquisition are rules governing the physical movement of goods from one Member State to another. Consequently, to obtain the exemption, physical movement of goods from the supplying Member State to another Member State must be established. This accords with the United Kingdom's submissions, and it remains for the supplier of the goods to furnish the proof that the conditions for zero rating are fulfilled. The conditions in UK law and in public notices will continue to govern the entitlement to zero rating.

The Court's decision also limits the Commissioners' ability to recover from the supplier, tax lost through incorrect zero rating in the circumstances of the Teleos case. In restricting the ability to assess in such cases, the court was balancing the benefit of legal certainty for suppliers who act in good faith with the need to have stringent conditions to prevent fraud and abuse. The good faith of the supplier, the steps they took, and whether they are established as not participating in fraud are critical factors in deciding whether they can be obliged to account for VAT after the event.

Indeed, the judgement makes it clear that it is not contrary to Community law to require the supplier to take every step which could be reasonably required of them to satisfy themselves that the transaction which they are effecting does not result in his participation in tax evasion. The judgement is therefore consistent with the line of ECJ cases which underpin HM-RC's approach to MTIC fraud and underlines that rights under EC VAT law cannot routinely be enjoyed where the taxpayer in question knew or could have known that they were participating in tax evasion.

CASES ON ALL FOURS

HMRC expect few cases to be on all fours with Teleos. Anyone who considers that an assessment for zero rating falls on the basis of the Teleos decision in the ECJ should make a claim subject to the time limits for such claims. Further information about making claims can be found in Public Notice 700/45 "How to correct VAT errors or make adjustments or claims" and Business Brief 28/04.

Commentary—*De Voil Indirect Tax Service* **V4.343**.

COMMISSION EARNED BY SUB-AGENTS IN THE TRAVEL INDUSTRY

11 October 2007. *HMRC Brief 62/07*

This Revenue & Customs Brief sets out a change in our interpretation of how VAT law applies to the treatment of commission earned by sub-agents in the travel industry.

Para 2.6 of Public Notice 709/6 "Travel agents and tour operators" states:

> "If you are acting as a sub-agent (that is an intermediary acting for another intermediary), then your services, which are supplied in the UK, are standard- rated."

There is no change if sub-agents provide services which facilitate the making of supplies, such as a simple introduction. In this case, the place of supply for this service is where the sub-agents are established. Where this is in the UK, their commission will be liable to VAT at the standard rate.

However, if sub-agents are involved in the making of arrangements for travel services, then the place of their supply will follow the normal rules for supplies by intermediaries. This will depend on:

– where the underlying arranged supply is made; and
– (where this is in the EU) whether the customer is EU VAT registered.

VAT Notice 741 "Place of supply of services" sets out these rules in more detail.

The liability of the sub-agents' supplies for which they receive the commission will follow that of the underlying supply. Where they are involved in the provision of specific supplies of zero-rated passenger transport, their commission for those transactions will also be zero-rated. Where they are involved in the provision of a package supplied by a UK tour operator under the Tour Operators' Margin Scheme, their commission will continue to be standard-rated.

The "making of arrangements for" travel services does not include supplies of market research, advertising, promotional or similar services. Supplies of these services will continue to be standard-rated, as will payments received from the providers of computerised reservations systems in respect of travel agents' use of these sites.

The vast majority of supplies made by sub-agents are to other VAT registered businesses, which are able to recover tax deducted. This change, therefore, will be broadly revenue neutral.

Businesses are not required to correct past declaration errors which were made on the basis of our earlier interpretation of the law. The second article of Business Brief 28/04 sets out our policy on correcting liability errors and gives more information on how to do this.

Businesses may apply the zero rate, where appropriate, with immediate effect, and otherwise should do so no later than 1 November 2007.

Commentary—*De Voil Indirect Tax Service* **V16.904**.

JP MORGAN FLEMING CLAVERHOUSE TRUST PLC – FUND MANAGEMENT SERVICES

5 November 2007. *HMRC Brief 65/07*

This Revenue & Customs Brief announces that HMRC have withdrawn from the appeal in *JP Morgan Fleming Claverhouse Trust plc*.

On 28 June 2007, the European Court of Justice (ECJ) delivered its judgment in this case which gave guidance for the VAT Tribunal to decide, on the facts, whether fund management services provided to investment trust companies (ITCs) should be exempt from VAT.

After careful consideration of the ECJ judgment, we now accept that fund management services supplied to ITCs are exempt and have withdrawn from the appeal. We remain of the view, published in HMRC Brief 58/07, that the judgment does not apply to funds other than ITCs.

SUPPLIES AFFECTED BY THIS DECISION

In an earlier ECJ judgment in Abbey National, it was ruled that the exemption for 'management' of funds covers not only investment management services, but also certain administrative services if, viewed broadly, they form a distinct whole and are specific to, and essential for, the management of the fund.

We published detailed guidance on this in Business Brief 07/06, but it should be noted that the Abbey judgment focused on authorised investment funds such as authorised unit trusts and open-ended investment companies. In this context, the court referred to the UCITS Directive, which sets out certain administrative functions that these funds are required to carry out.

Our revised policy was to exempt services, usually made up of several elements, forming single supplies which are recognisable in their own right as fund administration services. On the other hand, we made it clear that just because a service is a requirement of the regulations does not mean that it is exempt – for example, some legal services may be specific to and essential for the administration of the fund, but they remain legal services, not fund administration services.

Although ITCs are not subject to the same form of regulation, we believe the same principles should apply. For ITCs, services which are specific to, and essential for their administration (or provisions relating solely to ITCs) may be exempt if, viewed broadly, they form a distinct whole recognisable as a fund administration service. More generic management services, such as company secretarial services and accounting, remain taxable if they are not otherwise subsumed into a single composite supply of fund administration services.

IMPLEMENTATION

Businesses may exempt fund management services supplied to ITCs, but we cannot require this until such time as the UK law is amended. We expect to consult informally with key stakeholders in the coming weeks on possible legal changes in this regard.

CLAIMS FOR OVERSTATED OR OVERPAID VAT

Any claims for overstated or overpaid VAT on fund management services supplied to ITCs will now be dealt with in accordance with our Business Brief 28/04 – Correcting liability errors; Notice 700/45 – *How to correct VAT errors and make adjustments or claims*; and published guidance V1–33: VAT refunds – unjust enrichment – statutory interest – ex-gratia payments.

Commentary—*De Voil Indirect Tax Service* **V4.136H**.

TREATMENT OF THE CONSTRUCTION OF HOUSES OR FLATS IN THE GROUNDS OF EXISTING CARE HOMES, NURSING HOMES OR SIMILAR BUILDINGS

5 November 2007. *HMRC Brief 66/07*

This brief sets out HMRC's policy on the VAT treatment of the construction, and first major interest grant of, "independent living" units within the curtilage or grounds of residential care homes. (A "first major interest grant" is defined as the freehold sale or a lease in excess of 21 years, (20 years in Scotland.))

VAT PRs etc

In order for services of the construction, or first major interest grant, of such units to qualify for zero-rating, they must qualify either as buildings "designed as dwellings" or as buildings "intended for use solely for a relevant residential purpose", within the meaning of the these terms as defined in the VAT Act 1994.

Although "independent living" units generally have all of the physical characteristics of a "dwelling", the units only qualify for zero-rating if they meet all the conditions laid down in Note 2 to Group 5 of Schedule 8 to the VAT Act 1994. Where such units have a stipulation in their planning permission that they cannot be used separately from the care homes, of which they form a part, the construction of such units is ineligible for the zero rate, as is the first grant of a major interest in such units.

We have also been asked to consider whether the new units form a building (or buildings) that are "intended for use solely for a relevant residential purpose" thus qualifying the construction of the units for the zero rate.

In our view, the units do not qualify for the zero rate because, if personal care is provided to the occupants of the units, it is either not provided as a zero-rated home or institution would provide personal care or, if it is, it is provided as part of an existing home or institution.

Finally, we consider that such a unit would not qualify for zero-rating as "an institution which is the sole or main residence of at least 90 per cent of its residents", because the units are not institutions.

Commentary—*De Voil Indirect Tax Service* **V4.232**, **V4.411**.

THE DECISION OF THE TRIBUNAL IN INSURANCEWIDE.COM SERVICES LTD

21 November 2007. *HMRC Brief 69/07*

This concerns the VAT treatment of insurance introductory services following the VAT tribunal decision in *InsuranceWide.com Services Ltd (InsuranceWide)*. The tribunal found that certain internet services provided to insurers and brokers in connection with the arranging of insurance policies do not fall within the exemption for insurance related services provided by insurance brokers and agents and are liable to VAT at the standard rate.

BACKGROUND

InsuranceWide provides an online comparison website service, putting potential customers in touch with insurers via a click-through from its website to that of an insurer or insurance broker. It receives commission from the insurers based on the number of contracts that result from the introductions. Over the years, the services provided by InsuranceWide have changed as technology has developed.

In 2002 InsuranceWide introduced a system known as the InsuranceWide Wizard which automated the selection process by obtaining and recording the essential information required by insurers and applying that information to guide each prospective customer through to the most appropriate insurer or insurers. This information is discussed regularly with insurers to ensure it is kept up to date.

THE DECISION

The Tribunal found that none of the services provided by InsuranceWide fell within the VAT exemption because InsuranceWide was not an insurance agent. InsuranceWide specifically disclaimed being an agent on its website and was found to be playing no part in the negotiation of the contracts. Neither did InsuranceWide have the power to bind the insurance company which the tribunal found to be one of the indicators of an agency relationship (although not it itself determinative for VAT purposes).

Having found against the Appellant on this basis, the tribunal then went on to consider whether any of the services provided by InsuranceWide qualified as the "services of an insurance intermediary" (under UK law) or insurance "related services" (under EU law) which would have made them exempt had InsuranceWide been an insurance agent.

The tribunal found that, in performing the non-Wizard services, InsuranceWide's role was not that of a mediator between the parties to a contract of insurance. It found that InsuranceWide was "nothing more than an introducer and its role. . . . . cannot be properly distinguished from that of an advertiser in that via its website it had no interaction with either party beyond making the one aware of the other and providing a means of one contacting the other."

After the introduction of the Wizard, however, the tribunal found that InsuranceWide's services went beyond that of a mere promoter of, and introducer to, insurance companies and would qualify for exemption under both UK and EU law when provided by an insurance agent or broker. In particular the tribunal highlighted the regular negotiations with insurers about the range and price of products, the saving of time for both the insurers and would be insureds by referring only suitable applicants to appropriate insurers and assisting with the completion of forms.

IMPLICATIONS OF THE DECISION

The decision in InsuranceWide confirms HMRC's current published policy in this area (see in particular paragraph 10.5 of Notice 701/36, *Insurance*) and, as such, does not have implications for any of the insurance-related services that HMRC currently see as falling within the VAT exemption.

Whilst certain services provided via the internet were found to be liable to VAT, HMRC do not see the decision as applying to all internet services and accept that, where the necessary criteria are met, some internet services can fall within the VAT exemption and it is the arrangements between the parties and the nature of the services themselves that determines the VAT liability and not the means by which those services are delivered.

HMRC see the decision as applying, in particular, to advertising/promotional type services such as internet "click through" services and mail-shot and leaflet distribution services where the provider does little more than put one party in touch with the other and plays no part in any interaction between the parties once that introduction has been made. Such services are specifically excluded from the VAT exemption and are taxable regardless of whether (as with InsuranceWide's co-branded websites) the products are promoted in the name of the provider of the service, the provider is an insurance agent or broker by profession, or whether payment is made by fee or commission.

In circumstances (which would include certain "affinity" arrangements) where the provider is clearly acting as an agent of an insurer or insurers and is playing a more active role in arranging the policies than mere introduction – for example, negotiating terms and conditions of the insurance contacts, assisting with forms/queries and actively recommending/endorsing the insurance product/s – VAT exemption continues to apply.

Commentary—*De Voil Indirect Tax Service* **V4.123**.

INTRASTAT – THRESHOLDS FROM 1 JANUARY 2008

19 December 2007. *HMRC Brief 75/07*

This Revenue & Customs Brief article explains that the Intrastat thresholds will remain unchanged in 2008 from those set on 1 January 2007 and explains how businesses trading with other EU Member States will be affected by this.

INTRASTAT THRESHOLDS

- The exemption threshold remains at £260,000.
- The delivery terms threshold remains at £14,500,000.

BACKGROUND

Community legislation requires the UK to collect information on intra-EU trade for statistical purposes and sets minimum requirements for the quantity of trade covered. These requirements determine the level at which the exemption threshold is set in the UK. The same threshold is applied independently to arrivals (intra-EU imports) and dispatches (intra-EU exports).

Those traders with an annual intra-EU trade in goods above the specified exemption threshold are required to provide monthly statistical returns (Intrastat Supplementary Declarations).

Community legislation requires the UK to collect information to enable the accurate calculation of statistical value. These requirements determine the level at which the delivery terms threshold is set in the UK. The same threshold for delivery terms applies to arrivals and dispatches.

Traders with annual EU trade above the delivery terms threshold are required to supply additional information relating to delivery terms on their statistical returns.

FURTHER INFORMATION

Further information on trade statistics can be found online at www.uktradeinfo.com/ or by phoning uktradeinfo Customer Services on 01702 367485.

For further information and advice on submitting Intrastat declarations, please contact the National Advice Service 0845 010 9000.

Commentary—*De Voil Indirect Tax Service* **V5.276**.

PARTIAL EXEMPTION – CHESHIRE RACING TRIBUNAL DECISION

3 January 2008. *HMRC Brief 1/08*

This Revenue & Customs Brief article announces HMRC's revised policy about recovery of input tax on Satellite Information System (SIS) services received by bookmakers following the Tribunal decision in the case of *Cheshire Racing Ltd* (VTD 20283). It updates Article 1 in Business Brief 17/06 that also concerns SIS. It uses a number of specialist terms, which are fully explained in Public Notice 706, Partial Exemption.

BACKGROUND

SIS provides live coverage of horse and dog racing, real time odds, results information and commentary and opinion from pundits. Historically, HMRC's view was that this information related directly to the over the counter betting activity of Bookmakers, which is exempt for VAT purposes.

In the appeal of *Town and County Factors* (VTD 19616) the Tribunal found that there was a sufficient link between SIS costs and taxable supplies made, such that the costs were residual for partial exemption purposes. The Commissioners subsequently issued Business Brief 17/06 which set out how HMRC viewed the logic and wider application of the decision. The Business Brief stated that where the bookmaker contributed additional content to the SIS service so that it partly related to their taxable supplies, then the input tax incurred was residual for that bookmaker.

CHESHIRE RACING (VTD 20283)

Cheshire Racing Ltd disagreed with HMRC's view. They argued that input tax on SIS should be residual even though they did not add additional content. They felt that VAT incurred on the specialist TV services was partly recoverable because it had a direct and immediate link with taxable supplies from gaming machines, as well as betting.

In deciding in favour of Cheshire Racing Ltd, the Tribunal found as a fact there was a direct and immediate link between the content of the SIS broadcast and gaming machine income. This applied even when the bookmaker added no additional information to SIS.

HMRC'S POLICY FOLLOWING CHESHIRE RACING LTD

HMRC are not appealing the decision and now accepts that SIS services have a direct and immediate link to gaming machine supplies made by bookmakers as the SIS provides commentary relevant to those machines.

CLAIMS FOR UNDER-RECOVERED INPUT TAX

Bookmakers may wish to claim input tax which, in the light of this Revenue and Customs Brief, was incorrectly treated as exempt. Claims should be submitted to the Local Business Advice Centre. They must use the partial exemption method applicable to each accounting period unless there are exceptional circumstances as to why an alternative method is needed. In this case they should apply to HMRC to use an alternative special method. All claims are subject to the relevant time limits.

Further information about making claims can be found in Public Notice 700/45 How to correct VAT errors or make adjustments or claims and Business Brief 28/04.

Commentary—*De Voil Indirect Tax Service* **V4.131.**

THREE YEAR TIME LIMIT FOR VAT CLAIMS

20 February 2008. *HMRC Brief 7/08*

The recent House of Lords decisions in the cases of *Michael Fleming (t/a Bodycraft) v HMRC (Fleming)* and *Condé Nast Publications Ltd v HMRC (Condé Nast)* disapplied the three year time limit for input tax claims in respect of which the entitlement to deduct accrued before 1 May 1997.

HMRC consider that the terms of the judgment also apply to claims to recover VAT overpaid or overdeclared in accounting periods ending before 4 December 1996.

CLAIMS

As a result claims may now be made for:

- output tax overpaid or overdeclared in accounting periods ending before 4 December 1996
- input tax in respect of which the entitlement to deduct arose in accounting periods ending before 1 May 1997

Claims must be submitted to:

HM Revenue & Customs
"Fleming" Claims Team (Leeds)
Queens Dock
Liverpool
Merseyside L74 4AA

Telephone enquiries in relation to the submission of claims or to claims that have already been submitted to the Claims Team may be made on Tel 0113 389 4432.

Claims relating to accounting periods ending on or after 4 December 1996 (for output tax) or 1 May 1997 (for input tax) are capped at three years.

UNDERTAKINGS

Claims will now be paid, following verification, without the need to provide an undertaking to repay HMRC.

Claimants who have had their claims paid on condition that they provide an undertaking to repay in the event that the House of Lords found in favour of HMRC, are released from those undertakings. No further action is required by claimants.

FURTHER ANNOUNCEMENT

HMRC are still considering the full implications of the judgment and will make a further announcement in due course.

BACKGROUND

In 1996 the government reduced the time limit for claiming overpaid VAT to three years from the date of the overpayment. A similar three year time limit was also introduced for input tax claims in 1997. Both provisions had retrospective, as well as prospective, effect, ie they applied to claims that arose in accounting periods both before and after the enactment of the legislation. Neither contained transitional provisions to allow claims to be made for a limited period under the old rules, before the new time limits came into effect.

The absence of such transitional arrangements was held to breach Community law, in the ECJ judgment in Marks and Spencer plc in July 2002. In August and October 2002, HMRC sought to remedy the position by introducing an administrative transitional regime (Business Briefs 22/02 and 27/02). In January 2008 the House of Lords in Fleming and Condé Nast held that, in the absence of transitional arrangements in 1997, the three year cap had to be disapplied for input tax claims in respect of which the rights to deduct had accrued at 1 May 1997.

HMRC consider that the terms of the judgment are such that they cannot rely on the administrative transitional regime introduced for output tax claims. They accept that the three year cap must therefore be disapplied for such claims where the rights had accrued at 4 December 1996.

Commentary—*De Voil Indirect Tax Service* **V3.405**, **V5.159C**.

ACCESS TO INTRASTAT DATA

4 March 2008. *HMRC Brief 13/08*

This Revenue & Customs Brief announces the introduction of a new VAT regulation. This will make clear that HM Revenue & Customs (HMRC) may use for VAT purposes the data already collected for Intrastat purposes.

The new regulation will not require businesses to provide any additional information. Although it applies to those businesses which supply or acquire EC goods over the (current) annual threshold of £260,000 (net of VAT and Excise duty) and which are therefore required to submit monthly "Intrastat declarations", these businesses need take no action as a result of the change in the law, which comes into effect on 1 April 2008.

BACKGROUND

"Intrastat" is the EU-based system for the collection of statistics on the trade in goods between Member States.

Within the UK, intra-EU trade statistics are compiled from two sources:

– from the aggregate net value of EC supplies (sales) and acquisitions (purchases) which all VAT registered businesses are required to declare on their VAT returns, used to estimate the total value of trade;
– from detailed transaction information provided by those businesses, approximately 32,500 which supply or acquire EC goods over the (current) annual threshold of £260,000 (net of VAT and Excise duty) and which are therefore required to submit monthly "Intrastat declarations".

Data from these sources can support HMRC strategy to counter Missing Trader Intra-Community (MTIC) fraud, a sophisticated and systematic criminal attack on the VAT system, which has reduced VAT revenues by an estimated £2 billion to £3 billion in 2005/06 and £1 billion to £2 billion in 2006/07.

However, under current legislation the full extent to which this data can be used for HMRC VAT enforcement purposes is unclear. The position in law is therefore being regularised, so as to make clear that the data provided for Intrastat purposes is to be provided for VAT purposes as well.

ACTION REQUIRED

No action is required over and above that already required to submit Intrastat declarations. As of 1 April 2008, the data as provided on Intrastat declarations will be provided for both Intrastat and VAT purposes. Affected businesses are therefore still required to provide the information once only, in the same format and at no additional cost. They will not be required to store a second copy of the declaration in their VAT records. New Intrastat forms which make clear the dual purpose of the data in an amended heading to the form will be available shortly.

PENALTIES

Although any breach of the new VAT regulation will in principle become subject to a potential penalty under VAT provisions already in place, the VAT penalty provision does not apply where a person is convicted of an offence in relation to Intrastat. Accordingly, affected taxpayers cannot, once the new VAT regulation is in place, become liable to two penalties, under both VAT and Intrastat regimes for failing to submit the Intrastat declaration (or for completing it inaccurately).

Commentary—*De Voil Indirect Tax Service* **V5.276**, **V5.345**.

ANIMAL RESCUE CHARITIES – VAT LIABILITY OF THE SALE OF ABANDONED DOGS AND CATS

4 March 2008. *HMRC Brief 14/08*

This brief explains the VAT liability of the sale of abandoned animals by a charity following the Tribunal decision in the case of Gables Farm Dogs and Cats Home [*Gablesfarm Dog and Cats Home* VTD 20519].

BACKGROUND

Gables Farm Dogs and Cats Home is a charity that rescues lost, unwanted and homeless cats and dogs many of which are subsequently sold to new owners. It receives unwanted cats and dogs from owners as well as strays and abandoned animals given by local authority dog wardens, the police, and members of the public.

Subject to certain conditions the sale of donated goods by a charity is zero-rated and HMRC's view was that only animals given to the home by their original owners could be regarded as "donated" within the terms of the legislation.

The Tribunal found that the charity took steps to return genuinely lost animals to their owners and those it offered for re-homing had been deliberately abandoned. In these circumstances the animals given to the charity by the local authority, the police and members of the public were donated and therefore zero-rated when sold.

HMRC POLICY FOLLOWING GABLES FARM DOGS AND CATS HOME

HMRC are not appealing the Tribunal's decision and accept that charities selling animals in similar circumstances should zero-rate their supplies.

MAKING CLAIMS FOR PAST SALES

Charities that have accounted for and paid VAT on sales of animals that are now considered to be zero-rated may submit claims for overpaid tax to their Local Business Advice Centre. All claims are subject to the relevant time limits and unjust enrichment provisions.

More information about making claims can be found in VAT Notice 700/45 "How to correct VAT errors or make adjustments or claims" and Business Brief 28/04.

FURTHER INFORMATION

For further information and advice, please contact our Charities Helpline on 0845 302 0203.

Commentary—*De Voil Indirect Tax Service* **V4.261**.

VALUATION OF IMPORTED GOODS: CUSTOMS VALUATION DECLARATIONS AND GENERAL VALUATION STATEMENTS

11 March 2008. *HMRC Brief 16/08*

This Revenue and Customs Brief announces our plans to introduce changes to current procedures that require a valuation declaration form C105 or C109 to be completed by importers or their agents.

BACKGROUND

EC Regulations require that a declaration of particulars, relating to the customs value, shall accompany the customs entry made in respect of imported goods. The C105 is an official form on which the importer, or their agent, records information about the valuation of the imported goods in a single consignment for customs duty and import VAT purposes. Importers are required to provide a completed valuation declaration of particulars with their customs entries when the value of the imported goods exceeds a threshold limit of £6,500.

The C109 is a numbered document, the details of which are quoted on entry documents and used instead of individual valuation declarations for a period not exceeding three years.

REVISED PROCEDURE

So that you do not have to routinely provide information about your importations, we are relaxing the requirement for a valuation declaration to be completed for 99 per cent of all

VAT PRs etc

import entry declarations. In future, importers will only be required to complete a valuation declaration on request, for example in respect of import declarations examined by our officers on a post-importation audit.

The new procedure will also mean that there will be no need to complete and register General Valuation Statements, Form C109.

The changes will be introduced on 1 April 2008.

Further information can be found in Customs Information Paper (08)19.

NEW PENALTIES FOR ERRORS IN RETURNS AND DOCUMENTS

1 April 2008. *HMRC Brief 19/08*

INTRODUCTION

This brief explains how the new penalties will affect our customers and their advisers.

HM Revenue & Customs (HMRC) inherited a confusing variety of penalty charging powers. The new penalties are one of the first pieces of cross cutting legislation designed to make the tax system simpler and more consistent. It follows consultation with our customers and other interested parties during the Review of Powers, Deterrents and Safeguards.

The legislation aims to help those who try to comply, and come down hard on those who don't. The clear messages for customers are that:

– if they take reasonable care when completing their returns they will not be penalised;
– if they do not take reasonable care, errors will be penalised and the penalties will be higher if the error is deliberate;
– disclosing errors to us early will substantially reduce any penalty due.

TAXES AFFECTED

The new penalties are for errors on returns and documents initially for VAT, PAYE, National Insurance, Capital Gains Tax, Income Tax, Corporation Tax and the Construction Industry Scheme.

For these taxes, it applies to returns or other documents for tax periods starting on or after 1 April 2008 that are due to be filed on or after 1 April 2009. The legislation is Schedule 24 of Finance Act 2007.

WHEN CAN A PENALTY FOR INACCURACY BE CHARGED?

Two conditions must be satisfied before we can charge a penalty.

(1) The document given to HMRC must contain an inaccuracy that leads to:
  – an understatement of the person's liability to tax;
  – a false or inflated statement of a loss by the person;
  – a false or inflated claim to repayment of tax;
(2) The inaccuracy must be careless, deliberate or deliberate and concealed.

A penalty can also be charged where, in the absence of a return, we issue an assessment which is too low and the person does not take reasonable steps to tell us of the under-assessment within 30 days of the date of the assessment.

HOW IS THE PENALTY CALCULATED?

There is no penalty if a person takes reasonable care but submits an incorrect return. However, if the person later discovers the error but does not take reasonable steps to tell us about it, the inaccuracy will be treated as careless.

The penalty percentages are applied to the additional tax due as a result of correcting the error (known as the potential lost revenue). There is a different measure of potential lost revenue where the error results in an overstated loss:

– the penalty is up to 30 per cent of the potential lost revenue if the error is careless;

- the penalty is up to 70 per cent of the potential lost revenue if the error is deliberate;
- the penalty is up to 100 per cent of the potential lost revenue if the error is deliberate and the person conceals it.

The penalty chargeable where tax has been under-assessed because of the customer's failure to send us a return is 30 per cent of the potential lost revenue.

HOW CAN PENALTIES BE REDUCED?

There can be a substantial reduction in the level of penalty charged for unprompted disclosure of errors. A disclosure is unprompted if it is made at a time when the person making it has no reason to believe that HMRC has discovered, or is about to discover, the error.

Further reductions can be given based on the quality of the disclosure. The more a person tells, helps or gives access to HMRC the more the penalty may be reduced.

To calculate the reduction for disclosure we will consider three elements of disclosure. To what extent is the customer?

- telling HMRC about their error;
- helping HMRC work out what extra tax is due;
- giving HMRC access to their records to check their figures.

The reductions are made because we want to encourage people to come forward when they think there is a problem with their tax affairs, or they have not met a requirement.

REASONABLE CARE

Each person has a responsibility to take reasonable care. But what is necessary for each person to meet that responsibility has to be viewed in the light of their abilities and circumstances.

For example, we would not expect the same level of knowledge or expertise from a self-employed and unrepresented individual as from a large multi-national company. We expect a higher degree of care to be taken over large and complex matters than simple straightforward ones.

Every person is expected to make and keep sufficient records for them to provide a complete and accurate return. A person with simple, straightforward tax affairs needs to keep a simple system of records, which are followed and regularly updated. A person with larger and more complex tax affairs will need to put in place more sophisticated systems and maintain them equally carefully.

We believe it is reasonable to expect a person who encounters a transaction or other event with which they are not familiar to take care to check the correct tax treatment or to seek suitable advice. We expect people to take their tax seriously.

SOME PENALTIES MAY BE SUSPENDED

Suspension is intended to support those who try to meet their obligations by helping them to avoid penalties for inaccuracies in the future.

Only a penalty for failing to take reasonable care can be considered for suspension. Suspension conditions will be agreed and set and if they are met the penalty will be cancelled. If they are not met the penalty becomes payable. The period of suspension can be for up to two years.

For example, if a careless inaccuracy is due to poor record-keeping one of the conditions of suspension could be that specified improvements are made to the way records are kept. This will help the customer avoid future errors.

We will consider the taxpayer's general compliance behaviour, the level of disclosure and the nature of the inaccuracy before deciding whether to suspend the penalty.

OTHER TAXES

The 2008 Finance Bill makes provision to extend the new penalties to cover incorrect returns for the other taxes and duties HMRC administer. We expect the new provisions will apply for periods commencing on or after 1 April 2009 where the return is due to be filed on or after 1 April 2010 – see Budget Notice 96.

MORE INFORMATION

Please check the Frequently Asked Questions (FAQs) and the technical guidance in the Compliance Handbook on [www.hmrc.gov.uk/about/new-penalties/index.htmIssued 1 April 2008].

INTERPRETATION OF ARTICLE 13 OF THE PRINCIPAL VAT DIRECTIVE: "BODIES GOVERNED BY PUBLIC LAW" AND "SPECIAL LEGAL REGIME"

20 May 2008. *HMRC Brief 27/08*

HM Revenue and Customs has reconsidered its interpretation of the terms "bodies governed by public law" and "special legal regime" in the context of article 13(1) of the Principal VAT Directive (Directive 2006/112/EC) ("article 13(1)") as well as the application of this provision.

Our current interpretation is based on the decisions in the Court of Session's judgment in *Edinburgh Telford College (ETC)* [2006] CSIH 13 XA 18/05; XA 22/05, [2006] STC 1291, the High Court's judgment in *Riverside Housing Association (Riverside)* [2006] EWHC 2383 (CH), [2006] STC 2072 and the decision of the VAT and Duties Tribunal in *The Chancellors, Masters and Scholars of the University of Cambridge (Cambridge University)* LON/05/0958 (VTD 20610).

This Revenue & Customs Brief explains HMRCs' current thinking on the matter. While the Brief is of immediate interest to further and higher education providers, it may be relevant to other bodies as well.

BACKGROUND

1. Legal position

Under article 13(1), "states, regional and local government authorities and other bodies governed by public law" are not regarded as taxable persons when they engage in activities as "public authorities". Case law has confirmed that such public bodies engage as public authorities when they undertake their duties under a legal regime which applies to them and not to other bodies (a "special legal regime"). This is subject to certain mandatory exclusions and competition criteria.

This provision therefore only applies to the types of body specified, and only in the circumstances when they engage as public authorities. In any other circumstance the normal VAT rules apply.

2. ETC

ETC is a further education college providing further education as defined in the Further and Higher Education (Scotland) Act 1992 (amended by the F&HE (Scotland) Act 2005) and is funded by the Scottish Education Funding Council.

ETC argued that, when it provided further education courses for which it charged fees, it did so as a "public authority" within the meaning of article 13(1) so that it should not be treated as a taxable person in respect of that activity—taking the provision of such education outside the scope of VAT. There was no dispute over courses which are wholly funded through grants paid by the Scottish Further Education Funding Council which are outside the scope of VAT as the grant funding is not consideration for any supply either to the funding provider or to the students.

The Court of Session agreed with ETC, finding that the College's activities were undertaken under the umbrella of a special legal regime deriving from the Further & Higher Education (Scotland) Act 1992, the Scottish Further Education Funding Council (Establishment) (Scotland) Order 1998 and implemented in the funding agreement between the Scottish Further Education Funding Council and the College. The essence of the dispute was whether (as ETC argued) it is necessary to make judgements based on the wider legal regime governing the management and conduct of an activity, or (as HMRC argued) to focus solely upon the legal regime governing the delivery of a particular service. Although cases must be examined in the light of their own facts and on their own merits, HMRC accept that it is necessary to consider the wider legal regime.

The question of whether or not ETC was a body governed by public law was not considered by either the VAT and Duties Tribunal or the Court of Session because HMRC had accepted that the College was such a body. However, the High Court decision in Riverside has led HMRC to reconsider its interpretation of what is meant by a "body governed by public law" for the purposes of article 13(1) and to revise its policy in this area as set out below. This policy change will be reflected in changes to the current guidance on the meaning of a "body governed by public law" which is currently to be found at paragraph 3.7 of V1-14.

3. Riverside

Riverside is a large social housing provider registered with the Housing Corporation as a "Registered Social Landlord" (RSL). So far as is relevant hereto, Riverside argued that its activities were non-business on the basis that it was a body governed by public law for the purposes of article 13(1) and that the Housing Corporation rules, to which RSLs must adhere, amounted to a special legal regime. That contention was rejected by the Tribunal and the High Court.

Even though Riverside was subsidised by Government funds and required by statute to adhere to certain rules applying to RSLs, its supplies of social housing were nevertheless held to be made in the course of business.

In referring to article 13(1), the Tribunal stated that: "The provision clearly contemplates government organisations which are institutions of a democratic state and the European jurisprudence on the topic shows that the concept of a public body is to be narrowly construed. . . . . It is in my view clear from the legislation itself, interpreted in accordance with the jurisprudence of the Court of Justice, that the 'other bodies' contemplated by the article are those of a kind similar to government bodies, carrying out quasi-governmental functions, of which examples might be the Financial Services Authority and the Housing Corporation itself, with organisations such as the Institute of Chartered Accountants when undertaking its regulatory role. Riverside, by contrast, does not have a regulatory or similar role; it is itself the subject of regulation. It is a private sector organisation which happens to undertake functions on behalf of the state, but that does not make it a public body".

BODY GOVERNED BY PUBLIC LAW

In the light of the decision in Riverside, HMRC have concluded that the term "body governed by public law" in article 13(1) is narrow in application. HMRC consider that a body will only satisfy this criterion if it is a public sector body which forms a part of the UK's public administration, such as a government department, a local authority or a non-departmental public body. Article 13(1) is not intended to enable other bodies to claim special treatment merely because they have delegated powers, are regulated in some way by the State, are funded by public money or are subject to certain specific rules in the pursuit of their activities.

This view has recently been endorsed by the VAT and Duties Tribunal in the Cambridge University case.

Accordingly HMRC no longer accept that the generality of FE and HE providers are bodies governed by public law as defined in article 13(1).

A number of FE and HE bodies have sought to rely on article 13(1) to support an argument for entitlement to zero-rating under Group 5 of Schedule 8 and/or reduced rating under Schedule 7A to the VAT Act. FE and HE bodies should be aware that HMRC do not agree that such bodies can assume that they fall within this provision: rather it is necessary to examine the facts of each case separately.

Further, HMRC are of the view that, even were a body to come within article 13(1) in respect of a particular activity, that would serve only to take supplies in respect of that activity outside the scope of VAT and would not affect the liability of supplies made to that body.

Commentary—*De Voil Indirect Tax Service* **V2.108**.

LEARN HOW YOUR CLIENTS CAN AVOID PENALTIES

18 June 2008. *HMRC Brief 29/08*

We have published a learning package (www.hmrc.gov.uk/about/new-penalties/NPA/HTML/NPA_menu.html) to help agents and taxpayers understand the new penalty regime.

This package, published on our website, is also being rolled out to 28,000 of our staff.

VAT PRs etc

The module takes less than half an hour to complete and provides an overview of the new system.

It will help advisers understand the potential impact on their clients. During this financial year they have the opportunity to help their clients identify and correct potential errors and weaknesses in their systems before the new penalty regime starts from 1 April 2009.

THE NEW PENALTIES

The key points are:

– the new penalties are one of the first pieces of cross-cutting legislation designed to make the tax system simpler and more consistent;
– if taxpayers take reasonable care to get their tax right, we will not penalise them, even if they make a mistake;
– if they do not take reasonable care, errors will be penalised and the penalties will be higher if the error is deliberate;
– telling us about errors, especially if this is unprompted, can substantially reduce any penalty due.

Most people take care to fill in their tax returns and documents correctly. We want to encourage that and help them get it right. It uses penalties to stop people who do not take care from gaining an unfair advantage.

TAXES AFFECTED

The new penalties are for errors on returns and documents initially for Income Tax, VAT, PAYE and NICs paid by employers, Capital Gains Tax, Corporation Tax and the Construction Industry Scheme.

For these taxes, it applies to returns or other documents for tax periods starting on or after 1 April 2008 that are due to be filed on or after 1 April 2009. The relevant legislation is Schedule 24 of Finance Act 2007.

This year's Budget proposed to extend the new penalties to almost all the taxes we collect – see Budget Notice 96 – www.hmrc.gov.uk/budget2008/bn96.pdf.

MORE INFORMATION

In addition to the learning module, our internet page for new penalties, has frequently asked questions, a leaflet, and technical guidance, which are updated. There is an email address for queries.

HMRC Brief 19/08 also explains in more detail how the penalties work.

PARTIAL EXEMPTION: LAUNCH OF CONSULTATION

19 June 2008. *HMRC Brief 30/08*

This Revenue and Customs Brief article announces the launch of a consultation on ideas to simplify the VAT partial exemption rules to reduce compliance costs for businesses. The consultation invites comments and suggestions on the three partial exemption areas identified as simplification priorities by businesses:

– standard method;
– *de minimis* rules;
– Capital Goods Scheme (CGS).

It also invites comments on possibly combining partial exemption and business/non-business calculations.

Partly exempt businesses and their representatives are encouraged to participate to help cut compliance costs. Further information on partial exemption is available in Public Notice 706 "Partial Exemption".

BACKGROUND

VAT on costs relating to taxable supplies is recoverable, whereas VAT relating to exempt supplies is normally irrecoverable. A business that incurs VAT on costs relating to taxable and exempt supplies is partly exempt and must apply the partial exemption rules to calculate how much VAT it can recover.

There are around 140,000 partly exempt businesses including financial service providers, property companies, educational organisations, charities, gaming operators and undertakers. Around 120,000 of these, mainly smaller-sized businesses, operate the standard method, which is a simple turnover-based calculation set out in law.

Around 100,000 small partly exempt businesses benefit from being able to recover VAT relating to exempt supplies that is deemed insignificant under the *de minimis* rules. This is meant to relieve small businesses of the burden of restricting VAT relating to exempt supplies.

Some expenditure on capital items, mainly relating to land and buildings, falls within the CGS. This requires businesses to review the extent to which capital items are used in making taxable supplies for a period of up to ten years, making adjustments to previously recovered VAT where necessary. Most large businesses incur expenditure on capital items.

CONSULTATION

The consultation was launched on 19 June with publication of the consultation document on the HMRC website. Businesses and representative bodies are invited to suggest ways to simplify partial exemption and comment on a number of ideas for simplification. Responses from smaller-sized businesses and their representatives that regularly perform partial exemption calculations are particularly encouraged as they are likely to be affected most and have most to contribute. With this in mind, technical and legal content has been kept to a minimum. The consultation will end on 30 September 2008.

FURTHER INFORMATION

If you have any queries please contact Patrick Wilson on 020 7147 0595 or by email Patrick Wilson [see HMRC website for email form].

Commentary—*De Voil Indirect Tax Service* **V3.461**.

SET OFF WHERE RIGHT TO CLAIM OVERDECLARED TAX IS TRANSFERRED

27 June 2008. *HMRC Brief 31/08*

BACKGROUND

A new clause has been introduced into the Finance Bill currently before Parliament. The purpose of the new clause is to close off a potential avoidance opportunity that has arisen as a result of a recent judgment of the Court of Appeal.

In *Revenue & Customs Comrs v Midlands Co-operative Society* [2008] All ER (D) 121 (Apr), the Court held that a right to make a claim for overpaid or overdeclared VAT can be transferred, assigned or sold. Prior to this judgment, HM Revenue & Customs (HMRC) had taken the view that only the person who had overpaid or overdeclared the VAT was entitled to make a claim to recover it. Where a person makes such a claim HMRC are required to set-off against it any outstanding liabilities of the claimant.

The avoidance opportunity arises because there is no provision under current law for HMRC to set-off the liabilities of the person who originally overstated the VAT liability ("the original creditor") if the claim for the VAT overpaid or overdeclared is made by somebody else ("the current creditor"), as a result of the transfer of the right to make a claim. As a consequence, by transferring the right to make a claim, taxpayers can avoid the set-off procedures.

SET-OFF AND UNJUST ENRICHMENT

The new clause operates by putting the current creditor in the shoes of the original creditor for the purposes of setting off liabilities. It provides that, where the original creditor transfers the right to claim overpaid or overdeclared tax to the current creditor, the latter will not receive any more from HMRC than if the original creditor had made the claim.

Whilst the Midlands judgment concerned VAT, it has wider implications; the current procedure for claiming overpaid VAT is replicated for all of the indirect taxes administered by HMRC. The potential for avoidance therefore exists for all indirect taxes. We also consider that the avoidance opportunity may also exist in relation to claims for error or mistake relief for direct taxes.

The avoidance opportunity that arises as a result of this judgment is not restricted to set-off. HMRC has the power to refuse any indirect tax claim where it can show that meeting the claim would unjustly enrich the claimant, because the economic burden of the overcharged tax has been passed on to customers.

However, this defence against payment of a claim does not apply where the claimant was not the person who originally overpaid or overdeclared the tax being claimed. It is therefore possible for the original creditor to sidestep the unjust enrichment provisions by transferring the right to make a claim to another.

The new clause addresses this by again putting the current creditor in the shoes of the original creditor for the purposes of the unjust enrichment provisions. HMRC will be able to refuse to pay a current creditor's claim where they can establish that payment of the claim to the original creditor would have unjustly enriched that original creditor.

PRACTICAL EFFECTS OF THE NEW CLAUSE

The new clause does not make the current creditor liable for the debts of the original creditor. It simply ensures that the current creditor cannot receive a sum greater than the amount the original creditor would have received had they made the claim.

The new clause provides that the amount due from HMRC on a claim on a transferred right will be determined by first setting off the amount of the outstanding liabilities of the original creditor and then any liabilities of the current creditor. The set-off of the original creditor's amounts due to HMRC will discharge the obligations of the original creditor to HMRC and vice versa. Set-off will be of amounts still outstanding at the time when the claim is met.

A current creditor will be able to appeal to a Tribunal or to the Special Commissioners against a decision of HMRC to refuse to pay a claim in whole or in part. Any such appeal would be against the refusal to pay the claim or the decision to reduce it.

The provisions of the new clause will apply to all of the taxes (including excise) administered by HMRC. It will apply to all transfers of rights to make a claim for overpaid tax taking place on or after 25 June 2008.

Commentary—*De Voil Indirect Tax Service* **V5.159B**.

VAT EXEMPTION FOR FUND MANAGEMENT SERVICES

24 July 2008. *HMRC Brief 35/08*

At Budget 2008, it was announced that the VAT exemption for fund management services would be amended with effect from 1 October 2008. The amending legislation, explanatory memorandum, and draft guidance have now been published on our website. This Revenue & Customs Brief provides some detail about the amendment and information for businesses wishing to submit claims for overpaid VAT in the light of these changes.

BACKGROUND

EU VAT law exempts "the management of special investment funds as defined by Member States". The UK interpretation of this was challenged and, following the ECJ judgment in *JP Morgan Fleming Claverhouse Investment Trust plc*, we accepted that closed-ended investment undertakings, such as investment trust companies (ITCs), should be defined for the purposes of the exemption.

The amendment gives effect to this judgment in UK law and, in particular, defines "closed-ended collective investment undertaking" by reference to certain criteria which must be satisfied. These are that:

– its sole object is the investment of capital, raised from the public, wholly or mainly in securities;
– it manages its assets on the principle of spreading investment risk;
– all of its ordinary shares (of each class if there is more than one) or equivalent units are included in the official list maintained by the Financial Services Authority pursuant to section 74(1) of the Financial Services and Markets Act 2000; and
– all of its ordinary shares (of each class if there is more than one) or equivalent units are admitted to trading on a regulated market situated or operating in the United Kingdom.

For further details of this, you may wish to refer to the draft guidance.

CLAIMS FOR OVERSTATED OR OVERPAID VAT

Although the amended law comes into effect on 1 October 2008, it represents the situation as it should have been since 1 January 1990 when the exemption was first introduced. There is no requirement to make adjustments in respect of supplies made prior to 1 October 2008. However, businesses which have accounted for VAT on fund management services which qualify for exemption under the amended legislation may wish to submit claims to us for output tax over-accounted for (see VAT Notice 700/45 "How to correct VAT errors and make adjustments or claims").

All adjustments or claims are limited to a three-year period (except those that are subject to the recent House of Lords judgments in *Michael Fleming (t/a Bodycraft)* and *Condé Nast Publications Ltd*—see HMRC Brief 7/08). Businesses must be able to produce evidence that they have accounted for VAT on the relevant services and must be able to substantiate the amount claimed. Subject to the three-year limitation period, any claim should also be for all prescribed accounting periods in which the error occurred. Should a claim not take into account all errors or all affected accounting periods, then we will seek to set-off amounts owed to us for these periods against amounts claimed in other periods.

We may reject all or part of a claim if repayment would unjustly enrich the claimant. More details on "unjust enrichment" can be found at part 14 of VAT Notice 700/45, referred to above. All claims for overstated or overpaid VAT will be dealt with in accordance with our Business Brief 28/04— "Correcting liability errors".

Commentary—*De Voil Indirect Tax Service* **V4.136H**.

DEFAULT INTEREST AND NET ERRORS OF LESS THAN £2000

1 August 2008. *HMRC Brief 38/08*

The current practice, described in paragraph 2.4 of Notice 700/43 (Default Interest) and note 4 on form VAT 652, of not charging default interest on net errors of £2000 or less separately notified to HMRC, will continue until the end of August 2008. However, following the decision in *Wilkinson v Commissioners of Inland Revenue* [2005] UKHL 30, [2006] STC 270, this practice is not considered lawful and will be withdrawn with effect from 1 September 2008. This means therefore that all error notifications (previously known as voluntary disclosures) requiring an assessment may be subject to a default interest charge, irrespective of the amount involved. However as before, *de minimis* net errors can continue to be corrected on a VAT return and will not attract interest.

Commentary—*De Voil Indirect Tax Service* **V5.108**.

PARTIAL EXEMPTION—VAT ADJUSTMENTS WHEN HOUSE BUILDERS LET THEIR DWELLINGS BEFORE SELLING THEM

15 September 2008. *HMRC Brief 44/08*

We have published an Information Sheet 7/08 which provides guidance, including worked examples, on the VAT implications when house builders decide to temporarily let their dwellings before selling them.

This Information Sheet is in response to recent enquiries from the house building sector and takes account of the High Court decision in the joined cases of *Curtis Henderson and Briararch* [1992] STC 732 which arose in the early 1990s. The key points to which the Information Sheet refers are:

– if you temporarily let a dwelling before selling it, you may affect the VAT you can recover on your costs;
– many house builders who temporarily let a dwelling will not be affected but you need to check this to avoid making VAT mistakes;
– there is an easy way to check if you are affected by applying what we describe here as a "simple check for *de minimis*".

If you fail this check, you may have to:

VAT PRs etc

- adjust the VAT previously recovered on your submitted VAT returns;
- restrict the VAT to be recovered on your current and future VAT returns;
- both adjust your past VAT recovery and restrict your future VAT recovery.

If you need to adjust VAT previously recovered, exceptionally and if you prefer, you may be able to do this without contacting us.

FURTHER INFORMATION

Further information can be obtained from our website or through the National Advice service on Tel 0845 010 9000. Information Sheet 7/08 provides guidance and further detail is available and supersedes or compliments existing guidance, as appropriate.

Commentary—*De Voil Indirect Tax Service* **V3.461**.

VAT ON FUEL USED FOR PROPELLING PRIVATE PLEASURE CRAFT AND PRIVATE PLEASURE FLYING

17 October 2008. *HMRC Brief 52/08*

The reduced rate of VAT will continue to apply to supplies of fuel oil, gas oil and kerosene used as fuel for propelling private pleasure craft and kerosene used as fuel for private pleasure flying after 31 October 2008. This rate applies even though the derogations allowing reduced or nil excise duty rates have expired.

BACKGROUND

The reduced rate of VAT applies to supplies of fuel oil, gas oil and kerosene, which are used for domestic or charity non-business purposes, provided that the goods benefit from a rebated rate of excise duty. This includes supplies of not more than 2,300 litres, which are deemed to be supplied for domestic use.

However, from 1 November 2008:

- heavy oil (mainly red diesel, which is a gas oil) used as fuel for propelling private pleasure craft
- kerosene (avtur) used as fuel for private pleasure flying

Will effectively attract the full rate of excise duty (see HMRC Briefs 49/08 and 50/08). To enable the reduced VAT rate to continue, the excise duty criterion will be removed from these particular supplies.

LEGISLATION

The VAT (Reduced Rate) (Supplies of Domestic Fuel or Power) Order 2008 (SI 2008/2676) comes into effect on 1 November.

FURTHER INFORMATION

Further information can be obtained from our website or through the National Advice service on Tel 0845 010 9000. VAT Notice 701/19 "Fuel and power" will be updated in due course.

Commentary—*De Voil Indirect Tax Service* **V4.406**.

NEW ZERO-RATED DWELLINGS – WHETHER ARRANGEMENTS ARE ABUSIVE

28 October 2008. *HMRC Brief 54/08*

1. This brief is for house builders who have built or are building new dwellings with the intention, when they are completed, of selling either the freehold interest or a long lease of over 21 years (at least 20 years in Scotland) in each of the properties.

2. Several such house builders have sought guidance on whether HM Revenue & Customs (HMRC) considers certain transactions involving the supply of new dwellings to be abusive. This brief identifies those situations that HMRC considers not to be abusive.

BACKGROUND

3. The first grant of a major interest (freehold sale or a long lease of over 21 years (at least 20 years in Scotland)) of a new dwelling is zero rated. This allows the house builder to recover all

the input tax they have incurred in connection with the development (subject to the normal rules about blocked input tax) and to sell the dwelling without adding VAT.

4. In the current economic climate, many house builders have found that they are unable to sell new dwellings. For most, this leaves them with the choice of leaving them empty until they find a buyer, or renting them out in the short term while they wait for the housing market to recover in order to sell them.

5. Revenue & Customs Brief 44/08 and Information Sheet 07/08 (both published on 15 September 2008) provide guidance for house builders renting out new dwellings on short term lets while retaining the intention to sell a major interest in the dwellings when the markets recover. As those documents explain, short term lets of this kind can sometimes give rise to adjustments of input tax previously recovered.

APPROACH MADE

6. HMRC have been asked about the possibility that house builders might, in advance of any short term lets, make the first grant of a major interest in the completed dwellings to a connected person, who would not be a member of a VAT group with the house builder. This zero-rated sale might remove the need for the kind of adjustments explained in Information Sheet 07/08. The suggestion put to HMRC is that the connected person would then rent out the properties until such a time as they could be sold. The rentals would be exempt and not give rise to input tax deduction on ongoing costs including the costs of the eventual sale (for example estate agency and legal costs). However, deduction of the VAT associated with the original construction would have been secured. We have been asked whether we would see this arrangement as abusive from a VAT point of view. This brief does not attempt to address any other tax consequences that might flow from such transactions or any commercial or legal issues.

IS THIS INTENDED STRUCTURE ABUSIVE?

7. For a scheme to be abusive, it must (as well as having the essential aim of saving VAT) produce a result contrary to the purpose of the VAT legislation. HMRC believe that Parliament intended that the construction of new dwellings should be relieved from VAT. The first grant mechanism introduced by Parliament does achieve this but it relies on the assumption that there will always be a grant of a major interest around the time the dwelling is complete, so ensuring deduction of VAT on all appropriate costs.

8. In HMRC's view, the arrangement set out in paragraph 6 above does not produce a result contrary to the purpose of the legislation, but rather ensures that a transaction of the kind Parliament envisaged will actually take place at the appropriate time. That view rests on the assumption that the purpose of the zero rating provisions associated with new dwellings is to relieve fully from VAT the provision of precisely that – new dwellings. That means that all the costs (save on blocked goods such as washing machines, carpets etc – see Section 13 of Notice 708 Buildings and Construction for more details) associated with producing a new house should either not carry VAT, or carry VAT that is deductible in full.

9. However, whilst we believe it is the policy objective that new dwellings should be zero rated, that does not extend to other goods or services that might be packaged up with the supply of a dwelling. HMRC consider it abusive when a major interest is granted with an essential aim of deducting VAT on costs such as repair, maintenance and refurbishment of dwellings (other than for remedying defects in the original construction) the relief of those kinds of costs not falling within the policy objective as we see it. These types of arrangements are likely to be challenged.

SUMMARY

10. In short, HMRC agree that the arrangement outlined in paragraph 6 above is one that they would not see as abusive and so would not seek to challenge. However, if the VAT deducted goes beyond the VAT that would normally be deducted in relation to the supply of the new dwelling (for example VAT on costs such as repairs, maintenance or refurbishment, which is not normally deductible) such arrangements are likely to be challenged as abusive.

FURTHER INFORMATION

11. For further information and advice contact the HMRC VAT and Excise helpline on Tel 0845 010 9000.

Commentary—*De Voil Indirect Tax Service* **V4.233, V4.238**.

EXCESS CHARGES IN NON-LOCAL AUTHORITY CAR PARKS

8 December 2008. *HMRC Brief 57/08*

This Revenue & Customs Brief explains our revised policy on VAT on excess charges and other penalties levied in non-local authority car parks and what you should do if you have incorrectly accounted for VAT on such charges. Certain excess charges which have to date been regarded as further consideration for a taxable supply of parking are now regarded as outside the scope of VAT.

BACKGROUND

Business Brief 19/02 explained our policy on the VAT treatment of excess charges in off-street car parks following the tribunal case of *Bristol City Council* (LON/99/261, [VTD 17665]) ("BCC"). The Tribunal had concluded that excess charges levied by the Council in its off-street car parks were outside the scope of VAT because they were levied pursuant to the Road Traffic Regulation Act 1984 and were not part of the contract entered into between the driver and the council. We accepted that the decision would also apply to other local authorities operating off-street car parks under the same statutory framework.

However, where off-street car parks were not operated by local authorities, we considered that excess charges would normally be subject to VAT because they arose under the terms of the contract between the driver and car park operator. This followed the rationale adopted by the Tribunal in the case of *J G Leigh t/a Moor Lane Video* (LON/89/83X [VTD 5098]), which concerned additional charges for videos held by customers beyond the agreed period of hire.

REVISED POLICY

We have recently reconsidered that policy in the light of new legal advice and have concluded that, in the case of BCC, the Tribunal's decision was founded as much upon the contractual relationship as the statutory regime. Therefore, we now accept that there is a difference between the situation where the contract under which parking is supplied allows for an extension of the original terms, for which additional consideration will be payable, and the situation where the driver is not permitted to extend the original terms and a penalty for breach of contract ensues if this in fact happens. Thus, where a car park operator makes an offer of parking under clear terms and conditions, setting punitive fines for their breach, the fines constitute penalties for breaching the contract, rather than additional consideration for using the facilities. Consequently, they are outside the scope of VAT. Since the same contractual relationships arise between drivers and local authority car park operators as arise between drivers and other car park operators, we have also concluded that the VAT treatment of excess charges will be the same for all car park operators.

EXCESS CHARGES NOT SUBJECT TO VAT

The penalty charges that will no longer be subject to VAT are those that are levied where a driver is in breach of the terms of the contract with the car park operator. The commonest situations where a driver may be in breach of the contract are:

– no parking ticket on display;
– underpayment;
– overstaying purchased parking time;
– returning within a specified time;
– parking outside marked bays;
– parking in bays set aside for disabled drivers or parents with children.

EXCESS CHARGES SUBJECT TO VAT

Where the terms and conditions make it clear that the driver can continue to use the facilities after a set period upon payment of a further amount without being in breach of the contract – for example, no charge for an initial three hours parking but £70 if that period is exceeded – then the payment will be consideration for use of the facilities and subject to VAT.

EXCESS CHARGES RETAINED BY CONTRACTORS

Some parking site owners contract out the management and operation of their parking sites and allow the contractor to retain all or part of the penalties collected. Any such payments retained by the contractor will constitute further consideration for their services supplied to the parking site owner and are subject to VAT.

WHAT NEXT?

If you believe that you have accounted for VAT when you should not have done, you may make a claim for the overpaid tax in line with the provisions of Notice 700/45: "How to correct errors on your VAT Return". Please note that such claims will be subject to "capping" and may also be subject to the unjust enrichment provisions.

Commentary—*De Voil Indirect Tax Service* **V2.201**, **V3.104**.

MARKS & SPENCER PLC JUDGMENT: VAT CLAIMS AND UNJUST ENRICHMENT

19 February 2009. *HMRC Brief 5/09*

Marks & Spencer Plc v CRC [2009] UKHL 8 — *Judgment of the House of Lords — VAT claims made before 26 May 2005 no longer subject to unjust enrichment*

BACKGROUND

Where a business has accounted for too much VAT and makes a claim to recover it, HM Revenue & Customs (HMRC) can refuse to pay that claim if they can show that payment would unjustly enrich the claimant. However, until the law was changed in 2005, this unjust enrichment defence could only be used against a specific category of claimants. This meant that it was possible that a claim by one business could be refused whilst a similar claim from another business could not.

Marks & Spencer fell within the former category and challenged the discriminatory nature of the legislation.

THE HOUSE OF LORDS JUDGMENT

In light of the House of Lords judgment, issued on 4 February 2009 [*Marks and Spencer plc v Revenue and Customs Commissioners* [2009] All ER (D) 39 (Feb), [2009] STC 452], the unjust enrichment defence will no longer be used against any claim made before 26 May 2005 (the date on which the law was amended to remove the discrimination referred to above).

CLAIMS MADE BEFORE 26 MAY 2005

Claims made before 26 May 2005 that were refused by HMRC on the grounds of unjust enrichment and have still not been settled will now be paid, subject to verification. Claims where the unjust enrichment defence was not challenged or was upheld, in the courts, may be resubmitted for consideration, subject to the relevant time limits.

CLAIMS MADE ON OR AFTER 26 MAY 2005

As a result of the change in the law made in the Finance (No 2) Act 2005, which applies the unjust enrichment defence to all categories of claimants, the judgment of the House of Lords does not affect any claim made on or after 26 May 2005.

CLAIMS FOR RETROSPECTIVE APPLICATION OF EXTRA-STATUTORY CONCESSION (ESC) 3.35

23 February 2009. *HMRC Brief 6/09*

ESC 3.35 permits non-profit making membership bodies that supply a single package of benefits to their members to apportion their subscriptions to reflect the value and VAT liability of the individual benefits, without regard to whether there is one principal benefit.

A practical example is where the principal benefit of a membership subscription is standard-rated, but there are ancillary benefits which, if supplied in their own right, would be zero-rated

VAT PRs etc

and/or exempt. In such a case, the body may apportion the subscription to reflect the different elements, rather than treating the whole subscription as standard-rated.

HM Revenue & Customs (HMRC) is aware that some bodies have been using the ESC to rework previously submitted VAT returns, and have submitted claims for "overpaid" VAT. In our view, the ESC may not be used to make retrospective adjustments, as such returns were correct in law. HMRC will therefore reject any such claims.

In some cases the claims have alleged 100 per cent zero rating, due to the principal benefit being zero-rated. Such cases will be given due consideration by HMRC, provided the claim is based on the application of the law, as opposed to retrospective use of the ESC.

Commentary—*De Voil Indirect Tax Service* **V3.105**.

TRIBUNALS REFORM

16 March 2009. *HMRC Brief 10/09*

This Revenue & Customs Brief outlines the new tax appeals system and HMRC's new internal review process, due to be implemented from 1 April 2009.

INTRODUCTION

From 1 April 2009 there will be a major change to the current system of tax tribunals. To coincide with this, HMRC is changing the way it handles disagreements about tax. The new review process will help provide a more consistent approach to the way we seek to resolve disputes with those who disagree with appealable tax decisions made by HMRC.

At the moment, there are three main tribunals which deal with appeals against HMRC decisions. From April, these tribunals will be abolished and replaced by a single Tax Chamber in the First-tier Tribunal which will consider all disputes and hear appeals in relation to both direct and indirect tax.

NEW TRIBUNAL

The Tribunals, Courts and Enforcement Act 2007 introduced two new bodies, the First-tier Tribunal and the Upper Tribunal. Over time most existing tribunal jurisdictions including the tax tribunals will be transferring into the new bodies. The new system went live on 3 November 2008. These new statutory bodies are administered by the Tribunals Service which is part of the Ministry of Justice.

Both First-tier and Upper Tribunals are divided into "chambers" where similar types of appeal are heard. On 3 November when appeals formerly heard by the Social Security Appeals Tribunal successfully transferred to the First-tier Social Entitlement Chamber.

Tax appeals will transfer to a new First-tier Chamber, to be known as the Tax Chamber, on 1 April. A right of appeal against decisions of the First-tier Tax Chamber will also be created to a new chamber in the Upper Tribunal to be known as the Finance and Tax Chamber.

The First-tier Tribunal will deal with the vast majority of appeals, apart from a very small number of the most complex appeals that will transfer to the Upper Tribunal at first instance. The Upper Tribunal will mainly deal with appeals against decisions of the First-tier Tribunal. Work within each tier of the tribunal will be organised into specialist chambers, one of which will deal with tax.

The reforms will affect everyone who disagrees with one of our tax decisions and may wish to have it reviewed, or to make an appeal. As part of the reforms, the General Commissioners and Special Commissioners of Income Tax, the Section 706/704 Tribunal and the VAT & Duties Tribunals will be abolished after 31 March 2009 and their existing functions will transfer into the new First-tier Tax Chamber.

Some straightforward appeals will in future usually be dealt with on paper without the need for HMRC or customers to attend a hearing.

Where a hearing is needed the Tribunals Service will arrange this. Most appeals will be heard at one of a national network of tribunal hearing centres.

INTERNAL REVIEW

To coincide with tribunal reform, our customers will be entitled to request an internal review of appealable tax decisions. This new legal right to a review will replace reconsiderations and mandatory reviews in indirect taxes (mandatory reviews will remain for decisions about the restoration of seized goods).

Reviews will be optional and will be done by a trained review officer, who has not previously been involved with that decision, who will be able to offer a balanced and objective view. In the vast majority of cases the review officer will be outside the immediate line management chain of the decision maker.

We must complete reviews within 45 days (unless another period is agreed with the customer). If customers do not want a review, or if they do not agree with the result of the review, they can appeal to the tribunal for a decision.

FURTHER INFORMATION

You can find out more about tribunals reform and internal reviews from the Tribunals Reform Project (www.hmrc.gov.uk/about/tribunals-reform.htm) and more about changes to the tax tribunals from the Tribunals Service website (www.financeandtaxtribunals.gov.uk/taxAppealsModernisation.htm).

VAT STAFF HIRE CONCESSION

19 March 2009. *HMRC Brief 8/09*

As announced at Budget 2008 the VAT Staff Hire Concession, which applies to supplies of staff by employment bureaux, is to be withdrawn from 1 April 2009. This brief is intended to remind affected businesses of its withdrawal and to set out the VAT treatment that should be applied from 1 April. VAT Information Sheet 03/09 issued on 19 March 2009 contains more detailed guidance.

The concession is set out in Part A of the Statement of Practice in Notice 700/34 "Staff" and in Business Brief 2/04. It enables businesses making supplies of their own staff to exclude from the value of their supply the remuneration element and any PAYE (Pay As You Earn), National Insurance Contributions, pension contributions and similar payments relating to the worker provided such payments are made directly to the worker by the hirer, or a payroll company separate from the employment business supplying the staff. Such employment businesses have thus charged VAT solely on their profit margin and not on the full value of their supply.

Parts B and C of the Statement of Practice in Notice 700/34 "Staff" are unaffected and will not be withdrawn on 1 April 2009.

Business Brief 10/04 allowed employment bureaux that did not fall within the conditions of the Staff Hire Concession, because they made supplies of staff using self-employed workers, to choose whether to act as agents or principals for VAT purposes until the review of the Staff Hire Concession was completed. As announced at Budget 2008, this concession will also be withdrawn from 1 April 2009.

From 1 April 2009, in line with normal VAT principles, businesses making supplies of staff must charge and account for VAT on the full value of their supply. The correct VAT treatment following withdrawal is as follows:

If you act as a principal (eg employment business) in making a supply of staff using either:

- your own employees (which includes a director of your company) engaged under a contract of services
- self-employed workers who make their supplies to you under a contract for services

then VAT will be due on the full value of the supply (not just the profit margin).

If you act as an agent in providing introductory services of finding employment for workers or workers for your client and the workers enter into a direct contractual relationship with the client, who pays them, then VAT is due on your intermediary service only (based on your commission received). Such supplies are unaffected by the Staff Hire Concession and so will be unaffected by its withdrawal.

If you are making a supply of services other than staff, for example, supplies of care services, then your supply may qualify for exemption from VAT. See Notice 701/57 "Health professionals" for more information and the qualifying criteria. If your supply is of services other than staff it is unaffected by the Staff Hire Concession and so will be unaffected by its withdrawal.

If you are unsure of the correct VAT treatment of your supplies you should consult Notice 700/34 "Staff" and Notice 701/57 "Health professionals". You may also contact our National Advice Service Helpline on Tel 0845 010 9000, by email: National Advice Service Helpline, or in writing at:

HM Revenue & Customs
National Advice Service
Written Enquiries Section
Alexander House
Victoria Avenue
Southend
Essex SS99 1BD

Please include your VAT registration number and the name and address of your business in any correspondence. If you are not VAT registered please include your name and address.

Our Clearance procedure is also available in which we will give our view of the correct tax treatment of your transaction. You can use this procedure where you have demonstrated that there is material uncertainty and that the issue is commercially significant. For further guidance on this see "Clearance service for businesses—how to get certainty on significant business tax issues".

ACCOUNTING PROCEDURES AROUND 1 APRIL 2009

The normal time of supply (tax point) rules will apply. However, in respect of supplies spanning 1 April 2009, the Staff Hire Concession will be available to the extent that the service is performed prior to 1 April 2009. For example, if you raise an invoice or receive a payment on Friday 3 April, the concession will by then have been withdrawn. But you may, if you wish, account for VAT on the basis of the value of the services actually performed before and after the withdrawal of the concession, ie you may apportion the consideration for the services between:

– those services performed before 1 April, in respect of which the Staff Hire Concession is available;
– those services performed on or after 1 April, in respect of which the Staff Hire Concession will no longer be available.

Commentary—*De Voil Indirect Tax Service* **V3.221**.

EXTRA STATUTORY CONCESSION (ESC) 3.5—MISDIRECTION

27 March 2009. *HMRC Brief 15/09*

ESC 3.5 Misdirection gave the view of HM Revenue & Customs (HMRC) of the circumstances in which they would regard themselves as bound by incorrect advice given to customers in respect of Value Added Tax (VAT) and Insurance Premium Tax (IPT).

HMRC are required by law to collect all the taxes, duties and levies under their care, but they have a limited degree of discretion in specific circumstances. In recent years, there have been a number of cases before the courts which have defined the circumstances in which HMRC can regard themselves as bound by incorrect advice. More information is available on the Internet "When you can rely on advice provided by HMRC". ESC 3.5 Misdirection is therefore no longer necessary because it has been overtaken by other published guidance.

HMRC will not accept any further claims under this ESC from 1 April 2009. Customers who think they have received incorrect advice from HMRC in respect of VAT or IPT should see the guidance above for further help, or contact the National Advice Service on Tel 0845 010 9000. There will be no change in service to our customers, as they will still be able to ask us to consider their case if they feel they have been wrongly advised by HMRC.

This does not affect customers who think they have over declared tax, as such cases will continue to be considered under the relevant sections of the Value Added Tax Act 1994, and Finance Acts 1994 and 1997.

Commentary—*De Voil Indirect Tax Service* **V1.274**.

IMPLICATIONS TO THE BAD DEBT RELIEF CONDITIONS AS A RESULT OF THE TRIBUNAL DECISION IN TIMES RIGHT MARKETING LTD

31 March 2009. *HMRC Brief 18/09*

This brief announces a change in the treatment of VAT Bad Debt Relief claims made when the net VAT due on a return has not been paid or has been partly paid.

It follows the VAT Tribunal decision in Times Right Marketing Limited (TRML) (In Liquidation) LON/2006/1376.

BACKGROUND

If you make supplies of goods or services to a customer and have not been paid you may be able to claim relief from VAT on your bad debts. In order to claim relief you will have to satisfy all the conditions set out in HM Revenue & Customs (HMRC) Notice 700/18, 'Relief for VAT on bad debts'. One of the conditions is that you must already have accounted for and paid VAT on the supplies you want to claim bad debt relief on.

TRML appealed against a decision by HMRC to reject a claim for Bad Debt Relief (BDR) on the grounds that they had not originally paid the output VAT due. The Tribunal found that the deduction of input tax from output tax due should be seen as in effect payment of that output tax.

IMPLICATIONS OF THE DECISION

We now accept that where a BDR claim is made, payment will be taken to have been made to the extent that output tax is covered by deductible input tax.

The following examples provide further clarification. Please note these examples do not necessarily cover all scenarios that could arise. The amount of BDR to be claimed is included in Box 4 of the supplier's VAT Return, in the VAT period which covers the date they fulfill the conditions to make a claim, or a later period, subject to the usual time limits. For illustrative purposes this figure is shown separately here. It is assumed that all other BDR conditions have been satisfied.

£120,000 is taken to be the amount of VAT on bad debts over six months old at the time of the 2009–08 return.

Example 1 – Supplier has not paid net tax due in any period

	03/08	**06/08**	**09/08**
	£	**£**	**£**
Output tax	200,000	250,000	225,000
Input tax	110,000	112,000	111,000
BDR (in Box 4)			30,000 *
Net tax due	90,000	138,000	104,000
Tax paid	Nil	Nil	Nil

*Allowable BDR in period 09/08 is £30,000 calculated as follows:

VAT related to bad debts on supplies made in period 03/08—£120,000

Less unpaid net tax due in period 03/08 90,000

Maximum 03/08 bad debts available for relief six months later in period 09/08 30,000*

The amount of 03/08 BDR reclaimable in 09/08 has been restricted to the excess of input tax over output tax due on non-bad debt supplies, ie £110,000 input tax – £80,000 output tax.

Example 2 – Supplier has partly paid period 03/08 by the time of submitting their 09/08 return

VAT PRs etc

	03/08	06/08	09/08
	£	£	£
Output tax	200,000	250,000	225,000
Input tax	110,000	112,000	111,000
BDR (in Box 4)			50,000 *
Net tax due	90,000	138,000	84,000
Tax paid	Nil	Nil	Nil

*Allowable BDR claim in 09/08 is £50,000 calculated as follows:

VAT related to bad debts on supplies made in period 03/08 £120,000

Less unpaid net tax in period 03/08 70,000

Maximum 03/08 bad debts available for relief six months later in period 09/08 50,000*

The amount of 03/08 BDR reclaimable in 09/08 has been restricted to the excess of input tax over output tax due on non-bad debt supplies. £110,000 input tax – £60,000 (£80,000 – £20,000) output tax.

WHAT HAPPENS IF CHANGES OCCUR AFTER I HAVE MADE MY CLAIM, AS ABOVE?

Where BDR has been claimed on the basis of the interpretation of payment made as set out above, it is possible that the figures for tax paid or input tax due may change after the date of the claim. For example, as a result of additional payment of tax, or alterations to that period's input tax or output tax figures for the period by credit note or the correction of errors by voluntary disclosure or assessment.

In these circumstances the basis of the claim should be recalculated to see if the amount of BDR needs to be changed. If so, correction should be made on your next VAT Return, or if necessary by voluntary disclosure, subject to the normal time limits.

WHAT DOES THIS CHANGE MEAN?

This change in our policy only applies in circumstances relating to what constitutes paid for the purposes of claiming BDR. It does not alter the other conditions you need to satisfy before claiming BDR. It should be understood that BDR can only be reclaimed to the extent that the output tax has actually been paid. This brief clarifies what paid means. We will not be repaying in cash output tax that has not been paid to us in the first place on the original supplies. Revisions to HMRC guidance and Notice 700/18, 'Relief for VAT on bad debts' will be made in due course.

Taxpayers or their advisers who consider making retrospective claims for repayment of underclaimed BDR as a result of this brief are advised that normal BDR time limits apply. Claims must be made within three years and six months of either the date on which the consideration that was written off as BDR was due and payable or the date of the supply.

For further information on the matters covered in this brief or on BDR generally you should contact HMRC on 0845 010 9000.

Commentary—*De Voil Indirect Tax Service* **V5.156**.

PARTIAL EXEMPTION – CHANGES TO THE STANDARD METHOD

1 April 2009. *HMRC Brief 19/09*

This Revenue and Customs Brief article announces four changes to the partial exemption standard method that take effect from 1 April 2009.

(1) in-year provisional recovery rate
(2) early annual adjustment
(3) use-based option for new partly exempt businesses
(4) widening the scope of the standard method.

The changes are being made following responses to the consultation on ideas to simplify the partial exemption rules confirmed strong support for their implementation.

The first three changes are optional and businesses can benefit from them without seeking approval from HM Revenue & Customs (HMRC). Change four is compulsory and affects businesses that make:

– supplies of services to customers outside the UK
– certain financial supplies such as shares and bonds
– supplies made from establishments located outside the UK

FURTHER INFORMATION

Further information can be found in VAT Information Sheet 04/09 which supersedes or compliments existing guidance as appropriate. Legislation will shortly be published on the HMRC website.

Commentary—*De Voil Indirect Tax Service* **V3.461**.

CHANGES TO THE TOUR OPERATORS' MARGIN SCHEME

8 April 2009. *HMRC Brief 27/09*

This brief publicises changes to be made to the Tour Operators' Margin Scheme in order to comply fully with EU law. The changes are to take effect from 1 January 2010.

INTRODUCTION

This brief publicises changes to be made to the Tour Operators' Margin Scheme (TOMS) in order to comply fully with EU law. The changes are to take effect from 1 January 2010.

BRIEF OUTLINE OF THE SPECIAL SCHEME FOR TRAVEL AGENTS

The special scheme for travel agents is a VAT accounting scheme and simplification measure for tour operators and other travel service providers based in the EU. Under the normal VAT rules, those businesses buying and selling various elements of their travel packages in different Member States would be liable to register and account for VAT in each of the Member States concerned. The special scheme enables tour operators to register in just the Member State in which they are established, rather than in all Member States where they provide travel services, thus significantly reducing their administrative burdens. Under the scheme, the supply of a travel package is treated as a single supply taxable at the standard rate of VAT, and operators account for VAT on their profit margin in the Member State where they are established, but are prevented from recovering input tax incurred on scheme purchases.

BACKGROUND

The European Commission has written to the UK raising concerns about aspects of the UK's operation of the TOMS and opining that the UK arrangements in respect of these issues were not fully compatible with the VAT Directive (2006/112 EC).

Following legal advice, the UK has accepted that aspects of the scheme were not implemented properly and gave a commitment to amend the TOMS, in order to comply with European law. These aspects concern:

– supplies to business customers for subsequent resale
– supplies to business customers for their own consumption and supplies of educational school trips
– use of market values in respect of in house supplies

Separately, the European Commission commenced formal infraction proceedings against eight Member States for their operation of the TOMS. This did not include the UK.

CONSULTATION

As the UK had no option but to make these changes, HMRC consulted informally with industry representative bodies, the JVCC and other professional bodies in the three month period ended 31 August 2008. The consultation, by necessity, was limited in scope and its purpose was to

VAT PRs etc

ensure that the changes are introduced in as business-friendly a manner as possible, with an appropriate transitional period. HMRC considered that 1 April 2009 would be a reasonable implementation date for the changes but, as a result of responses to the consultation, decided that 1 January 2010 would give businesses more time to prepare for the changes. HMRC were unable to announce these changes earlier as we had to seek some further clarification from the European Commission.

CHANGES TO BE MADE

Supplies to business customers for resale (the "opt in")

As a concession (set out in paragraph 3.2 of Notice 709/5), HMRC has allowed tour operators who generally engage in normal holiday sales to the travelling public but occasionally sell to other travel businesses for onward resale the option of accounting for tax on the latter in the special scheme. This was intended to ease the administrative difficulties that operators might otherwise incur in having to use the normal VAT rules to account for occasional supplies of travel services to other businesses.

The UK has had to accept that the VAT Directive refers to supplies made to the "traveller". The "traveller" is the person who consumes the travel, and so the scheme should not be used when the travel service is sold to a person other than the traveller, such as when supplies are made to business customers for resale. Those tour operators affected will have to change their practices from 1 January 2010 to account for the VAT due under the normal VAT rules. In some cases, this may give rise to a requirement to register for VAT in other Member States.

Supplies to businesses for their own consumption and the provision of school trips ("the opt out")

The UK includes travel services which are supplied to other businesses for their own consumption in the special scheme.

However, tour operators have been allowed to opt out of the scheme in respect of such supplies. This has meant that business customers have been able to recover VAT charged on those supplies subject to the normal rules. HMRC has also treated the provision of school trips as a non business activity for VAT purposes and allowed them also to be excluded from the special scheme, enabling local authorities to recover the VAT charged in relation to Local Education Authority schools.

The Commission has clarified that the term "traveller" should not be restricted to the physical person who consumes a travel package, but also covers legal persons that consume the travel package, for example, businesses which pay for employee travel, and the supply of school trips to local authorities. Accordingly, Article 3(3) of the Value Added Tax (Tour Operators) Order 1987 will be revoked with effect from 1 January 2010. This means that from that date businesses receiving supplies of travel services from tour operators will no longer be able to recover VAT on such supplies. Those LEA schools that previously took advantage of the concession set out at paragraph 3.4 of Public Notice 709/5 will no longer be able to recover VAT on UK school trips purchased from tour operators. There will be no change for trips organised directly by a school, such as day trips involving coach transport to a zoo or museum. Non LEA schools (including Grant Maintained and Foundation schools) and youth clubs or colleges were not entitled to claim the concession, and are unaffected by this change.

MARKET VALUES

The current UK TOMS calculation (as detailed in Notice 709/5) requires the margin to be apportioned with reference to the actual costs incurred by the operator in putting together the package. However, the European Court of Justice (ECJ) decision in the case of *MyTravel* (C-291/03) [2005] STC 1617 ruled that, where it is possible to establish an appropriate market value for that part of the selling price which corresponds to the in house supplies, this should be used to apportion the selling price between in house and bought in components. The margin can then be calculated on each of these elements, and the tax computation completed accordingly.

The Court also said, however, that the cost based method could be used where this accurately reflected the actual structure of the package. The ECJ did not elaborate on what it meant by this term but HMRC consider that, as the cost based method assumes a fixed percentage mark up across all elements of the package, the tour operator's package would also have to be on a fixed mark up basis to meet this criterion. If it is not possible to determine a market value, tour operators can continue to use the current cost based method.

The ECJ left it to the national tax authorities and, where appropriate, the Courts, to assess whether it is possible to identify the part of the package corresponding to the in house services on the basis of their market value and, in this context, to determine the most appropriate market. Whilst the concept of market values is complex, and it is not always easy to determine exactly what a market value is in this context, drawing from the various Court findings, it would appear that certain parameters should be taken into account when deciding whether it is possible to establish such a value:

- The market value (selling price) must be within the context of the tour operator's business, eg a tour operator could not use the price of a scheduled airline flight in determining a market value of the flight forming part of a package holiday.
- The market value must be on a like-for-like basis, ie it should be determined on the basis of the price of similar services supplied by the taxable person, and not forming part of a package. If the taxable person does not provide similar services, it may be possible to use the price of services provided by other taxable persons, provided that they can be shown to be comparable.
- Across the board averages may be used if correctly weighted and reviewed regularly.

It is clear from this that market values need to be considered on a case by case basis. Where such values are to be used, they will simply slot into the current calculation method at the appropriate point. The tertiary legislation setting out the market value calculation will be included in the revised Public Notice 709/5 in due course. In the meantime, it is attached in draft as an annex to this brief, together with some examples of calculations (at the 17.5% rate of VAT) using market values. Although the tertiary legislation is not yet in place, in the light of the European Court decision, businesses may of course choose to use market values now where appropriate.

TOMS CALCULATION EXAMPLE 1 ALL IN HOUSE SUPPLIES CALCULATED BY MARKET VALUE

Package price £1000

Being the price paid for the full package by the holidaymaker

In-house MV SR £300

Being the market value of STD rate in-house supplied included in the package.

Bought-in SR cost £75

Bought-in ZR cost £250

Being the cost of the bought-in supplies that form part of the package

Using the matrix

Post the £1000 to box M1 and the £300 to box M2 of the market value matrix.

This works through to £700 in Box M5 which is then posted to Box 1 of the main margin scheme calculation.

The £75 is then posted to Box 2 and the £250 posted to Box 3.

The rest of the boxes can then be calculated based on the information (above) that has now been posted.

MARKET VALUE CALCULATION (ANNUAL ADJUSTMENT)

This section has the force of law and is referred to in paragraphs xx

This section only applies to packages or parts of packages being apportioned by the market value of the in-house element of the package. On completion of all the steps M1-M5 you must then follow the steps in the cost-based calculation in section 9, taking forward the figures from this section as instructed

Step	Boxes requiring "raw data" entry are in white, boxes which "process" that data are in grey.	
	Calculate the value of sales of margin scheme packages	
M1	Total the VAT-inclusive selling prices of all your designated travel services and margin scheme packages supplied during the financial year including any that are not "market value" packages.	1000
	Working out the market value	
M2	Total the VAT inclusive market value of the standard-rated in-house supplies at M1—carry forward this figure to step 21 of section 9	300
M3	Total the VAT inclusive market value of the zero- rated and outside the scope in-house travel services at M1—carry forward this figure to step 26 of section 9	-
M4	Total the VAT inclusive market value of the in-house supplies at step M2 + step M3	300
	Working out selling value of designated travel services and non-market value in-house supplies.	
M5	Deduct the total at step M4 from the total at step M1—carry forward this figure to step 1 of section 9	700

COST-BASED CALCULATION (ANNUAL ADJUSTMENT)

This section has the force of law and is referred to in paragraphs.

This section applies to packages being apportioned by reference to the costs of the in-house element of the package, and imports the figures calculated by the market value method in section 8, where that method is used for all or some of the travel packages. Do not include values already entered in section 8 unless explicitly stated

Step	Boxes requiring "raw data" entry are in white, boxes which "process" that data are in grey.	
	Working out the total sales of margin scheme packages	
1	Bring forward the total calculated at step M5 of section 8. If Section 8 is not used then enter the VAT-inclusive selling prices of your designated travel services and margin scheme packages supplied during the financial year.	700
	Working out the purchase prices of margin scheme supplies	
2	Total the VAT-inclusive purchase prices of the standard-rated designated travel services included in the total at step 1.	75

3	Total the VAT-inclusive purchase prices of the non standard-rated designated travel services (supplies enjoyed outside the EU) included in the total at step 1.	250
	Working out the direct costs of in-house supplies. Steps 4 to 7 can be ignored where a market value is applied to all in-house supplies under section 8	
4	Total the VAT-exclusive direct costs to you of the standard-rated in-house supplies included in step 1. Add a percentage of that amount equivalent to the standard rate of VAT.	-
5	Total the VAT-exclusive direct costs to you of the zero-rated in-house supplies included in step 1.	-
6	Total the VAT-inclusive direct costs to you of the exempt in-house supplies included in step 1. Deduct any input tax that you are entitled to recover on these costs.	-
7	Total the direct costs to you of the in-house supplies included in step 1 that are supplied outside the UK, exclusive of any VAT incurred on these costs that you are entitled to recover. Add to the total an uplift equivalent to the percentage VAT rate applicable to such supplies if you have accounted for VAT on these supplies to the VAT authorities in another member state.	-
	Working out the "costs" of agency supplies	
8	Total the VAT-inclusive amounts paid by you to your principals in respect of the agency supplies included in step 1 for which the consideration you receive is standard-rated	-
9	Total the VAT-inclusive amounts paid by you to your principals in respect of the agency supplies included in step 1 for which the consideration you receive is not standard-rated	-
	Working out the total margin	
10	Add the totals of costs at steps 2 to 9 inclusive.	325
11	Calculate the total margin for all the supplies included in step 1 by deducting the total at step 10 from the total at step 1.	375
	Apportioning the margin	
12	Calculate the margin for the standard-rated designated travel services by applying the following formula—	86.54
	total at step 2 x total at step 11 total at step10	

13	Calculate the margin for the zero-rated designated travel services by applying the following formula— total at step 3 x total at step 11 total at step 10 Steps 14 to 17 can be ignored where a market value is applied to all in-house supplies under section 8	288.46
14	Calculate the margin for the standard-rated in-house supplies by applying the following formula— total at step 4 x total at step 11 total at step 10	-
15	Calculate the margin for the zero-rated in-house supplies by applying the following formula— total at step 5 x total at step 11 total at step10	-
16	Calculate the margin for the exempt in-house supplies by applying the following formula— total at step 6 x total at step11 total at step 10	-
17	Calculate the margin for the in-house supplies made outside the UK by applying the following formula— total at step 7 x total at step 11 total at step10	-
18	Calculate the consideration for the standard-rated agency supplies by applying the following formula— total at step 8 x total at step 11 total at step 10	
19	Calculate the consideration for the non-standard-rated agency supplies by applying the following formula— total at step 9 x total at step 11 total at step 10	
	Working out your output tax	
20	Calculate the output VAT due on the designated travel services by applying the following formula— total at step 12 x the VAT fraction	12.89
21	Calculate the output VAT due on the standard-rated in-house supplies by applying the following formula— (total at step 4 + total at step 14 + total calculated at step M2 of section 8) x the VAT fraction.	44.68
22	Calculate the output VAT due on the standard-rated agency supplies by applying the following formula— total at step 18 x the VAT fraction	-
	Working out sales values	

23	Calculate the VAT-exclusive value of the standard-rated designated travel services by deducting the total at step 20 from the total at step 12.	73.65
24	Note the value of the zero-rated designated travel services at step 13	288.46
25	Calculate the VAT-exclusive value of your standard-rated in-house supplies by applying the following formula— (total at step 4 + total at step 14 + total calculated at step M2 of section 8)–total at step 21	255.32
26	Calculate the value of the zero rated supplies made within the scheme by applying the following formula— (total at step 5 + total at step 15 + total calculated at step M3 of section 8)	-
27	Calculate the value of your exempt in-house supplies made by applying the following formula— total at step 6 + total at step 16	-
28	Calculate the value of your in-house supplies which are supplied outside the UK by applying the following formula— total at step 7 + total at step 17	-
29	Calculate the total VAT exclusive value of the supplies— Total of steps 23 to 28. Include this total in box 6 of your VAT return.	617.43
	Working out the annual adjustment	
30	Calculate the total output VAT due on your designated travel services and margin scheme packages by adding the totals at steps 20 to 22 inclusive.	57.57
31	Total the provisional output VAT which has been accounted for during the financial year on the supplies included in the total at step 1.	-
32	Deduct the total at step 31 from the total at step 30. Include the resulting total in box 1 of your VAT return, either as a payable amount where the amount is positive or as a deductible amount where the amount is negative.	57.57

TOMS CALCULATION EXAMPLE 2 MIXTURE OF MARKET VALUE AND COST BASED IN HOUSE SUPPLIES

Package price £10,000

Being the price paid for the full packages by the holidaymaker

In-house MV SR £3,500

In-house MV ZR £1,000

Being the market value of in-house supplies included in the packages.

Bought-in SR cost £1,700

Bought-in ZR cost £0

Being the cost of the bought-in supplies that form part of the packages

In-house (non-MV) SR £100 + VAT =£117.50

In-house (non-MV) ZR £700

In-house (non-MV) Os £220

Agency SR £1000

Agency ZR £100

Using the matrix

Post the £10000 to box M1, the £3500 to box M2 and £1000 to box M3 of the market value matrix.

This works through to £5500 in Box M5 which is then posted to Box 1 of the main margin scheme calculation.

The £1700 is then posted to Box 2,

£117.50 to Box 4,

£700 to Box 5,

£220 to Box 7,

£1000 to Box 8,

£100 to Box 9

The rest of the boxes can then be calculated based on the information (above) that has now been posted.

MARKET VALUE CALCULATION (ANNUAL ADJUSTMENT)

This section has the force of law and is referred to in paragraphs xx

This section only applies to packages or parts of packages being apportioned by the market value of the in-house element of the package. On completion of all the steps M1-M5 you must then follow the steps in the cost-based calculation in section 9, taking forward the figures from this section as instructed

Step	Boxes requiring "raw data" entry are in white, boxes which "process" that data are in grey.	
	Calculate the value of sales of margin scheme packages	
M1	Total the VAT-inclusive selling prices of all your designated travel services and margin scheme packages supplied during the financial year including any that are not "market value" packages.	10000
	Working out the market value	
M2	Total the VAT inclusive market value of the standard-rated in-house supplies at M1—carry forward this figure to step 21 of section 9	3500
M3	Total the VAT inclusive market value of the zero- rated and outside the scope in-house travel services at M1—carry forward this figure to step 26 of section 9	1000

M4	Total the VAT inclusive market value of the in-house supplies at step M2 + step M3	4500
	Working out selling value of designated travel services and non-market value in-house supplies.	
M5	Deduct the total at step M4 from the total at step M1—carry forward this figure to step 1 of section 9	5500

COST-BASED CALCULATION (ANNUAL ADJUSTMENT)

This section has the force of law and is referred to in paragraphs.

This section applies to packages being apportioned by reference to the costs of the in-house element of the package, and imports the figures calculated by the market value method in section 8, where that method is used for all or some of the travel packages. Do not include values already entered in section 8 unless explicitly stated

Step	Boxes requiring "raw data" entry are in white, boxes which "process" that data are in grey.	
	Working out the total sales of margin scheme packages	
1	Bring forward the total calculated at step M5 of section 8. If Section 8 is not used then enter the VAT-inclusive selling prices of your designated travel services and margin scheme packages supplied during the financial year.	5500
	Working out the purchase prices of margin scheme supplies	
2	Total the VAT-inclusive purchase prices of the standard-rated designated travel services included in the total at step 1.	1700
3	Total the VAT-inclusive purchase prices of the non standard-rated designated travel services (supplies enjoyed outside the EU) included in the total at step 1.	-
	Working out the direct costs of in-house supplies. Steps 4 to 7 can be ignored where a market value is applied to all in-house supplies under section 8	
4	Total the VAT-exclusive direct costs to you of the standard-rated in-house supplies included in step 1. Add a percentage of that amount equivalent to the standard rate of VAT.	117.50
5	Total the VAT-exclusive direct costs to you of the zero-rated in-house supplies included in step 1.	700
6	Total the VAT-inclusive direct costs to you of the exempt in-house supplies included in step 1. Deduct any input tax that you are entitled to recover on these costs.	-

7	Total the direct costs to you of the in-house supplies included in step 1 that are supplied outside the UK, exclusive of any VAT incurred on these costs that you are entitled to recover. Add to the total an uplift equivalent to the percentage VAT rate applicable to such supplies if you have accounted for VAT on these supplies to the VAT authorities in another member state.	220
	Working out the "costs" of agency supplies	
8	Total the VAT-inclusive amounts paid by you to your principals in respect of the agency supplies included in step 1 for which the consideration you receive is standard-rated	1000
9	Total the VAT-inclusive amounts paid by you to your principals in respect of the agency supplies included in step 1 for which the consideration you receive is not standard-rated	100
	Working out the total margin	
10	Add the totals of costs at steps 2 to 9 inclusive.	3837.50
11	Calculate the total margin for all the supplies included in step 1 by deducting the total at step 10 from the total at step 1.	1662.50
	Apportioning the margin	
12	Calculate the margin for the standard-rated designated travel services by applying the following formula— total at step 2 x total at step 11 / total at step10	736.48
13	Calculate the margin for the zero-rated designated travel services by applying the following formula— total at step 3 x total at step 11 / total at step 10	-
	Steps 14 to 17 can be ignored where a market value is applied to all in-house supplies under section 8	
14	Calculate the margin for the standard-rated in-house supplies by applying the following formula— total at step 4 x total at step 11 / total at step 10	50.90
15	Calculate the margin for the zero-rated in-house supplies by applying the following formula— total at step 5 x total at step 11 / total at step10	303.26
16	Calculate the margin for the exempt in-house supplies by applying the following formula—	-

	total at step 6 x total at step11 total at step 10	
17	Calculate the margin for the in-house supplies made outside the UK by applying the following formula— total at step 7 x total at step 11 total at step10	95.31
18	Calculate the consideration for the standard-rated agency supplies by applying the following formula— total at step 8 x total at step 11 total at step 10	433.22
19	Calculate the consideration for the non-standard-rated agency supplies by applying the following formula— total at step 9 x total at step 11 total at step 10	43.32
	Working out your output tax	
20	Calculate the output VAT due on the designated travel services by applying the following formula— total at step 12 x the VAT fraction	109.69
21	Calculate the output VAT due on the standard-rated in-house supplies by applying the following formula— (total at step 4 + total at step 14 + total calculated at step M2 of section 8) x the VAT fraction.	546.36
22	Calculate the output VAT due on the standard-rated agency supplies by applying the following formula— total at step 18 x the VAT fraction	64.52
	Working out sales values	
23	Calculate the VAT-exclusive value of the standard-rated designated travel services by deducting the total at step 20 from the total at step 12.	626.79
24	Note the value of the zero-rated designated travel services at step 13	-
25	Calculate the VAT-exclusive value of your standard-rated in-house supplies by applying the following formula— (total at step 4 + total at step 14 + total calculated at step M2 of section 8)–total at step 21	3122.05
26	Calculate the value of the zero rated supplies made within the scheme by applying the following formula— (total at step 5 + total at step 15 + total calculated at step M3 of section 8)	2003.26

27	Calculate the value of your exempt in-house supplies made by applying the following formula— total at step 6 + total at step 16	-
28	Calculate the value of your in-house supplies which are supplied outside the UK by applying the following formula— total at step 7 + total at step 17	316.31
29	Calculate the total VAT exclusive value of the supplies— Total of steps 23 to 28. Include this total in box 6 of your VAT return.	6067.41
	Working out the annual adjustment	
30	Calculate the total output VAT due on your designated travel services and margin scheme packages by adding the totals at steps 20 to 22 inclusive.	720.57
31	Total the provisional output VAT which has been accounted for during the financial year on the supplies included in the total at step 1.	-
32	Deduct the total at step 31 from the total at step 30. Include the resulting total in box 1 of your VAT return, either as a payable amount where the amount is positive or as a deductible amount where the amount is negative.	720.57

TOMS CALCULATION EXAMPLE 3 PROVISIONAL CALCULATION

For the purpose of this exercise assume the year just gone is the summation of example 1 and example 2 Value of box 4 £117.50

Value of box 12 £823.02

Value of box 14 £50.90

Value of box 18 £433.22

Value of box M2 £3800

Total £5224.64

Value of box (M1) £11,000

Value of supplies this ¼ £3000

Using the matrix

Post the £5224.64 to box 1

Calculate the provisional percentage (47.49%) in box 2.

Post £3000 to box 3

Multiply £3000 x 47.5% to calculate provisional Std Rate supplies

Extract the VAT from that figure (7/47 in this example)

ACCOUNTING FOR VAT ON THE PROVISIONAL VALUE OF DESIGNATED TRAVEL SERVICES AND MARGIN SCHEME PACKAGES

THIS SECTION HAS THE FORCE OF LAW and is referred to in paragraphs

Step	Working out the provisional percentage		
1	Calculate the VAT-inclusive amount of your standard-rated supplies of designated travel services and margin scheme packages for the preceding financial year by adding the totals from steps 4, 12, 14 and 18 of section 9, together with the total M2 in the market value calculation in section 8.		5224.64
2	Calculate the VAT-inclusive standard-rated percentage of the total selling price of all your designated travel services and margin scheme packages for the preceding tax year by applying them one of following formulae— If you have used a market value to value in-house supplies total at step 1 of this section x 100 total at step M1 of section 8 If you have not used a market value to value in-house supplies total at step 1 of this section x 100 total at step 1 of section 9	47.5%	
	Working out the VAT return figures		
3	Total the VAT-inclusive selling prices of the designated travel services and margin scheme packages supplied during the prescribed accounting period.		3000
4	Calculate the provisional VAT-inclusive amount of your standard-rated supplies of designated travel services and margin scheme packages made during the prescribed accounting period by applying the following formula— total at step 3 x percentage at step 2		1424
5	Calculate the provisional amount of output VAT due for the prescribed accounting period by applying the following formula: total at step 4 x the VAT fraction		212.23

TERTIARY LAW

This section has the force of law and is referred to in paragraphs

TL1

1 This section shall come into effect on 1 January 1998.

2 Where a tour operator, in the same financial year, supplies:

- designated travel services or margin scheme packages which are to be enjoyed wholly outside the European Community
- designated travel services or margin scheme packages which are to be enjoyed wholly or partly within the European Community

the Commissioners of Customs and Excise may, on being given written notification by the tour operator no later than the due date for rendering his first VAT return for the financial year in which the supplies are to be made, allow the supplies under sub-paragraph (a) to be valued separately from those under sub-paragraph (b).

3 Where a tour operator, under paragraph 2 above, has separately valued supplies of designated travel services or margin scheme packages enjoyed wholly outside the European Community from supplies of designated travel services or margin scheme packages enjoyed wholly or partly within the European Community, the Commissioners of Customs and Excise may, on being given written notification by the tour operator no later than the due date for rendering his first VAT return for any subsequent financial year, allow supplies to be made in such subsequent financial year to be valued using the method specified at sections 8 and 9 of this Notice.

TL2

1 This section shall come into effect on 1 January 1998.

2 Where:

- a supply of goods or services is acquired by a tour operator for the purpose of supplying a designated travel service
- the value of the supply to the tour operator is expressed in a currency other than sterling

the tour operator must convert such value into sterling for the purposes of steps 2 and 3 of section 9 of this Notice or step 2 of section 11 of this Notice.

3 For the purposes of paragraph 2 above, the tour operator must use one of the following:

- the rate of exchange published in the Financial Times using the Federation of Tour Operators' base rate current at the time such supplies were costed by the person from whom the tour operator has acquired the goods or services
- the commercial rate of exchange current at the time that the supplies in his brochure were costed
- the rate published in the Financial Times on the date that the tour operator pays for the supplies
- the rate of exchange which was applicable to the purchase by the tour operator of the foreign currency which he used to pay for those supplies
- the period rate of exchange published by Customs and Excise for customs purposes in force at the time the tour operator pays for those supplies

4 Where the methods at paragraph 3(a) or (b) above are used, the tour operator must publish the rate in any brochure or leaflet in which these supplies are held out for sale.

5 The Commissioners of Customs and Excise may, on being given written notification by a tour operator no later than the due date for rendering his first return of his financial year, allow a different method to be used in that financial year from that used in the previous financial year.

TL3

1 This section shall come into effect on 1st January 2010.

2 Where possible the value of any in-house supplies shall be valued by reference to their market value and the value of designated travel services and agency supplies shall be determined by applying the formula set out in section 8 of this Notice (hereinafter referred to as the "market value calculation"), unless during the relevant period all such supplies are liable to VAT at the same rate, in which case the value shall be determined by applying the formula set out in section 11 of this Notice (hereinafter referred to as "the simplified calculation").

3 On completing the steps in the market value calculation the figures produced must be entered into the cost-based calculation as detailed in section 9 together with any packages, or parts of packages, for which the market value calculation is not being done.

4 Where the cost-based calculation in TL4 accurately reflects the structure of the package holidays you may opt to use the cost-based calculation for all packages regardless of whether a market value can be established for some or all of the packages and section 8 calculations may be ignored.

5 Where the market value calculation has been used a tour operator may only cease to use that method where it becomes impossible to continue to determine a market value of the supply in question or where the cost-based calculation accurately reflects the structure of the package.

TL4

1 Subject to Section TL1 and TL3 of section 13 of this Notice, the value of designated travel services, in-house supplies and agency supplies shall be determined by applying the formula set out in section 9 of this Notice (hereinafter referred to as the "cost-based calculation"), unless during the relevant period all such supplies are liable to VAT at the same rate, in which case the value shall be determined by applying the formula set out in section 11 of this Notice (hereinafter referred to as "the simplified calculation").

2 The provisional value of designated travel services, in-house supplies and agency supplies shall be determined in accordance with the formula set out in:

– section 10 of this Notice, where the cost-based calculation applies
– section 12 of this Notice, where the simplified calculation applies

3 A tour operator shall be required to account for VAT on the provisional value of his supplies of designated travel services, in-house supplies and agency supplies on the VAT return for the prescribed accounting period in which the supplies are made.

4 The difference between the amount of VAT due on the value of designated travel services, in-house supplies and agency supplies supplied during a tour operator's financial year, and the amount of VAT paid on the provisional value of those supplies, shall be adjusted by the tour operator on the VAT return for the first prescribed accounting period ending after the end of the financial year during which the supplies were made.

TL5

1 For the purpose of sections 8 to 13 of this Notice:

– (a) "in-house supply" means a supply by a tour operator which is neither a designated travel service nor an agency supply;
– (b) "market value" means the selling price of the in-house element of a "margin scheme package" were it to be sold independent of the package in an arms-length transaction to an unconnected person.
– (c) "cost based method" means the calculation in section 9 of this Notice.
– (d) "agency supply" means a supply arranged by a tour operator between two other persons, in the capacity of an agent or intermediary for either person, for which the tour operator receives a consideration, the value of which is not readily identifiable;
– (e) "margin scheme package" means a single transaction which includes one or more designated travel services;
– (f) "financial year" means a period corresponding to a tour operator's financial year for accounting purposes;
– (g) "direct costs" means costs which are directly and specifically attributable to the provision of in-house supplies, to the extent that they are so attributable;
– (h) "VAT fraction" has the same meaning as in Notice 700 The VAT Guide.

Commentary—*De Voil Indirect Tax Service* **V6.369**

REVERSE CHARGE ACCOUNTING FOR BUSINESSES TRADING IN MOBILE TELEPHONES AND COMPUTER CHIPS: RENEWAL OF EU DEROGATION

20 April 2009. *HMRC Brief 28/09*

WHO NEEDS TO READ THIS?

Businesses buying and/or selling any of the following goods:

(1) Mobile telephones
(2) Integrated circuit devices, such as microprocessors and central processing units, in a state prior to integration into end user products

BACKGROUND

The reverse charge for mobile phones and computer chips was implemented with effect from 1 June 2007 to remove the opportunity for fraudsters to use these goods to perpetrate missing trader intra-community (MTIC) carousel fraud. As an exception to the normal accounting rules for VAT the UK has a derogation from EU law to apply this anti-fraud measure, which runs until 30 April 2009. The Government announced in its Pre-Budget Report 2008 that it had applied for a renewal of the derogation. The purpose of this Revenue & Customs Brief is to provide:

(i) information on renewal of the derogation
(ii) guidance on the application of the reverse charge in the event that the renewal is not concluded by 30 April 2009

(I) RENEWAL OF THE DEROGATION

On 10 March 2009 the European Council of Finance Ministers (ECOFIN) agreed, in principle, to the renewal of the UK's derogation until April 2011. The Government is working with the Commission and the Member States to ensure that the legal text is adopted as soon as possible. We anticipate that it will be agreed within the next few weeks. Formal agreement to the renewal text, however, may not be concluded before 30 April, in which case there would be a short gap between the expiry of the derogation and its renewal. If there is a gap, it is expected to be temporary as we expect that the extension of the derogation will apply retrospectively from 1 May 2009 resulting in an unbroken legal vires for the reverse charge. UK law will therefore remain unchanged.

(II) APPLICATION OF THE REVERSE CHARGE

If there is a temporary gap in the derogation, businesses that make or receive business-to-business supplies of mobile phones and/or computer chips with a value of £5,000 or more should continue to apply the reverse charge. Suppliers should also continue to complete and submit Reverse Charge Sales lists for these supplies. Businesses that apply the reverse charge and comply with UK law will not be subject to any penalties as a consequence of any temporary gap in the EU derogation. If a business does not apply the reverse charge during any temporary gap in the derogation, it may be liable to pay to HM Revenue & Customs (HMRC) any tax lost or to have its input tax denied.

FURTHER INFORMATION

For further information on the reverse charge for mobile phones and computer chips please see Public Notice 735: "VAT Reverse charge for mobile phones and computer chips".

Commentary—*De Voil Indirect Tax Service* **V3.233, V3.425.**

TAX IMPLICATIONS OF THE VEHICLE SCRAPPAGE SCHEME

14 May 2009. *HMRC Brief 31/09*

The government announced at Budget 2009 the introduction of a temporary vehicle scrappage scheme. It is a voluntary scheme which will be administered by participating motor manufacturers and dealers, along with the Department for Business, Enterprise and Regulatory Reform (BERR). Information about it can be found on the BERR website and at Directgov – Motoring. You may also contact BERR's enquiry unit on Tel 020 7215 5000, or email the BERR Automotive Unit with "scrappage" entered in the subject heading.

A. VAT AND DIRECT TAX PROFITS IMPLICATIONS

Vehicles supplied under the scheme will be subject to the normal VAT and direct tax rules. The purpose of this brief is to explain how those rules apply to the £1,000 subsidy payable by BERR on qualifying supplies made under their scheme, plus the £1,000 discount paid by the manufacturer.

Manufacturers

If you are a manufacturer participating in the scheme you will be providing a £1,000 subsidy to the final consumer (over and above any other subsidy or discount you might provide), even though you have no direct contractual relationship with them. You may treat the VAT on your contribution as a discount to the output tax you have paid to HMRC on your sale of the car. You may therefore reduce your output tax by the appropriate VAT amount (which on a gross payment of £1,000 and the current standard rate of VAT of 15 per cent means £130.43). Any such adjustment should be made in the period in which it takes effect in the business records of the manufacturer. This treatment is in accordance with the decision of the European Court of Justice in *Elida Gibbs Ltd v Commissioners of Customs and Excise* [1996] STC 1387 and *Commission v Germany (Taxation)* [2003] STC 301. Guidance on the VAT treatment of such payments by manufacturers was given previously in Revenue and Customs Brief 08/07.

You must not reduce your output tax in respect of BERR's £1,000 contribution. Under the terms of the scheme, BERR will pay you £1,000, but you must pass it on to the dealer within 14 days who, in turn, is obliged to ensure that the final consumer receives the benefit of that sum. You are thus acting as a conduit, receiving and passing on BERR's third party payment to the dealer. The £1,000 subsidy provided by BERR is not a discount on the value of your supply, and so you should make no adjustment in respect of that payment.

For direct tax purposes BERR's £1,000 contribution has no overall effect on the trading profits of the manufacturer. The corresponding £1,000 payable by the manufacturer to the dealer will be an allowable deduction for the purposes of computing the profits of the manufacturing trade.

Dealers

If you are a dealer participating in the Scheme and the manufacturer uses the arrangements above, the cost of the new vehicle received by you is unaffected, and you should make no adjustments to the VAT you pay to the manufacturer, or claim from HMRC as input tax. As explained above, the manufacturer is not providing a £1,000 (or greater) discount to you as part of the Scheme – they are providing it to your customer. Your selling price for the vehicle has not changed and you must not reduce your output tax. Whatever your final VAT-inclusive ("On The Road") selling price of the new vehicle is, under the Scheme your customer pays £2,000 less, with the balance of the consideration being made up of the two £1,000 subsidies. Under the Scheme, it is important that it is clear to your customer that they are paying £2,000 less than would otherwise be the case – see Directgov – Motoring (www.direct.gov.uk/en/Motoring/BuyingAndSellingAVehicle/AdviceOnBuyingAndSelling AVehicle/DG_177693)

The effect of the Scheme on the dealer is neutral for the purposes of computing trading profits. The £2,000 reduction in the sale proceeds received from the customer is matched by the £2,000 trade receipt received in the form of the subsidies paid to the dealer under the scheme.

Customers

Customers buying a new vehicle under the scheme will pay £2,000 less for the vehicle, since BERR will be paying £1,000, and the vehicle manufacturer will be paying £1,000 towards the cost of the purchase. The subsidies will be settled between the manufacturer, dealer and BERR so you will not physically be paid these amounts.

If you are VAT-registered and buy a new car or van under the scheme, you may need to reduce your input tax in respect of the manufacturer's discount. However, you only need to consider this if you are entitled to claim VAT on the purchase of a vehicle — for example, on certain commercial vehicles, or a car that is intended to be used primarily as a taxi; driving instruction car, or self-drive hire (but see paragraph 3.1 of VAT Notice 700/64 "Motoring expenses"). If, under the normal VAT rules, you are entitled to reclaim the VAT you are charged on the purchase of a new vehicle and you buy one under the Scheme, you must reduce the input tax you claim in proportion to the manufacturer's discount. This is because, at the beginning of the chain of transactions culminating in your purchasing the vehicle, the manufacturer will have reduced its output tax. Therefore, since the manufacturer contributes £1,000 and the standard rate of VAT is 15 per cent, you must reduce your input tax by £130.43. You will not receive an amended invoice or credit note. This is the normal VAT treatment for business customers receiving such manufacturer's discounts – see Revenue and Customs Brief 08/07.

B. CAPITAL ALLOWANCES

A business purchaser of a vehicle under the scheme will only be able to claim capital allowances on the net cost to it (after the two subsidies have been deducted). However, the vehicle surrendered by the business consumer will be scrapped and therefore it has no value as a vehicle, in terms of the scrappage scheme. The two subsidies given as deductions from the purchase price will not constitute taxable disposal receipts for capital allowances purposes.

If you need further advice and are a large business with an allocated Customer Relationship Manager, you should consult them. Otherwise you should contact our National Advice Service Helpline on Tel 0845 010 9000, or by Enquiries.estn@hmrc.gsi.gov.uk, or by writing to:

HM Revenue & Customs
National Advice Service
Written Enquiries Section
Alexander House
Victoria Avenue
Southend
Essex SS99 1BD

Please include your VAT registration number and the name and address of your business in any correspondence. If you are not VAT registered please include your name and address.

HMRC'S POLICY FOLLOWING THE JUDGMENT IN NEWNHAM COLLEGE

9 June 2009. *HMRC Brief 33/09*

This Revenue and Customs Brief announces HM Revenue and Customs' (HMRC) revised interpretation of the law following the judgment of the House of Lords in the case of *The Principal and Fellows of Newnham College in the University of Cambridge* [2008] UKHL 23, [2008] 2 All ER 863. It also provides guidance for those businesses affected by the judgment.

THE ISSUE

The case before the House of Lords concerned whether Newnham was "in occupation" of the college library. If they were, their option to tax the library would be disapplied and their occupation would be for the purpose of making supplies of exempt education. Consequently, the VAT incurred on the rebuilding and refurbishment of the library would be irrecoverable. The House of Lords upheld the judgment of the Court of Appeal and found in Newnham's favour. They concluded that Newnham was not in occupation and, as a result, that their option to tax was not disapplied.

HMRC'S REVISED INTERPRETATION OF LAW

HMRC now accept that physical presence alone is not the correct test of occupation for the purposes of what is now VATA 1994 Schedule 10 Paragraphs 12 to 17 (the "anti-avoidance test"). Following the House of Lords judgment, a person is considered to be "in occupation" if, in addition to physical presence which occupation normally entails, they have the right to occupy the property as if they are the owner and to exclude others from enjoyment of such a right. This means a person must have actual possession of the land along with a degree of permanence and control. Such a right will normally result from the grant of a legal interest or licence to occupy. Occupation could also, however, be by agreement or de facto and it is therefore necessary to take account of the day to day arrangements, particularly where these differ from the contractual terms. An exclusive right of occupation is not a requirement; an agreement might, for example, allow for joint occupation. Equally, it is not necessary for a person to be utilising all of the land for all of the time for them to be considered as occupying it.

A person whose interest in land is subject to an inferior interest, such as to prevent him from having rights of occupation for the time being, is not "in occupation" for the purposes of the anti-avoidance test until the inferior interest expires. It should be noted, however, that an important feature of the test is that it is forward looking and takes account of the intended or expected occupation of the building at any time during the Capital Goods Scheme (CGS) adjustment period. As a result, a person who has granted an inferior interest but intends during that adjustment period to occupy the land himself would intend to be "in occupation" for the purposes of the anti-avoidance test and so must consider whether his intended occupation was for eligible purposes.

However, a person can ignore the following types of occupation for the purposes of the test:

1. Occupation which is purely for the purpose of making his rental supplies under the grant, since those are the very supplies whose liability he is trying to determine by applying the test. For example:

(a) occupation by the grantor between the date of the grant and the start of occupation by the tenant which is for the purpose of undertaking refurbishment or repairs,
(b) occupation by maintenance, security or reception staff (or similar), unless it is for the purpose of providing ongoing services separate from the letting itself.

2. Occupation at a future date, but within the CGS adjustment period, which is solely for the purpose of re-letting the property or making a fresh grant.

PRACTICAL IMPLICATIONS

Businesses that were wrongly denied input tax recovery may submit claims to their local Business Advice Centre. These will be subject to a three-year limitation period (four years from 1 April 2009, subject to a transitional period). All such adjustments or claims must take account of any underdeclared output tax as a result of incorrectly treating the option to tax as disapplied.

Further information about claims can be found in Notice 700/45 "How to correct VAT errors or make adjustments or claims".

Commentary—*De Voil Indirect Tax Service* **V4.116**.

VAT PRs etc

REVERSE CHARGE ACCOUNTING FOR BUSINESSES TRADING IN MOBILE TELEPHONES AND COMPUTER CHIPS: RENEWAL OF EU DEROGATION

18 June 2009. *HMRC Brief 34/09*

WHO NEEDS TO READ THIS?

Businesses buying and/or selling any of the following goods:

(1) Mobile telephones
(2) Integrated circuit devices, such as microprocessors and central processing units, in a state prior to integration into end user products

Further to Revenue & Customs brief 28/09 HMRC can now confirm that the Government's application to renew the derogation was formerly agreed on 5 May 2009 by the European Council of Finance Ministers (ECOFIN). The agreement has retroactive effect from 1 May 2009 meaning that legal vires for the reverse charge is unbroken.

BACKGROUND

The reverse charge for mobile phones and computer chips was implemented with effect from 1 June 2007 to remove the opportunity for fraudsters to use these goods to perpetrate missing trader intra-community (MTIC) carousel fraud. As an exception to the normal accounting rules for VAT the UK has a derogation from EU law to apply this anti-fraud measure, which ran until 30 April 2009. The Government announced in its Pre-Budget Report 2008 that it had applied for a renewal of the derogation.

On 10 March 2009 the ECOFIN agreed, in principle, to the renewal of the UK's derogation until April 2011 and it is this decision that has now been formerly ratified and published under Official Journal reference 2009/439/EC.

FURTHER INFORMATION

For further information on the reverse charge for mobile phones and computer chips please see Public Notice 735: VAT Reverse charge for mobile phones and computer chips.

CHANGES TO THE APPLICATION OF THE ZERO-RATE TO NEW BUILDINGS USED FOR A RELEVANT CHARITABLE OR RESIDENTIAL USE

June 2009 *HMRC Brief 39/09*

Note—Superseded by HMRC Brief 32/10, published 3-8-10, see also HMRC Brief 33/10, published 30-7-10.

"DUTCH BARGES" AND SIMILAR VESSELS DESIGNED FOR AND USED AS PERMANENT RESIDENTIAL ACCOMMODATION BY OWNERS

9 July 2009. *HMRC Brief 38/09*

WHO NEEDS TO READ THIS?

Businesses making supplies of:

– vessels to be used for permanent residential living by the owner;
– certain goods and services to the owners of vessels used for permanent residential living by the owner.

This brief also withdraws Section 4 of Business Brief 35/04 "VAT – clarification of the VAT liability of ships supplied to customers who intend to use them as residential accommodation".

BACKGROUND

"Qualifying ships" – are zero-rated for VAT purposes. A "qualifying ship" is defined as a ship which is not less than 15 gross tons and is neither designed nor adapted for use for recreation or pleasure. The law is set out in the Value Added Tax Act 1994, Schedule 8, Group 8, Item 1 and legal note A1(a).

"Houseboats" – are covered by a separate zero-rate. For VAT purposes, "houseboats" are boats designed as living accommodation that do not have, and cannot be fitted with, a means of propulsion. If a boat can be fitted with a means of propulsion, it is not a "houseboat". The law is set out in the Value Added Tax Act 1994, Schedule 8, Group 9, Item 2.

H M REVENUE & CUSTOMS (HMRC) POLICY

In the light of the High Court decision in the case of Lt Cmdr Colin Stone [2008] STC 2501, [2008] EWHC 1249 (Ch), HMRC are changing their long-standing policy on the liability of vessels used as residential accommodation, excluding houseboats, for VAT purposes. This case concerned the VAT liability of the supply of "Dutch barges" acquired for the purpose of being used as a permanent residence.

The High Court decided that the supply of the vessel was entitled to zero-rating under the terms of UK law, because it was designed to be lived in as a permanent home and, therefore, not designed for use as recreation or pleasure.

HMRC consider that many of these and similar vessels, although designed for use as a permanent residence, can also be designed for use as recreation or pleasure and are perfectly capable of being so used. It was never the intention that UK legislation should provide for the supply of such vessels to benefit from zero-rating but, following Tribunal and Court decisions over time, HMRC have found it increasingly difficult to apply a consistent and coherent policy around the borderlines in this area.

HMRC do not rule out a wider review of policy and legislation in this area. However, in the meantime, we have decided to treat Dutch barges and similar vessels that are designed and supplied for use as the permanent residence of the customer as qualifying ships and eligible for zero-rating. As vessels of less than 15 gross tons can never be zero-rated regardless of their design, the majority of narrow boats designed for permanent residential use will not meet this requirement and their supply will continue to be standard-rated.

As a result of this policy change some supplies of goods and services to the owners of such vessels may also be zero-rated by suppliers.

These include:

– repairs and maintenance of the vessel itself; this does not extend to the domestic equipment and fittings on board;

- modification or conversion of the vessel itself provided that it remains a qualifying ship after modification or conversion; this does not extend to domestic equipment and fittings;
- parts and equipment ordinarily installed or incorporated in the propulsion, navigation, communications or structure of a ship; this does not extend to domestic equipment and fittings.

Further details can be found in Notice 744C.

EVIDENCE OF INTENTION

In keeping with normal rules, suppliers will have to hold evidence to satisfy HMRC that the supply is entitled to zero-rating. This may be in the form of contractual or other documentary evidence. HMRC would also advise suppliers to obtain a declaration from their customers that the vessel is to be designed for use as a permanent residence and intended for such use. We would suggest that suppliers use the format set out for the Undertaking of Use in Notice 744C, adapted as necessary where the supply is one of the vessel itself. Customers should be aware that HMRC have powers to impose penalties where false documentation is used to obtain a tax advantage.

PAST SUPPLIES AND CLAIMS

Customers who have been previously charged VAT on a supply that is now covered by this policy must approach the person who made the supply to them to obtain a refund of VAT. They should not contact HMRC as we have no legal powers to refund tax direct to customers. Suppliers who wish to claim a refund of VAT charged to customers on a supply covered by this policy must submit their claims in accordance with the published rules and subject to the normal repayment, unjust enrichment and capping criteria to HMRC.

FURTHER INFORMATION

For further information on houseboats please see Public Notice 701/20: "VAT Caravans and Houseboats".

For further information on qualifying ships please read Public Notice 744C: "VAT Ships, aircraft and associated services".

For additional information on parts and equipment please read Information Sheet 15/07 "VAT: Supply of parts and equipment for qualifying ships and aircraft".

Or contact our National Advice Service Helpline on Tel 0845 010 9000, or by email, or by writing to: HM Revenue & Customs, National Advice Service, Written Enquiries Section, Alexander House, Victoria Avenue, Southend, Essex, SS99 1BD.

Commentary—*De Voil Indirect Tax Service* **V4.251, V4.275.**

DECISION OF THE HIGH COURT IN RESPECT OF RANK (MECHANISED CASH BINGO AND GAMING MACHINES)

14 July 2009. *HMRC Brief 40/09*

The High Court issued its decision in this case on 8 June 2009 – the judgment being in Rank's favour [see *Revenue and Customs Commissioners v The Rank Group* [2009] All ER (D) 65 (Jun)]. It confirmed that there had been a breach of fiscal neutrality in the tax treatment of the supply of mechanised cash bingo (MCB). This means that participation fees for playing MCB should have been exempt from VAT and businesses can now submit claims to HM Revenue & Customs (HMRC) for repayment of any output tax wrongly accounted for, subject to the guidelines below.

In relation to gaming machines, the High Court judgment relates to an appeal against an interim ruling of the VAT Tribunal. As the Tribunal has not yet ruled in respect of Rank's full appeal, HMRC will not at this time consider any claims relating to this issue.

BACKGROUND

Rank, which operates Mecca bingo halls, claimed there had been inconsistencies in the way VAT had been applied to the participation fees customers paid to play MCB and to the takings of gaming machines.

Last year the VAT Tribunal ruled there had been a breach of fiscal neutrality in the case of MCB as some participation fees were taxed while others were exempt. (Fiscal neutrality means that similar supplies must be treated the same for tax purposes to avoid any distortion of competition). The High Court has agreed with the Tribunal's decision that all participation fees for MCB should have been exempt from VAT.

The VAT Tribunal also issued an interim decision regarding the way HMRC taxed gaming machines, stating there had been a breach of fiscal neutrality in some cases and over a short period of time before the law was changed in December 2005.

IMPLICATIONS OF THIS JUDGMENT

HMRC will now consider claims for output tax wrongly accounted for by bingo operators on MCB participation fees.

As bingo duty is charged on the VAT-exclusive value of participation fees, this judgment will have an effect on bingo duty declarations although HMRC is still considering the precise implications. However, HMRC will now enforce those bingo duty assessments already made. Further assessments to bingo duty may be made as appropriate.

As the gaming machine case is continuing, with a VAT Tribunal hearing later this year, HMRC will not credit any claims on this issue.

MAKING CLAIMS OR ADJUSTMENTS

Where a business wishes to make a claim to HMRC for output tax wrongly accounted for in respect of MCB participation fees, they may do so, although evidence must be produced that output tax was accounted for, to substantiate the amount claimed.

All claims will be subject to the four-year time limit in section 80(4) of the VAT Act 1994 (as amended) and no claim for periods ending on or prior to 31 March 2006 will be considered. Correcting the error on your VAT return

Overdeclarations of output tax can also be corrected by adjusting the current VAT return if the net amount of all errors in the accounting periods being corrected is:

- £10,000 or less; or
- less than £50,000 and less than 1 per cent of the box 6 figure on the VAT return in which the adjustment is being effected

These de minimis levels apply to the entire "claim". Thus if your "claim" is for ten accounting periods, it is the net overdeclaration for all ten periods that must be within these levels.

Under regulation 34(1A) of the VAT Regulations 1995 (as amended), all adjustments must be made within four years after the end of the accounting period in which the overdeclaration was made but no accounting period can be adjusted if it ended on or before 31 March 2006.

FURTHER INFORMATION

Details of where to send your claim can be obtained from update 2 to VAT Notice 700/45 — "How to correct VAT errors and make adjustments or claims" from the HM Revenue & Customs National Advice Service on 0845 010 9000.

HMRC may reject all or part of a claim if repayment would unjustly enrich the claimant. More details on "unjust enrichment" can be found at part 14 of VAT Notice 700/45.

There may be direct tax implications where amounts of overdeclared output tax are repaid to businesses and your attention is drawn to R&C Brief 14/09 issued previously.

Where you are in any doubt about the correct treatment please contact the National Advice Service.

THREE-YEAR CAP FOR VAT CLAIMS – COURT OF SESSION DECISION IN SCOTTISH EQUITABLE

20 July 2009. *HMRC Brief 41/09*

Three-year cap for VAT claims — CRC v Scottish Equitable Plc (unreported) — Order of the Inner House of the Court of Session

THE JUDGMENT OF THE INNER HOUSE

In an Order handed down on 2 July, the court overturned the 2006 decision of the VAT and Duties Tribunal that the introduction of the three-year time limit without a transitional period in 1996 meant that it had never been lawfully enacted.

The Inner House held that the Tribunal was wrong to decide that the absence of transitional provisions, that enabled claims to be made under the old time limits before the new time limit took effect, meant that the provisions were void. The court stressed that it was well recognised that national legislation which breaches Community law is not void and noted that the Tribunal had failed to recognise the difference between rights to claim that accrued before the enactment of the three-year cap and those that accrued afterwards.

The Inner House followed the judgment of the House of Lords in *CRC v Fleming (t/a Bodycraft)* [2008] STC 324 in which the Law Lords held that the three-year time limit should be disapplied in relation to rights to claims that had accrued before its enactment and that that disapplication should continue until the expiry of an adequate, prospective transitional period.

There will be no application for leave to appeal to the House of Lords.

CURRENT CASE LAW ON TIME LIMITS

There are a number of judgments of the European Court of Justice (including *Marks & Spencer Plc v CCE* [2002] STC 1036) confirming that the imposition of reasonable time limits does not breach principles of Community law and that they are necessary to provide legal certainty for both the citizen and the state.

The judgment of the House of Lords in Fleming (referred to above) led to the enactment of section 121, Finance Act 2008. This provided businesses with a prospective transitional period of twelve months, ending on 31 March 2009, in which claims could be made for accounting periods ending before the introduction of the new time limits.

The Inner House in Scottish Equitable has taken the same view as the High Court in *Local Authorities Mutual Investment Trust v CCE* [2004] STC 246, which held that VAT claims for accounting periods ending after the enactment of the new time limit were properly capped.

STATUS OF VAT TIME LIMITS

All VAT claims are now capped at four years, or back to 1 April 2006, whichever is the shorter – see section 80(4) of the VAT Act 1994 as amended by Articles 2 and 6 of the Finance Act 2008, Schedule 39 (Appointed Day, Savings and Transitional Provisions) Order 2009, SI 2009/403 (output tax claims) and regulation 29(1A) of the VAT Regulations 1995 as amended by regulation 3 of the VAT (Amendment) Regulations 2009, SI 2009/586.

APPEALS ON-HOLD BEHIND THIS LITIGATION

A significant number of appeals to the First Tier Tribunal (Tax Chamber) are on-hold, pending the outcome of this litigation. Appellants will need to consider, in the light of the recent order, whether they wish to withdraw their appeal or proceed to a full hearing. HM Revenue & Customs are now taking steps to have these appeals restored to the Tribunal list so that, where necessary, a hearing date can be fixed.

Commentary—*De Voil Indirect Tax Service* **V3.405**, **V5.159C**.

PSYCHOLOGISTS' SERVICES

23 July 2009. *HMRC Brief 43/09*

With effect from 1 July 2009 practitioner psychologists are regulated by the Health Professionals Council meaning that any supplies of medical care they make became exempt from VAT from that date. Practitioner psychologists come under seven domains: clinical, counselling, educational, forensic, health, occupational, and sport/exercise. Psychologists who work purely in academic research and experimental psychology and who do not offer services to the general public are excluded from regulation meaning that there will be no change in the VAT treatment of their services.

By "medical care" we mean any service relating to the protection, maintenance or restoration of the health of the person concerned, including mental health. Medical care would include services such as counselling, working with children with emotional problems, dealing with criminals' behavioural problems or running stress management courses.

However, as is the case for all health professionals, the VAT exemption excludes services that are not primarily for the benefit of the patient, for example, assessing a patient's mental condition for legal reasons at the behest of a third party. This is because the primary purpose of such services is to enable a court to take a decision on whether the patient is fit to stand trial rather than any immediate concern about the patient's mental health.

Commentary—*De Voil Indirect Tax Service* **V4.146**.

CHANGES TO FORMS USED TO CLAIM VAT REFUNDS UNDER DIY REFUND SCHEME

31 July 2009. *HMRC Brief 45/09*

This Brief announces changes to the forms and guidance used by individuals who are claiming back VAT that they have incurred as DIY housebuilders and converters on the costs of their building work.

BACKGROUND

Since the first supply of new houses and newly converted non-residential properties into dwellings are zero-rated for VAT, the VAT DIY refund scheme seeks to ensure that VAT does not get added to the cost of such a development simply because an individual is building their own home.

Therefore, individuals who build new houses, or convert non-residential properties into dwellings, for personal use may recover VAT on certain building materials in the case of builders of new houses or certain building materials and services in the case of converters.

However, many applications are incomplete in terms of the information and evidence that they provide and some applicants have simply misunderstood what is required of them. This has meant that HM Revenue & Customs (HMRC) has to contact a significant number of claimants to obtain missing information, or further evidence, which feeds into delays in claimants receiving their refund while the information and evidence is awaited.

THE CHANGES

HMRC have made two key changes in their review of the operation of the scheme which will come into effect on 15 August 2009. Firstly, they have introduced two new claim forms; VAT 431NB for new houses and VAT 431C for conversions. This should ensure that the right information is provided for each type of development.

The questions are slightly different from the current form but these are designed to deal with many of the common issues that currently arise and so should lead to less queries being raised about the information on the forms.

Secondly, HMRC are withdrawing Notice 719 Refunds for "do-it-yourself" builders and converters and replacing it with separate dedicated guidance to support the completion of each of the new claim forms.

HMRC expects that the better information on clearer claim forms, together with the dedicated guidance, will reduce the number of claims requiring further information or evidence and that this will lead to most claimants receiving their refunds quicker than under the current system.

FURTHER INFORMATION

If you have any enquiries about this Brief, please contact the National Advice Service on Tel 0845 010 9000.

ZERO RATING OF EMISSIONS ALLOWANCES WITH EFFECT FROM 31 JULY 2009

31 July 2009. *HMRC Brief 46/09*

In response to the escalating threat of VAT fraud in connection with trading of emissions allowances (often called "carbon credits"), the Government has introduced legislation (SI

2009/2093) to zero rate the supply of emissions allowances within the UK with effect from 31 July 2009. This is an interim measure that the Government expects to remain in force until an EU-wide solution is implemented. It follows similar action taken by France and the Netherlands earlier in the summer. The UK has applied to the EU for a retrospective derogation to remove VAT from these products.

BACKGROUND

Emissions allowances or "carbon credits" are issued by governments under various schemes designed to cut carbon emissions by businesses. Within the European Economic Area, member states issue operators in the EU scheme with EU Allowances (EUA) — carbon credits — and further credits are auctioned by some governments (including the UK). The EUAs can be traded and there is also a secondary market in which anybody can trade, for example to speculate on the price of the credits. Operators (or "polluters") must ensure they have sufficient credits to cover their actual emissions at the end of April each year when these credits are "retired".

The opportunity for Missing Trader Intra-Community (MTIC) VAT fraud arises where standard-rated goods or services can effectively be traded VAT free between EU Member States. Up to now, most emissions allowances have been standard-rated in UK to UK transactions and VAT free when purchased from outside the UK by a UK based company. It is this VAT free source that provides the opportunity to perpetrate MTIC VAT fraud. It occurs where the UK company purchasing the emissions allowances from overseas sells them to another UK company, charges VAT but then fails to pay it over to HMRC and disappears.

The ability to trade freely in emissions allowances is an important feature of the EU Emissions Trading Scheme. However, the existence of a strong secondary cross-border market in emissions allowances generates very high volume, value and speed of trade. This, combined with the fact that EUAs are only surrendered once a year provides fraudsters with multiple opportunities to steal VAT following cross-border acquisitions.

EU LEGISLATION

Although there is currently no specific provision in EU law to introduce this measure, the UK Government believes that it is in the public interest that steps be taken now to prevent substantial potential losses to the Exchequer and to ensure that the legitimate market is not undermined by fraudulent trading. Although a number of other options were considered, zero rating was the only option that could be introduced quickly enough in the UK and without any significant impact on legitimate trade in the markets concerned.

SUPPLIES AFFECTED

The zero rate will apply to any transaction in EU emissions allowances and transferable units issued pursuant to the Kyoto Protocol. This will include over the counter spot trades, transactions for future delivery and options. Cross-border transactions are not affected.

TERMINAL MARKETS

Certain trades carried out on specific exchanges are currently treated as zero-rated based on the provisions of the Terminal Markets Order 1973 (TMO). This measure will effectively overlay those provisions and not affect them directly, except to the extent that transactions currently subject to VAT, such as when emissions allowances are consumed by members of the markets, will all become zero-rated.

TAX POINTS

The tax point for these supplies will be the earliest of either the transfer of title or payment. Therefore any amount purporting to be VAT on tax invoices dated from 31 July 2009 will not be recoverable as input tax.

WHAT IF I CAN'T STOP ACCOUNTING FOR VAT IN TIME?

We understand that this is extremely short notice for businesses to be able to change their systems in time and will bear this in mind when considering what action to take in cases where VAT has been charged or reclaimed when it should not have been. Such cases will be looked at on an individual basis. However, given that the fraud relies on VAT funnelling down supply chains to a potential fraudster, businesses are advised to stop paying VAT on affected purchases as soon as the zero rate comes into effect.

FURTHER INFORMATION

Please contact the National Advice Service on 0845 010 9000 or your nominated HMRC contact should you have one.

OPTION TO TAX LAND AND BUILDINGS–CORRECTION TO PREVIOUSLY PRINTED MATERIAL

14 August 2009. *HMRC Brief 51/09*

This HMRC Brief announces a correction to the tertiary law on opting to tax land and buildings with VAT.

This Revenue & Customs Brief ("R&C Brief"), announces a correction to the tertiary law as was published in VAT Information sheet 12/09 and Notice 742A – "Opting to tax land and buildings" (June 2008 edition). In both cases Condition 2, "the 20 year condition" of Box G was incorrectly reproduced. VAT Information Sheet 12/09 and R&C Brief 44/09 have been withdrawn and are being replaced with VAT Information sheet 14/09 and this R&C Brief. A description of the changes made to Schedule 10 of the VAT Act 1994 which came into effect on 1 August 2009 can be found in the attached Annex, see below.

BACKGROUND

On 1 June 2008, Schedule 10 of the VAT Act 1994 was replaced and at the same time, new tertiary legislation was introduced which was subsequently published in Notice 742A – Opting to tax land and buildings, (June 2008).

The new tertiary legislation in Box G of this notice, (paragraph 8.3.2), sets out the rules for revoking an option to tax without requiring the prior permission of the Commissioners. While the online version of Notice 742A contains the correct wording in Box G, the wording in the printed version is incorrect. The correct wording for condition 2, "the 20 year condition", in Box G is—

Box G

2	The 20 year condition The taxpayer or a relevant associate connected to the taxpayer held a relevant interest in the building or land which is: – after the time from which the option has effect; and – more than 20 years before the option is revoked.

The effect of the incorrect version of "the 20 year condition" would be to limit the ability of some businesses to revoke their option to tax without requiring the prior permission of the Commissioners.

Businesses are asked to use the version of Condition 2 above and as shown in the new corrected Information Sheet 14/09 when seeking automatic permission to revoke an option to tax after 20 years.

FURTHER INFORMATION

Further information can be obtained on HMRC's website or through the HM Revenue & Customs VAT and Excise Helpline on Tel 0845 010 9000 or +44 292 050 1261 for international enquiries.

ANNEX

The changes to Schedule 10 of VATA 1994 are as follows:

– minor changes to the operation of the option to tax
– changes to the connected persons rules

They came into effect on 1 August 2009 although some parts of the connected persons changes come into effect on 15 August 2009.

BACKGROUND

Schedule 10 to VATA 1994 deals primarily with the option to tax on land and buildings. Following a series of amendments necessary to block aggressive tax avoidance schemes, this legislation became increasingly more complex and was identified by business as a key area for simplification.

Schedule 10 was replaced on 1 June 2008 following extensive consultation. This new legislation was re-written in the "Tax Law re-write" style, which greatly improved the layout of the legislation as well as simplifying the language. The legislation also introduced guidance on how to revoke an option to tax after 20 years, a facility that became available to taxpayers on 1 August 2009.

MINOR CHANGES ARISING FROM THE OPERATION OF THE OPTION TO TAX

Following the introduction of the new Schedule 10, some unforeseen consequences were identified during HM Revenue & Customs' (HMRC) on-going discussions with business. As a result business and HMRC identified a number of minor amendments that were necessary to ensure that business is able to benefit as intended from the changes made as well as protect the revenue from future avoidance risks.

The changes that have been made include:

- Extension of the period for notification of the exclusion of a building from the effects of an option to tax to 30 days or such longer period as HMRC may allow.
- Denying automatic revocation under the six year rule, or on making a Real Estate Election ("REE"), where further supplies (for example, overages) will or may arise after revocation.
- Ensuring that all members of a VAT group are considered when options are revoked.
- Changes to the rules on REEs so that if there is more than one tax point for a supply, the option is made on the date of the first supply.
- Amending the capital item condition of the 20 year automatic revocation rules so that a taxpayer who meets all the other conditions can still have automatic revocation if the sum of all the remaining Capital Goods Scheme adjustments is £10,000 or less.
- Amending the rules on granting permission to revoke an option to tax after 20 years so as to enable the time of revocation to be tied to an event. This would allow revocation to be linked to say, the sale of a property.

Further details are contained in VAT Information Sheet 14/09

CHANGES TO THE CONNECTED PERSONS RULES

Several banks have become "connected" for the purposes of the s839 of the Income Taxes Act 1988 as a result of the Government taking shares in them. By being connected, certain anti–avoidance rules are triggered which has meant that unintended tax implications may arise on certain transactions. This amendment treats taxpayers as unconnected where their only connection (within the meaning of s 839 of the Income Taxes Act 1988) is because they are controlled by the Crown, a minister of the Crown, a Government Department or a Northern Ireland Department. These changes affect:

- the Option to Tax (paragraph 34 to Schedule 10 of the VAT Act)
- supplies of land for indeterminable consideration (Reg 84 of the VAT Regulations 1995)
- supplies of construction services (Reg 93 of the VAT Regulations 1995)
- continuous supplies of services ((Reg 94 of the VAT Regulations 1995)

HOW WILL THE CHANGES BE EFFECTED?

The changes to Schedule 10 were made by Treasury Order and became effective from 1 August 2009. The three changes to the VAT Regulations become effective from 15 August 2009.

A revised Public Notice 742A – "Opting to tax land and buildings" will be issued in due course.

Commentary—*Simon's Taxes* **E1.603**

RECOVERY BY LOCAL AUTHORITIES IN RESPECT OF VOLUNTARY AIDED SCHOOLS

18 August 2009. *HMRC Brief 53/09.*

HMRC has revised its policy on VAT recovery by local authorities under VAT Act 1994, s 33 on expenditure relating to capital works at voluntary aided schools.

This Revenue and Customs Brief explains our revised policy on VAT recovery by local authorities on expenditure relating to capital works at voluntary aided schools.

BACKGROUND

Under Section 33 of VAT Act 1994 ("Section 33") specified bodies, including local authorities, are entitled to recover VAT incurred on supplies made to them which relate to their non-business activities. Their provision of free education in state maintained schools is one such non-business activity.

However, governing bodies of maintained schools are separate legal entities and are not bodies specified in Section 33. Therefore any VAT they incur in relation to their non-business activities is not recoverable.

Where the local authority has a statutory duty to "defray" all expenses of maintaining a school, for example, community schools, then any VAT incurred on purchases made by it in connection with these schools is recoverable under Section 33.

However, in the case of voluntary aided schools the governing body retains statutory responsibility for certain capital expenditure, including when made from the school's delegated budget. Therefore, in respect of any supplies which fall within the prescribed definition of such expenditure, the supply will be made to the governing body, even where the expenditure is met from the school's delegated budget, and VAT incurred may not be recovered by the local authority. Governing bodies in England receive funding from the Department for Children, Schools and Families (DCSF) of up to 90 per cent of the cost of meeting these responsibilities (and there are similar arrangements in place in the devolved administrations).

Capital expenditure for which the governing body of a voluntary aided school is responsible is defined by DCSF as expenditure relating to:

- the existing buildings (internal and external)
- those buildings previously known as "excepted" (kitchens, dining areas, medical/dental rooms, swimming pools, caretakers dwelling houses)
- perimeter walls and fences, even if around the playing fields
- playgrounds
- furniture, fixtures and fittings – including ICT infrastructure and equipment
- other capital items (which can include capital work to boilers or other services)

REVISED POLICY

A local authority is allowed to contribute funding to a governing body to help it meet the cost of its responsibilities. We have to date accepted that local authorities can recover the VAT incurred on expenditure which is the responsibility of the governing bodies but which the authority funds. This is explained in Public Notice 701/30 paragraph 15.5 and "V1-14—Government and public bodies" and "V1-07 chapter 21; Education".

We have reviewed this policy, and we now realise that it goes beyond what Section 33 actually permits. Section 33 is confined to VAT incurred by local authorities etc on the goods and services that they purchase, not on the goods and services that another legal entity purchases. Therefore, with effect from 1 September 2009, with respect to projects initiated after this date, VAT may no longer be recovered by local authorities in these circumstances, as the supplies are not made to them (whether or not paid for from the delegated budget). We will consider, on their individual facts, cases where a project initiated after 1 September 2009 was funded on the basis of the previous policy.

A local authority may, however, continue to recover VAT on expenditure at a voluntary aided school for which the local authority is statutorily responsible, or where the local authority, rather than the governing body, procures a supply of works and pays for that supply from its own funds (for further details please refer to Public Notice 749 Local Authorities and similar bodies paragraph 7.1). In such cases HMRC accept that the local authority receives the supply in connection with its non business activities.

WHAT NEXT?

Guidance currently contained in Public Notice 701/30 paragraph 15.5 and "V1-14—Government and public bodies" and "V1-07 chapter 21; Education" will be amended to take account of this revised policy.

If you have any queries in relation to this, or any other tax matter, please contact the National Advice Service on Tel 0845 010 9000.

Commentary—*De Voil Indirect Tax Service* **V4.141.**

REGULATIONS TO RESOLVE DISPUTES ABOUT WHETHER DOCUMENTS ARE COVERED BY LEGAL PROFESSIONAL PRIVILEGE

18 August 2009. *HMRC Brief 54/09*

This Business Brief provides an overview of the new system contained in SI 2009/1916 that governs whether information HMRC has requested can be withheld due to legal professional privilege.

HM Revenue and Customs (HMRC) has published new regulations about whether information it has requested can be withheld due to legal professional privilege.

The regulations are in SI 2009/1916 the Information Notice—Resolution of Disputes as to Privileged Communications Regulations 2009, which became effective on 7 August 2009.

They apply where HMRC has given an information notice to a person and there is a dispute about whether the requested document can be withheld due to legal professional privilege. The aim is to provide a clear method to resolve these disputes.

HMRC will amend technical guidance and add new operational guidance to the Compliance Handbook in September 2009.

Meanwhile this Business Brief aims to give an overview of the new system.

BACKGROUND

The new compliance checks legislation is one of the first pieces of cross cutting legislation designed to make the tax system simpler and more consistent.

From 1 April 2009, under Schedule 36 of the 2008 Finance Act, HMRC has one set of powers covering Capital Gains Tax, Corporation Tax, the Construction Industry Scheme, Income Tax, PAYE and VAT to:

– visit business premises to inspect the premises, assets and records
– ask taxpayers and third parties for information and documents

One restriction of these powers is that an HMRC officer cannot require a person

– to provide privileged information
– to produce the privileged part of a document

Information is privileged if a claim to legal professional privilege or, in Scotland confidentiality of communications, could be maintained in legal proceedings.

This is a complex area of the law but, broadly speaking, privilege attaches to:

– documents containing confidential communications between lawyer and client for the purpose of obtaining or giving legal advice
– documents produced for the purpose of contemplated or actual litigation

INFORMATION NOTICE SENT IN CORRESPONDENCE

If an HMRC officer asks an unrepresented person for documents where legal professional privilege may be an issue, they should explain what documents may be protected by privilege.

The person or anyone acting on their behalf shall specify in a list each disputed document or type of document so they can be identified. They should send the list to HMRC by the deadline given in the information notice.

The officer should check the list and identify:

- items they accept are privileged
- documents they do not need to see
- documents that they still need to see

The officer then needs to contact Central Policy or the HMRC Solicitor for advice about items they still need to see. If Central Policy or the HMRC Solicitor agrees some of these documents are not covered by privilege the officer must then contact the person and:

- explain why they think the document is not privileged
- tell the person they must send the document unless they disagree with HMRC's view
- tell them what they need to do if they want the Tribunal to decide whether the document is subject to legal professional privilege

The person must make an application to the Tribunal within 20 working days of the date of the HMRC letter.

INFORMATION NOTICE GIVEN AT A VISIT

It will be unusual for an officer to give an information notice at a visit. They should only do so if it is reasonable and proportionate, and to address an identified risk.

If the person has an adviser the officer should give them the opportunity to contact them. If the person is unrepresented, and privilege may be an issue, the officer should explain what documents may be protected by legal professional privilege.

If there are disputed documents the person should place them in a container that prevents the documents being seen. They will then seal, label and sign the container. The officer will countersign and take custody of the container.

The officer must ensure that container, with its seal intact, reaches the Tribunal so it can resolve the dispute. Although the deadline is 42 working days they should aim to do this within 20 working days.

If the documents are in electronic form the officer may be prepared to accept copies – see Ch43360–www.hmrc.gov.uk/manuals/chmanual/ch23360.htm.

CONSULTATION

HMRC is grateful for the assistance it has had from the Law Society of England and Wales, and the Chartered Institute of Taxation. We will incorporate much of their feedback into the operational guidance.

BINGO DUTY—RANK HIGH COURT RULING ON 8 JUNE

21 August 2009. *HMRC Brief 55/09*

This Revenue & Customs Brief sets out HM Revenue & Customs' (HMRC) policy on bingo duty as a result of the *Rank* [2009] All ER (D) 65 (Jun) ruling, and it also reminds operators of their legal obligations for accounting for bingo duty.

BACKGROUND

The High Court ruled in the case of Rank that their Mechanised Cash Bingo (MCB) par fees were exempt from Value Added Tax because the way the UK had applied VAT to MCB par fees had resulted in a breach of fiscal neutrality.

HMRC has sought leave to appeal against the High Court ruling but until and if HMRC succeed in the appeal, the Rank High Court ruling has effect across all taxpayers in the same situation.

HMRC is now considering claims for VAT output tax wrongly accounted for by bingo operators on MCB participation fees. A Revenue & Customs Brief was issued, number 40/09 which explains the action HMRC is taking.

REVENUE & CUSTOMS BRIEF 40/09

The Brief also explained that HMRC was considering the impact of the High Court Ruling on bingo duty.

BINGO DUTY IMPLICATIONS

1 Bingo duty is calculated on bingo receipts (after any VAT due has been deducted) minus winnings. The High Court has ruled that MCB receipts are exempt from VAT. If VAT has been deducted from MCB receipts when calculating the amount of bingo duty due on returns already submitted then bingo duty has been underdeclared on those returns.

2 All businesses making bingo duty returns are required to include any underdeclarations of bingo duty made on previous returns (box 7 of the return, form BD510 refers). Following the High Court decision in Rank, HMRC requires businesses to make adjustments for any underdeclarations of bingo duty for returns in respect of prescribed accounting periods from September 2006 onwards if they have not already done so. If you have not already adjusted an earlier return then these adjustments should be made on your September 2009 bingo duty return.

Where HMRC has already assessed for the underdeclared duty, businesses need not make these adjustments. (Please see the explanatory notes to the return).

3 Subsequent bingo duty returns submitted will be scrutinised by HMRC for any additional duty included within box 7 of the return and returns received will be risk assessed. Returns may be selected for additional checks to be made. Some visits to businesses to check their accounting records may be made in conjunction with other work to check claims for repayments of VAT as a result of the Rank High Court Ruling.

4 If you fail to make the required adjustments and do not account for any underdeclaration, HMRC will assess for the bingo duty due. In addition, a failure to adjust your September 2009 bingo duty return may leave you liable to penalties.

5 HMRC maintains that its view of the law is correct and that MCB takings remain liable to VAT. However, both businesses and HMRC will need to protect their positions during the ongoing litigation. Businesses which make adjustments for bingo duty as required at Paragraph 2 above may wish to make claims to recover these amounts and appeal their subsequent refusal in the event that the current ruling is reversed in a higher court.

6 HMRC does not accept that the High Court ruling extends beyond MCB to encompass par fees charged on all bingo. However in order to protect our position we will raise protective assessments for bingo duty due in case it is finally determined that VAT is not due on any bingo par fees. Payment of these protective assessments will not be enforced until and unless the final legal position justifies such action.

Commentary—*De Voil Indirect Tax Service* **V4.131.**

GUIDANCE ON VAT AND EXCISE WRONGDOING PENALTIES

25 August 2009. *HMRC Brief 52/09*

This HMRC Brief outlines the VAT and Excise wrongdoing penalties contained in the Finance Act 2008. Full technical guidance is contained in the Compliance Handbook

INTRODUCTION

This Business Brief outlines the VAT and Excise wrongdoing penalties contained in the 2008 Finance Act (FA2008). There is full technical guidance on these and other penalties introduced in FA2007 and FA2008 in HMRC's Compliance Handbook (www.hmrc.gov.uk/manuals/chmanual/index.htm). The guidance on these particular penalties can be found at CH90000 onwards.

BACKGROUND

Under the review of HMRC's powers, deterrents and safeguards (www.hmrc.gov.uk/about/powers–appeal.htm) legislation has been introduced to align and modernise the framework under which HMRC administers the taxes and duties formerly handled by Customs and Excise and the Inland Revenue. The aim, developed through consultation, is to support those who seek to comply but come down hard on those who seek an unfair advantage through non-compliance.

HMRC inherited a number of different penalty regimes from Customs and Excise and the Inland Revenue. The law and practice relating to penalties varied not only between the two former departments but also between the various taxes and duties for which each department was responsible.

Finance Act 2007, s 97 and Sch 24 introduced a simpler and more consistent penalty system for inaccuracies in tax returns and other documents.

VAT PRs etc

Finance Act 2008, s 123 and Sch 41 extended and adapted the new penalty framework to introduce:

– In paragraph 1 of Schedule 41, a standard penalty regime across most HMRC taxes where a customer fails to register or notify us and as a result tax is due
– In paragraphs 2, 3 and 4 new penalties for various VAT and Excise Wrongdoings

We will cover the failure to notify penalties in a separate Business Brief.

VAT and Excise Wrongdoing penalties

From 1 April 2010 a new penalty regime applies where any person:

– makes an unauthorised issue of an invoice showing or including VAT
– misuses a product so that a higher rate of excise duty is payable, or supplies a product knowing that it will be used in such a way
– handles goods subject to unpaid excise duty.

The unauthorised issue of an invoice showing VAT for example occurs when someone who is not registered for VAT and who doesn't work for a VAT registered business, issues an invoice that includes an amount shown as VAT.

The penalties relating to use of a product which leads to a higher rate of excise duty becoming payable are concerned with the various duties on alcohol, tobacco and hydrocarbon oil products (such as petrol and diesel).

An example of misuse of a product is the use of red diesel in a road vehicle. Red diesel has a lower rate of duty and is cheaper than diesel legally sold for vehicles using the roads. The use of red diesel is restricted, for example to agricultural vehicles. Commercial hauliers who misuse red diesel can obtain a large commercial advantage over their competitors. The penalties help to deter such misuse.

We can also issue a wrongdoing penalty if someone handles goods for which excise duty is payable, if the correct excise duty has not been paid or deferred.

A supplier will be liable to a penalty under this provision if they:

– supply an excise product, and
– know that their customer will use it for a purpose that attracts a higher duty.

Handling goods includes:

– acquiring the goods
– being involved in carrying, removing, depositing or keeping the goods
– selling the goods

One example of handling goods that would lead to a penalty is buying cigarettes abroad and selling them in the UK without accounting for excise duty. Cigarettes can only be brought into the UK, without paying UK excise duty, if they are for your own use.

REASONABLE EXCUSE

We will not charge a penalty if we are satisfied that the person:

– has a reasonable excuse for a non–deliberate act, and
– if the excuse has ended, has remedied the act without unreasonable delay.

Reasonable excuse is likely to be an exceptional event beyond the individual's control such as:

– the death of a partner or close relative
– serious illness of the person. partner or close relative

Reasonable excuse does not apply where the failure to notify or wrongdoing is deliberate.

We would not normally accept the following as a reasonable excuse:

– lack of money
– reliance on another person

A person who supplies a product knowing that it will be misused is liable to a penalty whether or not they consider there is a reasonable excuse for their act. The supplier knows that the product will be misused, the supply is therefore a deliberate act and there is no exclusion for reasonable excuse.

HOW IT WORKS

If the person is not registered for VAT, we can assess a penalty for issuing an unauthorised VAT invoice in addition to recovering the amounts charged as though they were VAT.

Where a higher amount of excise duty becomes due as a result of a product having been misused we may assess a penalty as well as recovering the duty. We may also assess a penalty on any person who supplied the product, if they knew that it would be misused.

The amount of the penalty is a percentage of the VAT shown in the invoice or the extra excise duty due from any person. The percentage is determined by the behaviour that led to the act and any attempts that were made to conceal it. If the wrongdoing was:

- deliberate and concealed—maximum penalty 100%, minimum penalty 30%
- deliberate but not concealed—maximum penalty 70%, minimum 20%
- non-deliberate—maximum penalty 30%, minimum 10%.

The penalty is then reduced to take account of whether and to what extent the person has sought to disclose the wrongdoing to HMRC. This reduction depends on:

- whether the disclosure is unprompted or prompted, and
- the quality of the disclosure.

Reason for wrongdoing	*Disclosure*	*Minimum penalty*	*Maximum penalty*
Reasonable excuse	–	*No penalty*	*No penalty*
Careless	Unprompted	10%	30%
–	Prompted	20%	30%
Deliberate	Unprompted	20%	70%
–	Prompted	35%	70%
Deliberate &	Unprompted	30%	100%
concealed	Prompted	50%	100%

We will issue a penalty assessment. The person is entitled to a review of, and can appeal against (see HMRC1), our decision:

- that a penalty is payable, and/or
- the amount of the penalty.

AGENTS

Where an agent is acting for a person or company, they remain responsible for ensuring that no wrongdoing occurs. Examples of agents include employees, and advisers such as tax advisers.

That means the person or company can be penalised if the agent carelessly or deliberately:

- makes an unauthorised issue of an invoice with VAT,
- misuses a product so that a higher rate of excise duty is payable, or
- handles goods subject to unpaid excise duty,
- unless the person or company took reasonable care to avoid the wrongdoing committed by their agent.

We believe it is reasonable to expect the person or company to:

- set up systems and procedures to create and retain accurate records
- make accurate returns
- comply with the relevant legislation
- refrain from any wrongdoings, and
- meet their other tax obligations.

COMPANY OFFICERS

Where there is evidence to identify the officer or officers who caused a deliberate wrongdoing they will be liable for payment of all or part of the penalty where:

– there is evidence that the officer gained personally from the deliberate wrongdoing, or
– the company is insolvent, or
– there are grounds to suspect that the company will become insolvent, see CH98850.

Company officers are defined as a director or a secretary of the company.

MORE INFORMATION

– Compliance Handbook–www.hmrc.gov.uk/manuals/chmanual/index.htm
– New penalties internet page–www.hmrc.gov.uk/about/new–penalties/index.htm
– Q&A briefing on all penalty changes

Commentary—*De Voil Indirect Tax Service* **V5.345.**

VAT TREATMENT OF YACHT CHARTERING OR LEASING ACTIVITIES

27 August 2009. *HMRC Brief 56/09*

Further to HMRC Brief 11/07, the aim of this Brief is to clarify HMRC's view of the VAT treatment applying to the purchase and use (eg leasing and chartering) of pleasure craft and sets out HMRC's approach to artificial structures.

1 BACKGROUND AND AIM

In Revenue & Customs Brief 11/07 we announced our concerns relating to VAT schemes through which private individuals incur little or no VAT on the purchase of pleasure craft. We have since investigated a number of such schemes which typically involve artificial leasing or chartering structures.

There are also, of course, many bona–fide businesses who charter and lease pleasure craft. The aim of this Brief is to clarify our view of the VAT treatment applying to the purchase and use of pleasure craft and, in particular, the chartering and leasing of pleasure craft. We also set out our approach to artificial structures such as those described in Revenue & Customs Brief 11/07.

The term "pleasure craft" is used to describe motor and sailing yachts which are designed for recreational use. This guidance takes into account relevant case law including the ECJ's judgement in the case of *Halifax and others* C–255/02 (the Halifax case).

2 VAT REGISTRATION

Persons who are in business and are either making or intending to make taxable supplies, relevant EC acquisitions, distance sales or supplies of certain assets may be liable or entitled to register for VAT.

"Business" is defined in Section 94(1) of the VAT Act 1994 (VATA1994) as including any trade, profession or vocation. This definition is not designed to be exhaustive and the VAT meaning of business has emerged through the judgements of UK courts and the ECJ. Although the Principal VAT Directive refers to "economic activity" rather than "business" our domestic legislation must be interpreted so it conforms with the Directive. Consequently "business" and "economic activity" must be seen as having the same meaning.

A person carrying out yacht chartering or leasing is therefore only entitled to VAT registration (and the related entitlement to deduct input VAT) where the chartering or leasing is carried out in the course of an economic activity. We may ask for evidence to show that an economic activity is being pursued, either before registration is allowed or during subsequent verification.

The ECJ case of *Enkler* [C–230/94] shows that, where an asset is suitable for both business and for private purposes, then the Tax Authority has to consider all the circumstances in which it is used to determine whether it is actually used in the course of a business. The actual length of the period for which the vessel is hired, the number of customers and the amount of earnings are factors which, forming part of the circumstances of the case as a whole, may be taken into account, together with others. In addition the actual use should be compared with the circumstances in which the corresponding economic activity is usually carried out.

During any verification of entitlement to VAT registration we will look for evidence that a chartering or leasing activity has sufficient substance and continuity to meet the criteria set by the ECJ in *Enkler*. We will also consider the evidence in relation to the "business test" that emerged from the case of Lord Fisher QB [1981] STC 238, and the earlier case of *Morrison's Academy* CS1977, [1978] STC 1. The full circumstances in which the vessel is used will be considered and the onus will be on the registered person (or the applicant) to provide sufficient evidence to support a contention that the vessel is used in an economic activity.

3 VAT TREATMENT OF PRIVATE (NON–BUSINESS) USE OF A PLEASURE CRAFT

We are aware that the purchase of a pleasure craft is typically funded by a high net worth individual who agrees the specification with the supplier and who will use the vessel himself for some or all of the time that it is in service.

Such an individual may have legal ownership of the vessel in his own name or he may arrange for legal ownership to be held by a company (or other entity) which he may control, directly or indirectly.

WHEN AN INDIVIDUAL HAS LEGAL OWNERSHIP OF THE VESSEL IN HIS OWN NAME

If an individual has legal ownership of the vessel in his own name and uses it wholly for his own private use then there is no economic activity and he is not entitled to register for VAT.

MIXED BUSINESS AND PRIVATE USE

If an individual has legal ownership of the vessel in his own name and charters the vessel to others with sufficient continuity and substance to comprise an economic activity as well as using it himself then the vessel will be used partly for business and partly for private use.

If he is registered for VAT because of the business use he will incur VAT on goods (the vessel) that are intended for both business and private purposes.

He has a choice as to how to treat these goods for VAT purposes:

– He may treat them as a part business, part non–business asset, in which case the VAT incurred is only deductible to the extent that it relates to the taxable business activities [section 24(5) VATA 1994].
– He may treat them as a wholly business asset, the "Lennartz" approach, in which case the VAT incurred is treated as input tax and is deductible in full, subject to any partial exemption ("PE") restriction. However, VAT must then be accounted for when the goods are used for private purposes. Where a taxable person adopts the "Lennartz" approach he must do so at the time the input tax is incurred.

If the asset is subsequently sold within the UK, VAT will be due on that "portion" of the asset that is treated as business (in the circumstances described in 3.5.1 above) and on the whole of the asset (in the circumstances described in 3.5.2 above).

Further information on the application of the "Lennartz mechanism" is given in VAT Information Sheet 14/07.

WHEN AN INDIVIDUAL ARRANGES FOR LEGAL OWNERSHIP TO BE HELD BY A COMPANY (OR OTHER ENTITY)

The nature of the entity which owns a vessel does not, in itself, affect the VAT treatment of the vessel.

However, we are aware that structures involving a company (or an entity such as a limited liability partnership) have been used by individuals to obtain a VAT advantage. Put simply, this arises where an individual who has funded the purchase of a pleasure craft arranges for legal ownership of that vessel to be held by a company (or other entity) which registers for VAT as a chartering or leasing business and recovers VAT incurred on the purchase and operation of the vessel.

The individual's own use of the vessel is covered by charter or lease agreements issued to him in the name of the company. As a result it is claimed that there is no private use of the vessel.

We will consider the entitlement of such a company (or other entity) to VAT registration by applying the approach set out above to identify whether the chartering or leasing comprises an "economic activity".

The connection between the company and the user of the vessel does not in itself prevent the chartering or leasing being an economic activity. On the other hand, merely issuing charter agreements to the individual in the name of the company is not, alone, sufficient to create an economic activity. The full circumstances in which the vessel is used will be considered, as explained above.

We may also consider whether the structure amounts to an abusive practice by applying the tests identified by the ECJ in the Halifax case. More information on this aspect is given below.

4 APPLICATION OF THE PRINCIPLE OF PROHIBITING ABUSIVE PRACTICES

In recent years there have been significant developments in the case law of the ECJ concerning the application to VAT of the principle of prohibiting abusive practices. Of particular relevance are the ECJ's judgements in the Halifax case and in the case of Part Service Srl C–425/06.

From these cases it is clear that—

The principle of prohibiting abusive practices "applies to the sphere of VAT" (Halifax, paragraph 70). This means it applies to all aspects of VAT and not just the right to recover input tax. This was further demonstrated in the Part Service case which concerned avoidance of output tax.

The tests to establish whether an abuse exists are as follows:

> "For it to be found that an abusive practice exists, it is necessary, first, that the transactions concerned, notwithstanding formal application of the conditions laid down by the relevant provisions of the Sixth Directive [now the Principal VAT Directive] and of national legislation transposing it, result in the accrual of a tax advantage the grant of which would be contrary to the purpose of those provisions. Second, it must also be apparent from a number of objective factors that the essential aim of the transactions concerned is to obtain a tax advantage." (Halifax paragraph 86).

With regard to the first test ("contrary to purpose"), if the objective facts show that the economic reality underlying the structure is that an individual has purchased a pleasure craft for his own recreational use then, if no VAT is borne by that individual in relation to the purchase and use of the pleasure craft, that result may be contrary to article 1(2) of the Principal VAT Directive (*See Note 1 below*).

With regard to the second test, "essential aim" is determined by considering "the real substance and significance of the transactions concerned" taking account of "the purely artificial nature of those transactions and the links of a legal, economic and/or personal nature between the operators involved in the scheme for reduction of the tax burden" (Halifax paragraph 81).

It is important to note that "essential aim" is not a sole purpose test. There can be a finding of an abusive practice when the accrual of a tax advantage constitutes the principal aim of the transaction or transactions at issue (Part Service paragraphs 45 and 62).

The essential aim of the transactions concerned is determined from the objective facts of the case rather than the subjective aim or intention of the parties engaged in those transactions. It is an "objective" test which does not rely on establishing what the parties say their intention was (or what their subjective intention is found to have been). Instead, the essential aim is established by taking account of all the evidence and the commercial realities to determine what, viewed objectively, is the principal aim of the transactions viewed as a whole.

Where an abusive practice is found to exist then:

> "It follows that transactions involved in an abusive practice must be redefined so as to re–establish the situation that would have prevailed in the absence of the transactions constituting the abusive practice." (Halifax paragraph 94).

If we conclude that a structure meets the tests for an abusive practice then we will consider appropriate action to restore the situation that would have existed in the absence of the abusive transactions. This might include issuing assessments to disallow input tax and/or deregistration of the entity concerned. Such assessments might also give rise to interest charges and penalties.

5 POSSIBLE INDICATORS OF AN ABUSIVE PRACTICE

The existence of one or more of the following features might indicate an abusive structure (the list is not exhaustive–the indicators are illustrative of the points that we might take into account, together with others):

- The main user of a pleasure craft is the ultimate owner of the chartering or leasing entity.
- The main user of a pleasure craft funded the purchase of the vessel (directly or indirectly).
- The person who funded the purchase of a pleasure craft (directly or indirectly) uses the vessel for prolonged periods in the peak chartering season.
- The chartering of a pleasure craft to third parties would not, alone, be of sufficient continuity and substance to comprise an economic activity.
- The chartering or leasing entity shows significant ongoing losses in its financial statements.
- Charter fees or lease instalments due from the main user of a pleasure craft are paper transactions only (for example being offset against loans).
- Charter fees or lease instalments are below open market value.
- The terms of a lease differ significantly from normal commercial practice (for example, the duration of the lease is unusually long).

WHO CAN I CONTACT FOR FURTHER INFORMATION?

If you have a query for which you have been unable to find the answer within this publication, please contact HMRC's Advice Service for VAT on 0845 010 9000 (+44 208 929 0152 for International callers). The Advice Service VAT helpline is available from Monday to Friday, 8.00 am to 8.00 pm (GMT).

Note

(1) Article 1(2) states—"*The principle of the common system of VAT entails the application to goods and services of a general tax on consumption exactly proportional to the price of the goods and services, however many transactions take place in the production and distribution process before the stage at which the tax is charged.*"

Commentary—*De Voil Indirect Tax Service* **V3.212.**

PARTIAL EXEMPTION AFTER DECISION IN COMMUNITY HOUSING ASSOCIATION

7 September 2009. *HMRC Brief 57/09*

VAT: Partial exemption – policy in respect of payback claims in the light of the High Court decision in CHA

This Revenue and Customs Brief confirms HM Revenue & Customs (HMRC) policy on the VAT partial exemption "payback" rules following the High Court decision in the case of *Community Housing Association (CHA)* [2009] STC 1324. It uses a number of specialist terms which are explained more fully in Notice 706 "Partial exemption".

PAYBACK POLICY

VAT Regulation 109 in SI 1995/2518, "payback" allows a business to recoup input tax on costs that are incurred to make exempt supplies, but are instead used wholly or partly to make taxable supplies. Payback also applies to costs incurred for both taxable and exempt purposes, but actually used to make wholly taxable supplies. A payback claim cannot be made unless:

- the costs in question were not used as originally intended;
- the change of use arises after the end of the partial exemption longer period (if there is one);
- the change of use results in taxable supplies or both taxable and exempt supplies if the original intention had been to make a wholly exempt supply.

BACKGROUND TO THE CHA CASE

CHA is a housing association providing mainly rental housing, which is exempt for VAT purposes. CHA incurred input tax related to the construction of new dwellings for use in its business. CHA subsequently changed its operation by inserting a new subsidiary between itself and its suppliers. Then, having raised invoices to the subsidiary for the value of work undertaken on uncompleted projects prior to this change, CHA lodged a "payback" claim. They argued that input tax on costs for part completed projects incurred prior to the change were not used as originally intended and were now attributable to a taxable supply from CHA to the new subsidiary. HMRC rejected the claim on the grounds that there were no supplies of services between CHA and its subsidiary and, even if there were, the old costs did not become cost components of the supplies. The Tribunal agreed with HMRC.

HIGH COURT DECISION

The High Court overturned the Tribunal decision and allowed the payback claim. The High Court found as fact that CHA made supplies to its subsidiary and that the supplies transferred useful material and rights arising from the old supplies received by CHA. Based on these findings the High Court's decision was inevitable. HMRC have not appealed.

HMRC CONCLUSION

Supply covers a wide range of circumstances but there are some basic requirements that must apply before a supply can exist. The recipient of the supply must receive some benefit, he must provide some consideration and the consideration must be paid in return for the benefit.

Any business making a supply will incur costs in doing so. These are the cost components of the supply. Conclusions on what the cost components of any supply are will flow from an analysis of the nature of that supply. The mere raising of invoices and passing of funds between companies does not automatically create supplies. Careful analysis may be called for, especially if the companies are close associates.

Commentary—*De Voil Indirect Tax Service* **V4.123.**

HIGH COURT JUDGMENT IN INSURANCEWIDE/TRADER MEDIA GROUP

22 September 2009. *HMRC Brief 59/09*

This Brief explains the HMRC position following the High Court judgment in *Insurancewide-.com Services Ltd and Trader Media Group Ltd* [2009] EWHC 999 (Ch), (2009) Times, 5 June, [2009] SWTI 1724, [2009] All ER (D) 148 (May).

The High Court found against HMRC that supplies of insurance introductory services provided via the internet are exempt from VAT. HMRC has been granted leave to appeal this decision to the Court of Appeal.

BACKGROUND

The appeals of Insurancewide (IW) and Trader Media Group (TMG) concern the VAT liability of internet "click thru" services and whether introductory services such as this, that involve no intermediation of the contracts themselves, qualify as exempt insurance intermediary services.

The facts in each case are slightly different; IW is a comparison web-site providing "click thru" services to insurer or broker web-sites whereas TM provides "click thru" services from its Auto Trader car auction site to a third party co-branded broker web-site. Both are paid commission on successful take-up.

At tribunal, IW lost its appeal as they were found not to be acting as insurance agents at any time and appealed to the High Court. On the other hand, TM won its appeal as the tribunal found that their services constituted insurance intermediary services and HMRC appealed the decision to the High Court. Given the similarities in the two cases, the High Court agreed to hear the appeals jointly.

The High Court hearing took place in March 2009 and the judgment was released on 15 May. The Court found that IW and TMG were insurance intermediaries for the purposes of the VAT exemption and an act of introduction with no further involvement in the intermediation of the contract of insurance qualified for exemption as an insurance related service.

CLAIMS

Subject to the normal rules on capping and unjust enrichment, HMRC will pay claims for overpaid tax charged on insurance introductory services that follow the findings of the Court in IW/TMG. HMRC will raise protective recovery assessments under section 73(2) which will be enforced if HMRC are ultimately successful in the ongoing litigation.

Please note that HMRC see the judgment as applying to insurance introductory services only and do not see it as applying to introductory services relating to other financial contracts even if in other respects they are on "all fours" with IW/TMG. This is because, for services that fall within items 1 to 4 of the UK finance exemption, intermediaries are required to be both bringing together the parties and carrying work preparatory to the conclusion of the contract. A key aspect of the decision in IW/TMG was the fact that UK VAT insurance law allows exemption for businesses that are either bringing together the parties or carrying out work preparatory. Claims will not therefore be paid in respect of finance introductory services following this judgment.

FURTHER INFORMATION

Details of where to send your claim can be obtained from VAT Notice 700/45 How to correct VAT errors and make adjustments or claims from the HM Revenue & Customs Helpline on Tel 0845 010 9000.

HMRC may reject all or part of a claim if repayment would unjustly enrich the claimant. More details on "unjust enrichment" can be found at part 14 of VAT Notice 700/45 "How to correct VAT errors and make adjustments or claims".

Protective recovery assessments are covered in V1-35

There may be direct tax implications where amounts of over-declared output tax are repaid to businesses and your attention is drawn to R&C Brief 14/09 issued previously.

Where you are in any doubt about the correct treatment please contact the Helpline on Tel 0845 010 9000.

RELOCATION OF TELECOMS AND INTERNET SERVICE PROVIDERS AND BROADCASTERS

2 October 2009. *HMRC Brief 58/09*

HMRC explain their concerns where telecommunications businesses, internet providers and broadcasters move their place of supply from the UK to another Member State to obtain a more favourable VAT rate. All such arrangements will be carefully examined to determine if a fixed establishment still exists in the UK.

This Revenue & Customs Brief is of interest to all businesses within the telecommunications, Internet service provision and broadcasting sectors who claim to have moved or may consider moving the place of supply of their services from the UK to another Member State. The purpose of this Brief is to explain HM Revenue & Customs (HMRC) concerns and intended response and to encourage you to discuss these arrangements with your Customer Relationship Manager or the alternative contact given below.

HMRC are aware that some businesses within the telecommunications, Internet service provision and broadcasting sectors have implemented arrangements that claim to move the place of supply of their services from the UK to another Member State in order to take advantage of more favourable VAT rates.

The place of supply of telecommunications, Internet service provision and broadcasting services when provided to non-business customers in the EU is the place where the supplier is established. Some suppliers to the UK market claim to have reorganised their businesses so that the place of supply is no longer in the UK but another Member State.

HMRC accept that businesses have the freedom to choose where to locate and to enjoy any resultant benefits.

However, HMRC will carefully examine all such arrangements. Where HMRC consider that there are sufficient human and technical resources in the UK to form a fixed establishment from which the services are supplied, or where the entity purporting to make the supplies does not have a sufficient presence in the other Member State to be established there, HMRC will mount a robust challenge.

Any business wishing to discuss their arrangements should contact either their Customer Relationship Manager or Peter Langton at Large Business Service, 101 Victoria Street, Bristol, BS1 6DQ; Tel: 0117 9838317 in the first instance.

PARTIAL EXEMPTION—VAT DEDUCTION BY THEATRES ON PRODUCTION COSTS

14 October 2009. *HMRC Brief 65/09*

HMRC has revised its policy on input tax recovery on the costs of staging shows (production costs) for which the theatre's admissions are VAT exempt. It follows the Tribunal decision in *Garsington Opera Limited* (TC00045). Further information on partial exemption can be found in Public Notice 706.

THE DISPUTE

Garsington Opera incurred input tax on the costs of putting together its own "in-house" operatic performances at Garsington. HMRC maintained that the input tax was irrecoverable because whilst putting on operas was the core of Garsington's business, the production costs were directly and immediately linked only to exempt admissions. Garsington argued that the input tax was partly deductible (residual) because the production costs had a direct and immediate link not only to exempt admissions, but also to taxable supplies such as corporate sponsorship, touring (supplies of the production to an outside concert hall), programmes, CDs, intellectual property rights and the occasional supplies of production props and equipment.

THE TRIBUNAL DECISION

The Tribunal found for Garsington having identified a direct and immediate link between the production costs and both the exempt admission and the taxable supplies in issue. HMRC have not appealed this decision and has instead revised its policy on when theatres supplying exempt admission can treat input tax incurred on production costs as residual.

REVISED POLICY

It is an established principle of partial exemption that input tax is residual if the costs are "used or intended to be used" to make both taxable and exempt supplies. Costs are used if they have a direct and immediate link to supplies. Production costs will always be directly and immediately linked to exempt admissions to the show. Production costs only become partly deductible (residual) if there is a firm intention to make taxable as well as exempt supplies when the costs are incurred. Production costs are not "overhead costs" which are treated as residual because they relate to the organisation as a whole. Production costs only become residual if they relate to specific taxable supplies as well as exempt admissions. Examples of when production costs relate to taxable supplies include if a theatre has contracted to or intends to:

- Secure sponsorship – the sponsorship must relate to an event or a clearly defined run of events over a clearly defined time. Putting on the shows must be a condition of the sponsorship so that production costs become cost components of the sponsorship income. The intention may be evidenced by way of clear financial commitment.
- Tour the production – once again the intention may be evidenced by way of clear financial commitment.
- Record the show for later sale on CD or other media.

Production costs remain residual if an intention to make taxable supplies is frustrated. For example if production costs were treated as residual because of an intention to tour the show, the costs remain residual if the intended tour is later cancelled.

The intention to make taxable supplies must be a genuine intention. The mere aspiration or hope of making a taxable supply is insufficient to secure residual status. For example supplies of intellectual property or props/equipment created in a production are not sufficient to create a direct & immediate link in the absence of a firm intention at the time the costs were incurred that these costs would be used to make these supplies after their use in the show's run in the theatre.

Furthermore, residual status is not secured if the link to taxable supplies is indirect. For example, production costs do not become residual simply because the production is photographed for inclusion in the show programme which is a taxable supply. Likewise, the inclusion of synopses, lists of performers or performer profiles in a programme does not demonstrate that costs are directly and immediately linked to making the taxable supplies.

THE COURT OF APPEAL DECISION IN MAYFLOWER

In the similar case of *Mayflower Theatre Trust Ltd* [2007] STC 880 a direct and immediate link to programme sales was found in relation to "bought in" shows. This was because copyright information necessary for the programmes was obtained as part of the single supply of production services received from the touring company thus creating the direct and immediate link. If an individual actor or designer provides copyright information to a theatre/opera putting together a show "in house" as part of a single supply of their services this cost will also be residual. However it will not make other costs incurred residual.

The Mayflower decision also made clear that securing general corporate sponsorship does not make production costs residual even if the sponsorship package includes the provision of seats at performances. Likewise, catering supplies which arise as a consequence of admission do not make production costs residual.

IMPACT ON THEATRES

The vast majority of theatres use the partial exemption standard method to apportion residual input tax between taxable and exempt supplies. This works well provided VAT bearing costs are used in proportion to the value of supplies made. The standard method can work less well when significant residual costs do not relate to all of the taxable and exempt supplies made by the business.

Since 18 April 2002, if the standard method results in an over (or under) recovery of input tax which is classed as "substantial" then the recovery must be re-calculated in accordance with the "actual use" of the costs in question. This is known as the Standard Method Override (SMO). Further information on the SMO, including the definition of "substantial" can be found in the public notice and Information Sheet 4/02.

Where production costs are residual because of direct and immediate links to specific taxable supplies such as sponsorship or touring performances and those taxable supplies are small in comparison to the total taxable supplies of the theatre the SMO might be triggered and a "use-based" calculation required. In the case of theatres, the total taxable supplies may include substantial amounts of catering and refreshments for which the production is not a direct cost.

A "use-based" calculation is any calculation that fairly reflects how costs are used in making supplies. Calculations should be as simple as is possible whilst achieving a fair result. A fair calculation could be:

Recoverable input tax on production costs incurred in the tax year $= A \div (A + B) \times C$

Where:

A = Value of supplies in the year (such as sponsorship or touring) with a direct and immediate link from the production costs of any show.

B = Value of all box office sales in the year; and

C = Residual input tax incurred on production costs in the tax year.

Theatres operating the standard method where the SMO is likely to be triggered on a regular basis may wish to seek approval for a special method.

CLAIMS FOR UNDER-RECOVERED INPUT TAX

Theatres may wish to claim input tax which, in the light of this HMRC Brief, was incorrectly treated as exempt. They must use the partial exemption method in place when the input tax was incurred unless there are exceptional reasons why an alternative method is needed in which case full details should be submitted with the claim. Theatres using the standard method must consider the SMO when making a claim and all claims are subject to the normal time limits.

Further information about making claims can be found in Public Notice 700/45 How to correct VAT errors and make adjustments or claims.

Commentary—*De Voil Indirect Tax Service* **V4.176.**

VAT TREATMENT OF POSTAL SERVICES: ECJ DECISION IN TNT POST UK LTD

15 October 2009. *HMRC Brief 64/09*

EU law provides a mandatory exemption from VAT for supplies of postal services made "by the public postal services". In the UK, the application of this provision is limited to Royal Mail and covers all of Royal Mail's postal services. All other postal operators – both before and after full deregulation of the postal sector in the UK on 1 January 2006 – are required to charge VAT at the standard rate on their services.

Following a legal challenge to the scope of the exemption as applied in the UK, the European Court of Justice in the case of *TNT Post UK Ltd* [2009] STC 1438 has confirmed that Royal Mail, as the operator providing the public postal service, is the only postal body in the UK eligible to exempt postal services from VAT. However, it has also ruled that exemption applies to the public postal services (that is, Royal Mail) acting as such and does not apply to supplies made by Royal Mail for which the terms have been individually negotiated.

As a result, some postal services as supplied by Royal Mail – those which are individually negotiated or not subject to any price and regulatory control – which have been treated as exempt will become liable to VAT.

HM Revenue & Customs are currently in discussions with Royal Mail to establish precisely which of their services will be affected and further guidance will be issued once these discussions are complete. Any changes will be implemented from a future date and, in the meantime, all postal services provided by Royal Mail remain exempt from VAT.

For further information please contact the Helpline on 0845 010 9000.

Commentary—*De Voil Indirect Tax Service* **V4.126.**

LIABILITY OF PROPERTY SERVICE CHARGES FOLLOWING RLRE TELLMER (C-572/07)

27 October 2009. *HMRC Brief 67/09*

This Revenue & Customs Brief sets out HM Revenue & Customs' (HMRC) view of the judgment of the European Court of Justice ("ECJ") in the case of *RLRE Tellmer Property sro v Finanníeditelství v Ústí nad Labem* [2009] STC 2006 ("Tellmer") and confirms that the UK's current VAT treatment of service charges is unchanged following this decision.

BACKGROUND

The issue was whether the leasing of apartments and the related cleaning of the common parts of the apartment building formed a single exempt supply by the landlord, Tellmer. Tellmer argued this was the case but the Czech authorities argued that the cleaning services amounted to a separate taxable supply. The ECJ agreed that in the circumstances of Tellmer, the cleaning services could be separated from the property rental as a separate taxable supply.

In the UK, it is common for property leasing and letting to include the provision of service charges for, amongst other things, cleaning services; to this extent there is some parallel with Tellmer. HMRC's current policy is that where the service charge arises as a condition under a lease and is to be provided by the lessor (or his agent) without the lessee having a choice, then we treat the rent and the service charge as consideration for a single supply – this is the case in most property leasing. This follows the Judgment of the ECJ in the case of *Card Protection Plan Ltd v Customs and Excise Comrs* (Case C-349/96) [1999] STC 270 ("CPP") where the Court held that there is a single supply where one or more elements are to be regarded as constituting the principal supply, whilst one or more elements are to be regarded, by contrast, as ancillary supplies which share the tax treatment of the principal supply.

The ECJ sought to apply the principles established in the case of CPP, and in two more recent ECJ cases, *Levob Verzekeringen BV v Staatssecretaris van Financiën* (Case C-41/04) [2006] STC 766 and *Ministero dell'Economia e delle Finanze v Part Service Srl* (Case C-425/06) [2008] STC 3132, which also dealt with the issues of single and separate supplies. In reaching its judgment in the present case the ECJ concluded, on the basis of the limited facts available, that two separate supplies were made rather than a single indivisible supply. This must have been because, on the facts of the case, the tenants in the Czech Republic were not required to obtain the cleaning of the common parts from their landlord, but had a real option whether to ask their landlord to perform the cleaning of the common parts for additional consideration or to obtain those services themselves from a third party.

If, however, there is a requirement for service charges to be paid but the services are either provided by a different person to the lessor (or his agent) or they do not arise as a condition under the lease agreement, then HMRC's policy continues to be that in such circumstances these services are a separate supply from the lease. However, under certain circumstances, they can be treated as exempt by concession – see Notice 48, ESC 3.18.

IMPACT OF TELLMER

It is clear from the decision of the ECJ that *Tellmer* itself provided both the property leasing and the cleaning services to the tenants. However, the tenants had the choice of making an independent contract with a third party to provide the cleaning services. In the particular circumstances the court did not consider that the cleaning services were ancillary to the property letting and, as a result, concluded that they constituted a separate supply.

On this basis, since the UK only treats leasing of property and related service charges as a single supply, where the services are provided by the lessor (or his agent) as a condition under the lease agreement, HMRC consider that the findings in *Tellmer* are consistent with existing UK policy.

If you have any queries in relation to this, or any other tax matter, please contact the Helpline on Tel 0845 010 9000.

Commentary—*De Voil Indirect Tax Service* **V3.105.**

RETURN OF STANDARD RATE TO 17.5 PER CENT ON 1 JANUARY 2010 — MEASURES TO HELP BUSINESS

5 November 2009. *HMRC Brief 68/09*

This Brief explains two HMRC measures designed to assist businesses in implementing the return of the standard rate of VAT to 17.5 per cent. It also includes details of the consultation currently being carried out by the Department for Business, Innovation and Skills (BIS) about a proposal to amend the Price Marking Order 2004.

BACKGROUND

On 1 December 2008 the standard rate of VAT was temporarily reduced to 15 per cent. It reverts to 17.5 per cent on 1 January 2010. HMRC recognises that the date of the change may cause problems for certain businesses at a particularly busy time of year so we have introduced two measures to help business to implement the change. These are:

– special accounting arrangements for businesses operating beyond midnight on 31 December 2009
– the "light touch" to be operated by HMRC audit staff in dealing with errors arising out of the rate change.

Further details on each of these are provided below.

1. SPECIAL ACCOUNTING ARRANGEMENTS FOR BUSINESSES OPERATING BEYOND MIDNIGHT ON 31 DECEMBER 2009

Retailers

The temporary reduction of the standard rate of VAT to 15 per cent ends on 31 December 2009. As is normal with changes to the VAT rate, the return to 17.5 per cent will be effective from midnight on 31 December. However, HMRC recognises that making the necessary changes to account for VAT at 17.5 per cent may cause particular problems for certain businesses operating after midnight at what can be a particularly busy time of year. For example, it would not be practical for a pub, club, restaurant or hotel hosting a New Year's Eve celebration to stop serving customers at midnight in order to adjust their tills to account for VAT at 17.5 per cent and to amend their prices accordingly. In order to assist businesses in this position HMRC will allow them to account for VAT at 15 per cent on takings received up to the earlier of:

VAT PRs etc

- the end of trading of the 31 December session or
- 6am on the morning of 1 January 2010.

This treatment is subject to the following conditions:

- It is restricted to those businesses open at midnight on 31 December 2009 that account for VAT at the point of sale such as businesses on a retail scheme – pubs, shops, restaurants etc. It will not apply to:
  - mail order or on-line retailers; – businesses that account for VAT on the basis of VAT invoices issued; or
  - pre-payments for supplies of goods or services to be provided after 6am on 1 January 2010.
- It will not apply to sales made through coin operated or similar machines (vending, amusement or gaming machines etc). In these cases businesses must follow the normal rate change rules as set out in section 10.1 of the detailed rate change guidance (www.hmrc.gov.uk/vat/forms-rates/rates/rate-rise-guidance.pdf) and account for VAT based on the date that the machine is used or by apportionment if the machine does not record the date of usage.
- It will not apply to transactions made after midnight on 31 December that would have been caught by the rate change anti-forestalling legislation (Finance Act 2009, Schedule 3) had they been made before midnight. Any such supplies will be liable to VAT at 17.5 per cent. Further guidance on the anti-forestalling legislation is available below.
- HMRC may withdraw or restrict the application of this treatment in individual cases.

Telecommunications providers

As the hours around midnight on New Year's Eve are traditionally the busiest time of year for voice calls and text messages, it may similarly be difficult for telecommunications service providers to change their accounting and billing systems to take account of the change in the rate. HMRC will therefore allow VAT to be charged at 15 per cent on charges for voice calls and text messages that take place and are billed up to 6am on 1 January 2010.

2. THE LIGHT TOUCH

The following guidance has been given to HMRC VAT audit staff about the approach to adopt in relation to errors discovered in relation to the rate change:

What if businesses make mistakes implementing the change of rate (light touch)?

HMRC wants to encourage and assist businesses as they make the changes necessary to deal with the change in the standard rate.

If a business discovers that it has made material mistakes, it should correct them through the normal error correction process.

HMRC will however be operating a "light touch" in terms of errors made in the first VAT return after the change (where the error relates to a change of rate issue). This means that in our audit plans we will not target change of rate errors that are unlikely to lead to any material net revenue loss. And if we find errors which relate to a change of rate issue we will not seek an adjustment unless we have reason to suppose that there is an overall revenue loss.

For example, consider a fully taxable business which supplies standard-rated goods to a fully taxable customer and incorrectly charges 15 per cent rather than 17.5 per cent. As the detailed guidance makes clear, the customer should treat only 15 per cent of the tax exclusive (net) price as input tax. If the customer does this there will be no overall loss of tax. When auditing the supplier, HMRC will assume that the purchaser has followed the accounting documents unless there is good reason to suppose otherwise.

However, if the supply is or may be to a customer who is not able to recover VAT in full, then there is likely to be an overall loss of tax and HMRC will seek to adjust (issue an assessment) in the normal way.

In situations where HMRC do need to adjust (and issue an assessment) we will take into account the difficulties the business has faced in adjusting to the change in considering whether penalties apply.

3. BIS CONSULTATION ON PROPOSAL TO AMEND THE PRICE MARKING ORDER 2004

Traders are required to display clearly their prices inclusive of VAT. For a period up to 14 days, they are permitted under the Price Marking Order 2004 (SI 2004/102) to let consumers know, by way of a general notice, that an adjustment in price, to take account of the VAT change, will be made at the till.

BIS is consulting on its proposal to extend the length of time that traders can display a general notice, from 14 days to 28 days. Full details of the consultation, which closes on Monday 23 November 2009, can be obtained at [www.berr.gov.uk/consultations].

INTRASTAT—CHANGES FROM 1 JANUARY 2010

17 November 2009. *HMRC Brief 69/09*

This HMRC Brief announces changes to the Intrastat Exemption thresholds and details of other changes from 1 January 2010, including: all supplies of goods to British Embassies, Consulates and British armed forces bases situated in other Member States are excluded from Intrastat reporting (with the exception of the UK Sovereign Base Areas in Cyprus); emergency aid for disaster areas is no longer excluded from Intrastat reporting; and sales of new means of transport by VAT–registered businesses to private individuals in other Member States are no longer excluded from Intrastat reporting.

This Revenue and Customs Brief explains how businesses trading with other EU Member States could be affected by changes from 1 January 2010.

Changes in Intrastat thresholds from 1 January 2010

– The exemption threshold for arrivals is increased from £270,000 to £600,000
– The exemption threshold for dispatches is reduced from £270,000 to £250,000

Background

Community legislation requires the UK to collect information on intra–EU trade in goods for statistical purposes and sets minimum requirements for the quantity of trade covered.

Council Regulation (EC) No 638/2004 (The Intrastat Basic Regulation) requires EU Member States to collect data on a minimum percentage of the total value of their EU trade in goods. This regulation has been amended by Council Regulation (EC) No 222/2009. Please note that the minimum requirement for Member States to collect for their arrivals (intra–EU imports) has been reduced from 97 to 95%. The requirement for their dispatches (intra–EU Exports) remains at 97%.

These requirements determine the level at which the exemption thresholds, which are applied independently to arrivals and dispatches, are set in the UK. Those traders with an annual intra–EU trade in goods above the specified exemption thresholds are required to provide monthly statistical returns (Intrastat Supplementary declarations).

The threshold for arrivals has been increased to £600,000 as a result of the reduction in the coverage requirement to 95%. The threshold for dispatches has been reduced to £250,000 due to the current economic downturn and the consequent reduction in the number of UK businesses trading within the EU.

The revised thresholds ensure that the UK obtains the percentage coverage of the value of intra–EU trade required by Community legislation whilst at the same time ensuring that the number of businesses which are required to submit monthly information is kept to a minimum. The revised thresholds will be implemented by a Statutory Instrument. This instrument is being laid before Parliament in the coming weeks and, subject to Parliament having no objections to it, will come into force on 1 January 2010.

An Impact Assessment of the Simplification of Intrastat can be found at: Intrastat–simplification (www.hmrc.gov.uk/ria/091026–intrastat–simplification.pdf).

Other changes for 2010

The Intrastat Basic Regulation is implemented by Commission Regulation (EC) No 1982/2004. This regulation has been amended by two Commission Regulations to be published shortly in the official Journal.

The changes will be applied in the UK from 1 January 2010. As a result of this some of the reporting requirements have changed as follows:

- all supplies of goods to British Embassies, Consulates (whether or not benefiting from diplomatic immunity) and British armed forces bases situated in other Member States are excluded from Intrastat reporting (with the exception of the UK Sovereign Base Areas in Cyprus, which must continue to be reported with the partner country CY);
- emergency aid for disaster areas is no longer excluded from Intrastat reporting;
- sales of new means of transport by VAT–registered businesses to private individuals in other Member States are no longer excluded from Intrastat reporting; and
- the reporting Member State (for sales and purchases of vessels and aircraft, goods delivered to them and products of the sea) is determined according to where the entity that has "economic ownership" of the vessel or aircraft is established.

Information regarding these changes will be published on UK Trade info and in Notice 60 Intrastat General Guide. Where appropriate, the Trade Statistics unit will contact businesses affected by the changes to ensure that they are aware of the new requirement and will work with them to enable them to meet their obligations.

Further information

Further information on trade statistics can be found online at UK Trade info (www.uktradeinfo.com/index.cfm?&hasFlashPlayer=true) or by phoning UK Trade info Customer Services on 01702 367485.

ELECTRONIC LOTTERY TERMINALS

19 November 2009. *HMRC Brief 70/09*

This brief outlines HMRC policy in relation to the amusement machines known as "electronic lottery terminals" and their liability to VAT and Amusement Machine Licence Duty.

This Revenue & Customs Brief outlines HM Revenue & Customs (HMRC) policy in relation to amusement machines known as "electronic lottery terminals" and their liability to VAT and Amusement Machine Licence Duty (AMLD).

Background

HMRC is aware that certain gaming machines are being marketed as "electronic lottery terminals". The manufacturers argue that the product constitutes a lottery that is exempt from VAT and lottery duty, and outside the scope of AMLD. HMRC does not accept this as these "electronic lottery terminals" are completely different from the lottery ticket dispensers or vending machines typically found in members' clubs.

Guidance

Certain machines being marketed as "electronic lottery terminals" are gaming machines as they fall within the definitions of a gaming machine set out in section 23 of the VAT Act 1994 and s 25 of the Betting and Gaming Duties Act 1981.

Implications

Gaming machine income is standard–rated for VAT purposes, and depending on stake and prize limits, gaming machines are liable to AMLD.

What you need to do

You must account for VAT on any income you receive from an "electronic lottery terminal" and if you provide an "electronic lottery terminal" on any premises you must hold a valid AMLD licence before you make the machine available for play unless the machine falls within any of the exemptions.

If you have been operating an "electronic lottery terminal" that is liable for AMLD but have not obtained a licence, you should take action as follows:

- apply for a licence to cover future provision of the gaming machine for play
- include a voluntary declaration that you have provided a gaming machine for play without holding a valid licence for a specified period

You should do this by submitting a licence application form to HMRC Banking, St Mungo's Road, Cumbernauld, Glasgow, G70 5WY with a letter stating the period for which you have not held a valid licence. If you make a voluntary declaration you will avoid a penalty being imposed for the period when you did not hold a valid licence and we may issue you with a default licence and assessment for the unpaid duty. The Amusement Machine Licence Application can be downloaded from the HMRC website www.hmrc.gov.uk.

If you have not accounted for VAT correctly on your takings

You can correct underdeclarations of output tax by adjusting your current VAT return providing:

- the net value of errors found on previous returns does not exceed £10,000, or
- the net value of errors found on previous returns is between £10,000 and £50,000 but does not exceed one% of the box 6 (net outputs) VAT Return declaration due for the return period in which the errors are discovered.

You can find where to send your claim in VAT Notice 700/45 – How to correct VAT errors and make adjustments or claims.

If you are unsure whether your "electronic lottery terminal" is a gaming machine you should consult the HMRC Helpline on 0845 010 9000 with full details of the game before making the machine available for play.

If you do not agree that your "electronic lottery terminal" is a gaming machine and you take out an AMLD licence for the machine you will not be able to appeal. So if you do not agree that your "electronic lottery terminal" is a gaming machine you should contact HMRC on the Helpline on 0845 010 9000 with full details of the game. If HMRC think that your "electronic lottery terminal" is a licensable machine they will issue you with a default licence and assess for the outstanding duty and VAT. You will then be able to challenge the decision and ask for your appeal to be heard by an independent tribunal.

Further information

HMRC provides guidance in the following Notices which can be viewed on www.hmrc.gov.uk under "Quick Links" click on "library" then on publications and then on "Notices, Information Sheets and other reference materials.

- Notice 454 (October 2007) to help businesses decide whether their amusement machine is liable to Amusement Machine Licence Duty. Exemptions are covered in section 10.
- Notice 701/13 (June 2004) to explain how VAT applies to amusement and gaming machines.
- Notice 700/45 to explain how to correct VAT errors and make adjustments or claims.

CHANGES TO THE TOUR OPERATORS' MARGIN SCHEME—TRANSITIONAL PROVISIONS

4 December 2009. *HMRC Brief 74/09*

Revenue & Customs Brief 27/09 outlined changes to the Tour Operators' Margin Scheme (TOMS) which will take effect from 1 January 2010. This Revenue & Customs Brief sets out transitional arrangements in relation to supplies that straddle this date. These are necessary because the TOMS has its own rules with regard to the time of supply, deductibility of input tax and calculation of output tax due.

BACKGROUND

The TOMS is a mandatory scheme which applies to supplies made "for the direct benefit of the traveller", that is, the end customer. However, the UK has permitted businesses to opt out of the TOMS for supplies made to business customers for their own consumption, for example, business travel for employees, thus allowing business customers to recover input tax on such supplies. The UK has also allowed businesses to include within the TOMS, supplies made to other tour operators for onward resale, that is, supplies that are not being made for the direct benefit of the traveller. As announced in Revenue & Customs Brief 27/09, both of these arrangements are being withdrawn with effect from 1 January 2010. The transitional arrangements outlined in this Brief are designed to ensure that VAT is correctly accounted for on supplies that straddle this date.

TOMS TIME OF SUPPLY RULES

The TOMS has its own time of supply rules, which differ from the normal rules. These are set out at paragraph 4.14 and 4.15 of Public Notice 709/5. The operator must choose one of two methods to work out the tax point for margin scheme supplies and any in-house supplies sold within a margin scheme package. Method 1 uses the date of departure of the traveller or the first date on which the traveller occupies any accommodation, whichever happens first. Method 2 uses the date of receipt of payment of a certain size and a tax point is created when a payment is received which exceeds 20% of the selling price. A tax point is also created each time the payments received to date which have not already been accounted for exceed 20%, when added together.

INPUT TAX AND OUTPUT TAX

Under the TOMS, tour operators cannot recover any UK or EC VAT charged on the travel services bought in and resold – the suppliers of such goods and services account for tax on them in their own Member States. In turn, they account for VAT only on the margin achieved on their supplies under the TOMS, and not the full selling price.

EFFECT OF REMOVAL OF OPT-IN

Removal of the opt-in and application of the normal rules mean that, where tour operators have not previously recovered VAT on goods and services supplied to them for the direct benefit of the traveller, they may recover that VAT from 1 January 2010 for supplies being made after this date. Equally, from 1 January 2010 they should account for output tax on supplies made after this date on the full value of the supply (including payments received prior to 1 January 2010) in accordance with the normal time of supply rules. A VAT invoice must also be issued to customers. However, the customers, being themselves tour operators, will only be able to recover VAT if they are in turn supplying the travel services to another business for resale. If tour operators use the date of receipt of payments exceeding 20% of the selling price as their tax point (and have accounted for output tax at that time), they should also issue a belated VAT invoice in respect of those payments.

EFFECT OF REMOVAL OF OPT-OUT

Removal of the opt-out means that the TOMS rules must apply to supplies of designated travel services made after 1 January 2010. As the normal rules apply before that date, tour operators may recover VAT on supplies of goods or services received before 1 January 2010 for supplies being made for the direct benefit of the traveller after that date. The secondary legislation withdrawing the opt-out provides that the value of those supplies on which input tax is recovered cannot be included in the calculation of the margin for supplies being accounted for under the TOMS. Equally, tour operators using the opt-out should account for VAT under the normal rules where they issue a VAT invoice or receive a payment before 1 January 2010 for supplies of travel services being made by them to another taxable person. This means that the selling price which feeds into box 2 of the provisional calculation and box 1 of the annual calculation should reflect only the balance of the price payable on or after January 2010.

Commentary—*De Voil Indirect Tax Service* **V3.596**.

VAT AND BINGO DUTY—UPDATE ON IMPLICATIONS OF RANK LITIGATION IN RESPECT OF BINGO

10 December 2009. *HMRC Brief 75/09*

Revenue and Customs Comrs v The Rank Group [2009] All ER (D) 65 (Jun)

ABSTRACT

This HMRC Brief announces that, following the High Court decision in the case of Rank, HMRC now accepts that the judgment applies more widely to other forms of bingo played under the same sections of the Gaming Act as mechanised cash bingo.

Revenue & Customs Brief 40/09 was issued on 8 June 2009 following the High Court decision in the case of *Rank* ([2009] All ER (D) 65 (Jun)). This confirmed that participation fees for playing mechanised cash bingo (MCB) should have been exempt from VAT following the High Court's decision that there had been a breach of fiscal neutrality in the VAT treatment of this type of bingo.

Businesses were therefore invited to submit claims to HMRC for repayment of any VAT accounted for in respect of MCB and these are being dealt with. Revenue & Customs Brief 55/09 explained the effect these claims would have on businesses' liability to bingo duty.

Since then HMRC has received representations that the High Court judgment applies more widely to other forms of bingo played under the same sections of the Gaming Act as MCB. Having considered this carefully, HMRC accepts that the judgment has a wider application to other forms of bingo participation games. Claims for VAT accounted for on participation fees for other types of bingo, in addition to MCB, will now be considered, subject to the guidelines below. This means that the advice about bingo duty in Brief 55/09 now applies in relation to all bingo participation fees.

However, the Rank litigation continues, with the Court of Appeal due to hear HMRC's appeal in April 2010. If HMRC is successful either then or at a future date in a higher court, then any repayments made to businesses as a result of the High Court decision will need to be repaid, including interest.

Businesses may therefore prefer to wait until the final outcome of the litigation is known although protective claims can be lodged.

BACKGROUND

Rank, which operates Mecca bingo halls, claimed there had been inconsistencies in the way VAT had been applied to the participation fees customers paid to play MCB.

Last year the VAT Tribunal ruled there had been a breach of fiscal neutrality as some participation fees were taxed while others were exempt. Fiscal neutrality means that similar supplies must be treated the same for tax purposes to avoid any distortion of competition. The High Court agreed with the Tribunal's decision that all participation fees for MCB should have been exempt from VAT.

MAKING CLAIMS OR ADJUSTMENTS

Where a business wishes to make a claim to HMRC for output tax wrongly accounted for in respect of bingo participation fees, they may do so, although evidence must be produced that output tax was accounted for, to substantiate the amount claimed.

All claims are limited by section 80(4) of the VAT Act 1994 to four years. Until 1 April 2010, claims may be made going back to the accounting period ending on 30 April 2006. Claims for non-standard tax periods ending on or after 1 April 2006 are also in time.

CORRECTING THE ERROR ON YOUR VAT RETURN

Over-declarations of output tax can also be corrected by adjusting the current VAT return if the net amount of all errors in the accounting periods being corrected is:

- £10,000 or less, or
- less than £50,000 and less than 1% of the box 6 figure on the VAT return in which the adjustment is being effected.

These de minimis levels apply to the entire "claim". Thus if your "claim" is for 10 accounting periods, it is the net over-declaration for all 10 periods that must be within these levels. Under regulation 34(1A) of the VAT Regulations 1995 (as amended), all adjustments must be made within four years after the end of the accounting period in which the over-declaration was made. Until 1 April 2010, adjustments may be made going back to the accounting period ending on 30 April 2006. Adjustments for non-standard tax periods ending on or after 1 April 2006 are also in time.

CORRECTING THE ERROR ON YOUR BINGO DUTY RETURN

As explained in Revenue & Customs Brief 55/09 the High Court ruling that participation fees are exempt from VAT will mean that there has been an under-declaration of bingo duty. All businesses making bingo duty returns are required to include any under-declaration of duty made on previous returns (box 7 of the return, form BD510 refers). If you do not account for any under-declarations, HMRC will assess for the bingo duty due and you may become liable to penalties.

Where HMRC has already assessed for the undeclared duty, businesses need not make these adjustments. Revenue & Customs Brief 55/09 advised that we would not enforce any bingo duty assessments related to participation fees for bingo other than MCB. These assessments will now be enforced.

FURTHER INFORMATION

Details of where to send your claim can be obtained from update 2 to VAT Notice 700/45 "How to correct VAT errors and make adjustments or claims" from the HM Revenue & Customs Helpline on 0845 010 9000.

HMRC may reject all or part of a claim if repayment would unjustly enrich the claimant. More details on "unjust enrichment" can be found at part 14 of VAT Notice 700/45 "How to correct VAT errors and make adjustments or claims".

There may be direct tax implications where amounts of over-declared output tax are repaid to businesses and your attention is drawn to HMRC Brief 14/09 issued previously.

Where you are in any doubt about the correct treatment please contact the Helpline on Tel 0845 010 9000.

LENNARTZ ACCOUNTING–NEW POLICY FOLLOWING ECJ CASE

22 January 2010. *HMRC Brief 2/10*

INTRODUCTION

Last year, the ECJ in the case of *Vereniging Noordelijke Land-en Tuinbouw Organisatie v Staatssecretaris van Financien* (C-515/07) ([2009] STC 935) – VNLTO – considered whether or not *Lennartz* ([1995] STC 514) accounting can be used by a taxpayer who engages in activities that are not within the scope of VAT. As a result of this judgment, it is now clear that EU VAT legislation does not give, and has never given, a right to use Lennartz accounting in circumstances such as those of the VNLTO case.

WHO SHOULD READ THIS?

This Brief brings UK VAT policy in line with this judgment and should be read by anyone currently using, or intending to use, Lennartz accounting. It means that Lennartz accounting will only be available in the specific, limited circumstances set out below. HMRC's policy on Lennartz accounting as set out in Information Sheet 14/07 now has only limited application and should be read in conjunction with this Brief.

BACKGROUND

Guidance in Information Sheet 14/07 states that, where a taxable person incurs VAT on the cost of goods intended solely for business purposes, there is an entitlement to deduct the input tax incurred to the extent that it is used for making taxable supplies (or other supplies carrying a right to input tax deduction under section 26 of the VAT Act 1994). See paragraph 2.4 of Information Sheet 14/07 for the types of goods this policy applies to. If goods are used for both business and private/non-business purposes, there is a choice about how to treat them for VAT purposes, which must be made at the time they are acquired, namely:

– as a wholly non-business or private asset, in which case the VAT is not deductible;
– as a part business, part non-business asset, in which case the VAT incurred is only deductible to the extent that it relates to the taxable business activities (section 24(5) of the VAT Act 1994); or

- as a wholly business asset (the "Lennartz" approach) in which case the VAT incurred is treated as input tax and is deductible in full, subject to any partial exemption restriction; however, output tax must then be declared in so far as the goods are used for private/non-business purposes.

Lennartz accounting is not therefore available in cases where goods (including services used to create goods) are used wholly for business purposes.

ECJ DECISION

The case before the ECJ concerned an association - VNLTO - that promotes the interests of the agricultural sector. Its members, who are traders in that sector, pay a membership subscription to it, the greater part of which goes towards activities designed to promote their general interests. In addition to promoting those interests, VNLTO provides a number of individual services to its members for which it charges a fee.

Even though the activities of promoting members' interests are not subject to VAT, the ECJ held that this did not mean they were non-business activities. The ECJ stated that "business" in the context of Lennartz accounting extends beyond economic activities giving rise to supplies within the scope of VAT. It also includes use for any activity that forms part of the wider purpose of the taxable person's undertaking or enterprise, even those activities that are not economic activities (such as those outside the scope of VAT), and that are not normally regarded as "business" for UK VAT purposes.

IMPLICATIONS

From 22 January 2010, Lennartz accounting will only be available where:

(a) the goods are used in part for making supplies in the course of an economic activity that give a right to input VAT deduction (broadly, taxable supplies, supplies that would be taxable if made in the UK, or certain financial and insurance supplies to non-EC customers); and

(b) they are also used in part for the private purposes of the trader or his staff, or, exceptionally, for other uses which are wholly outside the purposes of the taxpayer's enterprise or undertaking.

From that date, where Lennartz accounting is not available, and goods are used (or to be used) for both economic activities and non-economic business activities, subject to the transitional provisions outlined below, the VAT incurred must be apportioned between these different activities on the basis of use (or intended use). The VAT attributed to the economic activities is input tax and is recoverable to the extent that the economic activities give rise to supplies with a right to input VAT deduction. The VAT attributed to the non-economic business activities is not input tax and cannot be recovered.

TAXPAYERS WITH ASSETS SUBJECT TO EXISTING LENNARTZ ACCOUNTING ARRANGEMENTS

Taxpayers for whom Lennartz accounting has, strictly speaking, never been available would normally be expected to unravel the mechanism and adjust both any input tax claimed and any output tax accounted for accordingly.

However, HMRC is committed to easing the administrative and financial burden on taxpayers who have already embarked on, and continue to operate, Lennartz accounting under HMRC's old policy.

Consequently, where a taxpayer has applied Lennartz accounting on the basis of HMRC's pre-VNLTO understanding of the law, the taxpayer may opt to continue using Lennartz accounting in respect of the assets concerned.

Taxpayers exercising this option must honour the full, ongoing commitment to account for output tax imposed under Lennartz accounting and HMRC will take action if a taxpayer fails to do so.

Those taxpayers who do not exercise this option must unravel the Lennartz accounting mechanism by adjusting both their output tax and corresponding input tax. They should write to their Client Relationship Manager within HMRC or the HMRC Written Enquiries Section at Alexander House, Victoria Avenue, Southend. SS99 1BD to discuss and agree a fair way of doing so. HMRC will not accept one-sided claims for repayment of the output tax only.

TAXPAYERS WHO HAVE COMMITTED TO PROJECTS ANTICIPATING THE AVAILABILITY OF LENNARTZ ACCOUNTING

Taxpayers who are not permitted to use Lennartz accounting must apportion VAT incurred for both economic and non-economic activities on the basis of use and intended use from the date of this announcement.

However, HMRC will consider claims from taxpayers who have already entered into binding commitments for projects on the understanding that Lennartz accounting will be available. Taxpayers should contact HMRC at the addresses above.

FLEMING CLAIMS

Some taxpayers (following the House of Lords' judgments in the cases of *Fleming and Condé Nast* [2008] All ER (D) 151 (Jan)) have submitted "Fleming" claims for Lennartz treatment for assets where VAT was incurred in accounting periods ending before 1 May 1997. No decisions on these claims were taken pending the issuing of this announcement. These claims will now be reviewed and, where appropriate, rejected if the taxpayer had not taken up the option to use Lennartz accounting at the time the input tax was incurred (where this was available) and/or where the VNLTO decision means that the claimants were not entitled to use Lennartz accounting as there was no EU law right to do so.

FURTHER INFORMATION

For further information please contact the Helpline on 0845 010 9000.

Commentary—*De Voil Indirect Tax Service* **V3.407**.

PARTIAL EXEMPTION – CHANGES TO THE DE MINIMIS RULES

8 March 2010. *HMRC Brief 10/10*

This Revenue & Customs Brief announces two changes to simplify the partial exemption *de minimis* rules that take effect from 1 April 2010:

– simplified tests
– annual test

The *de minimis* limit remains the same but the changes make it easier and less time-consuming for businesses to confirm their *de minimis* status.

The changes are being made following a consultation on ideas to simplify the partial exemption rules, which confirmed strong support for their implementation. They are optional and businesses can benefit from them without seeking approval from HM Revenue & Customs (HMRC).

Further information

Further information can be found in VAT Information Sheet 4/10 which supersedes or complements existing guidance as appropriate. Legislation will shortly be published on the HMRC website.

VAT STATUS OF UNIVERSITY TRADING SUBSIDIARY COMPANIES

12 March 2010 *HMRC Brief 9/10*

This Revenue & Customs Brief announces our revised policy with regard to the supply of education by a university subsidiary trading company. VAT Information Sheet 3/10 provides further detail.

SUMMARY

Following developments in VAT case law and in methods by which education is delivered by universities, we have reviewed our policy on the treatment of supplies of education delivered by companies that are owned or controlled by a university. This review has identified a need for a change in policy, and as a result the VAT liability of supplies of education will change in certain circumstances. The new policy applies to supplies made on or after the date of this Brief subject to transitional arrangements (see below).

WHO SHOULD READ THIS?

This Brief should be read by any university owned company that delivers education and any university owning such a company.

BACKGROUND

Supplies of education are exempt from VAT when provided by a UK university and any college, institution, school or hall of a university. (Note (1)(b), Group 6, Schedule 9, VAT Act 1994). Following the review, we have concluded that, in many cases where a university trading company provides education, they are acting as a 'college, institution, school or hall of a university.' As a consequence it is an 'eligible body' for the purposes of Group 6 Schedule 9 VATA 1994. This means that any education or training provided by the university subsidiary trading company is an exempt supply of education. Please see VAT Information Sheet 03/10 for further detail.

IMPLICATIONS

This policy change is limited to those companies that:

- are owned/controlled by a university;
- provide university level education leading to a qualification awarded by a university or a nationally recognised body;
- have close academic links with their parent university; for example, where students on the company's courses are registered/enrolled with the parent university, subject to its rules and regulations and awarded qualifications by it.

Please see VAT Information Sheet 3/10 for further detail.

Once a university subsidiary company is regarded as an eligible body within Note (1)(b):

(a) All supplies of education and vocational training provided by that company are exempt from VAT.

(b) Any supplies which fall within Group 6 of Schedule 9 VATA 94 should be treated as an exempt supply. (For example supplies of goods which are closely related to the supply of education under item 4.)

Other supplies, in particular consultancy services, provided by a subsidiary company of a university remain subject to VAT at the standard rate.

TRANSITIONAL ARRANGEMENTS

The policy change comes into effect formally from the date of this Brief. An affected company may also apply it with retrospective effect and make the relevant adjustments to its VAT accounting, subject to the statutory time limits.

However we recognise that many university companies have budgeted on the basis that their supplies would be taxed. Therefore, as a transitional measure, affected companies may continue to apply the old policy (that is taxation at the standard rate) to supplies, which are to be delivered before 1 August 2010.

If a tax point is created for courses (including closely related supplies) to be delivered both before and after 1 August 2010, only that part of the supply which comprises courses which are delivered before 1 August 2010 may be subjected to the previous policy that is taxed.

This transitional measure will not apply if used for tax avoidance purposes, including any attempts to forestall the impact of the policy change. In addition, any pre-invoicing and/or prepayments which have been made in anticipation of the issue of this Brief and which do not comprise the normal commercial practice of the company that is the company is attempting to create a tax point in anticipation of this formal announcement of the policy change will be considered to be tax avoidance and we will apply the policy change to any supplies covered by such pre-invoicing and/or prepayments delivered after 1 August 2010.

CAPITAL GOODS SCHEME

VAT Information Sheet 3/10 gives guidance on what, if any, impact this change of policy will have on capital items used by university owned or controlled companies in delivering university education.

FURTHER INFORMATION

For further information please contact: Dave O'Neil on 0191 4198971.

Commentary—*De Voil Indirect Tax Service* **V3.460, V3.465**.

LAND AND BUILDINGS: CHANGES TO THE OPERATION OF THE OPTION TO TAX AND UPDATED DEFINITIONS OF HOUSING ASSOCIATIONS

15 March 2010 *HMRC Brief 8/10*

This Revenue and Customs Brief announces three changes to Schedule 10 of the VAT Act 1994 which deals with the liability of supplies of land and buildings and one change to Group 5 to Schedule 8 of the VAT Act 1994 which deals with the zero-rate for construction services. These changes are:

– simplification of the operation of the option to tax,
– simplification of the 6 month "cooling-off" period to revoke an option to tax,
– and changes to the definition of a housing association.

These amendments all come into effect on 1 April 2010.

BACKGROUND

Schedule 10 to the VAT Act 1994 deals primarily with the option to tax on supplies of land and buildings. Following a series of amendments to block aggressive tax avoidance schemes, this legislation had become increasingly complex and was identified by business as a key area for simplification. Following consultation with business a re-written version of Schedule 10, in Tax Law Re-write style, was introduced on 1 June 2008. The revised version is easier to follow and employs a more logical layout and simplified language.

SIMPLIFICATION ARISING FROM THE OPERATION OF THE OPTION TO TAX

Following the introduction of the new Schedule 10, HMRC has continued to discuss with business ways in which the legislation could be further improved and simplified. In the course of our discussions additional concerns were also identified relating to certain aspects of the option to tax rules. As a result, a small number of minor amendments are being made which are intended to both simplify the legislation and facilitate business needs. A further change is also necessary as a result of the Housing and Regeneration Act 2008 and the redefining of the term "relevant housing association".

In making the changes set out below it was necessary to balance the business need for flexibility with the requirement that revenue should be protected.

The changes that have been made are as follows:

– occupation of minor parts of buildings (no more than 10 per cent of the total area) by persons that have provided finance for developments is now disregarded for the purposes of the option to tax anti-avoidance provision. A new sub-paragraph 15(3A) has been introduced into Schedule 10 and new tertiary legislation introduced, (see VAT Information Sheet 2/10: Annex A).
– the conditions for revoking an option to tax during the "cooling-off" period have been amended. The requirement that land must not have been used has been removed (Schedule 10 paragraph 23(1)(*b*)). The additional conditions set down in tertiary legislation have also been amended, (see VAT Information Sheet 2/10: Annex B).
– the definition of "relevant housing association" has been amended in Schedule 10 paragraph 10(3). The term "registered social landlord" will be replaced from 1 April for England only with "private provider of social housing" as defined by the Housing and Regeneration Act 2008. This consequential change ensures English housing associations continue to enjoy the same VAT reliefs as they do at present in common with housing

associations in the rest of the UK. A similar change is also being made in Group 5 to Schedule 8 of the VAT Act 1994 where we are also taking the opportunity to update the reference for Scotland as well.

More detailed explanations and amended tertiary legislation relating to the first two bullet points above are contained in VAT Information Sheet 2/10.

HOW WILL THE CHANGES BE EFFECTED?

All the changes to Schedule 10 and Group 5 to Schedule 8 are being made by separate Treasury Orders and will both be effective from 1 April 2010. The changes to tertiary legislation will also take effect from the same date.

A revised Public Notice 742A Opting to tax land and buildings will be issued in due course.

FURTHER INFORMATION

Further information can be obtained on our website www.hmrc.gov.uk or through the Helpline on Tel 0845 010 9000.

Information Sheet 2/10 provides guidance and further detail. It supersedes or complements existing guidance as appropriate. A revised Notice 742A "Opting to tax land and buildings" and new guidance will be available as soon as possible.

THE DECISION OF THE VAT TRIBUNAL IN RESPECT OF RANK (GAMING MACHINES) ISSUED DECEMBER 2009

16 March 2010 *HMRC Brief 11/10*

Revenue & Customs Brief 40/09 issued on 14 July 2009 advised of a High Court decision in the case of Rank, confirming there had been a breach of fiscal neutrality in the tax treatment of the supply of Mechanised Cash Bingo (MCB) and gaming machines.

In respect of gaming machines, as the judgment related to an appeal against an interim ruling of the VAT Tribunal, we advised that no claims for output tax wrongly accounted for would be considered until the Tribunal issued a final ruling in respect of Rank.

The First Tier Tribunal issued this in December 2009, finding that Fixed Odds Betting Terminals (FOBTs) were similar to, and in competition with, taxable gaming machines. We are appealing against this decision to the Upper Tribunal. Additionally, the Court of Appeal is due to hear the appeal against the earlier findings of both the VAT Tribunal and the High Court.

We intend, on the basis of the findings of both the VAT Tribunal and the High Court (and subject to the appeals), to consider those claims already received in respect of VAT paid on gaming machine takings.

BACKGROUND

Rank, which operates gaming machines, claimed there was inconsistency in the way VAT was applied to these, as compared with certain comparator machines and FOBTs which were exempt from VAT.

In 2008, the VAT Tribunal ruled there had been a breach of fiscal neutrality as a result of the difference in treatment. This ruling was upheld by the High Court last year although this itself is subject to a further appeal. The principle of fiscal neutrality requires similar supplies to be treated the same for tax purposes to avoid any distortion of competition.

The law was changed from 5 December 2005 and from that date the treatment of comparator machines, FOBTs and gaming machines has been the same (and subject to VAT).

IMPLICATIONS OF THIS JUDGMENT

As FOBTs came into commercial use in the United Kingdom in November 1998, this date agreed by the Tribunal, we will now consider existing claims submitted within required time limits for repayment of VAT paid on gaming machine takings for the period from 1 November 1998 to 5 December 2005.

Claims that have previously been rejected (for whatever reason) and which are not under appeal will not be considered. No new claims for the repayment of VAT paid for the period between 1 November 1998 and 5 December 2005 can be made.

The aim is to process all existing claims, where satisfactory evidence to support the claim has been provided, by 31 March 2011.

MAKING CLAIMS OR ADJUSTMENTS

Where a business has already made a claim to us for output tax wrongly accounted for in respect of gaming machines, this will be considered although further evidence may be requested.

All claims will be subject to the time limit in section 80(4) of the VAT Act 1994 – three years where the claim was made before 1 April 2009 or, where the claim was made on or after that date, four years or back to accounting periods ending on or after 1 April 2006 whichever is the shorter.

Protective assessments will also be issued under section 80(4A) of the VAT Act 1994 in order to allow us to recover any payments made should any appeals be successful.

There may be direct tax implications where amounts of over-declared output tax are repaid to businesses and your attention is drawn to Revenue & Customs Brief 14/09 issued previously.

FURTHER INFORMATION

We may reject all or part of a claim if repayment would unjustly enrich the claimant. More details on "unjust enrichment" can be found at part 14 of VAT Notice 700/45 "How to correct VAT errors and make adjustments or claims".

Where you are in any doubt about the correct treatment please contact the Helpline on 0845 010 9000.

Commentary—*De Voil Indirect Tax Service* **V4.131**.

PLACE OF SUPPLY OF FREIGHT TRANSPORT AND ASSOCIATED SERVICES: USED AND ENJOYED OUTSIDE THE EU

17 March 2010 *HMRC Brief 13/10*

This Revenue & Customs Brief announces a temporary administrative easement in relation to business to business (B2B) supplies of freight transport (or services closely associated with freight transport) which are physically performed wholly outside the EU.

WHO NEEDS TO READ THIS?

UK based businesses making or receiving supplies of freight transport (or services closely associated with freight transport) where the services are physically performed wholly outside the EU.

BACKGROUND

Until 1 January 2010, the place of supply of freight transport and associated services was the country where the activity physically took place, to the extent that it took place there. That meant that supplies physically performed outside the EU were outside the scope of VAT. Transportation related to imports to and exports from the EU could have a place of supply both within and outside the EU and, to the extent they were performed within the EU, the VAT liability was at zero rate.

From 1 January 2010, business to business (B2B) supplies of freight transport and associated services became subject to the new B2B general rule for place of supply of services — where the business customer belongs — regardless of the place of physical performance. This means that, where the customer is in the UK, the place of supply is the UK even if the supply physically takes place wholly outside the EU. As zero rating only applies to supplies in connection with EU imports and exports, the liability of supplies wholly outside the EU is standard-rated. That means that either the UK-based customer must perform a reverse charge for the supply (if the supplier is outside the UK) or the supplier needs to account for UK VAT on the supply.

HM REVENUE & CUSTOMS (HMRC) POLICY

We have become aware (via UK businesses and charities) that this change has had a real impact, either in terms of increasing administrative burdens (with no revenue impact for the UK) or, in some cases, resulting in a real VAT cost. We recognise that this change in law has produced an unintended anomaly in the treatment of supplies wholly enjoyed outside the EU, which may also be taxed locally in the place of performance.

With immediate effect, where a supply of freight transport (or services closely associated with freight transport) would be treated as supplied in the UK, it will not be treated as supplied in the UK if the use and enjoyment of the services is outside the EU. This administrative easement is being introduced as a temporary measure to allow time for consideration of a more permanent legislative solution.

PAST SUPPLIES AND CLAIMS

This treatment applies from 15 March 2010; it is not retrospective.

FURTHER INFORMATION

HMRC guidance will be updated to reflect this change.

If you have any further queries, please contact our VAT Helpline on Tel 0845 010 9000, or by email, or by writing to: HM Revenue & Customs National Advice Service, Written Enquiries Section, Alexander House, Victoria Avenue, Southend, Essex SS99 1BD

Commentary—*De Voil Indirect Tax Service* **V6.377**.

VAT PAYMENTS BY CHEQUE: IMPORTANT CHANGES WITH EFFECT FROM 1 APRIL 2010

17 March 2010 *HMRC Brief 14/10*

From 1 April 2010 all cheque payments sent by post will be treated as being received by HM Revenue & Customs on the date when cleared funds reach our bank account – not the date when we receive the cheque. This means that businesses must allow enough time for their payment to reach us and to clear into our bank account no later than the due date shown on their VAT return. A cheque takes three bank working days to clear – excluding Saturdays, Sundays, and bank holidays.

To allow for possible postal delays (for which we are not responsible) businesses should allow at least three working days for a cheque payment to reach us and a further three days for the payment to clear our bank account.

A business may be liable to a surcharge for late payment if a cheque payment does not clear by the due date shown on their VAT return.

This change does not affect any cheque payments made by Bank Giro. Payments by Bank Giro are treated as electronic which means that businesses will get up to an extra seven calendar days for the cleared payment to reach us (unless they use the Annual Accounting Scheme or are required to make Payments on Account).

THE REASON FOR THIS CHANGE

From 1 April 2010 businesses with an annual turnover of £100,000 or more (exclusive of VAT) and all newly registered businesses must file their VAT returns online and pay any VAT due electronically. The purpose of the change to the cheque clearance rules is to encourage compliance with the requirement to pay electronically by removing the cash flow advantage currently enjoyed by businesses paying by cheque. This change is also intended to make electronic methods of payment more attractive to those businesses who are not required to file their VAT returns online and pay electronically from 1 April.

We recommend that businesses make their VAT payments electronically as this is safe and secure and in, most cases, gives up to seven extra calendar days to pay or, if paying by Direct Debit, at least ten extra calendar days. This extra time does not apply to businesses if they use the Annual Accounting Scheme or are required to make Payments on Account. Please remember that if a VAT return is filed online then any VAT due must be paid electronically. To find out more about how to pay electronically use the link at the end of this Brief.

THE LEGAL BASIS FOR THE CHANGE

Section 58B of the VAT Act 1994 and section 95 of the Finance Act 2007 allow HMRC to make regulations to define when payments by cheque are regarded as made. The relevant regulation is regulation 5 of the Value Added Tax (Amendment) (No 4) Regulations 2009 which came into force on 1 December 2009 and applies to all cheque payments sent in the post to us on or after 1 April 2010.

FURTHER INFORMATION

For more information about paying VAT, payment deadlines and the full range of payment options go to "How to pay VAT" [on the HMRC website].

Commentary—*Simon's Taxes* **E4.11115**.

PROVISION OF HEALTH PROFESSIONALS, NURSING AUXILIARIES, CARE ASSISTANTS AND SUPPORT WORKERS BY EMPLOYMENT BUSINESSES: CLARIFICATION OF POLICY

18 March 2010 *HMRC Brief 12/10*

BACKGROUND

This brief aims to clarify our policy on the VAT treatment of supplies of health professionals, nursing auxiliaries, care assistants and support workers by employment businesses.

DEFINITIONS

The Employment Agencies Act 1973 defines an "employment business" as a "business (whether or not carried on with a view to profit and whether or not carried on in conjunction with any other business) of supplying persons in the employment of the person carrying on the business, to act for, and under the control of, other persons in any capacity". "Employment" is construed widely to include engagement on a contract of employment or a contract for services.

"Health professional" is an individual enrolled or registered on the appropriate statutory register including any and all of the following:

- Dentist or Dental Care Professional – an individual registered with the General Dental Council
- Doctor – an individual registered with the General Medical Council
- Nurse, midwife or community public health nurse – an individual registered with the Nursing & Midwifery Council
- Individuals registered by the Health Professions Council – including:
  - Arts Therapist
  - Biomedical Scientist
  - Chiropodist/Podiatrist
  - Clinical Scientist
  - Dietician
  - Occupational Therapist
  - Operating Department Practitioner
  - Orthoptist
  - Paramedic
  - Physiotherapist
  - Psychologist
  - Prosthetist/Orthotist
  - Radiographer
  - Speech & Language Therapist
- "Nursing auxiliary" – an individual who is not enrolled on any register of medical or health professionals but whose duties must include the provision of medical, as well as personal, care to patients.
- "Care assistant" is an individual who is not enrolled on any register of medical or health professionals but who provides both medical and personal care to the recipient.

- "Support worker" is an individual providing personal care and support services that may or may not be directly connected with the welfare of the recipient.
- "Medical care" – in the context of what is provided by nursing auxiliaries and care assistants, includes monitoring the health of patients, for example, by taking blood pressure and temperatures, as well as administering drugs to patients under the direct supervision of a health professional.
- "Personal care" – includes washing and dressing, feeding, helping people to mobilise, bed making, toileting etc., but does not include medical care.

EMPLOYMENT BUSINESSES IN THE HEALTH AND WELFARE SECTOR: BASIC VAT POSITION

Staff supplied by an employment business may be either employees of that business, or self-employed and engaged by an employment business. In both cases the workers' services are provided to the employment business, which in turn makes a supply of that worker to the client. If the worker comes under the direction and control of the client, this is a supply of staff. The employment business must therefore account for VAT when appropriate on the full charge to the client as in these circumstances it is acting as the "principal".

However, if the employment business maintains the direction and control of its staff to make a supply of welfare or medical services directly to the final consumer, we would see it as providing health or welfare services rather than merely a supply of staff. In these circumstances, subject to relevant criteria, we would see the business as making an exempt supply of welfare or health services – see Public Notices 701/2 "Welfare" and 701/57 "Health Professionals" and the section headed "Supplies of Contracted out Welfare Services" below.

SUPPLIES OF REGISTERED HEALTH PROFESSIONALS (OTHER THAN NURSES, MIDWIVES AND COMMUNITY PUBLIC HEALTH NURSES)

When an employment business supplies registered health professionals as a principal to a third party, where the health professional is working under the control and guidance of the third party, it is making a taxable supply of staff to that third party – not an exempt supply of healthcare or welfare services. It is the third party which is responsible for providing healthcare to the final patient, rather than the business supplying the staff which has no such responsibility.

A taxable supply of staff is made even where the employment business is responsible for ensuring that the workers it provides are properly trained and qualified when they work under the control of the third party.

SUPPLIES OF LOCUM GPS

Where an employment business supplies a locum GP to a practice, the employment business' only responsibility is to make a taxable supply of staff to the practice, not exempt healthcare to the final patient.

SUPPLIES OF NURSES, NURSING AUXILIARIES AND CARE ASSISTANTS BY STATE REGULATED AGENCIES

The nursing agencies' concession

By concession (HMRC regularly reviews these), nursing agencies (or employment businesses that provide nurses and midwives, as well as other health professionals) may exempt the supply of nursing staff and nursing auxiliaries supplied as a principal to a third party, if the supply is of:

- a person registered in the register of qualified nurses and midwives maintained under article 5 of the Nursing and Midwifery Order 2001
- an unregistered nursing auxiliary who is "directly supervised" by one of the above, or
- an unregistered nursing auxiliary, whose services are supplied to a hospital (NHS or private), hospice, care home with nursing under item 4 of Group 7, Schedule 9 VAT Act 1994 and form part of the care made to the patient.

The institution to which staff are supplied may be operated by a local authority, NHS body, charity or other organisation operating in the public or private sector.

To qualify for the concession, the employment business must be registered with one of the following organisations:

- Care Quality Commission (formerly known as the Commission for Social Care Inspection)
- Scottish Commission for the Regulation of Care
- Care Standards Inspectorate for Wales, or
- Northern Ireland Health and Personal Social Services Regulation and Improvement Authority.

For the supply of nursing auxiliaries or care assistants to benefit from the concession, they must undertake some direct form of medical care, such as administering drugs or taking blood pressures, for the final patient. The concession does not apply to supplies of general care assistants who are only involved in providing personal care such as catering, washing or dressing the patients or who are working in care homes without nursing where they do not require supervision by health professionals to provide their services.

However, where a state-regulated domiciliary care agency supplies the services of its care assistants directly to the final patient, we would see the agency as making an exempt supply of welfare services – see Public Notice 701/2 "Welfare" and the section headed "Supplies of contracted-out welfare services" below.

SUPPLIES OF CONTRACTED-OUT WELFARE SERVICES

As is clear from above, employment businesses in the welfare sector make a taxable supply of staff to third parties, such as local authorities, if the third party is legally responsible for the onward supply of providing care to the final recipient. This is subject to the nursing agencies' concession. The mere fact that an employment business is state-regulated does not mean that its supplies of staff are exempt if they are not covered by the nursing agencies concession.

However, when state-regulated welfare providers provide welfare services to the final consumer, these services remain exempt even if they are contracted and paid for by a local authority or other third party. For example, a local authority may contract out the provision of domiciliary care services for the elderly or disabled to a state-regulated domiciliary care agency. Although the local authority rather than the final consumer may pay the domiciliary care agency charities for the care services, for VAT purposes the care agency has still made an exempt supply of welfare services rather than staff to the local authority. This is because the care agency's staff will still be working directly to the agency itself throughout the provision of the services rather than to the local authority.

Exemption would also apply to cases where a local authority or other body subcontracts the provision of adult placement schemes. Under these schemes a "worker" provides personal care and/or support services to adults living with them or living in their own homes. Currently scheme providers need to be registered with the Care Quality Commission.

Sometimes local authorities make payments directly to people who have been assessed as needing help from social services, and who would like to arrange and pay for their own care and support services instead of receiving them directly from the local council. These arrangements are called direct payment schemes, and any welfare services provided to the recipient by a charity or state-regulated private institution or agency are again exempt from VAT.

THE WORDING OF TERMS AND CONDITIONS OF AGREEMENTS

We are aware that some employment businesses state in their contract terms that their staff are still working under their control and direction rather than the third party to which their staff are being supplied. If that is the case you are no longer acting as an "employment business" within the definition of the Employment Act 1976. You are reminded that the VAT liability of a supply is not determined conclusively by the terms of any contract or other documentation alone. If the wording of a contract does not reflect any changes in the way that the business actually operates in practice, the VAT liability of a taxable supply of staff will not change.

CORRECTING ERRORS

If businesses can demonstrate that they have taken reasonable steps to follow our previous guidance and that has resulted in their applying the wrong VAT treatment then we will take that into account when considering whether any corrective action is necessary.

FURTHER INFORMATION

Our public guidance will be updated in due course. If you are unsure of the correct VAT treatment of your supplies you should consult Notice 701/57 "Health professionals" and/or 700/34 "Staff".

You may also contact our Helpline on 0845 010 9000, by email, or by writing to: HM Revenue & Customs National Advice Service Written Enquiries Section Alexander House Victoria Avenue Southend Essex SS99 1BD.

Please include your VAT registration number and the name and address of your business in any correspondence.

Commentary—*De Voil Indirect Tax Service* **V4.146**.

Commentary—See also HMRC Brief 40/10, published 22-9-10 (consequential amendment to the nursing agency concession to allow VAT exemption of certain services provided by nursing agencies (the Nursing Agencies' Concession)).

CHANGES TO TIME LIMITS FOR ASSESSMENTS AND CLAIMS

19 March 2010 *HMRC Brief 16/10*

This Brief is a reminder of the new four-year time limit coming into effect on 1 April 2010 for direct taxes claims and assessments under self-assessment. This date also marks the convergence of the rules governing normal time limits for all the main direct and indirect taxes. For people outside self-assessment, the new time limits for repayment claims don't take effect until 1 April 2012.

INTRODUCTION

The compliance checks legislation introduced a new normal four year time limit for assessments and **claims**, from 1 April 2010, in schedule 39 of the Finance Act 2008.

Initially this affects:

– capital gains tax;
– corporation tax;
– income tax;
– PAYE;
– VAT.

Aligning these time limits where possible reduces compliance costs for customers and makes our compliance checks easier.

The new time limits come into effect on 1 April 2010 for direct taxes. The normal time limits for these taxes are decreasing from six years, or five years from the 31 January immediately following the tax year, to four years.

The new time limits came into effect on 1 April 2009 for VAT because the normal time limits for VAT are increasing from three to four years. There are transitional provisions for VAT. These provisions prevent out of time periods from coming back in time by disregarding a prescribed accounting period that ends on or before 31 March 2006. This means that by 1 April 2010 the four year time limit for VAT assessments will apply in full.

The new time limits apply to assessments and **claims** for the above taxes that are made after these dates regardless of the period the assessment or **claim** relates to.

REPAYMENT CLAIMS – SELF ASSESSMENT AND PAYE

. . .

CHANGES TO ASSESSMENT TIME LIMITS

–

[illegible] from 01 April 2010 for VAT assessments and **claims** are:

[illegible] – four years;

[illegible] years;

– Deliberate behaviour – 20 years;

from the end of the relevant tax period.

In particular, HMRC will no longer have 20 years to assess where a tax loss was attributable to negligent conduct which now equates to careless behaviour. However the 20 year time limit will still apply to cases of failure to notify, and certain failures in respect of tax avoidance schemes.

The new time limits do not affect:

– periods already out of date under the old time limits;
– the time limits for making enquiries into SA or CTSA returns;
– the time limits for making penalty determinations for direct tax;
– the time limits for assessing Class 1, 1A and 2 National Insurance Contributions; or
– the two-year rule and the evidence of facts rules for VAT assessments.

While the normal time limit for most assessments and determinations will be four years from the end of the relevant tax period, there are however many variations from this norm. The tables of time limits (www.hmrc.gov.uk/manuals/chmanual/ch56000.htm) in the appendices of the Compliance Handbook give a full summary.

For more information see the Compliance Handbook (www.hmrc.gov.uk/manuals/chmanual/ch50000.htm) chapter 50000.

Further indirect tax changes

For Indirect Tax the Finance Act 2009 schedule 51 introduced a new normal four-year time limit for assessments and **claims**, from 1 April 2010. This affects:

– Aggregates Levy
– Climate Change Levy
– Insurance Premium Tax
– Landfill Tax

The new limits from 1 April 2010 for the above taxes are:

– Normal time limit – four years
– Careless behaviour – four years
– Deliberate behaviour – 20 years

from the end of the relevant tax period.

The time limit for assessments and making **claims** was therefore increased with effect from 1 April 2010 from three years to four. However, in order to ensure that accounting periods that were out of time on 31 March 2010 are not brought back in time by the change, transitional arrangements have been put in place.

The technical guidance in the Compliance Handbook will be updated in due course to cover these further changes.

Commentary—*Simon's Taxes* **A6.708**.

CHANGES TO TREATMENT OF SPORTS-RELATED SERVICES FOLLOWING ECJ JUDGMENT IN CANTERBURY HOCKEY CLUB

29 March 2010 *HMRC Brief 15/10*

THE ISSUE

Changes to the VAT exemption for sports related services are being introduced from 1 September 2010. This will primarily affect affiliation fees charged by sports governing bo... to member clubs but the VAT treatment of other sports-related supplies may also be exempt ... not subject to

BACKGROUND

Certain services closely linked with and essential to sport or physic... when supplied by an eligible body (that is, essentially non-pr... commercial influence) to an individual taking part in sp...

In respect of affiliation fees charged by sports governing bodies to their member sports clubs, we have previously restricted the exemption to fees calculated on a per person basis (provided the services were closely linked to sport). Affiliation fees calculated by other methods, for example, on the basis of the club size or the number of teams fielded, were standard rated for VAT.

However, the ECJ in the case of *Canterbury Hockey Club and Canterbury Ladies' Hockey Club* (C-253/07) [2008] STC 3351 found that the exemption applies more widely. It has ruled that in the context of persons taking part in sport, the exemption includes services supplied to corporate persons and to unincorporated associations, provided that the supplies are closely linked and essential to sport, that they are supplied by non-profit making organisations and the true beneficiaries are individuals taking part in sport.

IMPLICATIONS

The ECJ ruling means that some supplies which were standard rated, for example because they were supplied to a corporate body or unincorporated association, may now be exempt from VAT if the services are closely linked and essential to sport and the true beneficiaries are individuals taking part in sport.

From 1 September 2010, eligible bodies meeting the conditions for exemption outlined in VAT Notice 701/45 "Sport" must exempt supplies where the true beneficiaries are persons taking part in sport, even if the supply is not made direct to an individual and irrespective of how the fee is calculated. Supplies made to commercial profit-making organisations do not meet the true beneficiary test and will not fall within the exemption for supplies of services closely linked and essential to sport.

Where the affiliation fee confers a number of benefits, which individually would be liable to different VAT treatment, the advice in section 4 of Notice 701/5 March 2002 will help determine whether there is a single or multiple supply. Where the conditions of Extra Statutory Concession 3.35 (apportionment of membership subscriptions to certain non-profit making bodies) are met governing bodies may continue to take advantage of the option to apportion their affiliation fees between the rates of VAT applicable to the individual elements.

The ECJ gave some examples of services that do not fall within the exemption, including advice about marketing and the obtaining of sponsors. These will be liable to the standard rate of VAT when ESC 3.35 is applied unless relief is available under another part of the VAT Act.

This policy change may also affect some other supplies closely linked and essential to sport by eligible bodies to corporate persons and unincorporated associations where the true beneficiary is a person taking part in sport. An example could be the letting of sports facilities to a club for the direct use of its members. In these circumstances, the supply is exempt if the club is non-profit making. Otherwise it will be taxable.

MAKING CLAIMS OR ADJUSTMENTS

The changes described above must be implemented from 1 September 2010 and there is no requirement to make adjustments in respect of supplies made prior to this date. However, any organisations wishing to implement the judgment before 1 September 2010 (and start exempting affected fees from an earlier date) are entitled to do so.

Where a business wishes to make a claim to us (under section 80 of the VAT Act 1994) for repayment of VAT incorrectly accounted for on sports related services, they may do so, subject to the conditions set out in Notice 700/45 "How to correct VAT errors and make adjustments or claims".

All claims will be subject to the four-year time limit in section 80(4) of the VAT Act 1994 and to the set-off provisions in section 81 of the VAT Act and section 130 of the Finance Act 2008.

There may be direct tax implications where amounts of over-declared output tax are repaid to businesses and your attention is drawn to Revenue & Customs Brief 14/10.

We may reject all or part of a claim if repayment would unjustly enrich the claimant. More details on making claims and "unjust enrichment" can be found in VAT Notice 700/45 "How to correct VAT errors and make adjustments or claims".

FURTHER INFORMATION

For further information and advice, please contact our Helpline on 0845 010 9000.

Commentary—*De Voil Indirect Tax Service* **V4.161**.

POSTAL SERVICES—CLAIMS FOR INPUT TAX

31 March 2010 *HMRC Brief 19/10*

INTRODUCTION

Following the European Court of Justice's (ECJ) decision in the case of TNT Post UK Ltd (see Revenue & Customs Brief 64/09), a number of businesses submitted claims (including "Fleming" claims) for a refund of VAT incurred on postal services purchased from Royal Mail. These have been held in abeyance by us pending discussions about the impact of the decision. These discussions have now been concluded and, as announced in Budget Note 48, certain services previously treated as exempt from VAT will become liable to VAT at the standard rate with effect from 31 January 2011. This brief is to advise that we will now begin considering these claims and the criteria which will be applied.

BACKGROUND

In essence, the ECJ confirmed that Royal Mail, as the operator providing the public postal service, is the only postal body in the UK eligible to exempt postal services from VAT. However, it further ruled that exemption applies to the public postal services (that is, Royal Mail), acting as such and does not apply to supplies where the terms have been individually negotiated. Accordingly, UK VAT law is being amended to bring it in line with the ECJ decision. The government intends to make the necessary legislative changes in a second Finance Bill 2010 to be introduced as soon as possible in the next Parliament.

SERVICES AFFECTED

In broad terms, the proposed changes will mean that any service which is individually negotiated or not subject to any price and regulatory control will become liable to VAT at the standard rate. This includes, but is not limited to:

- all individually negotiated services
- Parcelforce services
- door-to-door (unaddressed mail)
- mailroom services.

Services which Royal Mail is obligated to provide under, or pursuant to, the terms of its licence - and which are therefore subject to price and regulatory control – will remain exempt from VAT (subject to there being no individual negotiation). This means:

- services covered by Royal Mail's Universal Service Obligation (including stamped mail)
- regulated services
- access to its network for private postal operators

Detailed guidance on this can be found in our Technical Note issued on Budget Day.

HANDLING OF CLAIMS

To be valid, a claim must have included the information required, as set out in Notice 700/45 "How to correct VAT errors and make adjustments or claims". Claims that do not meet these basic criteria will be rejected.

Where a valid claim has been submitted, we will consider:

- the contractual arrangements between the claimant and Royal Mail over the period of the claim
- (in relation to "Fleming" claims only) developments in the postal market and related legislation over the period of the claim
- whether the supplies to which the claim relates would have been taxable at the standard rate under the new rules
- evidence that Input Tax has been incurred.

Unless they were made under the transitional provisions in section 121(2) of the Finance Act 2008 (Fleming claims), all claims will be subject to the four-year time limit in regulation 29(1A) of the VAT Regulations 1995.

FURTHER INFORMATION

For further information please contact the Helpline on Tel 0845 010 9000.

Commentary—*De Voil Indirect Tax Service* **V4.126**.

ZERO-RATING – CHANGES TO ZERO-RATE ON CARAVANS

15 April 2010 *HMRC Brief 20/10*

This Revenue & Customs Brief announces a change to the dimensions of caravan that will be eligible to be zero-rated.

EFFECT OF CHANGE

From 20 April 2010 the minimum width of caravan that will be eligible to be zero-rated will rise from 2.3 metres to 2.55 metres. The minimum length will remain unchanged at 7 metres.

All caravans less than 2.55 metres wide (and less than 7 metres long) will be subject to VAT at the standard rate – currently 17.5 per cent.

This change means that from 20 April 2010, the zero-rate will cease to apply to the sale of second hand caravans that are 2.55 metres wide or less and that were originally supplied zero-rated. HMRC are currently considering the VAT treatment of the sale of these second-hand caravans and will be issuing further guidance shortly.

BACKGROUND AND REASON FOR CHANGE

In essence, the ECJ confirmed that Royal Mail, as the operator providing the public postal service, is the only postal body in the UK eligible to exempt postal services from VAT. However, it further ruled that exemption applies to the public postal services (that is, Royal Mail), acting as such and does not apply to supplies where the terms have been individually negotiated. Accordingly, UK VAT law is being amended to bring it in line with the ECJ decision. The government intends to make the necessary legislative changes in a second Finance Bill 2010 to be introduced as soon as possible in the next Parliament.

SERVICES AFFECTED

The legislation for the zero-rate for caravans is contained in Group 9 of Schedule 8 to the VAT Act 1994 and is directly linked to Regulation 8 of the Road Vehicles (Construction and Use) Regulations 1986 which determines the maximum size of a trailer (including caravans) that may legally be towed by cars.

Following infraction proceedings by the European Commission, the UK now needs to permit the same width trailers (including caravans) to be towed by cars on the public highway as in other parts of Europe. The Department of Transport are therefore amending Regulation 8 of the Road Vehicles (Construction and Use) Regulations 1986 to increase the maximum trailer width from 2.3 metres to 2.55 metres with effect from 20 April 2010.

Since the zero rate for caravans is directly linked to the Road Vehicles (Construction and Use) Regulations 1986, any increase in the size of trailers (including. caravans) has an automatic corresponding impact on the zero rate for caravans. From 20 April 2010, any supply of a caravan with a width of less than 2.55 and with a length of less than 7 metres will be taxable at the standard rate (17.5 per cent).

An update to Public Notice 701/20 "Caravans and Houseboats" will be published in due course.

Further information may be obtained from the Helpline on 0800 010 9000.

Commentary—*De Voil Indirect Tax Service* **V4.275**.

TOUR OPERATORS' MARGIN SCHEME AND THE TREATMENT OF "HOTEL BILLBACK" TRANSACTIONS

25 May 2010 *HMRC Brief 21/10*

Following changes to the Tour Operators' Margin Scheme (TOMS) from 1 January 2010, this Revenue & Customs Brief sets out details of an agreement with representative bodies of the business travel sector about invoicing for supplies under the arrangement known as "hotel billback".

VAT PRs etc

TOMS is a special VAT accounting scheme applying to certain designated travel supplies such as accommodation and transport that are bought in and sold on by businesses. Under the scheme, businesses are unable to recover VAT charged on their purchases but account for VAT on their supplies only on their margin. This means that invoices for these supplies cannot show the VAT element, which becomes sticking tax to business customers.

Under the "hotel billback" arrangement, hotel booking agents book accommodation on behalf of their business client. The hotel issues a VAT invoice for the accommodation to the booking agents, who recover the VAT charged and then issue a VAT invoice to the business traveller, charging VAT on both the accommodation and their commission.

Without specific provisions in place, the VAT on such supplies should have been accounted for under the TOMS. Until the end of 2009, UK legislation provided for businesses making supplies of travel services to opt out of TOMS where the supplies were made to business customers for their own consumption, thus allowing the business customers to recover VAT on these supplies (subject to normal rules). However, with effect from 1 January 2010, a number of changes were introduced to the TOMS including withdrawal of the business to business opt out, to comply with EU law.

This means that hotel booking agents who receive invoices in their own name for hotel accommodation and recover the VAT charged must now account for VAT on their onward supplies under the TOMS and, in turn, their business customers will incur sticking tax.

However, it is entirely open to hotel booking agents to act in a disclosed capacity, with the hotels supplying accommodation direct to their business clients, rather than buy in and supply the accommodation themselves. Following separate approaches by the Hotel Booking Agents Association and the Guild of Travel Management Companies, we have agreed the arrangements detailed below where agents operate in this way. These arrangements are available generally to all business travel agents that wish to adopt them.

The agreed arrangements are:

- Invoices from hotels will be addressed c/o the hotel booking agent for payment. (This is to indicate that the invoice has been issued to the hotel booking agent in its capacity as an agent.)
- The booking field on the hotel invoice will identify the hotel guest, their employer and will ideally carry a unique reference number. (Until hotels can address their invoices directly to their business customers, it may be necessary for hotel booking agents to enter an employer identification number on the invoice.)
- The hotel booking agent will arrange for payment of the invoice(s) but will not recover the input tax thereon.
- The hotel booking agent will send the customer a payment request/statement of the expenditure incurred by the hotel booking agent on its behalf, separately identifying the value of its supplies, VAT, etc.
- The payment request/statement should say something along the lines of "The VAT shown is your input tax which can be reclaimed subject to the normal rules".
- The customer will use the payment request/statement as a basis for their input tax reclaim.
- The hotel booking agent will retain the original hotel invoices and these will be made available if evidence of entitlement is required by VAT staff.
- The hotel booking agent will send a VAT invoice for its own services, plus the VAT. This may be consolidated with the statement of hotel charges, or it can be a separate document.
- The hotel booking agent will charge its client the exact amount charged by the billback supplier, as a disbursement.

Commentary—*De Voil Indirect Tax Service* **V3.591, V6.262**.

PAY-PER-CLICK CHARITY ADVERTISEMENTS

7 June 2010 *HMRC Brief 25/10*

This Revenue & Customs Brief explains our revised policy on the VAT treatment of pay-per-click (PPC) charity advertising on sponsored links and other associated services.

BACKGROUND

PPC is used by organisations on search engines such as Google to encourage searchers to click on the organisation's link in priority to any other links on the results page following a search.

The organisation pays the search engine provider an agreed amount each time their website is accessed through the sponsored link. Supplies of advertisements for charities, when placed on a third party's website, and their design and production costs, attract the zero-rate of VAT under Schedule 8, Group 15, Item 8 and 8A–8C of VATA 1994. We have until now taken the view that a PPC-sponsored link is not an advertisement itself but simply a means of access to the charity's website. As such, we considered the costs of providing PPC were excluded from zero-rating by Note 10B to Group 15, Schedule 8 which excludes zero-rating on the costs of providing a charity's website. Following representations from charities that zero-rating should apply to PPC charity advertisements, we have reviewed our approach and concluded we should revise the VAT treatment of PPC advertising supplied to charities.

REVISED POLICY

We now accept that PPC-sponsored links appearing on search engine websites are advertisements for the purpose of Item 8 and 8A, and qualify for zero-rating when supplied to a charity. It follows that the supply of copyright and design services associated with such sponsored links fall within the zero-rating. However, we still maintain that services supplied by copywriters and designers for the purpose of search engine optimisation (structuring a website so that it contains as many keywords as possible) do not qualify for relief. We consider that these services entail the optimisation of the charity's own website, and so are specifically excluded from Item 8 by Note 10B to Group 15. The listing of a charity in the results of a search engine ("natural hits") does not constitute the promulgation of an advertisement for the purpose of Item 8 since the charity's name appears automatically, regardless of any action taken by or on behalf of a charity, and merely highlights text from the charity's own website.

MAKING CLAIMS OR ADJUSTMENTS

Businesses that have accounted for and paid VAT on supplies of charity advertisements that are now considered to be zero-rated may submit claims for overpaid tax. These will be subject to a transitional four year limitation period and "unjust enrichment" provisions. Guidance on how to make claims is contained in VAT Notice 700/45 "How to correct VAT errors or make adjustments or claims".

FURTHER INFORMATION

Detailed guidance on charity advertising can be found in VAT Notice 701/58 "Charity advertising and goods connected with collecting donations". If you are in any doubt about the correct treatment please contact the Charities Helpline on 0845 302 0203.

Commentary—*De Voil Indirect Tax Service* **V4.266**.

IMPLEMENTATION OF THE REVIEW OF HMRC POWERS AND RELATED WORK

8 June 2010 *HMRC Notice*

HMRC has published a summary of the legislation arising from its review of powers, deterrents and safeguards (penalties, compliance checks, time limits and interest) and the date these measures come into effect.

See also www.hmrc.gov.uk/about/powers-appeal.htm

Legislation:	Implementation date	Commencement Order
Penalties:		
ALIGNED AND MODERNISED PENALTIES FOR INCORRECT TAX RETURNS (IT, CGT, CT, VAT PAYE and NICs)		
Section 97 and Schedule 24 FA 2007	1 April 2008	SI 2008/568

Legislation:	Implementation date	Commencement Order
Penalties:		
ALIGNED PENALTIES FOR INCORRECT TAX RETURNS (OTHER TAXES: INSURANCE PREMIUM TAX, INHERITANCE TAX, STAMP DUTY LAND TAX, STAMP DUTY RESERVE TAX, PETROLEUM REVENUE TAX AND ENVIRONMENTAL TAXES: (AGGREGATES LEVY, CLIMATE CHANGE LEVY AND LANDFILL TAX).		
Section 122 and Schedule 40 FA 2008	1 April 2009	SI 2009/571
ALIGNED AND MODERNISED PENALTIES FOR FAILURE TO NOTIFY TAXABLE ACTIVITIES AND CERTAIN VAT AND EXCISE WRONGDOING.		
Section 123 and Schedule 41 FA 2008	1 April 2010	SI 2009/511
ALIGNMENT OF HMRC'S REGIMES FOR ENCOURAGING TIMELY FILING AND PAYMENT		
Section 106 and Schedule 55 FA 2009	anticipated: CIS: October 2011	
Section 107 and Schedule 56 FA 2009	anticipated: In-year PAYE/NIC: 6 April 2010	SI 2010/466: PAYE/IT SI 2010/721: PAYE/NIC
PUBLISHING DETAILS OF DELIBERATE TAX DEFAULTERS		
Section 94 FA 2009	1 April 2010	SI 2010/574
PENALTIES FOR OFFSHORE NON-COMPLIANCE		
Section 35 and Schedule 10 FA 2010	anticipated: 6 April 2011	
Compliance Checks:		
ALIGNED AND MODERNISED INFORMATION POWERS, RECORD KEEPING REQUIREMENTS AND TIME LIMITS FOR MAIN TAXES (IT, CT, CGT, VAT,PAYE)		
Section 113 and Schedule 36 FA 2008 (information & inspection powers),	1 April 2009	SI 2009/404
Section 114 FA 2008 (aligned computer records),	21 July 2008 (royal assent)	
Section 115 and Schedule 37 FA 2008 (record keeping),	1 April 2009	SI 2009/402
Section 118 and Schedule 39 FA 2008 (time limits).	1 April 2009	SI 2009/586 (VAT)
	1 April 2010	SI 2009/405
Section 119 FA 2008 (correction etc of tax returns)	1 April 2010	SI 2009/405
ALIGNED AND MODERNISED INFORMATION POWERS, RECORD KEEPING REQUIREMENTS AND TIME LIMITS (OTHER TAXES: INSURANCE PREMIUM TAX, INHERITANCE TAX, STAMP DUTY LAND TAX, STAMP DUTY RESERVE TAX, PETROLEUM REVENUE TAX AND ENVIRONMENTAL TAXES: (AGGREGATES LEVY, CLIMATE CHANGE LEVY AND LANDFILL TAX)		
Section 95 and Schedule 47 FA 2009 (amendments to information powers),	13 August 2009 (royal assent)	SI 2009/2035

Legislation:	Implementation date	Commencement Order
Penalties:		
Section 96 and Schedule 48 FA 2009 (mainly extension of inspection powers to other taxes),	1 April 2010	SI 2009/3054
Section 98 and Schedule 50 FA 2009 (record keeping, other taxes)	1 April 2010	SI 2010/815
Section 99 and Schedule 51 FA 2009 (time limits, other taxes).	Environmental taxes: 1 April 2010 & Other taxes: 1 April 2011	SI 2010/867
	Stamp duty reserve tax: 1 April 2011	SI 2010/664 (also amends SDRT inspection powers from 1 April 2010)
Secondary legislation:		
TIME LIMITS:		
- consequential changes to the 2002 Aggregates Levy Regulations	1 April 2010	SI 2010/642
- minor consequential changes to the 2001 Climate Change Levy Regulations	1 April 2010	SI 2010/643
Interest		
Harmonisation of interest rates	12 August 2009	SI 2009/2032
Introduce an aligned approach to charging and paying interest across HMRC's responsibilities		
Section 101 and Schedule 53	Not yet set	[See note following table]
Section 102 and Schedule 54 FA 2009.	Not yet set	[See note following table]

Note—The Finance Act 2009, Sections 101 to 103 (Appointed Day and Supplemental Provision) Order, SI 2010/1878 was made on 21 July 2010 and appoints 31 August 2010 as the day on which the interest regime contained in FA 2009 ss 101–103 comes into force for the purposes of bank payroll tax

Commentary—*Simon's Taxes* **Division A4.5**.

LIABILITY OF NON-COMPLIANCE CARBON CREDITS AND CARBON OFFSETTING SERVICES

16 June 2010 *HMRC Brief 28/10*

BACKGROUND

Revenue & Customs Brief 52/07 "Place of supply of trading allowances in greenhouse gas emissions" stated that further guidance would be issued on the VAT treatment of non-compliance carbon credits. This is covered in this Brief alongside the VAT treatment of carbon offsetting services. Revenue & Customs Brief 52/07 is no longer extant, having been superseded from May 2008 by guidance published in Notice 741 Place of Supply of Services (until December 2009) and since 1 January 2010 by the new Notice 741A Place of Supply of services.

SCOPE

This Brief covers the VAT treatment of supplies of carbon credits and services provided by carbon offset providers. For the purposes of this brief, "carbon offset providers" offer advice and/or the facility to reduce an individual's "carbon footprint".

CARBON CREDITS

Carbon credits fall into two categories:

- compliance market credits, which derive from the Kyoto Protocol and the EU Emissions Trading System ("EUETS");
- non-compliance credits, of which the most common example is the Verified Emission Reduction (VER).

The important distinction, for VAT purposes, between compliance market credits and VERs is that the former are capable of consumption of the type envisaged by the VAT system, and the latter are not. As VAT is a tax on consumption, this means that compliance market credits are subject to VAT, whilst VERs are outside the scope of VAT.

COMPLIANCE MARKET CREDITS

Compliance market credits are recognised under statutory "cap and trade" regimes. Polluting businesses which are subject to these regimes must hold, or obtain on the open market, and then "retire" sufficient emissions credits to cover their emissions. If they do not, then they will suffer financial penalties. The credits are consumed to enable businesses to engage in economic activity without penalty, and to meet their Kyoto commitments.

Kyoto and the EUETS provide for exacting verification and regulatory processes, which mean that both parties to a compliance market transaction are able to attribute a subjective value to the credit units. The credits are widely traded on national and international markets.

The motive of an individual paying for a credit does not matter, nor does it matter what is done with it. Thus if a private individual buys a compliance market credit, the supply of the credit to the individual is still taxable (even though the individual is not subject to any regime) because the credit is capable of consumption.

Examples of compliance market credits include Emission Reduction Units (ERUs), Certified Emission Reductions (CERs) and EU Allowances (EUAs).

VERIFIED EMISSION REDUCTIONS

A verified emission reduction (VER) is essentially a promise that carbon has been or may be reduced somewhere in the world. There may be a general benefit to the reputation of a business (good PR/marketing/corporate responsibility) in paying for a VER, but no particular service is rendered which can be identified as a cost component of the business. There is therefore no consumption. No service is being provided to an identifiable consumer and no benefit is being provided which is capable of forming a cost component of the activity of another person in the commercial chain.

Payment for a VER might produce a general social benefit, it might produce a specified result, or it might give rise to a legal relationship with reciprocal obligations. However, a taxable person's income is relevant for VAT purposes only if it constitutes the consideration for a supply of goods or services to a consumer. The mere fact that something is or may be done in exchange for a payment is insufficient to bring such a transaction within the VAT system. The public at large cannot constitute a specific recipient of the kind which must exist in order to give rise to a transaction chargeable to VAT.

Further, and in marked contrast to the situation with compliance market credits, we have seen no evidence of the existence of a genuine secondary trading market in VERs.

CARBON OFFSET SERVICES

There are a growing number of businesses providing carbon offsetting services. The range of services offered varies widely, but the VAT treatment of any individual transaction will depend on the particular arrangements. Because arrangements vary so widely, it is not considered practicable to provide anything beyond general advice in this brief.

In many situations, when a member of the public makes a payment to a carbon offset provider, there is no supply for VAT purposes. This is because there is no identifiable, direct benefit being received by the member of the public in return for their money.

Examples would be where a carbon offset provider makes a commitment that funds paid across by members of the public will be used to fund overseas projects, wind farms, development of environmentally friendly energy generation projects etc. without making any supply of direct benefit to the person making the payment. In such scenarios, the payment by the member of the public is outside the scope of VAT.

A common arrangement is where an airline offers its passengers the facility to offset the carbon emissions generated by their flights, perhaps via a third party carbon offset provider. Generally the passenger pays across an amount, calculated to be the cost of offsetting the resulting emissions, but receives no identifiable, direct benefit in return. There are a number of possible variants, including:

- the passenger has no choice, being obliged to pay the offsetting charge – the airline is making a single zero-rated supply of transport services;
- the offsetting service is optional, there is no administrative charge, and the entire payment goes to offset provision – the payment is outside the scope of VAT;
- the offsetting facility is optional, but a separate administration charge is made to the customer for providing the service – the admin charge is standard-rated, but the amount paid to offset provision is outside the scope of VAT.

In other situations, a carbon offset provider might make taxable supplies of carbon credits (supplies of compliance market credits are currently zero-rated), or of the purchase and "retirement" of compliance market credits (standard-rated), or of general advice on how an individual or a business can improve its energy efficiency (standard-rated).

INPUT TAX RECOVERY

Whether you are an offset provider, or simply a business incurring VAT in order to offset your own carbon emissions, you must follow the usual rules to determine whether any VAT incurred is Input Tax and the extent to which it is recoverable.

FURTHER INFORMATION

Further information can be obtained from the HMRC website contact the Helpline on Tel 0845 010 9000.

Commentary—*De Voil Indirect Tax Service* **V4.288**.

DIY HOUSEBUILDERS AND CONVERTERS VAT REFUND SCHEME – TREATMENT OF HOLIDAY HOMES

16 June 2010 *HMRC Brief 29/10*

This Brief announces a change to the treatment of claims received by us under the provisions of the above scheme in respect of holiday homes.

THE EFFECT OF THE CHANGE

Following a decision of the VAT Tribunal, we now accept that the DIY housebuilders and converters scheme applies to the construction of new holiday homes and to the conversion of non-residential buildings into holiday homes. Any refund of VAT is subject to the conditions of the scheme being met.

Guidance for the scheme is attached to application forms as follows:

- VAT 431NB: VAT refunds for DIY housebuilders (new houses);
- VAT431C: VAT refunds for DIY housebuilders (conversions).

BACKGROUND

Individuals who purchase the freehold or long leasehold (over 21 years or 20 years in Scotland) of new dwellings (either newly constructed or converted from non-residential buildings) receive those supplies zero-rated for VAT purposes. On the other hand, individuals who construct or convert non-residential buildings into dwellings for their own occupation, incur VAT on the purchase of building materials and, where conversions are concerned, on the purchase of any conversion services.

Where the dwellings are for their own (or a friend or relative's) occupation and are not constructed in the course or furtherance of a business, the individuals cannot register in order to recover the VAT and so, to this extent, are disadvantaged when compared to developers.

To address this issue, the DIY housebuilders and converters scheme, which was first introduced in 1974, refunds VAT incurred on the cost of building materials and (where appropriate) on conversion services for private individuals.

We have never applied the DIY housebuilders scheme to holiday homes since their supply by a developer attracts VAT at the standard rate. However, a recent decision of the VAT Tribunal (Mrs Irene Susan Jennings - TC00362) has found that the existing legislation does allow the same recovery of VAT on building materials for holiday homes that have been constructed by the individual for a non-business purpose.

As a consequence of this decision, we now accept that claims, for VAT incurred on building materials, may also be made for holiday homes that meet the necessary criteria.

We will also allow claims for a VAT refund on building materials and, where appropriate, services of conversion, where the work has involved the conversion of a previously non-residential building into a home.

HOW TO CLAIM

If you have not submitted a claim before in respect of your holiday home, then you may do so now providing the certificate of completion was issued within the last four years and three months from the date of this Brief. If your certificate of completion is older than this then we regret that your claim is out of time.

If you have, at any time, submitted a claim in relation to a holiday home which was refused in full or in part, for that reason, then you may now resubmit that claim if you wish.

If you are making a claim, please ensure you use the correct form as identified above.

The guidance to the forms is in the process of being amended to reflect this change in policy but the forms themselves will not require alteration.

Exceptionally, where you have submitted a claim in the past, we will accept the original claim form. All claim forms should be accompanied by:

- planning permission;
- certificate of completion;
- building plans;
- all original VAT invoices, bills and credit notes.

Please note that a claim cannot be considered unless the above evidence is provided.

Resubmitted claims should be sent, along with a covering note quoting this Brief, to:

HMRC DIY Claims Unit, Two Broadway Broad Street, Five Ways, Birmingham B15 1BG.

Further information may be obtained from our Helpline on Tel 0845 010 9000.

Commentary—*De Voil Indirect Tax Service* **V7.391**.

NEW PENALTY FOR FAILURE TO NOTIFY

18 June 2010 *HMRC Brief 30/10*

This Brief provides information on the penalty for failing to notify which applies to most taxes from 1 April 2010.

INTRODUCTION

This Business Brief explains the failure to notify penalty contained in Sch 41 of the 2008 Finance Act (FA 2008) which from 1 April 2010 can be applied to most taxes. There is full guidance on this penalty at CH70000 and CH500000 in the Compliance Handbook (www.hmrc.gov.uk/manuals/chmanual/index.htm).

FROM 1 APRIL 2010 THE PENALTY COULD BE APPLIED TO A FAILURE TO NOTIFY FOR:

Aggregates Levy
Air Passenger Duty
Alcoholic Liquor Duty
Amusement Machine Licence Duty
Bingo Duty
Capital Gains Tax
Climate Change Levy
Corporation Tax
Excise Duties
Gaming Duty
General Betting Duty
Hydrocarbon Oils Duty
Income Tax
Insurance Premium Tax
Landfill Tax
Lottery Duty
Pool Betting Duty
Remote Gaming Duty
Tobacco Products Duty
VAT

BACKGROUND

Under the review of HMRC's powers, deterrents and safeguards (www.hmrc.gov.uk/about/powers-appeal.htm) legislation has been introduced to align and modernise the framework under which we administer the taxes and duties formerly handled by Customs and Excise and the Inland Revenue.

We inherited a number of different penalty regimes from Customs and Excise and the Inland Revenue. The law and practice relating to penalties varied not only between the two former departments but also between the various taxes and duties for which each department was responsible.

Finance Act 2007, section 97 and Schedule 24 introduced a simpler and more consistent penalty system for inaccuracies in tax returns and other documents.

Finance Act 2008, section 123 and Schedule 41 has extended and adapted the new penalty framework to introduce:

- A standard penalty across most our taxes where a customer fails to register or notify us and as a result tax is due. Paragraph 1 of Schedule 41.
- Various VAT and Excise wrongdoing penalties. Paragraphs 2, 3 and 4 of Schedule 41 – see Revenue and Customs Brief 52/09.

FAILURE TO NOTIFY

Failure to notify occurs when someone fails to tell us on time that an event has happened that:

- gives rise to additional liability
- gives rise to chargeability
- means they need to register with us

These events could include:

- where a person has Income Tax, Capital Gains Tax or Corporation Tax to pay and we have not given them a notice to make a return
- when a person starts a new taxable activity
- when the turnover from an existing activity has reached a certain level
- when the nature of the activity changes

We will not charge a penalty if the person has a reasonable excuse for not telling us at the appropriate time, provided that they tell us without unreasonable delay after the excuse had ended.

DATES AND TIMES

The new failure to notify penalty regime applies to failures occurring on or after 1 April 2010. When you must notify us by depends on the type of tax and the declaration method involved. Examples are given in Appendix 1 at the end of this Brief of the most common taxes a self-employed person or small business is likely to encounter.

SIZE OF PENALTY

The amount of the penalty is a percentage of the tax that is unpaid at a specified date, or to which the person is liable for the relevant period. This tax is known as the "potential lost revenue".

The percentage is determined by the behaviour that led to the failure to notify and the behaviour after the failure has been established. Higher penalties are charged if the failure was deliberate, but the percentage can be reduced from the maximum for disclosure and the amount of help the person gives us in establishing the amount of tax unpaid.

BEHAVIOUR THAT LED TO THE FAILURE

The new penalty is designed to address the behaviour that caused the failure so that, within the deliberate category, the law provides for higher penalties in the most serious cases where the person has failed to notify us and has taken steps to conceal the need to notify.

The definition of the behaviour that led to the failure to notify will be:

	Maximum %	Prompted Minimum %	Unprompted Minimum %
Non-deliberate	30	20	10
Deliberate but not concealed	70	35	20
Deliberate and concealed	100	50	30

A disclosure is unprompted if at the time it is made the person had no reason to believe that we had discovered or were about to discover the failure. Otherwise it is a prompted disclosure.

We want to encourage people to join the tax system. If the failure is notified within 12 months of the tax becoming unpaid, the penalty for a non-deliberate failure to notify may be reduced for:

- a prompted disclosure from 20 per cent to 10 per cent
- an unprompted disclosure from 10 per cent to 0 per cent

BEHAVIOUR AFTER THE FAILURE HAS BEEN ESTABLISHED

The maximum penalty percentage is reduced by an amount that represents the quality of disclosure. The term "reduction for disclosure" replaces the terms "abatement" and "mitigation" used in previous penalty regimes. The first thing to consider about the quality of the disclosure is whether the disclosure was prompted or unprompted.

To calculate the reduction for disclosure you need to consider another three elements of disclosure:

- telling us about it – which involves admitting the failure, making a full disclosure and explaining how and why the failure occurred
- giving us help – which involves giving active assistance and actively engaging in quantifying the amount, as opposed to passive acceptance or obstruction
- volunteering any information relevant to the disclosure, such as allowing us access to records

APPEALING AGAINST A FAILURE TO NOTIFY PENALTY

When we have decided on the penalty we will issue a penalty assessment. The person is entitled to a review of, and can appeal against, our decision:

- that a penalty is payable
- the amount of the penalty

MORE INFORMATION

Compliance Handbook (www.hmrc.gov.uk/manuals/chmanual/index.htm).

New penalties internet page (www.hmrc.gov.uk/about/new-penalties/index.htm).

Q and A briefing on all penalty changes (www.hmrc.gov.uk/about/new-penalties/faqs.htm) Appendix 1.

EXAMPLES OF LATE NOTIFICATION

Below are some examples of when a failure to notify penalty may apply for the most common taxes.

INCOME THAT NEEDS TO BE DECLARED ON A SELF ASSESSMENT RETURN

. . .

VAT

A business that has exceeded the VAT registration threshold over the past 12 months, or expects to turnover the whole VAT threshold in the next 30 days, must tell us within 30 days.

Find out how and when to register for VAT (www.hmrc.gov.uk/vat/start/register/index.htm).

. . .

CHANGES TO EXCLUSION OF OPTION TO TAX ON BUILDINGS FOR RELEVANT RESIDENTIAL OR CHARITABLE PURPOSE

29 July 2010 *HMRC Brief 33/10*

Following the withdrawal of ESC 3.29 with effect from July 2010, HMRC will continue to accept that, where customer and supplier agree, the option to tax can be excluded on supplies of a building or part of a building that is to be used 95% or more for a relevant residential or charitable purpose in certain situations.

VAT: CHANGES TO THE EXCLUSION OF THE OPTION TO TAX ON SUPPLIES OF BUILDINGS TO BE USED SOLELY FOR A RELEVANT RESIDENTIAL OR RELEVANT CHARITABLE PURPOSE, (PARAGRAPHS 5, 6 AND 7 OF SCHEDULE 10 TO THE VAT ACT 1994 REFER)

In Revenue & Customs Brief 39/09, HM Revenue & Customs (HMRC) announced changes to the application of the zero rate to new buildings and that, following a review, the phrase "solely for a relevant residential or relevant charitable purpose" could incorporate a de minimis margin.

In order to avoid unnecessary disputes in marginal cases, HMRC accept that this statutory condition is satisfied for new buildings where the relevant use of the building by the charity or relevant residential user is 95 per cent or more. In light of this review, HMRC announced the withdrawal of Extra Statutory Concession (ESC) 3.29 and two related concessions as we considered them to be no longer necessary or appropriate.

However, ESC 3.29 also allowed charities to exclude the option to tax on supplies of buildings to them (other than parts used as an office) if they were solely used for a relevant charitable purpose. For consistency, HMRC accept that, where the customer and supplier agree, the option to tax can be excluded on supplies of a building or part of a building that is to be used 95 per cent or more for a relevant purpose in the following situations:

- where a building or part of a building (other than used as an office) will be used by a charity solely for a relevant charitable purpose (paragraph 7 of Schedule 10 to the VAT Act 1994 refers)
- where a grant is made in a building or part of a building designed solely for a relevant residential purpose (paragraph 5 of Schedule 10 to the VAT Act 1994 refers)
- where a grant in a building or part of a building is made to a person who intends to use the building solely for a relevant residential purpose (paragraph 6 of Schedule 10 to the VAT Act 1994 refers)

Commentary—*De Voil Indirect Tax Service* **V4.116**.

HMRC POSITION FOLLOWING CA JUDGMENT IN INSURANCEWIDE AND TRADER MEDIA GROUP

3 August 2010 *HMRC Brief 31/10*

HMRC is not appealing the judgment in the Insurancewide and Trader Media Group case and now accepts that insurance introductory services will be exempt from VAT when a provider is doing much more than acting as a "mere conduit" through which a potential customer is passed to a provider. This Brief sets out four conditions a provider of services will have to meet to qualify for exemption.

This Brief explains HM Revenue & Customs (HMRC) position following the Court of Appeal judgment in *Insurancewide.com Services Ltd and Trader Media Group Ltd* [2010] STC 1572 (Case ref A3/2009/1300).

The Court of Appeal found against HMRC and upheld the decision of the High Court that certain supplies of insurance introductory services provided via the internet are exempt from VAT. HMRC are not appealing this decision further.

BACKGROUND

The appeals of Insurancewide (IW) and Trader Media Group (TMG) concerned the VAT liability of internet "click-through" services and whether introductory services such as these, that involve no intermediation of the contracts themselves, qualify as exempt insurance intermediary services.

The facts in each case were slightly different in that:

- IW was a comparison website providing "click-through" services to insurer or broker websites, whereas
- TMG provided "click through" services from its Auto Trader car auction site to a 3rd party co-branded broker website

Both were paid commission on successful take-up.

IW lost its appeal at Tribunal as they were found not to be acting as an insurance agent at any time and appealed to the High Court. On the other hand, TM won its appeal as the Tribunal found that its services constituted insurance intermediary services and we appealed the decision to the High Court. Given the similarities in the two cases, the High Court agreed to hear the appeals jointly.

In May 2009 the High Court found that IW and TMG were insurance intermediaries for the purposes of the VAT exemption and an act of introduction, with no further involvement in the intermediation of the contract of insurance, qualified for exemption as an insurance related service.

THE COURT OF APPEAL JUDGMENT

On 22 April 2010 the Court of Appeal released its judgment. It held that it was not necessary for there to be intermediation of the insurance contracts and the introductory services provided by IW and TMG were exempt because they were doing much more than providing a mere "click-through" facility to a broker or insurer (that is, they were not acting as a "mere conduit"). In particular, the companies concerned were also fulfilling the following functions:

- they identified those looking for insurance and provided them with access to insurers who provided a range of competitive products
- they appraised and selected those insurers according to the competitiveness of their pricing and products and their level of consumer service

And, in addition to this:

- IW (in certain instances) also provided those seeking insurance with a means of directing them effectively and efficiently to the most appropriate insurers (whether directly or through an intermediary)
- TMG had input into the format of the co-branded broker website to which the customer was directed and into the composition of the insurer panel based on its understanding of the consumers using its website.

The Court concluded that IW and TMG were not acting as subcontractors and, taken overall, their relevant activities could be described as the business of bringing together insurers and those seeking insurance.

The Court also found that an insurance agent or broker is defined for the purposes of the VAT exemption by:

- what they do and not by how they choose to describe themselves
- whether or not they fall within the definition of an insurance intermediary for regulatory purposes

HMRC'S POSITION

In light of the conclusions of the Court of Appeal as outlined above, HMRC now accept that insurance introductory services will be exempt from VAT when a provider is doing much more than acting as a "mere conduit" through which a potential customer is passed to a provider. This can be demonstrated by all of the following four conditions being met:

(1) The services are provided by someone engaged in the business of putting insurance companies in touch with potential clients or more generally acting as intermediaries between the two parties (although this may not necessarily be their principal business activity).

(2) The business provides the means (that is, by way of an internet "click-through" or some other form of introduction) by which a person seeking insurance is introduced to a provider of insurance or to another intermediary in a chain leading to an insurance provider.
(3) That introduction takes place at the time a customer is seeking to enter into an insurance contract (although in some instances an insurance contract may not actually go on to be finally concluded).
(4) The introducer also plays a proactive part in putting in place the arrangements under which that introduction is effected.

For the purposes of condition 4 above, evidence that the introducer has been proactive in putting in place the arrangements under which the introduction is effected could, for example, take the form of some or all of the following:

- active endorsement of the insurer or the insurance product
- involvement in the selection of the insurance products and/or providers
- involvement in the process under which the insurance contract is entered into, even though the intermediation of the contact itself is undertaken by a 3rd party (for example, by having input into what questions should be asked of the prospective insured or the design of the 3rd party's website)
- negotiating a special rate for the insurance product/s on behalf of its customers or membership base
- some form of assessment of the customer's requirements so that they are directed to the most appropriate insurer for them

Previous case law has told HMRC that the means by which a business is remunerated for its services, that is, whether by fee or commission or some other means, is not determinative of the liability. Whilst remuneration based on successful take-up may indicate an introduction has taken place it is not enough in itself to determine exemption and it is always important to consider what is actually being done rather than how it is paid for.

Although the judgment specifically concerned insurance intermediary services, it does also provide some general guidance on the application of the exemption to finance intermediary services. It must be borne in mind, however, that the UK and EU law covering the exemption for finance intermediary services is different from that for insurance intermediary services. For example, for most finance intermediary services to be exempt, UK law requires businesses to be both bringing together a prospective customer with a product provider with a view to entering a contract for the provision of financial services **and** carrying out work preparatory to the conclusion of those contracts.

CLAIMS

Subject to the normal rules on capping and unjust enrichment, HMRC will pay claims for overpaid tax charged on insurance introductory services that fall within the findings of the Court of Appeal as outlined above.

FURTHER INFORMATION

Details of where to send your claim can be found in Notice 700/45 "How to correct VAT errors and make adjustments" or available on the HMRC internet or from the VAT Helpline on Tel 0845 010 9000.

We may reject all or part of a claim if repayment would unjustly enrich the claimant. More details on "unjust enrichment" can be found in Notice 700/45 "How to correct VAT errors and make adjustments or claims".

Where you are in any doubt about the correct treatment please contact the VAT Helpline on Tel 0845 010 9000.

Commentary—*De Voil Indirect Tax Service* **V4.123**.

VAT PRs etc

CHANGES TO THE APPLICATION OF THE ZERO-RATE TO NEW BUILDINGS USED FOR A RELEVANT CHARITABLE OR RESIDENTIAL USE

3 August 2010 *HMRC Brief 32/10*

This is a re-issued version of Brief 39/09, which announced a change in HMRC's interpretation of the legal provisions that apply the zero rate to new buildings used for a relevant charitable purpose, and the withdrawal of ESC 3.29 and two related concessions. The transitional period for the change ended on 1 July 2010.

This brief was originally published June 2009 under Revenue & Customs Brief 39/09.

This Brief announces a change in HM Revenue & Customs (HMRC) interpretation of the of the legal provisions that apply the zero rate to new buildings used for a relevant charitable purpose, and the withdrawal of Extra Statutory Concession (ESC) 3.29 and two related concessions. VAT Information Sheet 08/09 provides further detail.

BACKGROUND

A building intended to be used solely for a relevant charitable purpose (non-business use) can be zero-rated if the charity provides their developer with an appropriate certificate before the first supply is made.

If, however, the building is put to a business use within ten years of the building's completion, VAT must be paid to HMRC (a change in use charge) to reflect that the building has ceased to be eligible to benefit from the zero-rate.

The two related concessions, the "switching areas" concession (where the overall use of the building was unchanged) and the "look through" concession, (where the occupiers' use of the building was for a relevant charitable purpose) enabled some business use of a building to be disregarded.

OUTCOME OF REVIEW

Having fully considered the application of the provision and considered appropriate decisions of the higher courts, HMRC now recognise that the term "solely", as used in the phrase "solely for a relevant residential or relevant charitable purpose", can incorporate an appropriate de minimis margin. And in order to avoid unnecessary disputes in marginal cases, HMRC will accept that this statutory condition is satisfied if the relevant use of the building by the charity is 95 per cent or more.

In the light of this change of view, the ESC is no longer considered to be necessary or appropriate. It will therefore be withdrawn, subject to a 12 month transitional period, as described below.

WAY FORWARD

A person can now rely on this revised interpretation of "solely" that is, 95 per cent or more, to determine whether a building will be eligible for the zero rate or not.

For this purpose, use for a relevant charitable purpose does not have to be calculated using one of the three methods described in ESC 3.29. Any method may be used to calculate the qualifying use of the building, so long as it is fair and reasonable. Prior approval from HMRC for any method of calculation is not required.

If a building is zero rated as a result of applying this new interpretation, there will be a change of use charge if it ceases to be eligible within ten years of the buildings completion.

ESC 3.29 and the two connected concessions will now be withdrawn, subject to a 12 month transitional period starting on 1 July 2009. During this transitional period, charities will be able to continue to apply ESC 3.29, or choose to apply the revised interpretation of the statutory provision described above.

Further details are in VAT Information Sheet 08/09.

The meaning of the term "solely" will depend on the legal context in which it occurs and on the nature of the underlying transactions to which any particular piece of legislation is directed. The revised interpretation described above applies only to the construction of the phrase "solely for a relevant residential or relevant charitable purpose" as used in the context of Groups 5 and 6 of Schedule 8, Group 1 of Schedule 9 and Part 2 of Schedule 10 to the VAT Act 1994.

FURTHER INFORMATION

If you have any enquiries about this Brief, please contact the National Advice Service on Tel. **0845 010 9000** or, if a charity, the Charity Helpline on **0845 302 0203**.

Commentary—*De Voil Indirect Tax Service* **V4.232B**, **V3.248**.

PROPOSED REVERSE CHARGE ACCOUNTING FOR BUSINESSES TRADING IN EMISSIONS ALLOWANCES

24 August 2010. *HMRC Brief 35/10*

This Brief introduces the draft VAT legislation for a reverse charge in relation to business trading in emission allowances from 1 November 2010 in order to combat MTIC fraud. It also provides guidance on how the reverse charge will work.

Introduction

Budget Note 49 (24 March 2010) announced the introduction of legislation for a reverse charge with effect from 1 November 2010.

The purpose of this Brief is to share the draft legislation and provide guidance on how the reverse charge for emissions allowances will operate.

Who needs to read this?

Business selling or purchasing emissions allowances in the UK.

Background

A zero rate for emissions allowances was introduced on 31 July 2009 as an interim measure to halt rapidly escalating MTIC fraud in this area, pending agreement on a common EU-wide countermeasure (Revenue & Customs Brief 46/09). A Directive providing an option for all Member States to introduce a reverse charge was adopted in March 2010.

Timing and Scope of Implementation

With effect from 1 November 2010 (subject to Parliamentary process) the reverse charge accounting mechanism will apply to:

- a transfer of an allowance, as defined in Article 3 of Directive 2003/87/EC (concerning the EU emissions trading scheme)
- a transfer of an emission reduction unit which can be used by an operator for compliance with the scheme established by the Directive
- a transfer of a certified emission reduction which can be used by an operator for compliance with the scheme established by the Directive

The reverse charge will **not** apply to supplies of options for emissions allowances which are not covered by the EU legislation permitting the reverse charge.

At the same time the temporary zero rate for emissions allowances, including options, will be withdrawn. These changes do not affect the application of the Terminal Markets Order under which certain transactions on specified markets are zero-rated.

The reverse charge mechanism

Under the reverse charge accounting mechanism, it is the responsibility of the customer, rather than the supplier, to account to HM Revenue & Customs (HMRC) for VAT on supplies of the specified emission allowances. As is the case with the mobile telephone and computer chip reverse charge it will only apply to business to business transactions in the UK. However, there are two key differences between these measures, which are:

- there is no "de minimis" rule excluding supplies under £5,000 so the reverse charge applies to all specified supplies of emission allowances

– businesses will not be required to complete a Reverse Charge Sales List

Completion of the VAT Return

Suppliers of goods under reverse charge accounting must **not** enter in box 1 of the VAT Return any output tax on sales to which the reverse charge applies, but must enter the value of such sales in box 6.

Customers must enter in box 1 of the VAT Return the output tax on purchases to which the reverse charge applies, but must not enter the value of such purchases in box 6. They must reclaim the input tax on their reverse charge purchases in box 4 of the VAT Return and include the value of the purchases in box 7, in the normal way.

Invoicing

When making a sale to which reverse charge accounting applies, suppliers must:

– show all the information normally required to be shown on a VAT invoice
– annotate the invoice to make it clear that the reverse charge applies and that the customer is required to account for the VAT

The amount of VAT due under the reverse charge rules must be clearly stated on the invoice but should not be included in the amount shown as total VAT charged. The precise wording is not prescribed in law and discussions with business have highlighted the need to keep the annotation short. Either of the following would be acceptable:

– customer to pay output tax of £X to HMRC
– UK customer to pay O/T of £X to HMRC

Alternatively, any of the following would also be acceptable, provided that the amount of tax is shown elsewhere on the invoice (but not in box for total output tax charged):

– VAT Act 1994 Section 55A applies
– s 55A VATA 94 applies
– customer to account for the VAT to HMRC
– reverse charge supply — customer to pay the VAT to HMRC
– customer to pay VAT to HMRC
– UK customer to pay VAT to HMRC

Detailed guidance on the reverse charge mechanism can be found in Notice 735: "VAT reverse charge for mobile phones & computer chips".

Draft Legislation

Statutory instruments will bring the relevant changes into effect:

– the Value Added Tax (Section 55A) (Specified Goods and Excepted Supplies) Order, which specifies the supplies to which the reverse charge applies (Annex A)
– the Value Added Tax (Amendment) Regulations, which amend Regulations 38A, 55C(6) and 58(2)(g) of the VAT Regulations to reflect the fact that section 55A may now apply to supplies of services as well as goods (Annex B)
– The Value Added Tax (Emissions Allowances) Order, which removes the temporary zero rate (Annex C)

Drafts of these instruments as they are expected to be made are attached for information [see HMRC website].

Further information

Further information can be obtained from the HMRC website or by contacting the Helpline on 0845 010 9000.

Annex A

The Value Added Tax (Section 55A) (Specified Goods and Excepted Supplies) Order [not reproduced]

Annex B

The Value Added Tax (Amendment) Regulations [not reproduced]

Annex C

The Value Added Tax (Emissions Allowances) Order [not reproduced]

Commentary—*De Voil Indirect Tax Service* **V4.288, V3.233**.

LEISURE TRUSTS PROVIDING ALL INCLUSIVE MEMBERSHIP SCHEMES

3 September 2010 *HMRC Brief 37/10*

With effect from 1 April 2009, HMRC amended its interpretation of the law with the result that non-profit making bodies, including leisure trusts which were previously charging VAT on their all inclusive packages, will in the majority of cases have to treat them as exempt.

THE ISSUE

With effect from 1 April 2009 HMRC amended its interpretation of the law and therefore its guidance on the VAT treatment of membership schemes allowing unlimited access to leisure facilities in a leisure centre. Businesses that will be most affected are community leisure centres that are run by non-profit making trusts. Supplies made by commercial organisations are not affected and remain taxable at the standard rate.

This brief cancels Revenue & Customs Brief 50/07 and Revenue & Customs Brief 13/2009.

BACKGROUND

Supplies of services closely linked with and essential to sport or physical education, in which an individual takes part, are exempt from VAT when supplied by an "eligible body" (essentially a non-profit making body not subject to commercial influence) as set out in the Value Added Tax Act 1994, Schedule 9, Group 10 (Sport, Sports Competitions and Physical Education). Prior to 1 April 2009 HMRC's view was that where a scheme offered, over a period, unlimited use of a variety of both taxable and exempt facilities, typically in return for a monthly or annual payment, there was generally a single supply of the standard rated right to use the facilities. However, following representations from the leisure industry and taking into account the comments made in the Court of Appeal in *HMRC v Weight Watchers (UK) Ltd* [2008] STC 2313 about the typical consumer, we no longer see the supply as a right to use the services but as being the supply of underlying services.

The Weight Watchers case indicated that it is appropriate to look at the transaction from the viewpoint of the typical consumer, rather than the supplier. The extent of the linkage between the relevant transactions must be considered from an economic point of view. So regarded, the question then is whether it would be artificial to split the transaction into separate supplies. If it would be artificial, then there will be a single supply and the predominant element from the viewpoint of the typical consumer, will determine whether the supply is exempt or standard rated.

REVISED APPROACH

VAT liability depends on the nature of the supply which has to be decided at the time the all inclusive fee is paid. Where the supply is a single supply that would be artificial to split there can only be one overarching liability. In most cases, the typical consumer who purchases an all inclusive package will have access to a range of facilities at the leisure centre. Usually most of these facilities would, if supplied individually, be exempt as "services closely linked with and essential to sport or physical education in which the individual is taking part", (for example use of the swimming pool, showers, changing rooms). Therefore, in cases where the predominant reason for purchasing an all inclusive package is to use the range of available sports facilities, the single supply is exempt.

In some instances packages may include facilities that would be standard rated if supplied on their own, for example, sauna facilities. However, providing that the predominant reason that the typical consumer purchases the package is to use the (exempt) sports services, the supply of the package is still exempt.

VAT PRs etc

If the predominant reason a typical consumer purchases an all inclusive package is to make use of standard rated facilities the single supply is standard rated.

EFFECTS OF THE CHANGE

The effect of this change is that since 1 April 2009 non-profit making bodies, including leisure trusts which were previously charging VAT on their all inclusive packages, will in the majority of cases have to treat them as exempt. If businesses make both exempt and taxable supplies they will be partly exempt and will have to apply the partial exemption rules to determine how much of the input tax incurred on their costs can be deducted. The partial exemption rules are set out and explained in Notice 706 "Partial Exemption".

Notice 701/45 "Sport" will be amended in due course.

CAPITAL GOODS SCHEME (CGS) ITEMS; THE EFFECT OF THE CHANGE

The CGS applies to buildings and some items of computer hardware. It adjusts input tax claimed on building related capital expenditure for any changes in use over a ten year period. It includes both purchases of buildings and subsequent capital expenditure such as refurbishments. If a business is transferred as a going concern (TOGC) and a building subject to the CGS is one of the assets transferred then the new owner must continue the adjustments. The CGS rules are set out and explained in Notice 706/2 "The Capital Goods Scheme".

After affected bodies begin treating their supplies as exempt there will be an apparent change of use from taxable to exempt. However, the policy change represents what the true liability always was, assuming that sports providers have not changed the way they operate. The CGS adjusts the true amount that was initially claimable ignoring any errors that may have occurred whether they can be corrected or not. Therefore, no significant CGS adjustments are likely provided that the way sports facilities are supplied has not changed since any capital expenditure was incurred. If you are concerned that the CGS may significantly affect you then please contact your local VAT office.

If sports providers acquired a CGS building asset as part of a TOGC then the CGS may require adjustments if the previous owner deducted and was properly entitled to deduct input tax on the item. This is likely if the previous owner was a Local Authority. If you are concerned that these circumstances may apply to you then please contact the VAT Helpline on 0845 010 9000.

MAKING CLAIMS OR ADJUSTMENTS

The change described should have been implemented from 1 April 2009 and there is no requirement to make adjustments in respect of supplies made prior to that date. However, where a business wishes to make a claim to HMRC (under section 80 of the VAT Act 1994) for repayment of VAT incorrectly accounted for on sports services, they may do so, subject to the conditions set out in Notice 700/45 "How to correct VAT errors and make adjustments or claims". These will be subject to a transitional four year limitation period and "unjust enrichment" provisions.

Where you are in any doubt about the correct treatment please contact the VAT Helpline on 0845 010 9000.

Commentary—*De Voil Indirect Tax Service* **V3.105, V7.340**.

SUPPLIES OF NURSES, NURSING AUXILIARIES AND CARE ASSISTANTS BY STATE REGULATED AGENCIES

22 September 2010. *HMRC Brief 40/10*

This brief announces a consequential amendment to the nursing agency concession (previously detailed in HM Revenue & Customs (HMRC) Brief 12/10) that allows VAT exemption of certain services provided by nursing agencies (the Nursing Agencies' Concession).

With effect from 1 October 2010 (as a result of changes announced in the Health and Social Care Act 2008), the legal requirement for nursing agencies to be registered under the Care Quality Commission will cease and responsibility for quality standards will pass to those organisations that provide the regulated activity.

This consequential amendment ensures that nursing agencies that currently benefit from the concession continue to do so from 1 October 2010.

THE NURSING AGENCIES' CONCESSION

By concession (HMRC regularly reviews these), nursing agencies (or employment businesses that provide nurses and midwives, as well as other health professionals) may exempt the supply of nursing staff and nursing auxiliaries supplied as a principal to a third party, if the supply is of:

- a person registered in the register of qualified nurses and midwives maintained under article 5 of the Nursing and Midwifery Order 2001;
- an unregistered nursing auxiliary who is "directly supervised" by one of the above;
- an unregistered nursing auxiliary, whose services are supplied to a hospital (NHS or private), hospice, care home with nursing under item 4 of Group 7, Schedule 9 VAT Act 1994 and form part of the care made to the patient.

The institution to which staff are supplied may be operated by a local authority, NHS body, charity or other organisation operating in the public or private sector.

To qualify for the concession, the employment business must be registered with one of the following organisations:

- Care Quality Commission (formerly known as the Commission for Social Care Inspection);
- Scottish Commission for the Regulation of Care;
- Care Standards Inspectorate for Wales;
- Northern Ireland Health and Personal Social Services Regulation and Improvement Authority.

For the supply of nursing auxiliaries or care assistants to benefit from the concession, they must undertake some direct form of medical care, such as administering drugs or taking blood pressures, for the final patient. The concession does not apply to supplies of general care assistants who are:

- only involved in providing personal care such as catering, washing or dressing the patients;
- working in care homes without nursing where they do not require supervision by health professionals to provide their services.

However, where a state-regulated domiciliary care agency supplies the services of its care assistants directly to the final patient, we would see the agency as making an exempt supply of welfare services – see Public Notice 701/2 "Welfare" and the section headed "Supplies of contracted-out welfare services" below.

CONSEQUENTIAL CHANGES TO THE CONCESSION

From 1 October 2010, to qualify for the concession, the employment business must be registered with one of the following organisations:

- Care Quality Commission (or for supplies on or after 1 October 2010 would have been required to be registered with the Care Quality Commission prior to that date);
- Scottish Commission for the Regulation of Care;
- Care Standards Inspectorate for Wales; or
- Northern Ireland Health and Personal Social Services Regulation and Improvement Authority.

The Guidance will be updated in due course.

Further information may be obtained from the Helpline on 0800 010 9000.

Commentary—*De Voil Indirect Tax Service* **V4.146, V6.239**.

"ITALIAN REPUBLIC" CLAIMS FOR OVERPAID VAT

12 October 2010. *HMRC Brief 43/10*

This Brief gives information concerning a review by HM Revenue & Customs (HMRC) of the proper treatment of claims submitted as a result of the ECJ decision in *EC Commission v Italy (C-45/95)* [1997] STC 1062. The claims are for output tax over-declared on car sales where input tax was blocked on the purchase of the cars and typically involve the sale of demonstrator vehicles, courtesy cars and daily rental vehicles by businesses in the motor trade. A large number of such claims were submitted following the House of Lords decision in *Fleming/Condé Nast* [2008] STC 324. UK law on the input tax block was changed in 1999 and so these claims are for historic periods only.

Following a review of the implications of the ECJ decision in *Nordania Finans A/S and another v Skatteministeriet* [2008] STC 3314, HMRC is of the view that these claims did not take proper account of European case law on partial exemption. As a result HMRC is asking those businesses whose claims have not yet been paid to revise their claims to take account of the partial exemption implications. Where claims have already been repaid by HMRC without making adjustment for partial exemption HMRC is issuing recovery assessments subject to the appropriate time limits.

Further information on partial exemption can be found in Notice 706, "Partial Exemption", and the partial exemption section of HMRC VAT guidance.

BACKGROUND—OUTPUT TAX DECLARED ON CARS

Until 1 December 1999, input tax on new cars bought by businesses in the motor sector for use in their business before sale was blocked. To prevent double taxation when such cars were sold VAT was chargeable on the margin (if any) over the purchase price. However this still left some output tax payable in many cases. In 1997 the ECJ ruled that the only correct way of preventing double taxation of goods on which no input tax deduction was allowed is for the sale of the goods to be exempt from VAT. In response the former HM Customs & Excise issued Business Brief 23/97 in October 1997 inviting claims for overpaid VAT.

BACKGROUND—CLAIMING VAT EXEMPTION AND PARTIAL EXEMPTION

When UK law says a supply is taxable but European law says it is exempt taxpayers are entitled to claim exemption. However such claims must take into account the effect of the additional exempt supplies on the taxpayer's ability to deduct input tax (partial exemption).

The effect of partial exemption on motor sector businesses depends on whether cars owned by and used in the business for a limited time (such as demonstrators) can be treated for partial exemption purposes as capital goods used in the business. This is because the sale values of any such goods must be excluded from partial exemption calculations.

Until 2001 it was HM Customs and Excise's policy that demonstrator cars should not be classified as capital goods and therefore should be included in partial exemption calculations. This resulted in Italian Republic claims being reduced to take account of the partial exemption impact.

In 2001 however, the High Court ruled in *Customs and Excise Commissioners v JDL Ltd* [2002] STC 1 that demonstrator cars were capital goods used in a car dealer's business. It was therefore accepted that, other things being equal, "Italian Republic" claims for over-declared output tax need not take partial exemption into account. A number of claims have been repaid by HMRC on that basis.

THE ECJ DECISION IN NORDANIA FINANS, CASE C-98/07

In March 2008 the ECJ delivered its decision in the case of *Nordania Finans A/S and another v Skatteministeriet* [2008] STC 3314. This case concerned whether cars bought for leasing followed by sale were capital goods used in the business. Nordania's business model was to buy cars, lease them for a fixed period of eighteen months and then sell them at auction. Through these two ways of exploiting their assets they realised sufficient funds to cover their direct costs and overheads. The ECJ ruled that the exclusion of the sales, when the sales were an integral part of their business model, would distort Nordania's partial exemption calculations. The sales should therefore not be seen as sales of capital goods used in Nordania's business.

After due consideration, HMRC has concluded that Nordania has over-turned JDL. The sale of cars that were bought to be used in a motor sector taxpayer's business for a limited time and then sold is an integral part of that taxpayer's business. As such, based on Nordania, it would distort partial exemption calculations to exclude the sale, and the cars cannot be viewed as capital goods used in the business. As a result any claim for over-declared output tax arising from the "Italian Republic" case must take the impact of partial exemption on deductible input tax into account. Furthermore, in submitting an "Italian Republic" claim businesses make themselves partly exempt. Therefore it may also be necessary to consider partial exemption implications where there was no consideration of partial exemption when the Italian Republic claim was made and any other claims have subsequently been submitted following Fleming/Condé Nast and for the periods covered by the previous claim.

THE WAY FORWARD

Where businesses have invoked the Italian ECJ decision and any claims have not yet been paid HMRC will be writing to businesses inviting them to submit revised claims which take proper account of the partial exemption implications before any payment is made.

HMRC are reviewing claims which have been repaid without taking proper account of partial exemption and, in appropriate cases, issuing recovery assessments for repayment of tax and statutory interest subject to the time limits in the VAT Act 1994. Default interest will be charged where appropriate. Where payments have been made incorrectly and there is insufficient time to accurately establish the position before assessment time limits expire, HMRC will issue estimated assessments on a best judgement basis. Where this happens HMRC will remain open to working with the businesses concerned to establish the exact impact and amend assessments where appropriate.

Commentary—*De Voil Indirect Tax Service* **V3.461B**.

CHANGE IN THE TAX TREATMENT OF BUSINESS ENTERTAINMENT OF OVERSEAS CUSTOMERS

3 November 2010. *HMRC Brief 44/10*

HM Revenue & Customs (HMRC) has reviewed its policy on the treatment of business entertainment provided to overseas customers in the light of the European Courts of Justice (ECJ) judgment in the joined case of *Danfoss and AstraZeneca* (Case-371/07) [2009] STC 701.

THE UK POSITION ON THE ENTERTAINMENT OF OVERSEAS CUSTOMERS

The UK has blocked the recovery of input tax on business entertainment since the inception of VAT. The terms of the block denied recovery of such input tax except where the business entertainment was provided to an overseas customer. In 1988 UK law was amended to extend the block to cover all business entertainment including that provided to overseas customers. This change was made to align VAT law with changes introduced in relation to direct tax.

In the light of recent ECJ judgments HMRC has concluded that the UK's block on the recovery of input tax on the business entertainment of overseas clients is inconsistent with EU law. The Government intends to amend UK law shortly. In the meantime HMRC will consider claims for previously restricted VAT in respect of the entertainment of overseas customers, as a direct effect of EU law.

The block on recovering input tax on entertainment provided to anyone other than an overseas customer, for example, UK customers and non-UK business contacts who are not customers, remains effective and any VAT incurred on the costs of such entertainment cannot be recovered.

MAKING CLAIMS: TIME LIMITS

You may make claims in respect of input tax on the costs of entertaining overseas business customers, subject to the normal four year cap. HMRC announced in March 2009 that, pending the outcome of its review of policy in this area, it was inviting claims for such input tax incurred between 1 August 1988 (the date when UK law was amended) and 30 April 1997 (as prescribed following the *Fleming* judgement). HMRC will no longer accept claims for this period.

VAT incurred in future tax periods in respect of the entertainment of overseas business customers can be recovered in the usual way.

All claims are subject to the qualifications set out below.

MAKING CLAIMS: EVIDENCE REQUIRED

HMRC expects that, as a minimum, claims are supported by the following evidence:

- details of the overseas customers;
- the type of expenditure, for example, meals to support business meetings, etc;

VAT PRs etc

- the amount of VAT claimed;
- evidence that VAT has been incurred and not previously been deducted;
- if required for historical claims, evidence of the type of business entertainment the business normally excludes from recovery by reference to recently rendered tax periods.

WHAT VAT CAN BE RECOVERED IN RESPECT OF ENTERTAINMENT?

HMRC now takes the view that VAT incurred on the entertainment of overseas customers may be recovered under the terms of EU law. However, in some circumstances an output tax charge to reflect private use arises and cancels out any deductible input tax. Where that is the case, there is no benefit in making a claim, so in considering whether to claim you should also consider whether there is a charge to output tax.

PRIVATE USE CHARGE

The charge that taxes private use is intended to ensure that the taxable person, his/her staff and others do not achieve an advantage over private individuals simply because the taxable person is registered for VAT and can recover VAT incurred on costs. The ECJ has addressed the question of the applicability of such a charge and it is clear from two particular decisions that the circumstances under which an individual can benefit privately from a business expense without a private use charge arising should be very narrowly defined. The two cases – *Julius Fillibeck Sohne C-258/95* [1998] STC 513 and *Danfoss and AstraZeneca C-371/07* [2009] STC 701 – introduce separate tests that should be applied to private use of business expenditure; these are set out in more detail below. As no advantage arises if the VAT is not recovered by the taxable person there is no need to consider the applicability of the private use charge unless you intend to recover the VAT paid.

In the *Fillibeck Sohne* case an employer provided transport to his staff to get them from their homes to a construction site. As commuting expenditure is private, the Court was asked to consider whether having recovered tax on the cost of the transport it was appropriate to apply a charge to reflect the private use by the employees. The Court's starting point was that a charge applied in principle but they considered the particular facts of the case and concluded that because it was practically impossible for the employees to get to the site on their own a private use charge should not be applied. From this judgment we must therefore consider whether it is necessary for the taxable person to provide goods or services that are enjoyed privately in order for him to make his taxable supplies; this is the necessity test.

The joined case of *Danfoss and AstraZeneca* involved the provision of free meals to both employees and business contacts. In the context of the business having recovered VAT on the meals, the ECJ was asked to consider whether it was appropriate to apply a private use charge. The Court concluded that where the meals were provided for a strict business purpose no such charge should arise. In reaching this conclusion they carefully considered the circumstances of the free meals. In particular the lack of choice by the recipient of what, when and where to eat, the relatively basic nature of the fare and crucially the fact that the meals were provided to ensure the smooth running of business meetings; this is the strict business purpose test.

These cases set out the circumstances where it is and is not appropriate to apply a private use charge to a benefit provided by the business. HMRC considers that unless there is a necessity for the business to provide entertainment or there is a strict business purpose behind it, such as the facilitation of a meeting, it is appropriate to apply a private use charge to entertainment provided to overseas customers.

If you conclude that the entertainment you provide should trigger such a private use charge, HMRC suggests that you treat the VAT incurred as non-deductible instead, rather than claiming a deduction and offsetting this with an output tax charge. This approach is consistent with the view that VAT incurred on the entertainment of overseas customers should only be recovered where it is clearly used for the making of taxable supplies as well as being reasonable in scale and character.

We set out below a number of scenarios that should assist in deciding the correct VAT treatment of any expenditure that you have incurred on entertaining overseas customers.

Meetings in your office

HMRC considers that where you entertain overseas customers in your staff canteen or similar, and the entertainment is provided to facilitate a business meeting, then the VAT on such expenditure will be recoverable and no charge to reflect the private use will arise; we take the view that any private benefit derived by your overseas customer is accessory to the needs of your business. This approach satisfies the basic input tax recovery test by establishing a link between the expense and the taxable supplies that your business makes. It is also consistent with the approach adopted by the ECJ in assessing the applicability of any private use charge in that this expense has a strict business purpose.

External meetings/events

Where you cannot host meetings in the office because, for example, you have a large number of attendees or you have no in-house facilities, then you can still use the principles set out above to determine if your input tax is recoverable or there is a charge to output tax under the private use charge. The provision of basic refreshments at, for example, a training event or a meeting will be treated as if it were supplied by your own in-house canteen. However, where the provision goes beyond merely providing basic food and refreshment to facilitate the smooth running of the event, then you should not recover any input tax or, failing that, account for output tax under the private use charge.

Corporate hospitality events

Many businesses offer their customers or potential customers general entertainment and hospitality, for example, golf days, track days, trips to sporting events, evening meals, trips to night clubs. HMRC will generally not allow deduction of VAT in respect of these events or will require you to account for output tax, as such events are unlikely to have a strict business purpose and be necessary for the business to make its supplies.

Commentary—*De Voil Indirect Tax Service* **V7.437**.

REGULATIONS TO IMPLEMENT VAT TECHNICAL DIRECTIVE, VAT RATE INCREASE AND OTHER MISCELLANEOUS CHANGES

3 November 2010. *HMRC Brief 47/10*

INTRODUCTION

Budget Note 42 (22 June 2010) detailed the introduction of legislation to implement changes to the recovery of VAT for immoveable property, boats and aircraft to implement the EU VAT Technical Directive (Council Directive 2009/162/EU). As announced, the Capital Goods Scheme rules will be amended to allow for an adjustment mechanism, as required by the new EU VAT law.

The purpose of this Brief is to expose the draft legislation amending the VAT Regulations for a period of four weeks, to invite comments on it and to provide an explanation of the changes.

Alongside these amendments, HMRC intends to make other changes that are intended to simplify or update the current rules for the Capital Goods Scheme (CGS). HMRC will also regularise an existing Extra Statutory Concession linked to the option to tax and reaffirm an area of policy that has been the subject of litigation. There will also be two unrelated changes to the VAT Regulations which are required as a result of the standard VAT rate changing to 20 per cent from 4 January 2011.

WHO NEEDS TO READ THIS?

Taxpayers buying land, property, boats and aircraft on or after 1 January 2011; partly exempt taxpayers and those with non-business use of assets in the CGS; taxpayers acquiring CGS assets before they register for VAT; and representative members of VAT groups with CGS assets.

Taxpayers using the Flat Rate Scheme and taxpayers making supplies at the standard rate of VAT should read the section below on the increase in the VAT rate.

BACKGROUND

The key changes are outlined below. You will find more detailed information about the changes in Annex A; the draft legislation and explanatory note can be found at Annex B.

THE TECHNICAL DIRECTIVE

The Technical Directive requires all Member States to introduce an adjustment mechanism to take account of changes in use of certain assets when VAT recovery is restricted only to the business use of the assets (excluding any private use by the taxpayer or the taxpayer's staff) from 1 January 2011. In line with these requirements, HMRC intends to widen the scope of the current CGS so that it not only caters for changes between taxable and exempt business use (as now) but also for changes between business and non-business use of assets. This will mean businesses having to complete one adjustment mechanism rather than two.

Ships and aircraft costing £50,000 or more will be included in the CGS to ensure that taxpayers are able to adjust VAT recovery if use changes. Where these assets cost less than £50,000 they will not have the burden of undertaking any adjustments.

SIMPLIFICATION

While making these changes, HMRC will take forward the final phase of the three year programme of partial exemption and simplification proposals, on which business has been consulted. The key simplification measures proposed are:

- giving taxpayers the option of seeking approval for a combined method for dealing with taxable, exempt and non-business activities. Currently taxpayers can only apply for a special method to deal with taxable and exempt business activities. Introducing this option would streamline and simplify the VAT deduction process, give certainty and complement the Technical Directive changes;
- reducing the administrative burdens on taxpayers whose use of an asset changes only slightly - HMRC intends to legislate to ensure that insignificant CGS adjustments are disregarded, whether they favour HMRC or the taxpayer.

LEGISLATING FOR A CONCESSION

As part of its programme of regularising extra-statutory concessions, HMRC announced in April 2009 that it would be considering the future of one of its concessions, which allows VAT recovery under a CGS type calculation by a person who was not registered for VAT at the time they acquired a CGS asset. The draft legislation now covers this extra statutory concession, which will be withdrawn on the day the legislation takes effect. The concession links to the option to tax and is referred to in paragraph 9.4 of Notice 742A.

POLICY CLARIFICATION

HMRC has clarified in the draft legislation that the representative member of a VAT group is the owner for VAT purposes of all CGS items owned by companies while they are within the group. The legislation also clarifies who the owner is where there is a transfer of a going concern (TOGC) and other cases where there is a transfer without a VAT supply. There is no change to HMRC's policy in these areas and the new legislation aims only to put the matters beyond doubt.

INCREASE IN THE VAT RATE - CONSEQUENTIAL CHANGES

There are two consequential amendments required to implement the 4 January 2011 increase in the standard rate of VAT. This legislation establishes the invoicing requirements for the supplementary charge arising under the anti-forestalling legislation and sets the new rates and thresholds applicable under the Flat Rate Scheme (see "What to do if your flat rate percentage changes" www.hmrc.gov.uk/vat/start/schemes/flat-rate.htm).

TIMING

With the exception of the consequential changes required as a result of the VAT rate increase, which will take effect on 4 January 2011, all the amendments outlined above will take effect from 1 January 2011.

COMMENTS

If you would like to make any comments about the draft legislation please email Lara Pritchard by 30 November 2010.

FURTHER INFORMATION

Further information can be obtained from the HMRC website or by contacting the Helpline on 0845 010 9000.

ANNEX A: TECHNICAL NOTE ON PLANNED CHANGES

	Description of change		Implementing regulation (see draft legislation)
1.	Widening the scope of the CGS to include non-business VAT - brings VAT relating to non-business activities into the CGS and requires businesses to review their "business non-business" (BNB) calculation (in addition to the current requirement to review the PE calculation) at the end of each year for CGS items.		6, 14(i), and 16
2.	Define CGS items by reference to VAT-bearing capital expenditure (rather than input tax-bearing expenditure) - as the CGS is to be widened to include VAT relating to non-business activities, the definition of a CGS item should include the corresponding amount of VAT bearing expenditure relating to non- business activities (otherwise assets with significant non-business use might be excluded from the CGS).		12
3.	Widening the scope of the CGS to include ships and aircraft that cost £50k or more (VAT bearing capital expenditure) - this will replace the quarterly adjustments (for those taxpayers operating Lennartz accounting) with an annual CGS adjustment. Taxpayers whose ship or aircraft costs less than £50k will not be affected and will not undertake any adjustment to account for changes in use of their asset.		12
4.	Widening the scope of the clawback / payback rules to cater for changes in business use of assets - this change brings non-business activity into the clawback/payback rules (another adjustment mechanism). These rules apply where business related costs are provisionally claimed or not claimed on the basis of an intended supply, but before that intention comes to fruition, there is either a change of intention or the costs are actually used to make a supply of a different VAT treatment. The rules require that VAT on the relevant costs are reallocated. (So, for example, a business cannot claim back VAT on a cost that it intends to use for VAT exempt purposes. However, if there is a subsequent change of intention and the business decides to use the cost to make a taxable supply, it would be entitled to "clawback" (ie: recover) the VAT from HMRC.)		9
5.	Excluding costs incurred after 1 January from the value of deemed supplies under Lennartz accounting - this prevents costs (on assets falling within the Technical Directive) incurred on or after the 1 January from being included within the value of the Lennartz private use charge. This ensures that in transitional cases (an asset straddling 1 January), where the business has chosen to claim Lennartz accounting for the pre-Jan costs, then the Lennartz VAT on private use charge is computed by reference to just those costs. This prevents double taxation.		17
	Partial exemption / CGS simplification changes		
6.	Combined BNB PE method - gives taxpayers the option of seeking approval for a combined method for determining their BNB and PE calculations - effectively widening the scope of the current PE special method regime.		6, 7 and 8
7.	Ignoring insignificant CGS adjustments - a mandatory requirement that taxpayers using the CGS ignore insignificant adjustments where:		15
	–	total VAT bearing expenditure on CGS item is £1m or less and adjustment percentage is 10% or less; or	
	–	total VAT bearing expenditure on CGS item is £10m or less and adjustment percentage is 5% or less; or	

VAT PRs etc

	Description of change		Implementing regulation (see draft legislation)
	–	adjustment percentage is 1% or less.	
8.	Simplifying and clarifying the drafting of the legislation as follows:		12
	–	defining capital items - definitions have been reordered and changed - NB: there is a slight widening of the scope of the CGS in relation to the refurbishment, fitting out, alteration or extension of a civil engineering work (this ensures consistency with the definitions of other capital items and HMRC expects it to have minimal impact);	
	–	removing requirement for an extension to be more than 10% (one of the conditions for an alteration or extension of a building to qualify as a CGS item is that it creates at least 10% additional floor area). This change removes the 10% condition so businesses only need to consider total capital expenditure;	
	–	goods affixed to a building in the case of a refurbishment (under current rules expenditure on goods is only included within the value of a CGS item if they are affixed to a building). This change simplifies the rule by removing this condition so that a business only needs to consider total capital expenditure;	
	–	removes reference to self-supply charge prior to 1997 which is now redundant (certain changes in the use of buildings triggered a self-supply charge prior to 1 March 1997, which, in turn, created a capital item). This change removes such self-supply charges as they were no longer relevant with effect from 2008.	
9.	Clarifying legislation in light of case law to confirm the there a 3 elements to a capital item: the item, the owner's interest in the item and capital expenditure on the item - this aspect sets out more clearly what has been an area of some confusion.		11 and 12
10.	Simplifying and clarifying the drafting of the legislation that describes who is responsible for accounting for CGS adjustments in the event of a TOGC (transfer of a going concern) etc, and that where a taxpayer de-registers from VAT the adjustment is due on the final VAT return.		14(j) and (p)
11.	Clarifying the legislation in light of ECJ case law to cater for part-disposals of CGS items and consequential amendments. NB: the "old" disposal test has been removed as effectively redundant in light of change made in 1997.		14(e)
12.	Aligning the CGS period of adjustment with the time the owner has an interest in a capital item - in some cases, the period of time that a business has an interest in an asset is less than the required adjustment period under the CGS. This change aligns the period of adjustment with the interest in the asset to ensure a logical result.		13
13.	Defining the start of the CGS period of adjustment by reference to "first use" - this redefines the start date of the CGS period of adjustment by reference to first use (currently, there are various definitions including date of importations, acquisition, registration, first use and deemed supply).		13
	Legislating for the concession linked to the option to tax		
14.	Enables a person that was not registered for VAT at the time they acquired a CGS item to recover VAT in accordance with the CGS when it registers for VAT - thereby ensuring equal treatment with registered businesses. Consequential amendment required to 111 to ensure taxpayer does not reclaim the VAT twice.		10, 13 and 14(i)
	Confirmation of existing policy		

	Description of change	Implementing regulation (see draft legislation)
15.	To confirm existing policy that the owner of a capital item following a TOGC is the transferee, and representative member of a VAT group where the item is owned by a member of the group and they required to fulfil the obligations of the transferor or group member	11
	Consequential amendments for VAT rate change	
16.	The Flat Rate Scheme (FRS) needs to be amended to ensure that taxpayers using the FRS experience the same percentage increase as those using normal VAT accounting. The amendments ensure a straight mathematical recalculation of the flat rate percentages based on the forthcoming standard rate of 20%, and consequential changes to thresholds.	4
17.	Anti-forestalling legislation to prevent artificial avoidance seeking to exploit the change in the VAT rate was enacted as part of Finance Act (No 2) 2010. It counters forestalling by introducing a "supplementary charge to VAT" where a VAT invoice is issued or a prepayment received before 4 January 2011 but the provision of goods or services is to take place on or after that date. VAT of 17.5 per cent is due on the date of issue of the invoice or receipt of payment but, in certain circumstances, a supplementary charge of 2.5 per cent becomes due on the date that the standard rate increases to 20 per cent (or, if it arises on a grant of a right, on the date of the first exercise of the right on or after that date). The change here ensures that the invoicing requirements specified in regulations will apply in cases where this supplementary charge is triggered.	3

ANNEX B

Draft Value Added Tax (Amendment) Regulations 2010 [not reproduced]

Commentary—*De Voil Indirect Tax Service* **V3.212**.

PROPOSALS TO SIMPLIFY THE "CHANGE IN USE" PROVISIONS

7 December 2010. *HMRC Brief 49/10*

INTRODUCTION

This Brief announces a four week consultation period to consider proposals to simplify the "change in use" provisions (Paragraphs 35 to 37 of Part 2 of Schedule 10 to the Value Added Tax Act 1994).

From the date of implementation, the legislation will no longer have two adjustment mechanisms (each with its own rules on how to calculate and apply a tax charge) to apply to the two sets of circumstances where a "change in use" occurs.

Instead, there will be a single adjustment mechanism to be applied in all circumstances. It will be based on the:

– amount of VAT that would have been chargeable on the original supply (or supplies) had the building in question not been eligible for the zero rate
– proportion of the building that is affected by the change in use
– number of complete years that the building has been used solely for a qualifying purpose prior to the change in use

WHAT IS THE PURPOSE OF THE "CHANGE IN USE" PROVISIONS?

New buildings that are intended to be used solely for a relevant residential or relevant charitable purpose (a "qualifying purpose") are relieved of VAT on their construction or acquisition. A building that does qualify for that relief is expected to be used solely for that qualifying purpose for a period of, at least, ten years following completion of the building.

If the building ceases to be used solely for that "qualifying purpose" within that ten year period or if that use decreases, the "change in use" provisions allow HM Revenue & Customs (HMRC) to "claw back" some or all of the original relief.

Examples of how the current provisions work and how the proposed simplified provisions will work can be found at Annex A.

WHY DO WE WANT TO MAKE THIS CHANGE?

The current provisions are complex and, as can be seen from the examples at Annex A, produce uneven tax consequences. A change in use in one set of circumstances can produce a different tax charge to the one produced by a different set of circumstances even though, overall, the same percentage of the building continues to be used for a relevant use.

The new provisions will produce similar tax charges where use changes to a similar degree, regardless of the circumstances in which the change in use comes about.

A copy of the draft legislation can be found at Annex B.

WHO WILL BE AFFECTED BY THIS CHANGE?

This change will only affect buildings that cease to be used for a qualifying purpose after the implementation date or whose use for a qualifying purpose decreases after that date.

Charities are most likely to be affected by this change but owners of buildings used for a relevant residential purpose, such as care homes or old people's homes, may also be affected.

COMMENTS REQUIRED

A copy of the proposed draft legislation is attached. HMRC will be grateful for any comments on the legislation and their proposal. Please email any comments or observations to Stephen Lumby by 3 January 2011.

ANNEX A: EXAMPLES (BASED ON A STANDARD VAT RATE OF 20 PER CENT) OF HOW THE CURRENT "CHANGE IN USE" PROVISIONS WORK AND HOW THE PROPOSED SIMPLIFIED PROVISIONS WILL IMPACT

A £5 million new zero-rated building, consisting of five floors, was occupied by a charity for its own use. During the first five years it was used by them wholly for its non-business activities.

After five years it decides to change how it uses 20 per cent of the building.

The VAT consequences under current legislation will vary depending on the circumstances.

USED BY THAT CHARITY FOR BUSINESS PURPOSES

If one floor of the building is put to a business use by the charity, then a one-off self-supply charge of VAT of £100,000 will be due.

This has been calculated under the current provisions as follows:

The value of the original zero-rated supply (£5 million) multiplied by the part of the building that has ceased to be used for a qualifying purpose (20 per cent) multiplied by the remaining years left in the ten year period after the change (5 or 50 per cent) multiplied by the standard rate of VAT (20 per cent).

That is (£5m × 20% × 50% × 20%) = £100,000 VAT.

NB The charity can also recover the VAT charged, provided the business activity carried out in this area is fully taxable.

Impact of proposed change – none – charge would be calculated on the same basis as at present, resulting in a one-off self-supply charge of £100,000 VAT.

RENTED TO ANOTHER CHARITY FOR ITS NON-BUSINESS ACTIVITIES

Providing the rental to the other charity is non-business and the charity tenant uses the part rented to them solely for a relevant charitable use, then there is no change in use because the property is still used wholly for a non-business purpose. The owner of the building does not suffer a VAT cost.

RENTED TO A TENANT WHO USES IT FOR BUSINESS PURPOSES

If the property is let for five years to a tenant (including another charity) who does not use that part solely for a relevant charitable use, a change in use charge arises.

The charge is calculated by reference to any premium and rent charged.

Assuming a £200,000 premium, and an annual rent of £60,000, the change of use charge is £52,000 in the first year and £12,000 per annum in successive years (that is 20 per cent of £60,000 per annum) for a total of five years.

In total, the cost will be £100,000 VAT.

Different tax results are likely depending upon the length of the lease, whether there is a premium and the value of the rent.

Impact of proposed change – the annual charge based on rent charged is replaced by one-off liability based on 20 per cent overall changed use of the building, that is £5m × 20% × 50% × 20% = £100,000 VAT.

NB The charity can recover the VAT charged if it opts to tax the rent charged and that option is not disapplied.

ANNEX B

Draft Value Added Tax (Buildings and Land) Order 2011

NB The commencement date of the Order was 1 March 2011 as SI 2011/86.

Citation, commencement and effect

(1) This Order may be cited as the Value Added Tax (Buildings and Land) Order 2011 and shall come into force on [xxxx 2011].

(2) This Order has effect in relation to supplies made on or after [date].

Amendment of Schedule 10 to the Value Added Tax Act 1994

2. Schedule 10 to the Value Added Tax Act 1994 (buildings and land) is amended as follows.

3. For paragraphs 35 to 37 (residential and charitable buildings: change of use etc) and their headings substitute–

"Introductory

(1) This Part of this Schedule applies where one or more relevant zero-rated supplies relating to a building (or part of a building) have been made to a person ("P").

(2) In this Part of this Schedule–

"relevant zero-rated supply" means a grant or other supply which relates to a building (or part of a building) intended for use solely for–

(a) a relevant residential purpose, or

(b) a relevant charitable purpose,

and which, as a result of Group 5 of Schedule 8, is zero-rated (in whole or in part);

"relevant premises" means the building (or part of a building) in relation to which a relevant zero-rated supply has been made to P;

"relevant period", in relation to relevant premises, means 10 years beginning with the day on which the relevant premises are completed.

(3) Where P is a body corporate treated as a member of a group under sections 43A to 43D, any reference in this Part of this Schedule to P includes a reference to any member of that group.

Disposal of interest or change of use following relevant zero-rated supply

(1) Paragraph 37 applies on each occasion during the relevant period when–

(a) there is an increase in the proportion of the relevant premises falling within sub- paragraph (3) or (4), and

(b) as a result, the proportion of the relevant premises so falling ("R2") exceeds the maximum proportion of those premises so falling at any earlier time in the relevant period ("R1").

VAT PRs etc

(2) Sub-paragraph (1) is subject to sub-paragraph (9).

(3) The relevant premises fall (or part of the relevant premises falls) within this sub- paragraph if P has, since the beginning of the relevant period, disposed of P's entire interest in the relevant premises (or part).

(4) The relevant premises fall (or a part of the relevant premises falls) within this sub- paragraph if–

(a) those premises do not (or that part does not) fall within sub-paragraph (3), and

(b) those premises are not (or that part is not) being used by P for a relevant residential purpose or a relevant charitable purpose.

(5) Sub-paragraph (6) applies where-

(a) only a proportion of the use of the relevant premises (or the use of a part of those premises) by P is for a relevant residential purpose or a relevant charitable purpose, and

(b) that use is not confined to a part of those premises (or of that part) which is used solely for a relevant residential purpose or a relevant charitable purpose.

(6) Where this sub-paragraph applies, sub-paragraph (4) applies as if–

(a) the same proportion of the relevant premises (or part) were being used for a relevant residential purpose or a relevant charitable purpose, and

(b) the remainder of the relevant premises (or part) were not being used for a relevant residential purpose or a relevant charitable purpose.

(7) Subject to sub-paragraph (8), where the relevant premises are (or a part is) being used by P for a relevant residential purpose or a relevant charitable purpose but the premises (or part) is occupied by a person who is not using them (or it) for a relevant residential purpose or a relevant charitable purpose, the premises are not (or part is not) to be treated as being used by P for a relevant residential purpose or relevant charitable purpose.

(8) Sub-paragraph (7) does not apply if P is a charity using the relevant premises as a village hall or similarly in providing social or recreational facilities for a local community.

(9) Where P disposes of P's entire interest in all or part of the relevant premises ("the transferred premises") in the course of the transfer of a business as a going concern, and by virtue of an order under section 5(3), that disposal is not treated as a supply of goods or services, then–

(a) sub-paragraph (3) does not apply in respect of the disposal,

(b) from the time of the disposal, any relevant zero-rated supply in respect of the transferred premises made or previously treated as made to the transferor shall be treated as having been made to the transferee (and not the transferor),

(c) from the time of disposal, paragraphs 35 to 37 apply to the transferee (and not the transferor) in respect of the transferred premises,

(d) if one or more charges have arisen under paragraph 37 in relation to the relevant premises before the disposal, this paragraph and paragraph 37 apply in relation to the transferred premises and the remaining relevant premises as if the proportion of the premises in question falling within sub-paragraph (3) or (4) at the time of the disposal were such proportion (if any) as equates to a fair and reasonable part of the maximum proportion of the relevant premises so falling at any time in the relevant period before the disposal, and

(e) if a part is attributed to premises under sub-paragraph (d), paragraph 37(3)(b) (rather than paragraph 37(3)(a)) applies to the first deemed supply under paragraph 37 in relation to those premises which occurs after the disposal.

Charge to VAT

(1) Where this paragraph applies, P's interest, right or licence in the relevant premises held immediately prior to the time when the increase referred to in paragraph 36(1) occurs is treated for the purposes of this Part of this Schedule as–

(a) supplied to P for the purposes of a business which P carries on, and

(b) supplied by P in the course or furtherance of that business immediately prior to the time of that increase.

(2) The supply is taken to be a taxable supply which is not zero-rated as a result of Group 5 of Schedule 8.

(3) The value of the supply is taken to be-

(a) in the case of the first deemed supply under this paragraph, the amount obtained by the formula–

R2 x Y × ((10 – Z) / 10), and

(b) in the case of any subsequent deemed supply under this paragraph, the amount obtained by the formula–

(R2 - R1) × Y × ((10 – Z) / 10)

(4) For the purpose of sub-paragraph (3)–

(a) R1 and R2 have the meaning given by paragraph 36(1) (b),

(b) Y is the amount that yields an amount of VAT chargeable on it equal to–

(i) the VAT which would have been chargeable on the relevant zero-rated supply, or

(ii) if there was more than one supply, the aggregate amount of the VAT which would have been chargeable on the supplies,

had the relevant premises not been intended for use solely for a relevant residential purpose or a relevant charitable purpose, and

(c) Z is the number of whole years since the day on which the relevant premises were completed."

EXPLANATORY NOTE

(This note is not part of the Order)

This Order which comes into force on xxxx amends Schedule 10 to the Value Added Tax Act 1994 (c. 23) by substituting new paragraphs 35 to 37.

Paragraphs 35 to 37 make provision for when and how a charge to VAT will arise in circumstances where the construction of, or grant of an interest in, a building ("premises") has been zero-rated on the basis of its intended use ("a relevant purpose") and that use changes after the grant has been made.

Under the previous provisions, the charge to tax and the method of calculation of the charge differed depending on whether or not the recipient of the zero-rated supply subsequently granted an interest to a third party. Where a change in use occurred in an unidentifiable part of the premises, the charge arose on the entire premises or part of the premises.

Article 3 substitutes new paragraphs 35 to 37. The new paragraphs provide for a uniform application of the charge to VAT and a single method for its calculation as follows.

Paragraph 35 sets the context and provides additional definitions to aid interpretation. Paragraph 36 (1) provides for a charge to arise on each occasion that there is an increase in the use of the premises for a non-relevant purpose.

Paragraph 36(2) provides an exception to the circumstances in which a change in use charge applies.

Paragraph 36(3) provides there is a charge to VAT where a person disposes of the entire interest in the premises or in a part of the premises.

Paragraph 36(4) provides that there is a charge to VAT where an identifiable area of the premises, or of a part of the premises, is used for a non-relevant purpose.

Paragraphs 36(5) and (6) apply where use is made of the premises (or of part of the premises) for both a relevant and a non-relevant purpose. The proportion of use for a non- relevant purpose is to be calculated in the same proportion as if an identifiable part of the building were used for a non-relevant purpose.

Paragraph 36(7) provides that there is a charge to VAT where any person in occupation of the premises uses the premises (or part of the premises) for a non-relevant purpose.

Paragraph 36(8) provides an exception to the charge to VAT that arises under sub- paragraph (7) for charities using the premises as a village hall or for similar purposes.

Paragraph 36(9) applies where there has been a transfer of a business as a going concern. It disapplies the VAT charge that would otherwise arise on disposal and provides for the liability for a VAT charge that arises from a change in use subsequent to the transfer to be that of the transferee rather than the transferor. It also provides for any charges which arise prior to the transfer to be applied proportionately to the transferred premises and any remaining premises.

Paragraph 37 provides for the charge to VAT and makes provision as to how the supply is to be valued.

A full and final Impact Assessment has not been produced for this instrument as a negligible impact on the private or voluntary sectors is foreseen.

OPTION TO TAX FOR SUPPLIES OF LAND AND BUILDINGS – TWO PER-CENT OCCUPATION RULE

7 December 2010. *HMRC Brief 50/10*

INTRODUCTION

This Brief announces a four week consultation on draft legislation (see Annex A) which seeks to amend part of the option to tax anti-avoidance test for supplies of land & buildings contained in VATA 1994 Schedule 10 paragraphs 12 to 17. This Brief explains the proposed changes and invites comments. Subject to the consultation it is intended that the changes will be introduced in early 2011.

WHO NEEDS TO READ THIS?

Anyone who makes supplies of land and buildings which are subject to the anti-avoidance rule in VATA 1994 Schedule 10 paragraphs 12 to 17. See Notice 742A "Opting to tax land and buildings" section 13 for details about how the rule works and transactions that are likely to be affected.

BACKGROUND

Under the anti-avoidance provision in Schedule 10 of the VAT Act, an option to tax is disapplied where two key tests are satisfied:

- the grantor is a developer of the land
- the grantor or development financier intend or expect that the land will become "exempt land"

As a result of the disapplication of an option, the grantor's supplies are exempt from VAT. This can affect the amount of VAT the grantor is able to reclaim on costs.

The proposed amendment concerns the second of the above tests – the meaning of "exempt land". Under paragraph 15 of Schedule 10 VATA 1994 land is "exempt land" if it is to be occupied by the grantor, the "development financier" (a person who has provided finance for the purchase or development of the land) or a person connected to either the grantor or financier, and the occupation is not "wholly or substantially wholly for eligible purposes". To be in occupation for eligible purposes a person must be making predominantly taxable supplies (or supplies which entitle the person to input tax recovery). "Wholly or substantially wholly" is defined as at least 80 per cent.

The mechanistic nature of the anti-avoidance test has resulted in concerns about the effect of the measure on certain transactions. Following representations to HMRC the test was amended from 1 April 2010 and a new "10 per cent occupation test" was introduced, whereby occupation of no more than 10 per cent of a building by a person providing finance for its purchase or development is ignored. HMRC have now been made aware of instances where minor occupation by the grantor (or a connected person of the grantor) can cause an option to be disapplied even though there is no deliberate attempt to avoid tax. The proposed change addresses that concern by introducing a further "2 per cent occupation test" applicable where the grantor himself or a person(s) connected to the grantor is to be in occupation. The new rule is in addition to the existing 10 per cent rule and does not replace it.

HOW WILL THE "2 PER CENT OCCUPATION TEST" WORK?

Occupation of any part of a building by the grantor (even a very small proportion) normally counts as occupation for the purposes of the anti-avoidance test and can result in the option to tax being disapplied. Under the proposed change a grantor is not treated as in occupation where the conditions of the "2 per cent occupation test" are met (the conditions largely mirror those of the existing 10 per cent rule). The rule works as follows:

- There must be no intention or expectation at the time of the grant that the grantor or a person connected with the grantor will occupy more than 2 per cent of any building (or part of a building) included in the grant at any time during the grantor's CGS adjustment period. Where the grantor is in occupation together with a person connected to them, it is the combined occupation that counts towards the 2 per cent threshold, unless the occupation by either person meets the eligible purposes test in Schedule 10 paragraph 16.
- The proportion of the building occupied is to be calculated in relation to the whole of the single building or, where the grantor holds an interest in only part of the building, that part in which an interest is held immediately prior to the grant being made (this includes any part of the building in which an interest is held by a person(s) connected to the grantor.
- Where a number of buildings are included in the same grant, the rule is applied to each building on an individual basis. Where the 2 per cent threshold is exceeded in relation to any of the buildings, the conditions of the rule are not met. For the purpose of the rule a single building takes its meaning from VATA 1994 Schedule 10 sub-paragraphs 18(4) to (7).
- The rule is not satisfied where the person(s) occupy any land included in the grant which is not a building. However, occupation of land that falls within the curtilage of the building or is used for parking vehicles can be disregarded as long as such occupation is ancillary to the occupation of the building.
- For the purposes of calculating the percentage of the building occupied by a particular person the practices set out in the RICS "Code of Measuring Practice" are to be used. Further details about how this is applied are set out in paragraph 13.8.6 of Notice 742A Opting to tax land and buildings. As with the 10 per cent rule, HMRC will only require evidence of the calculation in cases where the area occupied is close to 2 per cent.

OCCUPATION BY REFERENCE TO ATMS

The way that occupation by reference to Automatic Teller Machines (ATMs) is treated will also be changed. Currently, occupation which is solely in the form of ATMs can be disregarded as a result of Schedule 10 sub-paragraph 16(7). Under the proposed changes the reference to ATMs in sub-paragraph 16(7) will be replaced by new references in paragraph 15. In future, occupation of land which is solely by reference to ATMs will not be treated as occupation for the purposes of the anti-avoidance test. In addition, occupation of any building which is solely by way of ATMs will be ignored for the purposes of both the 2 per cent and 10 per cent rules.

WHY ARE WE MAKING THESE CHANGES?

Following discussions with trade representatives and business we believe the changes will be seen as a welcome practical simplification of the anti-avoidance test. The amendments to paragraph 15 of Schedule 10 should ensure that the option to tax is not disapplied in cases where a grantor occupies very minor parts of buildings and should, as a result, help to facilitate business.

COMMENTS

If you would like to make any comments about the draft legislation please email Michael McLachlan by 3 January 2011.

FURTHER INFORMATION

Further information can be obtained from HMRC website or by contacting the Helpline on Tel 0845 010 9000.

ANNEX

Draft Value Added Tax (Buildings and Land) (No 2) Order 2011

Citation, commencement and effect

1. This Order may be cited as the Value Added Tax (Buildings and Land) Order 2011 and shall come into force on [xxxx 2011].

2. This Order shall have effect in relation to supplies made on or after [xxxx 2011] other than a supply arising from a grant made before [xxxx 2011].

Amendment of Schedule 10 to the Value Added Tax Act 1994

3. Schedule 10 to the Value Added Tax Act 1994 (buildings and land) is amended as follows.

4. In paragraph 15 (meaning of "exempt land": basic definition), for sub-paragraph (3A) substitute–

"(3A) Where a person ("P") is in occupation of the land at any time before the end of the relevant adjustment period as respects that land, P is treated for the purposes of sub-paragraph (2) as not in occupation of the land at that time if–

(a) the building occupation conditions are met at that time, or

(b) P's occupation of the land arises solely by reference to any automatic teller machine of P.".

5. In paragraph 15A (meaning of "exempt land": the building occupation conditions)-

(a) in sub-paragraph (1)(b)(ii) for "10%" substitute "the maximum allowable percentage";

(b) at the end of sub-paragraph (2) add–

"if that occupation is not wholly, or substantially wholly, for eligible purposes.";

(c) for sub-paragraph (4) substitute–

"(4) In sub-paragraph (1)(b)(ii)–

"the maximum allowable percentage" means–

(a) 2% where P is the grantor or a person connected with the grantor, and

(b) 10% where P is a development financier or a person connected with a development financier (but not also the grantor or a person connected with the grantor), and

"relevant building" means–

(a) a building any relevant interest in which is included in the grant, other than any part of such a building in which, immediately before the grant, neither the grantor nor any person connected with the grantor held a relevant interest, or

(b) any building P's occupation of which arises solely by reference to any automatic teller machine of P.".

(d) after sub-paragraph (6) insert–

"(6A) Sub-paragraph (5) of paragraph 15 (determination of whether occupation "wholly, or substantially wholly" for eligible purposes to be by reference to criteria in public notice) applies for the purposes of this paragraph.".

6. In paragraph 16 (meaning of "exempt land": eligible purposes) omit sub-paragraph 7.

EXPLANATORY NOTE

(This note is not part of the Order)

This Order amends paragraphs 15, 15A and 16 of Schedule 10 ("the Schedule") to the Value Added Tax Act 1994 (c. 23) ("the Act") and comes into force on [...] 2011. This Order has effect in relation to supplies made on or after [...] 2011 other than a supply arising from a grant made before that date.

Article 4 substitutes a new sub-paragraph (3A) in paragraph 15. The new provision provides that where a person ("P") is in occupation of the land at any time before the end of the relevant adjustment period as defined in the Schedule, P is treated as not in occupation of the land for the purposes of sub-paragraph (2) at that time if certain building occupation conditions are met, or if the occupation arises solely by reference any automatic teller machine of P.

Article 5 amends sub-paragraph (2) of paragraph 15A to provide that occupation by a person connected with P is treated as occupation by P unless that occupation is wholly, or substantially wholly, for eligible purposes. Article 5 also substitutes a new sub-paragraph (4) of paragraph 15A, and amends the building occupation conditions to introduce a "maximum allowable percentage" that P may occupy in order to be treated as not in occupation of the land. If P is a grantor or a person connected to the grantor, the maximum allowable percentage is 2%. If P is a development financier or person connected to a development financier, the maximum allowable percentage is 10%. The new sub-paragraph (4) also defines "relevant building", and excludes any building that P occupies solely by reference to any automatic teller machine of P. Sub-paragraph (5) applies the same criteria as paragraph 15(5) to determine whether occupation is wholly, or substantially wholly, for eligible purposes.

In the light of the amending provisions in Articles 4 and 5 which treat P as not being in occupation of land where it arises only as a result of any automatic teller machine of P, paragraph 16(7), which treated such occupation as occupation for eligible purposes, is no longer needed, and is therefore omitted.

A full and final Impact Assessment has not been produced for this instrument as a negligible impact on the private or voluntary sectors is foreseen.

CHANGES TO VAT IN JANUARY 2011

14 December 2010. *HMRC Brief 52/10*

This brief reminds businesses of two VAT changes that will take place in January 2011. These are:

- increase in the standard rate of VAT from 17.5 per cent to 20 per cent on 4 January 2011
- changes to the place of supply rules for cultural, artistic, sporting, scientific, educational, entertainment or similar activities supplied to relevant business customers on 1 January 2011.

1. CHANGE OF STANDARD RATE OF VAT TO 20 PER CENT

Businesses and consumers are reminded that the standard rate of VAT goes up from 17.5 per cent to 20 per cent on 4 January 2011.

The rate change only applies to the standard VAT rate. There are no changes to sales that are zero-rated or reduced-rated for VAT. Similarly, there are no changes to the VAT exemptions. Any sales you make at these rates are unaffected by this change.

PAYMENTS ON ACCOUNT REGIME

The VAT rate increase means that there will be consequential changes to the VAT Payment on Account (POA) thresholds. Under the POA, certain businesses are required to make monthly VAT payments. Since the VAT rate change will increase the VAT liabilities of businesses, the POA entry and exit thresholds will go up from £1.6m and £2m to £1.8m and £2.3m. The thresholds will change on 1 June 2011 for quarterly reviews and on 1 December 2011 for annual reviews. For further information on the POA see Notice 700/60 Payments on account on our website, go to www.hmrc.gov.uk

BUSINESSES – WHAT YOU MUST DO WHEN THE STANDARD VAT RATE CHANGES

For any sales of standard-rated goods or services that you make on or after 4 January 2011, you must charge VAT at the 20 per cent rate. The special arrangements for businesses trading on 31 December 2009 (when the standard rate reverted to 17.5 per cent) will not apply to this rate change.

If you have a cash business and calculate your VAT using the VAT fraction you must use the VAT fraction of 1/6 on your standard-rated VAT inclusive sales from 4 January 2011.

If your business issues VAT invoices, the normal rule is that you must use the new 20 per cent rate for all VAT invoices you issue on or after 4 January, which are issued within 14 days (or longer period that has been agreed with HMRC) of you providing the goods or services.

SUPPLIES THAT SPAN THE RATE CHANGE

If you supply goods or services before 4 January 2011, but issue a VAT invoice on or after that date, you can choose to charge VAT at 17.5 per cent.

VAT PRs etc

For continuous supplies of services where a contract started before 4 January, you can choose to charge the old rate, 17.5 per cent, on services actually performed before 4 January, and the new rate of 20 per cent on the value of services actually performed on or after.

BUSINESSES RECLAIMING VAT

From 4 January 2011, you may receive VAT invoices with the new 20 per cent rate, as well as VAT invoices with the old 17.5 per cent rate for goods or services you bought before the rate changed. In such cases, you should claim back VAT at the rate shown on the invoice.

COMPLETING A VAT RETURN

The deadlines for submitting VAT returns remain the same, so you should continue to submit VAT returns in the usual way – whether you send them monthly, quarterly or annually. For returns that span the change in rate, you will need to add together both the VAT on sales charged at 17.5 per cent and those charged at 20 per cent. You then put this total in box 1 of your VAT return.

COUNTERING ARRANGEMENTS DESIGNED TO TAKE ADVANTAGE OF THE VAT RATE CHANGE

In order to counter arrangements where businesses aim to take advantage of the VAT rate change by applying the 17.5 per cent VAT rate to goods or services to be delivered or performed on or after 4 January 2011, anti-forestalling legislation has been introduced. Further details can be found in the web link below.

GUIDANCE

HMRC has published detailed guidance on the rate change, which can be found at Business Link-VAT rate change (www.businesslink.gov.uk/bdotg/action/layer?topicId=1085334907&furlname=vatratechange&furlparam=vatratechange&ref=&domain=www.businesslink.gov.uk)

2. CHANGES TO THE PLACE OF SUPPLY RULES FOR CULTURAL, ARTISTIC, SPORTING, SCIENTIFIC, EDUCATIONAL, ENTERTAINMENT OR SIMILAR ACTIVITIES SUPPLIED TO RELEVANT BUSINESS CUSTOMERS

From 1 January 2011, as part of the changes to the cross border VAT rules (agreed at EU level in 2009), most business to business (B2B) supplies of cultural, artistic, sporting, scientific, educational, entertainment and similar services will be taxed where the customer is established, under the B2B general place of supply rule. However, supplies of admission to cultural, artistic, sporting, scientific, educational and entertainment events, and services ancillary to admissions (such as cloakrooms) will remain taxable where the event takes place. Business to consumer supplies (B2C) will be unaffected.

Admission will cover any payment that gives the right to attend an event even if it is covered by a season ticket or subscription. This includes payment to attend conferences, exhibitions and seminars even if they are of an educational nature. In-house events will fall within this rule as well as those open to the general public. Guidance on the place of supply rules can be found in VAT Notice 741A Place of supply of services on our website, go to www.hmrc.gov.uk

For further information on other VAT and Excise matters, you can also contact the Helpline on 0845 010 9000.

VAT: CHANGES TO LENNARTZ ACCOUNTING, THE CAPITAL GOODS SCHEME AND EXTRA STATUTORY CONCESSION TO BE WITHDRAWN

30 December 2010. *HMRC Brief 53/10*

This Brief provides information on the reduced availability of Lennartz accounting. From 1 January 2011, taxpayers buying land, property, ships, boats, other vessels or aircraft will be permitted to claim VAT only to the extent the asset is used for business purposes, subject to any partial exemption restriction. If use changes, ships, boats and other vessels and aircraft costing £50,000 or more will now be included in the Capital Goods Scheme.

INTRODUCTION

Changes to the VAT recovery rules in respect of land, property, boats (and other vessels) and aircraft were announced in 2010 (see Budget Note 42), along with amendments to the Capital Goods Scheme (CGS) rules to allow for an adjustment mechanism. These implement the EU VAT Technical Directive (Council Directive 2009/162/EU). The changes are made partly by primary law (Finance (No 3) Act 2010 section 19 and Schedule 8) and partly by secondary law (The VAT (Amendment) (No 4) Regulations 2010), taking effect from 1 January 2011.

HM Revenue & Customs (HMRC) also announced that alongside these amendments it would simplify or update the current rules for the CGS and that it would regularise an existing Extra Statutory Concession linked to the option to tax and reaffirm an area of policy that has been the subject of litigation (see Revenue & Customs Brief 47/10). Legislation relating to recovery of VAT on directors' accommodation is also removed.

Draft secondary legislation was published for comment in November and amended in light of responses. The new law takes effect from 1 January 2011.

WHO NEEDS TO READ THIS?

Taxpayers buying land, property, boats (as well as ships or other vessels) or aircraft on or after 1 January 2011; partly exempt taxpayers and those with non-business use of assets in the CGS; taxpayers acquiring CGS assets before they register for VAT; representative members of VAT groups with CGS assets; taxpayers using or intending to use Lennartz Accounting.

BACKGROUND

Under previous arrangements, VAT on land and property, boats and aircraft was recoverable upfront and in full on both the business and private use of the asset (subject to any partial exemption restriction). VAT was then payable over subsequent years in respect of the private use of the asset. This is known as "Lennartz" Accounting. The new legislation, introduced as a result of the new EU VAT law known as the Technical Directive, ensures that VAT recovery is restricted to the business use of the asset concerned, excluding any private use by the taxpayer or the taxpayer's staff. This VAT restriction does not affect owners of other types of asset.

The Technical Directive requires all Member States to introduce an adjustment mechanism to take account of changes in use of these assets when VAT recovery is restricted. The UK has adapted the existing CGS to provide for this adjustment mechanism.

HMRC took the opportunity, while making changes in this area, to take forward the final phase of a three year programme to simplify the partial exemption rules, on which business has been consulted. There are therefore a number of other aspects which simplify or update the rules in this area.

CONSULTATION

HMRC exposed draft secondary legislation for comment in Revenue & Customs Brief 47/10. All responses were considered carefully and, as a result of feedback, an aspect of the proposed simplification measures which HMRC had expected to be widely welcomed – legislation to ensure that insignificant CGS adjustments were disregarded – has now been removed.

There have been other minor changes to the draft legislation as a result of comments.

THE NEW LAW

The key changes are outlined below. Guidance on the changes will be published early in the new year. The new legislation and explanatory note can be found at Annex A.

From 1 January 2011, taxpayers buying land, property, ships, boats, other vessels or aircraft will be permitted to claim VAT only to the extent the asset is used for business purposes, subject to any partial exemption restriction. However, to help ensure a fair recovery of VAT if use changes, ships, boats and other vessels and aircraft costing £50,000 or more will now be included in the CGS.

The scope of the current CGS has been widened so that it not only caters for changes between taxable and exempt business use (as now) but also for changes between business and non-business use of assets.

As part of HMRC's drive to simplify and update the rules in this area, taxpayers now have the option of seeking approval for a combined method for dealing with taxable, exempt and non-business activities.

LEGISLATING FOR A CONCESSION

An Extra Statutory Concession, that allows VAT recovery under a CGS type calculation by a person who was not registered for VAT at the time a CGS asset was acquired, will be withdrawn from 1 January 2011. Taxpayers who registered for VAT before this date will still be able to rely on the concession whilst those registering for VAT on or after it will be able to recover the appropriate VAT under the revised CGS legislation.

References to the concession can be found in paragraph 9.4 of Notice 742A - Opting to Tax Land and Buildings (as well as HMRC VAT guidance on Land and Property (V1-8) paragraph 22.13.4 and Input Tax (V1-13) paragraph 6.9).

POLICY CLARIFICATION

HMRC has clarified in law that the representative member of a VAT group is the owner for VAT purposes of all CGS items owned by companies while they are within the group. The legislation also clarifies who the owner is where there is a Transfer Of a Going Concern (TOGC) and other cases where there is a transfer without a VAT supply. There is no change to HMRC's policy in these areas and the new legislation aims only to put the matters beyond doubt.

GUIDANCE

The secondary legislation and explanatory note can be found at Annex A. Q&A guidance on how the rules are applied in practice will be published early in the new year.

LENNARTZ ACCOUNTING

is now available only in very limited circumstances where, for assets other than land property, ships and aircraft, the goods are used in part:

- for making supplies in the course of an economic activity that give a right to input VAT deduction (broadly, taxable supplies, supplies that would be taxable if made in the UK or certain financial and insurance supplies to non-EC customers)
- in part for the private purposes of the taxpayer or his staff or, exceptionally, for other uses which are wholly outside the purposes of the taxpayer's enterprise or undertaking

Taxpayers who have embarked upon Lennartz Accounting in relation to an asset before 1 January 2011 must continue to operate it in respect of that asset. However, for land and property, ships and aircraft any VAT incurred on or after this date is recoverable only to the extent that the asset is used to make taxable supplies or other business supplies carrying input tax credit.

As a transitional measure, following a change in policy arising from an ECJ decision, many taxpayers who had incorrectly been permitted to use Lennartz Accounting were able to continue using this mechanism, unless they chose to unravel the Lennartz Accounting completely (see Revenue & Customs Brief 02/10). From 1 January 2011, any VAT incurred on land and property, ships and aircraft is recoverable only to the extent that the asset is used to make taxable supplies or other business supplies carrying input tax credit. From 1 July 2011, taxpayers who were incorrectly permitted to use Lennartz Accounting will be able to unravel only where normal assessing time limits still apply to the original claim.

HMRC will include more detailed information on the application of Lennartz Accounting with the guidance to be published early in the new year.

TIMING

The new law will take effect from 1 January 2011.

FURTHER INFORMATION

Further information can be obtained from the HMRC website or by contacting the Helpline on Tel 0845 010 9000.

ANNEX A

Statutory Instruments – SI 2010/3022 Value Added Tax, The Value Added Tax (Amendment) (No 4) Regulations 2010

Citation, commencement and effect

1. This Order may be cited as the Value Added Tax (Buildings and Land) Order 2011 and shall come into force on [xxxx 2011].
2. This Order shall have effect in relation to supplies made on or after [xxxx 2011] other than a supply arising from a grant made before [xxxx 2011].

Amendment of Schedule 10 to the Value Added Tax Act 1994

3. Schedule 10 to the Value Added Tax Act 1994 (buildings and land) is amended as follows.
4. In paragraph 15 (meaning of "exempt land": basic definition), for sub-paragraph (3A) substitute–

"(3A) Where a person ("P") is in occupation of the land at any time before the end of the relevant adjustment period as respects that land, P is treated for the purposes of sub-paragraph (2) as not in occupation of the land at that time if–

(a) the building occupation conditions are met at that time, or

(b) P's occupation of the land arises solely by reference to any automatic teller machine of P.".

5. In paragraph 15A (meaning of "exempt land": the building occupation conditions)-

(a) in sub-paragraph (1)(b)(ii) for "10%" substitute "the maximum allowable percentage";

(b) at the end of sub-paragraph (2) add–

"if that occupation is not wholly, or substantially wholly, for eligible purposes.";

(c) for sub-paragraph (4) substitute–

"(4) In sub-paragraph (1)(b)(ii)–

"the maximum allowable percentage" means–

(a) 2% where P is the grantor or a person connected with the grantor, and

(b) 10% where P is a development financier or a person connected with a development financier (but not also the grantor or a person connected with the grantor), and

"relevant building" means–

(a) a building any relevant interest in which is included in the grant, other than any part of such a building in which, immediately before the grant, neither the grantor nor any person connected with the grantor held a relevant interest, or

(b) any building P's occupation of which arises solely by reference to any automatic teller machine of P.".

(d) after sub-paragraph (6) insert–

"(6A) Sub-paragraph (5) of paragraph 15 (determination of whether occupation "wholly, or substantially wholly" for eligible purposes to be by reference to criteria in public notice) applies for the purposes of this paragraph.".

6. In paragraph 16 (meaning of "exempt land": eligible purposes) omit sub-paragraph 7.

EXPLANATORY NOTE

(This note is not part of the Order)

This Order amends paragraphs 15, 15A and 16 of Schedule 10 ("the Schedule") to the Value Added Tax Act 1994 (c. 23) ("the Act") and comes into force on [...] 2011. This Order has effect in relation to supplies made on or after [...] 2011 other than a supply arising from a grant made before that date.

Article 4 substitutes a new sub-paragraph (3A) in paragraph 15. The new provision provides that where a person ("P") is in occupation of the land at any time before the end of the relevant adjustment period as defined in the Schedule, P is treated as not in occupation of the land for the

VAT PRs etc

purposes of sub-paragraph (2) at that time if certain building occupation conditions are met, or if the occupation arises solely by reference any automatic teller machine of P.

Article 5 amends sub-paragraph (2) of paragraph 15A to provide that occupation by a person connected with P is treated as occupation by P unless that occupation is wholly, or substantially wholly, for eligible purposes. Article 5 also substitutes a new sub-paragraph (4) of paragraph 15A, and amends the building occupation conditions to introduce a "maximum allowable percentage" that P may occupy in order to be treated as not in occupation of the land. If P is a grantor or a person connected to the grantor, the maximum allowable percentage is 2%. If P is a development financier or person connected to a development financier, the maximum allowable percentage is 10%. The new sub-paragraph (4) also defines "relevant building", and excludes any building that P occupies solely by reference to any automatic teller machine of P. Sub-paragraph (5) applies the same criteria as paragraph 15(5) to determine whether occupation is wholly, or substantially wholly, for eligible purposes.

In the light of the amending provisions in Articles 4 and 5 which treat P as not being in occupation of land where it arises only as a result of any automatic teller machine of P, paragraph 16(7), which treated such occupation as occupation for eligible purposes, is no longer needed, and is therefore omitted.

A full and final Impact Assessment has not been produced for this instrument as a negligible impact on the private or voluntary sectors is foreseen.

VAT: ECJ JUDGMENT IN AXA UK PLC – DEBT COLLECTION

13 January 2011. *HMRC Brief 54/10*

ABSTRACT

HMRC is warning businesses that all payment related services falling within the definition of "debt collection" outlined by the ECJ in the AXA judgment are now liable to VAT at the standard rate, even if those services previously received a ruling from HMRC that they were exempt.

FULL TEXT

This brief explains the HM Revenue & Customs (HMRC) position following the ECJ judgment in AXA UK plc (case ref C-175/09). The case concerned the application of the VAT exemption in Article 135(1)(d) of the EU VAT Directive for:

– "transactions, including negotiation, concerning deposit and current accounts, payments, transfers, debts, cheques and other negotiable instruments, but excluding debt collection"
– the Court found that the services in AXA were specifically excluded from the exemption as "debt collection" and were therefore liable to VAT at the standard rate

BACKGROUND

AXA UK plc (AXA) is the representative member of a VAT group which includes a company Denplan Limited (Denplan). Denplan operates payment plans on behalf of dentists which offer patients the facility of paying for dental treatment by way of a fixed monthly charge. It was the VAT status of one of the supplies made by Denplan to the dentists in connection with the operation of this plan, ie collecting the payments using the Direct Debit payment method from the patients' bank accounts and accounting to the dentist for any payments received, that was the subject of the ECJ referral.

Both the VAT Tribunal and High Court agreed with AXA and found that there was a separate exempt supply of payment services falling within A135(1)(d). The Court of Appeal, however, decided the issue was not clear in current law and referred the case to the ECJ for a preliminary ruling.

The Court of Appeal asked a number of questions of the ECJ, all focussing in particular on the earlier ECJ judgment in SDC (case ref C-2/95) and the specific functions a business had to be carrying out to bring it within the VAT exemption.

The ECJ released its judgment in AXA on 28 October 2010 and, rather than answering each question individually, decided to consider all the questions together. The Court found that the supply AXA made to the dentists (which it summarised as the collection, processing and onward payment of sums of money due from third parties to the dentists) was specifically excluded from the A135(1)(d) exemption as "debt collection".

THE HMRC POSITION

The ECJ judgment in AXA now specifically defines what "debt collection" means for the purposes of the exclusions to the VAT exemption. The ECJ says in paragraph 34 of its judgment that:

- "... it is irrelevant that such service is supplied at the time when the debts concerned become due..."
- it then goes onto say that the words "debt collection" in Article 135(1)(d)
- "... cover the collection of debts of any nature, without limiting their application to debts which were not paid on their due date." and also cover "... debts which have not yet become due and which will be paid on the due date."

Following the AXA judgment, therefore, "debt collection" cannot be seen as applying solely to the service of chasing and recovering overdue payments on behalf of the creditor and all services principally concerned with collecting payments from the person owing them for the benefit of the entity to which those payments are owed (regardless of whether those payments are received before, on, or after their due date) fall within the exclusion to the exemption and are consequently liable to VAT at the standard rate.

Supplies which involve the collection of payments as a minor or ancillary function but which are principally concerned with other payment related transactions that fall within the Article 135(1) exemptions, for example the movement and settlement of payments between bank accounts, will not be affected by the AXA judgment and will continue to fall within the VAT exemption.

WHAT THIS MEANS FOR BUSINESSES

All payment related services falling within the definition of "debt collection" as outlined by the ECJ in the AXA judgment are now liable to VAT at the standard rate. If this applies to payment related services supplied by your business and your business has previously received a ruling from HMRC that those services fall within the VAT exemption (or it has previously been treating its services as exempt in line with HMRC's published policy in this area) then VAT must be applied to those services from the date of this brief.

FURTHER INFORMATION

Details of how to make any adjustments relating to previous VAT Return periods can be found in VAT Notice 700/45 How to correct VAT errors and make adjustments or claims and from the VAT Helpline on Tel 0845 010 9000.

Where you are in any doubt about the correct VAT treatment please contact the VAT Helpline on Tel 0845 010 9000.

VAT AND AMLD: ELECTRONIC LOTTERY MACHINES AND BINGO MACHINES

20 January 2011. *HMRC Brief 01/11*

ABSTRACT

This brief explains HMRC's position on electronic lottery machines following the decision in Oasis Technologies (UK) Limited (TC00581) and its treatment of electronic bingo machines.

FULL TEXT

This Brief explains HM Revenue & Customs' (HMRC's) position following the Tribunal decision in Oasis Technologies (UK) Limited (TC00581). It also explains the treatment of electronic bingo machines.

VAT PRs etc

1. LOTTERY MACHINES

VAT

The Tribunal agreed with HMRC that the Oasis Electronic Lottery Ticket Vending Machine (ELTVM) is a gaming machine. However, the Tribunal found that the Oasis ELTVM also grants the right to participate in a lottery and that the takings from this machine are exempt from VAT. HMRC is not appealing the decision.

BACKGROUND

Oasis hired out ELTVMs to private members' clubs and sold them virtual electronic lottery tickets for use in the machines. There was no issue concerning the liability of these supplies. The Tribunal appeal concerned the VAT liability of the supplies made by the clubs using these machines and whether they qualified for exemption from VAT.

An ELTVM displays a lottery ticket on-screen and shows whether a player wins a prize or not. The tickets are stored within an electronic pack of a finite number of pre-drawn winning and non-winning tickets. Packs of tickets are randomised securely prior to being supplied to clubs and are downloaded onto the hard drive of the ELTVM. The order in which tickets are displayed is fixed once downloaded and cannot be influenced by the player or club making the supply.

TRIBUNAL DECISION

The Tribunal released its decision on 1 July 2010. It held that the Oasis ELTVM is a gaming machine within Note 1(d) to Group 4 of Schedule 9, VAT Act 1994 and that it also grants the right to participate in a lottery within Item 2, Group 4 of Schedule 9. It ruled that the supplies made are exempt from VAT.

HMRC'S POSITION

In light of the conclusions of the Tribunal HMRC accept that a machine, whose operation is the same as that of the Oasis ELTVM, shall be treated as granting the right to participate in a lottery. The income thereof is VAT exempt.

The VAT exemption will apply to a machine having all of the following characteristics:

– the machine must provide a game of chance
– the tickets must be randomly distributed
– the player, operator or manufacturer must not be able to influence the order in which a ticket is revealed
– the result of the lottery must not be determined or influenced by means of the machine, and
– where groups of tickets have been pre-loaded into a machine, the machine may randomly select a new group when the current one is completed.

MAKING CLAIMS OR ADJUSTMENTS

When a business has overdeclared tax on its income from an electronic lottery terminal determined to fall within the findings of the Tribunal, HMRC will pay claims, subject to the normal rules on capping.

We may also reject all or part of a claim if repayment would unjustly enrich the claimant.

More details on how to submit a claim and "unjust enrichment" can be found in Notice 700/45 How to correct VAT errors and make adjustments

AMUSEMENT MACHINE LICENSING DUTY (AMLD)

While the Tribunal did not consider the liability of the machines to Amusement Machine Licence Duty (AMLD), it did find that the machines in question were gaming machines. This finding is consistent with HMRC's view that the machines are liable to AMLD.

HMRC is continuing to issue AMLD assessments on lottery machines without an appropriate AMLD licence.

If you do not agree that your "electronic lottery terminal" is a gaming machine you should phone the HMRC Helpline on 0845 010 9000 with full details of the game. If HMRC think that your "electronic lottery terminal" is a licensable machine we will issue you with a default licence and assess for the outstanding duty. You will then be able to challenge the decision by requesting a statutory review by HMRC or by appealing to an independent tribunal.

2. BINGO MACHINES

HMRC is aware that a number of manufacturers in the gaming industry have recently developed machines which are used to play an electronic version of bingo.

Where a machine meets the characteristics of bingo machines listed in guidance published by the Gambling Commission in June 2009 ("Key characteristics of bingo"), although some of the criteria are for regulatory purposes only, HMRC will accept that for VAT and gambling duties taxation the machine is designed or adapted for playing bingo.

The supply made thereof is exempt from VAT under Item 1, Group 4, of Schedule 9, VAT Act 1994.

If a machine will only allow playing of bingo, it does not require an AMLD licence.

FURTHER INFORMATION

For further information and advice please contact the Helpline on 0845 010 9000.

More information to help businesses decide whether their amusement machine is liable to AMLD can be found in Notice 454 Amusement Machine Licence Duty. Exemptions are covered in section 3.

HMRC'S POSITION FOLLOWING THE DECISION IN THE CASE OF JOHN PRICE

25 January 2011. *HMRC Brief 02/11*

ABSTRACT

This Brief explains HMRC's policy following the First Tier Tribunal decision in the case of John Price (TC/2010/01287). The Tribunal agreed with the appellant that roller blinds were "building materials" and the VAT could be recovered under the DIY Housebuilders and Converters VAT Refund Scheme.

FULL TEXT

This Brief explains HM Revenue & Customs' (HMRC) policy following the First Tier Tribunal decision in the case of John Price (TC/2010/01287).

The Tribunal agreed with the appellant that roller blinds were "building materials" as defined by Note 22 to Group 5 of Schedule 8 to the VAT Act 1994. As a result, the appellant was entitled to treat the VAT incurred on the purchase of the blinds as recoverable from HMRC under the provisions of the DIY Housebuilders and Converters VAT Refund Scheme (s 35 of the VAT Act 1994).

HMRC'S POSITION

HMRC's view remains unchanged in that roller blinds (and other "window furniture") are not "building materials" as defined and will not be changing its policy. The Tribunal chairman did not hear any evidence on the point of what is and what is not a "building material" for VAT purposes but reached his conclusion as a matter of judicial notice, that is, as a common sense fact.

Given the small amount of VAT at stake in this particular case, HMRC will not be appealing this decision further.

BACKGROUND

The construction of residential property is zero-rated for VAT purposes. The zero rate not only applies to the construction services but also to the "building materials" incorporated into the property by the person(s) supplying those construction services.

It has never been HMRC's policy that the zero rate should apply to all goods that were incorporated into residential property by builders during its construction. Their policy has always been to restrict the zero rate to those basic materials such as bricks, mortar, timber, glass etc., that make up the structure of a property and to those standard fittings and fixtures such as kitchen units, work surfaces, sinks and draining boards, wash hand basins, baths and toilets that enable the property to function.

To achieve the above result, "building materials" have been defined in law as meaning, in relation to any description of building, "goods of a description ordinarily incorporated by builders in a building of that description (or its site)". Certain goods are specifically excluded from the definition, for example, fitted furniture, electrical and gas appliances but with some exceptions made for kitchen furniture, boilers etc.

DIY house builders, to the extent that they purchase building materials and use their own (or others') labour to incorporate those materials into their properties, are unable to benefit from the above zero rate on "building materials". However, they can claim the VAT incurred on the purchase of those materials through a refund scheme. The restriction on the zero rate for building materials noted above also restricts the amounts of VAT recoverable through the refund scheme.

CHANGES TO THE OPTION TO TAX FOR SUPPLIES OF LAND AND BUILDINGS (ANTI-AVOIDANCE RULE)

25 January 2011. *HMRC Brief 03/11*

ABSTRACT

This Brief explains minor changes to the option to tax for land and buildings, and in particular the treatment of occupation by grantors. It follows the introduction of the new 2% occupation rule and a change to the way occupation by reference to ATMs is treated.

FULL TEXT

The introduction of a new "2 per cent occupation rule" and a change to the way that occupation by reference to Automatic Teller Machines is treated. See The Value Added Tax (Buildings and Land) Order 2011 (SI 2011/86)

1. INTRODUCTION

This Brief explains minor changes which are being made to the option to tax anti-avoidance rule. Currently the option to tax is disapplied where the grantor, or a person connected to the grantor, is in exempt occupation of the land (and the other conditions in the anti-avoidance rule are met). The changes to be introduced from 1 March 2011 mean that an option to tax will no longer be disapplied where the grantor or persons connected with the grantor only occupy minor parts of buildings (no more than two per cent) even if the other conditions of the anti-avoidance rule are met.

The treatment of Automatic Teller Machines (ATMs) is also being amended. From 1 March 2011 occupation of any building which is solely by way of ATMs will not be treated as occupation for the purposes of the anti-avoidance test.

2. WHO NEEDS TO READ THIS?

Anyone who makes supplies of land and buildings which are subject to the anti-avoidance rule in VATA 1994 Schedule 10 paragraphs 12 to 17. See Notice 742A Opting to tax land and buildings section 13 for details about how the rule works and transactions that are likely to be affected.

3. BACKGROUND

Under the anti-avoidance provision in Schedule 10 of the VAT Act, an option to tax is disapplied where two key tests are satisfied:

- the grantor is a developer of the land
- the grantor or development financier intends or expects that the land will become "exempt land".

As a result of the disapplication of an option, the grantor's supplies are exempt from VAT. This can affect the amount of VAT the grantor is able to reclaim on costs.

The amendment concerns the second of the above tests – the meaning of "exempt land". Under paragraph 15 of Schedule 10 VATA 1994 land is "exempt land" if it is to be occupied by the grantor, the "development financier" (a person who has provided finance for the purchase or development of the land) or a person connected to either the grantor or financier, and the occupation is not "wholly or substantially wholly for eligible purposes". To be in occupation for eligible purposes a person must be making predominantly taxable supplies (or supplies which entitle the person to input tax recovery). "Wholly or substantially wholly" is defined as at least 80 per cent.

The mechanistic nature of the anti-avoidance test has resulted in concerns about the effect of the measure on certain transactions. Following representations to HMRC the test was amended from 1 April 2010 and a new "ten per cent occupation test" was introduced. This allowed occupation of no more than ten per cent of a building by a person providing finance for its purchase or development to be ignored. HMRC have subsequently been made aware of instances where minor occupation by the grantor (or a person connected to the grantor) can cause an option to be disapplied even though there is no deliberate attempt to avoid tax. The change, which is effective from 1 March 2011, addresses that concern by introducing a further "two per cent occupation rule" applicable where the grantor himself or a person(s) connected to the grantor is to be in occupation. The new rule supplements the existing ten per cent rule.

4. DETAILS OF HOW THE NEW "2 PER CENT OCCUPATION RULE" WORKS

Occupation of any part of a building by the grantor (even a very small proportion) normally counts as occupation for the purposes of the anti-avoidance test and can result in the option to tax being disapplied. From 1 March 2011 all supplies arising from grants made on or after that date will be subject to the new "two per cent occupation rule". Under the proposed change a grantor is not treated as in occupation where the conditions of the "two per cent occupation rule" are met (the conditions largely mirror those of the existing ten per cent rule). The rule works as follows:

– there must be no intention or expectation at the time of the grant that the grantor or a person connected with the grantor will occupy more than two per cent of any building (part or all of which is included in the grant) at any time during the grantor's CGS adjustment period. Where the grantor is in occupation together with a person connected to them, it is the combined occupation that counts towards the two per cent threshold, unless the occupation by either person meets the eligible purposes test in Schedule 10 paragraph 16
– the proportion of the building occupied is to be calculated in relation to the whole of the single building (not just that part that is subject to the grant) or, where the grantor holds an interest in only part of the building, that part in which an interest is held immediately prior to the grant being made (this includes any part of the building in which an interest is held by a person(s) connected to the grantor
– where a number of buildings are included in the same grant, the rule is applied to each building on an individual basis. Where the two per cent threshold is exceeded in relation to any of the buildings, the conditions of the rule are not met. For the purpose of the rule a single building takes its meaning from VATA 1994 Schedule 10 sub-paragraphs 18(4) to (7)
– the rule is not satisfied where the person(s) occupy any land included in the grant which is not a building. However, occupation of land that falls within the curtilage of the building or is used for parking vehicles can be disregarded as long as such occupation is ancillary to the occupation of the building
– for the purposes of calculating the percentage of the building occupied by a particular person the practices set out in the RICS "Code of Measuring Practice" are to be used. Section 13 of Notice 742A Opting to tax land and buildings contains tertiary legislation setting out detailed rules about how the Code is to be applied. Further details about the method of calculation are given in paragraph 13.8.6 of Notice 742A Opting to tax land and buildings. As with the 10 per cent rule, HMRC will only require evidence of the calculation in cases where the area occupied is close to two per cent (between 0 and 7%)
– like the ten per cent occupation rule, the rule is based on the intention or expectation of the grantor at the time the grant is made and involves a forward look over the ten year period of the CGS. Where it is known at the time of the grant that further grants will be

made, the calculation must take account of the occupation that will result from those grants. The test is, however, a one-off test at the time of the grant

5. OCCUPATION BY REFERENCE TO ATMS

The way that occupation by reference to Automatic Teller Machines (ATMs) is treated will also be changed. Currently, occupation which is solely in the form of ATMs is treated as occupation for "eligible purposes" under Schedule 10 sub-paragraph 16(7). This means it can be ignored for the purposes of the anti-avoidance test. From 1 March 2011 an amendment to paragraph 15 of Schedule 10 will mean that occupation of any building which is solely by way of ATMs will not be treated as occupation for the purposes of the anti-avoidance test. As a result, sub-paragraph 16(7) will not be required and will be repealed.

6. FURTHER INFORMATION

Further information can be obtained from the HMRC website or by contacting the Helpline on 0845 010 9000

CONFIRMATION OF HMRC'S VIEW ON THE VAT TREATMENT OF COMMERCIALLY OPERATED SPORTS LEAGUES

9 February 2011. *HMRC Brief 04/11*

ABSTRACT

HMRC confirm that supplies made by commercial sports league providers are liable to the standard rate of VAT. If sports league providers feel they have been mislead by previous advice from HMRC officers, and they fulfil certain criteria, they should contact HMRC's Complaints Team.

FULL TEXT

It has been issued in response to enquiries from a number of organisations that run football leagues. The brief reflects what HMRC's policy has always been. It does not represent a change of policy.

BACKGROUND

There are a number of commercial organisations that run football and other sports leagues ("sports league providers"). Typically, a sports league provider will do most or all of the following:

- organise a league
- allocate fixtures to teams in the league
- provide pitches for teams to play on (some league providers own pitches, others rent them from other parties)
- provide referees
- determine results
- keep and publish scores and league tables
- award trophies to winning teams

Payments for such supplies are collected in a variety of ways. For example, the sports league provider may charge a one off "admin fee" to teams plus a "match fee" for each game that is played.

VAT LIABILITY

Some sports league providers have suggested that they are making supplies of land of a kind that are exempt under Group 1, Schedule 9 of the VAT Act 1994 (they rely on Note 16 to Group 1 which allows a series of lets of sports pitches to be exempt, subject to certain conditions). They consider that the essential nature of their supplies is one of pitch hire.

HMRC disagrees with this analysis. We consider that the supplies made by sports league providers consist of a bundle of elements, which are integral to each other, but that it cannot be said that there is one principal element to which all others are ancillary. In these circumstances, it is necessary to establish the character of the overarching supply to determine whether it falls within the exemption. In HMRC's view, the overarching supply is of participation in a sports league, not a supply of land.

It is therefore HMRC's view that the supplies made by commercial sports league providers are liable to the standard rate of VAT.

However, supplies made by certain non-profit making bodies may fall within the Group 10 sports exemption. For details of the conditions that must be met for the Group 10 exemption to apply, please see Notice 701/45 "Sport".

CLAIMS OF MISLEADING ADVICE BY HMRC

Some sports league providers have asked HMRC to consider whether they have been in receipt of misleading advice from HMRC officers in the past relating to the liability of their supplies. Such cases must be considered on an individual basis by the appropriate Complaints Team. We would recommend sports league providers to contact their Complaints Team if they:

– consider that they have been misled by HMRC in relation to the liability of their supplies
– have acted in accordance with the misleading representation
– would suffer real detriment if VAT was to be collected for past supplies

For information about our complaints procedure, go to www.hmrc.gov.uk, and under "quick links", select "Complaints".

CHANGE IN TAX TREATMENT OF BUSINESS ENTERTAINMENT OF OVERSEAS CUSTOMERS – DRAFT INSTRUMENT

25 February 2011. *HMRC Brief 09/11*

ABSTRACT

This brief announces a four week consultation on draft legislation which amends the VAT treatment of business entertainment expenses in the light of the ECJ's judgment in Danfoss and AstraZeneca. The change was announced in Revenue & Customs Brief 44/2010.

FULL TEXT

VAT: PROPOSED SECONDARY LEGISLATION TO IMPLEMENT THE CHANGE IN TAX TREATMENT OF BUSINESS ENTERTAINMENT OF OVERSEAS CUSTOMERS PREVIOUSLY ANNOUNCED IN REVENUE & CUSTOMS BRIEF 44/2010

Subject to the consultation it is intended that the changes will be introduced on 1 May 2011.

COMMENTS

If you would like to make any comments about the draft legislation please email David Webb by 28 March 2011.

FURTHER INFORMATION

Further information can be obtained from the HMRC website or by contacting the VAT Helpline on 0845 010 9000.

ANNEX A

2011/DRAFT VALUE ADDED TAX (INPUT TAX) (AMENDMENT) ORDER 2011

Made - - - - ***

Laid before the House of Commons ***

Coming into force - - ***

The Treasury make the following Order in exercise of the powers conferred by section 25(7) of the Value Added Tax Act 1994:

CITATION AND COMMENCEMENT

1. This Order may be cited as the Value Added Tax (Input Tax) (Amendment) Order 2011 and comes into force on 1st May 2011.

AMENDMENT TO THE VALUE ADDED TAX (INPUT TAX) ORDER 1992

(1) The Value Added Tax (Input Tax) Order 1992(SI 1992/3222) is amended as follows.

(2) In article 5(1) after the words "for the purposes of business entertainment" insert "unless the entertainment is provided for an overseas customer of the taxable person and is of a kind and on a scale which is reasonable, having regard to all the circumstances".

(3) After article 5(3) insert—

"(4) For the purposes of this article "overseas customer", in relation to a taxable person, means—

(a) any person who is not ordinarily resident nor carrying on a business in the United Kingdom or the Isle of Man and avails himself or herself, or may be expected to avail himself or herself, in the course of a business carried on by that person outside the United Kingdom and the Isle of Man, of any goods or services the supply of which forms part of the taxable person's business; and

(b) any person who is not ordinarily resident in the United Kingdom or the Isle of Man and is acting, in relation to such goods or services, on behalf of an overseas customer as defined in paragraph (a) above or on behalf of any government or public authority outside the United Kingdom and the Isle of Man.".

XX

XX

Two of the Lords Commissioners of Her Majesty's Treasury

8th April 2011

EXPLANATORY NOTE

(This note is not part of the Order)

The Value Added Tax (Input Tax) Order 1992 (SI 1992/3222) ("the 1992 Order") restricts recovery of Value Added Tax ("VAT") charged on certain goods and services. Article 5 of that Order restricts recovery of tax charged on any goods or services used for the purposes of business entertainment. This Order amends the 1992 Order.

Article 2 of this Order amends article 5(1) of the 1992 Order to allow recovery of VAT charged on business entertainment for an overseas customer when it is of a kind, and on a scale, reasonable in all the circumstances.

Article 3 of this Order inserts a new article 5(4) into the 1992 Order to provide a definition of overseas customer.

A full and final impact assessment has not been prepared for this instrument as it has a negligible impact on business, charities or voluntary bodies.

CLARIFICATION OF BUILDING CHANGE OF USE SIMPLIFIED PROVISIONS

21 March 2011. *HMRC Brief 13/11*

ABSTRACT

HMRC has published this Brief to clarify that the simplified VAT provisions for change of use will only apply to a building completed on or after 1 March 2011 and whose use changes on or after that date.

FULL TEXT

This Brief clarifies the introduction of simplified "change in use" provisions announced in RCB 05/11 VAT: Simplification of the "change in use" provisions for buildings zero-rated because they were intended to be used for a relevant residential and relevant charitable purpose.

In RCB 05/11, we announced a simplification in the "change in use" provisions.

We wish to make it clear that the simplified provisions will only apply to buildings completed on or after 1 March 2011, and whose use changes, from a qualifying one to a non-qualifying one, on or after 1 March 2011.

If the buildings were completed before 1 March 2011, the old "change in use" provisions will apply.

VAT Information Sheet 04/11 has been amended to reflect this clarification and to make other minor clarifications.

VAT GROUPING—ESC 3.2.2

25 March 2011. *HMRC Brief 16/11*

ABSTRACT

This Brief sets out HMRC's view on how ESC 3.2.2, which concerns reverse charges on VAT groups with overseas members, should be applied pending legislation to put the concession on a statutory footing. The government is to consult on the enactment of ESC 3.2.2 in May 2011.

FULL TEXT

VAT: reverse charges within VAT groups – legislating a VAT grouping Extra Statutory Concession (ESC 3.2.2)

1. INTRODUCTION

HM Revenue & Customs (HMRC) have a published Extra Statutory Concession (ESC) covering how a tax charge applicable to VAT groups should be calculated (ESC 3.2). HMRC is reviewing all its ESCs following the Wilkinson decision (*R v HM Commissioners of Inland Revenue ex p Wilkinson* [2005] UKHL 30). ESC3.2.2 is not "*Wilkinson*" compliant. The Government intends to legislate to give statutory effect to ESC 3.2.2. This Brief sets out how the ESC should be applied in the interim.

2. WHO NEEDS TO READ THIS?

This ESC affects UK VAT groups with an overseas member that buys services from persons outside the VAT group and uses them to make supplies to the UK members.

3. BACKGROUND

A VAT group comprises two or more corporate bodies under common control within a single VAT registration. A VAT group can contain members that are established overseas provided that they are also established in the UK. Transactions between members of a VAT group are normally disregarded for VAT purposes.

In the mid-1990s a VAT avoidance scheme allowed partly-exempt VAT groups to avoid paying VAT on certain services they bought in. The services involved were those where the VAT is accounted for by the customer. Services used in the UK would be bought by a VAT group member abroad so that UK VAT would not be charged (the supply being made outside the UK and thus outside the scope of UK VAT). The services would then be routed to the UK user via an intra-VAT group charge. As intra-VAT group charges were ignored for VAT purposes no VAT was chargeable at that point either. The net result was VAT-free services.

Anti-avoidance legislation was enacted in 1997 requiring a tax charge to be declared on certain supplies by the overseas members to the UK members of the group. The tax charge arose where:

– the supply incorporated services bought by the overseas member that would be treated as supplied here if bought by the UK members ("reverse charge services")

VAT PRs etc

– and the supply was taxable and itself would have been treated as supplied in the UK

The legislation applied the tax charge to the whole intra-group transaction whereas the avoidance scheme only related to services bought in from third parties.

4. THE PURPOSE OF THE ESC

ESC 3.2.2 was brought in to ensure that the anti-avoidance provision was limited to removing the tax advantage from such structures. The following is an extract from ESC 3.2.2:

> "...the amount of the tax charge...is calculated with reference to the value of the supply by the overseas member to the UK member. By concession, the value for calculating the tax charge may be reduced to the value of the Schedule 5 services purchased by the overseas group member, provided that the group is in a position to provide evidence in the UK of the value of those services, and that those services have not been undervalued."

The ESC works by restricting the tax charge to the value of reverse charge services bought in by the overseas member. These services were listed in Schedule 5 VAT Act 1994.

5. CHANGES TO PLACE OF SUPPLY OF SERVICES (POSS) RULES

On 1 January 2010 the POSS rules changed. The general rule determining where a supply was made for business to business transactions changed from the place where the supplier belongs to where the customer belongs. As a result of this change, Schedule 5 became redundant and was repealed.

6. HOW ESC 3.2.2 SHOULD BE APPLIED UNTIL IT IS LEGISLATED

Where a group makes use of this ESC, it should be applied in a way that maintains its intended effect. To achieve this, the reference to Schedule 5 should be read as a reference to the new general rule for supplies to businesses, in VATA 1994 s7A(2)(a). The ESC will continue to allow VAT groups to value the tax charge by reference to the services the overseas member has bought in that would now be treated as subject to UK VAT if the UK group member bought them direct. Evidence of the value of the services bought in, and that they have not been undervalued, will still be needed.

7. LEGISLATING ESC 3.2.2

The Government will commence a technical consultation with stakeholders in May 2011.

VAT TREATMENT OF SUPPLIES OF HOT FOOD MADE IN THE COURSE OF CATERING

1 April 2011. *HMRC Brief 19/11*

ABSTRACT

This Brief confirms HMRC's view of the VAT treatment of supplies of hot food made in the course of catering following judgment ECJ in four joined German cases.

FULL TEXT

INTRODUCTION

This Brief confirms HMRC's view of the VAT treatment of supplies of hot food made in the course of catering. It has been issued following the European Court of Justice (ECJ) judgment in the joined German cases of C-497/09, C-499/09, C501/09 and C-502/09 (*Manfred Bog* and others).

BACKGROUND

The ECJ ruled that the supply of food or meals freshly prepared for immediate consumption from snack stalls, mobile snack bars or in cinema foyers is a supply of goods within the meaning of Article 5 of the Sixth VAT Directive if a qualitative examination of the entire transaction shows that the elements of supply of services preceding and accompanying the supply of the food are not predominant. This is unlike the activities of a party catering service which are supplies of services within the meaning of Article 6 except in cases in which a party catering service does no more than deliver standard meals without any additional elements of supply of services.

Furthermore, the ECJ has held that the term "foodstuffs" in category 1 of Annex H to the Sixth Directive 77/ 388, as amended by Directive 92/111 (now category 1 of Annex 111 to the VAT Directive 2006/112), must be interpreted as also covering food and meals which have been prepared for immediate consumption by boiling, grilling, roasting, baking or other means.

The significance of the decision for German taxpayers is that certain supplies of hot food may now be eligible for the reduced rate.

HM REVENUE & CUSTOM'S (HMRC) POSITION

The UK treats most basic supplies of foodstuffs as zero rated but along with other specified items there is a specific exclusion from the zero-rate for supplies made in the course of catering. The Law (VAT Act 1994, Sch 8, Group 1, Note 3) goes further to specifically legislate for certain supplies of food that are for consumption on and off premises including the supply of hot food.

Article 110 of the VAT Directive 2006/112 allows the UK to retain its zero-rate for food as long as there are clearly defined social reasons and the supplies are for the benefit of the final consumer. There can be no extension to the zero-rate provisions and the Courts have determined that exemptions (including zero rating) must be construed strictly, but exceptions from the exemption (including Note 3) should not be construed restrictively.

The zero rating provisions form a specific legal framework and subject to the conditions of the derogation the UK has discretion as to what supplies fall within those provisions. Since the UK has specifically legislated to exclude supplies of hot food it is clear that the intention was not to include such supplies within the zero-rate.

CONCLUSION

HMRC considers that the ECJ judgment has no implications for the UK treatment of supplies of hot food and businesses should continue to treat their supplies in accordance with published guidance.

ACCOUNTING FOR ACQUISITION VAT ON INTRA-EU SUPPLIES—CHANGES TO THE "FALLBACK" PROVISIONS

17 May 2011. *HMRC Brief 20/11*

ABSTRACT

This brief contains details of changes that will affect you if you use a UK VAT registration for goods (including yachts) supplied between EU Member States without arriving in the UK. The changes are effective from 1 June 2011.

FULL TEXT

INTRODUCTION

This brief announces a change in VAT treatment where a business uses a UK VAT registration number (other than for triangulation purposes - see below) to secure zero-rating of goods sent from one EU Member State to another, without arriving in the UK.

Under what is often referred to as the "fallback" provision, use of a UK VAT registration number in these circumstances makes the customer liable to account for acquisition VAT in the UK. Significantly this does not cancel any liability to account for acquisition VAT in the Member State to which the goods are sent ("the Member State of arrival"). However, the UK VAT can be adjusted if VAT is accounted for correctly in the Member State of arrival.

The fallback rule is explained in paragraph 7.7 of Notice 725 (The Single Market). The change follows the judgement of the Court of Justice of the European Union (CJEU) in the joined cases of X (C-536/08) and Facet BV (C-539/08).

VAT PRs etc

THE CJEU DECISION

The issue before the CJEU arose from two similar cases. In each, supplies of computer goods were sourced from Member States other than the Netherlands and sent direct to customers located elsewhere in the EU. Dutch VAT registration numbers were used to secure zero-rating of the intra-EU supplies. The CJEU was asked to consider whether there was a right to deduct the acquisition VAT each of the taxpayers was required to account for under the Dutch equivalent of the fallback provision, as input tax.

In its decision the CJEU held that there could be no right to deduct acquisition VAT where it falls due under the fallback arrangements as the goods did not actually enter the Member State. In arriving at its decision the Court noted that if there were a right to deduct in these circumstances, it could jeopardise the operation of the normal rules as it would remove the incentive for the acquisition to be taxed in the Member State of arrival.

EFFECT OF THE DECISION

The decision provides a welcome clarification of what was previously an uncertain position. The liability to account for acquisition VAT where a UK VAT registration number is used in the course of an intra-EU supply of goods not involving removal to the UK remains unchanged. However, it is now clear that there is no right to recover the acquisition VAT as input tax. The only basis on which the UK VAT may be adjusted is where it can be demonstrated that acquisition VAT has been accounted for in the Member State of arrival.

TRIANGULATION SIMPLIFIED PROCEDURE

Use of a UK VAT registration number as part of the triangulation simplification arrangements (see section 13 of Notice 725) is unaffected.

IMPACT ON ACQUISITIONS OF YACHTS IN THE UK

In 1997 Customs & Excise agreed to arrangements under which a UK VAT registered business could account for acquisition VAT in the UK on a yacht purchased from a supplier in another Member State without the yacht arriving in the UK. This was announced in Business Brief 12/97 (see below) which also permitted input tax deduction subject to the normal rules.

Following the CJEU decision the UK acquirer may now no longer recover the UK acquisition VAT as input tax. For this reason the agreement will cease to have effect and so is to be withdrawn from 1 June 2011. After that date UK acquisition VAT accounted for on a yacht that does not arrive in the UK will no longer be recoverable as input tax. However, as a transitional measure, any UK VAT registered business who, before 1 June 2011, entered into a contract for the purchase of a yacht and who intended to adopt the procedure as agreed in Business Brief 12/97, may continue to rely on those arrangements (including recovery of the acquisition VAT as input tax, subject to the normal rules) when the yacht is eventually delivered. But this is subject their holding satisfactory evidence of the contract and the date that it was agreed.

EXTRACT FROM BUSINESS BRIEF 12/97

TAXABLE ACQUISITION OF YACHTS IN THE UNITED KINGDOM

Customs & Excise have agreed to introduce a temporary arrangement concerning the liability to account for VAT on the taxable acquisition of yachts in the United Kingdom, in certain limited circumstances. This follows representations made on behalf of owners of large yachts and is effective immediately.

Where a VAT-registered business in the United Kingdom buys a yacht from a supplier in another Member State, and the yacht is being removed from that Member State to the place where it will be hired on charter, acquisition VAT may be accounted for in the United Kingdom without the need for the yacht to actually come here. The normal rules will apply for recovery of any input tax that is incurred and for accounting for output tax on any supplies subsequently made.

This arrangement does not affect the VAT treatment of yachts being imported into the EU from third countries, and will be kept under review.

INTRODUCTION OF LEVY ON "SINGLE-USE" CARRIER BAGS IN WALES

22 June 2011. *HMRC Brief 23/11*

ABSTRACT

This HMRC Brief provides advice on the VAT treatment of the charge for carrier bags to be introduced in Wales from 1 October 2011, initially to be set at a minimum of 5 pence.

FULL TEXT

1. INTRODUCTION

The Welsh Assembly Government is to introduce a compulsory charge on "single-use" carrier bags which retailers must charge to customers in Wales, with effect from 1 October 2011.

This is not a HM Revenue & Customs measure, but it has implications for VAT and Direct Tax. This brief explains the basics of the charge and the tax implications.

2. WHO NEEDS TO READ THIS?

All retailers within Wales, and any retailers outside Wales who deliver goods to customers in Wales using "single-use" carrier bags.

3. BACKGROUND

The Welsh Assembly Government is to introduce a compulsory charge (initially to be set at a minimum of 5 pence) on single-use carrier bags which retailers in Wales must charge to their customers. Retailers outside Wales who deliver goods to customers in Wales using single-use carrier bags will also have to make the charge.

The relevant legislation (SI 2010/2880) will be effective from 1 October 2011 and full details of how the charge is to operate is contained in the draft guidance available from the Welsh Assembly Government website: wales.gov.uk/docs/desh/publications/110225carrierbagguidanceen.pdf.

4. VAT IMPLICATIONS

The charge is consideration for the bag and is taxable at the standard rate of VAT. In order that customers pay the same amount regardless of the VAT status of the business, the stated minimum charge (initially 5 pence) is the minimum total to be charged by non-VAT-registered businesses. The stated minimum charge will be deemed to include VAT when charged by a VAT-registered business.

Thus, for the avoidance of doubt, A VAT-registered business would charge 4.17 pence plus VAT.

Retail Scheme users should ensure that this is properly accounted through their scheme where applicable.

5. DIRECT TAX IMPLICATIONS

For the purposes of Corporation Tax and Income Tax, receipts from the compulsory charge on single-use carrier bags should be brought into account in calculating trading profits. The Welsh Assembly Government expects the proceeds to be used to fund good causes in Wales and relief may be available where the normal charitable donations/gift aid rules are met.

WITHDRAWAL OF BUSINESS BRIEF 28/04 ITEM 2 ISSUED 25 OCTOBER 2004

7 July 2011. *HMRC Brief 24/11*

ABSTRACT

This HMRC Brief announces that from 1 August 2011 Business Brief 28/04 item 2, "VAT — correcting liability errors", will be withdrawn to take account of the announcement concerning the VAT Misdirection Extra Statutory Concession 3.5 on 1 April 2009 in Revenue & Customs Brief 15/09.

VAT PRs etc

FULL TEXT

VAT — CORRECTING LIABILITY ERRORS MADE BY HMRC

Business Brief 28/04 item 2, "VAT — correcting liability errors", will be withdrawn with effect from 1 August 2011. This withdrawal is to take account of the announcement concerning the VAT Misdirection Extra Statutory Concession 3.5 on 1 April 2009 in Revenue & Customs Brief 15/09. This is available on the HM Revenue & Customs (HMRC) internet site at Revenue & Customs Brief 15/09.

Revenue & Customs Brief 15/09 confirmed that HMRC is bound by incorrect advice only in the circumstances explained in "When you can rely on information provided by HM Revenue & Customs (HMRC)". This is available on the HMRC internet site at When you can rely on information or advice provided by HM Revenue & Customs (HMRC): www.hmrc.gov.uk/pdfs/info-hmrc.htm.

Taxpayers will usually only be required to apply the new interpretation of the law from a current or future date that HMRC will announce when advising on the correct interpretation.

If, following HMRC's announcement of its new interpretation of the law, a business nevertheless chooses to correct historical errors, HMRC will accept the corrections providing all of the following conditions are met:

- all past errors are corrected
- the neutrality of the tax is respected
- the business is no better off and the Exchequer no worse off than they would have been if the mistaken interpretation had not been made

As explained in Business Brief 28/04, taxpayers will not usually be required to register in respect of previous supplies they had treated as exempt based on HMRC's interpretation of the law at the time of supply.

For example, a court rules that supplies previously regarded by HMRC as exempt were, and had always been, liable to VAT. HMRC would not usually require businesses affected by such rulings to register for VAT in relation to taxable supplies they made prior to the court decision. Businesses that choose to register for periods prior to the binding court decision on liability must satisfy the normal rules for VAT registration. They must also apply correct accounting procedures, including those for exempt supplies and associated input tax restrictions. They must also be able to submit supporting calculations and evidence any input tax deductions.

HMRC POSITION FOLLOWING THE TRIBUNAL DECISION IN *PAYMEX LTD*

20 July 2011. *HMRC Brief 27/11*

ABSTRACT

This brief explains the HMRC position following the First Tier Tribunal decision in *Paymex Ltd*, when the Tribunal upheld the appeal of *Paymex Ltd* that the liability of the services of Insolvency Practitioners when conducting and supervising consumer Individual Voluntary Arrangements are exempt from VAT.

FULL TEXT

This brief explains the HM Revenue & Customs (HMRC) position following the First Tier Tribunal decision in *Paymex Ltd* ([2011] UKFTT 350).

The Tribunal found against HMRC and upheld the appeal of Paymex Ltd that the liability of the services of Insolvency Practitioners when conducting and supervising consumer Individual Voluntary Arrangements are exempt from VAT. HMRC are not appealing this decision.

BACKGROUND

Paymex Ltd is the representative member of a VAT group which includes Blair Endersby. Blair Endersby provides Insolvency Practitioners (IPs) to run and maintain Individual Voluntary Arrangements (IVAs). An IVA is made and conducted in the context of a statutory framework and can only be conducted by a licensed IP. It enables an insolvent individual to make a proposal for an IVA with their creditors. The IP carries out two services; nominee services which involve the preparation of the proposal to be agreed between the debtor and their creditors, and supervisory services involving the supervision and monitoring of the agreement, including taking regular payments from the debtor and paying the creditors in accordance with the agreement.

TRIBUNAL DECISION

The Tribunal decided that the services of an IP, including both the nominee and supervisory stages, constitute a single exempt supply for VAT purposes. The Tribunal went on to decide that the two core elements were negotiation of debts and transactions concerning payments. Since it had found both core elements to be exempt, it was not necessary for the Tribunal to determine which of the supplies were dominant. However it stated that if it had been necessary for it to do so it would have found negotiation to be the "core" supply.

HMRC POSITION

HMRC will not be appealing this decision and subject to the normal rules on input tax adjustment, capping and unjust enrichment, HMRC will pay claims for overpaid tax charged on the services of Insolvency Practitioners that fall within the findings of this Tribunal decision.

FURTHER INFORMATION

Details of how to make any adjustments relating to previous VAT Return periods can be found in VAT Notice 700/45 How to correct VAT errors and make adjustments or claims and from the VAT Helpline on Tel 0845 010 9000.

Where you are in any doubt about the correct VAT treatment please contact the VAT Helpline on Tel 0845 010 9000.

CHANGES TO THE TREATMENT OF CERTAIN SUPPLIES MADE BY EMPLOYERS UNDER SALARY SACRIFICE ARRANGEMENTS FOLLOWING THE CJEU JUDGMENT IN CASE C-40/09

28 July 2011. *HMRC Brief 28/11*

ABSTRACT

Following the ECJ judgment in *Astra Zeneca*, where it was decided that provision of vouchers to staff amounted to a supply of services effected for consideration, HMRC considers that there is no longer a distinction between deductions from salary and a salary sacrifice. Therefore, the amount of salary foregone is consideration for supplies of the benefits whether provided under a salary sacrifice or by a deduction from salary.

FULL TEXT

1.1 BACKGROUND

Astra Zeneca (C-40/09) operated a flexible remuneration package scheme under which employees could opt to take part of their remuneration in the form of goods and/or services rather than as salary. The case before the Court of Justice of the European Union (CJEU) concerned the correct VAT treatment of high street shopping vouchers provided to employees as one of the options of the scheme.

The Court found that the provision of vouchers amounted to a supply of services effected for consideration. As a consequence, whilst Astra Zeneca was able to recover VAT incurred on acquiring the vouchers, output tax was due on the consideration received from its employees.

Although this case was concerned with the supply of vouchers to employees, the principles considered by the Court are of general application and will apply to other supplies of goods and services to employees.

1.2 THE UK POSITION ON THE PROVISION OF GOODS AND SERVICES VIA SALARY SACRIFICE OR DEDUCTIONS FROM SALARY

Following earlier decisions by the UK courts, HM Revenue & Customs' (HMRC) policy was to make a distinction between the VAT treatment of supplies of goods and services to employees by a deduction from salary, and those provided under a salary sacrifice arrangement.

1.2.1 DEDUCTION FROM SALARY

This occurs where an amount is deducted from an employee's pay in return for a supply of goods or services by the employer. Output tax has always been and continues to be due on the amount deducted from salary. Input tax is recoverable in accordance with the normal rules.

1.2.2 SALARY SACRIFICE

For VAT purposes "salary sacrifice" has a very narrow and specific meaning. It describes an arrangement such as in the Co-operative Insurance Society case [1992] (VTD 109) where an employee opts to receive services and forgoes part of their salary in return. The employee enters into a new employment contract or has their existing contract amended to reflect the new arrangement which they are tied into.

In relation to such schemes HMRC have, to date, accepted that the reduction in the salary did not constitute consideration for the benefits received and output tax was not due. Employers were able to recover the related VAT as input tax, subject to the normal rules.

In cases where the employee has been provided with the use of a good (for example a home computer) and opts to purchase it at the end of the scheme it has always been HMRC's view that VAT is due (where applicable) at that stage.

1.3 THE JUDGMENT OF THE CJEU

The Court considered whether the provision of the vouchers was a supply for a consideration. It found that there was a direct link between the provision of the retail vouchers by the company to its employees and the part of the cash remuneration which the employees gave up.

As far as arrangements involving deductions from salaries are concerned, the judgment supports HMRC's existing policy that these are consideration for a supply for VAT purposes.

However, HMRC considers that the rationale used by the CJEU goes wider than deductions from salary, and as a consequence of this there is no longer a distinction between deductions from salary and a salary sacrifice. Therefore, the amount of salary foregone is consideration for supplies of the benefits whether provided under a salary sacrifice or by a deduction from salary.

It is clear that the principles applied by the CJEU are not confined to vouchers, but are equally applicable to many other situations where employers offer benefits to their staff. Where the benefit is subject to VAT, output tax will be due from, and input VAT recoverable by the employer in accordance with the normal rules.

1.4 IMPLEMENTATION: REVISED VAT TREATMENT OF SALARY SACRIFICE

Businesses providing benefits under arrangements, which qualify as salary sacrifice schemes for VAT purposes, must account for output VAT on these supplies, where they are subject to VAT. In order to allow businesses time to make the necessary adjustments, HMRC will not require output tax to be accounted for on taxable benefits provided under salary sacrifice schemes, until 1 January 2012.

See the annex for details of how this change of practice will apply in particular circumstances.

2. VALUATION

In most cases the value of the benefit for VAT purposes will be the same as the amount of salary deducted or the amount foregone under a salary sacrifice arrangement. Where this is less than the true value (for example where employers supply the benefits at below what it cost to buy them in), the value should be based on the cost to the employer.

3. DIRECT TAX

HMRC considers that the judgement is limited to the application of VAT legislation. The principle derived from the CJEU decision is concerned with whether, in the context of the provision of a benefit by an employer to an employee as part of the remuneration, that constitutes a supply of services affected for consideration. There is no comparable concept within tax law applicable to the taxation of employment income and HMRC will not be amending the existing published guidance relating to employment income issues.

FURTHER ADVICE

Where you are in any doubt about the correct VAT treatment please contact the VAT Helpline on Tel 0845 010 9000.

ANNEX

4. EFFECT OF THE CJEU JUDGMENT IN PARTICULAR CIRCUMSTANCES

4.1 CYCLE TO WORK SCHEME

Under the Cycle to Work Scheme employers purchase bicycles and safety equipment and provide them to employees. Where this has been done under a salary sacrifice arrangement, the effect of the judgment is that employers must account for output tax based on the value of the salary foregone by the employee in exchange for the hire or loan of a bicycle.

Affected businesses should apply this treatment from 1 January 2012. Employers can continue to recover VAT on the purchase of the bicycle and associated equipment.

Employers who have provided bicycles under deduction from salary arrangements are unaffected by the judgment as payments received from employees have always been subject to VAT and will continue to be so.

VAT remains due when a bicycle is disposed of and its value should normally be based on the price of an identical or similar item, taking into account the age and condition etc.

We are aware that valuing bicycles has caused difficulties for Scheme operators and therefore, to reduce administration burdens, the table used to value bicycles for direct tax purposes may be used. This table provides valuations for bicycles based on the age and original price. Any bicycles that fall outside of the table (such as antique or specialist bicycles) should be valued using the normal VAT valuation rules. If businesses choose to use lower values, they may be challenged in which case evidence will be required to support the valuation.

4.2 FACE VALUE VOUCHERS

HMRC's published policy in relation to the provision of face value vouchers by employers to employees aligns with the judgment of the CJEU. In the case of supplies made under a deduction from salary arrangement input tax is recoverable but output tax must be declared. Where such vouchers have previously been provided under a salary sacrifice arrangement (as defined above) then input tax was claimable, subject to the normal rules, but output tax was due to the extent of the input tax claimed.

4.3 CHILDCARE VOUCHERS

Childcare vouchers are not directly affected by the judgment as they are not subject to VAT.

However, employers that incur administrative fees from their voucher provider have, to date, been permitted to recover VAT on those fees as a general business overhead. However, because the fees are directly attributable to the exempt supply of vouchers the normal partial exemption rules must be applied with the result that the VAT incurred may no longer be fully recoverable.

Affected businesses should apply this treatment from 1 January 2012.

4.4 FOOD AND CATERING PROVIDED BY EMPLOYERS

Employers may provide their staff with free or subsidised meals, snacks or drinks. Where employees pay for the meal etc, the normal VAT liability will apply.

If employees make no payment, VAT is not due (provided the benefit is available to all staff).

The judgment does not affect the VAT treatment where employees pay for their meals etc by a deduction from salary as VAT remains due.

However, from 1 January 2012 where employees pay for meals etc under a salary sacrifice arrangement, employers must account for VAT on the value of the supplies unless they are zero-rated. Subject to the normal rules, the employer can continue to recover the VAT incurred on related purchases.

HMRC are aware, that historically some employers have set up what they purport to be salary sacrifice arrangements to avoid VAT that is due on the consideration provided by employees for their meals, for example using electronic payments cards which record the value of consideration that is available to purchase meals. HMRC will continue to challenge such arrangements.

4.5 BENEFITS PROVIDED TO ALL EMPLOYEES FOR NO DEDUCTION OR REDUCTION FROM SALARY

The judgment only applies where an employee provides consideration in exchange for benefits. Where an employer provides, for example, a workplace gym which all employees may use for no deduction or reduction from their salary that will not fall within the scope of the judgment. Businesses may continue to recover VAT incurred on providing such facilities as a business overhead subject to the normal rules.

Separate charges to use facilities etc remain within the scope of VAT.

4.6 MOTOR CARS

Most businesses are prevented from recovering VAT in full on the purchase and leasing of company motor cars. The input tax block on cars (100 per cent on purcases and 50 per cent on leasing) means that employers do not account for output tax when cars are made available to employees. Where VAT recovery is restricted and output VAT is not due the judgment has no direct impact.

Where an employer suffers no input tax restriction, output tax remains due.

[See also: [2010] All ER (D) 32 (Oct)]

VAT LIABILITY OF GOLF CLUB GREEN FEES CHARGED TO NON-MEMBERS

27 July 2011. *HMRC Brief 30/11*

ABSTRACT

HMRC is seeking permission to appeal to the Upper Tribunal against the decision of the First-tier Tribunal in Bridport and West Dorset Golf Club. The Tribunal upheld the club's argument that restricting the VAT exemption in respect of green fees to club members only is contrary to EU law. HMRC's view remains that green fees charged to non-members are standard-rated and will treat all claims accordingly pending its appeal.

FULL TEXT

VAT: HMRC'S POSITION FOLLOWING THE FIRST-TIER TRIBUNAL DECISION IN THE CASE OF THE BRIDPORT AND WEST DORSET GOLF CLUB LIMITED (TC01214)

This brief explains HM Revenue & Customs' (HMRC's) position following the First-Tier Tribunal decision in the case of The Bridport and West Dorset Golf Club case (TC/2009/122260). The appeal concerned the VAT liability of green fees charged by the golf club to non-members.

BACKGROUND

Bridport and West Dorset Golf Club is a non-profit making members' golf club. The issue before the tribunal was whether the charges, known as green fees, made by the club to visiting non-members in return for the right to play golf are exempt from VAT or, as HMRC maintained, standard rated.

Under VATA 1994 Schedule 9 Group 10 Item 3, supplies by non-profit making bodies of services closely linked and essential to sport to individuals taking part in sport are exempt from

VAT. However, where the body operates a membership scheme, any supplies to individuals who are not members are excluded from the exemption and subject to VAT.

The tribunal concluded that by restricting the exemption to supplies made to members, the UK law was acting contrary to the purpose of the exemption in the Principal VAT Directive (or, in other words, had failed to "correctly implement its terms"). It was not persuaded by HMRC's argument that the exclusion applied to non-members was justified on grounds that it reduced distortion of competition. As a result, it agreed with the golf club that supplies to non-members of green fees were exempt from VAT.

HMRC'S POSITION

HMRC believes that the tribunal has erred in interpreting EU law and remains of the view that where clubs that run membership schemes make charges to non-members for the use of certain sporting facilities, such as green fees, the charges are standard rated. They have, as a result, sought permission to appeal to the Upper Tier Tribunal.

Decisions of the First-Tier Tribunal are binding only on the parties to the decision. Consequently, we do not propose to pay other claims already submitted and we are not inviting new claims in the wake of this decision. Any claims that are submitted will be rejected.

HMRC consider that businesses should continue to follow the guidance in Notice 701/45 Sport and standard-rate these types of supplies made to non-members of a membership club. Should any golf clubs decide to exempt their green fees on the basis of the First-Tier Tribunal's decision, HMRC will assess the underdeclared tax and enforce the assessments. Penalties may also be applicable in such cases.

HMRC'S POSITION FOLLOWING THE FIRST-TIER TRIBUNAL DECISION IN THE CASE OF REED EMPLOYMENT LIMITED

24 August 2011. *HMRC Brief 32/11*

ABSTRACT

This brief explains HMRC's policy following the First-Tier Tribunal decision in the case of Reed Employment Limited, which held that in providing temporary staff to its clients Reed was supplying introductory services rather than making supplies of staff.

FULL TEXT

1. BACKGROUND

This brief explains HM Revenue & Customs' (HMRC's) policy following the First-Tier Tribunal (FTT) decision in the case of TC01069 Reed Employment Limited (LON/2004/0130) (LNB News 12/04/2011 156).

The Tribunal held that in providing temporary staff to its clients Reed was supplying introductory services rather than making supplies of staff. Accordingly the company was only liable to account for VAT on the commission element of its charge and not on the overall amount paid by the client which included the wages paid to the temp and associated National Insurance contributions.

2. HMRC'S POSITION

As a judgment of the FTT Reed is only binding on the parties to the appeal. It was decided on its specific facts which involved an historic claim and concerned tax periods up to 1996. The Reed decision differs from the earlier judgment of the tribunal in Hays Personnel Services Ltd (LON/95/2610) in which the Tribunal determined that Hays was a principal and VAT was due on the whole consideration received.

HMRC therefore do not regard Reed as having any wider impact, particularly in relation to the VAT treatment that should apply to employment bureaux operating in the current market conditions and regulatory regime.

HMRC's view of the correct VAT treatment for employment bureaux remains that set out in VAT Information Note 03/09. In essence a bureau acting as an agent only has to account for

VAT on its commission whereas a bureau acting as a principal has to account for VAT on the full amount charged to clients including the temps' wages and employers' National Insurance contributions.

2.1 PRINCIPAL

In the context of employment bureaux a principal is the business making the supply of staff. The staff may be employees bound to the bureau by a contract of service or a self-employed worker making supplies to the bureau under a contract for services. In either case, the workers enter into a contract with the bureau making the supply of staff, which then makes an onward supply of those staff as principal to its client. VAT is due on the total consideration received by the bureau.

2.2 AGENT

If a bureau is not making a supply of staff as principal, but instead acts as an intermediary in finding work for work-seekers, or workers for its clients and:

— those two parties enter into a direct contractual relationship with each other

— the bureau (or any person with which it is connected) does not pay, or arrange to pay, the workers

— then the bureau is acting as an agent. The supply is not of staff but, rather, intermediary services of finding work-seekers employment. VAT is only due on the fee the bureau charges.

VAT: POSTAL AND POSTBUS SERVICES

16 September 2011. *HMRC Brief 34/11*

ABSTRACT

This Brief concerns consequential amendments to VATA 1994 and VAT Regs 1995, which are necessary to maintain the current VAT exemption for postal services following enactment of the Postal Services Act 2011 in June. The amendments are made by SI 2011/2085 and come into force on 1 October 2011.

FULL TEXT

CONSEQUENTIAL AMENDMENTS TO VAT LEGISLATION FOLLOWING THE IMPLEMENTATION OF THE POSTAL SERVICES ACT 2011

HM Revenue & Customs (HMRC) is amending the VAT legislation relating to supplies by a universal service provider of passenger transport and postal services, following the implementation of the Postal Services Act 2011 (PSA 2011). The amendments, which take effect on 1 October 2011, simply maintain the current VAT treatment of these supplies, but are necessary to reflect changes to the postal services regime.

PSA 2011, which received Royal Assent on 13 June 2011, provides for the introduction of a regulatory framework based on general authorisation to replace the licensing regime that was introduced under the Postal Services Act 2000 (PSA 2000). As Group 3 (Postal Services) of Schedule 9 (Exemptions) to the Value Added Tax Act 1994 refers to a licence duty that will no longer exist after the regulatory changes are made, HMRC are amending the legislation to maintain the scope of the VAT exemption for postal services. Similarly, HMRC are amending Group 8 (Transport) of Schedule 8 (Zero-Rating) to the Act to reflect the fact that PSA 2011 has superseded PSA 2000.

The amendments to the VAT legislation are being made by the Postal Services Act 2011 (Consequential Modifications and Amendments) Order 2011 (SI 2011/2085).

FURTHER ADVICE ON VAT DECISION IN *PAYMEX LIMITED*

21 September 2011. *HMRC Brief 35/11*

ABSTRACT

HMRC provides further information for insolvency practitioners on refund claims arising from the First-tier Tribunal decision in *Paymex Limited* (TC01210). This follows the initial response in Brief 27/2011, which confirmed that HMRC would not be appealing against the decision.

FULL TEXT

VAT TRIBUNAL DECISION IN THE CASE OF PAYMEX LIMITED V HMRC

HM Revenue & Customs (HMRC) recently issued a Business Brief (Revenue & Customs Brief 27/11 - LNB News 20/07/2011 25) in response to the VAT Tribunal decision in the case of Paymex Limited v HMRC (TC01210), dealing with the VAT liability of services provided by an Insolvency Practitioner (IP) in an Individual Voluntary Arrangement (IVA).

Following on from the above mentioned Business Brief, HMRC wishes to offer further clarification on the following points which may be of interest or concern to the insolvency profession:

1. GENERAL

- Although the Tribunal decision itself applied purely to consumer IVAs, HMRC considers that the terms of the Tribunal decision read across to all IVAs. The important point for IPs to consider here is not the specific type of IVA but rather whether the nature of the services they provide are covered by the terms of the *Paymex Limited* ruling.
- Although HMRC does not consider the terms of the Tribunal decision to be restricted to a particular type of IVA, the Tribunal decision does not deal with Company Voluntary Arrangements (CVAs) or Partnership Voluntary Arrangements (PVAs). If IPs consider, on the basis of the *Paymex Limited* ruling, that they have overpaid VAT arising from their role as supervisors of CVAs or PVAs and seek to reclaim such VAT, these claims will be rejected.

2. CLAIMS

- The effect of the Tribunal ruling is that IPs may have overpaid VAT where their services in an IVA are covered by the terms of the ruling. IPs affected are therefore entitled, but not obliged, to claim a refund of wrongly declared output VAT, under Section 80 of the VAT Act 1994. However, IPs may also have reclaimed input VAT in such cases to which, following the Tribunal ruling, they may not have been entitled. Refunds will only be issued for the balance of output VAT wrongly declared on the services in question less any input VAT wrongly deducted on the assumption that the supplies to which it was attributable were taxable.
- The input tax that will be deducted for the amount claimed will be both that input tax that was directly attributable to the supplies of services in question and, if the IP was already partially exempt, the appropriate percentage of the overhead or residual input VAT.
- Public Notice VAT 700/45 *How to correct VAT errors and make adjustments or claims* explains how to go about claiming a refund in this circumstance.
- If the IP was fully taxable for the period covered by the claim then making a claim for a refund of wrongly declared output VAT will have the effect of making them partially exempt for the period of the claim. In that event, they will have to calculate the percentage of overhead or residual input VAT that should have been blocked.
- Although input tax must be taken account of by IPs when claiming refunds of overdeclared VAT as above, HMRC will not seek to recover input tax previously overclaimed in the light of this ruling in any cases other than those in which a claim for a refund of overdeclared VAT is made. If the IP chooses not to "disturb the past", HMRC will not disturb it either. It is entirely a matter for the IP whether to claim a refund under Section 80 of the VAT Act or not. Nothing in VAT legislation obliges them to do so.

3. TIME LIMITS

- Claims for a refund of overdeclared VAT are subject to normal capping rules. Claims for repayment will therefore not be considered for periods ending more than four years before the date on which the claim is made.
- Any claim made under Section 80 of the VAT Act 1994 must set out the basis of the error and the amount being claimed and show how that amount has been calculated. The claimant must be able to provide copies of the documentation used in the calculation of the claim on request. An "estimated" claim, or a declared intention to lodge a claim at a future date, will not stop the clock running on the four year cap.

4. UNJUST ENRICHMENT

- HMRC can reject claims where they are able to show that the claimant would be unjustly enriched by payment of his claim.
- If an IP decides to claim a refund under Section 80 of the VAT Act and reimburse his customers under Section 80A and Regulations 43A to 43G of the VAT Regulation 1995, they must reimburse the total amount paid to them by HMRC in cash or by cheque. They are not entitled to deduct any amount by way of administration fee etc. This is expressly stipulated in Regulation 43C(b) of the VAT Regulations 1995, which states that "no deduction will be made from the relevant amount by way of fee or charge (howsoever expressed or effected)".
- Once the refund is paid into the IVA estate in its entirety, the refund then becomes an asset of the estate. Any subsequent question of IP's costs will be determined by the terms of the actual arrangement in accordance with insolvency legislation.

5. DIVIDENDS

Where IPs intend to declare additional dividends to creditors in IVAs from money refunded by HMRC, HMRC's Voluntary Arrangements Service is happy to accept one collated payment covering all of the IVAs concerned if possible, provided the IP can still identify the proportion of that dividend for individual IVAs.

HMRC hopes the above information assists the insolvency profession by further clarifying HMRC's view of the impact of the Tribunal ruling in this case. IPs may request further advice on the correct VAT treatment in individual cases by contacting the VAT Helpline on Tel 0845 010 9000.

FURTHER GUIDANCE ON THE TREATMENT OF SUPPLIES MADE BY EMPLOYERS UNDER SALARY SACRIFICE ARRANGEMENTS ON OR AFTER 1 JANUARY 2012

4 October 2011. *HMRC Brief 36/11*

ABSTRACT

This Brief provides further guidance to assist businesses with the implementation of changes to VAT accounting in relation to salary sacrifice arrangements announced in Revenue and Customs Brief 28/2011 on 28 July 2011.

FULL TEXT

HM Revenue & Customs (HMRC) recently issued a Business Brief (Revenue & Customs Brief 27/11 - LNB News 20/07/2011 24) in response to the VAT Tribunal decision in the case of *Paymex Limited v HMRC*, dealing with the VAT liability of services provided by an Insolvency Practitioner (IP) in an Individual Voluntary Arrangement (IVA).

1. This brief provides further guidance to assist businesses with the implementation of changes to VAT accounting in relation to salary sacrifice arrangements announced in Revenue and Customs Brief 28/11 (LNB News 28/07/2011 79) on 28 July 2011.

2. SALARY SACRIFICE AGREEMENTS IN PLACE BEFORE 28 JULY 2011 WHICH EXTEND BEYOND 31 DECEMBER 2011

For salary sacrifice agreements that were signed or otherwise agreed by the parties on or before 27 July 2011 and which extend beyond 31 December 2011, HM Revenue & Customs (HMRC) will allow amounts of salary foregone in return for taxable benefits to continue to be free of VAT until:

- The date that a fixed term agreement expires or the fixed number of salary sacrifice payments specified within the agreement are completed (if the agreement expires before 1 January 2012 any agreement subsequently entered into should follow the VAT treatment described in section 3 below).
- The date of an employee's annual salary/benefits review. HMRC will regard any salary sacrifice arrangements put in place after that date as a new agreement for VAT purposes which should follow the treatment described in section 3 below. This will be the case even if the employee continues to receive the same taxable benefits as before the review.
- The date of any other review or renegotiation that leads to a change in the provision of benefits under a salary sacrifice agreement or to a change in an employment contract.

Following one of the above events VAT will be due on any taxable benefits provided on or after 1 January 2012 by way of salary sacrifice.

3. SALARY SACRIFICE AGREEMENTS ENTERED INTO ON OR AFTER 28 JULY 2011

For agreements entered into on or after 28 July 2011 VAT must be accounted for in accordance with the guidance in Revenue and Customs Brief 28/11. With effect from 1 January 2012 VAT will be due on amounts of salary foregone in return for taxable benefits.

REMINDER OF FORTHCOMING WITHDRAWAL OF THREE EXTRA STATUTORY CONCESSIONS RELATING TO CARAVAN SITES

26 October 2011. *HMRC Brief 37/11*

ABSTRACT

This Brief reminds caravan site owners and their customers about the forthcoming withdrawal of three Extra Statutory Concessions relating to caravan sites. It also clarifies the effect of timing of invoices and payments on whether the concessions apply.

FULL TEXT

This Brief is for caravan site owners.

BACKGROUND

On 13 December 2010, HM Revenue & Customs (HMRC) announced its intention to withdraw three Extra Statutory Concessions relating to caravan sites with effect from 1 January 2012 (see Withdrawal of extra statutory concessions - LNB News 14/12/2010 29), which will result in changes to the VAT treatment of:

- recharges of business rates at holiday/leisure caravan sites
- recharges of non-metered water/sewerage rates at caravan sites
- one off charges for the first time connection to gas, electricity, water and sewerage

The purpose of this Brief is to remind caravan site owners and their customers about the forthcoming changes and to clarify the effect of the timing of invoices and payments on whether the concessions apply.

REASON FOR WITHDRAWAL

The House of Lords' decision in the Wilkinson (*R v HM Commissioners of Inland Revenue ex p Wilkinson* All ER (D) 68 (May)) case clarified the scope of HMRC's administrative discretion to make concessions that depart from the strict statutory position. HMRC has been reviewing its concessions in light of this decision. Although it is likely that the majority can remain as they are, some are thought to be beyond the scope of HMRC's discretion. Of these, some can be legislated to preserve their effect, others will need to be withdrawn.

After taking legal advice, HMRC has concluded that the three concessions that are subject of this Brief are beyond the scope of its discretion to make concessions. EU law does not permit the UK to introduce new legislation to preserve the effect of these concessions; therefore they need to be withdrawn.

VAT TREATMENT WITH EFFECT FROM 1 JANUARY 2012

From 1 January 2012, the concessions will be withdrawn and the following VAT treatment will apply:

- recharges of business rates will follow the VAT liability of the pitch fee (standard rated in the case of holiday/leisure sites)
- recharges of water/sewerage costs which are not metered to the individual customer at their pitch will follow the VAT liability of the pitch fee (generally standard rated, in the case of holiday/leisure sites; exempt, in the case of residential sites)
- one off charges for the first time connection to gas, electricity, water and sewerage will follow the liability of the pitch (exempt or standard rated) unless the site owner identifies and charges for individual consumption (that is, through metering to the individual pitch), in which case the charge will follow the liability of the utility (reduced rated for electricity and gas, zero rated for water and sewerage)

EFFECT OF TIMING OF INVOICES, PAYMENTS ETC ON VAT TREATMENT

HMRC has been asked to clarify the effect of the timing of invoices and payments and, for example, how to determine the VAT treatment when charges are made in 2011 that relate to services provided in 2012.

HMRC will allow the following treatment to apply. However, HMRC reserves the right to withdraw or restrict the application of this table where an attempt is made to use it for tax avoidance (for example, if a business raises an advance invoice in 2011 when it is not their normal practice to do so, HMRC may challenge this. HMRC will not challenge invoicing arrangements that are in accordance with a business's normal practice).

Type of supply

Connection charges	**VAT treatment**
Connection made before 1/1/12	Concession can be used, regardless of when invoiced or paid for
Connection made on or after 1/1/12	Concession can be used if invoiced or paid for before 1/1/12, otherwise concession does not apply

Type of supply

Business rates recharges	**VAT treatment**
Business rates recharges invoiced before 31/12/11	Concession can be used (subject to the conditions in paragraph 4.4, Notice 701/20 Caravans and houseboats)
Business rate recharges invoiced after 1/1/12	Concession does not apply

Type of supply

Water/sewerage charges	**VAT treatment**
Water/sewerage recharges invoiced before 31 December 2011	Concession can be used (subject to the conditions in paragraph 4.3, Notice 701/20 Caravans and houseboats)
Water/sewage charges invoiced after 1/1/12	Concession does not apply

FURTHER DETAILS ABOUT THE CONCESSIONS

RECHARGES OF BUSINESS RATES AT HOLIDAY/LEISURE CARAVAN SITES

BACKGROUND

Owners of holiday/leisure caravan sites are generally liable to pay non-domestic (business) rates to their Local Authority. It is common for such site owners to attribute and recharge a proportion of the rates to individual caravan owners using the official apportionment made by the Valuation Office (under a Regulation 4 Notice). Under the terms of paragraph 4.4, Notice 701/20 Caravans and Houseboats, HMRC currently allows such recharges to be treated as outside the scope of VAT. This treatment amounts to a "concession" because it has no legal basis.

EFFECT OF WITHDRAWAL

From 1 January 2012, where caravan site owners recharge a proportion of their business rates to individual caravan owners, the recharge will follow the same VAT liability as the pitch fee (usually standard rated, in the case of holiday/leisure sites).

RECHARGE OF WATER AND SEWERAGE RATES AT CARAVAN SITES

BACKGROUND

When a caravan site owner can identify the actual consumption of water and sewerage for individual pitches (that is, through metering at the individual pitch) and charges according to consumption, there is a separate zero rated supply of water and sewerage. In other circumstances, that is, where individual consumption cannot be identified, any charges for water and sewerage form part of the fee for occupation of the pitch and should follow the same VAT liability as the pitch (generally standard rated, in the case of holiday/leisure sites; exempt, in the case of residential sites). By concession, HMRC allows such charges to be treated as zero rated if the site owner's costs are apportioned on a fair and reasonable basis (paragraph 4.3, Notice 701/20 Caravans and houseboats).

EFFECT OF WITHDRAWAL

From 1 January 2012, charges made by caravan site owners for water and sewerage will remain zero rated if actual consumption can be identified (that is, through metering at the individual pitch). In other circumstances, charges will follow the VAT liability of the caravan pitch (generally standard rated, in the case of holiday/leisure sites; exempt, in the case of residential sites).

ESC 3.16 VAT: CONNECTION TO THE GAS OR ELECTRICITY MAINS SUPPLY

BACKGROUND

ESC 3.16 allows zero rating for, amongst other things, the first time connection to the gas or electricity mains supply of residential caravans. Under the terms of Notice 701/20 Caravans and houseboats, HMRC additionally allows concessionary zero rating for first time connection of holiday/leisure caravans to the gas or mains supply and for first time connection of caravans to water and sewerage, where the relevant charge is made by the caravan site owner.

EFFECT OF WITHDRAWAL

After the concession is withdrawn, charges made by caravan site owners for first time connection to electricity, gas, water and sewerage will be subject to the same VAT liability as the pitch (generally standard rated, in the case of holiday/leisure sites; exempt, in the case of residential sites) unless the site owner identifies and charges for the actual consumption of users (that is, through metering at the pitch), in which case, the connection charge will be subject to the same VAT liability as the supply of the utility (reduced rated for electricity and gas, zero rated for water and sewerage).

FURTHER INFORMATION

Further information about VAT and caravans can be found in Notice 701/20 Caravans and houseboats (LNB News 15/04/2010 1).

VAT SAILAWAY BOAT SCHEME - IMPORTANT CHANGE FROM 1 JANUARY 2012

22 November 2011. *HMRC Brief 38/11*

ABSTRACT

This Brief reminds customers that with effect from 1 January 2012 UK residents are no longer eligible to purchase a boat using the VAT Sailaway Boat Scheme.

FULL TEXT

WHO NEEDS TO READ THIS?

VAT-registered businesses who sell pleasure craft to private individuals under the Sailaway Boat Scheme.

WHAT IS THE CHANGE?

From 1 January 2012, the current concessionary treatment which allows a VAT-registered business to zero rate the supply of a sailaway boat to a UK resident who intends to keep it outside the European Community (EC) will be withdrawn. From this date the scheme can no longer be used for sales to UK residents.

However, a business can zero rate the supply of a boat to a UK resident provided that it meets the conditions for zero rating a direct export set out in paragraph 3.3 of Notice 703 *VAT: Export of goods from the United Kingdom* (LNB News 22/06/2005 46). In particular, this means that the business must undertake to export the boat themselves or make all the arrangements for the export and obtain satisfactory evidence of export within three months.

THE REASON FOR THIS CHANGE

The VAT Sailaway Boat Scheme allows overseas residents to obtain VAT refunds on vessels purchased for personal export to a destination outside the EU. Under extra-statutory concession 8.1, HM Revenue & Customs (HMRC) has allowed UK residents to purchase boats under the scheme. However, HMRC does not have the discretion to allow this concessionary treatment, and it is not possible to put the concession on a statutory basis as this would contravene EU law. The Government announced in December 2010 that the concession would be withdrawn on 1 January 2012 to allow businesses time to prepare for the change.

THE LEGAL BASIS FOR THE SCHEME

Article 146 of Directive 2006/112/EC permits zero rating of goods which are "...dispatched or transported to a destination outside the (European) Community by or on behalf of a purchaser not established within their respective territory...". The Article is given effect in Regulation 129 of the VAT Regulations 1995 (SI 1995/2518). Both the Article and the Regulation clearly exclude supplies to UK residents from the scope of zero rating.

FURTHER ADVICE

If you have any questions about this change, please contact Sarah Bush on Tel 0151 703 8950 or email Sarah Bush (www.hmrc.gov.uk/asplib/mailer/mailer_form.asp?dpt=SARAH_BUSH).

HMRC V THE RANK GROUP PLC - PRINCIPLE OF FISCAL NEUTRALITY

6 December 2011. *HMRC Brief 39/11*

ABSTRACT

Following the decision of the Court of Justice of the European Union in respect of questions referred by the Upper Tribunal and the Court of Appeal in the litigation between HMRC and the Rank Group plc, HMRC has withdrawn its appeal in respect of bingo. However, in respect of gaming machines, further consideration will be taken.

FULL TEXT

SUMMARY

Revenue & Customs Briefs 75/09 (issued 8 December 2009) and 11/10 (issued 10 March 2010) provided advice about the litigation between HM Revenue & Customs (HMRC) and the Rank Group plc considering the application of the principle of fiscal neutrality.

Following appeals by HMRC to both the Court of Appeal and the Upper Tribunal, both Courts referred questions to the Court of Justice of the European Union (CJEU) which issued its judgment on 10 November 2011.

READERSHIP

Bingo providers and gaming machine operators.

ACTION REQUIRED

For information only.

THE CJEU JUDGMENT

The CJEU confirmed the findings of the UK courts about the interpretation of the principle of fiscal neutrality. It confirmed that similar supplies from the point of view of the consumer should be taxed in the same way and that when considering whether there has been a breach of fiscal neutrality there is no need to apply a separate "competition" test, that is, it is not necessary to consider whether the supplies are in competition with each other. However, the CJEU also set out some tests for national courts to apply in deciding whether gaming machines are similar. In addition, it found that when determining whether there has been a breach of fiscal neutrality the actual tax treatment should be based on the legal position rather than any practice that may have been followed.

IMPLICATIONS

Bingo - In view of the CJEU's judgment, HMRC accept that the issue is now resolved in respect of bingo and our appeal in respect of this will be withdrawn. All valid claims received, further to Brief 75/09, have been paid, so the decision not to continue with litigation in respect of bingo means that HMRC will not be seeking any repayment of these amounts.

Gaming machines - HMRC believes that the judgment of the CJEU does not provide a final determination of the domestic litigation. Further consideration of the gaming machine appeals will now have to take place, with the parties and the domestic courts using the judgment of the CJEU for guidance. Accordingly, our appeals will continue. Brief 11/10 provided advice about claims relating to VAT accounted for on gaming machine takings between November 1998 and December 2005 and all valid claims have been paid. The judgment does not extend the findings of the UK courts to any other period, so any claims for periods prior to November 1998 and post-December 2005 will continue not to be paid.

BACKGROUND

The Rank Group claimed that the UK breached the principle of fiscal neutrality in respect of its taxation of gaming machines prior to December 2005 (when the legislation was changed to ensure all gaming machine takings were subject to VAT) and its taxation of certain bingo participation fees, particularly in relation to mechanised cash bingo (MCB).

The Tribunal ruled that in respect of MCB there had been a breach of fiscal neutrality because some participation fees were taxed and others were exempt from VAT and the supplies were identical. All bingo participation fees have been exempt from VAT since 2009.

The Tribunal also found that there was a breach of fiscal neutrality in respect of the tax treatment of gaming machines and similar non-gaming machines from mid-2003 and this period was extended back to November 1998 in a subsequent hearing.

The High Court supported these decisions so HMRC appealed to both the Court of Appeal and the Upper Tribunal (as the cases were at different stages) and they referred a number of questions to the CJEU.

RURAL FUEL DUTY RELIEF SCHEME

9 December 2011. *HMRC Brief 40/11*

ABSTRACT

This Brief gives information about the new Rural Fuel Duty relief scheme for retailers of road fuel on the Inner and Outer Hebrides, the Northern Isles, the Islands of the Clyde and the Isles of Scilly, which is being introduced on 1 January 2012. The Brief includes guidance on registration using Form HO80 and claiming the relief using Form HO81.

FULL TEXT

EXCISE DUTY: RURAL FUEL DUTY RELIEF SCHEME FOR ROAD FUEL ON THE INNER AND OUTER HEBRIDES, THE NORTHERN ISLES, THE ISLANDS OF THE CLYDE AND THE ISLES OF SCILLY

PURPOSE OF THIS BRIEF

This Brief gives information about a new Rural Fuel Duty relief scheme for retailers of road fuel on the Inner and Outer Hebrides, the Northern Isles, the Islands of the Clyde and the Isles of Scilly which is being introduced on 1 January 2012.

Retailers of road fuel within these areas will be eligible to register with HM Revenue & Customs (HMRC) to claim back five pence per litre (ppl) relief on unleaded petrol and diesel for retail sale within the eligible areas.

WHO NEEDS TO READ THIS?

Retailers of unleaded petrol and diesel sold as road fuel within the areas of the Inner and Outer Hebrides, the Northern Isles, the Islands of the Clyde and the Isles of Scilly.

BACKGROUND

The price of fuel in the Scottish islands is around 10 ppl higher than the average for the rest of the UK. In the Scilly Isles it is even higher at around 25 ppl above the UK average.

The higher price of fuel on the islands is due mainly to the high cost of selling fuel in these regions. This is because of higher transport and distribution costs for delivering fuel to the islands and the low volume of fuel sold, meaning that fuel retailers' fixed costs need to be spread over a lower volume of sales.

The five ppl relief will provide some help to consumers in the areas concerned who are faced with high costs of petrol and diesel.

A Council Decision on 24 November 2011 allowed a derogation from the Energy Products Directive (2003/96) in order to introduce the scheme.

WHO IS ELIGIBLE TO CLAIM RELIEF?

You can claim relief if you are a retailer of road fuel (unleaded petrol and diesel) within the Inner and Outer Hebrides, the Northern Isles, the Islands of the Clyde and the Isles of Scilly.

You are not eligible to register if you purchase fuel in bulk, for example, for your own business use.

HOW DOES THE RELIEF SCHEME WORK?

If you are a retailer of road fuel within the areas concerned you can register with HMRC to claim five ppl relief on fuel you purchase on or after 1 January 2012 for onward retail sale in the Inner and Outer Hebrides, the Northern Isles, the Islands of the Clyde and the Isles of Scilly. You can make claims on a monthly basis.

You will have 60 days following your registration to reduce the cost of every litre of road fuel sold by the equivalent amount of the relief claimed. This is so that all consumers in the areas concerned benefit from the reduction in fuel duty.

The 60 day period during which retailers are not required to pass on the relief is designed to help avoid initial cash flow problems.

HOW DO I REGISTER?

To register you need to complete form HO80: Registration to claim fuel duty relief (Scottish Islands and the Isles of Scilly), which is available on the HMRC website at customs.hmrc.gov.uk/channelsPortalWebApp/downloadFile?contentID=HMCE_PROD1_031799. The form can be completed electronically but must be printed and returned by post to:

HM Revenue & Customs
Mineral Oils Relief Centre
BP4002
Benton Park View
Longbenton
Newcastle-upon-Tyne NE981ZZ

You can also phone the Excise and Customs Helpline Tel 0845 010 9000 and ask them to send a form for you to complete and return.

A separate registration is needed for each retail premises.

HMRC will write to confirm that you are registered as a qualified claimant.

HOW DO I CLAIM THE RELIEF?

You need to register with HMRC to claim relief. HMRC will not accept a claim from any retailer who is not registered.

To claim the relief you need to complete form HO81: Claim for duty relief (Scottish Islands and Isles of Scilly), which will be available on the HMRC website in January 2012, in time for your first monthly claim. You will also be able to obtain a copy from the Excise and Customs Helpline Tel 0845 010 9000.

Claim periods will be based on a calendar month. You can only submit one claim per month. HMRC will pay the relief claimed within 30 days of receiving the claim.

WHAT INFORMATION WILL BE REQUIRED ON THE CLAIM FORM?

You will need to provide the following details of the fuel you have purchased and on which you are claiming relief:

- the date of the purchase
- the name of the supplier
- period of claim
- the reference of the purchase, such as invoice number
- total volume in litres of unleaded petrol purchased in the period
- total volume in litres of diesel purchased in the period
- the amount of the claim

HOW IS THE RELIEF CALCULATED?

The amount you can claim is:

- the volume in litres of unleaded petrol you purchased × five pence = A
- the volume in litres of diesel you purchased × five pence = B

Add A and B together to work out the total amount of your claim.

WHAT RECORDS MUST I KEEP?

You must keep evidence of all your purchases, such as invoices of road fuel on which your relief has been claimed. You will also need to keep your normal business records and produce them to HMRC if asked to do so.

DO I NEED TO SUBMIT EVIDENCE FOR MY RELIEF CLAIM WITH MY RETURN?

No. Please keep your documentary evidence as part of your records. HMRC will contact you if they wish to verify your claim.

HOW LONG WILL THE RELIEF SCHEME LAST?

The relief scheme is a pilot scheme which will be evaluated over a period of time to ensure that it is working effectively and that the price of fuel in the areas concerned has reduced.

This relief scheme is being implemented under the State Aid General Block Exemption Regulation No 800/2008.

WITHDRAWAL OF VAT ESC 3.16

9 December 2011. *HMRC Brief 43/11*

ABSTRACT

This Brief reminds taxpayers that VAT Extra Statutory Concession 3.16, which concerns zero-rating of charges for first-time connection to the gas or electricity mains supply, is being withdrawn from 1 January 2012. It sets out the circumstances under which connection charges may be zero-rated after 1 January and how the timing of connection, invoicing and payment around that date will affect whether or not the concession applies.

FULL TEXT

VAT: WITHDRAWAL OF EXTRA STATUTORY CONCESSION 3.16 - FIRST TIME CONNECTION TO THE GAS OR ELECTRICITY MAINS SUPPLY

SUMMARY

On 13 December 2010, HM Revenue & Customs (HMRC) announced its intention to withdraw Extra Statutory Class Concession 3.16 relating to first time connection charges to the gas or electricity mains supply, with effect from 1 January 2012 (see - Technical note on Withdrawal of extra statutory concessions (LNB News 14/12/2010 29).

The purpose of this Brief is to remind taxpayers about the forthcoming change and to clarify the effect of the timing of invoices and payments on whether the concession applies.

READERSHIP

Gas and electricity suppliers, independent connection providers.

ACTION

To be aware of the withdrawal of the concession and the related time of supply issues.

REASON FOR WITHDRAWAL

The House of Lords' decision in the Wilkinson case clarified the scope of HMRC's administrative discretion to make concessions that depart from the strict statutory position. HMRC is reviewing its concessions in light of this decision. The majority can remain as they are, but those that go beyond the scope of HMRC's discretion will be either legislated to preserve their effect or withdrawn.

After taking legal advice, HMRC has concluded that concession 3.16 is beyond the scope of its discretion to make concessions. EU law does not permit the UK to introduce new legislation to preserve the effect of the concession; therefore it needs to be withdrawn.

BACKGROUND TO THE CONCESSION

Before 1 April 1994, the supply of gas and electricity for domestic or non-business charity use was zero-rated. The zero-rating also applied to any connection charge made by the supplier (or someone in the same VAT group) who provided the utility, as this was ancillary to the supply of the utility. Any connection charge made in isolation from the supply of fuel of power to an existing building was standard-rated.

On 1 April 1994, the zero rate ceased to apply to the supply of gas and electricity. Without the concession, connection fees would now be reduced-rated if supplied by the supplier of the utility for domestic or non-business charity use to an existing building. The concession ensured that supplies made by the supplier of the utility used for a qualifying use would remain zero-rated.

The concession did not impact on any other supplies, meaning that any connection charges for supplies made independently of the utility to an existing building would remain standard rated.

SCOPE OF THE CONCESSION

The precise text of concession 3.16 is as follows:

"Connection to the gas or electricity mains supply, which would have been a zero-rated supply before 1 April 1994 by virtue of Group 7 of Schedule 5 to the Value Added Tax 1983, may continue to be treated as a zero-rated supply provided that:

(a) It is the first connection to the gas or electricity mains supply (as the case may be) of:

- a building, or part of a building, which consists of a dwelling or number of dwellings
- a building, or part of a building used solely for a relevant residential purpose (within the meaning of Note 4 to Group 7)
- a building, or part of a building, used by a charity otherwise than in the course or furtherance of a business
- a residential caravan (that is to say a caravan on a site in respect of which there is no covenant, statutory planning consent or similar permission precluding occupation throughout the year), or
- a houseboat (within the meaning of Group 6 to Note 7), and

(b) the person receiving the supply does not do so for the purpose of any business carried on by him."

VAT LIABILITY OF CONNECTION CHARGES FROM 1 JANUARY 2012

From 1 January 2012, the concession will be withdrawn. From that date, the treatment of one-off charges for the first time connection to gas and electricity will be as follows:

- If the supply of the connection and provision of the utility is made by the same person (or by members of the same VAT group) the connection charge will follow the treatment of the utility and be reduced rated.
- If the supplies are not made by the same person or if at the time of connection, the supplier of the utility has not been determined, the connection charge will continue to be standard rated (irrespective of who eventually provides the utility).
- The first time connection of a new dwelling or relevant residential or relevant charitable building to the gas or electricity mains supply is zero rated under Group 5 of Schedule 8 to the VAT Act 1994 if the connection is made as part of the construction of the building. (See Notice 708 Buildings and construction for further details).
- Works in connection with the means of providing fuel and power as part of the renovation or alteration of empty residential premises, or of the conversion of premises to a different residential use may be reduced - rated under Group 6 and Group 7 of Schedule 7A to the VAT Act 1994, if performed on the immediate site of the premises. (See Notice 708 Buildings and construction for further details).
- Grant-funded connection or reconnection to a mains gas supply relating to a qualifying person's sole or main residence is reduced-rated under Item 4 to Group 3 of Schedule 7A to the VAT Act 1994 (see Notice 708/6 Energy-saving materials for further details).

All other connections are standard rated.

TIMING OF INVOICES AND PAYMENTS

HMRC will allow the treatment detailed in the table below to apply. However, HMRC reserves the right to withdraw or restrict the application of this table where an attempt is made to use it for tax avoidance (for example, if a business raises an advance invoice in 2011 when it is not their normal practice to do so, HMRC may challenge this. HMRC will not challenge invoicing arrangements that are in accordance with a business's normal practice).

Type of supply	VAT treatment
Connection charges	

Connection made before 1 January 2012	Concession can be used, regardless of when invoiced or paid for
Connection made on or after 1 January 2012	Concession can be used if invoiced or paid for before 1 January 2012, otherwise concession does not apply

FURTHER INFORMATION

Further information about VAT on fuel and power can be found in Notice 701/19 Fuel and Power which will be amended in due course. For further details on how the withdrawal of the concession affects caravan sites - see Revenue & Customs Brief 37/2011.

WITHDRAWAL OF ZERO-RATING FOR ADAPTED MOTOR VEHICLES FROM 1 JANUARY 2012

19 December 2011. *HMRC Brief 41/11*

ABSTRACT

From 1 January 2012, the current concessionary arrangement, which allows zero-rating for a motor vehicle supplied to a disabled wheelchair user if the vehicle was adapted shortly after it was supplied to the disabled person, will no longer apply. The Government announced its intention to withdraw this concession in December 2010.

FULL TEXT

VAT: MOTOR VEHICLES ADAPTED AFTER INITIAL SUPPLY TO DISABLED PEOPLE - IMPORTANT CHANGE FROM 1 JANUARY 2012

WHO NEEDS TO READ THIS?

VAT registered businesses that sell motor vehicles to disabled wheelchair users.

WHAT IS THE CHANGE?

From 1 January 2012, the current concessionary arrangement which allows a motor vehicle supplied to a disabled wheelchair user to be treated as a zero rated supply, if the vehicle was adapted shortly after it was supplied to the disabled person, will no longer apply.

However, VAT zero-rating will continue to apply on motor vehicles that are adapted before the vehicle is supplied to a disabled wheelchair user provided all the other qualifying conditions for zero-rating are met.

THE REASON FOR THIS CHANGE

The UK VAT law allows a motor vehicle supplied to a disabled wheelchair user to be zero-rated provided it has been adapted before it is supplied to the disabled person. In addition, HM Revenue & Customs (HMRC) has allowed, by concession motor vehicles that are adapted shortly after they have been supplied to disabled persons to be zero-rated.

HMRC does not have the discretion to allow this concessionary treatment, and it is not possible to put the concession on a statutory basis as this would contravene EU law. There is no legal basis in EU law which would permit this concession to be introduced in UK legislation.

The Government announced in December 2010 that the concession would be withdrawn on 1 January 2012, to allow businesses a year to prepare for the change.

THE LEGAL BASIS FOR THE RELIEF

The current UK VAT legislation, under Items 2(f), 2A and Note 5L to Group 12, Schedule 8, VAT Act 1994, allows a motor vehicle to be zero-rated provided it has been adapted before it is supplied to a disabled wheelchair user for their personal use or to a charity that makes it available to such persons. The relevant legislation excludes the zero-rating of motor vehicles that are adapted after the supply has been made. This treatment goes beyond the scope of the statutory relief.

FURTHER INFORMATION

If you have any questions about this change, please contact VAT Disabled Reliefs Helpline on Tel 0845 302 0203.

WITHDRAWAL OF ZERO-RATING FOR ADAPTED PARTS AND ACCESSORIES FOR BOATS FROM 1 JANUARY 2012

19 December 2011. *HMRC Brief 42/11*

ABSTRACT

From 1 January 2012, the current concessionary arrangement which allows zero-rating for parts and accessories designed solely for use with boats adapted for use by disabled persons will no longer apply. The Government announced its intention to withdraw this concession in December 2010.

FULL TEXT

VAT: PARTS AND ACCESSORIES FOR BOATS SUPPLIED TO DISABLED PEOPLE AND CHARITIES - IMPORTANT CHANGE FROM 1 JANUARY 2012

WHO NEEDS TO READ THIS?

VAT registered businesses that sell parts and accessories for boats where the boats are designed or adapted for the personal use of a disabled person, or to charities that make them available for disabled persons.

WHAT IS THE CHANGE?

From 1 January 2012, the current concessionary arrangement which allows VAT zero-rating on the supply of parts and accessories designed solely for use in, or with, boats that are designed or permanently and substantially adapted for use by disabled persons will no longer apply.

However, VAT zero-rating continues to apply on supplies of:

— (a) boats that are designed or substantially and permanently adapted for the domestic or personal use of disabled persons
— (b) parts and accessories that are used in connection with repairs or maintenance to qualifying boats
— (c) parts and accessories that are included as part of the single supply of qualifying boats

THE REASON FOR THIS CHANGE

The UK VAT law allows parts and accessories designed solely for use in or with goods eligible for zero-rating in Items 2(a) to 2(g) of Group 12, Schedule 8 except for parts and accessories for use or with boats described in Item 2(i).

The concession has allowed parts and accessories that are not covered by the scope of the relief to be treated as zero-rated. HM Revenue & Customs does not have the discretion to allow this concessionary treatment, and it is not possible to put the concession on a statutory basis as this would contravene EU law. There

The Government announced in December 2010 that the concession would be withdrawn on 1 January 2012, to allow businesses a year to prepare for the change.

THE LEGAL BASIS FOR THE RELIEF

VAT zero-rating applies to parts and accessories designed solely for use in or with goods eligible for zero-rating in Items 2(a) to 2(g) of Group 12, Schedule 8, VAT Act 1994. Item 2(h) by default excludes parts and accessories for boats described in Item 2(i) to be zero rated.

FURTHER INFORMATION

If you have any questions about this change, please contact VAT Disabled Reliefs Helpline on Tel 0845 302 0203.

INTRASTAT THRESHOLDS AND CHANGES TO REPORTING PROCEDURES FROM 1 JANUARY 2012

23 December 2011. *HMRC Brief 44/11*

ABSTRACT

This Brief announces that Intrastat thresholds will remain unchanged in 2012 from those set in 2011 and also announces some changes to reporting procedures.

FULL TEXT

SUMMARY

This Revenue & Customs Brief announces that the Intrastat thresholds will remain unchanged in 2012 from those set in 2011.

It also announces some changes to reporting procedures to apply to Intrastat declarations with a reference period of January 2012 onwards and a change to the guidance found in Notice 60 Intrastat General Guide.

READERSHIP

Businesses that are required to submit declarations of their trade with other EU Member States using an Intrastat declaration. This is limited to those with intra-EU trade in excess of £600,000 per annum for Arrivals (EU imports) and/or £250,000 per annum for Dispatches (EU exports).

INTRASTAT THRESHOLDS

EXEMPTION THRESHOLDS

— the exemption threshold for dispatches remains at £250,000
— the exemption threshold for arrivals remains at £600,000.

DELIVERY TERMS THRESHOLD

— the delivery terms threshold remains at £16,000,000

CHANGES TO REPORTING PROCEDURES

The following changes apply for Intrastat declarations with a reference period of January 2012 onwards:

LOW VALUE CONSIGNMENT THRESHOLD

— the low value consignment threshold has been increased from £130 to £180

CHANGES TO DELIVERY TERMS CODES

If you are required to provide delivery terms information then you need to be aware that for Intrastat declarations with a reference period of January 2012 onwards, there are two new delivery terms codes for Intrastat purposes:

— DAT (Delivered at Terminal) which replaces DEQ
— DAP (Delivered at Place) which replaces DAF, DES and DDU

Information on these changes will be published on the uktradeinfo website (www.uktradeinfo.com/) and in Notice 60 Intrastat General Guide.

CLARIFICATION ON THE REPORTING OF PROCESSING TRADE

The Notice 60 Intrastat General Guide (Section 9) guidance on reporting goods sent for, or received after processing, will be amended for the January 2012 edition to make it clear that Nature of Transaction Codes (NoTCs) 40 and 50 must only be used if the goods subject to the processing do not change ownership.

BACKGROUND

EXEMPTION THRESHOLD

EU legislation requires the UK to collect information on intra-EU trade for statistical purposes and sets minimum requirements for the quantity of trade covered. These requirements determine the level at which the exemption thresholds are set in the UK. They are applied independently to arrivals (intra-EU imports) and dispatches (intra-EU exports).

If you are a VAT-registered business with annual intra-EU trade in goods above the specified exemption thresholds you are required to provide monthly statistical returns (Intrastat Supplementary Declarations).

DELIVERY TERMS THRESHOLD

EU legislation requires the UK to collect information to enable the accurate calculation of statistical value. These requirements determine the level at which the delivery terms threshold is set in the UK. The same threshold for delivery terms applies to arrivals and dispatches.

If your annual EU trade is above the delivery terms threshold you are required to supply additional information relating to delivery terms on your Intrastat declarations.

LOW VALUE CONSIGNMENT THRESHOLD

Low value transactions can be aggregated and classified to a single commodity code (9950 0000) provided these transactions have a value of £180 or less.

CHANGES TO DELIVERY TERMS THRESHOLDS

The International Chamber of Commerce have made changes to their Incoterms (international commercial terms). The Incoterms codes are also used as delivery terms codes for Intrastat purposes.

These changes see the introduction for Intrastat purposes of two new terms DAT and DAP which have replaced DAF, DES, DEQ and DDU.

FURTHER INFORMATION

Further information on trade statistics is available online at the uktradeinfo website (www.uktradeinfo.com/) or by phoning uktradeinfo Customer Services on Tel 01702 367485.

For further information and advice on submitting Intrastat declarations, please contact HM Revenue & Customs' VAT, Customs and Excise Helpline on Tel 0845 010 9000.

VAT - ZERO RATE - EXTRA CARE ACCOMMODATION

30 December 2011. *HMRC Brief 47/11*

ABSTRACT

This Brief confirms the VAT liability of the construction and first sale of dwellings that are linked to a separate provision of care. It reiterates the standard conditions for a first sale or long lease of such a dwelling to be zero rated.

FULL TEXT

SUMMARY

The purpose of this Brief is to clarify the VAT liability of the construction and first sale of dwellings that are linked to a separate provision of care (extra care accommodation).

READERSHIP

Those involved in the construction or development of dwellings that are linked to a separate provision of care.

ACTION REQUIRED

For information only.

MEANING OF "EXTRA CARE ACCOMMODATION"

For the purpose of this Brief extra care accommodation refers to self contained flats, houses, bungalows or maisonettes that are sold or let with the option for the occupant to purchase varying degrees of care to suit his or her needs as and when they arise. It does not apply to accommodation where the occupant needs care or supervision of a type typically provided by an institution (see "other types of accommodation" below).

CRITERIA FOR ZERO RATING: BUILDINGS DESIGNED AS DWELLINGS

Some planning authorities in England have classified extra care accommodation under Use Class C2 of the Town and Country Planning (Use Classes) Order 1987, rather than Use Class C3, which is the class that ordinarily applies to flats, houses, bungalows and maisonettes. While developments reviewed to date have all been in England, it is likely that similar issues may have arisen in developments in other parts of the UK where equivalent but not identical Use Classes apply.

However, HM Revenue & Customs (HMRC) is satisfied that the classification for planning purposes is not of itself determinative as to the nature of the building and so does not establish whether the building is "designed as dwellings" for the purpose of the VAT zero rate.

HMRC accepts, regardless of the Use Class, that extra care accommodation is "designed as a dwelling", and therefore its construction and first sale or long lease will be zero rated, *if* it meets all of the standard conditions, which are as follows:

— the dwelling consists of self-contained living accommodation
— there is no provision for direct internal access from the dwelling to any other dwelling or part of a dwelling
— the separate use of the dwelling is not prohibited by the terms of any covenant, statutory planning consent or similar provision
— the separate disposal of the dwelling is not prohibited by the terms of any covenant, statutory planning consent or similar provision
— statutory planning consent has been granted in respect of that dwelling and its construction or conversion has been carried out in accordance with that consent

OTHER TYPES OF ACCOMMODATION

This Brief is limited to extra care accommodation. HMRC intends to consider other types of accommodation and whether or not they too can be considered to be "designed as a dwelling" early in 2012.

Further information about these conditions and the VAT treatment of residential construction and development can be found in Notice 708 Buildings and construction (LNB News 03/03/2008 62) and HMRC's technical manual V1-08A: Construction.

USE OF REBATED FUEL IN VEHICLES UNDERTAKING SNOW CLEARANCE AND GRITTING WORK

5 January 2012. *HMRC Brief 45/11*

ABSTRACT

This Brief provides guidance on the use of red diesel by vehicles used for snow clearance/gritting following HMRC's review which considered whether there was scope for an extension of red diesel entitlement to vehicles used for certain community/charity activities. A consultation will take place in early 2012.

FULL TEXT

In October 2011 HM Revenue & Customs (HMRC) conducted a review which considered whether there was scope for the extension of rebated (red) diesel entitlement to vehicles undertaking certain community/charity activities. One aspect of community work considered was the use of tractors to perform road gritting activities.

The review recommended an extension to the current gritting rules to allow tractors to undertake such activity. Consequently, early in 2012, HMRC will begin the formal process of consulting stakeholders to determine whether legislation should be introduced to change the rules on the types of vehicles eligible to use red diesel for gritting.

Pending any legislative change, the rules as they now stand will continue to apply but, if, as in the last two winters, the UK experiences a period of sustained severe weather this winter, HMRC will adopt its previously successful policy of temporarily relaxing enforcement of those rules. If such a relaxation is considered necessary, HMRC will make the appropriate announcement on its website.

CURRENT RULES

Schedule 1 of the Hydrocarbon Oil Duties Act 1979 lists the categories of excepted vehicle. Excepted vehicles are those which are entitled to use rebated fuel. There are excepted vehicle categories for "Snow clearing vehicles" and "Gritters". The rules for qualification in each of these categories differ and are explained in the following paragraphs.

SNOW CLEARING

The law says that a snow clearing vehicle is an excepted vehicle when it is being used or going to or from the place where it is to be or has been used for the purpose of clearing snow from public roads by means of a snow plough or similar device.

This puts no restriction on the type of vehicle that can be used. Therefore, for example, a farm tractor with a snow plough fitted is entitled to use red diesel for clearing snow from the public road.

GRITTING

The law says that a vehicle qualifies in this category if it is constructed or adapted, and used, solely for the conveyance of machinery for spreading material on roads to deal with frost, ice or snow.

Qualification is restricted to vehicles designed and used only for gritting. Consequently, vehicles towing gritting equipment mounted on trailers or with detachable gritting equipment do not qualify. A farm tractor, for example, which is neither constructed nor used solely for such work, is not entitled to use red diesel for gritting public roads.

ADVICE

If you have any doubt about whether your vehicle qualifies to use red diesel, please phone the Excise and Customs Helpline on 0845 010 9000.

USE OF REBATED FUEL IN GRASS CUTTING VEHICLES

5 January 2012. *HMRC Brief 46/11*

ABSTRACT

This Brief provides guidance on the use of the use of tractors to perform grass cutting of rural communal land and recreation areas for no payment, following HMRC's review which considered whether there was scope for an extension of red diesel entitlement to vehicles used for certain community/charity activities. A consultation will take place in early 2012.

FULL TEXT

In October 2011 HM Revenue & Customs (HMRC) conducted a review which considered whether there was scope for the extension of red diesel entitlement to vehicles undertaking certain community/charity activities. One aspect of community work considered was the use of tractors to perform grass cutting of rural communal land and recreation areas for no payment. The review concluded that there should be no change to the current rules but that guidance should be published to help those concerned to understand when it is permitted to use red diesel in vehicles that are being used to cut grass.

Schedule 1 of the Hydrocarbon Oil Duties Act 1979 lists the categories of an excepted vehicle. Excepted vehicles are those which are entitled to use rebated fuel. Vehicles which meet the requirements of one of the following categories can use red diesel for cutting grass:

- unlicensed vehicles not used on public roads
- tractors
- mowing machines

The rules for qualification in each of these categories are explained in the following paragraphs.

UNLICENSED VEHICLES NOT USED ON PUBLIC ROADS

A vehicle that is not used on the public road and has no licence under the Vehicle Excise and Registration Act 1994 is an excepted vehicle. If a vehicle has become untaxed since 31 January 1998 it requires a Statutory Off-Road Notification (SORN). A vehicle for which a SORN has been made is eligible to use red diesel. Unlicensed vehicles that do not require a SORN may also use red diesel so long as they are kept off-road. Consequently, a tractor, mower or utility vehicle used for grass cutting which never goes on the public road can be fuelled on red diesel.

TRACTORS

To qualify in the "Tractors" excepted vehicle category the vehicle must be an agricultural tractor which the legislation defines as one that:

(a) is designed and constructed primarily for use otherwise than on roads, and
(b) is used on public roads solely for:
 (i) purposes relating to agriculture, horticulture or forestry;
 (ii) cutting verges bordering public roads; or
 (iii) cutting hedges or trees bordering public roads or bordering verges which border public roads.

In the view of HMRC, landscaping and the maintenance of recreational facilities are not agriculture, horticulture or forestry. This view is in accordance with the Memorandum of Agreement signed in January 2008 by HMRC, the Driver and Vehicle Licensing Agency, the National Farmers' Union, the National Association of Agricultural Contractors and the Confederation of Forest Industries, which defined the activities that qualify as being agriculture, horticulture or forestry. As a result, a tractor cannot use red diesel when travelling on the public road to or from a job involving grass cutting/maintenance work at golf courses, playing fields, parks, cemeteries or other grassed areas of a similar sort. However, a tractor can use red diesel to cut grass if the grass is being cultivated for harvesting as fodder or if it is growing on the verge of a public road.

MOWING MACHINES

In HMRC's opinion "mowing machine" means either a purpose-built mowing machine, or a vehicle which has been permanently adapted for the sole purpose of mowing. A tractor with mowing equipment attached to it is not a mowing machine, nor is a utilty vehicle to which mowing machinery can be temporarily attached. However, a vehicle consisting, for example, of a Land Rover chassis with permanently fixed grass cutters, designed and constructed for cutting grass and suitable solely for that purpose, would qualify in the mowing machine category.

SUMMARY

To summarise, rebated fuel can only be used to perform grass cutting where:

the vehicle is unlicensed and never uses the public road,

or

the vehicle is designed and constructed primarily for use other than on roads and the grass being cut is being cultivated as animal fodder or grows on the verge of a public road,

or

the vehicle is either a purpose-built mowing machine, or a vehicle which has been permanently adapted for the sole purpose of mowing.

A vehicle not included in the above descriptions is not eligible to use red diesel for cutting grass.

ADVICE

If you have any doubt about whether your vehicle qualifies to use red diesel, please phone the Excise and Customs Helpline on 0845 010 9000.

PRE-REGISTRATION CLAIMS FOLLOWING DE-REGISTRATION OF THE SAME LEGAL ENTITY

23 January 2012. *HMRC Brief 1/12*

ABSTRACT

This Brief is for information only and explains HM Revenue & Customs (HMRC) policy on claims for VAT on goods on hand at registration that are received from persons who were previously registered for VAT, de-registered and have now re-registered.

BACKGROUND

When taxable persons register for VAT they often bring assets into the tax system with them. There is a provision (regulation 111 of the VAT Regulations 1995) that allows VAT to be recovered on such assets within set time limits and with normal evidence of purchase, provided the assets were intended for business use when the VAT was incurred. The time limit for goods is four years and evidence is normally in the form of a VAT invoice.

Where a taxpayer de-registers due to reduced turnover they may have to declare output tax on goods on hand at de-registration on which they have claimed input tax, under Paragraph 8 of Schedule 4 of VATA 1994. This is a deemed self-supply when a person ceases to be VAT registered, to ensure that their future consumption of the assets (as a non-taxable person) is properly taxed.

If the business turnover increases again after de-registration the business may once again become a taxable person and have to register for VAT. If this occurs, and to the extent that the goods are still held and will be used in the new VAT registration, VAT on the deemed supply at de-registration can be considered when establishing an input tax claim under regulation 111.

As there will be no VAT invoice to support any such claim, HMRC's policy was that this precluded input tax deduction under the law. However the lack of any deduction offended neutrality (by precluding the possibility of effective input tax deduction on some of the cost components of taxed supplies). HMRC therefore allowed, by informal concession, claims for relief on goods on hand from persons who were previously registered for VAT under the same legal entity. This is set out in V1-13, para. 6.10.

HMRC POSITION

HMRC now consider that its discretion to allow alternative evidence as set out in regulation 29(2) of the VAT Regulations 1995 can be applied to claims under regulation 111 of the VAT Regulations 1995. HMRC has therefore revised its policy in this area and accepts that where proof that payment of VAT on the deemed supply was made to HMRC on de-registration, this will be accepted as alternative evidence in support of an input tax claim, allowing deduction under regulation 111 of the VAT Regulations 1995. As a result the concession is no longer needed and is withdrawn with immediate effect.

Please note that under regulation 111 such a deduction will not be available if outside the time limit specified (four years for goods) or if the goods were not intended for business use at the time of the deemed self-supply on de-registration. The most likely reason for this is that the business ceased altogether at this point.

Also Regulation 111 does not apply if the asset is a capital item falling within the capital goods scheme (land or buildings costing over £250,000, computer equipment, ships or aircraft costing over £100,000). Instead any input tax deduction must be under the capital goods scheme. For this purpose the cost may be the value of the self-supply or subsequent capital expenditure on the asset while not registered, depending on the circumstances. If the asset is a capital item then the four year limit does not apply. More information on the capital goods scheme can be found in Notice 706/2 Capital goods scheme and paragraph 13 covers registering with an existing item.

EMPLOYMENT INCOME – DEFINITION OF MOBILE PHONE (TREATMENT OF SMARTPHONES)

20 February 2012. *HMRC Brief 2/12*

ABSTRACT

This Revenue & Customs Brief announces a change in HMRC's application of ITEPA 2003, s 319(4) to smartphones, with them now being accepted to qualify as mobile phones rather than PDAs. The exemption from Income Tax in respect of an employer providing one mobile phone per employee, without any transfer of ownership occurring, will apply to smartphones from the start of 2012.

FULL TEXT

READERSHIP

This Revenue & Customs Brief is relevant to those employers that have:

– provided *just one* smartphone to their employees without transfer of ownership *and*
– treated that smartphone as a device that falls outside the meaning of "mobile phone" for the purposes of the exemption in section 319 Income Tax (Earnings and Pensions) Act 2003 ("ITEPA 2003") *and*
– included entries in form P11D and form P11D(b) for the benefit of the availability and use of that smartphone and for the corresponding Class 1A NIC liability (or included the benefit in a PAYE Settlement Agreement)

Instances where all three conditions are satisfied will be rare as in many cases employers and tax advisers have assumed that smartphones are already covered by the mobile phones exemption. Where employers have been aware of HM Revenue & Customs' (HMRC's) view that smartphones are not "mobile phones", employers are likely to have provided such devices in circumstances covered by the separate exemption in section 316 ITEPA 2003 for supplies and services used in employment duties. This exemption applies to certain categories of asset where the sole purpose for providing it is to enable the employee to perform the duties of the job, provided that private use is not significant. (For more technical detail on this exemption see the Employment Income Manual at EIM21611.)

HMRC is today announcing a change of view on the interpretation of section 319(4) ITEPA 2003, which deals with the definition of the term "telephone apparatus", which is used in the definition of "mobile phone" in section 319(2). Section 319 ITEPA provides an exemption from Income Tax in respect of the provision of one mobile phone per employee without any transfer of ownership.

BACKGROUND

Since the emergence of smartphones into the consumer mobile phones market from around late 2007 onwards, HMRC has considered that they were to be treated in the same way as set out in its previously published guidance about personal digital assistants ("PDAs"). This view was based on the understanding that smartphones were not devices that are designed or adapted for the *primary purpose* of transmitting and receiving spoken messages and used in connection with a public electronic communications service.

CHANGE OF VIEW

HMRC now considers that its application of the legislation to smartphones is incorrect.

HMRC now accepts that smartphones satisfy the conditions to qualify as "mobile phones". Developments in PDAs following the penetration of smartphones into consumer markets from late 2007 onwards mean that many modern consumer PDAs are now also likely to be smartphones. But this will not apply to devices that are solely PDAs.

It should be noted that this view applies to smartphones as configured and understood at the start of 2012. This is an area of rapidly changing technology and HMRC cannot be certain about the application of the definition of "mobile phone" to new forms of smartphone.

It should also be noted that there are many types of devices that have telephone functionality which do not qualify as mobile phones. The definition does not cover apparatus that is designed or adapted for a primary purpose other than transmitting or receiving spoken messages, even if that apparatus is also capable of being used in this way.

Examples of apparatus that does not fall within the definition of a mobile phone include satellite navigation devices, devices that are solely PDAs and tablet and laptop computers. In general, devices that use Voice Over Internet Protocol ("VOIP") systems to make and receive phone calls will not satisfy the primary purpose test.

GUIDANCE

As a result of the change of view set out above, the guidance at EIM21701, EIM21779 and EIM21780 is being updated. Amendments are also being made to the Expenses and Benefits A–Z and will be made in due course to booklet 480.

WHAT TO DO IF YOU ARE AFFECTED BY THIS BRIEF

EMPLOYERS

1. Where you provide a smartphone in 2011–12, treat it in the same way as any other mobile phone. Only include a benefit on form P11D for any mobile phones/smartphones that are either over and above the first one provided to the employee or that are provided to a member of the employee's family or household rather than to the employee personally.

2. If you provided a smartphone for 2010–11 and years back to 2007–08 *and* the three bulleted conditions listed under "Readership" are satisfied, you may wish to seek repayment of the Class 1A National Insurance contributions (NICs) liability in relation to the benefit of the smartphone.

3. You can do this by writing to HMRC with the following information for the tax years affected:

- the names and National Insurance numbers of the affected employees
- for each affected employee, confirmation of the smartphone benefit reported on form P11D
- details of the make and model of smartphone
- the calculation of the benefit
- confirmation of where this benefit was included in form P11D
- the amount of Class 1A NICs payable as shown on the original P11D(b)
- the revised amount of Class 1A NICs now payable after deducting the Class 1A NICs originally due on smartphones.

Please include a brief covering letter, with the heading "Employment income: mobile phones exemption - smartphones" and send the information to:

Customer Operations Employer Office
BP4009
Chillingham House
Benton Park View
Newcastle Upon Tyne NE98 1ZZ

4. HMRC will also use this information to identify any repayments of Income Tax that may be due to employees. In order that HMRC can act on this information and make any Income Tax repayments to your employees for 2007–2008 please provide the information in respect of 2007–2008 to HMRC by 31 July 2012. The time limits for repayment of Class 1A NICs liability are later, so if you comply with the dates for Income Tax, you will be within any time limits for claiming a refund of Class 1A NICs.

5. If you identify any affected employees for 2010–11, please check to see if you are also providing a form P11D for them for 2011–12.

- If you do provide a P11D for 2011–12 and you complete it as explained in paragraph 1 above, you don't need to provide HMRC with any additional information about smartphone provision in 2011-12.
- HMRC will automatically sort out 2011–12 and deal with any revision to the 2012-13 tax code when HMRC process 2011–12 P11Ds that you have completed on this basis.

6. However, if there are any affected employees for 2010–11 for whom the change of view on smartphones means you will not need to send a P11D for 2011–12 as there are now no benefits

or expenses to report on it please send a separate list of the names and employees affected. If you wish to complete forms P11D for other employees first, please send this information as soon as possible after you submit forms P11D for 2011–12. This will enable HMRC to sort out the position for 2011-12 and deal with any revision to the 2012–13 tax code. Please include a brief covering letter, with the heading "Employment income: smartphones – no P11D for 2011–12" and send the information to the address shown in paragraph 3 above.

7. Exceptionally, where the provision of a smartphone had been included in a PAYE Settlement Agreement for any of the tax years stated *and* the three bulleted conditions listed under "Readership" are satisfied you should write to:

HMRC Local Compliance
Specialist Employer Compliance
Dukes Court
Dukes Street
Woking
Surrey GU12 5XR

You should include with your repayment claim:

– confirmation that the three conditions were satisfied
– a copy of form P626 for each year where the provision of this benefit had been included
– a breakdown of the original calculation of tax and Class 1B NICs due for each year
– a detailed calculation of the amount to be refunded.

8. If you need help before writing to HMRC, please phone the Employer Helpline on 08457 143 143.

EMPLOYEES

1. If you think you may be affected by this Brief, you will need to check the position very carefully. Firstly you need to consider whether your employer treated smartphones differently to mobile phones and secondly gain confirmation that any smartphone provided was reported to HMRC by your employer as a taxable benefit. In most instances an employer-provided smartphone will *not* have been reported to HMRC as a taxable benefit. If you have been taxed on the benefit of the use of an employer-provided smartphone, this may be because the exemption (which can only cover one device) had already been used up by another mobile phone. In this case, the tax charge is correct, the change of view about smartphones has no effect and you will not be able to make a claim for repayment.

2. If you consider that you are due a repayment you should contact your employer to ask them to supply HMRC with the information detailed in the "Employers" section of this Brief.

3. If your employer or former employer does not supply the required information to HMRC, you will be able to contact HMRC direct and will need to demonstrate all the following:

– you were provided with *just one* smartphone without transfer of ownership to you
– your employer treated that smartphone as a device that falls outside the meaning of "mobile phone" for the purposes of the exemption in section 319 Income Tax (Earnings and Pensions) Act 2003 ("ITEPA 2003")
– the smartphone was not treated as being covered by the separate exemption for certain supplies and services used in employment duties
– your employer included an entry in form P11D for the benefit of the availability and use of that smartphone
– that you have paid tax on the benefit

4. You will also need to provide the information listed in the second, third, fourth and fifth bullets in paragraph 3 under the heading "Employers" above. You may need to ask your employer/former employer to provide you with some of this information.

5. The time limit for claiming repayment of overpaid income tax is four years from the last day of the relevant tax year. If you think you are due a repayment for 2007–2008, you will need to contact HMRC and provide the information for that year as soon as possible. HMRC will still consider claims made for 2007–2008 if they are made on or before 31 July 2012. For 2008–2009 the time limit is 5 April 2013 and for 2009–10 it is 5 April 2014.

6. You should not need to contact HMRC about 2011–12 as HMRC has asked employers to make sure that if the three conditions are satisfied that they do not include the smartphone on

your P11D for this year. As a consequence HMRC will automatically review the 2011–12 tax position after the end of the tax year when HMRC process your P11D information.

7. If you need advice or help, please look at the details for Income Tax enquiries for employees on the "Contact us" page on the HMRC website.

VAT LIABILITY OF CARAVAN PITCH RENTALS

27 February 2012. *HMRC Brief 5/12*

ABSTRACT

This Revenue & Customs Brief introduces new guidance on the VAT liability of caravan pitch rentals reflecting minor changes in effect from 1 March 2012. Sites that provide pitches for less than a year, are subject to an occupation restriction, or are on a holiday/leisure site may need to review their VAT liability. This guidance replaces paragraph 4.1 of Notice 701/20, which will be revised in due course.

FULL TEXT

PURPOSE OF THIS BRIEF

The purpose of this Brief is to introduce new guidance on the VAT liability of caravan pitch rentals, which reflects minor amendments effective from 1 March 2012.

READERSHIP

This Brief is for caravan site owners.

ACTION REQUIRED

Caravan site owners who currently supply exempt pitches in the circumstances described below (see "Who will be affected.....?") should check their VAT liability under the new guidance.

INTRODUCTION

This Brief introduces new guidance on the VAT liability of caravan pitch rentals. This new guidance reflects minor amendments that will take effect from 1 March 2012 as a result of legislation to put an existing concession on a formal basis (background information about the legislation can be found in the consultation document published on 13 December 2010 and the Summary of Responses (customs.hmrc.gov.uk/channelsPortalWebApp) to that document – the latter contains a link to the consultation document at the bottom of page 3).

There should be no change for the majority of caravan site owners. However, sites that currently supply exempt pitches in the circumstances described below (see "Who will be affected....?") should check their position under the new guidance.

WHO WILL BE AFFECTED BY THE MINOR AMENDMENTS?

You should review the VAT liability of your supplies if you currently treat caravan pitch fees as *exempt* in any of the following circumstances:

- the pitches are provided for less than a year
- the pitches are subject to an occupation restriction (such as a planning term stating "no caravan shall be lived in during February") which prevents them from being lived on at all times throughout the period for which the pitches are provided
- the pitches are on a holiday/leisure site

With effect from 1 March 2012, the criteria for treating your pitch fees as exempt will be stricter to ensure that only residential pitches qualify for exemption. Please see the new guidance below for details.

NEW GUIDANCE WITH EFFECT FROM 1 MARCH 2012

The guidance below is to replace paragraph 4.1 of Notice 701/20:

WHAT IS THE LIABILITY OF A CARAVAN PITCH?

Pitch fees or rents received for the granting of the right to caravan owners to keep their caravans on pitches are either exempt or standard-rated. Broadly speaking, the intention of the law is to exempt pitches for caravans used as principal private residences.

The following table will help you to decide the liability of your supply. Words highlighted in bold are defined in the "Notes" section at the bottom of the table.

Standard rated	**Exempt**
The provision of pitches:	The provision of pitches:
a) on *holiday/leisure sites*, regardless of how they are used, except for those pitches occupied by employees of site operators as their *principal private residences*	a) on *permanent residential sites* where caravans can be lived in at all times throughout the year
b) for *restricted occupancy periods*, except in the circumstances described in "(c)" to the right.	b) on sites for Travellers where the caravans are used as *principal private residences*
	c) for *restricted occupancy periods*, but only if — the site is not advertised or held out for holiday/leisure use, and — the pitch is intended to be used as the occupant's *principal private residence*
	d) any type of site (including *holiday/leisure sites*) if the pitch is occupied by a warden or other employee of the site operator as his or her *principal private residence*.

Notes and definitions

1) In determining whether a site is a "*holiday/leisure site*", HM Revenue & Customs (HMRC) will have regard to the way that the site is held out/advertised. In most cases, it will be clear from advertising material if a site is operated for holiday/leisure purposes.

2) A pitch is for a "*restricted occupancy period*" if it is either provided for less than a year or is subject to an *occupancy restriction*.

3) An "*occupancy restriction*" is any covenant (for example, agreement or term in a contract), statutory planning consent, site licence or similar permission, the terms of which prevent the person to whom the pitch is provided from occupying it by living in a caravan at all times throughout the period for which the pitch is provided (such as a condition that says "no caravan shall be lived in during February").

4) In the case of mixed use sites:
— any references above to "*holiday/leisure sites*" include holiday/leisure parts of mixed use sites
— any references to "*permanent residential sites*" include permanent residential parts of mixed use sites

5) HMRC will accept that a caravan is intended for use as a principal private residence if the site owner holds evidence such as, proof of listing on the Valuation Office Agency's (www.voa-.gov.uk/) council tax register, evidence that the occupier has received housing benefit to help with the pitch fee, or agreements or contracts that indicate that the caravan is intended to be used as the occupant's principal home.

Pitch agreements impose certain obligations upon site owners such as the construction of pitches, bases and the park infrastructure. If you raise a one-off charge which is directly related to these obligations it will follow the liability of the supply of the pitch.

The input tax that is attributable to these supplies should be determined accordingly. For information about input tax attribution, see Notice 706 "Partial exemption".

NEW NOTICE 701/20 TO BE PUBLISHED SHORTLY

The new guidance reproduced above will be incorporated into a revised version of Notice 701/20 Caravans and houseboats in due course.

VAT TRIBUNAL DECISION IN PAYMEX LIMITED V HMRC

1 March 2012. *HMRC Brief 3/12*

ABSTRACT

HMRC has changed its view on Paymex and insolvency practitioners' VAT claims, and will now accept claims relating to IVAs, CVAs, PVAs and protected trust deeds. Previously HMRC had stated that VAT claims for CVAs and PVAs would be rejected.

FULL TEXT

Revenue & Customs Brief 35/11 (LNB News 21/09/2011 12) published on 20 September 2011, dealt with the insolvency implications of the VAT Tribunal decision in the case of Paymex Limited, as we understood them at that time.

HM Revenue & Customs (HMRC) has subsequently undertaken a review of all insolvency processes in light of the Paymex ruling, to provide certainty to the insolvency profession as to where the exemption applies. Following completion of this review, it is HMRC's view that the VAT exemption arising from the Paymex ruling applies to:

- Individual voluntary arrangements
- Company voluntary arrangements
- Partnership voluntary arrangements
- Protected trust deeds (applicable only in Scotland)

Insolvency practitioner services in all other insolvency processes remain liable for VAT at the standard rate.

VAT ZERO-RATING OF PHOTO BOOKS - HARRIER LLC CASE

5 March 2012. *HMRC Brief 4/12*

ABSTRACT

HMRC has decided not to appeal the Tribunal decision in Harrier LLC and will now accept, subject to a couple of exceptions, that a photo book consisting of several pages, bound and with a cover stiffer than its pages, qualifies for zero-rating as a book.

FULL TEXT

VAT: HMRC'S POSITION FOLLOWING THE FIRST-TIER TRIBUNAL DECISION IN THE CASE OF HARRIER LLC (TC01562)

This brief is to confirm Her Majesty's Revenue and Customs' (HMRC) position following the decision in the case of Harrier LLC in the First Tier Tribunal. The case concerned the liability of photo books. The Tribunal found against HMRC with regard to most of the items in question and upheld Harrier's appeal that the photo books were zero-rated. HMRC have decided not to appeal the decision.

READERSHIP

Businesses who supply photo books.

BACKGROUND

Harrier provided customers with a photo book that comprised a number of photographs taken by the customer. Typically, the customer uploads his or her photographs and other images of text, drawings, handwritten text and so on to a third party website. The customer chooses the particular photo book template they desire and can arrange the layout of individual pages. Once the customer has completed their action they can then place their order. The order is electronically transmitted to Harrier who then produces the photo book using printing presses.

Harrier claimed that the photo books were zero-rated for VAT purposes as they fell within the definition of book under the law.

THE DECISION

The Tribunal decided that the majority of the items in question were books and dismissed HMRC's argument that the photo book was ancillary to a supply of services.

In making its decision the Tribunal took support from the High Court case of *Colour Offset Ltd* [1995], where it was found that a book has the minimum characteristics of having a significant number of leaves, usually of paper, held together by front and back covers usually more substantial than the leaves. The book must also be designed to be read or looked at.

Two items were found not to be books because they consisted of spiral binding and the pages had the quality and appearance of individual photographic prints.

HMRC POLICY GOING FORWARD

Subject to the exception below, HMRC accept that a photo book which possesses, as a minimum, several pages, a cover stiffer than its pages and is bound, will qualify for zero-rating as a book. The book must also be designed to be read or looked at.

HMRC would not see a photo book as falling within the zero rate if either:

- the photo book's pages have the appearance and quality of individual photographic prints; or
- the photo book that is held out for sale is capable of being dismantled, with individual pages that are removable or where individual pages can be easily removed without damaging the binding (for example, spiral binding).

This decision does not affect supplies where there is a predominate supply of services such as those where the customer is paying for and receiving photographic services that then result in the production of a "book". An example of this is in the Tribunal decision of Risbey's Photography Ltd, Digital Albums Ltd (decision number 20783) where it was found that Risbey's provision of a wedding package which consisted of making arrangements for photography, taking and viewing of photographs and a wedding book displaying a selection of photographs, was a supply of services and not one of goods.

We consider that in these instances the photographic service is the dominant supply and that the wedding book is ancillary to the supply of the services. Accordingly, there is a single supply of standard-rated services.

THE EFFECT OF THE DECISION

If you consider that the supplies that you make are on "all fours" with those of Harrier and the "books" that you supply have the characteristics described above then your supply is likely to be of a book and therefore zero-rated.

If they do not then it is likely that they will be taxable at the standard rate.

FURTHER INFORMATION

Details of how to make any adjustments relating to previous VAT Return periods can be found in VAT Notice 700/45 How to correct VAT errors and make adjustments or claims and from the VAT Helpline on 0845 010 9000.

Where you are in any doubt about the correct VAT treatment please contact the VAT Helpline.

CHANGE TO MONTHLY DEADLINE FOR INTRASTAT DECLARATIONS

16 March 2012. *HMRC Brief 7/12*

ABSTRACT

HMRC reminds businesses that with effect from 1 April 2012, Intrastat declarations must be submitted by the 21st day of the month. This change was announced in November 2011, following consultation, with regulations published in SI 2012/532.

FULL TEXT

SUMMARY

This Revenue & Customs Brief announces changes to the procedure for the submission of Intrastat declarations.

READERSHIP

Businesses that are required to submit declarations for their trade with other EU Member States using an Intrastat declaration. This is limited to those with intra-EU trade in excess of £600,000 per annum for arrivals (EU imports) and/or £250,000 per annum for dispatches (EU exports).

CHANGE TO THE MONTHLY DEADLINE FOR SUBMITTING DECLARATIONS

From 1 April 2012, Intrastat declarations must be submitted by the 21st day of the month. This means that your declarations will be due 21 days after the end of the month in which you have EU trade to declare. Therefore, HM Revenue & Customs (HMRC) must receive your March 2012 Intrastat declaration by 21 April.

ELECTRONIC SUBMISSION OF DECLARATIONS

From 1 April 2012, HMRC will not accept Intrastat declarations on paper forms C1500 and C1501.

You will need to provide your Intrastat declarations using online forms or other electronic formats, for example, Comma Separated Variable File (CSV off line form) or Electronic Data Interchange (EDI).

Information on submitting online can be found on the dedicated trade statistics website uktradeinfo (www.uktradeinfo.com/).

BACKGROUND

WHAT IS INTRASTAT?

Intrastat is the system for the collection of trade in goods between EU Member States for statistical purposes. All VAT-registered businesses that reach a set threshold, expressed in terms of annual value of intra-EU trade, are required to submit Intrastat supplementary declarations on a monthly basis.

WHY THE CHANGES ARE BEING MADE?

HMRC has been undertaking a programme to modernise the Intrastat system to take into account changing demands from users of Intrastat data and the Government's strategy to move to greater use of digital channels.

HMRC has brought forward the monthly deadline for businesses to submit Intrastat supplementary declarations to ensure that HMRC meets the legal deadline to submit data earlier to the EU. This also enables HMRC to make data available earlier to key Government users and to publish details of both EU and non-EU data at the same time.

In line with the Government's Digital Agenda, HMRC is implementing the mandatory submission of Intrastat supplementary declarations. This will enable HMRC to:

- provide a better and more cost effective service for customers submitting Intrastat supplementary declarations
- efficiently capture clean, easily processed data to help drive down costs for HMRC and its customers submitting paper declarations.

CONSULTATION OUTCOME

Between July 2010 and February 2011, HMRC informally consulted with Intrastat businesses to obtain information to help in the decision-making process and to identify how to help businesses comply with the changes.

Nearly 75 per cent of those still using the paper option who responded to the informal consultation on the mandatory electronic submission of Intrastat supplementary declarations said they would not have a problem moving over to electronic submission.

Information from the informal consultations on due date identified the 21st of the month as the most acceptable date for businesses balanced against HMRC's need to provide data earlier.

The majority of those consulted on the change to due date were confident that they would be able to adapt to this change in the first half of 2012, but there were strong views that January

2012 should be avoided. Therefore the changes, both to due date and mandatory electronic submission, will be implemented on 1 April 2012.

A summary of the informal consultation responses can be found in the Consultations section of HMRC's dedicated trade statistics website uktradeinfo (www.uktradeinfo.com/).

FURTHER INFORMATION

Further information on trade statistics is available online on the uktradeinfo website (www.uktradeinfo.com/) or by phoning uktradeinfo Customer Services on Tel 01702 367485.

For further information and advice on submitting Intrastat declarations, please contact the VAT Helpline on Tel 0845 010 9000.

CHANGING VAT LAW ON ROAD FUEL SCALE CHARGES

25 April 2012. *HMRC Brief 11/12*

ABSTRACT

Businesses may be able to claim a refund if they have charged employees for fuel provided for private use and accounted for VAT on an amount greater than the actual charge, for example based on fuel scale charges or the full cost of fuel provided. HMRC is advising businesses to account for VAT in future returns based on the amount they charge employees for private fuel. Current UK law in this respect does not comply with EU law and accordingly the government is consulting on changes to VAT fuel scale charges until 20 July 2012.

FULL TEXT

VAT: ROAD FUEL SCALE CHARGES (RFSCS) – LEGISLATING VAT EXTRA STATUTORY CONCESSIONS (ESCS) AND POSSIBLE CLAIMS FOR OVERPAID VAT

1. INTRODUCTION

HM Revenue & Customs (HMRC) operates a system of Road Fuel Scale Charges (RFSCs) to help businesses account for VAT when business road fuel is put to private use. This is a simplification measure that allows businesses to use a standardised scale charge to value private use fuel. Otherwise businesses would need to keep other records such as detailed records of private mileage.

Following the announcement in the Budget that the Government would be consulting on amendments to the legislation on the RFSC, HMRC has issued a Technical Note, "VAT: Road Fuel Scale Charges – changing UK law to comply with EU law and streamlining the scheme", available at customs.hmrc.gov.uk/channelsPortalWebApp/downloadFile?contentID=HMCE_PROD1_032032.

The changes to RFSC outlined in the Technical Note aim to maintain the overall benefits of the RFSC system. The changes will:

– bring into legislation the effect of two existing extra statutory concessions
– simplify the legislation and the process for the annual revalorisation of the scale charges
– withdraw one extra statutory concession
– correct a defect in the existing legislation

2. WHO NEEDS TO READ THIS?

VAT-registered businesses that use road fuel scale charge to account for VAT on fuel which has been acquired through their business but then used for private purposes.

3. IMPACT OF THE DEFECT IN EXISTING RFSC LEGISLATION

Under existing law, where a business has provided fuel to an employee for their private use and has made a charge for that fuel, they are required to account for VAT on the basis of the RFSC, unless they have accounted for VAT on the basis of detailed records of private mileage or the charge made was at least for the cost of the fuel. HMRC now recognises that there is a defect in this aspect of current law and that, where the business does make a charge for the private use of the fuel, the business should be given the option of accounting for VAT on the basis of the amount charged to the employee.

Businesses making a charge for private use of fuel may, until the defect has been corrected, account for VAT on this basis in future returns. Any businesses who consider that they have overpaid VAT as a result of this defect may submit a claim for repayment of the difference between the amount already accounted for and the amount due on the basis of the charge to the employee. All claims which are submitted to HMRC must be supported by proper evidence and are subject to the normal rules for claims. Further guidance on making claims can be found in Public Notice 700/45 *How to correct VAT errors and make adjustments or claims.*

CHANGES TO THE TREATMENT OF SINGLE PURPOSE FACE VALUE VOUCHERS

10 May 2012. *HMRC Brief 12/12*

ABSTRACT

This Brief sets out changes to the VAT rules for single-purpose face value vouchers, to be included in the current Finance Bill and given effect from 10 May 2012. The changes mean that all such face value vouchers will be taxed when they are issued, rather than on redemption as is currently the case. A single-purpose face value voucher is one that carries the right to receive only one type of goods or services, all subject to a single rate of VAT. Businesses issuing and redeeming the affected types of vouchers will not be required to account for VAT under the new rules until FA 2012 receives Royal Assent.

FULL TEXT

VAT: CHANGES TO THE TREATMENT OF SUPPLIES MADE IN CONNECTION WITH SINGLE PURPOSE FACE VALUE VOUCHERS FOLLOWING THE CJEU JUDGMENT IN CASE C-520/10

This Brief sets out changes to the VAT rules for certain types of face value vouchers as announced today by David Gauke, the Exchequer Secretary, in a Written Ministerial Statement. These changes will be included within the current Finance Bill and will have retrospective effect to 10 May 2012.

WHO NEEDS TO READ THIS?

Businesses involved in the sale of single purpose face value vouchers (see paragraph 1.4 below) or which provide goods or services in exchange for such vouchers. Other types of voucher are unaffected by the changes.

1.1 BACKGROUND

Lebara Limited operated a telecommunications business by which international telephone calls were made available to customers in other member states through the use of face value vouchers. Lebara sold the vouchers to distributors in other member states who then sold them on to other distributors or direct to the end customers. The case before the CJEU concerned the proper analysis of the supplies involved and how such services provided via vouchers should be taxed.

The Court found that, in circumstances such as these, there was a supply of services from Lebara to the distributors, but there was no supply by Lebara on redemption to the end customer. As a consequence, the UK legislation in VAT Act 1994, Schedule 10A for certain types of voucher is incompatible with EU law.

Although this case was concerned with the supply of telecommunications services via the use of a voucher, the principles considered by the Court are of general application and will apply to other single purpose vouchers that can be used to obtain only one type of good or service. However, it is HMRC's understanding that the majority of vouchers are unaffected.

VAT PRs etc

1.2 CONSEQUENCES OF THE JUDGMENT IN OUTLINE

As a consequence of the judgment, it has been necessary to amend the VAT treatment of certain types of face value vouchers. This has been in order to safeguard significant revenue and to prevent artificial VAT avoidance. Given the scale of this risk it has been necessary to implement these changes with immediate effect. However, businesses issuing and redeeming the affected types of vouchers will not be required to account for VAT under the new rules until the Finance Bill receives Royal Assent. They will then need to make an adjustment to cover the intervening period. Alternatively, businesses may opt to implement the changes straight away to avoid the need for an adjustment.

1.3 EXISTING TREATMENT FOR FACE VALUE VOUCHERS

The current rules for the treatment of face value vouchers are given in Schedule 10A to the VAT Act 1994. A face value voucher is any voucher, token or stamp that carries the right to receive goods or services to a value shown on it or contained within it. A face value voucher may be physical or electronic.

Under the existing rules there are two main types of face value vouchers: retailer vouchers and credit vouchers.

- A retailer voucher is a voucher issued by the same person who will redeem it. This includes, for example, gift tokens sold by a retailer for use in its own shops
- A credit voucher is any type of face value voucher that is issued by one person but which can be exchanged for goods and services from another person. This includes, for example, gift tokens sold by one company that can be exchanged for goods or services in a variety of high street shops.

All the consideration for all supplies of credit vouchers is currently disregarded with VAT being brought to account by the redeemer when the vouchers are exchanged for goods or services. With retailer vouchers the initial consideration on issue is disregarded but the vouchers are then taxed for subsequent supplies. Again the issuer is required to account for VAT on the supply when the voucher is redeemed.

1.4 AFFECTED VOUCHERS

As a result of the changes announced today, single purpose face value vouchers will be taxed when they are issued. This will affect all single purpose vouchers, whether credit, retailer or other types of voucher.

A single purpose face value voucher is one that carries the right to receive only one type of goods or services which are all subject to a single rate of VAT.

For example, where a prepaid telephone card can only be redeemed for telecommunication services it will be a single purpose voucher. Similarly a voucher that can be redeemed only for electronically supplied services will be a single purpose voucher even if the electronic service can have slightly different forms (e.g. streamed movies, music or games).

A book token that can be redeemed for zero rated books or standard rated e-books, will not be a single purpose voucher as it can be redeemed for more than one type of supply and they have different rates.

Further examples are given below.

1.5 THE NEW TREATMENT OF SINGLE PURPOSE VOUCHERS

As the announced changes remove single purpose vouchers from Schedule 10A, the special rules for face value vouchers will no longer apply.

Instead where a single purpose voucher is sold both initially and by retailers or distributors, it is treated as a supply of the goods or services for which it can be redeemed. This will apply whether the voucher is issued by the person from whom it can be redeemed or by a third party.

For example a telecommunications company produces vouchers that entitle the holder to £10 worth of telephone calls. It sells a voucher to a distributor for £8 and accounts for VAT on the £8. The distributor recovers the input tax and sells the voucher to a retailer for £9 and accounts for VAT on £9. The retailer recovers the input tax and sells the voucher to the final consumer for £10 and accounts for output tax on £10.

EXAMPLE 1 SINGLE PURPOSE VOUCHER

A UK provider of an online fantasy game sells face value vouchers that can be redeemed for game time or enhancements within the game (both standard rated electronic supplied services). The vouchers are sold to distributors in the UK, other Member States and non-EU countries who sell them on to consumers within their territory.

As the services for which the vouchers can be redeemed are of a single type and at the same rate of tax, they are single purpose vouchers. The supply by the game provider to the distributors is regarded as a supply of electronically supplied services and will be subject to UK VAT when supplied to UK distributors and outside of the scope when supplied to non-UK distributors.

EXAMPLE 2 SINGLE PURPOSE VOUCHER

A group discount provider sells face value vouchers to consumers which carry the right to specific services (for example, a manicure at a particular retailer). Even if contractually the provider is not the supplier of the services to the consumer, for VAT purposes there is a supply by the retailer to the provider and the provider to the consumer. VAT will be due from the provider when the voucher is issued, even if the voucher is never subsequently redeemed.

Other Examples of single purpose vouchers

- Prepaid telephone cards that can only be used for making calls
- Electronic download vouchers, where they can only be redeemed for downloads, electronic apps, file streaming or other electronically supplied services
- Group discount vouchers, where they are redeemed for a specific service or goods
- Vouchers for admission to amusement parks which cannot be exchanged for other goods and services in the park

1.6 OTHER TYPES OF VOUCHERS

For all vouchers that do not come within the definition of single purpose vouchers the current VAT treatment described in 1.3 continues.

EXAMPLE 3 OTHER TYPE OF VOUCHER

A cinema operator sells face value vouchers which can be redeemed for any services or goods provided in its venues, for example watching the film, buying popcorn or merchandise. As these are supplies of more than one type, such vouchers will not be affected by this change and the normal Schedule 10A rules will continue to apply.

EXAMPLE 4 OTHER TYPE OF VOUCHER

A restaurant offers face value vouchers that can be redeemed against the services provided by the restaurant which include both zero-rated cold take away food and standard rated meals inside the premises. As the vouchers can be redeemed for services which are at different rates of tax, they will not be affected by this change and the normal Schedule 10A rules will continue to apply.

Other Examples of vouchers that are not single purpose vouchers

- Shop vouchers for stores selling goods at different rates
- Book tokens which can also be exchanged for e-books
- Garden centre vouchers
- Multi-retailer vouchers
- Game console vouchers that can be redeemed for goods as well as downloading electronic products
- Hotel vouchers that can be used in more than one country or that can be used for other items added to the bill (e.g. newspapers)

1.7 TRANSITIONAL PROVISIONS

The changes announced by the Exchequer Secretary include transitional provisions. These apply where a single purpose voucher has been issued before 10 May 2012 (i.e. the consideration has been disregarded) but it is redeemed on or after this date.

The effect of the transitional provisions is to deem a supply for VAT purposes, by the person from whom the goods or services are obtained to the end user, where the supply to the end user is made in the UK. The value of the deemed supply will be the value of the goods or services obtained by use of the voucher. This provision ensures that the redeemer only accounts for the amount of VAT that it would have been required to under Schedule 10A.

So for example a telecommunications company produces a voucher with a face value of £10 that entitles the holder to 80 minutes of calls. It sold a voucher to a distributor for £8 on 1 April 2012 and, in accordance with the previous rules did not account for VAT. On 15 May the end customer who purchased the card uses it to make a 40 minute call – the company must account for VAT on £4. The next day the customer makes a 20 minute call – the company must account for VAT on £2. The customer makes no further calls after that so the company has no further VAT to account for.

1.8 FURTHER ADVICE

Given the definition of single purpose vouchers used by the CJEU, HMRC do not believe that the judgment will affect a large number of businesses. However we recognise the impact that the new rules will have on those that are affected and that it will take them time to adjust their business arrangements and accounting systems to cope. Businesses with an HMRC Customer Relationship Manager (CRM) should discuss with them any difficulties that they will have in complying with the new rules with a view to agreeing a workable solution.

Businesses that do not have a CRM are welcome to contact our specialist retail unit on 0113 272 9642 in order to discuss any problems that the changes might cause them, or in writing to:

HM Revenue and Customs
Retail Unit of Expertise
1 Munroe Court
White Rose Office Park
Millshaw park
Leeds LS11 0EA

OUT-OF-TIME CLAIMS FOR REPAYMENT OF INDIRECT TAXES

14 May 2012. *HMRC Brief 13/12*

ABSTRACT

The ECJ held in the recent case of *Banca Antoniana Popolare Veneta SpA* (Case C-427/10) that a bank's out-of-time VAT repayment claim against the Italian tax authorities succeeded because on the facts of the case the bank had been "totally deprived" of the opportunity to make a claim. In this Brief, HMRC states its view that the above case does not establish an automatic right for taxable persons to make out-of-time claims for repayment of wrongly accounted-for VAT simply because they have been legally required to make repayments to their customers.

FULL TEXT

Judgment of the Court of Justice of the European Union (ECJ) – Case C-427/10: *Banca Antoniana Popolare Veneta SpA v Ministero dell'Economia e delle Finanze and Agenzia delle Entrate* [2012] STC 526 (*Banca Antoniana*) – out-of-time claims for overdeclared indirect taxes

READERSHIP

This Brief is aimed predominantly at professional tax advisors and lawyers although it may be of interest to others.

While the judgment in *Banca Antoniana* concerned VAT, the judgment, and this Brief applies to all of the taxes previously administered by HM Customs & Excise.

BACKGROUND – CLAIMS FOR OVERPAID VAT AND TIME LIMITS

Where a person has accounted for tax contrary to EU law, he or she is entitled to make a claim to recover it - Case 199/82: *Amministrazione delle Finanze dello Stato v SpA San Giorgio* [1983] ECR 3595, [1985] 2 CMLR 658 at paragraph 12.

However, Member States are permitted to impose reasonable time limits on such claims provided that those time limits do not breach either the principle of effectiveness (the time limits must not be framed so as to render impossible or excessively difficult the exercise of EU law rights) or the principle of equivalence (they must not be less favourable than those relating to similar claims based on domestic law).

The imposition of such time limits on claims for repayment of overpaid or overdeclared tax does not, of itself, breach the principle of effectiveness even where it leads to the complete dismissal of the claim – Case C-188/95: *Fantask A/S & Ors v Industriministeriet (Erhvervsministeriet)* [1998] All ER (EC) 1 at paragraph 48.

Time limits as short as one year have been held to be reasonable by the ECJ – Case C-261/91: *Rosalba Palmisani v Istituto Nazionale della Previdenza Sociale (INPS)* [1997] ECR I-4025 at paragraph 29. The ECJ has already held that the time limits in the UK are reasonable (Case C-62/00: *Marks & Spencer Plc v CCE* [2002] STC 1036 at paragraph 35) and are not liable to make it excessively difficult or impossible in practice for claims to be made to recover amounts levied or collected by way of tax in breach of EU law. Since that judgment was delivered those time limits have been increased from three years to four.

ECJ JUDGMENT IN *BANCA ANTONIANA*

Banca Antoniana Popolare Veneta (the bank) is an Italian bank which, in accordance with the view of the Italian tax authority and the Italian courts, charged VAT on services supplied to its customers between 1984 and 1994.

In 1999 the Italian tax authority issued a circular stating that it was their view that these services ought to have been exempt from VAT. The bank's customers made claims against it for repayment of the VAT that it had wrongly charged to them and the bank was ordered by the Italian courts to pay those claims. The bank then made a claim against the Italian tax authority for the VAT that it had wrongly accounted for on the supplies to those customers.

Whilst the claims made by the customers against the Bank (Customers' Claims) were subject to a ten-year time limit, claims by the Bank against the tax authority (Taxable Persons' Claims) were subject to a time limit of two years from the date of payment or, if later, from the date on which the conditions for bringing the claim were met.

The Italian tax authority rejected the bank's claim on the grounds that the claim was made out-of-time and that decision was upheld by the courts.

The Italian Supreme Court referred a number of questions to the ECJ, essentially asking whether it is permissible in EU law to apply time limits to Customers' Claims that are longer than those applied to Taxable Persons' Claims.

The Court of Justice confirmed that rules of national law which apply a more generous time limit to Customers' Claims than to Taxable Persons' Claims do not breach the EU principle of effectiveness provided that the conduct of the national tax authority combined with the existence of the time limit does not have the effect that a person is *totally deprived* of the right to obtain a refund of VAT wrongly accounted for.

The ECJ found that, in all the circumstances of this case, the bank was, in fact, *totally deprived* of any opportunity to make a claim and the following factors were taken into account by the Court in reaching that conclusion:

- until the publication of the circular in February 1999, the tax authority had not considered that the VAT exemption applied
- the judgments of the Italian courts holding that it didn't had not been overturned
- the 1999 circular was retroactive and had the effect of moving the starting date for the time limit for claims back to the date on which the VAT was paid
- this had the effect that, when the circular was published, the two-year time limit for making claims against the tax authority for VAT wrongly accounted for between 1984 and 1994 had already expired
- at all times the bank acted as a prudent and alert economic operator
- on the facts of this case, the application of the time limits made it impossible or excessively difficult to make a claim against the tax authority and left the bank bearing the economic cost of the VAT which it had wrongly accounted for

HM REVENUE & CUSTOMS VIEW

In giving its judgment, the ECJ restated the well-rehearsed view that it is compatible with EU law for Member States to lay down reasonable time limits for making claims against the tax authority for tax collected contrary to EU law and that a two-year time limit is, in principle, sufficient.

HM Revenue & Customs' (HMRC) view is that this case is very fact-specific and that it does not automatically introduce an opportunity for taxable persons to make out-of-time claims for repayment of VAT wrongly accounted for in circumstances where they are legally required to make repayments of "tax" to their customers.

As noted above, the time limit has since been increased from three years to four. These time limits are clearly and publicly set out in statute and it is not open to HMRC retroactively to apply shorter or different time limits in such a way that it would have the effect of totally depriving a taxable person of a right to recovery. The fact that HMRC takes one view of the law does not prevent a taxable person from bringing a claim on another.

UPDATED SENIOR ACCOUNTING OFFICER GUIDANCE

11 June 2012. *HMRC Brief 16/12*

ABSTRACT

In this brief, HMRC draws attention to the publication in May 2012 of its Senior Accounting Officer Guidance Manual, which contains an updated version of guidance on the rules introduced by Finance Act 2009, Sch 46.

FULL TEXT

INTRODUCTION

HM Revenue & Customs (HMRC) has refreshed its guidance concerning the application of the Senior Accounting Officer (SAO) rules.

The updated guidance can be accessed via www.hmrc.gov.uk/manuals/saogmanual/index.htm.

Changes have been made to every section of the guidance, so it is not possible to list all the changes here. Although the terminology and structure has changed, there are few significant changes in policy. Specifically, the main updates in terms of HMRC's view are in respect of:

- The application of SAO rules during insolvency procedures. HMRC now believes that the SAO rules do apply in most cases where insolvency procedures were underway (see SAOG 11100+ and 15200).
- The meaning of the turnover test for banks and insurance companies. HMRC is now of the opinion that the word "turnover" takes its meaning from the Companies Act definition, and the test should be applied to all companies including banks and insurance companies (see SAOG 11232).
- HMRC no longer believes that companies are only within the SAO rules in relation to their UK activities (see SAOG 11210).
- HMRC now believes that there are no confidentiality/disclosure bars to prevent the disclosure of a late or the non-provision of an SAO certificate to a company (see SAOG 16500, 16600, 16610 and 16620).

WHO NEEDS TO READ THIS?

Companies, and their agents, that have previously fallen within the SAO rules and those that will fall within the SAO rules in line with the updated guidance.

APPLYING THE UPDATED GUIDANCE

There are a few areas in the updated guidance where HMRC has changed its interpretation of the SAO rules.

HMRC will not consider charging penalties where companies and SAOs have followed previous guidance for any period up to the first period commencing after the publication of this revised guidance. Additionally, HMRC will apply a "light touch" period to any companies that are brought into the SAO regime by its changed interpretation for the first period commencing after publication of the guidance - along the same lines as the "light touch" approach that was applied when the regime was introduced. Finally, HMRC will not charge any penalties for previous periods where one would seem to be due under the previous guidance, but which would not be due under the revised guidance.

Where HMRC's view has not changed there has been no need to update the content of the guidance and HMRC would expect companies and SAOs to continue to apply the SAO rules.

PLACE OF SUPPLY OF SERVICES CONNECTED TO LAND

2 August 2012. *HMRC Brief 22/12*

ABSTRACT

Following discussions at EU level, HMRC is changing its policy on the place of supply of three types of service: (1) stands at exhibitions; (2) storage of goods; and (3) airport lounges. Exhibition space packaged with certain accompanying services will no longer be treated as a supply of land. Storage space will only be treated as a supply of land where the supplier grants an exclusive right to use a specific area of a UK warehouse. Supplies of access to airport lounges, not currently treated as land-related, will become so. Services connected to land are subject to VAT in the country where the land is situated. The general rule is that services not connected to land are VATable where the customer is located. Businesses may continue to apply HMRC's old treatment for up to three months from the date of this brief (2 August 2012).

FULL TEXT

This Brief provides a statement of HM Revenue & Customs' (HMRC's) policy on the place of supply of services connected to land following discussions at EU level. It also details changes to HMRC's published policy in respect of the treatment of exhibition stands, storage and warehousing, and access to airport lounges.

The Brief is concerned only with determining the place of supply of these services. It does not affect HMRC's guidance or policy on the rate of tax that applies to any such supplies.

READERSHIP

This Brief is aimed at businesses that make or receive supplies of services connected to land and property. In particular it will affect businesses that:

- supply or buy in stands at exhibitions
- store goods for overseas customers
- provide access to airport lounges

BACKGROUND

The place of supply of services rules are an important concept in VAT as they are used to determine the country in which VAT is due so as to avoid either taxing the same supply twice or not taxing it at all. If a supply of services takes place in the UK then UK VAT will be due, but if the supply takes place in another EU Member State then it will be subject to VAT in that Member State.

In most cases where services are supplied by a business in the UK to a business customer in another Member State then no UK VAT is charged by the supplier. Instead the customer has to account for VAT in their own Member State using the "reverse charge". Similarly, most services supplied by UK businesses to business customers located outside the EU will not be subject to UK VAT.

However, in the case of services connected to land and property, Article 47 of the EU VAT Directive makes the service subject to VAT in the country where the land is situated. So, if the land is located in the UK, then UK VAT will be due. This VAT may be recovered by business customers, subject to the normal rules.

The changes to the place of supply rules from 1 January 2010 and 1 January 2011, highlighted differences in the treatment of certain supplies in various Member States. This has led to some businesses suffering double taxation. As it has not been possible to solve this issue in isolation, HMRC has been working with the Commission and EU Member States to try to agree the uniform application of Article 47 (services connected to land and property).

As a result of these discussions HMRC is changing aspects of its policy on the place of supply of:

– stands at exhibitions
– storage of goods
– airport lounges

Further details of these changes are given below.

WHAT DO WE MEAN BY LAND?

For the purpose of determining the place of supply, land means any:

– specific part of the earth, on, above or below its surface, over which title or possession can be created
– building or construction fixed to or in the ground above or below sea level which cannot be easily dismantled or moved
– item making up part of a building or construction and without which it is incomplete (such as doors, windows, roofs, staircases and lifts)
– item, equipment or machine permanently installed in a building or construction which cannot be moved without destroying or altering the building or construction

WHEN IS A SERVICE RELATED TO LAND?

In order for a service to be land related for determining the place of supply it must have a sufficiently direct connection with a specific piece of land.

This will include services:

– derived from land and where the land is a central and essential part of the service
– intended to legally or physically alter a property

EXAMPLES OF SERVICES RELATING TO LAND WHICH ARE SUBJECT TO VAT WHERE THE PROPERTY IS SITUATED

– Construction or demolition of a building or permanent structure (such as pipelines for gas, water or sewage).
– Surveying and assessing property.
– Valuing property, including for insurance or loan purposes.
– Providing accommodation in hotels, holiday camps, camping sites or timeshare accommodation.
– Maintenance, renovation and repair of a building (including work such as cleaning and decorating) or permanent structure.
– Property management services (but not the management of a property investment portfolio).
– Arranging the sale or lease of land or property.
– Drawing up of plans for a building or part of a building designated for a particular site.
– On-site security services.
– Agricultural work on land (including tillage, sowing, watering and fertilization).
– Installation and assembly of machines which, when installed, will form a fixture that cannot be easily dismantled or moved.
– The granting of rights to use all or part of a property (such as fishing or hunting rights and access to airport lounges).
– Legal services such as conveyancing and drawing up of contracts of sale or leases.
– Bridge or tunnel toll fees.
– The supply of space for the use of advertising bill-boards - for example the leasing of a plot of land or the side of a building to allow a billboard to be erected.
– The supply of plant and equipment together with an operator, to allow the customer to carry out work on land or property where the supplier has responsibility for the execution of work.

EXAMPLES OF SERVICES NOT RELATING TO LAND

– Drawing up of plans for a building or part of a building that do not relate to a particular site.
– Arranging the supply of hotel accommodation or similar services.
– Installation, assembly, repair or maintenance of machines or equipment which are not, and do not become, part of the land or property.
– Management of a property investment portfolio.

- Advertising services that involve the use of a billboard.
- The supply of equipment with an operator, *where it can be shown* that the supplier has no responsibility for the performance of the work.

STAND SPACE AT EXHIBITIONS AND CONFERENCES

Currently HMRC regards the supply of specific stand space at an exhibition or conference as a supply of land. This policy will continue where the service is restricted to the mere supply of space without any accompanying services.

However, where stand space is provided with accompanying services as a package, this package (stand and services) will no longer be seen as a supply of land with land related services but will be taxed under the general place of supply rule (customer location) when supplied to business customers.

Accompanying services provided as part of a package includes such things as the design and erection of a temporary stand, security, power, telecommunications, hire of machinery or publicity material.

STORAGE OF GOODS

Current HMRC policy is to see all supplies of storage space as land related. This will change so that where a supplier grants the right to use a specific area of a UK warehouse or storage area for the exclusive use of the customer to store goods, the service will be treated as relating to land and subject to VAT in the UK. However, where the supplier agrees to store goods but does not grant a right to a specific area for the exclusive use of the customer, this will not be seen as a land related supply but will be treated as falling within the general place of supply rule. In such cases business customers who belong outside the UK will not be liable to UK VAT.

AIRPORT LOUNGES

To date HMRC has not regarded the supply of access to airport lounges as a land related service. However, this policy will change and therefore VAT, if applicable, will be due in the country where the aircraft lounge is located.

CHANGES OF HMRC POLICY

Where businesses have been treating services in accordance with HMRC's earlier policy, they may continue to apply that treatment for a transitional period of up to three months from the date of this Brief in order to make adjustments to their systems and processes. However, businesses that wish to adopt the new treatment may do so immediately if they wish.

Although businesses may make adjustments for past periods, any VAT declared in accordance with HMRC's earlier policy, that would not have been due under the new interpretation, will not be entitled to a refund unless:

- it can be demonstrated that the customer has not recovered the VAT charge
- and any VAT repaid by HMRC will be refunded to the customer

If that is not the case then HMRC will consider the defence of unjust enrichment in deciding whether to make a repayment of the VAT declared.

WITHDRAWAL OF REDUCED VAT RATE FOR ENERGY SAVING MATERIALS

20 August 2012. *HMRC Brief 26/12*

ABSTRACT

The government has announced its intention to defend the UK's reduced rate for installation of energy saving materials in residential buildings, which is the subject of a formal challenge by the European Commission. The reduced rate for similar installations in charitable buildings is to be withdrawn from a date following Royal Assent to Finance Bill 2013 (likely to be 1 August 2013) and HMRC is asking businesses affected by the change to submit representations by 20 October 2012 about any particular problems this timetable might present. Where work on an installation has commenced before the date of withdrawal, the reduced rate will continue to apply to the whole installation.

VAT PRs etc

FULL TEXT

VAT - WITHDRAWAL OF THE REDUCED RATE OF VAT FOR ENERGY SAVING MATERIALS INSTALLED IN BUILDINGS USED FOR A RELEVANT CHARITABLE PURPOSE - INFRINGEMENT PROCEEDINGS BY THE EUROPEAN COMMISSION

PURPOSE OF THIS BRIEF

At Budget 2012, the Government announced its intention to withdraw the reduced rate for energy saving materials (ESM) installed in buildings used solely for a relevant charitable purpose. The Government is taking this action following pre-infraction communication with the European Commission (EC) who pointed out that this reduced rate is not permitted under European law. This Brief seeks views on two questions arising from the Budget 2012 announcement.

On 21 June 2012, the EC published a Reasoned Opinion which is the first public step in the process of taking infringement action against the UK in respect of its reduced rate for ESM (whether installed in residential accommodation or in buildings intended for use solely for a relevant charitable purpose). This Brief explains that the Government's view is that the reduced rate for the installation of ESM in residential accommodation is consistent with the VAT Directive and it will be defending this.

WHO NEEDS TO READ THIS?

Businesses in the construction sector who install ESM, charities that use buildings solely for a non-business use and anyone who manages a village hall or similar establishment.

BACKGROUND

The UK applies a reduced rate of VAT to the installation of ESM in various types of building. However, the EC has initiated legal proceedings against the UK on the basis that this reduced rate is not allowed in EU law and the UK is therefore in breach of its obligations as a Member State of the European Union.

The EC has commenced these proceedings on three grounds:

- that there is no specific provision in EU law to allow a reduced rate for ESM
- that the EU provisions on which the UK relies as the legal basis for the reduced rate (Category (10) of Annex III to the Principal VAT Directive) only apply where introduced "as part of a social policy", whereas the UK's relief for ESM has been introduced as part of an environmental policy, and
- that, in any event, the UK's relief is too wide as the EU provisions on which it relies apply only to housing, which does not include buildings used for a relevant charitable purpose

While the Government does not agree with the arguments in relation to the first two bullet points above, it has reluctantly accepted that the argument in the third bullet point is correct. Consequently, at Budget 2012, the Government announced its intention to withdraw this reduced rate from charitable buildings as part of Finance Bill 2013 and informed the EC of this.

The subsequent publication of the EC's Reasoned Opinion indicates that it intends to proceed with the infraction against the UK in any event. The Government will continue to defend the remainder of the reduced rate.

QUESTIONS

The Government intends to introduce legislation in Finance Bill 2013 to withdraw the reduced rate for ESM installed in buildings used for a relevant charitable purpose with the legislation to come into effect on the first day of the month following Royal Assent (likely to be 1 August 2013). However, HMRC seeks the views of those affected on the following questions:

(1) Does the proposed date (1 August 2013) for the removal of the reduced rate for the installation of ESM in relevant charitable buildings present any particular problems? If so, can you explain what they are and what alternatives you propose?

(2) Are there any particular factors that HMRC should take into account when making this change?

TRANSITIONAL RULES

Given that nearly a year's prior notice of the withdrawal of this relief has been given, the Government does not intend to provide for any additional transitional rules (subject to comments received on the questions above). However, where work has commenced for the installation of ESM before the date of withdrawal (provisionally 1 August 2013), the reduced rate will continue to apply to the whole installation even if part of that installation is performed after that date.

Responses should be sent by 20 October 2012 by email to Sandy Mackie or by post to:

Sandy Mackie
HMRC
VAT Liability Team
Room 3/34
3rd Floor
100 Parliament Street
London SW1A 2BQ

VAT: ADDRESSING BORDERLINE ANOMALIES – DETAILED INFORMATION SHEETS PUBLISHED

4 September 2012. *HMRC Brief 27/12*

ABSTRACT

HMRC has published seven information sheets containing guidance on the controversial VAT changes as finally enacted in FA 2012, Sch 26 and 27, relating to hot food and premises, caravans, sports nutrition drinks, listed buildings, hairdressers' chairs, self storage and anti-forestalling measures (for listed buildings and self storage). On 28 June 2012, the government published its responses and intended amendments to the measures as originally proposed in the "VAT Borderline Anomalies" consultation.

FULL TEXT

WHAT IS THIS ABOUT?

This brief announces publication of guidance covering the changes to address VAT borderline anomalies announced at Budget 2012. The changes take effect from 1 October 2012 (apart from caravans which takes effect from 6 April 2013).

The guidance takes the form of 7 information sheets covering each of the following areas:

- Hot food and premises (customs.hmrc.gov.uk/channelsPortalWebApp/downloadFile?contentID=HMCE_PROD1_032284)
- Caravans (customs.hmrc.gov.uk/channelsPortalWebApp/downloadFile?contentID=HMCE_PROD1_032283)
- Sports nutrition drinks (customs.hmrc.gov.uk/channelsPortalWebApp/downloadFile?contentID=HMCE_PROD1_032287)
- Listed buildings (customs.hmrc.gov.uk/channelsPortalWebApp/downloadFile?contentID=HMCE_PROD1_032282)
- Hairdressers' chairs (customs.hmrc.gov.uk/channelsPortalWebApp/downloadFile?contentID=HMCE_PROD1_032285)
- Self storage (customs.hmrc.gov.uk/channelsPortalWebApp/downloadFile?contentID=HMCE_PROD1_032286); and
- Anti-forestalling (relating to the listed building and self storage changes) (customs.hmrc.gov.uk/channelsPortalWebApp/downloadFile?contentID=HMCE_PROD1_032281)

WHO NEEDS TO READ IT?

Businesses that make supplies in the areas outlined above, and their advisers.

BACKGROUND

The Government announced at Budget 2012 that it was making a number of changes to address certain anomalies in the VAT system, to increase certainty for businesses, reduce compliance costs and to raise revenue.

WHAT IS BEING PUBLISHED?

Information sheets are being published to explain how each of the changes will work. These will be incorporated into HMRC's books of guidance as soon as possible.

WHAT IF I HAVE COMMENTS OR SUGGESTIONS ABOUT THESE INFORMATION SHEETS?

If you have comments or suggestions that you think will help to improve the content of this guidance please write to:

VAT Projects Team
HM Revenue & Customs
3rd Floor
100 Parliament Street
London SW1A 2BQ

Please note that this address is not for enquiries. If you have a question about the changes which is not covered in the information sheets please contact the VAT helpline on 0845 010 9000.

EXCISE DUTY: INCREASE IN RESTORATION FEE FOLLOWING THE SEIZURE OF A ROAD VEHICLE (FUEL OFFENCES)

26 October 2012. *HMRC Brief 29/12*

ABSTRACT

From 1 November 2012, the duty and VAT element of the restoration fee for road vehicles seized after being found with rebated fuel illegally in the fuel tank will be based on the total litre capacity of the vehicle's tank. Currently, this part of the fee is limited to the quantity of fuel actually in the tank at the time of seizure.

FULL TEXT

PURPOSE OF THIS BRIEF

This Brief gives information about changes to the way restoration fees are calculated and the increase in those fees following seizure of a road vehicle as a result of a fuel offence.

WHO NEEDS TO READ THIS?

This change *will not affect* the vast majority of road users who use fuel in their vehicles on which the full excise duty and VAT has been accounted for correctly. The changes will only affect those road users who are found to have rebated fuel illegally in the fuel tank of their road vehicle, whether private or commercial.

BACKGROUND

Rebated fuel bears a lower rate of excise duty than road fuel. It is not allowed to be used in vehicles using public roads other than in a limited number of "excepted vehicles", such as specified agricultural and construction vehicles, where use on the roads is incidental to the main use. The most common rebated fuel is "red diesel", but kerosene and "green diesel" from the Republic of Ireland are also included.

If a vehicle at the roadside is tested by HM Revenue & Customs (HMRC) and found to be illegally using rebated fuel or a road fuel substitute where the appropriate duty for road use has not been paid, the vehicle may be seized.

Under HMRC's current policy, it can be restored to the owner directly at the roadside on payment of a restoration fee, on condition that the fuel is changed at the first safe and practical opportunity.

In some cases, the vehicle may have to be seized pending further enquiries. These enquiries may lead to an audit to establish the extent of duty arrears and liability to penalties in respect of the detected vehicle and others owned or operated by the person responsible.

WHAT ARE THE CHANGES?

The restoration fee is currently made up of:

– an amount based on regulatory fixed penalties of £250, for unlawfully taking rebated fuel into a road vehicle and a further £250 for unlawfully using rebated fuel in a road vehicle
– an amount which is equal to the duty and VAT which *should* have been paid on the quantity of fuel found in the tank an amount to cover the storage and removal costs (in cases where the vehicle is removed)
– From 1 November 2012 the duty and VAT element of the restoration fee will be based on the *total litre capacity* of a vehicle's fuel tank, not the quantity of illicit fuel remaining in the vehicle's fuel tanks.

WHO WILL BE AFFECTED?

Anybody in charge of a vehicle on the road or at the roadside which is found with illegal traces of rebated fuel or a road fuel substitute where the appropriate duty for road use has not been paid in their vehicle's fuel tank will be liable to the increased fees. This includes both private and commercial vehicles.

WHY ARE THESE CHANGES BEING MADE?

Increasing the restoration fee will make it more of a deterrent to anybody considering using rebated fuel or a road fuel substitute where the appropriate excise duty for road use has not been paid.

The illegal use of these cheaper, rebated fuels places legitimate businesses at a disadvantage.

WHAT LEGISLATION IS BEING CHANGED OR INTRODUCED?

No changes to legislation are being made. HMRC is able to increase the amount of the fee without change to primary or secondary legislation.

TIMING

The changes come into effect on 1 November 2012.

FURTHER GUIDANCE

Further information relating to fuel for road and off road use can be found in Notice 75 Fuel for road vehicles (customs.hmrc.gov.uk/channelsPortalWebApp/channelsPortalWebApp.porta)

TRANSFER OF GOING CONCERN IN ROBINSON FAMILY LIMITED CASE

16 November 2012. *HMRC Brief 30/12*

ABSTRACT

HMRC confirms it will not be appealing the decision of the First-tier Tribunal in *Robinson Family Limited*, in which the Tribunal held that a transfer of a going concern (TOGC) had taken place for VAT purposes, even though the taxpayer had transferred only a part of the property used in their business. HMRC will now accept that the retention of a small reversionary interest in property transferred will not necessarily prevent the transaction from being a TOGC. Repayments of SDLT may also be due in respect of past transactions where taxpayers have relied on HMRC's existing guidance. HMRC is considering the SDLT aspect and further guidance will follow.

FULL TEXT

PURPOSE OF THIS BRIEF

The purpose of this Brief is to explain a change in HM Revenue & Customs' (HMRC's) position following the decision of the Tax Tribunal in the case of *Robinson Family Limited* ([2012] UKFTT 360 (TC), TC02046).

VAT PRs etc

READERSHIP

This Brief is for traders who enter into property transactions (other than solely as an occupier), and their advisers.

ACTION REQUIRED

To note the contents of this Brief.

INTRODUCTION

When the assets of a business (or part of a business) are transferred as a going concern, subject to certain conditions no supply of those assets takes place for VAT purposes. For this to happen, the purchaser must have the intention of using those assets to carry on the same kind of business as the seller. This is equally the case where the business is that of property development or property rental, and the asset sold is the property, but it can sometimes be less clear when a business is being transferred in these situations.

HMRC has interpreted the law as meaning that, for there to be the transfer of a property rental or property development business as a going concern ("TOGC"), the interest in land being transferred must be the same interest as that used by the transferor in his business. It followed from this interpretation that, if what was transferred was less than the transferor's full interest in the land, then the retained interest would prevent there having been the transfer of a property business as a going concern. For example, HMRC's guidance says that where a freeholder grants a 999 year lease the freeholder's business is not transferred as a going concern because of the interest retained.

In its decision in the case of *Robinson Family Limited,* the Tax Tribunal disagreed with this interpretation of the law in the facts of that case. *HMRC will not be appealing this decision.*

ROBINSON FAMILY LIMITED ("RFL")

RFL is a property development company which purchased a 125 year interest in a site owned by Belfast Harbour Commissioners, which it intended to develop into six units and grant sub-leases of these to third parties. The dispute between RFL and HMRC in the end concerned one unit which RFL had been negotiating to let. There was a restriction imposed by Belfast Harbour Commissioners against any sub-division of the site other than by way of the creation of sub-leases, so rather than sell its interest, RFL granted an interest of 125 years less three days to a purchaser subject to and with the benefit of the proposed letting.

HMRC relied solely on the argument that RFL could not have transferred all or part of its business as a going concern, because it did not assign the full term of its lease to the purchaser. HMRC's approach in the case reflected the guidance set out in the second bullet point in paragraph 6.3 of Notice 700/9 (April 2008): Transfer of business as a going concern:

> If you own the freehold of a property and grant a lease, even a 999-year lease, you are not transferring a business as a going concern. You are creating a new asset (the lease) and selling it while retaining your original asset (the freehold). This is true regardless of the length of the lease. Similarly, if you own a headlease and grant a sub-lease you are not transferring your business as a going concern.

The Tribunal found that, although RFL retained the headlease, that distant interest in a three day reversion and the small economic interest which it represented in no way altered the substance of the transaction. The substance of the transaction was to put the transferee business in a position where it was able to continue the previous lettings business of RFL. On this basis, the Tribunal found against HMRC.

WHAT THIS MEANS

In the light of the Tribunal's decision in the *Robinson Family case*, HMRC accepts that the fact that the transferor of a property rental business retains a small reversionary interest in the property transferred does not prevent the transaction from being treated as a TOGC for VAT purposes. Provided the interest retained is small enough not to disturb the substance of the transaction, the transaction will be a TOGC if the usual conditions are satisfied. In this context, the Tribunal's decision does not as such alter any other areas of HMRC's policy on TOGCs, but we are reviewing the policy on whether the surrender of an interest in land can sometimes result in a TOGC. HMRC is also reviewing whether properties which are used in a business other than property letting are affected by this change of policy.

The second bullet point in paragraph 6.3 of Notice 700/9 should be ignored, as we now accept that the creation of a new asset (a lease or sub-lease) and the retention of the original asset (the freehold or a superior lease) is not automatically incompatible with TOGC treatment. The Notice will be updated in due course.

HMRC will accept that a reversion retained by the transferor is sufficiently small for TOGC treatment to be capable of applying if the value of the interest retained is no more than 1 per cent of the value of the property immediately before the transfer (disregarding any mortgage or charge). Where more than one property is transferred at one time, this test should be applied on a property by property basis rather than for the entire portfolio.

If the interest retained by the transferor represents more than 1 per cent of the value of the property, HMRC will regard that as strongly indicative that the transaction is too complex to be a TOGC.

EXAMPLE

A Ltd owns the freehold of a building valued at £1m which A Ltd rents out commercially. A Ltd sells that property rental business by granting to B Ltd a 999 year lease under which A Ltd is entitled to receive a ground rent of £100 each year. The value of that right, together with any and all other rights retained by A Ltd, is £2,000. Provided all the normal conditions are satisfied, the transaction will be a TOGC, because HMRC will regard the 0.2 per cent interest retained as too small to disturb the substance of the transaction.

THE IMPACT OF THE DECISION

We accept there are situations where in the past customers did not regard a transaction as constituting a TOGC because of the guidance referred to. In some cases a building would have been sold where an option to tax had been exercised, and the relevant VAT charged and accounted for. SDLT would then have been payable on the VAT-inclusive amount. There are two questions to address where customers wish to retrospectively claim TOGC treatment on account of the Tribunal's decision in the Robinson Family.

Firstly, there is the difficulty that the relevant notification that an option to tax will not be rendered ineffective, will not have been given by the buyer to the seller. This is a legal requirement in articles 5(2A) and 5(2B) of the VAT (Special Provisions) Order 1995, and it is referred to in paragraph 11.2 of Notice 742A: Opting to tax land and buildings.

Provided the parties can satisfactorily evidence that *Article 5(2B) did not apply at the time of the transaction* and thus the requisite notification could have been given, we will accept that the legal requirement has been complied with.

Secondly, there is the question of whether an adjustment can be made to the SDLT already paid. We are considering this point and will provide further guidance on it soon.

RETROSPECTIVE CLAIMS

Details of how to make any adjustments relating to previous VAT Return periods can be found in VAT Notice 700/45 How to correct VAT errors and make adjustments or claims and from the VAT Helpline on 0845 010 9000.

Where you are in any doubt about the correct VAT treatment please contact the VAT Helpline.

Notice 700/45 How to correct VAT errors and make adjustments or claims (customs.hmrc.gov.uk/channelsPortalWebApp/downloadFile?contentID=HMCE_CL_000077)

REMOVAL OF VAT REGISTRATION THRESHOLD FOR BUSINESSES NOT ESTABLISHED IN THE UK

15 November 2012. *HMRC Brief 31/12*

ABSTRACT

With effect from 1 December 2012, businesses not established in the UK must register for UK VAT when they make supplies in the UK, regardless of value. FA 2012 introduced legislation to remove the registration threshold for non-established taxable persons, following the ECJ decision in the Schmelz case. Overseas businesses making only reverse charge supplies of services to the UK, or those only involved in distance sales or acquisitions are not, in most cases, affected by the change.

FULL TEXT

PURPOSE OF THIS BRIEF

To note that, from 1 December 2012, non-established taxable persons (NETPs) will no longer be able to benefit from the UK VAT registration threshold. They will be required to register for UK VAT when they make their first supply of goods or services here regardless of the value.

NETPs who are already making supplies here will be required to register for UK VAT with effect from 1 December 2012.

READERSHIP

This Brief is for NETPs and their agents.

BACKGROUND

The UK has always allowed its domestic VAT registration threshold (currently £77,000) to apply to NETPs who make taxable supplies in the UK, as well as to UK businesses. NETPs include, for example, non-UK traders at farmers' markets or Irish service suppliers working across the land border. However, a decision (Schmelz C-97/09) in the CJEU (the European Court of Justice) has confirmed that only businesses established in a Member State can benefit from its domestic VAT registration threshold.

Therefore, a new Schedule 1A to the VAT Act 1994 and other consequential changes were made in Finance Act 2012 and come into force on 1 December 2012.

From 1 December 2012, any non-established business which makes or intends to make taxable supplies in the next 30 days has 30 days from the date it formed that intention to notify HM Revenue & Customs (HMRC) that it is required to register for VAT. Businesses which become required to register in the UK on 1 December 2012 will have to notify HMRC of that fact by 30 December 2012.

A business not established in the UK will be required to register from the earliest of the date that it made or expected to make taxable supplies in the UK (but no earlier than 1 December 2012). Non-established businesses which are aware that they will need to be registered from 1 December 2012 (for example, because they are already making supplies in the UK under the current threshold) can provide advance notice to HMRC, and they will be registered for VAT from 1 December 2012.

Existing UK place of supply rules have not been changed. Overseas businesses making only reverse charge supplies of services to the UK will not normally be affected by the removal of the threshold. However, there are some exceptions that are taxable supplies in the UK where they are supplied to a private customer rather than to a business, for example, services in connection with land which is located in the UK or entertainment services when the performance takes place in the UK.

Overseas businesses only involved in distance sales or acquisitions are not affected by the removal of the VAT registration threshold.

Any NETP business which is required or entitled to register for VAT can apply for VAT registration either online or by completing form VAT 1.

More information on UK VAT registration can be found in Notice 700/1 Should I be registered for VAT? on the website. Where you are in any doubt about the correct treatment, please contact the VAT Helpline on Tel 0845 010 9000 or if calling from abroad on +44 2920 501 261.

Notice 700/1 Should I be registered for VAT? (customs.hmrc.gov.uk/channelsPortalWebApp/)

CHANGE IN VAT TREATMENT OF INSURANCE MIS-SELLING REVIEWS AND HELPLINE SERVICES

5 December 2012. *HMRC Brief 33/12*

ABSTRACT

HMRC is changing its policy on the treatment of supplies to insurers of pensions mis-selling review services and helpline services and will remove the current VAT exemption with effect from 1 April 2013, in response to a challenge by the European Commission. The change will not affect similar services involving Payment Protection Insurance (PPI) or Protection and Indemnity (P&I) Club managers, although HMRC will be revising its guidance on the latter. Businesses will not be required retrospectively to account for VAT on past supplies following removal of the exemption, but will not be able to recover input tax against those supplies that remain treated as exempt.

FULL TEXT

ENQUIRIES FROM THE EUROPEAN COMMISSION INTO THE UK'S VAT EXEMPTION OF INSURANCE MIS-SELLING REVIEWS AND HELPLINE SERVICES

PURPOSE OF THIS BRIEF

This Brief announces a change in the UK VAT treatment of supplies to insurers of certain mis-selling review services and helpline services following enquiries received from the European Commission ("the Commission").

WHO NEEDS TO READ THIS?

- Insurers
- Businesses that supply helpline services to insurers
- Businesses that might supply insurers with mis-selling review services in the future should further reviews be instigated by the regulatory authority.

This Brief does not affect businesses that supply banks and other lenders with Payment Protection Insurance ("PPI") mis-selling review services. PPI review services have always been subject to VAT and will not, therefore, be impacted by this change.

1.1 BACKGROUND

The UK currently exempts from VAT mis-selling review services and stand-alone helpline services supplied to insurers by insurance intermediaries, subject to certain conditions being met. This policy is set out in Paragraph 10.3 of Notice 701/36 Insurance (customs.hmrc.gov.uk/channelsPortalWebApp/channelsPortalWebApp.portal) and Paragraph 10.4 of Notice 701/36 Insurance (customs.hmrc.gov.uk/channelsPortalWebApp/channelsPortalWebApp.portal) and in sections VATINS5410 and VATINS5420 of the VAT Insurance guidance manual.

In both cases, the policy to exempt these services is based on UK case law (the relevant decisions are *Century Life Plc* [2000] EWCA Civ 366, which concerned the provision of pensions mis-selling review services by an insurance agent; and *C & V (Advice Line) Services Limited* VTD 17310, which concerned the services of a legal helpline that, amongst other things, advised insurance policyholders on the making of insurance claims).

The Commission has recently queried the UK's basis for treating such services as exempt and has expressed the view that the services are taxable in light of a number of recent judgments of the European Court of Justice ("ECJ") on the application of the EU VAT exemption to insurance related services.

Having reviewed the position, HM Revenue & Customs (HMRC) has concluded that the Commission is correct in its view that these services are taxable and that the UK case law which had previously indicated otherwise has now been superseded by subsequent decisions of the ECJ. Consequently HMRC has informed the Commission that its current policy to exempt these services will be amended from a future date.

VAT PRs etc

1.2 THE NEW VAT TREATMENT

1.2.1 PENSIONS MIS-SELLING REVIEW SERVICES

HMRC no longer accepts that exemption applies to the services described in Paragraph 10.3 of Notice 701/36 (customs.hmrc.gov.uk/channelsPortalWebApp/channelsPortalWebApp.portal) (Pensions mis-selling review services carried out on behalf of insurers) and in sections VATINS5410 and VATINS5420 of the VAT Insurance guidance manual. HMRC now considers all mis-selling review services to be liable to standard rated VAT.

There has been no change in the VAT treatment of PPI mis-selling review services. HMRC has always maintained that these services are liable to VAT at the standard rate and the VAT treatment for mis-selling reviews outlined in HMRC guidance has never applied to them. For the current exemption to apply the third party provider must be an insurance agent acting as an intermediary between an insurer and an insured party. This means that the insurer must be the party that is legally liable to have the reviews carried out and bear any claims for compensation or other redress. PPI reviews, however, are being carried out on behalf of banks and other lenders because, in this instance, they are the parties identified by the regulator as being liable for the mis-selling.

1.2.2 HELPLINE SERVICES

HMRC no longer accepts that exemption applies to the services described in paragraph 10.4 of Notice 701/36 (customs.hmrc.gov.uk/channelsPortalWebApp/channelsPortalWebApp.portal) (helplines supplied to insurers to provide assistance to insured parties on matters such as variations of contract and the making of claims).

However, if an insurance broker or agent provides helpline services to an insurer as part of a single supply which also includes the provision of exempt insurance related services (see section 9 of Notice 701/36 Insurance (customs.hmrc.gov.uk/channelsPortalWebApp/channelsPortalWebApp.portal)), the supply will have a single VAT liability which will be determined in accordance with its principal element (if there is a principal element to which other elements are ancillary) or its main focus or predominant nature. For example, if helpline services are provided as an ancillary part of a contract for exempt insurance related services, the supply will be exempt from VAT.

1.2.3 DATE FROM WHICH NEW POLICY TAKES EFFECT

Businesses that are affected by the change in policy are required to start accounting for VAT on any supplies made on or after 1st April 2013.

If they have relied on HMRC guidance to treat supplies as exempt in the past, they will not be required to retrospectively account for VAT on those supplies as long as they met the terms of the published policy. They will not, however, be able to recover any input tax against those supplies that remain treated as exempt.

The VAT Insurance guidance manual and Notice 701/36 will be updated in due course.

1.3. FURTHER INFORMATION ABOUT COMMISSION'S QUERY

In addition to querying the treatment of pensions mis-selling reviews and helpline services, the Commission has also queried HMRC's basis for applying exemption to the services of P&I Club Managers, as described in Paragraph 10.2.1, Notice 701/36 (customs.hmrc.gov.uk/channelsPortalWebApp/channelsPortalWebApp.portal). Having reviewed this matter, HMRC concluded that the services of P&I Club managers have been correctly treated as exempt but that the notice does not accurately portray the range of services that the managers actually provide. The Commission has accepted that, when correctly characterised, the services of P&I Club managers are properly exempt. The VAT insurance notice will be updated shortly to reflect the true position.

MOTOR VEHICLES FOR DISABLED PEOPLE – NEW HELPSHEETS

12 December 2012. *HMRC Brief 34/12*

ABSTRACT

This brief confirms the withdrawal of VAT Notice 701/59 and its replacement by two new helpsheets, VAT1615 and VAT1616, in December 2012.

FULL TEXT

PURPOSE OF THIS BRIEF

To note that, from 30 November 2012 HM Revenue & Customs (HMRC) is withdrawing VAT Notice 701/59 (March 2002) Motor vehicles for disabled people and replacing it with two new customer and dealer orientated help-sheets.

READERSHIP

All VAT-registered motor vehicle dealers and their agents and any customers who may be considering the purchase of a zero-rated, adapted motor vehicle or boat under this disability scheme.

BACKGROUND

The VAT zero rate relief for adapted motor vehicles for wheelchair users allows regular wheelchair users to purchase a motor vehicle that has been specifically designed or adapted to enable them to enter and drive (or otherwise be carried in) the vehicle at the zero rate of VAT, provided that the vehicle is for the domestic and personal use of the wheelchair user.

The current Notice is now ten years old and does not fully reflect HMRC's interpretation of the law.

WHAT IS CHANGING?

Two new help sheets have replaced the VAT Notice 701/59. One is aimed at dealers who sell vehicles and the other provides information and qualifying conditions for members of the public who are considering a purchase under this scheme.

The content of the new material remains largely unchanged from that contained in VAT Notice 701/59.

Download VAT 1615 "*About purchasing zero-rated adapted vehicles (Guidance for customers)*" (www.hmrc.gov.uk/helpsheets/vat1615.pdf)

Download VAT 1616 "*About purchasing zero-rated adapted vehicles (Guidance for suppliers)*" (www.hmrc.gov.uk/helpsheets/vat1616.pdf)

VOLUNTARY SCHEME FOR ADAPTED MOTOR VEHICLES AND BOATS

12 December 2012. *HMRC Brief 35/12*

ABSTRACT

This brief confirms that the voluntary scheme for traders to provide HMRC with information about their zero-rated sales of adapted motor vehicles and boats to disabled people opened for business on 30 November 2012.

FULL TEXT

PURPOSE OF THIS BRIEF

To note that, from 30 November 2012 HM Revenue & Customs (HMRC) is introducing a new voluntary scheme for motor and boat dealers. The purpose of the scheme is to gather information from traders about zero-rated sales of adapted motor vehicles and boats to disabled people.

READERSHIP

All VAT-registered motor vehicle and boat dealers who make sales under the zero-rated, adapted motor vehicle or boat disability scheme.

BACKGROUND

The VAT zero rate relief for adapted motor vehicles and boats for wheelchair users allows regular wheelchair users to purchase a motor vehicle or boat that has been specifically designed or adapted to enable them to enter and drive (or otherwise be carried in) the vehicle at the zero rate of VAT, provided that the vehicle is for the domestic and personal use of the wheelchair user.

HOW WILL THE SCHEME WORK?

This scheme for adapted motor vehicles and boats was announced at Budget 2012.

It is entirely voluntary. The aim of the scheme is to gather information from suppliers of vehicles and boats about the use of the VAT zero rate, on sales of motor vehicles and boats adapted for the use of wheelchair users.

Participating car dealerships and boat suppliers can provide information to HMRC by completing a survey form about their zero-rated motor vehicle and boat sales.

WHY DO YOU WANT US TO PROVIDE ADDITIONAL INFORMATION?

HMRC need further information in order to establish how often the relief is used, the types of adaptations required, the costs involved and the types of vehicles purchased.

HOW WILL THIS INFORMATION BE USED?

Currently HMRC has very little information about how much the relief is used.

HMRC will use the information to establish general trends, values and numbers. In addition it will help HMRC gain a better understanding of the current use of the relief to assist to improve guidance.

Read more about the voluntary scheme (www.hmrc.gov.uk/vat/sectors/motors/dvs.htm).

VAT: SUPPLIES MADE UNDER FINANCE LEASES FOLLOWING EON CASE

2 January 2013. *HMRC Brief 37/12*

ABSTRACT

This brief confirms that taxpayers who make finance lease supplies, or who receive such supplies in relation to business cars and block some of the input tax incurred from deduction should, for the time being, continue to treat hire supplies as set out in currently published HMRC guidance. HMRC still considering whether the decision of the European Court in EON Aset Menidjmunt (C-118/11) means that finance lease supplies are supplies of goods rather than supplies of services, but will not apply any future change of policy retrospectively.

FULL TEXT

VAT: SUPPLIES MADE UNDER FINANCE LEASES - EON ASET MENIDJMUNT - NO IMMEDIATE CHANGES TO WHETHER GOODS OR SERVICES - NO IMPACT ON INPUT TAX BLOCKED ON FINANCE LEASES OF CARS

PURPOSE OF THIS BRIEF

This brief confirms to taxpayers who make finance lease supplies, or who receive such supplies in relation to business cars and block some of the input tax incurred from deduction, that no current action is needed in relation to the EON case.

READERSHIP

Businesses that make supplies of capital goods under finance lease agreements and businesses that incur input tax on supplies of cars under finance lease agreements and block some of that input tax from deduction.

INTRODUCTION

Under UK VAT law hire purchase (HP) agreements are considered to be supplies of goods because they expressly envisage that title to the goods being hired will pass at the end of the hire term. Finance lease (FL) agreements do not provide for title to pass and are therefore treated as supplies of services.

The CJEU recently delivered its decision in the case of *EON Aset Menidjmunt*, C-118/11, (*EON*). Comments made in the decision suggest that, because the risks and rewards of ownership largely pass to the hirer in FL agreements, and because this is recognised in international accounting standards, supplies under FL agreements may be supplies of goods rather than supplies of services. This has created uncertainty in the finance leasing sector.

NO CHANGE OF TREATMENT AT THIS TIME

HM Revenue & Customs (HMRC) is considering representations made by industry representatives and has not reached a final conclusion on whether the EON decision means that FL supplies are supplies of goods rather than supplies of services or, if so, what features are decisive in determining whether a supply is of goods rather than of services. Until and unless HMRC make a contrary announcement taxpayers should continue to treat hire supplies as set out in currently published HMRC guidance. If there is any future change of policy then HMRC will only apply any changes from a future date and will not require taxpayers to make any retrospective accounting adjustments.

INPUT TAX BLOCK ON FL CARS

The EON decision has also raised questions in relation to the input tax block as it applies to FL cars. HMRC can confirm that whether the eventual VAT treatment of FL supplies is as goods or as services FL cars will continue to have a 50 per cent input tax block applied to them.

Where taxpayers are supplied cars for use in their business then unless the cars are stock in trade (for example, demonstrator cars at car showrooms), the car is central to their business (for example, driving instructors) or the car is not made available for private use, the input tax they incur is subject to a block on deduction. Normally input tax is wholly blocked but where the supply received is a "letting on hire" (such as under an FL) the block applies at 50 per cent, rather than at 100 per cent, of the tax incurred.

Whether FL supplies are eventually concluded to be supplies of goods, rather than supplies of services, will not affect the fact that they are "lettings on hire". Consequently no change to input tax blocked on FL supplies can be needed.

CONSULTATION ON WITHDRAWAL OF VAT EXEMPTION FOR RESEARCH SERVICES

20 December 2012. *HMRC Brief 38/12*

ABSTRACT

The UK government has accepted a European Commission decision that the VAT exemption for business supplies of research between eligible bodies (mainly government departments, schools, universities, charities and other public bodies) does not comply with EU law and plans to withdraw the exemption from 1 August 2013. In the meantime, HMRC is consulting on the impact of this withdrawal and on possible options to mitigate its effects.

FULL TEXT

VAT: PUBLICATION OF AN INFORMATION GATHERING CONSULTATION ON THE WITHDRAWAL OF THE EXEMPTION FOR BUSINESS SUPPLIES OF RESEARCH SERVICES BETWEEN ELIGIBLE BODIES

PURPOSE OF THIS BRIEF

The purpose of this Brief is to announce the publication of a consultation on the withdrawal of the VAT exemption for business supplies of research services between eligible bodies.

WHO SHOULD READ THIS BRIEF

All suppliers of business research and those that commission research.

BACKGROUND

The UK has received notification from the European Commission that its exemption for business supplies of research between eligible bodies does not comply with European legislation. The UK has accepted that this is the case and plans to withdraw the exemption from 1 August 2013.

HMRC have discussed the impact of withdrawal with representative bodies but have been unable to ascertain from these discussions the full impact on those affected.

In these discussions HMRC were informed that the impact of the withdrawal will be minimal when compared to the totality of all research conducted in the UK. Our best estimate is that it is likely to affect less than one per cent by value of all research undertaken in the UK.

The purpose of the consultation therefore is to gather information that will allow HMRC to assess more accurately the impact of the withdrawal of the exemption and to see whether there are any possible options to mitigate that impact.

WHO ARE ELIGIBLE BODIES?

Eligible bodies are generally Government departments, schools, universities, charities and other public bodies. It is only supplies of research between these bodies that will be affected. All other research will maintain its current VAT liability.

THE CONSULTATION

The consultation document is available on the HMRC website from 20 December 2012 at customs.hmrc.gov.uk/channelsPortalWebApp/downloadFile?contentID=HMCE_PROD1_032497.

VAT: CONNECTION CHARGES FOR WATER

28 December 2012. *HMRC Brief 40/12*

ABSTRACT

This brief concerns a change of HMRC's policy on the VAT liability of first-time connection charges for water and sets out the circumstances in which HMRC will treat these charges as either zero-rated or standard-rated supplies. The concession which allowed zero-rating for gas and electricity connection charges was withdrawn from January 2012 and this announcement on water charges follows a review of the extent to which these charges are similar.

FULL TEXT

This brief explains Her Majesty's Revenue and Customs' (HMRC) change of policy on the VAT liability of first time connection charges for water.

READERSHIP

Water companies, building contractors and plumbers.

ACTION

To be aware of HMRC's change of policy on water connection charges. This affects first time connection charges made by the same person who is supplying the water to the same customer.

BACKGROUND

Revenue & Customs Brief 43/11 announced that from 1 January 2012 one-off charges for the first time connection to gas and electricity made by the same person (or by members of the same VAT group) who supply the gas or electricity would follow the treatment of the utility and be reduced rated. Given the similarities, HMRC has now completed a review of first time connection charges for water.

LIABILITY OF FIRST CONNECTION CHARGES SUPPLIED WITH WATER

Where a customer contracts with a water supplier to provide mains water and that necessitates a first time connection to that water supply, the connection will be ancillary to the zero-rate supply of water providing the supplier of the water and connection are made by the same taxable person (or within the same VAT group) to the same customer.

However, if the customer is involved in a relevant industrial activity (e.g. manufacturing) the supply of the water and any connection will be standard rated. Further details are in Public Notice 701/16 paragraph 2.3)

First time connection of water pipe-work is standard rated if at the time of connection, no water supplier had been identified. The zero-rate only applies if in order to supply mains water for the first time, the supplier needs to carry out the connection (it is ancillary to the supply of water). However, where the connection is carried out for the first time without any reference to a water supplier, such work cannot be ancillary to the water supplier's supply. In such cases, the water connection will be a separate taxable supply from the supply of water.

LIABILITY OF CONNECTION CHARGES FOR REPLACEMENT WATER SUPPLIES

Any repairs, alterations or replacements carried out to existing pipe work of a water supply are standard rated.

The following table gives examples of the VAT liability of the connection charges for replacement supplies of water.

Replacement of lead piping or damaged pipework	Separate standard-rated supply
Water usage increases requiring a new additional mains connection.	Separate standard-rated supply
Water usage increases and existing mains connection is replaced with a new, larger capacity mains connection	Separate standard-rated supply
Relocation of existing water service pipe	Separate standard-rated supply
Existing building is demolished and replaced by new property or properties not being used for a relevant industrial activity.	Zero-rated, as being incidental to the new water supply
Property, not being used for a relevant industrial use, is on an existing common water supply and requires its own separate supply.	Standard-rated
Property is divided into multiple properties not being used for a relevant industrial purpose.	If there is still one water connection shared by the individual properties, the supply is standard-rated. Otherwise zero-rated.
Reconnection charges for existing properties	Standard-rated

CIVIL ENGINEERING WORKS SUPPLIED SEPARATELY FROM WATER

The new policy applies only where the provider of the connection is the same person who supplies the water (or a member of the same VAT group). If the connection is carried out by a third party, the supply will remain standard rated.

However, some supplies of civil engineering works provided in isolation from water can already be zero or reduced-rated under certain circumstances as follows:

Supply	**Liability**
The first time connection of a new dwelling or relevant residential or relevant charitable building to the water supply if the connection is made as part of the construction of the building.	Zero rated under item 2 of Group 5 of Schedule 8 to the VAT Act 1994.
The supply to a housing association of civil engineering works for connecting a property to the water supply being converted from commercial use to relevant residential use.	Zero-rated under item 3 of Group 5 of Schedule 8 to the VAT Act 1994.
The first time connection to a mains water supply in the course of construction of civil engineering works necessary for the development of a permanent park for residential caravans	Zero-rated under item 2(b) of Group 5 of Schedule 8 to the VAT Act 1994.

MAKING CLAIMS OR ADJUSTMENTS

Where a customer has paid VAT on a connection charge that should have been zero-rated and have been unable to deduct this VAT, they may approach their supplier for a refund of the VAT paid.

Where a supplier wishes to make a claim to HMRC (under section 80 of the VAT Act 1994) for repayment of VAT incorrectly accounted for, they may do so, subject to the conditions set out in Notice 700/45 How to correct VAT errors and make adjustments or claims.

All claims will be subject to the four-year time limit in section 80(4) of the VAT Act 1994 and to the set-off provisions in section 81 of the VAT Act and section 130 of the Finance Act 2008.

We may reject all or part of a claim if repayment would unjustly enrich the claimant.

More details on making claims and "unjust enrichment" can be found in Notice 700/45 *How to correct VAT errors and make adjustments or claims.*

FURTHER INFORMATION

For further information and advice, please contact our Helpline on 0845 010 9000.

VAT: ROOMS PROVIDED IN HOTELS OR SIMILAR ESTABLISHMENTS WITH CATERING

22 January 2013. *HMRC Brief 2/13*

ABSTRACT

In this brief, HMRC confirms its view that the provision of accommodation in an hotel or similar establishment for the purpose of catering is standard rated, regardless of whether the catering is provided by the operator of the hotel or by another person. This view is contained in the most recent version of Notice 709/3 (October 2011). Previously, HMRC treated the supply of the room only as exempt, where catering was supplied by a third party. HMRC will take no action to alter the treatment of relevant supplies made before 22 January 2013.

FULL TEXT

This brief confirms HM Revenue & Customs' (HMRC's) view of the VAT treatment of rooms provided in hotels and similar establishments for the purpose of supplies of catering. It is issued following the review and publication of Notice 709/3 Hotels and holiday accommodation.

READERSHIP

Anyone who provides rooms in hotels or similar establishments for the purpose of supplies of catering.

ACTION

Information only to ensure that all those affected are aware of HMRC's change of interpretation.

BACKGROUND

Supplies of land are normally exempt from VAT. However, this exemption does not apply to the provision of accommodation in hotels, inns, boarding houses and similar establishments, including accommodation in rooms provided for the purpose of supplies of catering, such as rooms provided by hotels for wedding receptions.

Normally, hotels (and similar establishments) supply both the venue and the catering. However, in some instances the catering may be supplied by third parties. When the previous version of the guidance was written, HMRC's view was that, where both the room and the catering were supplied by the hotel or similar establishment, the whole supply (including the provision of the room) would be standard rated. However, where the catering was supplied by a different person, the supply of the room only by the hotel would be exempt (unless the supplier had opted to tax). HMRC subsequently changed its view on this point, but did not update its guidance to reflect this.

HMRC'S INTERPRETATION OF THE LAW

HMRC published an updated version of Notice 709/3 Hotels and holiday accommodation in October 2011. Paragraph 4.1 of the updated Notice confirms that the provision of accommodation in an hotel, inn, boarding house or similar establishment for the purpose of catering is standard rated regardless of whether the catering is provided by the operator of the hotel, etc, or by another person.

WHAT THIS CHANGE MEANS

Where businesses have treated supplies as exempt from VAT in the past no assessments will be issued or action taken to correct the treatment of such supplies. All supplies should, however, be treated consistently with HMRC's revised interpretation from the date of this Revenue and Customs Brief.

FURTHER GUIDANCE

Notice 709/3 Hotels and holiday accommodation is available from HMRC's website.

SS/FS2A-SECURITIES IN RESPECT OF VAT AT RISK

4 March 2013. *HMRC Factsheet*

Factsheet for taxable persons from whom HMRC may require security against the risk they may not comply with their obligations to pay VAT.

Securities series (January 2013)

We have given you this factsheet either because we have told you that you may have to give security or because you must now give security. If you have a tax adviser, you may want to talk to them and show them any correspondence that we have given you.

Value Added Tax (VAT) law allows us to require a taxable person to give an amount of security if there is a serious risk that they will not pay VAT which is or becomes due. The relevant tax law is set out in paragraph 4(2)(a) of Schedule 11 to the VAT Act 1994.

WHAT A TAXABLE PERSON IS

A taxable person is a person or business that is registered or required to be registered for VAT as set out in section 3(1) of the VAT Act 1994.

WHO WE CAN ASK TO GIVE SECURITY

It is the taxable person who must give the security.

THE NOTICE OF REQUIREMENT TO GIVE SECURITY

If we require a taxable person to give security, we will issue them with a notice of requirement. This will show the amount of security required, and when it is required. It will also show the way in which the security must be given.

WHEN WE MAY ISSUE A NOTICE OF REQUIREMENT

We may send or give a notice of requirement to a taxable person if—

- in their previous or current business, they have failed to comply with their VAT obligations, or
- we have reason to believe that they might fail to comply with their VAT obligations.

SENDING A WARNING LETTER BEFORE THE NOTICE OF REQUIREMENT

Normally we will send a letter warning the taxable person that we may require security. However, if we believe that sending a warning letter will increase the risk that VAT will not be paid, we may send or give a notice of requirement without warning.

WHAT HAPPENS IF YOU ARE REQUIRED TO GIVE SECURITY AND DO NOT GIVE IT IN FULL

It is a criminal offence to continue to make or receive taxable supplies without giving the security shown on a notice of requirement. Taxable supplies mean the supply of any goods or services that are taxable. This includes supplies made between members of a group registration.

If we have sent or given you a notice of requirement and you continue to make taxable supplies without giving the security in full, we may prosecute you. In the event of a successful prosecution, you may have to pay a fine of up to £5,000 for each taxable supply you make without giving the security.

If you are involved in a business that continues to make or receive taxable supplies without giving the security, you may be prosecuted individually. You may also be personally responsible for paying any fines and compensation awarded by the court.

HOW WE CALCULATE THE AMOUNT OF SECURITY

We calculate the amount of security using a formula that has been approved by independent tribunals. That formula is based on—

- the amount of VAT paid or due to be paid by the business for a four or six month period
- plus an amount equal to any arrears of VAT from the current business.

If you make quarterly returns, we will require an amount of security based on the VAT we estimate you would have to pay over six months.

If you make monthly returns, we will require an amount of security based on the VAT we estimate you would have to pay over four months.

We calculate the amount of security using the most accurate information available to us at the time.

Note: Although we use the amount of any arrears of VAT as a way of calculating the amount of security, this does not affect the arrears. We will continue to pursue payment of any arrears in the normal way.

THE NOTICE OF DIRECTION

We can direct a taxable person to change the frequency of their VAT returns. This allows us to monitor the business activities more closely. We may issue a notice of direction to a taxable person that makes quarterly returns, telling them that they must change to monthly returns. Once we are satisfied that there is no longer a risk of VAT due not being paid, we may direct the taxable person to revert to quarterly returns.

A taxable person can also ask to move to monthly returns.

FORMS OF SECURITY THAT WE WILL ACCEPT

We will only accept the following forms of security—

- an electronic payment to a specified HM Revenue & Customs (HMRC) bank account
- a cheque or banker's draft
- a guarantee in the form of a performance bond authorised and approved by a financial institution
- a payment into a bank account held in the joint names of the taxable person and HMRC. If this option is used, you will not be able to make any withdrawals from this account without our approval.

We cannot accept property or items such as high value motor vehicles or boats as security.

If you need further information about the acceptable forms of security, please contact the office that has sent this factsheet to you.

TIME LIMITS FOR GIVING SECURITY

Once we send a notice of requirement to a taxable person, the law says that the security must be given immediately. We will allow what we consider to be a reasonable amount of time for the security to be arranged.

HOW LONG WE WILL HOLD THE SECURITY FOR

We normally hold security for VAT for at least 12 months for a business on monthly returns and 24 months for a business on quarterly returns. During this time we will monitor the tax affairs of the business. We will return the security when we consider there is no longer a risk that the business will fail to pay the VAT that is due or that may become due.

USING THE SECURITY TO PAY WHAT IS OWED

If a taxable person gives security and then fails to pay VAT that is due, we may use some or all of the security to pay what is owed. We may then require the taxable person to give further security.

When we no longer require the security for VAT we will check if the taxable person has any other debts with HMRC. If they do, we may then use the security to pay those debts.

Where there are no outstanding debts, we will return the security to the taxable person.

MAKING A TIME TO PAY ARRANGEMENT FOR ARREARS OF VAT

If a taxable person has arrears of VAT, agreeing a time to pay arrangement with us allows them to pay their arrears over an agreed period of time.

If you would like to make a time to pay arrangement with us, or would like more information about this, you should contact the office that sent you this factsheet.

If we agree a time to pay arrangement, we may consider withdrawing the notice of requirement to give security.

WHAT IF WE REQUIRE SECURITY FROM YOU AND YOU DISAGREE WITH OUR DECISION?

If we send you a notice of requirement and you disagree with our decision to require security from you, you have the right to an independent review of that decision. You should request a review within 30 days of the date of the notice of requirement to give security if you—

- think there are facts that may not have been fully considered, or
- can provide further information that you believe will alter our view.

If you prefer, you can appeal direct to an independent tribunal within 30 days of the date of the notice of requirement or, if you have opted for a review, within 30 days from the date of our letter telling you about the review decision.

You can find more information about appeals and reviews in factsheet HMRC1 HM Revenue & Customs decisions - what to do if you disagree. You can get this factsheet from our website, go to www.hmrc.gov.uk/factsheets/hmrc1.pdf or by phoning our orderline on 0845 900 0404.

You can find out more about tribunals on the Tribunals Service website. Go to www.tribunals-.gov.uk or you can phone them on 0845 223 8080.

WHAT IF YOU APPEAL TO AN INDEPENDENT TRIBUNAL AND CONTINUE TO MAKE TAXABLE SUPPLIES?

If you have appealed to an independent tribunal against a notice of requirement, and you continue to make or receive taxable supplies without giving the security we have asked for, you may still be prosecuted. However, to allow time for your appeal to be heard, we may agree to wait for the tribunal's decision before starting or continuing any prosecution action. If we agree to wait, we will write to tell you.

If the tribunal dismisses your appeal, or you withdraw it, we may decide to immediately start or re-start prosecution action.

How to give us security

You can give security by either—

- making a payment
- providing a guarantee in the form of a performance bond
- opening a joint bank account with us.

If you want to give us security by a performance bond or joint bank account, please contact the office that gave you this factsheet.

Before making a payment you should contact your bank or building society to confirm the services available to you, any daily value limits, how long they will take to transfer the money and the latest cut-off times for making a payment.

Details of how you can make a payment are shown below.

Through your own bank or building society by—

– Bacs Direct Credit
– internet/telephone banking
– Faster Payments, or
– CHAPS

You will need to give your bank or building society the following bank details—

— Sort code: 08-32-00

— Account number: 12000903

— Account name: HMRC Miscellaneous

— Reference: "Security" followed by your VAT Registration Number

By post

If you are unable to pay by any of the above methods, you can pay by post.

Make cheques payable to "HM Revenue & Customs only" followed by "Security" and your VAT Registration Number.

Post it to—

HM Revenue & Customs

Cumbernauld Accounting Team

St Mungo's Road

CUMBERNAULD G70 5WY

THIS FACTSHEET IS ONE OF A SERIES

For the full list of our security factsheets, go to www.hmrc.gov.uk/securitydeposit

SS/FS2B-SECURITIES IN RESPECT OF RELEASING A VAT CREDIT

4 March 2013. *HMRC Factsheet*

Factsheet for taxable persons from whom HMRC may require security before agreeing a large or unusual VAT repayment claim.

Securities series (January 2013)

We have given you this factsheet because you have asked us to release a Value Added Tax (VAT) credit to you, and we have agreed to do so on condition that security is given. If you have a tax adviser, you may want to talk to them and show them any correspondence that we have given you.

VAT law allows us to require a taxable person to give an amount of security if we believe that a large or unusual VAT repayment claim made by that person represents a risk to us and we need time to check the claim. The relevant tax law is set out in paragraph 4(1A) of Schedule 11 to the VAT Act 1994.

WHAT A TAXABLE PERSON IS

A taxable person is a person or business that is registered or required to be registered for VAT as set out in section 3(1) of the VAT Act 1994.

WHO WE CAN ASK TO GIVE SECURITY

It is the taxable person who must give the security.

THE NOTICE OF REQUIREMENT TO GIVE SECURITY

If we require a taxable person to give security, we will issue them with a notice of requirement. This will show the amount of security required, and when it is required. It will also show the way in which the security must be given.

WHEN WE MAY ISSUE A NOTICE OF REQUIREMENT

If a taxable person makes a large or unusual claim for a VAT credit that we need time to verify, we usually withhold payment of the credit until our checks are complete. However, if a taxable person asks us to release the VAT credit before our checks are complete, we may do so on the condition that they give security first. Before we issue a notice of requirement, we will write to the taxable person confirming—

- that we will release the VAT credit before we have completed our checks into it - subject to them giving security
- the amount of the security required
- the acceptable forms of security.

If the taxable person agrees to give security on this basis, we will then issue a notice of requirement.

WHAT HAPPENS IF YOU DO NOT GIVE SECURITY IN FULL

Once we issue a notice of requirement, the security must be given in full before we will release any of the VAT credit to you. If the security is not given in full, we will not release the VAT credit until we have checked and agreed the claim.

HOW MUCH SECURITY WILL BE REQUIRED

The amount of security we may require from you will be no more than the amount of the VAT credit that we are considering releasing.

FORMS OF SECURITY THAT WE WILL ACCEPT

We will only accept the following forms of security—

- a guarantee in the form of a performance bond, authorised and approved by a financial institution
- a payment into a bank account held in the joint names of the taxable person and HMRC. If this option is used, you will not be able to make any withdrawals from this account without our approval.

We cannot accept property or items such as high value motor vehicles or boats as security. If you need further information about the acceptable forms of security, please contact the office that has sent this factsheet to you.

HOW LONG WE WILL HOLD THE SECURITY FOR

We will hold the security until we have finished checking the claim to the VAT credit.

USING THE SECURITY

If we find that you were not entitled to some or all of the VAT credit, we may use some or all of the security to recover the credit already released to you.

WHAT IF YOU AGREE TO GIVE SECURITY AND THEN CHANGE YOUR MIND?

When you agree to give security, we will issue you with a notice of requirement. If you then change your mind and do not want to give the security you need to tell us. We will withdraw the notice of requirement and continue checking the VAT credit claim.

We will not release any repayment until our checks are finished.

HOW TO PAY A SECURITY

Where we have issued a notice of requirement as a condition of releasing a VAT credit, we can only accept the two methods of payment described under the heading Forms of security that we will accept.

Please contact the office that gave you this factsheet for more information.

THIS FACTSHEET IS ONE OF A SERIES

For the full list of our security factsheets, go to www.hmrc.gov.uk/securitydeposit

CC/FS12—PENALTIES FOR VAT AND EXCISE WRONGDOING

March 2013. *HMRC Factsheet*

This factsheet contains information about the penalties we may charge you for a VAT or Excise wrongdoing

VAT OR EXCISE WRONGDOINGS

VAT and Excise wrongdoings are when any person:

- who is not registered for VAT or is not authorised to issue VAT invoices, issues an invoice that includes an amount shown as VAT
- uses spirits or hydrocarbon oils for a purpose that attracts a higher rate of excise duty (this is called 'misuse'). For example, red diesel (normally used in farm machinery) carries a lower duty than diesel for road vehicles. If someone uses red diesel in a road vehicle, this is misuse, which is a wrongdoing
- supplies spirits or hydrocarbon oils knowing that they will be used in a way that means a higher rate of excise duty should have been paid. For example, the duty on fuel for domestic heating is lower than the duty on fuel for private boats. If someone supplies domestic heating fuel knowing that the purchaser will use it for a private boat, this is a wrongdoing because the supplier knows that the fuel will be used for a purpose that attracts a higher duty
- handles alcohol (all), tobacco or hydrocarbon oils on which there is unpaid excise duty or where the duty has not been deferred. Handling goods includes
    - acquiring possession of them
    - being involved in the carrying, removing, depositing or keeping of them, or
    - otherwise dealing with them.

For example, someone goes on holiday to France. They buy cigarettes and bring them back into the UK with the intention of selling them. As the cigarettes were not imported for their own use, they should have paid the duty on them. They have committed a wrongdoing. The person they sold the cigarettes to has also committed a wrongdoing for handling the goods.

WHEN WE MAY CHARGE A PENALTY FOR A WRONGDOING

We may charge you a penalty if you commit a wrongdoing and it results in VAT or Excise duty being due.

If you ask someone else, such as an employee or adviser, to do something on your behalf, you must do as much as you can to ensure that a wrongdoing does not occur. If you do not do this, we may charge you a penalty

WHEN WE WILL NOT CHARGE PENALTIES FOR A WRONGDOING

We will not charge a penalty for a wrongdoing if:

- you have a reasonable excuse for the wrongdoing, and
- the wrongdoing was not deliberate, and
- you notified us without unreasonable delay after your reasonable excuse ended.

What we mean by 'deliberate' is explained later in this factsheet.

A reasonable excuse is normally an unexpected or unusual event that is either unforeseeable or beyond your control. What is or is not a reasonable excuse depends on an individual's abilities and circumstances. Those abilities and circumstances may mean that what is a reasonable excuse for one person may not be a reasonable excuse for another. If you think you have a reasonable excuse please tell us. If we accept that you have a reasonable excuse, we will not charge a penalty.

DISCLOSING A WRONGDOING BEFORE WE FIND IT

If you tell us about a wrongdoing before you had any reason to believe that we were about to find it, we call this an 'unprompted disclosure'. If you tell us about a wrongdoing at any other time, we call it a 'prompted disclosure'. Once we have started a check, a disclosure can only be unprompted if, exceptionally:

- it is about a wrongdoing unrelated to what we are checking, and
- you had no reason to believe that we could have found it during our check.

The minimum penalty for an unprompted disclosure is lower than the minimum penalty for a prompted one.

WHAT YOU CAN DO TO REDUCE ANY PENALTIES WE MAY CHARGE

We can reduce the amount of any penalty we charge depending on our view of how much assistance you gave us. We refer to this assistance as the 'quality of disclosure' or as 'telling, helping and giving'.

Examples of telling, helping and giving include:

1. Telling:

- agreeing that there is a wrongdoing and telling us how and why it happened
- telling us everything you can about the extent of the wrongdoing as soon as you know about it
- answering our questions in full.

2. Helping:

- helping us understand your accounts or records
- replying to our letters quickly
- answering our questions in full
- agreeing to attend meetings, including any visits to your business premises, at a mutually convenient time
- checking your own records to identify the extent of the wrongdoing.

3. Giving:

- letting us see the documents we have asked for without unnecessary delay
- letting us see documents we may not know about, as well as those that we ask to see.

We will reduce the penalty by the maximum amount possible if you:

- tell us everything you can about any wrongdoing as soon as you know about it or you believe we are about to find it and
- do everything you can to help us correct it.

If you delay telling us, you may still be entitled to a reduction but it will be smaller.

If we do not need any help or records from you, we will give you the full reduction that the law allows for helping and giving.

LETTING US KNOW ABOUT ANY SPECIAL CIRCUMSTANCES

If there are any special circumstances that you believe the officer dealing with the check should take into consideration when calculating the penalty, you should let them know straightaway.

HOW WE WORK OUT THE AMOUNT OF A PENALTY

There are eight stages in working out the amount of any penalty. Each stage is explained in more detail below.

1. Calculating the amount of the potential lost revenue (PLR)

The penalty is a percentage of what we call the 'potential lost revenue'. Potential lost revenue (PLR) is the amount that arises as a result of the wrongdoing. The officer dealing with the check will explain how this is calculated.

VAT PRs etc

2. Determining our view of the 'behaviour'

When there is a wrongdoing, we will work with you to find out what caused it. We refer to this as the 'behaviour'. The type of behaviour will affect whether we charge a penalty and the amount of the penalty. The different types of behaviour are:

Non-deliberate

This is where you committed a wrongdoing but it was not deliberate or deliberate and concealed.

Deliberate

This is where you knew that you had committed a wrongdoing but did not attempt to conceal it.

Deliberate and concealed

This is where you knew that you had committed a wrongdoing and you took active steps to hide it from us

3. Deciding whether the disclosure was unprompted or prompted

This determines the minimum penalty percentage that we can charge. This is explained in more detail in the section of this factsheet titled 'Disclosing a wrongdoing before we find it

4. The penalty ranges

The penalty percentage will fall within a range. This range will depend on our view of the type of behaviour and whether the disclosure was unprompted or prompted. The following table shows the penalty ranges.

Type of behaviour	Unprompted disclosure	Prompted disclosure
Non-deliberate	10% to 30%	20% to 30%
Deliberate	20% to 70%	35% to 70%
Deliberate and concealed	30% to 100%	50% to 100%

There is also a separate penalty range for supplying a product knowing that it will be misused. This is shown below.

Type of behaviour	Unprompted disclosure	Prompted disclosure
Deliberate	30% to 100%	50% to 100%

If you have a reasonable excuse for a non-deliberate wrongdoing, we will not charge you a penalty.

5. Working out the reductions for the quality of disclosure (telling, helping and giving)

The quality of disclosure (or telling, helping, giving), determines where the penalty will fall within the penalty range. The reduction we give depends on how much assistance you give us. For:

- telling we give up to 30%
- helping we give up to 40%
- giving access to records we give up to 30%

6. Calculating the penalty percentage rate

The penalty percentage rate is determined by the penalty range and the reduction for the quality of disclosure.

Example

During a compliance check, we found a non-deliberate wrongdoing that the customer had not told us about before we started our check. When we told them about the wrongdoing, they agreed with us that they committed a wrongdoing. This was therefore a prompted disclosure.

The penalty range for a non-deliberate wrongdoing with a prompted disclosure is 20% to 30% of the 'potential lost revenue' (PLR).

The reduction for quality of disclosure (telling, helping and giving) was 70%.

To work out the penalty percentage rate, we first calculate the difference between the minimum and maximum penalty percentages.	30% minus 20% = 10
We then multiply that figure by the reduction for quality of disclosure to arrive at the percentage reduction	10 x 70% = 7%
We then deduct the percentage reduction from the maximum penalty percentage we can charge.	30% minus 7% = 23%
This gives us the penalty percentage rate	23%

7. Considering other reductions

Before calculating the amount of the penalty, we take into account any other reductions that are necessary. For example, where we have already charged another penalty on the same tax or duty.

8. Calculating the amount of the penalty

To calculate the amount of the penalty, we multiply the potential lost revenue (PLR) by the penalty percentage rate. For example, if the PLR in the example above was £3,000 and there were no other reductions, the penalty would be £690 (£3,000 x 23% = £690).

HOW WE TELL YOU ABOUT A PENALTY

We will write to you to tell you how much the penalty is and how we have worked it out. If there is anything about the penalty that you do not agree with, or if you think there is any information we have not already taken into account, you should tell us straightaway.

After taking account of anything you have told us, we will then send you a penalty assessment notice showing the amount due.

WHEN DIRECTORS AND/OR THE COMPANY SECRETARY MAY HAVE TO PAY A COMPANY'S PENALTY FOR DELIBERATE WRONGDOING

One or more of the directors and/or the company secretary may have to pay some or all of the company penalty if:

- the penalty is attributable to them, and either
- they have gained personally from a deliberate wrongdoing, or
- the company is, or we believe it is about to become insolvent, even if they did not gain personally from the deliberate wrongdoing.

If the company pays the penalty, we will not ask the directors or company secretary to pay it.

WHAT HAPPENS IF YOU HAVE DELIBERATELY DONE SOMETHING WRONG

If you give us a statement or documentation that you know to be false, you may be liable to prosecution.

Managing Deliberate Defaulters

If you have deliberately got your tax affairs wrong, we may need to monitor your tax affairs more closely. We have an enhanced monitoring programme called Managing Deliberate Defaulters. You can find more information about this in factsheet CC/FS14 Managing Deliberate Defaulters.

Publishing details of deliberate defaulters

In certain circumstances we may publish your details if you have deliberately got your tax affairs wrong. We cannot publish your details if you qualify for the maximum penalty reduction. You can find more information in factsheet CC/FS13 Publishing details of deliberate defaulters.

WHAT TO DO IF YOU DISAGREE

You can appeal against most of the decisions that we make. We will write and tell you when we make a decision that you can appeal against. We will also explain the decision and tell you what to do if you disagree. You will usually have three options.

Within 30 days you can:

- send new information or arguments to the officer you have been dealing with
- have your case reviewed by an officer who has not been involved in the check
- arrange for your case to be heard by an independent tribunal.

You can find more about this in factsheet HMRC1 HM Revenue & Customs decisions – what to do if you disagree. Details of how you can get a copy are in the right hand panel of this factsheet.

YOUR PRINCIPAL RIGHTS AND OBLIGATIONS

- You have the right to be represented. You can appoint anyone to act on your behalf. This includes professional advisers, friends, and so on.
- You have the right to consult your adviser. We will allow a reasonable amount of time for you to do so.
- We will protect information we obtain, receive or hold about you.
- We can only ask you for what is reasonable for us to carry out our check. What is reasonable will depend on the circumstances of the check.
- You have the right to complain if you believe that we have not treated you fairly.
- You have an obligation to take care to get things right.
- If you have an adviser, you must still take reasonable care to make sure that any returns, documents or details they send us on your behalf are correct.

Your Charter explains what you can expect from us and what we expect from you. For more information go to hmrc.gov.uk/charter

YOUR RIGHTS WHEN WE ARE CONSIDERING PENALTIES

The European Convention on Human Rights gives you certain important rights. If we are considering penalties, we will tell you. We will also tell you that these rights apply and ask you to confirm that you understand them. These rights are explained below.

- If we ask you any questions to help us decide whether to charge you a penalty, you have the right not to answer them. The amount of help that you give us when we are considering penalties is entirely a matter for you to decide.
- When deciding whether to answer our questions, you may want to get advice from a professional adviser – particularly if you do not already have one.
- If you disagree with us about the tax or any penalties we believe are due, you can appeal. If you appeal about both tax and penalties, you have the right to ask for both appeals to be considered together.
- You have the right to apply for funded legal assistance for dealing with any appeal against certain penalties.
- You are entitled to have the matter of penalties dealt with without unreasonable delay.

You can find more information about these rights in factsheet CC/FS9 The Human Rights Act and penalties.

CHANGES TO VAT PLACE OF SUPPLY RULES AND INTRODUCTION OF THE "MINI ONE-STOP-SHOP"

20 March 2013. *HMRC Notice*

HMRC has published a Q&A on changes to the VAT place of supply rules from 1 January 2015, which will make supplies of telecommunications, broadcasting and e-services taxable in the EU member state in which the consumer is located, rather than where the business is established. Legislation to implement the relevant EU law in the UK will be introduced in the 2014 Finance Bill. The "mini one-stop-shop" will give businesses the option of registering in just one place.

This briefing provides answers to common questions about—

- changes to the VAT place of supply rules affecting telecommunications, broadcasting and e-services from 1 January 2015; and
- the introduction of the mini one stop shop (MOSS).

Expressions of interest are also sought from smaller sized businesses to join a stakeholder group or to suggest issues to be covered in the full guidance. Please see Question and Answer 7 for details.

Q1 What are these changes?

A1 There are two changes. The first affects the VAT place of supply rules and will mean that supplies of telecommunications, broadcasting and e-services made by a business established in one EU member state to a private consumer located in another member state ("intra EU B2C supplies") will be taxed in the member state in which the consumer is located. These services are currently taxed where the business is established. This will ensure that these supplies are taxed fairly in the member state of consumption. The second change is the introduction of the Mini One Stop Shop (MOSS) which is an IT system being developed that will give businesses the option of registering in the UK from where they can account for VAT due in all member states by submitting a single return to HMRC.

Q2 When do these changes take effect?

A2 The place of supply changes take effect from 1 January 2015. Businesses will be able to register for MOSS with effect from October 2014 and the system will go fully live on 1 January 2015.

Q3 Why change the place of supply rules for telecommunications, broadcasting and e-services?

A3 The change ensures that supplies of telecommunications, broadcasting and e-services are taxed fairly in the member state of consumption. This means that businesses that provide these services to UK customers will charge and account for UK VAT.

Q4 Why introduce MOSS?

A4 Businesses that make intra EU B2C supplies of telecommunications, broadcasting and e-services will, unless they opt to register for MOSS, be required to register and account for VAT in every member state in which they have customers. MOSS will give these businesses the option of registering in just the UK and accounting for VAT on supplies to their customers in other member states using a single return submitted to HMRC, which will reduce administrative burdens.

Q5 How will these changes be implemented?

A5 The EU legislation for these changes is already in place and this will be incorporated into UK primary legislation by Finance Bill 2014.

Q6 Is HMRC consulting on these changes?

A6 Yes, HMRC has set up a working group with affected large businesses and their representatives, which meets regularly to discuss the practical application of these changes. HMRC will also publish draft legislation and a Tax Information and Impact Note as part of the consultation on draft Finance Bill clauses in autumn 2013.

Q7 I run a smaller sized business (SME) that makes supplies of affected services to private individuals in other member states; can I discuss the impact of these changes with HMRC?

A7 Yes, HMRC is very keen to establish a stakeholder group to represent the views of SMEs. If you are interested in joining this group please provide brief details about the type of activities you are involved in, or the types of businesses that you represent. Alternatively, if you would prefer not to join the group, HMRC would still like to hear about any issues that you have so that they can be considered when drafting full guidance - see Q10. In both cases please Email: moss.stakeholder@hmrc.gsi.gov.uk by 31 May 2013. Unfortunately, it may not be possible to respond to every Email or deal with specific queries at this time.

Q8 I run a small VAT registered business that supplies affected services (e.g. online information service) which I sell to private individuals located in the UK, France and Germany, will I be affected?

A8 Yes, while you will continue to account for VAT on your supplies to UK customers in the normal way, you will be required to register and account for VAT in France and Germany.

Alternatively, you have the option of registering for MOSS which will save you the need to register in France and Germany and allows you to account for VAT due in these countries by submitting a single return to HMRC.

Q9 What are telecommunications, broadcasting and e-services?

A9 A full description of these services will be set out in guidance.

Examples of telecommunications services include: fixed and mobile telephone services; videophone services; paging services; facsimile, telegraph and telex services; access to the internet and worldwide web.

Examples of broadcasting services include: radio and television programmes transmitted over a radio or television network, and live broadcasts over the internet.

Examples of e-services include: video on demand, downloaded applications (or "apps"), music downloads, gaming, e-books, anti-virus software and on-line auctions.

Q10 Where can I get more information about these changes?

A10 HMRC will publish full guidance on these changes on their website in advance of them taking effect on 1 January 2015.

LEVY ON "SINGLE-USE" CARRIER BAGS IN NORTHERN IRELAND

2 April 2013. *HMRC Brief 7/13*

ABSTRACT

This brief confirms that no VAT is due from retailers who charge only the minimum of 5 pence for each carrier bag under regulations coming into force in Northern Ireland on 8 April 2013. All receipts in respect of single-use carrier bags should be brought into account in calculating trading profits for income tax and corporation tax purposes.

FULL TEXT

INTRODUCTION

On 8 April 2013 a levy of 5 pence will be introduced on single use carrier bags supplied in Northern Ireland.

This Brief explains the VAT treatment of the levy.

LEGISLATIVE FRAMEWORK

The levy is being introduced under The Single Use Carrier Bags Charge Regulations (Northern Ireland) 2013 (which can be found at www.legislation.gov.uk/nisr/2013/4/introduction/made) which require retailers to charge a minimum of 5 pence for each single use carrier bag provided to customers. Retailers may charge a higher amount if they wish.

– Retailers are required to pay the "net proceeds" of their charges to the Department of Environment Northern Ireland (DoENI). In cases where a retailer charges the minimum of 5 pence, the full amount must be paid to DoENI.
– However, a retailer who charges more per bag must pay DoENI 5 pence less VAT (5p x 5/6 = 4.17p)

Certain bags are currently exempt from the levy, for example, "bags for life".

Detailed guidance on how the scheme operates is available from the DoENI website:

Guidance on the single use carrier bags charge regulations (Northern Ireland) 2013 (www.doeni.gov.uk/guidance_on_the_single_use_carrier_bags_charge_regulations__ni__2013.pdf).

VAT IMPLICATIONS

Where only the 5 pence levy is charged for a carrier bag and it is remitted in full to the DoENI, no VAT is due from the retailer in any circumstance.

However, where the charge exceeds 5 pence, then VAT is payable on the total amount where the bags are supplied by VAT registered businesses. For example, if a retailer charges 12 pence for a bag then VAT of 2 pence will be due from the retailer (12p x 1/6 = 2p).

If only the 5 pence levy is charged, then this amount should not be included in the DGT for any Retail Schemes. If taking the example above, 12 pence is charged, the bag should be treated as a standard rate good for Retail Schemes.

DIRECT TAX IMPLICATIONS

For the purposes of Corporation Tax and Income Tax, all receipts in respect of single-use carrier bags should be brought into account in calculating trading profits. A deduction for the "net proceeds" statutorily payable to DoENI is available. Figures should be adjusted for VAT when accounts are drawn up on a VAT-exclusive basis. For the avoidance of doubt, where only the minimum amount is charged, the VAT-exclusive price to be brought into account will be 5 pence per single bag as no VAT will be due.

VAT TREATMENT OF SERVICES TO EMPLOYERS IN CONNECTION WITH GROUP PERSONAL PENSIONS

17 April 2013. *HMRC Brief 9/13*

ABSTRACT

Businesses advising employers in relation to the setting up or administration of group personal pensions should charge VAT at the standard rate to employers on services rendered in return for "consultancy charges" or other fees. The FSA's Retail Distribution Review prevents employee benefit consultants and other pensions consultants from receiving commission-based remuneration with effect from 1 January 2013. Commission-only arrangements with pension providers have been common in the past. To fall within the finance or insurance exemptions, the provider must act as an intermediary between individual employees and the pension provider with a view to the conclusion of an individual pensions contract.

FULL TEXT

VAT: CORPORATE PENSIONS – FSA'S RETAIL DISTRIBUTION REVIEW - TREATMENT OF "CONSULTANCY CHARGES" FOR SERVICES SUPPLIED TO EMPLOYERS

PURPOSE OF THIS BRIEF

This Brief confirms the VAT implications of regulatory changes that will affect the way that Employee Benefit Consultants ("EBCs") and others providing services to employers for the setting up and administration of work place contract-based pensions will be remunerated in the future.

Services supplied to employers or Trustees in respect of occupational pension schemes held through trusts are not covered by this Brief.

WHO NEEDS TO READ THIS?

- Businesses (such as EBCs) that advise and assist employers and/or employees in connection with contract-based Group Personal Pension plans.
- Employers that receive these services.

ACTION TO TAKE

Businesses supplying the above services need to establish the following to determine the VAT treatment:

- what is the precise nature of the service supplied, and
- who is the recipient of that service?

Businesses that advise and assist employers in relation to the setting up and/or ongoing administration of Group Personal Pensions should charge standard rated VAT to employers on services provided to them in return for "consultancy charges" or other fees.

Employers should be aware that they will normally be able to recover the VAT that is charged to them on these services as input tax, subject to partial exemption and input tax rules (further information in paragraph 1.4 below).

The VAT treatment of services provided to employees will depend upon the nature of the services provided (further guidance can be found in the VATFIN and VATINS guidance manuals). Services to employees, even if paid for by the employer, will not generally attract input tax recovery.

1.1 BACKGROUND

Employers may seek advice and assistance from EBCs and other pension consultants on the setting up of and/or ongoing administration of workplace personal pensions. This market includes group personal pensions, group stakeholder pensions and group self-invested personal pensions – collectively referred to as GPP schemes.

Although some pension consultants have charged employers for such services (including advice and services provided to the employer's staff) in the past, it appears to have been more common for them to make no charge for these services, but to rely instead on commission paid by the pension provider.

As a result of the Financial Services Authority's (FSA's) Retail Distribution Review ("RDR"), EBCs and other pensions consultants have been banned from receiving commission based remuneration with effect from 1st January 2013 (subject to exceptions under transitional arrangements for clients engaged before this date). These businesses are now required to agree "consultancy charges" with the employer instead, which may in some cases be supplemented by separate fees charged directly to the employer.

1.2 ANALYSIS OF VAT LIABILITY

In order to fall within the finance or insurance exemptions, it is necessary for the provider to act as an intermediary (or one of the intermediaries) between the individual employees and the pension provider with a view to the conclusion of an individual pensions contract.

Based on the typical contractual arrangements reviewed by HMRC and its discussions with the pension consultants industry this does not appear to be the position in respect of the services currently provided by pension consultants in return for "consultancy charges". On the contrary, the "consultancy charge" is a fee paid in return for advisory, administration and other services supplied to the employer. The fact that the (net of VAT) "consultancy charges" are paid via the pension provider does not alter the VAT analysis. The same VAT analysis also applies to any separate fees charged to employers.

EBCs and other pensions consultants should therefore account for standard rated VAT on "consultancy charges" and any separate fees charged to employers for these services.

We understand the future use of consultancy charging is still under review and the position could change going forwards. If, therefore, the nature of the services remunerated by consultancy charges changes in future and it can be demonstrated those services meet the conditions for VAT exemption outlined above, any charges made for the provision of those services will be VAT exempt.

1.3 INVOICING ARRANGEMENTS

Consultancy charges are consideration for supplies of services by the pension consultant to the employer in respect of which the employer is liable to pay any VAT due. The pensions consultant is therefore required to provide a VAT invoice to the employer for taxable services provided to them that are remunerated by way of "consultancy charges". This is the case even though, in practice, the consultant will not receive the net charges from the employer but from the pension provider, who will deduct the charges from contributions and/or members' funds and remit them to the consultant.

1.4 EMPLOYERS' ENTITLEMENT TO RECOVER INPUT TAX

The VAT incurred on consultancy charges and other fees charged by EBCs and other pensions consultants in connection with the setting up and administration of corporate pension schemes will be recoverable as input tax by VAT registered employers that incur the costs in the course or furtherance of their business, subject to any necessary input tax restrictions.

If an employer makes exempt supplies, the amount of input tax that can be deducted may be restricted as, normally, input tax can only be deducted if it relates to taxable supplies. Further information on this is in Notice 706 *Partial exemption.*

UPDATE ON WITHDRAWAL OF EXEMPTION FOR SUPPLIES OF RESEARCH BETWEEN ELIGIBLE BODIES

26 April 2013. *HMRC Brief 10/13*

ABSTRACT

HMRC has provided guidance on where supplies of research between eligible bodies (mainly government departments, schools, universities and charities) will be outside the scope of VAT. This follows responses to the consultation on proposed withdrawal of the exemption for such supplies, on the basis that the exemption is contrary to EU law. Collaborative research and research conducted broadly for the public good will generally be outside the scope.

FULL TEXT

VAT: WITHDRAWAL OF THE VAT EXEMPTION FOR SUPPLIES OF RESEARCH BETWEEN ELIGIBLE BODIES – CONSULTATION UPDATE

PURPOSE OF THIS BRIEF

The purpose of this Brief is to update those engaged in research on developments arising from the consultation and to request further data from some of those who have already responded. The Summary of Responses will be published after this additional data has been provided.

WHO SHOULD READ THIS BRIEF

All suppliers of business research and those that commission research.

BACKGROUND

HM Revenue & Customs (HMRC) published the consultation December 2012 to gather information to allow them to assess more accurately the impact of the withdrawal of the exemption and to see whether there are any possible options to mitigate that impact.

The consultation has identified that there is a lack of clarity in the distinction between:

- supplies of research that are outside the scope of VAT, and
- those that are exempt business supplies which will be affected by the withdrawal

A number of respondents requested some clearer guidance on these differences.

While HMRC is grateful to the taxpayers that responded to the consultation, because of the difficulty expressed during the consultation that there is a lack of clarity between outside the scope of VAT research and business exempt research, HMRC is providing further guidance below and will be contacting those taxpayers who have already provided data to confirm their figures in light of this guidance.

COLLABORATIVE RESEARCH

HMRC has been made aware that a significant amount of research is collaborative – indeed, this seems common in the case of Research Council funding. Collaborative research is where several bodies (typically universities or other eligible bodies) get together to apply for grant funding to undertake a research project. It is not uncommon for one of the applicants to be shown as the head or lead body which deals primarily with the funding body including receiving funding which is passed to other applicant bodies for their contribution to the project. For ease, contracts are often concluded only in the name of the funding body and the lead research body even though this is a collaborative project.

HMRC will accept that in such cases of collaborative research, all research services provided by each of the bodies involved in the project are outside the scope of VAT, even if the funding may be passed on by the lead research body to others and that only the lead research body is party to the contract with the funding body.

VAT PRs etc

HMRC may ask for evidence that research bodies are participating in collaborative research; the best evidence of that will be the original application for funding which would, in many cases, show who all the collaborative partners are. However, HMRC will accept any alternative evidence that clearly demonstrates that the bodies concerned were participating in collaborative research.

CHANGES IN COLLABORATIVE PARTIES

HMRC can confirm that research bodies that are added to or are substituted in a collaborative research project once it has commenced (and so are not mentioned in the funding contract) would still be seen as parties to the collaborative project so that their supplies remain outside the scope of VAT.

FURTHER GUIDANCE

Although each individual contract must be considered on its own merits the following is a generic guide to assist in ascertaining the likely liability of the supplies that are made.

For there to be a supply of services for VAT purposes, there must be a direct and immediate link between consideration paid and a service provided. HMRC do not consider this to happen in the case of research which is funded, either by the public sector or by the charitable sector, for the wider public benefit. This was mentioned in the opinion of the Advocate General in Keeping Newcastle Warm (C-353/00).

Where a subsidy is granted by the donor to the recipient to enable a third party to obtain a specific service (or to obtain it more cheaply) this would, as a general rule, be a taxable transaction.

The main question to answer is whether the funding is the consideration or part of the consideration for any specific supply. If not, then it is outside the scope of VAT.

Situations where the funding will be outside the scope of VAT include:

- research which is funded for the "general public good" and there is no direct benefit for the funding body
- research which is funded for the general public good and is either not expected to generate any intellectual property (IP), or if it does then any reports or findings will be freely available to others
- where there is a "collaborative" agreement between different research institutions where all parties to the grant are named on the application
- where the funding flows through one named party – and they act purely as a conduit passing on the funds to others involved in the research project – the funding remains outside the scope of VAT

Where funding is provided to a named party for research that will either generate IP to be exploited by the funder and/or is not for the public good and they subsequently decide to sub-contract some of the research to an eligible body (for example a university), the initial funding to the named party (assuming an eligible body) will be taxable consideration for a supply.

PORTFOLIO MANAGEMENT FEES FOLLOWING ECJ DECISION IN DEUTSCHE BANK

25 June 2013. *HMRC Brief 11/13*

ABSTRACT

Following the decision of the ECJ in *Deutsche Bank* (C-44/11), HMRC has announced a change in its VAT treatment of fees charged for portfolio investment management services. With effect from 1 December 2013, HMRC will include periodic fees charged on a flat-fee basis for buying and selling on a client's behalf as part of a single, standard-rated, supply of portfolio management services. Currently, HMRC treats charges for purchases and sales as a separate, exempt, supply.

FULL TEXT

VAT: MODIFIED TREATMENT FOR CERTAIN PORTFOLIO MANAGEMENT FEES FOLLOWING A EUROPEAN COURT RULING

PURPOSE OF THIS BRIEF

This Brief modifies the current VAT treatment of certain supplies made by portfolio investment managers. This modification is needed to bring the current treatment into line with the European Court judgment in the case of *Deutsche Bank* (C-44/11).

WHO NEEDS TO READ THIS?

- Businesses providing portfolio investment management services
- Financial Advisors
- Businesses and other organisations, such as charities, that receive investment management services

BACKGROUND TO THE JUDGMENT

Deutsche Bank provided discretionary portfolio management services to individual investors. These services consisted of two elements:

(1) the activity of analysing and monitoring the assets owned by the investors in accordance with a strategy agreed with them, and

(2) the consequential activity of actually purchasing and selling financial securities on their behalf.

The investors paid a single annual portfolio management fee which included a separately identified charge for buying and selling securities. The issue before the Court was whether this charge constituted consideration for a separate exempt supply.

The Court decided that in the circumstances at issue in the case the two elements were parts of a single service and, as those elements were of equal weight and together formed a single supply of taxable portfolio management services, the entire fee was subject to VAT at the standard rate.

REVISED VAT TREATMENT

Whilst all portfolio management services are subject to VAT, the UK currently treats separate charges for effecting the purchase and sale of securities as exempt from VAT on the basis that they are consideration for separate supplies. This policy is set out in Paragraph 1.6 of Notice 701/49 *Finance* and in section VATFIN5800 of the VAT Finance guidance manual.

As a result of the judgment, it is clear that fees charged by portfolio managers on an annual or other periodic basis for the purchase and sale of securities can no longer be treated as exempt from VAT, regardless of whether or not a separate charge is made.

However, the ECJ in *Deutsche Bank* only considered the VAT position of periodic fees charged on a flat fee basis where there was no direct link to the transactions being executed. Where, therefore, fees are charged strictly on a transaction by transaction basis (that is, per purchase or sale of investments) exemption will continue to apply. This is conditional upon the portfolio management services being contracted for on that basis and the transaction charges being separately identified in any VAT invoice. This VAT treatment will apply irrespective of whether the portfolio is managed on a full discretionary or on an advisory basis.

Portfolio management services can be distinguished from other financial advisory services because there is an ongoing commitment to monitor and manage an individual client's investment portfolio to formulate investment decisions or recommendations. They should also be distinguished from investment fund management services (that is, the management of pooled investments within a fund structure) where VAT exemption is dependent upon the nature of the fund being managed.

Please see VATFIN7000 and VATINS5300 for guidance on VAT treatment of services provided by financial advisors and VATFIN5100-5400 for guidance on investment fund management services.

DATE FROM WHICH NEW TREATMENT TAKES EFFECT

This revised VAT treatment will apply from 1st December 2013.

Where you are in any doubt about the correct VAT treatment please contact the VAT Helpline on 0300 200 3700.

The HMRC guidance will be updated in due course.

LOSS-ADJUSTING SERVICES FOR MARINE AND AVIATION INSURANCE CLAIMS

3 July 2013. *HMRC Brief 13/13*

ABSTRACT

Loss-adjusting services supplied in the UK should always be standard rated. However, HMRC will not seek VAT on past supplies if businesses have applied the zero rate to loss-adjusting services relating to "qualifying" ships or aircraft where these services also involved a physical inspection. From 1 September 2013, HMRC will require all businesses to account for VAT on such services. This brief acknowledges that HMRC's existing guidance was misleading about services which required a physical inspection to be carried out.

FULL TEXT

VAT: LOSS ADJUSTING SERVICES SUPPLIED IN CONNECTION WITH MARINE AND AVIATION INSURANCE CLAIMS - INCORRECT APPLICATION OF THE ZERO-RATE

PURPOSE OF THIS BRIEF

This Brief confirms the VAT treatment of loss adjusting services supplied in connection with marine and aviation insurance claims and explains what action to take if you have failed to account for VAT in respect of such services in the past.

We are issuing this Brief because it appears that many businesses have been incorrectly treating such services as zero-rated surveys for VAT purposes.

WHO NEEDS TO READ THIS?

- Businesses that supply loss adjusting services in connection with marine or aviation insurance claims.
- Insurers that receive such loss adjusting services (including insurers that receive such services from abroad).
- Insurance brokers or agents acting in the marine and aviation insurance industry.

ACTION TO TAKE

Businesses that supply the relevant loss adjusting services should ensure that they account for VAT at the standard rate where the services are treated as supplied in the UK in accordance with the place of supply rules, and should review their retrospective VAT treatment in accordance with this Brief.

Insurers that receive these services from abroad should ensure that they account for standard rated VAT under the "reverse charge" and should also review their retrospective VAT treatment in accordance with this Brief.

Place of supply and the reverse charge are explained in Notice 741A "Place of supply of services" (customs.hmrc.gov.uk/channelsPortalWebApp).

BACKGROUND

The VAT Act 1994, Schedule 8, Group 8 provides that the zero-rate of VAT applies to certain services supplied in connection with "qualifying" ships and aircraft. HMRC's guidance on this subject is in Notice 744C "Ships, arcraft and associated services" (customs.hmrc.gov.uk/channelsPortalWebApp).

Amongst other things, the zero-rate covers surveying services or classification services supplied in connection with a "qualifying" ship or aircraft. This is explained in Notice 744C - paragraphs 9.5 and 9.6 (customs.hmrc.gov.uk/channelsPortalWebApp).

Some businesses have operated on the mistaken belief that loss adjusting services are zero-rated under this provision.

VAT LIABILITY - HMRC'S VIEW

SURVEYS

HMRC's view is that the zero-rate is restricted to surveys necessary to establish the seaworthiness, airworthiness or classification of a qualifying ship or aircraft to enable it to be registered and therefore meet the *direct needs* of the ship or aircraft. Such surveys by their nature require a physical inspection of the ship or aircraft. Certain surveys carried out under statutory authority may be outside the scope of VAT.

LOSS ADJUSTING

We do not consider loss adjusting services to fall within this zero-rate under any circumstances. It is our view that, although a supply of loss adjusting may contain an element of inspection, such inspections are not qualifying surveys for the purposes of the zero-rate.

In any event an inspection is just one of a number of elements that make up a supply of loss adjusting which will also include other elements such as establishing the facts, valuing the claim and determining the appropriate redress. The overarching or predominant nature of the supply is therefore not a surveying service. We consider the services to be single supplies of loss adjusting and liable to the standard rate of VAT to the extent that they are supplied in the UK. Such supplies do not meet the *direct needs* of the ship or aircraft; rather they meet the needs of the insurer in assessing the insurance claim.

PLACE OF SUPPLY OF LOSS ADJUSTING SERVICES

The place of supply of a loss adjusting service is where the customer belongs. Therefore, loss adjusting supplies made to non-UK located insurers will be outside the scope of UK VAT.

It is necessary to complete EC sales lists in relation to supplies of goods and services made to business customers based in the EC if those services would be liable to VAT if supplied in the UK. For information about this, see Notice 725 "The single market" - Section 17 (customs.hmrc.gov.uk/channelsPortalWebApp/channelsPortal).

LOSS ADJUSTING SERVICES RECEIVED FROM ABROAD

If a UK insurer receives loss adjusting services from abroad, the UK insurer will be required to account for standard rated VAT on the receipt of the services under the "reverse charge" procedure. For information about the reverse charge, see Notice 741A "Place of supply of services" - Section 18 (customs.hmrc.gov.uk/channelsPortalWebApp/channelsPortal).

WHAT TO DO ABOUT PAST SUPPLIES

SERVICES INVOLVING A PHYSICAL INSPECTION

We accept that our guidance about services which required a physical inspection to be carried out was misleading and that businesses had a legitimate expectation that these supplies were zero-rated.

Consequently, we do not require businesses to account for VAT on past supplies if they have incorrectly applied the zero-rate to loss adjusting services relating to "qualifying" ships or aircraft that involved a physical inspection. Businesses that have not already started to account for VAT on such supplies should start to do so from 1 September 2013.

SERVICES NOT INVOLVING A PHYSICAL INSPECTION

Businesses that applied the zero-rate to loss adjusting services that did not include a physical inspection are required to account for VAT, as set out in 1.6 below, unless they can demonstrate to their local Complaints Team that they were misled by HMRC and had a legitimate expectation that those supplies would be zero-rated. We would recommend businesses to contact their complaints team if they consider that they have been misled by HMRC in relation to the liability of their supplies have acted in accordance with the misleading representation would suffer real detriment if VAT was to be collected for past supplies.

However, we consider that legitimate expectation is less likely to apply to services not involving a physical inspection, because Notice 744C "Ships, aircraft and associated services" has, since 1997, made it clear that physical inspection is an essential condition to the zero-rate. The matter of whether we accept, in any individual case, that a business had a legitimate expectation will depend on the facts of the case.

For information about our complaints procedure, go to www.hmrc.gov.uk, and under "quick links", select "Complaints".

HOW TO ACCOUNT FOR UNDER DECLARED VAT

If, in light of this Brief, you have not accounted for VAT correctly in the past, please see Notice 700/45 "How to correct VAT errors or make adjustments or claims" (customs.hmrc.gov.uk/channelsPortalWebApp/) for guidance on how to make an adjustment.

We understand that some businesses will find it difficult to work out retrospectively to what extent their services were supplied in the UK, due to not having access to details of their insurance customers' locations. In cases of co-insurance, the issue is complicated further because there may be multiple customers based in multiple locations. HMRC will consider reasonable apportionment methods for any business that faces such difficulties - for example, apportionment based on sampling. Any proposal for an apportionment method should be submitted together with any error notification made in accordance with Notice 700/45.

JUDGMENT IN INVESTMENT TRUST COMPANIES AND COMMON LAW CLAIMS AGAINST HMRC

10 July 2013. *HMRC Brief 15/13*

ABSTRACT

This brief sets out the options for 'customers' in the Investment Trust Companies case to make mistake-based claims in restitution against HMRC for output tax wrongly charged, following the High Court judgments given in March 2012 and March 2013. These are not statutory claims under the taxes acts and must be made to the relevant court. Any repayments to 'customers' would be linked to a corresponding claim having been made by their 'suppliers' under VATA 1994, s80 within statutory time limits. Both parties have been given leave to appeal to the Court of Appeal.

FULL TEXT

Judgments of the High Court in Investment Trust Companies (in liquidation) v CRC [2012] EWHC 458 (Ch); [2012] STC 1150; [2012] All ER (D) 84 (Mar) & [2013] EWHC 665 (Ch); [2013] WLR (D) 125 (ITC)

Claims under section 80 of the VAT Act 1994 (section 80) (the VAT Act) – Claims by persons to whom VAT has been wrongly charged – Common law claims against HM Revenue & Customs (HMRC) by third parties – Whether HMRC is liable – Who can claim

PURPOSE OF THIS BRIEF

This Revenue & Customs Brief sets out, in the wake of the judgments of the High Court in ITC, HMRC's view of the situation where:

– a person (the Supplier) has charged an amount as VAT to their customers (the Customers) which ought not to have been charged
– they have passed the ultimate economic burden of that VAT charge on to those Customers so that the VAT has not been a cost to them and has not suffered any loss or damage to their business as a result, and
– owing to exceptional circumstances, the Customers are unable to get the amounts wrongly charged to them back from the Supplier

READERSHIP

This Revenue & Customs Brief is aimed primarily at professional tax advisors and lawyers although it may be of interest to others.

ACTION REQUIRED

This Revenue & Customs Brief is for information only.

HMRC does not require any action to be taken.

BACKGROUND – SECTION 80 CLAIMS

A person who makes taxable supplies (a Supplier) is required to register for VAT and to charge VAT (their output tax) on the supplies of goods and services that they make to their customers. Because they are making taxable supplies, they are entitled to deduct from the output tax for which they are liable the VAT that is charged to them (their input tax) by their suppliers.

If a person has accounted for output tax on goods or services they have supplied on the assumption that those supplies are properly taxable and later discover they are, in fact, exempt, they can make a clam under section 80 to recover the wrongly declared output tax. That claim is subject to statutory time limits (four years) and must be reduced by any input tax that was wrongly deducted.

Section 80 provides that only the person who accounted for the output tax is entitled to make a claim – Please note that it is possible to legally assign the right to make it to someone else under, for example, section 136(1) of the Law of Property Act 1925 (England & Wales), section 87(1) of the Judicature (Northern Ireland) Act 1978 or by an assignation in Scotland.

HMRC will reject a section 80 claim if they believe that the claimant would be unjustly enriched by the payment. Payment will unjustly enrich a claimant if:

- they passed the economic burden of the VAT charge on to their customers in the price charged to them, and
- they suffered no loss or damage to their business (for example, by loss of customers or of profits) as a result of having done so.

BACKGROUND – CLAIMS BY CUSTOMERS

Where a Customer believes that a Supplier has wrongly charged them VAT, their remedy is to bring a claim against their Supplier. This is a commercial matter and the right to claim against the Supplier will depend upon the terms of the contract under which the goods or services were supplied. In simple terms, the Customer has simply been overcharged by the Supplier.

Such claims are not statutory claims. They are not provided for in any of the tax legislation and will normally be subject to the time limits provided for in the relevant statute of limitations – see below.

There is no statutory provision which would enable the Customer to make a claim against HMRC.

BACKGROUND – ITC

In June 2007, the Court of Justice of the European Communities (ECJ) delivered its judgment in *JP Morgan Fleming Claverhouse Investment Trust Plc & Anor v CRC* [2008] STC 1180 ruling that supplies of fund management services were not liable to VAT at the standard rate but were exempt.

In the wake of that judgment, HMRC received, and paid, claims made under section 80 by fund managers (the Suppliers) for output tax overdeclared on supplies of fund management services made to investment trust companies (the Customers).

The Suppliers accepted, when they made their claims, that they had passed the economic burden of the wrongly charged VAT on to their Customers, that they had suffered no loss or damage to their business as a result and that, consequently, they would be unjustly enriched if they were allowed to keep any payments made to them by HMRC.

They undertook to reimburse to their Customers anything paid to them by HMRC.

However, as explained above, the Suppliers were not repaid by HMRC the total amount wrongly charged as VAT to their Customers. By way of example, assuming the output tax wrongly charged by the Supplier was £100 and the input tax wrongly deducted by them was £25, the latter was set against the former and the Supplier was repaid the net amount of £75 which they passed on to their Customers.

As a result, the amount wrongly charged to the Customers as VAT by their Suppliers exceeded the amount reimbursed to them.

Nine investment trust companies made common law claims in restitution against HMRC for the difference.

THE HIGH COURT'S JUDGMENT IN ITC

On 2 March 2012 and 26 March 2013, the High Court handed down its judgments.

Mr Justice Henderson held that:

- section 80 prevents any claim being made against HMRC by anyone other than the Supplier (in this case the fund managers)
- HMRC have been enriched at the expense of the investment trust companies to the extent of the full amount charged by the fund managers to the investment trust companies (that is, the £100 in the example given above)
- that enrichment had been unjust
- the investment trust companies could be said to have a common law claim in restitution against HMRC notwithstanding the fact that they had made no direct payment to HMRC.

He went on to hold that:

- the investment trust companies' primary remedy was to make a claim against the fund managers
- any such claim that they might make would, on the facts in this case, be excessively difficult or impossible in practice to enforce
- the investment trust companies have a directly effective EU law right to recover the balance of wrongly charged VAT from HMRC, and
- to that end they were entitled to make a mistake-based claim in restitution against HMRC.

It was accepted by all parties that the fund managers *had* passed the ultimate economic burden of the wrongly charged VAT on to the investment trust companies and had not suffered any loss or damage to their business as a result.

THE EFFECTS OF THE JUDGMENT

Both parties have been given leave to appeal to the Court of Appeal against the judgment of the High Court.

Customers who believe that they are entitled to bring claims on the basis of the judgment may do so. However, Mr Justice Henderson held that claims such as those made by the investment trust companies were claims of last resort. In any event, a Customer may *only* be entitled to make a claim direct against HMRC where they can show that:

- the tax was wrongly levied *in breach of EU law*
- the Supplier passed the wrongly charged tax on to them so that they ultimately bore the economic burden of it, and
- it is, *for reasons unrelated to the merits of the claim*, excessively difficult or impossible in practice for them to make a claim against their Supplier.

Claims *must* be brought in the relevant courts and *must* be particularised.

These judgments have *no application* in relation to duties, taxes and levies which have been collected by HMRC in breach of UK legislation but not in breach of EU law.

MAKING CLAIMS

These are not statutory claims for recovery of tax wrongly accounted for. They are not claims made under section 80 and are outside the jurisdiction of the First-Tier Tribunal.

In England and Wales and in Northern Ireland, these claims are mistake-based claims in restitution and must be brought in the High Court. Claims for less than £30,000 should be brought in the County Court.

In Scotland they are actions of repetition to recover an overpaid sum of money and can be brought in the Court of Session or the Sheriff Court. Claims for £5,000 or less must be brought in the Sheriff Court.

HMRC will normally agree to have claims founded on directly effective EU law rights, and falling within the scope of this Revenue & Customs Brief, stayed or sisted behind the litigation in ITC, but all claims *must* be particularised.

'Claims' submitted by writing to HMRC will be neither effective nor valid. HRMC is unable to do anything with them to validate them and they will not stop the clock for the purposes of the relevant time limits.

TIME LIMITS

Because these claims are not statutory claims and are not made under any provision of the VAT legislation, they are not subject to the time limits prescribed in the VAT Act but are subject to the time limits provided for in the various statutes of limitation in the three jurisdictions of the United Kingdom.

Those time limits are as follows:

– *England & Wales* – six years from the date on which the cause of action accrued or six years from the date on which the mistake giving rise to the cause of action was discovered or could have been discovered with reasonable diligence – sections 2 and 32(1)(c) of the Limitation Act 1980
– *Northern Ireland* – six years from the date on which the cause of action accrued or six years from the date on which the mistake giving rise to the cause of action was discovered our could have been discovered with reasonable diligence – Articles 6 and 71 of the Limitation (Northern Ireland) Order 1989, and
– *Scotland* – five years from the date on which the obligation arose (the date on which the payment was made by the Supplier to HMRC) unless the claimant can show that he was induced to refrain from making a claim by the words or actions of HMRC – section 6 of the Limitation and Prescription (Scotland) Act 1973.

In the circumstances with which this Revenue & Customs Brief is concerned, a cause of action normally accrues when a person pays an amount to another person which they ought not to have been required to pay.

IMPORTANT

It is important to note that the High Court held that the investment trust companies (the Customers) were only entitled to repayment of the VAT wrongly charged to them in the prescribed accounting periods for which the fund managers (their Suppliers) had themselves made claims which were in time under the statutory section 80 time limits.

They were not entitled to claim for amounts wrongly charged to them in prescribed accounting periods which were out-of-time when the fund managers made their claims.

In cases where a Supplier has accounted for VAT *in breach of EU law* but has not made a valid section 80 claim, it will not be possible for a Customer to make a claim against HMRC in respect of any period which is, at that point, outside the time limits for a section 80 claim.

The High Court said that the Customer can have no better claim, and no more advantageous time limits, than the Supplier had or would have had.

FURTHER INFORMATION

Claims of the type discussed in this Revenue & Customs Brief are outside the scope of HMRC's legislation and guidance manuals so that the National Advice Service and the Written Enquiries Teams are unable to advise potential claimants.

If you believe you may be entitled to make a claim, you should seek professional advice.

Guidance on reclaiming overpaid tax for taxpayers who *have* paid VAT to HMRC - including on time limits and unjust enrichment – can be found in Notice 700/45 *How to correct VAT errors and make adjustments or claims* and the *VAT Refunds Manual*.

VAT EXEMPTION FOR LABORATORY PATHOLOGY SERVICES PROVIDED BY STATE-REGULATED INSTITUTIONS

8 July 2013. *HMRC Brief 16/13*

ABSTRACT

HMRC has confirmed its current view that the supply of laboratory pathology services related to the provision of healthcare for individual patients is exempt from VAT. This applies to all state-regulated pathology laboratories, including where they supply services to non-NHS hospitals.

FULL TEXT

This brief provides clarification about Her Majesty's Revenue and Customs' (HMRC) policy on when laboratory pathology services are exempt from VAT.

READERSHIP

Health professionals, hospitals, hospices, nursing homes, pathology laboratories and any other state regulated institutions providing medical care. A state regulated institution includes any provider (including companies operated for profit) which requires approval, licensing, registration or exemption in relation to those activities.

ACTION

To be aware of HMRC's clarification of policy on supplies of laboratory pathology services.

BACKGROUND

As a result of the *Carter report on the review of NHS outsourcing services* (2006), which recommended the streamlining of NHS services, some NHS pathology services have been, or are being, outsourced to the private sector. HMRC consider that such services are exempt from VAT. Some suppliers of these services challenge that view. They think that such supplies are liable to VAT on the grounds that:

(a) they do not amount to diagnostic services, but merely provide information a third party to enable it to make a diagnosis, or
(b) the providers are not state-regulated institutions or are not making their supplies in a state-regulated institution.

HMRC'S CURRENT POSITION

Our policy (which reflects the decision of the European Court of Justice in the case of *LuP*: C-106/05) is that the supply of laboratory pathology services that directly relate to the provision of healthcare for individual patients is exempt from VAT. This applies to all businesses that are state-regulated and supply laboratory pathology testing services, whether they supply the services to the NHS or to independent hospitals.

HMRC's Notice 701/57 *Health professionals and pharmaceutical products* (section 2.3) explains what medical services are and which services performed by health professionals (including biomedical scientists and clinical scientists) are exempt from VAT.

HMRC's Notice 701/31 *Health institutions* (section 2.1) says that the exemption for care and treatment provided in qualifying institutions is exempt when either of the following conditions is met:

- the institution is a hospital.
- the institution is either a hospice or nursing home, and is either: approved, licensed or registered under the relevant social legislation, or exempted from obtaining such an approval or registration by the relevant legislation.

That Notice does not set out the full ambit of health institutions which HMRC consider are subject to the exemption. This Revenue and Customs Brief is designed to do this.

This Brief confirms that:

- state-regulated pathology laboratories are "qualifying health institutions", for the purposes of the health exemption.

– laboratories are providing exempt medical services when their services are connected with the protection, maintenance or restoration of the health of an individual.

The Guidance will be updated to reflect this in due course.

WHY ARE STATE-REGULATED PATHOLOGY LABORATORIES "QUALIFYING HEALTH INSTITUTIONS?"

An institution is "state-regulated" if it is approved, licensed, registered or exempted from registration by any Minister or other authority pursuant to legislation. A pathology laboratory which is state-regulated qualifies for the purposes of the exemption irrespective of the location from which it provides its services. It makes no difference whether it occupies premises with or within a hospital or in a separate location.

WHEN ARE STATE-REGULATED PATHOLOGY LABORATORIES PROVIDING EXEMPT MEDICAL CARE?

Services supplied by a pathology laboratory or other similar state-registered institutions are exempt if they are:

(a) made in respect of an individual.

(b) medical services, that is, they are connected with the protection, maintenance or restoration of the health of an individual. These include, but are not necessarily limited to:
   - tests performed as part of a routine check-up to confirm whether or not an individual has been exposed to a particular virus or is suffering from a certain medical condition
   - diagnostic services or services helping another health professional or health institution to make a diagnosis
   - tests to establish the overall health of patients to ensure that they are fit enough to have an operation
   - other tests provided as part of the medical treatment of a patient

WHEN ARE STATE-REGULATED PATHOLOGY LABORATORIES' SERVICES NOT COVERED BY THE HEALTH EXEMPTION?

Exemption does not apply when the services are not:

(a) concerned with the protection, maintenance or restoration of the health of specific patients, for example, the analysis of samples for general research purposes or for autopsies.

(b) performed primarily for the protection, maintenance or restoration of the health of the person concerned but are done solely to provide a third party with information necessary for taking a decision on non-medical matters such as insurance claims, or for legal purposes.

MAKING CLAIMS OR ADJUSTMENTS

Where a business has accounted for VAT on supplies of pathology services which qualify for exemption it may make a claim to HMRC (under *section 80* of the *VAT Act 1994*) for repayment of VAT incorrectly accounted for subject to the conditions set out in Notice 700/45 *How to correct VAT errors and make adjustments or claims* (customs.hmrc.gov.uk/channelsPortalWebApp/downloadFile?contentID=HMCE_CL_000077).

All claims are subject to the four-year time limit in *section 80(4)* of the *VAT Act 1994* and to the set-off provisions in *section 81* of the *VAT Act* and *section 130* of the *Finance Act 200* 8.

We may reject all or part of a claim if repayment would unjustly enrich the claimant.

More details on making claims and 'unjust enrichment' can be found in Notice 700/45 *How to correct VAT errors and make adjustments or claims* (customs.hmrc.gov.uk/channelsPortalWebApp/downloadFile?contentID=HMCE_CL_000077).

INSOLVENCY SERVICES AND TRIBUNAL DECISION IN *PAYMEX LIMITED*

8 July 2013. *HMRC Brief 17/13*

ABSTRACT

HMRC has clarified its guidance in the VAT Finance Manual on where services of insolvency practitioners in a voluntary arrangement will be standard-rated. Where a firm of insolvency practitioners acts only as supervisor and no-one from that firm has previously acted as nominee in the same matter, the supervisor's supplies should be standard-rated. For exemption to apply following the Tribunal decision in *Paymex Limited*, it will generally be necessary for the same firm to provide both nominee and supervisor.

FULL TEXT

In recent discussions the insolvency profession has drawn HM Revenue & Customs (HMRC) attention to an internal VAT Finance guidance relating to voluntary arrangements contained in VATFIN3260 (www.hmrc.gov.uk/manuals/vatfinmanual/VATFIN3260.htm) which states that

> "Where the IP acts only as the supervisor and has not previously acted as a Nominee then these supplies will be taxable at the standard rate."

Insolvency practitioners have asked HMRC to clarify this advice in light of the VAT Tribunal decision in the case of *Paymex Limited* and the subsequent HMRC Briefs published in response to the *Paymex* ruling, the content of which were agreed with the insolvency profession.

Revenue & Customs Brief 27/11 (www.hmrc.gov.uk/briefs/vat/brief2711.htm), issued in July 2011, contained the following paragraph under the heading "Tribunal Decision"

> "The Tribunal decided that the services of an IP, including both the nominee and supervisory stages, constitute a single exempt supply for VAT purposes. The Tribunal went on to decide that the two core elements were negotiation of debts and transactions concerning payments. Since it had found both core elements to be exempt, it was not necessary for the Tribunal to determine which of the supplies were dominant. However it stated that if it had been necessary for it to do so it would have found negotiation to be the "core" supply."

For the services of an IP to be covered by the *Paymex* ruling therefore, those services must constitute a single supply for VAT purposes including both the nominee and supervisory stages. Whilst there is no dispute that the nominee element of the supply is exempt for VAT purposes, HMRC does not accept that the supervisory stage, when provided alone, can always be deemed as exempt. The Tribunal Chairman did not specifically address this point as part of the *Paymex* ruling.

However, it should also be pointed out that the supply for VAT purposes in a voluntary arrangement is made by the IP firm, albeit through an individual IP. It is HMRC's view, therefore, that where an IP firm provides the services of a supervisor in a voluntary arrangement and no-one from that firm has previously acted as nominee in that particular voluntary arrangement then the supplies made by the supervisor remain taxable at the standard rate. HMRC regrets any confusion that may have arisen in the insolvency profession if this point was not made sufficiently clear in our previous correspondence.

Applying these principles to the following common situations, the VAT treatment will be:

– **If the nominee and supervisor are in the same firm** then their services to the debtor would comprise a single exempt supply.

– **Where a supervisor from a different firm is appointed either at the creditors meeting or subsequently as a successor IP**
The supervisor's fees will be standard rated.

– **Where a new firm acquires a portfolio of cases and a new supervisor is appointed.**
The supervisor's fees will be standard rated.

– **Where a new firm acquires a portfolio of cases but the supervisor moves across with the cases so remains in office.**
The supervisor's fees will be standard rated.

– The only exception would be if an IP can demonstrate that the core part of their service as supervisor is debt negotiation, in which case HMRC would consider exemption. However as this is usually not the prime purpose of the supervisor or the main role that a supervisor undertakes this situation is unlikely to arise in practice.

COMPANY VOLUNTARY ARRANGEMENTS

STAND-ALONE CVAS

Applying the principles of the *Paymex* decision, where an IP from the same firm acts as both nomine and supervisor so that his services constitute a single supply for VAT purposes and the core activity at the nominee stage consists of debt negotiation, then the supply will be exempt.

WHERE THE ADMINISTRATOR ACTS AS NOMINEE

If the CVA is part of an exit route from administration then it is unlikely that the administrator's activities prior to the beginning of the CVA would consist primarily of debt negotiation. The supervisor's fees would therefore be standard rated.

CONCLUSION

Generally, the VAT treatment will depend on the circumstances of the individual case measured against the above criteria, but much will always depend on the nature and characteristics of the services provided.

IPs who are uncertain about the correct VAT treatment of their fees in voluntary arrangement cases should either speak to the specific caseworker or contact the VAT Helpline on Tel 0845 010 900, to obtain advice.

TAX AVOIDANCE USING OFFSHORE ENTITIES — ECJ JUDGMENT IN *NEWEY*

10 July 2013. *HMRC Brief 18/13*

ABSTRACT

HMRC confirms it will continue to investigate what it considers to be artificial contractual relationships established for tax avoidance purposes and look through to the underlying economic reality of transactions. The recent ECJ decision in *Newey (t/a Ocean Finance)*, on a reference from the Upper Tribunal, gave support to the view that contractual terms are not necessarily decisive in the context of the Sixth VAT Directive.

PURPOSE OF THIS BRIEF

This brief updates taxpayers and their advisors on the recent decision of the European Court (CJEU) in *Paul Newey (trading as Ocean Finance)*, case C-653/11, [2013] All ER (D) 254 (Jun).

ACTION REQUIRED

For information only.

THE ISSUE

Mr Newey was a loan broker, established in the United Kingdom who arranged loans by UK lenders to UK borrowers. His services were exempt from VAT and as a result he could not recover VAT on advertising services supplied to him.

In order to avoid this irrecoverable VAT, Mr Newey set up a company, Alabaster (CI) Ltd, in Jersey, and granted it the right to use the business name Ocean Finance. Broking contracts were concluded between the lenders and Alabaster, and the broking commissions were paid not to Mr Newey, but to Alabaster. Alabaster then entered into a contract for the supply of advertising services.

HMRC took the view that, notwithstanding the contractual terms, the advertising services concerned were supplied to Mr Newey in the United Kingdom and were therefore taxable in the United Kingdom. The First Tier Tribunal allowed Mr Newey's appeal against that decision and HMRC appealed to the Upper Tribunal, which referred questions to the CJEU.

The CJEU decided that although contractual terms should be taken into consideration, they are not decisive. They may be disregarded where they do not reflect economic and commercial reality and are a wholly artificial arrangement set up with the sole aim of obtaining a tax advantage.

It is now for the Upper Tribunal to decide the case in light of this.

HMRC'S APPROACH

The guidance from the CJEU confirms HMRC's view that economic reality must be considered and that contractual relationships do not necessarily determine VAT issues. HMRC will continue to mount in-depth investigations where we believe that a tax advantage may have been claimed artificially.

VAT: TRANSITIONAL ARRANGEMENTS FOR WITHDRAWAL OF EXEMPTION FOR SUPPLIES OF RESEARCH BETWEEN ELIGIBLE BODIES

30 July 2013. *HMRC Brief 21/13*

ABSTRACT

As a transitional measure, the UK VAT exemption for business supplies of research between eligible bodies will continue to apply where a written contract was entered into before 1 August 2013, whether or not work has already commenced. The exemption is being withdrawn for all written contracts entered into on or after that date, in order to comply with EU law.

FULL TEXT

PURPOSE OF THIS BRIEF

The purpose of this Brief is to announce the transitional arrangements that will be implemented following the withdrawal on 1 August 2013 of the VAT exemption for research services between eligible bodies.

WHO SHOULD READ THIS BRIEF

Eligible bodies who supply business research services and those that commission research from eligible bodies.

BACKGROUND

The UK received notification from the European Commission that its exemption for business supplies of research between eligible bodies does not comply with European legislation. The UK has accepted that this is the case and will withdraw the exemption with effect from 1 August 2013.

HM Revenue & Customs published a consultation December 2012 to gather information to allow them to assess more accurately the impact that the withdrawal of the exemption would have and to establish whether there were any possible options to mitigate that impact.

TRANSITIONAL ARRANGEMENTS

The withdrawal will apply from 1 August 2013 to all written contracts that are entered into on or after that date.

The Government wants to mitigate the impact of the withdrawal of the exemption on supplies under existing contracts entered into before 1 August 2013.

For supplies of business research where the written contract was entered into before 1 August 2013, whether or not work has already commenced, the exemption will continue to apply to services within the scope of the contract.

The Government believes that these transitional arrangements will reduce the administrative burden on those bodies affected by the change.

FURTHER INFORMATION

VAT Information Sheet 11/13 is intended to assist those affected in distinguishing when a contract may be outside the scope of VAT or exempt from VAT. It will also explain in more detail how the transitional arrangements are intended to work and the restrictions on the scope of the arrangements.

RESPONSES DOCUMENT

The consultation responses document will also be published shortly on the GOV.UK website.

INSOLVENCY SERVICES - FURTHER CLARIFICATION OF TRIBUNAL RULING IN PAYMEX

4 September 2013. *HMRC Brief 25/13*

ABSTRACT

HMRC has issued this brief to give further clarification of its position on the VAT treatment of supervisors' fees in voluntary arrangements, in circumstances where the conditions for exemption as set out in the Paymex decision are not met. The brief also confirms that the same conditions for the exemption apply to trust deeds.

FULL TEXT

HMRC Revenue & Customs (HMRC) Brief 17/13 (www.hmrc.gov.uk/briefs/vat/brief1713.htm) published on 8 July 2013 further clarified the VAT treatment of supervisors' fees in light of the Paymex judgment, following on from Brief 27/11 (www.hmrc.gov.uk/briefs/vat/brief2711.htm) published on 19 July 2011 and Brief 35/11 (www.hmrc.gov.uk/briefs/vat/brief3511.htm) published on 20 September 2011.

In issuing Brief 17/13, HMRC did no more than re-state the existing legal position which was unaffected by the Paymex judgment. When handling any repayments of VAT HMRC takes into account all relevant circumstances of the case including published guidance before verifying the repayment as being appropriate.

The provisions of Brief 17/13 also apply to trust deeds in that the same firm of trustees must conduct the trust deed from the trustee's appointment through to its conclusion in order for the supply to constitute a single exempt supply for VAT purposes.

CHANGES TO RULES ON ZERO-RATING GOODS FOR INDIRECT EXPORT OUTSIDE THE EU

6 September 2013. *HMRC Brief 26/13*

ABSTRACT

From 1 October 2013, indirect exports of goods to customers established outside the UK may be zero-rated, even if the customer is registered for VAT in the UK. This change in policy, announced at Budget 2013 and consulted on between May and July, will be given effect by amending regulations (SI 2013/2241). Businesses may submit repayment claims to HMRC in respect of past transactions, subject to the four-year time limit.

FULL TEXT

PURPOSE OF THIS BRIEF

This Brief provides information on changes to certain rules for zero-rating supplies of goods for export outside the European Union (EU) that take effect from 1 October 2013.

ACTION TO TAKE

To be aware of the changes and how they impact on affected transactions.

BACKGROUND

In principle, no VAT is due on goods which are exported from the EU (referred to as zero-rating). Strict conditions must be met before sales can be zero-rated and those conditions are laid out in Public Notice 703 VAT: Export of goods from the United Kingdom.

Under EU VAT law (Article 146(1)(b) of Directive 2006/112), no VAT is due on indirect exports provided the overseas customer does not have a business establishment in the supplier's country

VAT PRs etc

(note: indirect exports occur where goods are collected, or arranged to be collected, by the overseas customer). The UK has implemented this condition into national law (Regulation 129 of VAT Regulations 1995) but with a further requirement that the customer is not registered for VAT in the UK. This is reflected in paragraph 3.4 of Public Notice 703 which excludes zero-rating where goods are supplied to a business registered for VAT in the UK.

EU law does not deny zero-rating where an indirect export takes place, and the customer is registered for VAT in the same country as the supplier but has no establishment in that country. Therefore, Regulation 129 of VAT Regulations 1995 will be amended from 1 October 2013 to ensure that UK law complies with EU law. The amendment will remove the current restriction in UK law which denies zero-rating where the customer is VAT registered in the UK. However, the condition relating to the business not having a business establishment in the UK still applies.

There is no change to the UK provisions for the zero-rating of goods exported directly out of the UK by the supplier.

REVISED VAT TREATMENT

The change to UK law means that (where an indirect export takes place) supplies made to any customer established outside the UK will be eligible for zero-rating even if that customer is VAT registered in the UK. Practical examples of the revised VAT treatment are shown below. In all cases, the conditions set out in Notice 703 (VAT: Export of goods from the UK) must be met.

EXAMPLE 1

A UK VAT registered business supplies goods to a customer established in the USA. That customer is also VAT registered in the UK but has no business establishment here. The customer arranges for the goods to be collected from the UK supplier for subsequent export outside the EU. *The supply is eligible for zero-rating as an indirect export. Regulation 129 of VAT Regulations 1995 will be amended to fully reflect the provisions of EU Law.*

EXAMPLE 2

A UK VAT registered business supplies goods to a customer established in China. That customer also has a business establishment in the UK and is VAT registered here. The goods are collected by the customer and exported outside the EU. *This is an indirect export involving a supply made to a customer who is established in the UK.As such, the criteria in the revised Regulation 129 of VAT Regulations 1995 is not met and the supply is not eligible for zero-rating.*

EXAMPLE 3

A UK VAT registered business supplies goods to a customer established in South Africa. That customer also has a business establishment in the UK and is VAT registered here. The goods are sent direct to a destination outside the EU by the UK supplier. *This is a direct export and the supply is eligible for zero-rating under the provisions of section 30(6) of VAT Act 1994.*

EXAMPLE 4

Customer (A) who is established in Canada orders goods from UK VAT registered supplier (B). The Canadian customer is also VAT registered in the UK but has no business establishment here. The UK supplier (B) sources the goods from another UK VAT registered supplier (C). The overseas customer (A) collects the goods from UK supplier (C) and subsequently exports those goods outside the EU. There are two separate supplies in this scenario - from UK supplier (C) to UK supplier (B) and from UK supplier (B) to Canadian customer (A). *The supply from (C) to (B) is a standard-rated supply and UK VAT is due. The final supply in this chain (from (B) to (A)) is eligible for zero-rating under the provisions of Regulation 129 of VAT Regulations 1995 (as amended).*

WHAT TO DO ABOUT PAST SUPPLIES

If affected businesses choose to correct past transactions and wish to make a claim to HMRC (under section 80 of the VAT Act 1994) for repayment of VAT incorrectly accounted for, they may do so, subject to the conditions set out in Notice 700/45 How to correct VAT errors and make adjustments or claims (www.customs.hmrc.gov.uk/channelsPortalWebApp/downloadFile?contentID=HMCE_CL_000077).

All claims will be subject to the four-year time limit in section 80(4) of the VAT Act 1994 and to the set-off provisions in section 81 of the VAT Act and section 130 of the Finance Act 2008.

We may reject all or part of a claim if repayment would unjustly enrich the claimant.

More details on making claims and 'unjust enrichment' can be found in Notice 700/45 How to correct VAT errors and make adjustments or claims (www.customs.hmrc.gov.uk/channelsPortalWebApp/downloadFile?contentID=HMCE_CL_000077).

In all cases, zero-rating of past supplies will only be appropriate if the supplier holds valid evidence to show that the goods have been exported. Guidance on acceptable evidence of export is set out in section 6 of public Notice 703 VAT: Export of goods from the United Kingdom. Additionally, for past transactions, the recipients of the supplies in question will need to make corresponding adjustments to the amount of input tax reclaimed.

FURTHER INFORMATION

Notice 703 (VAT: Exports of goods from the UK) provides detailed information on the rules for zero-rating a supply of goods for export to destinations outside the EU. This notice will be updated to reflect the changes outlined in this Brief.

For further information and advice, or where you are in any doubt about the correct VAT treatment please contact the VAT Helpline on 0300 200 3700.

WITHDRAWAL OF PARTIAL EXEMPTION CONCESSION FOR ROAD FUEL SCALE CHARGES

4 November 2013. *HMRC Brief 33/13*

ABSTRACT

This brief reminds taxpayers that the partial exemption concession on road fuel scale charges (RFSCs) will be withdrawn with effect from 1 January 2014. Partly-exempt businesses continuing to use RFSCs after that date must account for the full amount and recover input tax according to their agreed partial exemption method. The brief contains a suggested formula for calculating the recoverable input tax on road fuel, which businesses may use with HMRC's approval.

FULL TEXT

Withdrawal of partial exemption concession in relation to Road Fuel Scale Charges (RFSCs) - reminder of withdrawal and need to consider action

PURPOSE OF THIS BRIEF

The purpose of this Brief is to remind taxpayers that the partial exemption concession on Road Fuel Scale Charges (RFSCs) will be withdrawn with effect from 1 January 2014. Taxpayers who currently use the concession need to take action if they are to continue to achieve a fair result following withdrawal.

WHO SHOULD READ THIS BRIEF

Partly exempt taxpayers who use the RFSCs and the related partial exemption concession.

BACKGROUND

RFSCs are an optional way of calculating VAT on deemed supplies created when taxpayers allow business road fuel to be used for private journeys. They avoid the need to keep detailed mileage records to accurately calculate private usage.

Where taxpayers are partly exempt and VAT on road fuel is treated as residual declaring RFSCs can lead to unfair results. This is because output tax will be declared on the full value of private use fuel whereas input tax will only be claimable in part on that fuel according to the taxpayer's partial exemption recovery rate.

The concession corrects this unfairness by allowing the RFSCs to be reduced by applying the partial exemption recovery rate to them. This means that the output tax declared on private use fuel is consistent with the actual input tax deduction on that fuel. However HMRC needs to either withdraw concessions or bring them into law and this concession cannot be legislated.

CONSULTATION AND WITHDRAWAL OF CONCESSION

HMRC consulted on correcting errors in RFSCs and bringing associated concessions into law in summer 2012. The consultation set out that this concession would need to be withdrawn and asked whether any particular transitional arrangements would be needed. On 11 December 2012 HMRC published the summary of responses to that consultation, including its conclusions regarding this concession.

The summary announced that HMRC agreed that a long lead in time to the withdrawal was appropriate and that the concession was therefore to be withdrawn with effect from 1 January 2014.

FURTHER INFORMATION

Partly exempt businesses who wish to continue to use RFSCs from 1 January 2014 must account for the full amount of RFSCs applicable to their vehicles. Input tax on road fuel will continue to be recoverable in accordance with the business's agreed partial exemption method.

While HMRC consider that the following 'fuel sector' formula will give a similar overall VAT result to that realised under the concession, businesses may propose their own alternative.

The suggested formula to calculate the recoverable input tax on road fuel is as follows:

VAT ON FUEL SCALE CHARGES + ((VAT CHARGED ON FUEL PURCHASED IN THE PERIOD - VAT ON FUEL SCALE CHARGES) X PE RECOVERY RATE)

For example:

VAT on scale charge due - £300.00

VAT incurred on road fuel - £630.00

PE recovery rate 40%

Calculation =

300 + ((630 - 300) x 40%) =

300 + (330 x 40%) =

300 + (132.00) = £432.00 input tax recovery.

The effect of the suggested formula is consistent with the concession that is being withdrawn.

If as a result of the withdrawal of this concession or for any other reason businesses do consider that their current Partial Exemption Method will not give a fair and reasonable recovery of input tax they should contact HMRC requesting a new method. Until formal approval is granted businesses should not adopt this formula or make any other change to their partial exemption calculation method.

Along with any new method proposal businesses need to submit a declaration that the proposed method is fair and reasonable. The declaration needs to apply to the whole method not just the fuel sector. See Public Notice 706 Partial exemption for more information on the declaration.

Another option to ensure a fair and reasonable recovery of VAT following the withdrawal of the concession that does not require a new Partial Exemption Method is to keep accurate mileage records that would allow apportionment of the input tax incurred on road fuel so that only the portion relating to business use is included in the partial exemption calculation. No deemed supply would arise and so the RFSC would not apply.

Alternatively, where taxpayers have a very low partial exemption recovery rate they may prefer to claim no VAT on road fuel and also avoid the need to consider the RFSC.

REVERSE CHARGE FOR MOBILE TELEPHONES, COMPUTER CHIPS AND EMISSIONS ALLOWANCES

9 December 2013. *HMRC Brief 36/13*

ABSTRACT

HMRC confirms that the UK will continue to apply the reverse charge for mobile telephones, computer chips and emissions allowances at least until the end of 2018, following entry into force in August 2013 of the EU directive introducing the Reverse Charge Mechanism.

FULL TEXT

VAT: Reverse charge accounting for businesses trading in mobile telephones, computer chips and emissions allowances: continuation of current treatment. Withdrawal of partial exemption concession in relation to Road Fuel Scale Charges (RFSCs) - reminder of withdrawal and need to consider action

WHO NEEDS TO READ THIS?

Businesses buying and / or selling any of the following:

- mobile telephones
- integrated circuit devices, such as microprocessors and central processing units, in a state prior to integration into end user products
- emissions allowances, emissions reduction units and emissions reduction certificates

Further to EU Directive 2013/43/EU introducing the Reverse Charge Mechanism, HMRC can confirm that the UK will continue to apply the reverse charge for mobile telephones, computer chips and emissions allowances in their current forms. The Reverse Charge Mechanism allows these measures to run until the end of 2018.

BACKGROUND

The reverse charge for mobile phones and computer chips was implemented in the UK with effect from 1 June 2007 to remove the opportunity for fraudsters to use these goods to perpetrate missing trader intra-community (MTIC) carousel fraud. As an exception to the normal accounting rules for VAT, the UK secured agreement to derogate from EU law to apply this anti-fraud measure, which originally ran until 30 April 2009. The derogation was then renewed in 2009 and again in 2011.

A zero rate for emissions allowances was introduced on 31 July 2009 as an interim measure to halt rapidly escalating MTIC fraud in this area, pending agreement on a common EU-wide countermeasure. A Directive providing an option for all Member States to introduce a reverse charge was adopted in March 2010 and the UK's reverse charge for emission allowances was implemented with effect from 1 November 2010.

The EU legal base for the reverse charge for mobile telephones and chips has now been superseded by the Reverse Charge Mechanism. The Directive also has the effect of extending the period of validity of the reverse charge for carbon credits from 30 June 2015 to the end of 2018. However, no changes are required to UK law which will continue to apply in its current form.

The Reverse Charge Mechanism allows Member States the option to introduce a reverse charge without a derogation for other goods and services subject to MTIC fraud; these are: gas, electricity, games consoles, tablet PCs, laptops, industrial crops and raw and semi-finished metals.

FURTHER INFORMATION

For further information on the reverse charge please see Public Notice 735: VAT reverse charge on specified goods and services (customs.hmrc.gov.uk/channelsPortalWebApp/downloadFile?contentID=HMCE_PROD1_028649).

INTRASTAT CHANGES FROM 1 JANUARY 2014

16 December 2013. *HMRC Brief 38/13*

ABSTRACT

From 1 January 2014, the Intrastat arrivals threshold doubles from £600,000 to £1,200,000; the dispatches threshold remains unchanged at £250,000; and the delivery terms threshold increases from £16 million to £24 million.

FULL TEXT

PURPOSE OF THIS BRIEF

The purpose of this Brief is to explain how businesses, trading in goods with other EU Member States who are required to submit Intrastat declarations, will be affected by changes from 1 January 2014.

WHO SHOULD READ THIS BRIEF

VAT registered businesses that are required to submit declarations of arrivals (EU imports) trade received from other EU Member States and/or provide Delivery Terms information on an Intrastat declaration.

Changes to Intrastat thresholds from 1 January 2014

- the exemption threshold for arrivals is increased from £600,000 to £1,200,000
- the Delivery Terms threshold is increased from £16 million to £24 million
- the exemption threshold for dispatches (EU exports) remains unchanged at £250,000

BACKGROUND

ARRIVALS THRESHOLD

EU legislation requires the UK to collect information on intra-EU trade in goods for statistical purposes and sets minimum requirements for the quantity of trade covered.

Council Regulation (EC) No 638/2004 (as amended by Council Regulation (EC) No 222/2009) requires EU Member States to collect data on a minimum percentage of the total value of their EU trade in goods. This regulation has been amended by Council Regulation (EU) No 1093/2013 which reduces the minimum requirement which Member States are to collect for their arrivals (intra-EU imports) from 95% to 93%.

These requirements determine the level at which the exemption thresholds, which are applied independently to arrivals and dispatches, are set in the UK. If your annual intra-EU trade in goods is above the specified exemption thresholds you are required to provide monthly statistical returns (Intrastat declarations).

The exemption thresholds are set at a level that ensures the UK obtains the percentage coverage of the value of intra-EU trade required by EU legislation, whilst at the same time ensuring that the number of businesses which are required to submit monthly information is kept to a minimum.

The threshold for arrivals has been increased as a result of the reduction in the coverage requirement to 95%.

DELIVERY TERMS THRESHOLD

EU legislation requires the UK to collect information to enable the accurate calculation of statistical value. These requirements determine the level at which the Delivery Terms threshold is set in the UK. The same threshold for Delivery Terms applies to arrivals and dispatches.

If your annual EU trade is above the Delivery Terms threshold you are required to supply additional information relating to Delivery Terms on your Intrastat declarations.

FURTHER INFORMATION

Further information on Intrastat can be found on:

- www.uktradeinfo.com

- www.gov.uk
- Notice 60 Intrastat General Guide (customs.hmrc.gov.uk/channelsPortalWebApp/downloadFile?contentID=HMCE_CL_000267)

VAT AND GAMING MACHINES FOLLOWING *HMRC V THE RANK GROUP PLC*

22 January 2014. *HMRC Brief 1/14*

ABSTRACT

HMRC is taking action to recover VAT claimed by and repaid to gaming machine operators in accordance with guidelines issued in R&C Brief 11/2010 (March 2010), following the latest decision of the Court of Appeal in HMRC's favour over the definition of "gaming machines" in The Rank Group case. HMRC's action affects VAT repayments in relation to gaming machine takings for the period from 1 November 1998 to 5 December 2005.

FULL TEXT

VAT: FISCAL NEUTRALITY AND GAMING MACHINES - HM REVENUE AND CUSTOMS (HMRC) ACTION FOLLOWING THE DECISION OF THE COURT OF APPEAL IN THE CASE OF HMRC V THE RANK GROUP PLC.

1. SUMMARY

Revenue & Customs Briefs 75/09 (issued 8 December 2009), 11/10 (10 March 2010) and 39/11 (6 December 2011) provided updates about the ongoing litigation between HMRC and the Rank Group plc, in respect of the application of the European principle of fiscal neutrality to the VAT treatment of gaming machines between 1 November 1998 and 5 December 2005.

R&C Brief 11/10 advised that HMRC would pay any valid claims submitted by businesses in respect of the net amount of VAT paid on gaming machine takings during that period. The Brief also made clear that protective assessments would be issued under section 80(4A) of the VAT Act 1994 to allow HMRC to recover these amounts if we were successful at a later stage in the litigation and claims were paid on this basis in 2010 and 2011.

HMRC has now won in the Court of Appeal in relation to machines, including multi-player terminals, previously found to have not fallen within the legal definition of a gaming machine. The Court found that these machines did fall within the definition and so their takings at the time were taxable at the standard rate of VAT in the same way as other gaming machines and there was no breach of fiscal neutrality. In a second strand of the litigation relating to Fixed Odds Betting Terminals, the Upper Tribunal issued a decision on 4 October 2012 remitting the case back to the First Tier Tribunal for rehearing in light of the ruling of the European Court of Justice on 10 November 2011.

This means that legally there are now no adverse decisions against HMRC in respect of gaming machines. Therefore, HMRC will be recovering the amounts paid out in claims as per the terms of R&C Brief 11/10.

READERSHIP

Operators of gaming machines between November 1998 and December 2005 that received repayments of VAT from HMRC in respect of previously overpaid VAT on gaming machine takings.

2. ACTION REQUIRED

All businesses that made a claim and received a repayment from HMRC in accordance with R&C Brief 11/10 will be asked to repay the amount they received.

HMRC will write to all affected businesses individually setting out the amounts they received from HMRC. The letter will include guidance about how to repay the money. If you are unable to make the full payment by the due date you should contact HMRC and explain why you are unable to pay on time. HMRC will then discuss your circumstances with you.

HMRC will start writing to businesses in January 2014 and we expect that this work will take several months so you may not hear from us immediately.

3. FUTURE IMPLICATIONS

Litigation continues with the First Tier Tribunal still to hear the remitted case on the issue of the similarity of Fixed Odds Betting Terminals (FOBTs) to other machines. Rank has also petitioned the Supreme Court to be allowed to appeal the Court of Appeal decision.

HMRC will issue further guidance, as appropriate, as these strands of the litigation are concluded.

DEFINITION OF "STUDENT" FOR BUILDINGS CONSTRUCTED FOR RELEVANT RESIDENTIAL PURPOSE

31 January 2014. *HMRC Brief 3/14*

ABSTRACT

This brief contains revised guidance on the definition of "student" for the purposes of establishing zero-rating for construction of buildings used for a "relevant residential purpose", including student accommodation.

FULL TEXT

PURPOSE

This brief has been produced in order to clarify the definition of the term "student", which is significant when considering the VAT liability of construction works to buildings which are "used for a relevant residential purpose".

WHO SHOULD READ THIS?

The brief should be read by providers of residential accommodation to school pupils and students.

BACKGROUND

VAT relief is available for construction services in relation to particular new buildings, including those which are used for a relevant residential purpose, which includes student accommodation. Previous versions of the definition of the term "student" have been misinterpreted in a small number of cases. This revised guidance to replace VCONST15360 attempts to clearly set out HMRC's policy:

REVISED GUIDANCE

VCONST15360 - "RELEVANT RESIDENTIAL PURPOSE" - INTERPRETATION OF TERMS: NOTE (4)(D) TO GROUP 5 OF SCHEDULE 8 VATA - RESIDENTIAL ACCOMMODATION FOR STUDENTS OR SCHOOL PUPILS: WHAT IS A "STUDENT"?

Note (4)(d) includes, as a category of relevant residential purpose building, "residential accommodation for students or school pupils". Whereas the term "school pupil" is one that is reasonably clear and uncontroversial, the term "student" is less so and requires further clarification to assist in the determination of whether a building is intended for use for a relevant residential purpose for the purpose of obtaining VAT relief. For the avoidance of any doubt, VAT relief on the construction of residential accommodation for school pupils who are boarders will be subject to the same rules that apply to residential accommodation constructed for students.

The term "student" in this context refers to a person undertaking a course of educational study or instruction. It covers any person who is receiving education or vocational training from a university (or a centrally funded higher education institution or a further education institution) or from any other supplier who is providing similar, or the same type of, education or vocational training to a similar, or the same, academic standard.

Examples include (but are not necessarily limited to) individuals who have left school and are undertaking higher or further education or training with a view to:

(1) obtaining a generally recognised academic or professional qualification
(2) maintaining an existing professional qualification for which accreditation is received
(3) undertaking a course of study which, whilst not leading to a recognised qualification, has a high level of academic content and is intended to improve the knowledge and understanding of the student in an area of academic interest

The maintenance of existing professional qualifications would include Continuing Professional Development (CPD) applicable in cases where either:

- a professional body requires from its members the continuing recognition of a qualification
- an employer requires employees to maintain or improve relevant technical skills

Whilst it should be clear when an activity falls within the scope of one of the first two categories (as numbered above) it may be less clear when an activity falls within the scope of the third category. The following are examples which are intended to illustrate the kind of educational activity which is included:

- summer schools in which international students and others have the opportunity to undertake a programme of study comparable with the work done by full time students
- residential events the purpose of which is to show aspiring university applicants what it is like to study at university - whilst the academic content is high and the participants are school pupils, the purpose of their attendance is not either part of their A-level curriculum nor is it part of a programme which leads to a qualification
- English as a Foreign Language (EFL) courses (see paragraph 9.1 of Notice 701/30)
- academic conferences which offer development and ongoing learning to the academic staff of universities and colleges to ensure that academics are able to share ideas, learn from each other and embed the latest thinking into their own research and teaching

People who attend classes, often badged as "summer schools", which may offer a life-enhancing experience and promote greater cultural or spiritual awareness but the subject matter of which falls into the category of hobbies or leisure interests (for example pottery workshops, art or literature appreciation courses etc.) as opposed to receiving educational or vocational training to an academic standard, will not qualify as "students".

Whilst persons engaging in theological studies in order to become a minister of faith (such as a priest, rabbi or imam) will qualify as "students", those attending seminaries or religious retreats which do not serve this purpose but are intended primarily to foster or reinforce faith, are not considered to be receiving educational or vocational training to an academic standard and will not qualify as "students".

FURTHER INFORMATION

For further information please contact the VAT Helpline on telephone: 0300 200 3700.

The Helpline is available from 8.00 am to 6.00 pm, Monday to Friday.

If you have hearing difficulties, please ring the Textphone service on telephone: 0300 200 3719.

VAT ZERO-RATE ON BUILDINGS

31 January 2014. *HMRC Brief 4/14*

ABSTRACT

This Brief announces the issue of a VAT information Sheet providing updated guidance on the application of the zero-rate for VAT on buildings designed as dwellings and intended to be used for a "relevant residential purpose".

FULL TEXT

PURPOSE

This Brief announces the issue of VAT information Sheet 02/14 which updates and supersedes the relevant sections of Public Notice 708 and VAT Guidance VCONST.

The information sheet provides guidance on the application of the zero-rate for VAT on buildings that are:

- designed as a dwelling or dwellings
- intended to be used for a relevant residential purpose (RRP)

WHO SHOULD READ THIS?

All parties involved in the construction and supply of buildings that are intended to be used for a RRP but take the form of dwellings.

BACKGROUND

The zero-rate for dwellings is based on the design of the building and for RRPs based upon its use. HMRC accept that there may be instances where a building could qualify for zero-rating under both of these provisions at the same time. In such cases, a taxpayer is free to rely on either provision to achieve zero-rating for their building.

Following an informal consultation with representatives of professional bodies and the property sector, HMRC are publishing a VAT Information Sheet (02/14) in order to provide guidance on the application of the zero-rate for VAT on buildings that are designed as a dwelling or dwellings (meeting the conditions of Note 2 to Group 5 of Schedule 8 of the VAT Act 1994) and are also intended for use as a building used for a relevant residential purpose (RRP) (meeting the conditions of Note 4 to Group 5 of Schedule 8 of the VAT Act 1994).

VAT Information Sheet 02/14 (customs.hmrc.gov.uk/channelsPortalWebApp/downloadFile?contentID=HMCE_PROD1_033065)

WHO CAN I CONTACT FOR FURTHER INFORMATION?

For further information please contact the VAT Helpline on telephone: 0300 200 3700.

The Helpline is available from 8.00 am to 6.00 pm, Monday to Friday.

If you have hearing difficulties, please ring the Textphone service on telephone: 0300 200 3719.

TOUR OPERATORS MARGIN SCHEME

31 January 2014. *HMRC Brief 5/14*

ABSTRACT

This Brief explains HMRC's view that no immediate changes are required to the operation of TOMS in the UK following the recent decision of the CJEU in connection with the scheme in eight other member states. Based upon the CJEU's judgment, areas for possible review in the future may involve the inclusion of wholesale supplies, and calculations made on the basis of individual transactions, rather than using global figures for a whole year.

FULL TEXT

VAT: TOUR OPERATORS MARGIN SCHEME (TOMS) - POSITION FOLLOWING EUROPEAN COURT OF JUSTICE (ECJ) INFRACTION DECISIONS

PURPOSE OF THIS BRIEF

The purpose of this Brief is to explain how UK tour operators and other businesses supplying travel services will be affected by these ECJ decisions.

WHO NEEDS TO READ THIS BRIEF

Tour operators and other businesses who buy in and sell on various travel services, either on their own, or packaged with other supplies such as conference or training facilities.

Accountants, consultants and others who provide VAT advice to the businesses referred to above.

BACKGROUND

The Tour Operators Margin Scheme (TOMS) is a mandatory EU VAT accounting scheme for businesses which buy in and sell on certain travel services, such as passenger transport, hotel accommodation and car hire. Under normal VAT accounting rules, businesses which supply these services in several Member States would have to register, recover VAT on their costs, and account for VAT on their sales in each Member State in which they make supplies. Under TOMS, they cannot recover any VAT on the services they buy in, but only account for VAT on their profit margin in the Member State where they are established.

In the UK, we only apply TOMS to supplies to final consumers or to businesses for their own consumption (for example, business travel for employees). Travel services supplied to another business for onward sale ("wholesale" supplies) are subject to normal VAT rules.

We also require businesses to carry out their TOMS calculation annually using global figures for the year as a whole.

THE ECJ DECISIONS

The EU Commission initiated infraction proceedings against eight Member States (Spain, Poland, Italy, Czech Republic, Greece, France, Finland and Portugal) in connection with their operation of TOMS, and the ECJ released its decision in these proceedings on 26 September 2013 (C-189/11). The Court ruled that:

– wholesale supplies should be covered by TOMS
– the TOMS calculation should be carried out on an individual transaction basis

These decisions are binding on all Member States. However, after careful consideration, we have decided that there will be no changes to the operation of TOMS in the UK at this stage, and that businesses should continue to follow existing guidance. This is because:

– the EU Commission has indicated an intention to carry out a review of TOMS, which may result in significant changes to the scheme in future
– making changes now, which may be modified or reversed in future, would be particularly disruptive and costly for business

We will review this after a year.

DIRECT EFFECT

It is open for any business to apply direct effect and operate TOMS in accordance with the Court's decisions. For example, it is possible that some tour operators may gain a benefit from including wholesale supplies within TOMS, in which case they may choose to do so if they wish.

FURTHER INFORMATION

Full guidance on TOMS is given in VAT Notice 709/5, "*Tour Operators Margin Scheme*". The treatment of wholesale supplies is explained at paragraph 3.1, and details of the margin scheme calculation are at sections 5 and 8 to 12.

PENSION FUND MANAGEMENT COSTS FOLLOWING *PPG HOLDINGS* CASE

3 February 2014. *HMRC Brief 6/14*

ABSTRACT

HMRC is changing its policy on the recovery of input tax in relation to the management of defined-benefit occupational pension funds following the judgment of the CJEU in *PPG Holdings BV*. Employers may now be able to deduct VAT incurred in connection with investment management activities of the fund, in addition to the day-to-day administration of an occupational pension scheme.

FULL TEXT

1. PURPOSE OF THIS BRIEF

This brief sets out HM Revenue & Customs' (HMRC) position following the decision of the Court of Justice of the European Union (CJEU) in *Fiscale Eenheid PPG Holdings BV cs te Hoogezand (PPG)*. The case concerned an employer's entitlement to deduct VAT paid on services relating to the administration and management of a defined benefit pension scheme.

The CJEU ruled that, subject to certain conditions, the employer was entitled to deduct the VAT it paid on services relating to the administration of its employees' pensions and management of the assets of the pension fund set up to safeguard those pensions, where the pension fund was a legally and fiscally separate entity. The CJEU left it to the national court to determine whether those conditions were met in the case of *PPG*.

You can read the full text of the decision on the CURIA website.

1.1 READERSHIP

This Revenue and Customs Brief is aimed at:

- businesses and other taxable entities that provide pension schemes for their employees
- pension fund management providers
- trustees of occupational pension funds
- tax advisers.

1.2 BACKGROUND

PPG, a Dutch company, established a defined benefit pension scheme for its employees. PPG was required by law to establish a pension fund, which had to be legally and financially separate from PPG.

PPG received supplies of pension administration and investment management services from third parties, paid the cost of these services and did not pass the costs on to the pension fund. PPG deducted the VAT it paid on the administration and management fees as input tax. The Dutch tax authorities challenged this position, PPG appealed and the Dutch court referred two questions to the CJEU, which can be summarised as follows.

(1) Can an employer deduct the VAT incurred by it on administration and fund management services supplied to it in relation to the operation of a separate pension fund established for the benefit of its employees?

(2) Can the defined benefit pension fund in question be classified as a "special investment fund" so that the management of the fund was exempt from VAT?

CJEU DECISION

(1) The CJEU decided that an employer, like PPG, that has set up a pension fund that is legally and financially separate can deduct the VAT incurred on administration and pension fund management services, provided that there is a direct and immediate link between the services and the employer's own supplies.

(2) The CJEU did not answer the question concerning the liability of the pension fund management services as this point had already been addressed by the Court in the case of *Wheels Common Investment Fund Trustees and Others* C-424/11.

1.3 HMRC PREVIOUS POLICY

Until now, HMRC policy has been to distinguish between costs incurred in relation to the:

– setting up and day to day administration of occupational pension funds
– management of the investment activities of the fund.

HMRC previously allowed employers to deduct VAT incurred in relation to the general management (that is, administration) of an occupational pension scheme on the basis that these costs are overheads of the employer and thus have a direct and immediate link to their business activities.

In respect of investment management costs, HMRC considered these costs to be of the pension fund itself and to relate solely to the activities of the pension fund. To the extent that these inputs were deductible, they were deductible by the fund and/or trustees of the fund.

Where a single invoice was received covering both the administration of the pension fund and the management of the investments in the fund, HMRC allowed the employer to claim 30% of the VAT as relating to the general management of the scheme and the pension fund to claim 70% as relating to the investment management.

1.4 IMPLEMENTATION OF THE JUDGMENT

The CJEU has reiterated in *PPG* that, in order to deduct the VAT incurred on a cost, a business must establish a direct and immediate link between the supply received and the taxable supplies that the business makes. Whether there is a direct and immediate link will depend on whether the cost of the input services is incorporated in the price of the supplies made by the business. A cost may either be incorporated in the price of specific supplies or groups of supplies, or be part of its general costs and incorporated in the price of all the supplies made by the business. If a cost has a direct and immediate link to specific supplies or groups of supplies, then it cannot also be part of its general costs.

In respect of specific costs of investment management, these will have a direct and immediate link to the supplies of the investments themselves. For example, the costs of managing a property within a pension fund will have a direct and immediate link to the rental income derived from the property. They cannot therefore be general costs of the employer. A similar analysis can be applied to the financial investments. However, where the services received go further than the management of the investments, they may be general costs. Therefore, provided that the supply is received by the employer, the VAT incurred will potentially be deductible by the employer.

As a result, HMRC is changing its policy on the recovery of input tax in relation to the management of pension funds. This means that there are circumstances where employers may be able to claim input tax in relation to pension funds where they could not previously.

However HMRC will not accept that the VAT incurred in relation to pension fund management/administration is deductible by an employer in the following circumstances where the:

– supplies were not made to the employer (this includes, but is not limited to, consideration of whether the employer has commissioned and paid for the services)
– supply is limited to investment management services only (that is, it is not a combined supply of both investment management and pension administration services).

Additionally, where the employer receives the supply but the pension fund bears the cost of the services (whether by way of reimbursement or a set off against pension contributions), HMRC will require an equivalent amount of output VAT in respect of the amounts reimbursed to be accounted for. This amount is potentially deductible by the pension fund to the extent that it is engaged in taxable business activities.

Where an employer is engaged in non-business activities or makes exempt supplies, it will need to take these into account when deducting any VAT incurred and restrict its deduction accordingly. Further information on the treatment of non business activities can be found at chapter 4.6 of Notice 700, *The VAT Guide* and on partial exemption in Notice 706, *Partial exemption.*

Public Notice 700/17 *Funded Pension Schemes* will be updated shortly to reflect these changes in VAT treatment.

CLAIMS AND RETROSPECTIVE ACTION

From the date of this Brief, the policy outlined at 1.3 above will no longer apply, except as specified in the transitional rules below. The policy currently outlined in Notice 700/17 will be withdrawn with immediate effect except in circumstances where the pension fund is invoiced for services. In these circumstances, during a transitional period of six months, to allow time for businesses to adapt in response to this Brief, the pension fund and the employer may continue to agree to a 70/30 split on the terms set out in that Notice.

HMRC do not intend to take any action to correct the position in cases where the employer has deducted a proportion of the VAT under the existing treatment (outlined at 1.3 above) and the criteria outlined at 1.4 above were not met.

Businesses that provide pension schemes for their employees and receive supplies of services that fall within the criteria outlined at 1.4 above are entitled, but not obliged, to claim a refund of any input VAT which has not previously been claimed. Where a business has chosen to apply the 70/30 split, a claim for a refund would entail a recalculation of the amounts of input tax proper to the employer and the fund respectively.

Whilst the liability of management services in respect of defined benefit pension schemes has now been determined by the CJEU, a judgment on the liability of management services in respect of defined contribution pension schemes is expected soon from the CJEU in the case of *ATP Pension Service A/S* C-464/12. The CJEU may decide that VAT should not have been charged on such services. In such circumstances, HMRC will take the appropriate steps to protect their position in relation to input tax claimed for the management of defined contribution pension schemes. This will include the issuing of assessments to recover any VAT deducted that was incorrectly charged.

Public Notice VAT 700/45 *How to correct VAT errors and make adjustments or claims* explains how to go about claiming a refund in this circumstance.

Claims for under-declared input tax are subject to the normal capping rules. Claims for repayment will therefore not be considered for periods ending more than four years before the date on which the claim is made.

Any claim made must set out the basis of the error and the amount being claimed and show how that amount has been calculated. The claim should also make it clear whether the claim is in relation to VAT incurred in relation to a defined benefit or a defined contribution pension scheme. The claimant must be able to provide copies of the documentation used in the calculation of the claim on request. An "estimated" claim, or a declared intention to lodge a claim at a future date, will not stop the clock running on the four year cap.

All claims resulting from the changes outlined in this Brief should be sent to:

Email: vat.ppg.claims@hmrc.gsi.gov.uk
or by post to:

HMRC
VAT Repayments Team S0483
PO Box 200
BOOTLE L69 9AH

Businesses that have already made a claim will now have their claims processed. However, they may wish to provide details of their claim to the email address above to ensure claims are dealt with promptly.

CHANGE OF HMRC POLICY FOLLOWING *GOALS SOCCER CENTRES* CASE

17 February 2014. *HMRC Brief 8/14*

ABSTRACT

HMRC has announced a change in its policy on the VAT treatment of businesses providing sports pitches together with administration/management services for organised sports leagues and competitions. HMRC now accepts that such activities may, where operated in circumstances similar to Goals Soccer Centres, constitute separate exempt supplies of land and standard-rated supplies of administration services. This Brief now cancels R&C Brief 4/2011, which set out HMRC's former policy.

FULL TEXT

INTRODUCTION

This brief announces a change in HMRC policy following the First Tier Tribunal (FTT) decision in the case of *Goals Soccer Centres plc* [2012] UKFTT 576 (TC). This applies to all organisers of sports leagues and competitions in circumstances where pitches and league/competition management services are being supplied.

WHO NEEDS TO READ THIS?

Providers of pitches, both indoor and outdoor, used for league and cup competitions including traders who obtain pitches and associated facilities from third parties (such as local authorities, schools, sports clubs) and who administer/manage competitive sports leagues and competitions.

BACKGROUND

Goals Soccer Centres plc owned a sports centre with a number of five-a-side football pitches. It organised and administered competitive football leagues and competitions and charged the teams that participated. The business took the view that, for VAT purposes, this charge was for an exempt supply of land. HMRC disagreed and argued that the charge was for a taxable supply of the right to participate in an organised football league.

DECISION OF THE FTT

The FTT found that there were two separate supplies being made:

- a supply of land (the pitches) which was exempt as the relevant conditions were met, and
- a supply of administration and management services which was standard rated.

HMRC POLICY

HMRC accepts that the decision of the FTT is applicable to all traders who operate in circumstances akin to Goals Soccer Centres plc. This includes traders who hire the pitches from third parties such as local authorities, schools and clubs. However, exemption will only apply where there is a series of lets in accordance with the conditions set out in Note 16, Group 1, Schedule 9 of the VAT Act 1994. More details are provided in Chapter 5, VAT Notice 742 - *Land and Property*.

ACCOUNTING FOR VAT

Where a single price is charged to the customer, businesses will need to determine the value of the two different supplies to establish the correct amount of VAT due. Whatever method is adopted to do this, there must be sufficient documentary evidence kept to show how a business has arrived at a fair and reasonable apportionment. Paragraph 8.1 of the VAT Notice 700 - *The VAT Guide* gives more information. The business will also need to consider how much of the VAT it incurs is deductible, see Chapter 3, VAT Notice 706 - *Partial Exemption*.

WHAT IS BEING PUBLISHED?

Updated guidance on sports leagues to reflect HMRC change in policy, see VATLP19600. This Business Brief now cancels Business Brief 04/11.

DEREGISTRATION OF INSOLVENT BUSINESSES

6 April 2014. *HMRC Brief 13/14*

ABSTRACT

HMRC will no longer allow insolvency practitioners to cancel the VAT registration of insolvent businesses at an early stage following their appointment, but will now keep insolvent VAT registrations open until all trading has ceased and all assets are realised. Insolvency practitioners must render VAT returns and any payment due for each VAT period until the registration ceases.

FULL TEXT

HM Revenue & Customs (HMRC) has in the past allowed insolvency practitioners to cancel the VAT registration of the business they have been appointed over at an early stage and account for VAT on any subsequent supplies using form VAT 833 Statement of Value Added Tax on goods sold in satisfaction of a debt. As part of a review of this process, HMRC has received legal confirmation that a deregistered business can no longer issue a valid VAT invoice. This could result in VAT registered buyers of assets from insolvent businesses being denied claims for input tax on the purchase of the assets in question. Consequently, HMRC can no longer allow such "early" deregistration of insolvent businesses.

Even though trading may have ceased, VAT legislation requires a business to register and remain registered for VAT if that business is making taxable supplies above the VAT registration threshold. "Taxable supplies" in that context would include asset realisations by an insolvency practitioner. Consequently, HMRC will now keep insolvent VAT registrations open until all trading has ceased and all assets are realised (though an insolvent business has the same right as any other business to apply to deregister on the grounds that it is continuing to trade but below the VAT registration threshold, if that situation applies). Insolvency practitioners are required to render VAT returns and appropriate payment, if any, for each VAT period until the registration ceases.

HMRC is happy to work with insolvency practitioners to resolve any difficulties which may arise from this approach, particularly in cases where all trading has ceased but the insolvency practitioner is experiencing difficulties in selling a property on which there is an option to tax. Insolvency practitioners should discuss any such cases with the National Insolvency Unit in Liverpool.

The National Insolvency Unit Helpline may be contacted on 03000 540 808.

The Helpline is available from 8.30am to 5pm Monday to Thursday and 8.30am to 4pm on a Friday.

WITHDRAWAL OF CONCESSIONS FOR NEW STUDENT ACCOMMODATION AND DINING HALLS - WIDENING OF THE TRANSITIONAL RULES

7 April 2014. *HMRC Brief 14/14*

ABSTRACT

HMRC are announcing a widening of the transitional rules in relation to the ending of the VAT concessions for construction of new student accommodation and new dining halls and kitchens for students and school pupils, which will be withdrawn from 1 April 2015. In addition, clarification is made in relation to the terms "continued reliance on the concession" and "Late Certificates".

FULL TEXT

PURPOSE OF THIS BRIEF

This Brief announces revised transitional rules following the announcement by HM Revenue and Customs (HMRC) that concessions affecting:

– the construction of new student accommodation
– new dining halls and kitchens for students and school pupils

will be withdrawn from 1 April 2015.

WHO SHOULD READ THIS?

This Brief should read by those engaged in the construction or provision of new student accommodation which will be supplied to Higher Education Institutes (HEIs), and of new dining rooms and kitchens constructed at the same time as new residential accommodation for students and school pupils.

BACKGROUND

The construction of a building intended for use solely for a relevant residential purpose, and the first grant of a major interest in such a building by the person constructing it, are zero-rated.

As one of the conditions for zero-rating the user of the building must, before the supply is made, provide a certificate to the builder or developer as evidence that the building is intended to be used solely (at least 95%) for a relevant residential purpose.

In a Technical Note (www.hmrc.gov.uk/specialist/esc-withdrawal-tech-note.pdf) published on 31 January 2014, HMRC announced the withdrawal from 1 April 2015 of two concessions which allow:

– Higher Education Institutions (HEIs) to ignore vacation use when determining how new student accommodation is intended to be used
– dining rooms and kitchens to be zero-rated as residential accommodation for students and school pupils if they were used "predominantly" by the living-in students

Until 1 April 2015, those affected can choose either to use the concessions or rely on the statutory position.

TRANSITIONAL RULES

Following consultation with those affected, HMRC has widened the transitional rules which determine which student accommodation buildings that are not complete as at 1 April 2015 can rely on the concession. The revised rules are set out below.

Certificates which rely on the concession to meet the "solely" for a relevant residential purpose test (as student accommodation) will still be valid where:

- for construction services, the first supply is made before 1 April 2015 and relates to a meaningful start to the construction of the building by that date, and the works are expected to progress to completion without interruption (demolition or site clearance works will only be accepted where construction starts immediately afterwards).
- for the first grant of a major interest in new student accommodation, either:
  - a meaningful deposit (for example, on exchange of contracts) has been paid to the vendor (or their solicitor) before 1 April 2015 (options to purchase will not be accepted irrespective of intention)
  - an Agreement for Lease (or purchase) has been signed with the vendor or landlord before 1 April 2015 and a meaningful start to the construction of the building has taken place by that date, and the works are expected to progress to completion without interruption (demolition or site clearance works will only be accepted where construction starts immediately afterwards)

For single developments of more than one block of student accommodation constructed in phases, the above rules apply but:

- "meaningful start to the construction of the building" means "meaningful start to the construction of the first building"
- "expected to progress to completion without interruption" means "expected to progress to completion of all phases without interruption"

OTHER POINTS

"Continued reliance on the concession" - There are no changes to the rules set out in the technical note concerning the continued use of the concession for the purposes of the change in use charge. But in order to aid clarity, if you rely on the concession before 1 April 2015 then the concession will continue to apply until the building is no longer susceptible for consideration for a change in use charge (typically ten years from completion).

"Late Certificates" - If you can demonstrate to your supplier that at the time he made his supply, you had the intention that the building will be used in the way certified and that all the other conditions (including transitional rules) for zero-rating were met, then a certificate can be issued later than 1 April 2015 see para 16.6 of Notice 708 on Buildings and Construction.

WHO CAN I CONTACT FOR FURTHER INFORMATION?

For further information please contact the VAT Helpline on telephone: 0300 200 3700.

The Helpline is available from 8.00 am to 6.00 pm, Monday to Friday.

If you have hearing difficulties, please ring the Textphone service on telephone: 0300 200 3719.

VAT RETAIL EXPORT SCHEME NEXT STEPS

14 April 2014. *HMRC Brief 17/14*

ABSTRACT

HMRC will be contacting stakeholders during April to consider possible improvements to the processes behind tax-free shopping, including claim forms, overseas visitors' identification, signage at ports and airports and HMRC guidance. Any changes will be announced before the Summer, with some not taking effect until October 2014. Following consultation, work continues on a future digital solution.

FULL TEXT

PURPOSE OF THIS BRIEF

This brief updates stakeholders on the progress of HMRC's review of the VAT Retail Export Scheme and sets out the next steps.

WHO NEEDS TO READ THIS?

Retailers, VAT refund companies and other individuals or bodies with an interest in the VAT Retail Export Scheme.

BACKGROUND

The VAT Retail Export Scheme – also known as Tax Free Shopping – allows visitors from outside the European Union (EU) to claim a refund of VAT on goods they buy and export from the EU in their personal luggage.

It was announced at Budget 2013 that HMRC would review the scheme, with the key objectives of improving the customer experience and protecting VAT revenue. A formal consultation ran from 1 July to 30 September 2013.

In its response to the consultation, the Government acknowledged that a digital solution is the leading option for change and committed to continue exploring options for a digital solution. The Government is clear that to ensure value for money to the UK taxpayer, implementing a digital solution will be dependent on a strong business case and finding an acceptable means of funding.

Alongside this commitment, HMRC announced plans to work closely with stakeholders to bring about key improvements to the scheme in the interim.

NEXT STEPS ON THE DIGITAL SOLUTION

HMRC has continued to work on the detailed responses from the formal consultation and has analysed proposals for a wide range of possible digital solutions. This valuable information is helping to develop the case for a digital solution.

Since the consultation closed, HMRC has continued to be contacted by companies interested in developing a digital solution. Although these contributions were received too late to feature in the consultation response document, there will be an opportunity for these companies to participate in the review going forward. Interested parties can email resconsultation.idt@hmrc.gsi.gov.uk to be included as a stakeholder.

HMRC is currently looking carefully at digital systems in operation in some other EU Member States. This will ensure that we benefit from the experience of, and learn lessons from, our EU colleagues. It will help us determine whether any aspects of those systems might be suitable for the UK.

As this work develops, HMRC will look to determine a number of high-level business – or system – requirements for a digital Retail Export Scheme in the UK. This work will inform whether there is a case for a Market Engagement Exercise where HMRC would invite suppliers to participate in a forum to gain their views on our requirements and possible delivery options.

As stated in the response document, the key to delivering any digital solution will be finding an approach that guarantees value for money for the UK taxpayer supported by an acceptable means of funding the development.

IMPROVING THE CUSTOMER EXPERIENCE AND PROTECTING REVENUE

In April, HMRC will contact stakeholders to consider possible changes in the following areas:

- **claim form:** HMRC will look to simplify and standardise claim forms and also consider possible changes to the declaration and whether parts of the form could be completed away from the retailers premises
- **identification:** accepting alternative identification from overseas visitors
- **processes and signage:** improving these at airports and ports
- **HMRC guidance:** amendments to ensure it is up-to-date and accurate

To ensure certainty for businesses, HMRC aims to negotiate and announce the forthcoming changes with stakeholder groups before the busy summer period. To allow businesses time to make any necessary systems changes (for example, to the layout of the claim forms), some changes will take effect after the summer and by October 2014.

MEETING WITH STAKEHOLDERS

As part of the consultation, HMRC established three Stakeholder Interest Groups representing each of the main sectors using the Retail Export Scheme. These are retailers, refund companies and overseas visitors. HMRC will invite the participants of these groups to the next Open Forum session in May. The Forum will provide an update on the review, covering work on both the interim changes and the scoping of a digital solution, and there will be a Q&A session. Interested parties can email resconsultation.idt@hmrc.gsi.gov.uk to be included as a stakeholder.

NO EXTENSION OF VAT EXEMPTION TO COMMERCIAL HIGHER EDUCATION PROVIDERS

22 April 2014. *HMRC Brief 18/14*

ABSTRACT

Following public consultation and further discussions with the Department for Business, Innovation & Skills, HMRC has decided not to proceed with proposals first aired in 2012 to extend the VAT education exemption to commercial providers of higher education and further education.

FULL TEXT

1. PURPOSE OF THIS BRIEF

To announce the outcome of the review to consider extending the VAT exemption to for-profit providers of Higher Education (HE) and Further Education (FE).

2. WHO SHOULD READ THIS BRIEF

All providers of HE and FE whether they are for-profit, publicly funded or not-for-profit.

3. BACKGROUND

In September 2012, the Government issued a consultation entitled "*VAT: Consideration of the case to extend the education exemption to for-profit providers of Higher Education*" which invited comments on options that would enable for-profit providers of HE to exempt their supplies of HE where they exclusively provide this type of education. This followed an announcement at Budget 2012.

The number of responses was low, especially from for-profit providers, or potential providers, of HE. Overall, there was no overwhelming support for either of the options put forward. It was clear from the responses that businesses would prefer a solution that exempted both HE and FE training from VAT, and that there should, if at all possible, be a uniform basis of recognition of a commercial body as an eligible body, for both HE and FE.

In 2013, HM Revenue & Customs and the Department for Business, Innovation & Skills looked at alternative options and held a consultative workshop with interested parties.

4. OUTCOME

No solution was found that was acceptable to the majority of the for-profit education sector, and which also met Government objectives. The Government has therefore decided not to make any changes at the present time.

Some businesses would clearly benefit from an extension to the exemption, but on balance, the reasons not to extend the VAT exemption for education to for-profit providers weighed more heavily. These included:

- a lack of evidence that the change would bring more providers into the market, or increase price competition within the sector
- the impact on commercial providers who would need to exempt their education supplies and not be able to recover input tax, and also the impact on businesses purchasing training who would no longer be able to recover the VAT charged on training, and would likely be faced with higher costs
- recognition that a few commercial HE providers have achieved university status, and therefore benefit from the VAT exemption
- extending the exemption would be to create a number of winners and losers, and may not create an entirely level playing field

– the cost to the Exchequer of extending the exemption

The Government recognises that this news will be disappointing to some providers in the sector although others will be pleased to maintain the status quo.

5. WHO CAN I CONTACT FOR FURTHER INFORMATION?

For further information please contact the VAT Helpline on telephone: 0300 200 3700.

The Helpline is available from 8.00 am to 6.00 pm, Monday to Friday.

If you have hearing difficulties, please ring the Textphone service on telephone: 0300 200 3719.

HMRC APPEALS LITTLEWOODS DECISION ON COMPOUND INTEREST

6 May 2014. *HMRC Brief 20/14*

ABSTRACT

HMRC has received permission to appeal the High Court decision in favour of Littlewoods Retail Ltd and others on a claim for compound interest on overpaid VAT to the Court of Appeal. Pending the outcome of this appeal, HMRC will apply for a stay on any compound interest claims already lodged with the High Court or County Court and will refuse any new requests for compound interest.

FULL TEXT

HMRC'S POSITION FOLLOWING THE HIGH COURT JUDGMENT IN *LITTLEWOODS RETAIL LTD AND OTHERS* [2014] EWHC 868 (Ch)

This brief explains HM Revenue & Customs (HMRC) position following the High Court judgment in *Littlewoods Retail Ltd and Others* [2014] EWHC 868 (Ch) handed down on 28 March 2014.

The High Court found against HMRC deciding that Littlewoods claim for additional interest succeeded in full.

This finding was based on the "exceptional" circumstances specific to the Littlewoods claimants. It does not provide a clear basis that could be applied to other claimants or a formula for doing so.

No payments are due to other claimants at this stage.

BACKGROUND

Littlewoods Retail Limited and Others claimed a refund of overpaid VAT in respect of commissions on mail order sales. This VAT was repaid together with simple interest due under VAT Act 1994. They then argued that the interest already paid to them was not adequate and that they were entitled to compound interest both as a matter of European Community law and also as a matter of English domestic law.

HMRC's view is that there is no Community law right or domestic law right to compound interest and that section 78 of VATA 1994 provides an exhaustive statutory scheme by which only simple interest is payable.

The High Court ordered a reference to the Court of Justice of the European Union (ECJ) for a decision as to whether Community law required payment of compound interest. It was heard in the Grand Chamber of the ECJ on 22 November 2011.

The judgment of the European Court was delivered on 19 July 2012. The European Court ruled that there is no EU Law right to compound interest but returned the matter to the UK Courts to determine whether the UK's interest provisions comply with general EU principles.

HIGH COURT JUDGMENT

The issue was heard in the High Court during a 3 week hearing in October and November 2013. The Court considered the implications of the ECJ judgment and, as well as considering the national rules for payment of interest, the Court considered the quantum of any amount due if simple interest was found not to be adequate. Each side put forward a different approach to show how the benefit of overpaid tax might be quantified, if necessary. The High Court found compound interest to be due as claimed taking into account the "exceptional" circumstances of Littlewoods situation. The Court also held that that the current statutory provisions relating to VAT did provide an appropriate amount of interest in many cases.

HMRC'S POSITION

HMRC does not agree with the judgment and considers it to be at odds with the requirements of European law and how Parliament intended VAT law to work. Accordingly, this is not the end of the litigation as HMRC has received permission to appeal the judgment to the Court of Appeal.

In addition, after careful consideration, HMRC has concluded that the guidance provided by the judgment about the availability of compound interest is neither clear enough nor sufficiently general to be applied to other High Court claims for compound interest. Notably, the Court set a benchmark as to what the judgment of the ECJ required for adequate indemnity in relation to the Littlewoods claimants. In doing this the Court made reference to the specific facts relating to these claimants and the calculations appropriate to them. The Court went on to find that the simple interest paid to the Littlewoods claimants did not meet the aforementioned benchmark and therefore the claims succeeded in full. However, the Court did not provide a formula that could be generally applied to other claimants with other claims for compound interest. Nor did it alter the earlier finding of the Upper Tribunal that compound interest is not available consequent to an appeal to the Tribunal.

Further, in relation to a number of other claims, there are other significant strands of litigation still to be resolved before these claims can be considered in full with a view to possible settlement.

CLAIMS FOR COMPOUND INTEREST

In view of the above, HMRC will apply for any claims for compound interest already lodged with the High Court or County Court to continue to be stayed pending the final determination of the Littlewoods litigation.

HMRC's position in relation to Tribunal appeals is unchanged, namely that these should continue to be stood over until there has been a final determination as to the availability of compound interest in the United Kingdom.

Any new requests for compound interest will continue to be refused.

HMRC will reconsider their position in the event that their appeal to the Court of Appeal is unsuccessful.

ZERO-RATING OF DRUGS PRESCRIBED BY PHYSIOTHERAPISTS AND PODIATRISTS

23 May 2014. *HMRC Brief 21/14*

ABSTRACT

With effect from 21 May 2014, physiotherapists and podiatrists join the list of health professionals permitted to prescribe drugs which pharmacists and others authorised to dispense drugs can zero-rate.

FULL TEXT

ZERO-RATING OF THE DISPENSING OF DRUGS PRESCRIBED BY PHYSIOTHERAPISTS AND PODIATRISTS

PURPOSE

This Revenue & Customs Brief announces a consequential change to UK VAT law to permit the zero-rating of the dispensing of drugs prescribed by physiotherapists and podiatrists. This is as a result of changes introduced in The Human Medicines (Amendment) Regulations 2013.

WHO SHOULD READ THIS?

Physiotherapists and podiatrists, pharmacists and other health professionals who are authorised to dispense drugs.

BACKGROUND

Currently medical doctors, dentists and other health professionals authorised under the Human Medicines Regulations 2012 can prescribe medication.

Registered pharmacists or others with similar authorisation are already permitted to dispense zero-rated drugs and medicines to individuals for their personal use on prescription by virtue of Item 1 of Group 12 of Schedule 8 to the Value Added Tax Act 1994. Note 2B to Group 12 lists the health professionals who are permitted to prescribe drugs.

Physiotherapists and podiatrists are not currently listed and as such pharmacists cannot zero-rate the dispensing of drugs on prescription from these without the involvement of a doctor.

The Human Medicines (Amendment) Regulations 2013 came into force on 20 August 2013. It allows physiotherapists and podiatrists, after appropriate training, to prescribe certain drugs in their own right. As such, Group 12 is being updated to include these.

CHANGES TO LEGISLATION

A new statutory instrument 'SI 2014/1111 The Value Added Tax (Drugs and Medicines) Order 2014' will come into force. This Order amends the VAT Act 1994. It adds physiotherapists and podiatrists to the list of persons who can prescribe drugs which can be zero-rated by pharmacists or by other health professionals authorised to dispense drugs.

TIMING

The changes come into effect as of 21 May 2014.

UPDATE ON PENSION FUND MANAGEMENT COSTS FOLLOWING PPG HOLDINGS

27 May 2014. *HMRC Brief 22/14*

ABSTRACT

HMRC is reviewing again the VAT treatment of pension scheme administration and fund management services to take account of CJEU decisions in both *PPG Holdings* and the more recent *ATP Pension Services* case. These concerned deduction of VAT on investment management costs of defined benefit and defined contribution pension schemes respectively. Pending the outcome of the review, businesses may continue to use the transitional arrangements announced in R&C Brief 6/2014 for a 70/30 costs split between fund and employer in defined benefit cases.

FULL TEXT

VAT: CJEU JUDGMENT REGARDING DEDUCTION OF VAT ON PENSION FUND MANAGEMENT COSTS (PPG HOLDINGS BV)

PURPOSE OF THIS BRIEF

HM Revenue & Customs (HMRC) issued Revenue and Customs Brief 06/14 (RCB 06/14) to set out its position following the decision of the Court of Justice of the European Union (CJEU) in *PPG Holdings BV* (C-26/12) (*PPG*). This Revenue and Customs Brief is being issued to provide an update on HMRC's position following the CJEU's decision in *ATP Pension Services* (C-464/12) (*ATP*) and to extend the transitional period announced in RCB 06/14.

1.1 READERSHIP

This Revenue and Customs Brief is primarily aimed at:

- businesses and other taxable entities that provide pension schemes for their employees

- pension fund management providers
- pension scheme trustees
- tax advisers

1.2 BACKGROUND

PPG concerned an employer's entitlement to deduct VAT paid on services relating to the administration and management of a *defined benefit* pension scheme. The CJEU decided that, subject to certain conditions, the employer was entitled to deduct the VAT it paid on services relating to both the administration of its employees' pensions, and the management of the assets of the pension fund set up to safeguard those pensions in circumstances where the pension fund was a legally and fiscally separate entity. The CJEU left it to the National Court to determine whether those conditions were met in the case of *PPG*.

Before this decision, HMRC policy had been to allow employers to deduct VAT incurred in relation to the general management costs (the administration) of an occupational pension scheme, but not in relation to the investment management costs, as these latter costs were considered to be costs of the pension scheme itself. In addition, where a single invoice was received covering both the administration of the pension scheme and the management of the investments of the scheme, HMRC policy was to allow the employer to treat 30% of the VAT as relating to the general management of the scheme, and the pension scheme to treat the remaining 70% as relating to the investment management RCB 06/14 announced a change in HMRC policy following *PPG*. This stated that, subject to certain conditions as set out in the brief, an employer might be able to deduct some VAT incurred in relation to pension fund management/administration which HMRC had previously considered was not so deductible.

In addition, it outlined the process for submitting any claims and provided for a transitional period of six months during which, in specified circumstances, the pension fund and the employer could continue to agree a 70/30 split on the terms set out in VAT Notice 700/17 *Funded Pension Schemes*.

1.3 CURRENT POSITION

Following the publication of RCB 06/14, HMRC have had extensive discussions with industry representatives on how the new policy will apply. In addition to this, the CJEU has issued its decision in *ATP*. *ATP* concerned the VAT treatment of pension scheme administration services provided in relation to a *defined contribution* occupational pension scheme. The CJEU held that some of the services supplied by ATP could qualify for exemption on the basis that the scheme in that case was a "special investment fund" and that the services in question fell within the definition of "management" for the purposes of the VAT exemption which relates to such funds. It also found that certain services provided by ATP, which involved the movement of payments between parties, could qualify for exemption under a different provision of the finance exemptions as transactions concerning payments.

HMRC are now further reviewing the VAT treatment of pension scheme administration and fund management services to take account of both the *PPG* and *ATP* decisions and to consider whether to make any changes to the guidance outlined in Brief 06/14. Further guidance will be issued in the autumn on how both judgments are to be implemented (including a transitional period in which to make any changes). In the meantime, businesses may, if they wish, continue to use the transitional arrangements outlined in the 06/14 Brief.

Any new claims, whether for input tax following *PPG* or in relation to output tax following *ATP*, should be sent to:

Email: vat.ppg.claims@hmrc.gsi.gov.uk
or
by post to:
HMRC
VAT Repayments Team S0483
PO Box 200
BOOTLE L69 9AH

If they have not already done so, businesses that have already made a claim pending the outcome of any of the CJEU litigation concerning the VAT treatment of pension fund management services may wish to provide details of their claim to the email address above.

REVERSE CHARGE FOR WHOLESALE TRADING IN GAS AND ELECTRICITY

29 May 2014. *HMRC Brief 23/14*

ABSTRACT

The VAT reverse charge for wholesale supplies of gas and electricity within the UK, announced at Budget 2014, will apply from 1 July 2014. This brief contains guidance on how the reverse charge will operate, together with a draft order and set of draft regulations to implement the changes. The government announced at the Budget its intention to make this change to prevent missing trader intra-community fraud in the wholesale gas and electricity sectors.

FULL TEXT

VAT: INTRODUCTION OF A DOMESTIC REVERSE CHARGE FOR BUSINESSES WHOLESALE TRADING IN GAS AND ELECTRICITY

1. INTRODUCTION

In this year's Budget the government announced its plans to introduce a reverse charge accounting mechanism (domestic reverse charge) for wholesale supplies of gas and electricity within the UK. This is in response to the threat of missing trader intra-Community (MTIC) fraud in those supplies.

This brief announces the implementation date and publishes the associated draft legislation and guidance on how the domestic reverse charge for wholesale trading in gas and electricity will operate.

2. WHO NEEDS TO READ THIS?

Businesses registered or liable to be registered for VAT that buy or sell wholesale gas and electricity in the UK.

3. BACKGROUND

A domestic reverse charge means the customer receiving wholesale supplies of gas or electricity must account for the VAT due on these supplies on their VAT return rather than the supplier. The customer can deduct the VAT due on the supplies as input tax, meaning no net tax is payable to HM Revenue & Customs (HMRC), subject to the normal rules for reclaiming VAT. This removes the scope for fraudsters to steal the VAT due to HMRC and follows similar measures introduced in response to criminal threats for mobile telephones, computer chips and emissions allowances.

4. TIMING AND SCOPE OF IMPLEMENTATION

4.1 TIMING

The domestic reverse charge will apply to all affected supplies with effect from 1 July 2014. This means that supplies with a tax point on or after that date will be affected by the change.

HMRC recognises this timetable may be challenging for some businesses and will be adopting a "light touch" approach with regard to penalties to assist those who are making reasonable efforts to comply but may not be able to do so in time - see also paragraph 5.5.

4.2 SCOPE

Subject to certain exceptions, the domestic reverse charge will apply to all wholesale supplies of gas and electricity between counterparties established in the UK. This typically means wholesale supplies between UK counterparties under trading contracts (for example European Federation of Energy Traders contracts, Grid Trade Master Agreements and National Balancing Point contracts) and over the counter or spot contracts of:

- gas where it is gas supplied through a natural gas system situated within the territory of a member state or any network connected to such a system, or

- electricity

The domestic reverse charge will not apply to supplies of gas and electricity made under supply licence or metered arrangements to domestic and business premises (supplies for consumption). VAT registered businesses that do not resell or trade the gas or electricity will not be affected.

Examples of specific supplies or charges covered by the reverse charge are:

- balancing mechanism imbalance settlement charges, and other gas balancing or gas reconciliation charges
- electricity supplies under power purchase agreements (including Levy Exemption Certificates and/or Renewable Obligation Certificates to the extent these are under contract with the electricity even if invoiced separately)
- services supplied under a wholesale/trading contract that are ancillary to the supply of gas or electricity
- supplies to power stations and Combined Heating and Power plants will only be included in the domestic reverse charge where they are made by way of trading rather than for consumption only

4.3 EXCLUSIONS

The domestic reverse charge will not apply to:

- supplies made by an accredited feed in installation
- supplies currently zero-rated e.g. trades on terminal markets
- supplies to third party intermediaries & directed utilities for consumption by the directed utility or onward supply by the directed utility to an end user for consumption
- supplies that are contracted for separately from wholesale supplies of gas and electricity, for example transportation services, and
- businesses not registered and not liable to be registered for VAT

Examples of specific supplies or charges unaffected by the domestic reverse charge:

- distribution use of system charges
- transmission network use of system charges
- metering rental charges
- data collection charges
- balancing system use of system charges
- interconnector capacity charges
- gas storage charges
- gas network system charges
- payments made in respect of constraint contracts with National Grid
- balancing and settlement code charges (Elexon market operator charges)
- Levy Exemption Certificates and/or Renewable Obligation Certificates traded separately from the underlying electricity
- fees for exchange related settlement for example N2Ex fees.

The above list is not exhaustive.

5. THE DOMESTIC REVERSE CHARGE MECHANISM

5.1 HOW WILL IT WORK?

Under the domestic reverse charge, it is the responsibility of the customer, not the supplier, to account to HMRC for VAT on specified supplies of gas and electricity. As with the mobile telephone, computer chip and emissions allowances domestic reverse charge measures, it will only apply to business to business transactions in the UK where those businesses are registered or liable to be registered for VAT.

5.2 THE DE MINIMIS RULE AND REVERSE CHARGE SALES LIST

As is the case with the emissions allowances domestic reverse charge:

- there is no de minimis rule excluding supplies under £5,000 so the domestic reverse charge applies to all supplies of gas and electricity, unless those supplies are specifically excluded, and
- businesses will not be required to complete a Reverse Charge Sales List

5.3 THE VAT RETURN

Suppliers of goods under this domestic reverse charge must not enter in box 1 of the VAT return any output tax on sales to which the domestic reverse charge applies, but must enter the value of such sales in box 6.

Customers must enter in box 1 of the VAT return the output tax on purchases to which this domestic reverse charge applies, but must not enter the value of such purchases in box 6. They must reclaim the input tax on their domestic reverse charge purchases in box 4 of the VAT return and include the value of the purchases in box 7, in the normal way.

5.4 INVOICING

When making a supply to which the domestic reverse charge applies, suppliers must:

- show all the information normally required for a VAT invoice
- annotate the invoice to make clear that the domestic reverse charge applies and that the customer is required to account for the VAT

The amount of VAT due under the domestic reverse charge must be clearly stated on the invoice but should not be included in the amount shown as total VAT charged.

Under EC law and the VAT Regulations 1995, invoices for domestic reverse charge supplies, when the customer is liable for the VAT, must include the reference "reverse charge". The following examples fulfill the legal requirement:

- Reverse charge: VAT Act 1994 Section 55A applies
- Reverse charge: VAT Act 1994 Section 55A applies
- Reverse charge: Customer to pay the VAT to HMRC

5.5 PENALTIES

HMRC understands the difficulties businesses may have in implementing the domestic reverse charge and will, where there is no loss of tax, apply a light touch in dealing with errors that occur in the first six months after introduction.

6. CURRENT LAW AND DRAFT LEGISLATION

6.1 CURRENT LAW

- Section 1(2) of the VAT Act 1994 (VATA) makes the supplier liable for any VAT on supplies of goods or services.
- Section 55A of VATA provides that the recipient of a supply must account for the VAT due on supplies of a kind specified in an order made by the Treasury.
- EU legislation in Article 199a of Directive 2006/112/EC allows member states to provide for a domestic reverse charge for certain supplies of gas and electricity.

6.2 DRAFT LEGISLATION

Statutory instruments will bring the relevant changes into effect:

- the Value Added Tax (Section 55A) (Specified Goods and Excepted Supplies) Order 2014, which specifies the goods to which the reverse charge applies and the supplies which are excepted supplies for the purpose of section 55A (Annex A)
- the Value Added Tax (Amendment)(No 2) Regulations 2014, which amends Regulation 23A such that those who make supplies of gas and electricity to which the Value Added Tax (Section 55A) (Specified Goods and Excepted Supplies) Order 2014 applies, will not be required to make reverse charge sales statements (Annex B)

7. FURTHER INFORMATION

Detailed guidance on the other domestic reverse charges can be found in Notice 735: VAT reverse charge on specified goods and services. This will be updated to include guidance for gas and electricity.

Further information can be obtained from the HMRC website or by contacting the Helpline on telephone: 0845 010 9000.

ANNEX A

Not reproduced

ANNEX B

Not reproduced

SPORTING SERVICES SUPPLIED BY NON-PROFIT MAKING BODIES FOLLOWING BRIDPORT AND WEST DORSET GOLF CLUB

26 June 2014. *HMRC Brief 25/14*

ABSTRACT

This brief concerns how HMRC will deal with repayment claims arising from its revised policy following the recent CJEU decision in Bridport & West Dorset Golf Club. HMRC now accepts that supplies of sporting services to both members and non-members of non-profit making sports clubs can qualify to be treated as exempt from VAT. HMRC intends first to deal with repayment claims by members clubs who decide to reimburse non-members. Secondly, it will examine the scope for restricting repayments, on unjust enrichment grounds, to clubs who do not make such reimbursements.

FULL TEXT

VAT: SUPPLIES OF SPORTING SERVICES BY NON-PROFIT MAKING BODIES – IMPLICATIONS OF THE JUDGMENT BY THE EUROPEAN COURT IN BRIDPORT AND WEST DORSET GOLF CLUB LTD (C-495/12)

PURPOSE OF THIS BRIEF

This brief provides an update on HM Revenue & Customs (HMRC) policy following the decision by the Court of Justice of the European Union in Bridport & West Dorset Golf Club in December 2013. It explains HMRC's:

- interpretation of the judgment and the subsequent change to the policy
- approach to repayment claims by non-profit making golf clubs and other members' sports clubs in respect of VAT incorrectly charged to non-members

It also updates the position set out in Revenue & Customs Brief 30/11 issued 27 July 2011.

READERSHIP

Members' golf clubs and other non-profit making sports clubs and their advisers.

BACKGROUND

Bridport and West Dorset Golf Club is a non-profit making members' golf club. Under EU Law supplies by non-profit making bodies of services closely linked and essential to sport to persons taking part in sport are exempt from VAT. In UK law, where the body operates a membership scheme, any supplies to individuals who are not members are excluded from the exemption on the basis that the fees received represent 'additional income' for the purposes of EU Law.

The Bridport appeal concerned green fees paid by visitors (non-members) – Bridport had made a claim for repayment of VAT on green fees arguing that the exclusion of supplies made to non-members was not permissible under EU law.

The European Court of Justice (CJEU) found that where a supply is made by a non-profit making body it is immaterial whether it is provided to a member of the body or a visitor. It took the view that a Member State has no power to exclude certain groups of recipients of services from the benefit of the exemption -'additional income' could not be construed in such a way that it would lead to such a restriction in the scope of the exemption.

The CJEU also rejected the argument that the exclusion of supplies to non-members was permissible on the basis that it had the effect of reducing distortion of competition between members clubs and commercial organisations.

IMPLICATIONS OF THE JUDGMENT

As a result of the CJEU judgment, HMRC accepts that supplies of sporting services to both members and non-members of non-profit making sports clubs qualify to be treated as exempt from VAT. This is provided that the services are closely linked and essential to sport and are made to persons taking part in sport. HMRC will legislate by 1 January 2015 to reflect this.

HMRC will ensure any future changes comply with the decision of the CJEU.

CLAIMS FOR OVERPAID VAT

HMRC intends to deal in two phases with claims for the repayment of overpaid tax for previous periods:

I. PHASE 1. MEMBERS' CLUBS THAT DECIDE TO REIMBURSE NON-MEMBERS WHO WERE INCORRECTLY CHARGED VAT ON SPORTING SERVICES SUPPLIED TO THEM (INCLUDING MEMBERS' GOLF CLUBS THAT INCORRECTLY CHARGED VAT ON GREEN FEES) AND WILL ADOPT THE REIMBURSEMENT ARRANGEMENTS EXPLAINED IN SECTIONS 9 & 10 OF NOTICE NO. 700/45 'HOW TO CORRECT VAT ERRORS AND MAKE ADJUSTMENTS OR CLAIMS'.

Where a members' golf club or other non-profit making sports club considers it has overpaid VAT on sports related services it may make a claim to HMRC under section 80 of the VAT Act 1994 for repayment of VAT incorrectly accounted for. Such claims are subject to the conditions set out in Notice 700/45. This means that clubs will need to demonstrate that they have made arrangements to reimburse the VAT to non-members who actually paid it, and make a legally binding commitment to do so in a timely manner.

Claimants who intend to reimburse non-members need to ensure that their claim is adjusted to reflect any over claim of input tax by application of their partial exemption and/or capital goods scheme calculations as appropriate before advising HMRC they wish to proceed under Phase 1.

HMRC will meet eligible claims under the terms of sections 9 & 10 of Notice 700/45 providing the conditions are met. HMRC reserves the right to examine the quantum of the claim, including the requirement to apply revised partial exemption and capital goods scheme calculations as appropriate. All Phase 1 claims should be sent to the following address:

VAT Bridport Claims S0483
PO Box 200
BOOTLE L69 9AH

II. PHASE 2. CLUBS THAT DO NOT ADOPT REIMBURSEMENT ARRANGEMENTS

HMRC are examining the scope for restricting repayments to clubs not making arrangements to reimburse the paying non-members to avoid the unjust enrichment of members' clubs. Further advice will be issued on these claims after a conclusion has been reached on this point.

EXISTING CLAIMS

Where a submitted claim has already been rejected by HMRC and the claimant has not appealed, that claim cannot now be resubmitted. Any claims submitted now will be a new claim subject to the four-year time limit.

Rejected claims that were appealed to the First Tier Tribunal, however, are still open.

If a claimant wishes to claim any additional amounts in respect of non-members that were either overlooked or the result of calculation errors for accounting periods in the original claim, that claim can be amended. However, this only applies where the amendment is, for example, the correction of an arithmetical error or the inclusion of elements, non-members, etc. that were within the contemplation of the original claim. If the claimant wishes to claim for something not within the contemplation of the previous claims or for new accounting periods, a new claim will need to be submitted just for these items.

NEW CLAIMS

All new claims will be subject to the four-year time limit in section 80(4) of the VAT Act 1994.

Claims made should be adjusted for any amounts due to set-off under section 81(3) of the VAT Act 1994 (outstanding debts, assessments, etc.) and section 130 of the Finance Act 2008 (outstanding debts under any other head of taxation). In particular, claimants will need to adjust for any resultant over claim of input tax by application of the appropriate partial exemption calculation. In some cases, it may be necessary to revisit Capital Goods Scheme adjustments.

All new claims should be sent to the same address as for Phase 1 claims above.

ALL CLAIMS (WHETHER NEW OR EXISTING CLAIMS)

Finally, it should be noted that where amounts of overpaid output tax are repaid and not re-imbursed to affected customers, there may be direct tax implications. For example, trading income from non-members is taxable and therefore any surplus of non-member income that remains after the deduction of relevant expenses is liable to Corporation Tax.

HMRC SHARING OF NON-FINANCIAL VAT REGISTRATION DATA AND EXPORTER DATA

25 June 2014. *HMRC Brief 26/14*

ABSTRACT

The Government is seeking powers through the Small Business, Enterprise and Employment Bill which would permit HMRC to release non-financial VAT registration data and permit the release of exporter data as open data. HMRC consulted in July 2013 on proposals to share VAT registration data and is currently consulting until 19 September 2014 on the proposal to release a specific export data set.

FULL TEXT

PURPOSE OF THE BRIEF

HMRC data sharing measures are being taken forward in the Small Business, Enterprise and Employment Bill which was announced in the Queen's Speech on 4 June 2014 and published on 25 June 2014. The Government is seeking a power permitting HMRC to release non-financial VAT registration data for specific purposes (principally credit scoring) to a small number of qualifying parties (for example, credit reference agencies), and is seeking a power to make regulations (after consultation) to permit the release of exporter data as open data.

WHO NEEDS TO READ THIS?

VAT registered businesses and exporting businesses which may benefit from having their data shared, for example through an improved trade credit rating or through access to export data. Potential users of the data which is expected to be released.

SHARING OF NON-FINANCIAL VAT REGISTRATION DATA

VAT registration data is drawn from the data collected or created when traders register for VAT or update a registration. This data includes the VAT registration number (VRN), business and/or proprietor names, contact and status details (a full list is available at Annex C in the Government's consultation at the link below). The data is identifying data only: no financial or payment data of any kind is included.

The proposed legislation would give HMRC the power to release non-financial VAT registration data on a strictly controlled basis for these economically beneficial purposes: credit scoring, anti-fraud checking, and compliance with other financial regulation. Potential users include credit providers, credit reference agencies and other business information providers.

In July 2013, the Government consulted on proposals to share VAT registration data. HMRC also undertook a research project to assess the potential benefits from the use of VAT registration data. Both documents are available at the link below.

The research indicates that the use of VAT registration data for credit scoring by credit reference agencies would increase availability of trade credit to VAT registered businesses by up to £1.8

billion, with an estimated uptake of trade credit of between £0.7 billion - £1.4 billion. Smaller businesses, recently incorporated businesses and unincorporated businesses (e.g. sole traders) would be the main beneficiaries.

Data sharing will be subject to rigorous safeguards. Users will be selected on transparent criteria based on their ability to use the data for the permitted purposes and to comply with stringent requirements. There will be sanctions for data misuse, including a criminal sanction for unlawful disclosure of information relating to identifiable businesses. In addition, the agreements for release will contain rigorous rules and penalties for any breach, covering transfer, handling and use, storage and destruction of the data. Guidance will be published detailing the criteria for data sharing.

VAT registered businesses and their owners will be protected against intrusions on privacy, fraud and other impacts (eg, increased direct mail) by ensuring that the data can only be used for the permitted purposes and cannot be passed on to other users. No financial or payment data will be included in any release.

HMRC will not sell VAT registration data. It may recover costs associated with data sharing in line with Government guidance.

In parallel, HMRC will continue to explore options for the public release of a limited subset of VAT registration data as open data. HMRC will work with stakeholders to identify data which might be appropriate for a partial open data release. Release of a data field will not be considered where it would impinge on personal privacy or increase fraud risk.

Further background on the proposals and the documents referred to above: /www.gov.uk/government/consultations/sharing-and-publishing-data-for-public-benefit.

SHARING OF EXPORTER DATA

Information about exporters and the products they export is collected by HMRC from a customs declaration which has to be submitted to HMRC when goods are exported to non-EU countries.

The data being proposed for release as open data is the name and address of the exporter, description and commodity code of the goods and the month and year of export. No financial, duty or tax information is to be released.

Making a limited amount of export data available has the potential for it to be used in ways that could generate real public benefits without compromising the core principle of taxpayer confidentiality. There is increasing interest from both the public and private sectors in release of exporter data as a key information source to generate benefits. It would make exporters more visible in the global market place and significantly increase the ability for foreign buyers to search for and buy British products and help public and private sector efforts to provide better targeted and appropriate services to exporting businesses, especially SMEs.

This information is already largely in the public domain having being placed there by businesses themselves, for example in business directories and advertising on the internet and elsewhere, and on commercial stationery and invoices. However, the data is not always readily accessible or systematically available as a full set and may not always be managed and kept up to date. Release by HMRC of exporter data would provide a comprehensive source of accurate and up to date information.

HMRC has made similar information on importers available for over 25 years and we are not aware of any issues. Restricting proposals on publication of exporter data to a core set of similar, potentially less contentious but still valuable information would provide a credible minimum data release that could realise a range of benefits without compromising privacy or commercial confidentiality interests.

HMRC will be undertaking a full 12 week consultation on the proposal to release a specific export data set. This will be done in parallel with the passage of enabling legislation through Parliament and importantly before any regulation necessary to implement the measure is introduced.

The consultation: Sharing and publishing export data for public benefit: www.gov.uk/government/consultations/sharing-and-publishing-export-data-for-public-benefit.

NEXT STEPS

The measures are being taken forward in the Small Business, Enterprise and Employment Bill.

CHANGES IN POLICY ON TOGCS

9 July 2014. *HMRC Brief 27/14*

ABSTRACT

Following its consideration of the FTT decision in Robinson Family Ltd, HMRC has announced three shifts in policy: (1) accepting in principle that the surrender of a lease can be a transfer of a going concern (TOGC) for VAT purposes; (2) confirming that the change announced in R&C Brief 30/2012 on whether the grant of a lease can be a TOGC applies generally and is not confined to property letting businesses; and (3) accepting that a person acquiring a completed residential or charitable development as part of a TOGC inherits 'person constructing' status and is capable of making a zero-rated first grant of an interest.

FULL TEXT

This Brief explains a number of changes relating to the transfer of a business as a going concern (TOGC)

PURPOSE OF THE BRIEF

This Brief explains a number of changes relating to the transfer of a business as a going concern (TOGC):

- a change in HM Revenue & Customs' (HMRC's) policy on whether the surrender of a property lease can be a VAT-free TOGC
- to clarify the scope of certain aspects of the policy change announced in RC Brief 30/12
- to explain a change in policy concerning TOGCs of new residential and relevant charitable developments.

READERSHIP

This Brief is for those who transfer their business as a going concern together with an interest in property.

ACTION REQUIRED

To note the contents of this Brief and to treat future transactions accordingly.

SCOTLAND

For the purposes of this Brief all references to "surrender" of a lease include the renunciation of a lease in Scotland, all references to "assignment" of a lease include the assignation of a lease in Scotland and all references to a "reversion" retained by a transferor include the heritable title retained by the landlord in Scotland.

1. SURRENDER OF A PROPERTY LEASE

INTRODUCTION

When the assets of a business (or part of a business) are transferred as a going concern no supply of those assets takes place for VAT purposes. There are certain conditions to be met for the transfer not to be treated as a supply for VAT purposes, among which is that the buyer must intend to use the assets to carry on the same kind of business as the seller.

This intention can be relevant where:

- an occupier sells a business including the trading premises
- a landlord sells a property subject to tenancies
- in some cases where a developer sells a development that is currently in progress

Further guidance can be found in Notice 700/9 and in HMRC's manual Transfer of a going concern.

If the seller is a tenant, an outright disposal of the property might take the form either of an assignment of the lease or a surrender of the lease.

In an assignment, the buyer simply becomes the new tenant under the lease. HMRC has long accepted that, if the other conditions were met, the assignment of a lease with the benefit of a sublease could be a TOGC.

In a surrender, however, the buyer is the landlord, and the lease will normally merge with the landlord's existing interest in the land and will cease to exist. HMRC has historically taken the view that, where this happens, the transaction could not be a TOGC because the landlord would not use the same asset, the lease, in carrying on the business. This policy has now changed.

CHANGE OF POLICY

The Tribunal in *Robinson Family Limited* [2012] UKFTT 360 (TC), TC02046 held that the grant of a lease could in some circumstances be a TOGC, and indicated that "one must look to the substance of the transaction" rather than its form. In the light of that decision, we announced a change of policy on grants of leases in Revenue & Customs Brief 30/12, and said that we were reviewing the position with surrenders of leases. We have now concluded that review.

HMRC now considers that there is in principle no obstacle to the surrender of a lease being a TOGC, subject to all the normal conditions. This will apply, for instance, where a tenant subletting premises by way of business subsequently surrenders its interest in the property together with the benefit of the subtenants, or where a retailer sells its retailing business to its landlord. In substance the landlord has acquired the tenant's business. Note that this applies equally where the landlord's interest is held via one or more nominees, so that the transaction involves a transfer to the nominee(s) for the landlord's benefit.

SUPERSEDED GUIDANCE

This revised policy on the surrender of a property lease supersedes the guidance in HM-RC's manual at VTOGC6450, which will be amended shortly.

EFFECTIVE DATE

While this change of policy is immediate, we accept that there may be situations where customers need to make contractual or systems changes. In order to accommodate this, we are content for customers to delay implementing the change to 4 weeks from the date of this RCB provided that the transferor and transferee both agree to this.

RETROSPECTION: VAT

We accept there will be cases where in the past, businesses did not regard a surrender of a lease as constituting a TOGC in the light of HMRC's then policy, and may now be able to do so, subject to the normal time limits. In such circumstances VAT may have been charged where it need not have been.

Alternatively, input tax may have been restricted because the surrender was treated as an exempt supply.

Where VAT was charged, a difficulty is that the relevant notification (that an option to tax would not be rendered ineffective), will not normally have been given by the buyer (the landlord) to the seller (the tenant). This is a legal requirement in articles 5(2A) and 5(2B) of the VAT (Special Provisions) Order 1995, and it is referred to in paragraph 11.2 of Notice 742A: Opting to tax land and buildings.

Provided, however, that the parties can satisfactorily evidence that article 5(2B) did not apply at the time of the transaction and thus the requisite notification could have been given, we will accept that the legal requirement has been complied with.

Details of how to make any adjustments relating to previous VAT Return periods can be found in VAT Notice 700/45 *How to correct VAT errors and make adjustments or claims* and from the VAT Helpline on 0300 200 3700.

RETROSPECTION: SDLT

There may be situations where a past overpayment of VAT resulted in an overpayment of Stamp Duty Land Tax (SDLT), because SDLT was assessed on a value that incorrectly included VAT.

If a business believes that it has overpaid SDLT, it may make a claim for overpayment relief. The legislation relating to such claims is at schedule 10, paragraph 34, FA 2003.

The criteria that must be met and the exclusions from claims are set out at paragraph 34A of Schedule 10. Guidance can be found in the Stamp Duty Land Tax Manual (SDLTM) at SDLTM52500 and 54000.

Case G (liability calculated in accordance with practice generally prevailing - SDLTM54170) will not apply, and will therefore not exclude a claim where the amount of the chargeable consideration has been reduced as a result of the seller refunding the VAT.

Claims must be made within four years of the date of transaction. HMRC will be unable to accept any refund requests for transactions that took place more than four years before the date of claim. HMRC will also not refund SDLT unless the overpaid VAT has also been refunded.

2. CLARIFICATION OF POLICY CHANGE ANNOUNCED IN RC BRIEF 30/12

Revenue & Customs Brief 30/12 announced a change of policy on whether the grant of a lease could be a TOGC, but referred only to the transfer of a property rental business. We said then that we were reviewing whether the change of policy also affected properties used in a business other than property letting. An example would be where a retailer disposes of the retail business but transfers the premises by granting a lease.

We have completed this review, and concluded that the change of policy referred to in Revenue & Customs Brief 30/12 applies generally, and is not confined to property letting businesses. The same applies to the change of policy with respect to surrenders announced in this Revenue & Customs Brief.

In Revenue & Customs Brief 30/12, we also said that if the value of the interest retained by the transferor was no more than 1 per cent of the value of the property immediately before the transfer (disregarding any mortgage or charge) that this reversion would be sufficiently small that TOGC treatment could still apply.

This did not address the situation where the lease was of part of a building only.

We have been asked whether, in this case, the 1 per cent calculation considers the value of the entire building, or the value of the part over which the lease is granted.

It was always our intention that the calculation should be based on the relevant part of the building only, and that other areas of the building should be ignored in the calculation, as set out in the example below:

> A Ltd owns the freehold of a four-storey building, valued at £4m, which A Ltd rents out commercially. The freehold in each floor is worth £1m. A Ltd sells its property rental business in one of the floors by granting to B Ltd a 999 year lease of that floor, under which A Ltd is entitled to receive a ground rent of £100 each year. The value of that right, together with any and all other rights retained by A Ltd in that floor, is £2,000.
> A Ltd has retained 0.2 per cent of the value of its interest in the one floor, and 75.2 per cent of the value of its interest in the building as a whole. The 1 per cent figure mentioned in Revenue & Customs Brief 30/12 is to be considered in relation to the one floor alone. Provided all the normal conditions are satisfied, the transaction will be a TOGC, because HMRC will regard the 0.2 per cent interest retained as too small to disturb the substance of the transaction.

3. REVISION TO GUIDANCE CONCERNING TOGCS OF NEW DEVELOPMENTS OF DWELLINGS, RELEVANT RESIDENTIAL AND RELEVANT CHARITABLE BUILDINGS

The first grant of a major interest (freehold sale or long lease) in residential or relevant charitable property by the "person constructing" is generally zero-rated (as explained in Notice 708 *Buildings and construction and VCONST - Construction*). The zero rate is designed to ensure that the development of such properties is ordinarily, largely VAT free.

We have traditionally taken the view that "person constructing" status does not move to a person acquiring a completed building that is transferred as a going concern - this position is published in our technical manual in VCONST03560. However, recent cases in this area have highlighted that such transactions could lead to inequality of VAT treatment that is contrary to the purpose of the zero rate and could be in breach of the EU Principle of Fiscal Neutrality.

Having reviewed the position, we now accept that a person acquiring a completed residential or charitable development as part of a transfer of a going concern inherits 'person constructing' status and is capable of making a zero rated first major interest grant in that building or part of it as long as:

(a) a zero rated grant has not already been made of the completed building or relevant part by a previous owner (for this purpose, HMRC consider that the grant that gives rise to the TOGC should be disregarded);

(b) the person acquiring the building as a TOGC would suffer an unfair VAT disadvantage if its first major interest grants were treated as exempt (for example, a developer restructures its business. This entails the transfer (as a TOGC) of its entire property portfolio of newly constructed residential/charitable buildings to an associated company, which will make first major interest grants. If these were treated as exempt, the transferee might become liable to repay input tax recovered by the original owner on development costs under the Capital Goods Scheme or partial exemption "claw back" provisions and would incur input tax restrictions on selling fees that would not be suffered by businesses in similar circumstances - we would consider this to be an unfair disadvantage); and

(c) that person would not obtain an unfair VAT advantage by being in a position to make zero rated supplies (for example, by recovering input tax on a refurbishment of an existing building).

We will be amending our guidance in VCONST03560 in due course.

The above guidelines also apply in respect of "person converting" status (for buildings converted from non-residential to residential use) and "person substantially reconstructing" status (for substantially reconstructed listed buildings).

Although "person constructing" status may now transfer as part of the TOGC of a property, the "change of use provisions" would still need to be considered in the case of relevant residential and charitable buildings, i.e. the change in policy on person constructing does not dis-apply the change of use provisions.

Businesses are entitled to claim retrospective effect of this policy (subject to capping) if they fit within the above criteria.

ALTERNATIVES TO ONLINE FILING OF VAT RETURNS

29 July 2014. *HMRC Brief 29/14*

ABSTRACT

This brief concerns amending regulations which took effect from 1 July 2014, enabling HMRC to approve alternatives to electronic filing of VAT returns, including by phone and paper, for those unable to file online for reasons of age, disability or remoteness of location.

FULL TEXT

VAT: AMENDMENTS TO REGULATIONS FOR ONLINE FILING OF VAT RETURNS

WHO NEEDS TO READ THIS

VAT registered businesses who are unable to file their VAT returns online for reasons of age, disability or remoteness of location.

BACKGROUND

The vast majority of businesses were legally mandated to file their VAT returns online from 1 April 2012. Most have found it easy to make the transition from paper filing to online filing. However, some businesses contacted HMRC to explain their difficulties in filing VAT returns online. In such circumstances, we advise businesses of a range of digital assistance options to help them to meet their legal obligations. Such options include using public libraries, using computers owned by friends and family, using the services of an agent or, if none of these options are appropriate, using the existing Filing by Telephone service ("telephone filing").

FIRST TIER TRIBUNAL RULING

In response to appeals against the requirement to file online, the First-tier Tribunal (in the case of *L.H. Bishop Electrical Co Ltd* [2013] UKFTT 522 (TC)) ruled that UK VAT law failed to take account of a person's ability to comply on account of:

- age
- disability
- computer illiteracy (linked to age)
- remoteness of location

And, as such, was a breach of the European Convention on Human Rights (ECHR).

The judge also held that HMRC could not rely on the fact that telephone filing had been made available to certain businesses to cure the aforementioned human rights breach as it had not been legislated for or properly publicised.

CHANGES TO LEGISLATION

Following a formal consultation exercise, Regulation 25A of VAT Regulations 1995 (SI 1995/2518) has been amended to:

- enable HMRC to make a Commissioners' direction approving telephone filing as an alternative method of electronic filing for use by businesses that satisfy HMRC that it is not reasonably practicable for them to use the current method of online filing
- provide an additional exemption from electronic filing for businesses that satisfy HMRC that it is not reasonably practicable for them to use an online channel with the result that such businesses will be able to file on paper

TIMING

Changes to legislation took effect from 1 July 2014.

FURTHER INFORMATION

For further information please contact the VAT Helpline on Telephone: 0300 200 3700. The Helpline is available Monday to Friday, 8am to 6pm. If you have hearing difficulties you can use the Textphone service on 0300 200 3719.

VAT RECOVERY BY HOLDING COMPANIES FOLLOWING BAA DECISION

25 September 2014. *HMRC Brief 32/14*

ABSTRACT

HMRC has updated its VAT Input Tax Manual in relation to input tax recovery by holding companies, following the Court of Appeal decision in BAA Ltd. Although HMRC states its policy has not changed, the new guidance covers: when a shareholding is used as part of an economic activity; when VAT may be recoverable by a holding company; the effect of a holding company joining a VAT group; and how to treat mixed economic and non-economic activities. HMRC will review its policy again following the CJEU's judgments in two German cases, expected in approximately 12 to 18 months.

FULL TEXT

1. PURPOSE OF THIS BRIEF

This Revenue and Customs brief confirms that HM Revenue and Customs (HMRC) has reviewed its policy following the decision of the Court of Appeal in the case of *British Airport Authority (BAA)* ([2013] EWCA Civ 112) [2013] STC 752. The decision confirms that VAT is only recoverable where there is a direct and immediate link to taxable supplies. BAA was refused permission to appeal to the Supreme Court. For the purpose of this brief, "taxable supplies" includes supplies not charged to UK VAT, but which carry a right to input tax recovery.

Following this decision there is no change in HMRC's policy. However the facts in BAA related to particular circumstances and the decision does not address other commonly encountered issues relating to holding companies. HMRC has therefore updated its guidance to set out when HMRC considers that VAT recovery may be possible.

The revised guidance can be found at VAT Input Tax Manual.

Taxpayers should be aware that the German cases of *Larentia + Minerva & others* (C-108/14 and C-109/14) have been referred to the Court of Justice of the European Union (CJEU). The decision in those cases is likely to be relevant to the issues described in this brief and the guidance referred to in this brief. HMRC will review the policy contained in the guidance in the light of the CJEU's determination of this reference, which is expected in approximately 12 to 18 months.

2. BACKGROUND

A UK company, Airport Development and Investments Ltd (ADIL), which was owned by an investment consortium, made a bid to acquire the entire issued share capital of BAA plc. During this process ADIL received supplies of services in connection with the takeover bid. The takeover bid was successful and, subsequently, ADIL joined the BAA VAT group which then sought to recover the VAT that ADIL had incurred on those services.

The Court of Appeal noted that there are 2 conditions for the recovery of VAT. Firstly the tax must be incurred by a taxable person in the course of an economic activity. Secondly the goods and services on which the VAT is incurred must have a direct and immediate link with taxable supplies made by that person.

The Court of Appeal held that the BAA VAT group was not entitled to recover the VAT incurred on the costs of acquisition because when ADIL incurred the VAT:

- it was not carrying on an economic activity for VAT purposes, but was merely intending to takeover BAA plc by acquiring the shares in it, and
- there was no direct and immediate link between the services received by ADIL and the taxable supplies made by the BAA VAT group

The Court of Appeal found that ADIL did not make, nor intend to make, taxable supplies of goods or services at the time the VAT was incurred. Acquiring the shares had economic consequences, but that did not mean ADIL was engaged in an economic activity for VAT purposes.

3. NEW GUIDANCE COVERS THE FOLLOWING ISSUES

- when a shareholding is used as part of an economic activity
- when VAT may be recoverable by a holding company
- the effect of a holding company joining a VAT Group
- how to treat mixed economic and non-economic activities

DEVELOPING A DIGITAL SYSTEM FOR THE VAT RETAIL EXPORT SCHEME

26 September 2014. *HMRC Brief 34/14*

ABSTRACT

HMRC is inviting businesses wishing to be involved in development of a digital system for tax-free shopping (the VAT Retail Export Scheme) to register by 14 October 2014 for an event to be held later in October. HMRC consulted on proposals to improve the scheme between July and September 2013.

FULL TEXT

VAT RETAIL EXPORT SCHEME – MARKET ENGAGEMENT ON A DIGITAL SOLUTION

INTRODUCTION

Businesses interested in working with HM Revenue and Customs (HMRC) to develop a digital system to support the VAT Retail Export Scheme (RES) are invited to register for a forthcoming market engagement event.

This brief sets out the background to the event and explains how to register.

WHO NEEDS TO READ THIS?

Any business interested in working with HMRC to develop a digital VAT RES system.

BACKGROUND

The VAT Retail Export Scheme – known as Tax Free Shopping – allows visitors from outside the EU to claim a refund of VAT on goods they buy and export from the EU in their personal luggage.

HMRC has been reviewing the scheme since Budget 2013, with the key objectives of improving the customer experience and protecting VAT revenue. A formal consultation ran from 1 July to 30 September 2013.

The government's response to the consultation acknowledged that a digital solution was the leading option for change and committed to explore this. It was also noted that any digital solution would be dependent on a strong business case and finding an acceptable means of funding.

A number of interim improvements to the current operation of the scheme were also set out. This work is being taken forward and a separate communication will be sent to registered stakeholders in early October.

MARKET ENGAGEMENT EVENT

The next step in the development of a digital solution is a market engagement event which HMRC will host in October 2014. We will use the event to develop our requirements for a digital system and gain a better understanding of supplier capabilities and interest in helping to develop and fund a solution. Businesses interested in working with HMRC to develop and deliver a digital solution will be required to register to attend the market engagement event.

Details on how to register for the event, together with a summary of HMRC's evolving high-level requirements for a digital system, are contained in the Prior Information Notice. More details on the event will be provided to those who register.

If you have any queries about this update or the review, please email: resconsultation.idt@hmrc.gsi.gov.uk

LOK'NSTORE GROUP PLC DECISION ON CALCULATING DEDUCTIBLE VAT

10 October 2014. *HMRC Brief 35/14*

FULL TEXT

PURPOSE OF THIS BRIEF

This brief sets out HM Revenue and Customs' (HMRC) position following the decision of the Upper Tribunal (UT) in Lok'nStore Group PLC (LnS). The case concerned whether the Partial Exemption Special Method (PESM) proposed by LnS produced a more fair and reasonable result for calculating deductible VAT on overheads than the standard method.

The UT dismissed HMRC's appeal on the grounds that it could not find that that the First Tier Tribunal (FTT) had erred in law in concluding that the PESM produced a more fair and reasonable result than the standard method. HMRC is not appealing the decision, but does not intend to change its policy regarding floor space PESMs. HMRC does not consider that floor space methods are usually appropriate for the retail sector.

You can read the full text of the decision on the CURIA website: UKUT/TCC/2014/2881.1

BACKGROUND

LnS provides taxable self-storage facilities in purpose built stores. It also provides exempt insurance for stored goods to all customers who do not otherwise have adequate cover. The issue in this case was the amount of input VAT that could be recovered on general overhead costs, such as those incurred on the construction, maintenance and operation of its stores.

LnS proposed a PESM which involved a floor space allocation resulting in a 99.98% recovery rate for VAT on overheads. HMRC rejected this on the grounds that it did not provide for a better reflection of how the costs were used than the standard method.

Relying on the 'cost component of the price' test set out in AB SKF (C-29/08), the FTT concluded that the impact of the general overheads on the price of the insurance 'must be very small' and therefore these costs are only used to a very small extent for the supplies of insurance. It also found that the Appellant used the storage area of the buildings 'almost exclusively' for taxable storage. Accordingly it found that the proposed special method was fair and reasonable and better reflected use than the standard method, so allowed the appeal.

HMRC appealed to the UT on the grounds that the FTT had erred in law in that they had applied the wrong test, that they erred in their application of that test by stating that the price of insurance was set by reference to the market rate rather than the overhead costs, and that they erred in their approach to assessing economic use by adopting a method based on physical use.1.2

THE UPPER TRIBUNALS DECISION

Although the UT agreed that the FTT had indeed erred in law in applying the cost component test, it was not convinced that this led to an incorrect result.

In respect to the FTT's conclusion that the overhead costs were not cost components of the insurance, the UT reasoned that there were a number of possible ways to reach that conclusion and it was therefore impossible to conclude that the FTT had misdirected itself.

In relation to HMRC's argument that the FTT had relied on physical use rather than economic use, the UT said that although the use of the standard method appeared to be justified, it was unable to say that it was the only reasonably possible way of looking at the matter. For the above reasons, the appeal was dismissed.1.3

HMRC'S VIEW OF THE DECISION

HMRC's view of the decision The decision makes clear that whether an input cost is a cost component of an output is highly fact specific.

Despite upholding the FTT decision, the UT emphasised by reference to Etherton LJ in London Clubs that close attention must be paid to the facts of each case in understanding and assessing the economic or commercial reality underlying the use of the relevant VAT inputs.

In the LnS case, the FTT found that the VAT bearing costs in question were only cost components of insurance to a very slight extent. Where VAT bearing costs are used only slightly for exempt supplies, then HMRC agrees that a method which results in almost full recovery is appropriate.

However, the decision could be interpreted to suggest that a cost can only be a cost component of an output supply if the price of that output was set by reference to the cost. HMRC would not agree with that interpretation.

Even where the price of an output transaction is not set by reference to particular costs, those costs can still be incorporated into the price in that they contribute to its value. This was the conclusion of the Tribunal in TLLC Ltd v Revenue and Customs [2013] UKFTT 467 (TC).

Accordingly, although we are not challenging the UT decision in LnS, we do not consider that the decision has any further implications for our policy on floor space PESMs.1.4

HMRC'S POSITION

HMRC does not consider that floor space PESMs are normally appropriate for retail businesses. This view has not changed as a result of the LnS decision.

Businesses wishing to apply for a new or amended PESM similar to that in LnS will need to demonstrate that the overhead costs are not cost components of their exempt supplies, and that they do not intend to recover those costs through their exempt outputs.

VAT ZERO-RATING FOR MARSHMALLOW "SNOWBALLS"

14 October 2014. *HMRC Brief 36/14*

ABSTRACT

HMRC is changing its policy on the VAT treatment of marshmallow and chocolate "snowballs", following the recent decision of the FTT in *Lees of Scotland Ltd and Thomas Tunnock Ltd* that this type of confectionery possesses sufficient characteristics of a cake to be zero-rated.

FULL TEXT

1. PURPOSE OF THIS BRIEF

This brief sets out HM Revenue and Customs' (HMRC) position following the decision of the First Tier Tribunal. The case concerned the VAT liability of a food item and whether or not it was confectionary (standard rated) or a cake (zero-rated)?

2. READERSHIP

This Revenue and Customs brief is aimed at businesses that manufacture and/or sell this type of confectionery known as "snowballs" that are the same as those manufactured by Lees of Scotland and Thomas Tunnock Ltd.

3. BACKGROUND

Both taxpayers challenged a previous ruling that "snowballs" were standard rated confectionery by claiming they were also cakes and submitted voluntary disclosures for VAT they claimed was overcharged. HMRC disagreed with this view and so the matter was decided by the First Tier Tribunal.

4. THE TRIBUNAL DECISION

The Tribunal considered what factors should be considered when identifying whether a product is a cake. They used a number of factors derived from the authorities that fell to be weighted in the balance, namely:

- ingredients
- process and manufacture
- unpackaged appearance
- taste and texture
- circumstances of consumption
- packaging
- marketing
- self life
- name/description
- "how it behaves" after it is removed from packaging

In keeping with previous classification exercises the Tribunal acknowledged that there are no objective tests that can be imposed to determine whether a particular item of confectionery is or is not a cake, and that each case must turn on its own particular facts.

The Tribunal did not dispute that these snowball products are confectionery. After considering all of the above factors they accepted that whilst these snowballs do not have all of the characteristics of a cake they decided that they do have sufficient characteristics of a cake for them to be characterised as a cake. This means that they can be zero rated for VAT purposes.

5. CHANGES TO HMRC'S POLICY

HMRC consider that the borderline between confectionery and cake causes few problems, but with the ever changing selection of confectionery available there will always be some products whose status as cakes is not necessarily self-evident. These snowballs are an example of this type of product. The Tribunal has made its decision based upon the particular facts before them and HMRC have accepted that decision and will be updating their guidance in respect of this type of snowball in due course.

In this case a "snowball" was found to be a dome of marshmallow coated in any combination of the following:

- chocolate
- sugar strands
- carob
- cocoa
- coconut

which may or may not include a jam filling. Of course, products which are also called "snowballs" but not the same as those in this case may not be zero-rated.

VAT PRs etc

6. IMPLEMENTATION OF THE TRIBUNAL RULING

As a result of this Tribunal decision HMRC is changing its policy on the VAT classification of this type of snowball confectionery. Guidance and Public Notice 701/14 *Food* will be updated shortly to reflect these changes in VAT treatment.

7. CLAIMS AND RETROSPECTIVE ACTION

If you have supplied "snowballs" that are the same as those in this case, you may wish to refer to Public Notice VAT 700/45 "*How to correct VAT errors and make adjustments or claims*" explains how to go about claiming a refund. Any claims made will be subject to the unjust enrichment rules and the 4 year CAP in line with normal HMRC procedures.

EFFECT OF SKANDIA CASE ON VAT GROUPING RULES

13 October 2014. *HMRC Brief 37/14*

ABSTRACT

HMRC is considering what impact, if any, the CJEU judgment in *Skandia America Corp* has on the UK VAT grouping rules and will provide an update in due course. The case concerned services supplied from a main establishment in the US to its branch in Sweden, for which the court held the Swedish group was liable to VAT. The judgment did not consider the UK VAT grouping rules specifically, which differ from the Swedish rules.

FULL TEXT

1. PURPOSE OF THIS BRIEF

This revenue and customs brief outlines HM Revenue and Customs' (HMRC) position following the European Court of Justice (ECJ) judgment in *Skandia America Corp. (USA), filial Sverige* (C-7/13). The case concerned the interaction of VAT grouping rules on transactions between establishments of a business established both outside and inside Sweden. The ECJ found that the effect of the Swedish rules was that there was a taxable supply for VAT purposes. HMRC is considering whether the judgment has any application to UK grouping provisions, which are different to those in Sweden.

2. BACKGROUND

Skandia America Corporation is a company incorporated in the United States. It has a fixed establishment in Sweden. The Swedish branch became part of a Swedish VAT group.

The Swedish court referred 2 questions to the ECJ:

(i) whether supplies of services from a main establishment in a third country to its branch in a member state constitute taxable transactions when that branch belongs to a VAT group in the member state in which the branch is established; and, if so

(1) whether the person liable to pay the VAT is the supplier (the main establishment in the third country) or the recipient (the VAT group in the member state) of the services

The ECJ noted that under Swedish grouping provisions, the main establishment of Skandia America Corporation and the VAT group were separate taxable persons and accordingly found that the supplies in question constituted taxable transactions. Under the reverse charge procedures (Article 196 of the PVD), as the recipient of these services, the VAT group is liable for VAT.

3. IMPACT ON THE UK

It is important to note that the UK VAT grouping rules differ from the Swedish VAT grouping rules. The judgment did not consider what the position under the UK rules should be nor did it consider whether the Swedish rules were the only permissible VAT grouping rules. Accordingly we will need to consider carefully what impact, if any, this decision has on the UK rules and whether any changes to legislation are required.

4. ACTION TO TAKE

HMRC is carefully considering the decision and will provide a further update in due course. In the meantime, businesses should continue to follow existing guidance.

VAT: COMPULSORY CHARGE ON SINGLE-USE CARRIER BAGS IN SCOTLAND

16 October 2014. *HMRC Brief 38/14*

ABSTRACT

The Scottish Parliament introduced a compulsory 5p charge on single use carrier bags provided with goods supplied in or from Scotland with effect from 20 October 2014. The charge is consideration for the bag and is taxable at the standard rate of VAT. Receipts from the charge should be brought into account in calculating trading profits for corporation tax and income tax purposes.

FULL TEXT

INTRODUCTION

- from 20 October 2014 the Scottish Parliament will introduce a compulsory charge on single use carrier bags provided with goods supplied in or from Scotland
- this is not a HM Revenue and Customs measure. However, there are implications for VAT, Corporation Tax and Income Tax
- this brief explains the basics of the charge and the tax implications

WHO NEEDS TO READ THIS?

Suppliers of goods in Scotland who sell or deliver goods using single use carrier bags.

BACKGROUND

The Scottish Parliament is to introduce a compulsory charge on single use carrier bags set at a minimum of 5 pence. This charge will apply on single use carrier bags supplied with goods, supplied in or delivered from Scotland. The legislation takes effect from 20 October 2014.

VAT IMPLICATIONS

- where suppliers are liable to charge VAT, the amount they charge for a bag is tax inclusive at the standard rate of VAT. For a VAT registered business charging 5 pence, the taxable amount will be 4.17 pence and the VAT 83 pence
- suppliers using a Retail Scheme should ensure that VAT is properly accounted through their scheme
- non-VAT registered suppliers must still charge the same minimum amount of 5 pence

DIRECT TAX IMPLICATIONS

- for Corporation Tax and Income Tax, receipts from the compulsory charge on single use carrier bags should be brought into account in calculating trading profits
- the Scottish Government expects the proceeds to fund good causes in Scotland. Relief may be available where the normal charitable donations/gift aid rules are met

FURTHER INFORMATION

Information about how the charge will operate is available from the Scottish Parliament website: carrierbagchargescotland.org.uk/.

VAT PRs etc

VAT EXEMPTION FOR CATERING AND OTHER SERVICES LINKED TO EDUCATION

10 November 2014. *HMRC Brief 39/14*

ABSTRACT

HMRC will not alter its current policy on the VAT educational exemption until the Court of Appeal has delivered its judgment in the Brockenhurst College case next year, although it will consider claims and interim repayments based on the Upper Tribunal's decision. The FTT and UT have both held that supplies made by students to third parties were sufficiently closely related to exempt supplies of education. HMRC maintains that students must be the direct beneficiaries for the supplies to qualify for exemption.

FULL TEXT

PURPOSE OF THIS BRIEF

This brief sets out the HM Revenue and Customs' (HMRC) interim position following the decision of the Court of Appeal to grant leave to appeal against the UT's decision. The case concerned the VAT liability of restaurant meals provided to the public and charges for concerts and other performances put on by students as part of their further education courses.

READERSHIP

Colleges of further education and other education providers which provide goods or services to the public in the course of education or vocational training undertaken by students.

BACKGROUND AND FIRST TIER TRIBUNAL'S (FTT) DECISION

Brockenhurst College challenged a decision rejecting voluntary disclosures for:

(1) the supplies made from its restaurant, used for training chefs, restaurant managers and hospitality students. The claim was made on the basis that these were exempt supplies of education and not standard rated supplies of catering

(2) the tickets for concerts and other live performances put on by students as part of their educational courses. These were similarly claimed to be exempt

The FTT concluded that the supplies in question were exempt as being closely linked to education because:

(a) the College was an eligible body and so its principal supplies were exempt supplies of education

(b) the supplies were integral and essential to those principal exempt supplies

(c) the supplies were made at less than their cost

(d) the supplies were not advertised to the general public. Instead, there was a database of local groups and individuals who might wish to attend the restaurant or performances

(e) the supplies were not intended to create an additional source of income for the College

HMRC disagreed with the conclusion on the basis that the supplies were outside the education exemption because the students were not the beneficiaries of the supplies in question, but only benefitted from making them. HMRC appealed to the UT.

THE UT'S DECISION AND HMRC'S FURTHER APPEAL

The UT rejected HMRC's argument and agreed with the FTT. It held that the supplies were closely related to the exempt supplies of education because they enabled the students to enjoy better education. The requirement in the domestic law for the supplies to be for the direct use of the student was met because they were of direct benefit to him.

HMRC has subsequently appealed to the Court of Appeal and the hearing is to take place from 16 to 17 February 2015.

HMRC POLICY AND INTERIM IMPLEMENTATION OF THE TRIBUNAL RULING

There is no change to HMRC's policy that such supplies are outside the scope of the educational exemption because they are enjoyed by third parties not in receipt of education. This policy will not be reviewed until the Court of Appeal releases its judgment next year. In the meantime, HMRC will consider claims and make appropriate repayments based on the UT's decision where the circumstances are exactly the same. (HMRC are not making repayments in other circumstances such as where the supplies in question are linked to fully grant funded education). These repayments will be subject to protective assessments to cover the eventuality that the decision may be reversed in the Court of Appeal. However, Assessments will not be enforced unless and until that eventuality occurs.

CLAIMS AND RETROSPECTIVE ACTION

If you feel that you are entitled to a repayment based on the UT's decision:

- you may wish to refer to Public Notice VAT 700/45 'How to correct VAT errors and make adjustments or claims' which explains how to claim a refund
- your claim should be clearly identified as a "Claim Made Under the Upper Tribunal's Decision in Brockenhurst College HMRC Brief 39/14"
- any claims will be subject to an appropriate input tax restriction to recognise the additional exempt supplies and the four year time limit in line with HMRC procedures

FURTHER GUIDANCE

Public Notice 700/45 - How to correct VAT errors and make adjustments or claims.

INTEGRATION OF HMRC CLAIMS IN INSOLVENCIES

21 November 2014. *HMRC Brief 42/14*

FULL TEXT

PURPOSE OF THIS BRIEF

This brief is intended to alert the insolvency profession of upcoming changes in how HM Revenue and Customs (HMRC) deals with the tax affairs of insolvent taxpayers.

WHO NEEDS TO READ THIS

This brief is aimed at insolvency practitioners and official receivers.

BACKGROUND

HMRC was formed in 2005 following the merger of the former Inland Revenue and the former HM Customs & Excise. Both former departments had their own separate arrangements for lodging claims in UK insolvencies. Unfortunately, since the merger it's not been technically feasible to marry together the insolvency claim arrangements for the 2 former departments to produce a single claim encompassing all HMRC taxes and duties.

However, following an internal restructuring of insolvency processing work, HMRC will shortly be in a position to issue 'integrated' insolvency claims encompassing all HMRC debt. This will be achieved by centralising insolvency claims handling work at the following sites for the following insolvency types:

BANKRUPTCY/SEQUESTRATION, TRUST DEEDS, ADMINISTRATIVE RECEIVERSHIPS AND LIQUIDATIONS (EXCLUDING MEMBERS VOLUNTARY LIQUIDATIONS (MVL))

Insolvency Claims Handling Unit (ICHU)
Benton Park View
Longbenton
Newcastle
NE98 1ZZ

COMPANY ADMINISTRATIONS , MVL AND VOLUNTARY ARRANGEMENTS

Enforcement and Insolvency Service (EIS)
Durrington Bridge House

Barrington Road
Worthing
BN12 4SE

INFORMATION AND ACTION REQUIRED

This will affect insolvency practitioners as follows:

- insolvency practitioners should continue to complete a form VAT 769
- for new appointments in bankruptcies/sequestrations, trust deeds and liquidations (excluding MVL) the completed form VAT 769 should be sent to ICHU at the above address with immediate effect
- for new appointments in company administrations from 1 November 2014 onwards the completed form VAT 769 should be sent to EIS Worthing at the above address
- for new appointments in MVL from 1 December 2014 onwards the completed VAT 769 should be sent to EIS Worthing at the above address
- insolvency practitioners should ensure that the form VAT 769 they use is the version available on the HMRC website
- for company administrations, it will expedite processing of the form VAT 769 if it's accompanied by a Notice of Appointment 2.12
- unfortunately, due to the need to integrate VAT with the other HMRC taxes, details of any VAT debt owed by the insolvent business to HMRC may not be notified to the insolvency practitioner as quickly as has been the case in the past, so if the records of the business the insolvency practitioner is appointed over indicate a VAT debt to HMRC, please be patient as the integrated claim will be issued as soon as possible
- EIS Worthing will also take on responsibility for managing the post-appointment VAT account on company administrations for new appointments from 1 November 2014 and MVL for new appointments from 1 December 2014
- however, EIS Worthing won't be responsible for cancelling the VAT registration - requests for VAT deregistration for company administrations and MVL should be sent to:
  Grimsby Deregistration Unit
  Imperial House
  77 Victoria Street
  Grimsby
  DN31 1NH
- HMRC will require a dividend payment on the integrated claim, not on any separate components of the claim ie HMRC will no longer require a separate dividend payment for the VAT element of their claim - dividend payments should be sent to the appropriate office for the insolvency type as above
- the procedure for HMRC lodging claims in voluntary arrangements is unaffected by this change

HMRC expects that this change will be both cost effective and will help simplify insolvency practitioners interaction with the department. Any further changes in process that may become necessary as a result of the above transfer of work will be notified to the insolvency profession separately at the appropriate time.

VAT INPUT TAX RECOVERY ON PENSION FUND MANAGEMENT COSTS

26 November 2014. *HMRC Brief 43/14*

ABSTRACT

HMRC is changing its policy on input tax recovery in relation to investment management costs of pension schemes, following its review of the CJEU judgment in PPG Holdings. Broadly, HMRC will now accept that employers may deduct input tax in relation to fund management services where the employer is a party to the contract for those services and has paid for them. This Brief extends until 31 December 2015 the transitional period announced in R&C Briefs 6/2014 and 22/2014 during which the pension fund and employer may continue to apply a 70/30 costs split in line with previous HMRC policy. Separately, R&C Brief 44/2014 explains HMRC's change of policy on VAT exemption following the ATP Pension Service judgment.

FULL TEXT

1. PURPOSE OF THIS BRIEF

This brief sets out the position of HM Revenue and Customs (HMRC) following the decision of the Court of Justice of the European Union (CJEU) in *Fiscale Eenheid PPG Holdings BV cs te Hoogezand* (C-26/12) (PPG). The case concerned an employer's entitlement to deduct VAT paid on services relating to the administration of defined benefit pension schemes and the management of their assets.

Revenue and Customs Brief 6 (2014) set out HMRC's initial reaction to the judgment. However, following the subsequent decision in the case of *ATP Pension Service* (C-464/12) (ATP) and discussions with industry representatives HMRC issued Revenue and Customs Brief 22(2014) announcing that businesses could continue to use the transitional arrangements outlined in Revenue and Customs Brief 6(2014) whilst the VAT treatment of pensions was reconsidered.

This brief outlines the position of HMRC following that process and deals with the circumstances when an employer may deduct VAT that is charged on services provided in relation to pension schemes. A separate brief has been issued to explain the circumstances where VAT is not chargeable on such services following the ATP decision.

You can read the full text of the PPG and ATP decisions on the CURIA website: curia.europa.eu/.

2. READERSHIP

This brief is aimed at:

- businesses and other taxable entities that provide pension schemes for their employees
- pension fund management providers
- pension scheme trustees and pension providers
- tax advisers

3. BACKGROUND

PPG, a Dutch company, established defined benefit pension schemes for its employees which were required by law to be legally and financially separate from it.

PPG received supplies of services relating to the administration of the pensions and investment management of the assets of the pension fund from third parties on which VAT was charged. It paid the cost of these services itself and did not pass the costs on to the pension fund.

The CJEU decided that PPG was entitled to deduct the VAT incurred by it in such circumstances, provided that there was a direct and immediate link between the services and its own taxable supplies.

4. HMRC PREVIOUS POLICY

Until now, HMRC policy has been to distinguish between costs incurred in relation to the:

- setting up and day to day administration of occupational pension schemes
- investment management relating to the assets of occupational pension schemes

HMRC previously allowed employers to deduct VAT incurred in relation to the administration of an occupational pension scheme on the basis that these costs were overheads of the employer and thus had a direct and immediate link to the employer's business activities.

In respect of investment management costs, HMRC considered these costs to relate solely to the activities of the pension scheme. To the extent that these inputs were deductible, they were deductible by the scheme.

In some cases a single invoice was received covering both the administration of the pension scheme and the management of the investments. In such circumstances HMRC allowed the employer to claim 30% of the VAT as relating to the administration of the scheme and the pension scheme to claim 70% as relating to the investment management as an administrative simplification.

5. DEDUCTION BY THE EMPLOYER

As a result of the PPG judgment, HMRC is changing its policy on the recovery of input tax in relation to the management of pension schemes. This means that there are circumstances where employers may be able to claim input tax in relation to pension schemes where they could not do so previously.

VAT which is incurred on goods and services supplied to a taxable person is deductible if it is used for the onward taxable supplies of that person. The first stage in deciding whether the VAT on services may be deductible by an employer is to determine whether the services in question are supplied to the employer.

In the case of occupational pension schemes, there are normally 2 potential recipients of the supplies: the employer and the pension scheme through its trustees. The Courts have made clear that determining which of 2 persons is the recipient of a supply of services is a highly fact sensitive question that will depend upon consideration of all the circumstances in which the transaction in question took place. A fundamental criterion to be considered is economic reality and the most useful starting point is to examine the agreements between the parties. In this context, whilst the fact that a party pays for the supplies is not decisive, and payment may be third party consideration for supplies made to another party who is the actual recipient of the supplies, payment is an important indicator, particularly in cases where 2 parties use the services.

Accordingly, HMRC will not accept that the VAT incurred in relation to a pension scheme is deductible by an employer unless there is contemporaneous evidence that the services are provided to the employer and, in particular, the employer is a party to the contract for those services and has paid for them.

HMRC accepts that there are no grounds to differentiate between the administration of a pension scheme and the management of its assets, therefore there is no longer a need for any administrative simplification to deal with supplies involving both elements. In each case the employer will potentially be able to deduct input tax if it receives the supply of services.

In order to deduct, a business will require a valid VAT invoice. Where an employer is engaged in non-business activities or makes exempt supplies, it will need to take these into account when deducting any VAT incurred and restrict its deduction accordingly. Further information on the treatment of non-business activities can be found at chapter 4.6 of Notice 700, The VAT Guide and on partial exemption in Notice 706, Partial exemption.

If an employer receives a taxable supply of administration and investment management services and recharges them to the pension scheme, that recharge is consideration for an onward taxable supply. VAT is due accordingly. This amount is potentially deductible by the pension scheme to the extent that it is engaged in taxable business activities.

VAT Notice 700/17 Funded Pension Schemes will be updated shortly to reflect these changes in VAT treatment.

6. CLAIMS AND RETROSPECTIVE ACTION

RCB 6(2014) withdrew with immediate effect the policy currently outlined in Notice 700/17 and set out at 1.3 above except in circumstances where the pension scheme receives the services. In these circumstances, RCB 6(2014) and RCB 22(2014) provided a transitional period to allow time for businesses to adapt in response to HMRC's change in policy. This Brief extends that transitional period. During the transitional period, which will last until 31 December 2015, where the pension scheme receives the services the pension scheme and the employer may continue to agree to a 70/30 split on the terms set out in Notice 700/17. HMRC does not intend to take any action to correct the position in cases where the employer has properly deducted a proportion of the VAT under the existing treatment (outlined at 1.3 above) and the criteria outlined at 1.4 above were not met.

Businesses that provide pension schemes for their employees and receive supplies of services that fall within the criteria outlined at 1.4 above are entitled, but not obliged, to claim a refund of any input VAT which has not previously been claimed. Where a business has chosen to apply the 70/30 split, a claim for a refund would entail a recalculation of the amounts of input tax proper to the employer and the scheme respectively.

VAT Notice 700/45 How to correct VAT errors and make adjustments or claims explains how to go about claiming a refund in this circumstance.

Claims for under-declared input tax are subject to the normal capping rules. Claims for repayment will therefore not be considered for periods ending more than 4 years before the date on which the claim is made.

Any claim made must set out the basis of the error and the amount being claimed and show how that amount has been calculated. The claim should also make it clear whether the claim is for VAT incurred in relation to a defined benefit or a defined contribution (also known as money purchase) pension scheme and, if it is incurred in relation to a defined contribution pension scheme whether it is personal or occupational. The claimant must be able to provide copies of the documentation used in the calculation of the claim on request. An 'estimated' claim, or a declared intention to lodge a claim at a future date, will not stop the clock running on the 4 year cap.

All claims resulting from the changes outlined in this Brief should be sent to:

Email: vat.ppg.claims@hmrc.gsi.gov.uk

or by post to:

HMRC
VAT Repayments Team S0483
PO Box 200
Bootle L69 9AH

HMRC will now consider those claims for input tax made by businesses following the judgment in PPG. However, they may wish to provide details of their claim to the email address above to ensure that claims are dealt with promptly. In considering such claims account will be taken of claims by service providers that some supplies of administration/investment management were incorrectly taxed, as per the ATP Brief referred to above.

VAT EXEMPTION FOR PENSION FUND MANAGEMENT SERVICES

26 November 2014. *HMRC Brief 44/14*

ABSTRACT

Following its review of the CJEU judgment in ATP Pension Service, HMRC now accepts that pension funds meeting certain specific criteria are Special Investment Funds for the purposes of the fund management exemption. Management and administration services integral to the operation of such funds should therefore always have been exempt from VAT. This treatment will apply to funds containing the pooled assets of defined contribution occupational schemes as well as personal pension schemes. HMRC is still considering whether the judgment could have wider application, although taxpayers may rely directly on EU law to exempt services in accordance with this Brief pending amendments to UK legislation. Separately, R&C Brief 43/2014 sets out HMRC's revised policy on the right to deduct input tax on these services.

FULL TEXT

1. PURPOSE OF THIS BRIEF

This brief sets out the position of HM Revenue and Customs (HMRC) following the decision of the Court of Justice of the European Union (CJEU) in a Danish case concerning VAT and pension fund management services, ATP Pension Services (C-464/12) (ATP). The CJEU found that a pension fund which pooled investments from a number of defined contribution occupational pension schemes qualified as a Special Investment Fund (SIF) for the purposes of the VAT exemption for fund management services.

A separate Revenue and Customs brief has been issued that sets out HMRC's position on the right to deduct VAT charged on services supplied in connection with pension schemes following the CJEU's decision in PPG Holdings BV (C-26/12 (PPG).

2. READERSHIP

This Revenue and Customs brief is primarily aimed at:

- businesses and other organisations that provide pension schemes for their employees

- pension fund managers and administrators
- insurers and other pension providers
- pension scheme trustees
- tax advisers

3. BACKGROUND

ATP provided administration services in connection with a pension fund which pooled investments from a number of defined contribution occupational pension schemes. These services consisted of a number of functions aimed primarily at the operation and administration of accounts within the pension fund, including the handling of payments from employers and crediting pension contributions to an individual pension customer's account.

The Danish referring court asked the CJEU whether the fund administration services supplied by ATP could be viewed as exempt either as:

- the management of a SIF (under Article 135(1)(g) of the EU VAT Directive)
- transactions concerning deposit and current accounts or payments and transfers (under Article 135(1)(d) of the EU VAT Directive)

The case specifically concerned defined contribution (otherwise known as money purchase) pensions and did not concern the VAT treatment of services supplied in connection with defined benefit pensions. Services supplied in connection with defined benefit pensions were found by the CJEU in Wheels Common Investment Fund Trustees and Others (C-424/11) to fall outside the fund management exemption on the basis that the investment fund (which pools the assets of such a scheme/s) was not a SIF.

4. JUDGMENT

The CJEU concluded that a pension fund which pooled investments from a number of defined contribution pension schemes could be a SIF so that services supplied to it may be exempt fund management. This includes account administration services, such as those at issue in ATP, as long as they are 'essential' for the management of the fund.

The CJEU left it to the referring court to decide whether the services supplied by ATP were exempt transactions concerning payments and transfers but observed that such services may fall within that exemption. For information on the VAT exemption for payment and transfer services see the HMRC guidance manual Finance

5. HMRC PREVIOUS POLICY

Prior to the CJEU's judgment in ATP, HMRC did not consider pension funds of any kind to be SIFs and therefore treated services provided in connection with all types of pension fund as falling outside the VAT exemption for fund management services.

6. DEFINITION OF 'SPECIAL INVESTMENT FUND'

In light of the ATP judgment, HMRC now accepts that pension funds that have all of the following characteristics are SIFs for the purposes of the fund management exemption so that the services of managing and administering those funds should be, and always should have been, exempt from VAT:

- they are solely funded (whether directly or indirectly) by persons to whom the retirement benefit is to be paid (ie the pension customers)
- the pension customers bear the investment risk
- the fund contains the pooled contributions of several pension customers
- the risk borne by the pension customers is spread over a range of securities

In addition to funds that contain the pooled assets of defined contribution occupational pension schemes, such as that at issue in ATP, HMRC accepts that funds that contain the pooled assets of personal pension schemes and that have all of the above characteristics will also fall within the VAT exemption for fund management services.

A personal pension fund will not pool assets if an individual investor exercises an option to give directions as to how their contributions are invested (eg in specific assets and/or funds external to the pension fund) that overrides the investment powers of the trustee/pension provider.

HMRC does, however, accept that exemption could still apply to the fund where the costs of managing the assets of those investors who give such directions (ie the non-pooled assets) can be easily identified and excluded from exemption.

In respect of pension schemes that pay members' contributions into a number of different funds, exemption will only apply to services supplied in connection with funds that possess the characteristics outlined above. Where the contributions of a number of schemes are paid into a single fund, it will be necessary to consider whether that fund as a whole possesses all the characteristics set out above. Both such arrangements may be found in respect of hybrid pension schemes but will also apply in other circumstances.

Where investment management or administration services are supplied to a scheme that has a number of funds, some that posses the characteristics of a SIF and others that do not, to determine the correct VAT treatment of the services in question it will be necessary to apply the rules on single/multiple supplies outlined in HMRC guidance manual Supply and consideration.

7. DEFINITION OF 'MANAGEMENT'

Only fund management and administration services that are integral (ie specific and essential) to the operation of a pension fund will qualify for exemption. This may include the ATP type services of administering pension accounts in addition to those investment management and fund administration services that are already recognised as falling within the fund management exemption following *Abbey National* (C-169/04) and *GfBk* (C-275/11). In this context, the CJEU in Abbey National previously confirmed that the fund management exemption does not apply to fund supervisory services; and this remains the case.

8. SERVICES SUPPLIED IN RESPECT OF OTHER FUNDS

Exemption will only apply to charges made by third parties for services provided in connection with the management or administration of the contributions held in the pension fund itself. It will not apply to services provided in connection with any non-pension funds in which the contributions paid into the pension funds may have been invested; although the management of such funds may qualify for exemption on the basis that the fund is a SIF in its own right (eg an Authorised Unit Trust). The fact that some or all of the costs of managing non-pension funds is being borne by a qualifying pension fund (and ultimately by pension customers) will not bring services supplied in connection with non-qualifying investment funds, and charged to or on to pensions, within the fund management exemption.

9. IMPLEMENTATION OF THE JUDGMENT IN THE UK

UK legislation will be amended in due course to implement the ATP judgment. In the meantime, taxpayers may rely directly on EU law to exempt pension fund management or administration services in accordance with the policy outlined in this Brief.

HMRC is still considering whether the ATP judgment could have wider application and guidance will be issued if there are to be any further changes. In the meantime exemption should be applied in line with HMRC's current published policy.

10. CLAIMS AND RETROSPECTIVE ACTION

Businesses that have accounted for VAT on pension fund management services which qualify for exemption in accordance with HMRC's revised policy as set out in this Brief may, but are not obliged to, claim a refund of any output tax over-accounted for on these supplies - see VAT Notice 700/45 How to correct VAT errors and make adjustments or claims.

Claims are subject to the normal capping rules. Claims will therefore not be considered for periods ending more than 4 years before the date on which the claim is made. In support of claims, businesses must be able to produce evidence to demonstrate that they have accounted for VAT on the relevant services and must be able to substantiate the amount claimed. HMRC will not accept estimated claims.

Subject to the 4-year capping period, any claim should also cover all prescribed accounting periods in which the error occurred. Should a claim not take into account all errors or all affected accounting periods, then HMRC will seek to set-off amounts owed to it for these periods against amounts claimed in other periods.

HMRC may reject all or part of a claim if it takes the view that repayment would unjustly enrich the claimant (as it was not the claimant that bore the burden of the tax in question).

More information on 'unjust enrichment' can be found at Part 14 of VAT Notice 700/45, referred to above. All claims for overstated or overpaid VAT will be dealt with in accordance with Business Brief 28/04 'Correcting liability errors'.

Claims will be dealt with more quickly if they are accompanied by sufficient detail and evidence to enable the examination of each supply that the claimant contends should be exempt. This will include the detail of the services supplied (for example, that they are investment management), the basis upon which the claim is being made, who the supply is made to, what fund/funds the supply relates to and the value of each supply. It should also include details and evidence of whether the fund/s are pension funds (ie funds that only contain the investments of a pension scheme/s), whether the fund/s contain the investments of a defined benefit pension scheme, an occupational defined contribution pension scheme or a personal pension scheme, and of how the fund/s possess the characteristics of a SIF (as outlined above).

All claims resulting from the changes outlined in this Brief should be sent to:

Email: vat.atpclaims@hmrc.gsi.gov.uk

Or by post to:

HMRC
VAT Repayments Team S0483
PO Box 200
Bootle L69 9AH

HMRC will now consider claims already made by businesses following the ATP judgment that relate to output tax charged on services they have supplied in connection with funds that pool the investments of defined contribution pension schemes and which were clearly identified as such. Businesses that have made other claims for output tax charged on pension fund management services which they think may now be payable in whole or in part in accordance with the terms of this Brief are invited to provide details of the claims to the email address above. HMRC will not be able to consider these claims until such detail is provided.

ADDITIONAL GUIDANCE FOR MICRO BUSINESSES ON VAT MINI ONE-STOP-SHOP

10 December 2014. *HMRC Brief 46/14*

ABSTRACT

HMRC has issued additional guidance for small businesses below the UK VAT registration threshold on using the VAT mini one-stop-shop (MOSS) to account for cross-border supplies of digital services after 1 January 2015. The brief confirms that micro businesses registering for MOSS will not lose their UK VAT registration threshold, but will need to apply for UK VAT registration and complete a quarterly VAT return. Any VAT refund or expenses claims must be directly attributable to cross-border EU sales activities.

FULL TEXT

PURPOSE OF THIS BRIEF

This brief provides additional guidance to UK micro and small businesses who supply digital services to non-business customers in other EU member states about:

- how to comply with the new VAT rules for digital services that come into force on 1 January 2015
- how to register for HM Revenue and Customs (HMRC) VAT Mini One Stop Shop (MOSS) and still benefit from the UK's VAT registration threshold for sales to UK customers

WHO NEEDS TO READ THIS?

UK businesses that make cross-border Business to Consumer (B2C) supplies of digital services to customers in other EU member states, particularly micro and small businesses.

If you are a UK business and:

- are unsure whether the services you supply are 'digital services' covered by the new rules please read section 2
- are currently below the UK VAT registration threshold and want to register for MOSS to account for the VAT on your cross-border supplies please read section 3
- you want to understand the timescales that apply for registering for MOSS, please read section 4
- you want to understand what records you need to keep, please read section 5

SECTION 1: BACKGROUND

WHAT IS HAPPENING?

On 1 January 2015 the VAT rules for cross-border B2C supplies of 'digital services' (i.e. broadcasting, telecoms and e-services) will change. From that date, VAT must be accounted for in the member state where the customer normally lives, rather than where the supplier of the service is established. This means that sellers of digital services will no longer be able to unfairly undercut businesses in the UK by locating themselves in another EU member state with a lower VAT rate. You can find out more about these changes at VAT on digital services in the EU.

SECTION 2: DIGITAL SERVICES

WHAT SUPPLIES ARE COVERED BY THE CHANGES?

The changes apply to digital services. These are broadcasting, telecommunications and e-services that are electronically supplied.

It is unlikely that any small businesses supply broadcasting or telecommunications, but many will supply e-services to non-business customers in other EU member states and they will have to charge and account for VAT on their supplies.

SALES NOT AFFECTED BY THE CHANGE

Using the internet, or some electronic means of communication, just to communicate or facilitate trading does not necessarily mean that you are supplying e-services.

Using the internet for the following does not count:

- supplies of goods, where the ordering and processing are electronic
- supplies of physical books, newsletters, newspapers or journals
- services by lawyers and financial consultants who advise clients through e-mail
- booking services for entertainment events, hotel accommodation or car hire
- educational or professional courses, where the content is delivered by a teacher over the internet or an electronic network
- offline physical repair services of computer equipment
- advertising services in newspapers, on posters or on television

E-SERVICES WHICH ARE COVERED BY THE CHANGE IN RULES

The 1 January 2015 rule change only applies to e-services that are electronically supplied.

An e-service includes things like:

- images or text, such as photos, screensavers, e-books and other digitised documents e.g. pdf files
- music, films and games, including games of chance and gambling games, and of programmes on demand
- on-line magazines
- website supply or web hosting services
- distance maintenance of programmes and equipment
- supplies of software and software updates
- advertising space on a website

WHAT IS MEANT BY ELECTRONICALLY SUPPLIED?

This covers e-services which are automatically delivered over the internet, or an electronic network, where there is minimal or no human intervention. In practice, this means:

Where the sale of the digital content is entirely automatic - for eg a customer clicks the 'buy now' button on a website and the:

- content downloads onto their device
- customer receives an automated e-mail containing the content

Where the sale of the digital content is essentially automatic, and the small amount of manual process involved does not change the nature of the supply from an e-service. Examples of sales that are essentially automatic are where a customer clicks a "buy now" button on the website and the seller receives a notification and clicks a button, which:

- automatically sends an e-mail containing the digital content to the customer
- produces an e-mail pre-populated with the customer's details followed by the seller attaching the digital content and clicking 'send'

All e-services that are electronically supplied in the ways outlined above are categorised as 'digital services' and are covered by the rule change.

EXAMPLES OF ELECTRONIC SUPPLIES AND WHETHER OR NOT THEY ARE 'DIGITAL SERVICES'

Service	E-service?	Electronically supplied?	Covered by the new rules
Pdf document manually e-mailed by seller	Yes	No	No
Pdf document automatically e-mailed by seller's system	Yes	Yes	Yes
Pdf document automatically downloaded from site	Yes	Yes	Yes
Stock photographs available for automatic download	Yes	Yes	Yes
Live webinar	No	No	No
On-line course consisting of pre-recorded videos and downloadable pdfs	Yes	Yes	Yes
On-line course consisting of pre-recorded videos and downloadable pdfs plus support from a live tutor	Yes	No	No
Individually commissioned content sent in digital form e.g. photographs, reports, medical results	Yes	No	No
Link to online content or download sent by manual e-mail	Yes	Yes	Yes

SECTION 3: REGISTRATION FOR MOSS BY BUSINESSES CURRENTLY BELOW THE UK VAT REGISTRATION THRESHOLD (£81,000)

If you supply digital services to a customer in another EU member state, you must account for VAT to the tax authorities in that member state and at that member state's VAT rate.

So you do not have to register for VAT in every member state where you have customers, HMRC has developed a MOSS service for UK-based suppliers of digital services. You can find guidance on MOSS at Register for and use the VAT Mini One Stop Shop.

Although it is a condition of registering for the MOSS that you must have a UK VAT registration number to identify the business, you will not lose your UK VAT registration threshold.

WHO WILL THIS AFFECT?

These simplified VAT registration arrangements will only be available to you if:

- you are a UK-based supplier of digital services

- you wish to use the VAT MOSS
- your UK taxable turnover is below the UK-VAT registration threshold (currently £81,000)

HOW WILL THIS WORK?

If you make taxable supplies of digital services to customers in other EU member states, and your UK taxable turnover is below the UK VAT registration threshold, you may use the VAT MOSS to account for the VAT due in other EU member states but you do not need to account for and pay VAT on sales to your UK customers.

In these circumstances, you must:

- apply for UK VAT registration (see below)
- restrict any VAT refund claims you submit to HMRC to amounts directly attributable to your cross-border EU sales activities on which you will be accounting for VAT through MOSS (see Reclaiming VAT on your expenses and purchases below)

APPLYING FOR VAT REGISTRATION

You must apply for UK VAT registration.

When you are prompted to search for the correct business activity, you should select:

- search by business activity and then enter digital services in the following text box
- you will then be directed to select the business activity entitled supplies of digital services (below UK VAT threshold) under MOSS arrangements

Only follow this procedure:

- if you supply digital services to customers in other EU member states
- you wish to use the MOSS to account for VAT on those supplies
- your UK taxable turnover is below the VAT threshold

If these conditions do not apply, you should choose the Business Activity that best describes your business.

Following this process will ensure that HMRC can deal with your VAT registration application quickly.

RECLAIMING VAT ON YOUR EXPENSES AND PURCHASES

As you will not be charging VAT on your UK sales, any VAT you reclaim on your business expenses and purchases (see completing VAT returns below) must be either wholly attributable to your cross-border digital service supplies accounted for through MOSS, or only that proportion which is attributable to those sales.

For example, you might purchase a computer which you use to make all of your sales. If 60% of your sales are UK sales, and 40% of your sales are to customers in other EU member states, you would be able to recover 40% of the VAT charged on the purchase of the computer.

Please see further guidance on Reclaiming VAT.

You may also reclaim VAT on any business expenses incurred in other EU member states, provided these are directly related to your cross-border sales of digital services. To do this, you will need to complete a cross-border VAT refund application. There is guidance at VAT: refunds for UK businesses buying from other EU countries.

COMPLETING VAT RETURNS

UK VAT RETURN

You will need to complete a UK VAT return each quarter even if you are not charging VAT on your UK sales.

Unless you wish to reclaim VAT on business expenses or purchases in relation to your EU sales, you should enter '0' in every box on the return. If you do wish to reclaim VAT in relation to EU sales, you should complete boxes 4, 5 and 7.

You can find further guidance on completing the UK VAT return at VAT Returns.

VAT MOSS RETURN

You must declare any supplies of digital services to EU customers on the VAT MOSS return. You can view the guidance at Register for and use the VAT Mini One Stop Shop.

VAT MOSS return periods are calendar quarters (e.g. the first return period runs from 1 January to 31 March). Provided - when you registered for VAT – you selected the Business Activity entitled Supplies of digital services (below UK VAT threshold) under MOSS arrangements, HMRC will ensure that your UK VAT return period is aligned with the VAT MOSS return period, so you can complete both the UK return and the MOSS return at the same time.

WHAT IF MY UK TURNOVER EXCEEDS THE VAT REGISTRATION THRESHOLD?

It is important that you monitor your UK taxable turnover. If you exceed the VAT registration threshold (currently £81,000), you will need to start accounting for VAT on UK sales. There is information about how to calculate taxable turnover at Calculate VAT taxable turnover.

If you do not start to account for UK VAT at the right time, HMRC may assess any additional tax due.

SECTION 4: MOSS REGISTRATION AND USE IN 2015

MOSS REGISTRATION IN 2015

You can register for MOSS now, as this HMRC service is open and ready to use. You don't have to do it by 31 December 2014. Instead, you can wait until you sell your first digital service cross-border before applying to register. From 1 January, provided you notify HMRC and submit your VAT MOSS registration application by the 10th day of the month following your first digital service sale, the registration will be back-dated to the date of the first cross-border digital services sale. For example, if you sell your first cross-border digital service on 8 January 2015, you have until 10 February 2015 to submit your MOSS registration application to HMRC.

EU MEMBER STATES' VAT REQUIREMENTS

UK businesses registered for MOSS can find detailed information about the VAT requirements in every EU state, including the VAT rates and VAT invoicing requirements on the European Commission's website.

SECTION 5: RECORD KEEPING REQUIREMENTS

COLLECTING AND STORING INFORMATION ABOUT CUSTOMER LOCATION

MOSS registered businesses are required to collect and to keep in their records two pieces of evidence of where each customer normally lives. This helps demonstrate, if asked by the tax authorities, that the business has charged the correct rate of VAT to the customer. For many micro and small businesses this requirement can sometimes present a challenge. So, if you use a payment service provider to obtain payment for your digital service, HMRC suggests the following two step approach:

Step 1

When the customer places their order ask them to confirm either:

- the EU member state they usually live in
- their billing address

Step 2

When the customer pays for the product using the payment service provider, arrange for that provider to transmit the following two pieces of evidence to you:

- the customer's billing address
- the country code of the customer's bank or registered credit card

For confidentiality the payment service provider can remove the house number and street name from the billing address.

If the information on the EU member state where the customer is normally resident tallies, that will be sufficient to define the customer's location and you can record the details in your accounting records. However, if the information does not tally, you do not need to cancel the sale, but you must contact the customer and ask them to reconcile the discrepancy between the two sources of information.

WHAT ABOUT DATA PROTECTION?

As you have to keep customer records electronically you will need to register as a data controller with the Information Commissioner's Office (ICO), if you are not already registered. The current cost is £35 per year. The requirement to register is based on your place of business, and not the location of your customers; so you (as a UK business) will only have to register with the ICO in the UK, and not with the equivalent registrar in any other member state.

SECTION 6: HMRC GUIDANCE

HMRC is currently reviewing all its 2015 and MOSS guidance and all the material in this Revenue and Customs brief will be incorporated in that revised guidance.

INTRASTAT ARRIVAL THRESHOLD FROM 1 JANUARY 2015

10 December 2014. *HMRC Brief 47/14*

ABSTRACT

From 1 January 2015 the exemption threshold above which VAT-registered businesses must provide Intrastat arrivals declarations for EU imports will increase from £1,200,000 to £1,500,000. The exemption threshold for dispatches (EU exports) remains unchanged at £250,000.

FULL TEXT

PURPOSE OF THIS BRIEF

The purpose of this brief is to explain how businesses trading in goods with other EU member states, who are required to submit Intrastat arrival (EU imports) declarations, will be affected by a change to the Intrastat arrivals threshold from 1 January 2015.

WHO SHOULD READ THIS BRIEF

VAT-registered businesses that are required to submit declarations of arrivals trade received from other EU member states.

CHANGES TO INTRASTAT ARRIVALS THRESHOLD FROM 1 JANUARY 2015

From 1 January 2015 the exemption threshold for arrivals will increase from £1,200,000 to £1,500,000.

The exemption threshold for dispatches (EU exports) remains unchanged at £250,000.

BACKGROUND

Information on trade in goods between EU member states is collected by the Intrastat system. Member states are required by EU legislation to review annually their Intrastat exemption thresholds, below which businesses involved in such trade aren't required to submit Intrastat declarations.

All VAT-registered businesses are required to declare the value of their intra-EU trade in goods on their VAT returns. Businesses with an annual intra-EU trade above the thresholds (applied independently to arrivals and dispatches) are required to provide more detailed statistical returns.

The value of the thresholds are reviewed annually by HM Revenue and Customs (HMRC) to:

- accurately match the percentage coverage of the value of intra-EU trade required by EU legislation

VAT PRs etc

- ensure that the number of businesses required to submit monthly information is minimised

Following the annual review HMRC is able to increase the arrivals threshold from £1,200,000 to £1,500,000. The same review calculated that we should maintain the dispatches threshold at £250,000 to ensure we maintain the legislated percentage coverage for dispatches.

FURTHER INFORMATION

Further information on Intrastat can be found on the UKtradeinfo website and on GOV.UK.

PROMPT PAYMENT DISCOUNTS

22 December 2014. *HMRC Brief 49/14*

ABSTRACT

This brief provides guidance for businesses on how to account for VAT where a prompt payment discount is taken up after 1 April 2015, when new legislation takes effect for supplies requiring the issue of an invoice. Following consultation, HMRC confirmed that it will accept suitable alternatives to the issue of credit notes or revised invoices. This brief sets out the alternatives, including an example prompt payment discount invoice.

FULL TEXT

1. INTRODUCTION

PPD VAT legislation was amended earlier this year. This brief provides guidance on what to do when you raise or receive a VAT invoice offering a PPD from 1 April 2015 when the change takes effect.

2. WHO NEEDS TO READ THIS?

Suppliers who offer and customers who receive PPD where an invoice is issued.

3. BACKGROUND

A PPD is an offer by a supplier to their customer of a reduction in the price of goods and/or services supplied if the customer pays promptly; that is, after an invoice has been issued and before full payment is due. For example a business may offer a discount of 5% of the full price if payment is made within 14 days of the date of the invoice.

- at present, suppliers making PPD offers are permitted to put on their invoice, and account for, the VAT due on the discounted price, even if the full price (i.e. the undiscounted amount) is subsequently paid. Customers receiving PPD offers may only recover as input tax the VAT stated on the invoice.
- after the change, suppliers must account for VAT on the amount they actually receive and customers may recover the amount of VAT that is actually paid to the supplier.

Changes were made to UK legislation in the Finance Act 2014 in order to protect the revenue, and put it beyond doubt that UK legislation is aligned with EU legislation. The new legislation is at paragraph 4 below.

The change took effect on 1 May 2014 for supplies of broadcasting and telecommunication services where there was no obligation to provide a VAT invoice. For all other supplies the change takes effect on 1 April 2015.

A consultation took place between 17 June and 9 September 2014 asking businesses for their views and suggestions on how the changes should be implemented. In particular whether issuing credit or debit notes to evidence a change in the consideration would cause them difficulties. The Summary of Consultation Responses was published shortly after Autumn Statement 2014. We accepted that an alternative to issuing credit or debit notes was needed (see guidance below).

4. THE NEW LEGISLATION

The revised paragraph 4, Schedule 6, VATA 1994 is set out below:

4 (1) Sub-paragraph (2) applies where. (a) goods or services are supplied for a consideration which is a price in money, (b) the terms on which those goods or services are so supplied allow a discount for prompt payment of that price, (c) payment of that price is not made by instalments, and (d) payment of that price is made in accordance with those terms so that the discount is realised in relation to that payment. (2) For the purposes of section 19 (value of supply of goods or services) the consideration is the discounted price paid.

5. GUIDANCE

Suppliers:

(a) on issuing a VAT invoice, suppliers will enter the invoice into their accounts, and record the VAT on the full price. If offering a PPD suppliers must show the rate of the discount offered on their invoice (Regulation 14 of the VAT Regulations 1995 (SI 1995/2518)).

(b) the supplier will not know if the discount has been taken-up until they are paid in accordance with the terms of the PPD offer, or the time limit for the PPD expires.

(c) the supplier will need to decide, before they issue an invoice, which of the processes below they will adopt to adjust their accounts in order to record a reduction in consideration if a discount is taken-up.

(d) when adjustments take place in a VAT accounting period subsequent to the period in which the supply took place the method of adjustment needs to comply with Regulation 38 of the VAT Regulations 1995 (SI 1995/2518).

(e) suppliers may issue a credit note to evidence the reduction in consideration. In which case, a copy of the credit note must be retained as proof of that reduction.

(f) alternatively, if they do not wish to issue a credit note, the invoice must contain the following information (in addition to the normal invoicing requirements):

- the terms of the PPD (PPD terms must include, but need not be limited to, the time by which the discounted price must be made).
- a statement that the customer can only recover as input tax the VAT paid to the supplier.

Additionally, it might be helpful for invoices to show:

- the discounted price
- the VAT on the discounted price
- the total amount due if the PPD is taken up.

(g) if a business has adopted the option at (f), the VAT invoice, containing appropriate wording as described above, together with proof of receipt of the discounted price in accordance with the terms of the PPD offer (e.g. a bank statement) will be required to evidence the reduction in consideration, and the reduction to the supplier's output tax (in accordance with Regulation 38 of the VAT Regulations 1995).

(h) we recommend businesses use the following wording on the invoice:
"A discount of X% of the full price applies if payment is made within Y days of the invoice date. No credit note will be issued. Following payment you must ensure you have only recovered the VAT actually paid."

(i) if the discounted price is paid in accordance with the PPD terms, then the supplier must adjust their records to record the output tax on the amount actually received.

If the full amount is received no adjustment will be necessary.

Customers:

On receiving an invoice offering a PPD a VAT registered customer may recover the VAT charged, in accordance with VAT Regulation 29 of the VAT Regulations 1995.

As adjustments may take place in a VAT accounting period subsequent to the period in which the supply took place the method of adjustment needs to comply with Regulation 38 of the VAT Regulations 1995 (SI 1995/2518).

In practice this will mean:

(a) if the customer pays the full price they record it in their records and no VAT adjustment is necessary.

(b) if the customer pays the discounted price in accordance with the PPD terms on receipt of the invoice they may record the discounted price and VAT on this in their accounts and no subsequent VAT adjustment is necessary.

(c) if the customer does not pay when the invoice is first issued, they must record the full price and VAT in their records as shown on the invoice. If they subsequently decide to take-up the PPD then:

- if they have received an invoice setting out the PPD terms which states no credit note will be issued they must adjust the VAT in their records when payment is made. They should retain a document that shows the date and amount of payment (e.g. a bank statement) in addition to the invoice to evidence the reduction in consideration.
- if the supplier's invoice does not state that a credit note will not be issued, the customer must adjust the VAT they claim as input tax when the credit note is received. They must retain the credit note as proof of the reduction in consideration.

IMPORTS

The legislation in relation to prompt payments on imports has not changed; section 21(3) of VATA 1994 still applies.

PAYMENTS OUTSIDE PPD TERMS

Where a supplier receives a payment that falls short of the full price but which is not made in accordance with the PPD terms it cannot be treated as a PPD. The supplier must account for VAT on the full amount as stated on the invoice. If the amount not paid remains uncollected it will become a bad debt in the normal way. If a price adjustment is agreed later, then adjustment must be made in the normal way e.g. a credit note.

APPENDIX A - EXAMPLE PROMPT PAYMENT DISCOUNTS INVOICE

www.gov.uk/government/uploads/system/uploads/attachment_data/file/390184/appendix-rc49.pdf

VAT GROUPING RULES AND THE SKANDIA JUDGMENT

10 February 2015. *HMRC Brief 49/14*

ABSTRACT

HMRC has concluded that the CJEU judgment in Skandia does not require changes to the current UK VAT grouping rules. However, changes will be required to UK VAT accounting and VAT may become due where an overseas establishment of a UK group is situated in a member state which operates similar grouping provisions to Sweden, namely, that only the branch physically located in the country can belong to the VAT group. HMRC will confirm in due course which other member states this affects. The accounting changes will apply to services performed on or after 1 January 2016.

1. PURPOSE OF THIS BRIEF

Revenue and Customs Brief 37/2014 (13 October 2014) explained that HM Revenue and Customs (HMRC) was considering the effect of the judgment of the Court of Justice of the European Union (CJEU) in *Skandia America Corp. (USA), filial Sverige* (C-7/13) on the UK VAT grouping provisions. This brief notifies the outcome and provides further guidance.

2. WHO SHOULD READ THIS BRIEF

UK VAT-registered traders who are members of a VAT group in the UK or another EU member state, and have establishments (branches or head offices) in other member states.

3. BACKGROUND

Skandia America Corporation was a company incorporated in the United States, with a fixed establishment (a branch) in Sweden. The Swedish branch became part of a Swedish VAT group. The Swedish tax authority viewed services provided by Skandia America Corporation to its Swedish branch as taxable transactions. Skandia disagreed on the grounds that these were intra-company transactions and consequently not supplies for VAT purposes, following the decision in *FCE Bank* (C-210/04). The matter was referred to the CJEU.

The CJEU stated that under the Swedish grouping provisions only the branch that was physically located in Sweden could belong to a Swedish VAT group. The CJEU ruled that consequently the branch in Sweden became part of single taxable person (the group) different to the taxable person of the US head office. So the provision of IT services by the head office to its branch was a supply between 2 separate taxable persons and so liable to VAT. The Swedish VAT group had to account for VAT on those services under the reverse charge.

Under the UK's VAT grouping provisions, a body corporate such as a company must have an establishment in the UK to join a UK VAT group. However, unlike in Sweden, the whole body corporate is part of the VAT group, not just the establishment (branch or head office) in the UK. Therefore services provided between an overseas establishment and a UK establishment of the body are not normally supplies for UK VAT purposes, as they are transactions within the same taxable person

4. WAY FORWARD

The *Skandia* judgment did not consider the UK's different rules, which allow the whole body corporate into the UK group, and so did not rule this to be contrary to the VAT Directive. HMRC consequently does not consider that any changes to the UK grouping provisions are required.

The current grouping rules relating to UK VAT-grouped companies with overseas establishments will therefore be maintained. If an overseas company with a fixed establishment in the UK joins a VAT group, the whole legal entity (the company and its branches) becomes part of that taxable person.

However, UK VAT accounting will be affected and VAT may become due in the circumstances set out in the next section.

5. VAT CHANGES RESULTING FROM THE JUDGMENT

The implication of the *Skandia* judgment is that an overseas establishment of a UK-established entity is part of a separate taxable person if the overseas establishment is VAT-grouped in a member state that operates similar 'establishment only' grouping provisions to Sweden. This will be the case whether or not the entity in the UK is part of a UK VAT group. Businesses must treat intra-entity services provided to or by such establishments as supplies made to or by another taxable person and account for VAT accordingly:

- services provided by the overseas VAT-grouped establishment to the UK establishment will normally be treated as supplies made in the UK under place of supply rules, and subject to the reverse charge if taxable
- services provided by the UK establishment to the overseas VAT-grouped establishment will normally be treated as supplies made outside the UK under place of supply rules. Therefore they will need to be taken into account in ascertaining input tax credit for the UK establishment. If the supplies are reverse charge services, they should be reported on the trader's European Sales Listing of such supplies

If the UK entity is in a UK VAT group, the same applies to supplies between the overseas establishment and other UK VAT group members in UK. Under these circumstances the anti-avoidance legislation in VATA 1994, s 43(2A)–(2E) does not also apply, as the overseas establishment is not seen as part of the UK VAT group.

These changes of treatment do not require any change to UK law they follow automatically in circumstances where the overseas establishment is recognised as part of a separate taxable person.

HMRC will confirm which other member states will operate Swedish-style 'establishment only' VAT grouping following the *Skandia* decision as soon as possible, and update guidance accordingly.

6. WHEN WILL THE CHANGE TAKE EFFECT

This change in treatment must be applied to services performed on or after 1 January 2016. This will allow businesses time to adapt administrative and accounting procedures. Businesses may choose to apply the changes to services performed earlier than this date, provided they do so consistently for all services and establishments affected.

7. RELEVANT LEGISLATION

Article 11 of the Principal VAT Directive allows member states to treat two or more connected businesses established in the territory of that member state as a single taxable person (often called a VAT group). VAT grouping is enacted into UK legislation by VAT Act 1994, ss 43–43D.

DEDUCTING VAT ON PENSION FUND MANAGEMENT COSTS

26 March 2015. *HMRC Brief 8/15*

ABSTRACT

HMRC has confirmed it will accept tripartite contracts between the supplier, scheme trustees and employer as evidence to support an employer's entitlement to deduct VAT on fund management services in relation to defined benefit pension schemes. This brief sets out the specific arrangements that would need to exist under such contracts. HMRC will require the employer to have been issued with a valid VAT invoice for the full cost of the supply and to pay the service provider directly. R&Crief 43/2014 contains HMRC's policy following the CJEU decision in PPG Holdings BV. HMRC is considering the VAT deductibility of certain other types of service and intends to issue guidance in the Summer.

www.gov.uk/government/publications/revenue-and-customs-brief-8-2015-deduction-of-vat-on-pension-fund-management-costs

PURPOSE OF THIS BRIEF

This brief follows on from Revenue and Customs Brief 43 (2014) which set out the position of HM Revenue and Customs (HMRC) following the decision of the Court of Justice of the European Union (CJEU) in C-26/12 *Fiscale Eenheid PPG Holdings BV cs te Hoogezand (PPG)*.You can read the full text of the CJEU's decision in PPG on the CURIA website: curia.europa.eu.

This brief has been drafted following informal consultation with the pensions industry (including pension lawyers, managers and trustees) and outlines evidence that HMRC accepts meets the requirements outlined in the previous brief in order for employers offering DB pension schemes to achieve VAT deduction in respect of the costs of pension fund management services; in particular it considers the use of tripartite contracts.

This brief only relates to pension fund management services provided in respect of DB schemes. In specific circumstances pension fund management services supplied in respect of defined contribution pension schemes will be VAT exempt following the CJEU decision in C-464/12 *ATP Pension Services*. Further information on this can be found in Revenue and Customs Brief 44(2014).

HMRC has received enquiries in respect of the impact of the PPG decision on VAT recoverability relating to:

- other types of service (such as legal, actuarial and accounting services)
- other types of pension scheme (such as defined contribution and hybrid)
- VAT Groups that include a corporate trustee and a sponsoring employer
- trustees that charge employers to run their pension schemes

HMRC has been discussing these matters with interested parties and intends to provide further guidance in the summer.

READERSHIP

This brief is aimed at:

- employers that provide DB pension schemes for their employees
- the providers of pension fund management services
- pension scheme trustees
- tax advisers

BACKGROUND

Details of the *PPG* decision can be found in Revenue and Customs Brief 43 (2014). That brief also outlines the VAT treatment that applied prior to the *PPG* decision, the way that VAT treatment has changed as a result of the decision and the transitional arrangements that are currently in place.

In the case of funded DB pension schemes, which must be established under a trust, scheme trustees typically contract with third party service providers for the provision of pension fund management services. However, because benefits arising from DB pension schemes often form a central part of the sponsoring employer's staff remuneration package and the employer carries the ultimate burden of ensuring that there are sufficient funds with which to pay the promised benefits, all such services benefit the sponsoring employer as well as the pension scheme. This gives rise to the unique nature of DB pension provision and is a key factor in determining the recipient of the services supplied.

HMRC accepts, therefore, that for DB pension schemes there are normally 2 potential recipients of the supplies: the employer and the pension scheme through its trustees. Determining which party is the recipient of a supply of services is a fact sensitive question that will depend upon the circumstances in which the transaction took place. In particular, it is necessary to consider the economic reality of the arrangements and, whilst there are a number of factors to be taken into account, the most useful starting point for this is to examine the agreements between the parties.

Following the *PPG* decision, the factors to consider in order to determine the recipient of supplies (and therefore the party with the right to deduct) are outlined in detail in Revenue and Customs Brief 43 (2014). In particular, that brief makes it clear that it is necessary for the employer to both contract and pay for the services in order for it to be the recipient of the services for VAT purposes.

TRIPARTITE CONTRACTS

Since the publication of the Revenue and Customs Brief, some employers have expressed a concern that directly contracting for pension fund management services may sometimes be difficult owing to the regulatory context in which they operate. Accordingly they have asked whether HMRC will accept that tripartite contracts between the supplier, pension scheme trustees and employer meet the condition that the employer must contract for the services.

HMRC has considered the use of tripartite contracts specifically in the context of DB pension schemes where the regulatory regime requires the scheme to be established under a trust and it is the employer that ultimately bears the financial risks and benefits associated with the performance of the scheme.

Given the unique nature of these DB pension arrangements HMRC accepts that tripartite contracts can be used to demonstrate that the employer is the recipient of a supply of DB pension fund management services. An employer may therefore be able to deduct VAT incurred on these services in line with its residual recovery position where, as a minimum, the contract with the service provider evidences that:

- the service provider makes its supplies to the employer (albeit that the contract may recognise that, in the particular regulatory context in which DB schemes operate, the service provider may be appointed by, or on behalf of, the pension scheme trustees)
- the employer directly pays for the services that are supplied under the contract
- the service provider will pursue the employer for payment and only in circumstances where the employer is unlikely to pay (for example, because it has gone into administration) will it recover its fees from the scheme's funds or the pension scheme trustees
- both the employer and the pension scheme trustees are entitled to seek legal redress in the event of breach of contract, albeit that the liability of the service provider need not be any greater than if the contract were with the pension scheme trustees alone and any restitution, indemnity or settlement payments for which the service provider becomes liable may be payable in whole to the pension scheme trustees for the benefit of the pension scheme (for example in circumstance where the scheme is not fully funded)
- the service provider will provide fund performance reports to the employer on request (subject to the pension scheme trustees being able to stipulate that reports are withheld, for example where there could be a conflict of interest)

- the employer is entitled to terminate the contract, although that may be subject to a condition that they should not do so without the pension scheme trustees prior written consent (this can be in addition to any right that the pension scheme trustees may have to terminate the contract unilaterally)

In addition to the above, evidence that the pension scheme trustees agree that it is the employer who is entitled to deduct any VAT incurred on the services will reduce the potential for disputes.

PAYING AND RECHARGING OF COSTS

For an employer to be able to deduct any VAT, it will be necessary for them to be issued with a valid VAT invoice for the full cost of the supply and to pay the service provider directly for the full cost of the services. HMRC does not accept that an equivalent increase in contributions to the fund or any payment that is made by, or through, the fund constitutes payment by the employer.

If an employer recharges the net cost of those services to the pension scheme, that recharge is consideration for an onward taxable supply and VAT is due accordingly. This amount is potentially deductible by the pension scheme to the extent that the pension scheme is engaged in taxable business activities.

Pension scheme trustees and employers will normally regularly review the level of contributions required by the employer into its pension fund/s to ensure those funds are able to meet the forecast pension benefit commitments. HMRC accept that if adjustments are made to these contributions, to take account of the fact that it is the employer rather than the fund that is paying for certain costs, that does not constitute consideration for a supply by the employer to the pension fund. This is provided that there is no specific reduction equal to the actual costs that were incurred in any given period.

TRANSITIONAL PERIOD

The transitional period announced in Revenue and Customs Brief 43 (2014) will continue until 31 December 2015. In the meantime, businesses may continue to use the VAT treatment outlined in VAT Notice 700/17: *Funded Pension Schemes* should they choose, provided that both employer and pension scheme trustees agree the same treatment.

HMRC POSITION FOLLOWING JUDGMENT IN LITTLEWOODS RETAIL

23 June 2015. *HMRC Brief 9/15*

ABSTRACT

HMRC is seeking permission to appeal the Court of Appeal judgment in Littlewoods Retail, concerning a claim for compound interest on overpaid VAT, to the Supreme Court. Since the judgment was based on the circumstances specific to the Littlewoods claimants, HMRC does not regard it as generally applicable and will continue to ask for a stay of other compound interest claims already lodged and refuse new claims until litigation is final.

PURPOSE OF THIS BRIEF

This brief explains HM Revenue and Customs' (HMRC) position following the Court of Appeal judgment in Littlewoods Retail Ltd and others [2015] EWCA Civ 515 handed down on 21 May 2015.

The Court of Appeal found against HMRC deciding that Littlewoods claim for additional interest succeeded in full.

Like the High Court's earlier ruling this finding was based on the 'exceptional' circumstances specific to the Littlewoods claimants. It does not provide a clear basis that could be applied to other claimants or a formula for doing so.

No payments are due to other VAT compound interest claimants at this stage.

BACKGROUND

Littlewoods Retail Limited and others claimed a refund of overpaid VAT in respect of commissions on mail order sales. This VAT was repaid together with simple interest due under

VAT Act 1994. They then argued that the interest already paid to them was inadequate and that they were entitled to compound interest both as a matter of EC law and also as a matter of English domestic law.

HMRC's view is that there is no community law right or domestic law right to compound interest and that section 78 of VATA 1994 provides an exhaustive and adequate statutory scheme by which only simple interest is payable.

The High Court ordered a reference to the Court of Justice of the European Union (CJEU) for a decision as to whether community law required payment of compound interest. It was heard in the Grand Chamber of the CJEU on 22 November 2011.

The judgment of the European Court was delivered on 19 July 2012. The European Court ruled that there is no EU law right to compound interest but returned the matter to the UK courts to determine whether the UK's interest provisions comply with general EU principles, by providing the claimants with an adequate indemnity.

HIGH COURT JUDGMENT

The High Court considered the implications of the CJEU judgment and, as well as considering the national rules for payment of interest, the Court considered the total amount due if simple interest was found not to be adequate.

The Court found compound interest to be due as claimed, taking into account the 'exceptional' circumstances of Littlewoods' situation. The Court also held that that the current statutory provisions relating to VAT did provide an appropriate amount of interest in many cases.

COURT OF APPEAL JUDGMENT

The appeal was heard in March 2015. The judgment was released on 21 May 2015. The Court of Appeal supported the conclusions of the High Court but were careful to emphasise that their ruling applies to the specific circumstances of the Littlewoods claimants.

The judgment did not provide a general methodology for calculating the amount of interest which would give 'adequate indemnity' to the claimants. The court maintained that statutory provisions will provide an adequate amount of interest in many cases, therefore it is not the case that compound interest will always be payable where there has been an overpayment of tax.

HMRC'S POSITION

HMRC does not agree with the judgment and considers it to be at odds with the requirements of European law and how Parliament intended VAT law to work. Accordingly, this is not the end of the litigation as HMRC is seeking permission to appeal to the Supreme Court. It may, however, be a number of months before HMRC will know the outcome of its application for permission to appeal.

HMRC's view is that this ruling does not provide a clear method for calculating the level of interest which provides adequate indemnity to claimants. The Court of Appeal followed similar reasoning to the High Court, ruling that the claimants had a right to adequate indemnity, and this was not met by the statutory interest already paid. This was based on the facts and circumstances of those claimants. The litigation is not yet final so, given the Court of Appeal did not change the High Court judgment, the position taken by HMRC is unchanged.

The Court of Appeal, like the High Court, ruled that in many cases the statutory interest paid would be adequate and no further payments would be due. For any other claimant to succeed, the details of their claim would have to be considered in similar detail in a separate court hearing.

The Court of Appeal provided no further guidance on how claims to compound interest made through the Tribunal appeals process should be treated. Nor did it alter the earlier finding of the upper Tribunal that compound interest is not available consequent to an appeal to the Tribunal.

Further, in relation to a number of other claims, there are other significant strands of litigation still to be resolved before these claims can be examined and concluded.

As HMRC is seeking leave to appeal to the Supreme Court, the availability of compound interest in any circumstances remains in dispute.

CLAIMS FOR COMPOUND INTEREST

In view of the above, HMRC will apply for any claims for compound interest already lodged (and new claims) with the High Court or County Court to continue to be stayed pending the final determination of the Littlewoods litigation.

HMRC position in relation to Tribunal appeals is unchanged, namely that these should continue to be stood over until there has been a final determination as to the availability of compound interest in the UK.

Any new requests for compound interest will continue to be refused.

HMRC will reconsider their position in the event that permission to appeal to the Supreme Court is not granted.

An update to this brief will be issued in due course.

VAT ON DIRECT MARKETING SERVICES USING PRINTED MATTER

15 July 2015. *HMRC Brief 10/15*

ABSTRACT

HMRC regards supplies of printed matter combined with other services as supplies of standard-rated direct marketing services, not zero-rated delivered goods. HMRC accepts that its guidance in notice 700/24 was not clear and has agreed transitional arrangements to take no action in respect of incorrectly zero-rated separate single supplies of either addressed or unaddressed mail made prior to 1 August 2015. Anti-forestalling applies to payments or invoices after 9 June 2015 for deliveries to take place after 31 July 2015. Suppliers wishing to adopt the transitional arrangements must notify HMRC by 30 November 2015.

PURPOSE OF THIS BRIEF

This brief explains HM Revenue and Customs (HMRC) approach to supplies of direct marketing that have been wrongly treated as zero-rated supplies of delivered goods.

It sets out those circumstances where we will not take action to assess for past errors (see Transitional arrangements).

It also describes the settlement terms available to businesses whose supplies do not come within the scope of the transitional arrangements (see Printed matter supplied with other services).

WHO NEEDS TO READ THIS?

Anyone who makes or receives supplies of direct marketing services using printed matter.

ACTION TO TAKE

To be aware of the:

- correct VAT treatment of direct marketing services using printed matter
- transitional arrangements where direct marketing services using printed matter were treated incorrectly for VAT
- scope and time limit of an HMRC settlement offer for supplies that do not come within the scope of the transitional arrangements

BACKGROUND

HMRC has identified that a number of suppliers of printed matter combined with other services have been treating the supply as one of zero-rated delivered goods. In HMRC's view, these supplies should properly be characterised as a supply of standard-rated direct marketing services.

DIRECT MARKETING

Direct marketing via mail (addressed or unaddressed) or inserts in newspapers or magazines typically involves the production or acquisition of printed matter for distribution and any or all of the following services:

- posting or arranging the posting of customer mail such as publicity, advertising material or promotional goods to many recipients, including unaddressed mail (known as door drops)
- analysis or manipulation of data (either provided by the customer or sourced directly) for strategic or marketing reasons - for example, to target direct mail at specific groups based on geography, socio-economic factors or gender of recipients
- purchase or rental of third party mailing lists, including for amalgamation with customer's own lists
- analysis of own and customer data to produce reports on campaign results and advice on strategy

Following representations we accept that, in the context of direct marketing using printed matter, there have been occasions where what is to be treated as a zero-rated supply of delivered goods or a standard-rated service has been misunderstood based on the guidance provided in the former VAT Notice 700/24 Postage and delivery charges (1 April 2003).

In light of this we have published updated guidance in VAT Notice 700/24: postage, delivery charges and direct marketing and VAT Notice 701/10: zero-rating of books and other forms of printed matter to provide greater clarity.

We have also agreed with trade representatives a transitional period, which ends on 31 July 2015, for certain cases where businesses have treated supplies of direct marketing incorrectly for VAT.

TRANSITIONAL ARRANGEMENTS

Where there has been a misunderstanding by a supplier about the VAT treatment of direct marketing using printed matter, we will not take any retrospective action for supplies made prior to 1 August 2015 where the supplier has zero-rated a separate single supply consisting of either addressed or unaddressed mail only.

ADDRESSED MAIL

The supply of printing and mailing of zero-rated marketing material to recipients based on data (such as lists of customers) provided by the customer of the print supplier.

The following services may be treated as ancillary to this supply when they are supplied by the person who has the contract to supply the completed printed matter, provided that no other services are supplied with them:

- creative design, drafting and preparation of printed matter
- printing of direct mail packs using pre-sorted or unsorted data provided by the printing supplier's customer, so that the mail packs include names, addresses, postcodes and barcodes
- printing of direct mail packs and correction of data supplied by the printing supplier's customer - data correction includes only:
  - amendment in accordance with Royal Mail address format guidance
  - amendment to comply with the requirements of the Mail Preference Service
  - removal of 'gone-aways' and the deceased

UNADDRESSED MAIL (DOOR DROPS)

The transitional arrangements will only apply to door drops where it can be demonstrated that the supplier's service consisted only of the printing and delivery of zero-rated printed matter and the customer has instructed the supplier as to the timing and location of the deliveries.

Where a third party provides marketing services and the supply of these services is to the customer, the transitional arrangements apply, provided the other criteria above are met.

Where a third party provides marketing services and the supply is to the business which is providing printing and delivery of the material, the printing/delivery business will then be supplying those marketing services to the customer and the transitional arrangements will not apply.

If a business zero-rated supplies of door drops made prior to 1 August 2015 which fall within the scope of the transitional arrangements, it does not have to account for VAT on them. The business should retain any contracts/agreements, invoices or other contemporaneous evidence which demonstrate that the supply comprises printed matter and distribution services only. This evidence is required to demonstrate that the business has not:

- provided the door drops as part of a supply of direct marketing services
- been invoiced for services such as strategic, planning or other supplies (including determining the timing and location of deliveries) made to the customer by any third party unless they were treated as disbursements
- artificially split these supplies from other supplies it may have made to its customer

ADDRESSED AND UNADDRESSED MAIL

The transitional arrangements do not apply in cases where the arrangements are seen to be abusive or artificial. This includes forestalling, where a prepayment is made or an invoice issued after 9 June 2015 for deliveries to take place after 31 July 2015.

These transitional arrangements only apply to businesses which had misunderstood the guidance in the former VAT Notice 700/24 Postage and delivery charges (1 April 2003).

Businesses which had understood the guidance cannot seek to apply these transitional arrangements and HMRC will not repay VAT claimed in any Error Correction Notifications (ECN) which seek to claim the benefit of these arrangements.

IF YOU WISH TO ADOPT THE TRANSITIONAL ARRANGEMENTS

Suppliers must notify their intention to adopt the transitional arrangements to HMRC by 30 November 2015 by email to john.hegarty@hmrc.gsi.gov.uk or by post for the attention of:

John Hegarty
Local Compliance
HM Revenue and Customs
S0717
Newcastle NE98 1ZZ

The sender must be an 'authorised person' of the business. The email must acknowledge acceptance of the terms of the transitional arrangements as follows - '(Insert sender organisation and VAT registration number) intends to adopt the transitional arrangements set out in Revenue and Customs Brief 10 (2015) from the Commissioners of HMRC dated 15 July 2015.'.

Failure to notify an intention to adopt the transitional arrangements by 30 November 2015 will mean that a business will no longer be entitled to take advantage of them.

PRINTED MATTER SUPPLIED WITH OTHER SERVICES

Where a supplier has made supplies of direct marketing services prior to 1 August 2015 that are not within the scope of the transitional arrangements they may settle their outstanding VAT liabilities on the following terms.

For the purpose of the Settlement the supply of marketing services may be treated as multiple supplies of goods and services using the following analysis.

Zero-rating can be applied to the 'printed matter element' of the supply and any of the ancillary services described in paragraph 3.1 of VAT Notice 700/24: postage, delivery charges and direct marketing.

VAT at the standard rate must be accounted for on any other services supplied with the printed matter, including but not limited to:

- marketing
- promotional
- strategic
- planning
- response handling
- distribution
- media insert
- purchase of third party mailing lists
- data targeting analysis

- data cleansing
- other services not ancillary to the supply of printed matter

Where postal services were obtained from Royal Mail these will be taxed if they were subject to VAT when purchased by the supplier. They can be treated as a disbursement for the purposes of the Settlement if they were purchased as an exempt supply from the Royal Mail.

Where suppliers have charged a single price or where the supply includes the cost of in-house services (such as strategic, planning, management, response handling or similar) which comprise standard-rated services, then staff and other in-house costs must be directly attributed to the relevant supply of standard-rated services or the supply of printed matter wherever possible.

Where staff and other in-house costs are used for both standard and zero-rated supplies, then the value attributable to the zero-rated element must be apportioned between standard-rated and zero-rated supplies on a fair and reasonable basis (Section 31 VAT Notice 700: the VAT guide provides further information on how this may be done).

Suppliers who believe they have accounted for VAT correctly or have a clear ruling from HMRC which meets the tests for legitimate expectation do not have to accept the terms of the Settlement. HMRC may investigate these cases and matters will be dealt with in the normal way.

IF YOU WISH TO SETTLE

Suppliers must notify their acceptance to HMRC by 30 November 2015 by email to john.hegarty@hmrc.gsi.gov.uk or by post for the attention of:

John Hegarty
Local Compliance
HM Revenue and Customs
S0717
Newcastle NE98 1ZZ

The sender must be an 'authorised person' of the business. The email must acknowledge acceptance of the Settlement of the offer as follows - '(Insert sender organisation and VAT registration number) agrees to the terms and conditions of the Settlement as set out in Revenue and Customs Brief 10 (2015) from the Commissioners of HMRC dated 15 July 2015.'

Failure to accept the Settlement by 30 November 2015 will mean that a business will no longer be entitled to take advantage of the Settlement terms.

Where a supplier has notified acceptance, the Settlement is conditional on them submitting an ECN with a schedule on a VAT Return period basis for accounting periods from 1 August 2011 up to 31 July 2015. This must include the total of the disputed supplies, the value of the zero-rated supplies, the nature of the standard-rated supplies (data, insertion services, strategic, etc) and the relevant VAT due. Where a business which wishes to accept the Settlement is already being audited by HMRC, the terms of the Settlement will be reflected in any necessary changes to protective assessments already issued.

The information must either be emailed or posted to John Hegarty as above to reach him no later than 31 December 2015.

INTEREST

Adjustments will be subject to interest charges pursuant to s 74 of the VAT Act 1994.

PENALTIES

Each case will be judged on its own merits.

AVOIDANCE/ABUSE

Any attempt to exploit this Settlement in a manner which in HMRC's view amounts to tax avoidance or abuse will render the Settlement null and void.

VAT LIABILITY OF VERANDAHS SOLD WITH CARAVANS

30 July 2015. *HMRC Brief 12/15*

PURPOSE OF THIS BRIEF

This brief sets out the HM Revenue and Customs (HMRC) position following a decision of the Upper Tribunal. The case concerned the VAT liability of verandahs sold with caravans.

READERSHIP

Anyone who sells new or used caravans with verandahs - and their advisers.

BACKGROUND

The supply of a static caravan, excluding removable contents, can be reduced rated or zero-rated for VAT purposes, depending on its size and specification. HMRC considered that where the reduced or zero rate applied, it did not extend to a verandah or decking structure supplied at the same time. An optional verandah was considered by HMRC to be a separate standard-rated supply.

An appeal was made by Colaingrove Ltd on the grounds that they were making a single supply of a caravan with a verandah, and that as the verandah was ancillary to the caravan it should receive the same VAT treatment.

The First Tier Tribunal accepted that the verandah 'served' the static caravan. However it held that this type of verandah was:

- a structure in its own right, payment for which formed a substantial part of the total amount paid for the verandah and caravan taken together
- not integral or incidental to the static caravan
- an optional extra.

Therefore the Tribunal decided that there was a separate supply of the verandah which was subject to VAT at the standard rate.

Colaingrove Ltd appealed and the Upper Tribunal reversed the decision ruling that the sale of a static caravan with a verandah is a single supply for VAT purposes.

IMPLICATIONS OF THE UPPER TRIBUNAL DECISION

As a result of the Upper Tribunal decision, HMRC accepts that verandahs and decking structures sold with static caravans are to be treated as a single supply. Therefore the VAT liability of the verandah is the same as that of the caravan. Notice 701/20: caravans and houseboats will be updated to reflect this change.

CLAIMS AND RETROSPECTIVE ACTION

Notice 700/45: how to correct VAT errors and make adjustments or claims explains how to claim a refund.

Please note:

- claims are subject to the 4 year CAP in line with normal HMRC procedures
- the Business Income Manual provides further guidance for direct tax implications where amounts claimed are not fully reimbursed to affected customers
- claims made should be adjusted for any amounts due to set-off under Section 81(3) of the VAT Act 1994 (outstanding debts, assessments and so on) and Section 130 of the Finance Act 2008 (outstanding debts under any other head of taxation)
- further information can be obtained from the Contact HMRC pages

REDUCED RATE OF VAT FOR THE INSTALLATION OF ENERGY SAVING MATERIALS

31 July 2015. *HMRC Brief 13/15*

PURPOSE

The purpose of this brief is to explain the government's plans in respect of the decision of the European Court.

WHO SHOULD READ THIS?

This brief should be read by anyone who installs energy saving materials.

BACKGROUND

In 2012, the European Commission commenced infraction proceedings against the UK claiming that its application of the reduced rate for the installation of energy saving materials was not in accordance with EU law.

The European Court published its decision on 4 June 2015. The court agreed with the Commission that the UK had implemented the relief in a way that was not in accordance with EU law.

In essence, the court found that the UK had applied the reduced rate too widely. The reduced rate should be introduced as part of a social policy and should be targeted to those whom the policy is designed to help. A social policy cannot apply equally to everyone. In addition, the supplies must amount to a renovation or alteration of housing to be consistent with EU law potentially casting doubt on some of the installed goods currently subject to VAT relief.

CURRENT POSITION

The government is currently considering the implications of the decision.

If there are to be any legislative changes, they won't be implemented before Finance Act 2016. Until then, supplies of the installation of energy savings materials will continue to be reduced rated and any changes wont apply to future supplies and will not apply to supplies already made.

WHO CAN I CONTACT FOR FURTHER INFORMATION?

For further information please contact the VAT Helpline on Telephone: 0300 200 3700.

The VAT Helpline is available Monday to Friday, 8am to 6pm.

If you have hearing difficulties, please dial the Textphone service on Telephone: 0300 200 3719.

VAT Appeals etc

MAKING AN APPEAL

March 2015. Issued by the Tax Chamber of the First-tier Tribunal

1. HM COURTS & TRIBUNALS SERVICE

HM Courts & Tribunals Service is part of the Ministry of Justice and provides administrative support for the Tribunals' judiciary who hear cases and decide appeals. The tax appeals system was created on 1 April 2009, and this provides for tax appeals to be heard in a First-tier Tax Chamber, with a right of appeal with permission to the Upper Tribunal. The tax appeals system is totally independent of Her Majesty's Revenue and Customs (HMRC).

2. ABOUT THIS LEAFLET

This leaflet is designed to provide you with useful information about how to appeal against a decision of HMRC and how to make your appeal to the Tax Chamber of the First-tier Tribunal. We explain what decisions can be appealed against and how you may bring a case before the tax tribunal. This leaflet aims to give you the essential information you need to make your appeal, though it cannot cover all circumstances.

3. WHAT IS THE TAX TRIBUNAL?

The First-tier Tribunal is divided into several Chambers, one of which is the Tax Chamber. Throughout this leaflet this Tax Chamber is referred to as the tax tribunal. The tax tribunal hears the full range of appeals against HMRC decisions in relation to direct and indirect tax cases (explained in paragraph 4 below). It has a single set of procedural rules giving it the flexibility to deal with the whole range of tax matters from the straightforward to the complex.

The tax tribunal is completely independent of HMRC, and cases are heard by Judges and other Members who are qualified to hear cases. Annex A provides a list of the types of tax appeal the tribunal can deal with.

4. APPEAL RIGHTS

You can appeal only where the law gives you a right of appeal. Not every HMRC decision on a tax matter carries a right of appeal. When you do have a right of appeal the official letter from HMRC giving the decision will make this clear. The tribunal will determine, in doubtful cases, if it has the jurisdiction (which means the power) to deal with the dispute or not.

The main areas that the tribunal deals with are tax assessments and penalties. A list of the more common tax decisions made by HMRC that can be appealed to the tribunal can be found at Annex A. This is not a complete list and appeals against tax credit decisions are dealt with in the Social Entitlement Chamber and not by the tax tribunal.

Direct tax refers to tax that is usually levied directly off an organisation or an individual person, such as income tax or corporation tax. Indirect tax refers to tax that is usually levied on goods or services rather than on an individual or organisations, such as VAT or Customs Duties.

5. THE TRIBUNAL'S POWERS

In deciding whether to appeal or not, you need to know what the tribunal can and can't do for you. The tribunal does not have unlimited powers. It can only do what the law gives it the power to do. Sometimes, if it accepts that your appeal is valid, it can replace the decision you are appealing against with the decision it thinks should have been made. In other cases it can only direct HMRC to reconsider their decision. If it does not accept that your appeal is valid it will uphold the decision you are appealing against.

6. DECIDING WHETHER TO APPEAL

Before making your appeal, you should know that the tribunal cannot:

- Change the law. It has to apply the law as it stands, even if that leads to an outcome that you think is unfair
- Deal with administrative complaints about the conduct of HMRC officials. (If you are unhappy with the way HMRC have dealt with your tax affairs, please refer to their guidance on how to complain on the HMRC website www.hmrc.gov.uk/dealingwith/complain.htm.)

We cannot advise you whether you have a case or whether you are likely to win or lose your appeal nor can we tell you if you should appeal or not. HMRC, in their decision letter, will have told you whether you have a right of appeal to the tribunal.

Many people who make an appeal choose to get professional advice and support with it.

If you do decide to get advice, please do so at the earliest opportunity – when you are thinking about appealing. Please do not leave it until your appeal is well under way as we may not be able to put your appeal on hold whilst you are seeking representation. If you face a delay in getting advice please keep an eye on the timelimit for appealing.

In indirect tax appeals, the tax tribunal cannot hear an appeal that relates to disputed tax unless either you have paid or deposited the tax in dispute, or the Tribunal (or HMRC) have waived that requirement.

In direct tax, the payment of the tax in dispute is usually postponed pending the outcome of the appeal, and this is not an issue.

7. HARDSHIP CASES – APPLYING FOR YOUR APPEAL TO BE HEARD WITHOUT PAYMENT OF THE DISPUTED TAX

This relates to indirect tax only. The tribunal cannot hear an appeal which relates to disputed tax unless either you have paid or deposited the tax in dispute, or the Tribunal (or HMRC) have waived that requirement. If paying or depositing the disputed tax would cause you financial hardship, you should first write to HMRC asking them to waive the requirement. It is essential that you demonstrate your financial position to them so that they can consider the matter fully. If HMRC do not agree to waive the requirement, you may apply to the tribunal to consider the matter. If HMRC oppose your hardship request, we will arrange a tribunal hearing to decide whether or not to allow it.

To make an application for hardship to the tribunal after receiving HMRC's decision on the matter, you should complete the relevant section on the Notice of Appeal Form and send it to us.

8. WILL I BE EXPECTED TO PAY TO GO TO TRIBUNAL?

What follows applies to appeals and applications started since 1 April 2009.

What follows applies to appeals and applications started since 1 April 2009.

In most tax cases each side will pay their own costs. Your own costs in preparing your appeal will depend on the difficulty of your case and whether you decide to handle your appeal yourself or instruct a tax adviser such as a barrister, solicitor or accountant.

However, in certain circumstances, the Tribunal may order one side to pay costs to the other. Those circumstances can include the case where one side has behaved unreasonably in the way they have carried out the case. Costs awards in those circumstances are quite rare.

There is a special rule that additionally applies to cases categorised by the tribunal as 'complex', where the winning party can ask for the losing party to pay its costs. However, you can choose to opt out of this rule, so that each party pays their own costs except where one side has behaved unreasonably. If your appeal is categorised as complex, you will be notified of this as soon as it has been categorised and given information about the implications, including your right to opt out of the 'complex' costs rule.

For appeals started before 1 April 2009 the Tribunal has discretion to order that they continue to be covered by the rules which applied before April 1 2009. These old rules are as follows: the General Commissioner Rules (where no one was liable to pay the other side's costs), the Special Commissioner Rules (where costs could only be awarded for wholly unreasonable conduct) and the VAT and Duties Tribunal's Rules (where costs could always be awarded at the tribunal's discretion). Costs can only be awarded under the new rules for such appeals if they could have been awarded under the old rules.

Applications for costs should be requested in writing no later than 28 days after the date on which the Tribunal sends the decision notice or notice of withdrawal and should be accompanied by a schedule of the costs and expenses claimed.

Community Legal Advice and other help

Free legal assistance is not available in most tax appeals, see www.communitylegaladvice.org.uk However, if you are on a low income, you may be able to get free help, for example from

– a qualified lawyer or accountant (although most will wish to charge a fee)
– a Citizens Advice Bureau
– TaxAid at www.taxaid.org.uk
– TOP – TaxHelp for Older People at www.taxvol.org.uk which provides help to those over 60.

Any of the above are also able to refer your case to the Bar Pro Bono Unit. This is a charity which provides free legal assistance from volunteer barristers, see www.barprobono.org.uk. You cannot apply directly to the Unit, but if your adviser refers the case, and it is accepted, a barrister will act for you before the Tribunal. It is strongly recommended that you make contact with an adviser in good time before the date of your appeal, as it may otherwise be impossible to provide support. Because of resource constraints, the organisations listed above cannot guarantee that free legal help will be provided.

9. WHAT SHOULD I DO FIRST?

Before you can make your appeal, you must first have an appeal-able written decision from HMRC with which you disagree. HMRC will have informed you of your options if you disagree with a decision.

You should consider your options seriously before appealing, including asking HMRC to look again at the decision as many disagreements can be settled by discussion or correspondence with HMRC without you actually having to go to a tribunal. HMRC are able to offer a formal internal review of your decision by a reviewer who will have had no previous involvement with your dispute. If you do not wish to engage these processes you can still appeal directly to the tribunal.

10. TIME LIMIT FOR APPEALING

You will normally have 30 days to appeal a disputed HMRC decision. If you make use of HMRC's review process you will have 30 days to appeal from the date they tell you the outcome. The time limit runs from both the original decision and any decision following review. The letter you receive from HMRC, both the original decision and any decision following review, will confirm the time you have for appealing.

If you are making your appeal outside the time limit, you must give reasons to the tribunal in writing.

11. WHERE DO I OBTAIN A NOTICE OF APPEAL?

Appeals to the tax tribunal must be made in writing. When you decide to make your appeal to the tax tribunal, you are strongly advised to complete a Notice of Appeal form and send it to the address at the bottom of the form.

You can download the Notice of Appeal form from our website at www.justice.gov.uk/tribunals/tax. If you do not have access to the internet, please phone us on 0300 123 1024 and we will send you a copy.

12. COMPLETING THE NOTICE OF APPEAL

The Notice of Appeal form is an important document as the details contained in this form will be used to process your appeal to a tribunal hearing, and to ensure we convene a panel that is appropriate for determining your case. It helps the tribunal to consider your case fairly and also helps us contact you with information about how your appeal is progressing.

A separate information sheet with guidance notes on completing the Notice of Appeal is available on our website and will be sent to you with the Notice of Appeal if you ask us to send you one. Please phone us on 0300 123 1024 to request this.

The completed Notices of Appeal should be sent to:

HM Courts & Tribunals Service
First-tier Tribunal (Tax Chamber)
PO Box 16972
Birmingham B16 6TZ

If you prefer to complete the Notice of Appeal electronically, you can send it to us at: taxappeals@hmcts.gsi.gov.uk.

The tribunal will acknowledge receipt of your appeal in writing. You will be given a Tribunal Service Reference Number which you should quote whenever you contact us. At this stage, we will also notify HMRC of your appeal.

13. CASE CATEGORISATION

When you appeal to the tax tribunal, it will put your appeal in one of four categories: Default Paper, Basic, Standard or Complex. Which of the four categories your appeal is allocated to is dependent on the nature and complexity of your appeal.

When we acknowledge your appeal, we will tell you in writing which category your appeal has been allocated, and how your appeal will proceed. We will keep you or your representative informed of progress throughout your appeal. Please note, however, that if you have a representative, we will only send correspondence to them. If you disagree with the way your case has been categorised you should contact the tribunal.

Default Paper cases, by their nature, are generally decided by the tribunal after reading the Notice of Appeal and the other written material provided by you and HMRC. Default Paper cases are dealt with without a hearing, though you may ask for your appeal to be decided at a hearing. If you or HMRC request a hearing or it is decided there should be a hearing by the tribunal, you will be expected to attend. HMRC will also send a representative to the hearing.

Basic category appeals are dealt with at informal hearings (see paragraph 14 below).

The vast majority of appeals within the Standard and Complex categories will be registered at our Centre in Birmingham but will then be passed to other Tax tribunal offices in London, Manchester and Edinburgh. We will advise you in writing if we transfer your appeal.

Tax appeals are heard at a number of venues across the UK and we will, where possible, arrange for your appeal to be heard at a venue reasonably close to where you live or work. Sometimes, however, due to the size or complexity of an appeal, we may not be able to do this but we will let you know as soon as possible.

There may be occasions during the appeal process when judicial direction on your appeal will be sought. If this is required, we will inform you of the directions and any associated time limits which may apply. In more complex cases, you may be asked to attend a hearing at which a Judge will make directions.

14. STATEMENT OF CASE AND NEXT STEPS

The next step will usually be for the tribunal to request a statement of case from HMRC, except in relation to basic category cases. A statement of case is a written statement of HMRC's position on your case. It will normally contain information such as the legislation under which the appealed decision was made, HMRC's position on the case and any other relevant information associated with the appeal.

Default Paper category (where there is no hearing)

A case categorised as default paper is generally decided when the tribunal has read the Notice of Appeal and other written material provided by you and HMRC. When we have notified HMRC that you have made an appeal against a decision which falls into this category, HMRC have 42 days to provide a statement of case to the tribunal. When the statement of case has been prepared, HMRC will send a copy to you.

You may provide a written response to the statement of case within 30 days of it being sent to you. You should send your response, if you wish to make one, to us and send a copy to HMRC. Please remember to quote your Tribunal reference number when writing to us and your HMRC reference number when corresponding with them. Unless you have asked for an oral hearing, the case will be decided by the tribunal when you have provided your response, or if you do not provide one, when the 30 day time limit has expired. The tribunal will send you its response as soon as possible after considering your case.

Basic Category (where there is an informal hearing)

The tribunal does not normally require a statement of case to be produced by HMRC for cases categorised as Basic. If your case is categorised in this way it will be listed for a hearing. You are expected to attend the hearing, when you will be given the opportunity to put forward your case, show the Tribunal any relevant documents you have and, if you wish, call witnesses. HMRC will also attend, and they may put their case, produce documents and call witnesses at the hearing. The hearing will be informal, and the tribunal will usually tell you what it has decided at the end of the hearing.

Standard and Complex categories

When we have notified HMRC that you have made an appeal against a decision in the Standard and Complex categories, HMRC have 60 days to provide a statement of case to the tribunal. The statement of case will contain similar information to that described above for the default paper category, though the facts and issues are likely to be much more complex. As with default paper cases, when HMRC have prepared the statement of case they will send a copy to you.

You will normally have 42 days from receipt of the statement of case from HMRC in which to provide to the tribunal and HMRC a list of the documents which you will rely on at the tribunal hearing. HMRC also have to provide a list of documents and copy their list to you. The tribunal may also make any other direction at this time as to what may be required of you, and may determine that your case requires more intensive case management. You will have the opportunity to express your views on how your case should be managed.

15. WHEN AND WHERE WILL MY APPEAL BE HEARD?

Hearings in the tax tribunal take place at a network of venues across the UK and we will arrange your appeal, where possible, at a venue which is local to you.

If your appeal is categorised as Basic, Standard or Complex, you should attend your hearing. For more information about the process of informing you of your hearing, please see **paragraph 16** below.

16. NOTIFICATION OF HEARING

If your appeal is to be decided at a hearing, we will write to you notifying you of the date, time and venue of your hearing. We will give you at least 14 days notice of a hearing, unless both you and HMRC agree to a shorter period. However, we will usually give at least a month's notice.

You should tell us immediately in writing if the date we set for your tribunal hearing is not convenient and give the reasons why you cannot attend. We will then write to you to tell you whether your postponement request has been granted or not. For appeals in the Standard and Complex categories, we will ask you in advance about dates which are inconvenient for you. In these cases, the tribunal will be less willing to agree to a postponement, though it will do so for good reason, such as sudden illness.

Appellants in the Basic category appeals will usually be asked to attend at either 10:00 or 14:00 on the day of the hearing. In the Standard and Complex categories you will be given a set time to attend and the case may last a number of days.

The time to arrive at the venue is given in your notice of hearing letter, and it is the latest time by which you should arrive at the tribunal venue. If you are likely to be late for your hearing, please telephone us and we will relay a message to the tribunal.

For further information of what can happen at your hearing, please refer to the leaflet 'At your hearing'.

17. WITHDRAWALS OF APPEALS

You can withdraw your appeal at any time. Should you wish to withdraw your appeal, you should write to us immediately. If HMRC decide to concede the matter in dispute, they will write to both the tribunal and you.

ANNEX A: WHAT TYPE OF APPEALS DOES THE TAX TRIBUNAL DEAL WITH?

The tax tribunal deals with appeals against decisions about tax made by HMRC. These include:

Direct tax

- income tax
- corporation tax
- capital gains tax
- national insurance contributions
- statutory payments
- inheritance tax
- petroleum revenue tax
- student loans
- stamp duty land tax
- tax collected under Pay as You Earn and the Construction Industry Scheme

Indirect tax

- value added tax (VAT)
- customs duty
- excise duties including:
  - alcoholic liquor duties
  - hydrocarbon oils duties (ie petrol, diesel, heating fuel etc)
  - tobacco products duty
  - bingo duty
  - gaming duty
  - general betting duty
  - lottery duty
  - pool betting duty
  - remote gaming duty
- aggregates levy
- air passenger duty
- climate change levy
- insurance premium tax
- landfill tax

The tax tribunal also deals with appeals against decisions made by HMRC in relation to the Money Laundering Regulations 2007.

The above list contains the most common types of HMRC decisions.

GUIDANCE TO ACCOMPANY A DECISION FROM THE FIRST-TIER TRIBUNAL (TAX CHAMBER)

Issued by HM Courts & Tribunals Service First-tier Tribunal (Tax).

This guidance gives you information about what you can do to challenge a Tribunal's decision or apply to change a Tribunal's decision. It applies whether the decision has been made by the Tribunal at a hearing or whether the decision has been made on the papers alone.

This leaflet contains only a summary of the actions you can take following a Tribunal's decision. It is not an exhaustive statement of the law. You may wish to seek advice about your rights.

PLEASE NOTE

The rights to apply for permission to appeal to the Upper Tribunal, correcting and setting aside a decision are also available to Her Majesty's Revenue and Customs (HMRC). If you are outside a time limit, you may apply for an extension of time, explaining why your application is late and why you should be granted an extension of time.

THE DECISION

In every case, even if the decision has been given orally at a hearing, the Tribunal office will send a written notice of the decision to you, the appellant, and to HMRC. Unless the parties both agreed otherwise at the hearing, the decision will include either a summary of findings of fact and reasons for the decision, or full written findings and reasons.

APPEAL TO THE UPPER TRIBUNAL

If you think the Tribunal has made an error of law, you may apply for permission to appeal to the Upper Tribunal against the decision. The following are some examples of what is meant by "error of law".

- The Tribunal applied the law incorrectly
- The Tribunal conducted the proceedings in breach of the proper procedures
- The Tribunal failed to give adequate reasons for its decision

HOW DO I APPLY FOR PERMISSION TO APPEAL TO THE UPPER TRIBUNAL?

If you want to make an application for permission to appeal to the Upper Tribunal and you have not received full written findings of fact and reasons for the decision, you must apply to the Tribunal for these. The Tribunal office must receive your written application for the full reasons within 28 days after the date that the Tribunal sent the decision notice to you.

If, having considered the statement of reasons, you believe that the decision of the Tribunal was based on an error of law, you may then apply to us for permission to appeal against the decision to the Upper Tribunal.

Your application for permission to appeal must;

- be received in the Tribunal office no later than 56 days from the date the Tribunal sent you full written reasons; and
- must identify the decision of the Tribunal to which it relates, the alleged error or errors in the decision and state the result you are seeking.

You can apply to the Tribunal for permission to appeal to the Upper Tribunal by completing the 'Permission to Appeal form' which can be obtained, along with guidance on filling in the form, by telephoning 0845 223 8080 or downloaded from our website at www.justice.gov.uk/tribunals/tax

An application for permission to appeal will be considered by a Judge of the First-tier Tribunal (Tax chamber). The Judge will:

- First of all consider whether to review the decision and, if there is an error of law, make a fresh decision or arrange for your case to be re-decided (see Review below);
- Grant permission, in which case you can make your appeal to the Upper Tribunal; or
- Refuse permission, in which case you then have the option of applying directly to the Upper Tribunal for permission.

If the appeal proceeds to the Upper Tribunal, that Tribunal has the power to set aside the First Tier Tribunal's decision and give a fresh decision or refer the case to the First Tier Tribunal for re-hearing.

REVIEW

When the Tribunal receives an application for permission to appeal it will first consider whether to review the decision; that is, to determine whether the Tribunal decision contains an error of law. If, as a result of the review, the Tribunal decides there was an error of law in the decision we will write to you (and all other parties). We will write to give you the opportunity to make representations before any action is taken as a result of a review. This action could mean changing the decision against which you are appealing.

CORRECTIONS

If you think the decision notice contains an accidental error (for example the Tribunal may have written 2009 instead of 2008 as the applicable date) you may write to us asking for a correction to be made. This rule only applies to what might be called "slips of the pen".

SETTING ASIDE

If you think there has been an irregularity in the arrangements for dealing with your appeal, you may write to us to ask for the Tribunal s decision to be set aside (cancelled). Your application must be received by the Tribunal no later than 28 days after the day when the Tribunal sent you the decision.

Examples of irregularities in the arrangements could be that a document relating to your appeal was not considered by the Tribunal or some other procedural irregularity or you or your representative was not present. The Tribunal will set aside the decision if it is in the interests of justice to do so. If you are asking that the decision be set aside because you or your representative was not present, you must explain why. If you think there was an irregularity, you must tell us what it was.

APPEALING TO THE UPPER TRIBUNAL (TAX AND CHANCERY CHAMBER)

November 2014.

This leaflet describes how to appeal to the Upper Tribunal, explains what happens once an appeal has been made and lists the stages that take place before a judge decides an appeal.

INTRODUCTION

About this leaflet

This leaflet is to help both members of the public and advisors. It describes how to appeal to the Upper Tribunal (Tax and Chancery Chamber) from a decision given by the Tax Chamber and the Property Chamber (Land Registration) of the First-tier Tribunal, once you have asked the First-tier Tribunal judge for permission to appeal. It explains what will happen to an appeal to the Upper Tribunal (Tax and Chancery Chamber) once it has been made. It also lists the stages that take place before the judge decides an appeal. **However, it is only a guide and does not have legal status. It does not cover all aspects of every situation, nor does it provide a full interpretation of the procedural rules.**

This leaflet does not describe any of the procedures in the First-tier Tribunal or how to apply for permission to appeal to the First-tier Tribunal judge which is an essential first step in appealing to the Upper Tribunal (Tax and Chancery Chamber). This information is provided with the First-tier Tribunal decision notice.

At the end of this leaflet is a section in which the meaning of some words used in this leaflet, or in documents which you may receive from the Upper Tribunal (Tax and Chancery Chamber) Office, is explained. We recommend that you keep this leaflet for reference throughout your dealings with our office.

ABOUT THE UPPER TRIBUNAL (TAX AND CHANCERY CHAMBER)

What is the Upper Tribunal (Tax and Chancery Chamber)?

The Upper Tribunal is an appellate tribunal created by the Tribunals, Courts and Enforcement Act 2007. The Tax and Chancery Chamber is the part of the Upper Tribunal, which hears and decides appeals from decisions of the First-tier Tribunal in tax, charity and Land Registration cases, and cases arising from the Proceeds of Crime Act 2002. In most cases appeals are on a point of law.

The Tax and Chancery Chamber has taken over appellate work formerly dealt with in the High Court's Chancery Division. The Tax and Chancery Chamber consists of specialist judges appointed by the Lord Chancellor. Some are also judges in the Courts, including the High Court. **All judges are independent of, and in no way connected to Her Majesty's Revenue and Customs (HMRC) or the Charity Commission.**

The judges sitting in the Tax and Chancery Chamber decide appeals on a point of law from First-tier Tribunal decisions on issues such as amounts of tax or duty to be paid, matters relating to National Insurance contributions, Statutory Sick Pay and Statutory Maternity Pay entitlement and recovery, and cases in relation to certain anti-avoidance provisions under the Income Tax Act. The judges also decide appeals on onward appeals formerly dealt with by the Charity Tribunal and High Court; in addition they may also hear some particularly complex References. In Land Registration cases they can also hear appeals on the facts in limited circumstances.

As the Upper Tribunal (Tax and Chancery Chamber) judges give judicial decisions neither they, nor any of the staff in the Upper Tribunal (Tax and Chancery Chamber) office, can give legal advice. If you intend to appeal you may wish to seek legal advice.

Where are the offices of the Upper Tribunal (Tax and Chancery Chamber)?

The office of the Upper Tribunal (Tax and Chancery Chamber) is based in London and deals with applications for permission to appeal (leave to appeal for cases within Northern Ireland) and appeals against decisions made by the First-tier Tribunal in the UK. The administrative staff prepare case files for judges, arrange oral hearings and deal with correspondence and queries. The address of the office is:

Upper Tribunal (Tax and Chancery Chamber)
Fifth Floor
Rolls Building
Fetter Lane
London
EC4A 1NL
DX: 160042 Strand 4
Telephone (9am to 5pm): 020 7612 9700
Email: financeandtaxappeals@hmcts.gsi.gov.uk

If your First-tier Tribunal case was heard in Scotland or you live in Scotland you may send the form to the London office or the Scottish office:

The Upper Tribunal (Tax and Chancery Chamber)
George House
126 George Street
Edinburgh EH2 4HH

WHO CAN APPEAL TO THE UPPER TRIBUNAL (TAX AND CHANCERY CHAMBER)?

Appeals by tax payers, businesses and public bodies in tax and charity cases

Tax payers, businesses and public bodies who are parties at the First-tier Tribunal can appeal to the Upper Tribunal (Tax and Chancery Chamber) against the decision of that tribunal.

If you lost your case at the First-tier Tribunal you will normally be required to pay or repay any amounts due as a result of the tribunal decision, but in some exceptional cases this requirement may be suspended. You should speak to HM Revenue & Customs, the Serious Organised Crime Agency or the Charity Commission in the first instance if you think you should not be required to pay.

Appeals by Her Majesty's Revenue and Customs (HMRC), the Serious Organised Crime Agency (SOCA) or the Charity Commission in tax and charity cases

If you won your case at the First-tier Tribunal, it is still possible for the respondent (HMRC, SOCA or the Charity Commission) to appeal to the Upper Tribunal.

The rules about applying for the full written statement of reasons and permission to appeal are equally applicable to the respondent as to you. These rules are explained briefly in the sections **'Before you can appeal'** and **'How to appeal'**.

If the respondent is given permission to appeal you will be told by the First-tier Tribunal office. If they do, you will normally be paid or repaid amounts awarded to you by the First-tier Tribunal, but in some cases payment maybe suspended. You will be entitled to make comments in writing before the Upper Tribunal judge decides the appeal. You will also be able to ask for an oral hearing if you wish.

Appeals from decisions from in the First-tier Tribunal (Property Chamber) in Land Registration cases

Any party to a Land Registration case in the First-tier Tribunal's decision can appeal to the Upper Tribunal (Tax and Chancery Chamber) against the decision of that tribunal. In a case involving a disputed application to the Land Registry which has been referred to the tribunal, you should also ask for a 'stay' of the First-tier Tribunal's order and tell the Land Registry that you have done so if you want the Land Registry to agree not to implement the order pending any appeal.

BEFORE YOU CAN APPEAL

If you wish to challenge the decision of a First-tier Tribunal there are **various steps that you must have taken at that tribunal before you can appeal to the Upper Tribunal.** These will have been explained by the First-Tier Tribunal office in the information sent with the decision notice.

In particular you must have:

1. asked for a full written statement of the First-tier Tribunal's reasons for its decision (unless you have already received one); and

2. applied to the First-tier Tribunal judge for permission to appeal.

If you are appealing a Tax decision there is **56 day** time limit, and if you are appealing a Charity or Land Registration decision there is a **28 day** time limit in which to do so. This may be extended in certain circumstances. You should always ask for a written statement first (unless you have already received one), but if you do not, or you are refused one because you are too late, you must always ask the First-tier Tribunal judge for permission to appeal.

Please note: if you do not ask for a written statement within the time limit your chances of appealing may be lost or seriously limited.

REASONS (GROUNDS) FOR APPEALING

In most cases you can only appeal against the decision of a First-tier Tribunal if it was **wrong in law**. Examples of where the tribunal may be wrong in law include:

- The tribunal did not apply the correct law or wrongly interpreted the law.
- The tribunal made a procedural error.
- The tribunal had no evidence, or not enough evidence, to support its decision.
- The tribunal did not give adequate reasons for its decision in the written statement of its reasons.

This list is not exhaustive and the tribunal may be wrong in law for some other reason not mentioned here. If you are unsure whether the tribunal was wrong in law you may wish to seek legal advice.

In Land Registration cases it is also possible to appeal against the Tribunal's decision on the facts in limited circumstances.

You must always give full details of your reasons for appealing.

HOW TO APPEAL

In general

Once you have applied to the First-tier Tribunal judge for permission to appeal to the Upper Tribunal:

- If the First-tier Tribunal judge **refuses you permission, or does not admit your application,** you may apply to an Upper Tribunal (Tax and Chancery Chamber) judge for permission to appeal.
- If the First-tier Tribunal judge **grants you permission to appeal,** you should send your appeal to the Upper Tribunal (Tax and Chancery Chamber).

Details of what you need to do are set out below. They are also set out in the form for applying for permission or appealing to the Upper Tribunal (Tax and Chancery Chamber) and the notes which go with the form.

You **must** always have applied to a First-tier tribunal judge first.

How to apply to a judge in the Upper Tribunal (Tax and Chancery Chamber) for permission to appeal

If the First-tier Tribunal judge **refuses your application for permission** to appeal, **or does not admit** your application because you were late or because you did not have a written statement of reasons, you may apply for permission to appeal direct to the Upper Tribunal judge. **You must always have applied to the First-tier Tribunal judge first.**

The **First-tier Tribunal** will send you a letter or order telling you that the judge has refused you permission to appeal or refused to admit your application. You should then send your application to the Upper Tribunal (Tax and Chancery Chamber) so that it is received **no later than one month** after the date on the letter notifying you of the First-tier Tribunal judge's ruling. You should use the form which the First-tier Tribunal office will give you or, or which can be downloaded from our website at http://www.justice.gov.uk. If you cannot get a copy, you should write a letter setting out your reasons for appealing. You should enclose the necessary documents. These are:

- a copy of the decision issued by the First-tier Tribunal
- the letter or order from the First-tier Tribunal telling you that you have been granted or refused permission or that your application has not been admitted.

  You may ask for an oral hearing of your application for permission to appeal. If the Upper Tribunal judge grants your request you will be told the date and place, normally at least 14 days in advance.

  If you are late in applying for permission you must ask for an extension of time and explain why your application was not made in time. Unless the Upper Tribunal judge considers you should be granted an extension of time your application will not be admitted and **you will not be able to appeal.**

  If your application for permission to the First-tier Tribunal was not admitted because you were late or because you did not have a written statement, you should explain why your application was not made in time. The Upper Tribunal judge may only admit your application if the judge considers it is in the interests of justice. If the Upper Tribunal judge does **not admit your application you will not be able to appeal.**

  You may withdraw your application for permission to appeal at any time before it is decided. You just need to write a letter to the office of the Upper Tribunal (Tax and Chancery Chamber). If you later wish to ask for your application to be reinstated you should write to the Upper Tribunal (Tax and Chancery Chamber) office within one month. If you are late you may ask for an extension of time.

What happens if the Tax and Chancery Chamber judge refuses you permission to appeal?

The office will send you a copy of the judge's ruling refusing you permission to appeal, including the reasons.

If the judge decides your application for permission without an oral hearing and refuses you permission or gives permission on limited grounds or subject to conditions you may apply in writing within 14 days for the decision to be reconsidered at an oral hearing.

A refusal of permission to appeal may be set aside by the Upper Tribunal judge if there has been a procedural irregularity in the proceedings and the judge considers that it is in the interests of justice to do so. For example, if a document relating to the proceedings has gone astray or a party or his representative was not present at a hearing. An application to set aside must be made in writing **within one month.**

There is no right of appeal to the Court of Appeal (or the Court of Session in Scotland) against a refusal of permission to appeal or refusal to admit a late application. Also you cannot appeal against the decision of an Upper Tribunal judge to grant permission to appeal to someone else.

How to appeal to the Upper Tribunal (Tax and Chancery Chamber) once you have been granted permission to appea

If the First-tier Tribunal judge grants you permission to appeal, the First-tier Tribunal office will send you a letter or order telling you.

You should then send your appeal to the Upper Tribunal (Tax and Chancery Chamber) so that it is received **no later than one month** after the date of the letter notifying you of the First-tier Tribunal judge's ruling. You should use the form if you can. If not, just write a letter saying you wish to appeal and giving your reasons. **If you do not do this you may lose your opportunity to appeal.**

If you are late you must ask for an extension of time and should explain why your appeal was not made in time. Unless the Upper Tribunal judge considers you should be granted an extension of time your appeal will not be admitted and you will not be able to appeal.

If the Upper Tribunal judge grants you permission to appeal you will not normally have to make a separate appeal. You will be told by the office if you have to do so.

WHAT HAPPENS ONCE PERMISSION HAS BEEN GRANTED?

How the appeal will proceed

In general

Once you have appealed to the Upper Tribunal (Tax and Chancery Chamber), or a Tax and Chancery Chamber judge has granted you permission to appeal, the office will copy the appeal papers, including the notice of appeal to you and the other parties to the case (called respondents).

The Upper Tribunal judge will give reasons for granting permission to appeal (unless permission was granted by the First-tier Tribunal judge) and you will be told how the appeal is to proceed and any time limits.

You and the respondents may simply be asked whether you object to the Upper Tribunal deciding the appeal on a particular point. Otherwise the respondents will normally be asked for full comments on your appeal and you will be given the opportunity to reply.

If **HMRC, SOCA** or the **Charity Commission has appealed**, the Upper Tribunal (Tax and Chancery Chamber) office will ask you whether you have a representative and you (or your representative) will be asked if you wish to make comments on the appeal.

You should note that all comments or observations made by one party will be copied to all the other parties. At the same time the office will send out letters explaining what, if anything, needs to be done next.

Will there be an oral hearing of the appeal?

Appeals in the Upper Tribunal (Tax and Chancery Chamber) can be decided with or without an oral hearing. You may ask for an oral hearing of your appeal, giving your reasons.

If the appeal has been made by someone else and you are a respondent, and the judge decides to have an oral hearing you will be told about it and will be entitled to attend even if you did not ask for a hearing.

An Upper Tribunal judge can direct an oral hearing be held even though no one has asked for one.

Oral hearings are usually held in London, Manchester and Edinburgh. They are exceptionally held in other court centres if people are unable to travel.

If no oral hearing is held, the judge will give his or her decision on the appeal after considering the documents from the First-tier Tribunal as well as the grounds of appeal and the written comments made by all parties to the appeal to the Upper Tribunal (Tax and Chancery Chamber).

What will happen if there is an oral hearing?

Once the date for an oral hearing has been set, you will be sent a letter with details of the date, time and place.

You must normally be given at least 14 days notice of the date of a hearing unless both you and the respondent have agreed to shorter notice. However you will usually be given more notice.

Oral hearings are normally in public unless the judge directs a private hearing. However, it is unusual for members of the public to come to hearings. If you would like your hearing to be private, you should say why and the judge will decide this.

Your representative (if you have one) and any respondents to your appeal will also be entitled to attend the oral hearing and will be told about it.

The judge will not usually give a decision at the end of the hearing. It will be sent to you and all other parties after the hearing has taken place.

Where a case raises a particularly important or difficult point of law, it may be heard by three judges instead of one. However, this is very rare.

What you should do if you find you cannot attend an oral hearing

If you find that you will not be able to attend a hearing which has been fixed you should tell the Upper Tribunal (Tax and Chancery Chamber) office as soon as possible. **You should write unless the time is very short in which case you may telephone.** You should also be prepared to agree an alternative hearing date.

If you would like the hearing postponed you should say why and the judge will decide what should happen. **You should not assume a hearing will be cancelled because you have asked; a hearing once appointed remains on unless the tribunal states that it has been cancelled.** The judge may decide to go ahead with the hearing without you.

If you do not turn up at the hearing, the judge will decide whether to go ahead without you. **If you are delayed on your journey to the hearing, you should make every effort to ring the office to let them know immediately.**

What you should do if you wish to withdraw your appeal

Once you have been granted permission to appeal, you need the agreement of the Upper Tribunal to withdraw, so you should explain your reasons. If you then want your appeal to be reinstated you should write to the Upper Tribunal office within one month. If you are late you may ask for an extension of time.

If HMRC, SOCA or the Charity Commission has appealed you cannot withdraw from the appeal. You do not need to take any part but a decision will be made whether or not you do take part.

THE DECISION OF THE UPPER TRIBUNAL (TAX AND CHANCERY CHAMBER) ON THE APPEAL

The judge's decision

If there is no oral hearing the appeal papers will be sent to the Upper Tribunal judge to be decided once all the parties have made their written comments in accordance with the directions made by the judge.

The judge will always give his or her decision in writing. The Upper Tribunal (Tax and Chancery Chamber) office will send you a copy of the judge's decision. They will also send a copy to your representative if you have one and to the other parties to the appeal.

The judge must give reasons for the appeal being allowed or dismissed unless all the parties have agreed otherwise.

If the judge has sent the case back to be re-decided by the First-tier Tribunal, you will receive a letter from the First-tier Tribunal clerk.

If the Upper Tribunal judge dismisses your appeal, or the result of the appeal is not wholly favourable to you, you have the right to appeal to the Court of Appeal, or the Court of Session if you appeal was heard in Scotland. The office will send you a letter telling you about your right to appeal. There is more detail about this in the section **'What to do if you are dissatisfied with the decision of an Upper Tribunal (Tax and Chancery Chamber) judge'.**

If the Upper Tribunal judge allows your appeal or dismisses another party's appeal, that other party may wish to appeal to those courts.

PARTICULAR ISSUES WHICH MAY ARISE ON APPEALS

How much will it cost to appeal?

There is no fee payable for applying for permission to appeal or for appealing to the Upper Tribunal (Tax and Chancery Chamber).

The Upper Tribunal (Tax and Chancery Chamber) may order one party to pay another party's costs.

Representatives

It is open to you to have a representative to help you fill in the appeal form, deal with letters from the Upper Tribunal (Tax and Chancery Chamber) office, make and respond to submissions and appear in front of the judge for you if there is an oral hearing.

If you have a representative you must send the Upper Tribunal (Tax and Chancery Chamber) office written notice of your representative's name and address. If the person stops representing you, you must notify the Upper Tribunal (Tax and Chancery Chamber) office otherwise they are entitled to assume that you are still represented and will send documents to the representative and not to you.

You may instruct a solicitor, an accountant or any other person (qualified or not) to act as your representative.

Even if you do not have a representative to help you with the initial stages of your case you can bring another person to any oral hearing and, with the judge's permission, that person can act as your representative or assist you to present your case.

WHAT DO I DO IF I AM UNSATISFIED WITH THE DECISION OF THE UPPER TRIBUNAL?

In general

You may apply to the Upper Tribunal (Tax and Chancery Chamber) for a decision on an appeal to be set-aside on certain limited procedural grounds.

You may appeal to the Court of Appeal (or Court of Session in Scotland) against the decision of Upper Tribunal. **You need permission first.**

Any other party to the proceedings before the Upper Tribunal (Tax and Chancery Chamber) has the same right to appeal to the Court of Appeal/ Court of Session as you do.

How to apply for the decision of the Upper Tribunal (Tax and Chancery Chamber) to be set aside

A refusal of permission to appeal may be set aside by the Upper Tribunal (Tax and Chancery Chamber) judge if there has been a procedural irregularity in the proceedings and the judge considers that it is in the interests of justice to do so. For example, if a document relating to the proceedings has gone astray or a party or his representative was not present at a hearing. An application to set aside must be made in writing with reasons **within one month.**

How to appeal to the Court of Appeal/ Court of Session against an Upper Tribunal (Tax and Chancery Chamber) decision

Appeals from the Upper Tribunal (Tax and Chancery Chamber) are on a point of law only. If therefore the Upper Tribunal makes a finding of fact based on the evidence submitted in the appeal (or on the basis that you have not produced all the evidence to prove your case) there is no appeal against such findings of fact. HMRC, SOCA or the Charity Commission has a similar right of appeal if the Upper Tribunal finds in your favour.

To appeal to the Court of Appeal (Court of Session in Scotland) **you must have permission** from the Upper Tribunal, or if the Upper Tribunal refuses, from the Court.

An application for permission to appeal to the Court of Appeal or Court of Session must be received by the Upper Tribunal (Tax and Chancery Chamber) **within one month of the latest of:**

- written notice of the decision being sent to you; or
- your being notified of amended reasons for, or a correction of, the decision following review (see below); or
- your being notified that an application to set aside (made in time or with an extension of time) has not been successful.

The time limit may be extended by the Upper Tribunal judge.

You must make your application in writing identifying the alleged error or errors of law and stating the result you ask for.

How the Upper Tribunal (Tax and Chancery Chamber) considers your application for permission to appeal

On an application for permission to appeal, the Upper Tribunal (Tax and Chancery Chamber) may review the decision and may set it aside, amend the reasons for it or correct it if:

- when making the decision the judge overlooked a legislative provision or binding authority which could have had a material effect on the decision; or
- since the decision a higher court has made another decision binding on the Upper Tribunal which, if made before the decision, could have had a material effect on it.

The Upper Tribunal (Tax and Chancery Chamber) must notify the parties in writing of the outcome of any review.

If the Upper Tribunal takes any action on review without first giving every party an opportunity to make representations it must allow that party to apply for the action to be set aside and the decision to be reviewed again.

If the Upper Tribunal does not review, or on review decides not to alter the decision, it must decide whether to grant permission to appeal to the Court of Appeal. It must record the decision in writing and give reasons for refusing permission either completely or in respect of any grounds of appeal.

If you are refused permission to appeal by the Upper Tribunal (Tax and Chancery Chamber) you may renew your application in the Court of Appeal/ Court of Session.

If the Upper Tribunal (Tax and Chancery Chamber) grants you permission you will need to appeal to the Court of Appeal/ Court of Session.

The Court of Appeal/ Court of Session time limits are short so if you wish to renew your application or to appeal you should contact them as soon as possible.

The address for the Court of Appeal (England and Wales) is:

The Civil Appeals Office
Room E307
The Royal Courts of Justice
Strand
London
WC2A 2LL
Email: civilappeals.registry@HMCS.gsi.gov.uk

Further information of appealing to the Court of Appeal (Northern Ireland) can be found on their website, under 'legislation'. The address is: http://www.courtsni.gov.uk/en-GB/default.htm?UserPref=culture%5Een-GB

Information on applying to the Court of Session in Scotland is available under the Rules of the Court of Session, which can be found at http://www.scotcourts.gov.uk/index.asp

If you wish to appeal to the Court of Appeal/ Court of Session, you are advised to take legal advice, as you may become liable for costs.

THE MEANING OF WORDS

The following words are either used in this leaflet or may be used in documents you receive from the office of the Upper Tribunal (Tax and Chancery Chamber).

- An **appeal** is made by a person (or HMRC or SOCA) who has been given **permission to appeal.**
- An **appellant** is the person, or other body, who is appealing.
- The **Court of Appeal** in **London** is a higher court (for cases in England and Wales) to which you may be able to appeal against an Upper Tribunal (Tax and Chancery Chamber) decision.
- The **Court of Appeal** in **Belfast** is a higher court (for cases in Northern Ireland) to which you may be able to appeal against an Upper Tribunal (Tax and Chancery Chamber) decision.
- The **Court of Session** in **Edinburgh** is a higher court (for cases in Scotland) to which you may be able to appeal against an Upper Tribunal (Tax and Chancery Chamber) decision.

- A **Direction** is a written instruction by the Upper Tribunal (Tax and Chancery Chamber) judge on the procedure that must be followed. The judge will make a Direction at the beginning of an appeal as to the order in which the parties are to make their submissions and the time limits for doing so.
- **Oral hearings** are described in the section titled **'What happens once permission has been granted'**.
- **Permission to appeal** is the first essential step in the appeal process. If you do not have **permission** you will not be able to **appeal.**
- **A point of law, error of law and wrong in law**: examples are given in the section titled **'Reasons for appealing'**. You must bear in mind that there may be other points of law and if you are uncertain you may like to seek advice as described in that section.
- **A procedural error** is something that has gone wrong with the procedure in an appeal. The procedural rules in relation to appeals to the Upper Tribunal are set out in the Tribunal Procedure (Upper Tribunal) Rules 2008 as amended. However, only certain limited errors give you the right to have a decision **set aside**. These are set out in rule 43 of the Rules.
- A **Response** contains the observations made by a **respondent** in a written document answering the points made in an appeal or the points that the judge has raised in a **Direction. A response** may also be called **observations** or **submissions.**
- **A respondent** is a person who has a right to take part in or oppose an **appeal** that has been made to the Upper Tribunal (Tax and Chancery Chamber)
  - In Tax and Charity cases, respondents can be the HM Revenue & Customs (HMRC), Serious Organised Crime Agency (SOCA) or the Charity Commission.
  - In Land Registration cases, the respondent to an appeal is usually whoever won the case at the First-tier Tribunal.
- **A Submission** is made by any party in a written document answering the points made in an appeal or the points that the judge has raised in a **Direction. Submissions** may also be called **observations.**

GENERAL NOTE

The law governing the procedure on applications to the Upper Tribunal for permission to appeal and appeals is set out in the following documents:

- Tribunal Procedure (Upper Tribunal) Rules 2008
  - (SI number 2698, 2008)
  - http://www.opsi.gov.uk/si/si2008/uksi_20082698_en_1
- The Tribunal Procedure (Amendment) Rules 2009
  - (SI number 274, 2009)
  - http://www.opsi.gov.uk/si/si2009/uksi_20090274_en_1
- The Tribunal Procedure (Amendment No 2) Rules 2009 (SI number 1975, 2009).

Practice Directions

Practice Directions

IN THE SUPREME COURT OF ENGLAND AND WALES DIRECTION - CLASSES OF CASES SPECIFIED UNDER SECTION 18(6) OF THE TRIBUNALS, COURTS AND ENFORCEMENT ACT 2007

It is ordered as follows—

1. The following direction takes effect in relation to an application made to the High Court or Upper Tribunal on or after 3 November 2008 that seeks relief of a kind mentioned in section 15(1) of the Tribunals, Courts and Enforcement Act 2007 ("the 2007 Act").

2. The Lord Chief Justice hereby directs that the following classes of case are specified for the purposes of section 18(6) of the 2007 Act—

(a) Any decision of the First-Tier Tribunal on an appeal made in the exercise of a right conferred by the Criminal Injuries Compensation Scheme in compliance with section 5(l) of the Criminal Injuries Compensation Act 1995 (appeals against decisions on review); and

(b) Any decision of the First-tier Tribunal made under Tribunal Procedure Rules or section 9 of the 2007 Act where there is no right of appeal to the Upper Tribunal and that decision is not an excluded decision within paragraph (b), (c), or (f) of section 11(5) of the 2007 Act.

3. This Direction does not have effect where an application seeks (whether or not alone) a declaration of incompatibility under section 4 of the Human Rights Act 1998.

4. This Direction is made by the Lord Chief Justice with the agreement of the Lord Chancellor. It is made in the exercise of powers conferred by section 18(6) of the 2007 Act and in accordance with Part I of Schedule 2 to the Constitutional Reform Act 2005.

The Right Honourable Lord Judge

Lord Chief Justice of England and Wales

UPPER TRIBUNAL TRANSCRIPTS OF PROCEEDINGS

30 October 2008

TRANSCRIPTS OF PROCEEDINGS

1. At any hearing where the proceedings are recorded such recordings must be preserved by the Tribunal for six months from the date of the hearing to which the recording relates, and any party to the proceedings may, within that period, apply in writing for a transcript and a transcript must be supplied to that party.

2. If a transcript is supplied to a party under paragraph 1, that party must pay for the production and supply of the transcript unless they have applied in writing for, and the Tribunal has given, a direction that the transcript be produced and supplied at public expense.

3. The Tribunal may direct a transcript be supplied at public expense if satisfied that:

(a) a recording of the relevant proceedings is in existence; and

(b) the party making the application;

(i) has applied, or intends to apply, for permission to challenge the Upper Tribunal's decision in another court and has reasonable grounds for bringing or intending to challenge that decision; or

(ii) has been granted permission to challenge the Upper Tribunal's decision and has brought, or intends to bring, such proceedings; or

(iii) is a respondent to any such challenge to a decision of the Upper Tribunal in another court; and

(c) the transcript is necessary for the purpose of challenging the Upper Tribunal's decision; and

(d) the party's financial circumstances are such that that party cannot afford to pay for the transcript from their own income or funds.

4. Any transcript of proceedings directed to be supplied at public expense must be restricted to that part of the proceedings necessary for the purposes of any such challenge.

5. For the purposes of considering an application for a transcript at public expense, the Tribunal may give directions, for example, requiring the party to disclose details of their financial circumstances.

6. This Practice Direction is made by the Senior President of Tribunals with the agreement of the Lord Chancellor. It is made in the exercise of powers conferred by the Tribunals, Courts and Enforcement Act 2007.

LORD JUSTICE CARNWATH

SENIOR PRESIDENT OF TRIBUNALS

FIRST-TIER AND UPPER TRIBUNAL USE OF THE WELSH LANGUAGE IN TRIBUNALS IN WALES

30 October 2008

GENERAL

1. The purpose of this Practice Direction is to reflect the principle of the Welsh Language Act 1993 that in the administration of justice in Wales, the English and Welsh languages should be treated on a basis of equality.

2. In this Practice Direction "Welsh case" means a case which is before the Tribunal in which all "individual parties" are resident in Wales or which has been classified as a Welsh case by the Tribunal. An "individual party" is a party other than a Government Department or Agency. Where not all of the "individual parties" are resident in Wales the Tribunal will decide whether the case should be classified as a Welsh case or not.

USE OF THE WELSH LANGUAGE

3. In a Welsh case the Welsh language may be used by any party or witnesses or in any document placed before the Tribunal or (subject to the listing provisions below) at any hearing.

LISTING

4. Unless it is not reasonably practicable to do so a party, or their representative, must inform the Tribunal 21 days before any hearing in a Welsh case that the Welsh language will be used by the party, their representative, any witness to be called by that party or in any document to be produced by the party.

5. Where the proceedings are on appeal to the Upper Tribunal and the Welsh language was used in the Tribunal below, the Tribunal Manager must make arrangements for the continued use of the Welsh language in the proceedings before the Upper Tribunal.

6. Where practicable, a hearing in which the Welsh language is to be used must be listed before a Welsh speaking Tribunal and, where translation facilities are needed, at a venue with simultaneous translation facilities.

INTERPRETERS

7. Whenever an interpreter is needed to translate evidence from English into Welsh or from Welsh into English, the Tribunal Manager in whose tribunal the case is to be heard must ensure that the attendance is secured of an interpreter whose name is included in the list of approved interpreters.

WITNESSES

8. When a witness in a case in which the Welsh language may be used is required to give evidence on oath or affirmation the Tribunal must inform the witness that they may be sworn or affirm in Welsh or English as they wish.

9. This Practice Direction is made by the Senior President of Tribunals with the agreement of the Lord Chancellor. It is made in the exercise of powers conferred by the Tribunals, Courts and Enforcement Act 2007.

LORD JUSTICE CARNWATH

SENIOR PRESIDENT OF TRIBUNALS

FIRST-TIER TRIBUNAL CATEGORISATION OF CASES IN THE TAX CHAMBER

Practice Direction

29 April 2013

This Practice Statement has been made by the Chamber President to give guidance to the Tribunal and to Tribunal users on the practice adopted in relation to the categorisation of tax cases.

Introduction

Rule 23 of the Tribunal Procedure (First-tier Tribunal) (Tax Chamber) Rules 2009 provides that when the Tribunal receives a notice of appeal, application notice or notice of reference, the Tribunal must give a direction allocating the case to one of the categories set out in that Rule, namely,

- Default Paper cases (which will usually be disposed of without a hearing);
- Basic cases (which will usually be disposed of after a hearing, with minimal exchange of documents before the hearing);
- Standard cases (which will usually be subject to more detailed case management and be disposed of after a hearing); and
- Complex cases (to which special rules apply in relation to costs awards and eligibility for transfer to the Upper Tribunal).

The Tribunal may also at any time, either on the application of a party or on its own initiative, give a further direction re-allocating a case to a different category.

This Practice Statement sets out the practice of the Tribunal with regard to the allocation of tax cases. Nothing in it affects the powers or discretion of the Tribunal in relation to case categorisation generally, nor the ability of any party to an appeal to make any application regarding categorisation of that appeal. The fact that a case falls within the descriptions set out in this Practice Statement for a particular category does not mean that the case must, or will, be allocated to that category.

1. Default Paper cases

When the Tribunal receives a notice of appeal, application notice or notice of reference in one of the following types of cases, the Tribunal will allocate the case to the Default Paper category unless the Tribunal considers that there is a reason why it is appropriate to allocate the case to a different category.

(a) In relation to all taxes and duties, appeals against fixed penalties amounting to not more than £2000 for late filing of returns, statements, accounts or documents and late submission of notices of being chargeable to tax.

(b) Appeals against penalties amounting to not more than £2000 for late payment of any tax or duty.

2. Basic cases

When the Tribunal receives a notice of appeal, application notice or notice of reference in one of the following types of cases, the Tribunal will allocate the case to the Basic category unless the case is of a type listed in paragraph 1 (Default Paper cases) or the Tribunal considers that there is a reason why it is appropriate to allocate the case to a different category.

(a) Appeals—
  (i) against penalties for late filing of returns and documents and late payment of duties;
  (ii) against penalties for inaccurate returns or documents, except where the penalties are for deliberate action or cases where an appeal is also brought against the assessment of the tax to which the return or document relates;
  (iii) seeking the mitigation or reduction of penalties, and those in which a reasonable excuse is asserted;
  (iv) against information notices and penalties for non-compliance with information notices; and
  (v) against Pay As You Earn (PAYE) coding notices.

(b) Applications—
  (i) for permission to make or notify a late appeal;
  (ii) for an indirect tax appeal to be entertained without payment of tax or duty on grounds of hardship (hardship applications);
  (iii) for the postponement of the payment of tax pending the determination of an appeal; and
  (iv) for a direction that HMRC close an enquiry into a personal, partnership or company self-assessment return. or a direction that HMRC close an enquiry into a personal, partnership or company self-assessment return.

3. Standard cases

Any case that is not allocated to any of the Default Paper, Basic or Complex categories will be categorised as a Standard case.

4. Complex cases

Rule 23 provides that the Tribunal may allocate a case as a Complex case only if the Tribunal considers that the case—

(a) will require lengthy or complex evidence or a lengthy hearing;
(b) involves a complex or important principle or issue; or
(c) involves a large financial sum.

The Tribunal will assess whether, having regard to the nature of a particular case, any one or more of these criteria are satisfied. In making this assessment the Tribunal will take into account all the circumstances, including the implications of the costs-shifting regime (subject to the right of the taxpayer to opt out) and the fact that cases allocated to the Complex category are eligible, subject to various consents, to be transferred to the Upper Tribunal.

If on such an assessment the Tribunal considers that a case meets the stated criteria, it will, in the absence of special factors, allocate the case to the Complex category.

Colin Bishopp

President, First-tier Tribunal (Tax Chamber)

Practice Statements

Practice Statements

APPLICATIONS FOR PERMISSION TO APPEAL IN THE TAX CHAMBER AND THE TAX AND CHANCERY CHAMBER

Practice Statement

20 May 2015

FIRST-TIER TRIBUNAL and UPPER TRIBUNAL

This Practice Statement has been made by the Presidents of the Tax and Chancery Chamber and the Tax Chamber to give guidance to the tribunal and to tribunal users on the practice adopted in relation to the handling of applications for permission to appeal from the Tax Chamber to the Tax and Chancery Chamber, and from the Tax and Chancery Chamber to the relevant Court of Appeal or the Court of Session.

The Tribunal Procedure (First-tier Tribunal) (Tax Chamber) Rules 2009 (the "F-tT Rules") and the Tribunal Procedure (Upper Tribunal) Rules 2008 (the "UT Rules") provide for the making of applications for permission to appeal from the First-tier Tribunal to the Upper Tribunal, and set out a number of requirements which an applicant and the tribunals must meet. The rules are, however, silent on some other points.

In particular, the rules do not make it clear whether, and if so by whom and when, the other party to an appeal (in this Practice Statement referred to as the respondent) is to be notified that an application for permission to appeal has been filed, and they make no provision for the respondent to participate in the process, save in the event that the judge dealing with the matter decides to review the decision (see F-tT Rules 40 and 41, UT Rules 45 and 46). There is potential unfairness to a respondent who does not learn that a decision he thought had become final is the subject of an onward appeal until he receives a copy of the decision allowing an application for permission (see F-tT Rule 40(3), UT Rule 45(3)).

The practice which the Tax Chamber and the Tax and Chancery Chamber will apply (and which so far as possible reflects the practice in the civil courts), is as follows:

Applications to the First-tier Tribunal for permission to appeal

1 Every application to the First-tier Tribunal for permission to appeal which is in proper form will be copied to the respondent on receipt. An application in proper form is one which complies with all of the applicable requirements of F-tT Rule 39. An application not in proper form will be rejected. In particular, an applicant MUST first have received full reasons for the First-tier Tribunal's decision, MUST send a copy of the reasons with his application and MUST identify an error of law in that decision.

2 If the application is in time (see F-tT Rule 39(2) for the time limit) the application will at the same time be passed to a First-tier Tribunal judge for determination. The respondent will not be required, or invited, to make representations but will be assumed to support the decision which the applicant is seeking to appeal.

3 If the application is made out of time, but with an application in proper form for an extension of time (see F-tT Rule 39(4)), the respondent will be asked for observations in respect of the application for an extension. The Tribunal will send the applicant a copy of any observations it receives, to which the applicant may reply. If the application is opposed, the tribunal may decide to deal with it at an oral hearing.

4 If an extension of time is refused and the application for permission to appeal is not admitted, the applicant may apply to the Upper Tribunal for permission to appeal against that refusal: see UT Rule 21(2) and paragraph 8 below.

Practice Statements

5. Paragraphs 5, 6 and 7 below apply to applications which are in time, or where an extension of time has been granted.

6 If the judge decides to review the decision, the procedure spelt out in F-tT Rule 41 will be followed.

7 If the judge decides not to review the decision he will proceed immediately to deal with the application for permission to appeal. The application will normally be dealt with on the basis of the written application alone. Exceptionally the judge may arrange a hearing, which both parties will be invited (but not required) to attend. Neither an applicant nor a respondent has the right to an oral hearing of the application.

8 If permission to appeal is granted, a decision notice to that effect will be sent to the applicant and to the respondent. It is then for the applicant to file notice of appeal at the Upper Tribunal office within the time limit of one month from the date of the First-tier Tribunal's decision notice giving permission, and it MUST be include the information, and be accompanied by the prescribed documents (UT Rule 23(2)(a), (3) and (4)). The Upper Tribunal will send copies to the respondent.

Applications to the Upper Tribunal to appeal against a F-tT decision

9 If permission to appeal has been refused by the First-tier Tribunal or granted only on limited grounds, or the application to the First-tier Tribunal has not been admitted because it is out of time, the applicant may make a further application for permission to appeal to the Upper Tribunal. The application must be made within one month of the date of the First-tier Tribunal's decision notice refusing permission or refusing to admit the application (UT Rule 21(3)(b)). The application MUST include the information, and be accompanied by the documents, prescribed by UT Rule 21(4) and (5) and if the application to the First-tier Tribunal was not admitted because it was out of time MUST also comply with UT Rule 21(7). An incomplete application will be rejected.

10 Every application to the Upper Tribunal for permission to appeal which is in proper form will be copied to the respondent on receipt.

11 If the application is in time it will at the same time be passed to an Upper Tribunal judge for determination. The respondent will not be required, or invited, to make representations but will be assumed to support the decision which the applicant is seeking to appeal. The application will normally be dealt with on the basis of the written application alone. Exceptionally the judge may arrange a hearing, which both parties will be invited (but not required) to attend.

12 If the application is made out of time, but with an application in proper form for an extension of time (see UT Rule 21(6)), the respondent will be asked for observations in respect of the application for an extension. The Upper Tribunal will send the applicant a copy of any observations it receives, to which the applicant may reply. If the application is opposed, the tribunal may decide to deal with it at an oral hearing.

13 If permission to appeal is granted the application stands as the notice of appeal unless otherwise directed (see UT Rule 22(2)(b)) and the procedure spelt out by the UT Rules must thereafter be followed.

14 If permission to appeal is refused, in whole or in part, or if, without a hearing, the Upper Tribunal has refused to admit a late application for permission, the applicant may ask for a hearing at which the application is reconsidered. The hearing will be arranged as soon as practicable. The respondent will be invited, but not required, to attend and make representations.

15. If permission to appeal is refused by the Upper Tribunal after a hearing, there are limited circumstances in which an applicant may bring judicial review proceedings in the High Court against that decision under Rule 54.7A of the Civil Procedure Rules. Permission to bring judicial review proceedings will only be granted by the High Court in exceptional circumstances.

Applications to appeal against a decision of the Upper Tribunal

16 Where the Upper Tribunal has made a decision on an appeal from the First-tier Tribunal or has itself dealt with a case as a first-instance tribunal, the procedure for making an application for permission to appeal will be similar to that in paragraphs 1 and 2 above. Any application

to the Upper Tribunal for permission to appeal from a decision of the Upper Tribunal which is in proper form will be copied to the respondent on receipt. The application will be passed to an Upper Tribunal judge for determination without the respondent being required, or invited, to make representations.

17 The judge may decide to review the decision but only on the limited grounds set out in Rule 45 of the UT Rules. If the judge is unable, or decides not, to review the decision, a procedure similar to that in paragraph 6 above will be applied. If permission to appeal is granted, the appellant must then comply (in England and Wales) with the requirements of Part 52 of the Civil Procedure Rules applicable to appeals to the Court of Appeal (and in Scotland or Northern Ireland with the equivalent requirements of the Court of Session or Court of Appeal of Northern Ireland). If permission to appeal is refused, the appellant may make a further application to the Court of Appeal in accordance with Part 52 or, in Scotland, to the Court of Session and in Northern Ireland to the Court of Appeal of Northern Ireland.

18 In any case in which a professionally represented respondent wishes to attend an oral hearing and make submissions, a written outline of those submissions should be provided to the applicant and to the tribunal not less than 7 days before the hearing.

Mrs Justice Rose

President

Upper Tribunal

Tax and Chancery Chamber

Judge Colin Bishopp

President

First-tier Tribunal

Tax Chamber

DELEGATION OF FUNCTIONS TO STAFF IN RELATION TO THE TAX CHAMBER OF THE FIRST-TIER TRIBUNAL AND THE FINANCE AND TAX CHAMBER OF THE UPPER TRIBUNAL ON OR AFTER 1 APRIL 2009

10 March 2009

1. Paragraph 2 of this Practice Statement applies to cases in the Tax Chamber of the First-tier Tribunal. Paragraph 3 applies to cases in the Finance and Tax Chamber of the Upper Tribunal.

TAX CHAMBER OF THE FIRST-TIER TRIBUNAL

2. The Senior President of Tribunals hereby approves that a member of staff appointed under section 40(1) of the Tribunals, Courts and Enforcement Act 2007 may carry out any function of the First-tier Tribunal under the following rules of the Tribunal Procedure (First-tier Tribunal) (Tax Chamber) Rules 2009 where that member of staff has been authorised by the Chamber President of the Tax Chamber to exercise that particular function.

(a) Rule 5 (case management powers);
(b) Rule 23 (allocation of cases to categories); and
(c) Rule 32 (public and private hearings).

FINANCE AND TAX CHAMBER OF THE UPPER TRIBUNAL

3. The Senior President of Tribunals hereby approves that a member of staff appointed under section 40(1) of the Tribunals, Courts and Enforcement Act 2007 may carry out any function of the Upper Tribunal under rule 5 (case management powers) of the Tribunal Procedure (Upper Tribunal) Rules 2008 where that member of staff has been authorised by the Chamber President of the Finance and Tax Chamber to exercise that particular function.

LORD JUSTICE CARNWATH

SENIOR PRESIDENT OF TRIBUNALS

COMPOSITION OF TRIBUNALS IN RELATION TO MATTERS THAT FALL TO BE DECIDED BY THE TAX CHAMBER OF THE FIRST-TIER TRIBUNAL AND THE FINANCE AND TAX CHAMBER OF THE UPPER TRIBUNAL ON OR AFTER 1 SEPTEMBER 2009

27 August 2009

In this Practice Statement;

(a) "the 2007 Act" means the Tribunals, Courts and Enforcement Act 2007;
(b) "the 2008 Order" means the First-tier Tribunal and Upper Tribunal (Composition of Tribunal) Order 2008;
(c) "the 2009 Rules" means the Tribunal Procedure (First-tier Tribunal) (Tax Chamber) Rules 2009;
(d) "the Qualifications Order" means the Qualifications for Appointment of Members to the First-tier Tribunal and Upper Tribunal Order 2008;
(e) "the Upper Tribunal Rules" means the Tribunal Procedure (Upper Tribunal) Rules 2008;
(f) "Member" means a judge or other member;
(g) "Other member" means a member who is not a judge and has any of the qualifications set out in article 2(2)(f), (h), (i), 4(h), (i) of the Qualifications Order.

2. In exercise of the powers conferred by the 2008 Order the Senior President of Tribunals makes the following determinations and supplementary provision:—

TAX CHAMBER OF THE FIRST-TIER TRIBUNAL DEFAULT PAPER CASE

3. Subject to paragraph 10 a decision must be made by one judge or other member.

BASIC CASE

4. A decision that disposes of proceedings or determines a preliminary issue made at, or following, a hearing must be made by either one, two, or where the Chamber President considers it appropriate three, members each of whom is a judge or other member as determined by the Chamber President.

5. Where the Tribunal is constituted under paragraph 4 the "presiding member" for the purposes of article 7 of the 2008 Order will be chosen by the Chamber President.

6. Any other decision, including striking out a case under rule 8 of the 2009 Rules (except at, or following, a hearing) or giving directions under rule 5 of the 2009 Rules (whether or not at a hearing) must be made by one judge, or one other member who has been designated by the Chamber President to make such decisions.

STANDARD OR COMPLEX CASE

7. A decision that disposes of proceedings or determines a preliminary issue made at, or following, a hearing must be made by:

(a) one judge; or
(b) one judge and one or two members each of whom is a judge or other member as determined by the Chamber President.

8. Where the Tribunal is constituted under paragraph 7(b) the "presiding member" for the purposes of article 7 of the 2008 Order will be the judge. Where more than one judge is to decide the matter the "presiding member" will be chosen by the Chamber President.

9. Any other decision, including striking out a case under rule 8 of the 2009 Rules (except at, or following, a hearing) or giving directions under rule 5 of the 2009 Rules (whether or not at a hearing) must be made by one judge.

ALL CASES

10. Where the Tribunal has given a decision that disposes of proceedings ("the substantive decision"), any matter decided under, or in accordance with, rule 5(3)(l) or Part 4 of the 2009 Rules or section 9 of the 2007 Act must be decided by one judge, unless the Chamber President considers it appropriate that it is decided either by:—

(a) the same member or members of the Tribunal as gave the substantive decision; or
(b) a Tribunal, constituted in accordance with paragraphs 3 to 9, comprised of different members of the Tribunal to that which gave the substantive decision.

TAX AND CHANCERY CHAMBER OF THE UPPER TRIBUNAL

11. A decision that disposes of proceedings or determines a preliminary issue made at, or following, a hearing must be made by:

(a) one judge; or
(b) one judge and one or two members each of whom is a judge or other member as determined by the Chamber President.

12. Where the Tribunal is constituted under paragraph 11(b) the "presiding member" for the purposes of article 7 of the 2008 Order will be the judge. Where more than one judge is to decide the matter the "presiding member" will be chosen by the Chamber President.

13. Any other decision, including striking out a case under rule 8 of the Upper Tribunal Rules (except at, or following, a hearing) or giving directions under rule 5 of the Upper Tribunal Rules (whether or not at a hearing) must be made by one judge.

14. Where the Tribunal has given a decision that disposes of proceedings ("the substantive decision"), any matter decided under, or in accordance with, rule 5(3)(l) or Part 7 of the Upper Tribunal Rules or section 10 of the 2007 Act must be decided by the same member or members of the Tribunal as gave the substantive decision.

15. Paragraph 14 does not apply where complying with it would be impractical or would cause undue delay and, in such a case, the matter decided under, or in accordance with, rule 5(3)(l) or Part 7 of the Upper Tribunal Rules or section 10 of the 2007 Act must be decided by—

(a) if the substantive decision was given by more than one member of the Upper Tribunal and the presiding member or any other judge from that constitution is available, the members of the Upper Tribunal who gave the substantive decision and are available to decide the matter;
(b) otherwise, another judge of the Upper Tribunal nominated by the Chamber President.

LORD JUSTICE CARNWATH

SENIOR PRESIDENT OF TRIBUNALS

FORM OF DECISIONS AND NEUTRAL CITATION FIRST-TIER TRIBUNAL AND UPPER TRIBUNAL ON OR AFTER 3 NOVEMBER 2008
Practice Statement

31 October 2008

1. This Practice Statement sets out the arrangements for the neutral citation of decisions or written reasons (referred to in this Practice Statement simply as "decisions") of the First-tier Tribunal and Upper Tribunal from 3 November 2008. It follows international practice designed to facilitate their publication on the World Wide Web and their subsequent use by those who have access to it.

FORM OF DECISIONS

2. First-tier Tribunal and Upper Tribunal decisions must be prepared for delivery, or issued as approved decisions, with paragraph numbering.

NEUTRAL CITATIONS

3. In the Upper Tribunal a unique number will be issued for a decision, on request, by the Upper Tribunal Office. In the First-tier Tribunal requests for a unique number for a decision should be made to the Chamber President. If the Chamber President considers it appropriate, the decision will then be referred to the Upper Tribunal and a unique number will be issued by the Upper Tribunal Office.

4. The decisions will be numbered in the following way:

Upper Tribunal (Administrative Appeals Chamber): [200n] UKUT 1 (AAC)

First-tier Tribunal (Health Education and Social Care Chamber): [200n] UKFTT 1 (HESC)

First-tier Tribunal (Social Entitlement Chamber): [200n] UKFTT 2 (SEC)

First-tier Tribunal (War Pensions and Armed Forces Compensation Chamber): [200n] UKFTT 3 (WPAFCC)

5. There will be consecutive numbering of decisions in each of the First-tier Tribunal and the Upper Tribunal. Thus, the first three decisions of [2000n] delivered by the First-tier Tribunal would be numbered 1, 2, 3 irrespective of whether the case was allocated to HESC, SEC or WPAFCC.

6. Under these arrangements, paragraph 77 in Jones v Secretary of State for the Department of Work and Pensions, the tenth numbered decision of the year in the Upper Tribunal, would be cited:

Jones v Secretary of State for the Department of Work and Pensions [200n] UKUT 10 (AAC) at [77]

7. The paragraph number allotted by the Upper Tribunal Office should be used in all references to that decision.

8. Where anonymity was previously given to a party in a tribunal case, that practice will continue pending further review.

9. The neutral citation will be the official number attributed to the decision by the Tribunal and must always be used on at least one occasion when the decision is cited in a later decision or judgment. Once the decision is reported, the neutral citation will appear in front of any citation from the law report series. Thus:

Jones v Secretary of State for the Department of Work and Pensions [200n] UKUT 10 (AAC) at [77], [200n] 2 All ER 364, R(AF) 3/08

10. Given that this form of citation contains the official number given to each decision it is hoped that it will be reproduced wherever the decision is published.

LORD JUSTICE CARNWATH

SENIOR PRESIDENT OF TRIBUNALS

Anti-money Laundering

ANTI-MONEY LAUNDERING GUIDANCE
The Consultative Committee of Accountancy Bodies

2008

ANTI-MONEY LAUNDERING GUIDANCE FOR THE ACCOUNTANCY SECTOR

Guidance for those providing audit, accountancy, tax advisory, insolvency or related services in the United Kingdom, on the prevention of money laundering and the countering of terrorist financing. Issued by the Consultative Committee of Accountancy Bodies, in August 2008.

The Anti-Money Laundering Guidance for the Accountancy Sector has been approved by Treasury (excluding Appendix A — Supplementary guidance for the Tax Practitioner, which has been submitted for Treasury approval separately). Guidance which is approved by Treasury is "relevant guidance" within the meaning of the Money Laundering Regulations 2007. Courts must consider relevant guidance when determining whether an accountant's conduct gives rise to certain offences under either the Proceeds of Crime Act 2002 or the Money Laundering Regulations 2007. It is this guidance which practitioners should consider as authoritative when implementing and complying with anti-money laundering requirements.

The Guidance provides the accountancy sector with not only an interpretation of the requirements of the Money Laundering Regulations 2007 (which became effective from 15th December 2007) and primary legislation relating to money laundering and terrorist financing but also practical guidance on good practice for matters not prescribed in law.

This Guidance includes a number of minor changes made since the guidance was issued in December 2007 (following the publication of an exposure draft in October 2007).

The Guidance reflects not only law but the experience of practitioners. For more complex areas of customer due diligence, our guidance continues to be cross referred to the guidance notes issued by the Joint Money Laundering Steering Group. However, it is intended that, at least for most smaller practitioners, the guidance will be self contained and the need to refer to additional external material will be minimal.

To aid easy access, use is made of defined terms explained in a glossary and each section is prefaced with key points for quick reference.

Section 1 – About this Guidance

Key Points

- UK anti-*money laundering* regime requirements are set out in the Proceeds of Crime Act 2002 (*POCA)* (as amended by the Serious Organised Crime and Police Act 2005 (*SOCPA)*),the Money Laundering Regulations 2007 (*2007 Regulations)* and the Terrorism Act 2000 (*TA 2000)* (as amended by the Anti-Terrorism, Crime and Security Act 2001 (*ATCSA 2001)* and the Terrorism Act 2006 (*TA 2006*)).
- HM Treasury approval for this *Guidance* has been granted. As such the Courts must take it into account in deciding whether or not an offence has been committed under ss330-331, *POCA* or the *2007 Regulations* by an *individual* or *business* within its scope.

- *Businesses* and *individuals* should take account of this *Guidance* when acting in the course of business as auditors, *external accountants*, *insolvency practitioner* s and *tax adviser* s, and when acting in the course of business as trust and company service providers. Failure to do so could have serious legal, regulatory or professional disciplinary consequences.
- Where other professional or trade bodies have produced specialist *Guidance* concerning particular services or activities, *businesses* and *individuals* may need, to have regard to that *Guidance* as a supplement to this *Guidance*.

Introduction

1.1 Terms that appear in *italics* in this *Guidance* are explained in the Glossary.

1.2 This *Guidance* has been drafted to be consistent with the *Guidance* for the UK financial sector issued by the Joint Money Laundering Steering Group (*JMLSG*). Some of the material contained in this guide draws significantly on *JMLSG* wording, for which thanks are due to the *JMLSG*. The *JMLSG Guidance* is very comprehensive, and where *businesses* or *individuals* require further guidance, they may seek it from the *JMLSG Guidance*. *Businesses* and *individuals* carrying out *defined services* who follow the *JMLSG Guidance*, adapted for the circumstances in which they are practising, will be deemed to have followed this *Guidance*.

1.3 This *Guidance* has been prepared to assist accountants and related *businesses* and professionals in complying with their obligations, arising from United Kingdom legislation, in relation to the prevention, recognition and reporting of *money laundering*.

Businesses and Individuals within the Scope of this Guidance

1.4 The *Guidance* is addressed to *businesses* and *individuals* covered by Regulation 3 (1)(c) of the *2007 Regulations* ie, those who act in the course of a business carried on by them in the United Kingdom as an auditor, *external accountant*, *insolvency practitioner* or *tax adviser* (as defined in Regulation 3(4) to 3(8)), and those who act in the course of business as trust or company service providers under Regulation 3 (1)(e) of the *2007 Regulations* (as defined in Regulation 3(10)). These services are referred to together for the purpose of this *Guidance* as the *defined services*.

Businesses that provide both accountancy services and trust or company services and that are supervised by HMRC should generally follow the this *Guidance* but also have regard to 'Appendix 10: Supplementary guidance for trust or company services providers' of the HMRC guide 'MLR 8 — Preventing money laundering and terrorist financing'.

1.5 This *Guidance* is not addressed to *independent legal professional* s, even where they are acting as *tax adviser* s, *insolvency practitioner* s or trust or company service providers. *Independent legal professional* s should refer to *Guidance* issued by their professional body or *anti-money laundering supervisory authority*. Where *businesses* have sub-contracted parts of their work for clients to other *individuals* or *businesses* situated outside of the United Kingdom, it is likely that those others will be subject to local anti-money laundering law and not to United Kingdom law in respect of the work undertaken by them. However, the responsibility of United Kingdom *businesses* and *individuals* for compliance with the 2007 Regulations and *POCA and TA* in respect of the conduct of their business, and in respect of information or other matters coming to them in the course of conducting that business, remains whether or not parts of the work are sub-contracted.

1.6 Regulation 3(7) defines *external accountant* as someone who provides *accountancy services* by way of business to other persons, when providing such services. *The 2007 Regulations* do not define the term *accountancy services*. For the purpose of this *Guidance*, *Accountancy services* includes, any service provided under a contract for services (ie, not a contract of employment) which pertains to the recording, review, analysis, calculation or reporting of financial information.

1.7 Employees of organisations which are not providing *defined services* are outside the scope of this *Guidance*. Those employed in other *regulated sectors* (financial services, law firms, estate agents, high value dealers or casinos) should have regard to *Guidance* issued by the employer's trade or professional body or *anti-money laundering supervisory authority*. Employees are not engaged in the *regulated sector* for the purposes of the anti-*money laundering* legislation, if their employer is not acting in the *regulated sector*. Nor are those providing services privately on an unremunerated and voluntary basis, since those services will not have been provided 'by way of business'. Services provided in the course of employment or business in *defined services* will however be included, even if provided to the *client* on a probono or unremunerated basis.

1.8 All persons (including those outside the *regulated* sector) risk committing the *money laundering offences* and are required to report suspicions of *terrorist financing* formed in the course of their trade, profession or employment. However, those outside the *regulated sector* have no mandatory requirements for reporting knowledge or suspicions of non-terrorism related *money laundering* (although if they are themselves involved in the *money laundering*, reporting under s338, POCA (authorised disclosures) is required if the person is to benefit from the defence available in this regard under ss 327-329, POCA), or for maintaining anti-*money laundering* systems. Additional guidance on both the legal requirements and on the avoidance of *money laundering* risk, for accountants or tax advisers working outside the *regulated sector*, may be sought from an appropriate trade or professional body.

1.9 All *businesses* and *individuals* within the scope of this *Guidance* should have regard to its content, in respect of all *defined services*. Members and member firms of the *CCAB* member bodies and other professional bodies which adopt this *Guidance* should be aware that failure to take account of the provisions of this *Guidance* can give rise to a liability to disciplinary action. *Businesses* and *individuals* undertaking *defined services* who are supervised by HMRC should refer to the HMRC's web site to determine the likely effects of failure to take into account this *Guidance*.

1.10 It should also be noted that the way in which *businesses* and *individuals* apply the provisions of this *Guidance* will be likely to influence decisions by their professional bodies on whether they have complied with general ethical requirements, for example relating to integrity, the need to consider the public interest, or regulatory requirements.

1.11 *Businesses* and *individuals* may also need to have regard to *Guidance* issued by other standard setters, professional bodies or trade associations where this relates to particular specialist services. Additional *Guidance* should be read in conjunction with this *Guidance*. Such *Guidance* includes (but may not be limited to):

- Auditors – Auditing Practices Board Practice Note 12 'Money Laundering: Interim *Guidance* for Auditors in the UK'.
- *Tax advisers* — Supplementary Guidance for Tax Practitioners (Appendix A).

1.12 This *Guidance* does **not** deal with the specific requirements of the Financial Services Authority (*FSA*). Accordingly, those providing financial services and regulated by the *FSA* should additionally refer to *FSA* requirements, which incorporate anti-*money laundering Guidance* issued by the Joint Money Laundering Steering Group (*JMLSG*).

1.13 However, this *Guidance* **does** cover the requirements of firms providing services under the Designated Professional Body provisions of Part XX, section 326 of the Financial Services and Markets Act 2000, or otherwise providing financial services under the oversight of their professional body. Such activities for the purpose of this *Guidance* are included within the scope of *defined services*.

1.14 As well as '*business relationship*', the *2007 Regulations* refer to 'occasional transactions', ie, those outside the *business relationship* valued at over €15,000. 'Occasional transactions' is a cogent term in a banking context but is difficult to apply in the context of *accountancy services*. Therefore this *Guidance* uses only '*business relationship*', a more natural term for *accountancy and related services*, throughout.

Role of Supervisory Bodies

1.15 The 2007 Regulations require all businesses to be supervised by an appropriate antimoney laundering supervisory authority. For many businesses acting as external accountants and/or auditors, tax advisers or insolvency practitioners the supervisory authority will be the professional body to which they belong. A full list of approved supervisory authorities for the accountancy sector is set out in Schedule 3 to the 2007 Regulations, including all six CCAB member bodies and certain other accountancy and tax bodies. Those businesses that are not members of, or otherwise regulated by, one of the approved bodies will be supervised by HMRC. Where a business or individual is subject to more than one anti-money laundering supervisory authority the relevant anti-money laundering supervisory authorities may (Regulation 23 (2)) agree that one shall act in respect of that business or individual but they are not obliged to do so. Accordingly some businesses and individuals will continue to have to respond to more than one anti-money laundering supervisory authority.

Legal Requirements and Status of this Guidance

1.16 The legislation which embodies the UK anti-*money laundering* regime is contained in:

- The Proceeds of Crime Act 2002 (*POCA*) as amended by The Serious Organised Crime and Police Act 2005 (*SOCPA*) and relevant statutory instruments;

Practice Statements

- The Terrorism Act 2000 (*TA 2000*) (as amended by the Anti Terrorism Crime and Security Act 2001 (*ATCSA*) and the Terrorism Act 2006 (*TA 2006*)) and relevant statutory instruments; and
- The Money Laundering Regulations 2007 (*2007 Regulations*) and relevant statutory instruments.

POCA and *TA 2000* contain offences which may be committed by *individuals* or entities, whereas the *2007 Regulations* deal with the systems and controls which *businesses* are required to have and contain offences which may be committed by *businesses* as well as the key *individuals* within them.

1.17 Approval by HM Treasury has been granted in relation to this *Guidance*. This means the Courts must have regard to the *Guidance* in deciding whether *businesses* or *individuals* affected by it have committed an offence under the *2007 Regulations* or under ss330-331, *POCA*. Of course, this *Guidance* cannot be exhaustive. It may be necessary to seek advice either from trade or professional bodies, *anti-money laundering supervisory authorities* or other sources on issues and situations not covered by this *Guidance*.

1.18 This *Guidance* has been prepared on the basis that compliance with its requirements, and recommendations, will ensure compliance with relevant legislation and professional requirements. Within this *Guidance*, the term 'must' is used to indicate a legal or regulatory requirement and accordingly the use of this term indicates where following this *Guidance* is considered mandatory. *Businesses* and *individuals* may seek alternative interpretations of the UK *anti-money laundering* regime if they wish but they are recommended to consider the impact of any advice they receive on their obligations and be able to justify why they have preferred to implement an alternative interpretation. However, there are many instances where law and regulation does not prescribe the required actions. In such instances the term 'should' (and other terms suggesting possible ways in which *Businesses* and *Individuals* may approach matters subject to this *Guidance*) are used to indicate good practice methods that may be employed to meet statutory and regulatory requirements. *Businesses* and *individuals* need to consider the specific circumstances of their own situation in determining whether the suggested good practice methods are appropriate, or whether they consider alternative practices may be employed to achieve compliance with law and regulation. In all cases, *Businesses* and *individuals* need to be prepared to be able to explain to their anti-*money laundering supervisory authority* the rationale for their procedures and why they consider they are compliant with law and regulation.

1.19 Note that the UK anti-*money laundering* regime does not apply to some services that *businesses* may undertake and applying the regime's requirements to all their services may in these cases be unnecessarily costly. This *Guidance* assumes that many *businesses* will find it easier, and more effective, to apply the requirements to all their services. However, it is a decision for each *business* to take. Where *businesses* choose to outsource or subcontract work to non-regulated entities, they should bear in mind that they remain subject to the obligation to maintain appropriate risk management procedures to prevent *money laundering* activity. In that context, they should consider whether the subcontracting increases the risk that they will be involved in or used for money laundering, in which case appropriate controls to address that risk should be put in place.

1.20 Those involved in the provision of management consultancy services or interim management should be particularly alert to the possibility that they could be within the scope of the anti-*money laundering* regime to the extent they supply any of the *defined services* when acting under a contract for services in the course of business.

1.21 Throughout this *Guidance*, *businesses* and *individuals* subject to the provisions of the UK anti-*money laundering* regime through being covered in Regulation 3, *2007 Regulations* or Schedule 9 to *POCA* are referred to as being part of the *regulated sector*. Note that whilst *POCA* refers to those covered in Schedule 9 as 'regulated' persons and the *2007 Regulations* refer to those covered by Regulation 3 as 'relevant' persons, those included in the two categories are identical.

1.22 Throughout this *Guidance*, the *nominated officer* required to be appointed by a *business* under the *2007 Regulations* to receive disclosures in accordance with Part 7, *POCA* is referred to by the name commonly used in the *regulated sector* as a *Money Laundering Reporting Officer* or *MLRO*.

Section 2 – The Offences

Key Points

- The three *money laundering offences* are those contained in ss327-329, the Proceeds of Crime Act 2002 (*POCA*). The Terrorism Act 2000 (*TA 2000*) also creates similar offences relating to *terrorist financing*. In this *Guidance*, the term '*money laundering*' will encompass *terrorist financing* activities.

- Detailed *Guidance* as to the provisions of the *TA 2000* has not been provided as the requirements for the *regulated sector* are very similar to those contained in *POCA* which are described in detail. Reporting *of terrorist financing* suspicions is through the same channels *as money laundering* suspicions.
- The *money laundering* offences are framed very broadly and are designed to catch any activity in respect of *criminal property*, including possession of the proceeds of one's own *criminal conduct*.
- *Criminal conduct* is widely defined by s340, *POCA* to be conduct that is an offence in any part of the UK as well as conduct occurring elsewhere that would have been an offence if it had taken place in the UK. There are very limited exceptions to this for conduct which is both known to be legal in the country in which it is committed and which falls within the specific exceptions set out in orders made by the Secretary of State.
- *Criminal property* is defined by s340, *POCA* as being the benefit of *criminal conduct* where the alleged offender knows or suspects that the property in question represents such a benefit.
- *Terrorist property* is defined in s 14, *TA 2000* as money or property likely to be used for terrorist purposes, or the proceeds of commissioning or carrying out terrorist acts.
- The *money laundering* offences and the similar offences under *TA 2000* can be committed by any person, whether or not they are part of the *regulated sector*. Defences available to any person charged with such offences include reporting to the appropriate authorities and obtaining consent. *Individuals* working in any *business* can commit, subject to limited exemptions, the offence of failing to disclose *terrorist financing*.
- There are three further types of *POCA* offences relevant to *individuals* to whom this *Guidance* relates. These are the failing to disclose offences in ss330-331, *POCA* (NB: s332 contains a similar offence relating to *MLRO's* outside of the *regulated sector*); *tipping off* (s333A, *POCA*); and *prejudicing an investigation* (s342, *POCA*). There are similar offences in ss19-21A, *TA 2000*.
- The offence of failing to make a *money laundering* disclosure (often referred to as failing to report) can be committed by any *individual* working in the *regulated sector* or by an *MLRO* working in other *business*. The offence of *tipping off* is set out in s333A, *POCA* which applies to those in the *regulated sector* only The *POCA* offence of *prejudicing an investigation* can be committed by anyone. There are similar failing to disclose and *tipping off* offences contained in *TA 2000*.
- It is a criminal offence for a *business* not to comply with the *2007 Regulations*, if that *business* is within their scope. It is also an offence for any partner, director or officer of the *business*, to consent to or connive at the non-compliance or by neglect to cause noncompliance.

What is Money Laundering?

2.1 In UK law *money laundering* is defined very widely, and includes all forms of handling or possessing *criminal property*, including possessing the proceeds of one's own crime, and facilitating any handling or possession of *criminal property*. *Criminal property* may take any form, including in money or money's worth, securities, tangible property and intangible property. *Money laundering* can be carried out in respect of the proceeds of conduct that is an offence in the UK as well as most conduct occurring elsewhere that would have been an offence if it had taken place in the UK. For the purpose of this *Guidance*, *money laundering* is also taken to encompass activities relating to *terrorist financing*, including handling or possessing funds to be used for terrorist purposes as well proceeds from terrorism. Terrorism is taken to be the use or threat of action designed to influence government, or to intimidate any section of the public, or to advance a political, religious or ideological cause where the action would involve violence, threats to health and safety, damage to property or disruption of electronic systems. Materiality or de minimis exceptions are not available in relation to either *money laundering* or *terrorist financing* offences.

2.2 *Money laundering* activity may range from a single act, eg, being in possession of the proceeds of one's own crime, to complex and sophisticated schemes involving multiple parties, and multiple methods of handling and transferring *criminal property* as well as concealing it and entering into arrangements to assist others to do so. *Businesses* and *individuals* need to be alert to the risks of *clients*, their counterparties and others laundering money in any of its possible forms. The *business* or its *client* does not have to be a party to *money laundering* for a reporting obligation to arise (see section 3). Where criminal proceeds have already arisen, s340(11), *POCA* includes within the definition of *money laundering* any attempt, conspiracy or incitement to commit an offence under ss327-329, *POCA* as well as aiding, abetting, counselling or procuring an offence under ss327-329, *POCA*. In the case of *terrorist financing*, it is an offence to attempt to commit an offence under ss15-18, *TA 2000* even if *terrorist property* has not come into being, eg, under s15(1), *TA 2000* where the invitation to provide money or other property for *terrorist financing* is in itself an offence. Further, the definition of '*terrorist property*' means that all dealings with funds or property which are likely to be used for the purposes of terrorism, even if the funds are "clean" in origin, is a *terrorist financing* offence.

Money Laundering Offences

2.3 Sections 327-329 in the Proceeds of Crime Act (*POCA*) (as amended by the Serious Organised Crime and Police Act 2005 (*SOCPA*)) define the *money laundering* offences. **Anyone** can commit one of these. Conviction of any of these offences is punishable by up to 14 years imprisonment and/or an unlimited fine. A person commits a *money laundering* offence if he:

- **Conceals,**disguises, converts or transfers *criminal property*, or removes *criminal property* from England and Wales, or from Scotland or from Northern Ireland (s 327);
- Enters into or becomes concerned in an **arrangement** which he knows or suspects facilitates (by whatever means) the acquisition, retention, use or control of *criminal property* by or on behalf of another person (s 328); or
- **Acquires**, uses or has possession of *criminal property* except where adequate consideration was given for the property (s 329).

2.4 None of these offences are committed if:

- the persons involved did not know or suspect that they were dealing with the proceeds of crime; or
- a report of the suspicious activity is made promptly to an *MLRO* (an *internal report)* or direct to *SOCA* (a *suspicious activity report*, or *SAR)* under the provisions of 338, *POCA*, and (if the report is made before the act is committed) the appropriate consent is obtained before doing the act; *or*
- no report is made, there was a reasonable excuse for this failure (note that there is no *money laundering* case law on this issue and it is anticipated that only relatively extreme circumstances, such as duress, might be accepted); or
- the act is committed by someone carrying out a law enforcement or judicial function; or
- the conduct giving rise to the *criminal property* was reasonably believed to have taken place outside of the UK, and the conduct was in fact lawful under the criminal law of the place where it occurred, and the maximum sentence if the conduct had occurred in the UK would have been less than 12 months (except in the case of an act which would be an offence under the Gaming Act 1968, the Lotteries and Amusements Act 1976 or under ss23 or 25, *FSMA*, which will fall within the exemption even if the relevant sentence would be in excess of 12 months*)*. In this *Guidance*, this is referred to as the *overseas conduct exemption.*

2.5 It should be noted that the tests relating to overseas conduct (set out in SI 2006 No1070 and in Section 2.4, final bullet, of this *Guidance*) are complex and onerous. These are very stringent tests, and as such *individuals* and *businesses* need to be cautious in their application.

2.6 There is a further exemption for deposit taking bodies (accountancy *businesses* holding clients' money cannot use this exemption) who may continue to run an account containing *criminal property* where the each transaction is less than the threshold amount (currently £250) set out in s339A, *POCA*.

2.7 Note that ss15-18, Terrorism Act 2000 (*the TA 2000*) also create similar offences (*terrorist* offences) to those contained in ss 327–329, *POCA* but that there is no *overseas conduct exemption* or threshold amounts.

Offences of Failing to Disclose

2.8 *Individuals* in the *regulated sector* commit an offence if they fail to make a disclosure in cases where they have knowledge or suspicion, or reasonable grounds for suspicion, that *money laundering* is occurring. Disclosure must be made to their *MLRO* or direct to *SOCA* under ss 330, *POCA*. In this *Guidance*, disclosure to an *MLRO* is referred to as an *internal report* and to *SOCA* as a *suspicious activity report* or *SAR*. *MLROs* have a duty to make disclosures under s331, *POCA* if they have knowledge, suspicion or reasonable ground to suspect *money laundering* as a consequence of an *internal report*. The s 332 failure to disclose offence is similar and would apply to an *MLRO* in a business outside of the *regulated sector*, including an *MLRO* appointed to deal with reports emanating from non-regulated business within a *business* that conducted both regulated, and non-regulated services, in respect of suspicions arising from *internal reports*. This is not further addressed in this *Guidance*. These offences are punishable by imprisonment of up to 5 years and/or an unlimited fine.

2.9 Similar provisions regarding failure to disclose are contained in s 19, and 21A, *TA 2000*. The s19 failure to report offence is applicable to **anyone** in employment or business outside of the regulated sector, with s 21A being applicable to all those in the *regulated sector*.

The failure to disclose offence under Sections 330 and 331 POCA

2.10 The failure to disclose offence in s 330 is committed if an *individual* fails to make a report comprising the *required disclosure* as soon as is practicable either in the form of an *internal report* to his *MLRO* or in the form of a *SAR* to a person authorised by the Serious Organised Crime Agency *(SOCA)* to receive disclosures. The obligation to make the *required disclosure* arises when:

- a person knows or suspects, or has reasonable grounds for knowing or suspecting that another person is engaged in *money laundering*;
- the information or other matter on which the above is based came to him in the course of business in the *regulated sector*;
- he either can identify that other person, or has information concerning the whereabouts of the laundered property or the information he has may assist in identifying the person or the whereabouts of the property (the laundered property is that which forms the subject of the matter of the known or suspected *money laundering*).

2.11 An *MLRO* is obliged to report if he is satisfied that the information received in *internal report* s meets the tests set out in 2.10. An *MLRO* may commit the s331, *POCA* offence if he fails to pass on reportable information in *internal report* s that he has received, as soon as is practicable, to *SOCA*.

Required Disclosure

2.12 *Individuals* need to take care to ensure that any information held by them which is part of the *required disclosure*, ie, the identity of the suspect (if known), the information or other matter on which the knowledge or suspicion of *money laundering* (or reasonable grounds for such) is based and the whereabouts of the laundered property (if known) is passed as soon as is practicable to the *MLRO*. Additional information held by the *individual* which identifies other parties involved in or connected to the matter should also be given to the *MLRO*.

2.13 Further *Guidance* on the making of *SARs*,including the appropriate form and manner of reporting, is given in sections 5 and 6 below.

Defences and exemptions

2.14 There are defences to and exemptions from the failing to disclose offences as follows:

- there is reasonable excuse for not making a report (note that there is no *money laundering* case law on this issue and it is anticipated that only relatively extreme circumstances, such as duress and threats to safety, might be accepted); or
- the *privilege reporting exemption* (see sections 7.26 to 7.46 below) applies; or
- the *individual* does not actually know or suspect *money laundering* has occurred and has not been provided by his employer with the training required by the *2007 Regulations* (Regulation 21). If the employer has failed to provide the training, this is an offence on the part of the employer. The effect for the individual who has not been provided with training is that the objective test (of being required to report if there are 'reasonable grounds' for knowledge or suspicion) is removed; or
- it is known, or believed on reasonable grounds, that the *money laundering* is occurring outside the UK, and is not unlawful under the criminal law of the country where it is occurring.

In determining whether an offence has been committed under ss 330 and 331, the Courts must have regard to the content of this *Guidance* [Subject to HMT approval] when applied to an *individual* delivering *defined services* or to an *MLRO*.

2.15 Whilst an *individual* in the *regulated sector* has a duty to report, other persons may voluntarily report to *SOCA* and also receive the protections available both in terms of potentially creating a defence to a *money laundering* offence and also the protection against accusations of breach of confidentiality providing the report is properly made under the provisions of either of ss 337 and 338, *POCA* (See section 6.10) as appropriate.

Tipping Off

2.16 The offence of *Tipping off* was previously set out in s 333, *POCA*, but was removed by statutory instrument (effective from 26 December 2007) The s 333, *POCA* offence meant anyone not acting in the course of a business in the *regulated sector* could commit this offence which consisted of:

- knowing or suspecting that a report has been made either to an *MLRO* or to *SOCA* (under either s 337 or s 338, *POCA*); *and*
- making any disclosure which he knows or suspects is likely to prejudice any investigation that might follow that report.

There were limited exceptions relating to persons carrying out law enforcement or judicial functions, and to legal advisers acting in privileged circumstances provided the disclosure is not made with the intention of furthering a criminal purpose.

The penalty for this offence is a maximum of 5 years imprisonment, or an unlimited fine, or both.

2.17 Section 333, *POCA* is replaced by s 333A *POCA* which applies only to the *regulated sector*. The criminal offence of *tipping off* in s 333A, *POCA* arises where a person in the *regulated sector* discloses either:

- that a disclosure has been made by a person of information obtained in the course of a *regulated sector business* either to an *MLRO* or to *SOCA* (under either s 337 or s 338, *POCA*) or to any other person authorised by *SOCA* to receive disclosures, or to the police or HMRC and the disclosure is likely to *prejudice any investigation* that might be conducted following the disclosure referred to; or
- that an investigation into allegations that a *money laundering* offence has been committed, is being contemplated or is being carried out and the disclosure is likely to prejudice that investigation and the information disclosed came to the person in the course of a *business* in the *regulated sector.*

A *tipping off* offence will not be committed under s 333A, *POCA* if the person did not know or suspect that the disclosure was likely to *prejudice any investigation* that followed.

The penalty for this offence on summary conviction is a maximum of three months imprisonment, or a fine on scale 5, or both and on conviction on indictment to imprisonment for a term not exceeding two years, or a fine or both. There are a number of exceptions to this prohibition on revealing the existence of a report or an actual or contemplated investigation which are as follows:

- **Disclosures within an undertaking or group etc,** (s 333B): a person does not commit an offence if he makes a disclosure to another person employed by the same undertaking as him, and nor does an *independent legal professional* or a *relevant professional adviser* commit an offence if the disclosure is made to another *independent legal professional* or a *relevant professional adviser* where both the person making the disclosure and the person to whom it is made are in either an EEA state or a state imposing equivalent anti-*money laundering* requirements and those persons perform their professional activities within different undertakings that shares common ownership, management or control.
- **Other permitted disclosures between institutions etc** (s 333C): an *independent legal professional* or a *relevant professional adviser* does not commit an offence if he makes a disclosure to another person of the same kind from a different undertaking but of the same professional standing as himself (including as to duties of professional confidentiality and the protection of personal data) where the disclosure relates to the same *client* or former *client* of both advisers and involves a transaction or provisions of a service that involved them both, the disclosure is only made for the purpose of preventing a *money laundering* offence and the disclosure is made to a person in an EU Member State or a State imposing an equivalent money laundering requirements. This means that eg, an accountant may only disclose to another accountant, and not to a lawyer or another kind of *relevant professional adviser.*
- **Other permitted disclosures (general)** (s 333D): an offence is not committed if a disclosure is made to a *anti-money laundering supervisory authority* by virtue of the Money Laundering Regulations 2007 or for the purpose of the prevention, investigation or prosecution of a criminal offence in the UK or elsewhere, an investigation under *POCA*,or enforcement of any order of a court under *POCA*. In addition, and of importance to those who are *relevant professional advisers*, an offence is not committed by a *relevant*

professional adviser if he makes the disclosure to his *client* for the purpose of dissuading the *client* from engaging in conduct amounting to an offence.

2.18 Any of the *tipping off* offences contained in s 333A, *POCA* will only occur in the circumstances described, but there may be circumstances where a money launderer may be alerted to the possibility that a report will be or has been made or an investigation conducted, other than by a disclosure of such fact eg, by unexpected delay caused by waiting on *consent*. These have been distinguished in this *Guidance* by use of the phrase '*alerting a launderer*'. *Businesses* will also need to take care to guard against *alerting a launderer*,as part of their policies and procedures aimed at preventing operations related to *money laundering*.

2.19 A *tipping off* disclosure may be made in writing or verbally, and either directly or indirectly – including through inclusion of relevant information in published information. Considerable care is required in carrying out any communications with *clients* or third parties following a report. Before any disclosure is made relating to matters referred to in an *internal report* or *SAR*, it is important to consider carefully whether or not it is likely to constitute offences of *tipping* off or prejudicing an investigation. It is suggested that *businesses* keep records of these deliberations and the conclusions reached (sections 7.10 and 7.11).

2.20 However, *individuals* and *businesses* in the *regulated sector* will frequently need to continue to deliver their professional services and a way needs to be found to achieve this without falling foul of the *tipping off* offence. Section 333D(2) is of assistance in this regard (disclosure to his *client* for the purpose of dissuading the *client* from engaging in conduct amounting to a *money laundering* offence). More *Guidance* on acting for a *client* after a *money laundering* suspicion has been formed is given in section 9.

Practice Statements

Prejudicing an Investigation

2.21 This offence is set out in s 342, *POCA*. This offence is committed where a person:
- knows or suspects that a *money laundering*, confiscation or civil recovery investigation is being conducted or is about to be conducted; and
- makes a disclosure which is likely to *prejudice the investigation*; or
- falsifies, conceals or destroys documents relevant to the investigation, or causes that to happen.

As with *tipping off* offences, the person making the disclosure does not have to intend to prejudice an investigation for this offence to apply. However, there is a defence available if the person making the disclosure did not know or suspect the disclosure would be prejudicial, did not know or suspect the documents were relevant, or did not intend to conceal any facts from the person carrying out the investigation.

2.22 There are limited exceptions relating to persons carrying out law enforcement or judicial functions, and to legal advisers acting in privileged circumstances provided the disclosure is not made with the intention of furthering a criminal purpose.

2.23 Considerations similar to those set out under *tipping off* above apply in terms of how the offence may be committed and of taking precautions to ensure any disclosure made does not prejudice an investigation. *Businesses* should ensure they have sufficient document retention policies in place (see Section 3.9 of this *Guidance* – Record Keeping) to meet the needs of this section of *POCA* and the *2007 Regulations*, as well as their legal and professional obligations more generally.

Knowledge and Suspicion

Knowledge or suspicion?

2.24 An offence is committed by an *individual* in the *regulated sector* if he fails to report where he has knowledge, suspicion or reasonable grounds for suspecting *money laundering* activity. There is no definition of knowledge or suspicion within *POCA* and so interpretation of their meaning will rely on judgements in past legal cases, as well as this *Guidance* and on the ordinary meaning of the words.

2.25 Having knowledge means actually knowing that something is the case.

2.26 Case law suggests that suspicion is a state of mind more definite than speculation, but falls short of knowledge based on evidence. It must be based on some evidence, even if that evidence is tentative – simple speculation that a *client* may be *money laundering* is not sufficient grounds to form a suspicion. Similarly, a general assumption that low levels of crime (eg, not declaring all cash takings) are endemic in particular industry sectors does not amount to reasonable grounds for suspicion of particular *clients* operating in that sector.

2.27 A frequently used description is that '. . . A suspicion that something exists is more than a mere idle wondering whether it exists or not; it is a positive feeling of actual apprehension or mistrust, amounting to a "slight opinion, but without sufficient evidence"' (*Queensland Bacon PTY Ltd v Rees* [1966] 115 CLR 266 at 303, *per Kitto J*). In another more recent case, *Da Silva [2006] EWCA Crim 1654*, ' It seems to us that the essential element in the word "suspect" and its affiliates, in this context, is that the defendant must think that there is a possibility, which is more than fanciful, that the relevant facts exist. A vague feeling of unease would not suffice.'

2.28 *Money laundering* occurs only when *criminal property* has accrued to someone from a criminal act. In addition, it must be borne in mind that for property to be *criminal property* not only must it constitute a person's benefit from *criminal conduct*, but the alleged offender (ie, the person alleged to be laundering *criminal property*) must know or suspect that the property constitutes such a benefit. This means, for instance, that if someone has made an innocent error, even if such an error resulted in benefit and constituted a strict liability criminal offence, then the proceeds are not *criminal property* for the purposes of *POCA* and no *money laundering* offence has arisen until and unless the offender becomes aware of the error (eg, s 167(3), Customs and Excise Management Act 1979). *MLROs* need to consider carefully before reporting whether the information or other matter they intend to report meets these criteria. Examples of unlawful behaviour which may be observed, and may well result in advice to a *client* to correct an issue, but which are not reportable as *money laundering* are given below:

- offences where no proceeds or benefit results, such as the late filing of company accounts. However, *businesses and individuals* should be alert to the possibility that persistent failure to file accounts could represent part of a larger offence with proceeds, such as fraudulent trading or credit fraud involving the concealment of a poor financial position.
- misstatements in tax returns, for whatever cause, but which are corrected before the date when the tax becomes due.
- attempted frauds where the attempt has failed and so no benefit has accrued (although as this may still be a Fraud Act offence in England, Wales and Northern Ireland or the common law offence of fraud in Scotland, *individuals* and *businesses* may wish to consider reporting to their local police force or, once operational, the 'National Fraud Reporting Centre'). This includes '419' [1] letters and other attempted advanced fee frauds where there is no knowledge of benefit accruing. In the case of such letters, *individuals* and *businesses* may wish to consider following the guidance on the Metropolitan Police Fraud Alert internet pages (www.met.police.uk/fraudalert).

[1] Otherwise known as 'Nigerian scam' letters or equivalent

Where a *client* refuses to correct, or unreasonably delays in correcting, an innocent error that gave rise to proceeds and which was unlawful, *businesses* should consider what that indicates about the *client's* intent and whether the property has therefore now become *criminal property*.

Reasonable grounds for knowledge or suspicion

2.29 *Individuals* in the *regulated sector* must make an *internal report* or a *SAR*, as applicable, if there are 'reasonable grounds' for knowledge or suspicion, as well as actual knowledge or suspicion. This 'reasonable grounds' test creates an objective test – persons in the *regulated sector* will not be able to rely on an assertion of ignorance or naivety where this would not be reasonable to expect of a person with their training and position. For example, a person might be considered to have reasonable grounds for knowledge of *money laundering* if he had actual knowledge of, or possessed information which would indicate to a reasonable person, that another person was committing or had committed a *money laundering* offence; or had deliberately ignored the obvious inference from information (ie,. wilfully shutting one's eyes) known to him that another person was committing or had committed a *money laundering* offence. Please note that the interpretation of 'reasonable grounds' has not, as yet, been tested by the courts for the purposes of *POCA*.

2.30 'Reasonable grounds' should not be confused with the existence of higher than normal risk factors which may affect certain sectors or classes of persons. For example, cash-based *businesses* or complex overseas trust and company structures may be capable of being used to launder money, but this capability of itself is not considered to constitute 'reasonable grounds'.

2.31 Existence of higher than normal risk factors require increased attention to gathering and evaluation of 'know your *client*' information, and heightened awareness of the risk of *money laundering* in performing professional work, but do not of themselves require a report of suspicion to be made. For 'reasonable grounds' to come into existence, there needs to be sufficient information to advance beyond speculation that it is merely possible someone is laundering money, or a higher than normal incidence of some types of crime in particular sectors.

2.32 It is important that *individuals* do not turn a blind eye to information, but make reasonable enquiries such as a professional with their qualifications, experience and expertise might be expected to make in such a situation within the normal scope of their assignment or client relationship, and draw a reasonable conclusion such as may be expected of a person of their standing. *Individuals* should exercise a healthy level of professional scepticism, and if unsure of the action that should be taken, consult with their *MLRO* or otherwise in accordance with their *businesses'* procedures. If in doubt, *individuals* should err on the side of caution and make a report to their *MLRO*.

Non-compliance with the Money Laundering Regulations

2.33 It is a criminal offence for a *business* not to comply with the *2007 Regulations*, if it is within their scope. An offence may also be committed by any partner, director or officer of the *business*,who has consented to or connived at the non-compliance or where the non-compliance is attributable to his neglect.

2.34 The relevant offences are referred to below. *Individuals* and *businesses* should appreciate that there are a wide range of requirements in respect of which failure to comply could be considered to be a criminal offence.

2.35 The offences are set out in Regulation 45 and those which are relevant to the provision of *defined services* relate to:

- Regulation 7 – failure to apply *customer due diligence* measures
- Regulation 8 – failure to apply ongoing monitoring of *business relationships* and *customer due diligence*
- Regulation 9 – failure to comply with the requirements on timing of verification of identity of *clients* and any beneficial owner
- Regulation 11 – continuing with transaction/*business relationship* where unable to apply *customer due diligence* measures
- Regulation 14 – failure to apply enhanced *customer due diligence* and ongoing monitoring where required
- Regulation 18 – failing to follow a direction made by HM Treasury under this regulation (directions where *FATF* applies counter-measures)
- Regulation 19 – failure to keep the required records
- Regulation 20 – failure to establish, maintain, monitor and manage the required policies and procedures
- Regulation 21 – failure to take appropriate measures to provide the required training
- Regulations 26, 27 – failures regarding certain registration procedures where the Commissioners (HMRC) are the supervisory body (not applicable to those supervised by a body listed in Schedule 3)
- Regulation 33 – failure to comply with registration requirements specified by the Commissioners (not applicable to those supervised by a body listed in Schedule 3)

2.36 Further *Guidance* on compliance with the *2007 Regulations* is given in sections 3 to 7 below. As Treasury approval has been obtained the Courts are obliged to take into account compliance with this *Guidance*, in deciding whether an offence has been committed.

Section 3 — Anti Money Laundering Systems and Controls

Key Points

Under the Money Laundering Regulations 2007 (*2007 Regulations) businesses* are required to establish appropriate risk-sensitive policies and procedures in order to prevent activities related to *money laundering* and *terrorist financing* including those policies and procedures which provide for:

- identification and scrutiny of complex or unusually large transactions, unusual patterns of transactions with no apparent economic or lawful purpose and other activities regarded by the regulated person as likely to be of the nature of *money laundering* or *terrorist financing*;
- prevention of use of products favouring anonymity;
- determination of whether a *client* is a *PEP*;
- *customer due diligence*, ie, procedures designed to acquire knowledge about the firm's *clients* and prospective *clients* and to verify their identity as well as monitor *business relationships* and transactions;
- internal reporting including appointment of an *MLRO* to receive the *money laundering* reports required under the Proceeds of Crime Act 2002 (*POCA)* and the Terrorism Act *(TA 2000)* and a system for making those reports;

- record keeping, including details of *customer due diligence* and supporting evidence for *business relationships*, which need to be kept for five years after the end of a relationship and records of transactions, which also need to be kept for five years;
- internal control, risk assessment and management, compliance monitoring, management and communication; and
- in addition, *businesses* are required to take measures to make relevant employees aware of the law relating to *money laundering* and terrorist finance, and to train those employees in how to recognise and deal with transactions which may be related to *money laundering* or *terrorist financing*.

In order to ensure compliance is appropriately managed, *businesses* will need to ensure sufficient senior management oversight, appropriate analysis and assessment of the risks of *clients* and work/product types, systems for monitoring compliance with procedures and methods of communicating procedures and other information to personnel.

Introduction

3.1 *POCA* offences may be committed not only by *individuals* and *businesses* in the *regulated sector* but by any person. In contrast, the *2007 Regulations* impose obligations on *businesses* in the *regulated sector* as to the systems and controls they need to have in place to meet the requirements of the UK anti-money laundering regime. Under these regulations, not only must each *business* put anti-money laundering systems and controls in place but it also has a duty to ensure that relevant staff are aware of these systems and are appropriately trained. *Businesses* are explicitly required to monitor and manage their compliance with the *2007 Regulations*, to ensure continued observation of the requirements. 23

3.2 *Individuals* involved in the failure of *businesses* to meet their obligations under the *2007 Regulations* may be subject to criminal sanction, as may the *business* itself. Criminal sanctions for breach of the *2007 Regulations* only apply directly to the *individuals* working within a *business* when their neglect, connivance or consent has led to the failure to comply by the *business*.

The Requirements

3.3 The *2007 Regulations'* requirements of *businesses* are contained in the following Parts:

- customer due diligence (Part 2 of the 2007 Regulations); and
- record-keeping, procedures and training (Part 3 of the 2007 Regulations).

Systems

3.4 The *2007 Regulations* place requirements on *businesses* to have in place a wide range of systems in order to prevent operations related to *money laundering* or *terrorist financing*. The requirements cover the following issues. Where a separate section of this *Guidance* deals in detail with this matter, this is shown after the relevant heading, the other matters are dealt with in this section:

- *customer due diligence* and ongoing monitoring (see section 5 of this *Guidance*);
- reporting procedures (see sections 6 and 7 of this *Guidance*);
- record-keeping;
- internal control;
- risk assessment and management (see section 4 of this *Guidance*);
- compliance management; and
- communication.

3.5 The level of detail in the *2007 Regulations* as to what the requirements mean varies considerably, with *customer due diligence* being explained in some detail in Part 2 of the *2007 Regulations*, and with some detail being provided in respect of internal reporting procedures (Regulation 15) and record-keeping (Regulation 19). The *2007 Regulations* are less comprehensive on what is expected in respect of internal control, risk assessment and management, compliance management and communication.

3.6 *Businesses* need to establish systems that create an internal environment or culture in which people are aware of their responsibilities under the UK anti-money laundering regime and where they understand that they are expected to fulfil those responsibilities with appropriate diligence. In deciding what systems to install, a *business* will need to consider a range of matters including:

- the type, scale and complexity of its operations;
- the number of different business types it is involved in;
- the types of services it offers, and its *client* profiles;
- how it sells its services;
- the type of business transactions it becomes involved in or advises on; and
- the risks associated with each area of its *business* in terms of the risks of the *business* or its services being used for *money laundering* or terrorist operations, or the risks of its *clients* and their counterparties being involved in such operations.

3.7 *Businesses* should allocate responsibility for internal controls and effective risk management to a member of senior management, and should also ensure that the appointed *MLRO* has sufficient seniority and authority to carry out his task, whether or not these two functions are held by the same person. All *businesses* will need systems and controls, appropriate to the size and nature of their *business*, sufficient to achieve the following:

- determination and recording of the firm's systems for anti-money laundering awareness, *client* acceptance, *customer due diligence* and on-going monitoring requirements (including whether a customer is a *PEP*), consultation with and internal reporting to the *MLRO* (where applicable – sole practitioners with no staff and no associates are not required to have internal reporting procedures or an *MLRO*), and dissemination of such policies and procedures to all relevant staff;
- development and documentation of the firm's risk assessment of its *business*;
- training of all relevant staff, including systems and controls to ensure training is taken/attended and understood;
- methods for identification of topical update material and its dissemination as appropriate to senior management and other personnel;
- systems for periodic testing that policies and procedures comply with legislative and regulatory requirements;
- monitoring the compliance of the *business* with the policy and procedures including reporting to senior management on compliance and addressing any identified deficiencies.

3.8 In addition, *businesses* are recommended to maintain the following additional systems, for effective internal control and risk management:

- detailed documentation of policies and procedures in relation to matters not routinely a matter for *client* facing staff, such as *customer due diligence* for higher risk *clients*; information provision to senior management, training, awareness and compliance monitoring, and the role of the *MLRO*;
- provision in new product/service development processes for consideration of new services or business areas from an anti-*money laundering* perspective, and update of policy and procedure where appropriate;
- consideration at appropriate intervals of the *business* profile and whether the firm's risk assessment and/or policy and procedures require updating in response.

Appropriate systems might also include a policy of acceptance of new *clients* being reserved to partners or other senior personnel, who may wish to refer to the *MLRO* for advice, if it is proposed to accept *clients* from outside the usual and well understood *client* base of the firm.

Record-keeping

3.9 Records must be kept of *clients'* identity, the supporting evidence of verification of identity (in each case including the original and any updated records), the firm's *business relationships* with them (ie,. including any non-engagement related documents relating to the *client* relationship) and details of any occasional transactions and details of monitoring of the relationship. These records must be kept for five years after the end of the relevant *business relationships* or completion of the transactions. Care is needed to ensure retention of historic, as well as current records. *Businesses* are also recommended to store securely information relating to both *internal reports* and *SARs* for at least the same period, ie,. at least five years after receipt by the *MLRO*. Documentation of reports is dealt with in further detail in section 7 below. Shown below is a summary of record-keeping requirements specified in the *2007 Regulations* for *customer due diligence* and *business relationships*/occasional transactions and *Guidance* in respect of retention of internal reporting procedures and training records for which specific guidance is not given in the *2007 Regulations*.

Record	Retention period	Comments
Specified in the 2007 Regulations		

i) *Client* identification, including evidence of identity	**5 years** from end of *business relationship.*[2]	Care should be taken to ensure that records are not destroyed by one department, while another is still within the five year retention period or has undertaken new business with the *client*. Where a *business* is engaged with several different activities with a *client*, it may decide to keep details of *customer due diligence* within each part of the firm so engaged, or to maintain central files, depending on its internal organisation. Evidence of *client* identity can be held in a variety of forms, eg, in hard copy or in electronic form in accordance with the document retention policies employed within the *business*.
ii) *Business relationships*	**5 years** from the date when all activities in relation to the *business relationship* were completed — except in the case of particular transactions within that *business relationship* the retention period is 5 years from the date on which the transaction was completed	Records of *business relationships* and occasional transactions (ie,. client assignment working papers and related documents) also need to be maintained for 5 years from the end of the relationship or transaction. For particular transactions within a *business relationship*, the records for the particular transaction need only be retained for 5 years from the completion of that transaction. In the context of provision of *defined services* it would be reasonable to treat each engagement or assignment as a 'particular transaction'. As *businesses* will need to maintain records for a wide range of purposes that comply with both legal and professional requirements for retention of documentation, it is not anticipated that any special system should be needed but that the general document retention systems employed within the *business*, provided they meet these standards, should be sufficient.
Not specified in the 2007 Regulations		
iii) Suspicious activities	Not prescribed	Records of *internal reports*, the *MLRO's* consideration of them, any subsequent reporting decision and issues connected to consent, production of documents etc are a vital record as they may form the basis of a defence to accusations of *money laundering* and related offences. For this reason, it is recommended that such records are retained for at least 5 years after being made and possibly longer, at least whilst the *business relationship* continues. Records of *internal reports* are not considered to form part of *client* assignment working papers and so it is recommended that such records are kept, in a secure form separately from the *businesses'* normal methods for retaining *client* work documents. This is to guard against inadvertent disclosure to any party who may have or seek access to the *client* working paper files where the existence of otherwise of an *internal report* or *SAR* is not relevant to the purpose for which they are examining the files.
iv) Training	Not prescribed	We recommend that evidence of assessment of training needs and steps taken to meet such needs is retained. *Businesses* should determine a retention period in the light of their normal retention period for training and other internal records, but we recommend they be kept for at least 5 years in order to demonstrate a continuing compliance with current and previous regulations.

[2] As well 'business relationship', the *2007 Regulations* refer to 'occasional transactions', ie, those outside the *business relationship* valued at over €15,000. 'Occasional transactions' is a cogent term in a banking context but is difficult to apply in the context of *accountancy services*. Therefore this *Guidance* uses only '*business relationship*', a more natural term for *accountancy and related services*, throughout.

Reporting procedures

3.10 A *business's* internal procedures should clearly set out what is expected of *individuals* who form suspicions or obtain knowledge of possible *money laundering*. The reports can take any form specified by the *business* in internal procedures, eg, phone calls, emails, in writing, supplemented by copies of third party documents and working papers but *businesses* should ensure that, whatever forms the reporting takes, relevant personnel are aware of the procedures to be used. Consideration should be given to how to minimise the number of copies of reporting information held within a *business*. *Businesses* may wish to consider whether it is advisable to specify telephone or face to face contact with the *MLRO* as the preferred initial reporting step, with the reporting records being created by the *MLRO*, supplemented as necessary with copy information from *client* files.

3.11 It is recommended that all details of *internal reports* are held by the *MLRO* and excluded from *client* files. The duty to report is a matter which does not fall within the delivery of professional services to *clients* and accordingly reporting details are not required to be placed on *client* files. Exclusion of information from *client* files assists in avoiding inadvertent or inappropriate disclosure of information and provides some protection against the threat of *tipping off*. *Client* files should retain only that information relevant to, and required for, the professional work being undertaken. It should be noted that *anti-money laundering supervisory authorities* have an obligation under Regulation 24 (2) to make reports of suspicion. However, the law is not clear as to the interaction of the *POCA privilege reporting exemption* (Section 7.26–7.46) and the 2007 *Regulations* and unless this is resolved, there remains the risk of an *anti-money laundering supervisory authority* reporting a matter that was properly the subject of the *privilege reporting exemption*. Keeping internal reporting papers separate from *client* files may assist in mitigating this risk but is not a complete solution.

3.12 Further *Guidance* is given for *individuals*, on forming suspicions and making *internal reports* is given in section 6 and *Guidance* for *MLROs* in checking and validating *internal reports* and making *SARs* to *SOCA* in section 7.

Communication and Training

3.13 The *2007 Regulations* provide that all 'relevant' employees are required to be 'made aware' of law relating to *money laundering* and *terrorist financing*, and regularly given training in how to recognise and deal with transactions which may be related to *money laundering* or *terrorist financing*. Though the *2007 Regulations* contain no express requirement, it is considered to be best practice for these provisions to be applied to all partners in firms and to sole practitioners and it is likely to be necessary to train all *client*-facing staff (see section 3.15 below).

3.14 In considering a training plan, *businesses* need to keep in mind the objectives they are trying to achieve, which is to create an environment effective in preventing *money laundering* and which thereby helps protect *individuals* and the *business*.

3.15 When considering which staff may be considered relevant, *businesses* should consider not only those who have involvement in *client* work, but also, where appropriate, those who deal with the *business* finances, and those who deal with procuring services on behalf of the *business* and who manage those services. Accordingly, it is likely that all *client*-facing staff will be considered relevant and at least the senior support staff. *Businesses* may decide to provide comprehensive training to all relevant staff members, or may chose to tailor its provision to match more closely the role of the employees concerned. In particular, *MLROs* may require supplementary training, and members of senior management may also benefit from a customised approach or some supplementary training.

3.16 A training programme for relevant staff needs to contain content on the law and content which puts this into the context in which the *business* operates, to enable recognition of suspected *money laundering* in that context, and which illustrates the 'red flags' which staff should be aware of in conducting business. The core elements of law making up the UK anti-*money laundering* and anti-terrorism regime, are set out in this *Guidance* (in particular in section 2). In addition, *businesses* may wish to include reference to other elements of law where criminal penalties may be applied and where these relate directly to the work of the *individual* or *business*, eg, an *FSA* approved person might be expected to have a reasonable working knowledge of the parts of *FSMA 2000* relevant to his work. Whilst it is not necessary for relevant personnel to develop specialist knowledge of criminal law in general, they may reasonably be expected to apply the general legal and business knowledge which might normally be held by a person of their role and experience in determining whether to make a report to the *MLRO*.

3.17 Training also needs to cover how to deal with transactions which might be related to *money laundering* and *terrorist financing*. This would include training on the *businesses'* internal consultation and advisory systems (to assist *individuals* in assessing whether they have a valid suspicion) internal reporting systems and the *businesses'* expectations for confidentiality and the avoidance of *tipping off* and *alerting a money launderer*. Further *Guidance* on recognising *money laundering* by those undertaking *defined services* is given in section 6.

3.18 As regards the frequency of training, this is a matter for each *business* to consider. It may be influenced by changes in law, regulation or professional guidance, by new case law or national/international findings, or by a change in the profile and perceived risks of the *business*. Each *business* should consider the frequency of its training, possibly on an annual basis, and document its assessment as to whether the current training and state of awareness of employees is sufficient, or whether a supplement is needed. It may not be necessary to repeat the whole of a training programme on a regular basis, but it may be possible to provide concise update material which accomplishes the dual role of refreshing or expanding knowledge and generally reminding staff of the importance of effective anti-*money laundering* work.

3.19 Training methods may be selected to suit the size, complexity and culture of the *business*, and may be delivered in a variety of ways including face to face, self-study, e-learning and video, or a combination of methods. *Businesses* should keep records of attendance at, or completion of, training and are recommended to provide for some form of test or other confirmation of understanding of the training.

3.20 Should a *business* fail to make provision for the training of relevant employees, then under s330 (7), *POCA* a member of staff who does not know or suspect someone is engaged in *money laundering* gains a defence against the failure to disclose offence (ie, if there is only reasonable grounds for knowledge or suspicion and the staff member fails to make an *internal report*). However, such an omission is likely to open the *business* to the risk of prosecution for breach of the *2007 Regulations*. The significance of training records to both *individuals*, and *businesses* is reflected in the recommendation in section 3.9.

3.21 *Businesses* need to make arrangements to ensure new staff are trained as soon as possible after they join the *business*.

Section 4 – The Risk Based Approach

Key Points

- A risk based approach allows *businesses* to target resource and effort where the risk is greatest and, conversely, reduce requirements where the risk is low.
- *Businesses* must establish adequate and appropriate policies and procedures relating to risk assessment and management in order to prevent operations related to *money laundering* or *terrorist financing*.
- *Businesses* must—
  - (a) determine the extent of *customer due diligence* measures (section 5) on a risk-sensitive basis depending on the type of *client*, *business relationship*, or services to be provided;
  - (b) be able to demonstrate to their *anti-money laundering supervisory authorities* that the extent of *customer due diligence* measures is appropriate in view of the risks of *money laundering* and *terrorist financing*.
- *Businesses* are required to take a risk-based approach and have adequate measures to verify the identity of beneficial owners so that they are satisfied that they know who the beneficial owner is and what the control structure is in respect of a *client* who is other than a natural person (Regulation 5(1)(b)).
- *Businesses* are required to undertake scrutiny of transactions and other activities throughout the course of a *business relationship* to ensure consistency with *businesses' and individuals'* knowledge of the *client*, his business and risk profile.
- *Businesses* must also keep up-to-date the information collected in applying *customer due diligence* measures.
- *Businesses* must apply *customer due diligence* measures at appropriate times to existing *clients* on a risk-sensitive basis.

Risk Assessment and Management

Policies and Procedures

4.1 All *businesses* must have appropriate policies and procedures for assessment and management of the risk of the *business* being used for *money laundering*, of failing to recognise it where it occurs and report it when required. A risk-based approach to anti-*money laundering* incurs cost which is proportionate to this risk, focusing effort where it is needed and has most impact.

4.2 Professional firms are likely to already have in place policies and procedures to minimise professional, *client* and legal risk. Anti-money laundering procedures and policies may be integrated into existing risk management systems or be controlled separately. In either case, anti-*money laundering* policies and procedures should be valuable to *businesses*, in contributing to the control of risks to both *businesses* and *individuals* in this and other areas.

Risk profile

4.3 The development of a *money laundering* risk profile for the *business* enables a risk-based policy and approach to be developed, and thus to determine the most cost effective and proportionate way to manage and mitigate the *money laundering* and *terrorist financing* risks faced by the *business*. The risk profile of a *business* is determined by:

– identifying the *money laundering* and *terrorist financing* risks that are relevant to the *business*; and
– designing and implementing controls to manage and mitigate these risks, and record their operation.

Managing compliance

4.4 *Businesses* are required to monitor and manage their compliance with and internal communication of their policies and procedures and this includes their systems for risk assessment and management, as well as their other anti-*money laundering* policies and procedures (Regulation 20 (1)). All such systems should be managed through monitoring the operation of the controls, updating them where necessary and assessing whether they have been effective. *Businesses* may come into contact with activity in the *client's* business which they perceive as likely, by its nature, to be related to *money laundering* or *terrorist financing* (in particular, complex or unusually large transactions and all unusual patterns of transactions which have no apparent economic or visible lawful purpose). In those circumstances, *businesses* have a duty to pay special attention to such an activity.

4.5 *Businesses* can decide for themselves how to carry out their risk assessment, which may be simple or sophisticated depending on the nature of their practice. Where the practice is simple, involving few service lines, with most *clients* falling into similar categories, a simple approach may be appropriate for most *clients*, with the focus being on those *clients* that fall outside the norm.

4.6 A risk-based approach can never, by its nature, be an error–free system. However, it ensures the most cost effective results by directing the attention of *businesses* to the risks relating to different *clients* and services, in order to determine what level of knowledge and verification is required when establishing a *business relationship* and in conducting that relationship.

The Risk-based Approach

4.7 Each *business* needs to make a reasoned decision as to how it intends to manage *money laundering* risk. A risk-based approach does, however, enable a *business* to target its effort on conducting *customer due diligence* more effectively with increased depth of work being conducted where the risks are perceived, on a rational basis, to be higher.

4.8 Senior management engagement and commitment is needed to produce and embed a successful risk-based approach, and it also needs effective communication to all staff members who need to use it.

4.9 *Businesses* may assess the *money laundering* risks of:

– different products and services,
– *client* types and sectors, and
– the jurisdictions of *client* origin, funding, investment and conduct of business.

and apply a simple risk categorisation of low/normal/high on the basis of these categories. Such an approach is valid, and should be capable of minimising complexity, but needs to retain an element of discretion and flexibility where risk ratings may be raised or lowered with appropriate management input in response to particular or exceptional circumstances.

4.10 *Businesses* may also wish to consider the different types of risk to which they are exposed. These risks may include

– being used in an active sense to launder money through the handling of cash or assets,
– becoming concerned in an arrangement which facilitates *money laundering*, through the provision of investment services or the provision of trust or company services.

Practice Statements

– risks attaching to the *client* and/or those who trade with or otherwise interact with *clients* as regards their potential for involvement in *money laundering*.

4.11 A simple matrix prepared from a risk-assessment of the factors considered above may be prepared to provide a basic framework for the categorisation of *clients* and engagements, and to direct the depth and type of *customer due diligence* accordingly.

4.12 Chapter 4 of the *JMLSG Guidance* notes provides useful additional guidance on the risk-based approach

Developing and applying a risk based approach

4.13 In developing a risk-based approach, *businesses* need to ensure it is readily comprehensible and easy to use for all relevant staff. In cases of doubt or complexity, *businesses* may wish to consider putting in place procedures where queries may be referred to a senior and experienced person, eg, the *MLRO* for a risk-based decision which may vary from standard procedures.

4.14 To develop the approach it is necessary to review the *business* and consider what *money laundering* risks might attach to each service type, *client* type etc. One way to consider this in relation to the *defined services* is outlined below, but there are other approaches that may be equally or more valid depending on the type of *business*.

4.15 *Businesses* should consider first the type of risk presented:

– is the risk that the *business* might be used to launder money or provide the means to launder money? Examples might include handling *client* money, implementing company and trust structures, handling insolvent estates where assets are tainted by crime etc.
– is the risk that the *client* or its counterparties might be involved in *money laundering*? Examples might include *clients* who are *PEPs* (see section 5.27), or who are high profile and attract controversy or adverse comment in the public domain, or who are involved in higher risk sectors and jurisdictions (*eg*, those where corruption is known to be a higher risk), or who are known to be potentially involved in illegal activities, such as tax evaders seeking advice to resolve their affairs, and certain forensic work connected with fraud or other crime etc.

4.16 Consideration of these risk types should enable the *business* to draw up a simple matrix of characteristics of the *client* or service which are considered to present a higher than normal risk, and those which present a normal risk. Some may, by long acquaintance and detailed knowledge, or by their status (eg, listed, regulated and government entities as defined for the purpose of *simplified due diligence* in the *2007 Regulations*) be considered to present a lower than normal risk.

4.17 This matrix can then be incorporated into *client* acceptance procedures, and as step 1 of the *customer due diligence* process, allows a *money laundering* risk level to be assigned to ensure appropriate, but not excessive, *customer due diligence* work is carried out.

4.18 It is important for the approach adopted to incorporate a provision for raising the risk rating from low or normal to high if any information comes to light in conducting the *customer due diligence* that causes concern or suspicion.

4.19 In all cases, even where *clients* qualify for *simplified due diligence* under the terms of the *2007 Regulations*, or where they are considered low risk for other reasons, to assist in effective ongoing monitoring *businesses* should gather knowledge about the *client* to allow understanding of:

– who the *client* is
– where required, who owns it (including ultimate beneficial owners – see section 5.6)
– who controls it
– the purpose and intended nature of the *business relationship*
– the nature of the *client*
– the *client's* source of funds
– the *client's* business and economic purpose.

4.20 The information specified in the bullet points above are referred to in the remainder of this *Guidance* as 'know your client' or 'KYC' information which is one step in the *customer due diligence* process. However, *businesses* may avail themselves of the opportunity to conduct verification of identity on a simplified basis both under the terms of the *2007 Regulations*, where applicable, and otherwise where the accumulated knowledge of the *client* is considered sufficient to prove its identity on a risk-sensitive basis without collecting additional documents as might be required for a new *client* considered to present a normal risk (provided in both cases that any relevant requirements of the *2007 Regulations*, for example in relation to the identification of beneficial owners, are met).

4.21 *Businesses* need to set out clear requirements for collecting KYC information about the *client* and for conducting verification of identity, to a depth suitable to the assessment of risk. Set out in this *Guidance* are some high level guidelines as to how *businesses* might approach this. More detailed *Guidance* is contained in the *JMLSG Guidance* notes, Chapters 4 and 5.

Section 5 – Customer Due Diligence

Key Points

- Effective '*customer due diligence*' measures are an essential part of any system designed to prevent *money laundering* and are a cornerstone requirement of the Money Laundering Regulations 2007 (*2007 Regulations*).
- *Businesses* should take a **risk-based approach** to allow effort to be concentrated on higher risk areas (**also see section 4**). Risks must be assessed before the appropriate level of *customer due diligence* can be applied.
- *Customer due diligence* measures need to be carried out:
  * when establishing a business relationship,
  * when carrying out an occasional transaction,
  * where there is a suspicion of money laundering or terrorist financing; and
  * where there are doubts concerning the veracity of previous identification information.
- *Businesses* are required to ensure *customer due diligence* procedures are applied to all *clients*, both new and existing. *Customer due diligence* must be applied to existing *clients* (ie those existing prior to the *2007 Regulations* coming into force) at appropriate times on a risk-sensitive basis.
- **Before** entering a *business relationship*, *businesses* must:
  * identify and verify the *client's* identity using documents or information from reliable and independent sources.
  * identify the beneficial owner of the *client* (where there is one), including understanding the ownership and control structure of the *client* and verifying, according to risk, the identity of the beneficial owner(s).
  * obtain information on the purpose and intended nature of the *business relationship*.
- Verification of identity may in certain circumstances be conducted during the establishment of a *business relationship* if this is necessary not to interrupt the normal course of business and there is little risk of *money laundering* or *terrorist financing* occurring, provided the verification is completed as soon as practicable after contact is first established.
- **During** a *business relationship*, *businesses* must monitor activity on an ongoing basis. This includes scrutiny of transactions, source of funds and other elements of knowledge collected in the *customer due diligence* process, to ensure the new information is consistent with other knowledge of the *client* and keeping the documentation concerning the *client* and the relationship updated.
- *Businesses* can use a variety of tools and methods to conduct *customer due diligence*; the onus is on them to satisfy themselves and to be able to demonstrate to their *anti-money laundering supervisory authority* the appropriateness of their approach.

Why is this Important?

5.1 *Customer due diligence* measures are a key part of the anti-*money laundering* requirements. They ensure that *businesses* know who their *clients* are, ensure that they do not accept *clients* unknowingly which are outside their normal risk tolerance, or whose business they will not understand with sufficient clarity to be able to form *money laundering* suspicions when appropriate. If a *business* does not understand its *client's* regular business pattern of activity it will be very difficult to identify any abnormal business patterns or activities. In addition *businesses* must be in a position to supply the *client's* identity to *SOCA* should that *client* become the subject of a *SAR*.

5.2 Many *businesses* will have other procedures for *client* acceptance, for example to ensure compliance with professional requirements for independence and to avoid conflicts of interest.

Practice Statements

The requirements of the *2007 Regulations* may either be integrated with those procedures or addressed separately. In either case, initial *customer due diligence* information not only assists in acceptance decisions, but also enables the *business* to form well-grounded expectations of the *client*'s behaviour which provides some assistance in detecting potentially suspicious behaviour during the *business relationship*.

5.3 The processes required for compliance with *anti-money laundering* initial *customer due diligence* requirements contribute vitally to the overall picture of potential *clients* and appropriate risk assessment of them. However, a lack of concern raised during *customer due diligence* does not automatically mean that the *client* and engagement will remain in their initial risk category. Continued alertness for changes in the nature or ownership of the *client*, its business model, or its susceptibility to *money laundering* – or actual evidence of the latter — must be maintained.

What is Customer Due Diligence?

5.4 The *2007 Regulations* provide an outline of the required components of *customer due diligence* which *businesses* need to ensure are integrated into *client* acceptance processes and the continuing conduct of the *business relationship*. The required components are:

- identifying the *client* (ie, knowing who the *client* is) and verifying the identity of the *client* (ie, confirming that identity is valid by obtaining documents or other information from sources which are independent and reliable);
- identifying the beneficial owner(s) (see section 5.6) of a *client*, if there is one, so that the identity of the individual(s) who is the ultimate owner or controller is known, the ownership and control structure is understood and also that their identities are verified, as required, on a risk-sensitive basis; and
- information on the purpose and intended nature of the *business relationship*.

5.5 Whilst the *2007 Regulations* do indicate some cases where either *simplified due diligence* may be employed or *enhanced due diligence* must be employed, they do not specify, comprehensively, how to apply a risk-based approach in conducting *customer due diligence*. Section 4 of this *Guidance* provides a high level outline of the key elements of a risk-based approach. If further detail is required it is recommended that reference is made to the *JMLSG Guidance* notes which cover the subject in depth and, as HM Treasury approved *Guidance* for the financial services industry, may be considered as a reliable additional source of information in supplement to this *Guidance*.

What is a Beneficial Owner?

5.6 The *2007 Regulations* set out in some detail the meaning of 'beneficial owner' in terms of bodies corporate, partnerships, trusts and other legal entities/arrangements not falling into the three categories listed above as well as special provisions regarding estates of deceased persons and a catch all provision that, where not otherwise specified, defines the beneficial owner as the person who ultimately owns or controls the *client* or on whose behalf a transaction is being conducted. The provisions regarding beneficial ownership are set out in Regulation 6 and are summarised below:

- **Bodies corporate** –beneficial owner means any individual who, in respect of any body other than a company whose securities are listed on a *regulated investment market*, owns or controls, directly or indirectly including through bearer share holdings, more than 25% of the shares or voting rights in the body or who otherwise exercises control over the management of the body.
- **Partnerships** (other than limited liability partnerships established under the Limited Liability Partnerships Act 2000) — beneficial owner means any individual who ultimately is entitled to or controls (directly or indirectly) more than 25% of the capital or profits of the partnership or more than 25% of the voting rights in the partnership or who otherwise exercises control over the management of the partnership.
- **Trusts** — beneficial owner means any individual who is entitled to a *specified interest* in at least 25% of the capital of the trust property, or where a trust is not set up entirely for the benefit of persons with a *specified interest*, the class of persons in whose main interest the trust is set up or operates or any individual who has control (*a trust controller*) over the trust. Where a class of persons is identified, it is not a requirement for all members of that class to be separately identified.
- **Other entities and arrangements** (meaning an entity or arrangement which administers and distributes funds) – where the individuals who benefit from the entity or arrangement have been determined, beneficial owner means any individual who benefits from at least 25% of the property of the entity or arrangements. Where those benefiting have yet to be determined, beneficial owner means the class of persons in whose main interest the entity or arrangement is set up or operates or an individual who exercises control over at least 25% of the property of the entity or arrangement. Where a class of persons is the

beneficial owner, it is not a requirement for all members of that class to be separately identified. Note that where an individual is the beneficial owner of a body corporate which benefits from, or exercises control over, the property of an entity or arrangement, the individual is to be regarded as having that benefit or control and so is classed as the beneficial owner.

– **Estates of deceased persons** – the beneficial owner is considered to be the executor or administrator of the estate (full detail is shown in Regulation 6(8)).

5.7 The focus on identifying and, where appropriate, verifying the identity of beneficial owners is not only an important element of the required *customer due diligence* information, but is also an important factor in an effective risk-based approach to *client* acceptance. *Businesses* will need to be diligent in their enquiries in this field, taking into account that information may sometimes not be readily available from public record sources. This will necessitate a flexible approach to information gathering which will often involve direct enquiry of *clients* and their other advisers and professional service providers as well as undertaking public record searches in the UK and overseas.

Application and Timing of Customer Due Diligence Measures (when)

5.8 Identification and verification of identity procedures (together termed as "ID procedures") should normally be completed **before** entering into a *business relationship*. This applies also to occasional transactions. ID procedures are also required at other times, for example, when there is a suspicion of *money laundering* or *terrorist financing* or where there are doubts about the sufficiency of identification information already held. If it is concluded the information held is insufficient, the *business* should remedy this as soon as is practicable. Should a suspicion be developed about the *client*, *businesses* will need to consider whether they are satisfied that the information already held is sufficient and up to date or whether any additional or updated information is required in respect of the *client(s)* in question in order that the information required by Regulation 5 (customer due diligence) is met. In particular, in any case where suspicion is developed, *simplified due diligence* may no be longer be applied. This means if *simplified due diligence* had been applied, additional information will need to be collected in accordance with *businesses'* risk-based procedures. *Businesses* must bear in mind in conducting this *customer due diligence* work the need to avoid disclosing that a *money laundering* report has been made, or that an investigation is underway, or may be commenced (see section 2.17-2.21 Tipping Off).

5.9 The *2007 Regulations* allow for completion of ID procedures 'during the establishment of a *business relationship*' rather than before if the measures are completed as soon as practicable after the initial contact **but only** when such a process is necessary not to interrupt the normal conduct of business and there is little risk of *money laundering* or *terrorist financing* occurring. *Guidance* on how this might reasonably be applied in the case of provision of the *defined services* is provided below, although this is not intended to be prescriptive, or exclusive. *Businesses* should not complete any assignment for a *client* (eg, including transfer of *client* monies or delivery of work product) before *customer due diligence* has been carried out in full in accordance with the *businesses'* procedures.

5.10 If procedures are not completed before entering a *business relationship*, *businesses* and their *clients* may suffer considerable cost and inconvenience in having to terminate a relationship if ID procedures either cannot be completed, or where the results are unsatisfactory.

5.11 *Customer due diligence* should also be completed before undertaking occasional services for the *client* that do not form part of an ongoing *business relationship*. *Businesses* must understand why the *client* requires the service, the identities of other parties that might be involved, and any potential for *money laundering* that may arise.

When delay may be acceptable

5.12 In forming new *business relationships*, there are some cases where delay **may** be acceptable, such as in urgent insolvency appointments, and urgent appointments that involve ascertaining the legal position of a *client* or defending the *client* in legal proceedings.

5.13 In such cases, *businesses* should still gather enough information to allow them to at least form a basic assessment of the identity of the *client* and *money laundering* risk and to complete other acceptance formalities such as considering the potential for conflicts of interest.

5.14 In other cases, where the majority of information required has been collected before entering a *business relationship*, short time extensions to complete collection of remaining information may be acceptable, provided this is caused only by administrative or logistical issues, and not by any reluctance of the *client* to provide the information and is necessary not to interrupt the normal course of business. Such extensions should be exceptional, rather than the norm. It is recommended that such extensions of time are considered and agreed by a member of senior management or the *MLRO* to ensure the reasons for the extension are valid and do not give rise to concern over the risk category of the *client* or the potential for *money laundering* suspicion.

5.15 If evidence is delayed (rather than refused), *businesses* should consider;

– the credibility of the *client's* explanation,
– the length of delay,
– whether the delay is in itself reasonable grounds for suspicion of *money laundering* requiring a report to *SOCA* and/or a factor indicating against acceptance of the *client* and engagement, and
– documenting the reasons for delay and steps taken.

Non-compliance through client refusal

5.16 If a prospective *client* refuses to provide evidence of identity or other information properly requested as part of *customer due diligence*, the *business relationship* or occasional transaction must not proceed any further and any existing relationship with the *client* must be terminated (but see sections 5.56–5.59 on insolvency cases). Consideration must be given as to whether a report needs to be made to *SOCA* under *POCA* or *TA 2000*.

5.17 Where the appointment is of either a lawyer or *relevant professional advisor* in the course of ascertaining the legal position for the *client*, or performing the task of defending or representing the *client* in or concerning legal proceedings (including advice on instigating or avoiding proceedings) the requirement to cease acting and consider reporting to *SOCA* does not apply although *customer due diligence* information will still need to be collected within the time constraints in Regulation 9. *Businesses* are advised to consider the position very carefully before applying this exception to ensure that the type of work and their professional status fall within the definitions set out in Regulations 11(2) and (3).

Continuing customer due diligence

5.18 In addition to considerations before entering a *business relationship*, *customer due diligence* must be exercised on an ongoing basis during the relationship, as part of regular monitoring of *money laundering* risks or occasioned by the *client* undergoing significant changes. *Businesses* may wish to consider reviewing *customer due diligence* and other *client* information on a periodic basis, as well as in response to perceived risks.

5.19 Changes such as the appointment of new senior managers or shareholders and/ or controlling parties, changes in the *client's* strategy or changes of business profile should prompt *businesses* to re-apply *customer due diligence* procedures. These may differ from those adopted for a new *client*, and although there may be a change in focus the objective remains the same: to have a sound understanding of the *client's* identity and activities in order to assess risks of *money laundering* and to have accurate underlying records.

The Risk Based Approach to Client Due Diligence

5.20 Regulation 7(3) requires *customer due diligence* measures to be carried out on a risk-sensitive basis. This means that *businesses* need to consider how their risk assessment and management procedures (see section 3 above) flow through into their *client* acceptance and ID procedures, to give sufficient information and evidence, in the way most appropriate to the *business* concerned.

5.21 In addition, there are certain circumstances where the *2007 Regulations* themselves lay down categories where *simplified due diligence* or *enhanced due diligence* is appropriate, according to national and international assessments of the risk of *money laundering*.

Simplified due diligence

5.22 '*Simplified due diligence*' is a phrase used in the *2007 Regulations* (Regulation 13) which means that a *business* is not required to apply the *customer due diligence* measures laid out in Regulation 7, as set out in section 5.20 above, where the *business* has reasonable grounds for believing that a *client* falls into the relevant categories. *Businesses who* may be permitted to apply the *simplified due diligence* exemptions but who perceive other than a low risk of *money laundering* in a specific case, should consider applying their standard or *enhanced due diligence* processes. In any case where a *client* or potential *client* has been subject to *simplified due diligence* and a suspicion or *money laundering* or *terrorist financing* arises in relation to that *client*, the *simplified due diligence* provisions must no longer be applied and the *customer due diligence* requirements of Regulation 7 must be applied, subject to any *tipping off* issues.

5.23 The main categories of relevance to those providing *defined services* are:

- *credit* or *financial institutions* subject to the provisions of the *money laundering directive* or equivalent overseas requirements,
- companies listed on a regulated EEA market or equivalent overseas requirements subject to *specified disclosure obligations*,
- UK public authorities and certain public authorities in the EU and EEA (see Schedule 2 paragraph 2).

Simplified due diligence is also available for some categories of products and transactions which may be provided by financial institutions.

5.24 *Businesses* should set out clearly in their internal procedures what is considered to constitute reasonable grounds for a belief that a *client* can be made subject to *simplified due diligence*. Evidence should be obtained either as to the regulated status of the *credit* or *financial institution* (such as a print out from the regulator's official website or listing), or the listed status of the company (such as a print out from the exchange's official website or listing, or details of the listing obtained from a trusted, independent commercial provider of company information). With regard to public authorities, recourse to official government websites is recommended. In each case, where the body is not subject to UK, EC or EEA law, justification will also need to be recorded as to how the provisions and other conditions regarding *specified disclosure obligations* in respect of listed companies, and the check and balance procedures and other conditions in respect of public authorities outside the UK, have been met. Recourse to information provided from time to time by the *JLMSG* is recommended [ref to *JMLSG* source]. Where *simplified due diligence* applies, *businesses* are not required to apply standard *customer due diligence* measures. However, *businesses* must still carry out ongoing monitoring (see section 5.46) and appropriate KYC information should therefore still be obtained (see section 4.19).

Practice Statements

Enhanced due diligence

5.25 A risk-based approach to *customer due diligence* will identify situations which by their nature can present a higher risk of *money laundering* or *terrorist financing*. Regulation 14 sets out a general provision that *enhanced due diligence* must be applied in such situations and means that the *business* must obtain additional *customer due diligence* information about the *client*.

5.26 The *2007 Regulations* also specify that *enhanced due diligence* must be applied in a number of situations, of which two are relevant to providers of *defined services* and are outlined below:

- if a *client* has not been physically present for identification purposes, and if so, one or more additional measures must be taken to *enhance due diligence*, for example by, inter alia, either gathering additional documents, data or information, or taking additional steps to verify documents or obtain a confirmatory certificate from a *credit or financial institution* subject to the *money laundering directive*; and
- if a *business relationship* or occasional transaction is to be undertaken with a *politically exposed person (PEP)* in which case the *business* must provide for senior management approval for the relationship to be established, must take adequate measures to establish the source of wealth and funds which are involved and must conduct enhanced monitoring of any relationship entered into.

Politically exposed persons (PEPs)

5.27 The *2007 Regulations* define a *PEP* as a person '. . . who is or has, at any time in the preceding year been entrusted with a prominent public function by a state other than the United Kingdom, a community institution or an international body' or a family member or known close associate of such a person. Details of what are considered to be prominent public functions are shown in Schedule 2, paragraph 4(1)(a). For risk management and reputational risk reasons, *businesses* may wish to treat as *PEPs* individuals who held such positions more than a year ago. As regards establishing whether someone is considered to be a family member or known close associate, regard need only be had to information in the public domain or in the possession of the *business*. 'International body' is not defined, and due consideration should be given to the type, reputation and constitution of the body before excluding it or its representatives from *enhanced due diligence*. However, bodies such as the United Nations, NATO and *FATF* may reasonably be included within the definition of an international body for this purpose.

5.28 Under the *2007 Regulations*, *clients* who are *PEPs* must always be subject to the *enhanced due diligence* measures referred to in section 5.26 above.

5.29 *Businesses* are required to have risk sensitive measures in place to recognise *PEPs*. This can be a simple check conducted by enquiring of the *client* and perhaps using an internet search engine. *Businesses* that are likely to regularly undertake services for *PEPs* may need to subscribe to a specialist database. To the extent possible, *businesses* should be aware of any news during a *business relationship* that could change a *client's* status to *PEP*.

Prohibited relationships

5.30 The *2007 Regulations* set out circumstances which constitute prohibited relationships. In Regulation 16, correspondent banking relationships with *shell banks*, or a bank known to permit use of its accounts by a *shell bank* are prohibited. In addition, set up of anonymous accounts in the UK is prohibited, and *customer due diligence* must be applied to any existing accounts continuing in existence after 15 December 2007 before such an account is used.

5.31 All *businesses* must pay special attention to services or, where relevant, products or transactions that might allow anonymity and take measures to prevent their use in *money laundering* or terrorist activity. *Businesses* must include any such product or transaction within those requiring *enhanced due diligence*.

5.32 In addition, *businesses* must comply with any prohibition issued by HM Treasury in respect of any person, or State to which the Financial Action Task Force has decided to apply counter-measures (see also section 5.44). Directions may be given not to enter into *business relationships*, carry out *occasional transactions* or proceed with any such arrangements already in progress. The Government also issues advisory notices, against countries with material deficiencies in their anti-*money laundering* and counter *terrorist financing* (AML/CTF) regimes, based on the *FATF* Non- Cooperative Countries or Territories (NCCTs) list (consisting of countries with extremely ineffective AML/CTF legislation and systems which prevent them from adequately cooperating internationally in combating *money laundering* and *terrorist financing*) and other *FATF* concerns. An advisory notice requires that *businesses* and *individuals* in the UK should exercise caution when entering into *business relationships* in such countries. Advisory notices are available from the HM Treasury website under "press notices". *Businesses* may subscribe to receive press notices on the HM Treasury website.

Reliance on third parties

5.33 *Businesses* may rely on third parties, subject to the third parties' consent, to complete all or part of *customer due diligence* as set out below but they should be cautious in relying on third parties as they will remain liable for any failure to comply notwithstanding their reliance on a third party (See Regulation 17). *Businesses* should consider requiring copies of relevant information and documentation from the third parties, in order that they may satisfy themselves the information is sufficient.

5.34 Reliance may be made on persons who are:

- regulated *credit* or *financial institutions* (excluding money service businesses);
- professional lawyers, auditors, *external* accountants, *insolvency practitioner* s or *tax adviser* s;

'professionals' in the second of these categories must be regulated by one of the *anti-money laundering authorities* listed in Part 1 of Schedule 3 to the *2007 Regulations*, or be subject to equivalent regulation in an EEA or non-EEA state including mandatory professional registration recognised by law and supervision for compliance with requirements equivalent to the *money laundering directive*. *Businesses* may outsource their *customer due diligence* measures but remain liable for any failure in the *customer due diligence*.

5.35 Information on equivalence is very limited at present, but further information should [shortly be published by HM Treasury following an EU study].

5.36 Before reliance may be placed on one of those specified above, the other *individual* or *business* must agree to reliance being placed. If consent is obtained, the *individual* or *business* consenting to the reliance must take great care to ensure they have adequate systems in place to keep proper records and to respond to any request for these.

5.37 An *individual* or *business* consenting to be relied upon must, if requested, make available to the person relying as soon as is reasonably practicable:

- any information obtained about the *client* (and any beneficial owner) when applying *customer due diligence* measures; and/or
- copies of any identification and verification data and other documents on the identity of the *client* (and any beneficial owner) obtained when applying *customer due diligence* measures.

5.38 Before placing reliance, an *individual* or *business* seeking to rely must take steps to ensure the person being relied upon will provide the required information.

5.39 Any *individual* or *business* consenting to be relied upon must ensure the records of *customer due diligence* which become the subject of reliance are retained for 5 years from the date on which reliance commences.

5.40 Failure by a person who has been relied upon to comply with the requirements in relation to responding to requests for information, relying upon a person without having ensured they will provide the information required on request, or failing to keep the records required after reliance has been allowed are all criminal offences as set out in Regulation 45.

Where reliance is placed on a third party, *businesses* are not required to apply standard *customer due diligence* measures. However, *businesses* must still carry out ongoing monitoring (see section 5.46) and appropriate KYC information should therefore still be obtained (see section 4.19).

5.41 Whilst reliance may be a useful and efficient feature of a *customer due diligence* system between parties who are able to build a relationship of trust, it should not be entered into lightly. *Individuals* and *businesses* need to consider carefully whether they wish to be relied upon and before so consenting ensure:

– their *client* (and any other third party whose information would be disclosed) has no objection to their information being passed to the person seeking reliance; and
– that they have in place the necessary record-keeping systems.

Conducting Customer Due Diligence

'Know your client' or 'KYC'

5.42 The resources used to undertake effective *customer due diligence* are not prescribed. Various sources may be used to enhance a *business*' knowledge of their *client*, including direct discussion with the *client*, information (*eg*,websites, brochures, reports etc) prepared by the *client* and review of public domain information.

5.43 *Businesses* need to consider whether there are any particular steps they wish to specify for use in higher risk cases to increase the depth of *customer due diligence*, such as seeking out wider information from extensive internet and press searches concerning the potential *client*, its key counterparties, its sector and jurisdiction, or possibly using subscription databases which provide a quick way of accessing public domain information and in many cases provide links to persons or companies known to be associated with the potential *client* (see sections 5.54 to 5.55 on electronic identification).

5.44 *Businesses* might, as appropriate to their risk assessment, wish to check the names of *clients* against lists of persons subject to asset-freezing restrictions, including under financial sanctions and terrorism *financial restrictions*. HM Treasury maintains a consolidated list of persons designated as being subject to *financial restrictions* in force in the UK but recourse may be had to further lists such as those issued by the UN and the US Treasury Office of Foreign Assets Control or OFAC). Some electronic resources also include an automated check against this information as part of the product.

Specific customer due diligence prompts

5.45 It may be helpful for a list of questions or prompts to be incorporated into *customer due diligence* procedures. Examples are given at the end of this section (section 5A) which should be amended to suit the particular *business*' *client* base and services.

Ongoing monitoring

5.46 Ongoing monitoring of the *business relationship* is required. This comprises scrutiny of activity during the relationship, including enquiry into source of funds if needed, to ensure all is consistent with expected behaviour based on accumulated *customer due diligence* information. In addition, it is required that the documentation concerning the relationship (including *customer due diligence*) is kept updated as laid out in Regulation 8, *2007 Regulations*. The need to update *customer due diligence* information should be considered at appropriate times, following a risk based approach, according to the firm's knowledge of the *client* and changes in its circumstances or the nature of services provided by the firm. A firm also may wish to consider this need, on a more routine basis, as appropriate opportunities arise. Examples of such opportunities are:

– at the start of new engagements and when planning for recurring engagements;
– when a previously stalled engagement restarts;
– whenever there is a change of control and/or ownership of the *client*;

Practice Statements

- when there is a material change in the level, type or conduct of business; and
- where any cause for concern, or suspicion, has arisen (in such cases, care must be taken to avoid making any disclosure which could constitute *tipping off*).

Risk-based verification

5.47 Application of a risk-based approach is of considerable importance in verification, both to ensure a good depth of knowledge in higher risk cases, but also to avoid superfluous effort in lower or normal risk cases. Very extensive information is contained in the *JMLSG Guidance* notes. Reference to this is recommended, particularly for overseas *clients*, or those *clients* who have a legal form other than that of a UK private or public company, a UK partnership or LLP, or a UK government body.

5.48 With the more frequently encountered *client* types, ie individuals, UK private or public companies, UK partnerships or LLPs, a UK regulated *business*, or a UK government body, outline *Guidance* on a risk based approach to verification of identity is set out at the end of this section (section 5B).

Documentary evidence used in the verification of identity (How)

5.49 The purpose of verification of identity is to confirm and prove the information collected in so far as it relates to the identity of the *client*. Recourse to documents from independent sources is important. The amount of reliance that can be placed upon, and thus the strength of, particular forms of evidence varies.

5.50 The following are illustrative of a different of strength of various forms of documentary evidence starting with the highest:

- documents issued by a government department or agency or a Court (including documents filed at Companies House or overseas equivalent)
- documents issued by other public sector bodies or local authorities
- documents issued by *businesses* regulated by the Financial Services Authority or overseas equivalent
- documents issued by professionals regulated for anti-*money laundering* purposes by the bodies listed in Schedule 3 of the *2007 Regulations* or overseas equivalents
- documents issued by other bodies.

5. 51 In the case of individuals, documents from highly rated sources that contain photo identification as well as written details are a particularly strong source of verification of identity.

Certification and annotation

Certification

5.52 *Businesses* may wish to consider whether copies of original documents and copies of certified copies of original documents should be certified as true copies to demonstrate their provenance. *Businesses* may wish to create standard stamps or labels to apply to documents, which can then simply be filled in with name, signature and date. *Businesses* should have regard to the standing of the person certifying and may wish to consider specifying from whom certification may be accepted, for instance, *businesses* may decide to restrict acceptance to those documents certified by a person in the permitted categories for reliance (Regulation 17 of the *2007 Regulations*) which are broadly a credit or *financial institution* authorised by the *FSA*, a professionally qualified auditor, *external accountant, insolvency practitioner* or *tax adviser*, or *independent legal professional*, or their equivalent in EU countries and other countries which have equivalent law and provided in all cases that the person is subject to supervision as to his compliance with those requirements.

Annotation

5.53 This should be used when the document is as good as an original but is not the original itself. This particularly applies to printouts from the Internet, such as downloads from Companies House, regulator, stock exchange or government websites, or similar trustworthy business information sources. Each document so obtained should bear written evidence showing who printed it, when, from where and should be signed by the relevant person.

Electronic identification

5.54 There are now a number of subscription services that give access to databases of information on identity. Many of these services can be accessed on-line and are often used by *businesses* to replace or supplement paper verification checks. Subject to 5.55, this means *businesses* may use on-line verification as a substitute for paper verification checks for *clients* considered normal risk, supplemented by additional paper verification checks for higher risk *clients*,or vice versa.

5.55 Before using electronic databases, however, *businesses* should question whether the information supplied is sufficiently reliable, comprehensive and accurate. The following points should be considered before deciding to use an electronic source (either as part of a wider process or, where appropriate, on its own)[3]:

3 The JMLSG *Guidance* (Section 2, paragraphs 5.3.11 – 5.3.18) also covers indicators of good electronic identification resources.

– **Does the system draw on multiple sources?** A single source, *eg*,the Electoral Roll, is usually not sufficient. A system which uses both negative and positive data sources is generally more robust than one that does not.[4]
– **Are the sources checked across a period of time?** Systems that do not regularly update their data are generally prone to more inaccuracies than those that do.
– **Are there control mechanisms to ensure the quality and reliability of data?** Systems should have built-in checks that ensure the integrity of data and should ideally be transparent enough to show the results of these checks and their bearing on the integrity of data.
– **Is the information accessible?** Systems need to allow a *business* either to download and store the results of searches in appropriate electronic form, or to print off a hardcopy record containing all necessary details as to name of provider, source, date etc.

4 'Positive' data are those that prove an individual exists, e.g. name, current address, date of birth etc, whereas 'negative' data relate known incidents of fraud, including identity fraud, other known offences and registers of deceased persons.

Insolvency cases

5.56 In the context of insolvency work, the person or entity entering into the *business relationship* is considered to be the insolvent. *Insolvency practitioner* s are also referred to the *Guidance* provided by R3.[5]

5 www.r3.org.uk The Association of Business Recovery Professionals, better known as 'R3' (rescue, recovery, renewal).

5.57 An *Insolvency practitioner* should obtain verification of the identity of the person or entity over which he is appointed. Acceptable evidence of verification may include a court order, a court endorsed appointment, or an appointment made by a debenture holder or creditors meeting supported by a company search or similar. It is not always possible or necessary to obtain identification evidence direct from individuals or individual shareholders or directors in an appointment in respect of a company as their co-operation may not be forthcoming.

5.58 It is important for an officeholder to be sure about the identity of the person or entity over which he is taking appointment given the urgency of the situation and the necessity not to delay when this might risk dissipation of assets and erosion of value. However, completion of other KYC elements of *customer due diligence* may not be possible prior to appointment and should be completed as soon as practicable after appointment (if possible, usually within 5 working days).

5.59 *Insolvency practitioner* s post appointment have a very different relationship with the insolvent *client* than that with a normal audit or advisory *client* and have access to a very wide range of information which alters the need for traditional pre-appointment KYC. However, particular focus is needed before, and immediately after, appointment on considering the way the business has been operated and assessing the risk of assets being tainted by crime in which case it may well be necessary, but not as a matter of routine in every case, to apply to *SOCA* for *consent* to perform the normal range of duties of collection, realisation and distribution of assets (see section 8).

Section 5 A – Specific Prompts for Clients

These are suggested prompts only. In order to make the most use of these *businesses* should amend the text to suit their own *client* base and services offered.

A. For entities/businesses

(1) What is its purpose in entering into any transaction forming the basis of the proposed engagement or its purpose in seeking services where not related to a specific transaction?

(2) What are the entity's main trading and registered office addresses?

Practice Statements

(3) What are its business activities or purposes and sector?
(4) Who controls and manages it (ie, has executive power over the entity – this may be directors, shadow directors or others depending on the circumstances)?
(5) If the client is audited, were the accounts qualified and, if so, why?
(6) Name and check that the person(s) purporting to represent the entity is/are who they say they are.
(7) Who owns it — ultimate beneficial owner(s) and steps in between (at a minimum for companies provide details of any ultimate beneficial owners of more than 25% – for trusts, supply details of trustees and settlors and details of either beneficiaries with more than 25% interest, or the classes of beneficiary, and for collective investment funds or other similar arrangements provide details of the general partner and/or investment manager together with details of any person with more than 25% interest)?
(8) What is its business model/intended business model (ie, the mechanism by which a business intends to generate revenue and profits and serve its customers – in terms of broad principles)?
(9) What are the key sources of:
- income (eg, trading, investment etc); and
- capital (eg, public share offer, private investment etc)?

(10) The history and current (also forecast if readily available) scale of the entity's:
- earnings (eg, turnover and profits/losses); and
- net assets.

(11) The entity's geographical connections, so that you are in a position to ask such questions as "Why is it getting so much money from that place?" and "Why is it sending assets to that place?"
(12) Has the entity been subject to insolvency proceedings, or is it in course of being dissolved/struck-off, or has it been dissolved/struck-off?

B. For individuals

- His or her purpose in entering into any transaction forming the basis of the engagement or purpose in seeking services where not related to a specific transaction.
- Home address and, if applicable/different, trading address.
- His or her purpose in entering into any transaction forming the basis of the engagement or purpose in seeking services where not related to a specific transaction.
- The scale and sources of the individual's capital (past and future).
- The scale and sources of the individual's income (past and future).
- The type and sector of the individual's business activities.
- The individual's geographical connections, so that you are in a position to ask such questions as "Why is he getting so much money from that place?" and "Why is she buying assets from that place?"
- Has the individual been subject to bankruptcy proceedings?
  If after enquiry of the individual it is considered that the individual has been subject to bankruptcy proceedings, information can be obtained:
  - for England and Wales, on: www.insolvency.gov.uk/eiir/
  - for Scotland – call The Accountant in Bankruptcy on 0131 473 4600 (Search Team).
  - for Northern Ireland — call The Insolvency Service on 02890 251441 (Insolvency Search Department)
- Has the individual been disqualified as a director? Consult Companies House: www.companieshouse.gov.uk/ddir/

Section 5 B – Examples of Risk-based Verification

Set out below are examples of risk-based verification for some of the more common client types. For Guidance on other situations, reference should be had to the JMLSG Guidance Notes.

A. Individuals

Met face to face?

Yes and normal risk – obtain:

either: proof of identity – photo identity

or: proof of identity – non-photo identity and proof of address (Please note P.O. Boxes

are not acceptable addresses) or date of birth (can be electronic)

No and/or higher risk – obtain:

either: proof of identity – photo identity and an additional piece of evidence

or: proof of identity – non-photo identity, proof of address (Please note P.O. Boxes are

not acceptable addresses) or date of birth

Plus: an additional piece of evidence

Sources of evidence

List 1: Evidence of identity

Acceptable photo identity

- valid passport; or
- valid photocard driving licence (full or provisional); or
- national identity card (non-UK nationals issued by EEA member states and Switzerland); or

firearms certificate or shotgun licence; or

- identity card issued by the Electoral Office for Northern Ireland

Acceptable non-photo evidence of identity:

Documents issued by a government department, incorporating the person's name and residential address or their date of birth, *eg*,

- a current UK full driving licence old version (**not** provisional licences); or
- evidence of entitlement to a state or local authority funded benefit (including housing benefit and council tax benefit), tax credit, pension, educational or other grant; or
- documents issued by HMRC, such as PAYE coding notices and statements of account (NB: employer issued documents such as P60s are not acceptable)

List 2: Evidence of address or date of birth

instrument of a court appointment (such as a grant of probate, bankruptcy); or

- current council tax demand letter or statement; or
- current (within the last 3 months) bank statements, or credit/debit card statements issued by a regulated financial sector firm in the UK, EU or JMSLG equivalent jurisdiction (but not those printed off the internet); or

a file note of a visit by a member of the firm to the address concerned ("home visit"); or

- an electoral register search showing residence in the current or most recent electoral year (can be done via newcorp.192.com/search/index.cfm); or

a recent (last available) utility bill (gas, water, electricity, telephone – **not** mobile 'phone bills); it must be a bill or statement of account (**not** correspondence); or

- valid photocard driving licence (full or provisional); or
- a current UK full driving licence old version (**not** provisional licences); or
- evidence of entitlement to a state or local authority funded benefit (including housing benefit and council tax benefit), tax credit, pension, educational or other grant; or
- documents issued by HMRC, such as PAYE coding notices and statements of account (NB: employer issued documents such as P60s are not acceptable); or

• end of year tax deduction certificates.	a firearms/shotgun certificate; or • a solicitor's letter confirming recent house purchase or land registry confirmation (you must also verify the previous address).

B. Entities

i. Private company/LLP

Met a representative face to face?	**Yes and normal risk** – obtain: Full company search from a national companies registry (or equivalent information obtained through a commercial provider of registry information) *Or* Certified copies of taken from original documents evidencing details of incorporation or registration, registered office and list of directors and shareholders/members Identify any shareholder/member in the entity holding more than 25% of the equity (rights to either income, capital or voting), or if there is no holding over 25%, where considered appropriate on a risk sensitive basis, the largest holding. Repeat step above until appropriate ultimate beneficial owners have been identified.
	No and/or higher risk – obtain Select individual(s) and entities that is/are capable of exercising significant influence over this entity either as an appointed director, or as a shadow director or equivalent, **identify** it/them according to whether a legal or natural person Select any shareholder/member in the entity holding more than 25% of the equity (rights to either income, capital or voting), or where no holding over 25%, the largest holding **and identify** it/them according to whether a legal or natural person Repeat step above until appropriate ultimate beneficial owners have been verified. For all entities, if a money service business, verify HMRC registered number (obtain certified copy of certificate or call HMRC National Advice Service on 0845 0109000, Opt. 3)

ii. Listed or regulated entity

Obtain either a printout from the relevant regulator's or exchange's website (and annotate), or obtain direct written confirmation from the regulator or exchange, confirming the regulated or listed status of the entity (ensure basic details of name, address, any membership or registration details, and any disciplinary details where applicable are provided).

Additional verification steps are not generally considered necessary in such cases as these entities in the UK qualify for application of *simplified due diligence*.

iii. Government or similar bodies

Obtain and annotate evidence to confirm the body's:

– main place of operation; and
– the government or supra-national agency controlling it (government and supranational agency web-sites are a useful source of information)
– for Housing Associations, the printout must contain its registered number, registered company number (where appropriate) and registered address

Useful, trusted sites include:

UK Government information portal — www.direct.gov.uk/Homepage/fs/en

Housing Association Register — www.housingcorp.gov.uk

EU official site — www.europa.eu.int/

United Nations list of main bodies — www.un.org/aboutun/mainbodies.htm

USA government information portal — www.firstgov.gov/Agencies/Federal/All_Agencies/index-.shtml

Additional verification steps are not generally considered necessary in such cases as these entities in the UK qualify for application of *simplified due diligence.*

iv. Money Service business

Verify HMRC registered number (obtain certified copy of certificate or call HMRC National Advice Service on 0845 0109000, Opt. 3).

Section 6 — Reporting

Key Points

- *Suspicious activity reports* submitted by the *regulated sector* are an important source of information used by *SOCA* in meeting its harm reduction agenda, and by law enforcement more generally.
- *Businesses* are required to have procedures which provide for the nomination of a person *(*in this *Guidance* the *MLRO)* to receive disclosures (*internal reports*) under Part 7 of *POCA* and which require that everyone in the *business* complies with Part 7 of *POCA* in terms of reporting knowledge, suspicion or reasonable grounds for knowledge or suspicion of *money laundering*
- Failure to report in accordance with Part 7 of *POCA* where the relevant information or other matter has been obtained through the course of work in the *regulated sector* is a criminal offence which can be committed by any *individual* (s330, *POCA*), or by the *MLRO* (s331, *POCA*). There is a similar offence for *MLRO's* outside the *regulated sector* in s332, *POCA*.
- An *individual* other than the *MLRO* fulfils his reporting obligations by making an *internal report* to his *MLRO*.
- The *MLRO* is responsible for assessing *internal reports*, making further inquiries if need be (either within the *business* or using public domain information), and, if appropriate, filing *SARs* with *SOCA*.
- Where a *relevant professional advisor* forms knowledge or suspicion or reasonable grounds for such in 'privileged circumstances' no report should be made to *SOCA* unless this '*privilege reporting exemption*' is overridden by the crime/ fraud exception ie where the information or other matter is communicated to the *relevant professional advisor* with the intent of furthering a criminal purpose (Section 7.42 to 7.46).
- When reports are properly made they are 'protected' under s 337, *POCA* in that nothing in them shall be taken to breach any restriction on the disclosure of information, however imposed.
- A person who considers he may have engaged or is about to engage in *money laundering*, should make an 'authorised' disclosure (s 338, *POCA)*. Such a disclosure, provided it is made (and *SOCA's* consent to the act is obtained) before the act is carried out, or is made as soon as possible on the initiative of that person after the act is done and with good reason being shown for the delay, may provide a defence against charges of *money laundering*. When properly made such reports shall not be taken to breach any restriction on the disclosure of information, however imposed.
- *Consent* may be sought from *SOCA* under s 335, *POCA* (and confirmed to the *business* by the *MLRO* under s 336 *POCA*) to carry out activity that would otherwise be *money laundering* under ss 327-329 *POCA*. If granted, the *consent* provides complete protection against charges of *money laundering* but only in respect of the activity covered by the *consent*.

- *TA 2000* provides for broadly equivalent provisions regarding the reporting of knowledge, suspicion or reasonable grounds for such of *terrorist financing*. The definition of '*terrorist property*' is set out in s 14, *TA 2000* and the *terrorist offences* and provisions regarding reporting, *consent* and *tipping off* are set out in ss 15-21A.

What must be Reported?

6.1 Under ss 330-332, *POCA*, failing to report knowledge or suspicion, or reasonable grounds for such, of *money laundering* is a criminal offence (see section 2 of this *Guidance*, which outlines the offences and details of exemptions). The following must be reported, as soon as practicable. These are collectively known as 'the *required disclosure*':

- the identity of the suspect (if known);
- information or other matter on which the knowledge or suspicion of *money laundering* (or reasonable grounds for such) is based; and
- the whereabouts of the laundered property (if known)

6.2 Care is needed to ensure that any information held concerning identity (such as date of birth, passport number, address, registration numbers for companies and so on) is included within the report as well as details of the laundered property and its whereabouts, where known, and reasons for knowledge or suspicion.

6.3 Even if the name of a suspect is not known, any information available which may assist in identifying the suspect or the whereabouts of any of the laundered property must be included in the report, under the provisions of s 330 (3A), *POCA*. For example, even if the *business* does not have the name of the suspect, if the *business* is aware the *client* holds the detail the report needs to reflect this as information which may assist in identifying the suspect.

6.4 In cases where the suspect is not known, another subject should be included in the report, whether this is the victim or another subject associated with the activity. The fact that in these cases the subject of the report is not a suspect should be made clear in the report.

6.5 The disclosure requirement relates to any information coming to a person in the course of business in the *regulated sector*, and not just information relating to *clients* and their affairs. This means that reports made may be required on the basis of information not only about *clients*, but about potential *clients*, associates and counterparties of *clients*, acquisition targets and even employees of *businesses* in the *regulated sector*.

Types of Report

6.6 Reports made in accordance with the provisions of *POCA* are made under either s337 (protected disclosures) or s338 (authorised disclosures).

The Protected Disclosure

6.7 A protected disclosure is any report made by a person providing the *required disclosure*, based on information or other matter coming to their attention in the course of their trade, profession, business or employment, where this information has led to knowledge or suspicion (or reasonable grounds for such) that another person is engaged in *money laundering*.

6.8 A protected disclosure may be made by any person forming a *money laundering* suspicion, at work or carrying out professional activities, whether or not acting within the *regulated sector*. This means that any *individual* or *business*, or other organisation (such as a charity) meeting these conditions may make a voluntary report to *SOCA* in the public interest and benefit from the protections contained in s337, *POCA* against allegations of breach of confidentiality. In the *regulated sector*, such reports are compulsory (save where an exemption such as the *privilege reporting exemption* applies).

The Authorised Disclosure

6.9 An authorised disclosure is a report made by a person who makes the disclosure:

- before he has carried out a prohibited act (ie, done something which would constitute a *money laundering* offence under ss 327-329, *POCA*); or
- whilst he is doing the prohibited act, or after he has done such an act provided that when he started to do the act he didn't realise that it was *money laundering* (*ie*,did not realise that *criminal property* was involved) and made the report on his own initiative as soon as he knew or suspected *criminal property* was involved; or

– after he has done the prohibited act, provided that there was good reason for not reporting before he committed the act, and he made the report on his own initiative as soon as it was practicable to make it. There is no guidance in *POCA* as to what might constitute 'good reason', but this is likely to be applied narrowly.

Confidentiality protections

6.10 Any report properly made under the provisions of ss 337 and 338, *POCA* cannot be taken to breach any restriction on disclosure of information, however this is imposed. This means considerations of *client* or other duties of confidentiality must not impede reporting, unless the *privilege reporting exemption* applies (see section 7 below) where different considerations apply. Such protection does not exist for reports which are made founded only on speculation or made defensively, founded on generalities or 'just in case'.

Non-POCA reporting

6.11 This *Guidance* deals only with obligations under the UK anti-*money laundering* regime – *businesses* and *individuals* should have regard to other obligations they may have, such as reporting responsibilities under the Statements of Auditing Standards, statutory regulatory returns, and reports of misconduct of fellow members of professional bodies. In all cases, the risk of *tipping off* must be considered and avoided. Further *Guidance* on acting for *clients* who are the subject of *SARs* is given in section 9.

Recognising Money Laundering

The key elements

6.12 The anti-*money laundering* requirements only relate to criminal matters, that is those which attract criminal penalties. Other acts may be unlawful, but not criminal. This distinction is particularly important in areas of work where an array of penalties on both civil and criminal levels exist. An example of this is in relation to infringement of the requirements of the Companies Act where there is a mixture of issues attracting civil penalties and those attracting criminal penalties.

6.13 In most cases of suspicion, the reporter will have in mind a particular type of underlying or predicate *criminal conduct*. However, on occasion a transaction or activity may so obviously lack any normal economic rationale or business purpose as to lead to a suspicion that it may be linked to *money laundering* in the absence of any other credible explanation. *Individuals* should not hesitate to exercise professional scepticism and judgement and should report such matters if appropriate.

6.14 For a matter to be *money laundering*, there must not only be *criminal conduct*, but also proceeds or *criminal property*. These terms are described below.

Criminal conduct

6.15 *Criminal conduct* is that which constitutes an offence in any part of the UK or would do if it was committed in the UK. However, *businesses* and *individuals* should note that under the provisions of the *overseas conduct exception* (s 330(7)(A) *POCA)* there are limited exceptions to the requirement to report conduct occurring overseas – see sections 2.4 and 2.5.

6.16 Since UK law defines *money laundering* so widely, any *criminal conduct* which has resulted in any form of *criminal property* will also constitute *money laundering*. It is not expected that *individuals* will become expert in the very wide range of underlying or predicate criminal offences which lead to *money laundering* but they will be expected to recognise those that fall within the professional competence of their role but should use professional scepticism, judgement and independence as appropriate to identify offences.

6.17 If a person knowingly engages in criminal activity but does not successfully benefit from it, he may have committed some other offence (often fraud) but not *money laundering*. If an activity does not result in *criminal property* it cannot constitute a *money laundering* offence. Consequently, there is no obligation to file a *money laundering* report. However, *businesses* and *individuals* may wish to report the matter to the Police, or may have other reporting duties (such as those referred to in section 6.11 above).

Criminal property

6.18 *Criminal property* is the benefit derived from a person's criminal activity. Note that *criminal property* (or 'proceeds') can take any form. For example, cost savings from ignoring

Practice Statements

mandatory health and safety regulations (amounting to a criminal offence) savings as a result of tax evasion, and other less obvious financial benefits can also constitute *criminal property*. Where *criminal* property is used to acquire further assets these further assets themselves become *criminal property*. It is important to note that there is no de minimis level and thus *criminal property* is not identified by its value.

6.19 *POCA* defines *criminal property* in s 340(3)(b), *POCA* as 'property is *criminal property* if it constitutes a person's benefit from *criminal conduct* and the alleged offender knows or suspects, that it constitutes or represents such a benefit'.

Intent

6.20 Except for certain strict liability offences, *criminal conduct* requires an element of criminal intent. S 340(3)(b) of *POCA* means that an offender must know or suspect that property is criminal. Conduct which is an innocent error or mistake may be criminal where it constitutes a strict liability offence but will not also be *money laundering*.

6.21 If an *individual* or *business* knows or believes that a *client* is acting in error, the *individual* may approach the *client* and explain the situation and legal risks to him. However, once the criminality of the conduct is explained to the *client*, he must bring his conduct (including past conduct) promptly within the law to avoid a *money laundering* offence being committed. Where there is uncertainty about the legal issues, outside the competence of the *individual, clients* should be referred to an appropriate specialist or professional legal adviser.

6.22 Note that if there are reasonable grounds to suspect that a *client* knew or suspected that his/ its actions were criminal, a report must be made. Even if the *client* does not have the relevant intent, but *businesses* or *individuals* are aware that there is *criminal property*, consideration needs to be given to whether a report has to be made under s 338, POCA to avoid an offence under ss 327-329, POCA (see also section 6.27 and section 8).

Determining whether and when to report

6.23 There can be no hard and fast rules on how to recognise *money laundering*. It is important for all *individuals* to be alert to this issue and to apply their professional judgement and experience.

6. 24 *Individuals* need to consider whether activity or conduct observed in the course of business has the characteristics of *money laundering* and, therefore, warrants a report. Most *businesses* will include in their standard anti-*money laundering* systems and procedures arrangements to allow *individuals* to discuss whether the information they hold amounts to a reportable knowledge or suspicion, and *individuals* should take advantage of these arrangements where necessary.

6.25 *Individuals* must report promptly to the *MLRO* (or exceptionally direct to *SOCA*) once the requisite knowledge or suspicion has been formed, or reasonable grounds for such have come into existence. There are no external requirements for the format of an *internal report* and *businesses* may design their systems for *internal reporting* as they wish. *Internal reports* may be made orally or in writing, and may refer to *client* files or contain all the requisite information in a standard form, provided that all the information in the *required disclosure* and other information which the *business* requires under its procedures for the reporting of *money laundering* are reliably provided and recorded.

6.26 To decide whether or not a matter is suspicious *individuals* may need to make further enquiries (within the normal scope of the assignment or *business relationship*) of the *client* or their records. The anti-*money laundering* legislation does not prevent normal commercial enquiries being made to fulfil duties to *clients*, and such enquiries may also assist in understanding a matter to determine whether or not it is suspicious. However, investigations into suspected *money laundering* should not be conducted unless this is within the scope of the engagement, and information is limited to that to which the *individual* would normally be entitled in the course of business. Normal business activities should be maintained and such information or other matter which flows from this will form the proper basis of *internal reports* and *SARs*. To carry out additional investigations is unnecessary and could risk *alerting a money launderer.*

6.27 *Individuals* should be cautious and report to their *MLRO* if in doubt, but may wish to consider the following questions to assist their decision:

- Am I suspicious, or do I know, that activity I have seen is criminal and has caused someone to benefit from it in some way?
- Am I suspicious of an activity which, whilst I can't identify a specific *predicate offence*, is so unusual or lacking in normal commercial rationale that it causes suspicion that money is being laundered?

- If so, do I suspect a particular person or persons of having been involved in criminal activity (or do I know who undertook criminal activity), or does another person that I can name have details of this person(s) or information that might assist in identifying this person(s)?
- Do I know who might have received, or still be holding, the benefit of the criminal activity or where the *criminal property* might be located or have I got any information which might allow the property to be located?
- Do I think that the person(s) involved in the activity knew or suspected that the activity was criminal or do I think the activity arose from innocent error?
- Can I explain coherently what and who I am suspicious of, and why, either in terms of knowledge or suspicion that a *predicate offence* has been committed, or in terms of abnormal activities which may constitute *money laundering*?

Consideration must also be given to whether *individuals* or *businesses* have engaged, or intend to engage, in conduct which could constitute a *money laundering* offence under ss 327-329, POCA (eg, transferring *client* money that comprises *criminal property*). If so, this must also be reported to the *MLRO* as a report may be required under s 338, *POCA* and *consent* requested.

Practice Statements

How to Report

Internal reports to the MLRO

6.28 The *2007 Regulations* require *businesses* to maintain internal reporting procedures that allow any *individual* in the *business* to submit to the *MLRO* a report of knowledge or suspicion or reasonable grounds for such, of *money laundering*. Only by doing this can the *individual* fulfil his obligations under s 330, *POCA* (or in exceptional circumstances, reporting direct to *SOCA*). Of course, sole practitioners who do not employ any staff will simply make their own *SARs* directly to *SOCA*.

6.29 Under s 330, *POCA*, the *internal report* must reach the *MLRO* – a report to a line manager or other colleagues is not enough to comply with the legislation.[6] An *individual* may discuss his suspicion with managers or other colleagues to assure himself of the reasonableness of his conclusions but, other than in group reporting circumstances, the responsibility for reporting to the *MLRO* remains with him. It cannot be transferred to anyone else, however junior or senior they are.

6.30 Where a group (more than one *individual*) arrives at knowledge or reasonable suspicion together by consolidating their thoughts, a single *internal report* may be submitted, in terms agreed by those forming the suspicion and in the names of them all. This may occur, for example, where an engagement team has a reason to be suspicious.

6 Both the *2007 Regulations* and *POCA 2002* use the term 'nominated officer' for *MLRO*.

Reports to SOCA

6.31 The *MLRO* will be responsible for making decisions on whether the information contained in an *internal report* needs to be relayed to *SOCA* in the form of a *SAR*, and compiling and despatching the *SAR* to *SOCA* (section 7). The *MLRO* will also be responsible for determining whether *consent* is required to continue with the engagement or any aspect of it, and will usually be responsible for decisions on how business should be conducted pending receipt of *consent* (section 8).

Section 7 – The *MLRO* and Reporting to *SOCA*

Key Points

- The role of the *MLRO* carries significant responsibility and should be undertaken by a senior person within the *business* who has sufficient authority to take independent decisions, and who is properly equipped with sufficient knowledge, and resources, to undertake the role.
- The key role is that of receiving *internal reports*, and making *SARs* to *SOCA* as applicable, but *MLROs* may undertake other functions relating to the *businesses*' systems and controls in relation to its anti-*money laundering* activities.
- *Businesses* should make provision for delegates or deputies to cover any absence of the appointed *MLRO* and should ensure all relevant employees are aware of the reporting channels laid down by the *business*.

> – It is for *businesses* to determine the format of *internal reports*.
> – A *relevant professional adviser* who suspects or has reasonable grounds for knowing or suspecting that another person is engaged in *money laundering* is exempted from making a *money laundering* report where his knowledge or suspicion comes to him in privileged circumstances (the *privilege reporting exemption*).

The Role

7.1 The role of the *Money Laundering Reporting Officer* (*MLRO*) carries significant responsibility and should be undertaken by an appropriately experienced *individual*. Although there is no prescribed level of seniority, one of the principals of an accounting firm, or similar in other *businesses*, is likely to be suitable, or another senior and skilled person with sufficient authority to enable decisions to be taken independently. *MLROs* are **required** to:

- consider internal reports of money laundering;
- decide if there are sufficient grounds for suspicion to pass those reports on to SOCA in the form of a SAR, and, if so, to make that SAR; and
- act as the key liaison point with SOCA and law enforcement agencies including dealing with consent and disclosure issues.

MLROs **may** also take responsibility for:

- training within the *business*;
- advising on how to proceed with work once an *internal report* and/or *SAR* has been made in order to guard against risks of *tipping off* or *prejudicing an investigation*; and
- the design and implementation of internal anti-*money laundering* systems and procedures.

If this role is not undertaken by the *MLRO*, these responsibilities should be taken on by another sufficiently senior and skilled person within the *business*. This person should work closely with the *MLRO*.

7.2 The functions of an *MLRO* can be delegated, although this does not relieve that *MLRO* of his responsibility, and *businesses* should have contingency arrangements for discharging the duties of an *MLRO* during periods of absence or unavailability. It is recommended that *businesses* appoint an alternate or deputy *MLRO* for these situations and ensure that the reporting channels are well known to all relevant employees.

7.3 Like all individuals, MLROs can commit the money laundering offences as well as the related offences of failure to disclose, tipping off, and prejudicing an investigation.

Assessing Internal Reports

7.4 When first approached by a colleague with an *internal report*, there are two matters for immediate consideration. Rapid consideration is needed by the *MLRO* as to whether an application for *consent* is required (see section 8). In addition, the *MLRO* should first establish by discussion and review whether or not the *privilege reporting exemption* may apply, as this exemption significantly affects not only whether a *SAR* must be made under the legislation, but also whether it may be made. The *privilege reporting exemption* is limited to *relevant professional advisers*, and will not be available other than to members of well established professional bodies such as those listed in Schedule 3 to the *2007 Regulations* and who meet the requirements set out in s 330 (14), *POCA*. Further *Guidance* on the *privilege reporting exemption* is given in sections 7.26 to 7.46 below.

7.5 Once the *MLRO* receives an *internal report*, he must assess it and determine whether it meets the criteria laid down in s 331, *POCA* ie:

- does he know, suspect or have reasonable grounds to know or suspect that another person is engaged in *money laundering*; and
- did the information or other matter giving rise to the knowledge or suspicion come to him in a disclosure made under s 330, *POCA;* and
- does he know the name of the other person or the whereabouts of any laundered property from the s 330 disclosure; or
- can he identify the other person or the whereabouts of any laundered property from information or other matter contained in the s 330 disclosure; or
- does he believe, or is it reasonable for him to believe, that the information or other matter contained in the s 330 disclosure will or may assist in identifying the other person or the whereabouts of any laundered property.

7.6 In each case the *MLRO* should ensure the report contains all the relevant information known to the *individual(s)* making the report and records all necessary aspects as follows:

- who is making the report
- the date of the report
- who is suspected or information that may assist in ascertaining the identity of the suspect (which may simply be details of the victim and the fact that the victim knows the identity but this is not information to which the *business* is privy in the ordinary course of its work)
- who is otherwise involved in or associated with the matter and in what way
- what the facts are
- what is suspected and why
- information regarding the whereabouts of any *criminal property* or information that may assist in ascertaining it (which may simply be the details of the victim who has further information but this is not information to which the *business* is privy in the ordinary course of its work)
- what involvement does the *business* have with the issue in order that requirements for *consent*, the need for consideration of *tipping off* issues, basis of continuance of work and any other necessary guidance for engagement staff may be considered.

7.8 The *MLRO* may also wish to make reasonable enquiries of other *individuals* and systems within the *business*. Such enquiries may either have the effect of confirming the knowledge or suspicion, or reasonable grounds for such, or may provide additional material which enables the cause of suspicion to be eliminated at which point the matter may be closed without a *SAR* being issued.

7.9 In conducting his assessment, the *MLRO* may well wish to consider the criteria set out in section 6 [determining whether to report]. If the *MLRO* considers the information or other matter he has received in an *internal report* meets these criteria then a *SAR* to *SOCA* will be required unless either the *privilege reporting exemption* has been applied on the reporter seeking advice from the *MLRO* and not overridden by the crime/fraud exception or, on analysis of the *internal report* received, the *MLRO* determines that the *overseas conduct exemption* applies (sections 2.4 and 2.5).

The Reporting Record

7.10 It is vital for the control of legal risk that adequate records of *internal reports* are maintained, usually by the *MLRO*. These would normally be details of all *internal reports* made including details of the *MLRO's* handling of the matter, his requests for further information, assessments of the information received, decisions as to whether to conclude immediately or to wait for further developments or information, whether to make a *SAR* or not and on what grounds, any advice given to engagement teams as regards continuation of work and any *consent* requests made.

7.11 Details of *internal reports* submitted as *SAR* s should also be retained. For efficiency, and ease of reference for the *MLRO*, it is recommended that some form of index of reports is kept and internal reference numbers given. The records may be simple, or sophisticated, depending on the size of the *business* and the volume of reporting, but all need to contain broadly the same information and be supported by appropriate working papers. These records are important as they may subsequently be required to justify and defend the actions of an *individual* or *MLRO*. There is no prescribed form specified in *POCA* or elsewhere for *internal reports* to an *MLRO*.

Making External Reports

7.12 Once an *MLRO* has concluded a report is required, it should be prepared and submitted promptly to *SOCA*.

7.13 The requirement set out in *POCA* as to timing of reports is that a report should be made 'as soon as is practicable' after the information required is received. In practical terms, the interval between receiving an *internal report* and making a *SAR* will vary quite widely. Some matters may be disposed of very rapidly where all the information required to make a *SAR* is received with the first contact, and where this occurs a quick turnaround should be achieved. It is particularly important to work rapidly in matters where *consent* is required, or where '*money laundering* in action' is suspected, ie, another is engaged in current criminal activity which may provide law enforcement with opportunities to intervene. In other cases, where not all the required information is immediately to hand, or where there is material uncertainty as to whether the matter is reportable or not, the *MLRO* may reasonably chose to await further expected developments, and/or seek further information before making a reporting decision.

7.14 *MLROs* can use a variety of manners and methods of submission, to make reports such as:

- *SAR* on-line, using internet transfer
- Moneyweb, using extranet transfer
- Secure (encrypted email) using electronic file transfer by email
- Bulk reports in electronic form using CD etc for transfer
- Hard copy *SOCA* forms (obtainable on the internet or by post on request to *SOCA*) to be typed and submitted by post or fax

The manners most likely to be of relevance to those providing *defined services* are *SAR* on-line, Moneyweb and the hard copy forms, the other two manners and methods are normally only used by retail banks and others submitting very large quantities of reports. We recommend that *individuals* and *businesses* have regard to guidance on how to make reports published from time to time by *SOCA*. Details of *SOCA*'s preferred reporting methods are available from their web site at www.soca.gov.uk

7.15 Each of the manners contain compulsory fields which require information, where known, to be provided in accordance with the *required disclosure* provisions. These fields relate to the identity of the reporter, the details of subjects (to the extent known but at least one must be named whether as victim or suspect and the identity information known provided in the correct specified fields), and in the free text box (variously called 'reason for disclosure' or 'reason for suspicion') the whereabouts of the laundered property, where known, and the description of the reason for suspicion or knowledge.

7.16 Please note that currently there are no prescribed forms which *MLROs* must use. An offence for failing to use the prescribed manner and form for making a *SAR* is contained in s 339(1A), *POCA* but this section is not effective unless or until an order by the Secretary of State. We are not aware of any plans to prescribed manner and form in the immediate future.

7.17 In preparing *SARs*, *MLROs* should seek to present information in a way that is clear and succinct. In particular:

- the full name of the reporting *business* must be provided and the internal reference for the report should be provided in each case;
- identification information held by the *business* (name, address, date of birth, registration numbers etc) must be presented in the appropriate subject fields, and not simply incorporated into the 'reason for suspicion' text;
- where it assists in explaining the matter being reported, it may be appropriate to include a number of subjects in the report, providing such identification information as is known in the manner above for each of them;
- for each subject their role, as far as it is known, in the matter should be made clear and the options of flagging each subject as suspect/victim/unknown used as appropriate;
- where bank account/transaction details are available and relevant, these should be included in the appropriate fields;
- the activity observed should be explained clearly in the reasons for suspicion field, without using jargon or terms which might not be readily understood by nonaccountants and, as far as known, giving details of when events occurred;
- features of the activity which are unusual or are considered to denote either a *predicate offence* to *money laundering*, or *money laundering*, should be highlighted as such;
- such information held as to the whereabouts of any laundered property should be given;
- the information given in the reasons for suspicion field should be succinct; and
- the report should be submitted without any supporting documents and accordingly should be able to stand alone to explain the suspicion through provision of the information comprising the *required disclosure*.

7.18 If the *MLRO* so wishes, he may make use of the *SAR Glossary of Terms* provided by *SOCA* and incorporate the relevant terms in his report.

7.19 An important role for the *MLRO* on receipt of an *internal report* and on making a *SAR* is to advise engagement teams on how to continue their work and interact with the *client* to balance professional responsibilities, risk to the *business* and responsibilities under *POCA*. This area of work is examined in section 9.

Guarding confidentiality

7.20 If *clients* or third parties become aware that an *individual* or *business* has made a *SAR*, this can have adverse effects on *client* relationships and may ultimately endanger the security of staff members. Maintaining the confidentiality of *SARs* is important to *SOCA*[7]. Access to *SAR* information is now provided to end-users in law enforcement and similar agencies by *SOCA* only on condition that undertakings are taken as to compliance with Home Office guidance on preserving the confidentiality of *SARs*. (Home Office Circular 53 / 2005 'Money Laundering: The Confidentiality And Sensitivity Of Suspicious Activity Reports (*SARs*) And The Identity Of Those Who Make Them').

[7] The review into the future of the SAR regime, known as the Sir Stephen Lander Review, included recommendations regarding the importance of maintaining and improving confidentiality in the SAR regime.

7.21 *SOCA* has provided a reporting line for concerns over breach of confidentiality by end-users of reports and details may be found on www.soca.gov.uk/financialIntel/sarBreachLine.html.

7.22 Whilst it is reasonable for the *regulated sector* to expect *SOCA* to make strenuous efforts to protect the confidentiality of those who make *SARs*, reporters should also take such steps as are available to them to protect the confidentiality of *individuals* and *businesses* and the information reported.

7.23 In making reports, *MLROs* should disclose information relevant to the suspicion or knowledge of *money laundering* and information necessary to allow the reader to gain a proper understanding of the matters reported. It is recommended that reporters:

- refrain from including other confidential information where this is not required for compliance with obligations under *POCA*
- show the name of the *business*, *individual*, or *MLRO* submitting the report only once in the source ID field but nowhere else in the report;
- do not include names of personnel who made *internal reports* to the *MLRO*;
- only include parties as subjects where this information is necessary for an understanding of the report, or to meet the standards of the *required disclosure*; and
- highlight clearly in the reasons for suspicion/disclosure field any particular concern the reporter has about safety (in physical, reputational or other terms).

7.24 Whilst it is reasonable for an *MLRO* to answer questions from a *SOCA* officer or a law enforcement officer aimed simply at clarifying the content of a *SAR*, any further disclosure to *SOCA* or law enforcement or prosecuting agencies should normally only be undertaken in response to the exercise of a power to obtain information contained in relevant legislation, or in compliance with professional guidance on the balance of confidentiality and making disclosures in the public interest. This provides protection for the *MLRO* and the *business* against any allegation of breach of confidentiality.

7.25 A facility exists for any person to make voluntary disclosures to *SOCA* under s34, *SOCPA* provided that:

- the disclosure is made for the purposes of the exercise by *SOCA* of any of its functions (ss2-4, *SOCPA*);
- it is not a disclosure of personal data in contravention of the Data Protection Act 1998 where that personal data is not exempt from its provisions;
- it is not a disclosure prohibited by Part 1, Regulation of Investigatory Powers Act 2000 (relating to unlawful interception of communications).

If a disclosure meets these requirements, the person making the disclosure does not breach any duty of confidentiality or other restriction on the disclosure of information, however imposed. We recommend a cautious approach to disclosure under this section, as it is important to be sure that all the required conditions are met.

The Privilege Reporting Exemption

7.26 With effect from 21 February 2006, a *relevant professional adviser* who suspects or has reasonable grounds for knowing or suspecting that another person is engaged in *money laundering* is exempted from making a *money laundering* report where his knowledge or suspicion comes to him in privileged circumstances (the *privilege reporting exemption*). In such circumstances, provided that the information is not given to him with the intention (by his *client* or another person) of furthering a criminal purpose ('the crime/fraud exception' – see sections 7.42 to 7.46 below), s 330(6) affords the adviser a complete defence against a charge of failure to disclose (ie, to make a *SAR*). By implication, the exemption also means that in these circumstances a *business* should not make a *SAR*, as they are expected to be bound by the same standards of behaviour as is the case for legal professional advisers subject to legal professional privilege.

7.27 Discussions with the *MLRO* to seek advice about making a report under s 330, *POCA* shall not be taken to be an *internal report* when it was not intended as such, eg, if the person initiating the discussion believes the matter falls within the *privilege reporting exemption* and contacts the *MLRO* to confirm this. On receipt of such an approach, it is recommended the *MLRO* still collects the information which would otherwise be included in the *required disclosure* to enable careful consideration with the reporter of whether or not the matter falls within the *privilege reporting exemption* and, if it does, whether this is overridden by the crime/fraud exception. It is recommended that the *MLRO* documents the decision reached in this regard and the reasons for reaching that decision.

7.28 A *relevant professional adviser* is defined in the legislation as:

Practice Statements

- an accountant, auditor or *tax adviser* who is a member of a professional body which is established for accountants, auditors or *tax adviser* s (as the case may be); and which makes provision for;
  - (a) testing the competence of those seeking admission to membership of such a body as a condition for such admission; and
  - (b) imposing and maintaining professional and ethical standards for its members, as well as imposing sanctions for non-compliance with those standards.

The *privilege reporting exemption* also extends to persons in partnership with (or equivalent), or employed by, the *relevant professional adviser* to provide them with assistance or support. The information must come to these partners or employees in connection with this assistance or support and to the *relevant professional adviser* in privileged circumstances.

7.29 The legislation does not list which professional bodies meet the criteria listed in s 330 (14), but the *CCAB* member bodies meet those criteria and, accordingly, *individuals* who are members of a *CCAB* member body, those in partnership with such *individuals* in *businesses* regulated by the *CCAB* and the employees of such *businesses* and *individuals* are within the scope of the exemptions. If *businesses* or *individuals* are in any doubt as to whether these provisions apply to them, it is recommended that they seek legal advice.

7.30 However, the amendments referred to above affect only the duty to make *money laundering* reports and related disclosures under *POCA*. They do not in any way extend legal professional privilege to advice given by *relevant professional advisers* in any other circumstances. However, *businesses* and *individuals* need to be aware, when responding to requests for further information (sections 9.11 to 9.17), documents subject to a *client's* privilege are not disclosable.

7.31 If a *relevant professional adviser* considers that the information or other matter on which his knowledge or suspicion is based came to him in privileged circumstances, he is obliged to apply the *privilege reporting exemption* in s 330(6), *POCA* (unless the crime/fraud exception applies) and so has no discretion to make a *money laundering* report. This means that the *relevant professional adviser* could find himself in a situation where he might wish to make a report but is prevented from doing so. In such circumstances, he should consider whether he may continue to act, but in carrying out his decision will need to bear in mind the provisions of *POCA* relating to *prejudicing an investigation* (s 342, *POCA*).

7.32 Whether or not the *privilege reporting exemption* applies needs to be considered carefully, including a consideration as to whether the *relevant professional adviser* was working in privileged circumstances when the particular information or other matter came to him. This is an important consideration, as a *relevant professional adviser* may be providing a variety of services to a *client*, not all of which may create privileged circumstances for this purpose. Accordingly, it is strongly recommended that a careful record is maintained of the provenance of information considered when a decision is made on the applicability or otherwise of the *privilege reporting exemption*.

7.33 Set out below is a description of the two types of privileged circumstances and some examples of work which may fall within or outside of them.

Legal advice

7.34 For the privileged circumstances set out in s 330(10)(a) and (b), *POCA* to apply, the following conditions need to exist:

- there needs to be a confidential communication (written or oral) between the *relevant professional adviser* and his *client*, or a representative of the *client*, in which the *client* seeks or the *relevant professional adviser* gives legal advice;
- that communication must take place within the confines of a professional relationship between them, including an initial meeting which does not progress to a *business relationship*; and
- the communication must relate to legal advice (ie, advice concerning the rights, liabilities and obligations or remedies of the *client* under the law).

Litigation

7.35 For the privileged circumstance set out in s 330(10)(c), *POCA* to apply, the following conditions need to exist:

- there must be a confidential communication (written or oral) between the relevant professional advisor and the *client* or third party;
- the confidential communication must be made for the dominant purpose (ie, the overriding purpose) of being used in connection with actual, pending or contemplated litigation.

Defining contemplated litigation is difficult. In summary, it is usually necessary to be able to identify some act that gives rise to a cause of action in relation to which some threat of legal action has either been clearly intimated or is more than reasonably likely to follow. The party seeking to claim the benefit of litigation privilege must show that he was aware of circumstances that rendered litigation between himself and a particular person or class of persons a real likelihood rather than a mere possibility.

Examples of privileged circumstances

7.36 Examples where *relevant professional advisers* might frequently fall within privileged circumstances as regards legal advice privilege include, where this advice is delivered as part of the provision of a *defined service*:

- advice on taxation matters, where the *tax adviser* is giving advice on the interpretation or application of any element of tax law and in the process is assisting a *client* to understand his tax position;
- advice on the legal aspects of a take-over bid, for example on points under the Companies Act legislation;
- advice on duties of directors under the Companies Act;
- advice to directors on legal issues relating to the Insolvency Act 1986, *eg*, on the legal aspects of wrongful trading; and
- advice on employment law

7.37 Examples where *relevant professional advisers* might fall within privileged circumstances as regards litigation privilege include:

- assisting a *client* by taking witness statements from him or from third parties in respect of litigation;
- representing a *client*, as permitted, at a tax tribunal; and
- when instructed as an expert witness by a solicitor on behalf of a *client* in respect of litigation.

7.38 It should be noted that conducting audit work does not of itself give rise to privileged circumstances for this purpose, as the *relevant professional adviser* is neither providing legal advice, nor is he instructed in respect of litigation. Nor do routine book-keeping, accounts preparation or tax compliance assignments, though privileged circumstances may arise if the *client* requests or the adviser gives, legal advice on an informal basis, during the course of such an assignment

7.39 It is recommended that the reasons for the conclusion reached as to whether the *privilege reporting exemption* applies are carefully documented. If the *relevant professional adviser* decides it does apply, he must act in accordance with the *privileged reporting exemption* unless the crime/fraud exception applies. If in doubt, it is recommended that *businesses* and *individuals* seek professional or legal advice.

Recording and discussion with the MLRO

7.40 Even where the *client* service team believe that the *privilege reporting exemption* applies, *businesses* should consider whether all matters involving knowledge or suspicion of *money laundering* should still be referred to the *MLRO* for advice or to another appropriate person (see section 7.41 of this *Guidance*). Discussion of a matter with the *MLRO*, where the purpose of the discussion is the obtaining of advice about making a disclosure under s330, does not alter the applicability of the *privilege reporting exemption*. Given the complexity of these matters, and the need for considered and consistent treatment with adequate documentation of decisions made, a referral to and discussion with the *MLRO* is likely to be beneficial and is recommended. The *MLRO* may decide, with the reporter, to seek further appropriate advice.

7.41 Likewise reporters within a *business* are entitled to seek advice from an appropriate specialist (either a person within the *business* who would fall into the category specified in s330(7B) or an external adviser who himself is able to apply the *privilege reporting exemption*) without altering the applicability of the *privilege reporting exemption*.

The Crime/Fraud Exception

7.42 Before determining whether the *privilege reporting exemption* must be applied, consideration needs to be given to whether the exemption is lost through application of the crime/fraud exception. This exception, as set out in s 330(11), *POCA*, overrides the *privilege reporting exemption* which:

> 'does not apply to information or other matter which is communicated or given with the intention of furthering a criminal purpose'.

Practice Statements

This means that communications that would otherwise qualify under one or other of the above two types of privilege are not covered by the *privilege reporting exemption* where the communication was intended to facilitate or to guide someone (usually the *client* but possibly a third party) in the commission, or furtherance, of any crime or fraud. An example of this might be where tax advice was sought ostensibly to enable the affairs of a tax evader to be regularised but in reality was sought to aid continued evasion by improving the evader's understanding of the relevant issues.

7.43 The crime/fraud exception also applies where communication takes place between a *client* and his adviser in circumstances where the *client* is the innocent tool of a third party's criminal or fraudulent purpose. An example of this might be where a money launderer gives money to a family member, who is unaware of the source of that money, to purchase a property, for which purpose he communicates with his adviser.

7.44 The crime/fraud exception does not apply where the adviser is approached to advise on the consequences of a crime or fraud or similar conduct that has already taken place and where the *client* has no intention, in seeking advice, to further that crime or fraud. This means that a person who is concerned that he may be guilty of tax evasion can approach a *tax adviser* for legal advice in this regard without fear of the exception being invoked. This remains the case even if the potential *client* declines a *client* relationship having received the advice, and the adviser does not know whether the person will proceed to rectify his affairs. However, if the person behaves in a way that makes the adviser suspicious that he intends to use the advice to further his evasion, then a *money laundering* report could be required.

7.45 The crime/fraud exception is a difficult area and the Courts will not usually allow the exception to be invoked unless there is reasonably compelling circumstantial evidence available that demonstrates that the communications have in some way been intended to further the crime or the fraud. A mere speculation may not be sufficient as a basis to invoke it. It is strongly recommended that professional or legal advice is sought in all cases of doubt.

7.46 In summary, the following issues need to be considered before deciding whether to apply the *privileged reporting exemption*:

(a) Are those who received the information or other matter which gave rise to knowledge or suspicion of *money laundering relevant professional advisers* (s 330(14) and s 330(6)(b))?
(b) Was the *relevant professional adviser* acting in privileged circumstances (s330(10))?
(c) Was the information or other matter which gave rise to knowledge or suspicion of *money laundering* actually received in privileged circumstances (s 330(10)) and not in some other communication or situation?
(d) Was the information or other matter received or communicated with the intention of furthering a criminal purpose (*ie*,does the crime/fraud exception apply (s 330(10))?

If the answers to (a), (b), and (c) are yes, and the answer to (d) is no, the *privileged reporting exemption* must be applied. If the answer to (a), (b), and (c) are yes and the answer to (d) is yes, the crime fraud exception applies and a *money laundering* report must be made. Further advice should be sought from the relevant professional body or a lawyer in cases of doubt. This issue may be vital in balancing legal and professional requirements for confidentiality and for serving the public interest and the interests of *clients*. If doubts cannot be resolved through internal discussion, through access to normal sources of professional advice, *businesses* are strongly recommended to seek advice from a professional legal adviser with experience of these matters.

Section 8 – Consent

Key Points

- If a *business* or an *individual* believes an activity they are going to undertake would constitute a *money laundering* offence under ss 327-329 *POCA* then they must make an authorised disclosure under s 338, *POCA* (or have a reasonable excuse for not having made such a report); and
- If the authorised report was made before the *money laundering* activity took place, the reporter must receive an appropriate *consent* (s 335, *POCA*) before proceeding with the activity or an offence will be committed
- On receipt of the appropriate *consent* under s 335, *POCA*,an *MLRO* may then provide this *consent* to the *business* under the provisions of s 336, *POCA*
- Once a *consent* request is made, this may be granted by *SOCA* or given by default once 7 working days starting the working day after submission of the *consent* request (the 'notice period') has elapsed, or *consent* may be refused

- If *consent* is refused during the 7 working day notice period, a moratorium period of 31 days starts on the day notice of refusal is received during which the activity may not be undertaken unless and until the moratorium period expires.
- Once the moratorium has expired, then if no restraining action has been taken by law enforcement, the activity in question may be continued.

Matters for Consent

8.1 The *MLRO* needs to consider carefully when preparing to make a *SAR* whether continuation of activity by the *business* in respect of the subject matter of the *SAR* may potentially involve the *business* in carrying out an act which would constitute a *money laundering* offence.

8.2 Whilst this, on the face of it, appears relatively unlikely in the context of the *defined services* there are situations where *consent* issues do arise and careful consideration should be given to this possibility.

8.3 Before applying for *consent* it is important to consider whether the proposed activity is a matter to which *SOCA* is empowered to *consent*. *SOCA*'s power is strictly limited to being able to *consent* to activity that would otherwise be an offence under any of ss 327–329, *POCA*. In particular, it should be noted that *consent* may not be sought or given for offences under s 333A, *POCA* (*tipping off*) or s 342, *POCA* (*prejudicing an investigation*) or for any other *POCA* offence except those under ss 327–329, *POCA*. As well as having only restricted powers to consent to *POCA* offences, it does not have the power to *consent* to an act which would otherwise constitute the commission of any other criminal offence. Accordingly, it cannot give *consent* to *eg*,an adviser knowingly submitting a false VAT return on behalf of a *client* as this would be a separate criminal offence on the part of the adviser as well as an offence under s 328, *POCA*.

8.4 If in doubt as to whether a matter requires (or is eligible for) *consent* or not, either legal advice should be sought, or recourse had to helplines provided by the relevant supervisory bodies. Advice should not be sought from *SOCA* as they are not in a position to advise, although it will make clear if a matter falls outside of its powers.

8.5 Some of the more common instances where a *consent* may be required include:

- acting as an insolvency officeholder where there is knowledge or suspicion either that the assets may in whole or in part represent *criminal property*, or where the insolvent entity may enter into or become concerned in an arrangement under s 328, *POCA*
- designing and implementing trust and company structures for *clients*, including acting as trustees or company officers, where there is knowledge or suspicion that these structures are being, or may be about to be, used to launder money;
- acting on behalf of the *client* in the negotiation and implementation of transactions where these involve an element of *criminal property* being either bought or sold by a *client*, for example corporate acquisitions;
- handling money in *client* accounts which is suspected to be of criminal origin; and
- providing outsourced business processing for *clients* where money is suspected to be of criminal origin.

8.6 There will be some cases where *businesses* consider they no longer wish to act for the *client* in question and will decline to conduct the requested activity and possibly terminate the relationship. This is a matter for the *business* and not a matter for *consent*. However, this is unlikely to be the case in terms of insolvency appointments, or when acting for the innocent purchaser of assets of suspicious origin. *Businesses* may on occasion decide that undertaking an activity which might otherwise constitute an offence under ss 327-329, *POCA* may, at least in the short term, provided there is *consent*, be the most practical option even if there is no intention to continue acting for the *client* in the longer term. In particular, this might apply when monies are already held in *client* account and need to be returned to or paid away on the instructions of a known or suspected criminal and either a *consent* is required to enable transfer of monies away, or law enforcement confiscation activity is required to resolve the matter.

8.7 *Consent* requests must be clear as to the nature of the knowledge or suspicion of *money laundering* and specific as to the type and extent of the activity for which consent is requested, including how that activity would otherwise constitute an offence under ss327-329, *POCA*,or the *consent* request will not be accepted as a valid request by *SOCA* and no protection will be obtained.

8.8 *SOCA*'s priority in terms of dealing with *consent* issues are understandably focussed on those where there is an opportunity for law enforcement intervention either to confiscate assets or to prevent the commission of crime or acts of terrorism. Clearly, these may not entirely match with the priorities of the person requesting *consent*, who will be driven by *client* and transaction related considerations. To give the best chance of having a *consent* request processed rapidly, it is important to tick the *consent* box provided on the forms and it is recommended that any critical timescale attaching to the activity is explained clearly, and if the report is complex, a summary of key facts and the request is given at the beginning of the report, before explaining the supporting detail.

8.9 In terms of insolvency, *SOCA* are accustomed to dealing with *consent* requests from officeholders and, in general, officeholders should request *consent* to carry out their duties as an officeholder rather than attempting to request *consent* for specific transactions or activities. *SOCA* will try and provide a very rapid turnaround to such requests, as they recognise the unique position of a licensed officeholder acting as such. In order that *SOCA* can rapidly identify requests for *consent* from an insolvency officeholder, this should be made clear at the beginning of the report requesting *consent*, specifying the type of insolvency appointment as well as providing all the other required detail.

Constructive Trust

8.10 Where *client* assets or monies are held, and in forming knowledge or suspicion of *money laundering businesses* become concerned about potential third party claims to the assets or monies, appropriately qualified legal or professional advice should be sought. This is a complex area of law and any *SOCA consent* will not protect a *business* against the claims of a third party, but only against any accusation of *money laundering*. However, *SOCA* are aware of the need to avoid any unwarranted disadvantage accruing to the *regulated sector*, arising from issues of constructive trusts. Where constructive trusts could be an issue, *businesses* are strongly advised to draw this to the attention of *SOCA* when making a *SAR*, so that this can be taken into account in the way *SOCA* deals with the application for *consent*.

Suspension of Activity

8.11 Once a *consent* request has been made, the process must be adhered to and the activity that would otherwise be a *money laundering offence* refrained from unless and until *consent* has been received (or the notice period expired), or in the event *consent* has been refused, until the moratorium period has expired. Failure to do so risks prosecution either for a *money laundering* offence and/or, in the case of an *MLRO* giving *consent* for an activity to continue before he is entitled to do so, an offence under s336 (5) punishable by imprisonment and/or a fine.

8.12 It is appreciated that it is extremely difficult, in some cases, to explain to *clients* and other parties why activity has ceased in an unexpected fashion. Whilst *SOCA* will make every reasonable effort to deliver a rapid *consent*, in some cases the full 7 working days will be taken before a decision is reached whilst the matter is considered with law enforcement, and the potential for intervention in terms of confiscation, arrest etc is considered.

8.13 There is nothing in the legislation which provides for how a *business* may/may not deal with the issues arising from delay. There is nothing which requires a *business* to lie to *clients* or other parties, and clearly to lie would be unacceptable conduct for a professional, but *businesses* must take into account the provisions of the offences concerning *tipping off* and *prejudicing an investigation* when informing parties of delays. If the delay is such as to cause the *client* or other parties to question the *business* as to the reasons for delay, *businesses* may be well advised simply and persistently to refuse to enter into any discussion of the matter and explain that, with regret, they are unable at this point to discuss the matter further. Clearly, this is not a form of behaviour or communication with *clients* that would normally be engaged in, but the period after a request for *consent* has been made is an exceptional period, although frequently of very short duration and manageable in the normal course of business.

8.14 In exceptional circumstances, where an unexpected delay in carrying out a service for a *client* is likely to *alert a money launderer*, in a way that could bring harm to an *individual* or the *business* or could materially undermine a criminal investigation, *MLROs* are recommended to ask *SOCA* to be put in touch with the Law Enforcement Authority dealing with the situation, to discuss the circumstances.

Applying for and Receiving Consent

8.15 *Consent* may only be requested on the basis of a properly submitted *SAR*, made under the provisions of s 338, *POCA* (authorised disclosures). The '*consent* required' option should be selected on all methods of submission to alert *SOCA* to the request and enable them to prioritise appropriately. In cases of real urgency, a telephone call may also be made to alert *SOCA* to any special circumstances.

8.16 The *consent* request should be clear as to the reasons for knowledge or suspicion, the intended activity, and the nature of the consent requested. Great care is needed when requesting consent to cover the extent of the intended activity in a way that makes it clear to *SOCA* exactly what is being requested. Too narrow a *consent* request may mean repeated requests will be required causing issues of cost and efficiency to the *business* and possibly unnecessary *client* service impact. Too broad or ill-defined a *consent* may well result in *SOCA* having to refuse *consent* or possibly even determining the request is not validly made as it does not show clearly the act or acts to be undertaken which would otherwise be an offence under ss327-329, *POCA*.

8.17 *Consent* will frequently be received initially over the telephone from *SOCA*, and the name and contact number of the officer, and the *consent* reference should be noted on the *MLRO* records with the date and time of the call. Written confirmation ordinarily follows in due course but this may take several days and *MLROs* may rely on the telephone *consent*.

8.18 Once *consent* has been received by the *MLRO* under the provisions of s335 *POCA*, he should then (under the provisions of s 336, *POCA*) promptly inform the engagement team affected and give them clearance to continue their work, and any other guidance they might require as regards *money laundering* matters.

8.19 If a period of 7 working days, starting the first working day after the *consent* request is made (the notice period), has elapsed with no refusal having been received, consent is deemed to have been given and the activity may be allowed to continue.

Refusal of consent

8.20 If *consent* is refused during the notice period, then a further 31 days must elapse, starting with the day on which the consent is refused, before the activity may continue (the moratorium period). It may be that during either the notice period, or the moratorium period, that action is taken by law enforcement which means that the activity may no longer be able to be continued (eg, confiscation or other enforcement action may occur).

8.21 If no action has been taken to restrain the activity during the moratorium period, the activity may continue as planned.

Exemptions for Banks and Deposit Takers

8.22 The Serious Organised Crime and Police Act 2005 put in place a threshold provision in *POCA* (ss 327-329) that allows banks and deposit takers to continue to operate an account with an activity which potentially constitutes *money laundering* provided this relates to transactions worth £250 or less or as laid down from time to time in statutory instruments. Note that this change does not affect the requirement to report suspicions, does not constitute a 'de-minimis' provision, and is **not** available to providers of *defined services*.[8]

[8] See JMLSG *Guidance* for details on the change in thresholds for banks and deposit taking institutions.

Section 9 – Post SAR Actions

Key Points

- Once a *SAR* has been submitted, the *business* needs to consider whether or not the content of the *SAR* requires any change to, or even cessation in, any related *client* relationship.
- In addition, careful consideration needs to be given to reconciling the need to fulfil professional duties, whilst avoiding the risks of *tipping off*.
- A *SAR* may be followed by requests for further information from law enforcement or prosecuting agencies, both informal and by means of relevant orders. *Businesses* need to have in place procedures for checking the validity of requests, and for ensuring a proper response is made.

Continuing Work in Connection with a Reported Matter

Client relationships

9.1 *Businesses* do not have to stop working after submission of a *SAR* unless a *consent* has been requested, in which case all or part of *client* work may well require to be suspended until consent is received. In cases where *consent* has been requested and refused, the work which was the subject of the request will need to be suspended.

9.2 However, even where consent was not required, where a *SAR* involves a *client* as a suspect, *businesses* may wish to consider whether the behaviour observed is such that for professional reasons the *business* no longer wishes to act.

9.3 Generally, if following a report of suspicion a *business* wishes for its own commercial or ethical reasons to exit a relationship, there is nothing to prevent this provided the way the exit is communicated does not constitute *tipping off*. This also applies to the *prejudicing an investigation* offence outlined below.

9.4 If a decision is made to terminate a *client* relationship, a *business* should follow its normal procedures in this regard, whilst always bearing in mind the need to avoid *tipping off*.

Balancing professional work and POCA requirements

9.5 Normal commercial enquiries to understand a transaction carried out in the course of an engagement will not generally lead to *tipping off*, although care should be exercised to avoid either making a disclosure prohibited under ss 333A–333D, *POCA* (see section 2.19 of this *Guidance*) or making accusations or suggesting that any person is guilty of an offence. It is important to confine enquiries to those required in the ordinary course of business and not attempt to investigate a matter unless that is within the scope of the professional work commissioned.

9.6 Continuation of work may require discussion with *client* senior management of matters relating to suspicions formed. This may be of particular importance in audit relationships. Care must be taken to select appropriate, and non-complicit, members of senior management for such discussion whilst always bearing in mind the need to avoid *tipping off*.

9.7 In more complex circumstances, consultation with law enforcement may be necessary before enquiries are continued, but in most cases a common sense approach will resolve the issue. Note that neither *SOCA* nor law enforcement may give consent to *tipping off*, but discussions with them are still valuable.

9.8 *Businesses* may wish to consult the *MLRO* or other suitable specialist (for example a solicitor) regularly if there are *tipping off* concerns, and in particular it is important that before any document referring to the subject matter of a report is released to a third party the *MLRO* is consulted and, in extreme cases, law enforcement. Some typical examples of documents released to third parties are shown below as an aide memoire:

- public audit or other attest reports;
- public record reports to regulators;
- confidential reports to regulators (eg to the *FSA* under relevant auditing standards);
- provision of information to sponsors or other statements in connection with Rule 2.12 of the UK Stock Exchange Listing Rules;
- reports under the Companies Directors Disqualification Act 1986;
- reports under s 218 of the Insolvency Act 1986;
- Companies Act statements on resignation as auditors;
- professional clearance/etiquette letters;
- communications to *clients* of intention to resign.

9.9 In particular, audit resignations require statements to be filed at Companies House and the contents of such statements require careful consideration to ensure that statutory and professional duties are met, without including such information as may constitute *tipping off*. There is no legal mechanism for obtaining clearance from *SOCA* for the contents of such statements or other documents relating to resignation. However, *businesses* may well wish in cases of complexity to discuss the matter with *SOCA* or the relevant law enforcement agency in order to understand their perspective and document such discussion.

9.10 *MLROs* may on occasion need advice to assist them in formulating their instructions to the *business*. Legal advice may be sought from a suitably skilled and knowledgeable professional legal adviser, and recourse may also be had to helplines and support services provided by professional bodies. Discussion with *SOCA* and law enforcement may well be valuable, but *MLROs* should bear in mind these authorities are not able to advise, and nor are they entitled to dictate how professional relationships should be conducted.

Requests for Further Information

Requests from SOCA or Law Enforcement Agencies

9.11 *SOCA* or a Law Enforcement Authority may contact a *business* (usually the *MLRO*) or an *individual* to ask for further information about a *SAR* it/he has submitted. Before responding, it is recommended that a verification process is undertaken to ensure the person making contact is a bona fide member of *SOCA*/law enforcement. This may be most simply achieved by taking a caller's name and agency/force details, and then calling the main switchboard of the agency/force to be put through to the person.

9.12 To the extent that the request is simply aimed at clarifying the content of a *SAR*, *businesses/individuals* may respond without the need for any further process.

9.13 However, if the request is for production of documents, or provision of information additional to the *SAR*, it is recommended that *businesses/individuals* require the relevant agency to use its powers of compulsion before they respond. This is not intended to be non co-operative, and indeed *businesses/individuals* are recommended to engage in constructive dialogue with *SOCA*/law enforcement, including as to the content and drafting of the request, but is intended to protect *businesses/individuals* from allegations that they breached confidentiality. *Client* or other third party consent is not required in cases of compulsion, and nor should it be sought due to the risk of *tipping off*.

9.14 Before responding to orders for production of information, *businesses/individuals* should ensure they understand:

- the authority under which the request is made;
- the extent of the information requested;
- the required timing and manner of the production of information; and
- what information should be excluded *eg*,that subject to legal privilege,

If in any doubt, *businesses/individuals* should seek legal advice. *Businesses* should document their consideration of the issues.

9.15 None of the notices or orders will require the production of information that is subject to legal privilege or legal professional privilege. Terms used in the various relevant Acts of Parliament and the way the terms are defined vary slightly and it may be appropriate to take legal advice if unsure. The interaction of the *privilege reporting exemption* with the carve-outs for privileged material in the notices and orders outlined below is not clear, and has yet to be tested. This is a complex area of law. If *individuals* or *businesses* are unsure as to whether certain documents fall within the privileged category or not, they should not include these documents in initial disclosure and, before the expiry of the time allowed for disclosure, should inform the person to whom the information is to be provided that they believe they have material subject to privilege and request that, if they think it necessary to gain access to this material, the relevant agency appoint independent counsel to opine as to whether the material is disclosable, or not. The opinion of counsel may then be complied with.

9.16 Before passing across information to an officer, *businesses* should require the person identify themselves by eg showing a warrant card and a copy of the relevant order, or *businesses* may attend the premises of the relevant agency to hand over the information.

9.17 Orders for production of information may be received under a variety of legislation. In each case, production may be required in hard copy even where stored on a computer, or in electronic form where stored as such. Those which most commonly flow from *SARs* include the following:

- Production Orders under the provisions of *POCA*
  Production Orders are made under s354, *POCA*, and are made only by a judge in respect of a confiscation investigation, or a *money laundering* investigation. The maximum period for compliance will be 7 days starting with the day on which the order is made unless the judge thinks a shorter period should be applied. Failure to comply is treated as breach of a Court Order and penalties will be applied as such. There is no requirement to produce documents which are privileged, being material which a person would be entitled to refuse to produce on grounds of privilege in the High Court. For the interaction of this provision with the *privilege reporting exemption*, see section 9.15 of this *Guidance*.
- Disclosure Notices under the provisions of *SOCPA*
  A disclosure notice may be issued by an investigating authority (the Director of Public Prosecutions, the Director of Revenue and Customs Prosecutions and the Lord Advocate or their permitted delegates under s60, *SOCPA*) in respect of certain offences only. These are broadly those listed in Schedule 2 (Schedule 4 in Scotland) to *POCA*, offences under ss 15-18, *TA 2000*, certain duty offences, false accounting (s17, Theft Act 1968 in England and Wales) and certain matters concerning attempts at/conspiracy to commit certain offences. S61, *SOCPA* should be referred to in the case of any such notice being received to check it is in respect of a qualifying offence. ss62-65, *SOCPA* then set out the procedures in respect of the issue of the notice, and the response to it. The provisions of the notice will govern the extent of the information to be provided, and the timing, place and manner of disclosure. There is no requirement to produce documents or answer

questions where the matter is subject to legal professional privilege, or legal privilege (as defined in s412, *POCA*. For the interaction of this provision with the *privilege reporting exemption*, see section 9.15. Failure, without reasonable excuse, to comply is a criminal offence and penalties of up to two years imprisonment and/or an unlimited fine may be levied.

– S2 notices issued by the Serious Fraud Office under the provisions of the Criminal Justice Act 1987.

  Under s2, Criminal Justice Act 1987, staff authorised by the Director of the Serious Fraud Office have powers to require a person to answer questions, provide information or produce documents for the purposes of an investigation. Written notice is given where the Serious Fraud Office exercise these powers. In urgent cases, the Serious Fraud Office may require immediate compliance with a notice, but frequently will give a period of time for compliance. There is no requirement to produce documents which are privileged, being material which a person would be entitled to refuse to produce on grounds of privilege in the High Court. Failure to comply is a criminal offence punishable with imprisonment for up to 6 months and/or a fine not exceeding level 5 on the standard scale. For the interaction of this provision with the *privilege reporting exemption*, see section 9.15 of this *Guidance*.

Requests arising from a change of professional advisor (professional enquiries)

Requests regarding identification information

9.18 In such a case the disclosure request may be made under the provisions of Regulation 17, reliance, or the new adviser may simply want copies of identification evidence, in order to assist it in satisfying its own identification procedures. *Businesses* should not release confidential information without the *client's* consent. If reliance is being placed on the *business*, it should follow the guidance in section 5.36 above in relation to record keeping.

Requests for information regarding suspicious activity

9.19 In general, it is recommended that such requests are declined as the *tipping off* offence in the *regulated sector* greatly restricts the ability to make such disclosures. However, to the extent that the request is within the provisions of s 333C, *POCA* (section 2.19 of this *Guidance*) information may be provided (but there is no obligation to do so).

Data Protection Act — Subject Access Requests

9.20 Under the Data Protection Act 1998 *businesses* are exempted from disclosure under a subject access request where disclosure would be or is likely to be prejudicial to the prevention or detection of crime or the capture or conviction of offenders. Where personal data is held on a subject and relates to knowledge or suspicion of *money laundering* (ie, it has been processed for the purpose of the prevention or detection of crime) it is not required to be disclosed under a subject access request if disclosure may constitute a *tipping off* offence. This exception should be applied to internal **and SAR** reporting records.

9.21 Guidance has been issued by HM Treasury (www.hmtreasury.gov.uk/media/D/F/money_laundering.pdf) supporting the position that where granting access would amount to '*tipping off*' then the s29 Data Protection Act exemption would apply.

9.22 It is recommended that *businesses* document any considerations surrounding the decision to grant or refuse access to information requested in such circumstances (known as a 'subject access request').

Glossary

2007 Regulations	Statutory Instrument 2007 no 2157 — Financial Services "The Money Laundering Regulations 2007"
Alerting a money launderer	Disclosures that do not constitute *tipping off* but which nonetheless alert the money launderer to the suspicion regarding their activities.
Accountancy Services	*Accountancy services* includes for the purpose of this *Guidance* any service provided under a contract for services (ie, not a contract of employment) which pertains to the recording, review, analysis, calculation or reporting of financial information.

Anti-Money Laundering Supervisory Authority	Bodies identified by Regulation 23, *2007 Regulations* as being empowered to supervise the compliance of *individuals* and *businesses* with the *2007 Regulations*. The professional bodies designated as *anti-money laundering supervisory authorities* are listed in Schedule 3 to the *2007 Regulations*.
Businesses	A company, partnership or other organisation undertaking *defined services*. This includes accountancy practices, whether structured as partnerships, sole practitioners or corporate practices.
Business relationship	A business, professional or commercial relationship between a relevant person (ie someone to whom the Regulations 2007 apply) and a customer, which is expected by the relevant person, at the time when the contact is established, to have an element of duration.
CCAB	Consultative Committee of Accountancy Bodies: body representing the Institute of Chartered Accountants in England and Wales; the Institute of Chartered Accountants of Scotland; the Institute of Chartered Accountants in Ireland; the Association of Chartered Certified Accountants; the Chartered Institute of Management Accountants; and the Chartered Institute of Public and Finance and Accountancy.
Client	A person in a *business relationship*, or carrying out an occasional transaction, with a *business*.
Consent	Permission given, generally by *SOCA*, for the carrying out of any action that would constitute a *money laundering* offence in the absence of that permission. The definition and ruling legislation for the giving of consent is in s335, *POCA*, which also deals with the passing of the consent from the *MLRO* to the *individual* concerned (s336).
Credit institution	Has the meaning given by Regulation 3(2), *2007 Regulations*.
Criminal Conduct	Conduct that is an offence in any part of the UK as well as conduct occurring elsewhere that would have been an offence if it had taken place in the UK. There are very limited exceptions to this for conduct which is both known to be legal in the country in which it is committed and which falls within the specific exceptions set out in orders made by the Secretary of State.
Criminal Property	The benefit of *criminal conduct* where the alleged offender knows or suspects that the property in question represents such a benefit (s340, *POCA)*
Customer due diligence	The process by which KYC information is gathered, and the identity of a *client* is established and verified, for both new and existing clients.
Defined services	Activities carried on, in the course of business by *businesses* or *individuals* as an auditor, *external accountant*, *insolvency practitioner* or *tax adviser* (Regulation 3(c), *2007 Regulations)*, or as trust and company service providers (Regulation 3(e), *2007 Regulations*). It also includes persons providing services under the Designated Professional Body provisions of Part XX, s326 *FSMA 2000* or otherwise providing financial services under the oversight of their professional body.
EEA	European Economic Area countries, which are the European Union member states plus EFTA (European Free Trade Association) member states.
Enhanced due diligence	Additional due diligence steps that must be applied in situations where there is a higher risk of *money laundering* or *terrorist financing* and in a number of specific situations (Regulation 14), of which two are relevant to providers of *defined services;* where the *client* has not been physically present for identification purposes, if a *business relationship* or occasional transaction is to be undertaken with a politically exposed person *(PEP)*.
External accountant	Means a firm or sole practitioner who by way of business provides *accountancy services* to other persons, when providing such services (Regulation 3(7), *2007 Regulations*).
FATF	Financial Action Task Force, created by G7 nations to fight money laundering.
Financial institution	Has the meaning given by Regulation 3(3), *2007 Regulations*
Financial restrictions	See Glossary annex B
FSA	Financial Services Authority: statutory regulator of most financial services providers under the Financial Services and Markets Act 2000.
FSMA 2000	Financial Services and Markets Act 2000
Guidance	*Guidance* which is

(a) issued by a supervisory authority or any other appropriate body;
(b) approved by the Treasury; and
(c) published in a manner approved by the Treasury as suitable in their opinion to bring the *Guidance* to the attention of persons likely to be affected by it.

In this *Guidance*, the term has been used for *Guidance* for which Treasury approval has been applied, and is expected to be obtained, as well as that which already has Treasury approval. The circumstances in which Courts and others are required to take the *Guidance* into account in determining whether an offence has been committed are set out in *POCA* and the *2007 Regulations.*

Any use of the term "guidance" outside this definition, has not been italicised in this *Guidance.*

Individuals — Includes sole practitioners and the partners, directors, subcontractors, consultants and employees of *businesses.*

Independent legal professional — Provider of legal or notarial services as defined in Regulation 3(9) in the 2007 Regulations.

Internal Report — A report made to the *MLRO* in a *business.*

Insolvency practitioner — Means any person who acts as an *insolvency practitioner* within the meaning of s 388 Insolvency Act 1986 or Article 3 of the Insolvency (Northern Ireland) Order 1989 (Regulation 3(6), *2007 Regulations*).

JMLSG — Joint Money Laundering Steering Group: body representing UK Trade Associations in the Financial Services Industry and aiming to promote good anti-*money laundering* practices and give relevant practical *Guidance.*

Money laundering — For the purposes of this *Guidance*, *money laundering* is defined to include those offences relating to terrorist finance, which require to be *reported* under the *TA 2000*, as well as the *money laundering offences* as defined in *POCA.*

Money laundering directive — References in this *Guidance* are to the 3rd Money Laundering Directive (DIRECTIVE 2005/60/EC OF THE EUROPEAN PARLIAMENT AND OF THE COUNCIL of 26 October 2005 on the prevention of the use of the financial system for the purpose of money laundering and terrorist financing) available from: eurlex.europa.eu/LexUriServ/site/en/oj/2005/l_309/l_30920051125en00150036.pdf

MLRO — Money Laundering Reporting Officer. This term is used to describe the *nominated officer* appointed under Regulation 20(2)(d), *2007 Regulations* and as referred to in s 331, *POCA.*

Money Laundering Reporting Officer — see *MLRO* above

Money laundering offences — One of the three *money laundering offences* defined under ss327-329, *POC*

- **conceals**, disguises, converts or transfers *criminal property*, or removes *criminal property* from England and Wales, or from Scotland or from Northern Ireland (s 327);
- enters into or becomes concerned in an **arrangement** which he knows or suspects facilitates (by whatever means) the acquisition, retention, use or control of *criminal property* by or on behalf of another person (s 328); or
- **acquires**, uses or has possession of *criminal property* except where adequate consideration was given for the property (s 329).

Nominated Officer — Office required to be appointed by *businesses* carrying on business in the *regulated sector*. See *MLRO* above.

Overseas conduct exemption — Exemption from reporting requirement where an act is reasonably believed to have taken place outside of the UK, and the act was known to be lawful when committed under the criminal law of the place where the act was committed, and the maximum sentence if the act had been committed in the UK would have been less than 12 months (except in the case of an act which would be an offence under the Gaming Act 1968, the Lotteries and Amusements Act 1976 or under ss 23 or 25, *FSMA).*

PEPs	Politically exposed persons, as defined in the *2007 Regulations* paragraph 14(5) and paragraph 4(1)(a) of Schedule 2. See also sections 5.27 to 5.29 above.
POCA	Proceeds of Crime Act 2002
Prejudicing an investigation	A 'related' *money laundering* offence, defined under s 342, *POCA*. In summary, it captures the making of any disclosure that is likely to prejudice an investigation or falsifying, concealing, or destroying, any documents that are relevant to a *money laundering* investigation, or being complicit in such behaviour.
Predicate offence	Means the underlying offence or any offence as a result of which *criminal property* has been generated.
Privilege reporting exemption	An exemption from reporting suspicions formed on the basis of information received in privileged circumstances (see Sections 7.26–7.46 of this *Guidance*).
Regulated investment market	Within the EEA, has the meaning given by point 14 of Article 4(1) of the Markets in Financial Instruments Directive (MiFID); and outside the EEA, means a regulated financial market which subjects companies whose securities are admitted to trading to disclosure obligations which are contained in international standards and are equivalent to the specified disclosure obligations.
Regulated Sector	Defined in Proceeds of Crime Act Schedule 9 Part 1 (includes those who provide the *defined services*.
Relevant professional adviser	An accountant, auditor or *tax adviser* who is a member of a professional body which is established for accountants, auditors or *tax adviser* s (as the case may be); and which makes provision for (a) testing the competence of those seeking admission to membership of such a body as a condition for such admission; and (b) imposing and maintaining professional and ethical standards for its members, as well as imposing sanctions for non-compliance with those standards.
Required Disclosure	The identity of the suspect (if known), the information or other matter on which the knowledge or suspicion of *money laundering* (or reasonable grounds for such) is based and the whereabouts of the laundered property (if known).
SAR	Suspicious activity report made to *SOCA*
SAR Glossary of Terms	Glossary of terms used by *SOCA* to assist in relating/providing a theme to different SARs to increase effective mining of data by SOCA and Law Enforcement. The use of the terms is not mandatory.
Shell bank	means a *credit institution*, or an institution engaged in equivalent activities, incorporated in a jurisdiction in which it has no physical presence involving meaningful decision-making and management, and which is unaffiliated with a regulated financial group
Simplified due diligence	The phrase used in the *2007 Regulations* (Regulation 13) which means that a *business* is not required to apply the *customer due diligence* measures set out in Regulation 7 where the *business* has reasonable grounds for believing that a *client* falls into the relevant categories.
SOCA	Serious Organised Crime Agency. *SOCA* is an intelligence-led agency with law enforcement powers, responsible for reducing the social and individual harm of serious organised crime. Reports of known or suspected *money laundering* must be made to *SOCA*.
SOCPA	Serious Organised Crime and Police Act 2005
Specified disclosure obligations	See Annex A to the Glossary
Specified interest	A vested interest which is: • in possession or in remainder or reversion (or, in Scotland, in fee); and • defeasible or indefeasible.

Practice Statements

A 'vested interest' is an interest which to which an entitlement already exists (whether immediately — 'in possession'; or in the future, following the ending of another interest — 'in remainder' or 'in reversion'). It is in contrast to an interest which is merely 'contingent'; a contingent interest is an interest which will only arise on the happening of a particular event, such as surviving to a particular date or surviving a particular person. Determining whether an interest is vested or contingent requires careful analysis. For example, if a trust provides that A has a life interest, and that B has an interest which takes effect on A's death, both A and B will have vested interests and, if B does not survive A, B's interest will devolve as part of B's estate; however, if B's interest is expressed to take effect on A's death only if he (B) is then living, B's interest (which will fail if he predeceases A) is merely contingent.

A defeasible interest is one which may be defeated, generally by the exercise of a power under the trust deed; an indefeasible interest is one which cannot be defeated. In the examples given above, A and B both have indefeasible interests. It is important that a defeasible vested interest is not mistaken for a contingent interest. A defeasible vested interest will take effect unless and until it is defeated; a contingent interest on the other hand will not take effect unless and until the event on which it is contingent arises.

Suspicious Activity Report — Otherwise known as a *SAR*. *See SAR above*

TA 2000 — The Terrorism Act 2000 (as amended by the Anti-Terrorism, Crime and Security Act 2001 and the Terrorism Act 2006)

TA 2006 — The Terrorism Act 2006

Tax adviser — Means a firm or sole practitioner who by way of business provides advice about the tax affairs of other persons, when providing such services (Regulation 3(8), *2007 Regulations*). Tax compliance services, eg, assisting in the completion and submission of tax returns is, for the purpose of this *Guidance*, included within the term "advice about the tax affairs of other persons".

Terrorist financing — Means an offence under (Regulation 2 *2007 Regulations*):

(a) s 15 (fund raising), 16 (use and possession, 17 (funding arrangements), 18 (money laundering) or 63 (terrorist finance: jurisdiction), *TA 2000*;

(b) para 7(2) or (3), Schedule 3 to the Anti-Terrorism, Crime and Security Act 2001(a) (freezing orders);

(c) article 7, 8 or 10 of the Terrorism (United Nations Measures) Order 2006(b); or

(d) article 7, 8 or 10 of the Al-Qaida and Taliban (United Nations Measures) Order 2006(c).

Terrorist offences — The terrorist offences relate to fundraising (inviting another to provide money or other property with the intention or reasonable cause to suspect it is intended to be used for the purposes of terrorism), using or possessing terrorist funds (receiving or possessing money or other property with the intention or reasonable cause to suspect it is intended to be used for the purposes of terrorism), entering into funding arrangements (making arrangements as a result of which money or other property is or may be made available for the purposes of terrorism with the intention or reasonable cause to suspect it is intended to be used for the purposes of terrorism), money laundering, disclosing information relating to the commission of an offence (similar to *tipping off*), or failing to make a disclosure in the regulated sector. (ss19 and 21A *TA 2000* (as amended*))*

Terrorist property — Means:

(a) money or other property which is likely to be used for the purposes of terrorism (including any resources of a proscribed organisation),

(b) proceeds of the commission of acts of terrorism, and

(c) proceeds of acts carried out for the purposes of terrorism.

Tipping off — A 'related' *money laundering* offence for the regulated sector, defined under s 333A-D, *POCA*

Transaction — The provision of any advice by a *business* or *individual* to a *client* by way of business, or the handling of the *client's* finances by way of business.

Glossary Annex A – The Specified Disclosure Obligations

Details of the "Specified Disclosure Obligations" Referred to in Regulation 13 (3) MLR2007 Re Simplified Due Diligence

DIRECTIVE 2003/6/EC OF THE EUROPEAN PARLIAMENT AND OF THE COUNCIL of 28 January 2003 on insider dealing and market manipulation (market abuse)

Article 6

(1) Member States shall ensure that issuers of financial instruments inform the public as soon as possible of inside information which directly concerns the said issuers.

Without prejudice to any measures taken to comply with the provisions of the first subparagraph, Member States shall ensure that issuers, for an appropriate period, post on their Internet sites all inside information that they are required to disclose publicly.

(2) An issuer may under his own responsibility delay the public disclosure of inside information, as referred to in paragraph 1, such as not to prejudice his legitimate interests provided that such omission would not be likely to mislead the public and provided that the issuer is able to ensure the confidentiality of that information. Member States may require that an issuer shall without delay inform the competent authority of the decision to delay the public disclosure of inside information.

(3) Member States shall require that, whenever an issuer, or a person acting on his behalf or for his account, discloses any inside information to any third party in the normal exercise of his employment, profession or duties, as referred to in Article 3(a), he must make complete and effective public disclosure of that information, simultaneously in the case of an intentional disclosure and promptly in the case of a non-intentional disclosure.

The provisions of the first subparagraph shall not apply if the person receiving the information owes a duty of confidentiality, regardless of whether such duty is based on a law, on regulations, on articles of association or on a contract.

Member States shall require that issuers, or persons acting on their behalf or for their account, draw up a list of those persons working for them, under a contract of employment or otherwise, who have access to inside information. Issuers and persons acting on their behalf or for their account shall regularly update this list and transmit it to the competent authority whenever the latter requests it.

(4) Persons discharging managerial responsibilities within an issuer of financial instruments and, where applicable, persons closely associated with them, shall, at least, notify to the competent authority the existence of transactions conducted on their own account relating to shares of the said issuer, or to derivatives or other financial instruments linked to them. Member States shall ensure that public access to information concerning such transactions, on at least an individual basis, is readily available as soon as possible.

DIRECTIVE 2003/71/EC OF THE EUROPEAN PARLIAMENT AND OF THE COUNCIL of 4 November 2003 on the prospectus to be published when securities are offered to the public or admitted to trading and amending Directive 2001/34/EC

Article 3

Obligation to publish a prospectus

(1) Member States shall not allow any offer of securities to be made to the public within their territories without prior publication of a prospectus.

(2) The obligation to publish a prospectus shall not apply to the following types of offer:

(a) an offer of securities addressed solely to qualified investors; and/or

(b) an offer of securities addressed to fewer than 100 natural or legal persons per Member State, other than qualified investors; and/or

(c) an offer of securities addressed to investors who acquire securities for a total consideration of at least EUR 50000 per investor, for each separate offer; and/or

(d) an offer of securities whose denomination per unit amounts to at least EUR 50000; and/or

(e) an offer of securities with a total consideration of less than EUR 100000, which limit shall be calculated over a period of 12 months.

However, any subsequent resale of securities which were previously the subject of one or more of the types of offer mentioned in this paragraph shall be regarded as a separate offer and the definition set out in Article 2(1)(d) shall apply for the purpose of deciding whether that resale is an offer of securities to the public. The placement of securities through financial intermediaries shall be subject to publication of a prospectus if none of the conditions (a) to (e) are met for the final placement.

Practice Statements

(3) Member States shall ensure that any admission of securities to trading on a regulated market situated or operating within their territories is subject to the publication of a prospectus.

Article 5

The prospectus

(1) Without prejudice to Article 8(2), the prospectus shall contain all information which, according to the particular nature of the issuer and of the securities offered to the public or admitted to trading on a regulated market, is necessary to enable investors to make an informed assessment of the assets and liabilities, financial position, profit and losses, and prospects of the issuer and of any guarantor, and of the rights attaching to such securities. This information shall be presented in an easily analysable and comprehensible form.

(2) The prospectus shall contain information concerning the issuer and the securities to be offered to the public or to be admitted to trading on a regulated market. It shall also include a summary. The summary shall, in a brief manner and in non-technical language, convey the essential characteristics and risks associated with the issuer, any guarantor and the securities, in the language in which the prospectus was originally drawn up. The summary shall also contain a warning that:

(a) it should be read as an introduction to the prospectus;

(b) any decision to invest in the securities should be based on consideration of the prospectus as a whole by the investor;

(c) where a claim relating to the information contained in a prospectus is brought before a court, the plaintiff investor might, under the national legislation of the Member States, have to bear the costs of translating the prospectus before the legal proceedings are initiated; and

(d) civil liability attaches to those persons who have tabled the summary including any translation thereof, and applied for its notification, but only if the summary is misleading, inaccurate or inconsistent when read together with the other parts of the prospectus. Where the prospectus relates to the admission to trading on a regulated market of nonequity securities having a denomination of at least EUR 50000, there shall be no requirement to provide a summary except when requested by a Member State as provided for in Article 19(4).

(3) Subject to paragraph 4, the issuer, offeror or person asking for the admission to trading on a regulated market may draw up the prospectus as a single document or separate documents. A prospectus composed of separate documents shall divide the required information into a registration document, a securities note and a summary note. The registration document shall contain the information relating to the issuer. The securities note shall contain the information concerning the securities offered to the public or to be admitted to trading on a regulated market.

(4) For the following types of securities, the prospectus can, at the choice of the issuer, offeror or person asking for the admission to trading on a regulated market consist of a base prospectus containing all relevant information concerning the issuer and the securities offered to the public or to be admitted to trading on a regulated market:

(a) non-equity securities, including warrants in any form, issued under an offering programme;

(b) non-equity securities issued in a continuous or repeated manner by credit institutions,

(i) where the sums deriving from the issue of the said securities, under national legislation, are placed in assets which provide sufficient coverage for the liability deriving from securities until their maturity date;

(ii) where, in the event of the insolvency of the related credit institution, the said sums are intended, as a priority, to repay the capital and interest falling due, without prejudice to the provisions of Directive 2001/24/EC of the European Parliament and of the Council of 4 April 2001 on the reorganisation and winding up of credit institutions(14).

The information given in the base prospectus shall be supplemented, if necessary, in accordance with Article 16, with updated information on the issuer and on the securities to be offered to the public or to be admitted to trading on a regulated market.

If the final terms of the offer are not included in either the base prospectus or a supplement, the final terms shall be provided to investors and filed with the competent authority when each public offer is made as soon as practicable and if possible in advance of the beginning of the offer. The provisions of Article 8(1)(a) shall be applicable in any such case.

(5) In order to take account of technical developments on financial markets and to ensure uniform application of this Directive, the Commission shall, in accordance with the procedure referred to in Article 24(2), adopt implementing measures concerning the format of the prospectus or base prospectus and supplements.

Article 7

Minimum information

(1) Detailed implementing measures regarding the specific information which must be included in a prospectus, avoiding duplication of information when a prospectus is composed of separate documents, shall be adopted by the Commission in accordance with the procedure referred to in Article 24(2). The first set of implementing measures shall be adopted by 1 July 2004.

(2) In particular, for the elaboration of the various models of prospectuses, account shall be taken of the following:

(a) the various types of information needed by investors relating to equity securities as compared with non-equity securities; a consistent approach shall be taken with regard to information required in a prospectus for securities which have a similar economic rationale, notably derivative securities;

(b) the various types and characteristics of offers and admissions to trading on a regulated market of non-equity securities. The information required in a prospectus shall be appropriate from the point of view of the investors concerned for non-equity securities having a denomination per unit of at least EUR 50000;

(c) the format used and the information required in prospectuses relating to non-equity securities, including warrants in any form, issued under an offering programme;

(d) the format used and the information required in prospectuses relating to non-equity securities, in so far as these securities are not subordinated, convertible, exchangeable, subject to subscription or acquisition rights or linked to derivative instruments, issued in a continuous or repeated manner by entities authorised or regulated to operate in the financial markets within the European Economic Area;

(e) the various activities and size of the issuer, in particular SMEs. For such companies the information shall be adapted to their size and, where appropriate, to their shorter track record;

(f) if applicable, the public nature of the issuer.

(3) The implementing measures referred to in paragraph 1 shall be based on the standards in the field of financial and non-financial information set out by international securities commission organisations, and in particular by IOSCO and on the indicative Annexes to this Directive.

Article 8

Omission of information

(1) Member States shall ensure that where the final offer price and amount of securities which will be offered to the public cannot be included in the prospectus:

(a) the criteria, and/or the conditions in accordance with which the above elements will be determined or, in the case of price, the maximum price, are disclosed in the prospectus; or

(b) the acceptances of the purchase or subscription of securities may be withdrawn for not less than two working days after the final offer price and amount of securities which will be offered to the public have been filed.

The final offer price and amount of securities shall be filed with the competent authority of the home Member State and published in accordance with the arrangements provided for in Article 14(2).

(2) The competent authority of the home Member State may authorise the omission from the prospectus of certain information provided for in this Directive or in the implementing measures referred to in Article 7(1), if it considers that:

(a) disclosure of such information would be contrary to the public interest; or

(b) disclosure of such information would be seriously detrimental to the issuer, provided that the omission would not be likely to mislead the public with regard to facts and circumstances essential for an informed assessment of the issuer, offeror or guarantor, if any, and of the rights attached to the securities to which the prospectus relates; or

(c) such information is of minor importance only for a specific offer or admission to trading on a regulated market and is not such as will influence the assessment of the financial position and prospects of the issuer, offeror or guarantor, if any.

(3) Without prejudice to the adequate information of investors, where, exceptionally, certain information required by implementing measures referred to in Article 7(1) to be included in a prospectus is inappropriate to the issuer's sphere of activity or to the legal form of the issuer or to the securities to which the prospectus relates, the prospectus shall contain information equivalent to the required information. If there is no such information, this requirement shall not apply.

(4) In order to take account of technical developments on financial markets and to ensure uniform application of this Directive, the Commission shall, in accordance with the procedure referred to in Article 24(2), adopt implementing measures concerning paragraph 2.

Article 10

Information

(1) Issuers whose securities are admitted to trading on a regulated market shall at least annually provide a document that contains or refers to all information that they have published or made available to the public over the preceding 12 months in one or more Member States and in third countries in compliance with their obligations under Community and national laws and rules dealing with the regulation of securities, issuers of securities and securities markets. Issuers shall refer at least to the information required pursuant to company law directives, Directive 2001/34/EC and Regulation (EC) No 1606/2002 of the European Parliament and of the Council of 19 July 2002 on the application of international accounting standards(15).

(2) The document shall be filed with the competent authority of the home Member State after the publication of the financial statement. Where the document refers to information, it shall be stated where the information can be obtained.

(3) The obligation set out in paragraph 1 shall not apply to issuers of non-equity securities whose denomination per unit amounts to at least EUR 50000.

(4) In order to take account of technical developments on financial markets and to ensure uniform application of this Directive, the Commission may, in accordance with the procedure referred to in Article 24(2), adopt implementing measures concerning paragraph 1. These measures will relate only to the method of publication of the disclosure requirements mentioned in paragraph 1 and will not entail new disclosure requirements. The first set of implementing measures shall be adopted by 1 July 2004.

Article 14

Publication of the prospectus

(1) Once approved, the prospectus shall be filed with the competent authority of the home Member State and shall be made available to the public by the issuer, offeror or person asking for admission to trading on a regulated market as soon as practicable and in any case, at a reasonable time in advance of, and at the latest at the beginning of, the offer to the public or the admission to trading of the securities involved. In addition, in the case of an initial public offer of a class of shares not already admitted to trading on a regulated market that is to be admitted to trading for the first time, the prospectus shall be available at least six working days before the end of the offer.

(2) The prospectus shall be deemed available to the public when published either:

(a) by insertion in one or more newspapers circulated throughout, or widely circulated in, the Member States in which the offer to the public is made or the admission to trading is sought; or

(b) in a printed form to be made available, free of charge, to the public at the offices of the market on which the securities are being admitted to trading, or at the registered office of the issuer and at the offices of the financial intermediaries placing or selling the securities, including paying agents; or

(c) in an electronic form on the issuer's website and, if applicable, on the website of the financial intermediaries placing or selling the securities, including paying agents; or

(d) in an electronic form on the website of the regulated market where the admission to trading is sought; or
(e) in electronic form on the website of the competent authority of the home Member State if the said authority has decided to offer this service.

A home Member State may require issuers which publish their prospectus in accordance with (a) or (b) also to publish their prospectus in an electronic form in accordance with (c).

(3) In addition, a home Member State may require publication of a notice stating how the prospectus has been made available and where it can be obtained by the public.

(4) The competent authority of the home Member State shall publish on its website over a period of 12 months, at its choice, all the prospectuses approved, or at least the list of prospectuses approved in accordance with Article 13, including, if applicable, a hyperlink to the prospectus published on the website of the issuer, or on the website of the regulated market.

(5) In the case of a prospectus comprising several documents and/or incorporating information by reference, the documents and information making up the prospectus may be published and circulated separately provided that the said documents are made available, free of charge, to the public, in accordance with the arrangements established in paragraph 2. Each document shall indicate where the other constituent documents of the full prospectus may be obtained.

(6) The text and the format of the prospectus, and/or the supplements to the prospectus, published or made available to the public, shall at all times be identical to the original version approved by the competent authority of the home Member State.

(7) Where the prospectus is made available by publication in electronic form, a paper copy must nevertheless be delivered to the investor, upon his request and free of charge, by the issuer, the offeror, the person asking for admission to trading or the financial intermediaries placing or selling the securities.

(8) In order to take account of technical developments on financial markets and to ensure uniform application of the Directive, the Commission shall, in accordance with the procedure referred to in Article 24(2), adopt implementing measures concerning paragraphs 1, 2, 3 and 4. The first set of implementing measures shall be adopted by 1 July 2004.

Article 16

Supplements to the prospectus

(1) Every significant new factor, material mistake or inaccuracy relating to the information included in the prospectus which is capable of affecting the assessment of the securities and which arises or is noted between the time when the prospectus is approved and the final closing of the offer to the public or, as the case may be, the time when trading on a regulated market begins, shall be mentioned in a supplement to the prospectus. Such a supplement shall be approved in the same way in a maximum of seven working days and published in accordance with at least the same arrangements as were applied when the original prospectus was published. The summary, and any translations thereof, shall also be supplemented, if necessary to take into account the new information included in the supplement.

(2) Investors who have already agreed to purchase or subscribe for the securities before the supplement is published shall have the right, exercisable within a time limit which shall not be shorter than two working days after the publication of the supplement, to withdraw their acceptances.

DIRECTIVE 2004/109/EC OF THE EUROPEAN PARLIAMENT AND OF THE COUNCIL of 15 December 2004 on the harmonisation of transparency requirements in relation to information about issuers whose securities are admitted to trading on a regulated market and amending Directive 2001/34/EC

Article 4

Annual financial reports

(1) The issuer shall make public its annual financial report at the latest four months after the end of each financial year and shall ensure that it remains publicly available for at least five years.

(2) The annual financial report shall comprise:
(a) the audited financial statements;

(b) the management report; and
(c) statements made by the persons responsible within the issuer, whose names and functions shall be clearly indicated, to the effect that, to the best of their knowledge, the financial statements prepared in accordance with the applicable set of accounting standards give a true and fair view of the assets, liabilities, financial position and profit or loss of the issuer and the undertakings included in the consolidation taken as a whole and that the management report includes a fair review of the development and performance of the business and the position of the issuer and the undertakings included in the consolidation taken as a whole, together with a description of the principal risks and uncertainties that they face.

(3) Where the issuer is required to prepare consolidated accounts according to the Seventh Council Directive 83/349/EEC of 13 June 1983 on consolidated accounts [15], the audited financial statements shall comprise such consolidated accounts drawn up in accordance with Regulation (EC) No 1606/2002 and the annual accounts of the parent company drawn up in accordance with the national law of the Member State in which the parent company is incorporated.
Where the issuer is not required to prepare consolidated accounts, the audited financial statements shall comprise the accounts prepared in accordance with the national law of the Member State in which the company is incorporated.

(4) The financial statements shall be audited in accordance with Articles 51 and 51a of the Fourth Council Directive 78/660/EEC of 25 July 1978 on the annual accounts of certain types of companies [16] and, if the issuer is required to prepare consolidated accounts, in accordance with Article 37 of Directive 83/349/EEC.
The audit report, signed by the person or persons responsible for auditing the financial statements, shall be disclosed in full to the public together with the annual financial report.

(5) The management report shall be drawn up in accordance with Article 46 of Directive 78/660/EEC and, if the issuer is required to prepare consolidated accounts, in accordance with Article 36 of Directive 83/349/EEC.

(6) The Commission shall, in accordance with the procedure referred to in Article 27(2), adopt implementing measures in order to take account of technical developments in financial markets and to ensure the uniform application of paragraph 1. The Commission shall in particular specify the technical conditions under which a published annual financial report, including the audit report, is to remain available to the public. Where appropriate, the Commission may also adapt the five-year period referred to in paragraph 1.

Article 5

Half-yearly financial reports

(1) The issuer of shares or debt securities shall make public a half-yearly financial report covering the first six months of the financial year as soon as possible after the end of the relevant period, but at the latest two months thereafter. The issuer shall ensure that the halfyearly financial report remains available to the public for at least five years.

(2) The half-yearly financial report shall comprise:
(a) the condensed set of financial statements;
(b) an interim management report; and
(c) statements made by the persons responsible within the issuer, whose names and functions shall be clearly indicated, to the effect that, to the best of their knowledge, the condensed set of financial statements which has been prepared in accordance with the applicable set of accounting standards gives a true and fair view of the assets, liabilities, financial position and profit or loss of the issuer, or the undertakings included in the consolidation as a whole as required under paragraph 3, and that the interim management report includes a fair review of the information required under paragraph 4.

(3) Where the issuer is required to prepare consolidated accounts, the condensed set of financial statements shall be prepared in accordance with the international accounting standard applicable to the interim financial reporting adopted pursuant to the procedure provided for under Article 6 of Regulation (EC) No 1606/2002.
Where the issuer is not required to prepare consolidated accounts, the condensed set of financial statements shall at least contain a condensed balance sheet, a condensed profit and loss account and explanatory notes on these accounts. In preparing the condensed

balance sheet and the condensed profit and loss account, the issuer shall follow the same principles for recognising and measuring as when preparing annual financial reports.

(4) The interim management report shall include at least an indication of important events that have occurred during the first six months of the financial year, and their impact on the condensed set of financial statements, together with a description of the principal risks and uncertainties for the remaining six months of the financial year. For issuers of shares, the interim management report shall also include major related parties transactions.

(5) If the half-yearly financial report has been audited, the audit report shall be reproduced in full. The same shall apply in the case of an auditors' review. If the half-yearly financial report has not been audited or reviewed by auditors, the issuer shall make a statement to that effect in its report.

(6) The Commission shall, in accordance with the procedure referred to in Article 27(2), adopt implementing measures in order to take account of technical developments on financial markets and to ensure the uniform application of paragraphs 1 to 5 of this Article. The Commission shall, in particular:

(a) specify the technical conditions under which a published half-yearly financial report, including the auditors' review, is to remain available to the public;

(b) clarify the nature of the auditors' review;

(c) specify the minimum content of the condensed balance sheet and profit and loss accounts and explanatory notes on these accounts, where they are not prepared in accordance with the international accounting standards adopted pursuant to the procedure provided for under Article 6 of Regulation (EC) No 1606/2002.

Where appropriate, the Commission may also adapt the five-year period referred to in paragraph 1.

Article 6

Interim management statements

(1) Without prejudice to Article 6 of Directive 2003/6/EC, an issuer whose shares are admitted to trading on a regulated market shall make public a statement by its management during the first six-month period of the financial year and another statement by its management during the second six-month period of the financial year. Such statement shall be made in a period between ten weeks after the beginning and six weeks before the end of the relevant six-month period. It shall contain information covering the period between the beginning of the relevant six-month period and the date of publication of the statement. Such a statement shall provide:

– an explanation of material events and transactions that have taken place during the relevant period and their impact on the financial position of the issuer and its controlled undertakings, and

– a general description of the financial position and performance of the issuer and its controlled undertakings during the relevant period.

(2) Issuers which, under either national legislation or the rules of the regulated market or of their own initiative, publish quarterly financial reports in accordance with such legislation or rules shall not be required to make public statements by the management provided for in paragraph 1.

(3) The Commission shall provide a report to the European Parliament and the Council by 20 January 2010 on the transparency of quarterly financial reporting and statements by the management of issuers to examine whether the information provided meets the objective of allowing investors to make an informed assessment of the financial position of the issuer. Such a report shall include an impact assessment on areas where the Commission considers proposing amendments to this Article.

Article 14

(1) Where an issuer of shares admitted to trading on a regulated market acquires or disposes of its own shares, either itself or through a person acting in his own name but on the issuer's behalf, the home Member State shall ensure that the issuer makes public the proportion of its own shares as soon as possible, but not later than four trading days following such acquisition or disposal where that proportion reaches, exceeds or falls below the thresholds of 5 % or 10 % of the voting rights. The proportion shall be calculated on the basis of the total number of shares to which voting rights are attached.

(2) The Commission shall, in accordance with the procedure referred to in Article 27(2), adopt implementing measures in order to take account of technical developments in financial markets and to ensure the uniform application of paragraph 1.

Article 16

Additional information

(1) The issuer of shares admitted to trading on a regulated market shall make public without delay any change in the rights attaching to the various classes of shares, including changes in the rights attaching to derivative securities issued by the issuer itself and giving access to the shares of that issuer.

(2) The issuer of securities, other than shares admitted to trading on a regulated market, shall make public without delay any changes in the rights of holders of securities other than shares, including changes in the terms and conditions of these securities which could indirectly affect those rights, resulting in particular from a change in loan terms or in interest rates.

(3) The issuer of securities admitted to trading on a regulated market shall make public without delay of new loan issues and in particular of any guarantee or security in respect thereof. Without prejudice to Directive 2003/6/EC, this paragraph shall not apply to a public international body of which at least one Member State is member.

Article 17

Information requirements for issuers whose shares are admitted to trading on a regulated market

(1) The issuer of shares admitted to trading on a regulated market shall ensure equal treatment for all holders of shares who are in the same position.

(2) The issuer shall ensure that all the facilities and information necessary to enable holders of shares to exercise their rights are available in the home Member State and that the integrity of data is preserved. Shareholders shall not be prevented from exercising their rights by proxy, subject to the law of the country in which the issuer is incorporated. In particular, the issuer shall:

(a) provide information on the place, time and agenda of meetings, the total number of shares and voting rights and the rights of holders to participate in meetings;

(b) make available a proxy form, on paper or, where applicable, by electronic means, to each person entitled to vote at a shareholders' meeting, together with the notice concerning the meeting or, on request, after an announcement of the meeting;

(c) designate as its agent a financial institution through which shareholders may exercise their financial rights; and

(d) publish notices or distribute circulars concerning the allocation and payment of dividends and the issue of new shares, including information on any arrangements for allotment, subscription, cancellation or conversion.

(3) For the purposes of conveying information to shareholders, the home Member State shall allow issuers the use of electronic means, provided such a decision is taken in a general meeting and meets at least the following conditions:

(a) the use of electronic means shall in no way depend upon the location of the seat or residence of the shareholder or, in the cases referred to in Article 10(a) to (h), of the natural persons or legal entities;

(b) identification arrangements shall be put in place so that the shareholders, or the natural persons or legal entities entitled to exercise or to direct the exercise of voting rights, are effectively informed;

(c) shareholders, or in the cases referred to in Article 10(a) to (e) the natural persons or legal entities entitled to acquire, dispose of or exercise voting rights, shall be contacted in writing to request their consent for the use of electronic means for conveying information and, if they do not object within a reasonable period of time, their consent shall be deemed to be given. They shall be able to request, at any time in the future, that information be conveyed in writing, and

(d) any apportionment of the costs entailed in the conveyance of such information by electronic means shall be determined by the issuer in compliance with the principle of equal treatment laid down in paragraph 1.

(4) The Commission shall, in accordance with the procedure provided for in Article 27(2), adopt implementing measures in order to take account of technical developments in financial markets, to take account of developments in information and communication

technology and to ensure the uniform application of paragraphs 1, 2 and 3. It shall, in particular, specify the types of financial institution through which a shareholder may exercise the financial rights provided for in paragraph 2(c).

Article 18

Information requirements for issuers whose debt securities are admitted to trading on a regulated market

(1) The issuer of debt securities admitted to trading on a regulated market shall ensure that all holders of debt securities ranking pari passu are given equal treatment in respect of all the rights attaching to those debt securities.

(2) The issuer shall ensure that all the facilities and information necessary to enable debt securities holders to exercise their rights are publicly available in the home Member State and that the integrity of data is preserved. Debt securities holders shall not be prevented from exercising their rights by proxy, subject to the law of country in which the issuer is incorporated. In particular, the issuer shall:

(a) publish notices, or distribute circulars, concerning the place, time and agenda of meetings of debt securities holders, the payment of interest, the exercise of any conversion, exchange, subscription or cancellation rights, and repayment, as well as the right of those holders to participate therein;

(b) make available a proxy form on paper or, where applicable, by electronic means, to each person entitled to vote at a meeting of debt securities holders, together with the notice concerning the meeting or, on request, after an announcement of the meeting; and

(c) designate as its agent a financial institution through which debt securities holders may exercise their financial rights.

(3) If only holders of debt securities whose denomination per unit amounts to at least EUR 50000 or, in the case of debt securities denominated in a currency other than Euro whose denomination per unit is, at the date of the issue, equivalent to at least EUR 50000, are to be invited to a meeting, the issuer may choose as venue any Member State, provided that all the facilities and information necessary to enable such holders to exercise their rights are made available in that Member State.

(4) For the purposes of conveying information to debt securities holders, the home Member State, or the Member State chosen by the issuer pursuant to paragraph 3, shall allow issuers the use of electronic means, provided such a decision is taken in a general meeting and meets at least the following conditions:

(a) the use of electronic means shall in no way depend upon the location of the seat or residence of the debt security holder or of a proxy representing that holder;

(b) identification arrangements shall be put in place so that debt securities holders are effectively informed;

(c) debt securities holders shall be contacted in writing to request their consent for the use of electronic means for conveying information and if they do not object within a reasonable period of time, their consent shall be deemed to be given. They shall be able to request, at any time in the future, that information be conveyed in writing; and

(d) any apportionment of the costs entailed in the conveyance of information by electronic means shall be determined by the issuer in compliance with the principle of equal treatment laid down in paragraph 1.

(5) The Commission shall, in accordance with the procedure provided for in Article 27(2), adopt implementing measures in order to take account of technical developments in financial markets, to take account of developments in information and communication technology and to ensure the uniform application of paragraphs 1 to 4. It shall, in particular, specify the types of financial institution through which a debt security holder may exercise the financial rights provided for in paragraph 2(c).

Article 19

Home Member State control

(1) Whenever the issuer, or any person having requested, without the issuer's consent, the admission of its securities to trading on a regulated market, discloses regulated information, it shall at the same time file that information with the competent authority of its home Member State. That competent authority may decide to publish such filed information on its Internet site.

Where an issuer proposes to amend its instrument of incorporation or statutes, it shall communicate the draft amendment to the competent authority of the home Member State and to the regulated market to which its securities have been admitted to trading. Such communication shall be effected without delay, but at the latest on the date of calling the general meeting which is to vote on, or be informed of, the amendment.

(2) The home Member State may exempt an issuer from the requirement under paragraph 1 in respect of information disclosed in accordance with Article 6 of Directive 2003/6/EC or Article 12(6) of this Directive.

(3) Information to be notified to the issuer in accordance with Articles 9, 10, 12 and 13 shall at the same time be filed with the competent authority of the home Member State.

(4) In order to ensure the uniform application of paragraphs 1, 2 and 3, the Commission shall, in accordance with the procedure referred to in Article 27(2), adopt implementing measures. The Commission shall, in particular, specify the procedure in accordance with which an issuer, a holder of shares or other financial instruments, or a person or entity referred to in Article 10, is to file information with the competent authority of the home Member State under paragraphs 1 or 3, respectively, in order to:

(a) enable filing by electronic means in the home Member State;

(b) coordinate the filing of the annual financial report referred to in Article 4 of this Directive with the filing of the annual information referred to in Article 10 of Directive 2003/71/EC.

Article 30

Transitional provisions

(1) By way of derogation from Article 5(3) of this Directive, the home Member State may exempt from disclosing financial statements in accordance with Regulation (EC) No 95 1606/2002 issuers referred to in Article 9 of that Regulation for the financial year starting on or after 1 January 2006.

(2) Notwithstanding Article 12(2), a shareholder shall notify the issuer at the latest two months after the date in Article 31(1) of the proportion of voting rights and capital it holds, in accordance with Articles 9, 10 and 13, with issuers at that date, unless it has already made a notification containing equivalent information before that date. Notwithstanding Article 12(6), an issuer shall in turn disclose the information received in those notifications no later than three months after the date in Article 31(1).

(3) Where an issuer is incorporated in a third country, the home Member State may exempt such issuer only in respect of those debt securities which have already been admitted to trading on a regulated market in the Community prior to 1 January 2005 from drawing up its financial statements in accordance with Article 4(3) and its management report in accordance with Article 4(5) as long as

(a) the competent authority of the home Member State acknowledges that annual financial statements prepared by issuers from such a third country give a true and fair view of the issuer's assets and liabilities, financial position and results;

(b) the third country where the issuer is incorporated has not made mandatory the application of international accounting standards referred to in Article 2 of Regulation (EC) No 1606/2002; and

(c) the Commission has not taken any decision in accordance with Article 23(4)(ii) as to whether there is an equivalence between the abovementioned accounting standards and

– the accounting standards laid down in the law, regulations or administrative provisions of the third country where the issuer is incorporated, or

– the accounting standards of a third country such an issuer has elected to comply with.

(4) The home Member State may exempt issuers only in respect of those debt securities which have already been admitted to trading on a regulated market in the Community prior to 1 January 2005 from disclosing half-yearly financial report in accordance with Article 5 for 10 years following 1 January 2005, provided that the home Member State had decided to allow such issuers to benefit from the provisions of Article 27 of Directive 2001/34/EC at the point of admission of those debt securities.

Glossary Annex B

HM Treasury consolidated list of persons designated as being subject to financial restrictions.

This includes targets listed by the United Nations, European Union and United Kingdom under legislation relating to current financial restrictions regimes. The purpose of the HM Treasury list is to draw together in one place all the names of designated persons for the various financial restrictions regimes effective in the UK.

General legal requirements

The UK imposes financial restrictions on persons and entities following their designation at the United Nations and/or European Union. The UK also operates a domestic counterterrorism regime, where the Government decides to impose financial restrictions on certain persons and entities.

Financial restrictions in the UK are governed by various pieces of legislation. In all circumstances, where an asset freeze is imposed, it is unlawful to deal with the funds or other assets of the designated person or make payments to them or for their benefit

A list of all financial restrictions currently in force in the UK is maintained by the Treasury's Asset Freezing Unit. The Consolidated List of persons designated as being subject to financial restrictions can be found on the HM Treasury web site at: www.hmtreasury.gov.uk/financialsanctions

Further information on financial restrictions can also be found via this website.

There are specific financial restrictions targeted at the Al-Qaida network and Terrorism

Under the relevant legislation it is a criminal offence for any natural or legal person to:

(a) Deal with the funds of designated persons
(b) Make funds and economic resources, and in the case of Terrorism financial services, available, directly or indirectly to or for the benefit of designated persons, or
(c) Knowingly and intentionally participate in activities that would directly or indirectly circumvent the financial restrictions or enable or facilitate the commission of an offence relating to a) and b) above.

"Deal with" means:

(a) In respect of funds—
- Use, alter, move, allow access to or transfer
- Deal with in any other way that would result in any change in volume, amount, location, ownership, possession, character or destination, or
- Make any other change that would enable use, including portfolio management and

(b) In respect of economic resources -
- Use to obtain funds, goods or services in any way, including (but not limited to) by selling, hiring or mortgaging the resources.

The purpose of this legislation imposing financial restrictions is primarily to prevent the diversion of funds to terrorism and terrorist purposes.

HM Treasury has the power to grant licenses exempting certain transactions from the financial restrictions. Requests to disapply the financial restrictions in relation to a designated person are considered by the Treasury on a case-by-case basis to ensure that there is no risk of funds being diverted to terrorism. To apply for a licence, please contact the Asset Freezing Unit at HM Treasury using the contact details below.

Businesses

Businesses need to have appropriate policies and procedures in place to monitor payments in order to prevent breaches of the financial restrictions legislation.

For manual checking, businesses can register with the HM Treasury Asset Freezing Unit update service (directly or via a third party). If checking is automated, businesses will need to ensure that the relevant software includes checks against the latest consolidated list.

The Asset Freezing Unit may also be contacted to provide guidance and to assist with any concerns regarding financial restrictions at:

Asset Freezing Unit
Tel: 020 7270 5664/5454
Fax: 020 7451 7677
E mail: assetfreezingunit@hm-treasury.gov.uk

In the event that a customer or a payee is identified as a designated person payments must not proceed unless a licence is granted by the Treasury, as this would be a breach of the financial restrictions. The Treasury should be informed immediately and the transaction suspended pending their advice. No funds should be returned to the designated person. The firm may also need to consider whether there is an obligation also to report to SOCA under the Proceeds of Crime Act 2002 or the Terrorism Act 2000.

Written reports can be made to the Asset Freezing Unit at:

The Asset Freezing Unit
HM Treasury
1 Horse Guards Road London SW1A 2HQ

Appendix A
Supplementary Anti-money Laundering Guidance For The Tax Practitioner

Guidance for those providing tax services in the United Kingdom, on the prevention of money laundering and the countering of terrorist financing.

This Guidance is issued by

- **the Chartered Institute of Taxation,**
- **the Association of Taxation Technicians,**
- **the Institute of Chartered Accountants in England and Wales,**
- **the Association of Chartered Certified Accountants,**
- **the Chartered Institute of Management Accountants; and**
- **HM Revenue and Customs**

as an Appendix to the anti-money laundering guidance released by the Consultative Committee of Accountancy Bodies (CCAB).

This supplementary Guidance is not stand alone Guidance; it must be read in conjunction with the CCAB's anti money laundering guidance [see above] to which this Guidance is an appendix. It focuses on the interaction between anti money laundering compliance and tax offences and covers the issues that a tax practitioner is most likely to encounter in practice.

The comments received on the exposure draft of this guidance have been considered and incorporated where appropriate. HM Treasury has approved this guidance. This means that the Courts must consider the content of the Guidance when determining whether an accountant's or tax practitioner's conduct gives rise to an offence under either the Proceeds of Crime Act 2002, Terrorism Act 2000 or the Money Laundering Regulations 2007.

Issued on 25 June 2009

Glossary and interpretation

1.	**CCAB**	**The Consultative Committee of Accountancy Bodies**
	CDD	**Customer Due Diligence**
	CEMA	**Customs and Excise Management Act 1979**
	HMRC	**Her Majesty's Revenue and Customs**
	ICTA	**Income and Corporation Taxes Act 1988**
	JMLSG	**Joint Money Laundering Steering Group**
	MLR 2007	**Money Laundering Regulations 2007**
	MLRO	**Money Laundering Reporting Officer**
	POCA	**Proceeds of Crime Act 2002**
	SAR	**Suspicious Activity Report**
	SOCA	**The Serious Organised Crime Agency**
	TMA	**The Taxes Management Act 1970**

UK	**United Kingdom**
VATA	**Value Added Tax Act 1994**

2. Words importing the masculine gender include the feminine, words in the singular include the plural and words in the plural include the singular.

Note: This guidance is incomplete on its own. It must be read in conjunction with the CCAB's Anti Money Laundering guidance [above].

1. About this supplementary guidance

1.1 This supplementary guidance has been developed by the Chartered Institute of Taxation, the Association of Taxation Technicians, the Association of Chartered Certified Accountants, the Institute of Chartered Accountants in England and Wales, the Chartered Institute of Management Accountants and HMRC for professionals providing tax services.

1.2 This supplementary guidance uses the descriptive term 'tax practitioner' for someone in business offering tax services. The MLR 2007 uses the term 'tax adviser' and defines a tax adviser as

'a firm or sole practitioner who by way of business provides advice about the tax affairs of other persons, when providing such services'.

The meaning of 'advice' is widely interpreted. For the purpose of this and the CCAB guidance, tax compliance services, ie assisting in the completion and submission of tax returns, is included within the term. It was considered that, for the purposes of this supplementary guidance, the term 'tax practitioner' minimises the risk of someone assuming that MLR 2007 does not apply to their business because they provide tax compliance services.

1.3 The term 'tax' covers all direct and indirect taxes including duties.

1.4 A tax practitioner providing tax advice privately on an unremunerated or voluntary basis (for example as an unpaid volunteer with the Citizens Advice Bureau) does not come within the scope of the MLR 2007 as he is not providing his services 'by way of business'. However tax advice given by way of business is within the scope of MLR 2007 even if it is provided to the client on a pro bono or unremunerated basis. See also paragraph 1.6 of the CCAB guidance.

1.5 The Treasury has approved this guidance. As noted in the CCAB's guidance approval means that the Courts must have regard to the guidance in deciding whether businesses or individuals affected by it have committed an offence under the MLR 2007 or ss 330–331 POCA or s 21A of The Terrorism Act 2000..

2. How to use this supplementary guidance

2.1 This supplementary guidance is for professionals providing tax services. It focuses on the interaction between anti money laundering compliance or countering terrorist financing and tax offences and those issues that the tax practitioner is most likely to encounter. It is not intended to be a comprehensive guide to tax offences. It is not stand alone guidance – it must be read in conjunction with the CCAB AML guidance. The broad interpretation of 'tax adviser' means that this guidance cannot cover every aspect of tax work but the principles set out in the CCAB guidance and in this guidance apply to all taxes and duties.

2.2 A tax practitioner must have a clear understanding of his obligations under the anti Money Laundering legislation. Detailed guidance is given in the CCAB guidance as follows:

Section1	About this guidance
Section 2	The offences
Section 3	Anti money laundering systems and controls
Section 4	The risk based approach to Customer Due Diligence
Section 5	Customer Due Diligence
Section 6	Internal reporting
Section7	Role of MLRO and SAR reporting
Section 8	Consent

Practice Statements

Section 9 Post SAR actions

2.3 Where a tax practitioner is uncertain of his obligations under the anti-money laundering legislation he should seek specialist help.

3. Tax practitioners, MLR 2007 and POCA

3.1 The obligations placed on a tax practitioner under MLR 2007 and POCA are covered in the CCAB guidance.

3.2 Paragraph 1.14 of that guidance sets out the role of the supervisory authorities and advises tax practitioners who are in business of the requirement to be supervised by a supervisory authority.

3.3 A tax practitioner should be aware of HMRC's responsibility under MLR 2007 to regulate trust and company service providers, which may impinge upon the work they undertake for their clients. However if the tax practitioner is supervised by another supervisory authority for other tax and accounting services, that supervisory authority can act as supervisor for the trust and company service work.

3.4 Whilst this supplementary guidance focuses on tax offences, a tax practitioner should be aware of the potential need to report to SOCA (or to his firm's MLRO where he is not a sole practitioner) where he knows or suspects or has reasonable grounds for knowing or suspecting, on the basis of information which came to him in the course of his work as a tax practitioner, that another person is engaged in money laundering. This means that where, in the course of his work, a tax practitioner has knowledge or suspicion of proceeds derived from any crime (ie not restricted to tax crimes) a report may be required.

3.5 In particular, a tax practitioner should also take proper care, under Section 328 POCA, to ensure he does not become concerned in an arrangement which he knows or suspects facilitates (by whatever means) the acquisition, retention, use or control of criminal property by or on behalf of another person when assisting clients.

4. Overview of the tax sector

4.1 Tax work covers a broad range of activities from routine compliance work to complex tax planning.

4.2 Tax compliance includes the processing and submission of returns to the tax authorities.

4.3 Tax planning looks at advising on and structuring tax affairs in a tax efficient manner. This can sometimes involve the use of trusts, offshore entities and tax favourable regimes.

5. What are the money laundering risks in the tax sector?

5.1 The money laundering risk areas that a tax practitioner may encounter in practice include the following:

(a) Where a client's actions in respect of his tax affairs create proceeds of crime, for example:
   – a client's refusal to correct errors (both for the past and on an ongoing basis); or
   – a client's deliberate under declaration of profits/income/gain or deliberate over-statement of expenses/losses.

(b) Where during the course of dealing with a client's tax affairs a tax practitioner suspects or becomes aware that the client is holding proceeds of crime derived from criminal activity which may or may not be tax related.

5.2 The tax practitioner needs to be alert to the risk of assisting or facilitating the laundering of proceeds of crime whether through the evasion of taxes or otherwise. For example, where a client puts significant importance on maintaining the anonymity of beneficiaries or owners or in keeping confidential the structure of a complex plan ostensibly intended to minimise legally a tax liability, then the possibility that the funds involved are derived from the proceeds of crime should be kept in mind.

6. Tax offences

6.1 Introduction

6.1.1 There are a number of tax offences which can give rise to the proceeds of crime and SARs. These are discussed further below. When a tax practitioner has identified proceeds of crime, he (or his firm's MLRO where he is not a sole practitioner) should consider carefully whether the privilege reporting exemption applies before submitting a SAR. See section 12 below and section 7 of the CCAB guidance.

6.1.2 A tax practitioner is not required to be an expert in criminal law but would be expected to be aware of the boundaries between deliberate understatement or other tax evasion and simple cases of error or genuine differences in the interpretation of tax law and be able to identify conduct in relation to direct and indirect tax which is punishable by the criminal law. There will be no question of criminality where the client has adopted in good faith, honestly and without mis-statement a technical position with which HMRC disagrees.

6.1.3 The main areas where offences may arise in direct tax are:

– tax evasion, including making false returns (including supporting documents), accounts or financial statements or deliberate failure to submit returns;
– deliberate refusal to correct known errors; and less commonly
– failure to obtain consent under s 765 ICTA

6.2 Taxes Management Act 1970 ('TMA') tax 'offences'

6.2.1 The TMA provides a civil penalty regime covering both fraudulent and negligent conduct. It is only fraudulent or dishonest conduct which is reportable under POCA. The money laundering legislation is only concerned with the proceeds of criminal conduct. Therefore, it is only that conduct which the law treats as criminal offences which can lead to money laundering issues.

6.2.2 Where conduct may attract a civil penalty under the TMA but may also, on the particular facts, amount to criminal conduct then the conduct is criminal. By way of example, only, knowingly assisting in the preparation of an incorrect return etc could give rise to a civil penalty under s 99 TMA, but the conduct concerned would typically amount to a criminal offence (such as false accounting or cheating HMRC) as well. Any case where fraudulent conduct is suspected should be reported unless the privilege reporting exemption applies. See section 12 below and section 7 of CCAB guidance

6.3 Prosecution policy – the need to report

6.3.1 In the tax environment, there are many circumstances in which the tax authorities have a long and established practice of dealing with matters on a civil basis. A policy view is taken that this is a more cost effective approach and that the interest and penalties that can be charged on a civil basis constitute sufficient restitution and deterrent.

6.3.2 This is the case across direct tax and VAT where criminal prosecutions are very much the exception.

6.3.3 However, the practices or anticipated practices of HMRC are irrelevant to the reporting obligations under POCA. If a tax practitioner suspects that a criminal offence may have been committed, and that there may be or may have been proceeds, whether actual or prospective proceeds, then unless the privilege reporting exemption applies (see section 12 below and section 7 of the CCAB guidance), he is obliged to report to SOCA (or to his firm's MLRO where he is not a sole practitioner) irrespective of the fact that a criminal prosecution may in the member's view be highly unlikely in practice.

7. Reluctance to correct past errors

7.1 Innocent or negligent error – direct tax

7.1.1 It is not uncommon for tax practitioners to become aware of errors in or omissions in current or in past years from clients' tax returns or any calculations or statements appertaining to any liability or an underpayment of tax, for example because a payment date has been missed. If the tax practitioner has no cause to doubt that these came about as a result of innocent mistake or negligence then he will not have formed a suspicion. However, in some cases, the tax practitioner may form a suspicion that the original irregularity was criminal in nature and should make a report unless the privilege reporting exemption applies (see section 12 below and section 7 of the CCAB guidance).

7.2 Innocent or negligent error – indirect tax

7.2.1 In the case of indirect tax, see section 11 below on handling the original error.

7.3 Unwillingness or refusal to disclose to the tax authorities

7.3.1 Where a client indicates that he is unwilling or refuses to disclose the matter to HMRC in order to avoid paying the tax due, the client appears to have formed criminal intent and hence the reporting obligation arises unless the privilege reporting exemption applies (see section 12 below and section 7 of the CCAB guidance). A tax practitioner will need to be careful in applying the privilege exemption when the client has expressed clear intention to evade taxes and needs to consider whether the crime/fraud exception applies. The tax practitioner should also consider whether he can continue to act and consult his professional body's guidance on such matters. This paragraph applies equally to potential clients for whom the tax practitioner has declined to act.

7.4 Adjusting subsequent returns

7.4.1 Where the law permits the correction of small errors by subsequent tax adjustments, and the original error was not attributable to any criminal conduct, then the adjustment itself will not give rise to the need to report, since no crime will have been committed. However, it should be noted that the legislation does apply to any conduct which constitutes the laundering of the proceeds of any criminal offence however small the amount involved.

8. Intention to underpay tax

8.1.1 A client may suggest that he will in the future underpay tax which would be tax evasion and a money laundering offence when it occurs.

8.1.2 A tax practitioner can and should apply his professional body's normal ethical guidance to persuade the client to comply with the law. Should the client's intention in this regard still remain in doubt, the tax practitioner should consider carefully whether he can commence or continue to act.

8.1.3 A SAR may well be required in such cases once there are proceeds of crime, depending upon the facts and circumstances and whether the privilege reporting exemption applies (see section 12 below and section 7 of the CCAB guidance). As in 7.3.1 above a tax practitioner will need to be careful in applying the privilege exemption when the client has expressed clear intention to evade taxes.

9. Tax evasion

9.1 General

9.1.1 Where a tax practitioner knows or suspects, or has reasonable grounds for knowing or suspecting, that a client or other party is engaged in tax evasion in the UK or overseas, this will clearly amount to one or more of a number of possible criminal offences, such as theft, obtaining pecuniary advantage by fraud, false accounting, cheating HMRC, the offence of fraudulent evasion of income tax under s 144 Finance Act 2000 or a range of specific indirect tax offences (see section 11 below). Unless the privilege reporting exemption applies (see section 12 below and section 7 of the CCAB guidance) a tax practitioner should report the matter to SOCA (or to his firm's MLRO where he is not a sole practitioner) immediately.

9.1.2 If the suspected evasion is of taxes outside the UK, in circumstances which would be a criminal offence if the conduct occurred in the UK, this should also be reported immediately unless it is known to be lawful under the criminal law applying in that country and that conduct, if carried out in the UK, would attract a maximum sentence in the UK of less than twelve months, except as prescribed by order.

As in other cases, this is unless the privilege reporting exemption applies (see section 12 below and section 7 of the CCAB guidance). There are other very limited exceptions regarding the reporting of overseas criminal conduct; see 2.4 and 2.5 of CCAB guidance.

9.1.3 A tax practitioner can and should apply the principles set out in his professional body's normal ethical guidance to persuade the client to act properly. A tax practitioner will need to consider carefully whether he can continue to act if the client refuses to make a full disclosure to HMRC.

9.2 Civil Investigation of Fraud (CIF) Procedures

9.2.1 In circumstances where a potential or current client asks a member to act in the making of a CIF disclosure to HMRC a suspicion of tax evasion will often, but not always, arise.

9.2.2 A tax practitioner should be aware that notification to HMRC is not a substitute for a report to SOCA. Where appropriate a report must also be made to SOCA as soon as the tax practitioner has knowledge or suspicion or reasonable grounds for knowledge or suspicion that tax has intentionally not been paid when due. The tax practitioner (or his firm's MLRO where he is not a sole practitioner) should consider carefully whether the privilege reporting exemption applies (see section 12 below and section 7 of the CCAB guidance) before submitting a SAR.

9.2.3 There may be occasions where the tax practitioner does not hold sufficient information to make a detailed disclosure of his client's tax evasion to HMRC at the same time as he (or his firm's MLRO where he is not a sole practitioner) submits a SAR to SOCA. However the tax practitioner will be keen to protect his client's position by notifying HMRC of the tax evasion before SOCA does so that the case may be regarded as a voluntary disclosure. The practicalities of this situation are covered in a Question and Answer note agreed with HMRC attached as Appendix 1.

10. Failure to obtain Treasury consent – s 765 ICTA

10.1.1 This section is relevant to members who deal with transactions by companies with international aspects — those transactions that may require consent relate to the creation or issuing or transferring of shares or debentures.

10.1.2 Under s 766 ICTA 1988 companies, their officers and advisers may be guilty of criminal offences if a transaction requiring special consent under s 765(1) takes place without such consent. The person needs to know that the actions were unlawful under s 765(1) in order to be guilty of a criminal offence (s 766(1)). In practice this is of limited assistance in cases of innocent oversight because s 766(2) puts the burden of proof as to the person's state of knowledge on to the individual in the case of directors.

10.1.3 The next question is whether there are proceeds. If a client has undertaken a tax planning transaction for which Treasury consent was needed and would have been unlikely to have been granted, the tax not paid as a result of the planning would constitute proceeds from the crime. In other circumstances there may be no proceeds, but this will need to be considered on the facts. Where there are proceeds, the tax practitioner should finally consider whether the alleged offender knew or suspected that the proceeds arose from criminal conduct. The tax practitioner would usually advise the client that a criminal offence may have occurred, so that the client would then have the requisite knowledge.

10.1.4 When a tax practitioner realises that there has or may have been a breach of s 765 ICTA, he (or his firm's MLRO where he is not a sole practitioner) will need to consider making a SAR based on the factors discussed above. He should also bear in mind whether the privilege reporting exemption applies (see section 12 below and section 7 of the CCAB guidance). The tax practitioner should also consider what other action is appropriate, for example, advising the client to notify HMRC.

11. Indirect tax

11.1 Overview

11.1.1 Where indirect tax is concerned, innocent or negligent errors may be criminal offences as strict liability is imposed by such as167 (3) CEMA which provides:

> 'If any person –
>
> (a) makes or signs, or causes to be made or signed, or delivers or causes to be delivered to the Commissioners or any officer, any declaration, notice, certificate or other document whatsoever; or
>
> (b) makes any statement in answer to any question put to him by an officer which he is required by or under any enactment to answer,
>
> being a document or statement produced or made for any purpose of any assigned matter, which is untrue in any material particular, then, without prejudice to subsection (4) below, he shall be liable on summary conviction to a penalty of level 4 on the standard scale'.
>
> 'Assigned matter' is defined in section 1 of CEMA as meaning 'any matter in relation to which the Commissioners are for the time being required in pursuance of any enactment to perform any duties'.

11.1.2 This broadly makes most errors, however innocent, criminal offences in VAT and all other indirect taxes. The fact that VAT matters are in practice handled under the civil penalties regime in most circumstances is irrelevant (see section 6.3 above) to the fact that there is an offence under s 167(3) CEMA. However an innocent or negligent error will not fall to be classed as money laundering where the person making the error was not aware/did not suspect that they had committed a criminal offence.

Practice Statements

11.1.3 Property is only criminal property for the purposes of POCA if it not only constitutes or represents benefit from criminal conduct, but the 'alleged offender knows or suspects that it constitutes or represents such a benefit' (s340(3)POCA).

A client who has knowledge of s 167 CEMA will 'know or suspect' that they are in receipt of funds once they become aware of the error or mistake so the normal SAR regime applies. There is no presumption that the client is aware of the strict liability offence in s 167(3) and a practitioner does not have to investigate the client's knowledge, but should make a judgement based on his knowledge of the client. If a practitioner believes a report is necessary but that the client made an error or innocent mistake they should consider making reference to this opinion in any SAR they make.

11.1.4 Where the practitioner suspects that the irregularity may have amounted to tax evasion or tax fraud, the need to make a SAR should be considered on the usual basis and in the same way as for direct tax. There are large numbers of specific criminal offences in the indirect taxes legislation and these are outlined in paragraphs 11.2 and 11.3 below. However in essence they all amount to variations on tax evasion and involve some intent to avoid paying the correct amount of tax.

11.1.5 Unwillingness or refusal to correct indirect tax errors should be treated as set out in 7.3 above.

11.2 Other offences applicable across indirect tax

11.2.1 There is a range of crimes in the Customs and Excise legislation, covering such areas as:

- the bribing of a Commissioner, officer or appointed or authorised person;
- the obstructing of an officer performing any duty, or similar conduct;
- production, signing etc of untrue documents and statements;
- the counterfeiting or falsifying of documents;
- obstructing, or failing to assist in, the inspection of a computer;
- the breaching of conditions applied in respect of relief from VAT conferred on specified classes of persons, such as members of visiting forces; and
- the failure to furnish a supplementary declaration under the Intrastat procedure.

In addition there is the common law offence of Cheating the Public Revenue.

11.2.2 There are a number of other offences relating to particular indirect taxes and excise duties, such as stamp duty and stamp duty land tax, alcohol, tobacco products and mineral oil duties, betting and gaming duty, aggregates levy etc. The legislation in respect of these duties, taxes and levies provides the offences specific to them.

11.2.3 As VAT is the indirect tax most commonly advised upon by tax practitioners further details about specific offences applicable to VAT is given in 11.3 below.

11.3 Specific offences applicable in VAT

11.3.1 Fraudulent evasion of VAT (s 72(1) **VATA**)

A person who is knowingly concerned in, or is taking steps with a view to, the fraudulent evasion of VAT by him or any other person is liable under this offence. A person's conduct may amount to fraudulent evasion under this provision if he understates payments due to the Commissioners for a prescribed accounting period. In certain circumstances the over claiming of VAT (eg a refund in respect of bad debts) may also result in fraudulent evasion. If proceeds arose from such conduct, this would also constitute money laundering.

11.3.2 Production, furnishing or sending of false documents and statements (s 72 (3) **VATA**)

This involves the production, furnishing or sending of a false document with the intent to deceive. In addition, it includes knowingly or recklessly making a false statement. If proceeds arose from such conduct, this would also constitute money laundering.

11.3.3 Conduct which must have involved an offence (s 72(8) **VATA**)

Where a person's conduct during any specified period must have involved the commission by him of one or more of the offences listed above, then, regardless of whether the specifics of the offence(s) are known, he is guilty of an offence. The purpose of this provision is to cover cases where it can be proved that an offence has been committed during a period spanning a number of prescribed accounting periods, but it is not clear to what extent it was committed in any particular prescribed accounting period within the total period concerned. It is only one offence, even if it covers more than one period. If proceeds arose from such conduct, this would also constitute money laundering.

11.3.4 The possession and dealing in goods on which VAT has been evaded (s 72(10) VATA)

A person commits an offence, and is liable to penalties, if, having reason to believe that tax has been or will be evaded on them, he either acquires possession of any goods; deals with any goods; or accepts the supply of any services. If proceeds arose from such conduct, this would also constitute money laundering.

11.3.5 Supplying of goods or service without providing security (s 72(11) VATA)

A person who is required, under VAT Act 1994 Schedule 11 para 4(2), to give security for the further payment of VAT as a prerequisite for making taxable supplies and who makes those supplies without the provision of security, has committed an offence. If proceeds arose from such conduct, this would also constitute money laundering.

12. The privilege reporting exemption

12.1.1 A tax practitioner should be aware that the privilege reporting exemption does not apply to 'information or other matter which is communicated or given with the intention of furthering a criminal purpose'.

12.1.2 A tax practitioner should read this section in conjunction with paragraphs 7.26 – 7.46 of the CCAB guidance which covers the privilege reporting exemption and the crime/fraud exception in detail.

12.1.3 In summary a tax practitioner who is a professional legal adviser or a 'relevant professional adviser' who suspects or has reasonable grounds for knowing or suspecting that another person is engaged in money laundering is prohibited from making a money laundering report where the knowledge or suspicion comes to him in 'privileged circumstances'.

12.1.4 Relevant professional adviser is defined in s 330(14) POCA as follows:

> 'an accountant, auditor or tax adviser who is a member of a professional body which is established for accountants, auditors or tax advisers (as the case may be) and which makes provision for
>
> (a) testing of competence of those seeking admission to membership of such a body as a condition for such admission; and
>
> (b) imposing and maintaining professional and ethical standards for its members as well as imposing sanctions for non-compliance with those standards.'

12.1.5 The legislation does not list the professional bodies which meet the criteria but the CCAB bodies, the Chartered Institute of Taxation and the Association of Taxation Technicians meet the criteria and hence their members may be considered to be 'relevant professional advisers'

12.1.6 Privileged circumstances is defined at s 330 (10) POCA as

> 'Information or other matter comes to a professional legal adviser or other relevant professional adviser in privileged circumstances if it is communicated or given to him:
>
> (a) by (or by a representative of) a client of his in connection with the giving by the adviser of legal advice to the client;
>
> (b) by (or by a representative of) a person seeking legal advice from the adviser; or
>
> (c) by a person in connection with legal proceedings or contemplated legal proceedings.'

12.1.7 The CCAB gives guidance on when the privilege reporting exemption might apply. The CIOT and ATT took Counsel's opinion on the privilege reporting exemption and how it might affect their members. This advice included examples of when the privilege reporting exemption might apply and is unlikely to apply. Those examples together with the CCAB's are attached as Appendices 2 and 3.

13. Customer due diligence (CDD)

13.1.1 Customer due diligence and beneficial ownership is considered in detail in Section 5 of the CCAB guidance and a tax practitioner should refer to that guidance in the first instance. A tax practitioner should have regard to the financial restrictions list issued by the government and its advisory notices against countries with material deficiencies in their anti-money laundering and counter terrorist financing regimes. See paragraphs 5.32, 5.44 and Glossary

Annex B of the CCAB guidance for further details and HM Treasury's website at www.hm-treasury.gov.uk/documents/financial_services/sanctions/fin_sanctions_index.cfr

13.1.2 A tax practitioner may be called upon to advise another professional firm. Unless there is a clear agreement between the firms that the advising firm is intended to form a client relationship with the other firm's client, or unless the advising firm comes into contact with and/or enters into a dialogue with the other firm's client, the other firm is the client of the advising firm and accordingly must be made subject to CDD.

13.1.3 In cases where the advising firm's involvement is also with the other firm's client, then the other firm's client must also be made subject to CDD. It may be possible for the advising firm to rely on the other firm's CDD of the client but there are strict criteria which must be met; see paragraphs 5.33 – 5.41 of the CCAB guidance.

Appendix 1
Money Laundering and disclosures to HMRC: A Questions and Answers guidance note

This note is an updated version of a note originally agreed between HMRC, the Association of Taxation Technicians and the Chartered Institute of Taxation.

Object of note

To provide guidance about the practical effect of the money laundering legislation on disclosures of tax evasion by tax practitioners.

Questions and answers

(1) **Will the money laundering requirements make any difference to HMRC's willingness to use Code of Practice 9 or in local offices their willingness to come to a settlement without prosecution?**
HMRC have confirmed that the money laundering requirements will not affect enquiries under Code of Practice 9 or local office procedures.

(2) **Which government departments should I as a tax practitioner inform when I am approached by an individual who tells me that he wants to make a full disclosure of undeclared taxable income and/or gains?**
Traditionally, you as a tax practitioner, having taken instructions and collected all necessary information from your client, will have informed the relevant office within HMRC, depending on the circumstances.
But if you have reasonable grounds for knowing or suspecting that your client has intentionally evaded tax then the money laundering laws will also apply. You or your Money Laundering Reporting Officer (MLRO) if you have one, will be obliged also to make a report to SOCA in the specified form unless the privilege reporting exemption applies. Where you have a MLRO, you must notify him or her and they will in turn consider whether a report should be made to SOCA. See Section 7 of the CCAB anti money laundering guidance regarding the need to appoint a MLRO where you do not have one.

(3) **Should I make a report to SOCA when I receive a CoP 9 enquiry letter from HMRC?**
It is your knowledge or suspicion that counts rather than HMRC's suspicion. You should make up your own mind whether such a letter gives you grounds for making a report applying the criteria in Section 330 POCA 2002, ie do you know or suspect, or have reasonable grounds for knowing or suspecting, that the client is engaged in money laundering as defined at Chapter 2 of the CCAB anti money laundering guidance.

(4) **When should I make a report to SOCA?**
The money laundering legislation says that SOCA must be told 'as soon as is practicable after the information or other matter' that gave rise to the knowledge or suspicion was received.

(5) **It is possible that the potential client may not instruct me at all. Will HMRC monitor me as the tax practitioner named in the SOCA report to see if a disclosure emerges, and if so for how long?**
HMRC recognize that the potential client may go elsewhere (or nowhere) for advice. They have said they have no intention of monitoring reputable practitioners after SOCA reports have been submitted.

(6) **Once I have told SOCA, what happens next assuming no other agency is involved?**
SOCA will pass reports to a special intelligence unit within HMRC in the first instance. The unit will consider whether it is suitable for investigation towards criminal prosecution. If it is not, the case will either be considered for enquiry under a Civil Code

of Practice or be referred to HMRC's Centre for Research and Intelligence in Llanishen, Cardiff. Where it is considered appropriate to pass intelligence on to relevant staff in taxpayer-facing offices neither the fact that the intelligence has come from SOCA, nor the identity of the original source of the intelligence, is disclosed.

(7) **Does the need to report to SOCA before I am ready to tell HMRC affect the timing of my providing information to HMRC about my client's undeclared income and or gains? Although I have made a report to SOCA when approached by a potential client with a tax disclosure to make, I may not immediately be able to approach HMRC because I will have to be formally instructed and the approach to HMRC approved by the client. Collecting and collating the information will inevitably take time especially where several individuals or entities are involved. How long will HMRC regard as a reasonable period before the approach is made while leaving the option of using CoP 9 open?**

HMRC have confirmed that a delay would not jeopardise the CoP 9 approach where it would otherwise be available provided that the taxpayer is taking active steps to regularise their affairs. Doing nothing involves the risk that a CoP 9 enquiry may not be available and that prosecution may follow; or at least that penalty abatements are at risk.

One option, having obtained the client's permission, is to put down a marker by writing to HMRC, saying you have been instructed by a named client to act for them in coming to a settlement about undeclared income or gains. You would also provide a date by which you expect to be able to let HMRC have these details.

(8) **To which HMRC office should I send the marker letter?**

Under these circumstances all letters should be sent to the Centre for Research and Intelligence, Ty Glas Road, Llanishen, Cardiff, CF4 5YF.

(9) **How long a time period for providing the information would HMRC consider reasonable in my 'marker' notification?**

It will depend on the circumstances of each case but HMRC have indicated that they will take a reasonable approach.

Your estimated timetable will obviously depend on your assessment of the likely complexity of your client's affairs.

(10) **What happens if I miss my self-imposed deadline set out in my marker letter?**

HMRC appreciate that the information may be difficult to obtain. You should obviously inform HMRC if you wish to extend your self-imposed deadline. You will need to update HMRC from time to time to reassure them that the client is taking active steps to help you move matters forward.

(11) **What is the position where HMRC already had concerns about a taxpayer and the money laundering notification is the trigger for the raid or the launch of an investigation? HMRC may not be prepared to wait, possibly due to concerns that documents might be destroyed. Would a CoP 9 enquiry still be a possibility for my client if the normal conditions are met (for example if the raid does not indicate that my client is unsuitable for a CoP 9 enquiry)?**

HMRC have informed us that receipt of a report from SOCA or your 'marker' notification will not necessarily make them deviate from their proposed course of action. HMRC will look at the SOCA report in context of all other information available to them regarding a case when prioritizing the cases for investigation.

(12) **Will HMRC wait for a reasonable period of time before launching an enquiry on receipt of a report from SOCA?**

In the majority of cases, given the time it would take for SOCA to pass information to HMRC and for HMRC to consider what action to take, the time lag between the report to SOCA and the making of a voluntary disclosure to HMRC may not be an issue in practice. You should monitor the receipt of acknowledgements to track progress. If you are concerned you could consider the use of a marker letter as discussed above.

Appendix 2

Examples of when the privilege reporting exemption *might* apply

For the privilege reporting exemption to apply the information must come to a legal professional adviser or a relevant professional adviser in privileged circumstances. Whether the privilege reporting exemption applies will depend on the specific facts of the case. These examples are intended as general guidance only and are not a substitute for seeking legal advice in cases of doubt.

Examples included in the CCAB guidance

- advice on taxation matters, where the tax adviser is giving advice on the interpretation or application of any element of tax law and in the process is assisting a client to understand his tax position;
- advice on the legal aspects of a take-over bid, for example on points under the Companies Act legislation;
- advice on duties of directors under the Companies Act;
- advice to directors on legal issues relating to the Insolvency Act 1986, eg, on the legal aspects of wrongful trading; and
- advice on employment law.

Further examples based on advice given to the CIOT and ATT

- advice on how to order or structure a client's tax affairs in a tax efficient manner;
- advice on disclosure obligations to the tax authorities, including advice given in the context of compliance work on reporting requirements and situations where previously there may have been failure to disclose.
- Suspicions derived from pre-existing documents may be covered by the reporting exemption where those documents come to the tax practitioner in privileged circumstances. For example, if a client asked for tax advice on settling past tax under declarations and provided copies of bank statements or invoices or past tax returns in order that the tax adviser could advise, that information could be regarded as having come to the adviser in privileged circumstances.

Examples where relevant professional advisers might fall within privileged circumstances as regards litigation privilege include:

- assisting a client by taking witness statements from him or from third parties in respect of litigation;
- representing a client, as permitted, at a tax tribunal; and
- when instructed as an expert witness by a solicitor on behalf of a client in respect of litigation.

Appendix 3
Examples of when the privilege reporting exemption is unlikely to apply

Examples included in the CCAB guidance

It should be noted that conducting audit work does not of itself give rise to privileged circumstances for this purpose, as the relevant professional adviser is neither providing legal advice, nor is he instructed in respect of litigation. Nor do routine book-keeping, accounts preparation or tax compliance assignments, though privileged circumstances may arise if the client requests or the adviser gives legal advice on an informal basis during the course of such an assignment

Further examples based on advice given to the CIOT and ATT

- Information uncovered during tax compliance work, for example spotting that personal expenditure had been claimed as a business expense in a previous year.
- Information uncovered during a tax due diligence assignment or other agreed upon procedures exercise which is for the purposes of producing an evaluation report or an assurance based opinion (other than an audit) to the client or a third party.
- Information provided by or communications received direct from any third party particularly if no advice has been sought in respect of the underlying detailed content by the client. For example, receipt of information or communications when acting as the client's tax agent.
- Information received about the client's or a third party's affairs which is outside the scope of the tax services in respect of which the adviser has been engaged.

VAT Index

Defined words and phrases are listed separately at the end.

A

VAT Index

C

VAT Index

VAT Index

G

H

VAT Index

VAT Index

P

VAT Index

S

VAT Index

VAT Index

VAT Index

Y

Z

Words and phrases

Words in brackets indicate the context in which the word or phrase is used.

VAT Index

VAT Index